"Practically Indispensable" —*The New York Times*

The good, the bad—and the awful. Our 1991 edition brings you up to date and tells you what not to miss—and what to miss. It describes films so bad they're good, and so good they're legends. It identifies the all-time greats and classics—and the unforgettable duds. They're all listed here in alphabetical order, complete with all the essential information: director, stars, date, color or black-and-white, original length (so you'll know if the video has been cut), key songs (for musicals)—and a concise summary and capsule review of each film. **PLUS, a special symbol for films now available on videocassette.**

Leonard Maltin's
TV MOVIES AND VIDEO GUIDE

named "Best Reference Book of the Decade" by *Film Comment*

"HEAD AND SHOULDERS ABOVE THE REST!"
—*New York Post*

THE CREAM OF THE CROP . . . Written by one of film history's most devoted fans."—*Emmy Magazine*

"No other guide gives as much information as TV MOVIES." —*Harpers Magazine*.

"MOST RELIABLE!" —*Seattle Times*

"EASILY THE MOST COMPREHENSIVE WORK OF ITS KIND ANYWHERE. IT BELONGS NEXT TO EVERY TV AND VCR IN EVERY HOME."
—Larry King, *USA Today*

LEONARD MALTIN'S
TV MOVIES
AND VIDEO GUIDE
1991 Edition

LEONARD MALTIN'S
TV MOVIES
AND VIDEO GUIDE
1991 Edition

Edited by Leonard Maltin

ASSOCIATE EDITOR
Luke Sader

CONTRIBUTING EDITORS
Mike Clark
Rob Edelman
Alvin H. Marill
Bill Warren

VIDEO EDITOR
Casey St. Charnez

MANAGING EDITOR
Ben Herndon

A PLUME BOOK

PLUME
Published by the Penguin Group
Penguin Books USA Inc., 375 Hudson Street,
New York, New York 10014, U.S.A.
Penguin Books Ltd, 27 Wrights Lane,
London W8 5TZ, England
Penguin Books Australia Ltd, Ringwood,
Victoria, Australia
Penguin Books Canada Ltd, 2801 John Street,
Markham, Ontario, Canada L3R 1B4
Penguin Books (N.Z.) Ltd, 182–190 Wairau Road,
Auckland 10, New Zealand

Penguin Books Ltd, Registered Offices:
Harmondsworth, Middlesex, England

Published by Plume, an imprint of New American Library, a division of
Penguin Books USA Inc. Also published in a Signet edition.

First Plume Printing, November, 1990
10 9 8 7 6 5 4 3 2 1

Cover photo by Rex Hosea

 REGISTERED TRADEMARK—MARCA REGISTRADA

Printed in the United States of America

About the Editor

LEONARD MALTIN is one of the country's most respected film historians. After establishing himself with a series of definitive books (on topics ranging from Hollywood cameramen to the history of animated cartoons), he became known to an even wider audience as the film critic and historian on television's popular syndicated program *Entertainment Tonight*, along with the weekend edition *Entertainment This Week*. He also hosts a daily syndicated radio program, *Leonard Maltin on Video*, and serves as contributing editor of *Video Review* magazine. His books include *Of Mice and Magic: A History of American Animated Cartoons, The Great Movie Comedians, The Disney Films, The Art of the Cinematographer, Movie Comedy Teams, Selected Short Subjects (The Great Movie Shorts), The Whole Film Sourcebook*, and (as coauthor) *Our Gang: The Life and Times of the Little Rascals*. He is a member of The Authors Guild. For nine years he was the editor and publisher of *Film Fan Monthly* magazine; his articles have appeared in *The New York Times, Smithsonian, Saturday Review, TV Guide, Variety, Esquire, Film Comment*, and *American Film*. He lectures on film subjects around the country, and for nine years was a member of the faculty of the New School for Social Research in New York City. In 1976 he served as guest programmer for the Museum of Modern Art's Bicentennial Salute to American Film Comedy, and returned in 1985 to organize a tribute to Warner Bros. Cartoons. Most recently he has written and hosted a number of original homevideo programs, including *Leonard Maltin's Movie Memories, The Lost Stooges, Cartoons for Big Kids* and *Bugs and Daffy: The Wartime Cartoons*. He and his wife, Alice, are the proud parents of Jessica Bennett Maltin, a beautiful, budding movie buff.

The Associate Editors

LUKE SADER has been a movie buff for as long as he can remember. A graduate of Johns Hopkins University, he worked at CBS Cable *(Signature)* and CBS News *(The CBS Morning News)* in New York before heading west to Tinseltown. For the past few years he has been associated with the television show *Entertainment Tonight*, first as a researcher and presently as a Segment Director.

MIKE CLARK is currently senior film critic and homevideo columnist for the national newspaper *USA Today*, but he first came to prominence at the age of 10 when he appeared on the television quiz show *The $64,000 Question* as a film expert. Since then he has attended NYU's Graduate School of Cinema, been the film critic for the *Detroit Free Press*, and served as Director of the American Film Institute Theater in Washington, D.C.

ROB EDELMAN is the Director of Programming of Home Film Festival, which rents select videotapes by mail throughout the country. He has been the coordinator of National Film Programs at the American Film Institute, where he programmed film series in the institute's Washington, D.C. theater. His byline has appeared in *The New York Times, Washington Post, Variety, Premiere, American Film*, and the *International Film Guide*, and he has taught film courses at several schools, most recently Sacred Heart University. He is married to film archivist Audrey Kupferberg.

ALVIN H. MARILL is the author of the definitive reference work *Movies Made for Television*, and served for many years as Television Editor of *Films in Review* magazine. He has written books on such screen personalities as Katharine Hepburn, Errol Flynn, and Tyrone Power, as well as *Samuel Goldwyn Presents, The Complete Films of Edward G. Robinson, Robert Mitchum on the Screen*, and *More Theatre: Stage to Screen to Television*.

BILL WARREN is the author of the two-volume *Keep Watching the Skies*, which has been called "the most authoritative reference work on the fantasy cinema." He has written for *American Film, Starlog, Vendredi 13*, and *Cinefantastique*. He has contributed to *The New*

Encyclopedia of Science Fiction, two volumes on Stephen King, and the annual Science Fiction Writers of America Nebula Awards volumes. He was the Hollywood correspondent for the French television series *Fantasy* and is a "sysop" on GEnie, the commercial computer service.

CASEY ST. CHARNEZ is the buyer and public relations director for a chain of video stores in Santa Fe, New Mexico. He earned an M.A. in folklore and an M.A. and Ph.D. in movies from New York University. The author of *The Films of Steve McQueen,* he currently writes for both the *Santa Fe Reporter* and *The Hollywood Reporter.* An expert on dance and the Hollywood musical, he claims to keep several hundred thousand projects on the back burner.

BEN HERNDON began his association with *Entertainment Tonight* in 1987 in the research department and now works with Leonard Maltin in the preparation of segments for the show. A graduate of the UCLA Film History department, he got his professional start writing obituaries for *The Hollywood Reporter* but quit that job because deadlines were too vague. He has written for *Emmy, Twilight Zone Magazine,* and *Cinefantastique.* He is married to *The Simpsons* animation producer Margot Pipkin.

Introduction to 1991 Edition

It's that time again. I don't know how a year passes so quickly, but here I am, looking at a mass of scribbled notes and stacks of paper that constitute the additions and changes for the 1991 edition of our book.

Sometimes I worry we won't have enough to justify a brand-new edition. I don't know what I'm worried about; movies continue to be released at a staggering rate (not just in theaters, but on video, the elephant's graveyard for films no one would pay to watch on a theater screen). Older films continue to be unearthed, and given new life on TV and homevideo. And, sure enough, every year we find a dizzying amount of changes and corrections to make.

Yes, we do make mistakes, no matter how hard we work to avoid them. Last time we cited *I Could Go On Singing* as being available in a computer-colored version . . . when in fact the film was made in color! Oops.

Maintaining accuracy isn't easy. Several years ago I became curious about the inconsistent spelling of the name of rising young actor Daniel Day-Lewis; some sources used a hyphen, some didn't. A member of our crack research staff put in a transatlantic call to the actor's agent in London, who assured us there was *not* a hyphen, and based on that, we boldly refuted the growing number of sources that disagreed. Then, early this year, I had occasion to meet the (now) Oscar-winning actor at a Hollywood function, and I put the question to him directly: Is there or isn't there a hyphen in his name? "I'm so glad to have an opportunity to set the record straight," he replied. "Yes, there is." (A colleague of mine, overhearing the remark, told me that at one time he *didn't* use a hyphen, but got tired of people calling him Mr. Lewis. Whatever the case, I can find no better source than the gentleman himself. A hyphen there will be.)

As to additions: did you know that John Cleese made movies almost twenty years before *A Fish Called Wanda*? He's in 1968's *Interlude* and 1969's *The Best House in London*. Did you know that the 1950s hit *Blackboard Jungle* has no "The" in the title? Or that the sequel to 1933's *King Kong* is actually *The Son of Kong*—not just "Son of"? Did you know that Mel Gibson's first movie was a little Australian beach film called *Summer City*?—and yes, it's available on video here in the States.

With moviegoers' heightened awareness of Jessica Tandy, it's especially interesting to note that she played real-life husband Hume Cronyn's *daughter* in *The Green Years*, back in 1946! The emerging stardom of Miss Tandy's costar in *Driving Miss Daisy*, Morgan

Freeman, makes his early credits, like 1984's *Teachers* and 1985's *That Was Then . . . This Is Now*, more important than they would have seemed just a couple of years ago.

And, on another plateau of research, we've found film credits for standup comic-turned-movie star Andrew Dice Clay as far back as 1981's *Wacko*.

There are some questions and problems, however, that never seem to go away—and remain frustratingly constant in the preparation of this book. One is determining a film's correct title. Anyone examining ads for this past summer's megahit *Die Hard 2* would have sworn the full title was *Die Hard 2 Die Harder*. If you trusted some ads you might think it was simply called *Die Harder*. But our rule of thumb is to cite the film title that appears on screen, and there it simply says *Die Hard 2*; the words *Die Harder*, so prominent in all the ads, do not appear.

(That's not to say that whatever turns up on screen is 100 percent accurate. While watching a recent cable TV airing of 1940's *The Mummy's Hand* I noticed that not one but two of its cast names were misspelled: Eduardo "Cianelli" and Cecil "Kelloway." You can't win 'em all.)

There's a much more important problem to be reckoned with, however: what constitutes the "official" version of a film? Last year, director Tony Richardson arranged to reissue his long-unavailable 1963 movie *Tom Jones*, and decided to trim the picture by seven minutes; he felt the film needed some tightening for modern audiences. All well and good, but this is an Academy Award-winning picture; which version will continue to be shown in the years ahead? The one that earned it an Oscar in the first place, or the one prepared for reissue twenty-six years later?

That's just one example of many. Nowadays, many people regard the homevideo copy of a film to be its definitive version. What is one to say, then, about films that have been shortened or lengthened for video release—but continue to appear in their unaltered states when revived in theaters or shown on TV?

Universal/MCA has a long history of preparing alternate versions of its feature films for commercial television showings. Most recently, Cheech Marin's *Born in East L.A.* was lengthened for TV release, since it ran so short in theaters. One of our readers, who first saw the film on TV, and then purchased the videocassette, was furious to find that scenes she'd watched—and liked—on TV were "cut" from the video version. You see, it's almost always the original theatrical version that's issued on tape. (We received a similar letter about the 1970 *Diary of a Mad Housewife*, which plays quite differently on TV than it did in its theatrical release.)

But what of Steven Spielberg's *Close Encounters of the Third Kind*? The film we saw in theaters back in 1977 was revised by its director and rereleased three years later as *Close Encounters of the Third Kind: The Special Edition*. Then, when it made its network

TV debut, yet *another* version was edited together. It's the 1980 version that's been available on tape, but as we go to press, we're told that the 1977 cut (which we always liked just fine) is being reissued on laserdisc.

And on it goes. The British video distributor of *Aliens* has restored seventeen minutes of material that was cut just before its theatrical release. Does this help or hurt the film? Would it affect one's opinion of the picture? And which version is being shown in any given situation?

Moreover, which version should we be reviewing in these pages?

There can be no effective rule of thumb for *this* problem; we have to take each film on a case-by-case basis. For years we've carried a review of Sam Peckinpah's *Pat Garrett and Billy the Kid* based on its original theatrical showings in 1973. When we learned that the print airing on television had been changed considerably, we made note of that but did not alter our basic review. Then last year Peckinpah's much-discussed but never-seen "director's cut" of the film was finally released. Since we're told that it is the *only* version now being distributed, on television, on homevideo, and in revival theaters, it seems foolish not to put our original review in mothballs and deal with this print instead.

It certainly doesn't make things easy or clear—for us on this end *or* for the viewer. All we can do is promise to keep you as well informed as possible, so you can figure out what it is you're watching.

And that brings me to a continuing dilemma: how to judge a film. Time and again I've talked about the enormous difference between watching a film in a theater and seeing it on video. Within the past year I gave myself another dramatic demonstration. About eight years ago a revival theater in New York City, the beloved Regency, managed to obtain a print of Frank Capra's little-seen *Lady for a Day*, the Damon Runyon story about street woman Apple Annie and how an entire city conspires to fool her daughter into thinking she's wealthy and renowned. Since this screening constituted an event, my wife Alice and I played hooky from a deadline (for this book, in fact) and went to see it. There, surrounded by an eager and attentive audience, we were pulled into the magic spell of this film, a wish-fulfillment fantasy created in the depths of the Depression by Capra and his screenwriter Robert Riskin. We all cheered when it was over, and left the theater walking on Cloud Nine.

This past year, the film—still a rarity—turned up on cable TV, and we eagerly tuned it in, anxious to relive that wonderful experience. Instead, it fell flat. It had no buoyancy at all, and its conclusion now seemed contrived instead of charming. One can chalk some of this up to a second showing of a film that depends on surprise and freshness . . . but I think the greater problem was that of watching it alone on a small screen. *That movie came alive with an audience in a darkened theater.*

In another arena, several readers have written to complain about the "letterboxing" of the restored *Lawrence of Arabia* on video. They feel this does the film a disservice rather than a favor. Having watched the tape, I can understand their feelings. When I screened it, and saw the small but elongated image, with black on the top and bottom, the first thing I did was move six feet closer to my television set. At first, I found the format distracting, but once I got involved with the story, I stopped thinking about the letterbox, and by the time the sweeping desert scenes came on, I was glad I had the whole wide image, instead of a cropped version that filled the screen top to bottom.

Still, a television set is not the place to see that movie, or any big-scale epic. One can revisit an old favorite that way, I suspect, and still have a good time, but I shudder to think of anyone discovering the film for the first time in that format.

Movies were meant to be seen in a theater. Television (and homevideo, which uses a television set as its screen) simply cannot duplicate the experience. But since both television and video are here to stay, it's important to remember the difference in perception whenever you watch a film at home. Our reviews of new films are still based, for the most part, on theatrical showings. Please bear that in mind when you compare your own reaction after a video viewing.

And now, our rundown of how's, why's, and where's for this edition:

Alphabetization: Articles of speech—A, An, and The—are eliminated for the purpose of alphabetization, of course. (*The Awful Truth* is listed under *Awful Truth, The*.) Aside from that, film titles are listed in strict letter-by-letter spelling sequence. Separation of words and punctuation are ignored in this form of alphabetization; everything hinges on the letters. So, *Kingdom of the Spiders* comes before *King Kong*, because "d" comes before "k," and *Dr. Broadway* appears in a different spot than *Doctor at Large*. If you're confused at first, just let the alphabet be your guide, and you'll find the title you're looking for.

Films on Video: Every film available on homevideo is indicated with this symbol at the end of a review: ▼. Unfortunately videos, like books and records, often go "out of print" and become unavailable at different times. We cannot hope to keep track of these comings and goings, so we continue to list titles (like *Pinocchio*) which are not currently available, but which *do* exist on video and might still be found in certain stores. Also please see our new Guide to Locating Videos at the end of this introduction.

Accurate Titles: As previously mentioned, we try to determine the film's title as it appears on screen, not as it's listed in advertising. There was no number in the actual title of the last *Nightmare on Elm*

Street movie, though it was advertised as No. 5. Whereas the sequel to *The Stepfather* had a number, all right: a Roman numeral II on screen, but a 2 in all the newspaper ads! We also endeavor to catch up with mistakes and minutaie from the past: like placing the apostrophe in the correct (though not the obvious) position for the old Tyrone Power movie *Lloyd's of London.*

Year of Release: Our practice is to cite the year a film is first shown theatrically. For foreign films we list the year of release in the country of origin, which may vary anywhere from one to five years from their U.S. debut.

Country of Origin: We try to apply common sense to make this determination. So many films are multinational corporate projects these days it's hard to keep track, even with a score card!

Running Time: Here's a recent case study: just days apart, *The New York Times*, *Los Angeles Times*, *Daily Variety,* and *The Hollywood Reporter* listed completely different running times with their reviews of the Paul Newman movie *Blaze*—differing by as much as twelve minutes! What's more, according to the film's distributor, not one of those times was correct!! As you can see, the pursuit of accurate running times remains a frustrating exercise, but one we work very hard to perfect. We've revised a number of times on older films, as well, thanks to tips from our readers.

Ratings: Careful thought and consideration are given to every rating in this book, but there's still no way to translate the nuances of a critical opinion into numbers or stars. Fortunately, over the years, most of our readers have found their own way to use our ****-to-BOMB system as a barometer of their own taste. Always remember that these ratings are a form of shorthand, and they reflect an opinion that we propose as a guideline to watching films— not as the gospel.

Movies Made for Television: One Los Angeles television critic recently took us to task for using a separate ratings system for TV movies, comparing the practice to the outmoded use of separate drinking fountains in the South. We had no idea that what we were doing was nearly so earth-shattering! Each made-for-TV movie receives a full writeup and critique, with as many words of description, praise, or damnation as any other film; therefore, we honestly don't see any great shortcoming in dividing them into the categories of Below average, Average, and Above average. This way we can continue to deal with them as a breed apart from theatrical films, which we believe them to be.

Our listings do *not* include miniseries, plays produced on videotape, extended episodes of TV series, or so-called "movies" that are simply old TV episodes strung together.

Title Changes: Films that fail at the box office, and made-for-TV movies that need an extra boost, are often retitled. In the homevideo market the practice is rampant: Brian De Palma's early film with Robert De Niro, *Hi, Mom!* is now available on tape with the curious title *Confessions of a Peeping John*, while another early De Niro picture, *Born to Win* (which actually stars George Segal and Karen Black) is out on video as *Addict!* We try our best to keep up with these changes and cross-reference them for you.

Changes of Opinion: Face it, some films—even highly touted films of the past—don't hold up when you watch them again today . . . while others seem to improve with age. That being the case, we occasionally revise our reviews; some ratings are raised, others are lowered. Why cling to an opinion that simply isn't relevant anymore?

Addition of Older Titles and Obscure Movies: Much as we'd like to, it isn't possible to add every old Hollywood film that's being revived on cable TV. We *have* added quite a few, based in part on name value and in part on quality (don't miss the 1931 *Guilty Hands*, with Lionel Barrymore—a real sleeper).

As to newer titles, the number of grade B, C, and Z movies that continue to surface on video every year is positively staggering. Announcements of movies I've never heard of—with creditable, "name" actors—cross my desk every week. Does anybody watch them? Does anybody care? It's hard to say. Last year I made snide reference to two seemingly obscure titles I wasn't including—and discovered that a friend had appeared in one of them, and a colleague had seen and liked the other one! Suffice it to say that we can't include all of this sludge, but we have selected the most intriguing and nameworthy titles (for instance, *Madman*, a 1978 Israeli-made movie with future Oscar-winner F. Murray Abraham and, in her first leading role, Sigourney Weaver). After all, where else are you going to find out about them?

As always, I'm lucky to be surrounded by colleagues who love movies, care about detail and accuracy, and enjoy working on this book: Mike Clark, Rob Edelman, Alvin H. Marill, Luke Sader, Casey St. Charnez, and Bill Warren. Their work is supplemented by the contributions of Pete Hammond, Michael Scheinfeld, Jerry Beck, and Louis Black. And this year I owe a special debt of thanks to Ben Herndon, who assumed the post of Managing Editor with great skill and good humor.

Thanks go to such friends and cohorts as Kit Parker, Jon Mirsalis, Rita Guzman, Tom Murray, George Feltenstein, Richard F. May, Howard Green, Ronald Haver, Timothy Ryerson, Jonathan Stein, Spencer Green, Spencer Berger, and Rick Sheckman for making suggestions, finding errors, and always being there to answer questions and check facts.

My support system at New American Library includes Arnold Dolin, Hugh Rawson, Pat Lyons, Kenneth May, Helen Richards, and Kathy Murray. Without them the book wouldn't be in your hands. Without Patrick O'Connor and the late Robert Haynie, it wouldn't have come this far.

And without my wonderful wife Alice, none of this would be worthwhile. I love her very much.

I should like to add that this year, for the first time, I have taken into consideration the opinions of our four-year-old daughter Jessie on several films designed for children. She's not only a great test audience, but she's a lot of fun.

Finally, I want to thank our readers for their support, their interest, and their opinions. I'll take this opportunity to apologize for being unable to answer all the mail that comes in (the volume has grown to incredible proportions!), but please know that every letter is read and appreciated. Your comments, criticism, and corrections keep us all on our toes, and help us to continually improve our book. Thank you all . . . and see you next year!

Leonard Maltin

Mail-Order Sources for Video

Every week we receive letters from desperate readers trying to find favorite films on video. Obviously, in spite of the proliferation of video stores, many titles remain hard to find in some areas of the country. Therefore, we've decided to offer a select list of companies that sell (and in a few cases, rent) videotapes and discs by mail. As you will see, we've included some smaller organizations that specialize in certain film genres as well as large, comprehensive ordering services. It is our belief that this will lead those desperate film buffs to any video they seek.

Beta Library
836224 Promenade Station
Richardson TX 75083
214-385-2382
Truth in advertising for sure, with this suburban Dallas company dealing strictly in sales and mail order of Beta-format tapes. Some 500+ titles stocked. Free catalog.

The Blackhawk Catalog
5959 Triumph Street
Commerce, CA 90040-1688
800-826-2295 or 213-888-2229
Colorful sales catalog which bears the name of a venerable home-movie distributor. Blackhawk used to specialize in 8mm and 16mm films for the old-movie buff; now this video catalog runs the gamut of films available on tape, but still gives heavy emphasis to Hollywood classics. Offers sale prices on combo tape packages and runs frequent "specials."

BMG Video Club
6550 East 30th Street
Indianapolis, Indiana 46219-1194
no telephone number
Like so many book and record clubs, this one (an offshoot of various RCA record clubs) enrolls you with a great introductory deal (four tapes for the price of one) and then sends you a mailing nineteen times a year. After fulfilling your one-tape purchase obligation, you can choose from a mix of new offerings with no further requirements; for every tape you buy you can get another at half price.

Captain Bijou
POB 87
Toney AL 35773
205-852-0198
Sales of both mainstream and cult videos, including monsters, B-movies, Westerns, animation, and golden age TV, plus posters, comic books, collectibles, old radio shows, scripts, calendars, glossies, and books. A veritable mini-mall for the obsessed fan.

CBS Video Club
POB 1112
Terre Haute IN 47811-1112
800-544-4431
Yes, the "Take Any Six Movies for 89 cents Each" people who advertise in every *TV Guide*. They've got good prices, new releases, and great sales. Watch the ads closely until the tape you want turns up cheap. Then join the club . . . but just make sure you keep up with those mailers!

CinemaScoop
POB 9283
Santa Fe NM 87504-9283
Search service seeks out video labels for hard-to-find or out-of-print titles. 7 searches/$5.00 + SASE. Checks or money orders only.

Discount Video Tapes, Inc.
833-A N. Hollywood Way
POB 7122
Burbank CA 91510
818-843-3366
fax 818-843-3821
"Specializing in the rare and unusual," Woody Wise's VHS-only sales company does indeed carry titles you simply can't find anywhere else. Comedies, foreign, Westerns, serials, documentaries, silents, etc., etc. and another etc.

Eddie Brandt's Saturday Matinee
6310 Colfax Avenue
North Hollywood CA 91606
818-506-4242
fax 818-506-7722
A big video store with a big difference: the owner loves movies, with a stock reflecting both new-release taste and an affinity for the older. Mail-order rentals by the week, and sales as well. Catalog available.

Evergreen Video Society
213 W. 35th St., 2nd floor
New York NY 10001-4024
800-225-7783
212-714-9860
Sales and rentals of a couple thousand items that may not be in every hometown video store. Specialties include discontinued titles and label searches. Publishes its own news organ focusing on video rarities.

Facets Video
1517 W. Fullerton Ave.
Chicago IL 60614
800-331-6197
312-281-9075
fax 312-929-5437
A division of Facets Multimedia, a nonprofit arts organization founded in 1975. Video marketing manager Steve Bliss has an informed and all-encompassing selection of the known and the unknown for VHS home rental and/or purchase. Strong showing of independent American cinema, plus foreign, fine arts, instructional. Membership in Facets Cinematheque allows discounts. $4 for the oversized catalog.

Festival Films
2841 Irving Avenue South
Minneapolis, Minnesota 55408
612-870-4744
Devoted film buffs Ron and Chris Hall offer a connoisseur's collection of international cinema, including hard-to-find silent films, foreign titles, classics, and animation. Sales only. Many titles also available in 16mm.

Home Film Festival
POB 2032
Scranton PA 18501
800-258-3456 (national)
800-633-3456 (in PA)
Featuring "the best films you never saw," this well-regarded and trustworthy rental operation stocks recent and classic foreign films, independent works, documentaries, and Hollywood classics. Free information kit and film list.

Loonic Video
2022 Taraval St., # 6427
San Francisco CA 94116
415-526-5681
Wild and eclectic collection of inexpensive obscurities, concentrating on camp, antique comedy shorts, horror and sci-fi, cartoons, et al. $1.00 for the catalog, and well worth it.

Marshall Discount Video Service
3130 Edsel Drive # 328
Trenton MI 48183
313-671-5483
If you're looking for 50,000 movies to browse through, send $7 ($12 foreign) for Dave Marshall's extensive, exhaustive and exhausting catalog (laser list is another $2, or $6 foreign). Inventory is nothing less than staggering, all new, factory-sealed and guaranteed.

Movies Unlimited
6736 Castor Ave.
Philadelphia PA 19149
800-523-0823
215-722-8398
fax 215-725-3683
America's largest mail-order/phone-order video company. Weighty 654-page catalog displays 20,000 titles. $7.95 (+ $1.00 for separate laser list), of which $5.00 applies to first order of $25.00 or more. The definitive source for practically every currently available video in print.

National Ordering Service
800-626-9000
Over-the-phone credit card orders for many major labels.

PBS VideoFinders
1-900-860-9301
Operators available 9:00 A.M. to 9:00 P.M. Eastern Standard Time
VideoFinders is a paid telephone search service initiated by Los Angeles' Public Television station KCET. Originally the purpose was to lead viewers to video copies of 2,500 PBS programs available on tape; then the service expanded to include some 58,000 entertainment titles in current release. VideoFinders can provide answers on availability, cost, and distributor, and in many cases do the ordering for you. The charge is $2.00 for the first minute, then $1.00 for each additional minute. We're told the average call lasts three minutes. This is an excellent way to locate hard-to-find videos.

Sinister Cinema
POB 777
Pacifica CA 94044
415-355-5459
415-359-3292
Fascinating assemblage of over 900 offbeat offerings for genre fans. All titles sell for a flat $16.95, with a sincere effort made to acquire the best prints of known and obscure sci-fi, horror, sword and sandal, serials, Westerns, jungle adventures, silents, and schlock. Generally known as the genre buff's first stop.

Tamarelle's International Films
POB 11249
Chico CA 95926
800-356-3577 (national)
800-334-0136 (in CA)
916-895-3429
fax 916-343-9144
Specializing in sales of new and old foreign. In business for sixteen years, and certainly a good back-up source for the friends of the subtitle.

Video City Productions
4266 Broadway
Oakland CA 94611
800-847-8400 (national)
415-428-0202
fax 415-654-7802
Supplying the full range of customers from new video superstores to eager film fans, Video City stocks an arresting compendium of everything, and then some. $3 catalog.

Video Dimensions
530 West 23rd St.
New York, NY 10011
212-929-6135
Formerly a 16mm distributor of public-domain material, this small but savvy company offers a wide range of classics, foreign films, B Westerns, TV shows, and animation from its own source material. Free catalog.

Video Yesteryear
Box C
Sandy Hook, CT 06482
800-243-0987
203-426-2574
Offers more than 1,100 titles in the public domain, ranging from silent short subjects and features to television kinescopes. All tapes come from the company's own source material, which varies widely in terms of print quality. Many rare and obscure films in this collection.

Whole Toon Catalog
P.O. Box 369
Issaquah, WA 98027
206-391-8747
This is the best place for animation fans to do their one-stop shopping. Offers literally hundreds of animated programs, both classic and contemporary, with lively and informed descriptions of their content. Also sells books, posters, and cartoon memorabilia. Sales only.

Key to this Book

Each entry lists title and year of release. The letter "C" before a running time indicates that the film was made in color. "D:" indicates the name of the director. This is followed by a listing of the principal cast members. Alternate titles (if any) are noted at the end of the entry.

Ratings range from ****, for the very best, to *½, for the very worst. There is no * rating; instead, for these bottom-of-the-barrel movies, we use the citation BOMB.

Made-for-TV movies receive no star rating. They are indicated by the abbreviation TVM, and evaluated at the end of each entry as being Above average, Average, or Below average.

Films that are part of continuing series (particularly from the 1930s, 40s, and 50s) receive no ratings or individual writeups. Instead, the reader is referred back to special essay entries on such series as *Andy Hardy, Francis (the Talking Mule)*, and *Tarzan*.

▼ This symbol indicates the title is available on homevideo.

Aaron Loves Angela (1975) **C-98m.** ***
D: Gordon Parks, Jr. Kevin Hooks, Irene
Cara, Moses Gunn, Robert Hooks, Ernestine Jackson, Jose Feliciano. New York–
made variation on Romeo and Juliet set in
Harlem, with black boy (Kevin) in love
with Puerto Rican girl (Cara). OK combination of comedy, drama, violence, and
Feliciano's music.▼

Aaron Slick From Punkin Crick (1952)
C-95m. ** D: Claude Binyon. Alan Young,
Dinah Shore, Adele Jergens, Robert Merrill, Veda Ann Borg. Innocuous musical
satire of city slicker trying to fleece innocent widow Shore. Unmemorable score.

Abandoned (1949) **79m.** *½ D: Joe
Newman. Gale Storm, Dennis O'Keefe,
Raymond Burr, Marjorie Rambeau, Jeff
Chandler. Lukewarm tale of newspaperman
O'Keefe helping Storm find her sister's
illegitimate baby, and becoming involved
with adoption racket.

Abandon Ship! (1957-British) **100m.** ***
D: Richard Sale. Tyrone Power, Mai Zetterling, Lloyd Nolan, Stephen Boyd, Moira
Lister, James Hayter. Tyrone is officer suddenly in command of lifeboat holding survivors from sunken luxury liner. Tense
and exciting study of people fighting to
stay alive while exposed to savage seas
and each other. British title: SEVEN
WAVES AWAY.

Abbott and Costello Go to Mars (1953)
77m. *½ D: Charles Lamont. Robert
Paige, Mari Blanchard, Martha Hyer, Horace McMahon. Unimaginative vehicle has
Bud and Lou sailing through space with
escaped gangster, landing on Venus—despite
the film's title. Look quickly for Anita
Ekberg.

Abbott and Costello in Hollywood (1945)
83m. ** D: S. Sylvan Simon. Frances
Rafferty, Robert Stanton, Jean Porter,
Warner Anderson, Dean Stockwell. Uneven comedy with A&C as barber and
porter in Tinseltown. A few peeks behind
the scenes at MGM. Rags Ragland, Lucille Ball, Preston Foster, Butch Jenkins,
and director Robert Z. Leonard appear as
themselves. Officially titled BUD ABBOTT
AND LOU COSTELLO IN HOLLYWOOD.▼

Abbott and Costello in the Foreign Legion (1950) **80m.** ** D: Charles Lamont.
Patricia Medina, Walter Slezak, Douglass

Dumbrille. Unexceptional A&C vehicle
pitting them against nasty sergeant Slezak.
Best scene involves mirages in the desert.

Abbott and Costello in the Navy SEE:
In the Navy

Abbott and Costello Meet Captain Kidd
(1952) **C-70m.** ** D: Charles Lamont.
Charles Laughton, Hillary Brooke, Fran
Warren, Bill Shirley, Leif Erickson. Middling pirate spoof with too many lousy songs,
worth catching to see Laughton having the
time of his life in atypical low comedy.▼

**Abbott and Costello Meet Dr. Jekyll
and Mr. Hyde** (1953) **77m.** ** D: Charles
Lamont. Boris Karloff, Craig Stevens, Reginald Denny, Helen Westcott, John Dierkes.
Disappointing attempt to mix A&C with
Jekyll (Karloff) and Hyde (stuntman Eddie
Parker), with too few funny scenes. Special effects are film's main asset.▼

Abbott and Costello Meet Frankenstein
(1948) **83m.** ***½ D: Charles Barton.
Lon Chaney, Bela Lugosi, Lenore Aubert,
Jane Randolph, Glenn Strange, Frank Ferguson. Dracula (Lugosi) plans to put Lou's
brain in the Frankenstein Monster; werewolf Larry Talbot (Chaney) has his paws
full trying to convince the boys they're in
danger. All-time great horror-comedy still
works beautifully, mainly because the monsters play it straight. And, yes, that *is*
Vincent Price's voice at the end.▼

**Abbott and Costello Meet the Invisible
Man** (1951) **82m.** *** D: Charles Lamont.
Nancy Guild, Arthur Franz, Adele Jergens,
Sheldon Leonard. One of the team's best
vehicles, with Bud and Lou as detectives
helping boxer (Franz) who's been framed to
trap mobster Leonard, with aid of invisibility formula. Special effects are top-notch.

**Abbott and Costello Meet the Keystone
Kops** (1955) **79m.** ** D: Charles Lamont.
Fred Clark, Lynn Bari, Mack Sennett,
Maxie Rosenbloom, Frank Wilcox, Henry
Kulky, Sam Flint. Low-budget comedy
could have been better. Clark is fine as
conniving producer in this synthetic period-
piece of silent-movie days.

**Abbott and Costello Meet the Killer,
Boris Karloff** (1949) **84m.** **½ D: Charles
Barton. Lenore Aubert, Gar Moore, Donna
Martell, Alan Mowbray, James Flavin.
Pleasant blend of comedy and whodunit with
bodies hanging in closets and phony mystic
Karloff trying to do away with Costello.▼

Abbott and Costello Meet the Mummy (1955) 79m. **½ D: Charles Lamont. Marie Windsor, Michael Ansara, Dan Seymour, Kurt Katch, Richard Deacon. Amusing adventure with A&C getting mixed up with villainess Windsor, a valuable tomb, and a mummy who's still alive.

Abby (1974) C-92m. **½ D: William Girdler. Carol Speed, William Marshall, Terry Carter, Austin Stoker, Juanita Moore. Not-bad black variation on THE EXORCIST. Speed, wife of minister Carter and daughter-in-law of minister Marshall, is the possessed Abby.

ABC Murders, The SEE: **Alphabet Murders, The**

Abdication, The (1974-British) C-103m. ** D: Anthony Harvey. Peter Finch, Liv Ullmann, Cyril Cusack, Paul Rogers, Michael Dunn. Plodding historical drama of what happened to Sweden's Queen Christina when she abdicated to convert to Catholicism. Finch is the cardinal who must test her sincerity and with whom she falls in love.

Abduction (1975) C-100m. *½ D: Joseph Zito. Gregory Rozakis, Judith-Marie Bergan, David Pendleton, Leif Erickson, Dorothy Malone, Lawrence Tierney. Wealthy California coed is kidnapped by a group of leftists. Could be retitled "The Patty Hearst Story," though based on a novel (Harrison James's *Black Abductors*) written before the Hearst kidnapping.▼

Abduction of Kari Swenson, The (1987) C-100m. TVM D: Stephen R. Gyllenhall. Joe Don Baker, M. Emmet Walsh, Ronny Cox, Michael Bowen, Geoffrey Blake, Dorothy Fielding, Tracy Pollan. Moderately interesting drama about real-life biathlon champion Kari Swenson's abduction by mountain men in 1984 while training alone in the Montana wilderness. Average.▼

Abduction of Saint Anne, The (1975) C-78m. TVM D: Harry Falk. Robert Wagner, E. G. Marshall, Kathleen Quinlan, Lloyd Nolan, William Windom, Martha Scott, James Gregory. Cynical detective (Wagner) and Vatican bishop (Marshall) check reports that a mobster's daughter has miraculous powers and, if so, should be kidnapped by the church. Intriguing combination of religious drama and detective story, compromised by pedestrian telling. Also called THEY'VE KIDNAPPED ANNE BENEDICT. Average.▼

Abductors, The (1957) 80m. *½ D: Andrew McLaglen. Victor McLaglen, George Macready, Fay Spain, Gavin Muir. Boring account of men attempting to rob Lincoln's grave.

Abe Lincoln in Illinois (1940) 110m. **** D: John Cromwell. Raymond Massey, Gene Lockhart, Ruth Gordon, Mary Howard, Dorothy Tree, Minor Watson, Alan Baxter, Howard da Silva. First-rate Americana; sincere story of Lincoln's life and career is beautifully acted by Massey, with top support from Gordon as Mary Todd. Based on Robert Sherwood's Pulitzer Prize-winning play.▼

Abe Lincoln of Ninth Avenue, The SEE: **Streets of New York**▼

Abie's Irish Rose (1946) 96m. BOMB D: A. Edward Sutherland. Joanne Dru, Richard Norris, Michael Chekhov, Eric Blore, Art Baker. Outdated when written in 1920s and even worse now. Irish girl marries Jewish boy and families clash.

Abilene Town (1946) 89m. *** D: Edwin L. Marin. Randolph Scott, Ann Dvorak, Edgar Buchanan, Rhonda Fleming, Lloyd Bridges. Above-average Scott vehicle as patient sheriff tries to straighten out homesteader conflict out West after the Civil War. Also shown in computer-colored version.▼

Abominable Dr. Phibes, The (1971-British) C-94m. *** D: Robert Fuest. Vincent Price, Joseph Cotten, Hugh Griffith, Terry-Thomas, Virginia North. Above-average camp horror film in which Price, disfigured in a car wreck, seeks revenge on those he believes responsible for the death of his wife. Sequel: DR. PHIBES RISES AGAIN.▼

Abominable Snowman SEE: **Abominable Snowman of the Himalayas, The**

Abominable Snowman of the Himalayas, The (1957-British) 85m. **½ D: Val Guest. Forrest Tucker, Peter Cushing, Richard Wattis, Maureen Connell, Robert Brown. Intelligent tale of good man (Cushing) and corrupt man (Tucker) seeking the elusive title creature, with surprising results. Also known as ABOMINABLE SNOWMAN.

About Face (1952) C-94m. *½ D: Roy Del Ruth. Gordon MacRae, Eddie Bracken, Dick Wesson, Phyllis Kirk, Joel Grey. Dull comedy-musical remake of BROTHER RAT, about three friends in military academy, one of them secretly married. Grey's film debut.

About Last Night . . . (1986) C-113m. ** D: Edward Zwick. Rob Lowe, Demi Moore, James Belushi, Elizabeth Perkins, George DiCenzo, Michael Alldredge, Robin Thomas. True-to-life look at problems faced by a young couple fleeing the singles scene, biggest problem being his inability to make genuine emotional commitment to her. True-to-life doesn't make it terribly *interesting*, however. Expanded (and diluted) from David Mamet's one-act play *Sexual Perversity in Chicago*. Coscenarist Tim Kazurinsky appears briefly.▼

About Mrs. Leslie (1954) 104m. *** D: Daniel Mann. Shirley Booth, Robert Ryan, Marjie Millar, Alex Nicol. Flashbacks reveal romance between rooming-house owner (Booth) and business magnate (Ryan). Finely acted soaper; forgivable illogical coupling of stars.

Above and Beyond (1952) 122m. *** D: Melvin Frank, Norman Panama. Robert

Taylor, Eleanor Parker, James Whitmore, Jim Backus. Meaningful account of U.S. pilot who flew over Hiroshima with first atomic bomb; film focuses on his training and its effect on his personal life.

Above Suspicion (1943) **90m.** *** D: Richard Thorpe. Joan Crawford, Fred MacMurray, Conrad Veidt, Basil Rathbone, Reginald Owen, Richard Ainley. Crawford and MacMurray asked to do spy mission during European honeymoon on the eve of WW2. Pure escapism, with Joan more than a match for the Nazis.

Above the Law (1988) **C-99m.** ** D: Andrew Davis. Steven Seagal, Pam Grier, Sharon Stone, Henry Silva, Ron Dean, Daniel Faraldo, Thalmus Rasulala. Violence is the star of this slick but stupid actioner that attempts to make a pin-up boy/ superhero of real-life Aikido master Seagal, in his film debut (he also cowrote and coproduced). He's cast as a tough Chicago cop who's quick to employ his martial arts skills as he battles police corruption and drug dealing. His thesping makes Chuck Norris seem like Laurence Olivier.▼

Above Us the Waves (1956-British) **92m.** ††† D: Ralph Thomas. John Mills, John Gregson, Donald Sinden, James Robertson Justice. Utilizing documentary style, film relates account of unrelenting British attempt to destroy Nazi warship. Fine cast in exciting submarine drama.

Abraham Lincoln (1930) **97m.** **½ D: D. W. Griffith. Walter Huston, Una Merkel, Edgar Dearing, Russell Simpson, Cameron Prud'homme, Oscar Apfel, Henry B. Walthall. Huston is excellent in this sincere but static biography of Lincoln; can't match Griffith's silent masterpieces.▼

Abroad With Two Yanks (1944) **80m.** **½ D: Allan Dwan. William Bendix, Helen Walker, Dennis O'Keefe, John Loder, John Abbott. Bendix and O'Keefe are marines on the loose in Australia, both chasing Walker; breezy comedy.▼

Absence of Malice (1981) **C-116m.** *** D: Sydney Pollack. Paul Newman, Sally Field, Bob Balaban, Melinda Dillon, Luther Adler, Barry Primus, Josef Sommer, John Harkins, Don Hood, Wilford Brimley. A reporter (Field) is duped by a scheming government investigator into printing a story that discredits innocent Newman; while she hides behind the privilege of the press, he determines to get even. Absorbing drama by former reporter Kurt Luedtke with two charismatic star performances. Filmed in Miami.▼

Absent Minded Professor, The (1961) **97m.** *** D: Robert Stevenson. Fred MacMurray, Nancy Olson, Keenan Wynn, Tommy Kirk, Ed Wynn, Leon Ames, Elliott Reid. MacMurray discovers flubber (flying rubber) in this Disney audience-pleaser, but no one will believe him except Keenan Wynn, who tries to steal the substance. Broad comedy and bright special effects make this a lot of fun. Also shown in computer-colored version. Sequel: SON OF FLUBBER.▼

Absinthe SEE: **Madame X** (1929)

Absolute Beginners (1986-British) **C-107m.** **½ D: Julien Temple. Eddie O'Connell, Patsy Kensit, David Bowie, James Fox, Ray Davies, Ege Ferret, Anita Morris, Lionel Blair, Steven Berkoff, Mandy Rice-Davies, Sade Adu. Energetic, original musical set in London, 1958, when teenagers first came into their own. Highly stylized film (directed by music-video veteran Temple) suffers from two-dimensional characters and a misguided attempt to add substance by dealing with the rise of racism in England . . . but its virtues *almost* outweigh its shortcomings. Pulsating score supervised by jazz great Gil Evans; musical highlights from Sade ("Killer Blow") and jazz veteran Slim Gaillard ("Selling Out"). And don't miss that incredible opening shot! Adapted from Colin MacInnes' 1959 novel.▼

Absolution (1981-British) **C-105m.** **½ D: Anthony Page. Richard Burton, Dominic Guard, Dai Bradley, Billy Connolly, Andrew Keir, Willoughby Gray. Burton gives a commanding performance as a humorless, by-the-book priest who teaches at a boys' school, and falls victim to a snowballing practical joke played upon him by his pet student. Straightforward melodrama loses credibility toward the end. Written by Anthony Shaffer. Filmed in 1978, and unreleased in the U.S. until 1988, four years after Burton's death.▼

Abyss, The (1989) **C-140m.** *** D: James Cameron. Ed Harris, Mary Elizabeth Mastrantonio, Michael Biehn, Leo Burmester, Todd Graff, John Bedford Lloyd, J.C. Quinn, Kimberly Scott, Jimmie Ray Weeks, Chris Elliott. Spectacular underwater saga about an oil-rig crew that gets involved in a perilous mission to rescue a sunken nuclear sub. Better as futuristic adventure than as fantasy, with a couple of crises too many, but still a fascinating, one-of-a-kind experience. Great score by Alan Silvestri; Oscar winner for Visual Effects.▼

Acapulco Gold (1978) **C-105m.** ** D: Burt Brinckerhoff. Marjoe Gortner, Robert Lansing, Ed Nelson, John Harkins, Randi Oakes. Unexceptional drug-smuggling tale benefits from attractive location shooting on Hawaiian island of Kauai.

Accatone (1961-Italian) **116m.** *** D: Pier Paolo Pasolini. Franco Citti, Franca Pasut, Roberto Scaringella, Adele Cambria, Paolo Guidi, Silvana Corsini. Pasolini's first film is a vivid, unsentimental look at the desperate (and depressing) existence of pimps and petty thieves living in the slums of Rome. Bernardo Bertolucci was one of the assistant directors.▼

Accent on Youth (1935) **77m.** **½ D: Wesley Ruggles. Sylvia Sidney, Herbert Marshall, Phillip Reed, Holmes Herbert, Catharine Doucet, Astrid Allwyn. Trim comedy from Samson Raphaelson's play about middle-aged playwright pursued by his young secretary. A bit talky by modern standards, but quite watchable. Remade as MR. MUSIC and BUT NOT FOR ME.

Acceptable Risks (1986) **C-100m.** TVM D: Rick Wallace. Brian Dennehy, Kenneth McMillan, Christine Ebersole, Beah Richards, Richard Gilliland, Cicely Tyson. Surface-skimming drama about a domestic chemical plant disaster, reportedly written (by Norman Strum) before the actual 1984 incident in Bhopal, India. Average.

Accident (1967-British) **C-105m.** ***½ D: Joseph Losey. Dirk Bogarde, Stanley Baker, Jacqueline Sassard, Delphine Seyrig, Alexander Knox, Michael York, Vivien Merchant, Harold Pinter. Complex, thought-provoking script by Harold Pinter uses story (about Oxford professor who falls in love with a student) as just a foundation for examination of characters' thoughts and actions. A challenging film that operates on many levels; entire cast superb, including York in his first major film role.▼

Accidental Death (1963-British) **57m.** **½ D: Geoffrey Nethercott. John Carson, Jacqueline Ellis, Derrick Sherwin, Richard Vernon. Edgar Wallace suspenser with gimmick of letting the viewer guess the identity of the murderer in question.

Accidental Tourist, The (1988) **C-121m.** *** D: Lawrence Kasdan. William Hurt, Kathleen Turner, Geena Davis, Amy Wright, Bill Pullman, Robert Gorman, David Ogden Stiers, Ed Begley, Jr. Hurt gives an exquisite performance as a man shattered by the death of his son who only comes out of his shell when he meets a kooky, aggressive young woman (Oscar winner Davis) who couldn't be less his type. Finely wrought, extremely faithful adaptation of Anne Tyler's novel dares to take its time; may be too slow and quiet for some viewers but offers many rewards to those who can savor its qualities.▼

Accidents Will Happen (1939) **62m.** **½ D: William Clemens. Ronald Reagan, Gloria Blondell, Sheila Bromley, Dick Purcell, Addison Richards. Good little "B" picture about a young go-getting insurance claims adjuster who tries to blow the whistle on a phony-accident racket.

Accomplices, The (1959-Italian) **93m.** *½ D: Gianni Vernuccio. Sandro Luporini, Sandro Fizzotro, Annabella Incontrera, Jeannie. Lurid, minor film of love triangle, with resulting murder; unconvincing and pat.

Accursed, The (1958-British) **78m.** *½ D: Michael McCarthy. Donald Wolfit, Robert Bray, Jane Griffiths, Anton Diffring, Christopher Lee. Tepid whodunit involving the extinction of veterans of British military unit, and survivors' attempt to find killer.

Accused SEE: **Mark of the Hawk**

Accused, The (1948) **101m.** *** D: William Dieterle. Loretta Young, Robert Cummings, Wendell Corey, Sam Jaffe, Douglas Dick. Loretta accidentally becomes a murderess in this taut thriller of a woman on the run; good support from Cummings.▼

Accused, The (1988) **C-110m.** *** D: Jonathan Kaplan. Kelly McGillis, Jodie Foster, Bernie Coulson, Leo Rossi, Ann Hearn, Carmen Argenziano, Steve Antin, Tom O'Brien, Peter Van Norden. Public prosecutor McGillis deals with a gang-rape case in cut-and-dried fashion, until the victim demands full retribution for what she has suffered. Compelling drama inspired by a notorious real-life case and propelled by Foster's powerhouse, Oscar-winning performance as the provocative, foul-mouthed woman who gets her day in court. Only quibble: Was the climactic reenactment really necessary?▼

Accused of Murder (1956) **C-74m.** ** D: Joseph Kane. David Brian, Vera Ralston, Sidney Blackmer, Virginia Grey. Bland handling of police detective Brian, entranced with singer Ralston, involved in underworld killing.

Ace, The SEE: **Great Santini, The**▼

Ace Eli and Rodger of the Skies (1973) **C-92m.** ** D: Bill Sampson (John Erman). Cliff Robertson, Pamela Franklin, Eric Shea, Rosemary Murphy, Bernadette Peters, Alice Ghostley. Tepid tale of 1920s stunt flyer and son who tags along. Muddled film sat on studio shelf a long time; redoctoring didn't help. Story by Steven Spielberg. Peters' film debut.

Ace High (1969-Italian) **C-123m.** ** D: Giuseppe Colizzi. Eli Wallach, Terence Hill, Bud Spencer, Brock Peters, Kevin McCarthy, Steffen Zacharias. Awkwardly dubbed spaghetti Western tries to imitate Clint Eastwood-Sergio Leone epics, but director Colizzi lacks Leone's style. Hill plays a character named Cat Stevens, but there are no rock songs here.▼

Ace in the Hole SEE: **Big Carnival, The**

Ace of Aces (1933) **76m.** ** D: J. Walter Ruben. Richard Dix, Elizabeth Allan, Ralph Bellamy, Theodore Newton, Frank Conroy, William Cagney. Sculptor Dix has no use for flagwaving as America enters WW1; after being admonished by girlfriend Allan, he becomes a fighter pilot . . . and undergoes quite a personality change. Sincere in its anti-war point of view, but far too melodramatic. Coscripted by John Monk Saunders.▼

Aces High (1977-British) **C-104m.** *** D: Jack Gold. Malcolm McDowell, Christopher Plummer, Simon Ward, Peter Firth. Strong antiwar statement focusing on in-

[4]

doctrination of WW1 pilot Firth and his disillusioned squadron leader (McDowell). Solid British cast (with cameos by John Gielgud, Ray Milland, Trevor Howard, and Richard Johnson) and exciting aerial dogfight sequences highlight this remake of R. C. Sherriff's JOURNEY'S END.

Acorn People, The (1981) **C-100m. TVM** D: Joan Tewkesbury. Ted Bessell, LeVar Burton, Cloris Leachman, Dolph Sweet, Cheryl Anderson, Shawn Timothy Kennedy. Sensitive drama about the relationship between a camp counselor and a group of severely disabled children. Tewkesbury wrote the teleplay from Ron Jones's book, the title of which refers to the handmade acorn necklaces worn by the children, who affectionately refer to themselves as nuts. Above average.

Across 110th Street (1972) **C-102m.** ******* D: Barry Shear. Anthony Quinn, Yaphet Kotto, Anthony Franciosa, Richard Ward, Paul Benjamin, Ed Bernard, Antonio Fargas, Norma Donaldson, Gilbert Lewis. N.Y.C. police race the mobs to catch three blacks who, disguised as cops, stole $300,000 from a Mafia-controlled bank; mutual distrust of both black and Italian hoods is mirrored by differences between cops Quinn and Kotto. Exciting, well-paced, and extremely violent, with fine use of Harlem locations. Quinn was also co-executive producer.▼

Across the Bridge (1957-British) **103m.** ****½** D: Ken Annakin. Rod Steiger, David Knight, Bernard Lee, Eric Pohlmann. Agreeable study of panicky businessman Steiger on the run from authorities for stealing a fortune; taut performances.

Across the Great Divide (1977) **C-100m.** ****½** D: Stewart Raffill. Robert Logan, Heather Rattray, Mark Edward Hall, George "Buck" Flower. Innocuous tale of conman Logan and reluctant orphans Rattray and Hall, intent on traveling across the west to Oregon. Lots of horses, bears, deer, pretty scenery. From the makers of the WILDERNESS FAMILY films.▼

Across the Pacific (1942) **97m.** ****½** D: John Huston. Humphrey Bogart, Mary Astor, Sydney Greenstreet, Victor Sen Yung, Keye Luke, Richard Loo. Three MALTESE FALCON leads reteamed for enjoyable WW2 adventure. Bogart trails spies in Panama, has running battle of wits with Greenstreet, all the while romancing enticing Astor. Also shown in computer-colored version.

Across the Wide Missouri (1951) **C-78m.** ****½** D: William Wellman. Clark Gable, Ricardo Montalban, John Hodiak, Adolphe Menjou. Location filming helps pedestrian Western about pathfinders moving westward in 19th century.

Action for Slander (1938-British) **83m.** ****½** D: Tim Whelan. Clive Brook, Ann Todd, Margaretta Scott, Arthur Margetson, Ronald Squire, Athole Stewart, Percy Marmont, Francis L. Sullivan, Felix Aylmer, Googie Withers. Adequate drama about suave, stiff-upper-lip cavalry officer Brook, who feels his life is ruined when he's falsely accused of cheating at cards. Of interest mostly as an observation of the British class system and for Sullivan's forceful presence as Brook's lawyer.▼

Action in Arabia (1944) **72m.** ****½** D: Leonide Moguy. George Sanders, Virginia Bruce, Gene Lockhart, Robert Armstrong, Michael Ansara. OK low-budgeter, with reporter Sanders uncovering Nazi plot to gain Arab support in WW2.▼

Action in the North Atlantic (1943) **127m.** ******* D: Lloyd Bacon. Humphrey Bogart, Raymond Massey, Alan Hale, Julie Bishop, Ruth Gordon, Sam Levene, Dane Clark. Rousing tribute to WW2 merchant marine, with officers Bogart and Massey, seamen Hale and Levene, usual hothead Clark, and Gordon as Massey's wife. Also shown in computer-colored version.

Action Jackson (1988) **C-95m.** ****** D: Craig R. Baxley. Carl Weathers, Craig T. Nelson, Vanity, Sharon Stone, Thomas F. Wilson, Bill Duke, Robert Davi, Jack Thibeau. Strictly standard B movie fare pitting good guy Weathers (a cop) vs. bad guy Nelson. Plenty of explosions, car chases, corpses and noise.▼

Action of the Tiger (1957-British) **C-94m.** ****½** D: Terence Young. Van Johnson, Martine Carol, Herbert Lom, Anna Gerber, Sean Connery. Action packed, cliched adventure story with Johnson the virile American rescuing pro-Western refugees from Albania.

Act of Love (1953) **108m.** ******* D: Anatole Litvak. Kirk Douglas, Dany Robin, Barbara Laage, Robert Strauss. Sharply portrayed story of U.S. soldier (Douglas) romancing girl (Robin) in WW2 Paris, eventually deserting her, despite good intentions.

Act of Love (1980) **C-100m. TVM** D: Jud Taylor. Ron Howard, Robert Foxworth, Mickey Rourke, Jacqueline Brookes, Sondra West, David Spielberg, Gail Youngs, Mary Kay Place. Howard gives a sensitive portrayal of a man on trial for the mercy-killing of his paralyzed brother. Written by Michael De Guzman from the factual book by Paige Mitchell. Average.

Act of Murder, An (1948) **91m.** ******* D: Michael Gordon. Fredric March, Florence Eldridge, Edmond O'Brien, Geraldine Brooks. March is excellent as strict judge who must judge himself for saving his wife the anguish of illness by killing her; absorbing drama.

Act of Passion SEE: **Lost Honor of Kathryn Beck, The**▼

Act of the Heart (1970-Canadian) **C-103m.** ******* D: Paul Almond. Genevieve Bujold,

Donald Sutherland, Bill Mitchell, Monique Leyrac. Fascinating study of religious fanaticism manifesting itself in one young woman and her love for a Catholic priest. Beautifully atmospheric but ending deeply hurts film.

Act of Vengeance (1974) SEE: **Rape Squad**▼

Act of Vengeance (1986) **C-96m.** TVM D: John Mackenzie. Charles Bronson, Ellen Burstyn, Wilford Brimley, Hoyt Axton, Robert Schenkkan, Ellen Barkin. Bronson, sans mustache, in a rare television performance, is Jock Yablonski, the United Mine Workers official whose challenge to incumbent president Tony Boyle (Brimley) led to his and his family's murder. Passionless based-on-fact drama scripted by Scott Spencer. Made for cable. Average▼

Act of Violence (1949) **82m.** ******* D: Fred Zinnemann. Van Heflin, Robert Ryan, Janet Leigh, Mary Astor, Phyllis Thaxter, Berry Kroeger, Taylor Holmes. Stark, well-acted drama, with crippled, embittered Ryan stalking former senior officer Heflin, who betrayed his men while a POW. Fine vignette by Astor as a sympathetic call girl.

Act of Violence (1979) **C-100m.** TVM D: Paul Wendkos. Elizabeth Montgomery, James Sloyan, Sean Frye, Roy Poole, Biff McGuire, Linden Chiles. Plucky Ms. M in another of her traditional victim roles, showing true grit as a divorced career woman who's gang mugged. Graphic and remarkably arresting. Above average.

Act One (1963) **110m.** ****½** D: Dore Schary. George Hamilton, Jason Robards, George Segal, Eli Wallach, Sam Levene, Ruth Ford, Jack Klugman. Interesting for oddball cast, this fabrication of writer Moss Hart's autobiography lacks finesse or any sense of reality, but Robards is ideally cast as George S. Kaufman.

Actors and Sin (1952) **82m.** ****½** D: Ben Hecht, Lee Garmes. Edward G. Robinson, Eddie Albert, Marsha Hunt, Alan Reed, Dan O'Herlihy, Tracey Roberts, Rudolph Anders, Paul Guilfoyle, Jenny Hecht, John Crawford. Uneven two-part film: the overly melodramatic "Actor's Blood" concerns has-been thespian Robinson and his hardhearted (and murdered) Broadway star daughter Hunt; the more successful "Woman of Sin" details the plight of agent Albert, whose newest client is a 9-year-old (Hecht, Ben's daughter), who's penned a lascivious book.▼

Actor's Revenge, An (1963-Japanese) **C-114m.** ****½** D: Kon Ichikawa. Kazuo Hasegawa, Ayako Wakao, Fujiko Yamamoto, Ganjiro Nakamura, Raizo Ichikawa. Confusing tale of Kabuki actor Hasagawa getting back at a lord (Nakamura) responsible for the demise of his parents. Un-

evenly directed. Also known as THE REVENGE OF UKENO-JO.

Actress, The (1953) **91m.** ****½** D: George Cukor. Spencer Tracy, Jean Simmons, Teresa Wright, Anthony Perkins, Mary Wickes. Flavorful account based on Ruth Gordon's experiences as a teen-ager in early 20th-century Massachusetts, determined to become an acting star; Tracy is the irascible father. Perkins' film debut.

Ada (1961) **C-109m.** ******* D: Daniel Mann. Susan Hayward, Dean Martin, Wilfrid Hyde-White, Martin Balsam. Rags-to-riches soaper of poor Hayward maneuvering easygoing Martin to governor's mansion, using hellbent stamina to overcome political corruption. Hayward vs. Hyde-White in state senate is film's highlight.

Adalen 31 (1969-Swedish) **C-115m.** ******* D: Bo Widerberg. Peter Schildt, Kerstin Tidelius, Roland Hedlund, Stefan Feierbach. Strikers in a Swedish paper mill disagree over whether or not to make their case with violence; matters are further complicated when a striker's son falls in love with—and impregnates—the factory manager's daughter. Generally appealing mix of romance and history, though no one will ever mistake Widerberg (the director of ELVIRA MADIGAN) for a gritty filmmaker of social realism.

Adam (1983) **C-100m.** TVM D: Michael Tuchner. Daniel J. Travanti, JoBeth Williams, Martha Scott, Richard Masur, Paul Regina, Mason Adams. Compelling drama of true-life couple who, after the kidnap and murder of their child, lobby Congress to permit parents to use the FBI's national crime computer to help locate missing children. Script by Allan Leicht. Followed by sequel ADAM: HIS SONG CONTINUES. Above average.▼

Adam and Evalyn (1949-British) **92m.** ****½** D: Harold French. Jean Simmons, Stewart Granger, Wilfrid Hyde-White, Helen Cherry, Raymond Young. Pleasant but ordinary tale of gambler Granger and the daughter he adopts when a friend dies. British title: ADAM AND EVELYNE.

Adam and Evelyne SEE: **Adam and Evalyn**

Adam at 6 A.M. (1970) **C-100m.** ******* D: Robert Scheerer. Michael Douglas, Lee Purcell, Joe Don Baker, Grayson Hall, Charles Aidman, Meg Foster. Underrated film about young college professor from California who spends summer in Missouri working as a laborer. Authentic location footage and good performances by Purcell and Baker give rare, genuine feeling for the Midwest.▼

Adam Had Four Sons (1941) **81m.** ****½** D: Gregory Ratoff. Ingrid Bergman, Warner Baxter, Susan Hayward, Fay Wray, Richard Denning, Johnny Downs, June Lockhart. Handsome but predictable family saga about French governess Bergman watching

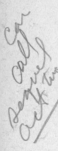

[6]

over Baxter's household after his wife's death. Bergman gives warm performance, and Hayward plays bad girl to the hilt.▼

Adam: His Song Continues (1986) C-100m. TVM D: Robert Markowitz. Daniel J. Travanti, JoBeth Williams, Richard Masur, Martha Scott, Raul Regina, Belinda Montgomery, Bob Gunton. Slightly less powerful (and actually rather dour) sequel to ADAM, with John and Reve Walsh (Travanti and Williams) continuing their efforts to create a national awareness of missing children. A roll call of missing youngsters followed this film in its premiere, similar to the (different) list at the conclusion of the original movie, which "found" literally dozens of the missing. Average.

Adam's Rib (1949) 100m. **** D: George Cukor. Spencer Tracy, Katharine Hepburn, Judy Holliday, Tom Ewell, David Wayne, Jean Hagen, Hope Emerson, Polly Moran, Marvin Kaplan, Paula Raymond, Tommy Noonan. Smart, sophisticated comedy (by Ruth Gordon and Garson Kanin) about husband and wife lawyers on opposing sides of the same murder case. One of Hollywood's greatest comedies about the battle of the sexes, with peerless Tracy and Hepburn supported by movie newcomers Holliday, Ewell, Hagen, and Wayne. Cole Porter contributed the song "Farewell, Amanda." Remade in Bulgaria in 1956 (in this version the heroine rebels against tradition as a result of her conversion to Marxism-Leninism!). Later a TV series. Also shown in computer-colored version.▼

Adam's Woman (1970-U.S.-Australian) C-116m. **½ D: Philip Leacock. Beau Bridges, John Mills, Jane Merrow, James Booth, Andrew Keir, Tracy Reed. Interesting if not altogether successful story of innocent Bridges suffering in 19th-century Australian penal colony. Although put on probation, he's still determined to escape.

Addict SEE: **Born to Win**▼

Addicted to His Love (1988) C-100m. TVM D: Arthur Allan Seidelman. Barry Bostwick, Polly Bergen, Colleen Camp, Erin Gray, Linda Purl, Dee Wallace Stone, Hector Elizondo, Peggy Lipton, Rosemary Forsyth. Rocky comedy/drama about a charming lothario who manages to juggle affairs with four women simultaneously until they band together to plot his downfall. Original title, SISTERHOOD, was more ironically apt. Average.

Adding Machine, The (1969-U.S.-British) C-100m. **½ D: Jerome Epstein. Milo O'Shea, Phyllis Diller, Billie Whitelaw, Sydney Chaplin, Julian Glover. Accountant becomes desperate upon learning he's to be replaced by a computer. This Elmer Rice comedy-fantasy is flawed but interesting. Diller has unusual straight role as harridan.

Address Unknown (1944) 72m. ** D: William Cameron Menzies. Paul Lukas,

Mady Christians, Morris Carnovsky, Carl Esmond, K.T. Stevens, Peter Van Eyck. Longtime American resident Lukas returns to his native Germany, and is all too easily swept up by Naziism. Offbeat visual style of director Menzies doesn't alleviate hollowness of this heavy-handed parable.

Adele Hasn't Had Her Supper Yet SEE: **Dinner for Adele**

Adios Amigo (1975) C-87m. ** D: Fred Williamson. Fred Williamson, Richard Pryor, Thalmus Rasulala, James Brown, Robert Phillips, Mike Henry. Offbeat Western comedy, written, produced, and directed by Williamson, who plays perennial patsy to con man Pryor. No sex or violence in this innocuous film; too bad it doesn't pull together better.▼

Adios, Sabata (1971-Italian-Spanish) C-104m. *½ D: Frank Kramer (Gianfranco Parolini). Yul Brynner, Dean Reed, Pedro Sanchez (Ignazio Spalla), Gerard Herter. Second Sabata Western finds Brynner subbing for Lee Van Cleef; otherwise, it's business as usual, with the gunslinger becoming involved with Mexican revolutionaries and helping himself to a cache of gold along the way. Sequel: THE RETURN OF SABATA.

Admirable Crichton, The (1957-British) C-94m. ** D: Lewis Gilbert. Kenneth More, Diane Cilento, Cecil Parker, Sally Ann Howes, Martita Hunt. Oft-filmed James Barrie classic wears thin: impeccable servant proves to be most resourceful when he and his aristocratic employers are ship-wrecked on an island. Retitled: PARADISE LAGOON.

Admiral Was a Lady, The (1950) 87m. ** D: Albert Rogell. Edmond O'Brien, Wanda Hendrix, Rudy Vallee, Steve Brodie. Ex-Wave Hendrix encounters quartet of fun-loving, work-hating men, all interested in courting her; weak.▼

Adolescent, The SEE: **L'Adolescente**

Adorable Creatures (1956-French) 108m. ** D: Christian-Jaque. Daniel Gelin, Martine Carol, Edwige Feuillère, Danielle Darrieux, Marilyn Buferd, Louis Seigner. Saucy, inconsequential study of life and love in Gallic country, focusing on bedroom romances.

Adorable Julia (1964-French) 94m. *** D: Alfred Weidenmann. Lilli Palmer, Charles Boyer, Jean Sorel, Thomas Fritsch. Charming rendering of Somerset Maugham's novel *Theatre*. Middle-aged actress dabbles in romances but allows nothing to interfere with career. Palmer and Boyer are admirable as wife-husband acting team.

Adulteress, The (1973) C-85m. BOMB D: Norbert Meisel. Eric Braeden, Greg Morton, Tyne Daly, Lynn Roth. Pro actors stuck in amateurish film that has stud Braeden servicing impotent old Morton's young wife Daly at her husband's request. Embarrassing, especially when the director tries for touches of Ingmar Bergman.▼

Advance to the Rear (1964) 97m. **½ D: George Marshall. Glenn Ford, Stella Stevens, Melvyn Douglas, Joan Blondell, Jim Backus, Andrew Prine. During Civil War, Northern soldier rejects are sent to Western territory. Stevens as Reb spy and Blondell as saucy worldly woman add only spice to predictable slapstick comedy.

Adventure (1945) 125m. ** D: Victor Fleming. Clark Gable, Greer Garson, Joan Blondell, Thomas Mitchell, Tom Tully, John Qualen, Richard Haydn. Gable's back, Garson's got him; they both sink in cumbersome comedy of seagoing roustabout and meek librarian. Not even breezy Blondell can save it.

Adventure for Two SEE: **Demi-Paradise, The**▼

Adventure in Baltimore (1949) 89m. ** D: Richard Wallace. Shirley Temple, John Agar, Robert Young, Josephine Hutchinson. Mild romancer of 1900s with Temple full of new-fangled notions, yet seeking old-fashioned romance.

Adventure in Diamonds (1940) 76m. ** D: George Fitzmaurice. George Brent, Isa Miranda, John Loder, Nigel Bruce. Tepid formula programmer dealing with jewel robberies in Africa.

Adventure in Manhattan (1936) 73m. **½ D: Edward Ludwig. Jean Arthur, Joel McCrea, Reginald Owen, Thomas Mitchell, Herman Bing. Bizarre blend of comedy and melodrama with the stars foiling planned bank robbery. Doesn't always work, but interesting.

Adventure in Washington (1941) 84m. ** D: Alfred E. Green. Herbert Marshall, Virginia Bruce, Gene Reynolds, Samuel S. Hinds, Ralph Morgan. Misleading title for tame account of Senator Marshall and his attempts to reform a delinquent youth who is working as a Senate page boy.

Adventure Island (1947) C-66m. ** D: Peter Stewart. Rory Calhoun, Rhonda Fleming, Paul Kelly, John Abbott. Weak remake of EBB TIDE with innocents marooned on island with self-made ruler, who is a maniac.▼

Adventure of Sherlock Holmes' Smarter Brother, The (1975) C-91m. **½ D: Gene Wilder. Gene Wilder, Madeline Kahn, Marty Feldman, Dom DeLuise, Leo McKern, Roy Kinnear, John LeMesurier. Wilder's first film as writer-director-star is mild spoof of Sherlockian adventures, as Sigerson Holmes becomes involved with music-hall songstress Kahn, a damsel in distress. DeLuise, as hammy opera star, adds film's liveliest moments. Made in England.▼

Adventurers, The (1952) SEE: **Fortune in Diamonds**

Adventurers, The (1970) C-171m. BOMB D: Lewis Gilbert. Bekim Fehmiu, Candice Bergen, Ernest Borgnine, Olivia de Havilland, Leigh Taylor-Young, Thommy Berg-gren, Rossano Brazzi, Jaclyn Smith. Three-hour challenge to the kidneys based on Harold Robbins' best-seller about fictional South American republic that has a new revolution every two minutes. Incredible mess wastes attractive cast.

Adventures at Rugby SEE: **Tom Brown's School Days** (1940)▼

Adventures in Babysitting (1987) C-99m. ** D: Chris Columbus. Elisabeth Shue, Maia Brewton, Keith Coogan, Anthony Rapp, Calvin Levels, Vincent Philip D'Onofrio, Penelope Ann Miller, Albert Collins. Shue, extremely winning in her first lead role, plays a teenager who takes her two babysitting charges into downtown Chicago to help get a friend out of a jam—and winds up in a snowballing series of wild adventures, à la FERRIS BUELLER'S DAY OFF. Young teens might go for it, but it's mediocre at best. Screenwriter Columbus' directing debut.▼

Adventures of a Taxi Driver (1976-British) C-89m. BOMB D: Stanley Long. Barry Evans, Judy Geeson, Adrienne Posta, Diana Dors, Liz Fraser. Tasteless, unfunny comedy about put-upon young cabdriver, his sexual exploits, and his involvement with jewel thieves.▼

Adventures of a Young Man SEE: **Hemingway's Adventures of a Young Man**

Adventures of Baron Munchausen, The (1989) C-126m. *** D: Terry Gilliam. John Neville, Eric Idle, Sarah Polley, Oliver Reed, Charles McKeown, Winston Dennis, Jack Purvis, Valentina Cortese, Jonathan Pryce, Bill Peterson, Peter Jeffrey, Uma Thurman, Alison Steadman, Sting, Robin Williams. The legendary tale spinner returns in a new interpretation of his exploits by director-cowriter Gilliam. Breathtaking special effects go hand in hand with Gilliam's outlandishly funny and far-out ideas; a visual feast that's worth staying with through its occasional lulls. The Baron's exploits were previously filmed in 1943 and (as THE FABULOUS BARON MUNCHAUSEN) in 1961.▼

Adventures of Barry McKenzie, The (1972-Australian) C-114m. **½ D: Bruce Beresford. Barry Crocker, Barry Humphries, Peter Cook, Spike Milligan. Melbournian Crocker, not particularly fond of the British, finds himself displaced in England. Broad, gross comedy, overlong, and a bit much for American audiences. Beresford's first film, from a cartoon strip by Humphries and Nicholas Garland. Sequel: BARRY MCKENZIE HOLDS HIS OWN.

Adventures of Buckaroo Banzai Across the Eighth Dimension, The (1984) C-103m. ** D: W. D. Richter. Peter Weller, John Lithgow, Ellen Barkin, Jeff Goldblum, Christopher Lloyd. Off-the-wall pulp fiction by Earl Mac Rauch about a hero who's a neurosurgeon, physicist, rocket-car driver, rock singer, and government troubleshooter. Should be fun, but it's just incoherent, like coming in at the *second* chapter of a Saturday matinee serial. Still, it has a fervent cult following. Also known as BUCKAROO BANZAI. ▼

Adventures of Bullwhip Griffin, The (1967) **C-110m.** *** D: James Neilson. Roddy McDowall, Suzanne Pleshette, Karl Malden, Harry Guardino, Richard Haydn, Hermione Baddeley, Bryan Russell. Bright Disney spoof of gold-rush sagas, with McDowall as Bostonian butler who learns to fend for himself in the wild and woolly West. Clever comic ideas and visual gimmickry make this fun.▼

Adventures of Captain Fabian (1951) **100m.** *½ D: William Marshall. Errol Flynn, Micheline Presle, Agnes Moorehead, Vincent Price. Soggy sea yarn has Flynn involved with accused murderess.▼

Adventures of Casanova (1948) **83m.** ** D: Roberto Gavaldon. Arturo de Cordova, Lucille Bremer, Turhan Bey, John Sutton. Very ordinary swashbuckler of Casanova de Cordova leading the oppressed people of Sicily against tyrannical rule; this one cries for color.

Adventures of Don Juan (1948) **C-110m.** *** D: Vincent Sherman. Errol Flynn, Viveca Lindfors, Robert Douglas, Alan Hale, Ann Rutherford, Raymond Burr. Handsome tongue-in-cheek swashbuckler has Errol stringing along countless maidens and even enticing the Queen (Lindfors); Oscar winner for Best Costumes.▼

Adventures of Ford Fairlane, The (1990) **C-96m.** *½ D: Renny Harlin. Andrew Dice Clay, Wayne Newton, Priscilla Presley, Morris Day, Lauren Holly, Maddie Corman, Gilbert Gottfried, David Patrick Kelly, Brandon Call, Robert Englund, Ed O'Neill, Tone Loc, Sheila E. Controversial standup comic Clay's first starring movie vehicle is an old-time private-eye yarn transplanted to the contemporary world of rock 'n' roll. Clay's got what it takes, but the film is clumsy, crude, and immature (just like his detective character). For rabid Clay fans only.

Adventures of Gallant Bess (1948) **C-73m.** ** D: Lew Landers. Cameron Mitchell, Audrey Long, Fuzzy Knight, James Millican. Mitchell is torn between his girl and his horse in this colorful but routine equestrian drama.▼

Adventures of Gerard, The (1970-British-Italian-Swiss) **C-91m.** BOMB D: Jerzy Skolimowski. Peter McEnery, Claudia Cardinale, Eli Wallach, Jack Hawkins, John Neville. Clumsy farce from Arthur Conan Doyle story about cocky but stupid officer who becomes fall guy for Napoleon's (Wallach) wartime strategy.

Adventures of Hajji Baba, The (1954) **C-94m.** **½ D: Don Weis. John Derek, Elaine Stewart, Thomas Gomez, Amanda Blake. Derek adds spark to OK desert tale of his romancing sheik's daughter, who's out to marry heir of rival kingdom.

Adventures of Hercules, The SEE: **Hercules II**▼

Adventures of Huckleberry Finn, The (1960) **C-107m.** *** D: Michael Curtiz. Tony Randall, Eddie Hodges, Archie Moore, Patty McCormack, Neville Brand. Good version of Twain's story with an appealing Hodges (Huck) and excellent Archie Moore (Jim). Assorted characters played by veterans Buster Keaton, Andy Devine, Judy Canova, John Carradine, Mickey Shaughnessy, and Sterling Holloway.

Adventures of Huckleberry Finn, The (1981) **C-100m.** TVM D: Jack B. Hively. Kurt Ida, Dan Monahan, Brock Peters, Forrest Tucker, Larry Storch, Lurene Tuttle, Mike Mazurki, Jack Kruschen. Huck and Tom again embark on their river escapade with runaway slave Jim in this "Classics Illustrated" interpretation. Average.▼

Adventures of Huckleberry Finn (1985) **C-105m.** *** D: Peter H. Hunt. Patrick Day, Jim Dale, Frederic Forrest, Lillian Gish, Barnard Hughes, Richard Kiley, Geraldine Page, Sada Thompson, Samm-Art Williams, Butterfly McQueen. Literate, enjoyable version of the Twain classic, with Day a smart, energetic Huck. Centers mostly on his relationship with Jim, the runaway slave (Williams); as richly rewarding for adults as for kids. Edited down from 240m. version, broadcast on PBS's *American Playhouse.*▼

Adventures of Ichabod and Mr. Toad, The (1949) **C-68m.** *** D: Jack Kinney, Clyde Geronimi, James Algar. Very entertaining animated doubleheader from Disney: a witty adaptation of Kenneth Grahame's *The Wind in the Willows,* about the puckish residents of Toad Hall, narrated by Basil Rathbone; and a broad, cartoony version of Washington Irving's *The Legend of Sleepy Hollow,* with a genuinely scary climax, narrated (and sung) by Bing Crosby. The two featurettes are released separately on homevideo. ▼

Adventures of Jack London, The SEE: **Jack London**▼

Adventures of Marco Polo, The (1938) **100m.** **½ D: Archie Mayo. Gary Cooper, Sigrid Gurie, Basil Rathbone, George Barbier, Binnie Barnes, Ernest Truex, Alan Hale. Lighthearted approach to famed explorer's life doesn't always work, but Cooper is pleasant and Rathbone's a good villain; sumptuous production. Look for Lana Turner as one of the handmaidens.

Adventures of Mark Twain, The (1944) **130m.** *** D: Irving Rapper. Fredric March, Alexis Smith, Donald Crisp, Alan Hale, C. Aubrey Smith, John Carradine, Percy Kilbride. This Hollywoodized story of Samuel Clemens's colorful life may not be great biography, but it's consistently entertaining—despite a penchant for biopic clichés.

Adventures of Mark Twain, The (1985) **C-90m.** ** D: Will Vinton. Voices of James Whitmore, Chris Ritchie, Gary Krug, Michele Mariana. Tom Sawyer, Huck Finn, and Becky Thatcher stow away on Mark Twain's amazing flying machine, heading for Halley's Comet in this clay-figure animated feature. Strangely disjointed, ineffectual feature incorporating pieces of Twain stories with an interesting (but unsettling) look at the darker side of the storyteller's personality. Interesting only for impressive use of Claymation technique throughout.▼

Adventures of Martin Eden, The (1942) **87m.** *** D: Sidney Salkow. Glenn Ford, Claire Trevor, Evelyn Keyes, Stuart Erwin, Dickie Moore. Sturdy Jack London tale of seaman aboard terror of a ship, writing account of sailing, fighting for literary recognition.

Adventures of Milo and Otis, The (1989-Japanese) **C-76m.** **½ D: Masanori Hata. Narrated by Dudley Moore. Cute film for kids about a dog and a cat who venture away from their farm and experience a variety of adventures. Not very strong on story but buoyed (in the American release version) by Moore's delightful narration. Original Japanese version, released in 1986, ran 90m.

Adventures of Nellie Bly, The (1981) **C-100m. TVM** D: Henning Schellerup. Linda Purl, Gene Barry, John Randolph, Raymond Buktenica, J. D. Cannon, Elaine Heilveil, Cliff Osmond. Trailblazing female journalist, well scrubbed for this fanciful "Classics Illustrated" adventure (and played with spunk by Purl), exposes corruption, sweatshop inhumanity, and insane-asylum brutality without mussing a hair on her head. Below average.▼

Adventures of Nick Carter (1972) **C-72m. TVM** D: Paul Krasny. Robert Conrad, Shelley Winters, Brooke Bundy, Broderick Crawford, Dean Stockwell, Pat O'Brien, Neville Brand, Pernell Roberts. Legendary private-eye Carter (Conrad) sets out to find out who bumped off good friend. Usual assortment of corrupt police types, millionaire robber baron, glamorous nightclub owner, etc.; emphasis on action, not mystery. Average.

Adventures of Picasso, The (1978-Swedish) **C-92m.** **½ D: Tage Danielsson. Gosta Ekman, Hans Alfredson, Margaretha Krook, Bernard Cribbins, Wilfred Brambell, Per Oscarsson, Lena Nyman, Lennart Nyman. Frantic slapstick, with actors impersonating the likes of Picasso, Dali, Apollinaire, Gertrude Stein, and Alice B. Toklas (the last two played by Cribbins and Brambell); occasionally funny but misses the mark.▼

Adventures of Robin Hood, The (1938) **C-102m.** **** D: Michael Curtiz, William Keighley. Errol Flynn, Olivia de Havilland, Basil Rathbone, Claude Rains, Patric Knowles, Eugene Pallette, Alan Hale, Herbert Mundin, Una O'Connor, Melville Cooper, Ian Hunter. Dashing Flynn in the definitive swashbuckler, winning hand of de Havilland, foiling evil prince Rains, dueling wicked Rathbone. Erich Wolfgang Korngold's outstanding score earned an Oscar, as did the art direction and editing. Scripted by Norman Reilly Raine and Seton I. Miller.▼

Adventures of Robinson Crusoe (1952-Mexican) **C-90m.** ***½ D: Luis Bunuel. Dan O'Herlihy, Jaime Fernandez. Colorful, entertaining adaptation of Daniel Defoe's classic story about a resourceful shipwreck victim, with some distinctive Bunuel touches; vivid performance by O'Herlihy, who got an Oscar nomination when film was given U.S. release in 1954. Excellent music score by Anthony Collins. Main title on film is ROBINSON CRUSOE.

Adventures of Sadie, The (1955-British) **C-88m.** **½ D: Noel Langley. Joan Collins, George Cole, Kenneth More, Robertson Hare, Hermione Gingold, Walter Fitzgerald, Hattie Jacques. Obvious sex satire relying on premise of Collins stuck on desert isle with love-hungry men. From an Ernest K. Gann novel. Original British title: OUR GIRL FRIDAY.

Adventures of Scaramouche, The (1964-French-Italian-Spanish) **C-98m.** ** D: J. Antonio Isasi-Isasmendi. Gerard Barray, Gianna Maria Canale, Michele Girardon, Yvette Lebon. Gallic rendering of Sabatini cloak-and-sword tale has action and wit, but not on grand scale.

Adventures of Sherlock Holmes (1939) **85m.** D: Alfred L. Werker. Basil Rathbone, Nigel Bruce, Ida Lupino, Alan Marshal, Terry Kilburn, George Zucco, E. E. Clive, Mary Gordon. SEE: **Sherlock Holmes** series.▼

Adventures of Tartu (1943-British) **103m.** **½ D: Harold S. Bucquet. Robert Donat, Valerie Hobson, Walter Rilla, Phyllis Morris, Glynis Johns. Improbable but well-acted account of British spy (Donat) trying to help Czech partisans destroy a poison gas factory manned by Nazis. Retitled: TARTU.▼

Adventures of the Queen (1975) **C-100m. TVM** D: David Lowell Rich. Robert Stack, David Hedison, Ralph Bellamy, Bradford Dillman, Sorrell Booke, Burr de Benning, John Randolph. Stack captains luxury cruise ship threatened with destruction as part of deadly vendetta against eccentric millionaire Bellamy. Predictable Irwin Allen disaster drama, filmed aboard the *Queen Mary*. Below average.

Adventures of the Wilderness Family, The (1975) **C-100m.** *** D: Stewart Raffill.

Robert F. Logan, Susan Damante Shaw, Hollye Holmes, Ham Larsen, Buck Flower, William Cornford. Good human-interest drama. Modern couple with two children forsake big city for life in magnificent but sometimes dangerous Rocky Mountain region. Followed by two look-alike sequels.▼

Adventures of Tom Sawyer, The (1938) C-77m. ***½ D: Norman Taurog. Tommy Kelly, Jackie Moran, Ann Gillis, May Robson, Walter Brennan, Victor Jory, Spring Byington, Margaret Hamilton. Entertaining David O. Selznick production of Mark Twain classic with more slapstick than Twain may have had in mind. Cave sequence with Injun Joe is unforgettable. Original running time 93m. Previously filmed in 1930, and again in 1973 (twice that year)—all under the title TOM SAWYER.▼

Adventuress, The (1946-British) 98m. *** D: Frank Launder. Deborah Kerr, Trevor Howard, Raymond Huntley, Liam Redmond, Harry Webster. A feisty Irish lass is persuaded to help a German agent during WW2—because it will hurt her sworn enemies, the British. Well-made, low-key film with touches of droll humor. British prints were originally 114m., which explains some abruptness in exposition. British title. I SEE A DARK STRANGER.▼

Advice to the Lovelorn (1933) 62m. **½ D: Alfred Werker. Lee Tracy, Sally Blane, Sterling Holloway, Jean Adair, Paul Harvey. Engaging comedy-drama capitalizing on Tracy's success in BLESSED EVENT; here he parlays a lonelyhearts column into business enterprise, with unexpected results. Loosely based on Nathanael West's *Miss Lonelyhearts*. Holloway excellent in key supporting role. Filmed again as LONELYHEARTS.

Advice to the Lovelorn (1981) C-100m. TVM D: Harry Falk. Cloris Leachman, Melissa Sue Anderson, Desi Arnaz, Jr., Lance Kerwin, Donna Pescow, Paul Burke, Tina Louise, Kelly Bishop, Rick Lenz. Cloris solves various domestic crises in her newspaper column but can't seem to handle her own; routine pilot to an unsold sitcom. Average.

Advise and Consent (1962) 139m. *** D: Otto Preminger. Henry Fonda, Don Murray, Charles Laughton, Walter Pidgeon, Peter Lawford, Gene Tierney, Franchot Tone, Lew Ayres, Burgess Meredith, Paul Ford, George Grizzard, Betty White. Long but engrossing drama of Washington wheeling and dealing, from Allen Drury novel. Cast is fine, with effective underplaying by Ayres and Tone standing out among more flamboyant performances by Laughton (his last film) and Grizzard. Also shown in computer-colored version.▼

Aerial Gunner (1943) 78m. ** D: William H. Pine. Richard Arlen, Chester Morris, Lita Ward, Jimmy Lydon, Keith Richards, Dick Purcell. Formula WWII action propaganda, pitting old rivals Arlen and Morris during basic training and competing for Ward's love. Partially salvaged by some energetic combat scenes.

Affair, The (1973) C-74m. TVM D: Gilbert Cates. Natalie Wood, Robert Wagner, Bruce Davison, Jamie Smith Jackson, Kent Smith, Frances Reid, Pat Harrington. Sensitive, careful handling of 30-ish female songwriter with polio (Wood) experiencing first love affair with lawyer (Wagner). Excellent cast, expert script by Barbara Turner. Above average.▼

Affair in Havana (1957) 77m. *½ D: Laslo Benedek. John Cassavetes, Raymond Burr, Sara Shane, Lila Lazo. Unexciting tale of songwriter in love with crippled man's wife. Filmed in Cuba.

Affair in Monte Carlo (1953-British) C-75m. ** D: Victor Saville. Merle Oberon, Richard Todd, Leo Genn, Peter Illing. Rich widow tries to convince gambler that romance is more rewarding than roulette. Monte Carlo backgrounds don't help.

Affair in Reno (1957) 75m. *½ D: R. G. Springsteen. John Lund, John Archer, Doris Singleton, Alan Hale. Inoffensive little film about detective Singleton falling in love with PR-man Lund.

Affair in Trinidad (1952) 98m. **½ D: Vincent Sherman. Rita Hayworth, Glenn Ford, Alexander Scourby, Torin Thatcher, Juanita Moore, Steven Geray. Hayworth and Ford sparkle as cafe singer and brother-in-law seeking their husband's murderer. Hayworth is most enticing.▼

Affairs in Versailles SEE: **Royal Affairs in Versailles**

Affairs of Annabel, The (1938) 68m. **½ D: Ben Stoloff. Lucille Ball, Jack Oakie, Ruth Donnelly, Bradley Page, Fritz Feld, Thurston Hall. Fair film industry satire, with Ball scoring as an actress and Oakie her scheming press agent whose publicity gimmicks always backfire. First of a short-lived series, followed by ANNABEL TAKES A TOUR.▼

Affairs of Cellini (1934) 80m. *** D: Gregory La Cava. Constance Bennett, Fredric March, Frank Morgan, Fay Wray, Jessie Ralph. March is excellent as roguish Renaissance artist who falls in love with Duchess. Lavish production, fine cast make this most entertaining. Lucille Ball plays a lady in waiting.

Affairs of Dobie Gillis, The (1953) 74m. *** D: Don Weis. Debbie Reynolds, Bobby Van, Hans Conried, Lurene Tuttle, Bob Fosse. Entertaining musicomedy based on Max Shulman's book of college kids. Debbie and Van a cute couple; Conried the dour prof. Later a TV series.

Affairs of Susan, The (1945) 110m. **½ D: William A. Seiter. Joan Fontaine, George Brent, Dennis O'Keefe, Don DeFore, Rita Johnson, Walter Abel. Fairly entertaining comedy of actress Fontaine who does more acting for her beaus than she does onstage.

Affair to Remember, An (1957) **C-115m.** **½ D: Leo McCarey. Cary Grant, Deborah Kerr, Richard Denning, Neva Patterson, Cathleen Nesbitt, Robert Q. Lewis, Charles Watts, Fortunio Bonanova. Middling remake of McCarey's LOVE AFFAIR. Bubbling shipboard comedy in first half, overshadowed by draggy soap-opera clichés and unnecessary musical numbers in N.Y. finale. Vic Damone croons title tune on soundtrack.

Affair With a Stranger (1953) 89m. **½ D: Roy Rowland. Victor Mature, Jean Simmons, Jane Darwell, Dabbs Greer, Olive Carey. Title figure is child adopted by couple on brink of divorce. Formula plot of marital seesaw; stars work well together.

Affectionately Yours (1941) 90m. ** D: Lloyd Bacon. Merle Oberon, Dennis Morgan, Rita Hayworth, Ralph Bellamy, George Tobias. Attractive triangle flounders in weak comedy of Morgan trying to win back wife Oberon, with interference from Hayworth. Bellamy is the poor sap again.

Africa Addio (1966-Italian) **C-122m.** *** D: Gualtiero Jacopetti, Franco Prosperi. Intriguing survey of contemporary Africa focusing on racial differences and variant tribal customs on the continent; overly gruesome at times. Recut and retitled AFRICA BLOOD AND GUTS.▼

Africa Blood and Guts SEE: **Africa Addio**▼

African Elephant, The (1972) **C-92m.** *** D: Simon Trevor. Excellent documentary on African wildlife centering on elephants and their sometimes strange habits. Released theatrically as KING ELEPHANT.

African Lion, The (1955) **C-75m.** ***½ D: James Algar. Narrated by Winston Hibler. Outstanding True-Life documentary is perhaps Disney's best. Naturalists Alfred and Elma Milotte filmed the African lion in his native habitat through a year's cycle of seasons. Filled with drama, excitement, color, humor. A gem.

✓ **African Queen, The** (1951) **C-105m.** **** D: John Huston. Katharine Hepburn, Humphrey Bogart, Robert Morley, Peter Bull, Theodore Bikel, Walter Gotell. Superb combination of souse Bogart (who won an Oscar) and spinster Hepburn traveling up the Congo during WWI, combating the elements and the Germans, and each other. Script by James Agee from C. S. Forester's novel; gorgeously filmed on location by Jack Cardiff.▼

African Treasure (1952) 70m. D: Ford Beebe. Johnny Sheffield, Laurette Luez, Lyle Talbot, Arthur Space, Smoki Whitfield. SEE: **Bomba, the Jungle Boy** series.

Africa Screams (1949) 79m. *** D: Charles Barton. Bud Abbott, Lou Costello, Hillary Brooke, Max Baer, Clyde Beatty, Frank Buck, Shemp Howard, Joe Besser. A&C go on safari in this funny outing full of wheezy but often hilarious gags and routines. Also shown in computer-colored version.▼

Africa—Texas Style! (1967) **C-106m.** **½ D: Andrew Marton. Hugh O'Brian, John Mills, Nigel Green, Tom Nardini, Adrienne Corri. Feature (which later spun off a TV series, *Cowboy in Africa*) doesn't offer much excitement, with O'Brian helping Mills preserve wild game in the dark continent.▼

After Hours (1985) **C-97m.** **½ D: Martin Scorsese. Griffin Dunne, Rosanna Arquette, Verna Bloom, Thomas Chong, Linda Fiorentino, Teri Garr, John Heard, Cheech Marin, Catherine O'Hara, Dick Miller, Bronson Pinchot. Ordinary guy goes through a series of bizarre experiences during one incredible night in N.Y.C. How much you enjoy this comic nightmare will depend on how closely you identify with Dunne—the only normal person in the picture!▼

After Midnight (1989) **C-90m.** *½ D: Ken and Jim Wheat. Jullian McWhirter, Pamela Segall, Ramy Zade, Nadine Van Der Velde, Marc McClure, Marg Helgenberger, Billy Ray Sharkey. Four coeds take turns telling the scariest story they know in this weak and predictable horror anthology . . . with a high violence quotient. This received limited theatrical release before heading to videoland.▼

After Midnight with Boston Blackie (1943) D: Lew Landers. Chester Morris, Ann Savage, George E. Stone, Richard Lane, Cy Kendall, George McKay. SEE: **Boston Blackie** series.

After Office Hours (1935) 75m. ** D: Robert Z. Leonard. Constance Bennett, Clark Gable, Stuart Erwin, Billie Burke, Harvey Stephens, Henry Travers, William Demarest, Katherine Alexander. Editor Gable tries to manipulate society girl Bennett while investigating shady Stephens. Gable's charm cannot overcome forgettable script (written by Herman J. Mankiewicz).

After the Fox (1966-British-Italian) **C-103m.** **½ D: Vittorio De Sica. Peter Sellers, Victor Mature, Britt Ekland, Martin Balsam. Not always successful comedy of Italian con man Sellers, who poses as a movie director. A must-see for Mature's performance as a fading romantic star with tremendous ego. Script by Neil Simon.▼

After the Promise (1987) **C-100m. TVM** D: David Greene. Mark Harmon, Diana

Scarwid, Rosemary Dunsmore, Donnelly Rhodes, Mark Hildreth, Trey Ames, Richard Billingsley. Surprisingly effective drama about an itinerant Depression-era carpenter's long struggle to regain custody of his four sons, who were institutionalized after their mother's death. Robert Lenski scripted from Sebastian Milito's story, based on actual events. Above average.▼

After the Rehearsal (1984-Swedish) C-72m. *** D: Ingmar Bergman. Erland Josephson, Ingrid Thulin, Lena Olin, Nadja Palmstjerna-Weiss, Bertil Guve. While staging the production of a Strindberg play a womanizing director is browbeaten by the actress daughter of an old lover, then a middle-aged actress/ex-lover who has fallen on tougher times. Short running time or not, you can exhaust yourself trying to figure out the relationships here. Small-screen viewing should make this original telefilm easier to take than it was in theatrical screenings. Fine acting.▼

After the Thin Man (1936) 113m. D: W. S. Van Dyke II. William Powell, Myrna Loy, James Stewart, Elissa Landi, Joseph Calleia. SEE: Thin Man series.▼

Afurika Monogatari (1981-Japanese) C-120m. BOMB D: Susumu Hani. James Stewart, Philip Sayer, Kathy, Eleanora Vallone, Heekura Simba. Pilot Sayer crashes plane in wilds of Africa, comes upon game preserve occupied by Stewart and granddaughter. Even old Jimmy is boring. Filmed in Kenya. Also known as A TALE OF AFRICA and THE GREEN HORIZON.▼

Against a Crooked Sky (1975) C-89m. ** D: Earl Bellamy. Richard Boone, Stewart Peterson, Geoffrey Land, Jewel Blanch, Henry Wilcoxon, Clint Ritchie. A boy searches for his sister, who's been kidnapped by Indians; simplistic, old-fashioned family western.▼

Against All Flags (1952) C-83m. **½ D: George Sherman. Errol Flynn, Maureen O'Hara, Anthony Quinn, Mildred Natwick. Flynn found his forte again as dashing British soldier who maneuvers way into pirate fortress, while managing to flirt with O'Hara. Remade as THE KING'S PIRATE.▼

Against All Odds (1984) C-128m. **½ D: Taylor Hackford. Rachel Ward, Jeff Bridges, James Woods, Alex Karras, Jane Greer, Richard Widmark, Dorian Harewood, Swoosie Kurtz, Saul Rubinek, Pat Corley, Bill McKinney, Kid Creole and the Coconuts. Unemployed jock needs cash, accepts a job from a sleazy ex-teammate to find his girlfriend, who's run off to Mexico. The plot thickens, in several directions, in this loose remake of OUT OF THE PAST (with Greer playing the mother of her character in the original). Hackford makes good stab at *film noir* feeling, but script is plot-heavy and unsatisfying. Best scene—a hair-raising race along Sunset Boulevard—is completely out of step with the rest of the film. An interesting misfire. Haunting title song by Phil Collins.▼

Against The Wind (1948-British) 96m. *** D: Charles Crichton. Robert Beatty, Simone Signoret, Jack Warner, Gordon Jackson, Paul Dupuis, James Robertson Justice. Taut, engrossing tale of British spies trained for mission inside occupied France during WW2. Documentary-style training scenes complement the dramatic story of resistance fighters.

Agatha (1979) C-98m. *** D: Michael Apted. Dustin Hoffman, Vanessa Redgrave, Timothy Dalton, Helen Morse, Celia Gregory, Paul Brooke. Fictional speculation on mystery writer Agatha Christie's famous 11-day disappearance in 1926; Redgrave is superb in this absorbing yarn, Hoffman strangely miscast as smooth American reporter who tracks her down.▼

Agatha Christie's A Caribbean Mystery SEE: **Caribbean Mystery, A.**

Agatha Christie's Dead Man's Folly SEE: **Dead Man's Folly**

Agatha Christie's Endless Night SEE: **Endless Night**▼

Agatha Christie's Murder with Mirrors SEE: **Murder with Mirrors**

Agatha Christie's Sparkling Cyanide SEE: **Sparkling Cyanide**

Agatha Christie's The Man in the Brown Suit (1989) C-100m. TVM D: Alan Grint. Rue McClanahan, Tony Randall, Edward Woodward, Stephanie Zimbalist, Ken Howard, Nickolas Grace, Simon Dutton. Contemporary adaptation (by Carla Jean Wagner) of Christie's 1924 novel about an American woman who becomes involved in a diamond theft and murder while traveling through the Middle East. Played much too broadly, with Zimbalist as a distaff Indiana Jones. Average.

Agatha Christie's Thirteen at Dinner SEE: **Thirteen at Dinner**

Age of Consent (1969-Australian) C-103m. **½ D: Michael Powell. James Mason, Helen Mirren, Jack MacGowran, Neva Carr-Glyn, Frank Thring. A put-upon artist escapes to the quietude of Australia's Great Barrier Reef, where he's inspired by a feisty young girl whom he persuades to pose for him. General amiability and pretty scenery help make up for clumsy comedy relief and gaps in story and characterization.

Agency (1981-Canadian) C-94m. *½ D: George Kaczender. Robert Mitchum, Lee Majors, Valerie Perrine, Saul Rubinek, Alexandra Stewart, Anthony Parr. Shifty Mitchum plots to gain political clout via information transmitted subliminally in television ads. Fascinating idea, but result is dull and unconvincing.▼

Agent 8¾ (1965-British) C-98m. *** D: Ralph Thomas. Dirk Bogarde, Sylva

Koscina, Leo McKern, Robert Morley, Roger Delgado, John LeMesurier. Released at height of James Bond craze, this spoof features Bogarde as a bumbling secret agent working in Czechoslovakia. Sometimes witty, bright comedy. Originally released in U.S. at 77m. Original British title: HOT ENOUGH FOR JUNE.

Agent for H.A.R.M. (1966) **C-84m.** *½ D: Gerd Oswald. Mark Richman, Wendell Corey, Carl Esmond, Barbara Bouchet, Martin Kosleck, Rafael Campos, Alizia Gur. Yet another secret agent adventure, definitely a lesser one, about investigation of scientist who is trying to combat spores that turn people into fungi. Shot as a TV pilot, but released to theaters instead.

Age-Old Friends (1989) **C-85m. TVM** D: Allan Kroeker. Hume Cronyn, Vincent Gardenia, Tandy Cronyn, Michele Scarabelli, Esther Rolle. Poignant tale of a sprightly nursing-home resident and his crochety buddy (who's drifting into senility) who try to exert their independence. Cronyn is aces, as usual, and his real-life daughter complements this sentimental adaptation by Bob Larby of his play, *A Month of Sundays*. Made for cable. Above average.▼

Agnes of God (1985) **C-98m.** ***½ D: Norman Jewison. Jane Fonda, Anne Bancroft, Meg Tilly, Anne Pitoniak, Winston Reckert, Gratien Gelinas. A young nun apparently became pregnant and murdered her own baby in the cloistered atmosphere of a convent, but court-appointed psychiatrist Fonda finds no easy explanations. Disturbing, not always satisfying, but electrified by three lead performances, and beautifully photographed by Sven Nykvist. Screenplay by John Pielmeyer, from his play.▼

Agony and the Ecstasy, The (1965) **C-140m.** **½ D: Carol Reed. Charlton Heston, Rex Harrison, Diane Cilento, Harry Andrews, Adolfo Celi. Huge spectacle of Michelangelo's artistic conflicts with Pope Julius II has adequate acting overshadowed by meticulous production. Short documentary on artist's work precedes fragmentary drama based on bits of Irving Stone's novel.▼

Aguirre: The Wrath of God (1972-German) **C-94m.** ***½ D: Werner Herzog. Klaus Kinski, Ruy Guerra, Del Negro, Helena Rojo, Cecilia Rivera, Peter Berling, Danny Ades. Powerful, hypnotic tale of deluded conquistador who leads a group of men away from Pizarro's 1560 South American expedition in search of seven cities of gold. Dreamlike film was shot on location in remote Amazon jungles; Kinski is perfect as the mad Aguirre. Filmed in both Germanand English-language versions; try to avoid the latter.▼

A-Haunting We Will Go (1942) **68m.** *½ D: Alfred Werker. Stan Laurel, Oliver Hardy, Dante the Magician, Sheila Ryan, John Shelton, Don Costello, Elisha Cook Jr. One of Stan and Ollie's poorest films, involving them with gangsters, a troublesome coffin, and a hokey stage magician. No magic in this turkey.

Ah, Wilderness (1935) **101m.** ***½ D: Clarence Brown. Wallace Beery, Lionel Barrymore, Aline MacMahon, Eric Linden, Cecilia Parker, Mickey Rooney, Frank Albertson, Bonita Granville. Rich Americana in this adaptation of Eugene O'Neill play about turn-of-the-century small-town life, focusing on boy who tackles problems of adolescence. Rooney, playing younger brother, took the lead in musical remake SUMMER HOLIDAY. Screenplay by Albert Hackett and Frances Goodrich.

Aida (1953-Italian) **C-96m.** **½ D: Clemente Fracassi. Sophia Loren, Lois Maxwell, Luciano Della Marra, Afro Poli, Antonio Cassinelli. Medium adaptation of the Verdi opera, of interest mostly for casting of Loren, in one of her earlier screen appearances, as the tragic Ethiopian princess. Her singing is dubbed by Renata Tebaldi.

Ain't Misbehavin' (1955) **C-82m.** **½ D: Edward Buzzell. Rory Calhoun, Piper Laurie, Jack Carson, Mamie Van Doren, Reginald Gardiner, Barbara Britton. Pleasant musical fluff about rowdy Laurie crashing high society when wealthy Calhoun falls in love with her.

Air America (1990) **C-112m.** ** D: Roger Spottiswoode. Mel Gibson, Robert Downey, Jr., Nancy Travis, David Marshall Grant, Lane Smith, Ken Jenkins, Burt Kwouk, Art La Fleur, Tim Thomerson. Pilots Mel and Bob are part of the C.I.A.'s smuggling operation in Laos during the Vietnam War. They crate anything and anyone anywhere—too bad they couldn't fly in a script doctor. Alleged action-comedy has few laughs and makes little sense. Even Gibson's patented swagger can't keep this one airborne.

Air Cadet (1951) **94m.** ** D: Joseph Pevney. Stephen McNally, Gail Russell, Alex Nicol, Richard Long, Rock Hudson. Standard training-recruit story, with McNally looking bored as head instructor.

Air Force (1943) **124m.** *** D: Howard Hawks. John Garfield, John Ridgely, Gig Young, Arthur Kennedy, Charles Drake, Harry Carey, George Tobias, Faye Emerson. Archetypal WW2 movie, focusing on archetypal bomber crew. Tough to stomach at times ("Fried Jap going down," chimes Tobias after scoring a hit), but generally exciting, well-done.▼

Air Mail (1932) **83m.** *** D: John Ford. Pat O'Brien, Ralph Bellamy, Russell Hopton, Slim Summerville, Frank Albertson, Gloria Stuart. Routine story of pioneer airmail pilots supercharged by fine aerial scenes and good cast. First-rate.

Airplane! (1980) **C-86m.** *** D: Jim

Abrahams, David Zucker, Jerry Zucker. Robert Hays, Julie Hagerty, Robert Stack, Lloyd Bridges, Peter Graves, Kareem Abdul-Jabbar, Leslie Nielsen, Lorna Patterson, Stephen Stucker. Very funny spoof of AIRPORT-type pictures (and Arthur Hailey's ZERO HOUR in particular), with a nonstop string of gags that holds up almost to the end (why carp?). Our favorite: the strange plight of Lt. Hurwitz. Stay tuned through final credits. Followed by AIRPLANE II: THE SEQUEL.▼

Airplane II: The Sequel (1982) **C-85m.** **½ D: Ken Finkleman. Robert Hays, Julie Hagerty, Lloyd Bridges, Peter Graves, William Shatner, Chad Everett. Mildly funny rehash of AIRPLANE (by a new writer-director), but can't match the quantity, or quality, of laughs in the original. Many cameos include Raymond Burr, Chuck Connors, Sonny Bono, Rip Torn.▼

Airport (1970) **C-137m.** ***½ D: George Seaton. Burt Lancaster, Dean Martin, George Kennedy, Helen Hayes, Jean Seberg, Jacqueline Bisset, Van Heflin, Maureen Stapleton, Barry Nelson, Dana Wynter, Lloyd Nolan, Barbara Hale. GRAND HOTEL plot formula reaches latter-day zenith in ultraslick, old-fashioned movie that entertains in spite of itself, detailing hectic winter night at metropolitan airport. Plastic performances dominate, with down-to-earth Kennedy, touching Stapleton, and nervous Heflin standing out. Helen Hayes won Oscar as impish stowaway. Based on the Arthur Hailey bestseller; followed by three sequels—so far.▼

Airport 1975 (1974) **C-106m.** *½ D: Jack Smight. Charlton Heston, Karen Black, George Kennedy, Efrem Zimbalist, Jr., Susan Clark, Helen Reddy, Gloria Swanson, Linda Blair, Dana Andrews, Sid Caesar, Myrna Loy, Nancy Olson, Roy Thinnes, Martha Scott. Yet another jetliner disaster epic, not worth your time unless you get your kicks watching a *Hollywood Squares*-type cast that includes Helen Reddy as a (singing) nun. Swanson plays herself in her final film. Look quickly for Sharon Gless.▼

Airport '77 (1977) **C-113m.** **½ D: Jerry Jameson. Jack Lemmon, Lee Grant, Brenda Vaccaro, George Kennedy, James Stewart, Joseph Cotten, Olivia de Havilland, Darren McGavin, Christopher Lee, Monte Markham, Chris Lemmon. All the cliches and stock characters are trucked out for another made-to-order disaster epic, not bad as these things go; Stewart's private luxury jet is sabotaged and sinks in the ocean, forcing daring rescue attempt. Lemmon brings conviction to his role as dedicated pilot. New footage added for network showing.▼

Airport '79 SEE: **Concorde, The—Airport '79**▼

Air Raid Wardens (1943) **67m.** ** D: Edward Sedgwick. Stan Laurel, Oliver Hardy, Edgar Kennedy, Jacqueline White, Horace (Stephen) McNally, Donald Meek. Weak, later Laurel and Hardy comedy. One potentially good scene with slow-burn Kennedy doesn't meet expectations.

AKA Cassius Clay (1970) **C-85m.** **½ D: Jim Jacobs. Narrated by Richard Kiley. Interesting documentary about the controversial heavyweight champion.

Akira (1988-Japanese) **C-124m.** *** D: Katsuhiro Otomo. Voices of Jimmy Flanders, Drew Thomas, Lewis Lemay, Barbara Larsen, Stanley Gurd, Jr. Bloody and violent animated science-fiction feature based on Japanese comic-book novel. A group of motorcycle-riding teenagers living in post-apocalyptic Neo-Tokyo tries to stop one of the gang who has run amok after becoming empowered with telekinetic powers in a government experiment. Technically spectacular and colorful animation is somewhat derailed by confusing storytelling and a cryptic ending. A must-see for adult animation buffs.

Aku Aku (1961) **C-86m.** **½ Documentary of anthropologist Thor Heyerdahl's trip to Easter Island and his encounters with the natives.

Aladdin and His Lamp (1952) **C-67m.** *½ D: Lew Landers. Patricia Medina, Richard Erdman, John Sands, Noreen Nash Poppycock, based on the juvenile fable, that will bore even the least discriminating children.

Alakazam the Great (1961) **C-84m.** **½ Voices of Jonathan Winters, Frankie Avalon, Arnold Stang, Sterling Holloway. Japanese-made cartoon is good children's entertainment; story centers on magical monkey's ambitious adventures, from bullfight in the pit of a volcano to an epic battle with Hercules of the Universe.▼

Alambrista! (1977) **C-110m.** ***½ D: Robert M. Young. Domingo Ambriz, Trinidad Silva, Linda Gillin, Ned Beatty, Julius Harris, Paul Berrones, Edward James Olmos. Boyish, naive Ambriz illegally crosses the U.S.-Mexican border and is exploited as he seeks work to support his family. Touching, fresh, insightful; director Young's first feature.

Alamo, The (1960) **C-161m.** *** D: John Wayne. John Wayne, Richard Widmark, Laurence Harvey, Richard Boone, Carlos Arruza, Frankie Avalon, Pat Wayne, Linda Cristal, Chill Wills. Long, and long-winded, saga of the Alamo, with plenty of historical name-dropping and speechifying. Worthwhile for final attack, a truly memorable movie spectacle. Fine score by Dimitri Tiomkin. Cut by 26m. after its L.A. premiere.▼

Alamo Bay (1985) **C-98m.** **½ D: Louis Malle. Amy Madigan, Ed Harris, Ho Nguyen, Donald Moffat, Truyer V. Tran, Rudy Young, Cynthia Carle. Well-made but strangely uninvolving film based on real-life conflict between Vietnamese immigrants and American fishermen on the Texas Gulf Coast.▼

Alamo: 13 Days to Glory, The (1987) **C-145m.** TVM D: Burt Kennedy. James Arness, Brian Keith, Raul Julia, Alec Baldwin, Lorne Greene, Isela Vega, Gene Evans, David Ogden Stiers, Fernando Allende, Ethan Wayne. Cliched rehash of the last days of Jim Bowie (Arness), Davy Crockett (Keith), Col. William Travis (Baldwin) and the valiant band of doomed Texans at the Alamo, with Lorne Greene doing a throwaway as Sam Houston. Raul Julia's flamboyant performance as Santa Anna, and robust battle scenes filmed by John Elsenbach, are on the plus side in this adaptation of J. Lon Tinkle's book, *Thirteen Days to Glory*. Average.

Alaska Seas (1954) **78m.** ** D: Jerry Hopper. Robert Ryan, Jan Sterling, Brian Keith, Gene Barry, Ross Bagdasarian. Crooks will be crooks, in insipid tale of north-country salmon canner who regrets rehiring former partner, now an ex-con. Remake of SPAWN OF THE NORTH.

Albuquerque (1948) **C-89m.** ** D: Ray Enright. Randolph Scott, Barbara Britton, Gabby Hayes, Lon Chaney, Russell Hayden. Good Western for Scott fans, with young man finally rebelling against overly strict uncle.

Al Capone (1959) **105m.** **½ D: Richard Wilson. Rod Steiger, Fay Spain, James Gregory, Martin Balsam, Nehemiah Persoff, Murvyn Vye. Good latter-day gangster biography with Steiger tirading as scarfaced Capone: good supporting cast, bringing back memories of Cagney-Robinson-Bogart films of the 30s.▼

Alcatraz: The Whole Shocking Story (1980) **C-200m.** TVM D: Paul Krasny. Michael Beck, Art Carney, Alex Karras, Telly Savalas, Ronny Cox, Will Sampson, Richard Lynch, Robert Davi, John Amos, Charles Aidman, James MacArthur, Peter Coyote. Straightforward prison drama about Clarence Carnes, said to be the youngest man ever sentenced to Alcatraz, and his decades of planning to escape. Ernest Tidyman's script swings wildly from intelligence to the hilarious simplicity of a '30s B movie. Carney gives a thoughtful performance as Robert Stroud, the legendary Birdman of Alcatraz, while Savalas chews up the scenery as a cellblock king. Originally shown in two parts. Average.

Alchemist, The (1985) **C-84m.** *½ D: James Amante (Charles Band). Robert Ginty, Lucinda Dooling, John Sanderford, Viola Kate Stimpson, Robert Glaudini. Minor rural horror flick is set in 1955. Ginty was cursed a century ago by Glaudini to live as an animal; he's ultimately saved by lovely Dooling, a lookalike of the 19th

century woman who came between the two men. Filmed in 1981.▼

Alexander (1968-French) **C-89m.** *** D: Yves Robert. Philippe Noiret, Francoise Brion, Marlene Jobert, Jean Carmet, Pierre Richard. Entertaining comedy about overworked, hilariously henpecked farmer Noiret and how he earns his liberation—not without the help of a cute, bright little dog. Occasionally silly but frequently inspired.

Alexander Hamilton (1931) **73m.** ** D: John Adolfi. George Arliss, Doris Kenyon, Montagu Love, Dudley Digges, June Collyer, Alan Mowbray, Charles Middleton. Episodic American historical drama of country's earliest financial wizard is interesting but quite stagy.

Alexander Nevsky (1938-Russian) **107m.** **** D: Sergei Eisenstein. Nikolai Cherkassov, Nikolai Okhlopkov, Alexander Abrikossov, Dmitri Orlov, Vassily Novikov. Epic tale of Cherkassov and Russian army repelling German invasion during the 13th century, a disturbing parallel to world situation at time of production. Magnificently visualized battle sequences, wonderful Prokofiev score. A masterpiece.▼

Alexander's Ragtime Band (1938) **105m.** **½ D: Henry King. Tyrone Power, Alice Faye, Don Ameche, Ethel Merman, Jack Haley, Jean Hersholt. Large-scale musical with stale plot but good stars and a flock of Irving Berlin songs: "Now It Can Be Told," "My Walking Stick," "I'm Marching Along with Time," title tune.

Alexander the Great (1956) **C-141m.** *** D: Robert Rossen. Richard Burton, Fredric March, Claire Bloom, Danielle Darrieux. Remarkable cast, intelligent acting, but a static epic, lacking essential sweep to make tale of Greek conqueror moving.▼

Alexander: The Other Side of Dawn (1977) **C-100m.** TVM D: John Erman. Leigh J. McCloskey, Eve Plumb, Earl Holliman, Juliet Mills, Jean Hagen, Lonnie Chapman. In sequel to DAWN: PORTRAIT OF A TEENAGE RUNAWAY, country-boy-turned-Hollywood-hustler (McCloskey) tries to find legitimate work in order to marry teen-aged prostitute (Plumb) he had hoped to regenerate, but gets involved with a homosexual football pro. Sordid tale, with McCloskey aping Jon Voight's MIDNIGHT COWBOY characterization. Average.▼

Alex and the Gypsy (1976) **C-99m.** **½ D: John Korty. Jack Lemmon, Genevieve Bujold, James Woods, Gino Ardito, Robert Emhardt, Titos Vandis. Meandering story of romance between bailbondsman Lemmon and gypsy Bujold who's accused of attempted murder. Some interesting ideas lost in the muddle of an indecisive film.

Alex in Wonderland (1970) **C-109m.** ** D: Paul Mazursky. Donald Sutherland,

Ellen Burstyn, Viola Spolin, Federico Fellini, Jeanne Moreau. Camera follows young film director Sutherland through tedium of his everyday life. Self-indulgent imitation of Fellini (who appears briefly) caused some wags to dub this film *1½*. Burstyn stands out as Sutherland's wife.

Alex: The Life of a Child (1986) **C-100m.** TVM D: Robert Markowitz. Craig T. Nelson, Bonnie Bedelia, Gennie James, Danny Corkill, Mark Withers. Melancholy dramatization of real-life sportswriter Frank Deford's book about his young daughter's losing battle with cystic fibrosis. Touching script by Carol Evan McKeand and Nigel McKeand. Average.

Alfie (1966-British) **C-114m.** ***½ D: Lewis Gilbert. Michael Caine, Shelley Winters, Julia Foster, Millicent Martin, Shirley Anne Field, Vivien Merchant, Denholm Elliott. Well-turned version of Bill Naughton play. Caine is superb as philandering Cockney playboy who can't decide if bachelor life is so bloody marvelous. Followed by ALFIE DARLING.▼

Alfie Darling (1975-British) **C-102m.** ** D: Ken Hughes. Alan Price, Jill Townsend, Joan Collins, Annie Ross, Sheila White, Rula Lenska. Forgettable sequel to ALFIE, with Price a most inadequate replacement for Michael Caine. This time around our hero falls for a chic magazine editor. Retitled OH, ALFIE for video.▼

Alfredo, Alfredo (1972-Italian) **C-98m.** *½ D: Pietro Germi. Dustin Hoffman, Stefania Sandrelli, Carla Gravina, Clara Colosimo, Daniele Patella, Duilio Del Prete. All-too-typical Italian comedy about a milquetoast who wins and weds a sexy woman, only to regret his conquest. Sole interest is observing Hoffman in this unusual setting (with a dubbed voice!). Originally 110m.

Alfred the Great (1969-British) **C-122m.** ** D: Clive Donner. David Hemmings, Michael York, Prunella Ransome, Colin Blakely, Julian Glover, Ian McKellen. Story of young leader of 9th-century England can't decide if it's a serious historical chronicle or broad swashbuckler; succeeds in neither department. Only highlight is series of meticulously filmed battle scenes; otherwise, ambitious script is boring.

✓ **Algiers** (1938) **95m.** *** D: John Cromwell. Charles Boyer, Sigrid Gurie, Hedy Lamarr, Joseph Calleia, Alan Hale, Gene Lockhart, Johnny Downs. Boyer as Pepe Le Moko falls in love with alluring Lamarr visiting Casbah district of Algiers: Calleia as police official, Lockhart as informer, stand out in well-cast romance. Remake of French PEPE LE MOKO, remade as CASBAH.▼

Alias a Gentleman (1948) **76m.** ** D: Harry Beaumont. Wallace Beery, Tom Drake, Dorothy Patrick, Gladys George,

Leon Ames. Minor saga of an aging jailbird (Beery) who doesn't want to see his daughter involved with shady characters like himself.

Alias Boston Blackie (1942) **67m.** D: Lew Landers. Chester Morris, Adele Mara, Richard Lane, George E. Stone, Lloyd Corrigan, Walter Sande, Larry Parks, Lloyd Bridges. SEE: **Boston Blackie** series.

Alias Bulldog Drummond SEE: **Bulldog Jack**

Alias Jesse James (1959) **C-92m.** *** D: Norman McLeod. Bob Hope, Rhonda Fleming, Wendell Corey, Jim Davis, Gloria Talbott. One of Hope's funniest has him an insurance salesman out West, mistaken for sharpshooter. Fleming is a lovely Western belle; the two do a cute song together. Many guests appear at the climax.

Alias Nick Beal (1949) **93m.** *** D: John Farrow. Ray Milland, Audrey Totter, Thomas Mitchell, George Macready, Fred Clark. Allegory of Devil (Milland) corrupting honest politician Mitchell with help of trollop Totter. Interesting drama with unusually sinister Milland.

Alias Smith and Jones (1970) **C-90m.** TVM D: Gene Levitt. Peter Deuel, Ben Murphy, John Russell, Earl Holliman, Forrest Tucker, James Drury, Susan Saint James. Reworking of BUTCH CASSIDY premise. Two bandits in American West find technology creeping up on them, making their job more difficult. Pilot for the TV series. Average.

Ali Baba and the Forty Thieves (1944) **C-87m.** **½ D: Arthur Lubin. Maria Montez, Jon Hall, Scotty Beckett, Turhan Bey, Kurt Katch, Andy Devine, Frank Puglia. Colorful escapism with rightful-prince Hall battling evil man who put him out of the way years ago; much footage reused in SWORD OF ALI BABA.

Ali Baba Goes to Town (1937) **81m.** *** D: David Butler. Eddie Cantor, Tony Martin, Roland Young, June Lang, John Carradine, Louise Hovick (Gypsy Rose Lee). Entertaining musical comedy sends Cantor back in time but retains topical jokes of 1937; nice production with Cantor in top form. Ends with modern-day movie premiere and glimpses of many stars, from Shirley Temple to Tyrone Power.

Alibi Ike (1935) **73m.** *** D: Ray Enright. Joe E. Brown, Olivia de Havilland, William Frawley, Ruth Donnelly, Roscoe Karns. Ingratiating baseball comedy by Ring Lardner, with Joe a tale-spinning pitcher who gets involved in various calamities. Young de Havilland is charming heroine in one of Joe's best vehicles.

Alice Adams (1935) **99m.** ***½ D: George Stevens. Katharine Hepburn, Fred MacMurray, Fred Stone, Evelyn Venable, Frank Albertson, Hattie McDaniel. Excellent small-town Americana with social-climbing girl finally finding love in person of unpretentious MacMurray. Booth Tarkington book becomes fine film, if not altogether credible. The dinner-table scene is unforgettable. Filmed before in 1923, with Florence Vidor.▼

Alice Doesn't Live Here Anymore (1975) **C-113m.** ***½ D: Martin Scorsese. Ellen Burstyn, Kris Kristofferson, Billy Green Bush, Alfred Lutter, Diane Ladd, Jodie Foster, Harvey Keitel, Vic Tayback, Valerie Curtin. Excellent look at a woman's odyssey to find herself and some measure of happiness after her husband dies, leaving her and a young son penniless. Kristofferson is gentle, well-meaning man who tries to win her love. Burstyn won well-deserved Oscar for Best Actress. Rich screenplay by Robert Getchell. Later reworked into a long-running TV sitcom called *Alice*.▼

Alice in the Cities (1974-German) **110m.** *** D: Wim Wenders. Rudiger Vogler, Yella Rottlander, Lisa Kreuzer, Chuck Berry. After wandering aimlessly across America, alienated journalist Vogler meets a woman—and finds himself saddled with her nine-year-old daughter when she mysteriously disappears. Intelligent, often hypnotic film reflects on the effect of American pop culture on post-war Europeans.▼

Alice in Wonderland (1933) **77m.** ** D: Norman Z. McLeod. Charlotte Henry, Richard Arlen, Gary Cooper, W.C. Fields, Cary Grant, Edward Everett Horton, Baby LeRoy, Edna May Oliver, Jack Oakie, many others. Top Paramount stars appear, disguised as various Lewis Carroll characters, in this slow-moving adaptation of the classic story. Fascinating because of its casting—Cooper as the White Knight, Fields as Humpty Dumpty, Grant as the Mock Turtle—but, overall, a bore. Screenplay by Joseph L. Mankiewicz and William Cameron Menzies.

Alice in Wonderland (1950-British) **C-83m.** ** D: Dallas Bower. Carol Marsh, Stephen Murray, Pamela Brown, Felix Aylmer, Ernest Milton. Static adaptation of Lewis Carroll classic with gimmick of mixing live action and puppets; most of the wit and charm are missing.▼

✓ **Alice in Wonderland** (1951) **C-75m.** *** D: Clyde Geronimi, Hamilton Luske, Wilfred Jackson. Voices of Kathryn Beaumont, Ed Wynn, Richard Haydn, Sterling Holloway, Jerry Colonna, Verna Felton, Bill Thompson. Entertaining, if somewhat aloof, rendering of Lewis Carroll's classic, with the Walt Disney animation team at its best bringing the Cheshire Cat, the Queen of Hearts, and the Mad Hatter to life. Episodic film is given major boost by strong personalities of Wynn, Colonna, Holloway, et al, and such tunes as "I'm Late" and "The Unbirthday Song." ▼

Alice's Adventures in Wonderland (1972) **C-96m.** *½ D: William Sterling. Fiona Fullerton, Michael Crawford, Ralph Richardson, Flora Robson, Peter Sellers, Dudley Moore, Michael Jayston. Tedious British film version of Lewis Carroll's classic proves Americans don't have a monopoly on making bad children's musicals. Waste of a good cast.▼

Alice's Restaurant (1969) **C-111m.** *** D: Arthur Penn. Arlo Guthrie, Pat Quinn, James Broderick, Michael McClanathan, Geoff Outlaw, Tina Chen. Guthrie's popular record inspired this odd blend of satire, whimsy, melodrama, and social commentary. Generally fun, with quizzically downbeat ending, showing freeform lifestyle of group of friends headed by Broderick and Quinn (as Alice).▼

Alice, Sweet Alice SEE: Holy Terror▼

Alien (1979) **C-117m.** **½ D: Ridley Scott. Tom Skerritt, Sigourney Weaver, John Hurt, Ian Holm, Harry Dean Stanton, Yaphet Kotto, Veronica Cartwright. Commercial spacecraft unwittingly takes on an alien being that wreaks merciless havoc on the crew. Space-age horror film reverts to 1950s formula story, but adds stomach-churning violence, slime, and shocks. Still, this is some people's idea of a good time. Oscar-winning effects. Inspired by IT! THE TERROR FROM BEYOND SPACE. Followed by ALIENS.▼

Alienator (1989) **C-92m.** ** D: Fred Olen Ray. Jan-Michael Vincent, John Phillip Law, Ross Hagen, Teagan, Dyann Ortelli, Jesse Dabson, Dawn Wildsmith, P. J. Soles, Robert Clarke, Richard Wiley, Leo V. Gordon, Robert Quarry. Gimlet-eyed Vincent, a cruel alien prison warden, sends unstoppable, Amazonian "hunter unit" Teagan after fugitive Hagen, who's crash-landed on Earth. Forest ranger Law and others help the desperate alien. OK sci-fi from the prolific Ray, with a great B-movie cast; looks like two movies overlapping.▼

Alien Nation (1988) **C-94m.** **½ D: Graham Baker. James Caan, Mandy Patinkin, Terence Stamp, Kevin Major Howard, Leslie Bevins. In the near future, a race of odd-looking aliens is slowly (and grudgingly) being integrated into society. World-weary L.A. cop Caan agrees to take one on as his partner, so he can track down the alien who killed his former sidekick. A great concept that doesn't quite pay off, despite many clever touches and terrific performances by Caan and Patinkin. Followed by a TV series.▼

Alien Predator (1987) **C-90m.** BOMB D: Deran Sarafian. Dennis Christopher, Martin Hewitt, Lynn-Holly Johnson, Luis Prendes, J.O. Bosso. Idiotic horror film is an imitation of THE ANDROMEDA STRAIN, with three teens vacationing in Spain, beset by monsters created by microbes from Skylab (which fell to Earth there in 1979). Both cast and special effects are terrible. Filmed in 1984.▼

Aliens (1986) **C-137m.** ***½ D: James Cameron. Sigourney Weaver, Carrie Henn, Michael Biehn, Paul Reiser, Lance Henriksen, Bill Paxton, Jenette Goldstein. Weaver, the sole human survivor from ALIEN, returns to planet that spawned the yukky creatures with a Marine squadron that's ready to wipe them out. Intense, exciting sequel directed by Cameron the same way he did THE TERMINATOR— once it gets going there's just no letup! Weaver is sensational in compelling lead role. The special effects won an Oscar. Director Cameron's original version of the film, running 17m. longer, has been released on video in the U.K.▼

Aliens Are Coming, The (1980) **C-100m.** TVM D: Harvey Hart. Tom Mason, Melinda Fee, Eric Braeden, Fawne Harriman, Caroline McWilliams, Max Gail, Ed Harris, Gerald McRaney. Slick sci-fi in the INVASION OF THE BODY SNATCHERS mold, with extraterrestrial beings from a dying planet possessing the bodies of earthlings. Average.▼

Alien's Return, The SEE: **Return, The**

Alien Thunder (1973-Canadian) **C-90m.** ** D: Claude Fournier. Donald Sutherland, Kevin McCarthy, Chief Dan George, Jean Duceppe, Jack Creely, Francine Racette. Mountie Sutherland chases Cree Indian accused of a sergeant's murder in this handsome but tedious actioner. Retitled DAN CANDY'S LAW.▼

Ali—Fear Eats the Soul (1974-German) **C-94m.** *** D: Rainer Werner Fassbinder. Brigitte Mira, El Hedi Ben Salem, Barbara Valentin, Irm Hermann, Rainer Werner Fassbinder. Widow Mira, in her 60s, falls in love with and marries an Arab 30 years her junior. Interesting, quietly effective Fassbinder film.▼

Al Jennings of Oklahoma (1951) **C-79m.** ** D: Ray Nazarro. Dan Duryea, Gale Storm, Dick Foran, Gloria Henry. Modest Western enhanced by Duryea in title role of gangster who serves his time and goes straight; sporadic action.

✓ **All About Eve** (1950) **138m.** **** D: Joseph L. Mankiewicz. Bette Davis, Anne Baxter, George Sanders, Celeste Holm, Gary Merrill, Thelma Ritter, Marilyn Monroe, Hugh Marlowe, Gregory Ratoff. Brilliantly sophisticated (and cynical) look at life in and around the theater, with a heaven-sent script by director Mankiewicz (based on the story "The Wisdom of Eve" by Mary Orr). Davis is absolutely perfect as an aging star who takes in an adoring fan (Baxter) and soon discovers that the young woman is taking over her life. Witty dialogue to spare, especially great when spoken by Sanders and Ritter. Six Oscars

include Best Picture, Director, Screenplay, and Supporting Actor (Sanders). Later musicalized on Broadway as *Applause*.▼

All American, The (1953) **83m.** ** D: Jesse Hibbs. Tony Curtis, Lori Nelson, Richard Long, Mamie Van Doren, Gregg Palmer, Stuart Whitman. Football is secondary aspect of typical romance story between two wholesome young people (Curtis and Nelson).

All-American Boy, The (1973) **C-118m.** ** D: Charles Eastman. Jon Voight, E. J. Peaker, Ned Glass, Anne Archer, Carol Androsky. Muddled drama about Olympic hopeful Voight's attempt to succeed as a boxer; striking locations of northern California, but that's all.

Allan Quatermain and the Lost City of Gold (1987) **C-99m.** BOMB D: Gary Nelson (additional scenes: Newt Arnold). Richard Chamberlain, Sharon Stone, James Earl Jones, Henry Silva, Robert Donner, Doghmi Larbi, Aileen Marson, Cassandra Peterson, Martin Rabbett. Cheapjack followup to 1985 version of KING SOLOMON'S MINES with the same two stars; Chamberlain returns to Africa in search of his brother, who's been tracking a lost white tribe. Post-production patchups are all too obvious—and they don't much help. Remake of the 1977 KING SOLOMON'S TREASURE. ▼

All Ashore (1953) **C-80m.** *½ D: Richard Quine. Mickey Rooney, Dick Haymes, Peggy Ryan, Ray MacDonald. Musical yarn of three gobs on shore leave finding gals, sinks despite Rooney's sprite spirit.

All at Sea (1958-British) **87m.** *** D: Charles Frend. Alec Guinness, Irene Browne, Percy Herbert, Harold Goodwin. Robust comedy that holds its own throughout. Guinness is admirable as seaman who can't bear sight of water but buys rundown house-laden pier, turning it into an amusement palace.

All Creatures Great and Small (1974-U.S.-British) **C-92m.** TVM D: Claude Whatham. Simon Ward, Anthony Hopkins, Lisa Harrow, Brian Stirner, Freddie Jones, T. P. McKenna. Gentle drama about rural English life, taken from James Herriot's autobiographical best-sellers (*If Only They Could Talk* and *It Shouldn't Happen to a Vet*). Ward plays the author in his younger days as apprentice to an eccentric veterinarian, wonderfully acted by Hopkins. Rich period piece. Script by Hugh Whitemore. Followed by a British TV series. Sequel: ALL THINGS BRIGHT AND BEAUTIFUL. Above average.▼

All Dogs Go to Heaven (1989) **C-85m.** *½ D: Don Bluth. Voices of Burt Reynolds, Loni Anderson, Judith Barsi, Dom DeLuise, Vic Tayback, Charles Nelson Reilly, Melba Moore. Bluth's colorful animation is only saving grace of this downbeat musical cartoon about an orphan "adopted" by an unlovable mutt (Reynolds) who has returned from heaven to do a good deed. Misguided film has some good moments (a musical sequence with a Cajun alligator), but combination of unappealing characters, confused storytelling, and forgettable songs makes this a major disappointment.▼

Allegheny Uprising (1939) 81m. *** D: William Seiter. John Wayne, Claire Trevor, George Sanders, Brian Donlevy, Robert Barrat, Moroni Olsen, Chill Wills. Wayne leads band of brave men against crooked Donlevy, tyrannical British captain Sanders in pre-Revolutionary colonies. Fine, unpretentious film; Trevor appealing as girl who goes after Wayne. Also shown in computer-colored version.▼

Allegro Non Troppo (1976-Italian) C-75m. *** D: Bruno Bozzetto. Animator Bozzetto's answer to Disney's FANTASIA is an uneven but imaginative collection of vignettes set to music by Debussy, Dvorak, Vivaldi, Stravinsky, and others, framed by heavy-handed live-action slapstick featuring an oafish orchestra-conductor. Best sequences: Sibelius' "Valse Triste," with a melancholy cat, and a chronicle of evolution set to Ravel's "Bolero."▼

All Fall Down (1962) 110m. *** D: John Frankenheimer. Warren Beatty, Eva Marie Saint, Karl Malden, Angela Lansbury, Brandon de Wilde. Improbable but absorbing William Inge script about narcissistic young man (Beatty), his admiring younger brother (de Wilde), indulgent parents (Lansbury and Malden), and the older woman (Saint) who suffers tragic results from loving him. Fine performances. Also shown in computer-colored version.

All God's Children (1980) C-100m. TVM D: Jerry Thorpe. Richard Widmark, Ned Beatty, Ossie Davis, Ruby Dee, Mariclare Costello, Ken Swofford, George Spell, Trish Van Devere. The provocative forced-busing issue has been molded into a sensitive drama about the tearing apart of friends, families, and a neighborhood. Widmark gives a fine performance as a judge who must decide the case. Script by William Blinn. Above average.▼

All Hands on Deck (1961) C-98m. ** D: Norman Taurog. Pat Boone, Buddy Hackett, Dennis O'Keefe, Barbara Eden. Innocuous musical comedy of free-wheeling sailors, Boone and Hackett, is lightweight entertainment.

All I Desire (1953) 70m. **½ D: Douglas Sirk. Barbara Stanwyck, Richard Carlson, Lyle Bettger, Lori Nelson, Maureen O'Sullivan. Family togetherness and home-town approval is answer to title, in period-piece uplifted by Stanwyck's valiant performance as erring mother of three who returns to her husband.

Alligator (1980) C-94m. *** D: Lewis Teague. Robert Forster, Robin Riker, Michael Gazzo, Perry Lang, Jack Carter, Henry Silva, Bart Braverman, Dean Jagger. If you've got to make a film about a giant alligator that's terrorizing Chicago, this is the way to do it—with a sense of fun to balance the expected violence and genuine scares. The knowing screenplay is by John Sayles; Silva does a hilarious self-parody as an egomaniacal Great White Hunter. Don't miss the graffiti in the final scene.▼

Alligator Named Daisy, An (1957-British) C-88m. **½ D: J. Lee Thompson. Diana Dors, Donald Sinden, Stanley Holloway, Roland Culver, Margaret Rutherford, Stephen Boyd. Dors reveals pleasing comic talent in fabricated account of salesman who mistakenly picks up someone else's alligator suitcase, leading to complications.

Alligator People, The (1959) 74m. **½ D: Roy Del Ruth. Beverly Garland, George Macready, Lon Chaney, Richard Crane, Frieda Inescort, Bruce Bennett. Garland searches for runaway husband and finds him at his family's Southern mansion—partly transformed into an alligator! Strictly routine.

Alligator Shoes (1981-Canadian) C-98m. **½ D: Clay Borris. Garry Borris, Ronalda Jones, Clay Borris, Rose Maltais-Borris, Len Perry. Clever but uneven fictionalized drama about the director's family, focusing on brother Garry's hustling and conning. Excellent use of working class Toronto locations.

All in a Night's Work (1961) C-94m. **½ D: Joseph Anthony. Dean Martin, Shirley MacLaine, Charlie Ruggles, Cliff Robertson. Featherweight (and often featherbrained) comedy about innocent office worker caught in compromising position with big-business exec, which leads to series of misunderstandings. Cast is filled with familiar character actors (Gale Gordon, Jerome Cowan, Jack Weston, et al). ▼

All Mine to Give (1957) C-102m. **½ D: Allen Reisner. Cameron Mitchell, Glynis Johns, Patty McCormack, Hope Emerson. Often touching story of pioneer family in Wisconsin determined to overcome all obstacles.▼

All My Darling Daughters (1972) C-73m. TVM D: David Lowell Rich. Robert Young, Eve Arden, Raymond Massey, Darleen Carr, Judy Strangis, Jerry Fogel, Darrell Larson, Sharon Gless. A judge's four daughters decide to get married on same day. Some amusing incidents. Followed by MY DARLING DAUGHTERS' ANNIVERSARY. Average.

All My Sons (1948) 94m. *** D: Irving Reis. Edward G. Robinson, Burt Lancaster, Mady Christians, Louisa Horton, Howard Duff, Arlene Francis, Lloyd Gough,

Henry (Harry) Morgan, Elisabeth Fraser. Arthur Miller's compelling drama of family discovering their father's unsavory business ethics during WW2 is well-acted, but quite verbose.

Allnighter, The (1987) **C-108m.** BOMB D: Tamar Simon Hoffs. Susanna Hoffs, Dedee Pfeiffer, Joan Cusack, Michael Ontkean, John Terlesky, James Anthony Shanta, Pam Grier, Mesach Taylor. Three female airheads stumble through assorted sexual hijinks during the final senior weekend at a Pacific party college. Grotesque in the AIDS era, though it would be a stinker anytime. Director Hoffs is the mother of the star, a member of The Bangles rock group.▼

All Night Long (1961-British) **95m.** **½ D: Basil Dearden. Patrick McGoohan, Marti Stevens, Betsy Blair, Keith Michell, Richard Attenborough. Fair updating of *Othello*, about an interracial couple, a white singer and black bandleader, and their Iago, a drummer (amusingly played by McGoohan). Guest musicians include Dave Brubeck, Charlie Mingus, and John Dankworth.

All Night Long (1981) **C-88m.** ***½ D: Jean-Claude Tramont. Gene Hackman, Barbra Streisand, Diane Ladd, Dennis Quaid, Kevin Dobson, William Daniels, Ann Doran. Married Hackman takes up with neighbor's wife Streisand after he's demoted to managing a downtown all-night drugstore, the clientele of which has torridly high weirdo quotient. Streisand is badly, if rather endearingly, miscast (she replaced Lisa Eichhorn after film was already in production), but Hackman is at the peak of his charm in this gentle, underrated comedy.▼

All of Me (1934) **75m.** ** D: James Flood. Fredric March, Miriam Hopkins, George Raft, Helen Mack, Blanche Frederici. Ineffectual melodrama of professor March yearning for open spaces and lover Hopkins learning about true devotion from gun moll Mack.

All of Me (1984) **C-93m.** *** D: Carl Reiner. Steve Martin, Lily Tomlin, Victoria Tennant, Madolyn Smith, Richard Libertini, Dana Elcar, Jason Bernard, Selma Diamond. The soul and spirit of a crotchety millionairess (Tomlin) enter the body of a young, idealistic lawyer (Martin) with often hilarious results. Uneven comedy-fantasy actually gets better as it goes along, and characters become more endearing. Martin's performance is a comic tour-de force.▼

Allotment Wives (1945) **83m.** ** D: William Nigh. Kay Francis, Paul Kelly, Otto Kruger, Gertrude Michael, Teala Loring. Mild sensationalism involving women who marry servicemen to collect their military pay; not one of Francis' better films.

All Over Town (1937) **62m.** **½ D: James W. Horne. Ole Olsen, Chic Johnson, Mary Howard, Harry Stockwell, Franklin Pangborn, James Finlayson. Low-budget shenanigans, with Olsen and Johnson trying to stage a show in a "jinxed" theater. Spotty, but has some funny moments.▼

All Quiet on the Western Front (1930) **105m.** **** D: Lewis Milestone. Lew Ayres, Louis Wolheim, John Wray, Slim Summerville, Russell Gleason, Ben Alexander, Beryl Mercer. Vivid, moving adaptation of Erich Maria Remarque's eloquent pacifist novel about German boys' experiences as soldiers during WWI. Time hasn't dimmed its power, or its poignancy, one bit. Scripted by Milestone, Maxwell Anderson, Del Andrews, and George Abbott. Academy Award winner for Best Picture and Director. Originally released at 140m., archivally restored to nearly that length in the 1980s. It's 130m. on home video. Sequel: THE ROAD BACK. Remade for TV a half century later.▼

All Quiet on the Western Front (1979) **C-150m.** TVM D: Delbert Mann. Richard Thomas, Ernest Borgnine, Patricia Neal, Ian Holm, Donald Pleasence. Solid remake of the vintage classic about young German soldiers in WWI and the grizzled veteran who teaches them to grow up fast in the trenches. Borgnine and Neal received Emmy nominations as did the film itself, adapted by Paul Monash from the Remarque novel. Above average.▼

All Screwed Up (1976-Italian) **C-105m.** *** D: Lina Wertmuller. Luigi Diberti, Nino Bignamini, Lina Polito, Sara Rapisarda. Appealing tragicomedy of two farmers trying to make it in the big city. Made between SEDUCTION OF MIMI and SEVEN BEAUTIES.▼

All's Fair (1989) **C-89m.** BOMB D: Rocky Lane. George Segal, Sally Kellerman, Robert Carradine, Jennifer Edwards, Jane Kaczmarek, John Kapelos, Lou Ferrigno. Dreadful comedy about some good-old-boy executives who spend their weekends playing macho war games, and end up taking on their wives and female counterparts in "battle." You'll be hard-pressed to find a comedy as unfunny as this.▼

All That Heaven Allows (1955) **C-89m.** *** D: Douglas Sirk. Jane Wyman, Rock Hudson, Agnes Moorehead, Virginia Grey, Conrad Nagel. When widow Wyman allows younger man Hudson to romance her, she faces the ire of friends and society. Nicely mounted production.

All That Jazz (1979) **C-123m.** **½ D: Bob Fosse. Roy Scheider, Jessica Lange, Ann Reinking, Leland Palmer, Cliff Gorman, Ben Vereen, Erzsebet Foldi, Sandahl Bergman, John Lithgow, Keith Gordon,

Ben Masters, Nicole Fosse, Theresa Merritt, Wallace Shawn. Director-choreographer Fosse's own 8½ casts a self-indulgent and largely negative look at his life; great show biz moments and wonderful dancing are eventually buried in pretensions, and an interminable finale which leaves a bad taste for the whole film. But that opening number (set to George Benson's recording of "On Broadway") is a wow!▼

All That Money Can Buy SEE: **Devil and Daniel Webster, The**▼

All the Brothers Were Valiant (1953) C-101m. **½ D: Richard Thorpe. Robert Taylor, Stewart Granger, Ann Blyth, Keenan Wynn, James Whitmore, Lewis Stone. Water-logged adventurer based on Ben Ames Williams' novel. Taylor and Granger lack conviction as New Bedford whalers having career and romantic conflicts.

All the Fine Young Cannibals (1960) C-112m. *½ D: Michael Anderson. Robert Wagner, Natalie Wood, Susan Kohner, George Hamilton, Pearl Bailey, Anne Seymour. Clichés abound in this romantic soap opera that was actually inspired by the life of jazz trumpeter Chet Baker (whose role is played here, somewhat improbably, by Wagner). British music group Fine Young Cannibals took its name from this film.

All the Kind Strangers (1974) C-78m. TVM D: Burt Kennedy. Stacy Keach, Samantha Eggar, John Savage, Robby Benson, Arlene Farber, Tim Parkison. Seven backwoods orphans turn remote farmhouse into prison for unsuspecting Keach and Eggar. Children want them to be their foster parents, or disappear permanently. Below average.▼

All the King's Horses (1934) 87m. ** D: Frank Tuttle. Carl Brisson, Mary Ellis, Edward Everett Horton, Katherine DeMille, Eugene Pallette. Mediocre musical about movie star who exchanges places with lookalike king, causing complications for both men, especially where l'amour is concerned.

All the King's Men (1949) 109m. **** D: Robert Rossen. Broderick Crawford, Joanne Dru, John Ireland, Mercedes McCambridge, John Derek, Shepperd Strudwick, Anne Seymour. Brilliant adaptation (by director Rossen) of Robert Penn Warren's Pulitzer Prize-winning novel about the rise and fall of a Huey Long-like senator, played by Crawford in the performance of his career. He and McCambridge (in her first film) won well-deserved Oscars, as did the film, for Best Picture.▼

. . . All the Marbles (1981) C-113m. *** D: Robert Aldrich. Peter Falk, Vicki Frederick, Laurene Landon, Burt Young, Tracy Reed, Ursaline Bryant-King, Claudette Nevins, Richard Jaeckel. There's no reason why this sloppily constructed, shallowly written movie—about a pair of beautiful female wrestlers and their two-bit manager—should be so entertaining, but it is. The climactic championship bout is a real audience-rouser. Retitled THE CALIFORNIA DOLLS. Aldrich's final film.▼

All the President's Men (1976) C-138m. **** D: Alan J. Pakula. Robert Redford, Dustin Hoffman, Jason Robards, Jack Warden, Martin Balsam, Hal Holbrook, Jane Alexander, Stephen Collins, Meredith Baxter, Ned Beatty, Robert Walden, Polly Holliday, F. Murray Abraham, Lindsay Ann Crouse. Redford and Hoffman play real-life *Washington Post* reporters Bob Woodward and Carl Bernstein, who persevered in their investigation of Watergate break-in that led to earthshaking scandal. Best elements of newspaper pictures, detective stories, and thrillers rolled into one superb movie. Robards and screenwriter William Goldman won Oscars.

All the Right Moves (1983) C-91m. **½ D: Michael Chapman. Tom Cruise, Craig T. Nelson, Lea Thompson, Charles Cioffi, Paul Carafotes, Christopher Penn. Amiable youth film about a goal-oriented high-school football player (Cruise) who runs afoul of his hotheaded—and equally ambitious—coach (Nelson). Location filming in Johnstown, Pa., adds flavor.▼

All These Women (1964-Swedish) C-80m. **½ D: Ingmar Bergman. Jarl Kulle, Harriet Andersson, Bibi Andersson, Allan Edwall. Satirical frolic involving woman-chasing cellist. He bargains with music critic to have biography written by agreeing to play writer's composition. Minor Bergman. Also known as NOW ABOUT ALL THESE WOMEN.

All the Way SEE: **Joker Is Wild, The**

All the Way, Boys (1973-Italian) C-105m. *½ D: Giuseppe Colizzi. Terence Hill, Bud Spencer, Cyril Cusack, Michele Antoine, Rene Koldehoff. Big comedown for the TRINITY boys; soggy comedy has them operating a ramshackle airplane in the Andes. Pathos overwhelms the slapstick, and it works about as well here as it did in most of Jerry Lewis's films.▼

All the Way Home (1963) 103m. ***½ D: Alex Segal. Jean Simmons, Robert Preston, Aline MacMahon, Pat Hingle, Michael Kearney, John Cullum, Thomas Chalmers. Outstanding filmization of the Tad Mosel play, set in 1915 Tennessee, an adaptation of James Agee's *A Death in the Family*. Preston is subdued in the pivotal role of a father and husband who is accidentally killed, leaving his loved ones to interpret the meaning of their lives before and after his death. Beautifully done, with Simmons offering an award-caliber performance as Preston's wife. Fine script by Philip Reisman, Jr.

All the Young Men (1960) 87m. **½ D: Hall Bartlett. Alan Ladd, Sidney Poitier, James Darren, Glenn Corbett, Mort Sahl. Hackneyed Korean war story with all the stereotypes present, mouthing the same old platitudes.

All Things Bright and Beautiful (1979-British) C-94m. **½ D: Eric Till. John Alderton, Lisa Harrow, Colin Blakely, Bill Maynard, Richard Pearson, Paul Shelley. Pleasant, inoffensive film for kids who like animals and can appreciate an entertainment devoid of car crashes. Kind-hearted veterinarian James Herriot (Alderton) tends to under-the-weather animals in Yorkshire at the end of the '30s. Based on two of Herriot's books, *Let Sleeping Vets Lie* and *Vet in Harness*, published in the U.S. as *All Things Bright and Beautiful*. A sequel to ALL CREATURES GREAT AND SMALL, made for American television. Also known as IT SHOULDN'T HAPPEN TO A VET.

All This, and Heaven Too (1940) 143m. *** D: Anatole Litvak. Bette Davis, Charles Boyer, Jeffrey Lynn, Barbara O'Neil, Virginia Weidler, Helen Westley, Walter Hampden, Henry Daniell, June Lockhart. Nobleman Boyer falls in love with governess Davis, causing scandal and death; stars do very well in elaborate filmization of Rachel Field book set in 19th-century France.▼

All This and World War II (1976) C-88m. ** D: Susan Winslow. Unusual documentary traces chronology of WW2 with Movietone newsreels and 20th Century-Fox feature film footage, all set to Beatles music! Not as bad as it sounds, but not particularly good either, because there is no point—or point of view.

All Through the Night (1942) 107m. *** D: Vincent Sherman. Humphrey Bogart, Conrad Veidt, Kaaren Verne, Jane Darwell, Frank McHugh, Peter Lorre, Judith Anderson, William Demarest, Jackie Gleason, Phil Silvers, Barton MacLane, Martin Kosleck. Bogart's gang tracks down Fifth Columnists (Veidt, Lorre, Anderson) in WW2 N.Y.C. Interesting blend of spy, gangster, and comedy genres, with memorable double-talk and auction scenes.

All Together Now (1975) C-78m. TVM D: Randal Kleiser. John Rubinstein, Glynnis O'Connor, Brad Savage, Helen Hunt, Dori Brenner, Bill Macy, Jane Withers. Fact-based tale of orphaned college student who has thirty days to prove himself a fit guardian for his younger brothers and sisters. Inspiring drama. Written by Jeff Andrus and Rubin Carson. Above average.

Almost a Bride SEE: Kiss For Corliss, A

Almost Angels (1962) C-93m. **½ D: Steve Previn. Peter Weck, Hans Holt, Fritz Eckhardt, Bruni Lobel, Vincent Winter, Sean Scully. Schmaltzy but entertaining

Disney film about two youngsters who become friends in the Vienna Boys Choir. Pleasant story, fine music.▼

Almost Human (1974-Italian) C-92m. BOMB D: Umberto Lenzi. Tomas Milian, Henry Silva, Anita Strindberg, Raymond Lovelock, Laura Belli. Sadistic punk Milian versus tired cop Silva. Not another gory horror film, just another clichéd crime melodrama. Originally titled THE KIDNAP OF MARY LOU.▼

Almost Perfect Affair, An (1979) C-93m. **½ D: Michael Ritchie. Keith Carradine, Monica Vitti, Raf Vallone, Christian De Sica, Dick Anthony Williams. Romantic comedy-drama about affair between naive American filmmaker and worldly wife of film producer; set against whirring backdrop of Cannes Film Festival, it will appeal mostly to film buffs and insiders.▼

Almost Summer (1978) C-88m. *½ D: Martin Davidson. Bruno Kirby, Lee Purcell, John Friedrich, Didi Conn, Thomas Carter, Tim Matheson. End-of-term frolics, and a cutthroat school election, are presented here in much the same fashion as BEACH BLANKET BINGO.

Almost You (1984) C-96m. *½ D: Adam Brooks. Brooke Adams, Griffin Dunne, Karen Young, Marty Watt, Christine Estabrook, Josh Mostel, Laura Dean, Miguel Piñero, Joe Silver, Joe Leon. Muddled, overlong, self-satisfied "romantic comedy" about Dunne's attempts to break out of his plodding existence with wife Adams in N.Y.C. Originally shown at 110m, which only made matters worse.▼

aloha, bobby and rose (1975) C-85m. ** D: Floyd Mutrux. Paul LeMat, Dianne Hull, Tim McIntire, Leigh French, Martine Bartlett, Robert Carradine, Eddie (Edward James) Olmos. OK melodrama follows predictable pattern as auto mechanic LeMat and girlfriend Hull are inadvertently drawn into crime, causing them to take it on the lam with the law in pursuit.▼

Aloha Means Goodbye (1974) C-100m. TVM D: David Lowell Rich. Sally Struthers, James Franciscus, Joanna Miles, Henry Darrow, Larry Gates, Frank Marth. Young woman fights for her life against rare blood disease and an unscrupulous doctor in need of heart-transplant donor, but manages to enjoy location beauty of Hawaii. Ludicrous. Below average.

Aloha Summer (1988) C-98m. ** D: Tommy Lee Wallace. Chris Makepeace, Yuji Okumoto, Don Michael Paul, Tia Carrere, Andy Bumatai, Lorie Griffin, Sho Kosugi. Well-meaning but bland story about six young American, Japanese, and Hawaiian boys coming of age on surfboards in Waikiki during the summer of 1959. There's nothing fresh here; in fact, the whole thing looks and feels as if it were made in 1959. The waves, however, are outtasight.▼

Aloma of the South Seas (1941) **C-77m.** ** D: Alfred Santell. Dorothy Lamour, Jon Hall, Lynne Overman, Philip Reed, Katherine DeMille. Still another sarong saga with native Hall sent to U.S. for education, returning when father dies to stop revolution on once peaceful island. Filmed before in 1927, with Gilda Gray.

Alone in the Dark (1982) **C-92m.** *½ D: Jack Sholder. Jack Palance, Donald Pleasence, Martin Landau, Dwight Schultz, Erland van Lidth de Jeude, Deborah Hedwall. Mental patients escape from a lunatic asylum and go on a rampage. If your IQ is 15, you might enjoy this.▼

Alone in the Neon Jungle (1988) **C-100m TVM** D: Georg Stanford Brown. Suzanne Pleshette, Danny Aiello, Priscilla Lopez, Joe Morton, Jon Tenney, Raymond Serra, Frank Converse, Georg Stanford Brown. Lady police captain vows to clean up a corrupt precinct in this OK variation on standard cop show plot. Average.

Alone on the Pacific (1963-Japanese) **C-100m.** *** D: Kon Ichikawa. Yujiro Ishihara, Kinuyo Tanaka, Masayuki Mori, Ruriko Asaoka, Hajime Hara. Stirring tale of youth (Ishihara) sailing the Pacific from Osaka to San Francisco by himself. Based on a true story. Original running-time: 104m. Also known as MY ENEMY, THE SEA.

Along Came a Spider (1969) **C-92m. TVM** D: Lee Katzin. Suzanne Pleshette, Ed Nelson, Andrew Prine, Brooke Bundy, Richard Anderson, Milton Selzer. Entertaining, occasionally moving drama featuring Pleshette as widow of research scientist torn between instincts and need for vengeance as she befriends scientist professor (Nelson) who had worked on same project that brought about deadly accident. Complete with nail-biting finish. Adapted by Barry Oringer from Leonard Lee's novel *Sweet Poison.* Originally broadcast at 73m. Above average.

Along Came Jones (1945) **90m.** *** D: Stuart Heisler. Gary Cooper, Loretta Young, William Demarest, Dan Duryea, Frank Sully, Russell Simpson. Three stars are most ingratiating in very low-key, leisurely Western spoof, with Cooper (who also produced) mistaken for notorious outlaw Duryea.▼

Along the Great Divide (1951) **88m.** **½ D: Raoul Walsh. Kirk Douglas, Virginia Mayo, John Agar, Walter Brennan. Douglas is appropriately tight-lipped as lawman determined to bring in his man, despite desert storm; some spectacular scenery.▼

Alphabet City (1984) **C-98m.** ** D: Amos Poe. Vincent Spano, Kate Vernon, Michael Winslow, Zohra Lampert, Jami Gertz, Raymond Serra. Slick, arty but shallow and practically plotless portrait of teenage hood-lum Spano, and his life on N.Y.C.'s Lower East Side. All imagery, no content.▼

Alphabet Murders, The (1966-British) **90m.** **½ D: Frank Tashlin. Tony Randall, Anita Ekberg, Robert Morley, Guy Rolfe, James Villiers. Odd adaptation of Agatha Christie's *The ABC Murders* (the film's original British title), with Hercule Poirot after a killer who seems to be doing in his victims in alphabetical order. Strange casting of Randall as the Belgian sleuth and a little too much slapstick make this more a curiosity than anything else. Margaret Rutherford makes a gag appearance as Miss Marple.

Alpha Caper, The (1973) **C-73m. TVM** D: Robert Michael Lewis. Henry Fonda, Leonard Nimoy, James McEachin, Larry Hagman, John Marley, Elena Verdugo, Noah Beery. Parole officer (Fonda), disenchanted with the System, convinces three paroled criminals to join him in an armored-car robbery scheme. Emphasis on action and suspense in mechanical narrative brightened only by good cast. Average.

Alpha Incident, The (1977) **C-84m.** ** D: Bill Rebane. Ralph Meeker, Stafford Morgan, John Goff, Carole Irene Newell. Government tries to cover up existence of a deadly organism that has been retrieved from Mars . . . but when radiation spreads, it's too late.▼

Alphaville (1965-French) **95m.** ** D: Jean-Luc Godard. Eddie Constantine, Anna Karina, Akim Tamiroff, Howard Vernon. Constantine, as super private-eye Lemmy Caution, is sent to futuristic city run by electronic brain to rescue scientist trapped there. Jumbled Godard epic, recommended for New Wave disciples only.▼

Alsino and the Condor (1982-Nicaraguan-Mexican-Cuban-Costa Rican) **C-89m.** *** D: Miguel Littin. Dean Stockwell, Alan Esquivel, Carmen Bunster, Alejandro Parodi, Delia Casanova. Idealistic young peasant (Esquivel) jumps out of a tree in the hope of flying; he becomes a hunchback, but learns to stand tall when he joins guerillas fighting in a Central American country. Certainly unsubtle, but far from uninteresting allegory, filmed in Nicaragua.▼

Altered States (1980) **C-102m.** **½ D: Ken Russell. William Hurt, Blair Brown, Bob Balaban, Charles Haid, Thaao Penghilis, Dori Brenner, Miguel Godreau, Drew Barrymore. A scientist (Hurt, in his film debut) becomes involved with primal research, using himself as guinea pig with mind-bending results. Talky and cerebral at first, then turns into a cross between THE WOLF MAN and THE TIME MACHINE, using state-of-the-art special effects. More successful as an assault on the senses than as a film, with thoroughly unappealing protagonists and a ludicrous story resolution. Paddy Chayefsky disowned his adaptation of his novel, which is now credited to his given name "Sidney Aaron." Look for John Larroquette as an X-ray technician.▼

Alvarez Kelly (1966) C-116m. **½ D: Edward Dmytryk. William Holden, Richard Widmark, Janice Rule, Victoria Shaw, Patrick O'Neal. Slow-moving Civil War tale. Holden is cattle driver who sells herd to Yankees, then is kidnapped by Reb Widmark who wants him to steal cattle for the South; incongruous love scenes thrown in.▼

Always (1985) C-105m. *** D: Henry Jaglom. Henry Jaglom, Patrice Townsend, Joanna Frank, Allan Rachins, Melissa Leo, Jonathan Kaufer, Bob Rafelson, Michael Emil, Andre Gregory. Often hilarious, but also insightful, comedy about what it means to be a couple. A trio of them—one about to get divorced, one about to get married, one solidly married—spend a July-4th weekend together. The first, by the way, is played by the director and Townsend, his own ex-wife. Like all of Jaglom's stream-of-consciousness films, this one's not for all tastes.▼

Always (1989) C-121m. **½ D: Steven Spielberg. Richard Dreyfuss, Holly Hunter, John Goodman, Brad Johnson, Audrey Hepburn, Roberts Blossom, Keith David, Marg Helgenberger. Slick remake of 1943's A GUY NAMED JOE, with Dreyfuss as a cocky pilot who specializes in dousing forest fires from the air, and Hunter as the dispatcher who loves him—and fears for his life. When he does in fact die, he returns in spirit form to guide a young pilot (Johnson) who wants to pursue the same career and the same woman. With Spielberg behind the camera and two charismatic stars, it's certainly entertaining but suffers from a serious case of The Cutes.▼

Always a Bride (1954-British) 83m. ** D: Ralph Smart. Peggy Cummins, Terence Morgan, Ronald Squire, James Hayter. Mild comedy of treasury officer romancing girl, aiding her dad to fleece others.

Always Goodbye (1938) 75m. **½ D: Sidney Lanfield. Barbara Stanwyck, Herbert Marshall, Ian Hunter, Cesar Romero, Lynn Bari, Binnie Barnes. Still another sacrificing mother tale—specifically, a remake of GALLANT LADY. Stanwyck is forced to give up her illicit child. Nicely done, but the same old story.

Always in My Heart (1942) 92m. *½ D: Jo Graham. Kay Francis, Walter Huston, Gloria Warren, Una O'Connor, Sidney Blackmer. Soaper of convict Huston returning to find wife Francis about to marry Blackmer and a daughter (Warren) who doesn't know him.

Always Leave Them Laughing (1949) 116m. **½ D: Roy Del Ruth. Milton

Berle, Virginia Mayo, Ruth Roman, Bert Lahr, Alan Hale. Berle is at home in tale of cocky comedian's ups and downs. Unfortunately, zesty opening leads into soggy drama. Lahr does his classic "stop in the name of the stationhouse" routine.

Always Together (1948) 78m. **½ D: Frederick de Cordova. Robert Hutton, Joyce Reynolds, Cecil Kellaway, Ernest Truex; guests Humphrey Bogart, Jack Carson, Dennis Morgan, Janis Paige, Alexis Smith. Innocuous fluff of dying millionaire Kellaway giving money to young Reynolds, then discovering he's quite healthy. Worthwhile only for amusing cameos by many Warner Bros. stars throughout film.

Amadeus (1984) C-158m. **½ D: Milos Forman. F. Murray Abraham, Tom Hulce, Elizabeth Berridge, Simon Callow, Roy Dotrice, Christine Ebersole, Jeffrey Jones. Abraham won well-deserved Oscar as composer Salieri, whose music never surpasses mediocrity, while a hedonistic young boor named Mozart expresses musical genius almost without trying! Literate, intelligent, exquisitely filmed (in Prague, by Miroslav Ondricek) . . . but fatally overlong and missing dramatic fire that distinguished Peter Shaffer's play (Shaffer rethought and rewrote it for the screen). Worth noting: Jones's wonderful performance as musical dilettante Emperor Joseph II. Winner of seven other Oscars, including Best Picture, Director, Screenplay, Art Direction.▼

Amarcord (1974-Italian) C-127m. ***½ D: Federico Fellini. Magali Noel, Bruno Zanin, Pupella Maggio, Armando Brancia, Giuseppe Lanigro, Josiane Tanzilli. Fellini's nostalgia trip to the Italy of his youth in the 1930s; warm, funny, poignant, bawdy episodes about love, sex, politics, family life, and growing up. Academy Award winner as Best Foreign Film.▼

Amateur, The (1982-Canadian) C-111m. BOMB D: Charles Jarrott. John Savage, Christopher Plummer, Marthe Keller, Arthur Hill, Ed Lauter, Nicholas Campbell, Graham Jarvis, John Marley. Savage is grossly miscast as a CIA computer whiz who hunts down the terrorists who seized the American Consulate in Munich and murdered his girlfriend. Complex and ultimately ridiculous spy thriller.▼

Amateur Night at the Dixie Bar and Grill (1979) C-100m. TVM D: Joel Schumacher. Victor French, Candy Clark, Louise Latham, Sheree North, Jamie Farr, Henry Gibson, Tanya Tucker, Don Johnson, Dennis Quaid. Multi-character comedy-drama written by Schumacher about country-western talent show at a Southern roadhouse. Surprisingly good vignettes in this film reminiscent of Robert Altman's NASHVILLE. Above average.

Amazing Adventure (1936-British) 70m. **½ D: Alfred Zeisler. Cary Grant, Mary

Brian, Henry Kendall, Leon M. Lion, Garry Marsh, John Turnbull. Grant inherits a fortune and, feeling guilty, sets out to earn his living instead. One of those The-Poor-Are-Smarter comedies typical of the era, and a rare opportunity to see Cary working on his home turf. Originally titled THE AMAZING QUEST OF ERNEST BLISS in Britain, ROMANCE AND RICHES in the U.S. E. Phillips Oppenheim's novel had been filmed before in England in 1920.▼

Amazing Colossal Man, The (1957) **80m.** ****½** D: Bert I. Gordon. Glenn Langan, Cathy Downs, James Seay, Larry Thor. Army officer who survives an atomic explosion starts growing; at sixty feet he attacks Las Vegas! Starts well but ends up as your standard monster-on-the-loose flick. Sequel: WAR OF THE COLOSSAL BEAST.

Amazing Dobermans, The (1976) **C-94m.** ****½** D: David & Byron Chudnow. James Franciscus, Barbara Eden, Fred Astaire, Jack Carter, Billy Barty. Engaging action comedy that has Bible-quoting ex-con-man Astaire's five remarkable Doberman pinschers help treasury agent Franciscus thwart a racketeer and his gang. Higher-budgeted sequel to THE DOBERMAN GANG and THE DARING DOBERMANS, aided by offbeat casting of Astaire.▼

Amazing Doctor Clitterhouse, The (1938) **87m.** ******* D: Anatole Litvak. Edward G. Robinson, Claire Trevor, Humphrey Bogart, Allen Jenkins, Donald Crisp, Gale Page. Amusing film of "method doctor" Robinson trying to discover what makes a crook tick; he joins Bogart's gang and becomes addicted.

Amazing Grace (1974) **C-99m.** ****** D: Stan Lathan. Moms Mabley, Slappy White, Moses Gunn, Rosalind Cash, Dolph Sweet. A few laughs in Philadelphia-made comedy about an elderly busybody who disrupts corrupt Baltimore politics. Mabley's only starring film; cameos by Butterfly McQueen, unrecognizable Stepin Fetchit.

Amazing Grace and Chuck (1987) **C-115m.** ***½** D: Mike Newell. Jamie Lee Curtis, Alex English, Gregory Peck, William L. Petersen, Joshua Zuehlke, Dennis Lipscomb, Lee Richardson. A 12-year-old Little League whiz decides to stop playing baseball until the world agrees to complete nuclear disarmament . . . and soon, other athletes around the world follow suit, as the protest escalates. Producer-writer David Field's Capraesque wish-fufillment fantasy is one of those films you either swallow wholeheartedly, or don't. It's dripping with good intentions, but just doesn't come off.▼

Amazing Howard Hughes, The (1977) **C-215m. TVM** D: William A. Graham. Tommy Lee Jones, Ed Flanders, James Hampton, Tovah Feldshuh, Lee Purcell, Jim Antonio, Sorrell Booke, Arthur Franz, Howard Hesseman, Ed Harris. Surprisingly colorless account of the reclusive millionaire's life. Jones' dull performance easily overshadowed by Flanders as associate Noah Dietrich, Feldshuh as Katharine Hepburn. Occasional intrigue in this ambitious production. Average.▼

Amazing Mr. Blunden, The (1972-British) **C-99m.** ******* D: Lionel Jeffries. Laurence Naismith, Lynne Frederick, Garry Miller, Rosalyn Landor, Marc Granger, Diana Dors, James Villiers. Dickensian fantasy about a genial ghost who takes two children back in time to help two mistreated tots. Colorful family film whose only liability is somewhat muddled storyline.▼

Amazing Mrs. Holliday, The (1943) **96m.** ****½** D: Bruce Manning. Deanna Durbin, Edmond O'Brien, Barry Fitzgerald, Arthur Treacher, Frieda Inescort. Lukewarm WW2 comedy-drama about dedicated missionary Durbin trying to sneak Chinese orphans into U.S. Durbin's song interludes offer respite from silly plot. Much of this was actually directed by Jean Renoir, but his and Durbin's plans for the film went awry.

Amazing Mr. Williams (1939) **80m.** ****½** D: Alexander Hall. Melvyn Douglas, Joan Blondell, Clarence Kolb, Ruth Donnelly. Douglas holds up his marriage to investigate murder in this satisfying comedy-mystery.

Amazing Mr. X, The (1948) **78m.** ****½** D: Bernard Vorhaus. Turhan Bey, Lynn Bari, Cathy O'Donnell, Richard Carlson, Donald Curtis. Phony mystic (Bey) teams up with supposedly dead man (Curtis) to dupe his wealthy "widow" (Bari). Modest but intriguing little film. Also known as THE SPIRITUALIST.

Amazing Quest of Ernest Bliss, The SEE: **Amazing Adventure**▼

Amazing Spider-Man, The SEE: **Spider-Man**▼

Amazing Transparent Man, The (1960) **58m. BOMB** D: Edgar G. Ulmer. Douglas Kennedy, Marguerite Chapman, James Griffith, Ivan Triesault. Tawdry cheapie in which a mad scientist makes a convict invisible to steal radioactive materials for him, but the upshot is more interested in testing his new power on a nearby bank. Stalwart Ulmer fans will wish they had the formula themselves.▼

Amazons (1984) **C-100m. TVM** D: Paul Michael Glaser. Jack Scalia, Madeline Stowe, Tamara Dobson, Jennifer Warren, Stella Stevens, William Schallert, Leslie Bevis, Peter Scolari. Lady surgeon stumbles onto a secret organization of women trying to take control of the government after one of her patients, an influential congressman, mysteriously dies. The plot's strictly comic book, but director Glaser is intent on dazzling in the manner of an up-and-coming Spielberg, and it's overkill. Below average.▼

Amazon Women on the Moon (1987) C/B&W-85m. *½ D: Joe Dante, Carl Gottlieb, Peter Horton, John Landis, Robert K. Weiss. Rosanna Arquette, Ralph Bellamy, Carrie Fisher, Griffin Dunne, Steve Guttenberg, Michelle Pfeiffer, Peter Horton, Sybil Danning, Ed Begley, Jr., Henny Youngman, Paul Bartel, Lou Jacobi, Howard Hesseman, B.B. King, Steve Allen, Steve Forrest, Russ Meyer, Arsenio (Hall), Phil Hartman, Joe Pantoliano, Rip Taylor, David Alan Grier, Angel Tompkins, Kelly Preston, Andrew Dice Clay, Mike Mazurki, Corinne Wahl. Series of unrelated skits in the KENTUCKY FRIED MOVIE vein, most of them astonishingly unfunny. Parody of CAT WOMEN OF THE MOON that punctuates the film is so exact that you might as well watch the original—it's just as funny. Best of all is the 1930s sex-film spoof with Bartel and Fisher, but that comes at the very end. Film was completed in 1986, unreleased for a year.▼

Ambassador, The (1984) C-90m. *** D: J. Lee Thompson. Robert Mitchum, Ellen Burstyn, Rock Hudson, Fabio Testi, Donald Pleasence, Michal Bat-Adam. Intelligent, entertaining thriller of American ambassador Mitchum, his adulterous wife Burstyn, and his attempts to peacefully mediate the Israeli-Palestinian crisis. Based on Elmore Leonard's novel *52 Pick-Up*, and remade just two years later under that name. Hudson's final theatrical film.▼

Ambassador's Daughter, The (1956) C-102m. **½ D: Norman Krasna. Olivia de Havilland, John Forsythe, Myrna Loy, Adolphe Menjou, Edward Arnold, Francis Lederer, Tommy Noonan, Minor Watson. Oomph is missing even though stars give all to uplift sagging comedy of de Havilland out for a fling in Paris, romanced by soldier Forsythe.▼

Amber Waves (1980) C-105m. TVM D: Joseph Sargent. Dennis Weaver, Kurt Russell, Mare Winningham, Penny Fuller, Fran Brill, Wilford Brimley. A rugged wheat farmer and an arrogant male model stranded in a small midwestern town clash over their opposing views of life, patriotism, and the work ethic. Engrossing character studies beautifully acted by Weaver, Russell, and Winningham, who won an Emmy for her rich performance as Weaver's daughter. Ken Trevey wrote the wonderful script; John Rubinstein composed the music. Above average.

Ambush (1949) 89m. **½ D: Sam Wood. Robert Taylor, John Hodiak, Arlene Dahl, Jean Hagen, Chief Thundercloud. Pat Western with Apaches vs. Cavalry, salvaged by star cast.

Ambush at Cimarron Pass (1958) 73m.

** D: Jodie Copeland. Scott Brady, Margia Dean, Baynes Barron, William Vaughn. Title tells all. Look for young Clint Eastwood.

Ambush at Tomahawk Gap (1953) C-73m. *½ D: Fred F. Sears. John Hodiak, John Derek, David Brian, Percy Helton, Maria Elena Marques. Standard oater has quartet of ex-convicts caught by Indian attack. One is left alive; he rides into sunset with newly-found squaw.

Ambush Bay (1966) C-109m. **½ D: Ron Winston. Hugh O'Brian, Mickey Rooney, James Mitchum, Harry Lauter. Lackluster adventures of marine group on Jap-held island during WW2 trying to help partisans—good cast wasted.

Ambushers, The (1968) C-102m. BOMB D: Henry Levin. Dean Martin, Senta Berger, Janice Rule, James Gregory, Albert Salmi, Kurt Kasznar, Beverly Adams. Do you really care that the first U.S. flying saucer will be sabotaged in space unless Matt Helm comes to the rescue? Third entry in the series may be the weakest, but few film scholars will want to take time making certain. Sequel: THE WRECKING CREW.▼

Ambush In Leopard Street (1961-British) 60m. *½ D: J. Henry Piperno. James Kenney, Michael Brennan, Bruce Seton, Norman Rodway. Listless crime tale involving heist of diamond shipment.

Ambush Murders, The (1982) C-100m. TVM D: Steven Hilliard Stern. James Brolin, Dorian Harewood, Alfre Woodard, Louis Giambalvo, John McLiam, Teddy Wilson, Antonio Fargas, Amy Madigan. Dramatization of book by Ben Bradlee, Jr., about a true-life white attorney who takes up the cause of a black activist accused of killing two white cops. Less gripping than talky. Average.▼

Amelia Earhart (1976) C-150m. TVM D: George Schaefer. Susan Clark, John Forsythe, Stephen Macht, Susan Oliver, Catherine Burns, Jane Wyatt, Charles Aidman. Intriguing portrait of a unique woman, her private and public careers, her search for fulfillment as a noted aviatrix. Susan Clark brings famed flier vibrantly to life as a pioneer in women's lib as well as aviation. Compliments, too, to Carol Sobieski for her excellent screenplay. Above average.

America (1924) 93m. *** D: D.W. Griffith. Neil Hamilton, Carol Dempster, Erville Alderson, Charles Emmett Mack, Lee Beggs, Frank McGlynn, Lionel Barrymore, Louis Wolheim. Impressive silent-film treatment of Revolutionary War, with fine battle scenes, period flavor, marred somewhat by silly love story; florid villainy by Barrymore. Still quite good. Originally 120m.

America (1986) C-83m. BOMB D: Robert Downey. Zack Norman, Tammy Grimes, Michael J. Pollard, Monroe Arnold, Richard Belzer, Liz Torres, Howard Thomashefsky, Laura Ashton. Downey lamely attempts to recapture the freewheeling satires of the 1960s (such as his classic PUTNEY SWOPE) with this amateurish tale of the loonies at a N.Y. cable TV station, whose signal is accidentally bounced off the moon, bringing them worldwide fame. Hopelessly dated; filmed in 1982.▼

America, America (1963) 168m. **** D: Elia Kazan. Stathis Giallelis, Frank Wolff, Elena Karam, Lou Antonio, John Marley, Estelle Hemsley. The dream of passage to America—as it unfolded for late 19th-century immigrants—is movingly captured by writer-director Kazan in this long, absorbing film, based on his uncle's experiences. Heartfelt and heart-rending, with impressive Oscar-winning art direction/set decoration by Gene Callahan.

America at the Movies (1976) C-116m. ** No director credited. Mindlessly amusing but ultimately pointless potpourri of clips from 83 American movies (YANKEE DOODLE DANDY, THE GRAPES OF WRATH, GIANT, etc.), originally produced by the American Film Institute as a Bicentennial project. Can anyone explain how FIVE EASY PIECES—which takes place in California oil fields and Puget Sound—shows up in a section devoted to "The Cities"? A similar lack of direction pervades throughout.▼

Americana (1981) C-91m. **½ D: David Carradine. David Carradine, Barbara Hershey, Michael Greene. Vietnam veteran Carradine attempts to rebuild a merry-go-round in rural Kansas town. Odd, thoughtful little drama, adequately directed by its star. Filmed in 1973.▼

American Anthem (1986) C-100m. *½ D: Albert Magnoli. Mitch Gaylord, Janet Jones, Michelle Phillips, R.J. Williams, Michael Pataki, Patrice Donnelly, Stacy Maloney, Maria Anz, Andrew White. Supremely corny, badly written tale of a gymnast with family problems which keep him from fulfilling his destiny. Inauspicious movie debut for Olympic gymnast Gaylord is strangely reminiscent of PURPLE RAIN, with the same music video approach to drama; Magnoli directed them both.▼

American Christmas Carol, An (1979) C-100m. TVM D: Eric Till. Henry Winkler, David Wayne, Dorian Harewood, Chris Wiggins, R. H. Thompson, Susan Hogan. A lot of facial putty turns "The Fonz" into Scrooge for this update of Dickens' classic set in a Depression-era New England town. Average.▼

American Commandos (1985) C-88m. BOMB D: Bobby A. Suarez. Christopher Mitchum, John Phillip Law, Franco Guerrero, Willie Williams, Ken Metcalfe. Poorly made action film about Vietnam war vets who go to the Golden Triangle in Southeast Asia on an anti-narcotics mission.

Opening scenes set in California are ridiculously simulated on Filipino locations. Original title: HITMAN. ▼

American Dream, An (1966) C-103m. **½ D: Robert Gist. Stuart Whitman, Eleanor Parker, Janet Leigh, Barry Sullivan, Lloyd Nolan. Distorted, watered-down Norman Mailer novel, dealing superficially with TV commentator who's wanted by underworld and police for murdering his wife; nightmare sequences are sterile.

American Dream (1981) C-74m. TVM D: Mel Damski. Stephen Macht, Karen Carlson, Michael Hershewe, Hans Conried, John McIntire, Scott Brady, Andrea Smith, John Malkovich. Superior pilot to the unfortunately short-lived family series about a man who moves his wife and children from an affluent Chicago suburb to a mixed inner-city neighborhood. Emmy nominations went to director Damski and to writers Ronald M. Cohen, Barbara Corday, and Ken Hecht. Above average.▼

American Dreamer (1984) C-105m. ** D: Rick Rosenthal. JoBeth Williams, Tom Conti, Giancarlo Giannini, Coral Browne, James Staley, Huckleberry Fox, C.B. Barnes. Misguided, miscast comedy-adventure yarn about a housewife who wins trip to Paris and (through circumstance) believes herself to be the daring heroine of a series of adventure thrillers. Cute idea (not dissimilar to ROMANCING THE STONE) that an otherwise able cast can't pull off.▼

American Empire (1942) 82m. **½ D: William McGann. Richard Dix, Leo Carrillo, Preston Foster, Frances Gifford, Guinn Williams. Dix and Foster join forces to develop cattle empire in Texas after Civil War, but not without problems. Pretty good outdoor actioner.▼

American Flyers (1985) C-114m. *** D: John Badham. Kevin Costner, David Grant, Rae Dawn Chong, Alexandra Paul, Janice Rule, Luca Bercovici, Robert Townsend, John Amos, Jennifer Grey. Two brothers—one of whom is dying—enter a grueling bicycle race marathon. Likable, sweet-natured, root-for-the-good-guys film, if a bit too pat and manipulative at times. Written by Steve Tesich, whose cycle theme fared even better in BREAKING AWAY.▼

American Friend, The (1977-U.S.-French-German) C-127m. *** D: Wim Wenders. Dennis Hopper, Bruno Ganz, Lisa Kreuzer, Gerard Blain, Jean Eustache, Sam Fuller, Nicholas Ray. Vague but suspenseful statement about American gangster films and the Americanization of European cinema and lifestyles, centering on a young German picture-framer (Ganz) hired to assassinate a mobster. Hopper is the title character, a mystery man; film directors Ray and Fuller appear as heavies. Based on Patricia Highsmith's *Ripley's Game*.▼

American Gigolo (1980) C-117m. BOMB

D: Paul Schrader. Richard Gere, Lauren Hutton, Hector Elizondo, Nina Van Pallandt, Frances Bergen. Schrader presents his weakest variation yet on his favorite theme, the seamy side of American life. Feeble morality play, posing as a thriller, is further undermined by neurasthenic acting and some of the unsexiest sex scenes of all time.▼

American Gothic (1988) C-90m. BOMB D: John Hough. Rod Steiger, Yvonne DeCarlo, Michael J. Pollard, Fiona Hutchison, Sarah Torgov, Mark Lindsay Chapman. Three couples off for an island weekend off the Seattle coast are forced to land at an unknown island dominated by murderous Ma and Pa (DeCarlo and Steiger) and their "kids" (grownups who've been kept mentally adolescent by their backward, backwoods parents). Populated exclusively by obnoxious characters; even Steiger can't help this one.▼

American Graffiti (1973) C-110m. ***½ D: George Lucas. Richard Dreyfuss, Ronny Howard, Paul LeMat, Charlie Martin Smith, Cindy Williams, Candy Clark, Mackenzie Phillips, Wolfman Jack, Harrison Ford, Bo Hopkins, Kathy Quinlan, Suzanne Somers, Joe Spano, Debralee Scott. Highly entertaining, insightful mosaic about youngsters "coming of age" after high-school graduation in 1962. Often hilarious, always on-target, this film made Dreyfuss a star and boosted many other careers. Re-edited to 112m. for 1978 reissue to play up latter-day stars. Sequel: MORE AMERICAN GRAFFITI.▼

American Guerilla in the Philippines (1950) C-105m. **½ D: Fritz Lang. Tyrone Power, Micheline Prelle, Tom Ewell, Jack Elam. If one ignores flaws in overpatriotic script, film is agreeable account of naval officer Power left behind enemy lines on WW2 Pacific island, helping natives combat Japanese.

American Harvest (1987) C-100m. TVM D: Dick Lowry. Wayne Rogers, Mariclare Costello, Fredric Lehne, Matt McCoy, John Anderson, Earl Holliman. Limp drama about family rivalries among itinerant wheat harvesters. The harvesting sequences, in fact, are the most interesting part of this film, providing grist for a solid half-hour documentary. Below average.

American Hot Wax (1978) C-91m. *** D: Floyd Mutrux. Tim McIntire, Fran Drescher, Jay Leno, John Lehne, Laraine Newman, Jeff Altman, Chuck Berry, Jerry Lee Lewis, Screamin' Jay Hawkins. Rose-colored story of controversial 1950s disc jockey Alan Freed. Uneven dramatically, but McIntire is excellent, period flavor is strong, and the original rock 'n' roll acts are fun to see.

American in Paris, An (1951) C-115m. ***½ D: Vincente Minnelli. Gene Kelly, Leslie Caron, Oscar Levant, Georges Guetary, Nina Foch. Joyous, original musical built around Gershwin score; dazzling in color. Plot of artist Kelly torn between gamine Caron and wealthy Foch is creaky, but the songs, dances, production are superb. Oscars include Best Picture, Story and Screenplay (Alan Jay Lerner), Cinematography (Alfred Gilks and John Alton), Scoring (Johnny Green and Saul Chaplin), Art Direction, Costume Design, and a special citation to Kelly.▼

Americanization of Emily, The (1964) 117m. ***½ D: Arthur Hiller. James Garner, Julie Andrews, Melvyn Douglas, James Coburn, Joyce Grenfell, Keenan Wynn, Judy Carne, Liz Fraser, Edward Binns, William Windom, Alan Sues. Garner is fall guy for U.S. admiral's master plan to have American naval officer first Normandy invasion victim, with predictable results. Cynical Garner-Andrews romance blends well with realistic view of life among U.S. military brass. Script by Paddy Chayefsky, from William Bradford Huie's novel. Also shown in computer-colored version.▼

American Justice SEE: Jackals▼

American Madness (1932) 81m. *** D: Frank Capra. Walter Huston, Pat O'Brien, Kay Johnson, Constance Cummings, Gavin Gordon. Huston is dynamic as a put-upon bank president in the depths of the Great Depression; vivid, upbeat film marred only by idiotic romantic subplot.

American Ninja (1986) C-95m. *½ D: Sam Firstenberg. Michael Dudikoff, Steve James, Judie Aronson, Guich Koock, John Fujioka, Don Stewart, John LaMotta. Low-grade martial-arts entry series set at U.S. Army base in Philippines, with beefy Dudikoff as a soldier who finds ample reason to use his deadly skills. James comes off well as Dudikoff's equally proficient Army pal. Followed by a pair of sequels.▼

American Ninja 2: The Confrontation (1987) C-89m. *½ D: Sam Firstenberg. Michael Dudikoff, Steve James, Larry Poindexter, Gary Conway, Jeff Weston, Michelle Botes, Michael Stone. Slight improvement over AMERICAN NINJA benefits from screen rapport of Dudikoff and James, as G.I. hunks who investigate disappearance of Marines on Caribbean island—where local druglord is training them for his own evil purposes. Bad guy Conway also co-scripted the film with actor James Booth.▼

American Ninja 3: Blood Hunt (1989) C-90m. BOMB D: Cedric Sundstrom. David Bradley, Steve James, Marjoe Gortner, Michele Chan, Calvin Jung. Tiresome—and, hopefully, last—entry in the series, with Bradley (replacing Michael Dudikoff as the hero) battling dastardly Gortner. Even martial arts fans will be bored.▼

Americano, The (1955) **C-85m.** **½ D: William Castle. Glenn Ford, Cesar Romero, Frank Lovejoy, Ursula Thiess, Abbe Lane. Good-guy Ford meets Brazilian badguys in standard Western, with change of scenery as major asset.▼

American Pop (1981) **C-97m.** **½ D: Ralph Bakshi. Voices of Ron Thompson, Marya Small, Jerry Holland, Lisa Jane Persky, Roz Kelly. Ambitious animated film, which follows 20th-century American music through pivotal characters in four generations. Bold graphics and a challenging narrative keep this interesting, if not always successful; animation buffs may wince at awkward rotoscoping (tracing from live action). Ultimate dilemma: the culmination of this heavily dramatic, multigenerational saga is the creation of punk rock!

American Romance, An (1944) **C-122m.** **½ D: King Vidor. Brian Donlevy, Ann Richards, Walter Abel, John Qualen, Stephen McNally. Long, flavorful story of immigrant steelworker's rise to wealth and power. Might have been a better film with someone more magnetic than Donlevy in the lead. Originally released at 151m.

American Roulette (1988-British-Australian) **C-102m.** BOMB D: Maurice Hatton. Andy Garcia, Kitty Aldridge, Robert Stephens, Al Matthews, Susannah York. Dreadful political thriller about the president of a Latin American country (Garcia), who also doubles as a poet, and his plight as he's hunted by a death squad while in exile in London. Poorly directed and crammed with plot holes; padded with scenes of Garcia racing through the London Underground, yet it's unclear as to who's chasing him.▼

American Success SEE: **American Success Company, The**

American Success Company, The (1979) **C-94m.** ** D: William Richert. Jeff Bridges, Belinda Bauer, Ned Beatty, Steven Keats, Bianca Jagger, John Glover. A contemporary fable about a young loser—in business and marriage—who decides to change his luck by emulating a macho prince. Offbeat in the extreme, often funny, but decidedly uneven. Filmed in Germany; based on a story by Larry Cohen. Richert has twice edited and reissued the film: in 1981 as AMERICAN SUCCESS, then in 1983 simply as SUCCESS.

American Tail, An (1986) **C-80m.** **½ D: Don Bluth. Voices of Dom DeLuise, Christopher Plummer, Nehemiah Persoff, Madeline Kahn, Phillip Glasser, John Finnegan, Cathianne Blore, Will Ryan. A young Russian mouse is separated from his family as they're about to arrive at their new homeland, America, in the late 19th century. Handsome, occasionally heart-tugging cartoon feature with a cute main

character—but serious flaws in the story department (why are there *three* climaxes?). Producer Steven Spielberg's first foray into animation, with Don Bluth and his team of one-time Disney artists.▼

American Tragedy, An (1931) **95m.** ** D: Josef von Sternberg. Phillips Holmes, Sylvia Sidney, Frances Dee, Irving Pichel, Frederick Burton, Claire McDowell. Straight-forward telling of Theodore Dreiser story about weak young man torn between poor girlfriend and beautiful, wealthy girl who falls in love with him. Sidney is ideally cast, but film is cold and uninvolving; certainly not as florid as remake A PLACE IN THE SUN.

American Way, The SEE: **Riders of the Storm**▼

American Werewolf in London, An (1981) **C-97m.** *** D: John Landis. David Naughton, Jenny Agutter, Griffin Dunne, John Woodvine, Brian Glover. A young man is bitten by a wolf on the British moors, with terrifying results. Not a spoof, but a full-blooded horror film that happens to have a sharp sense of humor—as well as a reverence for horror films past. Dynamite direction and script by Landis, startling Oscar-winning makeup effects by Rick Baker.▼

Americathon (1979) **C-86m.** BOMB D: Neil Israel. Harvey Korman, John Ritter, Nancy Morgan, Peter Riegert, Fred Willard, Zane Buzby, Richard Schaal, Elvis Costello, Chief Dan George, Tommy Lasorda, Jay Leno, Peter Marshall, Meat Loaf, Howard Hesseman. Unfunny comedy wastes great premise: in 1998, America must hold a telethon in order to raise money to save itself. Only spark is set by Buzby as Vietnamese punk-rocker. Narrated by George Carlin.▼

Amin—The Rise and Fall (1981-Kenya) **C-101m.** *½ D: Sharad Patel. Joseph Olita, Geoffrey Keen, Denis Hills, Leonard Trolley, Diane Mercier. Superficial, bloody potboiler chronicling the atrocities committed by Uganda dictator Idi Amin, played by look-alike Olita. For voyeurs only.▼

Amityville Curse, The (1990) **C-91m.** *½ D: Tom Berry. Kim Coates, Dawna Wightman, Helen Hughes, David Stein, Anthony Dean Rubes, Cassandra Gava, Jan Rubes. Attempt to cash in on the Amityville name with a strictly ho-hum story (based on Hans Holzer's book) about the house with a life of its own. Without interesting special effects there's no point to this one at all. Released directly to video.▼

Amityville Horror, The (1979) **C-117m.** *½ D: Stuart Rosenberg. James Brolin, Margot Kidder, Rod Steiger, Don Stroud, Murray Hamilton, Michael Sacks, Helen Shaver, Natasha Ryan, Val Avery, John Larch, Amy Wright, James Tolkan. Family moves into supposedly haunted Long Island home, finds that "supposedly" is inoperative. Based on Jay Anson's (supposedly) nonfiction best seller, film is yawn-inducing rehash of all the old schticks; not even good for laughs, with Steiger mercilessly hamming it up as local priest. Followed by a prequel, AMITYVILLE II: THE POSSESSION, a nonsequel, AMITYVILLE 3-D, and a TV movie.▼

Amityville II: The Possession (1982) C-104m. BOMB D: Damiano Damiani. Burt Young, Rutanya Alda, James Olson, Jack Magner, Diane Franklin, Andrew Prine, Ted Ross, Moses Gunn. Officially a prequel to THE AMITYVILLE HORROR, but actually just a ripoff. A loathsome lout (Young) moves into notorious Long Island house with his troubled family and all hell breaks loose. Alternately dull and disgusting.▼

Amityville: The Demon SEE: Amityville 3-D▼

Amityville 3-D (1983) C-105m. **½ D: Richard Fleischer. Tony Roberts, Tess Harper, Robert Joy, Candy Clark, John Beal, Leora Dana, John Harkins, Lori Loughlin, Meg Ryan. Thoroughly familiar retread of spirit-in-the-house formula, with Roberts as a Doubting Thomas who buys the dreaded Amityville house (seen in two otherwise unrelated films). Competence at every level keeps this from being trash; excellent 3-D effects too. Shown on TV as AMITYVILLE: THE DEMON; followed by TV movie AMITYVILLE: THE EVIL ESCAPES.▼

Amityville: The Evil Escapes (1989) C-100m. TVM D: Sandor Stern. Patty Duke, Jane Wyatt, Frederic Lehne, Norman Lloyd, Brandy Gold, Aron Eisenberg, Geri Betzler. Fourth in the series based on John G. Jones' horror thrillers is about par for the (TV) course, bringing into the "don't go in the attic/basement/pantry/front hall closet" genre a couple of frantic exorcists trying to save Duke & dodos. Retitled THE AMITYVILLE HORROR: THE EVIL ESCAPES—PART IV for video. Average.▼

Among the Living (1941) 68m. **½ D: Stuart Heisler. Albert Dekker, Susan Hayward, Frances Farmer, Harry Carey, Gordon Jones. Intriguing little B film about a deranged man, one of twins, kept isolated for years, who breaks loose and stirs up trouble. Some great moments, but film is a little too hurried and simplistic; Dekker is excellent in dual role.

Amor Bandido (1979-Brazilian) C-95m. *** D: Bruno Barreto. Paulo Gracindo, Cristina Ache, Paulo Guarnieri, Ligia Diniz, Flavio Sao Thiago. Tough drama of 17-year-old dancer-hooker Ache, estranged from cop father Gracindo, who takes up with baby-faced killer Guarnieri. Uncompromis-

ing and, ultimately, sad; based on one of Brazil's most notorious criminal cases.

Amorous Adventures of Moll Flanders, The (1965-British) C-126m. **½ D: Terence Young. Kim Novak, Richard Johnson, Angela Lansbury, George Sanders, Vittorio De Sica, Lilli Palmer, Leo McKern, Cecil Parker. Billed as female Tom Jones, Moll is far from thrilling. Fine cast romps through 18th-century England from bedroom to boudoir, but film needs more spice than Novak can muster. The two leads were married briefly in real life.

Amorous Mr. Prawn, The (1962-British) 89m. **½ D: Anthony Kimmins. Joan Greenwood, Cecil Parker, Ian Carmichael, Robert Beatty. Diverting fluff finds wife (Greenwood) of general (Parker) devising a scheme to obtain badly needed money so they can retire in style.

Amos (1985) C-100m. TVM D: Michael Tuchner. Kirk Douglas, Elizabeth Montgomery, Dorothy McGuire, Pat Morita, James Sloyan, Ray Walston. One-time baseball coach, now in his late seventies, finds himself confined to a nursing home against his will and crossing swords with the steely head nurse in this drama that shares many similarities with ONE FLEW OVER THE CUCKOO'S NEST (in which Douglas starred on Broadway). Peter Douglas (Kirk's son) produced, and Elizabeth Montgomery here plays a rare heavy. Average.▼

Amsterdam Affair (1968-British) C-91m. **½ D: Gerry O'Hara. Wolfgang Kieling, William Marlowe, Catherine von Schell, Pamela Ann Davy, Josef Dubin-Behrman. Inspector believes there's more to young woman's murder than supposed open-and-shut case against her lover would indicate. Passable thriller, pleasing Amsterdam locations.

Amsterdam Kill, The (1977) C-90m. **½ D: Robert Clouse. Robert Mitchum, Bradford Dillman, Richard Egan, Leslie Nielsen, Keye Luke. Tired drug bust movie gets a shot from Mitchum's presence as a retired narc who's lured back by a former colleague suspected of being part of an international dope ring.▼

Amsterdamned (1988-Dutch) C-113m. ** D: Dick Maas. Huub Stapel, Monique van de Ven, Serge-Henre Valcke, Hidde Maas, Wim Zomer. Elusive killer emerges by night from Amsterdam's canals to murder people at random; he's hunted by a police detective as determined as he is. Unusual setting and sleekness of production help disguise the fact that it's just another urban cop thriller, with slasher-movie overtones. Director Maas also wrote the script.▼

Amuck (1972-Italian) C-85m. **½ D: Silvio Amadio. Farley Granger, Barbara Bouchet, Rosalba Neri. Solid suspense thriller set in Venice with Granger as a mystery writer; new secretary Bouchet tries to find out what happened to her missing friend, his former secretary. Originally titled REPLICA OF A CRIME; unreleased in the U.S. until 1978.

Amy (1981) **C-100m.** *** D: Vincent McEveety. Jenny Agutter, Barry Newman, Kathleen Nolan, Chris Robinson, Lou Fant, Margaret O'Brien, Nanette Fabray, Lance LeGault, Lucille Benson. Sincere, entertaining Disney tale of Agutter leaving her husband in the early 1900s, teaching at a school for the handicapped. Though the film is targeted at kids, parents won't be bored. Made for TV, released to theaters instead.▼

Anastasia (1956) **C-105m.** **** D: Anatole Litvak. Ingrid Bergman, Yul Brynner, Helen Hayes, Akim Tamiroff. Inspired casting makes this film exceptional. Bergman won Oscar as amnesiac refugee selected by Brynner to impersonate surviving daughter of Russia's last czar. Confrontation scene in which Hayes as grand duchess must determine if girl is her relative is grand. Screenplay by Arthur Laurents based on Marcelle Maurette's play.▼

Anastasia: The Mystery of Anna (1986) **C-200m.** TVM D: Marvin J. Chomsky. Amy Irving, Olivia de Havilland, Omar Sharif, Jan Niklas, Claire Bloom, Edward Fox, Elke Sommer, Susan Lucci, Nicolas Surovy, Rex Harrison. Sumptuous retelling of the story of Anna Anderson, who claimed to have been the surviving daughter of Czarist Russia's Nicholas and Alexandra (played by Sharif and Bloom). James Goldman's literate script was based not on the familiar stage and screen tale of Anastasia of the 1950s but on Peter Kurth's book *Anastasia: The Riddle of Anna Anderson.* Originally shown in two parts. Above average.

Anatomist, The (1961-British) **73m.** ** D: Leonard William. Alastair Sim, George Cole, Jill Bennett, Margaret Gordon. Respected surgeon encourages corpse-stealing for experiments, causing rash of murders. Sim is wry in tame spooker.

Anatomy of a Marriage (1964-French) **193m.** **½ D: André Cayatte. Comprised of: "My Days with Jean-Marc" and "My Nights with Françoise." Jacques Charrier, Marie-Jose Nat, Georges Rivière, Macha Meril. Well-intentioned film which through its two parts attempts to analyze problems of young married couple from each one's point of view; becomes repetitious.

Anatomy of a Murder (1959) **160m.** **** D: Otto Preminger. James Stewart, Lee Remick, Ben Gazzara, Arthur O'Connell, Eve Arden, Kathryn Grant, George C. Scott, Orson Bean, Murray Hamilton. Long, exciting courtroom drama; daring when released, tamer now. Large cast is fine: O'Connell as drunken lawyer aroused by Stewart, Joseph Welch as judge (Welch was the famous Army-McCarthy hearings lawyer who later became a judge in real life), Scott as prosecuting attorney. But Stewart towers over all as witty, easygoing, but cagy defense lawyer. Fine Duke Ellington score.▼

Anatomy of a Seduction (1979) **C-100m.** TVM D: Steven Hilliard Stern. Susan Flannery, Jameson Parker, Rita Moreno, Ed Nelson, Michael LeClair. Romantic soaper about frosty divorcee's affair with bosom buddy's college-age son—who is also her own son's best friend. Average.▼

Anatomy of a Syndicate SEE: **Big Operator, The**

Anchors Aweigh (1945) **C-140m.** **½ D: George Sidney. Frank Sinatra, Kathryn Grayson, Gene Kelly, Jose Iturbi, Dean Stockwell, Pamela Britton. Popular '40s musical of sailors on leave doesn't hold up storywise, but musical numbers still good: Sinatra's "I Fall in Love Too Easily," Kelly's irresistible dance with Jerry the cartoon mouse.▼

And Baby Makes Six (1979) **C-100m.** TVM D: Waris Hussein. Colleen Dewhurst, Warren Oates, Maggie Cooper, Mildred Dunnock, Timothy Hutton, Allyn Ann McLerie. Middle-aged couple with three grown children face parenthood again. Dewhurst pulls this one up by its bootstraps. Script by Shelley List. Above average. Sequel: BABY COMES HOME.▼

And Baby Makes Three (1949) **84m.** ** D: Henry Levin. Robert Young, Barbara Hale, Robert Hutton, Billie Burke, Melville Cooper. OK comedy has Hale about to marry for second time, only to discover she's pregnant, and she really does want to stay married to Hubby #1 (Young).

Anderson Platoon, The (1967-French) **65m.** ***½ D: Pierre Schoendorffer. Superior chronicle of soldiers in American Army platoon fighting, living, and dying in Vietnam. Vivid, striking images, photographed at the front line. A Best Documentary Academy Award winner.▼

Anderson's Angels SEE: **Chesty Anderson, USN**▼

Anderson Tapes, The (1972) **C-98m.** *** D: Sidney Lumet. Sean Connery, Dyan Cannon, Martin Balsam, Ralph Meeker, Alan King, Margaret Hamilton, Christopher Walken, Garrett Morris. Fast-paced thriller of ex-con's master holdup plan, and strange electronic surveillances that have tracked him since he left prison. Climax is particularly exciting. Fine Quincy Jones score; Walken's film debut.▼

. . . And God Created Woman (1957-French) **C-92m.** **½ D: Roger Vadim. Brigitte Bardot, Curt Jurgens, Jean-Louis Trintignant, Christian Marquand, Georges Poujouly, Jean Tissier. Location shooting (at St. Tropez) and famous Bardot figure on display in simple tale of man-teaser finding it hard to resist temptation. Great cast clicks in Brigitte's best-known vehicle. Beware cuts. Remade (in name only) by Vadim in the U.S. in 1987.▼

And God Created Woman (1987) C-100m. *½ D: Roger Vadim. Rebecca De Mornay, Vincent Spano, Frank Langella, Donovan Leitch, Judith Chapman, Jaime McEnnan, Benjamin Mouton, David Shelley. Surprisingly tepid "variation" on director Vadim's one-time *scandale internationale* (see above). Luscious De Mornay marries carpenter Spano merely to secure her release from prison, then keeps him panting as she frolics with gubernatorial candidate Langella. Not all *that* different from Goldie Hawn's OVERBOARD; beware rock 'n' roll subplot.▼

And Hope to Die (1972-French) C-99m. *** D: René Clement. Robert Ryan, Tisa Farrow, Jean-Louis Trintignant, Lea Massari, Aldo Ray. Above-average caper with offbeat touches; gang hired to kidnap girl goes through with scheme even though she's already dead.▼

And I Alone Survived (1978) C-100m. TVM D: William A. Graham. Blair Brown, David Ackroyd, Vera Miles, G. D. Spradlin, James G. Richardson. Middling dramatization of Lauren Elder's account of her ordeal following a plane crash in the Sierra Nevadas in the spring of 1976. Underdeveloped and overdramatic. Average.▼

. . . And Justice for All (1979) C-117m. **½ D: Norman Jewison. Al Pacino, Jack Warden, John Forsythe, Lee Strasberg, Jeffrey Tambor, Christine Lahti, Sam Levene, Craig T. Nelson, Joe Morton. Lawyer Pacino single-handedly battles Maryland's judicial system. Outrageous satire mixes uncomfortably with painfully sad moments, in attempt to make biting statement on buying and selling of justice. Strong performances and good location photography cannot overcome weak script. Written by Barry Levinson and Valerie Curtin. Lahti's feature film debut.▼

And Millions Will Die (1973) C-96m. ** D: Leslie Martinson. Richard Basehart, Susan Strasberg, Leslie Nielsen, Tony Wager, Peter Sumner. Environmental crisis expert Basehart is called in when it's discovered that a madman has buried a time bomb filled with deadly nerve gas beneath the streets of Hong Kong. Lackluster suspense story.

And No One Could Save Her (1973) C-73m. TVM D: Kevin Billington. Lee Remick, Milo O'Shea, Jennie Linden, Frank Grimes, Liam Redmond, Paul Maxwell. Fern O'Neil, young American newlywed, almost goes crazy when immigrant husband disappears mysteriously in Ireland, leaving no traces. Written by Anthony Skene. Above average.

And Nothing But the Truth (1982-British)

C-90m. **½ D: Karl Francis. Glenda Jackson, Jon Finch, Kenneth Colley, James Donnelly, Emrys James, Karen Archer. An examination of the role and responsibility of the media, focusing on documentary filmmaker Jackson and reporter Finch at work on a TV magazine show. Earnest, and not without its merits, but basically ordinary; originally titled GIRO CITY, and released at 102m.▼

And Now For Something Completely Different (1972-British) C-89m. *** D: Ian McNaughton. Graham Chapman, John Cleese, Eric Idle, Terry Gilliam, Terry Jones, Michael Palin, Carol Cleveland, Connie Booth. First feature by the Monty Python troupe is a kind of "Greatest Hits" album, with some of the most popular sketches and animated bits from their long-running TV series. Fine introduction to their peculiar brand of humor includes "Dead Parrot," "The World's Deadliest Joke," "Upper-Class Twit of the Year," and memorable "Lumberjack Song."▼

And Now Miguel (1966) C-95m. *** D: James Clark. Pat Cardi, Michael Ansara, Guy Stockwell, Joe De Santis. Flavorful, leisurely paced account of young boy who wants to join his father on their summer mountain trip to graze sheep; set in Southwest. Produced by Robert Radnitz.

And Now My Love (1975-French) C-121m. ***½ D: Claude Lelouch. Marthe Keller, Andre Dussollier, Charles Denner, Carla Gravina, Gilbert Becaud, Charles Gerard. A what'll-he-do-next kind of extravaganza, in which Lelouch salutes life, love and the 20th century, using comedy, drama, and music to bring wealthy Keller and ne'er do well Dussollier together for the final fadeout. Film opens in b&w.▼

And Now the Screaming Starts! (1973-British) C-87m. ** D: Roy Ward Baker. Peter Cushing, Stephanie Beacham, Herbert Lom, Patrick Magee, Ian Ogilvy. Beacham weds Ogilvy and finds that she's living in a house that has been under a curse for years; OK horror drama with a good cast.▼

And Now Tomorrow (1944) 85m. **½ D: Irving Pichel. Alan Ladd, Loretta Young, Susan Hayward, Barry Sullivan, Beulah Bondi, Cecil Kellaway. Poor doctor Ladd falls in love with deaf socialite patient Young in this Rachel Field romance; sticky going at times.

And Quiet Flows the Don (1960-Russian) C-107m. *** D: Sergei Gerasimov. Ellina Bystritskaya, Pyotr Glebov, Zinaida Kirienko, Danilo Ilchenko. Faithful realization of Mikhail Sholokhov novel revolving around life of small village family during WW1 and postwar period. Absorbing study of social upheavals caused by revolution and war.

Andrei Rublev (1966-Russian) C/B&W-

185m. **** D: Andrei Tarkovsky. Anatoli Solonitzine, Ivan Lapikov, Nikolai Grinko, Nikolai Sergueiev. Brilliantly devised and directed account of the famous 15th century icon painter, focusing on an age-old conflict: should an artist participate in the political and social upheavals of the time, or should he simply record history with his brush? This magnificent film is worthy of comparison with the best of Eisenstein's historical dramas. Scripted by Tarkovsky and Andrei Milchakov-Konchalovsky; shelved by the Soviet authorities, and unseen until 1971.▼

Androcles and the Lion (1952) 98m. *** D: Chester Erskine. Jean Simmons, Alan Young, Victor Mature, Maurice Evans, Elsa Lanchester, Robert Newton. Shaw's amusing satire of ancient Rome can't be dampened by dull production retelling fable of Christian and lion he has befriended.▼

Android (1982) C-80m. *** D: Aaron Lipstadt. Klaus Kinski, Don Opper, Brie Howard, Norbert Weisser, Crofton Hardester, Kendra Kirchner. Entertaining sci-fi story about an almost-human android who's been working as assistant to mad scientist Kinski on a remote space station and learns he is about to be put out of commission. Charming, quirky ultra-low-budget film made on leftover sets from Roger Corman's BATTLE BEYOND THE STARS. Opper, who plays Max 404, also cowrote screenplay.▼

Andromeda Strain, The (1971) C-130m. **½ D: Robert Wise. Arthur Hill, David Wayne, James Olson, Kate Reid, Paula Kelly. Overlong sci-fi thriller in which small team of superscientists tries to isolate deadly strain of virus from outer space, racing against time and nuclear detonation. From Michael Crichton's novel.▼

And Soon the Darkness (1970-British) C-98m. ** D: Robert Fuest. Pamela Franklin, Michele Dotrice, Sandor Eles, John Nettleton, Clare Kelly. Moody thriller with sexual undertones. Franklin is one of two vacationing British nurses bicycling through rural France, menaced by mysterious sex murderer.▼

And So They Were Married (1936) 74m. **½ D: Elliott Nugent. Melvyn Douglas, Mary Astor, Edith Fellows, Dorothy Stickney, Jackie Moran, Donald Meek. Predictable but amusing little comedy with good co-stars.

And So They Were Married (1944) SEE: **Johnny Doesn't Live Here Any More**

And Suddenly It's Murder! (1964-Italian) 90m. **½ D: Mario Camerini. Alberto Sordi, Vittorio Gassman, Silvana Mangano. Frail but frantic minor comedy satire revolving around trip of couples on the Riviera, each suspected of murder.

And the Angels Sing (1944) 96m. **½ D: George Marshall. Dorothy Lamour, Fred MacMurray, Betty Hutton, Diana Lynn, Raymond Walburn, Eddie Foy Jr. Agreeable musical of singing sister act trying to make it big; MacMurray gives them their break. Brassy Hutton tries to steal the show.

And Then There Were None (1945) 98m. **** D: Rene Clair. Barry Fitzgerald, Walter Huston, Louis Hayward, Roland Young, June Duprez, C. Aubrey Smith, Judith Anderson, Mischa Auer, Richard Haydn. Highly suspenseful Agatha Christie yarn of ten people invited to lonely island where one by one they're murdered. Great script by Dudley Nichols complemented by superb visual ideas. Remade twice as TEN LITTLE INDIANS.▼

And the Ship Sails On (1984-Italian) C-138m. *** D: Federico Fellini. Freddie Jones, Barbara Jefford, Victor Poletti, Peter Cellier, Janet Suzman, Elisa Mai Nardi, Norma West, Paolo Paoloni. Uniquely Felliniesque ocean voyage, circa 1914, with an earnest journalist (Jones) acting as our "host" and introducing us to a variety of celebrated guests who have gathered for funeral voyage of great opera star. Flagrantly unrealistic, deliciously absurd, and somewhat uneven, but full of striking images and those indelible Fellini faces . . . plus an opening sequence that's absolutely mesmerizing.▼

Andy (1965) 86m. *** D: Richard C. Sarafian. Norman Alden, Tamara Daykarhonova, Zvee Scooler, Murvyn Vye. Touching insight into existence of retarded middle-aged man and his unique problems in N.Y.C. slum life.

Andy Hardy One of the most popular series of all time, the Hardy family first appeared in A FAMILY AFFAIR (1937) with Lionel Barrymore and Mickey Rooney as father and son. In 1938 YOU'RE ONLY YOUNG ONCE began the official series in the town of Carvel, with Rooney as Andy Hardy, typical American teen-ager, interested in cars and girls, Lewis Stone as Judge James Hardy, a stern but understanding father, Fay Holden as his "swell" mother, Cecilia Parker as Marian, his older sister striving to be a young lady, Sara Haden as Aunt Millie, and Ann Rutherford as Polly, the girlfriend who was often neglected for other prospects but to whom Andy always returned; George B. Seitz directed most entries in the series. Testament to the series' great appeal was the special Oscar given MGM "for its achievement in representing the American Way of Life." MGM used the films to springboard young starlets such as Judy Garland, Lana Turner, Esther Williams, Kathryn Grayson, and Donna Reed. The Andy Hardy films do not always wear well, with typical Rooney mugging and a plethora of 1940's slang dating them rather badly. In ine film Andy tells his dad "You can say hat again!" and the Judge replies, "Why should I say it again? Didn't you understand me the first time?" The sentimental nature of much of the series also doesn't fit into today's way of thinking, and in general the Hardy films serve mainly as reminders of an era in Hollywood and in America that is long gone. Indeed, when the cast, except Stone, was reunited, in 1958 for ANDY HARDY COMES HOME, the formula just didn't jell. What survives in the Hardy films is the very real talent that went into them.

Andy Hardy Comes Home (1958) **81m.** D: Howard W. Koch. Mickey Rooney, Patricia Breslin, Fay Holden, Cecilia Parker, Sara Haden, Joey Forman, Jerry Colonna, Vaughn Taylor, Frank Ferguson.

Andy Hardy Gets Spring Fever (1939) **85m.** D: W. S. Van Dyke II. Lewis Stone, Mickey Rooney, Cecilia Parker, Fay Holden, Ann Rutherford, Sara Haden, Addison Richards.

Andy Hardy Meets Debutante (1940) **86m.** D: George B. Seitz. Mickey Rooney, Lewis Stone, Judy Garland, Cecilia Parker, Ann Rutherford, Fay Holden, Diana Lewis, Sara Haden.

Andy Hardy's Blonde Trouble (1944) **107m.** D: George B. Seitz. Lewis Stone, Mickey Rooney, Fay Holden, Sara Haden, Herbert Marshall, Bonita Granville, Jean Porter, Keye Luke.

Andy Hardy's Double Life (1942) **92m.** D: George B. Seitz. Mickey Rooney, Lewis Stone, Cecilia Parker, Fay Holden, Ann Rutherford, Sara Haden, Bobby (Robert) Blake, William Lundigan, Susan Peters, Esther Williams.

Andy Hardy's Private Secretary (1941) **101m.** D: George B. Seitz. Mickey Rooney, Lewis Stone, Fay Holden, Ann Rutherford, Sara Haden, Kathryn Grayson, Ian Hunter, Gene Reynolds.

And Your Name Is Jonah (1979) **C-100m.** TVM D: Richard Michaels. Sally Struthers, James Woods, Randee Heller, Penny Santon, Titos Vandis. Earnest drama about couple trying to cope with young son disovered to be deaf after being wrongly institutionalized as retarded. Average.

Andy Warhol's Bad (1971) **C-100m.** **½ D: Jed Johnson. Carroll Baker, Perry King, Susan Tyrrell, Stefania Cassini, Cyrinda Foxe. Queens housewife supplements her facial-hair-removal business by running a murder-for-hire concern specializing in children and animals. Goes without saying that Warhol's most expensive film is inexecrable taste, but it frequently succeeds as a sick joke; Baker, at least, seems to be having a good time.▼

Andy Warhol's Dracula (1974-Italian-French) **C-93m.** ** D: Paul Morrissey. Udo Kier, Joe Dallesandro, Arno Juerging,

Vittorio De Sica, Maxime McKendry, Roman Polanski. Dracula (Kier) learns he must have blood of virgins (pronounced "where-gins") in order to survive. Companion piece to ANDY WARHOL'S FRANKENSTEIN is far less bloody and has some amusing bits . . . but it's still a long way from LOVE AT FIRST BITE. Originally released at 106m.; also known as BLOOD FOR DRACULA and YOUNG DRACULA.▼

Andy Warhol's Frankenstein (1974-Italian-German-French) **C-94m.** BOMB D: Paul Morrissey. Joe Dallesandro, Monique Van Vooren, Udo Kier, Srdjan Zelenovic, Dalila di Lazzaro. Mad baron Kier clones bodybeautiful monsters out of bloody human innards. Campy and disgusting, with severed heads and hands galore. Originally shown in 3-D. Also known as FLESH FOR FRANKENSTEIN.▼

Angel (1937) **91m.** ** D: Ernst Lubitsch. Marlene Dietrich, Herbert Marshall, Melvyn Douglas, Edward Everett Horton, Laura Hope Crews. Disappointing film for Dietrich-Lubitsch team about Marlene leaving husband Marshall for vacation, falling in love with Douglas. Not worthy of star trio.

Angel (1984) **C-92m.** *½ D: Robert Vincent O'Neil. Cliff Gorman, Susan Tyrrell, Dick Shawn, Rory Calhoun, John Diehl, Donna Wilkes. Wilkes is a straight-A high school student by day, Hollywood hooker by night—but despite "colorful" characters like drag queen Shawn, film goes nowhere, and remains inexplicably tame in terms of what it shows. Sequel: AVENGING ANGEL.▼

Angela (1955) **81m.** ** D: Dennis O'Keefe. Dennis O'Keefe, Mara Lane, Rossano Brazzi, Arnold Foa, Nino Crisman. Poor man's DOUBLE INDEMNITY has O'Keefe drawn into murder and double-dealing by seductive Lane. Standard programmer, filmed in Italy. O'Keefe also wrote the script.

Angela (1977-Canadian) **C-100m.** ** D: Boris Sagal. Sophia Loren, Steve Railsback, John Huston, John Vernon. Dreary story of the relationship between a woman and a younger man who turns out to be her son.▼

Angel and the Badman (1947) **100m.** *** D: James Edward Grant. John Wayne, Gail Russell, Harry Carey, Irene Rich, Bruce Cabot. First-rate Western with Russell humanizing gunfighter Wayne; predictable plot is extremely well handled. Also shown in computer-colored version.▼

Angel, Angel, Down We Go SEE: **Cult of the Damned**

Angel Baby (1961) **97m.** *** D: Paul Wendkos, Hubert Cornfield. George Hamilton, Salome Jens, Mercedes McCambridge, Joan Blondell, Henry Jones, Burt Reynolds. Penetrating exposé of evangelistic circuit plying backwood country; Jens in title role, Hamilton the promoter, McCambridge his shrewish wife—marvelous cameos by Blondell and Jones. Reynolds's film debut.▼

Angel City (1980) **C-100m. TVM** D: Philip Leacock. Ralph Waite, Paul Winfield, Jennifer Warren, Jennifer Jason Leigh, Mitchell Ryan. Stark contemporary drama about migrant workers who find themselves locked in a squalid labor camp. James Lee Barrett's script, from Patricia Smith's book, gives a good cast a gripping story to work with. Above average.

Angel Dusted (1981) **C-98m. TVM** D: Dick Lowry. Jean Stapleton, Arthur Hill, John Putch, Darlene Craviotto, Percy Rodrigues, Helen Hunt, Patrick Cassidy. Drama about a family crisis: the son goes berserk after smoking marijuana laced with angel dust. Stapleton is a standout, working here with her real-life son, John Putch (in his acting debut). Darlene Craviotto, who plays a psychiatrist, wrote the teleplay. Above average.

Angel Face (1953) **90m. **½ D: Otto Preminger. Robert Mitchum, Jean Simmons, Herbert Marshall, Mona Freeman, Leon Ames, Barbara O'Neil, Jim Backus. Title figure (Simmons) in slowly-paced film revealed as angel of death causing demise of those who love her.

Angel From Texas, An (1940) **69m. **½ D: Ray Enright. Eddie Albert, Wayne Morris, Rosemary Lane, Jane Wyman, Ronald Reagan, Ruth Terry, John Litel. Producers Morris and Reagan con innocent Albert into backing their show. Pleasant farce, nicely acted by the stars of BROTHER RAT. Based on George S. Kaufman's *The Butter and Egg Man,* filmed many times under different titles.

Angel Heart (1987) **C-113m. **½ D: Alan Parker. Mickey Rourke, Robert De Niro, Lisa Bonet, Charlotte Rampling, Stocker Fountelieu, Brownie McGhee, Michael Higgins, Charles Gordone, Kathleen Wilhoite. Two-bit private eye Rourke is hired by mysterious De Niro to track down a missing man, which leads him into a serpentine investigation—and a kind of emotional quicksand. An American Gothic yarn, full of striking, sensual, and frightening images, though after a while it bogs down. Intriguing, if not terribly appealing. A steamy sex scene was snipped (by seconds) to avoid an X-rating in the U.S.; it's restored in video version. Script by director Parker, based on the novel *Falling Angel* by William Hjortsberg.▼

Angel in a Taxi (1959-Italian) **95m. **½ D: Antonio Leonviola. Vera Cecova, Vittorio De Sica, Marietto, Gabriele Ferzetti, Roberto Risso. Marietto is the whole show in this cute if predictable comedy-fantasy of a six-year-old orphan who sees a photo of pretty ballerina Cecova—and decides that she's his mother. De Sica appears in three small but important roles.▼

Angel in Exile (1948) **90m. **½ D: Allan Dwan, Philip Ford. John Carroll, Adele Mara, Thomas Gomez, Barton MacLane, Alfonso Bedoya. Carroll heads for Arizona gold mine upon release from jail but has a change of heart when he's hailed as a religious figure by simple Mexican villagers. Unusual Republic semi-western.

Angel in Green (1987) **C-100m. TVM** D: Marvin J. Chomsky. Bruce Boxleitner, Susan Dey, Milo O'Shea, Pete Smith, Dan Lauria. Nun and army captain stuck on a remote Pacific Island—and don't let anyone tell you this isn't a new version of HEAVEN KNOWS, MR. ALLISON. Below average.

Angel in My Pocket (1969) **C-105m. ** D: Alan Rafkin. Andy Griffith, Lee Meriwether, Jerry Van Dyke, Kay Medford, Edgar Buchanan, Gary Collins. Fans of Griffith's TV series may enjoy homespun story of young minister trying to win confidence of new small-town parish. Predictable situations, cliché dialogue, with Van Dyke intolerable as obnoxious brother-in-law.

Angel Levine, The (1970) **C-104m. **½ D: Jan Kadar. Zero Mostel, Harry Belafonte, Ida Kaminska, Milo O'Shea, Eli Wallach, Anne Jackson, Gloria Foster. Touching, humorous, and sad. Black angel named Levine is on the outs with Heaven, so he tries to help poor old Morris Mishkin. A story often told, but seldom this well. Based on a story by Bernard Malamud.

Angel of Vengeance SEE: **Ms. 45**

Angelo, My Love (1983) **C-115m. *** D: Robert Duvall. Angelo Evans, Michael Evans, Steve "Patalay" Tsigonoff, Millie Tsigonoff, Cathy Kitchen. Fascinating journey into world of modern-day gypsies, with "story" loosely wrapped around precocious Angelo Evans, a remarkable young street hustler. Surprisingly successful attempt by Duvall (in his second directorial effort) to weave fictional story into real settings with nonprofessional cast. Incidentally, the two men who sing "Golden Days" in a restaurant scene are Duvall's brothers.▼

Angel on My Shoulder (1946) **101m. *** D: Archie Mayo. Paul Muni, Anne Baxter, Claude Rains, George Cleveland, Onslow Stevens. Entertaining fantasy of murdered convict Muni sent to earth by Devil as respected judge, and his efforts to outwit Satan while still in mortal form. Remade for TV.▼

Angel on My Shoulder (1980) **C-100m. TVM** D: John Berry. Peter Strauss, Richard Kiley, Barbara Hershey, Janis Paige, Seymour Cassel, Scott Colomby, Murray Matheson. Updated remake of the Paul

Muni fantasy, with tough-talking Strauss as a wrongfully executed Chicago hood sent on a new mission by Satan and having a devil of a time remaining evil. Average.▼

Angel on the Amazon (1948) 86m. *½ D: John H. Auer. George Brent, Vera Ralston, Constance Bennett, Brian Aherne, Fortunio Bonanova. Ludicrous "romance" with Vera in a state of eternal youth; good cast can't rescue clumsy story.

Angel River (1986) C-91m. *½ D: Sergio Olhovich Greene. Lynn-Holly Johnson, Salvador Sanchez, Janet Sunderland, Peter Matthey, Joey Shea. Blonde, innocent pioneer girl Johnson is kidnapped and raped by drunken bandido Sanchez. Will they fall in love? You bet—and you've seen it all before.

Angels' Alley (1948) 67m. D: William Beaudine. Leo Gorcey, Huntz Hall, Billy Benedict, David Gorcey. SEE: **Bowery Boys** series.

Angels' Brigade (1979) C-87m. ** D: Greydon Clark. Jack Palance, Neville Brand, Jim Backus, Pat Buttram, Alan Hale, Jr., Peter Lawford, Jacqueline Cole, Susan Kiger, Sylvia Anderson. Mindless entertainment about seven young women who team up and outfit a "super-van" to combat drug dealing. Lots of action.▼

Angels Die Hard (1970) C-86m. ** D: Richard Compton. Tom Baker, William Smith, Connie Nelson, R. G. Armstrong, Beach Dickerson, Rita Murray, Dan Haggerty, Bambi Allen, Michael Stringer, Gary Littlejohn. Average biker picture has Angels turning out to be good guys for a change as they save people in a mine disaster. Boasts an impressive cast of regulars from this genre.▼

Angels from Hell (1968) C-86m. *½ D: Bruce Kessler. Tom Stern, Arlene Martel, Ted Markland, Stephen Oliver, Paul Bertoya. Violent time-waster with Vietnam war hero Stern coming home to start a new motorcycle gang, tangling with rival bikers and police.

Angels Hard as They Come (1971) C-90m. *½ D: Joe Viola. James Iglehart, Gilda Texter, Gary Busey, Charles Dierkop, Gary Littlejohn, Larry Tucker, Sharon Peckinpah, Scott Glenn. Loosely structured road movie satirizes the format, but cannot rise above the cliches. Produced and co-written by Jonathan Demme (who claims this is a biker version of RASHOMON); Busey's film debut.▼

Angels in Disguise (1949) 63m. D: Jean Yarbrough. Leo Gorcey, Huntz Hall, Gabriel Dell, Mickey Knox, Jean Dean, Bernard Gorcey. SEE **Bowery Boys** series.

Angels in the Outfield (1951) 102m. *** D: Clarence Brown. Paul Douglas, Janet Leigh, Keenan Wynn, Donna Corcoran. Engaging fantasy as heavenly forces help Pittsburgh Pirates go on a winning streak.

Angels of Darkness (1956-Italian) 84m. ** D: Giuseppe Amato. Linda Darnell, Anthony Quinn, Valentina Cortese, Lea Padovani. Aimless account of life and love among unhappy inhabitants of Rome—waste of stars' abilities.

Angels One Five (1954-British) 98m. ** D: George More O'Ferrall. Jack Hawkins, Michael Denison, Dulcie Gray, John Gregson. Grounded for accidental plane mishap, British war pilot rebels against officers and friends, seeking to fly again.

Angels Over Broadway (1940) 80m. **½ D: Ben Hecht, Lee Garmes. Douglas Fairbanks, Jr., Rita Hayworth, Thomas Mitchell, John Qualen, George Watts. Mordant, ahead-of-its-time black comedy in which hustler Fairbanks decides to do "one good deed"—rescuing suicidal embezzler Qualen—aided by call-girl Hayworth and boozy Mitchell (who spouts reams of sardonic dialogue in a bravura performance). Hecht buffs will undoubtedly rate this higher, but despite impeccable production, it's just too offbeat (and pleased with itself about it) for most viewers.▼

Angel Street SEE: **Gaslight** (1940)

Angels Wash Their Faces, The (1939) 84m. **½ D: Ray Enright. Ann Sheridan, Dead End Kids, Frankie Thomas, Bonita Granville, Ronald Reagan, Margaret Hamilton, Marjorie Main. Protective sister Sheridan tries to clear brother Thomas' police record, but he joins Dead End Kids for more trouble. OK juvenile delinquent drama.

Angels With Dirty Faces (1938) 97m. ***½ D: Michael Curtiz. James Cagney, Pat O'Brien, Humphrey Bogart, Ann Sheridan, George Bancroft, Billy Halop, Leo Gorcey, Huntz Hall, Gabe Dell, Bobby Jordan, Bernard Punsley. Superior cast in archetypal tale of two playmates; one (Cagney) becomes a gangster, the other (O'Brien) a priest. The Dead End Kids come to idolize Cagney, much to O'Brien's chagrin. Rowland Brown's story was scripted by John Wexley and Warren Duff. Quintessential Warner Bros. melodrama, a favorite of parodists for decades. Also shown in computer-colored version.▼

Angel Unchained (1970) C-92m. ** D: Lee Madden. Don Stroud, Luke Askew, Larry Bishop, Tyne Daly, Aldo Ray, Bill McKinney. Biker Stroud joins a hippie commune. Dune buggy-riding cowboys don't like hippies, so it's Stroud's ex-buddies to the rescue. Anyway, the cast is interesting.

Angel Who Pawned Her Harp, The (1954-British) 76m. ** D: Alan Bromly. Felix Aylmer, Diane Cilento, Jerry Desmonde, Joe Linnane, Alfie Bass, David Kossoff, Sheila Sweet. Cilento, in her film debut, stars as an angel who visits earth and becomes involved in various people's lives. Slight, forgettable fare.

Angel Wore Red, The (1960) 99m. **½ D: Nunnally Johnson. Ava Gardner, Dirk Bogarde, Joseph Cotten, Vittorio De Sica. Sometimes engrossing tale of clergyman who joins the Spanish loyalist cause and his romance with a good-natured entertainer.

Angry Breed, The (1969) C-89m. BOMB D: David Commons. Jan Sterling, James MacArthur, William Windom, Jan Murray, Murray McLeod, Lori Martin, Melody Patterson. Vietnam veteran comes to Hollywood after discharge, gets mixed up with a group of motorcyclists. Twelfth-rate in all departments.

Angry Hills, The (1959) 105m. **½ D: Robert Aldrich. Robert Mitchum, Elisabeth Mueller, Stanley Baker, Gia Scala, Theodore Bikel, Sebastian Cabot. Mitchum shows vim in WW2 actioner as war correspondent plotting escape from Greece with valuable data for Allies.

Angry Red Planet, The (1959) C-83m. ** D: Ib Melchior. Gerald Mohr, Nora Hayden, Les Tremayne, Jack Kruschen, Paul Hahn. Martians sic incredible monsters on first Earth expedition to Mars. Lots of wild-eyed effects have given this film cult status. Filmed in odd "Cinemagic" process, which mostly turns everything pink.▼

Angry Silence, The (1960-British) 95m. *** D: Guy Green. Richard Attenborough, Pier Angeli, Michael Craig, Bernard Lee, Geoffrey Keene, Oliver Reed. Rewarding, unheralded film about brave stand by a simple Britisher who refuses to join wildcat strike, the repercussions he endures.

Anguish (1987-Spanish) C-89m. **½ D: Bigas Luna. Zelda Rubinstein, Michael Lerner, Talia Paul, Clara Pastor. Imaginative but overly violent horror film turns the action in on itself, as a mad-killer film unspools inside a theater where another mad killer is loose in the audience. Theatrical release carried warnings regarding use of subliminal effects on soundtrack. Well-recorded English dialogue.▼

Animal Behavior (1989) C-88m. BOMB D: H. Anne Riley. Karen Allen, Armand Assante, Holly Hunter, Josh Mostel, Richard Libertini, Alexa Kenin, Jon Matthews, Nan Martin. A man, a woman, a chimp, a campus—and let us all be thankful that Bonzo didn't live to see this. Allen, as a monkey researcher sweating out funding, delivers a most discomforting lemme-outa-here performance; this turkey was on the shelf for so long that the cops didn't even have to dust for prints. Incidentally, the director's name is a pseudonym; Jenny Bowen started the picture in 1984; producer Kjehl Rasmussen finished it.▼

Animal Crackers (1930) 98m. *** D: Victor Heerman. Groucho, Harpo, Chico,

and Zeppo Marx, Margaret Dumont, Lillian Roth, Louis Sorin, Hal Thompson, Robert Greig. Marx Brothers' second movie, adapted from Broadway success, suffers from staginess and musical comedy plotting, but gives the zany foursome plenty of comic elbow-room. "Story" has to do with stolen painting, but never mind: Groucho performs "Hooray for Captain Spaulding," Chico and Harpo play bridge, etc.▼

Animal Farm (1955-British) C-75m. *** D: John Halas, Joy Batchelor. Good straightforward animated-feature version of George Orwell's satire. Ending changed from original to make it more upbeat, but trenchant views of government still hold fast. Not a kiddie film.▼

Animal House SEE: **National Lampoon's Animal House**▼

Animal Kingdom, The (1932) 85m. *** D: Edward H. Griffith. Ann Harding, Leslie Howard, Myrna Loy, William Gargan, Neil Hamilton, Ilka Chase, Henry Stephenson. Publisher Howard, undergoing a crisis in values, has had a relationship with free-spirited artist Harding but marries manipulative, middle-class Loy. Sophisticated entertainment, still quite adult by today's standards, adapted from Philip Barry's play. Remade as ONE MORE TOMORROW.

Animals, The (1970) C-86m. *½ D: Ron Joy. Henry Silva, Keenan Wynn, Michele Carey, John Anderson, Joseph Turkel. Sadistic Western with routine performances and stereotyped plot. Pretty schoolteacher vows revenge on five brutes who raped and humiliated her after holding up her stagecoach. Similar to the later HANNIE CAULDER.

Animalympics (1979) C-80m. ** D: Steven Lisberger. Voices of Gilda Radner, Billy Crystal, Harry Shearer, Michael Fremer. Animated spoof of Olympics events and ubiquitous TV coverage by various anthropomorphic characters. Enough clever, funny material for a good short subject, but stretched to feature length. Cut to 48m. for network showings.▼

Anna (1951-Italian) 95m. **½ D: Alberto Lattuada. Silvana Mangano, Raf Vallone, Vittorio Gassman, Gaby Morlay. Thoughtful study of confused young woman who enters convent to avoid deciding which man she really loves, with fates forcing decision upon her.

Anna (1987) C-100m. **½ D: Yurek Bogayevicz. Sally Kirkland, Paulina Porizkova, Robert Fields, Ruth Maleczech, Stefan Schnabel, Larry Pine. Middle-aged Czech actress, once a star in her native country but now struggling to survive in N.Y.C., takes in an impoverished young immigrant and teaches her the ropes—only to see her succeed where she has failed. Intriguing little film misses the bull's-eye but still has much to offer, especially a riveting and heart-rending performance by Kirkland (who is *not* Czech). Supermodel Porizkova (who is) makes an impressive screen debut. ▼

Anna and the King of Siam (1946) **128m.** ***½ D: John Cromwell. Irene Dunne, Rex Harrison, Linda Darnell, Lee J. Cobb, Gale Sondergaard, Mikhail Rasumny. Sumptuous production chronicling the experiences of a British governess in 19th-century Thailand, and her battle of wits with strong-willed ruler. Based on Margaret Landon's book about real-life Anna Leonowens (renamed Anna L. Owens in the movie). Dunne and Harrison (in his Hollywood debut) are superb; won Oscars for Cinematography (Arthur Miller) and Art Director/Set Decoration. Screenplay by Talbot Jennings and Sally Benson. Later musicalized as THE KING AND I.

Annabel Takes a Tour (1938) **67m.** ** D: Lew Landers. Lucille Ball, Jack Oakie, Ruth Donnelly, Bradley Page, Ralph Forbes, Frances Mercer, Donald MacBride. Disappointing follow-up to THE AFFAIRS OF ANNABEL, with actress Ball going on tour with press agent Oakie. Second and last entry in series. ▼

Anna Christie (1930) **90m.** *** D: Clarence Brown. Greta Garbo, Charles Bickford, Marie Dressler, Lee Phelps, George Marion. Garbo is effective in her first talkie as girl with shady past finding love with seaman Bickford. Film itself is rather static. From the play by Eugene O'Neill. Filmed before in 1923, with Blanche Sweet. ▼

Anna Karenina (1935) **95m.** **** D: Clarence Brown. Greta Garbo, Fredric March, Freddie Bartholomew, Maureen O'Sullivan, May Robson, Basil Rathbone. Tolstoy's tragic love chronicle makes excellent Garbo vehicle, with fine support from March as her lover, Rathbone her husband, and Bartholomew, her adoring son. Filmed before with Garbo as LOVE. ▼

Anna Karenina (1948-British) **123m.** **½ D: Julien Duvivier. Vivien Leigh, Ralph Richardson, Kieron Moore, Hugh Dempster. Despite cast, strictly turgid adaptation of Tolstoy classic about married woman blindly in love with officer. ▼

Anna Karenina (1985) **C-150m.** TVM D: Simon Langton. Jacqueline Bisset, Christopher Reeve, Paul Scofield, Ian Ogilvy, Anna Massey, Judi Bowker. Glossy but overlong remake of Tolstoy classic with Scofield (as Karenin, Anna's dispassionate husband) acting rings around his co-stars. Average. ▼

Anna Lucasta (1958) **97m.** ** D: Arnold Laven. Eartha Kitt, Sammy Davis, Jr., Frederick O'Neal, Henry Scott, Rex Ingram. Tepid melodrama about promiscuous Kitt who leaves home when boyfriend learns her true morality. This all-black remake of 1949 film with Paulette Goddard is based on the play by Philip Yordan.

Annapolis Story, An (1955) **C-81m.** ** D: Don Siegel. John Derek, Diana Lynn, Kevin McCarthy, Pat Conway. Uninspired reuse of old service-school formula with Derek and McCarthy undergoing rigid training, both romancing Lynn. ▼

Anna to the Infinite Power (1983) **C-101m.** ** D: Robert Wiemer. Dina Merrill, Martha Byrne, Jack Gilford, Mark Patton, Donna Mitchell. Bright kid discovers that she is the result of a scientific cloning experiment and tries to find her "sisters," connected by telepathy. Mild science-fiction drama aimed at youngsters. ▼

Anne of Avonlea (1987-Canadian) **C-195m.** TVM D: Kevin Sullivan. Megan Follows, Colleen Dewhurst, Frank Converse, Schuyler Grant, Jonathan Crombie, Patricia Hamilton, Rosemary Dunsmore. Rare case of a sequel matching the original in near-perfection, focusing on Anne Shirley (Follows) at 18 as a teacher at Avonlea and dreaming of meeting her ideal man. Adapted by Sullivan from three Lucy Maud Montgomery books bringing the title character into adulthood: *Anne of Avonlea, Anne of the Island* and *Anne of Windy Poplars.* Originally shown in two parts. Also called ANNE OF GREEN GABLES: THE SEQUEL. Above average. ▼

Anne of Green Gables (1934) **79m.** **** D: George Nicholls, Jr. Anne Shirley, Tom Brown, O. P. Heggie, Helen Westley, Sara Haden. Utterly charming adaptation of L. M. Montgomery's book (filmed before in 1919) about a spirited orphan with a vivid imagination who endears herself to the older couple who take her in . . . and everyone else around her. Only the conclusion seems hurried and contrived. Anne Shirley took her professional name from the character she played in this film (until then she was known as Dawn O'Day). Followed by ANNE OF WINDY POPLARS. Remade for TV. ▼

Anne of Green Gables (1985-Canadian) **C-195m.** TVM D: Kevin Sullivan. Megan Follows, Colleen Dewhurst, Patricia Hamilton, Marilyn Lightstone, Charmion King, Rosemary Radcliffe, Jackie Burroughs, Richard Farnsworth. Lovely adaptation of the classic children's story chronicling young life of title character (Follows), from her adoption by bachelor farmer Matthew Cuthbert and his sister Marilla to her blossoming love for Gilbert Blythe. Shown in two parts, as ANNE OF GREEN GABLES: A NEW HOME and ANNE OF GREEN GABLES: A BEND IN THE ROAD. Followed by ANNE OF AVONLEA. Above average. ▼

Anne of Green Gables: The Sequel SEE: **Anne of Avonlea**▼

Anne of the Indies (1951) **C-81m.** **½ D: Jacques Tourneur. Jean Peters, Louis Jourdan, Debra Paget, Herbert Marshall. Peters isn't always believable as swaggering pirate, but surrounded by professionals and good production, actioner moves along.

Anne of the Thousand Days (1969) **C-145m.** *** D: Charles Jarrott. Richard Burton, Genevieve Bujold, Irene Papas, Anthony Quayle, Peter Jeffrey. Often inaccurate but totally engrossing, well-acted historical drama centering on Anne Boleyn and King Henry VIII. Lovely scenery, brilliant performance by Bujold, and Oscar-winning costumes by Margaret Furse.▼

Anne of Windy Poplars (1940) **88m.** ** D: Jack Hively. Anne Shirley, James Ellison, Henry Travers, Patric Knowles. Fair acting in tired story of teacher overcoming small-town prejudices. Follow-up to ANNE OF GREEN GABLES.

Annie (1982) **C-128m.** **½ D: John Huston. Albert Finney, Carol Burnett, Aileen Quinn, Bernadette Peters, Tim Curry, Ann Reinking, Geoffrey Holder, Edward Herrmann. Overblown adaptation of the Broadway musical hit about the Depression's most famous foundling (based on Harold Gray's "Little Orphan Annie" comic strip). Appealing performances by Quinn, as Annie, and Finney, as Daddy Warbucks, help buoy an uninspired—and curiously claustrophobic—production.▼

Annie Get Your Gun (1950) **C-107m.** *** D: George Sidney. Betty Hutton, Howard Keel, Louis Calhern, Edward Arnold, Keenan Wynn, Benay Venuta, J. Carrol Naish. Lively filming of Irving Berlin's Wild West show musical of Annie Oakley getting her man. Songs include "Anything You Can Do," "Doin' What Comes Naturally," "There's No Business Like Show Business."

Annie Hall (1977) **C-94m.** **** D: Woody Allen. Woody Allen, Diane Keaton, Tony Roberts, Paul Simon, Shelley Duvall, Carol Kane, Colleen Dewhurst, Christopher Walken, Janet Margolin. Woody's best film, an autobiographical love story with incisive Allenisms on romance, relationships, fame, N.Y.C. vs. L.A., and sundry other topics. Warm, witty, intelligent Oscar winner for Best Picture, Actress, Direction, Screenplay (Allen and Marshall Brickman). Look sharp and you'll spot future stars Jeff Goldblum (at the L.A. party), Shelley Hack (on the street), Beverly D'Angelo (on a TV monitor), and Sigourney Weaver (as Woody's date near the end of the picture).▼

Annie Oakley (1935) **88m.** *** D: George Stevens. Barbara Stanwyck, Preston Foster, Melvyn Douglas, Pert Kelton, Andy Clyde. Lively biography of female sharpshooter Stanwyck and her on-again off-again romance with fellow-performer Foster. Tight direction within episodic scenes, gives believable flavor of late 19th-century America. Moroni Olsen plays Buffalo Bill.▼

Annie's Coming Out SEE: **Test of Love, A**▼

Annihilator (1986) **C-100m. TVM** D: Michael Chapman. Mark Lindsay Chapman, Susan Blakely, Lisa Blount, Geoffrey Lewis, Catherine Mary Stewart, Brion James. Stylish but pedestrian series pilot about a newspaperman pursued by both the police and an army of automatons. Makeup artists Michael Westmore and Zoltan Elek, both Emmy nominated, are the real stars of this piece. Average.

Annihilators, The (1985) **C-84m.** BOMB D: Charles E. Sellier, Jr. Christopher Stone, Andy Wood, Lawrence Hilton-Jacobs, Gerrit Graham, Dennis Redfield, Paul Koslo. Formula vigilante tale of neighborhood folks in southern town who hire a bunch of Vietnam vets to protect them from local youth gangs. Nasty film with repellant violence. ▼

Anniversary, The (1968-British) **C-95m.** **½ D: Roy Ward Baker. Bette Davis, Sheila Hancock, Jack Hedley, James Cossins, Christian Roberts, Elaine Taylor. Human monster Davis uses date of wedding anniversary as excuse to reunite family, continue her stranglehold on them. Adapted from MacIlwraith stage play, black comedy emerges as vehicle for Davis' hammy performance.

Ann Jillian Story, The (1988) **C-100m. TVM** D: Corey Allen. Ann Jillian, Tony LoBianco, Viveca Lindfors, George Touliatos, Tim Webber, Pam Hyatt. Entertainer Jillian stars in her own biography dealing with her marriage to a Chicago vice cop, her successful career, and her battle with breast cancer. And she gets to sing four new songs too. In any event, it's ideally cast. Average.▼

Ann Vickers (1933) **72m.** **½ D: John Cromwell. Irene Dunne, Walter Huston, Bruce Cabot, Edna May Oliver, Conrad Nagel. Dunne becomes an unwed mother thanks to heel Cabot, eventually finds love with judge Huston. Leads are fine in adaptation of Sinclair Lewis novel, but film is more episodic than any movie has a right to be.▼

A Nos Amours (1984-French) **C-102m.** *** D: Maurice Pialat. Sandrine Bonnaire, Dominique Besnehard, Maurice Pialat, Evelyne Ker, Anne-Sophie Maille, Christophe Odent. A 15-year-old's casual promiscuity runs her family through the ringer, but they've got problems of their own—Pop's moving out, Mom's a screaming neurotic, and Brother's embraces are too hearty to be healthy. Dramatically uneven and somewhat of a downer, but Bonnaire creates a full-blooded, memorable character. Winner of France's César.▼

Another Country (1984-British) **C-90m.**
**½ D: Marek Kanievska. Rupert Everett, Colin Firth, Michael Jenn, Robert Addie, Cary Elwes, Anna Massey, Betsy Brantley. Faithful adaptation of Julian Mitchell's hit London play that speculates about the 1930s private-school experiences of Guy Burgess and Donald Maclean, who twenty years later were found to be spying for the Russians. Arguably more meaningful to British audiences, this examination of an oppressive existence that shuns any nonconformity makes for a pretty oppressive movie.▼

Another Dawn (1937) **73m.** **½ D: William Dieterle. Kay Francis, Errol Flynn, Ian Hunter, Frieda Inescort, Mary Forbes. Francis is torn between devotion to husband Hunter and officer Flynn in well-paced adventure story set at British army post in African desert.

Another 48 HRS (1990) **C-95m.** ** D: Walter Hill. Eddie Murphy, Nick Nolte, Brion James, Kevin Tighe, Ed O'Ross, David Anthony Marshall, Bernie Casey. Strictly by-the-numbers rehash of the first film, without its spontaneity, pizzazz, or humor: Nolte is forced to turn to Murphy (who's just being sprung from jail) to help him solve a case and save his police career. Watchable, but not terribly invigorating; must set some sort of record, however, for breaking more panes of glass than any movie in history.

Another Language (1933) **77m.** *** D: Edward H. Griffith. Helen Hayes, Robert Montgomery, Louise Closser-Hale, John Beal, Margaret Hamilton, Henry Travers. Vivid, devastating picture of American family life (based on Rose Franken's play), with Hayes as an outsider who marries Montgomery and faces hostility from matriarch Hale and her gossipy offspring.

Another Man, Another Chance (1977-French-U.S.) **C-132m.** **½ D: Claude Lelouch. James Caan, Genevieve Bujold, Francis Huster, Jennifer Warren, Susan Tyrrell. Virtual remake of Lelouch's A MAN AND A WOMAN, with late-1800s Western setting; Bujold and Caan are widow and widower who fall in love after losing their spouses. Mild-mannered to the point of distraction, and much too long.▼

Another Man's Poison (1952-British) **89m.** ** D: Irving Rapper. Bette Davis, Gary Merrill, Emlyn Williams, Anthony Steel. Hazy melodrama with a tame Davis performance as authoress who kills her escaped convict husband and is blackmailed by another con (Merrill) on the loose.

Another Part of the Forest (1948) **107m.**

*** D: Michael Gordon. Fredric March, Dan Duryea, Edmond O'Brien, Ann Blyth, Florence Eldridge, John Dall. Lillian Hellman's story predates THE LITTLE FOXES by tracing the Hubbard family's ruthlessness; unpleasant but well-acted movie.

Another Thin Man (1939) **105m.** D: W. S. Van Dyke II. William Powell, Myrna Loy, Virginia Grey, Otto Kruger, C. Aubrey Smith, Ruth Hussey, Nat Pendleton, Tom Neal, Sheldon Leonard, Marjorie Main. SEE: **Thin Man** series.▼

Another Time, Another Place (1958) **98m.**
**½ D: Lewis Allen. Lana Turner, Barry Sullivan, Glynis Johns, Sean Connery. Unconvincing melodrama; Turner suffers nervous breakdown when her lover is killed during WW2. Filmed in England.▼

Another Woman (1988) **C-84m.** ***½ D: Woody Allen. Gena Rowlands, Mia Farrow, Ian Holm, Blythe Danner, Gene Hackman, Betty Buckley, Martha Plimpton, John Houseman, Sandy Dennis, David Ogden Stiers, Philip Bosco, Harris Yulin, Frances Conroy. Woody ventures into Bergman territory again (with Ingmar's cameraman, Sven Nykvist, no less) with tremendous success. Rowlands plays a woman who has managed to live her life shielding herself from all emotions, until a series of incidents forces her to take stock. Searing, adult drama with a magnificent cast and many memorable moments . . . though like Allen's other dramas, it's not to everyone's taste.▼

Another Woman's Child (1983) **C-100m.**
TVM D: John Erman. Linda Lavin, Tony LoBianco, Joyce Van Patten, Doris Roberts, Ron Rifkin, Tracey Gold. Childless woman agonizes over role as stepmother to her husband's illegitimate daughter. Average.

A Nous la Liberte (1931-French) **87m.** ✓
**** D: Rene Clair. Raymond Cordy, Henri Marchand, Rolla France, Paul Olivier, Jacques Shelly, Andre Michaud. Classic satire on machinery and industrialization centering on the adventures of escaped prisoner Cordy, who becomes the owner of a phonograph factory, and his former friend from jail (Marchand), now a vagrant. Predates and equals MODERN TIMES in poignancy, with groundbreaking use of music. Arguably, Clair's masterpiece.▼

Anthony Adverse (1936) **141m.** ***½ D: Mervyn LeRoy. Fredric March, Olivia de Havilland, Donald Woods, Anita Louise, Edmund Gwenn, Claude Rains, Louis Hayward, Akim Tamiroff, Billy Mauch, Ralph Morgan, Henry O'Neill, Scotty Beckett, Luis Alberni. Blockbuster filmization of Hervey Allen bestseller (scripted by Sheridan Gibney) of young man gaining maturity through adventures in various parts of early 19th-century America, Mexico, et al. Gale Sondergaard won Oscar as Best Supporting Actress; rousing musical score by Erich Wolfgang Korngold and Tony Gaudio's cinematography also won.▼

Antonia: A Portrait of the Woman (1974) **C-58m.** ***½ D: Judy Collins, Jill Godmilow. Heartfelt documentary about conductor Antonia Brico and her struggle to triumph professionally over sexual prejudice within the symphonic community. Inspiring.

Antonio (1973) **C-81m.** ** D: Claudio Guzman. Trini Lopez, Larry Hagman, Noemi Guerrero, Pedro Becker, Marvin Walkenstein. South American village potter's life gets complicated after an eccentric Texas oilman gives him a car, so he sets out to return it. Good-hearted if empty-headed version of city mouse–country mouse fable. Hagman hams it up in pre-*Dallas* oilman role.▼

Antony and Cleopatra (1973) **C-160m.** *½ D: Charlton Heston. Charlton Heston, Hildegard Neil, Eric Porter, John Castle, Fernando Rey. Labor-of-love undertaking by Heston results in sluggish treatment of Shakespearean play, hampered by severe budgetary limitations.▼

Ants SEE: **It Happened At Lakewood Manor**▼

Any Gun Can Play (1967-Italian-Spanish) **C-103m.** BOMB D: Enzo G. Castellari. Edd Byrnes, Gilbert Roland, George Hilton, Kareen O'Hara, Pedro Sanchez, Gerard Herter. Bounty hunter Hilton, bandit Roland and bank official Byrnes vie for gold treasure. Silly spaghetti Western, filmed in Spain. Also known as FOR A FEW BULLETS MORE.▼

Any Man's Death (1990) **C-110m.** *½ D: Tom Clegg. John Savage, William Hickey, Mia Sara, Ernest Borgnine, Michael Lerner, James Ryan. Stultifying tale of a reporter who stumbles onto a Nazi war criminal in Africa, and has to deal with the issues raised by his discovery. Pretty interesting cast, but nothing else to recommend in this hollow moralistic drama.

Any Number Can Play (1949) **112m.** ** D: Mervyn LeRoy. Clark Gable, Alexis Smith, Wendell Corey, Audrey Totter, Mary Astor, Lewis Stone, Marjorie Rambeau. Low-key drama of gambling-house owner Gable, estranged from wife Smith and son Darryl Hickman. Good character roles breathe life into film.

Any Number Can Win (1963-French) **108m.** **½ D: Henri Verneuil. Jean Gabin, Alain Delon, Viviane Romance, Carla Marlier. Gabin leads bank robbery in Riviera resort. Comedy and suspense blend in "perfect crime" attempt.

Anyone Can Play (1968-Italian-French) **C-88m.** ** D: Luigi Zampa. Ursula Andress, Virna Lisi, Claudine Auger, Marisa Mell, Brett Halsey, Jean-Pierre Cassel. Aside from obvious good looks of four leading actresses, tale of adultery in Italy is not one of that country's better farces.

Any Second Now (1969) **C-97m.** TVM D: Gene Levitt. Stewart Granger, Lois Nettleton, Joseph Campanella, Dana Wynter, Katy Jurado, Tom Tully. Entertaining melodrama with Granger attempting to murder his wife when he realizes she's aware of his infidelity. Granger's TV movie debut. Above average.

Anything Can Happen (1952) **107m.** ** D: George Seaton. Jose Ferrer, Kim Hunter, Kurt Kasznar, Eugenie Leontovich. Smooth but schmaltzy adaptation of bestselling autobiographical book about Russian immigrant's new life.

Anything for Love SEE: **11 Harrowhouse**▼

Anything Goes (1936) **92m.** **½ D: Lewis Milestone. Bing Crosby, Ethel Merman, Charlie Ruggles, Ida Lupino, Grace Bradley, Arthur Treacher. Pleasant Crosby shipboard musical retain's Merman from the cast of the Broadway show, but scuttles much of the plot and most of Cole Porter's songs (except "You're the Top" and "I Get a Kick Out of You"). Remade in 1956. Retitled for TV: TOPS IS THE LIMIT.

Anything Goes (1956) **C-106m.** ** D: Robert Lewis. Bing Crosby, Jeanmaire, Donald O'Connor, Mitzi Gaynor, Phil Harris, Kurt Kasznar. Flat musical involving show business partners Crosby and O'Connor each signing a performer for the leading role in their next show. Sidney Sheldon's script bears little resemblance to the original Broadway show, though some Cole Porter songs remain. Crosby fared better in the 1936 film.

Anything to Survive (1990) **C-100m.** TVM D: Zala Dalen. Robert Conrad, Matthew LeBlanc, Ocean Hellman, Emily Perkins, Tom Heating, William B. Davis. A man and his three teenage children battle the elements for more than three weeks after being shipwrecked off the coast of Alaska. Gritty survival story adapted by Jonathan Rintels from Elmo Wortman's book *Almost Too Late*. Above average.

Any Wednesday (1966) **C-109m.** *** D: Robert Ellis Miller. Jane Fonda, Jason Robards, Dean Jones, Rosemary Murphy. Bedroom farce of N.Y.C. executive using his mistress' apartment for business deductions. Fonda is appropriately addled in unstagy sex comedy.▼

Any Which Way You Can (1980) **C-116m.** **½ D: Buddy Van Horn. Clint Eastwood, Sondra Locke, Geoffrey Lewis, William Smith, Harry Guardino, Ruth Gordon, Glen Campbell, Anne Ramsey, Logan Ramsey. This sequel to EVERY WHICH WAY BUT LOOSE is funnier, if no more intelli-

[42]

gent. Clint's climactic bare-fisted fight with Smith is a highlight, but the filmmakers wisely gave most of the laughs to the star's orangutan friend, Clyde.▼

Anzio (1968-French-Italian-Spanish) **C-117m.** ** D: Edward Dmytryk. Robert Mitchum, Peter Falk, Robert Ryan, Earl Holliman, Mark Damon, Arthur Kennedy, Reni Santoni, Patrick Magee. Undistinguished retelling of Allied invasion of Anzio; all-star cast, large-scale action, but nothing memorable. Also known as THE BATTLE FOR ANZIO.▼

Apache (1954) **C-91m.** ** D: Robert Aldrich. Burt Lancaster, Jean Peters, John McIntire, Charles (Bronson) Buchinsky. Pacifist Indian (Lancaster) learns might makes right from U.S. cavalry; turns to fighting one man crusade for his tribe's rights. Overacted and improbable (though based on fact).▼

Apache Ambush (1955) **68m.** ** D: Fred F. Sears. Bill Williams, Richard Jaeckel, Movita, Tex Ritter. So what else is new?

Apache Drums (1951) **C-75m.** *½ D: Hugo Fregonese. Stephen McNally, Coleen Gray, Willard Parker, Arthur Shields. Humdrum Western with gambler McNally coming to town's rescue when attacked by Indians.

Apache Gold (1965-German) **C-91m.** **½ D: Harald Reinl. Lex Barker, Mario Adorf, Pierre Brice, Marie Versini. A sort of Eastern-Western has good Indian atmosphere, plenty of action.

Apache Massacre SEE: Cry for Me, Billy

Apache Rifles (1964) **C-92m.** **½ D: William Witney. Audie Murphy, Michael Dante, Linda Lawson, John Archer, J. Pat O'Malley. Audie is stalwart cavalry captain assigned to corral renegading Apaches. Stock footage and plot mar potentials of actioner.

Apache Territory (1958) **C-75m.** *½ D: Ray Nazarro. Rory Calhoun, Barbara Bates, John Dehner, Carolyn Craig. Calhoun almost single-handedly routs rampaging Apaches and rescues defenseless Bates.

Apache Uprising (1966) **C-90m.** *½ D: R. G. Springsteen. Rory Calhoun, Corinne Calvet, John Russell, Lon Chaney, Gene Evans, Richard Arlen, Arthur Hunnicutt, Johnny Mack Brown, Jean Parker. No production values, but cast of familiar names may make it possible for some to sit through standard Western where Rory fights both Indians and outlaws.

Apache Warrior (1957) **74m.** ** D: Elmo Williams. Keith Larsen, Jim Davis, Michael Carr, Eddie Little. When an Indian leader's brother is killed, redskins go on the warpath. Nothing new.

Apache War Smoke (1952) **67m.** *½ D: Harold F. Kress. Gilbert Roland, Robert Horton, Glenda Farrell, Gene Lockhart, Bobby (Robert) Blake. Pat Western involving stagecoach robbery and Indian at-

tack on stage-line station. Good supporting cast wasted.

Apache Woman (1955) **C-83m.** BOMB D: Roger Corman. Lloyd Bridges, Joan Taylor, Lance Fuller, Morgan Jones, Paul Birch, Dick Miller, Chester Conklin. Government affairs expert Bridges attempts to ease tension between Apaches and whites, tangles with hellcat halfbreed Taylor. Sometimes hilariously bad, but mostly a bore.

Aparajito (1956-Indian) **108m.** ***½ D: Satyajit Ray. Pinaki Sen Gupta, Smaran Ghosal, Karuna Banerji, Kanu Banerji, Ramani Sen Gupta. The second of Ray's Apu trilogy is a moving, beautifully filmed story of life and death in a poor Indian family, with the son, Apu (Ghosal), trekking off to college in Calcutta. Also known as THE UNVANQUISHED.▼

Apartment, The (1960) **125m.** **** D: Billy Wilder. Jack Lemmon, Shirley MacLaine, Fred MacMurray, Ray Walston, Jack Kruschen, Edie Adams, David Lewis, Joan Shawlee. Superb comedy-drama that manages to embrace both sentiment and cynicism. Lemmon attempts to climb corporate ladder by loaning his apartment key to various executives, but it backfires when he falls for his boss's latest girlfriend. Fine performances all around, including MacMurray as an uncharacteristic heel. Oscar winner for Best Picture, Director, Screenplay (Wilder and I. A. L. Diamond), Editing (Daniel Mandell), Art Direction-Set Decoration, (Alexander Trauner, Edward G. Boyle). Later a Broadway musical, *Promises, Promises.* ▼

Apartment for Peggy (1948) **C-99m.** *** D: George Seaton. Jeanne Crain, William Holden, Edmund Gwenn, Gene Lockhart. Breezy story of newlyweds trying to live on college campus; old pros Gwenn and Lockhart steal film from young lovers.

Apartment Zero (1988-British) **C-124m.** *** D: Martin Donovan. Colin Firth, Hart Bochner, Dora Bryan, Liz Smith, Fabrizio Bentivoglio. Odd, intriguing psychological drama with political, moral, and sexual overtones. Fastidious film buff Firth's life is profoundly altered when he takes in freewheeling—and mysterious—Bochner as a boarder. Not for all tastes but extremely well acted and definitely worth a look. Set in Buenos Aires; scripted by Donovan and David Koepp. Shortened by 8 minutes for video by director.▼

Ape, The (1940) **62m.** ** D: William Nigh. Boris Karloff, Gertrude W. Hoffman, Henry Hall, Maris Wrixon. Low-budget shocker with mad doctor Karloff killing and experimenting with title character in order to save girl's life.▼

Ape Man, The (1943) **64m.** ** D: William Beaudine. Bela Lugosi, Louise Currie, Wallace Ford, Henry Hall, Minerva Urecal. Minor horror effort with Lugosi and cast overacting in story of scientist injecting himself to attain power of simian relatives. Followed by non-sequel, RETURN OF THE APE MAN.▼

Apocalypse Now (1979) C-150m. ***½ D: Francis Coppola. Marlon Brando, Robert Duvall, Martin Sheen, Frederic Forrest, Albert Hall, Sam Bottoms, Larry Fishburne, Dennis Hopper, G. D. Spradlin, Harrison Ford, Scott Glenn, Tom Mason, Colleen Camp. Coppola's controversial Vietnam war epic, based on Joseph Conrad's *Heart of Darkness*. Special agent Sheen journeys up river into Cambodia with orders to find and kill errant officer Brando, leading him (and viewer) on a mesmerizing odyssey of turbulent, often surreal encounters. Unfortunately, film's conclusion—when he does find Brando—is cerebral and murky. Still, a great movie experience most of the way, with staggering, Oscar-winning photography by Vittorio Storaro.▼

Apology (1986) C-98m. TVM D: Robert Bierman. Lesley Ann Warren, Peter Weller, John Glover, George Loros, Jimmie Ray Weeks, Christopher North, Harvey Fierstein. Seductive thriller involving a young Manhattan sculptress (who's creating an experimental art project), the psychotic killer pursuing her, and the determined detective trailing both. Occasionally far-fetched damsel-in-distress tale was written by playwright Mark Medoff. Made for cable. Average.▼

Appaloosa, The (1966) C-98m. **½ D: Sidney J. Furie. Marlon Brando, Anjanette Comer, John Saxon, Alex Montoya, Frank Silvera. Brooding Western set in 1870s with Brando trying to recover horse stolen from him by Mexican bandit; slowly paced, well photographed by Russell Metty.▼

Applause (1929) 78m. **½ D. Rouben Mamoulian. Helen Morgan, Joan Peers, Fuller Mellish, Jr., Henry Wadsworth, Dorothy Cumming. Revolutionary early talkie may seem awfully hokey to modern audiences (Morgan plays a fading burlesque queen with a two-timing boyfriend and an innocent young daughter just out of a convent), but Morgan's heart-rending performance, and innovative use of camera and sound by Mamoulian (in his film directing debut), make it a must for buffs.▼

Apple, The (1980) C-90m. BOMB D: Menahem Golan. Catherine Mary Stewart, Allan Love, George Gilmour, Grace Kennedy, Joss Ackland, Vladek Sheybal. Futuristic musical set in 1994, when a young couple's entry in songwriting contest is sabotaged by devilish Mr. Boogalow. As bad as it sounds—possibly worse.▼

Apple Dumpling Gang, The (1975) C-100m. ** D: Norman Tokar. Bill Bixby, Susan Clark, Don Knotts, Tim Conway, David Wayne, Slim Pickens, Harry Morgan. Disney Western comedy with gambler Bixby inheriting three children. Predictable doings sparked by Knotts and Conway as bumbling crooks.▼

Apple Dumpling Gang Rides Again, The (1979) C-88m. ** D: Vincent McEveety. Tim Conway, Don Knotts, Tim Matheson, Kenneth Mars, Elyssa Davalos, Jack Elam, Robert Pine, Harry Morgan, Ruth Buzzi. More of the same, with Knotts and Conway as bumbling outlaws in the Old West; usual Disney slapstick, without much zip or originality.▼

Appointment, The (1969) C-100m. **½ D: Sidney Lumet. Omar Sharif, Anouk Aimee, Lotte Lenya. Brilliant attorney falls in love with a girl who eventually ruins him. Soapy and long.

Appointment For Love (1941) 89m. **½ D: William Seiter. Charles Boyer, Margaret Sullavan, Rita Johnson, Reginald Denny, Ruth Terry, Eugene Pallette. Frothy comedy showcasing delightful stars: husband and wife with careers find happy marriage almost impossible.

Appointment In Berlin (1943) 77m. **½ D: Alfred E. Green. George Sanders, Marguerite Chapman, Onslow Stevens, Gale Sondergaard, Alan Napier. Another WW2 intrigue film, better than most, with Sanders joining Nazi radio staff to learn secret plans.

Appointment in Honduras (1953) C-79m. **½ D: Jacques Tourneur. Ann Sheridan, Glenn Ford, Zachary Scott, Jack Elam. Idealistic American (Ford) out to save Latin-American country, corrals villainous companions into helping crusade. Sheridan is not focal point, and a pity.▼

Appointment in London (1953-British) 96m. *** D: Philip Leacock. Dirk Bogarde, Ian Hunter, Dinah Sheridan, William Sylvester, Walter Fitzgerald, Bryan Forbes. Engrossing story of British bomber squadron in WW2, and high-pressured officer Bogarde who insists on flying dangerous mission in spite of orders to the contrary.

Appointment with a Shadow (1958) 73m. ** D: Richard Carlson. George Nader, Joanna Moore, Brian Keith, Virginia Field, Frank De Kova. Former ace reporter swears off alcohol and scoops big story.

Appointment With Danger (1951) 89m. *** D: Lewis Allen. Alan Ladd, Phyllis Calvert, Paul Stewart, Jan Sterling, Jack Webb, Harry Morgan. Ladd is a U.S. postal inspector aided by nun Calvert in cracking a case. Forget that part of the story; Webb and Morgan are the *villains* here, and *Dragnet* fans will be merrily amused. Best bit: Ladd ''dropping'' Webb on a handball court.

Appointment With Death (1988) C-108m. *½ D: Michael Winner. Peter Ustinov, Lauren Bacall, Carrie Fisher, John Gielgud, Piper Laurie, Hayley Mills, Jenny Seagrove, David Soul. Ustinov returns yet again as Agatha Christie's detective Hercule Poirot in this obvious, depressingly unsuspenseful mystery. It seems that greedy Laurie wants her late husband's money all for herself. How soon will she be murdered? And how soon will Poirot name her killer? Another loser from Winner; scripted by Anthony Shaffer, Peter Buckman and the director.▼

Appointment with Murder (1948) 67m. D: Jack Bernhard. John Calvert, Catherine Craig, Lyle Talbot, Jack Reitzen, Peter Brocco. SEE: **The Falcon** series.

Apprenticeship of Duddy Kravitz, The (1974-Canadian) **C-121m.** ***½ D: Ted Kotcheff. Richard Dreyfuss, Micheline Lanctot, Jack Warden, Randy Quaid, Joseph Wiseman, Denholm Elliott, Joe Silver. Mordecai Richler's vivid comedy-drama of an ambitious kid from Montreal's Jewish ghetto in the 1940s, determined to make good no matter how many toes he steps on. Pretentious bar mitzvah movie made by Duddy's "client," artsy director Elliott, is just one comic highlight.▼

Apprentice to Murder (1988) **C-94m.** ** D: R. L. Thomas. Donald Sutherland, Chad Lowe, Mia Sara, Knut Husebo, Rutanya Alda. Odd, affected, fact-based account of a practitioner of medieval medicine (Sutherland, in a disappointing performance), and his complex relationship with young Lowe. Filmed in Norway.▼

April Fools, The (1969) **C-95m.** ** D: Stuart Rosenberg. Jack Lemmon, Catherine Deneuve, Peter Lawford, Harvey Korman, Sally Kellerman, Myrna Loy, Charles Boyer. Attempt at old-fashioned romantic comedy is forced, unbelievable, unfunny. Lemmon is married businessman who decides to chuck it all to run away with Deneuve, who's wasted, along with Loy and Boyer.▼

April Fool's Day (1986) **C-88m.** ** D: Fred Walton. Deborah Foreman, Griffin O'Neal, Clayton Rohner, Thomas F. Wilson, Deborah Goodrich. Practical joker (Foreman) invites college pals to spend a weekend in her family's mansion on an off-coast island; one by one they're threatened and killed. Attempt to bring humor to FRIDAY THE 13TH formula isn't a total washout but doesn't quite click, either.▼

April in Paris (1952) **C-101m.** **½ D: David Butler. Doris Day, Ray Bolger, Claude Dauphin, Eve Miller, George Givot. Drab musical pegged on diplomat Bolger and showgirl Day having uninspired shipboard problems before reaching Paris.

April Love (1957) **C-97m.** **½ D: Henry Levin. Pat Boone, Shirley Jones, Dolores Michaels, Arthur O'Connell, Matt Crowley. Engaging musical with wholesome Boone visiting relatives' Kentucky farm, falling in love with neighbor Jones. Pat had a hit with the title tune. Previously filmed as HOME IN INDIANA.

April Morning (1988) **C-100m. TVM** D:

Delbert Mann. Tommy Lee Jones, Robert Urich, Chad Lowe, Susan Blakely, Rip Torn, Meredith Salenger. A teenage boy's coming of age on the eve of the American Revolution when the Colonists make their stand on the Lexington green. Well-crafted adaptation by James Lee Barrett of Howard Fast's 1961 novel. Above average.

April Showers (1948) **94m.** ** D: James V. Kern. Jack Carson, Ann Sothern, Robert Alda, S. Z. Sakall, Robert Ellis. Hackneyed backstage vaudeville yarn with Carson-Sothern teaming, splitting, reteaming, etc.

Aquarians, The (1970) **C-100m. TVM** D: Don McDougall. Ricardo Montalban, Jose Ferrer, Leslie Nielsen, Kate Woodville, Curt Lowens, Chris Robinson. Fair Ivan Tors production features Montalban as Dr. Luis Delgado, head of scientist/explorer operation using vessel capable of working at 15,000 feet below sea level. Average.

Arabella (1969-Italian) **C-91m.** *½ D: Adriano Barocco. Virna Lisi, James Fox, Margaret Rutherford, Terry-Thomas. Silly drawing-room black comedy in which Thomas plays four different roles, as various victims of Lisi's larceny.

Arabesque (1966) **C-105m.** *** D: Stanley Donen. Sophia Loren, Gregory Peck, Alan Badel, Kieron Moore, George Coulouris. Modern secret-agent escapism as Peck is drawn into espionage with Sophia, who was never more beautiful. Exciting, beautifully photographed, minus any message or deep thought.▼

Arabian Adventure (1979-British) **C-98m.** **½ D: Kevin Connor. Christopher Lee, Milo O'Shea, Puneet Sira, Oliver Tobias, Emma Samms, Peter Cushing, Mickey Rooney, Capucine. Just what the title says; colorful enough to entertain kids, with enough effects gimmicks and cameo performances to intrigue older viewers as well.

Arabian Nights (1942) **C-86m.** **½ D: John Rawlins. Jon Hall, Maria Montez, Sabu, Leif Erickson, Turhan Bey, Billy Gilbert, Shemp Howard, John Qualen, Thomas Gomez. Colorful, corny escapist stuff—beautifully mounted in Technicolor—about a dashing hero, an enslaved Sheherazade, and an evil caliph. The first teaming of Montez, Hall, and Sabu.

Arabian Nights (1974-Italian-French) **C-128m.** *** D: Pier Paolo Pasolini. Ninetto Davoli, Ines Pellegrini, Franco Citti, Tessa Bouche, Margarethe Clementi, Franco Merli. Several *Thousand and One Nights* tales are framed by the story of slave-girl Pellegrina, who becomes "king" of a great city. Dreamlike, exotic; the last and best of Pasolini's medieval trilogy. Running-time originally 155m., then 130m.▼

Arachnophobia (1990) **C-109m.** *** D: Frank Marshall. Jeff Daniels, Harley Jane

Kozak, John Goodman, Julian Sands, Stuart Pankin, Brian McNamara, Mark L. Taylor, Henry Jones, Peter Jason, James Handy. Fear of spiders is taken to extremes in this slick comic thriller from Steven Spielberg and Co. Small-town doctor Daniels (who hates spiders) and family play host to a wayward tropical arachnid that promptly sets up web in the barn out back. Essentially Grade Z movie fodder is socked across here by a big budget and spirited performances—from the stars and the human actors. Directorial debut of longtime Spielberg producer Marshall. Not recommended for anyone who's *ever* covered their eyes during a movie.

Archer—Fugitive From the Empire, The (1981) **C-100m. TVM** D: Nick Corea. Lane Caudell, George Kennedy, Belinda Bauer, Victor Campos, Kabir Bedi, John Hancock. Sword-and-sorcery pilot for brief series has a young wanderer seeking the sorcerer who can help him gain his rightful title. Corea's script stays at comic-strip level. Average; also known as FUGITIVE OF THE EMPIRE.▼

Arch of Triumph (1948) **114m. **½ D: Lewis Milestone. Ingrid Bergman, Charles Boyer, Charles Laughton, Louis Calhern. Sluggish drama of refugee Boyer falling in love with Bergman in WW2 France, based on Erich Maria Remarque's novel. Archivally restored to 131m. Remade for TV.▼

Arch of Triumph (1985) **C-95m. TVM** D: Waris Hussein. Anthony Hopkins, Lesley-Anne Down, Donald Pleasence, Frank Finlay. Remake of the old Bergman/Boyer wartime romance by Remarque is as lethargic as its predecessor; even color fails to bring it to life. Charles Israel wrote this adaptation. Average.

Are Husbands Necessary? (1942) **79m. ** D: Norman Taurog. Ray Milland, Betty Field, Patricia Morison, Eugene Pallette, Cecil Kellaway. And what about this film?

Arena (1953) **C-83m. ** D: Richard Fleischer. Gig Young, Jean Hagen, Polly Bergen, Henry (Harry) Morgan, Barbara Lawrence, Lee Aaker. Sappy, soapy story of rodeo star (Young) whose marriage is on the skids; film's only value is in realistic rodeo scenes, filmed on location in Arizona. Originally shown in 3-D.

Arena, The (1973) **C-83m. ** D: Steve Carver. Pam Grier, Margaret Markov, Lucretia Love, Paul Muller. Lavish (by Roger Corman standards) spectacle set in an ancient Rome in which all the gladiators are women. Rather surprisingly pro-feminist point of view, but Grier's and Markov's physiques remain the chief attractions. Retitled NAKED WARRIORS.

✓ **Are Parents People?** (1925) **60m. **½ D: Malcolm St. Clair. Betty Bronson, Adolphe Menjou, Florence Vidor, Lawrence Gray. Enjoyable silent with good cast; innocuous story of young Bronson bringing her estranged parents together. No great shakes, but fun.

Are You in the House Alone? (1978) **C-96m. TVM** D: Walter Grauman. Kathleen Beller, Blythe Danner, Tony Bill, Robin Mattson, Tricia O'Neil, Dennis Quaid. Predictable thriller about high school coed who is target of terror campaign. Unsatisfactory adaptation of Richard Peck's Edgar Mystery Award-winning novel. Average.▼

Are You With It? (1948) **90m. **½ D: Jack Hively. Donald O'Connor, Olga San Juan, Martha Stewart, Lew Parker. Bright little musical of math-whiz O'Connor joining a carnival.

Argentine Nights (1940) **74m. **½ D: Albert S. Rogell. Ritz Brothers, Andrews Sisters, Constance Moore, George Reeves, Peggy Moran, Anne Nagel. Boisterous musical comedy with the Ritzes fleeing the U.S., hooking up with troupe of entertainers in Argentina. Incoherent plotwise, but diverting.

Aria (1988-British) **C-90m. BOMB** D: Bill Bryden, Nicolas Roeg, Charles Sturridge, Jean-Luc Godard, Julien Temple, Bruce Beresford, Robert Altman, Franc Roddam, Ken Russell, Derek Jarman. John Hurt, Theresa Russell, Nicola Swain, Jack Kayle, Buck Henry, Anita Morris, Beverly D'Angelo, Elizabeth Hurley, Peter Birch, Julie Hagerty, Genevieve Page, Bridget Fonda, James Mathers, Linzi Drew, Tilda Swinton, Spencer Leigh, Amy Johnson. Godawful collection of short films by a cadre of internationally respected directors, each one supposedly inspired by an operatic aria. Precious few make sense, or even seem to match the music; some are downright embarrassing. Roddam's bittersweet Las Vegas fable (set to *Tristan und Isolde*), Beresford's sweet and simple rendering of Erich Wolfgang Korngold's *Die Totestadt* are among the better segments—relatively speaking. A pitiful waste of talent. Fonda's first film.▼

Arise, My Love (1940) **113m. *** D: Mitchell Leisen. Claudette Colbert, Ray Milland, Walter Abel, Dennis O'Keefe, Dick Purcell. News correspondent Colbert loves flyer-of-fortune Milland, who is working in war-torn Spain. Bright stars make Billy Wilder-Charles Brackett script seem better than it is; Benjamin Glazer and John S. Toldy received Oscars for their original story.

Arizona (1940) **127m. **½ D: Wesley Ruggles. Jean Arthur, William Holden, Warren William, Porter Hall, Paul Harvey. Lively story of determined woman battling corruption and plundering while trying to settle in new Arizona territory. Well done, but seems to go on forever.

Arizona Bushwhackers (1968) **C-86m. *½ D: Lesley Selander. Howard Keel,

Yvonne De Carlo, John Ireland, Marilyn Maxwell, Scott Brady, Brian Donlevy, Roy Rogers, Jr., James Craig. Confederate spy Keel takes job as sheriff in Arizona and routs Brady, who has been selling weapons to Apaches. Routine Western. Narration by James Cagney.

Arizona Mission SEE: **Gun the Man Down**

Arizona Raiders (1965) C-88m. **½ D: William Witney. Audie Murphy, Michael Dante, Ben Cooper, Buster Crabbe, Gloria Talbott. Murphy is confederate army officer heading Arizona rangers after Civil War, battling Quantrill's raiders.▼

Arizona Ripper SEE: **Bridge Across Time**▼

Arizona to Broadway (1933) 66m. ** D: James Tinling. James Dunn, Joan Bennett, Herbert Mundin, Sammy Cohen, Theodore von Eltz, J. Carrol Naish. Joan enlists carnival con-man Dunn's help in reclaiming money lost to gang of swindlers; predictable tale, remade as JITTERBUGS.

Arkansas Traveler, The (1938) 85m. ** D: Alfred Santell. Bob Burns, Fay Bainter, Jean Parker, Irvin S. Cobb, John Beal, Lyle Talbott, Dickie Moore, Porter Hall. Burns rambles into small town, keeps the local paper afloat, plays Cupid for the publisher's daughter and the Mayor's son. Pleasant entertainment relies on the charm of Bazooka Bob.

Armed and Dangerous (1986) C-88m. *½ D: Mark L. Lester. John Candy, Eugene Levy, Robert Loggia, Kenneth McMillan, Meg Ryan, Brion James, Jonathan Banks, Don Stroud, Steve Railsback. Lame comedy sticks talented costars with unappealing script about two bozos who wind up working for an armed security company—and tangling with a gangland boss (Loggia, wasted in a stereotype role). Even the chase finale is weak. ▼

Armed Response (1986) C-85m. ** D: Fred Olen Ray. David Carradine, Lee Van Cleef, Mako, Lois Hamilton, Ross Hagen, Brent Huff, Laurene Landon, Dick Miller, Michael Berryman. Modest actioner of Carradine and family becoming involved in a Chinatown war over a stolen jade art object. Cheapie benefits from a solid cast of both new and old B-movie favorites.▼

Armored Attack SEE: **North Star, The**▼

Armored Car Robbery (1950) 68m. *½ D: Richard Fleischer. Charles McGraw, Adele Jergens, William Talman, Steve Brodie. Inoffensive study of attempted large theft and the repercussions on those involved.▼

Armored Command (1961) 99m. ** D: Byron Haskin. Howard Keel, Tina Louise, Warner Anderson, Burt Reynolds. Bland war film with stars merely going through their paces.▼

Arnelo Affair, The (1947) 86m. ** D: Arch Oboler. John Hodiak, George Murphy, Frances Gifford, Dean Stock-

well, Eve Arden. Neglected wife drawn hypnotically to husband's client finally learns of his involvement in girl's murder.

Arnold (1973) C-100m. **½ D: Georg Fenady. Stella Stevens, Roddy McDowall, Elsa Lanchester, Shani Wallis, Farley Granger, Victor Buono, John McGiver, Patric Knowles. Bizarre horror comedy features novel deaths and offbeat humor, centering around luscious Stevens' marriage to corpse Norman Stuart.▼

Around the World in 80 Days (1956) C-167m. *** D: Michael Anderson. David Niven, Cantinflas, Shirley MacLaine, Robert Newton, Marlene Dietrich, all-star cast. Oscar-winning favorite has lost much of its charm over the years, but even so, Mike Todd's version of the Jules Verne tale offers plenty of entertainment, and more than forty cameo appearances offer plenty of star-gazing for buffs. Great Victor Young score was also an Oscar-winner, as was the screenplay adaptation (James Poe, John Farrow, S.J. Perelman), cinematography (Lionel Lindon) and editing (Gene Ruggiero, Paul Weatherwax). Remade as a TV miniseries.▼

Around the World in 80 Ways (1986-Australian) C-90m. **½ D: Stephen MacLean. Philip Quast, Allan Penney, Diana Davidson, Kelly Dingwall, Gosia Dobrowolska. Off-center Aussie farce about two brothers who contrive to spring their aging dad from his stultifying rest home and take him on an imaginary trip around the world. Wacky, and more than a bit crude at times, but likable throughout.▼

Around the World Under the Sea (1966) C-117m. ** D: Andrew Marton. Lloyd Bridges, Shirley Eaton, David McCallum, Brian Kelly, Keenan Wynn, Marshall Thompson. Several TV personalities appear together in this undistinguished underwater tour about testing earthquake warnings. Eaton adds femininity to otherwise all-male cast.

Arousers, The (1970) C-90m. *** D: Curtis Hanson. Tab Hunter, Nadyne Turney, Roberta Collins, Isabel Jewell. Little-known, case-history B movie with topnotch performance by Hunter as lonely Venice, California, psychopath who can't make love to women, so he ends up killing them. Unsung thriller packs a wallop; worth searching out. Originally released as SWEET KILL; also known as A KISS FROM EDDIE.▼

Arrangement, The (1969) C-120m. BOMB D: Elia Kazan. Kirk Douglas, Faye Dunaway, Deborah Kerr, Richard Boone, Hume Cronyn. Muddled, unpleasant film from Kazan's own novel about man fed up with Madison Avenue rat-race who suddenly goes berserk, reevaluates his life, family, surroundings. Good cast down the drain; Kerr's role is particularly demeaning.▼

Arrest Bulldog Drummond (1939) 57m. D: James Hogan. John Howard, Heather Angel, H. B. Warner, George Zucco, E. E. Clive, Reginald Denny, John Sutton. SEE: **Bulldog Drummond** series.▼

Arrivederci, Baby (1966) C-105m. *½ D: Ken Hughes. Tony Curtis, Rosanna Schiaffino, Lionel Jeffries, Zsa Zsa Gabor, Nancy Kwan. Comic theme about Bluebeard type who murders his wives for their money has been handled more successfully by others. Not very funny.

Arrowhead (1953) 105m. **½ D: Charles Marquis Warren. Charlton Heston, Jack Palance, Katy Jurado, Brian Keith, Milburn Stone. Apaches prefer war to peace, with many Indian vs. cavalry skirmishes; Heston and Palance are intense.▼

Arrow In the Dust (1954) 80m. ** D: Lesley Selander. Sterling Hayden, Coleen Gray, Keith Larsen, Tom Tully. Deserting horse soldier (Hayden) learns sterling virtues when he assumes identity of dead commanding officer, warding off Indian attack on passing wagon train.

Arrowsmith (1931) 99m. **½ D: John Ford. Ronald Colman, Helen Hayes, Richard Bennett, A. E. Anson, Claude King, Russell Hopton, Myrna Loy. Seriously flawed and illogical adaptation of Sinclair Lewis' novel about a dedicated young research doctor who spends most of his life facing the temptation of selling out. Worth seeing for some fine performances and stirring moments. Screenplay by Sidney Howard (who fared better with Lewis's *Dodsworth*). Originally 110m.; film was cut to 101m. for reissue, and has been restored in recent years to 99m.▼

Arruza (1972) C-75m. **½ D: Budd Boetticher. Narrated by Anthony Quinn. Interesting documentary, many years in production, about bullfighter Carlos Arruza. Ably photographed and edited, but the impact is nowhere near that of Boetticher's own fictional BULLFIGHTER AND THE LADY.▼

Arsenal Stadium Mystery, The (1939-British) 85m. *** D: Thorold Dickinson. Leslie Banks, Greta Gynt, Ian MacLean, Liane Linden, Anthony Bushell, Esmond Knight. Who is responsible for the murder of football star Bushell—right in the middle of a game? Eccentric, crackerjack Scotland Yard inspector Banks finds out. Neat little whodunit, and very British.▼

Arsene Lupin (1932) 84m. *** D: Jack Conway. John Barrymore, Lionel Barrymore, Karen Morley, John Miljan, Henry Armetta, Tully Marshall. Ripe detective yarn set in Paris: John is a gentleman, Lionel a detective, Morley a mystery woman. Which one is the title jewel thief? John and Lionel B. make a marvelous team in their first film together.

Arsenic and Old Lace (1944) 118m. ***½ D: Frank Capra. Cary Grant, Priscilla Lane, Raymond Massey, Peter Lorre, Jack Carson, Josephine Hull, Jean Adair, James Gleason, Grant Mitchell, John Alexander, Edward Everett Horton. Hilarious adaptation of Joseph Kesselring's hit play about two seemingly harmless old ladies who murder lonely gentlemen callers. Frantic cast is excellent, especially Lorre and Massey as unsuspecting murderers holed up in Brooklyn household. Made in 1941. Also shown in computer-colored version.▼

Arthur (1981) C-97m. ***½ D: Steve Gordon. Dudley Moore, Liza Minnelli, John Gielgud, Geraldine Fitzgerald, Jill Eikenberry, Stephen Elliott, Ted Ross, Barney Martin. Winning 1930s-style comedy, written by first-time director Gordon, who died the following year. Spoiled millionaire Moore must choose between continued wealth (in a planned marriage) and true love (with working-class waitress Minnelli). More genuine laughs than most recent comedies put together, and a memorable, Oscar-winning performance by Gielgud as Dudley's protective, acid-tongued valet; title song "Best That You Can Do (Arthur's Theme)" also earned a statuette. Followed by ARTHUR 2: ON THE ROCKS.

Arthur 2: on the Rocks (1988) C-110m. ** D: Bud Yorkin. Dudley Moore, Liza Minnelli, John Gielgud, Geraldine Fitzgerald, Stephen Elliott, Paul Benedict, Cynthia Sikes, Kathy Bates, Jack Gilford, Ted Ross, Daniel Greene. Arthur goes broke and his wife wants to adopt a baby. The cast tries, and there are some scattered laughs, but this schmaltzy sequel (executive produced by Moore) is a real disappointment. Gielgud "appears" briefly as a ghost. That's Dudley's wife, Brogan Lane, as Liza's hash-slinging colleague.▼

Arthur the King (1985) C-150m. TVM D: Clive Donner. Malcolm McDowell, Candice Bergen, Edward Woodward, Dyan Cannon, Lucy Gutteridge, Rupert Everett. The Arthurian saga, filtered through Lewis Carroll and a contemporary twist as Cannon tumbles down a rabbit hole into Camelot while wandering around Stonehenge. A bizarre adventure (glom Candice's fright wig!) and an unintentional hoot that sat for nearly three years before initial airing. Video title MERLIN AND THE SWORD; cut to 94m. Below average.▼

Artists & Models (1937) 97m. **½ D: Raoul Walsh. Jack Benny, Ida Lupino, Judy Canova, Gail Patrick, Richard Arlen, Martha Raye, Connee Boswell, Ethel Clayton. Lupino pretends to be a socialite in flimsy plot with uncharacteristic Benny and songs "Stop You're Breaking My Heart," "Whispers in the Dark." Vintage fun.

[48]

Artists and Models (1955) C-109m. *** D: Frank Tashlin. Dean Martin, Jerry Lewis, Shirley MacLaine, Dorothy Malone, Eva Gabor, Anita Ekberg. Overblown daffy-duo shenanigans spiced by feminine beauty and a few wacky sequences, with cartoonist Martin utilizing Lewis' far-out dreams for his strips.

Artists and Models Abroad (1938) 90m. *** D: Mitchell Leisen. Jack Benny, Joan Bennett, Mary Boland, Charley Grapewin, Yacht Club Boys, Joyce Compton. Breezy, entertaining froth of musical troupe stranded in Paris, perennially saved by conniving boss Benny. Yacht Club Boys sing incredible song, "You're Broke, You Dope."

Art of Crime, The (1975) C-78m. TVM D: Richard Irving. Ron Leibman, Jose Ferrer, David Hedison, Jill Clayburgh, Eugene Roche, Diane Kagan, Cliff Osmond, Mike Kellin. Gypsy antique dealer (Leibman) turns sleuth to clear friend accused of murder. Busted pilot adapted from Martin Smith's *Gypsy in Amber*, this comedy-drama is long on gypsy folklore and short on suspense. Average.

Art of Love, The (1965) C-99m. ** D: Norman Jewison. James Garner, Dick Van Dyke, Elke Sommer, Angie Dickinson, Ethel Merman, Carl Reiner. Ordinary comedy set in France, with a bemused cast headed by Van Dyke as a struggling artist who fakes death to increase the value of his work. Sommer is his virtuous girl, boisterous Merman a local madam with a yen for singing.

Ashanti (1979) C-117m. ** D: Richard Fleischer. Michael Caine, Peter Ustinov, Beverly Johnson, Kabir Bedi, Omar Sharif, Rex Harrison, William Holden. Beautiful wife (Johnson) of missionary-doctor Caine is kidnapped by slave trader Ustinov, prompting hot pursuit through the mideast. Tepid adventure yarn, despite great cast and promising story elements. Also known as ASHANTI: LAND OF NO MERCY.▼

Ashes and Diamonds (1958-Polish) 96m. ***½ D: Andrzej Wajda. Zbigniew Cybulski, Ewa Krzyzanowska, Adam Pawlikowski, Bogumil Kobiela, Waclaw Zastrzezynski. Stark, intelligent, perceptive account of the Resistance movement in Poland during the closing days of WW2. Cybulski, the Polish James Dean, came into his own with his portrayal of a young Resistance fighter. The last of Wajda's War trilogy, following A GENERATION and KANAL.▼

Ash Wednesday (1973) C-99m. BOMB D: Larry Peerce. Elizabeth Taylor, Henry Fonda, Helmut Berger, Keith Baxter, Margaret Blye. Liz undergoes a facelift to regain her youth, but she still looks older than Fonda. Sit through this one and you'll need surgery on your posterior.

As If It Were Raining (1963-French) 85m.

** D: Jose Monter. Eddie Constantine, Henri Cogan, Elisa Montes, Jose Nieto, Sylvia Solar. Constantine is at liberty in Spain, enmeshed in an embezzlement scheme; wooden yarn.

Ask Any Girl (1959) C-101m. *** D: Charles Walters. David Niven, Shirley MacLaine, Gig Young, Rod Taylor, Jim Backus, Elisabeth Fraser. Effervescent gloss of naive MacLaine coming to New York, discovering most men have lecherous designs on girls; she wants a husband, however.

As Long As They're Happy (1957-British) C-76m. *½ D: J. Lee Thompson. Janette Scott, Jean Carson, Diana Dors, Hugh McDermott, Jack Buchanan. Mini-musical involving daughter of staid British stockholder who falls for visiting song-and-dance man.

Asphalt Jungle, The (1950) 112m. ***½ D: John Huston. Sterling Hayden, Louis Calhern, Jean Hagen, James Whitmore, Sam Jaffe, John McIntire, Marc Lawrence, Marilyn Monroe. The plotting of a crime, and the gathering of a gang to pull it off; a taut, realistic film full of fine characterizations (especially Jaffe, and Monroe in a memorable bit). A model of its kind, frequently copied, and remade no less than three times (as THE BADLANDERS, CAIRO, COOL BREEZE). Scripted by Ben Maddow and Huston, from a W.R. Burnett novel. Also shown in computer-colored version ▼

Asphyx, The (1972-British) C-99m. *** D: Peter Newbrook. Robert Stephens, Robert Powell, Jane Lapotaire, Ralph Arliss, Alex Scott. Good fantasy plot has 19th-century scientist Stephens isolating the Asphyx, the spirit of death that appears around a person's body at times of imminent danger. In so doing, he becomes immortal. Lapotaire, who scored internationally on stage in *Piaf*, appears here as Stephens's daughter.▼

Assam Garden, The (1985-British) C-92m. *** D: Mary McMurray. Deborah Kerr, Madhur Jaffrey, Alec McCowen, Zia Mohyeddin, Anton Lesser. Quietly rewarding drama with Kerr in her best role in years (and first theatrical release since 1969's THE ARRANGEMENT), as a stuffy, long-repressed, just-widowed woman. While tending her husband's garden and dealing with his memory, she strikes up a curious complex friendship with Indian neighbor Jaffrey.▼

Assassin, The (1953-British) 90m. ** D: Ralph Thomas. Richard Todd, Eva Bartok, George Coulouris, Margot Grahame. Todd is detective on manhunt in postwar Venice; usual murders and romance result.

Assassin, The (1961-Italian) 105m. **½ D: Elio Petri. Marcello Mastroianni, Salvo Randone, Micheline Presle, Cristina Gajoni.

Engaging study of scoundrel Mastroianni implicated in a murder, broken by the police, proven innocent, with a wry ending. **Assassin** (1973-British) **C-83m.** ** D: Peter Crane. Ian Hendry, Edward Judd, Frank Windsor, Ray Brooks. Routine cold war espionage film, or, the loneliness of the long-distance assassin. **Assassin** (1986) **C-100m. TVM** D: Sandor Stern. Robert Conrad, Karen Austin, Richard Young, Jonathan Banks, Robert Webber. A bionic Frankenstein, reprogrammed to kill a series of government officials and top scientists, has to be terminated. Run-of-the-mill sci-fi entry notable only for the monster's resemblance to a California beach bum—and its prophetic name: Golem. Average.▼

Assassination (1987) **C-88m.** *½ D: Peter Hunt. Charles Bronson, Jill Ireland, Stephen Elliott, Jan Gan Boyd, Randy Brooks, Erik Stern, Michael Ansara, James Staley, Kathryn Leigh Scott. Bronson is a Secret Service bodyguard, Ireland the wife of the President, in this ridiculous, slapdash political thriller with more explosions than anything else. The First Lady is referred to here as One Mama!▼

Assassination Bureau, The (1969-British) **C-110m.** *** D: Basil Dearden. Oliver Reed, Diana Rigg, Telly Savalas, Curt Jurgens, Clive Revill. Fun tale based on Jack London story of secret club that eliminates unworthy people, until greed more than dedication begins to cloud the operation. **Assassination of Trotsky, The** (1972-French-Italian-British) **C-103m.** **½ D: Joseph Losey. Richard Burton, Alain Delon, Romy Schneider, Valentina Cortese. Last days of Russian rebel make for uneven melodrama of hunters and hunted. Burton's performance is strong but unconvincing.▼

Assassin of Youth (1937) **80m.** *½ D: Elmer Clifton. Luana Walters, Arthur Gardner, Dorothy Short, Earl Dwire, Fern Emmett. Another hokey marijuana exposé (this one a notch above the rest), about some fun-loving teens who smoke one too many reefers at one too many reefer parties. An intrepid investigative reporter poses as a soda jerk to expose their decadence. The short film within a film, THE MARIJUANA MENACE, is a hoot.▼

Assault (1971) SEE: **In the Devil's Garden**▼

Assault, The (1986-Dutch) **C-149m.** ***½ D: Fons Rademakers. Derek de Lint, Marc van Uchelen, Monique van de Ven, John Kraaykamp, Huub van der Lubbe, Elly Weller. A 12-year-old's family is liquidated in the final days of WW2, and he represses his memories and feelings while growing into manhood. Evocative performances and fine direction enhance a story that is both truthful and heartbreaking.

Long, but suspenseful, with many thought-provoking moments. Screenplay by Gerard Soeteman based on a novel by Harry Mulisch. Winner of the Best Foreign Language Film Oscar. A film not easy to forget.▼

Assault and Matrimony (1987) **C-100m. TVM** D: James Frawley. Jill Eikenberry, Michael Tucker, John Hillerman, Michelle Phillips, Joseph Cortese. Battling couple spends 100 frantic minutes trying to bump each other off, proving only that *L.A. Law*'s real-life marrieds Eikenberry and Tucker are adept at playing slapstick. Based on James Anderson's book. Average.▼

Assault Force SEE: **ffolkes**▼

Assault of the Rebel Girls SEE: **Cuban Rebel Girls**▼

Assault on Agathon (1975-British-Greek) **C-96m.** **½ D: Laslo Benedek. Nico Minardos, Nina van Pallandt, Marianne Faithfull, John Woodvine. Tepid drug-dealing thriller with spectacular Greek scenery overshadowing CIA man Minardos' efforts to nab Mr. Big.▼

Assault on a Queen (1966) **C-106m.** **½ D: Jack Donohue. Frank Sinatra, Virna Lisi, Tony Franciosa, Richard Conte, Reginald Denny. Sloppy Sinatra vehicle about big heist of H.M.S. *Queen Elizabeth's* vault.

Assault on Precinct 13 (1976) **C-90m.** ***½ D: John Carpenter. Austin Stoker, Darwin Joston, Laurie Zimmer, Martin West, Tony Burton, Nancy Loomis, Kim Richards, Henry Brandon. A nearly deserted L.A. police station finds itself under a state of siege by a youth gang in this riveting thriller, a modern-day paraphrase of Howard Hawks' RIO BRAVO. Writer-director Carpenter also did the eerie music score for this knockout.▼

Assault on the Wayne (1970) **C-90m. TVM** D: Marvin Chomsky. Joseph Cotten, Leonard Nimoy, Lloyd Haynes, Dewey Martin, William Windom, Keenan Wynn, Malachi Throne. Commander Philip Kettenring handed control of U.S. submarine *Anthony Wayne*, unaware of presence of enemy agents out to seize top-secret device. Good cast. Average.

Assignment, The (1977-Swedish) **C-94m.** **½ D: Mats Arehn. Christopher Plummer, Thomas Hellberg, Carolyn Seymour, Fernando Rey, Per Oscarsson, Walter Gotell. Modest drama of Swedish diplomat sent to mediate turbulent political situation in Latin American country.▼

Assignment In Brittany (1943) **96m.** ** D: Jack Conway. Pierre (Jean-Pierre) Aumont, Susan Peters, Richard Whorf, Margaret Wycherly, Signe Hasso, Reginald Owen. Aumont is lookalike for Nazi leader, uses this to his advantage working for French underground; patriotic WW2 melodrama. **Assignment K** (1968-British) **97m.** *½ D:

Val Guest. Stephen Boyd, Camilla Sparv, Michael Redgrave, Leo McKern, Jeremy Kemp, Robert Hoffman. Still another spy drama—this one a dull story about secret agent Boyd's disillusionment when he discovers that his girl and seemingly everyone he knows is a double agent.

Assignment: Kill Castro SEE: **Cuba Crossing▼**

Assignment: Munich (1972) **C-100m.** TVM D: David Lowell Rich. Richard Basehart, Roy Scheider, Lesley Warren, Werner Klemperer. Shady saloon owner in Germany helps U.S. government find gold stolen during WW2. Pilot for series *Assignment: Vienna.* Average.

Assignment—Paris (1952) **85m.** ** D: Robert Parrish. Dana Andrews, Marta Toren, George Sanders, Audrey Totter. Fitfully entertaining drama of reporter Andrews trying to link together threads of plot between Communist countries against the West. Filmed in Paris.

Assignment Redhead SEE: **Million Dollar Manhunt**

Assignment Terror (1970-Spanish-German-Italian) **C-86m.** BOMB D: Tulio Demicheli. Michael Rennie, Karin Dor, Craig Hill, Paul Naschy, Patty Shepard. Alien invader Rennie revives various earth monsters (including ersatz Frankenstein, Dracula, and Mummy) but socially conscious werewolf (Naschy) helps to combat his evil forces. Unwatchable stupidity.

Assignment to Kill (1968) **C-102m.** ** D: Sheldon Reynolds. Patrick O'Neal, Joan Hackett, John Gielgud, Herbert Lom, Eric Portman, Peter Van Eyck, Oscar Homolka. Private eye checks out shady corporation in Switzerland in this unrewarding thriller from the writer-director of TV's *Foreign Intrigue* series.

As Summers Die (1986) **C-87m.** TVM D: Jean-Claude Tramont. Scott Glenn, Jamie Lee Curtis, Bette Davis, John Randolph, Penny Fuller, Beah Richards, Ron O'Neal, John McIntire. Louisiana, 1959. Smalltown lawyer Glenn clashes with powerful local family when he tries to help a destitute black woman save her property. He finds unlikely allies in an eccentric old lady and her niece, both members of the greedy clan. Leisurely adaptation of Winston Groom's novel. The old Davis fire returns in her few scenes. Average.▼

As the Sea Rages (1960) **74m.** ** D: Horst Haechler. Maria Schell, Cliff Robertson, Cameron Mitchell. Seaman Robertson arrives in Greece planning a sponge-diving business and meets resistance from townfolk and the elements; muddled script. Filmed in Yugoslavia.

Astonished Heart, The (1950-British) **92m.** **½ D: Terence Fisher, Anthony Darnborough. Noel Coward, Celia Johnson, Margaret Leighton, Joyce Carey. Drawing-room melodrama about a married psychiatrist who succumbs to the wiles of another woman—an old schoolmate of his wife's—with unhappy results. One of Coward's lesser stories.

Astronaut, The (1971) **C-73m.** TVM D: Robert Michael Lewis. Monte Markham, Jackie Cooper, Susan Clark, Robert Lansing, Wally Schirra. Space officials involved in cover-up, ask ex-pilot to pose as lookalike astronaut who died on Mars. Average.

Astro-Zombies (1967) **C-83m.** BOMB D: Ted V. Mikels. Wendell Corey, John Carradine, Tom Pace, Joan Patrick, Rafael Campos. Demented Carradine creates the title monster in this, yet another nominee for worst picture of all time. Script by Mikels and Wayne Rogers (the same).▼

Asylum (1972-British) **C-92m.** *** D: Roy Ward Baker. Barbara Parkins, Sylvia Syms, Richard Todd, Peter Cushing, Barry Morse, Britt Ekland, Herbert Lom, Patrick Magee, Charlotte Rampling. Four fun chillers by Robert Bloch woven into puzzle that is solved at the conclusion of the fourth tale. Reissued in 1980 as HOUSE OF CRAZIES and trimmed to 86m.▼

As You Desire Me (1932) **71m.** **½ D: George Fitzmaurice. Greta Garbo, Melvyn Douglas, Erich von Stroheim, Hedda Hopper, Owen Moore. OK adaptation of Pirandello play about amnesiac (Garbo) who returns to husband she doesn't really remember. Never as compelling as it should be.

As You Like It (1936-British) **96m.** *** D: Paul Czinner. Elisabeth Bergner, Laurence Olivier, Sophie Stewart, Henry Ainley, Leon Quartermaine, Felix Aylmer. Olivier is solid (and handsome) as Orlando in this, his first attempt at the Bard on celluloid, but Bergner's Rosalind is more a matter of taste. Overall, an enjoyable production of this Shakespeare comedy.▼

As Young As You Feel (1951) **77m.** *** D: Harmon Jones. Monty Woolley, Thelma Ritter, David Wayne, Jean Peters, Constance Bennett, Marilyn Monroe. Marvelous cast enhances timely story of Woolley resenting retirement at age 65 and determined to alter corporate policy.

At Close Range (1986) **C-115m.** **½ D: James Foley. Sean Penn, Christopher Walken, Christopher Penn, Mary Stuart Masterson, Millie Perkins, Eileen Ryan, Alan Autry, Candy Clark, Tracey Walter, David Straithairn, Crispin Glover, Kiefer Sutherland. Brooding, but curiously unmoving, story about teenaged half-brothers who first get to know their no-account father, and come to realize what a dangerous person he is. Downbeat drama is marked by good acting, thoughtful filmmaking, but all-important emotional impact is muted. Based on a true incident.

At Gunpoint (1955) **C-81m.** **½ D: Alfred L. Werker. Fred MacMurray, Dorothy Malone, Walter Brennan, Tommy Rettig, Jack Lambert. MacMurray is well suited to role of peace-loving man drawn into gunplay by taunting outlaws.▼

Athena (1954) **C-96m.** **½ D: Richard Thorpe. Jane Powell, Debbie Reynolds, Edmund Purdom, Vic Damone, Louis Calhern, Evelyn Varden, Steve Reeves, Linda Christian. Back Bay lawyer (Purdom) and singer (Damone) romance two sisters living with eccentric grandparents. Wispy plot, average tunes.

Atlanta Child Murders, The (1985) **C-245m.** TVM D: John Erman. Jason Robards, James Earl Jones, Martin Sheen, Rip Torn, Morgan Freeman, Calvin Levels, Lynne Moody, Ruby Dee, Gloria Foster, Paul Benjamin, Andrew Robinson, Percy Rodrigues. Controversial but gripping docudrama by Abby Mann of the events leading to 1982 conviction of Wayne Williams following a wave of killings (primarily of children) in Atlanta's black community in late '70s. Robards and Torn are downright fascinating as opposing good-ole-boy attorneys. Originally shown in two parts. Above average.

Atlantic City (1944) **87m.** **½ D: Ray McCarey. Brad Taylor (Stanley Brown), Constance Moore, Charley Grapewin, Jerry Colonna, Adele Mara, Paul Whiteman & Orchestra, Louis Armstrong & Orchestra, Buck and Bubbles, Belle Baker, Dorothy Dandridge, Joe Frisco. Plethora of good musical numbers compensates for unoriginal plot about promoter who turns the Atlantic City pier into "the playground of America," starting pre-WWI. Taylor, who took his name from this (he was Stanley Brown at Columbia), and Moore adequately play Republic Pictures' John Payne-Alice Faye counterparts.

Atlantic City (1980-Canadian-French) **C-104m.** **** D: Louis Malle. Burt Lancaster, Susan Sarandon, Kate Reid, Michel Piccoli, Hollis McLaren, Robert Joy, Al Waxman. Rich character study of a city in transition, focusing on small-time losers who've stayed there too long and big-time dreamers who are just arriving. European in its ambience and storytelling approach, though its setting is an American resort. Lancaster gives one of his finest performances as an aging two-bit hood who's all style and no substance. Screenplay by John Guare. First shown abroad with the title ATLANTIC CITY, U.S.A.▼

Atlantis, the Lost Continent (1961) **C-90m.** *½ D: George Pal. Anthony Hall, Joyce Taylor, John Dall, Frank de Kova. Famed sci-fi producer George Pal's worst film is set on the island of Atlantis, in the time of ancient Greece. Heroic young fisherman becomes involved in tedious intrigue before, finally, the place sinks. Lots of stock footage, poor effects. Occasionally funny—too bad it's not on purpose.

Atlas (1961) **80m.** ** D: Roger Corman. Michael Forest, Frank Wolff, Barboura Morris, Walter Maslow, Christos Exarchos, Andreas Philippides. Praximedes convinces Olympic champion Atlas to represent him in battle, but Atlas eventually fights for the common folk. Only slightly hilarious low-budget Corman nonsense, filmed in Greece.

At Long Last Love (1975) **C-118m.** *½ D: Peter Bogdanovich. Burt Reynolds, Cybill Shepherd, Madeline Kahn, Duilio Del Prete, Eileen Brennan, John Hillerman, Mildred Natwick. Burt and Cybill are no Fred and Ginger. Bogdanovich's homage to 1930s Hollywood musicals has everything money can buy—including lavish sets and a Cole Porter score—but lacks the proper stars to put it over. Reedited for TV by the director.

At Mother's Request (1987) **C-200m.** TVM D: Michael Tuchner. Stefanie Powers, Doug McKeon, Frances Sternhagen, John Wood, Penny Fuller, Corey Parker, E. G. Marshall. Spotty drama about psychotic N.Y. socialite Frances Schreuder's manipulative efforts to have her millionaire father Franklin Bradshaw murdered. Jonathan Coleman's best-seller about the real-life events was the basis for Richard DeLong Adams' sluggish script. The same subject was approached later in a six-hour miniseries called NUTCRACKER: MONEY, MADNESS, MURDER (with Lee Remick) based on Shana Alexander's recounting of the events. Originally shown in two parts. Average.

Atoll K SEE: Utopia▼

Atom Age Vampire (1961-Italian) **87m.** BOMB D: Anton Giulio Majano. Alberto Lupo, Susanne Loret, Sergio Fantoni, Franca Parisi Strahl, Ivo Garrani. Mad professor restores dancer's disfigured face, then kills other women to obtain cells that will maintain her beauty. Hilariously bad; original running time 105m., video version 72m.▼

Atomic Brain, The SEE: Monstrosity▼

Atomic Cafe, The (1982) **88m.** *** D: Kevin Rafferty, Jayne Loader, Pierce Rafferty. Consistently chilling, occasionally hilarious, arguably monotonal compilation of U.S. government and "educational" propaganda shows how Americans of the 1950s Learned to Stop Worrying and Love the Bomb. One-of-a-kind is undeniably provocative, to say nothing of topical, but argues its point a little longer than necessary.▼

Atomic City, The (1952) **85m.** **½ D: Jerry Hopper. Gene Barry, Nancy Gates, Lydia Clarke, Lee Aaker. Tightly knit caper involving kidnapping of atomic scientist's son, well played by young Aaker.

Atomic Kid, The (1954) **86m.** *½ D:

Leslie Martinson. Mickey Rooney, Robert Strauss, Elaine Davis, Bill Goodwin. Rooney survives desert atomic blast, discovering he's radioactive. Slight spy comedy. Davis was Mrs. Rooney at the time. Story by Blake Edwards.▼

Atomic Man, The (1956-British) 78m. ** D: Ken Hughes. Gene Nelson, Faith Domergue, Joseph Tomelty, Peter Arne. Bland narrative of reporter and girlfriend involved in a mystery in which title character's experiments with radioactive materials have put him a few seconds into the future (allowing him to answer questions before they are asked). Yes, this is basically a spy melodrama.▼

Atomic Monster SEE: **Man-Made Monster**

Atomic Submarine, The (1959) 72m. ** D: Spencer Bennet. Arthur Franz, Dick Foran, Brett Halsey, Tom Conway, Bob Steele, Victor Varconi, Joi Lansing. In the near future, title sub investigates mysterious goings-on in the Arctic Circle. The culprit is an underwater flying saucer piloted by an alien! Typical Alex Gordon production, boasting lots of familiar character actors, is appealing and atmospheric. For diehard buffs.▼

Atonement of Gosta Berling, The (1924-Swedish) 91m. *** D: Mauritz Stiller. Lars Hanson, Greta Garbo, Ellen Cederstrom, Mona Martenson, Jenny Hasselquist, Gerda Lundequist. Memorable drama, from the Selma Lagerlof novel, about a defrocked priest (Hanson) and his love for a young married woman (a pleasingly plump Garbo, in the role which brought her to world attention). Stiller was, of course, Garbo's discoverer and mentor. Several longer versions run between 105m. and 165m. Also known as GOSTA BERLING'S SAGA.▼

Ator, the Fighting Eagle (1983) C-100m. BOMB D: David Hills. Miles O'Keeffe, Sabrina Siani, Ritza Brown, Edmund Purdom, Laura Gemser. Ridiculous Italian-made imitation of CONAN THE BARBARIAN has muscular O'Keeffe as the mythical title warrior, with beautiful blonde Siani along for the ride on his trek against evil. Followed by sequel THE BLADE MASTER.▼

Ator the Invincible SEE: **Blade Master, The**▼

✓ **Atragon** (1963-Japanese) 96m. ** D: Inoshiro Honda. Tadao Takashima, Yoko Fujiyama, Yu Fujiki, Horisho Koizumi. World is threatened by undersea kingdom in this juvenile sci-fi adventure, with enjoyable (if not believable) special effects.

At Sword's Point (1952) C-81m. **½ D: Lewis Allen. Cornel Wilde, Maureen O'Hara, Robert Douglas, Dan O'Herlihy, Alan Hale Jr., Blanche Yurka. Silly but likable variation on THE THREE MUSKETEERS with energetic cast, vivid technicolor settings.▼

Attack! (1956) 107m. *** D: Robert Aldrich. Jack Palance, Eddie Albert, Lee Marvin, Robert Strauss. Reenactment of the Battle of the Bulge, emphasizing a group of American soldiers "led" by cowardly captain Albert; tightly directed, avoids war-flick clichés.

Attack and Retreat SEE: **Italiano Brava Gente**

Attack Force Z (1981-Australian-Taiwanese) C-84m. **½ D: Tim Burstall. John Phillip Law, Sam Neill, Mel Gibson, Chris Haywood, John Waters. Taut little war drama: commandos set out to rescue survivors of a plane crash on a Japanese-held island during WW2.▼

Attack of the Crab Monsters (1957) 62m. ** D: Roger Corman. Richard Garland, Pamela Duncan, Russell Johnson, Leslie Bradley, Mel Welles, Ed Nelson. People are trapped on a shrinking island by intelligent, brain-eating giant crabs. Interesting early Corman thriller is hampered by a low budget—and some very silly monsters—but Charles B. Griffith's script has many ingenious ideas.

Attack of the 50 Ft. Woman (1958) 66m. BOMB D: Nathan Juran. Allison Hayes, William Hudson, Yvette Vickers, Roy Gordon. A harridan with a philandering husband has an alien encounter and grows to mammoth proportions. Hilariously awful sci-fi with some of the funniest special effects of all time.▼

Attack of the Giant Leeches (1959) 62m. *½ D: Bernard Kowalski. Ken Clarke, Yvette Vickers, Gene Roth, Bruno Ve Sota. Giant leeches in back waters of a Southern swamp take prisoners and suck their blood. Ludicrous hybrid of white trash and monster genres; screenplay by actor Leo Gordon. Also known as THE GIANT LEECHES.▼

Attack of the Killer Tomatoes (1980) C-87m. *½ D: John DeBello. David Miller, Sharon Taylor, George Wilson, Jack Riley, Rock Peace, The San Diego Chicken. Title and opening credits are the funniest things in this low-budget spoof of low-budget science-fiction, which cracks its one joke and then beats it to death for another eighty-five minutes. A staple at Worst Film Festivals, but nowhere nearly as hilarious as movies that aren't supposed to be. Followed by RETURN OF THE KILLER TOMATOES.▼

Attack of the Mayan Mummy (1963) 77m. BOMB D: Jerry Warren. Richard Webb, Nina Knight, John Burton, Steve Conte. Scientist gets patient to revert to former life and reveal site of ancient tomb in this grade-Z outing, comprised largely of Mexican horror-film footage.▼

Attack of the Phantoms SEE: **KISS Meets the Phantom of the Park**▼

Attack of the Puppet People (1958) 78m.

*½ D: Bert I. Gordon. John Agar, John Hoyt, June Kenney, Scott Peters. Low-class shocker about mad scientist who shrinks people; good performance by Hoyt, otherwise predictable and amateurish.

Attack of the Rebel Girls SEE: **Cuban Rebel Girls**▼

Attack on Fear (1984) **C-100m.** TVM D: Mel Damski. Paul Michael Glaser, Linda Kelsey, Kevin Conway, John Harkins, Alan Fudge, Barbara Babcock. Dramatization of how a married couple threw unwanted light on the cult workings of the Synanon Organization in their small-town weekly. Controversial material looks like it was watered down during the two years this film sat on the shelf. Average.

Attack on Terror: The FBI vs. the Ku Klux Klan (1975) **C-215m.** TVM D: Marvin J. Chomsky. Ned Beatty, John Beck, Billy Green Bush, Dabney Coleman, Andrew Duggan, Ed Flanders, George Grizzard, L. Q. Jones, Geoffrey Lewis, Maryln Mason, Wayne Rogers, Peter Strauss, Rip Torn. Docu-drama from FBI files, tying the murder of three civil rights workers in Mississippi in 1964 to the Klan after four-year investigation. Good cast and intelligent approach to basically formula plot. Calvin Clement's teleplay was based on Don Whitehead's book. Above average.

Attack on the Iron Coast (1968) **C-89m.** **½ D: Paul Wendkos. Lloyd Bridges, Andrew Keir, Sue Lloyd, Mark Eden, Maurice Denham. Canadian officer Bridges leads commando attack on German naval base in France during WW2. Capable if unsurprising action film, made in England.

Attempt to Kill (1961-British) **57m.** ** D: Royston Morley. Derek Farr, Tony Wright, Richard Pearson, Freda Jackson. Mild Edgar Wallace entry, salvaged by superior cast in predictable Scotland Yard manhunt caper.

Attention Bandits SEE: **Bandits**

At the Circus (1939) **87m.** **½ D: Edward Buzzell. Groucho, Chico and Harpo Marx, Margaret Dumont, Eve Arden, Nat Pendleton, Kenny Baker, Fritz Feld, Florence Rice. Not top-grade Marx Brothers, but some good scenes as they save circus from bankruptcy; highlight, Groucho singing "Lydia the Tattooed Lady."▼

At the Earth's Core (1976-British) **C-90m.** **½ D: Kevin Connor. Doug McClure, Peter Cushing, Caroline Munro, Cy Grant, Godfrey James, Sean Lynch. Colorful fantasy-adventure based on Edgar Rice Burroughs' novel. Inventor Cushing and protégé McClure bore their way from Victorian England to the center of the earth and encounter a lost world of prehistoric beasts and subhuman warriors. Competent special effects make this yarn palatable.▼

Attic, The (1979) **C-97m.** **½ D: George Edwards. Carrie Snodgress, Ray Milland, Rosemary Murphy, Ruth Cox, Francis Bay, Marjorie Eaton. Good cast helps this psychological thriller about a sheltered spinster's revolt against her tyrannical invalid father. A notch or two above routine.▼

Attica (1980) **C-100m.** TVM D: Marvin J. Chomsky. Charles Durning, George Grizzard, Glynn Turman, Anthony Zerbe, Henry Darrow, Joel Fabiani, Roger E. Mosley, Morgan Freeman. Gripping dramatization by James Henerson of the harrowing Attica Prison uprising of 1971. Taken from Tom Wicker's best-selling account, *A Time to Die*. Above average.▼

Attic: The Hiding of Anne Frank, The (1988) **C-100m.** TVM D: John Erman. Mary Steenburgen, Paul Scofield, Huub Stapel, Eleanor Bron, Miriam Karlin, Lisa Jacobs, Ronald Pickup. Steenburgen shines in her TV-movie debut as Miep Gies, the courageous Dutch woman who chose to hide her employer, Otto Frank, and his family from the Nazis. The Anne Frank story, told from a different perspective, artfully adapted by William Hanley from the Miep Gies book, *Anne Frank Remembered*. A beautifully crafted production made by top-of-the-line talent. Above average.

Attila (1958-Italian-French) **C-83m.** *½ D: Pietro Francisci. Anthony Quinn, Sophia Loren, Henri Vidal, Irene Papas. Inept spectacle with ridiculous script of Attila readying to conquer Rome.

At War with the Army (1950) **93m.** **½ D: Hal Walker. Dean Martin, Jerry Lewis, Polly Bergen, Angela Greene, Mike Kellin. In their first starring feature, Dean and Jerry are in the service, with some funny sequences, including memorable soda machine gag.▼

Audrey Rose (1977) **C-113m.** **½ D: Robert Wise. Marsha Mason, John Beck, Anthony Hopkins, Susan Swift, Norman Lloyd, John Hillerman. Overlong, underplayed reincarnation thriller. Mason and Beck are happily married couple until a stranger (Hopkins) tells them that their 12-year-old girl is his dead daughter returned to life. Script by Frank DeFelitta, from his novel.▼

Aunt Mary (1979) **C-100m.** TVM D: Peter Werner. Jean Stapleton, Martin Balsam, Harold Gould, Dolph Sweet, Robbie Rist, Anthony Cafiso, K. C. Martel. Inspirational true-life drama about Mary Dobkin, a physically handicapped Baltimore spinster who became a legend as a sandlot baseball coach. Stapleton sparkles. Above average.

Auntie Mame (1958) **C-143m.** ***½ D: Morton DaCosta. Rosalind Russell, Forrest Tucker, Coral Browne, Fred Clark, Roger Smith, Patric Knowles, Peggy Cass, Joanna Barnes, Pippa Scott. Colorful film version of Patrick Dennis' novel about his eccentric aunt, who believes that "life is a banquet, and most poor suckers are starving to death." Episodic but highly entertaining, sparked by Russell's tour-de-force performance. Musicalized as MAME.▼

Au Revoir Les Enfants (1987-French) C-103m. ***½ D: Louis Malle. Gaspard Manesse, Raphael Fejto, Francine Racette, Stanislas Carre de Malberg, Philippe Morier-Genoud, Francois Berleand. Deeply felt film based on an incident from Malle's youth, during WW2, when the headmaster of his Catholic boarding school decided to shield several Jewish children in the midst of Nazi-occupied France. Filled with telling details, the story unfolds at a deliberate pace, leading up to an emotionally devastating finale.▼

Aurora (1984) C-100m. TVM D: Maurizio Ponzi. Sophia Loren, Daniel J. Travanti, Edoardo Ponti, Philippe Noiret, Franco Fabrizi, Ricky Tognazzi, Anna Strasberg. A star turn for Sophia and her 11-year-old son, Edoardo (in his acting debut). She plays a woman who tricks her various former lovers into paying for an eye operation for the boy. The family affair also involves her stepson, Alex Ponti, as producer, and her niece, Allesandra Mussolini, granddaughter of Il Duce, in a small role. Ricky Tognazzi is veteran Italian actor Ugo's son, and Anna Strasberg is the widow of Lee (and stepmother of Susan), all of which is more interesting than the movie itself, which boasted four writers and even more production companies. Average.

Author! Author! (1982) C-110m. *** D: Arthur Hiller. Al Pacino, Dyan Cannon, Tuesday Weld, Eric Gurry, Alan King, Bob Dishy, Bob Elliott, Ray Goulding, Andre Gregory. Pacino's flaky wife walks out on him and their kids (mostly from her previous marriages) just as his new play is about to open on Broadway. Slight but winning little comedy, with likable performances all around. Written by playwright Israel Horovitz.▼

Autobiography of Miss Jane Pittman, The (1974) C-110m. TVM D: John Korty. Cicely Tyson, Barbara Chaney, Richard Dysart, Katherine Helmond, Michael Murphy, Odetta, Thalmus Rasulala. Acclaimed drama from Ernest J. Gaines' epic novel covering, through the memories of a fictional 110-year-old slave (Tyson), the black experience from the Civil War to the start of civil rights movement. Tyson's tour-de-force performance, Korty's subtle direction, and Tracy Keenan Wynn's intelligent script accounted for three of the nine Emmy Awards given to the film, one of the most ambitious ever made for television. Above average.▼

Autumn Leaves (1956) 108m. **½ D: Robert Aldrich. Joan Crawford, Cliff Robertson, Vera Miles, Lorne Greene. Middle-aged typist marries younger man (Robertson), only to discover he is mentally disturbed and already married. Stalwart performance by Crawford as troubled woman.▼

Autumn Sonata (1978-Swedish) C-97m. *** D: Ingmar Bergman. Ingrid Bergman, Liv Ullmann, Lena Nyman, Halvar Bjork, Gunnar Bjornstrand. Ingrid, a famed concert pianist, locks horns with daughter Ullmann when they visit for the first time in seven years. Director Bergman's drama is full of déjà vu, but Ingrid (in her final theatrical film) keeps it on the track most of the time. Sven Nykvist's photography is peerless.▼

Avalanche (1946) 70m. *½ D: Irving Allen. Bruce Cabot, Roscoe Karns, Helen Mowery, Veda Ann Borg. Programmer tale of murder and suspense at an isolated ski lodge; shoddy production.

Avalanche (1978) C-91m. ** D: Corey Allen. Rock Hudson, Mia Farrow, Robert Forster, Jeanette Nolan, Rick Moses, Barry Primus. Disaster at the newly opened ski resort where hard-driving tycoon Hudson is determined to double his not insubstantial investment while his ex-wife Mia is making whoopee with one of the locals championing ecology. Stodgy performances almost outweighed by special effects.▼

Avalanche Express (1979) C-88m. BOMB D: Mark Robson. Lee Marvin, Robert Shaw, Linda Evans, Maximilian Schell, Joe Namath, Mike Connors, Horst Buchholz. KGB head Shaw tries to defect on a Dutch train that's threatened by lots and lots of falling snow. Cast has enough stiffs in it to resemble audition time at the Hollywood Wax Museum. Sadly, final film for both Shaw and director Robson; in fact, most of Shaw's dialogue had to be dubbed by an impressionist.▼

Avanti! (1972) C-144m. ***½ D: Billy Wilder. Jack Lemmon, Juliet Mills, Clive Revill, Edward Andrews, Gianfranco Barra, Franco Angrisano. Sadly underrated comedy about stuffy Baltimore millionaire who falls in love with daughter of his late father's mistress when he comes to Italy to claim the old man's body. Closer to LOVE IN THE AFTERNOON than Wilder's satirical comedies; lovely scenery, wonderful performances by all, especially Revill as crafty hotel manager.

Avenger, The (1960-German) 102m. **½ D: Karl Anton. Ingrid Van Bergen, Heinz Drache, Ina Duscha, Maria Litto. Above-par shocker based on Edgar Wallace tale of bestial villain beheading several people, mailing them to appropriate recipients.▼

Avengers, The SEE: **Day Will Dawn, The** ▼

Avenging Angel (1985) C-93m. BOMB D:

Robert Vincent O'Neil. Betsy Russell, Rory Calhoun, Susan Tyrrell, Robert F. Lyons, Ossie Davis. Ex-teen prostitute, now college material, recruits pal Calhoun (still acting like the valedictorian at the Gabby Hayes Academy of Dramatic Arts) and takes to the street as an undercover cop. Follow-up to ANGEL proves conclusively that HEAVEN'S GATE is the only '80s film that can't rate a sequel. As proof, see ANGEL III: THE FINAL CHAPTER.▼

Avenging Force (1986) C-103m. **½ D: Sam Firstenberg. Michael Dudikoff, Steve James, John P. Ryan, James Booth, Bill Wallace, Karl Johnson. Dudikoff is retired secret agent Matt Hunter, who's forced into action when his one-time comrade (James), a black man running for office, is threatened by a right-wing terrorist group called Pentangle. A cut above the norm for the action/revenge genre, with exciting climax, and a truly heinous villain (well played by Ryan). Screenwriter James Booth also plays Dudikoff's former boss.▼

Aviator, The (1985) C-98m. ** D: George Miller. Christopher Reeve, Rosanna Arquette, Jack Warden, Sam Wanamaker, Scott Wilson, Tyne Daly, Marcia Strassman. Pioneer pilot Reeve crash-lands in the middle of some 1928 nowhere with whiny adolescent Arquette, then inexplicably falls in love with her while hunting food and warding off a bear. Dull Ernest Gann story barely made it (and understandably so) to theaters; director is the MAN FROM SNOWY RIVER—not MAD MAX—George Miller.▼

Aviator's Wife, The (1981-French) C-104m. ***½ D: Eric Rohmer. Philippe Marlaud, Marie Riviere, Anne-Laure Meury, Matthieu Carriere. Melancholy but charming story of young man's unhappy involvement with title character being interrupted by happy encounter with stranger in the park. Lovers of MAUD, CLAIRE, and CHLOE will be happy to find Rohmer in near-peak form after long layoff.

Awakening, The (1980) C-102m. *½ D: Mike Newell. Charlton Heston, Susannah York, Jill Townsend, Stephanie Zimbalist, Patrick Drury. Archeologist Heston enters the tomb of Egyptian Queen Kara, whose spirit enters the body of his newborn daughter. Need we continue? From a novel by Bram Stoker, filmed before as BLOOD FROM THE MUMMY'S TOMB.▼

Awakening of Candra, The (1983) C-100m. TVM D: Paul Wendkos. Blanche Baker, Cliff DeYoung, Richard Jaeckel, Jeffrey Tambor, Paul Regina. Dreary psycho drama based on sinister fisherman's real-life abduction of teenage bride Candra Torres during her camping-trip honeymoon in 1975. Made in 1981. Below average.▼

Away All Boats (1956) C-114m. **½ D: Joseph Pevney. Jeff Chandler, George Nader, Julie Adams, Lex Barker, Keith Andes, Richard Boone, David Janssen. Improbably heroic and overpartial slanting of America's participation in naval engagements during WW2 mar the movie's total effect.▼

Awful Dr. Orloff, The (1961-Spanish) 95m. ** D: Jess Franco. Howard Vernon, Conrado Sanmartin, Diana Lorys, Ricardo Valle, Perla Cristal. Medium spooker about deranged surgeon operating on a series of women, trying to find spare parts to revitalize his disfigured daughter. A long, disjointed Orloff series followed.

Awful Truth, The (1937) 92m. ***½ D: Leo McCarey. Irene Dunne, Cary Grant, Ralph Bellamy, Cecil Cunningham, Mary Forbes, Alex D'Arcy, Joyce Compton. Hilarious screwball comedy; Cary and Irene divorce, she to marry hayseed Bellamy, he to wed aristocratic Molly Lamont. Each does his best to spoil the other's plans. McCarey won an Oscar for his inspired direction. Screenplay by Vina Delmar. Based on a play by Arthur Richman previously filmed in 1925 and 1929; remade in 1953 as the musical LET'S DO IT AGAIN.

Babar The Movie (1989-Canadian-French) C-70m. *** D: Alan Bunce. Voices of Gordon Pinsent, Gavin Magrath, Elizabeth Hanna, Sarah Polley, Chris Wiggins. Entertaining feature-length cartoon based on the classic children's books by Jean and Laurent de Brunhoff. Strictly serviceable (and uninspired) animation is made up for by an engaging story line that's sure to appeal to young children.▼

Babbitt (1934) 74m. **½ D: William Keighley. Guy Kibbee, Aline MacMahon, Claire Dodd, Maxine Doyle, Minor Watson, Minna Gombell, Alan Hale, Berton Churchill. Sinclair Lewis's indictment of small-town blowhards is tranformed into a typical vehicle for blustery Kibbee and tower-of-strength MacMahon. Amusing but forgettable. Previously filmed in 1924.

Babe (1975) C-100m. TVM D: Buzz Kulik. Susan Clark, Alex Karras, Slim Pickens, Jeanette Nolan, Ellen Geer, Ford Rainey. Rich, absorbing film biography of Babe Didrickson Zaharias, America's foremost woman athlete, beautifully played by Clark (who won an Emmy for her performance). Ex-football star Karras offers a sensitive portrayal of her wrestler husband George, under Kulik's imaginative direction. The courageous Babe's tragic story leaves not a dry eye in the house, but secret ingredient here is taste. Adapted by Joanna Lee from the athlete's autobiography, *This Life I've Led*. Above average.

Babe Ruth Story, The (1948) 106m. *½ D: Roy Del Ruth. William Bendix, Claire Trevor, Charles Bickford, Sam Levene,

William Frawley. "Biography" is insult to famed baseball star; inept.▼

Babes in Arms (1939) 91m. **½ D: Busby Berkeley. Mickey Rooney, Judy Garland, Charles Winninger, Guy Kibbee, June Preisser, Douglas McPhail. Rodgers and Hart's musical, minus most of their songs, and one that's left, "Where or When," is trammeled to death. What remains is energetic but standard putting-on-a-show vehicle for Mickey and Judy. Dated fun. Originally ending was a production number spoofing Mr. and Mrs. Franklin D. Roosevelt, which was later removed for a 1948 reissue and never restored. Original running time 96m.▼

Babes in Bagdad (1952-U.S.-British-Spanish) **C-79m.** BOMB D: Edgar G. Ulmer. Paulette Goddard, Gypsy Rose Lee, Richard Ney, John Boles, Sebastian Cabot, Christopher Lee. Embarrassing, hokey costumer made even seedier by miscast veteran performers.

√ **Babes in Toyland** (1934) 73m. ***½ D: Gus Meins, Charles R. Rogers. Stan Laurel, Oliver Hardy, Charlotte Henry, Henry Kleinbach (Brandon), Felix Knight, Jean Darling, Johnny Downs, Marie Wilson. L&H version of Victor Herbert operetta looks better all the time, compared to lumbering "family musicals" of recent years. Stan and Ollie are in fine form, and fantasy element of Toyland—especially attack by Bogeymen—is excellent. Retitled MARCH OF THE WOODEN SOLDIERS. Originally released at 79m.▼

Babes in Toyland (1961) **C-105m.** **½ D: Jack Donohue. Ray Bolger, Tommy Sands, Annette Funicello, Henry Calvin, Gene Sheldon, Tommy Kirk, Ed Wynn, Ann Jillian. Colorful but contrived Disneyfication of Victor Herbert operetta has no substance or heart; classic songs, visual gimmicks, clowning of Calvin and Sheldon keep it afloat.▼

√ **Babes in Toyland** (1986) **C-150m.** TVM D: Clive Donner. Drew Barrymore, Richard Mulligan, Eileen Brennan, Keanu Reeves, Jill Schoelen, Pat Morita. Bloated remake of Victor Herbert's operetta—with only "Toyland" and "March of the Wooden Soldiers" remaining, alongside Leslie Bricusse's new score. Pulitzer Prize-winning playwright Paul Zindel wrote this adaptation. Stick with Stan & Ollie, who did it twice as well in half the time. Average.

Babes on Broadway (1941) 118m. **½ D: Busby Berkeley. Mickey Rooney, Judy Garland, Fay Bainter, Virginia Weidler, Richard Quine, Donna Reed. Showcase vehicle for Mickey and Judy's talents, with duo doing everything from imitations of Carmen Miranda and Bernhardt to minstrel numbers. Standout is Judy's "F.D.R. Jones." Film debut of Margaret O'Brien.▼

Babette Goes to War (1960-French)

C-103m. **½ D: Christian-Jaque. Brigitte Bardot, Jacques Charrier, Francis Blanche, Ronald Howard. Bardot is not at her forte playing lighthearted comedy. Flimsy WW2 account of French agent Bardot working for British, being sent back to France to help underground.

Babette's Feast (1987-Danish) **C-102m.** **** D: Gabriel Axel. Stephane Audran, Jean-Philippe Lafont, Gudmar Wivesson, Jarl Kulle, Bibi Andersson, Birgitte Federspiel, Bodil Kjer. Exquisite, delicately told tale of two beautiful young minister's daughters who pass up love and fame to remain in their small Danish village. They grow old, using religion as a substitute for living life . . . and then take in Parisian refugee Audran, a woman with a very special secret. Subtle, funny and deeply felt, with several wonderful surprises: an instant masterpiece that deservedly earned a Best Foreign Film Academy Award. Axel wrote the screenplay, from an Isak Dinesen short story originally published in the *Ladies Home Journal*. Don't miss this one.▼

Baby, The (1973) **C-102m.** ** D: Ted Post. Anjanette Comer, Ruth Roman, Marianna Hill. Social worker who gets in too deep with a man-child case, has to kill to keep "baby" at home with her.▼

Baby and the Battleship, The (1956-British) **C-96m.** **½ D: Jay Lewis. John Mills, Richard Attenborough, Andre Morell, Bryan Forbes, Lisa Gastoni, Michael Hordern, Lionel Jeffries, Gordon Jackson. Mildly amusing account of two sailors smuggling Italian baby aboard ship and their antics as they try to keep it hidden from top brass.▼

Baby Blue Marine (1976) **C-90m.** **½ D: John Hancock. Jan-Michael Vincent, Glynnis O'Connor, Katherine Helmond, Dana Elcar, Bert Remsen, Richard Gere, Art Lund. Norman Rockwell's America come to life, in bucolic tale of Marine dropout during WW2 who's mistaken for hero by residents of small town. Too bland to add up.

Baby Boom (1987) **C-103m.** *** D: Charles Shyer. Diane Keaton, Harold Ramis, Sam Shepard, Sam Wanamaker, James Spader, Pat Hingle, Britt Leach, Mary Gross, Victoria Jackson. Keaton is in top comic form as a supercharged business executive whose life changes dramatically when she "inherits" a baby. Amiable comedy takes well-aimed potshots at 1980s yuppie motherdom but remains agreeably sweet-natured from start to finish, which helps it through an occasional story lull. Written by Shyer and Nancy Meyers. Followed by a TV series.▼

Babycakes (1989) **C-100m.** TVM D: Paul Schneider. Ricki Lake, Craig Sheffer, Nada Despotovich, Paul Benedict, Betty Buckley, John Karlen. Middling remake of Percy

Adlon's German-language SUGARBABY gives cult chubbette Lake her first TV starring role as she searches for love, and zeroes in on hunky Sheffer. Average.

Baby Comes Home (1980) C-100m. TVM D: Waris Hussein. Colleen Dewhurst, Warren Oates, Mildred Dunnock, Devon Ericson, Fred Lehne, David Huffman, James Noble, Dena Dietrich. Middle-aged couple, having raised three children, find themselves parents again in this sequel to AND BABY MAKES SIX. Average.

Baby Doll (1956) 114m. ***½ D: Elia Kazan. Karl Malden, Carroll Baker, Eli Wallach, Mildred Dunnock, Lonny Chapman, Rip Torn. Starkly photographed on location in Mississippi, story revolves around a child bride, her witless and blustery husband, and a smarmy business rival bent on using both of them. Condemned by Legion of Decency when released, this Tennessee Williams story, although tame by today's standards, still sizzles. Film debuts of Wallach and Torn.▼

Baby Face (1933) 70m. **½ D: Alfred E. Green. Barbara Stanwyck, George Brent, Donald Cook, Margaret Lindsay, Douglass Dumbrille, John Wayne. Pre-Production Code item has Stanwyck bartending at a speakeasy, then literally sleeping her way floor by floor to the top of a N.Y.C. office building. Great first half gives way to sappily moralistic conclusion. Wayne's coat-and-tie bit—as one of the office help used by the heroine—is a hoot.

Baby Face Harrington (1935) 61m. **½ D: Raoul Walsh. Charles Butterworth, Una Merkel, Harvey Stephens, Nat Pendleton, Eugene Pallette. Mild-mannered Butterworth gets mixed up with gangsters in this pleasant comedy vehicle that takes its time getting started.

Baby Face Nelson (1957) 85m. ** D: Don Siegel. Mickey Rooney, Carolyn Jones, Cedric Hardwicke, Jack Elam, Ted De Corsia. Rooney gives flavorful performance in title role of gun-happy gangster in Prohibition-Depression days; low-budget product, but action-filled.

Baby, It's You (1983) C-105m. **½ D: John Sayles. Rosanna Arquette, Vincent Spano, Joanna Merlin, Jack Davidson, Nick Ferrari, Dolores Messina, Leora Dana, Sam McMurray, Tracy Pollan, Matthew Modine, Robert Downey, Jr., Caroline Aaron, Fisher Stevens. A middle-class Jewish girl is pursued by a working-class Italian Catholic boy who calls himself The Sheik in this slice-of-life set in 1960s New Jersey. Writer-director Sayles's eye for detail and ear for dialogue give his fine cast a solid foundation—but the script loses momentum after the characters graduate from high school. Story by coproducer Amy Robinson; Modine's film debut.▼

Baby M (1988) C-200m. TVM D: James Steven Sadwith. JoBeth Williams, John Shea, Dabney Coleman, Bruce Weitz, Robin Strasser, Anne Jackson, Bruce McGill, Jenny Lewis. One of the most famous custody battles of the '80s is intelligently played out with Williams giving a standout performance as surrogate mother Mary Beth Whitehead, who contractually agreed to conceive a child for William and Elizabeth Stern and then reneged when the baby was born. Shea won an Emmy for his passionate portrayal of Stern. Written by director Sadwith, this film contained, on its premiere, the longest epilogue crawl of any to date, explaining the progress of the case up to the very eve of its broadcast. Originally shown in two parts. Above average.

Baby Maker, The (1970) C-109m. ** D: James Bridges. Barbara Hershey, Colin Wilcox-Horne, Sam Groom, Scott Glenn, Jeannie Berlin. Childless couple hires young semi-hippie to have a baby by the husband when wife discovers she is sterile. Not a good way to make a living and not a very interesting film.▼

Baby . . . Secret of the Lost Legend (1985) C-95m. ** D: B.W.L. Norton. William Katt, Sean Young, Patrick McGoohan, Julian Fellowes, Kyalo Mativo. Old-fashioned yarn about discovery of a dinosaur family follows basic KING KONG outline—and the baby dino is sure to charm kids—but elements of racism, sexism, and much-too-casual violence just about kill it. TV title: DINOSAUR . . . SECRET OF THE LOST LEGEND.▼

Baby Sister (1983) C-100m. TVM D: Steven Hilliard Stern. Ted Wass, Phoebe Cates, Pamela Bellwood, Efrem Zimbalist, Jr., Virginia Kiser. Free-spirited college dropout goes on the make for her sister's boyfriend. Same plot used 53 years earlier in WHAT MEN WANT—and it hasn't improved with age. Below average.

Babysitter, The (1969) 70m. ** D: Don Henderson. Patricia Wymer, George E. Carey, Ann Bellamy, Cathy Williams, Robert Tessier, James McLarty. Low-budget drive-in fare is dated but still mildly enjoyable; young blonde babysitter seduces the district attorney and hilarity ensues. Lots of double duty on this one: Carey produced, McLarty wrote the script. Followed by nonsequel, WEEKEND WITH THE BABYSITTER.

Babysitter, The (1975-Italian-French-German) C-111m. BOMB D: Rene Clement. Maria Schneider, Sydne Rome, Vic Morrow, Robert Vaughn, Renato Pozzetto, Nadja Tiller, Carl Mohner. Misfired melodrama in which Schneider is innocently duped into participating in a kidnapping by her roommate (Rome). Schneider's walkthrough nonacting is abysmal, as is miscasting of chubby Italian comedian Pozzetto as her boyfriend. Retitled: WANTED: BABYSITTER.▼

Babysitter, The (1980) **C-100m.** **TVM** D: Peter Medak. Patty Duke Astin, William Shatner, Quinn Cummings, David Wallace, Stephanie Zimbalist, John Houseman. Psychological thriller about the infiltration of a family by a seemingly charming babysitter, who then exploits the vulnerabilities of each member. Promising premise, but a fraud in the end. Average.▼

Baby Snakes (1979) **C-166m.** BOMB D: Frank Zappa. Frank Zappa, Ron Delsener, Joey Psychotic, Donna U. Wanna, Frenchy the Poodle, Ms. Pinky's Larger Sister, Angel, Janet the Planet, Diva, John, Chris, Nancy. Excruciatingly overlong ego trip for musical maverick Zappa. In every fifth shot, it seems, Frankie is in close-up or a fan rushes up to him, kisses him, and screeches for joy. Zappa the producer should have fired Zappa the director, but Zappa the editor finally cut it down to 91m. for 1984 reissue. Bruce Bickford's clay animation is film's sole virtue.▼

Baby Take a Bow (1934) **76m.** ** D: Harry Lachman. Shirley Temple, James Dunn, Claire Trevor, Alan Dinehart, Ray Walker. Shirley's first starring vehicle seems one of her weakest today, but helped boost her career nonetheless; in typical little-miss-fixit fashion, she helps her excon father beat a bum rap. Also shown in computer-colored version.▼

Baby The Rain Must Fall (1965) **100m.** *** D: Robert Mulligan. Lee Remick, Steve McQueen, Don Murray, Paul Fix, Josephine Hutchinson, Ruth White. Much underrated account of ex-convict McQueen, returning to his wife and daughter, but unable to change his restless ways. Murray is sincere sheriff who tries to help. Screenplay by Horton Foote, from his play *The Traveling Lady*.▼

Bachelor and the Bobby-Soxer, The (1947) **95m.** *** D: Irving Reis. Cary Grant, Myrna Loy, Shirley Temple, Rudy Vallee, Ray Collins, Harry Davenport. Judge Loy orders playboy Grant to wine and dine her sister Temple, so the teen-ager will forget her infatuation for him. Breezy entertainment earned Sidney Sheldon an Oscar for his original screenplay. Also shown in computer-colored version.▼

Bachelor Apartment (1931) **77m.** **½ D: Lowell Sherman. Lowell Sherman, Irene Dunne, Mae Murray, Claudia Dell, Noel Francis, Bess Flowers. Sophisticated comedy about gay-blade Sherman shuffling his various girls back and forth; ancestor of COME BLOW YOUR HORN, etc.

Bachelor Father, The (1931) **90m.** **½ D: Robert Z. Leonard. Marion Davies, Ralph Forbes, C. Aubrey Smith, Doris Lloyd, Halliwell Hobbes, Ray Milland. Once dashing bachelor Smith, now old

and lonely, wants to know his three grown children. Staid but enjoyable adaptation of Edward Childs Carpenter's stage play.

Bachelor Flat (1961) **C-91m.** ** D: Frank Tashlin. Tuesday Weld, Richard Beymer, Celeste Holm, Terry-Thomas. Weld visits her mother's beach house and finds scientist Thomas at work; she moves in anyway and creates eventual havoc. Thomas has had better material; film's entertainment is all in his lap.

Bachelor in Paradise (1961) **C-109m.** ** D: Jack Arnold. Bob Hope, Lana Turner, Janis Paige, Jim Hutton, Paula Prentiss, Don Porter, Agnes Moorehead. Hope vehicle about the only bachelor in a community of married couples. Amusing, but not great. Hope has done better; Paige is fun as always.

Bachelor Mother (1939) **81m.** ***½ D: Garson Kanin. Ginger Rogers, David Niven, Charles Coburn, Frank Albertson, Ernest Truex. Rogers unwittingly becomes guardian for abandoned baby in this delightful comedy by Norman Krasna. Remade as BUNDLE OF JOY.▼

Bachelor Party, The (1957) **93m.** *** D: Delbert Mann. Don Murray, E. G. Marshall, Jack Warden, Patricia Smith, Carolyn Jones, Larry Blyden, Philip Abbott. Perceptive Paddy Chayefsky drama (originally a TV play) about bachelor party for groom-to-be Abbott, and its emotional effect on other married participants. Jones is exceptional as philosophical nympho.

Bachelor Party (1984) **C-106m.** ** D: Neal Israel. Tom Hanks, Tawny Kitaen, Adrian Zmed, George Grizzard, Robert Prescott. Amiable comedy about preparations for a raunchy bachelor party has real laughs for a while, then gets increasingly desperate and tasteless.▼

Back at the Front (1952) **87m.** **½ D: George Sherman. Tom Ewell, Harvey Lembeck, Mari Blanchard, Richard Long. Follow-up to UP FRONT, with Bill Mauldin's army goof-offs Willie and Joe scampering around post-WW2 Tokyo. Retitled: WILLIE AND JOE BACK AT THE FRONT.

Back Door to Heaven (1939) **85m.** *** D: William K. Howard. Wallace Ford, Aline MacMahon, Stuart Erwin, Patricia Ellis, Ken Smith, Van Heflin, Jimmy Lydon. Grim social drama focusing on hard life of poor boy and his reasons for choosing life of crime. Much talked about in its day; strong performances by all.▼

Back Door to Hell (1964) **68m.** **½ D: Monte Hellman. Jimmie Rodgers, Jack Nicholson, John Hackett, Annabelle Huggins, Conrad Maga. Mildly interesting film about WW2 reconnaissance mission in the Philippines; early collaboration of Nicholson and Hellman, who filmed FLIGHT TO FURY back to back with this.

Backfire (1950) **91m.** ** D: Vincent Sherman. Virginia Mayo, Gordon MacRae, Edmond O'Brien, Viveca Lindfors, Dane Clark, Ed Begley. OK mystery tale has MacRae search for missing friend through maze of murder and romance.

Backfire (1961-British) **59m.** ** D: Paul Almond. Alfred Burke, Zena Marshall, Oliver Johnston. Noel Trevarthen is insurance investigator solving arson and murder at a cosmetics firm; adequate programmer based on Edgar Wallace yarn.

Backfire (1987-U.S.-Canadian) **C-92m.** **½ D: Gilbert Cates. Karen Allen, Keith Carradine, Jeff Fahey, Bernie Casey, Dean Paul Martin, Dinah Manoff, Virginia Capers, Philip Sterling. Complicated plot with several surprises is best not revealed here, but it does involve wealthy, disturbed Vietnam vet Fahey, his wrong-side-of-the-tracks wife Allen, and mysterious drifter Carradine. Familiar story but well acted; builds up a fair amount of suspense. Good use of Canadian locations.▼

Back From Eternity (1956) **97m.** **½ D: John Farrow. Robert Ryan, Anita Ekberg, Rod Steiger, Phyllis Kirk. Moderately engrossing account of victims of plane crash, stranded in South American jungle, and their various reactions to the situation. OK remake of FIVE CAME BACK.▼

Back From the Dead (1957) **79m.** BOMB D: Charles Marquis Warren. Peggie Castle, Arthur Franz, Marsha Hunt, Evelyn Scott, James Bell. Castle is earnest as wife possessed by will of husband's dead first spouse, but cliché-ridden production makes everything ridiculous.

Background to Danger (1943) **80m.** *** D: Raoul Walsh. George Raft, Brenda Marshall, Sydney Greenstreet, Peter Lorre, Osa Massen, Kurt Katch. Slam-bang WW2 story with Raft swept into Nazi intrigue in Turkey; terrific car chase highlights fast-moving tale.

Backlash (1947) **66m.** ** D: Eugene Forde. Jean Rogers, Richard Travis, Larry Blake, John Eldredge, Leonard Strong, Robert Shayne, Louise Currie, Douglas Fowley. Standard programmer of man trying to frame his wife for murder he committed. Also shown in computer-colored version.

Backlash (1956) **C-84m.** **½ D: John Sturges. Richard Widmark, Donna Reed, William Campbell, John McIntire, Barton MacLane. Widmark is only survivor of Indian massacre; knowing the whereabouts of buried treasure, he is object of outlaw manhunt.

Backlash (1986-Australian) **C-88m.** **½ D: Bill Bennett. David Argue, Gia Carides, Lydia Miller, Brian Syron, Anne Smith. Well-meaning but muddled account of a young aborigine barmaid who's sodomized, then charged with the murder of her assailant, and finally treks across the outback in custody of two mindlessly jabbering cops. Bits of snappy dialogue and intriguing commentary on race relations, but far too much is left unexplained.▼

Backroads (1977-Australian) **C-61m.** ***½ D: Philip Noyce. Bill Hunter, Gary Foley, Zac Martin, Julie McGregor, Terry Camilleri. Aborigine Foley joins with loutish, self-centered white criminal Hunter, with tragic results. Superior drama is an incisive commentary on racism; in private life Foley is a radical black activist.

Back Roads (1981) **C-94m.** *½ D: Martin Ritt. Sally Field, Tommy Lee Jones, David Keith, Miriam Colon, Michael V. Gazzo, M. Emmet Walsh. Attractive leads are scant consolation for thoroughly unfunny comedy about a hooker and a drifter who find love on the road. Not as enjoyable as Hollywood's 10,000 previous derivations of the same script.▼

Backstage at the Kirov (1983) **C-80m.** *** D: Derek Hart. Galina Mezentxseva, Konstantin Zaklinsky, Altyani Assylmuratova, other dancers. Handsome, entertaining look at Leningrad's famed Kirov ballet troupe, behind the scenes and on-stage (performing "Swan Lake").▼

Back Street (1932) **89m.** *** D: John M. Stahl. Irene Dunne, John Boles, George Meeker, ZaSu Pitts, Arlette Duncan, June Clyde, William Bakewell, Doris Lloyd, Jane Darwell. Dunne shines in oft-filmed Fannie Hurst soaper of spirited young woman who becomes the mistress of Boles and must forever remain in the shadows. Dated, to be sure, but still entertaining. Remade in 1941 and 1961.

Back Street (1941) **89m.** *** D: Robert Stevenson. Charles Boyer, Margaret Sullavan, Richard Carlson, Frank McHugh, Tim Holt. Fine team of Boyer and Sullavan breathes life into Fannie Hurst perennial soaper of woman whose love for man doesn't die when he marries another.

Back Street (1961) **C-107m.** **½ D: David Miller. Susan Hayward, John Gavin, Vera Miles, Virginia Grey. Updated, lavish, unbelievable third version of Fannie Hurst's story of a woman's love for married man. Doesn't play as well as previous versions. Produced by Ross Hunter.▼

Back to Bataan (1945) **95m.** *** D: Edward Dmytryk. John Wayne, Anthony Quinn, Beulah Bondi, Fely Franquelli, Richard Loo, Philip Ahn, Lawrence Tierney. Good, sturdy WW2 action film with officer Wayne leading Filipino guerillas to victory in the South Pacific. Also shown in computer-colored version.▼

Back to God's Country (1953) **C-78m.** **½ D: Joseph Pevney. Rock Hudson, Marcia Henderson, Steve Cochran, Hugh O'Brian, Chubby Johnson. Sea captain Hudson and wife Henderson must face rigors of nature and villainy of Cochran in the Canadian wilds. Competent programmer, based on James Oliver Curwood's classic story.

Back to School (1986) **C-96m.** *** D: Alan Metter. Rodney Dangerfield, Sally Kellerman, Burt Young, Keith Gordon, Robert Downey, Jr., Paxton Whitehead, Terry Farrell, M. Emmet Walsh, Adrienne Barbeau, Ned Beatty, Severn Darden, Kurt Vonnegut, Jr. Bombastic, uneducated, self-made millionaire enrolls in college, in order to encourage his student son. That's all the premise necessary for this very entertaining comedy, full of hilarious Dangerfield one-liners. But the key to the film's success is that Rodney's character is so likable. Kellerman shines, too, as English professor who becomes the apple of his eye.▼

Back to the Beach (1987) **C-92m.** ** D: Lyndall Hobbs. Frankie Avalon, Annette Funicello, Lori Loughlin, Tommy Hinckley, Connie Stevens, Demian Slade; guest appearances by Don Adams, Bob Denver, Alan Hale, Jerry Mathers, Tony Dow, Barbara Billingsley, Edd Byrnes, Pee-wee Herman (Paul Reubens), Dick Dale and The Del-Tones. Frankie and Annette return to the scene of their youth—older but no wiser—as the parents of teens. The fun wears thin pretty fast in this uninspired comedy—despite the efforts of *six writers* (reportedly others worked without credit!) and the presence of 1950s and 60s TV sitcom stars in cameo roles. The songs are dull, too, though Annette's "Jamaica Ska" has its moments.▼

Back to the Future (1985) **C-116m.** *** D: Robert Zemeckis. Michael J. Fox, Christopher Lloyd, Crispin Glover, Lea Thompson, Wendie Jo Sperber, Marc McClure, Claudia Wells, Thomas F. Wilson, James Tolkan, Casey Siemaszko, Billy Zane, Jason Hervey. A teenager of the '80s travels back in time to the '50s, where he must arrange for his mismatched parents to meet—or else *he* won't exist! Wonderful, wacked-out time-travel comedy takes its time to get going, but once it does, it's a lot of fun, building to a frantic climax just like other Bob Gale–Robert Zemeckis scripts (USED CARS, I WANNA HOLD YOUR HAND, 1941). Lloyd is a particular standout as the crazed scientist who sets the whole story in motion. Huey Lewis, who sings film's hit song, "The Power of Love," has cameo as a high-school teacher. Produced by Steven Spielberg and company. Followed by two sequels.▼

Back to the Future Part II (1989) **C-107m.** ** D: Robert Zemeckis. Michael J. Fox, Christopher Lloyd, Lea Thompson, Thomas F. Wilson, Harry Waters Jr., Charles Fleischer, Joe Flaherty, Elisabeth Shue, James Tolkan, Casey Siemaszko. Joyless, frenetic follow-up to Part 1 which sends mad inventor Lloyd and young Fox back into their time-traveling DeLorean. Con-

siderable ingenuity, but hardly any laughs, and a surprising amount of unpleasantness. Works best toward the end when it creates a parallel existence to the climactic action in Part 1, but then it turns out to be a cliffhanger, advertising the upcoming Part 3! Talk about a cheat . . .▼

Back to the Future Part III (1990) **C-118m.** ***½ D: Robert Zemeckis. Michael J. Fox, Christopher Lloyd, Mary Steenburgen, Thomas F. Wilson, Lea Thompson, Elisabeth Shue, Matt Clark, Richard Dysart, Pat Buttram, Harry Carey, Jr., Dub Taylor, James Tolkan, ZZ Top. Delightful conclusion to this time-travel trilogy sends Fox back to the Old West, circa 1885, in search of Lloyd—hoping to change history and keep him from being shot in the back by a bad guy. The dormant movie Western gets a major dose of adrenaline from this high-tech, high-powered comic adventure, which offers great fun, dazzling special effects, and imagination to spare. There's real movie magic at work here.

Back to the Wall (1959-French) **94m.** ** D: Edouard Molinaro. Gerard Oury, Jeanne Moreau, Philippe Nicaud, Claire Maurier, Jean Lefebvre. As the adulterous wife, Moreau spins entertaining web of extortion and murder; satisfactory suspenser.

Backtrack (1969) **C-95m.** ** D: Earl Bellamy. Neville Brand, James Drury, Doug McClure, Peter Brown, Ida Lupino, Rhonda Fleming, Fernando Lamas. Maverick cowboy on the range. No more than an elongated version of a 1965 *Virginian* TV episode (which served as a pilot for the subsequent *Laredo* series).

Backwoods Massacre SEE: **Midnight** (1981)▼

Bad and the Beautiful, The (1952) **118m.** ***½ D: Vincente Minnelli. Kirk Douglas, Lana Turner, Dick Powell, Gloria Grahame, Barry Sullivan, Walter Pidgeon, Gilbert Roland. Captivating Hollywood story of ambitious producer (Douglas) told via relationships with actress Turner, writer Powell, director Sullivan. Solid, insightful, witty, with Lana's best performance to date. Five Oscars include Supporting Actress (Grahame), Screenplay (Charles Schnee). Minnelli and Douglas followed this a decade later with TWO WEEKS IN ANOTHER TOWN. Also shown in computer-colored version.▼

Bad Bascomb (1946) **110m.** ** D: S. Sylvan Simon. Wallace Beery, Margaret O'Brien, Marjorie Main, J. Carrol Naish, Marshall Thompson. Overlong Western with fine action scenes, overshadowed by incredibly syrupy ones with Beery and O'Brien.

Bad Blood (1981-New Zealand-British) **C-104m.** *** D: Mike Newell. Jack Thompson, Carol Burns, Denis Lill, Donna Akersten, Martyn Sanderson, Marshall Napier. Set during WW2, this provocative drama is a fact-based account of a back-woods farmer (Thompson) who shoots several people and is hunted in the New Zealand bush. The incident ends up being exploited by Lord Haw-Haw, the notorious Nazi propagandist.▼

Bad Blood (1987-French) **C-128m.** ** D: Leos Carax. Michel Piccoli, Denis Lavant, Juliette Binoche, Hans Meyer, Julie Delpy, Carroll Brooks, Serge Reggiani. Occasionally interesting but too often pretentious account of plot to pilfer a serum that's an antidote for an AIDS-like disease. Shot mostly in close-ups of faces, legs, etc., which eventually grows tiresome.

Bad Blood (1989) **C-104m.** ** D: Chuck Vincent. Gregory Patrick, Ruth Raymond, Linda Blair, Troy Donahue, Carolyn Van Bellinghen, Christina Veronica. Overlong, low-budget thriller with OK plot (reminiscent of Stephen King's *Misery*) about Patrick learning he's the long-lost son of eccentric, possessive millionairess Raymond; Blair is his victimized wife. Some good ideas, many bad ones—occasional scenes go on for minutes without cuts.▼

Bad Boy (1949) **86m.** **½ D: Kurt Neumann. Lloyd Nolan, Jane Wyatt, Audie Murphy, James Gleason, Martha Vickers. Juvenile delinquent rehabilitated by being sent to boys' ranch, where Nolan befriends him. Young Murphy is belligerently effective.

Bad Boys (1983) **C-123m.** *** D: Rick Rosenthal. Sean Penn, Reni Santoni, Esai Morales, Eric Gurry, Jim Moody, Ally Sheedy, Clancy Brown. Tough urban melodrama about juvenile prison, and a personal vendetta that reaches its peak within prison walls. Criticized by some as being amoral—and not always credible—but certainly scores on an emotional level. Sheedy's feature film debut.▼

Bad Company (1931) **75m.** **½ D: Tay Garnett. Ricardo Cortez, Helen Twelvetrees, John Garrick, Paul Hurst, Frank Conroy, Frank McHugh, Kenneth Thomson, Harry Carey. Fair curio with hood Cortez arranging for lawyer underling Garrick to wed naive Twelvetrees, sister of his rival. Deservedly not as famous as the other gangster pictures of its day.

Bad Company (1972) **C-93m.** ***½ D: Robert Benton. Jeff Bridges, Barry Brown, Jim Davis, David Huddleston, John Savage, Jerry Houser. Highly entertaining sleeper about two young drifters of wildly differing temperaments who rob their way West during the Civil War; aided immeasurably by Gordon Willis' subdued photography, Harvey Schmidt's piano score. Written by Benton and David Newman.▼

✓ **Bad Day at Black Rock** (1955) **C-81m.** ***½ D: John Sturges. Spencer Tracy, Robert Ryan, Anne Francis, Dean Jagger, Walter Brennan, John Ericson, Ernest Borgnine, Lee Marvin. Powerhouse cast in yarn of one-armed man (Tracy) uncovering skeleton in Western town's closet. Borgnine memorable as slimy heavy. Millard Kaufman expertly adapted Howard Breslin's story "Bad Time at Hondo." Excellent use of CinemaScope will be lost on TV.▼

Bad Dreams (1988) **C-84m.** BOMB D: Andrew Fleming. Jennifer Rubin, Bruce Abbott, Richard Lynch, Harris Yulin, Dean Cameron, Susan Barnes, E.G. Daily, Sy Richardson, Susan Ruttan, Charles Fleischer. Imitative horror flick about Rubin awakening as an adult after thirteen years in a coma (following her scrape with death as part of a suicide pact enacted by cult leader Lynch). Members of her therapy group are murdered one by one and she thinks Lynch's ghost is responsible. Chintzy effects, poor script and direction sink this one.▼

Bad For Each Other (1953) **83m.** **½ D: Irving Rapper. Charlton Heston, Lizabeth Scott, Dianne Foster, Mildred Dunnock, Marjorie Rambeau. Idealistic doctor Heston finds Pennsylvania mining town has more worthy patients than idle social set. Pouty Scott and wise Rambeau are good.

Badge of Marshal Brennan, The (1957) **76m.** *½ D: Albert C. Gannaway. Jim Davis, Arleen Whelan, Lee Van Cleef, Louis Jean Heydt. Uninspired account of criminal Davis mistaken as law enforcer, who redeems himself by corraling rustling gang.

Badge of the Assassin (1985) **C-100m.** TVM D: Mel Damski. James Woods, Yaphet Kotto, Alex Rocco, David Harris, Steven Keats, Larry Riley, Pam Grier, Rae Dawn Chong, Richard Bradford. Bristling police drama about real-life Manhattan assistant D.A. who directed campaign to locate a pair of cop killers of the '70s. Based by Lawrence Roman on the bestseller by Robert K. Tanenbaum (played with nervous intensity by Woods) and Philip Rosenberg. Above average.▼

Badge or the Cross, The SEE: **Sarge**

Badge 373 (1973) **C-116m.** *½ D: Howard W. Koch. Robert Duvall, Verna Bloom, Henry Darrow, Eddie Egan, Felipe Luciano, Tina Christiana. Very minor follow-up to THE FRENCH CONNECTION. Policeman Duvall tries to fight crime syndicate single-handedly in N.Y.C. Dull.▼

Bad Girl (1959-British) **100m.** *½ D: Herbert Wilcox. Anna Neagle, Sylvia Syms, Norman Wooland, Wilfrid Hyde-White, Kenneth Haigh, Julia Lockwood. Modest trivia enhanced by good cast involving teenager who becomes involved with sordid side of life. Retitled: TEENAGE BAD GIRL.▼

Bad Guys (1986) **C-86m.** BOMB D: Joel Silberg. Adam Baldwin, Mike Jolly, Michelle Nicastro, Ruth Buzzi, James Booth, Gene LeBell, Norman Burton. Shamelessly inane comedy about a pair of moronic young cops who become wrestlers after receiving their walking papers from the force. Predictably, a ringful of popular wrestlers also appear. Yecch!▼

Bad Influence (1990) **C-99m.** **½ D: Curtis Hanson. Rob Lowe, James Spader, Lisa Zane, Christian Clemenson, Kathleen Wilhoite, Tony Maggio. Spader befriends Lowe after the latter gets him out of a tense barroom confrontation, then finds this psychopathic leech calling the shots in his romantic—and professional—life. Slick, high-tech variation on STRANGERS ON A TRAIN knows which buttons to push. Lowe is passable, but he won't make you forget Robert Walker.▼

Bad Jim (1990) **C-90m.** ** D: Clyde Ware. James Brolin, Richard Roundtree, John Clark Gable, Harry Carey, Jr., Rory Calhoun, Ty Hardin, Pepe Serna, Bruce Kirby. Not-bad western has three good/bad men purchasing Billy the Kid's horse—and using it to pass themselves off as Billy's gang. Nice locations and welcome cast of veterans help make up for leisurely pace and lack of real action. Screen debut for Clark Gable's son, as the youngest of the bandit trio.▼

Badlanders, The (1958) **C-83m.** *** D: Delmer Daves. Alan Ladd, Ernest Borgnine, Katy Jurado, Claire Kelly. Turn-of-the-century Western set in Arizona with Ladd and Borgnine planning gold robbery, each trying to outsmart the other; nicely handled by all. Remake of THE ASPHALT JUNGLE.

Bad Lands (1939) **70m.** **½ D: Lew Landers. Noah Beery, Jr., Robert Barrat, Guinn Williams, Douglas Walton, Andy Clyde, Addison Richards, Robert Coote, Paul Hurst. Thinly disguised Western remake of THE LOST PATROL, about a posse stranded in the Arizona wilderness and trapped by Apaches. Painless and forgettable.

Badlands (1973) **C-95m.** **½ D: Terrence Malick. Martin Sheen, Sissy Spacek, Warren Oates, Ramon Bieri, Alan Vint. Stark, moody, moderately successful thriller inspired by the Starkweather-Fugate killing spree in the 50s. Well-cast film has cult following.▼

Badlands of Dakota (1941) **74m.** **½ D: Alfred E. Green. Robert Stack, Ann Rutherford, Richard Dix, Frances Farmer, Broderick Crawford, Hugh Herbert. Brothers Crawford and Stack fight over Rutherford, while Wild Bill Hickok (Dix) does fighting of another kind.

Badlands of Montana (1957) **75m.** *½ D: Daniel B. Ullman. Rex Reason, Beverly Garland, Keith Larsen, Jack Kruschen. Unimaginative oater leading up to inevitable climax of former buddies, sheriff and gunslinger, having shoot-out.

Bad Lord Byron (1951-British) **85m.** **½ D: David Macdonald. Dennis Price, Joan Greenwood, Mai Zetterling, Sonia Holm. Potentially exciting but static retelling of the life of 19th-century poet and lover, focusing on his many romances.

Bad Man, The (1941) **70m.** **½ D: Richard Thorpe. Wallace Beery, Lionel Barrymore, Laraine Day, Ronald Reagan, Henry Travers. Fairly good co-starring vehicle for Beery, as Western outlaw, and Barrymore, as former friend who depends on the bad man's loyalty.

Bad Man of Brimstone (1938) **90m.** ** D: J. Walter Ruben. Wallace Beery, Virginia Bruce, Dennis O'Keefe, Joseph Calleia, Lewis Stone, Guy Kibbee, Bruce Cabot. Low-grade Western vehicle is for Beery fans, with star as outlaw who is reformed by family revelation.

Badman's Country (1958) **68m.** **½ D: Fred F. Sears. George Montgomery, Buster Crabbe, Neville Brand, Malcolm Atterbury. Fictionalized Western history with name-dropping cast of characters. Sheriff Pat Garrett (Montgomery) joins with Wyatt Earp (Crabbe) and Buffalo Bill (Atterbury) for showdown with outlaw Butch Cassidy (Brand).

Bad Man's River (1972-Italian-Spanish) **C-89m.** ** D: Gene (Eugenio) Martin. Lee Van Cleef, James Mason, Gina Lollobrigida, Simon Andreu, Diana Lorys. Van Cleef is head of an outlaw gang repeatedly out-smarted by devilish Lollobrigida in this pallid comedy-Western made in Spain.▼

Badman's Territory (1946) **79m.** *** D: Tim Whelan. Randolph Scott, Ann Richards, Gabby Hayes, Ray Collins, Chief Thundercloud. Sheriff Scott is helpless when bandits flee across border into territory uncontrolled by government; good Western.▼

Bad Medicine (1985) **C-96m.** BOMB D: Harvey Miller. Steve Guttenberg, Alan Arkin, Julie Hagerty, Bill Macy, Curtis Armstrong, Julie Kavner, Joe Grifasi. Guttenberg can't get into any domestic medical schools, so he's forced to attend a dubious Central American institution run by Arkin. Cheap jokes and ethnic putdowns abound. Our prescription: skip it.▼

Bad Men of Missouri (1941) **74m.** *** D: Ray Enright. Dennis Morgan, Jane Wyman, Wayne Morris, Arthur Kennedy, Victor Jory, Alan Baxter. Younger brothers, enraged by Southern carpetbaggers, turn to lawless life in fictional Western, with good cast.

Bad News Bears, The (1976) **C-102m.** *** D: Michael Ritchie. Walter Matthau, Tatum O'Neal, Vic Morrow, Joyce Van Patten, Jackie Earle Haley, Alfred W. Lutter. Bright comedy about hopeless Little League baseball team that scores with an unlikely combination: a beer-guzzling coach (Matthau) and a female star pitcher

(O'Neal). Some of film's major appeal—young kids spouting four-letter words—will be lost on TV. Followed by two sequels and a TV series.▼

Bad News Bears Go To Japan, The (1978) **C-91m.** ** D: John Berry. Tony Curtis, Jackie Earle Haley, Tomisaburo Wakayama, George Wyner, Lonny Chapman. Curtis is good as a small-time hustler who sees money-making opportunity in the now-familiar baseball team. Third film was the kids' last, and it's easy to see why.▼

Bad News Bears in Breaking Training, The (1977) **C-100m.** **½ D: Michael Pressman. William Devane, Jackie Earle Haley, Jimmy Baio, Clifton James, Chris Barnes. Sentimental sequel to 1976 hit, with dirty talk largely absent. Star of the kids' baseball team, Haley heads for the Houston Astrodome and enlists the aid of estranged father Devane in coaching the misfits. Sporadically funny.▼

Bad Ronald (1974) **C-78m.** TVM D: Buzz Kulik. Scott Jacoby, Pippa Scott, John Larch, Dabney Coleman, Kim Hunter, John Fiedler. Family with three daughters moves into an old house unaware that it has a secret room occupied by psychopathic teenager who has murdered a taunting peer. Intriguing little thriller adapted by Andrew Peter Martin from the John Holbrook Vance novel. Above average.▼

✓ **Bad Seed, The** (1956) **129m.** *** D: Mervyn LeRoy. Nancy Kelly, Patty McCormack, Henry Jones, Eileen Heckart, Evelyn Varden, William Hopper. Stagy but spellbinding account of malicious child McCormack whose inherited evil "causes" deaths of several people. Fine performances; Maxwell Anderson's Broadway play was adapted by John Lee Mahin, with Kelly, McCormack, Jones, and Heckart recreating their stage roles. The corny "Hollywoodized" postscript is often cut but remains intact on the videocassette. Remade for TV.▼

Bad Seed, The (1985) **C-100m.** TVM D: Paul Wendkos. Blair Brown, Lynn Redgrave, David Carradine, Richard Kiley, David Ogden Stiers, Carrie Wells. Acceptable remake of 1956 thriller, though newcomer Wells isn't quite in the same league as child-star Patty McCormack. Carradine, though, is more sleazeball than creep. Average.

Bad Sleep Well, The (1960-Japanese) **135m.** *** D: Akira Kurosawa. Toshiro Mifune, Takeshi Kato, Masayuki Mori, Takashi Shimura, Akira Nishimura. Kurosawa effectively captures the spirit of 1940s Warner Bros. crime dramas in this engrossing tale of rising executive Mifune and corruption in the corporate world. Actually, it's a variation on *Hamlet*. Original version runs 151m.▼

Bad Taste (1988-New Zealand) **C-90m.** **½ D: Peter Jackson. Peter Jackson, Pete O'Herne, Mike Minett, Terry Potter, Craig Smith, Doug Wren, Dean Lawrie. Title is absolutely accurate in describing this gory comedy about callous alien fast-food entrepreneurs, here to harvest humanity, and battling it out with government hit squad. Quirky, fragmented direction matches subject matter and acting styles. Director Jackson also acted, wrote, edited, produced, and did the uneven but occasionally excellent makeup. A cult hit worldwide.▼

Bad Timing: A Sensual Obsession (1980-British) **C-129m.** ***½ D: Nicolas Roeg. Art Garfunkel, Theresa Russell, Harvey Keitel, Denholm Elliott, Daniel Massey. Mesmerizing melodrama triumphs over badly miscast male leads and occasional pretentiousness. Roeg's kinetic style brings the necessary passion to oddball story of a psychiatrist sexually engulfed by a self-destructive tramp. Russell is simply great, as is knockout background music from The Who, Keith Jarrett, and Billie Holiday.▼

Baffled (1972) **C-90m.** TVM D: Phillip Leacock. Leonard Nimoy, Susan Hampshire, Vera Miles, Rachel Roberts, Jewel Branch, Christopher Benjamin. Contrived but enjoyable race-against-time thriller by Theodore Apstein with Nimoy an American race driver whose visions convince an ESP expert (Hampshire) that people in vision are in danger. Above average.▼

Bagdad (1949) **C-82m.** ** D: Charles Lamont. Maureen O'Hara, Paul Christian, Vincent Price, John Sutton. Costume hijinks with O'Hara fetching if not believable as native chieftain's daughter seeking revenge for father's death in old Turkey.

Bagdad Cafe (1988-West German) **C-108m.** **½ D: Percy Adlon. Marianne Sägebrecht, CCH Pounder, Jack Palance, Christine Kaufmann, Monica Calhoun, Darron Flagg. Nearly plotless charmer from the director and star of SUGARBABY has Sägebrecht stranded in the California desert, making friends with the kooky folks who hang out at Pounder's roadside cafe. Palance provides a special treat portraying an ex-Hollywood set decorator who becomes obsessed with painting Sägebrecht's portrait. German version runs twenty minutes longer. Later a TV series.▼

Bahama Passage (1941) **C-83m.** **½ D: Edward Griffith. Madeleine Carroll, Sterling Hayden, Flora Robson, Leo G. Carroll, Mary Anderson. Scenery is chief asset of routine tale of lovely Madeleine meeting handsome Sterling in beautiful Bahama, with much hamming by Carroll and Robson. The stars later married in real life.

Bailiff, The SEE: Sansho the Bailiff ▼

Bailout at 43,000 (1957) **78m.** ** D: Francis D. Lyon. John Payne, Karen Steele, Paul Kelly, Richard Eyer, Constance Ford.

Dilemma of air force pilot Payne whose relief at not having to test new safety device is outweighed by coward-guilt complex. Routine material is not enhanced by flight sequences or romantic relief.

Bait (1954) **79m.** *½ D: Hugo Haas. Cleo Moore, Hugo Haas, John Agar, Emmett Lynn. A mining-camp ménage à trois, heavy-handed Haas at his worst, despite intriguing pre-credit prologue with Cedric Hardwicke as the Devil.

Bait, The (1973) **C-73m. TVM** D: Leonard Horn. Donna Mills, Michael Constantine, William Devane, June Lockhart, Thalmus Rasulala. Policewoman-widow (Mills) puts herself on line, demands assignment to rape-murder case. Adaptation of Dorothy Uhnak's novel has distasteful point of view, occasional suspense, unconvincing characters. Average.

Baja Oklahoma (1988) **C-105m. TVM** D: Bobby Roth. Lesley Ann Warren, Peter Coyote, Swoosie Kurtz, Billy Vera, Anthony Zerbe, Willie Nelson, Emmylou Harris, Alice Krige, Bob Wills, Jr. Lively adaptation of Dan Jenkins' funny novel of a smalltown Texas barmaid who is juggling her dreams of becoming a songwriter with her rocky romances. Loaded with local color and music stars like Billy Vera (of Billy and the Beaters), Willie Nelson (who co-write the title song with Jenkins), Emmylou Harris, Bob Wills, Jr. (as his dad), plus South African actress Alice Krige as Patsy Cline. Written by Jenkins and director Roth. Made for cable, but also briefly released to theaters. Above average.▼

Baker's Hawk (1976) **C-98m.** *** D: Lyman D. Dayton. Clint Walker, Burl Ives, Diane Baker, Lee H. Montgomery, Alan Young, Taylor Lacher. Fine family drama about young boy (Montgomery) who befriends hermitlike Ives, and comes of age as he participates in parents' struggle against vigilante forces. Beautifully filmed on location in Utah.▼

Baker's Wife, The (1938-French) **124m.** ***½ D: Marcel Pagnol. Raimu, Ginette Leclerc, Charles Moulin, Robert Vattier, Robert Brassac, Charpin. Abandoned by his wife for a shepherd, baker Raimu is unable to function; villagers, who love his bread as much as he loves his wife, bring back the wayward woman. Hilarious.▼

Balalaika (1939) **102m.** ** D: Reinhold Schunzel. Nelson Eddy, Ilona Massey, Charles Ruggles, Frank Morgan, Lionel Atwill, George Tobias. Plodding operetta of Russian revolution with little to recommend it.

Balboa (1986) **C-91m.** **½ D: James Polakof. Tony Curtis, Carol Lynley, Jennifer Chase, Chuck Connors, Lupita Ferrer, Sonny Bono, Catherine Campbell, Cassandra Peterson, Martine Beswicke, Henry Jones, Steve Kanaly. Road company version of TV soap *Dallas*, replete with guest star Kanaly from that series, is enjoyably silly. Curtis is the hissable tycoon in Balboa, out to pull off a real estate scam while everybody's sleeping with everyone else's mate; Chase is the bubble-headed beauty who learns the hard way how the decadent rich behave. Episodic structure (narrated by Beswicke) is the result of film being edited down from original (unsold) miniseries. Filmed in 1982. ▼

Balcony, The (1963) **84m.** ** D: Joseph Strick. Shelley Winters, Peter Falk, Lee Grant, Ruby Dee, Peter Brocco, Kent Smith, Jeff Corey, Leonard Nimoy. Low-budget, none-too-successful attempt to adapt Jean Genet play to the screen, with Winters as madam who maintains her brothel during a revolution. Grant stands out as Winters' lesbian confidante.▼

Ballad in Blue SEE: **Blues for Lovers**▼

Ballad of Andy Crocker, The (1969) **C-73m. TVM** D: George McCowan. Lee Majors, Joey Heatherton, Jimmy Dean, Agnes Moorehead, Marvin Gaye, Jill Haworth, Lisa Todd, Pat Hingle. Name in title refers to Vietnam veteran (Majors) returning to home town and reacting to major changes: former sweetheart now married, former business partner now crooked. Written by Stuart Margolin. Not quite a "ballad" but above average.

Ballad of a Soldier (1960-Russian) **89m.** *** D: Grigori Chukhrai. Vladimir Ivashov, Shanna Prokhorenko, Antonina Maximova, Nikolai Kruchkov. Effectively simple love story of Russian soldier on leave during WW2, who meets and falls in love with unaffected country girl.▼

Ballad of Cable Hogue, The (1970) **C-121m.** *** D: Sam Peckinpah. Jason Robards, Stella Stevens, David Warner, Strother Martin, Slim Pickens, L. Q. Jones, R.G. Armstrong. Peckinpah's lyrical, wholly enjoyable fable of loner who builds a life for himself in remote part of the Old West. Stevens has one of her best roles as whore who joins Cable Hogue in quest for the good life. Overlong.▼

Ballad of Gregorio Cortez, The (1982) **C-99m.** **½ D: Robert M. Young. Edward James Olmos, James Gammon, Tom Bower, Bruce McGill, Brion James, Alan Vint, Rosana DeSoto, Pepe Serna, William Sanderson, Barry Corbin. True story, told from several points of view, of 1901 incident in which a young Mexican killed an American sheriff, then managed to elude a 600-man posse for nearly two weeks! Authentic to the core—almost like being in a time capsule, in fact—but too subdued, especially in its portrayal of Cortez, whose plight isn't fully explained until the end of the film. Originally produced for PBS'

American Playhouse, then released to theaters a year later.▼

Ballad of Josie, The (1967) **C-102m.** **½ D: Andrew McLaglen. Doris Day, Peter Graves, George Kennedy, Andy Devine, William Talman. Uninspired Western spoof with widow Day running a ranch and trying to lead the good life.

✓ **Ball of Fire** (1941) **111m.** ***½ D: Howard Hawks. Gary Cooper, Barbara Stanwyck, Oscar Homolka, Dana Andrews, Dan Duryea, S. Z. Sakall, Richard Haydn, Henry Travers, Tully Marshall, Gene Krupa. Burlesque dancer moves in with eight prissy professors (led by Cooper) to explain ''slang'' for their new encyclopedia; delightful twist on *Snow White and the Seven Dwarfs* by screenwriters Billy Wilder and Charles Brackett. Remade (by same director) as A SONG IS BORN.▼

Baltimore Bullet, The (1980) **C-103m.** **½ D: Robert Ellis Miller. James Coburn, Omar Sharif, Bruce Boxleitner, Ronee Blakley, Jack O'Halloran, Calvin Lockhart. Pleasant enough film about major-league pool hustlers Coburn and Boxleitner, and their buildup to a high noon showdown with smoothie Sharif.▼

✓ **Bambi** (1942) **C-69m.** **** D: David Hand. Walt Disney's moving and exquisitely detailed animated feature about a deer, and how the phases of its life parallel the cycle of seasons in the forest. An extraordinary achievement, with the memorably endearing character of Thumper stealing every scene he's in.▼

Bambole! (1965-Italian) **111m.** ** D: Dino Risi. Luigi Comencini, Franco Rossi, Mauro Bolognini, Virna Lisi, Nino Manfredi, Elke Sommer, Monica Vitti, Gina Lollobrigida, Akim Tamiroff, Jean Sorel. Quartet of stories on Italian life that never sparkles. ''The Phone Call,'' ''Treatise on Eugenics,'' ''The Soup,'' ''Monsignor Cupid.'' Retitled: FOUR KINDS OF LOVE.

Bamboo Prison, The (1954) **80m.** ** D: Lewis Seiler. Robert Francis, Dianne Foster, Brian Keith, Jerome Courtland, E. G. Marshall, Earle Hyman. Superficial handling of loyal American soldier Francis posing as informer in North Korean P.O.W. camp to outwit enemy.

Bamboo Saucer, The (1968) **C-100m.** **½ D: Frank Telford. Dan Duryea, John Ericson, Lois Nettleton, Nan Leslie, Bob Hastings. Better-than-average low-budget sci-fier about American and USSR teams investigating a UFO spotting in mainland China. Nettleton's tongue-in-cheek portrayal of a Russian scientist aids considerably. Duryea's last film. Also known as COLLISION COURSE.▼

Banacek (1972) **C-100m. TVM** D: Jack Smight. George Peppard, Christine Belford, Don Dubbins, Murray Matheson, Ed Nelson, Ralph Manza. Boston-based insurance investigator T. Banacek (Peppard) assigned to unusual case of Brinks truck vanishing in middle of Texas highway. Some interesting situations, good direction. Interesting yarn served as pilot for TV series. Retitled DETOUR TO NOWHERE. Above average.

Banana Monster, The SEE: Schlock▼

Banana Peel (1965-French) **97m.** *** D: Marcel Ophuls. Jeanne Moreau, Jean-Paul Belmondo, Gert Frobe. Rogues cheat millionaire out of a small fortune in this engaging comedy.

Bananas (1971) **C-82m.** **** D: Woody Allen. Woody Allen, Louise Lasser, Carlos Montalban, Howard Cosell, Rene Enriquez, Charlotte Rae, Conrad Bain. Hilarious; the usual assortment of good jokes, bad jokes, bizarre ideas built around unlikely premise of Woody becoming involved in revolution south of the border. Funny score by Marvin Hamlisch; look for Sylvester Stallone as hoodlum, Allen Garfield as man on cross. ▼

Bananas Boat, The (1974-British) **C-82m.** BOMB D: Sidney Hayers. Doug McClure, Hayley Mills, Lionel Jeffries, Warren Mitchell, Dilys Hamlett. Heavy-handed farce about young boob's attempts to escape from troubled banana republic by piloting boat out of its harbor. Originally titled WHAT CHANGED CHARLEY FARTHING, running-time 101m.▼

Bandido (1956) **C-92m.** *** D: Richard Fleischer. Robert Mitchum, Zachary Scott, Ursula Thiess, Gilbert Roland, Rodolfo Acosta. Mitchum is gun supplier who tries to play both sides during 1916 Mexican rebellion; constant action, endless cat-and-mouse twists with rival Scott keep this one humming.

Bandit of Sherwood Forest, The (1946) **C-86m.** **½ D: George Sherman, Henry Levin. Cornel Wilde, Anita Louise, Jill Esmond, Edgar Buchanan. Colorful but standard swashbuckler with Wilde as son of Robin Hood carrying on in faithful tradition with the Merry Men.

Bandit of Zhobe, The (1959-British) **C-80m.** **½ D: John Gilling. Victor Mature, Anthony Newley, Norman Wooland, Anne Aubrey, Walter Gotell, Sean Kelly. Moderate actioner set in 19th-century India with Mature as native chief turned outlaw combatting the British.

Bandits, The (1967-Mexican) **C-89m.** ** D: Robert Conrad, Alfredo Zacharias. Robert Conrad, Jan-Michael Vincent, Roy Jenson, Pedro Armendariz, Jr., Manuel Lopez Ochoa. Ordinary Western about three cowboys, saved from the hangman's noose, who accompany their Mexican rescuer on various adventures south of the border. Unreleased here until 1979.▼

Bandits (1986-French) **C-98m.** ** D:

Claude Lelouch. Jean Yanne, Marie-Sophie L. (Lelouch), Patrick Bruel, Corinne Marchand, Charles Gerard. Yanne is a criminal, just released from prison, who's out to revenge his wife's murder and become reunited with daughter Marie-Sophie L. (director Lelouch's real-life wife). Sentimental drama downplays the thrills in favor of a nostalgic approach similar to Lelouch's superior HAPPY NEW YEAR, in which Gerard played virtually an identical sidekick role. Striking widescreen photography will suffer on TV.

Bandits of Corsica, The (1953) 81m. ** D: Ray Nazarro. Richard Greene, Paula Raymond, Raymond Burr, Lee Van Cleef. Pat costumer with Greene championing cause of the righteous.

Band of Angels (1957) C-127m. **½ D: Raoul Walsh. Clark Gable, Yvonne De Carlo, Sidney Poitier, Efrem Zimbalist, Jr., Patric Knowles. Flat attempt to make costume epic of Robert Penn Warren's Civil War novel; Gable is Southern gentleman with shady past, in love with high-toned De Carlo who discovers she has Negro ancestors. Poitier is resolute educated slave.

Band of Outsiders (1964-French) 97m. *** D: Jean-Luc Godard. Anna Karina, Sami Frey, Claude Brasseur, Louisa Colpeyn. Karina enlists the aid of two male hoods to swipe her aunt's stash, but as usual the supposed plot is only a jumping-off point for Godard's commentary on Hollywood melodramas and other twentieth-century artifacts. Among the more entertaining of the director's output; looks delightfully mellow today.▼

Band of the Hand (1986) C-109m. BOMB D: Paul Michael Glaser. Stephen Lang, Michael Carmine, Lauren Holly, John Cameron Mitchell, James Remar, Daniele Quinn. Five Miami punks are whipped into shape by a Vietnam vet, then form a vigilante unit to wipe out drug dealers. Moronic, way overlong junk from the creators of *Miami Vice*; Bob Dylan (*why*, Bob?) sings the title tune. ▼

Bandolero! (1968) C-106m. **½ D: Andrew V. McLaglen. James Stewart, Dean Martin, Raquel Welch, George Kennedy, Andrew Prine, Will Geer. Jimmy and Dino play outlaw brothers whose gang flees across Mexican border with Raquel as hostage. Not exactly like real life, but nice outdoor photography makes it passable escapism.▼

Band Wagon, The (1953) C-112m. **** D: Vincente Minnelli. Fred Astaire, Cyd Charisse, Oscar Levant, Nanette Fabray, Jack Buchanan. Sophisticated backstage musical improves with each viewing. Astaire plays a "washed-up" movie star who tries his luck on Broadway, under the direction of maniacal genius Buchanan. Musical highlights include "Dancing in the Dark," "Shine on Your Shoes," and "That's Entertainment" (all by Howard Dietz and Arthur Schwartz) and Astaire's Mickey Spillane spoof "The Girl Hunt."▼

Bang Bang SEE: Bang Bang Kid, The▼

Bang-Bang Kid, The (1968-Spanish-Italian) C-90m. **½ D: Stanley Prager. Guy Madison, Tom Bosley, Sandra Milo, Riccardo Garrone, Jose Caffaral. Offbeat lighthearted turn-of-the-century Western that pits an iron-handed sheriff against an unassuming bumbler and a gun-toting robot called The Bang-Bang Kid. Also known as BANG BANG.▼

Bang, Bang, You're Dead! (1966-British) C-92m. **½ D: Don Sharp. Tony Randall, Senta Berger, Terry-Thomas, Herbert Lom, Wilfrid Hyde-White. Unsuspecting Randall gets involved with Moroccan gangsters in OK spoof; good location shooting. Shown on TV as BANG BANG!

Bang the Drum Slowly (1973) C-97m. ***½ D: John Hancock. Michael Moriarty, Robert De Niro, Vincent Gardenia, Phil Foster, Ann Wedgeworth, Patrick McVey, Heather MacRae, Selma Diamond, Barbara Babcock, Tom Ligon, Nicolas Surovy, Danny Aiello. Touching study of two professional baseball players on fictional N.Y. team drawn to each other under unusual circumstance. Outstanding performances by two leads (Moriarty as hustling star pitcher, De Niro as simpleton catcher) in slightly longish, episodic script. Screenplay by Mark Harris, based on his 1956 novel; first dramatized on television, with Paul Newman. ▼

Bang You're Dead SEE: Game of Danger

Banjo Hackett: Roamin' Free (1976) C-100m. TVM D: Andrew V. McLaglen. Don Meredith, Ike Eisenmann, Jennifer Warren, Chuck Connors, Dan O'Herlihy, Gloria DeHaven, Anne Francis, L. Q. Jones, Jeff Corey, Jan Murray. Itinerant horse trader travels Old West with orphaned 9-year-old nephew in quest of the youngster's stolen Arabian mare. Episodic film benefits from Meredith's easygoing style, fine supporting cast. Average.

Banjo on My Knee (1936) 96m. *** D: John Cromwell. Barbara Stanwyck, Joel McCrea, Walter Brennan, Buddy Ebsen, Helen Westley, Walter Catlett, Tony Martin. Stanwyck's the whole show in riverboat saga, singing with Martin, dancing with Ebsen, scrapping with Katherine DeMille.

Bank Dick, The (1940) 74m. **** D: Eddie Cline. W. C. Fields, Cora Witherspoon, Una Merkel, Evelyn Del Rio, Jessie Ralph, Grady Sutton, Franklin Pangborn, Shemp Howard, Russell Hicks, Reed Hadley. Classic of insane humor loosely wound about a no-account who becomes a bank guard; Sutton as nitwit prospective son-in-law, Pangborn as bank examiner match the shenanigans of Fields. Screenplay by "Mahatma Kane Jeeves."▼

Banker, The (1989) C-95m. *½ D: William Webb. Robert Forster, Duncan Regehr, Shanna Reed, Jeff Conaway, Leif Garrett, Richard Roundtree, Deborah Richter. Title character (Regehr) is murdering and mutilating prostitutes; police sergeant Forster sets out to trap him. By-the-book programmer.▼

Bank Shot (1974) C-83m. *** D: Gower Champion. George C. Scott, Joanna Cassidy, Sorrell Booke, G. Wood, Clifton James, Bob Balaban, Bibi Osterwald. Fastpaced, engagingly nutty comedy with criminal mastermind Scott planning a literal bank robbery—making off with the entire building! Based on the novel by Donald Westlake, a sequel to *The Hot Rock* (with Scott in the role played by Robert Redford in the film version of that book).▼

Bannerline (1951) 88m. ** D: Don Weis. Keefe Brasselle, Sally Forrest, Lionel Barrymore, Lewis Stone. Brasselle is optimistic fledgling reporter who sparks civic pride into town fighting corruption; film marred by typecasting and clichéd plotline.▼

Banning (1967) C-102m. *** D: Ron Winston. Robert Wagner, Anjanette Comer, Jill St. John, Guy Stockwell, James Farentino, Susan Clark, Howard St. John, Mike Kellin, Gene Hackman, Sean Garrison, Logan Ramsey. Entertaining soap opera about corruption and infidelity in and about a swank L.A. golf club. Wagner is the pro with a past, St. John a love-hungry young woman. Music score by Quincy Jones.

Banyon (1971) C-97m. TVM D: Robert Day. Robert Forster, Darren McGavin, Jose Ferrer, Herb Edelman. Private-eye (and one-time cop) in hot water with police when girl is discovered murdered in his office with his gun. Standard, formula plot made interesting by 1930s-era atmosphere, unusually effective use of color and Ed Adamson's no-nonsense script. Above average; pilot for TV series.

Barabbas (1962) C-134m. *** D: Richard Fleischer. Anthony Quinn, Silvana Mangano, Arthur Kennedy, Jack Palance, Ernest Borgnine, Katy Jurado. Lavish production, coupled with good script (based on Lagerkvist's novel) and generally fine acting by large cast make for engrossing, literate experience. Overly long.▼

Barbados Quest SEE: **Murder on Approval**

Barbarella (1968-French-Italian) C-98m. **½ D. Roger Vadim. Jane Fonda, John Phillip Law, Anita Pallenberg, Milo O' Shea, David Hemmings, Marcel Marceau, Claude Dauphin. Midnight-movie favorite based on popular French comic strip about sexy 41st-century space adventuress. Not especially funny, but watchable, with Fonda's strip-tease during opening credits the principal reason for its cult status. Trivia footnote: rock group Duran Duran took its name from O'Shea's character. Also known as BARBARELLA, QUEEN OF THE GALAXY.▼

Barbarian, The (1933) 82m. ** D: Sam Wood. Ramon Novarro, Myrna Loy, Reginald Denny, Louise Closser Hale, C. Aubrey Smith, Edward Arnold. Overbaked account of sleazy, superficially charming Arab guide Novarro, who persistently pursues tourist Loy. Set in Egypt; lots of Myrna on display here—including a nude bathing scene. Screenplay by Anita Loos and Elmer Harris.

Barbarian and the Geisha, The (1958) C-105m. **½ D: John Huston. John Wayne, Eiko Ando, Sam Jaffe, So Yamamura. Twisting of 19th-century history allows Wayne as Ambassador Harris to romance Japanese beauty (Ando). Miscasting of Wayne is ludicrous, throwing costumer amuck.▼

Barbarian and the Lady, The SEE: **Rebel Son, The**

Barbarians, The (1987) C-87m. *½ D: Ruggero Deodato. David Paul, Peter Paul, Richard Lynch, Eva La Rue, Virginia Bryant, Sheeba Alahani, Michael Berryman. Staggeringly silly sword-and-sorcery saga starring two awesome-looking bodybuilders (brothers in real life), whose main achievement is keeping a straight face while mouthing their dialogue.▼

Barbaric Beast of Boggy Creek, The, Part II (1985) C-91m. ** D: Charles B. Pierce. Charles B. Pierce, Cindy Butler, Serene Hedin, Chuck Pierce, Jimmy Clem. Slight, forgettable story of anthropology professor Pierce, who leads an expedition to find the Boggy Creek monster. Although titled "Part II," this is the third journey to Boggy Creek, following THE LEGEND OF . . . and RETURN TO . . . Filmed in 1983. Formerly titled BOGGY CREEK II.

Barbarosa (1982) C-90m. *** D: Fred Schepisi. Willie Nelson, Gary Busey, Isela Vega, Gilbert Roland, Danny De La Paz, George Voskovec. Nelson is fine as legendary, free-spirited outlaw constantly on the lam, with able support from Busey as country boy who becomes his protégé. Solid Western, flavorfully directed by Schepisi.▼

Barbary Coast (1935) 90m. ***½ D: Howard Hawks. Miriam Hopkins, Edward G. Robinson, Joel McCrea, Walter Brennan, Frank Craven, Brian Donlevy. Lusty tale of San Francisco in the late 19th century with dance-hall queen Hopkins running head-on into big-shot Robinson. David Niven can be glimpsed as an extra.▼

Barbary Coast, The (1974) C-100m. TVM D: Bill Bixby. William Shatner, Dennis Cole, Lynda Day George, John Vernon, Charles Aidman, Michael Ansara, Neville Brand, Bill Bixby. Undercover agent Shatner and casino owner Cole comb boomtown San Francisco for an extortionist. Lighthearted adventure tale attempted to recapture the flair of TV's popular *Wild, Wild West*, later became short-lived series under same title. Average.▼

Barbary Coast Gent (1944) 87m. ** D: Roy Del Ruth. Wallace Beery, Binnie Barnes, John Carradine, Noah Beery, Sr., Frances Rafferty, Chill Wills, Donald Meek. Typical Beery vehicle, with good supporting cast, about smooth-talking bandit who goes straight.

Bare Essence (1982) C-200m. TVM D: Walter Grauman. Bruce Boxleitner, Linda Evans, Genie Francis, Lee Grant, Joel Higgins, Donna Mills, Belinda Montgomery, Tim Thomerson, François-Marie Benard, John Dehner, John Larroquette. Life among the glamorous folks in the perfume business. Soap opera supreme, from Meredith Rich's novel, that later spun off into a short-lived series. Originally shown in two parts. Average.

Barefoot Contessa, The (1954) C-128m. *** D: Joseph L. Mankiewicz. Humphrey Bogart, Ava Gardner, Edmond O'Brien, Marius Goring, Rossano Brazzi, Valentina Cortesa, Elizabeth Sellars, Warren Stevens. Cynical tale of beautiful Spanish dancer Gardner and how director Bogart makes her a Hollywood star. Mankiewicz's script is full of juicy dialogue, as usual. O'Brien won an Oscar as the press agent.▼

Barefoot Executive, The (1971) C-96m. ** D: Robert Butler. Kurt Russell, Joe Flynn, Harry Morgan, Wally Cox, Heather North, Alan Hewitt, John Ritter. Russell discovers chimp with ability to pick top-rated TV shows, and becomes vice-president of a network. Routine Disney slapstick.▼

Barefoot in the Park (1967) C-105m. *** D: Gene Saks. Robert Redford, Jane Fonda, Charles Boyer, Mildred Natwick, Herb Edelman, Mabel Albertson, Fritz Feld. Plotless, entertaining Neil Simon comedy finds Fonda and Redford as newlyweds in five-story walkup apartment. Running gag about climbing stairs grows thin, but film doesn't. Later a brief TV series (with an all-black cast!)▼

Barefoot Mailman, The (1951) C-83m. ** D: Earl McEvoy. Robert Cummings, Terry Moore, Jerome Courtland, Will Geer. Potentially engaging story of a first postal route in Florida bogs down in tale of former con-man (Cummings) tempted to fleece citizens of Miami with phony railroad stock; Moore is pert leading lady.

Barefoot Savage SEE: Sensualita

Barfly (1987) C-97m. *** D: Barbet Schroeder. Mickey Rourke, Faye Dunaway, Alice Krige, Jack Nance, J.C. Quinn, Frank Stallone. Surprisingly enjoyable portrait of L.A. lowlife, and a boozy, foolishly macho writer played with comic bravado by Rourke. Dunaway is exceptional as his

alcoholic soulmate. Based on the autobiographical writings of cult favorite Charles Bukowski, who can be glimpsed on one of the bar stools. Veteran character actor Fritz Feld has a lovely bit as a bum who gives Dunaway a light.▼

Barkleys of Broadway, The (1949) C-109m. *** D: Charles Walters. Fred Astaire, Ginger Rogers, Oscar Levant, Billie Burke, Gale Robbins. Astaire and Rogers reteamed after ten years in this witty Comden-Green script about show biz couple who split, then make up. Songs include "You'd Be Hard to Replace," "They Can't Take That Away from Me." Ginger reading "La Marseillaise" is a definite low point.▼

Barnaby and Me (1977-Australian) C-90m. TVM D: Norman Panama. Sid Caesar, Juliet Mills, Sally Boyden, John Newcombe. Harmless family comedy about American con man who gets involved with a girl and her pet koala bear. Average.▼

Barnacle Bill (1941) 98m. ** D: Richard Thorpe. Wallace Beery, Marjorie Main, Leo Carrillo, Virginia Weidler, Donald Meek, Barton MacLane. Beery and Main support basically run-of-the-mill material as old salt and woman trying to snare him into marriage.

Baron and the Kid, The (1984) C-100m. TVM D: Gary Nelson. Johnny Cash, Darren McGavin, Greg Webb, Tracy Pollan, June Carter Cash, Richard Roundtree, Claude Akins. Traveling pool hustler Cash joins forces with the son he never knew after the latter pops into his life. Like Kenny Rogers's THE GAMBLER, this is an uninspired expansion of Cash's hit song "The Baron." Average.▼

Baron Blood (1972-Italian) C-90m. **½ D: Mario Bava. Joseph Cotten, Elke Sommer, Massimo Girotti, Rada Rassimov, Antonio Cantafora, Alan Collins. Descendant of evil nobleman attempts "novel" rejuvenation principles. Standard plot livened by unusual settings and lighting. Retitled THE TORTURE CHAMBER OF BARON BLOOD. Original Italian version runs longer.▼

Baron Müenchhausen (1943-German) C-110m. *** D: Josef von Baky. Hans Albers, Brigitte Horney, Wilhelm Bendow, Leo Slezak, Ferdinand Marian. Lavish, impressive curio which tells of the legendary, free-spirited Baron, his exploits in Russia, Turkey, Venice, and elsewhere, and his quest for beautiful princesses and empresses. While the film is ostensibly an escapist entertainment, it does offer a depiction of the Baron as an heroic German: noble, shrewd, and ever loyal to the Fatherland. Produced on the order of Goebbels, Hitler's Minister of Propaganda and Public Enlightenment, to mark the 25th anniversary of UFA, the German production studio. This would make a fascinating (if overlong) double bill with Terry Gilliam's

THE ADVENTURES OF BARON MUNCHAUSEN.▼
Baroness and the Butler, The (1938) 75m. ** D: Walter Lang. William Powell, Annabella, Helen Westley, Henry Stephenson, Joseph Schildkraut, J. Edward Bromberg. Powell leads double life as Annabella's butler and member of parliament. He's fine as usual but script is rather thin.
Baron of Arizona, The (1950) 90m. **½ D: Samuel Fuller. Vincent Price, Ellen Drew, Beulah Bondi, Reed Hadley. Price has field day as landgrabbing scoundrel who almost gains control of Arizona in the 19th century.
Baron's African War, The (1943) 100m. **½ D: Spencer Bennet. Rod Cameron, Joan Marsh, Duncan Renaldo, Lionel Royce. Flavorful actioner set in WW2 Africa, with Cameron tackling sinister Nazis and Arabs with equal relish; quite well paced. Reedited from Republic serial SECRET SERVICE IN DARKEST AFRICA.
Barquero (1970) C-115m. *½ D: Gordon Douglas. Lee Van Cleef, Warren Oates, Forrest Tucker, Kerwin Mathews, Mariette Hartley. Bad-guy Oates, on the run after wiping out a town, has to deal with Van Cleef, a feisty ferry operator, in order to escape.
Barracuda (1978) C-90m. ** D: Harry Kerwin. Wayne-David Crawford, Jason Evers, Bert Freed, Roberta Leighton, Cliff Emmich. Chemical dumping affects fish and then people in small Florida community. Predictable formula film. Also known as THE LUCIFER PROJECT.▼
Barretts of Wimpole Street, The (1934) 110m. *** D: Sidney Franklin. Norma Shearer, Fredric March, Charles Laughton, Maureen O'Sullivan, Katherine Alexander, Una O'Connor, Ian Wolfe. Handsome, well-acted (if somewhat stodgy) MGM production of classic romance between Elizabeth Barrett and Robert Browning in 19th century England. Director Franklin remade this two decades later. Retitled for TV: FORBIDDEN ALLIANCE.
Barretts of Wimpole Street, The (1957-U.S.-British) C-105m. **½ D: Sidney Franklin. Jennifer Jones, John Gielgud, Bill Travers, Virginia McKenna. Tame interpretation of the lilting romance between poets Browning, Barrett, with actors bogged down in prettified fluff. Director Franklin fared better with this material in 1934.
Barricade (1939) 71m. ** D: Gregory Ratoff. Alice Faye, Warner Baxter, Charles Winninger, Arthur Treacher, Keye Luke, Moroni Olsen. Faye and Baxter are trapped in Chinese embassy and fall in love; rather tame.
Barricade (1950) C-75m. ** D: Peter Godfrey. Dane Clark, Ruth Roman, Raymond Massey, Robert Douglas. Clark pitted against Massey in gold-mining-camp Western lends a spark to usual battle of good vs. evil. Mild rehash of THE SEA WOLF.
Barrier (1966-Polish) 84m. **½ D: Jerzy Skolimowski. Joanna Szczerbic, Jan Nowicki, Tadeusz Lomnicki, Maria Malicka. Interesting view of youthful attitudes in Poland, combining reportage with fantasy elements. Not a total success, but still intriguing.
Barry Lyndon (1975-British) C-183m. ***½ D: Stanley Kubrick. Ryan O'Neal, Marisa Berenson. Patrick Magee, Hardy Kruger, Steven Berkoff, Gay Hamilton, Murray Melvin, Frank Middlemass, Andre Morell, Leonard Rossiter, Marie Kean, narrated by Michael Hordern. Exquisite, meticulously detailed period piece stars O'Neal as Thackeray's 18th-century Irish rogue-hero who covets success but lets it go to his head. Long, deliberately paced but never boring. Four Oscars include John Alcott's photography, Leonard Rosenman's adaptation of period music, Art Decoration-Set Decoration, and Costume Design. Screenplay by Kubrick.▼
Barry Mackenzie Holds His Own (1974-Australian) C-93m. *½ D: Bruce Beresford. Barry Crocker, Barry Humphries, Donald Pleasence, Dick Bentley, Louis Negin. Idiotic follow-up to THE ADVENTURES OF BARRY MACKENZIE, about oafish title character, his twin brother (both played by Crocker), and one Edna Everage (Humphries, in drag), who is kidnapped and taken to Transylvania.▼
Bar Sinister SEE: **It's a Dog's Life**
Bartleby (1972-British) C-78m. **½ D: Anthony Friedmann. Paul Scofield, John McEnery, Thorley Walters, Colin Jeavons, Raymond Mason. Herman Melville's great short story about 19th-century auditing clerk who refuses to leave job after he is fired is admirably attempted in modern-day update, even though story doesn't really lend itself to filming; Scofield is fine as bewildered but sympathetic boss.▼
Bashful Elephant, The (1962-German) 82m. BOMB D: Dorrell McGowan, Stuart E. McGowan. Molly Mack, Helmut Schmid, Kai Fischer, Buddy Baer. Supposedly a family film, this import spends more time on an elephant trainer's divorce than anything else. Not worth your time.
Basic Training (1985) C-88m. *½ D: Andrew Sugerman. Ann Dusenberry, Rhonda Shear, Angela Aames, Will Nye, Walter Gotell. Lamebrained raunch comedy about young woman who overcomes sexual harassment in the Pentagon by turning the tables on the lechers who surround her and her buxom colleagues. Pretty rank. Filmed in 1983.▼
Basileus Quartet (1982-French-Italian) C-118m. *** D: Fabio Carpi. Pierre Malet,

[70]

Hector Alterio, Omero Antonutti, Michel Vitold, Alain Cuny, Gabriele Ferzetti, Lisa Kreuzer. A violinist suddenly dies and his colleagues, who have lived only for music, must get on with their lives—which are profoundly altered by the young replacement for the deceased. Stark, quietly absorbing, beautifully realized.▼

Basket Case (1982) **C-91m.** **½ D: Frank Henenlotter. Kevin VanHentryck, Terri Susan Smith, Beverly Bonner, Robert Vogel, Diana Browne. Extremely self-conscious but intriguing tongue-in-cheek low-budget horror film about a twin who arrives in N.Y.C. from a small town carrying his deformed telepathic mutant brother in a basket. Some interesting animated sequences in this John Waters-ish film that boasts some effective horror moments. Followed by a sequel.▼

Bastard, The (1978) **C-200m. TVM** D: Lee H. Katzin. Andrew Stevens, Noah Beery, Peter Bonerz, Tom Bosley, Kim Cattrall, John Colicos, William Daniels, Buddy Ebsen, Lorne Greene, James Gregory, Olivia Hussey, Cameron Mitchell, Harry Morgan, Patricia Neal, Eleanor Parker, Donald Pleasence, William Shatner, Barry Sullivan, Keenan Wynn, Raymond Burr (narrator). Illegitimate Philip Kent searches through England and France for his birthright and is ultimately involved in the American Revolution. First of three TV adaptations of John Jakes's historical novels THE REBELS and THE SEEKERS later completed the trilogy. Also called THE KENT CHRONICLES. Originally shown in two parts. Average.

Bat, The (1959) **80m.** **½ D: Crane Wilbur. Vincent Price, Agnes Moorehead, Gavin Gordon, John Sutton, Lenita Lane, Darla Hood. Faithful adaptation of Mary Roberts Rinehart novel (filmed before in 1915, 1926 and—as THE BAT WHISPERS —in 1930), set in old gothic mansion. Fairly exciting yarn.▼

✓ **Bataan** (1943) **114m.** *** D: Tay Garnett. Robert Taylor, George Murphy, Thomas Mitchell, Lloyd Nolan, Lee Bowman, Robert Walker, Desi Arnaz, Barry Nelson. Realistically made drama of famous WW2 incident on Pacific Island; good combat scenes. Also shown in computer-colored version.▼

Bates Motel (1987) **C-100m. TVM** D: Richard Rothstein. Bud Cort, Jason Bateman, Gregg Henry, Khrystyne Haje, Moses Gunn. Misguided pilot to a proposed teen-oriented series; thankfully Hitchcock wasn't around to see what's become of the digs Norman Bates inherited in PSYCHO. Bates has handed the hostelry over to a fellow mental hospital inmate (Cort) who's being unleashed on the real world. (Even Tony Perkins boycotted this one.) Below average.

Bathing Beauty (1944) **C-101m.** **½ D:

George Sidney. Red Skelton, Esther Williams, Basil Rathbone, Ethel Smith, Xavier Cugat, Lina Romay, Harry James and His Orchestra. Esther's first starring vehicle gives Skelton and musical guest stars the spotlight most of the way, but does have a spectacular aquatic finale. Silly script, thankless role for Rathbone.

Batman (1966) **C-105m.** ** D: Leslie ✓ Martinson. Adam West, Burt Ward, Burgess Meredith, Cesar Romero, Frank Gorshin, Lee Meriwether, Neil Hamilton, Madge Blake, Reginald Denny. Quickly made feature to cash in on then-hot TV series pulls out all stops, features the Joker, Riddler, Penguin, and Catwoman trying to undo the caped crusader. Really misses the mark; the campy humor worked better in the TV series. Bears no relation to the 1989 blockbuster.▼

Batman (1989) **C-126m.** **½ D: Tim ✓ Burton. Jack Nicholson, Michael Keaton, Kim Basinger, Robert Wuhl, Pat Hingle, Billy Dee Williams, Michael Gough, Jack Palance, Jerry Hall, Tracey Walter, Lee Wallace. There's razzle-dazzle to spare in this dark, intense variation on Bob Kane's comic book creation—but there's also something askew when the villain (a particularly psychotic villain, played overboard by Nicholson) is so much more potent than the hero! Still, lots to grab your attention, including Anton Furst's Oscar-winning production design and Danny Elfman's terrific score. Prince contributes several songs.▼

Batmen of Africa (1936) **100m.** ** D: B. Reeves Eason, Joseph Kane. Clyde Beatty, Manuel King, Elaine Shepard, Lucien Prival. Diverting cliffhanger (Republic Pictures' first serial) ofBeatty leading expedition to jungle city torescue captured white girl; good special effects, primitive acting. Reedited movie serial: DARKEST AFRICA.

Bat People (1974) **C-95m.** *½ D: Jerry Jameson. Stewart Moss, Marianne McAndrew, Michael Pataki, Paul Carr, Arthur Space. A doctor is bitten by a bat while on his honeymoon, with expected results. Paltry horror entry from AIP, originally titled IT LIVES BY NIGHT.▼

Battered (1978) **C-100m. TVM** D: Peter Werner. Karen Grassle, LeVar Burton, Mike Farrell, Joan Blondell, Howard Duff, Chip Fields. Absorbing and disturbing drama interweaves three stories of wife-beating victims; Grassle also co-wrote this teleplay with Cynthia Lovelace Sears. Average.▼

***batteries not included** (1987) **C-106m.** ** D: Matthew Robbins. Hume Cronyn, Jessica Tandy, Frank McRae, Elizabeth Pena, Michael Carmine, Dennis Boutsikaris. Steven Spielberg's Amblin Productions has gone to the same well once too often. Cloying sci-fi fantasy has a "family" of small alien spacecrafts arrive from outer space to assist New Yorkers whose tenement is about to be demolished. Cronyn and Tandy do far more for the film than it does for them.▼

Battle at Apache Pass, The (1952) C-85m. **½ D: George Sherman. Jeff Chandler, John Lund, Beverly Tyler, Richard Egan, Hugh O'Brian, Jay Silverheels. Chandler reprises his BROKEN ARROW role as Cochise, who tries to prevent Indian wars but doesn't quite succeed.

Battle at Bloody Beach (1961) 83m. **½ D: Herbert Coleman. Audie Murphy, Gary Crosby, Dolores Michaels, Alejandro Rey. Sporadically exciting WW2 action with soldier Murphy locating his wife on a Pacific Island, involved with partisan cause and its leader.

Battleaxe, The (1962-British) 66m. ** D: Godfrey Grayson. Jill Ireland, Francis Matthews, Joan Haythorne, Michael Beint. Obvious sex farce with Matthews suing Ireland for breach of promise, Haythorne in title role supplying expected gags.

Battle Beneath the Earth (1967-British) C-91m. **½ D: Montgomery Tully. Kerwin Mathews, Viviana Ventura, Robert Ayres, Peter Arne, Al Mulock, Martin Benson. Silly but enjoyable pulp fantasy about Chinese plan to invade U.S. through network of tunnels.▼

Battle Beyond the Stars (1980) C-104m. **½ D: Jimmy T. Murakami. Richard Thomas, John Saxon, Robert Vaughn, Darlanne Fleugel, George Peppard, Sybil Danning, Sam Jaffe, Morgan Woodward. Not-bad space saga from Roger Corman, with good special effects and a John Sayles script that uses the reliable SEVEN SAMURAI/MAGNIFICENT SEVEN formula (with Vaughn from the SEVEN cast). Sets and special effects were reused for countless subsequent Corman cheapies.▼

Battle Beyond the Sun (1963) C-75m. ** D: Thomas Colchart. Edd Perry, Arla Powell, Andy Stewart, Bruce Hunter. Russian film NEBO ZOWET refashioned into American product by producer Roger Corman; story deals with rival space missions to Mars. Director Colchart is actually Francis Ford Coppola.▼

Battle Circus (1953) 90m. ** D: Richard Brooks. Humphrey Bogart, June Allyson, Keenan Wynn, Robert Keith, Philip Ahn. Soaper of doctor under fire during Korean war; Bogie saddled with bad script and syrupy June.

Battle Cry (1955) C-149m. *** D: Raoul Walsh. Van Heflin, Tab Hunter, Dorothy Malone, Anne Francis, Raymond Massey, Mona Freeman, Aldo Ray, James Whitmore, Nancy Olson, William Campbell, Fess Parker. Entertaining (if watered-down) version of Leon Uris WW2 Marine novel, focusing on servicemen in training, action, and in love. Hunter as wholesome soldier and Malone a love-hungry dame stand out in episodic actioner, which now seems less than daring. Film debut of Justus McQueen, who thereafter acted under the name of his character, L.Q. Jones.▼

Battle Flame (1959) 78m. *½ D: R. G. Springsteen. Scott Brady, Elaine Edwards, Robert Blake, Gordon Jones, Wayne Heffley, Richard Harrison. Programmer about Korean War and soldier Brady's romance with nurse Edwards.

Battle for Anzio, The SEE: Anzio▼

Battle for the Planet of the Apes (1973) C-92m. ** D: J. Lee Thompson. Roddy McDowall, Natalie Trundy, Severn Darden, Paul Williams, Claude Akins, John Huston. Substandard; fifth (and last) apes installment attempts to bring entire series fullcycle. Good footage from earlier films helps, but not much. A TV series followed.▼

Battle Force SEE: **Great Battle, The**▼

Battleground (1949) 118m. *** D: William Wellman. Van Johnson, John Hodiak, Ricardo Montalban, George Murphy, Marshall Thompson, Denise Darcel, Don Taylor, Richard Jaeckel, James Whitmore, James Arness, Scotty Beckett. Star-studded replay of Battle of the Bulge: division of American troops, their problems and reactions to war. Robert Pirosh's slick script, which was awarded an Oscar, lacks genuine insight into the characters; Paul C. Vogel also earned a statuette for his cinematography. Also shown in computer-colored version.▼

Battle Hymn (1956) C-108m. *** D: Douglas Sirk. Rock Hudson, Martha Hyer, Anna Kashfi, Dan Duryea, Don DeFore. Hudson turns in convincing performance as clergyman who returns to military duty in Korean War to train fighter pilots; expansive production values.

Battle in Outer Space (1960-Japanese) C-74m. *½ D: Inoshiro Honda. Ryo Ikebe, Kyoko Anzai, Leonard Stanford, Harold Conway. Unexciting sci-fi as Earth prepares for attack from outer space. Plenty of special effects.

Battle of Algiers, The (1965-Italian-Algerian) 123m. *** D: Gillo Pontecorvo. Yacef Saadi, Jean Martin, Brahim Haggiag, Tommaso Neri, Samia Kerbash. Straightforward drama about revolt against the French by Algerians from 1954-1962. Winner of many awards, but the objective, pseudo-documentary fashion in which it was filmed somewhat limits its dramatic power. Nonetheless, a good film.▼

Battle of Austerlitz, The (1960-French-Italian-Yugoslavian-Lichtensteiner) C-123m. *½ D: Abel Gance. Claudia Cardinale, Martine Carol, Leslie Caron, Vittorio De Sica, Jean Marais, Ettore Manni, Jack Palance, Orson Welles. International cast reenacts the epic of Napoleon's greatest battle in stultifying fashion. Drastic cutting from original length (166m.) and terrible dubbing job doom it. Originally titled AUSTERLITZ.▼

Battle of Britain (1969-British) C-132m.

[72]

** D: Guy Hamilton. Harry Andrews, Michael Caine, Trevor Howard, Curt Jurgens, Kenneth More, Laurence Olivier, Christopher Plummer, Michael Redgrave, Ralph Richardson, Robert Shaw, Susannah York. Superb aerial sequences, which will suffer on TV anyway, hardly redeem yet another "spot-the-star" WW2 epic, this time about British airmen who prevented threatened Nazi invasion.▼

Battle of El Alamein (1968-Italian-French) **C-105m.** ** D: Calvin Jackson Padget (Giorgio Ferroni). Frederick Stafford, Ettore Manni, Robert Hossein, Michael Rennie, George Hilton, Ira Furstenberg. Plenty of action as Italians and Germans, partners in an uneasy alliance, fight the British in the North African desert in 1942. Hossein plays Rommel, and Rennie does an unsympathetic Field Marshal Montgomery (the British are the villains in this one).▼

Battle of Mareth, The SEE: **Greatest Battle, The**▼

Battle of Neretva, The (1971-Yugoslavian-U.S.-Italian-German) **C-102m.** ** D: Veljko Bulajic. Yul Brynner, Sergei Bondarchuk, Curt Jurgens, Sylva Koscina, Hardy Kruger, Franco Nero, Orson Welles. Originally an Oscar nominee for Best Foreign Film, but when this $12 million spectacle about Nazi invasion of Yugoslavia was cut down from a nearly three-hour running time, it lost most of its coherency. Too bad.▼

Battle of Rogue River (1954) **C-71m.** ** D: William Castle. George Montgomery, Richard Denning, Martha Hyer, John Crawford. Much needed action sequence never comes in lopsided Western of Montgomery negotiating Indian truce as settlers seek statehood for Oregon in 1850s.

Battle of the Bulge (1965) **C-163m.** ** D: Ken Annakin. Henry Fonda, Robert Shaw, Robert Ryan, Telly Savalas, Dana Andrews, George Montgomery, Ty Hardin, Pier Angeli, Charles Bronson. Originally produced in Cinerama, this overinflated war drama about an important event cannot triumph over banal script. Read a good book on the subject instead.▼

Battle of the Commandos (1969-Italian) **C-94m.** ** D: Umberto Lenzi. Jack Palance, Curt Jurgens, Tomas Hunter, Diana Lorys, Wolfgang Preiss, Robert Hundar. Palance leads a small band of commandos on an assault on a powerful German cannon that has to be destroyed before the D-Day invasion. Also called LEGION OF THE DAMNED.▼

Battle of the Coral Sea (1959) **80m.** **½ D: Paul Wendkos. Cliff Robertson, Gia Scala, Teru Shimada, Patricia Cutts, Gene Blakely, Gordon Jones. Staunch Robertson is submarine captain on Japanese-held island during WW2, seeking to send vital data to U.S. fleet.

Battle of the River Plate SEE: **Pursuit of the Graf Spee**▼

Battle of the Sexes, The (1960-British) **84m.** *** D: Charles Crichton. Peter Sellers, Robert Morley, Constance Cummings, Jameson Clark. Sparkling British comedy with macabre overtones; Sellers is elderly Scotsman contemplating murder. Supporting cast keeps this moving.▼

Battle of the Villa Fiorita, The (1965-British) **C-111m.** **½ D: Delmer Daves. Maureen O'Hara, Rossano Brazzi, Richard Todd, Phyllis Calvert, Martin Stephens. Unconvincing soaper with O'Hara running off to Italy to carry on with widower Brazzi; predictable interference from each's children.

Battle of the Worlds (1961-Italian) **C-84m.** *½ D: Anthony Dawson (Antonio Margheriti). Claude Rains, Maya Brent, Bill Carter, Umberto Orsini, Jacqueline Derval. Rains adds some weight to this English-dubbed cheapie about scientists' frantic efforts to stop alien planet from colliding with Earth. Eerie atmosphere also helps a little.▼

Battleship Potemkin SEE: **Potemkin**▼

Battle Shock SEE: **Woman's Devotion, A**

Battlestar: Galactica (1979) **C-125m.** **½ D: Richard A. Colla. Richard Hatch, Dirk Benedict, Lorne Greene, Ray Milland, John Colicos, Patrick Macnee, Lew Ayres, Jane Seymour, Laurette Spang, Terry Carter. Feature cut down from first and fifth episodes of short-lived TV series; Greene is commander of starship taking survivors of doomed planet in search of new home. Belongs on small screen, where it's moderately interesting and John Dykstra's special effects come off best. Premiere originally telecast at 148m.▼

Battle Stations (1956) **81m.** *½ D: Lewis Seiler. John Lund, William Bendix, Keefe Brasselle, Richard Boone. Rehash about crew in WW2 Pacific and their preparation for fighting the Japs.

Battle Stripe SEE: **Men, The**▼

Battle Taxi (1955) **82m.** ** D: Herbert L. Strock. Sterling Hayden, Arthur Franz, Marshall Thompson, Joel Marston, Leo Needham. Ordinary tale of Korean War missions; strictly pedestrian.

Battletruck SEE: **Warlords of the 21st Century**▼

Battle Zone (1952) **82m.** ** D: Lesley Selander. John Hodiak, Linda Christian, Stephen McNally, Philip Ahn. Hodiak vies with McNally for Christian, with brief time out to fight Commies in static Korean War film.

Battling Bellhop SEE: **Kid Galahad** (1937)

Battling Hoofer SEE: **Something to Sing About**▼

Bat 21 (1988) **C-105m.** *** D: Peter Markle. Gene Hackman, Danny Glover, Jerry Reed, David Marshall Grant, Clayton Rohner, Erich Anderson, Joe Dorsey. Air Force Colonel and strategist Hackman has only seen the war from 30,000 feet, until he's up to Glover to get him out behind enemy lines. Now it's up to Glover to get him out before the NVC get him, and before his own forces carpet-bomb the area. Taut, compelling film, based on a true story, with fine acting all around. Costar Reed was executive producer and wrote some of the songs for the soundtrack.▼

Bawdy Adventures of Tom Jones, The (1976-British) **C-94m.** ** D: Cliff Owen. Nicky Henson, Trevor Howard, Joan Collins, Terry-Thomas, Arthur Lowe, Georgia Brown. Mild doings, based on London stage musical, can't hold a candle to 1963 classic. This time, Tom's (Henson) amorous adventures are pat and predictable, with Collins, as highwaywoman Black Bess, adding only zing.▼

Baxter (1973) **C-100m.** *** D: Lionel Jeffries. Patricia Neal, Scott Jacoby, Jean-Pierre Cassel, Lynn Carlin, Britt Ekland, Sally Thomsett, Paul Eddington. Well acted drama about young Jacoby's emotional problems and his relationship with speech therapist Neal, who tries to correct his lisp.

Bay Boy, The (1984-Canadian-French) **C-107m.** ** D: Daniel Petrie. Liv Ullmann, Kiefer Sutherland, Peter Donat, Mathieu Carriere, Isabelle Mejias, Alan Scarfe, Chris Wiggins, Leah Pinsent. Well-meaning but hopelessly predictable portrayal of a teenager (Sutherland, son of Donald), and his coming of age in rural Canadian community during 1930s. You've seen this one many times before; Ullmann in particular is one-dimensional as Sutherland's hardworking mother.▼

Bay Coven (1987) **C-100m.** TVM D: Carl Schenkel. Pamela Sue Martin, Tim Matheson, Barbara Billingsley, Jeff Conaway, Woody Harrelson, Susan Ruttan, James Sikking, Inga Swenson. Labored drama of modern-day witchcraft with yuppie couple moving into a quaint village and finding their neighbors part of an ancient witches' coven. Also known as STRANGERS IN TOWN. Average.

Bay of Saint Michel, The (1963-British) **73m.** ** D: John Ainsworth. Keenan Wynn, Mai Zetterling, Ronald Howard, Rona Anderson. Adequate actioner concerning trio of ex-commandos hunting for Nazi buried treasure, with expected conflicts and murders. Retitled: OPERATION MERMAID.

Baywatch: Panic at Malibu Pier (1989) **C-100m.** TVM D: Richard Compton. David Hasselhoff, Parker Stevenson, Shawn Weatherly, Gina Hecht, Billy Warlock, Monte Markham, Richard Jaeckel. Pilot feature about Southern California lifeguards and assorted damp damsels in distress.

The budget certainly didn't go for costumes judging from the skimpy bikinis—male and female. Later a TV series. Average.

Beach Ball (1965) **C-83m.** ** D: Lennie Weinrib. Edd Byrnes, Chris Noel, Robert Logan, Gale Gilmore, Aron Kincaid. Different group tries a beach picture, but it's essentially the same. Pretty girls, surfing, Edd in drag, and performances by The Supremes, Four Seasons, Righteous Bros., Hondells, Walker Bros.

Beach Blanket Bingo (1965) **C-98m.** *** D: William Asher. Frankie Avalon, Annette Funicello, Paul Lynde, Harvey Lembeck, Don Rickles, Linda Evans, Jody McCrea, Marta Kristen, John Ashley, Deborah Walley, Buster Keaton, Bobbi Shaw, Timothy Carey. Fifth BEACH PARTY movie is the best (and best known); amid various plot entanglements (parachuting, kidnapped singing idol Evans, mermaid Kristen), Lynde sneers at everybody, Rickles insults everybody, and Lembeck gets to sing before being cut into two halves by Carey's buzzsaw. For those so inclined, the ultimate wallow in '60s nostalgia. Sequel: HOW TO STUFF A WILD BIKINI.▼

Beach Boys: An American Band, The (1985) **C-103m.** ** D: Malcolm Leo. Ineffectual "authorized" bio of the Boys lacks focus and peters out after a delightful opening half hour. High points: numbers long excised from THE T.A.M.I SHOW, hilarious clip from THE GIRLS ON THE BEACH, wild TV appearance on a Bob Hope special.▼

Beachcomber, The (1938-British) **92m.** *** D: Erich Pommer. Charles Laughton, Elsa Lanchester, Tyrone Guthrie, Robert Newton, Dolly Mollinger. Disheveled bum Laughton, living on island paradise, is reformed by missionary Lanchester. Two stars (married in real-life) delightful in filmization of W. Somerset Maugham story originally titled VESSEL OF WRATH. The sole directorial outing of esteemed German producer (and Laughton partner) Pommer. Remade in 1955.▼

Beachcomber, The (1955-British) **C-82m.** *** D: Muriel Box. Glynis Johns, Robert Newton, Donald Sinden, Michael Hordern, Donald Pleasence. Remake of Somerset Maugham tale of South Sea island bum entangled with strait-laced sister of missionary is still flavorful.

Beaches (1988) **C-123m.** **½ D: Garry Marshall. Bette Midler, Barbara Hershey, John Heard, Spalding Gray, Lainie Kazan, James Read, Grace Johnston, Mayim Bialik, Marcie Leeds. Bittersweet saga of a thirty-year friendship that begins when two girls—one rich and pampered, the other poor and driven to show-biz success—meet on the beach at Atlantic City. As soap-opera storytelling it's just OK (not much depth to the characters and their motives, and at least two endings too many) but as a vehicle for Midler it's dynamite, with several opportunities for her to sing. Based on a novel by Iris Rainer Dart; Midler coproduced. Director Marshall features his on-screen "regulars" in a variety of cameo roles, including Hector Elizondo as a justice of the peace.▼

Beachhead (1954) C-89m. *** D: Stuart Heisler. Tony Curtis, Frank Lovejoy, Mary Murphy, Eduard Franz, Skip Homeier. Nicely handled action of marine quartet on dangerous mission in WW2.

Beach Party (1963) C-101m. ** D: William Asher. Frankie Avalon, Annette Funicello, Bob Cummings, Dorothy Malone, Harvey Lembeck, Jody McCrea, John Ashley, Morey Amsterdam, Candy Johnson, Eva Six. Anthropologist Cummings studies teenagers' "wild" behavior, but comes to learn they aren't so bad after all. First in long-running series is typical blend of slapstick and forgettable songs, as well as introduction of Lembeck's dopey Brando-biker takeoff, Eric Von Zipper. Sequel: MUSCLE BEACH PARTY.▼

Beach Patrol (1979) C-100m. TVM D: Bob Kelljan. Robin Strand, Jonathan Frakes, Christine DeLisle, Richard Hill, Paul Burke, Michael V. Gazzo. A *Rookies*-in-dune-buggies series pilot for action freaks and bikini watchers. Below average.

Beach Red (1967) C-105m. *** D: Cornel Wilde. Cornel Wilde, Rip Torn, Burr De Benning, Patrick Wolfe, Jean Wallace. Hard look at military life in South Pacific attempts to show ugly side of war. Likely to be watered down for TV.

Bear, The (1984) C-112m. ** D: Richard Sarafian. Gary Busey, Cynthia Leake, Harry Dean Stanton, Jon-Erik Hexum, Carmen Thomas, Cary Guffey, D'Urville Martin. Incredibly corny, old-fashioned Hollywood bio of famed collegiate football coach Paul "Bear" Bryant. Busey's sincere, gravel-voiced portrayal can't compensate for episodic, repetitive, and undramatic script.

Bear, The (1989-French) C-93m. *** D: Jean-Jacques Annaud. Bart, Douce, Jack Wallace, Tcheky Karyo, Andre Lacombe. Captivating and unusual film about a bear cub who is orphaned and forced to fend for itself, until it finds a new protector in a giant Kodiak—the tempting target for a pair of hunters. Filmed with utmost respect for animals and a real sense of nature's magnificence, there's still a level of manipulation in all of this that causes a bit of discomfort. Based on *The Grizzly King*, a 1916 novel by James Oliver Curwood.▼

Bear Island (1980-British-Canadian) C-118m. *½ D: Don Sharp. Donald Sutherland, Vanessa Redgrave, Richard Widmark, Christopher Lee, Barbara Parkins, Lloyd Bridges, Lawrence Dane. One of Alistair MacLean's best novels unfortunately became one of his worst films, mixing murder, intrigue and stolen bullion near the top of the world. Strong cast, capable director and scenic locations go for naught. Barely released to theatres.▼

Bears and I, The (1974) C-89m. *½ D: Bernard McEveety. Patrick Wayne, Chief Dan George, Andrew Duggan, Michael Ansara. Vietnam vet Wayne tries to soothe relations in North Woods between Indians and white bigots. Mild Disney film.▼

Beast, The (1988) C-109m. ** D: Kevin Reynolds. Jason Patric, Steven Bauer, George Dzundza, Stephen Baldwin, Don Harvey, Kabir Bedi, Erick Avari, Haim Gerafi. Soviet tank, cut off from its battalion in Afghan desert, tries to reach safety, while pursued by vengeful Afghan rebels. Eventually, a peace-minded Russian from the tank, left to die by his brutal commander, joins the rebels himself. Serviceable (if predictable) plot is undermined by ponderous pace and stereotyped characters. Filmed in Israel.▼

Beast from Haunted Cave (1960) 64m. ** D: Monte Hellman. Michael Forest, Sheila Carol, Frank Wolff, Richard Sinatra, Wally Campo. Economically shot (to say the least) by Roger Corman's company on scenic locations near Deadwood, South Dakota, this pits fleeing robbers against a mysterious, spiderlike monster. Charles B. Griffith script has some good dialogue, and Sinatra (Frank's nephew) and Carol showed promise. Monster created and played by actor Chris Robinson. Remake of NAKED PARADISE, with monster added.▼

Beast From 20,000 Fathoms, The (1953) 80m. ** D: Eugene Lourie. Paul Christian, Paula Raymond, Cecil Kellaway, Donald Woods, Lee Van Cleef, Ross Elliot. Prehistoric rhedosaurus wreaks havoc when thawed after an atom-bomb blast. Good Ray Harryhausen special effects. Suggested by the Ray Bradbury short story "The Fog Horn."

Beast in the Cellar, The (1971-British) C-87m. ** D: James Kelly. Beryl Reid, Flora Robson, John Hamill, T. P. McKenna, Tessa Wyatt. Two sisters hide their maniac brother in the cellar; performances of Reid and Robson brings movie to average level. British running time was 101m.▼

Beastmaster, The (1982) C-118m. ** D: Don Coscarelli. Marc Singer, Tanya Roberts, Rip Torn, John Amos, Rod Loomis. Yet another sword and sandal fantasy with Conan/Tarzan-clone hero who communicates with animals (including, believe it or not, some comedic ferrets), falls in love with slave girl Roberts and seeks revenge against evil priest (Torn) who killed his father. Cinematography by Oscar winner John Alcott (BARRY LYNDON).▼

Beast Must Die, The (1974-British) **C-93m.** *** D: Paul Annett. Calvin Lockhart, Peter Cushing, Charles Gray, Marlene Clark, Anton Diffring. New twists on the old werewolf theme make the difference. Millionaire sportsman Lockhart invites guests to his electronically bugged mansion, knowing one of them is a werewolf. Lockhart is overly mannered, while Cushing gains sympathy in his usual quiet but effective way. Like TEN LITTLE INDIANS, this movie gives the audience a minute to guess the killer's identity. Retitled BLACK WEREWOLF for home video.▼

Beast of Blood SEE: **Beast of the Dead**

Beast of Budapest, The (1958) 72m. *½ D: Harmon Jones. Gerald Milton, John Hoyt, Greta Thyssen, Michael Mills. Trite rendering of father vs. son conflict over politics, resolved when elder's death awakens son to truth about life in Communist Hungary.

Beast of Hollow Mountain, The (1956-Mexican-American) **C-80m.** **½ D: Edward Nassour, Ismael Rodriguez. Guy Madison, Patricia Medina, Eduardo Noriega, Carlos Rivas. Unusual combination of Western and monster-on-the-loose formula works well, with clever ending. Filmed in Mexico.

Beast of the City, The (1932) 87m. *** D: Charles Brabin. Walter Huston, Jean Harlow, Wallace Ford, Jean Hersholt, Dorothy Peterson, Tully Marshall, John Miljan, Mickey Rooney. "Instead of the glorification of gangsters, we need the glorification of policemen," reads President Hoover's opening statement, and this film delivers, in W. R. Burnett's solid, surprisingly gritty story, a sort of early DIRTY HARRY with a downbeat ending. Harlow is incredibly sexy as a gang moll.

Beast of the Dead (1970) **C-90m.** BOMB D: Eddie Romero. John Ashley, Eddie Garcia, Beverly Miller, Celeste Yarnall. Sequel to MAD DOCTOR OF BLOOD ISLAND, with that film's headless monster stalking natives on Pacific island while mad doctor plans new head transplant. Filmed in the Philippines. Originally titled BEAST OF BLOOD.

Beast of Yucca Flats, The (1961) 60m. BOMB D: Coleman Francis. Douglas Mellor, Tor Johnson, Barbara Francis. Johnson becomes a disfigured monster as a result of exposure to an A-bomb test. One of the worst films ever made, presented as a virtual silent film with voice-over narration. Subplot of a succession of voluptuous women being strangled bears little relation to the main story.

Beasts Are on the Streets, The (1978) **C-100m.** TVM D: Peter Hunt. Carol Lynley, Dale Robinette, Billy Green Bush, Philip Michael Thomas, Anna Lee. Dangerous beasts are accidentally set loose from wild animal park and thousands panic in nearby community. Intelligent story suffers from mediocre script. Average.

Beast with Five Fingers, The (1946) 88m. **½ D: Robert Florey. Robert Alda, Andrea King, Peter Lorre, Victor Francen, J. Carrol Naish. Intriguing if not entirely successful mood-piece about aging pianist and strange doings in his household. Lorre's confrontation with disembodied hand a horror highlight.

Beast Within, The (1982) **C-90m.** BOMB D: Philippe Mora. Ronny Cox, Bibi Besch, Paul Clemens, Don Gordon, R. G. Armstrong, L. Q. Jones. Besch was raped by hairy-legged "thing" while on honeymoon; her son (Clemens), now a teenager, commences killing, and killing, and killing. Oh, yes, he changes into a monster at one point, if you care.▼

Beat, The (1988) **C-98m.** *½ D: Paul Mones. John Savage, David Jacobson, Kara Glover, William McNamara, Jeffrey Horowitz. Well-meaning but painfully gauche drama of new kid Jacobson at a N.Y.C. high school dominated by street gangs, who brings poetry and mystical fantasy into his classmates' lives. Cast is earnest but treatment of generation gap issues is old-hat.▼

Beat Generation, The (1959) 95m. *½ D: Charles Haas. Steve Cochran, Mamie Van Doren, Ray Danton, Fay Spain, Louis Armstrong, Maggie Hayes, Jackie Coogan, Ray Anthony, Maxie Rosenbloom. Exploitation-type story of detective Cochran tracking down insane sexual assaulter; vivid sequences marred by hokey script. Retitled THIS REBEL AGE.

Beat Girl SEE: **Wild For Kicks**▼

Beatlemania (1981) **C-86m.** BOMB D: Joseph Manduke. Mitch Weissman, Ralph Castelli, David Leon, Tom Teeley. Awful, pretentious musical based on the equally awful, pretentious stage show, with lookalikes impersonating John, Paul, George, and Ringo. Turn off the tube and dust off your old copy of *Abbey Road*. Also known as BEATLEMANIA, THE MOVIE.▼

Beatrice (1988-French) **C-128m.** *** D: Bertrand Tavernier. Bernard Pierre Donnadieu, Julie Delpy, Nils Tavernier, Monique Chaumette, Robert Dhery, Michele Gleizer. Moody and well-mounted, if essentially ugly saga of the Hundred Years War; a father returns home from the front to bully his weakling son and engage his tougher (and beautiful) daughter in incest. Extremely violent and not for all tastes, but obviously the work of an outstanding filmmaker; try reconciling this with Tavernier's A SUNDAY IN THE COUNTRY. Also known as THE PASSION OF BEATRICE.▼

Beat Street (1984) **C-106m.** **½ D: Stan Lathan. Rae Dawn Chong, Guy Davis, Jon Chardiet, Leon W. Grant, Saundra

Santiago, Robert Taylor. Urban ghetto kids find creative outlets in painting graffiti, breakdancing, rapping, and developing new disco d.j. routines. A slicker version of WILD STYLE that places the old Mickey & Judy "let's put on a show" formula into a more realistic contemporary setting. Innocuous trend piece, coproduced by Harry Belafonte.▼

Beat the Devil (1954) 89m. *** D: John Huston. Humphrey Bogart, Jennifer Jones, Gina Lollobrigida, Robert Morley, Peter Lorre, Edward Underdown. Huston and Truman Capote concocted this offbeat, very funny satire of MALTESE FALCON-ish movies on location in Italy. Low-key nature of comedy eluded many people in 1954 and it immediately became a cult favorite, which it remains today.▼

Beau Brummel (1954-U.S.-British) C-113m. **½ D: Curtis Bernhardt. Stewart Granger, Elizabeth Taylor, Peter Ustinov, Robert Morley. Handsome cast in lavish production from Granger's rash of costume epics. Here, he's the famous 19th-century British Casanova-fop.

✓ **Beau Geste** (1939) 114m. *** D: William Wellman. Gary Cooper, Ray Milland, Robert Preston, Brian Donlevy, Susan Hayward, J. Carroll Naish, Albert Dekker, Broderick Crawford, Donald O'Connor. Scene-for-scene remake of famous 1926 silent film (with Ronald Colman) isn't quite as good but faithfully retells story of three devoted brothers serving in the Foreign Legion and battling martinent commander (Donlevy). Nothing can top that opening sequence! Based on the novel by P.C. Wren. Remade in 1966.▼

✓ **Beau Geste** (1966) C-103m. ** D: Douglas Heyes. Telly Savalas, Guy Stockwell, Doug McClure, Leslie Nielsen. The third version of Christopher Wren's adventure about honor in the French Foreign Legion is barely adequate, with brothers battling rampaging Arabs and sadistic commander Savalas.

Beau James (1957) C-105m. *** D: Melville Shavelson. Bob Hope, Vera Miles, Paul Douglas, Alexis Smith, Darren McGavin; narrated by Walter Winchell. Flavorful recreation of the political career of Mayor Jimmy Walker in 1920s N.Y.C., based on Gene Fowler's book. Hope is fine in basically noncomic performance. Guest appearances by Jimmy Durante, Jack Benny, George Jessel, Walter Catlett.

Beau Pere (1981-French) C-120m. ***½ D: Bertrand Blier. Patrick Dewaere, Ariel Besse, Maurice Ronet, Nicole Garcia, Nathalie Baye, Maurice Risch, Macha Meril. Piano player Dewaere is seduced by his determined stepdaughter, a 14-year-old childwoman (Besse), after the death of her mother. Thoughtful comedy-drama is sensitively, not exploitively, handled by director Blier.▼

Beauties of the Night (1954-French) 84m. **½ D: René Clair. Gerard Philipe, Martine Carol, Gina Lollobrigida, Magali Vendeuil. Diverting fantasy involving aspiring composer Philipe with a penchant for dreaming and wandering through various eras of history.

Beautiful Blonde from Bashful Bend, The (1949) C-77m. **½ D: Preston Sturges. Betty Grable, Cesar Romero, Rudy Vallee, Olga San Juan, Porter Hall, Sterling Holloway, El Brendel. Film was major flop in 1949, looks somewhat better today; broad Western farce has Grable a guntoting saloon girl mistaken for schoolmarm in hick town. Hugh Herbert hilarious as nearsighted doctor.▼

Beautiful But Deadly SEE: **Don Is Dead, The**▼

Beautiful Stranger SEE: **Twist of Fate** (1954)

Beauty and the Beast (1946-French) 92m. **** D: Jean Cocteau. Jean Marais, Josette Day, Marcel André. Cocteau's hauntingly beautiful rendition of this classic fable is great fantasy, great filmmaking—beguiling on any level.▼

Beauty and the Robot, The SEE: **Sex Kittens Go to College**

Beauty for Sale (1933) 87m. *** D: Richard Boleslawsky. Madge Evans, Alice Brady, Otto Kruger, Una Merkel, May Robson, Phillips Holmes, Eddie Nugent, Hedda Hopper, Florine McKinney, Isabel Jewell, Charles Grapewin. Entertaining soaper about beautiful girl whose job at high-society beauty salon leads to liaison with husband of wealthy customer. Evans never looked more beautiful, photographed here by James Wong Howe. Based on a Faith Baldwin story.

Be Beautiful But Shut Up (1957-French) 94m. ** D: Henri Verneuil. Mylene Demongeot, Henri Vidal, Isabelle Miranda. Unremarkable study of young hoods involved with smuggling and carefree living.

Beauty for the Asking (1939) 68m. *½ D: Glenn Tryon. Lucille Ball, Patric Knowles, Frieda Inescort, Donald Woods, Inez Courtney, Leona Maricle. It took five writers to concoct this flimsy drama about working girl Ball, who is jilted by moneyhungry Knowles; he comes crawling back after she invents an exclusive beauty cream. Watchable, but utterly forgettable, programmer.

Bebo's Girl (1964-Italian) 106m. **½ D: Luigi Comencini. Claudia Cardinale, George Chakiris, Mario Lupi, Dany Paris. At times memorable love story spotlighting Cardinale's decision to leave her new lover in order to reaffirm her attachment with first love, now serving a prison term.

Because He's My Friend (1978-Australian)

C-93m. TVM D: Ralph Nelson. Karen Black, Keir Dullea, Jack Thompson, Tom Oliver, Don Reid, Barbara Stephens. Sensitive drama about the plight of parents with a retarded child and the effect on their marriage. The youngster is especially well-played by Australian actor Warwick Poulsen. Above average.

Because of Him (1946) 88m. **½ D: Richard Wallace. Deanna Durbin, Franchot Tone, Charles Laughton, Helen Broderick, Donald Meek. Contrived comedy recalls Deanna's earlier (and better) vehicles as she schemes to become the protégé of Broadway star Laughton, with interference from playwright Tone. A few songs are shoehorned into the film as arbitrarily as most of the story elements.

Because of You (1952) 95m. *** D: Joseph Pevney. Loretta Young, Jeff Chandler, Alex Nicol, Frances Dee, Mae Clarke. Nifty tear-jerker has Young a parolee whose marriage is threatened by her past.

Because They're Young (1960) 102m. **½ D: Paul Wendkos. Dick Clark, Michael Callan, Tuesday Weld, Victoria Shaw, Doug McClure, James Darren, Warren Berlinger, Roberta Shore, Duane Eddy and the Rebels. Clark made his screen acting debut—if you really must know—in this ho-hum adaptation of John Farris' *Harrison High*. Mr. American Bandstand stars as an understanding do-gooder teacher, who attempts to help his troubled students.

Because You're Mine (1952) C-103m. ** D: Alexander Hall. Mario Lanza, James Whitmore, Doretta Morrow, Dean Miller, Paula Corday, Jeff Donnell, Spring Byington, Don Porter, Eduard Franz, Bobby Van. Opera star Lanza is drafted and falls in love with Morrow, the sister of his top sergeant (Whitmore). For Lanza fans only.

✓ **Becket** (1964) C-148m. **** D: Peter Glenville. Richard Burton, Peter O'Toole, John Gielgud, Donald Wolfit, Martita Hunt, Pamela Brown, Felix Aylmer. Stunning film, adapted by Edward Anhalt (who won an Oscar) from the Jean Anouilh play, centers on stormy friendship between Archbishop of Canterbury Thomas à Becket and his English King, Henry II. Superbly acted and magnificently photographed (by Geoffrey Unsworth) on location in England.▼

Becky Sharp (1935) C-83m. **½ D: Rouben Mamoulian. Miriam Hopkins, Frances Dee, Cedric Hardwicke, Billie Burke, Alison Skipworth, Nigel Bruce. Witty but sometimes ponderous adaptation of Thackeray's *Vanity Fair* with Hopkins as self-reliant girl whose sole concern is herself. Historically important as first full-Technicolor (3-color) feature, designed by Robert Edmond Jones (and photographed by Ray Rennahan). Long available to TV only in inferior 67m. Cinecolor reissue prints

(which rob the film of its greatest asset, full-color); archivally restored in 1985. Previously filmed (as VANITY FAIR) in 1923 and 1932.▼

Bed and Board (1970-French) C-97m. ***½ D: Francois Truffaut. Jean-Pierre Leaud, Claude Jade, Hiroko Berghauer, Daniel Ceccaldi, Claire Duhamel. Chapter Four of the Antoine Doinel story. Here, Doinel (Leaud) is married to Christine (Jade); he is confused, immature, becomes a father, and has an affair with Berghauer. Lovingly directed by Truffaut; Jacques Tati has an amusing cameo as M. Hulot. Followed by LOVE ON THE RUN.

Bedazzled (1967-British) C-107m. *** D: Stanley Donen. Peter Cook, Dudley Moore, Eleanor Bron, Raquel Welch, Alba. Cult film updating Faust legend is as sacrilegious as THE SINGING NUN and usually funnier. The laughs aren't always consistent, but the Cook-Moore team is terrific and Donen's direction stylish. And remember the magic words: "Julie Andrews!"▼

Bedelia (1946-British) 92m. **½ D: Lance Comfort. Margaret Lockwood, Ian Hunter, Barry K. Barnes, Anne Crawford, Jill Esmond. Naive Hunter marries a woman with a past, including (it turns out) several husbands who met mysterious ends. Absorbing but not terribly suspenseful. Based on a Vera Caspary novel.

Bedevilled (1955) C-85m. ** D: Mitchell Leisen. Anne Baxter, Steve Forrest, Simone Renant, Victor Francen. Bizarre yarn of chanteuse Baxter fleeing from murder scene, protected by Forrest, who's studying for priesthood; filmed in Paris.

Bedford Incident, The (1965) 102m. *** D: James B. Harris. Richard Widmark, Sidney Poitier, James MacArthur, Martin Balsam, Wally Cox, Eric Portman, Donald Sutherland. Strong Cold War story of authoritarian Navy captain (Widmark) scouting Russian subs near Greenland and the mental conflicts that develop on his ship. Poitier is reporter too good to be true, Balsam a sympathetic doctor disliked by Widmark. Cast excels in intriguing battle of wits.▼

Bedknobs and Broomsticks (1971) C-117m. *** D: Robert Stevenson. Angela Lansbury, David Tomlinson, Roddy McDowall, Sam Jaffe, Roy Snart, Cindy O'Callaghan, Ian Weighill. Elaborate Disney musical fantasy about amateur witch who helps British cause in WW2; no MARY POPPINS, but quite enjoyable, with Oscar-winning special effects and delightful animated cartoon sequences directed by Ward Kimball. Reissued at 98m.▼

Bedlam (1946) 79m. *** D: Mark Robson. Boris Karloff, Anna Lee, Ian Wolfe, Richard Fraser, Billy House, Jason Robards, Sr. Atmospheric Val Lewton chiller of courageous Lee trying to expose inadequate conditions at insane asylum, committed to one by institution head Karloff. Set in 18th-century London.▼

Bed of Roses (1933) 67m. ******* D: Gregory La Cava. Constance Bennett, Joel McCrea, Pert Kelton, John Halliday, Samuel S. Hinds, Franklin Pangborn. Smart pre-code comedy-drama with Bennett and Kelton released from reform school and on the make for plenty of 'umpchays with ashcay,' that is, until Bennett falls for riverboat skipper McCrea. Kelton is hilarious as a slinky, no-holds-barred 'bad girl' with an acid tongue, in her film debut.

Bedroom Window, The (1987) C-112m. ******* D: Curtis Hanson. Steve Guttenberg, Elizabeth McGovern, Isabelle Huppert, Paul Shenar, Carl Lumbly, Wallace Shawn, Frederick Coffin, Brad Greenquist. An innocent man offers to alibi for his boss' sexy wife, who witnessed an assault from his bedroom window after they make love. This apparently simple gesture snowballs into a web of crime and duplicity, in this attractive, sexy, and suspenseful Hitchcock homage. Guttenberg is no Cary Grant (or even James Stewart), but the film is consistently enjoyable—if not always absolutely believable.▼

Bedside Manner (1945) 72m. ****** D: Andrew L. Stone. Ruth Hussey, John Carroll, Charles Ruggles, Ann Rutherford, Claudia Drake, Renee Godfrey, Esther Dale. Carroll is pilot being treated by woman doctor Hussey; guess what happens? Routine, inoffensive romantic-comedy. Also known as HER FAVORITE PATIENT.

Bed-Sitting Room, The (British-1969) C-90m. ****½** D: Richard Lester. Rita Tushingham, Ralph Richardson, Peter Cook, Dudley Moore, Spike Milligan, Michael Hordern. Moderately successful black-comedy look at distorted, devastated England three years after nuclear war. A few funny bits, great cast, but film doesn't click. Marty Feldman makes his film debut in a brief bit.

Bedtime for Bonzo (1951) 83m. ****½** D: Frederick de Cordova. Ronald Reagan, Diana Lynn, Walter Slezak, Jesse White, Lucille Barkley. Often cited as the pinnacle of absurdity in Reagan's career, but in fact it's a cute, harmless little comedy about a professor who treats a chimp as his child for a heredity experiment. Reagan did not appear in the sequel, BONZO GOES TO COLLEGE.▼

Bedtime Story, A (1933) 87m. ****½** D: Norman Taurog. Maurice Chevalier, Helen Twelvetrees, Baby LeRoy, Adrienne Ames, Edward Everett Horton. Breezy Chevalier musical vehicle with Parisian playboy playing father to abandoned baby who interferes with his romancing.

Bedtime Story (1941) 85m. ******* D: Alexander Hall. Fredric March, Loretta Young, Robert Benchley, Allyn Joslyn, Eve Arden. Fine cast in sparkling comedy of playwright March trying to stop wife Young from retiring so she can star in his next play.

Bedtime Story (1964) C-99m. ****½** D: Ralph Levy. Marlon Brando, David Niven, Shirley Jones, Dody Goodman, Marie Windsor. Offbeat casting of stars provides chief interest in lackluster comedy of con men Brando and Niven competing for Jones' affection. Remade as DIRTY ROTTEN SCOUNDRELS.▼

Been Down So Long It Looks Like Up to Me (1971) C-90m. ***½** D: Jeffrey Young. Barry Primus, Linda DeCoff, David Browning, Susan Tyrrell, Philip Shafer, Bruce Davison, Raul Julia. Bland, dated film version of Richard Fariña's novel about hip 1960s-type trying to endure life on a 1958 campus.

Beer (1985) C-82m. ***½** D: Patrick Kelly. Loretta Swit, Rip Torn, Kenneth Mars, David Alan Grier, William Russ, Saul Stein, Dick Shawn. Unimaginative, ultimately tasteless spoof of Madison Avenue hype, with Swit as an ad agency executive who devises a highly successful commercial campaign to sell beer. Not so very far from reality—and not terribly funny.▼

Bees, The (1978) C-83m. ***½** D: Alfredo Zacharias. John Saxon, Angel Tompkins, John Carradine, Claudio Brook, Alicia Encinias. After THE SWARM, if you sincerely want to see this low-budget disaster film about killer bees, you get what you deserve. Filmed in Mexico.▼

Beetlejuice (1988) C-92m. ******* D: Tim Burton. Michael Keaton, Alec Baldwin, Geena Davis, Jeffrey Jones, Catherine O'Hara, Winona Ryder, Sylvia Sidney, Robert Goulet, Glenn Shadix, Dick Cavett, Annie McEnroe. Newly deceased couple in need of help coping with the afterlife, and obnoxious family who's moved into their home, get it in the form of renegade spirit Betelgeuse (Keaton, who pulls out all the stops). Fantastic effects make this a sort of live-action cartoon. Added treat: Sylvia Sidney as harried case worker in the hereafter. Great fun, and surprisingly good-natured in spirit. Music by Danny Elfman, with a strong assist from Harry Belafonte. Academy Award winner for makeup. Followed by an animated TV series.▼

Before and After (1979) C-100m. TVM D: Kim Friedman. Patty Duke Astin, Bradford Dillman, Barbara Feldon, Art Hindle, Rosemary Murphy, Kenneth Mars, Betty White. So-so comedy/drama about a housewife's battle with a weight problem that threatens her marriage. Average.

Before I Hang (1940) 71m. ****½** D: Nick Grinde. Boris Karloff, Evelyn Keyes, Bruce Bennett, Pedro de Cordoba, Edward Van

Sloan. Contrived but intriguing tale of prison scientist Karloff having youth serum backfire on him, driving him mad at odd moments.▼

Before I Wake SEE: **Shadow of Fear**

Before Winter Comes (1969-British) C-102m. **½ D: J. Lee Thompson. David Niven, Topol, Anna Karina, John Hurt, Anthony Quayle, Ori Levy. Topol is interpreter for British officer Niven in displaced persons' camp following WW2. Uneven comedy-drama with many touching moments, capturing plight of refugees. Topol's warmth shines in winning performance.

Beg, Borrow, or Steal (1973) C-73m. TVM D: David Lowell Rich. Mike Connors, Michael Cole, Kent McCord, Leonard Stone, Henry Beckman, Joel Fabiani. Three unemployed, handicapped men, failing to start own business, eventually devise plan to rob museum of priceless statue, unaware that second party has ideas of his own. Dismal miscasting of leads, forgettable action. Below average.

Beggarman, Thief (1979) C-200m. TVM D: Lawrence Doheny. Jean Simmons, Glenn Ford, Lynn Redgrave, Tovah Feldshuh, Andrew Stevens, Bo Hopkins, Jean-Pierre Aumont, Anne Francis, Anne Jeffreys, Robert Sterling, Susan Strasberg. Further travails of the Jordache family during the late '60s, set against tinselly Cannes Film Festival. High-grade soap opera in the tradition of its multipart predecessor, Irwin Shaw's RICH MAN, POOR MAN. Above average.

Beggar's Opera, The (1953-British) C-94m. *** D: Peter Brook. Laurence Olivier, Stanley Holloway, Dorothy Tutin, Daphne Anderson, Mary Clare, Hugh Griffith, Laurence Naismith. Celebrated stage director Brook made his film debut with this vivid, energetic version of John Gay's opera. Coproducer and star Olivier is somewhat miscast but more than makes up for it with his sly portrayal of a jailed highwayman who exaggerates his exploits into a musical revue.

Beginner's Luck (1983) C-85m. *** D: Frank Mouris. Sam Rush, Riley Steiner, Charles Homet, Kate Talbot, Mickey Coburn. Charming, refreshingly original little comedy about uptight, virginal law student Rush and his lusty upstairs neighbors (Steiner, Homet), with their friendship culminating in a zany ménage à trois. A trifle silly at times but often funny and attractively performed. ▼

Beginning of the End (1957) 73m. *½ D: Bert I. Gordon. Peggie Castle, Peter Graves, Morris Ankrum, Thomas Brown Henry. Awful sci-fi outing about giant grasshoppers (thanks to radiation) on the rampage; at the climax, they invade Chicago—but none too convincingly.

Beginning or the End, The (1947) 112m. *** D: Norman Taurog. Brian Donlevy, Robert Walker, Beverly Tyler, Audrey Totter, Hume Cronyn. Engrossing account of atomic bomb development, depicting both human and spectacular aspects.

Beguiled, The (1971) C-109m. *** D: Don Siegel. Clint Eastwood, Geraldine Page, Elizabeth Hartman, Jo Ann Harris, Darleen Carr, Pamelyn Ferdin. Offbeat, methodically paced story set in Civil War South. Wounded Eastwood brought to girls' school to recuperate; he becomes catalyst for flurry of jealousy and hatred. Unusual Eastwood fare, but for patient viewers, a rich, rewarding film.▼

Behave Yourself! (1951) 81m. ** D: George Beck. Farley Granger, Shelley Winters, William Demarest, Francis L. Sullivan. Strange casting of Granger and Winters as couple with dog wanted by criminal gang detracts from comic potential of this comedy.▼

Behind Enemy Lines (1985) C-100m. TVM D: Sheldon Larry. Hal Holbrook, Ray Sharkey, David McCallum, Maryam D'abo, Renee Soutendijk, Patricia Hodge. Flat WW2 actioner about an OSS attempt to spirit a Norwegian scientist from the Nazis begins flavorfully, but the moxie soon loses its fizz and everything goes in wildly different directions. Bring back Alan Ladd and William Bendix! Below average.

Behind Enemy Lines (1986) SEE: **P.O.W. The Escape**▼

Behind Locked Doors (1948) 62m. ** D: Oscar (Budd) Boetticher. Lucille Bremer, Richard Carlson, Douglas Fowley, Tom Browne Henry. Mishmash of judge on the lam seeking refuge in an insane asylum, and the reporter who tracks him down for the story.

Behind the Badge SEE: **Killing Affair, A** (1977)

Behind the Door SEE: **Man with Nine Lives, The**

Behind the Eight Ball (1942) 60m. ** D: Edward F. Cline. Ritz Brothers, Carol Bruce, Grace McDonald, Dick Foran, William Demarest, Johnny Downs. Entertainers get tangled in murder whodunit, with Demarest as determined detective. Typical nonsense plot squeezed in between musical numbers.

Behind the Front (1926) 60m. **½ D: A. Edward Sutherland. Wallace Beery, Mary Brian, Raymond Hatton, Richard Arlen, Tom Kennedy, Chester Conklin, Gertrude Astor. Entertaining silent army comedy, broadly played by buddies Beery and Hatton, supported by fine cast. Many devices have been reused countless times, but they're handled smoothly here.

Behind the High Wall (1956) 85m. ** D: Abner Biberman. Tom Tully, Sylvia Sidney, Betty Lynn, John Gavin. Intertwining yarn of grasping prison warden, his crippled wife (nicely played by Sidney), hidden money, and convict escape plan. Remake of THE BIG GUY.

Behind the Iron Curtain SEE: Iron Curtain, The▼

Behind the Mask (1932) 70m. ** D: John Francis Dillon. Jack Holt, Constance Cummings, Boris Karloff, Edward Van Sloan, Claude King. Secret-service man Holt tries to expose mysterious head of dope ring in this okay thriller, not a horror film despite presence of Karloff and Van Sloan.

Behind the Rising Sun (1943) 89m. **½ D: Edward Dmytryk. Margo, Tom Neal, J. Carrol Naish, Robert Ryan, Gloria Holden, Don Douglas, George Givot. Japanese man (Naish) urges his Americanized son (Neal) to become involved in Sino-Japanese war during 1930s, but doesn't like what happens as a result. Interesting for WW2-era point of view.▼

Behold a Pale Horse (1964) 118m. **½ D: Fred Zinnemann. Gregory Peck, Anthony Quinn, Omar Sharif, Mildred Dunnock, Christian Marquand, Raymond Pellegrin. Peck and Quinn wage an ideological battle in post-Spanish Civil War story of politics and violence that loses its focus and becomes confused talky film. Valiant try by all.▼

Behold My Wife (1935) 78m. ** D: Mitchell Leisen. Sylvia Sidney, Gene Raymond, Juliette Compton, Laura Hope Crews, Ann Sheridan. Raymond's snobbish family objects to his love for Indian maiden Sidney. Predictable wrong-side-of-the-reservation romance.

Being, The (1983) C-79m. *½ D: Jackie Kong. Martin Landau, Jose Ferrer, Dorothy Malone, Ruth Buzzi, Marianne Gordon Rogers, Murray Langston, Kinky Friedman, Johnny Dark. Creature spawned by nuclear waste terrorizes Idaho community. Humor is film's saving grace, but it isn't enough to overcome grade-Z script and production. Producer William Osco (Kong's then-husband) also costars under the name Rexx Coltrane. Filmed in 1980; briefly shown as EASTER SUNDAY.▼

Being There (1979) C-130m. **½ D: Hal Ashby. Peter Sellers, Shirley MacLaine, Melvyn Douglas, Jack Warden, Richard Dysart, Richard Basehart, James Noble, David Clennon. A childlike man (Sellers) chances to meet important, powerful people who interpret his bewildered silence as brilliance. Low-keyed black humor, full of savagely witty comments on American life in the television age, but fatally overlong. Adapted by Jerzy Kosinski from his own story. Douglas won Oscar as political kingmaker.▼

Bela Lugosi Meets a Brooklyn Gorilla (1952) 74m. BOMB D: William Beaudine. Bela Lugosi, Duke Mitchell, Sammy Petrillo,

Charlita, Muriel Landers, Ramona the Chimp. One of the all-time greats. Mitchell and Petrillo (the very poor man's Martin and Lewis) are stranded on a jungle island, where Lugosi is conducting strange experiments. Proceed at your own risk. Also known as THE BOYS FROM BROOKLYN.▼

Believe in Me (1971) C-90m. ** D: Stuart Hagmann. Michael Sarrazin, Jacqueline Bisset, Jon Cypher, Allen Garfield, Kurt Dodenhoff. Still another 70s film about drug addiction, and none too good; cleancut career girl Bisset becomes addicted to speed in the East Village. Performers do their best.

Believers, The (1987) C-114m. **½ D: John Schlesinger. Martin Sheen, Helen Shaver, Harley Cross, Robert Loggia, Elizabeth Wilson, Lee Richardson, Harris Yulin, Richard Masur, Carla Pinza, Jimmy Smits. Gripping, genuinely frightening story of widower and son who move to N.Y.C. and become involved (in more ways than one) with cultish religion of Santeria, which believes in the sacrifice of children. Well-crafted film knows how to manipulate its audience but shows no mercy, either: a boy sees his mother electrocuted in the very first scene!▼

Bell' Antonio (1962-Italian) 101m. **½ D: Mauro Bolognini. Marcello Mastroianni, Claudia Cardinale, Pierre Brasseur, Rina Morelli. OK Italian import of man ridiculed for his sexual impotence, saved by village girl who names him her lover.

Bell, Book and Candle (1958) C-103m. **½ D: Richard Quine. James Stewart, Kim Novak, Jack Lemmon, Ernie Kovacs, Hermione Gingold. John Van Druten play becomes so-so vehicle to showcase Novak as fetching witch who charms about-to-be-married publisher Stewart. Kovacs and Gingold supply their brands of humor.▼

Bellboy, The (1960) 72m. *** D: Jerry Lewis. Jerry Lewis, Alex Gerry, Bob Clayton, Sonny Sands. Amusing series of blackouts with Jerry as a bellboy at Fountainbleau in Miami Beach. No plot but a lot of funny gags. Milton Berle and Walter Winchell have guest appearances. Lewis's directorial debut.▼

Belle de Jour (1967-French-Italian) C-100m. **** D: Luis Bunuel. Catherine Deneuve, Jean Sorel, Michel Piccoli, Genevieve Page, Francisco Rabal, Pierre Clementi, George Marchal, Francoise Fabian. Bunuel's wry and disturbing tale of a virginal newlywed who works the day shift in a high-class Parisian brothel, unbeknownst to her patient husband. Bunuel's straight-faced treatment of shocking subject-matter belies the sharp wit of his script. Deneuve gives her finest, most enigmatic performance.

Belle Le Grand (1951) 90m. *½ D: Allan Dwan. Vera Ralston, John Carroll, William Ching, Muriel Lawrence. Weak Ralston vehicle has her a Western lady gambler willing to play any stakes to win back rambunctious Carroll. Look for James Arness in the fire scene.

Belle of New York, The (1952) **C-82m.** ****½ D:** Charles Walters. Fred Astaire, Vera-Ellen, Marjorie Main, Keenan Wynn, Alice Pearce. Uninspired musical set in Gay 90s N.Y.C. with Astaire a rich playboy chasing mission gal Vera-Ellen; Pearce adds comic touches. Songs include "Let A Little Love Come In."▼

Belle of the Nineties (1934) **73m.** ***** D:** Leo McCarey. Mae West, Roger Pryor, Johnny Mack Brown, Warren Hymer, Duke Ellington Orchestra. Mae struts, sings "My Old Flame," and heats up a gallery of admirers in amusing example of Western humor.

Belle of the Yukon (1944) **C-84m.** ****½ D:** William Seiter. Randolph Scott, Gypsy Rose Lee, Bob Burns, Dinah Shore, Charles Winninger, William Marshall, Guinn "Big Boy" Williams, Robert Armstrong, Florence Bates. Minor musical of saloon-owner Scott going straight at insistence of his girl (Lee); fast-moving, forgettable. Technicolor is film's best feature.

✓ **Belles of St. Trinians, The** (1955-British) **90m.** *****½ D:** Frank Launder. Alastair Sim, Joyce Grenfell, George Cole, Hermione Baddeley, Beryl Reid. Hilarious filmization of Ronald Searle's cartoons about completely crazy school for girls, run by dotty headmistress whose brother, a bookie, wants to use school to his advantage. Sim plays dual role in delightful madcap farce which spawned several sequels.▼

Belles on Their Toes (1952) **C-89m.** ***** D:** Henry Levin. Myrna Loy, Jeanne Crain, Debra Paget, Jeffrey Hunter, Edward Arnold, Hoagy Carmichael. Pleasing sequel to CHEAPER BY THE DOZEN focuses on Loy's lecture career and her ability to find romance while tending to her maturing brood. Twentieth Century-Fox backlot seen at its best recapturing 1900s America.

Belle Starr (1941) **C-87m.** ****½ D:** Irving Cummings. Randolph Scott, Gene Tierney, Dana Andrews, John Sheppard (Shepperd Strudwick), Elizabeth Patterson. Sophisticated Tierney miscast as notorious female outlaw in slowly paced account of her criminal career.

Belle Starr (1980) **C-97m. TVM D:** John A. Alonzo. Elizabeth Montgomery, Cliff Potts, Michael Cavanaugh, Fred Ward, Jesse Vint, Allan Vint, Geoffrey Lewis. The Old West's legendary bandit queen rides again, beautified by Montgomery and played with a none-too-convincing 1980 sensibility. Script by James Lee Barrett. Average.

Belle Starr's Daughter (1948) **86m.** **** D:** Lesley Selander. George Montgomery,

Rod Cameron, Ruth Roman, Wallace Ford, Isabel Jewell. Roman is title character, coming to rough Western town to avenge her mother's murder; fair Western.

Bell for Adano, A (1945) **103m.** *****½ D:** Henry King. Gene Tierney, John Hodiak, William Bendix, Glenn Langan, Richard Conte, Stanley Prager, Henry (Harry) Morgan, Hugo Haas, Fortunio Bonanova, Henry Armetta, Luis Alberni, Eduardo Ciannelli, Grady Sutton. John Hersey's moving narrative of American WW2 occupation of small Italian village; Hodiak is sincere commander, Bendix his aide, blonde Tierney the local girl he is attracted to. Scripted by Lamar Trotti (who also coproduced) and Norman Reilly Raine.

Bellissima (1951-Italian) **112m.** **** D:** Luchino Visconti. Anna Magnani, Walter Chiari, Tina Apicella, Gastone Renzelli, Alessandro Blasetti. Obvious drama about pushy, patronizing stage mother Magnani, obsessed to the point of hysteria with getting her cute, obedient little daughter into the movies. Loud when it should be tender, and ultimately tiresome.▼

Bellizaire the Cajun (1986) **C-100m.** ****½ D:** Glen Pitre. Armand Assante, Gail Youngs, Michael Schoeffling, Stephen McHattie, Will Patton, Nancy Barrett. Assante is well cast as a charismatic herbal dealer in love with the Cajun wife of a wealthy Anglo in this uneven and somewhat predictable drama about Anglo prejudice and violence against Cajuns in 19th-century Louisiana. Made with obvious enthusiasm on a low budget. Robert Duvall, credited as creative consultant, appears briefly as a preacher.▼

Bell Jar, The (1979) **C-107m.** ****½ D:** Larry Peerce. Marilyn Hassett, Julie Harris, Anne Jackson, Barbara Barrie, Robert Klein, Donna Mitchell. Sylvia Plath's virtually unfilmable novel about the crack-up of an overachiever in the 50s has a few powerful scenes and a good supporting performance by Barrie, but doesn't really come off. Hassett is well cast but fails to deliver the truly bravura performance this film needs.▼

Bellman and True (1988-British) **C-112m.** ****½ D:** Richard Loncraine. Bernard Hill, Kieran O'Brien, Richard Hope, Frances Tomelty, Derek Newark, John Kavanagh, Ken Bones. Meek computer programmer is drawn into an elaborate bank heist scheme, without ever realizing just how dangerous the people he's associating with can be. More a character study than a caper film, very low-key and very drawn-out, but with a number of rewarding moments and vignettes.▼

Bells SEE: **Murder by Phone**▼

Bells Are Ringing (1960) **C-127m.** ***** D:** Vincente Minnelli. Judy Holliday, Dean Martin, Fred Clark, Eddie Foy, Jr., Jean Stapleton, Ruth Storrey, Frank Gorshin,

Gerry Mulligan. Sprightly adaptation of Broadway musical hit by Betty Comden, Adolph Green, and Jule Styne, with Holliday recreating her starring role as an answering-service operator who falls in love with the man she's known only as a voice on the telephone. Songs include "Just in Time," "The Party's Over."▼

✓ **Bells of St. Mary's, The** (1945) **126m.** *** D: Leo McCarey. Bing Crosby, Ingrid Bergman, Henry Travers, William Gargan, Ruth Donnelly, Joan Carroll, Martha Sleeper, Rhys Williams. Amiable if meandering sequel to GOING MY WAY, with Father O'Malley assigned to a run-down parish where Bergman is the Sister Superior. Bing introduces the song "Aren't You Glad You're You?" Also shown in computer-colored version.▼

Belly of an Architect, The (1987-British-Italian) **C-108m.** **½ D: Peter Greenaway. Brian Dennehy, Chloe Webb, Lambert Wilson, Sergio Fantoni, Stephania Cassini, Vanni Corbellini. Highly personalized chronicle of an architect (Dennehy) and his wife (Webb), who arrive in Rome where he's to curate an exhibition. It's about architecture and art, obsession and omens, immortality and mortality; crammed with symbolism, striking visuals and beautiful cinematography by Sacha Vierny. Some will find it pretentious, others will be fascinated.

Beloved Enemy (1936) **86m.** *** D: H. C. Potter. Merle Oberon, Brian Aherne, Karen Morley, Henry Stephenson, Jerome Cowan, David Niven, Donald Crisp. High-class love story set during Irish Rebellion with Britisher Oberon in love with rebel leader Aherne.▼

Beloved Infidel (1959) **C-123m.** ** D: Henry King. Gregory Peck, Deborah Kerr, Eddie Albert, Philip Ober, Herbert Rudley, John Sutton, Karin Booth, Ken Scott. Ill-conceived casting of Peck as F. Scott Fitzgerald makes romance with Hollywood columnist Sheilah Graham (Kerr) in late 1930s more ludicrous than real; lush photography is only virtue of blunt look at cinema capital.

✓ **Beloved Rogue, The** (1927) **99m.** ***½ D: Alan Crosland. John Barrymore, Conrad Veidt, Marceline Day, Henry Victor, Lawson Butt, Mack Swain, Slim Summerville. Rousing, stunningly filmed story of poet-adventurer François Villon, his battle of wits with Louis XI (Veidt) and his swashbuckling romance with a damsel in distress. Has nothing to do with history; instead, an eye-filling, spirited, tongue-in-cheek costume tale with Barrymore in great form.

Below the Belt (1980) **C-98m.** *** D: Robert Fowler. Regina Baff, Mildred Burke, John C. Becher, Annie McGreevey, Jane O'Brien, Shirley Stoler, Dolph Sweet.

Waitress Baff seeks fortune and fame as a lady wrestler. Low-budget drama, filmed mostly in 1974; a sometimes fascinating portrait of people eking out existence on the edge of society. Based on a novel by Rosalyn Drexler.▼

Be My Guest (1965-British) **82m.** *½ D: Lance Comfort. David Hemmings, Stephen Marriot, Andrea Monet, Avril Angers, Joyce Blair, Jerry Lee Lewis, Nashville Teens. Young Hemmings uncovers attempt to mount a phony music contest, while his family takes over a seaside guest house. Trifling musical.

Ben (1972) **C-95m.** *½ D: Phil Karlson. Lee Harcourt Montgomery, Joseph Campanella, Arthur O'Connell, Rosemary Murphy, Meredith Baxter. WILLARD sequel finds sick youth befriended by Ben the rat. Title song (sung by young Michael Jackson) summed up situation but spared gory visuals that make this film so bad.▼

Bend of the River (1952) **C-91m.** *** D: ✓ Anthony Mann. James Stewart, Julia Adams, Arthur Kennedy, Rock Hudson, Lori Nelson, Jay C. Flippen, Harry Morgan. Compelling Western of 1840s Oregon, with bristling conflict between Stewart, outlaw-turned-wagon-train-scout, and Kennedy, his one-time comrade who hijacks settlers' supplies to turn a fast profit.▼

Beneath the Planet of the Apes (1970) ✓ **C-95m.** **½ D: Ted Post. James Franciscus, Kim Hunter, Maurice Evans, Linda Harrison, Charlton Heston, Victor Buono, Paul Richards, Thomas Gomez. Second APES film still has great sets, makeup and ideas, but somebody let it get away as Apes battle human mutants who survived a nuclear blast many years before. Followed by ESCAPE FROM . . .▼

Beneath the 12 Mile Reef (1953) **C-102m.** **½ D: Robert Webb. Robert Wagner, Terry Moore, Gilbert Roland, J. Carrol Naish, Richard Boone, Peter Graves. Romeo-Juliet-ish tale of sponge-diving families on Key West, Florida. Scenery outshines all. One of the first CinemaScope films.▼

Benefit of the Doubt, The (1967-British) **C-70m.** **½ D: Peter Whitehead. Eric Allan, Mary Allen, Jeremy Anthony, Noel Collins. Documentary shows British view of Vietnam War, featuring scenes from Peter Brook play US (Royal Shakespeare Company); thought-provoking at times. Retitled: US.

Bengal Brigade (1954) **C-87m.** ** D: Laslo Benedek. Rock Hudson, Arlene Dahl, Ursula Thiess, Torin Thatcher, Arnold Moss, Dan O'Herlihy, Michael Ansara. Low-level costumer with Hudson badly miscast as a British army officer working to thwart a Sepoy rebellion in India.

Bengazi (1955) **78m.** *½ D: John Brahm. Richard Conte, Victor McLaglen, Richard

Carlson, Mala Powers. Lackluster adventure of Powers and trio of men entrapped in desert shrine by marauding natives.

Ben-Hur (1926) **141m.** *** D: Fred Niblo. Ramon Novarro, Francis X. Bushman, May McAvoy, Betty Bronson, Claire McDowell, Carmel Myers, Nigel de Brulier. Biggest of all silent spectacles holds up quite well against talkie remake, particularly the exciting chariot race and sea battle (both directed by B. Reeves Eason); Novarro (as Judah) and Bushman (as Messala) give the performances of their careers. Trouble-plagued film was years in production, at a then-record cost of $4,000,000, but final result, despite a slow second half, is worth it. Filmed once before (in one reel!) in 1907.▼

Ben Hur (1959) **C-212m.** **** D: William Wyler. Charlton Heston, Jack Hawkins, Stephen Boyd, Haya Harareet, Hugh Griffith, Martha Scott, Sam Jaffe, Cathy O'Donnell. Gargantuan remake of Lew Wallace classic combines historical look at Palestine during the time of Christ with melodrama pitting two ex-friends, Judah Ben Hur and Messala, against each other. Heston and Griffith each received Oscars; film garnered nine others, including Picture, Director, Cinematography (Robert Surtees), Scoring (Miklos Rozsa), Art Direction/Set Decoration, Costumes, Editing, and Special Effects. Sea battle and chariot race (directed by Andrew Marton) among all-time great action scenes. Some prints run 165m.▼

Benjamin (1968-French) **C-100m.** BOMB D: Michel Deville. Catherine Deneuve, Michele Morgan, Pierre Clementi, Michel Piccoli, Francine Berge, Anna Gael, Jacques Dufilho, Odile Versois. Beautiful Deneuve, Morgan, cinematography; otherwise, boring tale of country boy Clementi's initiation into upper-class immorality. Also shown at 105m. and 108m.

Benji (1974) **C-86m.** ***½ D: Joe Camp. Peter Breck, Deborah Walley, Edgar Buchanan, Frances Bavier, Patsy Garrett. Instant classic of a remarkable dog (played by Higgins) who thwarts the kidnappers of two small children. Texas-made feature is ideal for family viewing. Sequel: FOR THE LOVE OF BENJI.▼

Benji the Hunted (1987) **C-88m.** *½ D: Joe Camp. Benji, Red Steagall, Frank Inn. Every dog has his day, but this talented canine deserves a better movie vehicle. Humans are incidental in this story of Benji surviving in the mountain wilds, and it looks as if they were incidental in making the film as well.▼

Benny and Barney: Las Vegas Undercover (1977) **C-76m.** TVM D: Ron Satlof. Terry Kiser, Timothy Thomerson, Jack Colvin, Jane Seymour, Jack Cassidy, Hugh O'Brian, Pat Harrington, Rodney Danger-

field, Marty Allen, George Gobel, Bobby Troup, Dick Gautier. Cops moonlight as Vegas performers to thwart kidnapping of top entertainer. Banal adventure; busted TV pilot. Below average.

Benny Goodman Story, The (1955) **C-116m.** **½ D: Valentine Davies. Steve Allen, Donna Reed, Herbert Anderson, Berta Gersten, Robert F. Simon, Sammy Davis, Sr., Gene Krupa, Lionel Hampton, Teddy Wilson. Typical Hollywood gloss about the bandleader's rise to fame and his romance with Reed; not exactly 100% factual, but the music is great. Additional guest performers include Harry James, Ziggy Elman and Martha Tilton. Goodman himself dubbed Allen's playing.▼

Benny's Place (1982) **C-100m.** TVM D: Michael Schultz, Louis Gossett, Jr., Cicely Tyson, David Harris, Bever-Leigh Banfield, Anna Maria Horsford, Terry Alexander. Powerful Gossett performance ignites this drama about a proud man who finds time nipping at his heels and his job threatened by younger men. Above average.

Benson Murder Case, The (1930) **69m.** D: Frank Tuttle. William Powell, Natalie Moorhead, Eugene Pallette, Paul Lukas, William Boyd, E.H. Calvert, May Beatty, Mischa Auer. SEE: **Philo Vance** series.

Bequest to the Nation, A SEE: **Nelson Affair, The**

Berkeley Square (1933) **84m.** *** D: Frank Lloyd. Leslie Howard, Heather Angel, Irene Browne, Beryl Mercer, Samuel S. Hinds. Intriguing fantasy of young American Howard finding himself in 18th-century London, living completely different life. Remade as I'LL NEVER FORGET YOU.

Berlin Affair (1970) **C-97m.** TVM D: David Lowell Rich. Darren McGavin, Fritz Weaver, Claude Dauphin, Brian Kelly. Spotty foreign intrigue thriller has OK performances in story of murder-for-hire organization. Music by Francis Lai. Situations implausible, forgettable. Below average.

Berlin Affair, The (1985-Italian-West German) **C-96m.** BOMB D: Liliana Cavani. Gudrun Landgrebe, Kevin McNally, Mio Takaki, Massimo Girotti, Philippe Leroy, Hanns Zischler, William Berger. English-language misfire adapts Junichiro Tanizuki's novel *The Buddhist Cross*. Director Cavani (of THE NIGHT PORTER) is slumming in Nazi Germany again for a tale of a lesbian love affair between Landgrebe and ambassador's daughter Takaki. Lifeless film isn't even sexy, quite surprising in view of the casting of A WOMAN IN FLAMES star Landgrebe. Original European running time was 115m.▼

Berlin Alexanderplatz (1980-German) **C-931m.** **** D: Rainer Werner Fassbinder. Gunter Lamprecht, Hanna Schygulla,

Barbara Sukowa, Gottfried John, Elisabeth Trissenaar, Brigitte Mira, Karin Baal, Ivan Desny. Monumental adaptation of Alfred Doblin's epic novel about German life in the late 1920s, focusing on a simple Everyman (Lamprecht), who has just been released from prison. He yearns for respectability but is led like a sheep by forces beyond his control into criminality and insanity. An epic if there ever was one, with stunning performances, cinematography (by Xaver Schwarzenberger), and direction. Originally produced for television in fourteen episodes. Filmed before in 1931.▼

Berlin Correspondent (1942) 70m. **½ D: Eugene Forde. Virginia Gilmore, Dana Andrews, Mona Maris, Martin Kosleck, Sig Ruman. American reporter Andrews risks his life so that his sweetheart and her professor-father can escape from Nazi Germany.

Berlin Express (1948) 86m. *** D: Jacques Tourneur. Merle Oberon, Robert Ryan, Charles Korvin, Paul Lukas, Robert Coote. Taut, suspenseful spy story set in post WW2 Europe. Members of several nations combine efforts to save German statesman kidnapped by Nazi underground.▼

Berlin Tunnel 21 (1981) C-150m. TVM D: Richard Michaels. Richard Thomas, Horst Buchholz, Jose Ferrer, Jacques Breuer, Nicolas Farrell, Ken Griffith, Ute Christensen. Thomas masterminds an escape under the Berlin Wall with the help of structural engineer Buchholz. John Gay's teleplay is based on Donald Lindquist's riveting novel. Above average.▼

Bermuda Depths, The (1978) C-100m. TVM D: Tom Kotani. Burl Ives, Leigh McCloskey, Julie Woodson, Carl Weathers, Connie Sellecca. A mysterious beauty and a colossal turtle puzzle some scientists but offer no challenge to the viewer; crummy sci-fi. Below average.

Bermuda Mystery (1944) 65m. ** D: Benjamin Stoloff. Preston Foster, Ann Rutherford, Charles Butterworth, Helene Reynolds. Mild account of strange murder and dead man's heirs' search to track down criminal.

Bernadette of Lourdes (1961-French) 90m. **½ D: Robert Darene. Daniele Ajoret, Nadine Alari, Pierre Arnoux, Blanchette Brunoy. Straightforward account of the peasant girl who saw a vision and was elevated to sainthood; unpretentious.

Bernardine (1957) C-95m. ** D: Henry Levin. Pat Boone, Terry Moore, Janet Gaynor, Dean Jagger, Walter Abel. Very weak look at teen-age life (all different now) marked return of Janet Gaynor to films after twenty years. Wholesome Pat Boone (in his film debut) sings and sings and sings. Eh!

Berserk (1967-British) C-96m. ** D: Jim

O'Connolly. Joan Crawford, Ty Hardin, Diana Dors, Michael Gough, Judy Geeson. Sadistic shocker with Crawford the shapely owner of a British circus, haunted by series of brutal murders. Supporting cast lacks verve.▼

Bert Rigby, You're a Fool (1989) C-94m. ** D: Carl Reiner. Robert Lindsay, Robbie Coltrane, Anne Bancroft, Corbin Bernsen, Cathryn Bradshaw, Bruno Kirby, Jackie Gayle. Writer-director Reiner conceived this deliberately old-fashioned musical comedy strictly as a showcase for the talents of Lindsay (who scored such a smash on stage in *Me and My Girl*), and that's its only value. He's a delight to watch—singing, dancing, and clowning as a jaunty British coal miner who wants to break into show business—but the well-meaning film is silly and contrived.▼

Best Boy (1979) C-111m. **** D: Ira Wohl. Poignant, beautifully filmed documentary about Wohl's 52-year-old mentally retarded cousin Philly and his family's struggle as he learns to relate to the outside world. Sequences related to his father's death and his visit backstage with Zero Mostel—together they sing "If I Were a Rich Man"—are especially moving. A Best Documentary Academy Award winner.▼

Best Defense (1984) C-94m. *½ D: Willard Huyck. Dudley Moore, Eddie Murphy, Kate Capshaw, George Dzundza, Helen Shaver, David Rasche. Unpleasant and unfunny comedy about defense-industry designer who inadvertently acquires blueprint sought by the KGB. "Strategic Guest Star" Murphy is no help.▼

Best Foot Forward (1943) C-95m. *** D: Edward Buzzell. Lucille Ball, William Gaxton, Virginia Weidler, Tommy Dix, Nancy Walker, Gloria DeHaven, June Allyson. Entertaining film of Broadway musical about movie-star Ball visiting small-town school for a lark; score includes "Buckle Down Winsockie." Harry James and his band do definitive "Two O'Clock Jump," Walker is dynamic plain Jane.▼

Best Friends (1982) C-116m. ** D: Norman Jewison. Burt Reynolds, Goldie Hawn, Jessica Tandy, Barnard Hughes, Audra Lindley, Keenan Wynn, Ron Silver, Carol Locatell. Lackluster comedy vehicle for two top stars, as screenwriters who function better as lovers than as husband and wife. Some funny vignettes with fine supporting cast (including Richard Libertini as Mexican justice-of-the-peace), but the lead characters aren't terribly interesting. Indulgent script by real-life "best friends" Barry Levinson and Valerie Curtin.▼

Best House in London, The (1969-British) C-105m. BOMB D: Philip Saville. David Hemmings, Joanna Pettet, George Sanders, Dany Robin, Warren Mitchell. Boring comedy about group of government officials in London who sponsor official bawdy house. Film didn't deserve "X" rating it got at the time. Look for John Cleese in a bit part.

Best Kept Secrets (1984) C-100m. TVM D: Jerrold Freedman. Patty Duke Astin, Frederic Forrest, Peter Coyote, Meg Foster, Howard Hesseman, Albert Salmi, Miriam Colon. Cop's wife stumbles onto the fact that her husband is under investigation when an undercover sting backfires. Average.▼

Best Little Girl in the World, The (1981) C-100m. TVM D: Sam O'Steen. Charles Durning, Eva Marie Saint, Jennifer Jason Leigh, Melanie Mayron, Viveca Lindfors, Jason Miller, David Spielberg, Lisa Pelikan, Ally Sheedy. Model teenager from a middle-class family suffers from anorexia nervosa—self-induced starvation—and is slowly killing herself. David Moessinger's teleplay, based on Steven Levenkron's novel, is especially well acted by Durning and Saint as the girl's desperate parents and Miller as her psychiatrist. Above average.▼

Best Little Whorehouse in Texas, The (1982) C-114m. ** D: Colin Higgins. Burt Reynolds, Dolly Parton, Dom DeLuise, Charles Durning, Jim Nabors, Robert Mandan, Lois Nettleton, Theresa Merritt, Noah Beery, Barry Corbin. Flashy but unsatisfying musical (based on hit Broadway show) about the pressures brought to bear on sheriff (Reynolds) to close a popular establishment called The Chicken Ranch—run by his ladyfriend. Dolly's a delight, and Durning has a showstopping number as the Governor, but every once in a while film actually tries to get serious and comes to a screeching halt.▼

Best Man, The (1964) 102m. *** D: Franklin Schaffner. Henry Fonda, Cliff Robertson, Edie Adams, Margaret Leighton, Shelley Berman, Lee Tracy, Ann Sothern, Gene Raymond, Richard Arlen, Mahalia Jackson. Sharp filmization of Gore Vidal's play about political conventioning with several determined presidential candidates seeking important endorsement; brittle, engrossing drama. Screenplay by Vidal.

Best of Enemies, The (1962-British) C-104m. *** D: Guy Hamilton. David Niven, Michael Wilding, Harry Andrews, Alberto Sordi, Noel Harrison. Nice counterplay between Niven and Sordi, who point out the futility of warfare in this study of WW2.

Best of Everything, The (1959) C-121m. *** D: Jean Negulesco. Hope Lange, Stephen Boyd, Suzy Parker, Diane Baker, Martha Hyer, Joan Crawford, Brian Aherne, Robert Evans, Louis Jourdan. Multifaceted fabrication about women seeking success and love in the publishing jungles of N.Y.C., highlighted by Crawford's performance as tough executive with empty heart of gold; from superficial Rona Jaffe novel.

Best of the Badmen (1951) C-84m. **½ D: William D. Russell. Robert Ryan, Claire Trevor, Robert Preston, Jack Buetel, Walter Brennan, Bruce Cabot. Band of outlaws (including James and Younger brothers) help former Union colonel Ryan in vendetta against detective Preston. Offbeat Western has more talk than action.

Best of the Best (1989) C-97m. BOMB D: Bob Radler. Eric Roberts, James Earl Jones, Sally Kirkland, Christopher Penn, Louise Fletcher, Phillip Rhee, John Dye. Yet another ROCKY-style rip-off in which five young men must overcome their differences before they can unite as the U.S. Karate Team and compete in an international match. Top-drawer cast is appallingly wasted.▼

Best of Times, The (1986) C-104m. **½ D: Roger Spottiswoode. Robin Williams, Kurt Russell, Pamela Reed, Holly Palance, Donald Moffat, Margaret Whitton, M. Emmet Walsh, Donovan Scott, R. G. Armstrong, Kirk Cameron. Williams has never lived down the moment he dropped winning pass in a high-school football game—so, twenty years later he fires up former teammate (Russell), the rival team, and his entire home town for a rematch. Some quirky, offbeat touches highlight Ron Shelton's script, and the wives (Reed, Palance) are a treat but seemingly surefire film becomes too strident (and too exaggerated) to really score. ▼

Best Place to Be, The (1979) C-200m. TVM D: David Miller. Donna Reed, Efrem Zimbalist, Jr., Stephanie Zimbalist, Mildred Dunnock, John Phillip Law, Betty White, Leon Ames, Coleen Gray, Timothy Hutton. Lavish "woman's" drama with enough plot threads to keep six soap operas running for months, taken Ross Hunter-style from Helen Van Slyke's long-time best seller and featuring Donna Reed in her widely heralded TV comeback following a 12-year absence. Elegant, but tiresome. Average.

Best Seller (1987) C-110m. ** D: John Flynn. James Woods, Brian Dennehy, Victoria Tennant, Allison Balson, Paul Shenar, George Coe, Anne Pitoniak. Dennehy, a cop-turned-author (à la Joseph Wambaugh), is approached by Woods to write the story of his former life as hit man for prominent businessman (Shenar) whose underworld tactics have long been covered up. Despite teaming of two terrific actors, film never quite cuts it, due to many holes in Larry Cohen's script—and Woods' largely unappealing character.▼

Best Things in Life Are Free, The (1956)

C-104m. **½ D: Michael Curtiz. Gordon MacRae, Dan Dailey, Ernest Borgnine, Sheree North, Tommy Noonan, Murvyn Vye. Typical of the antiseptic 1950s musicals, this film "recreates" the careers of Tin Pan Alley writers DeSylva, Brown, and Henderson. Highlight: North and Jacques D'Amboise dancing to "The Birth of the Blues."

Best Years of Our Lives, The (1946) **172m.** **** D: William Wyler. Fredric March, Myrna Loy, Teresa Wright, Dana Andrews, Virginia Mayo, Harold Russell, Hoagy Carmichael, Gladys George, Steve Cochran. American classic of three veterans returning home after WW2, readjusting to civilian life. Robert Sherwood's script from MacKinlay Kantor's book perfectly captured mood of postwar U.S., still powerful today. Seven Oscars include Best Picture, Wyler, March, Russell, Sherwood, Daniel Mandell's editing, Hugo Friedhofer's score. Russell, an actual veteran who lost his hands, also took home a second Oscar, a special award for bringing hope and courage to other veterans. Remade as TVM RETURNING HOME.▼

Betrayal (1974) **C-78m.** TVM D: Gordon Hessler. Amanda Blake, Tisha Sterling, Dick Haymes, Sam Groom, Britt Leach, Ted Gehring. Lonely widow Blake hires a young woman companion, unaware that the girl and her boyfriend are killer-extortionists who plan to make her their next victim. Standard suspense drama. Script by James Miller from Doris Miles Disney's novel *Only Couples Need Apply*. Average.

Betrayal (1978) **C-100m.** TVM D: Paul Wendkos. Lesley Ann Warren, Rip Torn, Richard Masur, Ron Silver, Bibi Besch, John Hillerman, Peggy Ann Garner. Young woman brings rape charges against her psychiatrist. Standard TV fare despite veering toward the lurid. Average.▼

Betrayal (1983-British) **C-95m.** *½ D: David Jones. Jeremy Irons, Ben Kingsley, Patricia Hodge. Harold Pinter's fascinating play about a triangle relationship—progressing *backward* in time—falls flat on screen, despite a powerhouse cast.▼

Betrayal from the East (1945) **82m.** ** D: William Berke. Lee Tracy, Nancy Kelly, Richard Loo, Abner Biberman, Regis Toomey, Philip Ahn. Americans vs. Japanese in usual flag-waving espionage film, no better or worse than most.▼

Betrayed (1944) SEE: **When Strangers Marry**

Betrayed (1954) **C-108m.** ** D: Gottfried Reinhardt. Clark Gable, Lana Turner, Victor Mature, Louis Calhern. Unconvincing WW2 espionage melodrama of Dutch underground. Filmed in Holland.

Betrayed (1988) **C-127m.** *½ D: Costa-Gavras. Debra Winger, Tom Berenger, John Heard, Betsy Blair, John Mahoney, Ted Levine, Jeffrey DeMunn, Albert Hall, David Clennon, Richard Libertini. Appalling botch of a film about the stupidest FBI undercover agent in movie history who's sent to sniff out white supremacists in America's heartland—but falls in love with her target instead. Important and genuinely upsetting subject matter is dealt with in pedantic terms. Even the moments of straight suspense are muffed! Winger's performance is virtually the only saving grace. Timothy Hutton can be seen fleetingly at the fairgrounds.▼

Betrayed by Innocence (1986) **C-100m.** TVM D: Elliot Silverstein. Barry Bostwick, Lee Purcell, Cristen Kauffman, Isaac Hayes, Paul Sorvino. Married filmmaker gets slapped with statutory rape charges when the coed who seduces him turns out to be a mature-for-her-age minor. Exploitive script, by-the-numbers performances. Below average.

Betrayed Women (1955) **70m.** *½ D: Edward L. Cahn. Carole Mathews, Beverly Michaels, Peggy Knudsen, Tom Drake, Sara Haden. Low-key filming of potentially volatile subject, sadistic treatment of inmates in women's prison.

Betsy, The (1978) **C-125m.** **½ D: Daniel Petrie. Laurence Olivier, Robert Duvall, Katharine Ross, Tommy Lee Jones, Jane Alexander, Lesley-Anne Down, Kathleen Beller, Edward Herrmann. Moderately enjoyable trash, adapted from Harold Robbins' novel about the multigenerational wheelings and dealings between an auto company patriarch and his family. Olivier's hamminess and Down's loveliness are the pluses here.▼

Betsy's Wedding (1990) **C-94m.** *** D: Alan Alda. Alan Alda, Joey Bishop, Madeline Kahn, Anthony LaPaglia, Catherine O'Hara, Joe Pesci, Molly Ringwald, Ally Sheedy, Burt Young, Julie Bovasso, Nicolas Coster, Bibi Besch, Dylan Walsh. Amusing social comedy about the plans, preparations, and events surrounding Ringwald's wedding—especially as they affect her father. One of writer-director-star Alda's better outings, a bit cluttered (and occasionally clumsy) but filled with enough truthful observations to strike a great many familiar chords.

Better a Widow (1969-Italian) **C-105m.** *½ D: Duccio Tessari. Virna Lisi, Peter McEnery, Gabriele Ferzetti, Jean Servais, Agnes Spaak. Italian underworld "comedy" is better forgotten.

Better Late Than Never (1979) **C-100m,** TVM D: Richard Crenna. Harold Gould, Tyne Daly, Strother Martin, Harry Morgan, Victor Buono, George Gobel, Lou Jacobi, Donald Pleasence, Larry Storch. The revolt of a bunch of senior citizens in a retirement home against house rules that limit their freedom is less funny than it could have been. And, yes, the fellow who sings the title song without credit is just who you think it is. Average.▼

Better Late Than Never (1982) **C-95m.** *½ D: Bryan Forbes. David Niven, Art Carney, Maggie Smith, Kimberly Partridge, Catherine Hicks, Melissa Prophet. Two ne'er-do-wells vie for acceptance by a 10-year-old heiress, who's a granddaughter to one of them. Nice locations in the South of France can't compensate for lightheaded script and waste of star talent.▼

Better Off Dead (1985) **C-98m.** **½ D: Savage Steve Holland. John Cusack, David Ogden Stiers, Kim Darby, Demian Slade, Scooter Stevens, Diane Franklin, Curtis Armstrong. Off-kilter comedy about teenage boy who's just lost the girl of his dreams. Frustrating film starts off with lots of funny, original gags—it even has a terrific "hamburger video" by clay-animation specialist Jimmy Picker—then it settles into much-too-conventional story and goes down the drain. Feature debut for writer-director Holland. ▼

Betty Blue (1986-French) **C-120m.** **½ D: Jean-Jacques Beineix. Jean-Hugues Anglade, Beatrice Dolle, Gerard Darmon, Consuelo de Havilland, Clementine Celarie, Jaques Mathou, Vincent Lindon. Handyman and dangerously schizoid sexpot maphop France practically waiting for her to crack up; when it finally happens, the grisly violence doesn't quite mesh with the light tone of what's come before. Well-photographed and sometimes quite funny, but ultimately much ado about nothing. If you're watching this for sex, don't miss the opening five minutes. Oscar nominee for foreign film.▼

Betty Ford Story, The (1987) **C-100m. TVM** D: David Greene. Gena Rowlands, Josef Sommer, Nan Woods, Concetta Tomei, Jack Radar, Brian McNamara. Rowlands' Emmy-winning performance, as the former First Lady who battled alcohol and prescription drugs, burnishes Karen Hall's adaptation of the book *The Times of My Life*, which Betty Ford wrote with Chris Chase. Above average.

Between Friends (1983) **C-100m. TVM** D: Lou Antonio. Elizabeth Taylor, Carol Burnett, Barbara Bush, Stephen Young, Henry Ramer, Bruce Grey, Charles Shamata. Two middle-aged divorcees from totally different backgrounds run into each other—literally—and become fast friends. Tour-de-force performances by the two leads, though it's stretching credibility that Carol is the desirable sex object and Liz has trouble getting guys. Adapted by producers Shelley List and Jonathan Estrin from List's novel, *Nobody Makes Me Cry*. Made for cable. Above average.▼

Between Heaven and Hell (1956) **C-94m.**

*** D: Richard Fleischer. Robert Wagner, Terry Moore, Broderick Crawford, Buddy Ebsen, Robert Keith, Brad Dexter, Mark Damon, Harvey Lembeck, Skip Homeier, L.Q. Jones, Carl Switzer, Frank Gorshin, Scatman Crothers. Conventional story of thoughtless Southern boy who matures during military experiences in WW 2.

Between Midnight and Dawn (1950) **89m.** ** D: Gordon Douglas. Edmond O'Brien, Gale Storm, Mark Stevens, Roland Winters, Madge Blake. Passable crimeland caper with cops battling escaped crooks.

Between the Darkness and the Dawn (1985) **C-100m. TVM** D: Peter Levin. Elizabeth Montgomery, Karen Grassle, James Naughton, Dorothy McGuire, Michael Goodwin. Woman awakens from a twenty-year coma and tries to catch up with the world, with Montgomery playing a beardless Rip Van Winkle and McGuire as her doting mom. Average.

Between the Lines (1977) **C-101m.** ***½ D: Joan Micklin Silver. John Heard, Lindsay Crouse, Jeff Goldblum, Jill Eikenberry, Bruno Kirby, Gwen Welles, Stephen Collins, Michael J. Pollard, Marilu Henner. Thoroughly enjoyable sleeper about the emotional problems of the staff of a Boston underground newspaper which is about to be purchased by a print tycoon. The performances by a then-unknown cast are first rate all the way.▼

Between Time and Eternity (1960-German) **C-98m.** **½ D: Arthur Maria Rabenalt. Lilli Palmer, Willy Birgel, Ellen Schwiers, Carlos Thompson. Palmer makes tear-jerker believable in story of middle-aged woman dying of rare disease, seeking romance and fun while she can.

Between Two Brothers (1982) **C-100m. TVM** D: Robert Lewis. Michael Brandon, Pat Harrington, Helen Shaver, Mary Jackson, Peter White, Brad Savage, Maggie Sullivan. One's a prominent social-climbing attorney, the other's a blue collar worker harboring guilt for their father's accidental death. Theirs is the grist for soaps. Average.

Between Two Women (1944) **83m.** D: Willis Goldbeck. Van Johnson, Lionel Barrymore, Gloria DeHaven, Keenan Wynn, Marilyn Maxwell, Keye Luke, Alma Kruger. SEE **Dr. Kildare** series.

Between Two Women (1986) **C-100m. TVM** D: Jon Avnet. Farrah Fawcett, Colleen Dewhurst, Michael Nouri, Bridgette Andersen, Danny Corkill, Steven Hill, Terry O'Quinn. A young wife trying to make a go of her marriage has to deal with her strong-willed mother-in-law living under the same roof. Gutsy performances by the two female stars spark this adaptation of Gillian Martin's novel *Living Arrows*. Dewhurst won an Emmy for her memorable work. Scripted by Larry Grusin and director Avnet. Above average.

Between Two Worlds (1944) **112m.** **½
D: Edward A. Blatt. John Garfield, Eleanor Parker, Sydney Greenstreet, Faye Emerson, Paul Henreid, Sara Allgood, Isobel Elsom, George Tobias, Edmund Gwenn. Updated remake of OUTWARD BOUND, with various deceased individuals aboard a ship that will take each one to heaven or hell. Flawed, but good acting by Warner Bros. star stock company makes it worthwhile.

Between Us Girls (1942) **89m.** ** D: Henry Koster. Kay Francis, Diana Barrymore, Robert Cummings, Andy Devine, John Boles, Scotty Beckett, Ethel Griffies. Chic Francis and daughter Barrymore both have romances at the same time in this OK comedy. Boles and Cummings are respective leads.

Beverly Hills Cop (1984) **C-105m.** ***½ D: Martin Brest. Eddie Murphy, Judge Reinhold, John Ashton, Lisa Eilbacher, Ronny Cox, Steven Berkoff, James Russo, Jonathan Banks, Stephen Elliott, Paul Reiser. Smart-mouthed Detroit cop, who never plays by the rules, goes to L.A. to track down an old friend's killers. Sassy, tough, and very funny vehicle for Murphy, who's in peak form as a guy who's never caught off guard. Deft blend of comedy and violent action, extremely well cast, with terrific song score to boot. Script by Daniel Petrie, Jr. Bronson Pinchot has hilarious scene-stealing role as gay art-gallery worker. Followed by a sequel.▼

Beverly Hills Cop II (1987) **C-102m.** ** D: Tony Scott. Eddie Murphy, Judge Reinhold, Jurgen Prochnow, Ronny Cox, John Ashton, Brigitte Nielsen, Allen Garfield, Dean Stockwell, Paul Reiser, Gil Hill, Robert Ridgley. Contrived, cold-hearted (and misogynistic) sequel has few laughs, mediocre music, and a ridiculous story: it manages to coast as far as it does on the strength of Murphy alone. All credibility goes out the window at the start when B.H. Captain Cox is seen talking to Murphy about a fishing trip. Are these the same characters we saw in the first film?▼

Beverly Hills Cowgirl Blues (1985) **C-100m. TVM** D: Corey Allen. James Brolin, Lisa Hartman, David Hemmings, Irena Ferris, Michael C. Gwynne, Alexa Hamilton, Lane Smith, Stuart Whitman. Lackadaisical cop movie mismatching a curvy lady detective from Laramie and a laid-back Beverly Hills policeman on the case of a killer from Wyoming. Average.

Beverly Hills Madam (1986) **C-100m. TVM** D: Harvey Hart. Faye Dunaway, Louis Jourdan, Melody Anderson, Donna Dixon, Terry Farrell, Marshall Colt, William Jordan. Flash and trash drama about a chic jet-setter and her stable of $1000-a-night call girls, with Faye giving it her loving-every-minute-of-it all. Average.▼

Beverly Hills Vamp (1989) **C-89m.** **½ D: Fred Olen Ray. Eddie Deezen, Britt Ekland, Tim Conway, Jr., Jay Richardson, Michelle Bauer, Robert Quarry, Dawn Wildsmith, Pat McCormick. Cheerfully cheap little film effectively spoofs itself while also being an entertaining vampire comedy. Jerry Lewis-oid Deezen is pitted against vampire madam Ekland and her three bloodsucking hookers.▼

Beware, My Lovely (1952) **77m.** **½ D: Harry Horner. Ida Lupino, Robert Ryan, Taylor Holmes, O. Z. Whitehead, Barbara Whiting. Widow Lupino hires Ryan as handyman, discovers he is psychopath; brooding and atmospheric.▼

Beware of Blondie (1950) **66m.** D: Edward Bernds. Penny Singleton, Arthur Lake, Larry Simms, Adele Jergens, Dick Wessel. SEE: **Blondie** series.

Beware of Children (1961-British) **80m.** *½ D: Gerald Thomas. Leslie Phillips, Geraldine McEwan, Julia Lockwood, Noel Purcell. Tedious attempt at lighthearted romp; young married couple transforms an inheritance of land into summer camp for all sorts of children, focusing on predictable pranks of youngsters.

Beware of Pity (1946-British) **102m.** **½ D: Maurice Elvey. Lilli Palmer, Albert Lieven, Cedric Hardwicke, Gladys Cooper. Maudlin but effective yarn of crippled young woman who finds romance and meaning to life.

Beware, Spooks! (1939) **68m.** ** D: Edward Sedgwick. Joe E. Brown, Mary Carlisle, Clarence Kolb, Marc Lawrence. Good fun as Brown solves mystery and becomes hero in Coney Island fun house.

Beware! The Blob (1972) **C-88m.** *½ D: Larry Hagman. Robert Walker, Richard Stahl, Godfrey Cambridge, Carol Lynley, Larry Hagman, Cindy Williams, Shelley Berman, Marlene Clark, Gerrit Graham, Dick Van Patten. They should have left it frozen in the Arctic. Weak comedy-sequel finds the gooey mess doing its thing once again. Also known as SON OF BLOB; reissued in 1982 with the tag line, "The Film That J.R. Shot!"▼

Bewitched (1945) **65m.** **½ D: Arch Oboler. Edmund Gwenn, Phyllis Thaxter, Henry Daniels, Jr., Addison Richards, Kathleen Lockhart. Interesting story of schizophrenic Thaxter who commits murder as one girl, doesn't recall it as the other.

Beyond a Reasonable Doubt (1956) **80m.** **½D: Fritz Lang. Dana Andrews, Joan Fontaine, Sidney Blackmer, Philip Bourneuf, Barbara Nichols. Far-fetched tale of man who pretends to be guilty of murder to get first-hand view of justice system, unable to prove himself innocent later on. Pale production values. Intriguing idea doesn't hold up.

Beyond Atlantis (1973-U.S.-Filipino) **C-89m.** *½ D: Eddie Romero. Patrick

Wayne, John Ashley, Leigh Christian, Lenore Stevens, George Nader, Sid Haig, Eddie Garcia, Vic Diaz. Low-budget fantasy about lost civilization, represented by amphibious humanoids; combines feminist subplot with philosophizing about modern extinction of cultures.▼

Beyond Evil (1980) C-94m. ** D: Herb Freed. John Saxon, Lynda Day George, Michael Dante, Mario Milano, Janice Lynde, David Opatoshu. Saxon and George move into an old house occupied by the spirit of a 100-year-old woman, who does not like this intrusion into her privacy. OK of its kind.▼

Beyond Forty SEE: Over Forty

Beyond Glory (1948) 82m. **½ D: John Farrow. Alan Ladd, Donna Reed, George Macready, George Coulouris. Predictable account of West Point captain Ladd, a WW2 veteran, on trial for misconduct; nicely done trivia. Also Audie Murphy's first film.

Beyond Mombasa (1957-U.S.-British) C-90m. ** D: George Marshall. Cornel Wilde, Donna Reed, Leo Genn, Ron Randell, Christopher Lee. Tame African adventure tale with Wilde seeking mysterious killers of his brother and clues to hidden uranium mine.

Beyond Reason (1977) C-83m. *½ D: Telly Savalas. Telly Savalas, Laura Johnson, Diana Muldaur, Marvin Laird, Bob Basso, Biff Elliot. Savalas made his writing-directing debut with this film about a psychologist who's going off the deep end. Never released theatrically, and it's easy to see why. Priscilla Barnes was replaced as leading lady but still turns up in several shots.▼

Beyond Reasonable Doubt (1980-New Zealand) C-127m. **½ D: John Laing. David Hemmings, John Hargreaves, Martyn Sanderson, Grant Tilly, Diana Rowan, Ian Watkin. Adequate docudrama chronicling the conviction on trumped-up charges of innocent farmer Arthur Thomas (Hargreaves) for a double murder. Hemmings is good as the hard-boiled cop who plants evidence that leads to Thomas's downfall. Based on a book by David Yallop.▼

Beyond the Bermuda Triangle (1975) C-78m. TVM D: William A. Graham. Fred MacMurray, Sam Groom, Donna Mills, Suzanne Reed, Dana Plato, Woody Woodbury. Retired businessman MacMurray probes into mysterious ship and plane disappearances off Florida coast after his friends and fiancee become involved. Foolish, two-dimensional mystery drama. Below average.▼

Beyond the Blue Horizon (1942) C-76m. ** D: Alfred Santell. Dorothy Lamour, Richard Denning, Jack Haley, Walter Abel, Elizabeth Patterson, Abner Biberman, Patricia Morison. Sarong queen Lamour turns out to be heiress to great fortune; witless film wastes more talent than usual.

Beyond the Door (1974-U.S.-Italian) C-94m. BOMB D: Oliver Hellman (Ovidio Assonitis). Juliet Mills, Richard Johnson, Elizabeth Turner, David Colin, Jr. Mills becomes pregnant with a fetus possessed by the Devil. Vulgar EXORCIST ripoff, complete with pea-green regurgitation, head spins, and Mercedes McCambridge-like voice. Warner Bros. even took legal action against the film, accusing its makers of plagiarism. Followed by the inevitable BEYOND THE DOOR II.▼

Beyond the Door II (1979-Italian) C-92m. *½ D: Mario Bava. Daria Nicolodi, John Steiner, David Colin, Jr., Ivan Rassimov. Corpse of dead man possesses his son, seeks vengeance on his wife. Nice directorial touches cannot save confusing, needlessly bloody EXORCIST clone; only resemblances to BEYOND THE DOOR I are cast member Colin and "possession" plot line.▼

Beyond the Door (1982-Italian) C-116m. ** D: Liliana Cavani. Marcello Mastroianni, Tom Berenger, Eleonora Giorgi, Michel Piccoli. Overbaked melodrama centering on complex relationship between jailed father Mastroianni and daughter Giorgi, complicated by arrival of American engineer Berenger.

Beyond the Fog SEE: **Horror on Snape Island**▼

Beyond the Forest (1949) 96m. ** D: King Vidor. Bette Davis, Joseph Cotten, David Brian, Ruth Roman, Dona Drake, Regis Toomey. Muddled murder story of grasping Davis, her small-town doctor husband (Cotten), and wealthy neighbor (Brian). Davis' overly mannered performance doesn't help. This is the film in which she utters the immortal line, "What a dump!"

Beyond the Law (1968-Italian) C-91m. ** D: Giorgio Stegani. Lee Van Cleef, Antonio Sabato, Lionel Stander, Bud Spencer, Gordon Mitchell, Ann Smyrner. Formula Western with a whole lot of Van Cleef and almost as much humor. Bad guy turns good guy, becomes sheriff long enough to get his hands on a shipment of silver, and then splits.▼

Beyond the Limit (1983) C-103m. *½ D: John Mackenzie. Michael Caine, Richard Gere, Bob Hoskins, Elpidia Carrillo, Joaquim De Almeida, A Martinez. Muddled adaptation of Graham Greene's *The Honorary Consul* with Gere miscast as British doctor who becomes involved with revolutionaries in South American country—and sexually involved with the ex-prostitute wife of boozy diplomat (well played by Caine). Slow, murky, completely uninvolving.▼

Beyond the Living (1978) C-88m. ** D: Al Adamson. Jill Jacobson, Geoffrey Land, Marilyn Joi, Mary Kay Pass. OK horrorpic in the CARRIE vein. Nurse is possessed by the spirit of a patient who died during surgery and begins killing the doctors who performed the operation. Best scene takes place in a foundry. Released to theatres as NURSE SHERRI.

Beyond the Poseidon Adventure (1979) **C-122m.** *½ D: Irwin Allen. Michael Caine, Sally Field, Telly Savalas, Peter Boyle, Jack Warden, Shirley Knight, Slim Pickens, Shirley Jones, Karl Malden, Mark Harmon, Veronica Hamel. Following THE SWARM, Caine teamed up with Irwin Allen for their second career killer in a row—a needless sequel about attempts to loot the vessel before it sinks.▼

Beyond Therapy (1987) **C-93m.** BOMB D: Robert Altman. Julie Hagerty, Jeff Goldblum, Glenda Jackson, Tom Conti, Christopher Guest, Genevieve Page, Cris Campion, Sandrine Dumas. Dreadful adaptation of Christopher Durang's paper-thin comic play about neurotic New York singles and their psychiatrists. Given that director and cast, it's hard to believe how awful this is—until you see for yourself! Filmed in Paris, though set in N.Y.C.▼

Beyond the Reef (1981) **C-91m.** ** D: Frank C. Clark. Dayton Ka'ne, Maren Jensen, Kathleen Swan, Keahi Farden, Joseph Ka'ne. In the wake of THE HURRICANE, Dino De Laurentiis produced this innocuous South Seas romance with two attractive leads. Old fashioned, to say the least. Completed in 1979. Also known as SHARK BOY OF BORA BORA and SEA KILLER.

Beyond the Time Barrier (1960) **75m.** ** D: Edgar G. Ulmer. Robert Clarke, Darlene Tompkins, Arianne Arden, Vladimir Sokoloff. Military pilot is thrust into 21st century, seeing tragic results of worldwide epidemic of 1970.▼

Beyond the Valley of the Dolls (1970) **C-109m.** *** D: Russ Meyer. Dolly Read, Cynthia Myers, Marcia McBroom, David Gurian, John LaZar, Michael Blodgett, Edy Williams, Erica Gavin, Phyllis Davis, Charles Napier, Strawberry Alarm Clock. Female rock trio attempts to make it (and make it and make it) in Hollywood. Time has been kind to raunchy in-name-only sequel to VALLEY OF THE DOLLS, screenplay by Roger Ebert, story by Meyer and Ebert, and picked by two prominent critics as one of the 10 best U.S. films 1968-78.▼

Beyond the Walls (1984-Israeli) **C-103m.** ** D: Uri Barbash. Arnon Zadok, Muhamad Bakri, Assi Dayan, Rami Danon, Boaz Sharambi. This potentially powerful drama about life in an Israeli prison, centering on the explosive relationship between Jewish and Arab convicts, is just a standard, predictable, noisy men-in-the-big-house yarn.

Incredibly, it earned Best Foreign Film Oscar nomination.▼

Beyond Tomorrow (1940) **84m.** **½ D: A. Edward Sutherland. Richard Carlson, Jean Parker, Harry Carey, C. Aubrey Smith, Charles Winninger, Maria Ouspenskaya, Rod LaRocque. Sensitive little drama of three wealthy men sharing Christmas with down-and-out Carlson and Parker, who fall in love.▼

Be Yourself (1930) **77m.** ** D: Thornton Freeland. Fanny Brice, Robert Armstrong, Harry Green, Gertrude Astor, Pat Collins. Contrived vehicle for Fanny as nightclub entertainer who falls in love with punchy prizefighter (Armstrong); silly story, overdose of sentiment leave too few moments for star to be herself.

B. F.'s Daughter (1948) **108m.** *½ D: Robert Z. Leonard. Barbara Stanwyck, Van Heflin, Charles Coburn, Richard Hart, Keenan Wynn, Margaret Lindsay. Disastrous film of J. P. Marquand novel, with Stanwyck the domineering girl ruining marriage to professor Heflin.

Bhowani Junction (1956-U.S.-British) **C-110m.** **½ D: George Cukor. Ava Gardner, Stewart Granger, Bill Travers, Abraham Sofaer. Set in post WW2 India; Gardner is half-caste torn between love of country and love for a British colonel. Based on John Masters novel, film was strikingly photographed on location.

Bible, The (1966-Italian) **C-174m.** BOMB D: John Huston. Michael Parks, Ullu Bergryd, Richard Harris, John Huston, Stephen Boyd, George C. Scott, Ava Gardner, Peter O'Toole, Franco Nero. Unsuccessful epic dealing with Adam and Eve, Cain and Abel, Noah and the Flood, etc. (first 22 chapters of Genesis). Only Huston himself as Noah escapes heavy-handedness. Definitely one time you should read the book instead.▼

Bicycle Thief, The (1949-Italian) **90m.** ✓ **** D: Vittorio De Sica. Lamberto Maggiorani, Lianella Carell, Enzo Staiola, Elena Altieri. Simple, realistic tale of working-man whose job depends on his bicycle, and the shattering week he spends with his young son after it is stolen. An honest, beautiful film that deservedly earned a special Academy Award (before foreign films had a category of their own); one of the all-time classics.▼

Big (1988) **C-102m.** ***½ D: Penny Marshall. Tom Hanks, Elizabeth Perkins, John Heard, Jared Rushton, Robert Loggia, David Moscow, Jon Lovitz, Mercedes Ruehl, Josh Clark, Tracy Reiner. A 12-year-old boy wishes he were "big"—and gets his wish, waking up the next morning in the body of a 30-year-old man! Charming fantasy tackles a rare modern-day subject—innocence—and pulls it off thanks to Hanks' superb, seemingly guileless performance, and Marshall's surefooted direction. A real treat. Written by coproducers Gary Ross and Anne Spielberg.▼

Bigamist, The (1953) **80m.** *** **D:** Ida Lupino. Edmond O'Brien, Joan Fontaine, Ida Lupino, Edmund Gwenn, Jane Darwell, Kenneth Tobey. Compassionate look at lonely man who finds himself married to (and in love with) two different women. Extremely well acted; one of Lupino's best directorial efforts and the only time she ever directed herself.

Big Bad Mama (1974) **C-83m.** *** **D:** Steve Carver. Angie Dickinson, Tom Skerritt, William Shatner, Susan Sennett, Robbie Lee, Dick Miller, Joan Prather, Royal Dano, Sally Kirkland. Sexy knock-off of BONNIE AND CLYDE has Angie and her two teen daughters spending as much time fooling around with partners Shatner and Skerritt as they do robbing banks. Angie's nude scenes make this a cable-TV favorite (and led to a sequel thirteen years later!). Flavorful score by David Grisman.▼

Big Bad Mama II (1987) **C-83m.** *½ **D:** Jim Wynorski. Angie Dickinson, Robert Culp, Danielle Brisebois, Julie McCullough, Bruce Glover. In this loosely linked sequel (more like a remake), Angie and her two daughters again shoot up rural, Depression-era America, robbing banks to avenge her husband's murder. Culp provides brief love interest. *Archie Bunker's Place* alumna Brisebois does a surprising topless scene.▼

Big Beat, The (1958) **C-81m.** ** **D:** Will Cowan. William Reynolds, Andra Martin, Gogi Grant, Rose Marie, Hans Conried, Jeffrey Stone, The Del Vikings, Fats Domino, The Diamonds, The Four Aces, Harry James, Mills Brothers. Reynolds is a record exec, Martin his secretary. The Big Bore—except for the vintage performances of Domino ("I'm Walking"), The Diamonds ("Little Darling") and company.

Big Bird Cage, The (1972) **C-88m.** **½ **D:** Jack Hill. Pam Grier, Anitra Ford, Sid Haig, Candice Roman, Vic Diaz, Carol Speed. Amusing spoof of Filipino prison films has pleasant team of Grier and Haig as thieving mercenaries who engineer a prison break from the outside. A follow-up to THE BIG DOLL HOUSE.▼

Big Black Pill, The (1981) **C-100m. TVM D:** Reza Badiyi. Robert Blake, JoBeth Williams, Neva Paterson, James Gammon, Veronica Cartwright, Edward Winter, Carol Wayne, Sondra Blake, Eileen Heckart, Wilford Brimley, Bubba Smith. The first of three pilot movies about a rugged private eye facing an unwarranted murder rap; created by Blake after shaking the "Baretta" image. Retitled JOE DANCER. Followed by THE MONKEY MISSION. Average.

Big Blockade, The (1942-British) **77m.** ** **D:** Charles Frend. Michael Redgrave, Leslie Banks, Will Hay, John Mills, Frank Cellier, Robert Morley, Alfred Drayton, Bernard Miles, Marius Goring, Michael Rennie, Michael Wilding. Dated propaganda chronicling Britain's economic blockade of Nazi Germany.

Big Blue, The (1988-U.S.-French) **C-119m.** ** **D:** Luc Besson. Rosanna Arquette, Jean-Marc Barr, Jean Reno, Paul Shenar, Sergio Castellito, Marc Duret, Griffin Dunne. Waterlogged chronicle of famed free diver Jacques Mayol (Barr), with Arquette redoing her DESPERATELY SEEKING SUSAN performance as a ditsy insurance investigator who falls for him. As much a psychological study as a drama of athletic competition—but who cares? Underwater photography is the main attraction here.▼

Big Bluff, The (1955) **70m.** ** **D:** W. Lee Wilder. John Bromfield, Martha Vickers. Robert Hutton, Rosemarie Bowe. Interesting premise poorly executed. Vickers is fatally ill girl married to fortune-hunter who seeks to murder her when she recovers from illness.▼

Big Bob Johnson and His Fantastic Speed Circus (1978) **C-100m. TVM D:** Jack Starrett. Charles Napier, Maud Adams, Constance Forslund, Robert Stoneman, William Daniels. Rambunctious comedy pitting a rag-tag auto racing team against a blackguard in Rolls-Royce for a run across Louisiana with a fortune at stake. Average.

Big Boodle, The (1957) **83m.** *½ **D:** Richard Wilson. Errol Flynn, Pedro Armendariz, Rossana Rory, Jacques Aubuchon. Seedy programmer emphasizing Flynn's career decline. Tame caper of gangsters and counterfeit money, set in Havana.

Big Bounce, The (1969) **C-102m.** ** **D:** Alex March. Ryan O'Neal, Leigh Taylor-Young, James Daly, Robert Webber, Lee Grant, Van Heflin. Muddle-headed tale of drifter O'Neal becoming involved with vixenish Taylor-Young, who has strange ideas of what to do for kicks.

Big Boy (1930) **69m.** **½ **D:** Alan Crosland. Al Jolson, Claudia Dell, Louise Closser Hale, Lloyd Hughes, Eddie Phillips, John Harron, Noah Beery. Jolson energetically recreates his 1925 stage success as Gus, black stable boy who hopes to ride the title horse in the Kentucky Derby. Jolie appears in blackface until the conclusion, when he sings "Tomorrow Is Another Day." A real curio, extremely dated, but fascinating nonetheless.

Big Brawl, The (1980) **C-95m.** **½ **D:** Robert Clouse. Jackie Chan, Jose Ferrer, Kristine DeBell, Mako, Ron Max. The martial arts are applied to '30s gangster movie set in Chicago. Appealing cast, lots of comedy, along with director and some of the production staff from ENTER THE DRAGON, make this a moderately successful chop-socky.▼

Big Broadcast, The (1932) 78m. *** D: Frank Tuttle. Bing Crosby, Kate Smith, George Burns, Gracie Allen, Stuart Erwin, Leila Hyams, Cab Calloway, Mills Brothers, Boswell Sisters. Failing radio station owned by Burns is saved by all-star show featuring Bing and many radio stars. Many offbeat, bizarre touches in standard love-triangle story make this a delight. Bing sings "Please," "Here Lies Love."

Big Broadcast of 1936, The (1935) 97m. **½ D: Norman Taurog. Jack Oakie, George Burns, Gracie Allen, Lyda Roberti, Henry Wadsworth, Wendy Barrie, C. Henry Gordon, Ethel Merman, Charlie Ruggles, Mary Boland, Bill "Bojangles" Robinson. Curious muddle of specialty acts and nonsensical "plot" involving radio station owner Oakie. Vignettes feature everyone from radio's original Amos 'n' Andy (Freeman Gosden and Charles Correll, in blackface) to the Vienna Boys Choir. Bing Crosby sings lovely "I Wished on the Moon."

Big Broadcast of 1937, The (1936) 102m. *** D: Mitchell Leisen. Jack Benny, George Burns, Gracie Allen, Bob Burns, Martha Raye, Shirley Ross, Ray Milland. Another plotless but enjoyable variety romp with many stars, plus guests Benny Goodman, Leopold Stokowski, Larry Adler, etc. Songs such as: "Here's Love In Your Eye," "La Bomba," "Night In Manhattan."

Big Broadcast of 1938, The (1938) 90m. ** D: Mitchell Leisen. W. C. Fields, Martha Raye, Dorothy Lamour, Shirley Ross, Lynne Overman, Bob Hope, Ben Blue, Leif Erickson. Hodgepodge of bad musical numbers from Tito Guizar to Kirsten Flagstad, notable only for Fields' few scenes, Hope and Ross's rendition of Oscar-winning "Thanks For The Memory." Hope's first feature.

Big Brown Eyes (1936) 77m. **½ D: Raoul Walsh. Joan Bennett, Cary Grant, Walter Pidgeon, Isabel Jewell, Lloyd Nolan. Bennett helps detective Grant trap a gang of notorious thieves in pleasing romantic mystery.

Big Bus, The (1976) C-88m. **½ D: James Frawley. Joseph Bologna, Stockard Channing, John Beck, Lynn Redgrave, Jose Ferrer, Ruth Gordon, Richard B. Shull, Sally Kellerman, Ned Beatty, Bob Dishy, Stuart Margolin, Richard Mulligan, Larry Hagman, Howard Hesseman, Harold Gould. Funny spoof of disaster films, using a super-duper Trailways bus; all expected cliches come in for ribbing, but film doesn't sustain its promising idea. Murphy Dunne hilarious as inane cocktail pianist.▼

Big Business (1988) C-97m. **½ D: Jim Abrahams. Bette Midler, Lily Tomlin, Fred Ward, Edward Herrmann, Michele Placido, Daniel Gerroll, Barry Primus, Michael Gross, Joe Grifasi, Mary Gross. Two sets of twins are mismatched and separated at birth; years later the girls who've grown up in the boonies come to N.Y.C. for a showdown with the conglomerate that's going to wipe out their little town, hardly dreaming that the corporation is run by their identical twins! Agreeable farce never really catches fire, though Bette is terrific as usual, and the special effects are quite remarkable.▼

Big Business Girl (1931) 75m. ** D: William A. Seiter. Loretta Young, Ricardo Cortez, Jack Albertson, Joan Blondell, Frank Darien. Young is cute and perky as a career-minded woman working her way up the corporate ladder while trying to help her singer-boyfriend and keeping her amorous boss at arm's length.

Big Cage, The (1933) 82m. **½ D: Kurt Neumann. Clyde Beatty, Anita Page, Mickey Rooney, Andy Devine, Vince Barnett, Raymond Hatton, Wallace Ford. Beatty plays himself in silly but watchable circus story; sappy love angle doesn't help, but supporting cast does, including Mickey as youngster who wants to be Just Like Beatty. Exciting animal footage was reused in countless subsequent films.

Big Caper, The (1957) 84m. **½ D: Robert Stevens. Rory Calhoun, Mary Costa, James Gregory, Robert Harris. Well-done account of Calhoun and Costa posing as married couple in small town in order to set up gang caper; realities of life reform them.

Big Carnival, The (1951) 112m. *** D: Billy Wilder. Kirk Douglas, Jan Sterling, Bob Arthur, Porter Hall, Frank Cady, Richard Benedict, Ray Teal, Gene Evans. Unrelenting cynicism is theme of hard-hitting Wilder drama of reporter Douglas, who capitalizes on Albuquerque mining tragedy. Not for all tastes, but biting and extremely well-acted. Originally titled ACE IN THE HOLE.

Big Chill, The (1983) C-103m. *** D: Lawrence Kasdan. Tom Berenger, Glenn Close, Jeff Goldblum, William Hurt, Kevin Kline, Mary Kay Place, Meg Tilly, JoBeth Williams, Don Galloway. Entertaining, surface-level look at a group of former college-radical friends who've dropped back into Society. Wonderful acting ensemble, irresistible soundtrack of 60s hits help camouflage weaknesses of script—which bears more than passing resemblance to John Sayles' RETURN OF THE SECAUCUS 7.▼

Big Circus, The (1959) C-108m. **½ D: Joseph M. Newman. Victor Mature, Red Buttons, Rhonda Fleming, Kathryn Grant, Vincent Price, Peter Lorre, David Nelson, Gilbert Roland, Howard McNear, Steve

Allen. Familiar but well-done circus story with exceptional cast (Lorre as a clown is worth the price of admission). Big-top action and intrigue is entertaining.

Big City, The (1937) **80m.** ****½** D: Frank Borzage. Spencer Tracy, Luise Rainer, Eddie Quillan, William Demarest, Regis Toomey, Charley Grapewin, Victor Varconi. Cabdriver Tracy and wife Rainer are pitted against crooked taxi bosses in well-acted but average film. Retitled: SKYSCRAPER WILDERNESS.

Big City, The (1948) **103m.** ****½** D: Norman Taurog. Margaret O'Brien, Robert Preston, Danny Thomas, George Murphy, Betty Garrett. Priest Preston, cantor Thomas, and cop Murphy "adopt" little O'Brien in this maudlin drama.

Big City Blues (1932) **65m.** ****½** D: Mervyn LeRoy. Joan Blondell, Eric Linden, Inez Courtney, Evalyn Knapp, Guy Kibbee, Humphrey Bogart, Ned Sparks. Polished Warner Bros. programmer of hayseed Linden encountering disillusionment and love in N.Y.C.

Big Clock, The (1948) **95m.** ******* D: John Farrow. Ray Milland, Charles Laughton, Maureen O'Sullivan, George Macready, Rita Johnson, Dan Tobin, Henry (Harry) Morgan. Tyrannical editor of crime magazine (Laughton) commits murder; his ace reporter (Milland) tries to solve case . . . and finds all the clues pointing to himself. Vibrant melodrama; taut script by Jonathan Latimore, from Kenneth Fearing's novel. Elsa Lanchester has hilarious vignette as eccentric artist. Remade as NO WAY OUT (1987).

Big Combo, The (1955) **89m.** ******* D: Joseph (H.) Lewis. Cornel Wilde, Jean Wallace, Brian Donlevy, Richard Conte, Lee Van Cleef, Robert Middleton, Earl Holliman, Helen Walker. Raw, violent *film noir* about persistent cop Wilde going up against cunning, sadistic racketeer Conte. A cult item, stylishly directed; Donlevy's demise is a highlight.▼

Big Country, The (1958) **C-166m.** ******* D: William Wyler. Gregory Peck, Burl Ives, Jean Simmons, Carroll Baker, Charlton Heston, Chuck Connors, Charles Bickford. Overblown Western has ex-sea captain Peck arrive to marry Baker, but forced to take sides in battle against Ives and sons over water rights. Heston as quick-tempered ranch foreman and Ives (who won an Oscar) as burly patriarch stand out in energetic cast. Jerome Moross' score has become a classic.▼

Big Cube, The (1969) **C-98m.** ***½** D: Tito Davison. Lana Turner, George Chakiris, Richard Egan, Dan O'Herlihy, Karin Mossberg. Absurd drama about relationship between beautiful young girl, her gigolo boyfriend, and her actress-mother at least offers some unintentional laughs. For camp followers only.

Big Deal on Madonna Street (1956-Italian) **91m.** *****½** D: Mario Monicelli. Vittorio Gassman, Marcello Mastroianni, Renato Salvatori, Rossana Rory, Carla Gravina, Toto. Classic account of misadventures of amateurish crooks attempting to rob a store; hilarious satire on all burglary capers. Retitled: BIG DEAL; remade as CRACKERS, and followed by a sequel, BIG DEAL ON MADONNA STREET . . . 20 YEARS LATER, which was actually released 30 years later! Also adapted for Broadway—unsuccessfully.▼

Big Doll House, The (1971) **C-93m.** ****½** D: Jack Hill. Judy Brown, Roberta Collins, Pam Grier, Brooke Mills, Pat Woodell, Sid Haig. Fast paced, tongue-in-cheek adventure shot in Philippines mixes sex, comedy, and violence in confrontation between sadistic warden and female prisoners. One of the earliest, most successful, and most influential of recent women-in-prison exploitation films. Followed by THE BIG BIRD CAGE.▼

Big Easy, The (1987) **C-108m.** ******* D: Jim McBride. Dennis Quaid, Ellen Barkin, Ned Beatty, John Goodman, Ebbe Roe Smith, Lisa Jane Persky, Charles Ludlam, Tom O'Brien, Grace Zabriskie, Marc Lawrence, Solomon Burke, Jim Garrison. Highly original crime yarn with steamy romance and unique New Orleans atmosphere neatly folded in. Quaid plays a stylish homicide detective who runs afoul of the new, uptight assistant D.A. (Barkin) while investigating a local mob murder; she soon finds herself romantically involved with him, even while they're at odds professionally. Sassy and sexy, with terrific Cajun music score. Written by Daniel Petrie, Jr.▼

Big Fisherman, The (1959) **C-180m.** ****½** D: Frank Borzage. Howard Keel, John Saxon, Susan Kohner, Herbert Lom, Martha Hyer, Ray Stricklyn, Alexander Scourby. Sprawling religious epic, from Lloyd Douglas' book about the life of St. Peter; seldom dull, but not terribly inspiring.

Big Fix, The (1978) **C-108m.** ******* D: Jeremy Paul Kagan. Richard Dreyfuss, Susan Anspach, Bonnie Bedelia, John Lithgow, F. Murray Abraham, Ofelia Medina, Fritz Weaver. Good vehicle for now-familiar Dreyfuss personality as he plays 1960s-campus-radical-turned-private-eye Moses Wine, and becomes involved in tangled whodunit in which a former hippie cult leader figures prominently. Screenplay by Roger L. Simon, based on his own novel. Look fast for Mandy Patinkin as a pool cleaner. Leon Redbone's "I Want to Be Seduced" is missing from video version.▼

Bigfoot (1987) **C-100m.** TVM D: Danny

Huston. Colleen Dewhurst, James Sloyan, Gracie Harrison, Joseph Maher, Adam Karl, Candace Cameron. A crusty anthropologist, two spunky youngsters, and a Sasquatch (Bigfoot, to you) and its mate are the elements of this Disney family adventure directed by Danny Huston, the legendary John's son. Extraspecial is the work of veteran makeup artist Robert Schiffer, who "created" the two Sasquatch. Average.

Big Gamble, The (1961) C-100m. **½ D: Richard Fleischer. Stephen Boyd, Juliette Greco, David Wayne, Sybil Thorndike. Not-too-convincing account of Irish adventurer and bride Greco who dally on the African Ivory Coast seeking to build their future the easy way.

Bigger Than Life (1956) C-95m. *** D: Nicholas Ray. James Mason, Barbara Rush, Walter Matthau, Robert Simon, Roland Winters. Compelling drama of teacher Mason who becomes hooked on drugs, and its devastating effects on him and his family. Mason also produced the film.

Biggest Battle, The SEE: **Greatest Battle, The**▼

Biggest Bundle of Them All, The (1968) C-110m. *½ D: Ken Annakin. Robert Wagner, Raquel Welch, Vittorio De Sica, Edward G. Robinson, Godfrey Cambridge. Supposedly a comedy, film is slapdash tale of amateur criminals who try to kidnap American gangster. Filmed in France and Italy.

Biggles: Adventures In Time (1986-British) C-108m. ** D: John Hough. Neil Dickson, Alex Hyde-White, Fiona Hutchinson, Peter Cushing, Marcus Gilbert. Curious, occasionally entertaining sci-fi adventure with Hyde-White inexplicably traveling through time from 1986 N.Y.C. to WW1 Europe . . . where he assists British flyboy Dickson. Based on characters created by Capt. W.E. Johns. Original British title: BIGGLES.▼

Big Guns SEE: **No Way Out** (1972)

Big Gusher, The (1951) 68m. *½ D: Lew Landers. Wayne Morris, Preston Foster, Dorothy Patrick, Paul Burns. Unshiny account of oil workers involved in hackneyed deadline to strike oil or lose all their savings.

Big Guy, The (1939) 78m. **½ D: Arthur Lubin. Jackie Cooper, Victor McLaglen, Ona Munson, Peggy Moran, Edward Brophy. Fairly interesting story of warden McLaglen given choice between wealth and saving innocent man from death penalty. Remade as BEHIND THE HIGH WALL.

✓ **Big Hand for the Little Lady, A** (1966) C-95m. *** D: Fielder Cook. Henry Fonda, Joanne Woodward, Jason Robards, Charles Bickford, Burgess Meredith. Excellent comedy centering on poker game in old West. Outstanding roster of character actors includes John Qualen, Paul Ford, and Robert Middleton. There's a neat surprise ending, too.

Big Hangover, The (1950) 82m. ** D: Norman Krasna. Van Johnson, Elizabeth Taylor, Leon Ames, Edgar Buchanan, Rosemary DeCamp, Gene Lockhart. Ambitious but noble war veteran Johnson, whose allergy to alcohol makes him drunk at inopportune moments, joins a staid law firm. How long will he remain there? And will he hook up with wealthy Taylor? Predictable, as well as silly and boring.

Big Heat, The (1953) 90m. *** D: Fritz Lang. Glenn Ford, Gloria Grahame, Jocelyn Brando, Lee Marvin, Carolyn Jones, Jeanette Nolan. Time has taken the edge off once-searing story of cop determined to bust city crime ring; famous coffee-hurling scene still jolts, and Grahame is excellent as bad-girl who helps Ford.▼

Big House, The (1930) 86m. *** D: ✓ George Hill. Wallace Beery, Chester Morris, Robert Montgomery, Lewis Stone, Karl Dane, Leila Hyams. The original prison drama, this set the pattern for all later copies; it's still good, hard-bitten stuff with one of Beery's best tough-guy roles. Won Oscars for Writing (Frances Marion) and Sound Recording.

Big House, U.S.A. (1955) 82m. **½ D: Howard W. Koch. Broderick Crawford, Ralph Meeker, Reed Hadley, Charles Bronson, Lon Chaney, Jr. Brutal account of kidnappers and extortion, and the FBI agents sent to track them down.

Big Jack (1949) 85m. ** D: Richard Thorpe. Wallace Beery, Marjorie Main, Edward Arnold, Richard Conte, Vanessa Brown. Beery's last film, rather flat; he and Main are vagabond thieves in colonial America, Conte a moralistic doctor.

Big Jake (1971) C-110m. ** D: George ? Sherman. John Wayne, Richard Boone, Maureen O'Hara, Patrick Wayne, Chris Mitchum, Bobby Vinton, Bruce Cabot. Uneasy combination of traditional Wayne Western and BUTCH CASSIDY-type spoof has Duke going after baddies who have kidnapped his grandson. Sounds as if it can't miss, but it does; excessively violent. Good performance by Boone.▼

Big Jim McLain (1952) 90m. **½ D: Edward Ludwig. John Wayne, James Arness, Nancy Olson, Veda Ann Borg, Hans Conried. One of the few dull Wayne films: story filmed in Hawaii tells of zealous government agent Wayne tracking down Communist spy ring.

Big Knife, The (1955) 111m. *** D: Robert Aldrich. Jack Palance, Ida Lupino, Shelley Winters, Rod Steiger, Ilka Chase, Wendell Corey. Clifford Odets' cynical view of Hollywood comes across well in hard-punching film, with fine portrayals that almost overcome stereotypes.

Big Land, The (1957) **C-92m.** **½ D: Gordon Douglas. Alan Ladd, Virginia Mayo, Edmond O'Brien, Julie Bishop. Cattle owners and grain farmers join together to bring railroad link to Texas; easygoing, familiar.

Big Leaguer, The (1953) **70m.** ** D: Robert Aldrich. Edward G. Robinson, Vera-Ellen, Jeff Richards, Richard Jaeckel. Baseball programmer of college-bound boy being scouted for the big diamond. Robinson wasted.

Big Lift, The (1950) **120m.** **½ D: George Seaton. Montgomery Clift, Paul Douglas, Cornell Borchers, O. E. Hasse. GI pilots involved in post-WW2 Berlin airlift and romance with German women. More interesting for on location photography than uneven story line.▼

Big Lobby, The SEE: **Rosebud Beach Hotel, The▼**

Big Mo SEE: **Maurie▼**

Big Mouth, The (1967) **C-107m.** **½ D: Jerry Lewis. Jerry Lewis, Harold Stone, Susan Bay, Buddy Lester, Del Moore, Paul Lambert. Typical Lewis effort, with Jerry involved in murder and search for missing treasure in Southern California.▼

Big Night, The (1951) **75m.** **½ D: Joseph Losey. John Barrymore, Jr., Preston Foster, Howland Chamberlain, Joan Lorring, Dorothy Comingore, Howard St. John. Brooding account of rebellious teenager Barrymore's emotional flare-up with humanity at large; well done.

Big Noise, The (1944) **74m.** BOMB D: Malcolm St. Clair. Stan Laurel, Oliver Hardy, Arthur Space, Veda Ann Borg, Bobby Blake, Jack Norton. L&H's worst film, about them delivering a bomb . . . and they do.

Big Operator, The (1959) **91m.** ** D: Charles Haas. Mickey Rooney, Steve Cochran, Mamie Van Doren, Mel Torme, Ray Danton, Jim Backus. Ray Anthony, Jackie Coogan. Rooney tries to add vim and vigor to title role as tough hood who goes on violent rampage when federal agents investigate his business activities. Paul Gallico story filmed before as JOE SMITH, AMERICAN. Retitled: ANATOMY OF A SYNDICATE.

Big Parade, The (1925) **141m.** **** D: King Vidor. John Gilbert, Renee Adoree, Hobart Bosworth, Claire McDowell, Claire Adams, Karl Dane. One of the best WW1 films ever; clean-shaven Gilbert a wonderful hero, Adoree an unforgettable heroine. Filled with memorable vignettes, and some of the most harrowingly realistic battle scenes ever filmed. A gem.▼

Big Parade of Comedy SEE: **MGM's Big Parade of Comedy**

Big Picture, The (1989) **C-100m.** **½ D: Christopher Guest. Kevin Bacon, Emily Longstreth, J. T. Walsh, Jennifer Jason Leigh, Michael McKean, Kim Miyori, Teri Hatcher, Dan Schneider, Jason Gould, Tracy Brooks Swope. Slight but good-natured comedy about Hollywood wheeling and dealing, with Bacon as a naive student filmmaker who's courted by a movie studio exec and swallowed whole into The System. Lots of inside jokes for Hollywood audiences. Very funny performance by Leigh as a dingbat, and many amusing cameos, including unbilled Martin Short as an agent. Guest's first feature as director (he also scripted with costar McKean).▼

Big Pond, The (1930) **75m.** **½ D: Hobart Henley. Maurice Chevalier, Claudette Colbert, George Barbier, Nat Pendleton. Claudette brings Maurice to America, where to make good he works in chewing gum factory. Chevalier charm overcomes trivia; song: "You Brought A New Kind Of Love To Me." Dialogue by Preston Sturges.

Big Punch, The (1948) **80m.** ** D: Sherry Shourds. Wayne Morris, Gordon MacRae, Lois Maxwell, Mary Stuart, Jimmy Ames, Anthony Warde. Boxer MacRae is falsely accused of murder, finds refuge with Morris, who has spurned ring for the pulpit. Serviceable melodrama.

Big Red (1962) **C-89m.** *** D: Norman Tokar. Walter Pidgeon, Gilles Payant, Emile Genest, Janette Bertrand, Doris Lussier. Charming, understated Disney drama of young boy who goes to work for wealthy dog fancier (Pidgeon) and becomes devoted to prize Irish setter. Fine family fare. Filmed in Canada.▼

Big Red One, The (1980) **C-113m.** ***½ D: Samuel Fuller. Lee Marvin, Mark Hamill, Robert Carradine, Bobby Di Cicco, Kelly Ward, Siegfried Rauch, Stephane Audran. Fuller returned to filmmaking after a long hiatus with this vivid, autobiographical account of a special infantry squadron and its intrepid sergeant during WW2. Hard to believe one film could pack so much into its narrative, but Fuller does it; a rich, moving, realistic, and poetic film.▼

Big Rip-Off, The (1975) **C-78m.** TVM D: Dean Hargrove. Tony Curtis, Brenda Vaccaro, Roscoe Lee Browne, Larry Hagman, John Dehner, Morgan Woodward. Conman Curtis plots elaborate swindle to recover ransom money from kidnappers of millionaire's wife. Reporter Vaccaro and night club performer Browne are his cohorts in this big rip-off of THE STING that evolved into Curtis' short-lived TV series *McCoy*. Average.

Big Risk, The (1960-French) **111m.** ** D: Claude Sautet. Jean-Paul Belmondo, Lino Ventura, Marcel Dalio, Sandra Milo. Too-leisurely-paced account of criminal on the lam, who for sake of his family gives himself up to police.

Big Rose: Double Trouble (1974) **C-78m.** TVM D: Paul Krasny. Shelley Winters,

Barry Primus, Lonny Chapman, Michael Constantine, Joan Van Ark, Peggy Walton. Detectives Winters and Primus are hired to expose team of con-artists blackmailing a wealthy contractor. It's fun watching Winters in unlikely role of private investigator; everything else is strictly formula. Below average.

Big Score, The (1983) **C-85m.** ** D: Fred Williamson. Fred Williamson, John Saxon, Richard Roundtree, Nancy Wilson, Ed Lauter, D'Urville Martin, Michael Dante, Joe Spinell. Barely adequate DIRTY HARRY clone with narc Williamson ignoring the rules and taking on thug Spinell. (In fact, this script was originally commissioned by Clint Eastwood for a Dirty Harry vehicle that never got made.)▼

Big Search, The SEE: **East of Kilimanjaro**

Big Shakedown, The (1934) **64m.** ** D: John Francis Dillon. Bette Davis, Ricardo Cortez, Glenda Farrell, Charles Farrell, Adrian Morris. Inconsequential tale. Davis rejects husband Farrell when he joins forces with mobster Cortez in cosmetic fraud.

Big Shot, The (1942) **82m.** **½ D: Lewis Seiler. Humphrey Bogart, Irene Manning, Susan Peters, Minor Watson, Chick Chandler, Richard Travis. OK grade-B gangster yarn with Bogey a three-time loser involved in robbery frameup and prison break.

Big Shots (1987) **C-90m.** **½ D: Robert Mandel. Ricky Busker, Darius McCrary, Robert Joy, Robert Prosky, Jerzy Skolimowski, Paul Winfield. So-so juvenile adventure about an inexperienced white boy and streetwise urban black who come together and become involved with dead bodies, hired killers and other mayhem.▼

Big Show, The (1961) **C-113m.** **½ D: James B. Clark. Esther Williams, Cliff Robertson, Nehemiah Persoff, Robert Vaughn. Drama of family conflict, similar to 1949's HOUSE OF STRANGERS, somehow set in a circus with swimmer Williams in a dramatic role. Glug!

Q **Big Sky, The** (1952) **122m.** *** D: Howard Hawks. Kirk Douglas, Dewey Martin, Elizabeth Threatt, Arthur Hunnicutt, Buddy Baer, Steven Geray, Hank Worden, Jim Davis. Camaraderie and conflict as furtrapper Douglas leads expedition up the Missouri River. Eventful, evocative film adapted from A. B. Guthrie, Jr.'s book by Dudley Nichols; well-directed by Hawks. Originally released at 141m. Also shown in computer-colored version.▼

Big Sleep, The (1946) **114m.** **** D: Howard Hawks. Humphrey Bogart, Lauren Bacall, John Ridgely, Martha Vickers, Louis Jean Heydt, Regis Toomey, Peggy Knudsen, Dorothy Malone, Bob Steele, Elisha Cook, Jr. Classic mystery thriller from Raymond Chandler's first novel; detective Philip Marlowe (Bogart) becomes involved with wealthy Bacall and her uncontrollable little sister Vickers. So convoluted even Chandler didn't know who committed one murder, but so incredibly entertaining that no one has ever cared. Powerhouse direction, unforgettable dialogue; script by William Faulkner, Jules Furthman and Leigh Brackett. Made in 1944, held back for general release (although prints of slightly different prerelease version still exist). Also shown in computer-colored version.▼

Big Sleep, The (1978-British) **C-100m.** ** D: Michael Winner. Robert Mitchum, Sarah Miles, Candy Clark, Oliver Reed, Richard Boone, James Stewart, Joan Collins, Edward Fox, John Mills, Harry Andrews, Richard Todd, Colin Blakely. Follow-up to FAREWELL, MY LOVELY is less a remake of the Hawks classic than a more faithful rendering of the Chandler novel, albeit updated and set in London. If you can get by that, it's tolerable, with a strong cast, fresh locations, and thankful lack of camp.▼

Big Steal, The (1949) **71m.** *** D: Don Siegel. Robert Mitchum, Jane Greer, William Bendix, Patric Knowles, Ramon Novarro. Well-made robbery caper set in Southwest and Mexico with Mitchum hustling after heisters, getting involved with enticing Greer. Full of terrific plot twists.

Big Store, The (1941) **80m.** ** D: Charles Riesner, Groucho, Chico and Harpo Marx, Tony Martin, Virginia Grey, Margaret Dumont, Douglass Dumbrille, Henry Armetta. Big comedown for Marxes in weak film of detective Groucho investigating crooked Dumbrille's department store. Low spot is Martin's ''The Tenement Symphony.''▼

Big Street, The (1942) **88m.** **½ D: Irving Reis. Henry Fonda, Lucille Ball, Barton MacLane, Eugene Pallette, Agnes Moorehead. Damon Runyon fable of timid busboy Fonda who devotes himself to disinterested nightclub singer Ball; wavers from good to too-sticky.▼

Big Time (1988) **C-87m.** *** D: Chris Blum. Tom Waits. Concert footage filmed at L.A.'s Wiltern Theater is combined with scenes of the chameleonlike Waits as various and sundry characters: you'll see Waits the sleazy lounge lizard, Waits the gravel-voiced crooner, and Waits the truly amazing performer. For Tom Waits fans, this is the next best thing to seeing him live.▼

Big Tip Off, The (1955) **79m.** *½ D: Frank McDonald. Richard Conte, Constance Smith, Bruce Bennett, Cathy Downs, James Millican, Dick Benedict. Occasionally confusing, ultimately forgettable programmer about newspaper columnist Conte and his dealings with hood Bennett and a fund-raising sham.

Big T.N.T. Show, The (1966) **93m.** ** D: Larry Peerce. David McCallum, Roger Miller, Joan Baez, Ike and Tina Turner, Bo Diddley, The Ronettes, Ray Charles,

The Lovin' Spoonful. Follow-up to THE T.A.M.I. SHOW casts a wider musical net, with lesser results, but Diddley, Tina Turner, and Ronnie Spector keep things pumping. Shot on tape, transferred to film; footage later reused in THAT WAS ROCK.

Big Top Pee-wee (1988) **C-90m.** **½ D: Randal Kleiser. Pee-wee Herman, Penelope Ann Miller, Kris Kristofferson, Valeria Golino, Susan Tyrrell, Albert Henderson, Kevin Peter Hall, Kenneth Tobey, voice of Wayne White. Farmer Pee-wee allows a traveling circus to stay on his property, and quickly develops circus fever—as well as a romance with the pretty trapeze artist (Golino). Quirky if overly bland comedy (cowritten and produced by Pee-wee's alter ego, Paul Reubens) has many clever moments, along with some curious ones. Ought to please kids and family audiences.▼

Big Town (1947) **60m.** ** D: William C. Thomas. Philip Reed, Hillary Brooke, Robert Lowery, Byron Barr. Standard story of newspaper reporter working with police to rid town of dangerous mob.

Big Town, The (1987) **C-109m.** ** D: Ben Bolt. Matt Dillon, Diane Lane, Tommy Lee Jones, Tom Skerritt, Lee Grant, Bruce Dern, Suzy Amis, David Grant. Small-town crapshooter with a "golden arm" comes to Chicago in the 1950s to become a big-time gambler, but still has a lot to learn. With that cast (and Lane as a stripper) it's easy to watch . . . but just as easy to forget.▼

Big Town After Dark (1947) **69m.** ** D: William C. Thomas. Philip Reed, Hillary Brooke, Richard Travis, Anne Gillis. OK drama of daring reporters walking into danger while trying to get lowdown on criminal gang. Retitled: UNDERWORLD AFTER DARK.▼

Big Trail, The (1930) **121m.** *** D: Raoul Walsh. John Wayne, Marguerite Churchill, El Brendel, Tully Marshall, Tyrone Power Sr., David Rollins, Ian Keith. Epic Western may seem creaky to some viewers, but remains one of the most impressive early talkies, with its grand sweep and naturalistic use of sound. Originally filmed in pioneer 70mm widescreen process called Grandeur. John Wayne was "discovered" for starring role, and already shows easygoing charm.▼

✓ **Big Trees, The** (1952) **C-89m.** **½ D: Felix Feist. Kirk Douglas, Eve Miller, Patrice Wymore, Edgar Buchanan. Douglas is staunch in so-so logging saga of lumbermen vs. homesteaders. Remake of VALLEY OF THE GIANTS.▼

Big Trouble (1985) **C-93m.** ** D: John Cassavetes. Peter Falk, Alan Arkin, Beverly D'Angelo, Charles Durning, Robert Stack, Paul Dooley, Valerie Curtin, Richard Libertini. Harried insurance salesman

Arkin needs money to put his three sons through Yale, so he becomes involved with ditsy D'Angelo in a plot to kill her loony husband (Falk). Pretty silly stuff, although the sardine-flavored liqueur does provide a couple of chuckles. Reteaming of talents from THE IN-LAWS had a troubled production, and barely received theatrical release. ▼

Big Trouble in Little China (1986) **C-99m.** *½ D: John Carpenter. Kurt Russell, Kim Cattrall, Dennis Dun, James Hong, Victor Wong, Kate Burton, Suzee Pai. Blowhard trucker Russell finds himself knee-deep in Chinatown intrigue (and mumbo-jumbo) when a friend's fiancée is kidnapped right in front of his eyes. High-tech INDIANA JONES-style adventure has heavy tongue-in-cheek attitude, but everything else about it is heavy, too . . . including Russell's John Wayne-ish swagger. Good electronic music score by director Carpenter.▼

Big Wave, The (1960-Japanese) **60m.** *½ D: Tad Danielewski. Sessue Hayakawa, Ichizo Itami, Mickey Curtis, Koji Shitara. Slowly paced account from Pearl Buck novel involving two boys who are childhood friends but later in life clash over their love for a local girl.

Big Wednesday (1978) **C-120m.** **½ D: John Milius. Jan-Michael Vincent, William Katt, Gary Busey, Lee Purcell, Patti D'Arbanville, Barbara Hale (Katt's real-life mother). Half of a good flick on surfing, Pacific Coast-style, early 60s. Up to midway point, a ridiculous comedy about macho Vincent and his fun-loving, destructive ways. As he and buddies Katt and Busey get older and action is brought up to 70s, dramatic content improves, and you sympathize with characters. Milius recut to 104m. for pay-TV release. Retitled SUMMER OF INNOCENCE for TV.▼

Big Wheel, The (1949) **92m.** **½ D: Edward Ludwig. Mickey Rooney, Thomas Mitchell, Spring Byington, Mary Hatcher, Allen Jenkins, Michael O'Shea. Rooney is determined race-car driver following in father's footsteps despite dad's death on track; familiar plot well done.▼

Big Zapper (1973-British) **C-94m.** *½ D: Lindsay Shonteff. Linda Marlowe, Gary Hope. Sean Hewitt, Richard Monette, Penny Irving. Tough blonde Marlowe is well cast in this low-grade comic strip adventure as a violent private eye with a trusty (and masochistic) sidekick named Rock.▼

Bikini Beach (1964) **C-100m.** **½ D: William Asher. Frankie Avalon, Annette Funicello, Keenan Wynn, Martha Hyer, Harvey Lembeck, Don Rickles, John Ashley, Jody McCrea, Meredith MacRae, Donna Loren, Candy Johnson, Timothy Carey, "Little" Stevie Wonder, Michael Nader. Third BEACH PARTY movie is second best, with Avalon in dual role as Frankie and a British singing rage called "The Potato Bug" (get it?). Relic of by-gone era. Followed by PAJAMA PARTY.▼

Bilitis (1977-French) **C-95m.** ** D: David Hamilton. Patti D'Arbanville, Mona Kristensen, Bernard Giraudeau, Mathieu Carriere, Gilles Kohler. Superficial story of young student D'Arbanville and her first romance. All imagery, no substance. Director Hamilton is best-known for his lush coffeetable photo books of nude women.▼

Bill (1981) **C-100m. TVM** D: Anthony Page. Mickey Rooney, Dennis Quaid, Largo Woodruff, Harry Goz, Anna Maria Horsford, Kathleen Maguire. The Mick is brilliant in the true story of Bill Sackter, a mentally retarded adult who is forced to cope with the world outside the mental institution where he has spent 46 years. Emmys went to Rooney and Corey Blechman's script (from the book by Barry Morrow). Above average. Sequel: BILL: ON HIS OWN.▼

Bill and Coo (1947) **C-61m.** *** D: Dean Riesner. Produced and narrated by Ken Murray. Charming, unique live-action film using trained birds in a story situation. A special Oscar winner, later reedited with new introductory material by Murray.▼

Bill & Ted's Excellent Adventure (1989) **C-90m.** ** D: Stephen Herek. Keanu Reeves, Alex Winter, George Carlin, Bernie Casey, Amy Stock-Poynton, Tony Camilieri, Dan Shor, Ted Steedman, Rod Loomis, Al Leong, Robert V. Barron. Inseparable teenage airheads, who are about to flunk their history course, are given the opportunity to go traveling through time to meet (and round up) such historical figures as Napoleon, Joan of Arc, and Abraham Lincoln. Radical! Reeves and Winter are great fun as Bill and Ted, but this goofy comedy never takes off as it should—and a potentially funny film falls flat.▼

Bill Cosby—"Himself" (1982) **C-105m.** **½ D: Bill Cosby. Likable in-concert film, featuring Cosby on the subjects of child rearing, human nature, family life. Pleasant but hardly "an event."▼

Billie (1965) **C-87m.** **½ D: Don Weis. Patty Duke, Warren Berlinger, Jim Backus, Jane Greer, Billy DeWolfe, Charles Lane, Dick Sargent. Airy comedy of tomboyish Duke and her athletic aspirations. Backus and Greer are her perplexed parents, Berlinger her boyfriend. Duke sings, runs, prances.

Billionaire Boys Club (1987) **C-200m.** **TVM** D: Marvin J. Chomsky. Judd Nelson, Fredric Lehne, Brian McNamara, Raphael Sbarge, John Stockwell, Barry Tubb, Stan Shaw, Jill Schoelen, James Sloyan, Ron Silver, James Karen. Dramatization of the real-life story of convicted killer Joe Hunt, whose manipulation of a group of

L.A. elitists into a get-rich-quick scheme led to murder. Look for an unbilled Shirley Knight as Hunt's dispassionate mother on the witness stand. Gy Waldron's nearly courtroom-bound script was adapted from Sue Horton's "forthcoming" book. Originally shown in two parts. Average.

Billion Dollar Brain (1967-British) **C-111m.** *** D: Ken Russell. Michael Caine, Karl Malden, Ed Begley, Oscar Homolka, Françoise Dorleac. Third in series which began with IPCRESS FILE finds Harry Palmer (Caine) again up to his neck in exciting espionage, this time in Scandinavia. Based on Len Deighton's novel.

Billion Dollar Hobo, The (1978) **C-96m.** *½ D: Stuart E. McGowan. Tim Conway, Will Geer, Eric Weston, Sydney Lassick, John Myhers, Frank Sivero. Dreary G-rated comedy about bumbling Conway becoming a hobo in order to qualify for inheritance.▼

Billion Dollar Threat, The (1979) **C-100m. TVM** D: Barry Shear. Dale Robinette, Ralph Bellamy, Keenan Wynn, Patrick Macnee, Ronnie Carol. Lighthearted pilot to proposed series involving a James Bondish superspy assigned to thwart the plans of a master agent threatening to destroy the planet. Written by Jimmy Sangster. Average.

Bill of Divorcement, A (1932) **69m.** *** D: George Cukor. John Barrymore, Katharine Hepburn, Billie Burke, David Manners, Henry Stephenson. Barrymore gives sensitive performance as man released from mental institution who returns to wife Burke and gets to know his daughter for the first time. Dated but worth seeing; notable as Hepburn's screen debut. Originally released at 75m.▼

Bill of Divorcement, A (1940) **74m.** **½ D: John Farrow. Maureen O'Hara, Adolphe Menjou, Fay Bainter, Herbert Marshall, Dame May Whitty, C. Aubrey Smith. Refilming of '32 drama follows it closely, but cast can't match the original's class. Retitled: NEVER TO LOVE.

Bill: On His Own (1983) **C-100m. TVM** D: Anthony Page. Mickey Rooney, Helen Hunt, Teresa Wright, Dennis Quaid, Largo Woodruff, Paul Leiber, Harry Goz. Rooney reprises his Emmy-winning role as Bill Sackter, a middle-aged mentally retarded man, in this nearly as luminous sequel to BILL. Above average.▼

Billy Budd (1962-U.S.-British) **112m.** ***½ D: Peter Ustinov. Robert Ryan, Peter Ustinov, Melvyn Douglas, Terence Stamp, Paul Rogers, David McCallum. Melville's classic good vs. evil novella set in British Navy, 1797. Naive, incorruptible seaman is courtmartialed for murder of sadistic master-ofarms. Film deals simply with heavier issues of morality. Sterling performances by all.▼

Billy Galvin (1986) **C-95m.** **½ D: John Gray. Karl Malden, Lenny Von Dohlen, Joyce Van Patten, Toni Kalem, Keith

Szarabajka, Alan North, Paul Guilfoyle, Barton Heyman. Well-meaning, fairly effective meat-and-potatos drama about title character (Von Dohlen), who wants to be a construction worker like his old man (Malden), a tough, obstinate codger who does everything to discourage him. Not without its share of moments, but also a bit too obvious. Good performances all around; an *American Playhouse* presentation.▼

Billy in the Lowlands (1979) C-88m. *** D: Jan Egleson. Henry Tomaszewski, Paul Benedict, David Morton, David Clennon, Ernie Loew. Diverting tale of young, working class Tomaszewski struggling for an identity, breaking out of jail to meet his estranged father. Filmed independently, in Boston; followed by thematically similar THE DARK END OF THE STREET.

✓ **Billy Jack** (1971) C-114m. *½ D: T. C. Frank (Tom Laughlin). Tom Laughlin, Delores Taylor, Clark Howat, Bert Freed, Julie Webb. Half-breed karate expert protects a free school imperiled by reactionary townspeople in this grass-roots hit. Seen today, its politics are highly questionable, and its "message" of peace looks ridiculous, considering the amount of violence in the film. Preceded by BORN LOSERS; followed by THE TRIAL OF BILLY JACK and BILLY JACK GOES TO WASHINGTON.▼

Billy Jack Goes to Washington (1977) C-155m. ** D: Tom Laughlin. Tom Laughlin, Delores Taylor, Sam Wanamaker, Lucie Arnaz, E.G. Marshall. Contrived update of MR. SMITH GOES TO WASHINGTON, with writer-director-star Laughlin, a supposed "everyman," fighting big-time corruption in the Senate. Basic story is still good, but it goes on forever.

Billy Liar (1963-British) 96m. ***½ D: John Schlesinger. Tom Courtenay, Julie Christie, Mona Washbourne, Ethel Griffies, Finlay Currie. Cast excels in story of ambitious but lazy young man caught in dull job routine who escapes into fantasy world, offering some poignant vignettes of middleclass life. Based on Keith Waterhouse novel and play.▼

Billy: Portrait of a Street Kid (1977) C-100m. TVM D: Steve Gethers. LeVar Burton, Ossie Davis, Dolph Sweet, Michael Constantine, Tina Andrews. Well-acted but predictable drama of a ghetto youth's dreams of escaping from his dismal existence. Especially good performance from Burton. Average.

Billy Rose's Diamond Horseshoe SEE: **Diamond Horseshoe**

Billy Rose's Jumbo (1962) C-125m. *** D: Charles Walters. Doris Day, Stephen Boyd, Jimmy Durante, Martha Raye, Dean Jagger. OK circus picture, at best during Rodgers and Hart songs, well-staged by Busby Berkeley. Durante (who had starred in the

1935 Broadway production) and Raye are marvelous. Songs include "The Most Beautiful Girl in the World," "My Romance," "This Can't Be Love." Also known as JUMBO.▼

✓ **Billy the Kid** (1930) 90m. **½ D: King Vidor. Johnny Mack Brown, Wallace Beery, Kay Johnson, Karl Dane, Roscoe Ates. Realistic early talkie Western with marshal Beery trying to capture outlaw Brown; some performances seem badly dated today. Originally shown in early widescreen process. Retitled: THE HIGHWAYMAN RIDES. Mgm o.k.

Billy the Kid (1941) C-95m. **½ D: ✓ David Miller. Robert Taylor, Brian Donlevy, Ian Hunter, Mary Howard, Gene Lockhart, Lon Chaney Jr. Cast looks uncomfortable in remake of 1930 Western, but plot is sturdy enough for OK viewing, with Taylor in title role and Donlevy as marshal.

Billy the Kid vs. Dracula (1966) C-95m. *½ D: William Beaudine. Chuck Courtney, John Carradine, Melinda Plowman, Virginia Christine, Walter Janovitz, Bing Russell, Harry Carey, Jr. Famed outlaw decides it's time to get married—but doesn't realize that his bride's uncle is a vampire. Campy nonsense.▼

Billy Two Hats (1974) C-99m. **½ D: ? Ted Kotcheff. Gregory Peck, Desi Arnaz, Jr., Jack Warden, Sian Barbara Allen, David Huddleston. Offbeat Western filmed in Israel, about a middle-aged Scot and a young half-Indian pursued by the law for bank robbery. Peck is appealing in unusual character role. Retitled THE LADY AND THE OUTLAW.

Biloxi Blues (1988) C-106m. *** D: Mike Nichols. Matthew Broderick, Christopher Walken, Matt Mulhern, Corey Parker, Casey Siemaszko, Markus Flanagan, Michael Dolan, Penelope Ann Miller, Park Overall. The further adventures of Eugene Jerome, Neil Simon's youthful alter ego introduced in BRIGHTON BEACH MEMOIRS. Here, WW2 is winding down, and Eugene (Broderick) forsakes Brooklyn for Biloxi, Miss., and ten grueling weeks of army basic training, where he comes that much closer to manhood. Quite wonderful, in its best moments. Followed on stage by *Broadway Bound.*▼

Bimbo the Great (1961-German) C-96m. *½ D: Harold Philipp. Claus Holm, Germaine Damar, Elma Karlowa, Marina Orschel. Hackneyed circus yarn of high-wire performer discovering wife's death was caused by his step-brother, with inevitable confession scene slightly spiced by potential big-top blaze.

Bingo Long Traveling All-Stars and Motor Kings, The (1976) C-110m. *** D: John Badham. Billy Dee Williams, James Earl Jones, Richard Pryor, Ted Ross, DeWayne Jessie, Stan Shaw. Bright, original comedy about baseball player Williams trying to buck owners of Negro National League in 1939 by starting his own razzle-dazzle team.▼

Biography of a Bachelor Girl (1935) 82m. *½ D: Edward Griffith. Ann Harding, Robert Montgomery, Edward Everett Horton, Edward Arnold, Una Merkel. A notorious woman is persuaded to write her memoirs by an aggressive magazine editor who falls in love with her in spite of the fact that she represents everything he loathes. Dreary, endlessly talky adaptation of S. N. Behrman play.

Bionic Showdown: The Six Million Dollar Man and the Bionic Woman (1989) C-100m. TVM D: Alan J. Levi. Lindsay Wagner, Lee Majors, Richard Anderson, Sandra Bullock, Jeff Yagher, Geraint Wyn Davies, Martin E. Brooks, Robert Lansing, Josef Sommer, Lee Majors II. Harmless bionic pap involving the older duo from the hit series and a younger twosome (for a possible new series) searching for a bionic spy who threatens glasnost at a U.S.-Soviet sports meet. If it weren't for all the slow-motion running, it could have been a half hour shorter. Average.

Birch Interval (1977) C-104m. *** D: Delbert Mann. Eddie Albert, Rip Torn, Ann Wedgeworth, Susan McClung, Brian Part. Eleven-year-old girl, sent to live with relatives in Amish country, finds out about life, love, suffering and compassion. Beautiful, sensitive film.▼

Bird (1988) C-160m. **½ D: Clint Eastwood. Forest Whitaker, Diane Venora, Michael Zelniker, Samuel E. Wright, Keith David, Michael McGuire, James Handy. Heartfelt biography of legendary saxophonist Charlie Parker, who revolutionized jazz music in the 1940s. While there's much music on hand, this is mostly the story of one man's drug addiction and self-destructive life, and as such, it goes on far too long, failing to balance its story with any real explanation of Parker's influence in the world of music. Excellent and believable performances help a great deal. That's really Parker's playing on the soundtrack, though all the accompanying music was rerecorded in 1988. (The film won an Oscar for sound recording.)▼

√ **Birdman of Alcatraz** (1962) 143m. *** D: John Frankenheimer. Burt Lancaster, Karl Malden, Thelma Ritter, Betty Field, Neville Brand, Edmond O'Brien, Hugh Marlowe, Telly Savalas. Pensive study of prisoner Robert Stroud who during his many years in jail became a world-renowned bird authority. Film becomes static despite imaginative sidelights to enlarge scope of action. 148m. version used for overseas release now turning up here.▼

Birdmen (1971) C-73m. TVM D: Philip Leacock. Doug McClure, Chuck Connors, Richard Basehart, Rene Auberjonois, Max Baer, Don Knight, Tom Skerritt. Uninteresting rehash of POW breakout plot. Captured Allies in German castle build glider to fly to freedom in Switzerland ten miles away. Average. Retitled ESCAPE OF THE BIRDMEN.

Bird of Paradise (1932) 80m. ** D: King Vidor. Joel McCrea, Dolores Del Rio, John Halliday, Skeets Gallegher, Lon Chaney Jr. Exotic but empty South Seas romance with McCrea as adventurer who falls in love with native-girl Del Rio. Handsome but unmoving; remade in 1951.▼

Bird of Paradise (1951) C-100m. ** D: Delmer Daves. Louis Jourdan, Debra Paget, Jeff Chandler, Everett Sloane. Jourdan's marriage to South Sea isle chief's daughter causes native uprising in grandly filmed but vapid tale. Remake of 1932 film.

Bird on a Wire (1990) C-110m. ** D: John Badham. Mel Gibson, Goldie Hawn, David Carradine, Bill Duke, Stephen Tobolowsky, Joan Severance, Jeff Corey. Star power is about all this lame actioncomedy has going for it, as drug-running murderers force Mel, who's been hiding in the F.B.I. witness relocation program, and Goldie, his onetime sweetheart, to take it on the lam. Script on a shoestring.

Birds, The (1963) C-120m. ***½ D: Alfred Hitchcock. Rod Taylor, Tippi Hedren, Suzanne Pleshette, Jessica Tandy, Veronica Cartwright, Ethel Griffies, Charles McGraw. Hitchcock's classic about a woman (Hedren) and mass bird attacks that follow her around isolated California community. Not for the squeamish; a delight for those who are game. Hold on to something and watch. Script by Evan Hunter, loosely based on Daphne du Maurier's story.▼

Birds and the Bees, The (1956) C-94m. ** D: Norman Taurog. George Gobel, Mitzi Gaynor, David Niven, Reginald Gardiner. Bland remake of THE LADY EVE about rich playboy who breaks off romance with cardshark girlfriend, but later decides he still loves her.▼

Birds, Bees and the Italians, The (1967-Italian) 115m. *** D: Pietro Germi. Virna Lisi, Gastone Moschin, Nora Ricci, Alberto Lionello. Very funny sex farce in which bed partners revolve as if on a merry-go-round.

Birds Do It (1966) C-95m. ** D: Andrew Marton. Soupy Sales, Tab Hunter, Arthur O'Connell, Edward Andrews, Beverly Adams, Frank Nastasi. Soupy's first starring vehicle has him under the spell of serum that enables him to fly. Fairly entertaining for kids.

Birds of Prey (1973) C-81m. TVM D: William Graham. David Janssen, Ralph Meeker, Elayne Heilveil, Harry Klekas, Sam Dawson. Good suspenser as Salt Lake City traffic-helicopter pilot Janssen witnesses bank robbery in progress, becomes inexorably involved. Above average.▼

Bird with the Crystal Plumage, The (1969-Italian-West German) **C-98m.** **½ D: Dario Argento. Tony Musante, Suzy Kendall, Eva Renzi, Enrico Maria Salerno, Mario Adorf, Renato Romano, Umberto Rano, Werner Peters. American writer living in Rome witnesses attempted murder in gallery; he and his mistress become involved in case. Uneven; best viewed on large screen. Reissued as THE PHANTOM OF TERROR.▼

Birdy (1984) **C-120m.** ***½ D: Alan Parker. Matthew Modine, Nicolas Cage, John Harkins, Sandy Baron, Karen Young, Bruno Kirby. Cage, reunited with schizophrenically silent Modine in an army hospital, flashes back to their adolescence in working-class Philadelphia and on Modine's lifelong desire to be a bird. William Wharton's allegorical novel, updated from WW2 to Vietnam, makes a surprisingly workable movie despite a weak "gag" ending. Terrific performances, with Modine a standout in a tricky, physically demanding role. Screenplay by Sandy Kroopf and Jack Behr.▼

Birgit Haas Must Be Killed (1981-French) **C-105m.** **½ D: Laurent Heynemann. Philippe Noiret, Jean Rochefort, Lisa Kreuzer, Bernard Le Coq. Unscrupulous police officer Noiret dupes innocent Rochefort into romancing former left-wing terrorist Kreuzer, intending to have her assassinated and hang the blame on Rochefort! Intriguing idea never really catches fire, despite honorable efforts; might have worked better if the two male stars had switched roles.▼

Birthday Party, The (1968-British) **C-127m.** *** D: William Friedkin. Robert Shaw, Patrick Magee, Dandy Nichols, Sydney Tafler, Moultrie Kelsall, Helen Fraser. Uncinematic film version of Harold Pinter's play about boarding house and its mysterious tenant (Shaw) is helped by good acting and playwright's usual superior dialogue.

Birth of a Nation, The (1915) **159m.** **** D: D. W. Griffith. Lillian Gish, Mae Marsh, Henry B. Walthall, Miriam Cooper, Robert Harron, Wallace Reid, Joseph Henabery. The landmark of American motion pictures. Griffith's epic story of two families during Civil War and Reconstruction is still fascinating. Sometimes the drama survives intact; other times, one must watch in a more historical perspective. Griffith's attitude toward Ku Klux Klan has kept this film a center of controversy to the present day.▼

Birth of the Beatles (1979) **C-100m.** TVM D: Richard Marquand. Stephen Mackenna, Rod Culbertson, John Altman, Ray Ashcroft, Ryan Mitchell, David Wilkinson, Brian Jameson. Dramatization of the early days

of John, Paul, George, and Ringo, and the fifth Beatle, Pete Best. Unfamiliar cast of lookalikes pretend to be the Fab Four, and the group Rain sings Beatles songs—but why accept substitutes? Average.

Birth of the Blues (1941) **85m.** *** D: Victor Schertzinger. Bing Crosby, Brian Donlevy, Carolyn Lee, Eddie (Rochester) Anderson, Mary Martin. Fiction about Crosby organizing jazz band in New Orleans has great music like "St. Louis Blues," "St. James Infirmary," "Melancholy Baby" and title tune to uplift fair story.

Biscuit Eater, The (1940) **83m.** *** D: Stuart Heisler. Billy Lee, Cordell Hickman, Helene Millard, Richard Lane, Lester Matthews. Warm, winning adaptation of James Street story about two boys—one white, one black—who take unwanted dog from litter and try to train him into champion bird dog. A B-picture that was regarded as the sleeper of the year. Remade in 1972.

Biscuit Eater, The (1972) **C-90m.** **½ D: Vincent McEveety. Earl Holliman, Lew Ayres, Godfrey Cambridge, Patricia Crowley, Beah Richards, Johnny Whitaker, George Spell. Wholesome but uninspired Disney remake of 1940 film with Whitaker and Spell as the young friends who devote themselves to training a champion bird dog.

Bishop Misbehaves, The (1935) **86m.** **½ D: E. A. Dupont. Edmund Gwenn, Maureen O'Sullivan, Norman Foster, Lucile Watson, Reginald Owen, Dudley Digges, Lillian Bond, Melville Cooper. Tongue-in-cheek mystery with Gwenn (in his first American film) as an English Bishop with a taste for detective stories who gets mixed up in a real jewel heist. Enjoyable but slow-paced.

Bishop Murder Case, The (1930) **91m.** D: Nick Grinde. Basil Rathbone, Leila Hyams, Roland Young, George T. Marion, Alec B, Francis, Zelda Sears, Bodil Rosing, Carroll Nye, Delmer Daves. SEE: **Philo Vance** series

Bishop's Wife, The (1947) **108m.** *** D: Henry Koster. Cary Grant, Loretta Young, David Niven, Monty Woolley, James Gleason, Gladys Cooper, Elsa Lanchester. Christmas fantasy of suave angel (Grant) coming to earth to help Bishop Niven and wife Young raise money for new church. Engaging performances by all.▼

Bitch, The (1979-British) **C-93m.** BOMB D: Gerry O'Hara. Joan Collins, Kenneth Haigh, Michael Coby, Ian Hendry, Carolyn Seymour, Sue Lloyd, John Ratzenberger. Weak entry in the Bimbo Chic genre, a follow-up to THE STUD, based on a book by Joan's sister, Jackie Collins. Joan gets involved in everything from smuggling to fixed horse racing in attempts to save her failing London disco, but who cares? And, yes, there is a title song.▼

Bite the Bullet (1975) **C-131m.** **** D: Richard Brooks. Gene Hackman, Candice Bergen, James Coburn, Ben Johnson, Ian Bannen, Jan-Michael Vincent, Robert Donner, Paul Stewart, Dabney Coleman, Sally Kirkland. Grand adventure in the classic tradition. Disparate types compete in a grueling, 600-mile horse race at the turn of the century; the finalists develop a grudging—and growing—respect for each other. Beautifully filmed on magnificent locations by Harry Stradling, Jr. Script by director Brooks.▼

Bitter Creek (1954) **74m.** *½ D: Thomas Carr. Bill Elliott, Carleton Young, Beverly Garland, Claude Akins, Jim Hayward. Tame happenings as Elliott seeks revenge for his brother's untimely death in the old West.

Bitter Harvest (1981) **C-100m. TVM** D: Roger Young. Ron Howard, Art Carney, Tarah Nutter, David Knell, Barry Corbin, Richard Dysart. Director Young and writer Richard Friedenberg received Emmy nominations for this illuminating drama about a young dairy farmer's race to identify a deadly chemical that is killing his cattle and bringing a strange illness to his child. Above average.▼

✓ **Bitter Rice** (1948-Italian) **107m.** *** D: Giuseppe De Santis. Silvana Mangano, Vittorio Gassman, Raf Vallone, Doris Dowling, Lia Corelli. Effective portrayal of the dreary, backbreaking existence of women toiling in the Po Valley rice fields, exploited by the rice growers and their go-betweens. The seductive Mangano, as a worker who betrays her comrades, became an international star.

Bitter Sweet (1933 British) **93m.** *** D: Herbert Wilcox. Anna Neagle, Fernand Graavey (Gravet), Miles Mander, Clifford Heatherley, Esme Percy, Ivy St. Helier, Pat Paterson, Kay Hammond. Noel Coward's first major work as a composer, filmed by the team of Wilcox-Neagle. Sentimental operetta creaks a bit, but the story of young love in 1880 Vienna is a must for musical theater buffs. Lovely score includes "If Love Were All" and "I'll See You Again." St. Helier vividly re-creates her London stage role of Manon la Crevette, written for her by Coward. Remade in 1940.▼

Bitter Sweet (1940) **C-92m.** *** D: W.S. Van Dyke II. Jeanette MacDonald, Nelson Eddy, George Sanders, Felix Bressart, Lynne Carver, Ian Hunter, Sig Ruman. Ignore plot, enjoy Noel Coward's songs in lavishly filmed operetta. Wonderful Herman Bing provides funniest scene as shopkeeper who hires Nelson and Jeanette to give his daughter music lessons. An earlier British version was filmed in 1933.▼

Bittersweet Love (1976) **C-92m.** *½ D: David Miller. Lana Turner, Robert Lan-

sing, Celeste Holm, Robert Alda, Scott Hylands, Meredith Baxter Birney. Excellent cast wasted on improbable story of young married couple (expecting a baby) suddenly discovering they are half-brother and sister. Termination of pregnancy and marriage are then talked to death.▼

Bitter Tea of General Yen, The (1933) **89m.** ***½ D: Frank Capra. Barbara Stanwyck, Nils Asther, Gavin Gordon, Toshia Mori, Richard Loo, Lucien Littlefield, Clara Blandick, Walter Connolly. May seem antiquated to modern audiences, but Capra's sensuous story of American woman's strange fascination with a Chinese warlord is still dazzling. A moody, beautifully atmospheric, sensitively performed film.

Bitter Tears of Petra Von Kant, The (1973-German) **C-119m.** ** D: Rainer Werner Fassbinder. Margit Carstensen, Hanna Schygulla, Irm Hermann, Eva Mattes, Karin Schaake, Gisela Fackelday. Wealthy lesbian fashion designer Petra Von Kant (Carstensen) worries over habits of inconsistent lover Schygulla and unmercifully bosses secretary Hermann. The action is limited to Petra's apartment, and the pace is annoyingly slow. Overrated by some.

Bitter Victory (1958-French) **82m.** *** D: Nicholas Ray. Richard Burton, Curt Jurgens, Ruth Roman, Raymond Pellegrin, Anthony Bushell, Christopher Lee. Strong WW2 story with Jurgens as unfit commander who receives undeserved citation for mission against Rommel's desert headquarters; Roman is his wife who's had prior affair with officer Burton. 103m. versions now in circulation are from British release of this film.

BJ and the Bear (1978) **C-100m. TVM** D: John Peyser. Greg Evigan, Claude Akins, Mills Watson, Penny Peyser, Julius Harris. Pilot to the hit series (that later spun off *Sheriff Lobo*) puts an independent trucker and his traveling buddy, a fun-loving chimp, at odds with a slightly corrupt sheriff who is involved with white slavery. Average.

Black Abbot, The (1963-German) **95m.** ** D: Franz Gottlieb. Joachim Fuchsberger, Dieter Borsche, Grit Bottcher, Eva Scholtz. Unearthly "Abbot" is on a killing rampage warding off those who approach country house with buried treasure underneath.

Black and White in Color (1977-French-African) **C-90m.** ***½ D: Jean-Jacques Annaud. Jean Carmet, Jacques Dufilho, Catherine Rouvel, Jacques Spiesser, Dora Doll. Unusual and witty story of self-satisfied Frenchmen at remote African trading post who are fired by sudden patriotism at outbreak of WW1, and decide to attack nearby German fort. Oscar winner as Best Foreign Film.▼

Black Angel (1946) **80m.** *** D: Roy William Neill. Dan Duryea, June Vincent,

Peter Lorre, Broderick Crawford, Wallace Ford. First-rate whodunit (by Cornell Woolrich) of Vincent trying to clear husband of charge that he murdered Duryea's wife. Imaginative film will have you glued to the screen all the way.

Black Arrow, The (1948) **76m.** *** D: Gordon Douglas. Louis Hayward, Janet Blair, George Macready, Edgar Buchanan, Paul Cavanagh. Superior swashbuckler with dashing knight Hayward, lovely heroine Blair, and villain Macready. Truly exciting finale with hero vs. villain in jousting tournament.▼

Black Arrow (1985) **C-93m.** TVM D: John Hough. Oliver Reed, Fernando Taylor, Benedict Taylor, Stephan Chase, Georgia Slowe, Donald Pleasence. Entertaining (though strangely inferior to the Louis Hayward version) adaptation of Robert Louis Stevenson's medieval swashbuckler, with villainous Reed getting top billing and more footage than the title character, played somewhat sedately by Chase. Made for cable by Disney. Average.▼

Black Bart (1948) **C-80m.** **½ D: George Sherman. Yvonne De Carlo, Dan Duryea, Jeffrey Lynn, Percy Kilbride. Enticing De Carlo steps between outlaws Duryea and Lynn, foiling their attempt to overthrow Wells Fargo company.

Blackbeard, the Pirate (1952) **C-99m.** ** D: Raoul Walsh. Robert Newton, Linda Darnell, William Bendix, Keith Andes, Richard Egan, Irene Ryan. Newton is rambunctious as 17th-century buccaneer, with lovely Darnell his captive; fun for a while, but Newton's hamming soon grows tiresome.▼

Blackbeard's Ghost (1968) **C-107m.** *** D: Robert Stevenson. Peter Ustinov, Dean Jones, Suzanne Pleshette, Elsa Lanchester, Joby Baker, Elliott Reid, Richard Deacon. Jones conjures up title character (Ustinov) who helps protect his descendants' home from being taken over by racketeers who want to make it a casino. Engaging slapstick comedy from Disney.▼

Black Beauty (1946) **74m.** **½ D: Max Nosseck. Mona Freeman, Richard Denning, Evelyn Ankers, Terry Kilburn, Arthur Space, J. M. Kerrigan. Second sound version of Anna Sewell's oft-filmed tale of little girl and her love for her horse is decent if unspectacular, with pleasing Dmitri Tiomkin score.▼

Black Beauty (1971-British) **C-106m.** **½ D: James Hill. Mark Lester, Walter Slezak, Peter Lee Lawrence, Ursula Glas. The story of a horse who passes from owner to owner; fails to capture the qualities that make Anna Sewell's novel a classic, but it's probably the best of several film versions.▼

Black Belly of the Tarantula (1972-Italian) **C-88m.** *½ D: Paolo Cavara. Giancarlo Giannini, Stefania Sandrelli, Barbara

Bouchet. Folks are being murdered in mysterious ways at health and beauty salon; none too exciting.

Black Belt Jones (1974) **C-87m.** **½ D: Robert Clouse. Jim Kelly, Gloria Hendry, Scatman Crothers, Alan Weeks, Nate Esformes. Black-oriented kung-fu mayhem from the team that made ENTER THE DRAGON. Kelly battles the Mafia to save his school of self-defense in Watts area of L.A. No gore, but lots of action and comedy.▼

Black Bird, The (1975) **C-98m.** BOMB D: David Giler. George Segal, Stephane Audran, Lionel Stander, Lee Patrick, Elisha Cook Jr., Felix Silla, Signe Hasso. Horrendously bad, unfunny takeoff on THE MALTESE FALCON, with Segal as Sam Spade, Jr., not saved by the presence of Patrick and Cook from the '41 cast.▼

Blackboard Jungle (1955) **101m.** ***½ D: Richard Brooks. Glenn Ford, Anne Francis, Vic Morrow, Louis Calhern, Sidney Poitier, Richard Kiley, Warner Anderson, Margaret Hayes, Emile Meyer, John Hoyt, Rafael Campos, Paul Mazursky. Excellent adaptation of Evan Hunter's novel (scripted by the director) of a teacher's harrowing experiences in N.Y.C. school system. Poitier memorable as a troubled youth. Hard-hitting entertainment. This was the first film to feature rock music—Bill Haley's "Rock Around the Clock" is played over the opening credits. Look for a young Jamie Farr (billed as Jameel Farah).▼

Black Book SEE: **Reign of Terror**

Black Caesar (1973) **C-96m.** **½ D: Larry Cohen. Fred Williamson, Art Lund, Julius W. Harris, Gloria Hendry, D'Urville Martin. Better-than-average gangster film follows rise to the top of shrewd, bloodthirsty black baddie. Sequel: HELL UP IN HARLEM.▼

Black Camel (1931) **71m.** D: Hamilton MacFadden. Warner Oland, Sally Eilers, Bela Lugosi, Victor Varconi, Robert Young, Dwight Frye, Mary Gordon. SEE: **Charlie Chan** series.

Black Castle, The (1952) **81m.** ** D: Nathan Juran. Richard Greene, Boris Karloff, Stephen McNally, Paula Corday, Lon Chaney Jr., John Hoyt. Uninspired gothic melodrama has Greene investigating disappearance of two friends who were guests of sinister Austrian count (McNally). Karloff reduced to colorless supporting role.▼

Black Cat, The (1934) **65m.** ***½ D: Edgar G. Ulmer. Boris Karloff, Bela Lugosi, David Manners, Jacqueline Wells (Julie Bishop), Lucille Lund, Henry Armetta. Polished horror film with bizarre sets, even more bizarre plot, loses a lot on TV, although confrontation of architect and devil-worshiper Karloff and doctor Lugosi is still fascinating. The first of Boris and Bela's many teamings.▼

[104]

Black Cat, The (1941) 70m. **½ D: Albert S. Rogell. Basil Rathbone, Hugh Herbert, Broderick Crawford, Bela Lugosi, Gale Sondergaard, Anne Gwynne, Gladys Cooper. Herbert and Crawford provide laughs, the others provide chills, in lively comedy-mystery not to be confused with earlier horror film. Look for Alan Ladd in a small role. Atmospheric photography by Stanley Cortez.

Black Cauldron, The (1985) C-80m. **½ D: Ted Berman, Richard Rich. Voices of Grant Bardsley, Susan Sheridan, Freddie Jones, John Byner, John Hurt. Disney's expensive, ambitious animated feature is a pretty good but unmemorable sword-and-sorcery tale about a young boy who must find powerful black cauldron before it falls into the hands of evil Horned King. Good storytelling for kids, with impressive effects animation for buffs. Supporting characters Gurgi (a good guy) and Creeper (a baddie) have all the best moments.

Black Christmas (1975-Canadian) C-98m. **½ D: Bob Clark. Olivia Hussey, Keir Dullea, Margot Kidder, John Saxon, Art Hindle, Douglas McGrath, Andrea Martin. Bizarre horror thriller about warped murderer in sorority house on Christmas Eve and two days following. Not bad; Kidder steals it as a nasty, foul-mouthed sorority sister. Also called SILENT NIGHT, EVIL NIGHT and STRANGER IN THE HOUSE.▼

Black Cross (1960-Polish) C-175m. ** D: Aleksander Ford. Urszula Modrzynska, Grazyna Staniszewska, Andrzej Szalawski, Henryk Borowski. Unremarkable account of Teutonic knights raiding Poland; notable only for detailed medieval settings, sterile presentation.

Black Dakotas, The (1954) C-65m. ** D: Ray Nazarro. Gary Merrill, Wanda Hendrix, John Bromfield, Noah Beery, Jr. Bland oater of greedy men who try to outwit the redskins and incite a war.

Black Devils of Kali, The SEE: **Mystery of the Black Jungle**

Black Dragon of Manzanar (1943) 100m. **½ D: William Witney. Rod Cameron, Roland Got, Constance Worth, Nino Pipitone, Noel Cravat. Sufficiently action-packed Republic cliff-hanger with Cameron as dynamic federal agent outdoing Oriental Axis agents during WW2. Reedited serial: G-MEN VS. THE BLACK DRAGON.

Black Dragons (1942) 61m. *½ D: William Nigh. Bela Lugosi, Joan Barclay, Clayton Moore, George Pembroke, Robert Frazer. Nazi doctor Lugosi has been altering the faces of some Japanese, to make them pass as Americans. Then topical chiller is now a sleep-inducing bore.▼

Black Eye (1974) C-98m. ** D: Jack Arnold. Fred Williamson, Rosemary Forsyth, Richard Anderson, Teresa Graves,

Cyril Delevanti. Involved action-mystery has black private detective Williamson investigating murders connected with a dope ring in Venice, Cal. Bret Morrison, radio's "The Shadow," plays a porno moviemaker. Standard fare.

Black Fist (1976) C-105m. **½ D: Timothy Galfas, Richard Kaye. Richard Lawson, Philip Michael Thomas, Annazette Chase, Dabney Coleman, Robert Burr. Coleman's gritty performance as a crooked cop elevates this standard blaxploitation drama about what happens when tough Lawson is hired by a crime boss as a streetfighter. Also known as, appropriately, THE BLACK STREETFIGHTER.

Black Fox, The (1962) 89m. ***½ D: Louis Clyde Stoumen. Narrated by Marlene Dietrich. Exceedingly taut, grim documentary tracing the rise and fall of Adolph Hitler, focusing on his use of power during Third Reich. Academy Award winner as best documentary feature.

Black Friday (1940) 70m. **½ D: Arthur Lubin. Boris Karloff, Bela Lugosi, Stanley Ridges, Anne Nagel, Anne Gwynne, Virginia Brissac. Well-made little chiller with Karloff putting gangster's brain into a professor's body. Jekyll-Hyde results are fascinating; Ridges excellent as victim. Lugosi has small, thankless role as gangster.

Black Fury (1935) 92m. *** D: Michael Curtiz. Paul Muni, Karen Morley, William Gargan, Barton MacLane, John Qualen, J. Carrol Naish, Vince Barnett. Hard-hitting Warner Bros. melodrama about union manipulation of coal miners, with Muni as robust "bohunk" who gets in over his head. Realistic, strikingly filmed, if a bit uneven dramatically. Muni's accent makes it tough to understand him at times. Based on a true story.▼

Black Girl (1972) C-97m. *** D: Ossie Davis. Brock Peters, Leslie Uggams, Claudia McNeil, Louise Stubbs, Gloria Edwards, Ruby Dee. One of the best black-oriented films concerns an aspiring dancer who joins with her two half-sisters in giving Uggams, who has been raised with them, a difficult time. Generally fine performances.

Black Gold (1947) C-92m. **½ D: Phil Karlson. Anthony Quinn, Katherine DeMille, Elyse Knox, Ducky Louie, Kane Richmond, Moroni Olsen, Raymond Hatton, Thurston Hall, Darryl Hickman. Effective, if sentimental, tale of Indian Quinn who discovers oil on his land and trains a Chinese orphan (Louie) to be the jockey for his beloved thoroughbred. Low-budget, but warmly acted, with excellent use of Cinecolor process. Quinn and DeMille were then husband and wife.

Black Gold (1963) 98m. ** D: Leslie Martinson. Philip Carey, Diane McBain, James Best, Claude Akins, Iron Eyes Cody.

Predictable search for oil set in Oklahoma, with standard villain and supposedly ironic outcome.

Black Gunn (1972) **C-98m.** ** D: Robert Hartford-Davis. Jim Brown, Martin Landau, Brenda Sykes, Luciana Paluzzi. Black nightclub owner goes after the Man when his brother is killed. Routine black actioner.

Black Hand (1950) **93m.** *** D: Richard Thorpe. Gene Kelly, J. Carrol Naish, Teresa Celli, Marc Lawrence, Frank Puglia. Kelly avenges his father's murder by the Black Hand society in turn-of-the-century N.Y.C. Atmospheric, well-made film with Kelly in a rare (and effective) dramatic performance.▼

Black Hole, The (1979) **C-97m.** **½ D: Gary Nelson. Maximilian Schell, Anthony Perkins, Robert Forster, Joseph Bottoms, Yvette Mimieux, Ernest Borgnine. U.S. expedition finds long-lost madman in space about to explore a "black hole." Disney studios' ambitious sci-fi effort is a throwback to 1957 Saturday matinee fodder, with thin story, cardboard characters. OK on that level—with great special effects—but should have been much better.▼

Black Horse Canyon (1954) **C-81m.** **½ D: Jesse Hibbs. Joel McCrea, Mari Blanchard, Race Gentry, Murvyn Vye. Diverting, gentle Western about rebellious black stallion and those who recapture him.

Black Jack SEE: **Wild in the Sky**

Blackjack Ketchum, Desperado (1956) **76m.** *½ D: Earl Bellamy. Howard Duff, Victor Jory, Maggie Mahoney, Angela Stevens. Former gunslinger must endure another shoot-out before returning to a peaceful way of life.

Black Knight, The (1954-U.S.-British) **C-85m.** **½ D: Tay Garnett. Alan Ladd, Patricia Medina, Andre Morell, Harry Andrews, Peter Cushing. Ladd lends some bounce to small budgeter about mysterious horseman championing King Arthur's cause in merry old England.

Black Legion (1936) **83m.** *** D: Archie Mayo. Humphrey Bogart, Erin O'Brien-Moore, Dick Foran, Ann Sheridan, Joe Sawyer. Factory worker Bogart becomes involved with Ku Klux Klan-ish group in powerful social drama, compactly told.

Black Like Me (1964) **107m.** *** D: Carl Lerner. James Whitmore, Roscoe Lee Browne, Lenka Petersen, Sorrell Booke, Will Geer, Al Freeman, Jr., Dan Priest, Raymond St. Jacques. Strong drama based on actual history of reporter who took drugs that allowed him to pass for black so he could experience racial prejudice firsthand. Some aspects of presentation are now dated, but basic themes are still timely.▼

Black Magic (1944) **67m.** D: Phil Rosen. Sidney Toler, Mantan Moreland, Frances Chan, Jacqueline de Wit, Claudia Dell,

Edward Earle, Joseph Crehan. Video release title MEETING AT MIDNIGHT. See **Charlie Chan** series.▼

Black Magic (1949) **105m.** **½ D: Gregory Ratoff. Orson Welles, Akim Tamiroff, Nancy Guild, Raymond Burr, Frank Latimore. Welles is predictably florid in chronicle of famous charlatan Cagliostro who seeks to rise to power in 18th century Italy. (He codirected this handsome film, uncredited.)▼

Blackmail (1929-British) **86m.** *** D: Alfred Hitchcock. Anny Ondra, Sara Allgood, John Longden, Charles Paton, Donald Calthrop, Cyril Ritchard. Young woman kills man who tries to rape her, then finds herself caught between investigating detective (who happens to be her boyfriend) and a blackmailer. Hitchcock's—and England's—first talking picture is still exciting, especially for fans and students of the director's work. Originally shot as a silent; that version, running 75m., also exists (and is significantly better). Incidentally, leading lady Ondra had a heavy accent, so her voice was dubbed for the talkie version.▼

Blackmail (1939) **81m.** **½ D: H. C. Potter. Edward G. Robinson, Gene Lockhart, Guinn Williams, Ruth Hussey, Esther Dale. Robinson is freed after serving stretch for crime he didn't commit; guilty Lockhart blackmails him in taut drama.

Black Mama, White Mama (1972-U.S.-Filipino) **C-87m.** ** D: Eddie Romero. Pam Grier, Margaret Markov, Sid Haig, Lynn Borden. Cliched, violent female rehash of THE DEFIANT ONES, as blonde Markov and black Grier escape chained together from a Filipino prison camp. Haig is hammy in cowboy costume. Story cowritten by Jonathan Demme.

Black Marble, The (1980) **C-113m.** **½ D: Harold Becker. Robert Foxworth, Paula Prentiss, Harry Dean Stanton, Barbara Babcock, John Hancock, Raleigh Bond, Judy Landers, James Woods, Michael Dudikoff, Anne Ramsey, Christopher Lloyd. Insightful but curiously unmemorable love story about sexy cop Prentiss and her new partner (Foxworth), an alcoholic romantic drowning in the reality of his job. Misses much of the humor that marked Joseph Wambaugh's novel.▼

Black Market Baby (1977) **C-100m.** TVM D: Robert Day. Linda Purl, Desi Arnaz Jr., Bill Bixby, Jessica Walter, David Doyle, Tom Bosley. Unmarried couple struggle with a black market adoption ring out to take their baby. Unpleasantly exploitive social drama done better as a sleazy B movie of yore. Based on the novel *A Nice Italian Girl* by Elizabeth Christman. Below average.

Black Moon Rising (1986) **C-100m.** BOMB D: Harley Cokliss. Tommy Lee

Jones, Linda Hamilton, Robert Vaughn, Richard Jaeckel, Bubba Smith, Lee Ving, William Sanderson. Vaughn's hot-car ring steals the Black Moon, one of those zoom-across-the-salt-flats dream machines no taller than a munchkin's shin; high-tech thief Jones pursues. Punk-rocker-turned-actor Ving wears a coat and tie, but that's about it for novelty value; this one deserves to get a Big Moon Rising. From a story by John Carpenter.▼

Black Narcissus (1946-British) **C-99m.** **** D: Michael Powell, Emeric Pressburger. Deborah Kerr, David Farrar, Sabu, Jean Simmons, Kathleen Byron, Flora Robson, Esmond Knight. Visually sumptuous, dramatically charged movie, from Rumer Godden novel, about nuns trying to establish a mission in a remote Himalayan outpost amid formidable physical and emotional challenges. One of the most breathtaking color films ever made (winning Oscars for cinematographer Jack Cardiff and art director Alfred Junge). Scenes in which Sister Superior Kerr recalls her former life, a key plot element, were originally censored from American prints.▼

Black Noon (1971) **C-73m.** TVM D: Bernard Kowalski. Roy Thinnes, Yvette Mimieux, Gloria Grahame, Lynn Loring, Ray Milland, Henry Silva. Traveling preacher and young wife stumble upon odd religious sect in American West. Last shot of film explains all. Average.

Black Oak Conspiracy (1977) **C-92m.** **½ D: Bob Kelljan. Jesse Vint, Karen Carlson, Albert Salmi, Seymour Cassel, Robert F. Lyons. Predictable action drama pitting an "average Joe" (Vint) against a crooked sheriff and unscrupulous land grabbers. Situations and dialogue are written to formula.▼

Black Orchid, The (1959) **96m.** **½ D: Martin Ritt. Sophia Loren, Anthony Quinn, Ina Balin, Jimmie Baird, Mark Richman, Naomi Stevens, Frank Puglia. Fabricated soaper of bumbling businessman (Quinn) romancing criminal's widow (Loren) and the problem of convincing their children that marriage will make all their lives better.▼

Black Orpheus (1959-French-Portuguese) **C-103m.** ***½ D: Marcel Camus. Breno Mello, Marpessa Dawn, Lea Garcia, Adhemar Da Silva, Lourdes De Oliveira. Street-car conductor Mello and country-girl Dawn fall in love in Rio de Janeiro during Carnival. Lyrical updating of the Orpheus and Eurydice legend is beautifully acted and directed. Oscar winner for Best Foreign Film; rhythmic score by Luis Bonfa and Antonio Carlos Jobim.▼

Blackout (1954-British) **87m.** ** D: Terence Fisher. Dane Clark, Belinda Lee, Betty Ann Davies, Eleanor Summerfield. Clark, down on his luck, makes some fast money

by agreeing to marry a pretty blonde—and then finds himself the patsy in a murder case. Ordinary programmer. Original British title: MURDER BY PROXY.

Blackout (1978-Canadian-French) **C-89m.** ** D: Eddy Matalon. Jim Mitchum, Robert Carradine, Belinda Montgomery, June Allyson, Jean-Pierre Aumont, Ray Milland. Violent story of criminals who terrorize apartment dwellers during N.Y.'s 1977 power blackout. Balanced with black comedy for so-so results.▼

Blackout (1985) **C-99m.** TVM D: Douglas Hickox. Richard Widmark, Keith Carradine, Michael Beck, Kathleen Quinlan, Gerald Hiken. Dogged cop pursues an amnesiac who holds the key to a long-ago murder. Made for cable. Average.▼

Black Patch (1957) **83m.** BOMB D: Allen H. Miner. George Montgomery, Diane Brewster, Leo Gordon, Sebastian Cabot. Inconsequential trivia with Montgomery as gun-toting sheriff out to clear his name.

Black Pirate, The (1926) **C-85m.** *** D: Albert Parker. Douglas Fairbanks, Sr., Billie Dove, Anders Randolf, Donald Crisp, Tempe Piggott, Sam De Grasse. Robust silent swashbuckler with Fairbanks a nobleman who turns pirate after being victimized by cutthroats. Filmed in early Technicolor process, but most extant prints are b&w.▼

Black Pirates, The (1954-Mexican) **C-72m.** **½ D: Allen H. Miner. Anthony Dexter, Martha Roth, Lon Chaney, Robert Clarke. Uninspired account of pirates searching for gold.

Black Rain (1989) **C-126m.** **½ D: Ridley Scott. Michael Douglas, Andy Garcia, Ken Takakura, Kate Capshaw, Yusaku Matsuda, Shigeru Koyama, John Spencer. Tough, violent, foulmouthed action yarn about street-worn N.Y.C. cop and his partner who are supposed to deliver a Japanese mobster to the cops in Osaka—and then wind up pursuing him on his own turf. Too long, too predictable at times, but slick and entertaining.▼

Black Rain (1989-Japanese) **123m.** *** D: Shohei Imamura. Yoshiko Tanaka, Kazuo Kitamura, Etsuko Ichihara, Shoichi Ozawa, Norihei Miki, Keisuke Ishida. Somber, restrained, and very moving story detailing ten years in the life of a family which survived Hiroshima, and the ways in which their bodies and souls are poisoned by the fallout—or "black rain." A quietly observant character study with a number of haunting images (in black & white).

Black Raven, The (1943) **64m.** *½ D: Sam Newfield. George Zucco, Wanda McKay, Noel Madison, Bob Randall (Bob Livingston), Byron Foulger. Paltry (and obvious) whodunit, with various people stranded at Zucco's inn during a storm. Glenn Strange is the comedy relief!▼

Black Rider, The SEE: Joshua▼

Black Rodeo (1972) C-87m. **½ D: Jeff Kanew. Archie Wycoff, Clarence Gonzalez, Pete Knight, Marval Rogers, Reuben Heura. Offbeat, frequently interesting documentary about a rodeo that takes place largely in Harlem; background music is performed by such stars as B.B. King, Ray Charles, Dee Dee Sharpe.

Black Room, The (1935) 67m. *** D: Roy William Neill. Boris Karloff, Marian Marsh, Robert Allen, Katherine DeMille, John Buckler, Thurston Hall. Excellent understated thriller of twin brothers (Karloff) and the ancient curse that dominates their lives. Features one of Karloff's best performances.▼

Black Rose, The (1950) C-120m. ** D: Henry Hathaway. Tyrone Power, Cecile Aubry, Orson Welles, Jack Hawkins, Michael Rennie, Herbert Lom, James Robertson Justice, Finlay Currie. Sweeping pageantry follows Saxon Power on Oriental adventures during 1200s; plodding film only somewhat redeemed by dynamic action scenes. Filmed in England and North Africa. Young Laurence Harvey has a bit part.

Black Sabbath (1964-Italian) C-99m. **½ D: Mario Bava. Boris Karloff, Mark Damon, Suzy Anderson, Jacqueline Pierreux. Italian three-part film hosted by Karloff, who appears in final episode about a vampire controlling an entire family. Other sequences are good, atmospheric.▼

Black Scorpion, The (1957) 88m. *½ D: Edward Ludwig. Richard Denning, Carlos Rivas, Mara Corday, Mario Navarro. Outstanding animation by KING KONG's Willis O'Brien is the highlight of this sci-fi thriller about giant arachids popping out of a volcano in Mexico. Basically a remake of the superior THEM!

Black Shield of Falworth, The (1954) C-99m. **½ D: Rudolph Maté. Tony Curtis, Janet Leigh, David Farrar, Barbara Rush, Herbert Marshall. Juvenile version of Howard Pyle novel, *Men of Iron;* Curtis unconvincing as nobility rising through ranks to knighthood in medieval England. Settings, supporting cast bolster production.

Black Sleep, The (1956) 81m. *½ D: Reginald LeBorg. Basil Rathbone, Akim Tamiroff, Lon Chaney, John Carradine, Bela Lugosi, Tor Johnson, Herbert Rudley. Big horror cast cannot save dull, unatmospheric tale of doctor performing brain transplants in remote castle. Laughable. Reissued as DR. CADMAN'S SECRET.

Black Spurs (1965) C-81m. *½ D: R. G. Springsteen. Rory Calhoun, Terry Moore, Linda Darnell, Scott Brady, Lon Chaney, Bruce Cabot, Richard Arlen. Ordinary Western with attraction of one-time movie stars including Darnell (her last film). Standard horse opera.

Black Stallion, The (1979) C-118m. *** D: Carroll Ballard. Kelly Reno, Mickey Rooney, Teri Garr, Clarence Muse, Hoyt Axton, Michael Higgins. Exquisitely filmed story of a young boy's adventures with a magnificent black stallion—from a dramatic shipwreck to a racing championship. Too slow at times, but still worthwhile, with many precious moments, and a lovely performance by Rooney as veteran horse trainer. Followed by 1983 sequel.▼

Black Stallion Returns, The (1983) C-93m. **½ D: Robert Dalva. Kelly Reno, Vincent Spano, Allen Goorwitz (Garfield), Woody Strode, Ferdinand Mayne, Jodi Thelen, Teri Garr. Fair action sequel with Reno, now a teenager, searching the Sahara for his Arabian horse. Those expecting the magic of the original will be disappointed. First-time director Dalva edited the 1979 film.▼

Black Streetfighter, The SEE: Black Fist

Black Sunday (1961-Italian) 83m. **½ D: Mario Bava. Barbara Steele, John Richardson, Ivo Garrani, Andrea Checchi. Intriguing story of the one day each century when Satan roams the earth. Steele is a witch who swears vengeance on the descendants of those who killed her hundreds of years ago. Beautifully atmospheric.▼

Black Sunday (1977) C-143m. *** D: John Frankenheimer. Robert Shaw, Bruce Dern, Marthe Keller, Fritz Weaver, Steven Keats, Bekim Fehmiu, Michael V. Gazzo, William Daniels. International terrorist organization plots to blow up the Super Bowl, enlists the aid of former Vietnam POW Dern, who pilots the TV blimp. Generally compelling adaptation (by Ernest Lehman, Kenneth Ross, Ivan Moffat) of the Thomas Harris bestseller, with Dern at his unhinged best. Splendid aerial photography.▼

Black Swan, The (1942) C-85m. *** D: Henry King. Tyrone Power, Maureen O'Hara, Laird Cregar, Thomas Mitchell, George Sanders, Anthony Quinn. Power makes a dashing pirate in this colorful swashbuckler, fighting Sanders and Quinn, rescuing O'Hara from their clutches. Leon Shamroy's cinematography deservedly earned him an Oscar.

Black Tent, The (1957-British) C-93m. ** D: Brian Hurst. Anthony Steel, Donald Sinden, Anna Maria Sandri, Donald Pleasence. Passable mixture of romance and action in the African desert as British soldier Steel romances native chief's daughters, helps tribe fight off Nazi attack.▼

Black Tights (1960-French) C-120m. *** D: Terence Young. Cyd Charisse, Moira Shearer, Zizi Jeanmaire, Cyd Sanders, Roland Petit. Narrated by Maurice Chevalier. Ballet fans will feast on this quartet of stunning performances, featuring some of the era's top dance talent. Our favorite: the ballet of Rostand's *Cyrano de Bergerac*, with Shearer a lovely Roxanne.▼

Black Tuesday (1954) 80m. *** D: Hugo Fregonese. Edward G. Robinson, Peter Graves, Jean Parker, Milburn Stone. Throwback to 1930-ish gangster films, with Robinson and Graves as escaped convicts being hunted by cops—nice gunplay, with Parker good as the moll.

Black Water Gold (1969) C-75m. TVM D: Alan Landsburg. Keir Dullea, Lana Wood, Ricardo Montalban, Bradford Dillman, France Nuyen, Aron Kincaid. Fairly intense (for TV) story of various forces vying for sunken Spanish galleon treasure of Panama Eagles. Above average.

Blackwell's Island (1939) 71m. **½ D: William McGann. John Garfield, Rosemary Lane, Dick Purcell, Victor Jory, Stanley Fields, Peggy Shannon, Leon Ames, Milburn Stone. Peppy little based-on-fact gangster film with crusading reporter Garfield attempting to nail tough but dimwitted mobster Fields.

Black Werewolf (1974) SEE: **Beast Must Die, The**

Black Whip, The (1956) 77m. *½ D. Charles Marquis Warren. Hugh Marlowe, Coleen Gray, Angie Dickinson, Sheb Wooley. Only spice to this oater is bevy of beautiful girls who are rescued by Marlowe.

Black Widow, The (1947) SEE: **Sombra, The Spider Woman**

Black Widow (1954) C-95m. ** D: Nunnally Johnson. Ginger Rogers, Van Heflin, Gene Tierney, George Raft, Peggy Ann Garner, Reginald Gardiner, Virginia Leith, Otto Kruger, Cathleen Nesbitt, Skip Homeier. Broadway producer Heflin takes young writer Garner under his wing, is naturally suspected when she turns up dead in his apartment. Glossy but dull adaptation of Patrick Quentin mystery, with remarkably poor performances by Rogers as bitchy star and Raft as dogged detective. Johnson also produced and wrote the screenplay.

Black Widow (1986) C-103m. **½ D: Bob Rafelson. Debra Winger, Theresa Russell, Sami Frey, Dennis Hopper, Nicol Williamson, Terry O'Quinn, D. W. Moffett, Lois Smith, Mary Woronov, Rutanya Alda, James Hong, Diane Ladd. Female investigator for the Justice Dept. becomes intrigued—then obsessed—by young woman who seduces, marries, and murders wealthy men. Handsome, stylishly crafted yarn, loaded with sexual tension, that stops just short of hitting the mark. Winger and Russell are both terrific. Photographed by Conrad Hall; effective music score by Michael Small. Amusing cameo by playwright David Mamet as one of Winger's poker-playing colleagues.▼

Black Windmill, The (1974-British) C-106m. **½ D: Don Siegel. Michael Caine, Joseph O'Conor, Donald Pleasence, John Vernon, Janet Suzman, Delphine Seyrig. Slick, craftsmanlike but generally undistinguished thriller, as espionage agent Caine tries to locate his son's kidnappers. Siegel has done better.▼

Black Zoo (1963) 88m. *½ D: Robert Gordon. Michael Gough, Virginia Grey, Jerome Cowan, Elisha Cook, Jeanne Cooper. Gough, head of private zoo, doubles as leader of cult of animal worshipers, leading to murders and various other surprises. Good cast flounders, but film has a moment or two. From the man who gave you I WAS A TEEN-AGE WEREWOLF.

Blacula (1972) C-92m. *** D: William Crain. William Marshall, Denise Nicholas, Vonetta McGee, Thalmus Rasulala, Ketty Lester, Elisha Cook, Jr., Gordon Pinsent. Dracula bit a Black Prince and now black vampire is stalking the streets of modern L.A. Some terrific shocks, and some very lively dialogue. Sequel: SCREAM, BLACULA, SCREAM.▼

Blade (1973) C-90m. **½ D: Ernest Pintoff. John Marley, Jon Cypher, Kathryn Walker, William Prince, John Schuck, Rue McClanahan. New York-made actioner about female-hating Cypher, who indulges in violent killings, and tough police Lt. Marley, who tracks him down. A bit pretentious and involved; fairly absorbing.▼

Blade in Hong Kong (1985) C-100m. TVM D: Reza Badiyi. Terry Lester, Keye Luke, Mike Preston, Jean-Marie Hon, Leslie Nielsen, Nancy Kwan, Anthony Newley, Ellen Regan. Action-adventure dealing with a private investigator (soap star Lester) from America and the Hong Kong underworld (run by Newley). Pilot for prospective series. Average.▼

Blade Master, The (1984-Italian) C-92m. *½ D: David Hills. Miles O'Keeffe, Lisa Foster (Lisa Raines), Charles Borromel, David Cain Haughton, Chen Wong. Silly sequel to ATOR THE FIGHTING EAGLE has O'Keeffe as the prehistoric warrior on a quest to protect the Earth from a primitive atomic bomb called the ''Geometric Nucleus.'' As in TARZAN, THE APE MAN, O'Keeffe wrestles with an oversize rubber snake, but film's silliest scene has him suddenly hang-gliding to storm an enemy castle. Original title: ATOR THE INVINCIBLE.▼

Blade Runner (1982) C-118m. *½ D: Ridley Scott. Harrison Ford, Rutger Hauer, Sean Young, Edward James Olmos, William Sanderson, Daryl Hannah, Joe Turkel, Joanna Cassidy, Brion James. In 21st century L.A., a former cop (Ford) is recruited to track down androids who have mutinied in space and made their way to Earth. A triumph of production design, defeated by a muddled script and main characters with no appeal whatsoever. However, the film has a fervent following. Loosely based on Philip K. Dick's novel *Do Androids Dream of Electric Sheep?* Futuristic stylings by Syd Mead and Lawrence G. Paull. Videocassette version runs 123m.▼

Blame It On Rio (1984) **C-100m.** **½ D: Stanley Donen. Michael Caine, Joseph Bologna, Valerie Harper, Michelle Johnson, Demi Moore, Jose Lewgoy. Caine has a fling with his best friend's sexy teenage daughter while vacationing in Rio de Janeiro. Caine's terrific, Johnson is voluptuous, but the script is kind of a sniggering TV sitcom, with a heavy-handed music score of too-familiar records. Written by Charlie Peters and Larry Gelbart. Remake of the French film ONE WILD MOMENT.▼

Blame It on the Night (1984) **C-85m.** *½ D: Gene Taft. Nick Mancuso, Byron Thames, Leslie Ackerman, Dick Bakalyan, Merry Clayton, Billy Preston, Ollie E. Brown. Plodding tale of rock star Mancuso, who attempts to buy the love of his ultrastraight, illegitimate, military cadet son. Based on a story by the director and Mick Jagger.▼

Blanche Fury (1948-British) **C-95m.** *** D: Marc Allegret. Stewart Granger, Valerie Hobson, Walter Fitzgerald, Michael Gough, Maurice Denham. Beautifully mounted gothic melodrama about a governess who marries into wealthy family, and the headstrong steward (Granger) who aspires to run the estate.

Blast-Off SEE: **Those Fantastic Flying Fools**▼

Blaze (1989) **C-119m.** **½ D: Ron Shelton. Paul Newman, Lolita Davidovich, Jerry Hardin, Gailard Sartain, Jeffrey DeMunn, Garland Bunting, Richard Jenkins, Robert Wuhl. Newman gives a flashy, uninhibited performance as Earl Long, the flamboyant governor of Louisiana in the 1950s who fell headlong in love with stripper Blaze Starr (Davidovich, in her first lead role). Seemingly surefire story, peppered with colorful characters and incidents, falls alarmingly flat after a while and never recovers. Real-life Blaze Starr appears fleetingly as Lily, the stripper whose shoulder Newman kisses backstage.▼

Blaze of Noon (1947) **91m.** **½ D: John Farrow. Anne Baxter, William Holden, Sonny Tufts, William Bendix, Sterling Hayden. Hokey story of Holden torn between his wife (Baxter) and true love, flying.

Blazing Forest, The (1952) **C-90m.** *½ D: Edward Ludwig. John Payne, Agnes Moorehead, Richard Arlen, William Demarest, Susan Morrow. Felling trees and romancing Moorehead's niece (Morrow) occupies Payne till big fire diverts him, but not the bored viewer.

Blazing Magnums SEE: **Strange Shadows in an Empty Room**▼

Blazing Saddles (1974) **C-93m.** ***½ D: ✓ Mel Brooks. Cleavon Little, Gene Wilder, Harvey Korman, Madeline Kahn, Slim Pickens, David Huddleston, Alex Karras, Burton Gilliam, Mel Brooks, John Hillerman, Liam Dunn, Carol Arthur, Dom DeLuise. Brooks's first hit movie is a riotous Western spoof, with Little an unlikely sheriff, Korman as villainous Hedley Lamarr, and Kahn as a Dietrich-like chanteuse. None of Brooks's later films have topped this one for sheer belly laughs. Richard Pryor was one of the screenwriters. Network TV version substitutes cutting-room floor footage for some of the original's raunchier gags.▼

Blessed Event (1932) **83m.** *** D: Roy Del Ruth. Lee Tracy, Mary Brian, Dick Powell, Emma Dunn, Frank McHugh, Allen Jenkins, Ned Sparks, Ruth Donnelly. Tracy's most famous role has him a Walter Winchell prototype whose spicy column makes him famous but also gets him in hot water; Powell makes film debut as crooner. Fast-moving, delightful.

Bless the Beasts and Children (1972) **C-109m.** *** D: Stanley Kramer. Billy Mumy, Barry Robins, Miles Chapin, Ken Swofford, Jesse White, Vanessa Brown. Exciting and well-intentioned, if repetitious, story of six young misfit boys, campers at a ranch, who attempt to free a captive herd of buffalo scheduled for slaughter. The Barry DeVorzon-Perry Botkin music that later became known as "Nadia's Theme" and the *Young and the Restless* theme originated here.▼

Blind Alley (1939) **71m.** **½ D: Charles Vidor. Chester Morris, Ralph Bellamy, Ann Dvorak, Joan Perry, Melville Cooper, Rose Stradner, John Eldredge. One of Hollywood's first attempts to illustrate psychological ideas. Morris is troubled gangster who holds psychiatrist Bellamy prisoner, and allows himself to be analyzed. Dated but interesting. Remade as THE DARK PAST.

Blind Alley (1984) SEE: **Perfect Strangers**▼

Blind Date (1934) **71m.** **½ D: Roy William Neill. Ann Sothern, Paul Kelly, Neil Hamilton, Mickey Rooney, Jane Darwell, Joan Gale. Sothern has her hands full choosing between mechanic Kelly and wealthy Hamilton in this pleasant little domestic comedy.

Blind Date (1959) SEE: **Chance Meeting**
Blind Date (1984) **C-100m.** **½ D: Nico Mastorakis. Joseph Bottoms, Kirstie Alley, James Daughton, Lana Clarkson, Keir Dullea. Dr. Dullea tests a portable machine that stimulates vision on blind Bottoms, causing Bottoms to become obsessed with capturing a psycho killer who's on

the loose. Solid cast perks up a contrived thriller, filmed in Greece. ▼

Blind Date (1987) C-93m. *½ D: Blake Edwards. Kim Basinger, Bruce Willis, John Larroquette, William Daniels, Phil Hartman, Alice Hirson, George Coe, Mark Blum, Graham Stark. Tiresome retread of all-too-familiar farcical material by Blake Edwards. Yuppie Willis takes Basinger out on a blind date, warned that she can't tolerate alcohol—and immediately gives her champagne. Alternately boring and grating. This was Willis' starring debut; guitarist Stanley Jordan makes a musical appearance. ▼

Blinded by the Light (1980) C-100m. TVM D: John A. Alonzo. Kristy McNichol, James Vincent McNichol, Anne Jackson, Michael McGuire, Jenny O'Hara, Phillip Allen, Keith Andes. Kristy tries to rescue her brother (played by real-life brother Jimmy) from a religious cult that has brainwashed him. Based on the novel by Robin F. Brancato. Average.

Blind Faith (1990) C-200m. TVM D: Paul Wendkos. Robert Urich, Joanna Kerns, Dennis Farina, Joe Spano, Robin Strasser, David Barry Gray, Jay Underwood, Doris Roberts. Plodding adaptation of Joe McGinniss' best-seller about real-life Rob Marshall, a model husband and father who killed his loving wife in 1984. Urich is good in an atypical role as a charming monster, but the film goes on too long. Originally shown in two parts. Average.

Blindfold (1966) C-102m. **½ D: Philip Dunne. Rock Hudson, Claudia Cardinale, Jack Warden, Guy Stockwell, Anne Seymour. Attractive cast falters in film that wavers from comedy to mystery. Slapstick scenes seem incongruous as Hudson engages in international espionage with a noted scientist. Shot partly in N.Y.C.

Blind Justice (1986) C-100m. TVM D: Rod Holcomb. Tim Matheson, Mimi Kuzyk, Philip Charles MacKenzie, Tom Atkins, Lisa Eichhorn. Freelance photographer's life turns into a nightmare when he's mistakenly arrested for armed robbery, kidnapping and rape in this pedestrian mistaken-identity drama. Average.▼

Blindman (1972-Italian) C-105m. ** D: Ferdinando Baldi. Tony Anthony, Ringo Starr, Agneta Eckemyr, Lloyd Batista. Blindman (Anthony) seeks revenge on man who stole fifty mail-order brides. Mindless entertainment, though any movie with Ringo as a slimy Mexican bandit can't be *all* bad.

Blind Man's Bluff SEE: **Cauldron of Blood**▼

Blind Rage (1978-Philippine) C-80m. *½ D: Efren C. Pinon. D'Urville Martin, Leo Fong, Tony Ferrer, Fred Williamson, Dick Adair. Five blind men attempt to rip off a

bank. Bright idea for an action-adventure spoof, but poorly handled.▼

Blind Spot (1947) 73m. *** D: Robert Gordon. Chester Morris, Constance Dowling, Steven Geray, Sid Tomack. Mystery writer Morris has to extricate himself from charge of murdering his publisher in this tight little mystery.

Blind Witness (1989) C-100m. TVM D: Richard Colla. Victoria Principal, Paul Le Mat, Stephen Macht, Matt Clark, Tim Choate. Blind woman is the sole witness to her husband's murder, but the legal system ignores the fact that her testimony against two suspects can be credible. Based on a story by blind actor/musician Tom Sullivan. Average.

Bliss (1985-Australian) C-111m. *½ D: Ray Lawrence. Barry Otto, Lynette Curran, Helen Jones, Miles Buchanan, Gia Carides, Tim Robertson. High-powered businessman has a major heart attack, sees himself dying, then revives—which changes his entire outlook on life. After a dynamic opening this stylized satire slows to a snail's pace and loses its thrust. Nevertheless, it was an Australian Academy Award winner and an international film festival favorite, so judge for yourself.▼

Bliss of Mrs. Blossom, The (1968-U.S.-British) C-93m. *** D: Joe McGrath. Shirley MacLaine, Richard Attenborough, James Booth, Freddie Jones, Bob Monkhouse, John Cleese. Oddball, original comedy with delicious performances. Wife of brassiere manufacturer keeps a lover in their attic for five years. Bogs down toward the end, but for the most part a delight.

Blithe Spirit (1945-British) C-96m. ***½ D: David Lean. Rex Harrison, Constance Cummings, Kay Hammond, Margaret Rutherford, Hugh Wakefield, Joyce Carey. Delicious adaptation of Noel Coward's comedy-fantasy about a man whose long-dead first wife appears to haunt—and taunt—him in his newly married life. Rutherford is wonderful as Madame Arcati, the medium; this earned an Oscar for its special effects. Scripted by the director, the producer (Anthony Havelock-Allan), and the cinematographer (Ronald Neame).▼

Blob, The (1958) C-86m. ** D: Irvin S. Yeaworth, Jr. Steven McQueen, Aneta Corseaut, Earl Rowe, Olin Howlin. Endearingly campy classic of cheap 50s sci-fi has "Steven" (in his first starring role) leading teenagers into battle to save their small town from being swallowed up by giant glop of cherry Jell-O from outer space. Not really all that good, but how can you hate a film like this? (Especially when Burt Bacharach composed the title song.) Sequel: BEWARE! THE BLOB. Remade thirty years later.▼

Blob, The (1988) C-95m. ** D: Chuck

Russell. Shawnee Smith, Donovan Leitch, Ricky Paull Goldin, Kevin Dillon, Billy Beck, Candy Clark, Joe Seneca. Needless, if undeniably gooey, remake about a man-made what's-it that wipes out the standard number of vagrants and oversexed teenagers on its way to enveloping a small town. Showstopper finds a restaurant employee getting pulled head first down a kitchen drain after foolishly attempting to "plunge" the Blob.▼

Blockade (1938) 85m. *** D: William Dieterle. Madeleine Carroll, Henry Fonda, Leo Carrillo, John Halliday, Vladimir Sokoloff, Reginald Denny. Vivid romance drama of Spanish Civil War with globe-trotting Carroll falling in love with fighting Fonda.

Block Busters (1944) 60m. D: Wallace Fox. Leo Gorcey, Huntz Hall, Gabriel Dell, Minerva Urecal, Noah Beery, Sr., Billy Benedict, Harry Langdon. SEE: **Bowery Boys** series.

Block-Heads (1938) 55m. *** D: John G. Blystone. Stan Laurel, Oliver Hardy, Patricia Ellis, Minna Gombell, Billy Gilbert, James Finlayson. Stan's been marching in a trench for twenty years—nobody told him WW1 was over! Ollie brings him home to find he hasn't changed. Top L&H.▼

Blockhouse, The (1973-British) C-90m. *½ D: Clive Rees. Peter Sellers, Charles Aznavour, Per Oscarsson, Peter Vaughan, Jeremy Kemp, Alfred Lynch. Dismal, downbeat story of laborers trapped in underground bunker when the Allies land at Normandy on D-Day.

Blonde Bait (1956-British) 70m. ** D: Elmo Williams. Beverly Michaels, Jim Davis, Joan Rice, Richard Travis, Paul Cavanagh, Thora Hird, Avril Angers, Gordon Jackson, April Olrich. Cheap, toothy blond bombshell Michaels excels as a Yank showgirl breaking out of a sedate British prison for women. British film, originally titled WOMEN WITHOUT MEN, was retitled, reedited, and reshot (with Davis, Travis, and Cavanagh added to the cast) for U.S. release.

Blonde Blackmailer (1958-British) 58m. BOMB D: Charles Deane. Richard Arlen, Susan Shaw, Constance Leigh, Vincent Ball. Hackneyed plot of innocent ex-con (Arlen) determined to prove innocence and find real killers.

Blonde Bombshell SEE: **Bombshell**

Blonde Crazy (1931) 79m. **½ D: Roy Del Ruth. James Cagney, Joan Blondell, Louis Calhern, Ray Milland, Polly Walters, Nat Pendleton. Dated fun with Cagney as small-time con-man who plays cat-and-mouse with big-time sharpie Calhern. Young Milland appears as businessman who marries Jimmy's girlfriend, Blondell.

Blonde Dynamite (1950) 66m. D: Wil-

liam Beaudine. Leo Gorcey, Huntz Hall, Gabriel Dell, Adele Jergens, Jody Gilbert. SEE: **Bowery Boys.**

Blonde Fever (1944) 69m. ** D: Richard Whorf. Philip Dorn, Mary Astor, Felix Bressart, Gloria Grahame, Marshall Thompson. Astor lends class to this mild account of widow on the loose in Europe finding love with Dorn, with Grahame as sultry competition.

Blonde From Peking, The SEE: **Peking Blonde**

Blonde In a White Car SEE: **Nude In a White Car**

Blonde Venus (1932) 97m. *** D: Josef von Sternberg. Marlene Dietrich, Herbert Marshall, Cary Grant, Dickie Moore, Sidney Toler. Episodic story of notorious Dietrich leading unsavory life to support herself and child. A triumph of style over content; this is the film where Marlene appears in an ape suit to sing "Hot Voodoo"! Most TV prints are missing opening sequence of Dietrich and friends skinny-dipping when Marshall happens along.▼

Blondie With a vast audience already familiar with the Chic Young comic strip, a Blondie series seemed like a shoo-in in 1938—and it was. The series, with Arthur Lake as Dagwood, Penny Singleton as Blondie, Larry Simms as Baby Dumpling (later Alexander), Marjorie Kent as Cookie, Jonathan Hale as Mr. Dithers (later Jerome Cowan as Mr. Radcliffe), and Daisy as Daisy, prospered for 12 years, spanning 28 episodes. As with most series, the first ones were the best—fresh, and original, with many clever touches belying the fact that they were low-budget films. By mid-1940s, however, with less capable directors and a fairly standard formula, the films became even more predictable, and the humor more contrived. Nevertheless, Blondie carried on with the same cast until 1951. Unlike some series, the Blondie films actually continued from one to the next, with Baby Dumpling growing up, starting school in the fourth film, taking the name of Alexander in the eleventh. Cookie is also born in the eleventh film, and Daisy has pups in the following one. Many interesting people pop up in the Blondie casts, such as Rita Hayworth in BLONDIE ON A BUDGET, Glenn Ford in BLONDIE PLAYS CUPID, Larry Parks and Janet Blair in BLONDIE GOES TO COLLEGE, Anita Louise in BLONDIE'S BIG MOMENT, and Adele Jergens in BLONDIE'S ANNIVERSARY. Many character actors appeared as well, with Irving Bacon usually playing the harried Bumstead mailman, Mr. Beasley. After nearly forty years of TV situation comedies, Blondie has lost some of its punch, but generally still stands out as an enjoyable, smoothly made series of comedies.

Blondie (1938) **69m.** D: Frank Strayer. Penny Singleton, Arthur Lake, Larry Simms, Gene Lockhart, Ann Doran, Jonathan Hale, Gordon Oliver, Stanley Andrews.

Blondie Brings Up Baby (1939) **67m.** D: Frank Strayer. Penny Singleton, Arthur Lake, Larry Simms, Danny Mummert, Jonathan Hale, Fay Helm, Peggy Ann Garner, Helen Jerome Eddy, Irving Bacon.

Blondie for Victory (1942) **70m.** D: Frank Strayer. Penny Singleton, Arthur Lake, Larry Simms, Majelle White, Stuart Erwin, Jonathan Hale, Danny Mummert.

Blondie Goes Latin (1941) **69m.** D: Frank Strayer. Penny Singleton, Arthur Lake, Larry Simms, Tito Guizar, Ruth Terry, Danny Mummert, Irving Bacon, Janet Burston.

Blondie Goes to College (1942) **74m.** D: Frank Strayer. Penny Singleton, Arthur Lake, Larry Simms, Jonathan Hale, Larry Parks, Janet Blair, Lloyd Bridges, Esther Dale, Adele Mara.

Blondie Has Servant Trouble (1940) **70m.** D: Frank Strayer. Penny Singleton, Arthur Lake, Larry Simms, Daisy, Danny Mummert, Jonathan Hale, Arthur Hohl, Esther Dale, Irving Bacon.

Blondie Hits the Jackpot (1949) **66m.** D: Edward Bernds. Penny Singleton, Arthur Lake, Larry Simms, Jerome Cowan, Lloyd Corrigan.

Blondie In Society (1941) **75m.** D: Frank Strayer. Penny Singleton, Arthur Lake, Larry Simms, Jonathan Hale, Danny Mummert, William Frawley, Edgar Kennedy, Chick Chandler.

Blondie in the Dough (1947) **69m.** D: Abby Berlin. Penny Singleton, Arthur Lake, Larry Simms, Marjorie Kent, Jerome Cowan, Hugh Herbert, Clarence Kolb, Danny Mummert.

Blondie Knows Best (1946) **69m.** D: Abby Berlin. Penny Singleton, Arthur Lake, Larry Simms, Marjorie Kent, Shemp Howard, Ludwig Donath, Jerome Cowan.

Blondie Johnson (1933) **67m.** ****½** D: Ray Enright. Joan Blondell, Chester Morris, Allen Jenkins, Claire Dodd, Earle Foxe, Arthur Vinton, Sterling Holloway, Mae Busch. Pretty good story of Depression victim Blondell vowing to stop at nothing to get ahead, working her way into a position of power in the underworld. Keeps shifting tone, from light to heavy, and doesn't quite pay off, but still entertaining.

Blondie Meets the Boss (1939) **58m.** D: Frank Strayer. Penny Singleton, Arthur Lake, Larry Simms, Dorothy Moore, Jonathan Hale, Stanley Brown, Inez Courtney, Don Beddoe.

Blondie of the Follies (1932) **90m.** ****½** D: Edmund Goulding. Marion Davies, Robert Montgomery, Billie Dove, Jimmy Durante, ZaSu Pitts, Sidney Toler, Louise Carter. Davies and Dove vie for the affection of Montgomery, while ascending to stardom in the Follies. Dramatically wobbly, but the musical numbers are fun. James Gleason fine as Marion's father. Best scene has Davies and Durante spoofing Garbo and Barrymore in GRAND HOTEL.

Blondie on a Budget (1940) **73m.** D: Frank Strayer. Penny Singleton, Arthur Lake, Larry Simms, Danny Mummert, Rita Hayworth, Don Beddoe, John Qualen, Fay Helm.

Blondie Plays Cupid (1940) **68m.** D: Frank Strayer. Penny Singleton, Arthur Lake, Larry Simms, Daisy, Jonathan Hale, Danny Mummert, Irving Bacon, Glenn Ford.

Blondie's Anniversary (1947) **75m.** D: Abby Berlin. Penny Singleton, Arthur Lake, Larry Simms, Marjorie Kent, Adele Jergens, Jerome Cowan, Grant Mitchell, William Frawley.

Blondie's Big Deal (1949) **66m.** D: Edward Bernds. Penny Singleton, Arthur Lake, Larry Simms, Jerome Cowan, Marjorie Kent, Collette Lyons, Ray Walker, Stanley Andrews, Alan Dinehart III.

Blondie's Big Moment (1947) **69m.** D: Abby Berlin. Penny Singleton, Arthur Lake, Larry Simms, Marjorie Kent, Jerome Cowan, Anita Louise, Danny Mummert, Jack Rice, Jack Davis.

Blondie's Blessed Event (1942) **69m.** D: Frank Strayer. Penny Singleton, Arthur Lake, Larry Simms, Norma Jean Wayne, Jonathan Hale, Danny Mummert, Hans Conried, Mary Wickes.

Blondie's Hero (1950) **67m.** D: Edward Bernds. Penny Singleton, Arthur Lake, Larry Simms, William Frawley, Iris Adrian, Edward Earle.

Blondie's Holiday (1947) **67m.** D: Abby Berlin. Arthur Lake, Penny Singleton, Larry Simms, Marjorie Kent, Jerome Cowan, Grant Mitchell, Sid Tomack, Jeff York, Mary Young.

Blondie's Lucky Day (1946) **75m.** D: Abby Berlin. Penny Singleton, Arthur Lake, Larry Simms, Marjorie Kent, Frank Jenks, Paul Harvey, Charles Arnt.

Blondie's Reward (1948) **67m.** D: Abby Berlin. Penny Singleton, Arthur Lake, Larry Simms, Marjorie Kent, Jerome Cowan, Gay Nelson, Danny Mummert, Paul Harvey, Frank Jenks.

Blondie's Secret (1948) **68m.** D: Edward Bernds. Penny Singleton, Arthur Lake, Larry Simms, Marjorie Kent, Jerome Cowan, Thurston Hall, Jack Rice, Danny Mummert, Frank Orth.

Blondie Takes a Vacation (1939) **61m.** D: Frank Strayer. Penny Singleton, Arthur Lake, Larry Simms, Danny Mummert, Donald Meek, Elizabeth Dunne, Robert Wilcox, Irving Bacon.

Blood Alley (1955) **C-115m.** ****½** D: William Wellman. John Wayne, Lauren Bacall, Paul Fix, Mike Mazurki, Anita Ekberg. Enjoyable escapism with Wayne, Bacall, and assorted Chinese escaping down river to Hong Kong pursued by Communists.▼

Blood and Black Lace (1964-Italian-French-German) **C-88m.** *½ D: Mario Bava. Cameron Mitchell, Eva Bartok, Mary Arden. Gruesome thriller about a sex murderer doing in fashion models. Wooden script and performances don't help. Fans of the genre will at least enjoy Bava's imaginative direction.▼

Blood & Guts (1978-Canadian) **C-93m.** ** D: Paul Lynch. William Smith, Micheline Lanctot, Henry Beckman, Brian Clark. Pat, predictable film about a wrestling troupe and the young tyro who joins it.▼

Blood and Lace (1971) **C-87m.** BOMB D: Philip Gilbert. Gloria Grahame, Melody Patterson, Milton Selzer, Len Lesser, Vic Tayback. Rock-bottom cheapie about murders tied in to corrupt orphanage. Don't bother.

Blood & Orchids (1986) **C-200m.** TVM D: Jerry Thorpe. Kris Kristofferson, Jane Alexander, Sean Young, Jose Ferrer, Susan Blakely, Richard Dysart, James Saito, William Russ. Fictional melodrama about a rape-assault trial set in 1930s Hawaii, involving racial prejudice and the islands' social caste system. Norman Katkov's script should have honed closer to his book, based on a real-life case. Kris is miscast as a laid-back detective, and Jane uncharacteristically camps it up as a local *grande dame*. Still, it looks good and has enough juice to make it watchable. Originally shown in two parts. Average.

Blood and Roses (1961-Italian) **C-74m.** **½ D: Roger Vadim. Mel Ferrer, Elsa Martinelli, Annette Vadim, Marc Allegret. This story of a jealous girl's obsession with her family's history of vampirism was based on Sheridan Le Fanu's *Carmilla*. Despite some effective moments, film does not succeed. Same story refilmed later as THE VAMPIRE LOVERS and THE BLOOD-SPATTERED BRIDE.

Blood and Sand (1922) **80m.** **½ D: Fred Niblo. Rudolph Valentino, Lila Lee, Nita Naldi, George Field, Walter Long, Leo White. Dated but still absorbing story of bullfighter Valentino torn between good-girl Lee and vampish Naldi. Scenes of hero being seduced are laughable, but bullfight material holds up well. Remade in 1941 and 1989.▼

Blood and Sand (1941) **C-123m.** *** D: Rouben Mamoulian. Tyrone Power, Linda Darnell, Rita Hayworth, Nazimova, Anthony Quinn, J. Carrol Naish, John Carradine, George Reeves. Pastel remake of Valentino's silent film about naive bullfighter who ignores true-love Darnell for temptress Hayworth. Slow-paced romance,

uplifted by Nazimova's knowing performance as Power's mother and beautiful color production, which earned cinematographers Ernest Palmer and Ray Rennahan Oscars. Remade in 1989▼

Blood and Steel (1959) **63m.** *½ D: Bernard Kowalski. John Lupton, James Edwards, Brett Halsey, John Brinkley. Routine study of U.S. navy men landing on Japheld island, and their assistance of the partisan cause to free the villagers from bondage.

Blood Arrow (1958) **75m.** *½ D: Charles Marquis Warren. Scott Brady, Paul Richards, Phyllis Coates, Don Haggerty. Uninspired tale of Mormon girl Coates trudging through Indian territory to obtain needed medicine, with usual Indian attacks.

Blood Barrier (1979-British) **C-86m.** **½ D: Christopher Leitch. Telly Savalas, Danny De La Paz, Eddie Albert, Michael Gazzo, Cecilia Camacho. Savalas plays a maverick border-patrolman who hates slimy Gazzo's exploitation of poor Mexicans, illegally trucked by Gazzo to California to be day laborers. Interesting drama isn't fully developed and suffers from pointless finale. Exteriors filmed in Mexico. Originally titled THE BORDER.▼

Blood Bath (1966) **80m.** *½ D: Stephanie Rothman, Jack Hill. William Campbell, Jonathan Haze, Sid Haig, Marissa Mathes, Lori Saunders, Sandra Knight. Another AIP paste-job, with half an hour from a Yugoslavian vampire film worked into tale of California artist who murders his models. Eerie atmosphere, some occasional frissons, but overall a mishmash. Shown on TV as TRACK OF THE VAMPIRE.▼

Blood Beach (1981) **C-89m.** ** D: Jeffrey Bloom. John Saxon, David Huffman, Mariana Hill, Otis Young, Stefan Gierasch, Burt Young. People are mysteriously disappearing into the sand at the local beach. Not very bloody, thank heavens, but not very good either.▼

Bloodbrothers (1978) **C-116m.** **½ D: Robert Mulligan. Richard Gere, Paul Sorvino, Tony Lo Bianco, Lelia Goldoni, Yvonne Wilder, Kenneth McMillan, Marilu Henner, Danny Aiello. Interesting if somewhat overblown drama about big-city construction workers. Best when actors have opportunity to underplay, e.g., Sorvino's touching story of baby son's death, Gere's interplay with young hospital patients. Gere stands out as son who wants to break away from family tradition. Recut to 98m. by Mulligan for pay-TV release; retitled A FATHER'S LOVE for network TV.▼

Blood Creature SEE: **Terror Is a Man**▼
Blood Demon, The SEE: **Torture Chamber of Dr. Sadism**▼

Bloodeaters (1980) **C-84m.** BOMB D: Chuck McCrann. Charles Austin, Beverly Shapiro, Dennis Helfend, Paul Haskin,

John Amplas. Government sprays reefer crops with herbicide; harvesters of the weed are transformed into marauding zombies. Cheap, nauseatingly bloody, low-budget horror film. Shot in Pennsylvania in 1979. Later called TOXIC ZOMBIES.

Blood Feud (1979-Italian) **C-112m.** ** D: Lina Wertmuller. Sophia Loren, Marcello Mastroianni, Giancarlo Giannini, Turi Ferro. Lawyer Mastroianni and hood Giannini both love Sicilian widow Loren, and she returns their favors. Loud, overblown, ineffective; set during the Fascist '20s. Also known as REVENGE, cut to 99m.▼

Blood Feud (1983) **C-200m.** TVM D: Mike Newell. Robert Blake, Cotter Smith, Danny Aiello, Edward Albert, Brian Dennehy, Ernest Borgnine, Jose Ferrer, Forrest Tucker, Michael V. Gazzo, Michael C. Gwynne, Nicholas Pryor, Sam Groom. Blake's in his glory as Jimmy Hoffa in this depiction of the lengthy conflict between the Teamsters Union leader and Robert Kennedy (played by newcomer Cotter Smith). Originally shown in two parts. Above average.

Blood For Dracula SEE: **Andy Warhol's Dracula**▼

Blood from the Mummy's Tomb (1972-British) **C-94m.** *** D: Seth Holt, Michael Carreras. Andrew Keir, Valerie Leon, James Villiers, Hugh Burden. Surprisingly satisfying chiller dealing with attempt at reincarnating ancient Egyptian high priestess. Based on Bram Stoker's *Jewel of the Seven Stars*. Remade as THE AWAKENING.

Bloodhounds of Broadway (1952) **C-90m.** **½ D: Harmon Jones. Mitzi Gaynor, Scott Brady, Mitzi Green, Michael O'Shea, Marguerite Chapman, Charles Buchinski (Bronson). Hick Gaynor becomes slick gal in N.Y.C., involved with pseudo-Damon Runyon folk; funny Green has too small a role. Songs include "I Wish I Knew." Runyon stories used as basis for 1989 film of the same name.

Bloodhounds of Broadway (1989) **C-93m.** ** D: Howard Brookner. Matt Dillon, Madonna, Jennifer Grey, Rutger Hauer, Randy Quaid, Julie Hagerty, Esai Morales, Anita Morris, Madeleine Potter, Ethan Phillips. Bland Damon Runyon tale chronicling the escapades of a gallery of gangsters, gamblers, and showgirl types on the Great White Way during New Year's Eve, 1928. The cast is game and there are some funny bits, but it's mostly a snooze. Documentary director Brookner's first fiction feature; he died prior to its release. William Burroughs—the subject of one of his earlier films—appears in a small role as a butler. A PBS *American Playhouse* theatrical production.▼

Blood Legacy (1971) **C-90m.** ** D: Carl Monson. John Carradine, Faith Domergue,

John Russell, Merry Anders, Jeff Morrow, Richard Davalos. To claim inheritance, heirs to a fortune must spend a night in a "haunted" house. Awfully familiar stuff, helped by a few good scenes, and a familiar cast of veterans. Also known as LEGACY OF BLOOD.▼

Bloodline (1979) **C-116m.** BOMB D: Terence Young. Audrey Hepburn, Ben Gazzara, James Mason, Michelle Phillips, Omar Sharif, Romy Schneider, Irene Papas, Gert Frobe, Beatrice Straight, Maurice Ronet. Hepburn finds her life endangered after inheriting a Zurich-based pharmaceutical company. Unbearable adaptation of Sidney Sheldon's novel, which was one of those best-sellers California blondes read on the beach when no one wants to play volleyball. Nearly forty minutes of footage was added for network showing. Officially released as SIDNEY SHELDON'S BLOODLINE.▼

Blood Mania (1970) **88m.** BOMB D: Robert O'Neil. Peter Carpenter, Maria De Aragon, Vicki Peters, Reagan Wilson, Alex Rocco. Avaricious woman kills her surgeon father—only to find that her sister is the beneficiary in his will. Low-budget sleaze.▼

Blood Money (1933) **65m.** *** D: Rowland Brown. George Bancroft, Frances Dee, Judith Anderson, Chick Chandler, Blossom Seeley. Lively, implausible story of underworld bail-bondsman Bancroft falling for thrill-a-minute socialite Dee, causing friction with Bancroft's female cohort (played by Anderson in incongruously gutsy, glamorous role). Dee's closing scene is a knockout. Look fast for Lucille Ball as Chandler's girlfriend at the racetrack.

Blood of Dracula (1957) **68m.** *½ D: Herbert L. Strock. Sandra Harrison, Gail Ganley, Jerry Blaine, Louise Lewis. Inoffensive programmer about girl being hypnotized into a life of vampirism.

Blood of Dracula's Castle (1967) **C-84m.** BOMB D: Al Adamson. John Carradine, Paula Raymond, Alex D'Arcy, Robert Dix, Barbara Bishop. Tacky low-budget mixture of vampirism and kinky sex, with Dracula and his bride "collecting" girls and chaining them up.▼

Blood of Fu Manchu, The (1968) **C-91m.** ** D: Jesus Franco. Christopher Lee, Richard Greene, Gotz George, Howard Marion Crawford, Shirley Eaton, Maria Rohm. Fourth in Lee's international FU MANCHU series, several pegs below its predecessors, finds him in the heart of the Amazon, injecting ten beautiful girls with a deadly potion and dispatching them to give the kiss of death to his enemies in various capitals. Also known as KISS AND KILL and AGAINST ALL ODDS. Sequel: CASTLE OF FU MANCHU. Released theatrically in the U.S. in black and white.▼

Blood of Ghastly Horror (1972) **C-87m.** BOMB D: Al Adamson. John Carradine, Kent Taylor, Tommy Kirk, Regina Carrol. Carradine stars as Dr. Van Ard, whose brain-transplant experiments lead to murder and mayhem. Ghastly indeed! Made in 1969, also known as THE FIEND WITH THE ATOMIC BRAIN, PSYCHO A GO-GO!, THE LOVE MANIAC, THE MAN WITH THE SYNTHETIC BRAIN, and THE FIEND WITH THE ELECTRONIC BRAIN.▼

Blood of Heroes, The (1990) **C-90m.** *½ D: David Peoples. Rutger Hauer, Joan Chen, Vincent Phillip D'Onofrio, Anna Katarina, Delroy Lindo. One-eyed Hauer and apprentice Chen are specialists at "juggers"—a kind of futuristic rugby where the scorer places a dog's skull atop a vertical stick on the opposing team's goal line. Stick to *Home Run Derby* reruns on ESPN instead; this may be the grimiest movie since C.H.U.D., which did, after all, take place in a sewer.

Blood of Others, The (1984) **C-176m.** TVM D: Claude Chabrol. Jodie Foster, Michael Ontkean, Sam Neill, Stephane Audran, Lambert Wilson, Jean-Pierre Aumont, Micheline Presle, Kate Reid. Dreadful adaptation of Simone de Beauvoir novel about young lovers in the resistance movement in war-torn Paris, incomprehensibly starring Foster and Ontkean in the leads, as French a twosome as money could buy. New Zealander Neill is equally difficult to accept as a suave German. (Where are you, Helmut Dantine, now that we need you?) Two flavor-saving graces: welcome sight of Aumont (as Ontkean's père) and Presle. Made for cable. Below average.▼

Blood of the Vampire (1958-British) **C-87m.** ** D: Henry Cass. Donald Wolfit, Barbara Shelley, Vincent Ball, Victor Maddern. Potentially vivid horror film weakened by slack production: doctor sent to prison hospital discovers the warden is an anemic mad scientist (need more be said?). Wolfit is made up here to resemble Bela Lugosi.▼

Blood on Satan's Claw, The (1971-British) **C-93m.** *** D: Piers Haggard. Patrick Wymark, Linda Hayden, Barry Andrews, Michele Dotrice, Tamara Ustinov. In 17th-century Britain a demon is unearthed which a group of evil farm children begin worshipping, sacrificing other children to it. Richly atmospheric horror film with erotic undertones, somewhat gruesome at times. Original British title: SATAN'S SKIN, running 100m. Retitled SATAN'S CLAW.
▼

Blood on the Arrow (1964) **C-91m.** *½ D: Sidney Salkow. Dale Robertson, Martha Hyer, Wendell Corey, Elisha Cook, Ted de Corsia. Humdrum Western dealing with Apache massacre and survivors' attempt to rescue their son held captive by redskins.

Blood on the Moon (1948) **88m.** *** D: Robert Wise. Robert Mitchum, Barbara Bel Geddes, Robert Preston, Walter Brennan, Phyllis Thaxter, Frank Faylen, Tom Tully, Charles McGraw, Tom Tyler. Straightforward Western tale (from a novel by Luke Short) about a drifter who's hired by his former partner to help him bilk some naive landowners. Mitchum sizes up the situation and decides he doesn't like it; Preston is an unrepentant villain. Watch for that great confrontation scene in a darkened barroom.▼

Blood on the Sun (1945) **98m.** *** D: Frank Lloyd. James Cagney, Sylvia Sidney, Wallace Ford, Rosemary DeCamp, Robert Armstrong. Cagney, in Japan during the 1930s, smells trouble coming but is virtually helpless; good melodrama. Also shown in computer-colored version.▼

Blood Relatives (1978-French-Canadian) **C-100m.** *** D: Claude Chabrol. Donald Sutherland, Aude Landry, Lisa Langlois, Laurent Malet, Micheline Lanctot, Stephane Audran, Donald Pleasence, David Hemmings. Barely released thriller about a secret, incestuous relationship with deadly consequences. Interesting cast and Chabrol's cold, scientifically masterful direction make this less unpleasant and gory than it might have been. Not released until 1981 in U.S.

Blood Rose (1969-French) **C-87m.** *½ D: Claude Mulot. Philippe Lemaire, Anny Duperey, Howard Vernon, Elisabeth Tessier, Michele Perello. An artist schemes to restore his wife's face, which was disfigured by fire; badly dubbed, low-grade French import.

Blood Simple (1984) **C-97m.** *** D: Joel Coen. John Getz, Frances McDormand, Dan Hedaya, Samm-Art Williams, M. Emmet Walsh. Flamboyant homage to *film noir* made on a shoestring by brothers Joel and Ethan Coen in Texas. A cuckolded husband hires a slimy character to kill his wife and her boyfriend . . . but that's just the beginning of this serpentine story. A visual delight, full of show-offy stylistics . . . just "a bit cold around the heart," to quote an earlier *noir* classic. ▼

Blood-Spattered Bride, The (1969-Spanish) **C-83m.** *½ D: Vicente Aranda. Maribel Martin, Simon Andreu, Alexandra Bastedo, Dean Selmier, Montserrat Julio. Newlyweds in secluded mansion are terrorized by a strange guest, the reincarnation of a murderess dead 200 years. Based on LeFanu's *Carmila*, but poorly done. Also shown as TIL DEATH DO US PART.▼

Blood Sport (1973) **C-73m.** TVM D: Jerrold Freedman. Ben Johnson, Larry Hagman, Gary Busey, Bill Lucking, David

Doyle, Mimi Saffian, Peggy Rea. Young boy (Busey) groomed by father to become pro football player in exceptional combination character study and drama. Written by Freedman. Above average.

Blood Sport (1986) **C-100m. TVM** D: Vincent McEveety. William Shatner, Heather Locklear, James Darren, Don Murray, Kim Miyori, Nobu McCarthy, Henry Darrow, Tim O'Connor, Keye Luke. TV movie expansion of the *T. J. Hooker* series, with Shatner and associates on assignment in Hawaii to protect a U. S. Senator who might be the target of an assassination. Average.

Bloodsport (1987) **C-92m.** ** D: Newt Arnold. Jean Claude Van Damme, Donald Gibb, Leah Ayres, Norman Burton, Forest Whitaker, Bolo Young. Belgian-born Van Damme joins the movie macho brigade in this story (based on true events) of American Ninja Frank Dux, the first westerner to win the Kumite, an international martial arts competition that tests its participants to their limits. Violent, low-budget action film has its moments.▼

Blood Suckers, The (1967) SEE: **Return from the Past**

Bloodsuckers (1970-British) **C-87m.** *½ D: Robert Hartford-Davis. Patrick Macnee, Peter Cushing, Alex Davion, Patrick Mower, Johnny Sekka, Medeline Hinde, Imogen Hassall, Edward Woodward. Confusing horror yarn about ancient vampire cult on Greek island of Hydra, somehow linked to sinister Oxford dons. Mishmash includes many narrated silent sequences and other evidence of considerable post-production tampering. ▼

Blood, Sweat and Fear (1975-Italian) **C-90m.** *½ D: Stevio Massi. Lee J. Cobb, Franco Gasparri, Giorgia Albertazzi, Sora Sperati. Plodding action drama involving a cat-and-mouse game between Cobb, as the brains behind a grand-scale drug operation, and Gasparri, as an ambitious young narcotics agent.

Blood Ties (1986-Italian) **C-120m.** *** D: Giacomo Battiato. Brad Davis, Tony Lo Bianco, Vincent Spano, Barbara De Rossi, Delia Boccardo, Ricky Tognazzi, Maria Conchita Alonso, Michael Gazzo. Uncompromising crime actioner about an innocent American (Davis), coerced by the mob into assassinating his Sicilian cousin (Lo Bianco), who's been investigating Mafia activities. Good job all around; originally a four-hour television movie.▼

Blood Vows: The Story of a Mafia Wife (1987) **C-100m. TVM** D: Paul Wendkos. Melissa Gilbert, Joe Penny, Talia Shire, Eileen Brennan, Tony Franciosa, Carmine Caridi. Young woman blinded by love finds that she's married into a Mafia family. Interestingly, the characters' Italian surnames were WASP-ized on the eve of the film's premiere, making for unintended humor. Average.

Blood Wedding (1981-Spanish) **C-72m.** *** D: Carlos Saura. Antonio Gades, Cristina Hoyos, Juan Antonio Jiminez, Pilar Cardenas, Carmen Villena. Gades' adaptation for ballet of Federico Garcia Lorca's classic tragedy, performed in full costume in a bare rehearsal hall. Saura's direction is best described as intimate in this happy union of dance and film.▼

Bloody Birthday (1986) **C-85m.** ** D: Ed Hunt. Susan Strasberg, Jose Ferrer, Lori Lethin, Melinda Cordell, Julie Brown, Joe Penny, Billy Jacoby, Michael Dudikoff. Three 10-year-old killer kids go on a rampage; they were born during a lunar eclipse. Formula horror fare "boasts" an unusually tasteless premise but lapses into the usual killing spree. Filmed in 1980.▼

Bloody Mama (1970) **C-90m.** *½ D: Roger Corman. Shelley Winters, Don Stroud, Pat Hingle, Robert De Niro, Clint Kimbrough, Robert Walden, Diane Varsi, Bruce Dern, Pamela Dunlap. Excellent performances cannot save sordid story of Ma Barker and her ugly brood. Film unsuccessfully mixes action narrative with psychological study.▼

Blossoms In the Dust (1941) **C-100m.** *** D: Mervyn LeRoy. Greer Garson, Walter Pidgeon, Felix Bressart, Marsha Hunt, Fay Holden, Samuel S. Hinds. Slick tear-jerker of Texas orphanage founded by Garson when she loses her own child, tastefully acted.

Blowing Wild (1953) **90m.** ** D: Hugo Fregonese. Gary Cooper, Barbara Stanwyck, Ruth Roman, Anthony Quinn, Ward Bond. Tempestuous Stanwyck is married to oil tycoon Quinn, but sets her sights on wildcatter Cooper, who's fully recovered from their one-time affair. Heated emotions can't warm up this plodding story, filmed in Mexico.▼

Blow Out (1981) **C-107m.** **½ D: Brian DePalma. John Travolta, Nancy Allen, John Lithgow, Dennis Franz, Peter Boyden. Intriguing variation on Antonioni's BLOWUP (with a similar title, no less!) set in Philadelphia, about a sound-effects man who records a car accident that turns out to be a politically motivated murder. Absorbing most of the way, but weakened by show-off camerawork and logic loopholes.▼

Blowup (1966-British-Italian) **C-111m.** ***½ D: Michelangelo Antonioni. Vanessa Redgrave, David Hemmings, Sarah Miles, Jill Kennington, Verushka, The Yardbirds. Writer-director Antonioni's hypnotic pop-culture parable of photographer caught in passive life-style. Arresting, provocative film, rich in color symbolism, many-layered meanings. Music by Herbie Hancock.▼

Blue (1968) **C-113m.** *½ D: Silvio Narizzano. Terence Stamp, Joanna Pettet, Karl Malden, Ricardo Montalban, Joe DeSantis, Sally Kirkland. Undistinguished, poorly written Western about American-born, Mexican-raised boy who trusts no one until bullet wounds force him to trust a woman.

Blue Angel, The (1930-German) 103m. ***½ D: Josef von Sternberg. Marlene Dietrich, Emil Jannings, Kurt Gerron, Rosa Valetti, Hans Albers. Ever-fascinating film classic with Jannings as stuffy professor who falls blindly in love with cabaret entertainer Lola-Lola (Dietrich), who ruins his life. Dietrich introduces "Falling in Love Again"; this role made her an international star. Robert Liebman scripted, from Heinrich Mann's novel *Professor Unrath*. Simultaneously shot in German and English versions; the former is obviously superior. Remade in 1959.▼

Blue Angel, The (1959) C-107m. *½ D: Edward Dmytryk. Curt Jurgens, May Britt, Theodore Bikel, John Banner, Ludwig Stossel, Fabrizio Mioni. Disastrous remake of Josef von Sternberg-Marlene Dietrich classic, from Heinrich Mann's novel of precise professor won over by tawdry nightclub singer.

Blue Bayou (1990) C-100m. TVM D: Karen Arthur. Alfre Woodard, Mario Van Peebles, Roy Thinnes, Keith Williams, Ashley Crow, Maxwell Caulfield, Cassie Yates, Elizabeth Ashley. Los Angeles D.A. Woodard and her troublesome teenage son relocate to New Orleans, where the boy can be supervised by his father, a cop who walked out on them years before. Pilot to prospective series scripted by former L.A. deputy D.A.-turned-TV executive Terry Louise Fisher. Average.

Bluebeard (1944) 73m. *** D: Edgar G. Ulmer. Jean Parker, John Carradine, Nils Asther, Ludwig Stossel, Iris Adrian, Emmett Lynn. Surprisingly effective story of incurable strangler Carradine, who falls for smart-girl Parker who senses that something is wrong.▼

Bluebeard (1962 French-Italian) C-114m. **½ D: Claude Chabrol. Charles Denner, Michele Morgan, Danielle Darrieux, Hildegarde Neff, Stephane Audran, Catherine Rouvel, Françoise Lugagne. Retelling of life of French wife-killer, far less witty than Chaplin's MONSIEUR VERDOUX. Original French title: LANDRU.▼

Bluebeard (1972) C-125m. ** D: Edward Dmytryk. Richard Burton, Raquel Welch, Virna Lisi, Joey Heatherton, Nathalie Delon, Karin Schubert. Burton doesn't make much of an impression as world's most famous ladykiller. Women are all beautiful, but script gives them little to do. International production.▼

Bluebeard's Eighth Wife (1938) 80m. ** D: Ernst Lubitsch. Claudette Colbert, Gary Cooper, David Niven, Edward Everett Horton, Elizabeth Patterson, Herman Bing. Contrived comedy about a woman determined to gain the upper hand over an oft-married millionaire. One of Lubitsch's weakest films, notable mainly for the way its two stars "meet cute." Script by Billy Wilder and Charles Brackett. Previously filmed in 1923.

Bluebeard's Ten Honeymoons (1960-British) 93m. ** D: W. Lee Wilder. George Sanders, Corinne Calvet, Jean Kent, Patricia Roc. Sanders enlivens OK chronicle of fortune hunter who decides that marrying and murdering a series of women is the key to financial success.

Blue Bird, The (1940) C-88m. ** D: Walter Lang. Shirley Temple, Spring Byington, Nigel Bruce, Gale Sondergaard, Eddie Collins, Sybil Jason. Released one year after THE WIZARD OF OZ, this lavish Technicolor fantasy (based on the famous play by Maurice Maeterlinck) has everything but charm. Even Shirley seems stiff. Filmed before in 1918, remade in 1976.▼

Blue Bird, The (1976-Russian-U.S.) C-99m. ** D: George Cukor. Todd Lookinland, Patsy Kensit, Elizabeth Taylor, Jane Fonda, Ava Gardner, Cicely Tyson George Cole, Will Geer, Robert Morley, Harry Andrews. Posh, star-studded but heavy-handed fantasy based on Maeterlinck's play about children seeking the bluebird of happiness. First co-production between U.S. and Russia is unbelievably draggy. Remake of 1940 film.

Blue Blood (1951) C-72m. *½ D: Lew Landers. Bill Williams, Jane Nigh, Arthur Shields, Audrey Long. Lackluster racehorse story with a few good moments by Shields as elderly trainer seeking comeback.

Blue City (1986) C-83m. BOMB D: Michelle Manning. Judd Nelson, Ally Sheedy, David Caruso, Paul Winfield, Scott Wilson, Anita Morris. Perfectly awful film about wiseguy kid who returns to Florida hometown after five years, discovers that his father was killed, and vows to avenge (and solve) his murder. Senseless and stupid; Nelson's unappealing character seems to possess a one-word vocabulary, and the word *isn't* fudge. Based on a good book by Ross McDonald.▼

Blue Collar (1978) C-114m. ***½ D: Paul Schrader. Richard Pryor, Harvey Keitel, Yaphet Kotto, Ed Begley, Jr., Harry Bellaver, George Memmoli. Punchy, muckraking expose melodrama with Pryor, Keitel, and Kotto delivering strong performances as auto workers who find that it isn't just management ripping them off—it's their own union. Schrader's directing debut.▼

Blue Dahlia, The (1946) 99m. *** D: George Marshall. Alan Ladd, Veronica Lake, William Bendix, Howard da Silva,

[118]

Hugh Beaumont, Doris Dowling. Exciting Raymond Chandler melodrama has Ladd returning from military service to find wife unfaithful. She's murdered, he's suspected in well-turned film.

Blue Denim (1959) 89m. *** D: Philip Dunne. Carol Lynley, Brandon de Wilde, Macdonald Carey, Marsha Hunt, Warren Berlinger, Roberta Shore. De Wilde and Lynley are striking as teen-agers faced with Carol's pregnancy. Generation gap problem and youths' naiveté date story, but believable performances make it worthwhile.

Blue de Ville (1986) C-100m. TVM D: Jim Johnston. Jennifer Runyon, Kimberley Pistone, Mark Thomas Miller, Alan Autry, Robert T. Prescott. Engagingly loopy cross-country odyssey in a mint-blue '59 Cadillac, with a Madonna-ish free spirit, her yuppie girlfriend, and a hitchhiking musician they pick up along the way. Offbeat and strangely endearing—with a no-name cast. Pilot to a prospective series. Written by Christopher Nelson and Edward D. Markley. Above average.

Blue Fin (1978-Australian) C-90m. ** D: Carl Schultz. Hardy Kruger, Greg Rowe, Elspeth Ballantyne, Liddy Clark, John Jarratt. Mild (but scenic) family outing about a father and son, not on the best of terms, who sail together in search of elusive tuna catch off Australia's southern coast.▼

Blue Gardenia, The (1953) 90m. *** D: Fritz Lang. Anne Baxter, Richard Conte, Ann Sothern, Raymond Burr, Jeff Donnell, George Reeves, Nat King Cole. Engaging murder caper with 1940s flavor. Baxter is accused of murdering wolfish Burr, decides to take columnist Conte's offer of help. Solid film with twist ending.

Bluegrass (1988) C-200m. TVM D: Simon Wincer. Cheryl Ladd, Brian Kerwin, Anthony Andrews, Mickey Rooney, Wayne Rogers, Diane Ladd, Shawnee Smith, Kieran Mulroney. Cheryl Ladd joins the horsey set struggling to become a top breeder. Entertaining soap opera of bluebloods and thoroughbreds, with a controversial foaling sequence that pulled the spotlight away from the actors—especially old horse-movie pro Rooney. Mart Crowley's teleplay was based on a novel by Borden Deal. Originally shown in two parts. Above average.

Blue Grass of Kentucky (1950) C-71m. ** D: William Beaudine. Bill Williams, Jane Nigh, Ralph Morgan. Routine account of horse-breeding families, their rivalry and eventual healing of old wounds when romance blooms between the younger generations.

Blue Hawaii (1961) C-101m. **½ D: Norman Taurog. Elvis Presley, Joan Blackman, Angela Lansbury, Roland Winters,

Iris Adrian. Agreeable Presley vehicle bolstered by Lansbury's presence as mother of soldier (Presley) returning to islands and working with tourist agency. Elvis performs one of his prettiest hits, "Can't Help Falling in Love."▼

Blue Iguana, The (1988) C-88m. BOMB D: John Lafia. Dylan McDermott, Jessica Harper, James Russo, Pamela Gidley, Tovah Feldshuh, Dean Stockwell, Yano Anaya, Flea, Michele Seipp. Amateurish spoof is a hybrid of B Western and *film noir*, with a down-and-out bounty hunter on a suicide mission to recover $20 million in contraband money from a gaggle of bad guys somewhere south of the border. This turkey barely made it to theaters; even an amusing cameo by Dean Stockwell can't save it.▼

Blue Knight, The (1973) C-103m. TVM D: Robert Butler. William Holden, Lee Remick, Joe Santos, Sam Elliott, David Moody, Jamie Farr, Vic Tayback. Holden gives gritty, Emmy-winning performance as Bumper Morgan, the hero of Joseph Wambaugh's best-selling novel about an aging L.A. street cop. Morgan's last four days on the job find him obsessed with finding a prostitute's killer, while his girlfriend (Remick) anxiously awaits the hour of his retirement. Well-done, authentic police story, superbly performed. Cut down from original four-part, 200-minute presentation. Above average.▼

Blue Knight, The (1975) C-78m. TVM D: J. Lee Thompson. George Kennedy, Alex Rocco, Glynn Turman, Verna Bloom, Michael Margotta, Seth Allen. Kennedy assumes role of Bumper Morgan (which he later played in weekly series) as he searches for killer of an aging fellow officer. Kennedy puts his own stamp on the role, but story and approach are definitely formula. Average.▼

Blue Lagoon, The (1949-British) C-101m. *** D: Frank Launder. Jean Simmons, Donald Houston, Noel Purcell, Cyril Cusack, Maurice Denham. Idyllic romance of Simmons and Houston, shipwrecked on tropic isle, falling in love as they grow to maturity; slowly paced but refreshing. Remade in 1980.

Blue Lagoon, The (1980) C-104m. *½ D: Randal Kleiser. Brooke Shields, Christopher Atkins, Leo McKern, William Daniels. Remake of the 1949 film is little more than CALIGULA for the heavy-petting set, as two children become sexually aware of each other after being shipwrecked on an island for several years. Nestor Almendros' photography can't save it.▼

Blue Lamp, The (1950-British) 84m. *** D: Basil Dearden. Jack Warner, Peggy Evans, Dirk Bogarde, Tessie O'Shea, Jimmy Hanley. Dandy manhunt thriller about Scotland Yard's search for murderer of policeman. Unpretentious and exciting.

Blue Light, The (1932-German) 77m. ** D: Leni Riefenstahl. Leni Riefenstahl, Mathias Weimann, Beni Fuhrer, Max Holzboer. Mysterious mountain-maiden Riefenstahl is loved and destroyed by artist Weimann. Slow, pretentious fable, also produced and cowritten by Riefenstahl. She recut film in 1952, and it is this version that's usually shown today.▼

Blue Lightning, The (1986) C-100m. TVM D: Lee Philips. Sam Elliott, Rebecca Gilling, Robert Culp, John Meillon, Robert Coleby, Max Phipps. San Francisco P.I. goes to Australia to retrieve a fabulous gem and is forced to do battle with a ruthless master criminal in the latter's Outback fortress. Average.▼

✓ **Blue Max, The** (1966) C-156m. **½ D: John Guillermin. George Peppard, James Mason, Ursula Andress, Jeremy Kemp, Carl Schell. Fantastic aerial photography and memorable Jerry Goldsmith score are the assets of this silly drama, taken from German point of view, about dogfighting in WW1. Steamy Peppard-Andress love scenes aren't bad either.▼

Blue Monkey (1987) C-98m. BOMB D: William Fruet. Steve Railsback, Gwynyth Walsh, Susan Anspach, John Vernon, Joe Flaherty, Robin Duke. Silly monster film set at hospital that's quarantined after a monster escapes. Poorly filmed in semidarkness. Title is meaningless and randomly selected; it was originally called GREEN MONKEY!▼

Blue Murder at St. Trinian's (1958-British) 86m. *** D: Frank Launder. Joyce Grenfell, Terry-Thomas, George Cole, Alastair Sim. Uncontrollable pupils at madcap school make a robber on the lam wish he'd never hidden out there; deft comedy.

Blueprint for Murder, A (1953) 76m. **½ D: Andrew L. Stone. Joseph Cotten, Jean Peters, Gary Merrill, Jack Kruschen, Mae Marsh. Whodunit has Peters as prime suspect of poison killings, with Cotten seeking the truth.

Blueprint for Robbery (1961) 87m. **½ D: Jerry Hopper. J. Pat O'Malley, Robert Wilkie, Robert Gist, Romo Vincent, Tom Duggan. Deliberately offbeat, low-key film of heist engineered by old-timer O'Malley; good moments put this above average, but overall result is unmemorable.

Blues Brothers, The (1980) C-130m. *** D: John Landis. John Belushi, Dan Aykroyd, The Blues Brothers Band, Cab Calloway, John Candy, Henry Gibson, Carrie Fisher, Charles Napier, Jeff Morris, Ray Charles, Aretha Franklin, James Brown, Kathleen Freeman. Engagingly nutty comedy about the title characters (deadpan musical performers introduced on TV's *Saturday Night Live*) trying to raise money to save their orphanage by reuniting their old band— and nearly destroying Chicago in the process. Off the wall from start to finish, with some fine music woven in, including wonderful numbers by Franklin and Calloway. Numerous cameos include Steven Spielberg, Frank Oz, Steve Lawrence, John Lee Hooker, Twiggy, and Paul Reubens (Pee-wee Herman).▼

Blues Busters (1950) 67m. D: William Beaudine. Leo Gorcey, Huntz Hall, Adele Jergens, Gabriel Dell, Craig Stevens, William Benedict. SEE: **Bowery Boys** series.

Blues for Lovers (1966-British) 89m. ** D: Paul Henreid. Ray Charles, Tom Bell, Mary Peach, Dawn Addams, Piers Bishop, Betty McDowall. Story of Charles (playing himself) and blind child is maudlin, but fans will like generous footage devoted to Ray's song hits, including "I Got a Woman" and "What'd I Say?" Also known as BALLAD IN BLUE.▼

Blues in the Night (1941) 88m. **½ D: Anatole Litvak. Priscilla Lane, Richard Whorf, Betty Field, Lloyd Nolan, Jack Carson, Elia Kazan, Wallace Ford, Billy Halop, Peter Whitney. Intriguing musical drama abandons early promise for soapy, silly melodramatics, in story of self-destructive musician (Whorf) and his band (young Kazan is featured as clarinetist). Good moments, wonderful Warner Bros. montages, but the great title song is never played once in its entirety!

Blue Skies (1946) C-104m. *** D: Stuart Heisler. Fred Astaire, Bing Crosby, Joan Caulfield, Billy De Wolfe, Olga San Juan, Frank Faylen. Astaire and Crosby play onetime show-biz partners and rivals in this paper-thin vehicle kept aloft by lots and lots of Irving Berlin songs. Highlights: Astaire's terrific "Puttin' on the Ritz," star duo's "A Couple of Song and Dance Men."

Blue Skies Again (1983) C-96m. **½ D: Richard Michaels. Harry Hamlin, Robyn Barto, Mimi Rogers, Kenneth McMillan, Dana Elcar, Marcos Gonzales. Friendly, well-meaning but ultimately minor-league chronicle of a young woman (Barto) attempting to play professional baseball.▼

Blue Steel (1990) C-102m. *½ D: Kathryn Bigelow. Jamie Lee Curtis, Ron Silver, Clancy Brown, Elizabeth Pena, Louise Fletcher, Philip Bosco. Stupid thriller with Curtis as a rookie cop stalked by a slick psycho (Silver) in N.Y.C. Laughably ludicrous dialogue is matched by preposterous story turns.▼

Blue Sunshine (1976) C-97m. **½ D: Jeff Lieberman. Zalman King, Deborah Winters, Mark Goddard, Robert Walden, Charles Siebert. Young man accused of murders eludes cops, discovers that apparently "random" killings derive from delayed drug reactions of ten-year-old college class. Offbeat psychological thriller, quite violent at times.▼

Blue Thunder (1983) **C-108m.** ** D: John Badham. Roy Scheider, Malcolm McDowell, Candy Clark, Daniel Stern, Warren Oates, Paul Roebling, Joe Santos. Slick action film built around L.A.'s police helicopter surveillance team. Fun at first, but gets stupider (and crueler) as film goes on—with villainous McDowell character especially ludicrous. Even escapist fare has to be believable on its own terms. Later a TV series.▼

Blue Veil, The (1951) **113m.** *** D: Curtis Bernhardt. Jane Wyman, Charles Laughton, Joan Blondell, Richard Carlson, Agnes Moorehead, Don Taylor, Audrey Totter, Everett Sloane, Cyril Cusack, Natalie Wood, Warner Anderson, Vivian Vance, Philip Ober. Wyman is self-sacrificing nursemaid whose life story is chronicled with intertwined episodes of her charges and their families.

Blue Velvet (1986) **C-120m.** ** D: David Lynch. Kyle MacLachlan, Isabella Rossellini, Dennis Hopper, Laura Dern, Hope Lange, Dean Stockwell, Jack Nance, Brad Dourif. Terminally weird, though flamboyantly original film about a young man's involvement in a small-town mystery involving a kinky nightclub singer, a sadistic kidnapper/drug dealer, and other swell folks. A highly individual look at the bizarre elements just behind the facade of a picture-perfect American town. Too audacious to be easily dismissed, but too strange to be easily enjoyed . . . yet this was one of the most critically praised movies of 1986! Lynch's use of widescreen will suffer on TV; the director also wrote this one. ▼

Blue Water, White Death (1971) **C-99m.** *** D: Peter Gimbel, James Lipscomb. Absorbing study of one of the sea's most colossal beasts, the great white shark.

Blue Yonder, The (1985) **C-105m. TVM** D: Mark Rosman. Peter Coyote, Art Carney, Huckleberry Fox, Dennis Lipscomb, Mittie Smith. Sentimental tale of a youngster who, obsessed with his granddad's exploits as a pioneer aviator, travels back in time to join in the long-ago adventures. Made for cable by Disney. Retitled TIME FLYER. Average.▼

Bluffing It (1987) **C-100m. TVM** D: James Sadwith. Dennis Weaver, Janet Carroll, Michelle Little, Robert Sean Leonard, Cleavant Derricks, Vickie Wauchope. Hardworking blue collar foreman comes to terms with his illiteracy and the fact that he's been bluffing his way through life. Johnny Cash tackled the same theme in 1981's THE PRIDE OF JESSE HALLAM. Average.

Blume in Love (1973) **C-117m.** **½ D: Paul Mazursky. George Segal, Susan Anspach, Kris Kristofferson, Marsha Mason, Shelley Winters, Paul Mazursky. Self-indulgent film about divorce-lawyer Segal refusing to accept fact that his wife (Anspach) has walked out on him, determining to win her back. Good look at modern marriages, but overlong, rambling; Kristofferson delightful as man who moves in with Anspach.▼

Boarding School (1977-German) **C-98m.** *½ D: Andre Farwagi. Nastassja Kinski, Gerry Sundquist, Kurt Raab, Sean Chapman. Sex comedy with Kinski in one of her first starring roles, as an American girl in an exclusive Swiss boarding school, circa 1956. She devises a ruse of the girls pretending to be prostitutes in order to seduce cute guys at nearby boy's school. Original title: THE PASSION FLOWER HOTEL. ▼

Boardwalk (1979) **C-98m.** **½ D: Stephen Verona. Ruth Gordon, Lee Strasberg, Janet Leigh, Joe Silver, Eli Mintz, Eddie Barth. Poignant view of elderly couple struggling to survive in decaying neighborhood missteps into DEATH WISH melodramatics for its finale. Fine performances, including Leigh as duty-bound daughter.

Boat, The SEE: **Das Boot**▼

Boat People (1983-Hong Kong-Chinese) **C-106m.** ***½ D: Ann Hui. Lam Chi-Cheung, Cora Miao, Season Ma, Andy Lau, Paul Ching. Harrowing, heartbreaking, highly provocative account of Japanese photojournalist Chi-Cheung's experiences in Vietnam after Liberation, particularly his friendship with 14-year-old Ma and her family.

Bob & Carol & Ted & Alice (1969) **C-104m.** *** D: Paul Mazursky. Natalie Wood, Robert Culp, Elliott Gould, Dyan Cannon, Horst Ebersberg, Greg Mullavey, Lee Bergere. Glossy look at modern lifestyles; ultrasophisticated couple (Wood & Culp) try to modernize thinking of their best friends (Gould & Cannon) about sexual freedom. Sharp observations, fine performances, marred by silly, pretentious finale. Mazursky's directorial debut. Later a short-lived TV series.▼

Bobbie Jo and the Outlaw (1976) **C-89m.** ** D: Mark L. Lester. Marjoe Gortner, Lynda Carter, Jesse Vint, Merrie Lynn Ross, Belinda Balaski, Gerrit Graham. Competent but excessively violent drive-in fare; bored carhop Carter hooks up with Marjoe and his gang for a robbing and killing spree. Noteworthy for a couple of glimpses of Lynda's left breast and the occasional film-buff in-joke (e.g., a tobacco-chewing deputy named Abel Gance), courtesy scripter Vernon Zimmerman.▼

Bobbikins (1960-British) **89m.** ** D: Robert Day. Max Bygraves, Shirley Jones, Steven Stocker, Billie Whitelaw. Gimmicky comedy with British singer Bygraves and

Jones the parents of an infant who talks like an adult. Not bad . . . but that awful title!

Bobby Deerfield (1977) **C-124m.** BOMB. D: Sydney Pollack. Al Pacino, Marthe Keller, Anny Duperey, Walter McGinn, Romolo Valli, Stephen Meldegg. Grand Prix race-car driver Pacino romances Florentine aristocrat Keller, who is dying of that unnamed disease that seems disproportionately to afflict movie heroines. Her suffering is nothing compared to the audience's; even Pacino is deadening. Recut to 99m. by Pollack for pay-TV release.▼

Bobby Ware Is Missing (1955) 67m. *½ D: Thomas Carr. Neville Brand, Arthur Franz, Jean Willes, Walter Reed. Tedious boy-hunt as his parents and sheriff track down kidnappers.

Bob Le Flambeur (1955-French) 102m. *** D: Jean-Pierre Melville. Roger Duchesne, Isabel Corey, Daniel Cauchy, Guy Decomble, Andre Garet, Gerard Buhr, Howard Vernon. Witty inversion of THE ASPHALT JUNGLE: hard-luck gambler Duchesne enlists pals in intricate plan to knock over Deauville casino, but everything is so stacked against them that we almost hope he'll call it off. Clever and atmospheric, blessed with eerily sexy Corey and a great closing line. Unreleased in the U.S. until 1982.▼

Bob Mathias Story, The (1954) 80m. *** D: Francis D. Lyon. Bob Mathias, Ward Bond, Melba Mathias, Paul Bryar, Ann Doran. Agreeable biography of star track athlete, his sports career, military duty, family life. Mathias turns in an engaging portrayal of himself.

Bobo, The (1967-British) **C-105m.** ** D: Robert Parrish. Peter Sellers, Britt Ekland, Rossano Brazzi, Adolfo Celi, Ferdy Mayne, Hattie Jacques. Misfire comedy casts Sellers as aspiring singing matador who's promised a booking if he can seduce Ekland, the most desirable woman in Barcelona, within three days. Filmed in Spain and Rome.▼

Boccaccio '70 (1962-Italian) **C-165m.** *** D: Vittorio De Sica, Luchino Visconti, Federico Fellini. Anita Ekberg, Sophia Loren, Romy Schneider, Peppino De Filippo, Dante Maggio, Tomas Milian. Trio of episodes: ''The Raffle''—timid soul wins a liaison with a girl as prize; ''The Job'' —aristocrat's wife takes a job as her husband's mistress; ''The Temptation of Dr. Antonio''—fantasy of puritanical fanatic and a voluptuous poster picture which comes alive. A fourth episode, directed by Mario Monicelli, was dropped for U.S. release.

Body and Soul (1947) 104m. **** D: Robert Rossen. John Garfield, Lilli Palmer, Hazel Brooks, Anne Revere, William Conrad, Joseph Pevney, Canada Lee. Most boxing films pale next to this classic (written by Abraham Polonsky) of Garfield working his way up by devious means, becom-

ing famous champ. Superb photography by James Wong Howe, and Oscar-winning editing by Francis Lyon and Robert Parrish. Remade in 1981.▼

Body and Soul (1981) **C-100m.** *½ D: George Bowers. Leon Isaac Kennedy, Jayne Kennedy, Peter Lawford, Michael V. Gazzo, Perry Lang, Kim Hamilton. Poor remake of the 1947 classic, with welterweight boxer Kennedy shunning corruption and becoming champion. Leon tries, but is defeated by his paper-thin screenplay. Muhammad Ali appears briefly as himself.▼

Body Chemistry (1990) **C-87m.** ** D: Kristine Peterson. Marc Singer, Lisa Pescia, Mary Crosby, David Kagen, H. Bradley Barneson, Doreen Alderman, Lauren Tuerk, Joseph Campanella. FATAL ATTRACTION clone about a married sexual-behavior researcher who strikes up a kinky, heated relationship with his lab partner after she comes on to him. When things get out of hand . . . well, if you saw the original, you know what happens. As a low-budget Roger Corman-factory ripoff, this isn't bad, but you've seen it all before. Pescia, in her film debut, is someone to watch out for.▼

Body Disappears, The (1941) 72m. ** D: Ross Lederman. Jeffrey Lynn, Jane Wyman, Edward Everett Horton, Marguerite Chapman. Not a very inspired mixture of comedy, suspense, and sci-fi, as Lynn is involved in invisible-making formula causing havoc with the police.

Body Double (1984) **C-109m.** *½ D: Brian DePalma. Craig Wasson, Gregg Henry, Melanie Griffith, Deborah Shelton, Guy Boyd, Dennis Franz. Gullible (and brainless) actor Wasson becomes obsessed with beautiful woman he's been eyeing through telescope and soon finds himself embroiled in labyrinthine murder plot. Another sleazy fetish film from DePalma, who not only rips off Hitchcock (again) but even himself (OBSESSION, DRESSED TO KILL, BLOW OUT). Some clever moments amid the sleaze, and a good performance by Griffith as porno actress.▼

Bodyguard (1948) 62m. ** D: Richard Fleischer. Lawrence Tierney, Priscilla Lane, Philip Reed, June Clayworth. Routine story of man accused of murder trying to clear himself. Based on a story cowritten by Robert Altman.

Body Heat (1981) **C-113m.** *** D: Lawrence Kasdan. William Hurt, Kathleen Turner, Richard Crenna, Ted Danson, J. A. Preston, Mickey Rourke. Hurt is a Florida lawyer whose brains work at half speed; Turner is a married socialite who turns on the heat and inspires him to bump off her husband. Over-derivative of 1940s melodramas at first, then goes off on its own path and scores. Turner's first film; Kasdan's directorial debut.▼

Bodyhold (1949) 63m. *½ D: Seymour

Friedman. Willard Parker, Lola Albright, Hillary Brooke, Allen Jenkins, Gordon Jones. Programmer of wrestler and girlfriend seeking to clean up corruption in the fight game.

Body of Evidence (1988) C-100m. TVM D: Roy Campanella II. Margot Kidder, Barry Bostwick, Tony Lo Bianco, Caroline Kava, Jennifer Barbour, David Hayward. Good suspense thriller about a wife who comes to suspect her pathologist husband might be the serial killer he is investigating. Crackerjack tale written by Cynthia Whitcomb and legendary baseball star Roy Campanella's director son. Above average.▼

Body Rock (1984) C-93m. *½ D: Marcelo Epstein. Lorenzo Lamas, Vicki Frederick, Cameron Dye, Ray Sharkey, Michelle Nicastro. Formula break-dancing movie (shot by the great Robby Muller!) casts beefy Lamas as hero/heel who suddenly dumps his best friend, his bf's quietly voluptuous sis, and other pals when he's hired to emcee a chic uptown club. Watching L.L. clomp to the beat is like watching Victor Mature do the boogaloo.▼

Body Slam (1987) C-89m. **½ D: Hal Needham. Dirk Benedict, Tanya Roberts, Roddy Piper, Capt. Lou Albano, Barry Gordon, Charles Nelson Reilly, Billy Barty, John Astin. Barely-released comedy, based on the successful rock 'n' roll/wrestling connection of the early 1980s, deserved better. Benedict is charming as an unscrupulous music promoter who latches onto wrestling as his meal ticket; "Rowdy" Roddy makes an engaging screen debut. Watch for cameos by many grapplers, including the Wild Samoans, Ric Flair and Bruno Sammartino.▼

Body Snatcher, The (1945) 77m. ***½ D: Robert Wise. Henry Daniell, Boris Karloff, Bela Lugosi, Edith Atwater, Russell Wade, Rita Corday. Fine, atmospheric tale from Robert Louis Stevenson story of doctor (Daniell) who is forced to deal with scurrilous character (Karloff) in order to get bodies for experiments. One of the classic Val Lewton thrillers.▼

Body Stealers SEE: Thin Air▼

Boeing Boeing (1965) C-102m. *** D: John Rich. Jerry Lewis, Tony Curtis, Dany Saval, Christiane Schmidtmer, Suzanna Leigh, Thelma Ritter. A surprisingly subdued Lewis is paired with Curtis in story of American newspaperman who runs swinging pad in Paris, constantly stocked with stewardesses, to the chagrin of housekeeper Ritter. Amusing.

Bofors Gun, The (1968) C-106m. *** D: Jack Gold. Nicol Williamson, Ian Holm, David Warner, Richard O'Callaghan, Barry Jackson, Donald Gee. British soldier, on the eve of his return home in 1950s, comes tragically face-to-face with a rebellious Irish gunner. Engrossing drama, well acted.

Boggy Creek II SEE: **Barbaric Beast of Boggy Creek, The, Part II**

Bogie (1980) C-100m. TVM D: Vincent Sherman. Kevin O'Connor, Kathryn Harrold, Ann Wedgeworth, Patricia Barry, Alfred Ryder, Donald May, Richard Dysart, Arthur Franz, Drew Barrymore. Unappealing biopic of Humphrey Bogart, boringly acted by players hired for their resemblance to Bogart, Bacall, and Mayo Methot; limply directed by Sherman, who years earlier directed several Bogart movies. Script by Daniel Taradash. Below average.▼

Bohemian Girl, The (1936) 70m. *** D: James Horne, Charles R. Rogers. Stan Laurel, Oliver Hardy, Thelma Todd, Antonio Moreno, Darla Hood, Jacqueline Wells (Julie Bishop), Mae Busch. Nifty comic opera with Stan and Ollie part of gypsy caravan. They adopt abandoned girl who turns out to be princess.▼

Bold and the Brave, The (1956) 87m. *** D: Lewis R. Foster. Wendell Corey, Mickey Rooney, Don Taylor, Nicole Maurey. Routine WW2 study of soldiers fighting in Italy, greatly uplifted by un-stereotyped performances; Rooney is outstanding.

Bolero (1934) 83m. **½ D: Wesley Ruggles. George Raft, Carole Lombard, Sally Rand, Gertrude Michael, William Frawley, Ray Milland. Silly, protracted story of cocky dancer's rise to fame is made fun by good stars and production values; dance sequences are first-rate, although much of Raft and Lombard's footwork is "doubled" by professionals. Rand, in a rare film appearance, performs her famous fan dance. Raft and Lombard reteamed for RUMBA.

Bolero (1981-French) C-173m. *½ D: Claude Lelouch. James Caan, Geraldine Chaplin, Robert Hossein, Nicole Garcia, Daniel Olbrychski, Evelyne Bouix. Boring tale of various characters of different nationalities and their love of music, set during a 50-year time span. The actors play more than one character, and the result is confusion.▼

Bolero (1984) C-104m. BOMB D: John Derek. Bo Derek, George Kennedy, Andrea Occipinti, Ana Obregon, Olivia d'Abo. Colossally boring sexual drama, for Bo-peepers only . . . though even voyeurs will be yawning during long stretches between nude scenes. Bo also produced the picture.▼

Bomba the Jungle Boy In 1949 producer Walter Mirisch, who has gone on to far greater things, decided to produce a series of low-budget adventure films based on a series of popular juvenile books about a boy who has grown up in the jungle. For this road-company Tarzan series he got Johnny Sheffield, who had played Boy in the Tarzan films, and director Ford Beebe, an expert at making something out of nothing. With a small studio backlot and plenty of footage of wild animals, BOMBA THE JUNGLE BOY emerged, a not-bad little adventure. The subsequent eleven films in the series, however, worked their way into a standard formula that by the last episodes was all too familiar. Bomba was made for younger audiences, and the films will probably still please the kids. As for adults, well, there have been worse films than the Bomba series.

Bomba and the Elephant Stampede SEE: **Elephant Stampede**

Bomba and the Hidden City SEE: **Hidden City, The**

Bomba and the Jungle Girl (1952) 70m. D: Ford Beebe. Johnny Sheffield, Karen Sharpe, Walter Sande, Martin Wilkins.

Bomba on Panther Island (1949) 76m. D: Ford Beebe. Johnny Sheffield, Allene Roberts, Lita Baron, Smoki Whitfield.

Bombardier (1943) 99m. *** D: Richard Wallace. Pat O'Brien, Randolph Scott, Anne Shirley, Eddie Albert, Walter Reed, Robert Ryan, Barton MacLane. Familiar framework of fliers being trained during WW2 comes off well with fast-moving script.▼

Bomba, The Jungle Boy (1949) 70m. D: Ford Beebe. Johnny Sheffield, Peggy Ann Garner, Smoki Whitfield, Onslow Stevens.

Bomb at 10:10 (1966-Yugoslavian) **C-86m.** ** D: Charles Damic. George Montgomery, Rada Popovic, Peter Banicevic, Branko Plesa. Thrown-together mishmash with Montgomery escaping from Nazi P.O.W. camp, plotting to help partisans and destroy prison leaders.▼

Bombers B-52 (1957) **C-106m.** **½ D: Gordon Douglas. Natalie Wood, Karl Malden, Marsha Hunt, Efrem Zimbalist, Jr., Dean Jagger. Ordinary love story between army pilot Zimbalist and Wood, with latter's sergeant father objecting, intertwined with good aerial footage of jet plane maneuvers.

Bomb in the High Street (1964-British) **60m.** **½ D: Terence Bishop. Ronald Howard, Terry Palmer, Suzanna Leigh. Unpretentious robbery caper involving phony bomb scare to divert authorities from site of crime.

Bombshell (1933) 95m. ***½ D: Victor Fleming. Jean Harlow, Lee Tracy, Frank Morgan, Franchot Tone, Una Merkel, Pat O'Brien, C. Aubrey Smith. Devastating satire of 1930s Hollywood, with Harlow a much-used star, Tracy an incredibly unscrupulous publicity director making her life hell. No holds barred. Retitled BLONDE BOMBSHELL.

Bombs Over Burma (1942) 62m. ** D: Joseph H. Lewis. Anna May Wong, Noel Madison, Dan Seymour, Richard Loo, Nedrick Young, Dennis Moore. Grade-B wartime saga of devoted Wong risking life for sake of China on espionage mission.

Bonanza: The Next Generation (1988) **C-100m.** TVM D: William F. Claxton. John Ireland, Robert Fuller, Barbara Anderson, Michael Landon, Jr., Brian A. Smith, John Amos, Peter Mark Richman, Gillian Greene. Reunion movie of sorts (none of the original stars are here) of the venerable 1959–1973 series. Ireland (his first starring role in a dog's age) is the late Ben Cartwright's seafaring brother who has taken over the Ponderosa and foolishly turned drilling rights over to land-grabbers, bringing Cartwright nephews to the rescue. Pilot to proposed series has Michael Landon's real-life son as the son of Little Joe, and Lorne Greene's daughter, Gillian, "introduced" as a love interest. Produced and written by David Dortort, creator of the original series, and directed by veteran William F. Claxton, also from *Bonanza*'s heyday. Average.

Bonjour Tristesse (1958) **C-94m.** *** D: Otto Preminger. Deborah Kerr, David Niven, Jean Seberg, Geoffrey Horne, Mylene Demongeot. Teen-ager does her best to break up romance between playboy widowed father and his mistress, with tragic results. Francoise Sagan's philosophy seeps through glossy production; Kerr exceptionally fine in soaper set on French Riviera.▼

Bonnie and Clyde (1967) **C-111m.** **** D: Arthur Penn. Warren Beatty, Faye Dunaway, Michael J. Pollard, Gene Hackman, Estelle Parsons, Denver Pyle, Gene Wilder, Dub Taylor. Trend-setting film about unlikely heroes of 1930s bank-robbing team has spawned many imitators but still leads the pack. Plunging from comedy to melodrama and social commentary, it remains vivid, stylish throughout. Screenplay by David Newman and Robert Benton. Parsons and cinematographer Burnett Guffey were Oscar winners. Wilder's first film.▼

Bonnie Parker Story, The (1958) **81m.** **½ D: William Witney. Dorothy Provine, Jack Hogan, Richard Bakalyan, Joseph Turkel. With the success of BONNIE AND CLYDE, this film takes on added luster, recounting the lurid criminal life of the female crook (Provine); low-budget production.

Bonnie Prince Charlie (1948-British) **C-118m.** ** D: Anthony Kimmins. David Niven, Margaret Leighton, Jack Hawkins, Judy Campbell, Morland Graham, Finlay Currie. Niven is Prince Charles of 16th-century Scotland in this draggy, overlong historical drama. The battle scenes are well-staged and the photography of Robert Krasker is excellent, but when the film was first released in England, it was considered a total disaster. Originally released at 140m., then cut to 118m. U.S. TV prints run 100m. and are in black and white.

Bonnie Scotland (1935) **80m.** **½ D: James Horne. Stan Laurel, Oliver Hardy, June Lang, William Janney, Anne Grey, Vernon Steele, James Finlayson. Plot sometimes gets in the way of L&H, but their material is well up to par; Stan and Ollie inadvertently join a Scottish military regiment stationed in the desert.▼

Bon Voyage! (1962) **C-130m.** *½ D: James Neilson. Fred MacMurray, Jane Wyman, Michael Callan, Deborah Walley, Tommy Kirk, Kevin Corcoran. Slow, drawn-out Disney comedy about "typical" American family's misadventures on trip to Europe. Aimed more at adults than kids, but too draggy and simple-minded for anyone.▼

Bon Voyage Charlie Brown (and Don't Come Back!) (1980) **C-75m.** *** D. Bill Melendez. Voices of Daniel Anderson, Casey Carlson, Patricia Patts, Arrin Skelley. Charlie Brown and company travel to France as exchange students. Cute animated entertainment for Peanuts devotees.▼

Bonzo Goes to College (1952) **80m.** ** D: Frederick de Cordova. Maureen O'Sullivan, Charles Drake, Edmund Gwenn, Gigi Perreau, Gene Lockhart, Irene Ryan, David Janssen. Follow-up to BEDTIME FOR BONZO has brainy chimp lead college football team to victory; good cast takes back seat to monkey-shines.

Boogens, The (1981) **C-95m.** BOMB D: James L. Conway. Rebecca Balding, Fred McCarren, Anne-Marie Martin, Jeff Harlan, John Crawford, Med Flory. The Boogens are scaly monsters who do away with character after character when a Colorado silver mine is reopened. As unappealing as its title.

Boogeyman, The (1980) **C-86m.** *** D: Ulli Lommel. Suzanna Love, Ron James, Michael Love, John Carradine, Raymond Boyden. Shards of mirror that "witnessed" horrible murder cause gruesome deaths. German art film actor-director Lommel lends unconventional angle to this combination of THE EXORCIST and HALLOWEEN. Effects are quite colorful, if somewhat hokey. Followed by BOOGEYMAN II.▼

Boogeyman II (1983) **C-79m.** BOMB D: Bruce Starr. Suzanna Love, Shana Hall, Ulli Lommel. Survivor of BOOGEYMAN goes to Hollywood to live with producer who is going to turn her life story into a movie. Moronic slasher film depends mostly on footage from BOOGEYMAN, amply used in flashbacks. Almost laughable.▼

Boogie Man Will Get You, The (1942) **66m.** **½ D: Lew Landers. Boris Karloff, Peter Lorre, Jeff Donnell, Larry Parks, Slapsy Maxie Rosenbloom, Maude Eburne, Don Beddoe, Frank Puglia. Good cast in lightweight cash-in on ARSENIC AND OLD LACE. Karloff is dotty scientist attempting to make supermen out of traveling salesmen while Donnell tries to turn his home into Colonial tourist trap; Lorre is screwy doctor/sheriff/notary/loan shark. No great shakes, but pleasant.

Book of Numbers (1973) **C-80m.** **½ D: Raymond St. Jacques. Raymond St. Jacques, Phillip Thomas, Freda Payne, Hope Clarke, D'Urville Martin, Gilbert Green. Uneven but sometimes enjoyable story of a black numbers-racket operation in a rural town during the Depression.

Boom! (1968-U.S.-British) **C-113m.** ** D: Joseph Losey. Elizabeth Taylor, Richard Burton, Noel Coward, Joanna Shimkus, Michael Dunn. Thud: Only film buffs who admire Losey's very original directorial style are likely to appreciate fuzzy adaptation of Tennessee Williams' *The Milk Train Doesn't Stop Here Anymore*. Fine location photography in Sardinia and Rome; good performance by Shimkus can't save this.

Boomerang (1947) **88m.** **** D: Elia Kazan. Dana Andrews, Jane Wyatt, Lee J. Cobb, Arthur Kennedy, Sam Levene, Robert Keith, Taylor Holmes, Ed Begley, Karl Malden, Cara Williams, Barry Kelley. Priest's murder brings rapid arrest of an innocent man; prosecuting attorney determines to hunt out real facts. Brilliant drama in all respects. Richard Murphy's taut screenplay, from Anthony Abbott's article "The Perfect Case," is based on a factual incident.

Boom in the Moon (1946-Mexican) **C-83m.** BOMB D: Jaime Salvador. Buster Keaton, Angel Grassa, Virginia Serret, Fernando Sotto, Luis Barreiro. Rock-bottom "comedy" vehicle for poor Buster as an innocent thought to be a modern-day Bluebeard, who then gets shanghaied to fly a rocketship to the moon. Filmed as A MODERN BLUEBEARD, and barely seen until its video release in the 1980s. ▼

Boom Town (1940) **116m.** *** D: Jack Conway. Clark Gable, Spencer Tracy, Claudette Colbert, Hedy Lamarr, Frank Morgan, Lionel Atwill, Chill Wills. No surprises in tale of get-rich-quick drilling for oil, but star-studded cast gives it life. Also shown in computer-colored version.▼

Boost, The (1988) **C-95m.** *½ D: Harold Becker. James Woods, Sean Young, John Kapelos, Steven Hill, Kelle Kerr, John Rothman, Amanda Blake, Grace Zabriskie. An anti-drug movie that's on the screen nearly an hour before you even realize it *is* an anti-drug movie. Woods is the hotshot salesman who goes to hell (and bankruptcy) via cocaine, with Young the sometime user who tries to stand by him. As with Jack Nicholson in THE SHINING, it's difficult to distinguish the "before" Woods from the "after" in this misfire.▼

Boot Hill (1969-Italian) **C-87m.** ** D: Giuseppe Colizzi. Terence Hill, Bud Spencer, Woody Strode, Victor Buono, Lionel Stander, Eduardo Ciannelli. Western ravioli representing another of the traditional teamings of blue-eyed, rock-jawed Hill and his bear of a sidekick Spencer. Uneven pasta of violence and comedy.▼

Bootleggers (1974) **C-101m.** ** D: Charles B. Pierce. Paul Koslo, Dennis Fimple, Slim Pickens, Jaclyn Smith, Chuck Pierce, Jr. Typical yahoo action comedy set in 1930s Arkansas with Koslo and Fimple trying to outsmart and outdo rival moonshining family while running their supplies to Memphis. Retitled BOOTLEGGERS' ANGEL to capitalize on Smith's later stardom.

Boots Malone (1952) **103m.** *** D: William Dieterle. William Holden, Johnny Stewart, Ed Begley, Harry Morgan, Whit Bissell. Holden comes alive in role of shady character who reforms when he trains Stewart to become a jockey.

Bop Girl (1957) **79m.** *½ D: Howard W. Koch. Judy Tyler, Bobby Troup, Margo Woode, Lucien Littlefield, Mary Kaye Trio, Nino Tempo. Psychologist Troup predicts that rock 'n' roll will lose its popularity to calypso. He was wrong. Also known as BOP GIRL GOES CALYPSO.

Bop Girl Goes Calypso SEE: **Bop Girl**

Border, The (1982) **C-107m.** **½ D: Tony Richardson. Jack Nicholson, Harvey Keitel, Valerie Perrine, Warren Oates, Elpidia Carrillo. Border patrolman Nicholson, spurred on by money-hungry spouse Perrine, begins taking payoffs from illegal Mexican aliens he's supposed to be arresting, eventually becomes emotionally involved with young mother Carrillo. Cast and storyline beg for Sam Peckinpah in his prime; film maintains mild interest, but never really takes off.▼

Border Incident (1949) **92m.** *** D: Anthony Mann. Ricardo Montalban, George Murphy, Howard da Silva, Teresa Celli, Charles McGraw. Tension-packed story of U.S. agents cracking down on wetback smuggling on Texas-Mexico border. Well directed, and uncompromisingly violent.

Borderline (1950) **88m.** **½ D: William Seiter. Fred MacMurray, Claire Trevor, Raymond Burr, Roy Roberts. Trevor and MacMurray work well together as law enforcers each tracking down dope smugglers on Mexican border, neither knowing the other isn't a crook.

Borderline (1980) **C-105m.** ** D: Jerrold Freedman. Charles Bronson, Bruno Kirby, Bert Remsen, Michael Lerner, Kenneth McMillan, Ed Harris, Wilford Brimley. Bronson, minus Jill Ireland, is a Border Patrol officer searching for a killer. Undis-

tinguished formula vehicle for Old Stone Face.▼

Border River (1954) **C-80m.** ** D: George Sherman. Joel McCrea, Yvonne De Carlo, Pedro Armendariz, Howard Petrie. Mildly intriguing Western about Rebel officer McCrea's mission to buy much-needed weapons from Mexicans to continue fight against Yankees.

Bordertown (1935) **90m.** *** D: Archie Mayo. Paul Muni, Bette Davis, Eugene Pallette, Margaret Lindsay. Fine drama of unusual triangle in bordertown cafe, with Davis as flirtatious wife of Pallette with designs on lawyer Muni; her overwrought scene on the witness stand is not easily forgotten. Used as basis for later THEY DRIVE BY NIGHT, but more serious in tone.

Borgia Stick, The (1967) **C-100m. TVM** D: David Lowell Rich. Don Murray, Fritz Weaver, Inger Stevens, Barry Nelson. Fairly grim suspense thriller by A. J. Russell exposing organized crime involvement in U.S. economy. Fine cast, particularly Weaver, works very well. Above average.

B.O.R.N. (1989) **C-92m.** ** D: Ross Hagen. Ross Hagen, Hoke Howell, P. J. Soles, William Smith, Russ Tamblyn, Amanda Blake, Rance Howard, Clint Howard, Claire Hagen, Kristine Gillespie, Dawn Wildsmith. Someone is kidnapping young people from the streets of L.A. to cut up as involuntary organ donors, but they didn't reckon with hero Hagen and his ex-cop pal Howell. Wild-eyed, bizarre action thriller has too many characters and too much gunfire but has its moments too. Title refers to "Body Organ Replacement Network."▼

Born Again (1978) **C-110m.** *½ D: Irving Rapper. Dean Jones, Anne Francis, Jay Robinson, Dana Andrews, Raymond St. Jacques, George Brent. If one is inspired by the religious rebirth of Pres. Nixon's Special Counsel (Charles Colson) after his Washington skullduggery, one might be absorbed by this one-dimensional film account. Others beware!▼

Born American (1986-U.S.-Finnish) **C-95m.** ** D: Renny Harlin. Mike Norris, Steve Durham, David Coburn, Thalmus Rasulala, Albert Salmi. The Cold War lives on as three young Americans vacationing in Finland accidentally cross the border into Russia, where they fight it out with the local troops. OK action scenes and personable young cast sugarcoat the heavy-handed political overtones. (In fact, this inconsequential film made headlines at the time of its release because it was banned in Finland!)▼

Born Beautiful (1982) **C-100m. TVM** D: Harvey Hart. Erin Gray, Ed Marinaro, Polly Bergen, Lori Singer, Ellen Barber, Judith Barcroft, Michael Higgins. Fair chronicle of young models trying to make big bucks in the Big Apple's fashion game. Average.▼

Born Free (1966-British) **C-96m.** ***½ D: James Hill. Virginia McKenna, Bill Travers, Geoffrey Keen, Peter Lukoye. Exceptional adaptation of the late Joy Adamson's book about Elsa the lioness, who was raised as a pet by two Kenya game wardens. Sincere, engrossing film, a must for family viewing. Oscars for Best Original Score (John Barry) and Title Song (Barry and Don Black). Followed by a sequel (LIVING FREE) and a brief TV series.▼

Born in East L.A. (1987) **C-87m.** *½ D: Cheech Marin. Cheech Marin, Daniel Stern, Paul Rodriguez, Jan-Michael Vincent, Kamala Lopez, Alma Martinez, Tony Plana. Third-generation American Hispanic gets caught in an immigration raid minus I.D. and is deported to Tijuana; it takes a tiresome hour and a half of screen time to get back. Nothing offensive about this but also nothing special; Rodriguez's dim-witted comedy relief is a particular drag. Based on Marin's popular Bruce Springsteen parody record. Expanded to 93m. for TV.▼

Born Innocent (1974) **C-100m. TVM** D: Donald Wrye. Linda Blair, Joanna Miles, Kim Hunter, Richard Jaeckel, Mary Murphy, Allyn Ann McLerie, Mitch Vogel. Graphic story of teenage girl's struggle to adjust to rigors of tough juvenile detention home. Uncompromising film, distinguished in its original showing by a realistic rape of Blair by her fellow inmates (now cut from film). Otherwise, played for the sensational. Average.▼

Born Losers (1967) **C-112m.** **½ D: T. C. Frank (Tom Laughlin). Tom Laughlin, Elizabeth James, Jeremy Slate, William Wellman, Jr., Robert Tessier. What seemed at the time just another biker film gained new interest in the 70s as the introduction of Billy Jack; he helps free young dropout James from the clutches of Slate's gang. Good action scenes, but Laughlin's use of violence as *an indictment of* violence is already present. Jane Russell makes a guest appearance as James' mother. Followed by BILLY JACK.▼

Born on the Fourth of July (1989) **C-144m.** ***½ D: Oliver Stone. Tom Cruise, Willem Dafoe, Raymond J. Barry, Caroline Kava, Kyra Sedgwick, Bryan Larkin, Jerry Levine, Josh Evans, Frank Whaley, Stephen Baldwin, John Getz, Tom Berenger, Abbie Hoffman. Relentlessly realistic and powerful saga of real-life Vietnam vet Ron Kovic, who joined the Marines as a gung-ho recruit in the 1960s and came home paralyzed from the chest down—only to endure an even greater ordeal of physical and mental rehabilitation before emerging as an antiwar activist. Stone cowrote the screenplay with Kovic, and spares us nothing in recreating some of America's most painful years, and Kovic's personal odyssey through them. This is his finest film to date. Cruise delivers a top-notch performance, and the drama is enhanced by a great John Williams score. Kovic can be seen in opening parade scene; Stone plays a TV reporter. Oscar winner for Best Director and Film Editing.▼

Born Reckless (1959) **79m.** *½ D: Howard W. Koch. Mamie Van Doren, Jeff Richards, Arthur Hunnicutt, Carol Ohmart, Tom Duggan. Rodeo star Richards divides his time between busting broncos and busting heads of lecherous old cowpokes trying to paw Mamie. Not bad enough to be really funny, but it has its moments; Mamie sings five of film's eight songs, including unforgettable "I'm Just a Nice, Sweet, Home-Type of Girl."

Born To Be Bad (1950) **94m.** **½ D: Nicholas Ray. Joan Fontaine, Robert Ryan, Joan Leslie, Mel Ferrer, Zachary Scott. Fontaine is a ruthless woman who gets her way by manipulating everyone around her. Good cast in somewhat overwrought drama.

Born To Be Loved (1959) **82m.** ** D: Hugo Haas. Carol Morris, Vera Vague (Barbara Jo Allen), Hugo Haas, Dick Kallman, Jacqueline Fontaine. Low-key yarn of poor-but-honest Morris and rich widow Vague seeking romance, helped by elderly music instructor Haas.

Born To Be Sold (1981) **C-100m. TVM** D: Burt Brinckerhoff. Lynda Carter, Harold Gould, Dean Stockwell, Ed Nelson, Lloyd Haynes, Donna Wilkes, Philip Sterling, Sharon Farrell. Social worker goes after an illegal baby-selling operation in this exploitive movie "suggested by" Lynn McTaggart's book *The Baby Brokers.* Average.

Born To Dance (1936) **105m.** *** D: Roy Del Ruth. Eleanor Powell, James Stewart, Virginia Bruce, Una Merkel, Sid Silvers, Frances Langford, Raymond Walburn, Buddy Ebsen. Powell bears out title in good Cole Porter musical with sensational footwork and fine songs: "Easy To Love," "I've Got You Under My Skin."▼

Born To Kill (1947) **92m.** *** D: Robert Wise. Claire Trevor, Lawrence Tierney, Walter Slezak, Audrey Long, Elisha Cook, Jr., Philip Terry. Murderer Tierney marries insecure Long, but can't stay away from her divorced sister Trevor. Supertough *film noir* is uncharacteristically meanspirited for director Wise, but is well put together nonetheless. A cult item.

Born to Kill (1974) SEE: **Cockfighter**▼

Born to Race (1988) **C-98m.** BOMB D: James Fargo. Joseph Bottoms, Marc Singer, George Kennedy, Marla Heasley, Antonio Sabato, Robert F. Logan, Dirk Blocker,

Michael McGrady. Silly tripe set against backdrop of North Carolina stock car races, where Heasley has brought her revolutionary prototype engine, and the "bad guys" set out to steal her blueprints. ▼

Born To Rock: The T.A.M.I. Show SEE: **That Was Rock▼**

Born to Win (1971) **C-90m.** **½ D: Ivan Passer. George Segal, Karen Black, Paula Prentiss, Jay Fletcher, Hector Elizondo, Robert De Niro. Unjustly neglected, but not altogether successful comedy-drama about ex-hairdresser in N.Y.C. and his $100-a-day heroin habit. Very well acted, particularly by Segal. Retitled ADDICT for video.▼

Born Yesterday (1950) **103m.** ***½ D: George Cukor. Judy Holliday, William Holden, Broderick Crawford, Howard St. John. Junk-dealer-made-good Crawford wants girlfriend (Holliday) culturefied, hires Holden to teach her in hilarious Garson Kanin comedy set in Washington, D.C. Priceless Judy repeated Broadway triumph and won Oscar for playing quintessential dumb blonde.▼

Borrowers, The (1973) **C-78m. TVM** D: Walter C. Miller. Eddie Albert, Judith Anderson, Tammy Grimes, Barnard Hughes, Beatrice Straight, Karen Pearson, Dennis Larson. Delightful adaptation by Jay Presson Allen of Mary Norton's fantasy about a family of little people only inches tall and the 8-year-old boy who disturbs their peaceful existence beneath the floorboards of the Victorian house into which his parents have brought him. This tape-to-film heartwarmer has a lovely Rod McKuen score augmenting charming performances by all. Above average.

Borsalino (1970-French) **C-125m.** *** D: Jacques Deray. Jean-Paul Belmondo, Alain Delon, Michel Bouquet, Catherine Rouvel, Francoise Christophe. PUBLIC ENEMY, French-style; delightful seriocomic film of two likable hoods who become gangland chieftains in 1930s Marseilles. Stars in top form; Claude Bolling's infectious music helps. Sequel: BORSALINO & CO.

Boss, The (1956) **89m.** *** D: Byron Haskin. John Payne, William Bishop, Gloria McGhee, Doe Avedon, Joe Flynn. Effective study of WW1 veteran returning to St. Louis and combatting corruption and crime; one of Payne's best performances as the city's underworld boss.

Boss's Son, The (1978) **C-97m.** *** D: Bobby Roth. Asher Brauner, Rudy Solari, Rita Moreno, Henry G. Sanders, James Darren, Richie Havens, Piper Laurie, Elena Verdugo. Good little independent feature by writer-director Roth about a young man who is reluctantly going into his father's business, a carpet factory. Credible and engaging.▼

Boss' Wife, The (1986) **C-83m.** *½ D:

Ziggy Steinberg. Daniel Stern, Arielle Dombasle, Fisher Stevens, Melanie Mayron, Lou Jacobi, Martin Mull, Christopher Plummer, Thalmus Rasulala, Robert Costanzo. Interesting cast falters in this tepid will-he-or-won't-he comedy about an ambitious young stockbroker (Stern) and the title lady (Dombasle), who's out to seduce him.▼

Boston Blackie Over a span of nine years, Chester Morris starred in fourteen films as Boston Blackie, a former thief now on the right side of the law but preferring to work for himself than for the police. He brought to the role a delightful offhand manner and sense of humor that kept the films fresh even when the scripts weren't. From MEET BOSTON BLACKIE (1941) to BOSTON BLACKIE'S CHINESE VENTURE (1949), Morris was Blackie. Regulars included Richard Lane as a frustrated police detective convinced that Blackie was up to no good, but always one step behind him; George E. Stone as Blackie's talkative dim-witted buddy; and Lloyd Corrigan as a dizzy millionaire pal who'd do anything for a lark. Top-flight directors Robert Florey and Edward Dmytryk got the series started, and when the films fell into less capable hands, Morris and company came to the rescue with consistently ingratiating performances. While no classics, the Boston Blackie films offer a great deal of fun.

Boston Blackie and the Law (1946) **69m.** D: D. Ross Lederman. Chester Morris, Trudy Marshall, Constance Dowling, Richard Lane.

Boston Blackie Booked on Suspicion (1945) **66m.** D: Arthur Dreifuss. Chester Morris, Lynn Merrick, Richard Lane, Frank Sully, Steve Cochran.

Boston Blackie Goes Hollywood (1942) **68m.** D: Michael Gordon. Chester Morris, George E. Stone, Richard Lane, Forrest Tucker, Constance Worth, Lloyd Corrigan, William Wright.

Boston Blackie's Chinese Venture (1949) **59m.** D: Seymour Friedman. Chester Morris, Joan Woodbury, Philip Ahn, Benson Fong.

Boston Blackie's Rendezvous (1945) **64m.** D: Arthur Dreifuss. Chester Morris, Nina Foch, Steve Cochran, Richard Lane, George E. Stone, Frank Sully.

Bostonians, The (1984) **C-120m.** ** D: James Ivory. Christopher Reeve, Vanessa Redgrave, Madeleine Potter, Jessica Tandy, Nancy Marchand, Wesley Addy, Linda Hunt, Wallace Shawn. Redgrave is perfectly cast as Henry James's 19th-century feminist heroine in this careful adaptation of his novel by Ruth Prawer Jhabvala . . . but the film itself, for all its period detail, is deadly slow and uninvolving. Reeve is in over his head as Redgrave's contrary cousin. ▼

Boston Strangler, The (1968) **C-120m.**

[128]

*** D: Richard Fleischer. Tony Curtis, Henry Fonda, George Kennedy, Mike Kellin, Hurd Hatfield, Murray Hamilton, Jeff Corey, Sally Kellerman, William Marshall, George Voskovec, William Hickey, James Brolin. Absorbing drama, semi-documentary-style, detailing rise, manhunt, capture, prosecution of notorious criminal. Curtis gives startling performance as killer. Complex multi-image technique may be lost on TV screen.▼

Botany Bay (1953) **C-94m.** **½ D: John Farrow. Alan Ladd, James Mason, Patricia Medina, Cedric Hardwicke. Based on Charles Nordhoff novel set in 1790s, picturesque yarn tells of convict ship bound for Australia, focusing on conflict between prisoner Ladd and sadistic skipper Mason, with Medina as Ladd's love interest.▼

Both Sides of the Law (1954-British) **94m.** *** D: Muriel Box. Peggy Cummins, Terence Morgan, Anne Crawford, Rosamund John. Documentary-style account of London policewomen and their daily activity. Unpretentious production allows for good natural performances.

Bottom of the Bottle, The (1956) **C-88m.** **½ D: Henry Hathaway. Van Johnson, Joseph Cotten, Ruth Roman, Jack Carson. Overblown melodramatics set in U.S.–Mexican border town, involving a seemingly respectable attorney and his alcoholic younger brother, a fugitive from prison.

Boudu Saved From Drowning (1932-French) **87m.** *** D: Jean Renoir. Michel Simon, Charles Granval, Marcelle Hania, Severine Lerczynska. Title tramp is rescued from the Seine and taken home by well-meaning book dealer; he eventually takes over household, then seduces both the wife and maid. Classic attack on complacency still holds up, with ratty-bearded Simon giving the performance of a lifetime. U.S. remake: DOWN AND OUT IN BEVERLY HILLS.▼

Boulevard Nights (1979) **C-102m.** ** D: Michael Pressman. Richard Yniguez, Marta Du Bois, Danny De La Paz, Betty Carvalho, Carmen Zapata, James Victor, Victor Millan. Sincere but uninspiring story of Chicano youth who yearns to move away from street-gang life, but drawn back because of hot-blooded young brother. Filmed in the barrios of L.A.▼

Bound for Glory (1976) **C-147m.** ***½ D: Hal Ashby. David Carradine, Ronny Cox, Melinda Dillon, Gail Strickland, John Lehne, Ji-Tu Cumbuka, Randy Quaid, M. Emmet Walsh. Life of folk singer-composer Woody Guthrie, superbly played by Carradine, with great feeling for 1936–40 period as Guthrie travels the country fighting and singing for the underdogs, victims of the Great Depression. Haskell Wexler's Oscar-winning photography is tops throughout, as is Leonard Rosenman's score adaptation (also an Oscar-winner). Beware of shorter prints.▼

Bounty, The (1984) **C-130m.** *** D: Roger Donaldson. Mel Gibson, Anthony Hopkins, Laurence Olivier, Edward Fox, Daniel Day Lewis, Bernard Hill, Liam Neeson. Handsome, well made retelling of history's most famous mutiny (*not* based on the Nordhoff-Hall book) paints Bligh as repressed and stubborn, not mad, and Christian as a dilettante with no real substance. Interesting all the way, but emotionally aloof. Great use of widescreen will suffer badly on TV.▼

Bounty Hunter, The (1954) **C-79m.** **½ D: Andre de Toth. Randolph Scott, Dolores Dorn, Marie Windsor, Howard Petrie. Scott is on his horse again, this time tracking down three murderers.

Bounty Killer, The (1965) **C-92m.** **½ D: Spencer G. Bennet. Dan Duryea, Rod Cameron, Audrey Dalton, Richard Arlen, Buster Crabbe, Fuzzy Knight, Johnny Mack Brown, Bob Steele, Bronco Billy Anderson. Western's chief interest is cast of old-timers from Hollywood oaters of years gone by. Unlike their previous vehicles, this is an adult, low-key Western minus happy ending. Interesting on both counts.

Bounty Man, The (1972) **C-73m.** TVM D: John Llewellyn Moxey. Clint Walker, Richard Basehart, John Ericson, Margot Kidder, Arthur Hunnicutt, Gene Evans. Surprisingly somber Western with nihilistic point of view. Man-hunter Kincaid (Walker) chases young killer to isolated valley town, in turn chased by gang of cutthroats. Jim Byrnes' script provides good complications. Above average.▼

Bourne Identity, The (1988) **C-200m.** TVM D: Roger Young. Richard Chamberlain, Jaclyn Smith, Anthony Quayle, Donald Moffat, Yorgo Voyagis, Denholm Elliott. An amnesiac spy runs all over Europe with a woman he's kidnapped trying to prove to the assassins dogging his footsteps that he's not really the man he appears to be. Exciting although somewhat convoluted adaptation by Carol Sobieski of Robert Ludlum's best-seller, with Tony Pierce Roberts' evocative photography helping immensely. Originally shown in two parts. Above average.

Bowery, The (1933) **90m.** *** D: Raoul Walsh. Wallace Beery, George Raft, Jackie Cooper, Fay Wray, Pert Kelton, Herman Bing. Raft is Steve Brodie, Beery a notorious saloon owner, Cooper his young nemesis in rowdy story of N.Y.C.'s Bowery during the Gay 90s. Kelton is marvelous as Beery's saloon soubrette.

Bowery at Midnight (1942) **63m.** ** D: Wallace Fox. Bela Lugosi, John Archer, Wanda McKay, Tom Neal, Dave O'Brien. Lugosi is kindly psychiatrist who leads double life as criminal mastermind in the Bowery. Also involves reviving the dead. Mild but atmospheric.▼

Bowery Battalion (1951) 69m. D: William Beaudine. Leo Gorcey, Huntz Hall, Donald MacBride, Virginia Hewitt, Russell Hicks.

Bowery Blitzkrieg (1941) 62m. D: Wallace Fox, Leo Gorcey, Bobby Jordan, Huntz Hall, Warren Hull, Charlotte Henry, Keye Luke, Bobby Stone.▼

Bowery Bombshell (1946) 65m. D: Phil Karlson. Leo Gorcey, Huntz Hall, Bobby Jordan, Billy Benedict, Sheldon Leonard, Emmett Vogan.

Bowery Boys, The Sidney Kingsley's Broadway play *Dead End* was a superior drama that cast a critical eye on big-city tenement slums. When Samuel Goldwyn brought it to the screen, he retained the services of the young performers who'd played the street kids on stage: Billy Halop, Bobby Jordan, Gabriel Dell, Huntz Hall, Leo Gorcey, and Bernard Punsley. Though Kingsley never intended to glorify hoodlums, these young actors made a tremendous impact on audiences, much as gangster antiheroes had earlier in the decade . . . and before long, The "Dead End Kids" were stars! Warner Bros. featured them in six films over the next few years with such costars as James Cagney (ANGELS WITH DIRTY FACES), Humphrey Bogart (CRIME SCHOOL), and John Garfield (THEY MADE ME A CRIMINAL). Most of these films maintained the *Dead End* stance of portraying these juvenile delinquents as victims of society, though some of this posturing rang hollow considering their shenanigans. Some of the gang also found work at Universal; a B picture called LITTLE TOUGH GUY launched a series of "Dead End Kids and Little Tough Guys" films, which included both original kids and newcomers. These vehicles were a motley and uneven bunch (CALL A MESSENGER, YOU'RE NOT SO TOUGH, HIT THE ROAD, MOB TOWN) randomly integrating action, melodrama, and juvenile comedy. Not only wasn't there the pointedness of *Dead End*; there was often no point at all. Universal even featured the group in two Saturday matinee serials, JUNIOR G-MEN and JUNIOR G-MEN OF THE AIR. Then, in 1940, producer Sam Katzman launched a low-budget series called *The East Side Kids* for Monogram Pictures, featuring Leo Gorcey and Bobby Jordan, who were later joined by fellow Dead Enders Huntz Hall and Gabriel Dell. These low-budget films stressed (grade-B) drama as much as comedy and had titles such as BOYS OF THE CITY, PRIDE OF THE BOWERY, LET'S GET TOUGH, and MR. WISE GUY. Gamblers, boxers, and Nazis figured promi-

nently, along with Bela Lugosi, who costarred in SPOOKS RUN WILD and GHOSTS ON THE LOOSE. The cast members began to hit their stride in these films, developing the camaraderie that was to make them enduringly popular. In 1946, Leo Gorcey took a hand in revamping the films, assumed the official starring role of Slip Mahoney, with Huntz Hall as his sidekick Sach Jones, and the series was rechristened *The Bowery Boys*. For several years' time these films (in the experienced hands of such veteran B-picture directors as William Beaudine) flirted with drama, as in HARD BOILED MAHONEY, IN FAST COMPANY, and JINX MONEY, but then decided to go all-out with broad juvenile comedy. Titles include HOLD THAT BABY, GHOST CHASERS, JALOPY, LOOSE IN LONDON, PRIVATE EYES, PARIS PLAYBOYS, and THE BOWERY BOYS MEET THE MONSTERS. Audiences enjoyed the results, and The Bowery Boys experienced a healthy run right into the 1950s, with veteran slapstick comedy writers and directors putting the aging delinquents through their paces. Leo Gorcey's father, Bernard, played Louie Dumbrowski, proprietor of the gang's ice-cream parlor hangout, and when he died in 1956, Gorcey left the series. Stanley Clements was brought in to replace him, for seven more generally lackluster comedies (HOT SHOTS, HOLD THAT HYPNOTIST, UP IN SMOKE) before the series finally breathed its last in 1958. Aimed primarily at kids, the best of the films retain that appeal today.

Bowery Boys Meet the Monsters, The (1954) 65m. Edward Bernds. Leo Gorcey, Huntz Hall, Bernard Gorcey, Lloyd Corrigan, Ellen Corby, John Dehner, Paul Wexler.

Bowery Buckaroos (1947) 66m. D: William Beaudine. Leo Gorcey, Huntz Hall, Bobby Jordan, Gabriel Dell, Billy Benedict.

Bowery Champs (1944) 62m. D: William Beaudine. Leo Gorcey, Huntz Hall, Billy Benedict, Bobby Jordan, Gabriel Dell, Anne Sterling, Evelyn Brent, Ian Keith.

Bowery to Bagdad (1955) 64m. D: Edward Bernds. Huntz Hall, Leo Gorcey, Joan Shawlee, Eric Blore.

Bowery to Broadway (1944) 94m. **½ D: Charles Lamont. Jack Oakie, Donald Cook, Maria Montez, Louise Allbritton, Susanna Foster, Turhan Bey, Andy Devine, Rosemary DeCamp, Frank McHugh, Ann Blyth, Leo Carillo, Evelyn Ankers, Peggy Ryan, Donald O'Connor. Film depends solely on its many guest stars for what entertainment it has; limp story of rival theatrical producers (Oakie, Cook) doesn't make it.

Boxcar Bertha (1972) C-97m. **½ D: ✓ Martin Scorsese. Barbara Hershey, David

Carradine, Barry Primus, Bernie Casey, John Carradine. Scorsese's first studio film is yet another BONNIE AND CLYDE cash-in, with small-town girl Hershey falling in with Carradine and his band of train robbers. Good of its kind, but buffs looking for embryonic Scorsese stylistics may be a little let down . . . although there *are* two minor characters named Michael Powell and Emeric Pressburger!▼

Boxer, The SEE: **Ripped Off**▼

Boy and His Dog, A (1975) C-87m. **½ D: L. Q. Jones. Don Johnson, Susanne Benton, Jason Robards, Alvy Moore, Helene Winston, Charles McGraw, Tiger, voice of Tim McIntire. Cult black comedy is definitely not a kiddie movie, despite its title. In the post-holocaust future, young punk Johnson, aided by his telepathic (and much smarter) dog, forages for food and women, is eventually lured into bizarre underground civilization. Faithful adaptation of Harlan Ellison's novella is hampered by low budget; still worthwhile for discriminating fans.▼

Boy and the Pirates, The (1960) C-82m. **½ D: Bert I. Gordon. Charles Herbert, Susan Gordon, Murvyn Vye, Paul Guilfoyle. OK fantasy-adventure for kids about a boy who is magically transported back to the days of pirates on the high seas. Vye is well cast as the main cutthroat.

Boy Cried Murder, The (1966-British) C-86m. **½ D: George Breakston. Veronica Hurst, Phil Brown, Beba Loncar, Frazer MacIntosh, Tim Barrett. A reworking of THE WINDOW set in Adriatic resort town. Youngster noted for his fabrications witnesses a murder; no one but the killer believes him.

Boy, Did I Get a Wrong Number! (1966) C-99m. BOMB D: George Marshall. Bob Hope, Elke Sommer, Phyllis Diller, Cesare Danova, Marjorie Lord. They sure did; result is worthless film that should be avoided. Absolutely painful.▼

Boy Friend, The (1971-British) C-135m. *** D: Ken Russell. Twiggy, Christopher Gable, Moyra Fraser, Max Adrian, Vladek Sheybal, Georgina Hale, Tommy Tune; cameo by Glenda Jackson. Director Russell's homage to Hollywood musicals works on several levels, from tacky matinee performance of a show to fantasy-world conception of same material, all loosely tied to Sandy Wilson's cunning spoof of 1920s musical shows. Busby Berkeley-ish numbers (choreographed by Gable) come amazingly close to spirit and execution of the Master himself. Originally released in U.S. at 110m.▼

Boyfriends and Girlfriends (1987-French) C-102m. *** D: Eric Rohmer. Emmanuelle Chaulet, Sophie Renoir, Anne-Laure Meury, Eric Viellard, Francois-Eric Gendron. The sixth of Rohmer's "Comedies and Proverbs" is a typically witty, perceptive, ironic account of two very different young women who strike up a friendship . . . and commence playing romantic musical chairs with a couple of men. Nobody can direct characters who are forever falling in and out of love quite like Eric Rohmer. Originally shown at film festivals as MY GIRLFRIEND'S BOYFRIEND (AMI DE MON AMI).▼

Boy From Indiana (1950) 66m. ** D: John Rawlins. Lon McCallister, Lois Butler, Billie Burke, George Cleveland. Modest horseracing yarn, with McCallister grooming his beloved horse while romancing Butler.

Boy From Oklahoma, The (1954) C-88m. **½ D: Michael Curtiz. Will Rogers, Jr., Nancy Olson, Lon Chaney, Anthony Caruso, Wallace Ford, Merv Griffin. Quiet Western film with Rogers as pacifist sheriff who manages to keep the town intact and romance Olson; good production values. Spun off as TV series *Sugarfoot*.

Boy in Blue, The (1986-Canadian) C-98m. ** D: Charles Jarrott. Nicolas Cage, Cynthia Dale, Christopher Plummer, David Naughton, Sean Sullivan, Melody Anderson. Humdrum, by-the-numbers tale of real-life 19th-century Canadian rowing champ Ned Hanlan; filled with stock characters, from faithful manager to "unattainable" love interest. Barely stays afloat.▼

Boy in the Plastic Bubble, The (1976) C-100m. TVM D: Randal Kleiser. John Travolta, Glynnis O'Connor, Robert Reed, Diana Hyland, Ralph Bellamy, Karen Morrow, John Friedrich, Buzz Aldrin, Anne Ramsey. Travolta is forced to live in an isolation bubble because he's been born without immunities. An engrossing look at a boy's coming of age under unusual—and challenging—circumstances. Script by Douglas Day Stewart, from his and Joseph Morgenstern's story. Above average.▼

Boy Meets Girl (1938) 86m. **½ D: Lloyd Bacon. James Cagney, Pat O'Brien, Marie Wilson, Ralph Bellamy, Frank McHugh, Dick Foran, Penny Singleton, Ronald Reagan. Screwball spoof of Hollywood sometimes pushes too hard, but has enough sharp dialogue, good satire in tale of two sharpster screenwriters to make it worthwhile. Script by Samuel and Bella Spewack, from their Broadway play.

Boy Named Charlie Brown, A (1969) C-85m. *** D: Bill Melendez. Voices of Peter Robbins, Pamelyn Ferdin, Glenn Gilger, Andy Pforsich. Peanuts gang makes surprisingly successful feature-film debut, with ingenious visual ideas adding to usual fun. Only debit: Rod McKuen's absurd songs.▼

Boy on a Dolphin (1957) C-111m. **½ D: Jean Negulesco. Alan Ladd, Clifton

Webb, Sophia Loren, Laurence Naismith. Grecian isles are backdrop to pedestrian sunken-treasure yarn. Loren, in U.S. film debut, cast as skindiver helping Ladd.▼

Boys, The (1961-British) **123m.** *** D: Sidney J. Furie. Richard Todd, Robert Morley, Felix Aylmer, Wilfred Brambell. Engrossing study of attorney (Todd) who trys to uncover motives for crimes allegedly committed by four teenagers.

Boys From Brazil, The (1978) **C-123m.** **½ D: Franklin J. Schaffner. Gregory Peck, Laurence Olivier, James Mason, Lilli Palmer, Uta Hagen, John Dehner, Rosemary Harris, Anne Meara, John Rubinstein, Denholm Elliott, Steven Guttenberg, David Hurst, Jeremy Black, Bruno Ganz, Walter Gotell, Michael Gough, Prunella Scales. Former Nazi chieftain Dr. Josef Mengele (Peck) has insidious plan to breed new race of Hitlers. Interesting but ultimately silly and unbelievable; definitely worth watching, though, for Olivier's brilliant, credible performance as aging Jewish Nazi-hunter. Based on Ira Levin novel.▼

Boys From Brooklyn, The SEE: **Bela Lugosi Meets a Brooklyn Gorilla**▼

Boys From Syracuse, The (1940) **73m.** **½ D: A. Edward Sutherland. Allan Jones, Joe Penner, Martha Raye, Rosemary Lane, Irene Hervey, Eric Blore. Disappointingly ordinary adaptation of Rodgers & Hart's Broadway musical based on Shakespeare's *Comedy of Errors,* but set in ancient Greece. Songs: "This Can't Be Love," "Falling In Love With Love."

Boys in Company C, The (1978) **C-127m.** *** D: Sidney J. Furie. Stan Shaw, Andrew Stevens, James Canning, Michael Lembeck, Craig Wasson, Scott Hylands, James Whitmore, Jr., Lee Ermey. Shaw (in a standout performance) whips a bunch of green Marine recruits into shape for combat in Vietnam; good, tough film focuses on stupidity of military brass and demoralization of the soldiers.▼

Boys in the Band, The (1970) **C-119m.** ***½ D: William Friedkin. Kenneth Nelson, Peter White, Leonard Frey, Cliff Gorman, Frederick Combs, Laurence Luckinbill, Keith Prentice, Robert LaTourneaux, Reuben Greene. Excellent filmization of Mart Crowley's landmark play about nine men at a birthday party: eight are gay, the ninth insists he's not. Often hilarious, frequently sad, but always thought provoking, and sensationally acted by the original stage cast; a rare case where a single, claustrophobic set is actually an asset. Avoid the shredded 108m. version released to commercial TV.▼

Boys Next Door, The (1985) **C-88m.** ** D: Penelope Spheeris. Maxwell Caulfield, Charlie Sheen, Christopher McDonald, Hank Garrett, Patti D'Arbanville, Moon Zappa. Alienated teens Caulfield and Sheen,

just about to graduate high school, go on a murder spree. A not-uninteresting portrait of desperation and hopelessness that ultimately fails because there's no real insight into the boys' behavior. ▼

Boys' Night Out (1962) **C-115m.** *** D: Michael Gordon. Kim Novak, James Garner, Tony Randall, Howard Duff, Janet Blair, Patti Page, Zsa Zsa Gabor, Howard Morris. Trio of married men and bachelor Garner decide to set up an apartment equipped with Novak. Script manages some interesting innuendos, with comic relief coming from Blair, Page, and Gabor.

Boys of Paul Street, The (1969-Hungarian-U.S.) **C-108m.** *** D: Zoltan Fabri. Anthony Kemp, Robert Efford, Gary O'Brien, Mark Colleano, John Moulder Brown. Allegory of children's battle for control of vacant lot in Budapest, from Ferenc Molnar's novel; eloquent statement on war in effective film. Filmed before in Hollywood as NO GREATER GLORY.

Boys of the City (1940) **65m.** D: Joseph H. Lewis. Bobby Jordan, Leo Gorcey, Dave O'Brien, Vince Barnett, George Humbert, Hally Chester. SEE: **Bowery Boys** series.

Boys Town (1938) **96m.** *** D: Norman Taurog. Spencer Tracy, Mickey Rooney, Henry Hull, Gene Reynolds, Leslie Fenton, Addison Richards, Edward Norris, Sidney Miller, Bobs Watson, Frankie Thomas. Tracy won Oscar as Father Flanagan, who develops school for juvenile delinquents; Rooney is his toughest enrolee. On the syrupy side but well done; Eleanore Griffin and Dore Schary also earned Oscars for their original story. Sequel: MEN OF BOYS TOWN.▼

Boy Ten Feet Tall, A (1963-British) **C-118m.** *** D: Alexander Mackendrick. Edward G. Robinson, Fergus McClelland, Constance Cummings, Harry H. Corbett. Colorful, charming film about orphaned boy traveling through Africa alone to reach his aunt, who lives in Durban. Cut to 88m. for American release, footage was restored for TV print. Originally titled SAMMY GOING SOUTH.

Boy! What a Girl (1946) **70m.** *** D: Arthur Leonard. Tim Moore, Duke Williams, Elwood Smith, Sheila Guyse, Betti Mays, Deek Watson and His Brown Dots, Big Sid Catlett, International Jitterbugs, Slam Stewart, Ann Cornell. Wonderfully entertaining independently produced musical comedy featuring all-black cast (with the exception of Gene Krupa). Scenario centers around a couple of producers attempting to win backing for their show. Moore is funny in drag; the jitterbugging is quite X-rated for 1946.▼

Boy Who Caught a Crook (1961) **72m.** ** D: Edward L. Cahn. Wanda Hendrix, Roger Mobley, Don Beddoe, Richard Crane,

Johnny Seven. Newsboy is menaced by bank robber who thinks the boy has the lost loot. Title tells rest.

Boy Who Could Fly, The (1986) C-114m. **½ D: Nick Castle. Lucy Deakins, Jay Underwood, Bonnie Bedelia, Fred Savage, Colleen Dewhurst, Fred Gwynne, Louise Fletcher. Sensitive girl moves to a new neighborhood and befriends an autistic (and mysterious) boy next door. Warm, well-intentioned film moves very slowly and makes uncomfortable turn from believable drama to fantasy—undermining much of its effectiveness. Good feelings and good performances (especially Bedelia and newcomer Deakins) help keep it aloft. Written by director Castle. ▼

Boy Who Cried Werewolf, The (1973) C-93m. ** D: Nathan Juran. Kerwin Mathews, Elaine Devry, Scott Sealey, Robert J. Wilke, Susan Foster. Boy discovers his own father has become a werewolf and is on the prowl. More like an adventure thriller than a horror movie, but not much good as anything. Odd werewolf makeup.

Boy Who Drank Too Much, The (1980) C-100m. TVM D: Jerrold Freedman. Scott Baio, Lance Kerwin, Ed Lauter, Mariclare Costello, Don Murray. Teenaged hockey player follows in his dad's footsteps by becoming an alcoholic. Average.

Boy Who Had Everything, The (1984-Australian) C-94m. ** D: Stephen Wallace. Jason Connery, Diane Cilento, Laura Williams, Lewis Fitz-Gerald, Ian Gilmour. Uneven, inconsequential account of sensitive first-year university student Connery, his relationships with his mother and girlfriend, and his growing pains. Jason is the son of Sean Connery and Diane Cilento (who plays his mom here).

Boy Who Stole a Million, The (1960-British) 64m. ** D: Charles Crichton. Maurice Reyna, Virgilio Texera, Marianne Benet, Harold Kasket. Family-type film of youth who gets involved in bank theft to help father with oppressive debts.

Boy With Green Hair, The (1948) C-82m. *** D: Joseph Losey. Dean Stockwell, Pat O'Brien, Robert Ryan, Barbara Hale. Thought-provoking fable of war orphan who becomes social outcast when hair changes color. ▼

Braddock: Missing in Action III (1988) C-101m. BOMB D: Aaron Norris. Chuck Norris, Aki Aleong, Roland Harrah III, Miki King. Dreary comic book sequel with Colonel Norris returning to Vietnam yet again, this time to look for his wife. Chuck even coscripted, with brother Aaron serving as director. ▼

Brady Girls Get Married, The (1981) C-100m. TVM D: Peter Baldwin. Robert Reed, Florence Henderson, Ann B. Davis, Maureen McCormick, Barry Williams, Christopher Knight, Mike Lookinland, Susan Olsen, Jerry Houser, Eve Plumb. Pilot to the short-lived *Brady Brides* series, which recycled *The Brady Bunch* (1969–74) with two of the girls marrying in a double wedding and sharing a rambling old house with their new husbands. Average.

Brady's Escape (1984-U.S.-Hungarian) C-96m. ** D: Pal Gabor. John Savage, Kelly Reno, Ildiko Bansagi, Laszlo Mensaros, Ferenc Bacs. Bland adventure yarn about a flier (Savage) shot down over Hungary during WW2, and how some Magyar cowboys help him to elude the Nazis. ▼

Brain, The (1965-German-British) 85m. *** D: Freddie Francis. Peter Van Eyck, Anne Heywood, Cecil Parker, Bernard Lee, Frank Forsyth, Jack MacGowran. Good remake of DONOVAN'S BRAIN, about scientist overtaken by dead man's brain kept "alive" in his laboratory. Original British title: VENGENCE. ▼

Brain, The (1969-French) C-100m. ** D: Gerard Oury. David Niven, Jean-Paul Belmondo, Bourvil, Eli Wallach, Silvia Monti, Fernand Valois. Fine international cast in OK caper comedy about a train heist masterminded by Niven. ▼

Brain Damage (1988) C-94m. *** D: Frank Henenlotter. Rick Herbst, Gordon MacDonald, Jennifer Lowry, Theo Barnes, Lucille Saint-Peter, Vicki Darnell. Extremely strange, oddly effective horror film about Herbst and a monster parasite that gives him psychedelic "highs" by injecting fluid into his brain. And that's not the half of it! Clever parable about drug addiction features a funny cameo by the star of Henenlotter's first film BASKET CASE. ▼

Brain Eaters, The (1958) 60m. ** D: Bruno Ve Sota. Joanna Lee, Jody Fair, Edwin Nelson, Alan Frost. Loosely based on Robert Heinlein's *Puppet Masters*, this has spongy brain creatures boring up from inner earth in a ship, attaching themselves to people's heads and turning them into mindless zombies. Some mildly scary moments. Look for early Leonard Nimoy cameo.

Brain from Planet Arous, The (1958) 70m. ** D: Nathan Juran. John Agar, Joyce Meadows, Robert Fuller, Henry Travis, Morris Ankrum, Tom Browne Henry. Giant floating brain (with eyes) takes over the body of scientist Agar as its first step in conquering Earth; meanwhile, policeman brain hides out in Agar's dog while waiting for the right moment to make the arrest. As you can see, this is not 2001 we're talking here, but it *is* fun in an idiotic sort of way, and Agar is pretty good under the circumstances. ▼

Brain Machine, The (1956-British) 72m. ** D: Ken Hughes. Patrick Barr, Elizabeth Allan, Maxwell Reed, Vanda Godsell. Average yarn about drug smuggling and those involved, one of them as the result of mind-shattering machine.

Brainstorm (1965) **114m.** ** D: William Conrad. Jeff Hunter, Anne Francis, Dana Andrews, Viveca Lindfors, Stacy Harris, Kathie Brown. Fair thriller about a determined man (Hunter) who attempts the perfect crime in order to eliminate Andrews and marry Francis. Contrived.

Brainstorm (1983) **C-106m.** *** D: Douglas Trumbull. Christopher Walken, Natalie Wood, Louise Fletcher, Cliff Robertson, Joe Dorsey, Jordan Christopher. Research scientists Walken and Fletcher perfect a sensory experience device—in the form of a headset—with explosive potential. Entertainingly old-fashioned "mad scientist" type story brought up to date, though it's best not to examine story too closely. Fletcher gives film's standout performance, but Wood, in her last film (she died during production in 1981) has a basically thankless role. Sure to lose most of its impact on TV, since Trumbull's state-of-the-art visual effects were designed for 70mm stereophonic showings.▼

Brain That Wouldn't Die, The (1963) **81m.** *½ D: Joseph Green. Herb (Jason) Evers, Virginia Leith, Adele Lamont, Leslie Daniel, Paula Maurice. Poorly produced tale of surgeon trying to find body to attach to fiancee's head (she was decapitated but still lives). Beware of shorter version, which eliminates most of the gore.▼

Brainwash SEE: Circle of Power▼

Brainwashed (1961-German) **102m.** ** D: Gerd Oswald. Curt Jurgens, Claire Bloom, Hansjorg Felmy, Albert Lieven. Austrian Jurgens' struggle to retain sanity while undergoing intense Nazi interrogation is basis of this psychological drama. Strong performances but weak story mars film.

Brainwaves (1982) **C-80m.** ** D: Ulli Lommel. Keir Dullea, Suzanna Love, Tony Curtis, Vera Miles, Percy Rodrigues, Paul Willson. Young woman, injured in an accident, receives the brain (and brainwaves) of a murdered girl and then is stalked by her killer. A glum-looking Tony Curtis is the modern-day Dr. Frankenstein in this pedestrian thriller.▼

Braker (1985) **C-75m.** TVM D: Victor Lobl. Carl Weathers, Joseph Bottoms, Anne Schedeen, Alex Rocco, Randall "Tex" Cobb, Peter Michael Goetz, Shanna Reed, Kristoffer Tabori, Ian McShane. Seasoned cop and young partner investigate a killing that involves them in Hollywood's music video and porno business. Series pilot that failed. Average.

Bramble Bush, The (1960) **C-105m.** **½ D: Daniel Petrie. Richard Burton, Barbara Rush, Jack Carson, Angie Dickinson. Charles Mergendahl's potboiler becomes superficial gloss with Burton, totally ill at ease, playing New England doctor returning to Cape Cod, where he falls in love with his dying friend's wife.

Branded (1950) **C-95m.** **½ D: Rudolph Maté. Alan Ladd, Mona Freeman, Charles Bickford, Joseph Calleia, Milburn Stone. Outlaws use carefree Ladd to impersonate rancher Bickford's long-missing son, leading to much different outcome than anticipated; action and love scenes balanced OK.▼

Brand New Life, A (1973) **C-74m.** TVM D: Sam O'Steen. Cloris Leachman, Martin Balsam, Marge Redmond, Gene Nelson, Mildred Dunnock, Wilfrid Hyde-White. Believable melodrama centering on middle-aged couple reacting to unexpected prospect of having first child. Remarkable script (by Jerome Kass and Peggy Chandler Dick) and performances. An impressive directorial debut by film editor O'Steen. Above average.

Brannigan (1975-British) **C-111m.** **½ D: Douglas Hickox. John Wayne, Richard Attenborough, Judy Geeson, John Vernon, Mel Ferrer, Ralph Meeker, Lesley-Anne Down. A criminal flees to London to avoid extradition, and Chicago cop Wayne pursues him. Overlong, but change of locale serves Duke well; highlight is amusing brawl in pub.▼

Brasher Doubloon, The (1947) **72m.** ** D: John Brahm. George Montgomery, Nancy Guild, Conrad Janis, Roy Roberts, Fritz Kortner. Rare coin seems to be object of several murders in very uneven Philip Marlowe detective mystery. Filmed before as TIME TO KILL.

Brass (1985) **C-100m.** TVM D: Corey Allen. Carroll O'Connor, Lois Nettleton, Jimmy Baio, Paul Shenar, Vincent Gardenia, Anita Gillette. O'Connor, in his first post-Archie Bunker TV role, is a N.Y.C. Chief of Detectives, involved with fictionalized versions of two headline-making Manhattan murder cases and some high-level departmental corruption. His ultra-low-key performance slows much of the action to a crawl in this pilot for a prospective series. Average.▼

Brass Bottle, The (1964) **C-89m.** ** D: Harry Keller. Tony Randall, Burl Ives, Barbara Eden, Edward Andrews, Ann Doran. Juvenile comedy-fantasy about genie Ives coming out of magic bottle to serve Randall. Leading lady Eden fared better when she went into a lamp herself on TV.

Brass Legend, The (1956) **79m.** *½ D: Gerd Oswald. Hugh O'Brian, Nancy Gates, Raymond Burr, Reba Tassell. Routine Western uplifted by Burr's villain role.

Brass Target (1978) **C-111m.** ** D: John Hough. John Cassavetes, Sophia Loren, George Kennedy, Max von Sydow, Robert Vaughn, Bruce Davison, Patrick McGoohan. Rambling thriller speculates that

Gen. Patton (Kennedy) was assassinated just after WW2 because of major gold heist perpetrated by his subordinates. Unfocused storyline is major liability; von Sydow is major asset as the killer.▼

Bravados, The (1958) C-98m. *** D: Henry King. Gregory Peck, Joan Collins, Stephen Boyd, Albert Salmi. Compelling Western starring Peck, seeking four men who raped and killed his wife, discovering that he has become no better than those he hunts. Joe De Rita (later Curly Joe of The Three Stooges) plays the hangman.▼

Brave Bulls, The (1951) 108m. *** D: Robert Rossen. Mel Ferrer, Miroslava, Anthony Quinn, Eugene Iglesias. Flavorful account of public and private life of a matador, based on Tom Lea book. Film admirably captures atmosphere of bullfighting. Some prints now available run 114m., with bullfight footage originally deemed too gruesome for U.S. audiences.

Brave Little Toaster, The (1987) C-80m. *** D: Jerry Rees. Voices of Jon Lovitz, Tim Stack, Timothy E. Day, Thurl Ravenscroft, Deanna Oliver, Phil Hartman. Entertaining animated feature about a group of humanized household appliances who embark on a perilous journey to find their young master. A welcome throwback to the cartoons of yore, with equal doses of heart and hip humor to please both kids and their parents. Some nice songs by Van Dyke Parks, too. Based on the novel by Thomas M. Disch.

Brave New World (1980) C-150m. TVM D: Burt Brinckerhoff. Keir Dullea, Bud Cort, Julie Cobb, Ron O'Neal, Lee Chamberlin, Kristoffer Tabori, Marcia Strassman, Dick Anthony Williams, Victoria Racimo. Disappointing adaptation of Aldous Huxley's novel about life 600 years in the future. Strange sci-fi mix of drama and comedy in Savageland. Average.

Brave One, The (1956) C-100m. *** D: Irving Rapper. Michel Ray, Rodolfo Hoyos, Fermin Rivera, Elsa Cardenas, Carlos Navarro, Joi Lansing. Predictable but charming tale of peasant-boy Ray and his love for Gitano, a valiant bull destined to meet his fate in the arena. Filmed in Mexico. "Robert Rich" (a pseudonym for blacklisted Dalton Trumbo) received a Best Original Story Academy Award, which went unclaimed until 1975.▼

Brave Warrior (1952) C-73m. *½ D: Spencer G. Bennet. Jon Hall, Jay Silverheels, Michael Ansara, Christine Larson. Inept yarn, set in 1800s Indiana, has Hall preventing Indian hostilities.

Bravos, The (1971) C-100m. TVM D: Ted Post. George Peppard, Peter Duel, Pernell Roberts, Belinda J. Montgomery, L. Q. Jones, Barry Brown, Vincent Van Patten. Standard Western centering around regular officer assigned to command small fort following end of Civil War. Average.

Brazil (1985) C-131m. *** D: Terry Gilliam. Jonathan Pryce, Kim Greist, Robert De Niro, Katherine Helmond, Ian Holm, Bob Hoskins, Michael Palin, Ian Richardson, Peter Vaughan. Dazzlingly different look at bleak future society (kind of a cross between 1984 and A CLOCKWORK ORANGE) where one hapless clerk (Pryce) clings to his ideals and dreams, including his Dream Girl (Greist). A triumph of imagination and production design, full of incredible black comedy . . . but also a relentless film that doesn't know when to quit: second half is often redundant and ineffectual. Gilliam cut film from 142m. for American release. Screenplay by Gilliam, Tom Stoppard, and Charles McKeown. ▼

Bread and Chocolate (1978-Italian) C-107m. ***½ D: Franco Brusati. Nino Manfredi, Anna Karina, Johnny Dorelli, Paolo Turco, Max Delys. Manfredi is marvelous as a Chaplinesque everyman, an optimistic lower-class worker who treks to Switzerland to make his fortune yet remains the eternal outsider. Memorable sequence in a chicken coop. Original running time: 111m.

Bread, Love and Dreams (1954-Italian) 90m. *** D: Luigi Comencini. Vittorio De Sica, Gina Lollobrigida, Marisa Merlini, Roberto Risso. Peppery comedy with spicy Gina vying for attention of town official De Sica.

Breaker! Breaker! (1977) C-86m. BOMB D: Don Hulette. Chuck Norris, George Murdock, Terry O'Connor, Don Gentry. Cheap, stupid actioner with some (occasional) intentional comedy. Little made of the CB craze as trucker Norris searches for kid brother Michael Augenstein in corrupt judge Murdock's speedtrap town.▼

Breaker Morant (1979-Australian) C-107m. ***½ D: Bruce Beresford. Edward Woodward, Jack Thompson, John Waters, Bryan Brown, Charles Tingwell, Vincent Ball, Lewis Fitz-Gerald. Potent drama based on the true story of three soldiers whose actions during the Boer War are used as fodder for a trumped-up court martial—in order to satisfy the political plans of the British Empire. Based on a play by Kenneth G. Ross. Winner of several Australian Academy Awards.▼

Breakfast at Tiffany's (1961) C-115m. ***½ D: Blake Edwards. Audrey Hepburn, George Peppard, Patricia Neal, Buddy Ebsen, Mickey Rooney, Martin Balsam, John McGiver. Charming film from Truman Capote's story, with Hepburn as Holly Golightly, small-town girl who goes mod in N.Y.C. Dated trappings don't detract from high comedy and winning romance. Screenplay by George Axelrod. Oscar-winner for Score (Henry Mancini) and Song, "Moon River" (Mancini and Johnny Mercer).▼

Breakfast Club, The (1985) **C-97m.** **½ D: John Hughes. Emilio Estevez, Judd Nelson, Molly Ringwald, Anthony Michael Hall, Ally Sheedy, Paul Gleason. A bold experiment in the era of teen raunch movies (written and directed by a man who's made more than his share): five kids sit and talk about themselves, during day-long detention. Alternately poignant, predictable, and self-important, but filled with moments of truth and perception.▼

Breakfast in Hollywood (1946) **91m.** *½ D: Harold Schuster. Tom Breneman, Bonita Granville, Beulah Bondi, Edward Ryan. Uninspired film derived from radio series of the same name; romantic plot offset by musical numbers with Spike Jones, The (Nat) King Cole Trio, and others.▼

Breakfast in Paris (1982-Australian) **C-86m.** *½ D: John Lamond. Barbara Parkins, Rod Mullinar, Jack Lenoir, Elspeth Ballantyne, Jeremy Higgins, Graham Stanley. Schlocky romance, with obnoxious fashion designer Parkins pursued by klutzy photographer Mullinar. The best thing about this is its title.▼

✓ **Breakheart Pass** (1976) **C-95m.** *** D: Tom Gries. Charles Bronson, Ben Johnson, Richard Crenna, Jill Ireland, Charles Durning, Ed Lauter. Slambang action Western, with second unit work by Yakima Canutt. Based on Alistair MacLean novel and set mainly on a train, it has Bronson as an undercover agent seeking gun runners and confronting a false epidemic. Highlight: incredible fight between Bronson and Archie Moore.▼

Breakin' (1984) **C-90m.** ** D: Joel Silberg. Lucinda Dickey, Adolfo (Shabba-Doo) Quinones, Michael (Boogaloo Shrimp) Chambers, Ben Lokey, Christopher McDonald, Phineas Newborn 3rd. Harmless FLASH-DANCE clone, but with the emphasis on breakdancing. Here, heroine Dickey waitresses rather than welds. A sequel (BREAK-IN' 2: ELECTRIC BOOGALOO) followed before the year was out.▼

Breakin' 2: Electric Boogaloo (1984) **C-94m.** *½ D: Sam Firstenberg. Lucinda Dickey, Adolfo (Shabba-Doo) Quinones, Michael (Boogaloo Shrimp) Chambers, Susie Bono. Two worthy adversaries—a toothy WASP developer who could rate a centerfold in *Forbes* and a young urban black whose earring is longer than a bola—clash when the former tries to bulldoze a community rec center. The 18 breakdancing standards include "Do Your Thang" and "Oye Mamacita."▼

Breaking All the Rules (1985-Canadian) **C-91m.** ** D: James Orr. Carl Marotte, Carolyn Dunn, Rachel Hayward. Minor PORKY's clone about youngsters' hijinks at an amusement park where robbers have stolen a prize to be given away. Dunn shines as a would-be punkster.▼

Breaking Away (1979) **C-100m.** ***½ D: Peter Yates. Dennis Christopher, Dennis Quaid, Daniel Stern, Jackie Earle Haley, Barbara Barrie, Paul Dooley, Robyn Douglass, Hart Bochner, Amy Wright, John Ashton. Winning, unpretentious film about four college-age friends in Bloomington, Indiana who don't know what to do with their lives; Dooley stands out in first-rate cast as Christopher's bewildered father. This sleeper hit really comes to life with an audience, may not play as well on TV. Steve Tesich's original screenplay won well-deserved Oscar; later spawned a brief TV series.▼

Breaking Glass (1980-English) **C-104m.** **½ D: Brian Gibson. Phil Daniels, Hazel O'Connor, Jon Finch, Jonathan Pryce, Peter-Hugo Daly, Mark Wingett. Rocker O'Connor rises from playing small London clubs to superstardom, finds success isn't everything. Good performances by O'Connor, Daniels (as her youthful manager), Pryce (as a junkie saxophone player) offset predictable story line.▼

Breaking Home Ties SEE: **Norman Rockwell's Breaking Home Ties**

Breaking In (1989) **C-91m.** **½ D: Bill Forsyth. Burt Reynolds, Casey Siemaszko, Sheila Kelley, Lorraine Toussaint, Albert Salmi, Harry Carey, Maury Chaykin, Steve Tobolowsky, David Frishberg. Low-key, off-center comedy about an aging safecracker who takes on a young protégé who's got a lot to learn about life, as well as his new profession. John Sayles' script, as interpreted by director Forsyth, is inventive and often quite funny . . . but not enough to keep this wispy film afloat. Reynolds is extremely good in his first character role.▼

Breaking Point, The (1950) **97m.** ***½ D: Michael Curtiz. John Garfield, Patricia Neal, Phyllis Thaxter, Wallace Ford, Sherry Jackson. High-voltage refilming of Hemingway's TO HAVE AND HAVE NOT, with Garfield as skipper so desperate for money he takes on illegal cargo. Garfield and mate Juano Hernandez give superb interpretations. Remade as THE GUN RUNNERS.

Breaking Point (1976-Canadian) **C-92m.** BOMB D: Bob Clark. Bo Svenson, Robert Culp, John Colicos, Belinda J. Montgomery, Stephen Young, Linda Sorenson. Svenson is pursued by Mafiosos after he testifies against them in court. Nothing new here.▼

Breaking Point (1989) **C-100m. TVM** D: Peter Markle. Corbin Bernsen, Joanna Pacula, John Glover, David Marshall, Lawrence Pressman. Unnecessary redo of George Seaton's middling WW2 spy yarn 36 HOURS. Bernsen is an Army officer the Nazis try pumping for info after convincing him he's in an American hospital and the war is long over. Made for cable. Average.▼

Breaking the Sound Barrier (1952-British) **109m.** ***½ D: David Lean. Ralph Richardson, Ann Todd, Nigel Patrick, John Justin, Dinah Sheridan, Denholm Elliott. Grade-A documentary-style story of early days of jet planes, and men who tested them; Richardson particularly good. Originally shown in England as THE SOUND BARRIER at 118m.

Breaking Up (1978) **C-100m. TVM** D: Delbert Mann. Lee Remick, Granville Van Dusen, Vicki Dawson, David Stambaugh, Meg Mundy, Frank Latimore. Effective drama about a sophisticated suburbanite forced to drastically change her life when her husband walks out on her and the kids. Remick superior as ever; director Mann and writer Loring Mandel each Emmy Award-nominated. Above average.

Breaking Up Is Hard to Do (1979) **C-150m. TVM** D: Lou Antonio. Robert Conrad, Ted Bessell, Jeff Conaway, Billy Crystal, Tony Musante, David Ogden Stiers, Bonnie Franklin, Susan Sullivan. Arresting if overlong drama dealing with separation and divorce from the man's point of view. The title comes from Neil Sedaka and Howard Greenfield's hit song, which Sedaka sings obligatorily over the credits. Above average.▼

Break in the Circle (1957-British) **C-69m.** *½ D: Val Guest. Forrest Tucker, Eva Bartok, Marius Goring, Guy Middleton. Unexciting chase tale has Tucker a boat owner thrust into helping to get scientist out of Communist Germany.

Break of Hearts (1935) **80m.** **½ D: Philip Moeller. Katharine Hepburn, Charles Boyer, John Beal, Jean Hersholt, Sam Hardy. Struggling composer Hepburn marries renowned conductor Boyer in this stale but well-acted romantic drama.▼

Breakout (1959-British) **99m.** **½ D: Don Chaffey. Richard Todd, Richard Attenborough, Michael Wilding, Dennis Price, Bernard Lee. Although format is now familiar, this remains an exciting story of British P.O.W.s attempting escapes from Axis prison camp during WW2. Fine performances all around. Retitled: DANGER WITHIN.

Breakout (1970) **C-100m. TVM** D: Richard Irving. James Drury, Kathryn Hays, Woody Strode, Sean Garrison, Red Buttons, Bert Freed. Prisoner Baker (Drury) creates two "foolproof" plans for escaping maximum security state pen so he can be reunited with wife (Hays) and $50,000 from bank robbery for which he was convicted. Good situations, adequate suspense. Above average.

Breakout (1975) **C-96m.** *** D: Tom Gries. Charles Bronson, Robert Duvall,

Jill Ireland, John Huston, Sheree North, Randy Quaid. Crisp action film generously laced with comedy touches has devil-may-care bush pilot Bronson taking on the job of spiriting Duvall, framed for murder, from a seedy Mexican prison. Awfully violent, though.▼

Breakthrough (1950) **91m.** **½ D: Lewis Seiler. David Brian, John Agar, Frank Lovejoy, Paul Picerni, William Self. Saga of men training for combat, their days of fighting and romancing; stark and satisfactory.

Breakthrough (1978-West German) **C-115m.** *½ D: Andrew V. McLaglen. Richard Burton, Robert Mitchum, Rod Steiger, Curt Jurgens, Klaus Loewitsch, Helmut Griem, Michael Parks. Superficial sequel to CROSS OF IRON, with the focus on the western front during WW2. German sergeant Burton becomes entangled in anti-Hitler conspiracy, saves the life of U.S. colonel Mitchum. Particularly disappointing, considering cast. Also known as SERGEANT STEINER.▼

Break to Freedom (1955-British) **88m.** ** D: Lewis Gilbert. Anthony Steel, Jack Warner, Robert Beatty, William Sylvester, Michael Balfour. Typical P.O.W.s escape-from-German-camp, uplifted by restrained acting.

Breathless (1959-French) **89m.** ***½ D: Jean-Luc Godard. Jean Seberg, Jean-Paul Belmondo, Daniel Boulanger, Liliane David. Belmondo is ideally cast as a Parisian hood who, accompanied by American girl (Seberg), is chased by police after stealing a car and killing a cop. Groundbreaking, influential New Wave tale with a classic romanticized gangster-hero and great candid shots of Paris life. Dedicated to Monogram Pictures, with a story by Francois Truffaut. Remade in 1983.▼

Breathless (1983) **C-100m.** ** D: Jim McBride. Richard Gere, Valerie Kaprisky, Art Metrano, John P. Ryan, William Tepper, Gary Goodrow. Remake of landmark 1959 Godard film follows basic outline of the original—an amoral punk on the lam from police—but lacks its sociological potency. Gere's kinetic performance is something to see, but his character, hooked on Jerry Lee Lewis music and "Silver Surfer" comics, soon grows tiresome.▼

Breath of Scandal, A (1960) **C-98m.** ** D: Michael Curtiz. Sophia Loren, John Gavin, Maurice Chevalier, Isabel Jeans, Angela Lansbury. Molnar's play *Olympia* is limp costume vehicle for Loren, playing a princess romanced by American Gavin. Chevalier and Lansbury vainly try to pump some life into proceedings.▼

Breed Apart, A (1984) **C-101m.** ** D: Philippe Mora. Rutger Hauer, Powers Boothe, Kathleen Turner, Donald Pleasence, John Dennis Johnston, Brion James.

Picturesque but illogical, uninvolving tale of famed mountain climber Boothe, hired to pilfer specimens of a new bald-eagle breed, and his entanglement with conservationist Hauer and fishing-supply store owner Turner.▼

Breezy (1973) **C-108m.** ** D: Clint Eastwood. William Holden, Kay Lenz, Roger C. Carmel, Marj Dusay, Shelley Morrison, Joan Hotchkis. Jaded middle-ager finds Truth with a teen-aged hippie in sappy romance. Fine performances by the leads only help up to a point.

Brenda Starr (1976) **C-78m. TVM** D: Mel Stuart. Jill St. John, Jed Allan, Sorrell Booke, Tabi Cooper, Victor Buono, Barbara Luna, Torin Thatcher. Intrepid comic strip newspaperwoman—played floridly by curvaceous St. John—becomes involved in voodoo, extortion, and strange doings in jungles of Brazil. Played too straight to be fun. Below average.

Brenda Starr (1989) **C-87m.** *½ D: Robert Ellis Miller. Brooke Shields, Tony Peck, Timothy Dalton, Diana Scarwid, Jeffrey Tambor, June Cable, Nestor Serrano, Kathleen Wilhoite, Charles Durning, Eddie Albert, Henry Gibson, Ed Nelson. This fiasco, based on Dale Messick's comic strip, sat on the shelf three years, and no wonder. Artist Peck enters the strip to talk Brenda out of quitting, is drawn into her adventuresome life. Film looks great, but story is aimless, uninvolving, and fizzles out. The creators have contempt for their source, always deadly in films like this.

Brewster McCloud (1970) **C-101m.** *** D: Robert Altman. Bud Cort, Sally Kellerman, Michael Murphy, William Windom, Shelley Duvall, Rene Auberjonois, Stacy Keach, John Schuck, Margaret Hamilton. Patently indescribable movie following exploits of owlish boy (Cort) whose ambition is to take wing and fly inside Houston Astrodome. Extremely bizarre; for certain tastes, extremely funny. Altman fans have head start.▼

Brewster's Millions (1945) **79m.** **½ D: Allan Dwan. Dennis O'Keefe, Helen Walker, Eddie "Rochester" Anderson, June Havoc, Gail Patrick, Mischa Auer, Joe Sawyer, Herbert Rudley. Bright, energetic filming of venerable George Barr McCutcheon comedy about ordinary guy (this time, a returning G.I.) who must spend a million dollars in a month's time in order to receive major inheritance. First filmed in 1914; remade in 1985.▼

Brewster's Millions (1985) **C-97m.** ** D: Walter Hill. Richard Pryor, John Candy, Lonette McKee, Stephen Collins, Jerry Orbach, Pat Hingle, Tovah Feldshuh, Joe Grifasi, Hume Cronyn. Seventh film version of venerable novel and play about a man who has one month to spend a million dollars. Surefire premise squelched by unfunny script and wooden direction. When Pryor and Candy can't make it work, you know there's something wrong.▼

Brian's Song (1970) **C-73m. TVM** D: Buzz Kulik. Billy Dee Williams, James Caan, Jack Warden, Judy Pace, Shelley Fabares. Exceptional film relating real-life relationship between Chicago Bears football players Brian Piccolo (Caan) and Gale Sayers (Williams), and tragedy which affects entire team when Piccolo develops cancer. Outstanding teleplay by William Blinn from Sayers' *I Am Third*. Beautiful score by Michel Legrand. A milestone of excellence in made-for-TV movies. Above average.▼

Bribe, The (1949) **98m.** ** D: Robert Z. Leonard. Robert Taylor, Ava Gardner, Charles Laughton, Vincent Price, John Hodiak. Taylor looks uncomfortable playing federal man who almost sacrifices all for sultry singer Gardner.

Bridal Path, The (1959-Scottish) **C-95m.** ***½ D: Frank Launder. Bill Travers, Bernadette O'Farrell, Alex MacKenzie, Eric Woodburn, Jack Lambert, John Rae. Charming film of young islander who goes to Scottish mainland in search of a wife. Enhanced by beautiful scenery in color.

Bride, The (1974) SEE: **House That Cried Murder, The**

Bride, The (1985) **C-118m.** **½ D: Franc Roddam. Sting, Jennifer Beals, Clancy Brown, David Rappaport, Geraldine Page, Anthony Higgins, Veruschka, Quentin Crisp. Revisionist remake of THE BRIDE OF FRANKENSTEIN brilliantly captures look and feel of a great gothic horror film—but fails to deliver on its promise of enlightened psychological approach to the story. Both Sting and Beals give one-note performances. Film is easily stolen by Rappaport, as midget who befriends Dr. Frankenstein's male monster (Brown); their sequences make film worth watching.▼

Bride and the Beast, The (1958) **78m.** BOMB D: Adrian Weiss. Charlotte Austin, Lance Fuller, Johnny Roth, Steve Calvert. A gorilla fancies the wife of an explorer. Screenplay by Edward D. Wood, Jr.; also known as QUEEN OF THE GORILLAS.

Bride Came C.O.D., The (1941) **92m.** **½ D: William Keighley. James Cagney, Bette Davis, Stuart Erwin, Eugene Pallette, Jack Carson, George Tobias. Unlikely comedy team in vehicle made enjoyable only by their terrific personalities; he's a flier, she's a runaway bride.

Bride Comes Home, The (1935) **82m.** **½ D: Wesley Ruggles. Claudette Colbert, Fred MacMurray, Robert Young, William Collier, Sr., Edgar Kennedy. Breezy fluff with wealthy Young competing against roughneck MacMurray for Claudette's affections in vintage comedy.

Bride Comes to Yellow Sky, The SEE: **Face to Face** (1952)

Bride for Sale (1949) 87m. **½ D: William D. Russell. Claudette Colbert, Robert Young, George Brent, Max Baer. Veteran star trio carries on despite thin story of female tax expert (Colbert) seeking wealthy spouse.

Bride Goes Wild, The (1948) 98m. **½ D: Norman Taurog. Van Johnson, June Allyson, Butch Jenkins, Hume Cronyn, Una Merkel, Arlene Dahl. Silly, sometimes funny tale of Johnson pretending to be Jenkins' father in order to woo Allyson; nice cast does its best.

Bride Is Much Too Beautiful, The (1958-French) 90m. **½ D: Fred Surin. Brigitte Bardot, Micheline Presle, Louis Jourdan, Marcel Amont. Gallic sex romp with BB a farm girl who becomes famous magazine model.▼

Bride of Boogedy (1987) C-100m. TVM D: Oz Scott. Richard Masur, Mimi Kennedy, Tammy Lauren, David Faustino, Howard Witt, Eugene Levy. Disney haunted-house comedy involving a fun-loving contemporary family and a fractious bride-seeking ghost. This followed an hour-long prospective series pilot from the previous year. Average.

✓ **Bride of Frankenstein** (1935) 75m. **** D: James Whale. Boris Karloff, Colin Clive, Valerie Hobson, Ernest Thesiger, Elsa Lanchester, Una O'Connor, E. E. Clive, Gavin Gordon, Douglas Walton, O. P. Heggie, Dwight Frye, John Carradine. Eye-filling sequel to FRANKENSTEIN is even better, with rich vein of dry wit running through the chills. Inimitable Thesiger plays weird doctor who compels Frankenstein into making a mate for his creation; Lanchester plays both the "bride" and, in amusing prologue, Mary Shelley. Pastoral interlude with blind hermit and final, riotous creation scene are highlights of this truly classic movie. Scripted by John L. Balderston and William Hurlbut. Marvelous Franz Waxman score, reused for many subsequent films. Followed by SON OF FRANKENSTEIN; remade as THE BRIDE.▼

Bride of the Gorilla (1951) 76m. ** D: Curt Siodmak. Raymond Burr, Barbara Payton, Lon Chaney, Jr., Tom Conway, Paul Cavanagh. Surprisingly watchable trash movie set on a jungle plantation, where hulking Burr marries sexy Payton—only to find himself the victim of a voodoo curse. Terrible but fun.▼

Bride of the Monster (1955) 69m. BOMB D: Edward D. Wood, Jr. Bela Lugosi, Tor Johnson, Tony McCoy, Loretta King, Harvey B. Dunne, George Becwar, Don Nagel, Bud Osborne. A dissipated Lugosi creates giant rubber octopus that terrorizes woodland stream. Huge Swedish wrestler Johnson provides added laughs as hulking manservant Lobo. Another hilariously inept Grade Z movie from the king of bad cinema. Sequel: NIGHT OF THE GHOULS.▼

Bride of Vengeance (1949) 91m. ** D: Mitchell Leisen. Paulette Goddard, John Lund, Macdonald Carey, Raymond Burr, Albert Dekker, Rose Hobart. Medium-warm costumer of medieval Italy with Goddard as the Borgia sent to do mischief but instead falling in love.

Bridesmaids (1989) C-100m. TVM D: Lila Garrett. Shelley Hack, Sela Ward, Stephanie Faracy, Audra Lindley, Brooke Adams, Jack Coleman. Four best friends reunite for a fifth's wedding, and try to resolve various loose ends in their relationships. Potentially interesting "woman's picture" gets muddled. Average.

Brides of Dracula, The (1960-British) C-85m. **½ D: Terence Fisher. Peter Cushing, Martita Hunt, Yvonne Monlaur, Freda Jackson, David Peel. Above-average entry in Hammer horror series, with the famed vampire's disciple (Peel) seeking female victims.

Brides of Fu Manchu, The (1966-British) C-94m. **½ D: Don Sharp. Christopher Lee, Douglas Wilmer, Marie Versini, Tsai Chin. Fu doesn't give up easily, still bent on conquering the world by forcing scientists to develop powerful ray gun. Sequel to FACE OF FU MANCHU, not as good, still diverting; followed by VENGEANCE OF FU MANCHU.

Bride Walks Out, The (1936) 81m. ** D: Leigh Jason. Barbara Stanwyck, Gene Raymond, Robert Young, Ned Sparks, Helen Broderick, Hattie McDaniel. Flimsy comedy; stars do their best with Stanwyck and Raymond trying to survive on his meager salary ▼

Bride Wore Black, The (1968-French) C-107m. ***½ D: Francois Truffaut. Jeanne Moreau, Claude Rich, Jean-Claude Brialy, Michel Bouquet, Michel Lonsdale, Charles Denner. Hitchcockian suspenser about Moreau tracking down and killing the quintet of men who accidentally killed her husband on their wedding day. Exciting, entertaining homage to The Master, right down to the Bernard Herrmann score (although Truffaut omitted the twist ending of Cornell Woolrich's novel).

Bride Wore Boots, The (1946) 86m. ** D: Irving Pichel. Barbara Stanwyck, Robert Cummings, Diana Lynn, Peggy Wood, Robert Benchley, Natalie Wood, Willie Best. Witless comedy of horse-loving Stanwyck saddled by Cummings, who does his best to win her total affection; they all try but script is weak.

Bride Wore Red, The (1937) 103m. ** D: Dorothy Arzner. Joan Crawford, Franchot Tone, Robert Young, Billie Burke, Reginald Owen. More fashion show than plot in this typical glossy Crawford soaper of girl who works her way up society ladder.

Bridge, The (1960-German) **100m.** ***
D: Bernhard Wicki. Folker Bohnet, Fritz
Wepper, Michael Hinz, Frank Glaubrecht.
Unrelenting account of teen-age boys drafted
into the German army in 1945, as last
resort effort to stem Allied invasion.

Bridge Across Time (1985) **C-100m.**
TVM D: E. W. Swackhamer. David
Hasselhoff, Stepfanie Kramer, Adrienne
Barbeau, Randolph Mantooth, Lindsay
Bloom, Clu Gulager, Rose Marie, Ken
Swofford. The spirit of Jack the Ripper
turns up in Arizona at the opening of the
reconstructed London Bridge. Cast gives a
straight-faced go at the investigation of
a series of grisly killings, giving this one
a semi-camp feel. Retitled ARIZONA RIP-
PER and (on video) TERROR AT LON-
DON BRIDGE. Average.▼

Bridge at Remagen, The (1969) **C-115m.**
✶✶½ D: John Guillermin. George Segal,
Robert Vaughn, Ben Gazzara, Bradford
Dillman, E.G. Marshall, Peter Van Eyck.
Well-acted film about group of Allies defending bridge toward the end of WW2
can't quite overcome familiar plot line;
lots of good explosions for those who
care.▼

Bridge of San Luis Rey, The (1944)
89m. ** D: Rowland V. Lee. Lynn Bari,
Nazimova, Louis Calhern, Akim Tamiroff,
Francis Lederer, Blanche Yurka, Donald
Woods. Thornton Wilder's moody, unusual
story of five people meeting doom on
a rickety bridge makes a slow-moving
film. Previously filmed in 1929.▼

Bridge on the River Kwai, The (1957-
British) **C-161m.** ✶✶✶✶ D: David Lean.
William Holden, Alec Guinness, Jack Haw-
kins, Sessue Hayakawa, Geoffrey Horne,
James Donald. British soldiers in Japanese
prison camp build a bridge as a futile
exercise while Holden plots to destroy it.
Psychological battles of will combined with
high-powered action sequences make this
a blockbuster. Seven Oscars include Picture, Director, Actor (Guinness), Cinematography (Jack Hildyard), Editing (Peter
Taylor), Scoring (Malcolm Arnold), and
Screenplay (by Carl Foreman and Michael
Wilson, based on Pierre Boulle's novel.
The writers were blacklisted, so Boulle—
who spoke no English—was credited with
the script!).▼

Bridger (1976) **C-100m. TVM** D: David
Lowell Rich. James Wainwright, Ben Murphy, Dirk Blocker, Sally Field, John Anderson, William Windom. Predictable western about legendary mountain man Jim
Bridger (Wainwright) who blazes a trail
through the Rockies to California in 1830.
Cliches and stereotypes bury the action element; subsequently cut to 78m. Average.

Bridges at Toko-Ri, The (1954) **C-103m.**
***½ D: Mark Robson. William Holden,
Grace Kelly, Fredric March, Mickey

Rooney, Robert Strauss, Earl Holliman.
Powerful, thoughtful drama, based on the
James Michener best-seller, focusing on
the conflicts and exploits of lawyer Holden
after he is recalled by the Navy to fly jets
in Korea. While the flying sequences are
exciting—the special effects earned an
Oscar—the ultimate futility of Korean War
is in no way deemphasized.▼

Bridge to Nowhere (1986-New Zealand)
C-86m. *½ D: Ian Mune. Bruno Lawrence, Alison Routledge, Philip Gordon,
Margaret Umbers, Stephen Judd, Shelley
Luxford, Matthew Hunter. Kiwi variation
on a familiar theme: backpacking kids raise
the ire of hermit Lawrence, causing a war
for survival. Well made but trite; features
a solid role for the ubiquitous star of New
Zealand films, Lawrence.▼

Bridge Too Far, A (1977-British) **C-175m.**
** D: Richard Attenborough. Dirk Bogarde,
James Caan, Michael Caine, Sean Connery,
Edward Fox, Elliott Gould, Gene Hackman,
Anthony Hopkins, Hardy Kruger, Laurence
Olivier, Ryan O'Neal, Robert Redford,
Maximilian Schell, Liv Ullmann, Arthur
Hill. Lifeless, overproduced version of the
fine Cornelius Ryan book about disastrous
1944 Allied airdrop behind German lines
in Holland. Some prints run 158m.▼

Bridge to Silence (1989) **C-100m. TVM**
D: Karen Arthur. Lee Remick, Marlee
Matlin, Michael O'Keefe, Josef Sommer,
Phyllis Frelich. Matlin (in her TV acting
debut) plays a hearing-impaired woman
trying to rebuild her life following a car
crash that killed her husband. Remick plays
her unfeeling mother who clashes with
Matlin over the fate of her young daughter. Good actors cannot overcome a predictable (and somewhat superficial) script.
Phyllis Frelich appears briefly in a sequence in which the Theatre of the Deaf
performs *The Glass Menagerie*. Average.

Bridge to the Sun (1961) **113m.** ***
D: Etienne Perier. Carroll Baker, James
Shigeta, James Yagi. Well-intentioned
telling of Southern girl Baker who marries
Japanese diplomat Shigeta and moves to
Japan at outbreak of WW2.

Brief Encounter (1945-British) **85m.** ****
D: David Lean. Celia Johnson, Trevor
Howard, Stanley Holloway, Cyril Raymond, Joyce Carey. Two ordinary people,
who happen to be married, meet at a train
station and find themselves drawn into a
short but poignant romance. Intense and
unforgettable, underscored by perfect use
of Rachmaninoff's *Second Piano Concerto*.
Adapted by Noel Coward from his one-act
play "Still Life" (from *Tonight at Eight-
thirty*). A truly wonderful film. Remade
as a TV movie.▼

Brief Encounter (1974) **C-103m. TVM**
D: Alan Bridges. Richard Burton, Sophia
Loren, Jack Hedley, Rosemary Leach, Ann

Firbank. Simply terrible remake of Noel Coward's story about a romantic liaison between two married people. Originally shown at 74m. Below average.▼

Brief Vacation, A (1973-Italian) **C-106m.** *** D: Vittorio De Sica. Florinda Bolkan, Renato Salvatori, Daniel Quenaud, Jose Maria Prada, Teresa Gimpera. Poorly educated woman leaves terrible job, despicable in-laws, and callous husband for a comparatively pleasant stay in a TB sanitorium. De Sica's sure-handed direction and Bolkan's knowing performance make this worth watching.

Brigadoon (1954) **C-108m.** *** D: Vincente Minnelli. Gene Kelly, Van Johnson, Cyd Charisse, Elaine Stewart, Barry Jones, Hugh Laing. Americans Kelly and Johnson discover magical Scottish village in this entertaining filmization of Lerner & Loewe Broadway hit. Overlooked among 1950s musicals, it may lack innovations but has its own quiet charm, and lovely score.▼

Brigand, The (1952) **C-94m.** ** D: Phil Karlson. Anthony Dexter, Anthony Quinn, Gale Robbins, Jody Lawrance. Dexter is lookalike for king and becomes involved with court intrigue; flat costumer.

Brigand of Kandahar, The (1965-British) **C-81m.** **½ D: John Gilling. Ronald Lewis, Oliver Reed, Duncan Lamont, Yvonne Romain, Catherine Woodville. Mostly nonsense set on British outpost in 1850s India with rampaging natives; good cast tries hard.

✓ **Brigham Young—Frontiersman** (1940) **114m.** **½ D: Henry Hathaway. Tyrone Power, Linda Darnell, Dean Jagger, Brian Donlevy, John Carradine, Jane Darwell, Jean Rogers, Mary Astor, Vincent Price. Well-intentioned but ludicrous depiction of Mormon leader with Jagger nominally in the lead, focus shifting to tepid romance between Power and Darnell; Astor all wrong as homespun wife.

Bright Eyes (1934) **83m.** **½ D: David Butler. Shirley Temple, James Dunn, Judith Allen, Jane Withers, Lois Wilson, Charles Sellon. Early Shirley, and pretty good, with juvenile villainy from Withers in tale of custody battle over recently orphaned Temple. Includes "On the Good Ship Lollipop."▼

Bright Leaf (1950) **110m.** **½ D: Michael Curtiz. Gary Cooper, Lauren Bacall, Patricia Neal, Jack Carson, Donald Crisp. Loose chronicle of 19th-century tobacco farmer (Cooper) building successful cigarette empire, seeking revenge on old enemies and finding romance.

Bright Lights (1935) **83m.** ** D: Busby Berkeley. Joe E. Brown, Ann Dvorak, Patricia Ellis, William Gargan, Joseph Cawthorn, Arthur Treacher. Rags-to-riches show business tale of husband and wife separating while trying to hit it big. Entertaining, but full of clichés.

Bright Lights, Big City (1988) **C-110m.** **½ D: James Bridges. Michael J. Fox, Kiefer Sutherland, Phoebe Cates, Swoosie Kurtz, Frances Sternhagen, Tracy Pollan, John Houseman, Charlie Schlatter, Jason Robards, Dianne Wiest, William Hickey. Everyone gets an A for effort on this adaptation of Jay McInerney's popular novel. Fox gives a good performance as the young Midwesterner whose life has started coming apart at the seams in N.Y.C., where he gets caught up in an endless cycle of drugs and nightlife. But the more cerebral aspects of the book (and some of its purple prose) don't translate to film . . . and it takes a long time to develop any real sympathy for Fox and his plight. Sutherland is convincingly smarmy as his druggie pal.▼

Brighton Beach Memoirs (1986) **C-110m.** **½ D: Gene Saks. Blythe Danner, Bob Dishy, Jonathan Silverman, Brian Drillinger, Stacey Glick, Judith Ivey, Lisa Waltz. Pleasant, if mostly undistinguished, adaptation of Neil Simon's celebrated autobiographical play about two families living under the same roof in 1937 Brooklyn. Oddly cast—Danner and Ivey play Jewish sisters—with attractive production design; Dishy underplays nicely as narrator Silverman's father. Followed by BILOXI BLUES and (on stage) Broadway Bound.▼

Brighton Rock (1947-British) **86m.** *** D: John Boulting. Richard Attenborough, Carol Marsh, Hermione Baddeley, William Hartnell, Harcourt Williams, Nigel Stock. Tour de force role for young Attenborough as loathsome, baby-faced gangster who finally gets his comeuppance. Notable for incredibly cynical trick ending. Screenplay by Terence Rattigan and Graham Greene from Greene's novel. U.S. title: YOUNG SCARFACE.

Brighton Strangler, The (1945) **67m.** ** D: Max Nosseck. John Loder, June Duprez, Michael St. Angel, Miles Mander, Rose Hobart, Gilbert Emery. Strained thriller of demented stage actor Loder with a strangling complex, set in England.▼

Bright Road (1953) **69m.** ** D: Gerald Mayer. Dorothy Dandridge, Harry Belafonte, Robert Horton, Philip Hepburn. Well-intentioned but labored tale of black teacher in small Southern town who tries to solve her young pupils' problems. Belafonte's film debut.

Bright Victory (1951) **97m.** *** D: Mark Robson. Arthur Kennedy, Peggy Dow, Julia (Julie) Adams, James Edwards, Will Geer, Nana Bryant, Jim Backus, Murray Hamilton, Richard Egan. Touching account of blinded ex-soldier who slowly readjusts to civilian life, even finding love. Potentially sticky subject handled well, with Kennedy excellent in lead role. Rock Hudson can be glimpsed as a soldier.

Brighty of the Grand Canyon (1967) **C-89m.** **½ D: Norman Foster. Joseph Cotten, Pat Conway, Karl Swensen, Dick Foran, Jason Clark. Harmless tale of a burro in the title locale; best for the kids.▼

Brimstone (1949) **C-90m.** ** D: Joseph Kane. Rod Cameron, Walter Brennan, Adrian Booth, Forrest Tucker, Jack Holt. Usual account of cattle-rustling and law enforcer who brings outlaws to justice.▼

Brimstone and Treacle (1982-British) **C-85m.** **½ D: Richard Loncraine. Sting, Denholm Elliott, Joan Plowright, Suzanna Hamilton. Strange, intriguing (but often unpleasant) film about a young man who worms his way into the lives of a vulnerable middle-class couple, whose daughter lies in a coma. Persuasive performance by Sting.▼

Bring 'Em Back Alive (1932) **65m.** **½ D: Clyde Elliott. Frank Buck plays Great White Hunter (and narrator) in this documentary curio, a great hit in its day and still interesting for its exciting jungle footage, as well as its often blatant phoniness. The inspiration for a same-named TV series fifty years later.

Bringing Up Baby (1938) **102m.** **** D: Howard Hawks. Cary Grant, Katharine Hepburn, Charlie Ruggles, May Robson, Barry Fitzgerald, Walter Catlett, Fritz Feld, Ward Bond. In her sole venture into slapstick, Hepburn plays a madcap heiress—"Baby" is her pet leopard—who sets her sights on absentminded zoologist Grant and inadvertently (?) proceeds to make a shambles of his life. Not a hit when first released, this is now considered the definitive screwball comedy and one of the fastest, funniest films ever made; grand performances by all. Screenplay by Dudley Nichols and Hagar Wilde, from Wilde's original story. More or less remade as WHAT'S UP, DOC?▼

Bring Me the Head of Alfredo Garcia (1974) **C-112m.** ** D: Sam Peckinpah. Warren Oates, Isela Vega, Gig Young, Robert Webber, Helmut Dantine, Emilio Fernandez, Kris Kristofferson. American piano player in Mexico gets involved with a smorgasbord of psychos; sub-par bloodbath doesn't even have the usual Peckinpah fast pace.▼

Bring Me the Head of Dobie Gillis (1988) **C-100m. TVM** D: Stanley Z. Cherry. Dwayne Hickman, Bob Denver, Connie Stevens, Sheila James, Steve Franken, William Schallert, Tricia Leigh Fisher, Scott Grimes. Dobie, Maynard and *The Many Loves of Dobie Gillis* pals 25 years later in this slight comedy that has fabulously rich Thalia Menninger coming back to town to urge high school beau Dobie to dump loving wife Zelda for her. Many from the original series returned at producer/

star (and CBS executive) Hickman's behest, with Connie Stevens coming aboard as Thalia (Tuesday Weld's original role), along with Connie's (and Eddie Fisher's) daughter, Tricia. Average.

Bring on the Girls (1945) **C-92m.** ** D: Sidney Lanfield. Veronica Lake, Sonny Tufts, Eddie Bracken, Marjorie Reynolds, Alan Mowbray, Grant Mitchell, Frank Faylen, Huntz Hall. Wealthy Bracken is unable to find a girl who isn't a golddigger, so he joins the Navy. Slight comedy, with music; best are numbers by dancer Johnny Coy and Spike Jones and his City Slickers. That's Yvonne De Carlo as the hatcheck girl.

Bring on the Night (1985-British) **C-97m.** *** D: Michael Apted. Sting, Omar Hakim, Darryl Jones, Kenny Kirkland, Branford Marsalis, Dolette McDonald, Janice Pendarvis, Trudie Styler, Miles Copeland. First-rate musical documentary about the formation of Sting's rock-jazz band, culminating in their first concert performance (performing the serious, often politically oriented material on the *Dream of the Blue Turtles* album). More than just a concert movie, thanks in large part to director Apted. Handsomely photographed by Ralf Bode. ▼

Bring Your Smile Along (1955) **C-83m.** ** D: Blake Edwards. Frankie Laine, Keefe Brasselle, Constance Towers, Lucy Marlow, William Leslie, Jack Albertson. Thin musical comedy of schoolteacher/songwriter Towers coming to N.Y.C. and hooking up with Brasselle both professionally and romantically. Laine records their songs, and he perks up the proceedings. This was Edwards' directing debut; he also wrote the script.

Brink of Life (1958-Swedish) **84m.** **½ D: Ingmar Bergman. Eva Dahlbeck, Ingrid Thulin, Bibi Andersson, Barbro Hiort af Ornas, Erland Josephson, Max von Sydow, Gunnar Sjoberg. Realistic, almost documentary-like chronicle of the lives of three women in a maternity ward. Meticulously filmed, but also gloomy and static; one of Bergman's lesser efforts.▼

Brink's Job, The (1978) **C-103m.** *** D: William Friedkin. Peter Falk, Peter Boyle, Allen Goorwitz (Garfield), Warren Oates, Gena Rowlands, Paul Sorvino, Sheldon Leonard. Entertaining, comically oriented account of the infamous 1950 Boston heist, masterminded by Falk and motley gang of accomplices. Excellent period and location flavor.▼

Brinks: The Great Robbery (1976) **C-100m. TVM** D: Marvin Chomsky. Carl Betz, Stephen Collins, Burr DeBenning, Michael Gazzo, Cliff Gorman, Darren McGavin, Art Metrano, Leslie Nielsen, Jenny O'Hara. Legendary Boston Brinks' holdup of January 17, 1950, is meticulously restaged, masterminded by McGavin and Gorman, and judged the perfect crime until solved by the FBI. Average.

Britannia Hospital (1982-British) **C-115m.** **½ D: Lindsay Anderson. Leonard Rossiter, Graham Crowden, Malcolm McDowell, Joan Plowright, Jill Bennett, Marsha Hunt, Frank Grimes, Roland Culver, Fulton Mackay, Vivian Pickles, Mark Hamill, Liz Smith, Alan Bates, Arthur Lowe. Absurdist comedy about a hospital beleaguered by labor woes, protest groups, impatient patients, a resident mad doctor, and an impending visit by the Queen Mother. Heavy-handed satire, but entertaining nonetheless, with some actors in continuing roles from Anderson's IF . . . and O LUCKY MAN!▼

Britannia Mews SEE: **Forbidden Street, The**

British Agent (1934) **81m.** *½ D: Michael Curtiz. Kay Francis, Leslie Howard, William Gargan, Philip Reed, J. Carrol Naish, Cesar Romero. British diplomat Howard falls for staunch Soviet Francis in 1917 Russia; a trite script sinks this turkey, which tries to combine romance and international intrigue.

British Intelligence (1940) **62m.** ** D: Terry Morse. Boris Karloff, Margaret Lindsay, Maris Wrixon, Holmes Herbert, Leonard Mudie, Bruce Lester. American nonsense about double-agent Lindsay encountering butler-spy Karloff in British official's home; far-fetched story. Remake of THREE FACES EAST (1930).▼

Broadcast News (1987) **C-131m.** *** D: James L. Brooks. William Hurt, Albert Brooks, Holly Hunter, Robert Prosky, Lois Chiles, Joan Cusack, Peter Hackes, Jack Nicholson. Appealing and intelligent comedy about a highly charged, neurotic woman who's a successful TV news producer, and her attraction to a pretty-boy anchorman who joins her network—and represents everything she hates about TV news. All three stars are fine, but Brooks is a special standout as an ace reporter, and Hunter's best friend, who's really in love with her. Nicholson (who won an Oscar for director Brooks' TERMS OF ENDEARMENT) contributes a funny unbilled performance as the network's star anchorman. Written by the director; set and filmed in Washington, D.C.▼

Broadminded (1931) **72m.** **½ D: Mervyn LeRoy. Joe E. Brown, William Collier, Jr., Margaret Livingston, Thelma Todd, Bela Lugosi, Ona Munson, Holmes Herbert. Pleasant Brown comedy with added spice of lovely Todd and hilarious cameo by Lugosi as man whose hot dog was stolen.

Broadway (1942) **91m.** *** D: William A. Seiter. George Raft, Pat O'Brien, Janet Blair, Broderick Crawford, Marjorie Rambeau, S.Z. Sakall. Raft recalls his days as a nightclub hoofer in this Prohibition era yarn (remake of 1929 film), full of colorful characters and incidents but not made with an eye toward believability. O'Brien is tough copper, Crawford a ruthless gangster.

Broadway Bad (1933) **61m.** **½ D: Sidney Lanfield. Joan Blondell, Ricardo Cortez, Ginger Rogers, Adrienne Ames. Chorus girl Blondell is unjustly maligned by husband, decides to milk bad publicity for all it's worth. A 1930s soap given first-class treatment.

Broadway Danny Rose (1984) **86m.** *** D: Woody Allen. Woody Allen, Mia Farrow, Nick Apollo Forte, Sandy Baron, Corbett Monica, Morty Gunty, Will Jordan, Milton Berle, Joe Franklin. Allen is wonderful as pathetic small-time manager who tries to boost career of over-the-hill singer Forte. Terrific casting, funny show-biz jokes but eventually wears a bit thin; a slight but amusing film.▼

Broadway Gondolier (1935) **98m.** **½ D: Lloyd Bacon. Dick Powell, Joan Blondell, Adolphe Menjou, Louise Fazenda, William Gargan, Grant Mitchell. Powell goes globetrotting so he'll be discovered by famous producer. Songs include: "Lulu's Back in Town."

Broadway Limited (1941) **74m.** ** D: Gordon Douglas. Dennis O'Keefe, Victor McLaglen, Marjorie Woodworth, ZaSu Pitts, Patsy Kelly, George E. Stone, Leonid Kinsky. Considering cast, a big disappointment, though innocuous entertainment: florid director Kinsky makes his new star (Woodworth) the center of publicity stunt that backfires.

Broadway Melody (1929) **104m.** **½ D: Harry Beaumont. Bessie Love, Anita Page, Charles King, Jed Prouty, Kenneth Thomson, Edward Dillon, Mary Doran. Early talkie musical curio about a pair of stage-struck sisters who seek fame on the Great White Way and fall for a charming song-and-dance man. This was the first musical to win a Best Picture Academy Award. Awfully dated today, but there's still a good score by Arthur Freed and Nacio Herb Brown: Title tune, "You Were Meant for Me," and "The Wedding of the Painted Doll." Some sequences originally in Technicolor; remade as TWO GIRLS ON BROADWAY.▼

Broadway Melody of 1936 (1935) **110m.** *** D: Roy Del Ruth. Jack Benny, Eleanor Powell, Robert Taylor, Una Merkel, Sid Silvers, Buddy Ebsen. Pleasant musicomedy with Winchell-like columnist Benny trying to frame producer Taylor via dancer Powell, whose solo spots are pure delight. Arthur Freed-Nacio Herb Brown songs: "You Are My Lucky Star," "Broadway Rhythm," "I've Got A Feelin' You're

Foolin,' " (which earned an Oscar for Dave Gould's dance direction).

Broadway Melody of 1938 (1937) 110m. **½ D: Roy Del Ruth. Robert Taylor, Eleanor Powell, Judy Garland, Sophie Tucker, Binnie Barnes, Buddy Ebsen, Billy Gilbert, Raymond Walburn. Not up to 1936 MELODY, with tuneful but forgettable songs, overbearing Tucker, and elephantine finale. Powell's dancing is great and Garland sings "Dear Mr. Gable."▼

Broadway Melody of 1940 (1940) 102m. *** D: Norman Taurog. Fred Astaire, George Murphy, Eleanor Powell, Frank Morgan, Ian Hunter, Florence Rice. Friendship and rivalry between dance partners Astaire and Murphy sparks this delightful, underrated MGM musical, with hilarious vignettes, fine performance from Astaire, outstanding Cole Porter songs, and matchless Astaire-Powell numbers like "Begin the Beguine." If only they'd tie up the plot a bit sooner.▼

Broadway Musketeers (1938) 62m. **½ D: John Farrow. Margaret Lindsay, Ann Sheridan, Marie Wilson, John Litel, Janet Chapman. Snappy, well-made B remake of THREE ON A MATCH is still interesting tale of three girls who grew up together in an orphanage and whose lives converge years later on Broadway.

Broadway Rhythm (1944) C-114m. ** D: Roy Del Ruth. George Murphy, Ginny Simms, Charles Winninger, Gloria De Haven, Nancy Walker, Ben Blue, Tommy Dorsey and Orch. Tedious, overlong MGM musical with plot (ex-vaudevillian Winninger at odds with producer-son Murphy) getting in the way of some good songs like "Amor," "All the Things You Are."

Broadway Serenade (1939) 114m. ** D: Robert Z. Leonard. Jeanette MacDonald, Lew Ayres, Ian Hunter, Frank Morgan, Rita Johnson, Virginia Grey, William Gargan, Katharine Alexander. Mediocre musical of songwriter Ayres and wife, singer MacDonald, having careers split up their marriage.

Broadway to Hollywood (1933) 85m. ** D: Willard Mack. Alice Brady, Frank Morgan, Jackie Cooper, Russell Hardie, Madge Evans, Mickey Rooney, Eddie Quillan. Three generations of show business (Cooper grows up to be Hardie, whose son, Rooney, grows up to be Quillan) in a story that's for the birds—but the acting is good, and some of the production numbers (lifted from MGM's famous 1930 extravaganza THE MARCH OF TIME) are interesting to see.

Brock's Last Case (1972) C-100m. TVM D: David Lowell Rich. Richard Widmark, Henry Darrow, Beth Brickell, David Huddleston, Will Geer, John Anderson, Michael Burns. N.Y.C. policeman disenchanted with big city life relocates in small town looking for peace and quiet but finds himself in same predicament. Decent premise doesn't work out. Average.

Broken Angel (1988) C-100m. TVM D: Richard T. Heffron. William Shatner, Susan Blakely, Roxann Biggs, Millie Perkins, Brock Peters, Erika Eleniak, Collin Davis. Undistinguished thriller has Shatner trekking through Southern California looking for his daughter, who has vanished after a gang shootout. Not too dissimilar from Brian Dennehy's quest in Germany in an earlier effort, A FATHER'S REVENGE. Below average.

Broken Arrow (1950) C-93m. *** D: Delmer Daves. James Stewart, Jeff Chandler, Debra Paget, Will Geer, Jay Silverheels. Authentic study of 1870s Apache Chief Cochise (Chandler) and ex-Army man (Stewart) trying to seek accord between feuding redskins and whites. Flavorful and effective; good action sequences. Chandler played Cochise again in THE BATTLE AT APACHE PASS. Later a TV series.▼

Broken Blossoms (1919) 95m. *** D: ✓ D. W. Griffith. Lillian Gish, Richard Barthelmess, Donald Crisp, Arthur Howard, Edward Piel. Dated but lovely film of Chinaman Barthelmess protecting frail Gish from clutches of evil Crisp; still creates a mood sustained by sensitive performances. One of Griffith's more modest, and more successful, films. Remade in England in 1936.▼

Broken Lance (1954) C-96m. ***½ D: Edward Dmytryk. Spencer Tracy, Robert Wagner, Jean Peters, Richard Widmark, Katy Jurado, Hugh O'Brian, Eduard Franz, Earl Holliman, E.G. Marshall. Tracy is superlative in tight-knit script (by Richard Murphy, from an Oscar-winning Philip Yordan story) about patriarchal rancher who finds he's losing control of his cattle empire and his family is fragmenting into warring factions. Remake of HOUSE OF STRANGERS (although it owes more to *King Lear!*).▼

Broken Land, The (1962) C-60m. ** D: John Bushelman. Kent Taylor, Dianna Darrin, Jody McCrea, Robert Sampson, Jack Nicholson, Gary Snead. Routine low-budget Western about a sadistic sheriff (Taylor) who browbeats just about everybody, including his deputy (McCrea) and the harmless son (Nicholson) of a notorious gunman.

Broken Lullaby (1932) 77m. *** D: Ernst Lubitsch. Lionel Barrymore, Nancy Carroll, Phillips Holmes, ZaSu Pitts, Lucien Littlefield, Emma Dunn. Excellent drama of French soldier who feels guilty for killing German during war, then falls in love with dead man's sweetheart. Retitled: THE MAN I KILLED.

Broken Promise (1981) **C-100m. TVM**
D: Don Taylor. Chris Sarandon, Melissa
Michaelsen, George Coe, McKee Anderson, David Haskell, Sondra West, Marc
Alaimo. Juvenile-court officer tries to cut
through red tape to keep five abandoned
children together as a family. Stephen
Kandel's script was based on a book by
Kent Hayes and Alex Lazzarino, which
dramatizes the plight of neglected children
in the foster-care system. Average.

Broken Rainbow (1985) **C/B&W-70m.**
*** D: Maria Florio, Victoria Mudd. Narrator: Martin Sheen. Historical voices: Burgess Meredith. Translator: Buffy Sainte-
Marie. Touching, biting, appropriately one-
sided, yet sometimes unnecessarily romanticized documentary about the relocation—
and resistance—of Navajo indians in Arizona. A Best Documentary Academy
Award-winner.

Broken Sky (1982-Swedish) **C-96m.** **½
D: Ingrid Thulin. Susanna Kall, Thommy
Berggren, Agneta Eckemyr, Margarethe
Krook. Ambitious but uneven account of
13-year-old Kall, in the process of breaking free from her childhood, and her relationships with various family members.
Thulin also wrote the script.

Broken Vows (1987) **C-100m. TVM** D:
Jud Taylor. Tommy Lee Jones, Annette
O'Toole, M. Emmet Walsh, Milo O'Shea,
David Groh, Madeleine Sherwood. A parish priest becomes involved with a murder
victim's girlfriend and is forced to question his vows of celibacy. Often confusing
adaptation of Dorothy Salisbury Davis'
mystery *Where the Dark Streets Go* by the
estimable James Costigan (who had his
name removed from the credits in favor of
the pseudonymous Ivan Davis). Average.

Bronco Billy (1980) **C-119m.** *** D: Clint
Eastwood. Clint Eastwood, Sondra Locke,
Geoffrey Lewis, Scatman Crothers, Bill
McKinney, Sam Bottoms, Dan Vadis, Sierra Pecheur. Enjoyable yarn about self-
styled cowboy hero who runs a fly-by-night
Wild West show and the spoiled heiress
who joins his entourage of escapees from
reality. Locke's rich-bitch character is a
bit hard to take, but neither she nor some
superfluous subplots can sour the charm of
this film.▼

Bronco Buster (1952) **C-81m.** **½ D:
Budd Boetticher. John Lund, Scott Brady,
Joyce Holden, Chill Wills, Casey Tibbs.
Minor story of rodeo star Lund helping
Brady learn the ropes, but forced to
fight him for Holden's love. Good rodeo
action.

Bronk (1975) **C-74m. TVM** D: Richard
Donner. Jack Palance, Henry Beckman,
Tony King, David Birney, Joseph Mascolo,
Joanna Moore, Dina Ousley, Chelsea
Brown. Honest cop Palance takes on mobsters and corrupt officials after accidental
death of partner during narcotics investigation. Palance plays Clint Eastwood in this
OK actioner. Pilot for the TV series, partially conceived by Carroll O'Connor.
Average.

Brontë (1983-Irish-U.S.) **C-88m.** *** D:
Delbert Mann. Julie Harris. Engrossing
performance by Harris portraying Charlotte Brontë in one-woman show recounting her life and family troubles via intimate,
first-person monologues. Unusual, literate
film benefits from all-location filming in
Ireland. Scripted by William Luce from
his radio play based on Brontë's own
writings.

Brontë Sisters, The (1979-French) **C-
115m.** **½ D: Andre Techine. Isabelle
Adjani, Marie-France Pisier, Isabelle
Huppert, Pascal Gregory, Patrick Magee.
Well-mounted but slightly sluggish portrait of the famous literary sisters and their
repressed lives. Worth watching mainly to
see three of France's most appealing actresses in one film. Also shot in English-
language version, which doesn't play as
well.

Brood, The (1979-Canadian) **C-90m.**
BOMB D: David Cronenberg. Oliver Reed,
Samantha Eggar, Art Hindle, Cindy Hinds,
Nuala Fitzgerald, Susan Hogan. Eggar eats
her own afterbirth while midget clones
beat grandparents and lovely young schoolteachers to death with mallets. It's a big,
wide, wonderful world we live in!▼

Brother, Can You Spare a Dime? (1975)
103m. **½ D: Philippe Mora. Documentary on 1930s has fuzzy point of view, and
no narration to tie footage together; it also
mixes newsreels and Hollywood clips. If
you know and like the period, the footage
will speak for itself and provide a certain
measure of entertainment.▼

Brother from Another Planet, The (1984)
C-104m. *** D: John Sayles. Joe Morton,
Darryl Edwards, Steve James, Leonard
Jackson, Maggie Renzi, Rosette Le Noire,
David Straithairn. Amiable, ingenious contemporary fantasy, filmed on a shoestring,
about a black visitor from another planet
who (like Chance in BEING THERE) impresses most of the people he meets because he doesn't say a word—and lets
them do all the talking! Falls apart toward
the end with a subplot about undoing some
drug dealers; but still worthwhile. Full of
fine dialogue by writer-director Sayles,
who, as usual, gives himself a funny role
(as one of the Brother's outer-space pursuers). ▼

Brotherhood, The (1968) **C-98m.** *** D:
Martin Ritt. Kirk Douglas, Alex Cord,
Irene Papas, Luther Adler, Susan Strasberg,
Murray Hamilton. Excellent story of Mafia
in changing times; tradition-bound Douglas clashes with younger brother Cord
who feels no ties to old-fashioned dic-

tates. Pre-GODFATHER, but in the same league.▼

Brotherhood of Justice (1986) **C-100m.** **TVM** D: Charles Braverman. Keanu Reeves, Lori Loughlin, Kiefer Sutherland, Joe Spano, Darren Dalton, Evan Mirand, Don Michael Paul. Vigilante society made up of teenaged high achievers is sent forth by the high school principal in this violence-for-violence-sake pilot. If you ever wondered what would happen if *Head of the Class* met *The Mod Squad*, this is your lucky day. Below average.▼

Brotherhood of Satan (1971) **C-92m.** **½ D: Bernard McEveety. Strother Martin, L. Q. Jones, Charles Bateman, Ahna Capri, Charles Robinson. Witches' coven takes over town in this horrifying little terror tale.▼

Brotherhood of the Bell, The (1970) **C-100m. TVM** D: Paul Wendkos. Glenn Ford, Rosemary Forsyth, Dean Jagger, Maurice Evans, William Conrad, Will Geer, Dabney Coleman. Ambitious but hollow story of Ford (in his TV dramatic debut) determined to investigate strange secret fraternity which is bigger and more powerful than he'd imagined. Average.

Brotherhood of the Rose (1989) **C-200m. TVM** D: Marvin J. Chomsky. Peter Strauss, Robert Mitchum, Connie Sellecca, David Morse, James B. Sikking, M. Emmet Walsh. Spies, counterspies, CIA moles and assorted international assassins lurk around every corner in this woefully overlong, nearly incomprehensible espionage tale adapted from David Morrell's book. Although almost every scene occurs in a different country, the entire mishmash was filmed in New Zealand. Originally shown in two parts. Below average.

Brotherhood of the Yakuza SEE: **Yakuza, The**▼

Brother John (1972) **C-94m.** *** D: James Goldstone. Sidney Poitier, Will Geer, Bradford Dillman, Beverly Todd, Paul Winfield. Highly entertaining tale of the Messiah's return—only no one knows that he's come, and that he's black.▼

Brotherly Love (1969-British) **C-112m.** *** D: J. Lee Thompson. Peter O'Toole, Susannah York, Michael Craig, Harry Andrews, Cyril Cusack, Judy Cornwell, Brian Blessed. Very funny study of strange relationships in upper-class British household. O'Toole and York are delightful. Original British title: COUNTRY DANCE.

Brotherly Love (1985) **C-100m. TVM** D: Jeff Bleckner. Judd Hirsch, Karen Carlson, George Dzundza, Barry Primus, Anthony Carnota, Ron Karabatsos, Lori Lethin. Successful businessman finds himself stalked by his murderous identical twin brother. Despite the estimable Ernest Tidyman's name on the script (adapted from William Blankenship's novel), this one has all the

earmarks of a bad "B" thriller from the '30s. Below average.▼

Brother Orchid (1940) **91m.** *** D: Lloyd Bacon. Edward G. Robinson, Ann Sothern, Humphrey Bogart, Ralph Bellamy, Donald Crisp, Allen Jenkins. Farfetched but entertaining yarn of racketeer Robinson who seeks "the real class" in life. Sothern delightful as his ever-faithful girlfriend.

Brother Rat (1938) **90m.** *** D: William Keighley. Priscilla Lane, Wayne Morris, Johnnie Davis, Jane Bryan, Eddie Albert, Ronald Reagan, Jane Wyman, William Tracy. Comedy of three pals at Virginia Military Institute isn't as fresh as it was in the 1930s, but still remains entertaining, with enthusiastic performances by all. Sequel: BROTHER RAT AND A BABY. Remade as ABOUT FACE.

Brother Rat and a Baby (1940) **87m.** **½ D: Ray Enright. Priscilla Lane, Wayne Morris, Eddie Albert, Jane Bryan, Ronald Reagan, Jane Wyman. Sassy follow-up to BROTHER RAT is not the same success, but still fun with three comrades graduating military school.

Brothers (1977) **C-104m.** **½ D: Arthur Barron. Bernie Casey, Vonetta McGee, Ron O'Neal, Renny Roker, Stu Gilliam, John Lehne. Well-intentioned story based on relationship between militant professor Angela Davis and literate black convict George Jackson during 1960s. Sloppy filmmaking and awkward scripting diminish impact of film's better moments.

Brothers in Arms (1989) **C-94m.** *½ D: George Jay Bloom III. Todd Allen, Charles Grant, Jack Starrett, Dedee Pfeiffer, Mitch Pileggi, Dan Bell, Shannon Norfleet. Uninteresting variation on DELIVERANCE pits estranged brothers against family of murderous religious fanatics in modern-day Rockies. Competent but unpleasant, and it goes on and on and on.▼

Brothers in Law, The (1957-British) **94m.** **½ D: Roy Boulting. Richard Attenborough, Ian Carmichael, Terry-Thomas, Jill Adams, Miles Malleson, Raymond Huntley. Misadventures of a young lawyer (Carmichael) fill this amiable British comedy.▼

Brothers-in-Law (1985) **C-75m. TVM.** D: E. W. Swackhamer. Mac Davis, Joe Cortese, Robert Culp, John Saxon, Daphne Ashbrook, Gerald S. O'Loughlin. Antagonistic brothers-in-law—a highway patrolman and a trucker—versus evil powermongers in this prospective pilot focusing on two guys who simply can't stand one another. Below average.▼

Brothers Karamazov, The (1958) **C-146m.** *** D: Richard Brooks. Yul Brynner, Maria Schell, Claire Bloom, Lee J. Cobb, Richard Basehart, William Shatner,

Albert Salmi. Set in 19th-century Russia, film version of Dostoyevsky's tragedy revolving about death of a dominating father (Cobb) and effect on his sons: fun-seeking Brynner, scholarly Basehart, religious Shatner, and epileptic Salmi. Exceptionally well-scripted by Brooks. William Shatner's first film.▼

Brothers O'Toole, The (1973) C-90m. ** D: Richard Erdman. John Astin, Steve Carlson, Pat Carroll, Hans Conried, Lee Meriwether, Allyn Joslyn, Jesse White. Strictly for the kids is this comedy Western. Actor turned director Erdman has a bit.▼

Brothers Rico, The (1957) 92m. **½ D: Phil Karlson. Richard Conte, Dianne Foster, Kathryn Grant, Larry Gates, James Darren. Incisive gangster yarn; Conte comes to N.Y.C. to counteract nationwide criminal gang's plot to eliminate his two brothers. Based on Georges Simenon novel, remade for TV as THE FAMILY RICO.

Brother Sun, Sister Moon (1973-Italian-British) C-121m. **½ D: Franco Zeffirelli. Graham Faulkner, Judi Bowker, Leigh Lawson, Alec Guinness, Valentina Cortese, Kenneth Cranham. Zeffirelli's wide-eyed youth-oriented slant on Francis of Assisi story runs hot and cold; some delicate, lovely scenes, but other ideas don't always come across. Songs by Donovan.▼

Broth of a Boy (1959-Irish) 77m. **½ D: George Pollock. Barry Fitzgerald, Harry Brogan, Tony Wright, June Thorburn, Eddie Golden. British TV producer hits upon scheme of filming birthday celebration of oldest man in the world, Irish villager Fitzgerald. The latter's battle to get cut of the pie is vehicle for study of human nature; quietly effective.▼

Browning Version, The (1951-British) 90m. ***½ D: Anthony Asquith. Michael Redgrave, Jean Kent, Nigel Patrick, Wilfrid Hyde-White, Ronald Howard, Bill Travers. Redgrave is superb as middle-aged boarding schoolteacher who realizes he's a failure, with an unfaithful wife and a new teaching position he doesn't want. Cast does full justice to Rattigan's play.

Brubaker (1980) C-132m. **½ D: Stuart Rosenberg. Robert Redford, Yaphet Kotto, Jane Alexander, Murray Hamilton, David Keith, Morgan Freeman, Matt Clark, Tim McIntire, Linda Haynes, M. Emmet Walsh, Richard Ward, Albert Salmi, John McMartin, Wilford Brimley. Earnest but predictable prison drama based on true story of reform-minded warden who dares to uncover skeletons in corrupt Southern prison system.▼

Brute Force (1947) 98m. ***½ D: Jules Dassin. Burt Lancaster, Hume Cronyn, Charles Bickford, Yvonne De Carlo, Ann Blyth, Ella Raines, Howard Duff, Whit Bissell, Jeff Corey, Sam Levene. Tingling,

hard-bitten prison film with its few cliches punched across solidly. Brutal captain Cronyn is utterly despicable, but you *know* he's going to get it in the end.

Brute Man (1946) 60m. *½ D: Jean Yarbrough. Tom Neal, Rondo Hatton, Jane Adams, Peter Whitney, Jan Wiley. Loosely based on star Hatton's own tragic life (he was handsome as a youth, became disfigured by acromegaly), this deals with a disfigured man who becomes a mad killer.▼

B.S. I Love You (1971) C-99m. *½ D: Steven Hillard Stern. Peter Kastner, Joanna Cameron, Louise Sorel, Gary Burghoff, Richard B. Shull, Joanna Barnes. Stale "youth" comedy about young ad-man who makes it with both mother and daughter is only for those who haven't seen THE GRADUATE or YOU'RE A BIG BOY NOW.

Bubble, The SEE: **Fantastic Invasion of Planet Earth**

Buccaneer, The (1938) 124m. *** D: Cecil B. DeMille. Fredric March, Franciska Gaal, Margot Grahame, Akim Tamiroff, Walter Brennan, Anthony Quinn. Typically entertaining epic-scale saga from DeMille, with florid performance by March as pirate-hero Jean Lafitte, who aids American cause during War of 1812. Good storytelling, and good fun. Remade in 1958.

Buccaneer, The (1958) C-121m. *** D: Anthony Quinn. Yul Brynner, Charlton Heston, Claire Bloom, Charles Boyer, Inger Stevens, Henry Hull, E.G. Marshall, Lorne Greene, Fran Jeffries, Woodrow (Woody) Strode. Starchy swashbuckler retelling events during War of 1812 when Andrew Jackson (Heston) is forced to rely on buccaneer Lafitte (Brynner) to stem the British invasion; action is spotty but splashy. Quinn's only film as director; executive produced by his then-father-in-law Cecil B. DeMille, who directed the 1938 original, and whose last film this was.▼

Buccaneer's Girl (1950) C-77m. ** D: Frederick de Cordova. Yvonne De Carlo, Philip Friend, Elsa Lanchester, Andrea King, Henry Daniell. Pure escapism with De Carlo cavorting as New Orleans singer and later leading forces to free pirate-friend from prison.

Buchanan Rides Alone (1958) C-78m. *** D: Budd Boetticher. Randolph Scott, Craig Stevens, Barry Kelley, Tol Avery, Peter Whitney, Manuel Rojas. Scott runs afoul of corrupt family in control of border town; taut B Western never runs out of plot twists.

Buck and the Preacher (1972) C-102m. ✓ **½ D: Sidney Poitier. Sidney Poitier, Harry Belafonte, Ruby Dee, Cameron Mitchell, Nita Talbot. Black-oriented Western of "hustler" preacher is long on getting to the action and short on staying with it. Good characterizations are major point of interest. Music by Benny Carter. Poitier's directorial debut.▼

Buckaroo Banzai SEE: **Adventures of Buckaroo Banzai Across the Eighth Dimension, The**▼

Buck Benny Rides Again (1940) 82m. *** D: Mark Sandrich. Jack Benny, Ellen Drew, Andy Devine, Phil Harris, Virginia Dale, Dennis Day, Eddie "Rochester" Anderson. Amusing Western spoof with Jack trying to convince Drew that he's a 100% cowboy. Radio colleagues help out, with Rochester supplying steady flow of funny dialogue.

Bucket of Blood, A (1959) 66m. *** D: Roger Corman. Dick Miller, Barboura Morris, Antony Carbone, Julian Burton, Ed Nelson, Bert Convy. Wimpy busboy impresses his coffeehouse betters with amazingly lifelike "sculptures." Writer Charles Griffith's predecessor to THE LITTLE SHOP OF HORRORS is nifty semi-spoof of dead-bodies-in-the-wax-museum genre. Nicely captures spirit of beatnik era; cult actor Miller's finest hour (he's reused his character's name, Walter Paisley, several times since).▼

✓ **Buck Privates** (1941) 84m. **½ D: Arthur Lubin. Bud Abbott, Lou Costello, Lee Bowman, Alan Curtis, Andrews Sisters, Jane Frazee, Nat Pendleton. Dated but engaging Army opus with Bud and Lou accidentally enlisting. Brassy songs (including Andrews Sisters' "Boogie Woogie Bugle Boy") and subplots get in the way, but A&C's routines are among their best; their first starring film.▼

Buck Privates Come Home (1947) 77m. *** D: Charles Barton. Bud Abbott, Lou Costello, Tom Brown, Joan Fulton (Shawlee), Nat Pendleton, Beverly Simmons, Don Beddoe. One of A&C's most enjoyable romps has boys returning to civilian life and trying to smuggle a young European orphan into this country. Climactic chase a highlight.

Buck Rogers SEE: **Destination Saturn**▼

Buck Rogers in the 25th Century (1979) C-89m. ** D: Daniel Haller. Gil Gerard, Pamela Hensley, Erin Gray, Tim O'Connor, Henry Silva, Joseph Wiseman, Felix Silla, voice of Mel Blanc. The legendary space hero returns, decked out in contemporary glibness, trying to prove he's not in league with intergalactic pirates. Much of the hardware and gadgetry (along with some footage) is from TV's expensive dud, BATTLESTAR GALACTICA, turned out by the same producers. Pilot for the TV series; released theatrically first.▼

Buckskin (1968) C-97m. *½ D: Michael Moore. Barry Sullivan, Joan Caulfield, Wendell Corey, Lon Chaney, John Russell, Barbara Hale, Barton MacLane, Leo Gordon. Land-baron Corey tries to force homesteaders

out of territory, but Marshal Sullivan is there to stop him in typical Western.

Buckskin Frontier (1943) 74m. ** D: Lesley Selander. Richard Dix, Jane Wyatt, Albert Dekker, Lee J. Cobb, Victor Jory, Lola Lane, Max Baer, Joe Sawyer, George Reeves. Unusual cast adds interest to this otherwise standard Western about railroad man Dix and his conflicts with proud Cobb (who fears for the demise of his freight company) and slimy Jory. Cobb, who's exactly the same age as Wyatt, is cast here as her father!▼

Bucktown (1975) C-94m. *½ D: Arthur Marks. Fred Williamson, Pam Grier, Thalmus Rasulala, Tony King, Bernie Hamilton, Art Lund. Repellent blaxploitation picture about war between whites and blacks in corruption-filled Southern town, which intensifies when blacks get into office and make things even worse.▼

Bud Abbott and Lou Costello in Hollywood SEE: **Abbott and Costello in Hollywood**▼

Bud and Lou (1978) C-100m. TVM D: Robert C. Thompson. Harvey Korman, Buddy Hackett, Michele Lee, Arte Johnson, Robert Reed. Major intent of this hackneyed biopic on Abbott and Costello is portraying Lou as an s.o.b., but its fatal flaw is Hackett and Korman's painfully unfunny renderings of classic A&C routines. Below average.▼

Buddy Buddy (1981) C-96m. *** D: Billy Wilder. Jack Lemmon, Walter Matthau, Paula Prentiss, Klaus Kinski, Dana Elcar, Miles Chapin, Joan Shawlee. Modest little black comedy about a hit-man whose current job is mucked up by an intrusive stranger. A simple farce, played to perfection by Lemmon and Matthau, adapted by Wilder and I.A.L. Diamond from the French film A PAIN IN THE A——.▼

Buddy Holly Story, The (1978) C-113m. ***½ D: Steve Rash. Gary Busey, Charles Martin Smith, Don Stroud, Maria Richwine, Amy Johnston, Conrad Janis, Dick O'Neill, William Jordan, Will Jordan (they're different actors), Fred Travalena, "Stymie" Beard. Busey gives an electrifying performance as the rock 'n' roll legend in this long but very satisfying musical drama, not quite the usual glossy Hollywood biography. Busey, Smith and Stroud sing and play "live," giving an extra dimension to Holly's hit songs; Joe Renzetti won an Oscar for Score Adaptation.▼

Buddy System, The (1984) C-110m. **½ D: Glenn Jordan. Richard Dreyfuss, Susan Sarandon, Nancy Allen, Jean Stapleton, Wil Wheaton, Edward Winter, Keene Curtis. Lonely kid (Wheaton) tries to play matchmaker between his single mom (Sarandon) and a grown-up friend, would-be novelist and gadget inventor Dreyfuss, but there are emotional complications. Nicely played but overly familiar (and overlong) romantic comedy.▼

Buffalo Bill (1944) **C-90m.** **½ D: William Wellman. Joel McCrea, Maureen O'Hara, Linda Darnell, Thomas Mitchell, Anthony Quinn, Edgar Buchanan, Chief Thundercloud, Sidney Blackmer. Colorful biography of legendary Westerner should have been much better, but still provides some fun and has good cast.▼

Buffalo Bill and the Indians, or Sitting Bull's History Lesson (1976) **C-120m.** ** D: Robert Altman. Paul Newman, Joel Grey, Kevin McCarthy, Burt Lancaster, Geraldine Chaplin, Harvey Keitel, Frank Kaquitts, Will Sampson. Altman makes the point that Buffalo Bill was a flamboyant fraud, then belabors it for two hours. Not without interest, but still one of the director's duller movies.▼

Buffet Froid (1979-French) **C-95m.** ***½ D: Bertrand Blier. Gerard Depardieu, Bernard Blier, Jean Carmet, Genevieve Page, Denise Gence, Carole Bouquet, Jean Benguigui, Michel Serrault. Strange, surreal, outrageously funny black comedy detailing the misadventures of hapless murderers Depardieu, Carmet, and Blier (the director's father). Brilliantly acted and directed; a treat.▼

Bug (1975) **C-100m.** ** D: Jeannot Szwarc. Bradford Dillman, Joanna Miles, Richard Gilliland, Jamie Smith Jackson, Alan Fudge, Patricia McCormack, Jesse Vint. Earthquake releases a disgusting variety of beetle from the earth, capable of setting people, animals, and objects on fire. Spray your set with Raid after watching this one. Produced by William Castle, whose last film this was.▼

Bugles in the Afternoon (1952) **C-85m.** **½ D: Roy Rowland. Ray Milland, Forrest Tucker, George Reeves, Helena Carter, Gertrude Michael. Standard tale of man branded coward (Milland) during Civil War, with Little Big Horn finale.▼

Bugle Sounds, The (1941) **101m.** ** D: S. Sylvan Simon. Wallace Beery, Marjorie Main, Lewis Stone, George Bancroft, Henry O'Neill, Donna Reed. Old-time sergeant Beery objects to progress in the army, bails cavalry out of trouble in finale. The usual.

Bugs Bunny/Road Runner Movie, The (1979) **C-92m.** **½ D: Chuck Jones, Phil Monroe. Bugs Bunny, Daffy Duck, Road Runner, Wile E. Coyote, Elmer Fudd, Porky Pig, Pepe LePew. New footage of Bugs Bunny surrounds this compilation of some of Chuck Jones' best Warner Bros. cartoon shorts. Not the best way to see these wonderful films, as the repetition grows tiresome, but still worthwhile. First shown in theaters as THE GREAT AMERICAN CHASE. Cut to 78m. for pay TV, and 48m. for network TV. Followed by THE LOONEY, LOONEY, LOONEY BUGS BUNNY MOVIE.▼

Bugs Bunny's 3rd Movie: 1001 Rabbit Tales (1982) **C-76m.** **½ D: David Detiege, Art Davis, Bill Perez. Yet another compilation of Warner Bros. cartoons, with better-than-average linking material. Some good episodes with Daffy Duck, Tweety and Sylvester, et al., plus Chuck Jones' classic "One Froggy Evening" (minus the punchline), but these are still better seen as individual shorts, and not as an ersatz feature film. Produced by Friz Freleng. Followed by DAFFY DUCK'S MOVIE: FANTASTIC ISLAND.▼

Bugs Bunny Superstar (1975) **C-91m.** *** D: Larry Jackson. Narrated by Orson Welles. Modestly produced compilation of 1940's Warner Bros. cartoons features interviews with the men who created some of the greatest animated films ever made—Bob Clampett, Friz Freleng, and Tex Avery—along with priceless home movies and behind-the-scenes material, as well as nine complete shorts, including A WILD HARE (the first real Bugs Bunny cartoon), CORNY CONCERTO, THE OLD GREY HARE, MY FAVORITE DUCK, and WHAT'S COOKIN' DOC?▼

Bugsy Malone (1976-British) **C-93m.** **½ D: Alan Parker. Scott Baio, Florrie Dugger, Jodie Foster, John Cassisi, Martin Lev. Unique musical spoof of Prohibition-era gangster films with all-kiddie cast; script cliches are intact, but the machine-guns shoot whipped cream instead of bullets. Beautiful production cannot escape coyness and doesn't hold up; plastic rendition of Paul Williams' score doesn't help.▼

Bulldog Drummond Hugh "Bulldog" Drummond, an ex-British army officer who yearned for adventure, was created in 1919 by "Sapper" (Herman Cyril McNeile); the character's film possibilities were realized and Drummond was the subject of several silent films. The definitive BULLDOG DRUMMOND was made in 1929 with dashing Ronald Colman in the lead and Claud Allister as his constant companion Algy; Colman also starred in a delightful sequel, BULLDOG DRUMMOND STRIKES BACK, which unfortunately is not available to TV. No one ever approached Colman's charm—or the wittiness of these first two scripts—in subsequent efforts (though the British spoof called BULLDOG JACK scored a bull's-eye in its own comic way, and other Britishers like Jack Buchanan and Ralph Richardson had a go at the role). The major series was made in the late 1930s by Paramount, with John Howard as Drummond, John Barrymore as Inspector Neilson of Scotland Yard, Reginald Denny as Algy, E.E. Clive as the butler Tenny, and a variety of girls as love interest for Howard. These were brief (around one hour), entertaining mysteries with such formidable villains as J. Carrol Naish, Anthony Quinn, George Zucco, and Eduardo Ciannelli. In the late 1940s Ron Randell and Tom Conway did two Drummonds each, which weren't bad but didn't catch on. The last one was CALLING BULLDOG DRUMMOND, a 1951 film with Walter Pidgeon in the lead and David Tomlinson as Algy; it was an enjoyable, slickly made film; it was only unfortunate that no one saw fit to continue the series beyond this point. (One attempt to revive the character was a flop: DEADLIER THAN THE MALE and SOME GIRLS DO, both with Richard Johnson.) Other older films that still pop up include such Drummonds as John Lodge and Ray Milland doing their bit in unremarkable but entertaining vehicles.

Bulldog Drummond (1929) **89m. D:** F. Richard Jones. Ronald Colman, Joan Bennett, Lilyan Tashman, Montagu Love, Lawrence Grant, Claud Allister.▼

Bulldog Drummond at Bay (1937-British) **62m. D:** Norman Lee. John Lodge, Dorothy Mackaill, Victor Jory, Claud Allister, Hugh Miller, Marie O'Neill, Brian Buchel.

Bulldog Drummond at Bay (1947) **70m.** D: Sidney Salkow. Ron Randell, Anita Louise, Pat O'Moore, Terry Kilburn, Holmes Herbert.

Bulldog Drummond Comes Back (1937) **64m.** D: Louis King. John Barrymore, John Howard, Louise Campbell, Reginald Denny, E. E. Clive, J. Carrol Naish, John Sutton, Helen Freeman.▼

Bulldog Drummond Escapes (1937) **65m.** D: James Hogan. Ray Milland, Guy Standing, Heather Angel, Porter Hall, Reginald Denny, E. E. Clive, Fay Holden, Clyde Cook, Walter Kingsford.▼

Bulldog Drummond in Africa (1938) **60m.** D: Louis King. John Howard, Heather Angel, H. B. Warner, J. Carrol Naish, Reginald Denny, Anthony Quinn, Michael Brooke.▼

Bulldog Drummond's Bride (1939) **55m.** D: James Hogan. John Howard, Heather Angel, H. B. Warner, Reginald Denny, Elizabeth Patterson, Eduardo Ciannelli.▼

Bulldog Drummond's Peril (1938) **66m.** D: James Hogan. John Barrymore, John Howard, Louise Campbell, Reginald Denny, E. E. Clive, Porter Hall, Elizabeth Patterson, Nydia Westman.▼

Bulldog Drummond's Revenge (1937) **60m.** D: Louis King. John Barrymore, John Howard, Louise Campbell, Reginald Denny, E. E. Clive, Nydia Westman, Lucien Littlefield, John Sutton.▼

Bulldog Drummond's Secret Police (1939) **56m.** D: James Hogan. John Howard, Heather Angel, H.B. Warner, Reginald Denny, Leo G. Carroll, Elizabeth Patterson.▼

Bulldog Drummond Strikes Back (1947) **65m. D:** Frank McDonald. Ron Randell, Gloria Henry, Pat O'Moore, Anabel Shaw, Terry Kilburn.

Bulldog Jack (1934-British) **73m. *** D:** Walter Forde. Jack Hulbert, Ralph Richardson, Fay Wray, Claude Hulbertson, Athole Fleming. British comedian Hulbert finds himself taking the place of ailing Bulldog Drummond on a sinister case. Fast and funny with some first-rate suspense as well; memorable climax set in the London underground system. Originally shown in the U.S. as ALIAS BULLDOG DRUMMOND, with all the comedy cut out!▼

Bull Durham (1988) **C-108m. *** D:** Ron Shelton. Kevin Costner, Susan Sarandon, Tim Robbins, Trey Wilson, Robert Wuhl, Jenny Robertson, Max Patkin. Smart, sassy film about minor-league North Carolina baseball team and its attentive, intelligent groupie (Sarandon) who feels it is her mission to live with one young player per season and help him mature. Costner is a hardened young veteran of the game whose job is to help one particular player—cocky, undisciplined, but talented pitcher Robbins. Literate and funny, if a bit sluggish at times, with some seriously sexy scenes near the end.▼

Bullet for a Badman (1964) **C-80m. **½** D: R. G. Springsteen. Audie Murphy, Darren McGavin, Ruta Lee, Skip Homeier, George Tobias, Bob Steele. Another revenge tale involving outlaw, his ex-wife, and a friend who married her.

Bullet for Joey, A (1955) **85m. **½** D: Lewis Allen. Edward G. Robinson, George Raft, Audrey Totter, Peter Van Eyck. Veteran cast improves caper about Communist agent attempting to kidnap U.S. nuclear scientist.

Bullet for Pretty Boy, A (1970) **C-91m. *½** D: Larry Buchanan. Fabian Forte, Jocelyn Lane, Astrid Warner, Michael Haynes. Tough punk (Pretty Boy Floyd) goes on violent rampage. Cheap and bloody, likely to be edited.

Bullet for Sandoval, A (1970-Italian-Spanish) **C-91m. ** D:** Julio Buchs. Ernest Borgnine, George Hilton, Alberto De Mendoza, Gustavo Rojo, Leo Anchoriz, Annabella Incontrera. Average foreign oater, with lots of action. Ex-Confederate Hilton plots revenge on don Borgnine, grandfather of Hilton's illegitimate son, for indirectly causing the baby's death.▼

Bullet for Stefano (1950-Italian) **96m. **** D: Duilio Coletti. Rossano Brazzi, Valentina Cortese, Carlo Campanini, Lillian Laine. Carefree young man (Brazzi) falls into life of crime and finds it pleasant; cast is engaging.

Bullet for the General, A (1967-Italian) **C-115m.** ** D: Damiano Damiani. Gian-Maria Volonte, Lou Castel, Klaus Kinski, Martine Beswick. Blond gringo joins marauding guerrillas and contributes to gory bloodletting. Not bad for the genre.▼

Bullet Is Waiting, A (1954) **C-82m.** **½ D: John Farrow. Jean Simmons, Rory Calhoun, Stephen McNally, Brian Aherne. Interesting human nature study hinging on sheriff's discovery that his prisoner is really innocent; nice desert locale.

Bulletproof (1988) **C-94m.** BOMB D: Steve Carver. Gary Busey, Darlanne Fluegel, Henry Silva, L.Q. Jones, R.G. Armstrong, Juan Fernandez, Rene Enriquez. L.A. cop Busey, who keeps the 39 bullets his body has taken in a bathroom mason jar, kamikazes across the Mexican border to rescue kidnapped army personnel (ex-love Fluegel included) from Silva's Soviet stooge. Preposterous, but you have to admire Silva for having kept the same act going for so many years; peroxided hair is simply not to Busey's advantage.▼

Bullets or Ballots (1936) **81m.** *** D: William Keighley. Edward G. Robinson, Joan Blondell, Barton MacLane, Humphrey Bogart, Frank McHugh. Cop Robinson pretends to leave police force to crack citywide mob ring run by MacLane. Good, tough gangster film.

Bullfighter and the Lady (1951) **87m.** ***½ D: Budd Boetticher. Robert Stack, Joy Page, Gilbert Roland, Katy Jurado, Virginia Grey, John Hubbard. Cocky American visiting Mexico decides that he wants to tackle bullfighting and enlists the aid of the country's leading matador with tragic results. The movies' best treatment of this subject, a fine, mature drama with unforgettable bullfighting scenes and an appealing love story as well. Roland has never been better; only the second leads (Grey, Hubbard) are a detriment. Produced by John Wayne. Boetticher's version of the film, running 124m., has now been restored, and it's even better than the shorter print. ▼

Bullfighters, The (1945) **61m.** ** D: Mal St. Clair. Stan Laurel, Oliver Hardy, Margo Woode, Richard Lane, Carol Andrews, Diosa Costello. One of better L&H later works, involving mistaken identity (Stan is lookalike for famous matador), subsequent nonsense in bull ring.▼

Bullies (1986-Canadian) **C-96m.** BOMB D: Paul Lynch. Jonathan Crombie, Janet Laine Green, Stephen B. Hunter, Dehl Berti, Olivia D'Abo, Bill Croft. Mindlessly violent garbage about a family of sadistic, booze-guzzling rednecks who terrorize a small town. ▼

Bullitt (1968) **C-113m.** ***½ D: Peter Yates. Steve McQueen, Robert Vaughn, Jacqueline Bisset, Don Gordon, Robert Duvall, Simon Oakland, Norman Fell, Victor (Vic) Tayback. Definitive McQueen antihero: police detective who senses something fishy behind assignment to guard criminal witness. Taut action-film makes great use of San Francisco locations, especially in now-classic car chase, one of the screen's all-time best; Oscar-winning editing by Frank Keller.▼

Bullshot (1983-British) **C-85m.** **½ D: Dick Clement. Alan Shearman, Diz White, Ron House, Frances Tomelty, Michael Aldridge, Ron Pember. Occasionally funny Monty Python-ish parody, with Shearman cast as one Captain Hugh "Bullshot" Crummond, a Bulldog Drummond caricature. Plenty of one-liners and slapstick, some humorous and some silly. The screenplay was adapted by Shearman, White, and House, from their stage play.▼

Bullwhip (1958) **C-80m.** ** D: Harmon Jones. Guy Madison, Rhonda Fleming, James Griffith, Don Beddoe. Madison is offered the choice of marrying Fleming or being hanged on phony murder charge; expected results.▼

Bundle of Joy (1956) **C-98m.** ** D: Norman Taurog. Eddie Fisher, Debbie Reynolds, Adolphe Menjou, Tommy Noonan. Labored musical remake of BACHELOR MOTHER has Reynolds as salesgirl who takes custody of a baby, causing scandal that boyfriend Fisher is child's father. Made when Debbie and Eddie were America's favorite couple.▼

Bunker, The (1981) **C-150m.** TVM D: George Schaefer. Anthony Hopkins, Piper Laurie, Richard Jordan, Susan Blakely, Cliff Gorman, James Naughton, Michael Lonsdale. Hopkins won an Emmy for his chilling portrayal of Adolf Hitler in this adaptation by John Gay of the James P. O'Donnell book depicting the Third Reich's final days. Piper Laurie was nominated for an Emmy Award for her performance as Magda Goebbels. Above average.

Bunny Caper, The (1974-British) **C-85m.** *½ D: Jack Arnold. Christina Hart, Jane Anthony, Drina Pavlovic, Jill Damas, Ed Bishop. Subpar sex comedy satirizing political intrigue during the Nixon/Kissinger era. An off-day assignment for noted sci-fi director Arnold. Also known as GAMES GIRLS PLAY and SEX PLAY.

Bunny Lake Is Missing (1965) **107m.** ** D: Otto Preminger. Laurence Olivier, Carol Lynley, Keir Dullea, Noel Coward, Martita Hunt, Finlay Currie, The Zombies. Aimless story of Lynley's child being kidnapped, subsequent investigation among several homosexual characters and assorted oddballs; pretty dreary going. Made in England.

Bunny O'Hare (1972) **C-91m.** *½ D: Gerd Oswald. Bette Davis, Ernest Borgnine, Jack Cassidy, Joan Delaney, Reva Rose,

John Astin. Bizarre, totally inept tale of bank robbers who look like hippies but are actually Davis and Borgnine. Don't bother watching.

Bunny's Tale, A (1985) **C-100m.** TVM D: Karen Arthur. Kirstie Alley, Cotter Smith, Deborah Van Valkenburgh, Joanna Kerns, Lisa Pelikan, Mary Woronov, Delta Burke, Diana Scarwid. Or, the time feminist Gloria Steinem masqueraded as a Playboy Bunny for an article she was writing in 1963. Average.

✓ **Buona Sera, Mrs. Campbell** (1968) **C-113m.** *** D: Melvin Frank. Gina Lollobrigida, Peter Lawford, Shelley Winters, Phil Silvers, Telly Savalas, Lee Grant, Janet Margolin. Bright comedy about Italian woman who's accepted money from three American men who all think they fathered her child during WW2. Now they're all coming back to Italy for Army reunion and "Mrs. Campbell" is in a state of panic. Good fun with top cast.

'burbs, The (1989) **C-103m.** ** D: Joe Dante. Tom Hanks, Bruce Dern, Carrie Fisher, Rick Ducommun, Corey Feldman, Wendy Schaal, Henry Gibson, Brother Theodore, Courtney Gains, Gale Gordon, Dick Miller. Strange new neighbors set a neighborhood abuzz, and lead several slightly cracked compadres to extreme measures so they can learn just what's going on behind closed doors. Comically warped view of suburban life takes far too much time to play out its paper-thin premise, and leads to (mostly) predictable results.▼

Burden of Dreams (1982) **C-94m.** ***½ D: Les Blank. Werner Herzog, Klaus Kinski, Claudia Cardinale, Jason Robards, Mick Jagger. Extraordinary documentary of the filming of Herzog's FITZCARRALDO in the Peruvian Amazon. Despite the filmmaker's high technology, his dream of completing the film is constantly thwarted by nature and clashing cultures. Some find this more compelling than FITZCARRALDO itself.▼

Bureau of Missing Persons (1933) **75m.** **½ D: Roy Del Ruth. Bette Davis, Lewis S. Stone, Pat O'Brien, Allen Jenkins, Ruth Donnelly, Hugh Herbert, Glenda Farrell, Alan Dinehart, George Chandler. Typically fast-paced—but strange—Warner Bros. programmer about big-city bureau of missing persons, where benevolent Stone plays God with the losers and hard-luck cases that come before him. Hip-shooting cop O'Brien is transferred there in hopes he'll mellow out, and we'll bet you a dollar six bits he dosen't. Davis is a mystery woman with whom he gets involved.

Burglar, The (1956) **90m.** **½ D: Paul Wendkos. Dan Duryea, Jayne Mansfield, Martha Vickers, Peter Capell, Mickey Shaughnessy, Phoebe Mackay. Odd little film noir about burglars Duryea and Mans-

field, who've grown up together, and their unpredictable accomplices in a bizarre burglary.

Burglar (1987) **C-102m.** *½ D: Hugh Wilson. Whoopi Goldberg, Bob Goldthwait, G.W. Bailey, Lesley Ann Warren, James Handy, Anne DeSalvo, John Goodman. Whoopi plays a cat burglar who accidentally witnesses a murder—and then tries to solve the crime, in order to clear herself. Unfunny, unsuspenseful, and completely unappealing comedy/mystery, with a superfluous, built-up secondary role for Goldthwait (who, if you're a fan, has a few good moments). Another waste of Whoopi's talent.▼

Burglars, The (1972-French) **C-117m.** **½ D: Henri Verneuil. Jean-Paul Belmondo, Omar Sharif, Dyan Cannon, Robert Hossein. Routine crime film set against lush Greek backdrop, with good cast. One good chase and it's all over. Remake of THE BURGLAR.

Burke and Wills (1986-Australian) **C-140m.** *** D: Graeme Clifford. Jack Thompson, Nigel Havers, Greta Scacchi, Matthew Fargher, Ralph Cotterill, Drew Forsythe, Chris Haywood. Impressive, larger-than-life historical drama chronicling the title characters' expedition through 1860 Australia, the first two men to cross the continent. Thompson is especially fine as Burke; another version of the saga was made the same year, titled WILLS AND BURKE.▼

Burma Convoy (1941) **72m.** **½ D: Noel Smith. Charles Bickford, Evelyn Ankers, Frank Albertson, Cecil Kellaway, Keye Luke, Turhan Bey. Neat little actioner of conflicting trucking interests involved in carrying needed supplies over the Burma Road during hectic days of WW2.

Burmese Harp, The (1956-Japanese) **116m.** ***½ D: Kon Ichikawa. Rentaro Mikuni, Shoji Yasui, Tatsuya Mihashi, Tanie Kitabayashi, Yunosuke Ito. Private Yasui volunteers to persuade a group of mountain fighters to surrender at the end of WW2 and undergoes a religious experience, becoming obsessed with desire to bury war casualties. Extraordinary antiwar drama is affecting and memorable if a bit overlong. Also known as HARP OF BURMA; remade by Ichikawa in 1985.▼

Burn! (1969-Italian-French) **C-112m.** *** D: Gillo Pontecorvo. Marlon Brando, Evaristo Marquez, Renato Salvatori, Tom Lyons, Norman Hill. Egomaniacal Sir William Walker (Brando) is sent by the British to instigate a slave revolt on a Portuguese-controlled sugar-producing Caribbean island. This political drama is visually striking but muddled, with a strong Brando performance. Ed Harris plays the same role in WALKER. Cut by 20m. before its U.S. release. Also known as QUEIMADA!▼

Burndown (1989) **C-87m.** *½ D: James Allen. Peter Firth, Cathy Moriarty, Michael McCabe, Hal Orlandini, Hugh Rouse. A murderous *and* radioactive rapist is stalking a Southern town, tracked by Sheriff Firth and his reporter/lover Moriarty. Bizarre accents, a slow pace, a dull plot, and a preposterously inconclusive ending obliterate interesting work by the actors. ▼

Burning, The (1981) **C-90m.** BOMB D: Tony Maylam. Brian Matthews, Leah Ayres, Brian Backer, Larry Joshua, Lou David. Awful FRIDAY THE 13TH ripoff (with Tom Savini's bloody makeup effects) about an old caretaker at a summer camp who takes his revenge in the usual way. Holly Hunter's screen debut. ▼

Burning Bed, The (1984) **C-100m.** TVM D: Robert Greenwald. Farrah Fawcett, Paul LeMat, Richard Masur, Grace Zabriskie, Penelope Milford, James Callahan. In a surprisingly effective performance Fawcett shows substance as a battered wife who sets her ex-husband on fire one night after living with his beatings and humiliations for years. Emmy nominations went to, among others, Fawcett and writer Rose Leiman Goldemberg, who based her script on Faith McNulty's book. One of the highest rated TV movies of all time. Above average. ▼

Burning Hills, The (1956) **C-94m** ** D: Stuart Heisler. Tab Hunter, Natalie Wood, Skip Homeier, Eduard Franz. Passive Hunter can't spark life into tired script based on a Louis L'Amour novel. Man on run from cattle thieves is sheltered by Wood, miscast as a half-breed Mexican girl.

Burning Man, The SEE: **Dangerous Summer, A** ▼

Burning Rage (1984) **C-100m.** TVM D: Gilbert Cates. Barbara Mandrell, Tom Wopat, Bert Remsen, John Pleshette, Carol Kane, Eddie Albert. If you can accept country singer Mandrell as a lady geologist sent by the government to put out fires in abandoned Appalachian coal mines, you deserve this slice of entertainment. Below average. ▼

Burning Secret (1988-U.S.-British-German) **C-106m.** **½ D: Andrew Birkin. Faye Dunaway, Klaus Maria Brandauer, David Eberts, Ian Richardson. Brandauer offers a splendid performance (as usual) as a charming, amoral baron, a WWI vet who's nursing a bayonet wound at a sanitarium. In order to get to Dunaway, he initiates a friendship with her impressionable, asthmatic 12-year-old son (Eberts). Generally compelling, and lushly filmed in Prague and Marienbad; however, Dunaway is miscast, and there are several key moments that simply don't work. Based on a Stefan Zweig short story; originally made in Germany in 1933 by Robert Siodmak, as BRENNENDES GEHEIMNIS. ▼

Burnt Offerings (1976) **C-115m.** ** D: Dan Curtis. Karen Black, Oliver Reed, Burgess Meredith, Eileen Heckart, Lee Montgomery, Dub Taylor, Bette Davis, Anthony James. Ordinary couple, with young son and aunt in tow, rent an old mansion as summer home, unaware that it's haunted. Strange occurrences lead to totally predictable "surprise" ending. A big buildup to nothing. From Robert Marasco's novel. ▼

Burn, Witch, Burn! (1962-British) **90m.** *** D: Sidney Hayers. Janet Blair, Peter Wyngarde, Margaret Johnston, Anthony Nicholls. Story of witchcraft entering lives of schoolteacher and his wife builds to shattering suspense, genuinely frightening climax. Filmed before as WEIRD WOMAN, this version scripted by Charles Beaumont and Richard Matheson. Later spoofed in WITCHES' BREW. Original British title: NIGHT OF THE EAGLE.

Bury Me an Angel (1971) **C-86m.** **½ D: Barbara Peeters. Dixie Peabody, Terry Mace, Joanne Jordan, Clyde Ventura, Dan Haggerty, Stephen Whittaker, Gary Littlejohn, Beach Dickerson. Tautly directed biker film, told from the woman's point-of-view; heroine sets out on the road, toting a shotgun and meaning business, to avenge her brother's murder. Haggerty is effective in small role as struggling artist. ▼

Bush Christmas (1947-Australian) **76m.** *** D: Ralph Smart. Chips Rafferty, John Fernside, Stan Tolhurst, Pat Penny, Thelma Grigg. Solid little adventure about some children who set out across the Australian bush in pursuit of horse thieves. Holds up quite nicely; kids should enjoy it. Remade in 1983.

Bushido Blade, The (1979-Japanese) **C-104m.** **½ D: Tom Kotani. Richard Boone, Frank Converse, James Earl Jones, Toshiro Mifune, Mako, Sonny Chiba, Laura Gemser. 19th-century Kung Fu action in Japan as Cmdr. Matthew Perry (Boone) leads a band of his men in the recovery of a treasured sword. Of note: Boone's last role; Mifune plays the Shogun, as he did in later TV miniseries. Also shown as THE BLOODY BUSHIDO BLADE. ▼

Bushwackers, The (1952) **70m.** *½ D: Rod Amateau. Dorothy Malone, John Ireland, Wayne Morris, Lawrence Tierney, Lon Chaney. Confederate army veteran forced into becoming gunman again; Malone wasted here. ▼

Business As Usual (1987-British) **C-89m.** **½ D: Lezli-An Barrett. Glenda Jackson, John Thaw, Cathy Tyson, Mark McGann, Eamon Boland, James Hazeldine, Buki Armstrong, Stephen McGann. Passionate but didactic pro-labor drama with Jackson as a Liverpool boutique manager whose arbitrary firing (after she's lodged a complaint about sexual harassment on behalf of an employee) escalates into a national cause celebre. One of the angry anti-Thatcher films of the late 80s; written by first-time feature director Barrett. Excellent performances help a one-sided script. ▼

Busman's Honeymoon SEE: **Haunted Honeymoon** (1940)

Bus Riley's Back in Town (1965) **C-93m.** **½ D: Harvey Hart. Ann-Margret, Michael Parks, Janet Margolin, Brad Dexter, Kim Darby, Jocelyn Brando, Larry Storch, David Carradine. Muddled William Inge script of folksy people in the Midwest. Parks, ex-sailor, returns home, torn by faltering ambitions and taunted by wealthy ex-girlfriend Ann-Margret. Character cameos make the film worthwhile.

Bus Stop (1956) **C-96m.** ***½ D: Joshua Logan. Marilyn Monroe, Don Murray, Arthur O'Connell, Betty Field, Eileen Heckart, Hope Lange, Hans Conried, Casey Adams. The film that finally proved Monroe really could act; excellent comedy-drama about innocent cowboy (Murray) who falls for saloon singer and decides to marry her—without bothering to ask. Fine performances by all, with MM's famed rendition of "That Old Black Magic" a highlight; adapted by George Axelrod from the William Inge play. Film debuts of Murray and Lange (who subsequently married). Some older TV prints are titled THE WRONG KIND OF GIRL. Later a brief TV series. ▼

Buster (1988-British) **C-102m.** **½ D: David Green. Phil Collins, Julie Walters, Larry Lamb, Stephanie Lawrence, Ellen Beaven, Michael Atwell, Ralph Brown, Christopher Ellison, Sheila Hancock, Martin Jarvis, Anthony Quayle. Buster Edwards, one of the men behind Britain's all-time biggest robbery, turns out to have been just a working-class stiff with big dreams and a bad track record of success, who wanted the good life for his wife and child. Singer Collins' starring film debut is a diverting (if forgettable) yarn, with Walters a good match as his loving, long-suffering spouse. Great soundtrack includes Collins' performances of "Two Hearts (One Mind)" and "Groovy Kind of Love." ▼

Buster and Billie (1974) **C-100m.** *½ D: Daniel Petrie. Jan-Michael Vincent, Joan Goodfellow, Pamela Sue Martin, Clifton James, Robert Englund. Blubbery account of high school romance in 1948 rural Georgia (the loosest girl in class is redeemed by love) can't overcome clichéd premise. ▼

Buster Keaton Story, The (1957) **91m.** *½ D: Sidney Sheldon. Donald O'Connor, Ann Blyth, Rhonda Fleming, Peter Lorre, Larry Keating. Weak fiction ignores the facts about silent-star Keaton, making up its own. More private life than on-screen moments are detailed with Blyth as

his true love and Fleming as a siren. Little comedy in this tale of a great comedian.

Busting (1974) **C-92m.** **½ D: Peter Hyams. Elliott Gould, Robert Blake, Allen Garfield, Antonio Fargas, Michael Lerner, Sid Haig, Cornelia Sharpe. Realistic if empty comedy-action-drama with Gould and Blake as unorthodox L.A. vice cops. Gay activists complained about film's few minutes of homosexual caricatures. Hyams, once a CBS-TV newsman, also did script. ▼

Bustin' Loose (1981) **C-94m** *** D: Oz Scott. Richard Pryor, Cicely Tyson, Robert Christian, Alphonso Alexander, Janet Wong. Despite the (expected) street language, this is at heart a family picture about an ex-convict who shepherds teacher Tyson and a busload of emotionally and physically handicapped youngsters to a new life. Best scene: a KKK band becomes putty in Pryor's hands. Filmed mostly in 1979, but not completed until 1981 because of Pryor's near fatal accident. Film debut for Broadway director Scott; Pryor coproduced and wrote the story. Later a TV series. ▼

Busy Body, The (1967) **C-90m.** **½ D: William Castle. Sid Caesar, Robert Ryan, Anne Baxter, Kay Medford, Jan Murray, Richard Pryor, Dom DeLuise, Godfrey Cambridge, Marty Ingels, Bill Dana, George Jessel. Broad, forced comedy involving gangsters and corpses, with Caesar as the patsy for Ryan's underworld gang. Supporting comics give film its funniest moments. Pryor's film debut.

Butch and Sundance: The Early Days (1979) **C-110m.** **½ D: Richard Lester. William Katt, Tom Berenger, Jeff Corey, John Schuck, Michael C. Gwynne, Brian Dennehy, Jill Eikenberry, Peter Weller, Arthur Hill. Prequel to BUTCH CASSIDY AND THE SUNDANCE KID has everything going for it—engaging performances, beautiful atmosphere and location photography—except a story. Pleasant enough but ultimately disappointing. ▼

Butch Cassidy and the Sundance Kid (1969) **C-112m.** **** D: George Roy Hill. Paul Newman, Robert Redford, Katharine Ross, Strother Martin, Henry Jones, Jeff Corey, George Furth, Cloris Leachman, Ted Cassidy, Kenneth Mars. Delightful seriocomic character study masquerading as a Western; outlaws Newman and Redford are pursued by relentless but remote sheriff's posse. Many memorable vignettes. Won Oscars for Cinematography (Conrad Hall), Original Score (Burt Bacharach), Song, "Raindrops Keep Fallin' On My Head" (Bacharach and Hal David), and William Goldman's original screenplay, which brims over with sharp dialogue. Followed a decade later by a prequel,

BUTCH AND SUNDANCE: THE EARLY DAYS.▼

Butcher, The SEE: Le Boucher

But I Don't Want to Get Married! (1970) **C-72m. TVM** D: Jerry Paris. Herschel Bernardi, Shirley Jones, Brandon Cruz, Nanette Fabray, June Lockhart, Tina Louise, Sue Lyon, Kay Medford, Harry Morgan, Joyce Van Patten, Teddy Eccles, Kathleen Freeman, Jerry Paris. Fair comedy features Bernardi as average-type father recently widowed finding himself irresistible to all sorts of women. Good cast works well with adequate material. Average.

Butley (1974-British) **C-127m. ****** D: Harold Pinter. Alan Bates, Jessica Tandy, Richard O'Callaghan, Susan Engel, Georgina Hale. Bates is superb in American Film Theatre presentation, recreating his 1971 London stage role as a teacher with sexual and other problems. Playwright Pinter made his film directing debut with this outrageous comedy by Simon Gray.

But Not For Me (1959) **105m. **** D: Walter Lang. Clark Gable, Carroll Baker, Lilli Palmer, Barry Coe, Lee J. Cobb, Thomas Gomez. Chic remake of ACCENT ON YOUTH dealing with theatrical producer Gable thwarting advances of young secretary Baker, deciding sophisticated Palmer is more logically suitable.

Buttercup Chain, The (1971-British) **C-95m. BOMB** D: Robert Ellis Miller. Hywel Bennett, Leigh Taylor-Young, Jane Asher, Sven Bertil Taube, Clive Revill, Michael Elphick. Cousins are raised together and find they needn't stop at kissing. Beautifully photographed in Spain, Sweden, and London; otherwise, an atrocity.

✓ **Butterfield 8** (1960) **C-109m. ***½** D: Daniel Mann. Elizabeth Taylor, Laurence Harvey, Eddie Fisher, Dina Merrill, Mildred Dunnock, Susan Oliver, Betty Field. Adaptation of O'Hara novel substitutes clichéd ending in tale of high-class prostitute wanting to go straight, convincing herself she's found Mr. Right. Film's major assets: great supporting cast and old-style performance by Taylor, who won Oscar.▼

Butterflies Are Free (1972) **C-109m. ****** D: Milton Katselas. Goldie Hawn, Edward Albert, Eileen Heckart, Mike Warren. Filmization of Leonard Gershe's Broadway play detailing blind boy's romance with kookie next-door neighbor (Hawn) and inevitable showdown with his overpossessive mother. Good light entertainment; Heckart won Best Supporting Actress Oscar.▼

Butterfly (1981-U.S.-Canadian) **C-107m. ** D: Matt Cimber. Stacy Keach, Pia Zadora, Orson Welles, Lois Nettleton, Edward Albert, James Franciscus, Stuart Whitman, Ed McMahon, June Lockhart, Paul Hampton. Trashy soap opera, based on James M. Cain's novel, with gold-digging sex-kitten Zadora seducing Keach, who is supposed to be her dad. Welles steals the film—not a difficult task—as a judge.▼

Butterfly Affair, The (1970-French-Italian) **C-100m. ** D: Jean Herman. Claudia Cardinale, Stanley Baker, Henri Charriere, Georges Arminel, Leroy Haynes, Joannin Hansen. Henri (PAPILLON) Charriere wrote this story of a diamond heist and a double cross; he also costars as the mastermind, but his performance, like the picture, is routine. Claudia, at her sexiest, adds some bright moments. Original title: POPSY POP.

Buy & Cell (1989) **C-95m. *½** D: Robert Boris. Robert Carradine, Michael Winslow, Malcolm McDowell, Lise Cutter, Randall "Tex" Cobb, Roddy Piper, Ben Vereen, Fred Travalena, Tony Plana, Michael Goodwin. Uninteresting would-be comedy set in prison, where a framed stockbroker secretly sets up a multi-million-dollar business with the help of stereotyped inmates. McDowell is the avaricious, crooked warden. Shot in Italy, set in U.S.▼

Buy Me That Town (1941) **70m. **½** D: Eugene Forde. Lloyd Nolan, Constance Moore, Albert Dekker, Sheldon Leonard, Barbara Allen (Vera Vague), Warren Hymer, Edward Brophy, Horace MacMahon, Russell Hicks. Clever little "B" comedy-drama about gangster (Nolan) who actually buys a bankrupt little village; he plans to use it as a hideout for law-breaker pals, but eventually becomes more civic-minded. Amusing and observant, with great cast full of veteran tough guys.

Bwana Devil (1952) **C-79m. *½** D: Arch ✓ Oboler. Robert Stack, Barbara Britton, Nigel Bruce, Paul McVey. Dud actioner was sparked theatrically as first commercial 3-D feature; man-eating lions set their teeth on railway workers in Africa.

By Candlelight (1934) **70m. ** D: James Whale. Paul Lukas, Elissa Landi, Nils Asther, Dorothy Revier, Lawrence Grant, Esther Ralston. Typical Continental fluff about valet who poses as his master to woo woman he believes is a countess. Leaden Lukas is so wrong for the part that he almost sinks the film, but a few Whale touches make it watchable; buffs may find it more to taste.

By Design (1981-Canadian) **C-88m ** D: Claude Jutra. Patty Duke Astin, Sara Botsford, Saul Rubinek, Sonia Zimmer. Lesbian fashion designer Astin decides she wants to be a mother. Potentially interesting subject matter is awkwardly handled; one of Astin's few bad performances.▼

Bye Bye Birdie (1963) **C-112m. ****** D: George Sidney. Janet Leigh, Dick Van Dyke, Ann-Margret, Maureen Stapleton, Paul Lynde, Jesse Pearson, Bobby Rydell, Ed Sullivan. Entertaining version of Broadway musical about drafted rock 'n' roll idol coming to small town to give "one last kiss" to one of his adoring fans. Lynde stands out as Ann-Margret's father. Songs include "Put on a Happy Face," "We Love You, Conrad," "Kids."▼

Bye Bye Blues (1989-Canadian) **C-116m.** *** D: Anne Wheeler. Rebecca Jenkins, Luke Cooper, Stuart Margolin, Kate Reid, Michael Ontkean, Wayne Robson, Robyn Stevan. Affectionate WW2 drama of Jenkins, proper, protected, and pregnant, who's stationed with her doctor-husband in India. Intensely moving story of how war affects the lives of those on the home front; if this doesn't give your tear ducts a workout, nothing will. Loosely based on the life of Wheeler's mother and a nice companion piece to her short documentary-drama, A WAR STORY, which tells of her father's plight as a POW.

Bye Bye Braverman (1968) **C-109m.** **½ D: Sidney Lumet. George Segal, Jack Warden, Joseph Wiseman, Sorrell Booke, Jessica Walter, Phyllis Newman, Zohra Lampert, Godfrey Cambridge, Alan King. To paraphrase one of the characters, this film, in the sum of its many parts, yields pleasure of a kind; but fuzzy, unresolved story of four Jewish intellectuals on their way to a friend's funeral is ultimately disappointing. Filmed in N.Y.C.

Bye Bye Brazil (1980-Brazil) **C-110m.** *** D: Carlos Diegues. Jose Wilker, Betty Faria, Fabio Junior, Zaira Zambelli. Bawdy comedy-drama about a troupe of traveling entertainers is really a travelogue of the country, from jungles to honky-tonk port towns. Not quite the total sensual pleasure of DONA FLOR AND HER TWO HUSBANDS, but still one of the best Brazilian imports.▼

Bye Bye Monkey (1978-French-Italian) **C-114m.** BOMB D: Marco Ferreri. Gérard Depardieu, Marcello Mastroianni, Gail Lawrence (Abigail Clayton), James Coco, Geraldine Fitzgerald, Mimsy Farmer, Clarence Muse. Sardonic, bleak comedy about a group of misfits in a decrepit area of Manhattan where rats seem about to displace humanity in all the buildings. Depardieu, irresistible to women as always, prefers the company of a chimpanzee he finds near the carcass of a giant ape, presumably left over from the remake of KING KONG. Good cast is wasted, including Fitzgerald, who also has a love scene with Depardieu. Filmed in English in N.Y.C.

By Love Possessed (1961) **C-115m.** *** D: John Sturges. Lana Turner, Efrem Zimbalist, Jr., Jason Robards, Jr., George Hamilton, Thomas Mitchell. Not true to James Gould Cozzens novel; ultraglossy romantic vehicle for Turner, whose lover is prominent New England attorney Zimbalist; personable cast.▼

By Rocket to the Moon SEE: **Woman in the Moon**▼

By the Light of the Silvery Moon (1953)

C-102m. **½ D: David Butler. Doris Day, Gordon MacRae, Leon Ames, Rosemary DeCamp, Mary Wickes, Billy Gray. Set in post WW1, this Booth Tarkington story finds returning soldier MacRae and fiancée Day readjusting to life. Ames wonderful as father thought to be romancing French actress, and Wickes delightful as family maid. Merv Griffin pops up in the closing scene. This old-fashioned musical was a sequel to ON MOONLIGHT BAY.

Cabaret (1972) **C-128m.** ***½ D: Bob Fosse. Liza Minnelli, Michael York, Helmut Griem, Joel Grey, Fritz Wepper, Marisa Berenson. Stylish film based on Fred Ebb-John Kander Broadway musical, from John van Druten's play *I Am a Camera*, now more a vehicle for Minnelli in her Oscar-winning performance as Sally Bowles, American girl caught up in phony glitter of prewar Berlin. Song numbers counterpoint dramatic narrative, including newly written "The Money Song," great duet for Minnelli and Oscar-winner Grey. Screenplay by Jay Presson Allen; the story's genesis was Christopher Isherwood's book *Goodbye to Berlin*. Won eight Academy Awards in all, including Director, Cinematography (Geoffrey Unsworth) and Score Adaptation (Ralph Burns). Beware of edited prints.▼

Cabinet of Caligari (1962) **104m.** **½ D: Roger Kay. Dan O'Herlihy, Glynis Johns, Richard Davalos, Lawrence Dobkin, Estelle Winwood, J. Pat O'Malley. Unimaginative remake of the 1919 German classic, removing all the mystery-exotic appeal; Johns tries hard as lady with bizarre nightmares in a mental institution.

Cabinet of Dr. Caligari, The (1919-German) **69m.** ***½ D: Robert Wiene. Werner Krauss, Conrad Veidt, Lil Dagover. Somewhat stiff but still fascinating German Expressionist film about "magician" Caligari and hypnotic victim who carries out his evil bidding. Landmark film still impresses audiences today.▼

Cabin in the Cotton, The (1932) **77m.** **½ D: Michael Curtiz. Bette Davis, Richard Barthelmess, Dorothy Jordan, Henry B. Walthall, Tully Marshall. Dated melodrama of sharecroppers with earnest Barthelmess almost led to ruin by Southern belle Davis; exaggerated, but interesting. Bette's immortal line: "Ah'd like to kiss ya, but Ah jes' washed mah hair."

Cabin in the Sky (1943) **100m.** *** D: Vincente Minnelli. Eddie "Rochester" Anderson, Lena Horne, Ethel Waters, Louis Armstrong, Rex Ingram, Duke Ellington and his Orchestra, The Hall Johnson Choir. Stellar black cast in winning (if somewhat racist) musical fable about forces of good and evil vying for the soul of Little Joe (Anderson). John Bubbles' dancing, Waters singing "Happiness Is a Thing Called

Joe'' (written especially for the film) among musical highlights. First feature for Minnelli (who, with Waters and Ingram, came from the Broadway production).▼

Cable Car Murder SEE: **Crosscurrent**

Caboblanco (1980) **C-87m.** ** D: J. Lee Thompson. Charles Bronson, Jason Robards, Dominique Sanda, Fernando Rey, Simon MacCorkindale, Camilla Sparv, Gilbert Roland, Denny Miller. Murky ripoff of CASABLANCA, with Bronson a barkeeper in Peru. Robards plays a Nazi, Rey a police captain, Sanda a Frenchwoman searching for her lover.▼

Cactus (1986-Australian) **C-93m.** **½ D: Paul Cox. Isabelle Huppert, Robert Menzies, Norman Kaye, Monica Maughan, Banduk Marika. Slow, deliberately paced story of Huppert's agony when her sight is impaired in an auto mishap and her growing relationship with blind Menzies. Of interest only when it sticks to the story, which isn't often enough.▼

Cactus Flower (1969) **C-103m.** **½ D: Gene Saks. Walter Matthau, Ingrid Bergman, Goldie Hawn, Jack Weston, Rick Lenz, Vito Scotti, Irene Hervey. Glossy comedy was pretty thin for Broadway, even thinner on film, with Bergman as prim nurse to dentist Matthau who blossoms when she realizes she's in love with him. Best moments belong to Hawn, who won Oscar for her first big role.▼

Caddie (1976-Australian) **C-107m.** **½ D: Donald Crombie. Helen Morse, Takis Emmanuel, Jack Thompson, Jacki Weaver, Melissa Jaffer. Adaptation of a popular Australian autobiography set in the late '20s and early '30s, which tells story of an independent-minded young woman determined to succeed on her own, despite the pressure of having two children to raise. Moments of insight and originality give way too often to cliché and overriding blandness. Morse is fine in lead role.▼

✓ **Caddy, The** (1953) **95m.** *½ D: Norman Taurog. Dean Martin, Jerry Lewis, Donna Reed, Fred Clark, Barbara Bates, Joseph Calleia. Weak Martin & Lewis vehicle about golf-nut Jerry coaching Dean to be a champion player. Dean sings "That's Amore."▼

Caddyshack (1980) **C-99m.** ** D: Harold Ramis. Chevy Chase, Rodney Dangerfield, Ted Knight, Michael O'Keefe, Bill Murray, Cindy Morgan, Sarah Holcomb, Scott Colomby, Brian Doyle-Murray, Chuck E. Rodent. ANIMAL HOUSE-type hijinks at a posh country club; another comedy where irreverence and destruction are a substitute for humor. Saving grace is Dangerfield, whose opening scenes are sidesplittingly funny. Followed by a sequel.▼

Caddyshack II (1988) **C-93m.** ** D: Allan Arkush. Jackie Mason, Dyan Cannon, Robert Stack, Dina Merrill, Chevy Chase, Dan Aykroyd, Randy Quaid, Jessica Lundy,

Jonathan Silverman, Chynna Phillips, Brian McNamara. In-name-only sequel to 1980 hit gets a big boost from Mason, who's extremely winning in the role of a plain-talking, self-made millionaire whose daughter wants to be accepted by the snooty crowd at a local country club. Unfortunately, film simply runs out of script (not to mention laughs) after a half hour or so.▼

Cadillac Man (1990) **C-97m.** **½ D: Roger Donaldson. Robin Williams, Tim Robbins, Pamela Reed, Fran Drescher, Zack Norman, Annabella Sciorra, Lori Petty, Paul Guilfoyle, Bill Nelson, Eddie Jones, Judith Hoag. Williams is terrific, as usual, playing an aggressive car salesman who may lose his job, his mistress, his other girlfriend, his Mafioso protector, and his daughter all during one eventful weekend. Wildly uneven film tests the mettle of even the staunchest Williams fans, swinging helter-skelter from comedy to melodrama, dragging and then picking up again. Infuriating at times, then occasionally redeemed by a great moment. Elaine Stritch appears unbilled as a grieving widow.▼

Caesar and Cleopatra (1946-British) ✓ **C-134m.** ** D: Gabriel Pascal. Claude Rains, Vivien Leigh, Stewart Granger, Flora Robson, Francis L. Sullivan, Cecil Parker. Two fine stars suffer through static, boring rendition of George Bernard Shaw's play, which seems to go on forever. Occasional wit and intrigue can't keep this afloat.▼

Cafe Express (1981-Italian) **C-89m.** **½ D: Nanni Loy. Nino Manfredi, Adolfo Celi, Vittorio Mezzogiorno, Luigi Basagaluppi, Silvio Spaccesi. Manfredi, virtually repeating his characterization in BREAD AND CHOCOLATE, is a Neapolitan working man who illegally sells coffee on the train from Milan to Naples. Sometimes funny and profound, more often trite. Manfredi, as usual, is fine. Originally ran 105m.▼

Cafe Metropole (1937) **84m.** **½ D: Edward H. Griffith. Loretta Young, Tyrone Power, Adolphe Menjou, Gregory Ratoff, Charles Winninger, Helen Westley. Young is courted by penniless playboy Power, who's passing bad checks and posing as a Russian prince. OK comedy, from a story by Ratoff.

Cafe Society (1939) **83m.** **½ D: Edward H. Griffith. Madeleine Carroll, Fred MacMurray, Shirley Ross, Jessie Ralph, Claude Gillingwater. This time around Carroll chases MacMurray to win husband on a bet; chic fluff.

Cage (1989) **C-101m.** BOMB D: Lang Elliott. Lou Ferrigno, Reb Brown, Michael Dante, Marilyn Tokuda, James Shigeta, Al Ruscio. Pointless, violent film provides viewers with the human equivalent of a cockfight as Ferrigno and Brown go at it in the Asian "sport" of cage fighting. A better title might have been THE INCREDIBLE HOKUM.▼

Caged (1950) **96m.** *** D: John Cromwell. Eleanor Parker, Agnes Moorehead, Ellen Corby, Hope Emerson, Jan Sterling, Jane Darwell, Gertrude Michael. Remarkable performances by entire cast in stark record of Parker going to prison and becoming hardened criminal after exposure to brutal jail life. Both Parker and Emerson were nominated for Academy Awards. Remade as HOUSE OF WOMEN.

Caged Fury (1948) **60m.** ** D: William Berke. Richard Denning, Sheila Ryan, Mary Beth Hughes, Buster Crabbe. Not bad low-budgeter about mad killer on the loose in a circus.

Caged Heat (1974) **C-84m.** **½ D: Jonathan Demme. Juanita Brown, Erica Gavin, Roberta Collins, Rainbeaux Smith, Barbara Steele, Toby Carr-Rafelson. Demme's first feature is tongue-in-cheek but otherwise typical women's prison flick, chiefly novel for being set in the U.S. instead of some banana republic, plus neat turn by Steele as wheelchair-bound warden. Has a sizable cult following, but not *that* much better than usual. Also known as RENEGADE GIRLS.▼

Cage of Gold (1950-British) **83m.** **½ D: Basil Dearden. Jean Simmons, David Farrar, James Donald, Madeleine Lebeau, Herbert Lom, Bernard Lee. Fair suspense yarn with sleazy Farrar, supposedly dead in a plane crash, attempting to blackmail wife Simmons, now remarried to Dr. Donald.

Cage Without a Key (1975) **C-100m. TVM** D: Buzz Kulik. Susan Dey, Jonelle Allen, Sam Bottoms, Michael Brandon, Anne Bloom, Karen Carlson. Teen-aged girl (Dey) innocently finds herself accomplice to robbery and murder when she accepts a ride with a stranger, and then is wrongly sentenced to jail. Tedious, run-of-the-cell-block tale resembles 1940s B-movie. Below average.

Cagney & Lacey (1981) **C-100m. TVM** D: Ted Post. Loretta Swit, Tyne Daly, Joan Copeland, Al Waxman, Ronald Hunter, Yvette Hawkins. Two women undercover cops crack a tough murder case involving a Hassidic diamond broker. An intelligent script and interesting relationship of the female police partners make this something more than just another cop show. Pilot to the hit series. Above average.

Cahill—U.S. Marshal (1973) **C-103m.** ** D: Andrew V. McLaglen. John Wayne, George Kennedy, Gary Grimes, Neville Brand, Marie Windsor, Harry Carey, Jr. Marshal Wayne's law enforcement duties are complicated as one of his sons threatens to enter a life of crime; routine, violent Western suffers from the same kind of

sermonizing that plagued most of the Duke's later films.▼

Cain and Mabel (1936) **90m.** ** D: Lloyd Bacon. Marion Davies, Clark Gable, David Carlyle (Robert Paige), Allen Jenkins, Roscoe Karns, Walter Catlett. Musical romance of prizefighter and showgirl; gargantuan production numbers add nothing to stale plot.

Caine Mutiny, The (1954) **C-125m.** **** D: Edward Dmytryk. Humphrey Bogart, Jose Ferrer, Van Johnson, Robert Francis, May Wynn, Fred MacMurray, E.G. Marshall, Lee Marvin, Tom Tully, Claude Akins. Naval officers Johnson and Francis mutiny against Capt. Queeg (Bogart) and are court-martialed in this exciting adaptation (by Stanley Roberts) of Herman Wouk's Pulitzer Prize novel. Followed by a TVM in 1988.▼

Caine Mutiny Court-Martial, The (1988) **C-100m. TVM** D: Robert Altman. Eric Bogosian, Jeff Daniels, Brad Davis, Peter Gallagher, Michael Murphy, Kevin J. O'Connor, Daniel Jenkins. Fine restaging of Herman Wouk's 1953 play, the heart of his Pulitzer Prize novel. Bogosian and Davis stand out in a fine ensemble as Defense Attorney Barney Greenwald and Lt. Cmdr. Phillip Queeg. Kudos to director Altman. Above average.

Cairo (1942) **101m.** ** D: W.S. Van Dyke II. Jeanette MacDonald, Robert Young, Ethel Waters, Reginald Owen, Lionel Atwill, Dooley Wilson. Musi-comedy spoof of WW2 spy films is strained, although stars are pleasant and production is well-mounted.

Cairo (1963-British) **91m.** **½ D: Wolf Rilla. George Sanders, Richard Johnson, Faten Hamama, John Meillon, Eric Pholmann, Walter Rilla. Mediocre remake of THE ASPHALT JUNGLE with the "surefire" caper aiming to steal King Tut's treasures from the Cairo Museum.

Cal (1984-British) **C-102m.** *** D: Pat O'Connor. Helen Mirren, John Lynch, Donal McCann, John Kavanagh, Ray McAnally, Stevan Rimkus, Kitty Gibson. Intelligent drama of modern-day Northern Ireland, with Lynch, 19, falling for older widow Mirren—despite his IRA involvement with her husband's murder. Strong performances, especially by Mirren; produced by David Puttnam.▼

Calaboose SEE: **Dudes Are Pretty People**

Calamity Jane (1953) **C-101m.** *** D: David Butler. Doris Day, Howard Keel, Allyn McLerie, Philip Carey, Gale Robbins, Dick Wesson. Entertaining musical with Doris at her bounciest as the tomboyish title character who maintains her sense of independence while falling for Wild Bill Hickok (Keel). Score includes the Oscar-winning "Secret Love."▼

Calamity Jane (1984) **C-100m. TVM** D:

James Goldstone. Jane Alexander, Frederic Forrest, David Hemmings, Ken Kercheval, Walter Olkewicz, Talia Balsam. Jane's exceedingly plain Jane is the centerpiece of this spirited feminist outlook of the Old West. No way will this ever be confused with the Doris Day musical version. Written by Suzanne Clauser. Above average.▼

Calamity Jane and Sam Bass (1949) C-85m. *½ D: George Sherman. Yvonne De Carlo, Howard Duff, Dorothy Hart, Lloyd Bridges, Milburn Stone. Tattered retelling of 19th-century cowgirl and Texas outlaw, with De Carlo and Duff a disinterested duo.

Calcutta (1947) 83m. **½ D: John Farrow. Alan Ladd, Gail Russell, William Bendix, June Duprez, Lowell Gilmore. Standard actioner with pilot Ladd avenging friend's murder.

California (1946) C-97m. **½ D: John Farrow. Barbara Stanwyck, Ray Milland, Barry Fitzgerald, Albert Dekker, Anthony Quinn, Julia Faye, George Coulouris. Ray is a wagonmaster with a past, Stanwyck a shady gal who makes good in this elaborately ordinary Western.

California Conquest (1952) C-79m. **½ D: Lew Landers. Cornel Wilde, Teresa Wright, John Dehner, Hank Patterson. Film deals with sidelight of American history. Californian Wilde et al under Spanish control help their ally against Russian attempt to confiscate the territory.

California Dolls, The SEE: . . . **All the Marbles**▼

California Dreaming (1979) C-92m. **½ D: John Hancock. Dennis Christopher, Glynnis O'Connor, Seymour Cassel, Dorothy Tristan, John Calvin, Tanya Roberts, Todd Susman, Alice Playten, Ned Wynn, Jimmy Van Patten, Stacey Nelkin, Marshall Efron. Revisionist beachparty movie finds nerd Christopher trying desperately to fit in with the surfing crowd, blind to the fact that their lives are even emptier than his. Strong drama sometimes bites off more than it can chew, but overall fairly compelling and surprisingly erotic; Wynn also wrote the screenplay.▼

California Girls (1985) C-100m. TVM D: Rick Wallace. Robby Benson, Martha Longley, Martin Mull, Charles Rocket, Ernie Hudson, Tawny Kitaen, Doris Roberts, Norman Alden, Zsa Zsa Gabor. Frisky romp about a bored auto mechanic from New Jersey who heads for California to meet girls and ends up in an offbeat affair with the woman of his dreams. Average.

California Gold Rush (1981) C-100m. TVM D: Jack B. Hively. Robert Hays, John Dehner, Henry Jones, Gene Evans, Ken Curtis, Victor Mohica, Cliff Osmond. "Classics Illustrated" look at Bret Harte's *The Luck of Roaring Camp* and *The Out-*

casts of Poker Flat as revisited by an adult Harte (Hays), now working for Captain John Sutter. Average.▼

California Kid, The (1974) C-78m. TVM D: Richard Heffron. Martin Sheen, Vic Morrow, Michelle Phillips, Stuart Margolin, Nick Nolte, Janit Baldwin. Taut, well-made thriller in which psychotic small town sheriff Morrow, who delights in punishing speeders by running them off hairpin mountain curves, is forced into a high-speed auto duel with Sheen, the hotrodding brother of one of the victims, played by Sheen's real-life brother Joe Estevez. Script by Richard Compton. Above average.

California Split (1974) C-108m. **½ D: Robert Altman. George Segal, Elliott Gould, Ann Prentiss, Gwen Welles, Joseph Walsh, Bert Remsen. Realistic but rambling look at two compulsive gamblers, their strange lifestyles, and the emptiness of winning. Altman's multi-channel soundtrack at its worst only adds to the muddle.

California Straight Ahead (1937) 67m. ** D: Arthur Lubin. John Wayne, Louise Latimer, Robert McWade, Theodore Von Eltz, Tully Marshall. Good little actioner with Wayne competing in cross-country race between trucks and train.

California Suite (1978) C-103m. *** D: Herbert Ross. Jane Fonda, Alan Alda, Maggie Smith, Michael Caine, Walter Matthau, Elaine May, Richard Pryor, Bill Cosby, Gloria Gifford, Sheila Frazier, Herb Edelman, Denise Galik. Four Neil Simon skits set at the Beverly Hills Hotel (and adapted from his Broadway hit). Oscar-winning Smith and husband Caine as gently bickering Britishers in town for Academy Awards come off best; Pryor and Cosby as unfunnily combative "friends" are the worst. Pleasant time-filler, with nice jazz score by Claude Bolling.▼

Caligula (1980) C-156m. *½ D: Tinto Brass. Malcolm McDowell, Peter O'Toole, Teresa Ann Savoy, Helen Mirren, John Gielgud, Guido Mannari. Filmdom's first $15 million porno (to say nothing of home) movie, produced by *Penthouse* and set in Rome A.G. (After Guccione), follows ruthless ruler through endless series of decapitations and disembowelings. Chutzpah and six minutes of not-bad hard-core footage earn this half a star for the faithful, but most viewers will be rightfully repelled. And besides, Jay Robinson does much better by the title character in THE ROBE and DEMETRIUS AND THE GLADIATORS. Reissued in 105m., R-rated version—which is considerably changed.▼

Call a Messenger (1939) 65m. D: Arthur Lubin. Billy Halop, Huntz Hall, William Benedict, David Gorcey, Robert Armstrong, Buster Crabbe, Victor Jory, El Brendel, Mary Carlisle. SEE: **Bowery Boys** series.

Callan (1974-British) C-106m. **½ D:

Don Sharp. Edward Woodward, Eric Porter, Carl Mohner, Catherine Schell, Peter Egan. Adequate drama of aging secret agent Woodward, demoted because he cares too much about his adversaries, assigned to kill a German businessman. Woodward had previously played same role on British TV.

Callaway Went Thataway (1951) 81m. **½ D: Norman Panama, Melvin Frank. Fred MacMurray, Dorothy McGuire, Howard Keel, Jesse White, Fay Roope, Natalie Schafer, Stan Freberg. Gentle spoof of early-TV "Hopalong Cassidy" craze, with Keel as lookalike who impersonates veteran cowboy star for promotional purposes; good fun until it starts getting serious. Several MGM stars make cameo appearances.

Caller, The (1989) C-97m. ** D: Arthur Allan Seidelman. Malcolm McDowell, Madolyn Smith. Strange two-character mystery set mostly in an isolated cabin in the woods; the verbal sparring partners are not what they seem to be. Partly effective, but goes on much too long; might have worked as a *Twilight Zone* episode. Shot in Italy in 1987.▼

Call Her Mom (1971) C-73m. TVM D: Jerry Paris. Connie Stevens, Van Johnson, Charles Nelson Reilly, Jim Hutton, Gloria DeHaven, Corbett Monica. Fraternity house takes on waitress as housemother and finds itself (and entire college) center of intense Women's Lib controversy. Needed better script. Average.

Call Her Savage (1932) 88m. **½ D: John Francis Dillon. Clara Bow, Gilbert Roland, Thelma Todd, Monroe Owsley, Estelle Taylor, Russell Simpson, Margaret Livingston. Wild comeback vehicle for indefatigable Clara Bow ranges from sharp comedy to teary-eyed soap opera, but it's never dull. Bow is amazingly sensual throughout, matched in brief confrontations with Todd; great fun for 1930s film buffs.

Call Him Mr. Shatter (1976-British) C-90m. *½ D: Michael Carreras. Stuart Whitman, Ti Lung, Lily Li, Peter Cushing, Anton Diffring. Hammer's entry into the Kung Fu market, begun by Monte Hellman, stars Whitman as a burned-out hit man on assignment in Hong Kong. Plenty of action, but nothing to hold it together; presence of three cinematographers is a tip-off to extensive production woes. Also known as SHATTER.▼

Callie & Son (1981) C-150m. TVM D: Waris Hussein. Lindsay Wagner, Jameson Parker, Dabney Coleman, Andrew Prine, Michelle Pfeiffer, James Sloyan. Rags-to-riches story of a woman's climb to wealth and power in Texas and her obsessive love for her teenaged son. Overlong, with a hint or two of kinkiness; written by best-selling author Thomas Thompson. Average.▼

Calling Bulldog Drummond (1951-U.S.-British) 80m. D: Victor Saville. Walter Pidgeon, Margaret Leighton, Robert Beatty, David Tomlinson. SEE: **Bulldog Drummond** series.

Calling Dr. Death (1943) 63m. ** D: Reginald LeBorg. Lon Chaney, Jr., Ramsay Ames, Patricia Morison, J. Carrol Naish, David Bruce. Ultra-low-budget mystery about a neurologist who is tormented by the realization that he may have killed his unfaithful wife during a moment of madness. First of the *Inner Sanctum* series.

Calling Dr. Gillespie (1942) 82m. D: Harold S. Bucquet. Lionel Barrymore, Donna Reed, Phil Brown, Nat Pendleton, Alma Kruger, Mary Nash, Charles Dingle. SEE: **Dr. Kildare** series.

Calling Dr. Kildare (1939) 86m. D: Harold S. Bucquet. Lew Ayres, Lionel Barrymore, Laraine Day, Nat Pendleton, Lana Turner, Samuel S. Hinds, Emma Dunn, Alma Kruger, Marie Blake, Phillip Terry, Donald Barry. SEE: **Dr. Kildare** series.

Calling Homicide (1956) 61m. *½ D: Edward Bernds. Bill Elliott, Don Haggerty, Kathleen Case, Myron Healey. Low-key detective yarn following detective Elliott's search for cop-killer.

Calling Northside 777 SEE: **Call Northside 777**

Calling Philo Vance (1940) 62m. D: William Clemens. James Stephenson, Margot Stevenson, Henry O'Neill, Edward Brophy, Ralph Forbes. SEE: **Philo Vance** series.

Call it a Day (1937) 89m. ** D: Archie Mayo. Olivia de Havilland, Ian Hunter, Alice Brady, Anita Louise, Peggy Wood, Frieda Inescort, Roland Young, Bonita Granville. Tiresome trivia about a British family's comic trials and tribulations during the course of an average day.

Call It Murder SEE: **Midnight** (1934)▼

Call Me (1988) C-96m. **½ D: Sollace Mitchell. Patricia Charbonneau, Patti D'Arbanville, Sam Freed, Boyd Gaines, Stephen McHattie, Steve Buscemi, John Seitz, David Strathairn. Horny reporter saddled with a lackluster boyfriend begins receiving obscene phone calls, and almost finds herself enjoying the experience. Very well acted by Charbonneau, but too many of the supporting roles are weakly cast; excessive melodrama detracts from what could have been a more compelling psychological study.▼

Call Me Bwana (1963) C-103m. ** D: Gordon Douglas. Bob Hope, Anita Ekberg, Edie Adams, Lionel Jeffries, Arnold Palmer. Hope and Adams on an African jungle safari encounter Ekberg and Jeffries—nothing much happens—the ladies are lovely.

Call Me Madam (1953) C-117m. *** D: Walter Lang. Ethel Merman, Donald

O'Connor, George Sanders, Vera-Ellen, Billy DeWolfe, Walter Slezak, Lilia Skala. Often stagy musical from Irving Berlin tuner based on Perle Mesta's life as Washington, D.C. hostess and Lichtenburg ambassadress. Merman is blowsy delight. Songs include "The Best Thing For You," "It's A Lovely Day Today," "You're Just in Love."

Call Me Mister (1951) **C-95m.** **½ D: Lloyd Bacon. Betty Grable, Dan Dailey, Danny Thomas, Dale Robertson, Benay Venuta, Richard Boone, Frank Fontaine, Jeffrey Hunter. Acceptable plot line helps buoy this musical. Soldier Dailey, based in Japan, goes AWOL to patch up marriage with Grable traveling with USO troupe. Bears little resemblance to the Broadway revue on which it's supposedly based. An unbilled Bobby Short sings "Going Home Train."

Call Northside 777 (1948) **111m.** ***½ D: Henry Hathaway. James Stewart, Richard Conte, Lee J. Cobb, Helen Walker, Moroni Olsen, E.G. Marshall. Absorbing drama of reporter Stewart convinced that convicted killer is innocent, trying to prove it; handled in semi-documentary style. Retitled: CALLING NORTHSIDE 777.

Call of the Wild (1935) **81m.** *** D: William Wellman. Clark Gable, Loretta Young, Jack Oakie, Reginald Owen, Frank Conroy. More Hollywood than Jack London, but this Yukon adventure/romance is lots of fun, and Owen is a fine snarling villain. Originally released at 95m. Remade in 1972 and as a TV movie in 1976.

Call of the Wild (1972) **C-100m.** **½ D: Ken Annakin. Charlton Heston, Michele Mercier, Maria Rohm, Rik Battaglia. Lackluster version of the Jack London adventure classic, produced by a multinational film combine and wasting the talents of a diverse cast. One redeeming quality: the striking Finnish scenery.▼

Call of the Wild, The (1976) **C-100m.** TVM D: Jerry Jameson. John Beck, Bernard Fresson, John McLiam, Donald Moffat, Michael Pataki, Billy Green Bush, Penelope Windust, Johnny Tillotson. Stark but quite graphic remake of Jack London's 1903 tale of gold fever and adventure in the Klondike. In this version, John Beck is eager greenhorn and Fresson is veteran prospector, but the star is sled dog named Buck, who faces the hazards of man as well as nature. Script by James Dickey. Above average.▼

Call Out the Marines (1942) **67m.** ** D: Frank Ryan, William Hamilton. Edmund Lowe, Victor McLaglen, Binnie Barnes, Paul Kelly, Dorothy Lovett, Franklin Pangborn. Tepid comedy, an updating of Lowe and McLaglen's Flagg and Quirt vehicles (and their last film together), with the boys tangling with waterfront seduc-

tress Barnes while on the trail of spies. There are several forgettable tunes (like "Zana Zaranda") to boot.▼

Call to Danger (1973) **C-74m. TVM** D: Tom Gries. Peter Graves, Stephen McNally, Diana Muldaur, Ina Balin, Michael Ansara, Clu Gulager, Tina Louise. Undercover investigator for Justice Department must rescue important witness kidnapped by the Mob. Grows increasingly implausible as plot unwinds. Average.

Caltiki, the Immortal Monster (1959-Italian) **76m.** ** D: Robert Hampton (Riccardo Freda). John Merivale, Didi Sullivan, Gerard Herter, Daniela Rocca. Set in Mexico, sci-fi has blob-ish fiend pursuing members of scientific expedition; poorly conceived but amusing. Photographed by Mario Bava.

Calypso Heat Wave (1957) **86m.** ** D: Fred F. Sears. Johnny Desmond, Merry Anders, Paul Langton, Michael Granger, Meg Myles, Joel Grey, The Treniers, The Tarriers, The Hi-Lo's, Maya Angelou, Darla Hood. Trite plot—crooked Granger takes over Langton's record company—takes a back seat to musical-dance performances by Desmond, Grey, Hi-Lo's, etc. A once-in-a-lifetime cast. Alan Arkin is one of The Tarriers.

Calypso Joe (1957) **76m.** *½ D: Edward Dein. Herb Jeffries, Angie Dickinson, Edward Kemmer, Stephen Bekassy, Laurie Mitchell, Lord Flea and His Calypsonians. Thin programmer about stewardess Dickinson and TV star Kemmer quarreling and making-up in a South American setting. Jeffries sings seven songs.

Camelot (1967) **C-178m.** *½ D: Joshua Logan. Richard Harris, Vanessa Redgrave, Franco Nero, David Hemmings, Lionel Jeffries. Appalling film version of Lerner-Loewe musical has only good orchestrations and sporadically good acting to recommend it; no one can sing and production looks cheap, in spite of big budget; this did, however, win Oscars for Costumes, Scoring, and Art Direction/Set Decoration. Film's nonstop use of close-ups may help it on TV.▼

Cameron's Closet (1989) **C-86m.** *½ D: Armand Mastroianni. Cotter Smith, Mel Harris, Scott Curtis, Chuck McCann, Leigh McCloskey, Kim Lankford, Tab Hunter. Pointlessly cluttered horror tale of a father whose constant mind experiments on his son have created an actual monster in the boy's closet. Lumbering in every way, with a dull monster created by Carlo Rambaldi.▼

Camila (1984-Argentine) **C-105m.** **½ D: Maria Luisa Bemberg. Susu Pecoraro, Imanol Arias, Hector Altiero. Shades of ELVIRA MADIGAN, in a story based on 19th-century Argentine fact, about a Jesuit priest and a young Catholic socialite who commit love on the lam as the authorities stalk them for 500 miles. Interesting, but never altogether compelling Foreign Film Oscar nominee.▼

Camille (1936) **108m.** ***½ D: George Cukor. Greta Garbo, Robert Taylor, Lionel Barrymore, Elizabeth Allan, Laura Hope Crews, Henry Daniell. Beautiful MGM production; in one of her most famous roles, Garbo is Dumas' tragic heroine who must sacrifice her own happiness in order to prove her love. Taylor is a bit stiff as Armand, but Daniell is a superb villain. Filmed before in 1915 (with Clara Kimball Young), 1917 (Theda Bara), and 1921 (Nazimova, with Rudolph Valentino as Armand).▼

Camille (1984-British) **C-100m.** TVM D: Desmond Davis. Greta Scacchi, Colin Firth, John Gielgud, Billie Whitelaw, Patrick Ryecart, Ben Kingsley, Denholm Elliott. Lavishly restaged for the umpteenth time, this candy-box production of Dumas's tragedy settles on a too-healthy courtesan. The version with the other Greta is still in front. Average.

Camille Claudel (1988-French) **C-149m.** ** D: Bruno Nuytten. Isabelle Adjani, Gerard Depardieu, Laurent Grevill, Alain Cuny, Madeleine Robinson, Katrine Boorman. Overblown biography of the French sculptress (Adjani), who has a "madness of mud" and who single-mindedly pursues her art; Depardieu plays Auguste Rodin, with whom she has a complex, turbulent relationship. Potentially provocative story is emotionally uninvolving, with an astonishing lack of depth. Wonderful production values and period detail, but all for naught. Cinematographer Nuytten's directorial debut. Original French running time 173m.

Camorra (1986-Italian) **C-115m.** **½ D: Lina Wertmuller. Angela Molina, Harvey Keitel, Daniel Ezralow, Francisco Rabal, Paolo Bonacelli, Isa Danieli. Complex tale of drug traffic, murder, and mayhem, focusing on the trials of ex-prostitute Molina; well-meaning in its depiction of how preteens are used and abused by drug kingpins. Generally better than the director's recent work, but miles below her gems of the 1970s.▼

Camouflage (1977-Polish) **C-106m.** ***½ D: Krzysztof Zanussi. Piotr Garlicki, Zbigniew Zapasiewicz, Christine Paul, Mariusz Dmochowski. Arrogant tenured professor Zapasiewicz challenges the independence of idealistic teaching assistant Garlicki at a summer school-camp for linguists. Pungently funny satire about conformity, the Communist hierarchy.

Campbell's Kingdom (1958-British) **C-102m.** ** D: Ralph Thomas. Dirk Bogarde, Stanley Baker, Michael Craig, Barbara Murray. Set in Canadian Rockies, big-budget adventure film focuses on landowner Bogarde's conflict with Baker et al, when latter seeks to build large dam near his property.

Camp on Blood Island, The (1958-British) **81m.** ** D: Val Guest. Andre Morell, Carl Mohner, Walter Fitzgerald, Edward Underdown. So-so gore as inhabitants rebel against brutal commander of prison compound. Followed by THE SECRET OF BLOOD ISLAND.

Campus Man (1987) **C-94m.** ** D: Ron Casden. John Dye, Steve Lyon, Morgan Fairchild, Kim Delaney, Kathleen Wilhoite, Miles O'Keeffe. Glossy but vacuous teen comedy of collegiate entrepreneur (i.e. hustler) who publishes a male beefcake calendar featuring his roommate, a hunky diver, and spawning all kinds of complications. Based on story of Arizona State University alumnus Todd Headlee (the film's associate producer), whose ASU calendar launched the nationwide craze.▼

Canadian Mounties vs. Atomic Invaders SEE: **Missile Base at Taniak**

Canadian Pacific (1949) **C-95m.** **½ D: Edwin L. Marin. Randolph Scott, Jane Wyatt, J. Carrol Naish, Victor Jory, Nancy Olson. Scott is railroad surveyor helping with construction of train link, fighting Indians while romancing Wyatt and Olson.

Canadians, The (1961) **C-85m.** ** D: Burt Kennedy. Robert Ryan, John Dehner, Torin Thatcher, John Sutton, Teresa Stratas. Cornball nonsense about Mounties who pacify war-happy Sioux. Film features Metropolitan Opera singer Stratas to no advantage. Filmed in Canada; Kennedy's first feature as director.

Canaris Master Spy (1954-German) **92m.** ** D: Alfred Weidenmann. O. E. Hasse, Martin Held, Barbara Rutting, Adrian Hoven. Potentially interesting account of German Intelligence leader during 1930s who tried to depose Hitler; meandering.

Canary Murder Case (1929) **81m.** D: Malcolm St. Clair. William Powell, Louise Brooks, James Hall, Jean Arthur, Charles Lane. SEE: **Philo Vance** series.

Can-Can (1960) **C-131m.** **½ D: Walter Lang. Frank Sinatra, Shirley MacLaine, Maurice Chevalier, Louis Jourdan, Juliet Prowse. Lackluster version of Cole Porter musical of 1890s Paris involving lawyer Sinatra defending MacLaine's right to perform "daring" dance in her nightclub. Chevalier and Jourdan try to inject charm, but Sinatra is blasé and MacLaine shrill. Songs: "C'est Magnifique," "I Love Paris," "Let's Do It," "Just One of Those Things."▼

Cancel My Reservation (1972) **C-99m.** BOMB D: Paul Bogart. Bob Hope, Eva Marie Saint, Ralph Bellamy, Forrest Tucker, Anne Archer, Keenan Wynn, Ned Beatty, Chief Dan George. Hope should have canceled this movie, a time-wasting turkey about a troubled talk-show host who gets involved in a murder case in Arizona. Based on a Louis L'Amour novel!▼

Candidate, The (1972) C-109m. *** D: Michael Ritchie. Robert Redford, Peter Boyle, Don Porter, Allen Garfield, Karen Carlson, Melvyn Douglas, Quinn Redeker, Michael Lerner, Kenneth Tobey. Keen-eyed political satire doesn't stray far from reality, which is its problem. Redford is idealist talked into running for Senate with promise of absolute integrity in campaign, since he's bound to lose—or is he? Oscar-winning screenplay by Jeremy Larner.▼

Candidate for Murder (1962-British) 60m. **½ D: David Villiers. Michael Gough, Erika Remberg, Hans Barsody, John Justin. Gough is deranged husband of actress Remberg, out to kill her; nicely told Edgar Wallace suspenser.

Candleshoe (1977) C-101m. *** D: Norman Tokar. David Niven, Jodie Foster, Helen Hayes, Leo McKern, Veronica Quilligan, Ian Sharrock, Vivian Pickles. Con man McKern tries to pass off orphan Foster as Hayes' heiress in order to locate hidden family treasure. Entertaining Disney comedy filmed in England, with Niven in fine form as disguise-laden butler.▼

Candy (1968-U.S.-Italian-French) C-115m. ** D: Christian Marquand. Ewa Aulin, Richard Burton, Marlon Brando, Charles Aznavour, James Coburn, John Huston, Walter Matthau, Ringo Starr, John Astin. Strained sexual satire about a nubile blonde who is attacked by every man she meets. Fair share of funny moments and bright performances (particularly by Burton and Astin), but not enough to sustain 115m. Adapted from Terry Southern and Mason Hoffenberg's book by Buck Henry.

Candy Man, The (1969) 98m. ** D: Herbert J. Leder. George Sanders, Leslie Parrish, Gina Ronan, Menolo Fabregas, Carlos Cortez. Routine kidnap drama filmed in Mexico City involving world-weary British drug pusher and American film star.▼

Candy Mountain (1987-Canadian-French-Swiss) C-91m. ** D: Robert Frank, Rudy Wurlitzer. Kevin J. O'Connor, Harris Yulin, Tom Waits, Bulle Ogier, Roberts Blossom, Leon Redbone, Dr. John, Joe Strummer, David Johansen (Buster Poindexter). Uneven account of has-been rocker O'Connor and his trip through America and Canada in search of elusive guitarmaker Yulin. Intriguing collaboration between photographer/filmmaker Frank, screenwriter Wurlitzer, and an eclectic cast of actors and musicians . . . but the results are too often dull.▼

Candy Stripe Nurses (1974) C-80m. *½ D: Allan Holleb. Candice Rialson, Robin Mattson, Maria Rojo, Kimberly Hyde, Dick Miller, Stanley Ralph Ross, Monte Landis, Tom Baker. Last of Roger Corman's five "nurse" pictures is tired sex comedy, focusing on antics of pretty volunteers; kept afloat by cast full of old hands at this sort of thing.

Can Ellen Be Saved? (1974) C-78m. TVM D: Harvey Hart. Leslie Nielsen, John Saxon, Michael Parks, Louise Fletcher, Kathy Cannon, Rutanya Alda, Bill Katt, Kathleen Quinlan. Exorcism movie in which Saxon is hired by parents of Cannon to save her from a fanatical religious commune. Unspectacular deprogramming drama that unfolds in totally predictable fashion. Below average.

Can Hieronymus Merkin Ever Forget Mercy Humppe and Find True Happiness? (1969-British) C-106m. *½ D: Anthony Newley. Anthony Newley, Joan Collins, Milton Berle, Connie Kreski, George Jessel, Stubby Kaye. Fellini-influenced mess about song-and-dance man who reviews his debauched past. Low-grade in all departments, though Connie reveals why she was "Playmate of the Year." Newley and Collins were then real-life husband and wife.

Cannery Row (1982) C-120m. **½ D: David S. Ward. Nick Nolte, Debra Winger, Audra Lindley, Frank McRae, M. Emmet Walsh, Sunshine Parker, Santos Morales, narrated by John Huston. Entertaining tug-of-war romance between baseball-player-turned-marine-biologist Nolte and drifter-turned-floozie Winger is hampered by sloppy, self-conscious direction, awkward continuity. Attractive performances by Nolte and Winger; great set design by Richard MacDonald. Based on John Steinbeck's *Cannery Row* and *Sweet Thursday*. Ward's directorial debut.▼

Cannibal Attack (1954) 69m. D: Lee Sholem. Johnny Weissmuller, Judy Walsh, David Bruce, Bruce Cowling. SEE: **Jungle Jim** series.

Cannibal Girls (1973-Canadian) C-84m. ** D: Ivan Reitman. Eugene Levy, Andrea Martin, Ronald Ulrich, Randall Carpenter, Bonnie Neison. Confused, convoluted low-budget Canadian import, an early effort by young talents Reitman, Levy, and Martin, has funny first half about a couple stranded in eerie town where there's a rather strange restaurant. Second half falls apart. Warning buzzer precedes gore scenes (which aren't much), and doorbell-like sound announces they're over.

Cannon (1970) C-100m. TVM D: George McCowan. William Conrad, Vera Miles, J.D. Cannon, Lynda Day, Earl Holliman. Overweight private-eye hired by wife of old friend to investigate husband's murder; case becomes linked to small-town corruption. Too many subplots make for confusion after halfway mark. Above average; pilot for TV series.

Cannonball (1976) **C-93m.** ** D: Paul Bartel. David Carradine, Veronica Hamel, Bill McKinney, Gerrit Graham, Robert Carradine, Belinda Balaski, Judy Canova, Carl Gottlieb. Rip-off of THE GUMBALL RALLY comes as close to plagiarism as any movie ever made. Funny moments are muted by unpleasant characters and inept stuntwork. As usual, many of Bartel's pals and coworkers appear in bits, including Sylvester Stallone, Roger Corman, and directors Martin Scorsese, Jonathan Kaplan, and Joe Dante.▼

Cannonball Run, The (1981) **C-95m.** BOMB D: Hal Needham. Burt Reynolds, Roger Moore, Farrah Fawcett, Dom De-Luise, Dean Martin, Sammy Davis, Jr., Terry Bradshaw, Jackie Chan, Bert Convy, Jamie Farr, Peter Fonda, Bianca Jagger, Molly Picon, Jimmy "The Greek" Snyder, Mel Tillis. Just what civilization needs—more Reynolds car-chase silliness, this one involving a cross-country auto race. Pretty unendurable, despite unusual cast (though rumor has it that the one responsible for casting Dino and Sammy as priests is still doing his Hail Marys). A rip-off of THE GUMBALL RALLY. Followed by CANNONBALL RUN II.▼

Cannonball Run II (1984) **C-108m.** BOMB D: Hal Needham, Burt Reynolds, Dom DeLuise, Shirley MacLaine, Marilu Henner, Dean Martin, Sammy Davis, Jr., Susan Anton, Catherine Bach, Ricardo Montalban, Jim Nabors, Charles Nelson Reilly, Telly Savalas, Jamie Farr, Jack Elam, Frank Sinatra, Sid Caesar, and many others. Sequel to 1981 box-office hit looks like someone's bad home movies. Amateurish action comedy with tons of tacky guest-star cameos. What a waste!▼

Cannon for Cordoba (1970) **C-104m.** **½ D: Paul Wendkos. George Peppard, Giovanna Ralli, Raf Vallone, Peter Duel, Don Gordon, John Russell. Peppard leads a band of soldiers against Mexican bandits on the Texas border ca. 1912, and tries to destroy stolen cannons. Standard action fare with a familiar ring.

Canon City (1948) **82m.** *** D: Crane Wilbur. Scott Brady, Jeff Corey, Whit Bissell, Stanley Clements, De Forrest Kelley. Solid crime thriller follows members of a prison break from a Colorado State jail in semidocumentary style. Strong and violent with excellent photography by John Alton.

Can She Bake a Cherry Pie? (1983) **C-90m.** *½ D: Henry Jaglom. Karen Black, Michael Emil, Michael Margotta, Frances Fisher, Martin Harvey Friedberg. Neurotic, unpredictable Black, whose husband has just left her, takes up with Emil, who never seems to stop talking. A couple of chuckles, but all the rest is rambling, superficial.▼

Can't Buy Me Love (1987) **C-94m.** **½ D: Steve Rash. Patrick Dempsey, Amanda Peterson, Courtney Gains, Tina Caspary, Seth Green, Sharon Farrell. Known as BOY RENTS GIRL during production, story has nerdy Dempsey paying senior heartthrob Peterson a hard-earned grand to pose as his girlfriend, correctly surmising his own stock will rise. Sentimental rendering of a terrific high school comedy premise. Peterson is excellent, Dempsey just adequate.▼

Canterbury Tale, A (1944-British) **124m.** *** D: Michael Powell, Emeric Pressburger. Eric Portman, Sheila Sim, John Sweet, Dennis Price, Esmond Knight, Charles Hawtrey, Hay Petrie. Curious and disarming film from the Powell–Pressburger writing-and-directing team draws on British eccentricities—and provincial flavor—to flesh out its simple story about three people whose lives cross in a small English village during the war. There's only the slightest tangent with the Chaucer work from which it draws its title. American version with added footage of Kim Hunter runs 95m. and doesn't retain the charm of the original.

Canterbury Tales, The (1971-Italian-French) **C-109m.** BOMB D: Pier Paolo Pasolini. Laura Betti, Ninetto Davoli, Pier Paolo Pasolini, Hugh Griffith, Josephine Chaplin, Michael Balfour, Jenny Runacre. Travelers recount four Chaucer stories—which, unfortunately, are enacted for the viewer. Tiresome, offensive, graphically sadistic, with Pasolini appearing as Chaucer. Italian-English cast; the second of the director's medieval trilogy.▼

Canterville Ghost, The (1944) **96m.** *** D: Jules Dassin. Charles Laughton, Margaret O'Brien, William Gargan, Rags Ragland, Una O'Connor, Robert Young, Peter Lawford, Mike Mazurki. Enjoyable fantasy of 17th-century ghost Laughton, spellbound until descendant Young performs heroic deed.▼

Can't Help Singing (1944) **C-89m.** **½ D: Frank Ryan. Deanna Durbin, Robert Paige, Akim Tamiroff, Ray Collins, Thomas Gomez. Durbin goes West to find her roaming lover; despite good cast and Jerome Kern songs, it's nothing much.

Can't Stop the Music (1980) **C-118m.** ** D: Nancy Walker. The Village People, Valerie Perrine, Bruce Jenner, Steve Guttenberg, Paul Sand, Tammy Grimes, June Havoc, Barbara Rush, Jack Weston, Leigh Taylor-Young. One or two catchy production numbers aren't enough to salvage otherwise stiff comedy about the music-publishing biz, though some will feel they *have* to see what V. People and Jenner are doing in same film. Gay subtext abounds, despite eye-boggling profile shots of Perrine.▼

Canyon Crossroads (1955) **83m.** **½ D: Alfred L. Werker. Richard Basehart, Russell Collins, Phyllis Kirk, Stephen Elliott. On-location filming in Colorado highlights this tale of uranium hunt, with Basehart quite convincing.

Canyon Passage (1946) **C-92m.** *** D: Jacques Tourneur. Dana Andrews, Brian Donlevy, Susan Hayward, Ward Bond, Andy Devine, Lloyd Bridges. Plotty, colorful Western mixing action, beautiful scenery, heated love relationships, and Hoagy Carmichael singing "Ole Buttermilk Sky." Well-made and entertaining.

Canyon River (1956) **C-80m.** *½ D: Harmon Jones. George Montgomery, Marcia Henderson, Peter Graves, Richard Eyer. Trite Western of Indian and rustler attacks on cattle drive.

Can You Feel Me Dancing? (1986) **C-100m. TVM** D: Michael Miller. Justine Bateman, Jason Bateman, Max Gail, Frances Lee McCain, Roger Wilson. Sensitive drama of a blind teenager's struggle to break free from her overly protective family. Inspired by the lives of Cheryl McMannis and Joe Nasser, both of whom have small but pivotal roles in the film uniting Justine Bateman and her brother, Jason, as sister and brother, and coproduced by their father, Kent Bateman. Written by the husband-and-wife team J. Miyoko Hensley and Steven Hensley. Above average.

Can You Hear the Laughter? The Story of Freddie Prinze (1979) **C-100m. TVM** D: Burt Brinckerhoff. Ira Angustain, Kevin Hooks, Randee Heller, Devon Ericson, Julie Carmen, Stephen Elliott. Affectionate account of the meteoric rise of the young comedian and his death by suicide in 1977. Average.▼

Cape Fear (1962) **105m.** *** D: J. Lee Thompson. Gregory Peck, Polly Bergen, Robert Mitchum, Martin Balsam, Lori Martin, Jack Kruschen, Telly Savalas. Well-paced suspenser as sadistic Mitchum seeks revenge on Peck and wife Bergen, highlighted by cat-and-mouse chase in Southern bayous. Based on John D. MacDonald's novel *The Executioners.*▼

Caper of the Golden Bulls, The (1967) **C-104m.** BOMB D: Russell Rouse. Stephen Boyd, Yvette Mimieux, Giovanna Ralli, Walter Slezak, Vito Scotti. Lots of bull but not much gold in this unendurable "thriller" about bank heist in Pamplona.▼

Cape Town Affair, The (1967) **C-103m.** ** D: Robert D. Webb. Claire Trevor, James Brolin, Jacqueline Bisset, Bob Courtney, Jon Whiteley, Gordon Milholland. Pedestrian remake of PICKUP ON SOUTH STREET, made in South Africa. Interest here is seeing Bisset and Brolin at the beginnings of their careers and Trevor making something different of the old Thelma Ritter role. Story deals with a Communist spy ring in Cape Town and an elusive envelope containing top secret microfilm.

Capone (1975) **C-101m.** BOMB D: Steve Carver. Ben Gazzara, Susan Blakely, Harry Guardino, John Cassavetes, Sylvester Stallone, Frank Campanella. Gazzara has cotton in his jowls and a cigar in his mouth, making most of the dialogue in this gangster saga incomprehensible—but that's OK, you've heard it all before. One big shootout is stock footage from THE ST. VALENTINE'S DAY MASSACRE.

Caprice (1967) **C-98m.** BOMB D: Frank Tashlin. Doris Day, Richard Harris, Ray Walston, Jack Kruschen, Edward Mulhare, Lilia Skala, Irene Tsu, Michael J. Pollard. Terrible vehicle for Doris as industrial spy plunged into international intrigue with fellow-agent Harris. Muddled, unfunny, straining to be "mod."

Capricorn One (1978) **C-124m.** *** D: Peter Hyams. Elliott Gould, James Brolin, Hal Holbrook, Sam Waterston, Karen Black, O. J. Simpson, Telly Savalas, Brenda Vaccaro, Denise Nicholas, David Huddleston, Robert Walden, David Doyle. Whirlwind contemporary adventure plays like a condensed Republic serial. First manned flight to Mars turns out to be a hoax, and when capsule supposedly burns up in re-entry, the astronauts suddenly realize they're expendable. Lots of great chases punctuated by Hyams' witty dialogue; not always plausible, but who cares?▼

Captain America (1979) **C-100m. TVM** D: Rod Holcomb. Reb Brown, Len Birman, Heather Menzies, Steve Forrest, Robin Mattson, Joseph Ruskin. Routine attempt to bring legendary comic book crimefighter to TV, this pilot has his ex-Marine son continuing the family tradition of righting wrongs by pursuing an archcriminal who's aiming a neutron bomb at Phoenix. Followed by another TV movie that same year. Below average.▼

Captain America II (1979) **C-100m. TVM** D: Ivan Nagy. Reb Brown, Len Birman, Connie Sellecca, Christopher Lee, Katherine Justice, Lana Wood, Christopher Carey. He's back, righting additional wrongs and defending America from terrorists who plan to use an accelerated aging drug to cripple the government. Average.▼

Captain Apache (1971) **C-94m.** ** D: Alexander Singer. Lee Van Cleef, Carroll Baker, Stuart Whitman, Percy Herbert. Violence in Old West laid on with a trowel. Filled with stereotypes.▼

Captain Blackjack (1951-U.S.-French) **90m.** ** D: Julien Duvivier. George Sanders, Herbert Marshall, Agnes Moorehead,

Patricia Roc, Marcel Dalio. American-French coproduction is pretty tacky tale about drug smuggling in the Mediterranean. Great cast, however, makes it worth a look. Filmed in Spain; released in France at 105m.▼

Captain Blood (1935) 99m. ***½ D: Michael Curtiz. Errol Flynn, Olivia de Havilland, Lionel Atwill, Basil Rathbone, Ross Alexander, Guy Kibbee. Flynn's first swashbuckler hits bullseye; he plays doctor forced to become a pirate, teaming for short spell with French cutthroat Rathbone, but paying more attention to proper young lady de Havilland. Original release print ran 119m. Also shown in computer-colored version.▼

Captain Blood (1960-French) C-95m. ** D: Andre Hunebelle. Jean Marais, Elsa Martinelli, Arnold Foa, Bourvil, Pierrette Bruno. Set in 17th-century France, this juvenile costumer deals with plot to overthrow throne of Louis XIII.

Captain Boycott (1947-British) 92m. **½ D: Frank Launder. Stewart Granger, Kathleen Ryan, Cecil Parker, Mervyn Johns, Alastair Sim. Poor Irish farmers band together to combat the abuses of their landlords in early 19th century; interesting but dramatically uneven, with misplaced components of humor and romance. Robert Donat appears briefly as Charles Parnell; Parker has title role.

Captain Carey, U.S.A. (1950) 83m. *** D: Mitchell Leisen. Alan Ladd, Wanda Hendrix, Francis Lederer, Russ Tamblyn. Nicely turned account of ex-military officer Ladd returning to Italy to uncover informer who cost lives of villagers. Theme song "Mona Lisa" won an Oscar.

Captain Caution (1940) 85m. ** D: Richard Wallace. Victor Mature, Louise Platt, Leo Carrillo, Bruce Cabot, Vivienne Osborne, Robert Barrat. OK action film of spunky Platt commandeering her father's ship into war; no messages, just fast-moving narrative.▼

Captain China (1949) 97m. ** D: Lewis R. Foster. John Payne, Gail Russell, Jeffrey Lynn, Lon Chaney, Edgar Bergen. Often listless sea yarn of Payne, seeking out persons responsible for his losing his ship's command.

Captain Clegg SEE: **Night Creatures**

Captain Eddie (1945) 107m. **½ D: Lloyd Bacon. Fred MacMurray, Lynn Bari, Charles Bickford, Thomas Mitchell, Lloyd Nolan, James Gleason. Routine aviation film doesn't do justice to exciting life of Eddie Rickenbacker; it's standard stuff.

Captain Falcon (1958-Italian) C-97m. *½ D: Carlo Campogalliani. Lex Barker, Rossana Rory, Anna Maria Ferrero, Carla Calo, Massimo Serato. Juvenile account of Barker (Captain Falcon) saving Rory and her principality from clutches of Serato.

Captain From Castile (1947) C-140m. *** D: Henry King. Tyrone Power, Jean Peters, Cesar Romero, Lee J. Cobb, John Sutton, Antonio Moreno. Power is driven to avenge the cruel treatment of his family by Sutton, eventually serves with Cortez (Romero) during the latter's conquest of Mexico. Color and romance; magnificently photographed on location by Charles Clarke and Arthur E. Arling, with an Alfred Newman score that ranks with Hollywood's very best. Peters' film debut.

Captain Fury (1939) 91m. *** D: Hal Roach. Brian Aherne, Victor McLaglen, Paul Lukas, June Lang, John Carradine. Australia serves as background in story of illustrious adventurer fighting evil head of penal colony.

Captain Hates the Sea, The (1934) 93m. ** D: Lewis Milestone. Victor McLaglen, John Gilbert, Walter Connolly, Wynne Gibson, Helen Vinson, Alison Skipworth, Leon Errol, Walter Catlett, Akim Tamiroff, Donald Meek, Arthur Treacher, The Three Stooges. Bizarre, seagoing GRAND HOTEL, with the accent on comedy; various romances and intrigues carry on under bored eye of disgruntled skipper Connolly. Once-in-a-lifetime cast does its best with mediocre script; Gilbert (ironically cast as a heavy drinker) gives a solid performance in his final film.

Captain Horatio Hornblower (1951-British) C-117m. *** D: Raoul Walsh. Gregory Peck, Virginia Mayo, Robert Beatty, Denis O'Dea, Christopher Lee. Exciting, well-produced sea epic based on C. S. Forester's British naval hero of the Napoleonic wars.

Captain Is a Lady, The (1940) 63m. ** D: Robert B. Sinclair. Charles Coburn, Beulah Bondi, Virginia Grey, Helen Broderick, Billie Burke, Dan Dailey. Thin little comedy of Coburn pretending to be a woman to accompany wife Bondi to old ladies' home.

Captain January (1936) 75m. **½ D: David Butler. Shirley Temple, Guy Kibbee, Slim Summerville, Buddy Ebsen, June Lang, Sara Haden. Straightforward, sentimental tale of orphaned Shirley, and the new truant officer who tries to separate her from her adoptive father, lighthouse keeper Kibbee. Short and sweet. Shirley and Ebsen sing and dance "At the Codfish Ball."▼

Captain John Smith and Pocahontas (1953) C-75m. *½ D: Lew Landers. Anthony Dexter, Jody Lawrance, Alan Hale, Jr., Douglass Dumbrille. Title tells all in pedestrian tale set in colonial America.

Captain Kidd (1945) 89m. ** D: Rowland V. Lee. Charles Laughton, Randolph Scott, Barbara Britton, Reginald Owen, John Carradine, Gilbert Roland, Sheldon Leonard. Even with Laughton, this is slow-going low-budget stuff.▼

[166]

Captain Kidd and the Slave Girl (1954) **C-83m.** ** D: Lew Landers. Anthony Dexter, Eva Gabor, Alan Hale, Jr., James Seay. Modest costumer has Dexter and Gabor in title roles romping the seas to find treasure for their benefactor.

Captain Kronos: Vampire Hunter (1974-British) **C-91m.** *** D: Brian Clemens. Horst Janson, John Carson, Caroline Munro, Shane Briant, John Cater, Lois Diane, Ian Hendry. Unique blend of horror and swashbuckler genres follows sword-wielding stranger as he stalks new breed of vampire across European countryside. Artsy, exciting, almost intoxicatingly atmospheric chiller has developed considerable following on both sides of the Atlantic; one of the best (and least typical) Hammer productions. Released in Britain as simply KRONOS.▼

Captain Lightfoot (1955) **C-91m.** *** D: Douglas Sirk. Rock Hudson, Barbara Rush, Jeff Morrow, Finlay Currie, Kathleen Ryan. Fine, flavorful costume adventure about 19th-century Irish rebellion and one of its dashing heroes. Beautifully filmed on location in Ireland.

Captain Mephisto and the Transformation Machine (1945) **100m.** **½ D: Spencer Bennet, Wallace Grissell, Yakima Canutt. Richard Bailey, Linda Stirling, Roy Barcroft, Kenne Duncan. Diverting cliffhanger with villain Barcroft in rare form as Mephisto, seeking ore deposits from underground hideout. Reedited from Republic serial MANHUNT OF MYSTERY ISLAND, its alternate title.

Captain Midnight SEE: **On the Air Live With Captain Midnight**▼

Captain Nemo and the Underwater City (1970) **C-105m.** **½ D: James Hill. Robert Ryan, Chuck Connors, Nanette Newman, Luciana Paluzzi. Average undersea fantasy centering around Captain Nemo who lives in an underwater fortress.

√ **Captain Newman, M.D.** (1963) **C-126m.** *** D: David Miller. Gregory Peck, Angie Dickinson, Tony Curtis, Eddie Albert, Jane Withers, Bobby Darin, Larry Storch, Bethel Leslie, Robert Duvall. Provocative, well-acted comedy-drama about dedicated Army psychiatrist Peck, battling bureaucracy and the macho military mentality on a stateside air base during WW2. Darin is particularly good as a troubled, ill-fated corporal. Based on Leo Rosten's best-selling novel.▼

Captain Pirate (1952) **C-85m.** **½ D: Ralph Murphy. Louis Hayward, Patricia Medina, John Sutton, Charles Irwin, George Givot, Ted de Corsia. Reformed pirate must return to his renegade ways in order to expose the imposter who is using his name; good-enough programmer based on Sabatini's *Captain Blood Returns*.

Captain Scarlett (1953) **C-75m.** *½ D:

Thomas Carr. Richard Greene, Leonora Amar, Nedrick Young, Edourado Noriega. Acceptable costumer with Greene properly dashing.▼

Captains Courageous (1937) **116m.** **** D: Victor Fleming. Spencer Tracy, Freddie Bartholomew, Melvyn Douglas, Lionel Barrymore, Mickey Rooney, John Carradine, Walter Kingsford, Charley Grapewin, Christian Rub. Spoiled richboy Bartholomew falls off cruise ship, rescued by Portuguese fisherman Tracy (who won Oscar for role). Boy learns to love seafaring on crusty Barrymore's fishing ship. Enthusiastic cast; top-notch production of Kipling's story. Scripted by John Lee Mahin, Marc Connelly, and Dale Van Every. Remade as a TV movie. Also shown in computer-colored version.▼

Captains Courageous (1977) **C-110m.** TVM D: Harvey Hart. Karl Malden, Jonathan Kahn, Ricardo Montalban, Fritz Weaver, Neville Brand, Fred Gwynne, Johnny Doran. OK redo of the Kipling classic, with the focus back on Captain Disko Troop (Malden) where it belongs. Young Kahn makes the rich kid an obnoxious snip. Montalban takes the old Spencer Tracy role which, without Tracy's overpowering presence, is cut down to size. Adaptation by John Gay. Average.

Captain Sindbad (1963) **C-85m.** **½ D: Byron Haskin. Guy Williams, Heidi Bruhl, Pedro Armendariz, Abraham Sofaer, Bernie Hamilton. Guy Williams is an energetic Sinbad in this elaborate, effects-filled but ponderous European fantasy.

Captain Sirocco SEE: **Pirates of Capri, The**

Captains of the Clouds (1942) **C-113m.** *** D: Michael Curtiz. James Cagney, Dennis Morgan, Alan Hale, Brenda Marshall, George Tobias. Cagney and company join Canadian air force as a lark, but prove their worth under fire. Colorful wartime drama.

Captain's Paradise, The (1953-British) **77m.** *** D: Anthony Kimmins. Alec Guinness, Yvonne De Carlo, Celia Johnson, Bill Fraser. Guinness has field day as carefree skipper who shuttles back and forth between wives in opposite ports. De Carlo and Johnson make a good contrast as the two women. Original British running time: 86m.▼

Captain's Table, The (1960-British) **C-90m.** ** D: Jack Lee. John Gregson, Peggy Cummins, Donald Sinden, Nadia Gray. Satisfactory comedy involving skipper of cargo vessel (Gregson) who is given trial command of luxury liner, and the chaos ensuing trying to keep order among crew and passengers.▼

Captain Tugboat Annie (1945) **60m.** ** D: Phil Rosen. Jane Darwell, Edgar Kennedy, Charles Gordon, Mantan Moreland, Pamela Blake, Hardie Albright, H.B. Warner. Annie sails again in low-budget epic which depends entirely on its stars, Darwell and Kennedy, for its flavor.

Captive City, The (1952) **90m.** ****½** D: Robert Wise. John Forsythe, Joan Camden, Harold J. Kennedy, Marjorie Crosland, Victor Sutherland, Ray Teal, Martin Milner. Small-town newspaper editor investigates local corruption when the law ignores situation. Earnest but undistinguished melodrama.

Captive Girl (1950) **73m.** D: William Berke. Johnny Weissmuller, Buster Crabbe, Anita Lhoest, Rick Vallin, John Dehner. SEE: **Jungle Jim** series

Captive Heart, The (1946-British) **108m.** *****½** D: Basil Dearden. Michael Redgrave, Mervyn Johns, Basil Radford, Jack Warner, Jimmy Hanley, Gordon Jackson, Ralph Michael, Rachel Kempson. Compelling examination of British P.O.W.s during WW2 and their German captors with controlled, flawless performance by Redgrave and excellent supporting cast. Patrick Kirwan's story was scripted by Angus MacPhail and Guy Morgan. Original British running time: 98m.

Captive Hearts (1987) **C-97m.** ****** D: Paul Almond. Noriyuki (Pat) Morita, Chris Makepeace, Mari Sato, Michael Sarrazin, Seth Sakai. American soldier shot down and taken prisoner in Japan during WW2 falls in love with a Japanese woman. If that sounds familiar, or simplistic, wait till you see the film! Easy to see why this barely made it to theaters.▼

Captive Wild Woman (1943) **61m.** ****½** D: Edward Dmytryk. John Carradine, Evelyn Ankers, Milburn Stone, Acquanetta, Martha MacVicar (Vickers), Lloyd Corrigan. Carradine turns an orangutan into beautiful woman (Acquanetta), who goes berserk with unrequited love. Good fun; Stone's animal-training scenes are stock footage of Clyde Beatty from THE BIG CAGE. Sequels: JUNGLE WOMAN, JUNGLE CAPTIVE.

Capture, The (1950) **81m.** ****½** D: John Sturges. Lew Ayres, Teresa Wright, Victor Jory, Duncan Renaldo. Straightforward account climaxing in Mexico: detective reinvestigates robbery to learn if he might have shot an innocent man.

Captured (1933) **72m.** ****½** D: Roy Del Ruth. Leslie Howard, Douglas Fairbanks, Jr., Paul Lukas, Margaret Lindsay. Fair story of honor and love, switching WW1 story from German prison camp, to warfront, to society England. Good cast major asset of production.

Car, The (1977) **C-95m.** ***½** D: Elliot Silverstein. James Brolin, Kathleen Lloyd, John Marley, Ronny Cox, R.G. Armstrong, John Rubinstein. Hokey thriller about a killer car demonically running down most of the cast. Unfortunately it takes over 90 minutes, while *Twilight Zone* once did a tidier, quite similar job in one third the time.▼

Caravan (1934) **101m.** ****½** D: Erik Charrell. Loretta Young, Charles Boyer, Jean Parker, Phillips Holmes, Louise Fazenda. Offbeat musical of royal Loretta forced to marry vagabond Boyer; main interest is curiosity in this not altogether successful film.

Caravans (1978-U.S.-Iranian) **C-123m.** ****½** D: James Fargo. Anthony Quinn, Jennifer O'Neill, Michael Sarrazin, Christopher Lee, Joseph Cotten, Barry Sullivan. Expensive-looking version of James Michener's contemporary desert epic about a search through the Middle East for the daughter (O'Neill) of a U.S. senator. Won't fool those who recognize it as just another updated version of THE SEARCHERS.

Carbine Williams (1952) **91m.** ******* D: Richard Thorpe. James Stewart, Jean Hagen, Wendell Corey, Paul Stewart, James Arness. Sturdy history of the inventor of famed gun, his problems with the law, and his simple family life. Stewart is most convincing in title role. Also shown in computer-colored version.▼

Carbon Copy (1981) **C-92m.** ****** D: Michael Schultz. George Segal, Susan Saint James, Denzel Washington, Jack Warden, Paul Winfield, Dick Martin, Tom Poston. Segal has hidden his identity as a Jew and become a successful corporate executive—until the arrival of his illegitimate 17-year-old son (Washington), who is black. Silly, uneven, but not uninteresting blend of comedy and social drama. Written by Stanley Shapiro.▼

Card, The SEE: **Promoter, The**▼

Cardiac Arrest (1980) **C-90m.** ****** D: Murray Mintz. Garry Goodrow, Mike Chan, Maxwell Gail, Susan O'Connell, Ray Reinhardt. Murderer is terrorizing San Francisco, removing the hearts of his victims, and the cops are stumped.▼

Cardinal, The (1963) **C-175m.** ****½** D: Otto Preminger. Tom Tryon, Romy Schneider, Carol Lynley, Maggie McNamara, John Saxon, John Huston, Robert Morse, Cecil Kellaway, Dorothy Gish, Burgess Meredith. Long, long story of an Irish-American's rise from priesthood to the college of Cardinals. Has some outstanding vignettes by old pros like Meredith, but emerges as an uneven, occasionally worthwhile film.▼

Cardinal Richelieu (1935) **83m.** ****½** D: Rowland V. Lee. George Arliss, Maureen O'Sullivan, Edward Arnold, Cesar Romero. Arliss etches another historical portrayal of France's unscrupulous cardinal who controlled Louis XIII (Arnold). Good cast supports star.

Care Bears Adventure in Wonderland!, The (1987-Canadian) **C-75m.** ** D: Raymond Jafelice. Voices of Bob Dermer, Eva Almos, Dan Hennessy, Jim Henshaw, Colin Fox. The Care Bears follow Alice through the looking glass in this typically bland kiddie outing, with music by John Sebastian.▼

Care Bears Movie, The (1985-Canadian) **C-75m.** ** D: Arna Selznick. Voices of Mickey Rooney, Georgia Engel. Songs by Carole King, John Sebastian. Animated feature based on heavily merchandised characters is strictly for toddlers, tough sledding for anyone older. Produced by Canadian Nelvana animation studio. Followed by two sequels and a TV series.▼

Care Bears Movie II, The: A New Generation (1986) **C-77m.** BOMB D: Dale Schott. Voices of Maxine Miller, Pam Hyatt, Hadley Kay. Your kids deserve better entertainment than this treacly stuff about the Kingdom of Caring. Prefab animation from the era of toy merchandising tie-ins.▼

Career (1959) **105m.** *** D: Joseph Anthony. Dean Martin, Anthony Franciosa, Shirley MacLaine, Carolyn Jones, Joan Blackman, Robert Middleton, Donna Douglas. Occasionally shrill, generally forceful presentation of an actor's (Franciosa's) tribulations in seeking Broadway fame; Jones is excellent as lonely talent agent.

Career Girl (1959) **C-61m.** *½ D: Harold David. June Wilkinson, Charles Robert Keane, Lisa Barrie, Joe Sullivan. Sloppy account of Wilkinson going to Hollywood, seeking screen career; sleazy production values.

Carefree (1938) **80m.** *** D: Mark Sandrich. Fred Astaire, Ginger Rogers, Ralph Bellamy, Luella Gear, Jack Carson, Franklin Pangborn. Madcap Rogers is sent to psychiatrist Astaire, and romance naturally blossoms; Fred and Ginger's most comic outing, wacky and offbeat, with good Irving Berlin score including "Change Partners," "I Used to Be Color Blind."▼

Careful, He Might Hear You (1983-Australian) **C-116m.** ***½ D: Carl Schultz. Wendy Hughes, Robyn Nevin, Nicholas Gledhill, John Hargreaves, Geraldine Turner. Involving drama about Depression-era custody battle between wealthy Hughes and working-class sister Nevin for their nephew, whose mother is dead and father has abandoned him. Manages to be credible yet larger-than-life at the same time, with wonderful shadings and observations. Effectiveness of its wide-screen camerawork will be lost on TV, alas. Based on a novel by Sumner Locke Elliott.▼

Caretaker, The SEE: **Guest, The**

Caretakers, The (1963) **97m.** *** D: Hall Bartlett. Robert Stack, Joan Crawford, Polly Bergen, Susan Oliver, Janis Paige, Constance Ford, Barbara Barrie, Herbert Marshall. At times incisive view of a West Coast mental hospital, marred by flimsy script and poor editing. Good characterizations by Crawford and Ford as nurses, Bergen and Paige as patients.

Carey Treatment, The (1972) **C-101m.** *** D: Blake Edwards. James Coburn, Jennifer O'Neill, Pat Hingle, Skye Aubrey, Elizabeth Allen, Alex Dreier. Good solid whodunit set in hospital, where doctor Coburn is determined to clear colleague of murder charge. O'Neill provides love interest in complicated but satisfying mystery, shot in Boston.

Cargo to Capetown (1950) **80m.** *½ D: Earl McEvoy. Broderick Crawford, John Ireland, Ellen Drew, Edgar Buchanan. Tramp steamer is setting for mild love triangle as Crawford and Ireland vie for Drew.

Caribbean (1952) **C-97m.** ** D: Edward Ludwig. John Payne, Arlene Dahl, Cedric Hardwicke, Francis L. Sullivan, Woody Strode. Costume vehicle set in 18th-century allows Payne to battle pirates and flirt with Dahl.

Caribbean Mystery, A (1983) **C-100m.** TVM D: Robert Lewis. Helen Hayes, Barnard Hughes, Jameson Parker, Season Hubley, Swoosie Kurtz, Stephen Macht, Beth Howland, Maurice Evans, Brock Peters. Miss Marple returns—delightfully played by Helen Hayes—to unmask the murderer of a retired British officer (Evans) at a posh resort in the Bahamas. Script by Sue Grafton and Steve Humphrey. Above average.

Cariboo Trail (1950) **C-81m.** **½ D: Edwin L. Marin. Randolph Scott, George "Gabby" Hayes, Bill Williams, Karin Booth, Victor Jory. Standard telling of conflict between cattlemen and settlers bringing civilization obliterating the grazing lands.

Carl Sandburg—Echoes and Silences (1982) **C-119m.** TVM D: Perry Miller Adato. John Cullum, Michael Higgins, Frances Conroy, Peter Michael Goetz, James Green. Top-notch biographical portrait of the celebrated, beloved American writer-historian, with Cullum (in the title role) and Adato effectively capturing the essence of Sandburg and his times. A PBS *American Playhouse* presentation. Above average.

Carlton-Browne of the F.O. SEE: **Man in a Cocked Hat**▼

Carly's Web (1987) **C-100m.** TVM D: Kevin Inch. Daphne Ashbrook, Cyril O'Reilly, Vincent Baggetta, Peter Billingsley, Bert Rosario, Jennifer Dale, Gary Grubbs. Painless comedy pilot about a lowly Justice Department clerk's unorthodox adventures in big-time crimebusting. Average.

Carmen (1983-Spanish) **C-102m.** *** D: Carlos Saura. Antonio Gades, Laura Del Sol, Paco de Lucia, Cristina Hayos, Juan Antonio Jimenez, Sebastian Moreno. Choreographer prepares dance production of Bizet's opera, but falls under spell of real-life Carmen he casts in leading role. Choreographer/star Gades and sensual Del Sol are superb, though dramatic impact dissipates somewhat during second half. A must for dance buffs.▼

Carmen (1984-French-Italian) **C-152m.** ** D: Francesco Rosi. Julia Migenes-Johnson, Placido Domingo, Ruggero Raimondi, Faith Esham, Jean-Philippe Lafont, Gerard Garino. Disappointing filmization of the Bizet opera is overbaked and unbelievably inept. Still, opera buffs will enjoy the music—if they close their eyes.▼

Carmen Jones (1954) **C-105m.** ***½ D: Otto Preminger. Dorothy Dandridge, Harry Belafonte, Pearl Bailey, Roy Glenn, Diahann Carroll, Brock Peters. Powerful melodrama adapted from Bizet's opera by Oscar Hammerstein II, with exciting music and equally exciting Dandridge as the ultimate femme fatale. Stars' singing voices are all dubbed— Dandridge's by opera star Marilyn Horne. Film debuts of Carroll and Peters.▼

Carnal Knowledge (1971) **C-96m.** *** D: Mike Nichols. Jack Nicholson, Candice Bergen, Arthur Garfunkel, Ann-Margret, Rita Moreno, Cynthia O'Neal, Carol Kane. Jules Feiffer's script details sexual attitudes and obsessions of two men from college through middle-age. Thought-provoking but depressing. Ann-Margret won acclaim for performance as Nicholson's kittenish mistress. Kane's film debut.▼

Carnegie Hall (1947) **134m.** **½ D: Edgar G. Ulmer. Marsha Hunt, William Prince, Frank McHugh, Martha O'Driscoll. Lame story about a pushy mother and her pianist son links magnificent concert performances by the cream of the classical music world: Artur Rubinstein, Leopold Stokowski, Jascha Heifetz, Rise Stevens, Lily Pons, Ezio Pinza, Jan Peerce, Gregor Piatigorsky, Bruno Walter and The New York Philharmonic. Some mediocre pop tunes are shoehorned into the proceedings, along with Vaughn Monroe and Harry James.

Carnival in Costa Rica (1947) **C-95m.** ** D: Gregory Ratoff. Dick Haymes, Vera-Ellen, Cesar Romero, Celeste Holm, Anne Revere, J. Carrol Naish. Despite fair cast, boring musical of trip to Costa Rica and the shenanigans of newlyweds and their quarreling parents.

Carnival of Souls (1962) **80m.** **½ D: Herk Harvey. Candace Hilligoss, Sidney Berger, Frances Feist, Herk Harvey, Stan Levitt, Art Ellison. Eerie little film of "phantom figure" pursuing Hilligoss after

she has seemingly drowned. Imaginative low-budget effort. Filmed mostly in Lawrence, Kansas. Original running-time: 91m.▼

Carnival Rock (1957) **75m.** ** D: Roger Corman. Susan Cabot, Dick Miller, Brian Hutton, The Platters, David Houston, David J. Stewart. Stewart, owner of a dilapidated nightclub, loves singer Cabot, who in turn loves gambler Hutton. Forgettable melodrama with The Platters, Houston, and others in musical cameos.▼

Carnival Story (1954) **C-95m.** ** D: Kurt Neumann. Anne Baxter, Steve Cochran, Lyle Bettger, George Nader, Jay C. Flippen. Hardened Baxter is involved with sleazy Cochran. "Nice guy" high diver Bettger takes her on as a protégée, and there are complications. When this romantic melodrama is not trashy, it's sluggish. Set in Germany, and not unlike E.A. Dupont's classic, VARIETY. A German version was also filmed, with Eva Bartok, Bernhard Wicki, and Curt Jurgens.▼

Carny (1980) **C-107m.** *** D: Robert Kaylor. Gary Busey, Jodie Foster, Robbie Robertson, Meg Foster, Bert Remsen, Kenneth McMillan, John Lehne, Elisha Cook, Craig Wasson. Striking, atmospheric film about a symbiotic pair of carnival hustlers and the teenage runaway who joins them on the road. Candid, intimate (and somewhat voyeuristic) look at seamy midway life, hurt by unsatisfying and abrupt conclusion. Rock star Robertson also produced and cowrote the film. Wonderful score by Alex North.▼

Carolina Cannonball (1955) **74m.** *½ D: Charles Lamont. Judy Canova, Andy Clyde, Jack Kruschen, Ross Elliott. Hicksville hokum with Canova involved with enemy agents and a missile that lands in her backyard.

Carousel (1956) **C-128m.** ***½ D: Henry King. Gordon MacRae, Shirley Jones, Cameron Mitchell, Barbara Ruick, Claramae Turner, Robert Rounseville, Gene Lockhart. Excellent filmization of Rodgers & Hammerstein's memorable adaptation of Ferenc Molnar's *Liliom*, with MacRae as rowdy carousel barker Billy Bigelow, who tries to change for the better when he falls in love with Jones. Excitement of wide-screen location filming will be minimized on TV, but moving characters, timeless songs ("If I Loved You," "Soliloquy," "You'll Never Walk Alone," etc.) remain. Script by Phoebe and Henry Ephron. Filmed before as LILIOM in 1930 and 1934.▼

Carpetbaggers, The (1964) **C-150m.** **½ D: Edward Dmytryk. George Peppard, Alan Ladd, Carroll Baker, Bob Cummings, Martha Hyer, Elizabeth Ashley, Lew Ayres, Martin Balsam, Audrey Totter, Archie Moore. Blowsy claptrap based on Harold

Robbins novel of millionaire plane manufacturer (Peppard) dabbling in movies and lovemaking à la Howard Hughes. Set in 1920s-30s; sex-ploitational values are tame. Ladd's last film; followed by prequel, NEVADA SMITH.▼

Carpool (1983) **C-100m. TVM** D: E. W. Swackhamer. Harvey Korman, Ernest Borgnine, Peter Scolari, T. K. Carter, Stephanie Faracy, Chuck McCann, Graham Jarvis. Lackluster comedy about a group of computer-matched carpoolers who stumble across a million dollars and then have to fight not only each other but gangsters and crooked cops to see who keeps the cash. Average.

Carrie (1952) **118m. **½ D: William Wyler. Jennifer Jones, Laurence Olivier, Miriam Hopkins, Eddie Albert, Mary Murphy. Jones passively plays title role in this turn-of-the-century story of farm girl who becomes famed actress. Olivier is excellent as her married lover. Based on Theodore Dreiser novel.

Carrie (1976) **C-97m. **½ D: Brian De Palma. Sissy Spacek, Piper Laurie, William Katt, John Travolta, Amy Irving, Nancy Allen, Betty Buckley, P.J. Soles, Priscilla Pointer. Evocative story of high school misfit degenerates into cheap, gory melodrama when Spacek's telekinetic powers are unleashed in revenge against those who have mocked her. De Palma borrows a great deal from Hitchcock, but has little of The Master's wit or subtlety. Screenplay by Lawrence D. Cohen, from Stephen King's novel. Debut film for Irving, Buckley and Soles. Later a stage musical.▼

Carrington, V. C. SEE: **Court Martial**▼
Carry on Admiral SEE: **Ship Was Loaded, The**

Carry on Camping (1972-British) **C-89m. ** D: Gerald Thomas. Sidney James, Kenneth Williams, Joan Sims, Barbara Windsor, Bernard Bresslaw, Terry Scott. The gang encounters hippie types at weekend campsite; usual double-entendre jokes in entry from never-ending series.

Carry on Cleo (1965-British) **C-92m. **½ D: Gerald Thomas. Amanda Barrie, Sidney James, Kenneth Williams, Joan Sims, Kenneth Connor, Charles Hawtrey. Diverting reworking of ancient history to serve as amusing satire on CLEOPATRA epic, sufficiently laced with hijinks by perennial misfits.▼

Carry on Doctor (1968-British) **C-95m. ** D: Gerald Thomas. Frankie Howerd, Kenneth Williams, Jim Dale, Barbara Windsor. Madcap group takes on medical profession. As usual, interest wanes after an hour and the amount of laughter varies quite a bit.▼

Carry on Henry VIII (1972-British) **C-90m. ** D: Gerald Thomas. Sidney James, Kenneth Williams, Joan Sims,

Charles Hawtrey, Barbara Windsor. Lecherous king, ribald times perfect milieu for "Carry On" gang's brand of farce; for fans only. Likely to be trimmed for TV.

Carry on Nurse (1959-British) **90m. *** D: Gerald Thomas. Kenneth Connor, Shirley Eaton, Charles Hawtrey, Hattie Jacques, Terence Longdon, Leslie Phillips, Joan Sims, Kenneth Williams, Wilfrid Hyde-White, Joan Hickson, Jill Ireland, Michael Medwin. Quite hilarious madcaps with series stock company involved in patients-vs.-hospital-staff battle of authority.▼

Carry on Sergeant (1959-British) **88m. ** D: Gerald Thomas. William Hartnell, Bob Monkhouse, Shirley Eaton, Eric Barker, Dora Bryan, Bill Owen, Kenneth Connor. This time around prankish misfits are the bane of Army officer's existence, who swears he'll make these recruits spiffy soldiers or bust.

Carry on Spying (1965-British) **88m. **½ D: Gerald Thomas. Kenneth Williams, Barbara Windsor, Bernard Cribbins, Charles Hawtrey, Eric Barker, Victor Maddern. Acceptable James Bond spoof with daffy novice spy-catchers on the hunt for enemy agents who stole secret formula.

Carson City (1952) **C-87m. ** D: Andre de Toth. Randolph Scott, Raymond Massey, Lucille Norman, George Cleveland. UK railroad story in 1870s West as construction engineer Scott battles to get the track down.

Cars That Ate Paris, The (1974-Australian) **C-91m. **½ D: Peter Weir. Terry Camilleri, John Meillon, Melissa Jaffa, Kevin Miles. The poor people of Paris (Paris, Australia, that is) keep the economy going by inducing traffic accidents and selling the spare parts/scrap metal. Iffy black comedy has its moments; must viewing for those who've followed Weir's directorial career step-by-step into the big leagues. Originally released in the U.S. at 74m, retitled THE CARS THAT EAT PEOPLE; full-length version finally made it here in 1984.▼

Cars That Eat People, The SEE: **Cars That Ate Paris, The**▼

Carter's Army (1969) **C-72m. TVM** D: George McCowan. Stephen Boyd, Robert Hooks, Susan Oliver, Roosevelt Grier, Paul Stewart, Moses Gunn, Richard Pryor, Billy Dee Williams. Southern Army captain handed company of all blacks with no prior combat experience to defend dam during WW2. Clichéd, despite good cast (including young Pryor). Below average.

Carthage in Flames (1959-Italian) **C-96m. ** D: Carmine Gallone. Jose Suarez, Pierre Brasseur, Anne Heywood, Illaria Occhini. Unremarkable mixture of love and intrigue set against backdrop of Rome-Carthage war of 2nd century B.C.; spirited action scenes.▼

Cartier Affair, The (1984) **C-100m. TVM**
D: Rod Holcomb. Joan Collins, David
Hasselhoff, Telly Savalas, Ed Lauter, Stephen Apostle Pec. TV sex goddess falls
for the charming thief who's out to rip off
her jewelry collection so he can pay off
debt to former prison cellmate. Collins not
only sends up her own public persona but
wears outfits she herself designed (and
takes credit for in the closing crawl).
Average.▼
Cartouche (1964-French-Italian) **C-115m.**
***½ D: Philippe De Broca. Jean-Paul
Belmondo, Claudia Cardinale, Odile Versois,
Philippe Lemaire, Marcel Dalio, Noel
Roquevert. Colorful, exciting exploits of
18th-century Frenchman and friends who
take over crime syndicate in Paris, eventually dedicating their lives to avenging death
of co-leader Venus (Cardinale). Rousing
action comedy; Cardinale and Belmondo
never better.
Car Trouble (1985-British) **C-93m.** *** D:
David Green. Julie Walters, Ian Charleson,
Vincenzo Ricotta, Stratford Johns, Hazel
O'Connor, Dave Hill. Low-key farce about
a hilariously hideous couple whose Bickerson-like marriage is put to the ultimate test
when he buys his dream car, and she goes
for a fateful spin. Walters and Charleson
are ideal, and the film offers some genuine
belly laughs. ▼
Car Wash (1976) **C-97m.** **½ D: Michael Schultz. Richard Pryor, Franklin
Ajaye, Sully Boyar, Ivan Dixon, George
Carlin, Irwin Corey, Melanie Mayron, The
Pointer Sisters, Garrett Morris, Antonio
Fargas. Boisterous look at L.A. car-wash
is light excuse for barely connected comedy set-pieces, involving various and sundry characters, and pulsating soul music
performed by Rose Royce. Often very
funny, but no awards for good taste; written by Joel Schumacher.▼
Casablanca (1942) **102m.** **** D: Michael Curtiz. Humphrey Bogart, Ingrid
Bergman, Paul Henreid, Claude Rains,
Conrad Veidt, Peter Lorre, Sydney Greenstreet, Dooley Wilson, Marcel Dalio, S.Z.
Sakall, Joy Page. Everything is right in
this WW2 classic of war-torn Casablanca
with elusive nightclub owner Rick (Bogart)
finding old flame (Bergman) and her
husband, underground leader Henreid,
among skeletons in his closet. Rains is
marvelous as dapper police chief, and
nobody sings "As Time Goes By" like
Dooley Wilson. Three Oscars include Picture, Director, and Screenplay (Julius &
Philip Epstein and Howard Koch). Our
candidate for the best Hollywood movie of
all time. Also shown in computer-colored
version.▼
Casanova (1987) **C-150m. TVM** D: Simon Langton. Richard Chamberlain, Faye
Dunaway, Sylvia Kristel, Ornella Muti,

Hanna Schygulla, Sophie Ward, Frank
Finlay. Lighthearted, often bawdy romp
providing another star turn for Chamberlain, as the legendary 18th-century lover,
and an international cast of lovelies as his
boudoir mates. Wittily written by George
MacDonald Fraser and directed with panache by Britisher Langton, but overlong.
Average.
Casanova & Co. (1976-Austrian-Italian-
French-German) **C-88m.** *½ D: Franz
Antel. Tony Curtis, Marisa Berenson, Sylva
Koscina, Hugh Griffith, Britt Ekland,
Marisa Mell, Umberto Orsini, Andrea
Ferreol, Victor Spinetti, Jean Bell, Olivia
Pascal, Lillian Muller. Misfired slapstick
romp debunks the legend with Curtis playing
dual roles of Casanova and a lookalike
commoner. Diverse female cast (including
former *Playboy* Playmates) disrobes at will,
while Tony in drag explicitly mocks his
classic SOME LIKE IT HOT role. Retitled SEX ON THE RUN.
Casanova Brown (1944) **94m.** **½ D:
Sam Wood. Gary Cooper, Teresa Wright,
Frank Morgan, Anita Louise, Isobel Elsom.
Cooper has divorced Wright, but now she's
pregnant; entertaining little comedy with
stars outshining material. Previously filmed
in 1930 and 1939 as LITTLE ACCIDENT.
Casanova in Burlesque (1944) **74m.** **½
D: Leslie Goodwins. Joe E. Brown, June
Havoc, Dale Evans, Lucien Littlefield, Ian
Keith. Shakespearean professor leads double life as burlesque clown; spirited little
comedy with Brown in good form.
Casanova's Big Night (1954) **C-86m.** ***
D: Norman Z. McLeod. Bob Hope, Joan
Fontaine, Audrey Dalton, Basil Rathbone,
Raymond Burr, Vincent Price. Lavish costumed fun with Bob masquerading as Casanova (Price) in Venice and wooing lovely
Fontaine.▼
Casanova '70 (1965-French-Italian) **C-113m.**
**½ D: Mario Monicelli. Marcello Mastroianni, Virna Lisi, Michele Mercier,
Marisa Mell, Marco Ferreri, Enrico Maria
Salerno. Dashing Major Mastroianni is only
interested in seducing women when there
is an element of danger involved. Modest,
though amusing.
Casa Ricordi SEE: **House of Ricordi**
Casbah (1948) **94m.** **½ D: John Berry.
Yvonne de Carlo, Tony Martin, Peter Lorre,
Marta Toren, Hugo Haas. Musical remake
of ALGIERS isn't bad, with Martin coming off surprisingly well amid good Harold
Arlen-Leo Robin tunes and colorful production; Lorre fine as determined police
detective after Martin in the Casbah.
Case Against Brooklyn, The (1958) **82m.**
*½ D: Paul Wendkos. Darren McGavin,
Maggie Hayes, Warren Stevens, Peggy
McCay. Unexciting little exposé yarn involves fledgling cop McGavin combatting
gambling syndicate in title borough.

Case Against Mrs. Ames, The (1936) 85m. **½ D: William Seiter. Madeleine Carroll, George Brent, Arthur Treacher, Alan Baxter, Beulah Bondi. D.A. Brent finds himself falling in love with beautiful Carroll, suspected of murdering her husband.

Case Closed (1988) C-100m. TVM D: Dick Lowry. Byron Allen, Charles Durning, Marc Alaimo, James Greene, Eddie Jones, Erica Gimpel. Half-baked cop flick cleaning up BEVERLY HILLS COP, putting in a road-company Eddie Murphy and plunking the whole mess down in Atlanta. A complete misfire for standup comic turned actor Allen, who also coproduced and wrote this one. Below average.

Case of Deadly Force, A (1986) C-100m. TVM D: Michael Miller. Richard Crenna, John Shea, Lorraine Toussaint, Frank McCarthy, Tom Isbell, Tate Donovan, Anna Maria Horsford. True story of a Boston attorney's struggle to clear the name of an innocent black man killed by police, after the force had stonewalled the investigation. Good production values enhance the strong story. Dennis Nemec adapted the book about the case by Lawrence O'Donnell, Jr., the son of the lawyer (well played, as usual, by Crenna). Above average.

Case of Dr. Laurent, The (1958-French) 91m. ** D: Jean-Paul le Chanois. Jean Gabin, Nicole Courcel, Sylvia Monfort, Michel Barbey. Film was exploited theatrically for its frank birth sequence, only small logical sequence in recounting life of country doctor Gabin who advocates natural childbirth.▼

Case of Jonathan Drew, The SEE: **Lodger, The** (1926)▼

Case of Mrs. Loring, The SEE: **Question of Adultery, A**

Case of Rape, A (1974) C-100m. TVM D: Boris Sagal. Elizabeth Montgomery, William Daniels, Cliff Potts, Rosemary Murphy, Ronny Cox, Patricia Smith. Middle-class housewife (Montgomery) reports being raped and finds that her ordeal has only begun, as the personal humiliations from the police, medical personnel, and the courts, and the waning trust from her husband (Cox) make her feel that she is the guilty one. Sensitively handled by Montgomery and director Sagal, but script, written by Robert E. Thompson, keeps veering toward the melodramatic. Look for Tom Selleck in a small role. Above average.

Case of the Curious Bride, The (1935) 80m. ** D: Michael Curtiz. Warren William, Margaret Lindsay, Donald Woods, Claire Dodd, Allen Jenkins, Wini Shaw. Shrill Perry Mason film takes offhanded approach to murder mystery with large doses of humor; Perry (William) is more interested in gourmet food than he is in the

case! Errol Flynn has small role as the victim in his second Hollywood film.

Case of the Hillside Stranglers, The (1989) C-100m. TVM D: Steven Gethers. Richard Crenna, Dennis Farina, Billy Zane, Tony Plana, James Tolkan, Karen Austin, Robert Harper. Crenna, so credible as detectives in innumerable TV movies, puts a spin on this one as the investigator of the real-life serial killers stalking women in and around L.A. in 1977–78. Unfortunately there's little to work with in director Gethers' talky script, which doesn't show any of the killings and wraps everything up too neatly. Average.

Case of the Red Monkey (1955-British) 73m. ** D: Ken Hughes. Richard Conte, Rona Anderson, Colin Gordon, Russell Napier. Acceptable police-on-the-case fare, tracking down murderers of atomic scientists.

Casey's Shadow (1978) C-117m. **½ D: Martin Ritt. Walter Matthau, Alexis Smith, Robert Webber, Murray Hamilton, Andrew A. Rubin, Stephen Burns. Lackadaisical family film about a ne'er-do-well horse trainer who has to raise three sons after his wife leaves him. Generally satisfactory, but should have been better.▼

Cash (1933-British) 73m. ** D: Zoltan Korda. Robert Donat, Wendy Barrie, Edmund Gwenn, Clifford Heatherley, Morris Harvey. Dull, disappointing comedy about ex-rich boy Donat, now working for a living, who becomes involved with pretty Barrie and scheming father Gwenn. Even Donat and Gwenn can't save it. The U.S. title was FOR LOVE OR MONEY; also known as IF I WERE RICH.▼

Cash McCall (1959) C-102m. **½ D: Joseph Pevney. James Garner, Natalie Wood, Nina Foch, Dean Jagger, E.G. Marshall, Henry Jones, Otto Kruger, Roland Winters. Garner is just right as business tycoon who adopts new set of values as he romances daughter (Wood) of failing businessman Jagger. Superficial film from Cameron Hawley novel.

Cash on Delivery (1956-British) 82m. ** D: Muriel Box. Shelley Winters, John Gregson, Peggy Cummins, Wilfrid Hyde-White. Story with a twist suffers from sloppy execution. Winters seeks to earn inheritance by preventing ex-husband's wife from having a child. Original title: TO DOROTHY A SON.

Casino (1980) C-100m. TVM D: Don Chaffey. Mike Connors, Barry Van Dyke, Gene Evans, Hedley Mattingly, Gary Burghoff, Joseph Cotten, Lynda Day George, Robert Reed, Barry Sullivan, Sherry Jackson. A recycling of Blake Edwards' old *Mr. Lucky* series and a pilot for a prospective new series starring Connors as the owner of a luxurious hotel/gambling palace. Edwards is billed as creative consultant. Average.▼

Casino Murder Case (1935) **85m.** D: Edwin L. Marin. Paul Lukas, Alison Skipworth, Donald Cook, Rosalind Russell, Arthur Byron. SEE: **Philo Vance** series.

Casino Royale (1967-British) **C-130m.** **½ D: John Huston, Ken Hughes, Robert Parrish, Joe McGrath, Val Guest. Peter Sellers, Ursula Andress, David Niven, Orson Welles, Joanna Pettet, Woody Allen, Deborah Kerr, William Holden, Charles Boyer, John Huston, George Raft, Jean-Paul Belmondo, Jacqueline Bisset. Gigantic, overdone spoof of James Bond films with Niven as the aging secret agent who relinquishes his position to nephew Allen and host of others. Money, money everywhere, but film is terribly uneven—sometimes funny, often not. Good score by Burt Bacharach, including hit song "The Look of Love."▼

Cassandra Crossing, The (1977-British) **C-127m.** *** D: George Pan Cosmatos. Richard Harris, Sophia Loren, Burt Lancaster, Ava Gardner, Martin Sheen, O.J. Simpson, John Phillip Law, Ingrid Thulin, Alida Valli, Lionel Stander. Entertaining disaster epic as train carrying plague approaches a weakened bridge. Filmed in France, Italy.▼

Cass Timberlane (1947) **119m.** **½ D: George Sidney. Spencer Tracy, Lana Turner, Zachary Scott, Tom Drake, Mary Astor, Albert Dekker. Overblown adaptation of Sinclair Lewis novel of esteemed judge trying to keep pace with new young wife; not Tracy's cup of tea.

Cast a Dark Shadow (1957-British) **84m.** *** D: Lewis Gilbert. Dirk Bogarde, Margaret Lockwood, Kay Walsh, Mona Washbourne. Bogarde is well cast as money-grasping wife-killer who is out to do in his latest mate, Lockwood; exciting throughout.

Cast a Giant Shadow (1966) **C-142m.** ** D: Melville Shavelson. Kirk Douglas, John Wayne, Frank Sinatra, Yul Brynner, Senta Berger, Angie Dickinson, James Donald, Luther Adler, (Chaim) Topol. Hokey bio of Arab-Israeli war hero Mickey Marcus has Kirk leaving Angie's bed to join Senta and several other less sexy freedom fighters. Guest roles by big names make film seem even sillier.▼

Cast a Long Shadow (1959) **C-82m.** *½ D: Thomas Carr. Audie Murphy, Terry Moore, John Dehner, James Best, Rita Lynn, Denver Pyle, Ann Doran. Murphy, troubled by shady past, is reformed by being given a ranch and building a new future; plodding oater.

Castaway (1987) **C-117m.** **½ D: Nicolas Roeg. Oliver Reed, Amanda Donohoe, Tony Rickards, Todd Rippon, Georgina Hale, Frances Barber. Scruffy Reed advertises for a "wife" to join him for a year on a desert island; Donohoe is the incongru-

ously vavavoomish adventure seeker who answers it. Visually splendid adaptation of Lucy Irvine's best-seller seems unlikely *as told*, though it remains a visceral experience, particularly for Roeg fans. Eventually overplays its hand.▼

Castaway Cowboy, The (1974) **C-91m.** ** D: Vincent McEveety. James Garner, Vera Miles, Robert Culp, Eric Shea, Elizabeth Smith, Gregory Sierra. Cowboy Garner is shipwrecked on Hawaiian island, runs into pretty widow and bad-guy Culp who wants her land. Old B-Western plot, Disney-fied on Hawaiian locations.▼

Castaways on Gilligan's Island, The (1979) **C-74m.** TVM D: Earl Bellamy. Bob Denver, Alan Hale, Jim Backus, Natalie Schafer, Russell Johnson, Dawn Wells, Judith Baldwin, Tom Bosley, Marcia Wallace. In the second of the "new" *Gilligan's Island* series, the shipwrecked gang decides to turn their tropical paradise into a tourist trap. Average.

Castillan, The (1963-Spanish) **C-129m.** **½ D: Javier Seto. Cesar Romero, Alida Valli, Frankie Avalon, Broderick Crawford, Spartaco Santoni. Strange grouping of actors are given little support by sticky script in costumer of nobleman leading his people against invaders.

Castle, The (1968-German-Swiss) **C-93m.** *** D: Rudolf Noelte. Maximilian Schell, Cordula Trantow, Trudik Daniel, Helmut Qualtinger. Appropriately vague filmization of Kafka's novel: "K" (Schell), a land surveyor, is called to a castle for work but is unable to gain admittance.▼

Castle in the Desert (1942) **62m.** D: Harry Lachman. Sidney Toler, Arleen Whelan, Richard Derr, Douglass Dumbrille, Henry Daniell, Victor Sen Yung. See: **Charlie Chan** series.▼

Castle Keep (1969) **C-105m.** *½ D: Sydney Pollack. Burt Lancaster, Peter Falk, Patrick O'Neal, Jean-Pierre Aumont, Scott Wilson, Al Freeman, Jr., Tony Bill, Bruce Dern, Astrid Heeren, Michael Conrad. Pretentious adaptation of William Eastlake's novel about eight soldiers on French border in WW2. Good cast, but film has no coherency.

Castle of Blood SEE: **Castle of Terror, The**▼

Castle of Evil (1966) **C-81m.** BOMB D: Francis D. Lyon. Scott Brady, Virginia Mayo, David Brian, Lisa Gaye, Hugh Marlowe. Electronic man belonging to dead chemist becomes unprogrammed at the reading of his master's will and starts killing the survivors. Producers should have taken the film's production costs and bought a candy bar instead.▼

Castle of Fu Manchu, The (1968) **92m.** BOMB D: Jess Franco. Christopher Lee, Richard Greene, Maria Perschy, Gunther Stoll, Howard Marion Crawford. Lee buries Fu Manchu with this one—the pits—experimenting with more deadly potions in his castle near Istanbul and parrying with his perennial adversary, Nayland Smith (Greene) of Britain's Home Office. Another international production. Originally released in the U.S. as ASSIGNMENT ISTANBUL.

Castle of Terror, The (1964-Italian-French) **85m.** ** D: Anthony Dawson (Antonio Margheriti). Barbara Steele, George Riviere, Margrete Robsahm, Henry Kruger, Montgomery Glenn, Sylvia Sorente. On a wager, poet spends the night in haunted castle. Atmospheric chiller. Remade by the same director as WEB OF THE SPIDER.▼

Castle of the Living Dead (1964-Italian-French) **90m.** ** D: Herbert Wise (Luciano Ricci). Christopher Lee, Gala Germani, Philippe Leroy, Jacques Stanislawski, Donald Sutherland. Lee is suitably cast as sinister Count Drago, who mummifies visitors to his gothic castle. Unexceptional horror fare, notable mainly as Sutherland's film debut.▼

Castle of the Walking Dead SEE: Torture Chamber of Dr. Sadism, The▼

Castle on the Hudson (1940) **77m.** *** D: Anatole Litvak. John Garfield, Pat O'Brien, Ann Sheridan, Burgess Meredith, Jerome Cowan, Henry O'Neill, Guinn "Big Boy" Williams, John Litel. Faithful but familiar remake of 20,000 YEARS IN SING SING, with tough, stubborn hood Garfield going up against dedicated, reform-minded warden O'Brien.

Cast the First Stone (1989) **C-100m.** TVM D: John Korty. Jill Eikenberry, Richard Masur, Elizabeth Ruscio, Joe Spano, Lew Ayres, Anne Schedeen, Salome Jens, Dick Anthony Williams. Small-town teacher (a former nun) is raped by a hitchhiker, becomes pregnant, and decides to keep the baby; then she's fired for immoral behavior! Pedestrian drama. Average.

Casual Sex? (1988) **C-97m.** **½ D: Genevieve Robert. Lea Thompson, Victoria Jackson, Stephen Shellen, Jerry Levine, Andrew Dice Clay, Mary Gross. Lightweight look at two young women who are looking for something more than a one-night stand—especially in these cautious times—and try their luck at a health and fitness spa. Slight but engaging contemporary comedy from young women's point of view, adapted from the play by Wendy Goldman and Judy Toll.▼

Casualties of War (1989) **C-113m.** ** D: Brian De Palma. Michael J. Fox, Sean Penn, Don Harvey, John C. Reilly, John Leguizamo, Thuy Thu Le, Erik King, Sam Robards. Vietnam War picture focusing on one patrol, led by off-the-wall Penn, and its inhumane treatment of an innocent Vietnamese girl. As the Voice of Reason,

Fox is well cast, but his clean-cut decency gets to be a bit much; Penn and Thu Le (the victim) are more effective. For all its good intentions, film has a jumbled, detached feel to it (though it's scripted by playwright David Rabe, a Vietnam veteran and author of *Sticks and Bones* and *Streamers*). Based on a real incident detailed in Daniel Lang's *New Yorker* article, subsequently published as a book ▼

Casualty of War, A (British-1990) **C-100m.** TVM D: Tom Clegg. Shelly Hack, David Threlfall, Amanda Burton, Richard Hope, Alan Howard, Clark Peters. Frederick Forsyth espionage thriller about a British ex-spy who goes undercover in Libya to foil a plot to furnish arms to the IRA. Average.

Cat, The (1966) **C-87m.** BOMB D: Ellis Kadison. Peggy Ann Garner, Barry Coe, Roger Perry, Dwayne Redlin. Humdrum account of boy separated from parents on camping trip, saved from rustler's wrath by wildcat he befriended.▼

Catalina Caper (1967) **C-84m.** *½ D: Lee Sholem. Tommy Kirk, Del Moore, Peter Duryea, Robert Donner, Ulla Stromstedt, Brian Cutler, Little Richard, The Cascades. There's little to recommend—not even Little Richard—in this forgettable beach-party item about college boys Kirk and Cutler on the trail of art thieves. Also known as NEVER STEAL ANYTHING WET.

Catamount Killing, The (1974-German) **C-93m.** ** D: Krzysztof Zanussi. Horst Buchholz, Ann Wedgeworth, Chip Taylor, Louise Clark, Patricia Joyce, Polly Holliday. German film made in Vermont with Polish director. Passably interesting story of two small-town people who try to pull off bank heist and then come to grips with themselves as criminals.▼

Cat and Mouse (1974) SEE: **Mousey**

Cat and Mouse (1975-French) **C-107m.** ***½ D: Claude Lelouch. Michele Morgan, Serge Reggiani, Philippe Leotard, Jean-Pierre Aumont, Valerie Lagrange. Anyone could've killed wealthy Aumont, philandering husband of Morgan, and Inspector Reggiani finds out who and why. Denouement is only letdown in this delightful comedy mystery, written, directed, and produced by master Lelouch. Dazzling views of Paris and the countryside. Released here in 1978.▼

Cat and the Canary, The (1927) **75m.** *** D: Paul Leni. Laura LaPlante, Tully Marshall, Flora Finch, Creighton Hale, Gertrude Astor, Lucien Littlefield. Delightful silent classic, the forerunner of all "old dark house" mysteries, with nice touch of humor throughout as heiress LaPlante and nervous group spend night in haunted house. Remade several times.▼

Cat and the Canary, The (1939) **72m.**

*** D: Elliott Nugent. Bob Hope, Paulette Goddard, Gale Sondergaard, John Beal, Douglass Montgomery, Nydia Westman, George Zucco. Entertaining remake of the venerable "old dark house" chiller, spiced with Hope's brand of humor. This film cemented his movie stardom and led to the even more successful scare comedy THE GHOST BREAKERS. Remade again in 1978.

Cat and the Canary, The (1978-British) C-90m. **½ D: Radley Metzger. Honor Blackman, Michael Callan, Edward Fox, Wendy Hiller, Olivia Hussey, Carol Lynley, Peter McEnery, Wilfrid Hyde-White. Entertaining remake of the old-dark-house staple, with a likable cast; reasonably faithful to the original, with the nicest twist being Hyde-White's method of communicating with his heirs.▼

Cat and the Fiddle, The (1934) 90m. *** D: William K. Howard. Jeanette MacDonald, Ramon Novarro, Frank Morgan, Charles Butterworth, Jean Hersholt. Delightful Jerome Kern-Oscar Hammerstein operetta, filled with sly comedy and clever ideas. Novarro is a struggling composer who forces his attentions on MacDonald; Morgan is "benefactor" who comes between them. Songs include "The Night Was Made for Love," "She Didn't Say Yes." Final sequence is in color.

✓ **Cat Ballou** (1965) C-96m. ***½ D: Elliot Silverstein. Jane Fonda, Lee Marvin, Michael Callan, Dwayne Hickman, Tom Nardini, John Marley, Reginald Denny, Jay C. Flippen. Funny Western spoof, with Fonda as Cat Ballou, notorious schoolteacher-turned-outlaw. Marvin copped an Oscar for his dual role as a drunken gunman and his twin, a desperado with an artificial nose. Nat King Cole and Stubby Kaye appear as strolling minstrels.▼

Catcher, The (1971) C-100m. TVM D: Allen H. Miner. Michael Witney, Jan-Michael Vincent, Tony Franciosa, Catherine Burns, David Wayne, Mike Kellin, Anne Baxter. Seattle policeman and Harvard grad join forces in locating fugitives, runaway husbands, missing children throughout U.S. Good locations main asset in otherwise unmemorable drama. Shot on videotape. Average.

Catch Me a Spy SEE: To Catch a Spy▼

Catch My Soul (1974) C-95m. *½ D: Patrick McGoohan. Richie Havens, Lance LeGault, Season Hubley, Tony Joe White, Susan Tyrrell, Delaney and Bonnie Bramlett. Jack Good's rock-opera adaptation of Shakespeare's *Othello*, with Havens as sanctimonious preacher and LeGault as his Iago is uninvolving, heavy-handed stuff. Some good music, but if the play's the thing, this one doesn't make it. Retitled: SANTA FE SATAN.

Catch-22 (1970) C-121m. **½ D: Mike Nichols. Alan Arkin, Martin Balsam, Richard Benjamin, Art Garfunkel, Jack Gilford, Bob Newhart, Anthony Perkins, Paula Prentiss, Martin Sheen, Jon Voight, Orson Welles, Buck Henry. Long, labored, expensive film of Joseph Heller's book halfway succeeds in capturing surrealist insanity of Army life during WW2. Heavy-handedness spoils potential, with good cast trying its best. Scripted by costar Henry.▼

Catch Us If You Can SEE: Having a Wild Weekend

Cat Creature, The (1973) C-72m. TVM D: Curtis Harrington. Meredith Baxter, David Hedison, Gale Sondergaard, Stuart Whitman, Keye Luke, John Carradine, Peter Lorre, Jr. Script by Robert Bloch and good direction combine in unusual horror tale of cat goddess possessing victims to gain access to gold amulet. Good suspense. Above average.

Cat Creeps, The (1946) 58m. BOMB D: Erle C. Kenton. Noah Beery, Jr., Lois Collier, Paul Kelly, Douglass Dumbrille, Rose Hobart. Lowest of low-grade horrors, with cat possessing dead girl's soul.

Catered Affair, The (1956) 93m. *** D: Richard Brooks. Bette Davis, Ernest Borgnine, Debbie Reynolds, Barry Fitzgerald, Rod Taylor. Davis sheds all glamour as Bronx taxi driver's wife wanting to give daughter ritzy wedding. Based on Paddy Chayefsky TV play. Also shown in computer-colored version.

Cat from Outer Space, The (1978) C-104m. **½ D: Norman Tokar. Ken Berry, Sandy Duncan, McLean Stevenson, Harry Morgan, Roddy McDowall, Ronnie Schell. Kids will probably like this Disney fantasy-comedy, though it holds few surprises: cat from another world seeks help from U.S. scientists to repair his spaceship, but military protocol and enemy spying get in the way. Ironically, plot has many similarities to later E.T.!▼

Cat Girl (1957-British) 69m. *½ D: Alfred Shaughnessy. Barbara Shelley, Robert Ayres, Kay Callard, Paddy Webster. Shelley is possessed by family curse which gives her a psychic link with ferocious leopard; rash of murders ensues. Pacing and low production values spoil it.

Catherine & Co. (1975-French-Italian) C-99m. ** D: Michel Boisrond. Jane Birkin, Patrick Dewaere, Jean-Pierre Aumont, Vittorio Caprioli, Jean-Claude Brialy. Slight sexual comedy about young girl who becomes prostitute and decides to incorporate herself. TV prints run 84m.▼

Catherine the Great (1934-British) 92m. ✓ **½ D: Paul Czinner. Douglas Fairbanks, Jr., Elisabeth Bergner, Flora Robson, Joan Gardner, Gerald Du Maurier. Lavish historical drama of Russian czarina whose life is spoiled by rigidly planned marriage. Slow-moving but interesting. Also known as THE RISE OF CATHERINE THE GREAT.▼

Catholics (1973) **C-78m. TVM** D: Jack Gold. Trevor Howard, Martin Sheen, Raf Vallone, Cyril Cusack, Andrew Keir, Michael Gambon, Leon Vitale. Powerful futuristic religious drama pitting strong-willed abbot Howard against emissary-of-change Sheen, sent by the Vatican to his secluded monastery. Wordy but thought-provoking; adapted by Brian Moore from his novel. Above average.▼

Catlow (1971) **C-103m.** **½ D: Sam Wanamaker. Yul Brynner, Richard Crenna, Leonard Nimoy, Daliah Lavi, Jo Ann Pflug, Jeff Corey. Outlaw tries to avoid interference on his way to $2 million gold robbery. Basically a comedy, with a surprisingly ebullient Brynner. Based on a Louis L'Amour novel.

Cat on a Hot Tin Roof (1958) **C-108m.** ***½ D: Richard Brooks. Elizabeth Taylor, Paul Newman, Burl Ives, Jack Carson, Judith Anderson, Madeleine Sherwood, Larry Gates. Southern patriarch Ives learns he is dying; his greedy family, except for son Newman, falls all over itself sucking up to him. Tennessee Williams' classic study of "mendacity" comes to the screen somewhat laundered but still packing a wallop; entire cast is sensational. Adaptation by Brooks and James Poe.▼

Cat o' Nine Tails, The (1971-Italian-German-French) **C-112m.** BOMB D: Dario Argento. Karl Malden, James Franciscus, Catherine Spaak, Cinzia De Carolis, Carlo Alighiero. Former newsman Malden, now blind, teams with reporter Franciscus to track down psycho killer in this gruesome murder mystery; graphic gore and sex, and badly dubbed, to boot.▼

Cat People (1942) **73m.** *** D: Jacques Tourneur. Simone Simon, Kent Smith, Tom Conway, Jack Holt, Jane Randolph. Storyline and plot elements don't hold up, but moments of shock and terror are undiminished in the first of producer Val Lewton's famous horror films. Smith falls in love with strange, shy woman (Simon) who fears ancient curse of the panther inside her. Followed by CURSE OF THE CAT PEOPLE. Remade in 1982.▼

Cat People (1982) **C-118m.** ** D: Paul Schrader. Nastassia Kinski, Malcolm McDowell, John Heard, Annette O'Toole, Ruby Dee, Ed Begley, Jr., Scott Paulin, John Larroquette. Virginal Kinski moves in with brother McDowell, a "cat man," and falls in love with zoo curator Heard as a black panther rampages through community. Sexy, bloody, technically well crafted, but uneven and ultimately unsatisfying; Schrader seems more concerned with camera angles and nudity than coherent storyline. Loosely based on the 1942 film.▼

Cat's Eye (1985) **C-93m.** *½ D: Lewis Teague. Drew Barrymore, James Woods, Alan King, Kenneth McMillan, Robert Hays, Candy Clark, James Naughton. Trio of heavy-handed Stephen King stories, short on irony, long on mean-spiritedness.▼

Cat's Paw, The (1934) **90m.** **½ D: Sam Taylor. Harold Lloyd, Una Merkel, George Barbier, Alan Dinehart, Grace Bradley, Nat Pendleton. Harold is a missionary's son, raised in China; he comes to U.S. a babe in the woods, is duped into running for mayor in big city by corrupt politicos who regard him as perfect patsy. Odd Capraesque comedy ends with strange denouement where Lloyd takes law into his own hands. A real curio. Edited for TV.

C.A.T. Squad (1986) **C-100m. TVM** D: William Friedkin. Joe Cortese, Jack Youngblood, Steve W. James, Patricia Charbonneau, Barry Corbin, Eddie Velez, Anna Maria Horsford. Disappointing return to television for director Friedkin, with STAR WARS weaponry mercifully getting in the way of uninteresting actors who make up an elite government counter-terrorist unit. Busted series pilot. Followed by a sequel. Below average. Retitled STALKING DANGER for video.▼

C.A.T. Squad: Python Wolf (1988) **C-100m. TVM** D: William Friedkin. Joe Cortese, Jack Youngblood, Steve James, Deborah Van Valkenburgh, Miguel Ferrer, Alan Scarfe. Government counter-terrorist group takes on a top-secret mission in South Africa to thwart a high-tech pirate's plans to illegally export radioactive materials. OK action followup to Friedkin's initial C.A.T. movie. Retitled PYTHON WOLF for homevideo. Average.▼

Cattle Annie and Little Britches (1980) **C-95m.** *** D: Lamont Johnson. Burt Lancaster, Rod Steiger, Amanda Plummer, Diane Lane, John Savage, Scott Glenn, Michael Conrad. Very pleasant little Western, which was thrown away by its distributor, Universal. In 1893, Eastern girls Plummer (Annie) and Lane (Britches) join the remnants of the Doolin-Dalton gang and inspire them to pull a few more jobs. Winning cast, including Plummer in her film debut. Based on Robert Ward's novel.

Cattle Drive (1951) **C-77m.** **½ D: Kurt Neumann. Joel McCrea, Dean Stockwell, Leon Ames, Chill Wills. Stockwell does well in role of bratty teen-ager who learns a sense of values from veteran cowhand McCrea on arduous cow drive.

Cattle Empire (1958) **C-83m.** ** D: Charles Marquis Warren. Joel McCrea, Gloria Talbott, Don Haggerty, Phyllis Coates. McCrea agrees to lead cattle drive, planning revenge on cattle owners who sent him to jail; OK Western.

Cattle King (1963) **C-88m.** ** D: Tay Garnett. Robert Taylor, Joan Caulfield,

Robert Loggia, Robert Middleton, Larry Gates, Malcolm Atterbury. Control of grazing land subject of standard Western confrontation saga, Taylor and Middleton squaring off in forgettable drama.

Cattle Queen of Montana (1954) **C-88m.** ****½** D: Allan Dwan. Barbara Stanwyck, Ronald Reagan, Gene Evans, Lance Fuller, Anthony Caruso, Jack Elam. Stanwyck battles to protect her livestock and property from plundering by Indians—and a ruthless villain (Evans). Reagan plays second fiddle to feisty Stanwyck here—but they're both done in by mediocre script. Beautiful scenery helps.▼

Cattle Town (1952) **71m.** ****** D: Noel Smith. Dennis Morgan, Philip Carey, Amanda Blake, Rita Moreno, Sheb Wooley, Merv Griffin. Both Warner Bros. and Morgan were at low points when this sad echo of a slick Western was churned out.

Cat Women of the Moon (1954) **64m.** ***½** D: Arthur Hilton. Sonny Tufts, Victor Jory, Marie Windsor, Bill Phipps, Douglas Fowley, Susan Morrow. All-star cast in tacky sci-fi entry about a moon expedition that discovers female civilization and its underground empire. Originally shown in 3D; also known as ROCKET TO THE MOON. Remade as MISSILE TO THE MOON.▼

Caught (1949) **88m.** ******* D: Max Ophuls. James Mason, Barbara Bel Geddes, Robert Ryan, Frank Ferguson, Curt Bois, Natalie Schafer. Compelling, intelligent story of young girl who marries powerful millionaire, tries to escape her shallow existence with him. Fine performances, skilled direction by Ophuls.▼

Caught in the Draft (1941) **82m.** ******* D: David Butler. Bob Hope, Dorothy Lamour, Lynne Overman, Eddie Bracken. The last thing movie-star Hope wants is to get drafted, but he accidentally enlists himself. Very funny service comedy.

Cauldron of Blood (1967-Spanish-U.S.) **C-95m.** ***½** D: Edward Mann (Santos Alcocer). Boris Karloff, Viveca Lindfors, Jean-Pierre Aumont, Jacqui Speed, Rosenda Monteros. Sordid, sleep-inducing tale of blind sculptor (Karloff) whose skeletal models are actually victims of his murdering wife. Also known as BLIND MAN'S BLUFF.▼

Cause for Alarm (1951) **74m.** ****½** D: Tay Garnett. Loretta Young, Barry Sullivan, Bruce Cowling, Margalo Gillmore. Young registers most convincingly as panic-stricken woman being framed for murder by her insane husband Sullivan.▼

Cavalcade (1933) **110m.** ******** D: Frank Lloyd. Diana Wynyard, Clive Brook, Herbert Mundin, Ursula Jeans, Margaret Lindsay, Beryl Mercer, Una O'Connor, Billy Bevan, Frank Lawton. Lavish Hollywood adaptation of Noel Coward's London stage success (which may remind many of TV's *Upstairs, Downstairs*) chronicling two families from eve of the 20th century to early 1930s. Nostalgic, richly atmospheric, but also sharply critical of war and the aftershocks that brought an end to a wonderful way of life. Oscar winner for Best Picture, Best Director, and "Interior Decoration" (it *is* handsome).

Cavalry Scout (1951) **C-78m.** ****** D: Lesley Selander. Rod Cameron, Audrey Long, Jim Davis, James Millican. Routine Western of scout Cameron tracking down stolen army goods and romancing Long.

Cave-In! (1983) **C-100m.** TVM D: Georg Fenady. Dennis Cole, Susan Sullivan, Ray Milland, Leslie Nielsen, Julie Sommars, James Olson, Lonny Chapman, Sheila Larkin. Disaster master Irwin Allen literally scraped bottom with this one, sending a tour party of familiar TV faces into a cavern with an escaped con and trapping them all in not one but *two* cave-ins. This one gathered dust on a shelf for more than four years before being foisted on viewers. Below average.

Caveman (1981) **C-92m.** ****½** D: Carl Gottlieb. Ringo Starr, Barbara Bach, John Matuszak, Shelley Long, Dennis Quaid, Avery Schreiber, Jack Gilford. Stoned-age spoof follows prehistoric Starr's adventures in One Zillion B.C. as a misfit who forms his own tribe, which is composed of outcasts from other caves. Dum-dum comedy saved by fantastic (and funny) special-effects dinosaurs created by David Allen.▼

Cave of Outlaws (1951) **C-75m.** ****** D: William Castle. Macdonald Carey, Alexis Smith, Edgar Buchanan, Victor Jory. Search for stolen gold leads ex-con, lawman, miner, et al. to title situation; Smith is wasted.

Cavern, The (1966) **83m.** ****½** D: Edgar G. Ulmer. Rosanna Schiaffino, John Saxon, Brian Aherne, Peter L. Marshall, Larry Hagman, Hans Von Borsody. Six soldiers are trapped for five months in cavern with luscious Schiaffino, but plot contrivance isn't handled badly in above-average programmer. The prolific director's swan song.

C.C. and Company (1970) **C-88m.** ***½** D: Seymour Robbie. Joe Namath, Ann-Margret, William Smith, Jennifer Billingsley, Teda Bracci, Greg Mullavey, Sid Haig, Bruce Glover, Wayne Cochran & the C.C. Riders. Broadway Joe gets sacked in his first starring role as a motorcyclist who tangles with Smith's biker gang while trying (not very hard) to fight off Ann-Margret's advances. Bracci's comedy relief is principal virtue, but the really big laughs are unintentional. Produced by Roger Smith (who also wrote the screenplay) and Allan Carr.▼

Cease Fire (1985) **C-97m.** ****½** D: David Nutter. Don Johnson, Lisa Blount, Robert F. Lyons, Richard Chaves, Rick Richards,

Chris Noel. Earnest drama about Vietnam vet who's still haunted by his experiences fifteen years later and unwilling to acknowledge that he has a problem. Sincere, poignant at times, but dramatically uneven. George Fernandez adapted script from his one-act play. ▼

Ceiling Zero (1935) **95m.** *** D: Howard Hawks, James Cagney, Pat O'Brien, June Travis, Stuart Erwin, Barton MacLane, Isabel Jewell. Irresponsible mail flier Cagney causes no end of grief for old pal (and boss) O'Brien, especially when he sets his sights on young pilot Travis. Typically machine-gun-paced Hawks drama belies its stage origins; one of the best Cagney-O'Brien vehicles. Based on the play by Frank "Spig" Wead; remade as INTERNATIONAL SQUADRON.

Celebration at Big Sur (1971) **C-82m.** ** D: Baird Bryant, Johanna Demetrakas. Joan Baez, Crosby, Stills, Nash and Young, Joni Mitchell, John Sebastian, Mimi Fariña. Lesser folk-rock documentary, filmed at 1969 Big Sur Festival, suffers from poor production values. Baez is highlighted, singing "I Shall Be Released," "Song for David," etc.

Celeste (1981-German) **C-107m.** *** D: Percy Adlon. Eva Mattes, Jurgen Arndt, Norbert Wartha, Wolf Euba, Leo Bardischewski. Slow-moving but stunningly photographed and detailed account of the relationship between Marcel Proust (Arndt) and his devoted housekeeper (Mattes). Based on the real Celeste's memoirs.

Cell 2455, Death Row (1955) **77m.** ** D: Fred F. Sears. William Campbell, Kathryn Grant, Vince Edwards, Marian Carr. Unsensational retracing of life of sex-offender Caryl Chessman and his bouts, while in prison, for retrials. Alan Alda later played Chessman in KILL ME IF YOU CAN.

Cemetery Girls SEE: **Velvet Vampire, The**▼

Centennial Summer (1946) **C-102m.** **½ D: Otto Preminger. Jeanne Crain, Cornel Wilde, Linda Darnell, Dorothy Gish, William Eythe, Constance Bennett, Walter Brennan. Leisurely, plush musical of Philadelphia Exposition of 1876, with sisters Crain and Darnell both after handsome Wilde; nice Jerome Kern score helps.

Centerfold Girls, The (1974) **C-93m.** *½ D: John Peyser. Andrew Prine, Tiffany Bolling, Aldo Ray, Ray Danton, Francine York, Jeremy Slate, Mike Mazurki, Dan Seymour. Fine cast of familiar faces helps routine tale of psycho Prine offing pinup girls.▼

Central Park (1932) **61m.** **½ D: John Adolfi. Joan Blondell, Guy Kibbee, Wallace Ford, Henry B. Walthall, Patricia Ellis, Charles Sellon. Blondell and Ford uplift this programmer as a pair of small-town kids making their way in the big city

who inadvertently become involved with gangsters. Set entirely in N.Y.C.'s Central Park.

Ceremony, The (1963) **105m.** **½ D: Laurence Harvey. Laurence Harvey, Sarah Miles, Robert Walker, Jr., John Ireland, Ross Martin, Lee Patterson, Noel Purcell. Mishmash about convicted killer rescued by brother who demands liaison with sister-in-law as reward.

Certain Fury (1985) **C-87m.** BOMB D: Stephen Gyllenhaal. Tatum O'Neal, Irene Cara, Nicholas Campbell, George Murdock, Moses Gunn, Peter Fonda. Atrocious film about two girls on the lam, featuring a pair of Academy Award winners (as the ads proclaimed) giving two of the worst performances in recent memory. Made in Canada.▼

Certain Smile, A (1958) **C-106m.** **½ D: Jean Negulesco. Rossano Brazzi, Joan Fontaine, Bradford Dillman, Christine Carere. Françoise Sagan's novella becomes overblown soap opera in romantic trivia between Parisian students Carere and Dillman, interrupted when she is beguiled by roué Brazzi; chic Fontaine is wasted.

Cervantes SEE: **Young Rebel**

Cesar (1933-French) **170m.** ***½ D: Marcel Pagnol. Raimu, Pierre Fresnay, Orane Demazis, Charpin, Andre Fouche, Alida Rouffe. Fanny's son (Fouche), now grown, learns that his father is Marius (Fresnay), not Panisse (Charpin). Raimu steals the film in the title role, particularly when he gives a poignant discourse on death. Third of Pagnol's trilogy, preceded by MARIUS and FANNY. All three were the basis of the play and movie FANNY (1961).▼

Cesar and Rosalie (1972-French-Italian-German) **C-104m.** *** D: Claude Sautet. Yves Montand, Romy Schneider, Sami Frey, Umberto Orsini, Eva Marie Meineke, Isabelle Huppert. Appealing stars in typically French story of a menage à trois relationship (a woman and her two lovers) and how it changes over the years.▼

Chad Hanna (1940) **C-86m.** ** D: Henry King. Henry Fonda, Dorothy Lamour, Linda Darnell, Guy Kibbee, Jane Darwell, John Carradine. Rather flat circus drama set in 19th-century New York; colorful but empty.

Chadwick Family, The (1974) **C-78m.** TVM D: David Lowell Rich. Fred Mac-Murray, Kathleen Maguire, Darleen Carr, Jane Actman, Stephen Nathan, Lara Parker. Undistinguished soap opera, with MacMurray moving from the dad of *My Three Sons* to patriarch of a clan consisting of wife Maguire, three daughters, one son, two sons-in-law, and the Chinese boyfriend of his youngest girl. Average.

Chained (1934) **76m.** **½ D: Clarence Brown. Joan Crawford, Clark Gable, Otto Kruger, Stuart Erwin, Una O'Connor, Akim Tamiroff. Chic formula MGM love triangle with Crawford torn between love for Gable and married lover Kruger.

Chained Heat (1983-U.S.-German) **C-95m.** BOMB D: Paul Nicolas. Linda Blair, John Vernon, Sybil Danning, Tamara Dobson, Stella Stevens, Louisa Moritz, Nita Talbot, Michael Callan, Henry Silva, Edy Williams. Innocent Blair finds herself in a prison where the warden has a hot tub in his office. Strictly for the 42nd Street grind-house crowd.▼

Chaingang Girls SEE: **Sweet Sugar**▼

Chain Lightning (1950) **94m.** ** D: Stuart Heisler. Humphrey Bogart, Eleanor Parker, Raymond Massey, Richard Whorf. Static account of jet pilot Bogart who reforms in an effort to win back Parker; flight scenes uninspired.

Chain of Evidence (1957) **64m.** *½ D: Paul Landres. Bill Elliott, Don Haggerty, James Lydon, Claudia Barrett. Programmer has dedicated cop Elliott track down real killer of businessman.

Chain Reaction (1980-Australian) **C-87m.** **½ D: Ian Barry. Steve Bisley, Arna-Maria Winchester, Ross Thompson, Ralph Cotterill, Patrick Ward. OK drama chronicling the repercussions of a nuclear plant accident on worker Thompson and couple (Bisley, Winchester) who assist him in trying to publicize danger.▼

✓ **Chairman, The** (1969) **C-102m.** **½ D: J. Lee Thompson. Gregory Peck, Anne Heywood, Arthur Hill, Alan Dobie, Conrad Yama. Lots of talk but little action in story of American scientist sent to Communist China on super-secret espionage mission.▼

Chalk Garden, The (1964-British) **C-106m.** *** D: Ronald Neame. Deborah Kerr, Hayley Mills, John Mills, Edith Evans, Felix Aylmer, Elizabeth Sellars. Very-high-class soap opera with good cast supporting story of teenager set on right path by governess Kerr; colorful production, quite entertaining. From Enid Bagnold play.▼

Challenge, The (1960) SEE: **It Takes a Thief**

Challenge, The (1970) **C-90m.** TVM D: Allen Smithee. Darren McGavin, Broderick Crawford, Mako, James Whitmore, Skip Homeier, Paul Lukas, Sam Elliott, Adolph Caesar. Odd sequence of events—returning orbital missile satellite crash-lands far from designated splashdown area; small Communist country's ship reaches it first and claims right of salvage—brings two nations to brink of nuclear war. Film's actual director is unknown ("Allen Smithee" is the standard pseudonym). Originally broadcast at 73m. Average.

Challenge (1974) **C-84m.** BOMB D: Martin Beck. Earl Owensby, William Hicks, Katheryn Thompson, Johnny Popwell. North Carolina-based Owensby's first film (which he also produced) amateurishly goes through the usual vengeance-for-killing-my-family paces. Opens with a printed crawl celebrating this as the return of "clean, decent entertainment," followed by Owensby blowing away half the cast with a shotgun. But don't worry—none of his victims is naked. Dreadful.▼

Challenge, The (1982) **C-112m.** **½ D: John Frankenheimer. Scott Glenn, Toshiro Mifune, Donna Kei Benz, Atsuo Nakamura, Calvin Young. Entertaining but sometimes pretentious actioner, with American boxer Glenn becoming involved in conflict between brothers Mifune and Nakamura over rights to family swords. Scripted by John Sayles and Richard Maxwell. Exteriors shot mostly in Kyoto; may be of interest to Japanophiles.▼

Challenge for Robin Hood, A (1968-British) **C-85m.** ** D: C. M. Pennington-Richards. Barrie Ingham, James Hayter, Leon Greene, Peter Blythe, Gay Hamilton, Alfie Bass. Hammer Films produced this inoffensive but undistinguished adventure yarn, which is of little interest except to children. Originally 96m.

Challenge of a Lifetime (1985) **C-100m.** TVM D: Russ Mayberry. Penny Marshall, Richard Gilliland, Jonathan Silverman, Mary Woronov, Paul Gleeson, Mark Spitz, Cathy Rigby-McCoy. Divorcée, spurred on by teenaged son, becomes obsessed with competing in Hawaii's Ironman Triathlon—or Penny's true grit in what appears to have been a personal real-life passion. Written by her friend, Peachy Markowitz. Average.▼

Challenger (1990) **C-150m.** TVM D: Glenn Jordan. Karen Allen, Barry Bostwick, Julie Fulton, Richard Jenkins, Brian Kerwin, Joe Morton, Keone Young, Lane Smith, Peter Boyle. Reverent chronicle of the Challenger space shuttle disaster in January 1986, with a flag-waving script by George Englund and the blessings of NASA. Average.

Challengers, The (1969) **C-100m.** TVM D: Leslie Martinson. Darren McGavin, Sean Garrison, Nico Minardos, Anne Baxter, Richard Conte, Farley Granger. Top professional racing drivers competing for Grand Prix; off track, for same girl. Embarrassing script. Below average.

Challenge To Be Free (1976) **C-88m.** **½ D: Tay Garnett. Mike Mazurki, Vic Christy, Jimmy Kane, Fritz Ford. Fur trapper is pursued by the law in Arctic surroundings; simple and simple-minded, best for younger viewers. Made in 1972 as MAD TRAPPER OF THE YUKON, this marked last film for veteran director Garnett, who appears briefly as Marshal McGee.▼

Challenge to Lassie (1949) **C-76m.** **½ D: Richard Thorpe. Edmund Gwenn, Donald Crisp, Geraldine Brooks, Reginald

Owen, Alan Webb, Ross Ford, Henry Stephenson, Alan Napier, Sara Allgood, Arthur Shields. Based-on-fact story, set in 19th-century Edinburgh, about a dog (actually a Skye terrier but played here by Lassie), who keeps returning to a churchyard where its master (Crisp) is buried. Pleasant trivia, with a fine character actor cast. Remade as GREYFRIARS BOBBY, which also features Crisp (as the cemetery caretaker).

Chamber of Horrors (1940-British) 80m. **½ D: Norman Lee. Leslie Banks, Lilli Palmer, Romilly Lunge, Gina Malo, Richard Bird, Cathleen Nesbitt. Low-budget horror comes over fairly well, with dastardly Banks making his house a mass morgue, menacing lovely Palmer. Based on Edgar Wallace story. Original title: THE DOOR WITH SEVEN LOCKS.▼

Chamber of Horrors (1966) C-99m. *½ D: Hy Averback. Patrick O'Neal, Cesare Danova, Wilfrid Hyde-White, Patrice Wymore, Suzy Parker, Marie Windsor, Tony Curtis. Wax museum provides setting for uneven mystery about mad killer on the loose. Intended for TV, it has mark of low-budget film plus two gimmicks: the "Horror Horn" and the "Fear Flasher."

Chameleons (1989) C-110m. TVM D: Glen A. Larson. Marcus Gilbert, Crystal Bernard, Mary Bergmann, John Standing, Stewart Granger. Comic action-adventure about the escapades of a self-styled crime-fighting superhero. Check out Granger sending up Batman! Pilot for a series (without Granger). Average.

✓ **Champ, The** (1931) 87m. ***½ D: King Vidor. Wallace Beery, Jackie Cooper, Irene Rich, Roscoe Ates, Edward Brophy, Hale Hamilton. Superb tearjerker about a washed-up prizefighter and his adoring son, played to perfection by Beery and Cooper (in the first of their several teamings). Simple, sentimental in the extreme, but extremely effective. Beery won an Oscar for his performance, as did Frances Marion for her original story. Remade in 1953 (as THE CLOWN) and 1979.

Champ, The (1979) C-121m. *½ D: Franco Zeffirelli. Jon Voight, Faye Dunaway, Ricky Schroder, Jack Warden, Arthur Hill, Strother Martin, Joan Blondell, Elisha Cook. Voight is too intelligent to convince as a dumb pug, and Dunaway, as a loving mother, looks as if she wants to bed down with her kid in hopeless remake of the 1931 sudser. Young Schroder cries (and cries) convincingly.▼

Champagne (1928-British) 93m. **½ D: Alfred Hitchcock. Betty Balfour, Jean Bradin, Gordon Harker, Ferdinand von Alten, Clifford Heatherley, Jack Trevor. Romantic escapades of irresponsible socialite Balfour whose father pretends he's broke to teach her a lesson. Overlong

silent Hitch is moderately entertaining with the usual quota of striking visuals.▼

Champagne Charlie (1944) 107m. **½ D: Cavalcanti. Tommy Trinder, Betty Warren, Stanley Holloway, Austin Trevor, Jean Kent, Guy Middleton. Splendid evocation of British music halls of the 1860s and their robust entertainers simply hasn't got enough story to last 107m. The songs are still great fun. Look for young Kay Kendall.

Champagne Charlie (1989-Canadian-French) C-200m. TVM D: Allen Eastman. Hugh Grant, Megan Gallagher, Megan Follows, Stephane Audran, R. H. Thomson, Georges Descrieres. Lushly mounted romantic drama about the man who introduced America to the joys of champagne in Abe Lincoln's day. Any fizz this might have had goes flat from overlength. Originally shown in two parts. Average.

Champagne for Caesar (1950) 99m. *** D: Richard Whorf. Ronald Colman, Celeste Holm, Vincent Price, Barbara Britton, Art Linkletter. Genius Colman becomes national celebrity on TV quiz show; sponsor Price sends temptress Holm to distract big winner. Enjoyable spoof, with Price hilarious as neurotic soap manufacturer.▼

Champagne Murders, The (1967-French) C-98m. *** D: Claude Chabrol. Anthony Perkins, Maurice Ronet, Stephane Audran, Yvonne Furneaux, Suzanne Lloyd, Catherine Sola. Sale of champagne company to U.S. conglomerate manipulated by various weird, competing types, complicated by murders which point to playboy (Ronet). Murder-mystery narrative backdrop for odd psychological drama; one-of-a-kind film was shot in both English- and French-language versions.

Champagne Waltz (1937) 87m. ** D: A. Edward Sutherland. Gladys Swarthout, Fred MacMurray, Jack Oakie, Herman Bing, Vivienne Osborne. Flyweight musical about rivalry between Vienna waltz palace and American jazz band next door gets sillier as it goes along; operatic Swarthout is saddled with mediocre songs, as well. Oakie's comedy relief most welcome.

Champ for a Day (1953) 90m. ** D: William Seiter. Alex Nicol, Audrey Totter, Charles Winninger, Hope Emerson, Henry (Harry) Morgan. Brooklyn boxer tracks down friend's murderer. Standard.

Champion (1949) 99m. ***½ D: Mark ✓ Robson. Kirk Douglas, Marilyn Maxwell, Arthur Kennedy, Ruth Roman, Paul Stewart, Lola Albright. Unscrupulous boxer punches his way to the top, thrusting aside everybody and everything. Douglas perfectly cast in title role; gripping film, with Oscar-winning editing (by Harry Gerstad).▼

Champions (1983-British) C-115m. **½ D: John Irvin. John Hurt, Edward Woodward, Jan Francis, Ben Johnson, Kirstie Alley, Peter Barkworth, Ann Bell, Judy

Parfitt. Formula drama of determined jockey Hurt battling cancer and hoping to make a comeback in the Grand National Steeplechase. The opening is reminiscent of CHARIOTS OF FIRE, the finale of ROCKY; however, the scenes with Hurt and his niece, and Hurt among children undergoing cancer treatment, are quite moving. Based on a true story.▼

Champions: A Love Story (1979) **C-100m. TVM** D: John A. Alonzo. Shirley Knight, Tony Lo Bianco, James Vincent McNichol, Joy LeDuc, Jennifer Warren, Richard Jaeckel. Teenagers, trying out for the national figure skating championships, fall in love; not unlike ICE CASTLES. Well written by John Sacret Young, photographed by Alonzo, acted—and skated. Above average.

Champions Forever (1989) **C-87m.** *** D: Dimitri Logothetis. Fascinating, insightful look back at the careers of five modern heavyweight boxing legends: Muhammad Ali, Joe Frazier, George Foreman, Larry Holmes, and Ken Norton. Interviews with each fighter are juxtaposed with classic footage of their respective ring battles together, with Ali the dominant presence throughout. Candor and a subtle pathos make the interviews as poignant as the boxing scenes are exciting. Though sobering to see the once verbose Ali reduced to a whispering giant, the early news clips of poetry-spouting Cassius Clay *are* the greatest. An absolute must for fight fans.▼

Chance at Heaven (1933) **70m.** ** D: William A. Seiter. Ginger Rogers, Joel McCrea, Marian Nixon, Andy Devine, Ann Shoemaker. Honest, hardworking McCrea leaves fiancée Ginger for spoiled society brat Nixon. Sincere performances and realistic small-town atmosphere are only virtues of this humdrum film.

Chance Meeting (1959-British) **96m.** **½ D: Joseph Losey. Hardy Kruger, Stanley Baker, Micheline Presle, Robert Flemyng, Gordon Jackson. Kafkaesque story of painter framed for girlfriend's murder. Intriguing little mystery becomes talky, loses initial momentum. British title: BLIND DATE.

Chance of a Lifetime, The (1943) **65m.** D: William Castle. Chester Morris, Eric Rolf, Jeanne Bates, Richard Lane, George E. Stone, Lloyd Corrigan. SEE: **Boston Blackie** series.

Chance of a Lifetime (1950-British) **89m.** *** D: Bernard Miles, Alan Osbiston. Basil Radford, Niall MacGinnis, Bernard Miles, Geoffrey Keen, Kenneth More, Julien Mitchell, Hattie Jacques. Nearly a landmark film by actor-director Miles, blending comedy and drama when a fed-up factory owner (Radford) agrees to turn over all management duties to his workers. Laborers, led by Miles and More, eventually learn how difficult it is to run a business. Outstanding performances and realistic location filming.

Chances (1931) **72m.** *** D: Allan Dwan. Douglas Fairbanks, Jr., Rose Hobart, Anthony Bushell, Mary Forbes, Holmes Herbert, William Austin. Entertaining, neatly acted drama of love and war, with soldier-brothers Fairbanks and Bushell both falling for Hobart. Fairbanks in particular is a standout.

Chances Are (1989) **C-108m.** *** D: Emile Ardolino. Cybill Shepherd, Robert Downey, Jr., Ryan O'Neal, Mary Stuart Masterson, Christopher McDonald, Josef Sommer, Joe Grifasi, Susan Ruttan, Fran Ryan, James Noble. A woman remains devoted to her husband years after his death . . . and then, one day, his spirit returns in the body of a much younger man. Surprisingly skillful blend of fantasy and romantic comedy manages to maintain its sweet-natured tone from start to finish. Appealing stars are supported by a gallery of top character actors. Written by Perry Howze and Randy Howze.▼

Chandler (1972) **C-88m.** *½ D: Paul Magwood. Warren Oates, Leslie Caron, Alex Dreier, Gloria Grahame, Mitchell Ryan. Private-eye falls in love with ex-mistress of racketeer. Substandard yarn.

Chandu the Magician (1932) **70m.** *½ D: William Cameron Menzies, Marcel Varnel. Edmund Lowe, Bela Lugosi, Irene Ware, Henry B. Walthall, Herbert Mundin. Spiritualist Chandu battles madman whose death ray threatens to destroy world; not as good as most serials of this genre, and even sillier. Disappointing.

Chanel Solitaire (1981-U.S.-French) **C-120m.** ** D: George Kaczender. Marie-France Pisier, Timothy Dalton, Rutger Hauer, Karen Black, Brigitte Fossey. Stylish but cliché-ridden biography of designer Coco Chanel, covering her first 38 years and focusing on her love life.▼

Changeling, The (1979-Canadian) **C-109m.** *** D: Peter Medak. George C. Scott, Trish Van Devere, Melvyn Douglas, John Colicos, Jean Marsh, Madeleine Thornton-Sherwood. Good, scary ghost story with Scott as recently widowed musician who moves into old house inhabited by spirit of a child who lived there 70 years ago.▼

Change of Habit (1969) **C-93m.** ** D: William Graham. Elvis Presley, Mary Tyler Moore, Barbara McNair, Jane Elliot, Leora Dana, Edward Asner, Doro Merande, Regis Toomey. Moore, a nun, is forced to choose between Dr. Presley and the church in substandard drama that at least represents slight change from typical Elvis fare. Presley's last screen role.▼

Change of Heart (1943) **90m.** ** D: Albert S. Rogell. John Carroll, Susan Hayward, Gail Patrick, Eve Arden, Melville Cooper, Walter Catlett, Dorothy Dandridge, Count Basie & Orchestra, Freddy Martin & Orchestra. Forgettable musical numbers abound in this romantic trifle of Carroll stealing songwriter Hayward's work. Of course, they fall in love. Originally titled HIT PARADE OF 1943.

Change of Mind (1969) **C-103m.** **½ D: Robert Stevens. Raymond St. Jacques, Susan Oliver, Janet MacLachlan, Leslie Nielsen, Donnelly Rhodes, David Bailey. In an emergency operation, the brain of a white district attorney is successfully transplanted into the body of a black man (St. Jacques). Racial-protest sci-fi thriller is contrived, to say the least, but strong cast and unusual premise keep it watchable. Filmed in Canada.

Change of Seasons, A (1980) **C-102m.** **½ D: Richard Lang. Shirley MacLaine, Anthony Hopkins, Bo Derek, Michael Brandon, Mary Beth Hurt, Ed Winter. College professor Hopkins, drowning in male menopause, has an affair with student Derek, so wife MacLaine decides to take a lover of her own. One of the better midlife crisis films of this period, though many thought its major asset was opening sequence of Bo bouncing in a hot tub. Cowritten by Erich Segal.▼

Chan Is Missing (1982) **80m.** *** D: Wayne Wang, Wood Moy, Marc Hayashi, Laureen Chew, Judy Mihei, Peter Wang, Presco Tabios. Wry, low-key comedy of cabdrivers Moy and Hayashi tracking down the mysterious Mr. Chan Hung, who absconded with their $4,000. Independently produced on shoestring budget and shot in San Francisco's Chinatown.▼

Chant of Jimmy Blacksmith, The (1978-Australian) **C-124m.** ***½ D: Fred Schepisi. Tommy Lewis, Freddy Reynolds, Ray Barrett, Jack Thompson, Peter Carroll, Elizabeth Alexander. Half-white aborigine Lewis, brought up by Methodist pastor, is caught between two cultures and exploited, with tragic results. Harrowing indictment of racism, a problem certainly not unique to U.S. Based on fact. Most U.S. prints run 108m.

Chaplin Revue, The (1958) **119m.** ***½ D: Charles Chaplin. Charlie Chaplin, Edna Purviance, Sydney Chaplin, Mack Swain. Three of Chaplin's best shorts strung together with his own music, narration, and behind-the-scenes footage: A DOG'S LIFE (1918), one of his loveliest films; SHOULDER ARMS (1918), a classic WW1 comedy; and THE PILGRIM (1923), his underrated gem about a convict who disguises as a minister.▼

✓ **Chapman Report, The** (1962) **C-125m.** **½ D: George Cukor. Efrem Zimbalist, Jr., Jane Fonda, Shelley Winters, Claire Bloom, Glynis Johns, Ray Danton, Ty Hardin. Slick, empty yarn about Kinsey-like sex researchers coming to suburban community to get statistical survey, with repercussions on assorted females. Potboiler material elevated by good performances and direction.

Chappaqua (1966) **C/B&W-92m.** ** D: Conrad Rooks. Jean-Louis Barrault, Conrad Rooks, William S. Burroughs, Allen Ginsburg, Ravi Shankar, Paula Pritchett, Ornette Coleman. Rooks, an alcoholic heroin addict, travels to Paris for a sleep cure and hallucinates while withdrawing. Autobiographical—and vague, surreal, phony. Prints of 82m. and 75m. also exist.

Chapter Two (1979) **C-124m.** ** D: Robert Moore. James Caan, Marsha Mason, Valerie Harper, Joseph Bologna. Neil Simon's autobiographical comedy-drama—one of his best Broadway plays—gets lost in screen translation. Caan is miscast as sharp-minded writer who's drawn into new romance (with Mason) before he's really recovered from death of his wife. Long, plastic, and unmoving.▼

Charade (1963) **C-114m.** ***½ D: Stanley Donen. Cary Grant, Audrey Hepburn, Walter Matthau, James Coburn, George Kennedy, Ned Glass, Jacques Marin. Suave comedy-mystery in Hitchcock vein, with Grant aiding widow Hepburn to recover fortune secreted by husband, being sought by trio of sinister crooks; set in Paris. Excellent screenplay by Peter Stone, score by Henry Mancini.▼

Charge at Feather River, The (1953) **C-96m.** **½ D: Gordon Douglas. Guy Madison, Vera Miles, Frank Lovejoy, Helen Westcott, Ron Hagerthy. One of many Westerns which literally threw action at viewers to utilize 3-D in its original release; now, just standard.

Charge of the Black Lancers (1961-Italian) **C-97m.** **½ D: Giacomo Gentilomo. Mel Ferrer, Yvonne Furneaux, Jean Claudio, Leticia Roman. Effective costumer, well-mounted and fast-paced. Claudio is traitor to country with his brother (Ferrer) leading patriots in defense of homeland.

Charge of the Lancers (1954) **C-74m.** ** D: William Castle. Paulette Goddard, Jean-Pierre Aumont, Richard Stapley. Stilted affair of gypsy Goddard and British officer Aumont finding romance in midst of Crimean War.

Charge of the Light Brigade, The (1936) **116m.** *** D: Michael Curtiz. Errol Flynn, Olivia de Havilland, Patric Knowles, Henry Stephenson, Nigel Bruce, Donald Crisp, David Niven. Thundering action based on Tennyson's poem, with climactic charge into certain death by British 27th Lancers cavalry. Lavish production values accent romantic tale of Flynn and de Havilland at army post in India. Also shown in computer-colored version.▼

Charge of the Light Brigade, The (1968-British) **C-130m.** **½ D: Tony Richardson. David Hemmings, Vanessa Redgrave, John Gielgud, Harry Andrews, Trevor Howard, Jill Bennett, Mark Burns. Exquisitely made, but ultimately disappointing drama of events leading up to British involvement in Crimean War. Stunning battle sequence cannot make up for dramatic loopholes in this story of military minds gone mad. Clever animated segments by Richard Williams.

Charge of the Model Ts, The (1979) C-94m. *½ D: Jim McCullough. John David Carson, Louis Nye, Arte Johnson, Herb Edelman, Carol Bagdasarian. Deplorable family-oriented comedy, filmed in Texas, about a German spy who tries to infiltrate the U.S. during WW1 with a specially equipped weapon-bearing automobile. Made in 1977.▼

Chariots of Fire (1981-British) C-123m. ***½ D: Hugh Hudson. Ben Cross, Ian Charleson, Nigel Havers, Nick Farrell, Alice Krige, Cheryl Campbell, Ian Holm, John Gielgud, Lindsay Anderson, Patrick Magee, Nigel Davenport, Dennis Christopher, Brad Davis. Absorbing and unusual drama based on true story of two men—devout Scottish missionary Eric Liddell, driven Jewish Cambridge student Harold Abrahams—who run in the 1924 Olympics. Fascinating probe of their motives, challenges, and problems, and a case study of repressed emotions even in the midst of exultation. Feature debut for director Hudson. Academy Award winner for Best Picture, Colin Welland's script, Vangelis' excellent score, and Milena Canonero's costumes.▼

Chariots of the Gods? (1974) C-98m. *** D: Harald Reinl. First of too many documentaries about ancient visitors from outer space who helped advance mankind's knowledge centuries ago. Well-made and filled with many natural beauties. Based on Erich Von Daniken's book.▼

Charles & Diana: A Royal Love Story (1982) C-100m. TVM D: James Goldstone. David Robb, Caroline Bliss, Christopher Lee, Rod Taylor, Margaret Tyzack, Mona Washbourne, Charles Gray, David Langton. One of two practically identical films about the romance and marriage of Britain's Prince Charles and Lady Diana Spencer, with two relative unknowns in the leads. For comparison see THE ROYAL ROMANCE OF CHARLES AND DIANA. Average.

Charleston (1978-Italian) C-91m. ** D: Marcello Fondato. Bud Spencer, James Coco, Herbert Lom. Title refers not to the dance and not to the city but to beefy Italian superstar Spencer as a flashy conman who supports his expensive tastes by parting rich American gangster Coco from his ill-gotten gains.

Charleston (1979) C-100m. TVM D: Karen Arthur. Delta Burke, Jordan Clarke, Richard Lawson, Lynne Moody, Patricia Pearcy, Martha Scott, Mandy Patinkin.

Unfortunate clone of GONE WITH THE WIND even has a pouty, self-centered Southern belle who looks like Vivien Leigh. Produced, directed, and written by women, but offers no insights—feminist or otherwise—on familiar material. Below average.

Charley and the Angel (1973) C-93m. **½ D: Vincent McEveety. Fred MacMurray, Cloris Leachman, Harry Morgan, Kurt Russell, Vincent Van Patten, Kathleen Cody. MacMurray learns he has only a short time left on earth from helpful angel (Morgan) and changes his hard ways with family. Lightly amusing Disney film, but the warmth and nostalgia seem artificial this time around.▼

Charley Hannah (1986) C-100m. TVM D: Peter H. Hunt. Robert Conrad, Shane Conrad, Christian Conrad, Joan Leslie, Red West, Stephen J. Cannell. Conrad and real-life sons star in this pilot about a hard-nosed Ft. Lauderdale cop who takes a teenage gang member under his wing after accidentally shooting another youth during a chase. TV producer Cannell's acting debut, as a Fagin-like drug dealer. Average.

Charley One-Eye (1973) C-107m. ** D: Don Chaffey. Richard Roundtree, Roy Thinnes, Nigel Davenport, Jill Pearson. Basically two-man show. Black Union Army deserter (Roundtree) and outcast Indian (Thinnes) thrown together in desert wasteland; gradual tragic relationship develops when outside forces interfere. Far too long; should've been a TV movie.

Charley's Aunt (1941) 81m. **½ D: Archie Mayo. Jack Benny, Kay Francis, James Ellison, Anne Baxter, Edmund Gwenn, Reginald Owen. Broad but surefire filming of Brandon Thomas play about Oxford student posing as maiden aunt, joke getting out of hand. Previously filmed six other times! Remade as musical WHERE'S CHARLEY?

Charley Varrick (1973) C-111m. ***½ D: Don Siegel. Walter Matthau, Joe Don Baker, Felicia Farr, John Vernon, Andy Robinson, Jacqueline Scott, Sheree North, Norman Fell, Woodrow Parfrey. Neatly contrived thriller with Matthau as a bank robber who discovers that his small-town take is actually laundered Mafia money. On target all the way, with a particularly satisfying wrap-up.▼

Charlie and the Great Balloon Chase (1981) C-100m. TVM D: Larry Elikann. Jack Albertson, Adrienne Barbeau, Slim Pickens, Moosie Drier, John Reilly, Pat Cooper, Ann Seymour, Bert Freed. Lighthearted family fare about a youngster who helps his retired granddad fulfill a dream of a transcontinental trip in a hot-air balloon. Average.▼

Charlie Bubbles (1968) C-91m. **½ D: Albert Finney. Albert Finney, Colin Blakely, Billie Whitelaw, Liza Minnelli. Finney's first directing attempt concerns itself with married writer who begins affair with his secretary. Not especially moving, but Minnelli's screen debut adds quite a bit of sparkle to film.

Charlie Chan Earl Derr Biggers' character of an Oriental detective on the Honolulu police force first appeared on the screen in 1926, but did not make an impression upon movie-goers until Warner Oland took over the role in 1931 with CHARLIE CHAN CARRIES ON. He essayed the part until his death in 1937, when he was replaced by Sidney Toler. Toler carried on for nine years, and upon his death was replaced in turn by Roland Winters, who starred for the last two years of the fading series. The early entries with Oland are the best, with CHARLIE CHAN AT THE OPERA and ON BROADWAY standing out; Toler's first attempts are quite good, especially CHARLIE CHAN AT TREASURE ISLAND (one of the best in the whole series) and IN PANAMA. But in the 1940s, with less interest and a change of studios, the series declined, and so did Toler. His last efforts, like DANGEROUS MONEY, were pretty bad, and Mr. Toler had aged considerably. The series gave out a dying gasp with Roland Winters, who was totally unsuited for the role. The last Chan film, SKY DRAGON, is unbearable. Despite their age, the early efforts remain fresh and entertaining today, with Charlie constantly at odds with his #1 or #2 son (Keye Luke and Sen Yung, respectively) and mouthing his famous words of wisdom: "Insignificant molehill sometimes more important than conspicuous mountain," etc. Today the Charlie Chan films offer a delightful change of pace and for the most part are highly recommended.

Charlie Chan and the Curse of the Dragon Queen (1981) C-97m. *½ D: Clive Donner. Peter Ustinov, Lee Grant, Angie Dickinson, Richard Hatch, Brian Keith, Michelle Pfeiffer, Roddy McDowall, Rachel Roberts, Paul Ryan, Johnny Sekka. Boring comedy wastes its talented cast. Ustinov is badly miscast, gives one of the worst performances of his career. Hatch is his clumsy half-Jewish, half-Oriental grandson. Paging Warner Oland.▼

Charlie Chan and the Golden Eye SEE: **Golden Eye, The**

Charlie Chan at Monte Carlo (1937) 71m. D: Eugene Forde. Warner Oland, Keye Luke, Virginia Field, Sidney Blackmer, Harold Huber, Louis Mercier, Robert Kent.

Charlie Chan at the Circus (1936) 72m. D: Harry Lachman. Warner Oland, Keye Luke, George and Olive Brasno, Francis Ford, Maxine Reiner, John McGuire, Shirley Deane, J. Carrol Naish.

Charlie Chan at the Olympics (1937) 71m. D: H. Bruce Humberstone. Warner Oland, Keye Luke, Katherine DeMille, Pauline Moore, C. Henry Gordon, Jonathan Hale, Allan Lane, John Eldredge.

Charlie Chan at the Opera (1936) 66m. D: H. Bruce Humberstone. Warner Oland, Boris Karloff, Keye Luke, Charlotte Henry, Thomas Beck, Gregory Gaye, Nedda Harrigan, William Demarest.▼

Charlie Chan at the Race Track (1936) 70m. D: H. Bruce Humberstone. Warner Oland, Keye Luke, Helen Wood, Thomas Beck, Alan Dinehart, Gavin Muir, Gloria Roy, Jonathan Hale.

Charlie Chan at the Wax Museum (1940) 63m. D: Lynn Shores. Sidney Toler, Sen Yung, C. Henry Gordon, Marc Lawrence, Joan Valerie, Marguerite Chapman, Ted Osborn, Michael Visaroff.▼

Charlie Chan at Treasure Island (1939) 75m. D: Norman Foster. Sidney Toler, Cesar Romero, Pauline Moore, Douglass Dumbrille, Billie Seward, Louis Jean Heydt, Charles Halton.

Charlie Chan in Black Magic SEE: **Black Magic** (1944)▼

Charlie Chan in City of Darkness (1939) 75m. D: Herbert I. Leeds. Sidney Toler, Lynn Bari, Richard Clarke, Pedro de Cordoba, Douglass Dumbrille, Lon Chaney, Jr., Leo G. Carroll.

Charlie Chan in Dangerous Money SEE: **Dangerous Money**

Charlie Chan in Egypt (1935) 65m. D: Louis King. Warner Oland, "Pat" Paterson, Thomas Beck, Rita Hayworth, Jameson Thomas, Frank Conroy, Nigel de Brulier, Paul Porcasi, Stepin Fetchit.

Charlie Chan in Honolulu (1938) 65m. D: H. Bruce Humberstone. Sidney Toler, Phyllis Brooks, Sen Yung, Eddie Collins, John King, Claire Dodd, George Zucco, Robert Barrat.

Charlie Chan in London (1934) 79m. D: Eugene Forde. Warner Oland, Ray Milland, Mona Barrie, Drue Leyton, Alan Mowbray, David Torrence, Madge Bellamy.

Charlie Chan in Meeting at Midnight SEE: **Black Magic** (1944)▼

Charlie Chan in Panama (1940) 67m. D: Norman Foster. Sidney Toler, Jean Rogers, Kane Richmond, Lionel Atwill, Mary Nash, Sen Yung, ChrisPin Martin.

Charlie Chan in Paris (1935) 72m. D: Lewis Seiler. Warner Oland, Mary Brian, Thomas Beck, Erik Rhodes, John Miljan, Minor Watson, John Qualen, Keye Luke, Henry Kolker.▼

Charlie Chan in Reno (1939) 70m. D: Norman Foster. Sidney Toler, Ricardo Cortez, Phyllis Brooks, Slim Summerville, Kane Richmond, Robert Lowery, Morgan Conway, Sen Yung.

Charlie Chan in Rio (1941) 60m. D: Harry Lachman. Sidney Toler, Mary Beth Hughes, Cobina Wright, Jr., Ted (Michael)

North, Victor Jory, Harold Huber, Sen Yung.▼

Charlie Chan in Shanghai (1935) 70m. D: James Tinling. Warner Oland, Irene Hervey, Russell Hicks, Keye Luke, Halliwell Hobbes, Charles Locher (Jon Hall).

Charlie Chan in the Secret Service (1944) 63m. D: Phil Rosen. Sidney Toler, Mantan Moreland, Gwen Kenyon, Benson Fong, Eddy Chandler.

Charlie Chan on Broadway (1937) 68m. D: Eugene Forde. Warner Oland, Keye Luke, Joan Marsh, J. Edward Bromberg, Leon Ames, Joan Woodbury, Douglas Fowley, Louise Henry, Donald Woods, Harold Huber.

Charlie Chan's Murder Cruise (1940) 75m. D: Eugene Forde. Sidney Toler, Sen Yung, Marjorie Weaver, Lionel Atwill, Robert Lowery, Don Beddoe, Leo G. Carroll.

Charlie Chan's Secret (1936) 71m. D: Gordon Wiles. Warner Oland, Rosina Lawrence, Charley Quigley, Henrietta Crosman, Edward Trevor, Astrid Allwyn.▼

Charlie Chaplin Carnival (1938) 100m. **** Four vintage comedies from Chaplin's 1916-17 peak period: BEHIND THE SCREEN, THE COUNT, THE FIREMAN, THE VAGABOND. First one is best, with leading lady Edna Purviance and oversized villain Eric Campbell. Some prints run 75m.▼

Charlie Chaplin Cavalcade (1938) 75m. **** More priceless gems from 1916-17 period: ONE A.M. (Chaplin's famous solo film), THE RINK, THE PAWNSHOP, THE FLOORWALKER. All great.▼

Charlie Chaplin Festival (1938) 96m. **** Best of the Chaplin compilations, which all suffer from obtrusive sound effects and music: THE ADVENTURER, THE CURE, EASY STREET, THE IMMIGRANT. Four of the greatest comedies ever made— don't miss them. Some prints run 75m.▼

Charlie Cobb: Nice Night for a Hanging (1977) C-100m. TVM D: Richard Michaels. Clu Gulager, Ralph Bellamy, Stella Stevens, Blair Brown, Pernell Roberts, Christopher Connelly, Tricia O'Neil. Lighthearted Western has Gulager, a resourceful private eye of the 1870s, battling those with evil plans for Brown, believed to be long-missing daughter of wealthy rancher Bellamy. Average.

Charlie McCarthy, Detective (1939) 65m. **½ D: Frank Tuttle. Edgar Bergen, Charlie McCarthy, Constance Moore, Robert Cummings, Louis Calhern, John Sutton, Harold Huber, Edgar Kennedy. Good comedy-whodunit with Bergen & McCarthy rivaling Inspector Kennedy's investigation.

Charlie Muffin (1979-British) C-109m. TVM D: Jack Gold. David Hemmings, Sam Wanamaker, Jennie Linden, Ian Richardson, Ralph Richardson, Pinkas Braun, Shane Rimmer. Literate, extremely entertaining tale of a shrewd, crafty—and very human—British espionage operative (Hemmings), who lives by his own rules and is in disfavor with his stuffy superiors, and his involvement with an "alleged" Soviet defector. The finale is a real stunner. Above average.

Charlie's Angels (1976) C-78m. TVM D: John Llewellyn Moxey. Kate Jackson, Farrah Fawcett-Majors, Jaclyn Smith, David Doyle, Diana Muldaur, Bo Hopkins, David Ogden Stiers, John Lehne, Tommy Lee Jones. Three attractive female detectives use their wiles to con the killer of a wealthy wine grower into revealing whereabouts of the body. Featherweight cop-show-with-a-twist that snowballed into one of the most popular TV series of the late 70s and began the Farrah Fawcett-Majors phenomenon. Average.

Charlie, the Lonesome Cougar (1968) C-75m. **½ No director credited. Narrated by Rex Allen. Ron Brown, Brian Russell, Linda Wallace, Jim Wilson. Average Disney animal adventure-comedy about a friendly cougar who lives in a lumber camp.▼

Charlotte Forten's Mission: Experiment in Freedom (1985) C-120m. TVM D: Barry Crane. Melba Moore, Mary Alice, Ned Beatty, Carla Borelli, Micki Grant, Moses Gunn, Anna Maria Horsford, Bruce McGill, Glynn Turman, Roderick Wimberly. Effectively simple, if obvious (and pretentiously titled), fact-based chronicle of a wealthy, educated Northern black woman (Moore), who comes to an island off the coast of Georgia to teach freed slaves during the Civil War. Screenplay by Samm-Art Williams. A PBS *American Playhouse* presentation. Average.

Charlotte's Web (1973) C-85m. *** D: Charles A. Nichols, Iwao Takamoto. Voices of Debbie Reynolds, Henry Gibson, Paul Lynde, Charles Nelson Reilly. Charming animated feature based on E.B. White classic of barnyard spider who befriends shy piglet. Above average for Hanna-Barbera cartoon studio.▼

Charly (1968) C-103m. ***½ D: Ralph Nelson. Cliff Robertson, Claire Bloom, Lilia Skala, Leon Janney, Dick Van Patten. Robertson won Oscar for fine work as retarded man turned into super-brain in scientific experiment (a role he first tackled on TV's *U.S. Steel Hour* in 1961). Bloom is sympathetic caseworker who becomes attached to Charly. Based on Daniel Keyes' *Flowers for Algernon*. First rate.▼

Charming Sinners (1929) 85m. *½ D: Robert Milton. Ruth Chatterton, Clive Brook, William Powell, Mary Nolan, Laura Hope Crews, Florence Eldridge. Obvious, creaky marital drama of Chatterton, whose philandering husband (Brook) has taken up with her best friend. To pique his jealousy, she pretends to become involved with former boyfriend Powell (who is wasted). Stiff direction does it in; based on Somerset Maugham's *The Constant Wife.*

Charro! (1969) **C-98m.** BOMB D: Charles Marquis Warren. Elvis Presley, Ina Balin, Victor French, Lynn Kellogg, Barbara Werle, Paul Brinegar. Attempt to change Presley's image by casting him in straight Western is total failure. Elvis sings only one song.▼

Chartroose Caboose (1960) **C-75m.** ** D: William "Red" Reynolds. Molly Bee, Ben Cooper, Edgar Buchanan, Mike McGreevey. Buchanan, an eccentric retired train conductor, shelters a young couple in his strange house, a converted caboose.

Chase, The (1946) **86m.** ** D: Arthur Ripley. Robert Cummings, Michele Morgan, Steve Cochran, Peter Lorre. Slow-moving second-rate story set in Cuba with Morgan running off from her husband. Based on a story by Cornell Woolrich.▼

✓ **Chase, The** (1966) **C-135m.** **½ D: Arthur Penn. Marlon Brando, Jane Fonda, Robert Redford, Angie Dickinson, Janice Rule, James Fox, Robert Duvall, E.G. Marshall, Miriam Hopkins, Martha Hyer. Intriguing, unsubtle drama of how prison escape by local boy (Redford) affects worthless Texas town and its sheriff (Brando). Based on a novel by Horton Foote. Notorious for behind-the-scenes conflicts with director Penn, screenwriter Lillian Hellman, and producer Sam Spiegel, it's not surprising that finished product misses the mark.▼

Chase (1985) **C-100m.** TVM D: Rod Holcomb. Jennifer O'Neill, Robert S. Woods, Michael Parks, Terence Knox, Cooper Huckabee, Richard Farnsworth. Female attorney and former lover find themselves on opposite sides in the murder case of her mentor when she's assigned to defend the killer. Average.▼

Chase a Crooked Shadow (1958-British) **87m.** *** D: Michael Anderson. Richard Todd, Anne Baxter, Herbert Lom, Alexander Knox. Heiress Baxter doubts her sanity when allegedly dead brother Todd appears to claim inheritance; exciting, Hitchcock-like melodrama.

Chase for the Golden Needles SEE: **Golden Needles**

Chase Me Charlie (1932) **61m.** ** Narrated by Teddy Bergman. Charlie Chaplin, Edna Purviance, Ben Turpin. Inept attempt to string early Chaplin shorts into story line—1914 material used is often weak.

Chasing Dreams (1982) **C-105m.** *½ D: Sean Roche, Therese Conte. David G. Brown, John Fife, Jim Shane, Matthew Clark, Lisa Kingston, Claudia Carroll,

Kevin Costner. Hopelessly hokey soaper of insecure, self-conscious farmboy Brown, who "finds" himself by playing college baseball. Of interest solely for early, brief appearance of Costner as Brown's older, medical-student brother.▼

Chastity (1969) **C-98m.** ** D: Alessio de Paola. Cher, Barbara London, Tom Nolan, Stephen Whittaker. Interesting story of girl who takes to the highway to find life of her own. Cher in solo acting debut is surprisingly good.

Chastity Belt, The SEE: **On My Way to the Crusades, I Met a Girl Who . . .**

Chato's Land (1972-Spanish-British) **C-110m.** **½ D: Michael Winner. Charles Bronson, Jack Palance, Richard Basehart, Jill Ireland. Posse seeks Indian Bronson in connection with marshal's murder; usual quota of blood in lengthy film.▼

Chattahoochee (1990) **C-98m.** ** D: Mick Jackson. Gary Oldman, Dennis Hopper, Frances McDormand, Pamela Reed, Ned Beatty, M. Emmet Walsh, William De Acutis, Lee Wilkof, Matt Craven, Gary Klar. Enervatingly straightforward account of man whose mental breakdown (actually post-Korea combat stress) wrongfully landed him in a Karloff caliber Florida institution. Standard "reform" drama—though based on fact—with Hopper's role (as a fellow patient) a glorified cameo; McDormand and Reed do all right as, respectively, Oldman's wife and crusading sister.

Chattanooga Choo Choo (1984) **C-102m.** ** D: Bruce Bilson. George Kennedy, Barbara Eden, Joe Namath, Melissa Sue Anderson, Bridget Hanley, Clu Gulager, Christopher McDonald, Davis Roberts, Tony Azito, Parley Baer. In order to collect inheritance, goofball Kennedy must restore the famous train and make one final 24-hour run from Pennsylvania Station. Spirited cast and slick production compensate somewhat for sitcom-level script. Rubber-limbed Azito is amazing as waiter who's never dropped a tray.▼

Chatterbox (1943) **76m.** **½ D: Joseph Santley. Joe E. Brown, Judy Canova, Rosemary Lane, John Hubbard, Gus Schilling, Chester Clute, Anne Jeffreys. Entertaining comedy of radio-cowboy Brown (not much of a hero in real life) visiting dude ranch for publicity purposes.

Che! (1969) **C-96m.** BOMB D: Richard Fleischer. Omar Sharif, Jack Palance, Cesare Danova, Robert Loggia, Woody Strode. Comic-book treatment of famed revolutionary became one of the biggest film jokes of 1960s. However, you haven't lived until you see Palance play Fidel Castro.▼

Cheap Detective, The (1978) **C-92m.** *** D: Robert Moore. Peter Falk, Ann-Margret, Eileen Brennan, Sid Caesar, Stockard Channing, James Coco, Dom DeLuise, Louise Fletcher, John Houseman,

Madeline Kahn, Fernando Lamas, Marsha Mason, Phil Silvers, Vic Tayback, Abe Vigoda, Paul Williams, Nicol Williamson. For Neil Simon and Peter Falk to parody Bogart movies like MALTESE FALCON is an easy task, but it's still pretty funny when not resorting to the obvious.▼

Cheaper by the Dozen (1950) C-85m. *** D: Walter Lang. Clifton Webb, Myrna Loy, Jeanne Crain, Mildred Natwick, Edgar Buchanan. Charming turn-of-the-century story of the Gilbreth children, twelve strong, their exacting father (well-played by Webb) and mother (Loy). Sequel: BELLES ON THEIR TOES.

Cheaper to Keep Her (1980) C-92m. BOMB D: Ken Annakin. Mac Davis, Tovah Feldshuh, Art Metrano, Ian McShane, Priscilla Lopez, Rose Marie, Jack Gilford, J. Pat O'Malley. Detective Davis is hired by lawyer Feldshuh to check out McShane and Gilford, who have been lax in their alimony checks. Sexist, racist, and obnoxious.▼

Cheaters, The (1945) 87m. *** D: Joseph Kane. Joseph Schildkraut, Billie Burke, Eugene Pallette, Ona Munson, Raymond Walburn, Ruth Terry. Excellent cast in enjoyable tale of wealthy family of snobs humanized by downtrodden actor they invite for Christmas dinner. Also known as THE CASTAWAY.

Check and Double Check (1930) 80m. BOMB D: Melville Brown. Freeman Gosden, Charles Correll, Sue Carol, Charles Norton, Ralf Harolde, Duke Ellington and His Band. Movie debut for radio's Amos 'n' Andy is a leaden-paced early talkie with stale script and precious little comedy; not nearly as good as a sample radio (or later TV) episode of the show.▼

Checkered Flag or Crash (1977) C-95m. ** D: Alan Gibson. Joe Don Baker, Susan Sarandon, Larry Hagman, Alan Vint, Parnelli Jones, Logan Clark. A 1,000 mile off-road race in the Philippines is the focal point of this unmemorable programmer; for car-action fans only.

Checking Out (1989) C-90m. *½ D: David Leland. Jeff Daniels, Melanie Mayron, Michael Tucker, Kathleen York, Ann Magnuson, Allan Havey, Jo Harvey Allen, Felton Perry, Alan Wolfe. When Daniels' best friend dies of a heart attack he suddenly turns into a raging hypochondriac, convinced the same thing will happen to him. After 90 minutes of this overblown black comedy you pray that it will. Familiar premise is botched, and features the seemingly impossible: a weak performance from Jeff Daniels.▼

Check Is in the Mail, The (1986) C-91m. ** D: Joan Darling. Brian Dennehy, Anne Archer, Hallie Todd, Chris Herbert, Michael Bowen, Nita Talbot, Dick Shawn. Ineffectual comedy about a beleaguered

family man who decides to beat the system by making his home self-sufficient. Episodic, slow-paced film wears out its sometimes likable ingredients.▼

Cheech & Chong's Next Movie (1980) C-99m. *½ D: Thomas Chong. Cheech Marin, Thomas Chong, Evelyn Guerrero, Betty Kennedy, Sy Kramer, Rikki Marin. After an auspicious debut in UP IN SMOKE, the pothead, put-on comic duo go seriously awry in this crude, incoherent film, which offers only sporadic laughs.▼

Cheech & Chong's Nice Dreams (1981) C-89m. ** D: Thomas Chong. Cheech Marin, Thomas Chong, Evelyn Guerrero, Stacy Keach, Dr. Timothy Leary. Episodic, generally below par C&C comedy finds them as owners of an ice-cream truck that fronts for more lucrative grass trade. Some hilarity involving a sexually jealous biker; Guerrero once again an apt comic foil.▼

Cheech & Chong's The Corsican Brothers (1984) C-90m. BOMB D: Thomas Chong. Cheech Marin, Thomas Chong, Roy Dotrice, Shelby Fiddis, Rikki Marin, Edie McClurg, Rae Dawn Chong, Robbi Chong. The boys (in three roles each) and their families (in one role each) star in their first non-drug (but still tasteless) comedy, an inept parody which seems all the more empty because of its magnificent French locations. Staggeringly unfunny even by C&C standards; the *previews* for START THE REVOLUTION WITHOUT ME have more laughs.▼

Cheers for Miss Bishop (1941) 95m. *** D: Tay Garnett. Martha Scott, William Gargan, Edmund Gwenn, Sterling Holloway, Sidney Blackmer, Mary Anderson, Dorothy Peterson. Sentimental story of schoolteacher Scott, devoting her life to teaching in small Midwestern town. Nicely done.▼

Cheetah (1989) C-84m. *** D: Jeff Blyth. Keith Coogan, Lucy Deakins, Collin Mothupi, Timothy Landfield, Breon Gorman, Ka Vundia, Kuldeep Bhakoo, Paul Onsongo. Two Southern California kids join their parents for several months in Kenya, make friends with a young Masai, and adopt an orphaned cheetah, which they raise as a pet. Simple story line is aimed squarely at kids, but it's believable and entertaining and teaches good lessons about tolerance and respect for the wild. A Disney release.▼

Cherokee Strip (1940) 86m. **½ D: Lesley Selander. Richard Dix, Florence Rice, Victor Jory, William Henry, Andy Clyde, George E. Stone. Solid if unsurprising little Western with quiet but determined Dix becoming marshal of small town, hoping to get the goods on crooked Jory and his gang.

Cherry 2000 (1988) C-93m. **½ D: Steve DeJarnatt. Melanie Griffith, Ben Johnson,

Harry Carey, Jr., David Andrews, Tim Thomerson, Pamela Gidley, Jennifer Mayo. Post-MAD MAX adventure about a female mercenary hired to bust into a 21st-century robot warehouse operated by psychos in what used to be the American Southwest. Derivative, but a bit more fun than its limited theatrical release might lead you to believe; Johnson and Carey are worth their combined weights in audience goodwill. Filmed in 1986.▼

Chesty Anderson, USN (1976) C-88m. ** D: Ed Forsyth. Shari Eubank, Rosanne Katon, Dorri Thomson, Marcie Barkin, Timothy Carey, Scatman Crothers, Frank Campanella, Fred Willard, Betty Thomas. Sexploitation comedy about female naval recruits is so timid that it keeps its lovely cast clothed even during physical exams! Good cast and production values, though. Retitled ANDERSON'S ANGELS for TV.▼

Cheyenne (1947) 100m. ** D: Raoul Walsh. Dennis Morgan, Jane Wyman, Janis Paige, Bruce Bennett, Alan Hale, Arthur Kennedy, Barton MacLane. Standard Western as gambler attempts to capture outlaw—instead spends time with outlaw's wife. Later a TV series. Retitled THE WYOMING KID.

Cheyenne Autumn (1964) C-145m. *** D: John Ford. Richard Widmark, Carroll Baker, Karl Malden, Dolores Del Rio, Sal Mineo, Edward G. Robinson, James Stewart, Ricardo Montalban, Gilbert Roland, Arthur Kennedy, Patrick Wayne, Elizabeth Allen, Victor Jory, John Carradine, Mike Mazurki, John Qualen, George O'-Brien. Sprawling, uneven, but entertaining John Ford Western (his last) about Cheyenne Indian tribe and its eventful journey back to original settlement after being relocated by the government. Dodge City sequence (with Stewart as Wyatt Earp) was cut after premiere engagements; recently restored for home video to 154m.▼

✓ **Cheyenne Social Club, The** (1970) C-103m. **½ D: Gene Kelly. Henry Fonda, James Stewart, Shirley Jones, Sue Ane Langdon, Elaine Devry. Jimmy inherits and runs a bawdy house in the Old West. Lots of laughs, but clichés run throughout.▼

Chicago Calling (1951) 74m. ** D: John Reinhardt. Dan Duryea, Mary Anderson, Gordon Gebert, Ross Elliot. Slim premise has Duryea sitting by telephone awaiting news of estranged family injured in car accident; mild tour de force.

Chicago Confidential (1957) 73m. **½ D: Sidney Salkow. Brian Keith, Beverly Garland, Dick Foran, Beverly Tyler, Elisha Cook. Keith and Garland make good protagonists in their crusade to clean up corruption and crime amid the labor unions of the Windy City.

Chicago Deadline (1949) 87m. **½ D: Lewis Allen. Alan Ladd, Donna Reed, June Havoc, Irene Hervey, Arthur Kennedy, Shepperd Strudwick. Potentially topnotch actioner bogs down in clichés, with Ladd as crusading reporter in corruption-filled city. Remade as FAME IS THE NAME OF THE GAME.

Chicago Story (1981) C-100m. TVM D: Jerry London. Vincent Baggetta, Dennis Franz, Kene Holiday, Jack Kehoe, Craig T. Nelson, Kristoffer Tabori, Gail Youngs. Pilot to the series, intertwining lawyer, cop, and doctor concepts, created and written by Eric Bercovici and directed by his *Shogun* associate. Intelligent drama has an innocent man charged with the sniper-wounding of a 10-year-old girl in a park. Above average.

Chicago Syndicate (1955) 83m. ** D: Fred F. Sears. Dennis O'Keefe, Abbe Lane, Paul Stewart, Xavier Cugat. Passable exposé film involving cleanup of Windy City rackets.

Chicken Chronicles, The (1977) C-95m. *½ D: Francis Simon. Steven Guttenberg, Ed Lauter, Lisa Reeves, Meridith Baer, Branscombe Richmond, Gino Baffa, Phil Silvers. Lowjinks of a high school senior, circa 1969, whose principal preoccupation is bedding the girl of his dreams. Guttenberg's film debut.▼

Chicken Every Sunday (1948) 91m. **½ D: George Seaton. Dan Dailey, Celeste Holm, Colleen Townsend, Alan Young, Natalie Wood. Easygoing turn-of-the-century Americana about get-rich-quick schemer Dailey and understanding wife Holm.

Chief Crazy Horse (1955) C-86m. **½ D: George Sherman. Victor Mature, Suzan Ball, John Lund, Ray Danton, Keith Larsen. Clichéd nonsense focusing on Mature in title role as idealistic tough redskin.

Chikamatsu Monogatari SEE: **Crucified Lovers**▼

Child Bride of Short Creek (1981) C-100m. TVM D: Robert Michael Lewis. Christopher Atkins, Diane Lane, Conrad Bain, Kiel Martin, Helen Hunt, Dee Wallace, Joan Shawlee. Unenthralling drama of a returning Korean vet's fight with his fundamentalist dad over the father's plan to add a teenage bride to his stable of wives in an isolated Arizona community where polygamy is practiced. Below average.▼

Child Is Born, A (1940) 79m. *** D: Lloyd Bacon. Geraldine Fitzgerald, Jeffrey Lynn, Gladys George, Gale Page, Spring Byington, Eve Arden. Smooth, touching remake of LIFE BEGINS about everyday life in maternity ward, involving prisoner Fitzgerald sent to hospital to have her child.

Childish Things SEE: **Confessions of Tom Harris▼**

Child Is Waiting, A (1963) **102m.** *** D: John Cassavetes. Burt Lancaster, Judy Garland, Gena Rowlands, Steven Hill, Bruce Ritchey. Poignant story of Lancaster's attempts to treat retarded children with the help of overly sympathetic Garland. Sensitive subject handled with honesty and candor.▼

Child Stealer, The (1979) **C-100m. TVM** D: Mel Damski. Beau Bridges, Blair Brown, Cristina Raines, David Groh, Eugene Roche, Marj Dusay. Well-acted drama about a young mother who battles to get her children back after her former husband kidnaps them. Script by Sue Milburn. Above average.

Child Under a Leaf (1974-Canadian) **C-88m.** ** D: George Bloomfield. Dyan Cannon, Joseph Campanella, Donald Pilon. Boring drama about an unhappily married woman who feels she cannot leave her husband for her lover.

Children, The (1980) **C-89m.** *½ D: Max Kalmanowicz. Martin Shakar, Gil Rogers, Gale Garnett, Jesse Abrams, Tracy Griswold, Joy Glacum. When mysterious gas from nuclear plant contaminates school bus, kids become radioactive and burn up whoever they hug. Dull movie with a few laughs and no suspense at all.▼

Children in the Crossfire (1984) **C-100m. TVM** D: George Schaefer. Julia Duffy, Charles Haid, David Huffman, Karen Valentine. Well-intentioned dramatization by Lionel Chetwynd about youngsters from Northern Ireland spending a summer in America degenerates into pedestrian tale with pat answers. Filmed partially in Dublin where Walter Lassally's creative photography gives it the kick of good Irish whiskey. Costar Haid also coproduced. Average.

Children Nobody Wanted, The (1981) **C-100m. TVM** D: Richard Michaels. Frederic Lehne, Michelle Pfeiffer, Matt Clark, Barbara Barrie, Noble Willingham. True-life drama of a young man's crusade to provide a family life for homeless youngsters. Average.

Children of a Lesser God (1986) **C-110m.** *** D: Randa Haines. William Hurt, Marlee Matlin, Piper Laurie, Philip Bosco, Alison Gompf, John F. Cleary, John Basinger. New teacher at school for the deaf is intrigued by an obviously intelligent but isolated young woman who works there as a janitor. The warmth of Hurt's performance, and the credibility of Matlin's, shine through this moving and unusual love story . . . though it lacks the edge and bite of Mark Medoff's play, on which it's based. An impressive feature-film directing debut for Haines. Matlin, also making

her film debut, won an Oscar. Filmed in New Brunswick. ▼

Children of An Lac, The (1980) **C-100m. TVM** D: John Llewellyn Moxey. Shirley Jones, Ina Balin, Beulah Quo, Alan Fudge, Ben Piazza, Lee Paul, Kieu Chinh, Vic Diaz. The story of three women (among them Ina Balin in her own real-life role) who try to evacuate hundreds of Vietnamese orphans just before the fall of Saigon. Lovely performance by veteran actress Quo. Blanche Hanalis wrote the teleplay from Balin's story. Above average.▼

Children of Divorce (1980) **C-97m. TVM** D: Joanna Lee. Barbara Feldon, Lance Kerwin, Stacey Nelkin, Billy Dee Williams, Olivia Cole, Zohra Lampert, Christopher Ciampa, Stella Stevens, Fritz Weaver, Greg Mullavey, Carmine Caridi, Mary-Robin Redd, Carmen Zapata. Drama about the impact of divorce on youngsters in three socially different families, written by director Lee. Average.▼

Children of Paradise (1944-French) **188m.** **** D: Marcel Carne. Jean-Louis Barrault, Arletty, Pierre Brasseur, Albert Remay, Maria Casares, Leon Larive. Story of love affair between pantomimist and beautiful woman is a classic film to see again and again.

Children of the Corn (1984) **C-93m.** *½ D: Fritz Kiersch. Peter Horton, Linda Hamilton, R. G. Armstrong, John Franklin, Courtney Gains, Robby Kiger. Laughable adaptation of Stephen King short-short story about young couple who stumble onto Iowa town that's been taken over by sinister juvenile cultists—and then, like all stupid couples in movies like this, fail to get out while the getting is good. Pretty tacky.▼

Children of the Damned (1964-British) **81m.** **½ D: Anton Leader. Ian Hendry, Alan Badel, Barbara Ferris, Patrick White, Bessie Love. Follow-up to VILLAGE OF THE DAMNED suffers from unimaginative account of precocious deadly children and their quest for power.

Children of the Lotus Eater SEE: **Psychiatrist: God Bless the Children**

Children of the Night (1985) **C-100m. TVM** D: Robert Markowitz. Kathleen Quinlan, Nicholas Campbell, Mario Van Peebles, Lar Park-Lincoln. Budding sociologist shelters teenage hookers seeking refuge from the streets in this exploitive drama based on the book by Dr. Lois Lee (portrayed by Quinlan). Average.

Children of Times Square, The (1986) **C-100m. TVM** D: Curtis Hanson. Howard E. Rollins, Jr., Joanna Cassidy, David Ackroyd, Griffin O'Neal, Larry B. Scott, Danny Nucci. Homeless runaways turn drug dealers in New York's Times Square under the watchful eye of Rollins as a modern-day Fagin. Exploitive but pedestrian drama, except for Rollins' change-of-pace characterization. Average.

Children Shouldn't Play With Dead Things (1972) **C-85m.** *½ D: Benjamin (Bob) Clark. Alan Ormsby, Anya Ormsby, Valerie Mauches, Jane Daly, Jeffrey Gillen. Young, kinky movie-makers take over a rural graveyard and unwittingly resurrect the evil dead. Weird.▼

Children's Hour, The (1962) **107m.** **½ D: William Wyler. Audrey Hepburn, Shirley MacLaine, James Garner, Miriam Hopkins, Fay Bainter, Karen Balkin, Veronica Cartwright. Updated version of Lillian Hellman's play is more explicit in its various themes, including lesbianism, than original THESE THREE, (also made by Wyler), but not half as good. Impact is missing, despite MacLaine and Hepburn as two teachers, Hopkins as meddling aunt, Bainter as questioning grandmother.

Child Saver, The (1988) **C-100m. TVM** D: Stan Lathan. Alfre Woodard, Michael Warren, Deon Richmond, Mario Van Peebles, Martin Balsam. Ambitious ad exec jeopardizes her career when she becomes preoccupied by a street kid. Woodard, as always, gives it everything—in this case, for naught. Below average.

Child's Cry (1986) **C-100m. TVM** D: Gilbert Cates. Lindsay Wagner, Peter Coyote, Taliesin Jaffe, Gerald S. O'Loughlin, Marlene Warfield. Social worker stumbles across child abuse. TV star Kate Jackson co-produced this as a starring vehicle for colleague and pal Lindsay Wagner. Average.

Child's Play (1972) **C-100m.** **½ D: Sidney Lumet. James Mason, Robert Preston, Beau Bridges, Ronald Weyland, Charles White, David Rounds, Kate Harrington, Jamie Alexander. Well-acted but somber and confusing account of rivalry between Catholic school professors Mason and Preston, and the seemingly senseless acts of violence perpetrated by some of their students. From the Robert Marasco play.

Child's Play (1988) **C-87m.** *** D: Tom Holland. Catherine Hicks, Chris Sarandon, Alex Vincent, Brad Dourif, Dinah Manoff, Tommy Swerdlow, Jack Colvin. Scary and clever horror thriller in which only young Vincent knows his new Chucky doll is really a monster, possessed with the spirit of dead murderer Dourif. His mom (Hicks) and the cop on the case (Sarandon) finally believe him but not before several deaths. Sleeper hit packs a wallop, with excellent special effects bringing the doll to life.▼

Chiller (1985) **C-100m. TVM** D: Wes Craven. Michael Beck, Beatrice Straight, Paul Sorvino, Laura Johnson, Dick O'Neill, Alan Fudge. Strange but not too unexpected things happen in this spooky tale when a young man, frozen in cryogenic

suspension, returns to life after ten years. Average.

Chilling, The (1989) **C-95m.** BOMB D: Deland Nuse and Jack A. Sunseri. Linda Blair, Dan Haggerty, Troy Donahue, Jack A. De Rieux, Ron Vincent. Amateurism, familiarity, and too many plot elements doom this ultracheap, Kansas City–made tale of cryogenic corpses turned into (yawn) cannibalistic zombies. At one point we see the shambling corpse of the Ayatollah Khomeni, surely some kind of first—but not a good kind.▼

Chilly Scenes of Winter SEE: **Head Over Heels**▼

Chimes at Midnight (1967-Spanish-Swiss) **115m.** *** D: Orson Welles. Orson Welles, Jeanne Moreau, Margaret Rutherford, John Gielgud, Marina Vlady. Welles combined parts of five Shakespeare plays with mixed results, with his own portrayal of Falstaff the most interesting aspect. Well cast, but limited budget hurt the effort; Ralph Richardson narrates. Also known as FALSTAFF.▼

China (1943) **79m.** ** D: John Farrow. Loretta Young, Alan Ladd, William Bendix, Philip Ahn, Iris Wong, Sen Yung. Pat wartime tale of mercenary Ladd who suddenly realizes his true allegiance while helping enemy.

China Clipper (1936) **85m.** **½ D: Ray Enright. Pat O'Brien, Beverly Roberts, Ross Alexander, Humphrey Bogart, Marie Wilson, Henry B. Walthall. O'Brien stars as man determined to develop trans-Pacific flights; usual plot of initial failure, grim determination, and neglected wife; fairly well done.

China Corsair (1951) **67m.** *½ D: Ray Nazzaro. Jon Hall, Lisa Ferraday, Ron Randell, Douglas Kennedy, Ernest Borgnine. Tinsel-like adventure of Hall's romancing, combating crooks aboard title ship. Borgnine's film debut.

China Doll (1958) **88m.** *½ D: Frank Borzage. Victor Mature, Li Li Hua, Bob Mathias, Stuart Whitman. Bizarre story line can't boost dull film of Mature accidentally buying Oriental wife whom he grows to love. When they are killed, daughter comes to U.S.A.

China Gate (1957) **97m.** *** D: Samuel Fuller. Gene Barry, Angie Dickinson, Nat King Cole, Paul Dubov, Lee Van Cleef, George Givot, Marcel Dalio. International soldiers under French command attack Communist munitions dumps in Indochina. Interesting subplots flesh out Fuller's dynamic action story, with early political view of Vietnam's internal strife.▼

China Girl (1942) **95m.** ** D: Henry Hathaway. Gene Tierney, George Montgomery, Lynn Bari, Victor McLaglen, Sig Ruman, Bobby (Robert) Blake, Ann Pennington, Philip Ahn. American photographer in mysterious Orient during WW2 is background for unbelievable adventure yarn; Bari best item in film.

China Girl (1987) C-88m. **½ D: Abel Ferrara. James Russo, Richard Panebianco, Sari Chang, David Caruso, Russell Wong. Atmospherically filmed romantic thriller about warring Chinese and Italian youth gangs in N.Y.C., with Panebianco and Chang as the star-crossed lovers. Director Ferrara, of TV's *Crime Story*, provides tremendous energy and some over-the-top violence.▼

China Lake Murders, The (1990) C-100m. TVM D: Alan Metzger. Tom Skerritt, Michael Parks, Nancy Everhard, Lauren Tewes, Bill McKinney, Lonny Chapman. A crazed big-city cop on vacation and a local lawman become adversaries during the investigation of serial murders in a small desert town. Well-made thriller written by N. D. Schreiner. Made for cable. Above average.

China 9, Liberty 37 (1978) C-102m. **½ D: Monte Hellman. Warren Oates, Fabio Testi, Jenny Agutter, Sam Peckinpah. Sluggish, mythicized Western in which railroad barons save a man from gallows in exchange for killing former gunfighter; gunfighter's wife falls for killer and helps do his dirty work. Title refers to signpost indicating distance to two nearby towns.

China Rose (1983) C-100m. TVM D: Robert Day. George C. Scott, Ali MacGraw, Michael Biehn, Denis Lill, David Snell, James Hong. American businessman Scott and Chinese-speaking guide MacGraw search for his long-lost son who disappeared during the Cultural Revolution in China. Good premise bludgeoned by miscasting, and unnecessary star-power. Average.

China Seas (1935) 90m. *** D: Tay Garnett. Clark Gable, Jean Harlow, Wallace Beery, Lewis Stone, Rosalind Russell, Dudley Digges, Robert Benchley, C. Aubrey Smith, Hattie McDaniel. Impossible to dislike film with that cast, even if the story—about mysterious goings-on and relationships on Gable's Singapore-bound ship—is ludicrous.▼

China Sky (1945) 78m. ** D: Ray Enright. Randolph Scott, Ruth Warrick, Ellen Drew, Anthony Quinn, Carol Thurston, Richard Loo. Slow-moving Pearl Buck story of dedicated doctor Scott fighting Japanese with Chinese comrades during WW2.▼

China's Little Devils (1945) 74m. ** D: Monta Bell. Harry Carey, Paul Kelly, Ducky Louie, Hayward Soo Hoo, Gloria Ann Chew. Patriotic yarn of Chinese waifs helping downed American pilots get going again.

China Syndrome, The (1979) C-123m. **** D: James Bridges. Jane Fonda, Jack Lemmon, Michael Douglas, Scott Brady, James Hampton, Peter Donat, Wilford Brimley, James Karen. Heartpounding drama about attempted cover-up of accident at California nuclear plant is as much a probe of television news as it is a story of nuclear power— and it scores bullseye on both fronts. There is no music score; story tension propels film by itself, along with solid performances by Fonda as TV reporter, Douglas (who also produced film) as radical cameraman, and especially Lemmon as dedicated plant exec. Screenplay by Mike Gray, T.S. Cook, and Bridges.▼

Chinatown (1974) C-131m. **** D: Roman Polanski. Jack Nicholson, Faye Dunaway, John Huston, Perry Lopez, John Hillerman, Darrell Zwerling, Diane Ladd, Burt Young, Bruce Glover. Bizarre, fascinating mystery in the Hammett-Chandler tradition (and set in the 1930s) with Nicholson as private eye led into a complex, volatile case by femme fatale Dunaway. Director Polanski appears briefly as the hood who knifes Nicholson. Oscar winner for Best Screenplay (Robert Towne). Sequel: THE TWO JAKES.▼

China Venture (1953) 83m. **½ D: Don Siegel. Edmond O'Brien, Barry Sullivan, Jocelyn Brando, Richard Loo, Philip Ahn. Exciting WW2 adventure film of marine group on mission to capture Japanese naval commander wanted by U.S. interrogation department.

Chinchero SEE: **Last Movie, The**

Chinese Cat, The (1944) 65m. D: Phil Rosen. Sidney Toler, Benson Fong, Joan Woodbury, Mantan Moreland, Sam Flint, John Davidson, Betty Blythe, Jack Norton, Ian Keith. SEE: **Charlie Chan** series.

Chinese Connection, The (1973-Chinese) C-107m. *** D: Lo Wei. Bruce Lee, Miao Ker Hsio. Violent Kung Fu film has Lee in Shanghai in early 1900s seeking vengeance on the murderers of his teacher. Graceful, powerful, humorous, and charismatic; Lee at his best.▼

Chinese Ring, The (1947) 67m. D: William Beaudine. Roland Winters, Warren Douglas, Victor Sen Yung, Mantan Moreland, Philip Ahn. SEE: **Charlie Chan** series.

Chino (1973-Italian) C-98m. **½ D: John Sturges. Charles Bronson, Jill Ireland, Vincent Van Patten, Marcel Bozzuffi, Fausto Tozzi, Melissa Chimenti. Offbeat Western that barely received theatrical release here in 1976; Bronson plays halfbreed whose attempts to maintain his horse ranch in peace are short-lived. Video title: THE VALDEZ HORSES.▼

Chip Off the Old Block (1944) 82m. ** D: Charles Lamont. Donald O'Connor, Peggy Ryan, Ann Blyth, Helen Vinson, Helen Broderick, Arthur Treacher, Patric Knowles, Ernest Truex. Innocuous war-

time musical of misunderstandings, climaxing in teenage romance and musical show.
Chisum (1970) **C-111m.** **½ D: Andrew V. McLaglen. John Wayne, Forrest Tucker, Christopher George, Ben Johnson, Glenn Corbett, Bruce Cabot, Patric Knowles, Lynda Day, Richard Jaeckel. Cattle-baron Wayne more catalyst than hero in handsomely produced, forgettable Western outing. Corrupt officials threaten to disrupt peaceful territory.▼

✓ **Chitty Chitty Bang Bang** (1968) **C-142m.** *½ D: Ken Hughes. Dick Van Dyke, Sally Ann Howes, Lionel Jeffries, Gert Frobe, Anna Quayle, Benny Hill. Children's musical about flying car is one big Edsel itself, with totally forgettable score and some of the shoddiest special effects ever. Loosely based on book by Ian Fleming.▼

Chloe in the Afternoon (1972-French) **C-97m.** ***½ D: Eric Rohmer. Bernard Verley, Zouzou, Francoise Verley, Daniel Ceccaldi. No. 6 of Rohmer's "Six Moral Tales" depicts married man's fascination with kooky girl during daylight hours. As Chloe, Zouzou becomes more alluring as film unwinds.▼

Chocolat (1988-French-German-Camaroon) **C-105m.** *** D: Claire Denis. Isaach de Bankolé, Giulia Boschi, François Cluzet, Cécile Ducasse, Jean-Claude Adelin, Jacques Denis, Mireille Perrier. Subtle, slowly paced slice-of-life about a young woman's memories of her childhood in French West Africa, where whites are masters and most blacks are servants. This very personal, autobiographical film (which first-time director Denis coscripted) is quietly rewarding.▼

Chocolate Soldier, The (1941) **102m.** ** D: Roy Del Ruth. Nelson Eddy, Rise Stevens, Nigel Bruce, Florence Bates, Dorothy Gilmore, Nydia Westman. Not the Oscar Straus operetta, but rather a remake of Molnar's THE GUARDSMAN. Eddy and Stevens are husband-wife opera stars; to test her fidelity, he disguises himself as a Cossack and woos her. Much too talky, and not enough music; remade as LILY IN LOVE.▼

Chocolate War, The (1988) **C-103m.** *** D: Keith Gordon. John Glover, Ilan Mitchell-Smith, Wally Ward, Bud Cort, Adam Baldwin, Jenny Wright, Doug Hutchinson. A Catholic boys school is divided by a power struggle between an idealistic student and a dictatorial acting headmaster, as each tries to deal with The Vigils, a secret society of schoolboys out for control. Chilling and impressive, well directed on a low budget by actor Gordon, who also adapted Robert Cormier's novel. Glover is wonderfully wicked.▼

Choice, The (1981) **C-100m.** TVM D: David Greene. Susan Clark, Mitchell Ryan, Jennifer Warren, Largo Woodruff, Paul Regina, Kathleen Lloyd, Lisa Jane Persky. Sudsy drama about a mother and daughter who both must make a decision about the latter's abortion. Average.▼

Choice of Arms (1981-French) **C-117m.** *** D: Alain Corneau. Yves Montand, Catherine Deneuve, Gerard Depardieu, Michel Galabru, Gerard Lanvin. Well-directed drama about retired gangster Montand forced into antagonistic relationship with young punk Depardieu, leading to reciprocal violence. Despite hostility, both men come to understand how similar they are. Good performances by excellent cast, especially Depardieu. Original French running time 135m.▼

Choice of Weapons SEE: **Dirty Knight's Work**

Choices (1981) **C-90m.** **½ D: Silvio Narizzano. Paul Carafotes, Victor French, Lelia Goldoni, Val Avery, Dennis Patrick, Pat Buttram. Partially deaf teenager Carafotes becomes alienated when prevented from playing football because of his handicap. Well-intentioned but obvious drama is helped by fine performances.▼

Choices (1986) **C-100m.** TVM D: David Lowell Rich. George C. Scott, Jacqueline Bisset, Melissa Gilbert. Self-righteous right-to-life judge comes face-to-face with the abortion issue when his much younger second wife and his unwed teenage daughter both have unwanted pregnancies. A glitzy soaper written by Judith Parker. Average.

Choices of the Heart (1983) **C-100m.** TVM D: Joseph Sargent. Melissa Gilbert, Martin Sheen, Mike Farrell, Helen Hunt, Peter Horton, Rene Enriquez, Pamela Bellwood. The story of Jean Donovan, the lay missionary killed in El Salvador in 1980 with three American nuns. Gilbert emerges as a young actress of depth here. Script is by John Pielmeier, author of AGNES OF GOD. Also titled IN DECEMBER THE ROSES WILL BLOOM AGAIN. Above average.

Choirboys, The (1977) **C-119m.** BOMB D: Robert Aldrich. Charles Durning, Louis Gossett, Jr., Perry King, Clyde Kusatsu, Stephen Macht, Tim McIntire, Randy Quaid, Chuck Sacci, Don Stroud, James Woods, Burt Young, Robert Webber, Jeanie Bell, Blair Brown, Michele Carey, Charles Haid, Joe Kapp, Barbara Rhoades, Jim Davis, Phyllis Davis, Jack DeLeon, David Spielberg, Vic Tayback, Michael Wills, George DiCenzo. Supposedly comic escapades of L.A. cops who relieve work pressures by raunchy doings. Foul-mouthed, foul-minded, heavy-handed film from book by Joseph Wambaugh, who disavowed this turkey.▼

Choke Canyon (1986) **C-94m.** **½ D: Chuck Bail. Stephen Collins, Janet Julian, Lance Henriksen, Bo Svenson, Victoria

Racimo, Nicholas Pryor. Fun sci-fi about stubborn cowboy physicist (!) who fights off corrupt industrialist's henchmen, trying to protect the environment against nuclear waste dumping on the eve of Halley's Comet's visit near Earth. Terrific aerial stuntwork.▼

C.H.O.M.P.S. (1979) **C-89m.** *½ D: Don Chaffey. Wesley Eure, Valerie Bertinelli, Conrad Bain, Chuck McCann, Red Buttons, Larry Bishop, Hermione Baddeley, Jim Backus. Cartoon-makers Hanna & Barbera struck out with this Disneyesque comedy about a young inventor (Eure) and his mechanical dog. Originally rated PG for mild profanities voiced by *another* dog in the film—then redubbed for kids' sake. Title is acronym for Canine HOMe Protection System.▼

Choose Me (1984) **C-106m.** ***½ D: Alan Rudolph. Genevieve Bujold, Keith Carradine, Lesley Ann Warren, Rae Dawn Chong, Patrick Bauchau, John Larroquette, John Considine. Outrageously inventive tale of the various relationships, truths, and lies that link radio sex-talk-show hostess Bujold, bar owner Warren, and mental hospital escapee Carradine, among others. This comedy-drama about the different roles that people play in life is a real kick, with a wonderful from-midnight-till-dawn feel and good performances by all. Evocative use of L.A. locations and Teddy Pendergrass songs. A companion piece to Rudolph's WELCOME TO L.A. and REMEMBER MY NAME.▼

Chopping Mall (1986) **C-76m.** *½ D: Jim Wynorski. Kelli Maroney, Tony O'Dell, John Terlesky, Russell Todd, Paul Bartel, Mary Woronov, Dick Miller, Karrie Emerson, Barbara Crampton, Suzee Slater, Gerrit Graham, Mel Welles. Updated imitation of 1973 TV movie TRAPPED has eight teenagers trapped overnight in a shopping mall where three malfunctioning guard robots go on a killing spree. Endless in-jokes and cameo roles (including Bartel and Woronov in their EATING RAOUL characters) fail to save a story that lapses into cliches. Originally titled: KILLBOTS.▼

Chorus Line, A (1985) **C-113m.** ** D: Richard Attenborough. Michael Douglas, Terrence Mann, Alyson Reed, Cameron English, Vicki Frederick, Audrey Landers, Gregg Burge, Nicole Fosse, Janet Jones. Auditionees for Broadway chorus line reveal their innermost thoughts and emotions in song and dance before a hard-boiled director (Douglas). Thoroughly uninspired, unmemorable filming of the landmark Broadway musical; watchable, especially if you never saw the play, but what can you say about a musical in which all the singing and all the dancing is mediocre? And the show's biggest number, "What I Did for Love," is treated as a throwaway!▼

Chorus of Disapproval, A (1988-British) **C-100m.** ** D: Michael Winner. Jeremy Irons, Anthony Hopkins, Prunella Scales, Sylvia Syms, Lionel Jeffries, Gareth Hunt, Patsy Kensit, Alexandra Pigg, Jenny Seagrove. Shy, simple-minded widower moves to a seaside town and joins an amateur theatrical troupe, in which romantic intrigues abound. Some pearly performances (especially Hopkins, as the director, and Scales, as his wife) can't overcome the slightness of the material and its faltering execution. Adapted from Alan Ayckbourn's stage play by the author and director Winner.▼

Chosen, The (1978-Italian-British) **C-105m.** BOMB D: Alberto De Martino. Kirk Douglas, Agostina Belli, Simon Ward, Anthony Quayle, Virginia McKenna, Alexander Knox. Nuclear power exec Douglas slowly realizes that his son (Ward) is the Antichrist, who plans to use nuclear power to bring on world destruction. There! We just saved you 105 minutes. Originally titled HOLOCAUST 2000.▼

Chosen, The (1981) **C-108m.** ***½ D: Jeremy Paul Kagan. Maximilian Schell, Rod Steiger, Robby Benson, Barry Miller, Hildy Brooks, Ron Rifkin, Val Avery. Excellent adaptation of Chaim Potok's novel, centering on friendship between Americanized Jew Miller and Hassidic Benson. Steiger, as Benson's rabbi father, gives his best performance in years, and even Robby isn't bad. Set in 1940s Brooklyn; later made into a Broadway musical.▼

Chosen Survivors (1974) **C-99m.** ** D: Sutton Roley. Jackie Cooper, Alex Cord, Richard Jaeckel, Bradford Dillman, Pedro Armendariz, Jr., Diana Muldaur, Barbara Babcock. Good cast in formula nonsense about group of people "selected" to survive future holocaust in underground shelter. Just one hitch: the shelter is invaded by vampire bats. Dialogue and characterizations from grade-Z movies of the past.

Christiane F. (1981-German) **C-124m.** **½ D: Ulrich Edel. Nadja Brunkhorst, Thomas Haustein, Jens Kuphal, Reiner Wolk. Grim, gruesome account of bored teenager Brunkhorst falling in with crowd of junkie-hustler Haustein. Well-meaning but uneven; based on a true story. Features unmemorable David Bowie concert sequence.▼

Christian Licorice Store, The (1971) **C-90m.** ** D: James Frawley. Beau Bridges, Maud Adams, Gilbert Roland, Anne Randall, Allen Arbus, McLean Stevenson. Quirky, dated comic study of tennis player Bridges looking for a meaning to life. Loaded with cameos, including directors Jean Renoir, Monte Hellman, Theodore J. Flicker, and James B. Harris. Filmed in 1969.

Christian the Lion (1976-British) **C-89m.** **½ D: Bill Travers, James Hill. Bill

Travers, Virginia McKenna, George Adamson, Anthony Bourke. Pleasant docudrama about the efforts of BORN FREE stars—and real-life wildlife expert George Adamson, whom Travers portrayed in earlier film—to return a lion born in London Zoo to its native habitat in Kenya. Expanded from 1971's THE LION AT WORLD'S END.▼

Christina (1974) C-98m. ** D: Paul Krasny. Barbara Parkins, Peter Haskell, James McEachin, Marlyn Mason, Barbara Gordon. Beautiful woman offers unemployed man $25,000 to marry her—in name only—but just as he's falling in love with her, she disappears. Murky suspenser filmed in Canada.▼

Christine (1983) C-111m. ** D: John Carpenter. Keith Gordon, John Stockwell, Alexandra Paul, Robert Prosky, Harry Dean Stanton, Christine Belford, Roberts Blossom, Kelly Preston. Stephen King bestseller about a '58 Plymouth with demonic powers never hits bullseye, despite a promising start that captures teenage life quite nicely.▼

Christine Jorgensen Story, The (1970) C-89m. BOMB D: Irving Rapper. John Hansen, Joan Tompkins, Quinn Redeker, John W. Hines, Ellen Clark. Ludicrous biography of famed 50s phenomenon is not exactly an in-depth study; one problem is that actor Hansen looks more masculine as female Christine and vice versa.

Christmas Carol, A (1938) 69m. *** D: Edwin L. Marin. Reginald Owen, Gene Lockhart, Kathleen Lockhart, Terry Kilburn, Barry MacKay, Lynne Carver, Leo G. Carroll, Ann Rutherford. Nicely done adaptation of Dickens' classic with Owen a well-modulated Scrooge, surrounded by good MGM players and period settings. Young June Lockhart makes her screen debut. Also shown in computer-colored version.▼

✓ **Christmas Carol, A** (1951-British) 86m. **** D: Brian Desmond-Hurst. Alastair Sim, Jack Warner, Kathleen Harrison, Mervyn Johns, Hermione Baddeley, Clifford Mollison, Michael Hordern, George Cole, Carol Marsh, Miles Malleson, Ernest Thesiger, Hattie Jacques, Peter Bull, Hugh Dempster. Superb film is too good to be shown only at Christmastime; always delightful Sim makes Scrooge a three-dimensional character in this faithful, heartwarming rendition of the Dickens classic. Screenplay by Noel Langley. Patrick Macnee plays young Marley. Original British title: SCROOGE.▼

Christmas Carol, A (1984) C-100m. TVM D: Clive Donner. George C. Scott, Nigel Davenport, Frank Finlay, Edward Woodward, Lucy Gutteridge, Angela Pleasence, Roger Rees, David Warner, Susannah York, Anthony Walters. Beautifully staged retelling of the Dickens classic with a memorable interpretation of Scrooge by Scott, by scott! Handsomely filmed in Shrewsbury, England. Script by Roger O. Hirson. Above average.

Christmas Coal Mine Miracle, The SEE: **Christmas Miracle in Caufield, U.S.A.**▼

Christmas Comes to Willow Creek (1987) C-100m. TVM D: Richard Lang. John Schneider, Tom Wopat, Kim Delaney, Zachary Ansley, Hoyt Axton. Feuding brothers (and onetime *Dukes of Hazzard*) get caught up in the Yuletide season when forced to truck gifts to a remote Alaskan village. Below average.▼

Christmas Eve (1947) 90m. *½ D: Edwin L. Marin. George Brent, George Raft, Randolph Scott, Joan Blondell, Virginia Field, Ann Harding, Reginald Denny. Slow-moving mixture of comedy and drama as foster sons discover evil intentions of relations to victimize Harding. Retitled: SINNER'S HOLIDAY.

Christmas Eve (1986) C-100m. TVM D: Stuart Cooper. Loretta Young, Ron Leibman, Trevor Howard, Arthur Hill, Patrick Cassidy, Season Hubley, Kate Reid. Young made her widely heralded return to acting after 23 years as an eccentric millionairess determined to bring her grown grandchildren, long estranged from their stuffy father, together for one final holiday celebration. A good cry is had by all. Written by Blanche Hanalis. Above average.

Christmas Evil SEE: **You Better Watch Out**▼

Christmas Gift, The (1986) C-100m. TVM D: Michael Pressman. John Denver, Jane Kaczmarek, Gennie James, Edward Winter, Pat Corley, Mary Wickes, James Callahan. Treacly holiday tale that asks you to accept country boy Denver as an embittered, widowed N.Y.C. architect who stumbles upon a modern-day *Brigadoon* world in the Colorado Rockies and discovers the true meaning of Christmas. He even gets a chance to sing. Average.

Christmas Holiday (1944) 92m. *** D: Robert Siodmak. Deanna Durbin, Gene Kelly, Gale Sondergaard, Gladys George, Richard Whorf. Somerset Maugham novel reset in America. Crime story with Durbin gone wrong to help killer-hubby Kelly; songs include "Spring Will Be A Little Late This Year."

Christmas in Connecticut (1945) 101m. **½ D: Peter Godfrey. Barbara Stanwyck, Dennis Morgan, Sydney Greenstreet, Reginald Gardiner, S.Z. Sakall, Robert Shayne, Una O'Connor. Airy fluff with Stanwyck, a chic magazine writer who's supposed to be an expert homemaker, forced to entertain a war veteran (Morgan) and her boss (Greenstreet) for the holidays. Standard studio corn it may be, but a wonderful treat for late-night viewing on Christmas Eve. Also shown in computer-colored version.▼

Christmas in July (1940) 67m. ***½ D: Preston Sturges. Dick Powell, Ellen Drew, Raymond Walburn, William Demarest, Ernest Truex, Franklin Pangborn. Top Sturges comedy about pauper Powell going on shopping spree mistakenly believing he has won big contest. Walburn and Demarest are at their best.▼

Christmas Kid, The (1968-Spanish) C-89m. ** D: Sidney Pink. Jeffrey Hunter, Louis Hayward, Gustavo Rojo, Perla Cristal, Luis Prendes. Average frijole Western about saddletramp's search for his true identity.▼

Christmas Lilies of the Field (1979) C-100m. TVM D: Ralph Nelson. Billy Dee Williams, Maria Schell, Fay Hauser, Judith Piquet, Hanna Hertelendy, Lisa Mann. Joyous followup to Nelson's Oscar-winning original of 15 years earlier, with Homer Smith turning up at the chapel he built in the Arizona desert and being conned once again by Mother Maria—this time to put up an orphanage and kindergarten. Above average.▼

Christmas Miracle in Caulfield, U.S.A. (1977) C-100m. TVM D: Jud Taylor. Mitchell Ryan, Kurt Russell, Andrew Prine, John Carradine, Karen Lamm, Melissa Gilbert. Coal miners trapped by an underground explosion on Christmas Eve. Mild drama by Dalene Young, taken from real life, but plays in standard TV fashion like a roadshow *Waltons*—right down to the off-camera narration by a younger member of the family and the final shot of home with the lights going out. Average. Retitled THE CHRISTMAS COAL MINE MIRACLE.▼

Christmas Mountain (1980) C-90m. ** D: Pierre Moro. Slim Pickens, Mark Miller, Barbara Stanger, Fran Ryan, Tina Minard, John Hart. An old cowboy finds the living spirit of Christmas with widow and her family in midst of blizzard of '88 out West. Minor holiday fare.

Christmas Star, The (1986) C-100m. TVM. D: Alan Shapiro. Edward Asner, Rene Auberjonois, Jim Metzler, Susan Tyrrell, Fred Gwynne, Alan North, Philip Bruns. Bearded con man Asner's holiday spirit is renewed by a couple of kids who believe that he really is Santa Claus in this Disney fantasy. Average.

Christmas Story, A (1983) C-98m. ***½ D: Bob Clark. Peter Billingsley, Darren McGavin, Melinda Dillon, Ian Petrella, Scott Schwartz, Tedde Moore. Humorist Jean Shepherd's delightful memoir of growing up in the 1940s and wanting nothing so much as a Red Ryder BB gun for Christmas. Shepherd narrates in the first person, and Billingsley portrays him (delightfully) as a boy. Truly funny for kids and grownups alike; wonderful period

flavor. Based on a portion of *In God We Trust, All Others Pay Cash.*▼

Christmas That Almost Wasn't, The (1966-Italian-U.S.) C-95m. *½ D: Rossano Brazzi. Rossano Brazzi, Paul Tripp, Lidia Brazzi, Sonny Fox, Mischa Auer. Santa Claus hijack makes for weak kiddie fare, none too thrilling for grownups either.▼

Christmas to Remember, A (1978) C-100m. TVM D: George Englund. Jason Robards, Eva Marie Saint, Joanne Woodward, George Perry, Bryan Englund. Sentimental Depression-era tale about an elderly farm couple who take in their city-bred adolescent grandson for the holidays. High-powered star cast elevates this already satisfying adaptation by Stewart Stern of Glendon Swarthout's novel, *The Melodeon.* Above average.▼

Christmas Tree, The (1969) 110m. *½ D: Terence Young. William Holden, Virna Lisi, Bourvil, Brook Fuller, Madeleine Damien. Sappy tear-jerker about relationship between young boy and his wealthy father when the latter learns his son's death is imminent. Cast is divided between those who overact and those who don't seem to care one way or the other. Retitled WHEN WOLVES CRY for homevideo.▼

Christmas Visitor, The (1987-Australian) C-98m. TVM D: George Miller. Dee Wallace Stone, John Waters, Charles Tingwell, Bill Kerr, Andrew Ferguson. Well-crafted holiday tale set in the drought-ridden Australian outback of the 1890s. Initially a coproduction with the Disney people for cable and known alternately (Down Under, at least) as BUSHFIRE MOON. Above average.

Christmas Wife, The (1988) C-73m. TVM D: David Jones. Jason Robards, Julie Harris, Don Francks, James Eckhouse, Patricia Hamilton, Deborah Grover. Sturdy character study by a couple of pros about a lonely widower who "hires" a woman to be his companion for a Christmas vacation at his comfortable mountain cabin. Reminiscent of the great "Golden Age of TV" dramas of yore, adapted from Helen Norris's short story by Katherine Ann Jones. Made for cable. Above average.▼

Christmas Without Snow, A (1980) C-100m. TVM D: John Korty. Michael Learned, John Houseman, Ramon Bieri, James Cromwell, Valerie Curtin, Ruth Nelson, Beah Richards. Heartwarming story, written by Korty, about a newly divorced woman's involvement in the lives of fellow church-choir members as they struggle to meet the demands of their perfectionist director. Above average.▼

Christopher Columbus (1949-British) C-104m. *** D: David Macdonald. Fredric March, Florence Eldridge, Francis L. Sullivan, Nora Swinburne, James Robertson Justice. Stark, slowly paced biography of 15th-century explorer, with earnest portrayal by March in title role; good period setting.

Christopher Strong (1933) **77m.** **½ D: Dorothy Arzner. Katharine Hepburn, Colin Clive, Billie Burke, Helen Chandler, Jack LaRue. Hepburn's an aviatrix in love with married Clive. Dated film intriguing for star's performance as headstrong, individualistic woman—and dig that silver lamé costume.▼

Christ Stopped at Eboli SEE: Eboli▼

Chrome and Hot Leather (1971) **C-91m.** BOMB D: Lee Frost. William Smith, Tony Young, Michael Haynes, Peter Brown, Marvin Gaye. Lurid time-waster about some motorcycle thugs who are responsible for a woman's death and her Green Beret fiancé (Young) who seeks revenge. If only he had been this effective back in Nam . . .

Chu Chu and the Philly Flash (1981) **C-100m.** BOMB D: David Lowell Rich. Alan Arkin, Carol Burnett, Jack Warden, Danny Aiello, Adam Arkin, Danny Glover, Sid Haig, Ruth Buzzi, Vito Scotti, Lou Jacobi. Maddeningly moronic comedy revolving around bum Arkin, show-biz failure Burnett, and a briefcase filled with secret government papers. A low point in the careers of its stars; Burnett isn't even funny in Carmen Miranda getup. Scripted by Barbara Dana (Mrs. Arkin).▼

Chubasco (1968) **C-100m.** **½ D: Allen H. Miner. Richard Egan, Christopher Jones, Susan Strasberg, Ann Sothern, Simon Oakland, Audrey Totter, Preston Foster. Young man working on tuna boat gets along with his skipper until he learns the boy has married his daughter; overlong but likable programmer filmed when Jones and Strasberg were married in real life.

Chuck Berry Hail! Hail! Rock 'n' Roll (1987) **C-120m.** ***½ D: Taylor Hackford. Chuck Berry, Keith Richards, Eric Clapton, Robert Cray, Etta James, Julian Lennon, Linda Ronstadt. Two delights in one: an overview of rock legend Chuck Berry's career—sparked by interviews with Richards, Clapton, Bo Diddley, Little Richard, Roy Orbison, The Everly Brothers, Willie Dixon, Bruce Springsteen, and the subject himself—and a climactic 60th birthday Berry concert held in his hometown of St. Louis. Whitewashes Berry's womanizing and early 1960s jail term, but his hot temper is much in evidence during some amusing skirmishes with concert producer Richards. Worthy of its title . . . if slightly overlong.▼

C.H.U.D. (1984) **C-90m.** BOMB D: Douglas Cheek. John Heard, Daniel Stern, Kim Greist, Brenda Currin, Justin Hall, Christopher Curry, Michael O'Hare, John Goodman. That's Cannibalistic Humanoid Underground Dwellers, folks—a band of ragtag derelicts who come up to street level at night to munch on human flesh.

Greist made this before BRAZIL, so she at least has an excuse—but what are Heard and Stern doing in this film? Grimy on all levels. Followed by a sequel.▼

C.H.U.D. II—Bud the Chud (1989) **C-84m.** BOMB D: David Irving. Brian Robbins, Bill Calvert, Gerrit Graham, Tricia Leigh Fisher, Robert Vaughn, Larry Cedar, Bianca Jagger, Larry Linville, Jack Riley, Norman Fell, June Lockhart. Teenagers swipe a corpse (Graham), unaware that it is a cannibalistic CHUD that passes on its tendencies to anyone it bites. Comedy sequel to straight original is far worse, but Graham is genuinely funny as the monster. Script credited to "M. Kane Jeeves."▼

Chuka (1967) **C-105m.** ** D: Gordon Douglas. Rod Taylor, John Mills, Ernest Borgnine, Luciana Paluzzi, James Whitmore, Angela Dorian, Louis Hayward. Good cast is wasted in routine Western about grizzled gunfighter who tries to promote peace between Indians and some undisciplined soldiers guarding nearby fort.

Chump at Oxford, A (1940) **63m.** **½ D: Alfred Goulding. Stan Laurel, Oliver Hardy, Wilfred Lucas, Forrester Harvey, James Finlayson, Anita Garvin. So-called feature is more like a series of barely related shorts; film is nearly half over before L&H even get to Oxford. Still quite funny, especially when they settle down in the Dean's quarters. A young Peter Cushing plays one of the boys' tormentors.▼

Chushingura (1962-Japanese) **C-108m.** ***½ D: Hiroshi Inagaki. Koshiro Matsumoto, Yuzo Kayama, Chusha Ichikawa, Toshiro Mifune, Yoko Tsukasa. Young lord Kayama is forced to commit hara kiri by corrupt feudal lord Ichikawa, and his forty-seven samurai retainers (or ronin) seek vengeance. This is the best-known version of an oft-filmed story, based on a real-life event: sprawling, episodic, exquisitely beautiful, if a bit slow. Sometimes referred to as the GONE WITH THE WIND of Japanese cinema. Originally released in Japan in two parts, running 204m.

Cimarron (1931) **124m.** **½ D: Wesley Ruggles. Richard Dix, Irene Dunne, Estelle Taylor, Nance O'Neil, William Collier, Jr., Roscoe Ates. Edna Ferber's saga about an American family and the effect of empire building on the American West, 1890–1915. Oscar winner for Best Picture and Best Screenplay (Howard Estabrook), it dates badly, particularly Dix's overripe performance—but it's still worth seeing. Remade in 1960.▼

Cimarron (1960) **C-147m.** **½ D: Anthony Mann. Glenn Ford, Maria Schell, Anne Baxter, Arthur O'Connell. Edna Ferber's chronicle of frontier life in Oklahoma between 1890-1915 becomes an indifferent sprawling soap opera unsalvaged by a few spectacular scenes.

Cimarron Kid, The (1951) **C-84m.** ** D: Budd Boetticher. Audie Murphy, Beverly Tyler, James Best, Yvette Dugay. Uninspired formula Western with Murphy in title role, persuaded to give up his criminal life by his sweetheart.

Cincinnati Kid, The (1965) **C-113m.** **½ D: Norman Jewison. Steve McQueen, Ann-Margret, Edward G. Robinson, Karl Malden, Tuesday Weld, Joan Blondell, Rip Torn, Jack Weston, Cab Calloway. Roving card-sharks get together in New Orleans for big poker game; side episodes of meaningless romance. Robinson, Blondell, and Malden come off best as vivid members of the playing profession. Script by Ring Lardner, Jr. and Terry Southern; Jewison replaced Sam Peckinpah as director.▼

Cinderella (1950) **C-74m.** ***½ D: Wilfred Jackson, Hamilton Luske, Clyde Geronimi. Voices of Ilene Woods, William Phipps, Eleanor Audley, Rhoda Williams, Lucille Bliss, Verna Felton. One of Walt Disney's best animated fairy tales spins the traditional story with some delightful comic embellishments, including a couple of mice named Gus and Jaq who befriend the put-upon heroine. Tuneful score includes "A Dream Is a Wish Your Heart Makes" and "Bibbidi Bobbidi Boo."▼

Cinderella Jones (1946) **88m.** ** D: Busby Berkeley. Joan Leslie, Robert Alda, S.Z. Sakall, Edward Everett Horton, Ruth Donnelly, Elisha Cook. Silly comedy of girl who must marry brainy husband to collect inheritance; good cast defeated by trivial script.

Cinderella Liberty (1973) **C-117m.** ***½ D: Mark Rydell. James Caan, Marsha Mason, Eli Wallach, Kirk Calloway, Burt Young, Bruce Kirby, Jr., Allyn Ann McLerie, Dabney Coleman, Sally Kirkland. Sensitive, original story by Darryl Ponicsan (based on his novel) about romance between simple, good-hearted sailor and a hooker with an illegitimate black son. Artfully mixes romance and realism, with sterling performances by Caan and Mason.▼

Cinderfella (1960) **C-91m.** **½ D: Frank Tashlin. Jerry Lewis, Ed Wynn, Judith Anderson, Anna Maria Alberghetti, Henry Silva, Count Basie. Jerry is the poor stepson turned into a handsome prince for a night by fairy godfather Wynn. Fairy tale classic revamped as a pretentious Lewis vehicle, with talky interludes and ineffectual musical sequences featuring Alberghetti.▼

Cindy (1978) **C-100m.** TVM D: William A. Graham. Clifton Davis, Charlaine Woodard, Scoey Mitchlll, Mae Mercer, Nell-Ruth Carter, Alaina Reed. Original musical updates Cinderella story to Harlem during WW2; delightful concoction from MTM team with multi-talented black cast. Above average.

Cinema Paradiso (1988-Italian-French) **C-123m.** ***½ D: Giuseppe Tornatore. Philippe Noiret, Jacques Perrin, Salvatore Cascio, Mario Leonardi, Agnese Nano, Leopoldo Trieste. A young boy is mesmerized by the movie theater in his small Italian town (in the years following WW2), and pursues a friendship with its crusty but warmhearted projectionist. Captivating, bittersweet film, with a perfect finale; Noiret and the boy (Cascio) are wonderful. Written by the director. After abortive Italian release in 1988 (at 155m.), film was shortened by a half-hour and awarded a Special Jury Prize at the 1989 Cannes Film Festival; it went on to win the Best Foreign Film Oscar.▼

Circle, The (1959-British) **84m.** **½ D: Gerald Thomas. John Mills, Derek Farr, Roland Culver, Wilfrid Hyde-White. Well-acted, neatly paced murder yarn involving London medico. Retitled: THE VICIOUS CIRCLE.

Circle of Children, A (1977) **C-100m.** TVM D: Don Taylor. Jane Alexander, Rachel Roberts, David Ogden Stiers, Nan Martin, Matthew Laborteaux. Beautifully acted drama about affluent suburbanite (Alexander) whose volunteer work with emotionally disturbed children fills the void in her life. Mary MacCracken's autobiographical novel served as the basis for this sensitive, intelligent, surprisingly unsentimental film. Jane Alexander's superb performance is matched by that of Rachel Roberts as a gifted, demanding teacher who regards the volunteer merely a hostess out of place. Script by Steven Gethers. Above average. Sequel: LOVEY: A CIRCLE OF CHILDREN, PART II.

Circle of Danger (1951-British) **86m.** **½ D: Jacques Tourneur. Ray Milland, Patricia Roc, Marius Goring, Hugh Sinclair. Straightforward account of Milland returning to England to ferret out brother's killers.

Circle of Deceit (1981-French-German) **C-108m.** **** D: Volker Schlondorff. Bruno Ganz, Hanna Schygulla, Jean Carmet, Jerzy Skolimowski, Gila von Weitershausen. Thoughtful, chilling, unrelentingly sober account of German journalist Ganz covering a Lebanese civil war, focusing on how he is affected by his experiences and his relationship with widow Schygulla. Actually filmed in Beirut against a backdrop of political turmoil; a superior film in every respect. Originally shown as FALSE WITNESS.

Circle of Deception, A (1961-British) **100m.** **½ D: Jack Lee. Bradford Dillman, Suzy Parker, Harry Andrews, Robert Stephens, Paul Rogers. At times engaging psychological yarn of WW2 espionage agent Dillman who breaks under Axis torture;

ironic climax. Dillman and Parker later married in real life.

Circle of Iron (1979) **C-102m.** **½ D: Richard Moore. David Carradine, Jeff Cooper, Roddy McDowall, Eli Wallach, Erica Creer, Christopher Lee. Strange, sometimes silly, but watchable blend of martial arts action and Zen philosophy; from an idea concocted by James Coburn and Bruce Lee. Cooper (looking like a California surfer) must pass rites of trial to find secret book of knowledge. Carradine plays four roles in this Stirling Silliphant-scripted fantasy, filmed in Israel as THE SILENT FLUTE.▼

Circle of Love (1964-French-Italian) **C-105m.** *½ D: Roger Vadim. Jane Fonda, Jean-Claude Brialy, Maurice Ronet, Jean Sorel, Catherine Spaak, Anna Karina, Marie Dubois, Claude Giraud, Francoise Dorleac. Undistinguished remake of Ophuls' classic LA RONDE: A seduces B, B makes love to C, C has an affair with D—circling all the way back to A. Screenplay by Jean Anouilh; original running time: 110m.▼

Circle of Power (1983) **C-103m.** **½ D: Bobby Roth. Yvette Mimieux, Christopher Allport, Cindy Pickett, John Considine, Julius Harris, Scott Marlowe, Fran Ryan, Walter Olkewicz, Danny Dayton, Denny Miller, Terence Knox. Intriguing—and disquieting—tale of businessmen and their wives who undergo EDT (Executive Development Training), which, as administered by Mimieux, turns out to be a horrifying and humiliating series of rituals. Based on actual events, believe it or not. Originally released as MYSTIQUE; also known as BRAINWASH and THE NAKED WEEKEND.▼

Circle of Two (1980-Canadian) **C-105m.** ** D: Jules Dassin. Richard Burton, Tatum O'Neal, Nuala FitzGerald, Robin Gammell, Patricia Collins, Kate Reid. Sixty-year-old artist has romantic but platonic relationship with 16-year-old student. Burton is OK, and Dassin does not go for the cheap thrill, but the result is slight and forgettable.▼

Circle of Violence (1986) **C-100m. TVM** D: David Greene. Tuesday Weld, Geraldine Fitzgerald, Peter Bonerz, River Phoenix, Philip Sterling. Woman caught in mid-life crisis turns on her mother, who is on the edge of senility, in this drama about parental abuse. Two lead actresses are undermined by pat script. Average.

Circumstantial Evidence (1945) **68m.** **½ D: John Larkin. Michael O'Shea, Lloyd Nolan, Trudy Marshall, Billy Cummings. Engaging programmer about efforts to save an innocent man from going to the electric chair.

Circus, The (1928) **72m.** ***½ D: Charles Chaplin. Charlie Chaplin, Merna Kennedy, Allan Garcia, Betty Morrissey, Harry Crocker. Not the "masterpiece" of THE GOLD RUSH or CITY LIGHTS, but still a gem; story has Charlie accidentally joining traveling circus, falling in love with bareback rider. Hilarious comedy, with memorable finale. Chaplin won a special Academy Award for "versatility and genius in writing, acting, directing and producing" this.▼

Circus Clown, The (1934) **63m.** ** D: Ray Enright. Joe E. Brown, Dorothy Burgess, Patricia Ellis, Lee Moran, Tom Dugan, William Demarest. Brown mixes comedy and drama in account of circus star whose father objects to his work.

Circus of Fear SEE: Psycho-Circus▼

Circus of Horrors (1960-British) **C-89m.** **½ D: Sidney Hayers. Anton Diffring, Erika Remberg, Yvonne Monlaur, Donald Pleasence. A most unethical plastic surgeon and nurse join bizarre circus to escape deformed patient threatening their lives; rousing horror film.▼

Circus World (1964) **C-135m.** **½ D: Henry Hathaway. John Wayne, Rita Hayworth, Claudia Cardinale, John Smith, Lloyd Nolan, Richard Conte. Made in Spain, film has nothing new to offer, but rehashes usual circus formula quite nicely. Climactic fire sequence is truly spectacular.▼

Cisco Pike (1972) **C-94m.** *** D: B. W. L. Norton. Kris Kristofferson, Karen Black, Gene Hackman, Viva!, Roscoe Lee Browne, Harry Dean Stanton. Surprisingly good drama about crooked cop Hackman getting mixed up with drug dealing, and blackmailing ex-rock star Kristofferson (among Kris's songs is "Lovin' Her Was Easier").

Citadel, The (1938-U.S.-British) **112m.** ***½ D: King Vidor. Robert Donat, Rosalind Russell, Ralph Richardson, Rex Harrison, Emlyn Williams, Penelope Dudley-Ward, Francis L. Sullivan. Superb adaptation of A. J. Cronin novel of impoverished doctor Donat eschewing ideals for wealthy life of treating rich hypochondriacs, neglecting wife and friends in the process; tragedy opens his eyes. Weak ending, but fine acting makes up for it. Frank Wead, Emlyn Williams, Ian Dalrymple, Elizabeth Hill, and John Van Druten all contributed to the script. Remade as a TV miniseries.▼

Citizen Kane (1941) **119m.** **** D: Orson Welles. Orson Welles, Joseph Cotten, Everett Sloane, Agnes Moorehead, Dorothy Comingore, Ray Collins, George Coulouris, Ruth Warrick, William Alland, Paul Stewart, Erskine Sanford. Welles' first and best, a film that broke all the rules and invented some new ones, with fascinating story of Hearst-like publisher's rise to power. The cinematography (by Gregg Toland), music score (by Bernard Herrmann), and Oscar-winning screenplay (by Welles and Herman J. Mankiewicz) are all first-rate. A stunning film in every way . . . and Welles was only 25 when he made it! Incidentally, the reporter with a pipe is Alan Ladd! ▼

Citizens Band SEE: **Handle with Care** (1977)▼

City, The (1971) C-100m. TVM D: Daniel Petrie. Anthony Quinn, Skye Aubrey; E.G. Marshall, Robert Reed, Pat Hingle, John Larch, Kaz Garas, Peggy McCay. Unengrossing drama of veteran Albuquerque mayor solving urban problems. Unconvincing situations, some pale performances; pilot for short-lived TV series. Below average.

City, The (1977) C-78m. TVM D: Harvey Hart. Robert Forster, Don Johnson, Ward Costello, Jimmy Dean, Mark Hamill, Susan Sullivan. Police drama with cops Forster and Johnson searching for a psychotic with a deadly grudge against a country singer. Below average.▼

City Across the River (1949) 90m. **½ D: Maxwell Shane. Stephen McNally, Thelma Ritter, Luis Van Rooten, Jeff Corey, Anthony (Tony) Curtis, Richard Jaeckel. Watered-down version of Irving Shulman's novel *The Amboy Dukes*, involving tough life in Brooklyn slums, with predictable hoods et al.

City After Midnight (1957-British) 84m. *½ D: Compton Bennett. Phyllis Kirk, Dan O'Herlihy, Petula Clark, Wilfrid Hyde-White, Jack Watling. Tame detective film of private eye O'Herlihy investigating death of antique dealer. British title: THAT WOMAN OPPOSITE.

City Beneath the Sea (1953) C-87m. **½ D: Budd Boetticher. Robert Ryan, Mala Powers, Anthony Quinn, Suzan Ball, Woody Strode. Inconsequential underwater yarn invigorated by Ryan and Quinn as deep-sea divers hunting treasure off Jamaican coast.

City Beneath the Sea (1970) C-98m. TVM D: Irwin Allen. Robert Wagner, Stuart Whitman, Rosemary Forsyth, Joseph Cotten, Richard Basehart, James Darren. It is 2053 A.D.: Colonists in first underwater city struggle through first year of attempted invasions, ocean horrors, and interpersonal squabbles. Better than average production values thanks to Irwin Allen. Script by John Meredyth Lucas. Above average.

City for Conquest (1940) 101m. *** D: Anatole Litvak. James Cagney, Ann Sheridan, Frank Craven, Arthur Kennedy, Donald Crisp, Frank McHugh, George Tobias, Elia Kazan, Anthony Quinn. Cagney makes this a must as boxer devoted to younger brother Kennedy (his adult film debut). Beautiful production overshadows film's pretentious faults. A rare chance to see young Kazan in an acting role, as a neighborhood pal turned gangster.

City Girl (1984) C-85m. *** D: Martha

Coolidge. Laura Harrington, Joe Mastroianni, Carole McGill, Peter Riegert, Jim Carrington, Geraldine Baron, Colleen Camp. Solid, uncompromising tale of a young woman (expertly played by Harrington) attempting to advance her career as a photographer, and her various, unsatisfactory relationships with men. Refreshingly realistic, and even funny; a winner. Peter Bogdanovich was executive producer.

City Heat (1984) C-97m. ** D: Richard Benjamin. Clint Eastwood, Burt Reynolds, Jane Alexander, Madeline Kahn, Rip Torn, Irene Cara, Richard Roundtree, Tony Lo Bianco, William Sanderson. Two macho stars do caricatures of themselves in this 1930s gangster/detective yarn that takes turns trying to be funny and serious (when they pour gasoline on a guy and set him on fire we're apparently supposed to find it funny). For diehard fans of Clint and Burt only.▼

City in Darkness SEE: **Charlie Chan in City of Darkness**

City in Fear (1980) C-150m. TVM. D: Allan Smithee. David Janssen, Robert Vaughn, Perry King, William Prince, Susan Sullivan, William Daniels, Mickey Rourke. A psycho-on-the-loose story, with Janssen (in his last role) as a burned-out columnist and Vaughn as circulation-hungry publisher who wants him to turn the killer into Page One news. Janssen's seldom been better; the pseudonymous director Allan Smithee is actually Jud Taylor. Script by Albert Ruben. Above average.▼

City Killer (1984) C-100m. TVM D: Robert Lewis. Gerald McRaney, Heather Locklear, Terence Knox, Peter Mark Richman, John Harkins, Jeff Pomerantz, Audrey Totter. Top-heavy with TV names (and veteran actress Totter) this pedestrian thriller about a love-crazed terrorist who takes out his frustrations by blowing up skyscrapers simply doesn't have the bang—although the demolitions are real. Below average.▼

City Lights (1931) 86m. **** D: Charles Chaplin. Charlie Chaplin, Virginia Cherrill, Harry Myers, Hank Mann. Chaplin's masterpiece tells story of his love for blind flower girl, and his hot-and-cold friendship with a drunken millionaire. Eloquent, moving, and funny. One of the all-time greats.▼

City Limits (1985) C-85m. BOMB D: Aaron Lipstadt. Darrell Larson, John Stockwell, Kim Cattrall, Rae Dawn Chong, John Diehl, Don Opper, James Earl Jones, Robby Benson, Danny De La Paz, Norbert Weisser. Disastrous sci-fi followup by the team that made ANDROID, an incoherent mess set 15 years in the future after a plague has devastated the planet, leaving roving youth gangs warring in MAD MAX fashion. Even a strong cast can't save this one, with most of the plot expressed in tacked-on narration by Jones. ▼

City News (1983) **C-65m.** *½ D: David Fishelson, Zoe Zinman. Elliot Crown, Nancy Cohen, Thomas Trivier, Richard Schlesinger, Valerie Felitto. Stream-of-consciousness story of alternative newspaper editor-publisher Crown who creates a comic strip based on his relationship with Cohen. A couple of chuckles, but mostly pretentious and silly; sloppily directed. Originally aired on PBS' *American Playhouse*.

City of Bad Men (1953) **C-82m.** ** D: Harmon Jones. Jeanne Crain, Dale Robertson, Richard Boone, Lloyd Bridges, Carl Betz. Robbers attempt to steal prizefight proceeds in 1890s Nevada; film combines Western with recreation of Jim Corbett-Bob Fitzsimmons fight bout.

City of Fear (1959) **81m.** *½ D: Irving Lerner. Vince Edwards, Lyle Talbot, John Archer, Steven Ritch, Patricia Blair. Programmer involving escaped convict Edwards sought by police and health officials; container he stole is filled with radioactive material, not money.

City of Fear (1966-British) **90m.** *½ D: Peter Bezencenet. Paul Maxwell, Terry Moore, Marisa Mell, Albert Lieven, Pinkas Braun. Tedious caper involving news reporter and refugee going to Hungary to smuggle out pro-Westerners.

City of Shadows (1955) **70m.** *½ D: William Witney. Victor McLaglen, John Baer, Kathleen Crowley, Anthony Caruso. Mild happenings about crafty newsboys involved with derelict racketeer McLaglen.

City of the Walking Dead (1983-Spanish-Italian) **C-92m.** *½ D: Umberto Lenzi. Mel Ferrer, Hugo Stiglitz, Laura Trotter, Francisco Rabal, Maria Rosaria Omaggio. Zombie-like monsters are on the prowl. If you've seen one . . . Filmed in 1980, and originally titled NIGHTMARE CITY.▼

City of Women (1981-Italian) **C-139m.** *** D: Federico Fellini. Marcello Mastroianni, Anna Prucnal, Bernice Stegers, Iole Silvani, Donatella Damiani, Ettore Manni. Marcello falls asleep on a train, dreams he has stumbled into an all-female society. Lavish fantasy could only have been made by one filmmaker; a Fellini feast or *déjà vu* o.d., depending on your mood and stamina.▼

City on a Hunt SEE: No Escape (1953)
City on Fire (1979-Canadian) **C-101m.** *½ D: Alvin Rakoff. Barry Newman, Henry Fonda, Ava Gardner, Shelley Winters, Susan Clark, Leslie Nielsen, James Franciscus, Jonathan Welsh. Dull, fill-in-the-blanks disaster film about citywide fire torched by a disgruntled ex-employee of local oil refinery. Good cast wasted. For pyromaniacs only.▼

City Streets (1931) **82m.** *** D: Rouben Mamoulian. Gary Cooper, Sylvia Sidney, Paul Lukas, Wynne Gibson, Guy Kibbee,

Stanley Fields, William (Stage) Boyd. Cooper is an unambitious carnival worker who's drawn into the underworld by his love for racketeer's daughter (Sidney). Stylish melodrama is more interesting for Mamoulian's innovative presentation (and the stunning camerawork of Lee Garmes) than for its predictable story. Lukas and Kibbee stand out in unusually smarmy characterizations. Notable, too, as Dashiell Hammett's only original screen story.

City That Never Sleeps (1953) **68m.** ** D: Albert S. Rogell. Edith Fellows, Leo Carrillo, Tommy Bond, Mary Gordon, Helen Jerome Eddy. Painless programmer with kindly Carrillo fighting for the interests of crippled orphan Fellows. Likable performances by the leads.

City That Never Sleeps (1953) **90m.** ** D: John H. Auer. Gig Young, Mala Powers, William Talman, Edward Arnold, Chill Wills, Marie Windsor, Paula Raymond. Standard melodrama of married Chicago patrolman Young almost giving up all for sake of tawdry café singer Powers. Location shooting helps.▼

City Under the Sea SEE: War Gods of the Deep
City Without Men (1943) **75m.** *½ D: Sidney Salkow. Linda Darnell, Michael Duane, Sara Allgood, Edgar Buchanan, Glenda Farrell, Leslie Brooks, Margaret Hamilton, Sheldon Leonard, Rosemary De Camp. Darnell is pretty, but this is a very routine lower-berth item about a boardinghouse near a prison where the women wait for their men to get out.

Clair de Femme (1979-French) **C-103m.** ** D: Costa-Gavras. Yves Montand, Romy Schneider, Romolo Valli, Lila Kedrova, Heinz Bennent. Slow-moving chronicle of the relationship between traumatized widower Montand and Schneider, who has been scarred by the death of her young daughter in an auto accident. Characters are one-dimensional, and film is gloomy, gloomy, gloomy. Based on novel by Romain Gary.

Claire's Knee (1971-French) **C-103m.** ***½ D: Eric Rohmer. Jean-Claude Brialy, Aurora Cornu, Beatrice Romand, Laurence De Monaghan, Michele Montel. No. 5 of Rohmer's "Six Moral Tales" has widest appeal. Young man about to be married is obsessed with a girl he doesn't even like, his attention focusing on her knee. Full of delicious relationships, but too talky for some viewers.▼

Clairvoyant, The (1934-British) **80m.** *** D: Maurice Elvey. Claude Rains, Fay Wray, Jane Baxter, Mary Clare, Athole Stewart, Felix Aylmer, Donald Calthrop. Moody, interesting psychic drama about a phony mind-reader who finds some of his predictions coming true. Nicely photographed by Glen MacWilliams, with Rains first-rate as usual. Also known as THE EVIL MIND.▼

Clambake (1967) **C-97m.** *½ D: Arthur Nadel. Elvis Presley, Shelley Fabares, Will Hutchins, Bill Bixby, Gary Merrill, James Gregory. Elvis is a millionaire's son who wants to make it on his own, so he trades places with water-skiing instructor Hutchins in Miami. One of Presley's weakest.▼

Clancy Street Boys (1943) **66m.** D: William Beaudine. Leo Gorcey, Huntz Hall, Bobby Jordan, Noah Beery, Sr., Lita Ward, Bennie Bartlett, Ric Vallin, Billy Benedict. SEE: **Bowery Boys** series.

Clan of the Cave Bear, The (1986) **C-98m.** *½ D: Michael Chapman. Daryl Hannah, Pamela Reed, James Remar, Thomas G. Waites, John Doolittle, Curtis Armstrong. World's first feminist caveman movie, minus the anthropological detail of Jean Auel's popular book. Hannah is perfectly cast as outsider who joins band of nomadic Neanderthals, but the story (such as it is) is alternately boring and unintentionally funny. Subtitles translate cave people's primitive tongue. Screenplay by John Sayles.▼

Clara's Heart (1988) **C-108m.** *½ D: Robert Mulligan. Whoopi Goldberg, Michael Ontkean, Kathleen Quinlan, Neil Patrick Harris, Spalding Gray, Beverly Todd, Hattie Winston. Whoopi plays a Jamaican domestic (think of Shirley Booth's *Hazel* with a reggae bias), a soft-spoken know-it-all who works for insufferable Maryland yuppies and their young, impressionable son (well played by Harris). The kind of movie best described as "nice" by undiscriminating viewers in search of blandness . . . and seemingly edited with a chainsaw.▼

Clarence and Angel (1980) **C-75m.** *** D: Robert Gardner. Darren Brown, Mark Cardova, Cynthia McPherson, Louis Mike, Leroy Smith, Lola Langley, Lolita Lewis. Aggressive, kung-fu-mad Angel (Cardova) befriends his new schoolmate, shy, illiterate Clarence (Brown), who has recently arrived in Harlem from South Carolina, and teaches him to read. Technically crude, but funny and touching; sequence in principal's office, in which Clarence's mother fakes reading a test score, is a gem.▼

Clarence, The Cross-Eyed Lion (1965) **C-98m.** **½ D: Andrew Marton. Marshall Thompson, Betsy Drake, Cheryl Miller, Richard Haydn, Alan Caillou. Basis for *Daktari* TV show is good family entertainment set in Africa with adventure and wholesome comedy well blended.

Clash by Night (1952) **105m.** *** D: Fritz Lang. Barbara Stanwyck, Paul Douglas, Robert Ryan, Marilyn Monroe, Keith Andes, J. Carrol Naish. Moody, well-acted Clifford Odets story of drifter Stanwyck settling down, marrying good-natured fisherman Douglas. Cynical friend Ryan senses that she's not happy, tries to take advantage. Andes and Monroe provide secondary love interest.▼

Clash of Steel (1962-French) **C-79m.** **½ D: Bernard Borderie. Gerard Barray, Gianna Maria Canale, Michele Grellier, Jean Topart. Thin plot involving overthrow of French king, Henry of Navarre, boosted by lively production and zesty swordplay.

Clash of the Titans (1981-British) **C-118m.** **½ D: Desmond Davis. Laurence Olivier, Harry Hamlin, Judi Bowker, Burgess Meredith, Sian Phillips, Maggie Smith, Claire Bloom, Ursula Andress, Tim Pigott-Smith. Juvenile fantasy-adventure based on Greek mythology. Olivier is Zeus, and Hamlin is his mortal son Perseus, who must face a variety of awesome challenges in pursuit of his destiny. Long and episodic, with some fine elements (the taming of Pegasus, the threat of Medusa—who can turn men into stone with one glance), but not enough guts or vigor to make it really special. As is, mainly for kids. Special effects by Ray Harryhausen.▼

Class (1983) **C-98m.** ** D: Lewis John Carlino. Rob Lowe, Jacqueline Bisset, Andrew McCarthy, Stuart Margolin, Cliff Robertson, John Cusack. Naive prep-school boy stumbles (almost literally) into affair with beautiful older woman, unaware of her identity. Slick but uneven mix of romance, comedy, and drama with one-dimensional characters and a decided lack of credibility. Some good moments lost in the shuffle.▼

Classified Love (1986) **C-100m.** TVM D: Don Taylor. Michael McKean, Stephanie Faracy, Dinah Manoff, Franc Luz, Paula Trueman, Barret Heins. Middling yuppie comedy about three Madison Avenue agency singles seeking meaningful relationships through the classifieds. "Suggested" by Sherri Foxman's popular book. Average.

Class of '44 (1973) **C-95m.** **½ D: Paul Bogart. Gary Grimes, Jerry Houser, Oliver Conant, Deborah Winters, William Atherton, Sam Bottoms. Sequel to SUMMER OF '42 is less ambitious, a lightly entertaining story centering on Grimes going to college, falling in love, growing up. Good period atmosphere.▼

Class of Miss MacMichael, The (1978-British) **C-99m.** *½ D: Silvio Narizzano. Glenda Jackson, Oliver Reed, Michael Murphy, Rosalind Cash, John Standing, Riba Akabusi, Phil Daniels. Echoes of TO SIR, WITH LOVE don't flatter this shrill comedy-drama of a dedicated teacher with a class full of social misfits.▼

Class of 1984 (1982) **C-93m.** ** D: Mark L. Lester. Perry King, Merrie Lynn Ross, Roddy McDowall, Timothy Van Patten, Stefan Arngrim, Al Waxman, Michael J. Fox. Thoroughly unpleasant, calculatedly campy melodrama about the harassment of high school teacher King by psychotic student Van Patten . . . with more than a few echoes of BLACKBOARD JUNGLE. As revenge movies go, the buzzsaw finale is not bad. Followed by CLASS OF 1999.▼

Class of 1999 (1990) C-98m. *½ D: Mark L. Lester. Bradley Gregg, Traci Lind, Malcolm McDowell, Stacy Keach, Patrick Kilpatrick, Pam Grier, John P. Ryan, Darren E. Burrows, Joshua Miller. Followup to CLASS OF 1984 from the same producer-director pictures high school of the near-future as Hell on Earth, with ultraviolent gang members meeting their match in a trio of androids who have been recruited as their teachers. Heavy-handed film wavers between high camp and taking itself seriously as a message movie! Keach goes overboard as a maniacal high school principal.

Class of Nuke 'Em High (1986) C-81m. BOMB D: Richard Haines, Samuel Weil. Janelle Brady, Gilbert Brenton, Robert Prichard, R. L. Ryan. Obnoxious horror comedy about a New Jersey high school near a nuclear waste spill that creates monsters and disgustingly transforms model teens Brady and Brenton. Sadistic gags are dehumanizing, masquerading as low-brow entertainment.▼

Class of '63 (1973) C-74m. TVM D: John Korty. Cliff Gorman, Joan Hackett, James Brolin, Woodrow Chambliss, Ed Lauter, Colby Chester, Graham Beckel. College reunion provides subtle setting for sad tale of dissolving marriage, bittersweet romance; unresolved ending. Full-blooded characters in absorbing, realistic melodrama by Lee Kalcheim. Above average.▼

Claudelle Inglish (1961) 99m. **½ D: Gordon Douglas. Diane McBain, Arthur Kennedy, Constance Ford, Chad Everett. Trite soaper derived from Erskine Caldwell tale of Southern farm gal who gives all to find excitement, with predictable consequences.

Claudia (1943) 91m. *** D: Edmund Goulding. Dorothy McGuire, Robert Young, Ina Claire, Reginald Gardiner, Olga Baclanova, Jean Howard. Warm comedy of young Claudia suddenly marrying, facing adult problems, learning a lot about life in short period; beautifully acted. McGuire, in film debut, recreates her Broadway role. Sequel: CLAUDIA AND DAVID.

Claudia and David (1946) 78m. *** D: Walter Lang. Dorothy McGuire, Robert Young, Mary Astor, John Sutton, Gail Patrick, Florence Bates. Enjoyable followup to CLAUDIA with McGuire and Young having a baby, adjusting to suburban life; engaging, well-acted.

Claudine (1974) C-92m. **½ D: John Berry. Diahann Carroll, James Earl Jones, Lawrence Hilton-Jacobs, Tamu, David Kru-

ger, Adam Wade. Slice-of-life comedy with a serious edge: Romance between garbageman Jones and young ghetto mother Carroll is charming and credible, but the problems of dealing with her six kids, and their collective poverty, can't be treated so lightly. "Upbeat" finale just doesn't ring true.

Claw Monsters, The (1955) 100m. *½ D: Franklin Adreon. Phyllis Coates, Myron Healey, Arthur Space, John Day, Mike Ragan. Latter-day Republic cliff-hanger is short on action, long on stock footage, in account of out-of-whack scientist guarding his diamond mines via superstitions and animal-skin-covered henchmen. Re-edited from serial PANTHER GIRL OF THE KONGO.

Clay Pigeon (1971) C-97m. *½ D: Tom Stern, Lane Slate. Tom Stern, Telly Savalas, Robert Vaughn, John Marley, Burgess Meredith, Ivan Dixon. Good cast in dull crime melodrama of Vietnam vet settling into drug scene, eventually experiencing change of heart and going after big-league pusher.

Clay Pigeon, The (1949) 63m. **½ D: Richard O. Fleischer. Bill Williams, Barbara Hale, Richard Loo, Richard Quine, Frank Fenton, Martha Hyer. Neat little actioner with Williams, a seaman accused of treason and of responsibility in the death of his friend, on the trail of the real culprit, a Japanese prison guard. Story by Carl Foreman, based on a true incident. ▼

Clean and Sober (1988) C-121m. *** D: Glenn Gordon Caron. Michael Keaton, Kathy Baker, Morgan Freeman, M. Emmet Walsh, Tate Donovan, Henry Judd Baker, Luca Bercovici, Claudia Christian, Pat Quinn, Ben Piazza. A young hustler enrolls in a drug rehabilitation program in order to duck out of sight for a while—refusing to admit to himself that he's an addict, too. Powerful drama showcases Keaton in an utterly believable performance, though the film's relentlessness makes it tough to watch.▼

Clean Slate SEE: Coup de Torchon▼

Clear All Wires (1933) 78m. **½ D: George Hill. Lee Tracy, Benita Hume, Una Merkel, James Gleason, Alan Edwards. Tracy enlivens this so-so story of a manipulative, globe-trotting journalist, who creates as much news as he covers; highlighted are his escapades while in Russia. Script by Bella and Sam Spewack, from their play.

Clear and Present Danger, A (1970) C-100m. TVM D: James Goldstone. Hal Holbrook, E. G. Marshall, Joseph Campanella, Jack Albertson, Pat Hingle, Mike Kellin, Jeff Corey. Son of retiring U.S. Senator risks political career in forthright determination to influence public opinion on air pollution. Some good dialogue, acting. Pilot for short-lived "The Senator" segment of *The Bold Ones*. Above average.

Cleo from 5 to 7 (1962-French) 90m. ***

[203]

D: Agnés Varda. Corinne Marchand, Antoine Bourseiller, Dorothée Blanck, Michel Legrand, Anna Karina, Eddie Constantine, Jean-Luc Godard. Intelligent, fluid account of Parisian songstress forced to reevaluate her life while awaiting vital medical report on her physical condition.▼

Cleopatra (1934) **95m.** ***½ D: Cecil B. DeMille. Claudette Colbert, Warren William, Henry Wilcoxon, Gertrude Michael, Joseph Schildkraut, C. Aubrey Smith, Claudia Dell, Robert Warwick. Opulent DeMille version of Cleopatra doesn't date badly, stands out as one of his most intelligent films, thanks in large part to fine performances by all. Top entertainment, with Oscar-winning cinematography by Victor Milner.▼

Cleopatra (1963) **C-243m.** ** D: Joseph L. Mankiewicz. Elizabeth Taylor, Richard Burton, Rex Harrison, Roddy McDowall, Pamela Brown, Martin Landau, Michael Hordern, Kenneth Haigh, Andrew Keir, Hume Cronyn, Carroll O'Connor. Saga of the Nile goes on and on and on. Definitely a curiosity item, but you'll be satisfied after an hour. Good acting, especially by Harrison and McDowall, but they are lost in this flat, four-hour misfire. Nevertheless earned Oscars, for cinematography, art direction-set decoration, costumes and special effects. Released to TV at 194m.▼

Cleopatra Jones (1973) **C-89m.** ** D: Jack Starrett. Tamara Dobson, Bernie Casey, Shelley Winters, Brenda Sykes, Antonio Fargas, Bill McKinney, Esther Rolle. Black bubblegum stuff with Dobson as karate-chopping government agent who goes after drug kingpins. Lots of action—and violence.▼

Cleopatra Jones and the Casino of Gold (1975) **C-96m.** **½ D: Chuck Bail. Tamara Dobson, Stella Stevens, Tanny, Norman Fell, Albert Popwell, Caro Kenyatta, Christopher Hunt. Wild, woolly, sexy, violent sequel to CLEOPATRA JONES. Stevens plays "The Dragon Lady," a tip-off on what to expect.▼

Cleopatra's Daughter (1960-Italian) **C-102m.** ** D: Richard McNamara. Debra Paget, Ettore Manni, Erno Crisa, Robert Alda, Corrado Panni. American actors are lost in this costumer, more intent on playing up sadistic sequences; intrigue at Egyptian court the highlight.

Climax, The (1944) **C-86m.** *** D: George Waggner. Boris Karloff, Gale Sondergaard, Susanna Foster, Turhan Bey, Thomas Gomez, Scotty Beckett. Tense Karloff vehicle of seemingly polished opera physician who is really a murderer; Foster gets to sing, too.

Climb an Angry Mountain (1972) **C-97m.** TVM D: Leonard Horn. Fess Parker, Barry Nelson, Joe Kapp, Stella Stevens, Marj Dusay, Clay O'Brien. Great location shooting (Northern California) enhances likable drama pitting tough sheriff (Parker) and

N.Y. cop against fugitive Indian holding sheriff's son hostage. Above average.

Clinging Vine, The (1926) **71m.** **½ D: Paul Sloane. Leatrice Joy, Tom Moore, Toby Claude, Robert Edeson, Dell Henderson. Handsome fluff about unfeminine executive (Joy) who becomes involved in business swindle, and falls in love.

Clinic, The (1982-Australian) **C-92m.** **½ D: David Stevens. Chris Haywood, Simon Burke, Rona McLeod, Gerda Nicolson, Suzanne Roylance, Veronica Lang, Pat Evison. Straightforward but much too obvious comedy-drama about the goings-on in a VD clinic operated by doctor Haywood.

Clinton and Nadine (1988) **C-110m.** TVM D: Jerry Schatzberg. Andy Garcia, Ellen Barkin, Morgan Freeman, Michael Lombard, John C. McGinley, Alan North, Brad Sullivan. Erotic, fast-paced drama about a small-time smuggler and high-class hooker who get mixed up in a plot to run guns to the Nicaraguan contras. Writer Robert Foster had his name removed at the last minute, with credit going to pseudonymous "Willard Walpole." Made for cable. Also known as BLOOD MONEY. Average.

Clipped Wings (1953) **65m.** D: Edward Bernds. Leo Gorcey, Huntz Hall, Bernard Gorcey, Mary Treen, Philip Van Zandt, Lyle Talbot. SEE: **Bowery Boys** series.

Clive of India (1935) **90m.** **½ D: Richard Boleslawski. Ronald Colman, Loretta Young, Colin Clive, Francis Lister, C. Aubrey Smith, Cesar Romero, Montagu Love, Leo G. Carroll. Colman is ideally cast as Robert Clive, the "man of destiny" who secured British rule in India at the sacrifice of his own personal happiness. More fanciful than factual, but entertaining and lavishly produced.

Cloak and Dagger (1946) **106m.** **½ D: Fritz Lang. Gary Cooper, Lilli Palmer, Robert Alda, Vladimir Sokoloff, Ludwig Stossel. Professor Cooper becomes a secret agent on his trip to Germany; Lang intrigue is not among his best, but still slick.▼

Cloak & Dagger (1984) **C-101m.** *** D: Richard Franklin. Henry Thomas, Dabney Coleman, Michael Murphy, John McIntire, Jeanette Nolan, Christine Nigra. Young Thomas gets involved with murderous espionage—but no one will believe him. Flawed but enjoyable reworking of THE WINDOW. Coleman's a delight in dual role as his father and his make-believe hero.▼

Cloak Without Dagger SEE: **Operation Conspiracy**

Clock, The (1945) **90m.** ***½ D: Vincente Minnelli. Judy Garland, Robert Walker, James Gleason, Keenan Wynn, Marshall Thompson, Lucille Gleason. Soldier Walker has two-day leave in N.Y.C., meets office worker Judy; they spend the day falling in love, encountering friendly milkman Gleason, drunk Wynn; charming little love story with beguiling Garland.▼

Clockmaker, The (1973-French) **C-105m.** ***½ D: Bertrand Tavernier. Philippe Noiret, Jean Rochefort, Jacques Denis, Julien Bertheau. Noiret is superb as a watchmaker who is forced to reevaluate his life after his son is arrested for murder. Meticulously directed; based on a novel by Georges Simenon.▼

Clockwise (1986-British) **C-96m.** **½ D: Christopher Morahan. John Cleese, Penelope Wilton, Alison Steadman, Stephen Moore, Sharon Maiden. Monty Python's Cleese is a school headmaster, obsessed with punctuality, en route to make a speech at a convention and constantly getting into trouble. A tour de force role that is a must for Cleese fans; others will be disappointed with the thinness of playwright Michael Frayn's script.▼

Clockwork Orange, A (1971) **C-137m.** ***½ D: Stanley Kubrick. Malcolm McDowell, Patrick Magee, Adrienne Corri, Aubrey Morris, James Marcus, Steven Berkoff, David Prowse. A scathing satire on a society in the not so distant future, with an excellent performance by McDowell as a prime misfit. Kubrick's vivid adaptation of Anthony Burgess's novel was too strong for some to stomach in 1971, and it remains potent today.▼

Clone Master, The (1978) **C-100m.** TVM D: Don Medford. Art Hindle, Robyn Douglass, Ed Lauter, Ralph Bellamy, John van Dreelen, Mario Roccuzzo. Biochemist clones himself thirteen times and sends the copies out to fight evil wherever it might exist. Pilot to a series that itself failed to get cloned. Average.

Clonus Horror, The SEE: **Parts: The Clonus Horror**▼

Close Call for Boston Blackie, A (1946) **60m.** D: Lew Landers. Chester Morris, Lynn Merrick, Richard Lane, Frank Sully, George E. Stone, Russell Hicks. SEE: **Boston Blackie** series.

Close Call for Ellery Queen (1942) **67m.** D: James Hogan. William Gargan, Margaret Lindsay, Ralph Morgan, Edward Norris. SEE: **Ellery Queen** series.

Close Encounters of the Third Kind (1977) **C-135m.** **** D: Steven Spielberg. Richard Dreyfuss, Francois Truffaut, Teri Garr, Melinda Dillon, Cary Guffey, Bob Balaban. Superb, intelligent sci-fi (written by Spielberg) about UFO mystery that leads to first contact with alien beings. Dreyfuss is perfect Everyman struggling with frustrating enigma that finally becomes clear. Powerhouse special effects throughout, plus John Williams's evocative score. Vilmos Zsigmond's impressive cinematography won an Oscar. Reedited by Spielberg to tighten midsection and add alien-encounter material to finale and reissued in 1980 at 132m. as THE

SPECIAL EDITION. (Then, for network showings, *all* existing footage was used!)▼

Closely Watched Trains (1966-Czech) **89m.** *** D: Jiri Menzel. Vaclav Neckar, Jitka Bendova, Vladimir Valenta, Libuse Havelkova, Josef Somr. Enjoyable but slightly overrated tragicomedy about naive apprentice train-dispatcher Neckar's attempts at sexual initiation during the German Occupation. Academy Award winner as Best Foreign Film.▼

Close to My Heart (1951) **90m.** *** D: William Keighley. Ray Milland, Gene Tierney, Fay Bainter, Howard St. John. Superior soaper; Tierney attaches herself to waif in Bainter's orphanage, but husband Milland won't allow adoption until child's background is traced.

Cloudburst (1951-British) **83m.** **½ D: Francis Searle. Robert Preston, Elizabeth Sellars, Harold Lang, Noel Howlett. Impressive little film of Preston, WW2 veteran working in British Foreign Office, seeking his wife's murderers.

Cloud Dancer (1980) **C-108m.** **½ D: Barry Brown. David Carradine, Jennifer O'Neill, Joseph Bottoms, Colleen Camp, Albert Salmi, Salome Jens, Nina Van Pallandt. Uneven tale of aerobatic-obsessed Carradine and his relationship with O'Neill. Nice—if too many flying sequences, hokey melodramatics. Filmed in 1978.▼

Cloud Waltzing (1987) **C-103m.** TVM D: Gordon Flemyng. Kathleen Beller, François-Eric Gendron, Paul Maxwell, Therese Liotard, Claude Gensac, David Baxt. Second in series of "Harlequin Romance Movies" adapted from the popular paperback bodice-busters and filmed in exotic European locations with an American actress in the lead, here it's a pretty journalist traveling to France to interview a reclusive but oh-so-handsome vintner. Average.▼

Clouded Yellow, The (1951-British) **85m.** *** D: Ralph Thomas. Jean Simmons, Trevor Howard, Barry Jones, Maxwell Reed, Kenneth More. Cast is exceptional in unpretentious murder-hunt film with Simmons seeking to prove her innocence.

Clouds Over Europe SEE: **Q Planes**

Clown, The (1953) **91m.** **½ D: Robert Z. Leonard. Red Skelton, Tim Considine, Jane Greer, Loring Smith, Philip Ober. Sentimental remake of THE CHAMP about a washed-up, self-destructive comic with a devoted son who looks out for him. Skelton's not bad in rare dramatic role; Considine is so good he overcomes some of the hokiness of script. Charles Bronson has a bit role in dice game scene.▼

Clown Murders, The (1975-Canadian) **C-96m.** *½ D: Martyn Burke. Stephen Young, Susan Keller, Lawrence Dane, John Candy, Gary Reineke, Al Waxman, Cec Linder. Melodrama set among the idle rich at a Halloween party where envious pals stage a fake kidnapping to botch pompous

Dane's real-estate deal. Clumsy thriller boasts comic Candy in early dramatic role (with his weight problem a running gag).▼

Clowns, The (1971-Italian) C-90m. ***½ D: Federico Fellini. Fellini's homage to circus clowns is itself a clownish spoof of documentary films, a funny, fully entertaining piece of fluff from this great director, who even makes fun of himself. Made for Italian TV.▼

Club, The (1980-Australian) C-99m. *** D: Bruce Beresford. Jack Thompson, Graham Kennedy, Frank Wilson, Harold Hopkins, John Howard. Thompson is excellent as a football coach in this searing drama about off-the-field politics in a football club. Screenplay by David Williamson, based on his play. Also known as PLAYERS.▼

Club Dead SEE: **Terror at Red Wolf Inn**

Club Havana (1945) 62m. ** D: Edgar G. Ulmer. Tom Neal, Margaret Lindsay, Don Douglas, Gertrude Michael, Isabelita (Lita Baron), Dorothy Morris, Ernest Truex. Roadshow GRAND HOTEL is very cheap production with little of interest.

Club Med (1986) C-100m. TVM D: Bob Giraldi. Jack Scalia, Linda Hamilton, Patrick Macnee, Janis Lee Burns, Jeff Kaake. Glossy but featherweight romantic drama set against the glitzy background of a popular tropical resort. Notable only as director Giraldi's TV movie debut after having made his mark in commercials and music videos. Below average.

Club Paradise (1986) C-104m. ** D: Harold Ramis. Robin Williams, Peter O'Toole, Rick Moranis, Jimmy Cliff, Twiggy, Adolph Caesar, Eugene Levy, Joanna Cassidy, Andrea Martin, Robin Duke, Mary Gross, Simon Jones. Pleasant cast in pleasant surroundings, lacking only a script and a few more laughs. Williams plays Chicago fireman who retires to West Indian island, goes halfies with native Cliff on turning ramshackle beachfront property into vacation resort. Writers even try to shoehorn a "serious" subplot about exploitation of the natives into the proceedings! Best of all is Cliff's almost nonstop music; his performance isn't bad, either.▼

Clue (1985) C-87m. **½ D: Jonathan Lynn. Eileen Brennan, Tim Curry, Madeline Kahn, Christopher Lloyd, Michael McKean, Martin Mull, Lesley Ann Warren, Colleen Camp, Lee Ving, Bill Henderson, Howard Hesseman. Silly comic whodunit based on the popular board game of the same name with all the familiar characters (Mrs. Peacock, Colonel Mustard, Miss Scarlet, et al) gathered for a murderous night in a Victorian mansion. Everyone tries very hard—*too* hard, since the script, by firsttime feature director Lynn, is so slim; addle-brained Brennan and puckish butler Curry come off best. When this played theatrically, audiences saw one of three alternate endings. On video, all three endings are shown in a row to total 96m.▼

Clue of the New Pin (1960-British) 58m. *½ D: Allan Davis. Paul Daneman, Bernard Archard, James Villiers, Catherine Woodville, Clive Morton. Old-fashioned Edgar Wallace yarn about "perfect crime," with Villiers a TV interviewer who tangles with murderer; ponderous.

Clue of the Silver Key (1961-British) 59m. **½ D: Gerald Glaister. Bernard Lee, Lyndon Brook, Finlay Currie, Jennifer Danie. Above-par Edgar Wallace yarn, highlighted by Lee's performance as determined Scotland Yard inspector unraveling series of murders.

Cluny Brown (1946) 100m. ***½ D: Ernst Lubitsch. Charles Boyer, Jennifer Jones, Peter Lawford, Helen Walker, Reginald Gardiner, C. Aubrey Smith, Reginald Owen, Richard Haydn. Delightful Lubitsch comedy of romance between plumber's daughter Jones and refugee Boyer in pre-WW2 England. Beautiful character performances help out.

C-Man (1949) 75m. ** D: Joseph Lerner. Dean Jagger, John Carradine, Harry Landers, Rene Paul. Acceptable programmer with Jagger as customs agent involved in murder and theft case.▼

C'mon, Let's Live a Little (1967) C-85m. BOMB D: David Butler. Bobby Vee, Jackie De Shannon, Eddie Hodges, John Ireland, Jr., Suzie Kaye, Bo Belinsky, Patsy Kelly, Kim Carnes. Folk singer Vee enrolls in college, romances De Shannon, is manipulated by student radical Ireland. Perfectly awful.

Coach (1978) C-100m. ** D: Bud Townsend. Cathy Lee Crosby, Michael Biehn, Keenan Wynn, Steve Nevil, Channing Clarkson, Sydney Wicks. Olympic gold medal winner Crosby is accidentally hired as a high-school basketball coach for boys. An exploitation film that turns out to be disappointingly tame and predictable.▼

Coach of the Year (1980) C-100m.TVM D: Don Medford. Robert Conrad, Erin Gray, Red West, Daphne Maxwell, Ed O'Bradovich, Ricky Paul, Alex Paez. Ex-pro-football star, wounded in Vietnam, volunteers to coach a ragtag team of young incorrigibles from his wheelchair. Conrad gives another strong performance in this busted pilot. Above average.

Coal Miner's Daughter (1980) C-125m. ✓ ***½ D: Michael Apted. Sissy Spacek, Tommy Lee Jones, Beverly D'Angelo, Levon Helm, Phyllis Boyens, Ernest Tubb. Rags-to-riches story of country singer Loretta Lynn is among the best musical bios ever made, though final quarter does slide over some "down side" details. Spacek won well-deserved Oscar (and did her own singing), but Jones, D'Angelo, and Helm (drummer for The Band) are just as good. Screenplay by Tom Rickman.▼

Coast Guard (1939) 72m. ** D: Edward

Ludwig. Randolph Scott, Frances Dee, Ralph Bellamy, Walter Connolly, Warren Hymer, Robert Middlemass, Stanley Andrews. Scott and Bellamy are hard-loving, hard-fighting guardsmen in love with Dee. When one of them is stranded in the snow after a plane crash, the other must decide whether to help or not. Routine but action-filled hokum with similarities to Capra's DIRIGIBLE.

Coast of Skeletons (1964-British) C-91m. ** D: Robert Lynn. Richard Todd, Dale Robertson, Heinz Drache, Marianne Koch, Elga Andersen, Derek Nimmo. Edgar Wallace's *Sanders of the River* is basis for largely rewritten tale of ex-officer hired to investigate scuttling of American tycoon's African diamond operation. Todd repeats role he played in SANDERS (DEATH DRUMS ALONG THE RIVER).

Coast to Coast (1980) C-95m. ** D: Joseph Sargent. Dyan Cannon, Robert Blake, Quinn Redeker, Michael Lerner, Maxine Stuart, Bill Lucking. A nutty woman (who's been institutionalized by her divorce-seeking husband) escapes from a sanitarium and travels cross-country with trucker Blake, who's got problems of his own. Strained road comedy, often abrasive, with occasional laughs.▼

Cobra, The (1968-Spanish-Italian) C-93m. BOMB D: Mario Sequi. Dana Andrews, Anita Ekberg, Peter Martell, Elisa Montes, Jesus Puente, Peter Dane. Awful melodrama has tough all-American secret service man Andrews fighting opium smuggling in the Middle East; Ekberg still can't act.▼

Cobra (1986) C-87m. *½ D: George P. Cosmatos. Sylvester Stallone, Brigitte Nielsen, Reni Santoni, Andrew Robinson, Lee Garlington, John Herzfeld, Art Le Fleur, Brian Thompson, David Rasche, Val Avery. Once more, Stallone wraps himself in the American flag and fights for the greater glory of mankind by going after criminal vermin; this time, he's a cop. Typical low-grade action fare, where all the other cops are stubborn dummies, and all the bad guys are repellent creeps. Some good action sequences.▼

Cobra Strikes, The (1948) 62m. ** D: Charles F. Reisner. Sheila Ryan, Richard Fraser, Leslie Brooks, Herbert Heyes. Weak low-budgeter about thief who meddles in inventor's workshop, complications that ensue.▼

Cobra Woman (1944) C-70m. *** D: Robert Siodmak. Maria Montez, Jon Hall, Sabu, Edgar Barrier, Lois Collier, Lon Chaney Jr., Mary Nash. Camp classic with Montez as twin sisters—one good, one evil. Technicolor fantasy-escape of the 1940s at its zenith.

Cobweb, The (1955) C-124m. ** D: Vincente Minnelli. Richard Widmark, Lauren Bacall, Gloria Grahame, Charles Boyer, Lillian Gish, John Kerr, Susan Strasberg, Oscar Levant, Tommy Rettig, Paul Stewart, Adele Jergens. Good cast in static soaper detailing the goings-on in psychiatric clinic headed by Dr. Widmark; of course, some of the personnel are more unbalanced than the patients. Scripted by John Paxton, produced by John Houseman. Film debuts of Strasberg and Kerr.

Coca-Cola Kid, The (1985-Australian) C-94m. **½ D: Dusan Makavejev. Eric Roberts, Greta Scacchi, Bill Kerr, Chris Haywood, Kris McQuade, Max Gilles, Rebecca Smart. Droll, sometimes wacky comedy about a hotshot Coca-Cola sales exec sent on mission to Australia, leading to various misadventures. Roberts's performance is strictly a matter of taste, and so is this offbeat, mildly satiric film. Sexy Scacchi is the best thing in the picture.▼

Cocaine and Blue Eyes (1983) C-100m. TVM D: E. W. Swackhamer. O. J. Simpson, Cliff Gorman, Candy Clark, Eugene Roche, Maureen Anderman, Cindy Pickett, Tracy Reed, Keye Luke. In this failed pilot, the Juice is a private eye in San Francisco who uncovers a drug-dealing operation while searching for a dead client's girlfriend. Average.

Cocaine Cowboys (1979) C-87m. BOMB D: Ulli Lommel. Jack Palance, Tom Sullivan, Andy Warhol, Suzanna Love, Pete Huckabee. Dreadful film about rock group that supports itself "between engagements" by dope smuggling; filmed at Warhol's Montauk home, where this film should remain.▼

Cocaine Fiends, The (1936) 68m. BOMB D: William A. O'Connor. Noel Madison, Lois January, Sheila Manners, Dean Benton, Lois Lindsay, Eddie Phillips. Dope peddler and mob front man, on the lam from the law, turns a young girl on to cocaine (which she believes is "headache powder") . . . and she's hopelessly addicted. Then her brother is taken "on a sleigh ride with some snow birds." Tawdry, hilariously awful and, in its way, a bit depressing; from the REEFER MADNESS school of filmmaking. Originally shown as THE PACE THAT KILLS.▼

Cocaine: One Man's Seduction (1983) C-100m. TVM D: Paul Wendkos. Dennis Weaver, Karen Grassle, David Ackroyd, Pamela Bellwood, James Spader, Jeffrey Tambor, Richard Venture. Weaver gives a devastating performance as a successful real estate agent who develops a cocaine habit during a temporary business slump and soon finds his career, marriage and life endangered. Script by Barry Schneider and David Goldsmith, however, veers toward the melodramatic. Average.▼

Cocaine Wars (1989) C-82m. *½ D: Hector Olivera. John Schneider, Kathy Witt, Royal Dano, Federico Luppi, Rodolfo Ranni, John Vitaly, Heidi Paddle, Nan

Grey, Edgar Moore. Low-grade actioner pitting undercover DEA agent Schneider against evil cocaine kingpin in South America; they seem to be ex-Nazis, which may be a first. Tedious and confusing.▼

Cockeyed Cavaliers (1934) 72m. *** D: Mark Sandrich. Bert Wheeler, Robert Woolsey, Thelma Todd, Dorothy Lee, Noah Beery, Franklin Pangborn. Colorful costume comedy with Wheeler & Woolsey trying to crash into society by posing as the King's physicians; lively mix of slapstick, puns, and music.▼

Cockeyed Cowboys of Calico County (1970) C-99m. ** D: Ranald MacDougall. Dan Blocker, Nanette Fabray, Jim Backus, Wally Cox, Jack Elam, Stubby Kaye, Mickey Rooney, Noah Beery, Marge Champion, Jack Cassidy. Great cast and waste of a movie. Turn-of-the-century progress in the Old West, but villains, varmints and saloons still remain. Originally made for TV, but released to theaters instead.

Cockeyed Miracle, The (1946) 81m. ** D: S. Sylvan Simon. Frank Morgan, Keenan Wynn, Cecil Kellaway, Audrey Totter, Marshall Thompson. Good cast carries weak material. Morgan returns from heaven to make up for financial error he made involving family.

Cockeyed World, The (1929) 118m. *½ D: Raoul Walsh. Victor McLaglen, Edmund Lowe, Lily Damita, El Brendel, Lelia Karnelly, Stuart Erwin. Sequel to WHAT PRICE GLORY? with McLaglen and Lowe as battling Marines Flagg and Quirt sent to South Sea island where fiery Damita captures their attention. Smash hit in 1929, it moves like molasses today, and is no match for GLORY.

Cockfighter (1974) C-83m. *** D: Monte Hellman. Warren Oates, Richard B. Shull, Harry Dean Stanton, Troy Donahue, Millie Perkins. Offbeat, violent but interesting drama of a man who trains fighting cocks in Georgia. Oates is silent until the very end, his thoughts serving as narration. Filmed in Georgia. Also called BORN TO KILL, WILD DRIFTER, GAMBLIN' MAN.▼

Cockleshell Heroes, The (1956-British) C-97m. ** D: Jose Ferrer. Jose Ferrer, Trevor Howard, Dora Bryan, Anthony Newley, Victor Maddern. Training of special task force troops during WW2 never jells into excitement.

Cocktail (1988) C-100m. ** D: Roger Donaldson. Tom Cruise, Bryan Brown, Elisabeth Shue, Lisa Banes, Laurence Luckinbill, Kelly Lynch, Gina Gershon, Ron Dean, Paul Benedict. Young hotshot comes to N.Y.C. to make his fortune, but winds up becoming a "hot" bartender instead, under the tutelage of self-styled barman/philosopher Brown. Cruise flashes his smile, Shue is cute, but that can't redeem the junior-high-school-level dramatics.▼

Cocktail Molotov (1980-French) C-100m. *** D: Diane Kurys. Elise Caron, Philippe Lebas, Francois Cluzet, Genevieve Fontanel, Henri Garcin, Michel Puterflam. Pleasant follow-up to PEPPERMINT SODA, with a trio of teenagers wandering through Europe at the time of the '68 student rebellion. Caron, Lebas, and Cluzet are attractive as the youngsters testing their wings.

Cocoanut Grove (1938) 85m. ** D: Alfred Santell. Fred MacMurray, Harriet Hilliard, Yacht Club Boys, Ben Blue, Rufe Davis, Billy Lee, Eve Arden. MacMurray's band just has to make good at Cocoanut Grove audition in this flimsy musical, with nine songs you'll never hear again.

Cocoanuts, The (1929) 96m. *** D: Joseph Santley, Robert Florey. Groucho, Harpo, Chico, Zeppo Marx, Kay Francis, Oscar Shaw, Mary Eaton, Margaret Dumont. The Marxes' first film suffers from stagy filming and stale musical subplot, but when the brothers have scenes to themselves it's a riot; highlights include hilarious auction, classic "viaduct" routine.▼

Cocoon (1985) C-117m. ***½ D: Ron Howard. Don Ameche, Wilford Brimley, Hume Cronyn, Brian Dennehy, Jack Gilford, Steve Guttenberg, Maureen Stapleton, Jessica Tandy, Gwen Verdon, Herta Ware, Tahnee Welch, Barret Oliver, Linda Harrison, Tyrone Power, Jr., Clint Howard. Florida senior citizens discover an actual fountain of youth in this warm, humanistic fantasy-drama, marred only by derivative and too literal science-fiction finale. What a pleasure to watch this cast at work! (Ameche won Best Supporting Actor Oscar.) Screenplay by Tom Benedek, from David Saperstein's novel; another impressive directing job by Howard. Followed by a sequel.▼

Cocoon: The Return (1988) C-116m. ** D: Daniel Petrie. Don Ameche, Jack Gilford, Gwen Verdon, Maureen Stapleton, Steve Guttenberg, Hume Cronyn, Jessica Tandy, Wilford Brimley, Elaine Stritch, Tahnee Welch, Courteney Cox. Disappointing follow-up in which the elderly earthlings return for a visit to their home planet. Most of the magic and warmth of the original are missing; while it's always a joy to see Ameche and company on screen, the actors are unable to transcend their material.▼

Code Name: Diamond Head (1977) C-78m. TVM D: Jeannot Szwarc. Roy Thinnes, France Nuyen, Ward Costello, Zulu, Don Knight, Ian McShane, Eric Braeden, Dennis Patrick. Undercover agent Thinnes scours Honolulu to find master spy McShane, hired by a foreign power to steal the formula for a deadly toxic gas. Assembly-line spy thriller hidden in exotic locales. Below average.▼

Code Name: Emerald (1985) **C-95m.** **
D: Jonathan Sanger. Ed Harris, Max von
Sydow, Horst Buchholz, Helmut Berger,
Cyrielle Claire, Eric Stoltz, Patrick Stewart, Graham Crowden. Old-fashioned WW2
espionage tale has Harris as a double agent
in plot to capture an Overlord (person with
information on the plans for the D-Day invasion). Credibility is undermined by miscasting of Stoltz, who looks way too young
to be an intelligence lieutenant and the target
Overlord. This was the first theatrical feature film produced by NBC TV network.▼
Code Name: Heraclitus (1967) **C-100m.**
TVM D: James Goldstone. Stanley Baker,
Leslie Nielsen, Jack Weston, Sheree North,
Signe Hasso, Kurt Kasznar, Ricardo Montalban. Dead man is "rebuilt" to become a
Cold War agent. Slick thriller crawling
with spies, counterspies and a gum-chewer
named Gannon (Baker) who may or may
not have come in from the cold. Expanded
from an episode of TV's *Chrysler Theater*.
Above average.
Codename: Kyril (1988-British) **C-230m.**
TVM D: Ian Sharp. Edward Woodward,
Ian Charleson, Denholm Elliott, Joss
Ackland, Richard E. Grant, John McEnery,
Peter Vaughan, James Laurenson, Catherine Neilson, Sven-Bertil Taube. Well-
crafted but overly complex (and long) spy
thriller with British Intelligence and the
KGB playing a cat-and-mouse game to
find the mole in each other's apparatus. A
basic course in spy jargon might have
helped us comprehend John Hopkins'
convoluted script, adapted from John Tren-
haile's *A Man Called Kyril*. Premiered on
American cable in two parts. Average.
Code Name: Minus One SEE: **Gemini Man**
Code Name, Red Roses (1969-Italian)
C-97m. **½ D: Fernando Di Leo. James
Daly, Pier Angeli, Michael Wilding, Peter
Van Eyck. The old "American saboteur
behind enemy lines" plot reenacted by a
pretty fair cast. Also called RED ROSES
FOR THE FUEHRER.
Code Name: Trixie (1973) **C-103m.** **
D: George Romero. Lane Carroll, W.G.
McMillan, Harold Wayne Jones, Lloyd
Hollar, Lynn Lowry. Biological plague
hits small Pennsylvania town. The Army
is called in to contain it, but townspeople
rebel and defy the soldiers. Gory but excit-
ing. Originally titled THE CRAZIES.▼
Codename: Wildgeese (1986-German-
Italian) **C-101m.** ** D: Anthony M. Dawson (Antonio Margheriti). Lewis Collins,
Lee Van Cleef, Ernest Borgnine, Klaus
Kinski, Mimsy Farmer. Action footage
redeems this cornball commando film of
Collins and mercenary troops sent to wipe
out a Far East drug stronghold. Good actors stuck with second-rate material here;

film is no relation to THE WILD GEESE
or its sequel.▼
Code of Scotland Yard (1948-British) **90m.**
** D: George King. Oscar Homolka, Muriel
Pavlow, Derek Farr, Kenneth Griffith. Man
escaped from Devil's Island runs seemingly
innocent antique shop. Nothing special.
Code of Silence (1985) **C-101m.** **½ D:
Andy Davis. Chuck Norris, Henry Silva,
Bert Remsen, Molly Hagan, Joseph Gu-
zaldo, Mike Genovese, Dennis Farina. Nor-
ris plays a loner on Chicago police force
who makes his own rules in dealing with
violent gang war. In other words, it's
"Dirty Chuckie." Formula action film,
and not bad.▼
Code of the Secret Service (1939) **58m.** *½
D: Noel Smith. Ronald Reagan, Rosella
Towne, Eddie Foy, Jr., Moroni Olsen, Edgar
Edwards, Jack Mower. Limp actioner with
Lt. Brass Bancroft (Reagan) tangling with
counterfeiters in Mexico. Second of a series,
following SECRET SERVICE OF THE AIR.
Code of Vengeance (1985) **C-100m. TVM**
D: Rick Rosenthal. Charles Taylor, Erin
Gray, Charles Haid, Randall "Tex" Cobb,
Keenan Wynn, Chad Allen, Lenka Peter-
son, Victor Mohica. Loner out of the Chuck
Norris school of acting gets involved in
war with gunrunners and dope smugglers in
the Southwest. Followed by a sequel, DAL-
TON: CODE OF VENGEANCE II, which
led to a *Dalton* TV series. Average.
Code Red (1981) **C-74m. TVM** D: J. Lee
Thompson. Lorne Greene, Andrew Ste-
vens, Sam J. Jones, Julie Adams, Martina
Deignan, Joe Maross, Robert Alda, Burr
DeBenning. The pilot of Irwin Allen's
adventure series about a family of big city
firefighters. Average.
Code 7 Victim 5 (1964-British) **C-88m.**
**½ D: Robert Lynn. Lex Barker, Ronald
Fraser, Walter Rilla, Dietmar Schonherr.
Moderate actioner with Barker investigat-
ing murder in South Africa; nicely paced.
Code 645 (1948) **100m.** ** D: Fred
Brannon, Yakima Canutt. Clayton Moore,
Roy Barcroft, Ramsay Ames, Drew Allen,
Tom Steele. Tame Republic cliff-hanger re-
lying on too much stock footage and pat
situations in contest between federal agents
and escaped arch-criminal with his own
master plan of destruction and success.
Reedited from serial G-MEN NEVER
FORGET.
Code Two (1953) **69m.** ** D: Fred Wilcox.
Ralph Meeker, Sally Forrest, Keenan Wynn,
Robert Horton, Jeff Richards. Three re-
cruits on L.A. motorcycle police force
face occupational hazards; when Richards
is killed, Meeker et al. seek to capture
those responsible.
Coffee, Tea or Me? (1973) **C-73m. TVM**
D: Norman Panama. Karen Valentine, John
Davidson, Michael Anderson Jr., Louise
Lasser, Lou Jacobi, Erica Hagen. Decent

comedy features Valentine as busy airline stewardess who, thru odd circumstance, has two husbands in separate continents. Weak resolution only liability. Above average.

Coffy (1973) **C-91m.** **½ D: Jack Hill. Pam Grier, Booker Bradshaw, Robert DoQui, William Elliott, Allan Arbus, Sid Haig. Fast-moving, generally agreeable trash about nurse who goes after junkies who turned her young sister into an addict; lots of nudity in Grier's biggest hit.▼

Cohen and Tate (1989) **C-85m.** *½ D: Eric Red. Roy Scheider, Adam Baldwin, Harley Cross, Cooper Huckabee. In this grim variation on O. Henry's "Ransom of Red Chief," Scheider and Baldwin, the hit men of the title, murderously kidnap young Cross, sole witness to a gang killing; story takes place almost entirely in their car. Clumsy irony, theatrical style, leaden illogic sink the film early. Scheider tries hard.▼

Cold Feet (1984) **C-96m.** ** D: Bruce van Dusen. Griffin Dunne, Marissa Chibas, Blanche Baker, Mark Cronogue, Joseph Leon, Marcia Jean Kurtz. A couple of chuckles are not enough to save this sluggish comedy about the courtship of Dunne and Chibas, who've been unlucky in love before. Baker steals the film as Dunne's flaky ex-wife.▼

Cold Feet (1989) **C-94m.** *½ D: Robert Dornhelm. Keith Carradine, Sally Kirkland, Tom Waits, Rip Torn, Bill Pullman, Kathleen York, Vincent Schiavelli. Carradine and Waits (the latter near-psychotic) squabble for hundreds of miles over a horse; marriage-hungry Kirkland is the flake who rounds out the threesome. Reminiscent in tone of coscripter Thomas McGuane's RANCHO DELUXE (which pops up on a theater marquee here)—but without the laughs; RANCHO'S Jeff Bridges has an unbilled scene as a smalltown bartender.▼

Colditz Story, The (1957-British) **97m.** ***½ D: Guy Hamilton. John Mills, Eric Portman, Christopher Rhodes, Lionel Jeffries, Bryan Forbes, Ian Carmichael, Richard Wattis, Anton Diffring, Theodore Bikel. Super-solid P.O.W. saga set in Germany's Colditz Castle, supposedly "escape-proof" but challenged by various European prisoners, and a hardy British group in particular.▼

Cold Night's Death, A (1973) **C-73m. TVM** D: Jerrold Freedman. Robert Culp, Eli Wallach, Michael C. Gwynne. Exceptional, offbeat mixture of psychological and physical terror in story of two scientists replacing dead predecessor in wasteland research laboratory. Watch out for that ending. Written by Christopher Knopf. Above average.

Cold River (1982) **C-94m.** *½ D: Fred G. Sullivan. Suzanne Weber, Pat Petersen, Richard Jaeckel, Robert Earl Jones, Brad Sullivan. The lovely Adirondack locations are the star of this paper-thin tale of Weber's and Petersen's adventures in the wilderness. Jaeckel is wasted.▼

Cold Room, The (1984) **C-95m. TVM** D: James Dearden. George Segal, Amanda Pays, Renee Soutendijk, Warren Clarke, Anthony Higgins. Rebellious college girl reluctantly accompanies her estranged writer-father to East Berlin and finds she's entered a time warp, with a hidden dissident in a secret room next to hers and the Gestapo nipping at her heels. Confused, lackadaisical adaptation of Jeffrey Caine's psychological thriller. Made for cable. Average.▼

Cold Sassy Tree (1989) **C-100m. TVM** D: Joan Tewkesbury. Faye Dunaway, Richard Widmark, Neil Patrick Harris, Frances Fisher, Lee Garlington, John Jackson. Handsome May-December romantic drama set in a sleepy Southern town at the turn of the century. An independent lady from up North causes a scandal when she decides to wed the local general-store owner just three weeks after he's been widowed. Dunaway and Widmark are a delight in this adaptation of Olive Ann Burns's novel (by director Tewkesbury). Made for cable. Above average.▼

Cold Steel (1987) **C-90m.** ** D: Dorothy Ann Puzo. Brad Davis, Sharon Stone, Jonathan Banks, Jay Acovone, Adam Ant, Eddie Egan. Standard actioner about cop Davis, whose father is murdered by disfigured psychotic Banks. Of course, he seeks revenge.▼

Cold Sweat (1971-French-Italian) **C-94m.** ** D: Terence Young. Charles Bronson, Liv Ullmann, James Mason, Jill Ireland, Michel Constantin, Gabriele Ferzetti. Richard Matheson's thriller *Ride the Nightmare* has been converted into a predictable action movie with Bronson as American expatriate in France forced into the drug trade by crime czar Mason.▼

Cold Turkey (1971) **C-99m.** *** D: Norman Lear. Dick Van Dyke, Pippa Scott, Tom Poston, Bob Newhart, Vincent Gardenia, Barnard Hughes, Edward Everett Horton, Jean Stapleton, Graham Jarvis. Bittersweet satire of contemporary America; minister Van Dyke leads township crusade to stop smoking, in order to win mammoth contest. Trenchant finale doesn't entirely gibe with rest of film: still worthwhile, with Bob & Ray hilarious as newscasters. Fine score by Randy Newman; Horton's last film. Made in 1969.▼

Cold Wind in August, A (1961) **80m.** **½ D: Alexander Singer. Lola Albright, Scott Marlowe, Herschel Bernardi, Joe De Santis. Offbeat account of tenement boy Marlowe having affair with stripper Albright; frank, flavorful tale.

Cole Younger, Gunfighter (1958) **C-78m.** ** D: R. G. Springsteen. Frank Lovejoy, James Best, Abby Dalton, Jan Merlin.

Modest actioner has gunfights to perk up trite account of 1870s Texas.

✓ **Collector, The** (1965) C-119m. *** D: William Wyler. Terence Stamp, Samantha Eggar, Maurice Dallimore, Mona Washbourne. Disturbing story of man who collects more than just butterflies, which is where Eggar fits in. Chilling, if not altogether believable.▼

Colleen (1936) 89m. *** D: Alfred E. Green. Dick Powell, Ruby Keeler, Joan Blondell, Hugh Herbert, Jack Oakie, Louise Fazenda, Paul Draper. Neglected Warner Bros. musical is quite good, with usual boy-meets-girl plot framing tasteful musical numbers: title tune, "An Evening With You," "Boulevardier from the Bronx." Includes perhaps-definitive Hugh Herbert performance.

College (1927) 65m. *** D: James W. Horne. Buster Keaton, Anne Cornwall, Flora Bramley, Harold Goodwin, Grant Withers, Snitz Edwards. Highbrow student Buster has to become an all-star athlete to please his girlfriend; episodic gag structure makes this less impressive than other Keaton features, but it's awfully funny.▼

College Coach (1933) 75m. **½ D: William Wellman. Dick Powell, Ann Dvorak, Pat O'Brien, Hugh Herbert, Herman Bing, Lyle Talbot. Well-paced tale of ruthless football coach O'Brien, neglected wife Dvorak, star player Powell who also likes chemistry. Look for John Wayne in a bit part.

✓ **College Confidential** (1960) 91m. *½ D: Albert Zugsmith. Steve Allen, Jayne Meadows, Mamie Van Doren, Walter Winchell, Herbert Marshall, Cathy Crosby, Conway Twitty, Ziva Rodann, Mickey Shaughnessy. Idiocy involving sociology professor Allen and what happens when he surveys the sexual activities of his students. "Special Guests" include Rocky Marciano, Sheilah Graham, Pamela Mason, and Earl Wilson.

College Holiday (1936) 88m. **½ D: Frank Tuttle. Jack Benny, George Burns, Gracie Allen, Mary Boland, Martha Raye, Marsha Hunt, Eleanore Whitney. Silly musicomedy about college types coming to bankrupt hotel where Boland is doing sex experiments.

College Humor (1933) 80m. *** D: Wesley Ruggles. Bing Crosby, Jack Oakie, Burns and Allen, Richard Arlen, Mary Carlisle, Mary Kornman, Joseph Sauers (Sawyer). College was never like this. Hokey, entertaining rah-rah musical with Bing a professor (!), Arlen and Oakie football stars; Carlisle and Kornman provide love interest. Songs: "Learn to Croon," "Down the Old Ox Road," among others.

College Swing (1938) 86m. *** D: Raoul Walsh. George Burns, Gracie Allen, Martha Raye, Bob Hope, Edward Everett Horton, Florence George, Ben Blue, Betty Grable, John Payne. Gracie hasn't been able to graduate from school in this entertaining collegiate musicomedy with top cast, forgettable songs like "What Did Romeo Say to Juliet?"

Collision Course (1968) SEE: **Bamboo Saucer**▼

Collision Course (1975) C-100m. TVM D: Anthony Page. Henry Fonda, E.G. Marshall, Lucille Benson, Lloyd Bochner, Ward Costello, Andrew Duggan, Russell Johnson, John Larch, John Randolph, Barry Sullivan, Richard Loo. Fonda is General Douglas MacArthur and Marshall is President Harry Truman in Ernest Kinoy's dramatic reconstruction of events surrounding their clash over methods to end the Korean War. Talky, static blend of fact and speculation. Average.

Colonel Blimp SEE: **Life and Death of Colonel Blimp, The**▼

Colonel Effingham's Raid (1945) 70m. **½ D: Irving Pichel. Charles Coburn, Joan Bennett, William Eythe, Allyn Joslyn, Elizabeth Patterson, Donald Meek. Entertaining little comedy of ex-officer Coburn fighting to save town's historical landmark; cast supports fair material.▼

Colonel Redl (1985-German-Hungarian-Austrian) C-149m. *** D: Istvan Szabo. Klaus Maria Brandauer, Armin Muller-Stahl, Gudrun Landgrebe, Jan Niklas, Hans-Christian Blech, Laszlo Mensaros, Andras Balint. Complex, fascinating account—inspired by John Osborne's *A Patriot for Me* as well as by actual historical evidence—of an ambitious, homosexual career soldier, whose ordinary family background does not hinder his rise to a position of high military rank in the Austro-Hungarian Empire prior to WWI. An incisive examination of the politics of power, highlighted by a superb Brandauer performance. Second in a trilogy, after MEPHISTO and followed by HANUSSEN.▼

Colorado Territory (1949) 94m. *** D: Raoul Walsh. Joel McCrea, Virginia Mayo, Dorothy Malone, Henry Hull, John Archer, Frank Puglia. Strong, fast-moving Western with McCrea an outlaw on the lam; remake of director Walsh's HIGH SIERRA, later remade as I DIED A THOUSAND TIMES.

Color Me Dead (1969-U.S.-Australian) C-97m. ** D: Eddie Davis. Tom Tryon, Carolyn Jones, Rick Jason, Patricia Connolly, Tony Ward. Story of a slowly poisoned man spending his last days tracking down his own murderer was done better as D.O.A. twenty years before.▼

Color of Money, The (1986) C-119m. *** D: Martin Scorsese. Paul Newman, Tom Cruise, Mary Elizabeth Mastrantonio, Helen Shaver, John Turturro, Bill Cobbs, Robert Agins, Forest Whitaker. Sharply made, nicely textured sequel to THE HUS-

TLER, with Newman's Fast Eddie Felson finding a younger, greener version of himself in small-time pool hotshot Cruise, whom he decides to promote for another shot at the big time. Hardboiled script by Richard Price, flashy direction by Scorsese, flamboyant camerawork by Michael Ballhaus, and top-notch performances by Cruise and especially Newman make this a must-see . . . though film's second half is protracted and disappointing, with a hoped-for climax that never occurs. Newman finally picked up an Academy Award for his fine work here. ▼

Color Purple, The (1985) **C-152m.** ***½ D: Steven Spielberg. Danny Glover, Whoopi Goldberg, Margaret Avery, Oprah Winfrey, Willard Pugh, Akosua Busia, Desreta Jackson, Adolph Caesar, Rae Dawn Chong, Dana Ivey. A black girl's life and hard times in the South, spanning some forty years: a sprawling saga of characters both frustrated and fulfilled, and at the center a Survivor. Spielberg's controversial interpretation of Alice Walker's Pulitzer Prize-winning book will either grab you emotionally (in which case you'll overlook its flaws) or leave you cold. Masterfully filmed from Menno Meyjes's script, with striking cinematography by Allen Daviau, moving music score by Quincy Jones (who also coproduced). Rich performances include screen debut for Winfrey. (Avery's singing was dubbed, by the way.)▼

Colors (1988) **C-120m.** *** D: Dennis Hopper. Sean Penn, Robert Duvall, Maria Conchita Alonso, Randy Brooks, Grand Bush, Don Cheadle, Rudy Ramos, Trinidad Silva. Penn and Duvall are well-matched as street cops assigned to gang detail in L.A. Their conflicts and experiences play out against the backdrop of nihilistic gang life in this realistic if unexceptional slice of life. Only serious flaw: unbelievable and unnecessary subplot with female lead Alonso. Hopper's 127m. version, altered by the theatrical distributor, is available on video.▼

Colossus of New York, The (1958) **70m.** ** D: Eugene Lourie. John Baragrey, Mala Powers, Otto Kruger, Robert Hutton, Ross Martin. Doctor implants dead son's brain into oversized robot with predictable chaos.

Colossus: The Forbin Project (1970) **C-100m.** *** D: Joseph Sargent. Eric Braeden, Susan Clark, Gordon Pinsent, William Schallert. Well-directed suspense thriller. Computer runs amok and uses its superior intelligence to sabotage man at every turn. Chilling and believable. Also titled THE FORBIN PROJECT.▼

Colt .45 (1950) **C-74m.** **½ D: Edwin L. Marin. Randolph Scott, Zachary Scott, Ruth Roman, Lloyd Bridges, Chief Thundercloud. The renowned title gun is star of this sometimes actionful Western. Retitled: THUNDERCLOUD.

Column South (1953) **C-85m.** ** D: Frederick de Cordova. Audie Murphy, Joan Evans, Robert Sterling, Ray Collins. OK mixture of Civil War and Indian fighting, as Union officer Murphy champions underdog redskins to prevent hostilities.

Coma (1978) **C-113m.** *** D: Michael Crichton. Genevieve Bujold, Michael Douglas, Elizabeth Ashley, Rip Torn, Richard Widmark, Lance LeGault, Lois Chiles. Someone is killing and stealing patients from a big-city hospital, and a woman doctor bucks male superiors to pursue her suspicions. Bujold and Widmark are well-matched adversaries in original suspenser that combines best of hospital pictures and mystery thrillers; scripted by director Crichton from Robin Cook's novel. Look for Tom Selleck in a bit part.▼

Comanche (1956) **C-87m.** ** D: George Sherman. Dana Andrews, Kent Smith, Linda Cristal, Nestor Paiva, Henry Brandon. Andrews is staunch as Indian scout seeking to patch redskin-cavalry hostilities. Film is pat Western.

Comancheros, The (1961) **C-107m.** *** D: Michael Curtiz. John Wayne, Stuart Whitman, Lee Marvin, Ina Balin, Bruce Cabot, Nehemiah Persoff. Well-paced Wayne actioner with Big John a Texas Ranger out to bring in gang supplying firearms and liquor to the Comanches. Curtiz' final film.▼

Comanche Station (1960) **C-74m.** *** D: Budd Boetticher. Randolph Scott, Nancy Gates, Claude Akins, Skip Homeier. Better-than-usual actioner with Scott leading a group through Indian lands, hoping to find his wife who has been kidnapped by redskins. Terse script by Burt Kennedy.

Comanche Territory (1950) **C-76m.** **½ D: George Sherman. Maureen O'Hara, Macdonald Carey, Will Geer, James Best, Edmund Cobb. Fictional bio of Western scout Jim Bowie (Carey) who helps Comanches save their lands from whiteskins.

Combat High (1986) **C-100m. TVM** D: Neal Israel. Keith Gordon, Wally Ward, George Clooney, Dana Hill, Robert Culp, Dick Van Patten, Jamie Farr, Sherman Hemsley, Richard Moll. Puerile comedy about a pair of teenage pranksters in a tough military academy. Below average.

Combat Squad (1953) **72m.** *½ D: Cy Roth. John Ireland, Lon McCallister, Hal March, Tris Coffin. Weak study of men in war; this time Korea.

Come and Get It (1936) **99m.** *** D: Howard Hawks, William Wyler. Edward Arnold, Joel McCrea, Frances Farmer, Walter Brennan, Andrea Leeds, Frank Shields, Mady Christians, Mary Nash. Arnold plays a self-made empire-builder who fights his way to the top in Wisconsin lumber business and sacrifices the one love of his life. Farmer has the best screen showcase of her career, in a dual role, as a blowsy saloon entertainer and (years later) her own daughter; Brennan won his first Best Supporting Actor Oscar playing Arnold's simple Swedish pal. Typically plotty, two-generation Edna Ferber saga. Reissued as ROARING TIMBER.▼

Come and See (1985-Russian) C-142m. ***½ D: Elem Klimov. Alexei Kravchenko, Olga Mironova, Lubomiras Lauciavicus. Thoroughly mesmerizing chronicle of the initiation of a young teen (impressively played by Kravchenko) into the horror and insanity of war, as the Nazis maraud through northwestern Russia in 1943. An extraordinary film about the need to maintain one's humanity and dignity no matter what the situation. Don't miss this one.▼

Comeback SEE: Love Is Forever

Comeback, The (1978-British) C-100m. BOMB D: Pete Walker. Jack Jones, Pamela Stephenson, David Doyle, Bill Owen, Sheila Keith, Richard Johnson. Gruesome story of American singer trying for showbiz comeback in England, drawn instead into chain of gory murders. Retitled: THE DAY THE SCREAMING STOPPED.▼

Comeback, The (1989) C-100m. TVM D: Jerrold Freedman. Robert Urich, Chynna Phillips, Mitchell Anderson, Brynn Thayer, Ronny Cox. Lethargic drama about a onetime football hero who returns home after twenty years to reestablish a relationship with the college-age son he hardly knows, and leaps into a hot and heavy affair with the boy's girlfriend. Average.

Come Back, Charleston Blue (1972) C-100m. ** D: Mark Warren. Raymond St. Jacques, Godfrey Cambridge, Jonelle Allen, Adam Wade, Peter DeAnda. Further adventures of Gravedigger and Coffin on their Harlem police beat. Loads of violence, no comedy; not nearly as good as original, COTTON COMES TO HARLEM. Fine Donny Hathaway score.

Comeback Kid, The (1980) C-100m. TVM D: Peter Levin. John Ritter, Susan Dey, James Gregory, Doug McKeon, Jeremy Licht, Rod Gist, Patrick Swayze. Romantic comedy with a heart features Ritter as a luckless big-league ballplayer who is talked into coaching a gang of underprivileged kids. Sort of a genteel BAD NEWS BEARS. Average.▼

✓ **Come Back, Little Sheba** (1952) 99m. ***½ D: Daniel Mann. Burt Lancaster, Shirley Booth, Terry Moore, Richard Jaeckel. William Inge play is emotional tour de force for Booth (who won an Oscar) as slovenly housewife coping with drunken ex-chiropractor husband (Lancaster) and boarder Moore, whose curiosity about her landlords sets drama in motion.

Come Back to the Five and Dime, Jimmy Dean, Jimmy Dean (1982) C-110m. **½ D: Robert Altman. Sandy Dennis, Cher, Karen Black, Sudie Bond, Kathy Bates, Marta Heflin. Girlfriends hold twenty-year reunion of a James Dean fan club they formed when he was filming GIANT in a nearby Texas town; the get-together becomes an occasion for personal and painful revelations. Strong performances, and director Altman's lively approach to filming Ed Graczyk's Broadway play, can't completely camouflage the fact that this is second-rate material. Cher's first film since CHASTITY in 1969.▼

Comeback Trail, The (1974) C-80m. *½ D: Harry Hurwitz. Chuck McCann, Buster Crabbe, Robert Staats, Ina Balin, Jara Kahout. Two-bit movie czar McCann stars faded cowboy hero Crabbe in a film, hoping the resulting disaster will salvage his studio. Dismal comedy, with occasional film buff in-jokes, and guest appearances by Henny Youngman, Irwin Corey, Hugh Hefner, Joe Franklin, and Monte Rock III. Never released theatrically.

Come Blow Your Horn (1963) C-112m. *** D: Bud Yorkin. Frank Sinatra, Lee J. Cobb, Molly Picon, Barbara Rush, Jill St. John, Tony Bill. Sinatra is good as a free-swinging bachelor with wall-to-wall girls and a nagging father (Cobb). He also sings the title song, and teaches kid brother (Bill) the ropes. From Neil Simon play.

Come Dance with Me! (1960-French) C-91m. **½ D: Michel Boisrond. Brigitte Bardot, Henri Vidal, Dawn Addams, Noel Roquevert. Fairly well blended mixture of mystery-comedy involving dentist accused of murdering a barroom pickup and his wife Bardot finding the real killer.

Comedians, The (1967) C-148m. **½ D: Peter Glenville. Elizabeth Taylor, Richard Burton, Alec Guinness, Peter Ustinov, Paul Ford, Lillian Gish, Raymond St. Jacques, James Earl Jones, Cicely Tyson. Excellent cast only partially salvages uninspired adaptation of Graham Greene's novel about political intrigue in Haiti, although film is more interesting today, since the departure of Duvalier. Beware 130m. prints.

Comedy Company, The (1978) C-100m. TVM D: Lee Philips. Jack Albertson, George Burns, Lawrence Hilton-Jacobs, Herbert Edelman, Joyce Van Patten, Susan Sullivan, Michael Brandon, Abe Vigoda. Drama about the efforts of an ex-vaudevillian to keep his failing nightclub alive as a showcase for aspiring comics. Average.

Comedy of Terrors, The (1964) C-84m. **½ D: Jacques Tourneur. Vincent Price, Peter Lorre, Boris Karloff, Basil Rathbone, Joe E. Brown, Joyce Jameson. Medium horror spoof with undertaker Price trying to hasten customers' demise, "helped" by bumbling assistant Lorre. Great cast; Richard Matheson wrote the screenplay.▼

Come Fill the Cup (1951) **113m.** **½ D: Gordon Douglas. James Cagney, Phyllis Thaxter, Raymond Massey, James Gleason, Gig Young. Cagney is quite restrained as ex-newspaperman seeking to conquer alcoholism. Fine performance by Gleason as helpful ex-drunk and by Young as drunken playboy.

Come Fly with Me (1963) **C-109m.** **½ D: Henry Levin. Hugh O'Brian, Pamela Tiffin, Dolores Hart, Karl Boehm, Lois Nettleton, Karl Malden. Flighty fluff of three stewardesses trying to catch husbands, becoming involved with three men on a trans-Atlantic flight. Glossy, easy to take.

Come Live with Me (1941) **86m.** *** D: Clarence Brown. James Stewart, Hedy Lamarr, Ian Hunter, Verree Teasdale, Donald Meek, Barton MacLane, Adeline de Walt Reynolds. Charming romantic comedy with starving writer Stewart marrying Lamarr so she won't be deported. Strong supporting cast, with Reynolds fine as Stewart's mother.

Come Next Spring (1956) **C-92m.** *** D: R. G. Springsteen. Ann Sheridan, Steve Cochran, Walter Brennan, Sherry Jackson. Arkansas Americana beautifully interpreted by intelligent acting, with Sheridan and Cochran overcoming nature and townfolks to make their farm go.

Come 'n' Get It SEE: **Lunch Wagon**▼

Come-On, The (1956) **83m.** ** D: Russell Birdwell. Anne Baxter, Sterling Hayden, John Hoyt, Jesse White. Baxter is dramatically fine as unscrupulous con woman involved with murder, but the story is hackneyed.

Come Out Fighting (1945) **62m.** D: William Beaudine. Leo Gorcey, Huntz Hall, Billy Benedict, Gabriel Dell, June Carlson. SEE: **Bowery Boys** series.

Comes a Horseman (1978) **C-118m.** **½ D: Alan J. Pakula. Jane Fonda, James Caan, Jason Robards, George Grizzard, Richard Farnsworth, Jim Davis, Mark Harmon. Starkly simple Western story (set in 1940s) about rival ranch owners whose roots are in the land. Low-key to the point of catatonia, but offers some beautiful tableaux and moving scenes.▼

Come September (1961) **C-112m.** *** D: Robert Mulligan. Rock Hudson, Gina Lollobrigida, Sandra Dee, Bobby Darin, Walter Slezak, Joel Grey. Frothy comedy about the younger generation (Darin and Dee) vs. the "older" folks (Hudson and Lollobrigida) at an Italian villa. Good fun, with some dated Darin vocals.

Come Spy with Me (1967) **C-85m.** *½ D: Marshall Stone. Troy Donahue, Andrea Dromm, Albert Dekker, Mart Hulswit, Valerie Allen, Dan Ferrone, Louis Edmonds. Except for those who want to tell their

friends they actually saw a film called COME SPY WITH ME starring Troy Donahue, this secret-agent flick about blond Dromm's attempts to solve murders of two Americans in the Caribbean isn't worth anyone's time. Smokey Robinson sings the title song!

Come to the Stable (1949) **94m.** *** D: Henry Koster. Loretta Young, Celeste Holm, Hugh Marlowe, Elsa Lanchester, Regis Toomey, Mike Mazurki. Young and Holm register well as French nuns living in New England, seeking aid from a variety of local characters in building a children's dispensary.

Comet over Broadway (1938) **69m.** *½ D: Busby Berkeley. Kay Francis, Ian Hunter, John Litel, Donald Crisp, Minna Gombell, Melville Cooper. Sappy, dated soap opera tells risible story of stage star Francis and the tragedy caused by her burning ambition. Not even a musical number to save it.

Comfort and Joy (1984-British) **C-105m.** *** D: Bill Forsyth. Bill Paterson, Eleanor David, C. P. Grogan, Alex Norton, Patrick Malahide, Rikki Fulton, Roberto Bernardi. Another quirky comedy from writer-director Forsyth (GREGORY'S GIRL, LOCAL HERO), though this one isn't as potent or consistent. Paterson plays a popular Scottish disc jockey who's going through some difficult changes in his personal life, then finds himself caught between two underworld families fighting for territorial rights to ice-cream vans! Entertaining and offbeat, though never as on-target as one might like it to be; Paterson is a delight.▼

Comic, The (1969) **C-94m.** **½ D: Carl Reiner. Dick Van Dyke, Michele Lee, Mickey Rooney, Cornel Wilde, Nina Wayne, Pert Kelton, Jeannine Riley. Sincere, well-meant seriocomedy about a silent-movie clown with a destructive ego. Artificial trappings surround truthful portrait (a composite of several real comics) by Van Dyke. Best of all: vivid recreations of silent comedies. Uneven; of interest mainly to film buffs.▼

Comin At Ya! (1981-Italian) **C-91m.** BOMB D: Ferdinando Baldi. Tony Anthony, Gene Quintano, Victoria Abril, Ricardo Palacios, Gordon Lewis. 3D spaghetti Western take-off features rats, bats, and blood, all hugged to death by the camera (and often in slow motion!). No redeeming sense of humor, either. It's films like this that killed 3D the first time around.

Coming Apart (1969) **110m.** *½ D: Milton Moses Ginsberg. Rip Torn, Viveca Lindfors, Megan McCormick, Lois Markle, Lynn Swann, Sally Kirkland. Fascinatingly bad drama about psychiatrist who sets up concealed movie camera in his apartment to record the messed-up lives of himself and women who visit him. Kirkland's most substantial screen role prior to ANNA in 1987.

Coming Attractions SEE: **Loose Shoes**▼
Coming Home (1978) C-127m. ***½ D: Hal Ashby. Jane Fonda, Jon Voight, Bruce Dern, Robert Carradine, Robert Ginty, Penelope Milford, David Clennon. Powerful look at the effect of Vietnam war on people at home. Fonda falls in love with paraplegic Voight while her husband (Dern) is overseas. Mature, gripping film, marred only by lapses into melodrama. Academy Awards went to Fonda, Voight, and writers Waldo Salt, Robert C. Jones, and Nancy Dowd.▼
Coming Out of the Ice (1982) C-100m. TVM D: Waris Hussein. John Savage, Willie Nelson, Ben Cross, Francesca Annis, Frank Windsor, Peter Vaughn. Cold retelling of the Victor Herman story, with Savage as a young Herman who suffered through nearly 20 years of torture, starvation and brutality in Siberia in the late 1930s. Willie Nelson turns up briefly (and somewhat jarringly) as a fellow prisoner and illustrates with ease what makes his screen personality unique. Average.▼
Coming-Out Party (1934) 79m. *½ D: John G. Blystone. Frances Dee, Gene Raymond, Alison Skipworth, Nigel Bruce, Harry Green. Tired tale of young socialite Dee in love with jazz musician, fighting her mother's ambitions for her to marry within social class.
Coming-Out Party (1961-British) 100m. **½ D: Ken Annakin. James Robertson Justice, Leslie Phillips, Stanley Baxter, Eric Sykes, Richard Wattis. P.O.W. comedy with prisoner Baxter impersonating lookalike Nazi commandant to help peevish scientist Justice escape camp. Original title: VERY IMPORTANT PERSON.
Comin' Round the Mountain (1951) 77m. *½ D: Charles Lamont. Bud Abbott, Lou Costello, Dorothy Shay, Kirby Grant, Joe Sawyer, Glenn Strange. Bud and Lou invade hillbilly country in this substandard comedy, with far too much footage of singing Shay.
Coming Through (1985-British) C-80m. ** D: Peter Barber-Fleming. Kenneth Branagh, Helen Mirren, Alison Steadman, Philip Martin Brown, Norman Rodway. Static tale of young D. H. Lawrence (Branagh), and his relationship with Frieda von Richthofer (Mirren), awkwardly paralleled with present-day story of young man who completely misses the point of Lawrence's writing. Sorely lacking the author's own fire and intensity.
Coming to America (1988) C-116m. *** D: John Landis. Eddie Murphy, Arsenio Hall, James Earl Jones, John Amos, Madge Sinclair, Shari Headley, Paul Bates, Allison Dean, Eriq LaSalle, Louie Anderson.

Cute change-of-pace film for Murphy, as the genteel prince of an African royal family who wants to choose his own wife, and decides that he will find her in America. Old-fashioned romantic comedy peppered with director Landis' in-jokes (including an update of TRADING PLACES, in which Murphy starred) and some surprise cameos. Watch the closing credits and see how much you caught.▼
Coming Up Roses (1986-British) C-93m. ** D: Stephen Bayly. Dafydd Hywel, Iola Gregory, Olive Michael, Mari Emlyn. Whimsical Welsh-language comedy concerns a group of townsfolk who band together to save a local cinema by growing mushrooms in the darkness of the empty theatre. Cute, but lacks the wit and sharp ensemble acting of the hilarious British comedies of the 1940s and 1950s.▼
Command, The (1954) C-88m. ** D: David Butler. Guy Madison, Joan Weldon, James Whitmore, Carl Benton Reid. Madison unflinchingly copes with smallpox epidemic and rampaging redskins as he leads troops and civilians through Wyoming Indian lands.
Command Decision (1948) 112m. ***½ D: Sam Wood. Clark Gable, Walter Pidgeon, Van Johnson, Brian Donlevy, Charles Bickford, John Hodiak, Edward Arnold, Marshall Thompson, Richard Quine, Cameron Mitchell, John McIntire. Taut, engrossing adaptation of the William Wister Haines stage hit, with Gable a Flight Commander who knows that, to win the war, he must send his men on suicide missions over Germany. Intriguing look at behind-the-scenes politics of the U.S. war effort. Screenplay by William Laidlaw and George Froeshel. Also shown in computer-colored version.
Command 5 (1985) C-100m. TVM D: E. W. Swackhamer. Stephen Parr, Wings Hauser, John Matuszak, William Russ, Sonja Smits, Gregory Sierra, Bill Forsythe, Robert F. Lyons. It's THE MAGNIFICENT SEVEN minus two in contemporary Arizona, trying to take back a small town from a band of mercenaries. Pilot for prospective series. Average.
Commando (1964-Italian) 90m. **½ D: Frank Wisbar. Stewart Granger, Dorian Gray, Fausto Tozzi, Carlos Casaravilla. Granger leads mission to rescue Algerian rebel leader, later learning ironic political significance. Satisfactory actioner.
Commando (1985) C-88m. ** D: Mark L. Lester. Arnold Schwarzenegger, Rae Dawn Chong, Dan Hedaya, Vernon Wells, David Patrick Kelly, Alyssa Milano, James Olson, Bill Duke. Exceptionally noisy comic-book yarn about retired special agent Schwarzenegger, who's forced to go back into action when vengeful goons kidnap his daughter. Film's sense of humor (cour-

tesy scripter Steven E. de Souza) is largely obliterated by all the noise and mindless violence. For undiscriminating action fans.▼

Commandos (1968-Italian-German) **C-89m.** ** D: Armando Crispino. Lee Van Cleef, Jack Kelly, Giampiero Albertini, Marino Masé, Pierre Paulo Capponi, Duilio Del Prete. Cliche-filled war drama with familiar plot; Italian commandos, led by a couple of stalwart Americans, must secure an important oasis in North African desert in advance of Allied landings.▼

Commando Squad (1987) **C-89m.** BOMB D: Fred Olen Ray. Brian Thompson, Kathy Shower, William Smith, Sid Haig, Ross Hagen, Robert Quarry, Mel Welles. Thompson and Shower (former *Playboy* Playmate of the Year) are government agents sent to Mexico to wipe out Smith's cocaine factory. Tiresome film features numerous screen veterans, including Marie Windsor and Russ Tamblyn.▼

Commandos Strike at Dawn, The (1942) **96m.** **½ D: John Farrow. Paul Muni, Anna Lee, Lillian Gish, Cedric Hardwicke, Robert Coote, Ray Collins, Rosemary De-Camp, Alexander Knox. Well-intentioned drama of Norwegian Muni aiding British commandos in attack on Nazis who have invaded Norway. Dated propaganda angle lessens impact today.▼

Common Ground (1990) **C-200m. TVM** D: Mike Newell. Jane Curtin, CCH Pounder, Richard Thomas, James Farentino, George Emelin, Erika Anderson. Disappointing dramatization of J. Anthony Lukas' Pulitzer Prize-winning book about the 60s/70s trauma surrounding desegregation of the Boston school system. Curtin, as a bigoted mom, and Pounder, as a mother from the ghetto projects, shine, but other roles suffer from miscasting and overdone Boston accents. Edward Hume's adaptation might have worked better in its originally intended seven-hour miniseries format. Originally shown in two parts. Average.

Communion (1977) SEE: **Holy Terror**▼
Communion (1989) **C-107m.** **½ D: Philippe Mora. Christopher Walken, Lindsay Crouse, Frances Sternhagen, Andreas Katsulas, Terri Hanauer, Joel Carlson, Basil Hoffman. Psychological thriller with Walken well cast as writer Whitley Strieber, who finds himself visited by strange creatures. Does he need a psychiatrist or an exorcist? A bit overlong, and the dramatic scenes between Walken and wife Crouse don't quite work, but still effectively scary while never gratuitously gory. Strieber adapted his own best-selling book, which he claims is true.▼

Companeros! (1971-Italian-Spanish-German) **C-105m.** ** D: Sergio Corbucci. Franco Nero, Tomas Milian, Jack Palance, Fernando Rey, Iris Berben, Karin Schubert. Swedish mercenary (Nero) seeks his fortune by running guns in revolution-racked Mexico at the turn of the century. Violent western fare.

Companions In Nightmare (1968) **C-99m. TVM** D: Norman Lloyd. Melvyn Douglas, Gig Young, Anne Baxter, Patrick O'Neal, Dana Wynter, Leslie Nielsen, William Redfield, Lou Gossett. Renowned psychiatrist (Douglas) invites hand-picked group of professionals to participate in group therapy experiment, unaware group includes dangerous psychotic. Performances can't hide film's contrived posturing. Average.

Company of Killers (1970) **C-88m.** ** D: Jerry Thorpe. Van Johnson, Ray Milland, John Saxon, Brian Kelly, Fritz Weaver, Clu Gulager, Susan Oliver, Diana Lynn, Robert Middleton. Gunman (Saxon) working for Murder, Inc. becomes target for his employers and big city police department after patrolman is shot down. Bites off more than it can chew.

Company of Wolves, The (1984-British) **C-95m.** ** D: Neil Jordan. Angela Lansbury, David Warner, Stephen Rea, Tusse Silberg, Sarah Patterson, Graham Crowden. Freudian, adult version of "Little Red Riding Hood," based on the premise that a wolf may not be what he seems. Intriguing idea mired in murky presentation; strange, slow, and unsatisfying.▼

Company She Keeps, The (1950) **81m.** **½ D: John Cromwell. Lizabeth Scott, Jane Greer, Dennis O'Keefe, Fay Baker, John Hoyt, Don Beddoe. Actors and unique love triangle spice this story of parole officer Scott and ex-con Greer both in love with O'Keefe.

Competition, The (1980) **C-129m.** *** D: Joel Oliansky. Richard Dreyfuss, Amy Irving, Lee Remick, Sam Wanamaker, Joseph Cali, Ty Henderson. Two young pianists, competing for the same prize, fall in love. Nothing much more than that, but smoothly done, with some excellent piano "faking." Screenwriter Oliansky's directing debut.▼

Compleat Beatles, The (1982) **C-120m.** *** D: Patrick Montgomery. Narrated by Malcolm McDowell. Absorbing chronicle of The Beatles and how they reflected (and often triggered) changes in our society during the 1960s and '70s. Filled with great Beatles songs, on the soundtrack and in performance. Intensely nostalgic and bittersweet for anyone who lived through that time. Originally produced for home video.▼

Compromising Positions (1985) **C-98m.** **½ D: Frank Perry. Susan Sarandon, Raul Julia, Edward Herrmann, Judith Ivey, Mary Beth Hurt, Joe Mantegna, Anne De Salvo, Josh Mostel. Long Island housewife becomes fascinated with the murder of a local dentist who (it turns out) was also an incredible womanizer. When it sticks to black comedy, the film is sharp and funny, but its other elements (male chauvinism, mystery, romance) don't pan out. Ivey has scene-stealing role as Sarandon's acid-tongued best friend. Screenplay by Susan Isaacs, from her novel.▼

Compulsion (1959) **103m.** ***½ D: Richard Fleischer. Orson Welles, Diane Varsi, Dean Stockwell, Bradford Dillman, E.G. Marshall, Martin Milner. Hard-hitting version of Leopold-Loeb thrill murder case of 1920s Chicago. Good characterizations, period decor, and well-edited courtroom scenes highlight picture.

Computercide (1982) **C-100m. TVM** D: Robert Michael Lewis. Joseph Cortese, Tom Clancy, Susan George, David Huddleston, Donald Pleasence. Lighthearted drama about THE FINAL EYE (the title when filmed in 1977), the last private eye on earth in the mid-1990s, unraveling a mystery in a utopian village where a noted scientist has vanished. A busted pilot that gathered dust on a shelf for a number of years—with good reason. Below average.

Computer Wore Tennis Shoes, The (1970) **C-91m.** ** D: Robert Butler. Kurt Russell, Cesar Romero, Joe Flynn, William Schallert, Alan Hewitt, Richard Bakalyan. The first of Disney's carbon-copy comedies with young Russell as the college whiz injected with a computer-brain, which poses threat to local gangster Romero. Standard slapstick. Followed by NOW YOU SEE HIM, NOW YOU DON'T.▼

Comrade X (1940) **90m.** **½ D: King Vidor. Clark Gable, Hedy Lamarr, Felix Bressart, Oscar Homolka, Eve Arden, Sig Ruman. NINOTCHKA-esque plot with American Gable warming up icy Russian Lamarr (a streetcar conductor). Synthetic romance tale never convinces; Bressart has great closing line, though.

Conan the Barbarian (1982) **C-129m.** **½ D: John Milius. Arnold Schwarzenegger, Sandahl Bergman, James Earl Jones, Gerry Lopez, Mako, Ben Davidson, Sven Ole Thorsen, Max von Sydow, Valerie Quennessen, Cassandra Gaviola, William Smith. The sword-wielding warrior seeks vengeance on the cult leader who enslaved him and massacred his village in this full-blooded (and bloody) adventure epic based on Robert E. Howard's pulp tales. Ron Cobb's spectacular production design and Basil Poledouris' vibrant score help make this superior to the many low-grade imitations it spawned. Also shown at 115m. and 123m. Sequel: CONAN THE DESTROYER.▼

Conan the Destroyer (1984) **C-103m.** *½ D: Richard Fleischer. Arnold Schwarzenegger, Grace Jones, Wilt Chamberlain, Mako, Tracey Walter, Sarah Douglas, Olivia

D'Abo. Lumbering attempt to jazz up Robert E. Howard's Hyborian Age hero with 80s-type fantasy and special effects—leading to ridiculous climax.▼

Con Artists, The (1977-Italian) **C-87m.** ** D: Sergio Corbucci. Anthony Quinn, Corinne Clery, Capucine, Adriano Celentano. Con man Quinn, recently sprung from prison, and his protégé Celentano, try to outwit the deadly Capucine. THE STING it ain't.▼

Concorde, The—Airport '79 (1979) **C-123m.** BOMB D: David Lowell Rich. Alain Delon, Susan Blakely, Robert Wagner, Sylvia Kristel, George Kennedy, Eddie Albert, Bibi Andersson, John Davidson, Andrea Marcovicci, Martha Raye, Cicely Tyson, Jimmie Walker, David Warner, Mercedes McCambridge. Wagner is a brilliant scientist, Kennedy and Andersson make love by the fire, Davidson's hair stays in place when the plane turns upside down, and McCambridge is a Russian gymnastics coach. Thank goodness Charo is around for credibility. Also known as AIRPORT '79. Nineteen minutes of footage was added for network TV.▼

Concrete Beat (1984) **C-78m. TVM** D: Robert Butler. John Getz, Darlanne Fluegel, Kenneth McMillan, Rhoda Gemignani, Van Nessa L. Clarke, Dean Santoro. Familiar newspaper scenario about a reporter who becomes involved in the lives of those on whom he's doing a story. Another failed pilot despite Getz's likable performance as nosy newshound. Average. ▼

Concrete Cowboys, The (1979) **C-100m. TVM** D: Burt Kennedy. Jerry Reed, Tom Selleck, Morgan Fairchild, Claude Akins, Gene Evans, Roy Acuff, Barbara Mandrell. Lighthearted mystery adventure about a couple of yahoos in Nashville who find themselves embroiled in an intricate blackmail scheme. Leisurely pace and amiable acting nearly cancel each other out. Pilot for a short-lived series. Average.▼

Concrete Jungle, The (1962-British) **86m.** **½ D: Joseph Losey. Stanley Baker, Margit Saad, Sam Wanamaker, Gregoire Aslan, Jill Bennett, Laurence Naismith, Edward Judd. Thoughtful filming of prison life focusing on escaped convict who doublecrosses pal. Baker is exceptionally able.

Concrete Jungle, The (1982) **C-99m.** *½ D: Tom DeSimone. Jill St. John, Tracy Bregman, Barbara Luna, Peter Brown, Aimee Eccles, Nita Talbot, Sondra Currie. Bregman's heel boyfriend gets her wrongly busted for drugs, leading to standard women's prison melodrama with St. John the kind of movie warden who is given glasses to show how uptight she is. Luna's performance as a hard-bitten prison vet is a cut above the others'. Followed by CHAINED HEAT.▼

Condemned (1929) **86m.** ** D: Wesley Ruggles. Ronald Colman, Ann Harding, Louis Wolheim, Dudley Digges, William Elmer. Attempt to depict social evils of Devils' Island with interspersed romantic plot, in stiff early talkie.

Condemned of Altona, The (1963) **114m.** **½ D: Vittorio De Sica. Sophia Loren, Fredric March, Robert Wagner, Maximilian Schell, Francoise Prevost. Sluggish pseudo-intellectual version of Jean-Paul Sartre play about post-WW2 Germany involving dying magnate (March), his two sons—one a playboy (Wagner) with an actress wife (Loren); the other an insane Nazi war criminal (Schell).

Condemned Women (1938) **77m.** **½ D: Lew Landers. Sally Eilers, Louis Hayward, Anne Shirley, Esther Dale, Lee Patrick, Leona Roberts, George Irving. Prison psychologist Hayward falls in love with inmate Eilers; no surprises in this B-picture, and not a lot of credibility either, but smooth performances and direction make it passable fare. Fans will enjoy seeing Patrick in an atypical role as the queen of this women's prison. Look for Jack Carson as an attendant.

Condominium (1979) **C-195m. TVM** D: Sidney Hayers. Barbara Eden, Dan Haggerty, Steve Forrest, Ralph Bellamy, MacDonald Carey, Dane Clark, Ana Alicia, Linda Cristal, Elinor Donahue, Don Galloway, Pamela Hensley, Arte Johnson, Jack Jones, Dorothy Malone, Nehemiah Persoff, Stuart Whitman. Condo sun-and-fun lovers' carefree life (and between-the-sheets activities) are threatened by a killer hurricane. Based on John D. MacDonald's best-selling novel. Average.

Condor (1986) **C-78m. TVM** D: Virgil L. Vogel. Ray Wise, Wendy Kilbourne, Craig Stevens, Victor Polizos, James Avery, Carolyn Seymour, Cassandra Gava. Secret agent teams with lady humanoid to thwart the plans of a diabolical woman prison escapee who's trying to gain access to the Pentagon's computers. Failed series pilot. Average.

Condorman (1981-British) **C-90m.** ** D: Charles Jarrott. Michael Crawford, Oliver Reed, James Hampton, Barbara Carrera, Jean-Pierre Kalfon, Dana Elcar. Cartoonist Crawford is transformed into Condorman, a comic book superhero who assists Soviet spy Carrera in her efforts to defect. Silly Disney film for only the most undiscriminating children.▼

Conduct Unbecoming (1975-British) **C-107m.** **½ D: Michael Anderson. Michael York, Richard Attenborough, Trevor Howard, Stacy Keach, Susannah York, Christopher Plummer. Quaintly old-fashioned drama of honor and outrage among the Bengal Lancers, where an officer's widow (York) is sexually attacked. Too

stuffy to be fun, yet too modern in other ways to be an antique; star performances are saving grace.▼

Coney Island (1943) **C-96m.** *** D: Walter Lang. Betty Grable, George Montgomery, Cesar Romero, Charles Winninger, Phil Silvers, Matt Briggs. Breezy, enjoyable turn-of-the-century musical of saloon entertainer Grable turned into famous musical star by hustling Montgomery. Remade with Grable seven years later as WABASH AVENUE.

Confess, Dr. Corda (1958-German) **81m.** ** D: Josef von Baky. Hardy Kruger, Elisabeth Mueller, Lucie Mannheim, Hans Nielsen. Tedious handling of story of Kruger circumstantially involved in death of his mistress, with his attempt to prove innocence at trial.

Confession (1937) **86m.** *** D: Joe May. Kay Francis, Basil Rathbone, Ian Hunter, Donald Crisp, Jane Bryan, Dorothy Peterson, Laura Hope Crews, Veda Ann Borg, Robert Barrat. Extremely stylish, well-acted soap opera in the MADAME X vein, with singer Francis recounting events leading up to her murder of oily Rathbone. Visually arresting, this looks more like a 1920s German film than a late 1930s Hollywood product; in fact, director May was a German émigré. Based very closely on the 1935 German film MAZURKA (which starred Pola Negri).

Confession, The (1970) **C-138m.** **½ D: Costa-Gavras. Yves Montand, Simone Signoret, Gabriele Ferzetti, Michel Vitold, Jean Bouise. True story of Czechoslovakian Communist Arthur London and his unjustified 1951 purge trial for treason; interesting tale well-acted by Montand, but film is as talky and overrated as Costa-Gavras' other efforts.

Confessional, The (1975-British) **C-104m.** *½ D: Pete Walker. Anthony Sharp, Susan Penhaligon, Stephanie Beacham, Norman Eshley, Sheila Keith. Lurid melodrama about a deranged priest. You've been warned. Originally titled HOUSE OF MORTAL SIN.▼

Confessions of a Married Man (1983) **C-100m. TVM** D: Steve Gethers. Robert Conrad, Jennifer Warren, Mary Crosby, Ann Dusenberry, Lance Guest, John Shepherd, Don Gordon. Loving husband and father, facing mid-life crisis, leaves his family for a younger woman. Average.

Confessions of a Nazi Spy (1939) **102m.** *** D: Anatole Litvak. Edward G. Robinson, Francis Lederer, George Sanders, Paul Lukas, Henry O'Neill, James Stephenson, Sig Ruman. Bristling drama of G-man Robinson investigating Nazi underground in U.S. Patriotic zest is forgivable.

Confessions of an Opium Eater (1962) **85m.** *½ D: Albert Zugsmith. Vincent Price, Linda Ho, Richard Loo, June Kim, Philip

Ahn, Victor Sen Yung. Bizarre low-budgeter. Price is hammy in tale of slave girls brought to San Francisco and the adventurer who aids them. Retitled: SOULS FOR SALE.

Confessions of a Peeping John SEE: **Hi, Mom!**

Confessions of a Police Captain (1971-Italian) **C-102m.** **½ D: Damiano Damiani. Martin Balsam, Franco Nero, Marilu Tolo, Claudio Gora. Interesting, sometimes ponderous drama of dedicated cop Balsam caught up in suffocating big-city corruption, as he tries to bring in an elusive criminal.▼

Confessions of a Window Cleaner (1974-British) **C-90m.** ** D: Val Guest. Robin Askwith, Anthony Booth, Linda Hayden, Bill Maynard, Dandy Nichols. British sex farce about voyeuristic window cleaner was dated when it came out; too obvious to be terribly funny. Followed by other CONFESSIONS films which weren't released here.

Confessions of Boston Blackie (1941) **65m.** D: Edward Dmytryk. Chester Morris, Harriet Hilliard, Richard Lane, George E. Stone, Lloyd Corrigan, Joan Woodbury. SEE: **Boston Blackie** series.

Confessions of Felix Krull, The (1958-German) **107m.** **½ D: Kurt Hoffman. Horst Buchholz, Lilo Pulver, Ingrid Andree, Susi Nicoletti. Waggish chronicle of charming rascal Buchholz rising in rank as Parisian hotel employee; based on Thomas Mann novel.

Confessions of Tom Harris (1972) **C-98m.** ** D: John Derek and David Nelson. Don Murray, Linda Evans, David Brian, Gary Clarke, Logan Ramsey. Offbeat, gritty study of a corrupt, amoral prizefighter, played by Murray, who also produced and wrote the story. Derek also photographed it. Filmed in 1966. First released in 1969 as CHILDISH THINGS.▼

Confidence (1979-Hungarian) **C-117m.** ***½ D: Istvan Szabo. Ildiko Bansagi, Peter Andorai, O. Gombik, Karoly Csaki, Ildiko Kishonti. Bansagi and Andorai, each separately married, fall in love while posing as husband and wife to elude the Germans during WW2. Striking, involving tale of trust and survival.

Confidential (1935) **67m.** **½ D: Edward L. Cahn. Donald Cook, Evalyn Knapp, Warren Hymer, J. Carrol Naish, Herbert Rawlinson, Theodore von Eltz, Morgan Wallace, Kane Richmond, Reed Howes. Fast-moving gangster programmer with G-man Cook going undercover to bust open a crime syndicate. Knapp is a sassy blonde; Hymer is a dumb lug with Brooklyn accent; Naish a cold-blooded killer. Good fun.▼

Confidential Agent (1945) **118m.** *** D: Herman Shumlin. Charles Boyer, Lauren Bacall, Peter Lorre, Katina Paxinou, Victor Francen, Wanda Hendrix. Boyer is Graham Greene's hero in engrossing spy

yarn of Spanish Civil War; he meets Bacall along the way; they battle enemy agents Lorre and Paxinou.

Confidentially Connie (1953) **74m.** **½ D: Edward Buzzell. Van Johnson, Janet Leigh, Louis Calhern, Walter Slezak, Gene Lockhart. Mild chuckles as pregnant wife Leigh schemes to get underpaid professor hubby (Johnson) to leave academic circles. Calhern as Van's rich Texan father is amusing.

Confidentially Yours (1983-French) **111m.** *** D: Francois Truffaut. Fanny Ardant, Jean-Louis Trintignant, Philippe Laudenbach, Caroline Sihol, Philippe Morier-Genoud, Xavier Saint Macary. Businessman is wanted for murder, and his spunky secretary takes on job of finding real killer while he hides out from the cops. Truffaut's final feature is airy mystery-comedy in the Hitchcock mold, based on an American novel (*The Long Saturday Night* by Charles Williams); beautifully shot in black & white by Nestor Almendros. No depth whatsoever, but lightly entertaining; Ardant is delightful. French title: VIVEMENT DIMANCHE! ▼

Confidential Report SEE: **Mr. Arkadin**▼

Confirm or Deny (1941) **73m.** **½ D: Archie Mayo. Don Ameche, Joan Bennett, Roddy McDowall, John Loder, Raymond Walburn, Arthur Shields. Love in an air-raid shelter with Ameche and Bennett as reporter and wireless operator; pleasant romance.

Conflagration SEE: **Enjo**

Conflict (1945) **86m.** **½ D: Curtis Bernhardt. Humphrey Bogart, Alexis Smith, Sydney Greenstreet, Rose Hobart, Charles Drake, Grant Mitchell. Far-fetched story of husband (Bogart) plotting to murder wife (Hobart) to marry her sister (Smith). Unconvincing plot not salvaged by good cast.

Conflict (1966) SEE: **Judith**

Conformist, The (1971-Italian-French-West German) **C-115m.** ***½ D: Bernardo Bertolucci. Jean-Louis Trintignant, Stefania Sandrelli, Dominique Sanda, Pierre Clementi, Pasquale Fortunato, Gastone Moschin. Disturbing blend of character study and historical context of 1930s. Repressing homosexual drives, Marcello Clerici strives for "acceptable" life as member of Italian Fascist secret service, and middle-class would-be wife chaser, until odd series of events make him a willing murderer. Film's overall mood uniquely tense.▼

Congo Crossing (1956) **C-87m.** ** D: Joseph Pevney. Virginia Mayo, George Nader, Peter Lorre, Michael Pate, Rex Ingram. OK adventure yarn set in Africa, involving wanted criminals and construction engineer's attempt to civilize the Congo territory.

Congo Maisie (1940) **70m.** D: H.C. Potter. Ann Sothern, John Carroll, Rita Johnson, Shepperd Strudwick, J.M. Kerrigan, E. E. Clive, Everett Brown. SEE: **Maisie** series.

Congratulations, It's a Boy (1971) **C-73m.** **TVM** D: William Graham. Bill Bixby, Diane Baker, Jack Albertson, Ann Sothern, Karen Jensen. Fairly entertaining vehicle for Bixby as swinging bachelor confronted by young man who claims to be his son. Average.

Conjugal Bed, The (1963-Italian) **90m.** *** D: Marco Ferreri. Ugo Tognazzi, Marina Vlady, Walter Giller, Linda Sini. Tognazzi is admirably suited to role of roué whose marriage to young beauty results in ironic twist of events.

Con Men, The SEE: Con Artists, The▼

Connecticut Yankee in King Arthur's Court, A (1949) **C-107m.** **½ D: Tay Garnett. Bing Crosby, Rhonda Fleming, William Bendix, Cedric Hardwicke, Henry Wilcoxon, Murvyn Vye, Virginia Field. Mark Twain's story becomes carefree Crosby musical, with Bing transported into past, branded a wizard. No great songs, but colorful production. Previously filmed in 1921 and 1931 (with Will Rogers); remade in 1979 (as UNIDENTIFIED FLYING ODDBALL) and as a TVM in 1989.▼

Connecticut Yankee in King Arthur's Court, A (1989) **C-100m.** **TVM** D: Mel Damski. Keshia Knight Pulliam, Jean Marsh, Rene Auberjonois, Emma Samms, Whip Hubley, Michael Gross. Girl from the MTV era is transported back to Arthurian England. Lame update of the classic Mark Twain tale (by playwright Paul Zindel), fashioned as a vehicle for the 10-year-old *Cosby* series costar. Average.

Connecting Rooms (1971-British) **C-103m.** ** D: Franklin Gollings. Bette Davis, Michael Redgrave, Alexis Kanner, Kay Walsh, Olga Georges-Picot, Leo Genn. Muddled melodrama of relationships in a rooming house. Davis is a street musician, Redgrave a former schoolmaster, and Kanner the rebellious youth who disrupts their equilibrium. Made in 1969, never released here.

Connection, The (1961) **103m.** ***½ D: Shirley Clarke. William Redfield, Warren Finnerty, Garry Goodrow, Jerome Raphael, James Anderson, Carl Lee, Roscoe Lee Browne, Jackie McLean. Searing, admirably acted drama of junkies awaiting arrival of their "connection" with heroin, and a documentary filmmaker (Redfield) filming them. Independently produced, based on Jack Gelber's stage play. Original running time 110m.; some prints run 93m.▼

Connection, The (1973) **C-73m. TVM** D: Tom Gries. Charles Durning, Ronny Cox, Zohra Lampert, Dennis Cole, Heather MacRae, Dana Wynter. Deliberately intricate tale of go-between (Durning) arranging meeting of jewel thief and insurance company representatives, capped by mad car chase on Manhattan's West Side. Flaw-

less pacing, great performances, good script by Albert Ruben. Above average.▼

Conquered City, The (1962-Italian) **C-87m.** **½ D: Joseph Anthony. David Niven, Ben Gazzara, Michael Craig, Martin Balsam, Lea Massari, Daniela Rocca. Niven and disparate international group are holed up in Athens hotel under siege in waning days of WW2; not-bad programmer released overseas as THE CAPTIVE CITY at 108m.

Conqueror, The (1956) **C-111m.** ** D: Dick Powell. John Wayne, Susan Hayward, Pedro Armendariz, Agnes Moorehead, Thomas Gomez, John Hoyt, William Conrad. Mongols vs. Tartars, and John Wayne vs. the silliest role of his career, Genghis Khan. Expensive epic has camp dialogue to spare. The film had a sobering real-life aftermath, however: it was shot on location in Utah near an atomic test site, and an alarming number of its cast and crew (including the stars) were later stricken by cancer.▼

Conquerors, The (1932) **86m.** ** D: William Wellman. Richard Dix, Ann Harding, Edna May Oliver, Guy Kibbee, Julie Haydon, Donald Cook. Unabashed rip-off of CIMARRON with Dix and Harding as newlyweds who go West to make their fortune, and build a banking empire that spans fifty years of ups and downs. Some good scenes lost in clichés in this epic saga. Retitled PIONEER BUILDERS.

Conqueror Worm, The (1968-British) **C-98m.** *** D: Michael Reeves. Vincent Price, Ian Ogilvy, Hilary Dwyer, Rupert Davies, Robert Russell, Patrick Wymark, Wilfred Brambell. As Matthew Hopkins, real-life witch-hunter during era of Cromwell, Price gives excellent nonhammy performance in underrated low-budget period thriller. Literate, balanced script pits him against young sympathetic lovers Ogilvy and Dwyer. Original British title: THE WITCHFINDER GENERAL.▼

Conquest (1937) **112m.** *** D: Clarence Brown. Greta Garbo, Charles Boyer, Reginald Owen, Alan Marshal, Henry Stephenson, Leif Erickson, Dame May Whitty. Boyer as Napoleon and Garbo as Polish countess Walewska in fairly interesting costumer with fine performances making up for not-always-thrilling script.

Conquest of Cochise (1953) **C-70m.** ** D: William Castle. John Hodiak, Robert Stack, Joy Page, John Crawford. Unspectacular Indian vs. cavalry, set in 1850s Southwest, as Stack and troops try to calm Cochise's (Hodiak) rampaging braves.

Conquest of Everest, The (1953-British) ✓ **C-78m.** *** No director credited. Outstanding, Oscar-nominated documentary chronicle of Edmund Hillary and company's successful expedition to the summit of Mount Everest. As dramatic as the most complexly plotted fiction; breathtaking photography by Thomas Stobart and George Love. ▼

Conquest of Space (1955) **C-80m.** **½ D: Byron Haskin. Eric Fleming, William Hopper, Ross Martin, Walter Brooke, Joan Shawlee. Despite some good special effects, this George Pal production about the first trip to Mars is hampered by a pedestrian script and an inappropriate emphasis on religion. A disappointment, based on Werner von Braun's book *The Mars Project.*

Conquest of the Planet of the Apes (1972) **C-87m.** **½ D: J. Lee Thompson. Roddy McDowall, Don Murray, Ricardo Montalban, Natalie Trundy, Severn Darden. Fourth APES feature shows how apes came to rebel and subsequently vanquish man. Loosely acted and often trite, but still interesting. Followed by BATTLE FOR THE PLANET OF THE APES.▼

Conrack (1974) **C-107m.** *** D: Martin Ritt. Jon Voight, Paul Winfield, Hume Cronyn, Madge Sinclair, Tina Andrews, Antonio Fargas. Pleasant film based on Pat Conroy's *The Water Is Wide*, about his attempts to bring common-sense education to backward black school on island off South Carolina. Subplot with hermit-like Winfield doesn't work, unfortunately.▼

Consenting Adults (1985) **C-100m. TVM** D: Gilbert Cates. Marlo Thomas, Martin Sheen, Barry Tubb, Talia Balsam, Ben Piazza, Corinne Michaels. Intelligent drama (by John McGreevey) about a family in turmoil when their "perfect" son discloses he's gay. Based on 1975 novel by Laura Z. Hobson. Above average.▼

Consolation Marriage (1931) **82m.** ** D: Paul Sloane. Irene Dunne, Pat O'Brien, John Halliday, Myrna Loy, Matt Moore, Lester Vail. Dunne and O'Brien are married after they're both jilted by their respective mates but years later must decide what to do when the former lovers return. Standard marital melodrama uplifted by considerably charming cast.▼

Conspiracy of Hearts (1960-British) **116m.** *** D: Ralph Thomas. Lilli Palmer, Sylvia Syms, Yvonne Mitchell, Ronald Lewis. Despite familiar situation of nuns sheltering refugee Jewish youths in Northern Italy, this film manages to be suspenseful and moving.

Conspiracy of Love (1987) **C-100m. TVM** D: Noel Black. Robert Young, Drew Barrymore, Elizabeth Wilson, Glynnis O'Connor, Mitchell Laurence. Treacly drama about a kindly barber, his beloved tomboy granddaughter, and her single-parent mother who wants to keep them apart because she feels her ex-father-in-law is a bad influence on the girl. Below average.▼

Conspiracy of Terror (1975) **C-78m.** **TVM** D: John Llewellyn Moxey. Michael Constantine, Barbara Rhoades, Mariclare

Costello, Roger Perry, David Opatoshu, Logan Ramsey. Husband-wife detective team investigates the case of a man who literally was scared to death and is confronted with satanism in suburbia. Comedy-drama, with "cute" touch of having the ethnically mixed pair working different shifts. Average.▼

Conspiracy to Kill SEE: **D.A.: Conspiracy to Kill**

Conspirator (1949-British) **85m.** **½ D: Victor Saville. Robert Taylor, Elizabeth Taylor, Honor Blackman, Wilfrid Hyde-White. Elizabeth is confronted by the fact that British husband Taylor is a Communist agent; story often better than stars.

Conspirators, The (1944) **101m.** **½ D: Jean Negulesco. Hedy Lamarr, Paul Henreid, Sydney Greenstreet, Peter Lorre, Victor Francen, Vladimir Sokoloff, George Macready, Monte Blue, Joseph Calleia. WW2 intrigue in Lisbon, with echoes of CASABLANCA; this one's no classic, but with that cast (and Hedy at her most beautiful) how bad can it be?

Constance (1984-New Zealand) **C-104m.** ** D: Bruce Morrison. Donogh Rees, Shane Briant, Judie Douglass, Martin Vaughan, Donald MacDonald, Mark Wignall. Muddled, forgettable tale of an ambitious, beautiful teacher (Rees), whose fantasy life is influenced by images from the Hollywood films she loves. She begins to act as if she's a character in a movie, with tragic result. Intriguing idea, but the film leaves no impression.

Constans SEE: **Constant Factor, The**

Constant Factor, The (1980-Polish) **C-96m.** *** D: Krzysztof Zanussi. Tadeusz Bradecki, Zofia Mrozowska, Malgorzata Zajaczkowska, Cezary Morawska. Idealistic mountain climber Bradecki refuses to kowtow to a hypocritical bureaucracy and winds up a window cleaner. Incisive, but not top-drawer Zanussi; filmed simultaneously with the director's CONTRACT.

Constant Husband, The (1955-British) **C-88m.** *** D: Sidney Gilliat. Rex Harrison, Margaret Leighton, Kay Kendall, Cecil Parker, Nicole Maurey, George Cole, Raymond Huntley, Michael Hordern, Robert Coote, Eric Pohlmann. Harrison, recovering from amnesia, realizes he's wed to more than one woman. Entertaining comedy, with sexy Rexy ideally cast (opposite real-life wife Kendall).

Constantine and the Cross (1962-Italian) **C-120m.** *** D: Lionello de Felice. Cornel Wilde, Christine Kaufmann, Belinda Lee, Elisa Cegani, Massimo Serato. Intelligent interpretation of 4th century A.D. Emperor (Wilde) battling Romans for Christianity. Good action.

Constant Nymph, The (1943) **112m.** ***½ D: Edmund Goulding. Charles Boyer, Joan Fontaine, Alexis Smith, Brenda Marshall, Charles Coburn, Dame May Whitty, Peter Lorre, Joyce Reynolds, Jean Muir, Montague Love, Edward (Eduardo) Ciannelli. Intensely romantic story of a Belgian gamine (Fontaine) who's madly in love with a self-serious and self-absorbed composer (Boyer), who marries a socialite (Smith) without ever realizing the depth of his own feelings for the younger girl. Touching, intelligent, and beautifully realized, with sweeping music by Erich Wolfgang Korngold. Margaret Kennedy's novel and play were adapted by Kathryn Scola. Filmed before in 1928 and 1934.

Consuming Passions (1988-U.S.-British) **C-98m.** *½ D: Giles Foster. Vanessa Redgrave, Jonathan Pryce, Tyler Butterworth, Freddie Jones, Sammi Davis, Prunella Scales, Thora Hird. Dumb dud of a satire about what happens when three men are accidentally shoved into a vat of chocolate in a candy factory . . . and chocolate lovers favor the resulting confections. Sounds a lot more promising than it plays; based on a play by Michael Palin and Terry Jones. ▼

Contempt (1963-French-Italian) **C-103m.** ***½ D: Jean-Luc Godard. Brigitte Bardot, Jack Palance, Michel Piccoli, Giorgia Moll, Fritz Lang. Perversely funny look at international moviemaking with Piccoli as a dramatist of integrity who gets mixed up with a vulgar producer (Palance) and director (Lang—playing himself) in a film version of *The Odyssey*. Producer Joseph E. Levine didn't seem to understand that Godard, who appears here as Lang's assistant, held *him* in contempt, making this film a highly amusing "in" joke. Bardot's appearance only adds to the fun.▼

Contest Girl (1966-British) **C-82m.** **½ D: Val Guest. Ian Hendry, Janette Scott, Ronald Fraser, Edmund Purdom, Linda Christian. Film well conveys glamorous and seamy sides of beauty-contest world. Purdom gives effective performance.

Continental Divide (1981) **C-103m.** ** D: Michael Apted. John Belushi, Blair Brown, Allen Goorwitz (Garfield), Carlin Glynn, Tony Ganios, Val Avery, Tim Kazurinsky. One of those "concept" movies that's all premise, no payoff: Belushi's a hard-hitting Chicago newspaper columnist, Brown's a self-reliant naturalist at home observing eagles in the Rockies. Can this romance survive? Interesting mainly to see Belushi playing such a "normal" and likable character. Written by Lawrence Kasdan, who obviously couldn't come up with a finish. Steven Spielberg was executive producer.▼

Continental Twist, The SEE: **Twist All Night**

Contraband (1940-British) **92m.** ***½ D: Michael Powell. Conrad Veidt, Valerie Hobson, Hay Petrie, Joss Ambler, Raymond Lovell, Esmond Knight, Peter Bull, Leo Genn. Superior spy yarn from the team of Michael Powell and Emeric Pressburger that's very much in the Hitchcock vein. Veidt is a Danish merchant sea captain, Hobson an enigmatic passenger—both get caught up with London spy ring. Though set in 1939, film hardly seems dated at all! That's Bernard Miles as a disgruntled smoker. Powell and Brock Williams adapted Pressburger's story. P&P had teamed up with Veidt and Hobson the previous year for THE SPY IN BLACK. Original U.S. title: BLACKOUT.

Contract (1980-Polish) **C-114m.** ***½ D: Krzysztof Zanussi. Leslie Caron, Maja Komorowska, Tadeusz Lomnicki, Magda Jaroszowna. Superb laced-in-acid comedy-satire centering on a wedding between the career-oriented son of a wealthy doctor and his none-too-eager bride. Zanussi incisively chides corrupt politicians and businessmen; Caron is memorable as a kleptomaniacal ballerina. Filmed simultaneously with the director's CONSTANS (THE CONSTANT FACTOR).

Contract on Cherry Street (1977) **C-150m.** TVM D: William A. Graham. Frank Sinatra, Harry Guardino, Martin Balsam, Henry Silva, Verna Bloom, Michael Nouri, Martin Gabel. Sinatra's first TV-movie (and first role after his seven-year "retirement") has him well cast as N.Y.C. police officer who takes on organized crime in his own fashion after his partner is gunned down. Aces to this fine thriller, adapted by Edward Anhalt from Philip Rosenberg's book. Above average.

Convention Girls (1978) **C-95m.** ** D: Joseph Adler. Nancy Lawson, Anne Sward, Carol Linden, Roberta White, Clarence Thomas. Executive suite-type maneuvering and soap-opera dramatics set against backdrop of Miami Beach toy convention (and the women hired to keep the conventioneers "entertained"). Closer in format to Robert Altman's NASHVILLE than the expected exploitation film.

Conversation, The (1974) **C-113m.** **** D: Francis Ford Coppola. Gene Hackman, John Cazale, Allen Garfield, Frederic Forrest, Cindy Williams, Michael Higgins, Elizabeth MacRae, Teri Garr, Harrison Ford. Brilliant film about obsessive surveillance expert (Hackman) who makes professional mistake of becoming involved in a case, and finds himself involved with murder and high-level power plays. Coppola's brilliant, disturbing script makes larger statements about privacy and personal responsibility. An unbilled Robert Duvall has a cameo. One of the best films of the 1970s.▼

Conversation Piece (1977-Italian) **C-122m.**

** D: Luchino Visconti. Burt Lancaster, Silvana Mangano, Helmut Berger, Claudia Marsani, Claudia Cardinale. Ponderous story of aging, aloof professor Lancaster who becomes involved with matron Mangano's hedonistic children and her young lover, Berger. All talk. Filmed in both English and Italian-language versions.

Convicted (1950) **91m.** **½ D: Henry Levin. Glenn Ford, Broderick Crawford, Dorothy Malone, Roland Winters, Ed Begley. Sincere account of prison warden's efforts to help unjustly convicted man, and those on the outside seeking actual killer. Remake of THE CRIMINAL CODE.

Convicted (1986) **C-100m.** TVM D: David Lowell Rich. Lindsay Wagner, Carroll O'Connor, John Larroquette, Laurie O'Brien, Caitlin O'Heaney, Burton Gilliam. Fact-based drama of a woman's five-year struggle to have her husband exonerated after he was falsely accused and convicted of rape. Average.▼

Convicted: A Mother's Story (1987) **C-100m.** TVM D: Richard Heffron. Ann Jillian, Gloria Loring, Kiel Martin, Fred Savage, Christa Denton, Veronica Redd. Mom goes to the slammer when slimy boyfriend lams with cash he had her "borrow" for him from work over the weekend. Below average.▼

Convicts Four (1962) **105m.** *** D: Millard Kaufman. Ben Gazzara, Stuart Whitman, Ray Walston, Vincent Price, Rod Steiger, Broderick Crawford, Sammy Davis, Jr., Jack Kruschen. Gazzara gives sincere portrayal as long-term prisoner who becomes professional artist. Oddball supporting cast. Retitled: REPRIEVE▼

Convoy (1978) **C-110m.** ** D: Sam Peckinpah. Kris Kristofferson, Ali MacGraw, Ernest Borgnine, Burt Young, Madge Sinclair, Franklyn Ajaye, Cassie Yates. Amiable comic-book movie based on the hit song about an independent trucker who leads protesting colleagues on a trek through the Southwest. Stupid script and blah acting redeemed somewhat by Peckinpah's punchy directorial style.▼

√ **Coogan's Bluff** (1968) **C-100m.** *** D: Don Siegel. Clint Eastwood, Lee J. Cobb, Susan Clark, Tisha Sterling, Don Stroud, Betty Field, Tom Tully. Arizona lawman Eastwood comes to N.Y.C. to show city cops a thing or two about tracking down a wanted man. Stylish action film, good location work. Sterling enjoyable as hippie. Later evolved into the *McCloud* TV series.▼

√ **Cook & Peary: The Race to the Pole** (1983) **C-100m.** TVM D: Robert Day. Richard Chamberlain, Rod Steiger, Diane Venora, Michael Gross, Samm-Art Williams. The struggles of two famed explorers as they trekked through the Arctic wasteland, each claiming to have reached the North Pole first. Low-key performances by the two

leads and starkness of the terrain make for relatively sluggish going. Average.

Cookie (1989) **C-93m.** *** D: Susan Seidelman. Peter Falk, Dianne Wiest, Emily Lloyd, Michael V. Gazzo, Brenda Vaccaro, Adrian Pasdar, Lionel Stander, Jerry Lewis, Bob Gunton, Ricki Lake. Droll comedy about a sassy teenager who gets to meet her mobster dad for the first time when he's sprung from prison after a long stretch. No fireworks here, but the performances are great fun to watch, especially Wiest as Falk's breathless mistress (and Lloyd's mother). Written by Nora Ephron and Alice Arlen.▼

Cook, The Thief, His Wife & Her Lover, The (1989-French-Dutch) **C-120m.** *** D: Peter Greenaway. Helen Mirren, Michael Gambon, Tim Roth, Richard Bohringer, Alan Howard. Another stylish, challenging piece of cinema from Greenaway that's set in a plush gourmet restaurant and details the various relationships between the title characters. This parable about love, revenge, and, most of all, greed is both funny and horrifying—and right on target. However, those who do not appreciate Greenaway's cinematic sensibility may be put off. Sacha Vierny's cinematography is an asset.▼

Cool and the Crazy, The (1958) **78m.** *** D: William Witney. Scott Marlowe, Gigi Perreau, Dick Bakalyan, Dick Jones. Fifties equivalent of REEFER MADNESS is a great unsung j.d. melodrama; reform school veteran introduces thirtyish-looking high schoolers to grass, turns them into psychotics. On-location Kansas City photography gives this one an authentic feel.

Cool Breeze (1972) **C-101m.** *½ D: Barry Pollack. Thalmus Rasulala, Judy Pace, Jim Watkins, Lincoln Kilpatrick, Sam Laws, Raymond St. Jacques. Routine remake of THE ASPHALT JUNGLE with plot line updated so that diamond robbery proceeds will go to set up a black people's bank.

Cooley High (1975) **C-107m.** *** D: Michael Schultz. Glynn Turman, Lawrence Hilton-Jacobs, Garrett Morris, Cynthia Davis, Corin Rogers, Maurice Leon Havis. Inner-city rip-off of AMERICAN GRAFFITI (set in Chicago, 1964) is nonetheless pleasing on its own terms, though only on the level of a good TV show. Lots of laughs. Later evolved into the *What's Happening!!* TV series.

Cool Hand Luke (1967) **C-126m.** ***½ D: Stuart Rosenberg. Paul Newman, George Kennedy, J.D. Cannon, Lou Antonio, Robert Drivas, Strother Martin, Jo Van Fleet, Wayne Rogers, Anthony Zerbe, Ralph Waite, Harry Dean Stanton, Dennis Hopper, Richard Davalos, Warren Finnerty, Morgan Woodward, Clifton James, Joe Don Baker. Modern slant on prison camps shows little change since Paul Muni; more irreverent, however, with memorably funny egg-eating contest. Top-notch film with Kennedy's Oscar-winning performance as prisoner.▼

Cool Million (1972) **C-100m. TVM** D: Gene Levitt. James Farentino, John Vernon, Barbara Bouchet, Jackie Coogan, Christine Belford, Lila Kedrova, Patrick O'Neal. International troubleshooter must locate genuine heiress of $50 million fortune when father dies under mysterious circumstances. Fantasy-world entertainment; pilot for the short-lived series. Average. Retitled MASK OF MARCELLA.

Cool Ones, The (1967) **C-95m. BOMB** D: Gene Nelson. Roddy McDowall, Debbie Watson, Gil Peterson, Phil Harris, Robert Coote, Glen Campbell, Mrs. Miller. Inane "musical" comedy spoofing trendy music business. Embarrassing on all counts, with broad performances. If you turn up your volume, you might hear a faint laugh track.

Coonskin (1975) **C-83m. **½ D: Ralph Bakshi. Barry White, Charles Gordone, Scatman Crothers, Philip (Michael) Thomas. Outrageous, original film about the status of blacks in America is told with live-action and animation vignettes, the best of which are sly parodies of the stories from Disney and Uncle Remus' SONG OF THE SOUTH. Very much in the Bakshi vein; uneven but worth a look. Retitled STREET-FIGHT for video.▼

Cop (1987) **C-110m. **½ D: James B. Harris. James Woods, Lesley Ann Warren, Charles Durning, Charles Haid, Raymond J. Barry, Randi Brooks, Annie McEnroe, Vicki Wauchope. Woods is excellent as usual in this otherwise familiar drama about a dedicated cop, his troubled marriage, and the difficulties he encounters while on a murder case. Woods and Harris coproduced.▼

Copacabana (1947) **92m. ** D: Alfred E. Green. Groucho Marx, Carmen Miranda, Andy Russell, Steve Cochran, Gloria Jean, Louis Sobol, Abel Green, Earl Wilson. Unengrossing musical comedy about wild complications when same girl applies for two jobs at nightclub; cast can't save it.▼

Copacabana (1985) **C-100m. TVM** D: Waris Hussein. Barry Manilow, Annette O'Toole, Joseph Bologna, Ernie Sabella, Estelle Getty, Silvana Gallardo. Campy Valentine to the backstage musicals Hollywood turned out in the 40s, with Manilow making his acting debut in a feature-length expansion of his 1978 hit record about a struggling songwriter and the chorus girl he falls for. Average.

Cop Au Vin (1984-French) **C-110m. ***½** D: Claude Chabrol. Jean Poiret, Stephane Audran, Michel Bouquet, Jean Topart, Lucas Belvaux, Pauline Lafont. Chabrol is in fine form in this diverting, neatly paced thriller about a young mail boy, his

widowed, invalid mother, and a greedy trio who attempt to evict them from their home. Murder brings a shrewd cop on the scene to investigate. Followed by a sequel, INSPECTOR LAVARDIN.

Cop Killers SEE: **Corrupt**▼

Cop on the Beat (1975) **C-78m. TVM** D: Virgil W. Vogel. Lloyd Bridges, Pat Crowley, Dane Clark, Jim Backus, Dean Stockwell, Della Reese, Janis Paige, Tom Drake, Edie Adams, Don Stroud, Hari Rhodes. Bridges is Joe Forrester, veteran plainclothes cop who voluntarily returns to uniform duty on his old beat to help solve a series of robbery-rapes in the rundown neighborhood. This evolved from TV's *Police Story* and served as a brief series for always reliable Bridges. Average.

Cop-Out (1968-British) **C-95m. **½ D: Pierre Rouve. James Mason, Geraldine Chaplin, Bobby Darin, Paul Bertoya, Ian Ogilvy, Bryan Stanton. OK murder mystery with dated generation-gap overtones. Reclusive lawyer Mason comes out of retirement to defend his daughter's boyfriend on trumped-up murder charge. Remake of 1942 French film STRANGER IN THE HOUSE.

Copper Canyon (1950) **C-83m. **½ D: John Farrow. Ray Milland, Hedy Lamarr, Macdonald Carey, Mona Freeman. Milland-Lamarr occasionally sparkle in this Western of post-Civil War days and movement West to find riches.

Cops and Robbers (1973) **C-89m. *** D: Aram Avakian. Cliff Gorman, Joseph Bologna, Dick Ward, Shepperd Strudwick, John P. Ryan, Ellen Holly, Dolph Sweet, Joe Spinell. Enjoyable Donald Westlake tale about two policemen who pull a million-dollar caper on Wall Street. Funny and exciting, with good location photography by David L. Quaid.▼

Cops and Robin, The (1978) **C-100m. TVM** D: Allen Reisner. Ernest Borgnine, Michael Shannon, John Amos, Carol Lynley, Natasha Ryan, Philip Abbott, Terry Kiser. The premise that began with FUTURE COP (with the same stars) and continued in the brief series that followed was given another shot here, with an aging street cop and his partner, a robot programmed to be the perfect policeman, assigned to protect the young daughter of a woman stalked by mobsters. Average.

Corey: For the People (1977) **C-79m. TVM** D: Buzz Kulik. John Rubinstein, Eugene Roche, Lana Wood, Ronny Cox, Richard Venture, Carol Rossen, Kip Niven, Joan Pringle. Rubinstein's a lowly assistant D.A., bucking the system—and looking for a series in this by-the-numbers pilot. Veteran writer Alvin Boretz scripted it. Average.

Corky (1972) **C-88m. **½ D: Leonard Horn. Robert Blake, Charlotte Rampling, Patrick O'Neal, Christopher Connelly, Ben

Johnson, Laurence Luckinbill. Blake's obsession for stock-car racing shuts out everything else in his life, including wife and friends. Good racing sequences, fairly absorbing character study. Originally titled LOOKIN' GOOD.

Cornbread, Earl and Me (1975) **C-95m.** **½ D: Joe Manduke. Moses Gunn, Bernie Casey, Rosalind Cash, Madge Sinclair, Keith Wilkes, Tierre Turner. Well-intentioned but overly melodramatic account of a black youth, on his way out of the ghetto on a basketball scholarship, who is innocently gunned down by police bullets. Fine performances and warm sense of black life evaporate in TV series clichés.▼

Cornered (1945) **102m.** *** D: Edward Dmytryk. Dick Powell, Walter Slezak, Micheline Cheirel, Nina Vale, Morris Carnovsky. High-tension drama with toughguy Powell in Buenos Aires tracking down the man who killed his wife during WW2; Powell in peak form.▼

Corn Is Green, The (1945) **114m.** ***½ D: Irving Rapper. Bette Davis, Nigel Bruce, John Dall, Joan Lorring, Rhys Williams, Rosalind Ivan, Mildred Dunnock. Thoughtful acting in this story of devoted middleaged teacher Davis in Welsh mining town coming to terms with her prize pupil. Emlyn Williams' play was adapted by Casey Robinson and Frank Cavett. Remade, beautifully, with Katharine Hepburn in 1979.▼

Corn Is Green, The (1979) **C-100m.** TVM D: George Cukor. Katharine Hepburn, Ian Saynor, Bill Fraser, Patricia Hayes, Anna Massey. Classy remake of the 1945 movie about a spinster teacher bringing education to North Wales mining community. Story is beginning to wear a bit, but glistens with Hepburn's tour-de-force performance (in her tenth and final teaming with director Cukor) and on-location filming. Above average.

Coronado (1935) **77m.** **½ D: Norman Z. McLeod. Johnny Downs, Betty Burgess, Jack Haley, Andy Devine, Leon Errol, Jacqueline Wells (Julie Bishop), Alice White, Eddy Duchin with his Orchestra. Unspectacular but pleasant B musical about wealthy, brash songwriter Downs, and his romantic escapades with singer Burgess one summer at a resort hotel. Haley and Devine lend support as a couple of hapless sailors.

Coroner Creek (1948) **C-93m.** **½ D: Ray Enright. Randolph Scott, Marguerite Chapman, George Macready, Sally Eilers, Edgar Buchanan. Good little Western: Scott seeks revenge on his fiancee's killer.▼

Corpse Came C.O.D., The (1947) **87m.** ** D: Henry Levin. George Brent, Joan Blondell, Adele Jergens, Jim Bannon, Leslie Brooks, Grant Mitchell, Una O'Connor. Two rival reporters attempt to solve mystery of dead body showing up at actress' residence. Strictly "B" material.

Corpse Vanishes, The (1942) **64m.** ** D:

Wallace Fox. Bela Lugosi, Luana Walters, Tristram Coffin, Elizabeth Russell, Vince Barnett, Joan Barclay, Angelo Rossitto. A cut above the average lowgrade thrillers Lugosi made for producer Sam Katzman. Bela is a scientist who kidnaps brides for the purpose of using their body fluids to rejuvenate wife Russell, an elderly countess.▼

Corregidor (1943) **73m.** ** D: William Nigh. Otto Kruger, Elissa Landi, Donald Woods, Frank Jenks, Rick Vallin, Wanda McKay, Ian Keith. Not a battle-action film but a routine love triangle set against wartime background, rather cheaply done.▼

Corridor of Mirrors (1948-British) **105m.** *** D: Terence Young. Eric Portman, Edana Romney, Barbara Mullen, Hugh Sinclair, Joan Maude, Lois Maxwell, Christopher Lee. Underrated "art" film, similar to Jean Cocteau's work of this period, has Portman well cast as an artist who lives in the past, surrounding himself with Renaissance-era objects. Beauteous Romney (whose acting is not so hot) is the woman he falls in love with, leading to tragic results. Stunning sets, photography, and musical score.

Corridors of Blood (1958-British) **86m.** **½ D: Robert Day. Boris Karloff, Betta St. John, Finlay Currie, Christopher Lee, Francis Matthews, Adrienne Corri, Nigel Green. Middling account of 19th-century British doctor who experiments with anesthetics, becomes addicted to the narcotics, and winds up a grave-robber to continue his experiments. Unreleased until the early 1960s, at which time Lee received higher billing than his supporting role warranted. Originally titled THE DOCTOR FROM SEVEN DIALS.▼

Corrupt (1983-Italian) **C-99m.** *** D: Roberto Faenza. Harvey Keitel, Nicole Garcia, Leonard Mann, John Lydon, Sylvia Sidney. Intriguing, entertaining psychological thriller about N.Y.C. policeman Keitel, his victimization by mysterious Lydon, and a hunt for a cop killer. Lydon used to be known as Johnny Rotten (of the punk rock group, The Sex Pistols). Fine performances; originally titled ORDER OF DEATH, with a 113m. running time, and also known as COP KILLERS▼

Corruption (1968-British) **C-91m.** ** D: Robert Hartford-Davis. Peter Cushing, Sue Lloyd, David Lodge, Kate O'Mara. Another film of famed surgeon who will stop at nothing to restore his love's destroyed beauty.

Corrupt Ones, The (1966-French-Italian-West German) **C-92m.** **½ D: James Hill. Robert Stack, Elke Sommer, Nancy Kwan, Christian Marquand, Werner Peters. Knock-about photographer Stack is befriended by stranger who gives him key (literally!) to ancient Chinese emperor's treasure. With better dialogue for its many grotesque characters, film could've been a knockout.▼

Corsican Brothers, The (1941) **112m.** *** D: Gregory Ratoff. Douglas Fairbanks Jr., Ruth Warrick, Akim Tamiroff, J. Carrol Naish, H. B. Warner, Henry Wilcoxon. Entertaining swashbuckler from Dumas story of twins who are separated, but remain spiritually tied. Fairbanks excellent in the lead, with strong support, ingenious photographic effects.▼

Corsican Brothers, The (1985) **C-100m.** TVM D: Ian Sharp. Trevor Eve, Geraldine Chaplin, Olivia Hussey, Nicholas Clay, Jean Marsh, Benedict Taylor, Simon Ward, Donald Pleasence. Eve is neither Cheech nor Chong, so it's OK to watch this handsome remake of the classic Dumas tale about brothers with a lifelong emotional bond. Robin Miller wrote the adaptation. Above average.

Corvette K-225 (1943) **99m.** *** D: Richard Rossen. Randolph Scott, James Brown, Ella Raines, Barry Fitzgerald, Andy Devine, Walter Sande, Richard Lane. First-rate war film with Canadian officer Scott fighting to save prominent navy destroyer from enemy attack; realistic actioner produced by Howard Hawks. Look quickly for Robert Mitchum.

Corvette Summer (1978) **C-105m.** ** D: Matthew Robbins. Mark Hamill, Annie Potts, Eugene Roche, Kim Milford, Richard McKenzie, William Bryant. High schooler Hamill falls for aspiring hooker Potts while in Vegas tracking down the person who stole the sports car restored by his shop class. Bland comedy drama offers Potts' disarmingly off-the-wall performance to keep your attention.▼

Cosmic Eye, The (1985) **C-76m.** *** D: Faith Hubley. Voices of Maureen Stapleton, Dizzy Gillespie, Sam Hubley, Linda Atkinson. Wonderfully imaginative, life-affirming animated feature about the needs, rights, and struggles of mankind, most especially children, around the world. A tapestry that includes pieces of earlier animated shorts by John and Faith Hubley, with music by such notables as Dizzy Gillespie, Benny Carter, and Elizabeth Swados.▼

Cosmic Man, The (1959) **72m.** *½ D: Herbert Greene. Bruce Bennett, John Carradine, Angela Greene, Paul Langton, Scotty Morrow. Mediocre sci-fi with now-you-see-me, now-you-don't title figure on a mission to earth.▼

Cosmic Monster, The (1958-British) **75m.** *½ D: Gilbert Gunn. Forrest Tucker, Gaby Andre, Martin Benson, Alec Mango, Wyndham Goldie, Hugh Latimer. Britain's only entry on the Giant Bug Movie Checklist is talky tale of a mad scientist whose magnetism experiments punch a hole in the ionosphere, letting in cosmic rays which enlarge insects in the woods. Gleefully ghoulish at times. On videotape also under original British title, THE STRANGE WORLD OF PLANET X.▼

Cosmo 2000: Planet Without a Name SEE: **Cosmos: War of the Planets**

Cosmos: War of the Planets (1977-Italian) **C-95m.** BOMB D: Al Bradley (Alfonso Brescia). John Richardson, Yanti Somer, West Buchanan, Kathy Christine, Max Karis, Percy Hogan. Unimpressive special effects and laughable performances dominate this confusing turkey set aboard a spaceship and on an unexplored planet. Don't say you weren't warned. Also known as WAR OF THE PLANETS and COSMO 2000: PLANET WITHOUT A NAME.

Cossacks, The (1959-Italian) **C-113m.** ** D: Giorgio Rivalta. Edmund Purdom, John Drew Barrymore, Giorgia Moll, Massimo Girotti. Heavy-handed historical tale set in 1850s Russia; Cossack Purdom and son Barrymore clash in loyalties to Czar Alexander II.

Cottage to Let (1941-British) **90m.** ** D: Anthony Asquith. Alastair Sim, John Mills, Leslie Banks, Michael Wilding, Carla Lehmann, Catherine Lacey. Good cast is wasted in this disappointing thriller about Nazi spies attempting to pilfer the plans for inventor Banks's secret bomb sight.

Cotter (1973) **C-94m.** **½ D: Paul Stanley. Don Murray, Carol Lynley, Rip Torn, Sherry Jackson. After tragic rodeo incident, unhappy Indian clown (Murray) struggles to reestablish himself in home town. Good cast in fair script that fares best in creating small-town atmosphere.

Cotton Candy (1978) **C-100m.** TVM D: Ron Howard. Charles Martin Smith, Clint Howard, Rance Howard, Leslie King, Kevin Lee Miller. Ron Howard directed (and co-wrote with brother Clint) this featherweight story about high school students who form a rock 'n' roll band in the 1970s. Average.

Cotton Club, The (1984) **C-127m.** **½ D: Francis Coppola. Richard Gere, Gregory Hines, Diane Lane, Lonette McKee, Bob Hoskins, James Remar, Nicolas Cage, Allen Garfield, Fred Gwynne, Gwen Verdon, Maurice Hines, Joe Dallesandro, Julian Beck, Jennifer Grey, Lisa Jane Persky, Tom Waits, Diane Venora, Woody Strode. Homage to the days of colorful gangsters and Harlem nightlife has style to spare and a wonderful soundtrack full of Duke Ellington music; (Gere plays his own cornet solos); all it needs is a story and characters whose relationships make some sense. Visually striking with good scenes scattered about; whether it's worth watching the whole film is strictly a matter of personal taste. In any case, the movie isn't nearly as interesting as the published stories about its tumultuous production! ▼

Cotton Comes to Harlem (1970) **C-97m.** *** D: Ossie Davis. Godfrey Cambridge, Raymond St. Jacques, Calvin Lockhart, Judy Pace, Redd Foxx, Emily Yancy, Cleavon Little. St. Jacques is Coffin Ed Johnson, Cambridge is Gravedigger Jones, black cops who suspect preacher Lockhart's back-to-Africa campaign is a swindle. Neatly combines action and comedy, with fine use of Harlem locales; from Chester Himes' novel. Sequel: COME BACK, CHARLESTON BLUE.

Couch, The (1962) **100m.** **½ D: Owen Crump. Shirley Knight, Grant Williams, Onslow Stevens, William Leslie. Bizarre yarn of psychopathic killer on the prowl while under analysis. Script by Robert Bloch from screen story cowritten by Blake Edwards.

Couch Trip, The (1988) **C-97m.** **½ D: Michael Ritchie. Dan Aykroyd, Walter Matthau, Charles Grodin, Donna Dixon, Richard Romanus, Arye Gross, David Clennon, Mary Gross. Amusing, if somewhat lackluster, comedy about a mental institution escapee who masquerades as a successful Beverly Hills psychiatrist and radio adviser. Some good laughs, served by a solid cast, but the story is pretty thin.▼

Counsellor-at-Law (1933) **82m.** **** D: William Wyler. John Barrymore, Bebe Daniels, Doris Kenyon, Onslow Stevens, Isabel Jewell, Melvyn Douglas, Thelma Todd, John Qualen, Mayo Methot, Vincent Sherman. Vivid adaptation of Elmer Rice play about rags-to-riches Jewish lawyer who cannot escape his background—and who begins to question his success when he learns his wife has been unfaithful. Barrymore gives one of his greatest performances in meaty, colorful role; Wyler keeps this comedy-drama moving at breakneck pace. Scripted by the playwright.

Countdown (1968) **C-101m.** ***½ D: Robert Altman. Robert Duvall, James Caan, Charles Aidman, Joanna Moore, Steve Ihnat, Barbara Baxley, Ted Knight, Michael Murphy. Near-flawless depiction of real-life trials and concerns of American astronauts, their wives, co-workers, leading to first flight to moon. Excellent ensemble performances, intelligent script, great use of mood. Dated technology only liability. An early gem from Altman.▼

Countdown at Kusini (1976-Nigerian) **C-101m.** ** D: Ossie Davis. Ruby Dee, Ossie Davis, Greg Morris, Tom Aldredge, Michael Ebert, Thomas Baptiste. Well-meaning treatment of liberation of fictional African country, "Fahari" (actually Lagos). Action and ideas are constantly swallowed up by romantic subplot. Film financed by DST Telecommunications, subsidiary of Delta Sigma Theta, world's largest black sorority.

Count Dracula (1970-Italian-Spanish-German) **C-98m.** **½ D: Jess Franco. Christopher Lee, Herbert Lom, Klaus Kinski, Frederick Williams, Maria Rohm, Soledad Miranda. Flawed but interesting low-budget adaptation of Bram Stoker novel which sticks close to its source; Lee turns in remarkably low-key performance. TV prints run 90m.▼

Count Dracula and His Vampire Bride (1973-British) **C-84m.** *½ D: Alan Gibson. Christopher Lee, Peter Cushing, Michael Coles, William Franklyn, Freddie Jones, Joanna Lumley. Last of the Hammer Films Dracula series is awfully tired, despite modern-day setting; the Count gets hold of a plague virus that can destroy mankind. Cut for U.S. release from original 88m. version called SATANIC RITES OF DRACULA.▼

Counter-Attack (1945) **90m.** **½ D: Zoltan Korda. Paul Muni, Marguerite Chapman, Larry Parks, Philip Van Zandt, George Macready, Roman Bohnen. Satisfactory WW2 movie of Allied fighters going behind enemy lines to sabotage German positions; no classic, but good.

Counterfeit Commandos SEE: **Inglorious Bastards**

Counterfeiters (1948) **73m.** **½ D: Peter Stewart. John Sutton, Doris Merrick, Hugh Beaumont, Lon Chaney, George O'Hanlon, Herbert Rawlinson. Not bad little actioner with Scotland Yard cop Sutton going undercover to nab counterfeiter Beaumont and his gang.

Counterfeit Killer, The (1968) **C-95m.** ** D: Josef Leytes. Jack Lord, Shirley Knight, Jack Weston, Charles Drake, Joseph Wiseman, Don Hanmer. Adapted from TV film THE FACELESS MAN, meandering actioner has Lord a secret service man infiltrating a counterfeit syndicate, with predictable results.

Counterfeit Plan, The (1957-British) **80m.** ** D: Montgomery Tully. Zachary Scott, Peggie Castle, Mervyn Johns, Sydney Tafler. Scott is appropriately nasty as escaped murderer who sets up international counterfeit syndicate.

Counterfeit Traitor, The (1962) **C-140m.** ***½ D: George Seaton. William Holden, Lilli Palmer, Hugh Griffith, Erica Beer, Werner Peters, Eva Dahlbeck. Holden runs around Europe as a double agent during WW2, falls in love with Palmer between various dangerous missions. Authentic backgrounds and fine cast. Based on true story.

Counterplot (1959) **76m.** ** D: Kurt Neumann. Forrest Tucker, Allison Hayes, Gerald Milton, Edmundo Rivera Alvarez, Jackie Wayne. Mundane hide-and-seeker set in Puerto Rico where Tucker is hiding out from police and his double-dealing attorney.

Counterpoint (1968) **C-107m.** *½ D: Ralph

Nelson. Charlton Heston, Maximilian Schell, Kathryn Hays, Leslie Nielsen, Anton Diffring. Absurd WW2 melodrama about symphony conductor captured by Nazi general, forced to put on private concert; Heston looks comfortable because he doesn't have to change facial expressions while conducting.

Counter Tenors, The SEE: **White Voices, The**

Countess Dracula (1972-British) **C-94m.** ** D: Peter Sasdy. Ingrid Pitt, Nigel Green, Peter Jeffrey, Lesley-Anne Down. Countess masquerades as her own daughter, needs blood to maintain facade of youth. OK shocker. Based on historical figure Elisabeth Bathory; has nothing to do with Dracula.

Countess From Hong Kong, A (1967-British) **C-108m.** *½ D: Charles Chaplin. Marlon Brando, Sophia Loren, Sydney Chaplin, Tippi Hedren, Patrick Cargill, Margaret Rutherford. Director-writer-composer (and bit-part actor) Chaplin's attempt to make old-fashioned romantic comedy sinks fast, though everybody tries hard. Sophia stows away in shipboard stateroom of diplomat Brando. Badly shot, badly timed, badly scored. A pity, particularly because this is Chaplin's cinematic swan song.

Countess of Monte Cristo, The (1948) **77m.** ** D: Frederick de Cordova. Sonja Henie, Olga San Juan, Dorothy Hart, Michael Kirby, Arthur Treacher. Sonja and Olga pretend to be royal visitors in this limp costume comedy.

Count Five and Die (1958-British) **92m.** **½ D: Victor Vicas. Jeffrey Hunter, Nigel Patrick, Ann-Marie Duringer, David Kossoff. WW2 espionage flick has Hunter an American agent working with British to mislead Nazis about Allied landing site.

Count of Bragelonne, The SEE: **Last Musketeer, The**

Count of Monte Cristo, The (1934) **119m.** ***½ D: Rowland V. Lee. Robert Donat, Elissa Landi, Louis Calhern, Sidney Blackmer, Raymond Walburn, O.P. Heggie, Luis Alberni, Irene Hervey. Superb filmization of classic story of Edmond Dantes, who spends years in prison unjustly but escapes to seek revenge on enemies who framed him. Donat leads excellent cast in rousing classic from Dumas' story.▼

Count of Monte Cristo, The (1954-French) **C-97m.** **½ D: Robert Vernay. Jean Marais, Lia Amanda, Roger Piquat. Serviceable rendition of Alexandre Dumas costume classic.

Count of Monte Cristo, The (1961-French) **C-90m.** **½ D: Claude Autant-Lara. Louis Jourdan, Yvonne Furneaux, Pierre Mondy, Bernard Dheran. Faithful adaptation of Dumas novel, but Jourdan hasn't the zest that Robert Donat gave the role in 1934. Originally 120m.

Count of Monte Cristo, The (1975) **C-100m. TVM** D: David Greene. Richard Chamberlain, Tony Curtis, Trevor Howard, Louis Jourdan, Donald Pleasence, Taryn Power, Kate Nelligan. Lavish costume drama with Chamberlain quite all right as a swashbuckling Edmond Dantes and Curtis as the villainous Mondego. Sidney Carroll's adaptation of Dumas holds its own against its many predecessors. Average.▼

Country (1984) **C-109m.** *** D: Richard Pearce. Jessica Lange, Sam Shepard, Wilford Brimley, Matt Clark, Therese Graham, Levi L. Knebel. Penetrating, believable look at modern farming family torn apart when government threatens to foreclose on loan and take their land away. It's the woman whose strength holds things together (and it's Lange who coproduced the film); all performances are first-rate, and William D. Wittliff's script neatly avoids pitfalls of cliché.▼

Country Dance SEE: **Brotherly Love** (1969)

Country Girl, The (1954) **104m.** ***½ D: George Seaton. Bing Crosby, Grace Kelly, William Holden, Anthony Ross. Kelly won an Oscar as wife of alcoholic singer (Crosby) trying for comeback via help of director (Holden). Crosby excels in one of his finest roles. Writer-director Seaton also won Academy Award for adaptation of Clifford Odets play.▼

Country Gold (1982) **C-100m. TVM** D: Gilbert Cates. Loni Anderson, Earl Holliman, Linda Hamilton, Cooper Huckabee, Dennis Dugan, Lee Richardson. ALL ABOUT EVE with a Nashville touch, as a country singer is "befriended" by a young woman. Cameos by country stars Mel Tillis, Barbara Mandrell, Stella Parton, Box Car Willie, The Bellamy Brothers and others. Average.

Country Music Holiday (1958) **81m.** ** D: Alvin Ganzer. Ferlin Husky, Zsa Zsa Gabor, Jesse White, Rocky Graziano, Cliff Norton, Clyde Woods, June Carter, The Jordanaires, Drifting Johnny Miller. A hillbilly's rise to fame; lots of songs and specialties dominate this curio.

Country Music Murders, The SEE: **Murder in Music City**

Count the Hours (1953) **76m.** ** D: Don Siegel. Teresa Wright, Macdonald Carey, Dolores Moran, Adele Mara. Trim but implausible story of ranch hand and pregnant wife. When police accuse them of murdering their employers, he takes blame so she can have their child.

Count Three and Pray (1955) **C-102m.** **½ D: George Sherman. Van Heflin, Joanne Woodward, Raymond Burr, Nancy Kulp. Atmospheric rural Americana in post-Civil War days, with Heflin exerting influence on townfolk as new pastor with reckless past. Woodward (making her film debut) as strong-willed orphan lass and Burr, the perennial villain, are fine.

Count Yorga, Vampire (1970) **C-91m.** *** D: Bob Kelljan. Robert Quarry, Roger Perry, Donna Anders, Michael Murphy, Michael Macready. Sophisticated, clever vampire (Quarry) establishes coven in modern-day Southern California. Fast-paced and convincing. Sequel: THE RETURN OF COUNT YORGA.▼

Count Your Blessings (1959) **C-102m.** ** D: Jean Negulesco. Deborah Kerr, Rossano Brazzi, Maurice Chevalier, Martin Stephens, Tom Helmore, Patricia Medina. Unfunny comedy that even Chevalier's smile can't help. Kerr marries French playboy Brazzi during WW2; he goes off philandering for years. Their child conspires to bring them together again.

Coup de Foudre SEE: **Entre Nous**▼

Coup de Grace (1976-French-German) **C-96m.** ** D: Volker Schlondorff. Margarethe von Trotta, Matthias Habich, Rudiger Kirschstein, Valeska Gert. Disappointing tale of a self-destructive countess (von Trotta, wife of the director), who wastes her life because the officer she loves does not reciprocate her feelings. Bleak, sometimes confusing film, not as emotional or involving as it should be.▼

Coup de Torchon (1981-French) **C-128m.** ***½ D: Bertrand Tavernier. Philippe Noiret, Isabelle Huppert, Stephane Audran, Irene Skobline, Eddy Mitchell, Jean-Pierre Marielle, Guy Marchand. Strong, disturbing black comedy, based on a novel by American Jim Thompson but reset in 1936 Equatorial Africa. Easygoing police chief (Noiret) of small colonial town is a doormat for everyone in sight, especially his wife; he gradually realizes he can use his position to gain vengeance with impunity. Fascinating film eventually overplays its hand, but enthralling most of the way, with marvelously shaded performance by Noiret. Also known as CLEAN SLATE.▼

Coupe de Ville (1990) **C-99m.** ** D: Joe Roth. Patrick Dempsey, Arye Gross, Daniel Stern, Alan Arkin, Annabeth Gish, Rita Taggart, Joseph Bologna, James Gammon. Obvious, forgettable formula tale of three warring brothers forced to deal with their feelings as they drive dad Arkin's car from Detroit to Florida. Set in 1963 and—guess what?—there are oldies on the soundtrack. Still, the sequence in which the boys debate the origin of, and words to, "Louie, Louie" is almost worth the price of admission.▼

Couple Takes a Wife, The (1972) **C-73m.** TVM D: Jerry Paris. Bill Bixby, Paula Prentiss, Valerie Perrine, Nanette Fabray, Robert Goulet, Myrna Loy, Larry Storch. Good cast works wonders with old-style situation: the Hamiltons (Bixby and Prentiss)

decide to take on "second wife," enabling Mrs. Hamilton to continue professional career. Written by Susan Silver. Above average.

Courage (1984) **C-90m.** BOMB D: Robert L. Rosen. Ronny Cox, Lois Chiles, Art Hindle, M. Emmet Walsh, Tim Maier, Lisa Sutton. Perfectly horrendous thriller about a trio of marathon runners taken prisoner by a citizen army in the New Mexico desert. Jog on. Also known as RAW COURAGE.▼

Courage (1986) **C-150m.** TVM D: Jeremy Kagan. Sophia Loren, Billy Dee Williams, Hector Elizondo, Val Avery, Ron Rifkin, Jose Perez, Dan Hedaya. Crackerjack drama about a real-life wife and mother who, heartbroken to discover her eldest son a drug addict, becomes an undercover operative for the Drug Enforcement Agency. Loren admirably dresses down to play a Queens, N.Y., housefrau for her gritty portrayal. E. Jack Neuman's solid screenplay is based on Michael Daly's 1984 *New York* Magazine piece, "Mother Courage." Above average.▼

Courage and the Passion, The (1978) **C-100m.** TVM D: John Llewellyn Moxey. Vince Edwards, Desi Arnaz, Jr., Don Meredith, Trisha Noble, Linda Foster, Robert Hooks, Monty Hall. Pilot about pilots who test jets and bring their personal problems to C.O. Edwards, who put this one together in hopes of having another hit series. Average.

Courage Mountain (1989-U.S.-French) **C-98m.** **½ D: Christopher Leitch. Juliette Caton, Charlie Sheen, Leslie Caron, Joanna Clarke, Nicola Stapleton, Jade Magri, Kathryn Ludlow, Jan Rubes, Yorgo Voyagis, Laura Betti, Urbano Barberini. Implausible though inoffensive updating of Johanna Spyri's *Heidi*, detailing what happens when the teenage girl is sent off to boarding school at the outset of WW1. Sheen is sorely miscast as Peter, her ever-loyal beau.▼

Courage of Black Beauty (1957) **C-77m.** ** D: Harold Schuster. John Crawford, Diane Brewster, J. Pat O'Malley, John Bryant. Wholesome programmer of Crawford and colt he is given.▼

Courage of Kavik, The Wolf Dog, The (1980) **C-100m.** TVM D: Peter Carter. Ronny Cox, John Ireland, Linda Sorenson, Andrew Ian McMillan, Chris Wiggins, John Candy. Uninspired, Canadian-made boy-and-his-sled-dog tale that won't do preteen viewers any harm. Average. Also known as KAVIK, THE WOLF DOG.▼

Courage of Lassie (1946) **C-92m.** **½ D: Fred Wilcox. Elizabeth Taylor, Frank Morgan, Tom Drake, Selena Royle, George Cleveland. Tasteful, folksy tale of Lassie used in WW2 as a killer dog, Taylor his mistress who reforms him into kindly animal once again.

Courageous Dr. Christian (1940) **67m.** ** D: Bernard Vorhaus. Jean Hersholt, Dorothy Lovett, Robert Baldwin, Tom Neal, Maude Eburne. The good doctor battles a town's indifference to its homeless and an epidemic that breaks out in shantytown. Typical entry in Hersholt's B-picture series.▼

Courageous Mr. Penn (1941-British) **79m.** ** D: Lance Comfort. Clifford Evans, Deborah Kerr, Dennis Arundell, Aubrey Mallalieu, D. J. Williams, O. B. Clarence. Repetition overwhelms this sometimes intelligent—but mostly dull—biography of Quaker William Penn. Highlighted are his trial for religious freedom and founding of the Pennsylvania colony. Original British title: PENN OF PENNSYLVANIA.▼

Court Jester, The (1956) **C-101m.** **** D: Norman Panama, Melvin Frank. Danny Kaye, Glynis Johns, Basil Rathbone, Angela Lansbury, Cecil Parker, Mildred Natwick, Robert Middleton, John Carradine. One of the best comedies ever made has Danny as phony jester who finds himself involved in romance, court intrigue, and a deadly joust. Delightfully complicated comic situations, superbly performed. And remember: the pellet with the poison's in the vessel with the pestle.▼

Court Martial (1955-British) **105m.** *** D: Anthony Asquith. David Niven, Margaret Leighton, Victor Maddern, Maurice Denham. Tense courtroom story of officer Niven accused of stealing military funds. The trial reveals provocations of grasping wife. A solid drama. Originally released as CARRINGTON, V.C.▼

Court-Martial of Billy Mitchell, The (1955) **C-100m.** *** D: Otto Preminger. Gary Cooper, Charles Bickford, Ralph Bellamy, Rod Steiger, Elizabeth Montgomery. Low-key drama about trial of military pioneer who in 1925 predicted Japanese attack on U.S. Steiger adds spark to slowly paced film as wily attorney; Montgomery made her movie debut here.▼

Courtney Affair, The (1947-British) **112m.** **½ D: Herbert Wilcox. Anna Neagle, Michael Wilding, Gladys Young, Coral Browne, Michael Medwin. Wealthy young man marries housemaid in this family saga that traces the years 1900-1945; amiable but soapy, this was a big hit in England. Original running time, 120m. Original title: THE COURTNEYS OF CURZON STREET.▼

Courtneys of Curzon Street, The SEE: **Courtney Affair, The**▼

Courtship of Andy Hardy, The (1942) **93m.** D: George B. Seitz. Lewis Stone, Mickey Rooney, Cecilia Parker, Fay Holden, Ann Rutherford, Sara Haden, Donna Reed, William Lundigan, Frieda Inescort. SEE: **Andy Hardy** series.

Courtship of Eddie's Father, The (1963) **C-117m.** *** D: Vincente Minnelli. Glenn Ford, Ronny Howard, Shirley Jones, Stella Stevens, Dina Merrill, Roberta Sherwood, Jerry Van Dyke. Cute family comedy with Howard trying to find wife for widower father Ford. Look sharp for Lee Meriwether as Glenn's assistant at work. Later a TV series.

Cousin, Cousine (1975-French) **C-95m.** *** D: Jean-Charles Tacchella. Marie-Christine Barrault, Victor Lanoux, Marie-France Pisier, Guy Marchand, Ginette Garcin, Sybil Maas. Barrault and Lanoux, married to others, become cousins by marriage and decide to go way beyond the kissing stage. Mild, easy-to-take comedy that became a surprise box-office sensation in U.S.—where it was later remade as COUSINS.▼

Cousins, The (1959-French) **112m.** ***½ D: Claude Chabrol. Jean-Claude Brialy, Gerard Blain, Juliette Mayniel, Claude Cerval, Genevieve Cluny. Complex, depressing, ultimately haunting tale of youthful disillusion, with decadent city boy Brialy and provincial cousin Blain competing for the affection of beauty Mayniel. Superbly directed by Chabrol.▼

Cousins (1989) **C-110m.** *** D: Joel Schumacher. Ted Danson, Isabella Rossellini, Sean Young, William Petersen, Lloyd Bridges, Norma Aleandro, George Coe, Keith Coogan, Gina de Angelis. A big family wedding sets the stage for romantic intrigues within two colorful clans. Highly enjoyable Americanization of the French hit COUSIN, COUSINE with charming performances by Danson, as a free-spirited soul, and Rossellini, as the married cousin to whom he's attracted.▼

Covenant (1985) **C-78m.** TVM D: Walter Grauman. Jane Badler, Kevin Conroy, Charles Frank, Whitney Kershaw, Bradford Dillman, Jose Ferrer, Michelle Phillips, Barry Morse. Earnestly played nonsense about wealthy (and marginally incestuous) Nob Hill family that lives with many dark secrets; for instance, its fortune was built on Nazi gold. Pilot to proposed series. Average.

Covenant with Death, A (1967) **C-97m.** ** D: Lamont Johnson. George Maharis, Laura Devon, Katy Jurado, Earl Holliman, Sidney Blackmer, Gene Hackman. Unjustly convicted murderer kills his hangman and is then found to be innocent of the first offense; what now? Interesting idea is handled too melodramatically to be effective.

Covered Wagon, The (1923) **98m.** **½ D: James Cruze. J. Warren Kerrigan, Lois Wilson, Alan Hale, Ernest Torrence. Slow-paced silent forerunner of Western epics, following a wagon train as it combats Indians and the elements; beautifully photographed, but rather tame today.▼

Cover Girl (1944) **C-107m.** *** D: Charles Vidor. Rita Hayworth, Gene Kelly, Lee Bowman, Phil Silvers, Jinx Falkenburg, Eve Arden, Otto Kruger, Anita Colby. Incredibly clichéd plot is overcome by loveliness of Rita, fine Jerome Kern-Ira Gershwin musical score (including "Long Ago and Far Away,") and especially Kelly's solo numbers. Silvers adds some laughs, but Eve Arden steals the film as Kruger's wise-cracking assistant.▼

Cover Girl and the Cop, The (1989) **C-100m. TVM** D: Neal Israel. Julia Duffy, Dinah Manoff, John Karlen, Parker Stevenson, Jonathan Frakes, Robert Picardo, Blair Underwood, David Carradine. Comedy whodunit unites a ditzy model and a streetwise policewoman who find themselves pursued by a killer. Average.

Cover Girls (1977) **C-78m. TVM** D: Jerry London. Jayne Kennedy, Cornelia Sharpe, Don Galloway, Vince Edwards, Sean Garrison, George Lazenby, Don Johnson. Two fashion models combine photo assignments with work as espionage agents. It's *Charlie's Angels* minus one, a rock-bottom rip-off that proves, as Red Skelton once said, "Imitation isn't the sincerest form of flattery, it's plagiarism." Below average.

Cover Me Babe (1970) **C-89m.** BOMB D: Noel Black. Robert Forster, Sondra Locke, Susanne Benton, Robert S. Fields, Ken Kercheval, Sam Waterston, Regis Toomey. Depressingly bad movie about student filmmaker who lets nothing stand in the way of gaining a contract.

Covert Action (1978-Italian) **C-95m.** *½ D: Romolo Guerrieri. David Janssen, Arthur Kennedy, Corinne Clery, Maurizio Merli, Stefano Satta Flores. Janssen is former CIA man whose life is imperiled after he writes a book about his experiences. Filmed in Greece.

Cow and I (1961-French) **98m.** *** D: Henri Verneuil. Fernandel, Rene Havard, Albert Remy, Bernard Musson. Country-style humor bolstered by Fernandel as peasant escaped from German farm prison, assisted by loyal cow.

Coward of the County (1981) **C-100m. TVM** D: Dick Lowry. Kenny Rogers, Frederic Lehne, Largo Woodruff, Mariclare Costello, Ana Alicia, Noble Willingham. Clyde Ware's script, based on the lyrics of one of Rogers's hit songs, has Kenny as a small-town Southern preacher whose nephew is deemed a coward because he refuses to join the Army during WW2. Average.▼

Cowboy (1958) **C-92m.** *** D: Delmer Daves. Glenn Ford, Jack Lemmon, Anna Kashfi, Brian Donlevy, Dick York. Intelligent, atmospheric Western based on Frank Harris' reminiscences as a tenderfoot.

Lemmon is Harris, with Ford as his stern boss on eventful cattle roundup.

Cowboy (1983) **C-100m. TVM** D: Jerry Jameson. James Brolin, Annie Potts, Ted Danson, Randy Quaid, George DiCenzo, Michael Pataki. Disillusioned teacher forsakes the big-city ghetto for a cattle ranch in this by-the-numbers contemporary Western. Average.

Cowboy and the Ballerina, The (1984) **C-100m. TVM** D: Jerry Jameson. Lee Majors, Leslie Wing, Christopher Lloyd, James Booth, Antoinette Bower, George de la Pena, Steven Ford, Anjelica Huston, John McIntire. With the tell-all title, one can hardly say more . . . except that it isn't very good! Below average.▼

Cowboy and the Lady, The (1938) **91m.** **½ D: H. C. Potter. Gary Cooper, Merle Oberon, Patsy Kelly, Walter Brennan, Fuzzy Knight, Harry Davenport. Aristocratic Oberon falls in love with rodeo star Cooper in mild comedy uplifted by stars.

Cowboy From Brooklyn, The (1938) **80m.** **½ D: Lloyd Bacon. Dick Powell, Pat O'Brien, Priscilla Lane, Dick Foran, Ann Sheridan, Johnnie Davis, Ronald Reagan, Emma Dunn. Powell can only get radio job if he proves he's an authentic cowhand. Silly musicomedy includes songs "Ride Tenderfoot Ride," title tune. Remade as TWO GUYS FROM TEXAS.

Cowboys, The (1972) **C-128m.** ** D: Mark Rydell. John Wayne, Roscoe Lee Browne, Bruce Dern, Colleen Dewhurst, Slim Pickens, Lonny Chapman, A Martinez, Robert Carradine, Allyn Ann McLerie. Well-produced but sluggish Western about aging rancher forced to take 11 youngsters with him on cattle drive; disappointing film whose message seems to be that violent revenge is good. Carradine's first film. Later a short-lived TV series.▼

Cow Country (1953) **82m.** ** D: Lesley Selander, Curtis Bishop. Edmond O'Brien, Helen Westcott, Peggie Castle, Raymond Hatton. Earnest Western of 1880s Texas, with debt-ridden ranchers overcoming all.

Cracker Factory, The (1979) **C-100m. TVM** D: Burt Brinckeroff. Natalie Wood, Perry King, Peter Haskell, Vivian Blaine, Juliet Mills, Marian Mercer, Shelley Long. Wood shines as a suicidal suburban housewife who's in and out of the asylum throughout this Richard Shapiro adaptation of Joyce Rebeta-Burditt's novel. Above average.▼

Crackers (1984) **C-92m.** ** D: Louis Malle. Donald Sutherland, Jack Warden, Sean Penn, Wallace Shawn, Trinidad Silva, Larry Riley, Christine Baranski, Charlaine Woodard, Irwin Corey. Remake of the classic caper comedy BIG DEAL ON MADONNA STREET, set in San Francisco, strives for the offbeat (in its motley collection of misfit characters) but forgets to go for the laughs, too.▼

Cracking Up (1983) **C-83m.** ****** D: Jerry Lewis. Jerry Who Else?, Herb Edelman, Zane Buzby; guest stars, Dick Butkus, Milton Berle, Sammy Davis, Jr., Foster Brooks, Buddy Lester. Jerry tries his hand at a sketch movie, playing various characters in assorted vignettes loosely tied to suicidal klutz seeking help from shrink Edelman. There are funny moments (some of them mildly risque), but Jerry refuses to believe that Less Is More. Originally titled SMORGASBORD; shelved after test engagements.▼

Crack in the Mirror (1960) **97m.** ******* D: Richard Fleischer. Orson Welles, Juliette Greco, Bradford Dillman, Alexander Knox. Welles, Greco, and Dillman enact contrasting dual roles in intertwining love triangles set in contemporary Paris, involving murder, courtroom trial, and illicit love; novelty eventually wears thin, marring Grade-A effort.

✓ **Crack in the World** (1965) **C-96m.** ****½** D: Andrew Marton. Dana Andrews, Janette Scott, Kieron Moore, Alexander Knox, Peter Damon. Believable sci-fi about scientists trying to harness earth's inner energy but almost causing destruction of the world; realistic special effects.

Crack-Up (1946) **93m.** ******* D: Irving Reis. Pat O'Brien, Claire Trevor, Herbert Marshall, Wallace Ford. Exciting Hitchcocklike thriller of art critic O'Brien who finds himself in hot water when he starts to investigate an art-forgery racket.

Cradle Will Fall, The (1983) **C-100m.** **TVM** D: John Llewellyn Moxey. Lauren Hutton, Ben Murphy, James Farentino, Charlita Bauer, Carolyn Ann Clark, Joe Ponazecki, Elvera Roussel, Peter Simon, Jerry ver Dorn. Gimmicky suspense drama involving lawyer Hutton, her doctor/lover Murphy, sinister gynecologist Farentino and various members of the long-running daytime soap *The Guiding Light*, with only so-so results. Based on the novel by Mary Higgins Clark. Average.▼

Craig's Wife (1936) **75m.** ******* D: Dorothy Arzner. Rosalind Russell, John Boles, Billie Burke, Jane Darwell, Dorothy Wilson, Alma Kruger, Thomas Mitchell. Russell scored first big success as domineering wife who thinks more of material objects than of her husband. Based on George Kelly play, remade as HARRIET CRAIG.▼

✓ **Cranes Are Flying, The** (1959-Russian) **94m.** *****½** D: Mikhail Kalatozov. Tatyana Samoilova, Alexei Batalov, Vasily Merkuryev, A. Shvorin. Lilting love story set in WW2 Russia. Doctor's son (Batalov) leaves his sweetheart (Samoilova) to join the army. She is seduced by his cousin, marries him, and from subsequent tragedies tries to rebuild her life.▼

Crash, The (1932) **58m.** ****** D: William Dieterle. George Brent, Ruth Chatterton,

Paul Cavanagh, Barbara Leonard, Henry Kolker, Lois Wilson. Chatterton is fine in this otherwise plodding drama about a self-centered, materialistic woman whose stock-broker husband (Brent) loses his fortune, and who wants to run off with Australian Cavanagh.

Crash! (1977) **C-85m.** ***½** D: Charles Band. Jose Ferrer, Sue Lyon, John Ericson, Leslie Parrish, John Carradine. Strange, unbelievable mixture of occult and car chase. Jealous invalid-husband Ferrer tries to kill wife Lyon, who uses demonic device to cause mayhem on her own.

Crash (1978) **C-100m.** **TVM** D: Barry Shear. William Shatner, Adrienne Barbeau, Eddie Albert, Brooke Bundy, Christopher Connelly, Lorraine Gary, George Maharis, Artie Shaw, Sharon Gless. Another plane goes down with a flight manifesto of TV familiars. This time the tale is based on fact (and covered similarly in the TV movie THE GHOST OF FLIGHT 401): dramatizing the jetliner disaster in the Florida Everglades in Dec. '72 and the rescue of 73 passengers. Average.

Crash Course (1988) **C-100m.** **TVM** D: Oz Scott. Jackée (Harry), Brian Bloom, Harvey Korman, Alyssa Milano, Charlie Robinson, Rob Stone, Tina Yothers, Dick Butkus, Ray Walston. Mildly amusing teenage romp involving a summer school Driver's Ed. class. Average.

Crash Dive (1943) **C-105m.** ****½** D: Archie Mayo. Tyrone Power, Anne Baxter, Dana Andrews, James Gleason, Dame May Whitty, Henry (Harry) Morgan. Submarine battleground just backdrop for love story; Power and Andrews both love young Baxter. Oscar-winner for special effects, film's main asset.

Crashing Las Vegas (1956) **62m.** D: Jean Yarbrough. Leo Gorcey, Huntz Hall, Jimmy Murphy, David Condon. SEE: **Bowery Boys** series.

Crash Landing (1958) **76m.** ***½** D: Fred F. Sears. Gary Merrill, Nancy Davis (Reagan), Irene Hervey, Roger Smith. Insipid revelations of passengers aboard plane facing possible crash landing into the ocean.

Crash of Silence (1953-British) **93m.** ******* D: Alexander Mackendrick. Phyllis Calvert, Jack Hawkins, Terence Morgan, Mandy Miller. Honest drama of young deaf girl (Miller) and her mother's dilemma: keep her at home or send her to a special school. Sensibly acted. Originally titled MANDY.

Crashout (1955) **90m.** ****½** D: Lewis R. Foster. William Bendix, Arthur Kennedy, Luther Adler, William Talman. Low-budget but interesting story of prison break headed by Bendix. Kennedy as humane gang member is fine.▼

Crater Lake Monster, The (1977) **C-74m.** BOMB D: William R. Stromberg. Richard Cardella, Glenn Roberts, Mark Siegel,

Kacey Cobb. Amateurish tale of carnivorous critter from Crater Lake (not the National Park) is climaxed by fine stop-motion animation of the menace, a plesiosaur. But it's too little and too late, making film of interest to genre buffs only. Even they will have a long wait for the fun.▼

Crawling Eye, The (1958-British) 85m. **½ D: Quentin Lawrence. Forrest Tucker, Laurence Payne, Janet Munro, Jennifer Jayne, Warren Mitchell. OK, if predictable, tale (adapted by Jimmy Sangster from British TV series *The Trollenberg Terror*) about cosmic cloud unleashing title creature on mountaintop. Hampered by low-grade special effects.▼

Crawling Hand, The (1963) 89m. *½ D: Herbert L. Strock. Peter Breck, Kent Taylor, Rod Lauren, Arline Judge, Richard Arlen, Allison Hayes, Alan Hale. Astronaut's disembodied hand instigates rash of stranglings in this amateurish rehash of THE BEAST WITH FIVE FINGERS. Good for a few (unintended) laughs, anyway.▼

Crawling Monster, The SEE: **Creeping Terror, The**▼

Crawlspace (1971) C-74m. TVM D: John Newland. Arthur Kennedy, Teresa Wright, Tom Harper, Eugene Roche, Dan Morgan. Retired couple living in New England take in odd young man to fill need for son; he takes up residence in house's cellar. Definitely offbeat combination of character study and psychological thriller. Adapted by Ernest Kinoy from Herbert Lieberman's novel. Above average.

Crawlspace (1986) C-82m. BOMB D: David Schmoeller. Klaus Kinski, Talia Balsam, Sally Brown, Barbara Whinnery. Shameless imitation of classic PEEPING TOM, as Kinski spies on young women from his apartment's hidden crawlspace area and then kills them, all as the legacy of his father having been a Nazi war criminal. ▼

Craze (1973-British) C-96m. *½ D: Freddie Francis. Jack Palance, Diana Dors, Julie Ege, Trevor Howard, Suzy Kendall, Michael Jayston, Dame Edith Evans. More laughs than horror as antique dealer Palance makes human sacrifices to African idol. Hugh Griffith and Howard wisely kid the material. Original British title: THE INFERNAL IDOL.▼

Crazies, The SEE: **Code Name: Trixie**▼

Crazy Desire (1964-Italian) 108m. ***½ D: Luciano Salce. Ugo Tognazzi, Catherine Spaak, Gianni Garko, Beatrice Altariba. Disarming fluff of Tognazzi enamoured of young funseekers, and Spaak in particular.

Crazy House (1943) 80m. *** D: Edward F. Cline. Ole Olsen, Chic Johnson, Martha O'Driscoll, Patric Knowles, Cass Daley, Percy Kilbride. Olsen & Johnson take over film studio to make epic in frantic musicomedy with guests galore: Basil Rathbone, Count Basie, Allan Jones, Edgar Kennedy, Billy Gilbert, Andy Devine, etc.

Crazy House (1975-British) C-90m. ** D: Peter Sykes. Ray Milland, Frankie Howerd, Rosalie Crutchley, Kenneth Griffith, Elizabeth McClennan. Horror spoof that fails as comedy but succeeds with the chills. Overage entertainer Howerd finds he's related to Milland's greedy family, which is being killed off for an inheritance. U.S. title: NIGHT OF THE LAUGHING DEAD.▼

Crazy Jack and the Boy SEE: **Silence**▼

Crazy Joe (1974-Italian-U.S.) C-100m. **½ D: Carlo Lizzani. Peter Boyle, Rip Torn, Fred Williamson, Eli Wallach, Paula Prentiss, Luther Adler. Crime drama based on the bloody career of New York racketeer Crazy Joe Gallo is tolerable, due to its cast. Henry Winkler can be seen as a mustached hoodlum.

Crazylegs (1953) 87m. *½ D: Francis D. Lyon. Elroy Hirsch, Lloyd Nolan, Joan Vohs, Louise Lorimer. Inconclusive fiction based on the football escapades of Elroy Crazylegs Hirsch with gridiron star playing himself.

Crazy Mama (1975) C-82m. *** D: Jonathan Demme. Cloris Leachman, Stuart Whitman, Ann Sothern, Jim Backus, Donny Most, Linda Purl, Bryan Englund, Merie Earle, Sally Kirkland. Joyous, unrelentingly kitschy celebration of '50s America (opportunity, rock 'n' roll, and the road), made during Demme's exploitation days, follows three generations of women (Sothern, Leachman, Purl) and the men they pick up, on an absurdist crime spree from California to old family homestead in Arkansas. Rough in places but overall a gem.▼

Crazy Moon (1986-Canadian) C-87m. *** D: Allan Eastman. Kiefer Sutherland, Peter Spence, Vanessa Vaughan, Ken Pogue, Eve Napier. Occasionally cliched, but still warm, winning little story of wealthy, alienated teen Sutherland and his romance with bright, independent—and deaf—salesgirl Vaughan. Originally titled HUGGERS.▼

Crazy Over Horses (1951) 65m. D: William Beaudine. Huntz Hall, Leo Gorcey, David Gorcey, William Benedict, Bernard Gorcey. SEE: **Bowery Boys** series.

Crazy People (1990) C-90m. ** D: Tony Bill. Dudley Moore, Daryl Hannah, Paul Reiser, Mercedes Ruehl, J.T. Walsh, Bill Smitrovich, Alan North, David Paymer, Dick Cusack, Ben Hammer. Stressed-out ad exec Moore devises a series of brutally honest (and very funny) advertisements, which prompt his partner to place him in a mental institution. Then, to everyone's amazement, the ads are a sensational success. Though the mock ads are quite funny, the film is bland and even dull. Everlikable Dudley chalks up a few extra points.▼

Crazy Quilt (1966) **75m.** *** D: John Korty. Ina Mela, Tom Rosqui, David Winters, Ellen Frye. Korty's first feature is almost a home movie, featuring arresting images but diffuse, whimsical (till it turns pompous in the final reels) story of girl's various romantic liaisons while her exterminator husband sits around and mopes. Filmed silent, with awkward postsynched dialogue; relies heavily upon Burgess Meredith's narration, unusual score by Peter Schickele.

Crazy Times (1981) **C-98m. TVM** D: Lee Philips. Michael Paré, David Caruso, Ray Liotta, Talia Balsam, Annette McCarthy, John Aprea, Sandra Giles, Bert Remsen, Amy Madigan. Nostalgic but rather charmless look at three teenage buddies who share the good times of 1955. Average.

Crazy World of Julius Vrooder, The (1974) **C-89m.** **½ D: Arthur Hiller. Timothy Bottoms, Barbara Hershey, George Marshall, Albert Salmi, Lawrence Pressman. Nobody likes this offbeat comedy of a confused Vietnam vet who acts insane to cope with a crazy world, but it has a certain charm. Veteran director Marshall returned to acting here shortly before his death.

Crazy World of Laurel and Hardy, The (1967) **83m.** **½ Narrated by Garry Moore. Unlike most L&H compilations, this one uses talkie material as well as silent footage; some good routines are fragmented, with too much lumped together, but Stan and Ollie survive nicely.

Created to Kill SEE: **Embryo**▼

Creation of the Humanoids (1962) **C-75m.** BOMB D: Wesley E. Barry. Don Megowan, Frances McCann, Erica Elliott, Don Doolittle. Years after an atomic war, human beings are about to be outnumbered by their subservient robots; anti-robot Megowan discovers a plot to replace people with robot duplicates. Andy Warhol loved this slow, stagy cheapie.▼

Creator (1985) **C-107m.** ** D: Ivan Passer. Peter O'Toole, Mariel Hemingway, Vincent Spano, Virginia Madsen, David Ogden Stiers, John Dehner, Jeff Corey. O'Toole once again plays a Lovable Eccentric (which he does to perfection), this time a university-based scientist who's trying to revive his long-dead wife and who serves as mentor for impressionable student Spano. Amiable but aimless adaptation of Jeremy Leven's novel, redeemed only by O'Toole's magnetism.▼

Creature (1985) **C-97m.** ** D: William Malone. Stan Ivar, Wendy Schaal, Lyman Ward, Robert Jaffe, Diane Salinger, Annette McCarthy, Klaus Kinski. Imitation of ALIEN is set on Saturn's moon Titan where nondescript cast is investigating life

forms discovered (fatally) by a previous mission. Guest star Kinski is funny, whether spouting gibberish or munching nonchalantly on a sandwich during otherwise tense scenes. Originally titled TITAN FIND. ▼

Creature From Black Lake (1976) **C-97m.** ** D: Joy Houck, Jr. Jack Elam, Dub Taylor, Dennis Fimple, John David Carson, Bill Thurman, Catherine McClenny. Two young men venture into Louisiana swamps, only to run smack into Bigfoot; not-bad low-budgeter follows familiar formula, with typically amusing performance by Elam. McClenny is Morgan Fairchild's sister.▼

Creature From the Black Lagoon (1954) **79m.** *** D: Jack Arnold. Richard Carlson, Julia (Julie) Adams, Richard Denning, Antonio Moreno, Whit Bissell, Nestor Paiva, Ricou Browning. Archetypal 50s monster movie has been copied so often that the edge is gone, but story of Amazon expedition encountering deadly Gill-Man is still entertaining, with juicy atmosphere, luminous underwater photography. Originally in 3-D, but just as good without it. Two sequels: REVENGE OF THE CREATURE and THE CREATURE WALKS AMONG US.▼

Creature From the Haunted Sea (1961) **74m.** *½ D: Roger Corman. Antony Carbone, Betsy Jones-Moreland, Edward Wain, E. R. Alvarez, Robert Bean. Gangster tries to cover crime wave by creating panic with story of sea monster . . . then real sea monster shows up. Roger Corman quickie comedy is not as freakish as his others. Costar Wain is actually Oscar-winning screenwriter Robert Towne. Remake of NAKED PARADISE.▼

Creature of Destruction (1968) **C-80m.** BOMB D: Larry Buchanan. Les Tremayne, Pat Delaney, Aron Kincaid, Scotty McKay. Mysterious hypnotist Dr. Basso (Tremayne) and pretty assistant predict murders at a country club; murders are committed by title monster, which rises from a lake. Excruciating, with hilariously illogical musical interludes. Remake of THE SHE CREATURE.

Creature of the Walking Dead (1965) **74m.** *½ D: Frederic Corte (Fernando Cortes). Rock Madison, Ann Wells, George Todd, Willard Gross, Bruno Ve Sota. Mad scientist brings his equally mad grandfather back to life, with Frankenstein-ish results, in this impoverished horror quickie. Made in Mexico in 1960, then "expanded" with new footage for American release by Jerry Warren.▼

Creatures SEE: **From Beyond the Grave**▼
Creatures of the Prehistoric Planet SEE: **Vampire Men of the Lost Planet**▼
Creatures the World Forgot (1971-British) **C-94m.** *½ D: Don Chaffey. Julie Ege, Tony Bonner, Robert John, Sue Wilson,

Rosalie Crutchley. Hammer Films gives us another prehistoric movie with no dinosaurs and little credibility.▼

Creature Walks Among Us, The (1956) **78m.** ** D: John Sherwood. Jeff Morrow, Rex Reason, Leigh Snowden, Gregg Palmer. Sequel to REVENGE OF THE CREATURE has Gill-man caged by humans, subjected to plastic surgery in hopes of humanizing him, returning to the ocean after a few mild tantrums.

Creature Wasn't Nice, The (1981) **C-88m.** *½ D: Bruce Kimmel. Cindy Williams, Bruce Kimmel, Leslie Nielsen, Gerrit Graham, Patrick Macnee, Ron Kurowski. Silly monster-loose-in-spaceship parody: Nielsen is the firm but obtuse commander, Macnee the loony scientist, Williams the only woman on board, etc. Believe it or not, this is a musical (one song is titled "I Want to Eat Your Face"). Also known as SPACESHIP.▼

Creature with the Atom Brain (1955) **70m.** ** D: Edward L. Cahn. Richard Denning, Angela Stevens, Gregory Gaye, Tristram Coffin. Passable hokum: scientist revives the dead via high-charged brain tissue, and these robots are used by gangster seeking revenge.

Creature with the Blue Hand (1970-German) **C-74m.** ** D: Alfred Vohrer. Klaus Kinski, Diana Kerner, Carl Lang, Ilse Page, Harold Leopold. OK Edgar Wallace story has innocent man accused of murders perpetrated by title creature.

Creeper, The (1948) **64m.** ** D: Jean Yarbrough. Onslow Stevens, Eduardo Ciannelli, June Vincent, Ralph Morgan, Janis Wilson. Stevens is mad doctor whose serum turns man into catlike killer.

Creeper, The (1978) SEE: **Rituals**▼

Creeping Flesh, The (1973-British) **C-94m.** *** D: Freddie Francis. Peter Cushing, Christopher Lee, Lorna Heilbron, George Benson. Well-intentioned, old-fashioned monster film on reincarnation of ancient evil spirit. Numerous subplots add to the fun.▼

Creeping Terror, The (1964) **75m.** BOMB D: Art J. Nelson. Vic Savage, Shannon O'Neill, William Thourlby, Louise Lawson, Robin James. Awful horror movie, poor on every conceivable (and inconceivable) level. Monster aptly described as a giant carpet absorbs humans into its body. When it's destroyed, another takes its place. Badly shot, with voice-over narration to make up for the loss of the soundtrack, on Lake Tahoe. Also known as THE CRAWLING MONSTER.▼

Creeping Unknown, The (1956-British) **78m.** *** D: Val Guest. Brian Donlevy, Margia Dean, Jack Warner, Richard Wordsworth. A spaceship returns to earth with only one man left on board; infested by an alien entity, he gradually transforms into a hideous monster. Tense, imaginative, adult; well acted by all concerned. Based on hit BBC-TV serial by Nigel Kneale. Also known under original British title, THE QUATERMASS EXPERIMENT. Followed by three sequels, beginning with ENEMY FROM SPACE.▼

Creepshow (1982) **C-120m.** ** D: George Romero. Hal Holbrook, Adrienne Barbeau, Fritz Weaver, Leslie Nielsen, Carrie Nye, E. G. Marshall, Viveca Lindfors, Ed Harris, Ted Danson, Gaylen Ross. Romero nicely captures the look of a comic book in this homage to 1950s E. C. Comics, but Stephen King's five "fantastic tales" of revenge and just desserts are transparent and heavy-handed (King himself stars in the second episode, as an ill-fated rube). The finale has hundreds of cockroaches bursting through the stomach of a man with an insect phobia (Marshall). If that's your cup of tea, tune in. Followed by CREEPSHOW 2.▼

Creepshow 2 (1987) **C-89m.** *½ D: Michael Gornick. Lois Chiles, George Kennedy, Dorothy Lamour, Tom Savini, Domenick John, Frank S. Salsedo, Holt McCallany, David Holbrook, Page Hannah. George A. Romero scripted this trio of Stephen King short stories, but their combined reputations can't lift this cheap-looking movie out of the muck. As in the much slicker CREEPSHOW, all the stories are juvenile and heavy-handed (a wooden Indian comes to life, a hitchhiker run over by a motorist lives on to terrorize her, etc.). King appears briefly as a truck driver.▼

Crescendo (1972-British) **C-83m.** *½ D: Alan Gibson. Stefanie Powers, James Olson, Margaretta Scott, Jane Lapotaire, Joss Ackland. Tiresome chiller has grad student Powers traveling to France for some research on a dead composer, becoming involved with his crazy family.

Crest of the Wave (1954-British) **90m.** **½ D: John Boulting, Roy Boulting. Gene Kelly, John Justin, Bernard Lee, Jeff Richards. Static account of navy officer Kelly joining British research group to supervise demolition experiments.

Cries and Whispers (1972-Swedish) **C-106m.** *** D: Ingmar Bergman. Harriet Andersson, Liv Ullmann, Ingrid Thulin, Kari Sylwan, Erland Josephson, George Arlin, Henning Moritzen. Beautifully photographed and acted drama about lives of a dying woman, her sisters and a servant girl was tremendous critical success, but may be too talky for some. Cinematographer Sven Nykvist won an Oscar.▼

Cries in the Night SEE: **Funeral Home**▼

Crime Against Joe (1956) **69m.** ** D: Lee Sholem. John Bromfield, Julie London, Henry Calvin, Patricia Blake. Standard find-the-actual-murderer fare.

Crime and Passion (1976) **C-92m.** *½ D:

[235]

Ivan Passer. Omar Sharif, Karen Black, Joseph Bottoms, Bernhard Wicki. Bizarre comedy-thriller set in Austrian Alps. Sharif is international financier who persuades secretary-mistress Black to wed industrialist Wicki for his money, then finds that they are both marked for death by the husband.▼

Crime and Punishment (1935) 88m. **½ D: Josef von Sternberg. Edward Arnold, Peter Lorre, Marian Marsh, Tala Birell, Elisabeth Risdon. Fascinating Hollywoodization of Dostoyevsky's novel about man haunted by murder he committed. Low-budget but full of inventive ideas by von Sternberg.

Crime and Punishment (1958-French) 108m. *** D: Georges Lampin. Jean Gabin, Marina Vlady, Ulla Jacobsson, Bernard Blier. Perceptive updating of Dostoyevsky novel set in Paris. Retitled: THE MOST DANGEROUS SIN.

Crime & Punishment, USA (1959) 78m. **½ D: Denis Sanders. George Hamilton, Mary Murphy, Frank Silvera, Marian Seldes, John Harding, Wayne Heffley. Trim, updated version of Dostoyevsky novel has Hamilton (film debut) a law student who becomes involved in robbery and murder.

Crime Boss (1972-Italian) C-93m. *½ D: Albert DeMartino. Telly Savalas, Antonio Sabato, Paola Tedesca. Crime czar Savalas takes on a young protege and lives to regret it. One of Telly's numerous Mafioso roles before sticking a lollipop in his mouth and a gold badge of the NYPD on his chest. Plodding and written to formula.

Crime Busters (1980-Italian) C-98m. *½ D: E. B. Clucher (Enzo Barboni). Terence Hill, Bud Spencer, Laura Gemser, Luciana Catenacci. Filmed in Miami, this cop-movie parody is a hair better than other Hill-Spencer efforts, but not a patch on the Trinity films; chief novelty derives from watching them go through their paces in a contemporary American setting. Bad dubbing doesn't help. Filmed in 1976 as TWO SUPERCOPS. Originally 115m.▼

Crime By Night (1944) 72m. **½ D: William Clemens. Jane Wyman, Jerome Cowan, Faye Emerson, Eleanor Parker, Creighton Hale. Good little murder mystery with detective Cowan unwittingly walking into murder case.

Crime Club (1973) C-73m. TVM D: David Lowell Rich. Lloyd Bridges, Victor Buono, Paul Burke, William Devane, David Hedison, Cloris Leachman, Belinda Montgomery, Barbara Rush, Martin Sheen, Richard Hatch. Forgettable mystery with Bridges using resources of government-related super-crime-organization to determine cause of the death of a friend's son. Average.

Crime Club (1975) C-78m. TVM D: Jeannot Szwarc. Scott Thomas, Eugene Roche, Robert Lansing, Biff McGuire, Barbara Rhoades, Michael Cristofer. Association of professionals who solve murders are faced with a loser who craves public recognition by confessing to series of icepick murders of young women. This one has "busted pilot" plastered all over it. Average.

Crime Doctor In 1943 Columbia Pictures took Max Marcin's successful radio show CRIME DOCTOR and initiated a film series of that name with Warner Baxter in the lead. The first film set the premise of an amnesia victim named Dr. Ordway becoming the country's leading criminal psychologist, later discovering that he was a gang leader himself before a blow clouded his memory. This idea served as the basis for ten fairly respectable, enjoyable mysteries, all starring Baxter as Ordway. Most of the films followed a standard whodunit formula, but were well acted and directed (by such people as William Castle and George Archainbaud), with competent players rounded up from Columbia's contract list. The films moved along briskly, most of them running barely over an hour. CRIME DOCTOR (1943) is interesting for its depiction of the origin of the character; CRIME DOCTOR'S GAMBLE takes him to Europe for an above-average murder hunt; and SHADOWS IN THE NIGHT has the distinction of refined George Zucco as an arch-fiend. Unremarkable but interesting, the Crime Doctor films held their own among the many mystery series of the day.

Crime Doctor (1943) 66m. D: Michael Gordon. Warner Baxter, Margaret Lindsay, John Litel, Ray Collins, Harold Huber, Don Costello, Leon Ames.

Crime Doctor's Courage, The (1945) 70m. D: George Sherman. Warner Baxter, Hillary Brooke, Jerome Cowan, Robert Scott, Lloyd Corrigan, Emory Parnell, Stephen Crane.

Crime Doctor's Diary (1949) 61m. D: Seymour Friedman. Warner Baxter, Lois Maxwell, Adele Jergens, Robert Armstrong.

Crime Doctor's Gamble, The (1947) 66m. D: William Castle. Warner Baxter, Micheline Cheirel, Roger Dann, Steven Geray, Marcel Journet.

Crime Doctor's Manhunt (1946) 61m. D: William Castle. Warner Baxter, Ellen Drew, William Frawley, Frank Sully, Claire Carleton, Bernard Nedell.

Crime Doctor's Strangest Case (1943) 68m. D: Eugene J. Forde. Warner Baxter, Lynn Merrick, Reginald Denny, Barton MacLane, Jerome Cowan, Rose Hobart, Gloria Dickson.

Crime Doctor's Warning, The (1945) 69m. D: William Castle. Warner Baxter, John Litel, Dusty Anderson, Coulter Irwin, Miles Mander, John Abbott.

Crime Does Not Pay (1962-French) 159m. **½ D: Gerard Oury. Pierre Brasseur, Gino Cervi, Danielle Darrieux, Gabriele Ferzetti, Annie Girardot, Michele Morgan,

Richard Todd. Interesting gimmick for three-part film—would-be-wife-killer goes to cinema showing trio of stories on murder: "The Spider's Web," "The Fenyrou Case," and "The Mask." Retitled: GENTLE ART OF MURDER.

Crime in the Streets (1956) 91m. **½ D: Donald Siegel. James Whitmore, John Cassavetes, Sal Mineo, Mark Rydell, Virginia Gregg, Denise Alexander, Will Kuluva, Peter Votrian, Malcolm Atterbury. Incisive if overlong drama of angry, alienated teen Cassavetes, who conspires to commit murder. Good performances by Cassavetes, Mineo and future director Rydell as his cronies, and Whitmore as an idealistic social worker. Adapted by Reginald Rose from his 1955 teleplay; Cassavetes, Rydell, and Kuluva repeat their TV performances.

Crime of Dr. Crespi, The (1935) 63m. ** D: John H. Auer. Erich von Stroheim, Dwight Frye, Paul Guilfoyle, Harriett Russell, John Bohn. Von Stroheim gets even with man who loves his girl by planning unspeakable torture for him. Low-grade chiller.▼

Crime of Dr. Hallet, The (1938) 68m. *½ D: S. Sylvan Simon. Ralph Bellamy, William Gargan, Josephine Hutchinson, Barbara Read, John King. Tedious story of jungle doctor working on fever cure who assumes assistant's identity when the latter dies in experiment. Remade as STRANGE CONQUEST.

Crime of Innocence (1985) C-100m. TVM D: Michael Miller. Andy Griffith, Diane Ladd, Ralph Waite, Shawnee Smith, Steve Inwood, Tammy Lauren, Jordan Charney. A fanatical judge tosses a couple of joy-riding teenage girls into the pokey to teach them and their parents a lesson and creates a nightmare for all involved. Average.

Crime of Passion (1957) 84m. **½ D: Gerd Oswald. Barbara Stanwyck, Sterling Hayden, Raymond Burr, Fay Wray, Virginia Grey. Stanwyck is rough and tough as grasping wife who'll do anything to forward hubby's career.

Crimes and Misdemeanors (1989) C-104m. ***½ D: Woody Allen. Caroline Aaron, Alan Alda, Woody Allen, Claire Bloom, Mia Farrow, Joanna Gleason, Anjelica Huston, Martin Landau, Jenny Nichols, Jerry Orbach, Sam Waterston. Film's title indicates the themes of two separate stories, which are neatly tied up in the final scene. Landau plays a married man who is desperate to cut off an adulterous relationship in this somberly tragic tale. Allen is an unhappy documentary filmmaker who's wooing attractive producer Farrow while making a film about her insufferably self-centered boss Alda, in a hilariously bittersweet story. Arguably Woody's most ambitious film, playing heavy drama against often uproarious com-

edy, and certainly one of his most passionately debated; a one-of-a-kind effort that only he could pull off. Daryl Hannah has an unbilled cameo as one of Alda's chippies.▼

Crime School (1938) 86m. **½ D: Lewis Seiler. Dead End Kids (Billy Halop, Bobby Jordan, Huntz Hall, Leo Gorcey, Bernard Punsley, Gabriel Dell), Humphrey Bogart, Gale Page. Bogart sets out to improve a reform school, but meets his match in the Dead End Kids. OK reworking of THE MAYOR OF HELL, weakened by the Kids' disreputable personalities and Bogart's unlikely casting as a do-gooder. Story rehashed again next year as HELL'S KITCHEN.

Crimes at the Dark House (1940-British) 69m. *** D: George King. Tod Slaughter, Sylvia Marriott, Hilary Eaves, Geoffrey Wardell, Hay Petrie. Slaughter is at his lip-smacking best in this adaptation of Wilkie Collins' *The Woman in White*. Old-fashioned melodrama without a whiff of condescension is not to all tastes, but for those with a liking for this rip-snorting stuff, this is one of the best. Typical line: "I'll feed your entrails to the pigs!"▼

Crimes of Dr. Mabuse, The SEE: **Testament of Dr. Mabuse, The**▼

Crimes of Passion (1984) C-101m. ** D: Ken Russell. Kathleen Turner, Anthony Perkins, John Laughlin, Annie Potts, Bruce Davison. Laughlin, trapped in a stale marriage, takes up with mysterious Turner—fashion designer by day, hooker by night. Watchable mess is given the subject matter, less out of control than other Russell movies. Turner actually gives a performance; Perkins amuses in one of his standard nutso roles. One of the two homevideo versions has several minutes of kinky footage originally seen only in Europe. ▼

Crimes of Stephen Hawke, The (1936-British) **½ D: George King. Tod Slaughter, Marjorie Taylor, D. J. Williams, Eric Portman, Ben Soutten. Florid melodrama with Slaughter deliciously ripe as kindly moneylender Hawke, secretly the murderous fiend known as Spine Breaker, for good reasons. Stodgy direction, in this case, is fully appropriate. Lower the rating if you can't stand barnstorming thrillers. Alternate title: STRANGLER'S MORGUE.▼

Crimes of the Heart (1986) C-105m. **½ D: Bruce Beresford. Diane Keaton, Jessica Lange, Sissy Spacek, Sam Shepard, Tess Harper, David Carpenter, Hurd Hatfield. Three Southern sisters, who are equally off-center, share their various woes and idiosyncrasies (along with pent-up jealousies and resentments) during a fateful reunion. Superior performances can't make a really good film out of Beth Henley's Pulitzer Prize-winning play, even though Henley wrote the screenplay herself.▼

Crime Wave (1954) **74m.** ** D: Andre de Toth. Sterling Hayden, Gene Nelson, Phyllis Kirk, Charles Bronson, Ted de Corsia, Richard Benjamin. Low-keyed telling of ex-con Nelson's attempt to go straight, despite insistence of crooks that he help on bank robbery; Hayden is toothpick-chewing cop.

Crimewave (1985) **C-83m.** **½ D: Sam Raimi. Louise Lasser, Paul L. Smith, Brion James, Sheree J. Wilson, Bruce Campbell, Reed Birney, Edward R. Pressman, Julius Harris. After a successful debut with EVIL DEAD, director Raimi pays tribute to slapstick comedy with this weird, almost incoherent crime story set in Detroit. Smith and James are well cast as grotesque goons on a robbery/killing spree. This exercise in style was cowritten by Raimi's pals, Joel and Ethan Coen, who made BLOOD SIMPLE and RAISING ARIZONA. Watch for producer Ed Pressman as a henpecked husband.▼

Crime Without Passion (1934) **72m.** *** D: Ben Hecht, Charles MacArthur. Claude Rains, Margo, Whitney Bourne, Stanley Ridges, Esther Dale, Leslie Adams. Bizarre, fascinating melodrama of callous lawyer Rains, jealous of Margo's escorts. Helen Hayes (Mrs. Charles MacArthur) and Fanny Brice have brief cameos in hotel lobby scene. And Slavko Vorkapich contributed that incredible opening montage.

Crime Zone (1988) **C-93m.** **½ D: Luis Llosa. David Carradine, Peter Nelson, Sherilyn Fenn, Michael Shaner, Orlando Sacha, Don Manor. Moody sci-fi set in repressive, stratified future society. Upper-caste Carradine recruits young lovers to commit crimes for a surprising reason. Profane, satiric, well-crafted low-budgeter, but loses its way before the finish. Shot in Peru!▼

Criminal Code, The (1931) **95m.** **½ D: Howard Hawks. Walter Huston, Phillips Holmes, Constance Cummings, Mary Doran, Boris Karloff, De Witt Jennings, John Sheehan. Warden Huston—tough but essentially fair—faces a dilemma when his daughter falls in love with prisoner Holmes. Creaky in parts, lively in others, but cast and director make this a must for buffs; Karloff footage here shows up in Peter Bogdanovich's TARGETS. Remade as PENITENTIARY in 1938 and CONVICTED in 1950.▼

Criminal Court (1946) **63m.** ** D: Robert Wise. Tom Conway, Martha O'Driscoll, Robert Armstrong, Addison Richards, June Clayworth, Pat Gleason, Steve Brodie, Robert Warwick. Disappointingly routine programmer finds O'Driscoll charged with murder of blackmailer Armstrong, defended by wily attorney Conway who is the real killer (by accident). Confusing mystery tale is one of Wise's minor early films.▼

Criminal Law (1989) **C-117m.** *½ D: Martin Campbell. Gary Oldman, Kevin Bacon, Karen Young, Joe Don Baker, Tess Harper, Elizabeth Sheppard. Weak suspense film, done in by an unsatisfying script and unbelievable story. Slick attorney Oldman (playing an American—and quite well) matches wits with wealthy psychopath Bacon in tale of serial murders in Boston. Unnecessarily pretentious, unintentionally funny, and, unfortunately, filmed nowhere near Boston.▼

Criminal Lawyer (1951) **74m.** *½ D: Seymour Friedman. Pat O'Brien, Jane Wyatt, Carl Benton Reid, Mary Castle. Alcoholic attorney O'Brien sobers up to defend friend saddled with homicide charge.

Criminal Life of Archibaldo de la Cruz, The (1955-Mexican) **91m.** ** D: Luis Bunuel. Ernesto Alonso, Miroslava Stern, Rita Macedo, Ariadna Walter, Rodolfo Landa, Andres Palma. Very minor psychological drama from Bunuel. As a boy, Archibaldo witnesses his governess' death and is fascinated by what he feels; as a man, he's obsessed with murder and dying. Much too talky; it sounds far more interesting than it plays.▼

Crimson Altar, The SEE: **Crimson Cult, The**

Crimson Blade, The (1963-British) **C-82m.** **½ D: John Gilling. Lionel Jeffries, Oliver Reed, Jack Hedley, June Thorburn, Duncan Lamont. OK swashbuckler features romance between two young people on opposite side of Cromwell's struggle for power in 17th century; good-looking Hammer production. Originally titled THE SCARLET BLADE.

Crimson Canary, The (1945) **64m.** **½ D: John Hoffman. Noah Beery Jr., Lois Collier, Danny Morton, John Litel, Claudia Drake, Steven Geray. Offbeat murder mystery with nightclub musicians the suspects, nicely done.

Crimson Cult, The (1968-British) **C-87m.** ** D: Vernon Sewell. Mark Eden, Virginia Wetherell, Christopher Lee, Boris Karloff, Michael Gough, Barbara Steele. Lackluster script and pacing major flaws in standard witchcraft thriller featuring aging Karloff as expert on black magic. Steele (in green makeup) as 300-year-old witch. Original British titles: CURSE OF THE CRIMSON ALTAR and THE CRIMSON ALTAR.

Crimson Ghost, The SEE: **Cyclotrode "X"**▼

Crimson Kimono, The (1959) **82m.** ** D: Samuel Fuller. Victoria Shaw, Glenn Corbett, James Shigeta, Anna Lee, Paul Dubov, Jaclynne Greene. Two L.A. detectives investigate a stripper's murder in this offbeat little film; more interesting for Sam Fuller buffs than general viewers, who may find story and treatment too low-key and meandering.

Crimson Pirate, The (1952) **C-104m.**
***½ D: Robert Siodmak. Burt Lancaster,
Nick Cravat, Eva Bartok, Torin Thatcher,
Christopher Lee. Lancaster and Cravat
swashbuckle their way across the Mediterranean in one of the great genre classics of
all time. Cult film offers loads of thrills
and laughs to both children and adults.▼
Crimson Romance (1934) **72m.** *** D:
David Howard. Ben Lyon, Sari Maritza,
Erich von Stroheim, Hardie Albright, James
Bush, William Bakewell, Herman Bing,
Bodil Rosing, Vince Barnett, Oscar Apfel,
Jason Robards, Sr., Brandon Hurst. Provocative drama of impetuous American
test pilot Lyon, whose German-born pal
returns to the Fatherland during WWI—
before America's involvement in the fra-
cas. He joins his friend in the German
military, and finds himself at odds with a
sadistic commandant (who else but von
Stroheim?).▼
Cripple Creek (1952) **C-78m.** **½ D:
Ray Nazarro. George Montgomery, Karin
Booth, Jerome Courtland, Richard Egan.
Government agents Montgomery and Court-
land track mining crooks by joining
gang in this OK Western.
Crisis (1950) **95m.** **½ D: Richard Brooks.
Cary Grant, Jose Ferrer, Paula Raymond,
Signe Hasso, Ramon Novarro, Antonio
Moreno, Leon Ames, Gilbert Roland. Melo-
drama of American doctor (Grant) held in
South American country to treat ailing
dictator (Ferrer); intriguing but slow.
Brooks's first film as director. Also shown
in computer-colored version.
Crisis at Central High (1981) **C-125m.**
TVM D: Lamont Johnson. Joanne Wood-
ward, Charles Durning, Henderson For-
sythe, William Russ, Calvin Levels. Dramat-
ic recreation of events surrounding the
1957 integration of Central High School in
Little Rock, Arkansas, with a stunning,
Emmy-nominated performance by Woodward as teacher Elizabeth Huckaby, who
found herself at the center of the tumult.
Richard Levinson and William Link based
their teleplay on Huckaby's journal. Above
average.▼
Crisis in Mid-air (1979) **C-100m.** TVM
D: Walter Grauman. George Peppard, Karen
Grassle, Desi Arnaz, Jr., Don Murray,
Martin Milner, Fabian Forte, Michael Constantine, Greg Morris. Overage air traffic
controller is accused of responsibility for a
midair collision. Timely topic unfortunately
run off the TV disaster drama assembly
line. Average.
Crisis in Sun Valley (1978) **C-100m.** TVM
D: Paul Stanley. Dale Robinette, Taylor
Lacher, Bo Hopkins, Tracy Brooks Swope,
John McIntire, Deborah Winters. Predictable adventure tale dealing with a stalwart
sheriff and his deputy in a sleepy ski resort
who first emerged in THE DEADLY TRI-

ANGLE. Middling action feature actually
combines two individual pilot films in hopes
of sparking some interest in a series to
have been called *Stedman*. Average.
Criss Cross (1949) **87m.** *** D: Robert
Siodmak. Burt Lancaster, Yvonne De Carlo,
Dan Duryea, Stephen McNally. Muted robbery yarn sparked by Lancaster and Duryea
each trying to do the other in. Anthony
(Tony) Curtis's film debut.▼
Critical Condition (1987) **C-107m.** BOMB
D: Michael Apted. Richard Pryor, Rachel
Ticotin, Ruben Blades, Joe Mantegna, Bob
Dishy, Sylvia Miles, Joe Dallesandro,
Randall "Tex" Cobb, Garrett Morris. Pryor
is a con artist who takes charge at a prison
hospital, with predictable results. He's in
good form, but the material just isn't there;
its semi-serious and sentimental threads
don't work at all, and the comedy is pretty
anemic.▼
Critical List, The (1978) **C-200m.** TVM
D: Lou Antonio. Lloyd Bridges, Melinda
Dillon, Buddy Ebsen, Barbara Parkins,
Robert Wagner, Ken Howard, Louis Gossett, Jr., Richard Basehart. Two pilot films
combined in search of a series for Bridges
as a hospital director whose tribulations
appeared to have been recycled from Dr.
Gillespie's files of yore. Bridges is earnest
and properly concerned, but movie is overlong. Average.
Critic's Choice (1963) **C-100m.** **½ D:
Don Weis. Bob Hope, Lucille Ball, Marilyn Maxwell, Rip Torn, Jessie Royce Landis, Marie Windsor, John Dehner. An in-
joke Broadway play diluted for movie
audience consumption. Lucy as a novice
playwright outshines Hope who plays her
drama critic hubby. Film emerges as tired,
predictable comedy, with best moments
contributed by supporting players.
Critters (1986) **C-86m.** BOMB D: Stephen Herek. Dee Wallace Stone, M. Emmet Walsh, Billy Green Bush, Scott Grimes,
Nadine Van Der Velde, Terrence Mann.
Sagebrushlike aliens with crummy ortho-
dontal work invade rural Kansas farmhouse, with the outerspace clone of an S&M
rock star in hot pursuit. Yet another GREM-
LINS ripoff is not as good as it sounds,
which pretty well says it all. Followed by a
sequel.▼
Critters 2: The Main Course (1988)
C-87m. BOMB D: Mick Garris. Scott
Grimes, Liane Curtis, Don Opper, Barry
Corbin, Tom Hodges, Sam Anderson, Lind-
say Parker, Herta Ware, Terrence Mann,
Roxanne Kernohan. More of the same . . .
this "main course" is better left uneaten.▼
"Crocodile" Dundee (1986-Australian)
C-98m. *** D: Peter Faiman. Paul Hogan,
Linda Kozlowski, John Meillon, David
Gulpilil, Mark Blum, Michael Lombard,
Irving Metzman. Amiable, laid-back Aussie
comedy (that became an enormous world-

wide hit) about an adventurer who shows a pretty American reporter around the bush country, then accompanies her to the equally strange terrain of New York City. Irresistibly simple and old-fashioned, with a sweetness that's rare in modern comedies. Hogan, making his movie debut, also cowrote the screenplay (reportedly inspired by TARZAN'S NEW YORK ADVENTURE). For American release quotation marks were added around CROCODILE—lest anyone think it was about a reptile! Followed by a sequel.▼

"Crocodile" Dundee II (1988-U.S.-Australian) **C-110m.** **½ D: John Cornell. Paul Hogan, Linda Kozlowski, John Meillon, Ernie Dingo, Hechter Ubarry, Juan Fernandez, Charles Dutton, Kenneth Welsh. Pleasant followup to the runaway hit reverses the original by opening in N.Y.C. and winding up in the bush country of Australia. This time the unflappable tracker runs afoul of an international drug kingpin. It's paced in such a leisurely way that after a while you wish they'd get on with it—especially when all suspense about the outcome is eliminated. Hogan's charisma carries this picture almost singlehandedly. Written by Hogan and his son Brett.▼

Cromwell (1970-British) **C-145m.** ** D: Ken Hughes. Richard Harris, Alec Guinness, Robert Morley, Dorothy Tutin, Frank Finlay, Timothy Dalton, Patrick Wymark, Patrick Magee. Turgid historical epic has everything money can buy, but no human feeling underneath. Harris is coldly unsympathetic as 17th-century Briton determined to rid England of tyrannical rule; one feels more sympathy for King Charles I (Guinness), which is not the idea. Great battle scenes, great cinematography and costume design, hampered by Harris and Oscar-winning amateurish music score.▼

Crook, The (1971-French) **C-120m.** *** D: Claude Lelouch. Jean-Louis Trintignant, Daniele Delorme, Charles Denner, Christine Lelouch. Very funny pop-art caper film of incurable thief, his successes and failures.

Crooked Hearts, The (1972) **C-74m.** TVM D: Jay Sandrich. Rosalind Russell, Douglas Fairbanks Jr., Ross Martin, Maureen O'Sullivan, Kent Smith, Michael Murphy, Penny Marshall, Dick Van Patten. Members of lonely hearts club stalked by mysterious con-artist supposedly involved with disappearances of wealthy widows. Good cast, good comedy. Russell's last film; script by A. J. Russell from Colin Watson's *Miss Lonelyhearts 4122*. Above average.

Crooked Road, The (1965-British) **86m.** **½ D: Don Chaffey. Robert Ryan, Stewart Granger, Nadia Gray, Marius Goring, George Coulouris. OK battle of wits be-

tween dictator Granger and newspaperman Ryan, who's got the goods on him.

Crooked Way, The (1949) **90m.** ** D: Robert Florey. John Payne, Sonny Tufts, Ellen Drew, Rhys Williams. Military hero Payne recovers from shellshock to be confronted by criminal past and his old gang seeking to eliminate him.

Crooked Web, The (1955) **77m.** *½ D: Nathan Juran. Frank Lovejoy, Mari Blanchard, Richard Denning, Richard Emory. Ponderous unspinning of government officer's ensnaring prime suspect to return to Germany, scene of the crime.

Crooks and Coronets (1969-British) **C-106m.** ** D: Jim O'Connolly. Telly Savalas, Edith Evans, Warren Oates, Cesar Romero, Harry H. Corbett. Crooks Savalas and Oates are hired to rob Evans' estate, but can't bring themselves to do it once they get to know her. Amiable but ordinary heist comedy. Also known as SOPHIE'S PLACE.▼

Crooks Anonymous (1962-British) **87m.** *½ D: Ken Annakin. Leslie Phillips, Stanley Baxter, Wilfrid Hyde-White, James Robertson Justice, Julie Christie. Cornball comedy with thief Phillips enrolling in Alcoholics Anonymous-type organization for hoods. Christie, in her film debut, plays Babette La Vern, a stripper.

Crosby Case, The (1934) **60m.** **½ D: Edwin L. Marin. Wynne Gibson, Alan Dinehart, Onslow Stevens, Warren Hymer, Skeets Gallagher. Former lovers have to clear themselves when police suspect them of murder. Good whodunit with interesting plot point—a hint of abortion.

Cross and the Switchblade, The (1972) **C-106m.** *½ D: Don Murray. Pat Boone, Erik Estrada, Jackie Giroux, Jo-Ann Robinson. Crusading minister Boone winds up in New York street-gang rumbles. Uneven, uninteresting, though sincere attempt at uplifting, moralistic filmmaking.▼

Cross Creek (1983) **C-122m.** *** D: Martin Ritt. Mary Steenburgen, Rip Torn, Peter Coyote, Dana Hill, Alfre Woodard, Joanna Miles, Ike Eisenmann, Cary Guffey. Leisurely paced but rewarding drama of writer Marjorie Kinnan Rawlings's endeavor to "find herself" by moving to remote Florida backwoods home—and dealing with the simple people around her. Wonderful performances and regional flavor—though Dalene Young's script takes more than a few liberties with the facts. Steenburgen's real-life husband Malcolm McDowell has cameo as famed editor Maxwell Perkins.▼

Crosscurrent (1971) **C-96m.** TVM D: Jerry Thorpe. Robert Hooks, Jeremy Slate, Robert Wagner, Carol Lynley, Simon Oakland, Jose Ferrer, John Randolph. Two cops in San Francisco go after the murderer of a cable car passenger. Good cast helps OK thriller. Also known as CABLE

CAR MURDER. Originally broadcast at 73m. Average.

Crossed Swords (1954-Italian) **C-86m.** *½ D: Milton Krims. Errol Flynn, Gina Lollobrigida, Cesare Danova, Nadia Gray. Unsuccessful attempt to recapture flavor of swashbucklers of 1930s; set in 16th-century Italy with Flynn out to save Gina and her father's kingdom.

Crossed Swords (1978) **C-113m.** ** D: Richard Fleischer. Mark Lester, Oliver Reed, Raquel Welch, Ernest Borgnine, George C. Scott, Rex Harrison, Charlton Heston. Lester is too old for his dual role in well-acted but flat version of Mark Twain's *The Prince and the Pauper.* Lavish sets, costumes, and Jack Cardiff's photography will suffer on TV. Also known as THE PRINCE AND THE PAUPER.▼

Crossfire (1947) **86m.** ***½ D: Edward Dmytryk. Robert Young, Robert Mitchum, Robert Ryan, Gloria Grahame, Paul Kelly, Richard Benedict, Sam Levene, Jacqueline White, Steve Brodie, Lex Barker. Engrossing film of insane ex-soldier leading city police in murderous chase. Anti-Semitic issue handled with taste, intelligence. Script by John Paxton, from Richard Brooks' novel *The Brick Foxhole.*▼

Crossfire (1975) **C-78m. TVM** D: William Hale. James Farentino, John Saxon, Patrick O'Neal, Pamela Franklin, Ramon Bieri, Herb Edelman, Lou Frizzell. Undercover cop Farentino infiltrates underworld to learn source of laundered money being used to corrupt city officials. Fairly conventional and muscular. Average.

Crossing Delancey (1988) **C-97m.** *** D: Joan Micklin Silver. Amy Irving, Reizl Bozyk, Peter Riegert, Jeroen Krabbe, Sylvia Miles, Suzzy Roche, George Martin, John Bedford Lloyd, Claudia Silver, Rosemary Harris, Amy Wright. Charming comedy about a self-reliant young N.Y.C. woman whose Jewish grandmother arranges for her to meet an eligible bachelor through the services of a marriage broker . . . much to her chagrin. Amusing, sometimes wistful look at the clash between old-world traditions and our modern way of life. Adapted by Susan Sandler, from her play.▼

Crossing the Mob (1988) **C-100m. TVM** D: Steven Hilliard Stern. Jason Bateman, Maura Tierney, Patti D'Arbanville, Louis Giambalvo, Robert Costanzo, Frank Stallone. Streetwise teen Bateman discovers working for mobster Stallone is his ticket out of his dead-end neighborhood, but finds he must also grapple with unexpected fatherhood. Average.

Cross My Heart (1946) **83m.** ** D: John Berry. Betty Hutton, Sonny Tufts, Rhys Williams, Ruth Donnelly, Iris Adrian, Michael Chekhov. Compulsive liar Hutton claims she's a killer so scrupulously honest lawyer husband Tufts can clear her and earn a reputation. Almost as bad as the comedy it's a remake of, TRUE CONFESSION.

Cross My Heart (1987) **C-90m.** ** D: Armyan Bernstein. Martin Short, Annette O'Toole, Paul Reiser, Joanna Kerns. The story of a date where everything goes wrong, mainly because both the man and the woman refuse to act natural and be themselves. Winning costars bring out the truthful observations in this comic script (by director Bernstein and Gail Parent), but it's just too slight, and too slow, to sustain itself.▼

Cross of Fire (1989) **C-200m. TVM** D: Paul Wendkos. John Heard, Mel Harris, David Morse, Lloyd Bridges, Kim Hunter, George Dzundza, Donald Moffat, Keith Szarabajka. Searing docudrama by writer Robert Crais about the rise and fall of Klan Grand Dragon and political bigwig D. C. Stephenson in 1920s Indiana. Originally shown in two parts. Above average.

Cross of Iron (1977-British-West German) **C-119m.** *** D: Sam Peckinpah. James Coburn, Maximilian Schell, James Mason, David Warner, Senta Berger, Klaus Lowitsch. Peckinpah's only war film, told from the viewpoint of Germans on the Russian front in 1943, is compelling without being particularly distinguished. The standard Peckinpah action scenes are excitingly done. European version runs 130m. Sequel: BREAKTHROUGH.▼

Cross of Lorraine, The (1943) **90m.** ***½ D: Tay Garnett. Jean-Pierre Aumont, Gene Kelly, Cedric Hardwicke, Richard Whorf, Joseph Calleia, Peter Lorre, Hume Cronyn. High-grade propaganda of WW2 POW camp with hero Aumont rousing defeated Kelly to battle; Whorf is dedicated doctor, Lorre a despicable Nazi, Cronyn a fickle informer.

Crossover Dreams (1985) **C-86m.** ** D: Leon Ichaso. Ruben Blades, Shawn Elliot, Tom Signorelli, Elizabeth Pena, Frank Robles, Joel Diamond. Salsa performer Blades starts shafting his pals, enjoying the good life, when he thinks his upcoming album is going to make him a smash with mainstream audiences . . . then the record flops. Standard backstage drama offers nothing beyond novel ethnicity, though Blades has real presence on camera.▼

Crossroads (1942) **84m.** *** D: Jack Conway. William Powell, Hedy Lamarr, Claire Trevor, Basil Rathbone, Margaret Wycherly, Felix Bressart, Sig Ruman. Smooth tale of French diplomat Powell victimized by heartless Rathbone, who capitalizes on Powell's having been an amnesiac.

Crossroads (1986) **C-96m.** **½ D: Walter Hill. Ralph Macchio, Joe Seneca, Jami Gertz, Joe Morton, Robert Judd, Harry Carey, Jr. Cocky young musician tracks down legendary bluesman in a Harlem hospital and agrees to bring him back to his Mississippi home in return for some long-lost songs. Promising idea turns into contrived formula film (with undeveloped subplot about the old-timer having sold his soul to the devil). Gets a shot in the arm from Ry Cooder's music score and Seneca's flavorful performance as the cranky old bluesman.▼

Crosstrap (1961-British) **62m.** *½ D: Robert Hartford-Davis. Laurence Payne, Jill Adams, Gary Cockrell, Zena Marshall. Juvenile thriller involving rival gangs of jewel thieves and murder.

Crosswinds (1951) **C-93m.** ** D: Lewis R. Foster. John Payne, Rhonda Fleming, Forrest Tucker, Robert Lowery. Payne tries to retrieve cargo of gold from plane that crashed in New Guinea, encountering head-hunters, crooks, and gorgeous Fleming.

Crowd, The (1928) **104m.** **** D: King Vidor. Eleanor Boardman, James Murray, Bert Roach, Daniel G. Tomlinson, Dell Henderson, Lucy Beaumont. Classic drama about a few happy and many not-so-happy days in the marriage of hard-luck couple. One of the greatest silent films; holds up beautifully.▼

Crowded Sky, The (1960) **C-105m.** **½ D: Joseph Pevney. Dana Andrews, Rhonda Fleming, Efrem Zimbalist, Jr., John Kerr, Troy Donahue, Patsy Kelly. Slick film focusing on emotional problems aboard jet liner and navy plane bound for fateful collision; superficial but diverting.

Crowd Roars, The (1932) **85m.** **½ D: Howard Hawks. James Cagney, Joan Blondell, Ann Dvorak, Eric Linden, Guy Kibbee, Frank McHugh. Exciting racing-driver tale with Cagney in typically cocky role, familiar plot devices, but well done by Warner Bros. stock company. Remade as INDIANAPOLIS SPEEDWAY.

Crowd Roars, The (1938) **92m.** **½ D: Richard Thorpe. Robert Taylor, Edward Arnold, Frank Morgan, Maureen O'Sullivan, William Gargan, Lionel Stander, Jane Wyman. Tippling Morgan gets son Taylor into fighting game, and involved with underworld chief Arnold in well-handled yarn. Remade as KILLER McCOY.

Crowhaven Farm (1970) **C-72m. TVM** D: Walter Grauman. Hope Lange, Paul Burke, Lloyd Bochner, John Carradine, Cindy Eilbacher. Middle-aged couple (Lange and Burke) inherit farm, move in to patch up strained marriage, eventually adopt child who becomes focal point in supernatural flashback story. Surprise ending in generally well-handled thriller. Written by John McGreevey. Above average.

Crucible, The (1957-French-East German) **140m.***** D: Raymond Rouleau. Simone Signoret, Yves Montand, Mylene Demongeot, Jean Debucourt, Raymond Rouleau.

If anything, Jean-Paul Sartre's version improves upon Arthur Miller parable of Salem witch trials in 17th-century New England; Signoret is outstanding. Also known as THE WITCHES OF SALEM.

Crucible of Horror (1971-British) **C-91m.** ** D: Viktors Ritelis. Michael Gough, Sharon Gurney, Yvonne Mitchell. Murdered man returns to haunt the living. Nothing new here.▼

Crucified Lovers, The (1954-Japanese) **100m.** ***½ D: Kenji Mizoguchi. Kazuo Hasegawa, Kyoko Kagawa, Yoko Minamida, Eitaro Shindo, Sakae Ozawa. Timid scrollmaker Hasegawa loves his master's wife (Kagawa), with tragic results. Superior performances, stunning direction; originally a marionette play written in 1715. Better known by its original Japanese title, CHIKAMATSU MONOGATARI.▼

Cruel Sea, The (1953-British) **121m.** ***½ D: Charles Frend. Jack Hawkins, Donald Sinden, Denholm Elliott, Stanley Baker, John Stratton, Virginia McKenna, Alec McCowen. Well-conceived documentary-style account of British warship during WW2 and its crew. Original British running time 126m.▼

Cruel Swamp SEE: **Swamp Women**▼

Cruel Tower, The (1956) **79m.** **½ D: Lew Landers. John Ericson, Mari Blanchard, Charles McGraw, Steve Brodie, Peter Whitney, Alan Hale Jr. Friendship, loyalty, jealousy, and fighting among a crew of highriggers; standard stuff, pretty well done.

Cruise into Terror (1978) **C-100m. TVM** D: Bruce Kessler. Dirk Benedict, Frank Converse, John Forsythe, Lynda Day George, Christopher George, Ray Milland, Hugh O'Brian, Stella Stevens. Shipboard terror involving an ancient sarcophagus and some evildoers among the all-star roster. Below average.▼

Cruising (1980) **C-106m.** *½ D: William Friedkin. Al Pacino, Paul Sorvino, Karen Allen, Richard Cox, Don Scardino, voice of James Sutorius. Cop Pacino goes underground to ferret out bloody killer of homosexuals in this distasteful, badly scripted film. Gay world presented as sick, degrading, and ritualistic. Filmed on authentic N.Y.C. locations.▼

Crusades, The (1935) **123m.** *** D: Cecil B. DeMille. Loretta Young, Henry Wilcoxon, Ian Keith, Katherine DeMille, C. Aubrey Smith. Love, action, and orgies galore in typical DeMille medieval spectacle that's good for fun, with Young a glamorous heroine.

Crusoe (1988) **C-91m.** *** D: Caleb Deschanel. Aidan Quinn, Ade Sapara, Warren Clark, Hepburn Grahame, Jimmy Nail, Tim Spall, Michael Higgins, Shane Rimmer. Solid version of the oft-filmed Defoe classic, with Quinn cast as the title character, a slave trader who's shipwrecked on a deserted isle, where he must deal with loneliness, isolation, survival; most intriguing of all is his evolving relationship with black warrior Sapara. Strikingly photographed by Tom Pinter, mostly in the Seychelles. ▼

Cry-Baby (1990) **C-85m.** **½ D: John Waters. Johnny Depp, Amy Locane, Susan Tyrrell, Polly Bergen, Iggy Pop, Ricki Lake, Traci Lords, Kim McGuire, Troy Donahue, Mink Stole, Joe Dallesandro, Joey Heatherton, David Nelson, Patricia Hearst, Willem Dafoe. Baltimore, 1954, and good-girl Locane is torn between her pristine roots and kids in black leather—especially the Elvis type (Depp) who'd love her to mount his cycle. More polished than Waters' previous HAIRSPRAY, but not as well focused and with less significant (if that can possibly be the term) subject matter. Uneven and exhausting, though performed with gusto; a few set pieces really deliver. ▼

Cry Baby Killer, The (1958) **62m.** *½ D: Jus Addiss. Harry Lauter, Jack Nicholson, Carolyn Mitchell, Brett Halsey, Lynn Cartwright, Ed Nelson. Nicholson's film debut is a Roger Corman quickie about juvenile delinquent who panics when he thinks he's committed murder. A curio at best, with coscripter Leo Gordon and Corman himself in bit parts. TV print runs 60m.

Cry Blood, Apache (1970) **C-82m.** BOMB D: Jack Starrett. Jody McCrea, Dan Kemp, Marie Gahua, Robert Tessier, Joel McCrea. Boring Western about some sadistic cowboys who look like hippies and lust after gold. The elder McCrea is wasted. ▼

Cry Danger (1951) **79m.** *** D: Robert Parrish. Dick Powell, Rhonda Fleming, Richard Erdman, Regis Toomey, William Conrad. Effective revenge yarn; ex-con Powell hunts down those responsible for his prison term. ▼

✓ **Cry for Happy** (1961) **C-110m.** **½ D: George Marshall. Glenn Ford, Donald O'Connor, Miiko Taka, Myoshi Umeki. Poor man's TEAHOUSE OF THE AUGUST MOON, involving Navy photography team in Tokyo using a geisha house for their home.

Cry for Help, A (1975) **C-78m. TVM** D: Daryl Duke. Robert Culp, Elaine Heilveil, Ken Swofford, Julius Harris, Chuck McCann, Michael Lerner, Bruce Boxleitner, Gordon Jump. Cynical radio talk-show host Culp rebuffs a phone-caller threatening suicide, then suspects she may have been serious and frantically tries to locate her with the help of his listeners. Neat initial concept is frittered away in standard rescue drama. Average.

Cry for Help: The Tracey Thurman

Story, A (1989) **C-100m. TVM** D: Robert Markowitz. Nancy McKeon, Dale Midkiff, Graham Jarvis, Yvette Heyden, Philip Baker Hall, Bruce Weitz. A battered woman unsuccessfully seeks police protection from her abusive husband and suffers a near fatal attack in broad daylight while the cops watch. McKeon is quite good as the real-life woman whose plight led to the adoption of Connecticut's Thurman Law. Beth Miller's script provides a harrowing indictment. Above average.

Cry for Love, A (1980) **C-100m. TVM** D: Paul Wendkos. Susan Blakely, Powers Boothe, Gene Barry, Edie Adams, Lainie Kazan, Charles Siebert, Herb Edelman, Patricia Barry. Amphetamine addict and divorced alcoholic meet, fall in love, and try to save each other from self-destruction. Literate drama adapted by Renée Taylor and Joseph Bologna from Jill Schary Robinson's autobiographical best-seller, *Bedtime Story*. Above average. ▼

Cry for Me, Billy (1972) **C-93m.** ** D: William A. Graham. Cliff Potts, Xochitl, Harry Dean Stanton, Don Wilbanks. Drifter falls in love with Indian girl, with tragic consequences, in this violent Western. Its title (and alleged year of release) keeps changing, but the film doesn't get any better. Also known as FACE TO THE WIND, as well as COUNT YOUR BULLETS, APACHE MASSACRE, and THE LONG TOMORROW. ▼

Cry for the Strangers (1982) **C-100m.** **TVM** D: Peter Medak. Patrick Duffy, Cindy Pickett, Lawrence Pressman, Claire Malis, Brian Keith, Robin Ignacio, Jeff Corey, Taylor Lacher. Who's stalking the visitors to a scenic Northwest vacation seaport village? It won't be much of a secret to mystery devotees. Below average.

Cry Freedom (1987-British) **C-157m.** *** D: Richard Attenborough. Kevin Kline, Penelope Wilton, Denzel Washington, Kevin McNally, John Thaw, Timothy West, Juanita Waterman, John Hargreaves, Alec McCowen, Zakes Mokae, Ian Richardson. Director Attenborough once again proves his facility as a storyteller with this sweeping and compassionate film about South African activist Steve Biko (well played by Washington) and his friendship with crusading newspaper editor Donald Woods (Kline). Unfortunately second half of film, minus the Biko character, loses momentum as it spends too much time on Kline and his family's escape from South Africa, but cannily injects flashbacks of Biko to steer it back on course. Attacked in some circles for its "armchair liberalism," film nevertheless brings attention to a worthy subject in the context of good drama. Screenplay by John Briley. Expanded by 23m. to fill a two-part TV time slot. ▼

Cry from the Streets, A (1959-British)

[243]

99m. *** D: Lewis Gilbert. Max Bygraves, Barbara Murray, Colin Peterson, Dana Wilson. Kathleen Harrison. Poignant handling of story about homeless London children and social workers who attempt to rehabilitate them; plot is forgivably diffuse and episodic.

Cry Havoc (1943) **97m.** *** D: Richard Thorpe. Margaret Sullavan, Joan Blondell, Ann Sothern, Fay Bainter, Marsha Hunt, Ella Raines, Frances Gifford, Diana Lewis, Heather Angel, Connie Gilchrist. Female volunteers join some overworked American nurses on beleaguered island of Bataan during WW2. Reveals its stage origins and incorporates expected clichés, but also presents pretty honest picture of war. Robert Mitchum has a bit part as a dying soldier.

Cry in the Dark, A (1988-U.S.-Australian) **C-121m.** ***½ D: Fred Schepisi. Meryl Streep, Sam Neill, Bruce Myles, Charles Tingwell, Nick Tate, Neil Fitzpatrick, Maurie Fields, Lewis Fitz-gerald. Astonishing true story of Lindy Chamberlin, an Australian woman accused of murdering her baby, despite her claims that the child was carried off by a dingo (wild dog). Writer-director Schepisi tells his story with almost documentary-like reality, eloquently attacking the process of trial by rumor that made Chamberlin and her husband the most maligned couple in Australia. Streep and Neill are heartbreakingly good.▼

Cry in the Night (1956) **75m.** **½ D: Frank Tuttle. Edmond O'Brien, Brian Donlevy, Natalie Wood, Raymond Burr. Capable cast enhances this tale of deranged man kidnapping girl from lover, with suspenseful police hunt ensuing.

Cry in the Wilderness, A (1974) **C-78m. TVM** D: Gordon Hessler. George Kennedy, Joanna Pettet, Lee H. Montgomery, Collin Wilcox-Horne, Roy Poole, Liam Dunn. Bitten by a rabid skunk, farmer Kennedy chains himself inside his barn to protect his family from his future madness, and then discovers that a flood is coming. Kennedy manipulates audience's terror quotient, while Pettet, as his young, helpless wife, handles hysteria factor. Average.

✓ **Cry of Battle** (1963) **99m.** **½ D: Irving Lerner. Van Heflin, Rita Moreno, James MacArthur, Leopoldo Salcedo. Uneven actioner set in Philippines with MacArthur as son of wealthy businessman who joins partisan cause, finding romance and sense ✓ of maturity.▼

✓ **Cry of the Banshee** (1970-British) **C-87m.** **½ D: Gordon Hessler. Vincent Price, Elisabeth Bergner, Essy Persson, Hugh Griffith, Hilary Dwyer, Sally Geeson, Patrick Mower. Witch Oona (Bergner) summons servant of Satan to avenge nobleman

(Price)'s bloody reign of witch-hunting. Confusion sets in midway.▼

Cry of the City (1948) **95m.** **½ D: Robert Siodmak. Victor Mature, Richard Conte, Fred Clark, Shelley Winters, Betty Garde, Debra Paget, Hope Emerson. Rehash of MANHATTAN MELODRAMA about childhood pals, one who becomes a cop, the other a criminal—slick but predictable.

Cry of the Hunted (1953) **80m.** ** D: Joseph H. Lewis. Vittorio Gassman, Barry Sullivan, Polly Bergen, William Conrad. Unnoteworthy chase film involving escaped convict Gassman being sought by lawman Sullivan, with a few atmospheric sequences set in Louisiana marshland.

Cry of the Innocent (1980) **C-105m. TVM** D: Michael O'Herlihy. Rod Taylor, Joanna Pettet, Nigel Davenport, Cyril Cusack, Walter Gotell, Alexander Knox. Aging former Green Beret vows to find the reason for a plane crash that killed his family as they vacationed in Ireland in this original Frederick Forsyth suspenser scripted by Sidney Michaels. Above average.▼

Cry of the Penguins (1971-British) **C-101m.** ** D: Al Viola. John Hurt, Hayley Mills, Dudley Sutton, Tony Britton, Thorley Walters, Judy Campbell. Can a womanizing young biologist find true happiness and redemption among an Antarctic colony of penguins? Do you care? Similar to later NEVER CRY WOLF—except in interest. Famed documentary filmmaker Arne Sucksdorff shot the fascinating but horrifying scenes of life and death among a penguin colony; an uncredited Roy Boulting reportedly directed the scenes with Hayley Mills. Original British title: MR. FORBUSH AND THE PENGUINS.

Cry of the Werewolf (1944) **63m.** ** D: Henry Levin. Nina Foch, Stephen Crane, Osa Massen, Blanche Yurka, Fritz Leiber. Gypsy girl hears the cry when it's proved her mother was a werewolf; OK low-grade thriller.

Cry Panic (1974) **C-78m. TVM** D: James Goldstone. John Forsythe, Earl Holliman, Ralph Meeker, Anne Francis, Claudia McNeil, Norman Alden. Forsythe plays a salesman caught in a personal nightmare after he accidentally kills a drunk with his car, and the body has disappeared. Modest little suspense drama. Average.▼

Cry Rape (1972) **C-73m. TVM** D: Corey Allen. Andrea Marcovicci, Peter Coffield, Greg Mullavey, Joseph Sirola, James Luisi, Anthony Costello, Lesley Woods. Two stories in one: first, the problems, indignities, frustrations in reporting rape to authorities; then, standard cops-chasing-suspects fare. Uneven but well done. Average.

Crystal Ball, The (1943) **81m.** ** D: Elliott Nugent. Paulette Goddard, Ray

Milland, Virginia Field, Gladys George, William Bendix, Ernest Truex. Weak comedy of beauty-contest loser who becomes fortune-teller; good players left stranded by stale material.

Crystal Heart (1987) **C-102m.** ** D: Gil Bettman. Tawny Kitaen, Lee Curreri, Lloyd Bochner, Simon Andreu, May Heatherly, Marina Saura. Young man who must live his life like the "boy in a bubble," confined to a controlled environment, develops a relationship with a sexy rock singer with whom he's fallen in love long-distance. Mild, predictable outing with music video segments from Kitaen.▼

Cry Terror (1958) **96m.** *** D: Andrew L. Stone. James Mason, Rod Steiger, Inger Stevens, Neville Brand, Angie Dickinson, Jack Klugman. Tight pacing conceals implausibilities in caper of psychopath Steiger forcing Mason to aid him in master extortion plot, filmed on N.Y.C. locations. Stevens good as Mason's frightened but resourceful wife. Also shown in computer-colored version.

Cry, the Beloved Country (1951-British) **111m.** ***½ D: Zoltan Korda. Canada Lee, Charles Carson, Sidney Poitier, Geoffrey Keen, Reginald Ngcabo, Joyce Carey. Back country Black minister goes to city in search of his son, now a criminal. First film to deal with Apartheid Policy and wretched living conditions of blacks in South Africa. Alan Paton's book was also basis for stage and film musical LOST IN THE STARS. Some TV prints run 96m.

Cry Tough (1959) **83m.** ** D. Paul Stanley. John Saxon, Linda Cristal, Joseph Calleia, Arthur Batanides, Joe De Santis, Barbara Luna, Frank Puglia. Saxon emotes well as Puerto Rican ex-con tempted back into criminal life by environment and his old gang. Torrid Saxon-Cristal love scenes shot for foreign markets gave film initial publicity.

Cry Uncle! (1971) **C-87m.** **½ D: John G. Avildsen. Allen Garfield, Madeleine de la Roux, Devin Goldenberg, David Kirk, Sean Walsh, Nancy Salmon. Private detective gets involved with murder, sex and blackmail in spoof of questionable taste; frequently hilarious, however.▼

Cry Vengeance (1954) **83m.** **½ D: Mark Stevens. Mark Stevens, Martha Hyer, Skip Homeier, Joan Vohs. Stevens lives up to title as innocent ex-con seeking gangsters who sent him to prison.▼

Cry Wolf (1947) **83m.** ** D: Peter Godfrey. Barbara Stanwyck, Errol Flynn, Geraldine Brooks, Richard Baschart, Jerome Cowan. Static adventure-mystery of Stanwyck attempting to untangle family secrets at late husband's estate.

Cuba (1979) **C-121m.** *** D: Richard Lester. Sean Connery, Brooke Adams, Jack Weston, Hector Elizondo, Denholm Elliott, Chris Sarandon, Lonette McKee. Entertaining adventure film/love story has mercenary Connery renewing an old affair with factory manager Adams, set against the fall of Batista in late '59. Director Lester is in pretty good form, with most scenes punctuated by memorable throwaway bits.▼

Cuba Crossing (1980) **C-90m.** BOMB D: Chuck Workman. Stuart Whitman, Robert Vaughn, Caren Kaye, Raymond St. Jacques, Woody Strode, Sybil Danning, Albert Salmi, Michael Gazzo. Tough Whitman becomes embroiled in a plot to kill Fidel Castro. Filmed in Key West, Florida, and at least the scenery is pretty. Retitled KILL CASTRO and ASSIGNMENT: KILL CASTRO. Also known as (believe it or not) THE MERCENARIES and SWEET VIOLENT TONY.▼

Cuban Love Song, The (1931) **80m.** **½ D: W.S. Van Dyke. Lawrence Tibbett, Lupe Velez, Ernest Torrence, Jimmy Durante, Karen Morley, Hale Hamilton, Louise Fazenda. Generally enjoyable, if slow-moving, musical-romance with fun-loving marine Tibbett (surprisingly effective as a romantic lead) tangling amorously with hot-tempered peanut vendor Velez in Havana—which of course is a cue for the song "The Peanut Vendor." Torrence and Durante are Tibbett's rowdy sidekicks.

Cuban Rebel Girls (1959) **68m.** BOMB D: Barry Mahon. Errol Flynn, Beverly Aadland, John McKay, Marie Edmund, Jackie Jackler. Flynn's last film is an embarrassment: playing himself, he aids Fidel Castro in his overthrow of Batista. Shot on location during the Castro revolution. Also known as ASSAULT OF THE REBEL GIRLS. Home video title: ATTACK OF THE REBEL GIRLS.▼

Cujo (1983) **C-91m.** *** D: Lewis Teague. Dee Wallace, Danny Pintauro, Daniel Hugh-Kelly, Christopher Stone, Ed Lauter, Mills Watson. Genuinely frightening adaptation of Stephen King thriller about a woman and her son terrorized by rabid dog. Builds slowly but surely to terrifying (but not gory) climax. Not for children.▼

Cul-De-Sac (1966-British) **111m.** *** D: Roman Polanski. Donald Pleasence, Francoise Dorleac, Lionel Stander, Jack MacGowran, Iain Quarrier, Jacqueline Bisset. Macabre comedy about two wounded gangsters who terrorize middle-aged milquetoast and his beautiful young wife. Not a total success, but good cast and stylish direction make it a winner. Some prints cut to 103m.

Culpepper Cattle Company, The (1972) **C-92m.** **½ D: Dick Richards. Gary Grimes, Billy "Green" Bush, Luke Askew, Bo Hopkins, Geoffrey Lewis, Wayne Sutherlin. A 16-year-old persuades trail

[245]

boss to take him along on cattle drive, becomes a man in the process. Fair but excessively violent western.▼

Cult of the Cobra (1955) **82m.** **½ D: Francis D. Lyon. Faith Domergue, Richard Long, Marshall Thompson, Jack Kelly, David Janssen. Minor camp masterpiece involves ex-servicemen being killed by exotic serpent lady Domergue.

Cult of the Damned (1970) **C-103m.** *½ D: Robert Thom. Jennifer Jones, Jordan Christopher, Holly Near, Roddy McDowall, Lou Rawls, Charles Aidman. Senseless story of lovers, and dozens of other things brewed into one wasteful vat. Also known as ANGEL, ANGEL, DOWN WE GO.

Curley (1947) **C-53m.** ** D: Bernard Carr. Larry Olsen, Frances Rafferty, Eilene Janssen, Walter Abel. Inconsequential juvenile nonsense about youngsters playing pranks on their schoolteacher. Originally part of HAL ROACH COMEDY CARNIVAL.▼

Curly Top (1935) **75m.** **½ D: Irving Cummings. Shirley Temple, John Boles, Rochelle Hudson, Jane Darwell, Rafaela Ottiano, Arthur Treacher. Shirley sings "Animal Crackers In My Soup" as she plays Cupid again, this time for sister Hudson and handsome Boles. Based on Jean Webster's DADDY LONG LEGS.▼

Curse, The (1987) **C-90m.** **½ D: David Keith. Wil Wheaton, Claude Akins, Cooper Huckabee, John Schneider, Amy Wheaton. Actor Keith steps behind the camera to direct this down-home horror flick: a deadly meteorite lands on a Tennessee farm, literally driving the folks crazy after contaminating their food. Loosely based on H.P. Lovecraft's novella *The Color Out of Space*, previously filmed as DIE, MONSTER, DIE!▼

Curse of Bigfoot, The (1972) **C-87m.** BOMB D: Don Fields. William Simonsen, Robert Clymire, Ruth Ann Mannella. Students unearth a dormant beast in this docudrama-style low-budgeter. A waste of time.

Curse of Dracula, The SEE: **Return of Dracula, The**

Curse of Frankenstein, The (1957-British) **C-83m.** **½ D: Terence Fisher. Peter Cushing, Christopher Lee, Hazel Court, Robert Urquhart, Valerie Gaunt, Noel Hood. OK retelling of original Shelley tale, with Cushing as Baron von Frankenstein, whose experimentation with creation of life becomes an obsession. First of Hammer Films' long-running horror series, and itself followed by six sequels, starting with REVENGE OF FRANKENSTEIN.▼

Curse of King Tut's Tomb, The (1980) **C-100m.** TVM D: Philip Leacock. Eva Marie Saint, Robin Ellis, Raymond Burr, Harry Andrews, Angharad Rees, Wendy Hiller, Tom Baker, Barbara Murray, Patricia Routledge. Sinister doings about some Egyptian diggings and the discovery of the Tutankhamen burial site. Paul Scofield narrates. Average.▼

Curse of the Black Widow (1977) **C-100m.** TVM D: Dan Curtis. Tony Franciosa, Donna Mills, Patty Duke Astin, June Lockhart, June Allyson, Sid Caesar, Vic Morrow, Roz Kelly, Jeff Corey. Chiller about the search for an elusive killer whose victims are wrapped in a spider-like web. Looks like Curtis had this script left over when his *Kolchak: The Night Stalker* series was cancelled. Average. Retitled: LOVE TRAP.▼

Curse of the Blood-Ghouls SEE: **Slaughter of the Vampires**▼

Curse of the Cat People, The (1944) **70m.** *** D: Gunther von Fritsch, Robert Wise. Simone Simon, Kent Smith, Jane Randolph, Elizabeth Russell, Ann Carter, Julia Dean. Follow-up to CAT PEOPLE creates wonderful atmosphere in story of lonely little girl who conjures up vision of Simon, her father's mysterious first wife. Despite title, not a horror film but a fine, moody fantasy. Produced by Val Lewton, written by DeWitt Bodeen. Wise's directing debut.▼

Curse of the Crimson Altar SEE: **Crimson Cult, The**

Curse of the Demon (1958-British) **83m.** ***½ D: Jacques Tourneur. Dana Andrews, Peggy Cummins, Niall MacGinnis, Maurice Denham, Athene Seyler. Andrews is a stuffily cynical psychologist who doesn't believe that series of deaths have been caused by ancient curse, but film convinces audience right off the bat and never lets up. Charles Bennett and producer Hal E. Chester adapted Montague R. James's story "Casting the Runes." Exceptional shocker, originally called NIGHT OF THE DEMON, and running 95m. in British version.▼

Curse of the Faceless Man (1958) **66m.** BOMB D: Edward L. Cahn. Richard Anderson, Elaine Edwards, Adele Mara, Luis Van Rooten. Silly sci-fi horror as gladiator encased in lava by eruption of Pompeii (yes, the hero has no face) comes back to life thinking he still has to rescue the woman he loves, conveniently reincarnated as the heroine.

Curse of the Fly, The (1965-British) **86m.** *½ D: Don Sharp. Brian Donlevy, Carole Gray, George Baker, Michael Graham, Jeremy Wilkins, Charles Carson. Third film based on THE FLY with scores of mutants and a mad doctor who mixes up scientific hodgepodge. Best forgotten.

Curse of the Living Corpse (1964) **84m.** ** D: Del Tenney. Helen Warren, Roy R. Sheider (Scheider), Margo Hartman, Hugh Franklin, Candace Hilligoss. Tepid old-dark-house murder mystery with dead man supposedly returning to "life" and committing series of killings. Scheider's film debut.▼

Curse of the Mummy's Tomb, The (1964-British) C-81m. ** D: Michael Carreras. Terence Morgan, Ronald Howard, Fred Clark, Jeanne Roland, George Pastell, Jack Gwillim, Dickie Owen (as the Mummy). Handsomely photographed but routine Hammer thriller featuring vengeful mummy at large in Victorian London, killing the usual profaners of the tomb in foggy surroundings. Most unusual twist: The (human) villain is in fact the Mummy's brother. Follow-up, not sequel, to THE MUMMY (1959).

Curse of the Pink Panther (1983) C-109m. *½ D: Blake Edwards. Ted Wass, David Niven, Robert Wagner, Herbert Lom, Joanna Lumley, Capucine, Robert Loggia, Harvey Korman, Burt Kwouk, Leslie Ash, Andre Maranne. Writer-director Edwards's pointless attempt to keep the Pink Panther series alive despite Peter Sellers's death—by putting young Wass through Sellers's sight-gag paces, and surrounding him with costars of earlier Panther films, who (all too obviously) shot their cameos at the same time as TRAIL OF THE PINK PANTHER. What a waste of time and talent! Niven's final film (with his voice dubbed by Rich Little).▼

Curse of the Stone Hand (1965) 72m. BOMB D: Jerry Warren, Carl Schlieppe. John Carradine, Sheila Bon, Ernest Walch, Katherine Victor, Lloyd Nelson. Americanized version of 1959 Mexican film tries to interweave two separate story elements with incoherent results.

Curse of the Swamp Creature (1966) C-80m. BOMB D: Larry Buchanan. John Agar, Francine York, Shirley McLine, Bill Thurman, Jeff Alexander. A geological expedition stumbles onto a mad doctor who's trying to evolve a man-monster. Low-budget junk.▼

Curse of the Undead (1959) 79m. ** D: Edward Dein. Eric Fleming, Michael Pate, Kathleen Crowley, John Hoyt, Bruce Gordon, Edward Binns. Once-novel mixture of horror-Western tale hasn't much zing. Mysterious stranger has vampirish designs on Crowley.

Curse of the Voodoo (1965-British) 77m. *½ D: Lindsay Shonteff. Bryant Halliday, Dennis Price, Lisa Daniely, Mary Kerridge. Modest film promises some exotic native black magic hi-jinks, but nothing worthwhile occurs.

Curse of the Werewolf, The (1961-British) C-91m. **½ D: Terence Fisher. Clifford Evans, Oliver Reed, Yvonne Romain, Anthony Dawson. Reed has wolf's blood and struggles to control the monster within him; it finally erupts when he is denied his girl's love. Eerie atmosphere pervades this good chiller.▼

Curse of the Yellow Snake, The (1963-German) 98m. **½ D: Franz Gottlieb. Joachim Fuchsberger, Eddi Arent, Brigitte Grothum, Charles Regnier, Werner Peters, Claus Holm. Edgar Wallace yarn dealing with anti-Western uprising by fanatic Oriental cult; eerie and atmospheric.▼

Curtain Call at Cactus Creek (1950) C-86m. **½ D: Charles Lamont. Donald O'Connor, Gale Storm, Vincent Price, Walter Brennan, Eve Arden. Sometimes foolish slapstick as O'Connor, touring with road show, gets involved with bank robbers and irate citizens of Arizona.

Curtains (1983-Canadian) C-89m. BOMB D: Jonathan Stryker (Richard Ciupka). John Vernon, Samantha Eggar, Linda Thorson, Anne Ditchburn, Lynne Griffin, Sandra Warren. Badly conceived and executed horror opus about murder at a film director's spooky old house where six actresses have gathered for an audition. Plethora of screen credits and use of pseudonym for director's name indicates production problems, which are certainly evident in finished product.▼

Curtain Up (1953-British) 81m. **½ D: Ralph Smart. Robert Morley, Margaret Rutherford, Kay Kendall, Joan Rice. Droll little film of rural repertory company battling among themselves as they prepare for their dramatic season.

Curucu, Beast of the Amazon (1956) C-76m. *½ D: Curt Siodmak. John Bromfield, Beverly Garland, Tom Payne, Harvey Chalk. One of the most infamous disappointments (for monster-loving kids) of the 1950s. Bromfield and Garland go after title monster, discover it is merely disguised Indian trying to scare people away. Boo hiss.

Custer of the West (1968-U.S.-Spanish) C-140m. **½ D: Robert Siodmak. Robert Shaw, Mary Ure, Jeffrey Hunter, Robert Ryan, Ty Hardin, Charles Stalnaker, Robert Hall, Lawrence Tierney. Fairly ambitious bio of famed general, originally in Cinerama, suffers from script that doesn't quite know how to characterize its subject. Some prints run 120m.

Cutter (1972) C-73m. TVM D: Richard Irving. Peter DeAnda, Cameron Mitchell, Robert Webber, Barbara Rush, Janet MacLachlan. Location shooting in Chicago can't help laughable black detective story with DeAnda starring as private eye searching for missing pro football quarterback. Look for Stepin Fetchit as a shoeshine man. Average.

Cutter and Bone SEE: **Cutter's Way**▼
Cutter's Trail (1969) C-100m. TVM D: Vincent McEveety. John Gavin, Marisa Pavan, Joseph Cotten, Beverly Garland. Respectable formula Western has Gavin returning to Santa Fe as marshal only to discover town intimidated by gang; only

people who'll help are mother and small boy. Above average.

Cutter's Way (1981) C-105m. **½ D: Ivan Passer. Jeff Bridges, John Heard, Lisa Eichhorn, Ann Dusenberry, Stephen Elliot, Nina Van Pallandt. Intriguing if not always satisfying film about a boozy, belligerent Vietnam vet (Heard) who prods his aimless friend (Bridges) into action after he's seen a man who may be a murderer. Low-key, sometimes enervating adaptation of Newton Thornburg's novel *Cutter and Bone* (this film's original title), enhanced by director Passer's eye for interesting detail.▼

Cyborg (1989) C-86m. BOMB D: Albert Pyun. Jean-Claude Van Damme, Deborah Richter, Vincent Klyn, Alex Daniels, Dayle Haddon, Blaise Loong, Rolf Muller. Van Damme plays a savior battling evil gangs who seem to enjoy various plagues and finding gruesome ways to murder people. Set, of course, in the near future. Even by the low standards of post-apocalyptic trash movies, this plumbs new depths. Repulsive.▼

Cyborg 2087 (1966) C-86m. ** D: Franklin Adreon. Michael Rennie, Wendell Corey, Eduard Franz, Karen Steele, Warren Stevens. Future Earth civilization sends cyborg—part machine, part human—back in time to 1960s so future can be changed. Good idea all but ruined due to unconvincing script and TV-style production.

Cyclone (1987) C-83m. ** D: Fred Olen Ray. Heather Thomas, Jeffrey Combs, Ashley Ferrare, Dar Robinson, Martine Beswicke, Robert Quarry, Martin Landau. TV star Thomas plays second fiddle to a high-tech motorcycle that's stolen by Landau's henchmen. Watch for numerous cameos including Huntz Hall, Troy Donahue, Russ Tamblyn and Michael Reagan.▼

Cycle Savages, The (1969) C-82m. BOMB D: Bill Brame. Bruce Dern, Melody Patterson, Chris Robinson, Maray Ayres, Scott Brady. Psychotic biker/white slaver Dern is displeased when artist Robinson opens his sketch pad, so he plans to crush the budding Rembrandt's hands. Sadism and torture galore; coproduced by deejay Casey Kasem and record exec Mike Curb, later the lieutenant governor of California.

Cyclops, The (1957) 75m. ** D: Bert I. Gordon. James Craig, Gloria Talbott, Lon Chaney Jr., Tom Drake. Expedition scours Mexico in search of Talbott's lost fiancé, discovers that radiation has transformed him into an enormous monster. Nothing much in this cheapie.▼

Cyclotrode "X" (1946) 100m. **½ D: William Witney, Fred Brannon. Charles Quigley, Linda Stirling, Clayton Moore, I. Stanford Jolley, Kenne Duncan. Well-paced cliff-hanger, with bouncy action as sinister Crimson Ghost tries to gain control of super-nuclear device. Reedited from Republic serial THE CRIMSON GHOST.▼

Cynara (1932) 78m. ** D: King Vidor. Ronald Colman, Kay Francis, Henry Stephenson, Phyllis Barry, Paul Porcasi. Badly dated film about British lawyer who has interlude with working girl while wife is away; Colman is good as usual.

Cynthia (1947) 98m. *½ D: Robert Z. Leonard. Elizabeth Taylor, George Murphy, S. Z. Sakall, Mary Astor, Gene Lockhart, Spring Byington, Jimmy Lydon. Sugary film of sickly girl Taylor finding outlet in music; good cast wasted.

Cyrano de Bergerac (1950) 112m. **** D: Michael Gordon. Jose Ferrer, Mala Powers, William Prince, Morris Carnovsky, Elena Verdugo. Ferrer received an Oscar for portraying the tragic wit, renowned for his nose but longing for love of a beautiful lady. Based on Edmond Rostand play of 17th-century Paris. Later modernized as ROXANNE. Also shown in computer-colored version.▼

Da (1988) C-102m. **½ D: Matt Clark. Barnard Hughes, Martin Sheen, Karl Hayden, Doreen Hepburn, William Hickey, Hugh O'Conor, Ingrid Craigie. Sheen returns to his native Ireland for his father's funeral, which triggers a series of remembrances of his irascible "da." Hugh Leonard's adaptation of his autobiographical stage comedy doesn't work as well on the screen, but remains a touching account of a father-son relationship that isn't interrupted by death. Hughes beautifully recreates his Tony-winning performance, and Sheen is equally good. Hepburn is marvelous as Hughes' pesky wife; Leonard appears briefly as a pallbearer. Filmed mostly on location in Ireland.▼

D.A.: Conspiracy to Kill (1970) C-100m. TVM D: Paul Krasny. Robert Conrad, Belinda Montgomery, William Conrad, Don Stroud, Steve Ihnat. Standard crime drama has energetic district attorney proving drugstore owner is robbery master-mind involved in murder. Unconvincing characters but fair action. Average.

Dad (1989) C-117m. ** D: Gary David Goldberg. Jack Lemmon, Ted Danson, Olympia Dukakis, Kathy Baker, Kevin Spacey, Ethan Hawke, Zakes Mokae, J. T. Walsh. Busy, distracted executive learns his father may be dying and rushes home; he winds up becoming his dad's caretaker and companion, and they grow closer than they've ever been. Genuinely affecting tearjerker turns sappy and "cute" at the midway point, almost negating Lemmon's fine performance. Why couldn't they have quit while they were ahead? Feature directing debut for TV sitcom producer Goldberg.▼

Dadah Is Death (1988) C-200m. TVM

D: Jerry London. Julie Christie, Victor Banerjee, Hugo Weaving, John Polson, Sarah Jessica Parker. Dramatization of real-life Australian Barbara Barlow's efforts to save her son from the gallows in Malaysia after he and a friend were arrested in 1986 for drug smuggling. Christie made her American TV-movie debut here, but most of the focus is on Aussie actors Weaving and Polson as the doomed pair. Overlong and occasionally harrowing drama filmed primarily in Macao. Average.

Daddy (1987) **C-100m. TVM** D: John Herzfeld. Dermot Mulroney, Patricia Arquette, John Karlen, Tess Harper, Trey Adams, Danny Aiello. Thoughtful "children having children" drama about two high schoolers unprepared for the reality of parenthood. Incisively written by director Herzfeld. Above average.

Daddy, I Don't Like It Like This (1978) **C-100m. TVM** D: Adell Aldrich. Talia Shire, Burt Young, Doug McKeon, Melanie Griffith, Erica Yohn. Youngster withdraws into his own world unable to cope with the bickering of his parents because of their unfulfilled dreams. Veteran director Robert Aldrich's daughter Adell made her own directing debut here, working with a somewhat pallid script by star Burt Young. Average.

Daddy Long Legs (1955) **C-126m.** **½ D: Jean Negulesco. Fred Astaire, Leslie Caron, Thelma Ritter, Fred Clark, Terry Moore, Larry Keating. Overlong musical remake of oft-filmed story about playboy (Astaire) anonymously sponsoring waif's education—then she falls in love with him. Some good dance numbers, and Johnny Mercer score highlighted by "Something's Got to Give." Previously filmed in 1919, 1931, and (as CURLY TOP) in 1935.

Daddy-O (1959) **74m.** BOMB D: Lou Place. Dick Contino, Sandra Giles, Bruno VeSota, Gloria Victor, Ron McNeil. Thugs recruit truck driver-singer Contino to drive a getaway car. Like wow, man, this flick's for squares. Also known as OUT ON PROBATION.

Daddy's Dyin'. . . Who's Got the Will? (1990) **C-95m.** **½ D: Jack Fisk. Beau Bridges, Keith Carradine, Beverly D'Angelo, Tess Harper, Judge Reinhold, Amy Wright, Patrika Darbo, Molly McClure, Bert Remsen. Affection, reminiscence, avarice, and hostility intermingle as a family of memorable oddballs gathers at the old Texas homestead to wait for their father to die and to find out what's in the will. Del Shores adapted his own stage play, and the results run from flat and predictable to sharp and funny; a terrific cast punches everything across.

Daddy's Gone A-Hunting (1969) **C-108m.** *** D: Mark Robson. Carol White, Paul Burke, Scott Hylands, Rachel Ames, Mala

Powers. Psycho stalks innocent young girl through streets of San Francisco. Some of the shocks may be lessened on TV screen, but still exciting thriller.▼

Daffodil Killer SEE: **Devil's Daffodil**

Daffy Duck's Movie: Fantastic Island (1983) **C-78m.** *½ D: Friz Freleng. Daffy Duck, Speedy Gonzales, Bugs Bunny, Yosemite Sam, Tweety and Sylvester, Pepe LePew, Foghorn Leghorn. Fourth and weakest of Warner Bros.' cartoon compilations. Linking material (spoofing TV's *Fantasy Island*) is flat, and few of the ten cartoon shorts included are better than average. Hardly Daffy's finest hour.▼

Daffy Duck's Quackbusters (1989) **C-72m.** *** D: Greg Ford, Terry Lennon. Voice of Mel Blanc. Perhaps the most watchable of the Warner cartoon-compilation films, with a clever bridging story incorporating the studio's many vintage horror-movie spoofs. Daffy Duck inherits a fortune and sets up a "ghost-busting" service with pals Bugs Bunny and Porky Pig. Contains the new short THE DUXORCIST and a cameo appearance by Egghead.▼

Daggers of Blood SEE: **With Fire and Sword**

Daisy Kenyon (1947) **99m.** **½ D: Otto Preminger. Joan Crawford, Dana Andrews, Henry Fonda, Ruth Warrick, Martha Stewart, Peggy Ann Garner. Love triangle starts intelligently, bogs down halfway into typical soapy histrionics (with a plot thread about child abuse surprising for its time). Good performances; handsomely filmed. Look sharp in the Stork Club scene for Walter Winchell, John Garfield, and Leonard Lyons.

Daisy Miller (1974) **C-91m.** **½ D: Peter Bogdanovich. Cybill Shepherd, Barry Brown, Cloris Leachman, Mildred Natwick, Eileen Brennan, Duilio Del Prete. Handsome, intelligent adaptation of Henry James' story misses the mark; the tone is cold, and Shepherd's hollow performance as a naive American courting European society in the late 1800s nearly sinks the film. Filmed in Italy.▼

Dakota (1945) **82m.** ** D: Joseph Kane. John Wayne, Vera Ralston, Walter Brennan, Ward Bond, Ona Munson, Hugo Haas. Sprawling Wayne vehicle with Duke involved in pioneer railroad territory dispute; Vera is his lovely wife!▼

Dakota (1988) **C-97m.** ** D: Fred Holmes. Lou Diamond Phillips, Eli Cummins, DeeDee Norton, Jordan Burton, Steve Ruge, John Hawkes. Well-meaning but slight, independently produced drama about a youth on the run (Phillips), who works on a Texas ranch and interrelates with various characters. Phillips, who served as associate producer, is the sole interest here; he made the film prior to attaining stardom in LA BAMBA.▼

Dakota Incident (1956) **C-88m.** **½ D: Lewis R. Foster. Linda Darnell, Dale Robertson, John Lund, Ward Bond. Indians attack stagecoach, leading to fight to the finish.▼

Dakota Lil (1950) **C-88m.** ** D: Lesley Selander. George Montgomery, Marie Windsor, Rod Cameron, Marion Martin, Wallace Ford. Pedestrian Western saved by Windsor's vitality in title role as crook who helps lawmen trap railroad thieves.

Daleks—Invasion Earth 2150 A.D. (1966-British) **C-84m.** **½ D: Gordon Flemyng. Peter Cushing, Bernard Cribbins, Andrew Keir, Ray Brooks, Jill Curzon, Roberta Tovey. Agreeable sequel to DR. WHO AND THE DALEKS, with the Earth threatened by Dalek aggressors. Retitled INVASION EARTH 2150 A.D.▼

Dallas (1950) **C-94m.** **½ D: Stuart Heisler. Gary Cooper, Ruth Roman, Steve Cochran, Raymond Massey, Antonio Moreno. Cooper returns to Big D. of post-Civil War days seeking revenge; finds love with Roman and gunplay from Cochran and other intended victims.

Dallas Cowboys Cheerleaders (1979) **C-100m. TVM** D: Bruce Bilson. Jane Seymour, Laraine Stephens, Bert Convy, Lauren Tewes, Pamela Susan Shoop, Katherine Baumann, Bucky Dent. Featherweight "inside story" about the famed cheerleading squad whose suggestive attire and movements spice many Sunday afternoon football halftime shows. It gets worse—there's another one. Below average.

Dallas Cowboys Cheerleaders II (1980) **C-100m. TVM** D: Michael O'Herlihy. John Davidson, Laraine Stephens, Roxanne Gregory, Duane Thomas, Julie Hill, Texie Waterman. Witless sequel to one of the highest-rated and most jiggly made-for-TV movies. For those deeply concerned, it focuses on the concocted conflicts the famed cheerleader squad faces while preparing dance routines for Super Bowl Sunday! Below average.

Dallas: The Early Years (1986) **C-150m. TVM** D; Larry Elikann. Larry Hagman, David Grant, Dale Midkiff, Molly Hagan, David Wilson, Hoyt Axton, Diane Franklin, Geoffrey Lewis, Marshall Thompson. Energetic "prequel" to the hugely successful series, with a cast of fresh faces playing earlier versions of the Ewing and Barnes clans from the Depression through the early 1950s. Larry Hagman, as J.R., is on hand briefly to spin the tale. Written by executive producer and creator of the series, David Jacobs. Above average.

Dalton: Code of Vengeance II (1986) **C-100m. TVM** D: Alan Smithee. Charles Taylor, Ed Bruce, Belinda Montgomery, Tony Frank, Donnelly Rhodes, Karen Landry, Alex Harvey. Vietnam vet-turned-loner David Dalton (Taylor) goes in pursuit of his now-crazed former C.O. who now leads a para-military band operating out of the Florida Everglades. Pseudonymously directed sequel to CODE OF VENGEANCE and forerunner of the short-lived *Dalton* series. Average.

Dalton Girls, The (1957) **71m.** *½ D: Reginald LeBorg. Merry Anders, Penny Edwards, Sue George, John Russell, Lisa Davis. Gimmick of female bandits wears thin in mild Western of Dalton Brothers' relatives carrying on in family tradition.

Damaged Lives (1937) **61m.** ** D: Edgar G. Ulmer. Diane Sinclair, Lyman Williams, Cecelia Parker, George Irving, Almeda Fowler, Jason Robards, Sr. Earnest melodrama preaching against the perils of extramarital flings which, in this case, leads to venereal disease. Definitely low-budget, but not the exploitation "camp" one would assume. Originally followed by a half-hour medical lecture on VD. Made in 1933, but unreleased for four years.

Dam Busters, The (1954-British) **102m.** ***½ D: Michael Anderson. Richard Todd, Michael Redgrave, Ursula Jeans, Basil Sydney. During WW2, British devise an ingenious plan to blow up Germans' Ruhr dam. Exciting and intelligent film. Original British running time: 119m.▼

Dames (1934) **90m.** *** D: Ray Enright. Joan Blondell, Dick Powell, Ruby Keeler, ZaSu Pitts, Hugh Herbert, Guy Kibbee, Phil Regan. Short on plot (let's-back-a-Broadway-musical) but top Busby Berkeley production ensembles like "I Only Have Eyes For You" and incredible "When You Were A Smile On Your Mother's Lips And A Twinkle In Your Daddy's Eye."▼

Damien—Omen II (1978) **C-107m.** **½ D: Don Taylor. William Holden, Lee Grant, Lew Ayres, Sylvia Sidney, Robert Foxworth, Jonathan Scott-Taylor, Leo McKern. Sequel to huge hit of 1976 is less effective, still has shock value from grisly murders, plus good work by Holden. Best scene is Ayres' death under an icy lake. Scott-Taylor is the demon child; Holden and Grant his stupidly unsuspecting kin. Taylor took over directing from Michael Hodges, who worked on screenplay. Followed by THE FINAL CONFLICT.▼

Damien: The Leper Priest (1980) **C-100m. TVM** D: Steven Gethers. Ken Howard, Mike Farrell, William Daniels, Wilfrid Hyde-White, David Ogden Stiers, Logan Ramsey, Roger Bowen, Irene Tsu. Disappointing drama based on the life of the Roman Catholic priest who dedicated himself to serving the Hawaiian leper colony on Molokai a century ago. A somewhat miscast, bewigged Howard replaced David Janssen, to whose memory this film is dedicated. Average.▼

Damnation Alley (1977) **C-91m.** *½ D:

Jack Smight. Jan-Michael Vincent, George Peppard, Dominique Sanda, Paul Winfield, Jackie Earle Haley. Five survivors of nuclear wipeout travel cross-country in search of civilization. Futuristic van in which they travel is more interesting than story or characters in this uninspiring sci-fi saga. Distantly related to the Roger Zelazny novel.▼

Damn Citizen (1958) **88m.** ****½** D: Robert Gordon. Keith Andes, Maggie Hayes, Gene Evans, Lynn Bari. Realistically told account of WW2 veteran (Andes) hired to wipe out corruption in state police.

Damned, The (1962) SEE: **These Are the Damned**

Damned, The (1969-Italian-West German) **C-146m.** ******* D: Luchino Visconti. Dirk Bogarde, Ingrid Thulin, Helmut Griem, Helmut Berger, Charlotte Rampling, Florinda Bolkan. Slow, grim drama depicting Nazi machinations and takeover of German industrialist family with few sympathetic characters. Beware cuts in controversial X-rated film.▼

Damned Don't Cry, The (1950) **103m.** ****½** D: Vincent Sherman. Joan Crawford, David Brian, Steve Cochran, Kent Smith, Richard Egan. Follow-up to FLAMINGO ROAD formula; Crawford is well cast as lower-class gal rising to wealth via wit and looks, discovering too late that a gangster's moll has no right to love and happiness.

Damn the Defiant! (1962-British) **C-101m.** ******* D: Lewis Gilbert. Alec Guinness, Dirk Bogarde, Maurice Denham, Nigel Stock, Richard Carpenter, Anthony Quayle. Bogarde vs. Guinness in stalwart tale of British warship during Napoleonic campaign. Production shows great attention to historic detail.▼

Damn Yankees (1958) **C-110m.** ******* D: George Abbott, Stanley Donen. Tab Hunter, Gwen Verdon, Ray Walston, Russ Brown, Jimmie Komack, Jean Stapleton, Nathaniel Frey. Aging, frustrated Washington Senators baseball fan says he'd sell his soul to see the club get one good hitter; a devilish Mr. Applegate appears to fulfill his wish, and transforms *him* into the club's new star. Faithful translation of hit Broadway musical (with Walston, Verdon, and others repeating their original roles) loses something along the way, and has a particularly weak finale, but it's still quite entertaining. Songs include "(You Gotta Have) Heart," "Whatever Lola Wants," and a mambo memorably danced by Verdon and choreographer Bob Fosse.▼

Damon and Pythias (1962-Italian) **C-99m.** ****** D: Curtis Bernhardt. Guy Williams, Don Burnett, Ilaria Occhini, Liana Orfei, Arnoldo Foa. Title reveals all in this routine costumer making legendary figures juvenile cardboard heroes.

Damsel in Distress, A (1937) **101m.** *******

D: George Stevens. Fred Astaire, George Burns, Gracie Allen, Joan Fontaine, Constance Collier, Reginald Gardiner, Montagu Love. Bright Gershwin musical set in London, with dancing star Astaire pursuing aristocratic heiress Fontaine. Burns and Allen have never been better—they even get to sing and dance. Songs include "Foggy Day in London Town," "Nice Work If You Can Get It." The clever "Fun House" sequence won an Oscar for Hermes Pan's dance direction.▼

D.A.: Murder One (1969) **C-100m. TVM** D: Boris Sagal. Robert Conrad, Howard Duff, Diane Baker, J. D. Cannon, Alfred Ryder, Scott Brady, Gerald S. O'Loughlin. Good cast struggles through Jack Webb production featuring Conrad as stereotyped deputy D.A. showing up his superiors in case involving insulin overdose. Average. Retitled MURDER ONE.

Dan Candy's Law SEE: **Alien Thunder**▼

Dance, Fools, Dance (1931) **81m.** ****½** D: Harry Beaumont. Joan Crawford, Cliff Edwards, Clark Gable, Earl Foxe, Lester Vail, Natalie Moorhead. Crawford, alone in the world, becomes reporter out to expose mobster Gable by winning him over. Interesting for early Gable-Crawford teaming; brisk drama.▼

Dance, Girl, Dance (1940) **90m.** ****½** D: Dorothy Arzner. Maureen O'Hara, Louis Hayward, Lucille Ball, Virginia Field, Ralph Bellamy, Maria Ouspenskaya, Mary Carlisle. Innocent young girl (O'Hara) aspires to be a ballerina, but self-centered Ball steers her toward burlesque instead. Film has won latter-day acclaim for feminist angles, especially O'Hara's closing speech; unfortunately, it's not as good as one would like it to be. Lucy is terrific as Bubbles.▼

Dance Hall (1941) **74m.** ***½** D: Irving Pichel. Carole Landis, Cesar Romero, William Henry, June Storey. Mild romantic musical with Romero, who runs a dance hall, falling in love with worker Landis.▼

Dance Hall (1950-British) **78m.** ****** D: Charles Crichton. Natasha Parry, Jane Hylton, Diana Dors, Petula Clark, Donald Houston, Bonar Colleano, Sydney Tafler, Kay Kendall, Geraldo, Ted Heath Band. Episodic tale of four factory girls' encounters and adventures at local dance hall. Nothing much.▼

Dance Little Lady (1955-British) **C-87m.** ****½** D: Val Guest. Mai Zetterling, Terence Morgan, Guy Rolfe, Mandy Miller, Eunice Gayson, Reginald Beckwith. Prima ballerina Zetterling is married to heel Morgan; after a car accident ends her career, he exploits the dancing talent of their daughter (Miller). Corny drama is aided by pleasant dance sequences.

Dance of Death (1968-British) **C-138m.** ******* D: David Giles. Laurence Olivier, Geraldine McEwan, Robert Lang, Malcolm

Reynolds, Janina Faye, Carolyn Jones. Film version of National Theatre production of August Strindberg's angst-laden play about an aging sea captain, notable chiefly for Olivier's fiery performance. Unreleased in U.S. until 1979.

Dance of the Dwarfs (1983) C-93m. *½ D: Gus Trikonis. Peter Fonda, Deborah Raffin, John Amos, Carlos Palomino. Female anthropologist (Raffin) searching for lost pygmy tribe in jungle hooks up with drunken helicopter pilot (Fonda) in this stupid AFRICAN QUEENish adventure shot in Phillipines. They encounter strange creatures, audience encounters boredom. Video version is titled JUNGLE HEAT. ▼

Dance of the Vampires SEE: **Fearless Vampire Killers, The or: Pardon Me, But Your Teeth Are in My Neck**

Dancers (1987) C-99m. *½ D: Herbert Ross. Mikhail Baryshnikov, Alessandra Ferri, Leslie Browne, Thomas Rall, Lynn Seymour, Victor Barbee, Mariangela Melato, Julie Kent. Trite, inexplicably bad movie about a ballet star/lothario (Baryshnikov, ideally cast) who's rehearsing a screen version of "Giselle," and becomes infatuated with an innocent young dancer. A waste of time. Baryshnikov, Browne and Ross collaborated ten years earlier on THE TURNING POINT. ▼

Dancers in the Dark (1932) 60m. **½ D: David Burton. Miriam Hopkins, Jack Oakie, George Raft, William Collier, Jr., Eugene Pallette, Lyda Roberti. Bandleader Oakie tries to kindle romance with taxi-dancer Hopkins, by sending her boyfriend (Collier) out of town, but doesn't reckon with gangster Raft falling for her too. Good stars help murky drama.

Dance with a Stranger (1985-British) C-101m. ***½ D: Mike Newell. Miranda Richardson, Rupert Everett, Ian Holm, Matthew Carroll, Tom Chadbon, Jane Bertish. Stylish, trenchant study of romantic self-destruction based on the true story of Ruth Ellis, who in 1955 became the last woman ever executed in Britain. Peaks with about a half hour to go, but Richardson, her leading men, and a haunting atmosphere more than compensate. Ellis' story was earlier told in YIELD TO THE NIGHT (BLONDE SINNER), with Diana Dors. ▼

Dance with Me Henry (1956) 79m. *½ D: Charles Barton. Lou Costello, Bud Abbott, Gigi Perreau, Rusty Hamer. Lowgrade Abbott and Costello involving the duo's ownership of run-down amusement park and two kids they've adopted; their last film together.

Dance 'Til Dawn (1988) C-100m. TVM D: Paul Schneider. Tempestt Bledsoe, Alyssa Milano, Brian Bloom, Tracy Gold, Mary Frann, Cliff DeYoung, Kelsey Grammer, Alan Thicke, Molly Cheek. Prom night pits a group of TV-star teens against their long-suffering TV-star parents. Average.

Dancing in the Dark (1949) C-92m. **½ D: Irving Reis. William Powell, Betsy Drake, Mark Stevens, Adolphe Menjou, Walter Catlett. Occasionally bubbly musical comedy with Powell hoping to cement good relations with film company by signing Broadway star; he becomes intrigued with talents of unknown girl, who turns out to be his daughter.

Dancing in the Dark (1986-Canadian) C-98m. ** D: Leon Marr. Martha Henry, Neil Munro, Rosemary Dunsmore, Richard Manette. Henry is impressive in this otherwise obvious, predictable account of a perfect, devoted wife, a meticulously controlled woman, and how she comes to have a mental breakdown. ▼

Dancing Lady (1933) 94m. **½ D: Robert Z. Leonard. Joan Crawford, Clark Gable, Franchot Tone, May Robson, Nelson Eddy, Fred Astaire, Robert Benchley, Ted Healy and his Stooges. Glossy backstage romance is best remembered for Astaire's film debut (he plays himself), dancing opposite a less-than-inspired Crawford. Show-biz story, three-cornered romance are strictly standard, but cast and MGM gloss add points. Funniest moments belong to the Three Stooges. Look fast for Eve Arden. ▼

Dancing Masters, The (1943) 63m. *½ D: Mal St. Clair. Oliver Hardy, Stan Laurel, Trudy Marshall, Robert Bailey, Matt Briggs, Margaret Dumont. L&H overcome by routine material, special effects that look phony. Robert Mitchum has bit as a hood.

Dancing Mothers (1926) 60m. **½ D: Herbert Brenon. Clara Bow, Alice Joyce, Dorothy Cumming, Norman Trevor. Sprightly account of Flapper Bow defying conventions as prototype of the Jazz Age. Silent film has simple plot but enthusiastic performances. ▼

Dancing on a Dime (1940) 74m. **½ D: Joseph Santley. Grace McDonald, Robert Paige, Virginia Dale, Peter Lind Hayes. Programmer musical with wispy plot allowing for McDonald et al. to do some dancing and vocalizing, such as "I Hear Music." Not bad.

Dandy in Aspic, A (1968-British) C-107m. ** D: Anthony Mann. Laurence Harvey, Tom Courtenay, Mia Farrow, Lionel Stander, Harry Andrews, Peter Cook. Wooden spy melodrama in which principals keep switching sides so rapidly it becomes impossible to follow. Mann died during filming; Harvey completed director's chores. ▼

Danger by My Side (1962-British) 63m. ** D: Charles Saunders. Anthony Oliver, Maureen Connell, Alan Tilvern, Bill Nagy. Connell hunts her brother's murderer by taking a job in a strip club; standard detective caper.

Danger Down Under (1988-U.S.-Australian) **C-100m. TVM** D: Russ Mayberry. Lee Majors, Rebecca Gilling, Martin Vaughan, William Wallace, Bruce Hughes, Morgan Lewis, Paul Chubb. Routine adventure has American horse breeder turn rancher in New South Wales, with Majors heading an otherwise all-Australian cast. Average.

Danger in Paradise (1977) **C-100m. TVM** D: Marvin Chomsky. Cliff Potts, John Dehner, Ina Balin, Bill Lucking, Jean-Marie Hon, Michael Mullins. Dreary action drama with stock characters—all unsympathetic. Prodigal son Potts battles wicked stepmother Balin, in cahoots with land developers, for control of ailing father's huge Hawaiian ranch estate. Pilot for TV series *Big Hawaii.* Below average.

Danger Island SEE: **Mr. Moto in Danger Island▼**

Danger Lights (1930) **73m.** ** D: George B. Seitz. Louis Wolheim, Jean Arthur, Robert Armstrong, Hugh Herbert, Robert Edeson, Frank Sheridan. Tough but kindhearted railroad supervisor Wolheim is engaged to marry Arthur, but she falls for younger, handsomer tramp-turned-engineer Armstrong. Predictable, with unmemorable race-against-the-clock finale.▼

Danger—Love at Work (1937) **81m.** **½ D: Otto Preminger. Ann Sothern, Jack Haley, Mary Boland, John Carradine, Edward Everett Horton, E. E. Clive, Stanley Fields. Wacky comedy of family headed by nutty Boland involved in shotgun wedding of Sothern and Haley.

Dangerous (1935) **72m.** **½ D: Alfred E. Green. Bette Davis, Franchot Tone, Margaret Lindsay, Alison Skipworth, John Eldredge, Dick Foran. Former star Davis, on the skids, is rehabilitated by Tone in good but syrupy tale, with flamboyant Oscar-winning performance by Davis. Remade as SINGAPORE WOMAN.▼

Dangerous Affection (1987) **C-100m. TVM** D: Larry Elikann. Judith Light, Jimmy Smits, Audra Lindley, Michael Parks, Bill O'Sullivan, Rhea Perlman, Joseph Hacker. Comedy thriller about a pregnant woman and her young son being stalked by a killer the boy can identify. Average

Dangerous Charter (1962) **C-76m.** *½ D: Robert Gottschalk. Chris Warfield, Sally Fraser, Richard Foote, Peter Forster, Chick Chandler. Fishermen become involved in heroin smuggling. Grade D all the way.▼

Dangerous Company (1982) **C-100m. TVM** D: Lamont Johnson. Beau Bridges, Carlos Brown, Karen Carlson, Jan Sterling, Kene Holiday, Ralph Macchio, Max Wright. Dramatization of the true story of Ray Johnson, his 27 years of violent crime and imprisonment (with various escapes and recaptures), and his rehabilitation. Listless script nearly undermines Bridges' tour-de-force performance. Based on Johnson's book *Too Dangerous to Be at Large.* Average.▼

Dangerous Corner (1934) **66m.** **½ D: Phil Rosen. Melvyn Douglas, Conrad Nagel, Virginia Bruce, Erin O'Brien Moore, Ian Keith, Betty Furness, Henry Wadsworth, Doris Lloyd. Interesting, well-acted adaptation of J.B. Priestley's play about a group of friends whose after-dinner conversation reveals the truth about an alleged suicide and theft committed years before; unique flashback structure and trick ending hold up.

Dangerous Crossing (1953) **75m.** **½ D: Joseph M. Newman. Jeanne Crain, Michael Rennie, Casey Adams, Carl Betz, Mary Anderson, Willis Bouchey. Well-acted suspenser has Crain a bride on ocean liner whose husband mysteriously disappears. Based on a John Dickson Carr story.

Dangerous Days of Kiowa Jones, The (1966) **C-83m. TVM** D: Alex March. Robert Horton, Diane Baker, Sal Mineo, Nehemiah Persoff, Gary Merrill, (Harry) Dean Stanton. Fair Western adventure features Horton in good performance as drifter agreeing to transport a pair of killers to jail. Average.

Dangerous Exile (1958-British) **C-90m.** ** D: Brian Desmond Hurst. Louis Jourdan, Belinda Lee, Keith Michell, Richard O'Sullivan. Jourdan is properly dashing in OK adventurer in which he saves royalty from execution during French revolution, aided by English lass (Lee).

Dangerous Female SEE: **Maltese Falcon, The** (1931)▼

Dangerous Friend, A SEE: **Todd Killings, The▼**

Dangerous Liaisons (1988) **C-120m.** ***½ D: Stephen Frears. Glenn Close, John Malkovich, Michelle Pfeiffer, Swoosie Kurtz, Keanu Reeves, Mildred Natwick, Uma Thurman, Peter Capaldi. In 18th-century France, an unscrupulous woman manipulates the lives of those around her, just for amusement, with the help of a like-minded count. Excellent adaptation of Christopher Hampton's play *Les Liaisons Dangereuses,* based on the famous period novel. Close is magnificent, Malkovich good (though miscast). Hampton's screenplay won an Oscar, as did the art direction and costumes. Same story filmed before in 1959 (as DANGEROUS LIAISONS 1960) and again in 1989 (as VALMONT).▼

Dangerous Love (1988) **C-96m.** BOMB D: Marty Ollstein. Lawrence Monoson, Brenda Bakke, Peter Marc, Teri Austin, Sal Landi, Anthony Geary, Elliott Gould. Someone is videotaping, and murdering, female members of a video dating club. A truly sloppy, stupid film. PEEPING TOM this ain't.▼

Dangerously Close (1986) C-95m. *½ D: Albert Pyun. John Stockwell, J. Eddie Peck, Carey Lowell, Bradford Bancroft, Don Michael Paul, Thom Mathews, Jerry Dinome, Madison Mason. Annoyingly muddled account of some rich, clean-cut young fascists who sadistically bully those in their school who are of the "wrong element." Slickly edited and photographed, and there's the germ of a serious theme—about the danger of blindly following leaders—but the result is sloppily plotted and laughably predictable.▼

Dangerously They Live (1942) 77m. **½ D: Robert Florey. John Garfield, Nancy Coleman, Raymond Massey, Moroni Olsen, Lee Patrick. When spy Coleman is captured by Nazis, doctor Garfield comes to her aid. Tried-and-true WW2 spy melodrama.

Dangerous Mission (1954) C-75m. *½ D: Louis King. Victor Mature, Piper Laurie, William Bendix, Vincent Price, Betta St. John. Laurie, witness to gang murder, flees N.Y.C. to Glacier National Park. Embarrassingly bad film was apparently edited with a buzz saw; if you must watch, look for Dennis Weaver in Bendix's office.

Dangerous Money (1946) 64m. D: Terry Morse. Sidney Toler, Gloria Warren, Victor Sen Yung, Rick Vallin, Joseph Crehan. Also known as CHARLIE CHAN IN DANGEROUS MONEY. SEE: **Charlie Chan** series.

Dangerous Moonlight (1941-British) 83m. *** D: Brian Desmond Hurst. Anton Walbrook, Sally Gray, Derrick de Marney, Keneth Kent. Intelligently presented account of concert pianist who becomes a member of a British bomber squadron during WW2; musical interludes well handled. Look for Michael Rennie in a small role. Retitled: SUICIDE SQUADRON.▼

Dangerous Moves (1984-Swiss) C-100m. *** D: Richard Dembo. Michel Piccoli, Alexandre Arbatt, Leslie Caron, Liv Ullmann, Daniel Olbrychski, Michel Aumont. Absorbing, thought-provoking film about international intrigue surrounding a world chess championship. Academy Award winner for Best Foreign Film.▼

Dangerous Orphans (1986-New Zealand) C/B&W-94m. ** D: John Laing. Peter Stevens, Jennifer Ward-Lealand, Michael Hurst, Ross Girven, Ian Mune, Zac Wallace, Grant Tilly. Slick but standard, bloody actioner about title trio and their vendetta against the thugs who wrecked their lives when they were boys. Plays like a TV series episode.▼

Dangerous Partners (1945) 74m. **½ D: Edward L. Cahn. James Craig, Signe Hasso, Edmund Gwenn, Andrey Totter, Mabel Paige. Craig and Hasso stumble into fortune in airplane accident; ensuing complications and chase are exciting.

Dangerous Passion (1990) C-100m. TVM D: Michael Miller. Carl Weathers, Billy Dee Williams, Lonette McKee, Elpidia Carrillo, Michael Beach. Pedestrian but violent action film harkening back to the "blaxploitation" 1970s, with he-man Weathers taking a job with crime boss Williams, getting himself seduced by latter's sexy wife, and spending the remaining reels on the run with her. Below average.

Dangerous Profession, A (1949) 79m. ** D: Ted Tetzlaff. George Raft, Pat O'Brien, Ella Raines, Jim Backus, Roland Winters, Robert Gist. Mystery yarn involving ex-bondsman, blackmail, and murder; not bad but standard.

Dangerous Pursuit (1990) C-100m. TVM D: Sandor Stern. Alexandra Powers, Gregory Harrison, Brian Wimmer, Elena Stiteler, Scott Valentine, Robert Prosky. Young woman who spent the night with a charming stranger (later discovered to be a paid assassin) finds herself being stalked by the same man when their paths cross several years later. Average.

Dangerous Summer, A (1981-Australian) C-100m. *½ D: Quentin Masters. Tom Skerritt, Ian Gilmour, James Mason, Wendy Hughes, Ray Barrett, Guy Doleman. Confusing, hilariously unsubtle drama about psychotic arsonist Gilmour attempting to torch a summer resort. Good cast looks collectively ill-at-ease. Originally titled THE BURNING MAN.▼

Dangerous to Know (1938) 70m. **½ D: Robert Florey. Akim Tamiroff, Anna May Wong, Gail Patrick, Lloyd Nolan, Harvey Stephens, Anthony Quinn. Neat little B about mobster Tamiroff fixing things so he can marry high-class Patrick; everything backfires.

Dangerous When Wet (1953) C-95m. ** D: Charles Walters. Esther Williams, Fernando Lamas, Jack Carson, Charlotte Greenwood, Denise Darcel. Williams is Midwestern lass hankering to win fame and fortune by swimming English Channel; Lamas romances her in between laps, Greenwood supplies brief comic moments.▼

Danger Route (1968-British) C-90m. ** D: Seth Holt. Richard Johnson, Carol Lynley, Barbara Bouchet, Sylvia Sims, Diana Dors, Harry Andrews, Gordon Jackson, Sam Wanamaker. Appearance (in both senses of the word) of Lynley and Bouchet give a little boost to typical secret-agent tale with several plot twists.

Danger Signal (1945) 78m. ** D: Robert Florey. Faye Emerson, Zachary Scott, Rosemary DeCamp, Bruce Bennett, Mona Freeman. No-account Scott comes between Emerson and her family in this routine drama; Scott is a most convincing heel.▼

Dangers of the Canadian Mounted SEE: **R.C.M.P. and the Treasure of Genghis Khan**

Danger Within SEE: **Breakout** (1959)

Daniel (1983) **C-130m.** *** D: Sidney Lumet. Timothy Hutton, Mandy Patinkin, Lindsay Crouse, Edward Asner, Ellen Barkin, Julie Bovasso, Tovah Feldshuh, Joseph Leon, Amanda Plummer, John Rubinstein. Excellent adaptation of E. L. Doctorow's *The Book of Daniel*, about the children of a couple patterned after Julius and Ethel Rosenberg who must confront their painful heritage in order to deal with their own lives in the protest-filled 1960s. Not without its flaws, but overall a provocative and extremely well-made film.▼

Daniel Boone (1936) **75m.** **½ D: David Howard. George O'Brien, Heather Angel, John Carradine, Ralph Forbes, Clarence Muse. OK action adventure detailing a chapter in the life of the legendary pioneer: his leading some settlers west from North Carolina into Kentucky. O'Brien is well cast in the title role.▼

Daniel Boone, Trail Blazer (1956) **C-76m.** **½ D: Albert C. Gannaway, Ismael Rodriquez. Bruce Bennett, Lon Chaney, Faron Young, Kem Dibbs. Generally well-acted low-budget version of life of famous frontier scout and his skirmishes with redskins. Filmed in Mexico.▼

Dante's Inferno (1935) **88m.** **½ D: Harry Lachman. Spencer Tracy, Claire Trevor, Henry B. Walthall, Alan Dinehart, Scotty Beckett. No Dante in this yarn of carnival owner who gets too big for his own good; just one scene showing Satan's paradise in good Tracy vehicle. Young Rita Hayworth dances in one scene.

Danton (1982-Polish-French) **C-136m.** **** D: Andrzej Wajda. Gerard Depardieu, Wojciech Pszoniak, Patrice Chereau, Angela Winkler, Boguslaw Linda. Literate, absorbing, knowing drama of Danton, Robespierre, and the Reign of Terror following the French Revolution. A brilliant film, with obvious parallels to contemporary political situation in Poland. Depardieu is magnificent in the title role.▼

Darby O'Gill and the Little People (1959) **C-93m.** ***½ D: Robert Stevenson. Albert Sharpe, Janet Munro, Sean Connery, Jimmy O'Dea, Kieron Moore, Estelle Winwood. Outstanding Disney fantasy about an Irish caretaker (Sharpe) who spins so many tales that no one believes him when he says he's befriended the King of Leprechauns. An utter delight, with dazzling special effects—and some truly terrifying moments along with the whimsy.▼

Darby's Rangers (1958) **121m.** **½ D: William Wellman. James Garner, Etchika Choureau, Jack Warden, Edward Byrnes, David Janssen. Garner does well in WW2 actioner as leader of assault troops in North Africa and Italy, focusing on relationship among his command and their shore romances.

Daredevil, The (1972) **C-70m.** ** D: Robert W. Stringer. George Montgomery, Terry Moore, Gay Perkins, Cyril Poitier, Bill Kelly. Offbeat, somewhat unappetizing actioner has heel Montgomery, a top racer, as driver for a dope ring. One of the odd twists has Poitier, a black mortician, cast as villain. Music by The Brooklyn Bridge.

Daring Dobermans, The (1973) **C-90m.** **½ D: Bryon Chudnow. Charles Knox Robinson, Tim Considine, David Moses, Claudio Martinez, Joan Caulfield. Sequel to THE DOBERMAN GANG provides amiable family viewing as the canines are trained for another daring heist by a new gang of crooks.▼

Daring Game (1968) **C-100m.** **½ D: Laslo Benedek. Lloyd Bridges, Nico Minardos, Michael Ansara, Joan Blackman. Not bad adventure tale of underwater expert (guess who?) in search of husband and daughter of his former girlfriend.▼

Daring Young Man (1942) **73m.** ** D: Frank Strayer. Joe E. Brown, Marguerite Chapman, William Wright, Roger Clark. Brown is able to make this formula Nazi spy chase comedy of passable interest; set in N.Y.C.

Dark, The (1979) **C-92m.** ** D: John (Bud) Cardos. William Devane, Cathy Lee Crosby, Richard Jaeckel, Keenan Wynn, Jacquelyn Hyde, Biff Elliott, Vivian Blaine. Fairly well made but predictable sci-fier; writer Devane and TV reporter Crosby take on a homicidal alien in a California town.▼

Dark Alibi (1946) **61m.** D: Phil Karlson. Sidney Toler, Mantan Moreland, Ben Carter, Benson Fong, Russell Hicks, Joyce Compton, Edward Earle. SEE: **Charlie Chan** series.

Dark Angel, The (1935) **110m.** *** D: Sidney Franklin. Fredric March, Merle Oberon, Herbert Marshall, Janet Beecher, John Halliday. Well-acted soaper of two men in love with same woman; fighting in WW1, one of them going blind.

Dark at the Top of the Stairs, The (1960) **C-123m.** *** D: Delbert Mann. Robert Preston, Dorothy McGuire, Eve Arden, Angela Lansbury, Shirley Knight. Superficial handling of William Inge play set in 1920s Oklahoma, revolving around Preston's family and neighbors, their problems and frustrations; still good. Arden and Lansbury come off best.

Dark Avenger, The SEE: **Warriors, The** (1955)▼

Dark City (1950) **88m.** **½ D: William

Dieterle. Charlton Heston, Lizabeth Scott, Viveca Lindfors, Dean Jagger, Jack Webb. In first major film role, Heston portrays alienated WW2 veteran-turned-gambler who becomes object of deranged killer. Scott and Webb uplift predictable casino-club-naked-city proceedings.

Dark Command (1940) 94m. *** D: Raoul Walsh. John Wayne, Claire Trevor, Walter Pidgeon, Roy Rogers, George "Gabby" Hayes, Marjorie Main. Pidgeon plays character patterned after 1860s renegade Quantrill, small-town despot who (in this story) launches his terror raids after clashing with newly elected marshal Wayne. Dramatically uneven, but entertaining.▼

Dark Corner, The (1946) 99m. *** D: Henry Hathaway. Lucille Ball, Clifton Webb, William Bendix, Mark Stevens, Reed Hadley, Constance Collier. Top-notch mystery with secretary Ball helping moody boss Stevens escape from phony murder charge. Well-acted, exciting *film noir.*▼

Dark Crystal, The (1983-British) C-94m. *** D: Jim Henson and Frank Oz. Performed by Jim Henson, Kathryn Mullen, Frank Oz, Dave Goelz, Brian Muehl, Jean Pierre Amiel, Kiran Shah. Elaborate fantasy—a cross between Tolkien and the Brothers Grimm—from the Muppets crew, with imaginative (and often grotesque) cast of characters enacting classic quest: a missing piece of the powerful Dark Crystal must be found or evil will take over the world. Takes time to warm up to, but worth the effort.▼

Dark Delusion (1947) 90m. D: Willis Goldbeck. Lionel Barrymore, James Craig, Lucille Bremer, Jayne Meadows, Warner Anderson. SEE: **Dr. Kildare** series.

Dark End of the Street, The (1981) C-90m. *** D: Jan Egleson. Laura Harrington, Henry Tomaszewski, Michelle Green, Lance Henriksen, Pamela Payton-Wright, Terence Grey, Al Eaton. Low-budget independent feature, shot in and around Boston, about white teenagers Harrington and Tomaszewski, who witness a black friend's accidental death. Realistic depiction of urban working-class lifestyle and problems. Fine performances, particularly by Harrington and Green (as her best friend).

Darker Side of Terror, The (1979) C-100m. TVM D: Gus Trikonis. Robert Forster, Adrienne Barbeau, Ray Milland, David Sheiner, John Lehne. Inept psychological thriller about a researcher who agrees to have himself cloned and then must fight his look-alike for his wife's affections. Below average.

Darker Than Amber (1970) C-97m. **½ D: Robert Clouse. Rod Taylor, Suzy Kendall, Theodore Bikel, Jane Russell, James Booth, Janet MacLachlan. OK action melo-

drama casts Taylor as John D. MacDonald's detective Travis McGee; he's after thugs who beat up Kendall. Good location photography in Miami and Caribbean.

Darkest Africa SEE: **Batmen of Africa**

Dark Eyes (1987-Italian) C-118m. ***½ D: Nikita Mikhalkov. Marcello Mastroianni, Silvana Mangano, Marthe Keller, Elena Sofonova, Pina Cei. Mastroianni gives a tour-de-force performance as a once-young, idealistic, aspiring architect, who settled for a life of wealth and ease after marrying a banker's daughter . . . and proved incapable of holding on to what's important to him. A rich, beautifully detailed, multileveled film that's at once sad, funny, and haunting. Based on short stories by Anton Chekhov.▼

Dark Eyes of London SEE: **Human Monster, The**▼

Dark Forces SEE: **Harlequin**▼

Dark Habits (1984-Spanish) C-116m. **½ D: Pedro Almodóvar. Cristina S. Pascual, Carmen Maura, Julieta Serrano, Marisa Paredes. Singer Pascual takes it on the lam after her lover ODs and finds herself in a convent crammed with wacky, free-spirited nuns. Funny, but not up to Almodóvar's later work.▼

Dark Hazard (1934) 72m. ** D: Alfred E. Green. Edward G. Robinson, Genevieve Tobin, Glenda Farrell, Henry B. Walthall, Sidney Toler. Robinson is bright spot of programmer about his precarious married life to Tobin, endangered by girlfriend Farrell and urge to gamble.

Dark Holiday (1989) C-100m. TVM D: Lou Antonio. Lee Remick, Norma Aleandro, Roy Thinnes, Ken Horton, Jim Antonio, Shanit Keter. A haughty American divorcee, on holiday in Istanbul, is tossed into prison for trying to "smuggle" out of the country some antiquities she innocently bought from street vendors. A highly sanitized, change-of-sex copy of MIDNIGHT EXPRESS, adapted from Gene LePere's personal account of her experience, *Never Pass This Way Again.* Average.

Dark Horse (1932) 75m. **½ D: Alfred E. Green. Warren William, Bette Davis, Guy Kibbee, Vivienne Osborne, Frank McHugh. Lively political spoof with nitwit Kibbee running for governor with help from campaign manager William and co-worker Davis.

Dark Intruder (1965) 59m. *** D: Harvey Hart. Leslie Nielsen, Judi Meredith, Mark Richman, Werner Klemperer, Gilbert Green, Charles Bolender. Uneven performances major liability in near-flawless supernatural thriller. Occult expert called in by San Francisco police in connection with series of weird murders. Intricate plot and exceptional use of time period blending with suspense make this a one-of-a-kind movie. Busted TV pilot given theatrical release.

Dark Journey (1937-British) **82m.** *** D: Victor Saville. Conrad Veidt, Vivien Leigh, Joan Gardner, Anthony Bushell, Ursula Jeans. Engrossing love story, set in WW1 Stockholm, about dress-shop-owner-double agent Leigh, who becomes involved with baron Veidt, the head of German Intelligence. Young Vivien is radiant.▼

Dark Mansions (1986) **C-100m. TVM** D: Jerry London. Joan Fontaine, Michael York, Paul Shenar, Melissa Sue Anderson, Linda Purl, Steve Inwood, Lois Chiles, Dan O'Herlihy, Raymond St. Jacques, Nicollette Sheridan, Grant Aleksander. Dreary contemporary gothic thriller about a shipbuilding clan in Seattle and the young woman (Purl) who finds herself up against supernatural forces when she moves into the family compound to chronicle its history. A prospective series pilot. Average.

Dark Mirror, The (1946) **85m.** *** D: Robert Siodmak. Olivia de Havilland, Lew Ayres, Thomas Mitchell, Richard Long, Charles Evans, Garry Owen. De Havilland plays twin sisters—one good, one disturbed—who are implicated in murder. One of Hollywood's post-WW2 forays into psychological drama; no longer fresh, but still entertaining. Remade for TV.▼

Dark Mirror (1984) **C-100m. TVM** D: Richard Lang. Jane Seymour, Stephen Collins, Vincent Gardenia, Hank Brandt, Ty Henderson, Jack Kruschen. Disappointing remake of the Olivia de Havilland good twin/evil twin murder thriller. Scripter Corey Blechman (BILL) painted this one with too broad a stroke; glum cast plays second fiddle to Jane and Jane, both overly flamboyant. Average.

Dark Night of the Scarecrow (1981) **C-100m. TVM** D: Frank De Felitta. Charles Durning, Robert F. Lyons, Claude Earl Jones, Lane Smith, Tonya Crowe, Larry Drake, Jocelyn Brando. Satisfying if predictable chiller about a young girl's innocent friendship with the town dummy, whose killing by a group of vigilantes leads to a series of inexplicable events. Above average.▼

Dark Obsession (1989-British) **C-87m.** BOMB D: Nicholas Broomfield. Gabriel Byrne, Amanda Donohoe, Michael Hordern, Judy Parfitt, Douglas Hodge, Sadie Frost, Ian Carmichael. Byrne and his buddies from the regiment run over a chambermaid after a night of drinking—and the only one who feels guilt about the death is the only one who will suffer. Documentary director Broomfield's first fiction feature is an obvious, boring parable about the amorality of the rich and titled. Even

Donohoe's frequent nudity quickly becomes dreary. Original British title DIAMOND SKULLS.

Dark of the Night (1985-New Zealand) **C-89m.** *** D: Gaylene Preston. Heather Bolton, David Letch, Gary Stalker, Danny Mulheron, Kate Harcourt, Michael Haigh. Bolton buys a used Jaguar that's seemingly haunted by its previous owner, a woman who was murdered. Entertainingly loopy psychological thriller that's also a keenly observed feminist fable about the frustrations and perils of a woman seeking independence in a "man's world." The original New Zealand title is MR. WRONG.

Dark of the Sun (1968-British) **C-101m.** *** D: Jack Cardiff. Rod Taylor, Yvette Mimieux, Jim Brown, Kenneth More, Peter Carsten, Andre Morell, Calvin Lockhart. Excellent cast in nerve-wracking actioner with Rod the leader of mercenary expedition to retrieve uncut diamonds and besieged refugees in Congo. One of Taylor's best pictures.

Dark Passage (1947) **106m.** *** D: Delmer Daves. Humphrey Bogart, Lauren Bacall, Bruce Bennett, Agnes Moorehead. Engrossing caper of escaped convict (Bogart) undergoing plastic surgery, hiding out at Bacall's apartment till his face heals. Stars outshine far-fetched happenings.▼

Dark Past, The (1948) **75m.** *** D: Rudolph Maté. William Holden, Nina Foch, Lee J. Cobb, Adele Jergens, Stephen Dunne. Absorbing narrative of mad killer holding psychologist prisoner and latter's attempts to talk sense into the maniac. Remake of BLIND ALLEY.▼

Dark Places (1974-British) **C-91m.** *½ D: Don Sharp. Christopher Lee, Joan Collins, Robert Hardy, Herbert Lom, Jane Birkin, Jean Marsh. Mild horror thriller. Hardy, heir to an insane murderer's estate, is possessed by his spirit, kills those who try to do him out of it.▼

Dark Sands (1937-British) **77m.** ** D: Thornton Freeland. Paul Robeson, Henry Wilcoxon, Wallace Ford, Princess Kouka, John Laurie. Weak drama with American deserter Robeson joining African desert tribe to avoid corporal punishment. Robeson again defeated by his material. Originally titled JERICHO.▼

Dark Secret of Harvest Home (1978) **C-200m. TVM** D: Leo Penn. Bette Davis, David Ackroyd, Rosanna Arquette, Rene Auberjonois, Norman Lloyd, Michael O'Keefe. Leisurely gothic horror tale set in New England village where Bette and other weirdos maintain ritualistic lifestyle, to the dismay of commercial artist who has moved his family there from Manhattan. Adapted from Thomas Tryon's novel *Harvest Home;* narrated in eerie fashion by Donald Pleasence. Above average.▼

Dark Side of Innocence, The (1976) **C-78m. TVM** D: Jerry Thorpe. Joanna Pettet, Anne Archer, John Anderson, Kim Hunter, Lawrence Casey, Claudette Nevins. Contemporary soap opera focusing primarily on Pettet, an affluent housewife oppressed by her domesticity, who walks out on her husband and two kids, and Archer, her sister embittered by a recent divorce. Average.

Dark Star (1974) **C-83m.** ****½** D: John Carpenter. Dan O'Bannon, Dre Pahich, Brian Narelle. Satiric, spaced-out version of 2001 with four wacko astronauts who think their mission is to bomb unstable planets. Enjoyable for sci-fi fans and surfers; stretches its shoestring budget pretty well. Carpenter's first feature, expanded from a college short he wrote with O'Bannon.▼

Darktown Strutters (1975) **C-85m.** ***½** D: William Witney. Trina Parks, Edna Richardson, Bettye Sweet, Shirley Washington, Roger E. Mosley, Stan Shaw, Christopher Joy. Poor spoof of black and white stereotypes. Story is about Parks attempting to find her kidnapped mother. Original running time: 90m. Retitled GET DOWN AND BOOGIE.▼

√ **Dark Victory** (1939) **106m.** *****½** D: Edmund Goulding. Bette Davis, George Brent, Humphrey Bogart, Geraldine Fitzgerald, Ronald Reagan, Cora Witherspoon, Henry Travers. Definitive Davis performance as spoiled socialite whose life is ending; Brent as brain surgeon husband, Fitzgerald as devoted friend register in good soaper. Bogart as Irish stable master seems out of place. Remade as STOLEN HOURS, then again in 1976. Also shown in computer-colored version.▼

Dark Victory (1976) **C-150m. TVM** D: Robert Butler. Elizabeth Montgomery, Anthony Hopkins, Michele Lee, Janet MacLachlan, Michael Lerner, John Elerick, Vic Tayback, Herbert Berghof. Updated version of Bette Davis classic has Montgomery as TV producer who falls in love with the doctor who tells her she has a brain tumor. Former four-hankie weeper now is curiously unaffecting, despite the professionalism of its cast. Updating failed to help the old chestnut, nor did subsequent slicing of an hour. Average.

Dark Waters (1944) **90m.** ****** D: Andre de Toth. Merle Oberon, Franchot Tone, Thomas Mitchell, Fay Bainter, Rex Ingram, John Qualen, Elisha Cook, Jr. Cast sinks into the bog (some literally) in confused film of/innocent girl staying with peculiar family.▼

Darling (1965-British) **122m.** *****½** D: John Schlesinger. Julie Christie, Dirk Bogarde, Laurence Harvey, Roland Curram, Jose Luis de Villalonga, Alex Scott, Basil Henson. Christie won Oscar as girl who rises from commonplace life to marry an Italian noble, with several unsatisfactory love affairs in between. Trendy, influential 60s film—in flashy form and cynical content. Frederic Raphael's script and costume designer Julie Harris also won Oscars.▼

Darling, How Could You (1951) **96m.** ****½** D: Mitchell Leisen. Joan Fontaine, John Lund, Mona Freeman, Peter Hanson. Chic stars brighten old-fashioned James Barrie play about teen-ager who thinks her mother (Fontaine) is having an affair.

Darling Lili (1970) **C-136m.** ******* D: Blake Edwards. Julie Andrews, Rock Hudson, Jeremy Kemp, Lance Percival, Jacques Marin, Michael Witney. Critically lambasted when first released, this entertaining spoof has Andrews and Hudson at their best, along with writer/director Edwards, keeping tongue-in-cheek but not becoming coy in telling story of German spy Julie posing as London entertainer during WW1, falling in love with squadron commander Hudson. Great fun, good music, including Johnny Mercer and Henry Mancini's lovely song "Whistling Away the Dark."

Darwin Adventure, The (1972) **C-91m.** ****½** D: Jack Couffer. Nicholas Clay, Susan Macready, Ian Richardson, Christopher Martin. Curious tale focusing on career of Charles Darwin and his theories on evolution of man.

D.A.R.Y.L. (1985) **C-99m.** ****½** D: Simon Wincer. Mary Beth Hurt, Michael McKean, Barret Oliver, Kathryn Walker, Colleen Camp, Josef Sommer, Steve Ryan, Danny Corkill. Childless couple adopts a little boy who turns out to be a highly sophisticated robot. Good premise undermined by incredibly bland presentation; young kids will probably enjoy it.▼

Das Boot (1981-German) **C-145m.** *****½** D: Wolfgang Petersen. Jurgen Prochnow, Herbert Gronemeyer, Klaus Wennemann, Hubertus Bengsch, Martin Semmelrogge, Bernd Tauber, Erwin Leder, Martin May. Realistic, meticulously mounted nail-biter chronicling a German U-boat on a mission during WW2, with Prochnow solid as its commander. Manages to embrace an anti-war message, as well. Based on Lothar-Guenther Buchheim's autobiographical novel. Originally shot as a six-hour TV miniseries. Well-dubbed American version is titled THE BOAT.▼

Date with an Angel (1987) **C-105m.** BOMB D: Tom McLoughlin. Michael E. Knight, Phoebe Cates, Emmanuelle Beart, David Dukes, Phil Brock, Albert Macklin. Aspiring musician Knight, about to be swallowed up by marriage and his future father-in-law's firm, finds salvation with the broken-winged angel who crashes into his pool on the night of his bachelor party.

Unbearable comic fantasy despite Beart's appropriately ethereal beauty.▼

Date with Death, A SEE: **McGuire Go Home!**

Date With Judy, A (1948) **C-113m.** **½ D: Richard Thorpe. Wallace Beery, Jane Powell, Elizabeth Taylor, Carmen Miranda, Xavier Cugat, Robert Stack, Scotty Beckett. Musicomedy of two teen-agers involved in family shenanigans; highlight is Beery dancing with Miranda. Songs include "It's a Most Unusual Day."▼

Date with the Falcon, A (1941) **63m.** D: Irving Reis. George Sanders, Wendy Barrie, Allen Jenkins, James Gleason, Mona Maris, Frank Moran. SEE: Falcon series.

Daughter of Darkness (1990) **C-100m.** TVM D: Stuart Gordon. Anthony Perkins, Mia Sara, Jack Coleman, Robert Reynolds, Dezso Garas, Mari Kiss, Ference Nemethy. Supernatural thriller about an American schoolteacher's search for her long-lost father in Eastern Europe that leads into the world of vampires. Tony's modern-day Dracula is not to be missed. Average.

Daughter of Dr. Jekyll (1957) **71m.** *½ D: Edgar G. Ulmer. John Agar, Gloria Talbott, Arthur Shields, John Dierkes. Silly spinoff on Robert Louis Stevenson's novel. Talbott thinks she is cursed with inheritance of part human, part monster. She's wrong; someone else has got hold of her daddy's secret formula. Madly scrambles vampire, werewolf, and Jekyll-Hyde story elements.▼

Daughter of Mata Hari SEE: **Mata Hari's Daughter**

Daughter of Rosie O'Grady, The (1950) **C-104m.** **½ D: David Butler. June Haver, Gordon MacRae, Debbie Reynolds, Gene Nelson, James Barton, S. Z. Sakall, Jane Darwell. Formula period musical with Haver in title role singing turn-of-the-century favorites. Talented MacRae is her love interest, and Sakall is forced to give another cuddly stereotype.

Daughter of Shanghai (1937) **63m.** **½ D: Robert Florey. Anna May Wong, Charles Bickford, Buster Crabbe, Cecil Cunningham, J. Carrol Naish, Anthony Quinn, Philip Ahn. Good-girl Wong seeks to expose illegal alien racket in tight-knit "B" actioner.

Daughter of the Dragon (1931) **72m.** **½ D: Lloyd Corrigan. Warner Oland, Anna May Wong, Sessue Hayakawa, Bramwell Fletcher, Francis Dade, Holmes Herbert. Oland is Dr. Fu Manchu in this entertaining, if familiar, adaptation of a Sax Rohmer story; the good doctor dispatches daughter Wong to commit murder, and she becomes entangled with Scotland Yard sleuth Hayakawa.

Daughter of the Mind (1969) **C-90m.** TVM D: Walter Grauman. Ray Milland, Gene Tierney, Don Murray, George Mac-

ready, Edward Asner, John Carradine. Professor Milland, convinced daughter is trying to communicate from beyond grave, hires parapsychologist; FBI steps in due to scientist's previous work with government. Wide-eyed and inconsequential. Adapted by Luther Davis from Paul Gallico's *The Hand of Mary Constable*. Originally broadcast at 73m. Average.

Daughter of the Streets (1990) **C-100m.** TVM D: Ed Sherin. Jane Alexander, Roxana Zal, Harris Yulin, Martha Scott, John Stamos, Brandon Maggart. Mom discovers her teenage daughter to be a prostitute, and vows to get her off the streets, in this shrill drama that pales in comparison to OFF THE MINNESOTA STRIP, done a decade earlier. Alexander was directed here by husband Sherin. Average.

Daughters Courageous (1939) **107m.** *** D: Michael Curtiz. John Garfield, Claude Rains, Fay Bainter, Priscilla Lane, Rosemary Lane, Lola Lane, Gale Page, May Robson, Donald Crisp, Frank McHugh. Enjoyable reworking of FOUR DAUGHTERS, featuring the same cast and chronicling what happens when wanderer Rains returns to the family he abandoned 20 years before. Garfield is fine as the brash charmer who's romancing Priscilla Lane.

Daughters of Darkness (1971-Belgian-French) **C-87m.** **½ D: Harry Kumel. Delphine Seyrig, Daniele Ouimet, John Karlen, Andrea Rau, Paul Esser, George Jamin, Joris Collet, Fons Rademakers. Sophisticated, witty, but cold tale of honeymooning couple meeting lesbian vampire Elisabeth Bathory (a real historical figure), becoming enmeshed in her schemes. Elegant, but pretentious and slow. Highly regarded by many. Also shown at 96m.▼

Daughters of Destiny (1954-French) **94m.** ** D: Marcel Pagliero. Claudette Colbert, Michele Morgan, André Clement, Daniel Ivernel. Over-blown, sluggish trio of tales telling of three famous women of history: Elizabeth I, Lysistrata, Joan of Arc.

Daughters of Joshua Cabe, The (1972) **C-73m.** TVM D: Philip Leacock. Buddy Ebsen, Karen Valentine, Lesley (Ann) Warren, Sandra Dee, Jack Elam, Leif Erickson, Don Stroud. New homesteading law and refusal of daughters to return West forces trapper Cabe (Ebsen) to hire three women to pose as his children. A TV timefiller. Followed by THE NEW DAUGHTERS OF JOSHUA CABE. Average.

Daughters of Joshua Cabe Return, The (1975) **C-78m.** TVM D: David Lowell Rich. Dan Dailey, Ronne Troup, Christina Hart, Brooke Adams, Dub Taylor, Carl Betz, Arthur Hunnicutt, Terry Wilson, Kathleen Freeman. Second sequel to 1972 movie with Dailey taking over as the rascally rancher, who, with the three shady ladies he has hired to pose as his daughters, is outwitted by the real dad of one of them, who holds her for a ransom Cabe cannot pay. Average.

Daughters of Satan (1972) **C-96m.** ** D: Hollingsworth Morse. Tom Selleck, Barra Grant, Tani Phelps Guthrie, Paraluman. Witches' curses, mumbo jumbo, and a lot of hokum as young girl is lured into witches' coven.▼

David (1979-German) **C-106m.** ***½ D: Peter Lilienthal. Mario Fischel, Walter Taub, Irene Vrkijan, Torsten Hentes, Eva Mattes. Jewish teenager Fischel manages to survive in Berlin during the Nazi reign of terror. Sometimes hard to follow, but still touching, haunting, powerful in its own quiet way. Based on a novel by Joel Konig.▼

David (1988) **C-100m. TVM** D: John Erman. Bernadette Peters, John Glover, Matthew Laurance, George Grizzard, Dan Lauria, Christopher Allport. Peters is Marie Rothberg, the single-minded woman dedicated to the well-being of her son after his father tried to burn him to death. Well-played drama based on an incredible real-life story. Adapted by Stephanie Liss from the book Rothberg wrote with Mel White. Above average.▼

David and Bathsheba (1951) **C-116m.** ** D: Henry King. Gregory Peck, Susan Hayward, Raymond Massey, Kieron Moore, James Robertson Justice, Jayne Meadows, John Sutton, George Zucco. Biblical epic with good production values but generally boring script; only fair performances.▼

David and Goliath (1961-Italian) **C-95m.** ** D: Richard Pottier, Ferdinando Baldi. Orson Welles, Ivo Payer, Edward Hilton, Eleonora Rossi-Drago, Massimo Serato. Juvenile spectacle based on biblical tale, with wooden script, bad acting, Welles as hefty King Saul.

✓ **David and Lisa** (1963) **94m.** *** D: Frank Perry. Keir Dullea, Janet Margolin, Howard da Silva, Neva Patterson, Clifton James. Independently made film about two disturbed teen-agers is excellent, sensitively played by newcomers Dullea and Margolin. Da Silva is fine as an understanding doctor.

✓ **David Copperfield** (1935) **130m.** **** D: George Cukor. Freddie Bartholomew, Frank Lawton, W.C. Fields, Lionel Barrymore, Madge Evans, Roland Young, Basil Rathbone, Edna May Oliver, Maureen O'Sullivan, Lewis Stone, Lennox Pawle, Elsa Lanchester, Una O'Connor, Arthur Treacher. Hollywood does right by Dickens in this lavishly mounted, superbly cast production, following David's exploits from youth to young manhood, with such unforgettable characterizations as Fields's Micawber, Rathbone's Mr. Murdstone, Young's Uriah Heep, and Oliver's Aunt Betsey. A treat from start to finish. Screenplay by Howard Estabrook and Hugh Walpole, the latter also portrays the vicar.▼

David Copperfield (1970) **C-110m. TVM** D: Delbert Mann. Robin Phillips, Susan Hampshire, Edith Evans, Michael Redgrave, Ralph Richardson, Laurence Olivier, Wendy Hiller, Emlyn Williams, Richard Attenborough. Top-drawer cast in moody new version of the classic. The giants of the English theater give what support they can to a rather limp script and an unanimated lead. Average.

David Harum (1934) **83m.** **½ D: James Cruze. Will Rogers, Louise Dresser, Evelyn Venable, Kent Taylor, Stepin Fetchit, Noah Beery, Charles Middleton. Foxy rancher Rogers plays matchmaker for Venable and Taylor, while spinning his own brand of folksy humor.

David Holzman's Diary (1968) **74m.** ***½ D: Jim McBride. L. M. Kit Carson, Eileen Dietz, Louise Levine, Lorenzo Mans. Superior, perceptively funny cinema verite feature about a serious young filmmaker who seeks truth by making a movie of his life. A classic of its kind.

Davy Crockett and the River Pirates (1956) **C-81m.** **½ D: Norman Foster. Fess Parker, Buddy Ebsen, Jeff York, Kenneth Tobey, Clem Bevans, Irvin Ashkenazy. Second CROCKETT feature strung together from two Disney TV shows; first half is comic riverboat race with Mike Fink (York), second half is more serious confrontation with Indians. Lightweight fun.▼

Davy Crockett, Indian Scout (1950) **71m.** ** D: Lew Landers. George Montgomery, Ellen Drew, Philip Reed, Chief Thundercloud. Humdrum wagon train saga which has nothing whatsoever to do with the legend of Davy C. (Montgomery plays one of his descendants.) Retitled INDIAN SCOUT.

Davy Crockett, King of the Wild Frontier (1955) **C-93m.** *** D: Norman Foster. Fess Parker, Buddy Ebsen, Basil Ruysdael, Hans Conried, William Bakewell, Kenneth Tobey. Originally filmed as three segments for Disney's TV show, this created a nationwide phenomenon in 1955; it's still fun today with Parker as famous Indian scout and Ebsen as his pal George Russel, whose adventures take them from Washington, D.C. to the Alamo.▼

Dawn at Socorro (1954) **C-80m.** **½ D: George Sherman. Rory Calhoun, Piper Laurie, David Brian, Kathleen Hughes, Edgar Buchanan, Alex Nicol. Calhoun is gunslinger wishing to reform, but fate forces inevitable shootout.

Dawning, The (1988-British) **C-97m.** **½ D: Robert Knights. Anthony Hopkins, Jean Simmons, Trevor Howard, Rebecca Pidgeon, Hugh Grant, Tara MacGowran. Set in Southern Ireland in 1920, this well-made but curiously ordinary drama chronicles the political turmoil of the time as perceived by a spirited, rapidly maturing

18-year-old girl (Pidgeon) who comes to the aid of a mysterious stranger (Hopkins). Howard's last film; he's cast as her wheelchair-bound grandfather.

Dawn of the Dead (1979) C-126m. ***½ D: George A. Romero. David Emge, Ken Foree, Scott Reiniger, Gaylen Ross, Tom Savini. Sequel-cum-remake of NIGHT OF THE LIVING DEAD is apocalyptic horror masterpiece; as zombie population increases, four people set up quasi-Utopian existence in barricaded shopping mall. Satiric, metaphorically rich adventure jerks viewers' emotions around with stunning ease, as zombies are, by turns, horrifying, heroic, made clownish, and even forgotten. Savini's hideously gory effects are mostly confined to the first and last half hours. Nontheatrical prints run 140m. Followed by DAY OF THE DEAD.▼

Dawn Patrol, The (1930) 82m. **½ D: Howard Hawks. Richard Barthelmess, Douglas Fairbanks Jr., Neil Hamilton, William Janney, James Finlayson, Clyde Cook. John Monk Saunders's Oscar-winning story of a beleaguered aerial squadron in WW1 France. Devotees of director Hawks prefer this to 1938 remake, but it doesn't hold up as well, particularly the stiff, overdrawn performances. Originally 95m. TV title: FLIGHT COMMANDER.

Dawn Patrol, The (1938) 103m. ***½ D: Edmund Goulding. Errol Flynn, Basil Rathbone, David Niven, Donald Crisp, Melville Cooper, Barry Fitzgerald. Remake of 1930 classic is fine actioner of WW1 flyers in France; Rathbone as stern officer forced to send up green recruits, Flynn and Niven as pilot buddies, all excellent.▼

Dawn: Portrait of a Teenage Runaway (1976) C-100m. TVM D: Randal Kleiser. Eve Plumb, Leigh J. McCloskey, Bo Hopkins, Georg Stanford Brown, Lynn Carlin, Marg DeLain, Joan Prather, Anne Seymour, William Schallert, Anne Ramsey. Fifteen-year-old Plumb turns to prostitution when she cannot find legitimate work after running away from her cocktail waitress mom Carlin. Serious social issue exploited for cheap sensationalism. Sequel: ALEXANDER: THE OTHER SIDE OF DAWN. Below average.

Day After, The (1983) C-120m. TVM D: Nicholas Meyer. Jason Robards, JoBeth Williams, Steve Guttenberg, John Cullum, John Lithgow, Bibi Besch, Lori Lethin, Amy Madigan, Jeff East. Chilling aftereffects of the catastrophic nuclear bombing of Lawrence, Kansas, in a potent drama written by Edward Hume. Probably the most controversial TV movie of its time, with unrelenting grimness, performances ranging from sturdy to overwrought, and a rare musical score by David Raksin, with Virgil Thompson's "The River" interpolated. Foreign theatrical and homevideo tape (but *not* video disc) versions run 126m. Cut by 23m. for network rerun. Above average.▼

Day and the Hour, The (1963-French-Italian) 115m. **½ D: René Clement. Simone Signoret, Stuart Whitman, Genevieve Page, Michel Piccoli, Reggie Nalder, Pierre Dux, Billy Kearns. In Nazi-occupied France, Signoret is a widow who becomes involved in the Resistance movement; Whitman is an American paratrooper trying to escape to Spain. ▼

Day at the Races, A (1937) 111m. ***½ D: Sam Wood. Groucho, Harpo and Chico Marx, Allan Jones, Maureen O'Sullivan, Margaret Dumont, Douglass Dumbrille, Sig Ruman. The Marxes wreak havoc at a sanitorium, where wealthy hypochondriac Dumont is the leading patient; often uproarious comedy features some of the trio's funniest set-pieces (Chico selling race tips, the seduction scene, etc.). A perfunctory storyline, and unmemorable songs, keep it from topping its immediate predecessor, A NIGHT AT THE OPERA . . . but the comedy content is sensational.▼

Daybreak (1939) SEE: **Le Jour Se Lève**▼
Daybreak (1946-British) 75m. ** D: Compton Bennett. Eric Portman, Ann Todd, Maxwell Reed, Edward Rigby, Bill Owen, Jane Hylton. Repressed Portman weds sultry Todd. He's out of town once too often . . . while oily, menacing Reed comes on the scene. Contrived *film noir* is only modestly entertaining.

Day Christ Died, The (1980) C-150m. TVM D: James Cellan Jones. Chris Sarandon, Colin Blakely, Keith Michell, Hope Lange, Jonathan Pryce, Barrie Houghton. Tedious retelling of the events leading to the Crucifixion. Sarandon's mannered and sullen Jesus is counterbalanced by Michell's colorful Pilate in this script by James Lee Barrett and Edward Anhalt, "suggested" by Jim Bishop's book. Average.

Daydreamer, The (1966) C-98m. *** D: Jules Bass. Ray Bolger, Jack Gilford, Margaret Hamilton, Paul O'Keefe, voices of Tallulah Bankhead, Boris Karloff, Burl Ives, Victor Borge, Terry-Thomas, Patty Duke. Partly animated story of Hans Christian Andersen as a 13-year-old who meets many of the fairy tale characters he later writes about. Surprisingly pleasant.▼

Day for Night (1973-French) C-120m. ***½ D: Francois Truffaut. Jacqueline Bisset, Jean-Pierre Aumont, Valentina Cortese, Francois Truffaut, Jean-Pierre Leaud, Alexandra Stewart, Dani, Nathalie Baye. Enjoyable fluff about a motion picture director (Truffaut) and his problems in trying to film a silly love story; bright performances and a loving look into the intricacies of filmmaking. Oscar winner as Best Foreign Film.▼

Day for Thanks on Waltons' Mountain,

A (1982) **C-100m. TVM** D: Harry Harris. Ralph Waite, Ellen Corby, Judy Norton-Taylor, Eric Scott, Jon Walmsley, Robert Wightman, Mary Beth McDonough, David W. Harper, Kami Cotler, Joe Conley, Ronnie Clare Edwards, Richard Gilliland, Melinda Naud. It looks like the Walton clan won't be together for Thanksgiving, though the outcome is never really in doubt. Average.

Day in the Death of Joe Egg, A (1972-British) **C-106m.** ***½ D: Peter Medak. Alan Bates, Janet Suzman, Peter Bowles, Sheila Gish, Joan Hickson. Excellent black comedy about a couple with a child who contemplate mercy-killing. Not a crowd-pleaser, but extremely well done. Peter Nichols adapted his own play.▼

Day Mars Invaded Earth, The (1962) **70m.** *½ D: Maury Dexter. Kent Taylor, Marie Windsor, William Mims, Betty Beall, Lowell Brown, Gregg Shank. Martians are exact doubles for scientist Taylor and family as they wreak havoc on pitiful earthlings. Minor sci-fi B pic.

Day of Anger (1969-Italian) **C-109m.** *½ D: Tonino Valerii. Lee Van Cleef, Giuliano Gemma, Walter Rilla, Christa Linder, Ennio Balbo, Lukas Ammann. Story of callous gunman and his relationship with young protege is below par, even for an Italian Western; only for the Van Cleef cult.

Day of Fury, A (1956) **C-78m.** *** D: Harmon Jones. Dale Robertson, Mara Corday, Jock Mahoney, Carl Benton Reid. Offbeat study of rebellious Robertson who can't cope with conventions of Western town he lives in.

Day of the Animals (1977) **C-98m.** **½ D: William Girdler. Christopher George, Lynda Day George, Leslie Nielsen, Richard Jaeckel, Michael Ansara, Ruth Roman. Fair action thriller in the nature-on-the-rampage mold, with a cast of back packers in the High Sierras at the mercy of hostile creatures crazed by the sun's radiation after the earth's ozone layer has been ecologically destroyed. Final score: beasts 7, cast 0 (in acting as well as survival). Also known as SOMETHING IS OUT THERE.▼

Day of the Bad Man (1958) **C-81m.** ** D: Harry Keller. Fred MacMurray, Joan Weldon, John Ericson, Robert Middleton. MacMurray is appropriately stiff in tame account of country judge holding off condemned man's brothers so scheduled hanging can occur.

Day of the Dead (1985) **C-102m.** ** D: George A. Romero. Lori Cardille, Terry Alexander, Joseph Pilato, Jarlath Conroy, Antone DiLeo Jr. Richard Liberty, Howard Sherman. Romero's creatures trap a female scientist with some army sexists in an underground bunker; she wants to "study" them, but the army balks at being zombie brunch. Third DEAD entry is relentlessly talky for over an hour, but Tom Savini's effects do give this a show-stopping finale. Easily the least of the series.▼

Day of the Dolphin, The (1973) **C-104m.** ** D: Mike Nichols. George C. Scott, Trish Van Devere, Paul Sorvino, Fritz Weaver, Jon Korkes, Edward Herrmann, John Dehner. Big-budget misfire about scientist Scott using his trained (and talking!) dolphins to foil an assassination plot. A waste of many talents, including scripter Buck Henry, who also provides the voices for the dolphins.▼

Day of the Evil Gun (1968) **C-93m.** ** D: Jerry Thorpe. Glenn Ford, Arthur Kennedy, Dean Jagger, John Anderson, Paul Fix, Nico Minardos, Royal Dano, (Harry) Dean Stanton. Very routine Western with Ford and Kennedy going after Indians who abducted the former's wife; Kennedy is smooth in likable-villain role he's played many times.

Day of the Jackal, The (1973-British-French) **C-141m.** ***½ D: Fred Zinnemann. Edward Fox, Alan Badel, Tony Britton, Cyril Cusack, Michel Lonsdale, Eric Porter, Delphine Seyrig, Derek Jacobi, Ronald Pickup. Exciting adaptation of Frederick Forsyth's best-seller about plot to assassinate De Gaulle and the painstaking preparations of the assassin. Beautifully filmed throughout Europe with a first-rate cast.▼

Day of the Locust, The (1975) **C-144m.** ***½ D: John Schlesinger. Donald Sutherland, Karen Black, Burgess Meredith, William Atherton, Geraldine Page, Richard A. Dysart, Bo Hopkins. Excellent adaptation of Nathanael West's sweeping novel about Hollywood's nether world in 1930s, seen mostly through eyes of a young artist (Atherton) who finds little glamor and a lot of broken-down people in Tinseltown. Disturbing, depressing . . . and absolutely fascinating. Script by Waldo Salt.▼

Day of the Outlaw (1959) **91m.** ** D: Andre de Toth. Robert Ryan, Burl Ives, Tina Louise, Alan Marshal, Nehemiah Persoff, Venetia Stevenson. Stark Western melodrama of outlaw Ives and gang taking over isolated Western town.

Day of the Triffids, The (1963-British) **C-95m.** **½ D: Steve Sekely. Howard Keel, Nicole Maurey, Janette Scott, Kieron Moore, Mervyn Johns. Meteor display blinds everyone who watched, while mutating experimental plants into giant, walking maneaters. Based on John Wyndham's classic sci-fi novel. Variable special effects.▼

Day of the Wolves (1973) **C-95m.** **½ D: Ferde Grofe Jr. Richard Egan, Martha Hyer, Rick Jason, Jan Murray. Ex-sheriff Egan tries to thwart bizarre attempt by strange group of men to isolate his town for three days, in order to pull off "perfect crime."▼

Day of Wrath (1943-Danish) **110m.** ***½

D: Carl Theodor Dreyer. Thorkild Roose, Lisbeth Movin, Sigrid Neiiendam, Preben Lerdorff, Anna Svierker. Strikingly composed drama about an old woman accused of being a witch and the curse that she puts on the pastor who is responsible for her burning. Serious, stark cinema, peerlessly photographed by Carl Andersson. Some prints run 95m.▼

Day One (1989) C-150m. TVM D: Joseph Sargent. Brian Dennehy, David Strathairn, Michael Tucker, Hume Cronyn, Richard Dysart, Hal Holbrook, Barnard Hughes, David Ogden Stiers, John McMartin. Strong but somewhat unwieldy drama (due to telescoping of events for time purposes) about the men who made first atomic bomb. Anchored by Dennehy as Gen. Leslie Groves, who supervised the project and wet-nursed the assorted scientists who bickered their way to its culmination. There's enough of a story here and a fascinating assortment of major figures that David Rintels' intelligent script (from Peter Wyden's book) could well have been expanded for another hour. Compare this to the theatrical film FAT MAN AND LITTLE BOY. Above average.

Days of Glory (1944) 86m. **½ D: Jacques Tourneur. Gregory Peck, Alan Reed, Maria Palmer, Lowell Gilmore, Tamara Toumanova. Sincere but plodding WW2 action pitting Russians against Nazis, memorable only as Peck's screen debut.▼

Days of Heaven (1978) C-95m. ***½ D: Terrence Malick. Richard Gere, Brooke Adams, Sam Shepard, Linda Manz, Robert Wilke, Jackie Shultis, Stuart Margolin. Exquisite mood piece about a turbulent love triangle set against midwestern wheat harvests at the turn of the century. Originally shown in 70mm, its visual beauty will be diminished on TV, leaving only the story—which is second priority here. Nestor Almendros won well-deserved Oscar for his cinematography.▼

Days of Thrills and Laughter (1961) 93m. **** Compiled by Robert Youngson. The third Youngson compilation of old movie clips is as funny and exciting as his first two. Scenes with Laurel and Hardy, Chaplin, the Keystone Kops, and others are hilarious, and action scenes with Doug Fairbanks and Pearl White are still fun. Nostalgic and thoroughly enjoyable.▼

Days of Thunder (1990) C-107m. ** D: Tony Scott. Tom Cruise, Robert Duvall, Randy Quaid, Nicole Kidman, Cary Elwes, Michael Rooker, Fred Dalton Thompson. Flashy, noisy race-car saga set in the South, brought to you by the filmmakers and star of TOP GUN. Depending on personal taste, viewer can a) savor crew chief Duvall's fine performance, b) revel in neurosurgeon/love interest Kidman's disdain for racing, c) sit back and soak up Cruise's charisma,

or d) count the clichés (cooked up by coauthors Cruise and Robert Towne). Gives new meaning to the term Formula One.

Days of Wine and Roses (1962) 117m. ***½ D: Blake Edwards. Jack Lemmon, Lee Remick, Charles Bickford, Jack Klugman, Alan Hewitt, Tom Palmer, Jack Albertson. Modern LOST WEEKEND set in San Francisco, with Lemmon marrying Remick and pulling her into state of alcoholism. Realistic direction and uncompromising writing combine for excellent results; poignant score by Henry Mancini, who also earned an Oscar for the title song with Johnny Mercer. Originally a television play, written by JP Miller.▼

Day That Shook the World, The (1977) C-111m. ** D: Veljko Bulajic. Christopher Plummer, Florinda Bolkan, Maximilian Schell. Plodding historical drama surrounding the events leading up to WW1 with the death of Archduke Ferdinand (Plummer) at Sarajevo. Yugoslavian-made with a humorless international cast, resulting in tedious though epic-sized chronicle.▼

Day the Bubble Burst, The (1982) C-150m. TVM D: Joseph Hardy. Richard Crenna, Blanche Baker, Robert Vaughn, Dana Elcar, Robert Hays, Bill Macy, Donna Pescow, Laurette Spang, Franklin Cover, Audra Lindley, Rue McClanahan, David Ogden Stiers, Caroline McWilliams. The personal lives of Wall Street wizards, average Joes, and jazz babies dovetail on Black Tuesday, when the stock market crashed. Written episodically and uninvolvingly by Stanley R. Greenberg (who was responsible for PUEBLO and THE MISSILES OF OCTOBER) from the best-seller by Gordon Thomas and Max Morgan-Witts. Average.

Day the Earth Caught Fire, The (1962-British) 99m. *** D: Val Guest. Edward Judd, Janet Munro, Leo McKern, Michael Goodliffe, Bernard Braden. Intelligent, absorbing sci-fi drama of gradual chaos that follows when atomic explosions start Earth spiraling toward the sun.▼

Day the Earth Moved, The (1974) C-78m. TVM D: Robert Michael Lewis. Jackie Cooper, Stella Stevens, Cleavon Little, William Windom, Beverly Garland, Lucille Benson, Kelly Thordsen. Aerial photographers Cooper and Little have less trouble predicting an imminent earthquake than in convincing some townspeople to get out before the walls come tumbling down on them. Modest thriller with competent performances and special effects. Average.

Day the Earth Stood Still, The (1951) 92m. **** D: Robert Wise. Michael Rennie, Patricia Neal, Hugh Marlowe, Sam Jaffe, Billy Gray, Frances Bavier, Lock Martin. Landmark science-fiction drama about dignified alien (Rennie) who comes to Earth to deliver anti-nuclear warning, stays to learn that his peaceful views are shared by most humans—but not all. Brilliantly acted, more timely than ever, with trenchant script by Edmund North, moody score by Bernard Herrmann. And remember: *Klaatu barada nikto!*▼

Day the Fish Came Out, The (1967-Greek-British) **C-109m.** BOMB D: Michael Cacoyannis. Tom Courtenay, Candice Bergen, Colin Blakely, Sam Wanamaker, Ian Ogilvy. Plot about the loss of two atom bombs over the Aegean Sea provides framework for disastrous comedy about homosexuals; combo of Candy Bergen plus whips, chains, and leather doesn't work.

Day the Hot Line Got Hot, The (1969) **C-92m.** *½ D: Etienne Perier. Robert Taylor, Charles Boyer, George Chakiris, Dominique Fabre, Gerard Tichy. Hollow attempt at topicality as secret agents mess up Moscow-Washington hot line, causing international crisis. Taylor's final film. Also known as HOT LINE.▼

Day the Loving Stopped, The (1981) **C-100m.** TVM D: Daniel Mann. Dennis Weaver, Valerie Harper, Dominique Dunne, James Canning, Ally Sheedy, Sam Groom, Stacey Glick. Two young girls experience the emotional turmoil of their parents' separation. Average.

Day the Screaming Stopped, The SEE: **Comeback, The**▼

Day the Sky Exploded, The (1958-Italian) **80m.** ** D: Paolo Heusch. Paul Hubschmid, Madeleine Fischer, Fiorella Mari, Ivo Garrani. Film doesn't live up to potential excitement as exploding missile in outer space sends debris to earth, causing chaos.

Day the Women Got Even, The (1980) **C-100m.** TVM D: Burt Brinckerhoff. Jo Ann Pflug, Georgia Engel, Tina Louise, Barbara Rhoades, Gerald Gordon, Rick Aviles, Julie Hagerty. Undistinguished comedy about four suburban housewives who band together to foil an unscrupulous talent agent's plan to blackmail them with compromising photos. Average.

Day the World Ended, The (1956) **82m.** ** D: Roger Corman. Richard Denning, Lori Nelson, Adele Jergens, Touch (Mike) Connors. Modest sci-fi involving survivors of radiation blast and interplay of human nature that causes friction among the group. And yes, there's a monster. Remade as YEAR 2889.

Day They Robbed the Bank of England, The (1960-British) **85m.** *** D: John Guillermin. Aldo Ray, Elizabeth Sellars, Peter O'Toole, Hugh Griffith, Kieron Moore, Albert Sharpe. IRA members plan to rob the Bank of England in this meticulous caper film.

Day Time Ended, The (1980) **C-79m.** ** D: John (Bud) Cardos. Jim Davis, Dorothy Malone, Christopher Mitchum, Marcy Lafferty, Scott Kolden, Natasha Ryan. Sci-fi mishmash about a family living in the

desert, who witness strange and terrifying phenomena. Badly scripted, and never really explained. Fine special effects by David Allen. Filmed in 1978 as TIME WARP.▼

Day-Time Wife (1939) **71m.** ** D: Gregory Ratoff. Tyrone Power, Linda Darnell, Warren William, Binnie Barnes, Wendy Barrie. Power and Darnell make an engaging couple, even in lightweight fare such as this: wife gets office job to see if work is really all play.

Dayton's Devils (1968) **C-107m.** ** D: Jack Shea. Rory Calhoun, Leslie Nielsen, Lainie Kazan, Hans Gudegast (Eric Braeden), Barry Sadler. Another heist film, this time about plot to rob an Air Force base of $2¼ million; Lainie's rendition of "Sunny" provides film's only special moment.▼

Day Will Dawn, The (1942-British) **99m.** *** D: Harold French. Hugh Williams, Griffiths Jones, Deborah Kerr, Ralph Richardson, Francis L. Sullivan, Roland Culver, Finlay Currie, Niall MacGinnis, Raymond Huntley, Patricia Medina. Solid WW2 adventure about foreign correspondent Williams and his involvement in destroying a German U-boat base in Norway. Kerr is fine in one of her early roles, as a young Norwegian lass who assists him. The treatment and screenplay are credited to Terrence Rattigan, Anatole de Grunwald, and Patrick Kirwen. Also known as THE AVENGERS.▼

D.C. Cab (1983) **C-99m.** **½ D: Joel Schumacher. Adam Baldwin, Charlie Barnett, Irene Cara, Anne DeSalvo, Max Gail, Gloria Gifford, DeWayne Jessie, Bill Maher, Whitman Mayo, Mr. T, Paul Rodriguez, Gary Busey, Marsha Warfield. Consistently likable, if loosely wound, comedy about a Washington taxi company staffed by misfits who get their act together when it really counts. After a few trims by TV censors it will be perfect for kids.▼

D-Day on Mars (1945) **100m.** ** D: Spencer Bennet, Fred Brannon. Dennis Moore, Linda Stirling, Roy Barcroft, James Craven, Bud Geary, Mary Moore. Average Republic nonsense keyed on action of dynamic Purple Monster fighting against alien forces bent on taking over earth; Stirling is the fetching heroine. Reedited from serial THE PURPLE MONSTER STRIKES.▼

D-Day the Sixth of June (1956) **C-106m.** *** D: Henry Koster. Robert Taylor, Richard Todd, Dana Wynter, Edmond O'Brien. Well executed study of the Normandy invasion during WW2, with massive action shots; film focuses on American officer Taylor and British leader Todd, their professional and personal problems.▼

Dead, The (1987) **C-83m.** *** D: John Huston. Anjelica Huston, Donal McCann,

Rachael Dowling, Cathleen Delany, Helena Carroll, Ingrid Craigie, Dan O'Herlihy, Frank Patterson, Donal Donnelly, Marie Kean, Maria McDernottroe, Sean McClory. All-Irish cast helps Huston bring James Joyce's short story (from *Dubliners*) to life, a vignette about a lively holiday dinner party in 1904, followed by a melancholy confrontation between a loveless husband and wife. Not for every taste, this finely embroidered film celebrates time, place, and atmosphere, without much discernible plot, but with a host of marvelous characterizations. Huston's last film as director was scripted by his son Tony.▼

Dead and Buried (1981) C-92m. **½ D: Gary A. Sherman. James Farentino, Melody Anderson, Jack Albertson, Dennis Redfield, Nancy Locke Hauser, Lisa Blount. Bizarre murders in a small New England town seem even stranger when the corpses come back to life. Gory but well-made chiller; from a Dan O'Bannon story.▼

Dead Are Alive, The (1972-Yugoslavian-German-Italian) C-98m. *½ D: Armando Crispino. Alex Cord, Samantha Eggar, John Marley, Nadja Tiller, Horst Frank, Enzo Tarascio. Confused, uninteresting suspenser dealing with series of murders that take place while archeologists are studying ancient tombs; Eggar is wasted.

Dead-Bang (1989) C-109m. *½ D: John Frankenheimer. Don Johnson, Penelope Ann Miller, William Forsythe, Bob Balaban, Tim Reid, Frank Military, Tate Donovan, Michael Higgins, Evans Evans. L.A. homicide detective Johnson tries to forget about his dismal home life by chasing nasty white supremacists around the West. Unpleasant, fact-based action film offers nothing you haven't seen before, except for the hero vomiting on a suspect.▼

Dead Calm (1989-Australian) C-96m. *** D: Philip Noyce. Sam Neill, Nicole Kidman, Billy Zane. A married couple, recovering from a family tragedy by spending some time on their yacht at sea, pick up a stranger who proceeds to terrorize them. Full-blooded thriller is so skillfully acted and directed that it enables you to gloss over its flaws—and forgive its slasher-movie-inspired finale. Based on a novel by Charles Williams.▼

Dead Don't Die, The (1975) C-78m. TVM D: Curtis Harrington. George Hamilton, Ray Milland, Linda Cristal, Ralph Meeker, Joan Blondell, James McEachin. Creaky 1930s thriller by Robert Bloch has Hamilton, out to clear his executed brother's name, clashing with a crazed zombie master who has hatched a plot to rule the world with his army of living dead. Below average.▼

Dead End (1937) 93m. ***½ D: William Wyler. Sylvia Sidney, Joel McCrea, Humphrey Bogart, Wendy Barrie, Claire Trevor,

Marjorie Main, Huntz Hall, Leo Gorcey, Gabriel Dell, Ward Bond, Billy Halop, Bernard Punsley, Allen Jenkins. Grim Sidney Kingsley play of slum life shows vignettes of humanity at breaking point in N.Y.C. tenements; extremely well directed, engrossing. Script by Lillian Hellman; magnificent sets by Richard Day. Film introduced the Dead End Kids, who appeared in the original Broadway production (see **Bowery Boys** entry for further details).▼

Dead End Kids (1986) C/B&W-90m. *** D: JoAnne Akalaitis. Ellen McElduff, Ruth Maleczech, George Bartenieff, David Brisbin, Terry O'Reilly. Effective, free-form dramatic narrative of the history of nuclear power—where it comes from and what it does—features some good performances and cohesive direction. Faithfully adapted from the off-Broadway production by Mabou Mines. Original score by David Byrne and additional music by Philip Glass, both of whom appear briefly. The full title is DEAD END KIDS: A STORY OF NUCLEAR POWER.

Deadfall (1968-British) C-120m. ** D: Bryan Forbes. Michael Caine, Giovanna Ralli, Eric Portman, Nanette Newman, David Buck. Jewel thief falls in love with beautiful woman who is married to her homosexual father. And you think you have problems? Overdirected film is not as interesting as it sounds.

Deadhead Miles (1972) C-93m. **½ D: Vernon Zimmerman. Alan Arkin, Paul Benedict, Hector Elizondo, Oliver Clark, Charles Durning, Larry Wolf, Barnard Hughes, Loretta Swit, Allen Garfield, Bruce Bennett, John Milius, Ida Lupino, George Raft. Plotless allegory about a trucker's experiences on the road, with unusual cast, loads of in-jokes. Unreleased and unseen for many years. A real curio, written by Zimmerman and Terrence Malick.

Dead Heat (1988) C-86m. BOMB D: Mark Goldblatt. Treat Williams, Joe Piscopo, Lindsay Frost, Darren McGavin, Vincent Price, Keye Luke, Clare Kirkconnell. Moronic, occasionally disgusting turkey with cops Williams and Piscopo confronted by criminals miraculously returning from the dead.▼

Dead Heat on a Merry-Go-Round (1966) C-104m. *** D: Bernard Girard. James Coburn, Camilla Sparv, Aldo Ray, Rose Marie, Severn Darden, Robert Webber. Involved but entertaining crime drama about an intricate plan to rob an airport bank. Watch for the surprise ending—and look quickly for Harrison Ford, in his film debut.▼

Deadlier Than the Male (1957-French) 104m. ** D: Julien Duvivier. Jean Gabin, Daniele Delorme, Lucienne Bogaert, Gerard Blain. Delorme encamps in ex-stepfather's home, planning to marry and then murder him; Gabin is stodgy as girl's intended victim.

Deadlier Than the Male (1967-British) **C-101m.** **½ D: Ralph Thomas. Richard Johnson, Elke Sommer, Sylvia Koscina, Nigel Green, Suzanna Leigh. Standard fare which half-heartedly resurrects Bulldog Drummond, trying to solve whodunit centering around two shapely suspects. Sequel: SOME GIRLS DO.

Deadliest Season, The (1977) **C-98m.** TVM D: Robert Markowitz. Michael Moriarty, Kevin Conway, Meryl Streep, Sully Boyar, Jill Eikenberry, Walter Mc-Ginn, Andrew Duggan, Patrick O'Neal, Mason Adams. Hard-hitting pro hockey drama about a defenseman (Moriarty) whose aggressiveness endears him to the fans and his bosses until he critically injures another player and is tried for manslaughter. Thought-provoking but violent Ernest Kinoy teleplay marred only by Moriarty's curiously mannered performance in leading role. This was Streep's first appearance on film. Above average.

Deadliest Sin, The (1956-British) **77m.** *½ D: Ken Hughes. Sydney Chaplin, Audrey Dalton, John Bentley, Peter Hammond. Good triumphing over evil is moral of this slight story of thief involved in murder.

Deadline (1987-German) **C-100m.** *½ D: Nathaniel Gutman. Christopher Walken, Hywel Bennett, Marita Marschall, Arnon Zadok, Amos Lavie. Convoluted political thriller with globe-trotting journalist Walken becoming enmeshed in various intrigues and lies in Lebanon. Strictly Grade-D stuff.▼

Deadline at Dawn (1946) **83m.** **½ D: Harold Clurman. Susan Hayward, Paul Lukas, Bill Williams, Joseph Calleia, Osa Massen, Lola Lane, Jerome Cowan, Steven Geray. Atmospheric but muddled murder mystery, with aspiring actress Hayward attempting to clear naive sailor Williams, who is suspected of murder. Clurman's only film as director. Screenplay by Clifford Odets, from a novel by William Irish (Cornell Woolrich).▼

Deadline: Madrid (1988) **C-100m.** TVM D: John Patterson. Brynn Thayer, Leigh Lawson, Joe Santos, J. Kenneth Campbell, Neva Patterson, Charles Cioffi, Marta Dubois, Miriam Colon. A foreign correspondent working out of Madrid teams up with her photojournalist ex-lover to expose a famine relief organization that's been running guns. Indifferently acted. A busted TV pilot. Below average.

Deadline U.S.A. (1952) **87m.** *** D: Richard Brooks. Humphrey Bogart, Ethel Barrymore, Kim Hunter, Ed Begley, Paul Stewart, Jim Backus. Biting account of newspaper's struggle to survive and maintain civic duty. Bogey is editor, Begley his assistant, Stewart a sports reporter who brings in wanted man; most enjoyable.

Deadlock (1969) **C-99m.** TVM D: Lamont Johnson. Leslie Nielsen, Hari Rhodes, Dana Elcar, Max Julien, Melvin Stuart, Ruby Dee, Aldo Ray. Intelligent study of election-year politics and ghetto turmoil. D.A. Washburn (Rhodes) accepts mayor's assignment to head special investigatory panel in death of newspaperman who had covered touchy racial issue. Excellent performances, realistic tension. Above average.

Deadly Affair, The (1967) **C-107m.** *** D: Sidney Lumet. James Mason, Simone Signoret, Maximilian Schell, Harriet Andersson, Harry Andrews, Lynn Redgrave, Kenneth Haigh, Roy Kinnear. Top-notch suspense tale with British agent Mason trying to unravel complicated mystery behind an agency official's suicide. Filmed in England and based on John Le Carre's novel *Call For The Dead.*

Deadly Bees, The (1967-British) **C-85m.** ** D: Freddie Francis. Suzanna Leigh, Guy Doleman, Catherine Finn, Katy Wild, Frank Finlay. High-powered shock scenes involving swarming bees are only worthwhile attraction in horror film marred by dull script.

Deadly Blessing (1981) **C-102m.** ** D: Wes Craven. Maren Jensen, Susan Buckner, Sharon Stone, Lois Nettleton, Ernest Borgnine, Jeff East, Lisa Hartman. Following her husband's murder, widow and two friends are terrorized, apparently by nearby repressive sect, headed by the father (Borgnine) of the dead man. Rural horror thriller has some good shocks but becomes confused and ultimately silly, especially the ending.▼

Deadly Business, A (1986) **C-100m.** TVM D: John Korty. Alan Arkin, Armand Assante, Michael Learned, Jon Polito, George Morfogen, James Rebhorn. Story of real-life ex-con Harold Kaufman who turned government informant after blowing the whistle on the illegal dumping of chemicals in New Jersey's waste-hauling business. Arkin gives another of his top-notch performances as suave garbage king Assante's bagman. Penetrating script by Al Ramrus. Above average.

Deadly Care (1987) **C-100m.** TVM D: David Anspaugh. Cheryl Ladd, Jason Miller, Jennifer Salt, Belinda Balaski, Peggy McCay, Silvana Gallardo. Downer about a critical-care nurse on downers, uppers, booze, and assorted substances, and her ultimate cry for help. Below average.

Deadly Companions, The (1961) **C-90m.** **½ D: Sam Peckinpah. Maureen O'Hara, Brian Keith, Steve Cochran, Chill Wills. Ex-army officer accidentally kills O'Hara's son and he makes amends by escorting the funeral procession through Indian country. Peckinpah's first feature is decent if unspectacular western.▼

Deadly Deception (1987) **C-100m. TVM** D: John Llewellyn Moxey. Matt Salinger, Lisa Eilbacher, Bonnie Bartlett, James Noble, Christopher Allport, Robert Harper. Bland psycho-thriller about a widower's desperate search for his infant son after his depressed wife's apparent suicide. Look for veteran actress Mildred Natwick in a rare single-scene acting return. Average.

Deadly Dream (1971) **C-73m. TVM** D: Alf Kjellin. Lloyd Bridges, Janet Leigh, Leif Erickson, Carl Betz, Don Stroud, Richard Jaeckel, Phillip Pine. Poor examination of dream-vs.-reality issue. Man has recurring and episodic dream that strange men belonging to "tribunal" chase after him. Adequate performances, but script and direction are real nightmare. Average.

Deadly Encounter (1982) **C-100m. TVM** D: William A. Graham. Larry Hagman, Susan Anspach, James Gammon, Michael C. Gwynne. Nonstop aerial action with Hagman as an ex-combat helicopter ace who's persuaded by old flame Anspach to help her flee from syndicate thugs. Great copter stunt work keeps this one moving briskly. Above average.

Deadly Eyes (1982) **C-93m. ** D: Robert Clouse. Sam Groom, Sara Botsford, Scatman Crothers, Lisa Langlois, Cec Linder. Overgrown rats on the warpath, with science teacher Groom and health official Botsford to the rescue. You've seen it all before. Originally titled, appropriately enough, THE RATS.▼

Deadly Force (1983) **C-95m. BOMB** D: Paul Aaron. Wings Hauser, Joyce Ingalls, Paul Shenar, Al Ruscio, Arlen Dean Snyder, Lincoln Kilpatrick. Ex-cop Hauser is on the trail of a killer; he's harassed by former colleague Kilpatrick, and trying to start over with estranged wife Ingalls. Rockbottom DIRTY HARRY clone.▼

Deadly Friend (1986) **C-92m. **½ D: Wes Craven. Matthew Laborteaux, Kristy Swanson, Anne Twomey, Michael Sharrett, Richard Marcus, Anne Ramsey. Inventive teenager, in love with the girl next door, revives her (à la Frankenstein) after she's killed. More heart, and more actual entertainment, than you'd expect from a Wes Craven horror film . . . though it's probably the only movie ever made in which someone is beheaded by a basketball! ▼

Deadly Game, The (1976) SEE: **Serpico: The Deadly Game**

Deadly Game (1977) **C-100m. TVM** D: Lane Slate. Andy Griffith, Mitzi Hoag, Claude Earl Jones, Sharon Spellman, Dan O'Herlihy, Morgan Woodward. Sequel to THE GIRL IN THE EMPTY GRAVE offers Griffith in further adventures of small town sheriff Abel Marsh. Here he investigates the destruction and scandal caused by chemical spillage from an army tanker truck. Average.▼

Deadly Games (1982) **C-95m. **½ D: Scott Mansfield. Sam Groom, Jo Ann Harris, Steve Railsback, Dick Butkus, Alexandra Morgan, Colleen Camp, Christine Tudor, June Lockhart, Denise Galik. Groom is a cop, Harris a reporter in routine mystery about a slasher on the loose. In-jokes come fast and furious in this very knowing film, keyed to a horror board game played by the principals. Final plot explanation is really stupid.▼

Deadly Harvest (1972) **C-73m. TVM** D: Michael O'Herlihy. Richard Boone, Patty Duke, Michael Constantine, Murray Hamilton, Jack Kruschen. Semi-idyllic existence of ex-spy-turned-grape-grower shattered when bomb shows up in his pickup truck. Frustratingly uneven; some good performances, some bad; occasional good mood, often too rushed. Adapted by Dan Ullman from Geoffrey Household's *Watcher in the Shadows*. Average.▼

Deadly Hero (1976) **C-102m. ** D: Ivan Nagy. Don Murray, Diahn Williams, James Earl Jones, Lilia Skala, George S. Irving, Conchata Ferrell, Charles Siebert, Dick A. Williams, Treat Williams, Joshua Mostel. Interesting premise: righteous cop (Murray) saves woman's life by killing her attacker (Jones) . . . but then woman begins to question the cop's motives. Performances outshine violent presentation. Treat Williams' film debut. Danny DeVito is also listed in the closing credits.▼

Deadly Hunt, The (1971) **C-74m. TVM** D: John Newland. Jim Hutton, Anjanette Comer, Tony Franciosa, Peter Lawford, Tim McIntire. Young businessman and wife (Hutton & Comer) on hunting trip discover themselves targets of paid assassins, caught in forest fire. Good location and stunt work major distinctions of acceptable chase-thriller, adapted by Jerrold Ludwig and Eric Bercovici from Pat Stadley's novel. Above average.

Deadly Illusion (1987) **C-87m. **½ D: William Tannen, Larry Cohen. Billy Dee Williams, Vanity, Morgan Fairchild, John Beck, Joseph Cortese, Dennis Hallahan, Joe Spinell. Fair programmer with Williams well cast as a detective framed in murder plot. Some humorous touches add to the proceedings. Cohen wrote the script; also known as LOVE YOU TO DEATH.▼

Deadly Impact (1985-Italian) **C-91m. **½ D: Larry Ludman (Fabrizio De Angelis). Bo Svenson, Fred Williamson, Marcia Clingan, John Morghen, Vincent Conte. Comfortable team of Svenson and Williamson try to enliven unbelievable crime caper in which a computer is used to tap into casinos' information systems in Las Vegas and predict when slot machines will pay off. Italian production was made in the U.S.A. in 1983.▼

Deadly Intentions (1985) **C-200m. TVM** D: Noel Black. Michael Biehn, Madolyn Smith, Morgana King, Jack Kruschen, Kevin McCarthy, Cliff De Young, Cloris Leachman. The psychopath plotting her murder, a young wife discovers, is her seemingly perfect husband, in this incredibly overlong thriller adapted by Andrew Peter Martin from William Randolph Stevens's book (and based on a true story). Originally shown in two parts. Average.

Deadly Is the Female SEE: **Gun Crazy**

Deadly Lessons (1983) **C-100m. TVM** D: William Wiard. Donna Reed, Larry Wilcox, David Ackroyd, Diana Franklin, Ally Sheedy, Donald Hotton, Deena Freeman. Crazed killer stalks exclusive girls school. Donna Reed, as headmistress, adds a misplaced touch of class to TV's contribution to slasher movie mania. Average.

Deadly Mantis, The (1957) **78m. ** D: Nathan Juran. Craig Stevens, William Hopper, Alix Talton, Donald Randolph. N.Y.C. is threatened again, here by giant insect heading south after Arctic tour de force; obligatory love story interrupts good special effects.

Deadly Messages (1985) **C-100m. TVM** D: Jack Bender. Kathleen Beller, Michael Brandon, Dennis Franz, Scott Paulin, Elizabeth Huddle, Charles Tyner. Chiller involving a terrified woman, a killer with murderous intentions, and an antique Ouija board. Plays like a send-up. Average.

Deadly Ray from Mars, The (1938) **99m. **½** D: Ford Beebe, Robert Hill. Buster Crabbe, Jean Rogers, Charles Middleton, Frank Shannon, Donald Kerr, Beatrice Roberts. Newly edited version of FLASH GORDON'S TRIP TO MARS serial. Flash, Dale Arden, and Dr. Zarkov seek mysterious force which drains nitrogen from earth's atmosphere, eventually discover Ming's behind it all. Uninspired handling of original footage. Video title: FLASH GORDON: MARS ATTACKS THE WORLD.▼

Deadly Silence, A (1989) **C-100m. TVM** D: John Patterson. Mike Farrell, Bruce Weitz, Charles Haid, Richard Portnow, Sally Struthers, Heather Fairfield, Wally Ward. Fact-based drama about a Long Island coed who hires a classmate to murder her abusive father. Clinical but cold telling of New York Times reporter Dena Kleiman's book, adapted by Jennifer Miller. Average.

Deadly Strangers (1974-British) **C-93m.** *** D: Sidney Hayers. Hayley Mills, Simon Ward, Sterling Hayden, Ken Hutchison, Peter Jeffrey. Lurid, exciting thriller about Mills offering a ride to young man, un-aware that a violent patient has escaped from a nearby mental hospital.▼

Deadly Thief SEE: **Shalimar**▼

Deadly Tower, The (1975) **C-100m. TVM** D: Jerry Jameson. Kurt Russell, Richard Yniquez, John Forsythe, Ned Beatty, Pernell Roberts, Clifton James, Paul Carr, Alan Vint, Pepe Serna, Maria Elena Cordero. Fact-based drama about Charles Whitman (Russell), who holed up in University of Texas tower in August, 1966, and fired at all in sight, killing 13 and wounding 33. Authentic, well-made recreation of the fateful event, with acting honors going to Yniquez as Mexican-American police officer and Beatty as passerby who reluctantly agrees to help him. Above average.▼

Deadly Trackers, The (1973) **C-110m.** BOMB D: Barry Shear. Richard Harris, Rod Taylor, Al Lettieri, Neville Brand, William Smith, Isela Vega. Deadly oater dwells on violence; Harris, Irish sheriff of a small Texas town, trails bank robber Taylor and gang to Mexico to avenge the deaths of wife and son. Sam Fuller wrote the story and was the original director.

Deadly Trap, The (1971-French-Italian) **C-96m.** BOMB D: Rene Clement. Faye Dunaway, Frank Langella, Barbara Parkins, Karen Glanguernon, Maurice Ronet. A deadly bore, about an industrious espionage organization that goes after one-time member Langella by harassing his emotionally fragile wife (Dunaway). Retitled DEATH SCREAM.▼

Deadly Treasure of the Piranha SEE: **Killer Fish**▼

Deadly Triangle, The (1977) **C-78m. TVM** D: Charles Dubin. Dale Robinette, Taylor Larcher, Geoffrey Lewis, Robert Lansing, Diana Muldaur, Linda Scruggs Bogart. Ex-Olympic skier turned sheriff investigates a murder in his resort town. Run-of-the-mill series pilot followed by CRISIS IN SUN VALLEY. Average.

Dead Man Out (1989) **C-86m. TVM** D: Richard Pearce. Danny Glover, Ruben Blades, Tom Atkins, Larry Block, Sam Jackson, Maria Ricossa. Searing drama about a psychiatrist who is hired by the state to "cure" an insane convict in order that the death sentence can be carried out. Gritty confrontational performances that give a contemporary sensibility to Stanley Kramer's PRESSURE POINT of 25 years earlier. Written by Ron Hutchinson. Made for cable. Above average.▼

Deadman's Curve (1978) **C-100m. TVM** D: Richard Compton. Richard Hatch, Bruce Davison, Pamela Bellwood, Susan Sullivan, Dick Clark, Wolfman Jack. Passable biography based on the meteoric tragedy-marred careers of Jan Berry and Dean Torrence, early '60s rock idols who popularized the Surfing Sound. Average.▼

Dead Man's Eyes (1944) **64m.** ** D: Reginald LeBorg. Lon Chaney Jr., Jean Parker, Paul Kelly, Thomas Gomez, Acquanetta. Interesting *Inner Sanctum* yarn of blind man (Chaney) accused of murdering girlfriend's father, whose announced intention was to bequeath his eyes to Chaney for transplant operation.

Dead Man's Float (1980-Australian) C-75m. **½ D: Peter Sharp. Sally Boyden, Greg Rowe, Jacqui Gordon, Rick Ireland, Bill Hunter, Sue Jones, John Heywood. Kids tangle with drug-smuggling adults. Unmemorable, though fast-moving and not unentertaining; for younger audiences.

Dead Man's Folly (1986) C-100m. TVM D: Clive Donner. Peter Ustinov, Jean Stapleton, Constance Cummings, Tim Pigott-Smith, Jonathan Cecil, Susan Woolridge, Christopher Guard, Nicollette Sheridan, Jeff Yagher. Hercule Poirot is enmeshed in an American novelist's murder hunt party which turns up real bodies. Constance Cummings makes a rare film appearance as a mysterious dowager. Contemporary adaptation of the Christie novel. Average.

Dead Men Don't Wear Plaid (1982) **89m.** ** D: Carl Reiner. Steve Martin, Rachel Ward, Reni Santoni, Carl Reiner, George Gaynes, Frank McCarthy. A one-joke movie, based on 1940s film noir melodramas, has detective Martin interacting with clips from various vintage films, and a very live client (Ward). Fun at first, but with no story and cardboard characters, it wears thin fast; film buffs will enjoy it more than the average viewer. Dedicated to famed costume designer Edith Head, whose final film this was.▼

Dead Men Tell (1941) **60m.** D: Harry Lachman. Sidney Toler, Sheila Ryan, Robert Weldon, Victor Sen Yung, Don Douglas, Kay Aldridge. SEE: **Charlie Chan** series.

Dead Men Tell No Tales (1971) C-73m. TVM D: Walter Grauman. Christopher George, Judy Carne, Patricia Barry, Richard Anderson. Engaging chase-thriller with sense of humor. Paid assassins mistake travel photographer (George) for real quarry. Carne stars as former girlfriend who decides to help hero. Above average.

Dead Men Walk (1943) **67m.** ** D: Sam Newfield. George Zucco, Mary Carlisle, Nedrick Young, Dwight Frye, Fern Emmett. Zucco plays brothers, one good, one evil, in this otherwise standard low-budget vampire tale—but it's hard to dismiss any horror film with Dwight Frye as a maniacal assistant.▼

Dead of Night (1945-British) **102m.** **** D: Cavalcanti, Basil Dearden, Robert Hamer, Charles Crichton. Mervyn Johns, Roland Culver, Antony Baird, Judy Kelly, Miles Malleson, Sally Ann Howes, Googie Withers, Ralph Michael, Michael Redgrave, Basil Radford, Naunton Wayne, Frederick Valk. Classic chiller involving gathering of people who have experienced dreams which seem to repeat themselves in reality; final sequence with Redgrave as a ventriloquist is a knockout. American theatrical version ran 77m., but complete edition has been restored for TV.▼

Dead of Night (1972) SEE: **Deathdream**▼

Dead of Winter (1987) C-100m. *** D: Arthur Penn. Mary Steenburgen, Roddy McDowall, Jan Rubes, William Russ, Ken Pogue, Wayne Robson. Down-on-her-luck actress is hired for a movie role by an eccentric man who lives in an eerie old mansion; eventually she realizes that she's being held prisoner. Somewhat predictable but extremely well-crafted thriller with crackerjack performances all around. Based, fairly transparently, on the 1940s B movie MY NAME IS JULIA ROSS: a key character name here is Julie Rose.▼

Dead Pigeon on Beethoven Street (1972-German) C-102m. **½ D: Samuel Fuller. Glenn Corbett, Christa Lang, Stephane Audran, Anton Diffring, Alex D'Arcy. Fast-paced, tongue-in-cheek Fuller thriller (financed by German TV) has Corbett on a detective mission, aided by lovely Lang (Mrs. Fuller in real life).

Dead Poets Society (1989) C-128m. *** D: Peter Weir. Robin Williams, Robert Sean Leonard, Ethan Hawke, Josh Charles, Gale Hansen, Dylan Kussman, Allelon Ruggiero, James Waterston, Norman Lloyd, Kurtwood Smith. Williams is a charismatic English teacher at a staid New England prep school in 1959, whose infectious love of poetry—and insistence that each boy "seize the day" and make the most of life—inspires his impressionable students, not always in the right direction. Well made, extremely well acted, but also dramatically obvious and melodramatically one-sided. Nevertheless, Tom Schulman's screenplay won an Oscar.▼

Dead Pool, The (1988) C-91m. **½ D: Buddy Van Horn. Clint Eastwood, Patricia Clarkson, Evan C. Kim, Liam Neeson, David Hunt, Michael Currie, Michael Goodwin. Fifth DIRTY HARRY movie finds Inspector Callahan investigating a bizarre death-threat list, while becoming involved (professionally and personally) with a female TV reporter. The story's pretty straightforward, the killing almost cartoonish, and the film surprisingly watchable (if not inspired). Eastwood's strong screen presence makes all the difference.▼

Dead Reckoning (1947) **100m.** *** D: John Cromwell. Humphrey Bogart, Lizabeth Scott, Morris Carnovsky, William Prince, Wallace Ford, Charles Cane. Bogart's fine as tough WW2 veteran solving soldier-buddy's murder. Well-acted drama.▼

Dead Ringer (1964) 115m. **½ D. Paul Henreid. Bette Davis, Karl Malden, Peter Lawford, Jean Hagen, George Macready, Estelle Winwood. A double dose of Davis, playing twin sisters (as she did earlier in A STOLEN LIFE) bearing a long-time grudge over a man, the sinister one trying to get even. Farfetched but fun; Bette's vehicle all the way, directed by her 1940s costar Paul Henreid. Remade for TV as THE KILLER IN THE MIRROR.

Dead Ringers (1988-Canadian) C-115m. **½ D: David Cronenberg. Jeremy Irons, Genevieve Bujold, Heidi Von Palleske, Barbara Gordon, Shirley Douglas, Stephen Lack. Fascinating but extremely unpleasant story of twin gynecologists who share each other's lives—and lovers. Notable mainly for a pair of superb performances by Irons, and the attendant movie trickery that makes us forget, at times, that we're watching one man play both roles. Based (believe it or not) on a true story!▼

Dead Run (1969) C-92m. ** D: Christian-Jaque. Peter Lawford, Countess Ira Furstenberg, George Geret. Stolen defense plans in Berlin and Rome. Dull, but Lawford and beautiful on-location filming help a bit.

Dead Solid Perfect (1988) C-95m. TVM D: Bobby Roth. Randy Quaid, Kathryn Harrold, Jack Warden, Corinne Bohrer, Larry Riley, DeLane Matthews, Bibi Besch, Brett Cullen. Quirky comedy/drama based on Dan Jenkins' best-seller about life and love on the pro golf circuit. Title refers to how it is when the golfer hits the ball at a perfect angle; film itself isn't quite. Made for cable. Average.

Dead Zone, The (1983) C-103m. *** D: David Cronenberg. Christopher Walken, Brooke Adams, Tom Skerritt, Herbert Lom, Anthony Zerbe, Colleen Dewhurst, Martin Sheen, Nicholas Campbell, Jackie Burroughs. Absorbing Stephen King story of young man who emerges from near-fatal accident with the gift (or curse) of second sight—being able to tell a person's fate just by making physical contact. Walken's moving, heartfelt performance is the core of involving, if sometimes meandering movie where (despite reputations of author King and director Cronenberg) the emphasis is not on blood-and-guts horror.▼

Deaf Smith and Johnny Ears (1973-Italian) C-91m. *** D: Paolo Cavara. Anthony Quinn, Franco Nero, Pamela Tiffin, Ira Furstenberg. Well-made "buddy Western" teams deaf-mute Quinn with upstart Nero as two common-man bystanders during a time of social upheaval in Texas. Beautifully photographed by Tonino Delli Colli. Originally titled LOS AMIGOS.

Dealers (1989-British) C-91m. **½ D: Colin Bucksey. Paul McGann, Rebecca De Mornay, Derrick O'Connor, John Castle, Paul Guilfoyle, Rosalind Bennett. These

"dealers" don't sell drugs but trade dollars for a London-based bank. Flashy, TV-inspired treatment of unexceptional story with reckless McGann sparring (and falling in love) with De Mornay. Good cast and novel setting help raise it slightly above the routine.▼

Dealing: or The Berkeley-to-Boston Forty-Brick Lost-Bag Blues (1972) C-99m. **½ D: Paul Williams. Robert F. Lyons, Barbara Hershey, John Lithgow, Charles Durning, Joy Bang. Dated but still watchable adaptation of Robert and Michael Crichton's lighthearted novel about Harvard law student who runs pot on the side. Lyons is pretty blah, but compensation is provided by Hershey as his free-thinking girlfriend and Lithgow as the head dope.

Deal of the Century (1983) C-99m. ** D: William Friedkin. Chevy Chase, Sigourney Weaver, Gregory Hines, Vince Edwards, Richard Libertini, William Marquez, Eduardo Ricard, Wallace Shawn. Attempted satire of international weapons merchants. Its leading characters are so cold-blooded and unappealing, and its script (by Paul Brickman) so disjointed, that the results are a mishmosh.

Dear America (1987) C/B&W-87m. TVM D: Bill Couturie. Narration by Robert De Niro, Michael J. Fox, Ellen Burstyn, Kathleen Turner, Tom Berenger, Willem Dafoe, Sean Penn, Matt Dillon, Kevin Dillon, Robin Williams, Howard Rollins, Jr., many others. Extremely moving account of the whos, whens and wheres of Vietnam, told via news footage and letters written by Americans fighting and dying in that most controversial war. Gut-wrenching human drama that makes excellent use of appropriate music, from 1960s rock classics to Bruce Springsteen's "Born in the U.S.A." An HBO production that also received a theatrical release. Based on the book of the same title edited by Bernard Edelman. Above average.▼

Dear Brat (1951) 82m. **½ D: William A. Seiter. Mona Freeman, Billy DeWolfe, Edward Arnold, Lyle Bettger. Another follow-up to DEAR RUTH has Freeman in title role involved with a crook trying to reform.

Dear Brigitte (1965) C-100m. **½ D: Henry Koster. James Stewart, Fabian, Glynis Johns, Cindy Carol, Billy Mumy, John Williams, Jack Kruschen, Alice Pearce, Jesse White, Ed Wynn. Guest: Brigitte Bardot. Good cast in OK family farce about an 8-year-old genius (Stewart's son, Mumy) with a crush on Brigitte Bardot (who makes a brief appearance at the end). Film tries hard to be whimsical but is contrived instead. Look fast for James Brolin as student spokesman.▼

Dear, Dead Delilah (1972) C-90m. *½

D: John Farris. Agnes Moorehead, Will Geer, Michael Ansara, Patricia Carmichael, Dennis Patrick. Low-budgeter about grisly competition for $600,000 buried somewhere around home of dying Moorehead. Filmed in Nashville, originally 95m. For axe-murder aficionados only.▼

Dear Detective (1977-French) C-105m. **½ D: Philippe De Broca. Annie Girardot, Philippe Noiret, Catherine Alric, Hubert Deschamps, Paulette Dubost. Girardot is fine as woman cop who becomes involved with old flame (pompous professor Noiret) as she hunts a killer. Sometimes funny, more often predictable and pointless. Remade in 1979 as a TV movie. Retitled DEAR INSPECTOR. Sequel: JUPITER'S THIGH.

Dear Detective (1979) C-90m. TVM D: Dean Hargrove. Brenda Vaccaro, Arlen Dean Snyder, Michael MacRae, John Dennis Johnston, Jack Ging, Stephen McNally, M. Emmet Walsh, Constance Forslund, R.G. Armstrong. Detective Vaccaro investigates killings of politicians, has romance with college professor Snyder. Forgettable mystery-comedy benefits from presence of Vaccaro. Remake of the 1977 feature; pilot for the TV series. Average.▼

Dear Heart (1964) 114m. *** D: Delbert Mann. Glenn Ford, Geraldine Page, Michael Anderson, Jr., Barbara Nichols, Angela Lansbury, Alice Pearce, Mary Wickes. Winning romance story with Ford and Page visiting N.Y.C. for conventions, falling in love; excellent characterizations with fine comedy supporting players.

Dear Inspector SEE: Dear Detective (1977)▼

Dear Mr. Wonderful (1982-German) C-115m. *** D: Peter Lilienthal. Joe Pesci, Karen Ludwig, Evan Handler, Ivy Ray Browning, Frank Vincent, Paul Herman, Tony Martin. Ruby Dennis (Pesci) owns a bowling alley-nightclub in Jersey City, thinks he's on the verge of crashing Las Vegas. The American Jewish working class experience, viewed with a European sensibility, doesn't ring true; still, a thoughtful portrait of a little man who must learn to take what life has to offer. The sequence with Martin is particularly memorable.

Dear Murderer (1947-British) 90m. **½ D: Arthur Crabtree. Eric Portman, Greta Gynt, Dennis Price, Maxwell Reed, Jack Warner, Hazel Court. Husband Portman kills wife's lover. All-too-familiar "perfect crime" melodrama sparked by fine Portman performance.

Dear Ruth (1947) 95m. **½ D: William D. Russell. Joan Caulfield, William Holden, Mona Freeman, Edward Arnold, Billy DeWolfe. Bouncy, naive comedy of errors with young girl pretending to be her older sister to impress soldier she corresponds with.

Dear Wife (1949) 88m. **½ D: Richard Haydn. Joan Caulfield, William Holden, Edward Arnold, Billy DeWolfe, Mona Freeman. Follow-up to DEAR RUTH focuses on Freeman's antics to get Holden elected to the state senate, although her politician father Arnold is seeking same position.▼

Death Among Friends (1975) C-78m. TVM D: Paul Wendkos. Kate Reid, John Anderson, A Martinez, Martin Balsam, Jack Cassidy, Paul Henreid, Pamela Hensley, William Smith, Lynda Day George, Denver Pyle. Affable lady police lieutenant tries to solve the murder of an international financier. Reid nearly succeeds in pulling this police story up from the predictable. Average. Retitled MRS. R.—DEATH AMONG FRIENDS.

Death and the Maiden SEE: Hawkins on Murder

Death at Love House (1976) C-78m. TVM D: E.W. Swackhamer. Robert Wagner, Kate Jackson, Sylvia Sidney, Joan Blondell, Dorothy Lamour, John Carradine, Bill Macy, Marianna Hill. "Nostalgia thriller" about obsession of young writer (Wagner) for long-dead movie queen who was supposed to have had an affair with his father and whose spirit reaches out from her glass tomb to destroy him. Creepy and unbelievable, but it's fun to see screen veterans and magnificent Harold Lloyd estate where this was filmed. Average.▼

Death Before Dishonor (1987) C-95m. ** D: Terry J. Leonard. Fred Dryer, Brian Keith, Paul Winfield, Joanna Pacula, Kasey Walker, Rockne Tarkington. Clichéd, by-the-numbers story of Marine gunnery sergeant Dryer (who keeps a picture of John Wayne from SANDS OF IWO JIMA on his wall), who singlehandedly battles Middle Eastern terrorists after they stage a massacre—and kidnap his superior (Keith). Lotsa stunts, little sense. ▼

Death Be Not Proud (1975) C-100m. TVM D: Donald Wrye. Arthur Hill, Jane Alexander, Robby Benson, Linden Chiles, Ralph Clanton, Wendy Phillips. Sterling version of John Gunther's 1949 account of his son's courageous battle against the brain tumor that killed him at 17. Perceptive portrayals by Hill as famed author and Benson as young Johnny, with a glowing one by Jane Alexander. Memorable true-life drama; scripted by the director. Above average.▼

Death Bite SEE: Spasms▼

Death Car on the Freeway (1979) C-100m. TVM D: Hal Needham. Shelley Hack, George Hamilton, Frank Gorshin, Peter Graves, Harriet Nelson, Barbara Rush, Dinah Shore, Abe Vigoda, Hal Needham.

Comely TV reporter goes after the maniac methodicallly terrorizing lone women drivers with his van on the L.A. freeways. Stunt work (supervised by Needham) more than compensates for nonacting of the leading lady. Average.

Death Collector (1975) **C-85m.** BOMB D: Ralph De Vito. Joseph Cortese, Lou Criscuolo, Joe Pesci, Bobby Alto, Frank Vincent, Keith Davis, Jack Ramage. Poor melodrama about Cortese's involvement with various hoods is of interest solely for early performance by Pesci. Also known as FAMILY ENFORCER.▼

Death Corps SEE: **Shock Waves**▼

Death Cruise (1974) **C-78m.** TVM D: Ralph Senensky. Richard Long, Polly Bergen, Edward Albert, Kate Jackson, Celeste Holm, Tom Bosley, Michael Constantine, Cesare Danova. Three couples win all-expenses-paid vacations, then realize on board ship that they are marked for death. Disaster drama sails along familiar seas. Below average.▼

Deathdream (1972-Canadian) **C-90m.** **½ D: Bob Clark. John Marley, Richard Backus, Lynn Carlin, Henderson Forsythe. Backus is Vietnam vet, thought dead, who returns to his family a virtual stranger with a murderous lust for blood. Grim, fairly shocking. Also known as DEAD OF NIGHT.▼

Death Drug (1978) **C-73m.** *½ D: Oscar Williams. Philip-Michael Thomas, Rosalind Cash, Vernee Watson, Frankie Crocker. Cliché-ridden saga of singer-songwriter whose life and career go to pieces after he becomes addicted to "angel dust." Home video release of this terrible low-budgeter is framed with new footage of *Miami Vice* star Thomas, including a music video!▼

Death Drums Along the River SEE: **Sanders**

Death Game (1977) **C-89m.** *½ D: Peter S. Traynor. Sondra Locke, Colleen Camp, Seymour Cassel, Beth Brickell. Unpleasant (and ultimately ludicrous) film about two maniacal lesbians who—for no apparent reason—tease, titillate, and torture a man in his own house. Filmed in 1974. Trivia fans: Sissy Spacek was one of the set decorators! Also known as THE SEDUCERS.▼

Death Hunt (1981) **C-97m.** ** D: Peter R. Hunt. Charles Bronson, Lee Marvin, Andrew Stevens, Angie Dickinson, Carl Weathers, Ed Lauter. Tough Mountie Marvin pursues proud, self-reliant trapper Bronson, innocent of a murder charge, across icy Canada. Good action, but not enough of it. Angie is wasted.▼

Death in California, A (1985) **C-200m.** TVM D: Delbert Mann. Cheryl Ladd, Sam Elliott, Alexis Smith, Fritz Weaver, Barry Corbin, Kerrie Keane, Granville Van Dusen, William Lucking. Pampered Beverly Hills socialite's boyfriend is murdered before her eyes, and she develops a love-hate relationship with the killer who has raped and terrorized her. Surprisingly gripping, considering the dubious premise, though it was based on fact. Joan Barthel's best-seller was adapted by E. Jack Neuman. Originally shown in two parts. Above average.

Death in Canaan, A (1978) **C-120m.** TVM D: Tony Richardson. Stefanie Powers, Paul Clemens, Tom Atkins, Brian Dennehy, Jacqueline Brookes, James Sutorius. Strong dramatization of the sensational Connecticut murder case involving a local teenager suspected of the mutilation murder of his mother. Richardson made his American TV directing debut here, and Clemens, son of actress Eleanor Parker, made his acting debut as Peter Reilly, the accused. Adapted by Thomas Thompson and Spencer Eastman from the book by Joan Barthel (played by Powers). Above average.

Death in Small Doses (1957) **79m.** *½ D: Joseph M. Newman. Peter Graves, Mala Powers, Chuck Connors, Merry Anders. Low-budget drama of narcotics use among truck drivers; dull presentation.

Death in Venice (1971-Italian) **C-130m.** ***½ D: Luchino Visconti. Dirk Bogarde, Mark Burns, Marisa Berenson, Bjorn Andresen, Silvana Mangano, Luigi Battaglia. Study of an artist, his loves, his homosexuality, and continuous search for beauty. Thomas Mann's slow-moving classic is splendidly brought to the screen. Music by Gustav Mahler (whom Bogarde is made up to resemble).▼

Death Kiss, The (1933) **75m.** *** D: Edwin L. Marin. Bela Lugosi, David Manners, Adrienne Ames, John Wray, Vince Barnett, Edward Van Sloan. Minor but entertaining whodunit set inside a movie studio, where an actor is killed while filming a scene. Nice atmosphere of a studio at work.▼

Deathline SEE: **Raw Meat**

Death Machines (1976) **C-90m.** BOMB D: Paul Kyriazi. Mari Honjo, Ron Marchini, Michael Chong, Joshua Johnson, Chuck Katzaian. Lady mobster Honjo and cronies kill for pay. Dismal exploitation actioner. Original running-time: 92m.▼

Deathmask (1984) **C-87m.** ** D: Richard Friedman. Farley Granger, Lee Bryant, John McCurry, Arch Johnson, Barbara Bingham, Danny Aiello, Ruth Warrick. Medical investigator Granger, haunted by the accidental drowning of his daughter, attempts to find the identity of a dead four-year-old boy. Might have been a good mystery-chiller, an effective study of a man obsessed, but done in by confusing direction, unnecessary exploitation elements. Video version is 103m.▼

Deathmaster, The (1972) C-88m. ** D: Ray Danton. Robert Quarry, Bill Ewing, Brenda Dickson, John Fiedler, Betty Ann Rees, William Jordan. Spellbinding stranger (Quarry) leads on a group of unsuspecting hippies; their "guru" turns out to be a vampire in this bloody, run-of-the-mill outing.

Deathmoon (1978) C-89m. TVM D: Bruce Kessler. France Nuyen, Robert Foxworth, Joe Penny, Barbara Trentham, Debralee Scott. Plodding tale of executive (Foxworth) tangling with a witch with supernatural powers while vacationing in Hawaii. Below average.▼

Death of a Centerfold: The Dorothy Stratten Story (1981) C-100m. TVM D: Gabrielle Beaumont. Jamie Lee Curtis, Bruce Weitz, Robert Reed, Mitchell Ryan, Tracy Reed, Bibi Besch. Exploitive, fact-based story of a starstruck teenager from Canada who goes to Hollywood looking for the big break, becomes Playmate of the Year, and finds tragedy. Stratten's sad story, scripted by Donald Stewart, was also utilized by Bob Fosse in STAR 80. Average.▼

Death of a Gunfighter (1969) C-100m. **½ D: Allen Smithee. Richard Widmark, Lena Horne, John Saxon, Michael McGreevey, Darleen Carr, Carroll O'Connor, Kent Smith. Downbeat but interesting Western drama of unwanted sheriff who refuses to be fired. Horne wasted as Widmark's occasional love interest. Directed by Robert Totten and Don Siegel, credited to fictitious Smithee.▼

Death of a Jew SEE: Sabra

Death of an Angel (1985) C-95m. ** D: Petru Popescu. Bonnie Bedelia, Nick Mancuso, Pamela Ludwig, Alex Colon, Irma Garcia. Inspirational misfire about newly ordained female priest Bedelia getting involved with Mexican religious charlatan Mancuso after her crippled daughter (Ludwig) runs away to join his flock. Well-meaning, well-acted effort is extremely hokey, with a fantasy ending that is wholly unbelievable.▼

Death of a Salesman (1951) 115m. ***½ D: Laslo Benedek. Fredric March, Mildred Dunnock, Kevin McCarthy, Cameron Mitchell, Howard Smith, Royal Beal, Jesse White. Arthur Miller's Pulitzer Prize-winning social drama of middle-aged man at end of emotional rope is transformed to the screen intact, with stagy flashbacks. March in title role can't fathom why business and family life failed; Dunnock is patient wife; McCarthy and Mitchell are disillusioned sons. Superb. Dunnock, Mitchell, and Smith recreate their Broadway roles; McCarthy, making his film debut, repeats the role he played on the London stage. Remade in 1985.

Death of a Salesman (1985) C-150m. TVM D: Volker Schlondorff. Dustin Hoffman, Kate Reid, John Malkovich, Stephen Lang, Charles Durning, Louis Zorich. Stunning though stylistic remounting of Hoffman's Broadway revival of the classic Arthur Miller play with most of the cast from that 1984 production. A landmark of its type. Executive-produced by Hoffman and Miller. Hoffman and Malkovich both won acting Emmys. Above average.▼

Death of a Scoundrel (1956) 119m. **½ D: Charles Martin. George Sanders, Yvonne de Carlo, Zsa Zsa Gabor, Victor Jory. Episodic chronicle of foreigner coming to U.S., ingratiating himself with an assortment of women whom he cons into helping him get ahead. Low-budget but fascinating.▼

Death of a Soldier (1986-Australian) C-93m. ** D: Philippe Mora. James Coburn, Bill Hunter, Mauric Fields, Belinda Davey, Max Fairchild. Yank soldier in 1942 Melbourne is strangling Aussie women; the U.S. Army—which desperately needs Allied help just after MacArthur's arrival there from the Philippines—wants to hang the assailant instead of providing the professional help he really needs. Based on fact, but not as interesting as it sounds; Coburn is the American MP who gets caught in the middle.▼

Death of Her Innocence SEE: Our Time

Death of Innocence, A (1971) C-73m. TVM D: Paul Wendkos. Shelley Winters, Arthur Kennedy, Tisha Sterling, Ann Sothern, John Randolph. Parents from Idaho (Winters & Randolph) journey to N.Y.C to attend daughter's murder trial; visit becomes major emotional experience for mother. Better than average script, by Joseph Stefano (from Zelda Popkin's novel), overblown performances, good direction. Above average.

Death of Me Yet, The (1971) C-73m. TVM D: John Llewellyn Moxey. Doug McClure, Darren McGavin, Richard Basehart, Rosemary Forsyth, Meg Foster, Dana Elcar. Happily married newspaper editor in small town, actually ex-spy for U.S. in Russia, suddenly questioned by government agent (McGavin) and sought by another agent. Good suspense, adequate performances. Above average.

Death of Ocean View Park, The (1979) C-100m. TVM D: E.W. Swackhamer. Mike Connors, Martin Landau, Diana Canova, Perry Lang, James Stephens, Caroline McWilliams, Mare Winningham. Hurricane levels a seaside amusement park on a holiday weekend, and lots of familiar TV personalities panic with conviction. Special effects are surprisingly mediocre, considering that an actual park was destroyed for the film. Average.

Death of Richie, The (1977) C-100m. TVM D: Paul Wendkos. Ben Gazzara,

Robby Benson, Lance Kerwin, Eileen Brennan, Charles Fleischer, Clint Howard. A family is torn apart by teenaged son's drug addiction. Gazzara is splendid as straight-arrow father who brings himself to kill the boy; intelligent script by John McGreevey from Thomas Thompson's nonfiction book *Richie* occasionally becomes maudlin. Homevideo version is titled RICHIE. Average.

Death of the Incredible Hulk, The (1990) **C-100m. TVM** D: Bill Bixby. Bill Bixby, Lou Ferrigno, Elizabeth Gracen, Philip Sterling, Barbara Tarbuck, Anna Katerina. David Banner takes a job with a scientist who may hold the key to his mysterious transformation into the Hulk. Is this *really* the end of the Big Green Guy? Only time will tell. Average.

Death on the Nile (1978-British) **C-140m. **½** D: John Guillermin. Peter Ustinov, Bette Davis, David Niven, Mia Farrow, Angela Lansbury, George Kennedy, Maggie Smith, Jack Warden, Lois Chiles, Olivia Hussey, Simon MacCorkindale, Jane Birkin, Jon Finch, Harry Andrews, I.S. Johar. Visually sumptuous but only marginally engrossing Agatha Christie mystery has Hercule Poirot (Ustinov) faced with a shipload of suspects after the murder of Chiles. A deserving Oscar winner for Anthony Powell's costume design; script by Anthony Shaffer. The first of Ustinov's portrayals of the Belgian detective.▼

Death Penalty (1980) **C-100m. TVM** D: Waris Hussein. Colleen Dewhurst, Dana Elcar, Joe Morton, David Labiosa, Dan Hedaya, Ted Ross. Slow-moving drama about a strong-willed psychologist's struggle to save a street-gang teenager from going to the electric chair for a double murder. Average.

Death Race (1973) **C-73m. TVM** D: David Lowell Rich. Lloyd Bridges, Doug McClure, Roy Thinnes, Eric Braeden, Dennis Rucker. Two Americans in wounded fighter plane vs. German tank separated from its squad; drawn-out, boring WW2 adventure. Below average.

Death Race 2000 (1975) **C-78m. **½** D: Paul Bartel. David Carradine, Simone Griffeth, Sylvester Stallone, Louisa Moritz, Mary Woronov, Don Steele, Joyce Jameson, Fred Grandy, Martin Kove, John Landis. Outrageous tongue-in-cheek action film about futuristic society where no-holds-barred auto race is the national sport, and points scored by running down pedestrians. Fast-paced fun, marred by unnecessary gore. Followed by DEATHSPORT.▼

Death Rage (1976-Italian) **C-98m. *½** D: Anthony M. Dawson (Antonio Margheriti). Yul Brynner, Barbara Bouchet, Martin Balsam, Massimo Ranieri. Brynner plays American hit man who's duped into agreeing to kill underworld kingpin in Naples.

All this picture kills is time. TV print runs 90m.▼

Death Ray 2000 (1981) **C-100m. TVM** D: Lee Katzin. Robert Logan, Ann Turkel, Maggie Cooper, Clive Revill, Ji-Tu Cumbuka, Dan O'Herlihy, Penelope Windust, Paul Mantee, Michele Carey. The pilot movie to the 1979–80 Robert Conrad series *A Man Called Sloane* has a flamboyant agent (here, Logan) and his associates ordered to retrieve an exotic device capable of destroying the world. Retitled T.P. SLOANE. Average.▼

Death Rides a Horse (1969-Italian) **C-114m. ** D: Giulio Petroni. Lee Van Cleef, John Phillip Law, Luigi Pistilli, Anthony Dawson (Antonio Margheriti). Long, drawn-out Italian revenge Western with Law seeking murderers of his family, unaware that his companion (Van Cleef) is one of them.

Death Ride to Osaka SEE: **Girls of the White Orchid**▼

Death Scream (1975) **C-100m. TVM** D: Richard T. Heffron. Raul Julia, John Ryan, Phillip Clark, Lucie Arnaz, Edward Asner, Art Carney, Diahann Carroll, Kate Jackson, Cloris Leachman, Tina Louise, Nancy Walker, Eric Braeden, Allyn Ann McLerie, Todd Susman, Tony Dow, Sally Kirkland. Thriller, based on Kitty Genovese murder in N.Y.C., involves fifteen neighbors who witnessed killing, did nothing to help, and refused to cooperate with police. Provocative theme deteriorates into formula cop story. Written by Stirling Silliphant. Retitled THE WOMAN WHO CRIED MURDER. Average.▼

Death Sentence (1974) **C-78m. TVM** D: E. W. Swackhamer. Cloris Leachman, Laurence Luckinbill, Nick Nolte, William Schallert, Alan Oppenheimer, Yvonne Wilder. Juror Leachman discovers that the wrong man is on trial for murder and finds her own life threatened by the real one— her husband. Not terribly convincing, to say the least. Below average.▼

Death Ship (1980-Canadian) **C-91m.** BOMB D: Alvin Rakoff. George Kennedy, Richard Crenna, Nick Mancuso, Sally Ann Howes, Kate Reid, Saul Rubinek. Luxury liner collides with "death ship." Survivors board "death ship." "Death ship" tries to murder survivors. Forget it.▼

Deathsport (1978) **C-82m. ** D: Henry Suso, Allan Arkush. David Carradine, Claudia Jennings, Richard Lynch, David McLean, Jesse Vint. Follow-up to DEATH RACE 2000 again puts Carradine into future world where he and Jennings battle destructo-cycles to survive. Not as campy or enjoyable as earlier film, though Claudia unclothed is a visual asset. TV prints run 76m.▼

Death Squad, The (1974) **C-78m. TVM**

D: Harry Falk. Robert Forster, Michelle Phillips, Claude Akins, Mark Goddard, Melvyn Douglas, Ken Tobey, Dennis Patrick. Tough ex-cop is recruited to root out rotten apples on police roster, a self-styled assassination squad that methodically executes criminals released on legal technicalities. If it all sounds familiar, refer to MAGNUM FORCE. Below average.▼

Death Stalk (1974) **C-78m. TVM** D: Robert Day. Vince Edwards, Anjanette Comer, Robert Webber, Carol Lynley, Vic Morrow, Neville Brand, Norman Fell. Two men desperately try to save their wives, abducted by four convicts fleeing in rubber rafts down treacherous river. Hokey suspense tale wastes good cast and splendid scenery, including the expected rapids-run. Below average.▼

Deathstalker (1984) **C-80m.** BOMB D: John Watson. Richard Hill, Barbi Benton, Richard Brooker, Lana Clarkson, Victor Bo, Bernard Erhard. Tacky sword-and-sorcery opus, good only for unintended laughs and gratuitous female nudity. Filmed in Argentina. Followed by a sequel.▼

Deathstalker II (1987) **C-77m.** ** D: Jim Wynorski. John Terlesky, Monique Gabrielle, John La Zar, Toni Naples, Maria Socas. Princess in exile (Gabrielle) is trying to regain her throne, with the aid of soldier of fortune Terlesky, in a medieval fantasyland. Filmed on the cheap in Argentina, picture was released directly to videocassette. Voyeurs will appreciate topless scenes by former model Gabrielle (in a dual role, no less). Watch for funny outtakes at the end.▼

Death Takes a Holiday (1934) **78m.** ***½ D: Mitchell Leisen. Fredric March, Evelyn Venable, Guy Standing, Gail Patrick, Helen Westley, Kent Taylor, Henry Travers, Katharine Alexander. Fascinating allegory about Death (March) entering the human world to discover what makes us tick, and falling in love. Maxwell Anderson, Gladys Lehman, and Walter Ferris adapted Alberto Casella's play. Remade as a TV movie.

Death Takes a Holiday (1971) **C-73m. TVM** D: Robert Butler. Melvyn Douglas, Myrna Loy, Yvette Mimieux, Monte Markham, Maureen Reagan. Silly update of 1934 version with Death (Markham) on Earth trying to understand why people cling to existence, falling in love with beautiful woman. Unbearable script, sloppy direction. Below average.

Death Trap (1976) SEE: **Eaten Alive!**▼

Deathtrap (1982) **C-116m.** ** D: Sidney Lumet. Michael Caine, Christopher Reeve, Dyan Cannon, Irene Worth, Henry Jones, Joe Silver. Playwright Caine, suffering through a series of flops, might just kill to take credit for novice author Reeve's new work; Cannon is Caine's hysterical wife. An overlong, second-rate SLEUTH, adapted

by Jay Presson Allen from Ira Levin's hit play. One sequence was added for original network showing.▼

Death Valley (1982) **C-87m.** *½ D: Dick Richards. Paul Le Mat, Catherine Hicks, Stephen McHattie, A. Wilford Brimley, Peter Billingsley, Edward Herrmann. Young Billingsley, a city boy, visits mom in Arizona, becomes entangled with psychotic criminal McHattie. Pretty bad, with a fine cast wasted.▼

Deathwatch (1980-French-German) **C-128m.** *** D: Bertrand Tavernier. Romy Schneider, Harvey Keitel, Harry Dean Stanton, Max von Sydow. Intelligent sci-fi drama. In a future civilization, TV producer Stanton uses Keitel—who has a camera in his brain—to film a documentary on terminally ill Schneider. A biting commentary on media abuse and manipulation, with solid performances, direction.▼

Death Weekend SEE: **House by the Lake**▼

Death Wish (1974) **C-93m.** *** D: Michael Winner. Charles Bronson, Hope Lange, Vincent Gardenia, Steven Keats, William Redfield, Stuart Margolin, Stephen Elliott, Olympia Dukakis, Christopher Guest, Eric Laneuville. Audience manipulation at its zenith: Businessman Bronson's wife and daughter are savagely raped, and his wife dies, turning mild-mannered liberal Bronson into a vigilante in N.Y.C. streets. Chilling but irresistible; a bastardization of the Brian Garfield novel, in which vigilantism as a deterrent to crime is not a solution but another problem. Music score by Herbie Hancock. One of those muggers is played by Jeff Goldblum, in his film debut. Followed by three sequels.▼

Death Wish II (1982) **C-93m.** BOMB D: Michael Winner. Charles Bronson, Jill Ireland, Vincent Gardenia, J. D. Cannon, Anthony Franciosa, Ben Frank, Robin Sherwood, Robert F. Lyons. Bronson's back in action, this time bringing his one-man vigilante act to L.A. Made by profiteers, not filmmakers; poorly directed to boot, with Charlie giving a wooden-Indian performance.▼

Death Wish 3 (1985) **C-90m.** *½ D: Michael Winner. Charles Bronson, Deborah Raffin, Ed Lauter, Martin Balsam, Gavan O'Herlihy, Kirk Taylor. Same old stuff, except that Bronson's "ordinary guy" vigilante character is no longer convincing; his entire immediate family was wiped out in the first two movies! ▼

Death Wish 4: The Crackdown (1987) **C-99m.** BOMB D: J. Lee Thompson. Charles Bronson, Kay Lenz, John P. Ryan, Perry Lopez, George Dickerson, Soon-Teck Oh, Dana Barron, Jesse Dabson. Cheapie entry in this worn-out series has a different director and an L.A. setting. This time vigilante Bronson's mission includes wiping out the gangs supplying crack.▼

Decameron, The (1970-Italian-French-West German) **C-111m.** **½ D: Pier Paolo Pasolini. Franco Citti, Ninetto Davoli, Angela Luce, Patrizia Capparelli, Jovan Jovanovic, Silvana Mangano, Pier Paolo Pasolini. An octet of tales from Boccaccio's *Decameron*, with Pasolini as Giotto, linking them up. Lively, earthy; the first of the director's trilogy of medieval stories.▼

Decameron Nights (1953-British) **C-87m.** ** D: Hugo Fregonese. Joan Fontaine, Louis Jourdan, Binnie Barnes, Joan Collins, Marjorie Rhodes. Distillation of robust medieval tales with Jourdan the story-spinning Boccaccio seeking fair Fontaine's love.▼

Deceivers, The (1988-British-Indian) **C-112m.** BOMB: D: Nicholas Meyer. Pierce Brosnan, Saeed Jaffrey, Shashi Kapoor, Helena Mitchell, Keith Michell, David Robb. Limp adventure saga of British officer Brosnan going undercover in colonial India to infiltrate a murderous brotherhood. Intriguing premise, deadening result; Brosnan simply fails to register. Produced, oddly enough, by Ismail Merchant.▼

Deception (1946) **112m.** ***½ D: Irving Rapper. Bette Davis, Claude Rains, Paul Henreid, John Abbott, Benson Fong. Acting duel de force by Davis and Rains as pianist and her jealous benefactor, with Henreid overshadowed by star duo.▼

Deceptions (1985) **C-200m.** TVM D: Robert Chenault, Melville Shavelson. Stefanie Powers, Barry Bostwick, Jeremy Brett, Sam Wanamaker, Gina Lollobrigida, Brenda Vaccaro, Joan Sims, Fabio Testi, James Faulkner. Delectable trash about identical twins—a bored jet-setter on the Continent and an unhappy New Jersey housewife—who swap identities and lives for a week. Not quite *Lifestyles of the Rich and Famous* but a fair approximation cloned by best-selling writer Judith Michael, who is actually the husband and wife novelist team of Judith Bernard and Michael Fain. Codirector Shavelson wrote the screenplay. Originally shown in two parts. Average.

Decision Against Time (1957-British) **87m.** **½ D: Charles Crichton. Jack Hawkins, Elizabeth Sellars, Eddie Byrne, Lionel Jeffries, Donald Pleasence. Hawkins is effective as test pilot giving all to save troubled craft for boss and to protect job future.

Decision at Sundown (1957) **C-77m.** **½ D: Budd Boetticher. Randolph Scott, John Carroll, Karen Steele, Noah Beery, John Litel. Scott tracks down man supposedly responsible for his wife's suicide in this odd but interesting Western.

Decision Before Dawn (1951) **119m.** *** D: Anatole Litvak. Richard Basehart, Gary Merrill, Oskar Werner, Hildegarde Neff. Werner is exceptional in realistic WW2

thriller of Nazi P.O.W. returning to Germany as American spy. Watch for Klaus Kinski in one of his earliest roles.

Decision of Christopher Blake, The (1948) **75m.** **½ D: Peter Godfrey. Alexis Smith, Robert Douglas, Cecil Kellaway, Ted Donaldson, John Hoyt. Insipid drama of child suffering from his parents' divorce.

Decks Ran Red, The (1958) **84m.** **½ D: Andrew L. Stone. James Mason, Dorothy Dandridge, Broderick Crawford, Stuart Whitman. Bizarre sea yarn with strange casting involves sailors' attempt to murder freighter captain and use vessel for salvage.

Decline of the American Empire, The (1986-Canadian) **C-101m.** *** D: Denys Arcand. Dominique Michel, Dorothée Berryman, Louise Portal, Geneviève Rioux, Pierre Curzi, Remy Girard, Yves Jacques, Daniel Brière, Gabriel Arcand. Witty, on-target account of how men and women feel about each other, and use each other, in their quests for pleasure and happiness. Focus is on a group of friends: The men prepare a gourmet dinner, while the women exercise in a health club, then they come together.▼

Decline and Fall of a Bird Watcher (1969-British) **C-86m.** ** D: John Krish. Robin Phillips, Colin Blakely, Leo McKern, Genevieve Page, Felix Aylmer, Robert Harris, Donald Wolfit, Patrick Magee. Uneven, often labored satirical farce about a young man who joins faculty of strange boys' school and becomes involved with manipulative older woman (Page). Adapted from Evelyn Waugh's novel.

Decline of Western Civilization, The (1981) **C-100m.** *** D: Penelope Spheeris. Alice Bag Band, Black Flag, Catholic Discipline, Circle Jerks, Fear, Germs, X. Funny, revealing documentary record of the whos, whats, and whys of the L.A. punk rock scene at the end of the 1970s: the music, performers, dancing, clubs, violence, desperation. An aptly titled chronicle. Much of cast now dead. Followed by a sequel.▼

Decline of Western Civilization Part II: The Metal Years, The (1988) **C-90m.** *** D: Penelope Spheeris. Joe Perry, Steven Tyler, Gene Simmons, Paul Stanley, Chris Holmes, Lemmy, Ozzy Osbourne, Faster Pussycat, Lizzy Borden, London, Odin, Seduce, Megadeth. Follow-up to definitive punk rock documentary concentrates more heavily on interviews, juxtaposing thoughts of seen-it-all veterans (Osbourne, Simmons, Perry and Taylor of Aerosmith) with young aspirants bucking formidable success odds. Sympathetic to its subjects without condoning the lifestyle it depicts; probably the only chance you'll ever get to see Osbourne cook breakfast.▼

Decoy for Terror (1970-Canadian) **C-90m.** *½ D: Erick Santamaria. William Kerwin, Jean Christopher, Neil Sedaka, Andree

Champagne, Mary Lou Collier. Talky low-budget film about an insane painter suspected of murdering his female models and a woman set as bait to catch him for the police. Originally titled THE PLAY-GIRL KILLER.▼

Deep, The (1977) **C-123m.** ** D: Peter Yates. Robert Shaw, Jacqueline Bisset, Nick Nolte, Louis Gossett, Eli Wallach, Robert Tessier. Endless film of Peter Benchley's novel about innocent couple who hit on treasure and drugs while scuba-diving off Bermuda coast. Gratuitous violence and titillation—not to mention unbelievable plot—sink this handsome production. NBC added 53m. for its first network showing.▼

Deep Blue Sea, The (1955-British) **C-99m.** **½ D: Anatole Litvak. Vivien Leigh, Kenneth More, Eric Portman, Emlyn Williams. Terence Rattigan play of marital infidelity and the repercussions on Leigh, frustrated well-married woman; slow-moving, but thoughtfully presented.

Deep Dark Secrets (1987) **C-100m.** TVM D: Robert Lewis. James Brolin, Melody Anderson, Pamela Bellwood, Morgan Stevens, Joe Spano. Murky melodrama about a sheltered woman who uncovers distressing secrets about her supposedly dead hubby's past. Average.▼

Deep End (1970-U.S.-German) **C-88m.** *** D: Jerzy Skolimowski. Jane Asher, John Moulder-Brown, Diana Dors, Karl Michael Vogler. Innocent 15-year-old Moulder-Brown, an attendant in a dreary public bath, falls in love with his 20-ish female counterpart (Asher). Well-made tragedy of obsessive love; set in London, with music by Cat Stevens.▼

Deep in My Heart (1954) **C-132m.** **½ D: Stanley Donen. Jose Ferrer, Merle Oberon, Helen Traubel, Doe Avedon, Tamara Toumanova, Paul Stewart, Douglas Fowley, Jim Backus; guest stars Walter Pidgeon, Paul Henreid, Rosemary Clooney, Gene and Fred Kelly, Jane Powell, Vic Damone, Ann Miller, Cyd Charisse, Howard Keel, Tony Martin. The life of composer Sigmund Romberg is not the stuff of high drama, but the film comes to life in various production numbers with MGM guest stars. Highlights include Kelly brothers' only appearance on film together, Charisse's exquisite and sensual dance number with James Mitchell, and an incredible number featuring Ferrer performing an entire show himself.▼

Deep in the Heart (1983-British) **C-101m.** *** D: Tony Garnett. Karen Young, Clayton Day, Suzie Humphreys, Ben Jones. Thought-provoking, if occasionally simplistic, drama about the evolution of a young woman (nicely played by Young) from passivity to violence, resulting from her

relationship with macho Texan Day. Originally titled HANDGUN.▼

Deep Red (1975-Italian) **C-98m.** **½ D: Dario Argento. David Hemmings, Daria Nicolodi, Gabriele Lavia, Macha Meril, Glauco Mauri, Clara Calamai. There's style to burn in senseless horror thriller with Hemmings on trail of sadistic psycho killer. Flashy, bizarre murders set to pounding rock soundtrack. Also known as THE HATCHET MURDERS; the original Italian version, titled PROFONDO ROSSO, is 20m. longer and much more violent.▼

Deep Six, The (1958) **C-105m.** **½ D: Rudolph Mate. Alan Ladd, Dianne Foster, William Bendix, Keenan Wynn, James Whitmore, Joey Bishop. Ladd is Quaker naval officer during WW2 who compensates for past inaction by heading dangerous shore mission; Bendix gives able support.▼

DeepStar Six (1989) **C-100m.** *½ D: Sean S. Cunningham. Greg Evigan, Nancy Everhard, Cindy Pickett, Miguel Ferrer, Taurean Blacque, Marius Weyers, Nia Peeples, Matt McCoy, Elya Baskin, Thom Bray, Ronn Carroll. In the near future, an undersea research and missile-installation base is threatened by a carnivorous swimming crustacean. Plodding, familiar story and talky script (not to mention an elaborate but unconvincing monster) sink this soggy sci-fi saga, which was the first of several such films to wash up in 1989.▼

Deep Valley (1947) **104m.** *** D: Jean Negulesco. Ida Lupino, Dane Clark, Wayne Morris, Fay Bainter, Henry Hull. Into Lupino's humdrum farm life comes a gangster from nearby prison camp; first rate cast in excellent drama.

Deep Waters (1948) **85m.** ** D: Henry King. Dana Andrews, Jean Peters, Cesar Romero, Dean Stockwell, Anne Revere, Ed Begley. Slick empty tale of fisherman Andrews and landlubber Peters brought together by cute little Stockwell.

Deer Hunter, The (1978) **C-183m.** **** D: Michael Cimino. Robert De Niro, John Cazale, John Savage, Meryl Streep, Christopher Walken, George Dzundza, Chuck Aspegren. Stunning film about young Pennsylvania steelworkers, their lives before, during, and after wartime duty in Vietnam. Long but not overlong, this sensitive, painful, evocative work packs an emotional wallop. Story by Cimino, Deric Washburn, Louis Garfinkle and Quinn Redeker; scripted by Washburn. Five Oscars include Picture, Director, Supporting Actor (Walken), Editing (Peter Zinner).▼

Deerslayer, The (1957) **C-78m.** *½ D: Kurt Neumann. Lex Barker, Forrest Tucker, Rita Moreno, Jay C. Flippen. James Fenimore Cooper's Leatherstocking novel of white man (Barker) raised by Indians is given pedestrian treatment, virtually all indoor sets and rear-screen projection.

Deerslayer, The (1978) **C-74m. TVM** D: Dick Friedenberg. Steve Forrest, Ned Romero, John Anderson, Victor Mohica, Joan Prather, Charles Dierkop. Trim "Classics Illustrated" treatment of the James Fenimore Cooper tale, a follow-up to a companion version of LAST OF THE MOHICANS also with Forrest and Romero as Hawkeye and Chingachgook. Later expanded to 100m. Average.▼

Def-Con 4 (1984) **C-89m. BOMB** D: Paul Donovan. Lenore Zann, Maury Chaykin, Kate Lynch, Tim Choate. It sounds like an industrial-strength roach killer, and it could use one. Three astronauts return to a post-holocaust earth run by some truly slimy punks. Next to C.H.U.D., the grimiest-looking movie in recent memory (at least *that* one had the excuse of taking place underground).▼

Defection of Simas Kudirka, The (1978) **C-100m. TVM** D: David Lowell Rich. Alan Arkin, Richard Jordan, Donald Pleasence, John McMartin, Shirley Knight. Absorbing drama, based on the Lithuanian seaman's abortive 1970 attempt at freedom by jumping ship in Portsmouth, New Hampshire. Arkin added another intriguing portrait to his personal acting gallery, and director Rich won an Emmy Award. Exceptionally well written by Bruce Feldman. Above average.

Defector, The (1966) **C-106m. **½** D: Raoul Levy. Montgomery Clift, Hardy Kruger, Roddy McDowall, David Opatoshu. Hackneyed Cold War spy trivia filmed in Europe, interesting only as Clift's last film; good cameo by McDowall.

Defence of the Realm (1985-British) **C-96m. ***½** D: David Drury. Gabriel Byrne, Greta Scacchi, Denholm Elliott, Ian Bannen, Bill Paterson, Fulton Mackay. Tough, obsessive journalist Byrne's investigative story causes a British MP to resign—but there's more to the case than he knows. A taut, extremely entertaining political thriller that also touches on the subject of journalistic responsibility and the public's right to know what its government is up to.▼

Defiance (1980) **C-102m. **½** D: John Flynn. Jan-Michael Vincent, Art Carney, Theresa Saldana, Danny Aiello. Fernando Lopez, Rudy Ramos. Gritty little film about rootless blue-collar loner Vincent, who single-handedly tames a vicious New York City street gang. A synthesis of '30s Warner Bros. melodramas, B Westerns, ON THE WATERFRONT, and BOARDWALK, with atmospheric direction and colorful supporting performances.▼

✓ **Defiant Ones, The** (1958) **97m. ****** D: Stanley Kramer. Tony Curtis, Sidney Poitier, Theodore Bikel, Charles McGraw,

Cara Williams, Lon Chaney, Jr. Engrossing story of two escaped convicts (Curtis and Poitier) shackled together as they flee from police in the South. Fine performances by Williams and Chaney as people they meet along the way. Academy Award-winning screenplay by Harold Jacob Smith and Nathan E. Douglas (blacklisted actor-writer Nedrick Young) and cinematography by Sam Leavitt. Remade for TV.▼

Defiant Ones, The (1986) **C-100m. TVM** D: David Lowell Rich. Robert Urich, Carl Weathers, Barry Corbin, Ed Lauter, Laurie O'Brien, Thalmus Rasulala, Wil Wheaton. OK scene-for-scene remake of the Stanley Kramer original, adapted for TV by James Lee Barrett. So which is better, watching this or colorizing the Tony Curtis/Sidney Poitier version? Average.

Déja Vu (1985) **C-95m. *½** D: Anthony Richmond. Jaclyn Smith, Shelley Winters, Claire Bloom, Nigel Terry. Smith and Terry relive the love affair they experienced in an earlier incarnation . . . then this supernatural thriller takes off on a whodunit storyline! Muddled, to say the least (and reminiscent of the 1980 film ECHOES), though Smith is quite beautiful in her dual role; her cinematographer husband directed the film.▼

Delancey Street: The Crisis Within (1975) **C-78m. TVM** D: James Frawley. Walter McGinn, Carmine Caridi, Michael Conrad, Lou Gossett, Mark Hamill, Barbara Bostock. Fact-based drama of San Francisco halfway house helping ex-cons and former junkies to get back on their feet. Earnest performances, admirable story by Robert Foster. Above average.

Deliberate Stranger, The (1986) **C-200m. TVM** D: Marvin J. Chomsky. Mark Harmon, Frederic Forrest, George Grizzard, Ben Masters, Glynnis O'Connor, M. Emmet Walsh, Bonnie Bartlett, Billy Green Bush, Lawrence Pressman. Highly charged drama about Ted Bundy, charismatic law school student sentenced to death for several Florida murders and suspected in the killing of at least 25 women in six states. Hesper Anderson adapted her script from Richard W. Larsen's book. Engrossing but overlong. Originally shown in two parts. Above average.

Delicate Balance, A (1973) **C-132m. **** D: Tony Richardson. Katharine Hepburn, Paul Scofield, Lee Remick, Kate Reid, Joseph Cotten, Betsy Blair. Edward Albee's Pulitzer Prize-winning play about a neurotic Connecticut family and the old friends who decide to move in with them indefinitely makes for stagy, uninvolving film, extraordinary cast notwithstanding. An American Film Theater Production.▼

Delicate Delinquent, The (1957) **100m. *** D: Don McGuire. Jerry Lewis, Martha Hyer, Darren McGavin, Horace Mc-

Mahon, Milton Frome. Jerry's first solo effort after splitting with Dean Martin has him as delinquent who becomes a cop with McGavin's help. Agreeable blend of sentiment and slapstick.▼

Delicious (1931) 106m. *½ D: David Butler. Janet Gaynor, Charles Farrell, El Brendel, Raul Roulien, Virginia Cherrill. Insipid romance; Janet as Irish colleen emigrating to N.Y.C. who falls in love with wealthy Farrell. Brief highlights in Gershwin score are bizarre dream sequence of Janet's welcome to America, and "New York Rhapsody."

Delightfully Dangerous (1945) 93m. **½ D: Arthur Lubin. Jane Powell, Ralph Bellamy, Constance Moore, Morton Gould Orchestra, Arthur Treacher, Louise Beavers. Pleasant froth of sisters Powell (sedate) and Moore (stripper) competing for Bellamy's love.

Delinquents, The (1957) 75m. ** D: Robert Altman. Tom Laughlin, Peter Miller, Richard Bakalyan, Rosemary Howard, Helene Hawley. Intriguingly awful exploitation drama about nice boy Laughlin, who becomes involved with a street gang because girlfriend Howard is too young to go steady. Definitely a relic of its era; Altman's first film, made in Kansas City, with Julia Lee singing "Dirty Rock Boogie."

Deliverance (1972) C-109m. **** D: John Boorman. Jon Voight, Burt Reynolds, Ned Beatty, Ronny Cox, Billy McKinney, Herbert "Cowboy" Coward, James Dickey. Superlative recreation of Dickey novel of four Atlanta businessmen who get more than they bargained for during a weekend canoe trip. McKinney and Coward are two of the most terrifying film villains in history; "Dueling Banjos" scene is equally memorable. Film debuts of Beatty and Cox. James Dickey adapted his own novel, and appears in the film as a sheriff. The director's son Charley Boorman (later star of THE EMERALD FOREST) plays Voight's son in this film.▼

Deliver Us From Evil (1973) C-78m. TVM D: Boris Sagal. George Kennedy, Jan-Michael Vincent, Bradford Dillman, Jack Weston, Jim Davis, Charles Aidman, Allen Pinson. Five "honest" men catch and kill a skyjacker during a camping trip and then get greedy about his $600,000 loot. So-so variation on THE TREASURE OF THE SIERRA MADRE. Average.

Delivery Boys (1986) C-91m. BOMB D: Ken Handler. Joss Marcano, Tom Sierchio, Jim Soriero, Nelson Vasquez, Jody Oliver, Mario Van Peebles, Kelly Nichols. Amateur-night break-dancing film about trio of pizza delivery boys' sexual misadventures en route to a big dance contest. If the cast of nonactors didn't sink this one, the crummy production values would have. Filmed in 1984.▼

Delphi Bureau, The (1972) C-99m. TVM D: Paul Wendkos. Laurence Luckinbill, Joanna Pettet, Celeste Holm, Bob Crane, Cameron Mitchell, Dean Jagger, Bradford Dillman. Fast-paced, sometimes effective cold-war thriller with U.S. in balance-of-power struggle. Shallow characterizations in this pilot for TV series; average.

Delta County, U.S.A. (1977) C-100m. TVM D: Glenn Jordan. Jim Antonio, Doney Oatman, Peter Donat, Joanna Miles, Jeff Conaway, Robert Hays, Lola Albright, Michele Carey. Contemporary drama dissecting life in rural Southern community, involving old-line families, traditional values and restless youth. PEYTON PLACE with a different accent. Average.

Delta Factor, The (1970) C-91m. ** D: Tay Garnett. Christopher George, Yvette Mimieux, Diane McBain, Ralph Taeger. OK Mickey Spillane tale about a private eye on a CIA mission to rescue a scientist imprisoned on an island.

Delta Force, The (1986) C-129m. **½ D: Menahem Golan. Chuck Norris, Lee Marvin, Martin Balsam, Joey Bishop, Robert Forster, Lainie Kazan, George Kennedy, Hanna Schygulla, Susan Strasberg, Bo Svenson, Robert Vaughn, Shelley Winters, Assaf Dayan. Surprisingly straightforward and straight-faced (considering that cast) account of terrorist plane hijack in the Middle East—until rescue climax when America's special squadron (led by Marvin and Norris) take on bad guys in comicbook style. Uneven, to say the least, but never boring. Filmed in Israel.▼

Delta Fox (1977) C-92m. ** D: Beverly and Ferd Sebastian. Richard Lynch, Priscilla Barnes, Stuart Whitman, John Ireland, Richard Jaeckel. Unremarkable action-chase opus about a smuggler on the run from Miami to L.A.▼

Delta Pi (1985) C-90m. ** D: Kevin Brodie. Ruth Gordon, Laura Brannigan, Joanna Dierek, Estrelita, Rebecca Forstadt, Candace Pandolfo, Kristi Somers, Eddie Deezen, James Marcel. Gordon adds her usual spark to this otherwise lackluster comedy as a sorority mom whose charges mud-wrestle to raise the funds to save their house. Originally titled MUGSY'S GIRLS.

Dementia 13 (1963) 81m. ** D: Francis Ford Coppola. William Campbell, Luana Anders, Bart Patton, Mary Mitchell, Patrick Magee. Gory horror film, set in Ireland, about a series of axe murders. Coppola's directorial debut—excluding his earlier nudie, TONITE FOR SURE—filmed for about 29¢ for Roger Corman, may be worth a look for curiosity's sake.▼

Demetrius and the Gladiators (1954) C-101m. **½ D: Delmer Daves. Victor Mature, Susan Hayward, Michael Rennie, Debra Paget, Anne Bancroft, Richard Egan,

Ernest Borgnine. Hokey sequel to THE ROBE has Emperor Caligula (Jay Robinson) searching for magic robe of Christ; Mature dallies with royal Hayward.▼

Demi-Paradise, The (1943-British) 115m. *** D: Anthony Asquith. Laurence Olivier, Penelope Dudley Ward, Leslie Henson, Marjorie Fielding, Margaret Rutherford, Felix Aylmer, Edie Martin, Joyce Grenfell, Jack Watling, Miles Malleson, John Laurie, Wilfrid Hyde-White, George Cole. Charming romantic comedy-satire with Olivier intriguingly cast as a Russian engineer who skeptically comes to England . . . and promptly becomes involved with Ward. Perceptive and, in its way, still-topical Anatole de Grunwald script gently chides people's prejudice against "foreigners." Marred only by the predictable finale. U.S. title: ADVENTURE FOR TWO.▼

Demon (1977) C-95m. **½ D: Larry Cohen. Tony Lo Bianco, Sandy Dennis, Sylvia Sidney, Deborah Raffin, Sam Levene, Richard Lynch, Mike Kellin. Weird, confusing shocker in which New York cop Lo Bianco investigates motiveless killings by ordinary people possessed by Christ-like demon. Some good scenes. Originally titled GOD TOLD ME TO.▼

Demon Barber of Fleet Street, The SEE: **Sweeney Todd, The Demon Barber of Fleet Street**▼

Demoniaque (1958-French) 97m. **½ D: Luis Saslavsky. Francois Perier, Micheline Presle, Jeanne Moreau, Madeleine Robinson. Perky yarn of French P.O.W. escaping and seeking refuge with girl his dead buddy romanced via the mails; girl believes him to be the letter-writer.

Demon Murder Case, The (1983) C-100m. TVM D: Billy Hale. Kevin Bacon, Liane Langland, Eddie Albert, Andy Griffith, Cloris Leachman, Richard Masur, Ken Kercheval, Joyce Van Patten, Charlie Fields. Demonologist Griffith, psychic Leachman, and priest Albert attempt to frighten the Devil out of young Fields. Also called THE RHODE ISLAND MURDERS. Average.

Demonoid, Messenger of Death (1981) C-78m. *½ D: Alfred Zacharias. Samantha Eggar, Stuart Whitman, Roy Cameron Jenson, Erika Carlson, Lew Saunders. Eggar and husband, while working Mexican mine, unearth a hand, which possesses him, wreaking terror and havoc. Insipid direction, a rotten script, and shoddy special effects get in the way of any suspense. Also known as MACABRA.▼

Demon Planet, The SEE: **Planet of the Vampires**▼

Demons (1986-Italian) C-89m. *½ D: Lamberto Bava. Urbano Barberini, Natasha Hovey, Paolo Cozza, Karl Zinny, Fiore Argento, Fabiola Toledo, Nicoletta Elmi. A horror film transforms its audience one by one into drooling, fanged "demons" who attack the remaining humans. Extremely gruesome and violent, a horror film for the 80s: no characterization, no logic, no plot. Achieved critical fame in some quarters. Director, who shows some visual style, is son of horror maestro Mario Bava. Cowritten and produced by Dario Argento. Followed by two sequels.▼

Demons 2 (1987-Italian) C-88m. ** D: Lamberto Bava. David Knight, Nancy Brilli, Coralina Cataldi Tassoni, Bobby Rhodes, Asia Argento, Virginia Bryant. Sequel is improvement on first film but highly derivative of NIGHT OF THE LIVING DEAD and THEY CAME FROM WITHIN. Demonic infection spreads among people in modern apartment building; they transform into fanged, clawed monsters and attack others. Like its predecessor, achieved great acclaim among gore fans.▼

Demon Seed (1977) C-94m. ***½ D: Donald Cammell. Julie Christie, Fritz Weaver, Gerrit Graham, Berry Kroeger, Lisa Lu. Intelligent futuristic thriller, provocatively written, stylishly directed, and well-acted, especially by Christie, the beauty terrorized by an ultra-sophisticated computer (voice of Robert Vaughn) that has decided to take over the world. As riveting as it is bizarre.▼

Dempsey (1983) C-150m. TVM D: Gus Trikonis. Treat Williams, Sam Waterston, Sally Kellerman, Victoria Tennant, Peter Mark Richman, Jesse Vint, Robert Harper, John McLiam, Bonnie Bartlett, James Noble. Earnest but plodding dramatization of the Manassa Mauler's colorful boxing career and his marriage to silent-screen star Estelle Taylor. A singularly humorless Williams punches his way through the story. Edward DiLorenzo scripted from Dempsey's autobiography. Average.▼

Dennis the Menace (1987) C-100m. TVM D: Doug Rogers. Victor DiMattia, William Windom, Patricia Estrinn, James W. Jansen, Barton Tinapp, Patsy Garrett. Anemic semi-resuscitation of the late 1950s-early 1960s series based on Hank Ketcham's comic strip with a group of dubiously talented youngsters, and veterans like Windom aboard for professionalism. Below average.

Den of Doom SEE: **Glass Cage, The**

Dentist in the Chair (1960-British) 84m. ** D: Don Chaffey. Peggy Cummins, Bob Monkhouse, Kenneth Connor, Eric Barker. Occasionally amusing shenanigans of dentists involved in crooked dealings, trying to undo their mischievous thefts.

Dentist on the Job SEE: **Get On With It**

Denver and Rio Grande, The (1952) C-89m. **½ D: Byron Haskin. Edmond O'Brien, Sterling Hayden, Dean Jagger, ZaSu Pitts, J. Carrol Naish. Another railroad rivalry Western as two competing companies battle elements and each other to complete tie-line through title area. Climax features an actual head-on collision between two steam locomotives.

Deported (1950) **80m.** **½ D: Robert Siodmak. Marta Toren, Jeff Chandler, Claude Dauphin, Carlo Rizzo. Engaging gangster yarn with Chandler deported to Italy, involved in the black market, but going straight to win Toren's love.

Deputies, The (1976) **C-100m.** TVM D: Virgil W. Vogel. Jim Davis, Don Johnson, Charles Martin Smith, Nicholas Hammond, Barbara Parkins, Glenn Corbett, Andrew Prine, Moses Gunn, Darleen Carr. Frontier lawman Davis and young deputies seek psychopath with vendetta against prostitutes. Old West melodrama best described as *The Rookies* on horseback. Average.

Deranged (1974) **C-82m.** **½ D: Jeff Gillen, Alan Ormsby. Roberts Blossom, Cosette Lee, Leslie Carlson, Robert Warner, Marcia Diamond. Blossom's neat performance uplifts this predictable shocker of a mother-obsessed farmer who preserves the old lady's corpse, then kills and stuffs other women to keep her company. Based on the same real-life case that inspired PSYCHO.

Derby (1971) **C-96m.** **½ D: Robert Kaylor. Charlie O'Connell, Eddie Krebs, Mike Snell, Christina Snell, Butch Snell. Documentary about roller derby stars and hopefuls is uneven; some scenes are vivid, others talky and dull. Provides a good look at one segment of Middle America. Filmed in Dayton, Ohio.▼

Derby Day (1952-British) **84m.** **½ D: Herbert Wilcox. Anna Neagle, Michael Wilding, John McCallum, Googie Withers. Diverting study of human nature, as an assortment of people intermingle at Epsom Downs race track. Retitled: FOUR AGAINST FATE.

Dersu Uzala (1975-Japanese-Russian) **C-140m.** ***½ D: Akira Kurosawa. Maxim Munzuk, Yuri Solomine. Simple, gentle gold hunter-guide Munzik teaches Russian explorer Solomine the rules of survival in Siberia; they develop mutual respect and friendship. A poignant, poetic examination of contrasting lives. Filmed in Russia; Best Foreign Film Oscar-winner.▼

De Sade (1969-U.S.-West German) **C-92m.** ** D: Cy Endfield. Keir Dullea, Senta Berger, Lilli Palmer, Anna Massey, John Huston. Fictionalized biography of world's most celebrated sexual and physical pervert. If you're expecting something raunchy, forget it. Pretty tepid stuff. Original running time: 113m.

Desert Attack (1960-British) **79m.** *** D: J. Lee Thompson. John Mills, Sylvia Syms, Anthony Quayle, Harry Andrews, Diane Clare. Well-handled psychological drama of British ambulance officer, two nurses, and a German soldier brought to-

gether in African desert. Original British version ICE COLD IN ALEX runs 132 m.

Desert Bloom (1986) **C-106m.** ***½ D: Eugene Corr. Jon Voight, JoBeth Williams, Ellen Barkin, Annabeth Gish, Allen Garfield, Jay D. Underwood. A perceptive, exquisitely realized memoir, set in 1951 Nevada—the dawn of the Atomic Age. The heroine is 13-year-old Gish, whose mother (Williams) only sees what she wants to and whose step-father (solidly acted by Voight) is an embittered, alcoholic WW2 hero reduced to running a gas station. Corr wrote the poignantly precise script from a story by Linda Remy and himself.▼

Desert Desperados (1959) **81m.** *½ D: Steve Sekely. Ruth Roman, Akim Tamiroff, Otello Toso, Gianni Glori, Unsuccessful mishmash of romance and unconvincing intrigue set in Egyptian desert; wasting Roman's most capable talents. Retitled: THE SINNER.

Deserter, The (1971-Italian-Yugoslav) **C-99m.** *½ D: Burt Kennedy. Bekim Fehmiu, John Huston, Richard Crenna, Chuck Connors, Ricardo Montalban, Ian Bannen, Brandon de Wilde, Slim Pickens, Woody Strode, Patrick Wayne. Dull cavalry pic about Indian fighting on Mexican border. Cast is capable, except for Fehmiu, who didn't improve after THE ADVENTURERS.▼

Desert Fox, The (1951) **88m.** *** D: Henry Hathaway. James Mason, Cedric Hardwicke, Jessica Tandy, Luther Adler. Mason standout as Field Marshal Rommel in sensitive account of his military defeat in WW2 Africa and disillusioned return to Hitler Germany. Mason repeated role in later DESERT RATS.▼

Desert Fury (1947) **C-95m.** **½ D: Lewis Allen. John Hodiak, Lizabeth Scott, Burt Lancaster, Mary Astor, Wendell Corey. Mild drama of love and mystery among gamblers, stolen by Astor in bristling character portrayal.

Desert Hawk, The (1950) **C-77m.** ** D: Frederick de Cordova. Yvonne De Carlo, Richard Greene, Jackie Gleason, Rock Hudson, George Macready. Pat Arabian desert tale, interesting for Gleason and Hudson in secondary roles.

Desert Hearts (1985) **C-93m.** **½ D: Donna Deitch. Helen Shaver, Patricia Charbonneau, Audra Lindley, Andra Akers, Dean Butler, Jeffrey Tambor. Uptight female professor comes to Reno to get a divorce in the 1950s and is pursued by a young woman who forces her to examine her own sexuality. Debut feature for writer-director Deitch (with a contemporary nod to THE WOMEN) has its moments, but characters are sketchily developed and story moves in fits and starts.▼

Desert Hell (1958) **82m.** ** D: Charles Marquis Warren. Brian Keith, Barbara

Hale, Richard Denning, Johnny Desmond. French Foreign Legion battles warring Arabs to save peace; very little of promised action given to viewer.

Desert Legion (1953) **C-86m.** ** D: Joseph Pevney. Alan Ladd, Richard Conte, Arlene Dahl, Akim Tamiroff. Mild Ladd vehicle of battling French Foreign Legion in a lost city; co-written by Irving Wallace.

Desert Patrol (1958-British) **78m.** **½ D: Guy Green. Richard Attenborough, John Gregson, Michael Craig, Vincent Ball. Staunch account of British patrol attempting to blow up Axis fuel dump before pending WW2 battle of El Alamein. Originally titled SEA OF SAND.

Desert Rats, The (1953) **88m.** *** D: Robert Wise. Richard Burton, James Mason, Robert Newton, Chips Rafferty. Fine WW2 actioner with Mason convincing as Field Marshal Rommel (repeating his role from DESERT FOX); Burton is British commando trying to ward off Germans in North Africa.

Desert Rats (1988) **C-78m. TVM** D: Tony Wharmby. Scott Plank, Scott Paulin, Dietrich Bader, Mark Thomas Miller, Geoffrey Lewis, Shanna Reed. Limp contemporary Western has a local rebel being appointed sheriff after he accidentally foils a bank robbery. Easy to see why this pilot got busted. Below average.

Desert Song, The (1953) **C-110m.** **½ D: H. Bruce Humberstone. Kathryn Grayson, Gordon MacRae, Steve Cochran, Raymond Massey, William Conrad, Dick Wesson. Third version of Sigmund Romberg operetta set in Africa creaks along on thin plot. American MacRae is secret leader of good natives (Riffs) in battle against evil Arabs. Songs: "The Riff Song," "One Alone." Previously filmed in 1929 and 1944.

Design for Living (1933) **90m.** ***½ D: Ernst Lubitsch. Gary Cooper, Fredric March, Miriam Hopkins, Edward Everett Horton, Franklin Pangborn. Hopkins leaves starving suitors Cooper and March to marry wealthy Horton in chic Ben Hecht adaptation of Noel Coward stage comedy with most of the witty innuendos left intact. Delightful, bore

Design for Scandal (1941) **85m.** **½ D: Norman Taurog. Rosalind Russell, Walter Pidgeon, Edward Arnold, Lee Bowman, Jean Rogers, Mary Beth Hughes, Guy Kibbee. Deft performances by stars in comedy of reporter Pidgeon doing sensational story involving prominent female judge Russell.

Designing Woman (1957) **C-118m.** *** D: Vincente Minnelli. Gregory Peck, Lauren Bacall, Dolores Gray, Sam Levene, Mickey Shaughnessy, Chuck Connors. Sportswriter and fashion designer marry and run head-on in this chic comedy reminiscent of the great Hepburn-Tracy vehicles. Bacall and Peck do their best; George Wells won an Oscar for Best Story and Screenplay.

Desire (1936) **96m.** *** D: Frank Borzage. Marlene Dietrich, Gary Cooper, John Halliday, William Frawley, Ernest Cossart, Akim Tamiroff, Alan Mowbray, Zeffie Tilbury. American car-designer Cooper falls in love with jewel thief Dietrich. Sophisticated romancer set in Spain; Marlene sings "Awake In a Dream." From the scintillating start to the finish, it bears the stylish stamp of its producer, Ernst Lubitsch.

Desiree (1954) **C-110m.** **½ D: Henry Koster. Marlon Brando, Jean Simmons, Merle Oberon, Michael Rennie, Cameron Mitchell, Elizabeth Sellars. Tepid, elaborate costumer: Brando plays a confused Napoleon, Simmons his seamstress love who marries another man; Oberon is quite lovely as Empress Josephine. Fiction and fact are muddled backdrop for rise and fall of the Emperor; few action scenes.▼

Desire in the Dust (1960) **102m.** **½ D: William F. Claxton. Raymond Burr, Martha Hyer, Joan Bennett, Ken Scott. Good casting carries this turgid soaper of a Southern aristocrat with a yen for politics, who tries to hide the shady past of some family members.

Desire Me (1947) **91m.** ** D: No director credited. Greer Garson, Robert Mitchum, Richard Hart, George Zucco, Morris Ankrum. Weak melodramatic romance with poor Garson caught between new love and old husband, presumed dead, who returns to make problems. Familiar story not helped by limp script. Directed mostly by George Cukor, who had his name removed after the studio tampered with it; Mervyn LeRoy and Jack Conway also had a hand in it.

Desire Under the Elms (1958) **114m.** **½ D: Delbert Mann. Sophia Loren, Anthony Perkins, Burl Ives, Frank Overton. Eugene O'Neill stage piece about family hatred and greed for land. Loren miscast as Ives' young wife in love with stepson Perkins, but she sparks some life into brooding account of 19th-century New England farm story.▼

Desk Set (1957) **C-103m.** ***½ D: Walter Lang. Spencer Tracy, Katharine Hepburn, Joan Blondell, Gig Young, Dina Merrill, Neva Patterson. Broadway play becomes a vehicle for Hepburn and Tracy, a guarantee for top entertainment. He's an efficiency expert automating her research department at a TV network; they clash, argue, and fall in love. Great fun.

Despair (1979-West German) **C-119m.** *** D: Rainer Werner Fassbinder. Dirk Bogarde, Andrea Ferreol, Volker Spengler, Klaus Lowitsch. Playwright Tom Stoppard's adaptation of the Nabokov novel concentrates too many of its wittiest lines in the first third, but the film still has its moments. Bogarde is brilliant as the Russian emigre who runs a German chocolate factory as Nazis start to take power.▼

Desperado (1987) **C-100m. TVM** D: Virgil W. Vogel. Alex McArthur, David Warner, Yaphet Kotto, Donald Moffat, Sydney Walsh, Robert Vaughn, Pernell Roberts, Gladys Knight. Umpteenth SHANE carbon centering on sullen, roving cowpoke taking on—with reluctance—a company-controlled mining town. Boosted, in part, by use of The Eagles hit song of the same name. Singer Knight, here "Pip"-less, makes her dramatic TV movie debut as a good-hearted madam. Novelist Elmore Leonard wrote this rather pedestrian pilot to a prospective series. Followed by RETURN OF DESPERADO. Average.

Desperado: Avalanche at Devil's Ridge (1988) **C-100m. TVM** D: Richard Compton. Alex McArthur, Alice Adair, Lise Cutter, Hoyt Axton, Rod Steiger. Roving cowboy, framed for murder, is offered freedom for finding the kidnapped daughter of town boss Steiger but discovers she's not what she seems to be. Average.

Desperado: Badlands Justice (1989) **C-100m. TVM** D: E. W. Swackhamer. Alex McArthur, John Rhys-Davies, James B. Sikking, Gregory Sierra, Robert O'Reilly, Patricia Charbonneau. Roving cowpoke with price on head uses a case of mistaken identity to become sheriff of a town terrorized by two corrupt businessmen. Average.

Desperado: The Outlaw Wars (1989) **C-100m. TVM** D: E. W. Swackhamer. Alex McArthur, Lise Cutter, Richard Farnsworth, Whip Hubley, Brad Dourif, Geoffrey Lewis. Fourth in the series of formula Westerns following the travails of a roving cowpoke who's slow to talk but quick on the trigger. Here he gets involved with scrungy bounty hunters and an overzealous reporter who wants to make him a legend. Average.

Desperadoes, The (1943) **C-85m.** *** D: Charles Vidor. Randolph Scott, Glenn Ford, Claire Trevor, Evelyn Keyes, Edgar Buchanan, Raymond Walburn, Guinn Williams. Pretty good Western; bandit Ford goes straight, joins forces with marshal Scott to clean up town.

Desperados, The (1969) **C-91m.** **½ D: Henry Levin. Vince Edwards, Jack Palance, George Maharis, Neville Brand, Sylvia Sims. Civil War deserters ravage the West. Not bad.▼

Desperados Are in Town, The (1956) **73m.** *½ D: Kurt Neumann. Robert Arthur, Kathy Nolan, Rhys Williams, Rhodes Reason. Bland oater of young man proving his worth by killing outlaws who murdered his friend.

Desperate (1947) **73m.** **½ D: Anthony

Mann. Steve Brodie, Audrey Long, Raymond Burr, Douglas Fowley, William Challee, Jason Robards, Sr. An honest truck driver is victimized by racketeers and forced to flee with his wife. Well-made little *film noir*, if not as good as director Mann's follow-ups (RAW DEAL, T-MEN, etc.). Also shown in computer-colored version.▼

Desperate (1987) **C-78m. TVM** D: Peter Markel. John Savage, Meg Foster, Chris Burke, Liane Langland, Andrew Robinson. Charter boat owner in Key West gets involved with Cuban gunrunners in this uncredited adaptation of Hemingway's *To Have and Have Not*, written by Michael Braverman as a prospective series pilot. Average.

Desperate Chance for Ellery Queen (1942) **70m.** D: James Hogan. William Gargan, Margaret Lindsay, Charley Grapewin, John Litel, Lilian Bond, James Burke, Jack LaRue. SEE: **Ellery Queen** series.

Desperate Characters (1971) **C-88m.** *** D: Frank D. Gilroy. Shirley MacLaine, Kenneth Mars, Gerald O'Loughlin, Sada Thompson, Jack Somack. Story of the horrors of day-to-day living in N.Y.C. is a bit too theatrical in origin, but benefits from excellent acting; one of MacLaine's best performances.

Desperate for Love (1989) **C-100m. TVM** D: Michael Tuchner. Christian Slater, Tammy Lauren, Brian Bloom, Veronica Cartwright, Scott Paulin, Billy Vera. Small-town Georgia teenage triangle that leads to tragedy when two best buddies are torn apart by a girl from the other side of the tracks. Pedestrian drama "inspired by actual events." Average.

Desperate Hours, The (1955) **112m.** ***½ D: William Wyler. Humphrey Bogart, Fredric March, Arthur Kennedy, Martha Scott, Dewey Martin, Gig Young, Mary Murphy, Robert Middleton. Extremely well acted account of escaped convicts terrorizing family household. Based on Joseph Hayes' novel and Broadway play, inspired by actual events.▼

Desperate Intruder (1983) **C-105m. TVM** D: Nick Havinga. Meg Foster, Nick Mancuso, Claude Akins, Robert Hogan, Stephen Keep, Lisa Jane Persky. Formula thriller: blind woman in isolated beach house takes in a mysterious stranger and falls for him, unaware that he's an escaped con and his sadistic buddy is on the way. Below average.

Desperate Journey (1942) **107m.** *** D: Raoul Walsh. Errol Flynn, Raymond Massey, Ronald Reagan, Nancy Coleman, Alan Hale, Arthur Kennedy, Albert Basserman. Spirited WW2 drama of American pilots stranded in Germany, struggling to cross border; propaganda interludes are forgivable.

Desperate Lives (1982) **C-100m. TVM**
D: Robert Lewis. Diana Scarwid, Doug
McKeon, Helen Hunt, William Windom,
Art Hindle, Tom Atkins, Sam Bottoms,
Diane Ladd, Dr. Joyce Brothers. Story of
brother and sister who become involved
with drugs in high school and their guidance counselor's battle against dope. Average.▼

Desperately Seeking Susan (1985) **C-104m.**
*** D: Susan Seidelman. Rosanna Arquette,
Madonna, Aidan Quinn, Mark Blum, Robert Joy, Laurie Metcalf, Steven Wright,
Richard Hell, Ann Magnuson, Richard Edson, John Lurie, Anne Carlisle, John
Turturro. Delightfully offbeat, original comedy about a bored suburban housewife
whose fascination with a kooky character
she's read about in the personal ads leads
to her being mistaken for the woman herself. Sort of an upscale underground film,
inventively directed by Seidelman, though
it doesn't sustain its buoyancy straight to
the end.▼

Desperate Man, The (1959-British) **57m.**
*½ D: Peter Maxwell. Jill Ireland, Conrad
Phillips, William Hartnell, Charles Gray.
Dull yarn of reporter Phillips and gal (Ireland) involved in tracking down a Sussex
crook; photography only virtue.

Desperate Miles, The (1975) **C-78m.**
TVM D: Daniel Haller. Tony Musante,
Joanna Pettet, Jeanette Nolan, Lynn Loring,
John Larch. Fact-based drama of disabled
Vietnam vet who makes grueling 130-mile
trip in wheelchair to prove his indepen-
dence. Sunk by maudlin, cliché-ridden script
and Musante's monotonous performance.
Below average.

Desperate Mission, The (1971) **C-100m.**
TVM D: Earl Bellamy. Ricardo Montalban,
Slim Pickens, Earl Holliman, Ina Balin,
Roosevelt Grier, Robert J. Wilke, Anthony
Caruso. Hokey Western with Montalban
as Joaquin Murietta, Mexican bandit-folk
hero portrayed here as a frontier Robin
Hood. Adequate performances, forgetta-
ble resolution. Average.

Desperate Moment (1953-British) **88m.**
**½ D: Compton Bennett. Dirk Bogarde,
Mai Zetterling, Philip Friend, Gerard Heinz.
Taut melodrama involving displaced person in post-WW2 Berlin falsely accused
of homicide; sensibly acted.

Desperate Ones, The (1968-Italian)
C-104m. **½ D: Alexander Ramati. Maximilian Schell, Raf Vallone, Irene Papas,
Theodore Bikel. Siberian labor camp escapees join Polish army. Okay if nothing
else is on.

Desperate Search (1952) **73m.** **½ D:
Joseph H. Lewis. Howard Keel, Jane Greer,
Patricia Medina, Keenan Wynn. Trim film
of two kids stranded in Canadian wastelands after plane crash, and their father's
efforts to find them.

Desperate Siege SEE: **Rawhide**▼
Desperate Voyage (1980) **C-95m. TVM**
D: Michael O'Herlihy. Christopher Plummer, Cliff Potts, Christine Belford, Lara
Parker, Nicholas Pryor, Jonathan Banks.
Plummer is marvelously evil as a modern-
day pirate who does his high-seas hijacking from a battered, diesel-powered fishing
boat. Alvin Sapinsley adapted his dandy
thriller from Ray Kytle's novel *Last Voyage of the Valhalla*. Above average.

Desperate Women (1978) **C-100m. TVM**
D: Earl Bellamy. Susan St. James, Dan
Haggerty, Ronee Blakley, Ann Dusenberry,
Max Gail. Three scrappy female prisoners, abandoned in the desert, team up with
laconic ex-gunslinger to outsmart a ratty
gang of desperadoes in this ragtag western
comedy. Average.▼

Destination America (1987) **C-100m.**
TVM D: Corey Allen. Bruce Greenwood,
Rip Torn, Joe Pantoliano, Corinne Bohrer,
Alan Autry. Blueblood forsakes the blue-
collar life he had taken out of spite, returns
to the patrician fold, and finds he's the
prime suspect in his estranged dad's murder. Pilot to a *Then Came Bronson*-type
series for Greenwood, who instead became a doctor on *St. Elsewhere*. Torn, as
his coldly distant dad, gives another fine
performance. Average.

Destination Fury (1961-French) **85m.** **
D: Giorgio Bianchi. Eddie Constantine,
Renato Rascel, Dorian Gray, Pierre Grasset.
Silly spy spoof with Constantine a double-
agent involved with Interpol.

Destination Gobi (1953) **C-89m.** **½ D:
Robert Wise. Richard Widmark, Don Taylor, Casey Adams, Murvyn Vye, Darryl
Hickman, Martin Milner. Unusual WW2
actioner involving U.S. naval men joining
forces with natives against Japanese assaults; nice action sequences.

Destination Inner Space (1966) **C-83m.**
** D: Francis D. Lyon. Sheree North,
Scott Brady, Gary Merrill, John Howard.
Undersea lab encounters an alien space-
ship and a pod that grows into an amphib-
ian monster. Routine but competent.

Destination Moon (1950) **C-91m.** **½
D: Irving Pichel. John Archer, Warner
Anderson, Tom Powers, Dick Wesson,
Erin O'Brien-Moore. One of the pioneer
sci-fi films, modestly mounted but still
effective. Won an Oscar for its special
effects. Produced by George Pal; coscripted
by Robert Heinlein. Woody Woodpecker
makes a "guest appearance."▼

Destination Saturn (1939) **91m.** **½ D:
Ford Beebe, Saul Goodkind. Buster Crabbe,
Constance Moore, Jackie Moran, Jack
Mulhall, Anthony Warde, C. Montague
Shaw. Newly edited version of BUCK
ROGERS serial. Buck and Buddy Wade,
revived from suspended animation by fu-
ture Earth scientists, fight Killer Kane and

his supergangsters. Uninspired handling of original footage.▼

Destination 60,000 (1957) 65m. BOMB D: George Waggner. Preston Foster, Pat Conway, Jeff Donnell, Coleen Gray. Worn-out premise of test pilots zooming through space, families waiting nervously on the ground.

Destination Tokyo (1943) 135m. *** D: Delmer Daves. Cary Grant, John Garfield, Alan Hale, John Ridgely, Dane Clark, Warner Anderson, William Prince. Suspenseful WW2 account of U.S. submarine sent into Japanese waters and interaction among crew. Commander Grant, seamen Garfield and Clark ring true. John Forsythe makes his film debut. Also shown in computer-colored version.▼

Destiny (1944) 65m. ** D: Reginald LeBorg. Gloria Jean, Alan Curtis, Frank Craven, Grace McDonald. Routine study of man sent to prison on homicide charge, and snowballing effects on his life. Expanded from a 30m. sequence originally shot by Julien Duvivier for FLESH AND FANTASY.

Destiny of a Spy (1969) C-99m. TVM D: Boris Sagal. Lorne Greene, Rachel Roberts, Anthony Quayle, James Donald, Patrick Magee, Patrick Newell. Dissatisfied Russian spy (Greene) reluctantly comes out of retirement, accepts assignment in London investigating death of British scientist. Effective subplot involving budding love affair with British double agent (Roberts). Good production. Adapted by Stanford Whitmore from John Blackburn's *The Gaunt Woman*. Above average.

Destroy All Monsters! (1968-Japanese) C-88m. ** D: Ishiro Honda. Akira Kubo, Jun Tazaki, Yoshio Tsuchiya, Kyoko Ai. All-star monster cast (from Toho Studios) teams up to combat alien forces bent on destruction. Godzilla, Mothra, Rodan, and other favorites are on hand in this juvenile epic.

Destroyer (1943) 99m. **½ D: William Seiter. Edward G. Robinson, Glenn Ford, Marguerite Chapman, Edgar Buchanan, Leo Gorcey, Regis Toomey, Ed Brophy. Predictable wartime drama of aging seaman Robinson shown up by novice Ford; of course Eddie comes through in the end.

Destructors, The (1968) C-97m. ** D: Francis D. Lyon. Richard Egan, Patricia Owens, John Ericson, Michael Ansara, Joan Blackman. Programmer nonsense with Egan a federal agent hunting international thieves who stole laser rubies.

Destructors, The (1974-British) C-89m. *** D: Robert Parrish. Anthony Quinn, Michael Caine, James Mason, Maureen Kerwin, Marcel Bozzufi, Maurice Ronet, Alexandra Stewart. Good Paris-localed crime melodrama with Quinn a U.S. drug agent out to stop kingpin Mason. An ani-

mated Caine is fine as a likable assassin. Original title: THE MARSEILLE CONTRACT.▼

Destry (1954) C-95m. **½ D: George Marshall. Audie Murphy, Mari Blanchard, Lyle Bettger, Lori Nelson, Thomas Mitchell, Edgar Buchanan, Wallace Ford. Audie is gun-shy sheriff who tames town and dance-hall girl without violence. The 1939 version—DESTRY RIDES AGAIN—is still unsurpassed. Later a TV series.

Destry Rides Again (1939) 94m. **** D: George Marshall. James Stewart, Marlene Dietrich, Charles Winninger, Brian Donlevy, Una Merkel, Mischa Auer, Allen Jenkins, Irene Hervey, Jack Carson, Billy Gilbert, Samuel S. Hinds. Slambang, action-filled Western satire, with Stewart taming rowdy town without violence and tangling with boisterous dance-hall girl Dietrich. Marlene sings "See What the Boys in the Back Room Will Have" in this Max Brand story, filmed before in 1932, then again in 1950 (as FRENCHIE), and in 1954 (as DESTRY). Screenplay by Felix Jackson, Gertrude Purcell, and Henry Myers.▼

Detective, The (1954) SEE: **Father Brown**▼

Detective, The (1968) C-114m. *** D: Gordon Douglas. Frank Sinatra, Lee Remick, Ralph Meeker, Jacqueline Bisset, William Windom, Al Freeman, Tony Musante, Jack Klugman, Robert Duvall. Trashy script, based on Roderick Thorpe's best-selling novel, pits cops against homosexuals; more than redeemed by fast, nononsense direction and good acting, particularly by Sinatra and Freeman.▼

Detective (1985-French) C-95m. ** D: Jean-Luc Godard. Claude Brasseur, Nathalie Baye, Johnny Hallyday, Laurent Terzieff, Jean-Pierre Leaud, Alain Cuny, Stephane Ferrara. The scenario takes a backseat in this talky, contrived *film noir homage* about a variety of characters and their business and intrigues in an elegant Paris hotel. The look and feel are uniquely of the director, but it's ultimately annoying, more a concept than a movie. Godard dedicated this to John Cassavetes, Edgar G. Ulmer, and Clint Eastwood!

Detective Kitty O'Day (1944) 63m. ** D: William Beaudine. Jean Parker, Peter Cookson, Tim Ryan, Veda Ann Borg. Parker adds bubbly zest as amateur sleuth who sets out to solve a crime; pleasant fluff on low-budget scale.

Detective Story (1951) 103m. ***½ D: William Wyler. Kirk Douglas, Eleanor Parker, Horace McMahon, William Bendix, Lee Grant, Craig Hill, Cathy O'Donnell, Bert Freed, George Macready, Joseph Wiseman, Gladys George, Frank Faylen, Luis van Rooten, Warner Anderson. Sidney Kingsley's once-forceful play about life at a N.Y.C. police precinct has lost much of its punch, but is still a fine film. Well cast, with Douglas a bitter detective, Parker his ignored wife, and Bendix, in one of his best roles, a sympathetic colleague. McMahon (the shrewd precinct head) Wiseman (an hysterical thief), and Grant (unforgettable as a frightened shoplifter) recreate their Broadway roles. This was Grant's first film—and also her last—before being blacklisted. Screenplay by Philip Yordan and Robert Wyler (the director's brother).▼

Detour (1945) 69m. **½ D: Edgar G. Ulmer. Tom Neal, Ann Savage, Claudia Drake, Edmund MacDonald, Tim Ryan, Esther Howard. Intriguing melodrama about hitchhiker who gets involved with femme fatale Savage, and murder. Ultracheap movie has deserved cult following.▼

Detour to Nowhere SEE: **Banacek**

Detroit 9000 (1973) C-106m. *½ D: Arthur Marks. Alex Rocco, Hari Rhodes, Vonetta McGee, Ella Edwards, Scatman Crothers. Cops pursue jewel thieves. Bloody blaxploitation entry with an integrated cast.▼

Devil, The SEE: **To Bed . . . Or Not To Bed**

Devil and Daniel Webster, The (1941) 85m. ***½ D: William Dieterle. Edward Arnold, Walter Huston, James Craig, Anne Shirley, Jane Darwell, Simone Simon, Gene Lockhart, John Qualen, H.B. Warner. Stephen Vincent Benet's story is a visual delight, with Huston's sparkling performance as Mr. Scratch (the Devil) matched by Arnold as the loquacious Webster. Oscarwinning score by Bernard Herrmann, cinematography by Joseph August, and special effects by Vernon L. Walker all superb. Screenplay by the author and Dan Totheroh. Even though current prints are cut from 112m. original, it's still a must. Also titled: ALL THAT MONEY CAN BUY and DANIEL AND THE DEVIL.▼

Devil and Max Devlin, The (1981) C-96m. ** D: Steven Hilliard Stern. Elliott Gould, Bill Cosby, Susan Anspach, Adam Rich, Julie Budd, David Knell. Gould returns to life to recruit three innocent souls for devil Cosby. Undistinguished Disney fare.▼

Devil and Miss Jones, The (1941) 92m. ***½ D: Sam Wood. Jean Arthur, Robert Cummings, Charles Coburn, Spring Byington, S.Z. Sakall, William Demarest. Delightful social comedy by Norman Krasna; millionaire Coburn masquerades as clerk in his own department store to investigate employee complaints. A must.▼

Devil and Miss Sarah, The (1971) C-73m. TVM D: Michael Caffey. Gene Barry, James Drury, Janice Rule, Donald Moffat, Logan Ramsey, Charles McGraw, Slim Pickens. Thoroughly predictable minor Western featuring battle for possession of

sanity by young bride: will Satanist outlaw Barry win out over husband? Below average.

Devil and the Deep (1932) 78m. **½ D: Marion Gering. Tallulah Bankhead, Gary Cooper, Charles Laughton, Cary Grant, Paul Porcasi. Overplayed but lush melodrama of Bankhead, her suitors Grant and Cooper, and jealous husband, submarine commander Laughton.

Devil and the Ten Commandments, The (1962-French) 143m. **½ D: Julien Duvivier. Michel Simon, Lucien Baroux, Claude Nollier, Dany Saval, Charles Aznavour. Episodic film in ten parts illustrating each of the commandments—too often superficial instead of cynical.

Devil at 4 O'Clock, The (1961) C-126m. **½ D: Mervyn LeRoy. Spencer Tracy, Frank Sinatra, Jean-Pierre Aumont, Kerwin Mathews, Barbara Luna. Static production, not saved by volcanic eruption climax, involving priest Tracy helping to evacuate children's hospital in midst of lava flow. Stars are lost in weak film.▼

Devil Bat, The (1941) 69m. ** D: Jean Yarbrough. Bela Lugosi, Suzanne Kaaren, Dave O'Brien, Guy Usher, Yolande Mallot, Donald Kerr. Lugosi raises bats and trains them to suck victim's blood on cue. One of Lugosi's more notorious pictures, and fairly entertaining. Also known as KILLER BATS. Remade as THE FLYING SERPENT. Sequel: DEVIL BAT'S DAUGHTER.▼

Devil Bat's Daughter (1946) 66m. ** D: Frank Wisbar. Rosemary La Planche, Molly Lamont, John James, Ed Cassidy. In this sequel to DEVIL BAT, La Planche is thought to have inherited the murderous tendencies of her late father, but in a bizarre turn of events, Dad turns out to have been a kindly researcher (contradicting the first film entirely!).▼

Devil Commands, The (1941) 65m. **½ D: Edward Dmytryk. Boris Karloff, Amanda Duff, Richard Fiske, Anne Revere, Ralph Penny, Dorothy Adams, Kenneth MacDonald. Improbable but intriguing chiller of scientist Karloff obsessed with idea of communicating with dead wife. Predictable but fun. Only debit: the absurd narration.

Devil Dogs of the Air (1935) 86m. ** D: Lloyd Bacon. James Cagney, Pat O'Brien, Margaret Lindsay, Frank McHugh. Tiresome potboiler with Marine Air Corps rivalry between Cagney and O'Brien. Their personalities, and good stunt-flying scenes, are only saving grace.

Devil Dog: The Hound of Hell (1978) C-100m. TVM D: Curtis Harrington. Richard Crenna, Yvette Mimieux, Kim Richards, Ike Eisenmann, Victor Jory, Martine Beswick. Chiller about a family falling under the spell of a dog imbued with the spirit of Satan. Love that title! Average.▼

Devil-Doll, The (1936) 79m. *** D: Tod

Browning. Lionel Barrymore, Maureen O'Sullivan, Frank Lawton, Robert Greig, Lucy Beaumont, Henry B. Walthall, Grace Ford, Rafaela Ottiano. Very entertaining yarn of Devil's Island escapee Barrymore shrinking humans to doll-size to carry out nefarious schemes.▼

Devil Doll (1964-British) **80m.** ******* D: Lindsay Shonteff. Bryant Halliday, William Sylvester, Yvonne Romain, Philip Ray. Obscure, underrated mystery features an eerily effective Halliday as a hypnotist-ventriloquist trying to transfer Romain's soul into that of a dummy, as he had already done with his onetime assistant. An exquisitely tailored, sharply edited sleeper. Coscripted by Erich von Stroheim.▼

Devil Girl from Mars (1954-British) **77m.** *½ D: David MacDonald. Patricia Laffan, Hugh McDermott, Hazel Court, Adrienne Corri, Peter Reynolds, Joseph Tomelty, John Laurie. Clad in black leather, Laffan lands in remote Scotland with her refrigeratorlike robot, hunting for human husbands! Hilariously solemn, high-camp British imitation of U.S. cheapies would be even funnier if it weren't rather dull and set-bound.▼

Devil Goddess (1955) **70m.** D: Spencer Bennet. Johnny Weissmuller, Angela Stevens, Selmer Jackson, William Tannen, Ed Hilton, William M. Griffith. SEE: **Jungle Jim** series.

Devil in Love, The (1968-Italian) **97m.** *½ D: Ettore Scola. Vittorio Gassman, Mickey Rooney, Claudine Auger, Ettore Manni, Annabella Incontrera. Gassman comes up from Hell during the French Renaissance to botch up an impending peace between Rome and Florence, but loses his powers when he falls for Auger. Comedy is both heavy-handed and unfunny, a bad combination.

Devil in the Flesh (1946-French) **110m.** ***½ D: Claude Autant-Lara. Gerard Philipe, Micheline Presle, Denise Grey, Jacques Tati. Exquisitely filmed, compassionate story of love affair between married woman and sensitive high school student during WW1. Controversial in its day because of sensual love scenes and cuckolding of soldier husband. Remade in 1986.▼

Devil in the Flesh (1986-Italian-French) C-**110m.** *** D: Marco Bellocchio. Maruschka Detmers, Federico Pitzalis, Anita Laurenzi, Riccardo De Torrebruna. Director Bellocchio remakes and updates the 1946 French classic as another of his studies of madness. Dutch actress Detmers burns up the screen as the going-nutty beauty torn between her terrorist boyfriend (De Torrebruna) and a handsome young boy (Pitzalis). Reportedly the first mainstream film in which a respected actress was involved in an explicitly pornographic sex scene. Available in both R- and X-rated versions.▼

Devil Is a Sissy, The (1936) **92m.** **½ D: W. S. Van Dyke. Freddie Bartholomew, Mickey Rooney, Jackie Cooper, Ian Hunter, Peggy Conklin, Katherine Alexander. Three top juvenile stars outclass their material in this rambling, episodic tale of tenement-district pals and British newcomer (Bartholomew) who tries to join their gang.

Devil Is a Woman, The (1935) **83m.** *** D: Josef von Sternberg. Marlene Dietrich, Lionel Atwill, Cesar Romero, Edward Everett Horton, Alison Skipworth. Sumptuous-looking film about alluring but heartless woman and the men who all but ruin their lives for her, set against backdrop of 19th century Spanish revolution. Hypnotic, if dramatically shaky; Luis Bunuel used same source material for THAT OBSCURE OBJECT OF DESIRE.

Devil Is a Woman, The (1975-Italian) C-**105m.** BOMB D: Damiano Damiani. Glenda Jackson, Adolfo Celi, Lisa Harrow, Claudio Cassinelli, Arnoldo Foa, Francisco Rabal. Ponderous, superficial melodrama: Jackson, the head of a religious hostel, casts spells over its "permanent residents." The convent is more like a psycho ward than a place for religious meditation. Indifferently acted, technically atrocious.

Devil Makes Three, The (1952) **96m.** ** D: Andrew Marton. Gene Kelly, Pier Angeli, Richard Egan, Claus Clausen. Kelly always seems pretentious in straight roles: here he's a soldier returning to Munich to thank family who helped him during WW2; he becomes involved with daughter Angeli and black market gangs.

Devil on Horseback (1954-British) **89m.** ** D: Cyril Frankel. Googie Withers, John McCallum, Jeremy Spenser, Liam Redmond, Meredith Edwards, Sam Kydd, Vic Wise, George Rose. Inconsequential racing yarn, with talented but cocky teen apprentice jockey Spenser attempting to bully his way to success. Coproduced by John Grierson.▼

Devil Pays Off (1941) **56m.** ** D: John H. Auer. J. Edward Bromberg, Osa Massen, William Wright, Margaret Tallichet. Meager account of one-time navy man trying to redeem his honor by tracking down espionage agents within the naval service.

Devils, The (1971-British) C-**109m.** **½ D: Ken Russell. Oliver Reed, Vanessa Redgrave, Dudley Sutton, Max Adrian, Gemma Jones, Murray Melvin, Michael Gothard. Fine performances save confused mixture of history, comedy, and surrealism in wide-eyed adaptation of Whiting play and Huxley book dealing with witchcraft and politics in 17th-century France. A mad movie, with fiery finale not for the squeamish.▼

Devil's Angels (1967) **C-84m.** *½ D: Daniel Haller. John Cassavetes, Beverly Adams, Mimsy Farmer, Leo Gordon. Killer cyclists head for outlaw sanctuary breaking everything in their way. Lurid and cheap.▼

Devil's Bait (1959-British) **58m.** *½ D: Peter Graham Scott. Geoffrey Keen, Jane Hylton, Gordon Jackson, Dermot Kelly. Intriguing if leisurely paced B film, about baker and his wife who accidentally put poison in their wares, trying to find purchasers.

Devil's Bride, The (1968-British) **C-95m.** *** D: Terence Fisher. Christopher Lee, Charles Gray, Nike Arrighi, Patrick Mower, Sarah Lawson, Paul Eddington. Taut filmization of Dennis Wheatley's novel. Duc de Richleau (Lee) assists young friend under spell of Mocate, ultra-evil Satanist. Watch out for that climax! Original British title: THE DEVIL RIDES OUT.

Devil's Brigade, The (1968) **C-130m.** ** D: Andrew V. McLaglen. William Holden, Cliff Robertson, Vince Edwards, Michael Rennie, Dana Andrews, Carroll O'Connor, Gretchen Wyler, Andrew Prine, Claude Akins, Richard Jaeckel, Paul Hornung, Patric Knowles, James Craig, Richard Dawson. Standard WW2 fare about reckless recruits fashioned into creditable fighting unit is rehashed here for more than two hours. Holden is wasted.

Devil's Brother, The (1933) **88m.** *** D: Hal Roach, Charles R. Rogers. Stan Laurel, Oliver Hardy, Dennis King, Thelma Todd, James Finlayson, Henry Armetta. L&H adaptation of operetta with King as romantic lead, a famous bandit, the boys as would-be assistants. One of their best. Originally titled FRA DIAVOLO.

Devil's Canyon (1953) **C-92m.** ** D: Alfred L. Werker. Virginia Mayo, Dale Robertson, Stephen McNally, Arthur Hunnicutt. Former marshal put in prison for shoot-outs, where he's entangled in prison riot. Photographed in 3-D.

Devil's Cargo (1948) **61m.** D: John F. Link. John Calvert, Rochelle Hudson, Roscoe Karns, Lyle Talbot, Tom Kennedy, Theodore Von Eltz. SEE: **The Falcon** series.

Devil's Daffodil, The (1961-British) **86m.** ** D: Akos Rathony. William Lucas, Penelope Horner, Christopher Lee, Ingrid van Bergen, Albert Lieven. Flabby entry in Edgar Wallace series, involving rash of murders linked with dope smuggling into England. Retitled: DAFFODIL KILLER.

Devil's Daughter, The (1972) **C-74m.** TVM D: Jeannot Szwarc. Belinda Montgomery, Shelley Winters, Robert Foxworth, Joseph Cotten, Jonathan Frid, Robert Cornthwaite. At funeral of mother, Montgomery is befriended by Winters, who claims long friendship with deceased; actually Montgomery is needed to fulfill pact in Devil-worshipping group. Great ROSEMARY'S BABY-ish premise rendered inconsequential by indifferent treatment. Written by Colin Higgins. Average.

Devil's Disciple, The (1959-British) **82m.** ***½ D: Guy Hamilton. Burt Lancaster, Kirk Douglas, Laurence Olivier, Janette Scott, Eva LeGallienne, Harry Andrews, Basil Sydney, George Rose, Neil McCallum, David Horne, Mervyn Johns. Sparkling adaptation of George Bernard Shaw's satire, set during American Revolution, with standout performances by star trio. Screenplay by John Dighton and Roland Kibbee.

Devil's Doorway (1950) **84m.** *** D: Anthony Mann. Robert Taylor, Louis Calhern, Paula Raymond, Marshall Thompson, Edgar Buchanan. Well-turned Western with offbeat casting of Taylor as Indian who served in Civil War, returning home to find that he must fight to right the injustices done against his people.

Devil's Eight, The (1969) **C-97m.** ** D: Burt Topper. Christopher George, Fabian, Ralph Meeker, Leslie Parrish. Federal agent helps six convicts escape from road gang to train them to smash moonshine rings. Undistinguished.

Devil's Eye, The (1960-Swedish) **90m.** **½ D: Ingmar Bergman. Jarl Kulle, Bibi Andersson, Nils Poppe, Sture Lagerwall. Confused account of the demon sending envoy Kulle to rob Andersson of her virginity; long morality dialogue uplifted by cast.▼

Devil's General, The (1956-German) **C-120m.** ***½ D: Helmut Kautner. Curt Jurgens, Marianne Cook (Koch), Victor De Kowa, Karl John, Eva-Ingeborg Scholz, Albert Lieven. Jurgens is outstanding as a German war hero aviator who becomes disenchanted with Hitler and Nazism. Allegedly based on fact.

Devil's Hairpin, The (1957) **C-82m.** **½ D: Cornel Wilde. Cornel Wilde, Jean Wallace, Mary Astor, Arthur Franz. Wilde is reckless sports car champion who learns fair play on the track; obligatory racing scenes are above average.

Devil's Henchman, The (1949) **69m.** ** D: Seymour Friedman. Warner Baxter, Mary Beth Hughes, Mike Mazurki, Harry Shannon. In this programmer, Baxter sets out to capture waterfront gang and becomes involved in murder.

Devil-Ship Pirates (1964-British) **C-89m.** **½ D: Don Sharp, Christopher Lee, Andrew Keir, Michael Ripper, John Cairney. Good little movie of stray Spanish ships conquering English countryside, unaware that the Armada has been defeated.

Devil's Imposter, The SEE: **Pope Joan**

Devil's in Love, The (1933) **71m.** **½ D:

William Dieterle. Loretta Young, Victor Jory, Vivienne Osborne, C. Henry Gordon, David Manners, J. Carrol Naish. Very odd, well-made film about doctor falsely accused of murder, efforts to clear his name. Bela Lugosi has good, small role as prosecuting attorney.

Devil's Island (1940) 62m. **½ D: William Clemens. Boris Karloff, Nedda Harrigan, James Stephenson, Adia Kuznetzoff, Will Stanton, Edward Keane. Above-average Karloff vehicle of innocent doctor exiled to Devil's Island, mistreated by supervisor Stephenson, saved in twist finish.

Devil's Mask, The (1946) 66m. ** D: Henry Levin. Jim Bannon, Anita Louise, Michael Duane, Mona Barrie, Ludwig Donath, Barton Yarborough. OK entry in short-lived I LOVE A MYSTERY series with Bannon as Jack Packard, Yarborough as Doc Young. Intriguing is far-fetched story involving shrunken heads and murder, spoiled by obvious identity of killer.

Devil's Men, The SEE: **Land of the Minotaur▼**

Devil's Messenger (1961-Swedish) 72m. *½ D: Curt Siodmak. Lon Chaney, Karen Kadler, John Crawford. Sultry girl is sent to earth to help Satan carry out master plan that will envelop the world; hazy plot, poor production values. Originally three episodes of unsold TV series #13 Demon Street.

Devil's Own, The (1966-British) C-90m. *** D: Cyril Frankel. Joan Fontaine, Kay Walsh, Alec McCowen, Ann Bell, Ingrid Brett, Gwen ffrangcon-Davies. Good Hammer chiller with Fontaine as headmistress of private school who learns that a student is to be sacrificed by a local voodoo cult. British title: THE WITCHES.

Devil's Party, The (1938) 65m. ** D: Ray McCarey. Victor McLaglen, William Gargan, Paul Kelly, Beatrice Roberts, Frank Jenks, Samuel S. Hinds. So-so melodrama of former Hell's Kitchen pals who reunite once a year . . . except this year one of them is murdered.▼

Devil's Playground (1937) 74m. **½: D: Erle C. Kenton. Richard Dix, Dolores Del Rio, Chester Morris, Pierre Watkin, Ward Bond. Good combination of action and romance with diver Dix discovering wife Del Rio in love with Morris; exciting underwater climax. Remake of 1928 Frank Capra film SUBMARINE.

Devil's Playground, The (1976-Australian) C-107m. *** D: Fred Schepisi. Arthur Dignam, Nick Tate, Simon Burke, Charles McCallum, John Frawley, Jonathan Hardy, Gerry Duggan. Young boys reaching puberty act out sexually while boarded at Roman Catholic school; meanwhile, their teachers have problems of their own. Pointed and well made, if a bit predictable.▼

Devil's Rain, The (1975) C-85m. **½ D: Robert Feust. Ernest Borgnine, Ida Lupino, William Shatner, Tom Skerritt, Eddie Albert, Keenan Wynn, Joan Prather. Offbeat approach to story of devil worshippers provides some effective horror and also some unintentional humor. Most of the cast melts in a memorable finale. John Travolta makes his debut in a bit part.▼

Devil's Undead, The SEE: **Nothing But the Night▼**

Devil's Wanton, The (1962-Swedish) 72m. **½ D: Ingmar Bergman. Doris Svenlund, Birger Malmsten, Eva Henning, Hasse Ekman. Sober account of desperate girl finding romance with another equally unhappy soul, reaffirming their faith in humanity.

Devil's Widow, The (1972) C-107m. ** D: Roddy McDowall. Ava Gardner, Ian McShane, Stephanie Beacham, Cyril Cusack, Richard Wattis, David Whitman, Madeline Smith. McDowall's directorial debut is a too-arty drama about aging Ava's attempts to keep her young lovers from straying too much. Formerly called TAMLIN.

Devil Thumbs a Ride, The (1947) 62m. ** D: Felix Feist. Lawrence Tierney, Ted North, Nan Leslie, Betty Lawford, Andrew Tombes, Harry Shannon. Mediocre B film stars Tierney as a bank robber who hitches a ride with North and involves him in criminal activity. Could have been better if it were less talky and more actionful.▼

Devil Times Five (1974) 90m. **½ D: Sean McGregor. Gene Evans, Sorrell Booke, Shelley Morrison, Dawn Lyn, Leif Garrett, Taylor Lacher. Five children who escape from state mental institution take refuge in Evans' winter retreat and terrorize its inhabitants. Not bad. Originally released as PEOPLETOYS; also known as PEOPLE TOYS and THE HORRIBLE HOUSE ON THE HILL.▼

Devil to Pay, The (1930) 73m. **½ D: George Fitzmaurice. Ronald Colman, Loretta Young, David Torrence, Myrna Loy, Mary Forbes, Paul Cavanagh. Early talkie shows its age, but Colman is fine in this drawing-room comedy.

Devil Within Her, The (1975-British) C-90m. *½ D: Peter Sasdy. Joan Collins, Eileen Atkins, Donald Pleasence, Ralph Bates, Caroline Munro, Hilary Mason, John Steiner. Collins's newborn baby is possessed. Another idiotic ROSEMARY'S BABY/EXORCIST rip-off. Also known as I DON'T WANT TO BE BORN.▼

Devonsville Terror, The (1983) C-82m. ** D: Ulli Lommel. Suzanna Love, Robert Walker, Donald Pleasence, Paul Wilson. Love (wife of German director Lommel) is the new teacher in the town of Devonsville, a burg haunted by a witch's curse from 300 years ago. Copycat horror film steals its climax directly from RAIDERS OF THE LOST ARK.▼

Devotion (1946) **107m.** **½ D: Curtis Bernhardt. Olivia de Havilland, Ida Lupino, Paul Henreid, Sydney Greenstreet, Nancy Coleman, Arthur Kennedy, Dame May Whitty. Powerful real-life story of Brontë sisters becomes routine love triangle with Henreid in the middle; intense, dramatic performances make it worthwhile. Made in 1943.

D. I., The (1957) **106m.** **½ D: Jack Webb. Jack Webb, Don Dubbins, Lin McCarthy, Jackie Loughery, Monica Lewis, Virginia Gregg, Barbara Pepper. Ostensibly realistic account of Marine basic training is today a wonderful exercise in high camp. Webb is emotionally empty sergeant trying to whip his raw recruits (most of them played by actual soldiers) into shape; stubborn Dubbins is the chief thorn in his side. Sequence where soldiers search for a "murdered" sand flea is priceless. Story reused 13 years later (but with a different outcome) for a TVM, TRIBES.▼

Diabolical Dr. Mabuse, The SEE: **Thousand Eyes of Dr. Mabuse, The**▼

Diabolique (1955-French) **107m.** ***½ D: Henri-Georges Clouzot. Simone Signoret, Vera Clouzot, Paul Meurisse, Charles Vanel, Michel Serrault. Tyrannical schoolmaster is bumped off by his long-suffering wife and mistress; they dump the body and return home . . . to be confronted with increasing evidence that they botched the job. Classic chiller builds slowly, surely to final quarter hour that will drive you right up the wall. A must. Also known as LES DIABOLIQUES; remade for TV as REFLECTIONS OF MURDER.▼

Diagnosis: Murder (1976-British) **C-95m.** *** D: Sidney Hayers. Chrisopher Lee, Judy Geeson, Jon Finch, Tony Beckley, Dilys Hamlett, Jane Merrow. Psychiatrist is drawn into bizarre sequence of events when his wife disappears and he is accused of murdering her. Solid little suspenser.

Dial Hot Line (1969) **C-100m. TVM** D: Jerry Thorpe. Vince Edwards, Chelsea Brown, Kim Hunter, Lane Bradbury, June Harding. Unconvincing lead performance by Edwards as head of psychiatric telephone service with story centering around three different young subjects. Later a short-lived TV series, *Matt Lincoln.* Average.

Dial M for Murder (1954) **C-105m.** *** D: Alfred Hitchcock. Ray Milland, Grace Kelly, Robert Cummings, John Williams, Anthony Dawson. Frederick Knott's suspense play of man plotting wife's murder and subsequent police investigation: superficial at best, but slick and entertaining. Filmed in 3D. Remade for TV.▼

Dial M for Murder (1981) **C-100m. TVM** D: Boris Sagal. Angie Dickinson, Christopher Plummer, Anthony Quayle, Michael Parks, Ron Moody, Gerry Gibson. Playwright Frederick Knott's mystery classic,

adapted by John Gay, about an ingenious murder conceived as the perfect crime given a straightforward refilming with many of Hitchcock's touches meticulously recreated. Average.

Dial 1119 (1950) **75m.** ** D: Gerald Mayer. Marshall Thompson, Virginia Field, Andrea King, Sam Levene, Keefe Brasselle. Modest suspenser hinged on plot of killer holding a group of bar patrons hostage.

Diamond Earrings SEE: **Earrings of Madame De . . . , The**▼

Diamond Head (1962) **C-107m.** **½ D: Guy Green. Charlton Heston, Yvette Mimieux, George Chakiris, France Nuyen, James Darren, Aline MacMahon, Elizabeth Allen. Soap opera set in Hawaii with Heston the domineering head of his family, whose dictates almost ruin their lives.▼

Diamond Horseshoe (1945) **C-104m.** *** D: George Seaton. Betty Grable, Dick Haymes, Phil Silvers, William Gaxton, Beatrice Kay, Carmen Cavallaro, Margaret Dumont. Colorful musical set in Billy Rose's famous cabaret, with Grable giving up luxury for medical student Haymes. Song "The More I See You." Original title: BILLY ROSE'S DIAMOND HORSESHOE.

Diamond Jim (1935) **93m.** *** D: A. Edward Sutherland. Edward Arnold, Jean Arthur, Binnie Barnes, Cesar Romero, Eric Blore. Big-budget biography of eccentric millionaire of 19th century whose appetite for money is only matched by love of food and Lillian Russell; Arthur has dual role in recreation of Gay 90s era. Most entertaining. Screenplay by Preston Sturges.

Diamond Queen, The (1953) **C-80m.** ** D: John Brahm. Fernando Lamas, Arlene Dahl, Gilbert Roland, Michael Ansara. Dahl is dazzling title figure over whom Lamas and Roland fight in costumer set in India.

Diamonds (1975-Israeli) **C-101m.** ** D: Menahem Golan. Robert Shaw, Richard Roundtree, Shelley Winters, Barbara (Hershey) Seagull, Shai K. Ophir. OK heist movie with Shaw in dual role, as diamond merchant who masterminds break-in at Tel Aviv diamond vault, and twin brother who designed the security system there. Good location work in Tel Aviv and Jerusalem.▼

Diamonds and Crime SEE: **Hi Diddle Diddle**

Diamonds Are Forever (1971-British) **C-119m.** ***½ D: Guy Hamilton. Sean Connery, Jill St. John, Charles Gray, Lana Wood, Jimmy Dean, Bruce Cabot, Bruce Glover, Putter Smith, Bernard Lee, Lois Maxwell, Desmond Llewellyn, Leonard Barr, Laurence Naismith. After a one-picture hiatus, Connery returned as James Bond in this colorful comic-book adventure set in Las Vegas; closer in spirit to Republic serials than Ian Fleming, but great fun.▼

Diamonds for Breakfast (1968-British)

C-102m. ** D: Christopher Morahan. Marcello Mastroianni, Rita Tushingham, Warren Mitchell, Elaine Taylor, Francisca Tu, Maggie Blye. Son of Russian nobleman tries to steal royal diamonds his father gambled away on the night of his birth. Offbeat comedy caper with fantasy elements just doesn't work, relies heavily on Mastroianni charm.

Diamond Skulls SEE: **Dark Obsession**

Diamond Trap, The (1988) **C-100m. TVM** D: Don Taylor. Howard Hesseman, Brooke Shields, Ed Marinaro, Twiggy, Darren McGavin, Dick O'Neill, Nicholas Pryor. Two N.Y.C. cops stumble on a major jewel heist that leads them on a merry chase in Merrie England. Would you believe Twiggy as a Scotland Yard detective? Average.

Diamond Wizard, The (1954-British) **83m.** ** D: Dennis O'Keefe. Dennis O'Keefe, Margaret Sheridan, Philip Friend, Allan Wheatley. OK caper of U.S. and British agents tracking down diamond counterfeiters.

Diane (1956) **C-110m.** **½ D: David Miller. Lana Turner, Pedro Armendariz, Roger Moore, Marisa Pavan, Sir Cedric Hardwicke, Henry Daniell. Although predictable, medieval romance has good cast, gorgeous sets and costumes, and comes off surprisingly well. Lana looks lovely, and Miklos Rozsa's score helps set the mood.

Diary of a Bachelor (1964) **88m.** *½ D: Sandy Howard. William Traylor, Dagne Crane, Joe Silver, Chris Noel, Paula Stewart. Meager pickings. Fiancee reads boyfriend's daily ledger and decides he'd better mend his ways; time passes and he has, but she's changed her way of life.

Diary of a Chambermaid (1946) **87m.** ** D: Jean Renoir. Paulette Goddard, Hurd Hatfield, Francis Lederer, Burgess Meredith, Judith Anderson, Irene Ryan, Florence Bates, Reginald Owen, Almira Sessions. Uneasy attempt at Continental-style romantic melodrama, with blonde Goddard as outspoken maid who arouses all sorts of emotions in her snooty household. Tries hard, but never really sure of what it wants to be. Meredith as nutsy neighbor and Ryan as timid scullery maid do their best to liven things; Meredith also coproduced and wrote the screenplay. Remade in 1964.▼

Diary of a Chambermaid (1964-French) **97m.** ***½ D: Luis Buñuel. Jeanne Moreau, Michel Piccoli, Georges Geret, Francoise Lugagne, Daniel Ivernel, Jean Ozenne. Remake of Jean Renoir's 1946 film concerns fascism in France in 1939 and how the bourgeoisie are viewed by maid Moreau. Sharp, unrelenting film from one of the great directors.▼

Diary of a Country Priest (1950-French) **120m.** ***½ D: Robert Bresson. Claude Laydu, Nicole Ladmiral, Jean Riveyre, Nicole Maurey, Andre Guibert, Martine Lemaire. The life and death of an unhappy young priest attempting to minister to his first parish in rural France. Slow-moving but rewarding, with brilliantly stylized direction. Bresson also scripted.▼

Diary of a Lost Girl (1929-German) **104m.** ***½ D: G. W. Pabst. Louise Brooks, Fritz Rasp, Josef Ravensky, Sybille Schmitz, Valeska Gert. Pabst and Brooks' followup to their PANDORA'S BOX is even more sordid, yet in some ways more intriguing: Louise is, in succession, raped, gives birth, is put in a detention home, then a brothel, inherits money, marries, is widowed . . . and writer Rudolf Leonhardt claims only the first half of his script was filmed. Fascinating nonetheless, with an explicitness that's still surprising; a must for devotees of German stylistics (and of course, Brooks). Heavily edited and feared lost, but fully restored version was reissued in 1984.▼

Diary of a Mad Housewife (1970) **C-103m.** **½ D: Frank Perry. Richard Benjamin, Frank Langella, Carrie Snodgress, Lorraine Cullen, Frannie Michel, Katherine Meskill. Interesting but pointless story of harried N.Y.C. wife finding much needed release via affair with self-centered Langella. Asinine husband Benjamin would drive anyone mad. Peter Boyle has prominent bit in final scene. Script by Eleanor Perry from Sue Kaufman's novel. "Alternate" version prepared for TV, with different footage, runs 95m.▼

Diary of a Madman (1963) **C-96m.** **½ D: Reginald Le Borg. Vincent Price, Nancy Kovack, Chris Warfield, Ian Wolfe, Nelson Olmstead. 19th-century magistrate Price is possessed by an evil spirit called the Horla, which compels him to murder. Colorful but routine. Based on a story by Guy de Maupassant.▼

Diary of Anne Frank, The (1959) **156m.** ***½ D: George Stevens. Millie Perkins, Joseph Schildkraut, Shelley Winters, Richard Beymer, Lou Jacobi, Diane Baker, Ed Wynn. Meticulously produced version of Broadway drama dealing with Jewish refugees hiding in WW2 Amsterdam. Unfortunately, Perkins never captures pivotal charm of title character, though Schildkraut is fine as father Frank. Winters won Supporting Actress Oscar as shrill Mrs. Van Daan, ever fearful of Nazi arrest, and the cinematography (William C. Mellor) and art direction-set decoration also earned Academy Awards. Frances Goodrich and Albert Hackett utilized Anne's diary for their stage play and its screen adaptation. Originally released at 170m. Remade as a TV movie.▼

Diary of Anne Frank, The (1980) **C-100m. TVM** D: Boris Sagal. Melissa Gilbert, Maximilian Schell, Joan Plowright,

[291]

Doris Roberts, James Coco, Scott Jacoby, Clive Revill. Straightforward but affecting remake of this still-powerful play, based on the 1959 Frances Goodrich-Albert Hackett script. A good showcase for young Gilbert in the title role, surrounded by a fine cast. Above average.

Diary of a Perfect Murder (1986) C-100m. TVM D: Robert Day. Andy Griffith, Lori Lethin, Alice Hirson, Kene Holliday, Steve Inwood, Jack Bannon, James McEachin, Lawrence Pressman, Billy Green Bush. Engaging mystery yarn introduced Andy Griffith as Ben Matlock, wily Harvard-bred Atlanta attorney who is senior partner in a father/daughter law firm. Pilot to the *Matlock* series, written by Dean Hargrove. Above average.

Diary of a Teenage Hitchhiker (1979) C-100m. TVM D: Ted Post. Dick Van Patten, Katherine Helmond, James Carroll Jordan, Charlene Tilton, Katy Kurtzman, Christopher Knight. Tawdry drama dramatizing the risk of soliciting rides from strangers. Below average.▼

Diary of Forbidden Dreams SEE: **What?**▼
Diary of Oharu SEE: **Life of Oharu**

Dick Tracy (1990) C-104m. *** D: Warren Beatty. Warren Beatty, Madonna, Al Pacino, Glenne Headly, Charlie Korsmo, Mandy Patinkin, Charles Durning, Paul Sorvino, William Forsythe, Seymour Cassel, Dustin Hoffman, Dick Van Dyke, Catherine O'Hara, James Caan, Michael J. Pollard, Estelle Parsons, James Tolkan, R.G. Armstrong. Colorful, high-style adaptation of the Chester Gould comic strip classic, with Beatty redefining the hawk-nosed, jut-jawed hero. Story is simple in the extreme, but there's so much to take in you really don't mind: a galaxy of guest stars as Gould's grotesque villains, eye-popping art direction and design, and Madonna singing new Stephen Sondheim songs (if a few too many). Standout: Pacino's hilarious, over-the-top performance as Big Boy Caprice.

Dick Tracy, Detective (1945) 62m. ** D: William Berke. Morgan Conway, Anne Jeffreys, Mike Mazurki, Jane Greer. Programmer entry about Chester Gould's square-jawed detective combatting crime; needed production values are lacking. Originally titled DICK TRACY.▼

Dick Tracy Meets Gruesome (1947) 65m. ** D: John Rawlins. Boris Karloff, Ralph Byrd, Anne Gwynne, Lyle Latell. Karloff is fun as Gruesome, who uses Dr. A. Tomic's experimental gas (which causes people to freeze in place) to commit daring bank robbery. Silly but watchable. Lex Barker has a bit role as ambulance driver.▼

Dick Tracy's Dilemma (1947) 60m. ** D: John Rawlins. Ralph Byrd, Lyle Latell, Kay Christopher, Jack Lambert, Ian Keith. RKO contract players abound in this Tracy

series entry; fast pacing makes predictable crime-solving satisfactory.▼

Dick Tracy Versus Cueball (1946) 62m. ** D: Gordon Douglas. Morgan Conway, Anne Jeffreys, Lyle Latell, Rita Corday, Dick Wessel. Ralph Byrd is definitive screen Tracy, but he isn't in this one; Conway does his best in OK entry in the Tracy series.▼

Dick Turpin (1925) 73m. *** D: John G. Blystone. Tom Mix, Kathleen Myers, Philo McCullough, Alan Hale, Bull Montana. Mix abandoned cowboy clothes to play famous English highwayman, but retained surefire formula of action and comedy in this enjoyable vehicle.

Did You Hear the One About the Traveling Saleslady? (1968) C-97m. BOMB D: Don Weis. Phyllis Diller, Bob Denver, Joe Flynn, Eileen Wesson, Jeanette Nolan, Bob Hastings, David Hartman, Charles Lane, Kent McCord. You've all heard it, so why bother watching this dud. For only the most fervent Diller fans.

Die! Die! My Darling! (1965-British) C-97m. **½ D: Silvio Narizzano. Tallulah Bankhead, Stefanie Powers, Peter Vaughan, Donald Sutherland, Yootha Joyce. Tallulah, in her last film, has field day as weirdo who keeps Powers under lock and key for personal vengeance against the death of her son. Engaging fun, especially for Bankhead devotees. Script by Richard Matheson. Original British title: FANATIC.▼

Die Hard (1988) C-131m. *** D: John McTiernan. Bruce Willis, Alan Rickman, Bonnie Bedelia, Alexander Godunov, Reginald Veljohnson, Paul Gleason, De'voreaux White, William Atherton, Hart Bochner, James Shigeta. Dynamite action yarn about a N.Y.C. cop who just happens to be visiting an L.A. highrise when it's commandeered by terrorist thieves. Great action scenes and stunts, with Richard Edlund's special effects, and a perfect part for Willis, who plays cat-and-mouse with bad guy Rickman. Marred only by over-length and too many needlessly stupid supporting characters. Followed by a sequel.▼

Die Hard 2 (1990) C-124m. *** D: Renny Harlin. Bruce Willis, Bonnie Bedelia, William Atherton, Reginald VelJohnson, Franco Nero, William Sadler, John Amos, Dennis Franz, Art Evans, Fred Dalton Thompson, Sheila McCarthy. Stupendously unbelievable—but very entertaining—sequel to the action hit; while waiting for his wife to land at Washington's Dulles airport, Willis dives head-first into trouble when he gets wind of an impending terrorist-type plot. Lots of violent, large-scale action, and lots of fun—just don't look for lots of logic. Based on Walter Wager's novel *58 Minutes.*

Die Laughing (1980) C-108m. BOMB D: Jeff Werner. Robby Benson, Linda Grovenor, Charles Durning, Elsa Lanchester, Bud Cort, Peter Coyote. Benson is the star, co-author, co-producer, and composer of this sophomoric black comedy and gives an excruciating performance as a cabbie who accidentally becomes implicated in the murder of a nuclear scientist. Cort is disgustingly oily as the fascist villain.▼

Die, Monster, Die! (1965) **C-80m.** ** D: Daniel Haller. Boris Karloff, Nick Adams, Freda Jackson, Suzan Farmer, Terence de Marney, Patrick Magee. Based on H. P. Lovecraft story, this thriller has Karloff a recluse who discovers a meteor which gives him strange powers. Good premise is not carried out well. Filmed in England. Remade as THE CURSE (1987).▼

Different Affair, A (1987) **C-100m. TVM** D: Noel Nosseck. Anne Archer, Tony Roberts, Bobby Jacoby, Stuart Pankin, Lenore Kasdorf, Beverly Todd, Ellen Geer. Plodding drama about radio talk show psychiatrist, her lover, and a foster child who comes into her life. Coproduced by Kenny Rogers. Below average.

Different Story, A (1978) **C-108m.** **½ D: Paul Aaron. Perry King, Meg Foster, Valerie Curtin, Peter Donat, Richard Bull, Barbara Collentine. Gays King and Foster get married to prevent his deportation, then fall in love. Sounds terrible, but first half is surprisingly good until film succumbs to conventionality in later scenes. Foster is terrific.▼

Digby—The Biggest Dog in the World (1974-British) **C-88m.** BOMB D: Joseph McGrath. Jim Dale, Spike Milligan, Milo O'Shea, Angela Douglas, Norman Rossington. Poor comedy-fantasy concerning liquid Project X, which causes sheepdog Digby to grow to huge proportions. Bad special effects, too. Written by Ted Key, creator of "Hazel," strictly for kids.▼

Dig That Uranium (1956) **61m.** D: Edward Bernds. Leo Gorcey, Huntz Hall, Bernard Gorcey, Mary Beth Hughes. SEE **Bowery Boys** series.

Dillinger (1945) **70m.** *** D: Max Nosseck. Edmund Lowe, Anne Jeffreys, Lawrence Tierney, Eduardo Ciannelli, Elisha Cook, Jr., Marc Lawrence. Solid ganster yarn written by Philip Yordan, one of the best B movies of its kind (though a key bank robbery is comprised of stock footage lifted from Fritz Lang's YOU ONLY LIVE ONCE).▼

Dillinger (1973) **C-96m.** *** D: John Milius. Warren Oates, Ben Johnson, Cloris Leachman, Michelle Phillips, Richard Dreyfuss, Harry Dean Stanton, Steve Kanaly. Heavily romanticized gangster movie is aided by some rough, violent gun battles. Story follows Dillinger midway through his bank-robbing career up until his death outside the Biograph Theatre.▼

Dime With a Halo (1963) **97m.** **½ D: Boris Sagal. Barbara Luna, Roger Mobley,

Paul Langton, Rafael Lopez, Manuel Padilla. Five poor Mexican kids steal ten cents from church collection plate and bet on a racehorse. Minor but winning little film.

Dimples (1936) **78m.** **½ D: William Seiter. Shirley Temple, Frank Morgan, Helen Westley, Robert Kent, Stepin Fetchit, Astrid Allwyn. Prime Shirley, with our heroine doing her best to save her destitute father, played by marvelous Morgan. Songs: "Oh Mister Man Up In The Moon," "What Did The Bluebird Say."▼

Dim Sum: a little bit of heart (1984) **C-89m.** *** D: Wayne Wang. Laureen Chew, Kim Chew, Victor Wong, Ida F.O. Chung, Cora Miao. Occasionally slow—there are one too many shots of empty rooms—but mostly wise, endearing tale of Chinese-Americans in San Francisco, focusing on the dynamics of a mother-daughter relationship. Characters may be distinctively Chinese, but there's a refreshing, knowing universality to this comedy.▼

Diner (1982) **C-110m.** *** D: Barry Levinson. Steve Guttenberg, Daniel Stern, Mickey Rourke, Kevin Bacon, Timothy Daly, Ellen Barkin, Paul Reiser, Michael Tucker. Problems of growing up are nicely synthesized by writer-director Levinson in this look at a group of friends who hang out in a Baltimore diner in the 1950s. Obviously made with care and affection; a real sleeper. Levinson's directorial debut and first film of Barkin and Reiser.▼

Dingaka (1965-South Africa) **C-98m.** **½ D: Jamie Uys. Stanley Baker, Juliet Prowse, Ken Gampu, Siegfried Mynhardt, Bob Courtney. Film focuses on contrasting white-black ways of life and the clashes of the two cultures; production bogs down in stereotypes.▼

Dinky (1935) **65m.** ** D: D. Ross Lederman, Howard Bretherton. Jackie Cooper, Mary Astor, Roger Pryor, Henry Armetta. Astor is framed, accused of fraud. She tries to keep it from hurting son Cooper in military school. Nothing special.

Dinner at Eight (1933) **113m.** **** D: George Cukor. Marie Dressler, John Barrymore, Wallace Beery, Jean Harlow, Lionel Barrymore, Lee Tracy, Edmund Lowe, Billie Burke, Madge Evans, Jean Hersholt, Karen Morley, Phillips Holmes, May Robson. Vintage MGM constellation of stars portray various strata of society in N.Y.C., invited to dine and shine; Harlow in fine comedy form, but Dressler as dowager steals focus in filmization of George Kaufman-Edna Ferber play. Scripted by three top writers: Herman Mankiewicz, Frances Marion, and Donald Ogden Stewart. Don't miss this one. Remade for cable TV.▼

Dinner at Eight (1989) **C-100m. TVM** D: Ron Lagomarsino. Lauren Bacall, Charles Durning, Ellen Greene, Harry Hamlin, John Mahoney, Marsha Mason, Joel

Brooks, Tim Kazurinsky. Update of the classic George S. Kaufman–Edna Ferber play about events leading up to a social climber's elegant dinner party. Bacall, in the Marie Dressler role (then a dowager, now a trash novelist) leads a first-rate cast . . . but this is no match for the original. Produced by Shelley Duvall. Made for cable. Average.▼

Dinner at the Ritz (1937-British) **77m.** **½ D: Harold Schuster. Annabella, Paul Lukas, David Niven, Romney Brent. Diverting murder whodunit with Annabella seeking the killer of her father; classy settings spice film.▼

Dinner for Adele (1978-Czech) **C-100m.** **½ D: Oldrich Lipsky. Michal Docolomansky, Rudolf Hrusinsky, Milos Kopecky, Nada Konvalinkova, Ladislav Pesek. Truly off-the-wall film festival favorite finds pulp hero Nick Carter (Docolomansky) in Prague in the year 1900 investigating murder spree that eventually leads to carnivorous plant named Adele. Tongue-in-cheek, gadget-laden film done in the style of a silent melodrama; worthwhile for those seeking the unusual, others beware. Originally titled NICK CARTER IN PRAGUE; also known as ADELE HASN'T HAD HER SUPPER YET.

Dino (1957) **94m.** **½ D: Thomas Carr. Sal Mineo, Brian Keith, Susan Kohner, Joe De Santis, Penny Stanton, Frank Faylen, Richard Bakalyan. Mineo at his rebellious best playing juvenile delinquent befriended by a girl (Kohner) and a social worker (Keith). Reginald Rose adapted his acclaimed TV play, and Mineo recreated his starring role.▼

Dinosaurus! (1960) **C-85m.** **½ D: Irvin S. Yeaworth, Jr. Ward Ramsey, Paul Lukather, Kristina Hanson, Alan Roberts. Interesting and unintentionally amusing story of hazards faced by caveman and two prehistoric monsters who are accidentally unearthed on an isolated tropical island.▼

Dion Brothers, The SEE: **Gravy Train**

Diplomaniacs (1933) **63m.** *** D: William A. Seiter. Bert Wheeler, Robert Woolsey, Marjorie White, Louis Calhern, Edgar Kennedy, Hugh Herbert. Genuinely odd but endearing nonsense musical comedy about barbers from Indian reservation sent to Geneva peace conference. Reminiscent of MILLION DOLLAR LEGS and DUCK SOUP, with memorable comic performances by Herbert—as wise-saying Chinese—and Calhern.▼

Diplomatic Courier (1952) **97m.** *** D: Henry Hathaway. Tyrone Power, Patricia Neal, Stephen McNally, Hildegarde Neff, Karl Malden. Power seeks to avenge friend's death in Trieste, becomes involved in international espionage. Cold War film is exciting, well acted. Look for Lee Marvin, Charles Bronson, and Michael Ansara in small, unbilled roles.▼

Dirigible (1931) **93m.** **½ D: Frank Capra. Jack Holt, Ralph Graves, Fay Wray, Hobart Bosworth, Roscoe Karns. Frank Wead story about Navy pilots' experimental use of dirigibles in the Antarctic has plenty of action and guts, but a sappy romantic story to weigh it down. On the whole, an interesting antique.

Dirt Bike Kid, The (1986) **C-90m.** **½ D: Hoite C. Caston. Peter Billingsley, Stuart Pankin, Anne Bloom, Patrick Collins, Sage Parker, Chad Sheets. Strictly formula teen melodrama, with young Billingsley taking on evil banker Pankin and some nasty bikers with the help of a very unusual Yamaha. Harmless and forgettable.▼

Dirt Gang, The (1972) **C-89m.** *½ D: Jerry Jameson. Paul Carr, Michael Pataki, Lee DeBroux, Jon Shank, Nancy Harris, T.J. Escott. Dirt is right; unremarkable motorcycle gang film.

Dirty Dancing (1987) **C-97m.** **½ D: Emile Ardolino. Jennifer Grey, Patrick Swayze, Jerry Orbach, Cynthia Rhodes, Jack Weston, Jane Brucker, Kelly Bishop, Lonny Price, Charles "Honi" Coles, Bruce Morrow. Superficial but audience-pleasing tale of spoiled teenage girl who learns something about real life—as well as a thing or two about dancing—during family vacation at a Catskills, N.Y., resort hotel in the early 1960s. Sparked by some hot dance numbers, and star-making performance of Grey (daughter of Joel) opposite actor-dancer Swayze. Most of the music is 1980s-style, not 1960s, but it seems to work. For a richer portrait of Catskills life see another 1987 release, SWEET LORRAINE. Oscar winner for best song: "(I've Had) The Time of My Life." Followed by a TV series.▼

Dirty Dingus Magee (1970) **C-90m.** *** D: Burt Kennedy. Frank Sinatra, George Kennedy, Anne Jackson, Lois Nettleton, Michele Carey, Jack Elam, John Dehner, Henry Jones, Harry Carey, Jr., Paul Fix. Broad, bawdy spoof with Sinatra as $10 outlaw whose attempts to make it big are slightly hindered by equally bungling sheriff Kennedy (not to mention assorted whores, Indians, and the U.S. Cavalry). Subtle it's not, but fast-paced and amusing, especially for Western buffs; Nettleton is a delight as Joanne Woodward-ish schoolmarm inappropriately named Prudence. Cowritten by Joseph Heller. TV prints run 79m.

Dirty Dishes (1978-French) **C-92m.** **½ D: Joyce Buñuel. Carole Laure, Pierre Santini, Catherine Lachens, Veronique Silver. Entertaining but obvious feminist comedy of Laure rebelling against her duties as a housewife. Director Buñuel is the late Luis Buñuel's daughter-in-law.

Dirty Dozen, The (1967) **C-150m.** ***½ D: Robert Aldrich. Lee Marvin, Ernest

Borgnine, Jim Brown, John Cassavetes, Robert Ryan, Charles Bronson, Donald Sutherland, George Kennedy, Telly Savalas, Ralph Meeker, Richard Jaeckel, Clint Walker, Trini Lopez. Box-office hit about 12 murderers, rapists, and other prisoners who get a chance to redeem themselves in WW2. Exciting, funny, and well acted, especially by Marvin and Cassavetes. Followed by a spate of inferior TV sequels and a series two decades later.▼

Dirty Dozen: The Deadly Mission, The (1987) C-100m. TVM D: Lee H. Katzin. Telly Savalas, Ernest Borgnine, Vince Edwards, Gary Graham, James Van Patten, Vincent Van Patten, Bo Svenson. The title tells all in this second TV sequel to Robert Aldrich's action classic of the big screen. Borgnine repeats the role he had in the previous two while Savalas, who was killed off in the original, returns in a different part, leading the mission to rescue six important scientists from the Nazis. Followed by THE FATAL MISSION. Average.

Dirty Dozen: The Fatal Mission, The (1988) C-100m. TVM D: Lee H. Katzin. Telly Savalas, Ernest Borgnine, Hunt Block, Jeff Conaway, Alex Cord, Erik Estrada, Ray "Boom Boom" Mancini, Heather Thomas. The third TV sequel to the mid-1960s classic has Savalas leading another Dirty Dozen against the Nazis—on the Orient Express! Twist here is having a female along on the mission. The series followed. Average.

Dirty Dozen: The Next Mission, The (1985) C-100m. TVM D: Andrew V. McLaglen. Lee Marvin, Ernest Borgnine, Richard Jaeckel, Ken Wahl, Larry Wilcox, Sonny Landham. Belated made-for-TV sequel to the hit 1967 movie with Marvin (recreating his original role along with Borgnine and Jaeckel) being coerced into forming another dirty dozen to foil a plot to kill Hitler! *The A-Team* had more believable plots. Followed by THE DEADLY MISSION. Below average.▼

Dirty Game, The (1966-Italian) 91m. **½ D: Terence Young, Christian-Jaque, Carlo Lizzani. Henry Fonda, Vittorio Gassman, Annie Girardot, Robert Ryan, Peter Van Eyck. Hodgepodge of stories dealing with espionage in post-WW2 era; none of episodes is convincing, stars don't help much.

Dirty Hands (1976-French) C-102m. ** D: Claude Chabrol. Rod Steiger, Romy Schneider, Paolo Giusti, Jean Rochefort, Hans Christian Blech. Laughable wife-and-lover-conspire-to-murder-husband melodrama; corpses keep turning up alive with boring regularity. However, some striking camera work, eerie sequences.▼

Dirty Harry (1971) C-102m. ***½ D: Don Siegel. Clint Eastwood, Harry Guardino, Reni Santoni, John Vernon, John Larch,

Andy Robinson. Riveting action film with Eastwood as iconoclastic cop determined to bring in psychotic killer Robinson, even if he has to break some rules. Brilliantly filmed and edited for maximum impact. Followed by MAGNUM FORCE, THE ENFORCER, SUDDEN IMPACT, and THE DEAD POOL.▼

Dirty Heroes (1969-Italian) C-105m. **½ D: Alberto DeMartino. Frederick Stafford, Daniela Bianchi, Curt Jurgens, John Ireland, Adolfo Celi, Michael Constantine. Wartime escape and revenge action drama—a poor man's DIRTY DOZEN—with a gang of ex-cons turned G.I.'s working behind enemy lines in Holland.▼

Dirty Knight's Work (1976-British) C-88m. ** D: Kevin Connor. John Mills, Donald Pleasence, Barbara Hershey, David Birney, Margaret Leighton, Peter Cushing. Anglo-American Birney enlists Mills' help in solving his father's murder, zeroes in on strange society of latter-day knights with vigilante tendencies. Offbeat and mildly diverting. Original title: TRIAL BY COMBAT. Also known as CHOICE OF WEAPONS.

Dirty Laundry (1987) C-79m. ** D: William Webb. Leigh McCloskey, Jeanne O'Brien, Frankie Valli, Sonny Bono, Nicholas Worth, Robbie Rist, Edy Williams, Carl Lewis, Greg Louganis. Odd cast (including Olympic champs Lewis and Louganis) is the only point of interest in this unmemorable comedy of innocent McCloskey becoming involved with gangsters.▼

Dirty Little Billy (1972) C-100m. *** D: Stan Dragoti. Michael J. Pollard, Lee Purcell, Charles Aidman, Richard Evans. Offbeat story based on early life of Billy the Kid. Grimy, muddy, adventurous; not a normal Western by any stretch of the imagination. Produced by Jack L. Warner!

Dirty Mary Crazy Larry (1974) C-93m. *** D: John Hough. Peter Fonda, Susan George, Adam Roarke, Vic Morrow, Roddy McDowall. Very fast action as racing driver Fonda, pickup George and mechanic Roarke demolish every car in sight while escaping with supermarket loot. Hardly a letup, and marred only by downbeat finale.▼

Dirty Money (1972-French) C-98m. **½ D: Jean-Pierre Melville. Alain Delon, Richard Crenna, Catherine Deneuve, Ricardo Cucciolla, Michael Conrad. Pedestrian melodrama of bank robbery and drug trafficking. Delon and Crenna are muscular, Deneuve and the scenery gorgeous.

Dirty Rotten Scoundrels (1988) C-110m. **½ D: Frank Oz. Steve Martin, Michael Caine, Glenne Headly, Anton Rodgers, Barbara Harris, Ian McDiarmid, Dana Ivey. A career con artist who fleeces women with great elan in the south of France must find a way to deal with crass new competition, in the person of American Martin.

Eventually they decide to compete to see who can dupe wide-eyed Headly first. Extremely pleasant but unremarkable comedy, a remake of the 1964 BEDTIME STORY, filmed on beautiful Riviera locations.▼

Dirty Tricks (1980-U.S.-Canadian) C-91m. *½ D: Alvin Rakoff. Elliott Gould, Kate Jackson, Rich Little, Arthur Hill, Nick Campbell, Angus McInnes. Harvard history professor Gould tussles with baddies over a letter written by George Washington. A comedy-thriller that is neither funny nor thrilling.

Disappearance, The (1977-Canadian) C-88m. ** D: Stuart Cooper. Donald Sutherland, Francine Racette, David Hemmings, David Warner, Christopher Plummer, John Hurt, Virginia McKenna, Peter Bowles. Slow-moving account of a hit-man's preoccupation with the disappearance of his wife. Strong Sutherland performance is obliterated by confusing script, pretentiously arty direction. Originally 100m.▼

Disappearance of Aimee, The (1976) C-110m. TVM D: Anthony Harvey. Faye Dunaway, Bette Davis, James Sloyan, James Woods, John Lehne, Lelia Goldoni, Barry Brown, Severn Darden. Period drama covering, through a courtroom hearing, the sensational disappearance and reappearance of the famed preacher, Aimee Semple McPherson, in 1926. Dunaway is fascinating as Aimee, Davis feisty as her mother in this absorbing, richly atmospheric dramatization. Above average.▼

Disappearance of Flight 412, The (1974) C-78m. TVM D: Jud Taylor. Glenn Ford, Bradford Dillman, Guy Stockwell, David Soul, Robert F. Lyons, Kent Smith, Jack Ging, Greg Mullavey. After two jets from commander Ford's unit mysteriously vanish while pursuing UFOs, he rips through military red tape to find out why the Air Force officially will not recognize the incident and stumbles onto a right-wing conspiracy. Average.

Disaster at Silo 7 (1988) C-100m. TVM D: Larry Elikann. Perry King, Ray Baker, Peter Boyle, Patricia Charbonneau, Michael O'Keefe, Joe Spano, Dennis Weaver. An Air Force technician races against time to prevent a devastating missile site explosion; fictionalized version of an actual 1980 event in the Midwest. Average.

Disaster on the Coastliner (1979) C-100m. TVM D: Richard Sarafian. Lloyd Bridges, Raymond Burr, Robert Fuller, Pat Hingle, E. G. Marshall, Yvette Mimieux, William Shatner, Paul L. Smith. Vengeful computer genius sets two passenger trains on a collision course in this fairly intelligent suspense thriller with lots of unplugged holes. Average.

Disc Jockey Jamboree SEE: **Jamboree**
Discreet Charm of the Bourgeoisie, The

(1972-French) C-100m. **** D: Luis Buñuel. Fernando Rey, Delphine Seyrig, Stephane Audran, Bulle Ogier, Jean-Pierre Cassel, Michel Piccoli. A Buñuel joke on his audience, using friends' attempts to have dinner party as excuse for series of surrealistic sequences. Reality and illusion soon blur into one, with delicious comic results. Oscar-winner as Best Foreign Film.▼

Disembodied, The (1957) 65m. *½ D: Walter Grauman. Paul Burke, Allison Hayes, Eugenia Paul, Robert Christopher. Standard voodoo chiller situated in dark jungle; usual results.

Dishonorable Discharge (1958-French) 105m. ** D: Bernard Borderie. Eddie Constantine, Pascale Roberts, Lino Ventura, Lise Bourdin. Variation on Hemingway's TO HAVE AND HAVE NOT, with Constantine skippering luxury ship loaded with hidden dope; flabby film.

Dishonored (1931) 91m. **½ D: Josef von Sternberg. Marlene Dietrich, Victor McLaglen, Lew Cody, Warner Oland, Gustav von Seyffertitz. Alluring Dietrich makes the most of a creaky script starring her as secret agent X-27 during WW1. Worth seeing for her masquerade as peasant girl.

Dishonored Lady (1947) 85m. *½ D: Robert Stevenson. Hedy Lamarr, Dennis O'Keefe, John Loder, William Lundigan, Natalie Schafer, Paul Cavanagh. Limp Lamarr vehicle of glamorous magazine art director accused of murder; ponderous.▼

Disorderlies (1987) C-86m. *½ D: Michael Schultz. The Fat Boys, Ralph Bellamy, Tony Plana, Anthony Geary, Marco Rodriguez, Troy Beyer. Get *down* with Ralph Bellamy, cast here as a Palm Beach millionaire about to be murdered for his estate by a conniving nephew and the valet; the title chubs—kind of a rap version of The Three Stooges—come to the rescue. Pretty desperate, but the ultimate in recent casting curios; Ralph gets an editorial assist via crosscutting during the more strenuous action scenes.▼

Disorderly Orderly, The (1964) C-90m. *** D: Frank Tashlin. Jerry Lewis, Glenda Farrell, Susan Oliver, Everett Sloane, Jack E. Leonard, Alice Pearce, Kathleen Freeman, Barbara Nichols, Milton Frome. First-rate slapstick and sight gags (including a wild chase finale) mix with cloying sentiment as Jerry runs amuck in a nursing home. Best scene: Jerry's suffering of "sympathy pains" as patient Pearce complains of her ills.▼

Disorganized Crime (1989) C-101m. *½ D: Jim Kouf. Hoyt Axton, Corbin Bernsen, Ruben Blades, Fred Gwynne, Ed O'Neill, Lou Diamond Phillips, Daniel Roebuck, William Russ, Marie Butler Kouf. Witless crime-chase comedy about a quartet of crooks waiting for leader Bernsen, who's plotted the perfect bank heist but has managed to get himself arrested. This one's no STAKEOUT (which was scripted by writer-director Kouf).▼

Dispatch From Reuters, A (1940) 89m. **½ D: William Dieterle. Edward G. Robinson, Edna Best, Eddie Albert, Albert Basserman, Gene Lockhart, Nigel Bruce, Otto Kruger. Watchable (if not always inspired) Warner Bros. biography of the man who started famous worldwide news agency by using pigeons to transmit information across the European continent.

Disputed Passage (1939) 87m. **½ D: Frank Borzage. Dorothy Lamour, Akim Tamiroff, John Howard, Victor Varconi, Keye Luke. Elisabeth Risdon, Philip Ahn. Average drama of conflict between scientists in their ideals. One believes that there's no place for marriage in science field.

Disraeli (1929) 89m. *** D: Alfred E. Green. George Arliss, Joan Bennett, Florence Arliss, Anthony Bushell, David Torrence, Ivan Simpson. Somewhat stagy but effective vehicle for Arliss, who won Oscar as cunning British prime minister:— a great statesman, devoted husband, and matchmaker (for Bennett and Bushell). Very much a one-man show.

Distance (1975) C-94m. **½ D: Anthony Lover. Paul Benjamin, Eija Pokkinen, James Woods, Bibi Besch, Hal Miller, Polly Holliday, Bruce Kornbluth. Impressive, though flawed, independently made drama detailing the problems of two army couples during the 1950s. Fine performances, particularly by Besch and Woods; Lover and producer George Coe were responsible for the classic short THE DOVE.

Distant Drums (1951) C-101m. ** D: Raoul Walsh. Gary Cooper, Mari Aldon, Richard Webb, Ray Teal. Tame actioner of Seminole Indians on warpath in early 19th-century Florida, with Cooper as stalwart swamp fighter. A reworking of the central story idea from director Walsh's WW2 saga OBJECTIVE BURMA.▼

Distant Harmony (1987) C-85m. **½ D: DeWitt Sage. Luciano Pavarotti, Kallen Esperian, Madelyn Renee. Disappointing documentary of opera superstar Pavarotti's 1986 visit to China. Has its moments, but lacks depth and insight . . . and pales beside FROM MAO TO MOZART: ISAAC STERN IN CHINA. Mainly for opera and Pavarotti fans.▼

Distant Thunder (1973-Indian) C-100m. *** D: Satyajit Ray. Soumitra Chatterji, Babita, Sandhya Roy, Gobinda Chakravarty, Romesh Mukerji. Famine strikes Bengal in 1942 and affects the lives of various families in many different ways. Harsh, vividly filmed tale in which one can almost feel the sand and wind blowing across the screen.▼

Distant Thunder (1988-U.S.-Canadian) C-114m. ** D: Rick Rosenberg. John Lithgow, Ralph Macchio, Kerrie Keane, Reb Brown, Janet Margolin, Dennis Arndt, Jamey Sheridan, Tom Bower. Well-intentioned but gooey soaper about yet one more emotionally troubled Vietnam vet (nicely played by the ever-reliable Lithgow), who lives alone in the wilderness, and whose long-abandoned son (Macchio) sets out to find him.▼

Distant Trumpet, A (1964) C-117m. **½ D: Raoul Walsh. Troy Donahue, Suzanne Pleshette, Kent Smith, Claude Akins, James Gregory. Paul Horgan's novel gets short-circuited in stock presentation of army men in the Old West combatting warring Indians while romancing women on the post; good supporting cast.

Distant Voices, Still Lives (1988-British) C-85m. *** D: Terence Davies. Freda Dowie, Peter Postlethwaite, Angela Walsh, Dean Williams, Lorraine Ashbourne. Strikingly visual evocation of England during the 1940s and '50s, a time when the corny, happy lyrics of popular songs can be contrasted to the drab, stultifying lives of the working class. Davies' autobiographical script mirrors the lives of his various family members, each of whom is brutalized by his irrationally cruel father. While there's little narrative structure and no depth to the characters, the haunting imagery makes this most worthwhile.▼

Diva (1982-French) C-123m. ***½ D: Jean-Jacques Beineix. Wilhelmenia Wiggins Fernandez, Frederic Andrei, Richard Bohringer, Thuy An Luu, Jacques Fabbri. Music-loving mailman bootleg-tapes the concert of a superstar diva who's never made a recording, finds himself in even hotter water when his possession is mixed up with a second tape that will incriminate gangsters. High-tech melodrama occasionally rubs your nose in its technique, but still makes for whale of a directorial debut by Beineix. Subway motorcycle chase is destined to become an action classic.▼

Dive Bomber (1941) C-133m. *** D: Michael Curtiz. Errol Flynn, Fred MacMurray, Ralph Bellamy, Alexis Smith, Robert Armstrong, Regis Toomey, Craig Stevens. Exciting, well-paced aviation film of experiments to eliminate pilot-blackout. Flynn, MacMurray, and Smith perform well in formula story.

Divided Heart, The (1954-British) 89m. *** D: Charles Crichton. Cornell Borchers, Yvonne Mitchell, Armin Dahlen, Alexander Knox, Michel Ray, Geoffrey Keen, Theodore Bikel. Intelligent study of dilemma faced by parents of foster child when real mother, thought dead, returns to claim her son. Set in Europe after WW2.

Divine Madness! (1980) C-95m. **½ D: Michael Ritchie. Bette Midler fanatics would probably up this rating a half-star or so, but unevenness and occasional oppressiveness of this concert film may even get to them. Some funny bits, but will someone tell her to quit desecrating rock'n'roll?▼

Divine Nymph, The (1979-Italian) **C-90m.** *½ D: Giuseppe Patroni Griffi. Marcello Mastroianni, Laura Antonelli, Terence Stamp, Michele Placido, Duilio Del Prete, Ettore Manni, Marina Vlady. Poor melodrama chronicling beautiful Antonelli's involvements with Marquis Mastroianni and Baron Stamp. Of interest only when Laura doffs her duds.▼

Divorce (1945) **71m.** ** D: William Nigh. Kay Francis, Bruce Cabot, Helen Mack, Craig Reynolds, Larry Olsen, Mary Gordon. Francis is city girl who returns to home town, enticing Cabot away from Mack and family; satisfactory programmer.

Divorce American Style (1967) **C-109m.** *** D: Bud Yorkin. Dick Van Dyke, Debbie Reynolds, Jason Robards, Jean Simmons, Van Johnson, Joe Flynn, Shelley Berman, Martin Gabel, Lee Grant, Pat Collins, Tom Bosley, Eileen Brennan. Highly entertaining comedy of Van Dyke and Reynolds finding more problems than they expected when they get divorced. Stars are unusually good in offbeat roles. Written by Norman Lear.

Divorcee, The (1930) **83m.** **½ D: Robert Z. Leonard. Norma Shearer, Chester Morris, Conrad Nagel, Robert Montgomery, Florence Eldridge. Stagy but interesting tale of young wife Shearer who puts up with husband Morris's flirtations until she decides to equal him. Shearer won an Oscar for this performance.

Divorce His—Divorce Hers (1973) **C-148m. TVM** D: Waris Hussein. Elizabeth Taylor, Richard Burton, Carrie Nye, Barry Foster, Gabriele Ferzetti. Adequate examination of husband-wife relationship in limbo, in two sections: first, through eyes of husband arriving in Rome, then through eyes of wife who has new lover. Uneven script has embarrassing moments, good performances. Average.▼

Divorce—Italian Style (1962-Italian) **104m.** ***½ D: Pietro Germi. Marcello Mastroianni, Daniela Rocca, Stefania Sandrelli, Leopoldo Trieste. Marcello can't stomach wife Rocca, so he schemes to wed sexy young Sandrelli. Hilarious, flavorful comedy, which earned an Oscar for its story and screenplay. The twist ending adds a perfect—and most ironic—touch.

Divorce of Lady X, The (1938-British) **C-91m.** **½ D: Tim Whelan. Merle Oberon, Laurence Olivier, Binnie Barnes, Ralph Richardson, Morton Selten, J.H. Roberts. Cute but extremely dated screwball comedy with lawyer Olivier forced to share a hotel room with mischievous Oberon. He becomes convinced he's the cause of her

pending divorce—even though she's not married.▼

Divorce Wars: A Love Story (1982) **C-100m. TVM** D: Donald Wrye. Tom Selleck, Jane Curtin, Candy Azzara, Joan Bennett, Maggie Cooper, Charles Haid, Viveca Lindfors, Philip Sterling, Joe Regalbuto. High-powered divorce attorney finds trouble at home beyond him in this remarkably intelligent drama about a failing marriage. Script by Wrye and Linda Elstad. Above average.

Dixie (1943) **C-89m.** *** D: A. Edward Sutherland. Bing Crosby, Dorothy Lamour, Billy DeWolfe, Marjorie Reynolds, Lynne Overman, Raymond Walburn, Eddie Foy, Jr., Grant Mitchell. Atmosphere overshadows plot in this biography of pioneer minstrel Dan Emmett, who wrote title song; Bing also sings "Sunday, Monday or Always."

Dixie: Changing Habits (1983) **C-100m. TVM** D: George Englund. Suzanne Pleshette, Cloris Leachman, Kenneth McMillan, John Considine, Geraldine Fitzgerald, Judith Ivey. Amusing tale of a flamboyant New Orleans bordello madam (Pleshette) who clashes with the Mother Superior (Leachman) of a local convent where she is sent for rehabilitation after her establishment is shut down. Pungently written by actor Considine and directed by Leachman's husband (both their sons also participated). Above average.▼

Dixie Dynamite (1976) **C-89m.** *½ D: Lee Frost. Warren Oates, Christopher George, Jane Anne Johnstone, Kathy McHaley, Wes Bishop, Mark Miller, R. G. Armstrong, Stanley Adams. Johnstone and McHaley wreak havoc on town after they are dispossessed from their farm and their moonshiner father is killed by a trigger-happy deputy. Sound familiar?▼

D.O.A. (1950) **83m.** *** D: Rudolph Mate. Edmond O'Brien, Pamela Britton, Luther Adler, Beverly Campbell (Garland), Lynn Baggett, William Ching, Henry Hart, Neville Brand. Surprisingly well-done suspenser involving O'Brien trying to find out who has given him a slow-acting poison and why. Music by Dmitri Tiomkin; shot almost entirely on the streets of L.A. and San Francisco. Remade in 1969 (as COLOR ME DEAD) and 1988. Also shown in computer-colored version.▼

D.O.A. (1981) **C-93m.** *½ D: Lech Kowalski. Sex Pistols, Dead Boys, Rich Kids, Generation X, Terry and the Idiots, X-Ray Spec, Nancy Spungen. Crummy documentary rip-off about the infamous punk rock band Sex Pistols. Of interest only for footage of the pathetic, now deceased Sid Vicious and girlfriend Nancy Spungen.▼

D.O.A. (1988) **C-100m. BOMB** D: Rocky Morton, Annabel Jankel. Dennis Quaid,

Meg Ryan, Daniel Stern, Charlotte Rampling, Jane Kaczmarek, Christopher Neame, Jay Patterson. Noisy and needless remake of the *film noir* original, transplanted to academia. Quaid is a college professor fed a slow-acting toxin in a dispute over a prized fiction manuscript; Ryan is an innocent student helping him pursue his "killer." Badly overdirected by the *Max Headroom* creators; obvious red herrings abound.▼

Doberman Gang, The (1972) **C-87m.** **½ D: Byron Chudnow. Byron Mabe, Julie Parrish, Hal Reed, Simmy Bow, Jojo D'Amore. Trim low-budget heist movie about a crook's ingenious plan to use six dobermans to pull off bank job. Dogs steal not only the loot but the picture, and starred in two sequels.▼

Doc (1971) **C-96m.** ** D: Frank Perry. Stacy Keach, Harris Yulin, Faye Dunaway, Michael Witney, Denver John Collins, Dan Greenburg. Well-crafted but unpleasant anti-Western, telling the story of Wyatt Earp and Doc Holliday in revisionist terms. Script by Pete Hamill.

Dock Brief, The (1962-British) **88m.** **½ D: James Hill. Peter Sellers, Richard Attenborough, Beryl Reid, David Lodge. Sellers is aging barrister who incompetently represents accused killer Attenborough with strange results; pleasant comic satire. Original U.S. title: TRIAL AND ERROR.

Docks of New Orleans (1948) **64m.** D: Derwin Abrahams. Roland Winters, Victor Sen Yung, Mantan Moreland, John Gallaudet, Virginia Dale. SEE: **Charlie Chan** series.

Docks of New York (1928) **76m.** **** D: Josef von Sternberg. George Bancroft, Betty Compson, Olga Baclanova, Mitchell Lewis, Clyde Cook, Gustav von Seyffertitz. Burly ship stoker Bancroft marries the attempted suicide victim he saved from the drink, first taking her for granted, then coming to love her. A rival to SUNRISE as the visual apogee of silent cinema, though the smoky hues of Sternberg's waterfront dive can fully be appreciated only on the big screen. Gaylord Carter's organ score on the videocassette version is a big plus. ▼

Docks of New York (1945) **61m.** D: Wallace Fox. Leo Gorcey, Huntz Hall, Billy Benedict, Gloria Pope, Carlyle Blackwell, Jr., Bud Gorman, George Meeker. SEE: **Bowery Boys** series.

Doc Savage: The Man of Bronze (1975) **C-100m.** **½ D: Michael Anderson. Ron Ely, Darrell Zwerling, Michael Miller, Pamela Hensley, Paul Wexler, Robyn Hilton, William Lucking, Paul Gleason, Eldon Quick, Janice Heiden. Film debut of Kenneth Robeson's pulp hero was sold (and accepted) as camp; in reality, it's a straight-faced period adventure that just came out at the wrong time. Story has Doc and his

Fabulous Five heading to South America to investigate his father's death, tangling with evil Captain Seas (Wexler). Fun for kids and buffs, with amusing score built around Sousa marches; final film of producer George Pal.▼

Doctor and the Devils, The (1985) **C-93m.** ** D: Freddie Francis. Timothy Dalton, Jonathan Pryce, Twiggy, Julian Sands, Stephen Rea. Serious-minded but unsuccessful (and unappealing) Gothic tale of grave robbers who supply a dedicated doctor who's content not to ask too many questions about their sources. Based on a 1940s screenplay by Dylan Thomas, revised by Ronald Harwood. Reminiscent of vintage Hammer horror films; no coincidence, with veteran Francis directing. Made in England.▼

Doctor and the Girl, The (1949) **98m.** **½ D: Curtis Bernhardt. Glenn Ford, Charles Coburn, Gloria DeHaven, Janet Leigh, Warner Anderson, Nancy Davis (Reagan). Ford is appropriately sterile as idealistic young doctor who married poor girl and practices medicine in slum area of N.Y.C.

Doctor at Large (1957-British) **C-98m.** **½ D: Ralph Thomas. Dirk Bogarde, Muriel Pavlow, Donald Sinden, James Robertson Justice, Shirley Eaton, Derek Farr, Michael Medwin, George Coulouris, Anne Heywood, Lionel Jeffries, Mervyn Johns, Ernest Thesiger. Another entry in pleasing series, with novice doctor Bogarde seeking staff position in wealthy hospital.▼

Doctor At Sea (1955-British) **C-93m.** **½ D: Ralph Thomas. Dirk Bogarde, Brigitte Bardot, Brenda de Banzie, James Robertson Justice, Maurice Denham, Michael Medwin, Raymond Huntley. Preferring the bachelor life, Bogarde signs on as ship's doctor on passenger-carrying freighter, in second entry of this entertaining series.▼

Doctor Blood's Coffin (1961-British) **C-92m.** **½ D: Sidney Furie. Kieron Moore, Hazel Court, Ian Hunter, Fred Johnson. Capable cast in well-paced chiller set in lonely village where people are being used for mysterious scientific experiments.▼

Doctor Death, Seeker of Souls (1973) **C-73m.** *½ D: Eddie Saeta. John Considine, Barry Coe, Cheryl Miller, Florence Marly, Jo Morrow. Cheap horror item about the transferring of souls by 1,000-year-old Considine. Few effective moments include The Three Stooges' Moe Howard in a gag bit.▼

Doctor Detroit (1983) **C-89m.** ** D: Michael Pressman. Dan Aykroyd, Howard Hesseman, T. K. Carter, Donna Dixon, Lynn Whitfield, Lydia Lei, Fran Drescher, Kate Murtagh, George Furth, Andrew Duggan, James Brown. Wimpy college professor becomes embroiled with pimps, prostitutes, and underworld intrigue, but the results are surprisingly bland, and only sporadically funny. Story by Bruce Jay Friedman. Aykroyd later married costar Dixon.▼

Doctor Dolittle (1967) C-144m. *½ D: Richard Fleischer, Rex Harrison, Samantha Eggar, Anthony Newley, Richard Attenborough, Peter Bull, Geoffrey Holder. Robert Surtees' photography is great, and that's it for this colossal musical dud that almost ruined its studio. The charm of Hugh Lofting's stories is gone. One merit: if you have unruly children, it may put them to sleep. Songs by Leslie Bricusse (including the Oscar-winning "Talk to the Animals") and choreography by Herbert Ross. This also earned an Academy Award for its special visual effects. Originally 152m.▼

Doctor Franken (1980) C-100m. TVM D: Marvin J. Chomsky. Robert Vaughn, Robert Perrault, David Selby, Teri Garr, Josef Sommer, Cynthia Harris. Contemporary rehash of Mary Shelley's Frankenstein saga tells, in this prospective series pilot, how a single-minded New York surgeon rebuilds a shattered body from spare parts he acquires at work. And it's acted perfectly straight! Average.

Doctor from Seven Dials, The SEE: **Corridors of Blood**▼

Doctor In Clover (1965-British) C-101m. ** D: Ralph Thomas. Leslie Phillips, James Robertson Justice, Shirley Anne Field, John Fraser, Joan Sims. New doctor, same old zany situations in sixth entry of series. Doctor studies nurses more than medicine. Not up to the others' standard.

Doctor In Distress (1963-British) C-102m. **½ D: Ralph Thomas. Dirk Bogarde, Samantha Eggar, James Robertson Justice, Mylene Demongeot, Donald Houston, Barbara Murray, Dennis Price, Leo McKern. Pompous chief surgeon falls in love for the first time, and his assistant tries to help the romance along while balancing his own love life. Another entertaining entry in comedy series. Bogarde's last appearance as Dr. Sparrow.▼

Doctor In Love (1960-British) C-93m. ** D: Ralph Thomas. Michael Craig, James Robertson Justice, Virginia Maskell, Carole Lesley, Leslie Phillips, Liz Fraser. Craig inherited Bogarde's role in DOCTOR series. This entry centers on young medic's inability to avoid romantic attachments.

Doctor in the House (1954-British) C-92m. ***½ D: Ralph Thomas. Dirk Bogarde, Muriel Pavlow, Kenneth More, Donald Sinden, Kay Kendall, James Robertson Justice, Donald Houston, Suzanne Cloutier, Geoffrey Keen, George Coulouris, Shirley Eaton, Joan Hickson, Richard Wattis. Hilarious comedy follows exploits of medical students intent on studying beautiful women and how to become wealthy physi-

cians. This delightful film (from Richard Gordon's stories) spawned six other "Doctor" movies, plus a TV series. Justice memorable as Sir Lancelot Spratt. Scripted by Gordon, Ronald Wilkenson, and costar Nicholas Phipps.▼

Doctor in Trouble (1970-British) C-90m. ** D: Ralph Thomas. Leslie Phillips, Harry Secombe, James Robertson Justice, Angela Scoular, Irene Handl, Robert Morley. Fair entry in the on-and-off British comedy series concerns Dr. Phillips' problems when he stows away on ocean liner; good supporting cast help a bit.▼

Doctor Satan's Robot (1940) 100m. **½ D: William Witney, John English. Edward (Eduardo) Ciannelli, Robert Wilcox, William Newell, Ella Neal, C. Montague Shaw. Ciannelli as mad Doctor Satan gives this Republic cliff-hanger a zingy flair, with Wilcox et al. battling the seemingly invincible robot who can even do a doubletake. Reedited from serial MYSTERIOUS DR. SATAN.▼

Doctor's Dilemma (1958-British) C-99m. *** D: Anthony Asquith. Leslie Caron, Dirk Bogarde, Alastair Sim, Robert Morley. Bubbly Shaw period play of young wife Caron conniving to convince medical specialists that her scoundrel husband is worth saving.

Doctors' Private Lives (1978) C-100m. TVM D: Steven Hilliard Stern. John Gavin, Donna Mills, Ed Nelson, Barbara Andersc·ı, Bettye Ackerman, John Randolph. Sudsy drama about the medical profession which spawned the mercifully brief (fourshow) hospital-based series in the spring of 1979. Average.

Doctor's Story, A (1984) C-100m. TVM D: Peter Levin. Howard E. Rollins, Jr., Art Carney, Charles Kimbrough, Viveca Lindfors, Uta Hagen, Jodi Thelen, Anna Maria Horsford. Young physician jeopardizes his marriage as well as his career by championing the rights of his geriatric patients. A prospective series pilot sparked by sturdy Rollins and veterans Carney, Lindfors, and Hagen (in a rare TV performance). Written by Ronald Rubin. Above average.

Doctors' Wives (1971) C-100m. *½ D: George Schaefer. Dyan Cannon, Richard Crenna, Gene Hackman, Rachel Roberts, Carroll O'Connor, Janice Rule, Diana Sands, Cara Williams, Ralph Bellamy. Super-sudsy soaper sparked by mysterious murder of cheating wife; glossy garbage. Scripted by a slumming Daniel Taradash.▼

Doctor Takes a Wife, The (1940) 89m. *** D: Alexander Hall. Ray Milland, Loretta Young, Reginald Gardiner, Gail Patrick, Edmund Gwenn, Frank Sully, Gordon Jones. Milland is mistaken for Young's husband, then forced to pretend he is.

Stars and material spark each other at a lively pace.▼

Doctor X (1932) **C-80m.** ** D: Michael Curtiz. Lionel Atwill, Fay Wray, Lee Tracy, Preston Foster, Robert Warwick, Mae Busch. Police have tracked the "full-moon strangler" to Atwill's experimental laboratory. Ludicrous Grand Guignol chiller (Wray's entrance has her screaming—for no reason at all) is a must for horror-film buffs because of its Anton Grot sets, special Max Factor makeup, and rich use of two-color Technicolor (though most TV prints are b&w) . . . but it creaks *badly* and seems much longer than it is.▼

Doctor, You've Got to Be Kidding (1967) **C-94m.** BOMB D: Peter Tewksbury. Sandra Dee, George Hamilton, Celeste Holm, Bill Bixby, Dick Kallman, Mort Sahl, Dwayne Hickman, Allen Jenkins. Dee would rather marry the boss than pursue singing career. Even *her* singing might have helped this alleged comedy.

✓ **Doctor Zhivago** (1965) **C-180m.** *** D: David Lean. Omar Sharif, Julie Christie, Geraldine Chaplin, Rod Steiger, Alec Guinness, Ralph Richardson, Tom Courtenay, Rita Tushingham. Overlong and overeverything film version of Boris Pasternak novel is nevertheless one of the most popular movies ever; most of the cast seems non-Russian, but there are some stirring scenes, great exodus sequence on train, and unforgettable performance by Christie. Five Oscars include Robert Bolt's script, Maurice Jarre's music, Freddie Young's cinematography. Originally released at 197m.▼

Dodes'ka-den (1970-Japanese) **C-140m.** **½ D: Akira Kurosawa. Yoshitaka Zushi, Tomoko Yamazaki, Hiroshi Akutagawa, Noboru Mitani. Episodic chronicle of life in a Tokyo slum; characters include a little boy who feeds himself and derelict dad by scrounging garbage—together, they visualize a dream house; a wan girl who makes artificial flowers to support her alcoholic stepfather; etc. Originally 244m.▼

✓ **Dodge City** (1939) **C-105m.** *** D: Michael Curtiz. Errol Flynn, Olivia de Havilland, Ann Sheridan, Bruce Cabot, Frank McHugh, Alan Hale, John Litel, Victor Jory, Ward Bond, Cora Witherspoon. Errol tames the West and de Havilland in entertaining large-scale Western, with Warner Bros. stock company giving good vignettes, and near-definitive barroom brawl. The principal inspiration for BLAZING SADDLES.▼

✓ **Dodsworth** (1936) **101m.** **** D: William Wyler. Walter Huston, Ruth Chatterton, Paul Lukas, Mary Astor, David Niven, Gregory Gaye, Maria Ouspenskaya, Spring Byington, Grant Mitchell. Superb adaptation of Sinclair Lewis novel about middle-aged American industrialist who retires, goes to Europe, where he and his wife find new set of values, and new relationships. Intelligently written (by Sidney Howard), beautifully filmed, extremely well acted, with Huston recreating his Broadway role. John Payne (billed as John Howard Payne) makes screen debut in small role. Won an Oscar for Interior Decoration (Richard Day). An unusually mature Hollywood film, not to be missed.▼

Dog, a Mouse and a Sputnik, A SEE: **Sputnik**▼

Dog and Cat (1977) **C-78m.** TVM D: Bob Kelljan. Lou Antonio, Kim Basinger, Matt Clark, Charles Cioffi, Richard Lynch, Dale Robinette, Dick Wesson. Flip streetwise detective and hip country girl he inherits as partner delve into porno business to nail kingpin. Offbeat characters and glib dialogue try to lift formula cop show out of the ordinary; pilot for the series. Created and co-written by Walter Hill. Average.▼

Dog Day (1983-French) **C-101m.** **½ D: Yves Boisset. Miou Miou, Lee Marvin, Jean Carmet, Victor Lanoux, David Bennent, Bernadette Lafont, Jean-Pierre Kalfon, Pierre Clementi, Tina Louise. Intriguing if gratuitously violent thriller about a tough but doomed American gangster on the lam (Marvin, well cast) who hides out on the farm of a depraved French family. Fairly effective as an ode to the mythical image of the American screen hood.▼

Dog Day Afternoon (1975) **C-130m.** ***½ D: Sidney Lumet. Al Pacino, John Cazale, Charles Durning, James Broderick, Chris Sarandon, Sully Boyar, Penny Allen, Carol Kane, Lance Henriksen, Dick Anthony Williams, Philip Charles Mackenzie. Incredible-but-true story of a loser (Pacino) who holds up a Brooklyn bank to raise money for his lover's sex-change operation, and sees simple heist snowball into a citywide incident. Pacino's performance and Lumet's flavorful N.Y.C. atmosphere obscure the fact that this is much ado about nothing. Frank Pierson won an Oscar for his screenplay (based on an article by P.F. Kluge and Thomas Moore).▼

Dog Eat Dog (1964-U.S.-Italian-German) **84m.** BOMB D: Gustav Gavrin. Cameron Mitchell, Jayne Mansfield, Dody Heath, Ivor Salter, Isa Miranda, Werner Peters, Pinkas Braun. Low-level, unintentionally funny potboiler of lust, greed, and depravity, with various characters intent upon making off with a stolen million dollars. A highlight: Jayne's constant complaining about her need for clean panties. Not released in the U.S. until 1966; various sources list Albert Zugsmith and Ray Nazarro as director.▼

Dog of Flanders, A (1959) **C-96m.** ** D: James B. Clark. David Ladd, Donald Crisp, Theodore Bikel, Max Croiset, Monique

Ahrens. Tear-jerker for children about a boy, his dog, and friends they make. Crisp and Bikel have good character roles.▼

Dogpound Shuffle (1975-Canadian) **C-95m.** *** D: Jeffrey Bloom. Ron Moody, David Soul, Pamela McMyler, Ray Stricklyn, Raymond Sutton. Unpretentious little fable about cynical ex-vaudevillian tap-dancer—now a bum—who must raise $30 to rescue his dog from the pound. Funny and wistful, with excellent character performance by Moody. Also known as SPOT.▼

Dogs (1976) **C-90m.** *½ D: Burt Brinckerhoff. David McCallum, George Wyner, Eric Server, Sandra McCabe, Sterling Swanson. Low-budget yawner about a pack of dogs on the prowl. Get out the flea powder.

Dogs in Space (1986-Australian) **C-105m.** BOMB D: Richard Lowenstein. Michael Hutchence, Saskia Post, Nique Needles, Deanna Bond, Chris Haywood. Noisy film from down under tries to encapsule the punk era of the late 1970s but merely becomes a tiresome slice-of-life peek at wayward youth. Title refers to the epochal effect of early space flights, including the Russian missions with dogs.▼

Dogs of War, The (1980-British) **C-102m.** *** D: John Irvin. Christopher Walken, Tom Berenger, Colin Blakely, Hugh Millais, Paul Freeman, JoBeth Williams. Appropriately mean if overly somber adaptation of the Frederick Forsyth best-seller about a mercenary who tangles with an Amin-like dictator in an African hellhole. Will not promote one-worldism, but Walken takes a screen beating nearly as impressively as Brando. British running time 118m.▼

Dog Soldiers SEE: **Who'll Stop the Rain**▼

Doing Life (1986) **C-100m.** TVM D: Gene Reynolds. Tony Danza, Jon DeVries, Alvin Epstein, Lisa Langlois, Rocco Sisto, Dawn Greenhalgh. Prison drama "inspired" by the real-life story of Jerry Rosenberg, convicted killer who beat the electric chair and became the nation's first jailhouse lawyer, eventually becoming the prisoners' spokesman during the Attica uprising. Adapted by Steve Bello from his book. Above average.

Doing Time (1979-British) **C-95m.** **½ D: Dick Clement. Ronnie Barker, Richard Beckinsale, Fulton Mackay, Brian Wilde, Peter Vaughan. Barker is a delight as a habitual prison inmate who inadvertently escapes—and wants back in! Reportedly not as funny as the TV series on which it's based, but that's usually the case with feature spinoffs. (The show was tried on American TV as *On the Rocks.*) Original British title: PORRIDGE.

Doin' Time (1985) **C-77m.** BOMB D: George Mendeluk. Jeff Altman, Dey Young, Richard Mulligan, John Vernon, Colleen Camp, Melanie Chartoff, Graham Jarvis, Pat McCormick, Eddie Velez, Jimmie Walker, Judy Landers, Mike Mazurki, Muhammad Ali. Shoddy, thoroughly obnoxious POLICE ACADEMY clone, set in the John Dillinger Memorial Penitentiary (yuk, yuk).▼

Doin' Time on Planet Earth (1988) **C-83m.** **½ D: Charles Matthau. Nicholas Strouse, Andrea Thompson, Hugh Gillin, Adam West, Candice Azzara, Hugh O'Brian, Matt Adler, Timothy Patrick Murphy, Roddy McDowall, Maureen Stapleton. Fresh-feeling but thin teen comedy about boy who feels *literally* alienated from his family and their Holiday Inn home: cheerful wackos West and Azzara convince him that he's really an alien born on Earth, destined to lead others back to the stars. Amusingly designed, inventively directed (by son of Walter Matthau), but aimless. ▼

Dolemite (1975) **C-88m.** *½ D: D'Urville Martin. Rudy Ray Moore, Jerry Jones, Lady Reed. Occasionally funny but amateurish vehicle for standup comedian Moore (who also produced the film), a stout nonactor who combines the personality of Mr. T with a rhyming rap routine. Karate gangster spoof is set in the milieu of black nightclubs where Moore performs.▼

$(Dollars) (1972) **C-119m.** ***½ D: Richard Brooks. Warren Beatty, Goldie Hawn, Gert Frobe, Robert Webber, Scott Brady. Top-notch caper thriller set in Germany with unusual chase that goes on for more than a fifth of the film. Awfully similar to PERFECT FRIDAY. Bouncy Quincy Jones score.▼

Doll Face (1945) **80m.** **½ D: Lewis Seiler. Vivian Blaine, Dennis O'Keefe, Perry Como, Carmen Miranda, Martha Stewart, Michael Dunne. Burlesque dancer Blaine makes good in the big time; pleasant musical with Como's hit "Hubba Hubba Hubba."▼

Dollmaker, The (1984) **C-150m.** TVM D: Daniel Petrie. Jane Fonda, Levon Helm, Amanda Plummer, Susan Kingsley, Geraldine Page. Fonda's glowing, Emmy-winning TV-movie debut, as a woman from the Kentucky hills who uproots her kids to follow her husband to a big-city job during WW2 and finds a new way of life using her natural whittling talents. Susan Cooper and Hume Cronyn (who wrote Broadway's *Foxfire* together) beautifully adapted Harriette Arnow's novel. Above average.▼

Dolls (1987) **C-77m.** ** D: Stuart Gordon. Ian Patrick Williams, Carolyn Purdy-Gordon, Carrie Lorraine, Guy Rolfe, Hilary Mason, Bunty Bailey, Cassie Stuart, Stephen Lee. OK horror from the director of RE-ANIMATOR has unsuspecting people

[302]

taking shelter from a storm in mansion owned by elderly couple who make murderous dolls. Nothing special here.▼

Doll's House, A (1973-British) **C-106m.** **½ D: Patrick Garland. Claire Bloom, Anthony Hopkins, Ralph Richardson, Denholm Elliott, Anna Massey, Edith Evans. Bloom and Hopkins give thoughtful performances in this rather stagy filmization of Ibsen's play. Still, the words are there and the play is a strong statement about women's (and all people's) rights to be human beings.▼

Doll's House, A (1973-British) **C-103m.** **½ D: Joseph Losey. Jane Fonda, David Warner, Trevor Howard, Delphine Seyrig, Edward Fox. Moderately successful, cinematic version of Ibsen play, worth a look for Fonda's controversial interpretation of a 19th-century liberated woman. Howard shines as the dying Dr. Rank.▼

Doll Squad, The (1973) **C-101m.** BOMB D: Ted V. Mikels. Michael Ansara, Francine York, Anthony Eisley, John Carter, Rafael Campos, Lisa Todd. Sexy York leads her all-female team against ex-CIA agent Ansara, out to rule the world. Poorly made and boring, with very little action. Interesting only as a forerunner to *Charlie's Angels*, with three girls who are sent on various missions; the smart one's even named Sabrina! Also known as HUSTLER SQUAD.▼

Dolly Sisters, The (1945) **C-114m.** **½ D: Irving Cummings. Betty Grable, John Payne, June Haver, S. Z. Sakall, Reginald Gardiner, Frank Latimore. Sassy hokum about popular vaudeville sister act with two lovely stars and a bevy of old song favorites, plus newly written "I Can't Begin to Tell You."

Dominick and Eugene (1988) **C-111m.** *** D: Robert M. Young. Tom Hulce, Ray Liotta, Jamie Lee Curtis, Todd Graff, Mimi Cecchini, Robert Levine, Bill Cobbs, David Strathairn. Heartrending story of a bright young intern (Liotta) and his devotion to a childlike twin brother (Hulce) who needs looking after. An overtly sentimental, sometimes melodramatic, but completely affecting story of love, compassion and responsibility. Hulce's performance as the sweet-natured, slow-witted Dominick is superb.▼

Dominique (1978-British) **C-100m.** ** D: Michael Anderson. Cliff Robertson, Jean Simmons, Jenny Agutter, Simon Ward, Ron Moody, Judy Geeson, Michael Jayston, Flora Robson, David Tomlinson, Jack Warner. Great cast tries its best in disappointing melodrama; crippled Simmons believes husband Robertson wants to drive her mad; she dies, but comes back to haunt him. Retitled DOMINIQUE IS DEAD.▼

Dominique Is Dead SEE: **Dominique**▼
Domino Kid, The (1957) **73m.** *½ D:

Ray Nazarro. Rory Calhoun, Kristine Miller, Andrew Duggan, Roy Barcroft. Revenge-oater with Calhoun returning to Lone Star State to seek killers of his family.

Domino Principle, The (1977) **C-97m.** BOMB D: Stanley Kramer. Gene Hackman, Candice Bergen, Richard Widmark, Mickey Rooney, Edward Albert, Eli Wallach. Muddled thriller about lunkhead Hackman's recruitment by a mysterious organization bent on political assassination. Bergen fails to convince as a lower-middle-class housewife.▼

Dona Flor and Her Two Husbands (1978-Brazilian) **C-106m.** ***½ D: Bruno Barreto. Sonia Braga, Jose Wilker, Mauro Mendoca, Dinorah Brillanti. Braga is torn between giving body and soul to the dead, irresponsible husband who keeps returning to earth, or to the considerate dullard who's become her new mate. Original fantasy is extremely sexy, with some of Braga's best scenes likely to be trimmed for noncable showings. Remade as KISS ME GOODBYE.▼

Dondi (1961) **100m.** BOMB D: Albert Zugsmith. David Janssen, Patti Page, David Kory, Walter Winchell, Gale Gordon. Adaptation of sentimental comic strip. Watch this film and you'll know why Janssen became a fugitive!

Don Is Dead, The (1973) **C-115m.** *½ D: Richard Fleischer. Anthony Quinn, Frederic Forrest, Robert Forster, Al Lettieri, Angel Tompkins, Ina Balin. Wars among Mafia families and heirs apparent to Mr. Big form the convoluted plot of this trashy, derivative gangster saga. Retitled BEAUTIFUL BUT DEADLY.▼

Don Juan (1926) **111m.** *** D: Alan Crosland. John Barrymore, Mary Astor, Willard Louis, Estelle Taylor, Helene Costello, Warner Oland, Montagu Love, Myrna Loy, Hedda Hopper. Entertaining swashbuckler, with Barrymore at his amorous best, surrounded by a top cast (including Oland as Cesare Borgia and Taylor as the infamous Lucretia) and lavish settings. Notable as the first silent film released with Vitaphone music and sound effects.

Don Juan Quilligan (1945) **75m.** **½ D: Frank Tuttle. William Bendix, Joan Blondell, Phil Silvers, Anne Revere, B. S. Pully, Mary Treen. Through mishap Bendix is married to two girls at same time; lightweight comedy.

Donkey Skin (1971-French) **C-90m.** *** D: Jacques Demy. Catherine Deneuve, Jacques Perrin, Jean Marais, Delphine Seyrig. Charming adaptation of Charles Perrault's fairy tale about widowed King who vows that his new Queen must be as beautiful as his first. Sumptuous color production, witty script by Demy.▼

Donner Pass: The Road to Survival (1978) **C-100m.** TVM D: James L. Conway.

Robert Fuller, Andrew Prine, Michael Callan, Diane McBain, John Anderson, John Doucette. "Classics Illustrated" version of the true-life travails of a wagon train of pioneers who were snowbound on their westward trek and forced to turn to cannibalism. Family adventure despite the grim underlying theme. Average.▼

Do Not Disturb (1965) **C-102m.** **½ D: Ralph Levy. Doris Day, Rod Taylor, Hermione Baddeley, Sergio Fantoni, Reginald Gardiner, Mike Romanoff, Leon Askin. Mild Day vehicle with Taylor as executive husband who brings her to suburban England. She meets suave Fantoni, enraging jealous hubby. Not up to her earlier fashion romps.

Do Not Fold, Spindle, or Mutilate (1971) **C-71m. TVM** D: Ted Post. Helen Hayes, Myrna Loy, Mildred Natwick, Sylvia Sydney, Vince Edwards, John Beradino. Four elderly ladies, practical-joke enthusiasts, create mythical girl for computer dating questionnaire, thirst for even more bizarre thrills. Way in which prank turns frightening could've been handled far, far better; otherwise, good performances. Average.

Donovan's Brain (1953) **83m.** *** D: Felix Feist. Lew Ayres, Gene Evans, Nancy Davis (Reagan), Steve Brodie. Scientist Ayres is overtaken by brain of dead industrialist which he has kept alive in his laboratory; intriguing story, modest but capable production. Story by Curt Siodmak filmed before as THE LADY AND THE MONSTER, and again as THE BRAIN.▼

Donovan's Reef (1963) **C-109m.** *** D: John Ford. John Wayne, Lee Marvin, Elizabeth Allen, Jack Warden, Cesar Romero, Dorothy Lamour, Mike Mazurki. Action-comedy bounces along with a good cast. Wayne and his freewheeling friends on a Pacific island are disrupted by Warden's grown daughter (Allen) who comes to visit. Lots of fun.▼

Don Quixote (1973) **C-107m.** *** D: Rudolf Nureyev, Robert Helpmann. Nureyev, Helpmann, Lucette Aldous, Australian Ballet. Fine ballet version of Cervantes' classic, choreographed by Nureyev, who plays barber Basilio; Helpmann is the wandering knight. Not just for ballet buffs.▼

Don's Party (1976-Australian) **C-91m.** ***½ D: Bruce Beresford. John Hargreaves, Pat Bishop, Graham Kennedy, Veronica Lang, Candy Raymond, Harold Hopkins. Powerful black comedy chronicling the interaction—sexual and otherwise—among a group of young suburbanites who get together to watch election returns. (Important note: In Australia, the "liberals" are actually the conservative party.) Stunning direction, top performances by all; biting script by David Williamson, from his play.▼

Don't Answer the Phone (1980) **C-94m.**

BOMB D: Robert Hammer. James Westmoreland, Flo Gerrish, Ben Frank, Nicholas Worth, Stan Haze. Another sadistic killer who's a Vietnam veteran. Don't watch this movie.▼

Don't Be Afraid of the Dark (1973) **C-74m. TVM** D: John Newland. Kim Darby, Jim Hutton, Pedro Armendariz, Jr., Barbara Anderson, William Demarest, Lesley Woods, Robert Cleaves. Young couple (Darby and Hutton) inherit strange house occupied by small creatures out to possess wife. Decent premise ruined by indifferent script, situations. Average.▼

Don't Bother to Knock (1952) **76m.** **½ D: Roy (Ward) Baker. Richard Widmark, Marilyn Monroe, Anne Bancroft, Jeanne Cagney, Elisha Cook, Jr., Gloria Blondell. Title has more punch than improbable yarn of mentally disturbed Monroe hired as babysitter in large hotel, saved from killing herself and charge by tough-but-good Widmark. Bancroft's film debut.

Don't Cry, It's Only Thunder (1982) **C-108m.** *** D: Peter Werner. Dennis Christopher, Susan Saint James, Roger Aaron Brown, Lisa Lu, Thu Thuy, James Whitmore, Jr. Dramatically uneven, but still moving account of G.I. Christopher and doctor Saint James' involvement with makeshift orphanage in Vietnam. Based on a true incident.▼

Don't Drink the Water (1969) **C-100m.** ** D: Howard Morris. Jackie Gleason, Estelle Parsons, Ted Bessell, Joan Delaney, Michael Constantine, Howard St. John, Avery Schreiber. Uninspired adaptation of Woody Allen play about American family held prisoner in Iron Curtain country of Vulgaria, and their desperate attempts to escape. Cast works hard, with sporadic results.▼

Don't Give Up the Ship (1959) **89m.** *** D: Norman Taurog. Jerry Lewis, Dina Merrill, Diana Spencer, Mickey Shaughnessy, Robert Middleton, Gale Gordon, Claude Akins. Top comedy with Jerry as an ensign who lost a battleship during war and doesn't remember how. Shaughnessy is pal who helps look for it underwater. One of Lewis' all-time best.

Don't Go in the House (1980) **C-82m.** BOMB D: Joseph Ellison. Dan Grimaldi, Robert Osth, Ruth Dardick, Charlie Bonet, Bill Ricci. Pyromaniac Grimaldi leads willing young women to their fiery deaths. Lurid junk.▼

Don't Go Near the Water (1957) **C-102m.** *½ D: Charles Walters. Glenn Ford, Gia Scala, Anne Francis, Fred Clark, Eva Gabor. Submerged comedy of sailors in the South Pacific of WW2 building a recreation hall. Clark, as a frustrated officer, is best thing in slow film.

Don't Go to Sleep (1982) **C-100m. TVM** D: Richard Lang. Dennis Weaver, Valerie

Harper, Ruth Gordon, Robert Webber, Claudette Nevins, Robin Ignacio, Kristin Cummings. Ned Wynn (Keenan's son) wrote this very effective shocker about a dead daughter reaching from the grave to take her family with her one by one. Above average.

Don't Just Stand There (1968) C-100m. **½ D: Ron Winston. Robert Wagner, Mary Tyler Moore, Harvey Korman, Glynis Johns, Barbara Rhoades. Frantic comedy with perky stars; Wagner and Moore try to unravel mystery of disappearance of authoress Johns after writing the first half of a new book. Players' vivacity makes script seem better than it is.

Don't Knock the Rock (1956) 84m. ** D: Fred F. Sears. Bill Haley and His Comets, Alan Freed, Little Richard, Alan Dale, The Treniers, Patricia Hardy. Rock 'n' roll star Dale returns to his hometown, encounters adult hostility. Of course, the elders are cheering the rockers by the finale. Little Richard sings "Long Tall Sally" and "Tutti Frutti."

Don't Knock the Twist (1962) 87m. BOMB D: Oscar Rudolph. Chubby Checker, Gene Chandler, Vic Dana, Linda Scott, Mari Blanchard, Lang Jeffries. The Dovells. Television producer Jeffries, with Checker's assistance, coordinates a twist show. Chandler, with cape, monocle and top hat, sings "Duke of Earl"; otherwise, you may want to twist your way to your TV set and turn the dial.

Dont Look Back (1967) 96m. ***½ D: D. A. Pennebaker. Bob Dylan, Joan Baez, Donovan, Alan Price, Albert Grossman, Allen Ginsberg. Candid documentary about Dylan's '65 concert tour of England, highlighted by his pseudo-hip personality, appearances by Baez and Grossman (Dylan's manager). Dylan performs "The Times They Are a Changin'," "Don't Think Twice, It's All Right," "It's All Over Now, Baby Blue," and "Subterranean Homesick Blues."▼

Don't Look Back: The Story of Leroy "Satchel" Paige (1981) C-98m. TVM D: Richard A. Colla. Louis Gossett, Jr., Beverly Todd, Cleavon Little, Ernie Barnes, Clifton Davis, John Beradino, Jim Davis, Ossie Davis, Hal Williams. The whitewashed story of legendary baseball star Paige, adapted from his book, *Maybe I'll Pitch Forever*. Colla replaced George C. Scott as director. Average.▼

Don't Look in the Basement (1973) C-95m. *½ D: S. F. Brownrigg. William McGee, Annie MacAdams, Rosie Holotik, Gene Ross, Jessie Lee Fulton, Camilla Carr. Amateurish horror thriller about inmates of secluded Florida insane asylum who contrive a bloody takeover.▼

Don't Look Now (1973-British) C-110m. *** D: Nicolas Roeg. Julie Christie, Donald Sutherland, Hilary Mason, Clelia Matania, Massimo Serato. Arty, overindulgent but gripping Daphne du Maurier occult thriller about parents of drowned child and their horror-laden visit to Venice; highlighted by memorably steamy love scene and violent climax.▼

Don't Make Waves (1967) C-97m. *** D: Alexander Mackendrick. Tony Curtis, Claudia Cardinale, Sharon Tate, Robert Webber, Mort Sahl, Jim Backus, Edgar Bergen. The one gem out of nine million bad Tony Curtis comedy vehicles; satire on Southern California has good direction, funny performance by Sharon Tate, and a catchy title song sung by the Byrds. Good fun.

Don't Push, I'll Charge When I'm Ready (1977) C-100m. TVM D: Nathaniel Lande. Enzo Cerusico, Sue Lyon, Cesar Romero, Dwayne Hickman, Jerry Colonna, Edward Andrews, Soupy Sales. Acceptable WW2 comedy has Italian P.O.W. in America drafted into Army. Filmed in 1969. Average.

Don't Raise the Bridge, Lower the River (1968) C-99m. ** D: Jerry Paris. Jerry Lewis, Terry-Thomas, Jacqueline Pearce, Bernard Cribbins, Patricia Routledge. Jerry plays American in England whose get-rich-quick schemes have put him on verge of divorce; mild Lewis comedy scripted by Max Wilk, from his novel.▼

Don't Take It to Heart (1945-British) 89m. *** D: Jeffrey Dell. Richard Greene, Patricia Medina, Richard Bird, Wylie Watson, Ernest Thesiger, Ronald Squire. Pleasant romantic comedy of ghost-ridden castle; Greene helps Medina and her townfolk overcome avaricious landowner.

Don't Touch the Loot SEE: **Grisbi**

Don't Trust Your Husband SEE: **Innocent Affair, An**

Don't Turn the Other Cheek (1973-Italian) C-93m. **½ D: Duccio Tessari. Franco Nero, Lynn Redgrave, Eli Wallach, Marilu Tolo, Horst Janson. Slapstick spaghetti Western detailing exploits of unlikely trio; a fiery, revolution-fomenting Irish journalist (Redgrave), a bogus Russian prince (Nero), and a seedy Mexican bandit (Wallach) with proverbial heart of gold.▼

Don't Worry, We'll Think of a Title (1966) 83m. BOMB D: Harmon Jones. Morey Amsterdam, Rose Marie, Joey Adams, Danny Thomas, Milton Berle, Nick Adams. Grade-Z shambles, despite many guest cameos by big TV and movie stars. Start worrying when you turn it on.

Doolins of Oklahoma, The (1949) 90m. **½ D: Gordon Douglas. Randolph Scott, George Macready, Louise Allbritton, John Ireland. Action-packed Western with Scott as head of the Doolin gang, who decides to give up his life of crime.

Doomed to Die (1940) 57m. *½ D: William Nigh. Boris Karloff, Grant Withers, Marjorie Reynolds, Melvin Lang, Guy

Usher. Fifth entry in the Mr. Wong series, with the detective on the trail of a shipping tycoon's killer and uncovering the whereabouts of some missing contraband bonds.▼

Doomsday Flight, The (1966) C-100m. TVM D: William Graham. Jack Lord, Edmond O'Brien, Van Johnson, Katherine Crawford, John Saxon, Michael Sarrazin, Edward Asner, Greg Morris, Richard Carlson, Don Stewart. Occasional suspense in Rod Serling-scripted story of madman (O'Brien) blackmailing airline, planting altitude activated bomb. As a thriller, pretty good; otherwise, characterization and dialogue clichéd. Notable for number of copycat bomb threats it allegedly inspired. Average.▼

Doomsday Machine, The (1972) C-88m. BOMB D: Lee Sholem, Harry Hope. Denny Miller, Mala Powers, Bobby Van, Ruta Lee, Grant Williams, Henry Wilcoxon. Tired cast in lumpy, stultifyingly boring melodrama about scientists on a space voyage who are constantly bickering.

Doomwatch (1972-British) C-92m. *** D: Peter Sasdy. Ian Bannen, Judy Geeson, George Sanders, John Paul, Simon Oates, Geoffrey Keen. Dr. Bannen investigates the effects of radioactivity on an island inhabited by a rather odd-acting population. Topical, thought-provoking mystery-thriller, not at all bad of its type. Based on the British TV series of the same name.▼

Door-to-Door Maniac (1961) 80m. *½ D: Bill Karn. Johnny Cash, Donald Woods, Cay Forrester, Pamela Mason, Midge Ware, Victor Tayback, Ronny Howard, Merle Travis. Cash and Tayback plot a bank robbery. Of interest only for the cast; also known as FIVE MINUTES TO LIVE.▼

Doorway to Hell (1930) 78m. *½ D: Archie L. Mayo. Lew Ayres, Charles Judels, Dorothy Matthews, Leon Janney, Robert Elliott, James Cagney, Kenneth Thomson. Antique, early-talkie gangster saga with Ayres improbably cast as ruthless Chicago underworld biggie and Cagney (billed sixth, in his second film) as his henchman.

Door With Seven Locks, The (1962-German) 96m. **½ D: Alfred Vohrer. Eddie Arent, Heinz Drache, Klaus Kinski, Adi Berber, Sabina Sesselman. Bizarre account of man who leaves in his will seven keys to treasure vault, with expected friction and murder; from Edgar Wallace story made before as CHAMBER OF HORRORS.

Doppelganger SEE: **Journey to the Far Side of the Sun**▼

Dorian Gray (1970-Italian-German-Lichtensteinian) C-93m. *½ D: Massimo Dallamano. Helmut Berger, Richard Todd, Herbert Lom, Marie Liljedahl, Margaret Lee. Trashy, slow-moving filmization of Oscar Wilde's novel, updated to the present: vain, immoral young man (Berger) ceases to grow older, while his portrait ages instead.

THE PICTURE OF DORIAN GRAY, released 25 years earlier, is vastly superior. Also known as THE SECRET OF DORIAN GRAY.▼

Do the Right Thing (1989) C-120m. *** D: Spike Lee. Danny Aiello, Ossie Davis, Ruby Dee, Richard Edson, Giancarlo Esposito, Spike Lee, Bill Nunn, John Turturro, Paul Benjamin, John Savage. Idealized, individualistic look at life in the black community of Bedford-Stuyvesant in Brooklyn, where a white-owned pizza parlor flourishes . . . and where circumstance leads to an outbreak of hostilities on a sweltering summer day. Entertaining and provocative, with a much-discussed (and troubling) finale. Writer-director Lee also stars as Mookie, the delivery boy; his real-life sister Joie plays his sister in the film.▼

Double, The (1963-British) 56m. ** D: Lionel Harris. Jeannette Sterke, Alan MacNaughton, Robert Brown, Jane Griffiths. Meandering Edgar Wallace yarn. MacNaughton, suffering from amnesia, seeks to unravel his life, revealing espionage plot.

Double Agent (1987) C-100m. TVM D: Mike Vejar. Michael McKean, John Putch, Susan Walden, Lloyd Bochner, Alexa Hamilton. Disney comic caper involving twins—one a suave, womanizing spy, the other an unsophisticated married clod called on to fill his brother's shoes when he disappears. Average.

Double Bunk (1960-British) 92m. *½ D: C. M. Pennington-Richards. Ian Carmichael, Janette Scott, Sidney James, Liz Fraser. Slapstick account of Carmichael and Scott navigating their houseboat down the Thames, with predictable sight gags.

Double Con SEE: **Trick Baby**

Double Confession (1950-British) 86m. ** D: Ken Annakin. Derek Farr, Joan Hopkins, Peter Lorre, William Hartnell, Kathleen Harrison, Naunton Wayne. Murky melodrama at a seaside resort: an innocent man tries to set someone else up as a murder suspect in his wife's mysterious death, only to get involved with some real killers.

Double Cross (1941) 66m. *½ D: Albert Kelley. Kane Richmond, Pauline Moore, Wynne Gibson. Mild account of cop seeking to get the goods on criminal gang; nothing unusual.

Double Cross (1949-Italian) 77m. **½ D: Riccardo Freda. Vittorio Gassman, Amedeo Nazzari, Gianna Maria Canale. Acceptable account of two crooks who doublecross each other, with the victim seeking revenge years later.

Double Cross (1956-British) 71m. ** D: Anthony Squire. Donald Houston, Fay Compton, Anton Diffring, Delphi Lawrence. Mild account of foreign agents involved in typical espionage plot to steal government secrets.

Double Crossbones (1951) **C-75m.** ** D: Charles Barton. Donald O'Connor, Helena Carter, Will Geer, Hope Emerson, Glenn Strange. O'Connor is would-be buccaneer who seeks to win his sweetheart and expose crooked city official. Light satire which doesn't quite come off.

Double Deal (1984-Australian) **C-90m.** *½ D: Brian Kavanagh. Louis Jourdan, Angela Punch-McGregor, Diana Craig, Warwick Comber, Peter Cummins. Idiotic drama about bored, married fashion model-designer Punch-McGregor who takes up with drifter Comber. Filmed in 1981.

Double Dynamite (1951) **80m.** ** D: Irving Cummings, Jr. Frank Sinatra, Jane Russell, Groucho Marx, Don McGuire. Star trio were at career low points when flat comedy was made; Sinatra is bank clerk accused of theft.▼

Double Exposure (1944) **63m.** ** D: William Berke. Chester Morris, Nancy Kelly, Jane Farrar, Richard Gaines. Fairly entertaining saga of girl who unwittingly takes photograph of murder.

✓ **Double Indemnity** (1944) **106m.** **** D: Billy Wilder. Barbara Stanwyck, Fred MacMurray, Edward G. Robinson, Porter Hall, Fortunio Bonanova, Jean Heather. Wilder-Raymond Chandler script (from the James M. Cain novel) packs fireworks in account of insurance salesman MacMurray coerced into murder plot by alluring Stanwyck and subsequent investigation by Fred's colleague Robinson. An American movie classic, with crackling dialogue throughout. Remade for TV, and the obvious inspiration for Lawrence Kasdan's BODY HEAT.▼

Double Indemnity (1973) **C-73m. TVM** D: Jack Smight. Richard Crenna, Lee J. Cobb, Samantha Eggar, Kathleen Cody, Arch Johnson, John Fiedler, Robert Webber. Remake of 1944 version with Eggar seducing insurance investigator Crenna into husband-murdering scheme. Follows original almost shot-for-shot, but overall effect is lifeless, unconvincing. Average.

Double Life, A (1947) **104m.** ***½ D: George Cukor. Ronald Colman, Signe Hasso, Edmond O'Brien, Shelley Winters, Ray Collins, Millard Mitchell. Colman gives a bravura, Oscar-winning performance as an actor whose stage roles spill over into his life—and now he's about to play Othello. Brilliant melodrama by Ruth Gordon and Garson Kanin, with wonderful New York theater flavor. Miklos Rozsa's fine score also won an Oscar.▼

Double Man, The (1967-British) **C-105m.** **½ D: Franklin Schaffner. Yul Brynner, Britt Ekland, Clive Revill, Anton Diffring, Moira Lister, Lloyd Nolan. Unconvincing spy thriller with Brynner playing both

unemotional C.I.A. agent *and* East German lookalike. Excellent photography by Denys Coop will suffer on TV.

Double McGuffin, The (1979) **C-89m.** **½ D: Joe Camp. Ernest Borgnine, George Kennedy, Elke Sommer, Rod Browning, Dion Pride, Lisa Whelchel, Jeff Nicholson, Michael Gerard, Vincent Spano. Teenagers stumble onto clues leading to assassination plot, but no one will believe them. Family-oriented thriller from creator of BENJI. Orson Welles explains film's title at the outset, for non-Hitchcock devotees.▼

Double Negative (1980-Canadian) **C-96m.** *½ D: George Bloomfield. Michael Sarrazin, Susan Clark, Anthony Perkins, Howard Duff, Kate Reid, Al Waxman, Elizabeth Shepherd. Confusing, annoying thriller with mentally tortured photojournalist Sarrazin attempting to track down his wife's murderer. Sarrazin is his usual bland self; Clark is wasted. Based on Ross MacDonald's *The Three Roads.*

Double Nickels (1977) **C-89m.** BOMB D: Jack Vacek. Jack Vacek, Patrice Schubert, Ed Abrams, Heidi Schubert, Mick Brennan. Amateurish noisemaker about a highway patrolman named Smokey who repossesses cars that are really stolen. Lots of speeding cars, little else.

Double or Nothing (1937) **95m.** **½ D: Theodore Reed. Bing Crosby, Martha Raye, Andy Devine, Mary Carlisle, William Frawley, Fay Holden, Frances Faye. Entertaining musical about four people given 30 days to double gifts of $5000. Several good specialty acts thrown in for good measure, and Bing sings "The Moon Got in My Eyes."

Double Standard (1988) **C-100m. TVM** D: Louis Rudolph. Robert Foxworth, Michele Greene, Pamela Bellwood, Christianne Hirt, James Kee. Improbable drama about a politically ambitious judge leading a secret life with two wives (and two families) in the same county. Below average.

Double Switch (1987) **C-100m. TVM** D: David Greenwalt. George Newbern, Elisabeth Shue, Michael Des Barres, Mariclare Costello, Barbara Rhoades, John Lawlor. Teenage rock star switches places with the winner of his look-alike contest in this contemporary Disney version of *The Prince and the Pauper.* Average.

Doubletake (1985) **C-200m. TVM** D: Jud Taylor. Richard Crenna, Beverly D'Angelo, Vincent Baggetta, Paul Gleason, Cliff Gorman, Drew Snyder, Lee Richardson, Priscilla Lopez, Jeffrey DeMunn, Corbin Bernsen. Solid cop drama involving a grisly double murder (in which the victims' heads were switched), high level police corruption, and a May-December romance. John Gay's script was based on William Bayer's novel, *Switch.* First of a series of Crenna-

Gorman cop movies. Originally shown in two parts. Above average.

Double Trouble (1962) SEE: **Swingin' Along**

Double Trouble (1967) **C-90m.** ** D: Norman Taurog. Elvis Presley, Annette Day, John Williams, Yvonne Romain, The Wiere Brothers, Chips Rafferty, Michael Murphy. Teen-age heiress falls for pop singer Presley when he's performing in England; usual Elvis fare, but he does sing "Long Legged Girl," one of his best post-Army tunes.▼

Double Wedding (1937) 87m. *** D: Richard Thorpe. William Powell, Myrna Loy, Florence Rice, Edgar Kennedy, Sidney Toler, Mary Gordon. Wackier than usual for Powell and Loy, as avant-garde painter and dress designer who want Loy's sister Rice to marry, but do it themselves.

Double Your Pleasure (1989) **C-100m.** TVM D: Paul Lynch. Jackée, Richard Lawson, Dan Hedaya, Harold Sylvester, Bill Fagerbaake, Cynthia Stevenson, Sharon Barr. Middling comedy about twin sisters who swap roles. One's a sassy waitress, the other a glamorous FBI agent trailing a shady business mogul. A showcase for the Mae West–like *227* star. Average.

Doubting Thomas (1935) 78m. *** D: David Butler. Will Rogers, Billie Burke, Alison Skipworth, Sterling Holloway, Andrew Tombes, Gail Patrick, Frank Albertson, John Qualen. Rogers is at his best as a small-town fellow who must deal with a variety of eccentric and pompous characters when his stagestruck wife Burke becomes involved with an amateur theatrical troupe. Often hilarious adaptation of George Kelly's play *The Torch Bearers,* with Skipworth in rare form as the play's directress.

Doughboys (1930) 79m. *½ D: Edward Sedgwick. Buster Keaton, Sally Eilers, Cliff Edwards, Edward Brophy, Victor Potel. One of Buster's worst films; a tiresome Army comedy. Obnoxious sergeant Brophy overrides few comic moments; some bright spots with "Ukulele Ike" Edwards.

Doughgirls, The (1944) 102m. **½ D: James V. Kern. Ann Sheridan, Alexis Smith, Jane Wyman, Eve Arden, Jack Carson, Charlie Ruggles, Alan Mowbray, Craig Stevens, Regis Toomey. Brittle comedy, still another variation on crowded-situation-in-wartime-Washington, with newlyweds Carson and Wyman on hectic honeymoon. Arden standout as Russian army officer.

Dove, The (1974) **C-105m.** **½ D: Charles Jarrott. Joseph Bottoms, Deborah Raffin, John McLiam, Dabney Coleman. Pleasant round-the-world adventure based on true story of 16-year-old who sails to every imaginable port. Filmed on location; produced by Gregory Peck.

Down Among the Sheltering Palms (1953) **C-87m.** ** D: Edmund Goulding. William Lundigan, Jane Greer, Mitzi Gaynor, David Wayne, Gloria DeHaven, Billy Gilbert, Jack Paar. Poor man's SOUTH PACIFIC recounts love problems of two U.S. army officers stationed in Pacific after WW2.

Down Among The Z Men (1952-British) 70m. ** D: Maclean Rogers. Harry Secombe, Peter Sellers, Carole Carr, Spike Milligan, Clifford Staton, Graham Stark, Miriam Karlin. Creaky vehicle for radio's The Goons in story of criminals who visit small town to steal a professor's secret scientific formula. Some good bits, especially Sellers doing impressions of Yank soldiers, but overloaded with dull song-and-dance numbers by a female chorus line.▼

Down and Out in Beverly Hills (1986) **C-103m.** **½ D: Paul Mazursky. Nick Nolte, Richard Dreyfuss, Bette Midler, Little Richard, Tracy Nelson, Elizabeth Pena, Evan Richards, Valerie Curtin, Mike the Dog. Bum moves in with neurotic, nouveau-riche Bev Hills family and takes over their lives. Slick, often funny, but unusually obvious satire for Mazursky (who also appears as one of Dreyfuss's fat-cat friends). Some good performances, though Mike the Dog easily steals the film. A remake of Renoir's BOUDU SAVED FROM DROWNING. Later a TV series.▼

Down Argentine Way (1940) **C-90m.** *** D: Irving Cummings. Don Ameche, Betty Grable, Carmen Miranda, Charlotte Greenwood, J. Carrol Naish, Henry Stephenson, Leonid Kinskey. Enjoyable 20th Century-Fox musical with Grable (in the movie that boosted her to stardom) falling in love with smooth Argentinian horse breeder Ameche. Miranda is terrific in her first American movie, performing infectious Brazilian songs with her own band . . . and look out for the Nicholas Brothers, who do a dynamite specialty number. Picture-postcard color throughout.▼

Down By Law (1986) 107m. **½ D: Jim Jarmusch. Tom Waits, John Lurie, Roberto Benigni, Ellen Barkin, Billie Neal, Rockets Redglare, Vernel Bagneris, Nicoletta Braschi. Third feature by writer-director Jarmusch is intriguing, amusing, and ever so slight, a look at three losers who wind up in jail together—and then make a break for it. Really comes alive when Italian comic Benigni turns up. Slow-moving, strikingly photographed (in black & white) by Robby Muller on location in Louisiana. Costars Lurie and Waits also provide music on the soundtrack. ▼

Downhill (1927-British) 95m. **½ D: Alfred Hitchcock. Ivor Novello, Ben Webster, Robin Irvine, Sybil Rhoda, Lillian Braithwaite, Isabel Jeans, Ian Hunter. Schematic silent film charts a man's slide downhill, beginning when, as a schoolboy, he is disowned by his family after an indiscretion with a girl, and later as an adult when his wife fritters away his unexpected inheritance. Major debit: the contrived happy ending. Lesser Hitchcock boasts the master's visual flair. Cowritten by Novello.

Downhill Racer (1969) **C-102m.** ******* D: Michael Ritchie. Robert Redford, Gene Hackman, Camilla Sparv, Karl Michael Vogler, Jim McMullan, Christian Doermer, Dabney Coleman. Vivid study of an empty life, with Redford as small-town egotist who joins U.S. Olympic ski team. Basically a character study; problem is an unappealing character. Dazzling ski scenes make lulls worth enduring.▼

Down Memory Lane (1949) **72m.** ******* D: Phil Karlson (new footage). Steve Allen, Franklin Pangborn, Frank Nelson, Mack Sennett; scenes of W. C. Fields, Bing Crosby, others. Allen decides to show old Sennett comedies on his TV show. OK framework for silent clips of Ben Turpin, Gloria Swanson, etc. Fields' classic THE DENTIST and Crosby's BLUE OF THE NIGHT both shown almost in toto, making silly Allen footage worth watching.

Downpayment on Murder (1987) **C-100m.** TVM D: Waris Hussein. Connie Sellecca, Ben Gazzara, David Morse, John Karlen, G.W. Bailey, Jonathan Banks, Sheila Larken. The estranged wife of a real-estate wheeler-dealer finds herself the prey of a hit man her schizo husband has hired. Average.

Downstairs (1932) **77m.** ****½** D: Monta Bell. John Gilbert, Paul Lukas, Virginia Bruce, Hedda Hopper, Reginald Owen, Olga Baclanova. Gilbert is quite good as a cad and scoundrel chauffeur who seduces his female employer as well as the butler's wife (Bruce, the real-life Mrs. Gilbert). Interesting MGM drama based on an original story by Gilbert himself. This was his best talkie showcase, aside from QUEEN CHRISTINA.

Down Three Dark Streets (1954) **85m.** ****½** D: Arnold Laven. Broderick Crawford, Ruth Roman, Martha Hyer, Marisa Pavan. Smoothly done interweaving episodes, pegged on FBI agent following through on trio of dead buddy's cases; Roman quite effective.

Down to Earth (1932) **73m.** ****½** D: David Butler. Will Rogers, Irene Rich, Dorothy Jordan, Mary Carlisle, Matty Kemp. Homer Croy's sequel to THEY HAD TO SEE PARIS has nouveau riche Midwesterner Rogers putting an end to his family's foolish spending by declaring that he's broke. OK Rogers vehicle, but not up to his best film efforts.

Down to Earth (1947) **C-101m.** ****** D: Alexander Hall. Rita Hayworth, Larry Parks, Marc Platt, Roland Culver, James Gleason, Edward Everett Horton. Terpsichore, the Goddess of Dance (Hayworth), comes to earth to help Parks with his mythological musical play. Rita's beauty is only asset of this hack musical, which appropriates Gleason, Horton and Culver characters from HERE COMES MR. JORDAN. Remade as XANADU.

Down to the Sea in Ships (1922) **83m.** ****½** D: Elmer Clifton. William Walcott, Marguerite Courtot, Clara Bow, Raymond McKee, J. Thornton Baston. Archaic plot line of romantic conflict in a whaling family enhanced by vivid atmosphere of on-location shooting in New England, striking photography on board actual whaling ships at sea. Also notable as Clara Bow's film debut.▼

Down to the Sea in Ships (1949) **120m.** ******* D: Henry Hathaway. Richard Widmark, Lionel Barrymore, Dean Stockwell, Cecil Kellaway, Gene Lockhart. Young Stockwell fulfills seafaring goal on crusty Barrymore's whaling ship, under guidance of sailor Widmark. Good atmospheric yarn.

Downtown (1990) **C-96m.** ****** D: Richard Benjamin. Anthony Edwards, Forest Whitaker, Joe Pantoliano, David Clennon, Penelope Ann Miller, Kimberly Scott, Art Evans, Rick Aiello. Naive white cop Edwards is transferred from easy suburban precinct to tough downtown area of Philadelphia and teamed with a sad, streetwise loner (Whitaker); together they go after a peculiar stolen-car ring. Uneasy mix of farce, melodrama, and buddy movie looks something like a pilot for a (bad) TV series.

Down Twisted (1987) **C-88m.** ***½** D: Albert Pyun. Carey Lowell, Charles Rocket, Trudi Dochtermann, Thom Matthews, Norbert Weisser, Linda Kerridge, Nicholas Guest. Unremittingly complicated, and unsatisfying, caper yarn with innocent young woman suddenly caught up in web of intrigue when she's thought to have a priceless artifact the bad guys are after. Echoes of other (better) movies abound, but this one adds nothing to the formula.

Do You Know the Muffin Man? (1989) **C-100m.** TVM D: Gilbert Cates. Pam Dawber, John Shea, Stephen Dorff, Anthony Geary, Matthew Laurance, Georgann Johnson, William Prince, Brian Bonsall. Drama about sexual abuse of preschoolers and how a cop's family copes with the trauma. The subject was far better handled in the later UNSPEAKABLE ACTS. Average.

Do You Love Me? (1946) **C-91m.** ****½** D: Gregory Ratoff. Maureen O'Hara, Dick Haymes, Harry James, Reginald Gardiner, Alma Kruger. Lightweight musical of bandsinger Haymes romancing college dean O'Hara.

Do You Remember Love (1985) **C-100m.** TVM D: Jeff Bleckner. Joanne Woodward, Richard Kiley, Geraldine Fitzgerald, Jim Metzler, Jordan Charney, Rose Gregorio, Susan Ruttan. Masterful performances by Woodward (who won the Emmy) and Kiley distinguish this exceptional drama about the effect on the family of a middle-aged college professor when she contracts Alzheimer's disease. Superb script by first-time author (and Emmy winner) Vickie Patik. Above average.

Do You Take This Stranger (1970) C-100m. TVM D: Richard Heffron. Gene Barry, Lloyd Bridges, Diane Baker, Joseph Cotten, Susan Oliver, Sidney Blackmer. OK drama featuring Barry as man who has million dollars within grasp if he can persuade another to assume his identity; terminal disease victim is likely candidate. Good complications, fair performances. Average.

Dozens, The (1981) C-78m. **½ D: Christine Dall, Randall Conrad. Debra Margolies, Edward Mason, Marian Taylor, Jessica Hergert, Ethel Michelson, Genevieve Reale. Tough, volatile young woman (Margolies) is released from prison, tries to rebuild her life. Not bad, but not particularly involving. Based on fact, and filmed in Boston.

✓ **Dracula** (1931) 75m. ***½ D: Tod Browning. Bela Lugosi, David Manners, Helen Chandler, Dwight Frye, Edward Van Sloan, Herbert Bunston, Frances Dade. Classic horror film of Transylvanian vampire working his evil spell on perplexed group of Londoners. Lugosi's most famous role with his definitive interpretation of the Count, ditto Frye as looney Renfield and Van Sloan as unflappable Professor Van Helsing. Sequel: DRACULA'S DAUGHTER.▼

Dracula (1958) SEE: **Horror of Dracula**▼

Dracula (1973) C-100m. TVM D: Dan Curtis. Jack Palance, Simon Ward, Nigel Davenport, Pamela Brown, Fiona Lewis, Penelope Horner, Murray Brown. The indomitable count of Transylvania lives in the person of Palance, who plays Bram Stoker's vampire king as a slightly pathetic figure, a victim of twisted fate. Sterling cast, Richard Matheson's faithful adaptation, and Oswald Morris' exceptional photography, rich in gothic touches, add to this classy new version of the old chestnut. Above average.▼

Dracula (1979) C-109m. *½ D: John Badham. Frank Langella, Laurence Olivier, Donald Pleasence, Kate Nelligan, Trevor Eve, Janine Duvitski, Tony Haygarth. Murky retelling of Bram Stoker classic, with Langella's acclaimed Broadway characterization lost amid trendy horror gimmicks and ill-conceived changes in original story. Filmed in England.▼

Dracula A.D. 1972 (1972-British) C-100m. ** D: Alan Gibson. Peter Cushing, Christopher Lee, Stephanie Beacham, Michael Coles, Christopher Neame, Caroline Munro. Farfetched, confusing tale of modern-day descendant of Dr. Van Helsing (Cushing) battling recently revived vampire (Lee). Somewhat jarring to see Dracula amid 1970s youth setting. Also known as DRACULA TODAY. Followed by THE SATANIC RITES OF DRACULA.

Dracula and Son (1979-French) C-78m. *½ D: Eduard Molinaro. Christopher Lee, Bernard Menez, Marie-Helene Breillat, Catherine Breillat, Jack Boudet, Geoffrey Carey. Limp horror satire chronicling the comic misadventures of the title vampire (Lee) and his bumbling offspring (Menez); they become rivals for the pretty heroine (Marie-Helene Breillat). Virtually destroyed by grotesquely inappropriate English dubbing.▼

Dracula Has Risen From The Grave ✓ (1968-British) C-92m. **½ D: Freddie Francis. Christopher Lee, Rupert Davies, Veronica Carlson, Barbara Ewing, Barry Andrews, Michael Ripper. Dracula runs afoul of small-town monsignor when he pursues the churchman's beautiful blonde niece. Pretty good Hammer horror, third in the series. Sequel: TASTE THE BLOOD OF DRACULA.

Dracula—Prince of Darkness (1966-British) C-90m. ** D: Terence Fisher. Christopher Lee, Barbara Shelley, Andrew Keir, Suzan Farmer. Sequel to HORROR OF DRACULA doesn't measure up. Lee is reincarnated as the evil Count who wreaks terror on a group of tourists in a secluded castle.

Dracula's Daughter (1936) 70m. *** D: Lambert Hillyer. Gloria Holden, Otto Kruger, Marguerite Churchill, Irving Pichel, Edward Van Sloan, Nan Grey, Hedda Hopper. Sequel to the Lugosi classic depicts vampirish activities of Holden, who has a decided taste for *female* victims; Pichel adds imposing support as her sinister manservant. Hillyer, normally a B-Western director, manages to imbue this chiller with a moody, subtly sensual quality.

Dracula's Dog (1978) C-90m. ** D: Albert Band. Jose Ferrer, Michael Pataki, Reggie Nalder, Jan Shutan, Libbie Chase, John Levin. Transylvanian vampire and bloodthirsty dog, endowed with vampirish traits by the original Count, go to L.A. to find Dracula's last living descendant. Horror cheapie with admittedly novel twist. Retitled ZOLTAN, HOUND OF DRACULA.▼

Dracula's Last Rites SEE: **Last Rites** (1980)▼

Dracula Today SEE: **Dracula A.D. 1972**

Dracula vs. Frankenstein (1971) C-90m. BOMB D: Al Adamson. J. Carrol Naish, Lon Chaney, Zandor Vorkov, Russ Tamblyn, Jim Davis, Anthony Eisley. Self-conscious comedy masquerading as horror film wasting talents of old-timers Naish and Chaney; Dracula makes deal with aging Dr. Frankenstein so as to have steady supply of blood. Regrettably, both Naish and Chaney's final film.▼

✓ **Dragnet** (1954) **C-89m.** *** D: Jack Webb. Jack Webb, Ben Alexander, Richard Boone, Ann Robinson, Stacy Harris, Virginia Gregg, Dennis Weaver. While investigating brutal murder, Sgt. Friday and Officer Frank Smith ignore 57 varieties of civil liberties; feature film version of classic TV show evokes its era better than almost anything. Highly recommended on a non-esthetic level.▼

Dragnet (1969) **C-97m.** **TVM** D: Jack Webb. Jack Webb, Harry Morgan, Vic Perrin, Virginia Gregg, Gene Evans, John Rosenboro. Friday and Gannon investigate series of murders of pretty models with vaguely identified male only suspect. Slightly better production than series; direction and dialogue same as show. Average.

Dragnet (1987) **C-106m.** **½ D: Tom Mankiewicz. Dan Aykroyd, Tom Hanks, Christopher Plummer, Harry Morgan, Alexandra Paul, Jack O'Halloran, Elizabeth Ashley, Dabney Coleman. Aykroyd is a comic reincarnation of Jack Webb, playing Sgt. Joe Friday's dense but dedicated nephew in this parody of Webb's memorable TV cop show. Hanks is fun as his freewheeling new partner, with Morgan, Webb's onetime sidekick, now promoted to captain of the L.A.P.D. Starts out quite funny, then goes flat . . . but the punchline is a howl. Aykroyd coscripted with Mankiewicz and Alan Zweibel.▼

Dragon Flies, The SEE: **Man from Hong Kong, The**

Dragonfly SEE: **One Summer Love**

Dragonfly Squadron (1954) **82m.** ** D: Lesley Selander. John Hodiak, Barbara Britton, Bruce Bennett, Jess Barker. Usual Korean War story, alternating between pilots in the air and their romantic problems on ground.▼

Dragon Murder Case (1934) **68m.** D: H. Bruce Humberstone. Warren William, Margaret Lindsay, Lyle Talbot, Eugene Pallette, Dorothy Tree. SEE: **Philo Vance** series.

Dragon Seed (1944) **145m.** **½ D: Jack Conway, Harold S. Bucquet. Katharine Hepburn, Walter Huston, Aline MacMahon, Turhan Bey, Hurd Hatfield, Agnes Moorehead, Frances Rafferty, J. Carrol Naish, Akim Tamiroff, Henry Travers. Well-meant but overlong film of Pearl Buck's tale of Chinese town torn asunder by Japanese occupation; fascinating attempts at Oriental characterization.▼

Dragonslayer (1981) **C-108m.** *** D: Matthew Robbins. Peter MacNicol, Caitlin Clarke, Ralph Richardson, John Hallam, Peter Eyre, Albert Salmi. Enjoyable fantasy-adventure about a sorcerer's apprentice who takes on the challenge of slaying a dragon—and finds he is in over his head. A bit scary and graphic for some kids. Filmed in England, Scotland, and Wales with a mostly British cast but American MacNicol in the lead—somewhat incongruously. Fine Alex North score.▼

Dragonwyck (1946) **103m.** **½ D: Joseph L. Mankiewicz. Gene Tierney, Walter Huston, Vincent Price, Glenn Langan, Anne Revere, Spring Byington, Henry (Harry) Morgan, Jessica Tandy. Period chiller set at a gloomy mansion on the Hudson, with good cast but episodic presentation. Mankiewicz's directorial debut; he also scripted from the Anya Seton story.

Dragoon Wells Massacre (1957) **C-88m.** ** D: Harold Schuster. Barry Sullivan, Dennis O'Keefe, Mona Freeman, Katy Jurado, Sebastian Cabot. Marauding Apaches force lawmen and renegades to join forces for self-protection; some action-packed scenes.

Drama of Jealousy, A SEE: **Pizza Triangle, The**

Dramatic School (1938) **80m.** **½ D: Robert B. Sinclair. Luise Rainer, Paulette Goddard, Alan Marshal, Lana Turner, Anthony Allen (John Hubbard), Henry Stephenson, Genevieve Tobin. Carbon-copy STAGE DOOR with Rainer the center of attraction as fanciful girl who makes good in both marriage and career; look for Ann Rutherford, Dick Haymes, Hans Conried in early bit roles.

Drango (1957) **92m.** ** D: Hall Bartlett, Jules Bricken. Jeff Chandler, Joanne Dru, Julie London, Donald Crisp. Chandler is Yankee Civil War veteran assigned to restore order to Southern town his command plundered. OK Western.

Draughtsman's Contract, The (1982-British) **C-103m.** ** D: Peter Greenaway. Anthony Higgins, Janet Suzman, Anne Louise Lambert, Hugh Fraser. Arrogant young artist takes commissions from the mistress of an estate in return for sexual favors; sumptuous-looking 17th-century tale, but cold and aloof. Will be of greater interest to fans of writer-director Greenaway.

Draw! (1984) **C-98m.** **TVM** D: Steven Hilliard Stern. Kirk Douglas, James Coburn, Alexandra Bastedo, Graham Jarvis, Derek McGrath, Len Birman. Two old pros give this lighthearted Western (filmed on the range in Alberta, Canada) the traditional college try. Kirk's an over-the-hill outlaw in this misfire, and Jimbo is his old nemesis, now a boozing lawman who challenges him to one last showdown. Made for cable. Average.▼

Dr. Black and Mr. White SEE: **Dr. Black, Mr. Hyde**▼

Dr. Black, Mr. Hyde (1976) **C-87m.** **½ D: William Crain. Bernie Casey, Rosalind Cash, Marie O'Henry, Ji-Tu

Cumbuka, Milt Kogan, Stu Gilliam. Black lab scientist Casey tests experimental serum on himself and turns into a white monster. No surprises, but not bad, either, with Casey doing first-rate job as Jekyll-Hyde character. Also known as THE WATTS MONSTER, DR. BLACK AND MR. WHITE.▼

Dr. Broadway (1942) **68m.** **½ D: Anthony Mann. MacDonald Carey, Jean Phillips, J. Carrol Naish, Richard Lane, Eduardo Ciannelli, Warren Hymer. Anthony Mann's first film is a decent little B mystery centering on Carey as Times Square doc and the assorted crooks and loonies he becomes involved with. Nicely done on a low-budget and featuring a rare performance by Phillips, Ginger Rogers's stand-in.

Dr. Bull (1933) **75m.** *** D: John Ford. Will Rogers, Marian Nixon, Ralph Morgan, Rochelle Hudson, Berton Churchill, Louise Dresser. Rogers in fine form as country doctor battling small-town pettiness as much as fighting illness. Stereotyped characters are perfect foils for Rogers' common-sense pronouncements; director Ford provides ideal atmosphere.

Dr. Christian Meets the Women (1940) **68m.** ** D: William McGann. Jean Hersholt, Dorothy Lovett, Edgar Kennedy, Rod La Rocque, Frank Albertson, Marilyn (Lynn) Merrick, Maude Eburne, Veda Ann Borg. Predictable but harmless series entry, with the good doctor exposing "Professor" La Rocque's diet and physical-culture scam.▼

✓ **Dr. Cook's Garden** (1970) **C-73m. TVM** D: Ted Post. Bing Crosby, Frank Converse, Blythe Danner, Abby Lewis, Barney Hughes, Bethel Leslie. Converse's return to Greenfield, Vermont, and the kindly doctor who raised him degenerates into cheap horror by halfway mark. Even Crosby as central character can't cut it. Adapted from play by Ira Levin. Below average.

✓ **Dr. Cyclops** (1940) **C-75m.** **½ D: Ernest Schoedsack. Albert Dekker, Thomas Coley, Janice Logan, Victor Kilian, Charles Halton. Title character (Dekker) shrinks humans to doll-size; the story is just OK, but the special effects (in color) are worth seeing.▼

Dream a Little Dream (1989) **C-99m.** *½ D: Marc Rocco. Corey Feldman, Meredith Salenger, Jason Robards, Piper Laurie, Harry Dean Stanton, William McNamara, Corey Haim. Yet another personality-exchange comedy—this one with Robards and Feldman switching bodies after a bike mishap. Perfectly dreadful.▼

Dreamboat (1952) **83m.** *** D: Claude Binyon. Ginger Rogers, Clifton Webb, Jeffrey Hunter, Anne Francis, Elsa Lanchester. Clever romp: silent-star Rogers cashes in on TV showings of her old movies, to chagrin of co-star Webb, now a distinguished professor. Scenes showing their old silent films are most enjoyable.

Dream Breakers (1989) **C-100m. TVM** D: Stuart Millar. Robert Loggia, Kyle MacLachlan, Hal Linden, D.W. Moffett, Charles Cioffi, John McIntire. Chicago building contractor Loggia joins forces with his two sons—an idealistic Harvard MBA and a dedicated parish priest—to take on power-hungry land developer Linden. Notable mainly for the casting against type of Loggia (as a good guy) and Linden (as the heavy). Average.

Dreamchild (1985-British) **C-94m.** **½ D: Gavin Millar. Coral Browne, Ian Holm, Peter Gallagher, Caris Corfman, Nicola Cowper, Jane Asher, Amelia Shankley, Shane Rimmer. Woman for whom Rev. Charles Dodgson (Lewis Carroll) invented his *Alice in Wonderland* stories comes to America at age 80 for the author's centenary, unable to understand the fuss, and fearful of her own repressed memories. Fascinating material seriously flawed by romantic subplot and ludicrous recreation of N.Y.C. setting and characters of the 1930s. Browne's superb performance makes it all worthwhile. Jim Henson's Creature Shop provided Wonderland characters. Written by Dennis Potter. ▼

Dream Date (1989) **C-100m. TVM** D: Anson Williams. Tempestt Bledsoe, Clifton Davis, Kadeem Hardison, Brandon Maggart, Ann Marie Johnson. Romantic fluff about a teenager on her first date and the overprotective father who feels a need to spy on the couple. Showcase for a battery of TV stars. Average.

Dreamer (1979) **C-86m.** ** D: Noel Nosseck. Tim Matheson, Susan Blakely, Jack Warden, Richard B. Shull, Barbara Stuart, Pedro Gonzalez-Gonzalez. Bowling, a sport only slightly more cinematic than isometric exercises, gets the ROCKY treatment in this bland rags-to-riches story. Having Matheson's bowling ball made of Flubber might have helped pick up the pace.▼

Dream for Christmas, A (1973) **C-100m. TVM** D: Ralph Senensky. Hari Rhodes, Beah Richards, Lynn Hamilton, George Spell, Juanita Moore, Joel Fluellen, Marlin Adams, Robert DoQui, Ta Ronce Allen, Clarence Muse. Inspirational story (by Earl *The Waltons* Hamner, Jr.) about black minister who takes his family from Arkansas to L.A. for his new assignment: a poor congregation in a church earmarked for demolition. Above average.▼

Dream Girl (1948) **85m.** ** D: Mitchell Leisen. Betty Hutton, Macdonald Carey, Virginia Field, Patric Knowles, Walter Abel, Peggy Wood. Hutton stars as female Walter Mitty with constant daydreams; lowbrow version of Elmer Rice play.

Dream House (1981) **C-100m. TVM** D: Joseph Hardy. John Schneider, Marilu Henner, Michael Gross, Remak Ramsey, Miguel Fernandes. Agreeable tale of a good old boy from Georgia who falls for a pretty Manhattan woman and decides to build his dream house in a N.Y.C. ghetto. Above average.

Dreaming Lips (1937-British) **93m.** **½ D: Paul Czinner, Lee Garmes. Elisabeth Bergner, Raymond Massey, Romney Brent, Joyce Bland, Charles Carson, Felix Aylmer. Glamorous, pampered Bergner, wife of orchestra conductor Brent, commences a romance with world-famous (but desperately lonely) violinist Massey. A bit overdone, and the ending is a disappointment, but it's entertaining most of the way. Good star vehicle for Bergner. ▼

Dreaming Out Loud (1940) **81m.** ** D: Harold Young. Lum 'n' Abner (Chester Lauck, Norris Goff), Frances Gifford, Frank Craven, Bobs Watson, Phil Harris. Radio comedians Lum 'n' Abner's screen debut is a very slight rural comedy-melodrama with music. The fabled proprietors of the Jot-Em-Down general store in Pine Ridge, Arkansas, get involved in the lives of various local residents . . . but movies never showed off this bucolic team at its best. ▼

Dream Lover (1986) **C-104m.** *½ D: Alan J. Pakula. Kristy McNichol, Ben Masters, Paul Shenar, Justin Deas, John McMartin, Gayle Hunnicutt, Matthew Penn. Abysmal thriller about young woman's attempts to expunge recurring nightmare from her mind through "dream therapy." Intensely unsettling film with an interesting idea torpedoed by snaillike pacing and sterile atmosphere. What Hitchcock could have done with this! ▼

Dream Maker, The (1964-British) **C-101m.** ** D: Don Sharp. Tommy Steele, Michael Medwin, Angela Douglas, Danny Williams, Dick Kallman, John Barry. Talent-scout Steele organizes a fundraising concert for an orphanage—and predictably becomes a star himself in the finale. Also known as IT'S ALL HAPPENING.

Dream Makers, The (1975) **C-78m. TVM** D: Boris Sagal. James Franciscus, Diane Baker, John Astin, Kenny Rogers, Mickey Jones, Jamie Donnelly, Devon Ericson, Steven Keats. College professor Franciscus leaves security of the campus to become recording company executive, only to be enmeshed in payola scandal. Muddled attempt at exposé of the recording industry; Rogers' acting debut. Below average.

Dream Merchants, The (1980) **C-200m. TVM** D: Vincent Sherman. Mark Harmon, Morgan Fairchild, Morgan Brittany, Eve Arden, Kaye Ballard, Vincent Gardenia, Red Buttons, Robert Culp, Howard Duff, Jose Ferrer, Robert Goulet, David Groh, Carolyn Jones, Fernando Lamas, Ray Milland, Jan Murray. Pedestrian tale of a young moviemaker's rise in the silent era. Based on the Harold Robbins novel. Originally shown in two parts. Average.

Dream of Kings, A (1969) **C-107m.** *** D: Daniel Mann. Anthony Quinn, Irene Papas, Inger Stevens, Sam Levene, Radames Pera, Val Avery. Emotional study of robust Quinn trying to find money to take ailing son to Greece. Vivid look at Greek community in Chicago; heart-rending story by Harry Alan Petrakis. Stevens exceptional as young widow attracted to Quinn. ▼

Dream of Passion, A (1978-Greek) **C-106m.** *½ D: Jules Dassin. Melina Mercouri, Ellen Burstyn, Andreas Voutsinas, Despo Diamantidou, Dimitris Papa-michael. Aside from Burstyn's powerhouse performance as an American jailed in Greece for killing her three children, this attempt to parallel her story with Medea's is the kind of idea that should never have left the story conference. Mercouri is typically hammy as the actress who takes up her cause. ▼

Dreams (1955-Swedish) **86m.** ** D: Ingmar Bergman. Eva Dahlbeck, Harriet Andersson, Gunnar Bjornstrand, Ulf Palme, Inga Landgre. Sometimes fascinating but mostly vague—and, ultimately lesser—Bergman drama, about photo agency head Dahlbeck and model Andersson, and their dreams, torments, crises, oppression, relations with men. Also known as JOURNEY INTO AUTUMN. ▼

Dreamscape (1984) **C-99m.** *** D: Joseph Ruben. Dennis Quaid, Max von Sydow, Christopher Plummer, Eddie Albert, Kate Capshaw, George Wendt, David Patrick Kelly. Quaid finds he can physically enter other people's dreams in this entertaining yarn; science-fantasy elements more successful than political intrigue subplot. ▼

Dreams Don't Die (1982) **C-100m. TVM** D: Roger Young. Ike Eisenmann, Trini Alvarado, Israel Juarbe, Mark Gordon, George Coe, Judi West, James Broderick, Paul Winfield. Teenagers in the urban drug-saturated war zone, with unrealistically pat solutions. Below average.

Dreams Lost, Dreams Found (1987) **C-102m. TVM** D: Willi Patterson. Kathleen Quinlan, David Robb, Betsy Brantley, Colette O'Neil, Charles Gray, Louise Breslin. Young American widow is drawn back to her Scottish heritage in this so-so drama, third in the "Harlequin Romance Movie" series. Made for cable. Average. ▼

Dreams of Gold: The Mel Fisher Story (1986) **C-100m. TVM** D: James Goldstone. Cliff Robertson, Loretta Swit, Scott Paulin, William Zabka, Steven Williams. Fact-based drama of treasure hunter Mel Fisher's 17-year search off the Florida

Keys for the wreck of a sunken 17th-century Spanish galleon, which yielded more than $200 million in riches. Average.

Dream Team, The (1989) C-113m. **½ D: Howard Zieff. Michael Keaton, Christopher Lloyd, Peter Boyle, Stephen Furst, Dennis Boutsikaris, Lorraine Bracco, Milo O'Shea, Philip Bosco, James Remar. Four mental-hospital patients become separated from their doctor while on a field trip to Yankee Stadium, and find themselves stranded in an even-larger looney bin called The Big Apple. Uneven farce seems inspired by ONE FLEW OVER THE CUCKOO'S NEST, and gets its mileage from the performances of its leading actors.▼

Dream Wife (1953) 101m. *½ D: Sidney Sheldon. Cary Grant, Deborah Kerr, Walter Pidgeon, Buddy Baer, Movita, Steve Forrest. Silly bedroom comedy about Grant "marrying" an Eastern princess for goodwill reasons. Cast is wasted. Also shown in computer-colored version.

√ **Dr. Ehrlich's Magic Bullet** (1940) 103m. ***½ D: William Dieterle. Edward G. Robinson, Ruth Gordon, Otto Kruger, Donald Crisp, Maria Ouspenskaya, Montagu Love, Sig Ruman, Donald Meek. Outstanding chronicle of 19th-century German scientist who developed cure for venereal disease. Robinson earnest in interpreting superior script by John Huston, Heinz Herald, and Norman Burnside; surprisingly compelling.

Dressed to Kill (1946) 72m. D: Roy William Neill. Basil Rathbone, Nigel Bruce, Patricia Morison, Edmond Breon, Carl Harbord, Patricia Cameron, Tom Dillon. SEE: **Sherlock Holmes** series. Also shown in computer-colored version.▼

Dressed to Kill (1980) C-105m. ***½ D: Brian De Palma. Michael Caine, Angie Dickinson, Nancy Allen, Keith Gordon, Dennis Franz, David Margulies, Brandon Maggart. High-tension melodrama about a psycho-killer who stalks two women—one a frustrated suburban housewife, the other a street-smart hooker who teams up with the first woman's son to trap the murderer. Writer-director De Palma works on viewer's emotions, not logic, and maintains a fever pitch from start to finish. Chilling Pino Donaggio score.▼

Dresser, The (1983-British) C-118m. ***½ D: Peter Yates. Albert Finney, Tom Courtenay, Edward Fox, Zena Walker, Eileen Atkins, Michael Gough, Cathryn Harrison. Excellent film adaptation of Ronald Harwood's play about an aging actor-manager (based on real-life Donald Wolfit) whose very survival depends on the constant pampering and prodding of his dresser—who lives vicariously through the old man's performances. Finney, as Sir, and Courtenay, as Norman the dresser, are simply superb. Yates' direction captures the look and feel of wartime England, and back-stage atmosphere of a small touring company, with uncanny ability. A must for anyone who loves acting and the theater.▼

Dressmaker, The (1988-British) C-89m. **½ D: Jim O'Brien. Joan Plowright, Billie Whitelaw, Peter Postlethwaite, Jane Horrocks, Tim Ransom. Medium account of two Liverpool sisters, one repressed (Plowright) and the other spirited (Whitelaw), and what happens when their naive, fragile niece falls for an American GI during WW2. Well acted, and starts off promisingly, but bogs down.▼

Dr. Faustus (1968-British) C-93m. ** D: Richard Burton, Nevill Coghill. Richard Burton, Andreas Teuber, Ian Marter, Elizabeth Taylor. Burton's retelling of Faustus legend lacks everything but a buxom Mrs. Burton in brief sequence as Helen of Troy. Strictly for their fans.▼

Dr. Fischer of Geneva (1983-British) C-110m. TVM D: Michael Lindsay-Hogg. Alan Bates, James Mason, Greta Scacchi, Clarissa Kaye, Hugh Burden, Cyril Cusack, Barry Humphries. Mason is magnificent in one of his last roles, as a rich man who cynically delights in manipulating people to demonstrate man's venality. At a "bomb party," where guests risk literally being blown up in opening their million-dollar party favors, future son-in-law Bates gives Mason his comeuppance. Features an excellent support performance by Kaye, Mason's real-life widow, as a greedy dowager. Based on a Graham Greene story. Above average.

Dr. Gillespie's Criminal Case (1943) 89m. D: Willis Goldbeck. Lionel Barrymore, Van Johnson, Donna Reed, Keye Luke, John Craven, Nat Pendleton, Marilyn Maxwell. SEE: **Dr. Kildare** series.

Dr. Gillespie's New Assistant (1942) 87m. D: Willis Goldbeck. Lionel Barrymore, Van Johnson, Susan Peters, Keye Luke, Richard Quine, Alma Kruger, Rose Hobart, Nat Pendleton, Stephen McNally, Marie Blake, Ann Richards. SEE: **Dr. Kildare** series.

Dr. Goldfoot and the Bikini Machine (1966) C-90m. ** D: Norman Taurog. Vincent Price, Frankie Avalon, Dwayne Hickman, Susan Hart, Fred Clark. Mad scientist tries to make a fortune manufacturing lifelike lady robots to marry wealthy men. Good chase scene, but otherwise just silly.▼

Dr. Goldfoot and the Girl Bombs (1966-Italian) C-85m. *½ D: Mario Bava. Vincent Price, Fabian, Franco Franchi, Moana Tahi, Laura Antonelli. Dumb sequel to DR. GOLDFOOT AND THE BIKINI MACHINE finds Price now backed by Red China, dropping actual girl bombs into the laps of unsuspecting generals.

Dr. Heckyl and Mr. Hype (1980) C-99m. **½ D: Charles B. Griffith. Oliver Reed, Sunny Johnson, Maia Danziger, Mel Welles, Virgil Frye, Jackie Coogan, Corinne Calvet.

Reed is a grotesquely ugly podiatrist who drinks a potion to commit suicide, instead turns into a handsome murderer. Moderately funny comedy, also written by Roger Corman veteran Griffith.

Drifter, The (1988) C-90m. **½ D: Larry Brand. Kim Delaney, Timothy Bottoms, Al Shannon, Miles O'Keeffe, Loren Haines, Thomas Wagner, Larry Brand. Interesting low-budget variation on the PLAY MISTY FOR ME/FATAL ATTRACTION formula as pretty costume designer Delaney picks up virile O'Keeffe hitchhiking, has a one-night affair, and is then hounded by him. Director Brand (who also plays the cop on the case) shows promise but film suffers from contrivance of having *three* psychotics on the loose.▼

Drifting Weeds SEE: **Floating Weeds**▼

Driftwood (1947) 90m. **½ D: Allan Dwan. Ruth Warrick, Walter Brennan, Natalie Wood, Dean Jagger, Charlotte Greenwood, Jerome Cowan, H. B. Warner, Margaret Hamilton. Small-town doctor adopts a young girl who's never experienced "civilization" before. Entertaining family film with standout performance by young Natalie.

Drive a Crooked Road (1954) 82m. ** D: Richard Quine. Mickey Rooney, Dianne Foster, Kevin McCarthy, Jack Kelly, Harry Landers. Quietly paced film of auto mechanic Rooney dreaming of being racing-car champ; instead becomes chump for gangsters, due to girlfriend.

Drive Hard, Drive Fast (1969) C-73m. TVM D: Douglas Heyes. Brian Kelly, Joan Collins, Henry Silva, Joseph Campanella, Karen Huston, Todd Martin. Odd murder drama with professional racing backdrop. Scheming wife (Collins) involves innocent man in husband's plan. Typical complications and doublecrosses in hohum script which cast can't save. Below average.

Drive, He Said (1972) C-90m. **½ D: Jack Nicholson. William Tepper, Karen Black, Michael Margotta, Bruce Dern, Robert Towne, Henry Jaglom. Confusing tale of youth alienation contains fine performances but loses itself in its attempt to cover all the bases; Dern is fabulous as gung-ho college basketball coach.

Drive-In (1976) C-96m. ** D: Rod Amateau. Lisa Lemole, Glen Morshower, Gary Cavagnaro, Billy Milliken, Lee Newsom, Regan Kee. Amiable low-budget trash about a night in the life of teenaged yahoos at a Texas drive-in during the unreeling of a campy disaster film (which takes up much of the screen time). Better after 20 beers.▼

Driver's Seat, The (1973-Italian) C-101m. *½ D: Giuseppe Patroni Griffi. Elizabeth Taylor, Ian Bannen, Mona Washbourne, Andy Warhol. Slow, tedious, complex melodrama with Taylor in one of her worst roles as psychotic spinster undergoing series of adventures as she seeks to keep date with lover-murderer.▼

Driver, The (1978) C-90m. *** D: Walter Hill. Ryan O'Neal, Bruce Dern, Isabelle Adjani, Ronee Blakley, Matt Clark, Felice Orlandi. Tense throwback to the Hollywood film noir era pits getaway driver O'Neal against creepy cop Dern. Oddball melodrama doesn't seem like much at the time, but has a way of staying with you afterwards. Great car chase sequences.▼

Driving Miss Daisy (1989) C-99m. *** D: Bruce Beresford. Morgan Freeman, Jessica Tandy, Dan Aykroyd, Patti LuPone, Esther Rolle. Genteel, entertaining adaptation of Alfred Uhry's stage play about a simple black man who's hired as chauffeur for a cantankerous old Southern woman, and winds up being her most faithful companion. A smooth and enjoyable ride, with fine performances by the two leads. Aykroyd is likable in an unusual "straight" role as Tandy's son, though you can never quite forget who's playing the part (especially with such obvious makeup). Oscar winner for Best Picture, Actress, Screenplay (by Uhry), and Makeup.▼

Dr. Jekyll and Mr. Hyde (1920) 63m. *** D: John S. Robertson. John Barrymore, Martha Mansfield, Brandon Hurst, Nita Naldi, Charles Lane, Louis Wolheim. One of several silent versions of famous tale, this one can hold its own next to the later March and Tracy filmings; Barrymore is superb as curious doctor who ventures into the unknown, emerging as evil Mr. Hyde. Bravura performance sparks well-made production.▼

Dr. Jekyll and Mr. Hyde (1932) 82m. *** D: Rouben Mamoulian. Fredric March, Miriam Hopkins, Rose Hobart, Holmes Herbert, Halliwell Hobbes. Exciting, floridly cinematic version of famous story with March in Oscar-winning portrayal of tormented doctor, Hopkins superb as tantalizing Ivy. Originally 98m., and censored for reissue.▼

Dr. Jekyll and Mr. Hyde (1941) 114m. *** D: Victor Fleming. Spencer Tracy, Ingrid Bergman, Lana Turner, Donald Crisp, Ian Hunter, Barton MacLane, C. Aubrey Smith, Sara Allgood. Tracy and Bergman are excellent in thoughtful, lush remake of Robert Louis Stevenson's classic, which stresses Hyde's emotions rather than physical horror. Also shown in computer-colored version.▼

Dr. Jekyll and Sister Hyde (1972-British) C-94m. **½ D: Roy Ward Baker. Ralph Bates, Martine Beswick, Gerald Sim, Lewis Fiander, Susan Broderick. Interesting twist to classic tale finds the good doctor discovering that his evil life is brought out in the form of a beautiful but dangerous woman. No thrills but fun;

resemblance between Bates and Beswick is remarkable. Released in Britain at 97m.▼

Dr. Kildare From 1938 to 1947, this MGM series, set in Blair General Hospital, was one of the most successful and entertaining of all. INTERNES CAN'T TAKE MONEY (1937, Paramount) was the first film based on Max Brand's characters, with Joel McCrea as Kildare, but it was not part of the series and did not use any of the later familiar roles. The first official entry, YOUNG DR. KILDARE, starred Lew Ayres as Kildare, Lionel Barrymore as Dr. Gillespie, Laraine Day (Mary Lamont), Alma Kruger (Nurse Molly Byrd), Walter Kingsford (Dr. Carewe, head of the hospital), Nat Pendleton (Joe Wayman, ambulance driver), Emma Dunn and Samuel S. Hinds (Dr. Kildare's benevolent parents), Nell Craig (Nurse Parker), Marie Blake (Sally, switchboard operator), Frank Orth (Mike), and George Reed (Conover). Indeed, the Kildare series has more running characters than most others. Laraine Day left the series after DR. KILDARE'S WEDDING DAY, and the parents left along with Lew Ayres after DR. KILDARE'S VICTORY. Van Johnson and Keye Luke spent several films trying to become Dr. Gillespie's assistant, with Marilyn Maxwell as love interest for Van. Philip Dorn tried out in CALLING DR. GILLESPIE, and James Craig finished the series with DARK DELUSION. Lionel Barrymore appeared in all of them as the crusty Dr. Gillespie, and supported those entries with lesser plots and casts, often by himself. Each film had at least three plots going at once, with a stress on comedy as well as non-gory hospital drama. None of the Kildare films is bad; a few are mediocre, but most of the films are quite enjoyable, with such interesting names as Lana Turner, Ava Gardner, Robert Young, and Red Skelton turning up from time to time.

Dr. Kildare Goes Home (1940) 78m. D: Harold S. Bucquet. Lew Ayres, Lionel Barrymore, Laraine Day, Samuel S. Hinds, Gene Lockhart, Nat Pendleton.

Dr. Kildare's Crisis (1940) 75m. D: Harold S. Bucquet. Lew Ayres, Lionel Barrymore, Laraine Day, Robert Young, Nat Pendleton, Walter Kingsford, Alma Kruger.

Dr. Kildare's Strange Case (1940) 76m. D: Harold S. Bucquet. Lew Ayres, Lionel Barrymore, Laraine Day, Shepperd Strudwick, Samuel S. Hinds, Emma Dunn, Nat Pendleton.▼

Dr. Kildare's Victory (1941) 92m. D: W. S. Van Dyke, II. Lew Ayres, Lionel Barrymore, Ann Ayars, Robert Sterling, Jean Rogers, Alma Kruger.

Dr. Kildare's Wedding Day (1941) 82m. D: Harold S. Bucquet. Lew Ayres, Lionel Barrymore, Laraine Day, Red Skelton,

Alma Kruger, Samuel S. Hinds, Nils Asther.

Dr. Mabuse: Der Spieler (The Gambler) (1922-German) 120m. ***½ D: Fritz Lang. Rudolf Klein-Rogge, Aud Egede Nissen, Gertrude Welcker, Alfred Abel, Lil Dagover, Paul Richter. Baroque tale about master criminal Mabuse (Klein-Rogge), who gambles with lives and fates, is an allegory of postwar German decadence. Brilliantly directed, designed, photographed; originally half of a two-part film, now shown separately.▼

Dr. Mabuse, King of Crime (1922-German) 93m. *** D: Fritz Lang. Rudolf Klein-Rogge, Aud Egede Nissen, Gertrude Welcker, Alfred Abel. Part Two of Lang's epic work DR. MABUSE, DER SPIELER, which follows various story threads and details Mabuse's descent into madness. Not as flamboyant as Part One, but still quite good. Director Lang later made THE TESTAMENT OF DR. MABUSE (1933) and THE THOUSAND EYES OF DR. MABUSE (1960).▼

Dr. Max (1974) C-78m. TVM D: James Goldstone. Lee J. Cobb, Janet Ward, Robert Lipton, David Sheiner, Katherine Helmond, Sorrell Booke. Irascible old G.P. remains dedicated to his less affluent patients in a run-down Baltimore neighborhood, tending to their personal and medical problems and those of his own family. Cobb is his usual larger-than-life self as the curmudgeonly medic. Average.

Dr. Minx (1975) C-94m. BOMB D: Hikmet Avedis. Edy Williams, Randy Boone, Harvey Jason, Marlene Schmidt, Alvy Moore, William Smith. Pitiful exploitation drama about Dr. Williams and her relationships with various men. Eternal starlet Edy's acting is abominable.▼

Dr. No (1962-British) C-111m. ***½ D: Terence Young. Sean Connery, Ursula Andress, Joseph Wiseman, Jack Lord, Bernard Lee, Lois Maxwell. First James Bond film is least pretentious, with meatier story, better all-round production of Ian Fleming caper. Bond investigates strange occurrences in Jamaica, encounters master-fiend Dr. No (Wiseman).▼

Drop-Out Father (1982) C-100m. TVM D: Don Taylor. Dick Van Dyke, Mariette Hartley, George Coe, William Daniels, Monte Markham, Arthur Rosenberg, Jacques Aubuchon, Rhea Perlman. Perceptive contemporary comedy about the effect on himself and his family when successful advertising executive Van Dyke decides to quit the rat race. Written and coproduced by Bob Shanks. Followed six years later by DROP-OUT MOTHER. Above average.

Drop-Out Mother (1988) C-100m. TVM D: Charles S. Dubin. Valerie Harper, Wayne Rogers, Carol Kane, Kim Hunter, Danny Gerard, Jane Eastwood, Alyson

Court, Bruce Gray. Tepid comedy tracing a successful lady executive's transition from big business to becoming housewife and mom. Follow-up by Bob and Ann Shanks to their far more cogent DROP-OUT FATHER six years earlier. Average.▼

Drowning By Numbers (1987-British) C-118m. ***½ D: Peter Greenaway. Joan Plowright, Bernard Hill, Juliet Stephenson, Joely Richardson. Another bizarre, fascinating celluloid put-on from Greenaway, about an obsessive coroner and his involvement with three generations of women from the same family. Stunningly filmed and very entertaining.

Drowning Pool, The (1976) C-108m. **½ D: Stuart Rosenberg. Paul Newman, Joanne Woodward, Anthony Franciosa, Murray Hamilton, Melanie Griffith, Richard Jaeckel, Gail Strickland, Linda Haynes. Newman returns as private eye Harper, (based on Ross MacDonald's Archer character) in slickly made but slow whodunit; here he is called to help former lover Woodward out of a jam. Screenplay by Tracy Keenan Wynn, Lorenzo Semple, and Walter Hill.▼

Dr. Phibes Rises Again (1972-British) C-89m. **½ D: Robert Fuest. Vincent Price, Robert Quarry, Valli Kemp, Fiona Lewis, Peter Cushing, Beryl Reid, Terry-Thomas, Hugh Griffith. Campy sequel to THE ABOMINABLE DR. PHIBES finds Price still looking for elixir to revive his dead wife, with Quarry hot on his trail throughout Egypt.▼

Dr. Popaul SEE: **High Heels**▼

Dr. Rhythm (1938) 80m. **½ D: Frank Tuttle. Bing Crosby, Mary Carlisle, Beatrice Lillie, Andy Devine, Laura Hope Crews, Sterling Holloway. Amiable but second-rate Crosby vehicle about doctor who masquerades as cop and falls in love with woman he's assigned to guard. Lillie adds her distinctive spark.

Dr. Scorpion (1978) C-100m. TVM D: Richard Lang. Nick Mancuso, Christine Lahti, Richard T. Herd, Roscoe Lee Browne, Denny Miller, Sandra Kerns. Silly comic book stuff abut a power-mad genius' plot to rule the world. Below average.

Dr. Socrates (1935) 70m. *** D: William Dieterle. Paul Muni, Ann Dvorak, Barton MacLane, Raymond Brown, Mayo Methot. Enjoyable film about small-town doctor Muni who unwillingly becomes official doctor for wounded mobsters. Offbeat role for Muni, unusually good one for MacLane as loudmouthed gangster. Remade as KING OF THE UNDERWORLD with Kay Francis in the Muni role!

Dr. Strange (1978) C-100m. TVM D: Philip DeGuere. Peter Hooten, Clyde Kusatsu, Jessica Walter, John Mills, Philip Sterling. Marvel Comics Group hero gets a shot at a series in this pilot dealing in the occult, with tongue firmly in cheek. Plot has him joining forces with a world weary sorcerer (played con brio by Sir John Mills) to stop a beautiful witch from adding to her collection of men's souls. Above average.▼

Dr. Strangelove or: How I Learned to Stop Worrying and Love the Bomb (1964-British) 93m. **** D: Stanley Kubrick. Peter Sellers, George C. Scott, Sterling Hayden, Slim Pickens, Keenan Wynn, Peter Bull, James Earl Jones. U.S. President must contend with the Russians and his own political and military leaders when a fanatical general launches A-bomb attack on U.S.S.R. Sellers plays the President, British captain, and mad inventor of the Bomb in this brilliant black comedy, which seems better with each passing year. Sellers' phone conversation with Soviet premier is classic. Outstanding cast, incredible sets by Ken Adam.▼

Dr. Syn (1937-British) 80m. **½ D: Roy William Neill. George Arliss, Margaret Lockwood, John Loder, Roy Emerton, Graham Moffatt. Arliss' final film finds aging star somewhat miscast as English vicar who rides at night as a pirate, but director Neill keeps things moving at his usual pace, and the atmosphere is rich. Remade twice in 1962—as NIGHT CREATURES, and DR. SYN, ALIAS THE SCARECROW.▼

Dr. Syn, Alias the Scarecrow (1962) C-98m. **½ D: James Neilson. Patrick McGoohan, George Cole, Tony Britton, Geoffrey Keen, Kay Walsh, Patrick Wymark. Agreeable Disney production made in England (and originally shown in three parts on the Disney TV show) about country vicar who in reality is a smuggler and pirate. McGoohan is well cast. Filmed before in 1937 with George Arliss; another 1962 version, NIGHT CREATURES, stars Peter Cushing.▼

Dr. Terror's Gallery of Horrors SEE: **Return from the Past**▼

Dr. Terror's House of Horrors (1965-British) C-98m. **½ D: Freddie Francis. Peter Cushing, Christopher Lee, Roy Castle, Donald Sutherland, Neil McCallum, Max Adrian, Edward Underdown, Ursula Howells, Jeremy Kemp, Bernard Lee. Don't let title steer you from this intelligent episodic thriller about a strange doctor (Cushing) who tells five men's fortunes on a train. Enjoyable horror-fantasy.▼

Drugstore Cowboy (1989) C-100m. ***½ D: Gus Van Sant, Jr. Matt Dillon, Kelly Lynch, James Remar, James Le Gros, Heather Graham, Beah Richards, Grace Zabriskie, Max Perlich, William S. Burroughs. Fascinating, completely credible look at the world of a junkie and his "family," who rob drugstores to support their habit. No preaching or moralizing here, which is precisely what gives the film its impact. Standout performances, particularly from Dillon and Lynch. Based on prison inmate James Fogle's unpublished autobiographical novel of the 1970s. Screenplay by Van Sant and Daniel Yost.▼

Drum (1976) **C-110m.** BOMB D: Steve Carver. Warren Oates, Ken Norton, Isela Vega, Pam Grier, Yaphet Kotto, John Colicos. Continuation of MANDINGO—a new and dreadful low in lurid characters and incidents. Norton in title role generates neither interest nor sympathy.▼

Drum, The SEE: Drums▼

Drum Beat (1954) **C-111m.** ** D: Delmer Daves. Alan Ladd, Audrey Dalton, Marisa Pavan, Robert Keith. Post-Civil War tale has Ladd as Indian fighter assigned to negotiate peacefully with warring Indian group.▼

Drums (1938-British) **C-99m.** *** D: Zoltan Korda. Sabu, Raymond Massey, Valerie Hobson, Roger Livesey, David Tree. Fine, colorful adventure with precocious Sabu rescuing British cavalry in 19th-century India; atmospheric and actionful. Originally titled THE DRUM. Original British running time: 104m.▼

Drums Across the River (1954) **C-78m.** ** D: Nathan Juran. Audie Murphy, Lisa Gaye, Walter Brennan, Lyle Bettger. Murphy ties in with gold-jumpers overrunning Indian land, redeems himself by joining forces against these men to achieve peace.

Drums Along the Mohawk (1939) **C-103m.** ***½ D: John Ford. Claudette Colbert, Henry Fonda, Edna May Oliver, John Carradine, Jessie Ralph, Arthur Shields, Robert Lowery, Ward Bond. John Ford richly captures flavor of Colonial life in this vigorous, appealing story of settlers in upstate N.Y. during Revolutionary War. Action, drama, sentiment, and humor are deftly interwoven in beautiful Technicolor production.▼

Drums in the Deep South (1951) **C-87m.** ** D: William Cameron Menzies. James Craig, Barbara Payton, Guy Madison, Barton MacLane, Craig Stevens. Stagnant Civil War yarn of West Pointers who find themselves fighting for opposite causes.▼

Drums of Tahiti (1954) **C-73m.** *½ D: William Castle. Dennis O'Keefe, Patricia Medina, Francis L. Sullivan, George Keymas. 3-D process only redeeming virtue of trite costumer. O'Keefe is footloose American who aids revolt against French annexation attempt of Tahiti.

Dr. Who and the Daleks (1965-British) **C-85m.** **½ D: Gordon Flemyng. Peter Cushing, Roy Castle, Jennie Linden, Roberta Tovey, Barrie Ingham. Pleasing feature inspired by the long-running British TV serial, with the Doctor and his young friends transported to another world where humans are threatened by robotlike Daleks. Followed by DALEKS—INVASION EARTH 2150 A.D.▼

Dry White Season, A (1989) **C-107m.** **½ D: Euzhan Palcy. Donald Sutherland, Janet Suzman, Zakes Mokae, Jurgen Prochnow, Susan Sarandon, Marlon Brando, Winston Ntshona, Thoko Ntshinga, Susannah Harker, Rowan Elmes. Disappointing film about South African apartheid, set in 1976, with Sutherland as a schoolteacher who slowly awakens to the appalling reality of how blacks are treated in his country. Crucially important subject matter is unfortunately presented in the context of a story that's contrived and dramatically hollow. Brando is magnetic (if somewhat askew) in a showy supporting role as an outspoken barrister.▼

DuBarry Was a Lady (1943) **C-101m.** *** D: Roy Del Ruth. Red Skelton, Lucille Ball, Gene Kelly, Virginia O'Brien, Rags Ragland, Zero Mostel, Donald Meek, George Givot, Louise Beavers, Tommy Dorsey and His Orchestra. Some idiot decided to scrap most of the original Cole Porter score, but see this if you've never thought Ball could look gorgeous; Karl Freund, who photographed her here, later became director of photography on *I Love Lucy*. High highs and low lows; plot piffle has Red downing a mickey, then dreaming he's Louis XV. Wildest bit: seeing Dorsey's orchestra—including Buddy Rich, Dick Haymes, and Jo Stafford—in wigs and period costume. Surviving Porter songs include "Friendship" and "Do I Love You?"▼

Du Barry, Woman of Passion (1930) **90m.** ** D: Sam Taylor. Norma Talmadge, William Farnum, Conrad Nagel, Hobart Bosworth, Alison Skipworth. Early sound version of oft-told tale about the life and loves of the famous 18th-century courtesan. Stiff and primitive but with fine art direction by William Cameron Menzies.

Du-beat-e-o (1984) **C/B&W-87m.** *½ D: Alan Sacks. Ray Sharkey, Joan Jett, Derf Scratch, Len Lesser, Nora Gaye. Outrageous, obnoxious, gimmicky punk collage about hip filmmaker Sharkey, who has been ordered by his mob financiers to complete his rock 'n' roll movie in 31 hours. Lots of energy, but it's all sorely misplaced.▼

Duchess and the Dirtwater Fox, The (1976) **C-103m.** *½ D: Melvin Frank. George Segal, Goldie Hawn, Conrad Janis, Thayer David, Roy Jenson, Bob Hoy. Dumb comedy about cardsharp Segal and dance-hall cutie Hawn teaming up in the Old West. Occasional laughs, inappropriate song interludes.▼

Duchess of Idaho (1950) **C-98m.** **½ D: Robert Z. Leonard. Esther Williams, Van Johnson, John Lund, Paula Raymond,

Amanda Blake, Eleanor Powell, Lena Horne. Williams' vehicle takes her to Sun Valley, where she's trying to help patch up roommate's romance but falls in love herself. MGM guest stars pep up the formula production.

Duck Soup (1933) 70m. **** D: Leo McCarey. Groucho, Harpo, Chico, Zeppo Marx, Margaret Dumont, Louis Calhern, Raquel Torres, Edgar Kennedy, Leonid Kinsky, Charles Middleton. The Marx Brothers' most sustained bit of insanity, a flop when first released, but now considered a satiric masterpiece. In postage-stamp-sized Freedonia, Prime Minister Rufus T. Firefly (Groucho) declares war on neighboring Sylvania just for the hell of it. Enough gags for five movies, but our favorite is still the mirror sequence. Zeppo's swan song with his brothers.▼

Duck, You Sucker (1972-Italian) C-138m. *** D: Sergio Leone. Rod Steiger, James Coburn, Romolo Valli, Maria Monti. Big, sprawling story of Mexican revolution, and how peasant thief Steiger gets talked into taking sides by Irish explosives expert Coburn. Tremendous action sequences; Leone's wry touches and ultra-weird Ennio Morricone score make it worthwhile diversion. Also known as A FISTFUL OF DYNAMITE, some prints of which run 121m. Released in Italy at 158m.▼

Dude Goes West, The (1948) 87m. ** D: Kurt Neumann. Eddie Albert, Gale Storm, James Gleason, Binnie Barnes, Gilbert Roland, Barton MacLane. Innocuous little comedy of Easterner Albert becoming a Western hero.

Dudes (1987) C-90m. BOMB D: Penelope Spheeris. Jon Cryer, Daniel Roebuck, Flea, Lee Ving, Catherine Mary Stewart. Incomprehensible, idiotic account of a trio of N.Y.C. punk rockers, and their fate when harassed by a gang of redneck killers in the Southwest. Thoroughly repugnant.▼

Dudes are Pretty People (1942) 95m. ** D: Hal Roach, Jr. Jimmy Rogers, Noah Beery, Jr., Marjorie Woodworth, Paul Hurst, Marjorie Gateson, Russell Gleason, Jan Duggan, Grady Sutton. A couple of itinerant cowboys move to a dude ranch when one of them falls for a flashy blonde. Pretty dull. This was originally one of producer Hal Roach's "Streamliner" featurettes, running 46m; for TV release it's been spliced to its equally dull sequel, CALABOOSE.

Duel (1971) C-90m. TVM D: Steven Spielberg. Dennis Weaver, Tim Herbert, Charles Peel, Eddie Firestone. Businessman driving rented car on lonely stretch of road begins to realize that the driver of a diesel truck (whom he cannot see) is out to get him. This TV movie put Spielberg on the map, and rightly so;

superb suspense film, from Richard Matheson's script. Originally telecast at 73m.; released theatrically in 1983 at 88m. Above average.▼

Duel at Apache Wells (1957) 70m. *½ D: Joe Kane. Anna Maria Alberghetti, Ben Cooper, Jim Davis, Bob Steele, Frank Puglia. Title tells more than all in standard oater.

Duel at Diablo (1966) C-103m. *** D: Ralph Nelson. James Garner, Sidney Poitier, Bibi Andersson, Dennis Weaver, Bill Travers. Aging Indians vs. Cavalry formula comes alive in this exciting Western; offbeat casting with tight direction. Some may find it too violent, but a must for action and Western fans.▼

Duel at Silver Creek, The (1952) C-77m. *½ D: Don Siegel. Audie Murphy, Stephen McNally, Faith Domergue, Susan Cabot, Gerald Mohr. Ponderous oater has Murphy as the "Silver Kid" helping marshal fight town criminals.

Duel at the Rio Grande (1962-Italian) C-93m. ** D: Mario Caiano. Sean Flynn, Danielle de Metz, Folco Lulli, Armando Calvo. Bland reworking of THE MARK OF ZORRO, with Flynn (Errol's son) uneasy in lead role.

Duel in Durango SEE: **Gun Duel in Durango**

Duel in the Jungle (1954-British) C-102m. **½ D: George Marshall. Dana Andrews, Jeanne Crain, David Farrar, George Coulouris, Wilfrid Hyde-White. Action-packed adventure of insurance investigator tracking allegedly dead man to Africa. Strong cast.

Duel in the Sun (1946) C-130m. *** D: King Vidor. Jennifer Jones, Joseph Cotten, Gregory Peck, Lionel Barrymore, Lillian Gish, Herbert Marshall, Walter Huston, Butterfly McQueen, Charles Bickford, Tilly Losch, Harry Carey. Producer-writer David O. Selznick's ambitious attempt to duplicate success of GONE WITH THE WIND: big, brawling, engrossing, often stupid sex-Western, with half-breed Jones caught between brothers Peck and Cotten. Great in color, with some memorable scenes and an unexpectedly bizarre finale. From the novel by Niven Busch.▼

Duellists, The (1977-British) C-101m. *** D: Ridley Scott. Keith Carradine, Harvey Keitel, Edward Fox, Cristina Raines, Robert Stephens, Diana Quick, Tom Conti, Albert Finney. Competent screen version of Joseph Conrad's The Duel concerns long-running feud between French officers Carradine and Keitel during the Napoleonic wars. Supporting players are more convincing than two leads, but film is among most staggeringly beautiful of its time. Director Scott's first feature.▼

Duel of Champions (1961-Italian) C-105m. ** D: Ferdinando Baldi. Alan

Ladd, Franca Bettoja, Franco Fabrizi, Robert Keith, Luciano Marin. Stodgy epic set in ancient Rome with bored-looking Ladd the Roman leader who challenges forces of Alba.▼

Duel of the Titans (1961-Italian) **C-88m.** ** D: Sergio Corbucci. Steve Reeves, Gordon Scott, Virna Lisi, Massimo Girotti. Reeves is Romulus and Scott is Remus in this fictional account of justice overcoming tyranny in ancient Rome.

Duet for Four (1982-Australian) **C-97m.** *½ D: Tim Burstall. Mike Preston, Wendy Hughes, Michael Pate, Diane Cilento, Gary Day, Arthur Dignam, Rod Mullinar. Middle-aged Preston's life is in turmoil: his wife has a lover, his mistress wants marriage, his daughter might be a drug addict, his business may be taken over. Weak drama does not delve beneath the surface of its characters.

Duet for One (1986) **C-107m.** **½ D: Andrei Konchalovsky. Julie Andrews, Alan Bates, Max von Sydow, Rupert Everett, Margaret Courtenay, Cathryn Harrison, Macha Meril, Liam Neeson. World-class violinist Andrews is stricken with multiple sclerosis, and her comfortable, rewarding life is shattered. Tom Kempinski based his two-character play (virtuoso and psychiatrist) on a real-life cellist, but for film it was opened up and, in the process, diluted. Husband Bates, therapist von Sydow, and rebellious protegé Everett are fine, but it's Andrews' gutsy performance that breathes life into the film. Made in England.▼

Duffy (1968-U.S.-British) **C-101m.** *½ D: Robert Parrish. James Coburn, James Mason, James Fox, Susannah York, John Alderton. Scummy crime comedy about two half-brothers who decide to rob their father of bank notes he is transporting by ship. A waste of everyone's talents and lovely location photography.

Duffy's of San Quentin (1954) **78m.** **½ D: Walter Doniger. Louis Hayward, Joanne Dru, Paul Kelly, Maureen O'Sullivan, George Macready. Low-keyed account of Warden Duffy's reforms within the famed prison. Followed by THE STEEL CAGE.

Duffy's Tavern (1945) **97m.** BOMB D: Hal Walker. Barry Sullivan, Marjorie Reynolds, Bing Crosby, Dorothy Lamour, Alan Ladd, Betty Hutton, Eddie Bracken, Veronica Lake, Robert Benchley, Paulette Goddard, Brian Donlevy. Disastrous "comedy" of radio character Ed Gardner trying to save Duffy's Tavern, Victor Moore trying to save his record company. No redeeming values despite guest appearances by several dozen Paramount stars.

Duke of West Point, The (1938) **109m.** **½ D: Alfred E. Green. Louis Hayward, Joan Fontaine, Tom Brown, Richard Carlson, Alan Curtis, Donald Barry. Predictable West Point saga of honor and love at the Academy is trite but entertaining, with Fontaine winning as the ingenue.

Dulcima (1971-British) **C-93m.** **½ D: Frank Nesbitt. Carol White, John Mills, Stuart Wilson, Bernard Lee, Sheila Raynor. Poor White moves in with and exploits wealthy old farmer Mills. OK melodrama benefits from solid work by the stars. Original running time: 98m.

Dulcimer Street (1948-British) **112m.** **½ D: Sidney Gilliat. Richard Attenborough, Alastair Sim, Stephen Murray, Fay Compton. Atmospheric account of a slum area of London and its inhabitants who champion one of their own accused of murder. Original British title: LONDON BELONGS TO ME.

Dulcy (1940) **64m.** *½ D: S. Sylvan Simon. Ann Sothern, Ian Hunter, Roland Young, Reginald Gardiner, Billie Burke, Lynne Carver, Dan Dailey, Jr. Pretty bad comedy of Chinese orphan mending new family's problems. Good cast with inferior material.

Dumbo (1941) **C-64m.** **** D: Ben Sharpsteen. Voices of Sterling Holloway, Edward Brophy, Verna Felton, Herman Bing, Cliff Edwards. One of Walt Disney's most charming animated films, about pint-sized elephant with giant-sized ears, and how his friend Timothy the Mouse helps build his confidence. Never a dull moment, but pink-elephants dream sequence is special treat. Frank Churchill and Oliver Wallace's scoring earned them Oscars.▼

Dummy (1979) **C-100m.** TVM D: Frank Perry. Paul Sorvino, LeVar Burton, Brian Dennehy, Rose Gregorio, Gregg Henry. Real-life account of the relationship between a deaf and dumb black youth accused of murder and the deaf court-appointed attorney who defended him in the precedent-setting Chicago trial. Tour-de-force roles for Sorvino, exceptionally good as the lawyer, and Burton. Ernest Tidyman's tidy script another plus. Above average.

Dune (1984) **C-140m.** *½ D: David Lynch. Kyle MacLachlan, Francesca Annis, Brad Dourif, Jose Ferrer, Linda Hunt, Freddie Jones, Richard Jordan, Virginia Madsen, Silvana Mangano, Kenneth McMillan, Jack Nance, Sian Phillips, Jurgen Prochnow, Paul Smith, Sting, Dean Stockwell, Max von Sydow, Sean Young. Elephantine adaptation of Frank Herbert's popular sci-fi novel set in the year 10,991. You know you're in trouble when film's opening narration (setting up the story) is completely incomprehensible! Visually imaginative, well cast, but joyless and oppressive—not to mention *long*. For devotees of Herbert's novel only. (A special 190-minute edition of the film was prepared from scratch for TV airings, under protest from director Lynch. It contains much new narration and footage that wasn't used in the theatrical version. The TV print credits the pseudonymous Allen Smithee as director.)▼

Dunera Boys, The (1985-Australian) C-150m. **½ D: Sam Lewin. Joseph Spano, Bob Hoskins, Joseph Furst, John Meillon, Warren Mitchell, Mary-Anne Fahey, Simon Chilvers, Steven Vidler, Moshe Kedem. Low-key, fact-based drama of Jewish refugees in England at the outset of WW2 who, because of their nationalities, are suspected of being Nazi spies and exiled to a POW camp in Australia. Hoskins plays a loutish fishmonger who's as English as Winston Churchill, but somehow is deported with the others. Fascinating subject matter is occasionally pointed, but film is overlong and uneven. Made for Australian television.▼

Dungeonmaster, The (1985) C-73m. *½ D: Rosemarie Turko, John Buechler, Charles Band, David Allen, Steve Ford, Peter Manoogian, Ted Nicolaou. Jeffrey Byron, Richard Moll, Leslie Wing, Blackie Lawless, Danny Dick. It took seven—count 'em, seven—directors to make this short, sour chronicle of a girl held hostage by a villain. Her savior (atrociously played by Byron) must overcome seven challenges. You have only one: to sit through this.▼

Dunkirk (1958-British) 113m. **½ D: Leslie Norman. John Mills, Robert Urquhart, Ray Jackson, Meredith Edwards. Documentary-style drama recounting 1940 evacuation of Allied troops, relying too much on newsreel footage. Original British running time: 135m.

Dunwich Horror, The (1970) C-90m. **½ D: Daniel Haller. Sandra Dee, Dean Stockwell, Ed Begley, Sam Jaffe, Lloyd Bochner, Joanna Moore, Talia Coppola (Shire). Adaptation of H.P. Lovecraft's novel about warlock Stockwell's sinister plans for girlfriend Dee. Often effective, but ending ruins the whole film.▼

Durant Affair, The (1962-British) 73m. *½ D: Godfrey Grayson. Jane Griffiths, Conrad Phillips, Nigel Green, Simon Lack. Flabby courtroom melodrama.

Dust (1985-French-Belgian) C-88m. ***½ D: Marion Hansel. Jane Birkin, Trevor Howard, John Matshikiza, Nadine Uwampa, Lourdes Christina Sayo, Rene Diaz. Birkin gives a fine performance as an unmarried woman, in need of love and affection, who murders her arrogant father (Howard) after he seduces the wife of his farm's black foreman. An intense, rewarding portrayal of isolation, oppression, and degradation.▼

Dust Be My Destiny (1939) 88m. **½ D: Lewis Seiler. John Garfield, Priscilla Lane,

Alan Hale, Frank McHugh, John Litel, Billy Halop, Henry Armetta, Stanley Ridges, Bobby Jordan, Charley Grapewin. Garfield is ideally cast as an alienated drifter who finds himself in jail, where he falls for vicious prison foreman's stepdaughter (Lane). The stars rise above their less-than-original material.

Dusty (1982-Australian) C-88m. *** D: John Richardson. Bill Kerr, Noel Trevarthen, Carol Burns, Nicholas Holland, John Stanton, Kate Edwards. Subtle, touching little film about a dingo (wild dog of the bush), who's captured while a puppy and eventually raised by an old man (Kerr). Adults will enjoy it as much as kids.▼

Dusty and Sweets McGee (1971) C-95m. ***½ D: Floyd Mutrux. Unconventional, no-holds-barred documentary detailing day-to-day life of various heroin addicts in Los Angeles area. Among real-life addicts and pushers shown is Billy Gray of TV's *Father Knows Best.*

Dutchman (1966-British) 55m. **½ D: Anthony Harvey. Shirley Knight, Al Freeman, Jr. Two-character allegory, based on LeRoi Jones's play, of confrontation between sadistic white trollop Knight and naive black Freeman in a subway car. Tense and well acted, but contrived.

Dying Room Only (1973) C-74m. TVM. D: Phillip Leacock. Cloris Leachman, Ross Martin, Ned Beatty, Louise Latham, Dana Elcar, Dabney Coleman. Couple traveling back to L.A. via desert by car stop off at roadside diner; husband mysteriously disappears. Excellent mood thanks to Richard Matheson's surprise-ending script, thoughtful direction, and small ensemble cast. Above average.▼

Dynamite (1929) 129m. *** D: Cecil B. DeMille. Conrad Nagel, Kay Johnson, Charles Bickford, Julia Faye, Joel McCrea. Enough plot for seven films in this silly but fascinating early talkie; aristocratic Johnson marries miner Bickford, who's about to be executed, to gain inheritance .. then Bickford is cleared. Typical DeMille entertainment.

Dynamite (1949) 69m. *½ D: William H. Pine. William Gargan, Virginia Welles, Richard Crane, Irving Bacon, Frank Ferguson, Mary Newton. Young commercial dynamiter Crane clashes with older colleague Gargan over affections of Welles in standard B-opus.▼

Dynamite Chicken (1971) C/B&W-76m. ** D: Ernie Pintoff. Richard Pryor, John Lennon, Yoko Ono, Sha Na Na, Ace Trucking Company, Joan Baez, Ron Carey, Andy Warhol, Paul Krassner, Leonard Cohen, Malcolm X, many others. Odd, dated pastiche of songs, skits, television commercial parodies and old movie clips, filmed when nudity and profanity on celluloid were still shocking. Worth a look alone for Pryor.▼

Each Dawn I Die (1939) 92m. *** D: William Keighley. James Cagney, George Raft, George Bancroft, Jane Bryan, Maxie Rosenbloom, Thurston Hall. Reporter Cagney is framed, sent to prison, where he meets tough-guy Raft. Good performances all around, but last half of film becomes outrageously improbable.▼

Eager Beavers SEE: **Swinging Barmaids**

Eagle, The (1925) 77m. *** D: Clarence Brown. Rudolph Valentino, Vilma Banky, Louise Dresser, Albert Conti, James Marcus, George Nichols. Valentino plays a sort of Russian Robin Hood in this entertaining costume picture, winning the hand of Vilma Banky while trying to outwit Czarina Dresser, angry because he snubbed her advances.▼

Eagle and the Hawk, The (1933) 68m. ***½ D: Stuart Walker. Fredric March, Cary Grant, Jack Oakie, Carole Lombard, Guy Standing, Douglas Scott. Well-produced antiwar film with reluctant hero March, co-pilot Grant, everyone's friend Oakie, society girl Lombard. Still timely. Originally 72m.

Eagle and the Hawk, The (1950) C-104m. **½ D: Lewis R. Foster. John Payne, Rhonda Fleming, Dennis O'Keefe, Thomas Gomez, Fred Clark. Contrived actioner set in 1860s Mexico-Texas with O'Keefe and Payne U.S. law enforcers stifling coup to make Maximilian ruler of Mexico; Fleming is fetching love interest.

Eagle Has Landed, The (1977) C-123m. *** D: John Sturges. Michael Caine, Donald Sutherland, Robert Duvall, Jenny Agutter, Donald Pleasence, Anthony Quayle, Jean Marsh, Sven-Bertil Taube, John Standing, Judy Geeson, Treat Williams, Larry Hagman. Action-packed wartime adventure taken from fanciful Jack Higgins bestseller about Nazi plot to kidnap Winston Churchill. Hardly a dull moment, thanks to solid cast and lively, twist-laden story. Original running time in England was 134m.▼

Eagle in a Cage (1971-British) C-98m. *** D: Fielder Cook. John Gielgud, Ralph Richardson, Billie Whitelaw, Kenneth Haigh, Moses Gunn, Ferdy Mayne. Fine drama of Napoleon in exile on St. Helena. Haigh is quite impressive in the title role, and is surrounded by a top cast. Screenplay by Millard Lampell.

Eagles Over London (1970-Italian) C-97m. **½ D: Enzo Castellari. Frederick Stafford, Van Johnson, Francisco Rabal, Evelyn Stewart, Christian Hay. German intelligence group infiltrates British High Command on the eve of Battle of Britain. Shopworn war drama.

Eagle Squadron (1942) 109m. **½ D: Arthur Lubin. Robert Stack, Eddie Albert, Diana Barrymore, Nigel Bruce, Jon Hall, Evelyn Ankers, Gladys Cooper, Mary Carr. Usual WW2 action and romance as young American fliers fought the war in the RAF. Good action scenes help average script.

Eagle's Wing (1979-British) C-111m. *½ D: Anthony Harvey. Martin Sheen, Sam Waterston, Caroline Langrishe, Harvey Keitel, Stephane Audran, John Castle, Jorge Luke. God never intended penguins to fly or the British to make Westerns. Dreary, artsy glop entangling half a dozen plots cribbed from other, better oaters; principal one involves seesawing between renegade Indian Waterston and trapper Sheen for possession of a magnificent white stallion. Billy Williams's lush cinematography doesn't help. Screenplay by John Briley (GANDHI). Most U.S. prints run 98m.▼

Earl Carroll Vanities (1945) 91m. **½ D: Joseph Santley. Dennis O'Keefe, Constance Moore, Eve Arden, Otto Kruger. Republic Pictures tried hard to give this musical class, but zest and production values are lacking; Arden adds her usual quips.

Earl of Chicago, The (1940) 85m. **½ D: Richard Thorpe. Robert Montgomery, Edward Arnold, Reginald Owen, Edmund Gwenn. Montgomery can't put over farfetched tale of Chicago mobster inheriting English title. His awkward performance strains film's credibility.

Early Frost, An (1985) C-100m. TVM D: John Erman. Gena Rowlands, Ben Gazzara, Sylvia Sidney, Aidan Quinn, D.W. Moffett, John Glover, Sydney Walsh. Emotion-packed drama about the effect on a family when their son breaks the news that he not only is gay but also has contracted AIDS. Terrific work by entire cast, bringing out the best of Ron Cowen and Daniel Lipman's solid, never maudlin, Emmy-winning script (based on Sherman Yellen's story). Above average.▼

Early to Bed (1936) 75m. **½ D: Norman Z. McLeod. Mary Boland, Charlie Ruggles, George Barbier, Gail Patrick, Robert McWade, Lucien Littlefield. Ruggles' sleepwalking involves him in shady adventure with gangsters. Boland and Ruggles are a perfect match.

Earrings of Madame de . . . , The (1954-French) 105m. ***½ D: Max Ophuls. Charles Boyer, Danielle Darrieux, Vittorio De Sica. Captivating story of fickle woman's regard for significant pair of earrings; masterfully filmed and acted. Also known as DIAMOND EARRINGS.▼

Earthbound (1981) C-94m. *½ D: James L. Conway. Burl Ives, Christopher Connelly, Meredith MacRae, Joseph Campanella, Todd Porter, Marc Gilpin, Elissa Leeds, John Schuck, Stuart Pankin. Average family from outer space lands in Middle America due to a faulty flying saucer.

Will dastardly government official Campanella shoot them? Trite, dumb, idiotic.

Earth Dies Screaming, The (1964-British) **62m.** **½ D: Terence Fisher. Willard Parker, Virginia Field, Dennis Price, Vanda Godsell. Grim thriller with invaders taking over remote village; packs great initial suspense but labors.

Earth Girls Are Easy (1989) C-**100m.** **½ D: Julien Temple. Geena Davis, Jeff Goldblum, Jim Carrey, Damon Wayans, Julie Brown, Michael McKean, Charles Rocket, Larry Linville, Rick Overton, Angelyne. Infectiously goofy musical comedy about aliens landing in the San Fernando Valley and being ushered into materialistic Southern California life by a ditsy manicurist. Not enough substance to sustain a feature film, but there are some good laughs, and an endearing performance by Davis. Costar Brown (who sings the airhead anthem " 'Cause I'm a Blonde") also cowrote the movie.▼

Earthling, The (1980-Australian) C-**102m.** **½ D: Peter Collinson. William Holden, Ricky Schroder, Jack Thompson, Olivia Hamnett, Alwyn Kurts. Holden, terminally ill, teaches Schroder, orphaned and lost, how to survive in the bush country. OK drama features much nature footage and will appeal mainly to kids. Originally released at 97m., later reedited and lengthened to 102m.▼

✓ **Earthquake** (1974) C-**129m.** BOMB D: Mark Robson. Charlton Heston, Ava Gardner, George Kennedy, Genevieve Bujold, Richard Roundtree, Lorne Greene, Barry Sullivan, Marjoe Gortner, Lloyd Nolan, Victoria Principal, Walter Matthau. Title tells the story in hackneyed disaster epic originally released in Sensurround. Marjoe as a sex deviate and Gardner as Lorne Greene's *daughter* tie for film's top casting honors. Additional footage was shot for inclusion in network showings. An Oscar winner for special effects.▼

Earth's Final Fury SEE: **When Time Ran Out . . .**

Earth*Star Voyager (1988) C-**200m.** TVM D: James Goldstone. Duncan Regehr, Brian McNamara, Julia Montgomery, Jason Michas, Tom Breznahan, Margaret Langrick, Sean O'Byrne, Lynnette Mettey. Disney sci-fier in *Star Trek* territory, with six young space cadets on an interstellar voyage 100 years into the future. Pilot to a prospective series. Originally shown in two parts. Average.

Earth II (1971) C-**100m.** TVM. D: Tom Gries. Hari Rhodes, Gary Lockwood, Tony Franciosa, Gary Merrill, Lew Ayres, Scott Hylands. Workable premise that doesn't lead anywhere; depiction of day-to-day operations of space station, with good performances battling forgettable dialogue. Average.

Earth vs. the Flying Saucers (1956) **82m.** ✓ *** D: Fred F. Sears. Hugh Marlowe, Joan Taylor, Donald Curtis, Morris Ankrum, Tom Browne Henry, voice of Paul Frees. Matter-of-fact presentation gives tremendous boost to familiar storyline (alien invaders order us to surrender peaceably—or else). Literate dialogue, subdued performances, and solid Ray Harryhausen effects make this a winner that belies its B origins nearly every step of the way.▼

Earthworm Tractors (1936) **69m.** **½ D: Ray Enright. Joe E. Brown, June Travis, Guy Kibbee, Dick Foran, Carol Hughes, Gene Lockhart, Olin Howland. Broad comedy with Joe as *Saturday Evening Post* character Alexander Botts, braggart and tractor salesman extraordinaire.▼

East End Chant SEE: **Limehouse Blues**

Easter Parade (1948) C-**103m.** ***½ D: Charles Walters. Judy Garland, Fred Astaire, Peter Lawford, Ann Miller, Jules Munshin. Delightful Irving Berlin musical about Astaire trying to forget ex-dance partner Miller while rising to stardom with Garland. Musical highlights include Astaire's solo "Stepping Out With My Baby," Miller's "Shaking the Blues Away," Fred and Judy's "A Couple of Swells," and the Fifth Avenue finale with Berlin's title song.▼

Easter Sunday SEE: **Being, The**▼

East of Borneo (1931) **76m.** *½ D: George Melford. Rose Hobart, Charles Bickford, Georges Renavent, Lupita Tovar, Noble Johnson. Headache-inducing melodrama about desperate Hobart, who treks into the jungle to find physician husband Bickford; he thinks she's cheated on him, and has become a cynical alcoholic. Dull and deadening.▼

East of Eden (1955) C-**115m.** **** D: ✓ Elia Kazan. James Dean, Julie Harris, Raymond Massey, Jo Van Fleet, Burl Ives, Richard Davalos, Albert Dekker. Emotionally overwhelming adaptation of the John Steinbeck novel about two brothers' rivalry for the love of their father; affects today's generation as much as those who witnessed Dean's starring debut. Van Fleet won Oscar as boys' mother. Screenplay by Paul Osborn. Remade as TV mini-series.▼

East of Elephant Rock (1977-British) C-**92m.** BOMB D: Don Boyd. Judi Bowker, John Hurt, Jeremy Kemp, Christopher Cazenove, Anton Rodgers. Inept period drama set in 1948 Malaya; final reel ripped off from W. Somerset Maugham's THE LETTER. Further sabotaged by campy songs on soundtrack as well as opening disclaimer, which invites viewers to "laugh and smile" at the film. Bowker is beautiful, as are Sri Lanka locations.▼

East of Kilimanjaro (1957-U.S.-British-Italian) C-**75m.** *½ D: Arnold Belgard, Edoardo Capolino. Marshall Thompson,

Gaby Andre, Fausto Tozzi, Kris Aschan, Rolf Aschan. Dull story of cameraman Thompson and efforts to halt virus affecting cattle in title region. Filmed in Africa. Original running time: 85m.; some prints 72m. Also known as THE BIG SEARCH.

East of Shanghai SEE: **Rich and Strange**▼

East of Sudan (1966-British) **C-84m.** ** D: Nathan Juran. Anthony Quayle, Sylvia Sims, Derek Fowlds, Jenny Agutter, Johnny Sekka. British trooper falls for English governess when he leads her and several others to safety from Arabs in 1880s; OK juvenile adventure.

East of Sumatra (1953) **C-82m.** **½ D: Budd Boetticher. Jeff Chandler, Marilyn Maxwell, Anthony Quinn, Suzan Ball, Peter Graves. Satisfactory actioner set on Pacific island. Chandler is mining engineer trying to prevent native uprising while romancing Maxwell; Quinn effective as villain. Based on a Louis L'Amour novel.

East of the River (1940) **73m.** **½ D: Alfred E. Green. John Garfield, Brenda Marshall, Marjorie Rambeau, William Lundigan, George Tobias, Jack LaRue, Douglas Fowley. Another variation of MANHATTAN MELODRAMA, with childhood pals Garfield and Lundigan growing up on opposite sides of the law. Rambeau is fine as Garfield's mother.

East Side Kids Meet Bela Lugosi, The SEE: **Ghosts on the Loose**▼

East Side of Heaven (1939) **90m.** **½ D: David Butler. Bing Crosby, Joan Blondell, Mischa Auer, Irene Hervey, C. Aubrey Smith, Baby Sandy. Cute Crosby comedy with songs; Bing becomes guardian of abandoned baby, croons title tune, "Sing A Song of Sunbeams."

East Side, West Side (1949) **108m.** **½ D: Mervyn LeRoy. Barbara Stanwyck, James Mason, Ava Gardner, Van Heflin, Cyd Charisse, Gale Sondergaard, William Frawley, Nancy Davis (Reagan). Stanwyck and Mason have pivotal roles as chic N.Y.C. society couple with abundant marital woes, stirred up by alluring Gardner and understanding Heflin. Static MGM version of Marcia Davenport's superficial novel.

Easy Come, Easy Go (1947) **77m.** **½ D: John Farrow. Barry Fitzgerald, Diana Lynn, Sonny Tufts, Dick Foran, Frank McHugh, Allen Jenkins. Fitzgerald is his usual self as a horseplayer who refuses to let daughter Lynn get married.▼

Easy Come, Easy Go (1967) **73m.** *½ D: John Rich. Elvis Presley, Dodie Marshal, Pat Priest, Elsa Lanchester, Frank McHugh, Pat Harrington. Presley's a frogman diving for buried treasure in this hackneyed comedy. Fortunately, he doesn't sing underwater. Yet he does get to perform such classics as "The Love Machine" and "Yoga Is As Yoga Does."▼

Easy Go SEE: **Free and Easy**

Easy Life, The (1963-Italian) **105m.** *** D: Dino Risi. Vittorio Gassman, Catherine Spaak, Jean-Louis Trintignant, Luciana Angiolillo. Gassman has proper joie de vivre for playing middle-aged playboy who introduces student Trintignant to life of frolic with tragic results; well-played and haunting.▼

Easy Living (1937) **86m.** *** D: Mitchell Leisen. Jean Arthur, Edward Arnold, Ray Milland, Franklin Pangborn, William Demarest, Mary Nash, Luis Alberni. Millionaire Arnold throws spoiled-wife's mink out the window; it drops on unsuspecting working girl Arthur. Arnold's son Milland, off making his career, falls in love. The girl: Arthur. Delightful comedy written by Preston Sturges.

Easy Living (1949) **77m.** *** D: Jacques Tourneur. Victor Mature, Lizabeth Scott, Lucille Ball, Sonny Tufts, Lloyd Nolan, Paul Stewart, Jeff Donnell, Jack Paar, Art Baker. Mature is aging football star who can't adjust to impending retirement—especially under constant pressure from grasping wife Scott. Intelligent film from Irwin Shaw story, with good performance from Lucy as team secretary in love with Mature.▼

Easy Money (1983) **C-95m.** **½ D: James Signorelli. Rodney Dangerfield, Joe Pesci, Geraldine Fitzgerald, Candy Azzara, Taylor Negron, Jennifer Jason Leigh, Tom Ewell. Working-class slob has one year to give up all his bad habits—drinking, overeating, smoking, gambling—in order to collect big inheritance. Dangerfield's first starring comedy vehicle is pleasant enough—with a refreshing amount of restraint for an 80s comedy. Final gag is right out of W. C. Fields.▼

Easy Prey (1986) **C-100m.** TVM D: Sandor Stern. Gerald McRaney, Shawnee Smith, Sean McCann, Susan Hogan, Kate Lynch. Exploitive fact-based drama about psychopathic kidnapper and serial killer Christopher Wilder and the teenage girl he drags with him on a cross-country ride of terror. Numbingly repulsive. Below average.

Easy Rider (1969) **C-94m.** ***½ D: Dennis Hopper. Peter Fonda, Dennis Hopper, Jack Nicholson, Karen Black, Luke Askew, Luana Anders, Robert Walker, Phil Spector. Low-budget film of alienated youth nearly ruined Hollywood when every studio tried to duplicate its success. Tale of two cyclists chucking it all and searching for "the real America," while inevitably dated, remains quite worthwhile, highlighted by fine Laszlo Kovacs photography, great rock soundtrack, and Nicholson's star-making performance as boozy lawyer who tags along. Written by Fonda, Hopper, and Terry Southern.▼

Easy to Love (1953) **C-96m.** **½ D:

Charles Walters. Esther Williams, Van Johnson, Tony Martin, John Bromfield, Carroll Baker. Pleasant Williams aquatic vehicle set at Florida's Cypress Gardens, with Johnson and Martin vying for her love. Spectacular production numbers by Busby Berkeley. Baker's first film.

Easy to Wed (1946) **C-110m.** **½ D: Edward Buzzell. Van Johnson, Esther Williams, Lucille Ball, Keenan Wynn, Cecil Kellaway. Remake of LIBELED LADY can't hold a candle to original, but remains passable comedy, with Lucy in one of her first major comedy showcases.

Easy Virtue (1927-British) **79m.** **½ D: Alfred Hitchcock. Isabel Jeans, Franklin Dyall, Eric Bransby Williams, Ian Hunter, Robin Irvine, Violet Farebrother. Jeans suffers nobly as the wife of an alcoholic and the lover of a suicide in this melodramatic silent Hitchcock. Laughable dramatics but imaginatively shot, based on a Noel Coward play.▼

Easy Way, The SEE: **Room For One More**

Eat a Bowl of Tea (1989) **C-104m.** *** D: Wayne Wang. Cora Miao, Russell Wong, Victor Wong, Lau Siu Ming, Eric Tsang Chi Wai. From 1924 until the end of WW2, most Chinese women were not allowed to accompany their menfolk who emigrated to the U.S. This charming but pointed ethnic comedy chronicles what happened when the ban was lifted, as American-born Russell Wong brings Chinese-born bride Miao to N.Y.C. A film that no one else but Wang could have made. A PBS *American Playhouse* theatrical production.▼

Eaten Alive (1976) **C-96m.** **½ D: Tobe Hooper. Neville Brand, Mel Ferrer, Carolyn Jones, Marilyn Burns, William Finley, Stuart Whitman. Ill-fated Hollywood debut feature by TEXAS CHAINSAW director Hooper is a garishly stylized, unrelentingly bizarre film about a psychopath (Brand) who has a crocodile living in the front yard of his hotel. Periodically guests who upset the management are fed to this pet. Originally titled DEATH TRAP; also known as STARLIGHT SLAUGHTER, LEGEND OF THE BAYOU, and HORROR HOTEL.▼

Eating Raoul (1982) **C-83m.** ***½ D: Paul Bartel. Paul Bartel, Mary Woronov, Robert Beltran, Susan Saiger, Buck Henry, Dick Blackburn, Edie McClurg, Ed Begley, Jr., John Paragon, Hamilton Camp. Delicious black comedy about the Blands, a super-square couple who lure wealthy swingers to their apartment and kill them, which both reduces the number of "perverts" and helps finance their dream restaurant. Sags a little here and there, but overall a bright, original, and hilarious satire; Paragon has a super bit as a sexshop owner. ▼

Eat My Dust! (1976) **C-90m.** *½ D: Charles Griffith. Ron Howard, Christopher Norris, Warren Kemmerling, Dave Madden, Rance Howard, Clint Howard, Corbin Bernsen. Nervewracking yarn about two young drivers unable to satisfy passion for speed. Hang on!▼

Eat the Peach (1986-Irish) **C-95m.** **½ D: Peter Ormrod. Stephen Brennan, Eamon Morrissey, Catherine Byrne, Niall Toibin, Joe Lynch, Tony Doyle. Two hard-luck friends in rural Ireland, suddenly unemployed, are inspired by a scene in Elvis Presley's movie ROUSTABOUT and decide to build a "wall of death" (a huge wooden cylinder in which they ride their motorcycles in a circuslike stunt). Can fame and fortune be far behind? Uniquely dour Irish sensibility permeates this uneven but engaging little film about hopes and dreams—even cockeyed ones like these. Director Ormrod and producer John Kelleher based their script on a true story.▼

Eat the Rich (1987-British) **C-88m.** BOMB D: Peter Richardson. Nosher Powell, Lanah Pellay, Fiona Richmond, Ronald Allen, Sandra Dorne. Literally tasteless black comedy about Pellay getting fired from his job in a restaurant, where he later returns leading a band of revolutionaries and begins serving human flesh on the menu. Many pointless cameos by the likes of Paul and Linda McCartney, Bill Wyman, Miranda Richardson and Koo Stark.▼

Ebb Tide (1937) **C-94m.** **½ D: James Hogan. Frances Farmer, Ray Milland, Oscar Homolka, Lloyd Nolan, Barry Fitzgerald, David Torrence. Hokey but entertaining outdoors picture with Nolan a madman on strange island. Remade as ADVENTURE ISLAND.

Eboli (1979-Italian) **C-120m.** ***½ D: Francesco Rosi. Gian Maria Volonte, Irene Papas, Paolo Bonicelli, Alain Cuny, Lea Massari. Slow-moving but rewarding chronicle of anti-Facist writer/artist Carlo Levi's exile in a small, primitive southern Italian mountain village during the mid-1930s. Stunningly directed, with Volonte perfect as Levi. Also known as CHRIST STOPPED AT EBOLI; most prints with this title run 210m.▼

Ebony, Ivory and Jade (1979) **C-78m.** TVM D: John Llewellyn Moxey. Bert Convy, Debbie Allen, Martha Smith, Claude Akins, Nina Foch, Ji-Tu Cumbuka. Las Vegas performer and two comely showgirls double as undercover agents to protect "guest" scientist Foch from terrorists in this routine pilot that never made it to series. Below average.▼

Echoes (1983) **C-89m.** **½ D: Arthur Allan Seidelman. Richard Alfieri, Nathalie Nell, Mercedes McCambridge, Ruth Roman, Gale Sondergaard, Mike Kellin, John Spencer. Art student Alfieri becomes obsessed by a dream in which his twin brother, who died before birth, is out to kill him. Intriguing premise, just adequate result.▼

Echoes in the Darkness (1987) C-250m. TVM D: Glenn Jordan. Peter Coyote, Stockard Channing, Robert Loggia, Peter Boyle, Cindy Pickett, Gary Cole, Zeljko Ivanek, Alex Hyde-White, Treat Williams. Intriguing if overlong dramatization of the 1979 "Main Line" murder case involving two teachers from an exclusive school in the Philadelphia suburbs, the killing of one of their colleagues and the disappearance of her two children. Joseph Wambaugh did the adaptation of his best-selling book, with Coyote playing the manipulative and bizarrely charming professor and Loggia the offbeat principal. Originally shown in two parts. Above average.▼

Echoes of a Summer (1976) C-99m. ** D: Don Taylor. Richard Harris, Lois Nettleton, Jodie Foster, Geraldine Fitzgerald, William Windom, Brad Savage. Another film in the "disease" genre, as 12-year-old Foster's stolid reaction to impending death inspires those around her. Overwritten tearjerker, but Jodie is always worth a look.

Echoes of Paradise (1987-Australian) C-92m. *½ D: Philip Noyce. Wendy Hughes, John Lone, Steven Jacobs, Peta Toppano, Rod Mullinar, Gillian Jones. Frustrated Hughes' husband cheats on her, so while in Thailand she liberates herself by commencing an affair with Balinese dancer Lone. Boring (though attractive) soaper is an unfortunate misfire for talented stars and director. Original Australian title: SHADOWS OF THE PEACOCK.▼

Echo Park (1986-Austrian-U.S.) C-93m. **½ D: Robert Dornhelm. Susan Dey, Thomas Hulce, Michael Bowen, Christopher Walker, Richard (Cheech) Marin, Cassandra Peterson, Timothy Carey. Small film set in older L.A. neighborhood, which follows the fortunes of three offbeat characters: a single mother/actress, a pizza delivery man/poet, and an Austrian weightlifter/TV hopeful. Bowen (as the latter) scores best in this mildly diverting film; first half is best.▼

Ecstasy (1933-Czech) 88m. **½ D: Gustav Machaty. Hedy Kiesler (Lamarr), Aribert Mog, Jaromir Rogoz, Leopold Kramer. Undistinguished but once-daring romantic drama is noteworthy mainly for famous footage of pre-Hollywood Lamarr in the buff.▼

Eddie and the Cruisers (1983) C-92m. ** D: Martin Davidson. Tom Berenger, Michael Paré, Joe Pantoliano, Matthew Laurance, Helen Schneider, Ellen Barkin. Ideal premise—whatever happened to the members of a legendary, innovative rock 'n' roll band of the 60s—buried by terrible script. Paré plays band's iconoclastic leader, who ran his car off a pier; Barkin is TV reporter who tries to piece together story, a la CITIZEN KANE . . . but there's no Rosebud here. Good song score by John Cafferty. Followed by a sequel.▼

Eddie and the Cruisers II: Eddie Lives! (1989) C-103m. BOMB D: Jean-Claude Lord. Michael Paré, Marina Orsini, Bernie Coulson, Matthew Laurance, Michael Rhoades, Anthony Sherwood. Now get this: Eddie Wilson did *not* die in a 1964 New Jersey car accident; he's living incognito in Montreal (where movies can be financed more cheaply) and is only surfacing now because the producers wanted a sequel. About as cinematically ambitious as a lesser Monogram Picture, though film's relatively few nonmusical moments allow for cameos by Bo Diddley, Martha Quinn, and Larry King. Eddie's life signs did not extend to the box office.▼

Eddie Cantor Story, The (1953) C-116m. *½ D: Alfred E. Green. Keefe Brasselle, Marilyn Erskine, Aline MacMahon, Marie Windsor. If Brasselle doesn't turn you off as Cantor, MacMahon's Grandma Esther or a putty-nosed young actor (Jackie Barnett) playing Jimmy Durante certainly will.

Eddie Macon's Run (1983) C-95m. **½ D: Jeff Kanew. Kirk Douglas, John Schneider, Lee Purcell, Leah Ayres, Lisa Dunsheath, Tom Noonan, John Goodman. Bumpy chase-and-car-crash picture that has wrongly convicted prison escapee Schneider (in his first starring role after attaining *Dukes of Hazzard* fame) trying to elude his relentless pursuer (Douglas) and make it to Mexico. Based on the novel by James McLendon. Goodman's film debut.▼

Eddie Murphy Raw (1987) C-93m. ** D: Robert Townsend. Occasionally uproarious but ultimately dispiriting Murphy concert film, shot at N.Y.C.'s Felt Forum. Best moments: the comic's imitations of Bill Cosby and Richard Pryor giving their opposing views on the crude tone of so much Murphy material. Worst: sexist slurs that too often predominate. Fades in the stretch; there's an amusing fictional prologue, "set" in the Murphys' home two decades ago.▼

Eddy Duchin Story, The (1956) C-123m. ** D: George Sidney. Tyrone Power, Kim Novak, Victoria Shaw, James Whitmore. Glossy Hollywood biography of pianist-bandleader of 30s-40s; Power tries hard (Carmen Cavallaro dubs at keyboard). Tearjerker ending and theme song memorable.

Edge of Darkness (1943) 120m. ***½ D: Lewis Milestone. Errol Flynn, Ann Sheridan, Walter Huston, Nancy Coleman, Helmut Dantine, Judith Anderson, Ruth Gordon, John Beal, Roman Bohnen. Intense, compelling drama of underground movement in Norway during Nazi takeover in WW2. Eye-popping camera work complements fine performances.

Edge of Doom (1950) **99m.** ** D: Mark Robson. Dana Andrews, Farley Granger, Joan Evans, Mala Powers, Adele Jergens. Granger reaches peak of histrionic despair in moody piece about young man baffled by poverty, religion, murder, and assorted other problems.

Edge of Eternlty (1959) **C-80m.** ** D: Don Siegel. Cornel Wilde, Victoria Shaw, Mickey Shaughnessy, Edgar Buchanan, Rian Garrick, Jack Elam. Deputy sheriff Wilde tracks killers to Grand Canyon, leading to shoot-out on mining buckets suspended on cables way above canyon.

Edge of Hell (1956) **76m.** *½ D: Hugo Haas. Hugo Haas, Francesca de Scaffa, Ken Carlton, June Hammerstein. Offbeat, minor film of pauper Haas, his beloved dog, and small boy who enters on the scene.

Edge of Sanity (1989-British) **C-90m.** *½ D: Gérard Kikoine. Anthony Perkins, Glynis Barber, Sarah Maur-Thorp, David Lodge, Ben Cole, Ray Jewers, Jill Melford, Lisa Davis, Noel Coleman. Grotesque, overwrought travesty on *Dr. Jekyll and Mr. Hyde* (Robert Louis Stevenson is not even credited). Jekyll (Perkins) *accidentally* discovers the Hyde formula, transforms only very slightly, and becomes Jack the Ripper. Tasteless, pointless, and unpleasant.▼

Edge of the City (1957) **85m.** **** D: Martin Ritt. John Cassavetes, Sidney Poitier, Jack Warden, Ruby Dee, Kathleen Maguire, Ruth White. Somber, realistic account of N.Y.C. waterfront life and corruption. Friendship of army deserter Cassavetes and dock worker Poitier, both conflicting with union racketeer Warden, provides focus for reflections on integration and integrity in lower-class society. Masterfully acted by all. Ritt's first film as director. Robert Alan Aurthur adapted his own 1955 TV play, *A Man Is Ten Feet Tall* (which was also film's British title), in which Poitier originated his role. Also shown in computer-colored version.

Edge of the World, The (1937-British) **74m.** *** D: Michael Powell. Niall MacGinnis, Belle Chrystall, John Laurie, Finlay Currie, Eric Berry. The life and death of an isolated Shetland island as it is evacuated of its citizens. Engrossing drama, filmed on the North Sea isle of Foula. Powell and those cast and crew still alive revisited the location 40 years later to film the documentary RETURN TO THE EDGE OF THE WORLD.

Edison, the Man (1940) **107m.** *** D: Clarence Brown. Spencer Tracy, Rita Johnson, Lynne Overman, Charles Coburn, Gene Lockhart, Henry Travers, Felix Bressart. Sequel to YOUNG TOM EDISON perfectly casts Tracy as earnest in-

ventor with passion for mechanical ingenuity. Facts and MGM fantasy combine well in sentimental treatment.

Edith and Marcel (1983-French) **C-104m.** *½ D: Claude Lelouch. Evelyne Bouix, Marcel Cerdan, Jr., Jacques Villeret, Jean-Claude Brialy, Francis Huster, Jean Bouise, Charles Aznavour. Passionless retelling of the love affair between singer Edith Piaf and middleweight boxer Marcel Cerdan, who died in a 1949 plane crash. Bouix and Cerdan, Jr., are bland in the title roles. Originally 162m.▼

Educating Rita (1983-British) **C-110m.** *** D: Lewis Gilbert. Michael Caine, Julie Walters, Michael Williams, Maureen Lipman, Jeananne Crowley, Malcolm Douglas. Entertaining adaptation of Willy Russell's stage play about a young working-class wife who wants to better herself, and selects boozy professor Caine as her tutor. Walters is excellent in her film debut (re-creating her stage role) and Caine has one of his best roles as her mentor.▼

Education of Sonny Carson, The (1974) **C-105m.** **½ D: Michael Campus. Rony Clanton, Don Gordon, Joyce Walker, Paul Benjamin, Ram John Holder. Interesting if overemotional drama of rebellious black youth in Brooklyn of the 50s and 60s, based on his autobiography.▼

Edward, My Son (1949-British) **112m.** *** D: George Cukor. Spencer Tracy, Deborah Kerr, Ian Hunter, James Donald, Mervyn Johns, Felix Aylmer, Leueen McGrath. Film recounts rocky marriage of Tracy and Kerr who discover they drove their son to suicide. Gimmicks of Tracy talking to viewer, title character never being shown, come off as forced.

Eegah! (1963) **C-92m.** BOMB D: Nicholas Merriwether (Arch Hall, Sr.). Arch Hall, Jr., Marilyn Manning, Richard Kiel, William Watters (Arch Hall, Sr.). Kiel, pre-James Bond, is a prehistoric giant who falls in love with teenager Manning. A staple at "All-Time Worst Film" festivals.▼

Effect of Gamma Rays on Man-in-the-Moon Marigolds, The (1972) **C-100m.** *** D: Paul Newman. Joanne Woodward, Nell Potts, Roberta Wallach, Judith Lowry. Woodward gives superb performance in tale of secluded boor of a mother and her two strange daughters. Screenplay by Paul Zindel from his Pulitzer Prize-winning play.

Egg and I, The (1947) **108m.** *** D: Chester Erskine. Claudette Colbert, Fred MacMurray, Marjorie Main, Louise Allbritton, Percy Kilbride, Richard Long, Donald MacBride, Samuel S. Hinds. Colbert is delightful as city girl who marries chicken farmer MacMurray and struggles to survive on his farm; first appearance of Ma and Pa Kettle. From Betty MacDonald's bestseller.▼

Egyptian, The (1954) **C-140m.** **½ D: Michael Curtiz. Edmund Purdom, Jean Simmons, Victor Mature, Gene Tierney, Michael Wilding, Peter Ustinov. Beautiful scenery and sets make for great atmosphere in otherwise uneven biblical spectacle. Some good acting by Purdom, others wasted.▼

Eiger Sanction, The (1975) **C-128m.** *½ D: Clint Eastwood. Clint Eastwood, George Kennedy, Vonetta McGee, Jack Cassidy, Thayer David, Heidi Bruhl, Reiner Schoene, Brenda Venus. Misfire of pseudo-James Bond material, often unintentionally funny. Thrilling mountain-climbing climax does not make up for film's many faults and ungodly length. Jack Cassidy as gay, treacherous spy contributes the only creative acting. Based on the novel by Trevanian.▼

8½ (1963-Italian) **135m.** **** D: Federico Fellini. Marcello Mastroianni, Claudia Cardinale, Anouk Aimee, Sandra Milo, Barbara Steele. Fellini's unique self-analytical movie casts Mastroianni as a filmmaker trying to develop a new project, amid frequent visions and countless subplots. A long, difficult, but fascinating film, overflowing with creative and technical wizardry. Certainly one of the most intensely personal statements ever made on celluloid. Oscar winner for Costume Design and as Best Foreign Language Film. Much imitated in recent years.▼

18 Again! (1988) **C-100m.** **½ D: Paul Flaherty. George Burns, Charlie Schlatter, Tony Roberts, Anita Morris, Red Buttons, Miriam Flynn, Jennifer Runyon. 81-year-old Jack Watson (92-year-old Burns) becomes 18 again via his grandson's body and a bump on the head. Sound familiar? What it lacks in originality is made up in part by Schlatter's utterly charming performance as the young George, and that fountain of youth Burns (who, alas, we see precious little of).▼

Eighteen and Anxious (1957) **93m.** ** D: Joe Parker. Martha Scott, Jim Backus, Mary Webster, William Campbell, Jackie Coogan. Oddball cast atones for amateurish muck about pregnant teen-ager forced to face life's realities.

Eight Iron Men (1952) **80m.** **½ D: Edward Dmytryk. Bonar Colleano, Lee Marvin, Richard Kiley, Nick Dennis, Arthur Franz, Mary Castle. WW2 actioner focusing on a group of soldiers, strain they undergo during continued enemy attack.

Eight Is Enough: A Family Reunion (1987) **C-100m.** TVM D: Harry Harris. Dick Van Patten, Willie Aames, Brian Patrick Clarke, Grant Goodeve, Dianne Kay, Connie Needham, Adam Rich, Lani O'Grady, Susan Richardson, Laurie Walters, Mary Frann. The cast of the hit series of the late 1970s returns for dad Van Patten's birthday (with Mary Frann substituting for Betty Buckley). Followed by AN EIGHT IS ENOUGH WEDDING in 1989. Average.

Eight Is Enough Wedding, An (1989) **C-100m.** TVM D: Stan Lathan. Dick Van Patten, Sandy Faison, Grant Goodeve, Joan Prather, Lani O'Grady, Laurie Walters, Willie Aames, Adam Rich, Jimmy Van Patten, Pat Van Patten, Eugene Roche. Title gives away the plot of this reunion movie in which the Bradford clan comes together for David's wedding. Most of the original cast members are back, save for Abby Bradford (played here by Sandy Faison). Average.

Eight Men Out (1988) **C-119m.** *** D: John Sayles. John Cusack, Clifton James, Michael Lerner, Christopher Lloyd, John Mahoney, Charlie Sheen, David Strathairn, D.B. Sweeney, Don Harvey, Michael Rooker, Perry Lang, James Read, Bill Irwin, Kevin Tighe, Studs Terkel, John Anderson, Maggie Renzi. Exquisitely detailed period piece about the infamous 1919 World Series, in which members of the Chicago White Sox agreed to throw the games in return for cash. Writer-director Sayles (who also appears as sportswriter Ring Lardner) hits all the bases, except perhaps in terms of emotion; the story doesn't have the impact it might have, though the actual baseball scenes are superb and the key performances (by Strathairn, Sweeney, and Cusack) are top-notch. Based on a book by Eliot Asinof.▼

8 Million Ways to Die (1986) **C-115m.** BOMB D: Hal Ashby. Jeff Bridges, Rosanna Arquette, Alexandra Paul, Randy Brooks, Andy Garcia. Dreary tale of alcoholic ex-cop who gets involved with high-priced call girl and her "friends" (a powerful pimp and a sleazy drug dealer). Slow, arid film populated by unpleasant and uninteresting characters.▼

Eight O'Clock Walk (1952-British) **87m.** **½ D: Lance Comfort. Richard Attenborough, Cathy O'Donnell, Derek Farr, Ian Hunter. Courtroom drama manages to create pace and tension, involving murder trial; nicely played by Attenborough.

Eight on the Lam (1967) **C-106m.** BOMB D: George Marshall. Bob Hope, Phyllis Diller, Jonathan Winters, Jill St. John, Shirley Eaton. Another of Hope's horrible 60s comedies casts him as a widower with seven children who finds $10,000; even Winters can't help this dud.

84 Charing Cross Road (1987) **C-97m.** ***½ D: David Jones. Anne Bancroft, Anthony Hopkins, Judi Dench, Jean De Baer, Maurice Denham, Eleanor David, Mercedes Ruehl, Daniel Gerroll. Loving, literate, and totally disarming film about the longtime correspondence, and growing friendship, between a feisty N.Y.C. woman and the British bookseller who provides her with the rare volumes she cherishes more than anything else in life. Affectionately detailed evocation of N.Y.C. and London over twenty years' time is capped by ideal performances. Based on the memoirs of Helen Hanff and the play adapted from her book. Screenplay by Hugh Whitemore.▼

84 Charlie Mopic (1989) **C-95m.** ******* D: Patrick Duncan. Jonathan Emerson, Nicholas Cascone, Jason Tomlins, Christopher Burgard, Glenn Morshower, Richard Brooks, Byron Thomas. Imaginative low-budget film provides fresh approach to life on the front line in Vietnam. Writer-director Duncan tells his story completely from the point of view of a combat cameraman who's assigned to follow a special seven-man reconnaissance unit on a dangerous mission. Lulls in pace are made up for by film's overall vitality, and commanding performances by cast of unknowns.▼

80 Steps to Jonah (1969) **C-107m.** ****** D: Gerd Oswald. Wayne Newton, Mickey Rooney, Jo Van Fleet, Keenan Wynn, Diana Ewing, Slim Pickens, Sal Mineo. A loner, running from the police, stumbles upon camp for blind children; new world changes his outlook on life. Major liability, casting of Newton in leading role.

80,000 Suspects (1963-British) **113m.** ****** D: Val Guest. Claire Bloom, Richard Johnson, Yolande Donlan, Cyril Cusack. Capable cast saddled with yarn of doctor (Johnson) and wife (Bloom) finding new love together while combating local small-pox outbreak.

Eijanaika (1981-Japanese) **C-151m.** *****½** D: Shohei Imamura. Shigeru Izumiya, Kaori Momoi, Masao Kusakari, Ken Ogata, Shigeru Tsuyuguchi, Mitsuko Baisho. Fascinating, compelling saga of corruption, politics, greed, power, deceit, focusing on experiences of peasant who has just returned to Japan after being shipwrecked and sent to America during the 1860s. Fine performances, with a memorable finale. Cut to 127m.; video release retains original running time.▼

El Alamein (1953) **67m.** ****** D: Fred F. Sears. Scott Brady, Edward Ashley, Rita Moreno, Michael Pate. No surprises in WW2 desert actioner with Brady heading group being attacked by Germans.

El Bruto (1952-Mexican) **83m.** ****** D: Luis Bunuel. Pedro Armendariz, Katy Jurado, Andres Soler, Rosita Arenas. Armendariz is conned by scheming boss into harassing tenants he unfairly wants to evict; seduced by the boss's lusty mistress (Jurado), he then falls in love with a girl whose father he accidentally murdered. Simplistic, quite unsubtle melodrama, a disappointment from a master filmmaker.▼

El Cid (1961) **C-184m.** ******* D: Anthony Mann. Charlton Heston, Sophia Loren, Raf Vallone, Genevieve Page, Hurd Hatfield. Mammoth spectacle with above-average script and acting in film of legendary Cid (Heston) who drove Moors from Spain. Music by Miklos Rosza.▼

El Condor (1970) **C-102m.** ****** D: John Guillermin. Jim Brown, Lee Van Cleef, Patrick O'Neal, Mariana Hill, Iron Eyes Cody, Elisha Cook, Jr. Slow western about two drifters in search of some gold supposedly buried in Mexican fortress; Hill looks good even with her clothes on.▼

El Dorado (1967) **C-126m.** ******* D: Howard Hawks. John Wayne, Robert Mitchum, James Caan, Arthur Hunnicutt, Edward Asner, Michele Carey, Christopher George, Charlene Holt, Paul Fix, R. G. Armstrong, Johnny Crawford, Robert Donner. Follow-up to RIO BRAVO finds aging gunfighter Wayne helping drunken sheriff pal Mitchum quell a range war. Typically smooth Hawks mix of comedy and action, with zesty Leigh Brackett script and exemplary performances, especially by Mitchum, Caan as young gambler who can't shoot, and George as ultra-cool hired gun.▼

Eleanor and Franklin (1976) **C-208m.** **TVM** D: Daniel Petrie. Jane Alexander, Edward Herrmann, Rosemary Murphy, Pamela Franklin, David Huffman, MacKenzie Phillips, Lilia Skala, Ed Flanders, Anna Lee, Linda Purl, Linda Kelsey, Lindsay Crouse. Outstanding performances by the two leads and all the supporting players (Rosemary Murphy won an Emmy for her Sara Delano Roosevelt) in this multi-award-winning production adapted by James Costigan from Joseph P. Lash's Pulitzer Prize best-seller about the Roosevelts from FDR's youth to his death in 1945. Director Petrie won an Emmy, and the film itself was named Outstanding Special of the Year. Above average.

Eleanor and Franklin: The White House Years (1977) **C-152m.** **TVM** D: Daniel Petrie. Jane Alexander, Edward Herrmann, Rosemary Murphy, Walter McGinn, Blair Brown, David Healy, Anna Lee, Mark Harmon, Linda Kelsey, Peggy McKay, Donald Moffat. Follow-up to award-winning TV portrait of the Roosevelts reunited most of the original cast and crew and practically duplicated the Emmy honors, with statuettes going to director Petrie and the program itself as Outstanding Special. This sequel concentrated on the lives of FDR and Eleanor during their 12-year residence at 1600 Pennsylvania Avenue. Written by James Costigan. Above average.

Eleanor, First Lady of the World (1982) **C-100m.** **TVM** D: John Erman. Jean Stapleton, E. G. Marshall, Coral Browne, Joyce Van Patten, Gail Strickland, Kenneth Kimmins, Richard McKenzie, Kabir Bedi. Stapleton glows as Eleanor Roosevelt in the years after FDR's death, emerging as an influential public figure on her own. Script by Caryl Ledner and Cynthia Mandelberg, from a story by Rhoda Lerman. Above average.

Eleanor Roosevelt Story, The (1965) **91m.** ***½ D: Richard Kaplan. Narrated by Archibald Macleish, Eric Sevareid, Francis Cole. Oscar-winning documentary account of the former First Lady, a great American citizen who overcame personal obstacles and became a beacon of human kindness. A most effective music score by Ezra Laderman.

Electra Glide in Blue (1973) **C-113m.** *** D: James William Guercio. Robert Blake, Billy Green Bush, Mitchell Ryan, Jeannine Riley, Elisha Cook, Jr., Royal Dano. Violent film about highway cop Blake making up in brains what he lacks in height. Striking action sequences and good characterizations.▼

Electric Dreams (1984) **C-95m.** **½ D: Steve Barron. Lenny Von Dohlen, Virginia Madsen, Maxwell Caulfield, voice of Bud Cort. Old-fashioned boy meets girl story told in rock-video terms, with a third corner to the love triangle: a jealous computer. Good idea gets sillier as it goes along.▼

Electric Horseman, The (1979) **C-120m.** **½ D: Sydney Pollack. Robert Redford, Jane Fonda, Valerie Perrine, Willie Nelson, John Saxon, Nicolas Coster, Wilford Brimley. Innocuous rip-off of LONELY ARE THE BRAVE tries to palm off Redford as a near-derelict who steals a $12 million thoroughbred from a Vegas hotel and heads for some grazing land. Pleasant, to be sure, but considering the people involved, a disappointment.▼

Electronic Monster, The (1957-British) **72m.** *½ D: Montgomery Tully. Rod Cameron, Mary Murphy, Meredith Edwards, Peter Illing. Cameron investigates actress' death, revealing strange experiments at a clinic; scientific gadgetry has its moments. Alternate title: ESCAPEMENT.▼

Elena and Her Men SEE: **Paris Does Strange Things**▼

Eleni (1985) **C-117m.** **½ D: Peter Yates. Kate Nelligan, John Malkovich, Linda Hunt, Oliver Cotton, Ronald Pickup, Rosalie Crutchley, Dimitra Arliss, Glenne Headly. *N.Y. Times* reporter gets himself assigned to Athens bureau so he can resolve life-long obsession with finding truth about his mother's execution by communists in Greece following WW2. Steve Tesich's script is based on Nicholas Gage's book—and life— but coldness of the lead character is just one reason this film remains aloof and uninteresting instead of being an emotional powerhouse. Nelligan plays Gage's mother in convincing flashback sequences.▼

Elephant Boy (1937-British) **80m.** *** D: Robert Flaherty, Zoltan Korda. Sabu, W.

E. Holloway, Walter Hudd, Allan Jeayes, Bruce Gordon, D. J. Williams. Interesting early-day docudrama about native boy (Sabu, in film debut) who claims he knows location of mythic elephant herd.▼

Elephant Gun (1959-British) **C-84m.** ** D: Ken Annakin. Belinda Lee, Michael Craig, Patrick McGoohan, Anna Gaylor, Eric Pohlmann, Pamela Stirling. Jungle love triangle has virtue of on-location shooting in Africa.

Elephant Man, The (1980) **125m.** ***½ D: David Lynch. Anthony Hopkins, John Hurt, Anne Bancroft, John Gielgud, Wendy Hiller, Freddie Jones. Moving dramatization of the story of John Merrick, a grotesquely deformed man shown compassion for the first time in his life by an eminent doctor in turn-of-the-century London. No relation to the Broadway play (in which one had to imagine how Merrick looked). Fine performances by all; rich Victorian atmosphere created by Lynch and veteran cameraman Freddie Francis—in beautiful black and white.▼

Elephant Stampede (1951) **71m.** D: Ford Beebe. Johnny Sheffield, Donna Martell, Edith Evanson, Martin Wilkins, Myron Healey, Leonard Mudie, Guy Kingsford. SEE: **Bomba the Jungle Boy** series.

Elephant Walk (1954) **C-103m.** ** D: William Dieterle. Elizabeth Taylor, Dana Andrews, Peter Finch, Abraham Sofaer. Overblown melodrama set on Ceylon tea plantation, with Taylor as Finch's new bride who must cope with environment and his father complex. Pachyderm stampede climax comes none too soon. Vivien Leigh, replaced by Taylor, can be seen in long shots.

Elevator, The (1974) **C-78m. TVM** D: Jerry Jameson. James Farentino, Roddy McDowall, Craig Stevens, Myrna Loy, Teresa Wright, Carol Lynley, Don Stroud, Barry Livingston. Standard amount of all-star thrills when a group of people are stuck between floors in high-rise building with claustrophobic thief (Farentino) trying to flee from his latest heist. Average.

11 Harrowhouse (1974-British) **C-98m.** *** D: Aram Avakian. Charles Grodin, Candice Bergen, James Mason, Trevor Howard, John Gielgud, Helen Cherry. Funny action spoof of heist films, as diamond merchant Grodin robs the world clearinghouse for gems. Grodin also adapted Gerald A. Browne's best-selling novel. Retitled: ANYTHING FOR LOVE.▼

11th Victim (1979) **C-100m. TVM** D: Jonathan Kaplan. Bess Armstrong, Max Gail, Harold Gould, Pamela Ludwig, Eric Burdon, Annazette Chase. Standard exploitation drama involving small town newswoman who goes to Hollywood looking for the killer of her prostitute sister. Average.

El Greco (1966-Italian-French) **C-95m.**
** D: Luciano Salce. Mel Ferrer, Rosanna
Schiaffino, Franco Giacobini, Renzo Gio-
vampietro, Adolfo Celi. Despite lavish trappings, story of painter reduced to soap-
opera terms falls flat. Beautiful color, but
no plot of any distinction.
Eliminators (1986) **C-96m.** *½ D: Peter
Manoogian. Andrew Prine, Denise Crosby,
Patrick Reynolds, Conan Lee, Roy Dotrice.
Woman scientist, white male guide, a ninja,
and an android team up to battle a mad-
genius industrialist who wants to take over
the world. Good to see an equal-opportunity
adventure, but this RAIDERS clone has
little to offer but low humor. Crosby is
Bing's granddaughter. ▼
Elizabeth of Ladymead (1948-British)
C-97m. *** D: Herbert Wilcox. Anna
Neagle, Hugh Williams, Michael Laurence,
Bernard Lee, Nicholas Phipps, Isabel Jeans.
Engaging comedy-drama in four episodes
from husband-wife team of Wilcox-Neagle.
Latter charming as English lady-of-the-
manor with mind of her own welcoming
home four husbands from four different
British wars. Star vehicle, unsuccessful
when released, quite intriguing today for its
depiction of woman's role in English mar-
riage and community. (Attention histori-
ans and feminists!) Some prints run 90m.
Elizabeth the Queen SEE: **Private Lives
of Elizabeth and Essex, The**▼
Ella Cinders (1926) 60m. *** D: Alfred
E. Green. Colleen Moore, Lloyd Hughes,
Vera Lewis, Doris Baker, Emily Gerdes,
Jed Prouty. Moore is in top form as the
much-abused stepdaughter of crochety old
Lewis, who wins a contest and treks off to
Hollywood to seek fame in the movies.
Bright and peppy, with Harry Langdon on
hand in a most amusing cameo. Based on a
popular comic strip. ▼
Ellery Queen Perhaps the most successful
series of detective stories ever written, the
Ellery Queen mysteries rank as one of the
least successful film series. A few scattered attempts to film Queen stories in the
1930s with Donald Cook and Eddie Quillan
never aroused much interest. Then in 1940,
Columbia began a series starring Ralph
Bellamy as Ellery Queen, Charley Grapewin
as his Inspector father, Margaret Lindsay
as his Girl Friday Nikki, and James Burke
as Inspector Queen's dim-witted aide. The
very first entry, ELLERY QUEEN, MAS-
TER DETECTIVE, belied its title by making Bellamy an incredible "comic" bumbler, an inexplicable characterization that
lasted through all of Bellamy's films in the
series. Heavy doses of comedy relief in
entries like ELLERY QUEEN AND THE
MURDER RING were not offset by solid
mystery angles, and the films, though only
one hour long, moved like molasses. A
switch in casting making William Gargan

the lead character in 1942 did not help
matters, with the actual suspects becoming
more obvious than ever. Gargan's three
efforts as Queen were undistinguished, and
his last episode, ENEMY AGENTS MEET
ELLERY QUEEN, was also the last in the
short-lived series. Consistent top-quality
casting with character actors like Eduardo
Ciannelli, Blanche Yurka, George Zucco,
Leon Ames, and former director Fred Niblo
could do nothing to offset the lifeless scripts
and turgid direction. None of the films in
the series is really worthwhile, a distinct
disappointment to the mystery fans who
came to regard the Ellery Queen stories as
top-grade in the mystery genre.
Ellery Queen (1975) **C-78m. TVM** D:
David Greene. Jim Hutton, David Wayne,
Ray Milland, Kim Hunter, Monte Markham,
John Hillerman, John Larch, Tim O'Connor.
Preoccupied sleuth Ellery helps his police
inspector dad in solving a fashion designer's
murder. The Ellery Queen mystery *The
Fourth Side of the Triangle* served as the
source for this entertaining, light-hearted
period detective movie that preceded the
well-crafted TV series. Written by Richard
Levinson and William Link. Above average.
Retitled TOO MANY SUSPECTS.
Ellery Queen and the Murder Ring (1941)
65m. D: James Hogan. Ralph Bellamy,
Margaret Lindsay, Charley Grapewin, Mona
Barrie, Paul Hurst, James Burke, Blanche
Yurka.
Ellery Queen and the Perfect Crime
(1941) **68m.** D: James Hogan. Ralph Bel-
lamy, Margaret Lindsay, Charley Grapewin,
Spring Byington, H. B. Warner, James
Burke.
Ellery Queen: Don't Look Behind You
(1971) **C-100m. TVM** D: Barry Shear.
Peter Lawford, Harry Morgan, Stefanie
Powers, E. G. Marshall, Coleen Gray,
Morgan Sterne, Skye Aubrey. Entertaining,
easily forgettable murder mystery has famed
detective taking over police-baffling Hydra
case. Relationship between Lawford and
Morgan starts out well but disappears as
film progresses. Based on *Cat of Many
Tales*. Average.
Ellery Queen, Master Detective (1940)
66m. D: Kurt Neumann. Ralph Bellamy,
Margaret Lindsay, Charley Grapewin,
James Burke, Michael Whalen, Marsha
Hunt.
Ellery Queen's Penthouse Mystery (1941)
69m. D: James Hogan. Ralph Bellamy,
Charley Grapewin, Margaret Lindsay,
James Burke, Anna May Wong, Eduardo
Ciannelli, Frank Albertson.
Elmer Gantry (1960) **C-145m.** ***½ D:
Richard Brooks. Burt Lancaster, Jean Sim-
mons, Dean Jagger, Arthur Kennedy, Shir-
ley Jones, Patti Page, Edward Andrews,
Hugh Marlowe, John McIntire, Rex In-
gram. Lancaster gives a vibrant Oscar-

winning performance as the salesman with the gift of gab who joins evangelist Simmons's barnstorming troupe in the 1920s Midwest. Jones won Academy Award as his jilted girlfriend turned prostitute; Brooks also won an Oscar for his sprawling screenplay from Sinclair Lewis's trenchant novel. ▼

Elmer the Great (1933) 74m. *** D: Mervyn LeRoy. Joe E. Brown, Patricia Ellis, Claire Dodd, Sterling Holloway, Jessie Ralph. Excellent Ring Lardner baseball comedy, filmed before as FAST COMPANY, of naive country boy who becomes ball star, gets involved with crooks at the same time.

El Norte (1983) C-139m. **** D: Gregory Nava. Aide Silvia Gutierrez, David Villalpando, Ernesto Cruz, Alicia del Lago, Eracio Zepeda, Stella Quan, Lupe Ontiveros. Sweeping, emotional saga of a brother and sister who leave their violence-torn village in Guatemala to find a better life in The North—El Norte. Getting to America is half the story; making a life there is the other half. Writer-director Nava presents a heightened sense of reality that removes this from the realm of documentary; a compassionate, heart-rending, unforgettable film. Cowritten and produced by Anna Thomas, for *American Playhouse.* ▼

Elopement (1951) 82m. ** D: Henry Koster. Clifton Webb, Anne Francis, Charles Bickford, William Lundigan, Reginald Gardiner. Tame proceedings despite Webb's arch performance as Francis' father, who disapproves of her marriage to Lundigan.

El Paso (1949) C-92m. ** D: Lewis R. Foster. John Payne, Gail Russell, Sterling Hayden, Gabby Hayes. Routine Western of post-Civil War Texas, with Payne an attorney who discovers gunplay more than words will rid town of crooks. Shown on TV in black and white.

El Super (1979) C-90m. *** D: Leon Ichaso, Orlando Jiminez-Leal. Raymundo Hidalgo-Gato, Zully Montero, Raynaldo Medina, Juan Granda, Hilda Lee. The trials of homesick exiled Cuban Hidalgo-Gato, who labors as an apartment-house super in Manhattan. Hidalgo-Gato is excellent as a comically sad outsider, still in transit after a decade away from his homeland. Reportedly the first Spanish-language film to be shot in N.Y.C. ▼

Elusive Corporal, The (1962-French) 108m. **½ D: Jean Renoir. Jean-Pierre Cassel, Claude Brasseur, Claude Rich, O. E. Hasse. Flavorful if predictable account of Frenchmen in German prison camp during WW2, determined to escape.

Elusive Pimpernel, The (1950-British) C-109m. *** D: Michael Powell, Emeric Pressburger. David Niven, Margaret Leighton, Cyril Cusack, Jack Hawkins, Arlette

Marchal, Robert Coote, Patrick Macnee. Colorful remake of THE SCARLET PIMPERNEL with Niven as British fop who secretly aids victims of Reign of Terror; lively fun. This was actually filmed as a musical; you can even tell where the numbers were cut!

Elvira Madigan (1967-Swedish) C-89m. *** D: Bo Widerberg. Pia Degermark, Thommy Berggren, Lennart Malmen, Nina Widerberg, Cleo Jensen. Combination of attractive stars, lovers-on-the-run theme, and lovely soft-focus photography made this click with public. Stylistically a bit too much like a shampoo commercial, but film has undeniable appeal, enhanced by canny use of Mozart music. ▼

Elvira, Mistress of the Dark (1988) C-96m. BOMB D: James Signorelli. Elvira (Cassandra Peterson), W. Morgan Sheppard, Daniel Greene, Susan Kellermann, Jeff Conaway, Edie McClurg, William Duell, Pat Crawford Brown. Peterson uncomfortably takes her TV horror host character to the big screen in this flimsy story of a TV host shaking up a small New England town which she's visiting to pick up an inheritance. Unfunny, one-joke script (cowritten by Peterson) keeps its attention firmly riveted to the star's ample chest. More yawns than yocks. ▼

Elvis (1979) C-150m. TVM D: John Carpenter. Kurt Russell, Shelley Winters, Pat Hingle, Season Hubley, Bing Russell, Ed Begley, Jr., Joe Mantegna. The Presley saga affectionately and believably retold, from his youth to his career as a club entertainer in 1969. Russell surprisingly effective as Elvis, whose songs were dubbed by country singer Ronnie McDowell. One of the highest rated TV movies ever—even outdrawing a rerun of GONE WITH THE WIND, shown opposite it at its premiere. Written by Anthony Lawrence. Some prints run 119m. Above average. ▼

Elvis and Me (1988) C-200m. TVM D: Larry Peerce. Dale Midkiff, Susan Walters, Billy Green Bush, Jon Cypher, Linda Miller, Anne Haney, Marshall Teague. The Presley saga, again, but this time based on his wife Priscilla's book (she's also one of the film's executive producers). Midkiff gets the King's moves pretty much down, though toward the end he looks more like Johnny Cash. Elvis' songs are performed by Ronnie McDowell (as they were in the other two Presley TV movies). Originally shown in two parts. Average. ▼

Elvis and the Beauty Queen (1981) C-100m. TVM D: Gus Trikonis. Don Johnson, Stephanie Zimbalist, Ann Dusenberry, Rick Lenz, John Crawford, Richard Herd, Ann Wedgeworth, Ruta Lee. The marketing of Elvis continues with this uninspired telling of Presley's romance with beauty queen Linda Thompson and their 5-year love affair. Average.

Elvis on Tour (1972) **C-93m.** ** D: Pierre Adidge, Robert Abel. Static study of rock 'n' roll's biggest super-star going through his paces at a series of U.S. concerts. Even the music is not up to standard.▼

Elvis: That's the Way It Is (1970) **C-97m.** *** D: Denis Sanders. Engaging look at Elvis Presley offstage, preparing major night-club act, culminating in opening-night performance in Las Vegas. Well-filmed if one-sided documentary paints vivid picture of Elvis as master showman.▼

Embassy (1972-British) **C-90m.** **½ D: Gordon Hessler. Richard Roundtree, Chuck Connors, Max von Sydow, Ray Milland, Broderick Crawford, Marie-Jose Nat. Spotty spy thriller about Russian defector von Sydow seeking asylum and the State Department's efforts to have agent Roundtree smuggle him out of the mideast under KGB man Connors' nose. Good cast works valiantly with contrived plot, talky script.▼

Embassy (1985) **C-100m. TVM** D: Robert Lewis. Nick Mancuso, Mimi Rogers, Richard Masur, Richard Gilliland, Blanche Baker, Eli Wallach, Sam Wanamaker, George Grizzard, Kim Darby, Lee Curreri. The tribulations and crises encountered by the (fictional) deputy chief of the American embassy in Rome (Mancuso) make up the assorted plots of this conventional thriller, a failed series pilot. Average.▼

Embraceable You (1948) **80m.** ** D: Felix Jacoves. Dane Clark, Geraldine Brooks, S. Z. Sakall, Wallace Ford. Tough-guy Clark injures young girl, then falls in love with her, in this sentimental romance.

Embryo (1976) **C-104m.** ** D: Ralph Nelson. Rock Hudson, Diane Ladd, Barbara Carrera, Roddy McDowall, Anne Schedeen. Sometimes interesting, sometimes repulsive horror sci-fi about woman and dog grown from fetuses outside the womb—with terrifying results. Retitled CREATED TO KILL.▼

Emerald Forest, The (1985) **C-113m.** *** D: John Boorman. Powers Boothe, Meg Foster, Charley Boorman, Dira Pass. American engineer spends ten years searching for his kidnapped son, who's been raised by primitive Amazon tribe. Fascinating look at a unique civilization, but lack of emotional empathy for the father and contrived storyline weaken overall impact. Still worthwhile. Script by Rospo Pallenberg; rich music score by Junior Homrich. And a completely convincing performance by young Boorman, son of the film's director. ▼

Emergency (1962-British) **63m.** ** D: Francis Searle. Glyn Houston, Zena Walker, Dermot Walsh, Colin Tapley. Adequate programmer dealing with Walker-Walsh

reaffirming their marriage while waiting for blood donor to save their daughter's life.

Emergency (1971) **C-100m. TVM** D: Jack Webb. Robert Fuller, Julie London, Bobby Troup, Randolph Mantooth, Kevin Tighe. Daily adventures, foibles of L.A. county paramedics unit and backup hospital personnel. Only difference between this and subsequent series is the running time. Average.

Emergency Call (1933) **61m.** ** D: Edward L. Cahn. William Boyd, Wynne Gibson, William Gargan, Betty Furness, Reginald Mason, Edwin Maxwell, George E. Stone. Boyd (pre-Hopalong Cassidy) is a naïve young surgeon who teams with sassy ambulance driver Gargan to battle racketeers trying to muscle in on hospital business. Minor programmer cowritten by Joseph L. Mankiewicz does have a certain appeal in its cheesy way.

Emergency Hospital (1956) **62m.** ** D: Lee Sholem. Margaret Lindsay, Byron Palmer, Walter Reed, Rita Johnson, John Archer, Jim Stapleton. The title tells all in this routine melodrama detailing the problems of patients and staff in a L.A. hospital during one 12-hour shift.

Emergency Room (1983) **C-100m. TVM** D: Lee H. Katzin. Sarah Purcell, LeVar Burton, Gary Frank, Gary Lockwood, Conchata Ferrell, Penny Peyser, Paul Stewart, Julia Sommars. Formula hospital drama mixing romance, operating room activities and hospital politics. Average.

Emergency Wedding (1950) **78m.** ** D: Edward Buzzell. Barbara Hale, Larry Parks, Una Merkel, Jim Backus, Queenie Smith. Sterile remake of YOU BELONG TO ME detailing jealous Parks who thinks new wife, doctor Hale, spends too much time with her male patients.

Emerson, Lake & Palmer in Concert (1981) **C-91m.** **½ D: Ron Kantor. Keith Emerson, Greg Lake, Carl Palmer. Adequate cinematic record of the veteran rock group in performance at Olympic Stadium in Montreal.

Emigrants, The (1971-Swedish) **C-148m.** *** D: Jan Troell. Max von Sydow, Liv Ullmann, Eddie Axberg, Allan Edwall. Solid if rambling tale of peasant farmer von Sydow, wife Ullmann, and fellow Swedes who emigrate to America in the 19th century. Sequel, THE NEW LAND, is even better; both have been edited together for TV, dubbed in English, and presented as THE EMIGRANT SAGA.

Emigrant Saga, The SEE: **Emigrants, The** and **New Land, The**

Emil and the Detectives (1964) **C-99m.** *½ D: Peter Tewksbury. Walter Slezak, Bryan Russell, Roger Mobley, Heinz Schubert, Peter Erlich, Cindy Cassell. Turgid Disney version of Erich Kastner's children's book about a young boy who is robbed and determines to nail the thief with the help of young detective friends. Filmed in Germany, where it was made before in 1931.▼

Emma (1932) **73m.** ***½ D: Clarence Brown. Marie Dressler, Richard Cromwell, Jean Hersholt, Myrna Loy, John Miljan, Leila Bennett. Beautiful film with Dressler at her best, as down-to-earth woman who works as housemaid-nanny for family and eventually marries widowed father (Hersholt). Sentimental movie never cloys, thanks to wonderful Marie. Frances Marion's story was scripted by Leonard Praskins and Zelda Sears.

Emma: Queen of the South Seas (1988-Australian) **C-200m. TVM** D: John Banas. Barbara Carrera, Steve Bisley, Thaao Penghlis, Hal Holbrook, Barry Quin, Rebecca Rigg, Gerard Kennedy, E. G. Marshall. Colorful story of strong-willed Emma Eliza Coe, daughter of a Samoan princess and the first U.S. Consul to that island in the mid-1800s. Half Victorian romance, half *Mutiny on the Bounty*, with such historical figures as Ulysses S. Grant (Marshall) and Kaiser Wilhelm thrown into the poi. Based on Geoffrey Dutton's historical novel. Originally shown in two parts. Average.

Emperor Jones, The (1933) **72m.** **½ D: Dudley Murphy. Paul Robeson, Dudley Digges, Frank Wilson, Fredi Washington, Ruby Elzy. Robeson plays Pullman porter who escapes from chain gang and improbably becomes King of a Carribbean island. Pretentious adaptation of Eugene O'Neill play derives its chief interest and value from Robeson himself. Look for Moms Mabley in bit part.▼

Emperor of Peru, The SEE: **Odyssey of the Pacific**▼

Emperor of the North (1973) **C-118m.** ***½ D: Robert Aldrich. Lee Marvin, Ernest Borgnine, Keith Carradine, Charles Tyner, Harry Caesar, Malcolm Atterbury, Simon Oakland, Matt Clark, Elisha Cook. Unusual, exciting (and heavily symbolic) action film set during the Depression. Sadistic conductor Borgnine will kill any tramp who tries to cop a ride on his train; legendary hobo Marvin announces he will be the first to succeed. Beautifully filmed in Oregon by Joseph Biroc; taut script by Christopher Knopf and typically muscular Aldrich direction make this a unique entertainment. Initially released as EMPEROR OF THE NORTH POLE.

Emperor of the North Pole SEE: **Emperor of the North**

Emperor's Candlesticks, The (1937) **89m.** **½ D: George Fitzmaurice. William Powell, Luise Rainer, Robert Young, Maureen O'Sullivan, Frank Morgan, Emma Dunn, Douglass Dumbrille. Powell and Rainer play cat-and-mouse as spies on opposite sides of the fence who (naturally) fall in love, in this enjoyable but wildly far-fetched story set in Czarist Russia and Vienna. Based on a novel by Baroness Orczy (who also wrote *The Scarlet Pimpernel*).

Emperor Waltz, The (1948) **C-106m.** **½ D: Billy Wilder. Bing Crosby, Joan Fontaine, Roland Culver, Lucile Watson, Richard Haydn, Sig Ruman. Lavish but standard Crosby musical set in Franz Joseph Austria (on Hollywood's backlots) with Bing selling record-players to royalty. Awfully schmaltzy material for writer-director Wilder.

Empire of Passion (1978-Japanese) **C-110m.** ** D: Nagisa Oshima. Kazuko Yoshiyuki, Tatsuya Fuji, Takahiro Tamura, Takuzo Kawatani. Peasant woman Yoshiyuki has affair with village good-for-nothing Fuji; they murder her husband, whose ghost returns to haunt them. Boring, despite interesting subject matter. A follow-up to IN THE REALM OF THE SENSES.

Empire of the Ants (1977) **C-90m.** ** D:✓ Bert I. Gordon. Joan Collins, Robert Lansing, Albert Salmi, John David Carson, Robert Pine, Jacqueline Scott. Laughable man-vs.-giant insects chiller from H. G. Wells' story. Vacationers on an isolated island find themselves at the mercy of voracious ants that have become monsters after feasting on a leaking barrel of radioactive waste.▼

Empire of the Sun (1987) **C-152m.** ** D: Steven Spielberg. Christian Bale, John Malkovich, Miranda Richardson, Nigel Havers, Joe Pantoliano, Leslie Phillips, Masato Ibu, Emily Richard, Rupert Frazer, Ben Stiller, Robert Stephens, Burt Kwouk. British boy, living a well-sheltered life in Shanghai, is separated from his parents and forced to fend for himself when Japan invades China at the outset of WW2. Sprawling, ambitious film with many striking scenes and images, and one enormous problem: We feel emotionally distant from the boy, even more so as the film goes on. What's more, Spielberg keeps setting up big, emotional crescendos (replete with crane camera shots and overbearing music by John Williams) that simply don't have the emotional content to warrant all that fuss. Tom Stoppard adapted J.G. Ballard's autobiographical novel (Ballard appears briefly in Beefeater costume in an early party scene).▼

Empire Strikes Back, The (1980) **C-✓ 124m.** **** D: Irvin Kershner. Mark Hamill, Harrison Ford, Carrie Fisher, Billy Dee Williams, Anthony Daniels, David Prowse, Peter Mayhew, Kenny Baker, Frank Oz, Alec Guinness, Clive Revill, Julian Glover, John Ratzenberger, voice of James Earl Jones. Smashing sequel to STAR WARS manages to top the original in its embellishment of leading characters' personalities, truly dazzling special effects (which earned a special Oscar) and nonstop spirit of adventure and excitement. (It *does* assume you've seen the first film.) Story threads include a blossoming romance between Han Solo and Princess Leia, the cosmic education of Luke Skywalker (by the mystical Yoda), an uneasy alliance with opportunistic Lando Calrissian, and a startling revelation from Darth Vader. Sequel: RETURN OF THE JEDI.▼

Employees Entrance (1933) **75m.** *** D: Roy Del Ruth. Warren William, Loretta Young, Wallace Ford, Alice White, Allen Jenkins. Zesty look at life in a department store and its ruthless, amoral manager. Gripping, funny, outrageous, and racy (made pre-Code). Based on a stage play.

Empty Canvas, The (1964-French-Italian) **118m.** *½ D: Damiano Damiani. Bette Davis, Horst Buchholz, Catherine Spaak, Isa Miranda, Lea Padovani, Daniela Rocca, Georges Wilson. Artist Buchholz is obsessed with model Spaak, eventually decorates her naked body with bank notes. Davis is his wealthy mother; hopefully, she was well paid for her time. Based on an Alberto Moravia novel.▼

Enchanted April (1935) **66m.** ** D: Harry Beaumont. Ann Harding, Frank Morgan, Katharine Alexander, Reginald Owen, Jane Baxter. Slightly overdone drama of four different women spending their vacation at same Italian villa.

Enchanted Cottage, The (1945) **92m.** **½ D: John Cromwell. Dorothy McGuire, Robert Young, Herbert Marshall, Mildred Natwick, Spring Byington, Hillary Brooke. Fantasy set in New England cottage where two misfits find love; sensitively handled, from Arthur Pinero play. Previously filmed in 1924. Some prints run 78m.▼

Enchanted Forest (1945) **C-78m.** **½ D: Lew Landers. Edmund Lowe, Brenda Joyce, Billy Severn, Harry Davenport, John Litel. Nicely done story of young boy who learns about life from old man who lives amid nature in the forest.▼

Enchanted Island (1958) **C-94m.** *½ D: Allan Dwan. Dana Andrews, Jane Powell, Don Dubbins, Arthur Shields. Miscast, low-budget version of Herman Melville's *Typee*. Andrews is deserter from American whaling ship who finds love with native girl Powell on South Sea island; some minor uprisings by local cannibals for good measure.▼

Enchantment (1948) **102m.** *** D: Irving Reis. David Niven, Teresa Wright, Evelyn Keyes, Farley Granger, Jayne Meadows, Leo G. Carroll. Weepy romancer with elderly Niven recalling his tragic love as he watches great niece Keyes' romance with Granger.

Encore (1952-British) **85m.** *** D: Pat Jackson, Anthony Pelissier, Harold French. Nigel Patrick, Roland Culver, Kay Walsh, Glynis Johns, Terence Morgan. Entertaining trilogy of Somerset Maugham stories: brothers try to outdo one another over money; grouchy matron almost ruins ship cruise; apprehensive circus performer faces a crisis.▼

Encounters in the Night SEE: **Intimate Encounters**

End, The (1978) **C-100m.** *** D: Burt Reynolds. Burt Reynolds, Sally Field, Dom DeLuise, Joanne Woodward, Kristy McNichol, Robby Benson, David Steinberg, Norman Fell, Carl Reiner, Pat O'Brien, Myrna Loy. Uneven but original black comedy by Jerry Belson about man who learns he's dying, and decides to commit suicide. DeLuise is achingly funny as Burt's schizophrenic sanitarium pal, and Reynolds' final soliloquy is great (in uncensored version).▼

Endangered Species (1982) **C-97m.** *½ D: Alan Rudolph. Robert Urich, JoBeth Williams, Paul Dooley, Hoyt Axton, Peter Coyote, Marin Kanter, Dan Hedaya, Harry Carey Jr., John Considine. Self-important, preachy story—based on a serious real-life situation—about a N.Y. cop's investigation of cattle mutilations in the Western U.S. Tries to be a thriller, but telegraphs all its punches.▼

Endless Game, The (1990-British) **C-105m.** TVM D: Bryan Forbes. Albert Finney, George Segal, Derek De Lint, Monica Guerritore, Ian Holm, John Standing, Kristin Scott Thomas, Anthony Quayle, Nanette Newman. British agent, seeking the truth behind the murder of a woman who'd been a onetime colleague and lover, finds himself knee-deep in international intrigue and political corruption. Convoluted spy thriller written by director Forbes. Quayle's last film appearance. Made for cable. Average.

Endless Love (1981) **C-115m.** BOMB D: Franco Zeffirelli. Brooke Shields, Martin Hewitt, Shirley Knight, Don Murray, Richard Kiley, Beatrice Straight, James Spader, Robert Moore, Penelope Milford, Jan Miner, Tom Cruise, Jami Gertz. Scott Spencer's deservedly praised novel about an obsessive romance between two teenagers is thoroughly trashed in textbook example of how to do everything wrong in a literary adaptation. Rightfully regarded as one of the worst films of its time. Cruise's film debut.▼

Endless Night (1971-British) **C-99m.** *** D: Sidney Gilliat. Hayley Mills, Hywel Bennett, Britt Ekland, George Sanders, Per Oscarsson, Peter Bowles, Lois Maxwell. Gripping Agatha Christie thriller about chauffeur (Bennett) who marries rich American girl (Mills) and moves into "dream house" which turns out to be more a nightmare. Also known as AGATHA CHRISTIE'S ENDLESS NIGHT.▼

Endless Summer, The (1966) **C-95m.** ******* D: Bruce Brown. Mike Hynson, Robert August. Superior documentary on surfing, filmed on location around the world, with a most diverting tongue-in-cheek narrative.▼

End of Desire (1962-French) **C-86m.** ****** D: Alexandre Astruc. Maria Schell, Christian Marquand, Pascale Petit, Ivan Desny. Schell is only bright light in De Maupassant tale of wife who discovers her husband loves her money and prefers to romance servant.▼

End of the Affair, The (1955-British) **106m.** ****½** D: Edward Dmytryk. Deborah Kerr, Van Johnson, John Mills, Peter Cushing, Michael Goodliffe. Graham Greene's mystic-religious novel about a wartime love affair in London loses much in screen version, especially from mismatched stars.

End of the Game (1976-German-Italian) **C-103m.** ******* D: Maximilian Schell. Jon Voight, Jacqueline Bisset, Martin Ritt, Robert Shaw, Gabriele Ferzetti, Donald Sutherland. Complex thriller about dying police commissioner Ritt, who for three decades has been trying to nail omnipotent criminal Shaw. Director Ritt, in a rare acting role, is excellent; Voight plays his assistant, and Sutherland appears as a dead man! Based on Friedrich Duerrenmatt's novel; retitled GETTING AWAY WITH MURDER for TV.

End of the Line (1987) **C-105m.** ****** D: Jay Russell. Wilford Brimley, Levon Helm, Mary Steenburgen, Barbara Barrie, Kevin Bacon, Holly Hunter, Bob Balaban, Clint Howard, Rita Jenrette, Howard Morris, Bruce McGill, Trey Wilson. Two lifelong Southern railroad workers, suddenly unemployed when their parent company abandons the rails for air freight, take off for the Chicago corporate headquarters in a stolen engine. Labor of love for executive producer Steenburgen begins promisingly, quickly degenerates into silly Capra-esque fantasy. Cast makes it a curio.▼

End of the River, The (1947-British) **80m.** ****** D: Derek Twist. Sabu, Bibi Ferreira, Esmond Knight, Torin Thatcher, Robert Douglas. Native boy Sabu fights for acceptance in white world; ambitious drama suffers from mediocre casting.

End of the Road (1970) **C-110m.** *****½** D: Aram Avakian. Stacy Keach, Harris Yulin, Dorothy Tristan, James Earl Jones, Grayson Hall, Ray Brock, James Coco. Keach and Jones give stinging performances in solid filmization of bizarre John Barth novel about unstable college instructor who becomes involved with the wife of a professor. Tristan is superb in crucial and difficult role.▼

End of the World (1977) **C-87m.** ****** D: John Hayes. Christopher Lee, Sue Lyon, Kirk Scott, Lew Ayres, Macdonald Carey, Dean Jagger, Liz Ross. Lee plays a priest and his sinister "double" in this strange sci-fi tale about imminent world destruction by alien invaders. Opens strong but drifts into dullness.

End of the World in Our Usual Bed in a Night Full of Rain, The SEE: **Night Full of Rain, A**

Enemies, A Love Story (1989) **C-119m.** *****½** D: Paul Mazursky. Anjelica Huston, Ron Silver, Lena Olin, Margaret Sophie Stein, Alan King, Judith Malina, Rita Karlin, Phil Leeds, Elya Baskin, Paul Mazursky. Quietly haunting film about an aloof Jewish intellectual (Silver) who managed to hide from the Nazis during WW2 and now, in 1949, leads a double life in Coney Island, N.Y., married to his wartime protector (Stein) and fooling around with a sexy married woman (Olin). Things get even more complicated when his first wife (Huston), who was thought dead, turns up. Typically quixotic Isaac Bashevis Singer material—full of irony, wit, and heartbreak—is beautifully realized by Mazursky (who cowrote the screenplay with Roger L. Simon) and a perfect cast. Kudos also to Pato Guzman for his incredibly evocative production design.▼

Enemy Agents Meet Ellery Queen (1942) **65m.** D: James Hogan. William Gargan, Gale Sondergaard, Margaret Lindsay, Charley Grapewin, Gilbert Roland. SEE **Ellery Queen** series.

Enemy Below, The (1957) **C-98m.** ******* D: Dick Powell. Robert Mitchum, Curt Jurgens, Theodore Bikel, Doug McClure, Russell Collins, David Hedison. Fine WW2 submarine chase tale, which manages to garner interest from usual crew interaction of U.S. vs. Germany in underwater action; the special effects for this earned Walter Rossi an Academy Award. Previously filmed in 1931 as THE SEAS BENEATH.▼

Enemy From Space (1957-British) **84m.** ******* D: Val Guest. Brian Donlevy, Michael Ripper, Sidney James, Bryan Forbes, John Longden, Vera Day, William Franklyn. Even better than the original, THE CREEPING UNKNOWN, this tense, scary science-fiction thriller concerns a secret alien invasion and BODY SNATCHERS-like takeovers of human beings. Donlevy is stern as Dr. Quatermass. Followed by FIVE MILLION YEARS TO EARTH.▼

Enemy General, The (1960) **74m.** ****½** D: George Sherman. Van Johnson, Jean-Pierre Aumont, Dany Carrel, John Van Dreelen. OSS officer Johnson and French resistance leader Aumont join forces to rescue Nazi general Van Dreelen who wants to defect to Allies; satisfactory handling of middling material.

Enemy Mine (1985) **C-108m.** ****½** D: Wolfgang Petersen. Dennis Quaid, Louis Gossett, Jr., Brion James, Richard Marcus.

Mortal space enemies are stranded together on a barren planet, forced to become friends in order to survive. Warmhearted science-fiction tale gets a bit too cuddly at times, but it's entertaining. Gossett's lizardlike makeup (by Chris Walas) is incredible; so is Rolf Zehetbauer's production design.▼

Enemy of the People, An (1977) **C-103m.** **½ D: George Schaefer. Steve McQueen, Charles Durning, Bibi Andersson, Richard Bradford, Robin Pearson Rose, Richard A. Dysart. Bearded scientist McQueen defies community by taking stand against polluted water system in Arthur Miller's adaptation of the Ibsen play. Sincere, plodding effort was a labor of love for McQueen, but understandably sat on the shelf for years and received only limited distribution. Still superior to the other films from McQueen's final period.

Enemy of the People, An (1989-Indian) **C-100m.** **½ D: Satyajit Ray. Soumitra Chatterjee, Dhritiman Chatterjee, Ruma Guhathakurta, Mamata Shankar, Dipankar Dey. Ray's first film in five years is an adaptation of the Ibsen play, updated and set in Bengal. Its message, about the perils of greed, religious fanaticism, and environmental pollution, may be topical, but the film is too static to have total impact. Still, there are enough flashes of Ray's brilliance to make it worthwhile. The director also scripted.

Enforcer, The (1951) **87m.** *** D: Bretaigne Windust. Humphrey Bogart, Zero Mostel, Ted de Corsia, Everett Sloane, Roy Roberts. Bogey is D.A. cracking down on crime ring led by Sloane in this raw drama, realistically done.▼

Enforcer, The (1976) **C-96m.** *** D: James Fargo. Clint Eastwood, Tyne Daly, Harry Guardino, Bradford Dillman, John Mitchum, DeVeren Bookwalter, John Crawford, Albert Popwell. Dirty Harry Callahan (Eastwood) has to contend with a female partner (Daly) as he goes after an underground terrorist group in San Francisco. Violent, bubble-gum-mentality script, but it's a formula that just seems to work. Followed by SUDDEN IMPACT.▼

England Made Me (1973-British) **C-100m.** *** D: Peter Duffell. Peter Finch, Michael York, Hildegard Neil, Michael Hordern, Joss Ackland. Unappreciated in its initial release, drama of a powerful financier in Nazi Germany of 1935 is absorbing, thoughtful fare. Made in Yugoslavia.

Enid is Sleeping (1990) **C-100m.** *** D: Maurice Phillips. Elizabeth Perkins, Judge Reinhold, Jeffrey Jones, Maureen Mueller, Rhea Perlman, Michael J. Pollard. Very black comedy about a woman who accidentally kills her much-hated sister—after being caught sleeping with her husband (who happens to be a police officer). Macabre humor may not be to everyone's

taste, but slapstick antics with the "dead" body and genuine character development put this leagues ahead of the similar WEEKEND AT BERNIE'S. Film was severely cut by its studio, then reclaimed (and put back in its original form) by its star and director; a particular triumph for Perkins, who's never been better.

Enigma (1982-British-French) **C-101m.** **½ D: Jeannot Szwarc. Martin Sheen, Brigitte Fossey, Sam Neill, Derek Jacobi, Michel Lonsdale, Frank Finlay. The KGB sends out five crack assassins to eliminate five Soviet dissidents; CIA agent Sheen (who's apparently seen NOTORIOUS once too often) tries to stop them by having ex-lover Fossey cozy up to top Russian agent Neill. Fine international cast does its best with so-so material; script by John Briley.▼

Enjo (1958-Japanese) **96m.** ***½ D: Kon Ichikawa. Raizo Ichikawa, Tatsuya Nakadai, Ganjiro Nakamura, Yoko Uraji, Tanie Kitabayashi. Troubled young novice priest Ichikawa cannot handle corruption around him and burns down a temple. Perceptive psychological study of a human being's destruction; based on a Yukio Mishima novel, fashioned around a true story. Also known as CONFLAGRATION.

Enola Gay: The Men, the Mission, the Atomic Bomb (1980) **C-150m.** TVM D: David Lowell Rich. Billy Crystal, Kim Darby, Patrick Duffy, Gary Frank, Gregory Harrison, Stephen Macht, Walter Olkewicz, Robert Pine, Ed Nelson, James Shigeta, Robert Walden, Henry Wilcoxon. The story of the crew that dropped the first atomic bomb, based on the reminiscences of the mission's leader, Paul Tibbets (played by Duffy). James Poe and Millard Kaufman wrote the dramatization. Average.▼

Enormous Changes at the Last Minute (1983) **C-115m.** **½ D: Mirra Bank, Ellen Hovde. Maria Tucci, Lynn Milgrim, Ellen Barkin, Ron McLarty, Zvee Scooler, Kevin Bacon, Jeffrey DeMunn, Sudie Bond. Three separate dramas about contemporary women living in N.Y.C., and their relationships with husbands, ex-husbands, lovers, parents, children. Ambitious but uneven; still, there are some good performances and touching moments. Screenplay by John Sayles with Susan Rice, based on the stories of Grace Paley. "Faith's Story" was filmed in 1978; "Virginia's Story" and "Alexandra's Story" were shot in 1982.▼

Ensign Pulver (1964) **C-104m.** ** D: Joshua Logan. Robert Walker, Jr., Burl Ives, Walter Matthau, Tommy Sands, Millie Perkins, Kay Medford. Flat sequel to MR. ROBERTS has Walker sinking in Jack Lemmon role amid synthetic seaboard-and-coral-isle-shenanigans. Disappointing film is worth noting for its large cast of future stars: Larry Hagman, Gerald O'Loughlin, Al Freeman, Jr., James Farentino, James Coco, Diana Sands, and Jack Nicholson.▼

Enter Arsene Lupin (1944) **72m.** ** D: Ford Beebe. Charles Korvin, Ella Raines, J. Carrol Naish, George Dolenz, Gale Sondergaard. Good supporting cast of villains gives zest to tame tale of naive heroine possessing a wealth of jewels.

Enter Laughing (1967) **C-112m.** ** D: Carl Reiner. Reni Santoni, Jose Ferrer, Shelley Winters, Elaine May, Jack Gilford, Janet Margolin, David Opatoshu, Michael J. Pollard, Don Rickles, Nancy Kovack, Rob Reiner. Reiner's funny semi-autobiographical Broadway play becomes bland screen comedy as youngster struggles to make it as an actor, despite all manner of problems in his way.▼

Enter Madame (1935) **83m.** **½ D: Elliott Nugent. Elissa Landi, Cary Grant, Lynne Overman, Sharon Lynne, Frank Albertson. Grant marries opera star Landi and winds up taking back seat to her career; pleasant romantic comedy.

Entertainer, The (1960-British) **97m.** ***½ D: Tony Richardson. Laurence Olivier, Brenda de Banzie, Roger Livesey, Joan Plowright, Daniel Massey, Alan Bates, Shirley Anne Field, Albert Finney, Thora Hird. Seedy vaudevillian (Olivier, recreating his stage role) ruins everyone's life and won't catch on. Film captures flavor of chintzy seaside resort, complementing Olivier's brilliance as egotistical song-and-dance man. Coscripted by John Osborne, from his play. Film debuts of Bates and Finney. Olivier and Plowright married the following year. Remade as a TV movie.▼

Entertainer, The (1975) **C-100m. TVM** D: Donald Wrye. Jack Lemmon, Ray Bolger, Sada Thompson, Tyne Daly, Allyn Ann McLerie, Michael Cristofer, Annette O'Toole, Mitch Ryan. Third-rate vaudevillian Archie Rice plays out his life in a seedy California burlesque house in the 1940s, vainly trying to emulate his once-famous father (Bolger) now living on faded memories. Lemmon is good, but no Olivier; Bolger is excellent as the father. Unrelenting drama punctuated by eight Marvin Hamlisch songs. Average.

Entertaining Mr. Sloane (1970-British) **C-94m.** **½ D: Douglas Hickox. Beryl Reid, Harry Andrews, Peter McEnery, Alan Webb. Acting by McEnery, Reid, and Andrews is extraordinary in story of young man who becomes involved with both brother and sister. Uneven adaptation of Joe Orton play.▼

Enter the Dragon (1973) **C-97m.** ***½ D: Robert Clouse. Bruce Lee, John Saxon, Jim Kelly, Ahna Capri, Yang Tse, Angela Mao. Almost perfect action film that forgets about plot and concentrates on mind-boggling action. Martial arts expert Lee (in last complete film role) infiltrates strange tournament on island fortress.▼

Enter the Ninja (1981) **C-94m.** *½ D: Menahem Golan. Franco Nero, Susan George, Sho Kosugi, Alex Courtney, Will Hare, Zachi Noy, Dale Ishimoto, Christopher George. Ninjitsu master Nero takes on greedy Christopher George and old rival Kosugi. Third-rate chop-socky actioner and certainly no ENTER THE DRAGON. Original running time: 99m. Followed by REVENGE OF THE NINJA.▼

Entity, The (1983) **C-115m.** ** D: Sidney J. Furie. Barbara Hershey, Ron Silver, Jacqueline Brooks, David Lablosa, George Coe, Margaret Blye, Alex Rocco. Woman is raped repeatedly by giant invisible mass. Her psychiatrist thinks it's all in the mind, until university parapsychologists manage to freeze the sex-crazed blob. Effectively sensational but atrociously exploitive horror movie supposedly based on actual incident.▼

Entre Nous (1983-French) **C-110m.** ***½ D: Diane Kurys. Miou Miou, Isabelle Huppert, Guy Marchand, Jean-Pierre Bacri, Robin Renucci, Patrick Bauchau. Moving, multi-layered story of two women who form a bond of friendship that lasts many years, takes many turns, and threatens their ineffectual husbands. Compassionate telling by Kurys of her own mother's story, with extraordinary performances all around. Original French title: COUP DE FOUDRE.▼

Equinox (1971) **C-80m.** ** D: Jack Woods. Edward Connell, Barbara Hewitt, Frank Boers, Jr. (Frank Bonner), Robin Christopher, Jack Woods, Fritz Leiber. Archaeology students confront Satanism—and mutant-like monsters—while searching for vanished professor. Late-1960s amateur film (directed by later special-effects Oscar winner Dennis Muren) was reworked for theatrical release, mixing movie clichés with good special effects. This film took several years to complete, and the young cast obviously ages in it.▼

Equus (1977) **C-138m.** **½ D: Sidney Lumet. Richard Burton, Peter Firth, Colin Blakely, Joan Plowright, Harry Andrews, Eileen Atkins, Jenny Agutter. Peter Shaffer's shattering play makes bumpy screen adaptation, its vivid theatricality lost on film; Burton, however, is superb as troubled psychiatrist trying to unlock deep-rooted problems of stable boy Firth.▼

Eraserhead (1978) **90m.** *** D: David Lynch. John (Jack) Nance, Charlotte Stewart, Allen Joseph, Jeanne Bates, Judith Anna Roberts, Laurel Near, V. Phipps-Wilson. Brooding experimental film full of repulsive imagery tells story of zombie-like misfit, his spastic girlfriend, and their half-human offspring. Bona fide cult film is full of surreal, nightmarish tangents. Feature film debut of director Lynch.▼

Erendira (1983-Mexican-French-German) **C-103m.** **½ D: Ruy Guerra. Irene Papas, Claudia Ohana, Michael Lonsdale, Oliver Wehe, Rufus. Strange does not begin to describe this fable of queenly Papas forcing beautiful, obedient granddaughter Ohana into prostitution in a vast, surreal desert. Ambitious and fluidly directed, but unmemorable; from a screenplay by Gabriel Garcia Marquez.▼

Eric (1975) **C-100m.** TVM D: James Goldstone. Patricia Neal, John Savage, Claude Akins, Sian Barbara Allen, Mark Hamill, Nehemiah Persoff, Tom Clancy. Sensitive weeper about athletic youth who, aware of his terminal illness, refuses to give up. Based on Doris Lund's book about her own teen-aged son, given dignity by the steady performances of Savage in title role and Neal as his valiant mother. Above average.▼

Eric Clapton and His Rolling Hotel (1981-British) **C-62m.** *½ D: Rex Pyke. Eric Clapton, Muddy Waters, George Harrison, Elton John. Below-average rock documentary of Clapton's '79 European tour.

Erik the Conqueror (1963-Italian) **C-81m.** ** D: Mario Bava. Cameron Mitchell, Alice Kessler, Ellen Kessler, Françoise Christophe. Unexceptional account of 10th-century Viking life, with Mitchell fighting for virtue and love. Released on video as THE INVADERS at 88m.▼

Erik the Viking (1989) **C-104m.** BOMB D: Terry Jones. Tim Robbins, Mickey Rooney, Eartha Kitt, Terry Jones, Imogen Stubbs, John Cleese, Antony Sher, Gordon John Sinclair, Freddie Jones. Robbins is a revisionist Erik, but quick—what's the Norse expression for "unwatchable satire"?▼

Ernest Goes to Camp (1987) **C-93m.** *½ D: John R. Cherry 3rd. Jim Varney, Victoria Racimo, John Vernon, Iron Eyes Cody, Lyle Alzado, Gailard Sartain, Daniel Butler, Hakeem Abdul-Samad. Ernest, an obnoxious dimwit popularized in a spate of TV commercials, is the star of this clumsy and unfunny comedy about a dumb cluck who wants to be a summer camp counselor in the worst way—and gets his wish. Aimed at children who aren't very bright. Followed by ERNEST SAVES CHRISTMAS.▼

Ernest Goes to Jail (1990) **C-82m.** ** D: John Cherry. Jim Varney, Gailard Sartain, Bill Byrge, Barbara Bush, Randall (Tex) Cobb, Barry Scott, Charles Napier. Third in the surprisingly successful series about Ernest P. Worrell finds out hero in prison as the result of a switch set up by an evil inmate lookalike (also played by Varney). Harmless, predictable, and hokey, the importance of seeing Ernest may depend on your age and I.Q.—if either is 12 or below this may be the movie for you.

Ernest Saves Christmas (1988) **C-89m.** *½ D: John Cherry. Jim Varney, Douglas Seale, Oliver Clark, Noelle Parker, Robert Lesser, Gailard Sartain, Billie Bird. The title character, who makes Gomer Pyle seem like Albert Einstein, attempts to help Santa Claus on Christmas Eve. This is one Christmas present to be opened with extreme caution . . . unless you're a fan of Ernest P. Worrell. Followed by ERNEST GOES TO JAIL.▼

Ernie Kovacs: Between the Laughter (1984) **C-100m.** TVM D: Lamont Johnson. Jeff Goldblum, Melody Anderson, Cloris Leachman, Madolyn Smith, John Glover, Edie Adams. Pioneering TV comic Ernie Kovacs' lesser publicized private agony—retrieving his two young daughters after their mother kidnapped them following a custody battle. Intriguing, once you get past the physical dissimilarity between Goldblum (as Kovacs) and the real Ernie, as well as the off-the-wall portrayal by Leachman of Kovacs' Hungarian mother. Melody Anderson plays Kovacs' second wife, Edie Adams, and Adams (here given credit as both "material supplier" and technical advisor) is seen briefly as Mae West. Average.▼

Errand Boy, The (1961) **92m.** **½ D: Jerry Lewis. Jerry Lewis, Brian Donlevy, Howard McNear, Sig Ruman, Fritz Feld, Iris Adrian, Kathleen Freeman, Doodles Weaver. Jerry on the loose in a movie studio has its moments. Long string of gags provide the laughter; veteran character actors produce the sparkle.▼

Escapade (1955-British) **87m.** *** D: Philip Leacock. John Mills, Yvonne Mitchell, Alastair Sim, Jeremy Spenser, Andrew Ray, Marie Lohr, Peter Asher. Mills is a professional pacifist whose life is anything but tranquil; his three sons, fearing that their parents are about to be divorced, react in a most unusual manner. Ambitious, insightful, solidly acted drama about the cynicism and hypocrisy of adults, contrasted with the idealism of youth. Stick with this one. ▼

Escapade in Japan (1957) **C-93m.** ** D: Arthur Lubin. Cameron Mitchell, Teresa Wright, Jon Provost, Roger Nakagawa, Philip Ober, Clint Eastwood. Location filming in Japan is the prime asset of this otherwise forgettable adventure of two young boys, one American and the other Japanese, and their search for the former's parents. Eastwood is cast as a serviceman named Dumbo!▼

Escape (1940) **104m.** *** D: Mervyn LeRoy. Norma Shearer, Robert Taylor, Conrad Veidt, Nazimova, Felix Bressart. Countess Shearer helps Taylor get his mother (Nazimova) out of German concentration camp before WW2; polished, with sterling cast.

Escape (1948-British) **78m.** ***** D: Joseph L. Mankiewicz. Rex Harrison, Peggy Cummins, William Hartnell, Norman Wooland, Jill Esmond. Compelling account of man sent to prison, unjustly in his opinion; his attempted escape climaxes narrative.

Escape (1970) **C-73m.** TVM D: John Llewellyn Moxey. Christopher George, Avery Schreiber, Marlyn Mason, William Windom, Gloria Grahame, John Vernon, William Schallert, Huntz Hall. After almost losing his life trying to prevent kidnapping of scientist, magician-adventurer, with help of sidekick and scientist's daughter (Mason), battles with mysterious mad scientist over plot to destroy Earth. Dumb characterizations, silly dialogue, passable action. Average.

Escape (1980) **C-100m.** TVM D: Robert Michael Lewis. Timothy Bottoms, Kay Lenz, Colleen Dewhurst, Allan Miller, Antonio Fargas, Miguel Angel Suarez. TV's answer to MIDNIGHT EXPRESS traces the true story of Dwight Worker, stashed for smuggling hash in Mexico, and his intricate breakout escapade. Dewhurst's patented "earth mother" turn, hatching the escape plot, gives Michael Zagar's script added zest, but the whole is predictable. Average.

Escape Artist, The (1982) **C-96m.** ** D: Caleb Deschanel. Griffin O'Neal, Raul Julia, Teri Garr, Joan Hackett, Gabriel Dell, Elizabeth Daily, Desiderio (Desi) Arnaz, Huntz Hall, Jackie Coogan. Maddeningly muddled tale of teen-ager O'Neal, an amateur magician, and the adults who attempt to exploit him. Griffin, son of Ryan and brother of Tatum, has a pleasing screen presence.▼

Escape from Alcatraz (1979) **C-112m.** *** D: Donald Siegel. Clint Eastwood, Patrick McGoohan, Roberts Blossom, Jack Thibeau, Fred Ward, Paul Benjamin. Straightforward, methodical telling of true story about 1962 breakout from supposedly impregnable prison. Vivid and credible throughout. Watch for Danny Glover.▼

Escape from Bogen County (1977) **C-100m.** TVM D: Steven Hilliard Stern. Jaclyn Smith, Mitchell Ryan, Michael Parks, Henry Gibson, Pat Hingle, Philip Abbott. Tawdry drama about a vicious political czar who strips his wife of her civil rights and imprisons her in their mansion when she threatens to expose his ruthlessness. Below average.

Escape from Crime (1942) **51m.** ** D: D. Ross Lederman. Richard Travis, Julie Bishop, Frank Wilcox, Rex Williams, Wade Boteler. Standard but fast-moving B picture about an ex-con who becomes a dare-

devil newspaper photographer; remake of James Cagney's PICTURE SNATCHER. Jackie "C." Gleason gets third billing but has just one scene!

Escape From East Berlin (1962) **94m.** ** D: Robert Siodmak. Don Murray, Christine Kaufmann, Werner Klemperer, Ingrid van Bergen, Karl Schell. East German chauffeur becomes determined to tunnel to West Berlin, to allow his family and new girlfriend to escape Communist domination. Dated and propagandistic but based on true events.

Escape From Fort Bravo (1953) **C-98m.** *** D: John Sturges. William Holden, Eleanor Parker, John Forsythe, Polly Bergen, William Demarest. Well-executed Western set in 1860s Arizona, balancing North-South conflict with whites vs. Indians, climaxed by tense redskin ambush.

Escape From Iran: The Canadian Caper (1981) **C-100m.** TVM D: Lamont Johnson. Gordon Pinsent, Chris Wiggins, Diana Barrington, Robert Joy, James B. Douglas, Tisa Chang. The true story of six Americans who escaped being taken hostage when the U.S. Embassy in Tehran was besieged, thanks to some daring Canadian Embassy officials. Inspiring Canadian-made film, written by Lionel Chetwynd, with a standout performance by Pinsent as Ambassador Ken Taylor. Above average.

Escape From New York (1981) **C-99m.** ** D: John Carpenter. Kurt Russell, Lee Van Cleef, Ernest Borgnine, Donald Pleasence, Isaac Hayes, Adrienne Barbeau, Harry Dean Stanton, Season Hubley. For a "fun" film this is pretty bleak. The year is 1997, Manhattan is a maximum-security prison, and a character named Snake Plissken (Russell) must effect a daring rescue from within its borders. Reminiscent in some ways of Carpenter's ASSAULT ON PRECINCT 13, which was smaller—and better.▼

Escape From Red Rock (1958) **75m.** *½ D: Edward Bernds. Brian Donlevy, Jay C. Flippen, Eilene Janssen, Gary Murray. Modest oater of rancher and girl involved in theft, being chased into Indian country by pursuing posse.

Escape From San Quentin (1957) **81m.** BOMB D: Fred F. Sears. Johnny Desmond, Merry Anders, Richard Devon, Roy Engel. Drab film has Desmond as runaway convict who decides to give himself and buddy up to police.

Escape from Sobibor (1987) **C-150m.** TVM D: Jack Gold. Alan Arkin, Joanna Pacula, Rutger Hauer, Hartmut Becker, Jack Shepherd. Searing drama detailing the largest prisoner escape from a WW2 Nazi death camp, with a memorable Arkin performance as the leader, and a terrific script by veteran writer Reginald Rose, based on

Richard Rashke's book. Top-notch production. Above average.

Escape From the Bronx (1985-Italian) **C-89m.** BOMB D: Enzo G. Castellari. Henry Silva, Valerie d'Obici, Mark Gregory, Timothy Brent, Paolo Malco. In this plodding sequel to 1990: THE BRONX WARRIORS, Silva attempts to kill off the inhabitants of the title N.Y.C. borough. Oh, yes, Gregory rehashes his role as "Trash."▼

Escape from the Dark SEE: **Littlest Horse Thieves, The**▼

Escape From the Planet of the Apes (1971) **C-98m.** *** D: Don Taylor. Roddy McDowall, Kim Hunter, Bradford Dillman, Natalie Trundy, Eric Braeden, William Windom, Sal Mineo, Ricardo Montalban. Third in series is best of the sequels, with the Apes in modern-day L.A.; ingeniously paves the way for 4th and 5th entries in series.▼

Escape From Zahrain (1962) **C-93m.** *½ D: Ronald Neame. Yul Brynner, Sal Mineo, Madlyn Rhue, Jack Warden, James Mason, Jay Novello. Plodding film of five prisoners escaping from jail in Mideastern country, being chased across desert. Nice photography at least.

Escape in the Desert (1945) **81m.** ** D: Edward A. Blatt. Philip Dorn, Helmut Dantine, Jean Sullivan, Alan Hale. Tame remake of THE PETRIFIED FOREST involving American flyer encountering Nazi at desert hotel.

Escape in the Fog (1945) **65m.** ** D: Oscar (Budd) Boetticher. Nina Foch, William Wright, Otto Kruger, Konstantin Shayne. Capable but unexceptional programmer of girl who has strange dream of murder being committed and encounters the dream victim in real life.

Escape Me Never (1947) **104m.** *½ D: Peter Godfrey. Errol Flynn, Ida Lupino, Eleanor Parker, Gig Young, Reginald Denny, Isobel Elsom. Sappy remake of 1935 Elisabeth Bergner vehicle, with Lupino as an itinerant waif (!) and Flynn as struggling composer who marries her but takes up with his brother's aristocratic fiancée (Parker). Forget it.

Escape of the Birdmen SEE: **Birdmen**

Escape to Athena (1979-British) **C-101m.** **½ D: George Pan Cosmatos. Roger Moore, Telly Savalas, David Niven, Claudia Cardinale, Richard Roundtree, Stefanie Powers, Sonny Bono, Elliott Gould, William Holden. Agreeable time-filler, with all-star cast in outlandish adventure yarn about WW2 POWs planning escape and art heist at the same time. Released in England at 125m.▼

Escape to Burma (1955) **C-87m.** ** D: Allan Dwan. Barbara Stanwyck, Robert Ryan, David Farrar, Murvyn Vye, Lisa Montell, Reginald Denny. Stanwyck rides herd over a tea plantation—and a pack of wild animals—but doesn't quite know how to deal with a wanted man who seeks refuge. Cast does what it can with pulp material.▼

Escape to Glory (1940) **74m.** *** D: John Brahm. Constance Bennett, Pat O'Brien, John Halliday, Alan Baxter, Melville Cooper. British ship is attacked by German sub at outbreak of WW2, giving pause to various passengers on-board—including a German doctor. Thoughtful, atmospheric B-picture with minimal amount of clichés.

Escape to Mindinao (1968) **C-95m.** TVM D: Don McDougall. George Maharis, Ronald Remy, Nehemiah Persoff, James Shigeta, Willi Coopman. Two American P.O.W.s break out of Japanese prison, must make it back to U.S. forces via Dutch black market freighter with valuable enemy decoder. Contrived, unbelievable resolutions; film should have been made for longer running time. Below average.

Escape to the Sun (1972-British-Israeli) **105m.** *½ D: Menahem Golan. Laurence Harvey, Josephine Chaplin, John Ireland, Lila Kedrova, Jack Hawkins, Clive Revill. Suspense tale about aftermath of unsuccessful attempt by Soviet Jews to hijack a plane wastes a capable cast.▼

Escape to Witch Mountain (1975) **C-97m.** *** D: John Hough. Eddie Albert, Ray Milland, Kim Richards, Ike Eisenmann, Donald Pleasence. Excellent Disney mystery-fantasy: two children with mysterious powers try to discover their origins, while being pursued by evil Milland, who wants to use their powers for his own purposes. Followed by sequel RETURN FROM WITCH MOUNTAIN.▼

Escape 2000 (1981-Australian) **C-92m.** BOMB D: Brian Trenchard-Smith. Steve Railsback, Olivia Hussey, Michael Craig, Carmen Duncan, Roger Ward. Repellently violent, unpleasant ripoff of THE MOST DANGEROUS GAME, set in future society where criminals are hunted in a controlled environment. Original title: TURKEY SHOOT. Video running time: 80m.▼

Escort for Hire (1960-British) **C-66m.** ** D: Godfrey Grayson. June Thorburn, Noel Trevarthan, Peter Murray, Jill Melford, Guy Middleton. Clichéd murder yarn, enhanced by Technicolor, with Trevarthan an out-of-work actor joining escort service, becoming involved in murder.

Escort West (1959) **75m.** **½ D: Francis D. Lyon. Victor Mature, Elaine Stewart, Faith Domergue, Reba Waters, Noah Beery, Leo Gordon, Rex Ingram. Fairly good Western with Confederate soldier and 10-year-old daughter heading West, encountering two women who survived renegade attack and saved Army payroll.

Espionage (1937) **67m.** **½ D: Kurt

Neumann. Edmund Lowe, Madge Evans, Paul Lukas, Ketti Gallion, Skeets Gallagher, Leonid Kinskey, Billy Gilbert. Slick goings-on in this fast-paced MGM B pic. Lowe and Evans are rival reporters on the trail of arms tycoon Lukas aboard the Orient Express.

Espionage Agent (1939) 83m. ** D: Lloyd Bacon. Joel McCrea, Brenda Marshall, George Bancroft, Jeffrey Lynn, James Stephenson, Martin Kosleck. Formula spy caper with McCrea and Marshall tracking down the head of notorious spy ring.

Esther and the King (1960-U.S.-Italian) **C-109m.** ** D: Raoul Walsh. Joan Collins, Richard Egan, Denis O'Dea, Sergio Fantoni. Cardboard biblical costumer pretends to recreate 4th-century B.C. Persia, with stony performances by Collins and Egan as the king and the Jewish maiden he wants to replace murdered queen. Filmed in Italy.

Esther Waters (1948-British) 108m. **½ D: Peter Proud. Dirk Bogarde, Fay Compton, Kathleen Ryan, Cyril Cusack, Mary Clare. Well-appointed account of rogue Bogarde involved with lovely damsels frequenting the racetracks; set in 19th-century England. Film bogs down into soaper of gloomy married life, marring initial zest.

Eternally Yours (1939) 95m. **½ D: Tay Garnett. Loretta Young, David Niven, Hugh Herbert, C. Aubrey Smith, Billie Burke, Broderick Crawford, ZaSu Pitts, Eve Arden. Wayout idea comes off fairly well; Young is married to magician Niven, thinks his tricks are taking precedence to their married life. Also shown in computer-colored version.▼

Eternal Sea, The (1955) 103m. **½ D: John H. Auer. Sterling Hayden, Alexis Smith, Dean Jagger, Virginia Grey. Well-played biography of Admiral John Hoskins' efforts to retain active command despite WW2 injury. Hayden is restrained in lead role; modest production values.

E.T. The Extra-Terrestrial (1982) **C-115m.** **** D: Steven Spielberg. Dee Wallace, Henry Thomas, Peter Coyote, Robert MacNaughton, Drew Barrymore, K.C. Martel, Sean Frye, Tom (C. Thomas) Howell. A 10-year-old boy (Thomas) befriends a creature from another planet that's been stranded on Earth. A warm, insightful story of childhood innocence, frustration, courage, and love . . . with a remarkable "performance" by E.T. An exhilarating experience for young and old alike. Screenplay by Melissa Mathison. John Williams won an Oscar for his soaring score, as did the sound and visual effects teams.▼

Eureka (1981) **C-130m.** ** D: Nicolas Roeg. Gene Hackman, Theresa Russell, Rutger Hauer, Jane Lapotaire, Ed Lauter, Mickey Rourke, Joe Pesci, Corin Redgrave. Klondike prospector becomes fabulously wealthy, watches his kingdom crumble 30 years later when his daughter's problems and Miami thugs converge on him at the same time. Odd drama, even for Roeg, that somehow climaxes with long, windy courtroom histrionics. Shelved by studio until "Classics" Division released it sporadically in 1985.▼

Europa '51 SEE: **Greatest Love, The**▼

Europeans, The (1979) **C-90m.** *** D: James Ivory. Lee Remick, Robin Ellis, Wesley Addy, Tim Choate, Lisa Eichhorn, Tim Woodward, Kristin Griffith. Meticulous film of Henry James novel vividly recreates 19th-century life in New England, as the arrival of two foreign cousins disrupts the stern-faced calm of a plain American family. Deliberately paced, but richly rewarding.▼

Eva (1965-British) 115m. *** D: Joseph Losey. Jeanne Moreau, Stanley Baker, Virna Lisi, Nona Medici, Francesco Rissone, James Villiers. Brooding account of writer Baker whose continued attraction for Eva (Moreau) causes wife (Lisi) to have tragic death. Premise isn't always workable, but Moreau is well cast as personification of evil.

Eve (1968-British-Spanish) **C-94m.** BOMB D: Jeremy Summers. Robert Walker, Jr., Celeste Yarnall, Herbert Lom, Christopher Lee, Fred Clark, Maria Rohm. Pilot is saved from Amazon savages by white jungle goddess who wields strange power over her subjects. Save yourself and don't watch.

Eve Knew Her Apples (1945) 64m. **½ D: Will Jason. Ann Miller, William Wright, Robert Williams, Ray Walker. Sprightly musical variation of IT HAPPENED ONE NIGHT, with Miller on the lam from her marriage-minded fiancé.

Evel Knievel (1972) **C-90m.** **½ D: Marvin Chomsky. George Hamilton, Sue Lyon, Bert Freed, Rod Cameron. Biography of daredevil motorcyclist contains some great action footage; modest but effective film. Shouldn't be confused with VIVA KNIEVEL! (in which Evel played himself).▼

Evelyn Prentice (1934) 80m. **½ D: William K. Howard. William Powell, Myrna Loy, Una Merkel, Rosalind Russell, Isabel Jewell, Harvey Stephens. Story of successful attorney who doesn't know his own wife is in trouble is too drawn-out, ultimately too implausible. Cast rises above material, but Cora Sue Collins is an obnoxious brat. Russell's first film. Remade as STRONGER THAN DESIRE.

Even Dwarfs Started Small (1968-German) 96m. *** D: Werner Herzog. Helmut Doring, Gerd Gickel, Paul Glauer, Erna Gschwnedtner, Gisela Hartwig. Unusual, disturbing, truly unsettling parable about dwarfs and midgets confined to a barren correctional institution who literally take over the asylum. Reminiscent of Tod Browning's FREAKS.

Evening in Byzantium (1978) **C-200m.** TVM D: Jerry London. Glenn Ford, Eddie Albert, Vince Edwards, Shirley Jones, Erin Gray, Harry Guardino, Patrick Macnee, Gregory Sierra, Michael Cole, Gloria DeHaven, George Lazenby, Christian Marquand, James Booth, Simon Oakland, Edward James Olmos. Fading movie producer Ford wheels and deals at the Cannes Film Festival as it is taken over by terrorists. Better than expected adaptation of Irwin Shaw's best seller. Originally shown in two parts. Above average.

Eve of St. Mark, The (1944) **96m.** *** D: John M. Stahl. Anne Baxter, William Eythe, Michael O'Shea, Vincent Price, Dickie Moore. Human focus on WW2 in tale of soldier Eythe and girl friend Baxter at outset of war; not always successful Maxwell Anderson story.

Evergreen (1934-British) **90m.** *** D: Victor Saville. Jessie Matthews, Sonnie Hale, Betty Balfour, Barry Mackay, Ivor MacLaren. British musical-comedy star's best known film is enjoyable fluff about young girl who becomes a stage sensation masquerading as her long-retired mother. Score includes Rodgers and Hart's "Dancing on the Ceiling."▼

Ever in My Heart (1933) **68m.** **½ D: Archie Mayo. Barbara Stanwyck, Otto Kruger, Ralph Bellamy, Ruth Donnelly, Frank Albertson. Stanwyck marries German immigrant Kruger, but their happiness is cut short by the outbreak of WW1. Beautifully acted weeper is a bit too hurried and simplistic to really score.

Ever Since Eve (1937) **79m.** *½ D: Lloyd Bacon. Marion Davies, Robert Montgomery, Frank McHugh, Patsy Kelly, Allen Jenkins, Louise Fazenda, Barton MacLane. Davies makes herself homely in order to avoid being harrassed on the job; dreary comedy tests the mettle of Warner Bros. stock cast. This was Marion's last film.

Every Bastard a King (1970-Israeli) **C-93m.** BOMB D: Uri Zohar. Pier Angeli, William Berger, Oded Kotler, Yehoram Gaon, Ori Levy. Story of journalist and his mistress, set against the 6-day Israeli-Egyptian War, is a slapdash effort with nothing to recommend it. Retitled EVERY MAN A KING for TV.

Everybody Does It (1949) **98m.** ***½ D: Edmund Goulding. Paul Douglas, Linda Darnell, Celeste Holm, Charles Coburn, Millard Mitchell. Exceptionally amusing yarn of aspiring singer Holm, harried husband Douglas, and prima donna Darnell. Celeste wants vocal career, Douglas gets one instead. Remake of WIFE, HUSBAND, AND FRIEND. Nunnally Johnson adapted his earlier screenplay (based on a James M. Cain story).

Everybody's All-American (1988) **C-127m.** *** D: Taylor Hackford. Jessica Lange, Dennis Quaid, Timothy Hutton, John Goodman, Carl Lumbly, Ray Baker, Savannah Smith Boucher, Patricia Clarkson. The twenty-five-year saga of a college football hero and his homecoming queen, who find a rocky road living happily ever after. Quaid seems too aware of the caricature he is about to become, but Lange's bittersweet performance rings true throughout and makes this film worth seeing. Based on Frank Deford's novel.▼

Everybody's Baby: The Rescue of Jessica McClure (1989) **C-100m.** TVM D: Mel Damski. Beau Bridges, Pat Hingle, Roxana Zal, Patty Duke, Will Oldham, Whip Hubley. An ensemble company reenacts the 1987 rescue of the 18-month-old tot who toppled into an abandoned well in rural Texas. A stunning example (thanks to writer David Eyre, Jr., and director Damski) of how an edge-of-your-seat thriller can be made from a headline-making event to which almost everyone knows the outcome. Above average.

Everybody Sing (1938) **80m.** ** D: Edwin L. Marin. Allan Jones, Judy Garland, Fanny Brice, Reginald Owen, Billie Burke, Reginald Gardiner. Shrill musical with stupid plot, unmemorable songs; good cast fighting weak material about nutty family involved in putting on a show. After loud finale you'll be waiting for a sequel called EVERYBODY SHUT UP.

Everybody Wins (1990) **C-98m.** BOMB D: Karel Reisz. Debra Winger, Nick Nolte, Will Patton, Jack Warden, Judith Ivey, Kathleen Wilhoite, Frank Converse, Frank Military. Private detective with an ax to grind ties his professional reputation to a schizoid small-town hooker who outbugs Bugs and Daffy. Arthur Miller's first screenplay since THE MISFITS (based on his one-act play "Some Kind of Love Story") gave fruit to this ironically titled fiasco; Winger flounders in a difficult—perhaps even unplayable—role.▼

Every Day's A Holiday (1937) **80m.** *** D: A. Edward Sutherland. Mae West, Edmund Lowe, Charles Butterworth, Charles Winninger, Walter Catlett, Lloyd Nolan, Louis Armstrong. Mae sells Herman Bing the Brooklyn Bridge, so police detective Lowe orders her to leave N.Y.C. She returns to help expose crooked police chief Nolan. Gay 90s setting for fast-moving West vehicle.

Every Girl Should Be Married (1948) **85m.** **½ D: Don Hartman. Cary Grant, Franchot Tone, Diana Lynn, Betsy Drake, Alan Mowbray. Airy comedy of girl (Drake) setting out to trap bachelor (Grant) into marriage; Tone has thankless "other man" role. Drake also "captured" Grant in real life; they were married soon after this film came out. Also shown in computer-colored version.▼

Every Home Should Have One SEE: **Think Dirty**▼

Every Little Crook and Nanny (1972) **C-91m.** ** D: Cy Howard. Lynn Redgrave, Victor Mature, Paul Sand, Austin Pendelton, John Astin, Dom DeLuise, Pat Harrington, Severn Darden. Good idea—the kidnapping of a mobster's son by nanny Redgrave—gets away in this comic crime-and-caper film. One bright spot: Mature's gangster portrayal.

Every Man a King SEE: **Every Bastard a King**

Every Man for Himself (1980-French-Swiss) **C-87m.** **½ D: Jean-Luc Godard. Isabelle Huppert, Jacques Dutronc, Nathalie Baye, Roland Amstutz, Anna Baldaccini. Self-conscious account of three characters whose lives are intertwined: Dutronc, who has left his wife for Baye; Baye, who is leaving Dutronc for life in the boondocks; and Huppert, country girl turned prostitute. Godard's "comeback" film was widely overrated, and certainly can't compare with his best work of the past.

Every Man for Himself and God Against All (1975-German) **C-110m.** **** D: Werner Herzog. Bruno S., Walter Ladengast, Brigitte Mira, Hans Musaus, Willy Semmelrogge, Michael Kroecher, Henry van Lyck. Man kept in confinement from birth mysteriously appears in 1820s Nuremberg. Poignant tale based on real incident explores his alternate vision of the world and his attempts to adjust to society. Herzog's best film (from his own screenplay) features stunning performance by Bruno S. as Kaspar Hauser. Also released as THE MYSTERY OF KASPAR HAUSER.▼

Every Man Is My Enemy (1967-Italian) **C-93m.** *½ D: Francesco Prosperi. Robert Webber, Elsa Martinelli, Jean Servais, Martina Berti, Pierre Zimmer. Mafia hitman Webber tries to pull off major diamond heist in Marseilles, with predictable complications.

Every Man Needs One (1972) **C-74m.** TVM D: Jerry Paris. Connie Stevens, Ken Berry, Gail Fisher, Steve Franken, Henry Gibson, Louise Sorel, Carol Wayne, Nancy Walker, Jerry Paris. Bachelor architect forced to eat words, hire "know it all" woman (Stevens) as assistant. Typical TV-style comedy complete with accommodating feminist slant. Average.

Every Night at Eight (1935) **81m.** **½ D: Raoul Walsh. George Raft, Alice Faye, Frances Langford, Patsy Kelly, Herman Bing, Walter Catlett. Forgettable trifle about Faye, Langford, and Kelly singing their way to fame with bandleader Raft. Dorothy Fields-Jimmy McHugh score includes "I Feel a Song Comin' On" and "I'm in the Mood for Love."

Everything But the Truth (1956) **C-83m.** ** D: Jerry Hopper. Maureen O'Hara, John Forsythe, Tim Hovey, Frank Faylen. When youngster Hovey joins truth pledge crusade at school, repercussions to his family and townfolk grow; cutesy.

Everything for Sale (1968-Polish) **C-105m.** *** D: Andrzej Wajda. Beata Tyszkiewicz, Elzbieta Czyzewska, Daniel Olbrychski, Andrzej Lapicki. Not top-drawer Wajda, but still an ambitious, fluidly directed examination of life on a movie set, the relationship between a director and his actors, and what happens when the leading man is accidentally killed. A very personal homage to Zbigniew Cybulski, Wajda's star of the '50s, who died in a freak mishap in 1967.

Everything Happens at Night (1939) **77m.** *** D: Irving Cummings. Sonja Henie, Ray Milland, Robert Cummings, Alan Dinehart, Fritz Feld, Jody Gilbert, Victor Varconi. One of Henie's best romantic skating vehicles, with Milland and Cummings as rival writers vying for her.

Everything I Have Is Yours (1952) **C-92m.** ** D: Robert Z. Leonard. Marge and Gower Champion, Dennis O'Keefe, Eduard Franz. Champions play dance team who finally get Broadway break, only to discover she's pregnant. Mild musical helped by stars' multitalents.

Everything's Ducky (1961) **81m.** ** D: Don Taylor. Mickey Rooney, Buddy Hackett, Jackie Cooper, Roland Winters. Nonsense of Rooney-Hackett teaming up with talking duck, with trio ending up on navy missile orbiting earth; strictly for kids.

Everything You Always Wanted to Know About Sex (But Were Afraid to Ask) (1972) **C-87m.** *** D: Woody Allen. Woody Allen, John Carradine, Lou Jacobi, Louise Lasser, Anthony Quayle, Tony Randall, Lynn Redgrave, Burt Reynolds, Gene Wilder, Jack Barry, Erin Fleming, Robert Q. Lewis, Heather MacRae, Pamela Mason, Sidney Miller, Regis Philbin, Geoffrey Holder, Jay Robinson, Robert Walden. Woody's most cinematic comedy, also most uneven, most tasteless. In multi-episode feature based very loosely on Dr. David Reuben's book, only a few segments stand out: final sequence inside male body is a gem.▼

Every Time We Say Goodbye (1986-Israeli) **C-95m.** **½ D: Moshe Mizrahi. Tom Hanks, Cristina Marsillach, Benedict Taylor, Anat Atzmon, Gila Almagor. Hanks' presence adds to this otherwise average soaper-romance, about an American flyer who falls for a Sephardic Jew (Marsillach) in WW2 Jerusalem.▼

Every Which Way But Loose (1978) **C-114m.** BOMB D: James Fargo. Clint Eastwood, Sondra Locke, Geoffrey Lewis,

Beverly D'Angelo, Ruth Gordon. Clint takes the first pickup truck to Stupidsville, with an orangutan as his best friend, in this bizarre change of pace for the action star. The clumsiest comedy of its year. Sequel: ANY WHICH WAY YOU CAN.▼

Evictors, The (1979) **C-92m.** *½ D: Charles B. Pierce. Michael Parks, Jessica Harper, Vic Morrow, Sue Ane Langdon, Dennis Fimple, Bill Thurman. Couple moves into eerie house, unaware of its violent history. Tired rehash of an all too familiar formula.▼

Evil, The (1978) **C-90m.** **½ D: Gus Trikonis. Richard Crenna, Joanna Pettet, Andrew Prine, Cassie Yates, Lynne Moody, Victor Buono, George O'Hanlon, Jr. Doctor Crenna rents "haunted" house to use as clinic, but he and associates are violently victimized by powers within. Slow-moving film covers familiar ground; some chills.▼

Evil Dead, The (1983) **C-85m.** **½ D: Sam Raimi. Bruce Campbell, Ellen Sandweiss, Betsy Baker, Hal Delrich, Sarah York. Five kids at mountain cabin chop each other to pieces when demons possess everything. Wildly stylish, ultra-low-budget movie made by precocious college students might be the grossest horror film ever. Borrowing inspiration from NIGHT OF THE LIVING DEAD, SUSPIRIA, THE EXORCIST and THE HOUSE ON HAUNTED HILL (just to name a few), it provides a deliriously imaginative roller coaster ride for those with strong stomachs. Followed by a sequel.▼

Evil Dead II (1987) **C-85m.** ** D: Sam Raimi. Bruce Campbell, Sarah Berry, Dan Hicks, Kassie Wesley, Theodore Raimi, Denise Bixler, Richard Domeier. Sequel provides "more of the same" with a similar plot about a cabin in the woods that turns out to be inhabited by evil spirits. Lots of gore and special effects, but at least there's some sense of style and humor. Almost on a par with the original.▼

Evil Eye, The (1962-Italian) **92m.** **½ D: Mario Bava. Leticia Roman, John Saxon, Valentina Cortese, Dante Di Paolo. Incredible but enjoyable chiller set in Rome, with Roman involved in a series of unsolved brutal murders.

Evil in Clear River (1988) **C-100m.** TVM D: Karen Arthur. Lindsay Wagner, Randy Quaid, Thomas Wilson Brown, Michael Flynn, Stephanie Dees, Carolyn Croft. Fictionalized drama about a real-life small-town housewife's crusade against a high school instructor who is espousing anti-Semitism in his classes. Average.

Evil in the Deep SEE: **Treasure of Jamaica Reef, The**▼

Evil Mind, The SEE: **Clairvoyant, The**▼

Evil of Frankenstein (1964-British) **C-84m.** ** D: Freddie Francis. Peter Cushing,

Duncan Lamont, Peter Woodthorpe, James Maxwell, Sandor Eles. Dr. F. thaws out his monster, with all-too-predictable consequences in this Hammer Films potboiler, a sequel to REVENGE OF FRANKENSTEIN. 97m. TV print makes matters worse; some scenes have been eliminated; terrible new footage showing frightened villagers has been added; new cast includes Steven Geray, Maria Palmer, William Phipps. Followed by FRANKENSTEIN CREATED WOMAN.▼

Evil Roy Slade (1971) **C-100m.** TVM D: Jerry Paris. John Astin, Edie Adams, Milton Berle, Pam Austin, Dom DeLuise, Mickey Rooney, Dick Shawn, Penny Marshall, John Ritter. Excellent cast tries hard in absurd attempt at bizarre Western comedy à la CAT BALLOU. Life and times of bumbling outlaw Slade and change in attitude after falling in love with beautiful girl (Austin). Script by Garry Marshall and Jerry Belson isn't bad; fault lies in what's done with it. Average.

Evilspeak (1982) **C-89m.** BOMB D: Eric Weston. Clint Howard, R. G. Armstrong, Joseph Cortese, Claude Earl Jones, Haywood Nelson, Charles Tyner. Orphan Howard is hassled by fellow students in military academy, seeks revenge with the help of black magic. Haven't we seen all this before?▼

Evil That Men Do, The (1984) **C-89m.** *½ D: J. Lee Thompson. Charles Bronson, Theresa Saldana, Joseph Maher, Jose Ferrer, Rene Enriquez, John Glover, Raymond St. Jacques, Antoinette Bower. Typical, violent Bronson entry, with Charlie a professional killer on the trail of a sadistic British doctor (Maher). For Bronson addicts only.▼

Evil Under the Sun (1982-British) **C-102m.** ** D: Guy Hamilton. Peter Ustinov, Jane Birkin, Colin Blakely, Nicholas Clay, Roddy McDowall, James Mason, Sylvia Miles, Denis Quilley, Diana Rigg, Maggie Smith, Emily Hone. Murder at a resort hotel, with Hercule Poirot (Ustinov) to the rescue. An all-star cast and top production values, but still blah. Based on the Agatha Christie novel, with a script by Anthony Shaffer; exteriors filmed in Majorca.▼

Evita Peron (1981) **C-200m.** TVM D: Marvin Chomsky. Faye Dunaway, James Farentino, Rita Moreno, Jose Ferrer, Pedro Armendariz, Jr., Michael Constantine, Signe Hasso, Katy Jurado, Robert Viharo, Jeremy Kemp, John Van Dreelen, Marvin Miller, Virginia Gregg. Dunaway gives a flamboyant portrayal of Argentina's charismatic First Lady, and Farentino (who replaced Robert Mitchum) is interesting as dictator Juan Peron, in this lengthy teleplay by Ronald Harwood. No relation to the Broadway musical, though the idea of doing this film was clearly inspired by its success. Average.

Ewok Adventure, The (1984) **C-100m. TVM** D: John Korty. Eric Walker, Warwick Davis, Fionnula Flanagan, Guy Boyd, Dan Fishman, Debbie Carrington, Burl Ives (narrator). Those furry characters from George Lucas's RETURN OF THE JEDI get their own movie and aid a couple of young space castaways who are searching for their parents. Lucas's maiden TV movie is jam-packed with the cinematic wizardry that has come to identify his work, although it tends to overshadow the story that he wrote. Sequel: EWOKS: THE BATTLE FOR ENDOR. Above average.

Ewoks: The Battle for Endor (1985) **C-100m.TVM** D: Jim and Ken Wheat. Wilford Brimley, Warwick Davis, Aubree Miller, Sian Phillips, Carel Struycken, Niki Botheloe, Eric Walker. An old hermit joins a little girl and her cuddly Ewok pal in a search for a nasty witch. Arresting (and expensive) George Lucas sequel to his earlier TV charmer THE EWOK ADVENTURE. Above average.▼

Excalibur (1981-British) **C-140m.** ***½ D: John Boorman. Nicol Williamson, Nigel Terry, Helen Mirren, Nicholas Clay, Cherie Lunghi, Corin Redgrave, Paul Geoffrey, Gabriel Byrne, Liam Neeson. Eccentric but spellbinding, sexually aware rendition of the King Arthur legend by a stylish filmmaker working at the peak of his powers. Magnificent production will lose much on small TV screen. Edited for TV to 119m.▼

Except For Me and Thee SEE: **Friendly Persuasion** (1975)▼

Ex-Champ (1939) **64m.** ** D: Phil Rosen. Victor McLaglen, Tom Brown, Nan Grey, Constance Moore. Routine programmer of boxer McLaglen trying to do good deed for his son, in dutch with the gambling syndicate.

Exclusive (1937) **85m.** **½ D: Alexander Hall. Fred MacMurray, Frances Farmer, Charlie Ruggles, Lloyd Nolan, Fay Holden, Ralph Morgan, Horace McMahon. Lively newspaper story has Farmer joining tabloid in direct competition with her father (Ruggles) and boyfriend (MacMurray), who are also reporters. Uneasy mix of comedy, romance, and melodrama.

Exclusive Story (1936) **75m.** **½ D: George B. Seitz. Franchot Tone, Madge Evans, Stuart Erwin, Joseph Calleia, Robert Barrat, J. Farrell MacDonald, Louise Henry. Fast-paced B-picture with Tone as newspaper attorney trying to get the goods on Calleia and falling in love with Evans.

Excuse My Dust (1951) **C-82m.** **½ D: Roy Rowland. Red Skelton, Sally Forrest, Macdonald Carey, Monica Lewis, William Demarest. Amiable Skelton musicomedy. Red invents automobile which almost costs

him his sweetheart; her father owns town livery stable.

Execution, The (1985) **C-100m. TVM** D: Paul Wendkos. Loretta Swit, Rip Torn, Jessica Walter, Barbara Barrie, Sandy Dennis, Valerie Harper, Robert Hooks, Michael Lerner. Five suburban women who survived the Holocaust plot the death of a former Nazi doctor after spotting him as a successful L.A. restaurateur. Exploitive drama that's doubly hard to accept with these actresses as German-accented concentration camp refugees. Below average.▼

Executioner, The (1970-British) **C-107m.** ** D: Sam Wanamaker. Joan Collins, George Peppard, Judy Geeson, Oscar Homolka, Charles Gray, Nigel Patrick, Keith Michell. Pedestrian thriller with British spy Peppard suspecting that colleague Michell is a double agent.▼

Executioner, Part II, The (1984) **C-85m.** BOMB D: James Bryant. Christopher Mitchum, Aldo Ray, Antoine John Mottet, Renee Harmon. Amateurish actioner, atrociously directed and acted, with homicide cop Mitchum hunting down a vigilante murderer. Has no connection to any other EXECUTIONER title.▼

Executioner's Song, The (1982) **C-200m. TVM** D: Lawrence Schiller. Tommy Lee Jones, Rosanna Arquette, Christine Lahti, Eli Wallach, Jordan Clark, Steven Keats, Richard Venture, Michael LeClair, Walter Olkewicz. Jones's electrifying, Emmy-winning portrayal of convicted killer Gary Gilmore and his efforts to get the state of Utah to carry out his death sentence in 1977 keeps this lengthy film sizzling. Equally as torrid: Arquette's erotic portrait of Gilmore's jailbait girlfriend, Nicole Baker. Norman Mailer adapted his own best seller. A 97m. version, originally released to theaters in Europe, contains some nudity. Originally shown in two parts. Above average.▼

Execution of Private Slovik, The (1974) **C-120m. TVM** D: Lamont Johnson. Martin Sheen, Mariclare Costello, Ned Beatty, Gary Busey, Matt Clark, Ben Hammer, Charles Haid. Solid drama enhanced by Sheen's beautiful performance as Eddie Slovik, the only American soldier since the Civil War to be executed for desertion (in 1945). Thoughtful, literate adaptation by Richard Levinson and William Link of William Bradford Huie's controversial book. Above average.

Executive Action (1973) **C-91m.** BOMB D: David Miller. Burt Lancaster, Robert Ryan, Will Geer, Gilbert Green, John Anderson. Excruciatingly dull thriller promised to clear the air about JFK's assassination but was more successful at clearing theaters. Ryan's last film.▼

Executive Suite (1954) **104m.** *** D: Robert Wise. William Holden, June Allyson, Barbara Stanwyck, Fredric March, Walter Pidgeon, Louis Calhern, Shelley Winters, Paul Douglas, Nina Foch, Dean Jagger. Slick, multifaceted story of company power struggle with top cast, from Cameron Hawley novel . . . though similar film PATTERNS is much better. Later a TV series.▼

Exile, The (1947) 95m. **½ D: Max Ophuls. Douglas Fairbanks, Jr., Maria Montez, Paule Croset (Rita Corday), Henry Daniell, Nigel Bruce, Robert Coote. OK swashbuckler with exiled king Fairbanks falling in love with common girl; guest appearance by Montez.

Ex-Lady (1933) 65m. **½ D: Robert Florey. Bette Davis, Gene Raymond, Frank McHugh, Claire Dodd, Ferdinand Gottschalk. Davis, looking sensational, plays an independent-minded woman who loves Raymond but doesn't believe in marriage. Provocative and sexy, stylishly filmed, but begins to drag and become conventional by the second half. A remake of ILLICIT, filmed just two years earlier!

Ex-Mrs. Bradford, The (1936) 80m. *** D: Stephen Roberts. William Powell, Jean Arthur, James Gleason, Eric Blore, Robert Armstrong. Chic à la THIN MAN comedy-mystery, with Powell teaming with ex-wife Arthur to crack a case.▼

Exodus (1960) C-213m. *** D: Otto Preminger. Paul Newman, Eva Marie Saint, Ralph Richardson, Peter Lawford, Lee J. Cobb, Sal Mineo, Hugh Griffith, Felix Aylmer, John Derek, Jill Haworth. Leon Uris' sprawling history of Palestinian war for liberation becomes sporadic action epic. Newman as Israeli resistance leader, Saint as non-Jewish army nurse aren't a convincing duo; supporting roles offer stereotypes. Best scene shows refugees escaping Cyprus detention center, running British blockade into homeland. Ernest Gold won an Oscar for his score.▼

Exo-Man, The (1977) C-100m. TVM D: Richard Irving. David Ackroyd, Anne Schedeen, A Martinez, Jose Ferrer, Harry Morgan, Kevin McCarthy, Jack Colvin, Donald Moffat. Paralyzed by the syndicate, physics professor Ackroyd creates a special "exo" suit to make him sufficiently mobile to take vengeance on his attackers. Disappointing and dull "superman" story. Below average.▼

Exorcist, The (1973) C-121m. ***½ D: William Friedkin. Ellen Burstyn, Max von Sydow, Linda Blair, Jason Miller, Lee J. Cobb, Kitty Winn, Jack MacGowran. Intense, well-mounted adaptation of William Peter Blatty's best-seller, calculated to keep your stomach in knots from start to finish. Blair is "normal" 12-year-old whose body is possessed by the Devil, Miller a troubled priest who attempts to confront the demon in her—and in himself. Oscar winner for Blatty's screenplay; vocal effects by Mercedes McCambridge. Followed by two sequels and countless imitations.▼

Exorcist II: The Heretic (1977) C-110m. *½ D: John Boorman. Richard Burton, Linda Blair, Louise Fletcher, Kitty Winn, James Earl Jones, Ned Beatty, Max von Sydow. Preposterous sequel to 1973 hit. Special effects are only virtue in this turkey about priest (Burton) trying to unravel mystery of demon still living inside Blair. Boorman recut the film (from 117m.) the day after its premiere, and made numerous changes—to no avail. Restored to 117m. for homevideo.▼

Experience Preferred . . . But Not Essential (1983-British) C-80m. *** D: Peter Duffell. Elizabeth Edmonds, Sue Wallace, Geraldine Griffith, Karen Meagher, Ron Bain, Alun Lewis, Robert Blythe. Simple, charming little film about a girl's experiences working as waitress for the summer at seaside resort hotel. June Roberts' script focuses on the blossoming of one young woman, while making humorous observations about the offbeat group of people around her. Short and sweet; made for British TV.▼

Experiment in Terror (1962) 123m. *** D: Blake Edwards. Glenn Ford, Lee Remick, Stefanie Powers, Ross Martin, Roy Poole, Ned Glass. Taut suspenser as F.B.I. agent Ford tracks down killer (Martin) who has kidnapped bank teller Remick's sister (Powers). Remick and Martin are extremely convincing. Great score by Henry Mancini.▼

Experiment Perilous (1944) 91m. *** D: Jacques Tourneur. Hedy Lamarr, George Brent, Paul Lukas, Albert Dekker, Margaret Wycherly, Julia Dean. Good melodrama in the GASLIGHT tradition, with beautiful Lamarr menaced by husband (Lukas), aided by doctor Brent.▼

Experts, The (1989) C-83m. ** D: Dave Thomas. John Travolta, Arye Gross, Charles Martin Smith, Kelly Preston, Deborah Foreman, James Keach, Jan Rubes, Brian Doyle Murray, Rick Ducommun. Fatally bland comedy about two Manhattan hipsters who are hired to open a nightclub in a small Nebraska town—which is really an exact replica of the hamlet built in the U.S.S.R. and used to train Russian spies. Weak in all respects, and peculiarly sentimental about the 1950s. Shot in Canada in 1987, and barely released to theaters.▼

Explorers (1985) C-109m. ** D: Joe Dante. Ethan Hawke, River Phoenix, Jason Presson, Amanda Peterson, Dick Miller, Robert Picardo, Mary Kay Place. Youngster hooked on science-fiction yearns to travel into space and gets his wish, with the help of a whiz-kid friend. Opens beautifully, takes its time developing story—then makes disastrous wrong turn in space that transforms film into a shaggy-dog joke! Director Dante has restructured film somewhat for cable TV and homevideo release. That version is 107m. ▼

Explosion (1969-Canadian) **C-96m.** *½ D: Jules Bricken. Don Stroud, Richard Conte, Gordon Thomson, Michele Chicoine, Cecil Linder, Robin Ward. Teenager haunted by his brother's death in Vietnam goes to Canada to avoid the draft, but drifts into crime instead. Heavy-handed melodrama. ▼

Explosive Generation, The (1961) **89m.** ** D: Buzz Kulik. William Shatner, Patty McCormack, Billy Gray, Steve Dunne. Shatner is high school teacher expelled for conducting sex talks in class.

Exposed (1983) **C-100m.** *½ D: James Toback. Nastassia Kinski, Rudolf Nureyev, Harvey Keitel, Ian McShane, Bibi Andersson, Ron Randell, Pierre Clementi, James Russo. Girl from the Midwest quits school, comes to N.Y.C., hits it big as a fashion model, then gets involved with enigmatic Nureyev and his plan to kill terrorist Keitel in Paris. Seems like three different movies— all of them strange. Nureyev's performance might best be described as overripe. That's writer-director Toback in the role of Kinski's professor/lover. ▼

Expresso Bongo (1960-British) **108m.** *** D: Val Guest. Laurence Harvey, Sylvia Syms, Yolande Donlan, Cliff Richard. Harvey is ideally cast as opportunist talent agent who almost makes the big time with bongo-playing discovery Richard, but bluffs himself back into small time. ▼

Exterminating Angel, The (1962-Mexico) **95m.** ***½ D: Luis Bunuel. Silvia Pinal, Enrique Rambal, Jacqueline Andere, Jose Baviera, Augusto Benedico, Luis Beristein. Guests at elegant dinner party cannot bring themselves to leave, begin to starve and die after several days. Wry assault on bourgeois manners by master surrealist Bunuel. ▼

Exterminator, The (1980) **C-101m.** BOMB D: James Glickenhaus. Christopher George, Samantha Eggar, Robert Ginty, Steve James, Tony Di Benedetto. Gore galore with Vietnam veteran Ginty aping Charles Bronson in DEATH WISH as he rubs out a gang who mugged and paralyzed a friend. If you love this film, good news—there's a sequel!▼

Exterminator II (1984) **C-88m.** BOMB D: Mark Buntzman. Robert Ginty, Mario Van Peebles, Deborah Geffner, Frankie Faison, Scott Randolph. Ginty and his blowtorch are back, hot after a gang whose most sadistic member is named X. Obnoxious, grade Z garbage.▼

Extra Girl, The (1923) **69m.** **½ D: F. Richard Jones. Mabel Normand, Ralph Graves, George Nichols, Anna Hernandez, Vernon Dent. Mack Sennett silent feature is far from prime, but still has its moments, thanks to classic comedienne Normand and an obliging lion.

Dramatic interludes in Hollywood rags-to-riches saga don't really work.▼

Extraordinary Seaman, The (1969) **C-80m.** BOMB D: John Frankenheimer. David Niven, Faye Dunaway, Alan Alda, Mickey Rooney, Juano Hernandez, Jack Carter, Manu Tupou, Barry Kelley. Extraordinarily muddled "comedy" of eccentric Niven piloting long-lost abandoned ship during WW2; shows signs of tampering from original conception of film. Barely received theatrical release. Only highpoints: clips from 1940s newsreels and Faye's eye makeup.

Extreme Close-Up (1973) **C-80m.** *½ D: Jeannot Szwarc. James McMullan, James A. Watson, Jr., Kate Woodville, Bara Byrnes, Al Checco, Antony Carbone. Ludicrous drama about snoopers and snooping equipment has topicality working for it, but that's all. Screenplay by Michael Crichton; retitled SEX THROUGH A WINDOW.▼

Extreme Prejudice (1987) **C-104m.** ** D: Walter Hill. Nick Nolte, Powers Boothe, Michael Ironside, Maria Conchita Alonso, Rip Torn, Clancy Brown, William Forsythe, Larry B. Scott. Boyhood friends Nolte and Boothe are now on opposite sides of the law, as Texas Ranger and drug kingpin on the Texas/Mexico border. Though its excesses (in characterization, music, and especially violence) are apparently deliberate, that doesn't make them any more entertaining . . . though it helps if you accept it as tongue-in-cheek.▼

Extremities (1986) **C-89m.** *½ D: Robert M. Young. Farrah Fawcett, James Russo, Diana Scarwid, Alfre Woodard. A woman is victimized by a taunting rapist in her own home but manages to turn the tables and trap him. William Mastrosimone adapted his own play, but what worked in a theater doesn't translate to film; Fawcett's adequate but one-note performance is another liability. ▼

Eye Creatures, The (1965) **80m.** *½ D: Larry Buchanan. John Ashley, Cynthia Hull, Warren Hammack, Chet Davis, Bill Peck. Gory horror film about title creatures and the intrepid band that tries to fight them off. Remake of INVASION OF THE SAUCER MEN.▼

Eye for an Eye, An (1966) **C-92m.** ** D: Michael Moore. Robert Lansing, Pat Wayne, Slim Pickens, Gloria Talbott. Oater with twist: two physically disabled men, who can function via teamwork as one sharpshooter, hunt down killers of older man's family. Video title TALION.▼

Eye for an Eye, An (1981) **C-106m.** ** D: Steve Carver. Chuck Norris, Christopher Lee, Richard Roundtree, Matt Clark, Mako, Maggie Cooper, Terry Kiser. Cop Norris's partner is killed by drug traffickers; he has nightmares, becomes a one-man army seeking vengeance against villain

Lee and his cronies. Silly and predictable, but delivers for formula fans.▼

Eye of the Cat (1969) C-102m. **½ D: David Lowell Rich. Michael Sarrazin, Gayle Hunnicutt, Eleanor Parker, Tim Henry, Laurence Naismith. Glossy but intriguing suspenser with seductive Hunnicutt teaming with Sarrazin to murder his aunt (Parker), who keeps a houseful of felines. Most terrifying scene has wheelchaired Parker tottering atop a San Francisco hill. Important note: new scenes were added to film for network TV showing to make it "less intense." Rating is based on original.

Eye of the Devil (1967-British) 92m. **½ D: J. Lee Thompson. Deborah Kerr, David Niven, Donald Pleasence, Edward Mulhare, Flora Robson, Emlyn Williams, Sharon Tate, David Hemmings, John Le Mesurier. Excellent cast in odd, low-key thriller set in France. The Marquis de Bellac (Niven) abruptly leaves wife in Paris to "do what he must" at ancestral estate near Bordeaux. Strange continuity due to cuts before initial release. Also titled: 13.

Eye of the Needle (1981) C-112m. *** D: Richard Marquand. Donald Sutherland, Kate Nelligan, Ian Bannen, Christopher Cazenove, Philip Martin Brown. Solid WW2 spy saga from Ken Follett's best-seller. Sutherland plays a super-cool German agent temporarily stranded on an island off the British coast, where he meets a lonely, sexually frustrated woman (Nelligan).▼

Eye of the Tiger (1986) C-90m. *½ D: Richard Sarafian. Gary Busey, Yaphet Kotto, Seymour Cassel, Bert Remsen, William Smith, Kimberlin Ann Brown, Denise Galik, Judith Barsi. Ex-con Busey's town is invaded by Hells Angels types, who sadistically murder his wife . . . so he goes on a one-man crusade for revenge. Sound familiar?▼

Eye on the Sparrow (1987) C-100m. TVM D: John Korty. Mare Winningham, Keith Carradine, Conchata Ferrell, Sandy McPeak, Kaaren Lee, Bianca Rose. Determined blind couple take on the establishment in a battle to adopt a child. Based-on-fact drama, well played by the two leads; written by Barbara Turner. Above average.

Eyes in the Night (1942) 80m. **½ D: Fred Zinnemann. Ann Harding, Edward Arnold, Donna Reed, Stephen McNally, Reginald Denny, Rosemary DeCamp, Mantan Moreland. Above-par mystery with Arnold as blind detective Duncan McClain helping Reed and Harding. The dog steals the picture. Director Zinnemann's feature film debut.

Eyes of a Stranger (1981) C-85m. BOMB. D: Ken Wiederhorn. Lauren Tewes, Jennifer Jason Leigh, John DiSanti, Peter DuPre, Gwen Lewis. Overweight creep DiSanti rapes and kills women, and the blood flows like wine; Tewes tracks him down, while her deaf, dumb, and blind sister (Leigh) is established as a potential victim. Utter trash.▼

Eyes of Charles Sand, The (1972) C-75m. TVM D: Reza Badiyi. Peter Haskell, Barbara Rush, Sharon Farrell, Bradford Dillman, Joan Bennett, Adam West, Ivor Francis. Despite excellent names connected with script (Henry Farrell & Stanford Whitmore), predictable, largely boring ESP-gimmicked mystery featuring troubled lead character (Haskell) who can flash onto future. Average.

Eyes of Hell (1961-Canadian) 83m. *½ D: Julian Roffman. Paul Stevens, Claudette Nevins, Bill Walker, Anne Collings, Martin Lavut, Jim Moran. Low-budget shocker—with 3-D sequences—about an ancient Aztec mask that causes wearer to hallucinate and murder. 3-D scenes were put together by famed montage expert Slavko Vorkapich. Originally released as THE MASK.▼

Eyes of Laura Mars (1978) C-103m. **½ D: Irvin Kershner. Faye Dunaway, Tommy Lee Jones, Brad Dourif, Rene Auberjonois, Raul Julia, Frank Adonis, Michael Tucker. A high-fashion photographer has frightening premonitions of grisly murders; some genuine suspense, lots of red herrings, and a silly resolution add up to an OK thriller . . . but Dunaway's kinky colleagues and their life-styles are a real turnoff. Co-written by John Carpenter.▼

Eyes of the Amaryllis, The (1982) C-84m. ** D: Frederick King Keller. Ruth Ford, Martha Byrne, Jonathan Bolt, Guy Boyd, Katharine Houghton. Young Byrne visits beachhouse of "mad" grandmother Ford, who awaits sign from her husband who was lost at sea 30 years before. Well-intentioned but slow-paced, uninvolving adaptation of Natalie Babbitt's story. Filmed on Nantucket Island.▼

Eyes of the Underworld (1943) 61m. **½ D: Roy William Neill. Richard Dix, Wendy Barrie, Lon Chaney, Lloyd Corrigan, Don Porter, Billy Lee, Marc Lawrence. Police chief Dix on the spot when mobster uncovers his old prison record; good crime story.

Eyes, the Mouth, The (1982-Italian-French) C-100m. ** D: Marco Bellocchio. Lou Castel, Angela Molina, Emmanuele Riva, Michel Piccoli, Antonio Piovanelli. Dreary, pretentious pap about the effect of a man's suicide on his actor-brother (Castel), mother (Riva) and pregnant lover (Molina). At one point Castel and Molina see FIST IN HIS POCKET, also directed by Bellocchio and starring Castel. We suggest the viewer do the same.▼

Eyes Without a Face, The SEE: **Horror Chamber of Dr. Faustus, The**▼

Eye Witness (1950-British) 104m. **½ D: Robert Montgomery. Robert Montgomery, Felix Aylmer, Leslie Banks, Michael

Ripper, Patricia Wayne (Cutts). Unpretentious yarn of American attorney Montgomery in London to defend friend accused of homicide, coping with contrasting British legal system while hunting title figure. Originally titled YOUR WITNESS.▼

Eyewitness (1970) SEE: **Sudden Terror**▼

Eyewitness (1981) **C-102m.** ** D: Peter Yates. William Hurt, Sigourney Weaver, Christopher Plummer, James Woods, Irene Worth, Kenneth McMillan, Pamela Reed, Steven Hill, Morgan Freeman. Slick but unsatisfying thriller about a building janitor who uses his second-hand knowledge of an unsolved murder to get close to a female TV news reporter with whom he's been infatuated. Steve Tesich's script is needlessly cluttered with minor characters and story twists.▼

Fabiola (1951-Italian) **96m.** **** D: Alessandro Blasetti. Michele Morgan, Henri Vidal, Michel Simon, Gino Cervi. Excellently produced and acted spectacle. Roman aristocracy plots massive Christian massacre before Constantine reaches Rome. Best of Italian spectacles, although cut quite a bit.

Fabulous Baker Boys, The (1989) **C-113m.** **½ D: Steve Kloves. Jeff Bridges, Michelle Pfeiffer, Beau Bridges, Elie Raab, Jennifer Tilly. Two brothers' fifteen-year partnership as a twin-piano nightclub lounge act is shaken by the addition of a feisty (and sexy) singer, who sparks changes in their act—and their relationship. Writer Kloves' directing debut is stylish and self-assured, with some great scenes and set-pieces, but it skimps on story—and never really fleshes out Jeff Bridges' sullen character. The real-life Bridges brothers are perfectly cast, and Pfeiffer is ideal. Her steamy rendition of "Makin' Whoopee" atop a piano is already considered a minor classic.▼

Fabulous Baron Munchausen, The (1961-Czech) **C-84m.** **½ D: Karel Zeman. Milos Kopecky, Jana Brejchova, Rudolph Jelinek, Jan Werich. Filmmaker Zeman (FABULOUS WORLD OF JULES VERNE) provides another visual delight here, but his episodic fantasy—which takes his hero from the inside of a whale to the surface of the moon—is stilted and uninvolving. Video title: THE ORIGINAL FABULOUS ADVENTURES OF BARON MUNCHAUSEN.▼

Fabulous Dorseys, The (1947) **88m.** ** D: Alfred E. Green. Tommy Dorsey, Jimmy Dorsey, Janet Blair, Paul Whiteman, William Lundigan. Limp "biography" of bandleading brothers, constantly arguing in between "Marie," "Green Eyes," and other hit songs. Musical highlight: a jam session with Art Tatum, Charlie Barnet, Ziggy Elman and Ray Bauduc.▼

Fabulous Joe, The (1947) **C-60m.** ** D: Bernard Carr, Harve Foster. Marie Wilson, Walter Abel, Margot Grahame, Donald Meek. Abel is typecast in this featurized segment from THE HAL ROACH COMEDY CARNIVAL. He's harassed husband who gains moral support from talking dog.▼

Fabulous Suzanne, The (1946) **71m.** ** D: Steve Sekely. Barbara Britton, Rudy Vallee, Otto Kruger, Richard Denning, Veda Ann Borg. Fair potential of romantic story of woman who has more luck at horses than with men doesn't come across, due to script and indifferent acting.

Fabulous World of Jules Verne, The (1958-Czech) **83m.** **½ D: Karel Zeman. Lubor Tolos, Arnost Navratil, Miroslav Holub, Zatloukalova. Zeman's ingenious visual effects, reproducing the look of 19th century engravings, outshine leaden enactment of fanciful sci-fi story by Verne. Released here in 1961 with Americanized names in credits and pointless introduction by Hugh Downs.▼

Face at the Window, The (1939-British) **65m.** **½ D: George King. Tod Slaughter, Marjorie Taylor, John Warwick, Robert Adair, Harry Terry. A fiendish killer known as "The Wolf" strikes terror in 1880s Paris. Who can it be? Surely not the Chevalier del Gardo (Slaughter), respected nobleman! And who is the hideous, drooling face at the window? Charming, well-produced blood-and-thunder melodrama, based on the frequently filmed play by F. Brooke Warren. The blessedly hammy Slaughter is in great form here.▼

Face Behind the Mask, The (1941) **69m.** *** D: Robert Florey. Peter Lorre, Evelyn Keyes, Don Beddoe, George E. Stone, John Tyrell. Model B film of immigrant Lorre having face disfigured in fire, donning mask, bitterly turning to life of crime. Extremely well done on slim budget.

Face in the Crowd, A (1957) **125m.** ***½ D: Elia Kazan. Andy Griffith, Patricia Neal, Anthony Franciosa, Walter Matthau, Lee Remick, Kay Medford. Perceptive script by Budd Schulberg about homespun hobo (Griffith) discovered by Neal and promoted into successful TV star. Cast gives life to fascinating story. Film debuts of Griffith and Remick. Look for young Rip Torn and Lois Nettleton. Many celebrities also appear as themselves, including Burl Ives, Mike Wallace, Betty Furness, Bennett Cerf, Faye Emerson, and Walter Winchell.▼

Face in the Rain, A (1963) **91m.** **½ D: Irvin Kershner. Rory Calhoun, Marina Berti, Niall MacGinnis, Massimo Giuliani. At times tense melodrama of Calhoun, U.S. spy, being hidden in Italy by partisan whose wife has been associating with Axis.

Face of a Fugitive (1959) **C-81m.** ** D: Paul Wendkos. Fred MacMurray, Lin Mc-

Carthy, Dorothy Green, James Coburn, Alan Baxter, Myrna Fahey. OK Western about MacMurray forced to start over again in a new town when he's falsely accused of murder; his past still haunts him.

Face of Fear, The (1971) C-72m. TVM D: George McCowan. Elizabeth Ashley, Ricardo Montalban, Jack Warden, Dane Clark, Burr DeBenning, Charles Dierkop. Young schoolteacher raised in Idaho learns she's to die of leukemia, journeys to San Francisco, eventually pays to be killed, then discovers she won't die. Very entertaining suspense film with wry humor, two well-drawn (for TV) characterizations, and believable dialogue. Adapted by Edward Hume from E. V. Cunningham's novel *Sally*. Above average.

Face of Fire (1959) 83m. *** D: Albert Band. Cameron Mitchell, James Whitmore, Bettye Ackerman, Royal Dano, Robert Simon, Richard Erdman. Unique adaptation of Stephen Crane short story *The Monster* about man disfigured while saving child from fire. Uneven cast, good direction.

✓ **Face of Fu Manchu, The** (1965-British) C-96m. *** D: Don Sharp. Christopher Lee, Nigel Green, James Robertson Justice, Howard Marion-Crawford, Tsai Chin, Walter Rilla. First of new series with Emperor Fu bent on conquering West. Great 1920s atmosphere, good international cast. Followed by THE BRIDES OF FU MANCHU.▼

Face of Marble (1946) 70m. ** D: William Beaudine. John Carradine, Claudia Drake, Robert Shayne, Maris Wrixon. Another mad doctor with new technique for bringing dead back to life. Carradine is good, others less impressive.

Face of Rage, The (1983) C-100m. TVM D: Donald Wrye. Dianne Wiest, George Dzundza, Graham Beckel, Jeffrey DeMunn, Raymond J. Barry, Danny Glover, John Glover, John Goodman, Thomas G. Waites. Rape victims come face-to-face with their attackers in an experimental therapy program. Hard-hitting, surprisingly honest film cowritten by Wrye and patterned fictionally after the acclaimed TV prison documentary, SCARED STRAIGHT. Above average.

Face of the Frog (1959-German) 92m. ** D: Harold Reinl. Joachim Fuchsberger, Fritz Rasp, Siegfied Lowitz, Joachen Brochmann. Lowitz is Inspector Elk tracking down the "Frog" in this routine Edgar Wallace actioner; serial-like techniques utilized. Retitled: FELLOWSHIP OF THE FROG.

Faces (1968) 130m. ***½ D: John Cassavetes. John Marley, Gena Rowlands, Lynn Carlin, Seymour Cassel, Fred Draper, Val Avery. Highly personal drama about assorted infidelities is one of the few Cassavetes films to make it with general public. Very powerful film with great acting, especially by Carlin and Cassel.

Face That Launched a Thousand Ships, The SEE: **Loves of Three Queens**

Face to Face (1952) 92m. **½ D: John Brahm, Bretaigne Windust. James Mason, Michael Pate, Robert Preston, Marjorie Steele. Quiet two-part film: Joseph Conrad's SECRET SHARER faithfully filmed with Mason as captain, Pate as fugitive; Stephen Crane's BRIDE COMES TO YELLOW SKY bland with Preston bringing bride Steele out West.▼

Face to Face (Swedish-1976) C-136m. *** D: Ingmar Bergman. Liv Ullmann, Erland Josephson, Gunnar Bjornstrand, Aino Taube-Henrikson, Kari Sylwan, Sif Ruud. Brilliant Ullmann performance and Sven Nykvist photography compensate somewhat for déjà vu feeling one gets from drama about woman psychiatrist who suffers severe nervous breakdown. As harrowing as they come; not for every taste or mood. Originally a four-part Swedish TV miniseries.

Face to Face (1990) C-100m. TVM D: Lou Antonio. Elizabeth Montgomery, Robert Foxworth, Lou Antonio, Ronald Lacey, Lydia Kigada, Richard Ngatia. Romantic comedy pitting an American paleontologist on an African dig against a rough-and-ready British miner staking out the same territory. Montgomery and Foxworth are a real-life couple off screen. Average.

Face to the Wind SEE: **Cry for Me, Billy**▼

Facts of Life, The (1960) 103m. *** D: Melvin Frank. Bob Hope, Lucille Ball, Ruth Hussey, Don DeFore. Sophisticated comedy with Bob and Lucy leaving their spouses for an interlude together. The two stars make a good team worth watching.

Facts of Life Down Under, The (1987) C-100m. TVM D: Stuart Margolin. Cloris Leachman, Lisa Whelchel, Nancy McKeon, Kim Fields, Mindy Cohn, Mackenzie Astin, Mario Van Peebles. If you liked *The Facts of Life* when the girls went to Paris, you'll flip over them when they journey to Australia. But then again . . . Below average.

Facts of Life Goes to Paris, The (1982) C-100m. TVM D: Asaad Kelada. Charlotte Rae, Lisa Whelchel, Nancy McKeon, Kim Fields, Mindy Cohn, Frank Bonner, Roger Til. The hit TV series thinly stretched to feature-length status with diminishing results despite a well-primed laugh track responding to the work of six writers. For diehard fans only. Below Average.

Fade-In (1968) C-93m. ** D: Allen Smithee (Jud Taylor). Burt Reynolds, Barbara Loden, Noam Pitlik, Patricia Casey, Jane Hampton, Joseph Perry. Odd little film made concurrently with BLUE, about love affair between film editor Loden and man she meets while working on location. Not very good, but a definite curio; never released theatrically.▼

Fade to Black (1980) **C-100m.** *½ D: Vernon Zimmerman. Dennis Christopher, Linda Kerridge, Tim Thomerson, Morgan Paull, Marya Small, Mickey Rourke. Weirdo film buff Christopher does in his enemies while dressed up as his favorite cinema villains. Interesting idea ruined by excessive violence, poor performance by Christopher. Marilyn Monroe lookalike Kerridge, as Christopher's girlfriend, is like a rose in a cesspool.▼

Fahrenheit 451 (1967) **C-111m.** *** D: Francois Truffaut. Julie Christie, Oskar Werner, Cyril Cusack, Anton Diffring, Jeremy Spenser, Bee Duffell, Alex Scott, Mark Lester. Odd and generally slow-going adaptation of Ray Bradbury sci-fi novel depicting future Earth civilization where all printed reading material is banned. Though viewer interest is held throughout, film has curiously reserved, unemotional feel to it. Truffaut's only film in English.▼

Failing of Raymond, The (1971) **C-73m.** TVM D: Boris Sagal. Jane Wyman, Dean Stockwell, Dana Andrews, Murray Hamilton, Tim O'Connor, Paul Henreid. Forgettable suspense drama about mental defective threatening high school teacher who flunked him in English. Film looks as if directed by hypnosis. Below average.

Fail-Safe (1964) **111m.** ***½ D: Sidney Lumet. Henry Fonda, Walter Matthau, Fritz Weaver, Dan O'Herlihy, Sorrell Booke, Larry Hagman, Frank Overton, Dom De-Luise. U.S. plane is accidentally ordered to bomb U.S.S.R., plunging heads of American and Russian governments into crisis of decisionmaking as time runs out. High-tension drama done with taste and intelligence, based on the Eugene Burdick–Harvey Wheeler best-seller.▼

Fair Wind to Java (1953) **C-92m.** **½ D: Joseph Kane. Fred MacMurray, Vera Ralston, Victor McLaglen, Robert Douglas, Philip Ahn. Hard-boiled skipper goes after treasure in the South Seas. Pretty good adventure yarn with Ralston surprisingly good as native love interest. Great climactic volcano explosion—though accompanying process-screen work is awful.

Faithful in My Fashion (1946) **81m.** ** D: Sidney Salkow. Donna Reed, Tom Drake, Edward Everett Horton, Spring Byington, Sig Ruman. Stale comedy-romance as soldier on leave discovers his girl engaged to someone else. Good cast in familiar settings.

Faithless (1932) **76m.** **½ D: Harry Beaumont. Tallulah Bankhead, Robert Montgomery, Hugh Herbert, Louise Closser Hale, Henry Kolker. Impoverished Bankhead tries to start life fresh after dismal past; polished soaper.

Fake, The (1953-British) **80m.** ** D: Godfrey Grayson. Dennis O'Keefe, Coleen

Gray, Guy Middleton, John Laurie. Famous painting is stolen, starting a police hunt; OK crime drama.

Fake-Out (1982) **C-96m.** *½ D: Matt Cimber. Pia Zadora, Telly Savalas, Desi Arnaz, Jr. Trifling combination crime drama/comedy/romance with Las Vegas performer Zadora pressured to rat on her gangster boyfriend. Pia is raped. Pia falls in love. There are car chases . . .▼

Fakers, The SEE: **Hell's Bloody Devils**

The Falcon Michael Arlen's debonair trouble-shooter, the Falcon, served as the basis for sixteen above-average mysteries in the 1940s, and while the series cannot be called unusual, one of its entries presented a perhaps-unique situation. George Sanders had played the character in three films when, in 1942, he decided to leave the series. In THE FALCON'S BROTHER it was arranged to put him out of the way so his brother could take over for him. What made the transition unique was that Sanders' real-life brother, Tom Conway, was the replacement; he carried on for nine subsequent films. John Calvert played the character in three final low-budget films which aren't really part of the main series. Various character actors came in and out of the series playing cronies of the Falcon, such as Allen Jenkins, Ed Brophy, Eddie Dunn, and Ed Gargan. James Gleason played a thick-witted inspector in the first few films, and Cliff Clark took over for the rest. In fact, some of the films had so much comedy relief, one yearned for some mystery relief from the comedy! One interesting gimmick in several films had a beautiful girl enter near the end of the picture to alert the Falcon to danger in a new location; this would lead into the next film in which the Falcon and the girl would embark upon the new mystery. One entry, THE FALCON TAKES OVER, was from a Raymond Chandler novel FAREWELL MY LOVELY which was remade as MURDER MY SWEET with Dick Powell as Philip Marlowe. Such young hopefuls as Wendy Barrie, Barbara Hale, Lynn Bari, Jane Greer, Harriet Hilliard, and Rita Corday (Paule Croset) appeared in the series from time to time; and to the everlasting glory of that great neurotic-character actor Elisha Cook, Jr., THE FALCON'S ALIBI cast him as a homicidal disk jockey!

Falcon and the Co-eds, The (1943) **68m.** D: William Clemens. Tom Conway, Jean Brooks, Rita Corday, Amelita Ward, Isabel Jewell, George Givot, Cliff Clark, Dorothy Malone (in a bit).

Falcon and the Snowman, The (1985) **C-131m.** **½ D: John Schlesinger. Timothy Hutton, Sean Penn, David Suchet, Lori Singer, Pat Hingle, Dorian Harewood, Mady Kaplan, Richard Dysart, Chris Makepeace. True story, based on Robert

Lindsay's book about two young men from affluent families who decide to sell government secrets to the Russians. Much food for thought here, but we never get to share Hutton's feelings, and that keeps this well-made film somewhat aloof. Standout: Penn's performance as a desperate, amoral, drugged-out kid. ▼

Falcon in Danger, The (1943) 70m. D: William Clemens. Tom Conway, Jean Brooks, Elaine Shepard, Amelita Ward, Cliff Clark, Ed Gargan.

Falcon in Hollywood, The (1944) 67m. D: Gorgon Douglas. Tom Conway, Barbara Hale, Veda Ann Borg, Sheldon Leonard, Frank Jenks, Rita Corday, John Abbott.▼

Falcon in Mexico, The (1944) 70m. D: William Berke. Tom Conway, Mona Maris, Nestor Paiva, Bryant Washburn, Emory Parnell.

Falcon in San Francisco, The (1945) 66m. D: Joseph H. Lewis. Tom Conway, Rita Corday, Edward Brophy, Sharyn Moffett, Fay Helm, Robert Armstrong.

Falcon Out West, The (1944) 64m. D: William Clemens. Tom Conway, Barbara Hale, Ed Gargan, Lyle Talbot, Chief Thundercloud, Joan Barclay, Minor Watson.

Falcon's Adventure, The (1946) 61m. D: William Berke. Tom Conway, Madge Meredith, Edward S. Brophy, Robert Warwick, Myrna Dell, Ian Wolfe.▼

Falcon's Alibi, The (1946) 62m. D: Ray McCarey. Tom Conway, Rita Corday, Vince Barnett, Jane Greer, Elisha Cook, Jr., Al Bridge, Jason Robards, Sr.

Falcon's Brother, The (1942) 63m. D: Stanley Logan. George Sanders, Tom Conway, Jane Randolph, Keye Luke, Charles Arnt.▼

Falcon's Gold (1982-Canadian) C-90m. TVM D: Bob Schulz. Simon MacCorkindale, John Marley, Louise Vallance, George Touliatos, Blanca Guerra, Jorge Reynaldo, Roger Cudney. Fantasy adventure pitting the good guys against the bad guys in a jungle search for an ancient golden treasure with mysterious hidden powers. Loosely based on Arthur Conan Doyle's *Challenger's Gold* and crossbred with RAIDERS OF THE LOST ARK, this colorful tale was announced as the first movie made for pay-TV. Also known as ROBBERS OF THE SACRED MOUNTAIN. Average.▼

Falcon Strikes Back, The (1943) 66m. D: Edward Dmytryk. Tom Conway, Harriet Hilliard, Jane Randolph, Edgar Kennedy, Cliff Edwards, Rita Corday, Wynne Gibson.

Falcon Takes Over, The (1942) 63m. D: Irving Reis. George Sanders, Lynn Bari, James Gleason, Allen Jenkins, Helen Gilbert, Ward Bond, Anne Revere, Hans Conried.▼

Fallen Angel (1945) 97m. **½ D: Otto Preminger. Alice Faye, Dana Andrews,

Linda Darnell, Charles Bickford, Anne Revere, Bruce Cabot, John Carradine. Andrews plans to dump wife Faye for Darnell, when latter is murdered; a change of pace for Faye, to say the least, but not terribly good.

Fallen Angel (1981) C-100m. TVM D: Robert Lewis. Dana Hill, Melinda Dillon, Richard Masur, Ronny Cox, David Hayward, Virginia Kiser, Shelby Leverington. Calculating drama about a child pornographer (Masur) who entices kids to pose for him. This not unexpectedly got a huge rating on its premiere, but less predictably won an Emmy nomination as Outstanding Drama Special. Average.▼

Fallen Idol, The (1948-British) 94m. ***½ D: Carol Reed. Ralph Richardson, Michele Morgan, Bobby Henrey, Sonia Dresdel, Jack Hawkins, Bernard Lee. Young boy idolizes a household servant who is suspected of murdering his wife. Exceptional realization of Graham Greene story, told in large part from the child's point of view. Also shown in computer-colored version.▼

Fallen Sparrow, The (1943) 94m. **½ D: Richard Wallace. John Garfield, Maureen O'Hara, Walter Slezak, Patricia Morison, Martha O'Driscoll, Bruce Edwards, John Miljan, John Banner, Hugh Beaumont. Entertaining if somewhat vague WW2 thriller with Garfield returning to N.Y.C. after fighting in the Spanish Civil War, only to find himself hunted by undercover Nazis. Promising material never really pans out.▼

Falling in Love (1984) C-107m. **½ D: Ulu Grosbard. Robert De Niro, Meryl Streep, Harvey Keitel, Jane Kaczmarek, George Martin, David Clennon, Dianne Wiest. Straightforward film about two married people who—against their better judgment—have an affair. BRIEF ENCOUNTER it's not, but De Niro and especially Streep lift it out of the ordinary.▼

Falling in Love Again (1980) C-103m. *½ D: Steven Paul. Elliott Gould, Susannah York, Stuart Paul, Michelle Pfeiffer, Kaye Ballard, Robert Hackman, Steven Paul. Amateurish slop wherein a frustrated Gould flashes back to his halcyon youth in the Bronx and his courtship of a WASP princess. Artificial, to say the least. Twenty-year-old producer-director-writer-actor Paul scores points for chutzpah, not talent, with this feature debut (which is also the screen debut for leading lady Pfeiffer).▼

Fall of the House of Usher (1960) SEE: House of Usher▼

Fall of the House of Usher, The (1982) C-101m. TVM D: James L. Conway. Martin Landau, Robert Hays, Charlene Tilton, Dimitra Arliss, Ray Walston, Peg Stewart. Amateurish retelling of the Edgar Allan Poe mystery thriller, filtered shamelessly through the Classics Illustrated mill—cardboard sets as well as acting included. Below average.▼

Fall of the Roman Empire, The (1964) **C-153m.** ***½ D: Anthony Mann. Sophia Loren, Stephen Boyd, James Mason, Alec Guinness, Christopher Plummer, Anthony Quayle, John Ireland, Mel Ferrer. Omar Sharif, Eric Porter. Intelligent scripting, good direction, and fine acting place this far above the usual empty-headed spectacle. Mason and Guinness are superb; several action sequences are outstanding. A winner all the way. Screenplay by Philip Yordan, Ben Barzman, and Basilio Franchina. Originally 172m.▼

False Face SEE: **Scalpel**▼

False Witness (1989) **C-100m. TVM** D: Arthur Allan Seidelman. Phylicia Rashad, Philip Michael Thomas, George Grizzard, Teri Austin, Robin Mattson, John Bennett Perry, James Sutorius. Ambitious assistant D.A. clashes with her lover/assistant as they go about solving a controversial rape case. Average.

Falstaff SEE: **Chimes at Midnight**▼

Fame (1980) **C-134m.** **½ D: Alan Parker. Irene Cara, Lee Curreri, Eddie Barth, Laura Dean, Paul McCrane, Barry Miller, Gene Anthony Ray, Maureen Teefy, Antonio Franceschi, Anne Meara, Albert Hague. The dreams, aspirations, struggles, and failures of students at N.Y.C.'s High School for Performing Arts should have made a great film, but this one just misses the mark, despite good ingredients and Oscar-winning music (by Michael Gore) and song (by Gore and Dean Pitchford). Moments of insight, excitement, and creativity eventually get lost in abrupt, disjointed continuity, which leaves a bushel of loose ends and unresolved ideas. Later a TV series.▼

Fame Is the Name of the Game (1966) **C-100m. TVM** D: Stuart Rosenberg. Tony Franciosa, Jill St. John, Jack Klugman, George Macready, Lee Bowman, Susan Saint James, Jack Weston, Robert Duvall, Nanette Fabray. Big-time magazine writer Franciosa investigates death of call girl; trail leads to various business and criminal types. Remake of CHICAGO DEADLINE. Later spawned TV series *The Name of the Game*. Average.

Fame Is the Spur (1946-British) **116m.** **½ D: John and Roy Boulting. Michael Redgrave, Rosamund John, Anthony Wager, Brian Weske. Thoughtful if slow-moving chronicle of a noted politician-diplomat who rises from poverty to fame.

Family, The (1970-Italian) **C-100m.** **½ D: Sergio Sollima. Charles Bronson, Jill Ireland, Telly Savalas, Michel Constantin, Umberto Orsini, George Savalas. Fast pacing fails to hide clichés in this action drama about an ex-con (Bronson) in single-minded hunt for the man who framed him and stole his girl. Lots of chefs involved in writing this brew, among them Lina Wertmuller. Also called VIOLENT CITY.▼

Family, The (1987-Italian) **C-127m.** *** D: Ettore Scola. Vittorio Gassman, Fanny Ardant, Stefania Sandrelli, Andrea Occhipinti, Jo Ciampa, Philippe Noiret. Episodic, revealing chronicle of eighty years in the life of an upper-middle-class Italian clan (with some characters portrayed through the decades by several different actors). An affectionate depiction, leisurely paced but well worth catching. Don't look for any sumptuous Roman exteriors: Scola never once strays from the family's apartment!▼

Family Affair, A (1937) **69m.** D: George B. Seitz. Lionel Barrymore, Mickey Rooney, Spring Byington, Cecilia Parker, Eric Linden, Julie Haydon, Sara Haden, Charley Grapewin. SEE: **Andy Hardy** series.

Family Business (1986-French) **C-98m.** **½ D: Costa-Gavras. Johnny Hallyday, Fanny Ardant, Guy Marchand, Laurent Romor, Remi Martin, Juliette Rennes, Caroline Pochon. Well-made but inconsequential comedy of professional safecracker Hallyday, whose wife, daughter, and (most tellingly) son are involved in various ways with his "career." The motivations of his spouse (Ardant), particularly in relation to their son, are utterly confounding.

Family Business (1989) **C-115m.** **½ D: Sidney Lumet. Sean Connery, Dustin Hoffman, Matthew Broderick, Rosana DeSoto, Janet Carroll, Victoria Jackson, Bill McCutcheon, Deborah Rush. Brainy Broderick, estranged from father Hoffman, enlists the aid of his grandfather Connery, a career criminal, to pull off a can't-miss heist. Worth seeing for three terrific performances by the charismatic leads, even though they're never quite believable as family—and the story lets them down. Further undermined by one of the most appalling music scores of recent memory, composed by Cy Coleman. Based on a novel by Vincent Patrick.▼

Family Enforcer SEE: **Death Collector**▼

Family Flight (1972) **C-73m. TVM** D: Marvin Chomsky. Rod Taylor, Kristoffer Tabori, Dina Merrill, Janet Margolin, Gene Nelson, Richard Roat. Family takes flying vacation to help ease failing home life, crash-lands, finds they must cooperate to fight for survival. Performances by three leads film's sole asset. Average.

Family for Joe, A (1990) **C-100m. TVM** D: Jeffrey Melman. Robert Mitchum, Maia Brewton, Jarrad Paul, Jessica Player, Barbara Babcock, David Nelson, John Mitchum. Four orphaned youngsters, about to be split up by the courts, recruit a homeless curmudgeon to pose as their grandfather to keep them together. Mitchum ambles through the light-hearted proceedings in this pilot to his first TV series. The film's a reworking of STICKIN' TOGETHER and the short-lived 1979 series that came from it, *The MacKenzies of Paradise Cove.* Average.

Family Game, The (1984-Japanese) **C-107m.** *** D: Yoshimitsu Morita. Yusaku Matsuda, Juzo Itami, Saori Yuki, Junichi Tsujita, Ichirota Miyagawa. Arrogant tutor is engaged to propel an indolent younger son into a classy school but ends up taking over entire household. Overlong, but original, satire of Japan's burgeoning middle class offers plenty of chuckles, insights into modern-day Japan.▼

Family Honeymoon (1948) **80m.** **½ D: Claude Binyon. Claudette Colbert, Fred MacMurray, Rita Johnson, Gigi Perreau. What could have been fine comedy turns out to be uneven farce as widow takes children on second honeymoon. Very good cast does its best.

Family Jewels, The (1965) **C-100m.** **½ D: Jerry Lewis. Jerry Lewis, Donna Butterworth, Sebastian Cabot, Robert Strauss, Milton Frome. Depending on your taste for Lewis, you'll either be in ecstasy or writhing on the floor in pain because he plays seven parts—all of them as potential guardians of little girl who is inheriting several million dollars.▼

Family Kovack, The (1974) **C-78m. TVM** D: Ralph Senensky. James Sloyan, Sarah Cunningham, Andy Robinson, Tammi Bula, Richard Gilliland, Renne Jarrett, Mary La Roche. Drama concerning the sort of efforts of a closely knit clan to prove oldest son innocent of bribery. Serviceable vehicle with competent cast that might have made a TV series but didn't; should not be confused with *The Family Holvak,* which did. Average.

Family Man, The (1979) **C-100m. TVM** D: Glenn Jordan. Edward Asner, Meredith Baxter Birney, Anne Jackson, Paul Clemens, Mary-Joan Negro, Martin Short. A happily married executive is torn between his infatuation for a beautiful young woman and his love for his wife and family. Daytime soap opera with prime prime-time cast. Average.

Family Nobody Wanted, The (1975) **C-78m. TVM** D: Ralph Senensky. Shirley Jones, James Olson, Katherine Helmond, Woodrow Parfrey, Claudia Bryar, Ann Doran. Impoverished minister and wife struggle to provide a home for their large brood of racially mixed, adopted children. Winning story tends to get cutesy, but stable performances keep it in line. Based on Helen Doss' best seller. Average.

Family of Spies (1990) **C-200m. TVM** D: Stephen Gyllenthal. Powers Boothe, Lesley Ann Warren, Graham Beckel, Gordon Clapp, John M. Jackson, Jeroen Krabbe. Boothe is a much-too-charming schemer in this drama recounting the true life of John Walker, Jr., the U.S. naval officer who became a spy for the Soviets and recruited his children and brother into his wing of espionage over two decades. Interesting, but ultimately tedious. Originally shown in two parts. Average.

Family Plot (1976) **C-120m.** **½ D: Alfred Hitchcock. Karen Black, Bruce Dern, Barbara Harris, William Devane, Ed Lauter, Cathleen Nesbitt, Katherine Helmond. Hitchcock coasts along in this tongue-in-cheek thriller. Harris is phony psychic who gets involved in a murder plot hatched by sinister Devane. Mildly entertaining but never credible. Ernest Lehman scripted Hitch's 54th and final film.▼

Family Reunion (1981) **C-200m. TVM** D: Fielder Cook. Bette Davis, J. Ashley Hyman, David Huddleston, John Shea, Roy Dotrice, David Rounds, Kathryn Walker, Roberts Blossom, Roberta Wallach, Jeff McCracken, Ann Lange, Paul Rudd. Schoolteacher, put out to pasture after 50 years, sets out to rediscover her far-flung family with a neighborhood youngster in tow (played by Davis's own grandson in his screen debut). Enough family characters are introduced to keep a prospective series going for years, but all eyes are firmly on Davis, especially when she uncovers sinister familial doings. Written by Allan Sloane. Above average.

Family Rico, The (1972) **C-73m. TVM** D: Paul Wendkos. Ben Gazzara, Sal Mineo, Jo Van Fleet, James Farentino, Sian Barbara Allen, Dane Clark, Leif Erickson, Jack Carter. Solid adaptation of Georges Simenon novel concerning torn loyalties of organized crime family leader. Good cast working with fairly realistic material. Above average. Filmed before as THE BROTHERS RICO.

Family Secret, The (1951) **85m.** **½ D: Henry Levin. John Derek, Lee J. Cobb, Erin O'Brien-Moore, Jody Lawrance. Good drama involving Cobb who defends man accused for crime which son committed.

Family Sins (1987) **C-100m. TVM** D: Jerrold Freedman. James Farentino, Jill Eikenberry, Andrew Bednarski, Mimi Kuzyk, Brent Spiner, Michael Durrell, Tom Bower. Grim psychological drama about a disciplinarian father whose bias toward one of his sons leads to family tragedy. Average.▼

Family Ties Vacation (1985) **C-100m. TVM** D: Will Mackenzie. Meredith Baxter Birney, Michael Gross, Michael J. Fox, Justine Bateman, Tina Yothers, Derek Nimmo, John Moulder Brown. The family of the hit television series *Family Ties* visits London—but should have stayed at home, judging from this lackluster "extension" movie. Even series fans will be disappointed. Below average.

Family Upside Down, A (1978) **C-100m.** TVM D: David Lowell Rich. Helen Hayes, Fred Astaire, Efrem Zimbalist, Jr., Pat Crowley, Patty Duke Astin. Affecting drama by Gerald DiPego about an elderly couple who become dependent on their grown children. Astaire won an Emmy Award and Hayes, Astin, and Zimbalist all received nominations. Above average.▼

Family Way, The (1966-British) **C-115m.** *** D: Roy Boulting. Hayley Mills, Hywel Bennett, John Mills, Marjorie Rhodes, Avril Angers, Murray Head. Winning comedy about young newlyweds' problems, including impotence, and difficulty of living in same house as his parents. This warm, gentle film was actually considered controversial in 1967 when released in U.S.! Music score by Paul McCartney.

Fan, The (1949) **89m.** ** D: Otto Preminger. Jeanne Crain, Madeleine Carroll, George Sanders, Richard Greene. Oscar Wilde's comedy of manners *Lady Windemere's Fan*, involving marital indiscretion and social-climbing in Victorian England, loses much of its wit in film version. Remake of 1925 silent.

Fan, The (1981) **C-95m.** *½ D: Edward Bianchi. Lauren Bacall, Michael Biehn, Maureen Stapleton, James Garner, Hector Elizondo, Anna Maria Horsford, Kurt Johnson, Griffin Dunne. Broadway actress Bacall is stalked by a psychotic admirer in this bloody, distasteful adaptation of the Bob Randall novel. Bacall's star appeal helps disguise the fact that this is just an exploitation cheapie in dress clothes.▼

Fanatic SEE: **Die! Die! My Darling!**▼

Fanatics, The (1957-French) **85m.** ** D: Alex Joffe. Pierre Fresnay, Michel Auclair, Gregoire Aslan, Betty Schneider. Occasionally taut tale of assassination plot on South American dictator, efforts of one rebel member to stop bomb explosion.

Fancy Pants (1950) **C-92m.** *** D: George Marshall. Mr. Robert Hope (formerly Bob), Lucille Ball, Bruce Cabot, Jack Kirkwood, Lea Penman, Eric Blore. Amusing remake of RUGGLES OF RED GAP with English valet Hope accompanying nouveau riche wildcat Lucy to her Western home.▼

Fandango (1985) **C-91m.** **½ D: Kevin Reynolds. Kevin Costner, Judd Nelson, Sam Robards, Chuck Bush, Brian Cesak, Marvin J. McIntyre, Suzy Amis. Five college pals have one last fling before moving on to face Real Life. Based on Reynolds's student film called PROOF, expanded to feature length under sponsorship of Steven Spielberg. Fresh and likable, if uneven.▼

Fan-Fan the Tulip (1951-French) **96m.** *** D: Christian-Jaque. Gerard Philipe, Gina Lollobrigida, Noel Roquevert, Olivier Hussenot, Marcel Herrard, Sylvie Pelayo. Most delightful satire of swashbuckling epics, with Philipe ideally cast

as the sword-wielding, love-hungry 18th-century Frenchman joining Louis XV's army. Retitled: SOLDIER IN LOVE.

Fanfare for a Death Scene (1964) **C-73m.** TVM D: Leslie Stevens. Richard Egan, Burgess Meredith, Viveca Lindfors, Telly Savalas, Tina Louise, Edward Asner. Special agent Egan hunts for vanished physicist whose secret formula is sought by the enemy. Atmospheric but standard spy tale spiked by New Orleans jazz with trumpeter Al Hirt. Average.

Fanny (1932-French) **120m.** ***½ D: Marc Allegret. Raimu, Pierre Fresnay, Charpin, Orane Demazis, Alida Rouffe. Marius (Fresnay) abandons Fanny (Demazis) with his child; with Cesar (Raimu) playing Cupid, she marries Panisse (Charpin). Second of Marcel Pagnol's charming trilogy, preceded by MARIUS and followed by CESAR. All three were the basis of the play and movie FANNY (1961).▼

Fanny (1961) **C-133m.** *** D: Joshua Logan. Leslie Caron, Maurice Chevalier, Charles Boyer, Horst Buchholz, Baccaloni, Lionel Jeffries. Gorgeously photographed and beautifully scored dramatic version of Marcel Pagnol's trilogy involving young girl left with child by adventure-seeking sailor. Chevalier and Boyer give flavorful performances.▼

Fanny and Alexander (1983-Swedish) **C-197m.** **** D: Ingmar Bergman. Pernilla Allwin, Bertil Guve, Gunn Wallgren, Allan Edwall, Ewa Froling, Jan Malmsjo, Erland Josephson, Harriet Andersson. Haunting, engrossing family saga set in turn-of-the-century Sweden; a summing up of Bergman's career (announced as his final film). Scenes of joy, exuberance, pain, torment, exquisitely expressed, and largely seen through the eyes of a young boy. This earned Oscars as Best Foreign Film, and for its costumes, art direction-set decoration, and Sven Nykvist's lovely cinematography. Edited from an even longer television mini-series.▼

Fanny By Gaslight SEE: **Man of Evil**

Fan's Notes, A (1972-Canadian) **C-100m.** ** D: Eric Till. Jerry Ohrbach, Burgess Meredith, Patricia Collins, Julia Ann Robinson, Rosemary Murphy. Confused, football-obsessed writer becomes disillusioned with the Great American Dream of success and conformity, and ends up in mental hospital. Unfortunate misfire of Frederick Exley's highly regarded novel.

Fantasies (1980) **C-100m.** TVM D: William Wiard. Suzanne Pleshette, Barry Newman, Robert Vaughn, Patrick O'Neal, Madlyn Rhue, Allyn Ann McLerie, Peter Bergman, Stuart Damon, John Gabriel, Robin Mattson, Robert S. Woods. Somebody's systematically knocking off the stars of a late-night soap opera (played by real-life daytime soap stars) and the show's creator Pleshette fears she may be next. Off-beat but flaccid whodunit. Average.

Fantasies (1981) **C-81m.** BOMB D: John Derek. Kathleen Collins (Bo Derek), Peter Hooten, Anna Alexiadis, Phaedon Gheorghitis, Therese Bohlin. Amateurish nonsense about Derek's and Hooten's efforts to renovate a Greek island into a tourist trap. Shot in 1973, when Bo was 16, as AND ONCE UPON A LOVE.▼

Fantasist, The (1986-Irish) **C-98m.** **½ D: Robin Hardy. Christopher Cazenove, Timothy Bottoms, Moira Harris, John Kavanagh, Mick Lally. Eerie tale of sexual repression among the Irish: country lass Harris moves to Dublin, where she's in danger of falling prey to Bottoms, who may be the notorious "phone call killer." Well done of its type, with Hardy effectively juxtaposing calm, quiet sequences with those of terror; however, some will find repugnant the graphic violence, and the idea that Harris is in some way intrigued by the goings-on.▼

Fantastica (1980-Canadian-French) **C-104m.** ** D: Gilles Carle. Carole Laure, Lewis Furey, Serge Reggiani, Claudine Auger, John Vernon. Laure, the star of a touring musical revue, loves impresario Furey, has an affair with ecologist Reggiani, and finds a political cause. Well intentioned, but far from fantastic.

Fantastic Invasion of Planet Earth (1966) **C-91m.** *½ D: Arch Oboler. Michael Cole, Deborah Walley, Johnny Desmond. Released theatrically in 3D, this plays like a padded *Twilight Zone* episode; young couple find themselves trapped in seemingly deserted town enclosed in a giant Baggie. The original title, THE BUBBLE, was far less misleading: there are no aliens and no "invasion" in evidence, and not much excitement, either. Originally 112m.

Fantastic Planet, The (1973-French) **C-72m.** **½ D: Rene Laloux. Interesting animated feature about futuristic planet where men are dominated by superdeveloped mechanized race. Worthwhile, but misses target by being static and aloof.▼

✓ **Fantastic Voyage** (1966) **C-100m.** ***½ D: Richard Fleischer. Stephen Boyd, Raquel Welch, Edmond O'Brien, Donald Pleasence, Arthur O'Connell, William Redfield, Arthur Kennedy, James Brolin. Tremendously entertaining science fiction story of medical team reduced to microscopic size, injected inside human body. Film's great effects will be lost on TV screen, but story and action will keep you glued to your seat nevertheless. Screenplay by Harry Kleiner, based on a story by Otto Klement and Jay Lewis Bixby. Won Oscars for art direction-set decoration and special visual effects.▼

Fantastic World of D. C. Collins, The (1984) **C-100m.** TVM D: Les Martinson. Gary Coleman, Bernie Casey, Shelley Smith, Fred Dryer, Marilyn McCoo, Philip Abbott, George Gobel, Michael Ansara. Daydreamer Coleman becomes a Walter Mitty mite while being pursued by secret agents seeking a videotape that was unknowingly slipped to him. Routine preteen adventure only for Gary's diehard fans. Below average.▼

Fantasy Island (1977) **C-100m.** TVM D: Richard Lang. Ricardo Montalban, Bill Bixby, Sandra Dee, Peter Lawford, Carol Lynley, Hugh O'Brian, Eleanor Parker, Victoria Principal, Dick Sargent. Dreams come true on mysterious millionaire Montalban's glamorous island paradise, where for $50,000 each, guests can live out their treasured fantasies. Derivative idea spawned the hit series. Below average.▼

Fantomas Against Scotland Yard (1966-French-Italian) **C-104m.** **½ D: Andre Hunebelle. Jean Marais, Louis De Funes, Mylene Demongeot, Henri Serre. Satirical cliffhanger-type adventure yarn, with Marais as super-criminal engaged in a number of athletic escapades. Retitled: FANTOMAS.

Far Country, The (1955) **C-97m.** *** D: Anthony Mann. James Stewart, Ruth Roman, Corinne Calvet, Walter Brennan, Jay C. Flippen, John McIntire, Harry Morgan. Cattleman Stewart, a confirmed loner, brings his herd to Alaska and finds nothing but trouble; solid Western saga set against colorful backdrop of mining camp towns.▼

Farewell Again (1937-British) **81m.** **½ D: Tim Whelan. Leslie Banks, Flora Robson, Sebastian Shaw, Patricia Hilliard. Neatly handled minor film detailing events in the lives of British soldiers on short leave before embarking for the front again.

Farewell, Friend (1968-French-Italian) **C-115m.** ** D: Jean Herman. Alain Delon, Charles Bronson, Olga Georges-Picot, Brigitte Fossey, Bernard Fresson. Mercenaries return to Marseilles following service in Algeria, team up for robbery, and inevitably clash. Ordinary and overlong. Retitled HONOR AMONG THIEVES.▼

Farewell, My Lovely (1975-British) **C-97m.** *** D: Dick Richards. Robert Mitchum, Charlotte Rampling, John Ireland, Sylvia Miles, Jack O'Halloran, Anthony Zerbe, Harry Dean Stanton, Sylvester Stallone. Third film version of Raymond Chandler novel tries too hard to evoke its period, but gets by anyway; Mitchum is appealing as a tired Philip Marlowe. Filmed before as MURDER, MY SWEET and THE FALCON TAKES OVER; followed by THE BIG SLEEP (1978).▼

Farewell to Arms, A (1932) **78m.** *** D: Frank Borzage. Helen Hayes, Gary Cooper, Adolphe Menjou, Mary Philips, Jack LaRue, Blanche Frederici. Lushly romantic adaptation of Hemingway novel about ill-fated WW1 romance between American soldier and British nurse; dated but well done. Charles Lang's exquisite cinematography won an Oscar. Remade in 1957.▼

Farewell to Arms, A (1957) C-152m. **½ D: Charles Vidor. Rock Hudson, Jennifer Jones, Vittorio De Sica, Alberto Sordi, Mercedes McCambridge, Elaine Stritch, Oscar Homolka. Overblown, padded remake has unconvincing leads, static treatment of WW1 story so romantically told in Hemingway novel. Hudson is American ambulance driver wounded in WW1 Italy who falls in love with nurse Jones.▼

Farewell to Manzanar (1976) C-105m. TVM D: John Korty. Yuki Shimoda, Nobu McCarthy, Clyde Kusatsu, Mako, Akemi Kikiumura, Pat Morita, James Saito. Factual story of one Japanese American family's internment in WW2 detention camp. Sad, often hidden slice of American history, beautifully directed by Korty and captured in the screenplay by Jeanne Wakatuski Houston (who lived it) and her husband James D. Houston, taken from their stirring book. Not to be missed. Above average.

Farewell to the King (1989) C-117m. ** D: John Milius. Nick Nolte, Nigel Havers, James Fox, Marilyn Tokuda, Frank McRae, Aki Aleong, William Wise. Disappointing actioner with Nolte an army deserter who becomes the leader of a Borneo tribe during WW2. His goals: to protect his people from the atrocities of the Japanese and the lies of the British. Intriguing premise, but the result sinks into cliché. Milius scripted, from Pierre Schoendoerffer's novel.▼

Far from Home (1989) C-86m. *½ D: Meiert Avis. Matt Frewer, Drew Barrymore, Richard Masur, Karen Austin, Susan Tyrrell, Anthony Rapp, Jennifer Tilly, Andras Jones, Dick Miller. Dumb killer-on-the-loose programmer with sexy teen Barrymore being stalked while vacationing with her father. Of interest only for Drew's casting in her first adolescent movie role.▼

Far from the Madding Crowd (1967-British) C-169m. ***½ D: John Schlesinger. Julie Christie, Peter Finch, Terence Stamp, Alan Bates, Prunella Ransome. Shamefully underrated adaptation of Thomas Hardy novel about beautiful woman and her profound effect on three men. Superb production, with brilliant photography by Nicolas Roeg, score by Richard Rodney Bennet, script by Frederic Raphael, and performances by Finch and Bates.▼

Far Horizons, The (1955) C-108m. **½ D: Rudolph Maté. Fred MacMurray, Charlton Heston, Donna Reed, Barbara Hale, William Demarest. Movie fiction about Lewis and Clark expedition, beautifully photographed; sporadic action; implausible love interest.

Farmer, The (1977) C-98m. BOMB D: David Berlatsky. Gary Conway, Angel Tompkins, Michael Dante, George Memmoli, Ken Renard. Sadistic, amateurish actioner set in Georgia just after WW2. Vet Conway tries to keep his farm going, gets mixed up with the syndicate. Lots of anachronistic errors, including the whole movie.

Farmer's Daughter, The (1940) 60m. ** D: James Hogan. Martha Raye, Charlie Ruggles, Richard Denning, Gertrude Michael, William Frawley. Not to be confused with later film, this one is about show business on the farm circuit, worthwhile only for Raye.

Farmer's Daughter, The (1947) 97m. ***½ D: H. C. Potter. Loretta Young, Joseph Cotten, Ethel Barrymore, Charles Bickford, Rose Hobart, Harry Davenport, Lex Barker, James Aurness (Arness), Keith Andes. Young won Oscar for her performance as headstrong Swedish girl who fights for congressional seat against the man she loves. Delightful comedy with excellent cast. Allen Rivkin and Laura Kerr adapted Juhni Tervataa's play *Hulda, Daughter of Parliament.* Later a TV series.▼

Farmer's Wife, The (1928-British) 97m. **½ D: Alfred Hitchcock. Jameson Thomas, Lillian Hall-Davies, Gordon Harker. A Hitchcock silent comedy. Farmer Thomas, unsuccessful at finding a bride, is secretly loved by devoted housekeeper Davies. Enjoyable rustic comedy, with screenplay by the director. Based on a play by Eden Philpotts.▼

Farmer Takes a Wife, The (1935) 91m. **½ D: Victor Fleming. Janet Gaynor, Henry Fonda, Charles Bickford, Slim Summerville, Jane Withers. Vintage romance of farmers living by the Erie Canal in 1800s; Fonda's first film, and he's still enjoyable as Gaynor's suitor. Remade in 1953.▼

Farmer Takes a Wife, The (1953) C-81m. ** D: Henry Levin. Betty Grable, Dale Robertson, Thelma Ritter, John Carroll, Eddie Foy, Jr. Musical remake of 1935 film is slow-paced account of life in 1800s along the Erie Canal.▼

Far North (1988) C-90m. *½ D: Sam Shepard. Jessica Lange, Charles Durning, Tess Harper, Donald Moffat, Ann Wedgeworth, Patricia Arquette, Nina Draxton. Shepard's directing debut, which he also scripted, is a pointless, artificial drama about the various members of a Minnesota family and what happens when patriarch Durning is almost killed by a wild horse. Good cast is wasted.▼

Far Out Man (1990) C-91m. BOMB D: Tommy Chong. Tommy Chong, Shelby Chong, Paris Chong, C. Thomas Howell, Martin Mull, Rae Dawn Chong, Judd Nelson. Labeled "A Tommy Chong Attempt," this vanity production is high on nepotism but short on laughs—or coherence. Chong plays a burned-out, leftover 1960s druggie who's trying to find his ex-lady and their child (played by their real-life counterparts). Longtime partner Cheech Marin contributes a cameo, but is sorely missed throughout the rest of the grungy film.▼

Farrell For the People (1982) **C-100m.** TVM D: Paul Wendkos. Valerie Harper, Ed O'Neill, Gregory Sierra, Eugene Roche, Judith Chapman, Steve Inwood, Kene Holliday, Dennis Lipscomb, Richard T. Herd. Harper's eager to make it as a prosecutor by taking on the case of an ex-con accused of murder and his celebrity author sponsor. This failed pilot built itself around the real-life case of convict Jack Henry Abbott and writer Norman Mailer. Average.

Fashions (1934) **78m.** *** D: William Dieterle. William Powell, Bette Davis, Verree Teasdale, Reginald Owen, Frank McHugh, Phillip Reed, Hugh Herbert. Trivial but enjoyable romp of con-man Powell and designer Davis conquering the Paris fashion world. Fine cast glides along with dapper Powell; Busby Berkeley's "Spin a Little Web of Dreams" number is great fun. Original title: FASHIONS OF 1934.▼

Fast and Loose (1930) **75m.** *½ D: Fred Newmeyer. Miriam Hopkins, Carol(e) Lombard, Frank Morgan, Ilka Chase, Charles Starrett. Stiff adaptation of a Broadway comedy about a society girl falling in love with an ordinary guy. Preston Sturges is credited with the dialogue. Hopkins' film debut; Lombard has a smallish role.

Fast and Loose (1939) **80m.** **½ D: Edwin L. Marin. Robert Montgomery, Rosalind Russell, Reginald Owen, Ralph Morgan, Sidney Blackmer. Average mystery about theft of Shakespearean manuscript during weekend stay at owner's estate.

Fast and Sexy (1960-Italian) **C-98m.** **½ D: Vittorio De Sica. Gina Lollobrigida, Dale Robertson, Vittorio De Sica, Carla Macelloni. Lollobrigida is fun-loving widow who returns to her village seeking new husband.

Fast and the Furious, The (1954) **73m.** ** D: Edwards Sampson, John Ireland. John Ireland, Dorothy Malone, Iris Adrian, Bruce Carlisle, Jean Howell, Larry Thor. Ireland is fugitive on the lam from murder frameup who jockeys Malone's sports car, with uninspired romantic interludes and cops-on-the-chase sequences. Produced and written by Roger Corman, this was the first film for American Releasing Corporation—soon to be the fabled AIP (American-International Pictures).

Fast Break (1979) **C-107m.** *** D: Jack Smight. Gabriel Kaplan, Harold Sylvester, Mike Warren, Bernard King, Reb Brown, Mavis Washington, Bert Remsen, Richard Brestoff, Rhonda Bates, K. Callan. Basketball coach Kaplan accepts post at midwestern college, but brings his N.Y.C. street players along with him. Perfect, innocuous TV fare, with some good laughs and exciting game climax.▼

Fast Charlie and the Moonbeam SEE: **Fast Charlie, The Moonbeam Rider**

Fast Charlie, The Moonbeam Rider (1979) **C-99m.** **½ D: Steve Carver. David Carradine, Brenda Vaccaro, L. Q. Jones, R. G. Armstrong, Jesse Vint. Period action comedy-drama about a WW1 deserter who enters the first long-distance motorcycle race. Appealing performance by Vaccaro as an early-day bike groupie and picturesque recreations of post-WW1 America are definite pluses. Also known as FAST CHARLIE AND THE MOONBEAM.

Fast Company (1938) **73m.** *** D: Edward Buzzell. Melvyn Douglas, Florence Rice, Louis Calhern, Claire Dodd, Nat Pendleton, George Zucco, Shepperd Strudwick. Neat little comedy-mystery in the THIN MAN mode. Douglas is a rare-book buff who does a little amateur sleuthing with wife Rice. TV title: THE RARE-BOOK MURDER.

Fast Company (1953) **67m.** ** D: John Sturges. Polly Bergen, Howard Keel, Marjorie Main, Nina Foch, Iron Eyes Cody. Not very exciting musical comedy about horse who prances to music, owned by racing enthusiast Bergen.

Fastest Guitar Alive, The (1968) **C-87m.** ** D: Michael Moore. Roy Orbison, Sammy Jackson, Maggie Pierce, Joan Freeman. Undercover Confederate spies steal a fortune from enemy right before the Civil War ends, then find they have to return it without anyone knowing; poor action tale. Worth catching only for novelty of Orbison's performance.

Fastest Gun Alive, The (1956) **92m.** *** D: Russell Rouse. Glenn Ford, Jeanne Crain, Broderick Crawford, Russ Tamblyn. Sincere Western with a moral. Ford is a peace-loving storekeeper trying to live down renown as gunslinger, but there's always someone waiting to challenge him. Also shown in computer-colored version.

Fast Food (1989) **C-92m.** **½ D: Michael A. Simpson. Clark Brandon, Randal Patrick, Tracy Griffith, Jim Varney, Michael J. Pollard, Traci Lords, Pamela Springsteen, Kevin McCarthy. Two perennial college students (and hucksters) start a fast-food operation with a twist: they lace their hamburgers with aphrodisiac sauce. A notch above the usual crude teen comedies, with Varney (aka Ernest P. Worrell) as the bad guy.▼

Fast Forward (1985) **C-110m.** *½ D: Sidney Poitier. John Scott Clough, Don Franklin, Tamara Mark, Tracy Silver, Cindy McGee, Gretchen F. Palmer, Irene Worth, Constance Towers. Eight squeaky-clean teens from Sandusky, Ohio, crash N.Y.C. in search of their Big Break in Show Biz. Despite the title, this film is stuck in the 1950s; break-dancing can't disguise such cornball stuff.▼

Fast Friends (1979) C-100m. TVM D: Steven Hilliard Stern. Carrie Snodgress, Dick Shawn, Edie Adams, Michael Parks, Jed Allan, Mackenzie Phillips, Vivian Blaine. Far from engrossing drama about a divorcee's struggle to make it on her own in the broadcasting game. Has definite curio interest for the casting of David Letterman as a comic who turns out to be funnier than talk-show host Shawn. Average.

Fast Lady, The (1962-British) C-95m. **½ D: Ken Annakin. James Robertson Justice, Leslie Phillips, Stanley Baxter, Kathleen Harrison, Julie Christie, Eric Barker. Enjoyable, modest farce of naive Baxter, a Scotsman living in England, learning how to drive an antique car—and how to woo Christie in the process. Julie, in her second film role, is thoroughly charming.

Fast Times at Ridgemont High (1982) C-92m. *** D: Amy Heckerling. Sean Penn, Jennifer Jason Leigh, Judge Reinhold, Robert Romanus, Brian Backer, Phoebe Cates, Ray Walston, Forest Whitaker, James Russo, Pamela Springsteen, Martin Brest. Brashly entertaining look at Southern California high school kids, who hang out at the Mall and think mostly about sex. Funny, surprisingly honest, with a very appealing cast and a memorable performance by Penn as a doped-out goofball named Spicoli. High-energy feature debut for director Heckerling, based on Cameron Crowe's factual book. Some footage of Sean Penn was added for pay TV—but songs on soundtrack changed, altering running time to 90m. Later a TV series. Film debuts of Eric Stoltz and Anthony Edwards.▼

Fast-Walking (1982) C-115m. **½ D: James B. Harris. James Woods, Tim McIntire, Kay Lenz, Robert Hooks, M. Emmet Walsh, Timothy Carey, Susan Tyrrell. Oddball prison picture, laced with black humor, stars Woods as Fast-Walking Miniver, mercenary prison guard who's hired to assassinate politico Hooks. McIntire gives a standout performance as a very cagey inmate in a film whose disparate elements (some of them quite interesting) never quite gel. ▼

Fast Workers (1933) 68m. *½ D: Tod Browning. John Gilbert, Robert Armstrong, Mae Clarke, Muriel Kirkland, Vince Barnett, Virginia Cherrill, Sterling Holloway. Abysmal film based on a play called *Rivets*, about construction workers who are friendly romantic rivals. Starts out snappy, then turns to turgid dramatics. Odd material for horror director Browning, too.

Fatal Attraction (1980) SEE: Head On▼

Fatal Attraction (1987) C-119m. **½ D: Adrian Lyne. Michael Douglas, Glenn Close, Anne Archer, Ellen Hamilton Latzen, Stuart Pankin, Ellen Foley, Fred Gwynne, Meg Mundy. Happily married man has a weekend fling with a sexy woman who turns out to be psychotic and proceeds to turn his (and his family's) life into a living hell. Audience-pleasing thriller telegraphs most of its suspense payoffs and features a finale that seems more appropriate to RAMBO. Still, it's extremely well acted and certainly holds your attention. The film's original ending, which was more subtle and intriguing (but dumped after an unsuccessful preview) may reportedly turn up on a future video release. James Dearden based his screenplay on his own British short subject, "Diversion."▼

Fatal Beauty (1987) C-104m. BOMB D: Tom Holland. Whoopi Goldberg, Sam Elliott, Ruben Blades, Harris Yulin, John P. Ryan, Jennifer Warren, Brad Dourif, Neill Barry, Richard (Cheech) Marin, Mike Jolly. One of Whoopi's several post-COLOR PURPLE blunders, an inexcusably awful concoction detailing her exploits as a narcotics cop. There's no shortage of gratuitous violence . . . and an antidrug message to rationalize its excesses. Some of the dialogue is mind-bogglingly awful.▼

Fatal Confession: A Father Dowling Mystery (1987) C-100m. TVM D: Christopher Hibler. Tom Bosley, Tracy Nelson, Susan Blakely, Leslie Nielsen, Peter Scolari, Sada Thompson, Stella Stevens, Mary Wickes. So-so adaptation by Donald Westlake featuring Ralph McInerny's mystery-solving parish priest in the Father Brown mold. This led to a series for Bosley, with Nelson as his streetwise nun sidekick. Average.

Fatal Desire (1953-Italian) 80m. ** D: Carmine Gallone. Anthony Quinn, Kerima, May Britt, Ettore Manni, Umberto Spadaro, voice of Tito Gobbi. Nonmusical version of Mascagni's opera *Cavalleria Rusticana*, about love, adultery, and revenge in small Sicilian town. Originally filmed in color and 3D, not released in U.S. until 1963 in b&w.

Fatal Hour, The (1940) 67m. *½ D: William Nigh. Boris Karloff, Marjorie Reynolds, Grant Withers, Charles Trowbridge, John Hamilton, Frank Puglia, Jason Robards, Sr. Slight mystery, fourth in the Mr. Wong series, with the detective becoming involved in the investigation of a cop's death.▼

Fatal Judgment (1988) C-100m. TVM D: Gilbert Cates. Patty Duke, Joe Regalbuto, Tom Conti, Philip Sterling, Jo Henderson. A licensed practical nurse is indicted for murdering a terminal patient. Drab presentation of a Massachusetts *cause celebre*, despite Conti's flamboyant portrayal of a hotshot defense attorney. Based on Gary Provost's *Fatal Dosage*, adapted by Gerald Green. Average.

Fatal Vision (1984) C-200m.TVM D: David Greene. Karl Malden, Eva Marie Saint, Gary Cole, Barry Newman, Andy Griffith, Gary Grubbs, Mitchell Ryan, Albert Salmi. Top-of-the-line filming of Joe McGinniss's book dealing with the murder case in which ex-Green Beret captain Jeffrey MacDonald was accused and then convicted of the murders of his wife and young daughters. Malden stands out in his Emmy-winning performance as MacDonald's father-in-law who, convinced of his guilt, relentlessly seeks justice. Pungent script by the prolific John Gay. Originally shown in two parts. Above average.▼

Fatal Witness, The (1945) 59m. *½ D: Lesley Selander. Evelyn Ankers, Richard Fraser, George Leigh, Barbara Everest, Frederick Worlock. Quickie mystery yarn with obvious plot about wealthy matron's murder, capture of culprit.

Fat City (1972) C-100m. *** D: John Huston. Stacy Keach, Jeff Bridges, Susan Tyrrell, Candy Clark, Nicholas Colasanto. Taut adaptation of Leonard Gardner's novel about tanktown boxer and his young protégé is Huston's best film in 20 years; Keach, Bridges, and Tyrrell are all fine.▼

Fate Is the Hunter (1964) 106m. **½ D: Ralph Nelson. Glenn Ford, Nancy Kwan, Rod Taylor, Suzanne Pleshette, Jane Russell, Wally Cox. One-note drama of investigation into cause of controversial plane crash. Good cast works with routine script.

Fate Takes a Hand (1961-British) 72m. **½ D: Max Varnel. Ronald Howard, Christina Gregg, Basil Dignam, Sheila Whittingham. Agreeable format about bag of mail recovered fifteen years after a robbery; effect of letters on recipients allows for five trim little tales.

Fat Guy Goes Nutzoid (1986) C-78m. BOMB D: John Golden. Tibor Feldman, Peter Linari, John MacKay, Douglas Stone. Tasteless comedy about two nerds who befriend a big, fat, retarded fellow, and his antics while on the loose in N.Y.C. Linari generates some sympathy as the big guy, but vulgar script makes fun of "retards." Surprisingly, the same filmmakers' next project was an authorized attempt to film J. P. Donleavy's classic novel *The Ginger Man*! Shot in 1983; originally titled ZEISTERS.▼

Father Brown (1954-British) 91m. *** D: Robert Hamer. Alec Guinness, Joan Greenwood, Peter Finch, Cecil Parker, Bernard Lee, Sidney James, Ernest Thesiger. Guinness is in rare form as G. K. Chesterton's clerical sleuth after stolen art treasures; another British gem, superbly cast. U.S. title: THE DETECTIVE.▼

Father Clements Story, The (1987) C-100m. TVM D: Ed Sherin. Louis Gossett, Jr., Malcolm-Jamal Warner, Carroll O'Connor, Rosetta LeNoire, Leon Robinson, Ron McClarty. Black priest from Chicago battles the Church hierarchy to stand by his convictions and adopt a teenager. Thoughtful, well-acted (particularly by Gossett) drama based on the life of the founder of "One Church-One Child" program. Teleplay by Arthur Heineman and Ted Tally. Above average.

Father Figure (1980) C-95m. TVM D: Jerry London. Hal Linden, Timothy Hutton, Jeremy Licht, Martha Scott, Cassie Yates. Widower tries to establish a relationship with two sons from whom he has been separated for five years. Affecting drama written by William Hanley from Richard Peck's novel. Above average.▼

Father Goose (1964) C-115m. *** D: Ralph Nelson. Cary Grant, Leslie Caron, Trevor Howard, Jack Good, Nicole Felsette. Grant goes native as shiftless bum on a South Seas island during WW2, who's persuaded to become a lookout for the Australian navy—and finds himself sheltering Caron and a gaggle of schoolgirls fleeing the Japanese. Lightweight and enjoyable. Oscar-winning script by Peter Stone and Frank Tarloff.▼

Father Is a Bachelor (1950) 84m. ** D: Norman Foster, Abby Berlin. William Holden, Coleen Gray, Mary Jane Saunders, Stuart Erwin, Sig Ruman. Vagabond Holden with five "adopted" kids meets Gray who wants to marry him; "cute" comedy.

Father Makes Good (1950) 61m. *½ D: Jean Yarbrough. Raymond Walburn, Walter Catlett, Barbara Brown, Gertrude Astor. Mild little film in Walburn series about smalltown man who purchases a cow to show his contempt for new milk tax.

Father of the Bride (1950) 93m. **** D: Vincente Minnelli. Spencer Tracy, Elizabeth Taylor, Joan Bennett, Billie Burke, Leo G. Carroll, Russ Tamblyn. Liz is marrying Don Taylor, but Dad (Tracy) has all the aggravation. Perceptive view of American life, witty script by Frances Goodrich & Albert Hackett, and peerless Tracy performance. Sequel: FATHER'S LITTLE DIVIDEND. Later a TV series. Also shown in computer-colored version.▼

Father's Homecoming, A (1988) C-100m. TVM D: Rick Wallace. Michael McKean, Brandon Douglas, Marcianne Warman, Jonathan Ward, Nana Visitor, Peter Michael Goetz. Drab pilot to a prospective series about students dealing with parental problems, class differences, coeducation, and puppy love at a New England boarding school. Filmed on location—in Atlanta. Below average.

Father's Little Dividend (1951) **82m.** *** D: Vincente Minnelli. Spencer Tracy, Joan Bennett, Elizabeth Taylor, Don Taylor, Billie Burke. Delightful sequel to FATHER OF THE BRIDE with same cast. Now Tracy is going to be a grandfather and he doesn't look forward to it. Also shown in computer-colored version.▼

Father's Love, A SEE: **Bloodbrothers**▼

Father's Revenge, A (1988) **C-100m.** TVM D: John Herzfeld. Brian Dennehy, Joanna Cassidy, Ron Silver, Anthony Valentine, Christoph M. Ohrt, Claudia Matschulla. Farfetched drama about an American father who hires a band of mercenaries to join him in the hunt for his stewardess daughter, who has been snatched by terrorists in West Germany. Always dependable Dennehy almost makes it plausible. Average.

Father's Wild Game (1950) **61m.** *½ D: Herbert I. Leeds. Raymond Walburn, Walter Catlett, Jane Darwell, Roscoe Ates, Ann Tyrrell. In this entry, Walburn is protesting inflation at the meat market and decides to hunt wild game himself.

Father Takes a Wife (1941) **79m.** **½ D: Jack Hively. Adolphe Menjou, Gloria Swanson, John Howard, Desi Arnaz, Helen Broderick, Florence Rice, Neil Hamilton. Pleasant little comedy about glamorous stage star (Swanson) who "settles down" and marries Menjou, but takes on opera singer Arnaz as her protege.

Father Takes the Air (1951) **61m.** *½ D: Frank McDonald. Raymond Walburn, Walter Catlett, Florence Bates, Gary Gray. Walburn is involved with local flying school, and accidentally captures a crook.

Father Was a Fullback (1949) **84m.** **½ D: John M. Stahl. Fred MacMurray, Maureen O'Hara, Betty Lynn, Rudy Vallee, Thelma Ritter, Natalie Wood. Wholesome comedy with most engaging cast. MacMurray is football coach with as many household problems as on the gridiron.

Fathom (1967) **C-99m.** *** D: Leslie H. Martinson. Raquel Welch, Tony Franciosa, Ronald Fraser, Greta Chi, Richard Briers, Clive Revill. Fast-paced, tongue-in-cheek spy caper with sky-diver Welch getting mixed up with dubious good-guy Franciosa. Great fun, with Revill's performance as eccentric millionaire stealing the show.

Fat Man, The (1951) **77m.** **½ D: William Castle. J. Scott Smart, Rock Hudson, Julie London, Clinton Sundberg, Jayne Meadows, Emmett Kelly. The star of radio's popular series of the same name appeared in this one-shot film adaptation as the corpulent gourmet/detective (created by Dashiell Hammett) whose investigation of a murder leads him to a circus for whodunit showdown.

Fat Man and Little Boy (1989) **C-126m.**

*** D: Roland Joffe. Paul Newman, Dwight Schultz, Bonnie Bedelia, John Cusack, Laura Dern, Ron Frazier, John C. McGinley, Natasha Richardson. Flawed but still arresting film about the development of the atomic bomb, personalizing the story by focusing on General Groves (Newman), the bullheaded Army officer who was handed the job; and the brilliant J. Robert Oppenheimer (Schultz), who organized the brain trust that created the bomb. One complaint: some decidedly non-1940s slang amid the dialogue.▼

Fatso (1980) **C-94m.** ** D: Anne Bancroft. Dom DeLuise, Anne Bancroft, Candice Azzara, Ron Carey, Michael Lombard, Sal Viscuso. Bancroft's first feature as writer-director is disappointing. Fat man DeLuise half-heartedly tries to reduce after the death of his obese cousin. Film veers unevenly between comedy and pathos, with a few too many excrement jokes, perhaps the uncredited contribution of Mel Brooks.▼

Fat Spy, The (1965) **C-75m.** *½ D: Joseph Cates. Phyllis Diller, Jack E. Leonard, Brian Donlevy, Jayne Mansfield, Jordan Christopher, The Wild Ones, Johnny Tillotson. Once-in-a-lifetime cast makes this a must for camp followers—and a sure thing to avoid for most other viewers. Fat Jack plays dual roles, in a story of a search for the Fountain of Youth. Filmed in Florida.

Fazil (1928) **88m.** ** D: Howard Hawks. Charles Farrell, Greta Nissen, Mae Busch, Vadim Uraneff, Tyler Brooke, John Boles. Strange casting of Farrell as desert sheik is just one oddity in this opulent romance. Visually stunning but dramatically farfetched. Silent film with original 1928 music score.

FBI Girl (1951) **74m.** ** D: William Berke. Cesar Romero, George Brent, Audrey Totter, Tom Drake, Raymond Burr. Title tells all in standard fare about federal agency tracking down extortion gang.

FBI 99 (1945) **100m.** ** D: Spencer Bennet, Wallace Grissell, Yakima Canutt. Marten Lamont, Helen Talbot, George J. Lewis, Lorna Gray, Hal Taliaferro. Satisfactory Republic cliffhanger involving federal agents' persistent attempts to overcome criminal syndicate planning robbery capers et al. Reedited from serial FEDERAL OPERATOR 99.

FBI Story, The (1959) **C-149m.** *** D: Mervyn LeRoy. James Stewart, Vera Miles, Murray Hamilton, Larry Pennell, Nick Adams, Diane Jergens, Joyce Taylor. Well-mounted fabrication of history of F.B.I. as seen through career of agent Stewart, allowing for episodic sidelights into action-packed capers and view of his personal life.

F.B.I. Story—The FBI Versus Alvin Karpis, Public Enemy Number One, The

(1974) **C-100m. TVM** D: Marvin Chomsky. Robert Foxworth, David Wayne, Kay Lenz, Gary Lockwood, Anne Francis, Harris Yulin, Chris Robinson, Eileen Heckart. Depression-era desperado Karpis (Foxworth) is hounded by J. Edgar Hoover (Yulin), who made a personal crusade of catching him. Authentically recreated dramatization in the old Warner Bros. pseudo-newsreel gangster style. Retitled THE FBI STORY—ALVIN KARPIS. Average.

Fear (1946) **68m.** *½ D: Alfred Zeisler. Peter Cookson, Warren William, Anne Gwynne, James Cardwell, Nestor Paiva. Rather tepid remake of Dostoyevsky's CRIME AND PUNISHMENT, suffering from low-budget production values.▼

Fear (1988) **C-96m.** *½ D: Robert A. Ferretti. Cliff DeYoung, Kay Lenz, Robert Factor, Scott Schwartz, Frank Stallone, Geri Betzler. Family on a camping trip is terrorized by escaped cons, headed by one more psychotic Vietnam veteran. Skip it.▼

Fear Chamber, The (1971-Mexican-U.S) **C-80m.** *½ D: Juan Ibanez and Jack Hill. Boris Karloff, Julissa, Carlos East, Isela Vega, Yerye Beirute. Strange film about a semi-living stone from volcano caves that requires fluid from a terrified person in order to communicate with humans; dedicated scientist Karloff and his assistants are all too eager to help. Though faintly better than the other three Mexican-American productions Karloff worked on in 1968 (just before his death), this is still awful.

Fear City (1984) **C-96m.** *½ D: Abel Ferrara. Tom Berenger, Billy Dee Williams, Jack Scalia, Melanie Griffith, Rossano Brazzi, Rae Dawn Chong, Joe Santos, Michael V. Gazzo, Jan Murray, Ola Ray, Maria Conchita Alonso. Incredibly sleazy look at Manhattan lowlife—violent and repellent in the extreme. Remarkably good cast for this kind of exploitation fodder.▼

Fear in the Night (1947) **72m.** *** D: Maxwell Shane. Paul Kelly, Ann Doran, Kay Scott, DeForest Kelley, Robert Emmett Keane. Nifty, exciting chiller involving man who commits murder while under hypnosis. Based on a story by Cornell Woolrich. Remade as NIGHTMARE (1956).▼

Fear in the Night (1972-British) **C-94m.** ** D: Jimmy Sangster. Judy Geeson, Joan Collins, Ralph Bates, Peter Cushing. A terrorized faculty wife. Nothing you haven't seen before.▼

Fear Is the Key (1972-British) **C-103m.** *½ D: Michael Tuchner. Barry Newman, Suzy Kendall, John Vernon, Dolph Sweet, Ben Kingsley. Confused, unsatisfying Alistair MacLean thriller about a man driven to extremes in pursuit of stolen booty—and revenge for the murder of his wife and child. Kingsley's debut, and only film appearance until GANDHI.

Fearless Fagan (1952) **79m.** ** D: Stanley Donen. Carleton Carpenter, Janet Leigh, Keenan Wynn, Richard Anderson, Ellen Corby, Barbara Ruick. Title character is circus lion who accompanies his dimwitted master (Carpenter) into the Army, with predictable results. Inconsequential comedy.

Fearless Frank (1967) **C-83m.** BOMB D: Philip Kaufman. Jon Voight, Monique Van Vooren, Joan Darling, Severn Darden, Anthony Holland, Lou Gilbert, David Steinberg, Nelson Algren. Naive country boy Voight treks off to the Big City, is murdered by gangsters, and is reincarnated as a superhero and his monsterlike clone. Pretentious satire is of interest only as a curio. Filmed in Chicago in 1965. Also known as FRANK'S GREATEST ADVENTURE and subsequently cut to 78m.

Fearless Vampire Killers or: Pardon Me, But Your Teeth Are in My Neck, The (1967-British) **C-98m.** ***½ D: Roman Polanski. Jack MacGowran, Roman Polanski, Sharon Tate, Alfie Bass, Ferdy Mayne, Terry Downes. Near-brilliant mixture of humor and horror: Professor Abronsius and assistant Alfred (great bumbling idiot team) attempt to destroy family of Slovonic vampires. Most revival theaters now show full 107m. version. Also known as DANCE OF THE VAMPIRES.▼

Fearmakers, The (1958) **83m.** **½ D: Jacques Tourneur. Dana Andrews, Dick Foran, Mel Torme, Marilee Earle. Well-done Communist witch-hunt theme as returning war veteran Andrews discovers subversives in his Washington D. C. ad agency.

Fear No Evil (1969) **C-98m. TVM** D: Paul Wendkos. Louis Jourdan, Bradford Dillman, Lynda Day, Marsha Hunt, Wilfrid Hyde-White, Carroll O'Connor. Antique mirror actually entrance to another supernatural world. Scientist (Dillman) buys it; after he dies in accident, fiancée learns it can bring him back. Good cast in moderately inventive, offbeat examination of magic. Followed by RITUAL OF EVIL. Written by Richard Alan Simmons. Above average.

Fear No Evil (1981) **C-96m.** ** D: Frank Laloggia. Stefan Arngrim, Elizabeth Hoffman, Kathleen Rowe McAllen, Frank Birney, Daniel Eden. Classic conflict between good and evil in this horror-gore film about a shy, retiring high-school student who turns out to be an incarnation of Lucifer. He viciously takes on his fellow students and his parents but is combated by two archangels.▼

Fear on Trial (1975) **C-100m. TVM** D: Lamont Johnson. George C. Scott, William Devane, Dorothy Tristan, John Houseman, Judd Hirsch, Lois Nettleton, Milt Kogan, Ben Piazza. Superb drama about blacklisting and subsequent libel trial of 1950s broadcaster John Henry Faulk. Scott etches another memorable portrait as attorney Louis Nizer; Devane is equally as fine as Faulk. David Rintels won an Emmy for his teleplay. Above average.

Fear Stalk (1989) **C-100m. TVM** D: Larry Shaw. Jill Clayburgh, Stephen Macht, Lynne Thigpen, Sandy McPeak, Lorna Luft, Sada Thompson. Middling thriller about a TV producer who discovers she's being stalked by a psycho seeking to take over her life. Average.

Fear Strikes Out (1957) **100m. ***** D: Robert Mulligan. Anthony Perkins, Karl Malden, Norma Moore, Adam Williams, Perry Wilson. Stark account of baseball star Jimmy Piersall and his bout with mental illness; Perkins is properly intense, with Malden superb as his domineering father.▼

Feathered Serpent, The (1948) **61m.** D: William Beaudine. Roland Winters, Keye Luke, Victor Sen Yung, Mantan Moreland, Carol Forman, Robert Livingston, Nils Asther. SEE: **Charlie Chan** series.

Federal Agents vs. Underworld Inc. SEE: **Golden Hands of Kurigal**

Federal Operator 99 SEE: **FBI 99**

Fedora (1978-German) **C-114m. **½** D: Billy Wilder. William Holden, Marthe Keller, Hildegarde Knef, Jose Ferrer, Frances Sternhagen, Henry Fonda, Michael York, Mario Adorf. Stylish but ponderous filmization of Thomas Tryon's short story about a producer's disastrous attempt to lure a Garbo-esque actress out of seclusion. Wilder's potshots at today's films and filmmakers might carry more weight if his own film were better.

Feds (1988) **C-91m. *½** D: Dan Goldberg. Rebecca De Mornay, Mary Gross, Fred Dalton Thompson, Ken Marshall, Larry Cedar. Pert female cop and her bookish roommate conquer male-chauvinistic colleagues during their struggle to make "the cut" at the FBI Academy. Unlike the POLICE ACADEMY farces, this is played fairly straight, perhaps in deference to Bureau cooperation; result is laughless—and thus, pointless—comedy.▼

Feet First (1930) **83m. **½** D: Clyde Bruckman. Harold Lloyd, Barbara Kent, Robert McWade, Lillianne Leighton, Henry Hall. Lloyd talkie tries to rekindle spirit of his silent comedies with middling results. Episodic film has some very funny moments, but Harold's building-ledge routine doesn't quite come off. Edited for TV.

Fellini Satyricon (1970-Italian) **C-129m. ***** D: Federico Fellini. Martin Potter, Hiram Keller, Max Born, Capucine, Salvo Randone. Opinions vary on merits of this visually stunning but overindulgent spectacle on ancient Rome, but if you love

Fellini, you'll be more receptive than most viewers to his unique panorama of colorful and bizarre characters.▼

Fellini's Casanova (1976-Italian) **C-158m. **½** D: Federico Fellini. Donald Sutherland, Tina Aumont, Cicely Browne, John Karlsen, Daniel Emilfork Berenstein. Uninvolving if opulent version of 18th-century lover's life, made entirely at Rome's Cinecitta Studios. Sutherland is enigmatic, the film stylized to a sometimes absurd degree. Nino Rota's music helps. Danilo Donati won an Oscar for his costumes.

Fellini's Roma (1972-Italian) **C-128m. ***** D: Federico Fellini. Peter Gonzales, Britta Barnes, Pia de Doses, Fiona Florence, Marne Maitland, Renato Giovannoli, Federico Fellini. Famed director's impressionistic ode to Eternal City of his youth, his adolescence, and the present—complete with fantasy sequence and usual carnival-of-life point of view.

Fellowship of the Frog SEE: **Face of the Frog**

Fellow Traveler (1989-British) **C-97m. ***** D: Philip Saville. Ron Silver, Hart Bochner, Imogen Stubbs, Daniel J. Travanti, Katherine Borowitz. Excellent political thriller detailing the plight and fate of a pair of childhood pals, one (Bochner) a movie star and the other (Silver) a scriptwriter, who are both blacklisted during the McCarthy era. Especially on target as a reflection of the temper of the 1950s, with a perceptive script by Michael Eaton. Produced by HBO, the BBC, and the British Film Institute.▼

Female (1933) **60m. ***** D: Michael Curtiz. Ruth Chatterton, George Brent, Ferdinand Gottschalk, Philip Faversham, Ruth Donnelly, Johnny Mack Brown, Lois Wilson, Gavin Gordon. Chatterton runs a major auto company with an iron hand—and tries to conduct her love life the same way—until independent-minded Brent comes along. Funny, fascinating role-reversal yarn with incredibly lavish set design—watch for the organist perched in Ruth's entrance foyer!

Female SEE: **Violent Years, The**▼

Female and the Flesh SEE: **Light Across the Street**

Female Animal, The (1958) **84m. **½** D: Harry Keller. Hedy Lamarr, Jane Powell, Jan Sterling, George Nader. Sad waste of Lamarr as mature Hollywood star who grapples with adopted daughter Powell over Nader.

Female Artillery (1973) **C-73m. TVM** D: Marvin Chomsky. Dennis Weaver, Ida Lupino, Sally Ann Howes, Linda Evans, Albert Salmi, Anna Navarro, Nina Foch. Boring adventure with comedy undertones features Weaver as man on run from gang, hiding stolen money with female wagon train, who, in turn, steal it from him to force him to lead them to nearby fort. Laughable resolution, negligible suspense, adequate performances. Average.

Female Instinct SEE: **Snoop Sisters, The**

Female Jungle (1956) **56m. **** D: Bruno VeSota. Jayne Mansfield, Lawrence Tierney, John Carradine, Kathleen Crowley, Rex Thorsen, Burt Carlisle, Bruno VeSota. Lukewarm melodrama of cop Tierney seeking the killer of an actress. Mansfield costars as a nymphomaniac; also known as THE HANGOVER.

Female on the Beach (1955) **97m. ***** D: Joseph Pevney. Joan Crawford, Jeff Chandler, Jan Sterling, Cecil Kellaway, Judith Evelyn, Natalie Schafer. Crawford makes this mystery believable as woman who suspects her lover (Chandler) may want to do her in. Sterling offers contrasting performance and fine support.

Female Trap, The SEE: **Name of the Game Is Kill, The**

Feminine Touch, The (1941) **97m. **½** D: W. S. Van Dyke, II. Rosalind Russell, Don Ameche, Kay Francis, Van Heflin, Donald Meek, Gordon Jones, Robert Ryan. Brittle comedy of author Ameche writing book on jealousy, finding himself a victim when he brings wife Russell to N.Y.C.; she suspects he's carrying on with glamorous Francis.

Feminine Touch, The (1956-British) **C-91m. **** D: Pat Jackson. George Baker, Belinda Lee, Delphi Lawrence, Adrienne Corri, Diana Wynyard. Undistinguished look at student nurses' experiences as they graduate to full-time hospital jobs. Also known as THE GENTLE TOUCH.

Feminist and the Fuzz, The (1970) **C-73m.** TVM D: Jerry Paris. Barbara Eden, David Hartman, Farrah Fawcett, Jo Anne Worley, Harry Morgan, Julie Newmar, Roger Perry, Penny Marshall. Contrived comedy throws two stereotypes—male chauvinist cop and Women's Libber—together as San Francisco apartment roommates with typical TV style resolution of initial differences. Average.

Fer-de-Lance (1974) **C-100m.** TVM D: Russ Mayberry. David Janssen, Hope Lange, Ivan Dixon, Jason Evers, Ben Piazza, Charles Robinson. Suspense tale about a submarine wedged below the sea, terrorized from within by deadly snakes. Ridiculous story and characters, with creepy-crawlers, for those who like that kind of thing. Below average.▼

Fernandel the Dressmaker (1957-French) **84m. **½** D: Jean Boyer. Fernandel, Suzy Delair, Françoise Fabian, Georges Chamarat. Undemanding plot has him wanting to be high-fashion designer rather than drab man's tailor.▼

Ferris Bueller's Day Off (1986) **C-103m. **½** D: John Hughes. Matthew Broderick, Alan Ruck, Mia Sara, Jeffrey Jones, Jennifer Grey, Cindy Pickett, Lyman Ward,

Edie McClurg, Charlie Sheen, Del Close. Saga of a cocky teenager's day of adventure while cutting classes. Starts off extremely funny, with on-target jabs at high school life, then wanders through heavy-handed slapstick and moody self-serious ruminations before regaining momentum for a bright finish. Typically uneven John Hughes script. Later a TV series.▼

Ferry Cross the Mersey (1965-British) **88m. **** D: Jeremy Summers. Gerry and The Pacemakers, Cilla Black, The Fourmost, Jimmy Saville. Gerry Marsden and The Pacemakers perform eight songs in this musical made to cash in on their popularity; most appropriately, they appear as a Liverpool band attempting to compete in a music contest.

Ferry to Hong Kong (1961-British) **C-103m. **½** D: Lewis Gilbert. Orson Welles, Curt Jurgens, Sylvia Syms, Jeremy Spenser. Welles and Jurgens have field day as straight-faced ferry boat skipper and drunken Austrian on trip to Macao. Film is otherwise just routine.▼

Feud, The (1989) **C-96m. ***** D: Bill D'Elia. Rene Auberjonois, Ron McLarty, Joe Grifasi, Scott Allegrucci, Gale Mayron, David Strathairn, Stanley Tucci, Lynne Killmeyer, Kathleen Doyle, Libby George. David Lynch meets Norman Rockwell in this oddly likable satire of 1950s small-town America, centering on a feud that erupts between two families in neighboring hamlets. Broadly played by its character-actor cast; this one has cult-status possibilities. Based on Thomas Berger's novel; coscripted by first-time director D'Elia.

Feudin' Fools (1952) **63m.** D: William Beaudine. Leo Gorcey, Huntz Hall, Dorothy Ford, Lyle Talbot, Benny Baker, Russell Simpson. SEE: **Bowery Boys** series.

Feudin', Fussin' and A-Fightin' (1948) **78m. **** D: George Sherman. Donald O'Connor, Marjorie Main, Percy Kilbride, Penny Edwards. Title and cast names tell all; loud and brassy.

Fever in the Blood, A (1961) **117m. **½** D: Vincent Sherman. Efrem Zimbalist, Jr., Angie Dickinson, Herbert Marshall, Don Ameche, Jack Kelly, Carroll O'Connor. Turgid dramatics focusing on murder trial which various candidates for governorship utilize to further political ambitions.

Fever Pitch (1985) **C-96m.** BOMB D: Richard Brooks. Ryan O'Neal, Catherine Hicks, Giancarlo Giannini, Bridgette Andersen, Chad Everett, John Saxon, William Smith. Anachronistic look at gambling fever with newspaper columnist (and "fever" victim) O'Neal. Embarrassingly bad; overwritten by veteran Brooks with declamatory dialogue from the *Dragnet* school of scripts.▼

Few Days at Weasel Creek, A (1981)

C-100m. TVM D: Dick Lowry. Mare Winningham, John Hammond, Colleen Dewhurst, Richard Farnsworth, Kevin Geer, Nicholas Pryor, Tracey Gold. Offbeat romantic adventure-drama about a farm lad who hits the road and hooks up with a freewheeling young woman bound for California in a house trailer. Durrell Royce Crays's interesting teleplay was based on Joanna Brent's book. Above average.

Few Days in the Life of I. I. Oblomov, A SEE: Oblomov▼

Few Days With Me, A (1988-French) **C-131m.** *** D: Claude Sautet. Daniel Auteuil, Sandrine Bonnaire, Jean-Pierre Marielle, Dominique Lavanant, Danielle Darrieux, Tanya Lopert. Intriguing chronicle of chameleonlike Auteuil, whose family owns a department-store chain, and the series of events that ensue upon his checking up on one outlet, located in a provincial town. Veers too much between comedy (some of which is hilarious) and drama.

ffolkes (1980) **C-99m.** *** D: Andrew V. McLaglen. Roger Moore, James Mason, Anthony Perkins, Michael Parks, David Hedison, Jack Watson, Lea Brodie. Moore has fun playing an eccentric counterterrorist hired by the British government when a team of terrorists threaten to blow up two North Sea oil rigs. Surprisingly little action *per se,* but an entertaining yarn. Retitled ASSAULT FORCE for TV. Also known as NORTH SEA HIJACK.▼

Fickle Finger of Fate, The (1967-Spanish) **C-91m.** *½ D: Richard Rush. Tab Hunter, Luis Prendes, Patty Shepard, Gustavo Rojo, Fernando Hilbeck. Low-budget comedy thriller about a American engineer who finds himself a patsy for smugglers trying to get some art objects out of Madrid.

Fiddler on the Roof (1971) **C-181m.** *** D: Norman Jewison. (Chaim) Topol, Norma Crane, Leonard Frey, Molly Picon, Paul Mann, Rosalind Harris, Michele Marsh, Neva Small, Candice Bonstein. Rousing, colorful location-filmed adaptation of Joseph Stein's hit play based on Sholem Aleichem stories of humble village of Anatevka. Topol is hearty as Tevye, trying to preserve Jewish heritage against growing odds. Sheldon Harnick-Jerry Bock score melodically performed; Isaac Stern's violin featured on soundtrack. Earned Oscars for Cinematography (Oswald Morris) and Scoring (John Williams). Reissued at 150m.▼

Field of Dreams (1989) **C-106m.** ***½ D: Phil Alden Robinson. Kevin Costner, Amy Madigan, Gaby Hoffman, Ray Liotta, Timothy Busfield, James Earl Jones, Burt Lancaster, Frank Whaley, Dwier Brown. Costner plays a novice farmer in Iowa who hears "a voice" that inspires him to build a baseball diamond on his property, in the hope of bringing the legendary baseball

star Shoeless Joe Jackson (whose career was cut short by the Black Sox scandal) back to life. A story of redemption and faith, in the tradition of the best Hollywood fantasies, with moments that are pure magic. Kudos to writer-director Robinson, who adapted W.P. Kinsella's book *Shoeless Joe,* for hitting (and maintaining) just the right note from start to finish. Lovely score by James Horner.▼

Fiendish Plot of Dr. Fu Manchu, The (1980-British) **C-108m.** BOMB D: Piers Haggard. Peter Sellers, Helen Mirren, Sid Caesar, David Tomlinson, Simon Williams, Steve Franken. Disastrous comedy features Sellers in a dual role, as the title character and as his archenemy, Scotland Yard detective Nayland Smith. Painfully unfunny and, sad to say, Sellers' last film.▼

Fiend Who Walked the West, The (1958) **101m.** **½ D: Gordon Douglas. Hugh O'Brian, Robert Evans, Dolores Michaels, Linda Cristal, Stephen McNally. Interesting if not altogether successful transposition of KISS OF DEATH to Western setting, with Evans ludicrous in the Widmark psycho role.▼

Fiend Without a Face (1958-British) **74m.** *½ D: Arthur Crabtree. Marshall Thompson, Kim Parker, Terence Kilburn, Michael Balfour, Gil Winfield. Scientist materializes thoughts in form of invisible brain-shaped creatures which kill people for food. Horrific climax; good special effects.▼

Fiend With the Atomic Brain, The SEE: Blood of Ghastly Horror▼

Fiend with the Electronic Brain, The SEE: Blood of Ghastly Horror▼

Fiercest Heart, The (1961) **C-91m.** ** D: George Sherman. Stuart Whitman, Juliet Prowse, Ken Scott, Raymond Massey, Geraldine Fitzgerald. Good cast and action-packed skirmishes with Zulus can't raise this programmer to any heights. Set in Africa.

Fiesta (1947) **C-104m.** ** D: Richard Thorpe. Esther Williams, Akim Tamiroff, Ricardo Montalban, John Carroll, Mary Astor, Cyd Charisse. Williams trades in her bathing suit for a toreador outfit in this weak musical opus.

15 Malden Lane (1936) **65m.** ** D: Allan Dwan. Claire Trevor, Cesar Romero, Douglas Fowley, Lloyd Nolan, Lester Matthews. Trevor lures Romero in order to crack his underworld gang in this satisfactory programmer.

Fifth Avenue Girl (1939) **83m.** ** D: Gregory LaCava. Ginger Rogers, Walter Connolly, Verree Teasdale, James Ellison, Tim Holt, Kathryn Adams. Tiresome social comedy with Rogers as homeless girl taken in by unhappy millionaire Connolly; even Ginger is lifeless in this film that purports to show that poor is better than rich if you've got a head on your shoulders.▼

Fifth Day of Peace, The (1972-Italian) **C-100m.** ** D: Guilliano Montaldo. Richard Johnson, Franco Nero, Bud Spencer, Michael Goodliffe, Helmut Schneider. Episodic story of several disillusioned WW1 German soldiers aimlessly wandering war-ravaged Italian countryside following the armistice.▼

Fifth Floor, The (1980) **C-90m.** BOMB D: Howard Avedis. Bo Hopkins, Dianne Hull, Patti D'Arbanville, Sharon Farrell, Mel Ferrer, Julie Adams, John David Carson. A few laughs don't compensate for derivative story of college disco dancer who is wrongly committed to an insane asylum. Collectors of screen dementia should study Hopkins's performance.▼

Fifth Missile, The (1986) **C-150m. TVM** D: Larry Peerce. Robert Conrad, Sam Waterston, Richard Roundtree, David Soul, Yvette Mimieux, Jonathan Banks, Art LaFleur. Naval officers Conrad and Waterston try to prevent WW3 when war games aboard a nuclear sub go haywire and Queeg-like commander Soul flips out. Muddled adaptation of the novel *The Gold Crew* by Thomas N. Scortia and Frank M. Robinson was filmed by a basically Italian crew in Malta—obviously without the U.S. Navy's cooperation—and probably would have been twice as coherent at half the length. Below average.

Fifth Musketeer, The (1979-Austrian) **C-103m.** **½ D: Ken Annakin. Beau Bridges, Sylvia Kristel, Ursula Andress, Cornel Wilde, Ian McShane, Lloyd Bridges, Alan Hale, Jr., Jose Ferrer, Helmut Dantine, Rex Harrison, Olivia de Havilland. Lavish, well-cast remake of THE MAN IN THE IRON MASK has nothing new to offer, but retells Dumas' story in capable fashion. Major points of interest: Austrian location work and veteran cast.▼

55 Days at Peking (1963) **C-150m.** *** D: Nicholas Ray. Charlton Heston, Ava Gardner, David Niven, Flora Robson, John Ireland, Paul Lukas, Jacques Sernas. Stars provide most of the interest in this confusing historical account of Boxer Rebellion in 1900s China.▼

Fifty Roads to Town (1937) **81m.** **½ D: Norman Taurog. Don Ameche, Ann Sothern, Slim Summerville, Jane Darwell, John Qualen, Stepin Fetchit, Oscar Apfel, Russell Hicks. Above-par comedy of Ameche and Sothern, both on the lam for different reasons, snowbound together in small inn.

52nd Street (1937) **80m.** ** D: Harold Young. Ian Hunter, Leo Carrillo, Pat Paterson, Kenny Baker, Ella Logan, ZaSu Pitts. Fictionalized story of how 52nd St. became nightclub row in the 1930s; soggy drama punctuated by appearances of some 52nd St. entertainers like Jerry Colonna, Georgie Tapps, Pat Harrington, Sr.

52 Miles to Midnight SEE: **Hot Rods to Hell**

52 Pick-Up (1986) **C-114m.** ** D: John Frankenheimer. Roy Scheider, Ann-Margret, Vanity, John Glover, John Trebor, Lonny Chapman, Kelly Preston, Clarence Williams III, Doug McClure. Self-made businessman is caught in web of blackmail and murder—and determines to break free by himself. Elmore Leonard's story is good, but the lead characters are cold, and film wallows too long in the sleazy, voyeuristic world of the bad guys. It also would have been better shorter. Same novel was adapted just two years earlier as THE AMBASSADOR. ▼

Fighter, The (1952) **78m.** **½ D: Herbert Kline. Richard Conte, Vanessa Brown, Lee J. Cobb, Roberta Haynes. Absorbing tale set in Mexico with Conte a boxer who uses winnings to buy arms to seek revenge for family's murder.

Fighter, The (1983) **C-96m. TVM** D: David Lowell Rich. Gregory Harrison, Glynnis O'Connor, Pat Hingle, Steve Inwood, Susan Kellerman, Justin Lord, Susan Ruttan. Predictable boxing film long a movie staple—with Harrison as an unemployed mill worker who straps on the gloves for the bucks. Average.

Fighter Attack (1953) **C-80m.** ** D: Lesley Selander. Sterling Hayden, J. Carrol Naish, Joy Page, Paul Fierro. Modest film uses flashback to recount Hayden's last important mission in Italy during WW2.▼

Fighter Squadron (1948) **C-96m.** ** D: Raoul Walsh. Edmond O'Brien, Robert Stack, John Rodney, Tom D'Andrea, Henry Hull. OK WW2 drama of dedicated flier O'Brien, has abundance of clichés weighing against good action sequences. Rock Hudson's first film.

Fight for Jenny, A (1986) **C-100m. TVM** D: Gilbert Moses. Philip Michael Thomas, Lesley Ann Warren, Jaclyn-Rose Lester, Jean Smart, Lynne Moody, Barbara Montgomery, Drew Snyder, William Atherton. Interracial southern couple faces a bruising custody battle over the wife's young daughter in this fact-based drama that's reminiscent of Larry Peerce's much-admired ONE POTATO, TWO POTATO. Average.

Fight for Life (1987) **C-100m. TVM** D: Elliot Silverstein. Jerry Lewis, Patty Duke, Morgan Freeman, Barry Morse, Jaclyn Bernstein, Gerard Parkes. Real-life dentist (Lewis, of all people) and wife fight to save their gravely ill daughter, an epileptic. Typical disease-of-the-week movie with a touch of truly offbeat casting. Average.

Fight For Your Lady (1937) **67m.** **½ D: Ben Stoloff. John Boles, Jack Oakie, Ida Lupino, Margot Grahame, Gordon Jones, Erik Rhodes, Billy Gilbert. Wrestling trainer Oakie takes over singer Boles' love life when he's jilted by tony Grahame in this fluffy but undeniably funny musical comedy. Rhodes is hilarious, as usual, as Spadissimo.

Fighting Back (1980) **C-100m. TVM** D: Robert Lieberman. Robert Urich, Art Carney, Bonnie Bedelia, Richard Herd, Howard Cosell, Simone Griffeth, Steve Tannen, Bubba Smith, The Pittsburgh Steelers. The story of Rocky Bleier, who overcame near-crippling war injuries in Vietnam to become a pro-football great. Average.

Fighting Back (1982) **C-98m.** **½ D: Lewis Teague. Tom Skerritt, Patti LuPone, Michael Sarrazin, Yaphet Kotto, David Rasche, Ted Ross, Pat Cooper. Producer Dino de Laurentiis pays a return visit to DEATH WISH territory; fed up with lackadaisical police, hotheaded South Philly deli owner (Skerritt, who's excellent) organizes Guardian Angels-like patrol to clean up criminal scum, but is unprepared for the complications which ensue. Certainly unpleasant, but fast, slick, and convincing; give these people credit for knowing which buttons to push. Sportscaster Donna DeVarona has a nice bit as a TV reporter.▼

Fighting Back (1982-Australian) **C-100m.** **½ D: Michael Caulfield. Lewis Fitz-Gerald, Paul Smith, Kris McQuade, Robyn Nevin, Caroline Gillmer. Ambitious if not entirely successful drama of teacher Fitz-Gerald trying to tame unruly, illiterate 13-year-old (Smith, excellent in his acting debut).

Fighting Chance, The (1955) **70m.** ** D: William Witney. Rod Cameron, Julie London, Ben Cooper, Taylor Holmes, Bob Steele. Standard fare. Horse trainer and jockey friend both fall in love with London and come to odds with each other.

Fighting Choice, A (1986) **C-100m. TVM** D: Ferdinand Fairfax. Beau Bridges, Karen Valentine, Patrick Dempsey, Frances Lee McCain, Lawrence Pressman. Teenager takes his parents to court to win the right to undergo a rare form of brain surgery to combat his epileptic seizures. From the folks at Disney. Average.

Fighting Coast Guard (1951) **86m.** **½ D: Joseph Kane. Brian Donlevy, Forrest Tucker, Ella Raines, John Russell. Better than usual entry in training-for-war film, mixing romance with WW2 military action.

Fighting Devil Dogs SEE: **Torpedo of Doom**▼

Fighting Father Dunne (1948) **93m.** **½ D: Ted Tetzlaff. Pat O'Brien, Darryl Hickman, Charles Kemper, Una O'Connor. Road company BOYS TOWN with O'Brien doing his usual competent work.▼

Fighting Fools (1949) **69m.** D: Reginald Le Borg. Leo Gorcey, Huntz Hall, Gabriel Dell, Frankie Darro, Lyle Talbot, Evelynne Eaton, Benny Bartlett, Bernard Gorcey. SEE: **Bowery Boys** series.

Fighting Guardsman (1945) **84m.** ** D: Henry Levin. Willard Parker, Anita Louise, Janis Carter, John Loder, Edgar Buchanan, George Macready, Lloyd Corrigan. OK costumer of oppressed Frenchmen rising against tyranny in days before French Revolution.

Fighting Kentuckian, The (1949) **100m.** **½ D: George Waggner. John Wayne, Vera Ralston, Philip Dorn, Oliver Hardy, Marie Windsor. Frontierland around 1810 is setting for two-fisted saga of Kentuckian (Wayne) combating land-grabbing criminals and courting Ralston, French General's daughter. Hardy makes rare solo appearance in character role. Also shown in computer-colored version.▼

Fighting Lawman, The (1953) **71m.** *½ D: Thomas Carr. Wayne Morris, Virginia Grey, Harry Lauter, John Kellogg, Myron Healey, Dick Rich. Grey tries to work with flimsy script as gal out to grab loot from robbers, pursued by sheriff.

Fighting Mad (1976) **C-90m.** **½ D: Jonathan Demme. Peter Fonda, Lynn Lowry, John Doucette, Philip Carey, Scott Glenn, Kathleen Miller. Typical revenge picture, with peaceable Fonda driven to violence by ruthless landowner who wants to take over his farm. On-target for this kind of entertainment.▼

Fighting Mad (1977-U.S.-Filipino) **C-96m.** *½ D: Cirio H. Santiago. James M. Iglehart, Jayne Kennedy, Leon Isaac (Kennedy), Joonie Gamboa, Leo Martinez, Armando Federico, Roberto Gonzalez. Routine actioner has Iglehart, left to die by his buddies during Vietnam War, captured by Japanese soldiers still fighting WW2. First released in 1981 to capitalize on the Kennedys' stardom.▼

Fighting Man of the Plains (1949) **C-94m.** **½ D: Edwin L. Marin. Randolph Scott, Bill Williams, Jane Nigh, Victor Jory. Scott seeks to avenge brother's murder, but kills the wrong man. OK Western, with Dale Robertson in first prominent role as Jesse James.

Fighting O'Flynn, The (1949) **94m.** **½ D: Arthur Pierson. Douglas Fairbanks, Jr., Richard Greene, Helena Carter, Patricia Medina. Enjoyable swashbuckler set in 1800s Ireland with Fairbanks and Greene vying in love and intrigue.

Fighting Prince of Donegal, The (1966) **C-112m.** *** D: Michael O'Herlihy. Peter McEnery, Susan Hampshire, Tom Adams, Gordon Jackson, Andrew Keir, Donal McCann. Fine Disney swashbuckler made in England, with McEnery as new head of Irish clan who tries to unite his country but runs afoul of villainous Jackson. Vivid, colorful fun.▼

Fighting Seabees, The (1944) **100m.** ***

[368]

D: Edward Ludwig. John Wayne, Susan Hayward, Dennis O'Keefe, William Frawley, Duncan Renaldo. Spirited WW2 saga of valiant Seabees Wayne and O'Keefe stationed in South Pacific, fighting over Hayward.▼

Fighting 69th, The (1940) 90m. **½ D: William Keighley. James Cagney, Pat O'Brien, George Brent, Jeffrey Lynn, Alan Hale, Frank McHugh, Dennis Morgan. Overripe WW1 tale mixes roughneck comedy, exciting battle action, sloppy sentiment, incredible characterizations (especially Cagney's) detailing exploits of famed Irish regiment. Also shown in computer-colored version.

Fighting Sullivans, The SEE: **Sullivans, The**

Fighting Trouble (1956) 61m. D: George Blair. Huntz Hall, Stanley Clements, Adele Jergens, Joseph Downing. SEE: **Bowery Boys** series.

Fighting Wildcats, The (1957-British) 74m. ** D: Arthur Crabtree. Keefe Brasselle, Kay Callard, Karel Stepanek, Ursula Howells. Innocuous intrigue set in London and Middle East involving gangsters. Original title: WEST OF SUEZ.

Fighting Youth (1935) 85m. **½ D: Hamilton MacFadden. Charles Farrell, June Martel, Andy Devine, J. Farrell MacDonald, Ann Sheridan, Edward Nugent. Commies vs. College Football! A genuinely bizarre bit of kitsch with subversive student Sheridan squaring off against anti-radical quarterback Farrell. Definitely one for the time capsule.

Figures in a Landscape (1970-British) C-95m. ** D: Joseph Losey. Robert Shaw, Malcolm McDowell, Henry Woolf, Christopher Malcolm, Pamela Brown. Capable leads and some amazing helicopter stunt work offer scant compensation for muddled allegory about two fugitives in an unnamed country pursued by an unnamed enemy. Barely released, and still difficult to catch; Losey fans will want to give a look.

File of the Golden Goose, The (1969-British) C-105m. ** D: Sam Wanamaker. Yul Brynner, Charles Gray, Edward Woodward, John Barrie, Adrienne Corri. Strictly formula effort with American agent and Scotland Yard man going undercover in London to get the goods on murderous counterfeiting gang.

File on Jill Hatch, The (1983-U.S.-British) C-180m. TVM D: Alastair Reed. Joe Morton, Frances Tomelty, Gloria Foster, Penny Johnson, Tim Woodward, John Atkinson. Tough and tender, refreshingly honest drama on relationships between the races, focusing on a black American soldier (Morton), who falls in love with and weds Englishwoman Tomelty during WW2. Their problems really begin when they come to the U.S. Originally presented over several evenings on PBS' *American Playhouse*. Above average.

File on Thelma Jordon, The (1949) 100m. **½ D: Robert Siodmak. Barbara Stanwyck, Wendell Corey, Joan Tetzel, Paul Kelly. Tough little *film noir* focusing largely on romance between D.A. Corey and murder suspect Stanwyck. Handsomely photographed. Retitled: THELMA JORDON.

Fillmore (1972) C-105m. *** D: Richard T. Heffron. Bill Graham, The Grateful Dead, It's a Beautiful Day, Santana, Jefferson Airplane, Quicksilver Messenger Service. Good rock documentary about Fillmore West's final days is made even better by extensive footage of its magnetic owner, Bill Graham, on the phone and on stage; one of the better rock films.▼

Final Assignment (1980-Canadian) C-92m. BOMB D: Paul Almond. Genevieve Bujold, Michael York, Burgess Meredith, Colleen Dewhurst, Alexandra Stewart. Television reporter Bujold takes on the KGB when she discovers the Russians are conducting scientific experiments on children. Schlock production, with Montreal an unsatisfactory substitute for Moscow; poor script, embarrassing performances.▼

Final Chapter—Walking Tall (1977) C-112m. BOMB D: Jack Starrett. Bo Svenson, Margaret Blye, Forrest Tucker, Lurene Tuttle, Morgan Woodward, Libby Boone. Yet another saga about true-life Tennessee sheriff Buford Pusser, and inferior to its predecessors. Despite title, this is not the final chapter; a TV movie (A REAL AMERICAN HERO) and series followed.▼

Final Conflict, The (1981) C-108m. *½ D: Graham Baker. Sam Neill, Rossano Brazzi, Don Gordon, Lisa Harrow, Mason Adams. The third and, happily, last of the OMEN trilogy has the anti-Christ Damien Thorn (Neill) thirtyish and the U.S. Ambassador to England. For genre addicts only.▼

Final Countdown, The (1980) C-104m. *** D: Don Taylor. Kirk Douglas, Martin Sheen, Katharine Ross, James Farentino, Ron O'Neal, Charles Durning. An aircraft carrier (the real-life *U.S.S. Nimitz*) enters a time-warp and finds itself in the Pacific just before the attack on Pearl Harbor. Familiar but satisfying fantasy yarn; perfect TV fare.▼

Final Crash, The SEE: **Steelyard Blues**▼

Final Days, The (1989) C-150m. TVM D: Richard Pearce. Lane Smith, Richard Kiley, David Ogden Stiers, Ed Flanders, Theodore Bikel, Graham Beckel, James B. Sikking, Gregg Henry. Well-acted drama about Richard Nixon, from Watergate to his resignation, with veteran character actor Smith doing the president to a turn, matched by Kiley's J. Fred Buzhardt, the Special

White House Counsel. Everyone else is reduced to a walk-on (although Bikel as Kissinger is really interesting casting). Craftily adapted by playwright Hugh Whitemore from the Bob Woodward–Carl Bernstein book. Above average.

Final Exam (1981) **C-90m.** *½ D: Jimmy Huston. Cecile Bagdadi, Joel S. Rice, Ralph Brown, Deanna Robbins, Sherry Willis-Burch. Killer stalks college kids. Not as bloody as most other entries in the genre, but still not very good.▼

Final Eye, The SEE: **Computercide**

Final Jeopardy (1985) **C-100m. TVM.** D: Michael Pressman. Richard Thomas, Mary Crosby, Jeff Corey, Jonathan Goldsmith, Michael Cavanaugh, Joey Sagal, Travis McKenna. Dumb chiller about an out-of-town couple's night of terror in the big town. Below average.

Final Notice (1989) **C-100m. TVM** D: Steven Hilliard Stern. Robert Urich, Melody Anderson, Jackie Burroughs, Louise Fletcher, David Ogden Stiers, Steve Landesburg. So-so thriller teaming a laid-back investigator with a pretty art librarian in the pursuit of a fiend who's mutilating books and then duplicating his crime with attractive women. Adapted by John Gay from Jonathan Valin's mystery novel. Made for cable. Average.

Final Option, The (1982-British) **C-125m.** BOMB D: Ian Sharp. Lewis Collins, Judy Davis, Richard Widmark, Robert Webber, Edward Woodward, Tony Doyle, John Duttine, Kenneth Griffith, Ingrid Pitt. Laughably ridiculous account of Britain's Special Air Services team and how one officer (Collins) goes underground—more or less—to infiltrate a terrorist gang with plans to take over the American Embassy. Lots of violence, but no brains in sight. Third-billed Widmark has precious little screen time, as the U.S. Secretary of State. Original British title: WHO DARES WINS.▼

Final Programme, The SEE: **Last Days of Man on Earth, The**▼

Final Terror, The (1981) **C-82m.** *½ D: Andrew Davis. John Friedrich, Adrian Zmed, Daryl Hannah, Rachel Ward, Mark Metcalf. Pretty bad dead-teenagers film set in the backwoods, of marginal interest for presence of latter-day stars in cast (though they don't get much of a showcase here).▼

Final Test, The (1953-British) **84m.** **½ D: Anthony Asquith. Jack Warner, Robert Morley, George Relph, Adrianne Allen. Droll, minor comedy of father-son rivalry over charming Allen.

Finders Keepers (1951) **74m.** **½ D: Frederick de Cordova. Tom Ewell, Julia (Julie) Adams, Evelyn Varden, Dusty Henley. Scatterbrained comedy that chugs down at end. Ewell and Varden enliven proceedings about a little boy who comes home with a cartful of money.

Finders Keepers (1984) **C-96m.** ** D: Richard Lester. Michael O'Keefe, Beverly D'Angelo, Louis Gossett, Jr., Ed Lauter, David Wayne, Pamela Stephenson, Brian Dennehy, John Schuck, Timothy Blake, Jim Carrey, Jack Riley. Wholehearted attempt at farce, involving stolen money, con artists in disguise, a bungling hit-man, and other promising ingredients, remains disappointingly flat. Lester manages a few neat sight gags, and Wayne is genuinely funny as the world's oldest train conductor.▼

Find the Lady (1976-Canadian-British) **C-79m.** *½ D: John Trent. Lawrence Dane, John Candy, Michel Rooney, Peter Cook, Alexandra Bastedo, Dick Emery. Pre-POLICE ACADEMY comedy highlights the antics of inept cops Dane and Candy, on the trail of a kidnapped socialite. A couple of genuine laughs, but it's mostly silly—and occasionally offensive. Candy and Dane played the same characters a year earlier in IT SEEMED LIKE A GOOD IDEA AT THE TIME.▼

Fine Madness, A (1966) **C-104m.** *** D: Irvin Kershner. Sean Connery, Joanne Woodward, Jean Seberg, Patrick O'Neal, Colleen Dewhurst, Renee Taylor. It's stubborn, nonconformist poet Connery versus the rest of society in this uneven but sometimes outrageously funny satire. Screenplay by Elliot Baker, from his novel.▼

Fine Mess, A (1986) **C-88m.** *½ D: Blake Edwards. Ted Danson, Howie Mandel, Richard Mulligan, Stuart Margolin, Maria Conchita Alonso, Jennifer Edwards, Paul Sorvino. A slapstick saga of two bumblers, with laughs few and far between. Familiar Blake Edwards trademarks, and the supposed inspiration of Laurel and Hardy's Oscar-winning short, THE MUSIC BOX, don't carry this very far.▼

Fine Pair, A (1969) **C-89m.** BOMB D: Francesco Maselli. Rock Hudson, Claudia Cardinale, Thomas Milian, Leon Askin, Ellen Corby, Walter Giller. N.Y.C. policeman Hudson falls for Cardinale, daughter of an old pal, and helps her rob some jewels in terrible comedy-thriller minus laughs or suspense.

Fingerman (1955) **82m.** ** D: Harold Schuster. Frank Lovejoy, Forrest Tucker, Peggy Castle, Timothy Carey, Glenn Gordon, Evelynne Eaton. Convincing performances uplift account of federal agents capturing liquor gang.▼

Finger of Guilt (1956-British) **85m.** **½ D: Joseph Losey. Richard Basehart, Mary Murphy, Constance Cummings, Roger Livesey, Mervyn Johns, Faith Brook. Film director Basehart is blackmailed by woman claiming to be his mistress, which threatens his career and marriage. Intriguing film with disappointing resolution; good look inside British film studio, however. Directed by blacklistee Losey under pseudonyms Alec Snowden/Joseph Walton. Originally released in England as THE INTIMATE STRANGER at 95m.

Finger on the Trigger (1965) **C-87m.** BOMB D: Sidney Pink. Rory Calhoun, James Philbrook, Todd Martin, Silvia Solar, Brad Talbot. Reb and Yankee vets join forces to secure buried treasure while holding off hostile Indians. Made in Spain.▼

Finger Points, The (1931) **88m.** **½ D: John Francis Dillon. Richard Barthelmess, Fay Wray, Regis Toomey, Robert Elliott, Clark Gable, Oscar Apfel. Vivid though meandering melodrama about crime reporter Barthelmess on the payroll of the mob. Wray is a newspaperwoman who urges him to go straight; Gable scores as a gang boss. One of the writers was W. R. Burnett.

Fingers (1978) **C-91m.** ***½ D: James Toback. Harvey Keitel, Jim Brown, Tisa Farrow, Michael V. Gazzo, Tanya Roberts, Marian Seldes, Danny Aiello, Ed Marinaro, Zack Norman. Crude but fascinating melodrama about an aspiring concert pianist who reluctantly "collects" on debts owed to his domineering father. Powerful, disturbing film is compellingly sensual and brilliantly acted, especially by Brown in a rare subdued role. Screenplay by the director.▼

Fingers at the Window (1942) **80m.** **½ D: Charles Lederer. Lew Ayres, Laraine Day, Basil Rathbone, Walter Kingsford, Miles Mander, James Flavin. Entertaining mystery of Ayres-Day tracking down maniac killer masterminding repeated axe murders.

Finian's Rainbow (1968) **C-145m.** ***½ D: Francis Ford Coppola. Fred Astaire, Petula Clark, Tommy Steele, Keenan Wynn, Al Freeman, Jr., Don Francks, Barbara Hancock. Whimsical Burton Lane-E. Y. Harburg musical fantasy about racial injustice was ahead of its time in the late '40s on Broadway, embarrassingly dated 20 years later, but Coppola and an attractive cast work wonders with it in this imaginatively filmed, widescreen winner—perhaps the best movie musical of its era. Harburg's lyrics remain elegant and witty, and Astaire is fun as the transplanted Irishman whose leprechaun comes to life in the American South. Try to see it in a theater.▼

Finishing School (1934) **73m.** **½ D: Wanda Tuchock, George Nicholls, Jr. Frances Dee, Bruce Cabot, Ginger Rogers, Beulah Bondi, Billie Burke, John Halliday. Interesting look at exclusive girls' school where hypocrisy reigns; wealthy Dee falls in love with struggling hospital intern Cabot.

Finish Line (1989) **C-100m.** TVM D: John Nicolella. James Brolin, Josh Brolin,

Mariska Hargitay, Kristoff St. John, John Finnegan, Billy Vera, Stephen Lang. Earnest father/son drama about a young track star's deadly involvement with muscle-building steroids. Brolin pere and fils play it too lackadaisically to sustain interest. Made for cable. Average.▼

Finnegan Begin Again (1985) **C-105m.** TVM D: Joan Micklin Silver. Mary Tyler Moore, Robert Preston, Sylvia Sidney, Sam Waterston, David Huddleston, Bob Gunton. Delightful comedy-drama about the unlikely relationship that blossoms between a widowed schoolteacher caught in a dead-end love affair with a married mortician and an aging newspaperman with a wife at home who's drifting into senility. Preston especially is an absolute joy. Made for cable. Above average.▼

Finnegan's Wake (1965) **97m.** ***½ D: Mary Ellen Bute. Page Johnson, Martin J. Kelly, Jane Reilly, Peter Haskell. James Joyce's classic story of Irish tavern-keeper who dreams of attending his own wake is brought to the screen with great energy and control.

Fire! (1977) **C-100m.** TVM D: Earl Bellamy. Ernest Borgnine, Vera Miles, Patty Duke Astin, Alex Cord, Lloyd Nolan, Ty Hardin, Donna Mills, Neville Brand, Gene Evans. Mountain community is threatened by forest fire started by convict to cover escape from road gang. Carefully structured suspense in the familiar Irwin Allen style. Average.▼

Fire and Ice (1983) **C-81m.** **½ D: Ralph Bakshi. Voices of Susan Tyrrell, Maggie Roswell, William Ostrander, Stephen Mendel. Muscular hero and buxom heroine become involved in power struggle between two warring world powers. Animated sword-and-sorcery saga is no worse (and arguably no better) than an average live-action entry, and benefits from graphic design by fabled illustrator Frank Frazetta, though the animation itself has been traced from live footage. Scripted by well-known comic book writers Roy Thomas and Gerry Conway.▼

Fire and Ice (1987-German) **C-83m.** BOMB D: Willy Bogner. Suzy Chaffee, John Eaves, narrated by John Denver. Loud, boring, interminable (even at 83m.) tale of skier "John" (Eaves), who romances skier "Suzy" (Chaffee) on the slopes. Bogner also produced, scripted, photographed, and designed the costumes. A real snooze, despite some good ski footage.▼

Fire and Rain (1989) **C-100m.** TVM D: Jerry Jameson. Charles Haid, John Beck, Tom Bosley, Penny Fuller, Robert Guillaume, David Hasselhoff, Dean Jones, Patti LaBelle, Angie Dickinson. Fact-based drama about the 1985 Delta Airlines crash in Dallas, with the well-known cast eschewing star turns for ensemble work. Made for cable. Average.▼

Fireball, The (1950) **84m.** *** D: Tay Garnett. Mickey Rooney, Pat O'Brien, Beverly Tyler, Marilyn Monroe, Milburn Stone, Glenn Corbett. Rooney's energetic performance carries this film. Orphan boy devotes himself to becoming big-time roller-skating champ.

Fireball 500 (1966) **C-92m.** BOMB D: William Asher. Frankie Avalon, Annette Funicello, Fabian, Chill Wills, Harvey Lembeck, Julie Parrish. Frankie is a stock-car racer who unknowingly transports moon-shine whiskey. Desperately in need of a beach ball.

Fireball Forward (1972) **C-100m. TVM** D: Marvin Chomsky. Ben Gazzara, Eddie Albert, Ricardo Montalban, Dana Elcar, L. Q. Jones, Anne Francis. Adequate WW2 story by Edmund North has Gazzara assuming command of "hard luck" division in France with usual subplots (traitor in the ranks, female journalist, etc). Holds its own. Could have been a theatrical movie; in fact, some of the combat footage is from PATTON (which North co-wrote). Above average.

Firebirds (1990) **C-85m.** BOMB D: David Green. Nicolas Cage, Tommy Lee Jones, Sean Young, Bryan Kestner, Dale Dye, Mary Ellen Trainor, J. A. Preston, Peter Onorati. High-tech Apache helicopters (with an assist from their pilots) take on South American drug cartels from the air. Standard military issue with a ruptured-duck script and absolutely no romantic chemistry between professional rivals Cage and Young. Jones doesn't exactly evoke memories of Gregory Peck in TWELVE O'CLOCK HIGH when he pep-talks Cage into a "full-tilt boogie for freedom and justice."

Firechasers, The (1970-British) **C-101m.** ** D: Sidney Hayers. Chad Everett, Anjanette Comer, Keith Barron, Joanne Dainton, Rupert Davies, John Loder. Strong production values in familiar story of insurance investigator hunting for arsonist.

Firecreek (1968) **C-104m.** **½ D: Vincent McEveety. James Stewart, Henry Fonda, Inger Stevens, Gary Lockwood, Dean Jagger, Ed Begley, Jay C. Flippen, Jack Elam, Barbara Luna. Somber Western has makings of a classic at outset, but goes astray, and goes on too long. Stewart is mild-mannered part-time sheriff in small town terrorized by Fonda and fellow plunderers. Beautifully photographed (by William H. Clothier), but unrelentingly downbeat.

Fire Down Below (1957-British) **C-116m.** **½ D: Robert Parrish. Rita Hayworth, Robert Mitchum, Jack Lemmon, Herbert Lom, Bernard Lee, Anthony Newley. Contrived but entertaining melodrama of Mitchum and Lemmon, owners of tramp boat, falling in love with shady Hayworth on voyage between islands.▼

Firefighter (1986) **C-100m. TVM** D: Robert Lewis. Nancy McKeon, Vince Irizarry, Barry Corbin, Amanda Wyss, James Whitmore, Jr., Ed Lauter. McKeon is real-life firefighter Cindy Fralick, the L.A. F.D.'s first woman member, and plays the part with pluck. Average.

Firefly, The (1937) **131m.** **½ D: Robert Z. Leonard. Jeanette MacDonald, Allan Jones, Warren William, Billy Gilbert, Henry Daniell, Douglass Dumbrille, George Zucco. Tried-and-true operetta moves slowly and goes on too long, but Jones' "Donkey Serenade" and Jeanette's vivacity remain enjoyable.

Firefox (1982) **C-124m.** *½ D: Clint Eastwood. Clint Eastwood, Freddie Jones, David Huffman, Warren Clarke, Ronald Lacey, Stefan Schnabel. Lamentably dull, slow-moving espionage yarn, with Eastwood as burned-out U.S. pilot who goes behind Russian lines to steal the Soviets' latest aeronautic marvel: a supersonic fighting plane. Jones wins the Charles Laughton Award for Eccentric Performances. Originally released at 137m.▼

Firehouse (1972) **C-73m. TVM** D: Alex March. Richard Roundtree, Vince Edwards, Andrew Duggan, Richard Jaeckel, Val Avery, Paul Le Mat. Tense situation develops when, after death of fireman, fire station accepts black rookie (Roundtree) as probational replacement. Resolution barely makes it, thanks to unusually fine combination of stock footage and studio work. Pilot for short-lived TV series. Above average.

Fire in the Sky, A (1978) **C-150m. TVM** D: Jerry Jameson. Richard Crenna, Elizabeth Ashley, David Dukes, Joanna Miles, Lloyd Bochner, Andrew Duggan. Disaster flick about a comet hurtling toward Phoenix, Arizona, is blessed with striking special effects and miniature work to offset the tedium of the multicharacter plot. Average.

Fire Maidens of Outer Space (1955-British) **80m.** BOMB D: Cy Roth. Anthony Dexter, Susan Shaw, Paul Carpenter, Harry Fowler, Sydney Tafler. Ultracheap space opera about astronauts who land on Jupiter's 13th moon and discover a society of young lovelies in need of male companionship (that's the polite term). Another in the So Bad It's Good Sweepstakes; you haven't lived until you've seen the Fire Maidens perform their ritual dance to "Stranger in Paradise."

Fireman Save My Child (1932) **67m.** ** D: Lloyd Bacon. Joe E. Brown, Evalyn Knapp, Lillian Bond, Guy Kibbee, Virginia Sale. Amusing Brown romp with Joe dividing his time between fire-fighting and baseball.

Fireman Save My Child (1954) **80m.** *½ D: Leslie Goodwins. Spike Jones, The

City Slickers, Buddy Hackett, Hugh O' Brian, Adele Jergens. Sloppy slapstick with Spike Jones et al manning fire station in 1900s San Francisco, running amuck when they receive a new fire engine. Originally intended for Abbott and Costello, who are still visible in some long shots.

Firemen's Ball, The (1968-Czech) **C-73m.** ** D: Milos Forman. Jan Vostrcil, Josef Sehanek, Josef Valnoha, Josef Kolb, Vaclav Stockel. Acclaimed comedy of small-town firemen's ball which turns into sprawling disaster apparently has elusive charm that completely escaped us.▼

Fire on the Mountain (1981) **C-100m. TVM** D: Donald Wrye. Ron Howard, Buddy Ebsen, Julie Carmen, Rossie Harris, Michael Conrad, Ed Brodow, Gary Graham, Will Hare. Crusty old-timer is joined by young land-speculator in his fight to hold onto the property the Army wants for a missile base. John Sacret Young's script was based on Edward Abbey's 1962 book. Average.

Fire Over Africa (1954) **C-84m.** ** D: Richard Sale. Maureen O'Hara, Macdonald Carey, Binnie Barnes, Guy Middleton, Hugh McDermott. O'Hara makes a pretty law enforcer traveling to Africa to track down dope-smuggling syndicate. Filmed on location.

Fire Over England (1937-British) **89m.** *** D: William K. Howard. Laurence Olivier, Flora Robson, Leslie Banks, Raymond Massey, Vivien Leigh, Tamara Desni, Morton Selten, Robert Newton, Donald Calthrop. Nice historical drama of British-Spanish conflict in 1500s with flawless performance by Robson (Queen Elizabeth), fine villainy by Massey, romantic support by Olivier and Leigh. Watch for James Mason in a small (unbilled) role.▼

Firepower (1979-British) **C-104m.** **½ D: Michael Winner. Sophia Loren, James Coburn, O. J. Simpson, Eli Wallach, Anthony Franciosa, George Grizzard, Vincent Gardenia, Victor Mature. Another international all-star action thriller, with beautiful people in beautiful locations (this time, the Caribbean). Inane, complicated story has Loren seeking revenge for murder of her chemist husband. Passable timefiller, especially on TV.▼

Fire Sale (1977) **C-88m.** BOMB D: Alan Arkin. Alan Arkin, Rob Reiner, Vincent Gardenia, Anjanette Comer, Kay Medford, Sid Caesar, Barbara Dana, Byron Stewart, Richard Libertini. Wretched black comedy about a department store owner and his two sons gives bad taste a bad name. Truly unbearable.

Fires on the Plain (1959-Japanese) **105m.** ***½ D: Kon Ichikawa. Eiji Funakoshi, Mantaro Ushio, Yoshihiro Hamaguchi, Osamu Takizawa. Japanese soldiers struggle to survive at the finale of the Philippine campaign during WW2; focus is on travails of tubercular Funakoshi, separated from his unit. Graphically realistic, disturbing, and depressing vision of damnation on earth, with a sobering antiwar message.▼

Firestarter (1984) **C-115m.** ** D: Mark L. Lester. David Keith, Drew Barrymore, George C. Scott, Martin Sheen, Heather Locklear, Art Carney, Louise Fletcher, Moses Gunn, Freddie Jones. Silly, sometimes laughable yarn about little girl whose parents acquired unusual mental powers as a result of a government experiment and who herself can set anything on fire at will. Lumbering story wastes a lot of acting talent, though it certainly gave employment to a number of stunt people and special effects technicians. Based on Stephen King's best seller.▼

Firewalker (1986) **C-104m.** BOMB D: J. Lee Thompson. Chuck Norris, Lou Gossett, Melody Anderson, Will Sampson, Sonny Landham, John Rhys-Davies, Ian Abercrombie. Anderson, hair perfectly intact throughout, hires Gossett and fellow mercenary Norris to find a hidden cache of loot she's imagined exists. Press releases described Norris' character as a "soldier-of-wacky-misfortune"; his light comedy skills recall a sportswriter's description of Yogi Berra playing third base—"like a man trying to put up a pup tent in a windstorm." Arguably Chuck's worst—but who wants to argue? ▼

Fire With Fire (1986) **C-103m.** **½ D: Duncan Gibbins. Craig Sheffer, Virginia Madsen, Jon Polito, Jeffrey Jay Cohen, Kate Reid, Jean Smart. Story of a forbidden love affair between a boy imprisoned at a juvenile detention facility and girl who *feels* imprisoned at Catholic girl's school nearby. Seems to move slowly, since there are no real surprises, but the leads are appealing and it's pleasant enough to watch . . . until ludicrous finale. Film buffs should note Ann Savage in the small role of Sister Harriet.▼

Fire Within, The (1963-French) **108m.** ***½ D: Louis Malle. Maurice Ronet, Lena Skerla, Yvonne Clech, Hubert Deschamps, Jeanne Moreau, Alexandra Stewart. Shattering study of alcoholism, as wealthy Ronet, released from a sanitarium after a breakdown, visits his old friends in Paris one last time. Probably Malle's best early film—photographed, scored (by Erik Satie), and acted to maximum effect—and with a minimum of self-pity.

First Affair (1983) **C-100m. TVM** D: Gus Trikonis. Loretta Swit, Melissa Sue Anderson, Joel Higgins, Kim Delaney, Amanda Bearse, Robin Morse. Romantic nonsense for soap wallowers. College freshman Anderson seduces English professor

Swit's husband after being hired as their baby-sitter. Below average.▼

First Blood (1982) **C-97m.** *½ D: Ted Kotcheff. Sylvester Stallone, Richard Crenna, Brian Dennehy, David Caruso, Jack Starrett. Ex-Green Beret is falsely arrested by smalltown cops, escapes and leads his pursuers into all kinds of booby traps in the "jungles" of the American Northwest. Throws all credibility to the winds about the time he gets off with only a bad cut after jumping from a mountain into some jagged rocks. And a kewpie doll to anyone who can understand more than three words of Sly's final monologue. Followed by RAMBO: FIRST BLOOD PART II.▼

Firstborn (1984) **C-103m.** ** D: Michael Apted. Teri Garr, Peter Weller, Christopher Collet, Corey Haim, Sarah Jessica Parker. Divorced mom is doing her best to raise two sons—until she lets her latest boyfriend (a real lout) move into the house and take over. Credible, if unappealing, drama leads to repellent conclusion, à la DEATH WISH, putting to waste the film's good qualities and performances.▼

First Comes Courage (1943) **88m.** **½ D: Dorothy Arzner. Merle Oberon, Brian Aherne, Carl Esmond, Fritz Leiber, Erik Rolf. Fairly good wartime film of Norwegian Oberon using her feminine wiles to extract secrets from Nazi officer.

First Deadly Sin, The (1980) **C-112m.** *** D: Brian G. Hutton. Frank Sinatra, Faye Dunaway, David Dukes, Brenda Vaccaro, Martin Gabel, James Whitmore. Sinatra's first starring feature after 10-year absence finds him in good form in adaptation of Lawrence Sanders' best-seller about an N.Y.C. cop who stalks a psycho during his wife's illness. Dunaway's near-comatose role couldn't be more thankless, but good supporting cast and moody Gordon Jenkins score make this one of Frank's better serious vehicles.▼

First Family (1980) **C-104m.** ** D: Buck Henry. Bob Newhart, Gilda Radner, Madeline Kahn, Richard Benjamin, Bob Dishy, Harvey Korman, Rip Torn, Austin Pendleton, Fred Willard, Julius Harris, Buck Henry. Almost laughless political satire, written by Henry, with Newhart a bumbling U.S. President, Kahn his inebriated First Lady, Radner their horny First Daughter. However, Newhart's conversation with African Ambassador Harris is a gem.▼

First Lady (1937) **82m.** *** D: Stanley Logan. Kay Francis, Anita Louise, Verree Teasdale, Preston Foster, Walter Connolly, Victor Jory, Louise Fazneda. Witty adaptation of the acerbic George S. Kaufman-Katherine Dayton play, with Francis as the ambitious wife of the Secretary of State (Foster), whom she's pushing into presidential campaign against corrupt judge

Connolly. Not very cinematic, but brightly acted by fine ensemble.

First Legion, The (1951) **86m.** *** D: Douglas Sirk. Charles Boyer, William Demarest, Lyle Bettger, Barbara Rush. Engrossing low-key account of Jesuit priest who is dubious about an alleged miracle occurring in his town. Boyer gives one of his best performances.▼

First Love (1939) **84m.** *** D: Henry Koster. Deanna Durbin, Robert Stack, Helen Parrish, Eugene Pallette, Leatrice Joy, Marcia Mae Jones, Frank Jenks. Charming Cinderella story of orphaned girl (Durbin) going to live with uncle and finding romance with Stack (in his film debut). Durbin sings "Amapola" and other songs; her first screen kiss (courtesy Stack) made headlines around the world.

First Love (1958-Italian) **103m.** ** D: Mario Camerini. Carla Gravina, Raf Mattioli, Lorella De Luca, Luciano Marin. Simple, unengrossing account of the pangs of adolescent love.

First Love (1970-British-French-Swiss) **C-90m.** *** D: Maximilian Schell. John Moulder-Brown, Dominique Sanda, Maximilian Schell, John Osborne. Original, often moving story of young lovers is total concept of Schell. While his direction often wanders, his script is extremely good.▼

First Love (1977) **C-92m.** ** D: Joan Darling. William Katt, Susan Dey, John Heard, Beverly D'Angelo, Robert Loggia, Swoosie Kurtz. Youthful romance between right-thinking college boy and girl who's involved with older man; muddled film with unsatisfying conclusion.▼

First Man Into Space (1959-British) **77m.** ** D: Robert Day. Marshall Thompson, Marla Landi, Robert Ayres, Bill Nagy, Carl Jaffe, Bill Edwards. Daring pilot, brother of hero, disobeys orders and becomes the title character, returning to Earth a dust-encrusted, blood-drinking monster. Better than it sounds.▼

First Men in the Moon (1964-British) **C-103m.** *** D: Nathan Juran. Edward Judd, Martha Hyer, Lionel Jeffries, Erik Chitty. Lavish adaptation of H. G. Wells novel is heavy-handed at times, overloaded with comic relief, but still worthwhile; good Ray Harryhausen special effects. Cameo appearance by Peter Finch.▼

First Monday in October (1981) **C-98m.** **½ D: Ronald Neame. Walter Matthau, Jill Clayburgh, Barnard Hughes, James Stephens, Jan Sterling, Joshua Bryant. Talky but OK adaptation of Jerome Lawrence–Robert E. Lee stage hit about Tracy-and-Hepburn-like clash of wills between first female member of the Supreme Court (a staunch conservative) and the most liberal of her brethren. Lost some of its novelty when it happened for real just before film was released, but still amusing; *Paper Chase* fans will enjoy Stephens virtually reprising his Hart role as Matthau's law clerk.▼

First Name: Carmen (1983-French-Swiss) **C-85m.** *** D: Jean-Luc Godard. Maruschka Detmers, Jacques Bonnaffe, Myriem Roussel, Christophe Odent, Jean-Luc Godard. Title character is a femme fatale, terrorist, and aspiring filmmaker, and Godard plays her uncle, a famous but "sick" and "washed-up" director named Jean-Luc Godard. Funny and compelling, if you like Godard's later work and can appreciate his point of view; otherwise, it will seem like a waste of time and celluloid.▼

First Nudie Musical, The (1976) **C-100m.** ** D: Mark Haggard, Bruce Kimmel. Stephen Nathan, Cindy Williams, Bruce Kimmel, Diana Canova, Alexandra Morgan, Leslie Ackerman. Basically a one-joke idea that wears thin despite an air of amiability: a desperate young filmmaker (Nathan) tries to rescue his studio by making a porno musical, complete with production numbers such as "Dancing Dildos." Best contributions come from those who keep their clothes on. Kimmel also scripted and wrote most of the songs.▼

First Power, The (1990) **C-99m.** *½ D: Robert Resnikoff. Lou Diamond Phillips, Tracy Griffith, Jeff Kober, Mykel T. Williamson, Elizabeth Arlen, Dennis Lipscomb. Cat-and-mouse battle between an L.A. cop and the spirit of an executed Devil's disciple who has the ability to pop in and out of other people's bodies. Very weak supernatural horror that fails to frighten, or offer anything fresh. Griffith is Melanie Griffith's half-sister.

First Spaceship on Venus (1960-German) **C-78m.** ** D: Kurt Maetzig. Yoko Tani, Oldrich Lukes, Ignacy Machowski, Julius Ongewe. Expedition goes to Venus following clues left by alien ship that exploded on Earth years before. They discover war-blasted landscape and still operating machines. Well produced but stilted. International coproduction was cut by an hour in the U.S., explaining the incoherent story line. From novel by Europe's most significant sci-fi writer, Stanislaw Lem, who repudiated the film.▼

First Steps (1985) **C-100m. TVM** D: Sheldon Larry. Judd Hirsch, Amy Steel, Kim Darby, Frances Lee McCain, John Pankow, James B. Sikking. A woman paralyzed in an auto accident and a dedicated bioengineer, who has been experimenting with computerized muscle "brains," team up to make her walk again. Inspired by the *60 Minutes* profile of Dr. Jerrold Petrofsky and one of his patients, Nan Davis. Average.

First Texan, The (1956) **82m.** **½ D: Byron Haskin. Joel McCrea, Felicia Farr, Jeff Morrow, Wallace Ford. McCrea is forceful as Sam Houston, leading Texans

in fight against Mexico for independence; good action sequences.

First 36 Hours of Dr. Durant, The (1975) **C-78m. TVM** D: Alexander Singer. Scott Hylands, Lawrence Pressman, Katherine Helmond, Dana Andrews, Renne Jarrett, Michael Conrad, Peter Donat, David Doyle. Idealistic surgical resident Hylands, during his first hectic 36 hours on call, confronts the realities of medical ethics with a life and a career at stake. Not bad, although the AMA might argue both the point and Stirling Silliphant's script. Average.

First Time, The (1952) **89m.** ** D: Frank Tashlin. Robert Cummings, Barbara Hale, Jeff Donnell, Mona Barrie, Cora Witherspoon. Predictable comedy pegged on young couple's many problems with raising a baby.

First Time, The (1969) **C-90m.** *½ D: James Neilson. Jacqueline Bisset, Wes Stern, Rick Kelman, Wink Roberts, Gerald Parkes. Combination of *Ozzie and Harriet* and WALK ON THE WILD SIDE concerns a teen-ager's sexual initiation. Artificial look at adolescence.▼

First Time, The (1982) **C-100m. TVM** D: Noel Nosseck. Susan Anspach, Jennifer Jason Leigh, Peter Barton, Edward Winter, Michael McKenzie, John Anderson, Krista Errickson, Harriet Nelson. Desperate mother clashes with teenaged daughter over their sexual mores, and can't understand why the youngster has run off with her boyfriend while she herself is looking for someone to bed down with. Average.

First Time, The (1983) **C-95m.** *** D: Charlie Loventhal. Tim Choate, Krista Errickson, Marshall Efron, Wendy Fulton, Raymond Patterson, Wallace Shawn, Wendie Jo Sperber, Cathryn Damon. Surprisingly intelligent, funny portrait of virginal, movie-loving college freshman Choate. A cut above other films of its type, and a promising debut for young Loventhal, a protege of Brian De Palma.▼

First To Fight (1967) **C-97m.** **½ D: Christian Nyby. Chad Everett, Marilyn Devin, Dean Jagger, Bobby Troup, Claude Akins, Gene Hackman. Conventional WW2 yarn with Everett the one-time hero who almost loses his courage on the battlefield.

First Traveling Saleslady, The (1956) **C-92m.** ** D: Arthur Lubin. Ginger Rogers, Barry Nelson, Carol Channing, David Brian, James Arness, Clint Eastwood. Rogers and Channing try to elevate this plodding comedy of girdle-sellers in the old West, but barely succeed. Carol and Clint make one of the oddest couples in screen history.

First Yank Into Tokyo (1945) **82m.** ** D: Gordon Douglas. Tom Neal, Barbara Hale, Marc Cramer, Richard Loo, Keye Luke, Leonard Strong, Benson Fong. Low-budget quickie made to be topical isn't so anymore, and it's not too good either; Neal undergoes plastic surgery, poses as Japanese soldier to help American POW escape.▼

First, You Cry (1978) **C-100m. TVM** D: George Schaefer. Mary Tyler Moore, Anthony Perkins, Richard Crenna, Jennifer Warren, Florence Eldridge, Don Johnson. Well-intentioned and well-received but curiously unenthralling dramatization of news correspondent Betty Rollin's book about her mastectomy, providing Moore with her first meaty dramatic role. Average.

Fish Called Wanda, A (1988) **C-108m.** **½ D: Charles Crichton. John Cleese, Jamie Lee Curtis, Kevin Kline, Michael Palin, Maria Aitken, Tom Georgeson, Patricia Hayes, Geoffrey Palmer. Fitfully funny farce about an uptight British barrister who becomes involved with a sexy con artist (Curtis), her mindlessly macho boyfriend (Kline), and their ambitious bank robbery and getaway scheme. Less outrageous than most Monty Python films, but Cleese's script still makes sure to include enough bad-taste gags to either repel or delight his audience, depending on one's personal point of view. Kline won an Oscar for his flamboyant comic performance.▼

Fish Hawk (1980-Canadian) **C-95m.** ** D: Donald Shebib. Will Sampson, Charlie Fields, Geoffrey Bowes, Mary Pirle, Don Francks, Chris Wiggins. Bland family film about an alcoholic Indian who tries to mend his ways—and becomes a companion to an impressionable young farm boy. This is the kind of unchallenging, inoffensive fare that gives G-rated movies a bad reputation.▼

Fish that Saved Pittsburgh, The (1979) **C-102m.** *½ D: Gilbert Moses. Julius Erving, James Bond III, Stockard Channing, Jonathan Winters, Margaret Avery, Jack Kehoe, Meadowlark Lemon, Nicholas Pryor, Flip Wilson, Kareem Abdul-Jabbar. Losing basketball team tries astrology to put them in winners' circle; low-grade comedy with disco soundtrack. Game hijinks are only saving grace.▼

F.I.S.T. (1978) **C-145m.** **½ D: Norman Jewison. Sylvester Stallone, Rod Steiger, Peter Boyle, Melinda Dillon, David Huffman, Tony Lo Bianco, Kevin Conway, Cassie Yates, Henry Wilcoxon, Brian Dennehy. Stallone's one-dimensional performance prevents this well-produced epic about a Hoffa-like labor kingpin from sustaining a strong first half. Peter Boyle does well with a role inspired by former Teamster boss Dave Beck.▼

Fistful of Chopsticks, A SEE: **They Call Me Bruce?**▼

✓ **Fistful of Dollars, A** (1964-Italian) **C-96m.** *** D: Sergio Leone. Clint Eastwood, Gian Maria Volonté, Marianne Koch, Wolfgang Lukschy, Mario Brega, Carol Brown. Sagebrush remake of YOJIMBO single-handedly invented the "spaghetti Western," made an international superstar of Eastwood, and boosted the careers of Leone and composer Ennio Morricone as well. Clint plays the laconic Man With No Name, a tough gunslinger manipulating (and manipulated by!) two rival families warring over small frontier town. Amusing, violent, and very stylish. Released in the U.S. in 1967. Sequel: FOR A FEW DOLLARS MORE.▼

Fistful of Dynamite, A SEE: **Duck, You Sucker**▼

Fist in His Pocket (1966-Italian) **105m.** **** D: Marco Bellochio. Lou Castel, Paola Pitagora, Marino Mase, Liliana Gerace, Pier Luigi Troglio. Brilliant one-of-a-kind about a mad family of epileptics whose protagonist kills his mother and drowns his younger brother, while his sis merely settles for repressed incest. One of the great, if largely unheralded, foreign films of the 60s, with Castel more than up to the demands of the difficult role.

Fist of Fear, Touch of Death (1980) **C-90m.** *½ D: Matthew Mallinson. Fred Williamson, Ron Van Clief, Adolph Caesar, Aaron Banks, Bill Louis. Boring chopsocky film chronicling the happenings at a Madison Square Garden martial arts tournament. Highlighted are short clips of legendary Bruce Lee.▼

Fist Right of Freedom SEE: **Fox and His Friends**▼

Fists of Fury (1972-Chinese) **C-103m.** ** ✓ D: Lo Wei. Bruce Lee, Miao Ker Hsiu, James Tien, Robert Baker. Kung Fu actioner finds honorable Bruce Lee defending honor by destroying world. Very violent.▼

Fitzcarraldo (1982) **C-157m.** **** D: Werner Herzog. Klaus Kinski, Claudia Cardinale, Jose Lewgoy, Miguel Angel Fuentes, Paul Hittscher. Vivid, fascinating portrait of a man obsessed (made by a man obsessed—see BURDEN OF DREAMS) who's determined to capture a shipping route on the Amazon, even though it means hauling a boat over a mountaintop, through hostile tribal territory. Then he's going to bring in grand opera! Astonishing and captivating movie, in spite of its length; admittedly not to everyone's taste.▼

Fitzwilly (1967) **C-102m.** **½ D: Delbert Mann. Dick Van Dyke, Barbara Feldon, Edith Evans, John McGiver, Harry Townes, John Fiedler, Norman Fell, Cecil Kellaway, Sam Waterston. Ordinary fluff about butler who has to rob Gimbel's on Christmas Eve to save his employer. Van Dyke's screen career was hurt by too many films like this one. Film debuts of Feldon and Waterston.

Five (1951) **93m.** *** D: Arch Oboler. ✓ William Phipps, Susan Douglas, James Anderson, Charles Lampkin, Earl Lee. Intriguing, offbeat film by famed radio writer-director Oboler about the survivors of a nuclear holocaust. Talky (and sometimes given to purple prose) but interesting. Filmed in and around Oboler's Frank Lloyd Wright home.

5 Against the House (1955) 84m. *** D: Phil Karlson. Guy Madison, Kim Novak, Brian Keith, Kerwin Mathews, William Conrad, Alvy Moore. "Perfect crime" caper has five friends set out to rob Reno, Nevada casino. Execution of robbery, along with gorgeous Novak, keep this film rolling along.

Five Angles on Murder SEE: **Woman in Question**

Five Ashore in Singapore SEE: **Singapore, Singapore**

Five Bloody Graves SEE: **Gun Riders**▼

5 Branded Women (1960) 106m. ** D: Martin Ritt. Van Heflin, Silvana Mangano, Jeanne Moreau, Vera Miles, Barbara Bel Geddes, Carla Gravina. Overambitious production, badly miscast, set in WW2 Middle Europe. Five girls scorned by partisans for consorting with Nazis prove their patriotism.

Five Came Back (1939) 75m. *** D: John Farrow. Chester Morris, Lucille Ball, Wendy Barrie, John Carradine, Allen Jenkins, Joseph Calleia, C. Aubrey Smith, Patric Knowles. This sleeper shows its age a bit, but remains interesting for colorful character studies among passengers on plane downed in Amazon jungle. Remade by Farrow as BACK FROM ETERNITY.▼

Five Card Stud (1968) C-103m. *½ D: Henry Hathaway. Dean Martin, Robert Mitchum, Inger Stevens, Roddy McDowall, Katherine Justice. Dino is a gambler and Mitchum virtually repeats his NIGHT OF THE HUNTER role in surprisingly disappointing Western; Maurice Jarre's Dr. Zhivago-on-the-range musical score doesn't help. Probably Hathaway's worst Western.▼

Five Corners (1988) C-92m. *** D: Tony Bill. Jodie Foster, Tim Robbins, Todd Graff, John Turturro, Elizabeth Berridge, Rose Gregorio, Gregory Rozakis, John Seitz. Moody piece about young people whose lives converge in a Bronx neighborhood in 1964. One of them, just released from prison, stirs trouble for the others. Unexpectedly melodramatic (which displeased some viewers) but potent and believable . . . and the only 1960s period film in recent memory not to flood the soundtrack with hit records in order to spark memories of that time. James Newton Howard's appropriately moody score is much more effective, anyway. Written by John Patrick Shanley.▼

Five Day Lover SEE: **Time Out for Love**
Five Days from Home (1978) C-109m. ** D: George Peppard. George Peppard, Neville Brand, Savannah Smith, Sherry Boucher, Victor Campos, Robert Donner.

Peppard breaks out of Louisiana prison, determined to reach L.A. and see his hospitalized son. Well-intentioned but improbable film.

Five Days One Summer (1983) C-108m. ** D: Fred Zinnemann. Sean Connery, Betsy Brantley, Lambert Wilson, Jennifer Hilary, Isabel Dean, Gerald Buhr, Anna Massey. Middle-aged man brings a young woman—ostensibly his wife—on Swiss vacation in the early 1930s where their hesitant relationship is explored against the natural drama of mountain climbing. Adaptation of a Kay Boyle story doesn't come off, despite impeccable production. Slow, ethereal, ultimately unsatisfying. Edited to 93m. for TV by director Zinnemann.▼

Five Desperate Women (1971) C-73m. TVM D: Ted Post. Robert Conrad, Anjanette Comer, Bradford Dillman, Joan Hackett, Denise Nicholas, Stefanie Powers. Forced character-study thriller has five female graduates of Brindley College reunited on rented island mansion stalked by mental hospital escapee. Typical newdangers-every-second approach can't hide formula plot. Average.

Five Easy Pieces (1970) C-98m. **** D: Bob Rafelson. Jack Nicholson, Karen Black, Billy Green Bush, Fannie Flagg, Susan Anspach, Sally Struthers, Ralph Waite. Brilliant character study of musician with great promise who gave up a career to work on an oil rig. Nicholson's performance is superb, but Black, Anspach, and Bush all contribute heavily. Helena Kallianiotes is hilarious as a malcontent hitchhiker. Beautifully written by Adrien Joyce (Carol Eastman).▼

Five Finger Exercise (1962) 109m. **½ D: Daniel Mann. Rosalind Russell, Jack Hawkins, Maximilian Schell, Richard Beymer, Lana Wood, Annette Gorman. Peter Shaffer's play suffers from change of locale and alteration of original ideas; now it becomes embarrassing soap opera of possessive mother in love with daughter's tutor. Stars are miscast but try their best.

Five Fingers (1952) 108m. *** D: Joseph L. Mankiewicz. James Mason, Danielle Darrieux, Michael Rennie, Walter Hampden, Richard Loo. Polished espionage film is endowed with fine Mason performance as unsuspected spy working for Germans during WW2.

Five Fingers of Death (1973-Chinese) C-102m. *½ D: Cheng Chang Ho. Lo Lieh, Wang Ping, Wang Ching-Feng. Only interesting in that it is the Kung Fu film that began the craze in America. Family honor defended with every part of the body except the mouth, which is horrendously dubbed.

Five Gates to Hell (1959) 98m. *½ D: James Clavell. Neville Brand, Benson Fong,

Shirley Knight, Ken Scott, John Morley, Dolores Michaels, Nancy Kulp, Irish McCalla. Overly melodramatic plot of American nurses captured by Chinese mercenaries and the various ordeals they undergo.

Five Golden Dragons (1967-British) **C-93m.** ** D: Jeremy Summers. Bob Cummings, Margaret Lee, Maria Perschy, Brian Donlevy, Christopher Lee, George Raft, Dan Duryea. Cummings is naive American caught up in international crime in Hong Kong; a most conventional actioner, not saved by veteran guest stars.▼

Five Golden Hours (1961-British) **90m.** **½ D: Mario Zampi. Ernie Kovacs, Cyd Charisse, George Sanders, Kay Hammond, Dennis Price. Comedy mishmash wavering between satire and slapstick as con man plots to utilize a witch to bedevil rich victims.

Five Graves to Cairo (1943) **96m.** ***½ D: Billy Wilder. Franchot Tone, Anne Baxter, Akim Tamiroff, Erich von Stroheim, Peter Van Eyck, Fortunio Bonanova. WW2 intrigue situated in Sahara oasis hotel run by Tamiroff and Baxter; Tone attempts to obtain secrets from visiting Field Marshal Rommel (von Stroheim). Billy Wilder-Charles Brackett script manages to incorporate wit and humor into genuinely exciting wartime yarn. A remake of HOTEL IMPERIAL.

Five Guns West (1955) **C-78m.** ** D: Roger Corman. John Lund, Dorothy Malone, Touch (Mike) Connors, Jack Ingram. Fair Corman western, which he co-scripted, about a group of Rebel soldiers who hold up a Yankee stagecoach. This was Corman's first film as director.

500 Pound Jerk, The (1972) **C-73m.** TVM D: William Kronick. James Franciscus, Alex Karras, Hope Lange, Howard Cosell, Victor Spinetti, Claudia Butenuth. Odd mixture of comedy and realism in lumpy tale of Olympic weight-lifter falling in love with Soviet athlete. Average.

Five Man Army, The (1970) **C-107m.** *½ D: Don Taylor. Peter Graves, James Daly, Bud Spencer, Tetsuro Tamba, Nino Castelnuovo. Ordinary adventure piece about five men who try to rob gold shipment being delivered to Mexican dictator in 1913; film is no WILD BUNCH.

Five Miles to Midnight (1963) **110m.** **½ D: Anatole Litvak. Tony Perkins, Sophia Loren, Gig Young, Jean-Pierre Aumont, Pascale Roberts. Jumbled murder mystery with Perkins convincing wife Loren to collect insurance money when it's thought he's been killed, with ironic results.

Five Million Years to Earth (1968-British) **C-98m.** *** D: Roy Ward Baker. James Donald, Barbara Shelley, Andrew Keir, Julian Glover, Maurice Good. Workers unearth spaceship and remains of alien crew in modern-day London. Good cast, great script complications, and suspense in fine example of what can be done on meager budget. Only subject matter will turn some viewers off. Originally released as QUATERMASS AND THE PIT, and far superior to the earlier QUATERMASS films; known in the U.S. as THE CREEPING UNKNOWN and ENEMY FROM SPACE. Followed by QUATERMASS CONCLUSION.

Five Minutes to Live SEE: **Door-to-Door Maniac**▼

Five of Me, The (1981) **C-100m.** TVM D: Paul Wendkos. David Birney, Dee Wallace, Mitchell Ryan, John McLiam, James Whitmore, Jr., Ben Piazza, Judith Chapman. Birney goes two up on Joanne Woodward in this male version of THE THREE FACES OF EVE, based on Henry Hawksworth's autobiographical book about how he battled four alter egos living in his body. Average.▼

Five on the Black Hand Side (1973) **C-96m.** **½ D: Oscar Williams. Clarice Taylor, Leonard Jackson, Virginia Capers, D'Urville Martin, Glynn Turman, Godfrey Cambridge. Black family comedy about patriarchal barber was once refreshing amidst many black exploitation films, now seems foolish.

Five Pennies, The (1959) **C-117m.** **½ D: Melville Shavelson. Danny Kaye, Barbara Bel Geddes, Tuesday Weld, Louis Armstrong, Bob Crosby, Harry Guardino, Ray Anthony, Shelley Manne, Bobby Troup. Danny plays jazz trumpeter Red Nichols in this sentimental biography. Only bright spots are musical numbers, especially duets with Kaye and Armstrong.

Five Star Final (1931) **89m.** *** D: Mervyn LeRoy. Edward G. Robinson. H. B. Warner, Marian Marsh, George E. Stone, Ona Munson, Boris Karloff, Aline MacMahon. Powerful drama of sensationalist newspaper sometimes falls apart with bad acting by second leads, but editor Robinson and unscrupulous reporter Karloff make it a must. Remade as TWO AGAINST THE WORLD.

Five Steps to Danger (1957) **80m.** ** D: Henry S. Kesler. Ruth Roman, Sterling Hayden, Werner Klemperer, Richard Gaines. By-now clichéd spy drama, enhanced by Roman and Hayden.

5,000 Fingers of Dr. T., The (1953) **C-88m.** *** D: Roy Rowland. Peter Lind Hayes, Mary Healy, Tommy Rettig, Hans Conried. Largely ignored, one of Hollywood's best fantasies, devised by Dr. Seuss. Boy has nightmare about cruel piano teacher (Conried) ruling over land where kidnapped youngsters are forced to play the piano. Song numbers slow action.

$5.20 an Hour Dream, The (1980) **C-**

100m. TVM D: Russ Mayberry. Linda Lavin, Richard Jaeckel, Nicholas Pryor, Pamela McMyler, Mayf Nutter. Feminist blue-collar drama, not dissimilar to NORMA RAE, about a divorced mother determined to get a higher-paying factory job on the traditionally all-male assembly line. Predictable at every turn. Average.

Five Weeks in a Balloon (1962) **C-101m.** **½** D: Irwin Allen. Red Buttons, Barbara Eden, Fabian, Cedric Hardwicke, Peter Lorre, Richard Haydn, Barbara Luna. Innocuous entertainment with formula script from Jules Verne tale of balloon expedition to Africa. Buoyed by fine cast, including veterans Billy Gilbert, Herbert Marshall, Reginald Owen, Henry Daniell.▼

Fixed Bayonets (1951) **92m.** **½** D: Samuel Fuller. Richard Basehart, Gene Evans, Michael O'Shea, Richard Hylton, Craig Hill. Taut Korean War drama of platoon cut off from the rest of its outfit; typical tough Fuller production. James Dean is one of the soldiers.

Fixer, The (1968) **C-132m.** **½** D: John Frankenheimer. Alan Bates, Dirk Bogarde, Georgia Brown, Hugh Griffith, Ian Holm, Jack Gilford, Elizabeth Hartman, David Warner, Carol White. Good acting helps, but Bernard Malamud's acclaimed novel fails on the screen; story of unjustly imprisoned Jewish handyman in turn-of-the-century Russia concerns itself too much with the thoughts of its main character to be effective as film.

Flame, The (1947) **97m.** ** D: John H. Auer. Vera Ralston, John Carroll, Robert Paige, Broderick Crawford, Henry Travers, Constance Dowling. Routine story of woman falling in love with intended victim of blackmail plot.

✓ **Flame and the Arrow, The** (1950) **C-88m.** *** D: Jacques Tourneur. Burt Lancaster, Virginia Mayo, Robert Douglas, Aline MacMahon, Nick Cravat. Bouncy, colorful action with Lancaster romping through his gymnastics as rebel leader in medieval Italy leading his people on to victory. Mayo is gorgeous heroine.▼

Flame and the Flesh, The (1954) **C-104m.** ** D: Richard Brooks. Lana Turner, Pier Angeli, Carlos Thompson, Bonar Colleano, Charles Goldner, Peter Illing. Pointless Turner vehicle filmed in Europe involving brunette Lana being romanced by continental Thompson, which causes a lot of misery.

Flame Barrier, The (1958) **70m.** *½ D: Paul Landres. Arthur Franz, Kathleen Crowley, Robert Brown, Vincent Padula. A satellite downed in jungle is discovered embedded in an ultra-hot alien organism. Fair cast tries hard in ineffectual story.

Flame Is Love, The (1979) **C-100m. TVM** D: Michael O'Herlihy. Linda Purl, Shane Briant, Timothy Dalton, Richard Johnson,

Joan Greenwood, Paul Lavers. Florid romantic melodrama about American heiress' encounters with love and intrigue in Paris while traveling to England to marry her sweetheart at the turn of the century. Perfunctory acting mars the filming of Barbara Cartland's popular novel. Average.▼

Flame of Araby (1951) **C-77m.** **½** D: Charles Lamont. Maureen O'Hara, Jeff Chandler, Maxwell Reed, Susan Cabot. O'Hara, looking fetching as ever, rides through this costumer of the Far East, involving battle over a prize horse.

Flame of Barbary Coast (1945) **91m.** **½** D: Joseph Kane. John Wayne, Ann Dvorak, Joseph Schildkraut, William Frawley, Virginia Grey. Hick rancher competes with slick Schildkraut for savvy saloon singer Dvorak; undemanding fluff, with Republic Pictures' version of the San Francisco earthquake.▼

Flame of Calcutta (1953) **C-70m.** *½ D: Seymour Friedman. Denise Darcel, Patric Knowles, Paul Cavanagh. Darcel champions her people's cause in this costumer set in India in 1750. Low-grade nonsense.

Flame of New Orleans, The (1941) **78m.** *** D: René Clair. Marlene Dietrich, Bruce Cabot, Roland Young, Laura Hope Crews, Mischa Auer, Andy Devine. Dietrich turns up in New Orleans and can have her pick of any man in town, can't decide between wealthy Young or hard-working Cabot. Picturesque, entertaining, Clair's first American film.

Flame of Stamboul (1951) **68m.** *½ D: Ray Nazarro. Richard Denning, Lisa Ferraday, Norman Lloyd, Nestor Paiva. Programmer about espionage in ancient title city.

Flame of the Islands (1955) **C-90m.** ** D: Edward Ludwig. Yvonne De Carlo, Howard Duff, Zachary Scott, Kurt Kasznar, Barbara O'Neil. Caribbean scenery and sultry De Carlo provide most of the spice in this tale of a cafe singer and the men who fall in love with her.▼

Flame Over India (1959-British) **C-130m.** *** D: J. Lee Thompson. Lauren Bacall, Kenneth More, Herbert Lom, Wilfrid Hyde-White. Fast-paced actioner set on northern frontier of India as British soldiers accompanied by governess Bacall seek to speed an Indian prince to safety aboard a run-down train. Originally titled NORTHWEST FRONTIER.

Flame Within, The (1935) **71m.** ** D: Edmund Goulding. Ann Harding, Herbert Marshall, Maureen O'Sullivan, Louis Hayward. Tired story of unrequited love. Young woman psychiatrist falls in love with patient, despite fact that she knows could never succeed.

Flaming Feather (1951) **C-?** Ray Enright. Sterling Hayden, Fc er, Barbara Rush, Arleen Whelan. Rousing Western as vigilantes rescue white woman from renegade Indians.

Flaming Frontier (1958-Canadian) **70m.** *½ D: Sam Newfeld. Bruce Bennett, Jim Davis, Paisley Maxwell, Cecil Linder, Peter Humphreys. Indian war is averted by half-breed army officer; very cheap Western.

Flamingo Kid, The (1984) **C-100m.** *** D: Garry Marshall. Matt Dillon, Richard Crenna, Hector Elizondo, Jessica Walter, Fisher Stevens, Janet Jones, Bronson Pinchot. Very likable film set in 1963, about a Brooklyn boy from a working-class family whose head is turned by a slick sharpie who holds court at the beach club where he works. Crenna, cast against type, scores a bull's-eye as the fat cat (and catches a glimpse of himself in *The Real McCoys* while testing his remote control TV in one scene). Nice coming-of-age story written by Neal Marshall (no relation to director Garry).▼

Flamingo Road (1949) **94m.** *** D: Michael Curtiz. Joan Crawford, Zachary Scott, Sydney Greenstreet, David Brian, Gertrude Michael, Gladys George. Crawford is excellent as tough carnival dancer ditched in small town where she soon is loving Scott and Brian and matching wits with corrupt politician Greenstreet. Remade as a TVM.

Flamingo Road (1980) **C-100m. TVM** D: Gus Trikonis. John Beck, Cristina Raines, Howard Duff, Morgan Fairchild, Kevin McCarthy, Barbara Rush, Mark Harmon, Stella Stevens, Woody Brown, Melba Moore, Dianne Kay, Mason Adams. Fair remake of the Joan Crawford oldie about the haves and the have-nots in a small Florida town into which an attractive carnival drifter stumbles. The TV series spun off from this version. Average.

Flaming Star (1960) **C-101m.** *** D: Don Siegel. Elvis Presley, Barbara Eden, Steve Forrest, Dolores Del Rio, John McIntire. Elvis is excellent as a half-breed Indian who must choose sides when his mother's people go on the warpath. No songs after the first ten minutes but lots of action; along with JAILHOUSE ROCK, Presley's best film.▼

Flap (1970) **C-106m.** ** D: Carol Reed. Anthony Quinn, Claude Akins, Tony Bill, Victor Jory, Shelley Winters. Uneven story of Indian outcast. You're supposed to pity Flapping Eagle, but script is so weak that the chances are you won't. At times funny, but supposedly tragic in its implications.

Flareup (1969) **C-100m.** **½ D: James Neilson. Raquel Welch, James Stacy, Luke Askew, Don Chastain, Ron Rifkin, Jeane Byron. Go-go dancer Raquel gets stalked from Las Vegas to L.A. by psychopathic ex-husband of friend who blames her for breakup of the marriage. Fast melodrama is helped by good location footage.

Flash and the Firecat (1975) **C-84m.** *½ D: Ferd and Beverly Sebastian. Roger Davis, Tricia Sembera, Dub Taylor, Richard Kiel, Joan Shawlee, Philip Bruns. Road-company Bonnie and Clyde try for one big heist; film's only novelty is the characters' use of dune buggies for transportation.▼

Flashback (1990) **C-108m.** *½ D: Franco Amurri. Dennis Hopper, Kiefer Sutherland, Carol Kane, Cliff De Young, Paul Dooley, Michael McKean, Richard Masur. Young straight-arrow FBI agent (Sutherland) is ordered to transport a recently captured "underground" political fugitive to the scene of his 60s' crime—disruption of a Spiro Agnew rally. Enervatingly predictable until its (surprisingly) bloody finale, though it's encouraging to see Hopper trim and in such fighting shape. Masur and McKean, who seem to be winging it, amuse as onetime political activists now trapped in a middle-class environment.▼

Flashdance (1983) **C-96m.** **½ D: Adrian Lyne. Jennifer Beals, Michael Nouri, Lilia Skala, Sunny Johnson, Kyle T. Heffner, Belinda Bauer. How to turn a rock video into a feature-length film—with glitzy images, high energy, an arresting music score (principally by Giorgio Moroder), and the stupidest story this side of Busby Berkeley. Still, this concoction about a girl with the perfect fantasy life (macho welder by day, sexy dancer by night, courted by the rich and handsome boss, watched over by a patron-saint ballerina) seemed to please a lot of people. Title song (by Moroder, Irene Cara, and Keith Forsey) won an Oscar.▼

Flash Gordon (1936) SEE: **Spaceship to the Unknown**▼

Flash Gordon (1980) **C-110m.** *** D: Mike Hodges. Sam J. Jones, Melody Anderson, Topol, Max von Sydow, Ornella Muti, Brian Blessed, Timothy Dalton, Mariangela Melato. Updated version of comic strip is better than expected, thanks to eye-filling production/costume design by Danilo Donati, amusing rock score by Queen. Jones and Anderson are liabilities as Flash and Dale Arden, but Muti's evil Princess Aura (who would make any male stray from Right) leads a strong supporting cast.▼

Flash Gordon Conquers the Universe SEE: **Purple Death from Outer Space**▼
Flash Gordon: Mars Attacks the World SEE: **Deadly Ray from Mars, The**
Flash Gordon's Trip to Mars SEE: **Deadly Ray From Mars, The**▼

Flash of Green, A (1984) **C-131m.** ** D: Victor Nunez. Ed Harris, Blair Brown, Richard Jordan, George Coe, Helen Stenborg, John Glover. Reporter in a small Florida coastal town gets in over his head when he plays footsie with a scheming county commissioner who's behind a shady land-fill development racket. Capable performances and refreshingly offbeat subject matter are eventually negated by the long running time and plot redundancies in the final third. Made for *American Playhouse* and produced by costar Jordan. Based on John D. MacDonald's book.▼

Flashpoint (1984) **C-94m.** ** D: William Tannen. Kris Kristofferson, Treat Williams, Rip Torn, Kevin Conway, Miguel Ferrer, Jean Smart, Roberts Blossom, Tess Harper. Two maverick Texas Border Patrol officers stumble into volatile territory when they discover a cache of money that figures in a long-dormant mystery. Intriguing overall premise (and good cast) defeated by uninteresting presentation. Bonus: the worst title song of 1984 (sung over closing credits).▼

Flatbed Annie & Sweetiepie: Lady Truckers (1979) **C-100m. TVM** D: Robert Greenwald. Annie Potts, Kim Darby, Harry Dean Stanton, Arthur Godfrey, Rory Calhoun, Billy Carter. Like the title says, with Potts and Darby as a pair of resourceful women acting like a pair of good ol' boys to keep their expensive rig out of the clutches of repossessors as well as hijackers. Video title: FLATBED ANNIE. Average.▼

Flatfoot SEE: **Knock Out Cop, The**▼

Flatliners (1990) **C-105m.** **½ D: Joel Schumacher. Kiefer Sutherland, Julia Roberts, Kevin Bacon, William Baldwin, Oliver Platt, Kimberly Scott. Offbeat but sophomoric supernatural drama (with touches of horror and humor) about medical students experimenting with life after death. Slick camerawork and effects can't camouflage the superficiality of the script, which undermines an intriguing idea.

Flat Top (1952) **C-83m.** **½ D: Lesley Selander. Sterling Hayden, Richard Carlson, Bill Phipps, Keith Larsen. Well-paced WW2 film of training of aircraft-carrier fighter pilots. Film integrates news footage successfully.▼

Flaxy Martin (1949) **86m.** **½ D: Richard Bare. Virginia Mayo, Zachary Scott, Dorothy Malone, Tom D'Andrea, Helen Westcott, Elisha Cook, Jr. Smooth melodrama of lawyer framed by client on a murder charge.

Flea in Her Ear, A (1968-U.S.-French) **C-94m.** ** D: Jacques Charon. Rex Harrison, Rosemary Harris, Louis Jourdan, Rachel Roberts. Unfunny farce about philandering barrister. Some of the slapstick gags go on interminably.

Fleet's In, The (1942) **93m.** *** D: Victor Schertzinger. Dorothy Lamour, William Holden, Betty Hutton, Eddie Bracken, Rod Cameron, Leif Erickson, Jimmy Dorsey Orchestra with Helen O'Connell, Bob Eberle. Bright wartime musical with reputed romeo Holden trying to melt iceberg Lamour. Bracken and Hutton (in her feature debut) provide laughs. Specialty numbers by Gil Lamb, Cass Daley; songs include "Tangerine," "I Remember You," title tune. Remake of 1936 LADY BE CAREFUL, remade as SAILOR BEWARE.

Flesh (1932) **95m.** *** D: John Ford. Wallace Beery, Karen Morley, Ricardo Cortez, Jean Hersholt, Herman Bing, John Miljan. Unusual, melancholy drama with Beery as simple-minded German wrestler in love with Morley—who tries to hide her shady relationship with no-good Cortez.

Flesh & Blood (1951-British) **102m.** ** D: Anthony Kimmins. Richard Todd, Glynis Johns, Joan Greenwood, Andre Morell, Freda Jackson, James Hayter, George Cole, Michael Hordern. Turbulent study of generations of family life, focusing on clashes and romances of parents and children. Set in Scotland.

Flesh & Blood (1979) **C-200m. TVM** D: Jud Taylor. Tom Berenger, Mitchell Ryan, Kristin Griffith, Denzel Washington, Suzanne Pleshette, John Cassavetes, Bert Remsen, Dolph Sweet. The rise and fall of a young street tough who becomes a heavyweight contender. Based on Pete Hamill's best seller (screenplay by Eric Bercovici), spiced with incest subplot, stunningly filmed by Vilmos Zsigmond. Originally shown in two parts. Above average.

Flesh + Blood (1985) **C-126m.** ** D: Paul Verhoeven. Rutger Hauer, Jennifer Jason Leigh, Tom Burlinson, Jack Thompson, Susan Tyrrell, Ronald Lacey, Brion James, Bruno Kirby. Rowdy adventure set in 16th century: Leigh is betrothed to young Prince Burlinson but falls into clutches of Hauer and his motley band of warriors. Plenty of flesh *and* blood, but it's all rather foul and nasty; Verhoeven (in his first American English-language effort) *does* score points for sheer audaciousness.▼

Flesh and Desire (1955-French) **94m.** ** D: Jean Josipovici. Rossano Brazzi, Viviane Romance, Peter Van Eyck, Jean-Paul Roussillon. Turgid farm romance tale of virile Brazzi's appearance setting into motion jealousy and murder.

Flesh and Fantasy (1943) **93m.** *** D: Julien Duvivier. Charles Boyer, Edward G. Robinson, Barbara Stanwyck, Robert Benchley, Betty Field, Robert Cummings, Thomas Mitchell, Charles Winninger. Three-part film of supernatural linked by Benchley; Field is ugly girl turned beauty by Cummings' love; Robinson's life is chang-by fortune-teller Mitchell; Boyer is chic circus star haunted by Stanwyck inson sequence, based on Oscar *Lord Arthur Saville's Crime,* interesting. Coproduced by L Boyer. A fourth episode was o fore release and subsequently expanded into a feature titled DESTINY.

Flesh and Flame SEE: **Night of the Quarter Moon**

Flesh and Fury (1952) **82m.** **½ D: Joseph Pevney. Tony Curtis, Jan Sterling, Mona Freeman, Wallace Ford, Harry Guardino. Curtis gives presentable performance as deaf prizefighter who seeks to regain hearing and love of decent girl.

Flesh and the Devil (1927) **112m.** *** D: Clarence Brown. John Gilbert, Greta Garbo, Lars Hanson, Barbara Kent, William Orlamond, George Fawcett, Eugenie Besserer. Garbo at her most seductive as temptress who comes between old friends Gilbert and Hanson. Pulsatingly romantic, beautifully filmed, probably the best Garbo-Gilbert love match. But talk about surprise endings!▼

Flesh and the Woman (1953-French-Italian) **C-102m.** ** D: Robert Siodmak. Gina Lollobrigida, Jean-Claude Pascal, Arletty, Raymond Pellegrin, Peter Van Eyck. Whole film is Lollobrigida, who plays dual roles; a Parisian whose corrupt ways cause her husband to join the Foreign Legion, and a lookalike prostitute in Algiers. Remake of Jacques Feyder's 1934 French film LE GRAND JEU.

Flesh Eaters, The (1964) **87m.** *½ D: Jack Curtis. Rita Morley, Martin Kosleck, Byron Sanders, Barbara Walken. Group trapped on island with deranged scientist is attacked by tiny but plentiful creatures that eventually make a giant monster. Occasionally tense, but gruesome and generally boring. Longer version on video.▼

Flesh Feast (1970) **C-72m.** BOMB D: B. F. Grinter. Veronica Lake, Phil Philbin, Heather Hughes, Chris Martell, Martha Mischon. Lake's final film (which she coproduced) is embarrassing, amateurish gorefest, likely to become a camp classic. As a mad scientist working on rejuvenation, she tortures Hitler to death at film's climax (maggots eat at his face in close-up), then addresses us directly, shouting a patriotic, anti-Nazi diatribe left over from THE GREAT DICTATOR.▼

Flesh for Frankenstein SEE: **Andy Warhol's Frankenstein**▼

Fletch (1985) **C-96m.** **½ D: Michael Ritchie. Chevy Chase, Dana Wheeler-Nicholson, Tim Matheson, Joe Don Baker, Richard Libertini, Geena Davis, M. Emmet Walsh, George Wendt, Kenneth Mars. Chase plays a smart-ass undercover reporter (with a penchant for disguises) who goes after major drug ring. Good mystery absolutely smothered in wisecracks, some funny, some tiresome; if you're not a fan of Chevy, stay clear! Watchable but never credible. Screenplay by Andrew Bergman from Gregory McDonald's novel. Followed by a sequel.▼

Fletch Lives (1989) **C-95m.** ** D: Michael Ritchie. Chevy Chase, Hal Holbrook, Julianne Phillips, Cleavon Little, R. Lee Ermey, Richard Libertini, Randall (Tex) Cobb, George Wyner, Patricia Kalember, Geoffrey Lewis, Richard Belzer. Chase returns as Fletch, the L.A. reporter with the multi-personality, in this silly sequel. He finds himself in Louisiana, dealing with a parade of stereotypical Southern morons. For diehard Chase fans only.▼

Flicks (1987) **C-76m.** BOMB D: Peter Winograd. Pamela Sue Martin, Joan Hackett, Martin Mull, Betty Kennedy, Paula Victor, Richard Belzer, Lincoln Kilpatrick. Lame homage to old films is structured as a night out at the movies, complete with coming attractions, cartoon, serial segments, and main feature. Unfunny writing sinks it all, with only mild diversions offered by a "Tom & Jerry" cartoon parody and a HOWARD THE DUCK forerunner about an alien moth pursuing a Bogart-type detective case on Earth. Filmed in 1981 but never released theatrically.▼

Flight (1929) **116m.** **½ D: Frank Capra. Jack Holt, Ralph Graves, Lila Lee, Alan Roscoe, Harold Goodwin, Jimmy de la Cruze. Dated story of battling buddies in the Marine flying corps, with some still-impressive aerial sequences. Costar Graves wrote the original story.

Flight Command (1940) **116m.** ** D: Frank Borzage. Robert Taylor, Ruth Hussey, Walter Pidgeon, Paul Kelly, Nat Pendleton, Shepperd Strudwick, Red Skelton, Dick Purcell. Hackneyed story with good cast as upstart Taylor tries to make the grade in naval flight squadron.

Flight Commander SEE: **Dawn Patrol, The** (1930)

Flight for Freedom (1943) **99m.** **½ D: Lothar Mendes. Rosalind Russell, Fred MacMurray, Herbert Marshall, Eduardo Ciannelli, Walter Kingsford. Pseudo-biography of Amelia Earhart has dynamic Russell as aviatrix whose devotion to flying alienates her from MacMurray.

Flight from Ashiya (1964) **C-100m.** ** D: Michael Anderson. Yul Brynner, Richard Widmark, George Chakiris, Suzy Parker, Shirley Knight. Slow movie dealing with three aviators in rescue attempt over Pacific. Big name cast will attract; stiff script.

Flight from Destiny (1941) **73m.** *** D: Vincent Sherman. Geraldine Fitzgerald, Thomas Mitchell, Jeffrey Lynn, James Stephenson, Mona Maris, Jonathan Hale. Well-acted tale of Mitchell, with short time to live, helping young couple by clearing young Lynn of charges brought against him; Fitzgerald a joy as Lynn's wife.

Flight Lieutenant (1942) **80m.** *½ D: Sidney Salkow. Pat O'Brien, Glenn Ford, Evelyn Keyes, Minor Watson, Larry Parks,

Lloyd Bridges, Hugh Beaumont. Commander Watson has sore memories of Ford's father (O'Brien), making life difficult; tired programmer.

Flight #90: Disaster on the Potomac (1984) **C-100m.** TVM D: Robert Michael Lewis. Richard Masur, Stephen Macht, Dinah Manoff, Donnelly Rhodes, Barry Corbin, Jamie Rose. Fairly engrossing dramatization of the fatal 1982 plane crash in Washington, D.C. A disaster movie that relies more on tension than familiar TV faces, and that gives it an edge. Average.

Flight Nurse (1954) **90m.** *½ D: Allan Dwan. Joan Leslie, Forrest Tucker, Jeff Donnell, Arthur Franz, Ben Cooper. Trite romantic triangle set against Korean War backdrop.

Flight of the Doves (1971-British) **C-105m.** ** D: Ralph Nelson. Ron Moody, Jack Wild, Dorothy McGuire, Stanley Holloway, Helen Raye, William Rushton. Calculated cuteness mars tale of two Liverpool children who flee to Ireland to visit their grandmother; good cast isn't seen to best advantage.

Flight of the Eagle, The (1982-Swedish) **C-139m.** *** D: Jan Troell. Max von Sydow, Goran Stangertz, S. A. Ousdal, Eva von Hanno. Beautifully shot true story about a foolhardy but heroic balloon mission to the North Pole in 1897 strives to become its country's national film epic, but falls short of greatness. Stays in the memory, however, despite the fact that the second half of a lengthy running time deals only with three men freezing to death in the snow. Simultaneously filmed as a miniseries for Swedish TV. An Oscar nominee for Best Foreign Film.▼

Flight of the Lost Balloon (1961) **C-91m.** *½ D: Nathan Juran. Marshall Thompson, Mala Powers, James Lanphier, Douglas Kennedy. Potentially interesting adventure drowns in low-budget telling of Thompson using balloon transport to travel across African wasteland to find missing explorer.

Flight of the Navigator (1986) **C-90m.** **½ D: Randal Kleiser. Joey Cramer, Veronica Cartwright, Cliff De Young, Sarah Jessica Parker, Matt Adler, Howard Hesseman. 12-year-old boy is whisked away by an alien spaceship and returns home eight years later—still a 12-year-old boy. That's when the adventure really begins. Yet another film featuring a youthful hero and a cute robot; adequate entertainment for kids. The voice of the robot, billed as Paul Mall, is actually Paul Reubens, a.k.a. Pee-wee Herman. ▼

✓ **Flight of the Phoenix** (1966) **C-147m.** ***½ D: Robert Aldrich. James Stewart, Richard Attenborough, Peter Finch, Hardy Kruger, Ernest Borgnine, Ian Bannen, Ronald Fraser, Christian Marquand, Dan Duryea, George Kennedy. A plane crash leaves a group of men stranded in the Arabian desert; film avoids clichés as tension mounts among the men. Stewart as the captain, Attenborough as the navigator stand out in uniformly fine cast.▼

Flight to Fury (1966) **76m.** ** D: Monte Hellman. Dewey Martin, Fay Spain, Jack Nicholson, Jacqueline Hellman, Vic Diaz. Odd group of adventurers headed for Philippines location and hidden diamonds when plane crashes. Low-budgeter has its points, but never really comes across. Initially released at 62 minutes, later reedited. ▼

Flight to Holocaust (1977) **C-100m.** TVM D: Bernard Kowalski. Patrick Wayne, Christopher Mitchum, Desi Arnaz, Jr., Sid Caesar, Rory Calhoun, Lloyd Nolan, Paul Williams, Fawne Harriman. Professional troubleshooters involved in freeing passengers of private plane that crashed and lodged in side of skyscraper. Contrived disaster-rescue tale with several second-generation film personalities competing with ludicrous special effects. Below average.

Flight to Hong Kong (1956) **88m.** ** D: Joseph M. Newman. Rory Calhoun, Barbara Rush, Dolores Donlon, Soo Yong. Standard fare of gangster in Far East preterring Rush to his smuggler friends; it almost costs him his life.

Flight to Mars (1951) **C-72m.** ** D: Lesley Selander. Marguerite Chapman, Cameron Mitchell, Virginia Huston, Arthur Franz. Adequate sci-fi about scientists and newspapermen who land on Mars and discover a lost civilization. Special effects hampered by modest budget.▼

Flight to Nowhere (1946) **75m.** BOMB D: William Rowland. Evelyn Ankers, Alan Curtis, Jack Holt, Jerome Cowan, Micheline Cheirel, John Craven, Inez Cooper, Hoot Gibson. Ultracheap, ultraboring account of former federal agent Curtis, who against his will becomes involved in an effort to recover a map of uranium deposits.▼

Flight to Tangier (1953) **C-90m.** **½ D: Charles Marquis Warren. Joan Fontaine, Jack Palance, Corinne Calvet, Robert Douglas. Fast-paced drama involving a cache of money aboard plane that has crashed, and the assorted people chasing after the loot.

Flim Flam Man, The (1967) **C-115m.** ✓ *** D: Irvin Kershner. George C. Scott, Sue Lyon, Michael Sarrazin, Harry Morgan, Jack Albertson, Alice Ghostley, Albert Salmi, Slim Pickens. Scott is engaging as a veteran Southern con-man who takes on young Sarrazin as apprentice in his travels, but finds the novice a bit too honest. Entertaining comedy.▼

Flipper (1963) **C-90m.** **½ D: James ✓ Clark. Chuck Connors, Luke Halpin, Kathleen Maguire, Connie Scott. Typical wholesome family fare about a boy who befriends a dolphin; kids will certainly enjoy it. Spun off into later TV series.▼

Flipper's New Adventure (1964) **C-103m.** ** D: Leon Benson. Luke Halpin, Pamela Franklin, Helen Cherry, Tom Helmore, Brian Kelly. Further exploits of everybody's favorite dolphin: Flipper and Halpin thwart escaped convicts' efforts to blackmail millionaire Helmore. Pleasant, inoffensive fare for kids, filmed in the Bahamas and Key Biscayne.

Flirtation Walk (1934) **97m.** **½ D: Frank Borzage. Dick Powell, Ruby Keeler, Pat O'Brien, Ross Alexander, Guinn Williams, Henry O'Neill. West Point plot is clichéd and trivial as usual as cadet Powell falls in love with officer's daughter Keeler; some fairly good numbers highlighted by "Mr. and Mrs. Is The Name."

Flirting with Fate (1938) **69m.** ** D: Frank McDonald. Joe E. Brown, Leo Carrillo, Beverly Roberts, Wynne Gibson, Steffi Duna, Stanley Fields, Charles Judels. Juvenile slapstick with Joe heading a vaudeville troupe stranded in South America. Carrillo fun as influential bandit, Duna's off-key singing good for a few laughs, but basically a weak comedy.

Floating Weeds (1959-Japanese) **C-119m.** ***½ D: Yasujiro Ozu. Ganjiro Nakamura, Machiko Kyo, Haruko Sugimura, Ayako Wakao. Struggling acting troupe visits remote island, where its leader (Nakamura) visits his illegitimate son and the boy's mother, with whom he had an affair years before. Powerful drama is meticulously directed, solidly acted. Ozu's first color film; he directed the same story, as a silent film, in 1934. Also known as DRIFTING WEEDS.▼

Flood! (1976) **C-100m. TVM** D: Earl Bellamy. Robert Culp, Martin Milner, Barbara Hershey, Richard Basehart, Carol Lynley, Roddy McDowall, Cameron Mitchell, Eric Olson, Teresa Wright. Cynical helicopter pilot Culp is pressed into reluctant service when a small town is devastated by a flood after a faulty dam bursts. Irwin Allen's first made-for-TV disaster movie, slick and predictable. Average.▼

Floods of Fear (1959-British) **82m.** ** D: Charles Crichton. Howard Keel, Anne Heywood, Cyril Cusack, Harry H. Corbett, John Crawford. Adequate drama about prisoner Keel on the lam, who performs heroic deeds during flood, later proving innocence and winning girl's love.

Flood Tide (1958) **82m.** **½ D: Abner Biberman. George Nader, Cornell Borchers, Michel Ray, Judson Pratt. Soapy mystery of an innocent man being convicted of murder on the say-so of a lame child, reputed to be a first-class liar.

Florodora Girl, The (1930) **80m.** *** D: Harry Beaumont. Marion Davies, Lawrence Gray, Walter Catlett, Louis John Bartels, Ilka Chase, Vivien Oakland, Jed Prouty, Sam Hardy. Charming piece of nostalgia with Marion only one of famed Floradora

Sextette of Gay 90s to spurn wealthy admirers and seek true love. Some scenes originally in color.

Florence Nightingale (1985) **C-150m. TVM** D: Daryl Duke. Jaclyn Smith, Claire Bloom, Timothy Dalton, Timothy West, Peter McEnery, Stephan Chase, Ann Thornton, Jeremy Brett. Flat portrait—with the accompanying folderol—of the legendary English noblewoman turned dedicated nurse in the Victorian Era. A lovingly photographed Smith gives it a decided go (her husband produced the film) with a mock English accent amid the remaining cast of true Britishers. Anna Neagle she's not. Average.

Florian (1940) **91m.** ** D: Edwin L. Marin. Robert Young, Helen Gilbert, Charles Coburn, Lee Bowman, Reginald Owen, Lucile Watson. Young and Gilbert, poor man and rich girl, marry, united by their love of horses.

Florida Special (1936) **70m.** ** D: Ralph Murphy. Jack Oakie, Sally Eilers, Kent Taylor, Frances Drake, J. Farrell MacDonald, Sam (Schlepperman) Hearn, Claude Gillingwater, Sidney Blackmer. Romance, mystery, and murder aboard southbound train. Song: "It's You I'm Talking About."

Florida Straits (1986) **C-97m. TVM** D: Mike Hodges. Raul Julia, Fred Ward, Daniel Jenkins, Jamie Sanchez, Victor Argo, Ilka Tanya Payan, Antonio Fargas. Julia leads a treasure hunt for gold buried in the Cuban jungle twenty years earlier during the Bay of Pigs invasion. Filmed on location in and around Myrtle Beach, S.C. Made for cable. Average.▼

Flower Drum Song (1961) **C-133m.** ** D: Henry Koster. Nancy Kwan, James Shigeta, Miyoshi Umeki, Juanita Hall, Benson Fong. Pleasant enough Rodgers and Hammerstein musical. No great songs, but listenable score and good choreography stringing together story of San Francisco's Chinatown. Major problem: it goes on too long.▼

Flower in His Mouth, The (1975-Italian) **C-113m.** *½ D: Luigi Zampa. Jennifer O'Neill, James Mason, Franco Nero, Orazio Orlando. O'Neill moves to small Italian town and finds its people paralyzed by fear, but unwilling to tell her why. Murky thriller isn't worth the time it takes to figure out.

Flowers in the Attic (1987) **C-95m.** ** D: Jeffrey Bloom. Louise Fletcher, Victoria Tennant, Kristy Swanson, Jeb Stuart Adams, Ben Granger, Lindsay Parker, Marshall Colt. Disappointing adaptation of the V.C. Andrews best-seller tones down the incest and sadomasochism of the story about four youngsters kept locked up by evil granny (Fletcher) in the family mansion. Material is strangely compelling nonetheless; benefits from effective casting.▼

Flowing Gold (1940) **82m.** **½ D: Alfred E. Green. John Garfield, Frances Farmer, Pat O'Brien, Raymond Walburn, Cliff

Edwards, Tom Kennedy. Dynamic Garfield in story that doesn't flow; standard fare in which he and O'Brien drill for oil and fight over Farmer.

Fluffy (1965) **C-92m. ** D: Earl Bellamy. Tony Randall, Shirley Jones, Edward Andrews, Ernest Truex, Howard Morris, Dick Sargent. Silly film dealing with professor Randall experimenting with a lion; he can't shake the beast, causing all sorts of repercussions, even winning Jones' affection.

Fly, The (1958) **C-94m. *** D: Kurt Neumann. Al (David) Hedison, Patricia Owens, Vincent Price, Herbert Marshall, Kathleen Freeman. Improbable but diverting sci-fi (screenplay by James Clavell!) about scientist who experiments with disintegration machine and has his atomic pattern traded with that of a fly. Memorable line: "Help me! Help me!" Two sequels—RETURN OF THE FLY and CURSE OF THE FLY. Remade in 1986.▼

Fly, The (1986) **C-100m. **½ D: David Cronenberg. Jeff Goldblum, Geena Davis, John Getz, Joy Boushel, Les Carlson. Goldblum is just right as slightly crazed scientist who tests himself in a genetic transporter machine—and starts to evolve into a human fly. Extremely intense, sharply written remake of the 1958 movie that (unfortunately) goes over the line to be gross and disgusting. Written by Charles Edward Pogue and director Cronenberg. An Oscar winner for makeup (Chris Walas, Stephan Dupuis). Followed by a sequel.▼

Fly II, The (1989) **C-104m. BOMB D: Chris Walas. Eric Stoltz, Daphne Zuniga, Lee Richardson, John Getz, Frank Turner, Ann Marie Lee, Gary Chalk, Saffron Henderson, Harley Cross, Matthew Moore. A case of "like father, like son"; too bad director Walas isn't like David Cronenberg. Stoltz, son of deceased Jeff Goldblum, has attained puberty at five with the intellect to match; now he's being unknowingly exploited by—here's a novel twist—the scientists in whose care he's entrusted. Alternately dull and messy but mostly dull; can Stoltz still move his neck muscles after having shlepped all that cranial makeup here and in MASK?▼

Fly Away Home (1981) **C-100m. TVM** D: Paul Krasny. Bruce Boxleitner, Tiana Alexandra, Michael Beck, Brian Dennehy, Lynne Moody, Olivia Cole, Edward Winter, Keye Luke. Writer-producer Stirling Silliphant's ambitious but unrewarding pilot for a weekly series about the Vietnam War as viewed by a combat cameraman and his cynical boss, head of a Saigon news bureau. Average.

Fly by Night (1942) **74m. **½ D: Robert Siodmak. Richard Carlson, Nancy Kelly, Albert Basserman, Walter Kingsford, Martin Kosleck, Miles Mander. Carlson is young doctor accused of murdering scientist who tracks down a Nazi spy ring in effort to clear himself. Fairly entertaining WW2 B propaganda, which aims for the Hitchcock style.

Flying (1986-Canadian) **C-94m. ** D: Paul Lynch. Olivia D'Abo, Rita Tushingham, Keanu Reeves, Jessica Steen, Renee Murphy. Minor imitation of FLASHDANCE has statuesque D'Abo overcoming a leg injury to become a medal-winning gymnast; Tushingham (with shocking carrot-colored hair) is her tough coach. This formula has whiskers, but D'Abo is easy to watch, even though her full figure is unconvincing for a gymnast.

Flying Aces SEE: Flying Deuces, The▼

Flying Deuces, The (1939) **65m. *** D: A. Edward Sutherland. Stan Laurel, Oliver Hardy, Jean Parker, Reginald Gardiner, Charles Middleton, James Finlayson. Stan and Ollie join the Foreign Legion so Ollie can forget unhappy romance; usual complications result. Good fun, faster paced than most L&H films, includes charming song and dance to "Shine On, Harvest Moon." Also known as FLYING ACES.▼

Flying Down to Rio (1933) **89m. *** D: Thornton Freeland. Dolores Del Rio, Gene Raymond, Raul Roulien, Ginger Rogers, Fred Astaire, Blanche Frederici, Eric Blore, Franklin Pangborn. Slim vehicle memorable for its scene of dancing girls cavorting on plane wings, plus Astaire and Rogers doing "The Carioca" in their first screen teaming.▼

Flying Fontaines, The (1959) **C-84m. **½ D: George Sherman. Michael Callan, Evy Norlund, Joan Evans, Joe De Santis, Roger Perry, Rian Garrick. Circus yarn involving egocentric high-wire artist Callan who covets one of the showgirls, and the repercussions involved.

Flying High (1931) **80m. **½ D: Charles F. Riesner. Bert Lahr, Charlotte Greenwood, Pat O'Brien, Kathryn Crawford, Charles Winninger, Hedda Hopper, Guy Kibbee. Dated, oddball comedy about harebrained inventor Lahr concocting an "aerocopter" machine; Lahr (in Hollywood debut) and Greenwood are fun together. Some De Sylva-Brown-Henderson songs carried over from Broadway production.

Flying High (1978) **C-97m. TVM** D: Peter Hunt. Kathryn Witt, Pat Klous, Connie Sellecca, Marcia Wallace, Jim Hutton. Middling comedy about airline stewardesses aloft and aground that spawned a brief series. Average.

Flying Irishman, The (1939) **72m. ** D: Leigh Jason. Douglas Corrigan, Paul Kelly, Robert Armstrong, Gene Reynolds. Routine biog, largely fictional, dealing with life of Douglas "Wrong Way" Corrigan.

Flying Leathernecks (1951) **C-102m. *** D: Nicholas Ray. John Wayne, Robert Ryan, Jay C. Flippen, Janis Carter, Don

Taylor, William Harrigan. Major Wayne is exceedingly tough on his Marines; executive officer Ryan thinks he should be a little nicer. Guess who wins this argument. Solid, if not especially original, WW2 actioner, with good aerial scenes and nice turn by Flippen as crafty sergeant.▼

Flying Missile, The (1950) 93m. ** D: Henry Levin. Glenn Ford, Viveca Lindfors, Henry O'Neill, Jerry Paris, Richard Quine. Clichéd WW2 story of commander Ford's attempt to modernize his fighting ship, with predictable results.

Flying Saucer, The (1950) 69m. *½ D: Mikel Conrad. Mikel Conrad, Pat Garrison, Russell Hicks, Denver Pyle. Pedestrian espionage tale set in Alaska; the lone flying saucer, disappointingly, is from Earth.▼

Flying Serpent, The (1946) 59m. ** D: Sherman Scott (Sam Newfield). George Zucco, Ralph Lewis, Hope Kramer, Eddie Acuff, Milton Kibbee. Zucco sole interest in B movie reminiscent of serials. Doctor protects Aztec treasure with prehistoric bird. Basically a remake of THE DEVIL BAT.

Flying Tigers (1942) 102m. *** D: David Miller. John Wayne, John Carroll, Anna Lee, Paul Kelly, Mae Clarke, Gordon Jones, James "Jimmie" Dodd. Good Wayne vehicle of famous Flying Tigers stationed in WW2 China. Exciting dog-fight scenes. Also shown in computer-colored version.▼

Flying Wild (1941) 62m. D: William West. Leo Gorcey, Bobby Jordan, Donald Haines, Joan Barclay, David Gorcey, Bobby Stone, Sunshine Sammy Morrison. SEE: **Bowery Boys** series.▼

FM (1978) C-104m. **½ D: John A. Alonzo. Michael Brandon, Martin Mull, Eileen Brennan, Cleavon Little, Cassie Yates, Alex Karras, Norman Lloyd, James Keach. Hip comedy (which could well have inspired TV's *WKRP*) about various conflicts at maverick radio station, chiefly against its profit-hungry parent company. More like a series of sketches than a movie, but film nicely captures feel of 70s L.A. and Mull (in his feature debut) is marvelous as the station's craziest dj. Good rock soundtrack, plus concert appearances by Linda Ronstadt, Jimmy Buffett, Tom Petty, and REO Speedwagon.

Fog, The (1980) C-91m. **½ D: John Carpenter. Adrienne Barbeau, Jamie Lee Curtis, Hal Holbrook, Janet Leigh, John Houseman, Tommy Atkins, Nancy Loomis, Charles Cyphers. Carpenter's follow-up to HALLOWEEN is a well-directed but obvious ghost story about a California coastal town cursed by a hundred-year-old shipwreck.▼

Fog Island (1945) 72m *½ D: Terry Morse. George Zucco, Lionel Atwill, Veda Ann Borg, Jerome Cowan, Sharon Douglas. Grade-B chiller situated at eerie mansion with usual gathering of people suspecting one another of murder and intrigue; Zucco and Atwill are potentially terrific team.▼

Fog Over Frisco (1934) 68m. **½ D: William Dieterle. Bette Davis, Lyle Talbot, Margaret Lindsay, Donald Woods, Henry O'Neill, Arthur Byron, Hugh Herbert, Alan Hale, William Demarest. Snappy melodrama of deceitful, thrill-a-minute party-girl Davis involved in stolen-securities scheme; stepsister Lindsay tries to help.

Folies Bergère (1935) 84m. *** D: Roy Del Ruth. Maurice Chevalier, Ann Sothern, Merle Oberon, Eric Blore, Ferdinand Munier. Entertainer Chevalier is asked to pose as aristocratic businessman, forcing him to temporarily desert fiery Sothern for elegant Oberon. Delightful musical is high-lighted by Busby Berkeleyish "Straw Hat" finale which won Dave Gould an Oscar for dance direction that year. Remade as THAT NIGHT IN RIO and ON THE RIVIERA.

Folies Bergère (1958-French) C-90m ** D: Henri Decoin. Jeanmaire, Eddie Constantine, Nadia Gray, Yves Robert. Slim plot allows for expansive cafe production numbers in tale of American crooner in Paris who almost loses wife when she becomes more successful in show biz than he.

Folks at Red Wolf Inn, The SEE: **Terror House** (1972)▼

Follow a Star (1960-British) 93m. *½ D: Robert Asher. Norman Wisdom, Jerry Desmonde, June Laverick. Flabby slapstick musical involving zany Wisdom as a cleaning store worker who is stagestruck.

Follow Me, Boys! (1966) C-131m. **½ D: Norman Tokar. Fred MacMurray, Vera Miles, Lillian Gish, Charlie Ruggles, Elliott Reid, Kurt Russell. Mile-high Disney corn about simple fellow who settles in small town during 1930s and starts Boy Scout troop, devoting his life to this inspiring pursuit. A little less syrup would have helped, but at least it's done with great conviction.▼

Follow Me Quietly (1949) 59m. *** D: Richard Fleischer. William Lundigan, Dorothy Patrick, Jeff Corey, Nestor Paiva, Charles D. Brown, Paul Guilfoyle. Solid little *film noir* about police manhunt for self-righteous psychopathic killer called The Judge. Packs style and substance into just 59 minutes.▼

Follow That Bird SEE: **Sesame Street Presents Follow That Bird**▼

Follow That Camel (1967-British) C-95m. **½ D: Gerald Thomas. Phil Silvers, Jim Dale, Peter Butterworth, Charles Hawtrey, Kenneth Williams, Anita Harris, Joan Sims. Silvers as conniving sergeant livens up otherwise standard CARRY ON outing with Foreign Legion setting.▼

Follow That Dream (1962) C-110m. **½ D: Gordon Douglas. Elvis Presley, Arthur

O'Connell, Anne Helm, Joanna Moore, Jack Kruschen, Simon Oakland. Presley and family move to southern Florida where they intend to homestead, despite all opposition. Easy-going comedy based on Richard Powell's *Pioneer Go Home*. Elvis sings "Home Is Where the Heart Is" and "On Top of Old Smokey"!▼

Follow That Woman (1945) **69m.** ** D: Lew Landers. Nancy Kelly, William Gargan, Regis Toomey, Ed Gargan, Byron Barr, Pierre Watkin. Predictable murder yarn, heightened by Kelly's sincerity as woman implicated in murder, Gargan her husband trying to solve case.

Follow the Boys (1944) **122m.** *** D: A. Edward Sutherland. Marlene Dietrich, George Raft, Orson Welles, Vera Zorina, Dinah Shore, W. C. Fields, Jeanette MacDonald, Maria Montez, Andrews Sisters, Sophie Tucker, Nigel Bruce, Gale Sondergaard. Universal Pictures' entry in all-star WW2 series has Raft organizing USO shows, Welles sawing Dietrich in half, MacDonald singing "Beyond The Blue Horizon," Fields doing classic pool-table routine, etc. Lots of fun.

Follow the Boys (1963) **C-95m.** ** D: Richard Thorpe. Connie Francis, Paula Prentiss, Ron Randell, Janis Paige, Russ Tamblyn. Dumb comedy unspiked by Francis' singing or antics as quartet of girls chase around the French Riviera seeking husbands.

Follow the Fleet (1936) **110m.** **** D: Mark Sandrich. Fred Astaire, Ginger Rogers, Randolph Scott, Harriet Hilliard (Nelson), Astrid Allwyn, Betty Grable. Delightful musical with sailors Astaire and Scott romancing sisters Rogers and Hilliard. Irving Berlin songs include "Let's Face the Music and Dance," "Let Yourself Go," "We Saw the Sea." A reworking of SHORE LEAVE, a 1925 Richard Barthelmess silent comedy, and the 1930 musical HIT THE DECK. That's Lucille Ball as Kitty.▼

Follow the Leader (1944) **64m.** D: William Beaudine. Leo Gorcey, Huntz Hall, Gabriel Dell, Joan Marsh, Mary Gordon, J. Farrell MacDonald, Billy Benedict. SEE: **Bowery Boys** series.

Follow the Sun (1951) **93m.** **½ D: Sidney Lanfield. Glenn Ford, Anne Baxter, Dennis O'Keefe, June Havoc. Fictionalized sports biography of golfer Ben Hogan with hokey dramatics to fill in lean spots.

Follow Your Dreams SEE: **Independence Day**▼

Folly to Be Wise (1952-British) **91m.** *** D: Frank Launder. Alastair Sim, Elizabeth Allan, Roland Culver, Martita Hunt. Generally amusing nonsense with Sim an Army chaplain trying to enliven service life with various unique entertainment programs.

Food of the Gods (1976) **C-88m.** ** D: Bert I. Gordon. Marjoe Gortner, Pamela Franklin, Ida Lupino, Jon Cypher, Ralph Meeker, Belinda Belaski. Fair-to-middling adaptation of H. G. Wells novel. Strange substance causes giant growth in wasps, worms, chickens and rats. Not for the squeamish. A remake of VILLAGE OF THE GIANTS, filmed by Gordon 11 years earlier.▼

Fool for Love (1985) **C-106m.** ** D: Robert Altman. Sam Shepard, Kim Basinger, Harry Dean Stanton, Randy Quaid. Altman's inventive direction tries to breathe life into what is ultimately a photographed play, Shepard's examination of two ex-lovers who find themselves inextricably bound together. Biggest problem is generating some level of interest in these characters. Very much of a piece with Shepard's other work; if you're a fan, you might adjust our rating upward.▼

Foolin' Around (1980) **C-111m.** ** D: Richard T. Heffron. Gary Busey, Annette O'Toole, Cloris Leachman, Eddie Albert, John Calvin, Tony Randall. Dumb 1950s-style comedy about a good-hearted klutz who pursues a wealthy girl, despite the fact that she's already engaged. Cardboard characters and clumsy slapstick.▼

Foolish Wives (1922) **107m.** *** D: Erich von Stroheim. Erich von Stroheim, Maud George, Mae Busch, Cesare Gravina, Malvine Polo. Von Stroheim's third film as director is a typically sophisticated, fascinating tale of seduction, fake counts, blackmail, suicide, lechery, and murder. Great photography by William Daniels and Ben Reynolds, and an incredible set depicting the Monte Carlo casino designed by von Stroheim and Richard Day.▼

Fool Killer, The (1965) **100m.** *** D: Servando Gonzalez. Anthony Perkins, Edward Albert, Dana Elcar, Henry Hull, Salome Jens, Arnold Moss. Set in post-Civil War South, film relates unusual adventures of runaway orphan (Albert) and his meeting with strange young man (Perkins). Interesting and offbeat.▼

Fools (1970) **C-97m.** BOMB D: Tom Gries. Jason Robards, Katharine Ross, Scott Hylands, Roy C. Jenson, Mark Bramhall. Wretchedly acted, written, and directed drama about love affair in San Francisco between horror movie star and beautiful, neglected wife of a lawyer. Story line is vaguely similar to PETULIA but the execution certainly isn't.▼

Fools for Scandal (1938) **81m.** **½ D: Mervyn LeRoy. Carole Lombard, Fernand Gravet, Ralph Bellamy, Allen Jenkins, Isabel Jeans, Marie Wilson. Generally a misfire, despite lovely Lombard as movie star who meets impoverished nobleman Gravet in Paris; Bellamy plays the sap again.

Fools' Parade (1971) **C-98m.** ** D: Andrew V. McLaglen. James Stewart, George Kennedy, Anne Baxter, Strother Martin, Kurt Russell, William Windom, Kathy Cannon. Another great Stewart performance can't save melodramatic treatment of Davis Grubb novel. Story of three ex-cons stalked by their former prison guard is unintentionally funny too many times to be taken seriously.

Footlight Glamour (1943) **75m.** D: Frank Strayer. Penny Singleton, Arthur Lake, Larry Simms, Ann Savage, Jonathan Hale, Thurston Hall. SEE: **Blondie** series.

Footlight Parade (1933) **104m.** ***½ D: Lloyd Bacon. James Cagney, Joan Blondell, Ruby Keeler, Dick Powell, Guy Kibbee, Ruth Donnelly, Hugh Herbert, Frank McHugh. Cagney plays a stage director who tries to outdo himself with spectacular musical numbers. Fast-paced Warner Bros. opus winds up with three incredible Busby Berkeley numbers back-to-back: "Honeymoon Hotel," "By a Waterfall," and "Shanghai Lil."▼

Footlight Serenade (1942) **80m.** *** D: Gregory Ratoff. Betty Grable, Victor Mature, John Payne, Jane Wyman, Phil Silvers, James Gleason, Mantan Moreland, Cobina Wright, Jr. Cute backstage musical with cocky boxer Mature turning to Broadway and trying to woo Grable, who's secretly engaged to Payne. Good fun.▼

Footloose (1984) **C-107m.** **½ D: Herbert Ross. Kevin Bacon, Lori Singer, John Lithgow, Dianne Wiest, Christopher Penn, Sarah Jessica Parker, John Laughlin, Elizabeth Gorcey, Frances Lee McCain. City kid moves to small town where dancing has been outlawed—and confronts hellfire minister (Lithgow) in effort to bring it back. Too much emphasis on hackneyed story in so-called musical (though the soundtrack did spawn a number of Top 10 hits). Bacon's charisma sparks innocuous film.▼

Footsteps (1972) **C-73m. TVM** D: Paul Wendkos. Richard Crenna, Joanna Pettet, Forrest Tucker, Clu Gulager, Ned Beatty, Allen Garfield, James Woods, Robert Carradine. OK study of monstrous Crenna arriving at success-starved college as assistant football coach, determined to eliminate all opposition. Good performances by entire cast, interesting point of view. Teleplay by Alvin Sargent and Robert E. Thompson from the novel *Paddy* by Hamilton Maule. Above average. Also titled: NICE GUYS FINISH LAST.

Footsteps in the Dark (1941) **96m.** **½ D: Lloyd Bacon. Errol Flynn, Brenda Marshall, Ralph Bellamy, Alan Hale, Lee Patrick, Allen Jenkins. Flashy comedy-mystery with Flynn as playboy doubling as independent detective.

Footsteps in the Fog (1955-British) **C-90m.** *** D: Arthur Lubin. Stewart Granger, Jean Simmons, Finlay Currie, Bill Travers, Ronald Squire. Cat-and-mouse battle involving servant girl who blackmails her employer for having murdered his wife. Fine acting, rich Victorian atmosphere.

Footsteps in the Night (1957) **62m.** *½ D: Jean Yarbrough. Bill Elliott, Don Haggerty, Eleanore Tanin, Zena Marshall. Programmer detective tale with Elliott solving the murder of a friend, occurring at a motel.

For a Few Bullets More SEE: **Any Gun Can Play**▼

For a Few Dollars More (1965-Italian) **C-130m.** *** D: Sergio Leone. Clint Eastwood, Lee Van Cleef, Gian Maria Volonté, Jose Egger, Mara Krup, Rosemarie Dexter, Klaus Kinski, Mario Brega. Sequel to A FISTFUL OF DOLLARS finds two gunslingers forming an uneasy alliance in their quest for outlaw Indio (Volonté)—although their reasons for chasing him are markedly different. Slightly draggy but still fun; don't miss the scene where Van Cleef strikes a match on the back of Kinski's neck! Trademark atmospheric score by Ennio Morricone. Released in the U.S. in 1967. Followed by THE GOOD, THE BAD, AND THE UGLY.▼

For All Mankind (1989) **C-90m.** *** D: Al Reinert. Oscar-nominated documentary on the Apollo moon flights, culled from a zillion hours of NASA footage and seamlessly edited into one representative journey. Impressive, and probably even a must—if a bit on the cold side; end credits inform us that film was shot "on location." Let us hope.

For Better, For Worse (1954-British) **C-83m.** **½ D: J. Lee Thompson. Dirk Bogarde, Susan Stephen, Cecil Parker, Dennis Price, Eileen Herlie, Athene Seyler, Thora Hird, Sidney James. Intelligently handled account of young married couple harassed by bills, in-laws, and marital adjustment.

For Better, For Worse (1974) SEE: **Zandy's Bride**

Forbidden (1932) **81m.** ** D: Frank Capra. Barbara Stanwyck, Adolphe Menjou, Ralph Bellamy, Dorothy Peterson, Henry Armetta. A spinster schoolteacher takes a cruise and falls in love with a man who can never marry her. Fine performances and stunning Joseph Walker photography buoy this BACK STREET soap opera until its ridiculous conclusion.

Forbidden (1953) **85m.** **½ D: Rudolph Maté. Tony Curtis, Joanne Dru, Lyle Bettger, Marvin Miller, Victor Sen Yung. Curtis and Dru are engaging in story of gangland chief seeking the whereabouts of girlfriend (Dru), hiring Curtis to find her.

Forbidden (1985) **C-116m. TVM** D: Anthony Page. Jacqueline Bisset, Jurgen Prochnow, Irene Worth, Peter Vaughan, Amanda Cannings, Avis Bunnage. Tortoise-paced drama about a German countess and a wimpish Jewish intellectual who have a forbidden love affair in Nazi Germany. Bisset (in her TV acting debut) is wildly miscast, although Prochnow, as the man she inexplicably hides from the SS for the duration, is fine. Written by Leonard Gross from his book *The Last Jews in Berlin*. Made for cable. Average.▼

Forbidden Alliance SEE: **Barretts of Wimpole Street, The** (1934)

Forbidden Cargo (1954-British) **83m.** **½ D: Harold French. Nigel Patrick, Elizabeth Sellars, Terence Morgan, Jack Warner, Greta Gynt, Joyce Grenfell, Theodore Bikel. Modest drama about customs agent Patrick clashing with dope-smuggling syndicate, enlivened by a solid cast.

Forbidden Dance, The (1990) **C-97m.** BOMB D: Greydon Clark. Laura Herring, Jeff James, Sid Haig, Richard Lynch, Barbara Brighton, Kid Creole. Brazilian jungle princess treks to America on behalf of her endangered rain forests, ends up on a coast-to-coast TV special as . . . a lambada dancer?!? Marginally lesser of two " 'L'-word" quickies that opened (and virtually closed) the same week. The inability of ex-Miss USA Herring to dance is good for a few stray chuckles.▼

Forbidden Fruit (1959-French) **97m.** **½ D: Henri Verneuil. Fernandel, Francoise Arnoul, Claude Nollier, Sylvie, Jacques Castelot. Unpretentious little film of Fernandel's touching love affair with a young maiden.

Forbidden Games (1951-French) **87m.** ***½ D: Rene Clement. Brigitte Fossey, Georges Poujouly, Louis Herbert. During WW2, young Parisian girl is orphaned and taken in by simple peasant family; she develops friendship with their youngest son, and shares with him a private world which the grownups cannot understand. Sad, intensely moving drama earned a Best Foreign Film Oscar.▼

Forbidden Island (1959) **C-66m.** *½ D: Charles B. Griffith. Jon Hall, Nan Adams, John Farrow, Jonathan Haze, Greigh Phillips. Sleazy film with Hall a skindiver seeking to find sunken treasure before a gang of crooks uncovers the loot.

Forbidden Love (1982) **C-100m. TVM** D: Steven H. Stern. Yvette Mimieux, Andrew Stevens, Lisa Lucas, Dana Elcar, Jerry Houser, Randy Brooks, Lynn Carlin, Hildy Brooks, John Considine. Tiresome older woman/younger man affair involving the same old pretty people who don't seem to have to work for a living. Below average.▼

Forbidden Paradise SEE: **Hurricane** (1979)▼

Forbidden Planet (1956) **C-98m.** ***½ D: Fred McLeod Wilcox. Walter Pidgeon, Anne Francis, Leslie Nielsen, Warren Stevens, Jack Kelly, Richard Anderson, Earl Holliman. Sci-fi version of Shakespeare's *The Tempest* remains one of the most ambitious and intelligent films of its genre; only slow, deliberate pacing works against it, as Nielsen and fellow space travelers visit planet where expatriate Pidgeon has built a one-man empire with daughter Francis and obedient Robby the Robot. Great effects, eerie electronic score. Beware 95m. reissue prints.▼

Forbidden Street, The (1949-British) **91m.** ** D: Jean Negulesco. Dana Andrews, Maureen O'Hara, Sybil Thorndike, Wilfrid Hyde-White, Fay Compton. Fanciful melodrama of wealthy O'Hara defying her family by marrying down-and-out artist Andrews. Set in 1870s England. Originally titled BRITANNIA MEWS.

Forbidden World (1982) **C-86m.** *½ D: Allan Holzman. Jesse Vint, June Chadwick, Dawn Dunlap, Linden Chiles, Fox Harris. Roger Corman-produced ALIEN rip-off is followup to (and uses sets from) his GALAXY OF TERROR as well as battle scenes lifted from his BATTLE BEYOND THE STARS. Lots of gore, weak special effects in this uneven work. Also known as MUTANT.▼

Forbidden Zone (1980) **76m.** *½ D: Richard Elfman. Herve Villechaize, Susan Tyrrell, Marie-Pascale Elfman, Viva. Pastiche film set in the Sixth Dimension, an underground kingdom ruled by Villechaize and Tyrrell. Mostly a collection of bizarre, campy musical numbers, done in the style of 1930s Max Fleischer cartoons. If only everything about the film weren't so *ugly!* Has an inevitable cult following. ▼

Forbin Project, The SEE: **Colossus: The Forbin Project**▼

Forced Entry (1984) **C-83m.** *½ D: Jim Sotos. Tanya Roberts, Ron Max, Nancy Allen, Robin Leslie. Trifling junk about a rapist-killer, and his attempt to victimize housewife Roberts. Shot in 1975 as THE LAST VICTIM; supposedly re-edited five years later.▼

Forced Vengeance (1982) **C-90m.** *½ D: James Fargo. Chuck Norris, Mary Louise Weller, Camilla Griggs, Michael Cavanaugh, David Opatoshu, Seiji Sakaguchi. Cliched karate nonsense with Norris, badly in need of an acting lesson, taking on mobster Cavanaugh. Set in Hong Kong.▼

Force Five (1975) **C-78m. TVM** D: Walter Grauman. Gerald Gordon, Nick Pryor, James Hampton, Bradford Dillman, David Spielberg, Leif Erickson. Hard-nosed veteran cop Gordon heads a special undercover squad of ex-cons to fight street crime using their specialized skills. It's THE DIRTY DOZEN minus seven in mufti. Below average.

Force: Five (1981) **C-95m.** ** D: Robert Clouse. Joe Lewis, Pam Huntington, Master Bong Soo Han, Richard Norton, Benny "The Jet" Urquidez. Lewis and company attempt to rescue girl from the clutches of religious-cult-head Han. Retread of Clouse's much-used martial arts formula, with gimmick of disparate five-person "team" as the collective hero. Remake of HOT POTATO.▼

Force of Arms (1951) **100m.** **½ D: Michael Curtiz. William Holden, Nancy Olson, Frank Lovejoy, Gene Evans, Dick Wesson. Updating of Hemingway's A FAREWELL TO ARMS to WW2 Italy, with unmemorable results. Reissued as A GIRL FOR JOE.

Force of Evil (1948) **78m.** *** D: Abraham Polonsky. John Garfield, Beatrice Pearson, Thomas Gomez, Roy Roberts, Marie Windsor, Howland Chamberlin. Rock-solid *film noir* about a racketeer's lawyer (Garfield, in a stunning performance), whose ideals have been obscured by his greed. Beautifully photographed (by George Barnes) and lit; this has become something of a cult item. Polonsky, who coscripted with Ira Wolfert, was blacklisted and didn't make another film until 1969's TELL THEM WILLIE BOY IS HERE.▼

Force of One, A (1979) **C-90m.** **½ D: Paul Aaron. Chuck Norris, Jennifer O'Neill, Clu Gulager, Ron O'Neal, James Whitmore Jr., Clint Ritchie, Pepe Serna. Followup to GOOD GUYS WEAR BLACK has karate champ Norris using his expertise to help California town combat drug trafficking. OK action fare.▼

Force 10 from Navarone (1978-British) **C-118m.** BOMB D: Guy Hamilton. Robert Shaw, Harrison Ford, Edward Fox, Franco Nero, Barbara Bach, Carl Weathers, Richard Kiel. Awful sequel to classic GUNS OF NAVARONE, poor in all departments, although Shaw, Ford, and Nero try to give it a lift. Mixed group (naturally), hindered by traitor Nero, attempt to blow a bridge vital to Nazis. They blew the film instead. Based on the Alistair MacLean novel.▼

Ford: The Man and the Machine (1987) **C-200m. TVM** D: Allan Eastman. Cliff Robertson, Hope Lange, Heather Thomas, Michael Ironside, R.H. Thomson, Chris Wiggins. A real lemon about Henry Ford, with a glum Robertson, a hand-wringing Lange (as Mrs. F.), and a vamping Thomas (as mistress Evangeline Cote) heading a Canadian cast in this plodding, episodic biography adapted from Robert Lacey's book. Originally shown in two parts. Below average.

Foreign Affair, A (1948) **116m.** ***½ D:

Billy Wilder. Jean Arthur, Marlene Dietrich, John Lund, Millard Mitchell, Peter Von Zerneck, Stanley Prager. Staid Arthur is sent to Berlin to investigate post-WW2 conditions, finds romance instead, with hot competition from Dietrich. Marlene sings "Black Market," "Ruins of Berlin," but Jean Arthur's Iowa State Song equally memorable in great Wilder comedy. Written by Charles Brackett, Billy Wilder, and Richard Breen.

Foreign Body (1986-British) **C-108m.** **½ D: Ronald Neame. Victor Banerjee, Warren Mitchell, Trevor Howard, Geraldine McEwan, Amanda Donohoe, Denis Quilley, Eve Ferret, Anna Massey. In a real casting switch, A PASSAGE TO INDIA star Banerjee has a field day as an itinerant Indian in London who poses as a doctor and soon finds all the women dying to get him into bed. Throwback to the style of 1950s British sex comedies was never given a chance to find an audience by its theatrical distributor. ▼

Foreign Correspondent (1940) **119m.** **** D: Alfred Hitchcock. Joel McCrea, Laraine Day, Herbert Marshall, George Sanders, Albert Basserman, Robert Benchley, Edmund Gwenn, Eduardo Ciannelli, Harry Davenport, Martin Kosleck. McCrea in title role caught in middle of spy ring with reporters Sanders and Benchley, innocent Day, suspicious father Marshall. Tremendously entertaining film with several Hitchcock showpieces. Scripted by Charles Bennett and Joan Harrison; dialogue by James Hilton and Benchley.▼

Foreign Exchange (1969-British) **C-72m. TVM** D: Roy (Ward) Baker. Robert Horton, Sebastian Cabot, Jill St. John, Eric Pohlmann, Dudley Foster, Clive Graham. So-called cynical exploits of American forced to work for British secret service in devious plan to have himself exchanged for former Russian defector jailed in England. If you miss one minute of plot, you'll probably be lost. Sequel to THE SPY KILLER. Average.

Foreign Intrigue (1956) **C-100m.** **½ D: Sheldon Reynolds. Robert Mitchum, Genevieve Page, Ingrid Thulin, Frederick O'Brady. Based on TV series, film has virtue of on-location shooting in Europe as unemotional Mitchum checks out the cause of his employer's death.

Foreman Went to France, The (1941-British) **88m.** **½ D: Charles Frend. Tommy Trinder, Clifford Evans, Constance Cummings, Robert Morley, Mervyn Johns, Gordon Jackson, Ernest Milton. Documentary-style tale of industrial engineer who journeys to France during WW2 to help save secret machinery from being confiscated by the Axis. Adapted from a J.B. Priestley story based on a true incident.▼

Forest Rangers, The (1942) **C-87m.** **½

D: George Marshall. Fred MacMurray, Paulette Goddard, Susan Hayward, Albert Dekker, Rod Cameron, Lynne Overman, Eugene Pallette. Hayward tries to show ranger MacMurray that he's made a mistake marrying wealthy Goddard in this OK romance with good action scenes. Introduced the hit song "I've Got Spurs That Jingle, Jangle, Jingle."

Forever (1978) **C-100m. TVM** D: John Korty. Stephanie Zimbalist, Dean Butler, John Friedrich, Beth Raines, Jordan Clarke, Diana Scarwid. Romantic drama about a teenage girl's first real love, adapted from Judy Blume's starry-eyed novel by A. J. Carothers. Average.▼

Forever Amber (1947) **C-140m.** ******* D: Otto Preminger. Linda Darnell, Cornel Wilde, Richard Greene, George Sanders, Jessica Tandy, Anne Revere, Leo G. Carroll. "Musical beds" costumer, taken from Kathleen Winsor's once-scandalous novel, about blonde Darnell's ascension to the court of Charles II. Lengthy but colorful and entertaining, with David Raksin's outstanding score.

Forever and a Day (1943) **104m. ****** D: René Clair, Edmund Goulding, Cedric Hardwicke, Frank Lloyd, Victor Saville, Robert Stevenson, Herbert Wilcox, Kent Smith. Brian Aherne, Robert Cummings, Ida Lupino, Charles Laughton, Herbert Marshall, Ray Milland, Anna Neagle, Merle Oberon, Claude Rains, Victor McLaglen, Buster Keaton, Jessie Matthews, Roland Young, C. Aubrey Smith, Edward Everett Horton, Elsa Lanchester, Edmund Gwenn. Eighty-odd British stars appear in episodic film of British house and its inhabitants over the years. Fine entertainment, once-in-a-lifetime cast.▼

Forever Darling (1956) **C-96m.** ****½** D: Alexander Hall. Lucille Ball, Desi Arnaz, James Mason, Louis Calhern. Ball's madcap antics nearly drive husband Arnaz to divorce, but guardian angel Mason saves the day. Contrived but enjoyable.

Forever Female (1953) **93m.** *****½** D: Irving Rapper. Ginger Rogers, William Holden, Paul Douglas, Pat Crowley, James Gleason. Top-notch show business comedy, with Rogers the star who finally realizes she is too old for the ingenue role, allowing writer Holden to cast Crowley in the part. Film captures flavor of the Broadway, summer stock milieux.

Forever, Lulu (1987) **C-85m. BOMB** D: Amos Kollek. Hanna Schygulla, Deborah Harry, Alec Baldwin, Annie Golden, Paul Gleason, Dr. Ruth Westheimer, Amos Kollek. Embarrassing, amateurish imitation of DESPERATELY SEEKING SUSAN has budding novelist Schygulla becoming embroiled in a real-life mystery in N.Y.C. involving drugs and killers. Despite her star billing in the title role, singing

star Harry makes only a brief cameo appearance. Complete misfire by Israeli director Kollek, who also turns in a poor acting job portraying Schygulla's agent. Baldwin's first film.▼

Forever My Love (1962-German) **C-147m.** ****½** D: Ernest Marischka. Romy Schneider, Karl Boehm, Magda Schneider, Vilma Degischer. Typical German confection dealing with 19th-century Austrian Emperor Franz Josef and Empress Elizabeth.

Forever Young, Forever Free (1976-South African) **C-85m.** ****½** D: Ashley Lazarus. Jose Ferrer, Karen Valentine, Muntu Ndebele, Norman Knox, Bess Finney, Simon Sabela. The adventures of a white orphan (Knox) and his black friend (Ndebele) who leave their South African village for N.Y.C when young Knox becomes ill. Entertaining, if a bit too sugar-coated. Also known as E LOLLIPOP and LOLLIPOP.

Forger of London (1961-German) **91m.** ****** D: Harald Reinl. Eddi Arent, Viktor de Kowa, Karin Dor, Hellmut Lange, Robert Graf. Scotland Yard investigates counterfeit gang tied in with prime suspect, an amnesiac playboy; from Edgar Wallace tale.

Forgiven Sinner, The (1961-French) **101m.** ****½** D: Jean-Pierre Melville. Jean-Paul Belmondo, Emmanuele Riva, Patricia Gozzi, Irene Tunc. Belmondo gives subdued, offbeat performance as clergyman trying to set shady woman onto the path of righteousness. Also known as LEON MORIN, PRIEST. Original French running time: 123m.

Forgotten, The (1989) **C-100m. TVM** D: James Keach. Keith Carradine, Steve Railsback, Stacy Keach, William Lucking, Mimi Maynard, Pepe Serna, Richard Lawson. Six Green Berets return from a Vietnam POW camp 17 years after the war's end for deprogramming in Europe, only to find themselves stalked by mysterious government agents. James Keach made his TV directing debut here (with wife Mimi Maynard and brother Stacy) and produced and cowrote the somewhat farfetched thriller with Railsback. Railsback in turn was coexecutive producer with Carradine. Made for cable. Average.▼

Forgotten Man, The (1971) **C-73m. TVM** D: Walter Grauman. Dennis Weaver, Anne Francis, Lois Nettleton, Andrew Duggan, Pamelyn Ferdin, Percy Rodrigues. North Vietnam escapee returns home and finds wife remarried, business sold, daughter adopted. Location-shot, film softpedals its anger. Good performances. Average.

Forgotten Woman (1939) **63m.** ****½** D: Harold Young. Sigrid Gurie, William Lundigan, Eve Arden, Elizabeth Risdon, Virginia Brissac. Overnight star (and overnight fadeout) Gurie is helpless woman, framed by influential gangsters, suffering on trial.

For Heaven's Sake (1926) 86m. **** D: Sam Taylor. Harold Lloyd, Jobyna Ralston, Noah Young, James Mason, Paul Weigel. Screamingly funny silent comedy has Lloyd a blase young millionaire whose crush on Ralston inspires him to help attract "customers" for her father's Bowery Mission. Even THE FRENCH CONNECTION hasn't dimmed the luster of Lloyd's chase climax on L.A. streets. Edited for TV and paired with abridged version of 1922 feature DR. JACK.

For Heaven's Sake (1950) 92m. **½ D: George Seaton. Clifton Webb, Joan Bennett, Robert Cummings, Edmund Gwenn, Joan Blondell. Droll fantasy with Webb and Gwenn two angels sent to earth to speed along the arrival of Bennett and Cummings' heavenly baby.

For Keeps (1988) C-98m. *½ D: John G. Avildsen. Molly Ringwald, Randall Batnikoff, Kenneth Mars, Miriam Flynn, Conchata Ferrell, Sharon Brown, Renee Estevez, Larry Drake. Studious teen Ringwald becomes pregnant, and must quickly face adult responsibilities. Subject matter is most worthwhile, but the result is predictable and phony. Tim Kazurinsky coauthored the screenplay.▼

For Ladies Only (1981) C-100m. TVM D: Mel Damski. Gregory Harrison, Patricia Davis, Dinah Manoff, Louise Lasser, Lee Grant, Marc Singer, Viveca Lindfors, Steven Keats. Struggling young actor takes a job as a male go-go dancer when he fails to achieve his initial goal. Ronald Reagan's daughter, Patricia Davis, makes her TV movie debut here, and Dinah Manoff costars with her mother, Lee Grant (although they share no scenes). Average.▼

For Love of Ivy (1968) C-102m. ** D: Daniel Mann. Sidney Poitier, Abbey Lincoln, Beau Bridges, Leon Bibb, Nan Martin, Lauri Peters, Carroll O'Connor. Family wants to keep maid, so they find her a beau; ho-hum black romance.▼

For Love or Money (1933) SEE: Cash▼
For Love or Money (1963) C-108m. **½ D: Michael Gordon. Kirk Douglas, Mitzi Gaynor, Gig Young, Thelma Ritter, William Bendix, Julie Newmar. Comedy strains to be funnier than it is. Widow Ritter hires lawyer Douglas to find spouses for her three daughters.

For Love or Money (1984) C-100m. TVM D: Terry Hughes. Suzanne Pleshette, Gil Gerard, Jamie Farr, Ray Walston, Lawrence Pressman, Barney Martin, Lori Lethin, Ray Buktenica, Mary Kay Place. Froth involving television game-show contestants played gamely (and undoubtedly just for the money) by the two leads and those supporting them. Average.▼

For Lovers Only (1982) C-100m. TVM

D: Claudio Guzman. Deborah Raffin, Andy Griffith, Gary Sandy, Sally Kellerman, Katherine Helmond, Robert Hegyes, Gordon Jump, Jane Kaczmarek, Tracy Pollan. A drydocked *Love Boat* with an unending parade of derivations on the familiar bringing-lovers-together-and-fulfilling-their-fantasies ploy. Below average.

For Me and My Gal (1942) 104m. **½ D: Busby Berkeley. Judy Garland, George Murphy, Gene Kelly, Marta Eggerth, Ben Blue, Horace (Stephen) McNally, Keenan Wynn, Richard Quine. Music sustains old-hat plot of vaudeville couple determined to play Palace, circa WW1. Kelly's film debut enhanced by he and Garland singing title tune, "When You Wore a Tulip," etc.▼

For Men Only (1952) 93m. ** D: Paul Henreid. Paul Henreid, Kathleen Hughes, Russell Johnson, James Dobson, Margaret Field, Vera Miles, Douglas Kennedy, O. Z. Whitehead. Sincere if obvious study of fraternity hazing that gets out of hand on a college campus. Retitled: THE TALL LIE.

Formula, The (1980) C-117m. ** D: John G. Avildsen. George C. Scott, Marlon Brando, Marthe Keller, John Gielgud, G. D. Spradlin, Beatrice Straight, Richard Lynch, John Van Dreelen. Amazingly matter-of-fact thriller about a cop who investigates a friend's murder and finds him linked to a mysterious plot involving a formula for synthetic fuel. Scott and Brando are always worth watching, but writer-producer Steve Shagan telegraphs all his punches.▼

For Pete's Sake (1974) C-90m. **½ D: Peter Yates. Barbra Streisand, Michael Sarrazin, Estelle Parsons, William Redfield, Molly Picon. Amiable, featherweight comedy about devoted wife who tries to raise money for her ambitious cab-driver husband, and gets involved with assorted nuts and underworld types. Streisand is fine in forgettable film.▼

For Queen and Country (1988-British) C-105m. *** D: Martin Stellman. Denzel Washington, Dorian Healey, Amanda Redman, Sea Chapman, Bruce Payne. Striking, laced-in-acid contemporary thriller of life in Thatcherite England. Washington is well cast as a former paratrooper who struggles for survival in an atmosphere of racism, poverty, and corruption—and then loses his British citizenship because of an immigration-law technicality. The director also cowrote screenplay.

Forsaking All Others (1934) 84m. ** D: W. S. Van Dyke II. Clark Gable, Joan Crawford, Robert Montgomery, Charles Butterworth, Billie Burke, Rosalind Russell. MGM superstars do their best with mediocre script. Gable stands by Joan for 20 years, but she never realizes that he loves her, and nearly marries Montgomery. Butterworth's droll humor most welcome in this soggy saga.

For Singles Only (1968) **C-91m.** BOMB D: Arthur Dreifuss. John Saxon, Mary Ann Mobley, Milton Berle, Lana Wood, Mark Richman, Chris Noel, The Nitty Gritty Dirt Band. Certainly not for those who like good movies. Two girls move into singles apartment where Berle is social director; result is film that features a rape, an attempted suicide, and several songs.

Fort Algiers (1953) **78m.** ** D: Lesley Selander. Yvonne De Carlo, Carlos Thompson, Raymond Burr, Leif Erickson. De Carlo romps through this adventure set in Algiers, dealing with villainous Arab leader inciting the natives to rebel.

✓ **Fort Apache** (1948) **127m.** *** D: John Ford. John Wayne, Henry Fonda, Shirley Temple, Pedro Armendariz, John Agar, Anna Lee, Victor McLaglen, Ward Bond. Fonda is effectively cast against type as stubborn martinet who rubs his own men— as well as neighboring Indians—the wrong way. First of Ford's cavalry trilogy tells its story slowly, deliberately, with time for comedy and telling characterizations. Followed by SHE WORE A YELLOW RIBBON. Also shown in computer-colored version.▼

Fort Apache, The Bronx (1981) **C-125m.** *** D: Daniel Petrie. Paul Newman, Edward Asner, Ken Wahl, Danny Aiello, Rachel Ticotin, Pam Grier, Kathleen Beller. Taut urban drama about a policeman's life in a ravaged N.Y.C. neighborhood; credible and exciting, with a fine star performance from Newman.▼

Fort Defiance (1951) **C-81m.** **½ D: John Rawlins. Dane Clark, Ben Johnson, Peter Graves, Tracey Roberts. Film focuses on human relations in between preparations for threatened Indian attacks.

Fort Dobbs (1958) **90m.** ** D: Gordon Douglas. Clint Walker, Virginia Mayo, Brian Keith, Richard Eyer. Rugged Walker is believable as hero who fights all obstacles in the old West to make decent life for himself and Mayo.

For the First Time (1959) **C-97m.** **½ D: Rudy Maté. Mario Lanza, Johanna Von Koszian, Kurt Kasznar, Zsa Zsa Gabor, Hans Sohnker. Lanza is typecast as fiery opera singer who falls in love with beautiful deaf girl in Capri. Not bad, with plenty of music to satisfy Lanza fans; this was his last film.

For the Love of Benji (1977) **C-84m.** *** D: Joe Camp. Benji, Patsy Garrett. Cynthia Smith, Allen Fiuzat, Ed Nelson, Peter Bowles, Bridget Armstrong. Moviedom's smartest pooch since Lassie in his second delightful screen adventure, this time scampering through the streets of Athens with

secret agents in pursuit, trying to get the formula tattoed on his paw. Fine family entertainment. Followed by OH, HEAVENLY DOG!▼

For the Love of It (1980) **C-100m.** TVM D: Hal Kanter. Deborah Raffin, Jeff Conaway, Barbi Benton, Don Rickles, Adam West, Tom Bosley, William Christopher, Norman Fell, Henry Gibson, Lawrence-Hilton Jacobs, Pat Morita, Jack Carter, Gil Lamb, Eddie Quillan, Lurene Tuttle. Madcap tale of a model and a lovestruck medical student, who find themselves pursued by a motley assortment of villains and government agents. Packed with stunts, sight gags, familiar TV faces, and frantic dialogue. Average.▼

For the Love of Mary (1948) **90m.** **½ D: Frederick de Cordova. Deanna Durbin, Edmond O'Brien, Don Taylor, Jeffrey Lynn. Airy fluff with Durbin a White House switchboard operator getting political figures and her own romance tangled up. Deanna's final film.

For the Love of Mike (1960) **C-84m.** **½ D: George Sherman. Richard Basehart, Stuart Erwin, Arthur Shields, Armando Silvestre. Mild happenings as Indian boy trains a horse, hoping to use prize money for a village shrine. Another intelligent Robert B. Radnitz production.

For Those Who Think Young (1964) **C-96m.** ** D: Leslie Martinson. James Darren, Pamela Tiffin, Tina Louise, Paul Lynde, Woody Woodbury, Ellen McRae (Burstyn). Witless plug for Pepsi is about low-jinks at college, undistinguished by Nancy Sinatra and Claudia Martin's presence, or cameos by George Raft, Robert Armstrong, Allen Jenkins et al.

Fort Massacre (1958) **C-80m.** ** D: Joseph M. Newman. Joel McCrea, Forrest Tucker, Susan Cabot, John Russell. McCrea is leader of troop platoon which constantly is entangled with redskin skirmishes.

Fort Osage (1952) **C-72m.** BOMB D: Lesley Selander. Rod Cameron, Jane Nigh, Douglas Kennedy, Iron Eyes Cody. Inept Grade-D Western involving perennial Indian uprisings.

Fortress (1985-Australian) **C-89m.** TVM D: Arch Nicholson. Rachel Ward, Sean Garlick, Rebecca Rigg, Robin Mason, Marc Gray, Beth Buchanan. Teacher and her students in Australia's outback turn the tables on vicious gang that has kidnapped them in this exceedingly violent but gripping tale. Made for cable. Average.▼

Fort Ti (1953) **C-73m.** ** D: William Castle. George Montgomery, Joan Vohs, Irving Bacon, James Seay. Best facet of this oater set during French-Indian war of 1760s is its 3-D gimmickry; otherwise, standard stuff.

Fortunate Pilgrim, The SEE: **Mario Puzo's The Fortunate Pilgrim**

Fortune, The (1975) **C-88m.** **½ D: Mike Nichols. Jack Nicholson, Warren Beatty, Stockard Channing, Scatman Crothers, Florence Stanley, Richard B. Shull. Nicholson and Beatty make like Laurel and Hardy in this uneven 1920s comedy about two bumblers who plan to murder a dizzy heiress to get her money. Worth seeing if only for Nicholson's wonderful comic performance. David Shire's period music is nice, too.

Fortune and Men's Eyes (1971-Canadian) **C-102m.** **½ D: Harvey Hart. Wendell Burton, Michael Greer, Zooey (David) Hall, Danny Freedman. Homosexuality in prison is the theme; sincere but exploitative, unpleasant.

Fortune Cookie, The (1966) **125m.** *** D: Billy Wilder. Jack Lemmon, Walter Matthau, Ron Rich, Cliff Osmond, Judi West, Lurene Tuttle. Biting Wilder comedy about TV cameraman (Lemmon) injured during football game and shyster lawyer (Matthau) who exaggerates damages for insurance purposes. Matthau's Oscar-winning performance hits home. Scripted by Wilder and partner I.A.L. Diamond.▼

Fortune in Diamonds (1952-British) **74m.** ** D: David MacDonald. Dennis Price, Jack Hawkins, Siobhan McKenna. Good cast of disparate types all thirsting for cache of gems hidden in the heart of African jungle. Retitled: THE ADVENTURERS.

Fortunes of Captain Blood (1950) **91m.** ** D: Gordon Douglas. Louis Hayward, Patricia Medina, George Macready, Terry Kilburn. This filming of Sabatini novel lacks flair and scope of the Flynn version. Costumer recounts tale of Irish doctor who becomes notorious pirate to revenge wrongdoings.

Fort Utah (1968) **C-83m.** *½ D: Lesley Selander. John Ireland, Virginia Mayo, Scott Brady, John Russell, Robert Strauss, James Craig, Jim Davis, Don "Red" Barry. Former gunfighter Ireland fights Brady, who is stirring up Indians around Fort Utah. See it only if you like the cast.

Fort Vengeance (1953) **75m.** *½ D: Lesley Selander. James Craig, Rita Moreno, Keith Larsen, Reginald Denny, Emory Parnell. Film lacks much-needed action in its account of Pacific Northwest and mounties chasing fur thieves, quelling Indian uprisings.

Fort Worth (1951) **C-80m.** ** D: Edwin L. Marin. Randolph Scott, David Brian, Phyllis Thaxter, Helena Carter. Scott learns that pen is not mightier than the sword; he's a gunslinger who becomes newspaper editor but can only rid town of outlaws via six-shooter.

Forty Carats (1973) **C-110m.** **½ D: Milton Katselas. Liv Ullmann, Edward Albert, Gene Kelly, Binnie Barnes, Deborah Raffin, Billy Green Bush, Nancy Walker. Bright Broadway comedy adapted from French farce suffers in transference to screen, mainly from miscasting of Ullmann as 40-ish New York divorcee, pursued by 20-ish Albert. Glossy, mildly amusing; pepped up by Barnes and Kelly.▼

Forty Deuce (1982) **C-89m.** *½ D: Paul Morrissey. Orson Bean, Kevin Bacon, Mark Keyloun, Harris Laskaway, Tommy Citera. Heavyhanded, poorly directed drama of teenage hustler Bacon attempting to sell runaway to wealthy Bean; complications arise when the boy overdoses on heroin. From an off-Broadway play by Alan Bowne.

48HRS. (1982) **C-97m.** ***½ D: Walter Hill. Nick Nolte, Eddie Murphy, Annette O'Toole, James Remar, Frank McRae, David Patrick Kelly, Sonny Landham, Brion James, James Keane, The Busboys. Slambang mix of action and comedy; weary cop Nolte springs Murphy out of the jug for two days to help him catch Murphy's escaped (and *really* disturbed) partner. Naturally, they hate each other's guts at first, but. . . . Murphy, in his screen debut, is nothing short of sensational, but so is Nolte in his low-key, raspy way; scene where Murphy terrorizes a redneck bar is the standout. Written by Roger Spottiswoode, Larry Gross, and Hill. Sequel: ANOTHER 48HRS.▼

Forty Guns (1957) **80m.** **½ D: Samuel Fuller. Barbara Stanwyck, Barry Sullivan, Dean Jagger, John Ericson, Gene Barry. Florid, wildly dramatic Sam Fuller Western with Stanwyck as self-appointed land baroness of Tombstone Territory—until marshal Sullivan shows up.

40 Guns to Apache Pass (1966) **C-95m.** ** D: William Witney. Audie Murphy, Michael Burns, Kenneth Tobey, Laraine Stephens, Michael Blodgett, Michael Keep. Standard Murphy Western with every horse-opera cliché intact: plot centers around missing shipment of rifles.

Forty Little Mothers (1940) **90m.** **½ D: Busby Berkeley. Eddie Cantor, Judith Anderson, Ralph Morgan, Rita Johnson, Bonita Granville, Diana Lewis. Second-rate Cantor vehicle casts him as reluctant school teacher. Veronica Lake is one of the mothers.

49th Man, The (1953) **73m.** **½ D: Fred F. Sears. John Ireland, Richard Denning, Suzanne Dalbert, Touch (Michael) Connors, Peter Marshall. Suspenseful account of federal agents tracking down foreign spies smuggling parts of atomic bomb into U.S. for later detonation.

Forty-Ninth Parallel (1941-British) **107m.** ***½ D: Michael Powell. Anton Walbrook, Eric Portman, Leslie Howard, Raymond Massey, Laurence Olivier, Glynis Johns, Niall MacGinnis, Finlay Currie. Taut, exciting WW2 yarn of Nazi servicemen whose

U-boat is sunk off the Canadian coast. Top-notch cast, rich suspense and characterizations. Oscar winner for Best Story (Emeric Pressburger). U.S. title: THE INVADERS. Original British running time: 123m.▼

41 Going on 30 (1988) **C-100m. TVM** D: Paul Schneider. Steve Eckholdt, Daphne Ashbrook, Adam Carl, Gabey Olds, Patrick Duffy, Harry Morgan, Loretta Swit, Alan Thicke, Dick Van Patten, Rick Rossovich. Disney comedy turning the PEGGY SUE GOT MARRIED plot around and turning a love-struck teenager into an adult, who then gets the chance to campaign for his pretty teacher's affections. Average.

Forty Pounds of Trouble (1963) **C-106m. **½** D: Norman Jewison. Tony Curtis, Phil Silvers, Suzanne Pleshette, Larry Storch, Howard Morris, Stubby Kaye, Claire Wilcox, Jack La Rue. "Cute" Curtis comedy of casino manager who "adopts" little girl with endless complications occurring. Disneyland locations enhance film and fine character actors pep it up. Carbon copy of LITTLE MISS MARKER.

✓ **Forty-Second Street** (1933) **89m. ****** D: Lloyd Bacon. Warner Baxter, Ruby Keeler, George Brent, Bebe Daniels, Dick Powell, Guy Kibbee, Una Merkel, Ginger Rogers, Ned Sparks, George E. Stone. The definitive backstage musical still has plenty of sass—along with its clichés. Ailing director Baxter puts everything into what may be his final show, then leading lady Daniels twists her ankle! Good thing Ruby Keeler's on hand. Harry Warren-Al Dubin songs include title tune, "Young and Healthy," "You're Getting to be a Habit With Me," "Shuffle Off to Buffalo." Busby Berkeley's ground-breaking production numbers are still sensational. Scripted by Rian James and James Seymour, from Bradford Ropes' story. Revived on the Broadway stage fifty years later. Also shown in computer-colored version.▼

43: The Petty Story SEE: **Smash-Up Alley**

Fort Yuma (1955) **C-78m. **** D: Lesley Selander. Peter Graves, Joan Taylor, Addison Richards, Joan Vohs. Indians go on warpath when their chief is killed. Occasionally good combat sequences.

For Us, the Living (1983) **C-90m. TVM** D: Michael Schultz. Howard Rollins, Jr., Irene Cara, Margaret Avery, Roscoe Lee Browne, Larry Fishburne, Janet MacLachlan, Dick Anthony Williams, Paul Winfield. Moving drama detailing the life and work of slain civil rights activist Medgar Evers (Rollins), adapted from a biography written by his widow, Myrtle (played here by Cara). A PBS *American Playhouse* presentation. Above average.▼

For Whom the Bell Tolls (1943) **C-130m.**

***½ D: Sam Wood. Gary Cooper, Ingrid Bergman, Akim Tamiroff, Arturo de Cordova, Joseph Calleia, Katina Paxinou, Vladimir Sokoloff, Mikhail Rasumny, Fortunio Bonanova. Hemingway story of U.S. mercenary Cooper fighting for Spain with motley crew of peasants, including Bergman; tense action, beautiful color, great love scenes, marvelous Victor Young score. Paxinou won Best Supporting Actress Oscar. Originally released at 170m.

For Your Eyes Only (1981-British) **C-127m. *** D: John Glen. Roger Moore, Carole Bouquet, (Chaim) Topol, Lynn-Holly Johnson, Julian Glover, Jill Bennett, Cassandra Harris, Desmond Llewelyn, Lois Maxwell, Walter Gotell. After years of space-age gadgetry, cartoon villains, female mannequins, and giants with steel teeth came this one-shot return to the old days of Ian Fleming minimalism. No other James Bond film has provoked so much debate among 007 fans (even us); judge for yourself. Undeniably exciting are spectacular chases and stunt work; debuting helmer Glen directed second-unit on several previous Bonds. Look for Charles Dance as a gunman.▼

For Your Love Only (1976-German) **C-97m. ** D: Wolfgang Petersen. Nastassia Kinski, Christian Quadflieg, Judy Winter, Klaus Schwarzkopf. Young student Kinski has an affair with a teacher, then kills the man who tries to blackmail and seduce her. Turgid soap opera. Made for German TV; theatrical release in 1982.

Foster and Laurie (1975) **C-100m. TVM** D: John Llewellyn Moxey. Perry King, Dorian Harewood, Talia Shire, Jonelle Allen, Roger Aaron Brown, Victor Campos, Rene Enriquez, Charles Haid, Eric Laneuville, David Proval. True-life story of two N.Y.C. cops killed in brutal ambush by militant extremist group attempting to terrorize the Police Department. More than a simple cop movie, this concentrates on characterization and the personal relationship between Italian Rocco Laurie (King) and his black partner, Gregory Foster (Harewood). Excellent performances. Look for James Woods as an addict. Above average.

Foul Play (1978) **C-116m. **½ D: Colin Higgins. Goldie Hawn, Chevy Chase, Burgess Meredith, Dudley Moore, Rachel Roberts, Eugene Roche, Marilyn Sokol, Billy Barty, Marc Lawrence, Brian Dennehy. Innocent woman gets caught in strange murder plot in San Francisco; no one believes her except detective Chase, who's falling in love with her. Likable stars, good fun, but protracted story, tasteless comedy, and Hitchcock plagiarism detract. Followed by a short-lived TV series.▼

Found Money (1983) **C-100m. TVM** D: Bill Persky. Dick Van Dyke, Sid Caesar,

Shelley Hack, Christopher Murney, William Prince, Ron Frazier, Barton Heyman. Thoughtful little satire winningly teams two comedy greats. Van Dyke is N.Y.C. bank executive, forced into early retirement, who uses new computer to clean out dormant accounts and donate the cash anonymously to deserving citizens; Caesar is fired bank guard who goes along until he sees how it's affecting the population. Written by Michael Fairman and Richard Sanders (both of *WKRP* fame), who gave themselves amusing cameos. Above average.

Fountain, The (1934) **83m.** **½ D: John Cromwell. Ann Harding, Brian Aherne, Paul Lukas, Jean Hersholt, Ian Wolfe. WW1 romance with Harding torn between former sweetheart Aherne and husband Lukas. Handsome but tedious.

Fountainhead, The (1949) **114m.** **½ D: King Vidor. Gary Cooper, Patricia Neal, Raymond Massey, Kent Smith, Robert Douglas, Henry Hull, Ray Collins, Jerome Cowan. Ambitious but confused version of Ayn Rand philosophic novel, spotlighting an idealistic architect's clash with compromises of big business; cast does what it can with the script.▼

Four Against Fate SEE: **Derby Day**
Four Bags Full (1956-French) **84m.** **½ D: Claude Autant-Lara. Jean Gabin, Bourvil, Jeanette Batti, Louis de Funes. Slender comedy vehicle for two top stars, involving duo who smuggle meat across French border during WW2.

Four Clowns (1970) **97m.** **** D: Robert Youngson. Laurel and Hardy, Buster Keaton, Charley Chase. A must for viewers of all ages: some of the best silent comedy ever. Interesting solo footage of Laurel and Hardy; Keaton's classic SEVEN CHANCES; hilarious sequences with underrated Chase including his best short, LIMOUSINE LOVE. One of compiler Youngson's very best efforts.

Four Dark Hours SEE: **Green Cockatoo, The**
Four Daughters (1938) **90m.** ***½ D: Michael Curtiz. Claude Rains, Rosemary Lane, Lola Lane, Priscilla Lane, Gale Page, John Garfield, Jeffrey Lynn, Frank McHugh, May Robson, Dick Foran. Believable, beautifully acted soaper of small-town life; four young women with musical father Rains have lives altered by four young men. Garfield is superb in first film, matched by fine cast. Remade as YOUNG AT HEART. Followed by two sequels.

Four Days in Dallas SEE: **Ruby and Oswald**
Four Days Leave (1950) **98m.** ** D: Leopold Lindtberg. Cornel Wilde, Josette Day, Simone Signoret, Alan Hale, Jr. Rather tame account of GI Wilde finding romance while on leave in Switzerland.

Four Desperate Men (1960-Australian)

104m. **½ D: Harry Watt. Aldo Ray, Heather Sears. Stark study of human nature as quartet of hardened thugs decide whether or not to set off huge bomb that would destroy Sydney harbor. Original title: THE SIEGE OF PINCHGUT.

Four Deuces, The (1975) C-87m. **½ D: William H. Bushnell, Jr. Jack Palance, Carol Lynley, Warren Berlinger, Adam Roarke, E. J. Peaker, Gianni Russo. Action comedy/drama involving Prohibition Era bootleggers. Palance is a gang lord whose mob and casino bear the film's title; Lynley is the moll he loves and fights for.▼

4D Man (1959) C-85m. **½ D: Irvin S. Yeaworth, Jr. Robert Lansing, Lee Meriwether, James Congdon, Guy Raymond, Robert Strauss, Patty Duke. Well-handled sci-fi of scientist who learns art of transposing matter, thus giving him power to pass through any substance.▼

Four Faces West (1948) **90m.** **½ D: Alfred E. Green. Joel McCrea, Frances Dee, Charles Bickford, Joseph Calleia. Quiet Western of fugitive pursued by determined sheriff, with cast giving intelligent interpretation to standard formula. Original, and more appropriate, title: THEY PASSED THIS WAY.▼

Four Fast Guns (1959) **72m.** *½ D: William J. Hole, Jr. James Craig, Martha Vickers, Edgar Buchanan, Brett Halsey, Paul Richards. Shoot-out of good vs. bad pits brother against brother.

Four Feathers, The (1939-British) C-115m. **** D: Zoltan Korda. Ralph Richardson, C. Aubrey Smith, June Duprez, Clive Baxter, John Clements, Jack Allen, Donald Gray. Grand adventure from A. E. W. Mason story of tradition-bound Britisher who must prove he's not a coward by helping army comrades combat Sudan uprising. Smith is just wonderful as talespinning army veteran. Originally released in Britain at 130m. Previously filmed in 1921 and 1928; remade as STORM OVER THE NILE and as a TVM.▼

Four Feathers, The (1977) C-110m. TVM D: Don Sharp. Beau Bridges, Robert Powell, Simon Ward, Richard Johnson, Jane Seymour, Harry Andrews. Robust retelling (fifth time around) of the great adventure classic. Adapted by Gerald DiPego. Dandy entertainment. Above average.▼

Four Flies on Grey Velvet (1972-Italian) C-101m. ** D: Dario Argento. Michael Brandon, Mimsy Farmer, Bud Spencer, Francine Racette. Unabsorbing psychological murder-mystery with performers who walk through their roles in a very disinterested fashion.

Four for Texas (1963) C-124m. *** D: Robert Aldrich. Frank Sinatra, Dean Martin, Anita Ekberg, Ursula Andress, Charles Bronson, Victor Buono, Richard Jaeckel,

Mike Mazurki, Jack Elam, The Three Stooges, Yaphet Kotto. Nonsensical Sinatra-Martin romp set in the old West, with their antics only outdone by Buono as villainous banker. Ekberg and Andress both outstanding scenery attractions.

Four Friends (1981) **C-115m.** ******* D: Arthur Penn. Craig Wasson, Jodi Thelen, Jim Metzler, Michael Huddleston, Reed Birney, James Leo Herlihy, Glenne Headly. A journey of self-discovery for an idealistic young Yugoslavian immigrant (Wasson), who lives through the turbulent American 1960s. Charming, coy, powerful, sentimental, and sometimes astonishingly old-fashioned—a real mixed bag, with many rewards and not a few flaws. Largely autobiographical script by Steve Tesich.▼

Four Frightened People (1934) **78m.** ****½** D: Cecil B. DeMille. Claudette Colbert, Herbert Marshall, Mary Boland, Leo Carrillo, William Gargan. Unspectacular DeMille vehicle of four disparate types lost in dense jungle. Colbert is plain Jane who gets prettier scene by scene; wry Boland steals the show.

Four Girls in Town (1956) **C-85m.** ******* D: Jack Sher. George Nader, Julie Adams, Gia Scala, Marianne Cook, Elsa Martinelli. Clichéd but absorbing account of four contrasting would-be stars coming to Hollywood seeking fame and romance; excellent musical score by Alex North.

Four Guns to the Border (1954) **C-82m.** ****½** D: Richard Carlson. Rory Calhoun, Colleen Miller, George Nader, Walter Brennan, Nina Foch. Better than usual handling of outlaws vs. Indians, with slight morality lesson for finale.

Four Horsemen of the Apocalypse, The (1921) **114m.** ******* D: Rex Ingram. Rudolph Valentino, Alice Terry, Alan Hale, Jean Hersholt, Nigel de Brulier, Wallace Beery. Famous silent spectacle cemented Valentino's popularity via legendary tango scene, but aside from that it's a relentlessly grim anti-war story of brothers who end up fighting on opposite sides during WWI. Extremely well made, with imagery that still staggers and message that cannot be overlooked. Based on the Blasco Ibanez novel. Remade in 1961.

Four Horsemen of the Apocalypse (1961) **C-153m.** ****½** D: Vincente Minnelli. Glenn Ford, Ingrid Thulin, Charles Boyer, Lee J. Cobb, Paul Henreid, Paul Lukas, Yvette Mimieux, Karl Boehm. Compared to silent version, this is glossy, padded trash, losing all sense of reality in its telling of a family whose members fight on opposite sides during WW2. Allegedly Angela Lansbury dubbed in Thulin's lines.▼

Four Hours to Kill (1935) **71m.** ******* D: Mitchell Leisen. Richard Barthelmess, Joe Morrison, Helen Mack, Gertrude Michael, Dorothy Tree, Ray Milland, Roscoe Karns,

John Howard, Noel Madison, Charles Wilson. Ingenious structure has film taking place entirely in a vaudeville theater (and lobby) where a killer (Barthelmess) escapes from the detective escorting him to execution, hoping to kill the stoolie who ratted on him. Norman Krasna's snappy script juggles numerous subplots in the GRAND HOTEL manner. Watch for director Leisen in a cameo as the orchestra leader.

Four Hundred Blows, The (1959-French) **99m.** ******** D: François Truffaut. Jean-Pierre Leaud, Patrick Auffay, Claire Maurier, Albert Remy. Captivating study of Parisian youth who turns to life of small-time crime as a reaction to derelict parents. First of Truffaut's autobiographical Antoine Doinel series; followed by the "Antoine et Colette" episode in LOVE AT TWENTY.▼

Four in a Jeep (1951-Swiss) **97m.** ****½** D: Leopold Lindtberg. Viveca Lindfors, Ralph Meeker, Joseph Yadin, Michael Medwin. On-location shooting in Vienna, Lindfors' creditable performance as refugee seeking international M.P.s help make this a diverting film.▼

Four Jacks and a Jill (1942) **68m.** ****** D: Jack Hively. Ray Bolger, Desi Arnaz, Anne Shirley, June Havoc, Eddie Foy, Jr., Jack Durant, Henry Daniell, Fritz Feld. Bright cast in a lackluster show-biz musical, a remake of STREET GIRL and THAT GIRL FROM PARIS.▼

Four Jills in a Jeep (1944) **89m.** ****½** D: William A. Seiter. Kay Francis, Carole Landis, Martha Raye, Mitzi Mayfair, Phil Silvers, Dick Haymes, Jimmy Dorsey and His Orchestra; guest stars Betty Grable, Alice Faye, Carmen Miranda, George Jessel. Contrived wartime entertainment with four leading ladies reenacting their actual experiences entertaining soldiers overseas (which Landis turned into a popular book of the same name). Some good musical moments but nothing to shout about.

Four Kinds of Love SEE: **Bambole!**

Four Men and A Prayer (1938) **85m.** ******* D: John Ford. Loretta Young, Richard Greene, George Sanders, David Niven, C. Aubrey Smith, William Henry, J. Edward Bromberg, Alan Hale, Reginald Denny, John Carradine. Compelling story of four brothers determined to unravel mystery behind their father's murder; handsome, well-paced production.

Four Mothers (1941) **86m.** ****½** D: William Keighley. Priscilla Lane, Rosemary Lane, Lola Lane, Gale Page, Claude Rains, Jeffrey Lynn, May Robson, Eddie Albert, Frank McHugh, Dick Foran. FOUR DAUGHTERS formula wearing thin in soapy tale of McHugh going bankrupt, whole family helping out.

Four Musketeers, The (1975) **C-108m.**

*** D: Richard Lester. Oliver Reed, Raquel Welch, Richard Chamberlain, Frank Finlay, Michael York, Christopher Lee, Jean-Pierre Cassel, Geraldine Chaplin, Simon Ward, Faye Dunaway, Charlton Heston. Second half of Lester's irreverent but amusing approach to Dumas with less emphasis on slapstick this time around. Rich cast in top form. Filmed in 1973, at the same time as THE THREE MUSKETEERS. Followed by THE RETURN OF THE THREE MUSKETEERS.▼

Four Poster, The (1952) **103m.** ***½ D: Irving Reis. Rex Harrison, Lilli Palmer. Jan de Hartog play is tour de force for stars who enact various phases of married couple's life; warm, witty script; superb performances enhanced by ingenious animated interludes by UPA studio. Later became the stage musical *I DO! I DO!*

Four Rode Out (1969) **C-99m.** *½ D: John Peyser. Pernell Roberts, Sue Lyon, Leslie Nielsen, Julian Mateos. Sheriff treks across New Mexican desert when accused of robbery and murder. Inferior Western.▼

Four's a Crowd (1938) **91m.** **½ D: Michael Curtiz. Errol Flynn, Olivia de Havilland, Rosalind Russell, Patric Knowles, Hugh Herbert. Lightheaded romance in which everyone loves another; straight comedy's a switch for Flynn, who proves he can handle genre well.

Four Seasons, The (1981) **C-107m.** *** D: Alan Alda. Alan Alda, Carol Burnett, Len Cariou, Sandy Dennis, Rita Moreno, Jack Weston, Bess Armstrong. Four stages of friendship among three middle-aged couples who vacation together. As comedy it scores, with a warmly winning cast, but like its main character, it professes to discuss serious issues while pulling back after just touching the surface. Scripted by Alda, who also made his feature directing debut; later developed into TV series.▼

Four Sided Triangle (1953-British) **81m.** BOMB D: Terence Fisher. James Hayter, Barbara Payton, Stephen Murray, John Van Eyssen, Percy Marmont.' Scientist invents a duplicating machine; hoping to solve romantic triangle, he duplicates the woman he and his best friend both love. Silly programmer.▼

Four Skulls of Jonathan Drake, The (1959) **70m.** ** D: Edward L. Cahn. Eduard Franz, Valerie French, Henry Daniell, Grant Richards, Paul Cavanagh, Howard Wendell. Acceptable horror fare involving centuries-old voodoo curse upon family and contemporary scientist who puts an end to the weird goings-on.

Four Sons (1928) **100m.** *** D: John Ford. James Hall, Margaret Mann, Earle Foxe, Charles Morton, Francis X. Bushman Jr., George Meeker. Ford's famous tearjerker about a Bavarian widow whose four beloved sons fight in WWI—one of

them on the American side. Simple and obvious but still effective. Remade in 1940.

Four Sons (1940) **89m.** **½ D: Archie Mayo. Don Ameche, Eugenie Leontovich, Mary Beth Hughes, Alan Curtis, George Ernest, Robert Lowery. Czech family affected by Nazi rise to power; not unlike MORTAL STORM, with sons choosing different allegiances. Remake of 1928 silent.

Fourteen Hours (1951) **92m.** *** D: Henry Hathaway. Paul Douglas, Richard Basehart, Barbara Bel Geddes, Debra Paget, Agnes Moorehead, Robert Keith, Howard da Silva, Jeffrey Hunter, Martin Gabel, Grace Kelly, Jeff Corey. Well-made suspense drama about a man threatening to jump off the ledge of a building, told in semidocumentary fashion. Look for Harvey Lembeck and Ossie Davis as cabbies, Joyce Van Patten as Paget's girlfriend. Grace Kelly's film debut.

Fourth Man, The (1979-Dutch) **C-104m.** ***½ D: Paul Verhoeven. Jeroen Krabbe, Renee Soutendijk, Thom Hoffman, Dolf De Vries, Geert De Jong. Sexy blonde hairdresser Soutendijk may or may not have murdered three husbands but definitely *does* screw up the mind of gay writer Krabbe when he tries to find out. Stylish dream-vs.-reality black comedy deserved its substantial art-house success; flashy direction and eroticism to spare. Unreleased in U.S. until 1984.▼

Fourth Protocol, The (1987-British) **C-119m.** **½ D: John Mackenzie. Michael Caine, Pierce Brosnan, Joanna Cassidy, Ned Beatty, Betsy Brantley, Peter Cartwright, David Conville, Matt Frewer, Ray McAnally, Ian Richardson, Anton Rodgers. Pretty good spy thriller adapted by Frederick Forsyth from his best-selling novel. Caine plays a British spy who's assigned to foil a Russian plot that would destroy relations between the U.S. and England by setting off a nuclear bomb near an American air base in the U.K. Brosnan does well as a Russian agent.▼

Fourth War, The (1990) **C-91m.** **½ D: John Frankenheimer. Roy Scheider, Jurgen Prochnow, Tim Reid, Harry Dean Stanton, Lara Harris, Dale Dye. Well-done but ever-so-familiar Cold War thriller in which an American colonel (Scheider) and his Soviet counterpart (Prochnow) engage in a private, potentially disastrous war. Best for fans of the genre. Stanton looks very out of place as Scheider's commanding general.

Four Ways Out (1954-Italian) **77m.** **½ D: Pietro Germi. Gina Lollobrigida, Renato Baldini, Cosetta Greco, Paul Muller, Enzio Maggio. Drama points up futility of a robbery by quartet who individually plan their own escapes, all to no avail.▼

Four Wives (1939) **110m.** **½ D: Michael Curtiz. Claude Rains, Eddie Albert,

Priscilla Lane, Rosemary Lane, Lola Lane, Gale Page, John Garfield, May Robson, Frank McHugh, Jeffrey Lynn. Sentimental but well-acted sequel to FOUR DAUGHTERS, further chronicling the lives and loves of the title quartet. Garfield appears briefly in flashback.

Fox, The (1968) **C-110m.** *** D: Mark Rydell. Sandy Dennis, Keir Dullea, Anne Heywood, Glyn Morris. Nicely crafted tale of two women who develop intimate relationship only to be split apart by an intruder who happens among them. Based on a D.H. Lawrence novella. Filmed in Canada.

Fox and His Friends (1975-German) **C-123m.** **** D: Rainer Werner Fassbinder. Rainer Werner Fassbinder, Peter Chatel, Karlheinz Bohm, Adrian Hoven, Ulla Jacobsson. Compassionate, politically astute melodrama by German wunderkind Fassbinder about gay lower-class carnival performer winning lottery fortune only to have his upper-class lover exploit him. Fassbinder is brilliant in title role. Also shown as FIST RIGHT OF FREEDOM.▼

Foxes (1980) **C-106m.** **½ D: Adrian Lyne. Jodie Foster, Cherie Currie, Marilyn Kagan, Kandice Stroh, Scott Baio, Sally Kellerman, Randy Quaid, Lois Smith. Four teenaged girls try coping with the standard non-*Our Town* problems brought by growing up today in San Fernando Valley. Capable cast; apparently sincere intentions undermined by choppy storyline that just isn't compelling enough.▼

Foxes of Harrow, The (1947) 117m. **½ D: John M. Stahl. Rex Harrison, Maureen O'Hara, Richard Haydn, Victor McLaglen, Vanessa Brown, Patricia Medina, Gene Lockhart. Lavish but lumbering tale of philanderer breaking up his marriage to seek affluence and fame in New Orleans in 1820. Pretty stale despite the trimmings.

Foxfire (1955) **C-92m.** **½ D: Joseph Pevney. Jane Russell, Jeff Chandler, Dan Duryea, Mara Corday, Barton MacLane. Russell battles cultural barriers when she impulsively marries Indian mining engineer Chandler while vacationing in Arizona. Not bad; the stars are well matched. Incidentally that's Chandler singing the title song on the sound track.

Foxfire (1987) **C-100m. TVM** D: Jud Taylor. Jessica Tandy, Hume Cronyn, John Denver, Gary Grubbs, Harriet Hall. Nicely realized filming of the Tandy-Cronyn Broadway production about an Appalachian farm family and the land of their roots. Tandy won an Emmy (to go with her Tony Award for the same part) as the elderly woman who refuses to leave her home in the hills where she communes with the ghost of her dead husband. Susan Cooper adapted the play she created with Cronyn. Above average.

Foxhole in Cairo (1961-British) 79m. **½ D: John Moxey. James Robertson Justice, Adrian Hoven, Peter Van Eyck, Neil McCallum. Sensibly told account of counterintelligence at work in Egypt during WW2 with British vs. Rommel's Nazis.

Foxiest Girl in Paris (1956-French) 100m. **½ D: Roger De Broin. Martine Carol, Michel Piccoli, Mischa Auer. Sultry Carol, a fashion model, becomes amateur sleuth to solve a robbery and a murder.

Foxtrap (1986-U.S.-Italian) **C-88m.** *½ D: Fred Williamson. Fred Williamson, Chris Connelly, Arlene Golonka, Donna Owen, Beatrice Palme, Cleo Sebastian, Lela Rochon. Low-budget actioner of Williamson hired to bring runaway Owen back home from Europe to her family. Little more than a fashion show by director Williamson spotlighting his favorite actor: Williamson. ▼

Foxtrot (1976-Mexican-Swiss) **C-91m.** ** D: Arturo Ripstein. Peter O'Toole, Charlotte Rampling, Max von Sydow, Jorge Luke, Helen Rojo, Claudio Brook. O'Toole and his wife flee Rumania in the late 1930s and retreat to an island paradise to isolate themselves from a world about to erupt into war. Shallow, predictable drama; filmed in Mexico. Alternate version with additional sex footage titled THE OTHER SIDE OF PARADISE.▼

Foxy Brown (1974) **C-94m.** *½ D: Jack Hill. Pam Grier, Peter Brown, Terry Carter, Kathryn Loder. Violence and little else in tale of nurse Grier and her vendetta against drug ring that killed her lover.▼

Fra Diavolo SEE: **Devil's Brother**

Fragment of Fear (1971-British) **C-96m.** ** D: Richard C. Sarafian. David Hemmings, Gayle Hunnicutt, Flora Robson, Wilfrid Hyde-White, Daniel Massey, Roland Culver, Adolfo Celi, Mona Washbourne. Hemmings is good in disappointing murder mystery that begins well, then falls apart. Photographed by the great Oswald Morris.

Framed (1947) 82m. ** D: Richard Wallace. Glenn Ford, Janis Carter, Barry Sullivan, Edgar Buchanan, Karen Morley. Title almost self-explanatory. Innocent man mistaken for robber is brought in, enabling real thief to escape.

Framed (1975) **C-106m.** **½ D: Phil Karlson. Joe Don Baker, Conny Van Dyke, Gabriel Dell, John Marley, Brock Peters, Roy Jenson. Railroaded to jail, Baker vows revenge on the corrupt cops who put him there. The writer, director, and star of WALKING TALL, old hands at this kind of action melodrama, make the most of the situation.▼

Frances (1982) **C-140m.** **½ D: Graeme Clifford. Jessica Lange, Kim Stanley, Sam Shepard, Bart Burns, Jeffrey DeMunn, Jordan Charney, Lane Smith. Biography of 1930s movie star Frances Farmer—who wound up in a barbaric insane asylum—chronicles her tragic life in some detail, but doesn't help us understand the reasons for her self-destructive tendencies. Well crafted but cold and depressing, despite impressive performances by Lange and Stanley, as Frances' crazed mother. Her story is also told in the TVM, WILL THERE REALLY BE A MORNING? and in the independent feature COMMITTED. Look for Kevin Costner, who has one line in an alley.▼

Francis (the Talking Mule) Never hailed as an artistic triumph, the Francis series made up for that in box-office receipts from 1950 to 1956. Based on a book by David Stern, each of the seven films dealt with a sincere but stupid young man (at West Point he is 687th in a class of 687) led into and out of trouble by a canny talking mule. The off-screen voice was Chill Wills, the on-screen bumbler was Donald O'Connor in all but the last film, which starred Mickey Rooney. O'Connor recently explained, "When you've made six pictures and the mule still gets more fan mail than you do . . ." Universal worked their contract starlets (Piper Laurie, Martha Hyer, Julia Adams, etc.) into the series as love interests, but the center of attraction was always the mule. The films, except the last one, were all about on a par: silly but amusing. The first six films were directed by Arthur Lubin, who went on to create a similar TV series called *Mr. Ed*, about a talking horse.

Francis (1950) 91m. D: Arthur Lubin. Donald O'Connor, Patricia Medina, ZaSu Pitts, Ray Collins, Anthony (Tony) Curtis.

Francis Covers the Big Town (1953) 86m. D: Arthur Lubin. Donald O'Connor, Gene Lockhart, Nancy Guild, Gale Gordon.

Francis Gary Powers: The True Story of the U-2 Spy Incident (1976) C-100m. TVM D: Delbert Mann. Lee Majors, Nehemiah Persoff, Noah Beery Jr., William Daniels, Lew Ayres, Brooke Bundy, Jim McMullen, Biff McGuire, James Gregory. Docu-drama about the pilot shot down over Russia during a spy mission. Majors does yeoman work as Powers, depicting the anguish he undergoes at the hands of Russian interrogator Persoff, excellent in his role. Despite its familiarity, story should have been more engrossing. Average.▼

Francis Goes to the Races (1951) 88m. D: Arthur Lubin. Donald O'Connor, Piper Laurie, Cecil Kellaway, Jesse White.

Francis Goes to West Point (1952) 81m. D: Arthur Lubin. Donald O'Connor, Lori Nelson, William Reynolds, James Best, Les Tremayne, David Janssen.

Francis in the Haunted House (1956) 80m. D: Charles Lamont. Mickey Rooney,

Virginia Welles, Paul Cavanagh, David Janssen.

Francis in the Navy (1955) 80m. D: Arthur Lubin. Donald O'Connor, Martha Hyer, Jim Backus, Paul Burke, David Janssen, Clint Eastwood, Martin Milner.▼

Francis Joins the Wacs (1954) 94m. D: Arthur Lubin. Donald O'Connor, Julia (Julie) Adams, Mamie Van Doren, Chill Wills, Lynn Bari, ZaSu Pitts.

Francis of Assisi (1961) C-111m. **½ D: Michael Curtiz. Bradford Dillman, Dolores Hart, Stuart Whitman, Cecil Kellaway, Finlay Currie, Pedro Armendariz. Lavish religious epic dealing with story of founder of school of monks with sympathetic performance by Dillman. Good cast and atmosphere. Script tends to sag at wrong moments.

Frankenstein (1931) 70m. ***½ D: James Whale. Colin Clive, Mae Clarke, Boris Karloff, John Boles, Edward Van Sloan, Dwight Frye, Frederick Kerr, Lionel Belmore. Definitive monster movie, with Clive as the ultimate mad scientist, creating a man-made being (Karloff) but inadvertently giving him a criminal brain. It's creaky at times, and cries for a music score, but it's still impressive . . . as is Karloff's performance in the role that made him a star. Long-censored footage, restored in 1987, enhances the impact of several key scenes, including the drowning of a little girl. Based on Mary Shelley's novel. Followed by BRIDE OF FRANKENSTEIN.▼

Frankenstein and the Monster from Hell (1974-British) C-93m. ** D: Terence Fisher. Peter Cushing, Shane Briant, Madeline Smith, Dave Prowse, John Stratton. Guess who runs a hospital for the criminally insane? Hammer's final entry in their Frankenstein cycle is amusing if you catch it in the right frame of mind.

Frankenstein Conquers the World (1966-Japanese) C-87m. ** D: Inoshiro Honda. Nick Adams, Tadao Takashima, Kumi Mizuno. Grade-C horror film, with Adams a scientist in Tokyo trying to combat giant, newly grown Frankenstein monster terrorizing the countryside; poor special effects.

Frankenstein Created Woman (1967-British) C-92m. ** D: Terence Fisher. Peter Cushing, Susan Denberg, Robert Morris, Barry Warren, Thorley Walters, Duncan Lamont. Sequel to EVIL OF FRANKSTEIN finds Dr. Frankenstein (Cushing) tring to put the soul of recently (and wrongly) executed man into body of scarred lover (Denberg). Everything goes wrong, including script. Followed by FRANKENSTEIN MUST BE DESTROYED!

Frankenstein '88 SEE **Vindicator, The**▼

Frankenstein General Hospital (1988) C/B&W-92m. BOMB D: Deborah Roberts. Mark Blankfield, Irwin Keyes, Kathy Shower, Katie Caple, Lou Cutell, Bobby

"Boris" Pickett. Ghastly comedy stars Blankfield as Dr. Bob Frankenstein, who's assembling a new Monster in the basement of the hospital where he's an intern. Crude, vulgar, and completely unfunny, this is the worst Frankenstein film ever made in English. At least that's a distinction.▼

Frankenstein Meets the Space Monster (1965) **78m.** BOMB D: Robert Gaffney. James Karen, David Kerman, Nancy Marshall, Marilyn Hanold. Low-grade horror entry dealing with interplanetary robot whose mechanism runs amuck as he goes berserk. Bizarre, Flash Gordon-esque aliens also involved. Has gained a peculiar cult reputation. Video title: MARS INVADES PUERTO RICO.▼

Frankenstein Meets the Wolf Man (1943) **72m.** *** D: Roy William Neill. Lon Chaney, Jr., Patric Knowles, Ilona Massey, Bela Lugosi, Maria Ouspenskaya, Lionel Atwill, Dennis Hoey, Rex Evans, Dwight Frye. Sequel to both GHOST OF FRANKENSTEIN and THE WOLF MAN finds werewolf Chaney seeking Dr. Frankenstein, hoping to be put out of his misery. He finds the scientist is dead—but the Monster isn't. Slick, atmospheric, fast-paced fun; Lugosi's only stint as the Monster. Followed by HOUSE OF FRANKENSTEIN.▼

Frankenstein Must Be Destroyed! (1970-British) **C-101m.** **½ D: Terence Fisher. Peter Cushing, Simon Ward, Veronica Carlson, Freddie Jones. Cushing is more cold-blooded here than usual, as he forces a young couple to help him in brain transplanting experiments. One of the best in the Hammer series. Followed by THE HORROR OF FRANKENSTEIN.

Frankenstein—1970 (1958) **83m.** BOMB D: Howard W. Koch. Boris Karloff, Tom Duggan, Jana Lund, Donald Barry. As last of the Frankenstein scientists, Karloff uses money from TV production shooting in his castle to revive original monster with atomic energy. Film is slow, monster unexciting, and Karloff unfortunately hammy.▼

Frankenstein's Daughter (1959) **85m.** BOMB D: Richard Cunha. John Ashley, Sandra Knight, Donald Murphy, Sally Todd, Harold Lloyd, Jr. Low-grade descendant of famed monster series with a new female horror-robot being created with typical results; tinsel sets.▼

Frankenstein: The True Story (1973) **C-200m.** TVM. D: Jack Smight. James Mason, Leonard Whiting, Michael Sarrazin, David McCallum, Jane Seymour, Michael Wilding, Margaret Leighton, Ralph Richardson, Agnes Moorehead, John Gielgud, Tom Baker. Epic retelling of Mary Shelley's frightmare with brilliant Christopher Isherwood screenplay; not quite the letter of the novel, but competes favorably with the immortal Karloff movies on the theme by sheer spectacle. Creature, played

stunningly by Sarrazin, is not the traditional stitched-together ogre, but a dashing Victorian rogue who proceeds to physically degenerate while various psychological avenues are explored. Marvelous cast in this thinking-man's horror movie. Above average.

Frankie and Johnny (1936) **66m.** BOMB D: Chester Erskine. Helen Morgan, Chester Morris, Lilyan Tashman, Florence Reed, Walter Kingsford. Dismally bad, cheaply made costume musical drama based on the old love-triangle song; even the great Morgan is undone. Made in 1934.▼

Frankie and Johnny (1966) **C-87m.** **½ D: Frederick de Cordova. Elvis Presley, Donna Douglas, Harry Morgan, Sue Ane Langdon, Nancy Kovack. Saloon song expanded into feature film story for Elvis. Riverboat setting, cohort Morgan, several pretty starlets, and tuneful songs (including "Down By the Riverside," "When the Saints Go Marching In") make this a satisfactory time-filler.▼

Frank's Greatest Adventure SEE: **Fearless Frank**

Frantic (1958-French) **90m.** **½ D: Louis Malle. Jeanne Moreau, Maurice Ronet, Georges Poujouly, Yori Bertin, Jean Wall. A man and woman plan to murder her husband, but fall short of committing a "perfect crime." Intriguing, but doesn't hold up. This was Malle's first nondocumentary feature as director. Music score improvised by Miles Davis.▼

Frantic (1988) **C-120m.** **½ D: Roman Polanski. Harrison Ford, Emmanuelle Seigner, Betty Buckley, John Mahoney, Jimmie Ray Weeks, Yorgo Voyagis, David Huddleston, Gerard Klein. American doctor is drawn into espionage, and the underworld, when his wife disappears on the first day of their trip to Paris. Carefully controlled suspense thriller never really cuts loose but keeps its grip thanks to Ford's believable performance.▼

Fraternity Row (1977) **C-101m.** *** D: Thomas J. Tobin. Peter Fox, Gregory Harrison, Scott Newman, Nancy Morgan, Robert Emhardt, Wendy Phillips. Well-done drama of campus life at exclusive Eastern college, 1954. Writer-producer Charles Gary Allison used USC students and crew, got professional Hollywood advice for polished look at tragic, fact-based, fraternity hazing. Cliff Robertson narrates, Don McLean did original score. Costar Newman is the late son of Paul Newman.

Fraternity Vacation (1985) **C-89m.** *½ D: James Frawley. Stephen Geoffreys, Sheree J. Wilson, Cameron Dye, Leigh McCloskey, Tim Robbins, John Vernon, Britt Ekland, Nita Talbot, Max Wright, Amanda Bearse. Two frat animals, saddled with a nerdy "brother"on a pleasure trip to Palm Springs, bet a rival they can be the first to score with an aloof, beautiful blond. Less strident, and thus less offensive, than many of its ilk, but still nothing to enrich our moviegoing heritage.▼

Fraulein (1958) **C-98m.** ** D: Henry Koster. Dana Wynter, Mel Ferrer, Dolores Michaels, Maggie Hayes. Bizarre tale of German girl in post-WW2 Berlin helping American soldier, then being held by the Communists. Wynter miscast.

Fraulein Doktor (1969-Italian-Yugoslavian) **C-102m.** *** D: Alberto Lattuada. Suzy Kendall, Kenneth More, Capucine, James Booth, Alexander Knox, Nigel Green, Giancarlo Giannini. Big cast and budget in rarely seen European antiwar film centering on career of real-life double-agent during WW1. Some of the battle sequences impressive. Same story has been filmed many times before, in Hollywood as STAMBOUL QUEST and in France as MADEMOISELLE DOCTEUR.

Freakmaker SEE: **Mutations, The**▼

Freaks (1932) **64m.** ***½ D: Tod Browning. Wallace Ford, Olga Baclanova, Leila Hyams, Roscoe Ates, Harry Earles. A unique movie about a traveling sideshow and the camaraderie of its unusual performers. Horror-film master Tod Browning gathered an incredible cast of real-life freaks for this bizarre and fascinating film. Many reissue prints are missing brief epilogue; also known as NATURE'S MISTAKES.▼

Freaky Friday (1977) **C-95m.** *** D: Gary Nelson. Barbara Harris, Jodie Foster, John Astin, Patsy Kelly, Dick Van Patten, Sorrell Booke, Marie Windsor, Charlene Tilton. Harris and Foster shine as mother and daughter who magically switch personalities for a day; their performances make this exceptional Disney fare, even though Mary Rodgers' script winds up with formula slapstick chase. The same premise was the basis of the 1948 movie VICE VERSA and several later Hollywood comedies (including LIKE FATHER, LIKE SON and the same-named VICE VERSA).▼

Freckles (1960) **C-84m.** *½ D: Andrew V. McLaglen. Martin West, Carol Christensen, Jack Lambert, Roy Barcroft, Ken Curtis, Steven Peck. Bland study of crippled youth who manages to be accepted as normal working member of lumber camp.

Free and Easy (1930) **92m.** **½ D: Edward Sedgwick. Buster Keaton, Anita Page, Robert Montgomery, Edgar Dearing, Lionel Barrymore, Dorothy Sebastian, Trixie Friganza. Interesting early-talkie musicomedy about Keaton becoming movie star; many guest appearances by Cecil B. DeMille, William Haines, *et al.* to boost uneven film. Retitled: EASY GO.

Freebie and the Bean (1974) **C-113m.** *½ D: Richard Rush. James Caan, Alan Arkin, Loretta Swit, Jack Kruschen, Mike Kellin. Some good action, but mostly repellent humor as San Francisco cops Arkin and Caan nearly wreck the city trying to get the goods on numbers racketeer Kruschen. Valerie Harper has a nice cameo as Arkin's Latin wife. Later a short-lived TV series.▼

Free, Blonde and Twenty One (1940) **67m.** *½ D: Ricardo Cortez. Lynn Bari, Mary Beth Hughes, Joan Davis, Henry Wilcoxon. Low-grade hokum about gold-digging gals on the make for wealthy men.

Freedom (1981) **C-100m. TVM** D: Joseph Sargent. Mare Winningham, Jennifer Warren, Tony Bill, Roy Thinnes, Peter Horton, Eloy Phil Casados, J. Pat O'Malley. Rebellious teenager takes off on a solitary journey through backroads America after being given her freedom by her family—and comes to understand the true meaning of having a home. Winningham gives another winning performance and sings six original songs written by Janis Ian. Above average.

Freedom Fighter (1988) **C-100m. TVM** D: Desmond Davis. Tony Danza, Neil Dickson, Geraldine James, David Robb, Colette Stevenson, David McCallum, Sid Caesar. GI in Berlin finds himself separated from East German girlfriend when the Berlin Wall goes up. Gerald DiPego's effective script was "suggested by" the book *The Berlin Wall* by Pierre Galante. Filmed in Berlin with a mostly British team on both sides of the camera. Average.

Freedom Riders, The SEE: **Undercover with the KKK**

Freedom Road (1979) **C-200m. TVM** D: Jan Kadar. Muhammad Ali, Kris Kristofferson, Ron O'Neal, Barbara-O Jones, Edward Herrmann, John McLiam, Ernest Dixon, Alfre Woodard. Lumbering adaptation of sprawling Howard Fast novel about an ex-slave's rise to U.S. Senator in Reconstruction Days, hampered by non-acting of Ali in the crucial lead. Ossie Davis provides dignified narration to Kadar's last film. Average.▼

Free for All (1949) **83m.** ** D: Charles Barton. Robert Cummings, Ann Blyth, Percy Kilbride, Ray Collins. Mild froth about Cummings inventing instant gasoline.

Free Soul, A (1931) **91m.** **½ D: Clarence Brown. Norma Shearer, Lionel Barrymore, Clark Gable, Leslie Howard, James Gleason. A hard-drinking, free-swinging attorney successfully defends gangster Gable on a murder rap—then finds to his dismay that his equally free-spirited daughter has fallen in love with him. Dated morality play-melodrama retains interest because of its cast and Barrymore's famous courtroom finale, which clinched him an Academy Award. Based on Adela Rogers St. Johns' book about her father. Remade as THE GIRL WHO HAD EVERYTHING.

Freeway (1988) **C-91m.** ** D: Francis Delia. Darlanne Fluegel, James Russo, Billy Drago, Richard Belzer, Michael Callan, Joey Palese, Steve Franken, Kenneth Tobey, Clint Howard. A nurse whose husband was the victim of a freeway shooting becomes obsessed with finding the Bible-quoting murderer, who habitually phones a radio psychiatrist from his car while cruising L.A. looking for new victims. Based on a novel but prompted by similar real-life crimes in L.A., this film is surprisingly nonexploitive, but slow and unconvincing as well. Fancy directorial touches seem hollow in this context.▼

Free, White and 21 (1963) **104m.** BOMB D: Larry Buchanan. Frederick O'Neal, Annalena Lund, George Edgley, Johnny Hicks, George Russell. Did black businessman O'Neal rape Lund? Who cares?▼

Free Woman, A (1972-German) **C-100m.** **½ D: Volker Schlondorff. Margarethe von Trotta, Friedhelm Ptok, Martin Luttge, Walter Sedlmayer. Von Trotta divorces Ptok, has trouble adjusting to life apart from husband and son as she tries to liberate herself from her traditional functions. Truthful but boring drama.

French Cancan SEE: **Only the French Can**▼

French Connection, The (1971) **C-104m.** **** D: William Friedkin. Gene Hackman, Fernando Rey, Roy Scheider, Tony Lo-Bianco, Marcel Bozzuffi. Fine action film detailing attempted international heroin smuggle into N.Y.C., and maverick detective who stops it. Five Oscars include Best Picture, Actor, Director, Screenplay (Ernest Tidyman) and Editing (Jerry Greenberg), the latter particularly for one of the most exciting car chases ever filmed. Followed by a sequel and, in 1986, a TV movie, POPEYE DOYLE.▼

French Connection II, The (1975) **C-119m.** **½ D: John Frankenheimer. Gene Hackman, Fernando Rey, Bernard Fresson, Jean-Pierre Castaldi, Charles Milot, Cathleen Nesbitt. Gruff N.Y. cop Popeye Doyle goes to Marseilles, determined to nail narcotics king (Rey) who eluded him in America. Enjoyable opening and riveting chase finale are separated by long, agonizing drug segment that weighs whole film down.▼

French Conspiracy, The (1973-French-Italian-German) **C-124m.** ** D: Yves Boisset. Jean-Louis Trintignant, Jean Seberg, Gian Maria Volonté, Roy Scheider, Michel Piccoli. Realistic but unexciting political drama centering around left-wing reporter Trintignant, pawn in a plot to assassinate Third World leader Volonté.

French Detective, The (1975-French) **C-93m.** *** D: Pierre Granier-Deferre. Lino Ventura, Patrick Dewaere, Victor Lanoux. Neat, entertaining police story

with Ventura a tough, independent, middle-aged cop who, with exuberant young partner Dewaere, determinedly pursues a hood working for politician Lanoux. ▼

Frenchie (1950) **C-81m.** ** D: Louis King. Joel McCrea, Shelley Winters, John Russell, John Emery, George Cleveland, Elsa Lanchester, Marie Windsor. When her father is murdered, Winters returns home and opens a saloon, planning revenge. Bland Western based on DESTRY RIDES AGAIN.

French Key, The (1946) **64m.** **½ D: Walter Colmes. Albert Dekker, Mike Mazurki, Evelyn Ankers, John Eldredge, Frank Fenton, Richard Arlen, Byron Foulger. Dekker gives mystery drama some class in this murder yarn.

French Lieutenant's Woman, The (1981-British) **C-123m.** ***½ D: Karel Reisz. Meryl Streep, Jeremy Irons, Leo McKern, Hilton McRae, Emily Morgan, Charlotte Mitchell, Lynsey Baxter. A scandalous romance between a gentleman and a tainted woman in Victorian England is contrasted with a contemporary affair between the actor and actress who are playing those roles in a movie. The juxtaposition is jarring at first, but becomes more engaging as the film progresses. Beautifully visualized, with rich period detail, superb performances; script by Harold Pinter, from John Fowles's novel.▼

French Line, The (1954) **C-102m.** ** D: Lloyd Bacon. Jane Russell, Gilbert Roland, Arthur Hunnicutt, Mary McCarty, Craig Stevens, Steven Geray, Joyce McKenzie, Paula Corday, Scott Elliot. Russell's bust in 3-D was the gimmick to sell this dull musical. All that's left is flat tale of wealthy Texas girl in Paris being romanced by Parisian. McCarty's wisecracking is a blessing. If you blink, you'll miss Kim Novak modeling a gown.▼

Frenchman's Creek (1944) **C-113m.** *** D: Mitchell Leisen. Joan Fontaine, Arturo de Cordova, Basil Rathbone, Nigel Bruce, Cecil Kellaway, Ralph Forbes, George Kirby. Colorful escapism of Fontaine romanced by dashing pirate de Cordova; good supporting cast. Based on a Daphne DuMaurier novel.

French Postcards (1979) **C-92m.** ** D: Willard Huyck. Blanche Baker, Miles Chapin, Debra Winger, Mandy Patinkin, Valerie Quennessen, David Marshall Grant, Marie-France Pisier, Jean Rochefort. Kind of follow-up to AMERICAN GRAFFITI from that film's authors (Huyck and Gloria Katz), detailing romantic misadventures of group of college students spending junior year abroad. Pleasant but forgettable comedy; worth checking out for cast full of future stars, many in their film debuts.▼

French Provincial (1974-French) **C-91m.** ** D: Andre Techine. Jeanne Moreau,

Michel Auclair, Marie-France Pisier, Claude Mann, Orane Demazis. Moreau, as a laundry woman who marries into a bourgeois family, shines in this otherwise flaky, superficially symbolic saga of economic change in France from the 1930s through 1970s.

French Quarter (1977) **C-101m.** *** D: Dennis Kane. Bruce Davison, Lindsay Bloom, Virginia Mayo, Alisha Fontaine, Lance LeGault, Laura Misch Owens, Ann Michelle, Becky Allen, Barry Sullivan, William Sims. Neglected drive-in treat is a genuine curiosity; tongue-in-cheek melodrama mixes PRETTY BABY plot with FRENCH LIEUTENANT'S WOMAN structure (but predates both!). Tale of young Fontaine, growing up as Storyville prostitute at the turn of the century, is paralleled by present-day story with same cast, linked by voodoo plot device. Ends bizarrely with narrator reminding us to "hang up your speakers and drive home safely." And Dick Hyman did the music!▼

French, They Are a Funny Race, The (1956-French) **83m.** ** D: Preston Sturges. Jack Buchanan, Noel-Noel, Martine Carol, Genevieve Brunet. Director-writer Sturges' last film is pretty much a misfire, with Buchanan as veddy-British major whose marriage to Frenchwoman sparks continuing nationalistic arguments. Original title: LES CARNETS DU MAJOR THOMPSON at 105m.

French Way Is, The SEE: **Love at the Top**

Frenzy (1972-British) **C-116m.** ***½ D: Alfred Hitchcock. Jon Finch, Barry Foster, Barbara Leigh-Hunt, Anna Massey, Alec McCowen, Vivien Merchant, Billie Whitelaw, Jean Marsh. Hitchcock in full gear, telling story of suave London strangler (Foster) and innocent man (Finch) suspected of crime wave. All classic Hitchcock elements are here, including delicious black humor, several astounding camera shots. Script by Anthony Shaffer.▼

Fresh From Paris (1955) **C-70m.** *½ D: Leslie Goodwins. Forrest Tucker, Margaret Whiting, Martha Hyer. Grade-C musical filmed at Moulin Rouge cafe in Hollywood, with tiresome musical interludes. Original title: PARIS FOLLIES OF 1956.

Fresh Horses (1988) **C-105m.** **½ D: David Anspaugh. Molly Ringwald, Andrew McCarthy, Patti D'Arbanville, Molly Hagan, Doug Hutchison, Ben Stiller, Leon Russom. Collegian McCarthy, engaged to a wealthy dullard, falls for Ringwald's underage no-no, a semi-shantytramp who lives across the river from his Cincinnati campus. Slightly better than expected, thanks to fine Midwest location work from the director of HOOSIERS. Ringwald isn't totally convincing in the kind of role Gloria Grahame invented.▼

Freshman, The (1925) **70m.** **** D: Sam

Taylor and Fred Newmeyer. Harold Lloyd, Jobyna Ralston, Brooks Benedict, James Anderson, Hazel Keener. One of Lloyd's best remembered films casts him as collegiate patsy who'll do anything to be popular on campus, unaware that everyone is making fun of him. Football game finale is one of several comic highlights. A real audience-rouser. Edited for TV.

Freshman, The (1990) **C-102m.** *** D: Andrew Bergman. Marlon Brando, Matthew Broderick, Maximilian Schell, Bruno Kirby, Penelope Ann Miller, Frank Whaley, Paul Benedict, B. D. Wong. New York University film student Broderick falls in with loony mob family headed by Brando in this infectious, off-center comedy. Not an outstanding film per se, but strong cast and New York flavor, plus Bergman's original and amusing screenplay, put it over. Best of all: Marlon's knockout performance (remind you of anyone?), and his rapport with Matthew.

Freud (1962) **120m.** ***½ D: John Huston. Montgomery Clift, Susannah York, Larry Parks, David McCallum, Susan Kohner, Eileen Herlie. Intelligent, unglamorous account of Sigmund Freud as young doctor, focusing on his early psychiatric theories and treatments and his struggle for their acceptance among Viennese medical colleagues. Fascinating dream sequence. Originally released at 139m. Also known as FREUD: THE SECRET PASSION.

Friday Foster (1975) **C-90m.** ** D: Arthur Marks. Pam Grier, Yaphet Kotto, Godfrey Cambridge, Thalmus Rasulala, Eartha Kitt, Jim Backus, Scatman Crothers, Ted Lange, Carl Weathers. Black bubblegum nonsense based on comic strip about fashion photographer who gets involved in mystery and intrigue; here she tries to foil assassination/conspiracy plot against black politicians.▼

Friday The Rabbi Slept Late SEE: **Lanigan's Rabbi**

Friday the 13th (1980) **C-95m.** *½ D: Sean S. Cunningham. Betsy Palmer, Adrienne King, Harry Crosby, Laurie Bartram, Mark Nelson, Jeannine Taylor, Kevin Bacon. Palmer, who figures in an admittedly bravura finale, slaughters teens holed up in woodsy summer camp. Young folks unexpectedly made this gory, cardboard thriller a box-office smash—one more clue to why SAT scores continue to decline. Rates higher than BOMB simply because it's slightly better than part 2. Followed by a seemingly never-ending series of sequels and a TV series.▼

Friday the 13th, Part 2 (1981) **C-87m.** BOMB D: Steve Miner. Betsy Palmer, Amy Steel, John Furey, Adrienne King, Kirsten Baker, Stu Charno, Warrington Gillette. More nubile campers, more bloody executions. If you loved Part 1 . . .▼

Friday the 13th Part 3 (1982) **C-96m.** **
D: Steve Miner. Dana Kimmell, Paul
Kratka, Tracie Savage, Jeffrey Rogers,
Catherine Parks, Larry Zerner. Strictly amateur night in terms of acting and writing,
but this entry deemphasizes explicit gore
in favor of shocks, and delivers a few—
especially in 3D.▼

Friday the 13th—The Final Chapter
(1984) **C-91m.** BOMB D: Joseph Zito.
Crispin Glover, Kimberly Beck, Barbara
Howard, E. Erich Anderson, Corey Feldman, Ted White, Bruce Mahler, Lawrence
Monoson. Why bother with a new script?
It worked three times before, and audiences flocked to this one as well, with the
usual onslaught of disgustingly gory murders. Jason finally gets his— except that
(title notwithstanding) the door is left open
for yet another sequel!▼

**Friday the 13th Part V: A New Begin-
ning** (1985) **C-102m.** BOMB D: Danny
Steinmann. John Shepard, Melanie Kinnaman, Shavar Ross, Richard Young, Carol
Lacatell. A clever title (after . . . THE
FINAL CHAPTER) for more gore galore,
as gruesome and disgusting as ever.▼

Friday the 13th, Part VI: Jason Lives
(1986) **C-87m.** BOMB D: Tom McLoughlin. Thom Mathews, Jennifer Cooke, David Kagan, Renee Jones, Kerry Noonan,
C.J. Graham. Jason's summer camp has
enjoyed years of tranquility after changing
its name, but watch out! If you really think
there's something to gain from watching
Jason rise from the grave again, better try
changing your own name and doing it in
secret. The pits. ▼

**Friday the 13th Part VII—The New
Blood** (1988) **C-88m.** *½ D: John Carl
Buechler. Lar Park Lincoln, Terry Kiser,
Susan Blu, Kevin Blair, Susan Jennifer
Sullivan, Elizabeth Kaitan. Makeup expert
Buechler fails to inject much life into this
endless series. Part VII has pretty, blonde
Lincoln foolishly traveling to Crystal Lake
(with her mom and her shrink) where her
talent for telekinesis brings the monstrous
Jason back up from his watery grave to kill
off lots more teens.▼

**Friday the 13th PART VIII: Jason Takes
Manhattan** (1989) **C-100m.** ** D: Rob
Hedden. Jensen Daggett, Kane Hodder,
Peter Mark Richman, Scott Reeves, Barbara Bingham, V. C. Dupree, Sharlene
Martin. The best film in the "Friday"
series, imaginatively directed and written
by Hedden, is still just a slasher film,
though less gruesome than most. Despite
the title, most of the film takes place on a
cruise ship. Too long and not really for
fans of the series.▼

Frieda (1947-British) **97m.** *** D: Basil
Dearden. David Farrar, Glynis Johns, Mai
Zetterling, Flora Robson, Albert Lieven.
Interesting study of Farrar bringing Ger-

man wife Zetterling back home to England,
and bigotry they encounter.▼

Friendly Enemies (1942) **95m.** **½
D: Allan Dwan. Charles Winninger, Charlie Ruggles, James Craig, Nancy Kelly.
Thoughtful minor film of conflicts between
lifelong friends when WW1 breaks out and
their German heritage leads to friction.

Friendly Fire (1979) **C-145m.** TVM D:
David Greene. Carol Burnett, Ned Beatty,
Sam Waterston, Dennis Erdman, Timothy
Hutton. Gripping if overlong Emmy-winning drama about a rural American couple
who try to cope with governmental indifference to learn the truth behind their son's
death in Vietnam. Burnett seems somewhat sullen in her one-note portrayal of
real-life war activist Peg Mullen, but Beatty
is outstanding as her husband. Script by
Fay Kanin. Above average.▼

Friendly Persuasion (1956) **C-140m.** ****
D: William Wyler. Gary Cooper, Dorothy
McGuire, Marjorie Main, Anthony Perkins, Richard Eyer, Robert Middleton, (Peter) Mark Richman, Walter Catlett, William Schallert. Charming account (from
Jessamyn West novel) of Quaker family
struggling to maintain its identity amid
confusion and heartbreak of Civil War.
Warm, winning performances in this beautifully made film. Music by Dimitri Tiomkin.
Though no screenplay credit appears, film
was written by blacklisted Michael Wilson. Remade for TV.▼

Friendly Persuasion (1975) **C-100m.** TVM
D: Joseph Sargent. Richard Kiley, Shirley
Knight, Clifton James, Michael O'Keefe,
Kevin O'Keefe, Tracie Savage, Sparky
Marcus. Picturesque, well-acted drama about
a gentle Quaker couple who risk their
lives to help a pair of runaway slaves
seeking freedom. Kiley and Knight compare admirably to Gary Cooper and Dorothy McGuire, who starred in 1956 film
classic. Retitled EXCEPT FOR ME AND
THEE. Above average.▼

Friends (1971-British) **C-102m.** BOMB
D: Lewis Gilbert. Sean Bury, Anicee
Alvina, Pascale Roberts, Sady Rebbot,
Ronald Lewis. Yucky early-teen romance
about French boy and girl who run off to
the seashore, set up housekeeping, and
have a baby . . . then Mommy and Daddy
show up to take them home. Popular in its
day, primarily due to Elton John song
score, but you can buy the album instead.
Sequel (!): PAUL AND MICHELLE.

Friends and Lovers (1931) **68m.** **½ D:
Victor Schertzinger. Adolphe Menjou, Laurence Olivier, Lili Damita, Erich von
Stroheim, Hugh Herbert. Unexceptional
film interesting only for its cast. Menjou
and Olivier are British officers stationed in
India, both in love with Damita. Von
Stroheim is fun to watch as Damita's sly,
conniving husband.

Friendship in Vienna, A (1988) **C-100m.** TVM D: Arthur Allan Seidelman. Edward Asner, Jane Alexander, Stephen Macht, Jenny Lewis, Kamie Harper, Rosemary Forsyth, Ferdinand Mayne, Jean Simmons (narrator). War clouds over Europe as seen through the eyes of a Jewish teenager whose best friend's Christian family helps her flee the Nazis. Meticulously produced, well-acted version of Doris Orgel's book *Devil in Vienna* adapted by Richard Alfieri. Made for cable by Disney. Above average.

Friendships, Secrets and Lies (1979) **C-100m.** TVM D: Ann Zane Shanks and Marlena Laird. Cathryn Damon, Shelley Fabares, Sondra Locke, Tina Louise, Paula Prentiss, Stella Stevens, Loretta Swit. Seven college sorority sisters relive the past when a baby's skeleton is discovered as the old house on campus is razed. Uninspired telling of Babs H. Deal's novel, *The Walls Come Tumbling Down,* with an all-female cast and virtually all-female production crew. Average.

Friends of Eddie Coyle, The (1973) **C-102m.** ***½ D: Peter Yates. Robert Mitchum, Peter Boyle, Richard Jordan, Steven Keats, Alex Rocco, Mitchell Ryan. Ultrarealistic depiction of criminals and police, as hardened con labors to supply guns and make deal with cops. Bleak nightmare picture of underworld enhanced by numerous Boston locations, flawless performances. Only liabilities: film's offbeat low-key narrative approach and finale. Adapted by Paul Monash from George V. Higgins's novel.

Fright (1971-British) **C-87m.** ** D: Peter Collinson. Susan George, Honor Blackman, Ian Bannen, John Gregson, George Cole, Dennis Waterman. Young baby-sitter (George) spends terror-filled evening at country house, menaced by mental hospital escapee. Contrived, mechanical direction and so-so script.▼

Frightened Bride, The (1953-British) **75m.** ** D: Terence Young. Andre Morell, Flora Robson, Mai Zetterling, Michael Denison, Mervyn Johns. Murder haunts a family when the youngest son becomes involved in homicide.

Frightened City, The (1962-British) **97m.** **½ D: John Lemont. Herbert Lom, John Gregson, Sean Connery, Alfred Marks, Yvonne Romain. Interesting inside look at a London racketeer amalgamating various city gangs for master plan syndicate.

Fright Night (1985) **C-105m.** *** D: Tom Holland. Chris Sarandon, William Ragsdale, Amanda Bearse, Roddy McDowall, Stephen Geoffreys, Jonathan Stark. Teenage boy enlists the aid of TV horror-movie host (and erstwhile actor) to kill suave, cunning vampire who's moved in next door. Entertaining, old-fashioned horror outing energized by Richard Edlund's spectacular special effects and highlighted by two wonderful performances, by McDowall and Sarandon. Written by director Holland. Followed by a sequel.▼

Fright Night Part II (1989) **C-104m.** ** D: Tommy Lee Wallace. Roddy McDowall, William Ragsdale, Traci Lin, Julie Carmen, Jonathan Gries, Russell Clark, Brian Thompson, Merritt Butrick, Ernie Sabella. Sister of the vampire who met a grisly end in FRIGHT NIGHT seeks revenge on the duo who destroyed him. More-of-the-same sequel is definitely a comedown from the earlier film, though well produced.▼

Fringe Dwellers, The (1986-Australian) **C-98m.** **½ D: Bruce Beresford. Kristina Nehm, Justine Saunders, Bob Maza, Kylie Belling, Denis Walker, Ernie Dingo. Ambitious young aborigine woman convinces her family to move out of their shantytown and into a prosperous, mostly white middle-class neighborhood in present-day Australia; the expected readjustment woes follow. Sincere, very well-acted drama (especially by Nehm) is undercut by sentimental, dramatically dishonest conclusion. Overall, worth a look.▼

Frisco Jenny (1933) **70m.** **½ D: William Wellman. Ruth Chatterton, Louis Calhern, Helen Jerome Eddy, Donald Cook, James Murray, Hallam Cooley, Pat O'Malley, Harold Huber, J. Carrol Naish. Chatterton's father and lover are killed in the San Francisco earthquake, but her problems have only begun. Loose retelling of MADAME X is a tailor-made Chatterton vehicle. Good atmosphere and smart dialogue overcome film's tendency to meander.

Frisco Kid (1935) **77m.** ** D: Lloyd Bacon. James Cagney, Margaret Lindsay, Ricardo Cortez, Lili Damita, Fred Kohler, George E. Stone, Donald Woods. Routine drama of Barbary Coast with Cagney fighting his way to the top, almost dethroned by local gangs but saved by blueblood Lindsay.

Frisco Kid, The (1979) **C-122m.** **½ D: Robert Aldrich. Gene Wilder, Harrison Ford, Ramon Bieri, Val Bisoglio, George Ralph DiCenzo, Leo Fuchs, Penny Peyser. Offbeat story of Polish rabbi crossing U.S. in 1850 and developing friendship with young bank robber. Wilder's performance, and some charming vignettes, make up for many other shortcomings.▼

Frisco Sal (1945) **94m.** ** D: George Waggner. Susanna Foster, Turhan Bey, Alan Curtis, Andy Devine, Thomas Gomez, Samuel S. Hinds. Tepid costume drama of Foster out West in California, determined to find her brother's killer.

Frisky (1955-Italian) **98m.** **½ D: Luigi Comencini. Gina Lollobrigida, Vittorio De Sica, Roberto Risso, Marisa Merlini. Lollobrigida provides sufficient sex appeal to carry simple tale of flirtatious village girl who beats out competition in winning heart of police official De Sica.

Friz Freleng's Looney Looney Looney Bugs Bunny Movie SEE: **Looney Looney Looney Bugs Bunny Movie▼**

Fritz The Cat (1972) **C-78m.** *** D: Ralph Bakshi. X-rated animated feature somewhat based on Robert Crumb's underground comics character. Flawed but engaging, irreverent look at radical-hip lifestyles of the 1960s, geared for people who experienced that era. Imaginatively conceived cartoon. Sequel: THE NINE LIVES OF FRITZ THE CAT.▼

Frogmen, The (1951) **96m.** *** D: Lloyd Bacon. Richard Widmark, Dana Andrews, Gary Merrill, Jeffrey Hunter, Robert Wagner, Jack Warden. Intriguing look at underwater demolition squads in action in the Pacific during WW2.

Frogs (1972) **C-91m.** **½ D: George McCowan. Ray Milland, Sam Elliott, Joan Van Ark, Adam Roarke, Judy Pace. Patriarchal Milland has been destroying bayou wildlife and now all the swamp critters are out to destroy his whole family. Dumb but enjoyable thriller.▼

From a Far Country: Pope John Paul II (1981-British-Italian-Polish) **C-100m.** TVM D: Krzysztof Zanussi. Cezary Morawski, Sam Neill, Christopher Cazenove, Warren Clarke, Lisa Harrow, Maurice Denham, Kathleen Byron. An earnest, somber—and boring—drama tracing the life of the man who would become Pope, from his boyhood through WW2. Ironically, its premiere coincided with the December 1981 crisis in Poland. Average.

From Beyond (1986) **C-85m.** **½ D: Stuart Gordon. Jeffrey Combs, Barbara Crampton, Ted Sorel, Ken Foree, Carolyn Purdy-Gordon, Bunny Summers, Bruce McGuire. The RE-ANIMATOR team returns to H. P. Lovecraft territory for this similarly demented film based on a scientist's search for a sixth sense . . . which, in time, causes his associates to go berserk. Takes its time getting revved up, but then cuts loose in outrageous fashion. As before, this is not for the squeamish, but if you liked RE-ANIMATOR . . .▼

From Beyond the Grave (1973-British) **C-97m.** *** D: Kevin Connor. Peter Cushing, Margaret Leighton, Ian Bannen, Donald Pleasence, David Warner, Diana Dors, Angela Pleasence, Nyree Dawn Porter, Lesley-Anne Down. Neat multistoried horror pic. Visitors to Cushing's little antique shop, Temptations Ltd., meet terrible fates. Leighton excels as a wacky clairvoyant. Retitled: CREATURES.▼

From Hell It Came (1957) **71m.** *½ D: Dan Milner. Tod Andrews, Tina Carver, Linda Watkins, John McNamara, Gregg Palmer, Robert Swan. Monstrous tree rises from grave of native chief's son, causing terror in South Seas village. As walkingtree movies go, this is at the top of the list.

From Hell to Borneo (1964) **C-96m.** ** D: George Montgomery. George Montgomery, Julie Gregg, Torin Thatcher, Lisa Moreno. Filmed in the Philippines, tale recounts Montgomery's efforts to maintain sanctity of his private island against aggressive crooks and smugglers.▼

From Hell to Texas (1958) **C-100m.** **½ D: Henry Hathaway. Don Murray, Diane Varsi, Chill Wills, Dennis Hopper. Sincere Western with Murray on the run with posse on his trail for accidentally killing a man.

From Hell to Victory (1979-French-Italian-Spanish) **C-100m.** ** D: Hank Milestone (Umberto Lenzi). George Peppard, George Hamilton, Horst Buchholz, Capucine, Sam Wanamaker, Jean-Pierre Cassel, Anny Duperey. Friends of various nationalities are torn apart by the coming of WW2. Undistinguished, superficial actioner.▼

From Here to Eternity (1953) **118m.** **** D: Fred Zinnemann. Burt Lancaster, Montgomery Clift, Deborah Kerr, Donna Reed, Frank Sinatra, Philip Ober, Ernest Borgnine, Mickey Shaughnessy, Jack Warden, Claude Akins, George Reeves. Toned-down but still powerful adaptation of James Jones' novel of Army life in Hawaii just before Pearl Harbor. Brilliantly acted by entire cast, including Sinatra in his "comeback" role as the pathetic soldier Maggio. Eight Oscars include Best Picture, Director, Screenplay (Daniel Taradash), Cinematography (Burnett Guffey), and Supporting Actors Sinatra and Reed. Remade in 1979 as a TV mini-series, which in turn spun off a brief series.▼

From Mao to Mozart: Isaac Stern in China (1980) **C-84m.** ***½ D: Murray Lerner. Isaac Stern, David Golub, Tan Shuzhen. Moving documentary about violinist Stern's '79 tour of China. Most memorably, he tutors talented Chinese students, encouraging them to *feel* their playing. Shuzhen, deputy director of the Shanghai Conservatory of Music, describes his incarceration during the Cultural Revolution. Deservedly won Best Documentary Academy Award.▼

From Nashville with Music (1969) **C-87m.** *½ D: Eddie Crandall. Marilyn Maxwell, Leo G. Carroll, (Pedro) Gonzalez-Gonzalez, Marty Robbins, Merle Haggard, Buck Owens. Some good C&W music, but one is better off buying the performers' albums instead of suffering through this story of N.Y.C. couple who go to the Grand Ole Opry by mistake.

From Noon Till Three (1976) **C-99m.** **½ D: Frank D. Gilroy. Charles Bronson, Jill Ireland, Douglas Fowley, Stan Haze, Damon Douglas, Anne Ramsey. Likably offbeat story (written by Gilroy) about a two-bit robber who enjoys a brief tryst with a woman who—after he is thought dead—fictionalizes their romance and turns him into a legendary hero. A kind of shaggy dog joke, which while pleasant, doesn't quite work. A nice change of pace for Bronson, though.

From Russia with Love (1963-British) **C-118m.** ***½ D: Terence Young. Sean Connery, Daniela Bianchi, Lotte Lenya, Pedro Armendariz, Robert Shaw, Bernard Lee, Lois Maxwell. Second James Bond film is one of the best; plenty of suspense and action, and one of the longest, most exciting fight scenes ever staged. Lenya makes a very sinister spy.▼

From the Dead of Night (1989) **C-200m.** TVM D: Paul Wendkos. Lindsay Wagner, Bruce Boxleitner, Robin Thomas, Robert Prosky, Diahann Carroll, Merritt Butrick, Joanne Linville. Fashion designer Wagner narrowly escapes death only to be pursued by "walkers," dead people who feel cheated that she didn't become one of them. Overlong adaptation by William Bleich of Gary Bradner's mystery-thriller, *Walkers*, although it does deliver a good number of chills. Originally shown in two parts. Above average.

From the Earth to the Moon (1958) **C-100m.** **½ D: Byron Haskin. Joseph Cotten, George Sanders, Debra Paget, Don Dubbins, Patric Knowles, Melville Cooper, Carl Esmond, Henry Daniell. Jules Verne's fiction doesn't float well in contrived sci-fi of early rocket flight to the moon. Veteran cast looks most uncomfortable.▼

From the Hip (1987) **C-112m.** BOMB D: Bob Clark. Judd Nelson, Elizabeth Perkins, John Hurt, Darren McGavin, Ray Walston, Dan Monahan, David Alan Grier, Nancy Marchand, Allan Arbus, Edward Winter. Once again, Nelson plays a character only a mother could love: a lawyer who's made a name for himself by winning a hopeless case through outrageous courtroom tactics. Now he's given another challenge: defending Hurt, who's accused of murder. Hurt's flamboyant performance can't save this mongrel of a movie.▼

From the Life of the Marionettes (1980-German) **C/B&W-104m.** ***½ D: Ingmar Bergman. Robert Atzorn, Christine Buchegger, Martin Benrath, Rita Russek, Lola Muethel, Walter Schmidinger, Heinz Bennent. Powerful, provocative drama about a respectable, successful businessman (Atzorn), who ravishes and strangles a prostitute. He has also been obsessed with killing his wife (Buchegger), with whom he constantly quarrels. Not coincidentally, both were minor characters in SCENES FROM A MARRIAGE.▼

From the Mixed-Up Files of Mrs. Basil E. Frankweiler (1973) **C-105m.** **½ D: Fielder Cook. Ingrid Bergman, Sally Prager,

Johnny Doran, George Rose, Georgann Johnson, Richard Mulligan, Madeline Kahn. Fanciful tale of New Jersey kids Prager and Doran who hide out in N.Y.C.'s Metropolitan Museum, creating a dream world and befriending recluse Bergman, seen too briefly. Best for children. Blanche Hanalis adapted E.L. Konigsburg's novel. Reissued as THE HIDEAWAYS.▼

From the Terrace (1960) **C-144m.** *** D: Mark Robson. Paul Newman, Joanne Woodward, Myrna Loy, Ina Balin, Leon Ames, Elizabeth Allen, Barbara Eden, George Grizzard. John O'Hara's ironic chronicle of young war veteran's rise to financial and social success is superficial film. Woodward is chic and Newman wooden; Loy is superb as drunken mother, Ames fine as bitter dad.▼

From This Day Forward (1946) **95m.** *** D: John Berry. Joan Fontaine, Mark Stevens, Rosemary DeCamp, Henry (Harry) Morgan, Arline Judge, Bobby Driscoll, Mary Treen. Agreeable soaper of Fontaine and Stevens readjusting their lives when he returns from war, and their struggle to get on in the world.

Front, The (1976) **C-94m.** **** D: Martin Ritt. Woody Allen, Zero Mostel, Herschel Bernardi, Michael Murphy, Andrea Marcovicci, Remak Ramsay, Joshua Shelley, Lloyd Gough. Bull's-eye comedy with serious theme. Allen is a schnook enlisted by blacklisted writers to put his name on their scripts during 1950s witch-hunt era, leading to various complications. Allen's casting is perfect, and Mostel is standout as "tainted" comic fighting for survival. Original script by blacklisted Walter Bernstein; Ritt, Mostel, Bernardi, Shelley, and Gough were also blacklisted in real life.▼

Frontier Gal (1945) **C-84m.** **½ D: Charles Lamont. Yvonne De Carlo, Rod Cameron, Andy Devine, Fuzzy Knight, Andrew Tombes, Sheldon Leonard, Clara Blandick. Sex in the West as saloon queen De Carlo falls in love with outlaw Cameron; no sympathy from villain Leonard in OK Western-comedy.

Frontier Gun (1958) **70m.** ** D: Paul Landres. John Agar, Robert Strauss, Barton MacLane, Morris Ankrum. Agar is honest sheriff who discovers that gunplay is only solution to town's crooks.

Frontier Hellcat (1966-German) **C-98m.** **½ D: Alfred Vohrer. Stewart Granger, Elke Sommer, Pierre Brice, Gotz George. Another Karl May *Winnetou* story, which captures flavor of Old West, recounting adventure of pioneers passing through Rockies.

Frontier Marshal (1939) **71m.** *** D: Alan Dwan. Randolph Scott, Nancy Kelly, Cesar Romero, Binnie Barnes, John Carradine, Lon Chaney, Jr., Chris-Pin Martin, Eddie Foy, Jr. Colorful retelling of events leading to legendary gunfight at the

O.K. Corral. Scott is fine as Tombstone's new marshal, Wyatt Earp, Romero is more moody than cold-blooded as Doc *Halliday*, and Kelly is the girl from his past who reminds Doc of his earlier, saner days as—an obstetrician! Many scenes and bits of dialogue were used in the 1946 remake, MY DARLING CLEMENTINE. Ward Bond, who plays Earp's brother in the later film, appears briefly as a cowardly town marshal.

Frontier Uprising (1961) 68m. *½ D: Edward L. Cahn. James Davis, Nancy Hadley, Ken Mayer, Nestor Paiva. Scout leading pioneers to West Coast in 1840s discovers that Mexico and U.S. are at war.

Front Page, The (1931) 103m. ***½ D: Lewis Milestone. Adolphe Menjou, Pat O'Brien, Mary Brian, Edward Everett Horton, Walter Catlett, Mae Clarke, George E. Stone. First filming of Hecht-MacArthur play is forceful, funny, and flamboyantly directed, with Menjou and O'Brien a good pair as battling editor and reporter in Chicago. Stands up quite well alongside remake HIS GIRL FRIDAY.▼

Front Page, The (1974) C-105m. *** D: Billy Wilder. Jack Lemmon, Walter Matthau, Carol Burnett, Susan Sarandon, Vincent Gardenia, David Wayne, Allen Garfield, Austin Pendleton, Charles Durning, Harold Gould, Herb Edelman, Dick O'Neill, Jon Korkes, Martin Gabel. Third filming of the Hecht-MacArthur play about wild and woolly Chicago newspapermen in the 1920s has hardly anything new to offer (except four-letter words) but remains an enjoyable vehicle for this fine cast. Only Burnett misses the boat as pathetic hooker Molly Malloy. Remade again(!) in 1988 as SWITCHING CHANNELS.

Front Page Story (1954-British) 99m. **½ D: Gordon Parry. Jack Hawkins, Elizabeth Allan, Eva Bartok, Martin Miller, Derek Farr. Solid performances enhance story of many problems confronting newspaper editor: pending divorce, murder, lost children, and a rebellious staff.

Front Page Woman (1935) 82m. **½ D: Michael Curtiz. Bette Davis, George Brent, Winifred Shaw, Roscoe Karns, Joseph Crehan. Breezy yarn of rival reporters Davis and Brent trying to outdo each other covering unusual fire story; prime ingenue Davis fare.

Frozen Dead, The (1967-British) C-95m. **½ D: Herbert J. Leder. Dana Andrews, Anna Palk, Philip Gilbert, Kathleen Breck, Karel Stepanek. Bizarre account of scientist Andrews who froze group of Nazi leaders, now trying to revive them and the Third Reich; sloppy production values mar tale. Released theatrically in b&w.

Frozen Ghost, The (1945) 61m. ** D: Harold Young. Lon Chaney, Evelyn Ankers, Milburn Stone, Douglass Dumbrille, Martin Kosleck, Elena Verdugo. Typical *Inner*

Sanctum nonsense about tormented hypnotist who stumbles into murder plot.

Fruit Machine, The (1988-British) C-103m. *** D: Philip Saville. Emile Charles, Tony Forsyth, Robert Stephens, Claire Higgins, Bruce Payne, Robbie Coltrane. Diverting contemporary thriller about two gay but very different Liverpool teens (Charles and Forsyth, in spirited performances) who witness a gangland murder and must flee for their lives. Scripted by Frank (LETTER TO BREZHNEV) Clarke. Video title: WONDERLAND.▼

F. Scott Fitzgerald and "The Last of the Belles" (1974) C-100m. TVM D: George Schaefer. Richard Chamberlain, Blythe Danner, Susan Sarandon, David Huffman, Ernest Thompson, Richard Hatch, James Naughton. Chamberlain is Scott and Danner is Zelda in this curious but well-acted intertwining of their real lives just after WWI and his writing of *The Last of the Belles* (acted by Sarandon and Huffman) to pay for a summer on the Continent. James Costigan wrote the screenplay as part of the same team that later did F. SCOTT FITZGERALD IN HOLLYWOOD. Above average.

F. Scott Fitzgerald in Hollywood (1976) C-100m. TVM D: Anthony Page. Jason Miller, Tuesday Weld, Julia Foster, Dolores Sutton, Susanne Benton, Michael Lerner, Tom Ligon, John Randolph, James Woods. Fitzgerald's Hollywood career, his marriage to the ill-fated Zelda (Weld is super), his affair with Sheilah Graham (Foster). Brilliant career made fuzzy by Miller's gloomy performance and James Costigan's muddled script, giving the viewer not much more than a broken-spirited and rather abusive alcoholic. A good opportunity passed up. Average.

F.T.A. (1972) C-94m. ** D: Francine Parker. Jane Fonda, Donald Sutherland, Len Chandler, Holly Near, Pamela Donegan, Michael Alaimo. Unusual, rarely-seen documentary of Fonda and Sutherland's *Free (or F——) the Army* revue, presented near Army bases and featuring antiwar skits and songs. Interesting only as a curio.

Fugitive, The (1947) 104m. ***½ D: John Ford. Henry Fonda, Dolores Del Rio, Pedro Armendariz, J. Carrol Naish, Leo Carrillo, Ward Bond. Brooding drama set in Mexico with revolutionist priest turned in by man who once sheltered him. Superbly photographed by Gabriel Figueroa.▼

Fugitive Family (1980) C-100m. TVM D: Paul Krasny. Richard Crenna, Diane Baker, Eli Wallach, Don Murray, Ronny Cox, Mel Ferrer, William Kirby Cullen. Drama about a government witness who is forced to take his family into hiding with new identities after testifying against a syndicate boss. Average.

Fugitive Kind, The (1959) 135m. **½

[409]

D: Sidney Lumet. Marlon Brando, Anna Magnani, Joanne Woodward, Maureen Stapleton, Victor Jory, R. G. Armstrong. Uneven filming of Tennessee Williams' *Orpheus Descending*, with strange casting. Wandering bum (Brando) arrives in Southern town, sparking romances with middle-aged married woman (Magnani) and spunky Woodward. Movie goes nowhere.▼

Fugitive Lovers (1934) 84m. ** D: Richard Boleslawski. Robert Montgomery, Madge Evans, Nat Pendleton, Ted Healy, C. Henry Gordon, The Three Stooges. Genially preposterous tale of runaway chorus girl and prison escapee who are drawn together during cross-country bus trip (all of it shot with "arty" camera angles). Moves like lightning to even *more* preposterous climax in snowbound Colorado.▼

Fugitive of the Empire SEE: **Archer—Fugitive From the Empire, The**▼

Fulfillment of Mary Gray, The (1989) C-100m. TVM D: Piers Haggard. Cheryl Ladd, Ted Levine, Lewis Smith, Sheila Kelley. Period romantic triangle about a turn-of-the-century farm woman, the husband who can't give her a child, and his brother who can. Average.

Full Circle SEE: **Haunting of Julia, The**▼

Full Confession (1939) 73m. ** D: John Farrow. Victor McLaglen, Sally Eilers, Joseph Calleia, Barry Fitzgerald. Mild yet effective yarn of clergyman who listens to a criminal's confessions and convinces him that he should go to the police to save innocent man accused of crime.

Fuller Brush Girl, The (1950) 85m. ** D: Lloyd Bacon. Lucille Ball, Eddie Albert, Jeff Donnell, Jerome Cowan, Lee Patrick. Low-grade slapstick with energetic Lucy as door-to-door salesgirl, mixed up with thieves.

Fuller Brush Man, The (1948) 93m. **½ D: S.Sylvan Simon. Red Skelton, Janet Blair, Don McGuire, Adele Jergens, Ross Ford, Hillary Brooke. Usual Skelton slapstick, with Red involved in murder while valiantly trying to succeed as a door-to-door salesman.▼

Full Exposure: The Sex Tape Scandal (1989) C-100m. TVM D: Noel Nosseck. Lisa Hartman, Anthony Denison, Jennifer O'Neill, Vanessa Williams, Peter Jurasik, Walter Olkiewicz, Jennifer Warren, John Anderson. Mini-skirted assistant DA joins forces with a cop to find out who's knocking off call girls after videotaping their trysts. Joins the family of ludicrously executed and dubiously acted time-wasters that makes a movie buff pine for an old-time "B" crime flick. Below average.

Full Metal Jacket (1987) C-116m. *** D: Stanley Kubrick. Matthew Modine, Adam Baldwin, Vincent D'Onofrio, Lee Ermey, Dorian Harewood, Arliss Howard, Kevyn Major Howard, Ed O'Ross. Adaptation of Gustav Hasford's *The Short Timers* is divided into two sections: a harrowing look at Marine basic training on Parris Island; and combat experiences in Vietnam. The first half is so strong (thanks in part to real-life former D.I. Ermey) that the second half suffers in comparison, as it covers more familiar ground, while keeping emotions in check. Still, it's compelling, well acted, and supremely well crafted, certainly in keeping with Kubrick's recurring theme of dehumanization. Filmed in England.▼

Full Moon High (1981) C-94m. *** D: Larry Cohen. Adam Arkin, Ed McMahon, Elizabeth Hartman, Roz Kelly, Bill Kirchenbauer, Kenneth Mars, Joanne Nail, Alan Arkin. Infectiously silly teenage werewolf comedy, with Arkin as a high-school football star whose strange, right-wing father (McMahon) takes him to Transylvania and inadvertently changes his life. Lots of off-the-wall laughs and cameos by various comedy performers.

Full Moon in Blue Water (1988) C-93m. ** D: Peter Masterson. Gene Hackman, Teri Garr, Burgess Meredith, Elias Koteas, Kevin Cooney, David Doty. Hackman is wallowing in self-pity over his drowned wife, as creditors duplicitously plot foreclosure on his coastal Texas bar. Also involved in the talky interchange are feisty bus driver Garr, Hackman's elderly father-in-law Meredith, and mentally shaky employee Koteas. This screen original by playwright Bill Bozzone feels like bad theater.▼

Full Moon in Paris (1984-French) C-102m. *** D: Eric Rohmer. Pascale Ogier, Fabrice Luchini, Tcheky Karyo, Christian Vadim, Virginie Thevenet. Neat little comedy from Rohmer about a headstrong young woman (Ogier), and her relationships with three men. Wonderful dialogue and characterizations, with a charming Ogier performance.▼

Full of Life (1956) 91m. *** D: Richard Quine. Judy Holliday, Richard Conte, Salvatore Baccaloni, Esther Minciotti. Holliday's antics as pregnant wife are almost matched by Baccaloni as excitable father-in-law with his own way of running things.

Full Treatment, The SEE: **Stop Me Before I Kill!**

Fun and Games (1980) C-100m. TVM D: Allen Smithee. Valerie Harper, Cliff De-Young, Max Gail, JoBeth Williams, Peter Donat, Art Hindle, Michael Nouri, Lloyd Gough. Sexual harassment on the job is faced obliquely and patly in this drama, from which the director withdrew his name, leaving credit to the prolific and pseudonymous Smithee. Average.

Funeral, The (1984-Japanese) C-124m. *** D: Juzo Itami. Nobuko Miyamoto, Tsutomu Yamazaki, Kin Sugai, Ichiro

Zaitsu, Nekohachi Edoya. Itami's debut feature is an on-target black comedy that chides solemn, traditional Japanese funeral rites. The scenario details what ensues when a modern family is compelled to hold a Buddhist funeral for its patriarch—who happened to own a brothel.▼

Funeral Home (1982-Canadian) **C-93m.** ** D: William Fruet. Lesleh Donaldson, Kay Hawtrey, Barry Morse, Dean Garbett, Stephen Miller, Harvey Atkin. Teenager Donaldson investigates when guests begin disappearing from grandmother Hawtrey's summer motel. OK of its type; also known as CRIES IN THE NIGHT.▼

Funeral in Berlin (1966) **C-102m.** ** D: Guy Hamilton. Michael Caine, Eva Renzi, Paul Hubschmid, Oscar Homolka, Guy Doleman. Second of three Harry Palmer films (based on Len Deighton's novels) featuring Caine as the British spy arranging for defection of Russian officer in charge of Berlin war security. Caine and Homolka are good, Renzi attractive, but slow-moving tale just doesn't click. Followed by BILLION DOLLAR BRAIN.▼

Funhouse, The (1981) **C-96m.** **½ D: Tobe Hooper. Elizabeth Berridge, Cooper Huckabee, Miles Chapin, Largo Woodruff, Sylvia Miles, William Finley, Kevin Conway. Intense drama about four teenagers who decide to spend night in funhouse of a sleazy traveling carnival. Once inside, there is sex, violence, suspense and an increasing tension as they encounter the unknown. Stylish visuals help create an eerie atmosphere in this not entirely successful chiller.▼

✓ **Fun in Acapulco** (1963) **C-97m.** **½ D: Richard Thorpe. Elvis Presley, Ursula Andress, Paul Lukas, Alejandro Rey. Scenery outshines story of Presley working as lifeguard and entertainer in Mexican resort city and performing the likes of "No Room to Rhumba in a Sports Car," "Bossa Nova Baby," and "You Can't Say No in Acapulco." Lukas is amusing as temperamental chef.▼

Funland (1986) **C-105m.** BOMB D: William Vanderkloot. David Lander, William Windom, Bruce Mahler, Robert Sacchi, Lane Davies, Mike McManus, Jan Hooks, Susan Ursitti. Limp mishmash about the various goings-on in an amusement park. Borrows elements of POLICE ACADEMY, M*A*S*H, PLAY IT AGAIN, SAM, and MAGIC—but all it adds up to is boredom.▼

Fun Loving SEE: **Quackser Fortune Has a Cousin in the Bronx**▼

Funny Face (1957) **C-103m.** ***½ D: Stanley Donen. Audrey Hepburn, Fred Astaire, Kay Thompson, Michel Auclair, Suzy Parker, Ruta Lee. Stylish and highly stylized musical with Astaire as fashion photographer who turns Hepburn into chic Paris model. Top Gershwin score ("How Long Has This Been Going On," "He Loves and She Loves," "S'Wonderful," title tune), striking use of color, entertaining performance by Thompson as magazine editor. Cinematography by Ray June and John P. Fulton. Leonard Gershe based his screenplay on an unproduced stage musical—and Astaire's role was based on Richard Avedon, who's credited as visual consultant.▼

Funny Farm, The (1982-Canadian) **C-95m.** ** D: Ron Clark. Miles Chapin, Eileen Brennan, Jack Carter, Tracy Bregman, Howie Mandel, Marjorie Gross, Lou Dinos, Peter Aykroyd. Young man from Ohio comes to L.A. to make it as a stand-up comic. Slow-moving film introduces many unknown comics who do short bits at a "comedy store" owned by Brennan. Some funny moments, but film as a whole is nothing much.▼

Funny Farm (1988) **C-101m.** **½ D: George Roy Hill. Chevy Chase, Madolyn Smith, Joseph Maher, Jack Gilpin, Brad Sullivan, MacIntyre Dixon. Oddly easygoing—and thus mildly endearing—Chase comedy about a N.Y. sportswriter who discovers, MR. BLANDINGS style, that country living isn't quite what it's cracked up to be. Has the look of quality (it was photographed by Miroslav Ondricek, designed by Henry Bumstead) but too many gags fizzle. Final episode is the best.▼

Funny Girl (1968) **C-155m.** *** D: William Wyler. Barbra Streisand, Omar Sharif, Kay Medford, Anne Francis, Walter Pidgeon, Lee Allen, Gerald Mohr. Streisand's Oscar-winning film debut as Fanny Brice, singer-comedienne whose unhappy private life contrasted comic antics onstage. Bad as biography, but first-rate as musical, including fine Bob Merrill-Jule Styne score, memorable tugboat finale to "Don't Rain on My Parade." Sequel: FUNNY LADY.▼

Funny Lady (1975) **C-137m.** **½ D: Herbert Ross. Barbra Streisand, James Caan, Omar Sharif, Roddy McDowall, Ben Vereen, Carole Wells. Sequel to FUNNY GIRL shows Fanny Brice at height of her career, meeting and marrying ambitious showman Billy Rose (Caan). Disjointed film has fine moments of music and comedy, but a cliché-ridden script to contend with.▼

Funnyman (1971) **C-98m.** *** D: John Korty. Peter Bonerz, Sandra Archer, Carol Androsky, Larry Hankin, Barbara Hiken, Gerald Hiken. Winning little film about improvising comic (Bonerz) who's nagged by the idea that he should be doing something more "important." Features great skits by The Committee and funny animated spoofs by director Korty.

Funny Thing Happened on the Way to the Forum, A (1966) C-99m. **½ D: Richard Lester. Zero Mostel, Phil Silvers, Buster Keaton, Jack Gilford, Michael Crawford, Annette Andre, Michael Hordern. Frenzied adaptation of Broadway musical about conniving slave (Mostel) in ancient Rome; tries too hard, comes off forced. Still, with great comic cast, there's plenty worth seeing. Self-spoof on song "Lovely" is a highlight; score by Stephen Sondheim.▼

Fun on a Weekend (1947) 93m. ** D: Andrew L. Stone. Eddie Bracken, Priscilla Lane, Tom Conway, Allen Jenkins, Arthur Treacher, Alma Kruger. Scatterbrain fluff as Bracken and Lane maneuver their way from penniless fortune to love and riches, all in the course of a day.

Fun With Dick and Jane (1977) C-95m. **½ D: Ted Kotcheff. Jane Fonda, George Segal, Ed McMahon, Dick Gautier, Allan Miller, John Dehner. Lightly amusing comedy about Segal losing his job, he and wife Fonda trying to cope with no income and finally turning to crime. Falls apart after promising start, becoming fragmented and pointless.▼

Furies, The (1950) 109m. **½ D: Anthony Mann. Barbara Stanwyck, Walter Huston, Wendell Corey, Gilbert Roland, Judith Anderson, Beulah Bondi, Thomas Gomez, Albert Dekker, Blanche Yurka, Wallace Ford. Well-directed but talky psychological Western, detailing Stanwyck's complex love-hate relationship with tyrannical cattle rancher father Huston (in his final role). Heavy going at times.

Further Adventures of Tennessee Buck, The (1988) C-88m. **½ D: David Keith. David Keith, Kathy Shower, Brant van Hoffman, Sydney Lassick, Tiziana Stella, Patrizia Zanetti. Fun imitation of the INDIANA JONES films is set in Borneo where ne'er-do-well Keith plays the big white hunter, on safari with Shower and her rich nerd husband van Hoffman. They meet up with a cannibal tribe whose women give Shower a vivid oil rubdown (the film's hightlight). Actor-director Keith maintains a breezy tone, and lovely Sri Lanka locations almost distract attention from beauteous Shower, former *Playboy* Playmate of the Year.▼

Further Adventures of the Wilderness Family, The (1978) C-105m. *** D: Frank Zuniga. Robert Logan, Susan D. Shaw, Heather Rattray, Ham Larsen, George (Buck) Flower, Brian Cutler. This clone of 1975's family hit ADVENTURES OF . . . has same cast, same elements, same magnificent Colorado scenery. So who's to argue with success? Also known as WILDERNESS FAMILY, THE, PART 2; followed by MOUNTAIN FAMILY ROBINSON.▼

Further Perils of Laurel and Hardy, The (1968) 99m. **½ D: Robert Youngson.

Laurel and Hardy, Charley Chase, Max Davidson, James Finlayson. Repetitious format of "episodes" dulls edge of great material, but still fun, with rare L&H silent footage, pleasing interludes by Chase and Davidson.▼

Fury (1936) 94m. ***½ D: Fritz Lang. Sylvia Sidney, Spencer Tracy, Walter Abel, Bruce Cabot, Edward Ellis, Walter Brennan, Frank Albertson. Still timely drama of lynch mobs and mob rule in small town, making hardened criminal of innocent Tracy, spoiling his love for sweetheart Sidney. Lang's first American film.

Fury, The (1978) C-118m. *** D: Brian De Palma. Kirk Douglas, John Cassavetes, Carrie Snodgress, Amy Irving, Fiona Lewis, Andrew Stevens, Charles Durning, Gordon Jump. Stylish trash about young woman (Irving) with psychokinetic powers, and Douglas' desperate attempt to save his similarly gifted son from being used—or destroyed. Bloody and violent—the ultimate litmus test for those who prefer form over content. Film debut of Daryl Hannah.▼

Fury at Furnace Creek (1948) 88m. ** D: H. Bruce Humberstone. Victor Mature, Coleen Gray, Glenn Langan, Reginald Gardiner, Albert Dekker. Ordinary Western tale of Mature erasing mar on father's career against formidable opposition.

Fury at Gunsight Pass (1956) 68m. ** D: Fred F. Sears, David Brian, Neville Brand, Richard Long, Lisa Davis. Occasionally actionful Western, in which outlaw gang takes over a town.

Fury at Showdown (1957) 75m. *½ D: Gerd Oswald. John Derek, John Smith, Carolyn Craig, Nick Adams. Peace-loving man branded a coward, must shoot it out to rescue his girl.

Fury at Smugglers Bay (1963-British) 92m. ** D: John Gilling. Peter Cushing, Michele Mercier, Bernard Lee, George Coulouris, Liz Fraser. Sea yarn of pirates scavenging passing ships and reaping rewards off the English coastline.

Fury of Hercules, The (1961-Italian) C-95m. ** D: V. Scega. Brad Harris, Brigitte Corey, Mara Berni, Carlo Tamberlani, Serge Gainsbourg. Harris is musclebound hero who helps Corey and her followers overcome evil ruler of their land; standard production.▼

Fury of the Congo (1951) 69m. D: William Berke. Johnny Weissmuller, Sherry Moreland, William Henry, Lyle Talbot. SEE: **Jungle Jim** series.

Fury of the Pagans (1963-Italian) 86m. ** D: Guido Malatesta. Edmund Purdom, Rossana Podesta, Livio Lorenzon, Carlo Calo. Routine adventure set in ancient Rome, with Purdom leading his tribe to victory and rescuing his true love.

Fury of the Wolf Man, The (1970-Spanish) C-80m. BOMB D: Jose Maria Zabalza.

Paul Naschy, Perla Cristal, Michael Rivers, Veronica Lujan, Mark Stevens. You'd be furious too if you had to appear in a film like this; English-dubbed garbage about scientist who turns into helpless werewolf.▼

Future Cop (1976) **C-78m. TVM** D: Jud Taylor. Ernest Borgnine, Michael Shannon, John Amos, John Larch, Herbert Nelson, Ronnie Clair Edwards. Boisterous veteran cop and his robot partner, programmed to be the perfect policeman, team up to track a gang of car thieves. Borgnine's blustering and Shannon's affability make the silly premise bearable if not workable—although it subsequently became a series. Average.▼

Future Cop (1985) **C-85m.** *** D: Charles Band. Tim Thomerson, Helen Hunt, Art La Fleur, Biff Manard, Anne Seymour, Richard Herd, Richard Erdman. Comedian Thomerson is cleverly cast as a low-budget version of Harrison Ford from BLADE RUNNER, sent back in time 300 years to 1985 L. A. to inhabit the body of one of his ancestors and change history to prevent a totalitarian state from coming into power. Sci-fi satire is most amusing and visually arresting. Originally titled TRANCERS.▼

Futureworld (1976) **C-104m.** *** D: Richard T. Heffron. Peter Fonda, Blythe Danner, Arthur Hill, Yul Brynner, Stuart Margolin, John Ryan. Suspenseful sequel to WEST-WORLD has overtones of INVASION OF THE BODY SNATCHERS as robot duplicates try to take over. Short on action but intelligently done.▼

Futz (1969) **C-92m.** *½ D: Tom O'Horgan. Seth Allen, John Bakos, Mari-Claire Charba, Peter Craig, Sally Kirkland. Director O'Horgan, whose youthful touch made this a mild off-Broadway hit, brings bizarre tale to screen with disastrous results. No plot worth describing, except that there's a man in love with a pig.▼

Fuzz (1972) **C-92m.** ** D: Richard A. Colla. Burt Reynolds, Raquel Welch, Yul Brynner, Jack Weston, Tom Skerritt, Peter Bonerz, Steve Ihnat, James McEachin, Bert Remsen. Oddball film tries to mix laughs and excitement, to be the M*A*S*H of police dramas, but doesn't have the style to pull it off; another disappointment for Reynolds fans. Script by Evan Hunter from one of his *87th Precinct* stories, written as "Ed McBain."▼

Fuzzy Pink Nightgown, The (1957) **87m.** ** D: Norman Taurog. Jane Russell, Ralph Meeker, Adolphe Menjou, Keenan Wynn, Fred Clark, Una Merkel. Mediocre comedy. When movie star is kidnapped, everyone thinks it's a publicity gag.

F/X (1986) **C-106m.** *** D: Robert Mandel. Bryan Brown, Brian Dennehy, Diane Venora, Cliff De Young, Mason Adams, Jerry Orbach, Joe Grifasi, Martha Gehman.

Movie special-effects man is hired to stage a phony "hit" with a mafia man the target—but quickly learns that he's been double-crossed. Fast-moving, entertaining yarn that's a lot of fun, as long as you don't think about it for a moment afterward. Dennehy and Grifasi make a hilarious pair of Mutt and Jeff cops.▼

Gable and Lombard (1976) **C-131m.** BOMB D: Sidney J. Furie. James Brolin, Jill Clayburgh, Allen Garfield, Red Buttons, Joanne Linville, Melanie Mayron. Pure tripe about offscreen romance of two great stars. Brolin and Clayburgh are game but one-dimensional; script and direction are hopeless.

Gabriela (1983-Brazilian-Italian) **C-102m.** ** D: Bruno Barreto. Marcello Mastroianni, Sonia Braga, Antonio Cantafora, Ricardo Petraglia. Obvious tale of barkeeper Mastroianni taking on luscious, free-spirited Braga as a cook and lover. Braga's body and smile are the main interests here. Based on Jorge Amado's novel, which was developed into a top soap opera on Brazilian television.▼

Gabriel Over the White House (1933) **87m.** *** D: Gregory La Cava. Walter Huston, Karen Morley, Franchot Tone, C. Henry Gordon, Samuel S. Hinds, Jean Parker, Dickie Moore. Dizzying Depression fantasy of crooked Huston elected President, experiencing mysterious change that turns him into Superpresident, determined to eliminate racketeers, find world peace. Bizarre, fascinating.

Gaby (1956) **C-97m.** **½ D: Curtis Bernhardt. Leslie Caron, John Kerr, Sir Cedric Hardwicke, Taina Elg. Remake of WATERLOO BRIDGE, telling of ballerina Caron and her romance with soldier Kerr in WW2 England; not up to original.

Gaby—A True Story (1987) **C-110m.** *** D: Luis Mandoki. Liv Ullmann, Norma Aleandro, Robert Loggia, Rachel Levin, Lawrence Monoson, Robert Beltran. Incredible true story of Gaby Brimmer, born with cerebral palsy to wealthy European refugee parents in Mexico, leaving her body almost completely paralyzed—but not affecting her mind. Levin, who is not disabled in real life, gives a stunning performance in the lead (matched by Monoson as her boyfriend), with Aleandro as a tower of strength as the woman who devotes her life to Gaby. An often painful but worthwhile film. Brimmer executive produced.▼

Gaily, Gaily (1969) **C-107m.** ** D: Norman Jewison. Beau Bridges, Melina Mercouri, Brian Keith, George Kennedy, Hume Cronyn, Margot Kidder, Wilfrid Hyde-White, Melodie Johnson. Ben Hecht's colorful memories of apprenticeship on Chicago newspaper are destroyed by silly, hollow script that even changes "Hecht" to "Harvey." Expensive sets, period flavor are only bright spots in contrived comedy. Kidder's film debut.

Galactic Gigolo (1988) **C-82m.** BOMB D: Gorman Bechard. Carmine Capobianco, Debi Thibeault, Ruth Collins, Angela Nicholas, Frank Stewart. Amateurish sci fi comedy of a broccoli from outer space (Capobianco) taking on human form and heading for Connecticut to try and bed down every woman in sight during his two-week vacation. Painfully unfunny example of regional filmmaking.

Galaxina (1980) **C-95m.** *½ D: William Sachs. Stephen Macht, Dorothy R. Stratten, James David Hinton, Avery Schreiber. Cheap STAR WARS/STAR TREK spoof reeks of low production values, boring scenario, and non-acting. Definitely not a vehicle for the late Ms. Stratten, though the film is of interest for her appearance as a robot.▼

Galaxy of Terror (1981) **C-80m.** *½ D: B. D. Clark. Edward Albert, Erin Moran, Ray Walston, Bernard Behrens, Zalman King, Sid Haig. Astronauts are killed off by monsters while on mission to aid spaceship marooned on another planet. A Grade D ALIEN clone. Also known as MINDWARP: AN INFINITY OF TERROR and PLANET OF HORRORS. Followed by FORBIDDEN WORLD.▼

Galileo (1973-British) **C-145m.** *** D: Joseph Losey. Topol, Edward Fox, Colin Blakely, Georgia Brown, Clive Revill, Margaret Leighton, John Gielgud, Michael Gough, Judy Parfitt, Patrick Magee, Tom Conti. Bertolt Brecht's play, whose 1947 U.S. premiere was staged by director Losey, turned into unremarkable but generally satisfactory film. Topol is a little much as the scientist whose theories of the universe confound the church, but supporting actors are excellent. An American Film Theatre Production.

Gallant Bess (1946) **C-101m.** ** D: Andrew Marton. Marshall Thompson, George Tobias, Jim Davis, Clem Bevans, Donald Curtis, Chill Wills. Blah MGM B-movie is a grown-up version of concurrent THE YEARLING—soldier takes army horse home with him; it eventually saves his life. The first MGM film produced in CineColor, if that's your idea of a milestone.

Gallant Blade, The (1948) **C-81m.** ** D: Henry Levin. Larry Parks, Marguerite Chapman, Victor Jory, George Macready. Colorful, standard swashbuckler with dashing Parks protecting French general from villainous plot.

Gallant Hours, The (1960) **111m.** *** D: Robert Montgomery. James Cagney, Dennis Weaver, Ward Costello, Richard Jaeckel. Sincere, low-key biog of Admiral Halsey played documentary-style. Cagney is reserved and effective, but production needs livening.

Gallant Journey (1946) **85m.** **½ D: William Wellman. Glenn Ford, Janet Blair, Charles Ruggles, Henry Travers, Arthur Shields, Selena Royle. Ford pioneers glider plane development in 19th century. OK, but not as stirring as it's meant to be.

Gallant Lady (1934) **86m.** ** D: Gregory LaCava. Ann Harding, Clive Brook, Otto Kruger, Tulio Carminati, Dickie Moore, Janet Beecher. Handsome but standard soaper about unwed Harding giving up baby for adoption, later hoping for second chance when adopted mother dies. Remade as ALWAYS GOODBYE.

Gallipoli (1981-Australian) **C-110m.** ***½ D: Peter Weir. Mark Lee, Mel Gibson, Bill Kerr, Robert Grubb, David Argue, Tim McKenzie. Youthful idealists Lee and Gibson enlist in the military, meet their fate in title WW1 battle. Engrossing human drama with meticulous direction, striking feel for period detail. Final freeze-frame shot is reminiscent of Robert Capa's classic Spanish Civil War photo of soldier at the moment of death.▼

Galloping Major (1950-British) **82m.** ** D: Henry Cornelius. Basil Radford, Jimmy Hanley, Janette Scott, A. E. Matthews. Uninspired comedy about horseracing, with slow-running nag winning the day.

Gal Who Took the West, The (1949) **C-84m.** ** D: Frederick de Cordova. Yvonne De Carlo, Charles Coburn, Scott Brady, John Russell. De Carlo is attractive as singer in 1890s Arizona who allows Brady and Russell to court her.

Gal Young 'Un (1979) **C-105m.** ***½ D: Victor Nunez. Dana Preu, David Peck, J. Smith, Gene Densmore, Jenny Stringfellow, Tim McCormick. Low-budget gem about Prohibition-era widow Preu charmed and then exploited by foppish hustler Peck. Effective performances, use of locales (near Gainesville, Florida), depiction of the era. Based on a story by Marjorie Kinnan Rawlings.▼

Gambit (1966) **C-109m.** *** D: Ronald Neame. Michael Caine, Shirley MacLaine, Herbert Lom, Roger C. Carmel, John Abbott. Gimmicky robbery yarn with scoundrel Caine hiring Eurasian MacLaine to carry out perfect heist of invaluable piece of sculpture; great fun.▼

Gambler, The (1974) **C-111m.** ** D: Karel Reisz. James Caan, Paul Sorvino, Lauren Hutton, Morris Carnovsky, Jacqueline Brookes, Burt Young, Carmine Caridi, Vic Tayback, Steven Keats, London Lee, M. Emmet Walsh, James Woods, Stuart Margolin. Misfire about college prof Caan's compulsion to gamble; much inferior to Altman's CALIFORNIA SPLIT. Written by James Toback.▼

Gambler, The (1980) SEE: **Kenny Rogers as The Gambler**▼

Gambler and the Lady, The (1952-

British) **71m.** *½ D: Patrick Jenkins, Sam Newfield. Dane Clark, Kathleen Byron, Naomi Chance, Meredith Edwards, Anthony Forwood, Eric Pohlmann. Tepid little drama of gambling man Clark who falls in love, altering his unorthodox way of life.

Gambler From Natchez, The (1954) **C-88m.** ** D: Henry Levin. Dale Robertson, Debra Paget, Thomas Gomez, Lisa Daniels. Set in 1840s, film focuses on Robertson's plot to eliminate trio of men who shot his father, a gambler caught cheating.

Gamblers, The (1969) **C-93m.** **½ D: Ron Winston. Suzy Kendall, Don Gordon, Pierre Olaf, Kenneth Griffith, Stuart Margolin, Faith Domergue. A team of card sharps work a cruise ship for high stakes; interesting international cast, nice views of Dubrovnik, resort town in Yugoslavia.

Gambler's Choice (1944) **66m.** ** D: Frank McDonald. Chester Morris, Nancy Kelly, Russell Hayden, Lee Patrick, Lyle Talbot, Sheldon Leonard. Another variation of MANHATTAN MELODRAMA—three kids grow up; one becomes a lawman, the other a shady gambler, the third the nice girl they both love.

Gambling House (1950) **80m.** ** D: Ted Tetzlaff. Victor Mature, Terry Moore, William Bendix, Cleo Moore, Ann Doran. At times overly melodramatic account of man acquitted for murder, facing deportation as undesirable alien.

Gambling Lady (1934) **66m.** **½ D: Archie Mayo. Barbara Stanwyck, Pat O'Brien, Claire Dodd, Joel McCrea, C. Aubrey Smith, Arthur Treacher. Family disapproves when wealthy McCrea marries gambler's daughter Stanwyck, but she proves her worth when McCrea encounters trouble.

Gamblin' Man SEE: **Cockfighter**▼

Game for Vultures (1979-British) **C-106m.** BOMB D: James Fargo. Joan Collins, Richard Harris, Richard Roundtree, Ray Milland, Jana Cilliers, Sven-Bertil Taube, Denholm Elliott, John Parsonson, Ken Gampu. Tired cast in a dreadful drama about racial strife in Rhodesia. The subject matter may be worthy, but the result couldn't be more ponderous.▼

Game Is Over, The (1966-French) **C-96m.** **½ D: Roger Vadim. Jane Fonda, Peter McEnery, Michel Piccoli, Tina Marquand, Jacques Monod. Fonda marries wealthy Piccoli, falls in love with and seduces his son (McEnery). Handsome, updated version of Zola's *La Curée* is not bad; at the time, best performance of Jane's career.▼

Gamekeeper, The (1980-British) **C-84m.** *** D: Kenneth Loach. Phil Askham, Rita May, Andrew Grubb, Peter Steels, Michael Hinchcliffe. Simple, effectively subtle tale of conservative young gamekeeper

Askham, who sublimates his anger at being unable to crack the British class system.

Game of Danger (1954-British) **88m.** **½ D: Lance Comfort. Jack Warner, Veronica Hurst, Derek Farr. Offbeat study of two youngsters involved in homicide, with strange effects on their lives. Original title: BANG YOU'RE DEAD.

Game of Death, A (1946) **72m.** *½ D: Robert Wise. John Loder, Audrey Long, Edgar Barrier, Russell Wade, Russell Hicks, Jason Robards (Sr.), Noble Johnson. Second official version of THE MOST DANGEROUS GAME—madman Barrier hunts humans shipwrecked on his island. Moves well, but indifferently acted; nowhere nearly as exciting as the original. Next remake: RUN FOR THE SUN.

Game of Death (1979) **C-102m.** **½ D: Robert Clouse. Bruce Lee, Gig Young, Hugh O'Brian, Colleen Camp, Dean Jagger, Kareem Abdul-Jabbar, Chuck Norris. Lee died midway through production of this karate thriller; six years later, Clouse reassembled the surviving actors and, with the use of doubles, completed the film. Standard fare until final, incredible half hour, when Lee goes one-on-one with each of the villains in some of the most explosive fight scenes ever filmed.▼

Games (1967) **C-100m.** **½ D: Curtis Harrington. Simone Signoret, James Caan, Katharine Ross, Don Stroud, Estelle Winwood. After arrival of mysterious Signoret at kinky newlywed N.Y.C. apartment, borderline pranks become deadly conspiracy. The trick: guess who's doublecrossing whom. Attempts at deeper meanings unfulfilling, despite good cast.

Games, The (1970-British) **C-97m.** *½ D: Michael Winner. Michael Crawford, Stanley Baker, Ryan O'Neal, Charles Aznavour, Jeremy Kemp, Elaine Taylor, Kent Smith, Sam Elliott, Mona Washbourne. Dull film on potentially interesting subject: preparation of four runners for grueling 26-mile marathon in the Olympics. Rafer Johnson plays one of the commentators.

Games Girls Play SEE: **Bunny Caper, The**

Game Show Models (1977) **C-89m.** ** D: David Neil Gottlieb. John Vickery, Diane Summerfield, Thelma Houston, Gilbert De Rush, Sid Melton, Dick Miller, Willie Bobo, Rae Sperling, Charles Champlin. Odd, sometimes effective mixture of satire and sexploitation, set in the lurid, behind-the-scenes world of TV game shows. A mishmash, but any drive-in movie with a supporting cast like that is at least worth the attempt.

Games Mother Never Taught You (1982) **C-100m.** TVM D: Lee Philips. Loretta Swit, Sam Waterston, Eileen Heckart, Ed Grover, Bill Morey, Christopher Allport,

Madlyn Rhue. Corporate gamesmanship becomes the first matter of business learned by the first female executive in an all-male office. So-so romantic comedy adapted from Betty Lehan Harragan's book by Liz Coe. Average.

Games of Desire (1968) **90m.** ** D: Hans Albin. Ingrid Thulin, Claudine Auger, Paul Hubschmid. Thulin is married to Sweden's ambassador to Greece, forced to make love with various men because her husband digs his male secretary. Tepid tale of depravity doesn't have many explicit scenes to cut for TV, which will make the film longer than anyone wants.

Gamma People, The (1956-British) **79m.** ** D: John Gilling. Paul Douglas, Eva Bartok, Leslie Phillips, Walter Rilla. Douglas and Phillips happen upon comic-opera country ruled by scientists trying to create geniuses; they do, but sometimes brainless "goons" also. Worse, the geniuses have no emotions. Peculiar Ruritanian sci-fi adventure.▼

Gammera, The Invincible (1966-Japanese-U.S.) **88m.** *½ D: Noriaki Yuasi. Brian Donlevy, Albert Dekker, John Baragrey. A giant, jet-propelled fire-breathing space turtle terrorizes the earth following atomic explosion. First in a series of juvenile sci-fi films.▼

Gandhi (1982-British-Indian) **C-188m.** ***½ D: Richard Attenborough. Ben Kingsley, Candice Bergen, Edward Fox, John Gielgud, Trevor Howard, John Mills, Martin Sheen, Rohini Hattangandy, Ian Charleson, Athol Fugard, Roshan Seth, Saeed Jaffrey, John Ratzenberger, Geraldine James, Michael Hordern, Marius Weyers. Sweeping account of the life and times of Mohandas K. Gandhi, who rose from a position of simple lawyer to become a nation's leader and a worldwide symbol of peace and understanding. Storytelling at its best, in the tradition of great Hollywood epics, though film's second half is less riveting than the first. Kingsley gives an unforgettable performance in the lead. Eight Oscars include Best Picture, Actor, Director, Screenplay (John Briley). Look for Daniel Day-Lewis as one of three youths who accost Gandhi in the street.▼

Gang Busters (1955) **78m.** ** D: Bill Karan. Myron Healey, Don C. Harvey, Sam Edwards, Frank Gerstle. Standard prison-life drama, focusing on breakout plan.▼

Gang's All Here, The (1943) **C-103m.** **½ D: Busby Berkeley. Alice Faye, Carmen Miranda, James Ellison, Charlotte Greenwood, Eugene Pallette, Edward Everett Horton, Benny Goodman, Sheila Ryan. Splashy wartime musical is terrible, but fun; Miranda in fine form with "The Lady in the Tutti Frutti Hat," a la Busby Berkeley; as an added kitsch treat, Benny Goodman sings!

Gangster, The (1947) **84m.** *** D: Gordon Wiles. Barry Sullivan, Belita, Joan Lorring, Akim Tamiroff, Harry Morgan, John Ireland, Fifi D'Orsay, Shelley Winters. Sullivan gives strong performance as man who falls victim to his slum environment and ends up a vengeful crook.

Gangster Boss (1959-French) **100m.** ** D: Henri Verneuil. Fernandel, Papouf, Gino Cervi. Buffoon Fernandel becomes involved with criminal gang when he accidentally snatches parcel containing stolen loot.

Gangster Story (1960) **65m.** **½ D: Walter Matthau. Walter Matthau, Carol Grace, Bruce McFarlan, Garrett Wallberg. Straightforward, tight little gangster chronicle, focusing on the crook's girlfriend who tries to reform him.

Gang That Couldn't Shoot Straight, The (1971) **C-96m.** ** D: James Goldstone. Jerry Orbach, Leigh Taylor-Young, Jo Van Fleet, Lionel Stander, Robert De Niro, Herve Villechaize. Film version of Jimmy Breslin's best-seller about some comical, twelfth-rate N.Y.C. crooks is well cast, but adapted in slapdash fashion and directed without much feeling for the material.

Gang War (1958) **75m.** **½ D: Gene Fowler, Jr. Charles Bronson, Kent Taylor, Jennifer Holden, John Doucette. Grade-B film tracing the savage events resulting from a teacher testifying against gang brutality.

Gang War (1962-British) **65m.** ** D: Frank Marshall. Sean Kelly, Eira Heath, David Davies, Sean Sullivan. Tame account of life among London gangsters.

Gangway for Tomorrow (1943) **69m.** ** D: John H. Auer. Margo, John Carradine, Robert Ryan, Amelita Ward, William Terry, Harry Davenport, James Bell, Charles Arnt, Wally Brown, Alan Carney. Lives of five workers in wartime munitions plant told in flashbacks; dated wartime fare with occasional bright moments. Written by Arch Oboler.

Garbage Pail Kids Movie, The (1987) **C-100m.** BOMB D: Rod Amateau. Anthony Newley, MacKenzie Astin, Katie Barberi. Crude live-action kiddie film "inspired" by the popular and controversial bubble-gum cards which feature creatures with names like Greaser Greg and Valerie Vomit. They all live in a garbage pail, where they are destined to be joined by the negative of this movie.▼

Garbo Talks (1984) **C-103m.** **½ D: Sidney Lumet. Anne Bancroft, Ron Silver, Carrie Fisher, Catherine Hicks, Steven Hill, Howard da Silva, Dorothy Loudon, Harvey Fierstein, Hermione Gingold. Silver sets out to fulfill his dying mother's last request: to meet Greta Garbo. Bancroft is a treat as the feisty mom, but film is just a series of vignettes, occasionally poignant but overall self-conscious and contrived, further undermined by Cy Coleman's saccharine score. That's writer-performer Betty Comden as Garbo in the last scene.▼

Garde A Vue (1981-French) **C-87m.** *** D: Claude Miller. Lino Ventura, Michel Serrault, Romy Schneider, Guy Marchand. Prominent lawyer Serrault, suspected of raping and murdering two girls, is interrogated by police inspectors Ventura and Marchand. Tense, involving drama, with fine performances by all.

Gardener, The SEE: **Seeds of Evil**▼

Garden Murder Case, The (1936) **62m.** D: Edwin L. Marin. Edmund Lowe, Virginia Bruce, Benita Hume, Douglas Walton, Nat Pendleton, Gene Lockhart. SEE: **Philo Vance** series.

Garden of Allah, The (1936) **C-80m.** ** D: Richard Boleslawski. Marlene Dietrich, Charles Boyer, Tilly Losch, Basil Rathbone, Joseph Schildkraut, Henry Kleinbach (Henry Brandon), John Carradine. Flagrantly silly romance set in the Algerian desert; full of ripe dialogue, troubled glances, beauty shots of Marlene in a variety of gorgeous sheaths and flowing gowns, and some wonderful Technicolor scenery (which helped win its cameramen, W. Howard Greene and Harold Rosson, special Oscar). It just isn't very good. ▼

Garden of Evil (1954) **C-100m.** **½ D: Henry Hathaway. Gary Cooper, Susan Hayward, Richard Widmark, Hugh Marlowe, Cameron Mitchell, Rita Moreno. Meandering adventure story set in 1850s Mexico, with trio escorting Hayward through bandit territory to save her husband.

Garden of the Finzi-Continis, The (1971-Italian) **C-95m.** **** D: Vittorio De Sica. Dominique Sanda, Lino Capolicchio, Helmut Berger, Fabio Testi, Romolo Valli. Exquisitely photographed drama about aristocratic Jewish family in WWII Italy which conveniently ignores the spectre of the concentration camp until it's too late. Sad, haunting film boosted Sanda to stardom and won an Oscar as Best Foreign Film.▼

Garden of the Moon (1938) **94m.** **½ D: Busby Berkeley. Pat O'Brien, Margaret Lindsay, John Payne, Johnnie Davis, Melville Cooper, Isabel Jeans, Penny Singleton. Nightclub owner O'Brien and bandleader Payne have running feud; plot is pleasant excuse to work in many Berkeley numbers: "Girlfriend Of The Whirling Dervish," "Love Is Where You Find It," title tune.

Gardens of Stone (1987) **C-111m.** **½ D: Francis Coppola. James Caan, Anjelica Huston, James Earl Jones, D. B. Sweeney, Dean Stockwell, Mary Stuart Masterson, Dick Anthony Williams, Lonette McKee, Sam Bottoms, Larry Fishburne. Well-acted story about life in Arlington National Cemetery's home guard during the thick of the Vietnam war—and one young soldier's determination to go into battle. Strong performances keep it going most of the way, but toward the end the dialogue sounds hollow, like the sentiment itself. Carmine Coppola's funereal music doesn't help. Jones steals the show in a warm-hearted role; young leading lady Masterson's real-life parents, Peter Masterson and Carlin Glynn, play her folks on screen.▼

Gargoyles (1972) **C-74m. TVM** D: B. W. L. Norton. Cornel Wilde, Jennifer Salt, Bernie Casey, Grayson Hall, Woodrow Chambliss, Scott Glenn. Anthropologist Wilde and daughter on trip to Mexico, stop off at wilderness curio station, come upon unusual skeleton. A very good beginning but deteriorates halfway through story. Flawless use of locations. Average.

Garment Jungle, The (1957) **88m.** **½ D: Vincent Sherman. Lee J. Cobb, Kerwin Mathews, Gia Scala, Richard Boone. Well-handled account of union-gangster corruption in dressmaking industry, with romantic interludes slowing down violent pace.

Gas (1981-Canadian) **C-94m.** BOMB D: Les Rose. Donald Sutherland, Susan Anspach, Howie Mandel, Sterling Hayden, Sandee Currie, Peter Aykroyd, Helen Shaver. Noisy, moronic garbage about the effect of a phony gas shortage on an "average" American town. Car crashes *ad nauseam*, with Sutherland wasted as Nick the Noz, a hip disc jockey.▼

Gaslight (1940-British) **84m.** ***½ D: Thorold Dickinson. Anton Walbrook, Diana Wynyard, Frank Pettingell, Cathleen Cordell, Robert Newton, Jimmy Hanley. First version of Patrick Hamilton's play about an insane criminal who drives his wife crazy in order to discover hidden jewels. What this version lacks in budget, compared to MGM remake, it more than makes up for in electrifying atmosphere, delicious performances, and a succinctly conveyed sense of madness and evil lurking beneath the surface of the ordinary. MGM supposedly tried to destroy the negative of this original when they made the remake, but it has survived and finally resurfaced to be appreciated in all its glory. Screenplay by A.R. Rawlinson and Bridget Boland. U.S. title: ANGEL STREET.

Gaslight (1944) **114m.** *** D: George Cukor. Ingrid Bergman, Charles Boyer, Joseph Cotten, Dame May Whitty, Angela Lansbury, Terry Moore. The bloom has worn off this classic chiller about a man trying to drive his wife insane, but lush production, Victorian flavor, and fine performances remain intact. Bergman won Oscar; Lansbury's film debut. Filmed before in 1940.▼

Gaslight Follies (1955) **110m.** *½ D: Joseph E. Levine. Charlie Chaplin, Douglas Fairbanks, Mary Pickford, Will Rogers. If it's possible to take priceless footage of Chaplin and his silent contemporaries and end up with a horrible hodgepodge, this film has done it. A mess.

Gas-s-s-s (1970) **C-79m.** *** D: Roger Corman. Bud Cort, Cindy Williams, Robert Corff, Ben Vereen, Talia Coppola (Shire), Elaine Giftos. Insane, often uproarious story focusing on reactions of youngsters in crisis: a gas kills everyone on Earth over 30 years of age. Reedited against Corman's wishes, causing much disjointedness, but stay with it. Also known as GAS-S-S-S . . . OR, IT MAY BECOME NECESSARY TO DESTROY THE WORLD IN ORDER TO SAVE IT.▼

Gate, The (1987) **C-92m.** ** D: Tibor Takacs. Stephen Dorff, Christa Denton, Louis Tripp, Kelly Rowan, Jennifer Irwin, Deborah Grove, Scot Denton. It's a boring weekend: Dorff is grounded, his sister is babysitting while the parents are away—then he and a pal discover the gate to hell in their suburban backyard. Worthless first half is somewhat redeemed by amusing special effects in the second; this low-budget horror film opened theatrically the same week as ISHTAR and came within about a hundred grand of beating it out as the No. 1 box-office attraction! Followed by a sequel.▼

Gate of Hell (1954-Japanese) **C-89m.** ***½ D: Teinosuke Kinugasa. Machiko Kyo, Kazuo Hasegawa, Isao Yamagata, Koreya Senda. Stark, stunning historical drama, set in 12th-century Japan, about a Samurai who falls in love with—and then tragically shames—a married woman. This beautiful production earned Oscars for Costume Design and Best Foreign Film.▼

Gates of Paris (1958-French) **103m.** **½ D: René Clair. Pierre Brasseur, Georges Brassens, Henri Vidal, Dany Carrel. Offbeat story of souse who gains a sense of importance when a criminal seeks refuge in his home.

Gateway (1938) **73m.** **½ D: Alfred L. Werker. Don Ameche, Arleen Whelan, Gregory Ratoff, Binnie Barnes, Gilbert Roland, Raymond Walburn, John Carradine. Irish immigrant Whelan pursued by various men during ocean crossing, becomes involved with gangster Roland. Formula story given interesting flavor by Ellis Island background.

Gathering, The (1977) **C-92m. TVM** D: Randal Kleiser. Edward Asner, Maureen Stapleton, Lawrence Pressman, Stephanie Zimbalist, Bruce Davison, John Randolph, Gregory Harrison, Veronica Hamel, Gail Strickland. Sentimental Emmy-winning Christmas drama of a man who seeks to reunite his shattered family for one final celebration before he dies. Asner is solid as usual, but Stapleton is simply luminous as the wife who had lost him in his drive

for success. Written by James Poe. Followed by THE GATHERING, PART II. Above average.▼

Gathering, Part II, The (1979) **C-98m. TVM** D: Charles S. Dubin. Maureen Stapleton, Efrem Zimbalist, Jr., Jameson Parker, Bruce Davison, Lawrence Pressman, Gail Strickland, Veronica Hamel. Soapy sequel in which a widow's Christmas reunion with her grown children is marred by the arrival of a new man in her life. Ed Asner's photograph throughout reminds all how glowing the original was. Average.▼

Gathering of Eagles, A (1963) **C-115m.** *** D: Delbert Mann. Rock Hudson, Rod Taylor, Mary Peach, Barry Sullivan, Kevin McCarthy, Henry Silva, Leif Erickson. Crisp Strategic Air Command drama with novelty of peacetime setting; Hudson gives one of his best performances as less than likable colonel whose wife struggles to adjust to being a military spouse. Good script by Robert Pirosh.▼

Gathering of Old Men, A (1987) **C-100m. TVM** D: Volker Schlondorff. Louis Gossett, Jr., Richard Widmark, Holly Hunter, Joe Seneca, Woody Strode, Papa John Creach, Julius Harris, Will Patton. Ensemble acting at its best in this wonderful drama about a group of old black men from rural Louisiana who take the first courageous step of their long lives by coming forward en masse to take responsibility for the killing of a white racist whom one of their members has shot. Scripted by Charles Fuller, from the novel by Ernest J. Gaines—the authors, respectively, of A SOLDIER'S STORY and THE AUTOBIOGRAPHY OF MISS JANE PITTMAN. Above average.

Gatling Gun, The (1972) **C-93m.** *½ D: Robert Gordon. Guy Stockwell, Woody Strode, Patrick Wayne, Robert Fuller, Barbara Luna, John Carradine, Pat Buttram, Phil Harris. Cavalry, renegade soldiers, Apaches, fight over Gatling gun. Standard, forgettable Western.▼

Gator (1976) **C-116m.** ** D: Burt Reynolds. Burt Reynolds, Jack Weston, Lauren Hutton, Jerry Reed, Alice Ghostley, Mike Douglas, Dub Taylor. Not-so-hot sequel to WHITE LIGHTNING, about attempts of Justice Dept. agent Weston and moonshiner ex-con Reynolds to get the goods on corrupt Southern politicians. Some good action shots but film is overlong and poorly constructed. Reynolds' directing debut.▼

Gator Bait (1976) **C-93m.** *½ D: Ferd and Beverly C. Sebastian. Claudia Jennings, Sam Gilman, Doug Dirkson, Clyde Ventura, Bill Thurman. All the menfolk are after the sexy swamp-girl called Desiree—but she has a surprise or two in store for them. A tedious tease of a film, with some moments of truly repellent violence.▼

Gauguin the Savage (1980) **C-125m. TVM** D: Fielder Cook. David Carradine, Lynn Redgrave, Barrie Houghton, Dame Flora Robson, Michael Hordern, Ian Richardson, Carmen Matthews, Bernard Fox. Plodding drama about the temperamental French painter who abandoned his wife and children to pursue a life of artistic freedom in Tahiti. A curiously cast Carradine is far from the Gauguin of Maugham's *The Moon and Sixpence.* Script by JP Miller. Average.

Gauntlet, The (1977) **C-109m.** **½ D: Clint Eastwood. Clint Eastwood, Sondra Locke, Pat Hingle, William Prince, Bill McKinney, Mara Corday. Eastwood stars as a none-too-clever cop escorting hooker Locke to trial; corrupt officials are determined to stop them, whatever the cost. Exciting at times, though its credibility factor is low.▼

Gay Adventure, The (1953-British) **87m.** *** D: Gordon Parry. Burgess Meredith, Jean-Pierre Aumont, Paul Valenska, Kathleen Harrison. Interestingly done yarn of trio of men in a train theorizing about pretty girl sitting across from them.

Gay Bride, The (1934) **80m.** ** D: Jack Conway. Carole Lombard, Chester Morris, ZaSu Pitts, Leo Carrillo, Nat Pendleton. Unsatisfying blend of comedy and melodrama with gold-digging Lombard hitching herself to succession of gangsters.

Gay Deception, The (1935) **77m.** **½ D: William Wyler. Francis Lederer, Frances Dee, Benita Hume, Alan Mowbray, Lennox Pawle, Akim Tamiroff, Luis Alberni, Lionel Stander. Romantic trifle of working girl (Dee) on spree in N.Y.C., pursued by proletarian-posing prince (Lederer). A slight comedy engagingly handled by Wyler.

Gay Desperado, The (1936) **85m.** **½ D: Rouben Mamoulian. Nino Martini, Ida Lupino, Leo Carrillo, Harold Huber, James Blakely, Stanley Fields, Mischa Auer. Jovial Mexican bandido Carrillo and his gang (who've learned how to be tough from watching Grade B gangster movies) recruit reluctant singer Martini and kidnap Lupino and her rich, wimpy boyfriend. Outlandishly silly and plays like a cartoon; some funny characterizations but mostly hard to take.

Gay Divorcee, The (1934) **107m.** ***½ D: Mark Sandrich. Fred Astaire, Ginger Rogers, Alice Brady, Edward Everett Horton, Erik Rhodes, Eric Blore, Betty Grable. Top Astaire-Rogers froth with usual needless plot and unusual musical numbers, including Oscar-winning "Continental" and Cole Porter's "Night and Day." Rhodes is memorable as would-be corespondent in divorce case. Incidentally, the Broadway hit on which this was based was called *The Gay Divorce,* but the Hollywood Produc-

tion Code wouldn't approve that sentiment!▼

Gay Falcon, The (1941) **67m.** D: Irving Reis. George Sanders, Wendy Barrie, Allen Jenkins, Anne Hunter, Gladys Cooper. SEE: **Falcon** series.

Gay Lady, The (1949-British) **C-95m.** **½ D: Brian Desmond Hurst. Jean Kent, James Donald, Hugh Sinclair, Lana Morris, Bill Owen, Michael Medwin. Lightweight costume picture about saucy entertainer who marries nobility; most notable aspect of film is its stunning use of Technicolor. Look fast for Christopher Lee as a dapper stage-door Johnnie. Original British title: TROTTIE TRUE.▼

Gay Purr-ee (1963) **C-86m.** **½ D: Abe Levitow. Voices of Judy Garland, Robert Goulet, Red Buttons, Hermoine Gingold, Paul Frees, Morey Amsterdam. Stylish cartoon from UPA studio, too sophisticated in many ways for kiddies. Adults will enjoy Garland and Goulet singing fairly good songs; broader characters played by others might attract youngsters. Original score by Harold Arlen and E. Y. Harburg.

Gay Sisters, The (1942) **108m.** ** D: Irving Rapper. Barbara Stanwyck, George Brent, Geraldine Fitzgerald, Gig Young, Nancy Coleman, Donald Crisp, Gene Lockhart, Anne Revere. Stanwyck secretly marries Brent to gain inheritance money in thin soaper, immensely aided by Fitzgerald and Coleman as her two sisters. Young derived his screen name from the character he plays in this.

Gazebo, The (1959) **100m.** *** D: George Marshall. Glenn Ford, Debbie Reynolds, Carl Reiner, Doro Merande, John McGiver, Mabel Albertson. Offbeat comedy involving murder and a backyard gazebo that covers up crime. Character actors McGiver and Merande wrap this up, but stars are competent. Also shown in computer-colored version.

Geisha Boy, The (1958) **C-98m.** **½ D: Frank Tashlin. Jerry Lewis, Marie McDonald, Sessue Hayakawa, Nobu McCarthy. Jerry, an inept magician, travels to the Far East, with disastrous consequences. Imaginative visual gags highspot this comedy. Film debut of Suzanne Pleshette.

Gemini Man (1976) **C-100m. TVM** D: Alan Levi. Ben Murphy, Katherine Crawford, Richard Dysart, Dana Elcar, Paul Shenar, Cheryl Miller. H. G. Wells' *The Invisible Man* recycled with Murphy as dare-devil secret agent whose transient invisibility (result of technological accident) makes him the bane of various saboteurs. Predictable spy show with fantasy element, later a short-lived TV series. Below average. Retitled CODE NAME: MINUS ONE and cut to 78m.

Gene Krupa Story, The (1959) **101m.**

**½ D: Don Weis, Sal Mineo, Susan Kohner, James Darren, Susan Oliver, Yvonne Craig, Lawrence Dobkin, Red Nichols, Buddy Lester. Hackneyed version of great drummer's life, his ups and downs, and his siege of dope addiction.▼

General, The (1927) **74m.** **** D: Buster Keaton. Buster Keaton, Marion Mack, Glen Cavender, Jim Farley, Joseph Keaton. One of Keaton's best silent features, setting comedy against true Civil War story of stolen train, Union spies. Not as fanciful as other Keaton films, but beautifully done; Disney did same story in 1956 as THE GREAT LOCOMOTIVE CHASE.▼

General Della Rovere (1960-Italian) **129m.** ***½ D: Roberto Rossellini. Vittorio De Sica, Hannes Messemer, Sandra Milo, Giovanna Ralli, Mary Greco, Linda Veras, Anne Vernon. Brilliantly acted account of De Sica forced to impersonate Axis general, with the role and situation going to his head; slowly paced but well-executed.▼

General Died at Dawn, The (1936) **97m.** ***½ D: Lewis Milestone. Gary Cooper, Madeleine Carroll, Akim Tamiroff, Dudley Digges, Porter Hall, William Frawley. Fine, atmospheric drama of Oriental intrigue, with mercenary Cooper falling in love with spy Carroll while battling evil warlord Tamiroff. Author John O'Hara has cameo as reporter on train.▼

General Spanky (1936) **71m.** ** D: Fred Newmeyer, Gordon Douglas. George "Spanky" McFarland, Billie "Buckwheat" Thomas, Carl "Alfalfa" Switzer, Phillips Holmes, Ralph Morgan, Irving Pichel, Rosina Lawrence, Louise Beavers. Sluggish Civil War story, balancing kiddie antics against an adult romance, was intended to showcase three Our Gang stars in a feature-film format; it's easy to see why there wasn't an encore. Buckwheat's role as a slave in search of a master may displease some contemporary audiences.

Generation, A (1954-Polish) **88m.** *** D: Andrzej Wajda. Ursula Modrzinska, Tadevsz Lomnicki, Zbigniew Cybulski. Strong, necessarily downbeat drama about the Polish Resistance during World War II and what happens when a young man falls in love with the woman who leads the Resistance group. Wajda's first film and the first of a trilogy that includes the even better KANAL and ASHES AND DIAMONDS. Young Roman Polanski is featured in the cast.

Generation (1969) **C-104m.** ** D: George Schaefer. David Janssen, Kim Darby, Carl Reiner, Peter Duel, Andrew Prine, James Coco, Sam Waterston. Darby helps otherwise dreary comedy based on Broadway play about just-married couple who infuriate the girl's father when husband plans to deliver their soon-to-arrive baby himself; plays like a TV sit-com.▼

Generation (1985) **C-100m. TVM** D: Michael Tuchner. Richard Beymer, Hanna Cutrona, Marta DuBois, Drake Hogestyn, Priscilla Pointer, Cristina Raines, Bert Remsen, Beah Richards, Kim Miyori. Futuristic tale about life, and a sport known as combat hockey, in the good old U.S. of A. at the turn of the millennium, 1999. Acceptable premise, though not as a series, for which this was a pilot. Average.

Genesis II (1973) **C-97m. TVM** D: John Llewellyn Moxey. Alex Cord, Mariette Hartley, Lynn Marta, Percy Rodrigues, Harvey Jason, Ted Cassidy. Disappointing sci-fi adventure. Cord is unique survivor of 20th-century holocaust as earth divides into two rival factions. Created by *Star Trek*'s Gene Roddenberry, but owes a great deal to FLASH GORDON. Reworked one year later as PLANET EARTH. Average.

Genevieve (1953-British) **C-86m.** ***½ D: Henry Cornelius. Dinah Sheridan, John Gregson, Kay Kendall, Kenneth More, Geoffrey Keen, Joyce Grenfell, Michael Medwin. Genteel comedy pits two couples and their vintage roadsters against one another in hilarious cross-country race. Best British Film of '53 with top-drawer performances. Music score by harmonica virtuoso Larry Adler.▼

Genghis Khan (1965) **C-124m.** *½ D: Henry Levin. Omar Sharif, Stephen Boyd, James Mason, Eli Wallach, Francoise Dorleac, Telly Savalas, Robert Morley, Yvonne Mitchell, Woody Strode. Laughable epic with gross miscasting and juvenile script, loosely based on legend of Mongol leader. No sweep or spectacle, but radiant Dorleac and earnest Sharif.

Genius at Work (1946) **61m.** *½ D: Leslie Goodwins. Wally Brown, Alan Carney, Lionel Atwill, Anne Jeffreys, Bela Lugosi, Marc Cramer. Radio detectives get involved in real-life murder schemes of Atwill. Brown & Carney's last film as Abbott & Costello-like team is pretty weak; Lugosi is wasted. Remake of SUPER SLEUTH.

Gentle Annie (1944) **80m.** ** D: Andrew Marton. Donna Reed, Marjorie Main, Harry Morgan, James Craig, Barton MacLane. Main vehicle about female outlaw with heart of gold.

Gentle Art of Murder SEE: **Crime Does Not Pay**

Gentle Giant (1967) **C-93m.** *** D: James Neilson. Dennis Weaver, Vera Miles, Clint Howard, Ralph Meeker, Huntz Hall. Feature film which hatched TV series *Gentle Ben* is appealing children's story of boy and his pet bear.▼

Gentle Gunman, The (1952-British) **86m.** *** D: Basil Dearden. Dirk Bogarde, John Mills, Elizabeth Sellars, Robert Beatty. Unpretentious actioner of Irish revolution and enthusiast whose attempt to prove his pariotism backfires.

Gentleman After Dark (1942) **77m.** **
D: Edwin L. Marin. Brian Donlevy, Miriam Hopkins, Preston Foster, Harold Huber. Hodgepodge yarn of man escaping prison to redeem honor of his daughter by killing his shady wife; good cast stifled by sloppy script. Remake of FORGOTTEN FACES.

Gentleman at Heart, A (1942) **66m.** **½
D: Ray McCarey. Cesar Romero, Carole Landis, Milton Berle, J. Carrol Naish, Richard Derr. Modest little comedy about bookie Romero discovering there's money in art forgery.

Gentleman Bandit, The (1981) **C-100m.**
TVM D: Jonathan Kaplan. Ralph Waite, Julie Bovasso, Jerry Zaks, Estelle Parsons, Joe Grifasi, Vincent Spano. Socially concerned Baltimore priest mistakenly arrested as a stickup man. Based on the true-life experience of Father Bernard Pagano, played by Waite with compassion. Average.▼

Gentleman Jim (1942) **104m.** ***½ D: Raoul Walsh. Errol Flynn, Alexis Smith, Jack Carson, Alan Hale, John Loder, William Frawley, Minor Watson, Ward Bond, Arthur Shields. Sassy biography of polished boxer Jim Corbett in fight game's early days. Flynn is dynamic in title role (reportedly his favorite), supported by colorful cast. Scripted by Vincent Lawrence and Horace McCoy.▼

Gentleman's Agreement (1947) **118m.** *** D: Elia Kazan. Gregory Peck, Dorothy McGuire, John Garfield, Celeste Holm, Anne Revere, June Havoc, Albert Dekker, Jane Wyatt, Dean Stockwell, Sam Jaffe. Sincere Academy Award-winning adaptation of Laura Z. Hobson's novel of writer (Peck) pretending to be Jewish, discovering rampant anti-Semitism. Holm won Supporting Actress Oscar as chic but lonely fashion editor, as did Kazan for his direction. Then-daring approach to subject matter is tame now. Screenplay by Moss Hart.

Gentlemen Marry Brunettes (1955) **C-97m.** ** D: Richard Sale. Jane Russell, Jeanne Crain, Alan Young, Rudy Vallee, Scott Brady. Anita Loos' follow-up to GENTLEMEN PREFER BLONDES has Russell and Crain, two sisters in show biz in Paris, trying to avoid romances. Not up to original.

Gentlemen Prefer Blondes (1953) **C-91m.** *** D: Howard Hawks. Jane Russell, Marilyn Monroe, Charles Coburn, Elliott Reid, Tommy Noonan, George "Foghorn" Winslow. Slick, colorful bauble of entertainment with two sassy leading ladies tantalizing the men of two continents; Marilyn is at her best as fortune-hunter Lorelei Lee, and Russell gives a sly, knowing comic performance as her pal. Based on the Broadway adaptation of Anita Loos' venerable story, with sprightly Leo Robin-

Jule Styne songs including "Diamonds Are a Girl's Best Friend." Sequel: GENTLEMEN MARRY BRUNETTES.▼

Gentle Rain, The (1966) **C-110m.** **½ D: Burt Balaban. Christopher George, Lynda Day, Fay Spain, Maria Helena Diaz, Lon Clark. Frigid N.Y.C. woman goes to Rio de Janeiro, falls for draughtsman who has been mute ever since he failed to save life of his former girlfriend in car crash. Fair.

Gentle Touch, The SEE: **Feminine Touch, The** (1956)

George McKenna Story, The (1986) **C-100m.** TVM D: Eric Laneuville. Denzel Washington, Lynn Whitfield, Akosua Busia, Richard Masur, Ray Buktenica, Virginia Capers. Real-life high school principal rejuvenates a failing inner-city South L.A. high school. Inspiring drama, well acted and directed by, respectively, Washington and Laneuville (costars of *St. Elsewhere*). Charles Eric Johnson wrote the straightforward script. Above average.

George Raft Story, The (1961) **106m.** **½ D: Joseph M. Newman. Ray Danton, Jayne Mansfield, Barbara Nichols, Julie London, Neville Brand, Frank Gorshin. Danton is good in title role of fast-moving account of Raft's rise from Broadway dancer to top Hollywood star. How much is true, who can say?

George Stevens: A Filmmaker's Journey (1984) **C-110m.** *** D: George Stevens, Jr. Katharine Hepburn, Cary Grant, Joel McCrea, Fred Astaire, Ginger Rogers, and Warren Beatty are among those who help create vivid documentary portrait of director Stevens, along with great clips from ALICE ADAMS, SWING TIME, GUNGA DIN, THE MORE THE MERRIER, A PLACE IN THE SUN, SHANE, GIANT, etc. Stevens, Jr., supplies personal insights, plus fascinating home movies taken by his father on film sets—and color footage shot during WW2 in Europe.▼

George Washington Slept Here (1942) **93m.** **½ D: William Keighley. Jack Benny, Ann Sheridan, Charles Coburn, Hattie McDaniel, Percy Kilbride, Franklin Pangborn. Brittle but dated comedy of N.Y.C. couple moving to the country and a dilapidated house. Benny essentially plays himself, smoothly. Sheridan is good straightwoman to the wacky, predictable turmoil. Based on the Kaufman-Hart play.

George White's Scandals (1934) **80m.** **½ D: George White, Thornton Freeland, Harry Lachman. Rudy Vallee, Jimmy Durante, Alice Faye, Adrienne Ames, Gregory Ratoff, Cliff Edwards, Dixie Dunbar, Gertrude Michael, George White. Idiotic backstage romance plot propels entertaining, expensive musical; Faye, in film debut, sings "Oh, You Nasty Man," one of several big production numbers.

George White's Scandals (1935) **83m.**

** D: George White. Alice Faye, James Dunn, Ned Sparks, Lyda Roberti, Cliff Edwards, Arline Judge, Eleanor Powell, George White, Benny Rubin. Tired show biz story of producer White seeing talented Alice in small-town show, bringing her (and her pals) to N.Y.C. where success poses problems. Story, songs all routine, but good cast gives it some life; Powell's dancing film debut. Retitled GEORGE WHITE'S 1935 SCANDALS.

George White's Scandals (1945) 95m. ** D: Felix E. Feist. Joan Davis, Jack Haley, Phillip Terry, Martha Holliday, Jane Greer. Mild musical heightened by Davis' zany antics, involving the usual show biz clichés. Slapstick helps hackneyed plot.▼

Georgia, Georgia (1972) C-91m. **½ D: Stig Bjorkman. Diana Sands, Dirk Benedict, Minnie Gentry. Black singer's involvement with white photographer and some American defectors. Interesting but uneven.▼

Georgia Peaches, The (1980) C-100m. TVM D: Daniel Haller. Tanya Tucker, Terri Nunn, Lane Smith, Sally Kirkland, Dennis Patrick, Burton Gilliam, Dirk Benedict. Roger Corman produced this comedy-action pilot about a trio of unlikely undercover government agents: a country singer, her sister (who runs the family auto-repair shop), and their macho moonshine-running pal. Retitled FOLLOW THAT CAR. Average.

Georgy Girl (1966-British) 100m. ***½ D: Silvio Narizzano. Lynn Redgrave, James Mason, Alan Bates, Charlotte Rampling, Bill Owen, Claire Kelly. Delightful, adult British comedy of modern-day morals, with Redgrave as ugly-duckling Georgy, Mason as the wealthy, aging married man who wants her for his mistress. Entire cast is excellent, with Rampling scoring as Georgy's bitchy roommate. Faithful adaptation of Margaret Forster novel.▼

Geronimo (1939) 89m. ** D: Paul H. Sloane. Preston Foster, Ellen Drew, Andy Devine, Gene Lockhart, Ralph Morgan, Marjorie Gateson, Chief Thundercloud. Run-of-the-mill Western marred by overuse of stock footage and bad process shots to simulate outdoor scenes. Lockhart getting just desserts is best item in trivial Indian vs. cavalry contest. Remake of LIVES OF A BENGAL LANCER.

Geronimo (1962) C-101m. **½ D: Arnold Laven. Chuck Connors, Kamala Devi, Ross Martin, Adam West, Pat Conway, Larry Dobkin. Exciting Indians-on-the-warpath tale, with Connors satisfactory in title role.

Gervaise (1956-French) 116m. *** D: Rene Clement. Maria Schell, Francois Perier, Suzy Delair, Armand Mestral. Splendidly acted version of Emile Zola tale of Schell struggling to keep her family going but finally succumbing to tawdry life of her drunken husband.▼

Getaway, The (1972) C-122m. *** D: Sam Peckinpah. Steve McQueen, Ali MacGraw, Ben Johnson, Sally Struthers, Al Lettieri, Slim Pickens. Exciting, enjoyable film built around a chase. Bank robber McQueen and wife MacGraw take it on the lam when robbery goes haywire. Many fine vignettes, including hair-raising episode on garbage truck. Written by Walter Hill.▼

Get Carter (1971-British) C-112m. *** D: Mike Hodges. Michael Caine, Ian Hendry, Britt Ekland, John Osborne, Tony Beckley, George Sewell. Lean, tough action melodrama with Caine as small-time gangster investigating his brother's death; good work by Caine, vivid seediness captured by writer-director Hodges. Remade one year later with black cast as HIT MAN.

Get Charlie Tully (1976-British) C-97m. *½ D: Cliff Owen. Dick Emery, Derren Nesbitt, Ronald Fraser, Pat Coombs, William Franklyn. Energetic, tasteless nonsense in which con man Emery frantically searches for four young women who have the location of negotiable bonds tattooed on their rear. The usually impeccable Frank Launder and Sidney Gilliat were executive producers.

Get Christie Love! (1974) C-100m. TVM D: William A. Graham. Teresa Graves, Harry Guardino, Louise Sorel, Paul Stevens, Andy Romano, Debbie Dozier. Shapely female cop goes undercover to crack a huge drug empire. Dorothy Uhnak's detective novel was the source, the later policewoman series was the result. Lots of action. Average.

Get Crazy (1983) C-92m. *** D: Allan Arkush. Daniel Stern, Malcolm McDowell, Gail Edwards, Allen Goorwitz (Garfield), Ed Begley, Jr., Miles Chapin, Lou Reed, Stacey Nelkin, Bill Henderson, Franklin Ajaye, Bobby Sherman, Fabian Forte, Lori Eastside, Lee Ving. Arkush's years working at Fillmore East rock palace form the basis for wonderful cartoonlike comedy set at a trouble-plagued New Year's Eve concert. Gags fly across the screen at machine-gun pace, interspersed with delightful musical numbers; superb take-offs on Mick Jagger (McDowell), Bob Dylan (Reed), and Muddy Waters (Henderson), plus many familiar rock stars and character actors in bits.▼

Get Hep to Love (1944) 71m. *½ D: Charles Lamont. Gloria Jean, Donald O'Connor, Jane Frazee, Robert Paige. Weak musical with precocious musical personality Jean running away to find happier home and singing career.

Get On With It (1961-British) 88m. ** D: C. M. Pennington-Richards. Bob Monkhouse, Kenneth Connor, Shirley Eaton, Eric Barker, Ronnie Stevens, Richard Wattis, Reginald Beckwith. Dental-school graduates Monkhouse and Stevens promote a new toothpaste. Intermittently funny. Also known as DENTIST ON THE JOB.

Get Out of Town (1962) **62m.** ** D: Charles Davis. Douglas Wilson, Jeanne Baird, Marilyn O'Connor, Tony Louis. Contrived account of ex-gangster returned home to locate his brother's killer.

Get Out Your Handkerchiefs (1978-French-Belgian) **C-109m.** ***½ D: Bertrand Blier. Gerard Depardieu, Patrick Dewaere, Carole Laure, Riton, Michel Serrault, Eleonore Hirt. Disarming black comedy about a man who will do almost anything to keep his sexually frustrated wife happy; highly unconventional. Oscar winner for Best Foreign Film.▼

Get Smart, Again! (1989) **C-100m.** TVM D: Gary Nelson. Don Adams, Barbara Feldon, Bernie Kopell, Dick Gautier, Robert Karvelas, King Moody, Harold Gould, Kenneth Mars, Roger Price, Fritz Feld. Maxwell Smart and Agent 99 are back with the old CONTROL gang for another battle with KAOS in this reunion movie of the landmark '60s series which, unfortunately, can't come up to the original. Average.

Getting Away From It All (1971) **C-74m.** TVM D: Lee Philips. Gary Collins, E. J. Peaker, Barbara Feldon, Larry Hagman, Jim Backus, Burgess Meredith, Vivian Vance, Randy Quaid, John Qualen. Two middle-aged, middle-class couples sell houses, quit work to find idyllic "back to nature" existence, decide to return to civilization. Contrived and infuriating, with unconvincing performances. Below average.

Getting Away With Murder SEE: **End of the Game**

Getting Even (1986) **C-90m.** **½ D: Dwight H. Little. Edward Albert, Audrey Landers, Joe Don Baker, Blue Deckert, Caroline Williams. Farfetched suspense film has industrialist Baker holding the city of Dallas hostage for $50 million ransom or he'll unleash a lethal poison gas. Albert and Landers are the government agents out to stop him. Rousing helicopter stunts give film a lift in the final reel. Originally titled: HOSTAGE: DALLAS. ▼

Getting Gertie's Garter (1945) **72m.** **½ D: Allan Dwan. Dennis O'Keefe, Marie McDonald, Barry Sullivan, Binnie Barnes, Sheila Ryan, J. Carrol Naish, Jerome Cowan. Similar to UP IN MABEL'S ROOM, a funny little comedy of O'Keefe trying to retrieve embarrassing memento without wife's knowledge.

Getting It Right (1989) **C-102m.** *** D: Randal Kleiser. Jesse Birdsall, Helena Bonham Carter, Peter Cook, Lynn Redgrave, Jane Horrocks, Richard Huw, John Gielgud, Shirley Anne Field, Pat Heywood, Judy Parfitt, Bryan Pringle. Sweetly comic story of a 31-year-old virgin and his attempts to cope with people—women in particular—seems mundane and meandering at first, and just gets better as it goes along. Some wonderful characterizations, especially Redgrave as a wealthy woman with a world-weary facade who just wants to be loved. Screenplay by Elizabeth Jane Howard, from her novel. Made in England by an American director and producer.▼

Getting Married (1978) **C-100m.** TVM D: Steven Hilliard Stern. Richard Thomas, Bess Armstrong, Van Johnson, Katherine Helmond, Mark Harmon, Fabian, Dena Dietrich. Romantic fluff set in a TV newsroom manned by lots of attractive people. Average.

Getting of Wisdom, The (1977-Australian) **C-100m.** **½ D: Bruce Beresford. Susannah Fowle, Hilary Ryan, Alix Longman, Sheila Helpmann, Patricia Kennedy, Barry Humphries, John Waters. A spirited, sensitive 13-year-old girl from the outback (Fowle) matures on her own terms at a snobbish Victorian ladies college. Fowle is miscast; however, the era is carefully recreated. Based on autobiographical novel by one Henry Handel Richardson.▼

Getting Physical (1984) **C-100m.** TVM D: Steven Hilliard Stern. Alexandra Paul, Sandahl Bergman, David Naughton, John Aprea, Robert Wagner, Sydney Penny, Franco Columbu. The first drama about women's bodybuilding is just FLASHDANCE with weights, as chunky Paul pumps iron to get her life together amid much tongue-clucking from family and friends. Endless working-out montages set to disco music lead up to ludicrous climax with Paul competing against real-life champs Rachel McLish, Candy Csencsits, and Lisa Lyons. Tries to be sympathetic, but fails even at that; catch the documentary PUMPING IRON II: THE WOMEN instead. Below average.▼

Getting Straight (1970) **C-124m.** **½ D: Richard Rush. Elliott Gould, Candice Bergen, Jeff Corey, Max Julien, Cecil Kellaway, Robert F. Lyons, Jeannie Berlin, John Rubinstein, Brenda Sykes, Harrison Ford. A period piece, but central issue of graduate student Gould choosing between academic double-talk and his beliefs remains relevant. Gould's personality propels glossy film. Written by Bob Kaufman.▼

Get to Know Your Rabbit (1972) **C-91m.** **½ D: Brian DePalma. Tom Smothers, John Astin, Suzanne Zenor, Samantha Jones, Allen Garfield, Katharine Ross, Orson Welles. Offbeat comedy was barely released, and heavily tampered with at that; starts with great premise of Smothers dropping out of establishment life to become tap-dancing magician, then loses itself along the way. Still has some inventive moments, funny ideas. Filmed in 1970.

Get Yourself A College Girl (1964) **C-88m.** *½ D: Sidney Miller. Chad Everett, Nancy Sinatra, Mary Ann Mobley, Dave Clark Five, The Animals. Songwriter who is undergraduate at a staid girls' school falls in love with a music publisher at resort hotel. Strictly for dropouts.

Ghidrah, the Three-Headed Monster (1965-Japanese) **C-85m.** **½ D: Inoshiro Honda. Yosuke Natsuki, Yuriko Hoshi, Hiroshi Koizumi, Emi Ito. Ingenious scripter works three favorites into plot (Mothra, Rodan, Godzilla). Trio champions people of Tokyo against rampaging title fiend.▼

Ghost, The (1963-Italian) **C-96m.** **½ D: Robert Hampton (Riccardo Freda). Barbara Steele, Peter Baldwin, Leonard Elliott (Elio Jotta), Harriet White. In 1910 Scotland, adulterous wife Steele and doctor-lover are seemingly haunted by the vengeful ghost of her crippled husband, whom they murdered. Measured, moody horror, let down by routine plot; still atmospheric and watchable. Follow-up to THE HORRIBLE DR. HICHCOCK.

Ghost (1990) **C-122m.** *** D: Jerry Zucker. Patrick Swayze, Demi Moore, Whoopi Goldberg, Tony Goldwyn, Rick Aviles, Vincent Schiavelli, Gail Boggs, Armelia McQueen, Phil Leeds. Overlong but enjoyable mix of fantasy, thriller, and romance. Swayze is killed, and when he learns (in his ghostly state) that he was the victim of a hit, he tries to warn his grieving wife that she's in danger too. Storefront medium Whoopi turns out to be the only one who can convey his messages to her. Swayze runs the gamut of expressions from A to B, but the relationships are credible and as a result the fantasy works.

Ghost and Mr. Chicken, The (1966) **C-90m.** **½ D: Alan Rafkin. Don Knotts, Joan Staley, Skip Homeier, Dick Sargent, Reta Shaw. Feather weight comedy with Knotts a would-be reporter seeking big scoop by spending night in supposedly haunted house.

Ghost and Mrs. Muir, The (1947) **104m.** ***½ D: Joseph L. Mankiewicz. Gene Tierney, Rex Harrison, George Sanders, Edna Best, Vanessa Brown, Anna Lee, Robert Coote, Natalie Wood. A lonely widow is romanced by the ghost of a sea captain in her "haunted" English cottage. Charming, beautifully made fantasy, a distant cousin to later TV sitcom; lovely score by Bernard Herrmann. Philip Dunne scripted, from the R.A. Dick novel.

Ghost Breakers, The (1940) **82m.** *** D: George Marshall. Bob Hope, Paulette Goddard, Richard Carlson, Paul Lukas, Anthony Quinn, Willie Best. More plot than usual for a Hope film as Bob and Paulette

investigate eerie Cuban mansion which she's inherited. Some real chills as well as laughs in this first-rate film. Remade as SCARED STIFF (1953).

Ghostbusters (1984) **C-107m.** *** D: Ivan Reitman. Bill Murray, Dan Aykroyd, Harold Ramis, Sigourney Weaver, Rick Moranis, Annie Potts, Ernie Hudson, William Atherton. The first multimillion-dollar scare comedy, about a trio of flaky "paranormal investigators" who go into business flushing out ghosts and spirits in N.Y.C.—and find their business booming! Engagingly offbeat, even subdued at times, with Murray's flippant personality nicely contrasting Richard Edlund's eye-popping special effects. Great fun all the way; written by Aykroyd and Ramis. Followed by a sequel and an animated TV series.▼

Ghostbusters II (1989) **C-102m.** *** D: Ivan Reitman. Bill Murray, Dan Aykroyd, Sigourney Weaver, Harold Ramis, Rick Moranis, Ernie Hudson, Peter MacNicol, David Margulies, Annie Potts. Amiable, entertaining sequel has the ghostbusting boys reteaming five years after their last adventure to save N.Y.C. from a slime attack of gargantuan proportions, generated by all the "negative energy" in the air of the Big Apple. Longish but good-natured, with some solid laughs along the way. Chloe Webb has a funny unbilled cameo as a guest on Murray's cable TV show.▼

Ghost Catchers (1944) **67m.** *** D: Edward F. Cline. Ole Olsen, Chic Johnson, Gloria Jean, Martha O'Driscoll, Leo Carrillo, Andy Devine, Walter Catlett, Lon Chaney, Jr. One of Olsen and Johnson's wackiest comedies, with duo as nightclub owners who help Southern colonel Catlett and his daughters, who have just moved into haunted house.

Ghost Chasers (1951) **69m.** D: William Beaudine. Leo Gorcey, Huntz Hall, Jan Kayne, Bernard Gorcey, Lloyd Corrigan, Billy Benedict. SEE: **Bowery Boys** series.

Ghost Comes Home, The (1940) **79m.** ** D: William Thiele. Frank Morgan, Billie Burke, Ann Rutherford, John Shelton, Reginald Owen, Donald Meek. Morgan, thought dead, returns to family which has been doing fine without him; cast does its best with fair material.

Ghost Dad (1990) **C-84m.** ** D: Sidney Poitier. Bill Cosby, Kimberly Russell, Denise Nicholas, Ian Bannen, Christine Ebersole, Barry Corbin, Salim Grant, Brooke Fontaine, Dakin Matthews, Dana Ashbrook, Arnold Stang. Overworked businessman (and widower) Cosby dies in a taxi accident, and learns he has only a few days to try to straighten out his finances so his three kids will be secure. Positive family message aside, this effects-laden fantasy plays like an extended sitcom. Younger kids may like it—others beware.

Ghost Dancing (1983) **C-100m. TVM** D: David Greene. Dorothy McGuire, Bruce Davison, Bo Hopkins, Richard Farnsworth, Bill Erwin, Wings Hauser, Victoria Racimo. McGuire shines in a rare latter-day performance as a widowed farmer-turned-activist, launching a one-woman war against the power company that has dammed up her valley's water supply. Phil Penningroth's original story won the annual "ABC Theatre Award." Above average.

Ghost Diver (1957) **76m.** *½ D: Richard Einfeld, Merrill G. White. James Craig, Audrey Totter, Nico Minardos, Lowell Brown. Programmer of underwater search for treasure city.

Ghost Fever (1987) **C-86m.** ** D: Alan Smithee (Lee Madden). Sherman Hemsley, Luis Avalos, Jennifer Rhodes, Deborah Benson, Diana Brookes, Myron Healey, Pepper Martin, Joe Frazier. Hemsley and Avalos make a comfortable comedy team as cops caught up with ghosts, notably one of a former slave owner (Martin). Slapstick occasionally triumphs over some tasteless material. Filmed principally in 1984, with director Madden uncredited (in favor of fictitious Smithee) following extensive re-shooting and re-editing.▼

Ghost Goes West, The (1936-British) **82m.** *** D: René Clair. Robert Donat, Eugene Pallette, Jean Parker, Elsa Lanchester. Pallette purchases castle haunted by ghost of fast-living ancestor of hero Donat in amusing fantasy-comedy penned by Robert Sherwood.▼

Ghost in the Invisible Bikini, The (1966) **C-82m.** *½ D: Don Weis. Tommy Kirk, Deborah Walley, Aron Kincaid, Quinn O'Hara, Nancy Sinatra, Claudia Martin, Harvey Lembeck, Jesse White, Susan Hart, Basil Rathbone, Boris Karloff, Patsy Kelly, Francis X. Bushman, Benny Rubin. Seventh (and final) BEACH PARTY movie failed to provide a shot in the arm with entirely new set of characters (save Lembeck's Eric Von Zipper); larger-than-usual roster of veteran movie greats might attract masochistic film buffs.

Ghost in the Noonday Sun (1973-British) **C-89m. BOMB** D: Peter Medak. Peter Sellers, Anthony Franciosa, Spike Milligan, Clive Revill, Peter Boyle, Richard Willis. Absolutely atrocious pirate comedy which understandably never got full-fledged theatrical release. Milligan, who's credited with "additional dialogue," appears in one sequence with his onetime *Goon Show* colleague Sellers, but even their chemistry can't save this turkey.▼

Ghost of a Chance (1987) **C-100m. TVM** D: Don Taylor. Dick Van Dyke, Redd Foxx, Geoffrey Holder, Brynn Thayer, Richard Romanus. Lightweight lark (from the "Here Comes Mr. Jordan" school of storytelling) with Foxx—in his TV movie debut—as a honkytonk piano player, accidentally shot by overambitious narco Van Dyke, but getting a reprieve from an angel emissary because it's not yet his time to go through the pearly gates. Pilot to a prospective series. Average.

Ghost of Dragstrip Hollow, The (1959) **65m. BOMB** D: William Hole, Jr. Jody Fair, Martin Braddock, Russ Bender, Leon Tyler, Elaine DuPont. Trite mixture of hot rod gangs and haunted house formulas, with most uneven results.

Ghost of Flight 401, The (1978) **C-100m. TVM** D: Steven Hilliard Stern. Ernest Borgnine, Gary Lockwood, Tina Chen, Kim Basinger, Eugene Roche, Beverly Todd. Supernatural mystery about the ghost (Borgnine) of the pilot of the plane that crashed in Florida Everglades around Christmas of 1972 and the legend of its presence in the cockpit of later flights. Taken from John C. Fuller's intriguing book. Average.

Ghost of Frankenstein, The (1942) **68m** **½ D: Erle C. Kenton. Cedric Hardwicke, Lon Chaney, Jr., Lionel Atwill, Ralph Bellamy, Bela Lugosi, Evelyn Ankers, Dwight Frye. Sequel to SON OF FRANKENSTEIN. Ygor (Lugosi) returns to foul Hardwicke's plan to replace the Monster's brain with that of educated man. Good cast manages to save stale plot. Followed by FRANKENSTEIN MEETS THE WOLF MAN.

Ghost of the China Sea (1958) **79m.** ** D: Fred F. Sears. David Brian, Lynn Bernay, Jonathan Haze, Norman Wright. Brian et al flee Japanese invasion of Philippines; nothing new here.

Ghost of Zorro (1959) **69m.** ** D: Fred C. Brannon. Clayton Moore, Pamela Blake, Roy Barcroft, George J. Lewis, Eugene Roth. Feature version of 1949 serial is a confusingly edited account of descendant of Zorro adopting same guise to combat outlaws destroying telegraph lines.

Ghost Ship, The (1943) **69m.** *** D: Mark Robson. Richard Dix, Russell Wade, Edith Barrett, Ben Bard, Lawrence Tierney. Offbeat Val Lewton melodrama about young man who signs on merchant ship run by power-crazy captain (Dix) who's obsessed with "authority." Absorbing mood-piece with unfortunately abrupt conclusion.

Ghost Ship (1952-British) **69m.** ** D: Vernon Sewell. Dermot Walsh, Hazel Court, Hugh Burden, John Robinson, Joss Ambler. Small-budget yarn about young couple purchasing a haunted yacht.▼

Ghosts—Italian Style (1969-Italian) **C-92m.** ** D: Renato Castellani. Sophia Loren, Vittorio Gassman, Mario Adorf, Margaret Lee, Aldo Guiffre, Francisco Tensi. Newlyweds Loren and Gassman move into haunted house. Weak vehicle for engaging stars.

Ghosts of Rome (1961-Italian) **C-105m.** **½ D: Antonio Pietrangeli. Marcello

Mastroianni, Belinda Lee, Sandra Milo, Vittorio Gassman, Franca Marzi. Scatterbrain antics of oddball characters inhabiting rundown house soon to be demolished, with prospects of finding new quarters frightening them all.

Ghosts on the Loose (1943) **65m.** D: William Beaudine. Leo Gorcey, Huntz Hall, Bobby Jordan, Bela Lugosi, Ava Gardner, Rick Vallin, Minerva Urecal. Also known as THE EAST SIDE KIDS MEET BELA LUGOSI. SEE: **Bowery Boys** series.▼

Ghost Story (1974) SEE: **Madhouse Mansion**▼

Ghost Story (1981) **C-110m.** **½ D: John Irvin. Fred Astaire, Melvyn Douglas, Douglas Fairbanks, Jr., John Houseman, Craig Wasson, Alice Krige, Patricia Neal, Ken Olin. Four elderly New Englanders are tormented by a 50-year-old secret, which now visits evil on one of their sons as well. Absorbing if not altogether satisfying simplification of Peter Straub's best-seller, which loses steam as it nears its resolution. Astaire's last film.▼

Ghost Town (1988) **C-85m.** **½ D: Richard Governor. Franc Luz, Catherine Hickland, Jimmie F. Skaggs, Penelope Windust, Bruce Glover, Blake Conway, Laura Schaefer. Imaginative fantasy thriller has modern-day Western sheriff Luz chosen to rid a century-old town of its curse by avenging its dead sheriff in HIGH NOON fashion. Fine special effects distinguish this modest sleeper.▼

Ghost Writer, The (1984) **C-80m. TVM** D: Tristam Powell. Rose Arrick, Claire Bloom, MacIntyre Dixon, Mark Linn-Baker, Cecile Mann, Sam Wanamaker, Joseph Wiseman. Literate but static adaptation of Phillip Roth's novel, about a famous writer who recalls his experiences when, as a young man, he visited an older, renowned author. Roth and director Powell co-wrote the screenplay. A PBS *American Playhouse* presentation. Average.

Ghoul, The (1933-British) **73m.** **½ D: T. Hayes Hunter. Boris Karloff, Cedric Hardwicke, Ernest Thesiger, Dorothy Hyson, Anthony Bushell, Ralph Richardson. England's answer to Hollywood's horror films: Egyptologist Karloff wishes to be buried with a jewel he believes will allow him eternal life. It's stolen, and he rises from the dead in search of the culprit. Slow going until Karloff's resurrection; then it really hums. Richardson's film debut. Remade as 1962 comedy NO PLACE LIKE HOMICIDE! Original 79m. version is available on video.▼

Ghoul, The (1975-British) **C-88m.** **½ D: Freddie Francis. Peter Cushing, John Hurt, Alexandra Bastedo, Gwen Watford, Veronica Carlson, Steward Bevan. Innocent people fall victim to a mysterious flesh-eating "monster" in Cushing's secluded home.

Fairly interesting, non-gory thriller, with Hurt as Cushing's crazed gardener.▼

Ghoulies (1985) **C-84m.** *½ D: Luca Bercovici. Peter Liapis, Lisa Pelikan, Michael Des Barres, Jack Nance, Peter Risch, Tamara de Treaux. Boring, ridiculous film about young man who invokes Satanic spirits in the form of gremlin-like creatures (who look like muppets dipped in shellac) at a creepy old mansion. Followed by two sequels.▼

Giant (1956) **C-201m.** **** D: George Stevens. Elizabeth Taylor, Rock Hudson, James Dean, Carroll Baker, Jane Withers, Chill Wills, Mercedes McCambridge, Dennis Hopper, Sal Mineo, Rodney (Rod) Taylor, Earl Holliman. Near-legendary epic based on Edna Ferber's novel about two generations of Texans holds up beautifully when not broken up into two nights on TV. Hudson's best performance, close to Taylor's best, and Dean's last film. Stevens won an Oscar for his direction.▼

Giant Behemoth, The (1959-British) **80m.** ** D: Eugene Lourie. Gene Evans, Andre Morell, John Turner, Leigh Madison, Jack MacGowran. Enormous radioactive dinosaur menaces England, finally invades London. Animation effects directed by Willis O'Brien are fine, but film is turgid.

Giant Claw, The (1957) **76m.** *½ D: Fred F. Sears. Jeff Morrow, Mara Corday, Morris Ankrum, Edgar Barrier. Lack of decent special effects ruins the running battle between colossal bird and fighter jets. Big bird is laughable.

Giant from the Unknown (1958) **77m.** *½ D: Richard E. Cunha. Edward Kemmer, Sally Fraser, Bob Steele, Morris Ankrum, Buddy Baer, Joline Brand, Billy Dix. Giant, depraved conquistador Baer, in suspended animation for centuries, is revived in California mountains, wreaking minor havoc. Cheap and silly.▼

Giant Gila Monster, The (1959) **74m.** *½ D: Ray Kellogg. Don Sullivan, Lisa Simone, Shug Fisher, Jerry Cortwright, Beverly Thurman, Don Flourney, Pat Simmons. Big, beaded lizard menaces small Texas town. Not as good as it sounds. Has a couple of wildly inappropriate songs.▼

Giant Leeches, The SEE: **Attack Of The Giant Leeches**▼

Giant of Metropolis, The (1962-Italian) **C-82m.** ** D: Umberto Scarpelli. Mitchell Gordon, Roldano Lupi, Bella Cortez, Liana Orfei. Uneven mixture of costumer and sci-fi with a dash of sadism, set in 10,000 B.C.▼

Giants of Thessaly, The (1960-Italian) **C-86m.** ** D: Riccardo Freda. Roland Carey, Ziva Rodann, Massimo Girotti, Alberto Farnese. Episodic sword-and-sandal account of Jason (Carey) and Orpheus (Girotti) seeking golden fleece, with expected clashes with monsters, evil women, etc.▼

Giant Spider Invasion, The (1975) **C-82m.**

BOMB D: Bill Rebane. Steve Brodie, Barbara Hale, Leslie Parrish, Alan Hale, Robert Easton, Bill Williams. Veteran cast can't do much for this tacky horror opus filmed in Wisconsin.

Gibbsville: The Turning Point of Jim Malloy SEE: **Turning Point of Jim Malloy, The**

G.I. Blues (1960) **C-104m.** **½ D: Norman Taurog. Elvis Presley, Juliet Prowse, Robert Ivers, Leticia Roman, Ludwig Stossel. Prowse's versatile performance as a cabaret dancer uplifts this standard Presley fare about a guitar-playing G.I. in West Germany. Elvis sings "Tonight Is So Right for Love," "Wooden Heart," "Blue Suede Shoes," and title song.▼

Gideon of Scotland Yard (1958-British) **C-91m.** *½ D: John Ford. Jack Hawkins, Dianne Foster, Cyril Cusack, Andrew Ray, James Hayter, Ronald Howard, Anna Massey, Anna Lee. A typical day in the life of a Scotland Yard inspector; Hawkins is likable but the film is unbelievably dull. A surprising dud from director Ford. British title: GIDEON'S DAY. Originally released theatrically in the U.S. in black and white.

Gideon's Day SEE: **Gideon of Scotland Yard**

Gideon's Trumpet (1980) **C-104m. TVM** D: Robert Collins. Henry Fonda, Jose Ferrer, John Houseman, Fay Wray, Sam Jaffe, Dean Jagger, Nicholas Pryor, William Prince, Dolph Sweet, Ford Rainey. Fonda is superb in the true story of a semiliterate Florida convict who changed the course of American legal history; Ferrer is equally fine as his powerful attorney, Abe Fortas. Script by David Rintels, from Anthony Lewis's book; produced by Houseman. Above average.▼

Gidget (1959) **C-95m.** **½ D: Paul Wendkos. Sandra Dee, James Darren, Cliff Robertson, Arthur O'Connell, Joby Baker, Yvonne Craig, Doug McClure. California teenage girl hits the beach one summer and falls in love with two surfer boys. Dee is spirited in the title role of this hit movie (based on Frederick Kohner's novel about his daughter), which led to a number of sequels and two different TV series!▼

Gidget Gets Married (1972) **C-73m. TVM** D: E. W. Swackhamer. Michael Burns, Monie Ellis, Don Ameche, Joan Bennett, Macdonald Carey, Corrine Camacho. Boring situation comedy (minus laugh track) featuring Burns and Ellis as young newlyweds in Glossop, Maryland; he an engineer, she a dissatisfied housewife. Tame humor, unbelievable plot. Below average.

Gidget Goes Hawaiian (1961) **C-102m.** ** D: Paul Wendkos. James Darren, Michael Callan, Deborah Walley, Carl Reiner, Peggy Cass, Eddie Foy, Jr. Inane follow-up has teenager off to the Islands, with embarrassing results for all.▼

Gidget Goes to Rome (1963) **C-101m.** ** D: Paul Wendkos. Cindy Carol, James Darren, Jessie Royce Landis, Cesare Danova, Jeff Donnell. Mild follow-up has fetching teen-ager off to Italy involved in predictable romancing.▼

Gidget Grows Up (1970) **C-75m. TVM** D: James Sheldon. Karen Valentine, Edward Mulhare, Paul Petersen, Nina Foch, Paul Lynde, Warner Anderson, Bob Cummings. Moving to N.Y.C. after short return to surfing life, Gidget takes job as U.N. guide, becomes involved in "first adult love affair." Romance never more unbelievable, nor dialogue more naive. Only Lynde has good material. Average.

Gidget's Summer Reunion (1985) **C-100m. TVM** D: Bruce Bilson. Caryn Richman, Dean Butler, Allison Barron, Don Stroud, Anne Lockhart, Vincent Van Patten, Johnny Yune, Don Murphy, Mary Frann. Another decade, another Gidget, and this time the little surfer girl's a married travel agent, still looking for the perfect wave with now-hubby Moondoggie. Pilot for new *Gidget* series. Average.

Gift, The (1979) **C-100m. TVM** D: Don Taylor. Glenn Ford, Gary Frank, Julie Harris, Allison Argo, Maggie Cooper, Tom Clancy, Kevin Bacon, M. Emmet Walsh. Poignant period piece (the '50s) about a sailor who returns to his old Brooklyn neighborhood on Christmas leave. Ford's eye-opening performance as his hard-drinking, Irish-brogued, peg-legged father makes this one shine. Based on Pete Hamill's autobiographical novella. Above average.

Gift, The (1982-French-Italian) **C-105m.** ** D: Michel Lang. Pierre Mondy, Claudia Cardinale, Clio Goldsmith, Jacques Francois, Cecile Magnet, Remi Laurent. Bank employees chip in to buy their colleague a surprise retirement gift: a beautiful prostitute. A "good clean sex farce," strained and silly, with no sex, very little nudity, and the improbable casting of beautiful Cardinale as Mondy's wife.▼

Gifted One, The (1989) **C-100m. TVM** D: Stephen Herek. Pete Kowanko, John Rhys-Davies, G. W. Bailey, Wendy Phillips, Khrystyne Haje, Gregg Henry. Umpteenth carbon of *The Fugitive* follows the odyssey of a young man with amazing powers who's searching for his birth mother while fleeing from an opportunistic think-tank bigwig who wants the secret he holds. A failed series pilot. Average.

Gift for Heidi, A (1958) **C-71m.** ** D: George Templeton. Douglas Fowley, Sandy Descher, Van Dyke Parks. Heidi learns the meaning of faith, hope, and charity. OK entertainment for youngsters. Inspired by Johanna Spyri's story.

Gift of Life, The (1982) **C-100m. TVM** D: Jerry London. Susan Dey, Paul LeMat, Edward Herrmann, Cassie Yates, Caroline

McWilliams, Priscilla Pointer, Art Lund, Michael Alldredge. Wife with two children becomes a surrogate mother, and faces family and social pressures, then has second thoughts about surrendering her baby to the adoptive parents. Similar to TOMORROW'S CHILD, which premiered at the same time. Average.

Gift of Love, The (1958) **C-105m.** ** D: Jean Negulesco. Lauren Bacall, Robert Stack, Evelyn Rudie, Lorne Greene, Anne Seymour. If you could put up with SENTIMENTAL JOURNEY you might bear this remake, which isn't even as good. Bacall dies but returns to earth as guiding spirit for her husband and daughter. Remade again for TV as SENTIMENTAL JOURNEY.

Gift of Love, The (1978) **C-100m. TVM** D: Don Chaffey. Marie Osmond, Timothy Bottoms, Bethel Leslie, June Lockhart, Donald Moffat, David Wayne, James Woods, Anne Ramsey. Sticky-sweet adaptation of O. Henry's *The Gift of the Magi* is a costume vehicle for Marie Osmond's acting debut. Veteran David Wayne is on hand to narrate in the guise of O. Henry. Average.

Gift of Love: A Christmas Story, The (1983) **C-100m. TVM** D: Delbert Mann. Lee Remick, Angela Lansbury, Polly Holliday, Joseph Warren, Michael Higgins, Mart Hulswit. Maudlin drama about one family's Christmas crisis that even Remick and Lansbury (as the put-upon lady and her mother) are hard-pressed to energize. Earl Hamner based his script on the short story *The Silent Stars Go By* by Bess Streeter Aldrich. Average.

Gig, The (1985) **C-92m.** *** D: Frank D. Gilroy. Wayne Rogers, Cleavon Little, Andrew Duncan, Jerry Matz, Daniel Nalbach, Warren Vache, Joe Silver, Jay Thomas. Perceptive, touching comedy-drama about dreams, compromises, disappointments—what it means to be alive. A group of middle-class, middle-aged men play jazz both to amuse themselves and to escape from the pressures of their lives; they are hired for their first professional engagement at a small resort, and the experience proves to be unexpectedly unsettling. Gilroy also wrote the script.▼

Gigantis, the Fire Monster (1959-Japanese) **78m.** ** D: Motoyoshi, Hugo Grimaldi. Hiroshi Koizumi, Setsuko Makayama, Mindru Chiaki. A new Godzilla, here called Gigantis, battles spiny Angorous, trashing another Japanese city. First sequel to GODZILLA, retitled: GODZILLA RAIDS AGAIN.▼

Gigi (1958) **C-116m.** **** D: Vincente Minnelli. Leslie Caron, Maurice Chevalier, Louis Jourdan, Hermione Gingold, Jacques Bergerac, Eva Gabor. Charming turn-of-the-century musical based on Colette's story of a French girl who's groomed to be a courtesan. Exquisitely filmed, perfectly cast, with memorable Lerner & Loewe score: title tune, "Thank Heaven for Little Girls," "I Remember it Well." Winner of nine Academy Awards including Best Picture, Director, Writing (Alan Jay Lerner), Cinematography (Joseph Ruttenberg), Costumes (Cecil Beaton), Song ("Gigi"), and Scoring (Andre Previn). Chevalier received an honorary Oscar for his career achievement.▼

Gigot (1962) **C-104m.** *** D: Gene Kelly. Jackie Gleason, Katherine Kath, Gabrielle Dorziat, Albert Remy, Yvonne Constant. Sentimental, well-acted tale of a deaf mute (Gleason) and a young girl in Paris. Simple film, well done; Gleason is excellent.

Gilda (1946) **110m.** *** D: Charles Vidor. Rita Hayworth, Glenn Ford, George Macready, Joseph Calleia, Steven Geray. Highly charged story of emotional triangle—mysterious South American casino owner Macready, his new man-Friday Ford, and Macready's alluring wife (Hayworth)—unfortunately cops out with silly resolutions. Rita has never been sexier, especially when singing "Put the Blame on Mame."▼

Gilda Live (1980) **C-90m.** **½ D: Mike Nichols. Gilda Radner, Father Guido Sarducci (Don Novello). Filmization of Radner's Broadway show, with the comedienne doing uncensored versions of her familiar *Saturday Night Live* TV characters. Best song: "Let's Talk Dirty to the Animals."▼

Gilded Lily, The (1935) **80m.** *** D: Wesley Ruggles. Claudette Colbert, Fred MacMurray, Ray Milland, C. Aubrey Smith, Edward Craven. Colbert has to choose between aristocratic Milland and down-to-earth MacMurray. Fine romantic fluff.

Gildersleeve's Ghost (1944) **64m.** ** D: Gordon Douglas. Harold Peary, Marion Martin, Richard LeGrand, Amelita Ward. Programmer entry in the *Great Gildersleeve* series, involving mixture of spooks and gangsters, with predictable results.

Gimme an 'F' (1984) **C-103m.** ** D: Paul Justman. Stephen Shellen, Mark Keyloun, John Karlen, Jennifer C. Cooke, Beth Miller, Daphne Ashbrook. Harmless but highly improbable account of the trials and tribulations of a spastic cheerleading squad and its overage instructor.▼

Gimme Shelter (1970) **C-91m.** **** D: David Maysles, Albert Maysles, Charlotte Zwerin. Rolling Stones, Jefferson Airplane, Melvin Belli. Outstanding documentary of the Rolling Stones and the famous Altamont Speedway free concert that resulted in chaos and murder. Chilling, beautifully handled, with the Stones performing their best songs of the period ("Satisfaction," "Sympathy for the Devil," "Brown Sugar," "Under My Thumb," etc.). ▼

Ginger and Fred (1986-Italian) **C-126m.**

*** D: Federico Fellini. Giulietta Masina, Marcello Mastroianni, Franco Fabrizi, Frederick Von Ledenberg, Martin Blau, Toto Mignone. Fellini satirizes TV, and the cult of instant celebrity, in this relaxed and amusing film. Ginger and Fred are, in fact, two small-time entertainers who used to *imitate* Rogers and Astaire and who are being reunited by an unctuous TV show. The targets are a bit obvious and the pace a bit leisurely, but the climactic sequence is fun, and the two stars are wonderful to watch, as always.▼

Ginger in the Morning (1973) **C-89m.** **½ D: Gordon Wiles. Sissy Spacek, Monte Markham, Mark Miller, Susan Oliver, Slim Pickens. So-so romantic comedy about a lonely salesman who picks up a comely hitchhiker. He's attracted to her young, fresh independence; she's drawn to his old-fashioned romanticism.▼

Girl, a Guy, and a Gob, A (1941) **91m.** ** D: Richard Wallace. George Murphy, Lucille Ball, Edmond O'Brien, Henry Travers, Franklin Pangborn, George Cleveland. Not very original triangle love story, with Ball undecided between Murphy and O'Brien. Produced by Harold Lloyd.▼

Girl Called Hatter Fox, The (1977) **C-100m.** TVM D: George Schaefer. Ronny Cox, Joanelle Romero, Conchata Ferrell, John Durren, Donald Hotten. Drama pitting medical science against witchcraft in the attempt to salvage a teen-aged Indian girl's life. Video title: LOST LEGACY. Average.▼

Girl Can't Help It, The (1956) **C-99m.** **½ D: Frank Tashlin. Tom Ewell, Jayne Mansfield, Edmond O'Brien, Julie London. One-joke film about press agent Ewell trying to hype gangster's girlfriend (Mansfield) to stardom. Some good Tashlin sight gags; classic performances by Fats Domino ("Blue Monday"), The Platters ("You'll Never Know"), Gene Vincent and His Blue Caps ("BeBop A Lula"), Little Richard ("She's Got It," "Ready Teddy," and "The Girl Can't Help It").▼

Girl Crazy (1943) **99m.** ***½ D: Norman Taurog. Mickey Rooney, Judy Garland, Gil Stratton, Robert E. Strickland, "Rags" Ragland, June Allyson, Nancy Walker, Guy Kibbee, Tommy Dorsey and his Orchestra. Rooney sent to small Southwestern school to forget girls, but meets Garland and that's that. Great Gershwin score includes "I Got Rhythm," "Embraceable You," "But Not For Me." Busby Berkeley (the film's original director) staged the finale. Filmed before in 1932; remade as WHEN THE BOYS MEET THE GIRLS.
▼

Girl for Joe, A SEE: **Force of Arms**
Girlfriends (1978) **C-88m.** *** D: Claudia Weill. Melanie Mayron, Anita Skinner, Eli Wallach, Christopher Guest, Bob Balaban, Viveca Lindfors, Mike Kellin. A young woman tries to cope with love, a career, and personal independence after her roommate/girlfriend leaves to get married. Mayron's warm, winning performance helps likable but uneven film over its rough spots.▼

Girl from Jones Beach, The (1949) **78m.** **½ D: Peter Godfrey. Ronald Reagan, Virginia Mayo, Eddie Bracken, Dona Drake, Henry Travers, Lois Wilson, Florence Bates. Breezy comedy about an artist who tries to find a living embodiment of the perfectly proportioned female in his illustrations. Capable romantic-comedy performance by Reagan.

Girl from Lorraine, The (1980-French-Swiss) **C-107m.** **½ D: Claude Goretta. Nathalie Baye, Bruno Ganz, Angela Winkler, Patrick Chesnais. Unemployed draughtswoman Baye, from the provinces, maintains her dignity in lonely, unfriendly Paris. Quietly rewarding drama with an extremely likable heroine; however, sometimes as dreary as some of the characters she meets. Originally titled LA PROVINCIALE.

Girl From Manhattan, The (1948) **81m.** ** D: Alfred E. Green. Dorothy Lamour, George Montgomery, Charles Laughton, Ernest Truex, Hugh Herbert, Constance Collier, Sara Allgood, George Chandler. Forgettable comedy-drama with model Lamour helping her uncle run his boarding house full of stereotypes. Passable time-killer.

Girl from Missouri, The (1934) **75m.** *** D: Jack Conway. Jean Harlow, Lionel Barrymore, Franchot Tone, Lewis Stone, Patsy Kelly, Alan Mowbray. Delightful fluff about good-girl Harlow trying to win a millionaire without sacrificing her integrity. Wise-cracking Kelly as her girlfriend is a treat.

Girl from Petrovka, The (1974) **C-104m.** ** D: Robert Ellis Miller. Goldie Hawn, Hal Holbrook, Anthony Hopkins, Gregoire Aslan, Anton Dolin. Old-fashioned comedy-drama about a bittersweet affair between American correspondent Holbrook and Russian Hawn. Filmed in Vienna and Hollywood, doubling for Moscow.▼

Girl from Scotland Yard, The (1937) **62m.** *½ D: Robert Vignola. Karen Morley, Robert Baldwin, Katherine Alexander, Eduardo Ciannelli, Milli Monti. Escapist story of girl trying to track down mysterious madman with destruction ray is poorly handled; not nearly as much fun as it might have been.

Girl from 10th Avenue, The (1935) **69m.** *** D: Alfred E. Green. Bette Davis, Ian Hunter, Colin Clive, Alison Skipworth, John Eldredge, Philip Reed, Katherine Alexander. Honest working girl Davis gets alcoholic, recently jilted society lawyer Hunter back on his feet; then his ex-girlfriend decides she wants him back. Davis shines in this engrossing soaper.

Girl-Getters, The (1966-British) 79m. *** D: Michael Winner. Oliver Reed, Jane Merrow, Barbara Ferris, Julia Foster. Realistic study of hoodlum youths at British seaside resort, their prankish games and romances; intelligently portrayed. Retitled: THE SYSTEM.

Girl Happy (1965) C-96m. **½ D: Boris Sagal. Elvis Presley, Shelley Fabares, Harold J. Stone, Gary Crosby, Joby Baker, Nita Talbot, Mary Ann Mobley, Chris Noel, Jackie Coogan. Formula Presley musical with tiresome plot of Elvis in Fort Lauderdale chaperoning Fabares, daughter of Chicago mobster.▼

Girl He Left Behind, The (1956) 103m. **½ D: David Butler. Tab Hunter, Natalie Wood, Jessie Royce Landis, Jim Backus. Reminiscent of SEE HERE PRIVATE HARGROVE, without any of the warmth or humor. Hunter is new recruit in Army.

Girl Hunters, The (1963) 103m. **½ D: Roy Rowland. Mickey Spillane, Lloyd Nolan, Shirley Eaton, Hy Gardner. Spillane plays his own fictional detective Mike Hammer in this rugged murder mystery, filmed in England.▼

Girl in a Million, A (1946-British) 81m. ** D: Francis Searle. Joan Greenwood, Hugh Williams, Yvonne Owen, Edward Lexy, Jane Hylton, Michael Hordern. Sometimes wacky comedy focusing on deaf mute who uses her charm to reform several cantankerous gentlemen.

Girl in a Swing, The (1989-U.S.-British) C-112m. BOMB D: Gordon Hessler. Meg Tilly, Rupert Frazer, Nicholas Le Prevost, Elspet Gray, Lorna Heilbron, Helen Cherry. Antique dealer marries a mysterious German woman after a whirlwind courtship and pays the consequences, surviving her hallucinations and related erratic behavior. Despite lots of simulated (and unrated) screen sex, this is absolutely unwatchable—though Frazer looks just enough like Regis Philbin to give this stinker some unexpected subtext.▼

Girl in Black Stockings, The (1957) 73m. ** D: Howard W. Koch. Lex Barker, Anne Bancroft, Mamie Van Doren, Ron Randell, Marie Windsor. Minor murder mystery with some nice touches and good performances; set at chic Utah resort.

Girl in Distress SEE: **Jeannie**

Girl in Every Port, A (1928) 62m. **½ D: Howard Hawks. Victor McLaglen, Robert Armstrong, Louise Brooks, Marcia Cassajuana, Myrna Loy, William Demarest, Natalie Joyce, Sally Rand. Lusty silent comedy about two swaggering sailor pals who travel the world brawling over anything—especially women. Pretty dated, but enthusiasm still puts it over; of special interest to Hawks buffs as the earliest

example of his "buddy-buddy" films. Remade as GOLDIE.

Girl in Every Port, A (1952) 86m. ** D: Chester Erskine. Groucho Marx, William Bendix, Marie Wilson, Don DeFore, Gene Lockhart. Nonsense of two gobs who hide a racehorse aboard ship. Good cast is wasted.▼

Girl in His Pocket (1957-French) 82m. **½ D: Pierre Kast. Jean Marais, Agnes Laurent, Genevieve Page. Strange tale of scientist who invents shrinking formula, changing his romantic life with unforetold complications.

Girl in Room 13 (1961) C-97m. *½ D: Richard Cunha. Brian Donlevy, Andrea Bayard, Elizabeth Howard, Victor Merinow, John Herbert. Low-grade private eye story set in Brazil, with Donlevy tracking down a murder and counterfeit gang.

Girl in the Empty Grave, The (1977) C-100m. TVM D: Lou Antonio. Andy Griffith, James Cromwell, Mitzi Hoag, Claude Earl Jones, Jonathan Banks, Robert F. Simon. Busted pilot in which small-town sheriff Abel Marsh (Griffith) doggedly pursues a murderer. There was, however, a sequel: DEADLY GAME. Below average.

Girl in the Kremlin, The (1957) 81m. ** D: Russell Birdwell. Lex Barker, Zsa Zsa Gabor, Jeffrey Stone, William Schallert. Espionage hokum involving Gabor in dual role as twins, one of whom is Stalin's mistress.

Girl in the Moon SEE: **Woman in the Moon▼**

Girl in the Painting (1948-British) 89m. *** D: Terence Fisher. Mai Zetterling, Robert Beatty, Guy Rolfe, Herbert Lom, Patrick Holt. Intriguing drama of serviceman involved in strange case of amnesiac girl seeking her lost past in Germany. Retitled: PORTRAIT FROM LIFE.

Girl in the Park, The SEE: **Sanctuary of Fear▼**

Girl in the Picture, The (1986-British) C-90m. ** D: Cary Parker. Gordon John Sinclair, Irina Brook, David McCay, Gregor Fisher, Caroline Guthrie, Paul Young. Slight, forgettable comedy about a young photographer (Sinclair), and his efforts to break up with pretty live-in girlfriend Brook. After he does, guess what? . . . He realizes he cannot live without her. ▼

Girl in the Red Velvet Swing, The (1955) C-109m. **½ D: Richard Fleischer. Ray Milland, Joan Collins, Farley Granger, Cornelia Otis Skinner, Glenda Farrell, Luther Adler. Glossy, fictionalized account of Evelyn Nesbit-Stanford White-Harry Thaw escapade of early 20th-century N.Y.C. Showgirl falls in love with prominent architect, which upsets mentally disturbed millionaire.

Girl in the Woods (1958) **71m.** *½ D: Tom Gries. Forrest Tucker, Maggie Hayes, Barton MacLane, Diana Francis. Lumbering tale of lumbermen's lives.

Girl in White, The (1952) **93m.** ** D: John Sturges. June Allyson, Arthur Kennedy, Gary Merrill, Mildred Dunnock, James Arness. Humdrum biography of Emily Dunning, the first woman to work as a doctor in a N.Y.C. public hospital.

Girl Most Likely, The (1957) **C-98m.** *** D: Mitchell Leisen. Jane Powell, Cliff Robertson, Keith Andes, Tommy Noonan, Kaye Ballard, Una Merkel. Musical remake of TOM, DICK AND HARRY comes off as bright, cheerful entertainment. A girl must decide which one of the trio she'll wed; Kaye Ballard does very well in supporting role. Choreography by Gower Champion.▼

Girl Most Likely to . . ., The (1973) **C-74m.** TVM D: Lee Philips. Stockard Channing, Edward Asner, Warren Berlinger, Suzanne Zenor, Larry Wilcox, Jim Backus, Fred Grandy, Carl Ballantine, Annette O'Toole. Clever black comedy co-scripted by Joan Rivers has ugly duckling made beautiful by plastic surgery, seeking revenge on men who made life miserable for her. Above average.

Girl Named Sooner, A (1975) **C-115m.** TVM D: Delbert Mann. Lee Remick, Richard Crenna, Don Murray, Anne Francis, Cloris Leachman, Susan Deer. Eight-year-old girl, raised by eccentric old woman in backwoods of Indiana, becomes the ward of a childless couple whose lives she enriches. Touching family entertainment, adapted from Suzanne Clauser's acclaimed 1972 novel, and well nigh stolen by Leachman as Old Mam, the feisty crone. Above average.

Girl Named Tamiko, A (1962) **C-110m.** **½ D: John Sturges. Laurence Harvey, France Nuyen, Martha Hyer, Gary Merrill, Michael Wilding. Miyoshi Umeki, Lee Patrick. Overblown soaper set in Tokyo. Harvey charms Hyer into proposing marriage so he can get U.S. citizenship. Nuyen is sweet Oriental whom Harvey really loves.

Girl Next Door, The (1953) **C-92m.** **½ D: Richard Sale. Dan Dailey, June Haver, Dennis Day, Cara Williams, Natalie Schafer. Pleasing musical of singing star Haver moving to new home and falling in love with neighbor Dailey, a cartoonist.

Girl of the Golden West, The (1938) **120m.** **½ D: Robert Z. Leonard. Jeanette MacDonald, Nelson Eddy, Walter Pidgeon, Leo Carrillo, Buddy Ebsen, Leonard Penn. Oft-produced tale of love affair of good-girl MacDonald and bandit Eddy, with tuneful Gus Kahn-Sigmund Romberg score that didn't produce any hits.▼

Girl of the Night (1960) **93m.** **½ D: Joseph Cates. Anne Francis, Lloyd Nolan,

Kay Medford, John Kerr. Francis gives a vivid performance as prostitute undergoing psychoanalysis.

Girl on a Motorcycle (1968-British-French) **C-91m.** *½ D: Jack Cardiff. Marianne Faithfull, Alain Delon, Roger Mutton, Marius Goring, Catherine Jourdan. Slick cinematography (by Cardiff) only asset to sleazy tale of Faithfull abandoning her husband, riding on her motorcycle to visit ex-lover Delon. From Andre Pieyre de Mandiargue's novel. Trimmed from original X-rated version titled NAKED UNDER LEATHER.▼

Girl on the Bridge (1951) **77m.** BOMB D: Hugo Haas. Hugo Haas, Beverly Michaels, Robert Dane, Johnny Close, Anthony Jochim. Typical Haasian look at Michaels as a so-called femme fatale and her effect on the men in her life.

Girl on the Late, Late Show, The (1974) **C-78m.** TVM D: Gary Nelson. Don Murray, Laraine Stephens, Bert Convy, Yvonne DeCarlo, Gloria Grahame, Van Johnson, Ralph Meeker, Cameron Mitchell, Mary Ann Mobley, Joe Santos, John Ireland, Walter Pidgeon, Sherry Jackson. Movieland murders follow TV producer Murray in his search for 50s film queen Grahame, who mysteriously vanished at the height of her career. Nostalgia buffs will find this a feast while detective nuts will spot the baddie early on. Average.

Girl Rush (1944) **65m.** *½ D: Gordon Douglas, Alan Carney, Wally Brown, Frances Langford, Paul Hurst, Vera Vague, Robert Mitchum. Dim-witted comedy with Carney and Brown starring as vaudeville troupers stranded in San Francisco during the gold rush. Langford is always good, but the film isn't.▼

Girl Rush, The (1955) **C-85m.** **½ D: Robert Pirosh. Rosalind Russell, Fernando Lamas, Eddie Albert, Gloria DeHaven, Marion Lorne. Russell inherits a Las Vegas casino and determines to make it go, romanced by Lamas. Minor musical numbers and forced gaiety are all too evident.

Girls, The (1968) **90m.** *** D: Mai Zetterling. Bibi Andersson, Harriet Andersson, Gunnel Lindblom, Gunnar Bjornstrand, Erland Josephson, Ulf Palme. Trenchant study of modern marriages and female roles, loaded with fantasy sequences. Fabulous cast drawn by actress-turned-director Zetterling from Ingmar Bergman's repertory company.

Girls About Town (1931) **82m.** *** D: George Cukor. Kay Francis, Joel McCrea, Lilyan Tashman, Eugene Pallette, Alan Dinehart, Louise Beavers. Title tells all in this Pre-Code comedy that stops just short of calling Francis and Tashman tarts. The latter (who died three years later) is likable in her best screen role, and gorgeous Travis

Banton costumes add to the fun. One of the best of the early Cukor films.

Girls' Dormitory (1936) **66m.** **½ D: Irving Cummings. Herbert Marshall, Ruth Chatterton, Simone Simon, Constance Collier, J. Edward Bromberg, Dixie Dunbar, Tyrone Power. Fairly standard tale of girl's infatuation for school head Marshall spotlights newcomer Simon, who does quite well, and young leading man Power in featured role.

Girls for Rent (1974) **C-92m.** BOMB D: Al Adamson. Georgina Spelvin, Susan McIver, Rosalind Miles, Preston Pierce, Robert Livingston, Kent Taylor. Low-budget quickie made to capitalize on Spelvin's success in the porno classic THE DEVIL IN MISS JONES; she's an evil hit lady in dreary film which deteriorates into chase filler.

Girls! Girls! Girls! (1962) **C-106m.** **½ D: Norman Taurog. Elvis Presley, Stella Stevens, Laurel Goodwin, Jeremy Slate, Benson Fong, Robert Strauss, Ginny Tiu. Presley is chased by a mass of girls and can't decide which one he prefers. Along the way, he sings "Return to Sender" and some other less memorable numbers (like "Song of the Shrimp").▼

Girl Shy (1924) **65m.** *** D: Fred Newmeyer, Sam Taylor. Harold Lloyd, Jobyna Ralston, Richard Daniels, Carlton Griffin. Enjoyable Lloyd vehicle mixes comedy, and sentiment with a spectacular chase finale. Harold is a small-town boy who's petrified of women but writes book on lovemaking secrets! Fantasy scenes of his love life mark highlight. Edited for TV.

Girls in Prison (1956) **87m.** *½ D: Edward L. Cahn. Richard Denning, Joan Taylor, Adele Jergens, Helen Gilbert, Lance Fuller, Jane Darwell, Raymond Hatton, Mae Marsh. Tawdry study of prison life with usual female stereotype prisoners.

Girls in the Night (1953) **83m.** ** D: Jack Arnold. Joyce Holden, Glenda Farrell, Harvey Lembeck, Patricia Hardy, Jaclynne Greene. Compact account of young people seeking to better their lives, blighted by N.Y.C. tenement existence.

Girls in the Office, The (1979) **C-97m.** TVM D: Ted Post. Susan Saint James, Barbara Eden, Tony Roberts, David Wayne, Penny Peyser, Joe Penny. Four women working in a Houston department store must choose between love and success in this standard romantic comedy. Average.

Girls Just Want to Have Fun (1985) **C-87m.** **½ D: Alan Metter. Sarah Jessica Parker, Lee Montgomery, Morgan Woodward, Jonathan Silverman, Helen Hunt, Holly Gagnier, Ed Lauter. Likable, upbeat teen comedy about girl with reactionary father who wants to enter dance contest. Clichés and contrivances are counterbalanced by believable portrayal of teen-

age girls, appealingly played by Parker and Hunt.▼

Girls of Huntington House, The (1973) **C-73m.** TVM D: Alf Kjellin. Shirley Jones, Mercedes McCambridge, Sissy Spacek, William Windom, Pamela Sue Martin, Darrell Larson. Weak melodrama takes place in school for unwed mothers where unmarried teacher finds herself drawn more and more to students' individual problems. Conceived from kids' point of view. Average.▼

Girls of Pleasure Island, The (1953) **C-95m.** ** D: F. Hugh Herbert, Alvin Ganzer. Leo Genn, Don Taylor, Gene Barry, Elsa Lanchester, Audrey Dalton. Unfunny comedy involving Genn and brood of daughters combating swarm of G.I.s who establish a base on their island.

Girls of the Night (1959-French) **114m.** **½ D: Maurice Cloche. Georges Marchal, Nicole Berger, Claus Holm, Kay Fischer, Gil Vidal. Sensible telling of plight of group of prostitutes, and clergyman who tries to help them.

Girls of the White Orchid (1983) **C-100m.** TVM D: Jonathan Kaplan. Jennifer Jason Leigh, Ann Jillian, Thomas Byrd, Mako, Carolyn Seymour, Richard Narita, Soon-Teck Oh. If it didn't take itself so seriously, this sleazy tale of young-girl-in-white-slavery-by-yellow-peril could have been a delicious send-up of Monogram B movies of the late '30s. Some nudity and sexual content have been added for the version shown on cable TV and homevideo. Retitled DEATH RIDE TO OSAKA. Below average.▼

Girls on Probation (1938) **63m.** *½ D: William McGann. Jane Bryan, Ronald Reagan, Anthony Averill, Sheila Bromley, Henry O'Neill, Elizabeth Risdon, Sig Rumann, Susan Hayward. Uninspired B picture about a young woman (Bryan) who can't seem to stay out of trouble with the law; Reagan is a lawyer who defends her and falls in love with her.

Girls on the Beach, The (1965) **C-80m.** *½ D: William N. Witney. Martin West, Noreen Corcoran, Peter Brooks, Lana Wood, The Beach Boys, Leslie Gore. Three coeds promise they'll get the Beatles to make a personal appearance and then have a mite of trouble delivering. The Beach Boys sing two tunes in this predictable comedy. Reissued as SUMMER OF '64.

Girls on the Loose (1958) **78m.** ** D: Paul Henreid. Mara Corday, Lita Milan, Barbara Bostock, Mark Richman. Drama unfolds account of Corday heading robbery gang, and eventual downfall.

Girls Town (1959) **92m.** *½ D: Charles Haas. Mamie Van Doren, Mel Torme, Paul Anka, Ray Anthony, Maggie Hayes, Cathy Crosby, Gigi Perreau, Gloria Talbott, Jim Mitchum, Elinor Donahue, Sheilah

Graham, The Platters, Harold Lloyd, Jr. Wisecracking bad girl Van Doren is sent to title correctional institution, where she learns that she doesn't have all the answers. Absurd in the extreme, but has definite camp value just for the cast alone . . . plus, Anka sings "Ave Maria"! As Mamie says, it's "cool, crazy, fantabulous." Retitled INNOCENT AND THE DAMNED.

Girl, the Gold Watch & Dynamite, The (1981) **C-100m. TVM** D: Hy Averback. Lee Purcell, Philip MacHale, Burton Gilliam, Zohra Lampert, Jack Elam, Gary Lockwood, Jerry Mathers, Richie Havens, Barney Phillips, Carol Lawrence, Tom Poston, Gene Barry, Morgan Fairchild. Pedestrian sequel to THE GIRL, THE GOLD WATCH & EVERYTHING, with further misadventures of the square heir to a foundering business and a time-stopping watch. Average.

Girl, the Gold Watch & Everything, The (1980) **C-100m. TVM** D: William Wiard. Robert Hays, Pam Dawber, Zohra Lampert, Ed Nelson, Maurice Evans, Peter Brown, Macdonald Carey, Jill Ireland. John D. MacDonald's fantasy about an unassuming fellow who inherits a gold watch with time-stopping powers is translated into a standard sitcom. Sequel: THE GIRL, THE GOLD WATCH & DYNAMITE. Average.

Girl Trouble (1942) **82m.** ** D: Harold Schuster. Don Ameche, Joan Bennett, Billie Burke, Frank Craven, Vivian Blaine. Pleasant frou-frou with Ameche and Bennett involved in business and romancing, with fine support from the adept scatterbrain Burke.

Girl Who Came Gift-Wrapped, The (1974) **C-78m. TVM** D: Bruce Bilson. Karen Valentine, Richard Long, Tom Bosley, Farrah Fawcett, Dave Madden, Louise Sorel. Country cutie Karen comes to big city looking for husband and setting her sights on bachelor Long, decides to give herself to him as a birthday present. Comic tale with large doses of leering sex and suggestive poses, but Karen looks great bikini-clad. Average.

Girl Who Couldn't Say No, The (1970-Italian) **C-83m.** ** D: Franco Brusati. Virna Lisi, George Segal, Lila Kedrova, Akim Tamiroff, Paola Pitagora, Felicity Mason. Square Segal and childhood friend Lisi fall for each other, but just can't maintain a permanent relationship; mild comedy.

Girl Who Had Everything, The (1953) **69m.** **½ D: Richard Thorpe. Elizabeth Taylor, Fernando Lamas, William Powell, Gig Young. Murky melodrama with top cast. Girl falls in love with criminal client of her attorney father. Remake of A FREE SOUL.

Girl Who Knew Too Much (1969) **C-96m.** ** D: Francis D. Lyon. Adam West, Nancy Kwan, Nehemiah Persoff, Robert Alda. Adventurer who is hired to find the killer of a syndicate boss discovers Communist plot to infiltrate organized crime.

Girl Who Spelled Freedom, The (1986) **C-100m. TVM** D: Simon Wincer. Wayne Rogers, Mary Kay Place, Kieu Chinh, Kathleen Sisk. A Disney delight about a real-life teenage Cambodian refugee who arrived in the States in 1979 speaking little English and went on to become a national spelling bee champion in just four years. Australian director Wincer and writers Christopher Knopf and David A. Simons do themselves proud. Above average.▼

Girl With a Suitcase (1960-Italian) **96m.** ***½ D: Valerio Zurlini. Claudia Cardinale, Jacques Perrin, Luciana Angelillo, Corrado Pani. Impressive Italian film of devoted but shady girl Cardinale following her ex-lover to Parma, only to fall in love with his adolescent brother. Confusing at times, but extremely well acted, worth seeing.

Girl with Green Eyes (1964-British) **91m.** *** D: Desmond Davis. Rita Tushingham, Peter Finch, Lynn Redgrave, T. P. McKenna, Marie Kean, Julian Glover. Moving drama of young farm-girl Tushingham falling in love with writer Finch, highlighted by winning Tushingham performance. Redgrave scores as her roommate. Filmed in Dublin.

Girl With the Red Hair, The (1981-Dutch) **C-116m.** **½ D: Ben Verbong. Renee Soutendijk, Peter Tuinman, Loes Luca, Johan Leysen, Robert Delhez, Ada Bouwman. Determined student Soutendijk becomes a killer of Nazi informers during WW2. Tense, chilling, sober, but overlong and too often slow; good score by Nicola Piovani helps move things along. Special color effect will be lost on TV. Based on a true story.

Girly SEE: **Mumsy, Nanny, Sonny and Girly**▼

Giro City SEE: **And Nothing But the Truth**▼

Git (1965) **C-90m.** *½ D: Ellis Kadison. Jack Chaplain, Heather North, Leslie Bradley, Richard Webb. Young boy and daughter of dog-breeder widower set out to train a renegade setter. Woof woof.▼

Give a Girl a Break (1953) **C-82m.** **½ D: Stanley Donen. Marge and Gower Champion, Debbie Reynolds, Kurt Kasznar, Larry Keating. Bland musical of a show producer, his emotional star, and the girl seeking the lead role.

Give 'Em Hell (1954-French) **90m.** **½ D: John Berry. Eddie Constantine, Mai Britt, Jean Danet, Jean Carmet. If not taken seriously, amusing gangster yarn of

Johnny Jordan (Constantine), with usual amount of fisticuffs and gunplay.

Give 'em Hell, Harry! (1975) **C-102m.** *** D: Steve Binder. James Whitmore. Straight reproduction of Whitmore's one-man stage triumph as Harry Truman, covering high points in both the political and personal life of our 33rd President. Videotaped and transferred to film for theatrical release, but original tape version used for TV.▼

Give Me a Sailor (1938) **80m.** **½ D: Elliott Nugent. Martha Raye, Bob Hope, Betty Grable, Jack Whiting, Clarence Kolb, J. C. Nugent. Fast-moving musicomedy of sailor Hope's complicated love affairs. Raye is always worth watching; undistinguished score.

Give Me Your Heart (1936) **87m.** **½ D: Archie Mayo. Kay Francis, George Brent, Roland Young, Patric Knowles, Henry Stephenson, Frieda Inescort, Helen Flint. Francis has a child by a married man, weds Brent yet still pines for her baby. Well made but all-too familiar drama, highlighted by Kay's glamorous wardrobe changes.

Give My Regards to Broad Street (1984-British) **C-108m.** ** D: Peter Webb. Paul McCartney, Bryan Brown, Ringo Starr, Barbara Bach, Linda McCartney, Tracey Ullman, Ralph Richardson. Vanity film for McCartney, with silly plot thread about a missing album tape connecting a number of music video-type numbers ("Ballroom Dancing," "No More Lonely Nights"). Some of the music is good (and McCartney reprises a couple of Beatles songs) but as a film it's a big snooze.▼

Give My Regards to Broadway (1948) **C-89m.** ** D: Lloyd Bacon. Dan Dailey, Charles Winninger, Nancy Guild, Charles Ruggles, Fay Bainter. Blah musical of old-time vaudevillian Winninger refusing to admit that the family act should break up.

Give Us Wings (1940) **62m.** D: Charles Lamont. Billy Halop, Huntz Hall, Gabriel Dell, Anne Gwynne, Bernard Punsley, Bobby Jordan, Wallace Ford, Victor Jory. SEE: **Bowery Boys** series.

Gizmo (1977) **C/B&W-77m.** **½ D: Howard Smith. Entertaining compilation of film clips on 20th-century "inventors" and their often outlandish contraptions. Good fun, though it can't quite sustain feature length.▼

Gladiator, The (1938) **70m.** **½ D: Edward Sedgwick. Joe E. Brown, Man Mountain Dean, June Travis, Dickie Moore, Lucien Littlefield. Timid boy (Brown) takes serum, becomes all-star hero at college. Simple, sincere, enjoyable.

Gladiator, The (1986) **C-100m. TVM** D: Abel Ferrara. Ken Wahl, Nancy Allen, Robert Culp, Stan Shaw, Rosemary For-

syth. One-man avenger of the road goes after his brother's hit-and-run killer whom the courts set free. Wahl goes the well-worn vigilante route in this pedestrian pilot to a prospective series. Below average.▼

Glass Alibi, The (1946) **70m.** ** D: W. Lee Wilder. Paul Kelly, Douglas Fowley, Anne Gwynne, Maris Wrixon, Jack Conrad. Satisfactory drama involving conman who thinks marrying a dying heiress is a sure bet, till he discovers she's recovering.

Glass Bottom Boat, The (1966) **C-110m.** *** D: Frank Tashlin. Doris Day, Rod Taylor, Arthur Godfrey, Paul Lynde, Eric Fleming, Alice Pearce, Ellen Corby, John McGiver, Edward Andrews, Dom De Luise, Dick Martin. Above-average Day nonsense, with widow Doris hired by research scientist Taylor as his biographer. He tries to seduce her; she's mistaken for a Russian spy. Godfrey is Day's father, skipper of the title vehicle. Lots of Tashlin's trademark slapstick.

Glass Cage, The (1964) **78m.** *½ D: Antonio Santean. John Hoyt, Elisha Cook, Arline Sax, Robert Kelljan. Programmer of burglar shot in self-defense and romance developing between police investigator and suspect. Retitled: DEN OF DOOM.

Glass House, The (1972) **C-73m. TVM** D: Tom Gries. Vic Morrow, Clu Gulager, Billy Dee Williams, Dean Jagger, Alan Alda, Kristoffer Tabori. Gripping account of what it's like to be in state prison, adapted from story by Truman Capote. Location-shot, with many real-life prisoners in supporting cast. Also known as TRUMAN CAPOTE'S THE GLASS HOUSE. Above average.▼

Glass Houses (1972) **C-90m.** ** D: Alexander Singer. Jennifer O'Neill, Bernard Barrow, Deirdre Lenihan, Ann Summers, Phillip Pine, Lloyd Kino. Low-grade drama about infidelity and incestuous desire is mildly interesting in a lurid kind of way; O'Neill's first film, but released after RIO LOBO and SUMMER OF '42.

Glass Key, The (1935) **80m.** *** D: Frank Tuttle. George Raft, Claire Dodd, Edward Arnold, Rosalind Keith, Ray Milland, Guinn Williams. Solid Dashiell Hammett story about politician Arnold getting involved in mysterious murder, Raft trying to dig out the facts. Drags during second half, but still quite good. Remade in 1942.

Glass Key, The (1942) **85m.** ***½ D: Stuart Heisler. Brian Donlevy, Veronica Lake, Alan Ladd, Joseph Calleia, William Bendix, Bonita Granville, Richard Denning. Fast-moving remake of 1935 film, with wardheeler Donlevy accused of murder, henchman Ladd bailing him out. Lake fine as mysterious love interest, Bendix effective as brutal bodyguard. Akira Kurosawa claims this was his inspiration for YOJIMBO. Dashiell Hammett novel neatly adapted by Jonathan Latimer.▼

Glass Menagerie, The (1950) **107m.** ******* D: Irving Rapper. Jane Wyman, Kirk Douglas, Gertrude Lawrence, Arthur Kennedy. More notable for its cast and intention than results. Slow-moving version of Tennessee Williams' drama of lame girl, her faded Southern belle mother, and idealistic brother, all living in their own fragile dream worlds. Remade twice.

Glass Menagerie, The (1973) **C-100m.** **TVM** D: Anthony Harvey. Katharine Hepburn, Sam Waterston, Joanna Miles, Michael Moriarty. Producer David Susskind and the entire four-member cast (Hepburn in her TV acting debut) deserve kudos for this superior version of the Tennessee Williams play (adapted by the playwright). Above average.

Glass Menagerie, The (1987) **C-134m.** ******* D: Paul Newman. Joanne Woodward, John Malkovich, Karen Allen, James Naughton. Respectable, well-made version of Tennessee Williams' now legendary play, with Woodward fine as Amanda Wingfield and Malkovich superb as son Tom. Woodward, Allen, and Naughton had appeared in two regional stage productions of Williams' play prior to making this film. A good—at times very good—picture, but by no means a great one.▼

Glass Mountain, The (1950-British) **94m.** ******* D: Henry Cass. Valentina Cortese, Michael Denison, Dulcie Gray, Sebastian Shaw. Beautifully-made film of a British composer who writes an opera, inspired by majestic Italian Alps. A treat for music-lovers, with many singers from La Scala appearing in opera sequence.

Glass Slipper, The (1955) **C-94m.** ****½** D: Charles Walters. Leslie Caron, Michael Wilding, Keenan Wynn, Estelle Winwood, Elsa Lanchester, Amanda Blake. Silky musical of Cinderella story with talky plot bogging down lilting fantasy dance and song sequences.

Glass Sphinx, The (1967-Italian-Spanish) **C-91m.** ***½** D: Luigi Scattini. Robert Taylor, Anita Ekberg, Gianna Serra, Jack Stuart, Angel Del Pozo, Jose Truchado. World-famous archeologist Taylor on trail of tomb of glass sphinx containing magic elixir; foreign agents have similar idea. Confusing and forgettable.

Glass Tomb, The (1955-British) **59m.** ****** D: Montgomery Tully. John Ireland, Honor Blackman, Geoffrey Keen, Eric Pohlmann, Sydney Tafler, Liam Redmond, Sam Kydd. Bizarre carnival backgrounds give this typical murder tale some spice.

Glass Tower, The (1957-German) **92m.** ****½** D: Harold Braun. Lilli Palmer, O. E. Hasse, Peter Van Eyck, Brigitte Horney, Hannes Messemer. Interesting study of overly jealous husband keeping beautiful wife Palmer a prisoner so she won't be tempted by other men; well acted.

Glass Wall, The (1953) **80m.** ****** D: Maxwell Shane. Vittorio Gassman, Gloria Grahame, Ann Robinson, Jerry Paris, Kathleen Freeman. Drama of refugee Gassman who illegally came to N.Y.C. and, rather than accept deportation, goes on the lam.

Glass Web, The (1953) **81m.** ******* D: Jack Arnold. Edward G. Robinson, John Forsythe, Kathleen Hughes, Marcia Henderson, Richard Denning, Hugh Sanders. Robinson is fine as criminal research authority for TV mystery show, who's caught up in murder utilized as basis for one of the programs. Kathleen Freeman and Beverly Garland have bits. Originally shot in 3-D.

Gleaming the Cube (1989) **C-104m.** ****** D: Graeme Clifford. Christian Slater, Steven Bauer, Ed Lauter, Micole Mercurio, Richard Herd, Charles Cyphers, Le Tuan, Minh Luong, Kieu Chinh. Rebellious young skateboarder sets out to find his brother's murderers with the help of a street-smart detective. Skateboard stunts are sensational, but the story is by-the-numbers TV stuff. The title, if you're curious, is skateboarding jargon for reaching the ultimate—which this movie never does.▼

Glen and Randa (1971) **C-94m.** ****½** D: Jim McBride. Steven Curry, Shelley Plimpton, Woodrow Chambliss, Garry Goodrow. Years after nuclear destruction of world, teenage lovers follow comic-book "clues" and look for Metropolis.▼

Glenn Miller Story, The (1954) **C-116m.** ✓ ******* D: Anthony Mann. James Stewart, June Allyson, Charles Drake, George Tobias, Harry Morgan, Frances Langford, Louis Armstrong, Gene Krupa. Marvelous music is most of this film, sentimental story the rest. All of Miller's hits played, many guest performers. Stewart is convincing as popular bandleader.▼

Glen or Glenda? (1953) **61m.** BOMB D: Edward D. Wood, Jr. Bela Lugosi, Dolores Fuller, Daniel Davis, Lyle Talbot, Timothy Farrell, "Tommy" Haynes, Charles Crafts, Conrad Brooks, Henry Bederski, George Weiss. Sensational but sincere "docu-fantasy" about transvestism could well be the worst movie ever made. Legendarily awful director Wood stars (under the name Daniel Davis) as Glen, who can't decide how to tell his fiancée he wants to wear her clothes. Dizzying hodgepodge of stock footage, demented dream sequences, and heartfelt plea for tolerance linked by campy Lugosi narrating from haunted house. "Bevare!" Even more inept and hilarious than Wood's infamous PLAN 9 FROM OUTER SPACE. Also released as I CHANGED MY SEX, I LED TWO LIVES, and HE OR SHE. Reissued at 67m.▼

Glitter Dome, The (1984) **C-95m. TVM**

D: Stuart Margolin. James Garner, Margot Kidder, John Lithgow, Colleen Dewhurst, John Marley, Stuart Margolin, Paul Koslo. Limp adaptation of Joseph Wambaugh's kinky novel about a pair of L.A. cops out to crack a film mogul's murder. Margolin not only directed but also co-produced, wrote the music, and co-starred with his buddy, Garner, on whose various series he'd also been a regular. Keep your eye on Kidder and her off-the-wall performance. Made for cable. Average.▼

Glitz (1988) **C-100m. TVM** D: Sandor Stern. Jimmy Smits, Markie Post, John Diehl, Madison Mason, Ken Foree, Robin Strasser. A Miami-based cop teams up with an Atlantic City lounge singer to track down a call girl's killer. Tepid dramatization of Elmore Leonard's best-selling detective novel. Average.▼

Global Affair, A (1964) **84m.** ****½** D: Jack Arnold. Bob Hope, Yvonne De Carlo, Robert Sterling, John McGiver, Lilo Pulver. Unwitty Hope vehicle has Bob in charge of a baby found at U.N., with female representative from each nation demanding the child.

Gloria (1980) **C-121m.** ****** D: John Cassavetes. Gena Rowlands, Buck Henry, John Adames, Julie Carmen, Lupe Guarnica. Ex-mob mistress goes on the lam with a young neighbor-boy after gangland hit-men wipe out his parents. Good-looking but way overlong melodrama, which Cassavetes may or may not be playing for laughs.▼

Glorifying the American Girl (1929) **87m.** ****½** D: Millard Webb, John Harkrider. Mary Eaton, Edward Crandall; and as themselves: Eddie Cantor, Helen Morgan, Rudy Vallee, Florenz Ziegfeld, Adolph Zukor, Otto Kahn, Texas Guinan, Mayor & Mrs. James Walker, Ring Lardner, Noah Beery, Norman Brokenshire, Johnny Weissmuller. Early talkie musical revue produced by Ziegfeld himself is a rather routine chorus-girl-trying-to-break-into-show-biz plot, but that is overshadowed by the sheer novelty of seeing such a dazzling and sometimes bizarre array of talent appearing as themselves. (Best of all: Helen Morgan.) Originally released with some two-color Technicolor sequences. Archivally restored to 96m.▼

Glory (1956) **C-100m.** ****** D: David Butler. Margaret O'Brien, Walter Brennan, Charlotte Greenwood, John Lupton. Bland horseracing story, with grown-up O'Brien as woman who owns champion horse.▼

Glory (1989) **C-122m.** ******** D: Edward Zwick. Matthew Broderick, Denzel Washington, Cary Elwes, Morgan Freeman, Jihmi Kennedy, Andre Braugher, John Finn, Donovan Leitch, John David Cullum, Bob Gunton, Cliff DeYoung. Exceptional story of America's first unit of black soldiers during the Civil War and the young, inexperienced Northerner (Broderick) who's given the job of training and leading them. Based in part on the letters of that young officer and brought to life with astonishing skill and believability. Grand, moving, breathtakingly filmed (by veteran cinematographer Freddie Francis) and faultlessly performed. One of the finest historical dramas ever made. Screenplay by Kevin Jarre. Jane Alexander (as Broderick's mother) and Raymond St. Jacques (as Frederick Douglass) appear unbilled. Oscar winner for Cinematography, Sound, and Supporting Actor (Washington).▼

Glory Alley (1952) **79m.** ****½** D: Raoul Walsh. Ralph Meeker, Leslie Caron, Gilbert Roland, Louis Armstrong, John McIntire. Just before the championship bout, boxer Meeker quits the fight game. Series of flashbacks tells his intriguing story. New Orleans backgrounds allow for some good musical interludes.

Glory Boy SEE: My Old Man's Place

Glory Brigade, The (1953) **82m.** ****** D: Robert D. Webb. Victor Mature, Alexander Scourby, Lee Marvin, Richard Egan, Alvy Moore. Passable Korean War actioner with good cast.

Glory Days (1988) **C-100m. TVM** D: Robert Conrad. Robert Conrad, Shane Conrad, Jennifer O'Neill, Stacy Edwards, Ed O'Ross. Another Conrad vanity project (as director and star for his own company with his son as costar, daughter as executive producer, wife in a small role, etc.) has him in the improbable role of a successful middle-aged business tycoon who decides to go back to college to fulfill his dream of becoming a football star. Average.

Glory! Glory! (1989) **C-210m. TVM** D: Lindsay Anderson. Richard Thomas, Ellen Greene, James Whitmore, Barry Morse, Winston Reckert. Broad, often slashing satire about TV evangelism with a dynamic but foul-mouthed female rock 'n' roller being brought in to save a money-machine mega-ministry from sinking under the leadership of the charismatic founder's straight-arrow son. Lots of truths, sight gags, rock music, sex, and Mike Fash's flashy camerawork. Written with a vengeance by Stan Daniels (of *The Mary Tyler Moore Show*), and directed to a turn by sharp-eyed Anderson. Made for cable; originally shown in two parts. Above average.▼

Glory Guys, The (1965) **C-112m.** ****** D: Arnold Laven. Tom Tryon, Harve Presnell, Michael Anderson, Jr., Senta Berger, James Caan, Slim Pickens, Wayne Rogers. Lumbering Cavalry western with a love triangle thrown in. Screenplay by Sam Peckinpah.▼

Glory Stompers, The (1967) **C-85m.** BOMB D: Anthony M. Lanza. Dennis Hopper, Jody McCrea, Chris Noel, Jock

Mahoney, Lindsay Crosby. Hopper, pre-EASY RIDER, stars as motorcycle-gang leader who wears a swastika patch and mouths lines like, "Hey, like, ya know, I wanna dance with you, baby." And, from Noel: "I just want something better than being a Stompers girl." Hilariously bad; see if you can count how many times Hopper says "man."▼

Glove, The (1978) C-91m. ** D: Ross Hagen. John Saxon, Rosey Grier, Joanna Cassidy, Joan Blondell, Jack Carter, Aldo Ray, Keenan Wynn. Violent action flick (with episodic comic diversions by various "guest" veterans), pitting a world-weary bounty hunter against a vengeful ex-con who commits mayhem with a leather-laced steel riot glove.▼

"G" Men (1935) 85m. ***½ D: William Keighley. James Cagney, Ann Dvorak, Margaret Lindsay, Robert Armstrong, Barton MacLane, Lloyd Nolan, William Harrigan. Although raised by an underworld figure, Cagney joins F.B.I. when a pal is killed by gangsters, puts his first-hand knowledge to use. Exciting film, beautifully shot by Sol Polito; prologue with David Brian added for 1949 reissue. Also shown in computer-colored version.

G-Men Never Forget SEE: **Code 645**
G-Men vs the Black Dragon SEE: **Black Dragon of Manzanar**

Gnome-Mobile, The (1967) C-90m. *** D: Robert Stevenson. Walter Brennan, Matthew Garber, Karen Dotrice, Richard Deacon, Tom Lowell, Sean McClory, Ed Wynn. Crusty businessman Brennan, his niece and nephew discover gnomes in redwood forest, try to protect them from freak-show entrepreneur, and land-destroyers. Lively Disney fantasy outing with top special effects, broad comedy highlights. Based on Upton Sinclair novel.▼

Go Ask Alice (1972) C-73m. TVM D: John Korty. Jamie Smith-Jackson, Andy Griffith, William Shatner, Julie Adams, Ruth Roman, Wendell Burton, Robert Carradine, Mackenzie Phillips, Charles Martin Smith. Strong performances, semi-documentary style combine in study of high school student's battle with drug addiction. Written by Ellen M. Violett. Above average.

Go-Between, The (1971-British) C-116m. ***½ D: Joseph Losey. Julie Christie, Alan Bates, Dominic Guard, Margaret Leighton, Michael Redgrave, Edward Fox. Beguiling film from L. P. Hartley story of boy who becomes messenger for love notes between aristocratic Christie and farmer Bates. Lushly filmed, full of nuances, fine performances. Script by Harold Pinter. A mood piece, not for all tastes.

GoBots: Battle of the Rock Lords (1986) C-75m. *½ D: Ray Patterson. Voices of Margot Kidder, Roddy McDowall, Mi-

chael Nouri, Telly Savalas. Hanna-Barbera and Tonka Toys present a 75-minute animated commercial about the war between good GoBots versus evil Renegades, and the struggle of innocent Rock people against wicked Rock Lords. Electronically altered soundtrack makes it difficult to hear big-name voice cast.▼

God Bless the Child (1988) C-100m. TVM D: Larry Elikann. Mare Winningham, Grace Johnston, Dorian Harewood, Charlaine Woodard, Obba Babatunde, L. Scott Caldwell. Winningham gives a beautifully modulated portrayal of a homeless single mother caught with her young daughter in a cycle of poverty. Powerful drama with a social conscience. Written by producer Dennis Nemec. Above average.

Godchild, The (1974) C-78m. TVM D: John Badham. Jack Palance, Jack Warden, Keith Carradine, Ed Lauter, Jose Perez, Fionnuala Flanagan, Bill McKinney. Seventh version (at least) of THE THREE GODFATHERS, with three Civil War prisoners, fleeing both Confederates and Apaches, risking freedom to become guardians of the baby they deliver for a dying woman in the desert. Peter B. Kyne's Western classic starkly recreated for TV, but John Ford's 1948 version still casts a mighty long shadow. Average.

Goddess, The (1958) 105m. *** D: John Cromwell. Kim Stanley, Lloyd Bridges, Steven Hill, Betty Lou Holland, Patty Duke. Absorbing biography of an ambitious girl seeking Hollywood fame. Author Paddy Chayefsky based his story on Marilyn Monroe; the film captures tragedy of the real-life Monroe with fine acting by Stanley and Bridges, among others. Film debuts of Stanley and Duke.▼

Goddess of Love (1960-Italian) C-68m. *½ D: W. Tourjansky. Belinda Lee, Jacques Sernas, Massimo Girotti, Maria Frau. Drivel concerning country girl who becomes prostitute when her lover is killed. Set in ancient times.

Goddess of Love (1988) C-100m. TVM D: Jim Drake. Vanna White, David Naughton, Amanda Bearse, John Rhys-Davies, Betsy Palmer, David Leisure, Little Richard. Hilariously bad movie marking the starring debut as Venus of Vanna White, letter-turner par excellence of TV's *Wheel of Fortune*. Will forever remain close to the bottom of the TV-movie barrel . . . but on its own terms, a must-see! Below average.

Godfather, The (1972) C-175m. ***½ D: Francis Ford Coppola. Marlon Brando, Al Pacino, James Caan, Richard Castellano, John Cazale, Diane Keaton, Talia Shire, Robert Duvall, Sterling Hayden, John Marley, Richard Conte, Al Lettieri, Abe Vigoda, Al Martino, Morgana King, Alex Rocco. The 1970s' answer to GONE WITH

THE WIND, from Mario Puzo's novel on the violent life and times of Mafia patriarch Don Corleone (Brando). Pulp fiction raised to the highest level; a film of epic proportions, masterfully done, and set to Nino Rota's memorable music. Absolutely irresistible. Academy Award winner for Best Picture, Actor (Brando), and Screenplay (Coppola and Puzo). Followed by two sequels.▼

Godfather, Part II, The (1974) **C-200m.** **** D: Francis Ford Coppola. Al Pacino, Robert Duvall, Diane Keaton, Robert De Niro, John Cazale, Talia Shire, Lee Strasberg, Michael V. Gazzo, G.D. Spradlin, Morgana King, Mariana Hill, Troy Donahue, Joe Spinell, Abe Vigoda, Fay Spain, Harry Dean Stanton, Danny Aiello, Roger Corman, James Caan. They said it couldn't be done, but cowriter-director Coppola made a sequel that's just as compelling. This one contrasts the life of melancholy "don" (Pacino) with early days of his father (De Niro) as an immigrant in N.Y.C. Winner of six Oscars including Best Picture, Director, Screenplay (Coppola, Mario Puzo), Supporting Actor (De Niro), Score (Nino Rota, Carmine Coppola), Art Direction/Set Decoration (Dean Tavoularis, Angelo Graham, George R. Nelson).▼

Godfather Saga, The (1977) **C-450m.** ***½ D: Francis Ford Coppola. A special marathon television version of THE GODFATHER and THE GODFATHER, PART II, intercutting the two films in linear fashion and adding leftover footage that didn't appear in theaters.▼

God Forgives, I Don't (1969-Italian-Spanish) **C-101m.** *½ D: Giuseppe Colizzi. Terence Hill, Bud Spencer, Frank Wolff, Gina Rovere, Jose Manuel Martin. In spite of colorful title, this spaghetti Western about an attempt to find some buried loot is like a thousand others. Hill's and Spencer's first film together.

God Is My Co-Pilot (1945) **90m.** **½ D: Robert Florey. Dennis Morgan, Raymond Massey, Andrea King, Alan Hale, Dane Clark, John Ridgely, Stanley Ridges, Donald Woods. Well-intentioned drama of WW2 pilots bogs down in clichés, still has many good scenes.

God Is My Partner (1957) **80m.** ** D: William F. Claxton. Walter Brennan, John Hoyt, Marion Ross, Jesse White, Nancy Kulp. Sincere but hokey little film of oldtimer who feels he owes a spiritual obligation which he can redeem by giving away his money.

God's Country (1946) **C-62m.** ** D: Robert E. Tansey. Buster Keaton, Robert Lowery, Helen Gilbert, William Farnum. Chief virtue of this flabby Western is Keaton trying to recreate some of his better pantomime skits.

God's Country (1985) **C-88m.** ***½ D: Louis Malle. Poignant, insightful, occasionally hilarious documentary look at life in Glencoe, Minnesota, a small, conservative farming community. There's priceless footage from the first frame to the last. Most of it was shot in 1979; Malle returned six years later to update the lives of his subjects.

God's Country and the Woman (1936) **C-80m.** ** D: William Keighley. George Brent, Beverly Roberts, Barton MacLane, Robert Barrat, Alan Hale, Joseph King. Routine tale of Brent and Roberts running rival lumber companies; color is only asset.

Godsend, The (1979-British) **C-93m.** ** D: Gabrielle Beaumont. Cyd Hayman, Malcolm Stoddard, Angela Pleasence, Patrick Barr. OMEN/EXORCIST-type horror film about an angelic little blonde girl who is left at a family farm on a rainy night by a strange woman. In the years that follow, death, disaster, and hostility are visited upon the family in this medium thriller.▼

God's Little Acre (1958) **110m.** *** D: Anthony Mann. Robert Ryan, Tina Louise, Aldo Ray, Buddy Hackett, Jack Lord, Fay Spain, Michael Landon. Effective Americana of Georgia farmers as seen by Erskine Caldwell, focusing on amusing as well as lusty, violent aspects of their existence.▼

Gods Must Be Crazy, The (1981-Botswana) **C-108m.** *** D: Jamie Uys. Marius Weyers, Sandra Prinsloo, N!xau, Louw Verwey, Michael Thys. Highly original, offbeat comedy about cultural clashes in Africa, involving a bushman who encounters civilization for the first time, a pretty schoolteacher whose new assignment is a remote village, and a bumbling scientist whose attempts to make her welcome result in slapstick catastrophes. Film itself is clumsy at times, but completely disarming. It didn't receive major U.S. release until 1984, but then became the biggest foreign box-office hit in history! Uys, who also wrote and produced, plays the reverend. Followed by a sequel.▼

Gods Must Be Crazy II, The (1989-U.S.-Botswana) **C-97m.** *** D: Jamie Uys. N!xau, Lena Farugia, Hans Strydom, Eiros, Nadies, Erick Bowen. Follow-up to the surprise smash-hit farce is just as funny and endearing. N!xau returns as the bushman; here, his two young children are accidentally transported to "civilization" by a pair of poachers, and he follows them with the expected, comic result. This started shooting in 1985 and sat on the shelf for several years.

Godspell (1973) **C-103m.** **½ D: David Greene. Victor Garber, David Haskell, Jerry Sroka, Lynne Thigpen, Katie Hanley, Robin Lamont. Sophomoric updating of Jesus' life with young bouncy disciples following their leader around modern-day New York. Energetic adaptation of popular stage musical; brilliant use of N.Y.C. locations, good score by Stephen Schwartz including "Day by Day," but hollow and unmoving.

God Told Me To SEE: **Demon**▼

Godzilla SEE: **Godzilla, King of the Monsters**▼

✓ **Godzilla, King of the Monsters** (1956-Japanese) **80m.** ****½** D: Terry Morse, Inoshiro Honda. Raymond Burr, Takashi Shimura, Momoko Kochi, Akira Takarada, Akihiko Hirata. A fire-breathing lizard threatens civilization: the special effects are the star in this, the original GODZILLA movie. Originally released in Japan in 1954 as GOJIRA, at 98m; over 20m. were eliminated, and inserts with Burr were added.▼

Godzilla 1985 (1985-Japanese) **C-91m.** BOMB D: Kohji Hashimoto, R. J. Kizer. Raymond Burr, Keiju Kobayashi, Ten Tanaka, Yasuko Sawaguchi, Shin Takuma. Supposed update of original GODZILLA yarn is just a retread, with the atomic-fueled monster threatening Tokyo all over again, and Burr back on hand in cheaply filmed insert sequences making like Greek chorus. Too straight to be funny; instead, the Big Fella is just a Big Bore.▼

Godzilla Raids Again SEE: **Gigantis the Fire Monster**

Godzilla on Monster Island (1972-Japanese) **C-89m.** ** D: Jun Fukuda. Hiroshi Ishikawa, Tomoko Umeda, Yuriko Hishimi, Minoru Takashima, Zan Fujita. Garbo talks? Ha! In this harmless, toylike movie, *Godzilla* talks, as he and spiny Angillus battle alien-summoned Ghidrah and new playmate Gigan, who has a buzz saw in his belly. Standard colorful Toho monster hijinks. Also known as GODZILLA VS. GIGAN.▼

Godzilla's Revenge (1969-Japanese) **C-69m.** **½ D: Inoshiro Honda. Kenji Sahara, Tomonori Yazaki, Machiko Naka, Sachio Sakai, Chotaro Togin, Yoshibumi Tujima. Fantasy of child daydreaming of adventures with Godzilla's son and other monsters. Battle scenes are mostly stock footage from GODZILLA VS. THE SEA MONSTER and SON OF GODZILLA. Good juvenile sci-fi.

Godzilla vs. Gigan SEE: **Godzilla on Monster Island**▼

Godzilla vs. Mechagodzilla SEE: **Godzilla vs. the Cosmic Monster**▼

Godzilla vs. Megalon (1976-Japanese) **C-80m.** *½ D: Jun Fukuda. Katsuhiko Sasaki, Hiroyuki Kawase, Yutaka Hayashi, Robert Dunham. Series sinks to new low as Godzilla teams up with robot superhero against Megalon and his pal Gigan. Incredibly cheap, with lots of unintended laughs. A hoho from Toho.▼

Godzilla vs. Monster Zero SEE: **Monster Zero**▼

Godzilla vs. Mothra SEE: **Godzilla vs. the Thing**▼

Godzilla vs. the Bionic Monster SEE: **Godzilla vs. the Cosmic Monster**▼

Godzilla vs. the Cosmic Monster (1974-Japanese) **C-80m.** ** D: Jun Fukuda. Masaaki Daimon, Kazuya Aoyama, Reiko Tajima, Barbara Lynn, Akihiko Hirata. Godzilla battles robot duplicate of himself, built by alien apes intent on conquering the world. He's helped this time by ancient Okinawan monster Kingseesar. Pokey until zappity-pow climax. Also known as: GODZILLA VS. THE BIONIC MONSTER, GODZILLA VS. MECHAGODZILLA.▼

Godzilla vs. the Sea Monster (1966-Japanese) **C-85m.** **½ D: Jun Fukuda. Akira Takarada, Toru Watanabe, Jun Tazaki, Kumi Mizuno, Hideo Sunazuka. Particularly colorful and lively entry in the series, with a yachtload of castaways helping captives of paramilitary villains. Meanwhile, Godzilla battles a stupendous shrimp. P.S.: Mothra also turns up.▼

Godzilla vs. the Smog Monster (1972-Japanese) **C-87m.** **½ D: Yoshimitu Banno. Akira Yamauchi, Hiroyuki Kawase, Toshio Shibaki. Godzilla freelances as do-gooder in ridding Japan of monster born of waste, fed on factory fumes and smog. Dubbed and daffy.▼

Godzilla vs. the Thing (1964-Japanese) **C-90m.** **½ D: Inoshiro Honda. Okira Takarada, Yuriko Hoshi, Hiroshi Koizumi, Yu Fujiki. Vivid special effects highlight battle between reptile Godzilla and Mothra, giant moth. TV title: GODZILLA VS. MOTHRA.▼

Go For Broke! (1951) **92m.** *** D: Robert Pirosh. Van Johnson, Gianna Maria Canale, Warner Anderson, Lane Nakano, George Miki. WW2 story with a twist: Johnson is commander of special U.S. squad made up of Japanese American G.I.'s.▼

Gog (1954) **C-85m.** ** D: Herbert L. Strock. Richard Egan, Constance Dowling, Herbert Marshall, John Wengraf. Is a series of deaths at scientific installation the result of equipment malfunction or sabotage? Title refers to one of a pair of nonhumanoid robots. OK sci-fi, originally in 3-D.

Goin' Cocoanuts (1978) **C-96m.** ** D: Howard Morris. Donny and Marie Osmond, Herbert Edelman, Kenneth Mars, Chrystin Sinclaire, Ted Cassidy, Marc Lawrence, Khigh Dhiegh, Harold Sakata. Bad guys go after Marie's necklace in Hawaii, but the villainy, like the story, is strictly kindergarten level. Kids may go for it . . . and of course, Donny and Marie get to sing.

Goin' Down the Road (1970-Canadian) **C-90m.** ***½ D: Donald Shebib. Doug McGrath, Paul Bradley, Jayne Eastwood, Cayle Chernin, Nicole Morin. Award-winning film made for less than $100,000 puts most Hollywood blockbusters to shame; modest tale of two unlucky Nova Scotians and their near-tragic finish packs a memorable punch. McGrath and Bradley are remarkably good.

Going Ape! (1981) **C-87m.** BOMB D: Jeremy Joe Kronsberg. Tony Danza, Jessica Walter, Stacey Nelkin, Danny De Vito, Art Metrano, Joseph Maher. Inept comedy, with Danza set to inherit $5 million if he cares for a trio of orangutans. Directional debut for screenwriter Kronsberg, who also penned Clint Eastwood's EVERY WHICH WAY BUT LOOSE—with an orangutan prominently featured.▼

Going Berserk (1983-Canadian) **C-85m.** BOMB D: David Steinberg. John Candy, Joe Flaherty, Eugene Levy, Alley Mills, Pat Hingle, Richard Libertini, Paul Dooley, Murphy Dunne, Dixie Carter, Ernie Hudson. Awesomely inept comedy about the misadventures of a young dolt (Candy) who's set to marry the daughter of a pompous congressman. Only a performer as likable as Candy could survive such a debacle as this; his *SCTV* colleagues Flaherty and Levy have little to do.▼

Going for the Gold: The Bill Johnson Story (1985) **C-100m.** TVM D: Don Taylor. Anthony Edwards, Dennis Weaver, Sarah Jessica Parker, Deborah Van Valkenburgh, Wayne Northrop. By-the-numbers dramatization of American downhill skier Bill Johnson from street smart punk (in Oregon) to winner at the 1984 Winter Olympics in Sarajevo, Yugoslavia. Average.▼

Going Hollywood (1933) **80m.** *** D: Raoul Walsh. Marion Davies, Bing Crosby, Fifi D'Orsay, Stuart Erwin, Ned Sparks, Patsy Kelly. Enjoyable fluff with Davies following crooner Crosby to Hollywood determined to win him away from tempestuous screen star D'Orsay. Kelly all but steals film from stars. Songs include "Temptation," "We'll Make Hay While the Sun Shines," and the title tune.

Going Home (1971) **C-97m.** *** D: Herbert B. Leonard. Robert Mitchum, Jan-Michael Vincent, Brenda Vaccaro, Jason Bernard, Sally Kirkland, Josh Mostel. Powerful, if downbeat, study of young man's troubled relationship with his father, who's just been released from prison after serving time for killing his wife.

Going in Style (1979) **C-96m.** ***½ D: Martin Brest. George Burns, Art Carney, Lee Strasberg, Charles Hallahan, Pamela Payton-Wright. Three retirees in Queens get more than they bargain for when they rob a bank in Manhattan to relieve their boredom. Unexpected gem from a 28-year-old filmmaker is predictably funny but unpredictably moving, with Burns standing out in a terrific cast.▼

Going My Way (1944) **126m.** **** D:

Leo McCarey. Bing Crosby, Barry Fitzgerald, Rise Stevens, Gene Lockhart, Frank McHugh, James Brown, Jean Heather, Stanley Clements, Carl Switzer, Porter Hall. Sentimental story of down-to-earth priest Father O'Malley (Crosby) winning over aging superior (Fitzgerald) and sidewalk gang of kids is hard to resist—thanks to the skills of writer-director McCarey, who won two Oscars. Academy Awards also went to Crosby, Fitzgerald, Best Picture, and Best Song: "Swinging on a Star." Sequel: THE BELLS OF ST. MARY'S.▼

Going Places (1938) **84m.** ** D: Ray Enright. Dick Powell, Anita Louise, Allen Jenkins, Ronald Reagan. Nonsensical musical with a variety of songs, steeplechase riding, and obligatory romantic interludes. Louis Armstrong and Maxine Sullivan introduce hit song "Jeepers Creepers."

Going Places (1974-French) **C-117m.** *** D: Bertrand Blier. Gerard Depardieu, Patrick Dewaere, Miou-Miou, Jeanne Moreau, Brigitte Fossey, Isabelle Huppert. Crude, overgrown juvenile delinquents Depardieu and Dewaere commit petty crimes, terrorize and share women. Funny, earthy, sometimes even lyrical examination of alienation; Moreau appears briefly as an ex-con who trysts with the boys.▼

Going Steady (1958) **79m.** *½ D: Fred F. Sears. Molly Bee, Bill Goodwin, Alan Reed, Jr., Irene Hervey. Uninspired happenings involving secretly married teenagers and the repercussions when in-laws discover fact.▼

Going to the Chapel (1988) **C-100m.** TVM D: Paul Lynch. Barbara Billingsley, Eileen Brennan, Joel Brooks, Mark-Linn Baker, John Ratzenberger, Michele Greene, Cloris Leachman, Scott Valentine, Dick Van Patten, Max Wright. All-star TV cast goes through routine comic paces trying to get a blissful couple down the aisle in spite of their feuding families. Average.

Going Undercover (1988) **C-88m.** *½ D: James Kenelm Clarke. Chris Lemmon, Jean Simmons, Lea Thompson, Mills Watson, Viveca Lindfors, Nancy Cartwright, Joe Michael Terry. Third-rate private-eye Lemmon is hired to keep an eye on rich brat Thompson during a trip to Europe—during which she's kidnapped. Obnoxious comedy was made in 1984, and (understandably) shelved.▼

Goin' South (1978) **C-109m.** *** D: Jack Nicholson. Jack Nicholson, Mary Steenburgen, Christopher Lloyd, John Belushi, Veronica Cartwright, Richard Bradford, Danny DeVito, Anne Ramsey. Amusing Western comedy, not for all tastes. Nicholson saving himself from lynch mob by marrying a spinster. Steenburgen is refreshingly offbeat and Belushi's disappointingly small role is a real hoot. Film debuts of Belushi and Steenburgen.▼

Goin' to Town (1935) **74m.** *** D: Alexander Hall. Mae West, Paul Cavanagh, Ivan Lebedeff, Marjorie Gateson, Tito Coral. Good West vehicle of dance-hall girl trying to crash society, highlight: Mae doing "Samson and Delilah" scenes.

Go Into Your Dance (1935) **89m.** ****½** D: Archie L. Mayo. Al Jolson, Ruby Keeler, Glenda Farrell, Helen Morgan, Patsy Kelly, Benny Rubin, Phil Regan, Barton MacLane. Flimsy backstage plot allows real-life husband and wife Jolson and Keeler (in their only film together) to sing and dance through seven listenable Harry Warren-Al Dubin tunes, including "About a Quarter to Nine" and "A Latin from Manhattan."

Go, Johnny, Go! (1958) **75m.** ****** D: Paul Landres. Jimmy Clanton, Alan Freed, Sandy Stewart, Chuck Berry, Jo-Ann Campbell, The Cadillacs, Ritchie Valens, Eddie Cochran, Harvey (Fuqua), The Flamingos, Jackie Wilson. Orphan Clanton, booted out of church choir for playing rock 'n' roll, is transformed by Freed into "Johnny Melody," teen idol. ("He's dreamy. Oh wow, he's the living end.") Not very good, but an artifact of its era. Berry, who acts as well as sings, performs "Memphis, Tennessee," "Little Queenie" and "Johnny Be Good," Cochran performs "Teenage Heaven," and Wilson does "You'd Better Know It."▼

Gold (1974-British) **C-120m.** ******* D: Peter Hunt. Roger Moore, Susannah York, Ray Milland, Bradford Dillman, John Gielgud. Grand-scale adventure yarn about plot to control price of gold on world market by destroying South African mine. Moore is stalwart hero. Long but entertaining.

Goldbergs, The (1950) **83m.** ****½** D: Walter Hart. Gertrude Berg, Philip Loeb, Eli Mintz, Betty Walker, David Opatoshu, Barbara Rush. Warm, human story of famous radio-TV Bronx family and their everyday problems. Retitled: MOLLY

✓ **Gold Diggers of 1933** (1933) **96m.** *****½** D: Mervyn LeRoy. Joan Blondell, Ruby Keeler, Aline MacMahon, Dick Powell, Guy Kibbee, Warren William, Ned Sparks, Ginger Rogers, Sterling Holloway. Another spectacular Busby Berkeley dance outing with familiar let's-produce-a-Broadway-show plot. Highlights: Blondell's "Forgotten Man," Rogers' "We're In The Money" (with pig-Latin chorus), chorus girls' "Shadow Waltz."▼

Gold Diggers of 1935 (1935) **95m.** ******* D: Busby Berkeley. Dick Powell, Adolphe Menjou, Gloria Stuart, Alice Brady, Glenda Farrell, Frank McHugh, Winifred Shaw. Big-scale Berkeley musical with stereotypes providing plot line and laughs between fantastic precision production numbers, including "The Words Are In My Heart," and classic, Oscar-winning "Lullaby of Broadway," sung by Wini Shaw.▼

Gold Diggers of 1937 (1936) **100m.** ****½**

D: Lloyd Bacon. Dick Powell, Joan Blondell, Glenda Farrell, Victor Moore, Lee Dixon, Osgood Perkins. Those gold-diggers won't give up; this time it's a group of insurance salesmen backing a show. Top song: "With Plenty of Money and You."

Gold Dust Gertie (1931) **66m.** ****½** D: Lloyd Bacon. Ole Olsen, Chic Johnson, Winnie Lightner, Dorothy Christy, Claude Gillingwater, Arthur Hoyt, Charley Grapewin. Olsen & Johnson are bathing-suit salesmen trying to elude their mutual ex-wife. Lightner is energetic as always in this absurd knockabout comedy with plenty of sexual innuendo.

Golden Age of Comedy, The (1957) **78m.** ******** D: Compiled by Robert Youngson. Laurel and Hardy, Carole Lombard, Ben Turpin, Will Rogers, Harry Langdon. Peerless grouping of some of silent comedy's greatest moments, including Rogers' classic spoofs of silent stars, and ending with Laurel and Hardy's legendary pie fight from "Battle of the Century."▼

Golden Arrow, The (1936) **68m.** ****½** D: Alfred E. Green. Bette Davis, George Brent, Eugene Pallette, Dick Foran, Carol Hughes, Catherine Doucet. Pleasant but featherweight comedy of "heiress" Davis and down-to-earth reporter Brent establishing marriage of convenience.

Golden Blade, The (1953) **C-81m.** ****½** D: Nathan Juran. Rock Hudson, Piper Laurie, Gene Evans, Kathleen Hughes. OK swashbuckler with Hudson going through gymnastics in Bagdad to save Laurie and help virtue triumph; strictly formula production.

Golden Boy (1939) **99m.** ****½** D: Rouben Mamoulian. Barbara Stanwyck, Adolphe Menjou, William Holden, Lee J. Cobb, Joseph Calleia, Sam Levene, Don Beddoe. Clifford Odets' narrative of music-minded boy who becomes prizefighter dates badly; Holden, in starring debut, still good, but Cobb blows the works with his Henry Armetta imitation.▼

Golden Child, The (1986) **C-96m.** BOMB D: Michael Ritchie. Eddie Murphy, Charlotte Lewis, Charles Dance, Victor Wong, Randall "Tex" Cobb, James Hong, J.L. Reate. Top candidate for the worst megahit of all time. A "perfect" child (Reate) is kidnapped despite his magical powers; as foretold by an ancient oracle, only Murphy can rescue him. Lewis is even more wooden than most ex-models; entire reels go by with nary a chuckle. A box-office smash—but have you ever met anyone who says they liked it?▼

Golden Coach, The (1952-Italian) **C-101m.** *****½** D: Jean Renoir. Anna Magnani, Odoardo Spadaro, Nada Fiorelli, Dante Rino, Duncan Lamont. Delightful film about an acting troupe touring South America in the 18th century and the amorous adventures of its leading lady. Theatrical and stylized, this is one of the great films about acting—and a stunning achievement in the use of color. Ironically, it was a flop when first released, then critically rediscovered.▼

Golden Earrings (1947) 95m. **½ D: Mitchell Leisen. Ray Milland, Marlene Dietrich, Murvyn Vye, Dennis Hoey, Quentin Reynolds. Incredible yet enjoyable escapism set in WW2 Europe has Milland joining gypsy Dietrich for espionage work; Dietrich most convincing. Gypsy Vye sings title song.

Golden Eye, The (1948) 69m. D: William Beaudine. Roland Winters, Victor Sen Yung, Tim Ryan, Wanda McKay, Bruce Kellogg, Evelyn Brent. Retitled MYSTERY OF THE GOLDEN EYE and CHARLIE CHAN AND THE GOLDEN EYE. SEE: **Charlie Chan** series.

Golden Gate (1981) C-100m. TVM D: Paul Wendkos. Jean Simmons, Richard Kiley, Perry King, Robyn Douglass, Mary Crosby, John Saxon, Melanie Griffith, Maggie Blye, Peter Donat. Slick soap-opera pilot about a publishing empire and the struggle to keep it out of an unscrupulous investor's hands. Written by Stirling Silliphant and acted by rote. Average.

Golden Gate Murders, The (1979) C-100m. TVM D: Walter Grauman. David Janssen, Susannah York, Tim O'Connor, Lloyd Bochner, Kim Hunter, Richard O'Brien. Gruff detective and pretty nun join forces to prove that a priest who fell from the Golden Gate Bridge was murdered and not a suicide. Accept initial premise of the cop/nun relationship, ignore the terrible studio recreation of the San Francisco landmark and you might have some fun. Being shown theatrically as SPECTER ON THE BRIDGE. Average.

Golden Girl (1951) C-108m. **½ D: Lloyd Bacon. Mitzi Gaynor, Dale Robertson, Dennis Day, Una Merkel. Undistinguished musical set in California during Civil War, with Gaynor portraying entertainer Lotta Crabtree who's intrigued by Rebel officer Robertson.

Goldengirl (1979) C-104m. ** D: Joseph Sargent. Susan Anton, Curt Jurgens, Robert Culp, Leslie Caron, Harry Guardino, Jessica Walter. Statuesque Anton is more or less turned into a robot so she can become a star in the Olympics. So-so. TV version runs 117m. (though it was originally planned for miniseries length—until the U.S. decided to boycott the Moscow Olympics).▼

Golden Gloves Story, The (1950) 76m. *½ D: Felix E. Feist. James Dunn, Dewey Martin, Kay Westfall, Kevin O'Morrison. Ordinary fare dealing with two boxers and the effects of the pending championship bout on their lives.

Golden Hands of Kurigal (1949) 100m. *½ D: Fred C. Brannon. Kirk Alyn, Rosemary La Planche, Roy Barcroft, Carol Forman, James Dale, Bruce Edwards. Spotty Republic cliff-hanger of federal agent (Alyn) rescuing missing archaeologist held by archcriminal. Reedited from serial FEDERAL AGENTS VS. UNDERWORLD INC.

Golden Hawk, The (1952) C-83m. ** D: Sidney Salkow. Rhonda Fleming, Sterling Hayden, John Sutton, Raymond Hatton. Frank Yerby's novel of Spanish-English fight against France in 17th century, set in Caribbean seas.

Golden Heist, The SEE: **Inside Out** (1975)▼

Golden Horde, The (1951) C-77m. ** D: George Sherman. Ann Blyth, David Farrar, George Macready, Henry Brandon, Richard Egan. Typical Arabian adventure set in 13th century, with Blyth using her brains to outwit invaders of her people's city.

Golden Idol, The (1954) 71m. D: Ford Beebe. Johnny Sheffield, Anne Kimbell, Paul Guilfoyle, Smoki Whitfield. SEE: **Bomba the Jungle Boy** series.

Golden Madonna, The (1949-British) 88m. **½ D: Ladislas Vajda. Phyllis Calvert, Michael Rennie, Tullio Carminati. Lively romantic yarn of Yankee lass inheriting an Italian villa and, aided by Rennie, seeking to retrieve a holy painting.

Golden Mask, The (1954-British) C-88m. **½ D: Jack Lee. Van Heflin, Wanda Hendrix, Eric Portman, Charles Goldner. Intelligent adventure yarn of people seeking fabulous treasure mask in Egyptian desert.

Golden Mistress, The (1954) C-82m. ** D: Joel Judge (Abner Biberman). John Agar, Rosemarie Bowe, Abner Biberman, Andre Narcisse. Agar comes to Bowe's rescue in hunting out alleged voodoo killers of her father.

Golden Moment: An Olympic Love Story, The (1980) C-200m. TVM D: Richard Sarafian. Stephanie Zimbalist, David Keith, Richard Lawson, Victor French, Merlin Olsen, Jack Palance, James Earl Jones, Nancy Marchand, Ed McMahon, Salome Jens. American athlete falls for pretty Russian gymnast at the 1980 Olympics. Obviously made to be tied in with the Olympic games—from which the U.S. withdrew! Cliché-ridden love-at-first-sight script further dooms it. Below average.

Golden Needles (1974) C-92m. ** D: Robert Clouse. Joe Don Baker, Elizabeth Ashley, Jim Kelly, Burgess Meredith, Ann Sothern. Everyone seems out of place in this Hong Kong-L.A. filmed action pic about a scramble for golden statue containing youth-restoring acupuncture needles. Silly. Retitled THE CHASE FOR THE GOLDEN NEEDLES.

Golden Rendezvous (1977) C-103m. ** D: Ashley Lazarus. Richard Harris, Ann

Turkel, David Janssen, Burgess Meredith, John Vernon, Gordon Jackson, Keith Baxter, Dorothy Malone, John Carradine. Attractive cast in pointless adaptation of Alistair MacLean's novel about gambling ship held hostage by terrorists. Retitled NUCLEAR TERROR for television.▼

Goldenrod (1977-Canadian) **C-100m.** **TVM** D: Harvey Hart. Tony LoBianco, Gloria Carlin, Donald Pleasence, Will Darrow MacMillan, Ian McMillan, Donnelly Rhodes. Sentimental tale of a crippled rodeo champ left with the responsibility of raising his two young sons alone. Well-acted drama produced by David Susskind and written by Lionel Chetwynd. Above average.▼

Golden Salamander, The (1951-British) **96m.** *** D: Ronald Neame. Trevor Howard, Anouk Aimee, Walter Rilla, Herbert Lom, Wilfrid Hyde-White. Courting a Tunisian girl, Howard becomes involved in gun smuggling; taut actioner.

Golden Voyage of Sinbad, The (1974-British) **C-104m.** *** D: Gordon Hessler. John Phillip Law, Caroline Munro, Tom Baker, Douglas Wilmer, Gregoire Aslan, John Garfield, Jr. Delightful rehash of earlier Sinbad adventures that evokes Saturday matinee fare of the 1950s, with Ray Harryhausen's finest "Dynamation" effects: a ship's figurehead comes to life, and a six-armed statue does sword-battle with Sinbad in action highlights. Grand entertainment.▼

Golden West, The (1932) **74m.** **½ D: David Howard. George O'Brien, Janet Chandler, Marion Burns, Arthur Pierson, Onslow Stevens. Solid Zane Grey story of O'Brien leaving town after feud killing, encountering Indians; son, raised as an Indian after father killed in massacre. Good "B+" Western.

✓ **Goldfinger** (1964-British) **C-111m.** ***½ D: Guy Hamilton. Sean Connery, Gert Frobe, Honor Blackman, Shirley Eaton, Bernard Lee, Lois Maxwell, Harold Sakata, Tania Mallett. Entertaining, exciting James Bond adventure, third in the series. Full of ingenious gadgets and nefarious villains, with hair-raising climax inside Fort Knox. Frobe (Goldfinger) and Sakata (Oddjob) are villains in the classic tradition.▼

Gold for the Caesars (1964-French-Italian) **C-86m.** *½ D: Andre de Toth. Jeffrey Hunter, Mylene Demongeot, Ron Randell, Massimo Giulio Bosetti, Ettore Manni. Still another Roman slave epic starring an American actor who'd look more at home in David and Ricky Nelson's fraternity; this time it's Jeffrey Hunter. Nothing special. Original French running time: 95m.

Goldie and the Boxer (1979) **C-100m.** **TVM** D: David Miller. O. J. Simpson, Melissa Michaelsen, Vincent Gardenia, Phil Silvers, Madlyn Rhue, Annazette Chase.

Pedestrian tale—fodder for countless B movies of yore—about a struggling fighter and an orphan who adopts him. Followed by a sequel. Below average.

Goldie and the Boxer Go to Hollywood (1981) **C-100m.** **TVM** D: David Miller. O. J. Simpson, Melissa Michaelsen, Roger Bowen, Reb Brown, Jack Gilford, James Gregory, Stubby Kaye, Sheila MacRae, Robert Mandan. Follow-up to the 1979 movie about a heavyweight champion and the 11-year-old girl who becomes his manager, and no better than the original. Below average.

Gold Is Where You Find It (1938) **C-90m.** **½ D: Michael Curtiz. George Brent, Olivia de Havilland, Claude Rains, Margaret Lindsay, John Litel, Barton MacLane. And gold-rush miners find it on California farmland, starting bitter feud in brisk film, perked by good cast.

Gold of Naples, The (1954-Italian) **107m.** ✓ *** D: Vittorio De Sica. Sophia Loren, Vittorio De Sica, Toto, Silvana Mangano, Paolo Stoppa. Four vignettes—poignant, perceptive, hilarious in turn: Loren as philandering wife of pizza baker; De Sica as avid card player upstaged by 8-year-old; Toto as Milquetoast family man; Mangano as prostitute involved in unusual marriage.

Gold of the Amazon Women (1979) **C-100m.** **TVM** D: Mark L. Lester. Bo Svenson, Anita Ekberg, Donald Pleasence, Richard Romanus, Maggie Jean Smith. Two fortune hunters stumble upon society of modern-day Amazons who follow the pair out of the jungle to downtown Manhattan. Silly B-minus movie stuff that brought '50s screen sex queen Ekberg out of obscurity. Below average.▼

Gold Raiders (1951) **56m.** *½ D: Edward Bernds. George O'Brien, The Three Stooges, Sheila Ryan, Clem Bevans, Lyle Talbot. Stooges add the only life to this flabby Western, with their usual shenanigans foiling the crooks and saving the day.▼

Gold Rush, The (1925) **82m.** **** D: ✓ Charlie Chaplin. Charlie Chaplin, Georgia Hale, Mack Swain, Tom Murray. Immortal Chaplin classic, pitting Little Tramp against Yukon, affections of dance-hall girl, whims of a burly prospector. Dance of the rolls, eating leather shoe, cabin tottering over cliff—all highlights of wonderful, timeless comedy. Chaplin reedited film in 1942; that version, with his narration and music, runs 72m.▼

Gold Rush Maisie (1940) **82m.** D: Edwin L. Marin. Ann Sothern, Lee Bowman, Slim Summerville, Virginia Weidler, Mary Nash, John F. Hamilton. SEE: **Maisie** series.

Goldstein (1965) **85m.** **½ D: Benjamin Manaster, Philip Kaufman. Lou Gilbert, Ellen Madison, Thomas Erhart, Benito Carruthers, Severn Darden, Nelson Algren.

[443]

The prophet Elijah (Gilbert) emerges from Lake Michigan, is pursued by sculptor Erhart. Odd, unsatisfying satire filmed in Chicago. Based on a story by Martin Buber. Original running time: 115m.

Goldwyn Follies, The (1938) **C-120m.** *½ D: George Marshall. Adolphe Menjou, Andrea Leeds, Kenny Baker, The Ritz Brothers, Zorina, Helen Jepson, Bobby Clark, Edgar Bergen & Charlie McCarthy. Dreadful hodgepodge as producer Menjou hires Leeds as ''Miss Humanity,'' to judge his movies from average person's point of view. She probably would have skipped this one. Ritz Bros. come off best, while Baker sings ''Love Walked In'' about thirty times. George Balanchine's ballet a matter of taste. Look for Alan Ladd as an auditioning singer.▼

Goliath Against the Giants (1961-Italian) **C-90m.** *½ D: Guido Malatesta. Brad Harris, Gloria Milland, Fernando Rey, Barbara Carrol. Juvenile cartoon characterizations in this sword-and-sandal, with Harris overcoming sea creatures, Amazons, and his people's enemies.▼

Goliath and the Barbarians (1960-Italian) **C-86m.** ** D: Carlo Campogalliani. Steve Reeves, Bruce Cabot, Giulia Rubini, Chelo Alonso, Arturo Dominici, Gino Scotti. Muscleman Reeves comes to the rescue of Italy by holding off rampaging hordes pressing down from the Alps.▼

Goliath and the Dragon (1960-Italian) **C-87m.** BOMB D: Vittorio Cottafavi. Mark Forest, Broderick Crawford, Gaby Andre, Leonora Ruffo. Baby-style fantasy costumer with embarrassing performances by all; poor special effects, with Forest challenging villainous Crawford.▼

Goliath and the Vampires (1964-Italian) **C-91m.** *½ D: Giacomo Gentilomo. Gordon Scott, Jacques Sernas, Gianna Maria Canale. Cloak-and-sandal nonsense; spotty special effects add only color to film.

Goliath Awaits (1981) **C-200m. TVM** D: Kevin Connor. Mark Harmon, Christopher Lee, Eddie Albert, John Carradine, Alex Cord, Robert Forster, Frank Gorshin, Jean Marsh, John McIntire, Jeannette Nolan, Emma Samms. Colony of survivors, trapped for over 40 years in the wreckage of an ocean liner torpedoed by a U-boat, is uncovered by oceanographer Harmon in this credibility-stretching tale. Originally shown in two parts. Average.

Go, Man, Go (1954) **82m.** **½ D: James Wong Howe. Dane Clark, Pat Breslin, Sidney Poitier, Edmond Ryan. Imaginative telling of the formation of Harlem Globetrotters and their rise as famed basketball team. A rare directorial effort by celebrated cinematographer Howe.

Go Masters, The (1982-Chinese-Japanese) **C-123m.** *** D: Junya Sato, Duan Jishun. Rentaro Mikuni, Sun Dao-Lin, Shen Guan-Chu, Misako Honno, Tsu Kasa Itoh. Sprawling, involving romance-mystery-suspenser, set between the 1920s and '50s and focusing on the relationships between two families, one Japanese and the other Chinese. Most fascinating is various characters' obsession with Go, a chesslike strategy game. The first Sino-Japanese co-production, and a smash hit in both countries.▼

Go Naked In the World (1961) **C-103m.** ** D: Ranald MacDougall. Gina Lollobrigida, Anthony Franciosa, Ernest Borgnine, Luana Patten. Turgid melodrama badly cast. Easy-loving Lollobrigida hooks Franciosa, much to his father's (Borgnine's) dismay.

Gone Are the Days (1963) **97m.** *** D: Nicholas Webster. Ossie Davis, Ruby Dee, Sorrell Booke, Godfrey Cambridge, Alan Alda, Beah Richards. Davis' satiric fable *Purlie Victorious* survives cheap film adaptation, thanks to buoyant performances and basic story: self-appointed preacher schemes to undo a despotic plantation owner, as a symbolic freeing of his people from the ways of the Old South. Alda's film debut.▼

Gone in 60 Seconds (1974) **C-103m.** ** D: H. B. Halicki. H. B. Halicki, Marion Busia, Jerry Daugirda, James McIntire, George Cole, Parnelli Jones, Gary Bettenhausen. Muddled drama about a car-theft ring is highlighted by a 40-minute-long chase sequence, which is well made—but so what?▼

Gone To Earth SEE: **Wild Heart, The**

Gone With the Wind (1939) **C-222m.** **** D: Victor Fleming. Clark Gable, Vivien Leigh, Leslie Howard, Olivia de Havilland, Thomas Mitchell, Barbara O'Neil, Victor Jory, Laura Hope Crews, Hattie McDaniel, Ona Munson, Harry Davenport, Ann Rutherford, Evelyn Keyes, Carroll Nye, Paul Hurst, Isabel Jewell, Cliff Edwards, Ward Bond, Butterfly McQueen, Rand Brooks, Eddie Anderson, Oscar Polk, Jane Darwell, William Bakewell, Violet Kemble-Cooper, Eric Linden, George Reeves. If not the greatest movie ever made, certainly one of the greatest examples of storytelling on film, maintaining interest for nearly four hours. Margaret Mitchell's story is, in effect, a Civil War soap opera, focusing on vixenish Southern belle Scarlett O'Hara, brilliantly played by Leigh; she won Oscar, as did the picture, McDaniel, director Fleming, screenwriter Sidney Howard (posthumously), many others. Memorable music by Max Steiner in this one-of-a-kind film meticulously produced by David O. Selznick.▼

Gong Show Movie, The (1980) **C-89m.** BOMB D: Chuck Barris. Chuck Barris, Robin Altman, Mabel King, Murray Langston, Jaye P. Morgan, Jamie Farr, Rip

Taylor. Barris created a bizarre TV show that belongs in a time capsule, but this movie (which dwells on Chuck's pressures and problems as host and producer of the show) belongs in the trash bin.

Good Against Evil (1977) **C-78m. TVM** D: Paul Wendkos. Dack Rambo, Dan O'Herlihy, Elyssa Davalos, Richard Lynch, John Harkins, Jenny O'Hara, Lelia Goldoni. Itinerant writer falls for woman chosen by satanic cult to bear the devil's child. O'Herlihy has flamboyant role as priest called upon to perform traditional exorcism in this silly supernatural thriller. Below average.

Goodbye Again (1961) **120m. ***** D: Anatole Litvak. Ingrid Bergman, Tony Perkins, Yves Montand, Jessie Royce Landis, Diahann Carroll. Francoise Sagan's chic soaper becomes teary Bergman vehicle of middle-aged woman having affair with Perkins, still craving playboy Montand. Set in Paris.▼

Goodbye Charlie (1964) **C-117m. *½** D: Vincente Minnelli. Tony Curtis, Debbie Reynolds, Pat Boone, Walter Matthau, Martin Gabel, Ellen McRae (Burstyn). Tasteless, flat version of George Axelrod's play; crude gangster dies and comes back to earth as Reynolds. Even Matthau struggles for laughs.

Goodbye, Children SEE: **Au Revoir, les Enfants**▼

Goodbye, Columbus (1969) **C-105m. ***** D: Larry Peerce. Richard Benjamin, Ali MacGraw, Jack Klugman, Nan Martin, Michael Meyers. Phillip Roth's stinging portrait of successful suburban Jewish family as seen through eyes of young man (Benjamin) who falls in love with daughter (MacGraw). Benjamin and MacGraw's first starring roles, but unknown Meyers steals the show as Ali's brother. Director's father Jan Peerce has a cameo role at a wedding; look for Jaclyn Smith as a model. Music composed and performed by The Association.▼

Goodbye, Franklin High (1978) **C-94m. **½** D: Mike MacFarland. Lane Caudell, Ann Dusenberry, Darby Hinton, Julie Adams, William Windom. A high-school senior faces various challenges and decisions involving a possible baseball career, a college education, his girlfriend, and his parents in this modest, likable film.

Goodbye Girl, The (1977) **C-110m. ***½** D: Herbert Ross. Richard Dreyfuss, Marsha Mason, Quinn Cummings, Paul Benedict, Barbara Rhoades. Neil Simon's warmest comedy to date puts young actor Dreyfuss and dumped-on divorcée Mason together as unwilling tenants of the same N.Y. apartment, explores their growing relationship. High-caliber script and performances to match; Dreyfuss won Oscar.▼

Goodbye, Miss 4th of July (1988) **C-90m.**

TVM D: George Miller. Louis Gossett, Jr., Chris Sarandon, Roxana Zal, Chantal Contouri, Chynna Phillips, Mitchell Anderson, Conchata Ferrell, Ed Lauter. Sentimental, true-life Disney drama about the coming of age of the idealistic teenage daughter of Greek immigrants in pre-WWI West Virginia, her family's relationship with an aging black ex-boxer and her later efforts to do her part in the great influenza epidemic. Based on the 1985 book by her brother. Made for cable. Average.

Goodbye, Mr. Chips (1939-U.S.-British) **114m. ***½** D: Sam Wood. Robert Donat, Greer Garson, Paul von Hernreid (Henreid), Terry Kilburn, John Mills. Donat won well-deserved Oscar for memorable portrayal of shy schoolmaster who devotes his life to "his boys," only coming out of his shell when he meets Garson. Extreme length works against film's honest sentiment, but Donat makes it all worthwhile. Based on James Hilton's novel; scripted by R.C. Sherriff, Claudine West, and Eric Maschwitz. Remade as a musical in 1969.▼

Goodbye, Mr. Chips (1969) **C-151m. **** D: Herbert Ross. Peter O'Toole, Petula Clark, Michael Redgrave, George Baker, Sian Phillips, Michael Bryant. Lumbering musical remake of 1939 classic. O'Toole is good as prim schoolteacher, but Clark's role as showgirl is shallow, ludicrous. Mediocre songs don't help; what emotion there is gets lost when film plods on to modern-day anticlimax. Ross' directorial debut. Some prints are 133m.

Goodbye, My Fancy (1951) **107m. ***** D: Vincent Sherman. Joan Crawford, Robert Young, Frank Lovejoy, Eve Arden. Congresswoman Crawford returns to her old college, more to see former boyfriend Young than to receive honorary degree. Lovejoy is callous newsman. Film debut of Janice Rule.

Good-bye, My Lady (1956) **95m. **½** D: William Wellman. Walter Brennan, Phil Harris, Brandon de Wilde, Sidney Poitier. James Street novel of small boy (de Wilde), an elderly man (Brennan), and the dog that brings joy into their lives is basis for easy going, poignant film, set in the South.▼

Goodbye, New York (1985-U.S.-Israeli) **C-90m. **½** D: Amos Kollek. Julie Hagerty, Amos Kollek, David Topaz, Aviva Ger, Shmuel Shiloh, Jennifer Babtist. Cute but slight, sometimes flat chronicle of New Yorker Hagerty, a Jewish American Princess of Irish extraction who finds herself penniless and stranded in Israel where she eventually adjusts to life on a kibbutz and gets to know a part-time soldier (Kollek).▼

Goodbye, Norma Jean (1976) **C-95m. BOMB** D: Larry Buchanan. Misty Rowe, Terence Locke, Patch Mackenzie, Preston Hanson. Sleazy look at adolescent Marilyn

Monroe and her rocky road to stardom; what will have to be cut for TV will leave behind even less reason to watch this piece of tripe.▼

Goodbye People, The (1984) **C-104m.** *½ D: Herb Gardner. Judd Hirsch, Martin Balsam, Pamela Reed, Ron Silver, Michael Tucker, Gene Saks. Absolute torture (adapted by Gardner from his own play) about Balsam's begging-for-bankruptcy scheme to open a tropical drink stand on some ill-located beach property. Gardner's A THOUSAND CLOWNS may strike some as sentimental and dated, but this one doesn't even have comedy to carry it. A mawkish disaster, long on the shelf.▼

Goodbye Pork Pie (1981-New Zealand) **C-105m.** *** D: Geoff Murphy. Kelly Johnson, Tony Barry, Claire Oberman, Bruno Lawrence, John Beach, Frances Edmond. Amiable comedy/road movie about a pair of alienated men, one (Johnson) still in his teens and the other (Barry) about twice his age, who trek across New Zealand in a stolen car with the police on their trail.▼

Goodbye, Raggedy Ann (1971) **C-73m.** TVM D: Fielder Cook. Mia Farrow, Hal Holbrook, John Colicos, Martin Sheen, Marlene Warfield. Tear-jerker fluctuates between convincing scenes and unintentional comedy. Overly sensitive Hollywood starlet on brink of suicide must change her notions of success. Average.

Good Companions, The (1957-British) **C-104m.** *** D: J. Lee Thompson. Eric Portman, Celia Johnson, Hugh Griffith, Janette Scott, John Fraser, Joyce Grenfell, Bobby Howes, Rachel Roberts, Thora Hird, Mona Washbourne, Alec McCowen, John Le Mesurier, Anthony Newley, Shirley Ann Field. Fabulous cast adds luster to this lightweight, entertaining chronicle of a group of individuals who combine their resources to save a failing "concert party" (musical troupe). Based on a novel by J. B. Priestley; originally filmed in 1933 with Jessie Matthews, Edmund Gwenn, and John Gielgud.

Good Dame (1934) **74m.** *½ D: Marion Gering. Fredric March, Sylvia Sidney, Jack LaRue, Helene Chadwick, Noel Francis, Russell Hopton. March and Sidney deserve better than this: tired story of carnival huckster redeemed by the love of a good woman.

Good Day for a Hanging (1958) **C-85m.** **½ D: Nathan Juran. Fred MacMurray, Maggie Hayes, Robert Vaughn, Denver Pyle. Straightforward account of MacMurray taking over for slain sheriff and bringing in killer, only to find townspeople don't care if murderer is sentenced.

Good Die Young, The (1954-British) **100m.** ** D: Lewis Gilbert. Laurence Harvey, Gloria Grahame, Richard Basehart, Stanley Baker, Margaret Leighton,

John Ireland, Joan Collins. Solid cast fails to enhance standard robbery tale, with a quartet of strangers coming together to commit a holdup.

Good Earth, The (1937) **138m.** **** D: Sidney Franklin. Paul Muni, Luise Rainer, Walter Connolly, Charley Grapewin, Jessie Ralph, Tilly Losch, Keye Luke, Harold Huber. Mammoth Pearl Buck novel recreated in detail, telling story of greed ruining lives of simple Chinese farming couple. Rainer won Oscar as the ever-patient wife of Muni, as did Karl Freund for his cinematography. Screenplay by Talbot Jennings, Tess Slesinger, and Claudine West. The special effects are outstanding.▼

Good Fairy, The (1935) **97m.** ***½ D: William Wyler. Margaret Sullavan, Herbert Marshall, Frank Morgan, Reginald Owen, Alan Hale, Beulah Bondi, Cesar Romero. Sparkling romantic comedy, adapted from Molnar play by Preston Sturges; wide-eyed Sullavan tries to act as "good fairy" to struggling lawyer Marshall, while hotly pursued by wealthy Morgan. Hilarious, charming; movie spoof near beginning is priceless. Remade as I'LL BE YOURS.

Good Father, The (1987-British) **C-90m.** **½ D: Mike Newell. Anthony Hopkins, Jim Broadbent, Harriet Walter, Fanny Viner, Simon Callow, Joanne Whalley, Michael Byrne. Hopkins is excellent in the role of a father who loses custody of his child and takes out his incredible anger by befriending Broadbent and funding latter's court case to regain *his* kid's custody. Callow is terrific as an unscrupulous lawyer. Dramatically uneven, but worth a look. Made for British TV, film suffers technically from its grainy lab blowup.▼

Good Fellows, The (1943) **70m.** ** D: Jo Graham. Cecil Kellaway, Mabel Paige, Helen Walker, James Brown. Pleasant fluff about a man who neglects his family in favor of a beloved fraternal lodge.

Good Fight, The (1983) **C/B&W-98m.** ***½ D: Mary Dore, Sam Sills, Noel Buckner. Incisive, often moving documentary of the 3,200 American men and women who were among 40,000 volunteers battling Fascism in the Spanish Civil War. Franco may have won and they may have been harassed by their own government, but they are ultimately both authentic American patriots and survivors. Cut to 85m. for PBS showings.▼

Good Girls Go to Paris (1939) **75m.** **½ D: Alexander Hall. Melvyn Douglas, Joan Blondell, Walter Connolly, Alan Curtis, Isabel Jeans, Clarence Kolb. Spunky waitress Blondell will do anything to visit France; she sees a meal ticket in wealthy Curtis, but really loves professor Douglas. OK comedy.

Good Guys and the Bad Guys, The (1969)

C-91m. **½ D: Burt Kennedy. Robert Mitchum, George Kennedy, David Carradine, Tina Louise, Douglas Fowley, Lois Nettleton, Martin Balsam, John Carradine. Mild Western comedy-drama has aging marshall Mitchum going after lifelong foe Kennedy, who has been abandoned by his outlaw gang for being over the hill.

Good Guys Wear Black (1979) **C-96m.** ** D: Ted Post. Chuck Norris, Anne Archer, James Franciscus, Lloyd Haynes, Dana Andrews, Jim Backus. Norris jumps feet first through a windshield and threatens to rearrange the face of bellman Backus— all in the name of national security. Silly political paranoia thriller kills time easily enough. Follow-up: A FORCE OF ONE.▼

Good Humor Man, The (1950) **79m.** **½ D: Lloyd Bacon. Jack Carson, Lola Albright, Jean Wallace, George Reeves, Richard Egan. Rambunctious antics with Carson in title role, getting involved in murder plot, aided by gang of "Captain Marvel Kids."

Good Luck, Miss Wyckoff (1979) **C-105m.** BOMB D: Marvin J. Chomsky. Anne Heywood, Donald Pleasence, Robert Vaughn, Carolyn Jones, Dorothy Malone, Ronee Blakley, John Lafayette, Earl Holliman. Repressed schoolteacher's first taste of sex comes via rape, in awkward adaptation of William Inge novel. Good cast generally wasted. Retitled THE SIN and THE SHAMING.▼

Good Morning, Babylon (1987-Italian-U.S.) **C-115m.** *** D: Paolo and Vittorio Taviani. Vincent Spano, Joaquim De Almeida, Greta Scacchi, Desiree Becker, Charles Dance, Omero Antonutti, David Brandon. Two Italian brothers, whose artisan family has shaped and restored cathedrals for generations, come to America in 1915 and wind up working for D.W. Griffith on his epic film INTOLERANCE. A valentine to the early days of moviemaking, and a statement about the immortality of art, be it sculpture or film. Beguilingly naive, like the period (and the people) it depicts, with a surprising turn of events for its denouement. Dance is a standout as D.W. Griffith.▼

Good Morning, Miss Dove (1955) **C-107m.** *** D: Henry Koster. Jennifer Jones, Robert Stack, Marshall Thompson, Chuck Connors, Jerry Paris, Mary Wickes, Robert Douglas. For several generations, small town spinster schoolteacher has touched and helped shape lives of her students. Now hospitalized, her past is revealed through flashbacks. Sentimental, warm, and wonderful.

Good Morning, Vietnam (1987) **C-120m.** *** D: Barry Levinson. Robin Williams, Forest Whitaker, Tung Thanh Tran, Chintara Sukapatana, Bruno Kirby, Robert Wuhl, J.T. Walsh, Noble Willingham, Floyd Vivino. Williams is the whole show here, playing an Army disc jockey who turns Armed Forces radio inside out when he's brought to Saigon in 1965. His manic monologues are so uproarious that they carry the rest of the film, which has a weakly developed "story" and often irrelevant musical interludes. Apparently the real-life Adrian Cronauer, on whom story was based, wasn't nearly as funny or outrageous as Williams.▼

Good Mother, The (1988) **C-103m.** ** D: Leonard Nimoy. Diane Keaton, Liam Neeson, Jason Robards, Ralph Bellamy, Teresa Wright, James Naughton, Asia Vieira, Joe Morton, Katey Sagal, Tracy Griffith, Charles Kimbrough. Keaton is excellent as usual in the role of a divorced woman who finds sexual fulfillment for the first time in her life . . . but unwittingly jeopardizes her ability to raise her daughter in the process. Tedious adaptation of the Sue Miller novel.▼

Good Neighbor Sam (1964) **C-130m.** *** D: David Swift. Jack Lemmon, Romy Schneider, Edward G. Robinson, Michael Connors, Dorothy Provine, Neil Hamilton, Joyce Jameson. Good comedy of Lemmon's adventures pretending he's not married to his real wife but to luscious neighbor Schneider. Plenty of sight gags and chase scenes make this a lot of fun.▼

Good News (1947) **C-95m.** **½ D: Charles Walters. June Allyson, Peter Lawford, Patricia Marshall, Joan McCracken, Mel Torme. Average 1920s college campus musical with last-minute touchdowns, complicated subplots all neatly coming together at the end. Bright score includes "Varsity Drag," "The French Lesson." Remake of 1930 version of this DeSylva-Brown-Henderson show.▼

Goodnight, My Love (1972) **C-73m. TVM** D: Peter Hyams. Richard Boone, Barbara Bain, Michael Dunn, Victor Buono, Gianni Russo. Down-and-out detective team have visit from seemingly innocent blonde who wants fiancé found. Not quite MALTESE FALCON takeoff as claimed, film (also written by Hyams) has offbeat point of view with timeless atmosphere, excellent direction. Above average.

Good Sam (1948) **128m.** ** D: Leo McCarey. Gary Cooper, Ann Sheridan, Ray Collins, Edmund Lowe, Joan Lorring, Ruth Roman. Almost complete misfire, despite cast and director. Cooper is an incurable good Samaritan in this lifeless comedy. Some prints run 113m.▼

Good Sport, A (1984) **C-100m. TVM** D: Lou Antonio. Lee Remick, Ralph Waite, Sam Gray, Richard Hamilton, Dan Frazer, Antonio Fargas, Tracy Pollan, Joe Morton. Lee and Ralph go the Tracy-Hepburn route in this amiable (uncredited) update of WOMAN OF THE YEAR. She's a chic fashion editor; he's a boozing sports columist; together they form an unlikely mutual admiration society and swear off any hanky panky—at least till the fadeout. Average.

Good, the Bad, and the Ugly, The (1967-Italian-Spanish) **C-161m.** ***½ D: Sergio Leone. Clint Eastwood, Lee Van Cleef, Eli Wallach, Rada Rassimov, Mario Brega, Chelo Alonso. Third and best of Leone's "Dollars" trilogy, set during Civil War; three disparate low-lifes search for Confederate government treasure chest, each possessing only partial whereabouts. Long, funny, and flamboyant, with memorable Ennio Morricone score; the quintessential spaghetti Western. Followed by ONCE UPON A TIME IN THE WEST.▼

Good Time Girl (1950-British) **81m.** *½ D: David MacDonald. Jean Kent, Dennis Price, Herbert Lom, Flora Robson. Inoffensive trivia about young girl prevented from wayward life by a judge's telling of tragic fate of another teen-ager.

Good Times (1967) **C-91m.** **½ D: William Friedkin. Sonny and Cher, George Sanders, Norman Alden, Larry Duran. Back when the singing duo was considered kooky, they made this enjoyable little film, with Sonny fantasizing their potential movie roles and he and Cher singing "I've Got You, Babe." Friedkin's first film . . . Cher's, too.

Good to Go (1986) **C-87m.** ** D: Blaine Novak. Art Garfunkel, Robert Doqui, Harris Yulin, Reginald Daughtry, Richard Brooks, Hattie Winston. Forgettable fare about journalist Garfunkel, who's framed on a rape-murder charge. Of interest mainly for its go-go music, which came out of the Washington D.C. ghetto . . . and did *not* become the national music fad of its time. Highlighted are the performances of such go-go groups as Redds & the Boys, Trouble Funk, Chuck Brown & the Soul Searchers, among others. Retitled SHORT FUSE for home video.▼

Good Wife, The (1986-Australian) **C-92m.** **½ D: Ken Cameron. Rachel Ward, Bryan Brown, Sam Neill, Steven Vidler, Jennifer Claire, Bruce Barry. Isolated, bored wife Ward becomes obsessed with the new man in town (Neill). Predictable and a bit slow but also well made and well acted. Overall, a very mixed bag. Original Australian title: THE UMBRELLA WOMAN.▼

Goonies, The (1985) **C-111m.** **½ D: Richard Donner. Sean Astin, Josh Brolin, Jeff Cohen, Corey Feldman, Kerri Green, Martha Plimpton, Ke Huy Quan, John Matuszak, Anne Ramsey, Joe Pantoliano. A bunch of kids go in search of hidden treasure in this old-fashioned adventure yarn (from a story by Steven Spielberg, who may have recalled Our Gang's MAMA'S LITTLE PIRATE). Big, lively, and exceptionally noisy, aimed squarely at kids, with a likable bunch of kids onscreen.

Also makes appropriate use of Max Steiner's swashbuckling theme from ADVENTURES OF DON JUAN.▼

Goose and the Gander, The (1935) **65m.** ** D: Alfred E. Green. Kay Francis, George Brent, Genevieve Tobin, John Eldredge, Claire Dodd. Woman's story of high-living Francis keeping an eye on ex-husband Brent.

Gor (1988) **C-95m.** *½ D: Fritz Kiersch. Urbano Barbarini, Oliver Reed, Rebecca Ferratti, Larry Taylor, Graham Clarke, Arnold Vosloo, Chris Du Plessis, Paul L. Smith, Jack Palance. Ordinary sword-and-sorcery adventure in which meek American professor is magically whisked off to "counter-Earth" Gor, where he becomes a hero and battles chuckling, tyrannical Reed. Based on the first in "John Norman's" series of Edgar Rice Burroughs-inspired adventure fantasies. Palance's role is just a cameo setting up the sequel, OUTLAW OF GOR.▼

Gordon's War (1973) **C-90m.** *** D: Ossie Davis. Paul Winfield, Carl Lee, David Downing, Tony King. When a Vietnam vet comes home to find his wife hooked on drugs, he trains four-man army to destroy the pushers. Good action, but gets lost toward the end.▼

Gore Vidal's Billy the Kid (1989) **C-100m.** TVM D: William A. Graham. Val Kilmer, Duncan Regehr, Wilford Brimley, Julie Carmen, Michael Parks, Rene Auberjonois, Albert Salmi. William Bonney was a likable but misunderstood teenager who happened to get caught up in a range war, became embittered and went bad . . . according to Vidal, whose earlier go at Billy the Kid was a 1950s teleplay that became a Paul Newman movie, THE LEFT-HANDED GUN. This one is similarly interesting if unremarkable. The author has a cameo as a minister at graveside. Made for cable. Average.▼

Gore Vidal's Lincoln (1988) **C-200m.** TVM D: Lamont Johnson. Sam Waterston, Mary Tyler Moore, John Houseman, Richard Mulligan, John McMartin, Ruby Dee, Cleavon Little, Jeffrey DeMunn, James Gammon, Deborah Adair, Robin Gammell. Thoughtful performances by Waterston (as a pensive Abe) and Moore (as an unsteady Mary Todd) firmly ground this slow-moving personal portrait of the two, from the day they came to Washington to the day they left for the President's burial in Springfield. Earnestly adapted by Ernest Kinoy from Vidal's best-seller, with a fine music score by Ernest Gold, and Emmy-winning direction by Johnson. Originally shown in two parts. Above average.

Gorgeous Hussy, The (1936) **102m.** **½ D: Clarence Brown. Lionel Barrymore, Joan Crawford, Robert Taylor, Franchot Tone, Melvyn Douglas, James Stewart. Star-studded cast in strained historical drama of Andrew Jackson's belle, who disgraces herself and those connected with her. Crawford et al are beautifully costumed in well-appointed settings.

Gorgo (1961-British) **C-78m.** ******* D: Eugene Lourie. Bill Travers, William Sylvester, Vincent Winter, Bruce Seton, Joseph O'Conor. Good sci-fi story of captured baby sea monster put into London circus and gigantic parent coming to rescue it. Exciting special effects.▼

Gorgon, The (1964-British) **C-83m.** ****½** D: Terence Fisher. Peter Cushing, Christopher Lee, Richard Pasco, Barbara Shelley, Michael Goodliffe. A spirit inhabits the body of beautiful girl and gives her gaze that turns others to stone. Atmospheric.▼

Gorilla SEE: **Nabonga**▼

Gorilla, The (1939) **66m.** ****** D: Allan Dwan. The Ritz Brothers, Anita Louise, Patsy Kelly, Lionel Atwill, Bela Lugosi, Joseph Calleia. Disappointing comedy-whodunit with the Ritz Brothers as fumbling detectives prowling around old-darkhouse in search of murderer. Lugosi is wasted. Filmed before in 1930.▼

Gorilla at Large (1954) **C-84m.** ******* D: Harmon Jones. Cameron Mitchell, Anne Bancroft, Lee J. Cobb, Raymond Burr, Peter Whitney, Lee Marvin, Warren Stevens. Offbeat murder mystery at amusement park, with exceptionally able cast. Filmed in 3-D.

Gorilla Man, The (1942) **64m.** ****** D: D. Ross Lederman. John Loder, Ruth Ford, Marian Hall, Richard Fraser, Creighton Hale. Title is misleading. Pro-Nazis try to discredit RAF pilot by linking him with series of brutal murders. Grade-B material with adequate acting.

✓**Gorillas in the Mist** (1988) **C-129m.** ******* D: Michael Apted. Sigourney Weaver, Bryan Brown, Julie Harris, John Omirah Miluwi, Iain Cuthbertson, Constantin Alexandrov, Waigwa Wachira. Absorbing drama based on the life of Dian Fossey, who journeyed to Africa in 1967 and, with no prior experience, set out to document the vanishing breed of mountain gorillas for *National Geographic.* Her transformation from diligent researcher to obsessive madwoman is a bit more abrupt than it ought to be, but it's still a good film, and Weaver is compelling in the lead.▼

Gorky Park (1983) **C-128m.** ******* D: Michael Apted. William Hurt, Lee Marvin, Brian Dennehy, Ian Bannen, Joanna Pacula, Alexander Knox. Absorbing murder mystery set in Russia, where police investigator Hurt doggedly pursues the case of three bodies buried in Gorky Park. Lots of twists and turns, vivid atmosphere (with Helsinki doubling for Moscow) . . . marred somewhat by unconvincing romance and protracted finale. From the novel by Martin Cruz Smith.▼

Gorp (1980) **C-90m.** BOMB D: Joseph Ruben. Michael Lembeck, Dennis Quaid, Philip Casnoff, Fran Drescher, David Huddleston, Robert Trebor, Julius Harris. Sophomoric, depressingly unfunny drug-oriented comedy set in a summer camp. Makes MEATBALLS seem like *Hamlet*; for people who think the word "Quaalude" is automatically funny.▼

Gospel (1982) **C-92m.** *****½** D: David Leivick, Frederick A. Ritzenberg. James Cleveland and the Southern California Community Choir, Walter Hawkins and the Hawkins Family, Mighty Clouds of Joy, Shirley Caesar, Twinkie Clark and the Clark Sisters. Inspiring, tremendously entertaining concert film spotlighting top gospel performers. Each number is more rousing than the last.▼

Gospel According to St. Matthew, The (1966-Italian-French) **135m.** ******** D: Pier Paolo Pasolini. Enrique Irazoqui, Margherita Caruso, Susanna Pasolini, Marcello Morante, Mario Socrate. Unconventional, austere film on life and teachings of Christ, based solely on writings of the Apostle, Matthew. Amateur cast (including director's mother) is expressive and moves with quiet dignity. Ironically, director of this masterpiece was a Marxist.▼

Gospel According to Vic, The (1985-British) **C-92m.** ****** D: Charles Gormley. Tom Conti, Helen Mirren, David Hayman, Brian Pettifer, Jennifer Black. Very minor comedy of Catholic schoolteacher Conti and the series of miracles that befall him. Mirren is wasted as a music teacher/love interest. Also known as HEAVENLY PURSUITS.▼

Gospel Road, The (1973) **C-83m.** ****½** D: Robert Elfstrom. Johnny Cash, June Carter, Robert Elfstrom. Musical journey through Holy Land follows story of Jesus from his birth to his death and resurrection. Sincere but not especially good.▼

Gossip Columnist, The (1979) **C-100m.** TVM D: James Sheldon. Kim Cattrall, Bobby Vinton, Robert Vaughn, Dick Sargent, Conrad Janis, Joe Penny, Martha Raye, Bobby Sherman, Sylvia Sidney, Lyle Waggoner, Steve Allen, Jayne Meadows, Jack Carter, Jim Backus. Idealistic political journalist is assigned to replace a legendary news-hen. Slickly done but strictly ho-hum, despite the shine from Raye's turn as a faded night-club singer. Average.

Gosta Berling's Saga SEE: **The Atonement of Gosta Berling**▼

Gotcha! (1985) **C-101m.** ****½** D: Jeff Kanew. Anthony Edwards, Linda Fiorentino, Nick Corri, Alex Rocco, Marla Adams, Klaus Loewitsch, Christopher Rydell. Nerdy college kid goes to Paris on vacation, meets seductive older woman who involves him in espionage in East Berlin. Very nearly a good movie, with some sharp dialogue to start, but loses its appeal as it loses its credibility.▼

Go Tell It On The Mountain (1984) C-97m. TVM D: Stan Lathan. Paul Winfield, James Bond III, Olivia Cole, Rosalind Cash, Ruby Dee, Linda Hopkins, Alfre Woodard. This drama about a young black boy's efforts to gain the approval of—and, later, understand—his stern, unrelenting stepfather is poignant, intelligent, and well acted. Adapted from James Baldwin's semiautobiographical novel; a PBS *American Playhouse* presentation. Above average.

Go Tell the Spartans (1978) C-114m. ***½ D: Ted Post. Burt Lancaster, Craig Wasson, Jonathan Goldsmith, Marc Singer, Joe Unger, David Clennon, Dolph Sweet, James Hong. Perceptive, moving Vietnam War picture, set in early '64; Burt shines as "advisory group" commander who is already starting to have his doubts about the conflict. More realistic in dialogue and situation than other, more publicized, popular films on the subject. Wendell Mayes's cynically funny script is right on target. Based on Daniel Ford's novel *Incident at Muc Wa*.▼

Gotham (1988) C-100m. TVM D: Lloyd Fonvielle. Tommy Lee Jones, Virginia Madsen, Colin Bruce, Kevin Jarre, Denise Stephenson, Frederic Forrest. A down-on-his-luck private eye gets involved with a dead beauty's ghost when hired by a wealthy financier to get the woman (his late wife) to stop harassing him for money. Funny, bizarre, erotic—although the usually reliable Jones seems to be wondering what his character's all about. Made for cable. Average.▼

Gothic (1986-British) C-90m. ** D: Ken Russell. Gabriel Byrne, Julian Sands, Natasha Richardson, Miriam Cyr, Timothy Spall. That night in 1816 when Mary Shelley (author of *Frankenstein*) and Dr. Polidori (*The Vampyre*) were inspired to write their gothic classics—previously depicted in THE BRIDE OF FRANKENSTEIN—is given the wild Ken Russell treatment here. Too weird for some, too highbrow for many horror fans, no doubt, but full of Russell's hallucinatory visuals. Richardson (daughter of Tony Richardson and Vanessa Redgrave) makes an impressive screen debut. The same story was told two years later in HAUNTED SUMMER.▼

Go to the Light (1988) C-100m. TVM D: Mike Robe. Linda Hamilton, Richard Thomas, Piper Laurie, Ned Beatty, Brian Bonsall, Joshua Harris, Rosemary Dunsmore. A family faces the approaching death of a hemophiliac child who has contracted AIDS. Well-intentioned, but an unrelenting downer. Average.

Government Girl (1943) 94m. **½ D: Dudley Nichols. Olivia de Havilland, Sonny Tufts, Anne Shirley, Jess Barker, James Dunn, Paul Stewart, Agnes Moorehead. Tufts has clear field in wartime Washington, but de Havilland gets him; that's about it for this breezy comedy.

Go West (1940) 81m. ** D: Edward Buzzell. Groucho, Chico, and Harpo Marx, John Carroll, Diana Lewis, Walter Woolf King, Robert Barrat. Big letdown from Marxes, until hilarious train-ride climax. Occasional bits sparkle through humdrum script.▼

Go West, Young Girl (1978) C-74m. TVM D: Alan J. Levi. Karen Valentine, Sandra Will, Stuart Whitman, Richard Jaeckel, David Dukes, John Payne. Lighthearted Western pits a peppery young woman from back East and a cavalry officer's widow against gamblers, bounty hunters, and leering lawmen as they go in search of Billy the Kid. Average.

Go West, Young Man (1936) 82m. *** D: Henry Hathaway. Mae West, Randolph Scott, Warren William, Alice Brady, Elizabeth Patterson, Lyle Talbot, Isabel Jewell. Movie queen Mae is stuck in the sticks, but passes time nicely with handsome farm-boy Scott. Not top-notch West, but still fun.

Grace Kelly (1983) C-100m. TVM D: Anthony Page. Cheryl Ladd, Lloyd Bridges, Diane Ladd, Alejandro Rey, Ian McShane, William Schallert, Marta DuBois, Salome Jens. Cardboard valentine to Princess Grace that reportedly was given her blessing shortly before her death in late 1982. Ladd poses prettily as Grace and McShane postures somewhat unsteadily as Rainier, but Bridges (who worked with the real Grace in HIGH NOON) manages to give some dimension to Jack Kelly, her father. Cynthia Mandelberg's script is somewhat pat, but fun can be gathered from watching the parade of Hollywood personalities who are impersonated—including veteran actress Edith Fellows turning up as famed costume designer Edith Head. Average.

Grace Quigley (1985) C-87m. *½ D: Anthony Harvey. Katharine Hepburn, Nick Nolte, Elizabeth Wilson, Chip Zien, Kit Le Fever, William Duell, Walter Abel. Abysmal misfire that manages to be both bland and tasteless, about lonely, elderly Hepburn, who hires hit man Nolte to kill her—and then others of her set who would all rather be dead. Filmed in 1983, first shown at 1984 Cannes Film Festival at 102m. However, another version of this exists, titled THE ULTIMATE SOLUTION OF GRACE QUIGLEY and put together by its scriptwriter, A. Martin Zweiback. Despite an uneven second half, it is a touching, funny, surreal black comedy about the problems of the elderly and the right of choice. This cut runs 94m and is rated **½. ▼

Gracie Allen Murder Case, The (1939) 74m. D: Alfred E. Green. Gracie Allen,

Warren William, Ellen Drew, Kent Taylor, Jerome Cowan, Judith Barrett, Donald MacBride, William Demarest, H.B. Warner. SEE: **Philo Vance** series

Grad Night (1980) C-85m. *½ D: John Tenorio. Joe Johnson, Barry Stoltze, Suzanna Fagan, Sam Whipple, Caroline Bates. Mindless bedlam on high-school graduation night. All-too-typical youth comedy.

Graduate, The (1967) C-105m. **** D: Mike Nichols. Anne Bancroft, Dustin Hoffman, Katharine Ross, Murray Hamilton, William Daniels, Elizabeth Wilson, Brian Avery, Norman Fell, Marion Lorne, Alice Ghostley. A landmark film of the late 60s that's still just as pungent— and funny—as ever. Hoffman, in his first major film role, plays ultra-naive college grad who's seduced by a middle-aged woman, then falls in love with her daughter. Perfect song score by Simon and Garfunkel. Script by Buck Henry (who plays the desk clerk) and Calder Willingham from Charles Webb's novel. Nichols won Best Director Oscar. Look fast for Mike Farrell in the hotel lobby, and Richard Dreyfuss in Berkeley rooming house.▼

Graduation Day (1981) C-96m. BOMB D: Herb Freed. Christopher George, Patch Mackenzie, E. Danny Murphy, Michael Pataki, E. J. Peaker, Vanna White. A bloody FRIDAY THE 13TH clone, done with no talent or imagination.▼

Grambling's White Tiger (1981) C-100m. TVM D: Georg Stanford Brown. Bruce Jenner, Harry Belafonte, LeVar Burton, Dennis Haysbert, Deborah Pratt, Ray Vitte. The story of Jim Gregory, a California high-school football star quarterback who becomes the only white player on all-black Grambling College's team. Olympic-athlete-turned-actor Jenner is somewhat miscast as a high schooler, but Belafonte, in his TV acting debut, is solid as legendary Coach Eddie Robinson in this so-so dramatization of Bruce Behrenberg's book *My Little Brother Is Coming Tomorrow.* Average.▼

Grand Central Murder (1942) 73m. **½ D: S. Sylvan Simon. Van Heflin, Patricia Dane, Cecilia Parker, Virginia Grey, Samuel S. Hinds, Sam Levene, Tom Conway. Slick, fast-moving B whodunit, with Heflin investigating actress' murder on private train car at Grand Central Station.

Grand Duel, The (1972-Italian) C-92m. *½ D: Giancarlo Santi. Lee Van Cleef, Peter O'Brien, Marc Mazza, Jess Hahn, Horst Frank. Typically spare spaghetti Western with mysterious gunman Van Cleef becoming guardian angel to a man wrongly accused of murder.

Grand Highway, The (1987-French) C-104m. *** D: Jean-Loup Hubert. Anemone, Richard Bohringer, Antoine Hubert, Vanessa Guedj, Christine Pascal. Fine, subtle, slice-of-life tale of a fragile nine-year-old boy (Hubert, son of the director) and his experiences while spending three weeks in a rural village while his mother is off giving birth. Young Guedj is a delight as the tomboy who becomes his friend.▼

Grand Hotel (1932) 113m. **** D: Edmund Goulding. Greta Garbo, Joan Crawford, John Barrymore, Wallace Beery, Lionel Barrymore, Lewis Stone, Jean Hersholt. Vicki Baum's novel of plush Berlin hotel where "nothing ever happens." Stars prove the contrary: Garbo as lonely ballerina, John B. her jewel-thief lover, Lionel B. a dying man, Crawford an ambitious stenographer, Beery a hardened businessman, Stone the observer. Best Picture Oscar winner; a must. Plot reworked many times (in HOTEL BERLIN, WEEKEND AT THE WALDORF, etc.). Later a Broadway musical.▼

Grand Illusion (1937-French) 111m. **** D: Jean Renoir. Jean Gabin, Pierre Fresnay, Erich von Stroheim, (Marcel) Dalio, Dita Parlo, Carette. Renoir's classic treatise on war, focusing on French prisoners during WW1 and their cultured German commandant. Beautiful performances enhance an eloquent script.▼

Grand Jury (1977) C-100m. *½ D: Christopher Cain. Bruce Davison, Meredith MacRae, Leslie Nielsen, Barry Sullivan, Sharon Thomas. Dull drama about Davison and MacRae becoming unintentionally entangled in insurance hijinks.

Grandma's Boy (1922) 81m. *** D: Fred Newmeyer. Harold Lloyd, Mildred Davis, Anna Townsend, Charles Stevenson, Noah Young, Dick Sutherland. Lloyd's first great success casts him as a mousy small-town type inspired to fight for his girl—and his honor—by his grandma's tales of family heritage. Still entertaining. Edited for TV and paired with condensed version of 1921 feature A SAILOR-MADE MAN.

Grand National Night (1953-British) 81m. ** D: Bob McNaught. Nigel Patrick, Moira Lister, Beatrice Campbell, Betty Ann Davies, Michael Hordern, Noel Purcell. Melodramatic murder yarn involving the horsey set in northern England. Hordern, as a police inspector, gives the most interesting performance. One tip: pay close attention to the surname of leading man Patrick's character.

Grand Prix (1966) C-175m. ** D: John Frankenheimer. James Garner, Eva Marie Saint, Yves Montand, Toshiro Mifune, Brian Bedford, Jessica Walter, Francoise Hardy. Big cast is saddled with rambling script about personal lives of auto racers and their loves; use of split screen and spectacular sequences won't mean much on TV. Deservedly won Oscars for its teams of editors and sound effects people.▼

[451]

Grand Slam (1933) 67m. **½ D: William Dieterle. Loretta Young, Paul Lukas, Frank McHugh, Glenda Farrell, Helen Vinson, Roscoe Karns, Walter Byron. Breezy, semisatirical look at early '30s bridge-tournament stars Young and Lukas as a couple who find love and luck. Interesting use of slow motion and freeze frame for finale.

Grand Slam (1968-Italian-U.S.) C-120m. *** D: Giuliano Montaldo. Edward G. Robinson, Janet Leigh, Adolfo Celi, Klaus Kinski, Georges Rigaud, Robert Hoffman. International jewel-heist film, with all the trappings. Nothing new, but smoothly done, most enjoyable.

Grand Theft Auto (1977) C-85m. ** D: Ron Howard. Ron Howard, Nancy Morgan, Marion Ross, Pete Isacksen, Barry Cahill. Howard's directorial debut (he also co-scripted with his actor-father Rance) is typical unsophisticated car-crash action fare, no better or worse than most.▼

Grandview, U.S.A. (1984) C-97m. **½ D: Randal Kleiser. Jamie Lee Curtis, C. Thomas Howell, Patrick Swayze, Jennifer Jason Leigh, Ramon Bieri, Carole Cook, Troy Donahue, William Windom, Elizabeth Gorcey, Michael Winslow. So-so slice of Americana, focusing on several characters in archetypal Midwestern town: a young boy coming of age, an independent young woman trying to make it on her own running her father's demolition-derby business, and a lovesick sap who's her ace driver. Passable time-filler but nothing more.▼

✓ **Grapes of Wrath, The** (1940) 129m. **** D: John Ford. Henry Fonda, Jane Darwell, John Carradine, Charley Grapewin, Dorris Bowden, Russell Simpson, John Qualen. Steinbeck Americana of Okies moving from dust bowl to California during Depression, lovingly brought to screen. Fonda, as ex-con, is unforgettable in role of his life. Darwell, as determined family head, and Ford won well-deserved Oscars. Written for the screen and produced by Nunnally Johnson. Don't miss this one.▼

Grasshopper, The (1970) C-95m. *** D: Jerry Paris. Jacqueline Bisset, Jim Brown, Joseph Cotten, Corbett Monica, Ramon Bieri. Episodic but fairly compelling chronicle of how a beautiful 19-year-old from British Columbia ends up as a burned-out Vegas call girl at age 22. Better than expected melodrama actually features Brown in a sympathetic role. Video title: PASSING OF EVIL, THE▼

Grass Is Always Greener Over the Septic Tank, The (1978) C-100m. TVM D: Robert Day. Carol Burnett, Charles Grodin, Alex Rocco, Linda Gray, Robert Sampson, Vicki Belmonte. The Erma Bombeck book loses some of its humor in this still-amiable translation to the screen, telling of a N.Y.C. couple who decide to swap the hassle of big city living for suburbia. Originally intended to test the waters as a possible Burnett series. Average.▼

Grass Is Greener, The (1960) C-105m. *** D: Stanley Donen. Cary Grant, Deborah Kerr, Robert Mitchum, Jean Simmons. Chic drawing-room fare that suffers from staginess. Grant-Kerr marriage is threatened by Simmons and Mitchum romancing the two, respectively.▼

Grass Is Singing, The (1981-British-Swedish) C-108m. *** D: Michael Raeburn. Karen Black, John Thaw, John Kani, John Moulder Brown, Patrick Mynhardt. Black is excellent as a lonely woman who marries farmer Thaw and cannot adjust to life in the African woodland. Filmed in Zambia; based on a novel by Doris Lessing. Released in U.S. in 1984 as KILLING HEAT.▼

Grave Robbers from Outer Space SEE: **Plan 9 from Outer Space**▼

Gravy Train, The (1974) C-96m. **½ D: Jack Starrett. Stacy Keach, Frederic Forrest, Margot Kidder, Barry Primus, Richard Romanus, Denny Miller. OK blend of fast-moving action and comedy as West Virginia brothers Keach and Forrest develop a liking for crime. Also known as THE DION BROTHERS.

Grayeagle (1978) C-104m. **½ D: Charles B. Pierce. Ben Johnson, Iron Eyes Cody, Lana Wood, Jack Elam, Paul Fix, Alex Cord. Interesting if flawed rehash of THE SEARCHERS with Johnson tracking the Indian (Cord) who kidnapped his daughter. Good classic Western style an asset, sluggish pacing a drawback. Produced, directed, written by Pierce, who also appears.▼

Gray Lady Down (1978) C-111m. ** D: David Greene. Charlton Heston, David Carradine, Stacy Keach, Ned Beatty, Ronny Cox, Rosemary Forsyth. Tired drama about rescue of nuclear submarine, captained by Heston. Good special effects, and colorful performance by Carradine as designer of experimental diving craft. Look for Christopher Reeve as one of the officers.▼

Grazie Zia SEE: **Thank You, Aunt**

Grease (1978) C-110m. *** D: Randal Kleiser. John Travolta, Olivia Newton-John, Stockard Channing, Jeff Conaway, Didi Conn, Eve Arden, Sid Caesar, Joan Blondell, Edd Byrnes, Alice Ghostly, Dody Goodman, Lorenzo Lamas, Michael Tucci. Energetic, imaginative filming of long-running Broadway show that fantasizes life in the 1950s; spirited cast, clever ideas, and Patricia Birch's choreography make it fun. Hit songs (written for the movie) include: "You're the One That I Want," "Hopelessly Devoted To You," and title number, sung by Frankie Valli. Followed by a sequel.▼

Grease 2 (1982) C-114m. BOMB D: Patricia Birch. Maxwell Caulfield, Michelle Pfeiffer, Adrian Zmed, Lorna Luft, Didi Conn, Eve Arden, Sid Caesar, Dody Goodman, Tab Hunter, Connie Stevens. Mindless sequel to the musical hit; opens with a great back-to-school number, then goes downhill. Pedestrian music, clumsy comedy, uncharismatic leads; only the supporting players (like newcomer Luft and veteran Arden) shine through. Inauspicious directing debut for choreographer Birch.▼

Greased Lightning (1977) **C-94m.** ** D: Michael Schultz. Richard Pryor, Beau Bridges, Pam Grier, Cleavon Little, Vincent Gardenia, Richie Havens, Julian Bond. Spirited cast does little to enliven plodding, episodic bio of Wendell Scott, the first black racing car driver. A waste of Pryor, both dramatically and comically.▼

Greaser's Palace (1972) **C-91m.** *** D: Robert Downey. Allan Arbus, Albert Henderson, Luana Anders, George Morgan, Larry Moyer, Michael Sullivan, James Antonio, Ron Nealy. Super-offbeat Jesus Christ parody with Western setting. Drifter (Arbus) discovers "true identity" and heals "sick" cowboys in crazy, tiny town.▼

Great Adventure, The (1953-Swedish) **73m.** ***½ D: Arne Sucksdorff. Anders Norberg, Kjell Sucksdorff, Arne Sucksdorff. Outstanding story told in semidocumentary style covering four seasons of a boy's life on a farm. Written, directed, edited, and photographed by an Oscar-winning filmmaker with a special gift for capturing animal life.▼

Great Adventure, The (1975-Italian-Spanish) **C-87m.** ** D: Paul Elliotts (Gianfranco Baldanello). Jack Palance, Joan Collins, Fred Romer (Fernando Romero), Elisabetta Virgili, Manuel de Blas, Remo de Angelis. Middling tale, taken from Jack London, of a boy and his dog trying to make it in the wilds of gold-rush Alaska—fighting the odds, marauding wolves, sinister town boss Palance, dancehall queen Collins.▼

Great American Beauty Contest, The (1973) **C-74m. TVM** D: Robert Day. Eleanor Parker, Bob Cummings, Louis Jourdan, Joanna Cameron, Susan Damante, Tracy Reed, Farrah Fawcett. Offbeat, behind-the-scenes look at present-day big-time pageant, complete with sordid intrigues, rumors of rigging, etc., enlivened by social-commentary point of view. Good performances, especially Parker's. Above average.

Great American Broadcast, The (1941) **92m.** **½ D: Archie Mayo. Alice Faye, John Payne, Jack Oakie, Cesar Romero, The Four Ink Spots, James Newill, Mary Beth Hughes. Fictional fun of development of radio industry, with such musical

guests as zany Wiere Brothers. Entertaining; bright cast.▼

Great American Cowboy, The (1974) **C-90m.** *** D: Kieth Merrill. Narrated by Joel McCrea. Exciting documentary on rodeo life focuses on rodeo superstar Larry Mahan and his competition with newcomer Phil Lyne. Oscar-winner as Best Documentary Feature.▼

Great American Pastime, The (1956) **89m.** ** D: Herman Hoffman. Tom Ewell, Anne Francis, Ann Miller, Dean Jones, Ruby Dee. Ewell manages to work some enthusiasm into this programmer about Little League baseball and its effect on suburban families.

Great American Traffic Jam, The SEE: **Gridlock**▼

Great American Tragedy, A (1972) **C-73m. TVM** D: J. Lee Thompson. George Kennedy, Vera Miles, William Windom, Hilarie Thompson, Kevin McCarthy, James Woods, Tony Dow. Family experiences economic realities of life when aerospace engineer (Kennedy) gets laid off. Staunch middle-class point of view. OK performances, upbeat ending. Average.

Great Balloon Adventure, The SEE: **Olly, Olly, Oxen Free**▼

Great Balls of Fire! (1989) **C-102m.** **½ D: Jim McBride. Dennis Quaid, Winona Ryder, Alec Baldwin, Lisa Blount, Trey Wilson, John Doe, Steve Allen. Slick, highly stylized cartoon about the rise (and temporary fall) of '50s rocker Jerry Lee Lewis, a twice-married hellraiser whose doom was sealed when he took his 13-year-old second cousin as wife No. 3. Quaid's amusing, but verrrry broad lead performance is balanced by Ryder's more even-keeled portrayal of cousin Myra. Reasonably entertaining but falls far short of its potential. That's Lewis' real voice, though Quaid *is* playing the piano.▼

Great Bank Hoax, The (1977) **C-89m.** **½ D: Joseph Jacoby. Richard Basehart, Burgess Meredith, Paul Sand, Ned Beatty, Michael Murphy, Charlene Dallas, Arthur Godfrey. Unremarkable but diverting comedy, a Watergate allegory about bank officials who try to cover up embezzlement by arranging an even bigger theft. Also known as THE GREAT GEORGIA BANK HOAX; originally titled SHENANIGANS.▼

Great Bank Robbery, The (1969) **C-98m.** *½ D: Hy Averback. Zero Mostel, Kim Novak, Clint Walker, Claude Akins, Akim Tamiroff, Larry Storch. Bogus preacher and company, Mexican gang led by Tamiroff, and local outlaws all compete for control of the town of Friendly. Spoof of Westerns is a total dud. Be warned.

Great Battle, The (1978-German-Yugoslavian) **C-97m.** BOMB D: Humphrey Longan (Umberto Lenzi). Helmut Berger,

Samantha Eggar, Giuliano Gemma, John Huston, Stacy Keach, Henry Fonda, Edwige Fenech. Amateurish muddle about WW2 combines tired vignettes with well-known stars, dubbed sequences with others, and newsreel footage narrated by Orson Welles. A waste of everybody's time. Also known as BATTLE FORCE.▼

Great Brain, The (1978) **C-82m.** *** D: Sidney Levin. Jimmy Osmond, James Jarnigan, Len Birman, Pat Delaney, Fran Ryan, John Fredric Hart. Ambling but enjoyable family film produced by The Osmonds from John D. Fitzgerald's award-winning book. Young Jimmy plays a Tom Sawyer-ish con artist at the turn of the century.

Great British Train Robbery, The (1967-Germany) **104m.** *** D: John Olden, Claus Peter Witt. Horst Tappert, Hans Cossy, Gunther Neutze, Isa Miranda. Absorbing true study of mammoth robbery of British mails by an ingenious band of outlaws.

Great Caruso, The (1951) **C-109m.** *** D: Richard Thorpe. Mario Lanza, Ann Blyth, Jarmila Novotna, Dorothy Kirsten. Biographical fiction about the legendary singer, entertainingly done. Fine music makes clichés endurable.▼

Great Cash Giveaway Getaway, The (1980) **C-105m.** TVM D: Michael O'Herlihy. George Hamilton, David Kyle, Elissa Leeds, Albert Salmi, Richard Bull, James Keach, Audrey Totter. Hamilton is a suave heavy who wants to nail the two teenagers who've gone on a spending spree with the quarter-million dollars he gained in a drug-smuggling deal. Sounds like an old Bowery Boys plot recycled. Below average.

Great Catherine (1968-British) **C-98m.** *½ D: Gordon Flemyng. Peter O'Toole, Jeanne Moreau, Zero Mostel, Jack Hawkins, Akim Tamiroff. Terrible adaptation of George Bernard Shaw's comedy about Catherine the Great wastes capable cast; wait for revival of Dietrich's THE SCARLET EMPRESS.

Great Chase, The (1963) **77m.** ***½ Narrated by Frank Gallop. Buster Keaton, Douglas Fairbanks, Sr., Pearl White, Richard Barthelmess, Lillian Gish. Entertaining silent-film compilation of great chase scenes from THE MARK OF ZORRO, WAY DOWN EAST, etc., with most of film devoted to Keaton's classic, THE GENERAL. Score composed by harmonica virtuoso Larry Adler.▼

Great Dan Patch, The (1949) **94m.** **½ D: Joseph M. Newman. Dennis O'Keefe, Gail Russell, Ruth Warrick, Charlotte Greenwood. Acceptable yarn of legendary trotting horse and his phenomenal harness racing career.▼

Great Day (1945-British) **94m.** **½ D: Lance Comfort. Eric Portman, Flora Robson, Sheila Sim, Isabel Jeans, Walter Fitzgerald, Philip Friend. English village readies itself for visit by Eleanor Roosevelt. Somber, effective study of the courageous women who helped Britain win WW2.▼

Great Day in the Morning (1956) **C-92m.** **½ D: Jacques Tourneur. Virginia Mayo, Robert Stack, Ruth Roman, Alex Nicol, Raymond Burr. Good cast, beautiful color scenery help so-so story of pre-Civil War Colorado, when gold rush fever and separationist sentiments clashed.▼

Great Diamond Robbery, The (1953) **69m.** ** D: Robert Z. Leonard. Red Skelton, Cara Williams, James Whitmore, Dorothy Stickney, Steven Geray. Limp vehicle buoyed by Skelton. Red is hoodwinked by jewel thief who wants him to recut huge diamond.

Great Dictator, The (1940) **128m.** ***½ D: Charles Chaplin. Charles Chaplin, Paulette Goddard, Jack Oakie, Reginald Gardiner, Maurice Moscovich, Billy Gilbert, Henry Daniell. Chaplin's first full talkie; unusual comedy combines slapstick, satire, and social commentary, as he plays dual role of Jewish ghetto barber and dictator Adenoid Hynkel of Tomania. Unique, surprisingly effective film also features Oakie in unforgettable portrayal of "Benzino Napaloni" of rival country Bacteria.▼

Great Escape, The (1963) **C-168m.** **** D: John Sturges. Steve McQueen, James Garner, Richard Attenborough, Charles Bronson, James Coburn, David McCallum, Donald Pleasence, James Donald, Gordon Jackson, John Leyton. Allied P.O.W.s plot massive escape from German prison camp. Based on true story, this blockbuster was beautifully photographed by Daniel Fapp on location in Germany. Rip-roaring excitement with marvelous international cast; script by James Clavell and W.R. Burnett, from Paul Brickhill's book. Rousing score by Elmer Bernstein. Followed by a TV sequel twenty-five years later.▼

Great Escape II: The Untold Story, The (1988) **C-200m.** TVM D: Paul Wendkos, Jud Taylor. Christopher Reeve, Anthony Denison, Charles Haid, Judd Hirsch, Michael Nader, Donald Pleasence. The '60s action classic was unnecessarily defiled here by vaguely remaking the original film in the first two hours and then adding a two-hour what-happened-then addendum. Reeve is bland as a German-speaking American-born British officer(!) who leads the survivors on a hunt after the war for their captors. Of interest: Pleasence, one of the would-be great escapees in the original, here as an SS baddie. Originally shown in two parts. Average.

Greatest, The (1977) **C-101m.** *½ D: Tom Gries. Muhammad Ali, Ernest Borgnine, John Marley, Robert Duvall, James Earl Jones, Roger E. Mosley, Ben Johnson, Paul Winfield, Lloyd Haynes, Dina Merrill, David Clennon. Potentially exciting screen bio of the great heavyweight champ becomes an episodic mess suffering from a script devoid of dramatic focus and ham-handed direction. Ironically, Mosley's performance as Sonny Liston has the charisma Ali's lacks. Soundtrack features George Benson's "The Greatest Love of All."▼

Greatest Battle, The SEE: **Great Battle, The**▼

Greatest Gift, The (1974) **C-100m. TVM** D: Boris Sagal. Glenn Ford, Julie Harris, Lance Kerwin, Harris Yulin, Charles Tyner, Dabbs Greer. Rural, poverty-stricken preacher (Ford) battles ruthless sheriff (Yulin) and restless church deacons in struggle to support family in small Southern town in 1940. Sentimental, homespun, with a violent turn. Adapted by Abby Mann (as "Ben Goodman") from Jack Farris' novel *Ramey*. Subsequently it spun off a series, *The Family Holvak*. Above average.

Greatest Love, The (1951-Italian) **116m.** *½ D: Roberto Rossellini. Ingrid Bergman, Alexander Knox, Giulietta Masina, Teresa Pellati, Sandro Frachina. Unusual, slow-moving story of a wealthy woman who feels compelled to help people, in order to restore meaning to her own life after her son's death. Originally titled EUROPA '51.

Greatest Show on Earth, The (1952) **C-153m.** ***½ D: Cecil B. DeMille. Betty Hutton, Charlton Heston, Cornel Wilde, Dorothy Lamour, Gloria Grahame, James Stewart, Henry Wilcoxon, Lawrence Tierney, Lyle Bettger. Big package of fun from DeMille, complete with hokey performances, clichés, big-top excitement, and a swell train wreck. Stewart well cast as circus clown with mysterious past. Some funny surprise guests appear. Oscar winner for Best Picture and Story.▼

Greatest Story Ever Told, The (1965) **C-141m.** **½ D: George Stevens. Max Von Sydow, Charlton Heston, Carroll Baker, Angela Lansbury, Sidney Poitier, Shelley Winters, John Wayne, Ed Wynn, Jose Ferrer, Van Heflin, Claude Rains, Telly Savalas, many others. Some of the most spectacular scenes ever filmed lose all validity because of incessant cameos that run throughout film. Would *you* believe John Wayne as a Roman centurion supervising Christ's crucifixion? Originally shown at 260m., then at 195m.▼

Greatest Thing That Almost Happened, The (1977) **C-100m. TVM** D: Gilbert Moses. Jimmie Walker, James Earl Jones, Deborah Allen, Tamu, Kevin Hooks, Saundra Sharp, Valerie Curtin. Tearjerker involving a high school athlete stricken with leukemia and his insensitive father who never had time for him. Average.

Great Expectations (1934) **C-100m.** **½ D: Stuart Walker. Jane Wyatt, Phillips Holmes, George Breakston, Henry Hull, Florence Reed, Alan Hale, Francis L. Sullivan. Acceptable version of Dickens' story about a young boy and unknown benefactor is dwarfed by '46 classic. Sullivan plays Jaggers in both films. ▼

Great Expectations (1946-British) **118m.** **** D: David Lean. John Mills, Valerie Hobson, Bernard Miles, Francis L. Sullivan, Finlay Currie, Martita Hunt, Anthony Wager, Jean Simmons, Alec Guinness, Ivor Barnard, Freda Jackson, Torin Thatcher, Eileen Erskine, Hay Petrie. One of the greatest films ever made, a vivid adaptation of Dickens's tale of a mysterious benefactor making poor young orphan a gentleman of means. Opening graveyard sequence is a gem. Oscars went to cinematographer Guy Green and art director John Bryan. Lean, Kay Walsh, Cecil McGivern, and producers Anthony Havelock-Allan and Ronald Neame all contributed to script. Filmed before in 1934, and again in 1974. Jean Simmons played Miss Havisham in a 1989 miniseries remake.▼

Great Expectations (1974-U.S.-British) **C-103m. TVM** D: Joseph Hardy. Michael York, Sarah Miles, James Mason, Margaret Leighton, Robert Morley, Anthony Quayle, Joss Ackland, Rachel Roberts, Heather Sears, Peter Bull. OK remake of the Dickens classic; originally produced as a musical, but songs have been deleted. Anyway, OLIVER! it ain't. Average.

Great Flamarion, The (1945) **78m.** **½ D: Anthony Mann. Erich von Stroheim, Mary Beth Hughes, Dan Duryea, Stephen Barclay, Lester Allen, Esther Howard. Better than most of von Stroheim's cheapies, this one has him double-crossed by circus star Hughes to make way for Duryea.▼

Great Gabbo, The (1929) **95m.** ** D: James Cruze. Erich von Stroheim, Don Douglas, Betty Compson, Margie Kane. The idea of von Stroheim as an egomaniacal ventriloquist is irresistible, but the story is slim, predictable, and stiffly done—padded out by lots of big and unintentionally hilarious musical numbers. A curio for film buffs. Based on Ben Hecht story; some sequences originally in color.▼

Great Gambini, The (1937) **70m.** **½ D: Charles Vidor. Akim Tamiroff, Marian Marsh, Genevieve Tobin, William Demarest, Reginald Denny, Roland Drew. Engaging low-budget film, with Tamiroff starring as magico who predicts deaths, becomes his own victim.

Great Garrick, The (1937) **91m.** *** D:

James Whale. Brian Aherne, Olivia de Havilland, Edward Everett Horton, Melville Cooper, Lionel Atwill, Lana Turner, Marie Wilson. Members of the Comédie Française perpetrate a hoax to deflate the ego of pompous David Garrick (Aherne) in this entertaining, fictionalized yarn about real-life British actor.

Great Gatsby, The (1949) 92m. **½ D: Elliott Nugent. Alan Ladd, Betty Field, Macdonald Carey, Barry Sullivan, Ruth Hussey, Shelley Winters, Howard da Silva. Misguided adaptation of F. Scott Fitzgerald's book about a mysterious young millionaire who crashes Long Island society in the 1920s. Too talky and much too literal-minded. Ladd is pretty good, but Field (as Daisy Buchanan) gives a strangely petulant performance. Filmed before in 1926 and again in 1974.

Great Gatsby, The (1974) C-144m. **½ D: Jack Clayton. Robert Redford, Mia Farrow, Bruce Dern, Karen Black, Scott Wilson, Sam Waterston, Lois Chiles, Howard da Silva, Edward Herrmann, Patsy Kensit. Bland adaptation of F. Scott Fitzgerald's jazz-age novel about a golden boy in Long Island society; faithful to the book, and visually opulent, but lacks substance and power. Script by Francis Ford Coppola; Theoni V. Aldredge's costumes and Nelson Riddle's score earned Oscars.▼

Great Georgia Bank Hoax, The SEE: **Great Bank Hoax, The**▼

Great Gilbert and Sullivan, The (1953-British) C-105m. ***½ D: Sidney Gilliat. Robert Morley, Maurice Evans, Eileen Herlie, Peter Finch, Martyn Green. Highly flavorful biography of operetta composers with many highlights from their works. Original British title: THE STORY OF GILBERT AND SULLIVAN.

Great Gildersleeve, The (1943) 62m. ** D: Gordon Douglas. Harold Peary, Nancy Gates, Freddie Mercer, Mary Field, Jane Darwell, Thurston Hall. First of series based on famous radio character Throckmorton P. Gildersleeve is moderately amusing nonsense, as Gildy enters local politics and avoids spinster Field.▼

Great Guns (1941) 74m. ** D: Monty Banks. Stan Laurel, Oliver Hardy, Sheila Ryan, Dick Nelson, Edmund MacDonald. Later L&H Army comedy is weak, not as bad as some but far below their classic films. Look quickly for Alan Ladd.▼

Great Guy (1936) 75m. ** D: John G. Blystone. James Cagney, Mae Clarke, James Burke, Edward Brophy, Henry Kolker, Bernadene Hayes, Edward McNamara. Second-rate Cagney in low-budget production about inspector crusading against corruption in meat business.▼

Great Houdinis, The (1976) C-100m. TVM D: Melville Shavelson. Paul Michael Glaser, Sally Struthers, Ruth Gordon, Vivian Vance, Adrienne Barbeau, Peter Cushing, Bill Bixby, Jack Carter, Nina Foch, Maureen O'Sullivan, Wilfrid Hyde-White, Clive Revill, Geoffrey Lewis. Drama about life and times of the famed illusionist-escape artist whose career masks obsession with the occult. Brisk direction and literate script (both by Shavelson), wonderful performance by Gordon as Houdini's possessive mother. Above average.

Great Ice Rip-Off, The (1974) C-78m. TVM D: Dan Curtis. Lee J. Cobb, Gig Young, Grayson Hall, Robert Walden, Matt Clark, Geoffrey Lewis. Grumpy retired cop Cobb matches wits with jewel thief Young and his gang during cross-country bus chase. Light-hearted suspense caper, tossed off by a couple of old pros and, uncharacteristically, occult-horror director Curtis. Above average.

Great Impostor, The (1960) 112m. **½ D: Robert Mulligan. Tony Curtis, Edmond O'Brien, Arthur O'Connell, Gary Merrill, Frank Gorshin. Incredible story of Ferdinand Demara, who succeeded in a variety of professional guises. Film is episodic and pat.▼

Great Jesse James Raid, The (1953) C-74m. **½ D: Reginald Le Borg. Willard Parker, Barbara Payton, Tom Neal, Wallace Ford. Generally action-packed tale blending fact and legend about the notorious outlaw and his last big robbery caper.

Great Jewel Robber, The (1950) 91m. ** D: Peter Godfrey. David Brian, Marjorie Reynolds, John Archer, Warren Douglas. Brian chomps through title role; film recounts his many criminal capers.

Great John L., The (1945) 96m. **½ D: Frank Tuttle. Greg McClure, Linda Darnell, Barbara Britton, Lee Sullivan, Otto Kruger, Wallace Ford, George Matthews, Rory Calhoun. Not bad little biography of famous boxer's rise and fall, his two loves and unhappy end.

Great K&A Train Robbery, The (1926) 53m. ***½ D: Lewis Seiler. Tom Mix, Dorothy Dwan, William Walling, Harry Grippe, Tony. Silent screen's most popular cowboy star in one of his greatest films: rollicking fun, filmed on magnificent locations in Colorado.

Great Lie, The (1941) 107m. *** D: Edmund Goulding. Mary Astor, Bette Davis, George Brent, Lucile Watson, Hattie McDaniel, Grant Mitchell, Jerome Cowan. Brent marries Davis when alliance with Astor is annulled. He is lost in plane crash, leaving Davis and pregnant Astor to battle each other and the elements. Well-mounted soaper won Astor an Oscar as fiery concert pianist.▼

Great Locomotive Chase, The (1956) C-85m. *** D: Francis D. Lyon. Fess

Parker, Jeffrey Hunter, Jeff York, John Lupton, Eddie Firestone, Kenneth Tobey. True story of Andrews' Raiders (filmed before by Buster Keaton as THE GENERAL) comes to life in colorful Disney film; Parker is famous Union spy who leads a rowdy band in capturing and "kidnapping" a Confederate railroad train during Civil War. Retitled ANDREWS' RAIDERS.▼

Great Lover, The (1949) 80m. *** D: Alexander Hall. Bob Hope, Rhonda Fleming, Roland Young, Roland Culver, George Reeves, Jim Backus. Vintage Hope; Bob's a boy scout leader on ship filled with his troop, luscious Fleming, and murderer Young.▼

Great Man, The (1956) 92m. ***½ D: Jose Ferrer. Jose Ferrer, Dean Jagger, Keenan Wynn, Julie London, Jim Backus, Ed Wynn. Well-loved TV star dies and Ferrer prepares memorial show, only to discover star was a despicable phony. Hardbitten look at TV industry; top performances by senior and junior Wynns. Ferrer and Al Morgan adapted Morgan's novel.

Great Manhunt, The (1950-British) 97m. *** D: Sidney Gilliat. Douglas Fairbanks, Jr., Glynis Johns, Jack Hawkins, Herbert Lom. Genuine suspenser; American doctor tries to flee Middle European country after he discovers its real leader has been assassinated and replaced with a double. Originally released in England as STATE SECRET at 104m.

Great Man's Lady, The (1942) 90m. **½ D: William Wellman. Barbara Stanwyck, Joel McCrea, Brian Donlevy, Thurston Hall, K. T. Stevens, Lucien Littlefield. Saga of the West is no great shakes as McCrea dreams of oil wells, Donlevy takes his girl. Stanwyck ages to 100 years to frame story.

Great Man's Whiskers, The (1971) C-100m. TVM D: Philip Leacock. Dennis Weaver, Ann Sothern, John McGiver, Harve Presnell, Beth Brickell, Cindy Eilbacher. Weak comedy-drama about President Lincoln rerouting train tour after receiving letter from 10-year-old girl urging him to grow whiskers. Political aspect of plot doesn't work; historically unbelievable, too. Below average.

Great Man Votes, The (1939) 72m. ***½ D: Garson Kanin. John Barrymore, Peter Holden, Virginia Weidler, Donald MacBride, William Demarest. Simple, sincere, delightful film of Barrymore, once a professor, now a souse, fighting for custody of his children, suddenly elevated to new stature when election-time rolls around. MacBride fun as small-time politico, Demarest an energetic campaign promoter.

Great McGinty, The (1940) 81m. *** D: Preston Sturges. Brian Donlevy, Muriel Angelus, Akim Tamiroff, Allyn Joslyn, William Demarest, Louis Jean Heydt, Arthur Hoyt. Sturges' directorial debut (and Oscar-winning screenplay) isn't up to his later comedy classics, but Donlevy is excellent as bum who is manipulated into governor's chair by crooked political machine—then blows it all when he tries to be honest. Typically sharp dialogue, plus fine work by Sturges' stock company of character actors.▼

Great Meadow, The (1931) 78m. **½ D: Charles Brabin. John Mack Brown, Eleanor Boardman, Lucille LaVerne, Anita Louise, Gavin Gordon, Guinn Williams, Russell Simpson, John Miljan. Naive and primitive but still compelling story of Virginians who undertake mountainous trek to settle new land in Kentucky, circa 1777. Fairly authentic drama gives a real sense of the hardship these pioneers endured.

Great Mike, The (1944) 70m. ** D: Wallace Fox. Stuart Erwin, Robert (Buzz) Henry, Marion Martin, Carl Switzer, Pierre Watkin. Sloppy comedy-drama of horse-racing, with Erwin as lovable rogue who trains unlikely horse to win big race.

Great Missouri Raid, The (1950) C-83m. ** D: Gordon Douglas. Wendell Corey, Macdonald Carey, Ellen Drew, Ward Bond, Anne Revere. Another account of the infamous outlaws, James brothers and Younger brothers.▼

Great Moment, The (1944) 83m. ** D: Preston Sturges. Joel McCrea, Betty Field, Harry Carey, William Demarest, Franklin Pangborn, Grady Sutton, Louis Jean Heydt, Jimmy Conlin. Confused biography of anesthesia inventor wavers from comedy to drama; ineffectual, filled with frustrating flashbacks. Very offbeat for writer-director Sturges, although film was taken out of his hands and re-edited. Filmed in 1942.

Great Mouse Detective, The (1986) C-80m. *** D: John Musker, Ron Clements, Dave Michener, Burny Mattinson. Voices of Vincent Price, Barrie Ingham, Val Bettin, Susanne Pollatschek, Candy Candido, Eve Brenner, Alan Young, Melissa Manchester. Brisk animated adaptation of Eve Titus' book, *Basil of Baker Street,* about a Sherlockian mouse who matches wits with the nefarious Prof. Ratigan (whose role is performed with gusto by Price). Not much depth to this Disney cartoon feature, but it *is* a lot of fun.

Great Muppet Caper, The (1981-British) C-95m. *** D: Jim Henson. The Muppet Performers (Jim Henson, Frank Oz, Dave Goelz, Jerry Nelson, Richard Hunt), Charles Grodin, Diana Rigg, John Cleese, Robert Morley, Peter Ustinov, Jack Warden. The Muppets try to solve a London jewel robbery in their second feature-film. Clever gags and ideas plus hilarious musical numbers with Miss Piggy make up for meandering script with more than its share of slow spots.▼

Great Niagara, The (1974) **C-78m. TVM** D: William Hale. Richard Boone, Michael Sacks, Randy Quaid, Jennifer Salt, Burt Young. Offbeat outdoor adventure about a bitter, obsessed old cripple (Boone) who endangers his sons' lives by forcing them to challenge Niagara Falls in a barrel to continue a family tradition. Evocative drama, set in the Depression 30s with generous supply of thrills. Average.

Great Northfield, Minnesota Raid, The (1972) **C-91m. **½ D: Philip Kaufman. Cliff Robertson, Robert Duvall, Luke Askew, R. G. Armstrong, Dana Elcar, Donald Moffat, John Pearce, Matt Clark, Wayne Sutherlin, Elisha Cook. New-style Western showing famous robbery scheme from seamy side. Vivid portraits of Younger brothers, James brothers, but muddled point of view.▼

Great O'Malley, The (1937) **71m. ***½ D: William Dieterle. Pat O'Brien, Humphrey Bogart, Ann Sheridan, Donald Crisp, Mary Gordon, Frieda Inescort, Sybil Jason. Syrupy film of ruthless cop O'Brien and poor man Bogart who has lame daughter and turns to crime to support her. Pretty sticky stuff.

Great Outdoors, The (1988) **C-90m. ***½ D: Howard Deutch. Dan Aykroyd, John Candy, Stephanie Faracy, Annette Bening, Chris Young, Ian Giatti, Hilary Gordon, Rebecca Gordon, Robert Prosky. Joyless scattershot comedy about the disintegration of the Candy clan's summer vacation by the uninvited appearance of boorish in-law Aykroyd and family. Written by John Hughes, apparently with something else on his mind.▼

Great Profile, The (1940) **82m. ***½ D: Walter Lang. John Barrymore, Mary Beth Hughes, Gregory Ratoff, John Payne, Anne Baxter, Lionel Atwill, Edward Brophy. Barrymore on downslide provides some laughs in self-parodying tale of aging, conceited actor.

Great Race, The (1965) **C-150m. **½ D: Blake Edwards. Tony Curtis, Natalie Wood, Jack Lemmon, Peter Falk, Keenan Wynn, Larry Storch, Dorothy Provine, Arthur O'Connell, Vivian Vance, Ross Martin, George Macready. Long, sometimes funny, often labored comedy, not the greatest ever made, as advertised. Duel sequence and barroom brawl are highlights, but pie fight falls flat, other gimmicks don't work. Definitely a mixed bag; one good song, "The Sweetheart Tree."▼

Great Rock and Roll Swindle, The (1980-British) **C-103m. *** D: Julien Temple. Malcolm McLaren, Johnny Rotten, Sid Vicious, Steve Jones, Paul Cook, Ronnie Biggs, Liz Fraser. Fascinating portrait of outrageous punk-rock group The Sex Pistols, featuring Johnny Rotten and the late Sid Vicious.

Great Rupert, The (1950) **86m. **½ D: Irving Pichel. Jimmy Durante, Terry Moore, Tom Drake, Queenie Smith, Frank Orth, Jimmy Conlin, Chick Chandler. Agreeable comedy-fantasy about a trained squirrel who finds a cache of money and gives it to impoverished vaudevillian Durante and his family. Durante is at his best, but story runs out of steam before it's through. Produced by George Pal; director Pichel appears in a brief bit.

Great Santini, The (1979) **C-116m. **½ D: Lewis John Carlino. Robert Duvall, Blythe Danner, Michael O'Keefe, Lisa Jane Persky, Stan Shaw, Theresa Merritt, David Keith. Character study of a career Marine who, in 1962, is "a warrior without a war," except for the one he wages with his adolescent son. Compelling performances give this film its meat, but dramatic structure and resolutions are not nearly as strong. Adapted by Carlino from Pat Conroy's novel. Also known as THE ACE.▼

Great Scout and Cathouse Thursday (1976) **C-102m. **½ D: Don Taylor. Lee Marvin, Oliver Reed, Robert Culp, Elizabeth Ashley, Howard Platt, Strother Martin, Sylvia Miles, Kay Lenz. Broad unsubtle comedy set in Colorado of 1908 involves swindles, defanged snake, kidnapped prostitutes, and robbery of proceeds from big boxing match. Could have been funnier, although Reed is a delight as an Indian(!).▼

Great Sinner, The (1949) **110m. **½ D: Robert Siodmak. Gregory Peck, Ava Gardner, Melvyn Douglas, Walter Huston, Ethel Barrymore. Murky romance lavishly produced, meandering along with tale of Peck saving Gardner from drowning in gambling fever—then catching it himself.

Great Sioux Massacre, The (1965) **C-91m. **½ D: Sidney Salkow. Joseph Cotten, Darren McGavin, Philip Carey, Julie Sommars, Nancy Kovack, John Matthews, Frank Ferguson. Good acting enhances this version of Custer's last stand.

Great Sioux Uprising, The (1953) **C-80m. **½ D: Lloyd Bacon. Jeff Chandler, Faith Domergue, Lyle Bettger, Glenn Strange. Chandler as ex-Yankee officer is adequate in formula Western about threatened Indian war.

Great Smokey Roadblock, The (1976) **C-84m. **½ D: John Leone. Henry Fonda, Eileen Brennan, John Byner, Dub Taylor, Susan Sarandon, Melanie Mayron, Austin Pendleton. Innocuous story of aging trucker (Fonda) attempting one perfect cross-country run before his truck is repossessed; his haul is a houseful of evicted prostitutes. Some nice vignettes. Originally titled THE LAST OF THE COWBOYS, running 106m. Co-produced by Sarandon.▼

Great Spy Mission, The SEE: **Operation Crossbow**

Great St. Louis Bank Robbery, The (1959) 86m. *½ D: Charles Guggenheim, John Stix. Steve McQueen, David Clarke, Crahan Denton, Molly McCarthy, James Dukas. Modest robbery caper with virtue of McQueen in cast.

Great St. Trinian's Train Robbery, The (1966-British) C-94m. ** D: Frank Launder, Sidney Gilliat. Frankie Howerd, Reg Varney, Richard Wattis, Dora Bryan. Overly droll entry in popular series begins with the real Great Train Robbery, then injects political satire with usual hijinks as the crooks' hiding place for the loot becomes the new site for infamous girls' school. Alastair Sim's presence is sorely missed.▼

Great Texas Dynamite Chase, The (1977) C-90m. *½ D: Michael Pressman. Claudia Jennings, Jocelyn Jones, Johnny Crawford, Chris Pennock, Tara Strohmeier. A pair of sexy female bank robbers take to the roads in this all-too-typical low-budget outing.▼

Great Train Robbery, The (1979-British) C-111m. *** D: Michael Crichton. Sean Connery, Donald Sutherland, Lesley-Anne Down, Alan Webb, Malcolm Terris, Robert Lang. Stylish fun as an elegant trio conspire to pull off the greatest heist of all time, in the mid-1800s: stealing shipment of gold from a moving train! Crichton based his script on true incident, filmed it against beautiful British countryside. British title: THE FIRST GREAT TRAIN ROBBERY.▼

Great Victor Herbert, The (1939) 84m. **½ D: Andrew L. Stone. Allan Jones, Mary Martin, Walter Connolly, Lee Bowman, Susanna Foster, Jerome Cowan. Music overshadows plot in this lightweight romance about two young singers and the famed composer. Many of Herbert's most popular songs ("Ah, Sweet Mystery of Life," "March of the Toys," etc.) are included.

Great Waldo Pepper, The (1975) C-107m. *** D: George Roy Hill. Robert Redford, Bo Svenson, Bo Brundin, Susan Sarandon, Geoffrey Lewis, Edward Herrmann, Margot Kidder, Scott Newman. Boxoffice disappointment from director of BUTCH CASSIDY and THE STING is a much more personal film, even though brilliantly photographed story of aviation pioneers wavers uncomfortably between slapstick and drama. Worth a look.▼

Great Wall, A (1986) C-100m. **½ D: Peter Wang. Peter Wang, Sharon Iwai, Kelvin Han Yee, Li Qinqin, Hy Xiaoguang. Good-natured story of culture clash that results when Chinese-American family makes its first trip to mainland China. Amiable but hardly inspired. First U.S.-Chinese coproduction is also Wang's first

feature as cowriter, director, and star (he played the chef in CHAN IS MISSING by Wayne Wang—no relation).▼

Great Wallendas, The (1978) C-100m. TVM D: Larry Elikann. Lloyd Bridges, Britt Ekland, Taina Elg, Cathy Rigby, Michael McGuire, John Van Dreelen. Straightforward drama based on the legendary circus family of high-wire artists whose career has been stalked by tragedy. Enthralling when up in the air. Average.▼

Great Waltz, The (1938) 102m. **½ D: Julien Duvivier. Luise Rainer, Fernand Gravet, Miliza Korjus, Hugh Herbert, Lionel Atwill, Curt Bois. Music outdoes drama in this elaborately produced biography of composer Johann Strauss, with plenty of waltzes covering up a standard triangle tale. Joseph Ruttenberg's lovely cinematography earned an Oscar.

Great Waltz, The (1972) C-135m. BOMB D: Andrew L. Stone. Horst Buchholz, Mary Costa, Rossano Brazzi, Nigel Patrick, Yvonne Mitchell, James Faulkner. Bio of Johann Strauss is unintentionally funny in the way director Stone's SONG OF NORWAY was, but after 135 minutes, even the laughs begin to subside. Filmed on location in Austria.

Great War, The (1959-Italian-French) 118m. ** D: Mario Monicelli. Vittorio Gassman, Alberto Sordi, Silvana Mangano, Folco Lulli. Uneven, episodic comedy-drama of two gold-bricking pals during WW1, somewhat reminiscent of WHAT PRICE GLORY? but not nearly as good. Released here in 1961.▼

Great White Hope, The (1970) C-101m. *** D: Martin Ritt. James Earl Jones, Jane Alexander, Lou Gilbert, Joel Fluellen, Chester Morris, Robert Webber, R. G. Armstrong, Hal Holbrook, Beah Richards, Moses Gunn. Supercharged adaptation of Broadway success with Jones and Alexander (in her film debut) repeating stage roles as Jack Jefferson, famed heavyweight champion, and white mistress. Not a boxing film or social doctrine, but emotional character study. Holds up until final scene, which doesn't ring true.▼

Great Ziegfeld, The (1936) 176m. ***½ D: Robert Z. Leonard. William Powell, Myrna Loy, Luise Rainer, Frank Morgan, Fanny Brice, Virginia Bruce, Reginald Owen, Ray Bolger, Stanley Morner (Dennis Morgan). Spectacular, immensely entertaining biography of flamboyant impresario Florenz Ziegfeld, with Powell quite dashing in the title role. However, Rainer (as Anna Held) is no less than stunning, and won an Academy Award; her telephone scene is a classic. This also won Oscars for Best Picture and Dance Direction (the "A Pretty Girl Is Like A Melody" number, supervised by Seymour Felix).▼

Greed (1924) 140m. **** D: Erich von

Stroheim. Gibson Gowland, ZaSu Pitts, Jean Hersholt, Chester Conklin, Dale Fuller. Powerful adaptation of Frank Norris' novel *McTeague*, about a simple man whose wife's obsession with money eventually drives him to madness. Even though von Stroheim's film was taken from him and severely cut by the studio (it originally ran eight hours), this remains a stunning work, one of the greatest of all silent films. The final sequences in Death Valley are unforgettable.▼

Greeks Had a Word for Them, The (1932) **79m.** *** D: Lowell Sherman. Joan Blondell, Ina Claire, Madge Evans, David Manners, Lowell Sherman. Vintage comedy of three gold-digging girls looking for husbands; still entertaining although redone several times, including HOW TO MARRY A MILLIONAIRE. Retitled: THREE BROADWAY GIRLS.▼

Greek Tycoon, The (1978) **C-106m.** *½ D: J. Lee Thompson. Anthony Quinn, Jacqueline Bisset, Raf Vallone, Edward Albert, Charles Durning, Camilla Sparv, James Franciscus. Pointless fabrication about romance and marriage of Aristotle you-know-who and a certain president's widow. Beautiful settings add only luster to tepid script that doesn't even rate as good trash. Videocassette version runs 112m.▼

Green Archer, The (1961-German) **95m.** **½ D: Jurgen Roland. Gert Frobe, Karin Dor, Klausjurgen Wussow, Edith Teichman. Nicely paced actioner with plenty of excitement as masked archer eliminates his victims, baffles police; from Edgar Wallace novel.

Green Berets, The (1968) **C-141m.** BOMB D: John Wayne, Ray Kellogg. John Wayne, David Janssen, Jim Hutton, Aldo Ray, Raymond St. Jacques, Bruce Cabot, George Takei, Jack Soo, Patrick Wayne, Mike Henry. Politics aside, this overlong, incredibly clichéd salute to the Special Forces has enough absurd situations and unfunny comedy relief to offend anyone; don't miss now-famous final scene, where the sun sinks into the East.▼

Green Cockatoo, The (1937-British) **65m.** ** D: William Cameron Menzies. John Mills, Rene Ray, Robert Newton, Charles Oliver, Bruce Seton. Considering credentials of this film (story by Graham Greene, director Menzies, etc.) the results are particularly disappointing: song-and-dance man Mills tries to unravel mystery surrounding murder of his brother (Newton). Originally titled FOUR DARK HOURS.

Green Dolphin Street (1947) **141m.** **½ D: Victor Saville. Lana Turner, Van Heflin, Donna Reed, Richard Hart, Frank Morgan, Edmund Gwenn. If only for its glossy production values and Oscar-winning special effects, this plodding costumer has merit. Story of two sisters (Turner, Reed)

after the same man in New Zealand is tedious; set in 19th century.▼

Greene Murder Case, The (1929) **69m.** D: Frank Tuttle. William Powell, Florence Eldridge, Ulrich Haupt, Jean Arthur, Eugene Pallette. SEE: **Philo Vance** series.

Green-Eyed Blonde, The (1957) **76m.** ** D: Bernard Girard. Susan Oliver, Tommie Moore, Juanita Moore, Evelyn Scott, Roy Glenn. Oliver in title role is properly rebellious as teenager involved in homicide and her own tragic end.

Green Eyes (1976) **C-100m.** TVM D: John Erman. Paul Winfield, Rita Tushingham, Jonathan Lippe, Victoria Racimo, Royce Wallace, Claudia Bryar. Disillusioned ex-GI returns to Vietnam to search for the son he left behind with his common-law prostitute wife. Poignant drama by David Seltzer with a moving performance by Winfield. Above average.▼

Green Fire (1954) **C-100m.** **½ D: Andrew Marton. Grace Kelly, Stewart Granger, Paul Douglas, John Ericson, Murvyn Vye. Hokum about love and conflict between emerald prospector (Granger) and coffee-plantation owner (Kelly), set in Colombia, South America. Attractive stars, hot love scenes, slimy villain (Vye).

Green For Danger (1946-British) **93m.** **** D: Sidney Gilliat. Alastair Sim, Sally Gray, Trevor Howard, Rosamund John, Leo Genn, Judy Campbell, Megs Jenkins. Exciting whodunit set in a rural English emergency hospital during WW2. Tension neatly counterbalanced by droll wit of Sim as implacable Scotland Yard inspector; a must-see classic. Written by Gilliat and Claude Curney.

Greengage Summer, The SEE: **Loss of Innocence**

Green Glove, The (1952) **88m.** **½ D: Rudolph Maté. Glenn Ford, Geraldine Brooks, Cedric Hardwicke, George Macready. Occasionally interesting tale of Ford returning to France to find cache of gems he hid during WW2, becoming involved in murder.

Green Goddess, The (1930) **80m.** ** D: Alfred E. Green. George Arliss, Alice Joyce, H. B. Warner, Ralph Forbes, Reginald Sheffield, Nigel de Brulier, Ivan Simpson. Campy early talkie, with Arliss a self-righteous potentate who holds innocent Britishers prisoner. The closing line is a gem. A remake of Arliss' 1923 silent film.

Green Grass of Wyoming (1948) **C-89m.** **½ D: Louis King. Peggy Cummins, Robert Arthur, Charles Coburn, Lloyd Nolan. Atmospheric tale of rival horse-breeding families; the usual, but nicely done. Sequel to THUNDERHEAD—SON OF FLICKA, based on a novel by Mary O'Hara.

Green Grow the Rushes (1951-British) **80m.** *** D: Derek Twist. Richard Burton, Honor Blackman, Roger Livesey, Geoffrey Keen, Archie Duncan. Delightful comedy of villagers trying to hide their whiskey-smuggling from government agents.

Green Hell (1940) 87m. **½ D: James Whale. Douglas Fairbanks, Jr., Joan Bennett, Alan Hale, John Howard, George Bancroft, Vincent Price, George Sanders. Standard jungle-expedition film worthwhile for fine cast.

Green Ice (1981-British) C-115m. ** D: Ernest Day. Ryan O'Neal, Anne Archer, Omar Sharif, Domingo Ambriz, John Larroquette. Emerald smuggling, with good guy O'Neal, bad guy Sharif, Archer the woman in between. Painless time-killer.▼

Green Light, The (1937) 85m. **½ D: Frank Borzage. Errol Flynn, Anita Louise, Margaret Lindsay, Cedric Hardwicke, Henry O'Neill, Spring Byington, Erin O'Brien-Moore. Genuinely odd blend of melodrama, religion, purple prose, and medical drama with Flynn as an idealistic doctor who makes a career sacrifice and then tries to understand the larger meaning of his life. Adaptation of a Lloyd C. Douglas novel is entertaining enough but awfully hard to swallow seriously.

Green Man, The (1957-British) 80m. *** D: Robert Day. Alastair Sim, George Cole, Terry-Thomas, Jill Adams, Avril Angers. Droll comedy of a seemingly timid clockmaker who prefers his part-time job as paid assassin.

Green Mansions (1959) C-101m. **½ D: Mel Ferrer. Audrey Hepburn, Anthony Perkins, Lee J. Cobb, Sessue Hayakawa, Henry Silva, Nehemiah Persoff. W. H. Hudson's romance set in South America suffers from miscast Hepburn as Rima the Bird Girl, whom fate decrees shall not leave her sanctuary. Perkins properly puzzled as male lead.

Green Pastures, The (1936) 90m. ***½ D: William Keighley, Marc Connelly. Rex Ingram, Oscar Polk, Eddie Anderson, Frank Wilson, George Reed, Abraham Gleaves, Myrtle Anderson. All-black cast in Marc Connelly fable of life in heaven, and biblical stories which give more meaning to Adam, Noah, and Moses than many so-called biblical films. Ingram is fine as "de Lawd."▼

Green Promise, The (1949) 93m. **½ D: William D. Russell. Marguerite Chapman, Walter Brennan, Robert Paige, Natalie Wood. Grim little film of Brennan and his four children trying to eke out a living on their farm; unpretentious and engaging.▼

Green Room, The (1978-French) C-95m. ** D: Francois Truffaut. Francois Truffaut, Nathalie Baye, Jean Daste, Jean-Paul Moulin, Jeanne Lobre. Truffaut stars as a death-obsessed journalist who converts a run-down chapel into a memorial for his deceased WW1 comrades. Dreary, lifeless, disappointing, with Truffaut's character engulfed in his own rhetoric. Based on writings of Henry James; coscripted by Truffaut and Jean Gruault.▼

Green Scarf, The (1955-British) 96m. *** D: George More O'Ferrall. Michael Redgrave, Ann Todd, Kieron Moore, Leo Genn. Imaginative handling of blind man accused of homicide, defended by aging attorney; set in Paris.

Green Slime, The (1969-Japanese-U.S.) C-88m. *½ D: Kinji Fukasaku. Robert Horton, Richard Jaeckel, Luciana Paluzzi, Bud Widom. On space station, title substance—exposed to blood—grows into red-eyed, tentacled monsters that quickly multiply and threaten to spread to Earth. Not as much fun as it sounds.

Greenwich Village (1944) C-82m. **½ D: Walter Lang. Carmen Miranda, Don Ameche, William Bendix, Vivian Blaine, Felix Bressart, Tony and Sally DeMarco, The Four Step Brothers. Silly but amiable musical about a "serious" composer (Ameche) persuaded to adapt his songs for a Broadway revue starring Blaine. When it's supposed to be 1922 N.Y.C. and Carmen Miranda turns up, you know not to expect stark realism. Look fast in both party scenes to spot The Revuers (Betty Comden, Adolph Green, Judy Holliday, Alvin Hammer).

Green Years, The (1946) 127m. **½ D: Victor Saville. Charles Coburn, Tom Drake, Hume Cronyn, Gladys Cooper, Dean Stockwell, Jessica Tandy, Norman Lloyd, Wallace Ford. Sentimental A. J. Cronin weeper of orphaned Irish lad and his experiences growing up with his mother's family in Scotland. Coburn is wonderful as his great-grandfather, an irascible teller of tall tales. Tandy plays Cronyn's *daughter* here.

Greetings (1968) C-88m. *** D: Brian De Palma. Jonathan Warden, Robert De Niro, Gerrit Graham, Richard Hamilton, Megan McCormick, Allen Garfield. Loose, informal, improvisational satire about the draft, sex, the counterculture. Exudes a late '60s N.Y.C.-Greenwich Village ambience not to be found in any Hollywood feature. Sequel: HI, MOM!▼

Gregory's Girl (1981-Scottish) C-91m. *** D: Bill Forsyth. Gordon John Sinclair, Dee Hepburn, Chic Murray, Jake D'Arcy, Alex Norton, John Bett, Clare Grogan. Bright, winning comedy of wimpy teenager Sinclair's love for Hepburn, who takes his place on the school soccer team. Enjoyable, if perhaps a bit overrated.▼

Gremlins (1984) C-111m. ** D: Joe Dante. Zach Galligan, Phoebe Cates, Hoyt Axton, Frances Lee McCain, Polly Holliday, Glynn Turman, Dick Miller, Keye Luke, Scott Brady, Judge Reinhold, Jackie Joseph. A teenager's unusual new pet spawns a legion of vicious, violent monsters who turn picture-postcard town into living hell. A comic nightmare film that's a cross between Capra's IT'S A WONDERFUL LIFE and THE BLOB, with more film-buff in-jokes than one can count . . . but the comedy is negated by too-vivid violence and mayhem. Cameos range from animator Chuck Jones to Robby the Robot—but you have to look fast for executive producer Steven Spielberg. Howie Mandel is the voice of Gizmo. Followed by a sequel.▼

Gremlins 2 The New Batch (1990) C-106m. *** D: Joe Dante. Zach Galligan, Phoebe Cates, John Glover, Robert Prosky, Robert Picardo, Christopher Lee, Haviland Morris, Dick Miller, Jackie Joseph, Gedde Watanabe, Keye Luke, Kathleen Freeman. Not so much a horror film as a goofy sendup of itself, this sequel turns the slimy creatures loose in N.Y.C. Filled with gags, movie in-jokes, satiric barbs, and gratuitous cameo appearances. Glover is especially funny as a Donald Trump/Ted Turner type, and Lee is a delight as a genetic scientist. Be sure to stay with this through the closing credits.

Grendel, Grendel, Grendel (1980-Australian) C-90m. **½ D: Alexander Stitt. Voices of Peter Ustinov, Keith Michell, Arthur Dignam, Ed Rosser, Bobby Bright, Ric Stone. Crude but appealing animation highlights this fable about Grendel, a medieval monster only a mother could love, and his observations about the creatures he calls "man"—who murder and pillage. Based on a novel by John Gardner.▼

Grey Fox, The (1982-Canadian) C-92m. *** D: Phillip Borsos. Richard Farnsworth, Jackie Burroughs, Wayne Robson, Ken Pogue, Timothy Webber. Low-key account of real-life robber Bill Miner, who switched from stagecoaches to trains after spending thirty-three years in jail. Director Borsos may be just a bit too laid back, but Farnsworth's charming and commanding performance makes up for that. The scene in which he watches THE GREAT TRAIN ROBBERY is a gem.▼

Greyfriars Bobby (1961) C-91m. **½ D: Don Chaffey. Donald Crisp, Laurence Naismith, Alex Mackenzie, Kay Walsh, Duncan Macrae, Gordon Jackson. British Disney film based on true story of a Skye terrier who became "neighborhood pet" in Edinburgh during 19th century through unusual circumstances. Great charm, fine performances offset by slow pacing. A remake of CHALLENGE TO LASSIE, which also features Crisp (who played the dog's master in the earlier film). ▼

Grey Gardens (1976) C-95m. *** D: David and Albert Maysles. Tasteless, suspect, but riveting documentary about Edith Bouvier Beale (79) and daughter Edie (57)—aunt and cousin of Jacqueline Onassis—filmed in their rotting, filthy 28-room mansion in East Hampton, N.Y., which was officially declared a health hazard. Fascinating for voyeurs, but film would have had more depth had we been given a better picture of mother and daughter in their youth.▼

Greystoke: The Legend of Tarzan, Lord of the Apes (1984) C-129m. *** D: Hugh Hudson. Christopher Lambert, Andie MacDowell, Ian Holm, Ralph Richardson, James Fox, Cheryl Campbell, Ian Charleson, Nigel Davenport. Retelling of Tarzan tale, liberally adapted from Edgar Rice Burroughs' original. Infant son of shipwrecked couple is raised by apes, discovered at manhood by a Belgian explorer, and returned to civilization—and his doting grandfather (Richardson, who's just wonderful in his final film performance). At its best in the jungle scenes, with Rick Baker's incredible makeup effects; more sluggish back in Britain, and hampered by all-too-obvious signs of prerelease cutting. Leading lady MacDowell's voice was dubbed by Glenn Close.▼

Gridlock (1980) C-100m. TVM D: James Frawley. Desi Arnaz, Jr., John Beck, Noah Beery, Rene Enriquez, Shelley Fabares, Phil Foster, James Gregory, Lisa Hartman, Michael Lerner, Rue McClanahan, Ed McMahon, Christopher Norris, Al Molinaro, Allen Sues, Vic Tayback, Abe Vigoda, Lyle Waggoner, Marcia Wallace, Howard Hesseman. Comic chaos involving a highway full of TV stars as the L.A. freeway system grinds to a halt following a series of freak accidents. Retitled THE GREAT AMERICAN TRAFFIC JAM. Average.▼

Griffin and Phoenix: A Love Story (1976) C-100m. TVM D: Daryl Duke. Peter Falk, Jill Clayburgh, John Lehne, Dorothy Tristan, Ben Hammer, John Harkins. Tearjerker about two doomed people sharing a brief but buoyant affair. The stars do wonders brightening a maudlin tale. Average.▼

Grim Reaper, The (1981-Italian) C-81m. *½ D: Joe D'Amato. Tisa Farrow, Saverio Vallone, Vanessa Steiger, George Eastman. Tourist Farrow and companions are stalked by killer on a Greek island. Trifling shocker.▼

Grip of the Strangler SEE: **Haunted Strangler, The**▼

Grisbi (1953-French) 94m. **½ D: Jacques Becker. Jean Gabin, Jeanne Moreau, Rene Dary, Lino Ventura, Dora Doll. Gabin is tough in unorthodox tale of Parisian underground, involving gold heist and its mysterious disappearance. Retitled: DON'T TOUCH THE LOOT.

Grissly's Millions (1944) 54m. **½ D: John English. Paul Kelly, Virginia Grey, Don Douglas, Elisabeth Risdon. Programmer involving murder of wealthy man and the typical manhunt for the killer; smoothly done.

Grissom Gang, The (1971) **C-127m.** ***
D: Robert Aldrich. Kim Darby, Scott Wilson, Irene Dailey, Tony Musante, Ralph Waite, Connie Stevens, Robert Lansing, Wesley Addy. Outlandish, extremely violent comic-book thriller set in the 1920s. Heiress Darby is kidnapped by family of drooling grotesques, whose leader (Wilson) starts to fall in love with her. Very funny if you appreciate the Aldrich sense of humor; otherwise, solid action fare. Remake of 1948 British film NO ORCHIDS FOR MISS BLANDISH.▼

Grizzly (1976) **C-92m.** ** D: William Girdler. Christopher George, Andrew Prine, Richard Jaeckel, Joan McCall, Joe Dorsey. OK rip-off of JAWS about an 18-foot, 2000-pound grizzly bear who launches series of attacks on campers in national park. Might be subtitled "Claws." Also known as KILLER GRIZZLY.▼

Groom Wore Spurs, The (1951) **80m.** **
D: Richard Whorf. Ginger Rogers, Jack Carson, Joan Davis, Stanley Ridges. Occasionally zesty comedy of attorney Rogers marrying cowboy actor Carson, divorcing him, but coming to his defense in criminal case.

Groove Tube, The (1974) **C-75m.** **½
D: Ken Shapiro. Ken Shapiro, Lane Sarasohn, Chevy Chase, Richard Belzer, Mary Mendham, Bill Kemmill. Sometimes funny, sometimes stupid collection of satirical episodes about television. Definitely has its heart in the right place, but a mixed bag. Originally X-rated, later trimmed; Chase's feature debut.▼

Gross Anatomy (1989) **C-107m.** **½ D: Thom Eberhardt. Matthew Modine, Daphne Zuniga, Christine Lahti, Todd Field, John Scott Clough, Alice Carter, Robert Desiderio, Zakes Mokae. So-so tale of doctor-in-training Modine, who doesn't take his studies as seriously as he should. Not bad, but not particularly distinguished; Lahti is wasted as the aspiring doctors' demanding instructor. Viewers who've attended medical school may appreciate this more.▼

Grounds for Marriage (1950) **91m.** **½
D: Robert Z. Leonard. Van Johnson, Kathryn Grayson, Paula Raymond, Barry Sullivan, Lewis Stone. Cutesy musicomedy of opera star Grayson and her ex-husband, physician Johnson.

Groundstar Conspiracy, The (1972-Canadian) **C-96m.** **½ D: Lamont Johnson. George Peppard, Michael Sarrazin, Christine Belford. When explosion smashes secret space project, espionage work first begins. Tightly made, but poor dialogue.▼

Ground Zero (1987-Australian) **C-109m.** *** D: Michael Pattinson, Bruce Myles. Colin Friels, Jack Thompson, Donald Pleasence, Natalie Bate, Simon Chilvers,

Neil Fitzpatrick, Bob Maza, Peter Cummins. Cameraman learns that his father may have died because he saw—and photographed—too much during British A-bomb testing in Australia in the 1950s. Exciting political paranoia thriller, though sluggish in spots. Pleasence is excellent in supporting role as hermitlike survivor of those tests. A fictional story based on factual events.▼

Group, The (1966) **C-150m.** *** D: Sidney Lumet. Candice Bergen, Joan Hackett, Elizabeth Hartman, Shirley Knight, Joanna Pettet, Mary-Robin Redd, Jessica Walter, Kathleen Widdoes, James Broderick, Larry Hagman, Richard Mulligan, Hal Holbrook. Uneven, but generally good adaptation of Mary McCarthy's high-class soap opera about eight graduates of Vassar-type college. Knight and Hackett stand out in excellent cast. Film debuts of Bergen, Hackett, Pettet, Widdoes, and Holbrook.▼

Group Marriage (1972) **C-85m.** **½ D: Stephanie Rothman. Victoria Vetri, Claudia Jennings, Aimee Eccles, Zack Taylor, Jeff Pomerantz, Jayne Kennedy, Milt Kamen. Engaging drive-in comedy with something to say. Group of young Californians sets up a communal housekeeping situation, gradually adding new members. Needless to say, the neighbors are less than thrilled. Nicely done, with most attractive cast.▼

Grunt! The Wrestling Movie (1985) **C-90m.** BOMB D: Allan Holzman. Jeff Dial, Robert Glaudini, Marilyn Dodds Farr, Greg Magic Schwartz. Would-be documentary spoof about a fabled wrestler named Mad Dog Joe De Curso; designed to cash in on 1980s wrestling mania lands with a thud. Ugh! ▼

Guadalcanal Diary (1943) **93m.** ***½ D: Lewis Seiler. Preston Foster, Lloyd Nolan, William Bendix, Richard Conte, Anthony Quinn, Richard Jaeckel. Richard Tregaskis' hot-off-the-wire account of Marines fighting for vital Pacific base becomes one of best WW2 actioners; large, competent cast.▼

Guardian, The (1984) **C-102m. TVM** D: David Greene. Martin Sheen, Louis Gossett, Jr., Arthur Hill, Tandy Cronyn, Maury Chaykin, Kate Lynch. Writers Richard Levinson and William Link have concocted a provocative, though ultimately flawed, what-price-personal-safety tale pitting ultraliberal apartment dweller Sheen against no-nonsense military type Gossett, who is hired as the building's security guard following a series of break-in murders. Made for cable. Above average.▼

Guardian, The (1990) **C-93m.** ** D: William Friedkin. Jenny Seagrove, Dwier Brown, Carey Lowell, Brad Hall, Miguel Ferrer, Natalia Nogulich, Pamela Brull, Gary Swanson. Yuppie couple hires a nanny for their newborn child, but we know there's something odd about her: she feeds babies to a tree in a nearby gully. Friedkin's first return to horror after THE EXORCIST has a few good scenes, but a ludicrous story and a humorless approach. Seagrove is very good in an almost unplayable role. Cowritten by the director from novel *The Nanny* by Dan Greenburg.

Guardsman, The (1931) 89m. *** D: Sidney Franklin. Alfred Lunt, Lynn Fontanne, Roland Young, ZaSu Pitts, Maude Eburne, Herman Bing. The Lunts' only starring film is charming tour de force from Molnar's comedy of jealous husband testing his wife's fidelity. Remade as THE CHOCOLATE SOLDIER and LILY IN LOVE.

Guerrillas in Pink Lace (1964) C-96m. *½ D: George Montgomery. George Montgomery, Valerie Varda, Roby Grace, Joan Shawlee. Poorly produced yarn filmed in Philippines about Montgomery and group of showgirls on the lam from Manila and the Japanese.

Guess Who's Coming to Dinner (1967) C-108m. *** D: Stanley Kramer. Spencer Tracy, Katharine Hepburn, Sidney Poitier, Katharine Houghton, Cecil Kellaway, Beah Richards, Roy E. Glenn, Sr., Virginia Christine. Glossy tale of mixed marriage as Houghton (Hepburn's real-life niece) brings home fiancé Poitier to meet her perplexed parents. Fluff is given strength by Oscar-winning Hepburn, and Tracy in his last film appearance. William Rose also took home an Oscar for his story and screenplay.▼

Guess Who's Sleeping in My Bed? (1973) C-74m. TVM D: Theodore Flicker. Barbara Eden, Dean Jones, Kenneth Mars, Susanne Benton, Reta Shaw, Todd Lookinland. Ex-husband too lazy to find work ingratiates his way into former wife's house, stays there with his family and all but ruins her sex life. Entertaining comedy with likable performances. Above average.

Guest, The (1964-British) 105m. *** D: Clive Donner. Alan Bates, Donald Pleasence, Robert Shaw. Derelict Pleasence invades the world of mentally ill Shaw and his sadistic brother Bates. Superior cast and superb performances, but claustrophobically directed by Donner. Screenplay by Harold Pinter, based on his play *The Caretaker*, which was also this film's title in Britain.

Guest in the House (1944) 121m. *** D: John Brahm. Anne Baxter, Ralph Bellamy, Aline MacMahon, Ruth Warrick, Scott McKay, Marie McDonald, Jerome Cowan, Margaret Hamilton, Percy Kilbride. Atmospheric, occasionally gripping melodrama about neurotic young Baxter and her effect on the family of her betrothed. Bellamy is extremely attractive in a rare

romantic lead, and Anne goes all out in this Eve Harrington–like characterization.▼

Guest Wife (1945) 90m. **½ D: Sam Wood. Claudette Colbert, Don Ameche, Dick Foran, Charles Dingle, Grant Mitchell, Wilma Francis. Breezy comedy depends on stars for flair; they do just fine, with Claudette posing as Ameche's wife to husband Foran's chagrin.▼

Guide for the Married Man, A (1967) C-89m. ***½ D: Gene Kelly. Walter Matthau, Inger Stevens, Robert Morse, Sue Ane Langdon, Claire Kelly, Elaine Devry; guest stars Lucille Ball, Jack Benny, Polly Bergen, Joey Bishop, Sid Caesar, Art Carney, Wally Cox, Jayne Mansfield, Hal March, Louis Nye, Carl Reiner, Phil Silvers, Terry-Thomas, Ben Blue, Ann Morgan Guilbert, Jeffrey Hunter, Marty Ingels, Sam Jaffe. Consistently funny, imaginative adult comedy of Morse trying to teach faithful husband Matthau the ABC's of adultery, with the aid of many guest stars who demonstrate Morse's theories. Joke of it all is that Matthau is married to gorgeous Inger Stevens!▼

Guide for the Married Woman, A (1978) C-100m. TVM D: Hy Averback. Cybill Shepherd, Charles Frank, Barbara Feldon, Eve Arden, George Gobel, Bill Dana, John Hillerman, Bonnie Franklin, John Byner, John Beradino, Mary Frances Crosby. There's a smile or two to be had as lots of familiar TV faces pop up to help daydreaming housewife Shepherd looking for some innocent romance to spice up her life. A belated, so-so follow-up by writer Frank Tarloff to his very funny A GUIDE FOR THE MARRIED MAN. Average.▼

Guilt of Janet Ames, The (1947) 83m. *** D: Henry Levin. Rosalind Russell, Melvyn Douglas, Sid Caesar, Betsy Blair, Nina Foch, Charles Cane, Harry Von Zell. Good casting highlights well-done film of Russell at the end of her rope when husband dies and she seeks the cause.

Guilty, The (1947) 70m. **½ D: John Reinhardt. Bonita Granville, Don Castle, Wally Cassell, Regis Toomey. At times engaging murder yarn; twin sisters clash over their love for Castle.

Guilty Bystander (1950) 92m. **½ D: Joseph Lerner. Zachary Scott, Faye Emerson, Mary Boland, Sam Levene, Kay Medford. Down-and-out ex-house detective finds new zest for life when estranged wife reports their child kidnapped.

Guilty Conscience (1985) C-100m. TVM D: David Greene. Anthony Hopkins, Blythe Danner, Swoosie Kurtz. Top-notch though talky three-person psychological drama crafted by Richard Levinson and William Link, dealing with a self-centered lawyer who debates with his alter ego about the ramifications in killing his haughty wife for his sexy mistress. Above average.

Guilty Hands (1931) **71m.** *** D: W. S. Van Dyke. Lionel Barrymore, Kay Francis, Madge Evans, William Bakewell, C. Aubrey Smith, Polly Moran, Alan Mowbray. Former D.A. Barrymore tells unscrupulous lothario Mowbray that he'll kill him—and get away with it—if he dares to go through with his plan to marry Lionel's daughter. First-rate whodunit-style drama with imaginative camerawork, a solid script, some real plot twists, and an unusually lively performance from Barrymore.

Guilty of Innocence: The Lenell Geter Story (1987) **C-100m.** TVM D: Richard T. Heffron. Dorian Harewood, Dabney Coleman, Paul Winfield, Hoyt Axton, Dennis Lipscomb, Debbi Morgan, Marshall Colt, Victor Love. Straight-ahead dramatization of the real-life story (as reported on *60 Minutes*) of a young black engineer from Dallas and his efforts to overturn the life sentence he received for a fast-food store armed robbery he did not commit. Average.

Guilty of Treason (1949) **86m.** **½ D: Felix E. Feist. Charles Bickford, Paul Kelly, Bonita Granville, Richard Derr. Splendidly acted account of the famed Cardinal Mindszenty trial in Hungary, marred by low production values.

Guilty or Innocent: The Sam Sheppard Murder Case (1975) **C-150m.** TVM D: Robert Michael Lewis. George Peppard, Barnard Hughes, Walter McGinn, William Windom, Nina Van Pallandt, Paul Fix, William Dozier, George Murdock, Claudette Nevins, Kathleen Crawford, John Crawford. Peppard is famed Cleveland osteopathic surgeon convicted in 1954 of the murder of his wife, then retried twelve years later. Striking performance by McGinn as F. Lee Bailey, the flamboyant lawyer whose defense in retrial of Sheppard made him courtroom superstar. Above average.

Gulag (1985-British) **C-129m.** TVM D: Roger Young. David Keith, Malcolm McDowell, David Suchet, Warren Clarke, John McEnery. An American sportscaster is railroaded by the KGB into a Russian labor camp. Harrowing prison drama similar to COMING OUT OF THE ICE. Made for cable. Average.▼

Gulliver's Travels (1939) **C-74m.** **½ D: Dave Fleischer. Singing voices of Lanny Ross, Jessica Dragonette. Max Fleischer's feature-length cartoon version of Jonathan Swift tale suffers from weak scripting, never getting audience involved in story. Town-crier Gabby is obnoxious, but he's got film's most memorable song, "All's Well."▼

Gulliver's Travels (1977-British-Belgian) **C-80m.** *½ D: Peter R. Hunt. Richard Harris, Catherine Schell, Norman Shelley, Meredith Edwards, voices of Julian Glover, Murray Melvin, Bessie Love, others. Un-

imaginative retelling of the Jonathan Swift classic. Part live-action, part animation; the songs are the most forgettable since LOST HORIZON.▼

Gulliver's Travels Beyond the Moon (1966-Japanese) **C-78m.** ** D: Yoshio Kuroda. OK animated feature has Gulliver and companions going into outer space; acceptable kiddie fare.

Gumball Rally, The (1976) **C-107m.** *** D: Chuck Bail. Michael Sarrazin, Tim McIntire, Raul Julia, Normann Burton, Gary Busey, Nicholas Pryor, Susan Flannery, Steven Keats, J. Pat O'Malley, Harvey Jason, Joanne Nail, Vaughn Taylor, Tricia O'Neil, Med Flory. First of the cross-country road-race comedies is still the only good one, with genuinely funny characters, great cars, and loads of cartoonlike action. Julia steals the film as lecherous Italian who throws out his rear-view mirror because "what's behind me is not important." Ripped off that same year by CANNONBALL, then later by the CANNONBALL RUN series.▼

Gumshoe (1972-British) **C-88m.** **½ D: Stephen Frears. Albert Finney, Billie Whitelaw, Frank Finlay, Janice Rule, Carolyn Seymour. Whimsical crime-comedy of small-time British vaudevillian who has seen too many Bogart films and decides to play private eye. Finney also produced.▼

Gun, The (1974) **C-78m.** TVM D: John Badham. Stephen Elliott, Jean Le Bouvier, Wallace Rooney, David Huffman, Pepe Serna, Edith Diaz. Odyssey of an American handgun—like the legendary overcoat in TALES OF MANHATTAN—forms this episodic story sketching the dramatic changes in the lives of its various owners. Absorbing film with no stars, just sterling character actors, gripping Richard Levinson-William Link script, and taut direction. Above average.

Gun and the Pulpit, The (1974) **C-78m.** TVM D: Daniel Petrie. Marjoe Gortner, Slim Pickens, David Huddleston, Geoffrey Lewis, Estelle Parsons, Pamela Sue Martin, Jeff Corey. Evangelist-turned-actor Marjoe is a gunslinger who masquerades as a preacher and fights for law and order in both guises. Average.

Gun Battle at Monterey (1957) **67m.** *½ D: Carl G. Hittleman, Sidney A. Franklin, Jr. Sterling Hayden, Pamela Duncan, Mary Beth Hughes, Lee Van Cleef, Byron Foulger, Ted de Corsia. Unremarkable oater with stern Hayden the gunslinger out for revenge against former friend.

Gun Belt (1953) **C-77m.** **½ D: Ray Nazarro. George Montgomery, Tab Hunter, Helen Westcott, Jack Elam. Notorious outlaw trying to go straight is implicated in crime by his old gang.

Gun Brothers (1956) **79m.** ** D: Sidney Salkow. Buster Crabbe, Ann Robinson,

Neville Brand, Michael Ansara. Innocuous Western of two brothers, one who becomes a rancher, the other an outlaw who wants to go straight.

Gun Crazy (1949) 86m. ***½ D: Joseph H. Lewis. Peggy Cummins, John Dall, Berry Kroeger, Morris Carnovsky, Annabel Shaw, Harry Lewis, Nedrick Young. Knockout of a sleeper in the BONNIE AND CLYDE tradition, stylishly (and sometimes startlingly) directed. Cummins is femme fatale who leads gun-crazy Dall into life of crime. Story and screenplay by MacKinlay Kantor. Also known as DEADLY IS THE FEMALE.

Gun Duel in Durango (1957) 73m. ** D: Sidney Salkow. George Montgomery, Steve Brodie, Bobby Clark, Mary Treen. Montgomery must wipe out his outlaw gang before he can reform. Retitled: DUEL IN DURANGO.

Gunfight, A (1971) C-90m. **½ D: Lamont Johnson. Kirk Douglas, Johnny Cash, Jane Alexander, Raf Vallone, Karen Black, Keith Carradine. Off-beat western about two aging gunfighters who meet and decide to sell tickets for a winner-take-all final shootout. Cash is good in his acting debut.▼

Gunfight at Comanche Creek (1964) C-90m. *½ D: Frank McDonald. Audie Murphy, Colleen Miller, Ben Cooper, DeForest Kelley, Jan Merlin, John Hubbard. Undistinguished Western with detective Murphy infiltrating a gang of outlaws who force wanted men to participate in their robberies and then kill them to collect reward money.

Gunfight at Dodge City, The (1959) C-81m. ** D: Joseph M. Newman. Joel McCrea, Julie Adams, John McIntire, Nancy Gates, Richard Anderson, James Westerfield. McCrea plays Bat Masterson, who cleans up gangster-ridden town with ironic results.

Gunfight at the O.K. Corral (1957) C-122m. *** D: John Sturges. Burt Lancaster, Kirk Douglas, Rhonda Fleming, Jo Van Fleet, John Ireland, Lee Van Cleef, Frank Faylen, Kenneth Tobey, DeForest Kelley, Earl Holliman, Dennis Hopper, Martin Milner, Olive Carey. Stimulating Western filled with tense action sequences in recreation of Doc Holliday-Wyatt Earp battle with Clanton gang. Written by Leon Uris. Frankie Laine sings title song.▼

Gunfighter, The (1950) 84m. ***½ D: Henry King. Gregory Peck, Helen Westcott, Millard Mitchell, Jean Parker, Karl Malden, Skip Homeier, Verna Felton, Ellen Corby, Richard Jaeckel, Alan Hale, Jr. Peck is most impressive as gunslinger trying to overcome his bloody past. A top-notch Western scripted by William Bowers and William Sellers, from a story by Bowers and Andre de Toth. Catch this one!▼

Gunfighters (1947) C-87m. **½ D: George Waggner. Randolph Scott, Barbara Britton,

Dorothy Hart, Bruce Cabot, Charles Grapewin, Forrest Tucker. Strictly average story of gunfighter who vows never again to spill blood. Good cast, but there must be fifty like this one.

Gunfighters, The (1987-Canadian) C-100m. TVM D: Clay Borris. Art Hindle, Reiner Schoene, Tony Addabbo, George Kennedy, Michael Kane, Lori Hallier. Lackluster Canadian-made oater pitting an uninteresting trio of related individualists against a bullying empire builder. A pilot to a proposed series. Below average.

Gunfight in Abilene (1967) C-86m. **½ D: William Hale. Bobby Darin, Emily Banks, Leslie Nielsen, Michael Sarrazin. Undistinguished post-Civil War account of gun-shy Darin, town sheriff, taking up arms against outlaws.

Gunfire (1950) 60m. *½ D: William Berke. Don Barry, Robert Lowery, Wally Vernon, Pamela Blake. Flabby Western cashing in on the Jesse James legend, as a man resembling Frank James commits a series of robberies.

Gunfire at Indian Gap (1957) 70m. *½ D: Joseph Kane. Vera Ralston, Anthony George, George Macready, John Doucette, Barry Kelley, Glenn Strange. Exactly what the title implies, with lovely Ralston to boot.

Gun for a Coward (1957) C-73m. **½ D: Abner Biberman. Fred MacMurray, Jeffrey Hunter, Janice Rule, Chill Wills, Dean Stockwell, Josephine Hutchinson. MacMurray is rancher with two younger brothers, each with contrasting personalities, leading to predictable results.

Gun Fury (1953) C-83m. **½ D: Raoul Walsh. Rock Hudson, Donna Reed, Phil Carey, Lee Marvin, Neville Brand, Leo Gordon. Hudson goes after men who have kidnapped his fiancée (Reed); formidable villainy, beautiful Arizona locations. Originally shown in 3-D.▼

Gunga Din (1939) 117m. **** D: George Stevens. Cary Grant, Victor McLaglen, Douglas Fairbanks, Jr., Joan Fontaine, Sam Jaffe, Eduardo Ciannelli, Montagu Love, Abner Biberman, Robert Coote. *The* Hollywood action-adventure yarn, vaguely based on Rudyard Kipling's famous poem, about three soldier-comrades in 19th century India who battle the savage Thugee when they aren't busy carousing and getting into trouble. Water boy Jaffe saves the day. Splendid comic adventure whose story is credited to Ben Hecht and Charles MacArthur (who based the relationships of the central characters on the same marriage/rivalry device used in *The Front Page*); scripted by Joel Sayre and Fred Guiol. For years most prints ran 96m., until the film was archivally restored. Also shown in computer-colored version.▼

Gung Ho! (1943) 88m. **½ D: Ray Enright. Randolph Scott, Grace McDonald, Alan Curtis, Noah Beery Jr., J. Carrol Naish, David Bruce, Robert Mitchum, Sam Levene. Typical WW2 action film is marked by outrageous jingoism, celebrating the bloodthirsty misfits of the ''gung ho'' squadron as great American patriots. A jaw-dropping experience. Also shown in computer-colored version.▼

Gung Ho (1986) C-111m. *** D: Ron Howard. Michael Keaton, Gedde Watanabe, George Wendt, Mimi Rogers, John Turturro, Soh Yamamura, Sab Shimono, Clint Howard, Michelle Johnson. Cocky Keaton convinces Japanese company to reopen shuttered auto factory in his economically depressed hometown—but doesn't count on culture clash that follows. Extremely lightweight but entertaining comedy from the writing-directing team responsible for NIGHT SHIFT and SPLASH. Later a TV series.▼

Gun Glory (1957) C-89m. ** D: Roy Rowland. Stewart Granger, Rhonda Fleming, Chill Wills, James Gregory. Granger is reformed gunslinger rejected by his community until outlaw rampage allows him to redeem himself.

Gun Hawk, The (1963) C-92m. **½ D: Edward Ludwig. Rory Calhoun, Rod Cameron, Ruta Lee, John Litel, Rod Lauren, Lane Bradford. Outlaw Cameron attempts to reform Lauren, who's heading for criminal life.

Gun in the House, A (1981) C-100m. TVM D: Ivan Nagy. Sally Struthers, David Ackroyd, Dick Anthony Williams, Jeffrey Tambor, Allen Rich, Millie Perkins. Woman is prosecuted for the handgun murder of an intruder in her house. Average.▼

Gunman's Walk (1958) C-97m. *** D: Phil Karlson. Van Heflin, Tab Hunter, Kathryn Grant, James Darren. Rancher Heflin tries to train sons Hunter and Darren to be respectable citizens, but clashing personalities cause outburst of violence. Tight-knit Western.

Gunmen from Laredo (1959) C-67m. BOMB D: Wallace MacDonald. Robert Knapp, Jana Davi, Walter Coy, Paul Birch, Don C. Harvey. Hackneyed hunt-the-real-killer Western.

Gunmen of the Rio Grande (1965-Italian) C-86m. ** D: Tulio Demicheli. Guy Madison, Madeleine LeBeau, Carolyn Davys, Massimo Serato. Madison portrays Wyatt Earp, who helps heroine ward off schemes of grasping mine owner.

Gun Moll SEE: **Jigsaw** (1949)▼

Gunn (1967) C-94m. *½ D: Blake Edwards. Craig Stevens, Laura Devon, Edward Asner, Sherry Jackson, Helen Traubel, Albert Paulsen. Unsuccessful attempt to recapture flavor of *Peter Gunn* TV series; Herschel Bernardi, Lola Albright sorely missed, along with quiet understatement and wit that made it memorable. New

story is tasteless, violent whodunit involving curious madam. Screenplay by Edwards and William Peter Blatty. Revived again for TV in 1989 as PETER GUNN.

Gunpoint (1966) C-86m. ** D: Earl Bellamy. Audie Murphy, Joan Staley, Warren Stevens, Edgar Buchanan. Murphy as sheriff gathers a posse to catch outlaw gang who have kidnapped saloon girl.

Gun Riders (1970) C-98m. BOMB D: Al Adamson. Jim Davis, Scott Brady, Robert Dix, John Carradine. Ruthless gunman terrorizes settlers one more time, but his heroic counterpart is there to stop him. Cast is full of Western veterans, but they're not much help. Also known as FIVE BLOODY GRAVES and LONELY MAN.▼

Gunrunner, The (1984-Canadian) C-92m. *½ D: Nardo Castillo. Kevin Costner, Sara Botsford, Paul Soles, Gerard Parkes, Ron Lea, Mitch Martin, Larry Lewis, Aline Van Dine, Ruth Dahan. Murky gangster melodrama about idealistic Costner, seeking guns for Chinese rebellion during the 1920s, returning to native Canada and becoming involved with liquor smugglers. Tedious, to say the least, this film was (understandably) shelved until Costner's stardom prompted a 1989 video release . . . but even he isn't very good in this one.▼

Gun Runners, The (1958) 83m. ** D: Don Siegel. Audie Murphy, Eddie Albert, Patricia Owens, Everett Sloane, Jack Elam. Murphy is involved with gun-smuggling to Cuba; standard plot stolen from TO HAVE AND HAVE NOT.

Guns at Batasi (1964-British) 103m. **½ D: John Guillermin. Richard Attenborough, Jack Hawkins, Mia Farrow, Flora Robson, John Leyton. Acting is all in this intelligent if predictable account of British military life in present-day Africa.▼

Guns for San Sebastian (1968) C-111m. ** D: Henri Verneuil. Anthony Quinn, Anjanette Comer, Charles Bronson, Sam Jaffe, Silvia Pinal. Quinn plays a popular bandit who helps Mexican village defeat some Yaqui Indians after he is mistaken for a priest, but his personal magnetism isn't enough to combat ridiculous script.

Guns, Girls and Gangsters (1959) 70m. ** D: Edward L. Cahn. Mamie Van Doren, Gerald Mohr, Lee Van Cleef, Grant Richards, Elaine Edwards, John Baer, Carlo Fiore, Paul Fix, W. Beal Wong. Classic 1950s trash, with the pneumatic Mamie in her prime as a Vegas nightclub singer drawn into scheme to rip off an armored truck carrying casino winnings. Vigorous direction and diverting cast make this more enjoyable than expected.

Gunsight Ridge (1957) 85m. ** D: Francis D. Lyon. Joel McCrea, Mark Stevens, Joan Weldon, Addison Richards, Slim Pickens. Townsfolk finally band together to rid themselves of outlaws; OK Western.

Gunslinger, The (1956) **C-83m.** *½ D: Roger Corman. John Ireland, Beverly Garland, Allison Hayes, Martin Kingsley. Strange little Western of female marshal trying to maintain law and order in outlaw-ridden town.▼

Gunsmoke (1953) **C-79m.** **½ D: Nathan Juran. Audie Murphy, Susan Cabot, Paul Kelly, Charles Drake, Jack Kelly. Compact Western with Murphy reforming to run a ranch and marry his employer's daughter.

Gunsmoke in Tucson (1958) **C-80m.** **½ D: Thomas Carr. Mark Stevens, Forrest Tucker, Gale Robbins, Gail Kobe, Bill Henry. Sheriff vs. outlaw brother in Arizona territory; not bad.

Gunsmoke: Return to Dodge (1987) **C-100m. TVM** D: Vincent McEveety. James Arness, Amanda Blake, Buck Taylor, Fran Ryan, Earl Holliman, Steve Forrest. Matt Dillon and Miss Kitty meet up again in Dodge City 12 years after the end of the long-running series that spanned two television decades. It's nice to greet old friends in the agreeable oater that this proves to be, involving much of the original talent, although Chester and Doc are sorely missed. Script by Jim Byrnes. Followed by GUNSMOKE: THE LAST APACHE. Above average.

Gunsmoke: The Last Apache (1990) **C-100m. TVM** D: Charles Correll. James Arness, Richard Kiley, Michael Learned, Amy Stock-Poynton, Geoffrey Lewis, Joe Lara, Joaquin Martinez, Hugh O'Brian. Matt Dillon goes in search of the 21-year-old daughter he never knew, who has been kidnapped by Apaches. This second GUNSMOKE movie is a patent reworking of Arness mentor John Wayne's THE SEARCHERS, with Learned recreating a role she played years ago on the *Gunsmoke* series as Dillon's one-time love—the missing girl's mother. Average.

Guns of a Stranger (1973) **C-91m.** BOMB D: Robert Hinkle. Marty Robbins, Chill Wills, Dovie Beams, Steve Tackett. Robbins is The Drifter, a singing cowboy, in super-boring family film. Paging Gene Autry.

✓**Guns of August, The** (1964) **99m.** *** D: Nathan Kroll. Straightforward documentary about World War I spans the period from Edward VII's funeral (1910) through the final Armistice eight years later. Highly competent, if not exceptional, adaptation of Barbara Tuchman's best-seller utilizes lots of rare combat footage from the time. Worth a look.▼

Guns of Darkness (1962) **95m.** **½ D: Anthony Asquith. David Niven, Leslie Caron, David Opatoshu, James Robertson Justice, Eleanor Summerfield, Ian Hunter.

Civilized drama of Niven searching for life's meaning, set in South America.

Guns of Fort Petticoat, The (1957) **C-82m.** *** D: George Marshall. Audie Murphy, Kathryn Grant, Hope Emerson, Jeff Donnell, Isobel Elsom. Most enjoyable Western, with Army deserter Murphy supervising a group of Texas women in the art of warfare against pending Indian attack.

Guns of Navarone, The (1961) **C-157m.** ***½ D: J. Lee Thompson. Gregory Peck, David Niven, Anthony Quinn, Stanley Baker, Anthony Quayle, James Darren, Irene Papas, Gia Scala, James Robertson Justice, Richard Harris. Explosive action film about Allied commandos during WW2 plotting to destroy German guns; high-powered adventure throughout this first-rate production, highlighted by Oscar-winning special effects. Script by Carl Foreman from the Alistair MacLean novel. Sequel: FORCE 10 FROM NAVARONE.▼

Guns of the Black Witch (1961-Italian) **C-83m.** ** D: Domenico Paolella. Don Megowan, Silvana Pampanini, Emma Danieli, Livio Lorenzon. Tepid account of pirate leader Megowan out to avenge his father's death; Pampanini his love interest. Set in 17th-century Caribbean.

Guns of the Magnificent Seven (1969) **C-106m.** **½ D: Paul Wendkos. George Kennedy, Monte Markham, James Whitmore, Reni Santoni, Bernie Casey, Joe Don Baker, Scott Thomas, Michael Ansara, Fernando Rey. Third time out, the "Seven" plot to free Mexican revolutionary leader from a well-guarded fortress. Nothing new, but well done, with plenty of action.▼

Guns of the Timberland (1960) **C-91m.** **½ D: Robert D. Webb. Alan Ladd, Jeanne Crain, Gilbert Roland, Frankie Avalon. Pat telling of loggers vs. townpeople.

Guns, Sin and Bathtub Gin SEE: **Lady in Red, The**▼

Gun That Won the West, The (1955) **C-71m.** ** D: William Castle. Dennis Morgan, Paula Raymond, Richard Denning, Robert Bice. Harmless Grade-B Western of cavalry's use of Springfield rifles to put down Indian uprising.

Gun the Man Down (1956) **78m.** ** D: Andrew V. McLaglen. James Arness, Angie Dickinson, Robert Wilke, Emile Meyer. Wounded outlaw swears vengeance on cohorts who left him during holdup. Retitled: ARIZONA MISSION.

Guru, The (1969) **C-112m.** ** D: James Ivory. Michael York, Rita Tushingham, Utpal Dutt, Saeed Jaffrey, Mudhur Jaffrey. Sincere but uninvolving story of rock star York who goes to India to learn sitar, meditation from guru Dutt. Director Ivory dwells on Indian lifestyle, settings; Tushingham provides welcome lighter moments in slow-moving film.

Gus (1976) **C-96m.** *** D: Vincent Mc-

Eveety. Edward Asner, Don Knotts, Gary Grimes, Tim Conway, Liberty Williams, Dick Van Patten, Dick Butkus. Football-kicking mule catapults a last-place team to victory; crooks try to kidnap Gus with usual results, including slapstick chase through a supermarket. Entertaining Disney comedy.▼

Gus Brown and Midnight Brewster (1985) **C-75m. TVM** D: James Fargo. John Schneider, Ron Glass, Teri Copley, Scoey Mitchlll, Faye Hauser, Harvey Vernon. Mildly amusing period piece about a pair of returning G.I. buddies—a hayseed and a big-city hustler—out to make their fortune by racing greyhounds. Pilot for a prospective series. Average.

Guts and Glory: The Rise and Fall of Oliver North (1989) **C-200m. TVM** D: Mike Robc. David Keith, Annette O'Toole, Barnard Hughes, Peter Boyle, Amy Stock-Poynton, Bryan Clark, Donald Craig. Straightforward account of the life and career of Oliver North, from the beginnings of his military career through his indictment for involvement in the Iran-Contra scandal in Washington, D.C. Attempt at telling a "balanced" story about this controversial figure doesn't come off. Originally shown in two parts. Average.

Guyana: Cult of the Damned (1980-Mexican-Spanish-Panamanian) **C-90m.** *½ D: Rene Cardona, Jr. Stuart Whitman, Gene Barry, John Ireland, Joseph Cotten, Bradford Dillman, Jennifer Ashley, Yvonne De Carlo. Not easy to turn the awesomeness of the Jonestown tragedy—where cult followers committed mass suicide—into lackluster drama, but that's what they've done here.

Guyana Tragedy: The Story of Jim Jones (1980) **C-192m. TVM** D: William A. Graham. Powers Boothe, Ned Beatty, Irene Cara, Veronica Cartwright, Rosalind Cash, Brad Dourif, Meg Foster, Diane Ladd, Randy Quaid, Ron O'Neal, Diana Scarwid, Madge Sinclair, LeVar Burton, James Earl Jones, Colleen Dewhurst. Gripping recreation of the late '70s tragedy in which more than 900 cult followers of Rev. Jim Jones (played with magnetism by Boothe) committed mass suicide in a jungle clearing. Kudos to Beatty, as Congressman Leo J. Ryan, to Jones, in a riveting cameo as Father Divine, and to the huge cast. Boothe won an Emmy for his performance. Script by Ernest Tidyman. Above average.▼

Guy Called Caesar, A (1962-British) **62m.** *½ D: Frank Marshall. Conrad Phillips, George Moon, Phillip O'Flynn, Maureen Toal. Sloppy account of gangsters on the loose in England, with the inevitable showdown with cops.

Guy Named Joe, A (1943) **120m.** **½ D: Victor Fleming. Spencer Tracy, Irene Dunne, Van Johnson, Ward Bond, James Gleason, Lionel Barrymore, Barry Nelson,

Esther Williams, Don DeFore. Good cast flounders in meandering fantasy about WW2 pilot Tracy coming back to Earth to give young serviceman Johnson a hand in his romance with Tracy's girlfriend Dunne. Remade in 1989 as ALWAYS.▼

Guys and Dolls (1955) **C-150m.** *** D: Joseph L. Mankiewicz. Frank Sinatra, Marlon Brando, Jean Simmons, Vivian Blaine, Stubby Kaye, B. S. Pully, Veda Ann Borg, Sheldon Leonard, Regis Toomey. Lavish Hollywoodization of classic Broadway musical based on Damon Runyon's colorful characters with Blaine, Kaye, Pully, and Johnny Silver reprising their stage performances and Brando making a not-bad musical debut as gambler Sky Masterson. Tuneful Frank Loesser score includes "If I Were a Bell," "Luck Be a Lady," Blaine's memorable "Adelaide's Lament," and Stubby's showstopping "Sit Down, You're Rockin' the Boat." ▼

Guy Who Came Back, The (1951) **91m.** ** D: Joseph M. Newman. Paul Douglas, Linda Darnell, Joan Bennett, Don DeFore, Zero Mostel. Cast is above such material but does well by it: ex-football star tries to "find himself."

Guy With a Grin SEE No Time for Comedy

Gymkata (1985) **C-90m.** BOMB D: Robert Clouse. Kurt Thomas, Tetchie Agbayani, Richard Norton, Edward Bell. Champion gymnast Thomas stars in this silly martial-arts potboiler, shot in Yugoslavia by the folks who brought you ENTER THE DRAGON. Amateurish stuff, based on Dan Tyler Moore's novel, *The Terrible Game.*▼

Gypsy (1962) **C-149m.** *** D: Mervyn LeRoy. Rosalind Russell, Natalie Wood, Karl Malden, Paul Wallace, Betty Bruce, Parley Baer, Ann Jillian. Entertaining screen version of bittersweet Broadway musical about the ultimate stage mother, Mama Rose, and her daughters Baby June (Havoc) and Gypsy Rose Lee. Can't lose with that Stephen Sondheim–Jule Styne score, including "Everything's Coming Up Roses," "Let Me Entertain You," "Small World" (though "Together, Wherever We Go" was cut from the film, alas).▼

Gypsy and the Gentleman, The (1958-British) **C-107m.** **½ D: Joseph Losey. Melina Mercouri, Keith Michell, Patrick McGoohan, Flora Robson. Mercouri as fiery gypsy makes a spicy drama of her love affair with a member of the nobility.

Gypsy Colt (1954) **C-72m.** **½ D: Andrew Marton. Donna Corcoran, Ward Bond, Frances Dee, Larry Keating. Tender little film of faithful horse who returns to mistress after parents have sold it to racing stable. Remake of LASSIE COME HOME.

Gypsy Fury (1951-Swedish-French) **63m.**

** D: Christian-Jaque. Viveca Lindfors, Christopher Kent, Romney Brent, Johnny Chabot, Lauritz Falk. Fable about gypsy and the aristocratic lover who gives up all to marry her.

Gypsy Girl (1966-British) **C-102m.** **½ D: John Mills. Hayley Mills, Ian McShane, Laurence Naismith, Geoffrey Bayldon. Brooding account of backward Hayley Mills finding her first romance with McShane; atmospheric but meandering. Originally titled SKY WEST AND CROOKED.

Gypsy Moths, The (1969) **C-110m.** *** D: John Frankenheimer. Burt Lancaster, Deborah Kerr, Gene Hackman, Scott Wilson, Bonnie Bedelia, William Windom, Sheree North. Story of three skydivers in Kansas captures the Midwest well; Kerr, Wilson and Bedelia help raise potential soap opera to the level of "personal drama."

Gypsy Wildcat (1944) **C-75m.** ** D: Roy William Neill. Maria Montez, Jon Hall, Nigel Bruce, Leo Carrillo, Gale Sondergaard, Douglass Dumbrille. Lowbrow saga of princess raised by gypsies; colorful, splashy, but routine. James M. Cain was one of the writers!

Hadley's Rebellion (1984) **C-96m.** ** D: Fred Walton. Griffin O'Neal, William Devane, Charles Durning, Adam Baldwin, Lisa Lucas. Another teenage-problem picture, this one centering on wrestling-obsessed O'Neal. While it doesn't exploit its characters, it's still bland and superficial.▼

Hail SEE: **Hail to the Chief** ▼

Hail! Hail! Rock 'n' Roll SEE: **Chuck Berry Hail! Hail! Rock 'n' Roll**▼

Hail, Hero! (1969) **C-97m.** *½ D: David Miller. Michael Douglas, Arthur Kennedy, Teresa Wright, John Larch, Louise Latham, Charles Drake, Peter Strauss, Deborah Winters, Virginia Christine, John Qualen, Carmen Zapata. Talky, overblown drama about a well-scrubbed hippie (Douglas) who confronts his family as he sorts out his feelings about Vietnam war. Notable only as screen debuts for Douglas and Strauss, and a rare film contribution by musician Gordon Lightfoot, who composed and sings two songs. Originally 100m.▼

Hail, Mafia (1965) **89m.** **½ D: Raoul Levy. Henry Silva, Jack Klugman, Eddie Constantine, Elsa Martinelli, Micheline Presle. Fairly interesting melodrama about hired killers going after a witness to gangland mayhem; film has some good European players and nice photography by Raoul Coutard.

Hail Mary (1985-French-Swiss) **C-107m.** *½ D: Jean-Luc Godard. Myriem Roussel, Thierry Rode, Philippe Lacoste, Manon Anderson, Juliette Binoche. Boring, overblown updating of the story of Christ's birth, with Mary a student/basketball player/

gas station attendant and Joseph her cabdriver boyfriend; although still a virgin, she finds herself pregnant. This film sparked much controversy and was even condemned by the Pope; however, all the fuss was much ado about very little. A variety of running times have been credited to this film, so beware; has been screened with THE BOOK OF MARY, an infinitely superior featurette about a girl and her bickering parents, directed by Godard associate Anne-Marie Mieville.▼

Hail the Conquering Hero (1944) **101m.** **** D: Preston Sturges. Eddie Bracken, Ella Raines, Raymond Walburn, William Demarest, Bill Edwards, Elizabeth Patterson, Jimmy Conlin, Franklin Pangborn, Jack Norton, Paul Porcasi, Al Bridge. Frail Bracken, rejected by army, is mistaken for war hero by home town. Satirical Sturges at his best, with Demarest and Pangborn stealing much of the proceedings.

Hail to the Chief (1973) **C-85m.** **½ D: Fred Levinson. Dan Resin, Richard B. Shull, Dick O'Neill, Joseph Sirola, Patricia Ripley, Gary Sandy, Willard Waterman. Paranoid President Resin gleefully becomes dictator of the land. Good cast and some hilarious bits—but the result is not as funny as it could be. Filmed in 1970. Also known as HAIL and WASHINGTON, B.C.▼

Hair (1979) **C-121m.** **½ D: Milos Forman. John Savage, Treat Williams, Beverly D'Angelo, Annie Golden, Dorsey Wright, Don Dacus, Cheryl Barnes, Nicholas Ray, Charlotte Rae, Miles Chapin. James Rado-Gerome Ragni-Galt MacDermot's hit musical play celebrated the 60s as the Age of Aquarius; unfortunately, it's now a period piece and its impact considerably muffled. Story of straitlaced midwesterner who falls in with N.Y. hippies has exciting musical moments, but doesn't hang together. Choreography by Twyla Tharp. Among the singers: Nell Carter, Melba Moore, Ellen Foley, and Ronnie Dyson.▼

Hairspray (1988) **C-96m.** *** D: John Waters. Sonny Bono, Ruth Brown, Divine (Harris Glenn Milstead), Colleen Fitzpatrick, Michael St. Gerard, Debbie Harry, Ricki Lake, Leslie Ann Powers, Jerry Stiller, Shawn Thompson, Pia Zadora, Ric Ocasek, John Waters. Shock/schlock merchant Waters goes PG, with irresistible nostalgia satire about the integration of a TV teen dance program in 1962 Baltimore. "Name" performances include Harry as the shellac-haired mother of a deposed local celebrity, Zadora as a pot-smoking Bohemian, Brown as the owner of an r & b record store, and director Waters as the deranged psychiatrist. Loses steam toward the end, but still fun. Rich sound track mixes chestnuts and deservedly unearthed oldies.▼

Hairy Ape, The (1944) **90m.** ** D: Alfred Santell. William Bendix, Susan Hayward, John Loder, Alan Napier, Dorothy Comingore, Eddie Kane. One-note drama of bestial ship stoker Bendix's obsession with wealthy, bitchy passenger Hayward. Disappointing version of Eugene O'Neill play.▼

Half a Hero (1953) **71m.** ** D: Don Weis. Red Skelton, Jean Hagen, Charles Dingle, Willard Waterman, Mary Wickes, Polly Bergen. Subdued Skelton vehicle written by Max Shulman casts him in situation-comedy mold, as N.Y. magazine writer who tries suburban life for background on story. Pretty bland.

Half Angel (1951) **C-77m.** **½ D: Richard Sale. Loretta Young, Joseph Cotten, Cecil Kellaway, Jim Backus. Pleasant comedy of Young blessed with sleepwalking troubles, leading to romantic complications.

Half A Sixpence (1967) **C-148m.** *½ D: George Sidney. Tommy Steele, Julia Foster, Penelope Horner, Cyril Ritchard, Grover Dale. Boisterous but cardboard musical based on show adapted from H. G. Wells' *Kipps*, about draper's assistant who inherits fortune, tries to crash society. Colorfully filmed in England, but totally without charm.

Half-Breed, The (1952) **C-81m.** ** D: Stuart Gilmore. Robert Young, Janis Carter, Jack Buetel, Barton MacLane, Reed Hadley, Porter Hall. Unscrupulous profiteer incites Apaches to attack white settlers in this predictable Western.

Half-Human (1955-Japanese) **70m.** *½ D: Inoshiro Honda, Kenneth Crane. John Carradine, Morris Ankrum, Russ Thorson, Robert Karns. Americans Carradine and Ankrum are spliced into Japanese film about an abominable snowmanlike monster and his son(!). There are indications that the original Japanese film might be OK. This version isn't. Almost no dubbing, just Carradine's narration.▼

Half Moon Street (1986) **C-90m.** BOMB D: Bob Swaim. Michael Caine, Sigourney Weaver, Keith Buckley, Patrick Kavanagh, Nadim Sawalha, Angus MacInnes. Intriguing premise has Weaver playing a Ph.D researcher by day and glorified call girl by night, Caine a British diplomat who becomes an extra special client. Sounds as if it can't miss, but is worthless on every level; perennially fresh Weaver gives the first stilted performance of her career. Adapted from *Doctor Slaughter,* the first half of Paul Theroux's two-part novella *Half Moon Street.* ▼

Half-Naked Truth, The (1932) **77m.** *** D: Gregory LaCava. Lupe Velez, Lee Tracy, Eugene Pallette, Frank Morgan. Delightful comedy about wiseguy carnival pitchman (Tracy) scheming to make Velez an instant celebrity; plenty of laughs, and wonderful performance by Morgan as neurotic Ziegfeld-ish producer.

Half Shot at Sunrise (1930) **78m.** **½ D: Paul Sloane. Bert Wheeler, Robert Woolsey, Edna May Oliver, Dorothy Lee, George MacFarlane. Pretty funny Wheeler and Woolsey comedy (their first starring vehicle) has them as WWI soldiers AWOL in Paris and featured in a variety of misogynistic episodes as the military police close in. Best of all: the mock ballet. ▼

Half Slave, Half Free SEE: **Solomon Northrup's Odyssey** ▼

Halfway House, The (1943-British) **95m.** **½ D: Basil Dearden. Mervyn Johns, Glynis Johns, Francoise Rosay, Tom Walls, Alfred Drayton, Sally Ann Howes. Pleasant but low-key fantasy of disparate people brought together at mysterious country inn run by quiet but all-seeing Johns and his daughter.

Hallelujah (1929) **106m.** ***½ D: King Vidor. Daniel L. Haynes, Nina Mae McKinney, William Fountaine, Everett McGarrity, Victoria Spivey. King Vidor's early talkie triumph, a stylized view of black life focusing on a Southern cotton-picker who becomes a preacher but retains all-too-human weaknesses. Dated in some aspects and unabashedly melodramatic, but still quite moving. Beautifully filmed on location, with some outstanding musical sequences.

Hallelujah I'm a Bum (1933) **82m.** ***½ D: Lewis Milestone. Al Jolson, Madge Evans, Frank Morgan, Harry Langdon, Chester Conklin, Tyler Brooke, Edgar Conner. Fascinating Depression curio about a hobo who tries to "reform" for the sake of a beautiful girl. Provocative, politically savvy script by Ben Hecht and S. N. Behrman, rhyming dialogue and lovely songs by Rodgers and Hart (who also make cameo appearances as photographers, following the cornerstone-laying scene), and winning performances all around. Beware edited prints (reissue title: THE HEART OF NEW YORK) and the frequently screened British version, cut and redubbed as HALLELUJAH I'M A TRAMP.▼

Hallelujah Trail, The (1965) **C-165m.** **½ D: John Sturges. Burt Lancaster, Lee Remick, Jim Hutton, Brian Keith, Martin Landau, Donald Pleasence, Pamela Tiffin. Narrated by John Dehner. Remick is rambunctious temperance leader out to stop cavalry-guarded shipment of whiskey en route to thirsting Denver miners; amiable but lumbering western satire goes on and on. Originally released in Cinerama.

Halliday Brand, The (1957) **77m.** **½ D: Joseph H. Lewis. Joseph Cotten, Viveca Lindfors, Betsy Blair, Ward Bond. Brooding Western about rancher whose domination of family and workers leads to gunplay and revenge. Weak script; strong performances.

Halloween (1978) **C-93m.** *** D: John Carpenter. Donald Pleasence, Jamie Lee Curtis, Nancy Loomis. P. J. Soles, Charles Cyphers, Kyle Richards. Low-budget chiller about psychotic murderer who struck on Halloween as a child, and threatens to do so again 15 years later. Well-made, with lots of scares, plus in-joke references for film buffs. Followed by several sequels and myriad clones.▼

Halloween II (1981) **C-92m.** *½ D: Rick Rosenthal. Jamie Lee Curtis, Donald Pleasence, Charles Cyphers, Jeffrey Kramer, Lance Guest, Pamela Susan Shoop. Explicitly bloody sequel is as bad as any of HALLOWEEN's countless clones, with maniac continuing to stalk Curtis on the same night on which the original ends. Scripted by John Carpenter and Debra Hill.▼

Halloween III: Season of the Witch (1983) **C-96m.** BOMB D: Tommy Lee Wallace. Tom Atkins, Stacey Nelkin, Dan O'Herlihy, Ralph Strait, Michael Currie. Genuinely repellent 80s-style horror film, with gore galore (after a slow start), about a maniacal plot to murder millions of children on Halloween. Nice, huh? No relation to either of the earlier HALLOWEEN films, but owes more than a bit to INVASION OF THE BODY SNATCHERS.▼

Halloween 4: The Return of Michael Myers (1988) **C-88m.** ** D: Dwight H. Little. Donald Pleasence, Ellie Cornell, Danielle Harris, George P. Wilbur, Michael Pataki, Beau Starr, Kathleen Kinmont. Unkillable monster is back, this time mindlessly headed for his hometown to murder his niece (young Harris). Standard horror thriller is technically well made but offers little novelty.▼

Halloween 5 (1989) **C-96m.** *½ D: Dominique Othenin-Girard. Donald Pleasence, Danielle Harris, Donald L. Shanks, Wendy Kaplan, Ellie Cornell, Jeffrey Landman. Slightly more plot than before but still just a sequential slaughter of teenagers as Michael Myers (Shanks) again sets out to kill his young niece (Harris). Routine and plodding, with too many endings and unnecessary setup for sequel.

Halls of Anger (1970) **C-96m.** **½ D: Paul Bogart. Calvin Lockhart, Janet Mac-Lachlan, James A. Watson, Jr., Rob Reiner, Jeff Bridges, Edward Asner. Standard violence-in-school story, but with a racial angle. No better or worse than a dozen other similar films.

Halls of Montezuma (1950) **C-113m.** **½ D: Lewis Milestone. Richard Widmark, Walter (Jack) Palance, Robert Wagner, Jack Webb, Reginald Gardiner, Karl Malden, Philip Ahn. Grim WW2 actioner dealing with marine action in the Pacific. Good cast makes stereotypes acceptable.▼

Hallucination Generation (1966) **90m.** BOMB D: Edward Mann. George Montgomery, Danny Stone, Renate Kasche, Tom Baker, Marianne Kanter, Steve Rowland. Silly melodrama about American hippies in Spain, and their introduction to crime. Don't miss the LSD sequence, shot in color.

Hal Roach Comedy Carnival SEE: Curley▼

Hal Roach Comedy Carnival SEE: Fabulous Joe, The▼

Hambone and Hillie (1984) **C-89m.** **½ D: Roy Watts. Lillian Gish, Timothy Bottoms, Candy Clark, O. J. Simpson, Robert Walker, Jack Carter, Alan Hale, Anne Lockhart. Elderly Gish loses her devoted mutt at an airport and he races cross-country to find her. Sugar-coated soaper is no dog, but is also no BENJI.▼

Hamburger Hill (1987) **C-110m.** ** D: John Irvin. Anthony Barrile, Michael Patrick Boatman, Don Cheadle, Michael Dolan, Don James, M.A. Nickles, Courtney B. Vance. Cold, clinical, yet occasionally preachy recreation of some true-life 1969 Vietnam carnage, with troops of the 101st Airborne Division encountering the enemy in mutual slaughter for the title reward. Authentic, with expertly staged battle scenes—but limited in its emotional power. Scripted by Jim Carabatsos.▼

Hamburger . . . The Motion Picture (1986) **C-90m.** BOMB D: Mike Marvin. Leigh McCloskey, Dick Butkus, Randi Brooks, Chuck McCann, Jack Blessing, Charles Tyner. Anyone who watches a movie with this title deserves whatever he gets.▼

Hamlet (1948-British) **153m.** **** D: Laurence Olivier. Laurence Olivier, Eileen Herlie, Basil Sydney, Felix Aylmer, Jean Simmons, Stanley Holloway, Peter Cushing. Brilliant adaptation of Shakespeare's play about Danish prince "who just couldn't make up his mind." Hauntingly photographed in Elsinore, Denmark. Won Oscars for Best Picture, Best Actor (Olivier), Art Direction-Set Decoration and Costumes.▼

Hamlet (1969-British) **C-114m.** **½ D: Tony Richardson. Nicol Williamson, Gordon Jackson, Anthony Hopkins, Judy Parfitt, Mark Dignam, Marianne Faithfull. Richardson and Williamson moved their boisterous interpretation of the Shakespeare play from stage to screen with only fair results; perhaps the irritating overuse of close-ups will play better on TV. Interesting casting of Faithfull as Ophelia.▼

Hammer (1972) **C-92m.** *½ D: Bruce Clark. Fred Williamson, Bernie Hamilton, Vonetta McGee, William Smith, Charles Lampkin. Black boxer takes on the syndicate in fast, but mindless melodrama. Some violence may be cut.

Hammerhead (1968-British) **C-99m.** *½ D: David Miller. Vince Edwards, Judy

Geeson, Diana Dors, Peter Vaughan, Beverly Adams. Weak James Bond carbon copy, tale of supercriminal pursued by soldier of fortune.

Hammersmith Is Out (1972) **C-108m.** ** D: Peter Ustinov. Elizabeth Taylor, Richard Burton, Peter Ustinov, Beau Bridges, Leon Askin, Leon Ames, John Schuck, George Raft. Grotesque comedy about mental patient, his male nurse, and a hash slinger proves once again that Liz and Dick would do anything for money; cast has more fun than viewers in this variation on the Faust legend.▼

Hammett (1983) **C-97m.** *** D: Wim Wenders. Frederic Forrest, Peter Boyle, Marilu Henner, Elisha Cook, R. G. Armstrong, Richard Bradford, Roy Kinnear, Lydia Lei, Sylvia Sidney, Samuel Fuller, Royal Dano. Wenders' first American film is a real treat for detective buffs: an adaptation of Joe Gores' fiction about famed author Dashiell Hammett's involvement in a real-life mystery (elements of which would find their way into his later stories). You couldn't ask for a more faithful re-creation of 1930s studio look; a magnificent-looking (and sounding) film. Several years in production, with much of it reportedly reshot by executive producer Francis Coppola, but final result is seamless.▼

Hamster of Happiness, The SEE: **Second-Hand Hearts**

Hand, The (1960-British) **60m.** *½ D: Henry Cass. Derek Bond, Ronald Leigh Hunt, Reed De Rouen, Ray Cooney. Slowly paced murder caper, with Scotland Yard tracking down one-armed killer; a few gruesome scenes.

Hand, The (1981) **C-104m.** *½ D: Oliver Stone. Michael Caine, Andrea Marcovicci, Annie McEnroe, Bruce McGill, Viveca Lindfors, Rosemary Murphy, Mara Hobel. Cartoonist Caine's drawing hand is severed in auto accident, which destroys his career and places additional strain on his shaky marriage. Life becomes even more nightmarish when the hand returns on a murderous spree; unfortunately it didn't get Caine or writer-director Stone and save them from this embarrassment.▼

Handful of Dust, A (1988-British) **C-118m.** ***½ D: Charles Sturridge. James Wilby, Kristin Scott Thomas, Rupert Graves, Judi Dench, Anjelica Huston, Alec Guinness, Pip Torrens, Cathryn Harrison. Rich adaptation of Evelyn Waugh's ironic story about a doomed marriage among England's smart set in the early 1930s, and the unexpected results for both the stiflingly tradition-bound husband (brilliantly and movingly played by Wilby) and the nonchalantly selfish wife (perfectly essayed by Thomas). Superior script by Tim Sullivan, Derek Granger, and Sturridge is matched by an unerring eye for period detail.▼

Handgun SEE: **Deep in the Heart**▼

Hand in Hand (1960-British) **75m.** **½ D: Philip Leacock. Loretta Parry, Philip Needs, John Gregson, Sybil Thorndike. Good film with a moral for children, about a Jewish girl and a Catholic boy who become friends and learn about each other. Adults may find it hard to take at times.

Handle With Care (1958) **82m.** **½ D: David Friedkin. Dean Jones, Joan O'Brien, Thomas Mitchell, John Smith, Walter Abel. Earnest minor film about law student Jones investigating crime within the town where classmates are assigned mock grand-jury work.

Handle With Care (1977) **C-98m.** *** D: Jonathan Demme. Paul LeMat, Candy Clark, Ann Wedgeworth, Marcia Rodd, Charles Napier, Alix Elias, Roberts Blossom. Fine character studies and vignettes make up for shortcomings in bright, original film. Loosely revolves around LeMat and his obsession with C.B. radio; subplot with bigamist truckdriver is hilarious. Written by Paul Brickman. Originally released as CITIZENS BAND.▼

Handmaid's Tale, The (1990) **C-109m.** **½ D: Volker Schlondorff. Natasha Richardson, Robert Duvall, Faye Dunaway, Aidan Quinn, Elizabeth McGovern, Victoria Tennant, Blanche Baker, Traci Lind. Intriguing story set in a near-future world in which young, healthy white women are brainwashed to become bearers of babies for a new, "pure" generation. Richardson must overcome the jealousy of an infertile wife (Dunaway) while fending off the advances of her high-powered husband (Duvall). Interesting elements abound, but the film might best be described as sterile. Scripted by Harold Pinter from the novel by Margaret Atwood. David Dukes appears unbilled as a doctor.▼

Hand of the Gallows SEE: **Terrible People, The**

Hands Across the Table (1935) **80m.** *** D: Mitchell Leisen. Carole Lombard, Fred MacMurray, Ralph Bellamy, Astrid Allwyn, Marie Prevost. Lombard sparkles as fortune-hunting manicurist who has to choose between MacMurray and Bellamy.

Hands of a Stranger (1962) **86m.** **½ D: Newton Arnold. Paul Lukather, Joan Harvey, Irish McCalla, Barry Gordon, Michael Rye. Unacknowledged fourth version of THE HANDS OF ORLAC, with a pianist receiving a hand-transplant from a criminal, causing him to go berserk.

Hands of a Stranger (1987) **C-200m.** TVM D: Larry Elikann. Armand Assante, Blair Brown, Beverly D'Angelo, Michael Lerner, Philip Casnoff, Arliss Howard. Manipulative filming of Robert Daley's best-seller about an ambitious detective, obsessed with finding his wife's rapist, who becomes romantically involved with a lady D.A. Scripted by playwright Arthur Kopit. Originally shown in two parts. Average.

Hands of Orlac, The (1960-British-French) **95m.** ** D: Edmond T. Greville. Mel Ferrer, Lucile Saint-Simon, Christopher Lee, Dany Carrel, Felix Aylmer, Basil Sydney, Donald Wolfit, Donald Pleasence. Pianist gets hand transplant from a strange doctor—and finds he has the impulse to kill. Flat remake of Maurice Renard's famous story, filmed before in 1924 and (as MAD LOVE) in 1935. French-language version runs 105m. Also known as HANDS OF THE STRANGLER.

Hands of the Ripper (1971-British) **C-85m.** **½ D: Peter Sasdy. Eric Porter, Angharad Rees, Jane Merrow, Keith Bell, Derek Godfrey. Early believer in Freud tries to help young daughter of Jack the Ripper. Great atmosphere, solid performances, but after good start, dissolves into series of bloody murders. Not bad—but hampered by addition of psychiatrist "explaining" main character for TV prints.▼

Hands of the Strangler SEE: Hands of Orlac, The▼

Handyman, The (1980-Canadian) **C-99m.** ***½ D: Micheline Lanctot. Jocelyn Berube, Andree Pelletier, Jannette Bertrand, Paul Dion, Marcel Sabourin. Shy, boyish, romantic Berube—he's not exactly short, but other men seem to tower over him—has a love affair with a married woman. A sad, beautifully made little film about people who can never get what they want because they are unable to take stands.

Hangar 18 (1980) **C-93m.** *½ D: James L. Conway. Darren McGavin, Robert Vaughn, Gary Collins, James Hampton, Philip Abbott, Joseph Campanella, Pamela Bellwood, Steven Keats, Tom Hallick, William Schallert. This Sunn Classic Picture alleges that the U.S. government is concealing a captured UFO. Slickly made, but about as credible as THE THREE STOOGES IN ORBIT; shown on TV as INVASION FORCE with new ending that undermines entire film!▼

Hanged Man, The (1964) **C-87m. TVM** D: Don Siegel. Edmond O'Brien, Vera Miles, Robert Culp, Gene Raymond, J. Carrol Naish, Brenda Scott. Man sets out to avenge murder of friend, winds up at New Orleans Mardi Gras where he meets young woman. Culp and Miles stand out in otherwise OK cast but film overall seems insignificant. Remake of RIDE THE PINK HORSE. Average.▼

Hanged Man, The (1974) **C-78m. TVM** D: Michael Caffey. Steve Forrest, Dean Jagger, Cameron Mitchell, Sharon Acker, Will Geer, Brendon Boone. Gunslinger Forrest miraculously survives his own execution and becomes an Old West soldier

of fortune. Interesting idea routinely told. Average.▼

Hang 'em High (1968) **C-114m.** **½ D: Ted Post. Clint Eastwood, Inger Stevens, Ed Begley, Pat Hingle, Arlene Golonka, James MacArthur, Ruth White, Ben Johnson, Charles McGraw, Bruce Dern, Alan Hale Jr., Dennis Hopper. Slick American attempt at spaghetti Western comes off fairly well. Eastwood survives his own hanging, swears vengeance on nine men who lynched him. Fine supporting cast; nice cameo by cowboy veteran Bob Steele as dungeon prisoner.▼

Hanging by a Thread (1979) **C-200m. TVM** D: Georg Fenady. Sam Groom, Patty Duke Astin, Bert Convy, Burr DeBenning, Donna Mills, Cameron Mitchell. Party of friends dangle above a mountain gorge in a disabled tram reliving the past in this bloated Irwin Allen disaster flick that could have been resolved in 90 minutes or less. Originally shown in two parts. Average.

Hanging Tree, The (1959) **C-106m.** *** D: Delmer Daves. Gary Cooper, Maria Schell, Karl Malden, George C. Scott, Karl Swenson, Ben Piazza, Virginia Gregg. Literate, low-key Western with outstanding performance by Schell as a blind girl nursed by Cooper, a frontier doctor with a past. Not for all tastes. Scott's first film.

Hangman, The (1959) **86m.** ** D: Michael Curtiz. Robert Taylor, Tina Louise, Fess Parker, Jack Lord, Mickey Shaughnessy, Shirley Harmer. Rugged Taylor is the lawman who must buck the entire Western town defending a man wanted for murder.

Hangman's House (1928) **72m.** *** D: John Ford. June Collyer, Larry Kent, Earle Foxe, Victor McLaglen, Hobart Bosworth. Florid melodrama of frustrated romance and family honor, elevated by sumptuous production and Ford's sure direction. Steeplechase scene predates the one in THE QUIET MAN, and ironically, you can spot young John Wayne as a spectator along the railing!

Hangman's Knot (1952) **C-81m.** **½ D: Roy Huggins. Randolph Scott, Donna Reed, Claude Jarman, Jr., Richard Denning, Lee Marvin. Above-par Scott Western involving Rebs robbing gold shipment and officer Scott deciding they should return it.

Hangmen Also Die (1943) **131m.** **½ D: Fritz Lang. Brian Donlevy, Walter Brennan, Anna Lee, Gene Lockhart, Dennis O'Keefe. OK WW2 drama written by Bertolt Brecht; lethargic Donlevy performance as assassin of notorious Nazi leader; exciting climax including frame-up of Lockhart.

Hangover, The SEE: Female Jungle
Hangover Square (1945) **77m.** *** D: John Brahm. Laird Cregar, Linda Darnell, George Sanders, Glenn Langan, Faye Marlowe, Alan Napier, Frederic Worlock.

Cregar (in his final film) is delicious as unhinged composer who goes off his top and kills women whenever he hears loud noises. Barre Lyndon's script bears little relation to the Patrick Hamilton novel, but result is still entertaining, with superb Victorian London sets and evocative Bernard Herrmann score.

Hangup (1974) **C-94m.** ** D: Henry Hathaway. William Elliott, Marki Bey, Cliff Potts, Michael Lerner, Timothy Blake. Disappointing black-oriented actioner about a drug racket; Hathaway has done many fine films, but this, his last, isn't one. Bey is good as a doomed prostitute. Also known as SUPERDUDE.

Hanky Panky (1982) **C-110m.** *½ D: Sidney Poitier. Gene Wilder, Gilda Radner, Kathleen Quinlan, Richard Widmark, Robert Prosky, Josef Sommer, Johnny Sekka. Innocent architect Wilder is chased by spies, cops, etc. Predictable, barely funny comedy-thriller, with Radner miscast as the love interest. (The film was intended to be a followup to STIR CRAZY, but Richard Pryor's part was rewritten for Gilda.) You've seen it all before, and better.▼

Hannah and Her Sisters (1986) **C-106m.** ***½ D: Woody Allen. Woody Allen, Michael Caine, Mia Farrow, Carrie Fisher, Barbara Hershey, Lloyd Nolan, Maureen O'Sullivan, Daniel Stern, Max von Sydow, Dianne Wiest, Tony Roberts, Sam Waterston, Julie Kavner, Julia Louis-Dreyfus, John Turturro, Joanna Gleason, Bobby Short. Allen strikes gold as he examines some typically interesting and neurotic New Yorkers whose lives intertwine. Superbly cast with Woody in peak form as Farrow's hypochondriac ex-husband; Wiest in a powerhouse performance as Mia's self-consumed, self-destructive sister. There's also an atypical Allen touch of warmth, even sentiment, as frosting on the cake—all of it set to some wonderful old songs. Academy Award winner for Best Supporting Actor (Caine), Best Supporting Actress (Wiest), and Woody's Original Screenplay.▼

Hannah Lee SEE: **Outlaw Territory**

Hanna K. (1983-French) **C-108m.** ** D: Constantine Costa-Gavras. Jill Clayburgh, Jean Yanne, Gabriel Byrne, Mohammed Bakri, David Clennon. Intriguing but unsatisfying melodrama about flaky lawyer Clayburgh and her conflicting relationships with ex-husband Yanne, Israeli district attorney Byrne and Palestinian Bakri, who's attempting to reclaim his ancestral home. A source of controversy because of its pro-Palestinian stand, but on artistic terms a major disappointment from Costa-Gavras.▼

Hanna's War (1988) **C-148m.** *½ D: Menahem Golan. Ellen Burstyn, Maruschka Detmers, Anthony Andrews, Donald Plea-

sence, David Warner, Denholm Elliott, Vincenzo Ricotta, Ingrid Pitt. The true story of Hungarian freedom fighter Hanna Senesh (Detmers), based in part on her diaries, is a misguided mess. The young, Jewish WW2 martyr deserved a far better production than this overlong, uninspiring melodrama. Hanna's prison-issue designer blouses don't help matters.▼

Hannibal (1960-U.S.-Italian) **C-103m.** ** D: Edgar G. Ulmer. Victor Mature, Rita Gam, Gabriele Ferzetti, Milly Vitale. Cardboard costume saga follows Hannibal and his elephants across the Alps and into Rome . . . but *you* may not last that long.

Hannibal Brooks (1969-British) **C-101m.** **½ D: Michael Winner. Oliver Reed, Michael J. Pollard, Wolfgang Preiss, Helmut Lohner, Karin Baal, Peter Karsten. Pleasant, forgettable film of British P.O.W. Reed assigned to evacuate valuable elephant from Munich zoo during WW2; forced to go on foot, he turns trip into escape plan. Wavers from comedy to melodrama, with Pollard major comic character; good action climax.

Hannie Caulder (1972-British) **C-85m.** **½ D:. Burt Kennedy. Raquel Welch, Robert Culp, Ernest Borgnine, Jack Elam, Strother Martin, Christopher Lee, Diana Dors. Bizarre, mystical Western about raped/widowed/homeless woman who begs bounty hunter Culp to teach her to shoot so she can seek vengeance. Neat idea to have bad guys Borgnine, Elam, and Martin play it a la The Three Stooges, but laughter is vitiated by their gory killings. Nice cameo by Lee as sympathetic gunsmith.

Hanoi Hilton, The (1987) **C-130m.** *½ D: Lionel Chetwynd. Michael Moriarty, Paul LeMat, Jeffrey Jones, Lawrence Pressman, Stephen Davies, David Soul, Rick Fitts, Aki Aleong, Gloria Carlin. What may have been a sincere effort to dramatize the plight of American POWs in Vietnam becomes an unbearably dull, impossibly overlong, and embarrassingly cliched drama, which does a real disservice to its subject . . . and throws in right-wing polemics and potshots at Jane Fonda to boot.▼

Hanover Street (1979) **C-109m.** ** D: Peter Hyams. Harrison Ford, Lesley-Anne Down, Christopher Plummer, Alec McCowen, Richard Masur, Michael Sacks. WW2 romance between married Englishwoman and American soldier who's sent on daring mission behind enemy lines is slick but contrived and unconvincing. Script by director Hyams.▼

Hans Christian Andersen (1952) **C-120m.** **½ D: Charles Vidor. Danny Kaye, Farley Granger, Jeanmaire, Roland Petit, John Qualen. Melodic Frank Loesser score ("Inchworm," "Ugly Duckling," "Thumbelina," etc.) can't save musical biography of vagabond tale-teller. Some TV prints run 104m. Glossy and completely fabricated—has no relation to real Andersen's life story.▼

Hanussen (1988-German-Hungarian) **C-120m.** ***½ D: Istvan Szabo. Klaus Maria Brandauer, Erland Josephson, Ildiko Bansagi, Walter Schmidinger, Karoly Eperjes. Brandauer offers a compelling performance as the title character, a WW1 Austrian soldier who is shot in the head—and develops the ability to read minds and foretell the future. An intriguing, insightful, based-on-fact tale; third in a trilogy, following MEPHISTO and COLONEL REDL.▼

Happening, The (1967) **101m.** ** D: Elliot Silverstein. Anthony Quinn, George Maharis, Michael Parks, Robert Walker, Faye Dunaway, Milton Berle, Oscar Homolka, Jack Kruschen, Clifton James, Eugene Roche. Lighthearted and lightheaded caper story centering around kidnapping of a now respectable former gangster (Quinn). Turns unpleasantly serious towards end. Dunaway's film debut. The title song became a No. 1 hit for The Supremes.

Happiest Days of Your Life, The (1950-British) **81m.** *** D: Frank Launder. Alastair Sim, Margaret Rutherford, Guy Middleton, Joyce Grenfell, Richard Wattis, Laurence Naismith. Funny comedy involving a boys' school sharing quarters with a displaced girls' academy, with frantic situations resulting. Launder and John Dighton scripted, from the latter's play.

Happiest Millionaire, The (1967) **C-118m.** **½ D: Norman Tokar. Fred MacMurray, Tommy Steele, Greer Garson, Geraldine Page, Gladys Cooper, Hermione Baddeley, Lesley Ann Warren, John Davidson. Lively but overlong and uninvolving Disney musical (the last film he personally oversaw) about Philadelphia household of eccentric millionaire Anthony J. Drexel Biddle (MacMurray). Lightly entertaining. Originally tradescreened at 164m., then released at 141m.; reissued in 1984 at 159m.▼

Happily Ever After (1978) **C-100m. TVM** D: Robert Scheerer. Suzanne Somers, Bruce Boxleitner, Eric Braeden, John Rubinstein, Ron Hayes. In her first starring role, Suzanne is an aspiring singer torn between hitting it big in Las Vegas or running off with the hick who's smitten with her. Below average.

Happily Ever After (1990) **C-74m.** ** D: John Howley. Voices of Irene Cara, Edward Asner, Carol Channing, Dom DeLuise, Phyllis Diller, Zsa Zsa Gabor, Linda Gary, Jonathan Harris, Michael Horton, Sally Kellerman, Malcolm McDowell, Tracey Ullman, Frank Welker. All-star voice cast gives major boost to this otherwise undistinguished sequel to the story of

Snow White, who's surrounded here by dwarfelles. Produced by Filmation Studios with noticeably better animation than their Saturday morning product can boast.

Happiness SEE: **Le Bonheur**

Happiness Ahead (1934) **86m.** **½ D: Mervyn LeRoy. Dick Powell, Josephine Hutchinson, Frank McHugh, John Halliday, Allen Jenkins, Ruth Donnelly. Pleasant little film about wealthy heiress pretending to be poor when she meets likable working-stiff Powell. No production numbers, really, but several nice songs, including "Pop Goes Your Heart."

Happiness Cage, The (1972) **C-94m.** **½ D: Bernard Girard. Christopher Walken, Joss Ackland, Ralph Meeker, Ronny Cox, Marco St. John, Tom Aldredge. Uneven but thought-provoking drama about doctor in Germany who utilizes shock treatment on soldiers to stabilize aggressive behavior. Also known as THE MIND SNATCHERS.▼

Happy (1983) **C-100m. TVM** D: Lee Philips. Dom DeLuise, Dee Wallace, Henry Silva, Jack Gilford, Tony Burton, Bill Morey, David DeLuise, Carol Arthur DeLuise. Rotund Dom goes dramatic as a down-on-his-luck TV clown who gets involved in a gangland rubout and tracks the gunman himself when the cops bungle the case. Average.

Happy Anniversary (1959) **81m.** **½ D: David Miller. David Niven, Mitzi Gaynor, Carl Reiner, Loring Smith, Monique Van Vooren, Patty Duke, Elizabeth Wilson. Funny but strained comedy of married couple Niven and Gaynor being embarrassed by daughter Duke telling the nation on TV show that father was indiscreet in his younger days.

Happy Birthday, Gemini (1980) **C-107m.** ** D: Richard Benner. Madeline Kahn, Rita Moreno, Robert Viharo, Alan Rosenberg, Sarah Holcomb, David Marshall Grant, Timothy Jenkins. Disappointing adaptation of Albert Innaurato's long-running Broadway play *Gemini*, centering on young man's sexual identity crisis. Colorful stage characters are lost on film.

Happy Birthday to Me (1981-Canadian) **C-108m.** BOMB D: J. Lee Thompson. Melissa Sue Anderson, Glenn Ford, Tracy Bregman, Jack Blum, Matt Craven, Lawrence Dane, Sharon Acker. Is or is not Anderson killing off her classmates at Crawford Academy because they inadvertently caused her mother's death four years earlier? More killings, more blood, more exploitation; Ford, as Anderson's psychiatrist, must have been desperate for the work.▼

Happy Birthday, Wanda June (1971) **C-105m.** *** D: Mark Robson. Rod Steiger, Susannah York, George Grizzard, Don

[476]

Murray, William Hickey, Pamelyn Ferdin, Steven Paul. Stagy but enjoyable film of Kurt Vonnegut, Jr.'s play about male chauvinist explorer who returns home after seven years, finds his wife matured (and engaged), and his values now obsolete. Fine performances of Vonnegut's funny black-humor situations and dialogue; Hickey hilarious as Steiger's Jerry Lewis-esque buddy.

Happy Ending, The (1969) **C-112m.** **½ D: Richard Brooks. Jean Simmons, John Forsythe, Lloyd Bridges, Shirley Jones, Teresa Wright, Dick Shawn, Nanette Fabray, Robert (Bobby) Darin, Tina Louise. Initially intriguing view of modern marriage drones on interminably, as Simmons walks out on husband and family trying to find herself. Michel Legrand score highlighted by "What Are You Doing the Rest of Your Life?"▼

Happy Endings (1983) **C-100m. TVM** D: Jerry Thorpe. Lee Montgomery, Jill Schoelen, Sarah Nevin, Robbie Kiger, Oliver Clark, Robin Gammell, Carol Mayo Jenkins, Laura Dern. Eighteen-year-old college dropout struggles to keep the family together after his parents' deaths. Writer/producer Christopher Beaumont (one of the guiding hands behind TV's *Fame*) based this on his own experience. Heartwarming but predictable television fare. Average.

Happy Endings (1983) **C-96m. TVM** D: Noel Black. John Schneider, Catherine Hicks, Ana Alicia, Joseph Hacker III, Bibi Osterwald, Matthew Faison, Murphy Cross. Pleasant but perfunctory romantic comedy about a twosome, rebounding from broken love affairs, who meet and go for the currently "in" Meaningful Relationship. Average.

Happy Go Lovely (1951-British) **C-87m.** ** D: H. Bruce Humberstone. David Niven, Vera-Ellen, Cesar Romero, Bobby Howes, Diane Hart. Minor musical about producer who hires a chorus girl hoping that her boyfriend has money to invest in the show.▼

Happy Go Lucky (1943) **C-81m.** **½ D: Curtis Bernhardt. Mary Martin, Dick Powell, Eddie Bracken, Betty Hutton, Rudy Vallee, Mabel Paige. Happy little musical has Martin chasing millionaire Vallee on Caribbean cruise; no great songs, but spirited cast keeps it moving.

Happy Hooker, The (1975) **C-96m.** ** D: Nicholas Sgarro. Lynn Redgrave, Jean-Pierre Aumont, Lovelady Powell, Nicholas Pryor, Elizabeth Wilson, Tom Poston, Conrad Janis, Mason Adams, Anita Morris. Xaviera Hollander's best-seller about her rise as N.Y.C.'s most prominent madam is so heavily sanitized that one wonders just what audience scripter William Richert had in mind, but it's moderately amusing,

and the cast seems to be having a good time. Followed by two fictitious sequels.▼

Happy Hooker Goes Hollywood, The (1980) **C-85m.** *½ D: Alan Roberts. Martine Beswicke, Chris Lemmon, Adam West, Phil Silvers, Richard Deacon, Lindsay Bloom, Army Archerd, Edie Adams. Now Xaviera is a brunette; she and her girls rush to the aid of a corruption-riddled movie studio in this limp rehash of SILENT MOVIE. Fine comic cast is wasted, although film buffs might enjoy seeing cult actors Beswicke and Dick Miller in bed together.▼

Happy Hooker Goes to Washington, The (1977) **C-89m.** *½ D: William A. Levey. Joey Heatherton, George Hamilton, Ray Walston, Jack Carter, Phil Foster, Billy Barty, David White. Xaviera (a *blonde* this time) is called before Congress to answer charges that sex is ruining the country and subsequently gets involved in a CIA escapade. A few chuckles here and there, but overall, more silly than sexy; Hamilton and writer Bob Kaufman did considerably better with their next film, LOVE AT FIRST BITE.▼

Happy Is the Bride (1957-British) **84m.** ** D: Roy Boulting. Ian Carmichael, Janette Scott, Cecil Parker, Terry-Thomas, Joyce Grenfell, John Le Mesurier, Eric Barker, Athene Seyler. Remake of 1940's QUIET WEDDING, a mild farce about a young couple's headaches as their families prepare for their nuptials. Seyler repeats her role from the original as a helpful aunt.

Happy Land (1943) **73m.** **½ D: Irving Pichel. Don Ameche, Frances Dee, Harry Carey, Ann Rutherford, Cara Williams, Richard Crane, Henry (Harry) Morgan, Dickie Moore. Sincere but not always successful Americana of grieving father learning meaning of war as he questions his son's death in WW2. Five-year-old Natalie Wood's first feature.

Happy Landing (1938) **102m.** **½ D: Roy Del Ruth. Sonja Henie, Don Ameche, Cesar Romero, Ethel Merman, Jean Hersholt, Billy Gilbert. Predictable Henie vehicle is not up to her other musicals. Pilot Ameche lands near her home; romance blossoms instantly.

Happy Mother's Day, Love George (1973) **C-90m.** ** D: Darren McGavin. Patricia Neal, Cloris Leachman, Bobby Darin, Ron Howard, Simon Oakland. Unconvincing horror tale, despite some clever attempts by director McGavin to spice it up. Strange doings in seaside house include two great gory murders, but everything else is weak. Retitled: RUN, STRANGER, RUN.▼

Happy New Year (1973-French) **C-112m.** *** D: Claude Lelouch. Lino Ventura, Francoise Fabian, Charles Gerard, Andre Falcon. Two thieves plot a robbery, but one falls hard for the liberated charmer who runs the antique shop next to the target. Bright romantic caper film is easy to take. Remade in Hollywood in 1987. Retitled: THE HAPPY NEW YEAR CAPER.▼

Happy New Year (1987) **C-85m.** **½ D: John G. Avildsen. Peter Falk, Wendy Hughes, Charles Durning, Tom Courtenay, Joan Copeland. Falk is a treat to watch in this pleasant Americanization of Claude Lelouch's French comedy caper about a pair of sophisticated crooks and their plans to hit a jewelry store in West Palm Beach, Florida. Film was plagued with production problems (evidenced by abundance of narration and abruptness of certain sequences) and barely received theatrical release after sitting on the shelf for a year. Australian Hughes is charming in her first American film; Lelouch makes a cameo appearance in the opening scene.▼

Happy New Year Caper, The SEE: **Happy New Year** (1973)▼

Happy Road, The (1957) **80m.** **½ D: Gene Kelly. Gene Kelly, Barbara Laage, Michael Redgrave, Bobby Clark, Brigitte Fossey. Two single parents—American Kelly and Frenchwoman Laage—are drawn together when their children run away from school together. Pleasant but minor family fare, enhanced by location filming in French countryside.

Happy Thieves, The (1962) **88m.** **½ D: George Marshall. Rex Harrison, Rita Hayworth, Joseph Wiseman, Gregoire Aslan, Alida Valli. Sad pairing of star duo, out of place in museum theft caper, set in Spain.

Happy Time, The (1952) **94m.** **½ D: Richard Fleischer. Charles Boyer, Louis Jourdan, Marsha Hunt, Linda Christian, Bobby Driscoll. Pleasant nostalgia dealing with everyday events in life of a typical family, set in 1920s Canada.

Happy Together (1989) **C-102m.** ** D: Mel Damski. Patrick Dempsey, Helen Slater, Dan Schneider, Marius Weyers, Barbara Babcock. Slight, predictable romantic comedy in which college students Dempsey and Slater are accidentally paired as roommates. You can just guess how this one turns out.▼

Happy Years, The (1950) **C-110m.** *** D: William Wellman. Dean Stockwell, Scotty Beckett, Darryl Hickman, Leo G. Carroll, Margalo Gillmore, Leon Ames. High-spirited boy in turn-of-the-century prep school finds he has trouble fitting in. Familiar comedy-drama, adapted from Owen Johnson's *Lawrenceville Stories*, is hardly typical Wellman fare, but well enough done. Robert Wagner makes his film debut.

Harbor Lights (1963) **68m.** BOMB D: Maury Dexter. Kent Taylor, Jeff Morrow, Miriam Colon, Allan Sague. Cheap film of intrigue, with B picture perennial Taylor. Congratulations to anyone who

can find some relation between title and what goes on in film.

Harbor of Missing Men (1950) **60m.** *½ D: R. G. Springsteen. Richard Denning, Barbra Fuller, Steven Geray, George Zucco, Ray Teal, Percy Helton. Unsparkling Republic Pictures programmer with Denning innocently involved with jewel smuggling.

Hardbodies (1984) **C-87m.** BOMB D: Mark Griffiths. Grant Cramer, Gary Wood, Michael Rapport, Sorrells Pickard, Teal Roberts, Roberta Collins, Courtney Gaines, Joyce Jameson. Three middle-aged clods rent a beach house and hire young stud Cramer to teach them how to score. A really good, sexy film could've been made from the *Penthouse* article, but this amateurish mess isn't it; even the girl-watching palls after ten minutes or so. Made for cable TV, but released to theatres first. Followed by a sequel.▼

Hardbodies 2 (1986) **C-95m.** BOMB D: Mark Griffiths. Brad Zutaut, Fabiano Udinio, James Karen, Alba Francesca, Roberta Collins. Topless tease about the daily misfortunes of an American film crew shooting an inane romance in Greece; has there ever been another time in film history when the idea of a sequel to something called HARDBODIES would have been discussed? Still, if you're partial to airplane commode jokes . . . ▼

Hard Boiled Mahoney (1947) **63m.** D: William Beaudine. Leo Gorcey, Huntz Hall, Betty Compson, Bobby Jordan, Gabriel Dell, Billy Benedict, David Gorcey. SEE: **Bowery Boys** series.

Hardcase (1971) **C-74m.** TVM D: John Llewellyn Moxey. Clint Walker, Stefanie Powers, Pedro Armendariz, Jr., Alex Karras, Luis Mirando. Interesting period Western featuring Walker as soldier of fortune who joins up with Mexican revolutionaries, discovers wife amongst them. Dialogue not bad, situations sometimes believable. Otherwise, pace of film too rushed. Average.

Hard Choices (1986) **C-90m.** **½ D: Rick King. Margaret Klenck, Gary McCleery, John Seitz, John Sayles, John Snyder, Martin Donovan, Spalding Gray. Teenager jailed for innocent involvement in a robbery and shooting is befriended by a young female social worker, who has more problems of her own than she cares to admit. Interesting independently produced feature loses its footing as story progresses; strongest asset is Sayles' offhanded performance as the bad guy. Made in 1984. ▼

Hard Contract (1969) **C-107m.** **½ D: S. Lee Pogostin. James Coburn, Lee Remick, Lilli Palmer, Burgess Meredith, Patrick Magee, Sterling Hayden, Karen Black. Hired killer Coburn starts to have self-doubts when a woman (Remick) humanizes him. Film is too concerned with

making an "important statement" to become particularly entertaining or involving.
Hardcore (1979) **C-108m.** **½ D: Paul Schrader. George C. Scott, Peter Boyle, Season Hubley, Dick Sargent, Leonard Gaines, David Nichols. Calvinistic Midwesterner Scott (in powerful performance) searches for teenage daughter who's inexplicably dropped out. He's heartsick after viewing porno film starring her, and his journey into netherworld of prostitution and porn is at times fascinating, sad, and repellent. Marred by unbelievable conclusion.▼

Hard Country (1981) **C-104m.** **½ D: David Greene. Jan-Michael Vincent, Kim Basinger, Michael Parks, Gailard Sartain, Tanya Tucker, Ted Neeley, Daryl Hannah, Richard Moll. Good ole boy Vincent works all day, parties all night; his girlfriend (Basinger) wants to marry him, but also wants out of Texas. Overshadowed by URBAN COWBOY, but not bad and done with conviction. Music by Michael Martin Murphey. Film debuts of Basinger and Nashville star Tucker.▼

Hard Day's Night, A (1964-British) **85m.** **** D: Richard Lester. John Lennon, Paul McCartney, George Harrison, Ringo Starr, Wilfrid Brambell, Norman Rossington, John Junkins, Victor Spinetti, Anna Quayle. First Beatles film is director Lester's idea of a typical day in the group's life. He lets his imagination run wild; result is a visual delight, with many Beatles songs on the soundtrack (including "Can't Buy Me Love," "And I Love Her," "I Should Have Known Better," and the title tune). Original screenplay by Alun Owen. Reissued in 1982 with a short prologue. ▼

Hard Driver SEE: **Last American Hero, The**▼

Harder They Come, The (1973-Jamaican) **C-98m.** *** D: Perry Henzell. Jimmy Cliff, Janet Barkley, Carl Bradshaw, Ras Daniel Hartman, Bobby Charlton. Country-boy Cliff comes to Kingston to make it as a singer; ironically, it isn't until he turns to a life of crime that his record starts to climb the charts. Crude but powerful film almost single-handedly launched reggae music's popularity in America; still a major cult favorite. Terrific song score includes "You Can Get It If You Really Want," "Many Rivers to Cross," title tune.▼

Harder They Fall, The (1956) **109m.** ***½ D: Mark Robson. Humphrey Bogart, Rod Steiger, Jan Sterling, Mike Lane, Max Baer, Edward Andrews. Bogart's last feature casts him as cynical sportswriter-turned-press agent who realizes for the first time how badly prizefighters are manipulated by their unfeeling managers. Powerful drama by Budd Schulberg.▼

Hard, Fast and Beautiful (1951) **79m.** ** D: Ida Lupino. Claire Trevor, Sally Forrest, Carleton Young, Robert Clarke, Kenneth Patterson. Domineering mother pushes daughter into world of competitive tennis. Straightforward story, awkwardly filmed (and acted) at times. Director Lupino and Robert Ryan make cameo appearances.

Hard Feelings (1981) **C-110m.** *** D: Daryl Duke. Carl Marotte, Charlaine Woodard, Grand Bush, Vincent Buffano, Allan Katz, Lisa Langlois. Intelligent, entertaining, moving tale of young, confused Marotte, his problems at home and school and friendship with a straightforward black girl (appealingly played by Woodard). Set in 1963, with good juxtaposition of white suburban and black urban cultures.

Hardhat and Legs (1980) **C-105m. TVM** D: Lee Philips. Kevin Dobson, Sharon Gless, Bobby Short, Jacqueline Brookes, Ray Serra, W. T. Martin. Engaging comedy-drama written by Garson Kanin and Ruth Gordon that tosses together a girl-watching construction worker and a beauty who happens to teach sex education. Well cast, delightfully acted. Above average.▼

Hard Knocks (1980-Australian) **C-85m.** *** D: Don McLennan. Tracey Mann, John Arnold, Bill Hunter, Max Cullen, Tony Barry. Gritty, powerful drama centering on the efforts of ex-con Mann to straighten out her life, highlighted by a brilliant, multifaceted lead performance.▼

Hard Knox (1984) **C-100m. TVM** D: Peter Werner. Robert Conrad, Red West, Bill Erwin, Shane Conrad, Dean Hill, Dianne B. Shaw, Joan Sweeny. Conrad, a career Marine flyer, has the unhappy choice of a desk job, or the leadership of a military school running amok with young misfits. Obviously, a series pilot. Average.▼

Hardly Working (1981) **C-91m.** ** D: Jerry Lewis. Jerry Lewis, Susan Oliver, Roger C. Carmel, Deanna Lund, Harold J. Stone, Steve Franken, Buddy Lester. Jerry's "comeback" (filmed in Florida in 1979) is typical lamebrain comedy (about an unemployed circus clown who bumbles from one job to another), but an older Jerry wavers between playing the oafish kid of yore and a more "mature" character. In any case, not a very good movie; the opening montage from earlier films is much funnier than anything that follows. Trimmed from European release length.▼

Hard Man, The (1957) **C-80m.** ** D: George Sherman. Guy Madison, Lorne Greene, Valerie French, Trevor Bardette. Madison is earnest sheriff who falls in love with murdered rancher's widow.

Hard Ride, The (1971) **C-93m.** **½ D: Burt Topper. Robert Fuller, Sherry Bain, Tony Russel, Marshall Reed, Biff Elliot, William Bonner. Ex-sergeant Fuller accompanies the body of a black buddy home from Vietnam and tries to persuade the vet's white sweetheart and the Indian leader of his motorcycle gang to attend his funeral. Not just another cycle flick, and not bad.

Hard Times (1975) **C-97m.** *** D: Walter Hill. Charles Bronson, James Coburn, Jill Ireland, Strother Martin, Maggie Blye, Michael McGuire. Bronson is a tight-lipped streetfighter and Coburn is the sharpster who arranges his bare-knuckled bouts in 1930s New Orleans. Colorful (but violent) entertainment. Hill's directorial debut.▼

Hard to Get (1938) **80m.** *** D: Ray Enright. Dick Powell, Olivia de Havilland, Charles Winninger, Allen Jenkins, Bonita Granville, Penny Singleton. Good variation on spoiled-rich-girl-meets-poor-but-hardworking-boy idea. Winninger, as Olivia's wealthy father, and Singleton, as their maid, are hilarious. Film is full of great supporting comics (Grady Sutton, Thurston Hall, Arthur Housman, etc.), and includes "You Must Have Been a Beautiful Baby."

Hard to Handle (1933) **78m.** **½ D: Mervyn LeRoy. James Cagney, Mary Brian, Ruth Donnelly, Allen Jenkins, Emma Dunn, Claire Dodd, Robert McWade. Cagney sparkles in this otherwise so-so Depression-era comedy as a fast-talking promoter/hustler who courts pretty Brian; Donnelly is aces as her mom. The "Grapefruit Acres" and diet schemes are homages of sorts to Cagney's legendary scene with Mae Clarke in PUBLIC ENEMY.

Hard to Hold (1984) **C-93m.** *½ D: Larry Peerce. Rick Springfield, Janet Eilber, Patti Hansen, Albert Salmi, Bill Mumy. Pampered rock star collides (literally) with spirited young woman who doesn't know—or care—who he is . . . so naturally he falls in love with her. Tiresome romance designed as star vehicle for teen idol Springfield, and retitled "Hard to Watch" by some wags.▼

Hard to Kill (1990) **C-95m.** ** D: Bruce Malmuth. Steven Seagal, Kelly LeBrock, Bill Sadler, Frederick Coffin, Bonnie Burroughs, Zachary Rosencrantz, Dean Norris. Police detective Seagal uncovers a major political corruption ring and is shot and left for dead; when he awakens from a seven-year coma, he's ripe for revenge. Full of the usual violence and chases for this genre, but Seagal is up to the game and fun to watch. LeBrock, who nurses him back to health, is the real-life Mrs. Seagal.▼

Hard Traveling (1985) **C-107m.** **½ D: Dan Bessie. J. E. Freeman, Ellen Geer, Barry Corbin, James Gammon, Jim Haynie. Occasionally touching but ultimately disappointing drama about a gentle, decent, but uneducated and disadvantaged man (Freeman) who finds love and stability with widow Geer, but commits murder when unable to support her. Done in by

too many flashbacks; lacks that special spark that might have made it memorable. Based on the novel *Bread and a Stone* by Alvah Bessie, father of the director. ▼

Hard Way, The (1942) **109m.** *** D: Vincent Sherman. Ida Lupino, Dennis Morgan, Joan Leslie, Jack Carson, Gladys George, Julie Bishop. Intriguing but artificial story of strong-willed Lupino pushing younger sister Leslie into show business career. Holds up until improbable finale, although it seems unlikely that Broadway would cheer Leslie as the greatest discovery of the age. Morgan and Carson match Lupino's fine performance.

Hardys Ride High, The (1939) **80m.** D: George B. Seitz. Lewis Stone, Mickey Rooney, Cecilia Parker, Fay Holden, Ann Rutherford, Sara Haden, Virginia Grey, Marsha Hunt, William T. Orr. SEE: **Andy Hardy** series.

Harem (1985-French) **C-113m.** *½ D: Arthur Joffe. Nastassja Kinski, Ben Kingsley, Dennis Goldson, Zohra Segal, Michel Robin, Julette Simpson. Thin, boring drama about Arab prince Kingsley, who kidnaps Kinski and adds her to his harem. Solid production values can't take the place of a coherent scenario and fully fleshed-out characterizations.▼

Harem (1986) **C-200m.** TVM D: Billy Hale. Nancy Travis, Art Malik, Sarah Miles, Yaphet Kotto, Cherie Lunghi, Omar Sharif, Ava Gardner. A richly evocative hoot about an American damsel-in-distress being sold to Turkish sultan Sharif for his harem, where she finds murder, intrigue, imperious, jealous #1 wife Gardner, and a white knight riding to the rescue. This one had a record *seven* producers! Look instead for John Milius' vaguely similar but superior adventure romance THE WIND AND THE LION. Originally shown in two parts. Below average.

Harem Girl (1952) **70m.** ** D: Edward Bernds. Joan Davis, Peggie Castle, Arthur Blake, Minerva Urecal. Wacky Davis does her best to enliven slim vehicle about her substituting for a princess.

Harlan County, U.S.A. (1977) **C-103m.** ***½ D: Barbara Kopple. Gripping, human documentary (an Academy Award winner) about the strike of Kentucky mine workers against the Eastover Mining Company, a subsidiary of Duke Power. Memorable scene of miner and Brooklyn cop having a "conversation."▼

Harlem Globetrotters, The (1951) **80m.** ** D: Phil Brown. Thomas Gomez, Dorothy Dandridge, Bill Walker, Angela Clarke. Vehicle built around famed basketball team, with a few romantic interludes.

Harlem Globetrotters on Gilligan's Island, The (1981) **C-100m.** TVM D: Peter Baldwin. Bob Denver, Alan Hale, Jr., Russell Johnson, Dawn Wells, Connie

Forslund, Jim Backus, Natalie Schafer, Scatman Crothers, Martin Landau, Barbara Bain, The Harlem Globetrotters. In the third of their "comeback" movies years after the original series was relegated to that great boob tube in the sky, Gilligan and gang are visited by the Globetrotters, a mad scientist and his assistant, and a squad of basketball-playing robots. Below average.

Harlem Nights (1989) **C-115m.** ** D: Eddie Murphy. Eddie Murphy, Richard Pryor, Redd Foxx, Danny Aiello, Berlinda Tolbert, Della Reese, Jasmine Guy, Michael Lerner. The proprietor of an after-hours club in 1930s Harlem (Pryor) and his adopted son (Murphy) try standing up to a white mobster who's determined to cut in on their take or put them out of business. Murphy's debut as writer-director is skimpily scripted and completely devoid of energy. Even Pryor's effortless charisma can't breathe much life into this one.▼

Harlequin (1980-Australian) **C-96m.** **½ D: Simon Wincer. Robert Powell, David Hemmings, Carmen Duncan, Broderick Crawford, Gus Mercurio, Alan Cassell. Faith-healer Powell helps politician Hemmings's son, who has leukemia; however, his wife (Duncan) is also attracted to the healer. Middling drama updating story of Rasputin, Nicholas, and Alexandra. Retitled DARK FORCES.▼

Harlow (1965) **C-125m.** **½ D: Gordon Douglas. Carroll Baker, Peter Lawford, Red Buttons, Michael Connors, Raf Vallone, Angela Lansbury, Martin Balsam, Leslie Nielsen. Slick, colorful garbage will hold your interest, but doesn't ring true. Baker could never match the real Harlow, but Vallone and Lansbury are good as her stepfather and mother.▼

Harlow (1965) **109m.** ** D: Alex Segal. Carol Lynley, Efrem Zimbalist, Jr., Barry Sullivan, Hurd Hatfield, Ginger Rogers, Hermione Baddeley, Lloyd Bochner, Audrey Totter, John Williams, Robert Strauss. Amateurish off-the-cuff tedium loosely based on screen star of the 1930s. Rogers as Mama Harlow is best. This quickie production made news in 1965 because it was produced in an unusual manner: staged as a live television show, and transferred to kinescope film.

Harness, The (1971) **C-100m. TVM** D: Boris Sagal. Lorne Greene, Julie Sommars, Murray Hamilton, Louise Latham, Lee Harcourt Montgomery, Henry Beckman, Joan Tompkins, Robert Karnes. Fairly strong, Steinbeck-based love story: Greene as middle-aged widower, Sommars as young woman. Good location filming, believable script. Above average.

Harold and Maude (1972) **C-90m.** ***½ D: Hal Ashby. Bud Cort, Ruth Gordon, Vivian Pickles, Cyril Cusack, Charles Tyner,

Ellen Geer. Black comedy focuses on loving relationship between 20-year-old Cort, who's obsessed with death, and 79-year-old swinger Gordon. Dismissed at time of release, this has become a cult favorite, and the cornerstone of writer Colin Higgins' reputation. Cort's phony suicides are hilarious. Music by Cat Stevens.▼

Harold Lloyd's World of Comedy (1962) **94m.** *** Compiled by Harold Lloyd. Harold Lloyd, Bebe Daniels, Mildred Davis. Delightful comedy scenes show why Lloyd was so popular in the 1920s. Highlights include classic building-climbing episode and other great sight gags. A real gem.

Harold Robbins' The Betsy SEE: **Betsy, The**▼

Harold Robbins' The Pirate (1978) **C-200m. TVM** D: Kenneth Annakin. Franco Nero, Anne Archer, Olivia Hussey, Ian McShane, Christopher Lee, James Franciscus, Eli Wallach, Stuart Whitman, Michael Constantine, Armand Assante. Expensively mounted and deliciously lurid romantic pap in the best Robbins tradition, set against a backdrop of Arab-Israeli intrigue, with Nero playing a tempestuous Jewish-born, Arab-raised oil sheik with a frosty American wife and a daughter who grows up to become a PLO fanatic. Tedious and predictable. One interesting note: Archer's real-life mom (Marjorie Lord) plays her mother here. Script by Julius J. Epstein. Average. Also known as THE PIRATE. Later cut to 150m.

Harper (1966) **C-121m.** ***½ D: Jack Smight. Paul Newman, Lauren Bacall, Julie Harris, Shelley Winters, Robert Wagner, Janet Leigh, Arthur Hill, Pamela Tiffin, Robert Webber, Strother Martin, Harold Gould. High-grade action-mystery has Newman as private eye hired by Bacall to investigate disappearance of her husband; blowsy Winters, frustrated Harris are involved in fast-paced, sophisticated yarn. Screenplay by William Goldman, from Ross MacDonald's *The Moving Target.* Sequel: THE DROWNING POOL.▼

Harper Valley P.T.A. (1978) **C-102m.** ** D: Richard Bennett. Barbara Eden, Ronny Cox, Nanette Fabray, Susan Swift, Ron Masak, Louis Nye, Pat Paulsen, Audrey Christie, John Fiedler, Bob Hastings. Bubble-gum comedy based on the hit song about small-town mother who arouses local wrath for her free-thinking ways and retaliates with series of elaborate revenges. Not exactly Noel Coward, but cast full of old pros ekes some chuckles out of the threadbare material. Later a TV series.▼

Harp of Burma SEE: **Burmese Harp, The**▼

Harpy (1970) **C-100m. TVM** D: Gerald Seth Sindell. Hugh O'Brian, Elizabeth Ashley, Tom Nardini, Marlyn Mason, Mark Miller. Extremely odd (and near brilliant)

combination of character study and horror show, most of it occurring at architect's desert home involving ex-wife, ranch assistant, and architect himself. Formula bloody ending, in mysterious tale of passion, actually works. Above average.

Harrad Experiment, The (1973) **C-88m.** **½ D: Ted Post. Don Johnson, James Whitmore, Tippi Hedren, B. (Bruno) Kirby, Jr., Laurie Walters, Robert Middleton, Victoria Thompson. Fair adaptation of offbeat best-seller by Robert Rimmer in which experimental coed college pushes policy of sexual freedom. Two pairs of relationships singled out as in book, but film actually should've been longer! Improvisational group Ace Trucking Co. appears as itself. Melanie Griffith (Hedren's daughter) was an extra in this—at age 14. Look for young Gregory Harrison. Sequel: HARRAD SUMMER.▼

Harrad Summer (1974) **C-103m.** **½ D: Steven H. Stern. Richard Doran, Victoria Thompson, Laurie Walters, Robert Reiser, Bill Dana, Marty Allen. Fair sequel to THE HARRAD EXPERIMENT, about sex-education school for young students, which sends them home, where they can apply what they've learned.▼

Harriet Craig (1950) **94m.** *** D: Vincent Sherman. Joan Crawford, Wendell Corey, Lucile Watson, Allyn Joslyn, Ellen Corby. Remake of CRAIG'S WIFE is well cast, with Crawford in title role of perfectionist wife who'll stop at nothing to have her house and life run as she wishes.

Harry and Son (1984) **C-117m.** ** D: Paul Newman. Paul Newman, Robby Benson, Joanne Woodward, Ellen Barkin, Wilford Brimley, Judith Ivey, Ossie Davis, Morgan Freeman. Newman directed, coproduced and cowrote this contrived, meandering drama about the relationship between a widower father (who's just lost his job—and his self-respect) and son (who hasn't gotten his life in order yet). Newman isn't really convincing as the old man; Benson has played the younger role a bit too often.▼

Harry and the Hendersons (1987) **C-110m.** **½ D: William Dear. John Lithgow, Melinda Dillon, Margaret Langrick, Joshua Rudoy, Kevin Peter Hall, David Suchet, Lainie Kazan, Don Ameche, M. Emmet Walsh. Family encounters a Bigfoot-type monster in the woods and takes it home, thinking it's dead. When it comes alive, the family finds itself becoming attached to the hairy fellow. Amusing but fatally overlong, this sweet-natured variation on E.T., THE EXTRA TERRESTRIAL runs hot and cold; best recommended for kids. Lithgow is terrific as always. Rick Baker's makeup earned an Academy Award.▼

Harry and Tonto (1974) **C-115m.** *** D: Paul Mazursky. Art Carney, Ellen Burstyn, Chief Dan George, Geraldine Fitzgerald,

Larry Hagman, Arthur Hunnicutt, Joshua Mostel, Melanie Mayron, Herbert Berghof, Barbara Rhoades. An old man takes a cross-country trip with his cat as companion. Art Carney won an Oscar for his performance in this bittersweet, episodic comedy.▼

Harry and Walter Go to New York (1976) **C-123m.** ** D: Mark Rydell. James Caan, Elliott Gould, Diane Keaton, Michael Caine, Charles Durning, Lesley Ann Warren, Val Avery, Jack Gilford, Carol Kane. Lavish but lopsided period farce with Caan and Gould as low-grade vaudevillians in the 1890s who wind up trying their luck as safecrackers in N.Y. Spirited but strenuous comedy misses the mark. Nice art direction by Harry Horner.▼

Harry Black and the Tiger (1958-British) **C-107m.** BOMB D: Hugo Fregonese. Stewart Granger, Barbara Rush, Anthony Steel, I. S. Johar. Moldy jungle film tangled in the underbrush, with confusing flashbacks. Filmed in India. Sorry, Harry.▼

Harry in Your Pocket (1973) **C-103m.** *** D: Bruce Geller. James Coburn, Michael Sarrazin, Trish Van Devere, Walter Pidgeon. Engaging story of group of superpickpockets and how they prey upon innocent victims. Pidgeon steals the film as sleazy professional crook.

Harry's Hong Kong (1987) **C-100m.** TVM D: Jerry London. David Soul, Mike Preston, Mel Harris, Jan Gan Boyd, Lisa Lu, David Hemmings. In this series pilot, Soul attempts to transfer Rick Blaine from his short-lived *Casablanca* series to the Orient, playing a white-suited Hong Kong-based soldier of fortune—with just as little panache. Below average.

Harry's War (1981) **C-98m.** **½ D: Kieth Merrill. Edward Herrmann, Geraldine Page, Karen Grassle, David Ogden Stiers, Salome Jens, Elisha Cook. Easygoing postman Herrmann battles the IRS after his aunt (Page) is unfairly billed for $190,000 in back taxes. Capra-esque one-man-against-the-bureaucracy tale is sometimes touching but mostly overbaked. Herrmann performs earnestly; Merrill also wrote the screenplay.▼

Harry Tracy, Desperado (1982-Canadian) **C-100m.** **½ D: William A. Graham. Bruce Dern, Helen Shaver, Michael C. Gwynne, Gordon Lightfoot. Saga of outlaw who lives by his own moral code. A bit laid-back but worthwhile for Dern's fine performance and vivid recreation of Western life at the turn of the century.▼

Hart to Hart (1979) **C-100m.** TVM D: Tom Mankiewicz. Robert Wagner, Stefanie Powers, Lionel Stander, Roddy McDowall, Jill St. John, Stella Stevens, Eugene Roche, Clifton James. Wagner and Powers play jet-setters who, in true Nick and Nora Charles fashion, dabble in detective work to solve the mysterious death of a close friend at a glamorous health spa. Pilot for hit series also offers a gag walk-on by Natalie Wood, billed in closing credits with her real name, Natasha Gurdin. Average.

Harum Scarum (1965) **C-86m.** **½ D: Gene Nelson. Elvis Presley, Mary Ann Mobley, Fran Jeffries, Michael Ansara, Jay Novello, Philip Reed, Theo Marcuse, Billy Barty. Visiting the Middle East gives usual Presley musical formula a change of scenery, via back-lot desert locations.▼

Harvest (1937-French) **105m.** **** D: Marcel Pagnol. Gabriel Gabrio, Orane Demazis, Fernandel, Edouard Delmont, Henri Poupon. Simple, stark tale of peasants Gabrio and Demazis struggling against all odds to till the land and give life to the earth. Magnificent, with Fernandel memorable as Demazis' comical husband.▼

Harvey (1950) **104m.** ***½ D: Henry Koster. James Stewart, Josephine Hull, Peggy Dow, Charles Drake, Cecil Kellaway, Victoria Horne, Jesse White, Wallace Ford, Ida Moore. Stewart gives one of his best performances as tippler Elwood P. Dowd, whose companion is a six-foot invisible rabbit named Harvey (actually, he's 6 feet, 3 inches). Hull won Oscar as distraught sister. Mary Chase and Oscar Brodney adapted Chase's Pulitzer Prizewinning play. Hull, Horne, and White recreate their Broadway roles, with White making his film debut.▼

Harvey Girls, The (1946) **C-101m.** *** D: George Sidney. Judy Garland, Ray Bolger, John Hodiak, Angela Lansbury, Preston Foster, Virginia O'Brien, Marjorie Main, Kenny Baker, Cyd Charisse. Westward expansion brings with it Fred Harvey's railroad station restaurants, and proper young waitresses who have civilizing influence on rowdy communities. Silly script made entertaining by good cast and a few musical highlights (like Oscar-winning "Atchison, Topeka, and the Santa Fe").▼

Harvey Middleman, Fireman (1965) **C-75m.** ** D: Ernest Pintoff. Gene Troobnick, Hermione Gingold, Patricia Harty, Arlene Golonka, Will MacKenzie, Charles Durning. Low-key comedy about mildmannered fireman trying to coordinate fantasy and real life; amiable but unfocused film was animator Pintoff's first live-action feature.

Has Anybody Seen My Gal? (1952) **C-89m.** **½ D: Douglas Sirk. Charles Coburn, Piper Laurie, Rock Hudson, Gigi Perreau, Lynn Bari, William Reynolds, Larry Gates, Skip Homeier. Pleasant, lightweight 1920s nostalgia about rich old Coburn planning to leave his fortune to the family of a woman who turned down his marriage proposal years earlier. Coburn's performance is the whole show; look fast for James Dean.

Hasty Heart, The (1949-British) **99m.**

***½ D: Vincent Sherman. Ronald Reagan, Patricia Neal, Richard Todd, Anthony Nicholls, Howard Crawford. Sensitive film version of John Patrick play, focusing on proud Scottish soldier who discovers he has short time to live and friendships he finally makes among his hospital mates.

Hatari! (1962) **C-159m.** ***½ D: Howard Hawks. John Wayne, Elsa Martinelli, Red Buttons, Hardy Kruger, Gerard Blain, Bruce Cabot. Marvelous lighthearted action film of wild-animal trappers in Africa, with just-right mixture of adventure and comedy. Wayne is at his best. Notable Henry Mancini score. Filmed in Tanganyika; title is Swahili for "Danger!"▼

Hatchet Man, The (1932) **74m.** **½ D: William Wellman. Edward G. Robinson, Loretta Young, Dudley Digges, Blanche Frederici, Leslie Fenton. Fascinating yarn about Chinatown tongs, and Robinson's attempts to Americanize himself. Potent melodrama, once you get past obvious barrier of Caucasian cast.

Hatchet Murders, The SEE: **Deep Red**▼

Hatfields and the McCoys, The (1975) **74m. TVM** D: Clyde Ware. Jack Palance, Steve Forrest, Richard Hatch, Karen Lamm, James Keach, Joan Caulfield. Drama about the petty thievery and the ill-starred love that changed sporadic violence into the legendary feud of the 1880s. Palance and Forrest are the patriarchs of the opposing clans. Average.▼

Hatful of Rain, A (1957) **109m.** *** D: Fred Zinnemann. Eva Marie Saint, Don Murray, Anthony Franciosa, Lloyd Nolan, Henry Silva, Gerald S. O'Laughlin, William Hickey. Realistic melodrama of the living hell dope addict Murray undergoes, and the effects on those around him; fine performances. Scripted by Michael V. Gazzo, from his play.

Hats Off (1936) **70m.** ** D: Boris Petroff. Mae Clarke, John Payne, Helen Lynd, Luis Alberni, Skeets Gallagher, Franklin Pangborn. Minor musical about the travails of rival press agents. The supporting actors, particularly Alberni and Gallagher, fare best here. Payne's first starring role.

Hatter's Castle (1941-British) **90m.** **½ D: Lance Comfort. Deborah Kerr, James Mason, Robert Newton, Emlyn Williams. Fine cast must support fair material in tale of poor man who relentlessly pursues his dream of social acceptance; from A. J. Cronin's novel.

Hatter's Ghost, The (1982-French) **C-120m.** *½ D: Claude Chabrol. Michel Serrault, Charles Aznavour, Monique Chaumette, Aurore Clement. Disappointing murder mystery from Chabrol, based on a Georges Simenon novel. Tailor Aznavour learns that nephew Serrault is a mass killer, but is too scared to inform the police. Potentially exciting thriller is badly handled.

Haunted (1984) C-118m. TVM D: Michael Roemer. Brooke Adams, John De-Vries, Trish Van Devere, Ari Meyers. Uninteresting, overbaked drama about a young woman (Adams) attempting to come to terms with her past as she visits her adoptive mother (Van Devere). Fine performances really cannot save it. Scripted by Roemer; a PBS *American Playhouse* presentation. Average.

Haunted by Her Past (1987) C-100m. TVM D: Michael Pressman. Susan Lucci, John James, Marcia Strassman, Finola Hughes, Robin Thomas, Douglas Seale, Madeleine Sherwood. Romantic pap about a woman possessed by a century-old spirit. Devotees of the soap stars who fill the cast should eat this one up. Average.

Haunted Honeymoon (1940-British) 83m. **½ D: Arthur B. Woods. Robert Montgomery, Constance Cummings, Leslie Banks, Seymour Hicks, Robert Newton, Googie Withers. Famed amateur criminologist Lord Peter Wimsey (Montgomery) marries mystery writer (Cummings) and settles down to quiet honeymoon—until murder enters the picture and demands their involvement. Montgomery miscast as Dorothy L. Sayers' witty sleuth. Originally titled BUSMAN'S HONEYMOON.

Haunted Honeymoon (1986) C-82m. BOMB D: Gene Wilder. Gene Wilder, Gilda Radner, Dom DeLuise, Jonathan Pryce, Paul L. Smith, Peter Vaughan, Bryan Pringle. Tediously unfunny "scare movie" farce inspired by old Bob Hope/Red Skelton comedies; set in an old dark house full of creepy people (with one great gag lifted from Fred MacMurray's MURDER, HE SAYS). When you put Dom DeLuise in drag and still can't get laughs, you know something's wrong. ▼

Haunted House of Horror, The SEE: **Horror House**

Haunted Palace, The (1963) C-85m. **½ D: Roger Corman. Vincent Price, Debra Paget, Lon Chaney, Jr., Frank Maxwell, Leo Gordon, Elisha Cook, Jr., John Dierkes. When a man arrives in New England town to claim family castle, he discovers the town populated by mutants and the castle under an ancestor's evil spell, which soon possesses him. Good-looking but minor film from Corman's Edgar Allan Poe cycle; screenplay by Charles Beaumont, based mainly on H. P. Lovecraft's *The Strange Case of Charles Dexter Ward.*

Haunted Strangler, The (1958-British) 81m. **½ D: Robert Day. Boris Karloff, Anthony Dawson, Elizabeth Allan, Derek Birch, Jean Kent. Offbeat yarn of mystery writer investigating case of murderer hung twenty years ago, with dismaying results. Originally titled GRIP OF THE STRANGLER.▼

Haunted Summer (1988) C-106m. **½

D: Ivan Passer. Phillip Anglim, Laura Dern, Alice Krige, Eric Stoltz, Alex Winter. Flawed film version of Anne Edwards' novel about the fabled and emotional meeting between poets Lord Byron and Percy Shelley, novelist Mary Godwin and Dr. John Polidori in Italy in 1816. The psychedelic '60s had nothing on *this* "summer of love" and experimentation. Beautifully filmed, and better than Ken Russell's similar GOTHIC, but it's still forced and unconvincing.▼

Haunting, The (1963) 112m. ***½ D: Robert Wise. Julie Harris, Claire Bloom, Richard Johnson, Russ Tamblyn, Lois Maxwell, Fay Compton. Ninety-year-old New England house is setting for chosen group being introduced to the supernatural, with hair-raising results. See it with a friend! Filmed in England; Nelson Gidding adapted Shirley Jackson's *The Haunting of Hill House.*▼

Haunting of Julia, The (1976-British-Canadian) C-96m. ** D: Richard Loncraine. Mia Farrow, Keir Dullea, Tom Conti, Jill Bennett, Robin Gammell, Cathleen Nesbitt. Occult thriller about a young woman who tries to start a new life after the death of her daughter and moves into a house inhabited by a troubled spirit. A good (if familiar) start, but soon lapses into unsatisfying contrivance. From a Peter Straub story. Originally titled FULL CIRCLE.▼

Haunting of Sarah Hardy, The (1989) C-100m. TVM D: Jerry London. Sela Ward, Michael Woods, Roscoe Born, Polly Bergen, Morgan Fairchild. Newly married heiress is terrorized by the ghost of her dead mother who is haunting the family mansion. Made for cable. Average.

Haunting Passion, The (1983) C-100m. TVM D: John Korty. Jane Seymour, Gerald McRaney, Millie Perkins, Ruth Nelson, Paul Rossilli, Ivan Bonar. Surprisingly effective and rather erotic thriller, written by Michael Berk and Douglas Schwartz, about a woman who moves into an old house with her new husband, only to find herself pursued by the ghost of the former occupant's dead lover. Seductive Seymour is smashing. Above average.▼

Haunts (1977) C-98m. *** D: Herb Freed. May Britt, Cameron Mitchell, Aldo Ray, William Gray Espy, Susan Nohr. You have to stay with it to appreciate this offbeat horror pic fully, but it's well worth the effort. Writers Anne Marisse and Herb Freed and a good cast have vividly captured small-town atmosphere when a series of murders grips the countryside. As a farm woman with demons of her own, Britt gives the best performance of her erratic career.▼

Haunts of the Very Rich (1972) C-72m. TVM D: Paul Wendkos. Lloyd Bridges, Cloris Leachman, Edward Asner, Anne

[484]

Francis, Tony Bill, Donna Mills, Robert Reed, Moses Gunn. Mixed up reworking of NO EXIT premise. Seven vacationers agree to be flown to tropical paradise, even though they aren't told exactly where they are. Offbeat location work only asset in otherwise plainly acted, unimaginatively scripted allegory. Forget about ending. Average.▼

Hauser's Memory (1970) **C-100m. TVM** D: Boris Sagal. Robert Webber, Susan Strasberg, David McCallum, Leslie Nielsen, Lilli Palmer. Psychological thriller based on Curt Siodmak story; scientist McCallum injects himself with another man's brain fluid, enabling him to relive man's WW2 experiences. Filmed in Europe. Average.

Have Rocket, Will Travel (1959) **76m.** **½ D: David Lowell Rich. The Three Stooges, Jerome Cowan, Anna Lisa, Bob Colbert. Good slapstick with the Stooges accidentally launched into space, where they meet a unicorn and become national heroes. This was the trio's first starring feature after being rediscovered on TV.

Having a Wild Weekend (1965-British) **91m.** **½ D: John Boorman. Dave Clark Five, Barbara Ferris, Lenny Davidson, Rick Huxley, Mike Smith, Denis Payton, David Lodge. Just as The Dave Clark Five tried to steal some of the Beatles' thunder, this fast-paced trifle tried to capture success of A HARD DAY'S NIGHT. The Five star as stuntmen who, along with a model (Ferris), search for a dream island. Songs include "Having a Wild Weekend," "Catch Us If You Can," "I Can't Stand It." Director Boorman's first film. Originally titled CATCH US IF YOU CAN.

Having Babies (1976) **C-100m. TVM** D: Robert Day. Desi Arnaz, Jr., Adrienne Barbeau, Ronny Cox, Harry Guardino, Tom Kennedy, Vicki Lawrence, Richard Masur, Greg Mullavey, Linda Purl, Jan Sterling, Karen Valentine, Abe Vigoda, Jessica Walter. Drama interweaving stories of four couples as they experience childbirth by the "natural" Lamaze method. Topical subject, familiar TV faces, dumb dialogue. Followed by two sequels and then a weekly series. Average.

Having Babies II (1977) **C-100m. TVM** D: Richard Michaels. Tony Bill, Cliff Gorman, Carol Lynley, Paula Prentiss, Wayne Rogers, Nicholas Pryor, Lee Meriwether, Susan Sullivan, Rhea Perlman, Rosanna Arquette. Another dose of emotional crises involving birth, adoption and first love affecting the lives of several couples. The usual multi-character suds capped by actual birth of twins. Average.

Having Babies III (1978) **C-100m. TVM** D: Jackie Cooper. Susan Sullivan, Dennis Howard, Beverly Todd, Mitchell Ryan, Patty Duke Astin, Jamie Smith Jackson,

Phil Foster. Third trip to the delivery room before the series that quickly was retitled *Julie Farr, M.D.* (for Sullivan's character) and tried in several formats over subsequent seasons. Movie gave Astin another of her many Emmy nominations. Average.

Having It All (1982) **C-100m. TVM** D: Edward Zwick. Dyan Cannon, Barry Newman, Hart Bochner, Melanie Chartoff, Sylvia Sidney. Bicoastal woman has two husbands—one in N.Y.C., the other in L.A.—in this change-of-sex update of Alec Guinness's wry THE CAPTAIN'S PARADISE. Below average.▼

Having Wonderful Crime (1945) **70m.** **½ D: A. Edward Sutherland. Pat O'Brien, George Murphy, Carole Landis, Lenore Aubert, George Zucco. Lighthearted mystery of trio of friends investigating magic act which ended in murder; nonstop silliness is strained at times.▼

Having Wonderful Time (1938) **71m.** **½ D: Alfred Santell. Ginger Rogers, Douglas Fairbanks, Jr., Peggy Conklin, Lucille Ball, Lee Bowman, Eve Arden, Red Skelton. Big cast in OK film about Catskills resort hotel; Ginger wants culture on summer vacation but gets Doug instead. Skelton does some funny routines in his feature film debut.▼

Hawaii (1966) **C-171m. *** D: George Roy Hill. Julie Andrews, Max von Sydow, Richard Harris, Torin Thatcher, Gene Hackman, Carroll O'Connor, Jocelyne LaGarde, John Cullum, George Rose, Michael Constantine. Sprawling filmization of James Michener's novel plays well on TV, where cutting actually helps. Story (adapted by Dalton Trumbo and Daniel Taradash) follows growth of Hawaii in 1800s as fierce but well-intentioned missionary tries to bring religion to the undeveloped islands. Uneven but generally entertaining epic. Originally released at 189m.; some prints 151m. Look for Bette Midler as a passenger on the Hawaii-bound ship. Sequel: THE HAWAIIANS.▼

Hawaiians, The (1970) **C-134m. *** D: Tom Gries. Charlton Heston, Geraldine Chaplin, John Phillip Law, Tina Chen, Alec McCowen, Mako. Sequel to HAWAII is epic narrative of seafaring Heston returning home to a restless, changing Hawaii. Film follows several decades of relationships, conflict, hardship, progress, sex, leprosy—you name it. Compelling, colorful storytelling, with outstanding performance by Chen.

Hawaii Five-O (1968) **C-100m. TVM** D: Paul Wendkos. Jack Lord, Nancy Kwan, Leslie Nielsen, Andrew Duggan, Lew Ayres, James Gregory. Supposedly realistic depiction of high-tension police force headed by taskmaster McGarrett (Lord) trying to uncover deadly Chinese

[485]

weapon hidden aboard tramp steamer. Pilot for TV series. Average.

Hawkins on Murder (1973) **C-74m. TVM** D: Jud Taylor. James Stewart, Bonnie Bedelia, Margaret Markov, Strother Martin, Kate Reid, David Huddleston, Antoinette Bower, Robert Webber, Charles McGraw. Pilot for Stewart's TV series surrounds likable star with good cast in OK mystery/ courtroom drama by David Karp about heiress accused in triple murder. Some scenes were shot at lavish Harold Lloyd estate. Above average. Retitled DEATH AND THE MAIDEN.

Hawk of the Wilderness SEE: Lost Island of Kioga

Hawk the Slayer (1980-British) **C-93m.** *½ D: Terry Marcel. Jack Palance, John Terry, Bernard Bresslaw, Ray Charleson, Peter O'Farrell, Harry Andrews, Roy Kinnear, Ferdy Mayne. Brothers Palance and Terry vie for a magical family sword in this period costumer. Labored, with gimmicky direction.▼

Hawmps! (1976) **C-113m.** ** D: Joe Camp. James Hampton, Christopher Connelly, Slim Pickens, Jack Elam, Denver Pyle. Amusing idea based on real life incident: camels trained as Army mounts in Texas desert. Some comedy results, but how far can you stretch one idea? Originally released at 126m.▼

Haywire (1980) **C-200m. TVM** D: Michael Tuchner. Lee Remick, Jason Robards, Deborah Raffin, Dianne Hull, Hart Bochner, Linda Gray, Dean Jagger, Richard Johnson. Provocative drama based on Brooke Hayward's best-seller about growing up in a celebrated but ill-fated family in which glamor and good times met head-on with tragedy. Remick is actress Margaret Sullavan, and Robards is her husband, famous show-business agent/producer Leland Hayward. Brooke's brother William Hayward (sensitively played here by Bochner) produced the movie. Above average.

Hazard (1948) **95m.** ** D: George Marshall. Paulette Goddard, Macdonald Carey, Fred Clark, Stanley Clements. Routine comedy of private-eye Carey following Goddard, falling in love in the process.

Hazard of Hearts, A (1987-British) **C-100m. TVM** D: John Hough. Diana Rigg, Edward Fox, Helena Bonham Carter, Fiona Fullerton, Neil Dickson, Marcus Gilbert, Christopher Plummer, Stewart Granger, Anna Massey, Eileen Atkins. Florid Gothic drama from the vast library of Barbara Cartland romance novels, about a petulant young virgin lost in a card game by her wealthy father to a lecherous nobleman, falling under the spell of a mysterious marquis. On and on it goes, in sumptuous but ultimately tedious splendor, highly budgeted by Lord Grade. Average.

Head, The (1959-German) **92m.** ** D:

Victor Trivas. Horst Frank, Karin Kernke, Michel Simon, Helmut Schmid, Dieter Eppler. Old-fashioned chiller involving head-transplants, with obligatory murders and blood-drenched revenge; extremely eerie but not very convincing.▼

Head (1968) **C-86m.** *** D: Bob Rafelson. The Monkees, Terry (Teri) Garr, Vito Scotti, Timothy Carey, Logan Ramsey, Frank Zappa, Jack Nicholson. Far-out film debut for TV rock group was written (or concocted) by Rafelson and Nicholson before they made big splash with FIVE EASY PIECES; this overlooked item is a delightful explosion of crazy ideas with no coherent plot, many old film clips, some good songs, and such unlikely guest stars as Sonny Liston and Victor Mature. Well worth seeing.▼

Headhunter (1990) **C-92m.** ** D: Francis Schaeffer. Kay Lenz, Wayne Crawford, John Fatooh, Steve Kanaly, June Chadwick, Sam Williams. Seeking the Nigerian tribe that fled Africa, a decapitating demon breezes into Miami, creating problems for cops Lenz and Crawford. Unoriginal and routinely made. Shot in South Africa.▼

Headin' For Broadway (1980) **C-89m.** *½ D: Joseph Brooks. Rex Smith, Terri Treas, Vivian Reed, Paul Carafotes, Gene Foote. Astonishingly amateurish film by writer-director-producer-composer Brooks about four young hopefuls auditioning for a Broadway musical. Looks like a film they tried to save in the editing room; it didn't work.

Heading for Heaven (1947) **71m.** *½ D: Lewis D. Collins. Stuart Erwin, Glenda Farrell, Irene Ryan, Milburn Stone, Selmer Jackson, Janis Wilson. Soggy account of well-meaning Erwin trying to build model middle-income-bracket community, but being fleeced by racketeers.

Headless Ghost, The (1958-British) **61m.** BOMB D: Peter Graham Scott. Richard Lyon, Liliane Sottane, David Rose, Clive Revill, Carl Bernard, Trevor Barnett. Brainless horror-comedy with students investigating a haunted castle.

Headline Hunters (1955) **70m.** ** D: William Witney. Rod Cameron, Julie Bishop, Ben Cooper, Raymond Greenleaf. Uninspired tale of fledgling reporter tracking down big-city racketeers. Remake of 1940 BEHIND THE NEWS.

Headlines of Destruction (1955-French) **85m.** ** D: John Berry. Eddie Constantine, Bella Darvi, Paul Frankeur, Walter Chiari. Interesting concept poorly executed; Darvi is defense attorney involved with Constantine in trial of man accused of murder.

Head of a Tyrant (1958-Italian) **C-83m.** ** D: Fernando Cerchio. Massimo Girotti, Isabelle Corey, Renato Baldini, Yvette Masson. Humdrum spectacle involving siege

[486]

of Bethulia by Assyrians, with Corey playing the legendary Judith.

Head Office (1986) **C-86m.** ** D: Ken Finkleman. Judge Reinhold, Eddie Albert, Jane Seymour, Danny De Vito, Rick Moranis, Don Novello, Michael O'Donoghue, Wallace Shawn, Lori-Nan Engler. Naive Reinhold is hired by world's most powerful multinational conglomerate after his father pulls strings, falls for board chairman's renegade daughter. Episodic, wildly uneven comedy wastes good cast, though Novello, Albert, and O'Donoghue have their funny moments, Seymour some sexy ones.▼

Head On (1980-Canadian) **C-98m.** ** D: Michael Grant. Sally Kellerman, Stephen Lack, John Huston, Lawrence Dane, John Peter Linton. Strange comedy-drama with Kellerman and Lack meeting after a car accident, fulfilling each other's sex fantasies by acting out bizarre games. Ambitious but unsuccessful. Retitled FATAL ATTRACTION for U.S. release in 1985.▼

Head Over Heels (1979) **C-97m.** **½ D: Joan Micklin Silver. John Heard, Mary Beth Hurt, Peter Riegert, Kenneth McMillan, Gloria Grahame, Nora Heflin, Griffin Dunne. Low-key story of Heard's obsession with winning back former girlfriend Hurt; the kind of film that engenders strictly personal reactions—it will either charm or annoy you. Based on Ann Beattie's novel CHILLY SCENES OF WINTER, and re-issued under that name at 93m. Jazz harmonica great Toots Thielemans is prominently featured on the soundtrack.▼

Healers, The (1974) **C-100m.** TVM D: Tom Gries. John Forsythe, Kate Woodville, Season Hubley, Pat Harrington, Anthony Zerbe, Beverly Garland, John McIntire. Hospital drama with the harassed director of a medical center (Forsythe) at the core. Performances are adequate, the plot written to formula. Another busted pilot. Average.

Health SEE: **H.E.A.L.T.H.**

H.E.A.L.T.H. (1979) **C-102m.** ** D: Robert Altman. Carol Burnett, Lauren Bacall, Glenda Jackson, James Garner, Dick Cavett, Paul Dooley, Henry Gibson, Alfre Woodard, Donald Moffat. Offbeat political satire using health-food convention in Florida hotel as basis for various backroom shenanigans. Non-Altman buffs may like this more than devotees; Woodard steals the film—no easy feat considering that incredible cast—as hotel's ultra-patient manager. Shelved for two years, finally released by another distributor. Title is acronym for Happiness, Energy, And Longevity Through Health.

Hear Me Good (1957) **80m.** *½ D: Don McGuire. Hal March, Joe E. Ross, Merry Anders, Jean Willes. Trivia concerning a fixed beauty contest.

Hear No Evil (1982) **C-100m.** TVM D: Harry Falk. Gil Gerard, Bernie Casey, Wings Hauser, Mimi Rogers, Christina Hart, Brion James, Ron Karabatsos. Ex-cop left stone deaf by a bike gang he'd been trying to nail on drugs, goes after the baddies on his own, with the help of his one-time partner, a therapist, and a "hearing ear" dog. Pilot to a prospective series. Average.

Hearse, The (1980) **C-100m.** ** D: George Bowers. Trish Van Devere, Joseph Cotten, David Gautreaux, Donald Hotton, Med Flory, Donald Petrie. Passably engrossing yarn right off the woman-in-distress/house-inhabited-by-spirits assembly line, with an unsatisfying conclusion.▼

Hearst and Davies Affair, The (1985) **C-100m.** TVM D: David Lowell Rich. Robert Mitchum, Virginia Madsen, Fritz Weaver, Doris Belack. Lush but lackadaisical drama about the relationship between publishing magnate William Randolph Hearst and actress Marion Davies, whitewashed for television. Average.

Heart (1987) **C-90m.** *½ D: James Lemmo. Brad Davis, Frances Fisher, Steve Buscemi, Robinson Frank Adu. Dreary, stereotypical boxing tale about has-been fighter Davis—complete with dishonest manager—who's pitted against a rival ten years his junior.▼

Heartaches (1981-Canadian) **C-93m.** **½ D: Donald Shebib. Margot Kidder, Annie Potts, Robert Carradine, Winston Rekert, George Touliatos, Guy Sanvido. Pregnant Potts abandons husband Carradine—who is not the baby's father—and becomes the unwilling buddy of man-hunting screwball Kidder. Fine lead performances spark this minor comedy.▼

Heartbeat (1946) **102m.** ** D: Sam Wood. Ginger Rogers, Jean-Pierre Aumont, Adolphe Menjou, Basil Rathbone, Melville Cooper. So-so drama of lady pickpocket and diplomat who eventually fall for each other; benefits from good cast.

Heart Beat (1980) **C-109m.** *½ D: John Byrum. Nick Nolte, Sissy Spacek, John Heard, Ray Sharkey, Anne Dusenberry, Kent Williams, Tony Bill, Steve Allen. Hapless chronicle of the relationship between Jack Kerouac (Heard) and Carolyn (Spacek) and Neal (Nolte) Cassady. Byrum's flaky script (based more on fiction than on fact) has no continuity whatsoever. Sharkey stands out as the Allen Ginsbergesque Ira; good period score by Jack Nitzsche. Watch for John Larroquette.▼

Heartbeeps (1981) **C-79m.** *½ D: Allan Arkush. Andy Kaufman, Bernadette Peters, Randy Quaid, Kenneth McMillan, Melanie Mayron, Christopher Guest, voice of Jack Carter. Two robots fall for each other in this misfired futuristic comedy. Students of makeup might want to take a peek at Stan Winston's work.▼

Heartbreaker (1983) **C-90m.** ** D: Frank Zuniga. Fernando Allende, Dawn Dunlap, Peter Gonzales Falcon, Michael D. Roberts, Miguel Ferrer, Pepe Serna, Rafael Campos. Chicano Allende falls for WASP Dunlap amid an ambience of custom-fitted automobiles. Lackluster independent production is annoyingly devoid of insight into the culture it depicts. Look fast for Patty "Apollonia" Kotero.▼

Heartbreakers (1984) **C-98m.** **½ D: Bobby Roth. Peter Coyote, Nick Mancuso, Carole Laure, Max Gail, James Laurenson, Carol Wayne, Kathryn Harrold, Jamie Rose. Moody, provocative film about two male friends (avant-garde artist Coyote, second-generation businessman Mancuso) seeking creative and sexual fulfillment and trying to define their relationships with others. Highly personal, occasionally insightful film invites highly personal reactions. Bull's-eye performances, great use of L.A. locations.▼

Heartbreak Hotel (1988) **C-93m.** **½ D: Chris Columbus. David Keith, Tuesday Weld, Charlie Schlatter, Jacque Lynn Colton, Angela Goethals, Chris Mulkey, Karen Landry. A reliable test of your whimsy quotient, as an Ohio teen (Schlatter) kidnaps Elvis in 1972, then transports him home to the divorced mom (Weld) who's carried a torch for the King since the mid-1950s. Keith's Presley, like the entire film, is fun, though the premise is so hard to swallow that you're likely to go with this—or reject it—all the way. Pair this with WILD IN THE COUNTRY or ROCK, ROCK, ROCK for a compatible VCR double bill.▼

Heartbreak Kid, The (1972) **C-104m.** *** D: Elaine May. Charles Grodin, Cybill Shepherd, Jeannie Berlin, Eddie Albert, Audra Lindley. Neil Simon's supreme comedy of embarrassment, adapted from Bruce Jay Friedman's short story "A Change of Plan." Jewish boy (Grodin) gets married (to Berlin) but meets beautiful WASP blonde (Shepherd) on honeymoon, and determines to juggle plans. Either hilarious or horrifying, depending on your point of view; directed for maximum impact by May, whose daughter plays Grodin's bride.▼

Heartbreak Ridge (1986) **C-130m.** **½ D: Clint Eastwood. Clint Eastwood, Marsha Mason, Everett McGill, Moses Gunn, Eileen Heckart, Bo Svenson, Boyd Gaines, Mario Van Peebles, Arlen Dean Snyder. Eastwood is so enjoyable to watch, as a hell-raising career marine sergeant who whips a squadron of young recruits into shape, that he makes this predictable and protracted film worthwhile. But it's still pretty thin stuff and takes longer to play

out than the real-life invasion of Grenada it depicts. ▼

Heartburn (1986) **C-108m.** *** D: Mike Nichols. Meryl Streep, Jack Nicholson, Jeff Daniels, Maureen Stapleton, Stockard Channing, Richard Masur, Catherine O'Hara, Steven Hill, Milos Forman, Karen Akers, Anna Maria Horsford, Mercedes Ruehl, Joanna Gleason, Yakov Smirnoff. Nora Ephron adapted her own best-selling (and autobiographical) book about a sophisticated couple whose marriage seems just fine until she learns he's been having an affair—while she's pregnant! Lightweight, superficial story is supercharged by two charismatic stars, who make it a must-see. Director Forman makes his acting debut in minor supporting role.▼

Heart Condition (1990) **C-95m.** **½ D: James D. Perriott. Bob Hoskins, Denzel Washington, Chloe Webb, Roger E. Mosley, Ja'net Dubois, Alan Rachins, Ray Baker, Jeffrey Meek. Superficial but entertaining yarn about a crass, bigoted L.A. cop who gets a heart transplant and learns, to his dismay, that the donor was the slick black lawyer he'd been stalking. What's more, the deceased appears as a ghost/ companion who wants the cop to help avenge his murder. Outlandish premise made palatable by its two dynamic leads.▼

Heart Is a Lonely Hunter, The (1968) **C-125m.** **½ D: Robert Ellis Miller. Alan Arkin, Sondra Locke, Laurinda Barrett, Stacy Keach, Chuck McCann, Cicely Tyson. Good acting by Arkin and entire cast helps this rambling adaptation of Carson McCullers' novel about the way a deaf mute helps those around him; film would have been better as a period-piece. Film debuts of Locke and Keach.▼

Heartland (1979) **C-96m.** ***½ D: Richard Pearce. Rip Torn, Conchata Ferrell, Barry Primus, Lilia Skala, Megan Folson, Amy Wright. Simple, well-told story of hearty Americans surviving the rigors of frontier life, circa 1910. Ferrell plays a young widow who accepts a job as housekeeper for dour rancher Torn in the wilds of Wyoming. Well-acted, well-filmed, and beautifully understated; based on the actual diaries of a pioneer woman.▼

Heartland Reggae (1980-Canadian) **C-87m.** BOMB D: J. P. Lewis. Bob Marley and the Wailers, Peter Tosh, Jacob Miller and the Inner Circle Band, Althea and Donna. Shoddy documentary of '78 concert commemorating a visit to Jamaica by Haile Selassie. Even the music can't save it.▼

Heart Like a Wheel (1983) **C-113m.** **½ D: Jonathan Kaplan. Bonnie Bedelia, Beau Bridges, Leo Rossi, Hoyt Axton, Bill McKinney, Anthony Edwards, Dean Paul Martin, Paul Bartel, Dick Miller, Terence Knox. Well-made but curiously uninspiring bio of race-car driver Shirley

Muldowney, who had to fight sexism—and the conflict of career vs. marriage—to become a champion on the track. Bedelia's performance is outstanding, but disjointed narrative—particularly where her relationship with racer Connie Kalitta (Bridges) is concerned—is a handicap.▼

Heart of a Champion: The Ray Mancini Story (1985) C-100m. TVM D: Richard Michaels. Robert Blake, Doug McKeon, Mariclare Costello, Tony Burton, Ray Buktenica, James Callahan. Lightweight champion Ray "Boom Boom" Mancini fights for the title he felt his dad would have won had WW2 not cut short the latter's promising career. The more interesting story would have been the old man's. Incidentally, the fight sequences were staged by film's executive producer, Sylvester Stallone. Average.▼

Heart of Dixie (1989) C-95m. *½ D: Martin Davidson. Ally Sheedy, Virginia Madsen, Phoebe Cates, Treat Williams, Don Michael Paul, Kyle Secor, Francesca Roberts, Kurtwood Smith, Richard Bradford, Barbara Babcock. Forgettable story of Alabama college sorority in the late 1950s and one girl's awakening to larger realities of life—including the mistreatment of blacks in the South. Superficial and uninvolving, to say the least.▼

Heart of Glass (1976-German) C-93m. *** D: Werner Herzog. Josef Bierbichler, Stefan Autter, Clemens Scheitz, Volker Prechtel, Sonia Skiba. A glassblower has died without revealing the secret formula of his craft, and this has a profound, disturbing effect on his fellow townspeople. Thematically muddled but visually stunning; crammed with stark, graphic, beautiful images. Based on a Bavarian legend; Herzog each day put his cast into a hypnotic trance, to attempt to achieve an effect of collective hysteria.▼

Heart of Midnight (1988) C-93m. *½ D: Matthew Chapman. Jennifer Jason Leigh, Peter Coyote, Gale Mayron, Sam Schacht, Denise Dummont, Frank Stallone, Brenda Vaccaro. Psychological thriller about a young woman teetering on the edge of sanity, who inherits a seedy sex club which attracts a sick clientele. Good performance by Leigh, and artsy approach to subject, are minor diversions in this muddled and unpleasant film. Written by the director.▼

Heart of Steel (1983) C-100m. TVM D: Donald Wrye. Peter Strauss, Pamela Reed, John Doucette, Barry Primus, John Goodman, Gary Cole. Strauss gives another top-notch performance as a laid-off steelworker striving to put food on the family table as the American dream crumbles. Fine script by his producing partner, Gary DeVore, goes right to the core of a contemporary social issue. Above average.

Heart of the Matter, The (1954-British)

105m. *** D: George More O'Ferrall. Trevor Howard, Elizabeth Allan, Maria Schell, Denholm Elliott. Graham Greene's novel of inner and outward conflict set in South Africa, with Howard as police officer on verge of mental collapse.

Heart of the Stag (1984-New Zealand) C-91m. ** D: Michael Firth. Bruno Lawrence, Mary Regan, Terence Cooper, Anne Flannery. Lawrence is mysterious stranger who signs on as a farmhand and disrupts incestuous relationship of Cooper and his redheaded daughter Regan. Pretentious drama benefits from good acting and a tense musical score by Leonard Rosenman.▼

Hearts and Armour (1982-Italian) C-101m. ** D: Giacomo Battiato. Tanya Roberts, Barbara De Rossi, Zeudi Araya, Rick Edwards, Leigh McCloskey, Ron Moss. Well-mounted but confusing fantasy based on the 1516 classic *Orlando Furioso* by Ludovico Ariosto. De Rossi is a sexy female warrior in knight's armor fighting in the war between Christians and Moors. American stars such as Roberts and McCloskey add little to a film (also shot in TV miniseries form) aimed at an international audience.▼

Hearts and Minds (1974) C-110m. ***½ D: Peter Davis. Oscar-winning documentary about our misguided involvement in Vietnam was political hot potato for awhile, but may rate more frequent showings now that the country has caught up with it. Packs a wallop, regardless of one's political persuasion.▼

Hearts Divided (1936) 87m. ** D: Frank Borzage. Marion Davies, Dick Powell, Charlie Ruggles, Claude Rains, Edward Everett Horton, Arthur Treacher. Davies is French girl and Powell is Napoleon's brother in OK musical romance.

Hearts of Fire (1987) C-95m. BOMB D: Richard Marquand. Fiona (Flanagan), Rupert Everett, Bob Dylan, Julian Glover, Suzanne Bertish, Ian Dury, Richie Havens, Larry Lamb, Maury Chaykin. Perfectly dreadful account of the rise of a rock singer (Fiona), and her relationships with her mentors: a British pop star (Everett) and a cynical, retired rock legend (who else but Dylan). Dylan's first screen appearance since 1977's RENALDO AND CLARA; Marquand's final credit as director. This turkey played briefly in England in 1987, and was released to video in 1990. There are 19 songs on the soundtrack (but none memorable enough to raise its rating).▼

Hearts of the West (1975) C-102m. *** D: Howard Zieff. Jeff Bridges, Andy Griffith, Donald Pleasence, Blythe Danner, Alan Arkin, Richard B. Shull, Herb Edelman. Offbeat comedy about starry-eyed Bridges who comes to Hollywood in the 1930s hoping to be a Western writer, winds up starring in cheap cowboy films instead. Enjoyable but low-key.▼

Hearts of the World (1918) 122m. **½ D: D. W. Griffith. Lillian Gish, Dorothy Gish, Robert Harron, Kate Bruce, Ben Alexander, George Fawcett, George Siegmann. Griffith's epic of WW1, shot in England and France; melodramatic story of a young man gone to war, the sufferings of his family and homeland, was made as propaganda to convince America to enter WW1. Dorothy Gish has fine comedy role, young Noel Coward a small part as man with wheelbarrow and villager, Erich von Stroheim a lusty German. For these highlights, other good moments, worth seeing.▼

Heartsounds (1984) C-135m. TVM D: Glenn Jordan. Mary Tyler Moore, James Garner, Sam Wanamaker, Wendy Crewson, David Gardner, Carl Marotte. Justifiably acclaimed weeper, a wonderfully acted version of Martha Weinman Lear's bestseller dealing with her life when her doctor-husband suffers a series of debilitating heart attacks. Fay Kanin wrote the script and Norman Lear, the author's cousin, produced. The two leads give the best performances of their careers. Above average.

Heart To Heart (1978-French) C-110m. *** D: Pascal Thomas. Daniel Ceccaldi, Laurence Ligneres, Anne Caudry, Michel Galabru, Elisa Servier. Fifteen years in the life of a family, recalled by daughter-sister Caudry. Sometimes episodic, but mostly a light, cheerful, well-acted comedy.

Heat (1972) C-100m. *** D: Paul Morrissey. Sylvia Miles, Joe Dallesandro, Andrea Feldman, Pat Ast, Ray Vestal. Andy Warhol meets SUNSET BOULEVARD in this hot and heavy tale of unemployed actor Dallesandro taking up with faded star Miles. Even non-fans of the Warhol group might like this.▼

Heat (1987) C-101m. BOMB D: R. M. Richards. Burt Reynolds, Karen Young, Peter MacNicol, Howard Hesseman, Neill Barry, Diana Scarwid, Joe Mascolo, Alfie Wise. Dim, dingy, scattershot film (written by William Goldman, of all people) about a Las Vegas tough, whose exact livelihood is never defined, but who knows how to handle the low-lifes—and teaches "protege" MacNicol all he knows. So what?▼

Heat and Dust (1983-British) C-130m. *** D: James Ivory. Julie Christie, Greta Scacchi, Christopher Cazenove, Julian Glover, Susan Fleetwood, Shashi Kapoor, Madhur Jaffrey, Barry Foster, Zakir Hussain, Patrick Godfrey. Englishwomen Scacchi and great-niece Christie, sixty years apart, fall in love with India and become pregnant by natives—yet still remain outsiders in a land they can never fully comprehend. Intelligent drama, highlighted by lovely performances. Screenplay by Ruth Prawer Jhabvala, from her novel.▼

Heathers (1989) C-102m. **½ D: Michael Lehmann. Winona Ryder, Christian Slater, Shannen Doherty, Lisanne Falk, Kim Walker, Penelope Milford, Glenn Shadix, Lance Fenton. Sharp, somewhat smug satire of high school social strata, with Ryder in a terrific performance as a girl who hangs out with the school's bitch-queens but doesn't feel quite comfortable about their reign of terror. Outrageous black humor works at first, but isn't sustained by an uneven script that goes far astray. Slater is commanding in his Jack Nicholsonesque performance. Feature debut for director Lehmann and writer Daniel Waters is an instant cult-type film, with many virtues as well as flaws.▼

Heat of Anger (1971) C-74m. TVM D: Don Taylor. Susan Hayward, James Stacy, Lee J. Cobb, Fritz Weaver, Bettye Ackerman, Tyne Daly. Familiar blend of courtroom stereotypes in story of assured lady attorney teaming up with young lawyer in defense of accused murderer (with construction site as crime's setting). Good cast cannot redeem script by usually superior Fay Kanin. Average.

Heat of Desire (1980-French) C-90m. ** D: Luc Beraud. Patrick Dewaere, Clio Goldsmith, Jeanne Moreau, Guy Marchand, Pierre Dux, Jose-Luis Lopez Vasquez. Happily married university professor is whisked away for spontaneous sex by mysterious, loose-living free spirit, who soon destroys his marriage and scuttles his career. Silly but sometimes sexy heavy-breather, with several screen-filling shots of Goldsmith's ample frame. U.S. release: 1984.▼

Heat's On, The (1943) 80m. ** D: Gregory Ratoff. Mae West, Victor Moore, William Gaxton, Lester Allen, Mary Roche, Hazel Scott, Xavier Cugat, Lloyd Bridges. Mae is a musical-comedy star involved with conniving producers in this flat, low-budget nightclub musical. The heat's certainly off; West's last film until MYRA BRECKINRIDGE in 1970.

Heat Wave (1954-British) 68m. *½ D: Ken Hughes. Alex Nicol, Hillary Brooke, Paul Carpenter, Sidney James. Tame murder yarn, with Brooke the sultry dame involved in homicide.▼

Heat Wave! (1974) C-78m. TVM D: Jerry Jameson. Ben Murphy, Bonnie Bedelia, Lew Ayres, David Huddleston, John Anderson, Robert Hogan, Dana Elcar. Young clerk and his pregnant wife struggle to escape from a catastrophic heat wave. The cast sweats this one out in standard style. Average.

Heatwave (1983-Australian) C-99m. *** D: Phillip Noyce. Judy Davis, Richard Moir, Chris Haywood, Bill Hunter, John Gregg, Anna Jemison. Radical Davis protests destruction of neighborhood for $100 million redevelopment project by firm which might have mob connections. Situation further complicated by attraction between her and project architect Moir in this Aussie counterpart to CHINATOWN. Based on a real-life incident, which also inspired THE KILLING OF ANGEL STREET.▼

Heaven (1987) C-80m. ** D: Diane Keaton. Nothing if not bizarre, this personal project of Keaton's intersperses oddly shot interviews with non sequitur clips from old movies on the subject of Heaven: how to get there, what it will be like, if it exists, etc. Clips range from METROPOLIS to THE HORN BLOWS AT MIDNIGHT . . . but what's the point?▼

Heaven Can Wait (1943) C-112m. ***½ D: Ernst Lubitsch. Gene Tierney, Don Ameche, Charles Coburn, Marjorie Main, Laird Cregar, Spring Byington, Allyn Joslyn, Eugene Pallette, Signe Hasso, Louis Calhern. Excellent comedy-fantasy, set in the 1880s. Ameche, who believes he's lived a life of sin, recalls his past as he requests admission to Hades. Witty Samson Raphaelson script helps make this a delight. Based on the play *Birthdays* by Laszlo Bus-Fekete.▼

Heaven Can Wait (1978) C-100m. *** D: Warren Beatty and Buck Henry. Warren Beatty, Julie Christie, Jack Warden, Dyan Cannon, Charles Grodin, James Mason, Buck Henry, Vincent Gardenia. Gentle, pleasing remake of HERE COMES MR. JORDAN with Beatty as good-natured football player who is taken to heaven ahead of schedule, and has to return to "life" in another man's body. Amiable but never moving, with Christie miscast as the woman who inspires Beatty. Screenplay by Beatty and Elaine May.▼

Heaven Help Us (1985) C-104m. *** D: Michael Dinner. Donald Sutherland, John Heard, Andrew McCarthy, Mary Stuart Masterson, Kevin Dillon, Malcolm Danare, Jennie Dundas, Kate Reid, Wallace Shawn, Philip Bosco, Patrick Dempsey, Christopher Durang. Very funny evocation of Catholic high school life in Brooklyn, circa 1965, with solid ring of truth throughout. Shawn has hilarious cameo as priest who kicks off school dance with denunciation of lust. Impressive feature debuts for writer Charles Purpura and director Dinner. ▼

√ **Heaven Knows, Mr. Allison** (1957) C-107m. *** D: John Huston. Deborah Kerr, Robert Mitchum. Marvelous, touching tale of nun Kerr and Marine Mitchum stranded together on a Japanese-infested Pacific island during WW2. Solid performances by the stars.

Heavenly Bodies (1985-Canadian) C-89m. BOMB D: Lawrence Dane. Cynthia Dale, Richard Rebiere, Walter George Alton, Laura Henry, Stuart Stone. The world's first Aerobics Musical, and with any luck, the last.▼

Heavenly Body, The (1943) 95m. ** D: Alexander Hall. Hedy Lamarr, William Powell, James Craig, Fay Bainter, Henry O'Neill, Spring Byington. Hedy is heavenly, but script is silly; astronomer Powell suspects neglected wife Lamarr of being unfaithful with air-raid warden Craig.

Heavenly Days (1944) 71m. ** D: Howard Estabrook. Fibber McGee and Molly (Jim and Marion Jordan), Barbara Hale, Eugene Pallette, Gordon Oliver. Mild entry in famed radio comedians' series, with the lovable married couple off to Washington to help run the Senate.

Heavenly Kid, The (1985) C-89m. *½ D: Cary Medoway. Lewis Smith, Jason Gedrick, Jane Kaczmarek, Richard Mulligan, Mark Metcalf. Embarrassingly amateurish fantasy-comedy about a greasy teen of the early '60s who dies in a chicken race and can't get into heaven—until he makes amends on earth by helping out a young nerd in the 1980s. Film's better moments come toward the end, but by then you may have bailed out.▼

Heavenly Pursuits SEE: **Gospel According to Vic, The** ▼

Heaven Only Knows (1947) 95m. **½ D: Albert S. Rogell. Robert Cummings, Brian Donlevy, Jorja Curtwright, Marjorie Reynolds, Bill Goodwin, John Litel, Stuart Erwin. Strictly standard Western with fantasy touches as angel Cummings descends to earth to help soulless gambler. Good cast but nothing new. Retitled: MONTANA MIKE.

Heavens Above! (1963-British) 105m. *** D: John and Roy Boulting. Peter Sellers, Cecil Parker, Isabel Jeans, Eric Sykes. Wry satire on British clergy life, with Sellers top-notch as the reverend who becomes bishop in outer space. Originally released at 118m.▼

Heaven's Gate (1980) C-149m. ** D: Michael Cimino. Kris Kristofferson, Christopher Walken, Isabelle Huppert, Jeff Bridges, John Hurt, Sam Waterston, Brad Dourif, Joseph Cotten, Geoffrey Lewis, Richard Masur, Terry O'Quinn, Mickey Rourke. Writer-director Cimino's now-notorious spectacle is missing just one thing: a story. It deals, more or less, with the conflict between immigrant settlers of 19th century Wyoming and the ruthless American empire-builders who want them eliminated. Stunningly photographed (by Vilmos Zsigmond) on magnificent locations, with incredible period detail—all to little effect, since the narrative, character motivations, and soundtrack are so hopelessly muddled. Originally shown at 219m.▼

Heaven with a Barbed Wire Fence (1939) 62m. **½ D: Ricardo Cortez. Jean Rogers, Glenn Ford, Raymond Walburn, Marjorie Rambeau, Richard Conte. Good little romance with down-and-out Rogers and Ford deciding to marry despite many obstacles. Ford's feature debut.

Heaven with a Gun (1969) **C-101m.** **½ D: Lee H. Katzin. Glenn Ford, Carolyn Jones, Barbara Hershey, John Anderson, David Carradine. Peace-loving man is forced to return to world of violence in the Old West when danger threatens. Uneven.

Heavy Metal (1981-Canadian) **C-90m.** *** D: Gerald Potterton. Voices of Richard Romanus, John Candy, Joe Flaherty, Don Francks, Eugene Levy, Harold Ramis, John Vernon. Episodic animated feature is uneven, but great fun on a mindless, adolescent level. Sexy sci-fi stories and vignettes in a variety of graphic styles, many set to rock music. Our favorites: "Harry Canyon," about a N.Y.C. cabbie of the future, and "Den," a boy's macho fantasy. Film is actually the work of many animation studios, directors, and writers around the world.

Heavy Petting (1988) **C-80m.** **½ D: Obie Benz. David Byrne, Sandra Bernhard, Allen Ginsberg, Ann Magnuson, Spalding Gray, Josh Mostel, Laurie Anderson, John Oates, Abbie Hoffman, Jacki Ochs. ATOMIC CAFE–style look at sexual mores in the 1950s, punctuated by celebrity interviews and highlighted by hysterical period film clips. Scattershot quasi-documentary lacks strong point of view, but it's tough to knock a film in which such "witnesses" as David Byrne, William S. Burroughs, and Zoe Tamerlis (of MS. 45 cultdom) offer their views on teen dating.▼

Heavy Traffic (1973) **C-76m.** ***½ D: Ralph Bakshi. X-rated animated feature is somewhat pretentious and largely gross in telling story of young New Yorker depressed by sights and sounds around him, finding refuge at drawing-board. Dazzling cinematic treatment, with often revolutionary combination of live-action and animation. Some brilliant set-pieces within loose story framework.▼

Hedda (1975-British) **C-104m.** **½ D: Trevor Nunn. Glenda Jackson, Peter Eyre, Timothy West, Jennie Linden, Patrick Stewart. Royal Shakespeare Company production of Ibsen's *Hedda Gabler* attains a modicum of vitality from Jackson's showy performance in the title role. So-so.▼

Heidi (1937) **88m.** **½ D: Allan Dwan. Shirley Temple, Jean Hersholt, Arthur Treacher, Helen Westley, Mady Christians, Sidney Blackmer, Sig Ruman, Marcia Mae Jones, Mary Nash. Classic children's story set in 19th-century Switzerland is good vehicle for Shirley, playing girl taken from grandfather (Hersholt) to live with cruel

Nash. Nice tear-jerker for children. Also shown in computer-colored version.▼

Heidi (1952-Swiss) **98m.** *** D: Luigi Comencini. Elsbeth Sigmund, Heinrich Gretler, Thomas Klameth, Elsie Attenoff. Faithful, flavorful retelling of Johanna Spyri's children's classic.

Heidi (1965-Austrian-German) **C-95m.** *** D: Werner Jacobs. Eva Marie Singhammer, Gertraud Mittermayr, Gustav Knuth, Lotte Ledi. Fine retelling of classic children's story about young girl who leaves her cozy home in Swiss Alps for adventures in the world below.▼

Heidi (1968) **C-110m.** **TVM** D: Delbert Mann. Maximilian Schell, Jean Simmons, Michael Redgrave, Walter Slezak, Jennifer Edwards, Peter Van Eyck. Well-made version of the classic story, with Edwards (daughter of Blake Edwards) leading a good cast. Script by Earl Hamner Jr. of *The Waltons* fame. Above average.▼

Heidi and Peter (1955-Swiss) **C-89m.** **½ D: Franz Schnyder. Heinrich Gretler, Elsbeth Sigmund, Thomas Klameth, Anita Mey. Further adventures of Johanna Spyri's characters, involving flood threatening Heidi's village.

Heidi's Song (1982) **C-94m.** *½ D: Robert Taylor. Voices of Lorne Greene, Sammy Davis, Jr., Margery Gray, Michael Bell, Peter Cullen. Animated feature from Hanna-Barbera studio reprises all-too familiar Heidi tale. Despite songs by Sammy Cahn and Burton Lane, awkward continuity, lifeless animation and an excess of cute animals leave this little better than most Saturday morning fare.▼

Heimat (1984-German) **C/B&W-940m.** ✓ *** D: Edgar Reitz. Marita Breuer, Dieter Schaad, Rudiger Weigang, Karin Rasenack, Willi Burger, Gertrud Bredel, Mathias Kniesbeck, Michael Kausch. No, that running time is not a typo! This is an ambitious epic, almost 16 hours in length, about life in a provincial German village between 1919 and 1982. First few hours are generally more compelling than the last. Has its boring stretches, and after a while it does seem like a glorified soap opera, but at its best, perceptive, comic, even poetic. Gernot Roll's cinematography is exquisite.

Heiress, The (1949) **115m.** **** D: William Wyler. Olivia de Havilland, Ralph Richardson, Montgomery Clift, Miriam Hopkins, Vanessa Brown, Mona Freeman, Ray Collins, Selena Royle. Henry James' novel *Washington Square* receives superlative screen treatment with Oscar-winning de Havilland as spinster wooed by fortune-hunter Clift in 19th century N.Y.C. Aaron Copland's music score also won an Oscar. Adapted by Ruth and Augustus Goetz from their stage play.▼

Heist, The (1972) **C-73m.** **TVM** D: Don

McDougall. Christopher George, Elizabeth Ashley, Howard Duff, Norman Fell, Michael Bell, Robert Mandan. Tough cop (Duff) is convinced armored car guard Craddock (George) engineered bank robbery via clever alibi, even though film clearly shows man innocent. Predictable resolution, fair performances, and closing sequence that must be seen to be believed. Average.

Heist, The (1979-Italian) **C-85m.** **½ D: Sergio Gobbi. Charles Aznavour, Virna Lisi, Robert Hossein. Typical cop-chasing-gangster mishmash wastes its cast but is distinguished by some great stunt driving. Video version runs 92m.▼

Heist, The (1989) **C-97m. TVM** D: Stuart Orme. Pierce Brosnan, Tom Skerritt, Wendy Hughes, Robert Prosky, Noble Willingham. Ex-con devises intricate race-track robbery to exact revenge on his former partner, who had framed him in an emerald-smuggling deal. Entertaining yarn with a first-rate cast, including transplanted Australian leading lady Hughes. Made for cable. Average.

He Knows You're Alone (1981) **C-94m.** *½ D: Armand Mastroianni. Don Scardino, Caitlin O'Heaney, Elizabeth Kemp, Tom Rolfing, Patsy Pease, Tom Hanks, Dana Barron, Paul Gleason. Yet another entry in slice-and-dice genre, this one with minor novelty of brides-to-be as victims. A bit less bloody than others of its ilk; otherwise, business as usual. Hanks' film debut.▼

He Laughed Last (1956) **C-77m.** **½ D: Blake Edwards. Frankie Laine, Lucy Marlow, Anthony Dexter, Dick Long, Alan Reed, Jesse White, Florenze Ames, Henry Slate. Marlow is a 1920s flapper who inherits a gangster's nightclub in this colorful spoof of Prohibition era crime stories. Laine even gets to croon a couple of songs.

Helen Morgan Story, The (1957) **118m.** **½ D: Michael Curtiz. Ann Blyth, Paul Newman, Richard Carlson, Gene Evans, Alan King, Cara Williams. Fiction about dynamic 1920-30s torch singer, overfocusing on her romances and alcoholism: Blyth never captures the star's pathos or greatness. She's dubbed by Gogi Grant.

✓ **Helen of Troy** (1955) **C-118m.** ** D: Robert Wise. Stanley Baker, Rossana Podesta, Brigitte Bardot, Jacques Sernas, Cedric Hardwicke, Harry Andrews. Sweeping pageantry, but empty script spoils this version of story about the woman who caused the Trojan War. Filmed in Italy.

Hell and High Water (1954) **C-103m.** **½ D: Samuel Fuller. Richard Widmark, Bella Darvi, Victor Francen, Cameron Mitchell, Gene Evans, David Wayne, Stephen Bekassy, Richard Loo. Uneven mixture of romance, espionage, and a demolition caper, stemming from U.S. sub's mission to Arctic; originally released in CinemaScope, which gave tame film some novelty.

Hell Below (1933) **105m.** **½ D: Jack Conway. Robert Montgomery, Walter Huston, Madge Evans, Jimmy Durante, Robert Young, Sterling Holloway, Eugene Pallette. Vintage submarine drama surpasses many more elaborate efforts; Huston is captain, Montgomery his seaman nemesis.

Hell Below Zero (1954) **C-91m.** ** D: Mark Robson. Alan Ladd, Joan Tetzel, Basil Sydney, Stanley Baker. Tepid adventure yarn casting Ladd as helper of Tetzel, who commands a whaling vessel while searching for her dad's killer. Made in England.

Hell Bent for Leather (1960) **C-82m.** **½ D: George Sherman. Audie Murphy, Felicia Farr, Stephen McNally, Robert Middleton. Western focuses on battle of power between reward-hungry sheriff and innocent man mistaken for killer.

Hellbound: Hellraiser II (1988-British) **C-97m.** *½ D: Tony Randel. Ashley Laurence, Clare Higgins, Kenneth Cranham, Imogen Boorman, Sean Chapman, Doug Bradley, William Hope. Confusing, tedious sequel begins immediately after first film ends. Teenage heroine literally goes to Hell in effort to rescue ill-fated father, but encounters opposition from her revived stepmother and an occult-obsessed psychiatrist. Hell, however, is a boring, dusty labyrinth. Almost as gruesome as the first film, but nowhere near as entertaining.▼

Hellcamp SEE: **Opposing Force**▼

Hell Canyon Outlaws (1957) **72m.** ** D: Paul Landres. Dale Robertson, Brian Keith, Rossana Rory, Dick Kallman, Buddy Baer. Triumph against outlaw forces in the Old West; that's it.

Hellcats of the Navy (1957) **82m.** **½ D: Nathan Juran. Ronald Reagan, Nancy Davis (Reagan), Arthur Franz, Harry Lauter, Selmer Jackson. Satisfactory actioner of WW2 exploits of U.S. submarine and its crew. Ronald and Nancy Reagan's only screen appearance together.▼

Hell Divers (1932) **113m.** ** D: George Hill. Wallace Beery, Clark Gable, Conrad Nagel, Dorothy Jordan, Marjorie Rambeau, Marie Prevost, Cliff Edwards. Beery and Gable are boisterous rivals in the Naval Air Force in this often lively but overlong MGM effort, with some still-exciting aerial action. Watch for young Robert Young as a sailor.

Hell Drivers (1958-British) **91m.** **½ D: Cy Endfield. Stanley Baker, Herbert Lom, Peggy Cummins, Patrick McGoohan, Jill Ireland, Gordon Jackson, David McCallum, Sean Connery. Taut account of ex-con trucker carrying heavy cargoes over rugged roads and trying to expose boss's racket. Original British running time: 108m.

Heller in Pink Tights (1960) **C-100m.** **½ D: George Cukor. Sophia Loren, Anthony Quinn, Margaret O'Brien, Steve Forrest, Edmund Lowe. Colorful tale of theatrical troupe that travels throughout the Old West—with the law often in pursuit. Based on a Louis L'Amour novel.▼

✓ **Hellfighters** (1969) **C-121m.** ** D: Andrew V. McLaglen. John Wayne, Katharine Ross, Jim Hutton, Vera Miles, Bruce Cabot, Jay C. Flippen. Comic-book adventure about men who fight oil fires is made endurable by good cast.▼

Hellgate (1952) **87m.** **½ D: Charles Marquis Warren. Sterling Hayden, Joan Leslie, James Arness, Ward Bond. Offbeat account of Hayden falsely sent to prison, and strange manner in which he redeems himself during prison breakout. Reworking of THE PRISONER OF SHARK ISLAND. Same story covered in the later TV movie, THE ORDEAL OF DR. MUDD.

Hellhole (1985) **C-95m.** *½ D: Pierre de Moro. Ray Sharkey, Judy Landers, Mary Woronov, Marjoe Gortner, Edy Williams, Terry Moore, Rick Cox, Lynn Borden. Innocent Landers is caught inside women's sanitarium where strange experiments are being conducted. They should have tried to conjure up a better script. Pretty bad, even for the genre.▼

Hellinger's Law (1981) **C-98m.** TVM D: Leo Penn. Telly Savalas, Melinda Dillon, Rod Taylor, James Sutorius, Morgan Stevens, Ja'net DuBois, Roy Poole, Tom McFadden, Kyle Richards. Flamboyant lawyer is hired to defend the mob's accountant accused of killing a TV newscaster in this pilot for a prospective Savalas series. Average.

Hell in Korea (1956-British) **81m.** **½ D: Julian Amyes. Ronald Lewis, Stephen Boyd, Victor Maddern, George Baker, Robert Shaw, Stanley Baker, Harry Andrews, Michael Medwin, Michael Caine, Percy Herbert. Standard drama about small United Nations patrol tangling with Chinese; interesting to see Caine in his first film and Shaw in his second. Also known as A HILL IN KOREA.

✓ **Hell in the Pacific** (1968) **C-103m.** *** D: John Boorman. Lee Marvin, Toshiro Mifune. Two men, one American, one Japanese, confront each other on deserted Pacific island during WW2. Gripping idea well executed, with two dynamic actors; only the finale disappoints.▼

Hellions, The (1962-British) **C-87m.** **½ D: Ken Annakin. Richard Todd, Anne Aubrey, Lionel Jeffries, Zena Walker, Jamie Uys, Marty Wilde. Western revenge plot transferred to 19th-century South Africa; inevitable shoot-out intact.

Hell Is for Heroes (1962) **90m.** *** D:

Donald Siegel. Steve McQueen, Bobby Darin, Fess Parker, Harry Guardino, James Coburn, Mike Kellin, Nick Adams, Bob Newhart. Tough, taut WW2 film about a small squadron forced to hold off a German attack by pretending they're larger— and more powerful—than they really are. Takes its time getting started but builds in intensity to a riveting climax. Only incongruous note: presence of young Newhart, who even interpolates a variation on one of his telephone monologues into the story! Cowritten by WW2 specialist Robert Pirosh.▼

Hell Night (1981) **C-101m.** *½ D: Tom DeSimone. Linda Blair, Vincent Van Patten, Peter Barton, Jenny Neumann, Kevin Brophy, Suki Goodwin, Jimmy Sturtevant. How's this for originality? Four college fraternity/sorority pledges must spend a night in Garth Mansion, which is haunted by ghost of retarded killer. Unfortunately, reports of his death were greatly exaggerated. What appears to be the usual teenage hack-'em-up has no nudity or explicit violence, making one wonder just what audience they had in mind. Extremely dull.▼

Hello Again (1987) **C-96m.** ** D: Frank Perry. Shelley Long, Judith Ivey, Gabriel Byrne, Corbin Bernsen, Sela Ward, Austin Pendleton, Carrie Nye, Robert Lewis, Madeleine Potter, Thor Fields. Long Island housewife chokes to death but is brought back to life by her witchlike sister one year later . . . and soon discovers that she can't simply pick up her life where she left off. Contemporary comedy written by Susan Isaacs doesn't develop its own premise with any logic or momentum, and quickly sags. Long tries her best.▼

Hello, Dolly! (1969) **C-146m.** **½ D: Gene Kelly. Barbra Streisand, Walter Matthau, Michael Crawford, E. J. Peaker, Marianne McAndrew, Tommy Tune, Louis Armstrong. Splashy cinema treatment of smash Broadway play with Jerry Herman's popular score. Dolly Levi insists on playing matchmaker, even when it's she herself who gets matched. Overblown and unmemorable, but colorful diversion. Based on Thornton Wilder's *The Matchmaker* (previously filmed in 1958). Some prints run 118m.▼

Hello Down There (1969) **C-98m.** *½ D: Jack Arnold. Tony Randall, Janet Leigh, Jim Backus, Roddy McDowall, Ken Berry, Merv Griffin, Richard Dreyfuss. So-called comedy about family living in experimental underwater home might entertain children if you pay them to watch it. Reissued as SUB-A-DUB-DUB.

Hello Elephant (1952-Italian) **78m.** *½ D: Gianni Franciolini. Vittorio De Sica, Sabu, Maria Mercader, Nando Bruno. Misfire of comedy-satire involving royalty who bestows an elephant on one of his subjects as a fitting reward. Retitled: PARDON MY TRUNK.▼

Hello Frisco, Hello (1943) **C-98m.** ** D: H. Bruce Humberstone. Alice Faye, John Payne, Jack Oakie, Lynn Bari, Laird Cregar, June Havoc, Ward Bond. Hackneyed musicomedy of Payne getting too big for his britches as Barbary Coast entrepeneur; Oscar-winning song, "You'll Never Know." Big comedown from earlier musicals with star trio.

Hello-Goodbye (1970-British) **C-107m.** BOMB D: Jean Negulesco. Michael Crawford, Curt Jurgens, Genevieve Gilles, Ira Furstenberg, Lon Satton. Abysmal love triangle which goes nowhere and makes no sense. Awful, loose, and annoying.

Hello Mary Lou: Prom Night II (1987-Canadian) **C-96m.** **½ D: Bruce Pittman. Lisa Schrage, Michael Ironside, Wendy Lyon, Justin Louis. No relation to PROM NIGHT except in title. Lyon, who looks great in or out of costume, is possessed by the spirit of a murdered prom queen and becomes her instrument of revenge.▼

Hell on Devil's Island (1957) **74m.** *½ D: Christian Nyby. Helmut Dantine, William Talman, Donna Martell, Rex Ingram, Alan Lee. Unlurid exposé of unsavory working conditions in prison mining operations.

✓ **Hell on Frisco Bay** (1955) **C-98m.** **½ D: Frank Tuttle. Alan Ladd, Edward G. Robinson, Joanne Dru, William Demarest, Fay Wray, Jayne Mansfield. Thirties-style gangster film recounting the exposure of crime syndicate and its head; actionful, with good cast.▼

Hello Sister (1933) **62m.** **½ D: Erich von Stroheim, Alfred Werker. James Dunn, Boots Mallory, ZaSu Pitts, Minna Gombell. Innocuous boy-meets-girl story of special interest to film buffs. Originally filmed by von Stroheim as WALKING DOWN BROADWAY; later reedited, partially refilmed; enough bizarre touches remain to reveal von Stroheim's touch, however.

Hello Sucker (1941) **60m.** *½ D: Edward Cline. Peggy Moran, Tom Brown, Walter Catlett, Hugh Herbert. Dingy little film of Moran and Brown acquiring vaudeville booking agency, making it a success and finding love with one another.

Hellraiser (1987-British) **C-94m.** **½ D: Clive Barker. Andrew Robinson, Clare Higgins, Ashley Laurence, Sean Chapman, Oliver Smith, Robert Hines. Robinson and Higgins move into a roomy British dwelling, unaware that his half brother—and her former lover—is hiding upstairs in a kind of gelatinous/skeletal state; soon the beast is forcing her to lure stray men back to the house so he can replenish himself with their blood. Grisly but stylish directorial debut by famed horror novelist Barker;

ugly fun all the way. Followed by HELL-BOUND: HELLRAISER II.▼

Hell's Angels (1930) **127m.** ***½ D: Howard Hughes. Ben Lyon, James Hall, Jean Harlow, John Darrow, Lucien Prival, Roy Wilson. Hughes' expensive, indulgent WW1 aviation film is in a class by itself; slow-moving and sometimes corny storywise, but unmatched for aerial spectacle. Also the film that launched Harlow ("Would you be shocked if I put on something more comfortable?") to stardom. Two-color Technicolor party scene and tinted night sequences were restored in 1989. James Whale, credited as dialogue director, actually wrote and directed much of the film. Beware shorter prints.

Hell's Angels Forever (1983) **C-92m.** ** D: Richard Chase, Kevin Keating, Leon Gast. Superficial quasi-documentary portrait of the Hell's Angels, with no real information on, or insight into, the notorious cycle gang.▼

Hell's Angels on Wheels (1967) **C-95m.** **½ D: Richard Rush. Adam Roarke, Jack Nicholson, Sabrina Scharf, Jana Taylor, John Garwood. Excellent photography by then-unknown Laszlo Kovacs, and Nicholson's characterization as gas station attendant named Poet, make this one tough to resist on a trash level. Famed Angel Sonny Barger is credited as technical advisor.▼

Hell's Bloody Devils (1970) **C-92m.** ** D: Al Adamson. Broderick Crawford, Scott Brady, John Gabriel, Kent Taylor, John Carradine, Robert Dix, Keith Andes, Jack Starrett, Anne Randall, Vicki Volante. Traveling the low road to action with, believe it or not, a gang of sadistic bikers, a band of neo-Nazis, the Vegas mob, a sinister dude named Count von Delberg—all beating one another to a bloody pulp. Add to this a cast loaded with veteran actors and, incredibly, a score by Nelson Riddle! Later retitled THE FAKERS; then SMASHING THE CRIME SYNDICATE.

Hell's Crossroads (1957) **73m.** ** D: Franklin Adreon. Stephen McNally, Peggie Castle, Robert Vaughn, Barton MacLane. Oater involving members of the James Brothers outlaw gang.

Hell's Five Hours (1958) **73m.** ** D: Jack L. Copeland. Stephen McNally, Coleen Gray, Vic Morrow, Maurice Manson. Several people are held prisoners at missile depot by Morrow, bent on blowing the place sky-high.

Hell's Half Acre (1954) **91m.** **½ D: John H. Auer. Wendell Corey, Evelyn Keyes, Elsa Lanchester, Nancy Gates, Philip Ahn, Keye Luke, Marie Windsor. A woman seeks her long-missing husband in Honolulu, where he's established a new identity. Some interesting vignettes in this

OK melodrama, definitely above-par for a Republic picture.

Hell's Highway (1932) **62m.** **½ D: Rowland Brown. Richard Dix, Tom Brown, C. Henry Gordon, Charles Middleton, Rochelle Hudson, Oscar Apfel, Stanley Fields, Fuzzy Knight, Clarence Muse. Dix, serving time on a blatantly misrun chain gang, has to change his escape plans when his kid brother is brought in as prisoner. Though it pales alongside I AM A FUGITIVE FROM A CHAIN GANG (released just a few months later), this highly melodramatic tale still has much to recommend it: it's tough, raw (touching on everything from racial prejudice to homosexuality), and pictorially striking. Biggest disappointment: the finale.

Hell Ship Mutiny (1957) **66m.** *½ D: Lee Sholem, Elmo Williams. Jon Hall, John Carradine, Peter Lorre, Roberta Haynes, Mike Mazurki, Stanley Adams. Hall looks bored in rehash of South Sea tale of ship captain overcoming sinister forces exploiting the natives.

Hell's Horizon (1955) **80m.** ** D: Tom Gries. John Ireland, Marla English, Bill Williams, Hugh Beaumont, Jerry Paris, Kenneth Duncan. Interaction among men of bombing squad in the Korean War.

Hell's House (1932) **72m.** ** D: Howard Higgin. Junior Durkin, Pat O'Brien, Bette Davis, Junior Coghlan, Charley Grapewin, Emma Dunn. Low-budget quickie about naive kid who takes rap for bootlegger and goes to poorly run boys' reformatory. Interesting mainly for early appearances of O'Brien and Davis.▼

Hell's Island (1955) **C-84m.** **½ D: Phil Karlson. John Payne, Mary Murphy, Francis L. Sullivan, Eduardo Noriega, Paul Picerni. Tough-talking melodrama about Payne's pursuit of stolen gem, and relationship with deceitful former girlfriend; script has echoes of THE MALTESE FALCON, and even a Sydney Greenstreet figure in the person of Sullivan.

Hell's Kitchen (1939) **81m.** **½ D: Lewis Seiler, E. A. Dupont. Ronald Reagan, Stanley Fields, Grant Mitchell, Margaret Lindsay, Dead End Kids. Ex-con Fields goes straight, tries to bail Dead End Kids out of their usual trouble, sets them on the right road. Remake of THE MAYOR OF HELL.

Hell's Long Road (1963-Italian) **C-89m.** **½ D: Charles Roberti. Elena Brazzi, Kay Nolandi, Berto Frankis, Bela Kaivi, Marcello Charli. Offbeat costume sudser set in ancient Rome during rule of Nero (Frankis), focusing on personal life of arch senator (Charli) and romance with splendiferous Brazzi; vivid settings.

Hell's Outpost (1954) **90m.** ** D: Joseph Kane. Rod Cameron, Joan Leslie, Chill Wills, John Russell. Cameron is ambitious miner in this sturdy little film; Leslie is the fetching love interest.

Hellstrom Chronicle, The (1971) **C-90m.** **½ D: Walon Green. Lawrence Pressman. Documentary about man's impending struggle against insects won at Cannes and somehow beat THE SORROW AND THE PITY for the Oscar, but sappy narration and repetitive structure lessen its effect. Still, microphotography is incredible, and film enjoyed brief vogue as a "head" movie.▼

Hell to Eternity (1960) **132m.** **½ D: Phil Karlson. Jeffrey Hunter, David Janssen, Vic Damone, Patricia Owens, Sessue Hayakawa. Straightforward drama based on true story of WW2 hero Guy Gabaldon, who was raised by Japanese foster parents; battle scenes galore.▼

Hell Town (1985) **C-100m.** **TVM** D: Don Medford. Robert Blake, Jeff Corey, James Gammon, Zitto Kazann, Vonetta McGee, Whitmán Mayo, Isabel Grandin, Fran Ryan. Blake's a scrappy ex-con who is now a ghetto priest in this *Baretta*-with-a-turned-around-collar project that became a subsequent short-lived TV series. Average.

Hell Up in Harlem (1973) **C-96m.** BOMB D: Larry Cohen. Fred Williamson, Julius W. Harris, Gloria Hendry, Margaret Avery, D'Urville Martin. Excessively violent, poorly filmed sequel to BLACK CAESAR as Fred makes N.Y.C. a decent place to live by annihilating all who stand in his way.▼

Hell with Heroes, The (1968) **C-95m.** **½ D: Joseph Sargent. Rod Taylor, Claudia Cardinale, Harry Guardino, Kevin McCarthy, Peter Duel, William Marshall. OK pulp fiction about WW2 flyers Taylor and Duel who run air-cargo service, become involved with notorious smuggler Guardino and his mistress (Cardinale). Unprofound, but slickly done.

Hellzapoppin (1941) **84m.** *** D: H. C. Potter. Ole Olsen, Chic Johnson, Martha Raye, Mischa Auer, Jane Frazee, Hugh Herbert, Robert Paige, Shemp Howard, Elisha Cook Jr. Famous madcap Broadway show is conventionalized by Hollywood, with romantic subplot and too many songs, but still has many inspired moments of lunacy, from a throwaway CITIZEN KANE gag to the mutterings of Hugh Herbert.

Help! (1965-British) **C-90m.** ***½ D: Richard Lester. John Lennon, Paul McCartney, George Harrison, Ringo Starr, Leo McKern, Eleanor Bron, Victor Spinetti, Roy Kinnear, Patrick Cargill. Crazy, funny film, the Beatles' second. Lots of wild gags, many songs (including "Ticket to Ride," "Another Girl," "You've Got to Hide Your Love Away," title tune). The story: a religious sect attempts to recover a sacrificial ring from Ringo. Written by Charles Wood and Marc Behm.▼

Help Me Dream (1981-Italian) **C-112m.**
*** D: Pupi Avati. Mariangela Melato,
Anthony Franciosa, Paola Pitagora, Jean-
Pierre Leaud, Alexandra Stewart. Intriguing,
original, winningly nostalgic musical ro-
mance centering on affable American flyer
Franciosa hiding out with Italian Melato
and children in a farmhouse during WW2.
An ode to an idealized America, with
period songs and choreography by Hermes
Pan.

Help Wanted: Kids (1986) **C-100m. TVM**
D: David Greenwalt. Cindy Williams,
Bill Hudson, Chad Allen, Hillary Wolf,
John Dehner, Joel Brooks, Miriam Flynn.
Squeaky-clean Disneyana about a pair of
yuppie ad executives who hire a couple of
kids and play the "perfect" family, in
order to keep their new jobs. Williams and
Hudson are real-life wife and husband.
Average.

Help Wanted: Male (1982) **C-100m. TVM**
D: William Wiard. Suzanne Pleshette, Gil
Gerard, Bert Convy, Dana Elcar, Harold
Gould, Caren Kaye, Ed Nelson. Career
woman hires a sportswriter to help her
become a mother after finding that her
boyfriend isn't up to it. Max Shulman
wrote this sniggering romantic comedy.
Average.▼

Helter Skelter (1976) **C-194m. TVM** D:
Tom Gries. George DiCenzo, Steve Railsback, Nancy Wolfe, Marilyn Burns, Christina Hart, Cathey Paine, Alan Oppenheimer, Skip Homeier, David Clennon, Paul
Mantee, Sidney Clute. Electrifying film of
prosecutor Vincent Bugliosi's best-seller,
adapted by JP Miller, about the trackdown
and trial of Charles Manson and his spaced-
out "family" in California. Serious, intense, and frightening; a vivid performance
by Railsback as Manson. Originally shown
in two parts. Above average.▼

He Married His Wife (1940) **83m.** ** D:
Roy Del Ruth. Joel McCrea, Nancy Kelly,
Roland Young, Mary Boland, Cesar Romero. McCrea doesn't want to bear the
expense of divorce; solution is obvious,
and so is most of the film.

**Hemingway's Adventures of a Young
Man** (1962) **C-145m.** ** D: Martin Ritt.
Richard Beymer, Diane Baker, Paul New-
man, Corinne Calvet, Fred Clark, Dan
Dailey, James Dunn, Juano Hernandez,
Arthur Kennedy, Ricardo Montalban, Su-
san Strasberg, Jessica Tandy, Eli Wallach,
Simon Oakland, Michael (J.) Pollard.
Loosely based on autobiographical data
from his stories, this pretentious, drawn-
out memory of the famed author is over-
blown, cornball, and embarrassing. Fine
cast mostly wasted. Also known as just
ADVENTURES OF A YOUNG MAN.

Henderson Monster, The (1980) **C-105m.
TVM** D: Waris Hussein. Jason Miller,
Christine Lahti, Stephen Collins, David
Spielberg, Nehemiah Persoff, Larry Gates.
Miller is an egotistical Nobel Prize-winning
scientist in this static gene-splicing drama
that dissolves into romantic-triangle pap.
Script by Ernest Kinoy. Average.▼

Hennessy (1975-British) **C-103m.** **½
D: Don Sharp. Rod Steiger, Lee Remick,
Richard Johnson, Trevor Howard, Peter
Egan, Eric Porter. Interesting but unbe-
lievable thriller about Irish man whose
wife and child are killed in Belfast vio-
lence, stirring him to plan bombing of
Parliament on opening day when the Royal
Family attends.▼

Henry Aldrich Teen-aged Henry Aldrich
was Paramount's answer to MGM's Andy
Hardy series, and while the Aldrich films
were less popular, less prestigious, and
shorter-lived, they were then, and remain
today, well-crafted, entertaining little films,
without any of the pretentiousness and
calculated coyness that marred the Hardy
series. Henry and group were the invention of Clifford Goldsmith, whose play
WHAT A LIFE opened in 1938 on Broadway, spawning a radio series with Ezra
Stone repeating his stage role of Henry. In
1939, Paramount turned the hit play into a
pleasant film, retaining Betty Field (as
Henry's plain-jane girlfriend) and Vaughan
Glaser (as dour principal Mr. Bradley)
from the original cast, but bypassing Ezra
Stone in favor of Jackie Cooper, and casting Eddie Bracken as Henry's pal Dizzy.
Best of all, Paramount assigned their writing team of Billy Wilder and Charles
Brackett to provide the script—an unlikely
pair for such Middle American doings, but
welcome nonetheless. Two years passed
before the studio decided to turn the Aldrich movie into a regular series, a decision strengthened no doubt by the continuing
popularity of the radio show. In 1941,
Jackie Cooper and Eddie Bracken repeated
their roles in a second outing, LIFE WITH
HENRY, a typically silly but likable effort. Then Paramount cast a newcomer,
Jimmy Lydon, in the key role of Henry
and surrounded him with a new supporting
cast for a string of actual series films:
Charles Smith as his laconic but shifty pal
Dizzy, John Litel as his stern father, Olive
Blakeney as his forgiving mother, and
welcome Vaughan Glaser as the forever-
pouting principal. A new director, ex-film
editor Hugh Bennett, was added to com-
prise the working unit that turned out nine
films over the next four years. The Aldrich
films, timed around 70 minutes, fell into a
pattern that proved generally successful:
putting hopelessly blundering Henry into
an increasingly complicated series of mishaps which would alienate him from his
parents, sometimes his friends, and often
the entire town, before culminating in a
major action and/or slapstick climax in

which Henry would be vindicated. In HENRY ALDRICH FOR PRESIDENT the finale is a wild airplane ride; in HENRY AND DIZZY it's a runaway motorboat; in HENRY ALDRICH, BOY SCOUT it's a cliff-hanger rescue; and best of all, in HENRY ALDRICH, EDITOR there is a truly exciting fire sequence. The films are consistently well-paced and slickly filmed, never belying their modest budgets, and filled with engaging players: Mary Anderson as Henry's girlfriend in several entries (later replaced by Diana Lynn, and other less notable starlets); Frances Gifford as a movie star who accepts Henry's prom invitation as a publicity stunt in HENRY ALDRICH GETS GLAMOUR, Fritz Feld as a famous musician whose Stradivarius is accidentally "borrowed" by Henry in HENRY ALDRICH SWINGS IT; Lucien Littlefield as an antagonistic teacher in two of the episodes; June Preisser as a vamp in HENRY ALDRICH FOR PRESIDENT; and Vera Vague as a potential wife for Mr. Bradley in HENRY ALDRICH PLAYS CUPID. Best of all is Francis Pierlot as a character called Nero Smith, a pyromaniac who announces his intentions to Henry, leading to suspicions and troubles galore in perhaps the best series entry, HENRY ALDRICH, EDITOR. HENRY ALDRICH'S LITTLE SECRET is the last and easily the weakest film of the nine Lydon pictures, but the other eight maintain a surprisingly good standard of filmmaking quality and good, lightweight entertainment. The players fill their often silly roles with the kind of conviction that gets an audience involved, but the scripts take sly winks at the same audience every once in a while to reassure us that it's not to be taken too seriously (the name of the resort near Centerville is Lake Wopacotapotalong). Henry Aldrich later went on to a short-lived TV series with Bobby Ellis in the lead, but to most people, Jimmy Lydon is best identified with the role of America's dumbest high-schooler—dumb, yet in an odd way, endearing.

Henry Aldrich, Boy Scout (1944) **66m.** D: Hugh Bennett. Jimmy Lydon, Charles Smith, John Litel, Olive Blakeney, Joan Mortimer, Darryl Hickman, Minor Watson, Richard Haydn.
Henry Aldrich, Editor (1942) **71m.** D: Hugh Bennett. Jimmy Lydon, Charles Smith, John Litel, Olive Blakeney, Rita Quigley, Vaughan Glaser, Francis Pierlot.
Henry Aldrich for President (1941) **73m.** D: Hugh Bennett. Jimmy Lydon, Charles Smith, June Preisser, Mary Anderson, Martha O'Driscoll, Dorothy Peterson, John Litel, Rod Cameron, Lucien Littlefield, Kenneth Howell.
Henry Aldrich Gets Glamour (1943) **75m.** D: Hugh Bennett. Jimmy Lydon, Charles Smith, John Litel, Olive Blakeney, Diana Lynn, Frances Gifford, Gail Russell, Bill Goodwin, Vaughan Glaser.
Henry Aldrich Haunts A House (1943) **73m.** D: Hugh Bennett. Jimmy Lydon, Charles Smith, John Litel, Olive Blakeney, Joan Mortimer, Vaughan Glaser, Jackie Moran, Lucien Littlefield.
Henry Aldrich Plays Cupid (1944) **65m.** D: Hugh Bennett. Jimmy Lydon, Charles Smith, John Litel, Olive Blakeney, Diana Lynn, Vaughan Glaser, Vera Vague, Barbara Jo Allen, Paul Harvey, Barbara Pepper.
Henry Aldrich's Little Secret (1944) **75m.** D: Hugh Bennett. Jimmy Lydon, Charles Smith, Joan Mortimer, John Litel, Olive Blakeney, Ann Doran, John David Robb, Tina Thayer, Sarah Edwards.
Henry Aldrich Swings It (1943) **64m.** D: Hugh Bennett. Jimmy Lydon, Charles Smith, John Litel, Olive Blakeney, Mimi Chandler, Vaughan Glaser, Marion Hall, Fritz Feld, Beverly Hudson.
Henry and Dizzy (1942) **71m.** D: Hugh Bennett. Jimmy Lydon, Charles Smith, Mary Anderson, John Litel, Olive Blakeney, Maude Eburne, Vaughan Glaser, Shirley Coates, Olin Howland, Minerva Urecal, Trevor Bardette.
Henry VIII and His Six Wives (1973-British) **C-125m.** ***½ D: Waris Hussein. Keith Michell, Donald Pleasence, Charlotte Rampling, Jane Asher, Lynne Frederick. Adapted from BBC-TV series, historical pageant divides time evenly among the wives, Rampling and Frederick coming off best. Michell is exceptional as the King.
Henry V (1945-British) **C-137m.** **** D: Laurence Olivier. Laurence Olivier, Robert Newton, Leslie Banks, Renee Asherson, Esmond Knight, Leo Genn, Ralph Truman. Olivier's masterful rendition of Shakespeare play is a cinematic treat, filmed in rich color and framed by ingenious presentation of a typical performance at the Globe Theater during 1500s. This earned Olivier a special Academy Award "for his outstanding achievement as actor, producer, and director in bringing HENRY V to the screen." ▼
Henry V (1989-British) **C-137m.** ***½ D: Kenneth Branagh. Kenneth Branagh, Derek Jacobi, Brian Blessed, Alec McCowen, Ian Holm, Richard Briers, Robert Stephens, Robbie Coltrane, Christian Bale, Judi Dench, Paul Scofield, Michael Maloney, Emma Thompson, Geraldine McEwan. Stunning revitalization of Shakespeare's play about the warrior-king, with Branagh (in an incredible directorial debut) breathing fire and meaning into the worthy text. A different reading from Olivier's but no less impressive; when he finishes his speech before leading his men into battle at Agincourt, you're ready to enlist! Supporting cast is peppered with familiar

faces from the elite of British theater and film. Oscar winner for Costume Design.▼

Henry IV (1984-Italian) **C-95m.** ** D: Marco Bellochio. Marcello Mastroianni, Claudia Cardinale, Luciano Bartoli, Latou Chardons, Leopoldo Trieste. Disappointing update of Pirandello's brilliant satirical play on the nature of madness and illusion. When a nobleman falls off his horse, he comes to believe he's Emperor Henry IV . . . or does he? The two stars do what they can to extract a few moments of lucidity from the confusion, but the result is generally unrewarding.▼

Henry: Portrait of a Serial Killer (1990) **C-90m.** ***½ D: John McNaughton. Michael Rooker, Tracy Arnold, Tom Towles. Unpleasant, unexploitive, and brilliantly directed portrayal of diseased minds (not just Henry's), loosely based on the life of self-confessed Texas mass murderer Henry Lee Lucas. As disturbing as Michael Powell's PEEPING TOM, which it in many ways resembles. Definitely not for everyone, with some very graphic scenes; a powerful (if minimalist) movie experience. Screenplay by director McNaughton and Richard Fire. Filmed in 1986.▼

Henry, the Rainmaker (1949) **64m.** *½ D: Jean Yarbrough. Raymond Walburn, Walter Catlett, William Tracy, Mary Stuart. Mild little comedy of homey Walburn who develops a "scientific" way to make rain. First in short-lived "Father" series starring Walburn; followed by LEAVE IT TO HENRY.

Her Adventurous Night (1946) **76m.** **½ D: John Rawlins. Dennis O'Keefe, Helen Walker, Tom Powers, Fuzzy Knight. Youngster with wild imagination fabricates tale of murder and crime, causing parents to go to jail and the youth's life put in peril.

Her Alibi (1989) **C-94m.** **½ D: Bruce Beresford. Tom Selleck, Paulina Porizkova, William Daniels, James Farentino, Hurd Hatfield, Patrick Wayne, Tess Harper, Joan Copeland. Successful mystery writer hopes to cure his career slump by providing a fake alibi for accused murderer Porizkova (by putting her up in his dreamy country home and observing her behavior). Amiable but awkwardly directed comedy benefits from attractive leads and amusing supporting cast; would you believe Wayne in a ponytail and loud golf pants?▼

He Ran All the Way (1951) **77m.** **½ D: John Berry. John Garfield, Shelley Winters, Wallace Ford, Selena Royle, Gladys George, Norman Lloyd. Taut but predictable thriller with on-the-lam cop killer Garfield hiding out in Winters' home. Garfield's final film.

Herbie Goes Bananas (1980) **C-100m.** *½ D: Vincent McEveety. Charlie Martin Smith, Steven W. Burns, Cloris Leachman, John Vernon, Elyssa Davalos, Harvey Korman, Richard Jaeckel, Alex Rocco, Fritz Feld. Fourth Disney LOVE BUG epic finds Smith and Burns driving ol' '53 toward a race in Brazil, but encountering all sorts of "hilarious" obstacles along the way. One amusing scene where the VW turns matador; otherwise, strictly scrap metal. Last of the theatrical features, but a TV series followed.▼

Herbie Goes to Monte Carlo (1977) **C-91m.** ** D: Vincent McEveety. Dean Jones, Don Knotts, Julie Sommars, Roy Kinnear, Jacques Marin. Spy ring hides diamond in Herbie the Volkswagen's gas tank while Jones is racing in Europe. Disney's LOVE BUG formula is starting to run out of gas.▼

Herbie Rides Again (1974) **C-88m.** **½ D: Robert Stevenson. Helen Hayes, Ken Berry, Stefanie Powers, Keenan Wynn, John McIntire, Huntz Hall. OK sequel to THE LOVE BUG with similar special effects, as Herbie the Volkswagen tries to help Hayes and Berry steer clear of evil Alonzo Hawk (Wynn). Typical Disney slapstick.▼

Her Brother (1960-Japanese) **C-98m.** **½ D: Kon Ichikawa. Keiko Kishi, Hiroshi Kawaguchi, Kinuyo Tanaka, Masayuki Mori. Troublesome family is brought together when immature brother-son Kawaguchi contracts tuberculosis; central to the scenario is his warm relationship with his older sister (Kishi). Sentimental drama.

Her Cardboard Lover (1942) **93m.** *½ D: George Cukor. Norma Shearer, Robert Taylor, George Sanders, Frank McHugh, Elizabeth Patterson. Tired comedy that chic Shearer, in her final screen appearance, is unable to salvage.

Hercules (1959-Italian) **C-107m.** **½ D: Pietro Francisci. Steve Reeves, Sylva Koscina, Gianna Maria Canale, Fabrizio Mioni, Ivo Garrani, Gina Rovere, Luciana Paoluzzi (Paluzzi). Prototype of all cloak-and-sandal pictures to come: Reeves is musclebound mythical hero who undergoes myriad of ordeals for woman he loves. Sequel: HERCULES UNCHAINED.▼

Hercules (1983-Italian) **C-98m.** *½ D: Lewis Coates (Luigi Cozzi). Lou Ferrigno, Mirella D'Angelo, Sybil Danning, Ingrid Anderson, William Berger, Brad Harris, Rossana Podesta. Silly, special-effects-laden epic with Hercules (Ferrigno) attempting to rescue kidnapped Princess Anderson. However, the ex-Incredible Hulk is undeniably well cast. Followed by a sequel.▼

Hercules II (1985-Italian) **C-90m.** *½ D: Lewis Coates (Luigi Cozzi). Lou Ferrigno, Milly Carlucci, Sonia Viviani, William Berger, Carlotta Green, Claudio Cassinelli. Sequel to HERCULES (1983). Recommended for nondiscriminating viewers too young to read this. Also known as THE ADVENTURES OF HERCULES.▼

Hercules Against Rome (1960-Italian) **C-87m.** ** D: Piero Pierott. Alan Steel, Wandisa Guida, Livio Lorenzon, Daniele Vargas. Steel fights a series of unconvincing villains to protect the late emperor's daughter.

Hercules Against the Moon Men (1964-Italian) **C-88m.** ** D: Giacomo Gentilomo. Alan Steel, Jany Clair, Anna-Maria Polani, Nando Tamberlani. Steel is muscular hero who frees people of Samar from control of magical lunar people holding them in bondage; potential action never occurs.▼

Hercules Against the Sons of the Sun (1963-Italian) **C-91m.** ** D: Osvaldo Civirani. Mark Forest, Anna Pace, Giuliano Gemma, Andrea Rhu. Setting is pre-Columbian America, but the adventure is the same as usual.

Hercules and the Captive Women (1963-Italian) **C-87m.** ** D: Vittorio Cottafavi. Reg Park, Fay Spain, Ettore Manni, Marlo Petri. Cardboard costumer with Park vs. Spain, the despotic ruler of Atlantis.▼

Hercules in New York (1970) **C-91m.** *½ D: Arthur Allan Seidelman. Arnold Stang, Arnold Strong (Schwarzenegger), Taina Elg, James Karen, Deborah Loomis, Ernest Graves, Tanny McDonald. Hercules journeys to Earth from Mt. Olympus and gets mixed up with wrestling promoters—and mobsters—in this lumbering comedy. Inept, but irresistible for the opportunity to watch a young, badly dubbed Schwarzenegger in his movie debut. Reissued as HERCULES—THE MOVIE at 82m, and HERCULES GOES BANANAS at 75m. For TV release a three-minute prologue has been added. Aren't you glad you asked?▼

Hercules in the Haunted World (1961-Italian) **C-83m.** ** D: Mario Bava. Reg Park, Christopher Lee, Leonora Ruffo, Giorgio Ardisson, Ida Galli. Occasionally sparked by atmospheric settings, this sword-and-sandal epic narrates adventures of Park in the devil's kingdom.▼

Hercules, Samson and Ulysses (1965-Italian) **C-85m.** ** D: Pietro Francisci. Kirk Morris, Richard Lloyd, Liana Orfei, Enzo Cerusico. Title alerts one for gymnastics of trio of legendary musclemen.

Hercules Unchained (1960-Italian) **C-101m.** ** D: Pietro Francisci. Steve Reeves, Sylva Koscina, Primo Carnera, Sylvia Lopez. Par for the muscleman hero entry, dealing with rescue of his bride-to-be.▼

Here Comes Every Body (1973) **110m.** *½ D: John Whitmore. Dull documentary about encounter groups in California is only for those with an extraordinary interest in the subject.

Here Comes Mr. Jordan (1941) **93m.** **** D: Alexander Hall. Robert Montgomery, Evelyn Keyes, Claude Rains, Rita Johnson, Edward Everett Horton, James Gleason, John Emery. Excellent fantasy-comedy of prizefighter Montgomery accidentally sent to heaven before his time, forced to occupy a new body on earth. Hollywood moviemaking at its best, with first-rate cast and performances; Harry Segall won an Oscar for his original story, as did Sidney Buchman and Seton I. Miller for their screenplay. Characters used again in DOWN TO EARTH; film remade as HEAVEN CAN WAIT in 1978. Look fast for a young Lloyd Bridges.▼

Here Comes the Groom (1951) **113m.** *** D: Frank Capra. Bing Crosby, Jane Wyman, Franchot Tone, Alexis Smith, James Barton, Anna Maria Alberghetti. Crosby contrives to keep former fiancée Wyman from marrying millionaire Tone in this lightweight musical outing. Guest appearances by Louis Armstrong, Dorothy Lamour, Phil Harris, and Cass Daley, plus Oscar-winning song, "In the Cool, Cool, Cool of the Evening."▼

Here Comes the Navy (1934) **86m.** **½ D: Lloyd Bacon. James Cagney, Pat O'Brien, Gloria Stuart, Dorothy Tree, Frank McHugh. Enjoyable but standard tale of cocky Cagney who becomes navy hero; nothing new, but well done.

Here Come the Co-eds (1945) **87m.** **½ D: Jean Yarbrough. Bud Abbott, Lou Costello, Peggy Ryan, Martha O'Driscoll, June Vincent, Lon Chaney, Donald Cook. Pretty zany Abbott and Costello comedy of two wacky caretakers turning formerly staid girls' school on its ear.

Here Come the Girls (1953) **C-78m.** **½ D: Claude Binyon. Bob Hope, Arlene Dahl, Rosemary Clooney, Tony Martin, Fred Clark, Robert Strauss, the Four Step Brothers. At times amusing romp with Hope a naive show biz-ite who becomes involved with killer on the loose.

Here Come the Littles (1985-Luxembourg) **C-72m.** *½ D: Bernard Deyries. Voices of Jimmy E. Keegan, Bettina Bush, Donovan Freberg, Hal Smith. Silly, boring animated effort about tiny people with tails who live in the walls of big peoples' houses and their adventures with a 12-year-old boy. Spawned from the popular books and TV series. ▼

Here Come the Marines (1952) **66m.** D: William Beaudine. Leo Gorcey, Huntz Hall, Bernard Gorcey, Gil Stratton, Jr., Arthur Space, Tim Ryan. SEE: **Bowery Boys** series.▼

Here Come the Nelsons (1952) **76m.** ** D: Frederick de Cordova. Ozzie, Harriet, David and Ricky Nelson, Rock Hudson, Ann Doran, Jim Backus, Barbara Lawrence, Sheldon Leonard, Gale Gordon. Expanded version of radio's *Adventures of Ozzie & Harriet,* spotlighting a series of typical, comical situations. Light, predictable fare that paved the way for the long-running TV series.

Here Come the Tigers (1978) **C-90m.** *½ D: Sean S. Cunningham. Richard Lincoln, James Zvanut, Samantha Grey, Manny Lieberman, William Caldwell. Kids will have no trouble pinning this as a shameless ripoff of THE BAD NEWS BEARS—and nowhere near as good. Also known as MANNY'S ORPHANS.▼

Here Come the Waves (1944) **99m.** *** D: Mark Sandrich. Bing Crosby, Betty Hutton, Sonny Tufts, Ann Doran, Catherine Craig. Zippy wartime musicomedy of singer Crosby joining the navy. Hit song "Ac-cent-u-ate the Positive" is performed in blackface!

Here Is My Heart (1934) **77m.** **½ D: Frank Tuttle. Bing Crosby, Kitty Carlisle, Roland Young, Alison Skipworth, Reginald Owen. Bing's a radio star in love with princess Carlisle in this flimsy little musical. Songs include "Love Is Just Around the Corner."

Her Enlisted Man SEE: **Red Salute**

Here We Go Again (1942) **76m.** ** D: Allan Dwan. Edgar Bergen and Charlie McCarthy, Jim and Marian Jordan (Fibber McGee and Molly), Harold Peary (The Great Gildersleeve), Ginny Simms, Bill Thompson, Isabel Randolph, Gale Gordon, Mortimer Snerd. Follow up to LOOK WHO'S LAUGHING finds Fibber and Molly on a cross-country trip for their 20th anniversary, getting involved in mild antics at resort hotel with rest of radio gang. Competent, easy-to-take comedy, but nothing special.

Here We Go Round the Mulberry Bush (1968-British) **C-96m.** **½ D: Clive Donner. Barry Evans, Judy Geeson, Angela Scoular, Sheila White, Vanessa Howard, Denholm Elliott. British teen-ager Evans is hung up on girls, but finds his pursuits a constant dead-end. Amusing, often clever adolescent romp; music by Stevie Winwood & Traffic, Spencer Davis Group.

Her Favorite Patient SEE: **Bedside Manner**

Her First Romance (1951) **73m.** *½ D: Seymour Friedman. Margaret O'Brien, Allen Martin, Jr., Jimmy Hunt, Sharyn Moffett. O'Brien's first grown-up role and her first screen kiss are only assets of this plodding summer camp story.

Her Highness and the Bellboy (1945) **112m.** **½ D: Richard Thorpe. Hedy Lamarr, Robert Walker, June Allyson, Carl Esmond, Agnes Moorehead, Rags Ragland. Sentimental fluff of N.Y.C. bellboy Walker, crippled girlfriend Allyson, captivating Princess (Lamarr) he escorts; a bit creaky.

Her Husband's Affairs (1947) **83m.** *½ D: S. Sylvan Simon. Lucille Ball, Franchot Tone, Edward Everett Horton, Mikhail Rasumny, Gene Lockhart, Nana Bryant. Pretty sterile comedy about Ball learning not to poke into husband's business affairs.

He Rides Tall (1964) **84m.** **½ D: R. G. Springsteen. Tony Young, Dan Duryea, Madlyn Rhue, George Petrie. Stark Western about a sheriff forced to shoot it out with foster-father's son.

Her Jungle Love (1938) **C-81m.** **½ D: George Archainbaud. Dorothy Lamour, Ray Milland, Lynne Overman, J. Carrol Naish, Dorothy Howe (Virginia Vale). Flyers Milland and Overman stranded on tropical isle with Lamour; Ray teaches her how to kiss; Naish tries to destroy everyone in this escapist fare.

Her Kind of Man (1946) **78m.** ** D: Frederick de Cordova. Dane Clark, Janis Paige, Zachary Scott, Faye Emerson, George Tobias. Lukewarm drama of young singer with gangster background making good in Big City and falling in love with gossip columnist. Fair cast.

Her Life as a Man (1984) **C-100m. TVM** D: Robert Ellis Miller. Robyn Douglass, Robert Culp, Marc Singer, Laraine Newman, Joan Collins, Miriam Flynn. Female reporter lands job as a sportswriter by disguising herself as a man in this lighthearted addition to the drag genre popularized by TOOTSIE and VICTOR/VICTORIA. Douglass makes a pretty good-looking guy in this Joanna Crawford adaptation of Carol Lynn Mithers' based-on-a-true-story *Village Voice* article. Average.▼

Her Lucky Night (1945) **63m.** ** D: Edward Lilley. Andrews Sisters, Martha O'Driscoll, Noah Beery, Jr., George Barbier, Grady Sutton, Ida Moore. Minor comedy with singing trio seeking romance at any cost.

Her Majesty, Love (1931) **75m.** *½ D: William Dieterle. Marilyn Miller, W. C. Fields, Leon Errol, Ford Sterling, Chester Conklin, Ben Lyon, Virginia Sale. Unbearable musical with sweet Miller in love with Lyon in old Berlin. Errol as persistent suitor, Fields as juggling father, provide only uplifting moments.

Her Man Gilbey (1948-British) **89m.** **½ D: Harold French. Albert Lieven, Margaret Rutherford, Peggy Cummins, Martin Miller. Capable cast nicely handles contrived yarn of quartet of people whose lives intertwine in Geneva.

Hero, The (1972) **C-97m.** **½ D: Richard Harris. Richard Harris, Romy Schneider, Kim Burfield, Maurice Kaufman, Yossi Yadin. Old-fashioned film about a soccer star and the young boy who idolizes him; partly filmed in Israel.▼

Hero Ain't Nothin' But a Sandwich, A (1978) **C-105m.** **½ D: Ralph Nelson. Cicely Tyson, Paul Winfield, Larry B.

Scott, Helen Martin, Glynn Turman, David Groh. Well-meaning drama (from Alice Childress' book) about intelligent but alienated black ghetto youth who takes up drugs. Moralistic film may get PTA recommendations, but doesn't really deliver: young Scott's performance is major asset.▼

Hero and the Terror (1988) **C-96m.** *½ D: William Tannen. Chuck Norris, Brynn Thayer, Steve W. James, Jack O'Halloran, Ron O'Neal, Billy Drago. Flat melodrama proves to be an unwise change of pace for action star Norris, here playing a "sensitive" police detective who must exorcise his personal demons by doing battle one last time with his larger-than-life maniac nemesis O'Halloran. The film's novelist and cowriter, former actor Michael Blodgett, has an endless cameo in a restaurant scene.▼

Hero At Large (1980) **C-98m.** **½ D: Martin Davidson. John Ritter, Anne Archer, Bert Convy, Kevin McCarthy, Harry Bellaver, Anita Dangler. Unemployed actor Ritter is mistaken for do-gooding "Captain Avenger"; political hucksters Convy and McCarthy attempt to co-opt him. Winning if naive satire. Look briefly for Kevin Bacon.▼

Herod the Great (1960-Italian) **C-93m.** *½ D: Arnaldo Genoino. Edmund Purdom, Sylvia Lopez, Sandra Milo, Alberto Lupo. Juvenile account of ruler of ancient Judea, his warring and his jealousy of wife's admirers.▼

Heroes, The (1972-Italian) **C-99m.** ** D: Duccio Tessari. Rod Steiger, Rod Taylor, Rosanna Schiaffino, Claude Brasseur, Terry-Thomas. A middling script sinks this forgettable actioner about a motley crew that bands together to pull off a heist of "lost" military money.

Heroes (1977) **C-113m.** **½ D: Jeremy Paul Kagan. Henry Winkler, Sally Field, Harrison Ford, Val Avery, Olivia Cole, Hector Elias. Innocuous film marked Winkler's first starring role, as crazy Vietnam vet who chases a dream of wealth and success cross-country; Field is appealing as the girl he meets and wins along the way.▼

Heroes for Sale (1933) **73m.** *** D: William A. Wellman. Richard Barthelmess, Loretta Young, Aline MacMahon, Robert Barrat, Grant Mitchell, Douglass Dumbrille, Charles Grapewin, Ward Bond. Potent melodrama with Barthelmess as an American Everyman who manages to survive one calamity after another—from morphine addiction (as a result of a WW1 injury) to job-hunting during the Depression—and continues to endure, like the country itself. Ambitious script by Wilson Mizner and Robert Lord tackles everything from the hypocrisy of hero worship to Commu-

nism! A fascinating social document of the early 1930s.

Heroes of Telemark, The (1965-British) **C-131m.** **½ D: Anthony Mann. Kirk Douglas, Richard Harris, Michael Redgrave, Mervyn Johns, Eric Porter. Douglas and Harris spend more time battling each other than the Nazis overrunning Norway in this pictorially striking (filmed on location), predictable blow-up-the-German-factory yarn.

Hero in the Family (1986) **C-100m. TVM** D: Mel Damski. Christopher Collet, Cliff De Young, Annabeth Gish, Darleen Carr, M. Emmet Walsh. Disney adventure about a teenager's efforts to turn things around after discovering that his astronaut dad's mind has been transferred into a chimp's body during a mishap in space. Average.

Hero's Island (1962) **C-94m.** **½ D: Leslie Stevens. James Mason, Kate Manx, Neville Brand, Rip Torn, Warren Oates, Brendan Dillon, (Harry) Dean Stanton. Peculiar mixture of adventure and soap opera set on 18th-century island near North Carolina, involving pirates and homesteaders.

Her Panelled Door (1951-British) **84m.** *** D: Ladislas Vajda. Phyllis Calvert, Edward Underdown, Helen Cherry, Richard Burton. During an air raid Calvert is shellshocked, forgetting her past, leading to dramatic results. Thoughtful study.

Her Primitive Man (1944) **79m.** *½ D: Charles Lamont. Robert Paige, Louise Allbritton, Robert Benchley, Edward Everett Horton. Grade-C flick with Paige pretending to be a savage to win love of anthropologist Allbritton.

Her Secret Life (1987) **C-100m. TVM** D: Buzz Kulik. Kate Capshaw, Jeroen Krabbe, Gregory Sierra, Valerie Mahaffey, James Sloyan, Cliff De Young. Ex-spy turned housewife and schoolteacher is coerced into staging a one-woman invasion of Cuba to snatch her former lover from a Castro prison. So-so drama that's almost *Scarecrow and Mrs. King* minus Scarecrow. Average.

Her Sister's Secret (1946) **86m.** **½ D: Edgar G. Ulmer. Nancy Coleman, Margaret Lindsay, Felix Bressart, Regis Toomey, Philip Reed, Henry Stephenson. Young woman discovers she's pregnant after brief affair. Fair weeper with competent cast.

Hers to Hold (1943) **94m.** ** D: Frank Ryan. Deanna Durbin, Joseph Cotten, Charles Winninger, Nella Walker, Gus Schilling, Ludwig Stossel, Irving Bacon. Grown-up Durbin is in love with serviceman Cotten in undistinguished romance, brightened by Deanna's singing. Songs: "Begin The Beguine," etc.

Her 12 Men (1954) **C-91m.** ** D: Robert Z. Leonard. Greer Garson, Robert Ryan, Barry Sullivan, Richard Haydn, James

Arness, Tim Considine, David Stollery. Maudlin script has Greer as dedicated teacher in boys' school. A failed attempt to repeat the success of GOODBYE, MR. CHIPS.

He's a Cockeyed Wonder (1950) **77m.** *½ D: Peter Godfrey. Mickey Rooney, Terry Moore, William Demarest, Ross Ford, Mike Mazurki. Bland Rooney film has him as energetic young man who captures a gang of robbers and gets to marry his boss' daughter.

He's Fired, She's Hired (1984) **C-100m. TVM** D: Marc Daniels. Wayne Rogers, Karen Valentine, Elizabeth Ashley, Howard Rollins, Jr., Martha Byrne, Mimi Kuzyk. Comedy about an upwardly mobile couple in which the wife becomes an ad exec (despite absolutely no experience) when hubby gets bounced from his high-paying job. Average.

He's My Girl (1987) **C-104m.** ** D: Gabrielle Beaumont. T.K. Carter, David Hallyday, Misha McK, Jennifer Tilly, David Clennon. A few amusing moments cannot save this silly comedy about Carter dressing in drag to accompany pal Hallyday on a free trip to Hollywood. Lots of energy, but it's mostly for naught.▼

He's Not Your Son (1984) **C-100m. TVM** D: Don Taylor. Donna Mills, Ken Howard, Ann Dusenberry, Michael C. Gwynne, George Coe, Dorothy Malone, John James. Pedestrian soaper about two married couples who learn that their infant sons were inadvertently switched at the hospital. Average.

He Stayed for Breakfast (1940) **89m.** ** D: Alexander Hall. Loretta Young, Melvyn Douglas, Una O'Connor, Eugene Pallette, Alan Marshal. NINOTCHKA and COMRADE X in reverse, as Russian Douglas is Americanized by beautiful Young; trivial.

Hester Street (1975) **92m.** ***½ D: Joan Micklin Silver. Steven Keats, Carol Kane, Mel Howard, Dorrie Kavanaugh, Doris Roberts, Stephen Strimpell. Young Jewish immigrant (Kane) joins her husband in N.Y.C. at turn of the century, only to find that he has forsaken his Old World ways and expects her to do the same. Disarmingly simple story, outstanding period flavor.▼

He Walked by Night (1948) **79m.** *** D: Alfred L. Werker. Richard Basehart, Scott Brady, Roy Roberts, Whit Bissell, Jack Webb. Grade-A drama of killer hunted by police; told in semi-documentary style (and, as film buffs know, partially directed by Anthony Mann). Effective performances by all.▼

He Was Her Man (1934) **70m.** ** D: Lloyd Bacon. James Cagney, Joan Blondell, Victor Jory, Frank Craven, Sarah Padden. Disappointing drama of safecracker Cagney on the lam, meeting Blondell, who's engaged to fisherman Jory. One of Cagney's weakest Warner Bros. vehicles.

He Who Gets Slapped (1924) **85m.** *** D: Victor Seastrom. Lon Chaney, Norma Shearer, John Gilbert, Tully Marshall, Marc McDermott, Ford Sterling. Brilliant scientist tries to bury personal tragedy under mask of circus clown, who falls in love with beautiful bareback rider (Shearer). Famous story becomes Pagliacci-type vehicle for Chaney.

He Who Rides a Tiger (1966-British) **103m.** ** D: Charles Crichton. Tom Bell, Judi Dench, Paul Rogers, Kay Walsh, Ray McAnally. Cat burglar is nice to children and is further softened by love, but he still has professional problems; OK programmer.

Hex (1973) **C-92m.** *½ D: Leo Garen. Keith Carradine, Tina Herazo (Cristina Raines), Hilarie Thompson, Gary Busey, Robert Walker, Dan Haggerty, John Carradine, Scott Glenn. Off-the-wall bike movie that involves a motorcycle gang with occultism in post-WWI Nebraska. You've got to be high to go for this one.▼

Hey Babu Riba (1986-Yugoslavian) **C-109m.** *** D: Jovan Acin. Gala Videnovic, Relja Basic, Nebojsa Bakocevic, Marko Todorovic, Dragan Bjelogrlic, Milos Zutic. Perceptive film combines nostalgia and political commentary in flashback story of four men recalling their pranks in the early 1950s when all were in love with dream girl Videnovic. Film buffs will appreciate picture being built around kids' fascination with Esther Williams in BATHING BEAUTY; also features vintage footage from the sexy Swedish classic SHE ONLY DANCED ONE SUMMER.▼

Hey Boy! Hey Girl! (1959) **81m.** *½ D: David Lowell Rich. Louis Prima, Keely Smith, James Gregory, Henry Slate, Asa Maynor, Sam Butera and The Witnesses. Minor low-budget musical about a singer (Smith) who will join Prima and the Witnesses only if they appear at a church bazaar. Louis sings the unforgettable "A Banana Split for My Baby (And a Glass of Water for Me)."

Hey Good Lookin' (1982) **C-86m.** *½ D: Ralph Bakshi. Voices of Richard Romanus, David Proval, Jesse Welles, Tina Bowman. Animated feature dips into "nostalgia" for street gangs in 1950s Brooklyn, and a sense of deja vu hangs over the proceedings. More interesting visually than Bakshi's other later films, because this one wasn't completely traced from live-action footage, but as entertainment it's vulgar and pointless. Originally made in 1975, then largely redone for 1982 release.▼

Hey, I'm Alive! (1975) **C-78m. TVM** D: Lawrence Schiller. Edward Asner, Sally Struthers, Milton Selzer, Hagan Beggs, Maria Hernandez, Claudine Melgrave. Fact-based drama about two plane crash survivors who spent 49 days in the Yukon wilderness subsisting on melted snow while awaiting rescue. Good work by Asner and Struthers. Average.▼

Hey, Let's Twist! (1961) **80m.** BOMB D: Greg Garrison, Joey Dee, The Starliters, Peppermint Loungers, Jo Ann Campbell, Zohra Lampert, Teddy Randazzo, Allan Arbus. Let's not. This minor film about the rise, decline, and rise of the Peppermint Lounge nightclub came out at the height of the Twist dance rage and wasn't very good then . . . now it's just a bad way to kill 80 minutes.

Hey, Rookie (1944) **77m.** **½ D: Charles Barton. Larry Parks, Ann Miller, Condos Brothers, Joe Sawyer, Jack Gilford, Selmer Jackson. Typical let's put-on-a-show-for-the-servicemen, with Miller's dancing and several specialty acts.

Hey There It's Yogi Bear (1964) **C-89m.** ** D: William Hanna, Joseph Barbera. Voices of: Mel Blanc, J. Pat O'Malley, Julie Bennett, Daws Butler, Don Messick. First full-length cartoon from Hanna-Barbera studio stars Yogi Bear in amusing musical tale for younger folk.▼

H. G. Wells' New Invisible Man SEE: **New Invisible Man, The**

Hiawatha (1952) **C-80m.** *½ D: Kurt Neumann. Vincent Edwards, Keith Larsen, Michael Tolan, Yvette Dugay. Juvenile low-budget version of the Longfellow classic.

Hickey and Boggs (1972) **C-111m.** **½ D: Robert Culp. Robert Culp, Bill Cosby, Rosalind Cash, Sheila Sullivan, Isabel Sanford, Ta-Ronce Allen, Lou Frizzell. Tough melodrama by Walter Hill about two weary, hard-luck private eyes whose search for a missing girl brings death to almost everyone around them. Well made but extremely violent and downbeat; will come as a surprise to fans of the stars' tongue-in-cheek antics on their *I Spy* TV series. Many now-familiar faces appear in bits: Robert Mandan, Michael Moriarty, Vincent Gardenia, James Woods, and Ed Lauter.

Hidden, The (1987) **C-96m.** *½ D: Jack Sholden. Michael Nouri, Kyle MacLachlan, Ed O'Ross, Clu Gulager, Claudia Christian, Clarence Felder, William Boyett, Richard Brooks. L.A. cop Nouri has the kind of week Jack Webb never had—pursuing an outer-space ghoul who implants himself ALIEN-style into the bodies of victims, causing them to commit violent crimes. High-concept mating of horror and urban jungle genres grows increasingly silly, with MacLachlan as the good-guy alien giving Nouri an assist.▼

Hidden City, The (1950) **71m.** D: Ford Beebe. Johnny Sheffield, Sue England, Paul Guilfoyle, Leon Belasco, Smoki

Whitfield. SEE: **Bomba the Jungle Boy** series.

Hidden Eye, The (1945) **69m.** **½ D: Richard Whorf. Edward Arnold, Frances Rafferty, Ray Collins, Paul Langton, Raymond Largay, William Phillips. Follow-up to EYES IN THE NIGHT, with blind detective Arnold making good use of other senses to solve murder mystery; fast-moving, entertaining mystery.

Hidden Fear (1957) **83m.** *½ D: Andre de Toth. John Payne, Alexander Knox, Conrad Nagel, Natalie Norwick. On-location filming in Copenhagen is chief virtue of mild hunt-down-the-murderer plot.

Hidden Fortress, The (1958-Japanese) **126m.** ***½ D: Akira Kurosawa. Toshiro Mifune, Misa Uehara, Minoru Chiaki, Kamatari Fujiwara, Susumu Fujita, Takashi Shimura. Autocratic young Princess Uehara and loyal general Mifune must make dangerous journey to their homeland with royal fortune, with only bare minimum of help from two bumbling misfits hoping to make off with a share of the gold. Solid comedy-adventure with great deadpan performance by Mifune; one of Kurosawa's personal favorites. Acknowledged by George Lucas as a primary inspiration for STAR WARS. Some U.S. prints cut to 90m.; released in Japan at 139m., and reissued in the U.S. in 1984 at that length.▼

Hidden Homicide (1959-British) **70m.** *½ D: Tony Young. Griffith Jones, James Kenney, Patricia Laffan, Bruce Seton, Charles Farrell. Circumstantial evidence makes writer think he's a murderer.

Hidden Room, The (1949-British) **98m.** *** D: Edward Dmytryk. Robert Newton, Sally Gray, Naunton Wayne, Phil Brown, Michael Balfour, Olga Lindo. Very effective suspenser involving Newton's plan to eliminate a man threatening his marriage; nifty climax. Retitled: OBSESSION.▼

Hideaways, The SEE: **From the Mixed-Up Files of Mrs. Basil E. Frankweiler**▼

Hide in Plain Sight (1980) **C-98m.** *** D: James Caan. James Caan, Jill Eikenberry, Robert Viharo, Joe Grifasi, Barbra Rae, Kenneth McMillan, Josef Sommer, Danny Aiello. Caan made a creditable directing debut with this true story about a divorced man whose children are swept away by the U.S. government when their new father is moved underground by the Justice Department's witness relocation program. Straightforward and well done.▼

Hideous Sun Demon, The (1959) **74m.** *½ D: Robert Clarke. Robert Clarke, Patricia Manning, Nan Peterson, Patrick Whyte, Fred La Porta, Bill Hampton. Doctor exposed to radiation discovers that sunlight turns him into ghastly lizard creature. Hideously low-budget production stars the director himself as demon of title.▼

Hide-Out (1934) **83m.** **½ D: W. S. Van

Dyke. Robert Montgomery, Maureen O'-Sullivan, Edward Arnold, Elizabeth Patterson, Whitford Kane, Mickey Rooney, C. Henry Gordon, Edward Brophy. Big-city racketeer recovers from gunshot wound on idyllic farm where he falls in love (of course) with fetching O'Sullivan. Opens and closes great, with some humdrum stuffing in between; wonderful supporting cast (including Henry Armetta and Herman Bing as nightclub co-owners!). Remade in 1941 as I'LL WAIT FOR YOU.▼

Hideout, The (1961-French) **80m.** **½ D: Raoul Andre. Marcel Mouloudji, Yves Vincent, Francis Blanche, Louise Garletti. Diverting account of Mouloudji seeking refuge in an insane asylum during WW2, kept there as a patient.

Hi Diddle Diddle (1943) **72m.** **½ D: Andrew L. Stone. Adolphe Menjou, Martha Scott, Pola Negri, Dennis O'Keefe, Billie Burke, June Havoc, Walter Kingsford. OK screwball comedy of young lovers and wacky con-artist parents, notable for appearance of silent-screen vamp Negri. Also known as DIAMONDS AND CRIME.

Hiding Out (1987) **C-98m.** ** D: Bob Giraldi. John Cryer, Keith Coogan, Annabeth Gish, Gretchen Cryer, Oliver Cotton, Anne Pitoniak. Silly, thoroughly unbelievable teen comedy-thriller about stockbroker Cryer, who's on the lam from thugs. He hides out by dying his hair and becoming an instant high-school senior. Jon's real-life mother, actress/writer Gretchen Cryer, plays Aunt Lucy.▼

Hiding Place, The (1975) **C-145m.** **½ D: James F. Collier. Julie Harris, Eileen Heckart, Arthur O'Connell, Jeanette Clift, Robert Rietty, Pamela Sholto. Well-meaning, sometimes effective, but draggy, predictable story of Dutch Christians aiding Jews in WW2. Produced by Billy Graham's Evangelistic Association.▼

High and Dry (1954-British) **93m.** **½ D: Alexander Mackendrick. Paul Douglas, Alex Mackenzie, James Copeland, Abe Barker. Satisfactory, minor yarn about U.S. financier Douglas in conflict with the captain of broken-down ship carrying valuable cargo; static at times. Originally titled THE MAGGIE.

✓ **High and Low** (1962-Japanese) **142m.** *** D: Akira Kurosawa. Toshiro Mifune, Tatsuya Mihashi, Yutaka Sada, Tatsuya Nakadai, Kyoko Kagawa. Carefully paced study of business executive Mifune, who is financially ruined when he nobly pays ransom money to kidnappers who mistakenly stole his chauffeur's son. Based on an Ed McBain story; one color sequence.▼

High and the Mighty, The (1954) **C-147m.** ***½ D: William A. Wellman. John Wayne, Claire Trevor, Laraine Day, Robert Stack, Jan Sterling, Phil Harris, Robert Newton, David Brian, Paul Kelly. Granddaddy of

all the airborne disaster films, and more fun than most of them put together: a GRAND HOTEL cast of characters boards a flight from Hawaii to the mainland, little dreaming of the trouble in store. Corny and predictable but great fun, bolstered by Dimitri Tiomkin's Oscar-winning music. Written by Ernest K. Gann.

High Anxiety (1977) **C-94m.** **½ D: Mel Brooks. Mel Brooks, Madeline Kahn, Cloris Leachman, Harvey Korman, Dick Van Patten, Ron Carey, Howard Morris, Murphy Dunne, Jack Riley, Charlie Callas. Affectionate, well-made but uneven spoof of Hitchcock films with Brooks as psychiatrist who walks into trouble as new head of sanitarium. Isolated moments of great comedy bolster so-so film.▼

High-Ballin' (1978-U.S.-Canadian) **C-100m.** **½ D: Peter Carter. Peter Fonda, Jerry Reed, Helen Shaver, Chris Wiggins, David Ferry, Chris Longevin. Good-buddy truckdrivers Fonda and Reed battle a rival kingpin's goons who want to force them off the road for good. Predictable action fare, with added spice from female trucker Shaver.▼

High Barbaree (1947) **91m.** ** D: Jack Conway. Van Johnson, June Allyson, Thomas Mitchell, Marilyn Maxwell, Cameron Mitchell. Navy flier's life story told in flashback as he awaits rescue in plane in ocean. Good cast in inferior story.

High Command, The (1937-British) **90m.** **½ D: Thorold Dickinson. Lionel Atwill, Lucie Mannheim, Steven Geray, James Mason, Allan Jeayes, Wally Patch. Crime melodrama set at an African military outpost. Atwill is a general caught up in a blackmailing scheme that leads to murder. An early role for Mason.▼

High Commissioner, The (1968-British) **C-93m.** *½ D: Ralph Thomas. Christopher Plummer, Rod Taylor, Lilli Palmer, Camilla Sparv, Daliah Lavi, Clive Revill, Franchot Tone. Wonderful cast is wasted in tired spy thriller about diplomat involved in murder at height of Cold War negotiations. British title: NOBODY RUNS FOREVER.

High Cost of Loving, The (1958) **87m.** **½ D: Jose Ferrer. Jose Ferrer, Gena Rowlands, Joanne Gilbert, Jim Backus, Edward Platt, Werner Klemperer. Lots of familiar faces in this very mild romantic comedy about tensions that threaten marriage of Ferrer and Rowlands. Enjoyable but innocuous semi-satire. Rowlands' film debut.

High Country, The (1981-Canadian) **C-101m.** BOMB D: Harvey Hart. Timothy Bottoms, Linda Purl, George Sims, Jim Lawrence, Bill Berry, Walter Mills. Feeble drama about obnoxious escaped con Bottoms and illiterate Purl eluding pursuers in the mountains.▼

High Crime (1973-Italian) **C-100m.** **
D: Enzo G. Castellari. Franco Nero, James
Whitmore, Fernando Rey, Delia Boccardo.
Energetic but superficial action drama with
narcotics cop Nero going up against Mafioso
Rey. You've seen it all before.▼

High Desert Kill (1989) **C-100m. TVM**
D: Harry Falk. Chuck Connors, Anthony
Geary, Marc Singer, Micah Grant. Offbeat sci-fi thriller involving four hunters in
the New Mexico badlands whose bodies
and minds are invaded by a supernatural
force. Written by T. S. Cook (THE CHINA
SYNDROME). Made for cable. Above
average.

Higher and Higher (1943) **90m.** **½ D:
Tim Whelan. Michele Morgan, Jack Haley,
Frank Sinatra, Leon Errol, Marcy McGuire,
Victor Borge, Mary Wickes, Mel Torme.
Bright, breezy, generally witless musical,
with good cheer compensating for lack of
material, as once-wealthy Errol schemes
with his own servants to raise money.
Sinatra's songs are fine: "The Music
Stopped," "I Couldn't Sleep a Wink Last
Night." This was his starring debut.▼

Higher Ground (1988) **C-100m. TVM**
D: Robert Day. John Denver, Meg Wittner,
David Renan, John Rhys-Davies, Martin
Kove, Richard Masur. Ex-FBI agent Den-
ver decides to become a bush pilot in
Alaska and stumbles into a drug-smuggling
operation. A prospective series pilot for
Denver. Below average.

High Flight (1958-British) **C-89m.** *½ D:
John Gilling. Ray Milland, Bernard Lee,
Kenneth Haigh, Anthony Newley. Stale
British drama of recruits in training for the
RAF—not as good as Milland's I WANTED
WINGS. Last reel, in the air, only exciting
part.

High Frequency (1988-Italian) **C-105m.**
** D: Faliero Rosati. Vincent Spano, Oliver Benny, Anne Canovas, Isabelle Pasco,
David Brandon. Satellite relay station attendant Spano and young ham operator Benny see
a murder on a satellite monitor and try to
warn a woman they believe will be the killer's
next victim. Ersatz REAR WINDOW lifts
ideas—but not substance—from the Hitchcock classic. Italian production released
with English-language soundtrack.▼

High Fury (1947-British) **71m.** ** D:
Harold French. Madeleine Carroll, Ian Hunt-
er, Michael Rennie, Anne Marie Blanc.
Standard film of couple quarreling over
adopting war orphan. Nice locations in
Switzerland. Originally titled WHITE CRA-
DLE INN.

High Heels (1972-French) **C-100m.** **½
D: Claude Chabrol. Jean-Paul Belmondo,
Mia Farrow, Laura Antonelli, Daniel
Ivernel. Well-acted but disappointing Chabrol comedy-mystery about a playboy doctor (Belmondo) attracted to women other
men find unappealing. Originally titled

DR. POPAUL. Also known as SCOUN-
DREL IN WHITE.▼

High Hell (1958-British) **87m.** **½ D:
Burt Balaban. John Derek, Elaine Stewart,
Rodney Burke, Patrick Allen. Mine owner's wife has an affair with husband's
partner; trio snowbound for winter fight
about it.

High Hopes (1988-British) **C-112m.** ***½
D: Mike Leigh. Philip Davis, Ruth Sheen,
Edna Dore, Philip Jackson, Heather Tobias,
Lesley Manville, David Bamber. Extraordinary slice-of-life comedy-drama about
love, alienation, and responsibility, centered on a young, laid-back working-class
couple, his aged mother and manic sister.
Writer-director Leigh offers a provocative,
highly original view of life's misfits in
modern-day England, and offers food for
thought along with some very hearty
laughs.▼

High Ice (1980) **C-97m. TVM** D: Eugene S. Jones. David Janssen, Tony Musante, Madge Sinclair, Dorian Harewood,
Warren Stevens, Gretchen Corbett, Allison Argo, James G. Richardson. Dandy
thriller about the rescue of three weekend
climbers from a tiny mountainside ledge,
pitting gruff veteran ranger Janssen against
by-the-book army colonel Musante. Above
average.▼

Highlander (1986) **C-111m.** *½ D: Russell Mulcahy. Christopher Lambert, Roxanne Hart, Clancy Brown, Sean Connery,
Beatie Edney, Alan North. Immortal being
is tracked from 16th-century Scotland to
modern-day America by his eternal arch-
enemy. Interesting notion made silly and
boring. Connery, at least, shows some
style in smallish role as Lambert's survival
tutor. Not hard to guess that director
Mulcahy cut his teeth on rock videos:
relentlessly showy camera moves may cause
you to reach for the Dramamine. Ran
17m. longer outside U.S. (and reportedly
made more sense).▼

High Lonesome (1950) **C-81m.** ** D:
Alan LeMay. John Barrymore, Jr., Chill
Wills, Lois Butler, Jack Elam. Moody
little drama set in the West with Barrymore a brooding youth involved with killers.

Highly Dangerous (1951-British) **88m.**
**½ D: Roy Baker. Dane Clark, Marius
Goring, Margaret Lockwood, Wilfrid Hyde-
White, Olaf Pooley, Eric Pohlmann. Clark
is American reporter accompanying scientist (Lockwood) on secret mission; well
paced.

High Midnight (1979) **C-100m. TVM** D:
Daniel Haller. Mike Connors, David Birney,
Christine Belford, Granville Van Dusen,
George DiCenzo. Blue collar worker Birney
seeks revenge for the murder of his family
in a mistaken no-knock drug raid and stalks
Connors, head of the narcotics squad re-
sponsible. Average.

High Mountain Rangers (1987) **C-100m.** TVM D: Robert Conrad. Robert Conrad, Christian Conrad, Shane Conrad, Tony Acierto, P.A. Christian, Timothy Mac-Lachlan, Roy Conrad. Action drama about a special squad of rangers working in the High Sierras is a true family affair. Robert Conrad cowrote, directs, and stars with his two real-life sons. Daughter Joan produced for the Conrad production outfit. Pilot to the series. Average.

✓ **High Noon** (1952) **84m. ****** D: Fred Zinnemann. Gary Cooper, Grace Kelly, Lloyd Bridges, Thomas Mitchell, Katy Jurado, Otto Kruger, Lon Chaney. Retiring sheriff Cooper feels responsibility to ungrateful town when challenged by gunfighter. Legendary Western highlighted by Oscar-winning Dimitri Tiomkin-Ned Washington song ("Do Not Forsake Me, Oh My Darlin' ") and, Tiomkin score, plus memorable cameos by character actors. Cooper won an Oscar, as did Elmo Williams and Harry Gerstad for their editing, which enabled the story to unfold in "real time," as the grandfather's clock in that hotel lobby will verify. Followed by a TV sequel.▼

High Noon, Part II: The Return of Will Kane (1980) **C-100m.** TVM D: Jerry Jameson. Lee Majors, David Carradine, J. A. Preston, Pernell Roberts, M. Emmet Walsh, Katherine Cannon, Michael Pataki. Majors takes the role of Will Kane here, which picks up where the Gary Cooper movie left off. In this long-delayed (and seemingly unnecessary) sequel, he has to strap on his guns again to face down the bounty-hunting marshal who replaced him. Average.▼

✓ **High Plains Drifter** (1973) **C-105m. ***** D: Clint Eastwood. Clint Eastwood, Verna Bloom, Marianna Hill, Mitchell Ryan, Jack Ging, Stefan Gierasch. Moody, self-conscious but compelling story of drifter hired by townspeople to protect them from vengeful outlaws who have just been released from prison. Half-serious, half tongue-in-cheek, with great role for midget Billy Curtis.▼

Highpoint (1980-Canadian) **C-88m.** BOMB D: Peter Carter. Richard Harris, Christopher Plummer, Beverly D'Angelo, Kate Reid, Peter Donat, Saul Rubinek. Confused and sloppy comedy thriller (reedited by a film doctor) has Harris as an accountant mixed up in a CIA plot and international intrigue. It's all an excuse for frequent chases culminating in a poorly photographed stunt fall off the needle tower in Toronto. ▼

High Pressure (1932) **74m. ***** D: Mervyn LeRoy. William Powell, Evelyn Brent, Frank McHugh, George Sidney, Guy Kibbee, Evalyn Knapp, Ben Alexander. Slam-bang con-man caper stars Powell as hilarious scheming promotor trying to sell artificial rubber. Typical nonstop Warner Bros. early talkie farce.

High Price of Passion, The (1986) **C-100m.** TVM D: Larry Elikann. Richard Crenna, Karen Young, Sean McCann, Terry Tweed, Steven Flynn. Sleazy retelling of the exploits of a real-life Tufts University professor driven to murder by his infatuation with a young hooker. A misguided venture for the always reliable Crenna, as well as the entire supporting cast of Canadian actors. Below average.

High Risk (1981) **C-94m. **½** D: Stewart Raffill. James Brolin, Cleavon Little, Bruce Davison, Chick Vennera, Anthony Quinn, Lindsay Wagner, James Coburn, Ernest Borgnine. Presposterous movie about group of normal Americans becoming mercenaries, flying to South America, parachuting into jungle to rip off dope dealers .. and that's just the beginning, because they soon run into bandidos. Ridiculous story, but good fun.▼

High Road to China (1983) **C-120m. **** ✓ D: Brian G. Hutton. Tom Selleck, Bess Armstrong, Jack Weston, Wilford Brimley, Robert Morley, Brian Blessed. Low road to escapism, with Selleck (in his first major starring feature) as a boozy ex-WW1 aerial ace hired by heiress Armstrong to find her father. Strictly mediocre, with substandard action scenes, and the flattest dialogue this side of the Great Wall.▼

High School Caesar (1960) **72m. **** D: O'Dale Ireland. John Ashley, Gary Vinson, Lowell Brown, Steve Stevens, Judy Nugent, Daria Massey. Rich kid Ashley, whose parents are too busy for him, gets a chip on his shoulder the size of the Rock of Gibraltar . . . and sets up his own little crime empire in school. Actually, not bad of its type.▼

High School Confidential! (1958) **85m.** ✓ ***½** D: Jack Arnold. Russ Tamblyn, Jan Sterling, John Drew Barrymore, Mamie Van Doren, Diane Jergens, Ray Anthony, Jerry Lee Lewis, Jackie Coogan, Charles Chaplin, Jr., Lyle Talbot, William Wellman, Jr., Michael Landon. Amateurish, hilariously awful marijuana exposé, with young undercover agent Tamblyn obtaining evidence against dope pushers. A most fascinating cast. Retitled YOUNG HELLIONS; followed by COLLEGE CONFIDENTIAL!▼

High School U.S.A. (1983) **C-100m.** TVM D: Rod Amateau. Michael J. Fox, Nancy McKeon, Todd Bridges, Lauri Hendler, Dana Plato, Bob Denver, Tony Dow, Angela Cartwright, Dwayne Hickman, Elinor Donahue, David Nelson. Mediocre sitcom about the class(room) wars showcasing a cast load of contemporary young TV faces along with television child stars of the previous generation. Average.▼

High Season (1987-British) **C-92m.** ** D: Clare Peploe. Jacqueline Bisset, James Fox, Irene Papas, Sebastian Shaw, Kenneth Branagh, Lesley Manville, Robert Stephens. Romantic misfire has Bisset (stunningly lovely as always) as a photographer residing in Rhodes who becomes involved with obnoxious tourists, a spy, and her egotistical ex-hubbie Fox. Fluff offers little more than luscious views of Bisset and the Greek island setting.▼

High Sierra (1941) **100m.** *** D: Raoul Walsh. Humphrey Bogart, Ida Lupino, Alan Curtis, Arthur Kennedy, Joan Leslie, Henry Hull, Henry Travers, Barton MacLane, Jerome Cowan, Cornel Wilde. Bogey is Mad Dog Earle, killer with a soft heart on the lam from police, in rousing (if not exactly credible) gangster caper. Lupino as the moll and Leslie as the lame innocent Bogart befriends offer interesting contrast. Screenplay by John Huston and W.R. Burnett based on Burnett's novel. Remade as I DIED A THOUSAND TIMES, and in Western garb as COLORADO TERRITORY. Also shown in computer-colored version.▼

High Society (1955) **61m.** D: William Beaudine. Leo Gorcey, Huntz Hall, Bernard Gorcey, Amanda Blake, David Condon (Gorcey), Addison Richards, Paul Harvey, Bennie Bartlett. SEE: **Bowery Boys** series.

High Society (1956) **C-107m.** *** D: Charles Walters. Bing Crosby, Grace Kelly, Frank Sinatra, Celeste Holm, Louis Calhern, Louis Armstrong, Sidney Blackmer. Fluffy remake of PHILADELPHIA STORY is enjoyable, but has lost all the bite of the original. Kelly is about to marry John Lund when ex-hubby Crosby arrives, along with reporters Sinatra and Holm. Cole Porter songs include "True Love," "Did You Evah?" "You're Sensational," plus Bing and Satchmo's "Now You Has Jazz." Grace Kelly's last acting role.▼

High Spirits (1988) **C-97m.** BOMB D: Neil Jordan. Peter O'Toole, Daryl Hannah, Steve Guttenberg, Beverly D'Angelo, Liam Neeson, Peter Gallagher, Jennifer Tilly, Ray McAnally, Donal McCann, Connie Booth, Liz Smith. Two yuppie stereotypes and a pair of 200-year-old ghosts romp around in an Irish castle threatened with foreclosure, with O'Toole—looking a bit ghostly here himself—playing ring master. Head-splitting farce full of collapsing sets and lots of wind-machine action; cast members complained that film's producers crudely altered the original whimsical intentions of writer-director Jordan. Unbearable.▼

High Stakes (1989) **C-102m.** ** D: Amos Kollek. Sally Kirkland, Robert LuPone, Richard Lynch, Sarah Gellar, Kathy Bates, W. T. Martin. A stripper/prostitute tries to retrieve her daughter from the Mob, while falling in love with a Wall Street speculator. A B-movie script with an A performance by Kirkland. Filmed as MELANIE ROSE and sent almost directly to video under this nondescript title.▼

High Terrace (1956-British) **77m.** ** D: Henry Cass. Dale Robertson, Lois Maxwell, Derek Bond, Eric Pohlmann. Fledgling actress is implicated in murder in minor drama.

High Tide (1947) **72m.** **½ D: John Reinhardt. Lee Tracy, Don Castle, Julie Bishop, Regis Toomey, Anabel Shaw, Francis Ford. Low-budget gets good mileage from players convincingly relating story of newspaper's attempts to prevent racketeers taking over city.

High Tide (1987-Australian) **C-101m.** **½ D: Gillian Armstrong. Judy Davis, Jan Adele, Claudia Karvan, Colin Friels, John Clayton, Frankie J. Holden, Monica Trapaga, Mark Hembrow. Quietly emotional story of a woman who inadvertently encounters the teenage daughter she abandoned years ago. Truthfully told, well acted, and set against bleakness of an Australian coastal town, but hampered by a leading character we don't necessarily care about. It's fun to see Davis in the opening scenes playing a backup singer for a crummy Elvis impersonator!▼

High Time (1960) **C-103m.** **½ D: Blake Edwards. Bing Crosby, Fabian, Tuesday Weld, Nicole Maurey. Middling Crosby vehicle has Bing a widower resuming college career and trying to be one of the boys; forced comedy.

High Treason (1952-British) **93m.** **½ D: Roy Boulting. Andre Morell, Liam Redmond, Mary Morris. Well-handled drama involving complex caper to instigate chaos in English industrial life via high-explosive bomb.

High Velocity (1977) **C-105m.** ** D: Remi Kramer. Ben Gazzara, Paul Winfield, Britt Ekland, Keenan Wynn, Alejandro Rey, Victoria Racimo. Hard-nosed Vietnam vets are hired to spring an international executive who's been kidnapped. Standard action fare, unworthy of good cast.▼

High Voltage (1929) **57m.** *½ D: Howard Higgin. William Boyd, Owen Moore, Carol(e) Lombard, Diane Ellis, Phillips Smalley, Billy Bevan. Main attraction in this deadening, laughably predictable antique is a very young Lombard (who was then billed as "Carol," without the final "e"), as one of a group of diverse individuals stranded in the wilderness after a snowstorm; she's a prisoner, in the custody of sheriff (Moore), who falls for tough guy (Boyd).▼

High Wall (1947) **99m.** *** D: Curtis Bernhardt. Robert Taylor, Audrey Totter, Herbert Marshall, Dorothy Patrick, H. B.

Warner, Warner Anderson. Well-paced mystery of former air force bomber pilot who attempts to establish innocence in murder case by working with psychiatrist.

Highway Dragnet (1954) **71m.** ** D: Nathan Juran. Richard Conte, Joan Bennett, Wanda Hendrix, Reed Hadley, Mary Beth Hughes. Tawdry caper of Conte trying to prove his innocence of a murder rap. This was Roger Corman's first film, as cowriter and coproducer.

Highwayman, The (1951) **C-82m.** **½ D: Lesley Selander. Charles Coburn, Wanda Hendrix, Philip Friend, Cecil Kellaway, Victor Jory. Filmization of famous poem, involving innkeeper's daughter in love with nobleman who masquerades as bandit to help the oppressed; set in 1760s England.

Highwayman, The (1987) **C-100m. TVM** D: Doug Heyes. Sam Jones, Claudia Christian, Stanford Egi, Wings Hauser, Jimmy Smits, Theresa Saldana, G. Gordon Liddy. Undercover cop declares war on small-town corruption. Scaled-down Schwarzenegger-style mayhem with the help of a high-tech eighteen wheeler in this pilot to the series. Average.

Highwayman Rides, The SEE: Billy the Kid (1930)

Highway 301 (1950) **83m.** ** D: Andrew L. Stone. Steve Cochran, Virginia Grey, Robert Webber, Richard Egan. Good little gangster film relating robbery capers in straightforward manner.

Highway to Battle (1960-British) **71m.** ** D: Ernest Morris. Gerard Heinz, Margaret Tyzack, Peter Reynolds, Richard Shaw. Trim little film set in 1935 England involving Nazi diplomats who try to defect, chased by Gestapo agents.

High, Wide, and Handsome (1937) **112m.** **½ D: Rouben Mamoulian. Irene Dunne, Randolph Scott, Dorothy Lamour, Elizabeth Patterson, Charles Bickford, Raymond Walburn, Alan Hale, Akim Tamiroff, William Frawley. Jerome Kern-Oscar Hammerstein old-time musical of determined Scott drilling for oil in 19th-century Pennsylvania, fighting corrupt Hale. Corny plot put over by energetic cast; result is entertaining. Songs include "The Folks Who Live On The Hill."

High Wind in Jamaica, A (1965-British) **C-104m.** *** D: Alexander Mackendrick. Anthony Quinn, James Coburn, Dennis Price, Gert Frobe, Lila Kedrova, Nigel Davenport, Kenneth J. Warren. Excellent cast and intelligent script about group of children who reveal their basic natures when left adrift aboard a pirate vessel. Score composed by harmonica virtuoso Larry Adler.

Hi, Good Lookin' (1944) **62m.** ** D: Edward Lilley. Harriet Hilliard, Eddie Quillan, Kirby Grant, Betty Kean, Roscoe Karns, Ozzie Nelson and His Orchestra,

Jack Teagarden and His Orchestra, Delta Rhythm Boys, Tip, Tap and Toe. Lightweight musical programmer serves as a showcase for Hilliard as she attempts to become a radio star with help of Grant. Pleasant songs and specialty acts make it palatable.

Hijack (1973) **C-73m. TVM** D: Leonard Horn. David Janssen, Keenan Wynn, Ronald Feinberg, Lee Purcell, Jeanette Nolan, William Schallert. Two truckdrivers, unaware of nature of cargo, menaced by criminals not afraid of going all the way for possession of government secret material. Janssen and Wynn work well together, but script full of implausible situations and resolution. Average.

Hilda Crane (1956) **C-87m.** ** D: Philip Dunne. Jean Simmons, Guy Madison, Jean-Pierre Aumont, Judith Evelyn, Evelyn Varden. Twice-divorced Simmons returns to the college town that used to be her home, starts the local gossips to fluttering with her behavior. Not much overall, but with one real claim of distinction: Simmons' character is surprisingly liberated for her time, making her one of the 1950s' more interesting screen heroines.

Hill, The (1965) **122m.** ***½ D: Sidney Lumet. Sean Connery, Harry Andrews, Ian Hendry, Michael Redgrave, Ian Bannen, Alfred Lynch, Ossie Davis, Roy Kinnear, Jack Watson. Powerful drama of military prison camp, with superb performances by all. One problem: British actors bark at each other and much dialogue is unintelligible to American ears (though if you can make it through the first reel, hang on). Written by Ray Rigby. Also shown in computer-colored version.

Hillbillys in a Haunted House (1967) **C-88m.** *½ D: Jean Yarbrough. Ferlin Husky, Joi Lansing, Don Bowman, John Carradine, Lon Chaney, Jr., Basil Rathbone, Molly Bee, Merle Haggard, Sonny James. Country singers Husky and Lansing spend a night in an old mansion, become involved with an espionage ring. Moronic comedy with an elderly, tired cast; a follow-up to LAS VEGAS HILLBILLYS. Sorry to say, Rathbone's last film.▼

Hill in Korea, A SEE: Hell in Korea

Hills Have Eyes, The (1977) **C-89m.** **½ D: Wes Craven. Susan Lanier, Robert Houston, Virginia Vincent, Russ Grieve, Dee Wallace, Martin Speer, Michael Berryman. Typical American family on camping trip is harassed by savage, cannibalistic mutants. Above average of its type, with compact direction and plenty of amusing plot twists. Extremely gory film has acquired a cult following. Followed by a sequel.▼

Hills Have Eyes Part II, The (1985-U.S.-British) **C-88m.** BOMB D: Wes Craven. Michael Berryman, John Laughlin,

Tamara Stafford, Kevin Blair, John Bloom. Lame sequel has a group of young motocross enthusiasts stranded in the desert, preyed upon by primitive family. Loaded with flashback footage from 1977 film, including one sequence ludicrously purporting to be a recollection by a dog! Filmed in 1983. ▼

Hills of Home (1948) **C-97m.** *** D: Fred M. Wilcox. Edmund Gwenn, Donald Crisp, Tom Drake, Janet Leigh. Fine Lassie movie about doctor convincing Scottish father to urge son to study medicine.

Hills Run Red, The (1966-Italian) **C-89m.** ** D: Carlo Lizzani. Thomas Hunter, Henry Silva, Dan Duryea, Nando Gazzola. Civil War Western of stolen payrolls; poorly dubbed and loosely acted.

Hill 24 Doesn't Answer (1955-Israeli) **102m.** *** D: Thorold Dickinson. Edward Mulhare, Haya Harareet, Michael Wager, Michael Shillo, Arieh Lavi. Evocative if occasionally schmaltzy drama, played in flashbacks, of the fight for modern Israel, centering on the stories of four soldiers defending a hill outside Jerusalem during the 1948 war. ▼

Hi, Mom! (1970) **C/B&W-87m.** ***½ D: Brian De Palma. Robert De Niro, Allen Garfield, Lara Parker, Jennifer Salt, Gerrit Graham, Charles Durning. Sequel to GREETINGS! is funny satire of the late '60s, with Vietnam veteran De Niro making dirty movies and bombing apartment houses. Video title: CONFESSIONS OF A PEEPING JOHN. ▼

✓ **Hindenburg, The** (1975) **C-125m.** ** D: Robert Wise. George C. Scott, Anne Bancroft, William Atherton, Roy Thinnes, Gig Young, Burgess Meredith, Charles Durning, Richard A. Dysart, Robert Clary, Rene Auberjonois, Katherine Helmond. Intriguing premise, that 1937 airship disaster was an act of sabotage, undermined by silly Grand Hotel-type characters and unexciting denouement combining original newsreel footage and newly-shot material. This earned special Oscars for its visual and sound effects. Five minutes were added to film for network showing. ▼

Hi, Nellie! (1934) **75m.** **½ D: Mervyn LeRoy. Paul Muni, Glenda Farrell, Ned Sparks, Robert Barrat, Kathryn Sergava, Hobart Cavanaugh, Berton Churchill, Douglass Dumbrille. Minor but enjoyable newspaper yarn with Muni as hard-hitting editor who's punished by being assigned to advice-to-the-lovelorn column. Loses initial momentum with gangland subplot, but it's still entertaining. Remade as LOVE IS ON THE AIR, YOU CAN'T ESCAPE FOREVER, and THE HOUSE ACROSS THE STREET.

Hippodrome (1961-German) **C-96m.** **½ D: Herbert Gruber. Gerhard Reidmann, Margit Nunke, Willy Birgel, Mady Rahl,

Walter Giller. Atmospheric circus mystery yarn, integrating varied circus acts with tale of murder and lust under big top.

Hips, Hips, Hooray (1934) **68m.** *** D: Mark Sandrich. Bert Wheeler, Robert Woolsey, Dorothy Lee, Thelma Todd, Ruth Etting, George Meeker. One of Wheeler & Woolsey's best vehicles is a lavish, risqué musical comedy about their attempts to save Todd's ailing beauty business. Wild production numbers, plus a nice song from Etting, "Keep Romance Alive." ▼

Hired Gun, The (1957) **63m.** **½ D: Ray Nazarro. Rory Calhoun, Anne Francis, Vince Edwards, John Litel, Chuck Connors. Francis is fetching as condemned killer Calhoun determines to prove innocent.

Hired Hand, The (1971) **C-93m.** *** D: Peter Fonda. Peter Fonda, Warren Oates, Verna Bloom, Robert Pratt, Severn Darden. First-rate photography by Vilmos Zsigmond and good performances by Oates and Bloom aid this offbeat, sometimes pretentious Western about cowboy who goes to work for the wife he deserted seven years before. TV prints run 98m., and include a scene with Larry Hagman. ▼

Hired Wife (1940) **93m.** *** D: William A. Seiter. Rosalind Russell, Brian Aherne, Virginia Bruce, Robert Benchley, John Carroll. Secretary Russell marries boss Aherne for business reasons; then the fun begins. Hilarious trifle with cast of comedy experts.

Hireling, The (1973-British) **C-108m.** ***½ D: Alan Bridges. Robert Shaw, Sarah Miles, Peter Egan, Elizabeth Sellars, Caroline Mortimer, Patricia Lawrence. Artistic adaptation of L. P. Hartley novel of stifling class system of England. Chauffeur (Shaw) helps upper-class woman (Miles) out of mental depression, mistakenly assumes she's interested in him. Ensemble British cast, good direction. Screenplay by Wolf Mankowitz.

Hi-Riders (1978) **C-90m.** BOMB D: Greydon Clark. Mel Ferrer, Stephen McNally, Darby Hinton, Neville Brand, Ralph Meeker, Diane Peterson. Obnoxious melodrama about a group of drag racers and the young boy and girl who join them. ▼

Hiroshima, Mon Amour (1960-French) **88m.** ***½ D: Alain Resnais. Emmanuele Riva, Eiji Okada, Stella Dassas, Pierre Barband. Thoughtful study of French movie actress and Japanese architect whose sensual love affair in 1950 Hiroshima evokes strange memories of the past and thoughts of the future. ▼

His Brother's Wife (1936) **90m.** ** D: W. S. Van Dyke, II. Barbara Stanwyck, Robert Taylor, Jean Hersholt, Joseph Calleia, John Eldredge, Samuel S. Hinds. Glossy soaper of dedicated scientist Taylor scorning Stanwyck, who marries his brother

Eldredge for spite. Stanwyck and Taylor married in real-life three years later.

His Butler's Sister (1943) **94m.** ** D: Frank Borzage. Deanna Durbin, Franchot Tone, Pat O'Brien, Evelyn Ankers, Elsa Janssen, Akim Tamiroff, Walter Catlett, Alan Mowbray. Great opening (Iris Adrian and Robin Raymond as the Sunshine Twins) and moving finale (Deanna's stunning rendition of "Nessun Dorma" from *Turandot*), but in between, a tired Durbin vehicle with Tone as an aloof Broadway composer.

His Double Life (1933) **67m.** **½ D: Arthur Hopkins. Roland Young, Lillian Gish, Montague Love, Lucy Beaumont, Lumsden Hare. Slight, moderately entertaining tale about a shy but famous artist (Young), who is more than pleased to settle down with middle-class spinster Gish when he is thought dead. Based on Arnold Bennett's play *Buried Alive,* filmed three times in the silent era. Remade far more successfully as HOLY MATRIMONY.▼

His First Command (1929) **61m.** ** D: Gregory La Cava. William Boyd, Dorothy Sebastian, Gavin Gordon, Helen Parrish, Alphonse Ethier, Howard Hickman, Paul Hurst. Slow-moving romantic drama with Boyd offering an awkward performance as a playboy who enlists in the army to win the affection of colonel's daughter Sebastian. Forgettable.▼

His Girl Friday (1940) **92m.** **** D: Howard Hawks. Cary Grant, Rosalind Russell, Ralph Bellamy, Gene Lockhart, Helen Mack, Ernest Truex, Clarence Kolb, Porter Hall, Roscoe Karns, Abner Biberman, Cliff Edwards, John Qualen, Frank Jenks, Billy Gilbert. Splendid comedy remake of THE FRONT PAGE with Grant as conniving editor, Russell as star reporter (and his ex-wife), Bellamy as mama's boy she's trying to marry amid hot murder story. Terrific character actors add sparkle to must-see film, scripted by Ben Hecht and Charles Lederer. Remade (with the same gender twist) in 1988 as SWITCHING CHANNELS.▼

His Kind of Woman (1951) **120m.** *** D: John Farrow. Robert Mitchum, Jane Russell, Vincent Price, Tim Holt, Raymond Burr, Charles McGraw, Marjorie Reynolds, Jim Backus. Mitchum blindly goes to Mexico for a payoff of 50 grand, discovers he's the soon-to-be-dead chump whose identity will help deported gangster Burr re-enter the country. Cult film is overlong, but its spoofing of he-man heroics predates the more celebrated BEAT THE DEVIL by three years; Price is hilarious as a ham actor.▼

His Majesty O'Keefe (1953) **C-92m.** **½ D: Byron Haskin. Burt Lancaster, Joan Rice, Benson Fong, Philip Ahn, Grant Taylor. Another athletic Lancaster buccaneer romp, set in the South Seas.

His Mistress (1984) **C-100m. TVM** D: David Lowell Rich. Robert Urich, Cynthia Sikes, Julianne Phillips, Linda Kelsey, Mark Shera, Tim Thomerson, Sachi Parker. Plodding sudser about a high-powered industrialist involved in an unhappy marriage and an affair with an ambitious junior executive in his company. Parker, daughter of Shirley MacLaine, here made her TV movie debut. Below average.

History Is Made at Night (1937) **97m.** ***½ D: Frank Borzage. Charles Boyer, Jean Arthur, Leo Carrillo, Colin Clive, Ivan Lebedeff, George Meeker, Lucien Prival, George Davis. Arthur, fleeing from a jealous husband she doesn't love, falls in love with Parisian headwaiter Boyer. Elegant, adult romantic drama, seamlessly directed by Borzage, with incredible shipboard climax and flawless performances by the two leads.▼

History of Mr. Polly, The (1949-British) **96m.** *** D: Anthony Pelissier. John Mills, Sally Ann Howes, Finlay Currie, Betty Ann Davies, Edward Chapman, Megs Jenkins, Juliet Mills. Worthy adaptation of H. G. Wells novel about timid draper's clerk (Mills) and his relationships with women—notably a shrewish cousin and a jolly innkeeper. Amusing and enjoyable Victorian comedy.

History of the World—Part 1 (1981) **C-92m.** *½ D: Mel Brooks. Mel Brooks, Gregory Hines, Dom DeLuise, Madeline Kahn, Harvey Korman, Cloris Leachman, Ron Carey, Sid Caesar, Pamela Stephenson, Mary-Margaret Humes, Howard Morris, Spike Milligan, many guest stars. Narrated by Orson Welles. Scattershot comedy wanders from the Stone Age to Roman Empire to French Revolution, dispensing gags that range from hilarious to hideous. After a while there's no more momentum, and it all just lies there, despite the efforts of a large comic cast. Caesar scores highest as a caveman in opening scenes. Hines' film debut.▼

His Woman (1931) **80m.** ** D: Edward Sloman. Gary Cooper, Claudette Colbert, Douglass Dumbrille, Harry Davenport. Stiff, early-talkie romance between skipper Cooper and passenger, nurse Colbert.

Hit! (1973) **C-134m.** *** D: Sidney J. Furie. Billy Dee Williams, Paul Hampton, Richard Pryor, Gwen Welles. Detailed and overlong, but exciting story of black U.S. agent who seeks revenge on top drug importers in Marseilles who are indirectly responsible for his daughter's death.

Hit, The (1984-British) **C-98m.** *** D: Stephen Frears. Terence Stamp, John Hurt, Tim Roth, Laura Del Sol, Bill Hunter, Fernando Rey. Sly, offbeat film about a criminal stool pigeon (Stamp) who's been in hiding for ten years but whose time has just run out: two hit men have tracked him down. Sharp, often very funny, and doggedly unpredictable. Written by Peter Prince; memorable theme music by Eric Clapton, assisted by Roger Waters.▼

Hit and Run (1957) **84m.** BOMB D: Hugo Haas. Hugo Haas, Cleo Moore, Vince Edwards. Trash involving Haas' efforts to rid himself of wife's young boyfriend.

Hit and Run (1982) **C-93m.** ** D: Charles Braverman. Paul Perri, Claudia Cron, Will Lee, Bart Braverman, E. Brian Dean, Donald Symington. All gloss, no substance in this implausible drama of cabdriver Perri's entanglement with mysterious, beautiful passenger Cron and murder. Also known as REVENGE SQUAD.▼

Hitched (1971) **C-73m. TVM** D: Boris Sagal. Tim Matheson, Sally Field, Neville Brand, Kathleen Freeman, Don Knight, Slim Pickens, Denver Pyle. Lame, predictable Western with comedy undertones featuring two newlyweds thwarting half-hearted crooked deal. Sequel to LOCK, STOCK AND BARREL. Below average.

Hitcher, The (1986) **C-97m.** **½ D: Robert Harmon. Rutger Hauer, C. Thomas Howell, Jennifer Jason Leigh, Jeffrey DeMunn, John Jackson. Hitchhiker Hauer keeps reappearing in Howell's life—is he real, or an hallucination? Reminiscent of other movies, except all those other movies (DUEL, NIGHT OF THE HUNTER) are better. Not without interest, but some of the violence is genuinely grisly and unappealing.▼

Hitchhike! (1974) **C-78m. TVM** D: Gordon Hessler. Cloris Leachman, Michael Brandon, Henry Darrow, Cameron Mitchell, John Elerick, Linden Chiles. Lonely middle-aged vacationer is unaware that the young hitchhiker she has picked up just killed his stepmother. Below average.

Hitch-Hiker, The (1953) **71m.** *** D: Ida Lupino. Edmond O'Brien, Frank Lovejoy, William Talman, Jose Torvay. Tense account of two vacationing businessmen held captive by a psychopath. Generally regarded as Lupino's best directorial achievement.▼

Hit Lady (1974) **C-78m. TVM** D: Tracy Keenan Wynn. Yvette Mimieux, Joseph Campanella, Clu Gulager, Dack Rambo, Keenan Wynn. Mimieux wrote this one and stars as a successful artist who moonlights (in bikini) as a ruthless syndicate assassin. Middling gangster flick with a twist told in its title. Average.▼

✓ **Hitler** (1962) **107m.** **½ D: Stuart Heisler. Richard Basehart, Cordula Trantow, Maria Emo, Martin Kosleck, John Banner, Carl Esmond. Basehart gives a cerebral interpretation to the career of the leader of the Third Reich.▼

Hitler—Dead or Alive (1943) **70m.** ** D: Nick Grinde. Ward Bond, Dorothy Tree, Warren Hymer, Paul Fix, Russell Hicks,

Felix Basch, Bobby Watson. Low-budget nonsense, with con-men shooting for high stakes by attempting to kill Hitler.▼

Hitler Gang, The (1944) **101m.** **½ D: John Farrow. Robert Watson, Martin Kosleck, Victor Varconi, Luis Van Rooten, Sig Ruman, Tonio Selwart, Ludwig Donath. Historical drama of Hitler's rise to power had greatest impact on WW2 audiences but is still fairly interesting, though dwarfed by recent documentaries.

Hitler's Children (1943) **83m.** *** D: ✓ Edward Dmytryk, Irving Reis. Tim Holt, Bonita Granville, Kent Smith, Otto Kruger, H. B. Warner, Lloyd Corrigan. Engrossing exploitation film of young people forced to live life of horror in Nazi Germany. Quite sensational in its day.▼

Hitler's Gold SEE: **Inside Out** (1975)▼

Hitler's Madman (1943) **84m.** **½ D: Douglas Sirk. Patricia Morison, John Carradine, Alan Curtis, Ralph Morgan, Howard Freeman, Ludwig Stossel, Edgar Kennedy. Sensationalistic saga based on true story of small Czech village destroyed by Nazis, and commander Heydrich, assassinated by determined Czechs. Look for Ava Gardner in a small part.

Hitler's S.S.: Portrait in Evil (1985) **C-150m. TVM** D: Jim Goddard. John Shea, Bill Nighy, Lucy Gutteridge, David Warner, Jose Ferrer, Tony Randall, Carroll Baker. The tale of two brothers in Nazi Germany—one an S.S. storm trooper, the other an S.S. officer. Of interest are Randall's Putzi, an effeminate nightclub entertainer similar to Joel Grey's master of ceremonies in CABARET, and Warner's Reinhard Heydrich, whom he earlier portrayed in HOLOCAUST. Average.

Hitler: The Last Ten Days (1973-British- ✓ Italian) **C-108m.** ** D: Ennio de Concini. Alec Guinness, Simon Ward, Adolfo Celi, Diane Cilento, Gabriele Ferzetti, Eric Porter, Doris Kunstmann. Strange treatment of Hitler's final tyrannies is grimly amusing at times; muddled film doesn't really work.▼

Hit List (1989) **C-87m.** ** D: William Lustig. Jan-Michael Vincent, Lance Henriksen, Rip Torn, Leo Rossi, Jere Burns, Ken Lerner, Harriet Hall. Familiar urban thriller of ordinary guy whose child is mistakenly kidnapped by cold-eyed hit man working for flamboyant mobster Torn. Hero teams up with the real target, an informer. Lots of violent action. Torn and Henriksen are good, but you've seen it all before.▼

Hit Man (1972) **C-90m.** ** D: George Armitage. Bernie Casey, Pamela Grier, Lisa Moore, Don Diamond. Reworking of GET CARTER in black mold. Big rubout is key to crime story, and it loses steam before long.

Hitman (1985) SEE: **American Commandos**▼

Hit Parade of 1943 SEE: **Change of Heart**

Hit the Deck (1955) **C-112m.** **½ D: Roy Rowland. Jane Powell, Tony Martin, Debbie Reynolds, Ann Miller, Vic Damone, Russ Tamblyn, Walter Pidgeon, Kay Armen, Gene Raymond. Second-string MGM musical of sailors on shore leave is pleasant time-filler, no more, with nice Vincent Youmans songs like "Hallelujah," "Sometimes I'm Happy," "More Than You Know." Filmed before in 1930.▼

Hit the Ice (1943) **82m.** **½ D: Charles Lamont. Bud Abbott, Lou Costello, Ginny Simms, Patric Knowles, Elyse Knox, Sheldon Leonard, Marc Lawrence, Joseph Sawyer. Bud and Lou are newspaper photographers involved with gang of thugs in zany comedy with good gags on skating rink.▼

Hit the Road (1941) **61m.** D: Joe May, Gladys George, Barton MacLane, Billy Halop, Huntz Hall, Gabriel Dell, Bernard Punsley, Bobs Watson, Evelyn Ankers, Charles Lang, Shemp Howard, Walter Kingsford. SEE: **Bowery Boys** series.

Hitting a New High (1937) **85m.** **½ D: Raoul Walsh. Lily Pons, Jack Oakie, Edward Everett Horton, Lucille Ball, Eric Blore, Eduardo Ciannelli. Title refers to Pons' voice, not the film per se; fluffy musical romance relies on supporting cast for entertainment.

Hi'ya, Chum (1943) **61m.** *½ D: Harold Young. Ritz Brothers, Jane Frazee, Robert Paige, June Clyde, Edmund MacDonald. Entertainers find themselves in small boomtown, and open a restaurant there. Weak musical comedy, if that's what you want to call it.

H-Man, The (1958-Japanese) **C-79m.** ** D: Inoshiro Honda. Kenji Sahara, Yumi Shirakawa, Akihiko Hirata, Koreya Senda. Good special effects marred by dumb script involving radioactive liquid causing havoc in Tokyo, subplot of cops vs. underworld.▼

H. M. Pulham, Esq. (1941) **120m.** ***½ D: King Vidor. Hedy Lamarr, Robert Young, Ruth Hussey, Charles Coburn, Van Heflin, Fay Holden, Bonita Granville. Intelligent, mature, and witty film (based on John P. Marquand story) about a man who's lived his life as he was supposed to—not as he chose to. Lamarr is excellent as the spirited career woman who coaxes proper Bostonian Young out of his shell, ever so briefly.

Hobo's Christmas, A (1987) **C-100m.** TVM D: Will Mackenzie. Barnard Hughes, Gerald McRaney, Wendy Crewson, William Hickey, Helen Stenborg, Lee Weaver. Comfortable Yuletide tale about a wizened old hobo's holiday reunion with the family he walked out on twenty years earlier. Only a Scrooge could dislike this one,

especially with Hughes' crafty performance. Average.▼

Hobson's Choice (1954-British) **107m.** *** D: David Lean. Charles Laughton, John Mills, Brenda de Banzie, Daphne Anderson, Prunella Scales, Richard Wattis. Laughton is overbearing owner of bootshop in 1890s who's decided whom his daughters shall marry, in spite of their own preferences. Handsome production is delightfully well acted; remade as a TVM in 1983.▼

Hobson's Choice (1983) **C-100m.** TVM D: Gilbert Cates. Richard Thomas, Sharon Gless, Jack Warden, Lillian Gish, Bert Remsen. Colorful but miscast period piece about a stubborn shoestore owner whose free-spirited daughter rebels by marrying one of his employees. Despite the resetting to multi-hued New Orleans of 1914 and the brief presence of delightful Lillian Gish as a spunky customer, the choice here is David Lean's 1954 version. Average.▼

Hockey Night (1984-Canadian) **C-77m.** **½ D: Paul Shapiro. Megan Follows, Rick Moranis, Gail Youngs, Yannick Bisson, Henry Ramer, Sean McCann, Rum Johnston. A girl goalie makes the boys' hockey team in a small Canadian town. Unexceptional but still likable, and ideal nonexploitation fare for pre- and early teens.▼

Hoffman (1970-British) **C-116m.** *** D: Alvin Rakoff. Peter Sellers, Sinead Cusack, Jeremy Bulloch, Ruth Dunning. Very odd, low-key dual character study with Sellers blackmailing attractive young bride-to-be to spend weekend with him. Slightly overlong; great performances.

Hog Wild (1980-Canadian) **C-97m.** *½ D: Les Rose. Michael Biehn, Patti D'Arbanville, Tony Rosato, Angelo Rizacos, Martin Doyle, Matt Craven. Dumb comedy about humorously nasty bikers who harass teenagers. Predictable, low-grade production benefits from spirited performances, especially Rosato as incoherently mumbling gang leader The Bull.▼

Holcroft Covenant, The (1985-British) **C-112m.** ** D: John Frankenheimer. Michael Caine, Anthony Andrews, Victoria Tennant, Lilli Palmer, Mario Adorf, Michael Lonsdale. Muddy, twisty, unbelievable tale from Robert Ludlum novel. Caine's late father (a comrade-in-arms of Adolf Hitler) has left a fortune behind, supposedly to make amends for his wrongdoing— and leading Caine on a globe-trotting series of adventures. Just old-fashioned enough to be watchable—but not very good.▼

Hold Back the Dawn (1941) **115m.** ***½ D: Mitchell Leisen. Charles Boyer, Olivia de Havilland, Paulette Goddard, Victor Francen, Walter Abel, Rosemary DeCamp. First-rate soaper with Billy Wilder-Charles Brackett script of gigolo Boyer marrying spinsterish Olivia to get into U.S. That's director Leisen playing himself in the Hollywood soundstage sequence. Catch this one.

Hold Back the Night (1956) **80m.** ****½** D: Allan Dwan. John Payne, Mona Freeman, Peter Graves, Chuck Connors. Korean War officer Payne recounts facts about bottle of liquor he always has with him.

Hold Back Tomorrow (1955) **75m.** *½ D: Hugo Haas. Cleo Moore, John Agar, Frank de Kova, Harry Guardino, Jan Englund. Strange B-film concerning condemned murderer who marries a girl on the night before his execution.

Hold 'Em Jail (1932) **74m.** **½ D: Norman Taurog. Bert Wheeler, Robert Woolsey, Betty Grable, Edgar Kennedy, Edna May Oliver, Roscoe Ates. Silly comedy about privileged prisoners (Wheeler & Woolsey) at Kennedy's Bidemore Prison who start competitive football team. Some good laughs.▼

Hold 'Em Navy (1937) **64m.** ** D: Kurt Neumann. Lew Ayres, Mary Carlisle, John Howard, Benny Baker, Elizabeth Patterson. Ayres and Howard on the gridiron, with Carlisle the love interest. Boolah, boolah!

Hold On! (1966) **C-85m.** *½ D: Arthur Lubin. Peter Noone, Herman's Hermits, Sue Ane Langdon, Karl Green, Shelley Fabares. Will NASA name a spaceship after Herman's Hermits? That's the burning question in this awful musical, set while the group is on a U.S. tour. One of their songs is titled "A Must to Avoid," which just about sums up this loser.

Hold That Baby! (1949) **64m.** D: Reginald Le Borg. Leo Gorcey, Huntz Hall, Gabriel Dell, Frankie Darro, Billy Benedict, John Kellogg, Anabel Shaw, Bernard Gorcey. SEE: **Bowery Boys** series.

Hold That Blonde (1945) **76m.** ** D: George Marshall. Eddie Bracken, Veronica Lake, Albert Dekker, Frank Fenton, George Zucco, Donald MacBride. OK comedy, sometimes strained, of kleptomaniac Bracken tangling with sultry thief Lake.

Hold That Co-ed (1938) **80m.** *** D: George Marshall. John Barrymore, George Murphy, Marjorie Weaver, Joan Davis, Jack Haley, George Barbier. Good musicomedy supercharged by Barrymore as windy politician; he makes the whole film.

Hold That Ghost (1941) **86m.** *** D: Arthur Lubin. Bud Abbott, Lou Costello, Richard Carlson, Joan Davis, Mischa Auer, Evelyn Ankers, Marc Lawrence, Shemp Howard, Ted Lewis, The Andrews Sisters. Prime A&C, with the boys inheriting a haunted house. Fine cast includes hilarious Davis as professional radio screamer. Highlight: the moving candle.▼

Hold That Hypnotist (1957) **61m.** D: Austen Jewell. Huntz Hall, Stanley Clements, Jane Nigh, David Condon. SEE: **Bowery Boys** series.

Hold That Line (1952) **64m.** D: William Beaudine. Leo Gorcey, Huntz Hall, John Bromfield, Veda Ann Borg, Pierre Watkin. SEE: **Bowery Boys** series.

Hold the Dream (1986) **C-200m. TVM** D: Don Sharp. Jenny Seagrove, Stephen Collins, Deborah Kerr, John Mills, Claire Bloom, James Brolin, Suzanna Hamilton, Nigel Havers, Liam Neeson. Sequel to the popular miniseries of Barbara Taylor Bradford's *A Woman of Substance,* continuing the story of fabulously wealthy Emma Harte (Kerr), now an octogenarian, and her efforts to turn over her business empire to her favorite granddaughter (Seagrove, who played young Emma in the original). Bradford herself wrote the script, and her husband was executive producer, both taking on tasks not assumed on the superior predecessor. Originally shown in two parts. Average.▼

Hold Your Man (1933) **86m.** *** D: Sam Wood. Jean Harlow, Clark Gable, Stuart Erwin, Elizabeth Patterson, Blanche Frederici. Delightful film that effectively makes the transition from comedy to drama with Harlow falling for jailbound Gable. The stars are at their best here.

Hole In the Head, A (1959) **C-120m.** ** D: Frank Capra. Frank Sinatra, Edward G. Robinson, Eleanor Parker, Carolyn Jones, Thelma Ritter, Eddie Hodges, Keenan Wynn, Joi Lansing. Sticky story of a ne'er-do-well (Sinatra) and his son (Hodges) doesn't seem sincere. Only distinction is Oscar-winning song, "High Hopes."▼

Holiday (1930) **96m.** *** D: Edward H. Griffith. Ann Harding, Robert Ames, Mary Astor, Edward Everett Horton, Hedda Hopper, Monroe Owsley. This rediscovered version of Philip Barry's play about nonconformity is a pleasant surprise; an unstodgy early talkie with casting that in some cases (Astor, Owsley) even tops the more famous 1938 version (Horton plays the same role in both movies!).

Holiday (1938) **93m.** ***½ D: George Cukor. Katharine Hepburn, Cary Grant, Doris Nolan, Lew Ayres, Edward Everett Horton, Henry Kolker, Binnie Barnes, Jean Dixon, Henry Daniell. Fine, literate adaptation of Philip Barry's play (filmed before in 1930) about nonconformist Grant confronting stuffy N.Y.C. society family, finding his match in Hepburn (who had understudied the role in the original Broadway company a decade earlier). Screenplay by Donald Ogden Stewart and Sidney Buchman. Delightful film.▼

Holiday Affair (1949) **87m.** *** D: Don Hartman. Robert Mitchum, Janet Leigh, Wendell Corey, Gordon Gebert. Well-done Christmas season story about widow Leigh, her small son, and two contrasting men courting her.▼

Holiday Camp (1948-British) **97m.** **½

D: Ken Annakin. Dennis Price, Flora Robson, Jack Warner. Pleasantly handled account of life and love at British summer resort; atmospheric, with good characterizations.

Holiday for Lovers (1959) **C-103m.** **½
D: Henry Levin. Clifton Webb, Jane Wyman, Jill St. John, Carol Lynley, Paul Henreid, Gary Crosby, Jose Greco. Arch Dr. Webb and Wyman escort attractive daughters on South American vacation, with predictable mating.

Holiday for Sinners (1952) **72m.** **½ D: Gerald Mayer. Gig Young, Janice Rule, Keenan Wynn, William Campbell. Strange goings-on at Mardi Gras as several people try to forget their troublesome lives and have a good time.

Holiday in Havana (1949) **73m.** ** D: Jean Yarbrough. Desi Arnaz, Mary Hatcher, Ann Doran, Steven Geray, Minerva Urecal, Sig Arno. Typical low-budget show-biz musical that takes place mostly in Cuba, with Desi as a fledgling band leader.

Holiday in Mexico (1946) **C-127m.** ***
D: George Sidney. Walter Pidgeon, Ilona Massey, Roddy McDowall, Jose Iturbi, Xavier Cugat, Jane Powell. Engaging, well-cast musical comedy of daughter of ambassador falling for noted musician.

Holiday Inn (1942) **101m.** *** D: Mark Sandrich. Bing Crosby, Fred Astaire, Marjorie Reynolds, Virginia Dale, Walter Abel, Louise Beavers. Entertaining musical built on paper-thin plot about a romantic triangle, and the establishment of a country inn that's open only on holidays. That's the cue for a raft of Irving Berlin holiday songs (there's even one for George Washington's birthday!) including the timeless Oscar-winner "White Christmas." Good fun, and snappier than partial remake WHITE CHRISTMAS.▼

Hollow Image (1979) **C-100m. TVM** D: Marvin J. Chomsky. Robert Hooks, Saundra Sharp, Dick Anthony Williams, Hattie Winston, Morgan Freeman. Black career girl is torn between her chic new life in the world of fashion and her roots in Harlem with an old beau. Occasionally pretentious black awareness movie with standout performances by Williams and Freeman. A winner for first-time dramatist Lee Hunkins. Above average.

Hollow Triumph (1948) **83m.** *** D: Steve Sekely. Paul Henreid, Joan Bennett, Eduard Franz, Leslie Brooks. Tense melodrama of killer assuming identity of lookalike doctor. Retitled: THE SCAR.▼

Holly and the Ivy, The (1953-British) **80m.** *** D: George More O'Ferrall. Ralph Richardson, Celia Johnson, Margaret Leighton, Denholm Elliott, Hugh Williams, Roland Culver. Straightforward adaptation of Wynyard Browne play revolving around Christmas holiday with Richardson, the small-town cleric, learning about his three grown-up children; nicely acted.

Hollywood Boulevard (1936) **70m.** **½
D: Robert Florey. John Halliday, Marsha Hunt, Robert Cummings, Mae Marsh, C. Henry Gordon, Esther Ralston, Frieda Inescort, Esther Dale, Albert Conti, Charles Ray, Francis X. Bushman, Maurice Costello, Betty Compson. Halliday is vain former star who writes his memoirs for *Confidential*-type magazine, affecting lives of daughter Hunt, ex-girlfriend Ralston. Slow-moving drama is saved by sometimes crisp, perceptive dialogue, presence of silent stars Marsh, Bushman, Ray, etc. Gary Cooper appears briefly as himself.

Hollywood Boulevard (1976) **C-83m.** **½
D: Joe Dante, Allan Arkush. Candice Rialson, Mary Woronov, Rita George, Jeffrey Kramer, Dick Miller, Paul Bartel. Shameless low-budgeter splices shots from various Roger Corman films into the "story" of a would-be actress who goes to work for some schlock moviemakers. Engaging nonsense and some funny gags (especially for film buffs and Corman devotees)—though not enough to completely hide the fact that this *is* a schlock movie. Miller and Bartel are great fun as an agent and a motivation-minded director. Don't miss gag after closing credits.▼

Hollywood Canteen (1944) **124m.** **½
D: Delmer Daves. Bette Davis, John Garfield, Joan Leslie, Robert Hutton, Dane Clark, Janis Paige; many guest stars including Joan Crawford, Ida Lupino, Barbara Stanwyck, Eddie Cantor, Jack Carson, Eleanor Parker, Alexis Smith, S. Z. Sakall. Amiable all-star silliness set in Hollywood's real-life haven for WW2 servicemen, featuring cofounders Davis and Garfield. Hutton plays G.I. with a crush on lovely Leslie. Best bits: Peter Lorre and Sydney Greenstreet; Jack Benny and violinist Joseph Szigeti. Roy Rogers introduces "Don't Fence Me In," later reprised by the Andrews Sisters.

Hollywood Cavalcade (1939) **C-96m.** ***
D: Irving Cummings. Alice Faye, Don Ameche, Al Jolson, Mack Sennett, Stuart Erwin, Buster Keaton, Mary Forbes, Chester Conklin, Rin-Tin-Tin, Jr. First half a delight, with Don bringing Alice to Hollywood in silent days with flavorful recreation of old-time comedies; remainder of film bogs down in phony dramatics.

Hollywood Detective, The (1989) **C-100m. TVM** D: Kevin Connor. Telly Savalas, Helen Udy, George Coe, Joe Dallesandro, Tom Reese, James Green. Savalas sends up his "Kojak" image as an out-of-work former TV detective who takes on a real case in order to pay the rent, with the help of a ditsy girl Wednesday (that's her name) and the down-and-out ex-writer of his old

[515]

show. A cute idea that should have panned out better. Average.

Hollywood Hotel (1937) **109m.** **½ D: Busby Berkeley. Dick Powell, Rosemary Lane, Lola Lane, Ted Healy, Johnnie "Scat" Davis, Alan Mowbray, Frances Langford, Louella Parsons, Hugh Herbert, Glenda Farrell, Edgar Kennedy. Silly, paper-thin plot about Powell winning Hollywood talent contest but finding stardom elusive, buoyed by bright Johnny Mercer-Richard Whiting score, including "Hooray for Hollywood" and historic numbers by the Benny Goodman band ("Sing Sing Sing") and quartet (with Gene Krupa, Lionel Hampton, Teddy Wilson). Ronald Reagan has brief bit as radio announcer.

Hollywood Knights, The (1980) **C-95m.** *½ D: Floyd Mutrux. Tony Danza, Michelle Pfeiffer, Fran Drescher, Leigh French, Randy Gornel, Robert Wuhl, Stuart Pankin, P. R. Paul, Richard Schaal, Debra Feuer. A punk answer to AMERICAN GRAFFITI, which follows a band of high-school hell-raisers on Halloween Night, 1965, when their favorite drive-in hangout is about to close. Sophomoric humor to spare, only a small part of it funny. Danza's feature debut.

Hollywood or Bust (1956) **C-95m.** **½ D: Frank Tashlin. Dean Martin, Jerry Lewis, Anita Ekberg, Pat Crowley. Starstruck Lewis teams up with gambler Martin on trek to crash the movie capital; typical comedy by the frantic team. Dean and Jerry's last film together opens with Jerry's "tribute" to movie fans around the world.▼

Hollywood Party (1934) **68m.** **½ No director credited. Jimmy Durante, Laurel and Hardy, Lupe Velez, Polly Moran, Charles Butterworth, Eddie Quillan, June Clyde, George Givot, Jack Pearl, Ted Healy and The Three Stooges, many others. Musical comedy hodgepodge built around screen star Durante throwing a gala party. Romantic subplot is for the birds, but Stan and Ollie battling fiery Velez, Durante as Schnarzan, befuddled Butterworth and opening title tune make it worthwhile. Richard Boleslawski, Allan Dwan, Roy Rowland directed various scenes without credit; TV print runs 63m., and is missing appearance by Mickey Mouse and color Disney cartoon HOT CHOCOLATE SOLDIERS.

Hollywood Revue of 1929, The (1929) **130m.** ** D: Charles Riesner. Conrad Nagel, Jack Benny, John Gilbert, Norma Shearer, Joan Crawford, Laurel and Hardy, Bessie Love, Lionel Barrymore, Marion Davies, Buster Keaton, Marie Dressler, Polly Moran, many others. MGM's all-star revue introducing its silent-film stars as talkie personalities, cohosted by Benny and Nagel. Definitely a curio for film buffs, rough sledding for others. TV print at 116m.

is missing some material; several scenes originally filmed in color.

Hollywood Shuffle (1987) **C-82m.** **½ D: Robert Townsend. Robert Townsend, Anne-Marie Johnson, Starletta Dupois, Helen Martin, Craigus R. Johnson. Uneven but enjoyable comedy about young black actor trying to get a foothold in Hollywood, but running into problems of stereotyping at every turn. Townsend (who also directed and cowrote, with Keenen Ivory Wayans) is so appealing, and his message is so dead on-target, that it's hard to dislike this film, even though it's strictly hit-or-miss.▼

Hollywood Story (1951) **77m.** **½ D: William Castle. Richard Conte, Julia (Julie) Adams, Richard Egan, Henry Hull. Trying to solve an old murder, producer makes a picture on the subject, hoping to uncover culprit.

Hollywood Vice Squad (1986) **C-100m.** BOMB D: Penelope Spheeris. Trish Van Devere, Ronny Cox, Frank Gorshin, Leon Isaac Kennedy, Carrie Fisher, Ben Frank, Robin Wright. Stupid comic variation on VICE SQUAD with Van Devere asking help of the cops to find her runaway daughter, who's now a hooker and heroin addict.▼

Holocaust 2000 SEE: **Chosen, The** (1978)▼

Holy Matrimony (1943) **87m.** *** D: John M. Stahl. Monty Woolley, Gracie Fields, Laird Cregar, Una O'Connor, Alan Mowbray, Melville Cooper, Franklin Pangborn. Delightful tale of artist Woolley assuming late butler's identity to avoid publicity, finding many complications. Remake of 1933 film HIS DOUBLE LIFE.

Holy Terror (1977) **C-96m.** ** D: Alfred Sole. Brooke Shields, Tom Signorelli, Louisa Horton, Paula Sheppard, Mildred Clinton, Linda Miller, Lillian Roth. Does 12-year-old Alice (Sheppard) kill her sister, parents, aunt, etc.? OK murder mystery is noteworthy mainly as Shields's feature debut—and she's bumped off in the first reel. Filmed on location in Paterson, New Jersey; cameo appearance by Roth as a pathologist. Original running time: 108m. Also known as ALICE, SWEET ALICE and COMMUNION.▼

Hombre (1967) **C-111m.** *** D: Martin Ritt. Paul Newman, Fredric March, Richard Boone, Diane Cilento, Cameron Mitchell, Barbara Rush, Martin Balsam. Interesting Western (from an Elmore Leonard story) of Indian-raised Newman trying to survive in white man's world in Arizona circa 1880. Encounters with various characters on a stagecoach provide basis for film's action and drama; well acted, entertaining.▼

Home at Seven (1953-British) **85m.** *** D: Ralph Richardson. Ralph Richardson,

Margaret Leighton, Jack Hawkins, Campbell Singer. Taut thriller involving bank clerk who can't account for a day in his life when a murder and a bank robbery occurred. Retitled: MURDER ON MONDAY.

Home Before Dark (1958) **136m.** ******* D: Mervyn LeRoy. Jean Simmons, Dan O'Herlihy, Rhonda Fleming, Efrem Zimbalist, Jr. Shiny but poignant telling of Simmons' readjustment to life after nervous breakdown; on-location shooting in Massachusetts.

Homebodies (1974) **C-96m.** ****½** D: Larry Yust. Frances Fuller, Ian Wolfe, Ruth McDevitt, Paula Trueman, Peter Brocco, William Hansen. Bizarre horror-comedy will depend on one's taste for scenario. Elderly tenants of condemned building resort to murder to keep their home. Good cast, including Douglas Fowley as the builder. Made in Cincinnati.▼

Homeboy (1988) **C-118m.** ****½** D: Michael Seresin. Mickey Rourke, Christopher Walken, Debra Feuer, Thomas Quinn, Kevin Conway, Antony Alda, Ruben Blades. Downbeat, rainy tale of aging, alcoholic boxer Rourke, his relationship with flashy, philosophical crook Walken, and his romance with a carousel owner. Very well made, with fine, quirky performances by the leads, but so unrelentingly grim it can scarcely be called entertainment.▼

Homecoming (1948) **113m.** ****** D: Mervyn LeRoy. Clark Gable, Lana Turner, Anne Baxter, John Hodiak, Ray Collins, Cameron Mitchell. Gable and Turner have exciting WW2 romance in the trenches, but that can't support 113 minutes of dreary drama; one of Gable's lesser efforts.

Homecoming, The (1973) **C-111m.** *****½** D: Peter Hall. Cyril Cusack, Ian Holm, Michael Jayston, Vivien Merchant, Terence Rigby, Paul Rogers. Jayston, long separated from his London family, brings wife Merchant home to meet his father and two brothers. Film version of the Harold Pinter play is among the most satisfactory of all stage-to-screen adaptations. An American Film Theater Production.

Homecoming—A Christmas Story, The (1971) **C-120m.** TVM D: Fielder Cook. Patricia Neal, Edgar Bergen, Ellen Corby, Andrew Duggan, Josephine Hutchinson, Cleavon Little, Dorothy Stickney, Richard Thomas, William Windom, David Huddleston. Patricia Neal is Olivia Walton in her first TV movie, the forerunner to the long-running series *The Waltons*. Teleplay by Earl Hamner, Jr., was adapted from his own novel, which previously had been converted into SPENCER'S MOUNTAIN. Corby, Thomas, and a number of the other young players continued in *The Waltons* for years. Above average.▼

Home Fires (1987) **C-230m.** TVM D: Michael Toshiyuki Uno. Guy Boyd, Amy Steel, Max Perlich, Juliette Lewis, Whitby Hertford, Mitchell Laurence. A four-day odyssey in the life of a 1980s family. Dramatically sound but as uneventful as the average household. Made for cable and originally shown in two parts. Average.

Home Fires Burning (1989) **C-100m.** TVM D: Glenn Jordan. Barnard Hughes, Sada Thompson, Robert Prosky, Bill Pullman, Elizabeth Berridge, Neil Patrick Harris. Endearing slice of Americana set in a small Georgia town, with Hughes wonderful as a cantankerous, opinionated local editor shaken by the winds of change in his life as WW2 is ending. Written by Robert Inman, based on his novel. Above average.

Home for the Holidays (1972) **C-74m.** TVM D: John Llewellyn Moxey. Eleanor Parker, Sally Field, Jessica Walter, Julie Harris, Jill Haworth, Walter Brennan. Four daughters protect aging, vulnerable Brennan from a homicidal maniac during a Christmas reunion. Not bad, but you've seen it all before. Average.▼

Home Free All (1983) **92m.** ****½** D: Stewart Bird. Allan Nicholls, Roland Caccavo, Lorry Goldman, Maura Ellyn, Shelley Wyant. Nicholls is appealing in this comedy-drama about an ex-hippie radical, a child of the 50s and 60s desperately lost in the 80s. Some hilarious moments but not as incisive as intended.▼

Home from the Hill (1960) **C-150m.** ******* D: Vincente Minnelli. Robert Mitchum, Eleanor Parker, George Peppard, George Hamilton, Luana Patten, Everett Sloane, Constance Ford. Overlong but generally satisfying drama about Southern landowner's conflicts with his wife and two sons—one of them illegitimate. Typical MGM gloss seems at odds with gritty subject matter; noteworthy for giving the two Georges their first big break.

Home in Indiana (1944) **C-103m.** ******* D: Henry Hathaway. Walter Brennan, Jeanne Crain, June Haver, Charlotte Greenwood, Lon McCallister, Ward Bond, Willie Best, George Cleveland. Typical horse-racing saga gets a good rehashing here with colorful production and sincere performances; climactic race is well-handled. Remade as APRIL LOVE.

Home Is the Hero (1959-Irish) **83m.** ****½** D: Fielder Cook. Walter Macken, Eileen Crowe, Arthur Kennedy, Joan O'Hara. Modest yarn with Abbey Theatre group, telling story of ex-con (Macken) trying to pick up pieces of home-life.

Home Is Where the Heart Is SEE: **Square Dance**▼

Home Movies (1979) **C-90m.** ***½** D: Brian DePalma. Keith Gordon, Nancy Allen, Kirk Douglas, Gerrit Graham, Vincent Gardenia, Mary Davenport. Flaky farce reminiscent of DePalma's early work. Nebbish Gordon, an "extra in his own life," is given Star Therapy treatment by egomaniacal director Douglas (who has his own life filmed constantly), and sets out to woo Allen away from his nutsy older brother (Graham). Original in concept but tiresome in execution, although nobody eats a hamburger like Allen. Most of the production crew was made up of DePalma's filmmaking students from Sarah Lawrence College.▼

Home of the Brave (1949) **85m.** *** D: Mark Robson. James Edwards, Douglas Dick, Steve Brodie, Jeff Corey, Lloyd Bridges, Frank Lovejoy. More daring when made than now, but still hard-hitting account of black soldier Edwards suffering more abuse from fellow G.I.'s than the enemy while on a mission during WW2. From an Arthur Laurents play.▼

Home of the Brave (1986) **C-90m.** *** D: Laurie Anderson. Laurie Anderson, Adrian Belew, Richard Landry, Joy Askew, Dolette McDonald, Janice Pendarvis, William S. Burroughs. Concert film pretty well duplicates what fans of performance artist Anderson have been seeing for years; mix of music and provocative visuals doesn't quite add up to another STOP MAKING SENSE, but it's a generally rewarding introduction for the uninitiated. Mostly accessible, but the middle-section will test your openness to unconventional music.

Homer (1970) **C-91m.** *½ D: John Trent. Don Scardino, Alex Nicol, Tisa Farrow, Lenka Peterson, Ralph Endersby, Trudy Young. Well-meaning but cliché-ridden drama about small-town teen-ager, generation gap, Vietnam War protests, rock music, sex. You've seen it all before.

Homer & Eddie (1990) **C-99m.** BOMB D: Andrei Konchalovsky. James Belushi, Whoopi Goldberg, Karen Black, Ernestine McClendon, Nancy Parsons, Anne Ramsey, Beah Richards. He's been mentally impaired since getting smacked in childhood by a flying baseball; she's dying of brain cancer; theirs is an odyssey-by-auto punctuated by service-station knock-offs and a musical interlude where they dance with paper bags on their heads. Not to be confused with Homer & Jethro or Flo & Eddie, though you may be praying for any and all to show up.▼

Homestretch, The (1947) **C-96m.** ** D: H. Bruce Humberstone. Cornel Wilde, Maureen O'Hara, Glenn Langan, Helen Walker, James Gleason. Harmless film of romance between young girl and horse-owner suffers from uneven acting and script.

Home, Sweet Homicide (1946) **90m.** ** D: Lloyd Bacon. Peggy Ann Garner, Randolph Scott, Lynn Bari, Dean Stockwell. Nothing-special comedy-mystery, as children of mystery writer solve local murder and find husband for their mother.

Home to Stay (1978) **C-74m.** TVM D: Delbert Mann. Henry Fonda, Michael McGuire, Frances Hyland, David Stambaugh, Kirsten Vigard. Sentimental tale of a teenager and the trip she takes with her spirited grandfather to keep him from being sent to a home for the aged. Fonda, as usual, is dignity personified in this Canadian-filmed story taken from Janet Majerus' *Grandpa and Frank.* Above average.▼

Hometown Story (1951) **61m.** ** D: Arthur Pierson. Jeffrey Lynn, Donald Crisp, Marjorie Reynolds, Alan Hale, Jr., Marilyn Monroe, Barbara Brown, Melinda Plowman, Glenn Tryon. Obvious programmer of recently defeated pol Lynn, who blames big business for his loss and tries to defame manufacturer Crisp. Of interest mostly for Monroe's supporting role as one of Lynn's employees.▼

Hometown USA (1979) **C-93m.** BOMB D: Max Baer. Gary Springer, David Wilson, Brian Kerwin, Pat Delaney, Julie Parsons, Sally Kirkland. Yet another nostalgic look at teenagers in the late 1950s is just a sloppy, sleazy, unfunny AMERICAN GRAFFITI rip-off.▼

Homeward Bound (1980) **C-100m.** TVM D: Richard Michaels. David Soul, Moosie Drier, Barnard Hughes, Judith Penrod, Jeff Corey, Carmen Zapata. Drama involving a divorced man, his long-estranged father, and his incurably ill teenaged son during one special summer at the grandfather's vineyard. Written by Burt Prelutsky, it has an especially touching performance by Hughes. Fred Karlin's score won an Emmy nomination. Above average.▼

Homework (1982) **C-90m.** *½ D: James Beshears. Joan Collins, Michael Morgan, Shell Kepler, Lanny Horn, Lee Purcell, Carrie Snodgress, Wings Hauser, Mel Welles, Beverly Todd, Betty Thomas. Atrocious, wildly inconsistent "comedy" about a teenage boy's sexual awakening—and embarrassment. Filmed mostly in 1979, it underwent major surgery, including attempt to simulate nude scenes with Joan Collins (using an alleged double) so it could be promoted as a young boy–older woman sex comedy à la PRIVATE LESSONS and MY TUTOR.▼

Homicidal (1961) **87m.** **½ D: William Castle. Jean Arless, Patricia Breslin, Glenn Corbett, Eugenie Leontovich, Alan Bunce, Richard Rust. One of Castle's less gimmicky shockers, about pretty but rather strange young nurse who presides over creepy household consisting of mute stroke victim and decidedly unmacho young man. Shamelessly steals a great deal from PSYCHO, and much of the dialogue is ludicrous, but still manages to deliver some shudders.

Homicide Bureau (1939) 58m. *½ D: C. C. Coleman, Jr. Bruce Cabot, Rita Hayworth, Robert Paige, Marc Lawrence, Richard Fiske, Moroni Olsen. Cabot plays a brash detective who's in perennial hot water with his superiors in this humdrum B picture. Rita's role as a lab technician is small—and dull.

Hondo (1953) C-84m. *** D: John Farrow. John Wayne, Geraldine Page, Ward Bond, Michael Pate, James Arness, Rodolfo Acosta, Leo Gordon, Lee Aaker. Rousing, well-done Western with Wayne the tough, wily cavalry scout who comes upon Page and her young son living in the wilderness, unalarmed about a pending Apache uprising. Good script by James Edward Grant, from a story by Louis L'Amour. Originally shown in 3D. Later a short-lived TV series.

Honey (1981-Italian-Spanish) C-84m. *½ D: Gianfranco Angelucci. Clio Goldsmith, Catherine Spaak, Fernando Rey, Donatella Damiani, Susan Scott, Luc Merenda. Utterly confusing chronicle of writer Spaak forcing editor Rey to read her manuscript about the sexual awakening of young Goldsmith—or so it seems.▼

Honeyboy (1982) C-100m. TVM D: John Berry. Erik Estrada, Morgan Fairchild, James McEachin, Robert Costanza, Yvonne Wilder, Phillip R. Allen, Robert Alan Browne, Hector Elizondo. Rehash of every cliched fight movie Hollywood ever made, with Estrada trying to box his way out of the barrio to overnight fame and fortune. Average.▼

Honeychile (1951) C-90m. *½ D: R. G. Springsteen. Judy Canova, Eddie Foy, Jr., Alan Hale, Jr., Walter Catlett. Cornball stuff involving Canova in the music-publishing business.

Honey, I Shrunk the Kids (1989) C-93m. *** D: Joe Johnston. Rick Moranis, Matt Frewer, Marcia Strassman, Kristine Sutherland, Thomas Brown, Jared Rushton, Amy O'Neill, Robert Oliveri. Cute comedy-fantasy about a quartet of kids who accidentally trigger Moranis' experimental ray gun and find themselves reduced to microscopic size—and stranded across the yard from their home. Enjoyable family fare, with engaging special effects (by such whizzes as Phil Tippet and David Allen).▼

Honeymoon (1947) 74m. ** D: William Keighley. Shirley Temple, Franchot Tone, Guy Madison, Lina Romay, Gene Lockhart, Grant Mitchell. Unmemorable mixture of romance and comedy in story of G.I. who longs for fiancée in Mexico during three-day pass. Good cast fails to make film click.

Honeymoon (1959-Spanish) C-90m. ** D: Michael Powell. Anthony Steel, Ludmilla Tcherina, Antonio, Rosita Segovia. Muddled romancer intertwined with ballet sequences, from the director of THE RED SHOES. Steel, on wedding trip with Tcherina, encounters Antonio who tries to court the ex-ballerina. Excerpts from ballets *Los Amantes de Teruel* and *El Amor Brujo.*

Honeymoon Academy (1990) C-94m. *½ D: Gene Quintano. Kim Cattrall, Robert Hays, Leigh Taylor-Young, Charles Rocket, Lance Kinney, Christopher Lee. Time waster about a secret agent (Cattrall) who tries to take time off for a honeymoon in Madrid, but finds herself involved in espionage business all the same. Attempt at lighthearted chase comedy/romance doesn't come off . . . and incidentally, the film's title has nothing to do with the story.

Honeymoon Ahead (1945) 60m. ** D: Reginald Le Borg. Allan Jones, Raymond Walburn, Grace McDonald, Vivian Austin. Nonsensical trivia involving kindly prisoner (head of convicts' choir) and his involvement with the world outside the big walls.

Honeymoon for Three (1941) 77m. **½ D: Lloyd Bacon. Ann Sheridan, George Brent, Charlie Ruggles, Osa Massen, Walter Catlett, Jane Wyman. Breezy comedy of novelist Brent warding off female admirers by pretending to be married; Sheridan is his witty, amorous secretary.

Honeymoon Hotel (1964) C-89m. *½ D: Henry Levin. Robert Goulet, Jill St. John, Nancy Kwan, Robert Morse, Elsa Lanchester, Keenan Wynn. Asinine shenanigans with bachelors Goulet and Morse arriving at resort for newlyweds. Lanchester is fun despite all.

Honeymoon in Bali (1939) 95m. *** D: Edward H. Griffith. Fred MacMurray, Madeleine Carroll, Allan Jones, Osa Massen, Helen Broderick, Akim Tamiroff. Funny romantic boy-chases-girl film, with MacMurray after beautiful Carroll with interference from aristocratic Jones. Also known as MY LOVE FOR YOURS.▼

Honeymoon Killers, The (1970) 108m. *** D: Leonard Kastle. Shirley Stoler, Tony LoBianco, Mary Jane Higby, Doris Roberts. True story of couple who murder "lonelyhearts" women after stripping them of their savings. Terse and chilling.▼

Honeymoon Lodge (1943) 63m. ** D: Edward Lilley. David Bruce, Harriet Hilliard, June Vincent, Rod Cameron, Franklin Pangborn, Andrew Tombes, Ozzie Nelson and His Orchestra, Veloz and Yolanda, Tip, Tap and Toe. Innocuous musical centers on Bruce and Vincent's romantic complications at a country resort. Slim pretext for some amusing songs and dances by Ozzie & Harriet and others.

Honeymoon Machine, The (1961) C-87m. **½ D: Richard Thorpe. Steve McQueen, Jim Hutton, Paula Prentiss, Brigid Bazlen, Dean Jagger, Jack Weston. Pleasant comedy with a spirited cast about two sailors who find a way to beat the roulette table in Monte Carlo. Easy to take, easy to forget.

Honeymoon with a Stranger (1969) **C-88m. TVM** D: John Peyser. Janet Leigh, Rossano Brazzi, Joseph Lenzi, Cesare Danova, Barbara Steele, Eric Braeden. After blissful wedding night, American newlywed discovers husband missing and strange man claiming to be genuine article. Routine story enhanced by location filming in Spain. Originally broadcast at 74m. Average.

Honey Pot, The (1967) **C-131m.** **½ D: Joseph L. Mankiewicz. Rex Harrison, Susan Hayward, Cliff Robertson, Capucine, Edie Adams, Maggie Smith, Adolfo Celi. Director/writer Mankiewicz updates *Volpone* in sly blend of high comedy and whodunit. Harrison pretends to be dying, sends for former mistresses to see their reactions; hoax evolves into elaborate murder scheme. Never as amusing as one would like it to be. Also known as IT COMES UP MURDER.▼

Honeysuckle Rose (1980) **C-119m.** *** D: Jerry Schatzberg. Willie Nelson, Dyan Cannon, Amy Irving, Slim Pickens, Joey Floyd, Charles Levin, Priscilla Pointer, Mickey Rooney, Jr., Diana Scarwid. Appealing, low-key film about a country music star and his lifestyle at home in Texas and on the road, which begins to come apart when he starts fooling around with the young daughter of his longtime musical sidekick. Lots of good music by Willie, fiddler Johnny Gimble, and guest star Emmylou Harris. Officially based on INTERMEZZO, believe it or not! Retitled ON THE ROAD AGAIN.▼

Hong Kong (1951) **C-92m.** ** D: Lewis R. Foster. Ronald Reagan, Rhonda Fleming, Nigel Bruce, Marvin Miller. Mediocre account of Reagan trying to heist a valuable antique from orphaned girl but going straight before finale. Strictly backlot Hong Kong.

Hong Kong Affair (1958) **79m.** *½ D: Paul F. Heard. Jack Kelly, May Wynn, Richard Loo, Lo Lita Shek. Kelly is the Yank who comes to the Orient to investigate his property holdings, getting more than he bargained for.

Hong Kong Confidential (1958) **67m.** **½ D: Edward L. Cahn. Gene Barry, Beverly Tyler, Allison Hayes, Noel Drayton. Harmless B film about Anglo-American agents rescuing a kidnapped Arabian prince.

Honkers, The (1972) **C-102m.** **½ D: Steve Ihnat. James Coburn, Lois Nettleton, Slim Pickens, Anne Archer, Richard Anderson, Joan Huntington, Jim Davis. Theme about aging rodeo performer was handled better in J. W. COOP and JUNIOR BONNER; actor Ihnat died shortly after directing this film.

Honky (1971) **C-89m.** **½ D: William A. Graham. Brenda Sykes, John Nielson, William Marshall, Maia Danziger, Marion Ross, Lincoln Kilpatrick. Not-bad drama of budding romance between black Sykes and white Nielson, and the problems they encounter. Score by Quincy Jones.▼

Honky Tonk (1941) **105m.** **½ D: Jack Conway. Clark Gable, Lana Turner, Frank Morgan, Claire Trevor, Marjorie Main, Albert Dekker, Chill Wills. Good-gal Lana loves gambler Gable in romantic Western that's fun for a spell, then drags into talky marathon. Morgan and Wills offer fine character performances. Remade for TV.

Honky Tonk (1974) **C-90m. TVM** D: Don Taylor. Richard Crenna, Stella Stevens, Margot Kidder, Will Geer, John Dehner, Geoffrey Lewis, Gregory Sierra. Pleasant remake of Gable-Turner vehicle with smooth cast enacting con man/respectable lady/dance-hall girl triangle. Average.

Honky Tonk Freeway (1981) **C-107m.** ** D: John Schlesinger. William Devane, Beverly D'Angelo, Beau Bridges, Jessica Tandy, Hume Cronyn, Geraldine Page, George Dzundza, Teri Garr, Joe Grifasi, Howard Hesseman, Paul Jabara. An absurdist view of contemporary America, in fragmented vignettes of various oddballs whose lives converge in Ticlaw, Florida, a tiny town determined to attract tourists despite the lack of an exit ramp from the new freeway. As a statement on life, it's a failure; as a silly comedy, it sometimes succeeds. Reminiscent (in its narrative style) of NASHVILLE.▼

Honkytonk Man (1982) **C-122m.** *½ D: Clint Eastwood. Clint Eastwood, Kyle Eastwood, John McIntire, Alexa Kenin, Verna Bloom, Matt Clark, Barry Corbin. The kind of film that gives "change-of-pace" a bad name. Clint is Depression-era country singer hoping to make it to the Grand Old Opry before he dies of leukemia; son Kyle plays his nephew, who tags along to keep an eye on him. Artificial and overlong; many music greats appear in bits, including Marty Robbins, who provides film's sole touching moment and, ironically, died himself only days before the picture opened.▼

Honolulu (1939) **83m.** **½ D: Edward Buzzell. Eleanor Powell, Robert Young, George Burns, Gracie Allen, Rita Johnson, Willie Fung, Sig Ruman, Ruth Hussey. Standard musical about mistaken identities. Screen idol changes places with plantation owner.

Honor Among Thieves SEE: **Farewell, Friend**▼

Honor Thy Father (1971) **C-100m. TVM** D: Paul Wendkos. Joseph Bologna, Raf Vallone, Brenda Vaccaro, Richard Castellano, Joe De Santis, Gilbert Green, Marc Lawrence. Extraordinary slice-of-life presentation of day-to-day operations of organized crime family, written (primarily) around Bill Bonanno character. Adapted from Gay Talese's book by Lewis John Carlino. Within TV restrictions, not bad. Above average.▼

Hoodlum, The (1951) 61m. ** D: Max Nosseck. Lawrence Tierney, Allene Roberts, Marjorie Riordan, Lisa Golm. Once a crook, always a crook is plot of this caper about ex-con planning bank robbery.▼

Hoodlum Empire (1952) 98m. **½ D: Joseph Kane. Brian Donlevy, Claire Trevor, Forrest Tucker, Vera Ralston, Luther Adler. Cast is sufficiently versed in format to make this exposé of a crime syndicate better than average.▼

✓ **Hoodlum Priest, The** (1961) 101m. *** D: Irvin Kershner. Don Murray, Larry Gates, Keir Dullea, Logan Ramsey, Cindi Wood. Based on real-life clergyman who devoted himself to trying to help would-be criminals, focusing on Murray's efforts to rehabilitate delinquent Dullea (in film debut); splendidly acted. Murray coproduced and cowrote (latter under pseudonym Don Deer).

Hoodlum Saint, The (1946) 91m. **½ D: Norman Taurog. William Powell, Esther Williams, Angela Lansbury, James Gleason, Rags Ragland, Lewis Stone, Emma Dunn. Modest film benefits from good Powell performance as cynic who sees The Light.

Hook, The (1963) 98m. *** D: George Seaton. Kirk Douglas, Robert Walker, Jr., Nick Adams, Nehemiah Persoff. Film examines men at war (Korean) and the taking of one life, face-to-face, as opposed to killing many in battle. Earnest, thought-provoking. Music by harmonica virtuoso Larry Adler.

Hooked Generation (1969) C-92m. BOMB D: William Grefe. Jeremy Slate, Willie Pastrano, Steve Alaimo, John Davis Chandler, Socrates Ballis. Narcotics peddlers slaughter their Cuban contacts, and kidnap innocent victims; poor excuse for a film.

Hook, Line & Sinker (1969) C-91m. BOMB D: George Marshall. Jerry Lewis, Peter Lawford, Anne Francis, Pedro Gonzalez, Jimmy Miller, Kathleen Freeman. Potentially funny premise about supposedly dying man who runs up $100,000 in credit card debts, only to discover he's healthy, is totally botched; even Lewis fans will be bored.

Hooper (1978) C-100m. *** D: Hal Needham. Burt Reynolds, Jan-Michael Vincent, Sally Field, Brian Keith, John Marley, James Best, Adam West, Robert Klein. Lighthearted look at aging ace Hollywood stunt man Reynolds, his freewheeling life-style, and the young tyro who gets him to try the biggest stunt of all.▼

Hooray for Love (1935) 72m. *** D:

Walter Lang. Ann Sothern, Gene Raymond, Bill Robinson, Maria Gambarelli, Pert Kelton, Fats Waller. Modest but very entertaining backstage musical with Sothern and Raymond the pleasing romantic leads, Robinson and Waller contributing fine musical specialties, Kelton adding laughs as aspiring soprano.

Hoosiers (1986) C-114m. *** D: David Anspaugh. Gene Hackman, Barbara Hershey, Dennis Hopper, Sheb Wooley, Fern Parsons, Brad Boyle, Steve Hollar, Brad Long, David Neidorf. Hackman gets a last-chance job coaching a small-town Indiana high school basketball team in the 1950s, and faces the dual challenge of bringing the team to the state championship—and redeeming himself. Thoroughly ingratiating (and just as thoroughly calculated), this well-made slice of Americana is hard to resist. Hackman is terrific as usual; Hopper is fine in a showy role as an alcoholic basketball nut. Written by Angelo Pizzo.▼

Hoosier Schoolboy (1937) 62m. ** D: William Nigh. Mickey Rooney, Anne Nagel, Frank Shields, Edward Pawley, William Gould. Routine low-budget rural tale of young delinquent Rooney saved from his alcoholic father and life of poverty by teacher Nagel.

Hootenanny Hoot (1963) 91m. ** D: Gene Nelson. Peter Breck, Joby Baker, Ruta Lee, Pam Austin, Johnny Cash, Sheb Wooley, The Brothers Four, Judy Henske. Predictable comedy about college hootenanny show brought to TV is made bearable only by presence of Cash and other country/folk performers. One of producer Sam Katzman's "topical" low-budgeters.

Hoover Vs. the Kennedys: The Second Civil War (1987) C-200m. TVM D: Michael O'Herlihy. Jack Warden, Nicholas Campbell, Robert Pine, Barry Morse, Heather Thomas, Richard Anderson, Le-Land Ganett, Marc Strange. Cryptic, episodic, slanted drama about a contentious J. Edgar Hoover and his unsparing battles with JFK and Bobby Kennedy. Totally miscast from top to bottom, especially Warden as a dyspeptic Hoover, Anderson as a lanky Lyndon Johnson, Pine as a studied JFK, and Morse as an English-accented Joe Kennedy, although Thomas' Marilyn Monroe nearly hits the mark. Originally shown in two parts. Made for cable. Below average.

Hope and Glory (1987-British) C-113m. ***½ D: John Boorman. Sarah Miles, David Hayman, Derrick O'Connor, Susan Wooldridge, Sammi Davis, Ian Bannen, Sebastian Rice-Edwards, Jean-Marc Barr, Annie Leon. A loving look back at British family life during the first years of WW2, as seen through the eyes of a young boy to whom the whole thing is a great adven-

[521]

ture. Boorman's autobiographical tale is funny, moving and richly detailed; no one has captured the experience of living through the London air raids and bombings so well. Charley Boorman (the director's son, who starred in THE EMERALD FOREST) appears briefly as a German pilot who's been shot down.▼

Hoppity Goes to Town (1941) **C-77m.** ****½ D:** Dave Fleischer. Pleasant animated feature about residents of bug-ville and their various problems—living in a human world, and threatened by villainous C. Bagley Beetle. Good-looking but uncompelling story-wise, with unmemorable Frank Loesser–Hoagy Carmichael score. Originally titled MR. BUG GOES TO TOWN.▼

Hopscotch (1980) **C-104m.** ***** D:** Ronald Neame. Walter Matthau, Glenda Jackson, Sam Waterston, Ned Beatty, Herbert Lom. Entertaining contrivance about a maverick CIA operative who's fed up with his idiotic boss (Beatty) and decides to teach him a lesson by publishing his volatile memoirs. Barely believable, but fun to watch, thanks largely to Matthau. From the novel by Brian Garfield, who coproduced and coscripted the film.▼

Horizons West (1952) **C-81m.** ****½ D:** Budd Boetticher. Robert Ryan, Julia (Julie) Adams, Rock Hudson, Raymond Burr, James Arness, John McIntire, Dennis Weaver. Standard Western of brothers Ryan and Hudson on opposite sides of the law; the latter attempts to block the former's efforts to ruthlessly acquire power in post–Civil War Texas.▼

Horizontal Lieutenant, The (1962) **C-90m.** ****½ D:** Richard Thorpe. Jim Hutton, Paula Prentiss, Miyoshi Umeki, Jim Backus, Jack Carter, Marty Ingels, Charles McGraw. Artificial service comedy set on WW2 Pacific island involving army officer Hutton's capture of innocuous supply thief.

√ **Horn Blows at Midnight, The** (1945) **78m.** ***** D:** Raoul Walsh. Jack Benny, Alexis Smith, Dolores Moran, Allyn Joslyn, Reginald Gardiner, Guy Kibbee, John Alexander, Margaret Dumont, Franklin Pangborn. Enjoyable, original comedy-fantasy about an angel (Benny) sent to destroy earth with a blast from Gabriel's horn. Broad, funny, no classic, but not the turkey Benny so often joked about either. Franklin Pangborn is especially funny as a flustered hotel detective.

Hornets' Nest (1970) **C-110m.** ****½ D:** Phil Karlson. Rock Hudson, Sylva Koscina, Sergio Fantoni, Jacques Sernas, Giacomo Rossi Stuart, Tom Felleghi. Hudson and group of Italian children plot to blow up Nazi-controlled dam. Reasonably well done and exciting.

Horrible Dr. Hichcock, The (1962-Italian) **C-76m.** ****½ D:** Robert Hampton (Ricardo Freda). Robert Flemyng, Barbara Steele, Teresa Fitzgerald, Maria Teresa Vianello. Unaware her doctor husband is a (gulp!) necrophiliac, woman accompanies him to the mansion where his first wife apparently died twelve years earlier during sexual games. Eerie, handsome horror, with undertones of Poe. British version, TERROR OF DR. HICHCOCK, runs 88m. and is also available on tape. Followed by THE GHOST.▼

Horrible House on the Hill, The SEE: **Devil Times Five**▼

Horror at 37,000 Feet (1972) **C-73m.** **TVM D:** David Lowell Rich. William Shatner, Roy Thinnes, Buddy Ebsen, Tammy Grimes, Lynn Loring, France Nuyen. OK fantasy premise disintegrates into forgettable suspense drama of ancient evil aboard transatlantic commercial flight. Below average.

Horror Castle (1963-Italian) **C-83m.** ***½ D:** Anthony Dawson (Antonio Margheriti). Christopher Lee, Rossana Podesta, George Riviere, Jim Nolan, Anny Belli Uberti. Chiller about a demented WW2 victim running rampant in a Rhine castle, using assorted torture chamber devices on unsuspecting people. The effect is numbing. Also known as THE VIRGIN OF NUREMBERG and TERROR CASTLE. British title: THE CASTLE OF TERROR.▼

Horror Chamber of Dr. Faustus, The (1959-French-Italian) **88m.** ***** D:** Georges Franju. Pierre Brasseur, Alida Valli, Edith Scob. Moody horror film, a classic in some circles, about a brilliant but crazed plastic surgeon (Brasseur) and his fate after disfiguring his daughter. Originally titled LES YEUX SANS VISAGE (THE EYES WITHOUT A FACE).▼

Horror Creatures of the Prehistoric Planet SEE: **Vampire Men of the Lost Planet**▼

Horror Express (1972-Spanish-British) **C-88m.** ***** D:** Eugenio Martin. Christopher Lee, Peter Cushing, Telly Savalas, Silvia Tortosa, Jorge Rigaud, Helga Line. Crackerjack horror movie, ingeniously staged and well acted by the genre's superstars. Turn-of-the-century chiller has a long-frozen monster coming to life while being transported from Asia to the West. Lee and Cushing are rival anthropologists aboard the train and Savalas is a power-crazed Cossack officer. Also known as PANIC ON THE TRANS-SIBERIAN EXPRESS.▼

Horror High SEE: **Twisted Brain**▼

Horror Hotel (1960-British) **76m.** ****½ D:** John Moxey. Dennis Lotis, Christopher Lee, Betta St. John, Patricia Jessel, Venetia Stevenson. Seventeenth-century witch burned at the stake maintains an inn to lure victims for blood sacrifice to the devil. Not bad of its type. Original British title: THE CITY OF THE DEAD.▼

Horror Hotel (1976) SEE: **Eaten Alive!**▼
Horror House (1969-British) **C-79m.** *½
D: Michael Armstrong. Frankie Avalon,
Jill Haworth, Dennis Price, George Sewell,
Gina Warwick, Richard O'Sullivan. Be-
low-standard thriller using dog-eared "let's-
spend-a-night-in-a-haunted-house" script.
Frankie should have stayed on the beach
with Annette. Original British title: THE
HAUNTED HOUSE OF HORROR
Horror Island (1941) **60m.** **½ D: George
Waggner. Dick Foran, Leo Carrillo, Peggy
Moran, Fuzzy Knight, John Eldredge, Lewis
Howard, Iris Adrian. Fast-paced, divert-
ing B-thriller film has various colorful
types converging at isolated manor; one by
one, they're stalked and murdered.
Horror of Dracula (1958-British) **C-82m.**
*** D: Terence Fisher. Peter Cushing,
Christopher Lee, Melissa Stribling, Mi-
chael Gough, Carol Marsh, John Van
Eyssen, Valerie Gaunt, Miles Malleson.
Probably Hammer Films' best shocker, a
handsomely mounted retelling of the Stoker
tale, with fantasy elements deemphasized.
Lee is smooth as the Count, and Cushing
perfect as tireless Professor Van Helsing.
Script by Jimmy Sangster; full-blooded
score by James Bernard. Released in
Britain as DRACULA; followed by six
sequels, the first of which was DRACULA
—PRINCE OF DARKNESS.▼
Horror of Frankenstein, The (1970-
British) **C-95m.** ** D: Jimmy Sangster.
Ralph Bates, Kate O'Mara, Graham Jones,
Veronica Carlson, Bernard Archard, Den-
nis Price, Joan Rice. New kind of Dr.
Frankenstein: he arranges murder of fa-
ther, cheats on his lover, kills his best
friend, while creating new, laughable monster. For aficionados only. Followed by
FRANKENSTEIN AND THE MONSTER
FROM HELL.▼
Horror of Party Beach, The (1964) **72m.**
BOMB D: Del Tenney. John Scott, Alice
Lyon, Allen Laurel, Marilyn Clark, Eula-
belle Moore. Radioactive waste is dumped
off-shore, resulting in scaly monsters who
disrupt the sand-surf-and-sun fun of a bunch
of Connecticut beach bunnies. One of the
earliest anti-nuclear warning films, although
for some strange reason the message fails
to come across. Billed as "The First Hor-
ror Musical" by its producers, who evi-
dently never saw Liberace in SINCERELY
YOURS.▼
Horror of the Blood Monsters SEE: **Vampire Men of the Lost Planet**▼
Horror on Snape Island (1972-British)
C-85m. BOMB D: Jim O'Connolly. Bryant
Halliday, Jill Haworth, Anna Palk, Jack
Watson, Mark Edwards, Derek Fowlds.
One of the horrors is a series of brutal
murders masterminded by lunatic; another
one is the film itself. Retitled TOWER OF
EVIL and BEYOND THE FOG.▼

Horror Planet (1982-British) **C-86m.**
BOMB D: Norman J. Warren. Robin Clark,
Jennifer Ashley, Stephanie Beacham, Ste-
ven Grives, Barry Houghton, Victoria
Tennant, Judy Geeson. Obnoxious, gory
garbage about male and female space trav-
elers and their discovery of a crawling
terror. Interesting cast wasted in this awful
ALIEN clone. The original title is INSEM-
INOID. ▼
Horrors of the Black Museum (1959-
British) **C-95m.** **½ D: Arthur Crabtree.
Michael Gough, June Cunningham, Gra-
ham Curnow, Shirley Ann Field, Geoffrey
Keen. Gruesome sequences highlight chiller
about writer who uses his hypnotized helper
to commit a series of killings.
Horse Feathers (1932) **68m.** ***½ D:
Norman Z. McLeod. Groucho, Harpo,
Chico, and Zeppo Marx, Thelma Todd,
David Landau, Robert Greig, Nat Pendle-
ton. Groucho is head of Huxley College,
building up football team to play rival
Darwin U. in crazy Marx nonsense. The
password is "swordfish." Originally released at 70m.▼
Horse in the Gray Flannel Suit, The
(1968) **C-113m.** *** D: Norman Tokar.
Dean Jones, Diane Baker, Lloyd Bochner,
Fred Clark, Ellen Janov, Kurt Russell.
Cheerful Disney comedy about advertising
man (Jones) who finds a way to link his
daughter's devotion to horses with an ad
campaign.▼
Horsemasters, The (1961) **C-87m.** ** D:
William Fairchild. Annette Funicello, Janet Munro, Tommy Kirk, Donald Pleasence, Tony Britton, Jean Marsh, John Fraser, Millicent Martin. Minor family fare
(originally shown in two parts on the Disney TV show) about Annette learning
horsemanship—and trying to overcome her
fear of jumping—at an exclusive British
riding school. Filmed in England and released as a feature in Europe.▼
Horsemen, The (1971) **C-109m.** **½ D:
John Frankenheimer. Omar Sharif, Leigh
Taylor-Young, Jack Palance, David De,
Peter Jeffrey. Sharif enters grueling buzkashi
tournament to please his demanding father
(Palance) and prove his machismo. Old-
fashioned action-adventure mixes uncomfortably with soul-searching in Dalton
Trumbo's script. Filmed in Afghanistan
and Spain. Beautiful photography by Claude
Renoir.▼
Horse Named Comanche, A SEE: **Tonka**▼
Horse's Mouth, The (1958-British) **C-93m.**
***½ D: Ronald Neame. Alec Guinness,
Kay Walsh, Renee Houston, Mike Morgan, Michael Gough, Ernest Thesiger. Joyce
Cary's wry novel is admirably handled,
with Guinness as the eccentric painter living on the cuff, seeking oddball surfaces to
use for his more ambitious paintings.
Guinness also wrote the screenplay.▼

[523]

Horse Soldiers, The (1959) **C-119m.** **½
D: John Ford. John Wayne, William
Holden, Constance Towers, Althea Gibson,
Hoot Gibson, Anna Lee, Russell Simpson,
Ken Curtis, Denver Pyle, Strother Martin,
Hank Worden. Ford's only feature set dur-
ing the Civil War, based on actual incidents.
Union Colonel Wayne leads sabotage party
deep into Rebel territory, accompanied by
somewhat pacifistic doctor Holden. Large-
scale actioner rates only a "medium" by
Ford buffs; others may like it better.▼
Horse Without a Head, The (1963)
C-89m. *** D: Don Chaffey. Leo McKern,
Jean-Pierre Aumont, Herbert Lom, Pa-
mela Franklin, Vincent Winter. Excellent
cast in entertaining British-made Disney
film (first shown in two parts on the Disney TV show) about kids mixed up with
bad guys on the trail of stolen loot stashed
in a discarded toy horse. First-rate family
fare. ▼
Hospital, The (1971) **C-103m.** ***½ D:
Arthur Hiller. George C. Scott, Diana Rigg,
Barnard Hughes, Nancy Marchand, Richard Dysart, Stephen Elliott, Roberts Blossom,
Robert Walden, Lenny Baker, Frances
Sternhagen, Stockard Channing. Sardonically funny view of modern city hospital
where bitterly discouraged doctor (Scott)
is drawn into chaos by crazy girl (Rigg)
and her scheming father. Paddy Chayefsky's
Oscar-winning script makes fun of serious
situation by turning it into Marx Brothers-
ish lunacy; ultimate truth in what's being
said leaves viewer somewhat sad.▼
Hostage, The (1967) **C-84m.** **½ D:
Russell S. Doughton, Jr. Don O'Kelly,
(Harry) Dean Stanton, John Carradine,
Ron Hagerthy, Ann Doran. Well-done
low-budget film about a six-year-old who
stows away on moving van driven by
two murderers. Shot entirely on location
in Iowa.▼
Hostage (1983-Australian-German) **C-90m.**
*½ D: Frank Shields. Kerry Mack, Ralph
Schicha, Judy Nunn, Clare Binney. Young,
carefree Mack is blackmailed into marriage by Nazi Schicha, and her life becomes
hell on earth. Intriguing scenario, based on
a true story and set in the 70s, but the
result is disjointed, repetitive, boring. Original title: HOSTAGE: THE CHRISTINE
MARESCH STORY; the videocassette title is SAVAGE ATTRACTION.▼
Hostage (1987) **C-95m.** ** D: Hanro Mohr.
Wings Hauser, Karen Black, Kevin Mc-
Carthy, Nancy Locke (Hauser), Robert
Whitehead, Gerhard Hametner. When a
planeload of innocents is kidnapped by
Arab terrorists, Hauser and McCarthy enlist ex-soldiers for a rescue mission. Black
is very funny in role of a movie star tired
of being a sex symbol. Filmed in South
Africa.▼
Hostage (1988) **C-100m. TVM** D: Peter

Levin. Carol Burnett, Carrie Hamilton,
Leon Russom, Annette Bening, Priscilla
Caroline Smith, Doris Belack. Aside from
the novelty of Burnett starring with real-
life actress-daughter Hamilton, there's little substance in this story of a lonely
widow and the teenage escaped con who
had kidnapped her. Average.
Hostage: Dallas SEE: **Getting Even**▼
Hostage Flight (1985) **C-100m. TVM** D:
Steven Hilliard Stern. Ned Beatty, Barbara
Bosson, Rene Enriquez, Jack Gilford,
John Karlen, Kristina Wayborn, Ina Balin,
Dee Wallace Stone, Mitchell Ryan. Terrorists take over a plane in flight but
are unprepared for their hostages' reactions. (There are two endings to this
one: the tempered one shown by the net-
work in its premiere and a more radical
one that the producers favored, to be used
in overseas theatrical showings and subse-
quent ones, by choice, in syndication.)
Average.
Hostage Heart, The (1977) **C-100m. TVM**
D: Bernard McEveety. Bradford Dillman,
Loretta Swit, Vic Morrow, Cameron
Mitchell, Belinda J. Montgomery, Sharon
Acker, George DiCenzo, Paul Shenar, Carl
Weathers. Terrorists break into a hospital
operating room and hold a billionaire, un-
dergoing a heart operation, for millions in
ransom. Familiar premise given interest-
ing twist, but the characters are stereotyped.
Average.
Hostages (1943) **88m.** ** D: Frank Tuttle.
Luise Rainer, William Bendix, Roland
Varno, Oscar Homolka, Katina Paxinou,
Paul Lukas. Routine tale of underground
movement in WW2; Bendix outshines Rainer
acting-wise.
Hostage: The Christine Maresch Story
SEE: **Hostage** (1983)▼
Hostage Tower, The (1980) **C-105m.**
TVM D: Claudio Guzman. Peter Fonda,
Billy Dee Williams, Keir Dullea, Douglas
Fairbanks, Jr., Rachel Roberts, Celia John-
son, Maud Adams, Britt Ekland. Alistair
MacLean's adventure thriller (his first writ-
ten for television) has a flamboyant crimi-
nal masterminding the capture of the Eiffel
Tower and the holding of the U.S. Presi-
dent's visiting mother for $30 million ran-
som. The fast pacing fails to mask the
silliness of it all. Average.▼
Hostile Guns (1967) **C-91m.** **½ D: R.
G. Springsteen. George Montgomery,
Yvonne De Carlo, Tab Hunter, Brian
Donlevy, John Russell. U.S. marshal, transporting prisoners to penitentiary, discovers
that female prisoner is a woman he once
loved. Typical.▼
Hot Blood (1956) **C-85m.** *½ D: Nicholas Ray. Jane Russell, Cornel Wilde, Luther Adler, Joseph Calleia. Jane Russell
shakes her tambourines and drives Cornel

Wilde, in this supremely silly (not to mention unbelievable) gypsy yarn.

Hot Box, The (1972) **C-85m.** ** D: Joe Viola. Margaret Markov, Andrea Cagan, Ricky Richardson, Laurie Rose, Charles Dierkop. Filipino-shot women's prison film adequately runs through the standard changes, as heroines break out and foment a local revolution. Cowritten and produced by Jonathan Demme.▼

Hot Car Girl SEE: **Hot Rod Girl**

Hot Dog . . . The Movie (1984) **C-96m.** *½ D: Peter Markle. David Naughton, Patrick Houser, Tracy N. Smith, John Patrick Reger, Frank Koppola, Shannon Tweed. Hijinks at a ski resort: an updating of '60s Beach Party-type movies, just as dumb, but now much raunchier. Good ski sequences, but that's about it. Film is so titled to avoid confusion with HOT DOG . . . THE OPERA.▼

Hotel (1967) **C-124m.** ** D: Richard Quine. Rod Taylor, Catherine Spaak, Karl Malden, Melvyn Douglas, Richard Conte, Michael Rennie, Merle Oberon, Kevin McCarthy. Adaptation of still another Arthur Hailey multicharactered novel is not all that inferior to AIRPORT, but that's faint praise; Douglas has some good scenes. Later a TV series.▼

Hotel Berlin (1945) **98m.** **½ D: Peter Godfrey. Helmut Dantine, Andrea King, Raymond Massey, Faye Emerson, Peter Lorre, Alan Hale. GRAND HOTEL author Vicki Baum tries again with sundry characters based in hotel during decline of Nazi Germany; good cast makes it generally interesting.

Hotel Colonial (1987-Italian-U.S.) **C-104m.** BOMB D: Cinzia Torrini. John Savage, Rachel Ward, Robert Duvall, Massimo Troisi. International mishmash wastes a good cast in downbeat tale of Savage going to Colombia to investigate the death of his brother, aided by embassy attaché Ward and thwarted by evil Duvall. Pretty Mexican scenery is film's only merit.▼

Hotel for Women (1939) **83m.** ** D: Gregory Ratoff. Linda Darnell, Ann Sothern, Elsa Maxwell, Lynn Bari, Sidney Blackmer, Alan Dinehart. Weak film about group of manhunting girls, noteworthy only as Darnell's film debut. Originally titled ELSA MAXWELL'S HOTEL FOR WOMEN.

Hotel Imperial (1939) **67m.** ** D: Robert Florey. Isa Miranda, Ray Milland, Reginald Owen, Gene Lockhart, Albert Dekker. Miranda encounters intrigue while searching for man responsible for her sister's death; fairly entertaining drama. Troubled film was years in production, with numerous cast, director and title changes. A remake of 1927 silent film, this film was in turn remade as FIVE GRAVES TO CAIRO.

Hotel New Hampshire, The (1984) C-110m. *** D: Tony Richardson. Rob Lowe, Jodie Foster, Beau Bridges, Nastassja Kinski, Paul McCrane, Jennie Dundas, Dorsey Wright, Matthew Modine, Wilford Brimley, Amanda Plummer, Wallace Shawn, Anita Morris. Faithful adaptation of John Irving's sprawling seriocomic novel about an unconventional family and its bizarre adventures—social, sexual, and political—on both sides of the Atlantic. Some fine vignettes and good performances make this worth watching, though characters eventually wear out their welcome.▼

Hotel Paradiso (1966-British) **C-96m.** **½ D: Peter Glenville. Alec Guinness, Gina Lollobrigida, Robert Morley, Akim Tamiroff. Pretentious farce of manners is only fitfully amusing; meek Guinness tries to carry on his rendezvous with gorgeous neighbor Gina, but everything interferes.

Hotel Reserve (1944-British) **79m.** *** D: Lance Comfort, Max Greene, Victor Hanbury. James Mason, Lucie Mannheim, Herbert Lom, Patricia Medina, Anthony Shaw, David Ward. Suspenseful, moody film about visitor at French resort during WW2 accused of being Nazi spy, trying to prove innocence. Based on Eric Ambler novel.▼

Hotel Sahara (1951-British) **96m.** **½ D: Ken Annakin. Yvonne De Carlo, Peter Ustinov, David Tomlinson, Roland Culver. Pleasant fluff about North African hotel owner and beautiful fiancée who must shift "loyalties" every time new army marches into town during WW2.

Hotel Terminus: The Life and Times of Klaus Barbie (1987) **C-267m.** ***½ D: Marcel Ophuls. Sobering, Oscar-winning documentary about the infamous Nazi war criminal who, decades after WW2, was expelled from Bolivia and returned to France for trial. Filled with incisive interviews with key individuals in his life. A fine companion piece to Ophuls' THE SORROW AND THE PITY.▼

Hot Enough for June SEE: **Agent 8¾**

Hot Lead SEE: **Run of the Arrow**

Hot Lead and Cold Feet (1978) **C-90m.** *** D: Robert Butler. Jim Dale, Darren McGavin, Karen Valentine, Jack Elam, Don Knotts, John Williams. Amiable Disney Western spoof with lots of slapstick features British comic Dale in three roles: tough patriarch, tougher gunfighter son, and meek twin, a Salvation Army lad. The brothers participate in a wild obstacle race to gain possession of the town, then to defeat villainous Mayor McGavin. Good Oregon location filming.▼

Hot Line (1969) SEE: **Day the Hot Line Got Hot, The**▼

Hotline (1982) **C-96m.** TVM D: Jerry Jameson. Lynda Carter, Steve Forrest, Granville Van Dusen, Monte Markham, James Booth, Harry Waters, Jr. Carter takes a job answering phones at a crisis center and finds herself stalked by an unknown psychotic caller. Average.▼

Hot Millions (1968-British) **C-105m.** *** D: Eric Till. Peter Ustinov, Maggie Smith, Karl Malden, Bob Newhart, Robert Morley, Cesar Romero. Wry piece of fluff about Ustinov using a computer to siphon off big bucks from huge American conglomerate. Good performers aid pleasant romp, which became one of the biggest sleepers of its year.

Hot News (1953) **68m.** *½ D: Edward Bernds. Stanley Clements, Gloria Henry, Ted de Corsia, Veda Ann Borg. Programmer tale of dedicated newspaperman cleaning up crime syndicate involved in sporting events.

Hot Paint (1988) **C-100m. TVM** D; Sheldon Larry. Gregory Harrison, John Larroquette, Cyrielle Claire, John Glover, Jonathan Cecil, Julie Bovasso. A pair of amateur hustlers inadvertently steal a Renoir from the Mob and spend the next ninety minutes frantically trying to unload it. Fitfully amusing but increasingly tiresome. Average.

Hot Pepper (1933) **76m.** **½ D: John G. Blystone. Victor McLaglen, Edmund Lowe, Lupe Velez, El Brendel. Another reprise of feud between Flagg (McLaglen) and Quirt (Lowe) from WHAT PRICE GLORY?, now civilians involved in nightclub, with spitfire Velez the woman they fight over. Constant wisecracks are a bit forced, but stars milk script for all it's worth.

Hot Potato (1976) **C-87m.** *½ D: Oscar Williams. Jim Kelly, George Memmoli, Geoffrey Binney, Irene Tsu, Judith Brown. Idiotic action film in which karate expert Kelly and two cohorts try to rescue kidnapped Senator's daughter from Oriental villain. Comic-book stuff. Filmed in Thailand. Remade as FORCE: FIVE.▼

Hot Pursuit (1987) **C-93m.** *½ D: Steven Lisberger. John Cusack, Robert Loggia, Wendy Gazelle, Jerry Stiller, Monte Markham, Shelley Fabares. Student Cusack, grounded by bad grades, has been prevented from taking a dream vacation with the family of his wealthy girlfriend. Then he gets last-minute reprieve from a kindly prof, and tries to catch up with them on the road. Silly comedy will probably remind you of Cusack's earlier THE SURE THING—and the comparison isn't favorable (somehow you don't expect machinegun fire at the end). Loggia's performance as a boat captain should put him in the running for the next Long John Silver movie.▼

Hot Resort (1985) **C-92m.** BOMB D: John Robins. Tom Parsekian, Michael Berz, Bronson Pinchot, Daniel Schneider, Frank Gorshin, Marcy Walker, Debra Kelly, Samm-Art Williams, Victoria Barrett, Dana Kaminsky, Mae Questel. Vulgar comedy adheres to the Cannon Films formula of young guys on the make, this time spending the summer working at a resort hotel on the Caribbean island of St. Kitts. There's pretty scenery and prettier girls but few laughs. Costar Pinchot later badmouthed this one after his career perked up. ▼

Hot Rock, The (1972) **C-105m.** *** D: Peter Yates. Robert Redford, George Segal, Ron Leibman, Paul Sand, Zero Mostel, Moses Gunn, William Redfield, Charlotte Rae, Topo Swope. Light, funny caper comedy where inept robbers blunder every step of carefully planned jewel heist. Best bit: the raid on the police station. Screenplay by William Goldman from Donald Westlake's novel; followed by BANK SHOT.▼

Hot Rod (1979) **C-100m. TVM** D: George Armitage. Gregg Henry, Robert Culp, Pernell Roberts, Robin Mattson, Grant Goodeve. Local dragstrip championship pits a free-wheeling outsider against the son of the town boss who has the race fixed. Lots of revving engines and screeching tires drown out the dumb dialogue. Also known as REBEL OF THE ROAD. Average.▼

Hot Rod Gang (1958) **72m.** *½ D: Lew Landers. John Ashley, Gene Vincent, Jody Fair, Steve Drexel. Low-budget relic of its era, about hot-rod-happy Ashley joining Vincent's band to earn money to enter big race.

Hot Rod Girl (1956) **75m.** BOMB D: Leslie Martinson. Lori Nelson, Chuck Connors, John Smith, Frank Gorshin, Roxanne Arlen, Dabbs Greer. Tedious trash with Nelson, in title role, helping to crack down on city hot-car racing.▼

Hot Rod Rumble (1957) **79m.** *½ D: Leslie Martinson. Brett Halsey, Richard Hartunian, Joey Forman, Leigh Snowden. Title tells all in this formula programmer of juvenile delinquents.

Hot Rods to Hell (1967) **C-92m.** **½ D: John Brahm. Dana Andrews, Jeanne Crain, Mimsy Farmer, Laurie Mock. Fast-paced actioner has Andrews and family tormented by hot-rod-happy juvenile delinquents. Original title: 52 MILES TO MIDNIGHT.

H.O.T.S. (1979) **C-95m.** *½ D: Gerald Seth Sindell. Susan Kiger, Lisa London, Pamela Jean Bryant, Kimberly Cameron, Lindsay Bloom, Mary Steelsmith, Angela Aames, Danny Bonaduce, Ken Olfson. Lame-brained knock-off of ANIMAL HOUSE with two sororities at each other's throats until they settle their differences with a strip football game. Leering sexploitation fare at least has gorgeous girls and decent production, making this best watched with the sound off. Written by two women, believe it or not, one of them actress Cheri Caffaro (whose husband produced the film).▼

Hot Shots (1956) **61m.** D: Jean Yarbrough.

Huntz Hall, Stanley Clements, Joi Lansing, Phil Phillips. SEE: **Bowery Boys** series.

Hot Spell (1958) 86m. ** D: Daniel Mann. Shirley Booth, Anthony Quinn, Shirley MacLaine, Earl Holliman, Eileen Heckart, Warren Stevens. Quinn—not just a pig but a blue-ribbon hog—cheats on wife Booth, who spouts irritating platitudes like Hazel on speed. Well-acted but dated drama about the breakup's effect on their children; MacLaine shines as the daughter who gets dumped by boyfriend Stevens because she can't advance his career. Set in New Orleans.▼

Hot Spot SEE: **I Wake Up Screaming**▼

Hot Stuff (1979) C-87m. **½ D: Dom DeLuise. Dom DeLuise, Suzanne Pleshette, Jerry Reed, Luis Avalos, Ossie Davis, Marc Lawrence. Four Miami cops set up a "Sting"-like operation to fence stolen goods. Unexceptional but pleasant trifle that surprises by treating its characters as real human beings instead of cartoon stereotypes. Cowritten by Donald Westlake.▼

Hot Summer Night (1957) 86m. **½ D: David Friedkin. Leslie Nielsen, Colleen Miller, Edward Andrews, Claude Akins, Paul Richards. Offbeat story about reporter seeking an interview with leader of robbery gang.

Hot to Trot (1988) C-83m. BOMB D: Michael Dinner. Bob Goldthwait, Virginia Madsen, Dabney Coleman, Cindy Pickett, Jim Metzler, Tim Kazurinsky, Gilbert Gottfried, Jack Whitaker; voices of John Candy, Burgess Meredith. Here's a fresh concept for the 1980s: a comedy about a talking horse. Goldthwait plays a semi-imbecile who gets stock tips from a whinnying pal with the voice of John Candy. As comedies go, this is the equivalent of Black Monday. Coleman, courtesy of the makeup department, wears a pair of horse teeth here; they *are* funny.▼

Houdini (1953) C-106m. **½ D: George Marshall. Tony Curtis, Janet Leigh, Torin Thatcher, Ian Wolfe, Sig Ruman. Fanciful biography of famed escape artist; more fiction than fact, perhaps better this way.

Hound-Dog Man (1959) C-87m. *** D: Don Siegel. Fabian, Carol Lynley, Stuart Whitman, Arthur O'Connell, Dodie Stevens, Betty Field, Royal Dano, Margo Moore, Claude Akins, Edgar Buchanan, Jane Darwell, L.Q. Jones. Pleasant tale of Southern country boys Fabian (in film debut) and Whitman courting Stevens and Lynley. Fabian is surprisingly good; of course, he also sings.

Hound of the Baskervilles, The (1939) 80m. D: Sidney Lanfield. Basil Rathbone, Nigel Bruce, Richard Greene, Wendy Barrie, Lionel Atwill, John Carradine, Beryl Mercer, Mary Gordon, E. E. Clive, Ralph Forbes, Ivan Simpson. SEE: **Sherlock Holmes** series.▼

Hound of the Baskervilles, The (1959-British) C-84m. *** D: Terence Fisher. Peter Cushing, Christopher Lee, Andre Morell, Maria Landi, Miles Malleson, John LeMesurier. Cushing is well cast as Sherlock Holmes in this atmospheric Hammer Films adaptation of the Conan Doyle classic.▼

Hound of the Baskervilles, The (1972) C-73m. TVM D: Barry Crane. Stewart Granger, William Shatner, Bernard Fox, John Williams, Anthony Zerbe, Jane Merrow. Ludicrous remake of Conan Doyle spellbinder with casting the least of its problems. Nuance, tension, situation all made trivial by script, pacing, production values. For masochists only. Below average.

Hound of the Baskervilles, The (1977-British) C-84m. BOMB D: Paul Morrissey. Dudley Moore, Peter Cook, Denholm Elliott, Joan Greenwood, Spike Milligan, Jessie Matthews, Roy Kinnear. Dreadful spoof of Conan Doyle story scripted by Cook (who plays Sherlock Holmes), Moore (as both Watson and Holmes's mother), and director Morrissey. After a few initial laughs it descends into dreariness and never recovers. What a waste of talent! The U.S. version runs 78m., with sequences out of order.▼

Hound of the Baskervilles, The (1983-British) C-101m. TVM D: Douglas Hickox. Ian Richardson, Donald Churchill, Martin Shaw, Denholm Elliott, Brian Blessed, Ronald Lacey, Eleanor Bron, Edward Judd, Glynis Barber, Nicholas Clay. Best version of the Doyle classic to date with excellent use of locations. Richardson is an energetic, witty Holmes, though story requires him to be offstage much of the time. Well paced, stylish, and atmospheric, this deserved theatrical release but didn't get it. Above average.

Hour Before the Dawn, The (1944) 75m. ** D: Frank Tuttle. Franchot Tone, Veronica Lake, John Sutton, Binnie Barnes, Henry Stephenson, Mary Gordon, Nils Asther. Polished, empty WW2 romance-espionage, with Tone falling for Nazi spy Lake; unlikely casting doesn't help.

Hour of Decision (1957-British) 81m. ** D: C.M. Pennington Richards. Jeff Morrow, Hazel Court, Anthony Dawson, Lionel Jeffries, Carl Bernard, Mary Laura Wood. Morrow is newspaperman who tracks down murderer of fellow columnist, discovering his wife was involved with the man.

Hour of Glory SEE: **Small Back Room, The**▼

Hour of the Assassin (1987) C-93m. ** D: Luis Llosa. Erik Estrada, Robert Vaughn, Alfredo Alvarez Calderon, Lourdes Berninzon. OK political thriller has Estrada called back from L.A. to South

American nation of San Pedro to assassinate the newly elected democratic president. Vaughn is the CIA agent assigned to stop him. Filmed in Peru. ▼

Hour of the Gun (1967) **C-100m.** ** D: John Sturges. James Garner, Jason Robards, Robert Ryan, Albert Salmi, Charles Aidman, Steve Ihnat, Jon Voight. Western about Ike Clanton and the Earp Brothers after O.K. Corral shoot-up begins well, becomes increasingly tedious. Robards has a good time as Doc Holliday; flavorful score by Jerry Goldsmith. Voight's film debut. ▼

Hour of the Wolf (1968-Swedish) **88m.** *** D: Ingmar Bergman. Liv Ullmann, Max von Sydow, Erland Josephson, Gertrud Fridh, Gudrun Brost. Lesser Bergman about painter von Sydow, wife Ullmann, and apparitions he sees when they retreat to deserted island. The acting, as usual, is first-rate.

Hour of 13, The (1952) **79m.** **½ D: Harold French. Peter Lawford, Dawn Addams, Roland Culver, Colin Gordon. Mystery yarn set in 1890s London, with Lawford a ritzy thief who develops a heart of gold in order to do a good deed for society. Remake of 1934 film THE MYSTERY OF MR. X.

Hours of Love, The (1965-Italian) **89m.** **½ D: Luciano Salce. Ugo Tognazzi, Emmanuele Riva, Barbara Steele, Umberto D'Orsi, Mara Berni. Pleasant little sex farce proving the adage that illicit love is sweeter than blessed marriage.

House (1986) **C-93m.** BOMB D: Steve Miner. William Katt, George Wendt, Richard Moll, Kay Lenz, Michael Ensign, Susan French, Mary Stavin. Horror novelist Katt, simultaneously suffering from the split-up of his marriage, son's disappearance, and Vietnam memories, is plagued by demonic fantasies when he moves to the Victorian home where his aunt hanged herself. Cluttered, derivative horror schlock from FRIDAY THE 13TH veterans; talk about a low interest rate . . . Followed by HOUSE II: THE SECOND STORY. ▼

House II: The Second Story (1987) **C-88m.** BOMB D: Ethan Wiley. Arye Gross, Jonathan Stark, Royal Dano, Lar Park Lincoln, Bill Maher, John Ratzenberger. A followup rather than a sequel to HOUSE, this incoherent mess is, if anything, a step down. Another young hero moves into another weird house, and finds himself involved with living-dead gunslingers, crystal skulls, Aztec sacrifices, pterodactyls, and a sword-wielding electrician. Busy, but chaotic and boring. ▼

House Across the Bay, The (1940) **86m.** **½ D: Archie Mayo. George Raft, Joan Bennett, Lloyd Nolan, Gladys George, Walter Pidgeon, June Knight. Raft's out to get Pidgeon, who has taken wife Bennett

from him while he's been in jail. Familiar but exciting film. ▼

House Across the Street, The (1949) **69m.** ** D: Richard Bare. Wayne Morris, Janis Paige, James Mitchell, Alan Hale, Bruce Bennett. Routine remake of Paul Muni's HI, NELLIE, with Morris as newspaperman on the scent of a murder. Paige is peppery as love interest.

Houseboat (1958) **C-110m.** ***½ D: Melville Shavelson. Cary Grant, Sophia Loren, Martha Hyer, Harry Guardino, Eduardo Ciannelli, Murray Hamilton. Loren becomes Grant's housekeeper and takes his three motherless kids in hand. Predictable romance ensues, in this delightful comedy. Guardino hilarious as houseboat handyman. ▼

House by the Lake, The (1977-Canadian) **C-89m.** *½ D: William Fruet. Brenda Vaccaro, Don Stroud, Chuck Shamata, Richard Ayres, Kyle Edwards. Violent, ugly thriller of four morons led by Stroud who invade weekend retreat of lovers Vaccaro and Shamata. Stroud and Vaccaro are good, though. Originally titled DEATH WEEKEND. ▼

House by the River, The (1950) **88m.** *** D: Fritz Lang. Louis Hayward, Jane Wyatt, Lee Bowman, Ann Shoemaker, Kathleen Freeman. Strange, moody tale of larcenous husband (Hayward) who spins web of evil that involves his wife (Wyatt) and brother (Bowman). Overwrought at times—particularly near the end—but full of fascinating touches, striking atmosphere.

House Calls (1978) **C-98m.** ***½ D: Howard Zieff. Walter Matthau, Glenda Jackson, Art Carney, Richard Benjamin, Candice Azzara, Dick O'Neill, Thayer David. Matthau plays recently widowed doctor who tries to woo feisty Jackson without sacrificing his independence, in this laughing-out-loud contemporary comedy. Cowritten by Max Shulman and Julius J. Epstein. Carney hilarious as addle-brained head of surgery at Matthau's hospital. Later a TV series. ▼

Housekeeper, The SEE: **Judgment in Stone, A** ▼

Housekeeper's Daughter, The (1939) **79m.** ** D: Hal Roach. Joan Bennett, Victor Mature, Adolphe Menjou, William Gargan. Pleasant murder mystery enhanced by chic Bennett, who helps crack a homicide case. Mature's film debut.

Housekeeping (1987) **C-116m.** **½ D: Bill Forsyth. Christine Lahti, Sara Walker, Andrea Burchill. Two orphaned girls meet their aunt for the first time when she comes to live with them; she turns out to be a free spirit who shuns responsibility and has a profound effect on the sisters' own relationship. Forsyth's first American film, set in the 1950s, is a quiet, offbeat, and melancholy story that unfolds like a novel but lacks a certain momentum. Still, there are many touching moments. Lahti is wonderful as always, and the girls (both movie newcomers) are excellent. Based on Marilynne Robinson's book.▼

House of Bamboo (1955) C-102m. **½ D: Samuel Fuller. Robert Ryan, Robert Stack, Shirley Yamaguchi, Cameron Mitchell, Sessue Hayakawa. Picturesque if not credible story of army officers and Japanese police tracking down a gang of former soldiers working for a well-organized syndicate.

House of Cards (1969) C-105m. ** D: John Guillermin. George Peppard, Inger Stevens, Orson Welles, Keith Michell, Ralph Michael, Maxine Audley. Down-and-out boxer/adventurer (Peppard) hired by rich widow (Stevens) to tutor her young son becomes pawn of Fascist millionaires and generals intent on retaking Europe. Sound familiar? One good chase, though.

House of Crazies SEE: **Asylum**▼

House of Dark Shadows (1970) C-96m. *** D: Dan Curtis. Jonathan Frid, Grayson Hall, Kathryn Leigh Scott, Roger Davis, Joan Bennett, John Karlen, Thayer David, Louis Edmonds, Nancy Barrett. Feature version of popular TV serial, recounting vampire Barnabas Collins' (Frid) quest for a cure so he can wed lovely Scott. Nothing new script-wise, but beautiful locations, flashy direction and camerawork, and some nice jolts make it an enjoyable chiller. Followed by NIGHT OF DARK SHADOWS.▼

House of Dracula (1945) 67m. **½ D: Erle C. Kenton. Onslow Stevens, Lon Chaney, Jr., John Carradine, Martha O' Driscoll, Jane Adams, Lionel Atwill, Glenn Strange, Skelton Knaggs. Sequel to HOUSE OF FRANKENSTEIN takes different tack: Stevens tries "real" science to cure various Universal monsters, but finds that some of their bad habits begin to rub off. Acting, direction, and eerie set design compensate for overly ambitious script, hasty resolution.

House of Evil (1971-Mexican-U.S.) C-80m. BOMB D: Juan Ibanez and Jack Hill. Boris Karloff, Julissa, Andres Garcia, Angel Espinosa, Beatriz Baz. The old heirs-being-killed-one-by-one story, involving crazy composer Karloff, his old house, killer toys, and an organ melody that heralds death. One of four films Karloff made back to back in 1968, constituting his last film work; all four are bad, but this is the worst of the lot.

House of Exorcism, The SEE: **Lisa and the Devil**▼

House of Fear (1939) 67m. **½ D: Joe May. William Gargan, Irene Hervey, Alan Dinehart, Walter Woolf King, Dorothy Arnold, El Brendel, Harvey Stephens, Robert Coote. Murderer stalks N.Y.C. theater; offbeat show business character in pretty good whodunit. Remake of 1929 film THE LAST WARNING.

House of Fear, The (1945) 69m. D: Roy William Neill. Basil Rathbone, Nigel Bruce, Dennis Hoey, Aubrey Mather, Paul Cavanagh, Holmes Herbert, Gavin Muir. SEE: **Sherlock Holmes** series.▼

House of Frankenstein (1944) 71m. **½ D: Erle C. Kenton. Boris Karloff, J. Carroll Naish, Lon Chaney, Jr., John Carradine, Elena Verdugo, Anne Gwynne, Lionel Atwill, Peter Coe, George Zucco, Glenn Strange, Sig Rumann. Episodic all-star monster opus linked by evil scientist Karloff and hunchback Naish posing as traveling horror show operators. First half has them dealing with Dracula, second picks up where FRANKENSTEIN MEETS THE WOLF MAN left off. Contrived, to say the least, but tough to dislike. Strange's first appearance as the Frankenstein Monster. Sequel: HOUSE OF DRACULA.

House of Fright SEE: **Two Faces of Dr. Jekyll, The**

House of Games (1987) C-102m. *** D: David Mamet. Lindsay Crouse, Joe Mantegna, Mike Nussbaum, Lilia Skala, J.T. Walsh, Willo Hausman, Ricky Jay, Meshach Taylor. Uptight female psychiatrist (and best-selling author) becomes involved with a slick confidence man and his "team," and quickly gets in over her head. Fascinating Hitchcockian tale by David Mamet, which also marks his film directing debut. Many of his stage cronies are on hand, notably Mantegna, in a dynamic performance, and Crouse, who is also Mamet's wife.▼

House of God, The (1979) C-108m. *½ D: Donald Wrye. Tim Matheson, Charles Haid, Bess Armstrong, Michael Sacks, Lisa Pelikan, George Coe, Ossie Davis, Howard Rollins, Jr., James Cromwell, Sandra Bernhard. Misfire black comedy about bunch of young interns coming to grips with reality of hospital pressures. A few scattered laughs, but mostly a waste of terrific (and then-unknown) talent. Adapted by Wrye from Samuel Shem's novel; never released theatrically.

House of Horrors (1946) 65m. ** D: Jean Yarbrough. Bill Goodwin, Robert Lowery, Virginia Grey, Rondo Hatton, Martin Kosleck. Slightly below average horror meller. Frustrated artist (Kosleck) uses fiend The Creeper to knock off critics. Laughable script, adequate acting.

House of Intrigue, The (1959-Italian) C-94m. **½ D: Duilio Coletti. Curt Jurgens, Dawn Addams, Folco Lulli, Dario Michaelis, Philippe Hersent. WW2 espionage caper with pleasing on-location European backgrounds.

House of Mortal Sin SEE: **Confessional, The**▼

House of Mystery (1961-British) **56m.**
**½ D: Vernon Sewell. Jane Hylton, Peter
Dyneley, Nanette Newman, Maurice Kaufman, John Merivale. Nifty little story of
haunted house, with its new owners learning the mysterious history of the premises;
supernatural played up well.

House of Numbers (1957) **92m.** **½ D:
Russell Rouse. Jack Palance, Barbara Lang,
Harold J. Stone, Edward Platt. Palance
plays dual role as man seeking to spring
gangster brother from prison and take his
place.

House of 1,000 Dolls (1967-British-Spanish)
C-83m. *½ D: Jeremy Summers. Vincent
Price, Martha Hyer, George Nader, Anne
Smyrner, Wolfgang Kieling, Sancho Garcia, Maria Rohm. Vacationing couple in
Tangiers befriended by young man convinced that his fiancée has been abducted
into white slavery ring. Incredible dialogue,
with Price walking through film in a daze.

House of Ricordi (1956-Italian) **C-117m.**
** D: Carmine Gallone. Paolo Stoppa,
Roland Alexandre, Marta Toren, Roldano
Lupi. Passable biography of well-known
music-publishing house, set in the 18th
century, with many musical interludes.
Retitled: CASA RICORDI.

House of Rothschild (1934) **88m.** *** D:
Alfred L. Werker. George Arliss, Boris
Karloff, Loretta Young, Robert Young,
Florence Arliss, C. Aubrey Smith. Elaborate, entertaining chronicle of famed banking family, with Arliss as Nathan Rothschild
at time of Napoleonic Wars, Loretta his
daughter, R. Young her suitor, Karloff as
civilized villain. Finale originally shot in
color.

House of Seven Corpses, The (1973)
C-90m. ** D: Paul Harrison. John Ireland, Faith Domergue, John Carradine,
Carol Wells, Charles McCauley, Jerry
Stricklen. A film crew uses a supposedly
haunted house for location work on a horror film, and learns to regret it; low-budget,
but not bad.▼

House of Seven Gables, The (1940) **89m.**
*** D: Joe May. George Sanders, Margaret Lindsay, Vincent Price, Nan Grey,
Alan Napier, Cecil Kellaway, Dick Foran.
Good adaptation of Hawthorne's classic
novel. Set in 17th-century New England,
jealous brother sends sister's fiancée to
prison. Fine performances.

House of Strangers (1949) **101m.** *** D:
Joseph L. Mankiewicz. Edward G. Robinson, Susan Hayward, Richard Conte, Luther Adler, Efrem Zimbalist, Jr., Debra
Paget, Hope Emerson, Esther Minciotti.
Dynamic drama of ruthless financier Robinson who uses his four sons to suit his
own schemes. Unique plot line has been
utilized for many subsequent films in various disguises—most memorably, five years
later in the Western BROKEN LANCE.

House of the Black Death (1965) **80m.**
*½ D: Harold Daniels. Lon Chaney, Jr.,
John Carradine, Andrea King, Tom Drake,
Dolores Faith, Sabrina. Warlock holds people captive in a creepy old house; terribly
dragged out, grade-Z stuff.

House of the Long Shadows (1983-British)
C-96m. *½ D: Pete Walker. Vincent Price,
Christopher Lee, Peter Cushing, Desi
Arnaz, Jr., John Carradine, Sheila Keith,
Julie Peasgood, Richard Todd. Arnaz, Jr.
single-handedly sinks this sixth screen version of George M. Cohan's spoof, SEVEN
KEYS TO BALDPATE, miscast as a mystery writer staying the night in a spooky
mansion on a bet with Todd. Notable only
for its historic teaming of four all-time
horror masters, all wasted in small roles.
▼

House of the Seven Hawks, The (1959)
92m. **½ D: Richard Thorpe. Robert
Taylor, Nicole Maurey, Linda Christian,
Donald Wolfit, David Kossoff, Eric Pohlmann. Diverting account of skipper Taylor
involved in shipboard murder and hunt for
long-lost Nazi loot. Made in England.

House of Unclaimed Women SEE: **School
for Unclaimed Girls**

House of Usher (1960) **C-85m.** ***½ D:
Roger Corman. Vincent Price, Mark Damon, Myrna Fahey, Harry Ellerbe. First-rate horror film based on classic tale by
Edgar Allan Poe. When beautiful young
girl's suitor arrives to ask her hand in
marriage, the doors of the house of Usher
fling open, and terror begins. Filmed several times before and since, but never this
effectively; first of Corman's eight Poe
adaptations. Also known as FALL OF
THE HOUSE OF USHER.▼

House of Wax (1953) **C-88m.** *** D:
Andre de Toth. Vincent Price, Frank
Lovejoy, Phyllis Kirk, Carolyn Jones, Paul
Cavanagh, Charles Buchinsky (Bronson).
Remake of MYSTERY OF THE WAX
MUSEUM stars Price as vengeful sculptor
who rebuilds his fire-destroyed showplace
by using human victims as wax figures.
Jones excellent as an early victim. The
most popular of the era's 3-D films, a
status it retains today. Love that paddle-ball man!▼

House of Women (1962) **85m.** **½ D:
Walter Doniger. Shirley Knight, Andrew
Duggan, Constance Ford, Barbara Nichols, Margaret Hayes, Virginia Gregg. Trite
rendition of conditions in a women's prison
elevated by good cast and fast pacing.
Remake of CAGED.

House on Carroll Street, The (1988)
C-100m. ** D: Peter Yates. Kelly McGillis,
Jeff Daniels, Mandy Patinkin, Christopher
Rhode, Jessica Tandy, Jonathan Hogan,
Trey Wilson. McGillis, who's just lost her
job after being branded a subversive during the McCarthy era, stumbles onto a

[530]

strange espionage plot that's being covered up, and gradually persuades FBI agent Daniels that she's on to something big. Finely detailed period piece set in 1950s N.Y.C. starts off well, then chucks its relevance (and believability) for a melodramatic finale filmed à la Hitchcock at Grand Central Station . . . leaving a passel of plot holes and unanswered questions. A real disappointment from onetime blacklisted writer Walter Bernstein. Patinkin is excellent as Roy Cohn-type attorney.▼

House on Garibaldi Street, The (1979) C-100m. TVM D: Peter Collinson. Topol, Martin Balsam, Janet Suzman, Nick Mancuso, Leo McKern. Textbook spy thriller about the capture of Adolph Eichmann by Israeli agents in Argentina in 1960; good, but nearly drowns itself in polemics. Filmed in Spain. Average.▼

House on Greenapple Road, The (1970) C-113m. TVM D: Robert Day. Christopher George, Janet Leigh, Julie Harris, Tim O'Connor, Walter Pidgeon, Barry Sullivan, Keenan Wynn, Lynda Day, Edward Asner. Entertaining police mystery set in suburban California town, supposedly illustrating average town police practices and state government politics. Mild-mannered husband (O'Connor) fears for life of promiscuous wife (Leigh). Too confused for own good by halfway mark. Pilot for the *Dan August* TV series. Average.

✓ **House on Haunted Hill** (1958) 75m. *** D: William Castle. Vincent Price, Carol Ohmart, Richard Long, Alan Marshal, Elisha Cook, Jr., Carolyn Craig, Leona Anderson. Zillionaire Price offers group of people $50,000 each if they'll spend a night in spooky old mansion with murder-laden history; he even provides loaded guns as party favors. Campy fun; probably the Castle film which holds up best on TV.▼

House on Marsh Road, The SEE: Invisible Creature, The

House on 92nd St., The (1945) 88m. ***½ D: Henry Hathaway. William Eythe, Lloyd Nolan, Signe Hasso, Gene Lockhart, Leo G. Carroll, Lydia St. Clair. Exciting, trend-setting documentary-style drama—based on fact and staged on actual locations—about FBI counterespionage activities during WW2: Nazi agents, operating in N.Y.C., attempt to pilfer part of the atom bomb formula. Charles G. Booth earned an Oscar for his original story.

House on Skull Mountain, The (1974) C-89m. *½ D: Ron Honthaner. Victor French, Janee Michelle, Jean Durand, Mike Evans, Xernona Clayton. Voodoo man Durand is on the loose in the title abode. Black horror entry (but with a white hero!) is not particularly bloody, but also not particularly good.▼

House on Telegraph Hill, The (1951) 93m. **½ D: Robert Wise. Richard Basehart, Valentina Cortese, William Lundigan, Fay Baker. Good cast in intriguing tale of WW2 refugee assuming dead woman's identity so that she can come to San Francisco where wealthy relatives reside.

House Party (1990) C-100m. *** D: Reginald Hudlin. Christopher Reid, Robin Harris, Christopher Martin, Martin Lawrence, Tisha Campbell, A. J. Johnson, Paul Anthony. Infectiously good natured comedy about urban black teenagers and the events leading up to (and following) a house party one night. Upbeat and imaginative, cast with real-life music rappers (including Reid, who plays the leading role of Kid). A solid feature debut for young writer-director Hudlin.▼

House That Cried Murder, The (1974) C-85m. **½ D: Jean-Marie Pelissie. Robin Strasser, John Beal, Arthur Roberts, Iva Jean Saraceni. Strasser has some surprises in store for Roberts when he is unfaithful on their wedding day. Pretty scary thriller; also known as THE BRIDE.

House That Dripped Blood, The (1971-British) C-101m. **½ D: Peter Duffell. John Bennett, John Bryans, Denholm Elliott, Joanna Dunham, Tom Adams, Peter Cushing, Christopher Lee, Nyree Dawn Porter, Jon Pertwee, Ingrid Pitt. Entertaining four-part horror film written by Robert Bloch with a bit too much tongue in cheek, revolving around suitably creepy-looking mansion purchased by new, hesitant owner. Best segments: first and last.▼

House That Screamed, The (1970-Spanish) C-94m. *½ D: Narciso Ibanez Serrador. Lilli Palmer, Chistina Galbo, John Moulder-Brown, Mary Maude, Candida Losada. Grisly horror at a home for troubled girls, where disciplinarian Palmer and her sex-starved son (Brown) make life difficult—to say the least—for the young ladies.

House That Would Not Die, The (1970) C-72m. TVM D: John Llewellyn Moxey. Barbara Stanwyck, Michael Anderson, Jr., Doreen Lang, Richard Egan, Katherine Winn, Mabel Albertson. Thriller built around Revolutionary era haunted house. With longer running time, Henry Farrell-scripted story could've been great. One or two unusual situations, otherwise nothing new. Average.

House Where Evil Dwells, The (1982) C-88m. ** D: Kevin Connor. Edward Albert, Susan George, Doug McClure, Amy Barrett, Mako Hattori, Toshiyuki Sasaki, Toshiya Maruyama. American family moves into stylish old house in Kyoto, Japan, ignoring warnings that it's haunted by ghosts of doomed 19th-century love triangle. A few new twists can't relieve familiar formula, and general air of silliness. Quite violent at times.▼

Housewife (1934) 69m. ** D: Alfred E. Green. Bette Davis, George Brent, Ann

Dvorak, John Halliday, Ruth Donnelly. Little punch in story of struggling copywriter Brent deserting wife Dvorak for old-flame Davis (playing unsubtle vamp).

Houston Story, The (1956) **79m. **½** D: William Castle. Gene Barry, Barbara Hale, Edward Arnold, Paul Richards, Jeanne Cooper. Barry portrays greedy oil worker who plans to take over crime syndicate involved in stealing oil.

Houston: The Legend of Texas (1986) **C-150m. TVM** D: Peter Levin. Sam Elliott, Michael Beck, Bo Hopkins, Devon Ericson, Michael C. Gwynne, G. D. Spradlin, William Russ, James Stephens. Episodic drama covering thirty years in the life of colorful statesman and battle hero Sam Houston should have been a shorter ripsnorter. Look sharp toward the end for an unbilled Katharine Ross, Elliott's real-life wife. Average.

Houston, We've Got a Problem (1974) **C-78m. TVM** D: Lawrence Doheny. Robert Culp, Clu Gulager, Sandra Dee, Gary Collins, Ed Nelson, Sheila Sullivan, Steve Franken. Fictionalized account of the flight of ill-fated Apollo 13 and the traumatic effect the spacecraft explosion has on the flight controllers. No-nonsense performances mesh with real-life tragedy. Average.

Howard Beach: Making a Case for Murder (1989) **C-100m. TVM** D: Dick Lowry. Daniel J. Travanti, William Daniels, Joe Morton, Cliff Gorman, Bruce Young, Dan Lauria. Straightforward docudrama detailing the inflammatory case about the 1986 death of a black man in the white, blue-collar Queens, N.Y.C., community of Howard Beach and the efforts of state prosecutor Joe Hynes to bring it to trial. Average.

Howards of Virginia, The (1940) **122m. **½** D: Frank Lloyd. Cary Grant, Martha Scott, Cedric Hardwicke, Alan Marshal, Richard Carlson, Paul Kelly, Irving Bacon. Historical account of Revolutionary War is OK, but too long for such standard retelling.▼

Howard the Duck (1986) **C-111m. BOMB** D: Willard Huyck. Lea Thompson, Jeffrey Jones, Tim Robbins, Paul Guilfoyle. Steve Gerber's sarcastic comic-book creation is (unwisely) turned into a live-action character for this hopeless mess of a movie set in Cleveland. Gargantuan production produces gargantuan headache. Executive produced, but disowned, by George Lucas.▼

How Awful About Allan (1970) **C-72m. TVM** D: Curtis Harrington. Anthony Perkins, Julie Harris, Joan Hackett, Kent Smith, Robert H. Harris. Guilt-ridden blind mental patient Perkins thinks release from hospital and closeness to sister (Harris) will cure him. Considering talent connected with script, direction, and cast, a major disappointment. Below average.

How Do I Love Thee? (1970) **C-110m. *½** D: Michael Gordon. Jackie Gleason, Maureen O'Hara, Shelley Winters, Rosemary Forsyth, Rick Lenz, Clinton Robinson. Pleasant cast can't do much for sloppily sentimental film about Gleason's inability to relate to his son, a philosophy professor. Plays like a TV show, and a bad one at that.

How Funny Can Sex Be? (1976-Italian) **C-97m. **½** D: Dino Risi. Giancarlo Giannini, Laura Antonelli, Alberto Lionello, Duilio Del Prete, Paola Barbone, Carla Mancini. Eight bawdy episodes on love, sex, and marriage. More misses than hits, but buoyed by Giannini's comic prowess and Antonelli's tantalizing beauty. Released here after Giannini's success in Wertmuller films.

How Green Was My Valley (1941) **118m. ****** D: John Ford. Walter Pidgeon, Maureen O'Hara, Donald Crisp, Anna Lee, Roddy McDowall, John Loder, Sara Allgood, Barry Fitzgerald, Patric Knowles, Rhys Williams (who also narrates). Moving drama from Richard Llewellyn's story of Welsh coal miners, centering on Crisp's large, close-knit family. Beautifully filmed, lovingly directed, winner of five Academy Awards: Best Picture, Director, Supporting Actor (Crisp), Cinematography (Arthur Miller), Art Director. Screenplay by Philip Dunne. ✓

How I Got into College (1989) **C-89m. **** D: Savage Steve Holland. Anthony Edwards, Corey Parker, Lara Flynn Boyle, Finn Carter, Charles Rocket, Christopher Rydell, Brian Doyle-Murray. Aimless senior applies to a small college because his high-achiever dream girl is doing the same, and gets caught up in the cutthroat recruitment machine. Mild execution of ripe satirical premise, buoyed by fantasy set pieces associated with director Holland's previous work. Has its moments, but not enough of them.▼

How I Spent My Summer Vacation (1967) **C-100m. TVM** D: William Hale. Robert Wagner, Lola Albright, Peter Lawford, Walter Pidgeon, Jill St. John. Muddy tale tells in flashback Wagner's singleminded efforts to prove himself to (and take revenge on) Lawford, who humiliated him years ago. Below average.

How I Won the War (1967-British) **C-109m. ***** D: Richard Lester. Michael Crawford, John Lennon, Roy Kinnear, Jack MacGowran, Michael Hordern. Often hilarious study of one man's military career and strange way he has of reminiscing by distorting the truth.▼

Howling, The (1981) **C-91m. ***** D: Joe Dante. Dee Wallace, Patrick Macnee, Dennis Dugan, Christopher Stone, Belinda Balaski, Kevin McCarthy, John Carradine, Slim Pickens, Elisabeth Brooks, Dick Miller. A female TV news reporter is sent to a strange California encounter-group community to recover from a sexual trauma, unaware that virtually everyone there is a werewolf. A hip, well-made horror film, brimming with film-buff jokes (almost every character is named after a werewolf movie director) and Rob Bottin's amazing wolf transformations. Only complaint: Why set the horror against such a patently bizarre backdrop? Co-scripter John Sayles has a funny cameo as a morgue attendant. Followed by three so-called sequels.▼

Howling II: Your Sister Is a Werewolf (1985) **C-90m.** BOMB D: Philippe Mora. Christopher Lee, Annie McEnroe, Reb Brown, Sybil Danning, Marsha A. Hunt, Ferdy Mayne. Ridiculous sequel is set in Transylvania where unlikely siblings Danning and Lee head up a family of werewolves. Attempt at sending up the genre falls flat.▼

Howling III (1987-Australian) **C-94m.** ** D: Philippe Mora. Barry Otto, Imogen Annesley, Dasha Blahova, Max Fairchild, Frank Thring, Michael Pate, Barry Humphries. OK horror spoof stars Annesley, a Kim Basinger-like beauty, as an Australian marsupial werewolf, who gives birth to a cute little creature that lives in a pouch on her belly. Unusual addition to werewolf genre features some funny cameos, including Thring as an Alfred Hitchcock-style director.▼

Howling in the Woods, A (1971) **C-100m.** TVM D: Daniel Petrie. Barbara Eden, John Rubinstein, Vera Miles, Larry Hagman, Tyne Daly, Ford Rainey, Ruta Lee. Complicated double conspiracy only revelation in thriller involving disillusioned wife vacationing with relatives at Lake Tahoe lodge, and husband not far behind. Average.▼

How Sweet It Is! (1968) **C-99m.** *½ D: Jerry Paris. James Garner, Debbie Reynolds, Maurice Ronet, Paul Lynde, Marcel Dalio, Terry-Thomas. Married couple with teen-age son goes to Europe to revitalize themselves, but Mom starts to dally with sexy Frenchman. Bland comedy looks like a TV show and is about as memorable.▼

How the West Was Won (1962) **C-155m.** ***½ D: John Ford, Henry Hathaway, George Marshall. George Peppard, Debbie Reynolds, Carroll Baker, James Stewart, Henry Fonda, John Wayne, Gregory Peck, All-Star Cast; narrated by Spencer Tracy. Blockbuster epic about three generations of Western pioneers isn't same experience on TV it was on Cinerama screen, but great cast, first-rate photography and lovely Alfred Newman score still make it top entertainment. Peppard stands out with excellent portrayal. This won Oscars for Story and Screenplay (James R. Webb) and Editing (Harold F. Kress).▼

How to Beat the High Co$t of Living (1980) **C-110m.** *½ D: Robert Scheerer. Susan Saint James, Jane Curtin, Jessica Lange, Richard Benjamin, Cathryn Damon, Fred Willard, Dabney Coleman, Eddie Albert, Art Metrano, Garrett Morris. Thoroughly blah caper comedy by Bob Kaufman about three housewives who plot a heist at the local shopping center. Worth a glance to see Coleman in rare romantic lead . . . and Saint James and Curtin years before they clicked together as *Kate and Allie*.▼

How to Be Very, Very Popular (1955) **C-89m.** **½ D: Nunnally Johnson. Betty Grable, Robert Cummings, Charles Coburn, Sheree North, Fred Clark, Alice Pearce, Orson Bean. Grable and North on the lam hide in a college fraternity in this semi-remake of SHE LOVES ME NOT. Sheree does wild "Shake, Rattle and Roll" number, stealing Grable's spotlight. This was Betty's last movie.

How to Break Up a Happy Divorce (1976) **C-78m.** TVM D: Jerry Paris. Barbara Eden, Hal Linden, Peter Bonerz, Marcia Rodd, Harold Gould, Liberty Williams. Madcap comedy involving a pretty divorcee trying to win back her ex-husband by playing on his jealousy and dating a slick man-about-town. Sight-gag-happy farce loaded with quickie comic bits. Average.▼

How to Commit Marriage (1969) **C-95m.** ** D: Norman Panama. Bob Hope, Jackie Gleason, Jane Wyman, Maureen Arthur, Tim Matheson, Leslie Nielsen, Tina Louise, Irwin Corey. Above average for later Hope movies, but still a far cry from great comedy. Hope and Wyman are about to divorce when their daughter announces plans to marry Gleason's son. "Mod" elements of script were already dated when film came out.

How to Frame a Figg (1971) **C-103m.** ** D: Alan Rafkin. Don Knotts, Joe Flynn, Elaine Joyce, Edward Andrews, Yvonne Craig. Simplistic chap (Knotts) finds trouble behind every doorway as he is made patsy for crooked politicians. Usual unsubtle Knotts comedy.

How to Get Ahead in Advertising (1989-British) **C-95m.** **½ D: Bruce Robinson. Richard E. Grant, Rachel Ward, Richard Wilson, Jacqueline Tong, John Shrapnel, Susan Wooldridge, Mick Ford. Advertising hotshot Grant is under so much pressure—and has become so negative about his manipulative profession—that his anxiety brings forth a talking boil on his shoulder with a mind of its own! Certifiably weird comedy by writer-director Robinson (reunited with the star of his first film, WITHNAIL AND I) has its share of funny and bizarre moments, but its attack on advertising is so heavy handed that as satire it fizzles.▼

How to Make a Monster (1958) **74m.** BOMB D: Herbert L. Strock. Robert Harris, Walter Reed, Gary Clarke, Paul Brinegar. Dismal chiller involving studio makeup artist who goes berserk and turns his creations into zombie-like killers. Final 18m. of film is in color.

How to Make It SEE: **Target: Harry**

How to Marry a Millionaire (1953) **C-95m.** *** D: Jean Negulesco. Marilyn Monroe, Betty Grable, Lauren Bacall, William Powell, Rory Calhoun, David Wayne, Alex D'Arcy, Fred Clark, Cameron Mitchell. Terrific ensemble work in dandy comedy of three man-hunting females pooling resources to trap eligible bachelors. Nunnally Johnson scripted and produced this remake of THE GREEKS HAD A WORD FOR THEM, which is preceded by Alfred Newman conducting his famed "Street Scene" theme (a prologue designed to show off stereophonic sound).▼

How to Murder a Rich Uncle (1957-British) **80m.** **½ D: Nigel Patrick. Charles Coburn, Nigel Patrick, Wendy Hiller, Anthony Newley, Katie Johnson, Athene Seyler. Amusing cash-in on THE LADY-KILLERS, with nouveau poor British family deciding to knock off visiting American relative Coburn for his money, succeeding only in doing themselves in. No classic, but entertaining. Script by John Paxton; Michael Caine has a tiny bit.

How to Murder Your Wife (1965) **C-118m.** *** D: Richard Quine. Jack Lemmon, Virna Lisi, Terry-Thomas, Eddie Mayehoff, Claire Trevor, Sidney Blackmer, Max Showalter, Jack Albertson, Mary Wickes. Engaging comedy that almost holds up to finale. Cartoonist Lemmon marries Lisi while drunk and spends rest of picture devising ways to get rid of her. Mayehoff is standout as Lemmon's lawyer friend.▼

How to Pick Up Girls! (1978) **C-100m.** TVM D: Bill Persky. Desi Arnaz, Jr., Bess Armstrong, Fred McCarren, Polly Bergen, Richard Dawson, Alan King, Abe Vigoda, Deborah Raffin. Naive small towner (McCarren) comes to the Big Apple and stumbles onto the secret of successful girl-chasing to the dismay of his sophisticated buddy (Arnaz) from back home, now a full-time swinger. Amiable sitcom treatment of Eric Weber's funny book. Average.▼

How to Save a Marriage (And Ruin Your Life) (1968) **C-108m.** *½ D: Fielder Cook. Dean Martin, Stella Stevens, Eli Wallach, Anne Jackson, Betty Field, Jack Albertson. Typical 1960s sex farce has swinging bachelor Dino mistaking Stella for his best friend's mistress, with predictable complications. Stevens wasted again.

How to Steal a Million (1966) **C-127m.** *** D: William Wyler. Audrey Hepburn, Peter O'Toole, Charles Boyer, Eli Wallach, Hugh Griffith. Hepburn and O'Toole are a delightful match in this sophisticated comedy about a million-dollar theft in a Paris art museum. Boyer, O'Toole's boss, and Griffith, Hepburn's father, are equally good.

How to Steal an Airplane (1971) **C-100m.** TVM D: Leslie Martinson. Peter Deuel, Clinton Greyn, Sal Mineo, Katherine Crawford, Claudine Longet. Good combination of action and laughs as American and Welshman plan to get back at playboy son of Latin dictator. Offbeat casting, script. Filmed in 1968. Retitled: ONLY ONE DAY LEFT BEFORE TOMORROW. Above average.

How to Stuff a Wild Bikini (1965) **C-90m.** ** D: William Asher. Annette Funicello, Dwayne Hickman, Brian Donlevy, Buster Keaton, Mickey Rooney, Harvey Lembeck, Beverly Adams, Jody McCrea, John Ashley, Bobbi Shaw. The fatigue is palpable in this sixth BEACH PARTY movie, which tries out another new leading man (with Frankie Avalon again shunted to a cameo role). As usual, the veterans—especially Rooney—help liven things a little, but overall, pretty mediocre. Followed by GHOST IN THE INVISIBLE BIKINI.▼

How to Succeed in Business Without Really Trying (1967) **C-121m.** ***½ D: David Swift. Robert Morse, Michele Lee, Rudy Vallee, Anthony Teague, Maureen Arthur, Sammy Smith. Delightful, original musical from Broadway hit about ambitious window-washer (Morse) who uses wiles, and a handbook, to rise to prominence in Vallee's Worldwide Wicket Co. Superb farce, good Frank Loesser songs (including "Brotherhood of Man" and "I Believe in You"), imaginative staging of musical numbers.▼

Huckleberry Finn (1931) **80m.** **½ D: Norman Taurog. Jackie Coogan, Mitzi Green, Junior Durkin, Eugene Pallette, Jackie Searl, Clarence Muse, Jane Darwell. Life on the Mississippi with Huck, Tom Sawyer, and Becky Thatcher. Charming but very, very dated; a follow-up to previous year's TOM SAWYER, with same cast.

Huckleberry Finn (1939) **90m.** *** D: Richard Thorpe. Mickey Rooney, Walter Connolly, William Frawley, Rex Ingram, Lynne Carver. Subdued Rooney fine, Ingram excellent as Huck and Jim in classic Mark Twain tale of early 19th-century America; Connolly and Frawley are amusing as riverboat con-artists. Also shown in computer-colored version.▼

Huckleberry Finn (1974) **C-118m.** ** D: J. Lee Thompson. Jeff East, Paul Winfield, Harvey Korman, David Wayne, Arthur O'Connell, Gary Merrill. Little of Mark Twain is left in this handsome but empty-headed musical version of his classic story. Score by Richard and Robert Sherman is as forgettable as their script.

Huckleberry Finn (1975) **C-78m.** TVM D: Robert Totten. Ron Howard, Donny Most, Antonio Fargas, Jack Elam, Merle Haggard, Royal Dano, Rance Howard,

Clint Howard. Folksy treatment of the classic by Twain (played by Dano), minus the social criticism and sinister aspects of the literary adventure favorite. Above average.▼

Hucksters, The (1947) 115m. *** D: Jack Conway. Clark Gable, Deborah Kerr, Sydney Greenstreet, Adolphe Menjou, Ava Gardner, Keenan Wynn, Edward Arnold. Glossy dig at advertising and radio industries, with Gable battling for integrity among yes-men. Greenstreet memorable as despotic head of soap company; Kerr's first American movie.

Hud (1963) 112m. **** D: Martin Ritt. Paul Newman, Patricia Neal, Melvyn Douglas, Brandon de Wilde, John Ashley. Excellent story of moral degradation set in modern West, with impeccable performances by all. Neal won Best Actress Oscar as family housekeeper who doesn't want to get involved with no-account Newman. Douglas received Best Supporting Oscar as Newman's ethical, uncompromising father, and James Wong Howe's cinematography also earned a statuette. Irving Ravetch and Harriet Frank, Jr. scripted from Larry McMurtry's novel *Horseman, Pass By*.▼

Hudson's Bay (1940) 95m. **½ D: Irving Pichel. Paul Muni, Gene Tierney, Laird Cregar, John Sutton, Virginia Field, Vincent Price, Nigel Bruce. Muni's good, but life of founder of Hudson Bay fur-trading company lacks punch. Expansive production.

Hue and Cry (1947-British) 82m. *** D: Charles Crichton. Alastair Sim, Jack Warner, Frederick Piper, Jack Lambert, Joan Dowling. Rowdy youngsters turn tables on crooks who've been using their newspaper to pass coded information. Great fun.▼

Huey Long (1985) C/B&W-88m. ***½ D: Ken Burns. Entertaining, thoroughly fascinating documentary portrait of Huey Long, controversial Depression-era Louisiana governor and one of the most intriguing personalities in American history. Crammed with priceless footage; a must.

Huggers SEE: **Crazy Moon**▼

Hugo the Hippo (1976) C-90m. **½ D: William Feigenbaum. Voices of Burl Ives, Marie and Jimmy Osmond, Robert Morley, Paul Lynde. OK children's cartoon musical about a youngster's attempt to save a hippo from extinction in ancient Zanzibar.▼

Huk (1956) C-84m. *½ D: John Barnwell. George Montgomery, Mona Freeman, John Baer, James Bell. Philippine-made hokum about Montgomery returning to the Islands to revenge his dad's murder.

Human Comedy, The (1943) 118m. ***½ D: Clarence Brown. Mickey Rooney, Frank Morgan, Jackie "Butch" Jenkins, James Craig, Marsha Hunt, Fay Bainter, Ray Collins, Darryl Hickman, Donna Reed, Van Johnson. Memorable Americana, faithfully adapted from William Saroyan's sentimental Oscar-winning story of life in a small town during WW2. Unfolds like a novel, with many lovely vignettes, and one of Rooney's best performances as a teenager with growing responsibilities. Screenplay by Howard Estabrook. P.S.: Keep an eye out for those three soldiers on leave: Barry Nelson, Don DeFore, and Robert Mitchum! Also shown in computer-colored version.▼

Human Desire (1954) 90m. **½ D: Fritz Lang. Glenn Ford, Gloria Grahame, Broderick Crawford, Edgar Buchanan, Kathleen Case, Diana DeLaire. Lang's follow-up to THE BIG HEAT is a well-directed but muddled account of railroad engineer Ford, just back from Korea, who becomes mixed up with married Grahame and murder. Based on Zola's *La Bête Humaine*, filmed in 1938 by Jean Renoir.▼

Human Duplicators, The (1965) C-82m. ** D: Hugo Grimaldi. George Nader, Barbara Nichols, George Macready, Dolores Faith, Hugh Beaumont, Richard Arlen. An alien giant paves the way for a major invasion by duplicating people—but then falls in love. Some imagination here, but low-budget production sinks it.▼

Human Experiments (1980) C-82m. *½ D: Gregory Goodell. Linda Haynes, Geoffrey Lewis, Ellen Travolta, Aldo Ray, Jackie Coogan, Darlene Carviotto. As the title says . . .▼

Human Factor, The (1975-British-Italian) C-96m. *½ D: Edward Dmytryk. George Kennedy, John Mills, Raf Vallone, Rita Tushingham, Barry Sullivan, Arthur Franz. Violent, bloody chronicle of Kennedy tracking down the killers of his family. Decent cast wasted.▼

Human Factor, The (1979) C-115m. ** D: Otto Preminger. Nicol Williamson, Iman, Derek Jacobi, Richard Attenborough, Robert Morley, Ann Todd, John Gielgud. Dry, unexciting filmization of Graham Greene's spy novel about a British double agent (Williamson) who's forced to defect to Russia. Top cast, script by Tom Stoppard, but results are mediocre.

Human Feelings (1978) C-96m. TVM D: Ernest Pintoff. Nancy Walker, Billy Crystal, Pamela Sue Martin, Squire Fridell, Jack Carter, Donna Pescow, Armand Assante. Inspired by OH, GOD!, this series pilot casts Walker as God and Crystal as an eager young angel who has six days to clean up Las Vegas. Good performers do their best with middling material. First telecast at 74m., with a laugh track that was eliminated when the film was expanded for its initial network repeat. Average.

Human Highway (1982) **C-88m.** *½ D: Bernard Shakey (Neil Young), Dean Stockwell. Neil Young, Russ Tamblyn, Dennis Hopper, Sally Kirkland, Dean Stockwell, Charlotte Stewart, Devo. Young and Tamblyn run a gas station in the middle of nowhere in this wacked-out, anti-nuke comedy. Notable for footage of Young in concert plus rock group Devo performing with a red, radioactive glow about them (caused by the nuclear power plant in the vicinity).

Human Jungle, The (1954) **82m.** **½ D: Joseph M. Newman. Gary Merrill, Jan Sterling, Paula Raymond, Emile Meyer, Regis Toomey, Chuck Connors. Documentary-style account of a typical day at a busy police precinct house; nicely done.

Human Monster, The (1939-British) **73m.** ** D: Walter Summers. Bela Lugosi, Hugh Williams, Greta Gynt, Edmon Ryan, Wilfred Walter. Absurd, sometimes engaging Edgar Wallace tale of evil Lugosi using blind men as pawns in elaborate murder scheme. Original title: DARK EYES OF LONDON.▼

Humanoids from the Deep (1980) **C-80m.** *** D: Barbara Peeters. Doug McClure, Ann Turkel, Vic Morrow, Cindy Weintraub, Anthony Penya, Denise Galik. Mutated salmon monsters with penchant for bikinied beachgoers commit rape and other (graphic) mayhem in small oceanside town. Fast, occasionally hilarious gutter trash from the Roger Corman stable. The finale is not for squeamish viewers.▼

Humongous (1981-Canadian) **C-93m.** *½ D: Paul Lynch. Janet Julian, David Wallace, Janit Baldwin, John Wildman, Joy Boushel, Layne Coleman. Slow-moving horror film opens with brutal rape and follows with every cliche in the book. A group of youths who wreck their boat on a small island are picked off one at a time by a raving manbeast. Most of the action occurs in complete darkness and you never even get a good look at the monster.▼

Humoresque (1946) **125m.** ***½ D: Jean Negulesco. Joan Crawford, John Garfield, Oscar Levant, J. Carrol Naish, Craig Stevens, Tom D'Andrea, Peggy Knudsen, Paul Cavanagh. Ambitious violinist Garfield gets involved with wealthy, unstable patroness Crawford. No cardboard soap opera this; superb performances, handsome production, hilarious support from Levant, and a knockout finale. Perhaps Crawford's finest hour. Young Robert Blake plays Garfield as a child, and that's Isaac Stern's violin on the soundtrack. Filmed before in 1920.

✓ **Hunchback of Notre Dame, The** (1923) **93m.** *** D: Wallace Worsley. Lon Chaney, Patsy Ruth Miller, Ernest Torrence, Tully Marshall, Norman Kerry. Lavish filming of Hugo classic, capturing flair of medieval Paris and strange attraction of outcast Chaney for dancing girl (Miller). Silent classic holds up well, with Chaney's makeup still incredible.▼

Hunchback of Notre Dame, The (1939) **115m.** ***½ D: William Dieterle. Charles Laughton, Sir Cedric Hardwicke, Thomas Mitchell, Maureen O'Hara, Edmond O'Brien, Alan Marshal, Walter Hampden, Harry Davenport, George Zucco, Curt Bois, George Tobias, Rod LaRoque. Superb remake of Lon Chaney silent is even better than the original. Laughton, as Victor Hugo's misshapen bell-ringer Quasimodo, is haunting and unforgettable. Magnificently atmospheric studio recreation of medieval Paris also a big plus. Film debut of Edmond O'Brien, and U.S. debut of Maureen O'Hara. Also shown in computer-colored version.▼

Hunchback of Notre Dame, The (1957-French) **C-104m.** **½ D: Jean Delannoy. Gina Lollobrigida, Anthony Quinn, Jean Danet, Alain Cuny. Quinn makes a valiant try in lead role, but film misses scope and flavor of Victor Hugo novel.

Hunchback of Notre Dame, The (1982) **C-150m. TVM** D: Michael Tuchner. Anthony Hopkins, Derek Jacobi, Lesley-Anne Down, Robert Powell, John Gielgud, David Suchet, Gerry Sundquist, Tim Pigott-Smith, Alan Webb, Roland Culver. Rousing new production of the Victor Hugo classic, adapted by John Gay. Highlighted by Hopkins's carefully shaded portrait of Quasimodo and production designer John Stoll's detailed replica of Paris's Notre Dame Cathedral, built on the backlot of Pinewood Studios outside London. Above average.▼

Hunger, The (1983) **C-97m.** *½ D: Tony Scott. Catherine Deneuve, David Bowie, Susan Sarandon, Cliff DeYoung, Beth Ehlers, Dan Hedaya. Kinky trash masquerading as a horror film, with Deneuve as a vampire who needs fresh blood to survive. Bowie's quite good as Deneuve's companion—with an aging scene that's the film's highlight. As for the rest, beware, unless seeing Deneuve and Sarandon in bed together is your idea of a good time. Look for Ann Magnuson and Willem Dafoe in small roles.▼

Hungry Hill (1947-British) **92m.** ** D: Brian Desmond Hurst. Margaret Lockwood, Dennis Price, Cecil Parker, Jean Simmons, Eileen Herlie, Siobhan McKenna. Based on Daphne DuMaurier's book focusing on 19th-century Irish family with their vices and virtues highlighted; capable cast, with Herlie and McKenna making their film debuts.

Hunk (1987) **C-102m.** ** D: Lawrence Bassoff. John Allen Nelson, Steve Levitt, Deborah Shelton, Rebeccah Bush, James

Coco, Robert Morse, Avery Schreiber. Youthful nerd sells his soul to become a full-fledged California hunk—but still has to deal with the Devil (Coco) and his beautiful emissary (Shelton). Silly stuff benefits from an attractive and colorful cast.▼

Hunted, The (1948) 67m. **½ D: Jack Bernhard. Preston Foster, Belita, Pierre Watkin, Edna Holland. Trim minor film with Foster a cop out to reform girlfriend Belita; efficiently produced.

Hunted (1952) SEE: **Stranger In Between, The**

Hunted, The (1974) SEE: **Touch Me Not**▼

Hunted Lady, The (1977) C-100m. TVM D: Richard Lang. Donna Mills, Robert Reed, Lawrence Casey, Andrew Duggan, Will Sampson, Alan Feinstein. Undercover police woman flees for her life after being framed by mobsters. Predictable pilot movie melding elements from *The Fugitive* and *Police Woman*. Average.▼

Hunter (1971) C-73m. TVM D: Leonard Horn. John Vernon, Steve Ihnat, Fritz Weaver, Edward Binns, Sabrina Scharf, Barbara Rhoades. Enemy brainwash scheme uncovered when government agent survives racetrack crackup. But for what purpose? Sloppy, mechanical pace ruins good premise. Average.

Hunter, The (1980) C-97m. BOMB D: Buzz Kulik. Steve McQueen, Eli Wallach, Kathryn Harrold, LeVar Burton, Ben Johnson. Incomprehensible bio of real-life contemporary bounty hunter Ralph (Pappy) Thorson has plot holes that Hannibal could have led elephants through. McQueen's last film and probably his worst.▼

Hunters, The (1958) C-108m. **½ D: Dick Powell. Robert Mitchum, Robert Wagner, Richard Egan, Mai Britt, Lee Phillips. Veteran pilot Mitchum falls for wife of younger flyer Phillips—who crashes behind enemy lines. Fair of its type.▼

Hunters Are for Killing (1970) C-100m. TVM D: Bernard Kowalski, Bernard Girard. Burt Reynolds, Melvyn Douglas, Suzanne Pleshette, Martin Balsam, Larry Storch, Peter Brown. Ex-con (Reynolds), after drifting around for 3 years, decides it's time to return to home town, tyrannical father who refused to come to his aid during murder trial, woman he loves, etc. Uneven film fluctuates from scene to scene. Not bad, in all. Average.

Hunters of the Reef (1978) C-100m. TVM D: Alex Singer. Michael Parks, Mary Louise Weller, William Windom, Felton Perry, Steve Macht, Katy Kurtzman. Rival salvage crews vie for sunken treasure in shark infested waters. Busted pilot using concept and characters created by Peter (JAWS) Benchley is predictable action adventure. Average.

Hunt for Red October, The (1990) C-135m. ***½ D: John McTiernan. Sean Connery, Alec Baldwin, Scott Glenn, Sam Neill, James Earl Jones, Joss Ackland, Richard Jordan, Peter Firth, Tim Curry, Courtney B. Vance, Jeffrey Jones. Exciting, complex thriller from the best-seller by Tom Clancy. Connery stars as a Soviet submarine captain who may (or may not) be planning to defect to the U.S. during the maiden voyage of a supersecret nuclear sub; Baldwin is the American intelligence ace who tries to anticipate his every move. Long, potentially confusing at times, but always manages to make a course correction in the nick of time . . . and deliver another direct hit.▼

Hunting Party, The (1971) C-108m. BOMB D: Don Medford. Oliver Reed, Candice Bergen, Gene Hackman, Simon Oakland, L. Q. Jones, Ronald Howard, G. D. Spradlin. When his wife is kidnapped and raped by Reed and his gang, Hackman sets out to kill them one by one. Fine cast wasted in repellently violent Western that adds nothing new to tired plot, unless you count the bordello-equipped train.

Hunt the Man Down (1950) 68m. ** D: George Archainbaud. Gig Young, Lynne Roberts, Willard Parker, Gerald Mohr, Paul Frees. Ordinary whodunit with Young as public defender trying to solve a murder case.▼

Hunt to Kill SEE: **White Buffalo, The**▼

Hurricane, The (1937) 102m. ***½ D: John Ford. Dorothy Lamour, Jon Hall, Mary Astor, C. Aubrey Smith, Raymond Massey, Thomas Mitchell, John Carradine, Jerome Cowan. First-rate escapism on isle of Manikoora, where idyllic native life of Hall and Lamour is disrupted by vindictive governor Massey. Climactic hurricane effects have never been equaled. Lovely score by Alfred Newman. Disastrously remade in 1979.▼

Hurricane (1974) C-78m. TVM D: Jerry Jameson. Larry Hagman, Martin Milner, Jessica Walter, Barry Sullivan, Will Geer, Frank Sutton, Michael Learned, Lonny Chapman, Patrick Duffy. Vivid hurricane footage easily outshines a GRAND HOTEL-like collection of stereotyped characters trapped in disaster area. Below average.▼

Hurricane (1979) C-119m. BOMB D: Jan Troell. Jason Robards, Mia Farrow, Max von Sydow, Trevor Howard, Dayton Ka'ne, Timothy Bottoms, James Keach. Look what just blew in: a $22 million remake of the 1937 classic that may well put you to sleep! Retitled FORBIDDEN PARADISE for TV.▼

Hurricane Island (1951) C-70m. *½ D: Lew Landers. Jon Hall, Marie Windsor, Marc Lawrence, Edgar Barrier. Low-budget nonsense involving the fountain of youth and female buccaneer.

Hurricane Smith (1952) C-90m. ** D: Jerry Hopper. Yvonne De Carlo, John

Ireland, James Craig, Forrest Tucker. Romance and a search for gold are the substance of this tale involving a ship beached on a South Sea island.

Hurry Sundown (1967) **C-142m.** ** D: Otto Preminger. Michael Caine, Jane Fonda, John Phillip Law, Diahann Carroll, Robert Hooks, Faye Dunaway, Burgess Meredith, Robert Reed, George Kennedy, Frank Converse, Loring Smith, Beah Richards, Madeleine Sherwood, Rex Ingram, Jim Backus. Often ludicrous, overripe melodrama with ruthless Southerner Caine determined to buy up cousin's land, stopping at nothing to achieve goal. A curio for Fonda and Caine's offbeat casting, not to mention Horton Foote as one of the scripters. Jane's saxophone "solo," though, is worth checking out.

Hurry Up, or I'll Be 30 (1973) **C-88m.** ** D: Joseph Jacoby. John Lefkowitz, Linda De Coff, Ronald Anton, Maureen Byrnes, Danny DeVito. Mild low-budget comedy about efforts of schnook (Lefkowitz) to get his life in order before he hits 30. Made in New York.▼

Husbands (1970) **C-138m.** **½ D: John Cassavetes. Ben Gazzara, Peter Falk, John Cassavetes, Jenny Runacre, Jenny Lee Wright, Noelle Kao. Cassavetes' follow-up to FACES is not nearly as good; story deals with trio of middle-aged buddies who take off for Europe when their best friend dies. Some good scenes, but plagued by Cassavetes' habitual self-indulgence. Originally released at 154m.

Hush . . . Hush, Sweet Charlotte (1965) **133m.** *** D: Robert Aldrich. Bette Davis, Olivia de Havilland, Joseph Cotten, Agnes Moorehead, Cecil Kellaway, Victor Buono, Mary Astor, Bruce Dern. Macabre story of a family with a skeleton in its closet, confusing at times but worth watching for its cast. Bette is Olivia's victimized cousin; Cotten is Olivia's boyfriend.▼

Hussy (1980-British) **C-95m.** *½ D: Matthew Chapman. Helen Mirren, John Shea, Murray Salem, Paul Angelis, Jenny Runacre. Muddled, poorly directed melodrama centering on hooker Mirren, boyfriend Shea, and illicit drugs. Mirren tries, but cannot rise above the material.▼

Hustle (1975) **C-120m.** BOMB D: Robert Aldrich. Burt Reynolds, Catherine Deneuve, Ben Johnson, Paul Winfield, Eileen Brennan, Eddie Albert, Ernest Borgnine, Jack Carter, Catherine Bach. Pretentious, foul-mouthed and foul-minded story about an L.A. cop and a high-class call-girl who dream of escaping from their gritty life but never make it. This one's the pits.▼

Hustler, The (1961) **135m.** **** D: Robert Rossen. Paul Newman, Jackie Gleason, Piper Laurie, George C. Scott, Myron McCormick, Murray Hamilton, Michael Constantine, Jake LaMotta, Vincent Gar-

denia. Newman is outstanding as disenchanted drifter and pool hustler who challenges legendary Minnesota Fats (Gleason). Dingy pool-hall atmosphere is vividly realized in this incisive film. Cinematographer Eugen Shuftan won an Oscar for his work. Followed years later by sequel, THE COLOR OF MONEY.▼

Hustler of Muscle Beach, The (1980) **C-97m.** TVM D: Jonathan Kaplan. Richard Hatch, Kay Lenz, Veronica Hamel, Jeannette Nolan, Joe Santos, Bobby Van, Kenneth McMillan, Jack Carter. N.Y.C. hustler heads west and gets involved in the unique world of bodybuilders and iron pumpers. Average.

Hustler Squad SEE: **Doll Squad, The**▼

Hustling (1975) **C-100m.** TVM D: Joseph Sargent. Lee Remick, Jill Clayburgh, Monte Markham, Alex Rocco, Dick O'-Neill, Burt Young, Melanie Mayron. Searing drama by Fay Kanin about prostitution racket, well-acted by Remick as an investigative reporter (à la Gail Sheehy, who wrote the book on which this was based) and Clayburgh, giving a gritty portrait of a hooker. Played for the sensational. Above average.▼

Hypnotic Eye, The (1960) **79m.** ** D: George Blair. Jacques Bergerac, Merry Anders, Marcia Henderson, Allison Hayes. Partially successful chiller of theatrical mesmerizer with penchant for having female victims disfigure themselves.

Hysterical (1983) **C-87m.** BOMB D: Chris Bearde. William, Mark and Brett Hudson, Cindy Pickett, Richard Kiel, Julie Newmar, Bud Cort, Robert Donner, Murray Hamilton, Clint Walker, Franklin Ajaye, Charlie Callas, Keenan Wynn, Gary Owens. Lame parody of AMITYVILLE/EXORCIST type pictures that hoped to launch the Hudson Brothers on a screen career, and didn't.▼

I Accuse! (1958-British) **99m.** **½ D: Jose Ferrer. Jose Ferrer, Anton Walbrook, Emlyn Williams, Viveca Lindfors, David Farrar, Leo Genn, Herbert Lom, Harry Andrews, Felix Aylmer, George Coulouris, Donald Wolfit. Sincere but pretentious treatment of the treason trial of Alfred Dreyfus (Ferrer), with Williams as his defender, Emile Zola. Screenplay by Gore Vidal.

I Aim at the Stars (1960) **107m.** *** D: J. Lee Thompson. Curt Jurgens, Victoria Shaw, Herbert Lom, Gia Scala. Low-key fictional history of Nazi missile scientist Werner Von Braun and his problems adjusting to life in America.

I Am a Camera (1955-British) **98m.** ***½ D: Henry Cornelius. Julie Harris, Laurence Harvey, Shelley Winters, Ron Randell, Patrick McGoohan, Peter Prowse. Intelligent adaptation of John van Druten's play (itself based on Christopher Isherwood stories) about pre-war Berlin, with Harris a delight as a fun-loving young woman who'll accept anything from anyone. Basis for the Broadway musical and film CABARET.▼

I Am a Dancer (1973) **C-93m.** *** D: Pierre Jourdan, Bryan Forbes. Documentary on Rudolf Nureyev is handled a little better than many dance films and may interest a larger audience than usual; includes shots of rehearsals and lots of footage with Margot Fonteyn.▼

✓ **I Am a Fugitive from a Chain Gang** (1932) **93m.** **** D: Mervyn LeRoy. Paul Muni, Glenda Farrell, Helen Vinson, Preston Foster, Edward Ellis, Allen Jenkins. Still packs a wallop after all these years, with Muni as innocent man brutally victimized by criminal justice system. Haunting finale is justly famous. Scripted by Sheridan Gibney and Brown Holmes, from Robert E. Burns' autobiographical story. Shown on TV as I AM A FUGITIVE; Burns' plight is also dramatized in the made for cable TVM THE MAN WHO BROKE 1,000 CHAINS.▼

I Am a Thief (1935) **64m.** ** D: Robert Florey. Mary Astor, Ricardo Cortez, Dudley Digges, Robert Barrat, Irving Pichel. Stilted adventure of jewel thieves and insurance fraud set on Orient Express. Good cast can't save indifferent script.

I Am the Cheese (1983) **C-95m.** **½ D: Robert Jiras. Robert MacNaughton, Hope Lange, Don Murray, Robert Wagner, Cynthia Nixon, Lee Richardson, John Fiedler, Sudie Bond. Paper-thin but occasionally appealing tale of alienated teenager MacNaughton, who has witnessed his parents' death, and the fantasies and realities of his life while under psychiatric care. From Robert Cormier's novel.▼

I Am the Law (1938) **83m.** **½ D: Alexander Hall. Edward G. Robinson, Otto Kruger, Wendy Barrie, John Beal, Louis Jean Heydt, Fay Helm, Barbara O'Neil. No surprises in this story of D.A. Robinson fighting corrupt city government, but it's done so smoothly you forget you've seen it before. Don't miss E.G. dancing the Big Apple at the beginning.▼

I Believe In You (1952-British) **93m.** **½ D: Michael Relph, Basil Dearden. Cecil Parker, Celia Johnson, Harry Fowler, Godfrey Tearle, Laurence Harvey, Joan Collins. Intelligent study of methods used by probation officers to reform their charges; tight editing.

I Bury the Living (1958) **76m.** *** D: Albert Band. Richard Boone, Theodore Bikel, Peggy Maurer, Herbert Anderson. Crisp little chiller about cemetery manager who finds he may have power of life and death by sticking white (or black) pins into a map of the graveyard.

I Can Get It for You Wholesale (1951) **90m.** *** D: Michael Gordon. Susan Hay-

ward, Dan Dailey, Sam Jaffe, George Sanders. Jerome Weidman's flavorful novel about N.Y.C. garment industry, with Hayward the fiery designer who'll cheat anybody to get ahead. Retitled: ONLY THE BEST.

Ice Castles (1979) **C-109m.** *** D: Donald Wrye. Lynn-Holly Johnson, Robby Benson, Colleen Dewhurst, Tom Skerritt, Jennifer Warren, David Huffman. Successful ice skating career of Iowa farm girl is interrupted after she is blinded in freak accident. Tops for the disease/affliction genre, with well-photographed skating sequences and good performances by all.▼

Ice Cold in Alex SEE: **Desert Attack**

Ice Follies of 1939 (1939) **82m.** **½ D: Reinhold Schunzel. Joan Crawford, James Stewart, Lew Ayres, Lewis Stone, Bess Ehrhardt, Lionel Stander, Roy Shipstad, Eddie Shipstad. Cast elevates routine story of Stewart trying to put over big ice show while his wife becomes a movie star. This was not exactly a career high point for any of the leading players. Final musical number is in color.

Iceland (1942) **79m.** ** D: H. Bruce Humberstone. Sonja Henie, John Payne, Jack Oakie, Felix Bressart, Osa Massen, Joan Merrill. Labored love story defeats this Henie musical, although skating and singing interludes are pleasant; song standard, "There Will Never Be Another You."

Iceman (1984) **C-99m.** ***½ D: Fred Schepisi. Timothy Hutton, Lindsay Crouse, John Lone, Josef Sommer, David Straithairn, Danny Glover. A Neanderthal man is found frozen in ice, and scientists manage to bring him back to life, but only young Hutton is interested in him as a human being and not a lab specimen. Fascinating and credible science fiction made all the more involving by Schepisi's fine direction. Haunting music score by Bruce Smeaton and a remarkable performance as the caveman by Lone.▼

Iceman Cometh, The (1973) **C-139m.** ***½ D: John Frankenheimer. Lee Marvin, Fredric March, Robert Ryan, Jeff Bridges, Martyn Green, Moses Gunn, Bradford Dillman, Evans Evans. Remarkably successful film of Eugene O'Neill's play about assorted barflies in a 1912 saloon; Marvin's Hickey is only adequate, but Ryan dominates an outstanding supporting cast. An American Film Theatre production. This was March's last film.

Ice Palace (1960) **C-143m.** **½ D: Vincent Sherman. Richard Burton, Robert Ryan, Carolyn Jones, Martha Hyer, Jim Backus, Ray Danton, Shirley Knight, Diane McBain, Karl Swenson, George Takei. Typically sprawling (and silly) Edna Ferber saga of two men whose friendship turns to bitter rivalry, and whose lives parallel the development of Alaska through the 20th century. Watchable, to be sure, but hokey from start to finish.▼

Ice Pirates, The (1984) **C-91m.** ** D: Stewart Raffill. Robert Urich, Mary Crosby, Michael D. Roberts, John Matuszak, Anjelica Huston, Ron Perlman, John Carradine, Robert Symonds. Spoofy blend of space opera and swashbuckler, set in an arid future where water has become the most precious of commodities. Script vacillates between clever and half-baked; claustrophobic direction (which won't help on TV) keeps this from being anything more than a passable rainy-afternoon flick.▼

Ice Station Zebra (1968) **C-148m.** **½ D: John Sturges. Rock Hudson, Ernest Borgnine, Patrick McGoohan, Jim Brown, Tony Bill, Lloyd Nolan. Standard Cold War nail-biter with all-male cast has Hudson a sub commander sailing for North Pole to await orders, not knowing that Cold War incident will ensue; McGoohan a British agent out to trap a Russian spy. Based on the Alistair MacLean novel; originally in Cinerama. Infamous as Howard Hughes' favorite movie!▼

Icicle Thief, The (1989-Italian) **C-90m.** **½ D: Maurizio Nichetti. Maurizio Nichetti, Caterina Sylos Labini, Heidi Komarek, Renato Scarpa. Ingenious satire of contemporary commercialism—and disrespect for the art of film on television—has Nichetti's *Bicycle Thief*-type drama being presented on TV with so many commercials that soon no one can separate the program from the ads . . . including the actors in the film! Nichetti plays with his audience, often amusingly, but also pulls the rug out from under them a bit too often.

I Confess (1953) **95m.** **½ D: Alfred Hitchcock. Montgomery Clift, Anne Baxter, Karl Malden, Brian Aherne, Dolly Haas, O. E. Hasse. A priest (Clift) hears a murderer's confession and is himself accused of the crime. Lesser Hitchcock film, made on location in Quebec, is nevertheless intriguing for its stark photography and symbolism.▼

I Could Go on Singing (1963-British) **C-99m.** **½ D: Ronald Neame. Judy Garland, Dirk Bogarde, Jack Klugman, Aline MacMahon, Gregory Phillips. Garland is famed singer returning to England to claim illegitimate son living with real father (Bogarde). Garland is exceptional in singing sequences revealing the true Judy; sadly, this was her last film.▼

I Could Never Have Sex With Any Man Who Has So Little Respect For My Husband (1973) **C-86m.** ** D: Robert McCarty. Carmine Caridi, Lynne Lipton, Cynthia Harris, Andrew Duncan, Dan Greenburg. Talky but amusingly offbeat comedy written by humorist Greenburg. A study of

guilt as two couples are stuck together on vacation on Martha's Vineyard.

I Cover Big Town (1947) **63m.** ** D: William C. Thomas. Philip Reed, Hillary Brooke, Robert Lowery, Robert Shayne, Louis Jean Heydt. Uninspired mystery has female reporter solving complicated murder case. Uneven cast. Retitled: I COVER THE UNDERWORLD.

I Cover the Underworld (1947) SEE: **I Cover Big Town**

I Cover the Underworld (1955) **70m.** *½ D: R. G. Springsteen. Sean McClory, Ray Middleton, Lee Van Cleef, Joanne Jordan. Republic pictures programmer of clergyman whose twin brother is an about-to-be-released gangster.

I Cover the War (1937) **68m.** ** D: Arthur Lubin. John Wayne, Gwen Gaze, Major Sam Harris, James Bush, Don Barclay. Second-rate pulp fiction about correspondent Wayne tangling with Arab rebel leader.

I Cover the Waterfront (1933) **70m.** **½ D: James Cruze. Ben Lyon, Claudette Colbert, Ernest Torrence, Hobart Cavanaugh, Maurice Black, Purnell Pratt, Wilfred Lucas. Dated but still entertaining yarn about tired but persistent waterfront reporter Lyon, who romances free-spirited Colbert to trap her father (Torrence), who has been smuggling Chinese immigrants. How long will it take for him to actually fall in love? Considered pretty raw in its day. ▼

I'd Climb the Highest Mountain (1951) **C-88m.** *** D: Henry King. Susan Hayward, William Lundigan, Rory Calhoun, Barbara Bates, Gene Lockhart. Touching story of 1900s family life in Georgia, reflecting Americana at its best.

Ideal Husband, An (1948-British) **C-96m.** **½ D: Alexander Korda. Paulette Goddard, Michael Wilding, Diana Wynyard, C. Aubrey Smith, Glynis Johns, Michael Medwin. Oscar Wilde's drawing room comedy receives classy presentation but is slow-moving.

I Deal in Danger (1966) **C-89m.** **½ D: Walter Grauman. Robert Goulet, Christine Carere, Donald Harron, Werner Peters. Feature version of TV series *Blue Light* involves adventures of Goulet pretending to be Nazi convert in order to help Allies.

Identity Unknown (1945) **71m.** **½ D: Walter Colmes. Richard Arlen, Cheryl Walker, Roger Pryor, Bobby Driscoll, Lola Lane, Ian Keith, John Forrest, Sara Padden. Occasionally moving but uneven psychological drama about a soldier with amnesia, who treks around the country attempting to discover his identity. The scenes with young Driscoll, who thinks Arlen's his dad, are a highlight.▼

I, Desire (1982) **C-100m. TVM** D: John Llewellyn Moxey. David Naughton,

Dorian Harewood, Brad Dourif, Marilyn Jones, Barbara Stock, Arthur Rosenberg, James Victor. Credit the cast for playing this one straight: An obsessed coroner's aide becomes suspicious of a Hollywood hooker who turns out to be a vampire. And there's not a tongue to be spied in cheek! Average.

I Died a Thousand Times (1955) **C-109m.** ** D: Stuart Heisler. Jack Palance, Shelley Winters, Lori Nelson, Lee Marvin, Earl Holliman, Lon Chaney. Overblown remake of Bogart's HIGH SIERRA with Palance as mad killer with soft spot for crippled girl (Nelson). Winters is his moll in this gangster run-through.

Idiot, The (1960-Russian) **C-122m.** **½ D: Ivan Pyrlev. Julia Borisova, Yuri Yakovlev, N. Podgorny, L. Parkhomenko, R. Maximova, N. Pazhitnov. Faithful if not inspired adaptation of Dostoyevsky novel of tormented soul and his peculiar interactions with others.

Idiot's Delight (1939) **105m.** *** D: Clarence Brown. Norma Shearer, Clark Gable, Edward Arnold, Charles Coburn, Joseph Schildkraut, Burgess Meredith, Virginia Grey. Disparate characters—including a tacky vaudevillian and his one-time flame, who's come up in the world—are forced to share each other's company in a hotel near the Italian border as WW2 is about to erupt. Robert E. Sherwood's Pulitzer Prize-winning play is badly dated, an interesting period piece, notable for its pacifist ideals . . . but frankly more interesting for Gable's famous song-and-dance routine to "Puttin' on the Ritz."▼

Idol, The (1966) **107m.** ** D: Daniel Petrie. Jennifer Jones, Michael Parks, John Leyton, Jennifer Hilary, Guy Doleman. Trash about worthless type who makes it with both mother and girl of his best friend; interesting only as chance to see latter-day Jones and watch Parks try to ape James Dean. Filmed in England.

Idolmaker, The (1980) **C-119m.** **½ D: Taylor Hackford. Ray Sharkey, Tovah Feldshuh, Peter Gallagher, Paul Land, Joe Pantoliano, Maureen McCormick, Olympia Dukakis. Fictionalized bio of rock producer Bob Marcucci, who guided (pushed?) Frankie Avalon and Fabian to stardom in the late '50s. A great idea overcome by a script that builds momentum and then drops the ball. Good performances, sharp direction, though little period flavor (even in rock vet Jeff Barry's slick music score).▼

I Don't Care Girl, The (1953) **C-78m.** **½ D: Lloyd Bacon. Mitzi Gaynor, David Wayne, Oscar Levant, Warren Stevens. Premise of George Jessel preparing film biography of Eva Tanguay is vehicle to recreate facets in life of the vaudeville star.

I Don't Want to Be Born SEE: **Devil Within Her, The**▼

I Dood It (1943) **102m.** ** D: Vincente Minnelli. Red Skelton, Eleanor Powell, Richard Ainley, Patricia Dane, Lena Horne, Hazel Scott, Jimmy Dorsey and Orchestra. Strained, overlong musicomedy about a tailor and his movie-star sweetheart; good songs include "Star Eyes" and "Taking a Chance on Love," but patchwork film lifts its big finale from Powell's earlier BORN TO DANCE! A remake (more or less) of Buster Keaton's SPITE MARRIAGE.

I'd Rather Be Rich (1964) **C-96m.** **½ D: Jack Smight. Sandra Dee, Maurice Chevalier, Andy Williams, Robert Goulet, Gene Raymond, Charles Ruggles, Hermione Gingold, Allen Jenkins, Rip Taylor. Airy remake of IT STARTED WITH EVE. Dee finds substitute fiancé to please dying grandfather who wants to see her happy. Only Chevalier-Gingold scenes have spice.

I Dream of Jeannie (1952) **C-90m.** ** D: Allan Dwan. Ray Middleton, Bill Shirley, Muriel Lawrence, Lynn Bari, Louise Beavers, James Kirkwood. Fictional biog of Stephen Foster, 19th-century American composer, suffers from low-budget Republic production.

I Dream of Jeannie: 15 Years Later (1985) **C-100m. TVM** D: William Asher. Barbara Eden, Wayne Rogers, Bill Daily, Hayden Rorke, MacKenzie Astin, Dori Brenner, Andre DeShields, Dody Goodman. Nostalgic revival of the popular series of the mid-1960s finds the genie Jeannie in blissful domesticity and svelte Barbara still an eyeful in her now navel-showing harem duds. The stars, though (Rogers in for Larry Hagman), disconcertingly wait in vain for the laugh track to catch up with them—and it wasn't included! Pilot for proposed new series. Average.

I Dream Too Much (1935) **95m.** **½ D: John Cromwell. Lily Pons, Henry Fonda, Eric Blore, Lucille Ball, Osgood Perkins. One of Pons' typical operatic vehicles; she and Fonda are married couple with career problems.▼

I Drink Your Blood (1970) **C-88m.** ** D: David Durston. Bhaskar, Jadine Wong, Ronda Fultz, George Patterson. To get revenge on sadistic band of hippies, young boy gives them meat pies infected with rabies and they go homicidally crazy.

I Eat Your Skin (1964) **82m.** BOMB D: Del Tenney. William Joyce, Heather Hewitt, Betty Hyatt Linton, Dan Stapleton, Walter Coy, Robert Stanton. Scientifically-created zombies menace two-fisted hero on Caribbean island. Worthless. First released in 1970.▼

I Escaped from Devil's Island (1973) **C-89m.** BOMB D: William Witney. Jim

[541]

Brown, Christopher George, Paul Richards, Rick Ely, Richard Rust, Jan Merlin. Produced by the Corman boys (Roger and Gene) in Mexico and the Caribbean, this actioner is an insult to vet director Witney's standing with buffs who know his earlier work. Violent, vulgar.

I Escaped from the Gestapo (1943) **75m.** ** D: Harold Young. Dean Jagger, John Carradine, Mary Brian, William Henry, Sidney Blackmer, Ian Keith. Low-budget WW2 thriller; title tells the story. Retitled: NO ESCAPE.

if. . . . (1969-British) **C/B&W-111m.** **** D: Lindsay Anderson. Malcolm McDowell, David Wood, Richard Warwick, Robert Swann, Christine Noonan, Arthur Lowe. Magnificent, surrealistic study of students at boarding school who plot revolution—or do they? Originally X-rated, later trimmed for wider acceptance.▼

If a Man Answers (1962) **C-102m.** **½ D: Henry Levin. Sandra Dee, Bobby Darin, Micheline Presle, John Lund, Cesar Romero, Stefanie Powers, Christopher Knight, Charlene Holt. Trite pap of Dee and Darin (then married in real life) trying to outdo each other with jealousy-baiting antics.

If Ever I See You Again (1978) **C-105m.** *½ D: Joe Brooks. Joe Brooks, Shelley Hack, Jimmy Breslin, Jerry Keller, George Plimpton, Danielle Brisebois. Producer-director-writer-composer-arranger-conductor Brooks' followup to his mediocre YOU LIGHT UP MY LIFE is even worse; this time he stars, as a songwriter trying to rekindle old flame with Hack (in her starring movie debut). Breslin should stick to his typewriter.▼

If He Hollers, Let Him Go (1968) **C-106m.** *½ D: Charles Martin. Raymond St. Jacques, Kevin McCarthy, Barbara McNair, Dana Wynter, Arthur O'Connell, John Russell, Ann Prentiss, Royal Dano. Prison escapee St. Jacques tries to clear himself of false rape-murder charge. Lots of clichés, plus McNair's celebrated nude scenes.

If I Had a Million (1932) **83m.** ***½ D: James Cruze, H. Bruce Humberstone, Stephen Roberts, William A. Seiter, Ernst Lubitsch, Norman Taurog, Norman Z. McLeod. Gary Cooper, George Raft, Mary Boland, Charles Laughton, W. C. Fields, Wynne Gibson, Gene Raymond, Charlie Ruggles, Alison Skipworth, Jack Oakie, Frances Dee, Richard Bennett. Wealthy Bennett gives that sum to various people to see their reactions; all the episodes are good, but the most famous are Laughton's worm-turning and Fields' revenge on road hogs.

If I Had My Way (1940) **94m.** **½ D: David Butler. Bing Crosby, Gloria Jean, Charles Winninger, El Brendel, Allyn Joslyn, Claire Dodd. Title tune is chief asset of pleasant but standard Crosby vehicle in which he helps little Gloria find her guardian, vaudevillian Winninger.

If I'm Lucky (1946) **79m.** ** D: Lewis Seiler. Perry Como, Carmen Miranda, Phil Silvers, Vivian Blaine. Lukewarm musical with Harry James' band involved in political campaign; Miranda is good as always. Remake of THANKS A MILLION.

If It's Tuesday, It Still Must Be Belgium (1987) **C-100m. TVM** D: Bob Sweeney. Claude Akins, Bruce Weitz, Courteney Cox, Stephen Furst, Anna Maria Horsford, Peter Graves, Kiel Martin, Kene Holiday, David Leisure, Tracy Nelson, Richard Moll, Doris Roberts. Americans on a European bus tour in this less-than-sophisticated comedy "inspired by" the 1969 movie. Average.

If It's Tuesday, This Must Be Belgium (1969) **C-99m.** *** D: Mel Stuart. Suzanne Pleshette, Ian McShane, Mildred Natwick, Murray Hamilton, Sandy Baron, Michael Constantine, Norman Fell, Peggy Cass, Joan Collins. Funny study of Americans abroad on quickie tour; filmed throughout Europe. Host of cameos sprinkled throughout. Rehashed as a TV movie in 1987.

If I Were Free (1933) **66m.** **½ D: Elliott Nugent. Irene Dunne, Clive Brook, Nils Asther, Henry Stephenson, Vivian Tobin, Tempe Pigott, Lorraine MacLean, Laura Hope Crews, Halliwell Hobbes. Dunne and Brook shine as lovers trying to break away from their respective failing marriages. First-rate cast and production do wonders with tearjerker material.

If I Were King (1938) **101m.** *** D: Frank Lloyd. Ronald Colman, Frances Dee, Basil Rathbone, Ellen Drew, C. V. France, Henry Wilcoxon, Heather Thatcher, Sidney Toler. Preston Sturges script of roguish poet Francois Villon (Colman) in battle of wits with King Louis XI (Rathbone) plays with facts but makes good entertainment.

If I Were Rich SEE: Cash▼

I Found Stella Parish (1935) **84m.** ** D: Mervyn LeRoy. Kay Francis, Ian Hunter, Paul Lukas, Sybil Jason, Jessie Ralph, Barton MacLane. Shady actress with a past (Francis) comes to U.S. with her daughter (Jason) hoping for a quiet future; mild soaper.

I.F. Stone's Weekly (1973) **62m.** ***½ ✓ D: Jerry Bruck, Jr. Loving, concise documentary of the maverick Washington journalist is often funny and always moving. Narrated by Tom Wicker.

If Things Were Different (1980) **C-100m. TVM** D: Robert Lewis. Suzanne Pleshette, Tony Roberts, Don Murray, Arte Johnson, Chuck McCann, Dan Shor. Slick drama about a suburban housewife who's at wits end trying to hold her family together when hubby has a nervous breakdown. Suzanne's valiant but the lady as written is just too perfect. Average.▼

If This Be Sin (1949-British) **98m.** ** D: Gregory Ratoff. Roger Livesey, Myrna Loy, Peggy Cummins, Richard Greene, Elizabeth Allan. Maudlin multi-love-affair story set on isle of Capri. Original British title: THAT DANGEROUS AGE.

If Tomorrow Comes (1971) **C-73m. TVM** D: George McCowan. Patty Duke, Frank Liu, James Whitmore, Anne Baxter, Pat Hingle, Mako. California, 1941: young girl falls in love with Japanese-American; due to prejudices and tense atmosphere, they keep marriage secret. Enter Pearl Harbor. Typically stereotyped, one-sided; film's point of view and overall feel designed not to offend anyone. Average.

If Winter Comes (1947) **97m.** ** D: Victor Saville. Walter Pidgeon, Deborah Kerr, Angela Lansbury, Binnie Barnes, Janet Leigh, Dame May Whitty, Reginald Owen. Good cast fails to enliven wooden drama of young man who finds happiness by following code of honor; set in England.

If You Could Only Cook (1935) **70m.** *** D: William A. Seiter. Herbert Marshall, Jean Arthur, Leo Carrillo, Lionel Stander, Alan Edwards. Arthur and Marshall are superb team in comedy of wealthy couple pretending to be mobster Carrillo's maid and butler.

If You Could See What I Hear (1982-Canadian) **C-103m.** ** D: Eric Till. Marc Singer, R. H. Thompson, Sarah Torgov, Shari Belafonte Harper, Douglas Campbell, Helen Burns. Well-intentioned but overly cute, ultimately unreal biography of Tom Sullivan (Singer), the writer, composer, athlete, TV personality and Renaissance man who happens to be blind.▼

If You Knew Susie (1948) **90m.** **½ D: Gordon Douglas. Eddie Cantor, Joan Davis, Allyn Joslyn, Charles Dingle. Weak film of show biz couple is a delight for Cantor-Davis fans but pointless for others.▼

I Hate Actors (1986-French) **C/B&W-90m.** **½ D: Gerard Krawrzyk. Jean Poiret, Michel Blanc, Bernard Blier, Michel Galabru, Guy Marchand, Dominique Lavanant. Cute, slight little satire on Hollywood, with a series of murders comically disrupting the filming of a costume epic; agent Poiret is the prime suspect. Based on a novel by Ben Hecht and filmed mostly in beautiful black-and-white; set in Tinseltown, yet all of the dialogue's in French. Look very carefully for Gerard Depardieu.

I Hate Blondes (1981-Italian) **C-89m.** *** D: Giorgio Capitani. Enrico Montesano, Jean Rochefort, Corinne Clery, Marina Langner, Paola Tedesco, Ivan Desny. Funny comedy about ghostwriter Montesano, whose work inspires a series of real-life heists.

Crammed with sight gags; highlighted by a sequence in which Montesano searches for stolen jewels at a party.

I Hate Your Guts! SEE: **Intruder, The** (1961)▼

I Have Seven Daughters SEE: **My Seven Little Sins**

I Heard the Owl Call My Name (1973) **C-74m. TVM** D: Daryl Duke. Tom Courtenay, Dean Jagger, Paul Stanley, Marianne Jones, George Clutesi. Young Anglican priest is posted to a remote Indian village in British Columbia. Beautiful film translation of Margaret Craven book. Above average.▼

I, Jane Doe (1948) **85m.** *½ D: John H. Auer. Ruth Hussey, John Carroll, Vera Ralston, Gene Lockhart, John Howard, John Litel. Ludicrous courtroom "drama" of murderess Ralston, with the victim's wife (Hussey) defending her.

Ike: The War Years (1978) **C-196m. TVM.** D: Melville Shavelson, Boris Sagal. Robert Duvall, Lee Remick, Dana Andrews, J. D. Cannon, Darren McGavin, Paul Gleason, Laurence Luckinbill, Wensley Pithey, Ian Richardson, William Schallert. Duvall is four-stars as Eisenhower, fighting WW2 and having a war-time romance with his driver, Kay Summersby, sparklingly played by Remick. Originally aired as IKE in a six-hour miniseries form. Above average.▼

I Killed Rasputin (1967-French-Italian) **C-95m.** *½ D: Robert Hossein. Gert Frobe, Peter McEnery, Geraldine Chaplin, Robert Hossein, Ira Furstenberg, Ivan Desny. Well-mounted but ponderous story of the man who befriended and then murdered Rasputin; Frobe is simply awful.▼

Ikiru (1952-Japanese) **143m.** **** D: Akira Kurosawa. Takashi Shimura, Nobuo Kaneko, Kyoko Seki, Miki Odagiri, Yunosuke Ito. Minor bureaucrat Shimura, dying of cancer, searches for meaning in his life. Thoughtful, poignant examination of loneliness, with a brilliant performance by Shimura, but awfully depressing.▼

I Know My First Name Is Steven (1989) **C-200m. TVM** D: Larry Elikann. Cindy Pickett, John Ashton, Corin "Corky" Nemec, Ray Walston, Barry Corbin, Arliss Howard. Well-executed recounting of the case of Steven Staynor, who was snatched off the street in 1972 at age seven and held captive by a loner, only to escape seven years later and try to adjust to the family and life he had long forgotten—and whom he thought had forgotten him. A sad postscript: the real-life Staynor died in a motorcycle accident just months after this film's initial broadcast. Written by JP Miller and Cynthia Whitcomb. Originally shown in two parts. Above average.▼

I Know Where I'm Going (1945-British) **91m.** **** D: Michael Powell, Emeric

Pressburger. Wendy Hiller, Roger Livesey, Finlay Currie, Pamela Brown, Valentine Dyall, Petula Clark. Simple film of headstrong girl (Hiller) who plans to marry for money, stranded in Scottish seacoast town for a week, where she meets and slowly falls in love with Livesey. Very little plot, but an abundance of charm and wit. A quiet gem. Beautifully scripted by the filmmakers.

I Know Why the Caged Bird Sings (1979) **C-100m. TVM** D: Fielder Cook. Diahann Carroll, Ruby Dee, Paul Benjamin, Roger E. Mosley, Esther Rolle, Madge Sinclair, Constance Good, Art Evans. Black writer Maya Angelou's remembrances of her childhood in the Depression-era South. Good is more than good as young Maya and Rolle is a tower of strength as the grandmother who raises her. Scripted by Leonora Thuna, Ralph B. Woolsey, and Angelou, from her book. Above average.▼

Il Bidone SEE: **Swindle, The**▼

Il Grido SEE: **Outcry, The**▼

I Like Money (1962-British) **C-97m.** **½ D: Peter Sellers. Peter Sellers, Nadia Gray, Herbert Lom, Leo McKern, Martita Hunt, John Neville, Michael Gough, Billie Whitelaw. Subdued satirical remake of TOPAZE, with Sellers the timid schoolteacher who becomes an unscrupulous businessman.

I Like Your Nerve (1931) **69m.** *½ D: William McGann. Douglas Fairbanks, Jr., Loretta Young, Henry Kolker, Edmund Breon, Boris Karloff. Devil-may-care Fairbanks breezes into Latin country and sets his sights on Loretta—even though she's already promised in marriage. Tiresome comic romance. Karloff has tiny role as a butler named Luigi!

I Live for Love (1935) **64m.** **½ D: Busby Berkeley. Dolores Del Rio, Everett Marshall, Guy Kibbee, Allen Jenkins, Berton Churchill. Lesser Berkeley musical concerns backstage romance between Del Rio and Marshall. A couple of OK songs, but unfortunately no dancing.

I Live My Life (1935) **92m.** ** D: W. S. Van Dyke II. Joan Crawford, Brian Aherne, Frank Morgan, Aline MacMahon, Eric Blore. Crawford and Aherne are in love, but she's flighty and he's an archeologist. Glossy and empty.

I'll Be Home for Christmas (1988) **C-100m. TVM** D: Marvin J. Chomsky. Hal Holbrook, Eva Marie Saint, Courteney Cox, Peter Gallagher, Nancy Travis, Jason Oliver. Well-acted (if manipulative) holiday drama about one WW2 family in a small New England town, written by Blanche Hanalis but owing a lot to Saroyan's *The Human Comedy*. Above average.

I'll Be Seeing You (1944) **85m.** **½ D: William Dieterle. Ginger Rogers, Joseph Cotten, Shirley Temple, Spring Byington, Tom Tully, John Derek. Overblown David Selznick schmaltz. Rogers, convict home on parole, meets disturbed soldier Cotten; they fall in love.

I'll Be Yours (1947) **93m.** **½ D: William A. Seiter. Deanna Durbin, Tom Drake, Adolphe Menjou, William Bendix, Franklin Pangborn. Pleasant but undistinguished remake of THE GOOD FAIRY with Deanna in hot water after telling white lie to wealthy and amorous Menjou.

I'll Cry Tomorrow (1955) **117m.** ***½ D: Daniel Mann. Susan Hayward, Richard Conte, Jo Van Fleet, Ray Danton, Eddie Albert, Margo. Superlative portrayal by Hayward of star Lillian Roth, her assorted marriages and alcoholic problems. Everything a movie biography should be. Helen Rose won an Oscar for her costumes. Also shown in computer-colored version.▼

Illegal (1955) **88m.** **½ D: Lewis Allen. Edward G. Robinson, Nina Foch, Hugh Marlowe, Jayne Mansfield, Albert Dekker, Ellen Corby, DeForest Kelley, Howard St. John. Former D.A. Robinson becomes criminal attorney with gangster client, but lays reputation—and life—on the line to defend former assistant Foch for homicide. Valiant attempt to recapture spark of earlier Robinson vehicles; remake of THE MOUTHPIECE.▼

Illegal Entry (1949) **84m.** **½ D: Frederick de Cordova. Howard Duff, Marta Toren, George Brent, Gar Moore. Harsh narrative of federal agent assigned to uncover smuggling racket.

Illegally Yours (1988) **C-102m.** BOMB D: Peter Bogdanovich. Rob Lowe, Colleen Camp, Harry Carey, Jr., Kenneth Mars, Kim Myers. Juror Lowe is shocked to see that defendant Camp was once the girl he lusted for in elementary school, and snoops around on his own to clear her of the charge. Barely released, painfully unfunny farce, with Bogdanovich still trying to palm himself off as Howard Hawks; how bizarre to see pratfalling Lowe (in glasses) aping Ryan O'Neal in WHAT'S UP DOC? —who, in turn, was aping Cary Grant in BRINGING UP BABY.▼

I'll Get By (1950) **C-83m.** **½ D: Richard Sale. June Haver, William Lundigan, Gloria DeHaven, Dennis Day, Thelma Ritter. Remake of TIN PAN ALLEY, involving songwriter and his girlfriend; Jeanne Crain, Victor Mature and Dan Dailey make guest appearances.

I'll Get You (1953-British) **79m.** ** D: Seymour Friedman, Peter Graham Scott. George Raft, Sally Gray, Clifford Evans, Reginald Tate, Patricia Laffan. OK gangster yarn of Raft (FBI man) and Gray (British Intelligence) cracking a kidnapping syndicate. Originally titled ESCAPE ROUTE.

I'll Give a Million (1938) **72m.** ** D Walter Lang. Warner Baxter, Lynn Bari

Jean Hersholt, John Carradine, Peter Lorre. Amusing little idyll of rumor that an eccentric millionaire is posing as a hobo, causing droll results.

Illicit (1931) 81m. ** D: Archie Mayo. Barbara Stanwyck, James Rennie, Ricardo Cortez, Joan Blondell, Charles Butterworth. Stanwyck fears that marriage with Rennie will destroy their love, and is proven correct, in this silly film. Remade two years later as EX-LADY.

Illicit Interlude (1951-Swedish) 94m. **½ D: Ingmar Bergman. Maj-Britt Nilsson, Alf Kjellin, Birger Malmsten, Georg Funkquist. Moody film using flashback retells Britt-Nilsson's romance with now-dead lover, and its relationship to her present frame of mind. Original title: SUMMER-PLAY; also known as SUMMER INTERLUDE.▼

Ill Met By Moonlight SEE: **Night Ambush**▼

I'll Never Forget What's 'is Name (1967-British) C-99m. ***½ D: Michael Winner. Orson Welles, Oliver Reed, Carol White, Harry Andrews, Marianne Faithfull, Peter Graves. Excellent comedy-drama in which one man rebels against his good life and tries vainly to go back to simpler days.

I'll Never Forget You (1951) C-90m. **½ D: Roy (Ward) Baker. Tyrone Power, Ann Blyth, Michael Rennie, Dennis Price, Beatrice Campbell. American (Power) working in London is transported back to 18th century, where he falls in love with Blyth. Remake of BERKELEY SQUARE. Opens in b&w, switches to color.

I'll Remember April (1945) 63m. *½ D: Harold Young. Gloria Jean, Kirby Grant, Samuel S. Hinds, Milburn Stone, Addison Richards, Mary Forbes. Jean lacks verve as goodie-goodie vocalist out to solve crime for which Dad was blamed.

I'll See You in My Dreams (1951) 110m. **½ D: Michael Curtiz. Doris Day, Danny Thomas, Frank Lovejoy, Patrice Wymore, James Gleason. Warner Bros. formula musical biography at its hokiest: trite telling of Gus Kahn's life and times; songs include "Ain't We Got Fun," "It Had to Be You."

I'll Take Romance (1937) 85m. **½ D: Edward H. Griffith. Grace Moore, Melvyn Douglas, Stuart Erwin, Helen Westley, Margaret Hamilton. Silly story of opera star Moore kidnapped by agent Douglas has lovely title tune, operatic arias to keep it moving along.

I'll Take Sweden (1965) C-96m. ** D: Frederick de Cordova. Bob Hope, Dina Merrill, Tuesday Weld, Frankie Avalon, Jeremy Slate. Pseudo-sexy Hope vehicle, with everyone frantic over life and love; witless proceedings.

I'll Tell the World (1945) 61m. ** D: Leslie Goodwins. Lee Tracy, Brenda Joyce, Raymond Walburn, June Preisser, Thomas Gomez, Howard Freeman, Lorin Raker. Minor comedy with idea-man Tracy saving Walburn's failing radio station.

Illusions (1983) C-100m. TVM D: Walter Grauman. Karen Valentine, Brian Murray, Ben Masters, Wayne Tippitt, Joe Silver. High fashion designer gets entangled in international intrigue while searching for her supposedly dead husband in France. Average.

Illustrated Man, The (1969) C-103m. ** D: Jack Smight. Rod Steiger, Claire Bloom, Robert Drivas, Don Dubbins, Jason Evers, Tim Weldon, Christie Matchett. Young wanderer Drivas meets tattooed man Steiger, searching for the strange woman (Bloom), who "illustrated" his entire body. The wanderer sees futuristic stories in three of the illustrations, all of which also star Steiger and/or Bloom and Drivas. Disappointing, slow-paced adaptation of stories from Ray Bradbury's well-regarded collection. A few good moments but weak overall.▼

I Love a Bandleader (1945) 70m. ** D: Del Lord. Phil Harris, Leslie Brooks, Walter Catlett, Eddie Anderson, Frank Sully, Pierre Watkin. Formula claptrap about meek Harris who becomes a swinging bandleader; actors' natural abilities rise above material.

I Love a Mystery (1945) 70m. **½ D: Henry Levin. Jim Bannon, Nina Foch, George Macready, Barton Yarborough, Carole Mathews, Lester Matthews. Bizarre, entertaining whodunit based on popular radio show, with Bannon as Jack Packard, Yarborough as Doc Young. This one involves strange Oriental cult, and a prophecy of doom for bewildered Macready.

I Love a Mystery (1973) C-100m. TVM D: Leslie Stevens. Ida Lupino, David Hartman, Les Crane, Jack Weston, Terry-Thomas, Hagan Beggs, Don Knotts. Depressing attempt at adventure-comedy in spoof of old-time radio series features three detectives representing insurance company in search for missing billionaire; instead they find they've been lured to island. Filmed in 1967. Below average.

I Love a Soldier (1944) 106m. ** D: Mark Sandrich. Paulette Goddard, Sonny Tufts, Beulah Bondi, Mary Treen, Barry Fitzgerald. Reteaming of Goddard and Tufts after their hit in SO PROUDLY WE HAIL! doesn't match original; story examines problems of wartime marriages.

I Loved a Woman (1933) 91m. BOMB D: Alfred E. Green. Edward G. Robinson, Kay Francis, Genevieve Tobin, J. Farrell MacDonald, Robert Barrat. Robinson plays meat-packing plant owner whose life is destroyed by enticing, ambitious opera singer Francis. Absurd story moves like molasses; dialogue is good only for (unintended) laughs.

I Love Melvin (1953) C-76m. **½ D:

Don Weis. Donald O'Connor, Debbie Reynolds, Una Merkel, Allyn Joslyn, Jim Backus, Richard Anderson, Noreen Corcoran. Cute musical comedy. O'Connor tries to get to first base with Reynolds by pretending he can get her picture on the cover of *Look* magazine.

I Love My . . . Wife (1970) **C-95m.** **
D: Mel Stuart. Elliott Gould, Brenda Vaccaro, Angel Tompkins, Dabney Coleman, Joan Tompkins. The kind of comedy for which the word "vehicle" was invented. Rarely funny chronicle of Gould's lifelong sexual hangups suffers from witless script, bland direction.▼

I Love Trouble (1948) **94m.** *** D: S. Sylvan Simon. Franchot Tone, Janet Blair, Janis Carter, Adele Jergens, Glenda Farrell. Flippant mystery with private-eye Tone romancing Blair while searching for her missing sister-in-law.

I Love You (1981-Brazilian) **C-104m.** *½
D: Arnaldo Jabor. Sonia Braga, Paulo Cesar Pereio, Vera Fischer, Tarcisio Meira, Maria Lucia Dahl, Regina Case. Silly, pretentiously arty chronicle of relationship between Braga and Pereio, each of whom tries to manipulate the other. Sonia, however, is lovely to look at.▼

I Love You Again (1940) **99m.** ***½ D: W. S. Van Dyke II. William Powell, Myrna Loy, Frank McHugh, Edmund Lowe, Donald Douglas, Nella Walker. Hilarious story of amnesiac Powell—solid citizen in a small town—reverting to former life as con-man, but trying to forestall divorce proceedings by "his" wife (Loy). Ingenious script by Charles Lederer, George Oppenheimer and Harry Kurnitz.

I Love You, Alice B. Toklas (1968) **C-93m.** ***½ D: Hy Averback. Peter Sellers, Jo Van Fleet, Leigh Taylor-Young, Joyce Van Patten. Excellent comedy about the freaking out of mild-mannered L.A. lawyer. Sellers has never been better. Written by Larry Tucker and Paul Mazursky.▼

I Love You, Goodbye (1974) **C-78m.** TVM D: Sam O'Steen. Hope Lange, Earl Holliman, Michael Murphy, Patricia Smith, Kerry Shuttleton, Brian Andrews. Frustrated suburban housewife decides to leave her family to make it on her own. Gentle feminist drama, well-acted by Lange. Average.

I Love You, I Love You Not SEE: Together?▼

I Love, You Love (1961-Italian) **C-84m.** **½ D: Alessandro Blasetti. Marny Trio, Fattini and Cairoli, Don Yada's Japanese Dance Troupe, The Benitez Sisters. Documentary-style survey of love in various capitals of the world, occasionally spiced by imaginative use of footage.

I Love You Perfect (1989) **C-100m.** TVM D: Harry Winer. Susan Dey, Anthony John Dennison, Alley Mills, David Wilson, Tim Scott. An unlikely pair of lovers have their relationship tested when the woman gets devastating medical news. A bittersweet tale played with an incongruous light touch up to the final reel. Average.

I Love You to Death (1990) **C-96m.** **½ D: Lawrence Kasdan. Kevin Kline, Tracey Ullman, Joan Plowright, River Phoenix, William Hurt, Keanu Reeves, James Gammon, Victoria Jackson, Miriam Margolyes, Heather Graham. Lumpy black comedy about a gregarious Italian-American pizzeria owner whose constant womanizing remains a secret to his wife—until one day when she learns the truth, and then attempts to murder him, with spectacular lack of success. Kline is fun to watch, and Plowright is hilarious as his mordant, Slavic mother-in-law, but unfortunately, the film goes flat. Director Kasdan plays a lawyer in the closing scenes, and Kline's real-life wife Phoebe Cates has an unbilled part as one of his one-night-stands. Incidentally, this seemingly fanciful story is based on a real-life couple!

Image, The (1990) **C-110m.** TVM D: Peter Werner. Albert Finney, John Mahoney, Kathy Baker, Swoosie Kurtz, Marsha Mason, Spalding Gray. In this first cousin to NETWORK, a top TV news anchorman (Finney) chases the ratings at all costs, until a falling out with his longtime pal and a Savings & Loan scandal bring him disillusionment. Provocative, well-acted, but ultimately empty. Made for cable. Average.

Imagemaker, The (1986) **C-93m.** ** D: Hal Wiener. Michael Nouri, Jerry Orbach, Jessica Harper, Anne Twomey, Farley Granger, Maury Povich. The President's ex-media adviser, still reeling from his wife's death, has an audio tape that could incriminate his former boss; genuine or bogus, people are literally dying to get their hands on it. A muddled mess, though a sometimes entertaining one; high point is a hilariously melodramatic scene on a Washington talk show. Twomey good as an ambitious TV news reporter. ▼

Images (1972-U.S.-British) **C-101m.** ***½ D: Robert Altman. Susannah York, Rene Auberjonois, Marcel Bozzuffi, Hugh Millais, Cathryn Harrison. Difficult but fascinating film about a troubled woman who tries to sort out her life; images of reality and fantasy clash in a kind of continuous hallucination. Off-putting at first, but worth the effort to hang on. Filmed in Ireland.

Imagine: John Lennon (1988) **C-103m.** **½ D: Andrew Solt. Narrated by John Lennon. Unusual documentary, produced by Solt and David L. Wolper, assembled from 240 hours of footage from Yoko Ono's personal archives. Not exactly a puff job, but a bit discomforting given the obvious calculation that went into the project. Not to be missed are Lennon's confrontations with Al Capp and journalist Gloria Emerson.▼

I'm All Right Jack (1959-British) **104m.** ***½ D: John Boulting. Ian Carmichael, Terry-Thomas, Peter Sellers, Richard Attenborough, Margaret Rutherford, Dennis Price, Irene Handl, Miles Malleson. Carmichael works for his uncle and unwittingly upsets an elaborate and crooked business scheme in this memorable comedy. Sellers wonderful as labor leader. Scripted by Frank Harvey, John Boulting, and Alan Hackney, from Hackney's novel *Private Life*. Produced by Roy Boulting.▼

I-Man (1986) **C-100m.** TVM D: Corey Allen. Scott Bakula, Ellen Bry, Joey Cramer, John Bloom, John Anderson, Herschel Bernardi. Cabbie, son, and family dog find themselves pursued by villains after mysteriously becoming "indestructible." Disney movie pilot to a prospective series. Average.

I Married a Centerfold (1984) **C-100m.** TVM D: Peter Werner. Teri Copley, Timothy Daly, Diane Ladd, Bert Remsen, Anson Williams, Todd Susman. Swinger flips for centerfold model—and what else is new? Truly a time filler and, in Copley's case, an eye filler. Average.▼

I Married a Communist (1950) **73m.** **½ D: Robert Stevenson. Laraine Day, Robert Ryan, John Agar, Thomas Gomez, Janis Carter. Gomez is murderous Communist who blackmails shipping executive Ryan over past activities in this wildly "patriotic" film. Interesting, if not credible. Retitled WOMAN ON PIER 13.

I Married a Monster from Outer Space (1958) **78m.** **½ D: Gene Fowler, Jr. Tom Tryon, Gloria Talbott, Ken Lynch, John Eldredge, Jean Carson, Maxie Rosenbloom. One of the silliest titles in film history obscures pretty good little rehash of INVASION OF THE BODY SNATCHERS: Talbott notices that husband Tryon (as well as some of his friends) has been behaving very peculiarly of late. Some nice, creepy moments in chiller which has slowly developed a cult following.▼

I Married an Angel (1942) **84m.** ** D: W. S. Van Dyke II. Jeanette MacDonald, Nelson Eddy, Edward Everett Horton, Binnie Barnes, Reginald Owen, Douglass Dumbrille. Playboy Eddy dreams that he marries an angel (MacDonald) in this bizarre adaptation of Rodgers and Hart musical. This was MacDonald and Eddy's last film together. Songs include "Spring Is Here," title tune.▼

I Married a Shadow (1982-French) **C-110m.** *** D: Robin Davis. Nathalie Baye, Francis Huster, Richard Bohringer, Madeleine Robinson, Guy Trejan. Engrossing if sometimes overwrought drama of abandoned, pregnant Baye taking on the identity of another after a train wreck. Baye is radiant, particularly in the scenes with her newborn baby. Based on a Cornell Woolrich story previously filmed as NO MAN OF HER OWN (1950).

I Married a Witch (1942) **76m.** *** D: René Clair. Fredric March, Veronica Lake, Robert Benchley, Susan Hayward, Cecil Kellaway, Elizabeth Patterson. Witch burned in Salem centuries ago (Lake) comes back to haunt descendants of Puritan (March) who sent her to her death. Saucy comedy-fantasy based on a story by Thorne (*Topper*) Smith. Good special effects, too.▼

I Married a Woman (1958) **84m.** ** D: Hal Kanter. George Gobel, Diana Dors, Adolphe Menjou, Jessie Royce Landis. Lackluster events concerning harassed ad man Gobel who'd rather spend time with his gorgeous wife than overtime at the office. Look fast for young Angie Dickinson.▼

I Married Wyatt Earp (1983) **C-100m.** TVM D: Michael O'Herlihy. Marie Osmond, Bruce Boxleitner, John Bennett Perry, Ross Martin, Jeffrey DeMunn, Allison Arngrim. Title tells all, though the memoirs of singer-actress Josephine Marcus, who left a middle-class Jewish family to pursue a career, and then became the legendary lawman's wife, should have provided more interesting fare. Made in 1981, which explains posthumous credit for Ross Martin. Average.

I'm Dancing as Fast as I Can (1982) **C-107m.** **½ D: Jack Hofsiss. Jill Clayburgh, Nicol Williamson, Dianne Wiest, Daniel Stern, Joe Pesci, Geraldine Page, James Sutorius, Cordis Heard, Richard Masur, Ellen Greene, John Lithgow. Successful Valium-addicted TV documentary filmmaker Clayburgh undergoes harrowing ordeal when she quits pills cold-turkey. Searing because of subject matter, but not particularly well made; still, Clayburgh and costars are first-rate. Screenplay by David Rabe (Clayburgh's husband), based on Barbara Gordon's memoir.▼

I Met Him in Paris (1937) **86m.** **½ D: Wesley Ruggles. Claudette Colbert, Melvyn Douglas, Robert Young, Lee Bowman, Mona Barrie, Fritz Feld. Prolonged romantic comedy dependent entirely on charm of its stars. Vacationing Colbert, in Paris, then Switzerland, has to choose from Bowman, Young, and Douglas (you guess who wins out).

I Met My Love Again (1938) **77m.** **½ D: Arthur Ripley, Joshua Logan. Joan Bennett, Henry Fonda, Dame May Whitty, Alan Marshal, Louise Platt, Alan Baxter, Tim Holt. Familiar soaper of young girl Bennett running off with amorous author, with tragic consequences; acting surpasses script.

I'm From Missouri (1939) **80m.** ** D: Theodore Reed. Bob Burns, Gladys George,

Gene Lockhart, William Henry, George P. Huntley, Judith Barrett, Patricia Morison. Homespun Burns sails to England with a load of Army mules and encounters London society. Episodic, occasionally funny comedy.

I'm Gonna Git You Sucka (1988) **C-87m.** ******* D: Keenen Ivory Wayans. Keenen Ivory Wayans, Bernie Casey, Antonio Fargas, Steve James, Isaac Hayes, Jim Brown, Ja'net DuBois, Dawnn Lewis, John Vernon. Hip spoof of '70s blaxploitation films with Wayans (who also wrote and directed) as Jack Spade, vowing to avenge the death of his brother, who died of an o.g. (overdose of gold chains). Loose and good-natured, with some laugh-out-loud gags. Jim Brown and Isaac Hayes, who made so many straight-faced films of this kind, contribute some of the funniest moments. Look for Wayans' compatriot Robert Townsend in a cameo.▼

Imitation General (1958) **88m.** ****½** D: George Marshall. Glenn Ford, Red Buttons, Taina Elg, Dean Jones, Kent Smith, Tige Andrews. Travesty of what WW2 was all about has Ford taking place of killed superior officer, saving day and winning Elg.

Imitation of Life (1934) **109m.** ****½** D: John M. Stahl. Claudette Colbert, Warren William, Rochelle Hudson, Louise Beavers, Fredi Washington, Ned Sparks, Alan Hale, Henry Armetta. Believable but dated first version of Fannie Hurst's soaper of working-girl Colbert who makes good with Beavers' pancake recipe; Washington is fine as latter's daughter who passes for white. Ultrasentimental.

Imitation of Life (1959) **C-124m.** *****½** D: Douglas Sirk. Lana Turner, John Gavin, Sandra Dee, Dan O'Herlihy, Susan Kohner, Robert Alda, Juanita Moore, Mahalia Jackson, Troy Donahue. Plush remake of Fannie Hurst story, with Turner as career-driven actress; Moore is the good-hearted black woman who shares her life, and whose troubled daughter (Kohner) passes for white. Fine performances and direction overcome possible soapiness to make this quite credible and moving.▼

Immediate Family (1989) **C-95m.** ****½** D: Jonathan Kaplan. Glenn Close, James Woods, Mary Stuart Masterson, Kevin Dillon, Linda Darlow, Jane Greer, Jessica James, Mimi Kennedy. Well-off professional marrieds yearn for a child and hook up with a pregnant, underprivileged teenager via an adoption agency. Watchable change of pace from a pair of often angstridden leads but more slick and rose-colored than need be. Masterson stands out in a solid acting quartet.▼

Immigrants, The (1978) **C-200m. TVM** D: Alan J. Levi. Stephen Macht, Sharon Gless, Aimee Eccles, Richard Anderson, Ina Balin, Lloyd Bochner, Kevin Dobson, Roddy McDowall, Pernell Roberts, John Saxon, Susan Strasberg, Barry Sullivan, Yuki Shimoda. Son of Italian immigrants becomes a shipping magnate in turn-of-the-century San Francisco and claws his way into Nob Hill society. Based on Howard Fast's novel. Originally shown in two parts. Average.

Immortal, The (1969) **C-75m. TVM** D: Joseph Sargent. Christopher George, Jessica Walter, Barry Sullivan, Carol Lynley, Ralph Bellamy. Uneven mixture of sci-fi (from James Gunn novel) and drama. Racetrack driver discovers blood contains freak antibodies making him immune to aging process. Complications and subplots need far more running time. Average; pilot for the series.

Immortal Bachelor, The (1979-Italian) **C-95m.** ****½** D: Marcello Fondato. Monica Vitti, Giancarlo Giannini, Vittorio Gassman, Claudia Cardinale, Renato Pozzetto. Cleaning woman Vitti is on trial for killing philandering husband Giannini; jury member Cardinale decides she'd prefer him to her boring husband (Gassman). Slight Neapolitan comedy, with a fine cast wasted.▼

Immortal Battalion, The SEE: **Way Ahead, The**▼

Immortal Monster, The SEE: **Caltiki, The Immortal Monster**

Immortal Sergeant, The (1943) **91m.** ****½** D: John M. Stahl. Henry Fonda, Maureen O'Hara, Thomas Mitchell, Allyn Joslyn, Reginald Gardiner, Melville Cooper. OK wartime drama of inexperienced corporal (Fonda) who is forced to take command of patrol in Africa after sergeant dies.▼

Immortal Story, The (1969-French) **C-63m.** ******* D: Orson Welles. Orson Welles, Jeanne Moreau, Roger Coggio, Norman Ashley. Interesting tale of merchant who contrives to make sailor's myth of seducing a wealthy man's wife come true. Generally well done and, at times, dazzling; originally made for French television.

I'm No Angel (1933) **87m.** *****½** D: Wesley Ruggles. Mae West, Cary Grant, Edward Arnold, Gertrude Michael, Kent Taylor. West in rare form as star of Arnold's sideshow who chases after playboy Grant; highlight is Mae's courtroom plea.

I, Mobster (1958) **80m.** ****½** D: Roger Corman. Steve Cochran, Lita Milan, Robert Strauss, Celia Lovsky. Rugged account of gangster Cochran and events in his crime-filled life.▼

I, Monster (1972-British) **C-74m.** ****** D: Stephen Weeks. Christopher Lee, Peter Cushing, Mike Raven, Richard Hurndall, George Merritt, Kenneth J. Warren. Good, atmospheric production and ensemble performances cannot completely redeem boring adaptation of Stevenson's *Dr. Jekyll and Mr. Hyde*. This time, early student of Freud develops serum to relieve human inhibitions. Film was intended to be shown in 3D, which explains some of the unusual camera shots.

Impact (1949) 111m. *** D: Arthur Lubin. Brian Donlevy, Ella Raines, Helen Walker, Charles Coburn, Anna May Wong, Robert Warwick, Mae Marsh. Nice-guy Donlevy's wife is cheating on him. She and her lover plot to do him in . . . but there are complications. Entertaining, thoughtful drama will keep you guessing at every turn.▼

Impasse (1970) C-100m. **½ D: Richard Benedict. Burt Reynolds, Anne Francis, Vic Diaz, Jeff Corey, Lyle Bettger, Rodolfo Acosta. OK actioner with Reynolds and pals seeking out a cache of gold bullion on Corregidor.

Impatient Heart, The (1971) C-100m. TVM D: John Badham. Carrie Snodgress, Michael Brandon, Michael Constantine, Marian Hailey, Hector Elizondo. Young social worker seems to be able to solve everyone's problems except her own. Fair melodrama by Alvin Sargent with strong lead performances. Above average.

Impatient Years, The (1944) 91m. **½ D: Irving Cummings. Jean Arthur, Lee Bowman, Charles Coburn, Edgar Buchanan, Harry Davenport, Grant Mitchell, Jane Darwell. Thin comedy of soldier Bowman returning to civilian life with wife Arthur, finding trouble readjusting.

Imperative (1982-German) C/B&W-96m. *** D: Krzysztof Zanussi. Robert Powell, Brigitte Fossey, Leslie Caron, Sigfrit Steiner, Matthias Habich. Unusual, intense chronicle of math professor Powell's attempt to find spiritual understanding. Occasionally overdone but still provocative and worthwhile.

Imperfect Lady, The (1947) 97m. ** D: Lewis Allen. Teresa Wright, Ray Milland, Cedric Hardwicke, Virginia Field, Anthony Quinn, Reginald Owen. Undistinguished drama of Parliament member falling in love with ballerina in London during 1890s.

Imperial Venus (1962-French-Italian) C-120m. ** D: Jean Delannoy. Gina Lollobrigida, Stephen Boyd, Raymond Pellegrin, Micheline Presle, Gabriele Ferzetti, Massimo Girotti. Lumpy spectacle about how Paolina Bonaparte, Napoleon's hot-blooded sister, spread her charms around practically his entire army in her lust for power.▼

Impersonator, The (1961-British) 64m. ** D: Alfred Shaughnessy. John Crawford, Jane Griffiths, Patricia Burke, John Salew, Yvonne Ball. Satisfactory chiller programmer of murder in a small village, with Crawford trying to clear himself; offbeat climax.

Importance of Being Earnest, The (1952-

British) C-95m. *** D: Anthony Asquith. Michael Redgrave, Michael Denison, Richard Wattis, Edith Evans, Margaret Rutherford, Joan Greenwood, Dorothy Tutin. Oscar Wilde's peerless comedy of manners set in Victorian England is given admirable treatment by most able cast.▼

Impossible Object SEE: **Story of a Love Story**

Impossible Spy, The (1987-U.S.-British) C-96m. TVM D: Jim Goddard. John Shea, Eli Wallach, Michal Bat-Adam, Rami Danon, Sasson Gabay, Chaim Girafi. Absorbing spy thriller about Elie Cohen, an Egyptian-born Israeli who is persuaded to become a government agent and winds up leading a double life—as a mild-mannered (mostly absentee) husband and father in Israel, and as a wealthy businessman who infiltrates the highest levels of the Syrian government. Fascinating story based on the exploits of a real-life Israeli hero. Made for cable, and originally shown at 89m. Above average.▼

Impossible Years, The (1968) C-92m. BOMB D: Michael Gordon. David Niven, Lola Albright, Chad Everett, Ozzie Nelson, Cristina Ferrare. Stupid, leering sex farce based on the hit Broadway play about psychiatrist who has problems of his own with nubile young daughter; the most obscene G-rated film of all.

Imposter, The (1975) C-78m. TVM D: Edward M. Abroms. Paul Hecht, Nancy Kelly, Meredith Baxter, Jack Ging, Barbara Baxley, John Vernon, Edward Asner. Ex-Army intelligence officer Hecht accepts $5000 to impersonate a man targeted for assassination. Routine movie and projected series pilot. Average.

Imposter, The (1984) C-100m. TVM D: Michael Pressman. Anthony Geary, Lorna Patterson, Jordan Charney, Penny Johnson, Billy Dee Williams. Hard-to-swallow tale of a con man who talks his way into job as high school principal so he can wipe out the student drug problem. Produced by Gloria Monty, the guiding hand behind several daytime soap operas, and onetime actress Nancy Malone. Below average.▼

Impostor, The (1944) 95m. **½ D: Julien Duvivier. Jean Gabin, Richard Whorf, Allyn Joslyn, Ellen Drew, Peter Van Eyck, Ralph Morgan. Well-acted but ordinary story of patriotic Frenchman who escapes prison, assumes new identity to join WW2 fight again. Retitled: STRANGE CONFESSION.

Improper Channels (1981-Canadian) C-92m. **½ D: Eric Till. Alan Arkin, Mariette Hartley, Sarah Stevens, Monica Parker, Harry Ditson. OK comedy with oddball architect Arkin erroneously accused of child abuse. Stevens, as his 5-year-old daughter, is cute; Hartley, as his estranged wife, is wasted.▼

Impulse (1974) **C-91m.** BOMB D: William Grefe. Ruth Roman, William Shatner, Harold Sakata, Kim Nicholas, Jennifer Bishop, James Dobson. Distasteful Floridamade cheapie with Shatner overacting as a child-molester. Truly awful. Originally titled WANT A RIDE, LITTLE GIRL?▼

Impulse (1984) **C-91m.** *½ D: Graham Baker. Tim Matheson, Meg Tilly, Hume Cronyn, John Karlen, Bill Paxton, Amy Stryker. Matheson visits girlfriend Tilly in a small farming community, finds the citizens are robbing banks, shooting children, urinating on cars. Plodding reverse variation on INVASION OF THE BODY SNATCHERS—here, everyone exhibits *too much* emotion.▼

Impulse (1990) **C-108m.** *** D: Sondra Locke. Theresa Russell, Jeff Fahey, George Dzundza, Alan Rosenburg, Nicholas Mele, Eli Danker, Charles McCaughan, Lynne Thigpen, Shawn Elliott. Half-standard, half-fresh, and always tough: honest narc Russell, moonlighting as an L.A. streetwalker for the vice squad, briefly but fatefully yields to corruption after lousy hours and failed relationships combine to wear her down. Underrated sleeper doesn't exactly expand parameters of the cop genre, but benefits from a memorable central character; arguably Russell's best performance to date.▼

Impure Thoughts (1985) **C-87m.** **½ D: Michael A. Simpson. Brad Dourif, Lane Davies, Terry Beaver, John Putch, Joe Conley, Mary McDonough, Mary Nell Santacroce, narration by Dame Judith Anderson. A quartet of men have died; they meet in Purgatory and recall their lives together as Catholic school students when JFK was president and no one had ever heard of Vietnam. Occasionally funny and insightful, with some truly wonderful moments, but it just doesn't hold together.▼

Inadmissible Evidence (1968-British) **96m.** **½ D: Anthony Page. Nicol Williamson, Eleanor Fazan, Jill Bennett, Peter Sallis, David Valla, Eileen Atkins. John Osborne's play about barrister who has reached saturation point with everyone and everything preserves Williamson's fine stage performance, but result is still photographed play, not a film.

In a Lonely Place (1950) **91m.** ***½ D: Nicholas Ray. Humphrey Bogart, Gloria Grahame, Frank Lovejoy, Robert Warwick, Jeff Donnell, Martha Stewart. Mature, powerful drama about a feisty, self-destructive screenwriter (Bogart) who has an affair with starlet Grahame while trying to clear himself of a murder rap. Excellent performances in this study of two turbulent characters set against realistic and cynical Hollywood backdrop. Written by Andrew Solt.▼

In a Shallow Grave (1988) **C-92m.** BOMB D: Kenneth Bowser. Michael Biehn, Maureen Mueller, Michael Beach, Patrick Dempsey, Thomas Boyd Mason. Gloomy, slow-moving tale of WW2 veteran Biehn, disfigured at Guadalcanal, who has retreated to his family's desolate Virginia homestead to brood about his condition (and wallow in self-pity). Biehn tries hard but is overpowered by film's snail-like pacing and bizarre, romantic story line (involving drifter Dempsey, whose character is weird in the extreme). One of the oddest and most maudlin dramas ever made. An *American Playhouse* coproduction.▼

In a Year of Thirteen Moons (1978-German) **C-129m.** ***½ D: Rainer Werner Fassbinder. Volker Spengler, Ingrid Caven, Gottfried John, Elisabeth Trissenaar, Eva Mattes. Extraordinary performance by Spengler in the difficult role of a pathetic transsexual conceived and abandoned by his mother while her husband was in a prison camp. Powerful, disturbing tale of loneliness, alienation, rejection, winningly directed by Fassbinder.

In Broad Daylight (1971) **C-73m.** TVM D: Robert Day. Richard Boone, Suzanne Pleshette, Stella Stevens, Fred Beir, John Marley, Whit Bissell. Recently blinded movie star (Boone) discovers wife's infidelity, plots double murder. Excellent cast in straightforward, no-nonsense suspense film written by Larry Cohen. Above average.

In Caliente (1935) **84m.** ** D: Lloyd Bacon. Dolores Del Rio, Pat O'Brien, Edward Everett Horton, Leo Carrillo, Glenda Farrell. Pedestrian romantic comedy filmed in Agua Caliente, with fast-talking magazine editor O'Brien wooing dancer Del Rio. Horton's comic relief is the saving grace, along with Busby Berkeley's production numbers for "Muchacha" and "The Lady in Red" (sung by Wini Shaw, with a novelty chorus by Judy Canova).

In Celebration (1975-British) **C-110m.** *** D: Lindsay Anderson. Alan Bates, James Bolam, Brian Cox, Constance Chapman, Gabrielle Day, Bill Owen. Overly theatrical but still taut, vivid drama depicting the pain, anger, and intense relationship of three brothers who return to the coal mining town of their youth for their parents' 40th anniversary. Based on a play by David Storey, which Anderson had directed on the stage; an American Film Theatre production.▼

Incendiary Blonde (1945) **C-113m.** *** D: George Marshall. Betty Hutton, Arturo de Cordova, Charlie Ruggles, Albert Dekker, Barry Fitzgerald, Mary Phillips, Bill Goodwin. Hollywoodized biography of 1920s nightclub queen Texas Guinan is Hutton all over. Plenty of old-time songs.

Inchon (1982-Korean-U.S.) **C-105m.** BOMB D: Terence Young. Laurence Olivier, Jacqueline Bisset, Ben Gazzara, Toshiro

Mifune, Richard Roundtree. Empty-headed Korean war epic produced by Rev. Sung Myung Moon's Unification Church. Olivier looks like a wax museum figure in his makeup as Gen. Douglas MacArthur. Laughable script punctuated by epic-scale battle scenes. Cut from original 140m. length.

Incident, The (1967) 107m. *** D: Larry Peerce. Tony Musante, Martin Sheen, Beau Bridges, Jack Gilford, Thelma Ritter, Brock Peters, Ruby Dee, Ed McMahon, Diana Van Der Vlis, Mike Kellin, Jan Sterling, Gary Merrill, Donna Mills. Tough, brutal story of two drunken hoods who terrorize passengers in N.Y.C. subway. Well made but unpleasant—and still topical. Film debuts of Sheen and Mills.▼

Incident, The (1990) C-100m. TVM D: Joseph Sargent. Walter Matthau, Susan Blakely, Robert Carradine, Peter Firth, Barnard Hughes, Harry Morgan, William Schallert. Matthau is first-rate as a small-town lawyer during WW2 who becomes a pariah when he's forced to defend a German POW in a murder trial. Written by Michael and James Norell. Matthau's TV movie debut. Above average.

Incident at Crestridge (1981) C-100m. TVM D: Jud Taylor. Eileen Brennan, Pernell Roberts, Bruce Davison, Sandy McPeak, Cliff Osmond. Modern-day Western about a woman who decides to clean up her politically corrupt town by running for sheriff. Average.

Incident at Dark River (1989) C-100m. TVM D: Michael Pressman. Mike Farrell, Tess Harper, Helen Hunt, Arthur Rosenberg, Philip Baker Hall, K Callan, Nicolas Coster. Blue-collar worker takes on a local battery factory after his daughter is poisoned by toxic-waste pollution. Albert Ruben's earnest, environmentally indicting script is too pat. Made for cable. Average.

Incident at Midnight (1963-British) 58m. ** D: Norman Harrison. Anton Diffring, William Sylvester, Tony Garnett, Martin Miller. Based on Edgar Wallace short story, film deals with drugstore hangout of dope addicts and gangsters who ply their trade there; trim yarn.

Incident at Phantom Hill (1966) C-88m. **½ D: Earl Bellamy. Robert Fuller, Dan Duryea, Jocelyn Lane, Claude Akins. Solid little Western about greedy trio chasing after horde of gold, combating Indians, the elements and each other.

Incident in San Francisco (1970) C-98m. TVM D: Don Medford, Richard Kiley, Chris Connelly, Leslie Nielsen, Phyllis Thaxter, John Marley, Ruth Roman, Tim O'Connor, Claudia McNeil. Middle-aged businessman (Kiley) cannot prove innocence in assault-case-turned-murder, but young newspaperman (Connelly) attempts single-handed crusade. Well executed, but script unconvincing at wrong moments. Forget about ending. Above average.

Incident on a Dark Street (1972) C-73m. TVM D: Buzz Kulik. James Olson, Richard Castellano, William Shatner, David Canary, Robert Pine, Gilbert Roland. Uneven but interesting crime-actioner detailing typical day-in-the-life of a big city D.A. office, centering on murder of man as he left nightclub. OK performances, fair resolution. Average.

In Cold Blood (1967) 134m. **** D: Richard Brooks. Robert Blake, Scott Wilson, John Forsythe, Paul Stewart, Gerald S. O'Loughlin, Jeff Corey, Will Geer. Excellent semidocumentary adaptation of Truman Capote's book, tracing stories of two young killers (Blake, Wilson), their motives and eventual arrest after slaughtering innocent family. Incisive, engrossing, unsensational; masterful script, direction by Brooks, fine black-and-white photography by Conrad Hall.▼

In Country (1989) C-120m. *½ D: Norman Jewison. Bruce Willis, Emily Lloyd, Joan Allen, Kevin Anderson, John Terry, Peggy Rea, Judith Ivey, Richard Hamilton, Patricia Richardson, Jim Beaver. Disappointing, poorly executed film of Vietnam vet Willis (in a change-of-pace dramatic role) and niece Lloyd, two Kentuckians trying to come to terms with the war. Willis is good as a cynical, shell-shocked recluse, but script, from Bobbie Ann Mason's acclaimed novel, is flawed; character relationships are uneven, and too many questions are left unanswered (like Willis' medical condition). Beautifully handled concluding scenes, leading up to Washington, D.C. Veterans Memorial visit, can't redeem film.▼

Incredible Hulk, The (1977) C-100m. TVM D: Kenneth Johnson. Bill Bixby, Susan Sullivan, Jack Colvin, Lou Ferrigno, Susan Batson, Charles Siebert. Sci-fi adventure drama in the Jekyll-Hyde mold, taken from Marvel Comics. Bixby plays the hapless scientist whose radiation experiments turn him into a homeless wanderer and powerful seven-foot monster (Ferrigno) when enraged. Good for some thrills and laughs. Pilot for the series, and followed by several TVM versions, starting with THE RETURN OF THE HULK. Average.▼

Incredible Hulk Returns, The (1988) C-100m. TVM D: Nicholas Corea. Bill Bixby, Lou Ferrigno, Jack Colvin, Lee Purcell, Charles Napier, Steve Levitt, John Gabriel, Eric Kramer. Research scientist David Banner and his superhero alter ego The Hulk return to do battle with a thawed-out but klutzy Viking named Thor, sent after them by power-hungry industrialists trying to steal Banner's latest experiment. Less a pilot for a resurrected Hulk series than one for the newest Marvel Comics character, Thor. Followed by THE TRIAL OF THE INCREDIBLE HULK. Average.▼

Incredible Invasion SEE: **Sinister Invasion**▼

Incredible Journey, The (1963) **C-80m.** *** D: Fletcher Markle. Emile Genest, John Drainie, Tommy Tweed, Sandra Scott. Entertaining, well-made Disney story of three pets—two dogs and a cat—who make 250 mile journey across Canada on their own to be with their family of humans.▼

Incredible Journey of Doctor Meg Laurel, The (1979) **C-150m. TVM** D: Guy Green. Lindsay Wagner, Jane Wyman, Dorothy McGuire, Gary Lockwood, Brock Peters, Andrew Duggan, James Woods. Lady doctor returns from the big city to bring modern medicine to her kinfolk in Appalachia of the '30s and runs afoul of the local medicine woman (Miss Jane Wyman, as she is billed). Average.▼

Incredible Melting Man, The (1978) **C-86m.** *½ D: William Sachs. Alex Rebar, Burr DeBenning, Myron Healey, Michael Aldredge, Ann Sweeney, Lisle Wilson. Rebar is only survivor of outer space mission which has turned his body into a melting muck. Cheap, old-fashioned B horror film whose only saving grace is Rick Baker's excellent makeup effects.▼

Incredible Mr. Limpet, The (1964) **C-102m.** ** D: Arthur Lubin. Don Knotts, Jack Weston, Carole Cook, Andrew Duggan, Larry Keating. Knotts plays a milquetoast who dreams of becoming a fish—and miraculously gets his wish (turning into an animated cartoon figure). What's more, he helps the Navy spot Nazi submarines during WW2. Innocuous family fare goes on too long.▼

Incredible Petrified World, The (1958) **78m.** BOMB D: Jerry Warren. John Carradine, Allen Windsor, Phyllis Coates, Lloyd Nelson, George Skaff. Four people explore the ocean in diving bell and are plunged into land of catacombed tunnels. Don't get trapped into watching it.▼

Incredible Rocky Mountain Race (1977) **C-100m. TVM** D: James L. Conway. Christopher Connelly, Forrest Tucker, Larry Storch, Whit Bissell, Bill Zuckert, Mike Mazurki, Jack Kruschen. Madcap Western involving a cross-country grudge race between young Mark Twain (Connelly) and his longtime rival, Mike Fink (Tucker). Average.▼

Incredible Sarah, The (1976) **C-106m.** ** D: Richard Fleischer. Glenda Jackson, Daniel Massey, Yvonne Mitchell, Douglas Wilmer, David Langton, Simon Williams. Broadly sketched portrait of legendary French actress Sarah Bernhardt; Jackson chews the scenery in a flamboyant performance, but someone should have chewed up the script instead. Filmed in England.▼

Incredible Shrinking Man, The (1957) **81m.** *** D: Jack Arnold. Grant Williams, Randy Stuart, April Kent, Paul Langton, William Schallert, Billy Curtis. Outstanding special effects highlight intelligent story. Williams' mysterious shrinkage forces him to view the world—and himself—in a different light than ever before. Existential script by Richard Matheson, from his novel.▼

Incredible Shrinking Woman, The (1981) **C-88m.** ** D: Joel Schumacher. Lily Tomlin, Charles Grodin, Ned Beatty, Henry Gibson, Elizabeth Wilson, Mark Blankfield, Pamela Bellwood, Mike Douglas. Semi-spoof of SHRINKING MAN with Tomlin in three roles, principally as a suburban housewife whose constant exposure to household products causes her to dwindle; she becomes a media darling, then the target of an evil corporation. Never as funny or pointed as it would like to be, but worth catching for really peculiar color schemes and an amazing performance by Rick Baker as a gorilla named Sidney.▼

Incredible Two-Headed Transplant, The (1971) **C-88m.** *½ D: Anthony M. Lanza. Bruce Dern, Pat Priest, Casey Kasem, Albert Cole, John Bloom, Berry Kroeger. The head of an insane murderer is attached to the head of a mental retardate. Which head made this film?▼

Incredibly Strange Creatures Who Stopped Living and Became Mixed-Up Zombies, The (1963) **C-82m.** **½ D: Ray Dennis Steckler. Cash Flagg (Ray Dennis Steckler), Brett O'Hara, Atlas King, Sharon Walsh, Madison Clarke, Son Hooker. Legendary (thanks to that title) low-budget horror film about hideous goings-on at a carny sideshow, with lots of rock numbers thrown in. Truly bizarre film features gorgeously saturated color, awful acting, hideous dialogue, haunting atmosphere and little plot. Cinematography by Joe Micelli (author of *American Cinematographers' Manual*) with very young Laszlo Kovacs and Vilmos Zsigmond helping. Also known as THE TEENAGE PSYCHO MEETS BLOODY MARY.▼

"In" Crowd, The (1988) **C-96m.** **½ D: Mark Rosenthal. Donovan Leitch, Jennifer Runyon, Scott Plank, Joe Pantoliano, Bruce Kirby, Wendy Gazelle, Page Hannah. Surprisingly likable look at the lives and loves of those guys and gals who danced their hearts out on daily TV dance shows in the 1960s. Not as hip as John Waters' similarly themed HAIRSPRAY but fun anyway. Leitch is the son of '60s recording star Donovan.▼

Incubus, The (1982-Canadian) **C-90m.** BOMB D: John Hough. John Cassavetes, Kerrie Keane, Helen Hughes, Erin Flannery, Duncan McIntosh, John Ireland. Repulsive, poorly made horror thriller about sex murders in small Wisconsin town.▼

In December the Roses Will Bloom Again SEE: **Choices of the Heart**

In Defense of Kids (1983) **C-100m. TVM** D: Gene Reynolds. Blythe Danner, Sam Waterston, Joyce Van Patten, Georg Stanford Brown, Beth Ehlers. Attorney Danner chucks her job to defend kids in trouble with the law. Average.

Independence (1987) **C-100m. TVM** D: John Patterson. John Bennett Perry, Isabella Hofman, Sandy McPeak, Macon McCalman, Amanda Wyss, Stephanie Dunnam, Anthony Zerbe. Busted series pilot about an Old West sheriff dedicated to avenging the massacre of his family and protecting the frontier town he single-handedly tamed. Offbeat touches include overlapping dialogue, fast-paced intercutting, and the melding of comedy and drama— elements that earmarked creative consultant Michael Kozoll's earlier TV series *Hill Street Blues*. Average.

Independence Day (1983) **C-110m. ** D: Robert Mandel. Kathleen Quinlan, David Keith, Frances Sternhagen, Cliff De-Young, Dianne Wiest, Josef Sommer, Bert Remsen, Richard Farnsworth, Brooke Alderson, Noble Willingham, Susan Ruttan. Interesting but unfocused little picture about a young woman who's aching to leave her claustrophobic hometown but held back (in part) by romance with car mechanic Keith. Subplot about battered wife (superbly played by Wiest) seems to be a separate film altogether. Shown on TV as FOLLOW YOUR DREAMS.▼

✓ **Indestructible Man, The** (1956) **70m. ** D: Jack Pollexfen. Lon Chaney, Jr., Marian Carr, Casey Adams, Ross Elliott, Stuart Randall. Man returns from the dead seeking revenge on robbery cohorts who betrayed him; OK science-fiction.▼

✓ **Indiana Jones and the Last Crusade** (1989) **C-127m. **½ D: Steven Spielberg. Harrison Ford, Sean Connery, Denholm Elliott, Alison Doody, John Rhys-Davies, Julian Glover, River Phoenix, Michael Byrne, Alex Hyde-White. Follow-the-numbers adventure spectacle has Ford in fine form and Connery adding panache as Indy's archeologist father, whose mysterious disappearance (while searching for the Holy Grail) sets the story in motion. This deliberately old-fashioned Saturday matinée yarn has everything money can buy, but never really generates a sense of wonder and excitement. A definite improvement over the second Indiana Jones outing, but it still bears the mark of one too many trips to the well.▼

Indiana Jones and the Temple of Doom (1984) **C-118m. ** D: Steven Spielberg. Harrison Ford, Kate Capshaw, Ke Huy

Quan, Amrish Puri, Roshan Seth, Philip Stone, Dan Aykroyd. Headache-inducing prequel to RAIDERS OF THE LOST ARK, following further exploits of 1930s archaeologist/adventurer . . . only this time he's got a weaker story and wimpier heroine. Re-creates (and outdoes) a bunch of great cliffhanger stunts, but never gives us a chance to breathe . . . and tries to top the snake scene in RAIDERS by coming up with a variety of new "gross-out" gags. Followed by INDIANA JONES AND THE LAST CRUSADE.▼

Indianapolis Speedway (1939) **82m. ** D: Lloyd Bacon. Pat O'Brien, Ann Sheridan, John Payne, Gale Page, Frank McHugh, John Ridgely, Regis Toomey. Routine but watchable remake of Howard Hawks's THE CROWD ROARS, about the rivalry between brothers O'Brien and Payne on the racetrack. James Cagney's patented cockiness, the best thing about the original, is what's missing here.

Indian Fighter, The (1955) **C-88m. *** D: Andre de Toth. Kirk Douglas, Walter Matthau, Elsa Martinelli, Walter Abel, Lon Chaney. Exciting account of Douglas leading wagon train through rampaging Indian country.

Indian Love Call SEE: **Rose Marie** (1936)▼

Indian Paint (1964) **C-91m. ** D: Norman Foster. Johnny Crawford, Jay Silverheels, Pat Hogan, Robert Crawford, Jr., George J. Lewis. Fifteen-year-old Arikara (Crawford), his foal, and his coming-to-manhood. Harmless, forgettable.▼

Indian Scarf, The (1963-German) **85m. ** D: Alfred Vohrer. Heinz Drache, Gisela Uhlen, Corny Collins, Klaus Kinski. Edgar Wallace suspenser, with heirs to an estate being strangled one by one during sojourn at benefactor's country home.

Indian Scout SEE: **Davy Crockett, Indian Scout**

Indian Tomb, The (1959-German) **C-97m. **½ D: Fritz Lang. Debra Paget, Paul Hubschmid, Walther Reyer, Claus Holm, Sabine Bettmann, Rene Deltman. The pace picks up a bit in this second of Lang's Indian diptych, chronicling the events leading up to lovers Paget and Hubschmid's escape from the clutches of maharajah Reyer. Paget's exotic dance is a highlight. This and Part One (THE TIGER OF ESCHNAPUR) were originally dubbed, edited down to 95m., and released as JOURNEY TO THE LOST CITY.

Indian Uprising (1952) **C-75m. ** D: Ray Nazarro. George Montgomery, Audrey Long, Carl Benton Reid, Robert Shayne. Geronimo on the warpath again.

Indict and Convict (1973) **C-100m. TVM** D: Boris Sagal. George Grizzard, Reni Santoni, Susan Howard, Ed Flanders, Eli Wallach, William Shatner, Harry Guardino.

Drama traces investigation of deputy DA Shatner, accused of murdering his wife and her lover, although he was 150 miles away at the time. Good cast sparks courtroom action under judge Myrna Loy. Above average.

Indiscreet (1931) **81m.** *½ D: Leo McCarey. Gloria Swanson, Ben Lyon, Barbara Kent, Arthur Lake, Monroe Owsley. Tiresome romantic comedy-drama with Swanson trying to keep her scarlet past from Lyon. Art deco sets, and Gloria's rendition of two DeSylva-Brown-Henderson songs, aren't compensation enough for sitting through this one. Original running time 92m.▼

Indiscreet (1958) **C-100m.** *** D: Stanley Donen. Cary Grant, Ingrid Bergman, Cecil Parker, Phyllis Calvert, David Kossoff, Megs Jenkins. Bergman is renowned actress whom American playboy Grant romances and can't forget. Delightful comedy based on Norman Krasna play *Kind Sir*. Made in England. Remade as a TV movie.▼

Indiscreet (1988) **C-100m.** TVM D: Richard Michaels. Robert Wagner, Lesley-Anne Down, Maggie Henderson, Robert McBain, Jeni Barnett. Bland remake of the Cary Grant-Ingrid Bergman film which, slight as it was, had Cary and Ingrid to make it sparkle. Below average.

Indiscretion of an American Wife (1953-U.S.-Italian) **63m.** **½ D: Vittorio DeSica. Jennifer Jones, Montgomery Clift, Gino Cervi, Richard Beymer. Turgid melodrama set in Rome's railway station, with Jones the adulterous wife meeting lover Clift for one more clinch. DeSica's original 87m. version, titled TERMINAL STATION, was restored in 1983.▼

Indomitable Teddy Roosevelt, The (1983) **C-94m.** *** D: Harrison Engle. Narrated by George C. Scott. Excellent and innovative documentary about the remarkable, larger-than-life figure who became our 26th president. Artfully mixes newsreel footage with meticulous recreations featuring Bob Boyd in the role of T.R. Set to the stirring music of John Philip Sousa.▼

In Enemy Country (1968) **C-107m.** ** D: Harry Keller. Tony Franciosa, Anjanette Comer, Guy Stockwell, Paul Hubschmid, Tom Bell, Emile Genest. So-so programmer of WW2 intrigue, set in France and England, filmed on Universal's backlot. Not very convincing.

I Never Promised You a Rose Garden (1977) **C-96m.** *** D: Anthony Page. Bibi Andersson, Kathleen Quinlan, Reni Santoni, Susan Tyrrell, Signe Hasso, Diane Varsi, Dennis Quaid. Intelligent adaptation of Hannah Green's book about her treatment for schizophrenia as a teenager, focusing on relationship between her (Quinlan) and dedicated psychiatrist (Andersson). Graphic, clinical approach is often disturbing.▼

I Never Sang for My Father (1970) **C-93m.** ***½ D: Gilbert Cates. Melvyn

Douglas, Gene Hackman, Dorothy Stickney, Estelle Parsons, Elizabeth Hubbard, Lovelady Powell. Sensitive adaptation of Robert Anderson play about grown man (Hackman) faced with problem of caring for elderly father (Douglas). Fine job all around, but extremely depressing. Scripted by the playwright.▼

Infamous Crimes SEE: **Philo Vance Returns**

In Fast Company (1946) **61m.** D: Del Lord. Leo Gorcey, Huntz Hall, Jane Randolph, Judy Clark, Bobby Jordan. SEE: **Bowery Boys** series.

Infernal Idol, The SEE: **Craze**▼

Inferno (1953) **C-83m.** **½ D: Roy Baker. Robert Ryan, Rhonda Fleming, William Lundigan, Henry Hull, Carl Betz, Larry Keating. Fleming plots rich husband Ryan's demise, with surprising results. Good desert sequences. Originally in 3-D. Remade as a TV movie, ORDEAL.

Inferno (1980-Italian) **C-107m.** **½ D: Dario Argento. Leigh McCloskey, Irene Miracle, Sacha Pitoeff, Daria Nicolodi, Eleonora Giorgi, Veronica Lazar, Alida Valli. American returns to N.Y. from studies in Rome to investigate the gruesome murder of his sister, and discovers ''evil mothers'' wreaking supernatural havoc on both sides of Atlantic. Surreal, hypnotic shocker by Italian horror maestro Argento is short on sense, but long on style.▼

Infidelity (1987) **C-100m.** TVM D: David Lowell Rich. Kirstie Alley, Lee Horsley, Laurie O'Brien, Robert Englund, Courtney Thorne-Smith. With this title you expect suds and you get it, along with a pair of attractive but dull leads as yuppies with marital woes. Below average.

Information Received (1962-British) **77m.** ** D: Robert Lynn. Sabina Sesselman, William Sylvester, Hermione Baddeley, Edward Underdown. Potentially effective seesaw cat-and-mouse account of criminals Sesselman and Sylvester each trying to kill the other.

Informer, The (1935) **91m.** **** D: John Ford. Victor McLaglen, Heather Angel, Preston Foster, Margot Grahame, Wallace Ford, Una O'Connor, Joseph Sawyer. Masterpiece study of human nature tells of hard-drinking McLaglen, who informs on buddy to collect reward during Irish Rebellion. Powerful drama, based on Liam O'Flaherty's novel, with a memorable Max Steiner score. McLaglen won Best Actor Oscar, as did Ford, Steiner, and Dudley Nichols (for Best Screenplay). Filmed before in England in 1929. Remade as UP TIGHT.▼

Informers, The SEE: **Underworld Informers**

In For Treatment (1979-Netherlands) **C-99m.** ***½ D: Eric van Zuylen, Marja Kok. Helmert Woudenberg, Frank Groothof, Hans Man In't Veld, Marja Kok, Joop

Admiraal. Simple, pointed, powerful story of a middle-aged man who checks into a hospital for tests but is really dying of cancer; he must deal with a distant, maddeningly impersonal hospital system. Hard to watch because of the subject, but still poignant and never maudlin; a production of the Werkteater, a Dutch theater collective.

Infra-Man (1976-Hong Kong) **C-92m.** *** D: Hua-Shan. Li Hsiu-hsien, Wang Hsieh, Yuan Man-tzu, Terry Liu, Tsen Shu-yi, Huang Chien-lung, Lu Sheng. Princess Dragon Mom (Liu) and her odd assortment of monster underlings attempt to take over the earth—and it's Infra-Man (Hsiu-hsien) to the rescue. Action-packed, with gloriously corny dialogue (dubbed), outlandish costumes and sets, adequate special effects. Great fun.▼

Inglorious Bastards (1978-Italian) **C-100m.** ** D: Enzo G. Castellari. Ian Bannen, Bo Svenson, Fred Williamson, Peter Hooten, Michael Pergolani. Five soldiers about to be court-martialled during WW2 take off through France, hoping to make the Swiss border. Far-fetched story with a few good action scenes. Retitled COUNTERFEIT COMMANDOS.

In God We Tru$t (1980) **C-97m.** BOMB D: Marty Feldman. Marty Feldman, Peter Boyle, Louise Lasser, Richard Pryor, Andy Kaufman, Wilfrid Hyde-White, Severn Darden. Naive monk Feldman treks to L.A. to raise money for his monastery. A comedy that is tragically unfunny—including Pryor, who plays God. Feldman also co-wrote the script.

In Harm's Way (1965) **165m.** **½ D: Otto Preminger. John Wayne, Kirk Douglas, Patricia Neal, Tom Tryon, Paula Prentiss, Henry Fonda, Dana Andrews, Brandon de Wilde, George Kennedy, Carroll O'Connor, Slim Pickens, Larry Hagman, Bruce Cabot, Jill Haworth, many others. Overlong, overacted, and overly pretentious story of Navy man who goes out to capture strategic islands held by Japanese during WW2.▼

Inheritance, The (1947-British) **98m.** *** D: Charles Frank. Jean Simmons, Derrick DeMarney, Derek Bond, Katina Paxinou, Esmond Knight. Well-appointed chiller, with Simmons as innocent preyed upon by corrupt uncle; situated in Victorian London and Paris. Based on a novel by Sheridan Le Fanu. Original British title: UNCLE SILAS.

Inheritance, The (1976-Italian) **C-105m.** **½ D: Mauro Bolognini. Anthony Quinn, Dominique Sanda, Fabio Testi, Adriana Asti, Luigi Proietti. Moody melodrama about dying patriarch (Quinn) who wants to disown everyone but his calculating daughter-in-law (Sanda), who offers him sexual comforts. Well-acted, handsome production with emphasis on eroticism. Originally 121m.▼

Inherit the Wind (1960) **127m.** ***½ D: Stanley Kramer. Spencer Tracy, Fredric March, Gene Kelly, Florence Eldridge, Dick York, Harry Morgan, Donna Anderson, Elliot Reid, Claude Akins, Noah Beery, Jr., Norman Fell. Vocals by Leslie Uggams. Absorbing adaptation of Jerome Lawrence–Robert E. Lee play based on notorious Scopes Monkey Trial of 1925, when Clarence Darrow defended and William Jennings Bryan prosecuted a schoolteacher arrested for teaching Darwin's Theory of Evolution. All names are changed (Kelly's character is based on acid-tongued H.L. Mencken), but the issue is real and still relevant. An acting tour de force, with solid support from Morgan as the judge, Reid as a lawyer, Eldridge as March's devoted wife. Only offbeat casting of Kelly doesn't quite come off. Screenplay by Nathan E. Douglas (Nedrick Young) and Harold Jacob Smith. Remade as a TV movie.▼

Inherit the Wind (1988) **C-100m.** TVM D: David Greene. Kirk Douglas, Jason Robards, Jean Simmons, Darren McGavin, Megan Follows, Kyle Secor, John Harkins. Pallid version of the memorable Broadway play thrown awry by clashing acting styles of the two stars, and the elimination of some key scenes involving supporting characters. Ubiquitous writer John Gay did this adaptation and Peter Douglas (Kirk's son) produced. Average.

Initiation of Sarah, The (1978) **C-100m.** TVM D: Robert Day. Kay Lenz, Shelley Winters, Kathryn Crosby, Tony Bill, Elizabeth Stack, Morgan Brittany, Tisa Farrow. Occult tale surrounding a college sorority initiation; one of the coeds falls under the spell of a witch (Winters). Average.▼

In-Laws, The (1979) **C-103m.** *** D: Arthur Hiller. Peter Falk, Alan Arkin, Richard Libertini, Nancy Dussault, Penny Peyser, Arlene Golonka, Michael Lembeck, Ed Begley, Jr. Wacky comedy about a dentist (Arkin) who becomes involved in the bizarre intrigues of his daughter's father-in-law-to-be (Falk), who claims to be a CIA agent. Andrew Bergman's script is commendably unpredictable from start to finish; Libertini is hilarious as Latin dictator with a Señor Wences fetish. Enjoyable music score by John Morris. ▼

In Like Flint (1967) **C-114m.** **½ D: Gordon Douglas. James Coburn, Lee J. Cobb, Jean Hale, Andrew Duggan. Weak sequel to OUR MAN FLINT finds our hero going against secret society of women plotting to take over the world.

In Like Flynn (1985) **C-100m.** TVM D: Richard Lang. Jenny Seagrove, Murray Crutchley, Maury Chaykin, Robert Webber, Eddie Albert, William Conrad, William Gray Espy. A ROMANCING THE STONE clone with a minor change of sex. Pilot for a prospective series. Average.

In Love and War (1958) **C-111m.** **½ D: Philip Dunne. Robert Wagner, Dana Wynter, Jeffrey Hunter, Hope Lange, Bradford Dillman, Sheree North, France Nuyen, Mort Sahl. WW2 film in 1940s style, tracing the effects of war on three soldiers; handsome cast uplifts soaper.

In Love and War (1987) **C-100m. TVM** D: Paul Aaron. Jane Alexander, James Woods, Dr. Haing S. Ngor, Richard McKenzie, Concetta Tomei. Graphic but strangely uninvolving dramatization of the book by U.S. Navy Commander James B. Stockdale and his wife Sybil about their lives when he, for eight years, was being tortured as a POW during the Vietnam War and she was waging a fight back home as an organizer of POW wives. Average.

In Love with an Older Woman (1982) **C-100m. TVM** D: Jack Bender. John Ritter, Karen Carlson, Jamie Ross, Robert Mandan, Jeff Altman, George Murdock, Robert Townsend. Ingratiating bittersweet romantic comedy several notches above the routine mature lady-younger man movie that the title suggests, sparked by the two lead performances. David Kaufelt's novel *Six Months with an Older Woman* was the basis for Michael Norell's witty script. Above average.▼

Inmates: A Love Story (1981) **C-100m. TVM** D: Guy Green. Kate Jackson, Perry King, Shirley Jones, Tony Curtis, Pamela Reed, Paul Koslo, Fay Hauser, Penelope Allen. Credit everyone for playing this one straight, considering it's about a coed prison! Relish Curtis's flamboyant small-time hood and Jones's scenery-chewing send-up of Ida Lupino's hard-as-nails prison matron. Average.

In Name Only (1939) **94m.** *** D: John Cromwell. Carole Lombard, Cary Grant, Kay Francis, Charles Coburn, Helen Vinson, Peggy Ann Garner. Solid soaper with wealthy, married Grant falling for widowed Lombard, trying desperately to obtain a divorce from bitchy, manipulative social climber Francis. Beautifully acted by all. ▼

In Name Only (1969) **C-75m. TVM** D: E. W. Swackhamer. Michael Callan, Ann Prentiss, Paul Ford, Eve Arden, Elsa Lanchester, Ruth Buzzi, Chris Connelly. Several marriages set up by young Callan and Prentiss are discovered illegal; couples must be found and remarried. Rehash of WE'RE NOT MARRIED (which also featured Arden) is pleasant comedy, if not taken too seriously, thanks to good cast, dialogue. Script by Bernard Slade. Above average.

Inner Sanctum (1948) **62m.** ** D: Lew Landers. Charles Russell, Mary Beth Hughes, Lee Patrick, Nana Bryant. Satisfactory low-budgeter based on famous radio show, with fortune-teller predicting tragedy for a young girl on a train.▼

Innerspace (1987) **C-120m.** **½ D: Joe Dante. Dennis Quaid, Martin Short, Meg Ryan, Kevin McCarthy, Fiona Lewis, Vernon Wells, Robert Picardo, Wendy Schaal, Harold Sylvester, William Schallert, Henry Gibson, Orson Bean, Kevin Hooks, Kathleen Freeman, Dick Miller, Ken Tobey. Diverting tale of rambunctious Navy test pilot (Quaid) who undergoes miniaturization experiment and is accidentally injected into the body of hypochondriac Short. Heady combination of science fiction and comedy, with an off-the-wall sensibility that keeps things unpredictable . . though tightening would have helped. Short is a delight as the comic hero. Oscar winner for Best Visual Effects.▼

Innocent, The (1979-Italian) **C-115m.** **** D: Luchino Visconti. Giancarlo Giannini, Laura Antonelli, Jennifer O'Neill. Director Visconti's final film is among his greatest, a lavishly mounted tragedy about a Sicilian aristocrat who has the tables turned on him by the luscious wife he has chosen to ignore.▼

Innocent, The (1985-British) **C-101m.** **½ D: John Mackenzie. Andrew Hawley, Tom Bell, Kika Markham, Clive Wood, Kate Foster, Miranda Richardson. Medium drama about a young boy (Hawley) on the edge of puberty, growing up in a Yorkshire town during the Depression. Occasionally striking but too often slow.

Innocent Affair, An (1948) **90m.** ** D: Lloyd Bacon. Fred MacMurray, Madeleine Carroll, Buddy Rogers, Rita Johnson, Alan Mowbray, Louise Allbritton, Anne Nagel. Outmoded marital sex comedy of love and jealousy, bolstered by teaming of MacMurray and Carroll—their fifth and final pairing. Retitled: DON'T TRUST YOUR HUSBAND.

Innocent and the Damned SEE: **Girls Town**

Innocent Bystanders (1973-British) **C-111m.** **½ D: Peter Collinson. Stanley Baker, Geraldine Chaplin, Donald Pleasence, Dana Andrews, Sue Lloyd, Derren Nesbitt. Baker plays James Bond-like character involved in international manhunt for Russian scientist who has escaped from Siberia. Well-made but standard fare, with heavy doses of sadism and violence.

Innocent Love, An (1982) **C-100m. TVM** D: Roger Young. Melissa Sue Anderson, Doug McKeon, (Steven) Rocky Bauer, Christoff St. John, Pat Finley, John Colenback. Romance blossoms between a fourteen-year-old math genius and the nineteen-year-old coed he's tutoring in this derivation of the "older woman" movie cycle of the early '80s. Average.

Innocent Man, An (1989) **C-113m.** ** D: Peter Yates. Tom Selleck, F. Murray Abraham, Laila Robins, David Rasche, Richard Young, Badja Djola. Happily married airline mechanic is mistaken for a drug contact by a pair of on-the-take cops who've burst into his home; victim gets a hearty course of "Slammer 101" after both slugs frame him. Slick and soft at the center, despite some potentially compelling script elements; not too strong on credibility, either.▼

Innocents, The (1961-British) **100m.** ***½ D: Jack Clayton. Deborah Kerr, Michael Redgrave, Peter Wyngarde, Megs Jenkins, Pamela Franklin, Martin Stephens. First-rate thriller based on Henry James' *The Turn of the Screw*, with Kerr as governess haunted by specters that may or may not be real. Script by William Archibald and Truman Capote, brilliantly realized on film. Photographed by Freddie Francis.

Innocents in Paris (1953-British) **93m.** *** D: Gordon Parry. Alastair Sim, Ronald Shiner, Claire Bloom, Margaret Rutherford, Claude Dauphin, Laurence Harvey, Jimmy Edwards, Richard Wattis, Louis de Funes, Christopher Lee. Most engaging comedy about seven diverse types crossing the channel to France, each having wacky adventures. Original British running time 102m.

Inn of the Damned (1974-Australian) **C-118m.** **½ D: Terry Bourke. Judith Anderson, Alex Cord, Michael Craig, Joseph Furst, Tony Bonner, John Meillon. Bounty hunter Cord investigates the disappearances of travelers at an inn operated by sickies Anderson and Furst. Fair of its type, uplifted immeasurably by Anderson's entertaining performance.

Inn of the Frightened People (1971-British) **89m.** ** D: Sidney Hayers. Joan Collins, James Booth, Ray Barrett, Sinead Cusack, Tom Marshall, Kenneth Griffith. Parents of young girl who was raped and murdered take revenge on man they believe to be guilty. Sordid, low-budget thriller with some interesting moments. British title: REVENGE. Also known as TERROR FROM UNDER THE HOUSE.▼

✓**Inn of the Sixth Happiness, The** (1958) **C-158m.** *** D: Mark Robson. Ingrid Bergman, Curt Jurgens, Robert Donat, Ronald Squire, Athene Seyler, Richard Wattis. True story of English missionary and how she leads children on dangerous journey through enemy territory in pre-WW2 China. Bergman is wonderful and Donat memorable in final screen performance. Simple, effective score by Malcolm Arnold.▼

Inn on the River, The (1962-German) **95m.** **½ D: Alfred Vohrer. Joachim Fuchsberger, Klaus Kinski, Brigitte Grothum, Richard Much. Remake of THE RETURN OF THE FROG, this Edgar Wallace yarn involves series of brutal murders on the waterfront by the "Shark's" gang.

In Old California (1942) **88m.** ** D: William McGann. John Wayne, Binnie Barnes, Albert Dekker, Helen Parrish, Patsy Kelly, Edgar Kennedy, Dick Purcell, Harry Shannon. Wayne moves into Western town controlled by shifty Dekker, with inevitable confrontation.▼

In Old Chicago (1938) **95m.** ***½ D: Henry King. Tyrone Power, Alice Faye, Don Ameche, Alice Brady, Andy Devine, Brian Donlevy, Phyllis Brooks, Tom Brown, Berton Churchill, Sidney Blackmer, Gene Reynolds, Bobs Watson. Lavish periodpiece building up to Chicago fire of 1871; Oscar-winning Brady is Mrs. O'Leary, whose sons Power, Ameche, and Brown find their own adventures in the Windy City. Scripted by Lamar Trotti and Sonya Levien, based on a story by Niven Busch. Originally released at 115m.

In Old Kentucky (1935) **86m.** **½ D: George Marshall. Will Rogers, Dorothy Wilson, Bill "Bojangles" Robinson, Russell Hardie, Louise Henry, Charles Sellon. Story is as old as the hills—a family feud—but Rogers' natural charm and Bojangles' fantastic footwork make it most enjoyable. Rogers' last film.

In Old Oklahoma SEE: **War of the Wildcats, The**▼

In Our Hands (1984) **C-90m.** *** No director credited. Impressive documentary record of the June 1982 anti-nuclear rally in N.Y.C. Many speeches and musical performances; appearances by Helen Caldicott and Benjamin Spock, Pete Seeger, Carly Simon, Peter, Paul & Mary, Holly Near, Roy Scheider, Ellen Burstyn, Jill Clayburgh, Orson Welles, Meryl Streep, and dozens of others.▼

In Our Time (1944) **110m.** **½ D: Vincent Sherman. Ida Lupino, Paul Henreid, Nazimova, Nancy Coleman, Mary Boland, Victor Francen, Michael Chekhov. Lupino and Henreid try to save Poland from Nazi takeover in plush soaper that seeks to be meaningful propaganda; Nazimova is touching as Henreid's aristocratic mother. Never quite hits the mark.

In Person (1935) **85m.** **½ D: William Seiter. Ginger Rogers, George Brent, Alan Mowbray, Grant Mitchell, Samuel S. Hinds, Joan Breslau. In between TOP HAT and FOLLOW THE FLEET, Rogers made this formula romantic comedy about a movie star who hides away from the crowds and finds romance with Brent. Trivial, but pleasant.▼

In Praise of Older Women (1978-Canadian) **C-108m.** BOMB D: George Kaczender. Tom Berenger, Karen Black, Susan Strasberg, Helen Shaver, Alexandra Stewart, Marilyn Lightstone. Hungarian stud recalls nearly two decades' worth of conquests, all of whom are paraded across the screen in various stages of undress. Strasberg and Stewart are particularly praiseworthy, but nothing else is in this tease of a movie.▼

Inquiry, The (1987-Italian) **C-107m.** **½ D: Damiano Damiani. Keith Carradine, Harvey Keitel, Phyllis Logan, Lina Sastri. Intriguing story treats the resurrection of Christ as a mystery thriller. Carradine is a hardnosed investigator sent from Rome to find out what happened to the missing body of Jesus Christ; an official cover-up is presumed. Offbeat point of view holds interest. Excellent dubbing of the Italian supporting characters, but it's still distracting to hear Keitel's Bronx accent as Pontius Pilate.▼

In Search of America (1970) **C-72m. TVM** D: Paul Bogart. Carl Betz, Vera Miles, Ruth McDevitt, Jeff Bridges, Renne Jarrett, Howard Duff, Kim Hunter, Tyne Daly, Sal Mineo. Bridges stuns family when he refuses to go to college, eventually convinces entire family to reexamine their goals. Game attempt at relevance can't cut it, despite efforts by large, distinguished cast. Script by Lewis John Carlino. Average.

In Search of Gregory (1970-British) **C-90m.** ** D: Peter Wood. Julie Christie, Michael Sarrazin, John Hurt, Adolfo Celi, Paola Pitagora. Muddled film set in Geneva, about two potential lovers who fantasize about, but never meet, each other.

In Search of Historic Jesus (1980) **C-91m.** BOMB D: Henning G. Schellerup. John Rubinstein, John Anderson, Nehemiah Persoff, Andrew Bloch, Morgan Brittany, Walter Brooke, Royal Dano, Lawrence Dobkin. Sunn Classic drivel about Jesus and the Shroud of Turin. Film should be retitled "In Search of Morons Who Will Believe Anything." Narrated ominously by Brad Crandall.▼

In Search of Noah's Ark (1976) **C-95m.** *½ D: James L. Conway. Narrated by Brad Crandall. Cheaply made documentary reveals "new evidence" that Noah's ark really existed. Premise may hold your attention.▼

In Search of the Castaways (1962) **C-100m.** **½ D: Robert Stevenson. Hayley Mills, Maurice Chevalier, George Sanders, Wilfrid Hyde-White, Michael Anderson, Jr., Keith Hamshire. Expedition tries to locate missing sea captain, in journey that encounters fire, flood, earthquake and other disasters. Disney adaptation of Jules Verne suffers from muddled continuity; good cast does its best.▼

In Self Defense (1987) **C-100m. TVM** D: Bruce Seth Green. Linda Purl, Yaphet Kotto, Terry Lester, Billy Drago. Gail Edwards, Rick Lenz. Spunky Purl, who witnessed a triple murder, arms herself

against the assailant when the cops prove ineffectual. Average.

Inseminoid SEE: **Horror Planet**▼

Inserts (1976-British) **C-99m.** BOMB D: John Byrum. Richard Dreyfuss, Jessica Harper, Veronica Cartwright, Bob Hoskins, Stephen Davies. Pretentious, unending nonsense played out by five characters on one set: decaying Hollywood mansion in early thirties where once-famous director now makes porno films. Dreadful. The British version runs 117m.▼

Inside Daisy Clover (1965) **C-128m.** **½ D: Robert Mulligan. Natalie Wood, Robert Redford, Christopher Plummer, Roddy McDowall, Ruth Gordon, Katherine Bard. Potentially biting account of Wood's rise as Hollywood star in 1930s misfires; pat situations with caricatures instead of people.

Inside Detroit (1955) **82m.** ** D: Fred F. Sears. Dennis O'Keefe, Pat O'Brien, Margaret Field, Mark Damon. Ordinary exposé-style narrative of corruption in automobile industry.

Inside Job (1946) **65m.** ** D: Jean Yarbrough. Preston Foster, Ann Rutherford, Alan Curtis, Jimmy Moss. Sensible minor film of struggling young marrieds tempted to enter life of crime to solve their financial problems.

Inside Moves (1980) **C-113m.** **½ D: Richard Donner. John Savage, David Morse, Diana Scarwid, Amy Wright, Tony Burton, Bill Henderson, Bert Remsen, Harold Russell. Offbeat drama about a young suicide survivor (Savage) who falls in with a group of upbeat misfits and learns about self-esteem. A well-meaning film with some excellent performances and emotional highpoints but a few too many story flaws—including the final scene. This was Russell's first film since THE BEST YEARS OF OUR LIVES.▼

Inside Out (1975-British) **C-97m.** **½ D: Peter Duffell. Telly Savalas, James Mason, Robert Culp, Aldo Ray, Charles Korvin. Savalas engineers break-in at maximum security prison in East Germany to free notorious war criminal who knows whereabouts of a secret cache of gold. Not bad international caper. Retitled HITLER'S GOLD and THE GOLDEN HEIST.▼

Inside Out (1986) **C-87m.** **½ D: Robert Taicher. Elliott Gould, Howard Hesseman, Jennifer Tilly, Beah Richards, Dana Elcar, Nicole Norman. Sad little film about a man whose problems only begin with his agoraphobia—his irrational fear of being in public places. An interesting story that after a while, like its main character, has nowhere to go. Still, the vignette about the homeless man in the hallway is quite touching.

Inside Story, The (1948) **87m.** ** D: Allan Dwan. Marsha Hunt, William Lundigan, Charles Winninger, Gail Patrick.

Warm, minor film set in Depression days in Vermont, involving sudden circulation of large amount of money.
Inside Straight (1951) 89m. **½ D: Gerald Mayer. David Brian, Arlene Dahl, Barry Sullivan, Mercedes McCambridge. Study of greed and corruption as ambitious man rises to fortune in 1870s San Francisco only to find life empty.
Inside the Mafia (1959) 72m. **½ D: Edward L. Cahn. Cameron Mitchell, Elaine Edwards, Robert Strauss, Jim L. Brown, Ted de Corsia, Grant Richards. Gunblasting account of the Black Hand organization, with cast having field-day.
Inside the Third Reich (1982) C-250m. TVM D: Marvin J. Chomsky. Rutger Hauer, John Gielgud, Maria Schell, Blythe Danner, Trevor Howard, Viveca Lindfors, Derek Jacobi, Randy Quaid, Stephen Collins, Ian Holm, Elke Sommer, Renee Soutendjik, Robert Vaughn, Zoe Wanamaker, Mort Sahl. Jarring adaptation of Albert Speer's autobiography with a stellar cast headed by Dutch actor Hauer in his American TV debut. Jacobi is a standout as Adolf Hitler. Written and produced by E. Jack Neuman. Originally shown in two parts. Above average.▼
Inside the Walls of Folsom Prison (1951) 87m. ** D: Crane Wilbur. Steve Cochran, David Brian, Philip Carey, Ted de Corsia. Moderately successful account of crusade to improve harsh penitentiary conditions.
Insignificance (1985-British) C-105m. ***½ D: Nicolas Roeg. Gary Busey, Tony Curtis, Theresa Russell, Michael Emil, Will Sampson. Striking, gloriously cinematic examination of the meaning of fame in America and the perils of atomic warfare. The stars are cast as unnamed celebrities—a ballplayer, senator, actress, and professor—who resemble Joe DiMaggio, Joseph McCarthy, Marilyn Monroe, and Albert Einstein, and meet in a N.Y.C. hotel room in 1953. At once funny, ironic, thought-provoking. Wonderfully acted by all. ▼
In Society (1944) 75m. ** D: Jean Yarbrough. Bud Abbott, Lou Costello, Marion Hutton, Arthur Treacher, Thomas Gomez, Thurston Hall, Kirby Grant. Minor A&C, with the boys as plumbers mistaken for members of society; hectic slapstick finale. Includes chase footage lifted from NEVER GIVE A SUCKER AN EVEN BREAK.
Inspector Calls, An (1954-British) 80m. *** D: Guy Hamilton. Alastair Sim, Arthur Young, Olga Lindo, Eileen Moore. J. B. Priestley's play detailing British police detective Sim's investigation of girl's suicide. Via flashbacks he learns a family's responsibility for her fate. Clever plot finale.
Inspector Clouseau (1968) C-94m. ** D:

Bud Yorkin. Alan Arkin, Delia Boccardo, Frank Finlay, Patrick Cargill, Beryl Reid, Barry Foster. Scotland Yard calls on inept French detective to crack potential robbery; in spite of Arkin's talents, Peter Sellers is too well identified with the role (from other Pink Panther movies) for one to fully accept this characterization. Besides, film isn't particularly funny. Made in England.
Inspector General, The (1949) C-102m. *** D: Henry Koster. Danny Kaye, Walter Slezak, Barbara Bates, Elsa Lanchester, Gene Lockhart, Alan Hale, Walter Catlett. Kaye plays a buffoon who pretends to be a visiting bureaucrat in an Eastern European village. Entertaining musical adaptation of the Gogol story.▼
Inspector Maigret (1958-French) 110m. **½ D: Jean Delannoy. Jean Gabin, Annie Girardot, Oliver Hussenot, Jeanne Boitel. Famed French detective must track down notorious woman-killer. Retitled: WOMAN-BAIT.
Inspiration (1931) 74m. **½ D: Clarence Brown. Greta Garbo, Robert Montgomery, Lewis Stone, Marjorie Rambeau, Beryl Mercer, Oscar Apfel. Lesser Garbo about beautiful Parisian woman whose past makes her decide to leave Montgomery, even though she still loves him. Garbo has had much better material than this modern version of Alphonse Daudet's *Sappho*.
Instant Justice (1987-Gibraltar) C-101m. **½ D: Christopher Bentley (Denis Amar) Michael Paré, Tawny Kitaen, Peter Crook, Charles Napier. Solid action scenes spark routine drama of young marine Paré resigning his commission to go after the killers of his sister. Kitaen is the beautiful call girl who reluctantly helps him. Originally titled: MARINE ISSUE. ▼
Institute for Revenge (1979) C-78m. TVM D: Ken Annakin. Sam Groom, Lauren Hutton, Lane Binkley, Leslie Nielsen, Ray Walston, George Hamilton, Robert Coote. Tongue-in-cheek sci-fi about a sophisticated computer that assigns human operatives to correct wrongs against the defenseless and non-violently bring in the evildoers. Pilot to a prospective series. Average.
Insurance Man, The (1985-British) C-77m. *** D: Richard Eyre. Robert Hines, Daniel Day Lewis, Jim Broadbent, Hugh Fraser, Tony Haygarth. Dramatically uneven yet still ambitious, impressive account of a young dyeworker named Franz (Hines), whose body develops a rash, and his dealings with both the bureaucracy and a man named Mr. Kafka (Day Lewis), a claims assessor who also writes. A tribute to Kafka and his work, with a screenplay by Alan Bennett.
In Tandem (1974) C-78m. TVM D: Bernard Kowalski. Claude Akins, Frank Converse, Sondra Blake, Richard Angarola,

Ann Coleman, Janis Hansen, Titos Vandis. Tough veteran and young college-educated partner, gypsy truckers, get involved in a labor dispute in citrus country. Rugged performances led to subsequent *Movin' On* series (this film's subsequent title). Average.

Intent to Kill (1958-British) **89m.** **½ D: Jack Cardiff. Richard Todd, Betsy Drake, Herbert Lom, Warren Stevens. Potboiler about attempted assassination of Latin American dictator who has gone north for brain surgery.

Interiors (1978) **C-93m.** ***½ D: Woody Allen. Diane Keaton, Geraldine Page, E. G. Marshall, Maureen Stapleton, Kristin Griffith, Mary Beth Hurt, Richard Jordan, Sam Waterston. Woody Allen's first screen drama as writer-director is an Ingmar Bergmanesque study of a family full of unhappy, frustrated men and women; this drama of anguished lives is not for all tastes, but extremely well done.▼

Interlude (1957) **C-90m.** **½ D: Douglas Sirk. June Allyson, Rossano Brazzi, Marianne Cook (Koch), Jane Wyatt, Francoise Rosay. Adequate tearjerker of Allyson falling in love with Continental composer Brazzi, whose wife refuses to accept the situation. Remake of WHEN TOMORROW COMES, and remade in 1968 under same title.

Interlude (1968-British) **C-113m.** *** D: Kevin Billington. Oskar Werner, Barbara Ferris, Virginia Maskell, Donald Sutherland, Nora Swinburne, Alan Webb, John Cleese. Charming, sentimental tale of symphony conductor and reporter who have an affair; told in flashback. Previously filmed as WHEN TOMORROW COMES and INTERLUDE (1957).

Intermezzo (1936-Swedish) **88m.** *** D: Gustav Molander. Gosta Ekman, Inga Tidblad, Ingrid Bergman, Bullen Berglund, Britt Hagman. Young pianist Bergman and famous—but married—violinist Ekman fall in love. Ingrid is ravishing in her sixth Swedish film; its remake, three years later, was to be her Hollywood debut. Coscripted by Molander, and based on his story.▼

Intermezzo (1939) **70m.** ***½ D: Gregory Ratoff. Leslie Howard, Ingrid Bergman, Edna Best, Cecil Kellaway, John Halliday. One of the best love stories ever filmed, as married Howard, renowned violinist, has an affair with musical protegee Bergman (in her first English-speaking film). Short and sweet, highlighted by Robert Henning-Heinz Provost love theme. Originally titled INTERMEZZO, A LOVE STORY; Bergman played the same role in Gustav Molander's Swedish version. Remade, after a fashion, as HONEYSUCKLE ROSE.▼

Internal Affairs (1988) **C-200m. TVM** D: Michael Tuchner. Richard Crenna, Kate Capshaw, Cliff Gorman, Lee Richardson,

Dennis Boutsikaris, Danton Stone. Followup to Crenna's earlier DOUBLETAKE has him returning with Gorman to ferret out corrupt cops and solve another grisly murder. William Bayer, who wrote the novel on which the earlier film was based, provides a compelling original teleplay here. Originally shown in two parts. Above average.

Internal Affairs (1990) **C-117m.** ** D: Mike Figgis. Richard Gere, Andy Garcia, Nancy Travis, Laurie Metcalf, Richard Bradford, William Baldwin, Michael Beach. Smarmy, overripe, and overlong drama about a young cop who joins L.A.'s Internal Affairs Dept. and becomes obsessed with nailing a cocky, corrupt officer (Gere) who's a past master at manipulating people. Intriguing ideas get lost, and illogic takes over pretty quickly.▼

International Airport (1985) **C-100m TVM** D: Charles S. Dubin, Don Chaffey. Gil Gerard, Berlinda Tolbert, Pat Crowley, Cliff Potts, Bill Bixby, Susan Blakely, George Grizzard, George Kennedy, Vera Miles, Robert Reed, Connie Sellecca, Susan Oliver, Robert Vaughn. The standard periodic white-knuckles flight for a cast of familiars (and what's a disaster movie involving an airplane if George Kennedy's not around?) though this one unaccountably needed *two* directors to traffic the assorted actors. Pilot for proposed series. Average.

International House (1933) **70m.** ***½ D: A. Edward Sutherland. W. C. Fields, Peggy Hopkins Joyce, Stuart Erwin, George Burns, Gracie Allen, Bela Lugosi, Franklin Pangborn, Rudy Vallee, Sterling Holloway, Cab Calloway, Baby Rose Marie. Offbeat, delightful film with early television experiment bringing people from all over the world to large Oriental hotel. Spotlight alternates between Fields and Burns & Allen, all in rare form, with guest spots by various radio entertainers. Short and sweet, a must-see film. Calloway sings the memorable "Reefer Man."▼

International Lady (1941) **102m.** **½ D: Tim Whelan. Ilona Massey, George Brent, Basil Rathbone, Gene Lockhart. Massey is a femme fatale spy, Brent the U.S. government agent involved in cracking espionage ring. Superficial but entertaining.

International Settlement (1938) **75m.** ** D: Eugene Forde. George Sanders, Dolores Del Rio, June Lang, Dick Baldwin, Leon Ames, John Carradine, Harold Huber. Mediocre tale of Shanghai intrigue with Sanders masquerading as notorious smuggler, pursued by various crooks and sultry Del Rio.

International Squadron (1941) **87m.** **½ D: Lothar Mendes. Ronald Reagan, James Stephenson, Olympe Bradna, William

Lundigan, Joan Perry, Julie Bishop, Cliff Edwards. Air Force straightens out no-account Reagan and turns him into fighting ace. Standard war story, a remake of CEILING ZERO.

International Velvet (1978-British) **C-127m.** *** D: Bryan Forbes. Tatum O'Neal, Christopher Plummer, Anthony Hopkins, Nanette Newman, Dinsdale Landen. Long overdue sequel to NATIONAL VELVET has Velvet (Newman) a grown woman with a live-in lover (Plummer) and a niece (O'Neal) primed to follow in her footsteps as an Olympic horsewoman. Too lengthy and shunned by the critics, but deftly played by Hopkins and Plummer; exquisitely filmed, entertaining.▼

Internecine Project, The (1974-British) **C-89m.** ** D: Ken Hughes. James Coburn, Lee Grant, Harry Andrews, Ian Hendry, Michael Jayston, Keenan Wynn. Lackluster espionage drama with Coburn as opportunist who tries to eliminate skeletons in his closet by having a handful of industrial spies kill each other off.▼

Internes Can't Take Money (1937) **77m.** D: Alfred Santell. Barbara Stanwyck, Joel McCrea, Lloyd Nolan, Stanley Ridges, Lee Bowman, Irving Bacon, Pierre Watkin, Charles Lane, Fay Holden. SEE: **Dr. Kildare** series.

Interns, The (1962) **120m.** *** D: David Swift. Michael Callan, Cliff Robertson, James MacArthur, Nick Adams, Suzy Parker, Haya Harareet, Stefanie Powers, Buddy Ebsen, Telly Savalas, Glossy, renovated DR. KILDARE soap opera, kept afloat by an interesting young cast. Followed by sequel THE NEW INTERNS.▼

Interrupted Journey (1949-British) **80m.** **½ D: Daniel Birt. Richard Todd, Valerie Hobson. Eerie film about Todd involved in bizarre dream concerning his marital life and its present complexities.▼

Interrupted Melody (1955) **C-106m.** *** D: Curtis Bernhardt. Eleanor Parker, Glenn Ford, Roger Moore, Cecil Kellaway, Ann Codee, Stephan Bekassy. Fine biography of Marjorie Lawrence, Australian opera star, who made a comeback after being crippled by polio. Eileen Farrell sings for Parker. William Ludwig and Sonya Levien won Oscars for their story and screenplay.

Interval (1973-Mexican) **C-84m.** ** D: Daniel Mann. Merle Oberon, Robert Wolders, Claudio Brook, Russ Conway, Charles Bateman, Barbara Ransom. A globetrotting woman who keeps running from her past finds true love with a much younger man (Wolders, who became Oberon's husband in real life). Drippy May-December romance, filmed in Mexico and produced by Oberon, whose last film this was.▼

In the Cool of the Day (1963-British) **C-89m.** **½ D: Robert Stevens. Jane Fonda, Peter Finch, Angela Lansbury, Arthur Hill, Constance Cummings. Finch loves Fonda although he's married to Lansbury. Turgid soaper filmed largely in Greece.

In the Custody of Strangers (1982) **C-100m.** TVM D: Robert Greenwald. Martin Sheen, Jane Alexander, Emilio Estevez, Kenneth McMillan, Ed Lauter, Matt Clark, John Hancock, Virginia Kiser. Thoughtful drama about a middle-class family's ordeal when their teenage son (Sheen's real-life son, Estevez) is jailed on drunk charges with hardened criminals and the parents can't get him out. Written by Jennifer Miller. Above average.▼

In the Devil's Garden (1971-British) **C-89m.** *½ D: Sidney Hayers. Suzy Kendall, Frank Finlay, Freddie Jones, Lesley-Anne Down, James Laurenson, Tony Beckley. Undistinguished thriller of rapist-killer in girls' school; of interest mainly for the presence of Down, in an early role as one of the victims. Also known as ASSAULT and TOWER OF TERROR.▼

In the French Style (1963) **105m.** **½ D: Robert Parrish. Jean Seberg, Stanley Baker, Addison Powell, James Leo Herlihy, Philippe Forquet, Claudine Auger. Two short stories by Irwin Shaw are basis for this overlong account of American girl who discovers transient affairs are marring her life.

In the Glitter Palace (1977) **C-100m.** TVM D: Robert Butler. Chad Everett, Barbara Hershey, Anthony Zerbe, Howard Duff, David Wayne, Tisha Sterling. Sleazy murder melodrama in which lawyer/detective Everett is dragged into the case of a lesbian charged with killing her blackmailer. Below average.

In the Good Old Summertime (1949) **C-102m.** *** D: Robert Z. Leonard. Judy Garland, Van Johnson, S. Z. "Cuddles" Sakall, Spring Byington, Clinton Sundberg, Buster Keaton. Musical remake of THE SHOP AROUND THE CORNER, with Garland and Johnson the pen pals who fall in love. Not up to most MGM Garland vehicles, but pleasant. That's young Liza Minnelli with Judy in the finale.▼

In the Heat of the Night (1967) **C-109m.** **** D: Norman Jewison. Sidney Poitier, Rod Steiger, Warren Oates, Lee Grant, Scott Wilson, Larry Gates, Quentin Dean, James Patterson, Anthony James, William Schallert. Redneck Southern sheriff grudgingly accepts help from big-city black detective in solving bizarre murder. Marvelous social thriller hasn't dated one bit—tough, funny, and atmospheric, with unbeatable acting and splendid Quincy Jones score. Five Oscars include Best Picture, Actor (Steiger), Screenplay (Stirling Silliphant), Editing (Hal Ashby). Poitier reprised his character in THEY CALL ME *MISTER* TIBBS! and THE ORGANIZATION. Followed by a TV movie and a series 20 years later.▼

In the Line of Duty: The F.B.I. Murders (1988) **C-100m.** TVM D: Dick Lowry. Ronny Cox, Bruce Greenwood, Michael Gross, Doug Sheehan, David Soul, Teri Copley. Thriller based on the events leading up to the bloody 1986 Miami shootout between a pair of scrungy killers and the F.B.I. The climactic showdown here set new standards for TV violence in much the way that BONNIE AND CLYDE had done for movies in its day. Written by Tracy Keenan Wynn. Above average.

In the Matter of Karen Ann Quinlan (1977) **C-100m.** TVM D: Glenn Jordan. Brian Keith, Piper Laurie, David Huffman, Biff McGuire, David Spielberg, Stephanie Zimbalist, Louise Latham. Docu-drama exploring legal, moral and ethical aspects of the case of New Jersey woman whose parents (Keith and Laurie) argued her right to die with dignity and wanted life-saving machines turned off after she lapsed into a coma and suffered brain damage. Good performances, talky script, tiresome movie. Average.

In the Meantime, Darling (1944) **72m.** ** D: Otto Preminger. Jeanne Crain, Eugene Pallette, Mary Nash, Cara Williams, Reed Hadley, Frank Latimore. Whimsical comedy of rich-girl Crain "roughing it" when she marries soldier Latimore. That's a young Blake Edwards jitterbugging with Jeanne.

In the Money (1958) **61m.** D: William Beaudine. Huntz Hall, Stanley Clements, Patricia Donahue, Paul Cavanagh. SEE: **Bowery Boys** series.

In the Mood (1987) **C-99m.** **½ D: Phil Alden Robinson. Patrick Dempsey, Talia Balsam, Beverly D'Angelo, Michael Constantine, Betty Jinette, Kathleen Freeman, Peter Hobbs, Edith Fellows. Engaging if low-key comedy based on true story of 1944's "woo woo kid" Sonny Wisecarver, a 15-year-old California boy who made headlines because of his affairs with two "older" women, one of whom he actually married. Dempsey is ideal in the lead, and Robinson's script is delightfully wry, but film lacks a certain punch. The real-life Wisecarver appears as a mailman in newsreel sequence (which is narrated by an uncredited Carl Reiner). Wonderful score by Ralph Burns, incorporating many vintage songs.▼

In the Name of the Pope King (1977-Italian) **C-105m.** *** D: Luigi Magni. Nino Manfredi, Danilo Mattei, Carmen Scarpitta, Giovannella Grifea, Carlo Bagno. Manfredi gives one of the best performances of his career in this moving tale, set in the mid-19th century, of a magistrate to the pontifical state whose son is suspected of terrorism.▼

In the Navy (1941) **85m.** **½ D: Arthur Lubin. Bud Abbott, Lou Costello, Dick Powell, The Andrews Sisters, Claire Dodd, Dick Foran. Bud and Lou are somehow in the Navy; Lou has hallucinations and nearly wrecks the entire fleet by playing captain. Powell and Andrews Sisters provide songs, and Costello shows Abbott how $7 \times 13 = 28$.

In the Realm of the Senses (1976-Japanese-French) **C-105m.** **½ D: Nagisa Oshima. Tatsuya Fuji, Eiko Matsuda, Aio Nakajima, Meika Seri. Sexually insatiable Matsuda will do anything to possess husband Fuji. Explicit, controversial, often erotic and well acted, but overall a pretentious film.▼

In The Shadow of Kilimanjaro (1986-U.S.-British-Kenya) **C-97m.** BOMB D: Raju Patel. John Rhys-Davies, Timothy Bottoms, Michele Carey, Irene Miracle, Calvin Jung, Don Blakely, Patty Foley. There's a drought in the African bush, so 90,000 baboons are looking for dinner—and begin attacking humans. A ponderous, obvious, stupid movie that's also unnecessarily, disgustingly gory. Filmed on location in Kenya and based on a series of true events.▼

In the Spirit (1990) **C-94m.** ** D: Sandra Seacat. Marlo Thomas, Elaine May, Peter Falk, Jeannie Berlin, Olympia Dukakis, Melanie Griffith, Michael Emil, Christopher Durang. Oddball throwback to black comedies of the 1970s, as mystic Thomas and house guest May get targeted by the mysterious killer who's murdered the prostitute next door. Packed with characters and performances that tend to grate on the nerves, though it is fun to see Thomas and May doing Abbott and Costello (or is it a neurotic version of Lucy and Ethel?). Griffith has just one scene.▼

In the Wake of a Stranger (1958-British) **69m.** ** D: David Eady. Tony Wright, Shirley Eaton, Danny Green, Harry H. Corbett, Willoughby Goddard, Barbara Archer. Sailor implicated in murder tries to clear himself; just fair.

In the White City (1983-Swiss-Portuguese) **C-108m.** ***½ D: Alain Tanner. Bruno Ganz, Teresa Madruga, Julia Vonderlinn, Jose Carvalho. Involving, thought-provoking, Kafkaesque tale of seaman Ganz's experiences while in Lisbon, highlighted by his relationship with chambermaid Madruga. The work of a filmmaker in complete command of his art.

In This House of Brede (1975) **C-100m.** TVM D: George Schaefer. Diana Rigg, Judi Bowker, Gwen Watford, Pamela Brown, Denis Quilley, Nicholas Clay. Sophisticated London businesswoman chucks it all to become a Benedictine nun. Rigg gives her usual sublime performance in this moving James Costigan adaptation of Rumer Godden's novel. Above average.

In This Our Life (1942) **97m.** *** D: John Huston. Bette Davis, Olivia de

Havilland, George Brent, Dennis Morgan, Charles Coburn, Frank Craven, Billie Burke, Hattie McDaniel, Lee Patrick. Fine drama of neurotic family with husband-stealing Davis ruining sister's (de Havilland's) life, and eventually her own; Davis at histrionic height. Based on Ellen Glasgow novel. Walter Huston has cameo role as bartender in one scene.▼

Intimacy (1966) 87m. *½ D: Victor Stoloff. Jack Ging, Nancy Malone, Joan Blackman, Barry Sullivan, Jackie de Shannon. Grade-C drama may get more interesting response on TV than it deserves, since plot involves the spying on a Washington official by hidden cameras. Remade as THE WASHINGTON AFFAIR.

Intimate Agony (1983) C-100m. TVM D: Paul Wendkos. Anthony Geary, Judith Light, Mark Harmon, Arthur Hill, Brian Kerwin, Penny Fuller, Robert Vaughn. Idealistic doctor (daytime soap star Geary) tries to find out who's spreading herpes through arrogant developer Vaughn's summer resort. As a "disease of the week" drama, this one's the pits. Below average.

Intimate Contact (1987-British) C-140m. TVM D: Waris Hussein. Claire Bloom, Daniel Massey, Abigail Cruttenden, Mark Kingston, Sylvia Syms, Sally Jane Jackson. Strong AIDS drama, well played by Massey and Bloom as a senior executive and his wife who discover he's contracted the disease while on a weekend business trip. Powerful stuff, written by Alma Cullen. Shown initially on cable in two parts. Above average.▼

Intimate Encounters (1986) C-100m. TVM D: Ivan Nagy. Donna Mills, James Brolin, Cicely Tyson, Veronica Cartwright, Gary Bayer, Mitchell Anderson. A woman whose marriage has gone stale because of an inattentive husband begins fantasizing about sexual encounters with strangers. Mills coproduced this one herself. Also known as ENCOUNTERS IN THE NIGHT. Below average.

Intimate Lighting (1965-Czech) 72m. *** D: Ivan Passer. Vera Kresadlova, Zdenek Brezusek, Karel Blazek, Jaroslava Stedra, Jan Vostrcil, Vlastmila Vlkova, Karel Uhlik. Unpretentious, day-in-the-life story of two old friends, professional musicians, reuniting after long absence at country home. Excellent performances.

Intimate Stranger, The SEE: **Finger of Guilt**

Intimate Strangers (1977) C-100m. TVM D: John Llewellyn Moxey. Dennis Weaver, Sally Struthers, Tyne Daly, Larry Hagman, Melvyn Douglas, Quinn Cummings, Rhea Perlman. Overlong drama about a battered wife and the destruction of a marriage. Offbeat roles for its two stars plus a sparkling cameo by Douglas as

Weaver's mean old buzzard of a father. Average.▼

Intimate Strangers (1986) C-100m. TVM D: Robert Ellis Miller. Teri Garr, Stacy Keach, Cathy Lee Crosby, Priscilla Lopez, Justin Deas, Max Gail, Max Barabas. Nurse returns from Vietnam POW camp after ten years, with Asian son in tow, hoping to start new life with her husband—who's made a new life of his own in the meantime (with a new lover). Average.

Intolerance (1916) 123m. **** D: D. W. Griffith. Lillian Gish, Robert Harron, Mae Marsh, Constance Talmadge, Bessie Love, Seena Owen, Alfred Paget, many others. Surely one of the all-time great movies, although be prepared for melodrama, preaching, and some hokey title cards. Man's inhumanity to man and his sins are examined in series of four interlocking tales from Babylonian times to modern day. (Non-TV prints shown at silent-film speed run as much as 208m.!)▼

Into the Blue (1950-British) 83m. *½ D: Herbert Wilcox. Michael Wilding, Odile Versois, Jack Hulbert, Constance Cummings, Edward Rigby. Dreary comedy about stowaway Wilding and his adventures on a yacht. Retitled MAN IN THE DINGHY.

Into the Fire (1987-Canadian) C-93m. ** D: Graeme Campbell. Susan Anspach, Olivia d'Abo, Art Hindle, Lee Montgomery. Old-fashioned murder/sex triangle thriller has the novelty of a wintry Canadian setting where lodge owner Anspach is an impressive seductress. Almost outdone by one too many plot twists. Precocious d'Abo is also a stunning, contrasting femme fatale.▼

Into the Homeland (1987) C-115m. TVM D: Lesli Linka Glatter. Powers Boothe, C. Thomas Howell, Cindy Pickett, Paul LeMat, David Caruso, Shelby Leverington. Boozing ex-cop's search for his missing teenage daughter leads him to a violent band of white supremists. Interesting, if flawed, feature film debut for director Glatter with a script by Anna Hamilton Phelan, author of MASK. Made for cable. Average.▼

Into the Night (1985) C-115m. *** D: John Landis. Jeff Goldblum, Michelle Pfeiffer, Richard Farnsworth, Irene Papas, Kathryn Harrold, Paul Mazursky, Roger Vadim, Dan Aykroyd, David Bowie, Bruce McGill, Vera Miles, Clu Gulager. Engaging, episodic film about a middle-class nerd who helps a beautiful woman who's being chased by killers. Convoluted story filled with offbeat vignettes and colorful characters, many of them played by Hollywood directors (Don Siegel, Jonathan Demme, Jack Arnold, Lawrence Kasdan, Paul Bartel, David Cronenberg, Richard Franklin, Colin Higgins, Andrew Marton,

Amy Heckerling). Landis himself is very funny as one of the Iranian bad guys. Probably more appealing to film buffs than general audiences.▼

Into Thin Air (1985) **C-100m. TVM** D: Roger Young. Ellen Burstyn, Robert Prosky, Sam Robards, Tate Donovan, Caroline McWilliams, Nicholas Pryor, John Dennis Johnston. Fact-based drama of a Canadian teenager's disappearance while driving to summer school in Colorado. Burstyn's dedicated portrayal of his single-minded mother is matched by Prosky's work as a dogged, retired detective who agrees to look for the boy. Script by George Rubio. Above average.▼

Intrigue (1947) **90m.** ** D: Edwin L. Marin. George Raft, June Havoc, Helena Carter, Tom Tully, Marvin Miller, Dan Seymour, Philip Ahn. Predictable Raft vehicle of ex-military man with mar on his record turning Shanghai crime ring over to cops to clear himself.

Intrigue (1988) **C-100m. TVM** D: David Drury. Scott Glenn, Robert Loggia, William Atherton, Martin Shaw, Cherie Lunghi, Eleanor Bron. U.S. intelligence agent Glenn is recruited to smuggle old colleague Loggia out of Moscow (where he had defected some years earlier) and then learns that murder is part of his orders. Average.▼

Intruder, The (1955-British) **84m.** **½ D: Guy Hamilton. Jack Hawkins, Hugh Williams, Michael Medwin, Dennis Price, Dora Bryan. Hawkins is resolute army veteran who digs into past to discover why one of his old military group went astray.

Intruder, The (1961) **80m.** *** D: Roger Corman. William Shatner, Frank Maxwell, Beverly Lunsford, Robert Emhardt, Leo Gordon, Jeanne Cooper. Racist Shatner drifts from one small Southern town to another inciting townspeople to riot against court-ordered school integration. Corman's only "message" film—and one of his few box-office flops—still packs a punch; low budget and location filming aid authenticity. Script by Charles Beaumont. Reissued as I HATE YOUR GUTS! and SHAME.▼

Intruder in the Dust (1949) **87m.** *** D: Clarence Brown. David Brian, Claude Jarman, Jr., Juano Hernandez, Porter Hall, Elizabeth Patterson. Black man (Hernandez, in a solid performance) is accused of murder in a Southern town, and a gathering mob wants to lynch him. First-rate adaptation of William Faulkner novel.▼

Intruders, The (1970) **C-95m. TVM** D: William Graham. Don Murray, Edmond O'Brien, John Saxon, Anne Francis, Gene Evans, Edward Andrews, (Harry) Dean Stanton, Harrison Ford. Half breed ex-con Billy Pye (Saxon) returns to Medelia to become lawman, vindicate himself from frame-up. Many subplots and characters to get into, but nothing comes together. Average.

Intruder Within, The (1981) **C-100m. TVM** D: Peter Carter. Chad Everett, Joseph Bottoms, Jennifer Warren, Rockne Tarkington, Lynda Mason Green, Paul Larson. Strange doings on an isolated oil rig when a primeval creature from the depths begins menacing the crew. Fair chiller. Average.▼

Invader, The SEE: **Old Spanish Custom, An**▼

Invaders, The SEE: **Forty-Ninth Parallel**▼

Invaders from Mars (1953) **C-78m.** *** D: William Cameron Menzies. Helena Carter, Arthur Franz, Jimmy Hunt, Leif Erickson, Hillary Brooke, Bert Freed. Stylish sci-fi told from little boy's point of view, as he alone witnesses invasion of aliens who capture and brainwash residents of small average town. Remade in 1986.▼

Invaders from Mars (1986) **C-100m.** *½ D: Tobe Hooper. Karen Black, Hunter Carson, Timothy Bottoms, Laraine Newman, James Karen, Louise Fletcher, Bud Cort, Jimmy Hunt. Remake of '50s fantasy favorite about a boy's nightmarish experiences when aliens land in his back yard and overtake everyone around him—even his parents. Starts fine, rapidly goes downhill toward utter disaster. Hunt, the youngster in the original film, plays a police chief here; the boy this time is real-life son of costar Black.▼

Invasion (1966-British) **82m.** **½ D: Alan Bridges. Edward Judd, Yoko Tani, Lyndon Brook, Eric Young, Anthony Sharp, Stephanie Bidmead. Entertaining little sci-fi flick involving interplanetary travelers forced to land on earth, and their conflict with humans.

Invasion Earth 2150 A.D. SEE: **Daleks—Invasion Earth 2150 A.D.**▼

Invasion Force SEE: **Hangar 18**▼

Invasion of Johnson County, The (1976) **C-100m. TVM** D: Jerry Jameson. Bill Bixby, Bo Hopkins, John Hillerman, Billy Green Bush, Stephen Elliott, Luke Askew. City slicker and country bumpkin versus land barons and their gunslingers to foil a land-grab scheme in the Old West. Offbeat hoss-opera with a witty script and enough action to please every western fan. Predates HEAVEN'S GATE, which tells the same basic story. Above average.

Invasion of Privacy, An (1983) **C-100m. TVM** D: Mel Damski. Valerie Harper, Cliff DeYoung, Tammy Grimes, Carol Kane, Richard Masur, Jerry Orbach, Peter Michael Goetz, Jeff Daniels. Provocative drama about a newly divorced vacationer's tribulations after being raped by one of the locals. Elaine Mueller's well-turned script was based on Joan Taylor's book *Asking for It*, but gets compromised. Average.

Invasion of the Animal People (1962) **73m.** *½ D: Virgil Vogel, Jerry Warren. Robert Burton, Barbara Wilson, Sten Gester, Bengt Bomgren. John Carradine is narrator and American link for Swedish-made 1960 production about rampaging monster who escapes from spaceship and terrorizes Lapland. Low-grade nonsense.▼

Invasion of the Bee Girls (1973) **C-85m.** *** D: Denis Sanders. Victoria Vetri, William Smith, Anitra Ford, Cliff Osmond, Wright King, Ben Hammer. Wonderfully campy (and sexy) sci-fi outing about a strange force that's transforming women into dangerous creatures who you-know-what men to death in a small California town. Written by Nicholas Meyer pre-SEVEN PERCENT SOLUTION.▼

Invasion of the Body Snatchers (1956) **80m.** ***½ D: Don Siegel. Kevin Mc-Carthy, Dana Wynter, Larry Gates, King Donovan, Carolyn Jones, Virginia Christine. Classic, influential, and still very scary science-fiction (with McCarthy-era subtext) about small-town residents who are being replaced by inert duplicates hatched from alien "pods." Tense script by Daniel Mainwaring from Jack Finney's *The Body Snatchers*; Sam Peckinpah can be glimpsed as a meter reader. Reissued in 1979 at 76m., minus unnecessary, studio-imposed prologue and epilogue with Whit Bissell and Richard Deacon. Remade in 1978. Also shown in computer-colored version.▼

Invasion of the Body Snatchers (1978) **C-115m.** *** D: Philip Kaufman. Donald Sutherland, Brooke Adams, Leonard Nimoy, Jeff Goldblum, Veronica Cartwright. Chilling remake of 1956 classic with many new twists and turns; unfortunately, it runs out of steam and offers one climax too many. Kevin McCarthy and Don Siegel, star and director of original film, have significant cameo roles . . . but look fast for Robert Duvall. Weird score by Denny Zeitlin.▼

Invasion of the Saucer Men (1957) **69m.** *½ D: Edward L. Cahn. Steve Terrell, Gloria Castillo, Frank Gorshin, Raymond Hatton, Ed Nelson. Slow paced, minor sci-fi comedy about bulbous-headed aliens trying to pin the death of one of them on a teenager. Cheap, but has some atmosphere and Paul Blaisdell's outlandish aliens. Remade as THE EYE CREATURES.

Invasion, U.S.A. (1952) **74m.** *½ D: Alfred E. Green. Gerald Mohr, Peggie Castle, Dan O'Herlihy, Phyllis Coates, Robert Bice, Tom Kennedy, Noel Neill. Red Scare movie depicting full-fledged invasion of America by "The Enemy" —while Mohr romances Castle. Hopelessly cheap and ineffectual, using tons of stock footage showing actual air battles and bombings. Trivia note: Both women who played Lois Lane on TV's *Superman* series appear in the cast.

Invasion U.S.A. (1985) **C-107m.** BOMB D: Joseph Zito. Chuck Norris, Richard Lynch, Melissa Prophet, Alex Colon. Political-paranoia action film about retired CIA agent (Norris) who gets back on the job when Russian terrorists invade Florida, trying to overtake entire country by causing panic and turmoil. Repellent in the extreme.▼

Investigation of a Citizen Above Suspicion (1970-Italian) **C-115m.** *** D: Elio Petri. Gian Maria Volonte, Florinda Bolkan, Salvo Randone, Gianni Santuccio, Arturo Dominici. Oscar-winning foreign film about powerful police chief who slashes the throat of his mistress, then waits entire movie to see if he'll be caught. Interesting, but not overly gripping. Superbly creepy score by Ennio Morricone.

Invincible Six, The (1968) **C-96m.** **½ D: Jean Negulesco. Stuart Whitman, Elke Sommer, Curt Jurgens, James Mitchum, Ian Ogilvy. Energetic action film about a motley crew on the lam who come to the aid of isolated villagers under the thumb of a bandit gang. It's THE MAGNIFICENT SEVEN transplanted to present-day mid-East in this Iranian-made production.▼

Invisible Agent (1942) **81m.** ** D: Edwin L. Marin. Ilona Massey, Jon Hall, Peter Lorre, Cedric Hardwicke, J. Edward Bromberg, John Litel. Hall plays agent fighting Nazis with invisibility. Fun for the kids; dialogue is witless.

Invisible Boy, The (1957) **85m.** **½ D: Herman Hoffman. Richard Eyer, Diane Brewster, Philip Abbot, Harold J. Stone. One of the earlier sci-fi flicks to deal with unwieldy computers gone berserk and power-happy; not bad. Also features Robby the Robot (from FORBIDDEN PLANET).

Invisible Creature, The (1959-British) **70m.** ** D: Montgomery Tully. Sandra Dorne, Patricia Dainton, Tony Wright. Oddball little film of ghost that interferes with homicide plot in eerie English mansion. Retitled: THE HOUSE ON MARSH ROAD.

Invisible Dr. Mabuse, The (1961-German) **89m.** **½ D: Harald Reinl. Lex Barker, Karin Dor, Siegfried Lowitz, Wolfgang Preiss, Rudolf Fernau. Well-paced entry in arch-villain series, with U. S. detective Barker in Germany to track down killer, involved with Mabuse (Preiss); offbeat setting enhances film.

Invisible Ghost, The (1941) **64m.** ** D: Joseph H. Lewis. Bela Lugosi, Polly Ann Young, John McGuire, Clarence Muse, Terry Walker, Betty Compson. Low-grade horror about domineering wife who hypnotizes her husband into murder plot.▼

Invisible Invaders (1959) **67m.** *½ D: Edward L. Cahn. John Agar, Jean Byron, Robert Hutton, Philip Tonge, John Carradine, Hal Torey. Invisible aliens from the moon possess corpses and attack the living; holed up in a cave, scientists race against time to stop them. Cheap, silly, and boring.

Invisible Kid, The (1988) **C-95m.** BOMB D: Avery Crounse. Jay Underwood, Karen Black, Wally Ward, Chynna Phillips, Brother Theodore, Mike Genovese, Jan King. High-school dolt stumbles onto invisibility formula, which enables him to poke into the girls' locker room and such. Crude in all respects.▼

✓ **Invisible Man, The** (1933) **71m.** ***½ D: James Whale. Claude Rains, Gloria Stuart, Una O'Connor, William Harrigan, E. E. Clive, Dudley Digges, Dwight Frye. H. G. Wells' fantasy brilliantly materializes on screen in tale of mad scientist who makes himself invisible, wreaking havoc on British country village. Rains' starring debut is dated but still enjoyable.▼

Invisible Man, The (1975) **C-78m. TVM** D: Robert Michael Lewis. David McCallum, Melinda Fee, Jackie Cooper, Henry Darrow, Alex Henteloff, Arch Johnson. Contemporized version of the H. G. Wells classic about a scientist who learns the secret of invisibility but later runs into complications. Should have disappeared before becoming a series. Below average.

Invisible Man Returns, The (1940) **81m.** *** D: Joe May. Cedric Hardwicke, Vincent Price, John Sutton, Nan Grey, Cecil Kellaway, Alan Napier. Fine follow-up to exciting original, with Price going invisible to clear himself of murder charge.▼

Invisible Man's Revenge, The (1944) **77m.** **½ D: Ford Beebe. Jon Hall, Alan Curtis, Evelyn Ankers, Leon Errol, John Carradine, Gale Sondergaard, Ian Wolfe, Billy Bevan. Hall made invisible by doctor to obtain estate; he then kills doctor after being refused visibility. Better-than-average cast saves rather innocuous script.

Invisible Menace, The (1938) **55m.** ** D: John Farrow. Boris Karloff, Marie Wilson, Regis Toomey, Henry Kolker, Eddie Craven, Eddie Acuff, Charles Trowbridge. Not a horror/fantasy film, as the title implies, but a Grade B whodunit set at a military installation, with Karloff as the woebegone prime suspect. Wilson supplies incongruous comedy relief, while the FBI is rather poorly represented by Cy Kendall. Remade as MURDER ON THE WATERFRONT.

Invisible Monster, The SEE: **Slaves of the Invisible Monster**

Invisible Ray, The (1936) **81m.** **½ D: Lambert Hillyer. Boris Karloff, Bela Lugosi, Frances Drake, Frank Lawton, Walter Kingsford, Beulah Bondi. Scientist Karloff contracts radiation that gives him

touch of death, and slowly deteriorates his mind. Interesting yarn, but a notch below other Karloff-Lugosi vehicles.▼

Invisible Stripes (1939) **82m.** *** D: Lloyd Bacon. George Raft, Jane Bryan, William Holden, Flora Robson, Humphrey Bogart, Paul Kelly, Moroni Olsen, Tully Marshall. Earnest account of parolee Raft trying to go straight, protecting brother Holden from gangster Bogart; subdued acting is effective.

Invisible Woman, The (1941) **72m.** *** D: A. Edward Sutherland. John Barrymore, Virginia Bruce, John Howard, Charlie Ruggles, Oscar Homolka, Margaret Hamilton, Donald MacBride, Edward Brophy, Shemp Howard, Charles Lane, Thurston Hall. Great cast in likable comedy about screwy professor Barrymore turning model Bruce invisible, arousing the curiosity of playboy sponsor Howard, as well as the more monetary interests of gangster Homolka. Slick and sprightly, with Ruggles terrific as Howard's long-suffering butler; Maria Montez has a bit as one of Bruce's fellow models.

Invisible Woman, The (1983) **C-100m. TVM** D: Alan J. Levi. Bob Denver, Alexa Hamilton, David Doyle, George Gobel, Anne Haney, Harvey Korman, Jonathan Banks, Garrett Morris, Richard Sanders. Reporter Hamilton starts fading out after spilling some chemicals on herself in biochemist uncle Denver's lab and puts her occasional invisibility to use in chasing big story of a huge art heist. Done by the *Gilligan's Island* people and pretty much at that level, right down to the laugh track. Busted pilot shot on videotape. Below average.

Invitation (1952) **84m.** **½ D: Gottfried Reinhardt. Van Johnson, Dorothy McGuire, Louis Calhern, Ray Collins, Ruth Roman. Society tearjerker decked out in MGM gloss about invalid McGuire; her father (Calhern) tries to buy Johnson to romance dying daughter. Memorable theme by Bronislau Kaper (which was originally used in A LIFE OF HER OWN).

Invitation to a Gunfighter (1964) **C-92m.** ✓ **½ D: Richard Wilson. Yul Brynner, George Segal, Janice Rule, Pat Hingle, Brad Dexter. Cast surpasses turgid, talky script about town that hires gunslinger to kill an outcast, with surprising results.▼

Invitation to Happiness (1939) **95m.** **½ D: Wesley Ruggles. Irene Dunne, Fred MacMurray, Charles Ruggles, William Collier, Sr., Eddie Hogan. Ordinary story, well acted: society girl marries fighter, but marriage can't survive because of his driving ambition in boxing ring.

Invitation to Hell (1984) **C-100m. TVM** D: Wes Craven. Robert Urich, Joanna Cassidy, Susan Lucci, Kevin McCarthy, Patricia McCormack, Joe Regalbuto. The *Faust* story with a contemporary twist and daytime soap vixen Lucci playing the Devil herself, out to nab the souls of space scientist Urich and family. Average.▼

Invitation to the Dance (1957) **C-93m.** **½ D: Gene Kelly. Gene Kelly, Igor Youskevitch, Claire Sombert, David Paltenghi, Daphne Dale, Claude Bessy, Tommy Rall, Carol Haney, Tamara Toumanova, Belita. Kelly's ambitious film tells three stories entirely in dance. Earnest but uninspired, until final "Sinbad" segment with Kelly in Hanna-Barbera cartoon world. Music by Jacques Ibert, Andre Previn, and Rimsky-Korsakov. Filmed in 1952.▼

In Which We Serve (1942-British) **115m.** **** D: Noel Coward, David Lean. Noel Coward, John Mills, Bernard Miles, Celia Johnson, Kay Walsh, Joyce Carey, Michael Wilding, James Donald, Richard Attenborough. Unlike many WW2 films, this masterpiece doesn't date one bit; superb film about men on a British fighting ship, told through flashback. Written, codirected, and scored by costar Coward (who was given a special Oscar "for his outstanding production achievement"). Lean's first directing credit. Film debuts of Johnson, Attenborough, young Daniel Massey and infant Juliet Mills.▼

I Ought to Be in Pictures (1982) **C-107m.** ** D: Herbert Ross. Walter Matthau, Ann-Margret, Dinah Manoff, Lance Guest, Lewis Smith, Martin Ferrero. Poor formula Neil Simon sitcom, adapted from his play: 19-year-old Brooklynite Manoff hitches to L.A. to make it in movies—and establishes connection with her father (Matthau), screenwriter turned gambler-drinker. Matthau and Manoff do their best; Ann-Margret wasted as Walter's mistress.▼

I Passed for White (1960) **93m.** ** D: Fred M. Wilcox. Sonya Wilde, James Franciscus, Pat Michon, Elizabeth Council, Griffin Crafts, Isabelle Cooley. Exploitation film handled with slight dignity involving light-skinned black woman and her rich white boyfriend.

Ipcress File, The (1965-British) **C-108m.** ***½ D: Sidney J. Furie. Michael Caine, Nigel Green, Guy Doleman, Sue Lloyd, Gordon Jackson. First and best of Len Deighton's Harry Palmer series, with Caine as unemotional Cockney crook turned secret agent, involved in grueling mental torture caper. Eerie score by John Barry; two sequels—FUNERAL IN BERLIN and BILLION DOLLAR BRAIN.▼

I Promise to Pay (1937) **65m.** **½ D: D. Ross Lederman. Chester Morris, Helen Mack, Leo Carrillo, Thomas Mitchell, John Gallaudet, Wallis Clark. Snappy little programmer about likable, scrupulously honest family man Morris who's taken in by loan sharks. Enjoyable (if not quite credible).

I Remember Mama (1948) **134m.** ***½

D: George Stevens. Irene Dunne, Barbara Bel Geddes, Oscar Homolka, Philip Dorn, Cedric Hardwicke, Edgar Bergen, Rudy Vallee, Barbara O'Neil, Florence Bates, Ellen Corby. Beautifully realized, exquisitely detailed filming of John Van Druten's play, based on Kathryn Forbes' memoirs about growing up with her Norwegian immigrant family in San Francisco. A bit long, but richly rewarding, with top performances in each and every role. Screenplay by DeWitt Bodeen. Followed by the TV series *Mama*.▼

Irene (1940) **104m.** **½ D: Herbert Wilcox. Anna Neagle, Ray Milland, Roland Young, Alan Marshal, May Robson, Billie Burke, Marsha Hunt, Arthur Treacher, Tommy Kelly. Pleasant remake of venerable musical (done as a silent film with Colleen Moore) minus most of the songs. Wealthy playboy Milland romances working-girl Neagle; some offbeat touches make it pleasing. "Alice Blue Gown" sequence originally filmed in color.

Irish Eyes Are Smiling (1944) **C-90m.** **½ D: Gregory Ratoff. June Haver, Monty Woolley, Dick Haymes, Anthony Quinn, Maxie Rosenbloom, Veda Ann Borg. Colorful corn about Ernest R. Ball, composer of famous Irish songs, with pleasant cast and familiar tunes.

Irish in Us, The (1935) **84m.** ** D: Lloyd Bacon. James Cagney, Pat O'Brien, Olivia de Havilland, Frank McHugh, Allen Jenkins. Pretty stale comedy about rivalry between policemen and prizefighters, with good cast to hold one's interest.

Irishman, The (1978-Australian) **C-108m.** *** D: Donald Crombie. Michael Craig, Simon Burke, Robin Nevin, Lou Brown, Andrew Maguire. Effective, wonderfully acted drama of teamster Craig, his wife and sons, and his refusal to accept change and progress during the 1920s. A touching portrait of a family in turmoil.▼

Irish Whiskey Rebellion (1972) **C-93m.** ** D: J. C. Works (Chester Erskine). William Devane, Anne Meara, Richard Mulligan, David Groh, Judie Rolin, William Challee, Stephen Joyce. Pedestrian action tale of Irish rum-running during America's Prohibition era hoping to raise money for IRA struggles back home. Strong performances by all.

Irma la Douce (1963) **C-142m.** **½ D: Billy Wilder. Shirley MacLaine, Jack Lemmon, Lou Jacobi, Herschel Bernardi, Joan Shawlee, Hope Holiday, Bill Bixby. Wilder's straight comedy adaptation of Broadway musical is a Parisian fairytale for adults. Gendarme Lemmon falls for prostitute MacLaine and will do anything to keep her for himself. Red Light District is vividly recreated, but reteaming of stars and director can't equal THE APARTMENT. André Previn won an Oscar for his scoring. Look fast for young James Caan in walk-on.▼

Iron Curtain, The (1948) **87m.** *** D: William Wellman. Dana Andrews, Gene Tierney, June Havoc, Berry Kroeger, Edna Best. Excellent cast and intelligent direction make this Cold War espionage story set in Canada of superior caliber. Retitled: BEHIND THE IRON CURTAIN.

Iron Eagle (1986) **C-119m.** *½ D: Sidney J. Furie. Louis Gossett, Jr., Jason Gedrick, David Suchet, Tim Thomerson, Larry G. Scott, Caroline Lagerfelt, Jerry Levine, Michael Bowen. Dum-dum comic-book movie about an 18-year-old who commandeers an F-16 fighter jet and flies to the Middle East (playing rock music on his Walkman all the way) in order to save his dad, who's been taken prisoner. Full of jingoistic ideals, dubious ethics, and people who die and miraculously come back to life. Not boring, just stupid. Followed by a sequel.▼

Iron Eagle II (1988-Canadian-Israeli) **C-105m.** *½ D: Sidney J. Furie. Louis Gossett, Jr., Mark Humphrey, Stuart Margolin, Alan Scarfe, Sharon H. Brandon, Maury Chaykin. Equally idiotic sequel, with General Gossett recruiting pilot Humphrey to team with his Soviet counterparts on a secret mission in the Mideast. Humphrey may be a Tom Cruise clone, but the film makes TOP GUN seem like FROM HERE TO ETERNITY.▼

Iron Glove, The (1954) **C-77m.** **½ D: William Castle. Robert Stack, Ursula Thiess, Richard Stapley, Charles Irwin, Alan Hale, Jr. Typical swashbuckler about 18th-century England and Prince James, pretender to the throne.

Iron Horse, The (1924) **119m.** *** D: John Ford. George O'Brien, Madge Bellamy, Cyril Chadwick, Fred Kohler, Gladys Hulette, J. Farrell MacDonald. Epic-scale silent film about building of transcontinental railroad, intertwined with predictable human-interest subplots involving surveyor O'Brien, sweetheart Bellamy, traitor Kohler, etc. Storywise, film may seem hackneyed today, but it's important to note that this movie *invented* what later became clichés.

Iron Major, The (1943) **85m.** **½ D: Ray Enright. Pat O'Brien, Ruth Warrick, Robert Ryan, Leon Ames, Russell Wade, Bruce Edwards. Good biography of Frank Cavanaugh, who in civilian life was famous football coach, in WW1 became a military hero; O'Brien is convincing in lead.▼

Iron Man (1931) **73m.** ** D: Tod Browning. Lew Ayres, Jean Harlow, Robert Armstrong, John Miljan, Eddie Dillon. Routine early talkie of prizefighter Ayres and gold-digging wife Harlow (who hadn't clicked yet in films). Manager-pal Armstrong is only one who sees through her.

Remade in 1937 (as SOME BLONDES ARE DANGEROUS) and 1951.

Iron Man (1951) **82m.** **½ D: Joseph Pevney. Jeff Chandler, Evelyn Keyes, Stephen McNally, Joyce Holden, Rock Hudson, Jim Backus. Remake of Harlow film focuses more on boxer (Chandler) and his unhappy rise in the boxing world.

Iron Mask, The (1929) **87m.** *** D: Allan Dwan. Douglas Fairbanks, Belle Bennett, Marguerite De La Motte, Dorothy Revier, Vera Lewis, William Bakewell, Nigel de Brulier, Ullrich Haupt. Entertaining Dumas tale later filmed as THE MAN IN THE IRON MASK told from point of view of D'Artagnan (Fairbanks), who becomes Louis XIV's protector from birth to later time when scheming Rochefort (Haupt) tries to pass off twin brother as heir to throne. Lavish silent swashbuckler originally had talkie sequences. Most current prints are of the 1940 reissue with narration by Douglas Fairbanks, Jr.▼

Iron Mistress, The (1952) **C-110m.** **½ D: Gordon Douglas. Alan Ladd, Virginia Mayo, Joseph Calleia, Phyllis Kirk. Spotty Western adventure of Jim Bowie (Ladd), who invented the famed two-edged knife.

Iron Petticoat, The (1956) **C-87m.** **½ D: Ralph Thomas. Bob Hope, Katharine Hepburn, James Robertson Justice, Robert Helpmann, David Kossoff. Curious comedy made in England tries to update NINOTCHKA theme with Hepburn as humorless Russian and Hope as American military man who tries to win her over. Stars' surprising rapport is film's chief value; mediocre script and direction kill the rest.

Iron Sheriff, The (1957) **73m.** *½ D: Sidney Salkow. Sterling Hayden, Constance Ford, John Dehner, Kent Taylor, Darryl Hickman. Marshal Hayden sets out to prove son is not guilty of murder.

Ironside (1967) **C-98m.** TVM D: James Goldstone. Raymond Burr, Geraldine Brooks, Gene Lyons, Don Galloway, Don Mitchell, Barbara Anderson. Excellent performance by Burr and tight direction highlight sympathetic, suspenseful story of San Francisco police inspector shot and paralyzed by sniper, reacting to public pressure and friends who rally 'round him. Above average. Pilot for the hit series.

Iron Triangle, The (1989) **C-91m.** ** D: Eric Weston. Beau Bridges, Haing S. Ngor, Johnny Hallyday, Liem Whatley, James Ishida. A U.S. army captain, serving in Vietnam in 1969, is captured by a 17-year-old Vietcong soldier, and the pair develop a bond. Intriguing as a look at the war from the side of the "enemy," but the result is confused and slight.▼

Ironweed (1987) **C-144m.** **½ D: Hector Babenco. Jack Nicholson, Meryl Streep, Carroll Baker, Michael O'Keefe, Diane

Venora, Fred Gwynne, Margaret Whitton, Tom Waits, Jake Dengel, Joe Grifasi. William Kennedy adapted his Pulitzer Prize-winning novel about street people, set in Albany, New York, in 1938. Nicholson plays a man haunted by his past, trying to come to terms with the life he turned his back on years ago. Streep is his longtime companion who, like him, can't stay off the bottle for long. Babenco's first American film is strong on atmosphere and filled with haunting images . . . but it's long and unremittingly bleak, with a few too many dramatic peaks. The salvation is Nicholson and Streep, whose rich performances are a privilege to watch.▼

Iroquois Trail, The (1950) 85m. ** D: Phil Karlson. George Montgomery, Brenda Marshall, Dan O'Herlihy, Glenn Langan. Too often flabby account of French and Indian War, lacking sufficient plot motivation and action sequences.

Irreconcilable Differences (1984) C-117m. *** D: Charles Shyer. Ryan O'Neal, Shelley Long, Drew Barrymore, Sam Wanamaker, Allen Garfield, Sharon Stone. Bittersweet comedy about a bright young couple who marry and prosper, until success in Hollywood causes them to lose sight of what's really important in their lives. Result: Their ten-year-old daughter sues them for divorce! Perceptive script by Nancy Meyers and first-time director Shyer, with especially funny jabs at Hollywood. Also the only film in recent memory to drop the name of Sig Rumann!▼

Isabel's Choice (1981) C-100m. TVM D: Guy Green. Jean Stapleton, Richard Kiley, Peter Coyote, Betsy Palmer, Mildred Dunnock. The choice in this drama by Oliver Hailey is between career and marriage for a widowed secretary when her boss, whom she has helped climb the corporate ladder, is forced into early retirement. If anybody really cares, that is. Average.

Isadora (1969-British) C-131m. ***½ D: Karel Reisz. Vanessa Redgrave, James Fox, Jason Robards, Ivan Tchenko, John Fraser, Bessie Love, Cynthia Harris. Extremely long but gripping study of Isadora Duncan, first of modern dancers and most prominent free-thinker of her time. Interesting technique and carefully studied performances combine together in this offbeat biography. Originally titled THE LOVES OF ISADORA. That version, which runs 168m., was withdrawn shortly after release and only restored in 1987.▼

I Sailed to Tahiti with an All Girl Crew (1968) C-95m. *½ D: Richard L. Bare. Gardner McKay, Fred Clark, Diane McBain, Pat Buttram, Edy Williams. One of the all-time camp classics, if only for its title. Unfortunately, film doesn't live down to its expectations.

I Saw What You Did (1965) 82m. *** D:

William Castle. Sara Lane, Andi Garrett, John Ireland, Joan Crawford, Leif Erickson, Patricia Breslin. Tense, gimmick-free Castle shocker about two teenage girls who dial phone numbers at random and whisper film's title; one of their "victims" is Ireland—who's just murdered his wife! Look out! Remade for TV.

I Saw What You Did (1988) C-100m. TVM D: Fred Walton. Shawnee Smith, Tammy Lauren, Candace Cameron, Robert Carradine, David Carradine. Bland remake of William Castle's 1965 thriller about a pair of teenagers menaced by a psychotic killer after playing a telephone prank on him. Average.

I See a Dark Stranger SEE: Adventuress, The▼

I Sent a Letter to My Love (1981-French) C-96m. ***½ D: Moshe Mizrahi. Simone Signoret, Jean Rochefort, Delphine Seyrig. A woman (Signoret) cares for her paralyzed brother (Rochefort); through a newspaper personals column, they unknowingly begin a romantic correspondence. Perceptive character study, highlighted by brilliant Signoret performance; fine work by Rochefort and Seyrig (as their spinsterish friend).▼

Ishi: The Last of His Tribe (1978) C-150m. TVM D: Robert Ellis Miller. Dennis Weaver, Eloy Phil Casados, Devon Ericson, Joseph Running Fox, Lois Red Elk, Michael Medina. Absorbing drama traces the life of the last Yahi Indian from childhood to his early death, and his friendship with an anthropologist (Weaver). Interesting adaptation of Theodora Kroeber's book was started by Dalton Trumbo (who died while writing it) and completed by his son Christopher. Above average.

I Shot Jesse James (1949) 81m. ** D: Samuel Fuller. Preston Foster, Barbara Britton, John Ireland, Reed Hadley, J. Edward Bromberg. Flamboyant directorial touches (in Fuller's first film) cannot redeem essential dullness of story about Bob Ford, the man who plugged Jesse in the back.

Ishtar (1987) C-107m. ** D: Elaine May. Warren Beatty, Dustin Hoffman, Isabelle Adjani, Charles Grodin, Jack Weston, Tess Harper, Carol Kane, Aharon Ipale. The HEAVEN'S GATE of movie comedies made headlines because of its huge expense and costly delays, but the only thing wrong with it is that it isn't very funny. Beatty and Hoffman go the Hope and Crosby route as a couple of untalented singer-songwriters who get involved with international intrigue in North Africa (shades of ROAD TO MOROCCO!). A blind camel and a flock of vultures steal the show. Paul Williams' deliberately awful songs are funny, too, but not funny enough to overcome the flatness of director May's script.▼

Island, The (1962-Japanese) 96m. *** D:

Kaneto Shindo. Nobuko Otowa, Taiji Tonoyama, Shinji Tanaka, Masanori Horimoto. Engrossing documentary-style study of peasant family living on rocky island near Japan, struggling to survive. Visually stunning film contains not a single word of dialogue.▼

Island, The (1980) **C-114m.** BOMB D: Michael Ritchie. Michael Caine, David Warner, Angela Punch McGregor, Frank Middlemass, Don Henderson, Jeffrey Frank. Absolutely awful thriller about magazine reporter who investigates strange doings in the Caribbean and winds up a prisoner of primitive island tribe. You know you're in trouble when David Warner plays the most normal guy on the island! Peter Benchley scripted from his own novel.▼

Island at the Top of the World, The (1974) **C-93m.** **½ D: Robert Stevenson. David Hartman, Donald Sinden, Jacques Marin, Mako, David Gwillim, Agneta Eckemyr. Disney's attempt to score again in Jules Verne territory misses bullseye; simplistic, derivative story of Arctic expedition which stumbles across "lost" Viking civilization is mainly for kids.▼

Island Claws (1980) **C-82m.** BOMB D: Hernan Cardenas. Robert Lansing, Steve Hanks, Nita Talbot, Barry Nelson, Jo McDonnell, Martina Deignan. Florida-lensed horror stinker (never released theatrically) blames a nuclear reactor spill for causing crabs to become giant-sized and start killing people. Very talky, cheap and unscary; Roger Corman's ATTACK OF THE CRAB MONSTERS is a lot more fun. Retitled: NIGHT OF THE CLAW.▼

Islander, The (1978) **C-100m. TVM** D: Paul Krasny. Dennis Weaver, Sharon Gless, Peter Mark Richman, Bernadette Peters, Robert Vaughn, Sheldon Leonard. Lawyer Weaver retires to Hawaii to run a hotel, but soon finds himself involved with a variety of characters in various degrees of trouble with the law. OK series pilot. Average.▼

Island in the Sky (1953) **109m.** **½ D: William Wellman. John Wayne, Lloyd Nolan, James Arness, Andy Devine, Walter Abel, Allyn Joslyn. Clichéd survival story of a downed transport plane and its crew under the staunch leadership of Wayne, set in Greenland during WW2. Unconvincing and talky most of the way. Written by Ernest K. Gann.▼

Island in the Sun (1957) **C-119m.** ** D: Robert Rossen. James Mason, Joan Fontaine, Dorothy Dandridge, Joan Collins, Michael Rennie, Diana Wynyard, John Williams, Stephen Boyd, Harry Belafonte. Misfire adaptation of Alec Waugh's book about idyllic West Indies island torn by racial struggle. Good cast can't do much with unconvincing script.▼

Island of Desire (1952-British) **C-103m.**

*½ D: Stuart Heisler. Linda Darnell, Tab Hunter, Donald Gray, John Laurie, Sheila Chong. Sun-drenched, romantic WW2 drama of nurse, Marine, and injured pilot all washed ashore on tropical desert island. Parched performances. British title: SATURDAY'S ISLAND.▼

Island of Doomed Men (1940) **67m.** ** D: Charles Barton. Peter Lorre, Robert Wilcox, Rochelle Hudson, George E. Stone, Don Beddoe, Kenneth MacDonald. Low-grade melodrama even Lorre can't save as man who traps unsuspecting victims on island, turns them into his slaves.

Island of Dr. Moreau, The (1977) **C-104m.** *** D: Don Taylor. Burt Lancaster, Michael York, Nigel Davenport, Barbara Carrera, Richard Basehart. Handsomely produced remake of ISLAND OF LOST SOULS with Lancaster heading a solid cast as demented doctor who has spent years creating half-man, half-beast "humanimals," Good horror-fantasy chiller, based on H.G. Wells' story.▼

Island of Lost Men (1939) **63m.** *½ D: Kurt Neumann. Anna May Wong, J. Carrol Naish, Eric Blore, Ernest Truex, Anthony Quinn, Broderick Crawford. Generally dull mystery of Wong searching for Oriental general along the waterfront. A few atmospheric scenes, but stilted dialogue throughout.

Island of Lost Souls (1933) **70m.** ***½ D: Erle C. Kenton. Charles Laughton, Bela Lugosi, Richard Arlen, Stanley Fields, Kathleen Burke, Leila Hyams. Strong adaptation of H. G. Wells's story of a mad scientist isolated on a remote island, where he transforms jungle beasts into half-human "mansters." Laughton hams it up a bit, but despite more explicit horror films of late, this retains its frightening aura, particularly in the grisly finale. Remade as THE ISLAND OF DR. MOREAU.

Island of Lost Women (1959) **71m.** ** D: Frank Tuttle. Jeff Richards, Venetia Stevenson, John Smith, Diane Jergens, Alan Napier, June Blair. Plane forced down on remote island leads to complications with scientist and daughters who inhabit the jungle isle.

Island of Love (1963) **C-101m.** **½ D: Morton Da Costa. Robert Preston, Tony Randall, Giorgia Moll, Walter Matthau, Betty Bruce. Dud attempt to make bubbly romantic comedy. Filmed in Greece.

Island of Terror (1967-British) **C-90m.** ** D: Terence Fisher. Peter Cushing, Edward Judd, Carole Gray, Niall MacGinnis. Sci-fi tale about cancer research gone wild and mutations that result is directed and acted by veterans of the field, but result is nothing special.

Island of the Blue Dolphins (1964) **C-93m.** *½ D: James B. Clark. Celia Kaye, George Kennedy, Ann Daniel, Carlos Romero,

Larry Domasin. True story of Indian girl (Kaye) abandoned on small island, befriended only by wild dogs. Set in early 19th century. Well meaning but not very good.▼

Island of the Burning Damned SEE: **Island of the Burning Doomed**▼

Island of the Burning Doomed (1967-British) **C-94m.** **½ D: Terence Fisher. Christopher Lee, Peter Cushing, Patrick Allen, Sarah Lawson, Jane Merrow, William Lucas. Aliens cause a massive heatwave during winter. Good sci-fi, with Lee and Cushing at their best. Also known as ISLAND OF THE BURNING DAMNED and NIGHT OF THE BIG HEAT.▼

Island of the Doomed SEE: **Man-Eater of Hydra**

Island of the Lost (1967) **C-91m.** *½ D: John Florea; Underwater sequences, Ricou Browning. Richard Greene, Luke Halpin, Mart Hulswit, Jose De Vega, Robin Mattson, Irene Tsu. Anthropologist Greene takes his family on an expedition to find an uncharted South Sea isle but becomes shipwrecked. Clean-cut, highly innocuous travelogue from the Ivan Tors studio, cowritten by Tors and actor Richard Carlson. Underwater expert Browning appeared with Carlson years before in CREATURE FROM THE BLACK LAGOON. ▼

Island Princess, The (1955-Italian) **C-98m.** ** D: Paolo Moffa, Marcello Mastroianni, Silvana Pampanini, Gustavo Rojo. Rather hackneyed yarn set in 1500s, with Mastroianni a Spanish captain falling in love with princess of the Canary Islands.

Island Rescue (1952-British) **87m.** ** D: Ralph Thomas. David Niven, Glynis Johns, George Coulouris, Barry Jones, Noel Purcell. Lukewarm comedy involving rescue of cows from German-occupied island during WW2. Original British title: APPOINTMENT WITH VENUS.

Island Sons (1987) **C-100m. TVM** D: Alan J. Levi. Timothy Bottoms, Joseph Bottoms, Samuel Bottoms, Benjamin Bottoms, David Wohl, Claire Kirkconnell, Kim Miyori. The four acting Bottoms brothers play four battling brothers struggling to preserve the family dynasty following their dad's mysterious disappearance. By-the-numbers Hawaiian-based action pilot. Average.

Islands in the Stream (1977) **C-105m.** **½ D: Franklin J. Schaffner. George C. Scott, David Hemmings, Claire Bloom, Susan Tyrrell, Gilbert Roland, Richard Evans. Film version of Hemingway novel about an island-dwelling sculptor and his three sons begins well but falls apart completely in the final third. Still one of the better adaptations of this author, with one of Scott's best performances.▼

Island Woman (1958) **72m.** *½ D: William Berke. Marie Windsor, Vincent Edwards, Marilee Earle, Leslie Scott, Maurine Duvalier, George Symonette. Sailboat captain Edwards falls for tourist Earle, while her aunt (Windsor) connives to win him for herself. Dull; spiced with calypso music.

Isle of Forgotten Sins (1943) **82m.** ** D: Edgar G. Ulmer. John Carradine, Gale Sondergaard, Sidney Toler, Frank Fenton, Rita Quigley, Veda Ann Borg, Rick Vallin, Betty Amann, Tala Birell. Standard programmer with deep sea divers Carradine and Fenton going up against conniving ship captain Toler over a gold treasure. As usual, Ulmer's direction is much better than the material. Based on his short story; retitled MONSOON.▼

Isle of Fury (1936) **60m.** ** D: Frank McDonald. Humphrey Bogart, Margaret Lindsay, Donald Woods, Paul Graetz, Gordon Hart, E. E. Clive. Mild remake of Somerset Maugham novel NARROW CORNER, involving love triangle on South Sea island; early Bogart.

Isle of Lost Women SEE: **99 Women**▼

Isle of Sin (1960-German) **63m.** *½ D: Johannes Kai. Christiane Nielsen, Erwin Strahl, Jan Hendriks, Slavo Schwaiger. Trite tale of passengers on plane which crashes on deserted island, with expected friction between types.

Isle of the Dead (1945) **72m.** *** D: Mark Robson, Boris Karloff, Ellen Drew, Marc Cramer, Katherine Emery, Helene Thimig, Jason Robards. Eerie horror tale of assorted characters stranded on Greek island during quarantine. Good Val Lewton production.▼

Isle of the Snake People SEE: **Snake People**▼

Is My Face Red? (1932) **66m.** **½ D: William A. Seiter. Ricardo Cortez, Helen Twelvetrees, Jill Esmond, Robert Armstrong, Sidney Toler, ZaSu Pitts. Cortez does well as a wisecracking, Walter Winchell-like columnist. Some snappy dialogue, but film really goes nowhere—and main character is such a total heel that our sympathies aren't with him when script demands they should be. That's director Seiter as the ship's purser.

Isn't It Romantic? (1948) **87m.** ** D: Norman Z. McLeod. Veronica Lake, Mary Hatcher, Mona Freeman, Billy DeWolfe, Patric Knowles, Roland Culver, Pearl Bailey. No.

Isn't It Shocking? (1973) **C-73m. TVM** D: John Badham. Alan Alda, Louise Lasser, Edmond O'Brien, Ruth Gordon, Will Geer, Dorothy Tristan, Lloyd Nolan. Virtually everything clicks in brilliant, oddball comedy-mystery about series of bizarre murders disrupting usual day-to-day routine of small New England town's police department. Excellent cast, script (by Lane Slate) and direction. A film to remember. Above average.

Is Paris Burning? (1966-French-U.S.) 173m. ** D: René Clement. Jean-Paul Belmondo, Charles Boyer, Leslie Caron, Jean-Pierre Cassel, Claude Dauphin, Alain Delon, Kirk Douglas, Glenn Ford, Gert Frobe, Daniel Gelin, Yves Montand, Simone Signoret, Robert Stack, Orson Welles. Rambling pseudo-documentary-style recreation of WW2 France, showing liberation of Paris and Nazis' attempt to burn the city. Cameos by international players confuse blotchy film made in Europe. Screenplay by Gore Vidal and Francis Ford Coppola, from the Larry Collins-Dominique Lapierre book.

Istanbul (1957) **C-84m.** ** D: Joseph Pevney. Errol Flynn, Cornell Borchers, John Bentley, Torin Thatcher, Nat King Cole. Unsatisfying drama of adventurer Flynn returning to title city to find cache of gems, discovering his old girlfriend still alive. Remake of SINGAPORE.

Istanbul (1990-Turkish-Swedish) **C-88m.** BOMB D: Mats Arehn. Timothy Bottoms, Twiggy, Emma Kilberg, Robert Morley, Lena Endre, Sverre Anker Ousdal. Journalist Bottoms arrives in Istanbul with his daughter to seek information on family of his wife's son, but becomes enmeshed in confusing intrigue. Twiggy is a mystery woman. Murky, clumsy, impenetrable international coproduction is about as interesting as watching camel spit dry.▼

Istanbul Express (1968) **C-94m.** TVM D: Richard Irving. Gene Barry, John Saxon, Senta Berger, Mary Ann Mobley, Tom Simcox. Trans-Europa Express main scene of action in tired espionage adventure film featuring Barry as one of several spies vying for research notes of deceased scientist. Script by Richard Levinson and William Link. Average.

I Stand Condemned (1935-British) 75m. **½ D: Anthony Asquith. Harry Baur, Laurence Olivier, Penelope Dudley Ward, Robert Cochran, Morton Selten, Athene Seyler. Inconsequential story of jealous Russian framing young officer as a spy, to eliminate him from rivalry over woman. Worth seeing for young, dashing Olivier. British title: MOSCOW NIGHTS.▼

Is There Sex After Death? (1971) **C-97m.** *** D: Jeanne and Alan Abel. Buck Henry, Alan Abel, Marshall Efron, Holly Woodlawn, Earle Doud. Crude but funny satire of porn films. Famous hoaxer Abel (who, with his wife, also produced and scripted) plays a traveling sexologist; Efron hilarious as an X-rated film director.▼

It (1927) 72m. **½ D: Clarence Badger. Clara Bow, Antonio Moreno, William Austin, Jacqueline Gadsdon (Jane Daly), Priscilla Bonner. Bow is dazzling in this otherwise ordinary tale of a spirited, gold-digging department-store salesgirl with designs on her handsome boss (Moreno).

Based on Elinor Glyn's trendy story of the same title; Madame Glyn appears briefly as herself. Look for Gary Cooper in a walk-on as a reporter.▼

It (1967) 96m. ** D: Herbert J. Leder. Roddy McDowall, Jill Haworth, Ernest Clark, Paul Maxwell, Aubrey Richards. McDowall brings hulking stone statue— the Golem, no less—to life and soon finds it makes a great murderer. Kill it! Filmed in England.

It Ain't Hay (1943) 80m. **½ D: Erle C. Kenton. Bud Abbott, Lou Costello, Patsy O'Connor, Grace McDonald, Leighton Noble, Cecil Kellaway, Eugene Pallette, Eddie Quillan. Pretty good A&C from Damon Runyon story of racehorse Teabiscuit; good supporting cast helps.

I Take These Men (1983) **C-100m.** TVM D: Larry Peerce. Susan Saint James, John Rubinstein, James Murtaugh, Adam West, Dee Wallace, Brian Dennehy, Hermione Baddeley, Steve Garvey. Engaging comedy about a bored suburban wife who spends her anniversary party first asking for a divorce and then fantasizing about marriage to three others. Average.

I Take This Woman (1940) 97m. ** D: W. S. Van Dyke II. Spencer Tracy, Hedy Lamarr, Verree Teasdale, Kent Taylor, Laraine Day, Mona Barrie, Jack Carson. Disappointing soaper with dedicated doctor Tracy sacrificing all for Lamarr, who at first isn't grateful. Not up to stars' talents.

Italian Connection, The (1973-Italian) **C-92m.** ** D: Fernando Di Leo. Henry Silva, Woody Strode, Mario Adorf, Luciana Paluzzi, Sylva Koscina, Adolfo Celi. Violent gangster meller has Milanese hood Adorf set up by gang boss Celi for the blame in a six million dollar heroin heist. For action fans only. Video title: MANHUNT.▼

Italian Job, The (1969-British) **C-101m.** **½ D: Peter Collinson. Michael Caine, Noel Coward, Maggie Blye, Benny Hill, Tony Beckley, Raf Vallone. $4,000,000 in gold bullion's the object in average caper film about prison-based mastermind Coward's plan to divert authorities in Turin, Italy, causing "history's biggest traffic jam." Wild chases galore, plus truly bizarre ending, but characterizations are pat, forgettable.

Italiano Brava Gente (1965-Italian) 156m. *** D: Giuseppe De Santis. Arthur Kennedy, Peter Falk, Tatyana Samoilova, Rafaelle Pisu, Andrea Checchi. Expansive chronicle of Italian-Russian warfront during WW2, focusing on a variety of strata of soldiers and civilians. Much edited since European opening. Retitled: ATTACK AND RETREAT.

It All Came True (1940) 97m. **½ D:

Lewis Seiler. Ann Sheridan, Humphrey Bogart, Jeffrey Lynn, ZaSu Pitts, Jessie Busley, Una O'Connor, Grant Mitchell, Felix Bressart. Offbeat story combines comedy, drama, music, and sentiment as gangster Bogart hides out in quaint boarding house. Fine showcase for Sheridan, who sings "Angel in Disguise" and "The Gaucho Serenade."

It Always Rains on Sunday (1948-British) **92m.** ***½ D: Robert Hamer. Googie Withers, Edward Chapman, Sydney Tafler, Jane Hylton, Alfie Bass, Hermione Baddeley. Excellent mosaic of characters whose lives intertwine in a drab London neighborhood.

√ **It Came from Beneath the Sea** (1955) **80m.** *** D: Robert Gordon. Kenneth Tobey, Faith Domergue, Donald Curtis, Ian Keith, Harry Lauter. Breathtaking special effects highlight this sci-fi thriller. Huge octopus emerges from Pacific Ocean and wreaks havoc on San Francisco. First film made by Ray Harryhausen-Charles H. Schneer team.▼

It Came from Hollywood (1982) **C-80m.** *½ D: Malcolm Leo, Andrew Solt. Dan Aykroyd, John Candy, Cheech and Chong, Gilda Radner. Contemporary comedy stars are spectacularly *unfunny introducing and narrating clips from some of Hollywood's worst movies—most of which are funny enough without additional wisecracks. What's more, this pointless, poorly constructed compilation includes scenes from *good* movies like WAR OF THE WORLDS and THE INCREDIBLE SHRINKING MAN! Even so, howlers like MARS NEEDS WOMEN and PLAN 9 FROM OUTER SPACE still offer some genuine laughs.▼

√ **It Came From Outer Space** (1953) **81m.** *** D: Jack Arnold. Richard Carlson, Barbara Rush, Charles Drake, Russell Johnson, Joe Sawyer, Kathleen Hughes. Intriguing science-fiction based on a Ray Bradbury story. An alien ship crashes in the Arizona desert; its passengers assume the identities of nearby townspeople so they can effect repairs unnoticed—they think. Remarkably sober for its era, with crisp performances and real restraint, even in its use of 3-D.▼

It Came Upon the Midnight Clear (1984) **C-100m.** TVM D: Peter H. Hunt. Mickey Rooney, Scott Grimes, Barrie Youngfellow, George Gaynes, Gary Bayer, William Griffis, Christina Pickles, Hamilton Camp, Elisha Cook, Annie Potts, Lloyd Nolan. The Mick's an ex-cop turned angel who goes home to the Big Apple to cheer up the town during Christmas and help his grandson from California see what an old-fashioned Yule was like. The Rooney artistry, alas, can do only so much, and the story remains earthbound. Average.▼

It Came Without Warning SEE: **Without Warning**

It Comes Up Murder SEE: **Honey Pot, The**▼

It Conquered the World (1956) **68m.** **½ D: Roger Corman. Peter Graves, Beverly Garland, Lee Van Cleef, Sally Fraser. Low-budget sci-fi which intelligently attempts to create atmospheric excitement in yarn of carrot-shaped monster from Venus, Paul Blaisdell's finest creation. One of Corman's best early quickies, well acted and interesting but awkwardly plotted. Remade as ZONTAR, THE THING FROM VENUS.

It Couldn't Happen to a Nicer Guy (1974) **C-78m.** TVM D: Cy Howard. Paul Sorvino, Michael Learned, Bob Dishy, Adam Arkin, Ed Barth, Roger Bowen. Farce about a mild-mannered salesman who has trouble convincing anyone he has been raped at gunpoint by a beautiful woman. Silly, but versatile Sorvino manages to pull it off. Average.

It Grows on Trees (1952) **84m.** ** D: Arthur Lubin. Irene Dunne, Dean Jagger, Richard Crenna, Les Tremayne. Dunne's last feature is slim vehicle of wife who discovers backyard foliage is blossoming crisp money.

It Had To Be You (1947) **98m.** **½ D: Don Hartman, Rudolph Maté. Ginger Rogers, Cornel Wilde, Percy Waram, Spring Byington, Ron Randell. Rogers has severe indecision before every scheduled marriage, until dream-lover Wilde appears. Airy, fanciful comedy.

It Had to Happen (1936) **79m.** ** D: Roy Del Ruth. George Raft, Leo Carrillo, Rosalind Russell, Alan Dinehart, Arline Judge. Italian immigrant Raft working his way to political power in N.Y.C., trying to romance upper-class Russell.

I Thank a Fool (1962-British) **C-100m.** ** D: Robert Stevens. Susan Hayward, Peter Finch, Diane Cilento, Cyril Cusack, Kieron Moore, Athene Seyler. Dreary, far-fetched story about Hayward spending a year and a half in prison for mercy-killing, then becoming involved with lawyer Finch, who prosecuted her case, with bizarre results.

It Happened at Lakewood Manor (1977) **C-100m.** TVM D: Robert Sheerer. Lynda Day George, Robert Foxworth, Myrna Loy, Suzanne Somers, Bernie Casey, Brian Dennehy. Insects on the rampage, or what happens when the traditional stellar TV cast vacationing at a secluded lodge tampers with Mother Nature. Predictable horrors, and the squeamish are forewarned. Also known as PANIC AT LAKEWOOD MANOR and ANTS. Average.▼

It Happened at the World's Fair (1963) **C-105m.** *** D: Norman Taurog. Elvis Presley, Joan O'Brien, Gary Lockwood, Yvonne Craig. Entertaining Presley vehicle set at Seattle World's Fair, with Elvis and O'Brien brought together by little Ginny Tiu. Listenable tunes (including "One Broken Heart for Sale," "A World of Our Own" and "Happy Ending") help make this most enjoyable. Young Kurt Russell, who later played Elvis in a TV movie, has a small role.▼

It Happened Here (1966-British) **95m.** *** D: Kevin Brownlow, Andrew Mollo. Pauline Murray, Sebastian Shaw, Fiona Lelard, Honor Fehrson. Imaginative fable of Britain taken over by the Nazis during WW2, made in semidocumentary style by two ingenious young filmmakers. Brits keep a stiff upper lip during fascist persecution; leading lady Murray is the odd woman out, as a nurse thought to be collaborating with the enemy. Subject of a documentary followup in 1974: IT HAPPENED HERE AGAIN.

It Happened in Athens (1962) **C-92m.** ** D: Andrew Marton. Jayne Mansfield, Trax Colton, Lili Valenty, Maria Xenia, Bob Mathias, Nico Minardos. Silly, juvenile charade made somewhat watchable by Mansfield in a variety of revealing costumes as an actress who agrees to marry the winner of the marathon at the 1896 Olympics. Previewed at 100m.

It Happened in Brooklyn (1947) **105m.** ** D: Richard Whorf. Frank Sinatra, Kathryn Grayson, Jimmy Durante, Peter Lawford, Gloria Grahame. Hokey musical of group of Brooklynites trying to make it big in show biz; all coating, no substance. Some good songs, including "Time After Time" and wonderful Sinatra-Durante duet, "The Song's Gotta Have Heart."

It Happened One Christmas (1977) **C-112m. TVM** D: Donald Wrye. Marlo Thomas, Wayne Rogers, Orson Welles, Cloris Leachman, Barney Martin, Karen Carlson, Doris Roberts. IT'S A WONDERFUL LIFE with change of sex only proves how wonderful the original by Frank Capra was—and is. This one goes on forever, and that's just one of the problems. Anyway, earnestly made. Average.

✓ **It Happened One Night** (1934) **105m.** **** D: Frank Capra. Clark Gable, Claudette Colbert, Walter Connolly, Roscoe Karns, Alan Hale, Ward Bond. Legendary romantic comedy doesn't age a bit. Still as enchanting as ever, with reporter Gable and runaway heiress Colbert falling in love on rural bus trip. Hitch-hiking scene, the Walls of Jericho, other memorable scenes remain fresh and delightful. First film to win all five major Oscars: Picture, Actor, Actress, Director, and Screenplay (Robert Riskin). Remade as musicals EVE KNEW HER APPLES and YOU CAN'T RUN AWAY FROM IT.▼

It Happened One Summer SEE: **State Fair** (1945)

It Happened on 5th Avenue (1947) **115m.** ** D: Roy Del Ruth. Don DeFore, Ann Harding, Charlie Ruggles, Victor Moore, Gale Storm, Grant Mitchell. Overlong comedy about elegant N.Y.C. mansion taken over by thoughtful bum, who invites horde of friends and real owner in disguise to be his guests.

It Happened to Jane (1959) **C-98m.** **½ D: Richard Quine. Doris Day, Jack Lemmon, Ernie Kovacs, Steve Forrest, Teddy Rooney, Russ Brown, Mary Wickes, Parker Fennelly. Breezy, likable comedy: Doris runs a Maine lobstery, and Jack is her lawyer; together they tangle with ultracheap villain Kovacs (who hams mercilessly). Also known as TWINKLE AND SHINE.

It Happened Tomorrow (1944) **84m.** *** D: René Clair. Dick Powell, Linda Darnell, Jack Oakie, Edgar Kennedy, John Philliber, Edward Brophy, George Cleveland, Sig Ruman, Paul Guilfoyle. Diverting if somewhat static fantasy yarn about a turn-of-the-century reporter who gets inside track on *tomorrow's* headlines, leading to unexpected complications. Low-key, often charming.

It Happens Every Spring (1949) **87m.** ***½ D: Lloyd Bacon. Ray Milland, Jean Peters, Paul Douglas, Ed Begley. Clever little comedy of chemistry professor (Milland) accidentally discovering a chemical mixture which causes baseballs to avoid all wooden surfaces, namely bats. A most enjoyable and unpretentious picture.

It Happens Every Thursday (1953) **80m.** *** D: Joseph Pevney. Loretta Young, John Forsythe, Frank McHugh, Edgar Buchanan. Warm comedy about married couple who buy small-town newspaper and try every method conceivable to make it click.

I, the Jury (1953) **87m.** ** D: Harry Essex. Biff Elliot, Preston Foster, Peggie Castle, Elisha Cook, Jr., John Qualen. Undistinguished Mickey Spillane caper with Mike Hammer seeking his friend's killer. Originally in 3D; remade in 1982 in 2D.

I, the Jury (1982) **C-111m.** ** D: Richard T. Heffron. Armand Assante, Barbara Carrera, Alan King, Laurene Landon, Geoffrey Lewis, Paul Sorvino, Judson Scott. Mickey Spillane's hard-boiled Mike Hammer seems out of place in this updated remake, though contemporary levels of violence and nudity suit the material. Lots of action and some truly beautiful women help camouflage the holes in Larry Cohen's script; Assante is a sulky Hammer.▼

It Lives Again (1978) **C-91m.** *½ D: Larry Cohen. Frederic Forrest, Kathleen Lloyd, John Ryan, John Marley, Andrew Duggan, Eddie Constantine. Sequel to IT'S ALIVE offers not one but three murderous babies. More of a horror film than a thriller—and not a very good one. Constantine's first American film in many years.

Also known as IT'S ALIVE II, and followed by IT'S ALIVE III: ISLAND OF THE ALIVE.▼

It Lives by Night SEE: **Bat People**▼

It Nearly Wasn't Christmas (1989) C-100m. TVM D: Burt Brinckerhoff. Charles Durning, Ted Lange, Wayne Osmond, Annette Marin, Risa Schiffman. Durning is Santa Claus, and he's sick and tired of making chimney deliveries to unappreciative families. Undemanding Yuletide timepasser concocted by the Osmond Family (Wayne costars, Jimmy coproduced, Merrill and Jimmy cowrote the title song, which Wayne sings). So where are Donny and Marie? Average.

It Only Happens to Others (1971-French-Italian) C-88m. ** D: Nadine Trintignant. Marcello Mastroianni, Catherine Deneuve, Serge Marquand, Dominique Labourier, Catherine Allegret. Loss of young child causes happily married couple to withdraw from society. Heavy on the syrup.

It's a Big Country (1951) 89m. **½ D: Charles Vidor, Richard Thorpe, John Sturges, Don Hartman, Don Weis, Clarence Brown, William Wellman. Ethel Barrymore, Keefe Brasselle, Gary Cooper, Nancy Davis (Reagan), Gene Kelly, Keenan Wynn, Fredric March, Van Johnson, James Whitmore. Dore Schary's plug for America uses several pointless episodes about the variety of people and places in U.S. Other segments make up for it in very uneven film. Narrated by Louis Calhern.

It's a Bikini World (1967) C-86m. *½ D: Stephanie Rothman. Deborah Walley, Tommy Kirk, Bob Pickett, Suzie Kaye, The Animals, The Gentrys. Superlover Kirk loves bikinied Debbie, but she doesn't dig him until he masquerades as an intellectual. Not among the best of its kind, if there even *is* a best of its kind. The Animals, however, do perform "We Gotta Get Out of This Place."

It's a Date (1940) 103m. **½ D: William A. Seiter. Deanna Durbin, Walter Pidgeon, Kay Francis, Eugene Pallette, Lewis Howard, S. Z. Sakall, Samuel S. Hinds, Cecilia Loftus. Durbin faces unique growing pains when she's offered a Broadway role intended for her mother (Francis) and then is courted by a man her mother's age (Pidgeon). Star trio shines brightly in this enjoyable contrivance, which unfortunately goes on too long and ends (incongruously) with Deanna singing "Ave Maria"! Remade as NANCY GOES TO RIO.

It's a Dog's Life (1955) C-88m. **½ D: Herman Hoffman. Jeff Richards, Edmund Gwenn, Dean Jagger, Sally Fraser. Film uses gimmick of having the canine star tell his life story from slums to luxury. Retitled: BAR SINISTER.

It's A Gift (1934) 73m. **** D: Norman Z. McLeod. W. C. Fields, Baby LeRoy, Kathleen Howard, Tommy Bupp, Morgan Wallace. Fields is a grocery store owner who goes West with his family. Beautiful comedy routines in one of the Great Man's unforgettable films. Charles Sellon as a blind man, T. Roy Barnes as a salesman looking for Carl LaFong, contribute some hilarious moments. A remake of Fields' silent film IT'S THE OLD ARMY GAME.▼

It's A Great Feeling (1949) C-85m. **½ D: David Butler. Dennis Morgan, Doris Day, Jack Carson, Bill Goodwin. Gentle spoof of Hollywood with Carson's ego making filming difficult for himself and partner Morgan; guest appearances by many Warner Bros. players and directors, including Joan Crawford, Gary Cooper, Jane Wyman, Sydney Greenstreet, Danny Kaye, Edward G. Robinson, Eleanor Parker, Patricia Neal, and Ronald Reagan.

It's a Great Life (1943) 75m. D: Frank Strayer. Penny Singleton, Arthur Lake, Larry Simms, Hugh Herbert, Jonathan Hale, Danny Mummert, Alan Dinehart. SEE: **Blondie** series.

It's a Joke, Son (1947) 63m. ** D: Ben Stoloff. Kenny Delmar, Una Merkel, June Lockhart, Kenneth Farrell, Douglass Dumbrille. Folksy comedy featuring further exploits of Senator Claghorn (Delmar) from the Fred Allen radio show.▼

It's Alive! (1974) C-91m. **½ D: Larry Cohen. John Ryan, Sharon Farrell, Andrew Duggan, Guy Stockwell, James Dixon, Michael Ansara. Schlocky thriller about a baby who goes on a murderous rampage. Has a devoted following, but not for all tastes. Effective score by Bernard Herrmann. Sequels: IT LIVES AGAIN and IT'S ALIVE III: ISLAND OF THE ALIVE.▼

It's Alive II SEE: **It Lives Again**▼

It's Alive III: Island of the Alive (1987) C-91m. **½ D: Larry Cohen. Michael Moriarty, Karen Black, Laurene Landon, Gerrit Graham, James Dixon, Neal Israel, Macdonald Carey. Part 3 makes serious comments on issues ranging from the AIDS crisis to abortion as Moriarty, father of a monster baby, succeeds in preventing society from exterminating all the monster infants who are quarantined on a desert island. Wild fun, loaded with dark humor.▼

It's All Happening SEE: **Dream Maker, The**

It's Always Fair Weather (1955) C-102m. *** D: Gene Kelly, Stanley Donen. Gene Kelly, Dan Dailey, Michael Kidd, Cyd Charisse, Dolores Gray, David Burns. Three WW2 buddies meet ten years after their discharge and find they have nothing in common. Pungent Comden and Green script falls short of perfection but still has wonderful moments, and some first-rate musical numbers. Best: the ash-can dance, although clever use of wide-screen is lost on TV.▼

It's a Mad Mad Mad Mad World (1963) **C-154m.** **½ D: Stanley Kramer. Spencer Tracy, Edie Adams, Milton Berle, Sid Caesar, Buddy Hackett, Ethel Merman, Mickey Rooney, Dick Shawn, Dorothy Provine, Phil Silvers, Jonathan Winters, Peter Falk, Jimmy Durante, Terry-Thomas, Eddie "Rochester" Anderson, William Demarest, many guest stars. Supercomedy cast in attempt at supercomedy, about group of people racing to find hidden bank loot under watchful eye of detective Tracy. Big, splashy, generally funny, but bigness doesn't equal greatness. Originally shown in Cinerama process at 192m.▼

It's a Pleasure! (1945) **C-90m.** ** D: William A. Seiter. Sonja Henie, Michael O'Shea, Bill Johnson, Marie McDonald, Gus Schilling, Iris Adrian. Skater Henie and hockey player O'Shea get married but can't seem to break the ice; pretty weak.

It's a Small World (1950) **68m.** ** D: William Castle. Paul Dale, Lorraine Miller, Will Geer, Steve Brodie, Todd Karns. Truly strange B-movie stars Dale (a deejay in real life) as a midget who suffers a succession of life's hard knocks until finally becoming "adjusted" and even finding romance in a circus. Director Castle (who appears in a cameo as a cop) makes it interesting but unnecessarily nasty for the little guy.

It's A Wonderful Life (1946) **129m.** **** D: Frank Capra. James Stewart, Donna Reed, Lionel Barrymore, Thomas Mitchell, Henry Travers, Beulah Bondi, Frank Faylen, Ward Bond, Gloria Grahame, H.B. Warner, Frank Albertson, Todd Karns, Samuel S. Hinds, Mary Treen, Sheldon Leonard, Ellen Corby. Sentimental tale of Stewart, who works all his life to make good in small town, thinking he's failed and trying to end his life. Guardian angel Travers comes to show him his mistake. Only Capra and this cast could pull it off so well; this film seems to improve with age. Capra, Frances Goodrich, Albert Hackett, and Jo Swerling expanded Philip Van Doren Stern's short story "The Greatest Gift" (which had originally been written by Stern as a Christmas card!). Remade for TV as IT HAPPENED ONE CHRISTMAS. Also shown in computer-colored version.▼

It's a Wonderful World (1939) **86m.** *** D: W. S. Van Dyke II. Claudette Colbert, James Stewart, Guy Kibbee, Nat Pendleton, Frances Drake, Edgar Kennedy, Ernest Truex, Sidney Blackmer, Hans Conried. Screwball comedy with Colbert a runaway poetess, Stewart a fugitive chased by cops Pendleton and Kennedy. Very, very funny, with Stewart having a field-day. Scripted by Ben Hecht, from his and Herman J. Mankiewicz' story. We swear by our eyes!

It Seemed Like a Good Idea at the Time (1975-Canadian) **C-106m.** ** D: John Trent. Anthony Newley, Stefanie Powers, Isaac Hayes, Lloyd Bochner, Yvonne De Carlo, Henry Ramer, Lawrence Dane, John Candy. Tired comedy with a mostly tired cast, centering on Newley's attempts to woo back his remarried ex-wife. Dane and Candy appear as a pair of bumbling cops, characters they replayed a year later in FIND THE LADY.

It's Good to Be Alive (1974) **C-100m.** TVM D: Michael Landon. Paul Winfield, Lou Gossett, Ruby Dee, Ramon Bieri, Joe DeSantis, Ty Henderson, Lloyd Gough. The Roy Campanella story, beginning with the baseball star's crippling automobile accident in 1958. Especially strong performances by the three leads make this rewarding viewing. Above average.▼

It Should Happen to You (1954) **87m.** *** D: George Cukor. Judy Holliday, Peter Lawford, Jack Lemmon, Michael O'Shea, Vaughn Taylor. Raucous comedy about publicity-seeking actress (Holliday) who has her name plastered on billboards in N.Y.C. with deft results. Lemmon's first film.▼

It Shouldn't Happen to a Dog (1946) **70m.** **½ D: Herbert I. Leeds. Carole Landis, Allyn Joslyn, Margo Woode, Henry (Harry) Morgan, Reed Hadley, Jean Wallace. Fluff of fast-talking reporter, policewoman, and a troublesome dog.

It Shouldn't Happen to a Vet SEE: **All Things Bright and Beautiful**

It's in the Air (1935) **80m.** ** D: Charles Reisner. Jack Benny, Una Merkel, Ted Healy, Nat Pendleton, Mary Carlisle, Grant Mitchell. Uncharacteristic Benny as con-artist who goes to ex-wife Merkel for help. Fair comedy; mainly a curiosity item.

It's in the Bag (1945) **87m.** *** D: Richard Wallace. Fred Allen, Binnie Barnes, Robert Benchley, Sidney Toler, Jack Benny, Don Ameche, Victor Moore, Rudy Vallee, William Bendix. Story similar to THE TWELVE CHAIRS with flea-circus promoter Allen entitled to inheritance; plot soon goes out the window in favor of unrelated but amusing episodes, including hilarious encounter between Allen and Benny.▼

It's Love Again (1936-British) **83m.** *** D: Victor Saville. Robert Young, Jessie Matthews, Sonnie Hale, Ernest Milton, Robb Wilton, Sara Allgood. Lighter-than-air musical-comedy vehicle for Matthews following her success with Saville on EVERGREEN. Young is wise-guy publicity man who dreams up idea of creating an imaginary socialite, until Matthews steps out of the chorus line to fill the role. Funny, charming and imaginatively done, with several pleasant songs.▼

It's Love I'm After (1937) **90m.** *** D: Archie Mayo. Bette Davis, Leslie Howard, Olivia de Havilland, Patric Knowles,

Eric Blore, Bonita Granville, Spring Byington, Veda Ann Borg. Delightful, witty comedy of ego-struck actor Howard and his fiancée/co-star Davis, who explodes when he becomes involved with infatuated admirer de Havilland. Reminiscent in spirit of TWENTIETH CENTURY; Blore is marvelous as Howard's ultradedicated valet.

It's My Turn (1980) **C-91m.** *** D: Claudia Weill. Jill Clayburgh, Michael Douglas, Charles Grodin, Beverly Garland, Steven Hill, Teresa Baxter, Joan Copeland, John Gabriel, Jennifer Salt, Daniel Stern, Dianne Wiest. Enjoyable, low-key romantic comedy-drama about a young woman trying to balance her life as a career woman, mate, and daughter. A quirky and consistently surprising little film with good performances, especially from Grodin as Clayburgh's aloof lover. Film debut of Dianne Wiest.▼

It's Never Too Late (1956-British) **C-95m.** **½ D: Michael McCarthy. Phyllis Calvert, Guy Rolfe, Sarah Lawson, Peter Illing, Patrick Barr. Pleasant frou-frou about Calvert becoming famed writer, caught between choice of being good mother or living a celebrity's life.

It's Not the Size That Counts (1974-British) **C-90m.** BOMB D: Ralph Thomas. Leigh Lawson, Elke Sommer, Denholm Elliott, Vincent Price, Judy Geeson, George Coulouris, Harry H. Corbett, Milo O'Shea. Abominable sequel to PERCY, even worse than the original, if that's possible, with Lawson replacing Hywel Bennett as penis-transplant recipient. Originally titled PERCY'S PROGRESS.▼

It's Only Money (1962) **84m.** *** D: Frank Tashlin. Jerry Lewis, Joan O'Brien, Zachary Scott, Jack Weston, Jesse White, Mae Questel. TV repairman Jerry wants to be a detective like his idol (White!), so he sets out to locate a missing heir—and guess who it turns out to be? Slick mystery-comedy is one of Lewis' best vehicles, thanks to solid script (by John Fenton Murray) and direction, fine cast, and memorable climax involving runaway army of robot lawn mowers.

It's Showtime (1976) **C/B&W-86m.** *** No director credit. Enjoyable compilation of animal sequences from movies, reaching back to Rin Tin Tin's silent films. Maximum footage from NATIONAL VELVET and LASSIE COME HOME, but everything—from canine version of "Singin' in the Rain" to Bonzo the Chimp being bottle-fed by Ronald Reagan—is great fun.

It Started in Naples (1960) **C-100m.** **½ D: Melville Shavelson. Clark Gable, Sophia Loren, Vittorio De Sica, Marietto, Paolo Carlini, Claudio Ermelli. Gable is American lawyer, in Italy to bring nephew back to America, but Aunt Sophia won't

agree. Star duo never clicks as love match, but they do their best.

It Started with a Kiss (1959) **C-104m.** **½ D: George Marshall. Glenn Ford, Debbie Reynolds, Eva Gabor, Fred Clark, Edgar Buchanan, Harry Morgan. Airy comedy about wacky Reynolds and her army officer husband Ford, trying to make a go of marriage, set in Spain.

It Started with Eve (1941) **90m.** *** D: Henry Koster. Deanna Durbin, Charles Laughton, Robert Cummings, Guy Kibbee, Margaret Tallichet, Walter Catlett. Delightful romantic comedy; Deanna poses as Cummings' fiancee to please his dying father (Laughton). Trouble starts when Laughton shows signs of recovery. Remade as I'D RATHER BE RICH.

It's Tough to Be Famous (1932) **79m.** *** D: Alfred E. Green. Douglas Fairbanks, Jr., Mary Brian, Walter Catlett, Lilian Bond, Terrence Ray, David Landau. Pungent story of naval hero who becomes a much-manipulated media celebrity against his wishes. Done with usual Warner Bros. pizazz—and still surprisingly timely.

It's Trad, Dad! SEE: **Ring-a-Ding Rhythm**

It's Your Move (1968-Italian-Spanish) **C-93m.** ** D: Robert Fiz. Edward G. Robinson, Terry-Thomas, Adolfo Celi. Good cast aids limp tale of Englishman who uses lookalikes for four bank tellers to pull off robbery.

It Takes a Thief (1960-British) **90m.** ** D: John Gilling. Jayne Mansfield, Anthony Quayle, Carl Mohner, Edward Judd. Mansfield is gangland leader with big heist in the workings; supporting cast uplifts flick. Original title: THE CHALLENGE.

It Takes All Kinds (1969-U.S.-Australian) **C-98m.** ** D: Eddie Davis. Robert Lansing, Vera Miles, Barry Sullivan, Sid Melton, Penny Sugg. Fair double-cross drama about Miles' shielding of Lansing when he accidentally kills sailor in a brawl in Australia. Nothing special.

It Takes Two (1988) **C-79m.** **½ D: David Beaird. George Newbern, Leslie Hope, Kimberly Foster, Barry Corbin, Anthony Geary, Frances Lee McCain. Romantic comedy concerning a would-be groom with cold feet who suddenly decides to warm them up by splurging on the car of his dreams (and the sexy saleswoman, too). Bright, often amusing film with promising cast of attractive newcomers in the leads.▼

It! The Terror from Beyond Space (1958) **69m.** *½ D: Edward L. Cahn. Marshall Thompson, Shawn Smith, Kim Spalding, Ann Doran. Mild sci-fi of space ship returning to earth with a most unwelcome creature stowed away on it. This was the inspiration for ALIEN.

Ivanhoe (1952) **C-106m.** *** D: Richard

Thorpe. Robert Taylor, Joan Fontaine, Elizabeth Taylor, Emlyn Williams, George Sanders, Robert Douglas, Finlay Currie, Felix Aylmer, Francis de Wolff, Guy Rolfe, Norman Wooland, Basil Sydney. Almost a classic spectacular, marred by draggy scripting of Walter Scott's epic of England in Middle Ages, in days of chivalrous knights; beautifully photographed on location in Great Britain. Remade as a TVM.▼

Ivanhoe (1982) C-150m. TVM D: Douglas Camfield. James Mason, Anthony Andrews, Sam Neill, Michael Hordern, Olivia Hussey, Lysette Anthony, Julian Glover, John Rhys-Davies. Robust, florid adaptation (by John Gay) of the Scott classic. Stunningly photographed by John Coquillon and enthusiastically played by a standout cast, especially Mason as Isaac of York. Above average.▼

Ivan the Terrible, Part One (1943-Russian) **96m.** **** D: Sergei Eisenstein. Nikolai Cherkasov, Ludmila Tselikovskaya, Serafina Birman. Film spectacle of the highest order. Eisenstein's incredibly lavish, detailed chronicle of Czar Ivan IV's life from coronation to defeat to reinstatement, forging fascinating image of the man and his country. Enhanced by Prokofiev's original score. Heavy going, but worthwhile; the story continues in IVAN THE TERRIBLE, (PART TWO).▼

Ivan the Terrible, Part Two (1946-Russian) **88m.** ***½ D: Sergei Eisenstein. Nikolai Cherkassov, Serafina Berman, Mikhail Nazvanov, Pavel Kadochnikov, Andrei Abrikosov. Continuation of the saga of Czar Ivan IV, in which he takes on the boyars in a battle for power. Impressive film is just a shade below its predecessor. Banned by Stalin because of Eisenstein's controversial depiction of Ivan's secret police, and not released until 1958. (The director had planned to shoot Part Three—which, needless to say, he never did.) The banquet-dance sequence was originally in color.▼

I've Always Loved You (1946) C-117m. *** D: Frank Borzage. Philip Dorn, Catherine McLeod, William Carter, Maria Ouspenskaya, Felix Bressart. Lavish romancer with classical music background; Ouspenskaya stands out in cast.

I've Heard the Mermaids Singing (1987-Canadian) C-81m. **½ D: Patricia Rozema. Sheila McCarthy, Paule Baillargeon, Ann-Marie McDonald, John Evans. Wistful, original comedy-drama about a young woman who's never really been successful at anything but manages to land a job as assistant to a chic, intelligent art gallery owner whom she comes to idolize. McCarthy's winning and empathetic performance, in her film debut, keeps us hooked even when the movie starts to wander, which it does, more than once, before redeeming

itself with the final shot. A slight but impressive first feature for writer-director Rozema.▼

I've Lived Before (1956) 82m. **½ D: Richard Bartlett. Jock Mahoney, Leigh Snowden, Ann Harding, John McIntire, Raymond Bailey. Strange small-budget film about pilot who thinks he is an aviator who died in WW1.

I Vitelloni (1953-Italian) **104m.** **** D: Federico Fellini. Alberto Sordi, Franco Interlenghi, Franco Fabrizi, Leopoldo Trieste. Magnificent comedy-drama—arguably Fellini's masterpiece—about five shiftless male adolescents in a small Adriatic town who have to cope with emerging adulthood. Film's episodic structure brings to mind AMERICAN GRAFFITI; its love of humanity anticipates the director's own AMARCORD two decades later. In any event, a lovely film.▼

Ivory Ape, The (1980) C-96m. TVM D: Tom Kotani. Jack Palance, Cindy Pickett, Steven Keats, Earle Hyman, Derek Partridge. The search for a snow-white gorilla that has been spirited from the African jungles to Bermuda by a crooked white hunter makes this one resemble a tacky Saturday matinee serial. Average.

Ivory Hunter (1951-British) C-107m. **½ D: Harry Watt. Anthony Steel, Dinah Sheridan, Harold Warrender, William Simons. Documentary-ish account of establishment of Mount Kilimanjaro Game Preserve Park in Africa. Retitled: WHERE NO VULTURES FLY.

Ivy (1947) 99m. **½ D: Sam Wood. Joan Fontaine, Patric Knowles, Herbert Marshall, Richard Ney, Cedric Hardwicke, Lucile Watson. Average drama of murderess snared in her own seemingly faultless plans. Good cast gives film added boost.

I Wake Up Screaming (1941) 82m. *** D: H. Bruce Humberstone. Betty Grable, Victor Mature, Carole Landis, Laird Cregar, William Gargan, Alan Mowbray. Entertaining whodunit with Grable and Mature implicated in murder of Betty's sister (Landis), pursued by determined cop Cregar. Twist finish to good mystery. Remade as VICKI; originally titled HOT SPOT.▼

I Walk Alone (1947) 98m. ** D: Byron Haskin. Burt Lancaster, Lizabeth Scott, Kirk Douglas, Wendell Corey, Kristine Miller, George Rigaud, Marc Lawrence. A prison term changes Lancaster's outlook on life, and return to outside world makes him bitter. Good cast, weak film.

I Walked with a Zombie (1943) 69m. ***½ D: Jacques Tourneur. Frances Dee, Tom Conway, James Ellison, Edith Barrett, Christine Gordon, Theresa Harris, James Bell. Nurse Dee comes to Caribbean island to treat zombie-like wife of troubled Conway, finds skeletons in family closet, plus local voodoo rituals and legends that cannot be ignored. Exceptional Val Lewton chiller with rich atmosphere, mesmerizing story. Loosely adapted from *Jane Eyre*!▼

I Walk the Line (1970) **C-95m.** **½ D: John Frankenheimer. Gregory Peck, Tuesday Weld, Estelle Parsons, Ralph Meeker, Lonny Chapman. Rural sheriff Peck falls for moonshiner's daughter Weld, thereby destroying both his professional and personal life. Offbeat but aimless drama, helped by excellent Weld performance. Johnny Cash sings five songs.

I Wanna Hold Your Hand (1978) **C-104m.** *** D: Robert Zemeckis. Nancy Allen, Bobby DiCicco, Marc McClure, Susan Kendall Newman, Theresa Saldana, Eddie Deezen, Wendie Jo Sperber, Will Jordan. Teenagers connive to get tickets for the Beatles' first appearance on *The Ed Sullivan Show*. If this original comedy seems occasionally silly and overbearing, that's the price it pays for being a generally accurate portrayal of a raucous event. Comedian Jordan is as hilariously Sullivanlike as ever. Steven Spielberg was executive producer.▼

I Want a Divorce (1940) **75m.** **½ D: Ralph Murphy. Joan Blondell, Dick Powell, Gloria Dickson, Frank Fay, Dorothy Burgess, Jessie Ralph, Harry Davenport, Conrad Nagel. Powell and Blondell have just gotten married but already they're beginning to wonder in this light comedy. The two stars were married at the time in real life, too.

I Wanted Wings (1941) **131m.** ** D: Mitchell Leisen. Ray Milland, William Holden, Wayne Morris, Brian Donlevy, Constance Moore, Veronica Lake, Hedda Hopper. Stale plot of three men undergoing air force training served to introduce Lake as star material; that remains only real point of interest. However, the special effects for this did garner an Oscar.

I Want Her Dead SEE: **W**▼

I Want to Keep My Baby (1976) **C-100m.** TVM D: Jerry Thorpe. Mariel Hemingway, Susan Anspach, Jack Rader, Lisa Mordente, Dori Brenner, Vince Baggetta, Rhea Perlman. Pregnant teenager decides to have her child and raise it herself. Social drama written by Joanna Lee and acted with intelligence and vitality, despite a touch of sensationalism. Above average.

I Want to Live! (1958) **120m.** ***½ D: Robert Wise. Susan Hayward, Simon Oakland, Virginia Vincent, Theodore Bikel. Hayward won an Oscar for her gutsy performance as prostitute-crook Barbara Graham who (according to the film) is framed for murder and goes to gas chamber. Smart presentation, fine acting, memorable jazz score by Johnny Mandel. Nelson Gidding and Don Mankiewicz based their script on

articles about Graham. Remade as a TV movie.▼

I Want to Live (1983) **C-100m.** TVM D: David Lowell Rich. Lindsay Wagner, Martin Balsam, Pamela Reed, Harry Dean Stanton, Seymour Cassel, Dana Elcar, Robert Ginty, Don Stroud, Barry Primus, Ken Swofford, Anne Ramsey. Wagner's portrayal of B-girl Barbara Graham who went to the gas chamber in San Quentin in 1955 after being convicted of a robbery murder is only a shadow of Susan Hayward's Oscar-winning one in this remake. Average.

I Want What I Want (1972-British) **C-91m.** **½ D: John Dexter. Anne Heywood, Harry Andrews, Jill Bennett, Nigel Flatley, Paul Rogers. Interesting little piece about sexual crisis in the life of man who wants a sex-change operation.▼

I Want You (1951) **102m.** *** D: Mark Robson. Dana Andrews, Dorothy McGuire, Farley Granger, Peggy Dow, Robert Keith, Mildred Dunnock, Martin Milner, Ray Collins, Jim Backus. Dated yet still touching Americana detailing effects of the Korean war on a small-town family. An artifact of its era, with fine performances all around. Screenplay by Irwin Shaw.

I Was a Communist for the FBI (1951) **83m.** **½ D: Gordon Douglas. Frank Lovejoy, Dorothy Hart, Philip Carey, James Millican. Documentary-style counterspy caper, low key and effective.

I Was a Mail Order Bride (1982) **C-100m.** TVM D: Marvin J. Chomsky. Valerie Bertinelli, Ted Wass, Sam Wanamaker, Karen Morrow, Kenneth Kimmins, Holland Taylor. Sophomorically cutesy comedy whose plot can be summed up in six words—and they're all in the title. Director Chomsky, with credits ranging from ROOTS to HOLOCAUST, must have done this one as a lark. Below average.

I Was a Male War Bride (1949) **105m.** *** D: Howard Hawks. Cary Grant, Ann Sheridan, Marion Marshall, Randy Stuart, William Neff, Ken Tobey. Delightful comedy of errors has French Army officer Grant trying to accompany WAC wife Sheridan back to U.S. with hilarious results. Grant in drag makes this one worth watching.

I Was an Adventuress (1940) **81m.** **½ D: Gregory Ratoff. Vera Zorina, Erich von Stroheim, Richard Greene, Peter Lorre, Sig Ruman. Jewel thief Zorina goes straight, marries Greene, but can't shake off former associates von Stroheim, Lorre, et al. With that cast, it should have been better.

I Was an American Spy (1951) **85m.** **½ D: Lesley Selander. Ann Dvorak, Gene Evans, Douglas Kennedy, Richard Loo, Philip Ahn, Lisa Ferraday. Dvorak is chanteuse in Manila who helps combat

Japanese attack in WW2 spy story, elevated by veteran star. Song: "Because of You."
I Was a Shoplifter (1950) 82m. **½ D: Charles Lamont. Scott Brady, Mona Freeman, Charles Drake, Andrea King, Anthony (Tony) Curtis. Fair programmer with cop Brady going undercover to bust open a shoplifting gang. Look for Rock Hudson as a department-store detective.
I Was a Spy (1933-British) 83m. ** D: Victor Saville. Madeleine Carroll, Conrad Veidt, Herbert Marshall, Gerald du Maurier, Edmund Gwenn, Donald Calthrop, Nigel Bruce. Unmemorable account of espionage agent Carroll, a Belgian nurse who aids the British after her country is overrun by the Germans during WW1. Veidt is perfectly cast as a German commandant.▼
I Was a Teenage Boy SEE: **Something Special**▼
I Was a Teenage Frankenstein (1957) 72m. *½ D: Herbert L. Strock. Whit Bissell, Gary Conway, Phyllis Coates, Robert Burton. Campy junk about mad scientist who pulls young Conway from an auto wreck and "repairs" him. Doesn't live up to that title; worth catching only for Bissell's immortal line, "Answer me! You have a civil tongue in your head! I know—I sewed it in there!" One sequence is in color.
I Was a Teen-age Werewolf (1957) 70m. ** D: Gene Fowler, Jr. Michael Landon, Yvonne Lime, Whit Bissell, Vladimir Sokoloff, Guy Williams. The title tells all in this curious mating of horror movies and juvenile delinquency melodramas. Marred by low production values; memorable for Landon's presence.
I Was a Teenage Zombie (1987) C-92m. BOMB D: John E. Michalakias. Michael Ruben, George Seminara, Steve McCoy, Cassie Madden. Low-grade horror spoof concerns teen zombie Ruben battling McCoy, the zombie version of a drug pusher who's been preying on adolescents. Amateur night at the movies.▼
I Was Happy Here SEE: **Time Lost and Time Remembered**
I Was Monty's Double (1958-British) 100m. ***½ D: John Guillermin. M. E. Clifton-James, John Mills, Cecil Parker, Marius Goring, Michael Hordern, Leslie Phillips, Bryan Forbes. Exciting, true WW2 story of actor persuaded to pose as Gen. Montgomery in order to divert German intelligence in North Africa. Cast is first-rate.
I Will Fight No More Forever (1975) C-100m. TVM D: Richard T. Heffron. James Whitmore, Ned Romero, Sam Elliott, Nick Ramus, Emilio Delgado, Linda Redfearn. Moving dramatization of the historical confrontation between Chief Joseph, trying to lead his tribe of Nez Perce Indians off the reservation to safety in Canada, and the U.S. Government, which sent the cavalry out to stop the migration. Written by Jeb Rosebrook and Theodore Strauss. Above average.▼

I Will, I Will . . . For Now (1976) C-96m. ** D: Norman Panama. Elliott Gould, Diane Keaton, Paul Sorvino, Victoria Principal, Robert Alda, Warren Berlinger. Fair satire on frigidity, infidelity, marriage counselling and a sex clinic. Gould and ex-wife Keaton spend film rediscovering each other.▼
I Wonder Who's Killing Her Now? (1976) C-87m. **½ D: Steven H. Stern. Bob Dishy, Joanna Barnes, Bill Dana, Vito Scotti. Luckless husband (Dishy) hires someone to bump off his wife (Barnes) to collect insurance money, then tries to call it off; uneven but often funny farce, written by Woody Allen's one-time collaborator Mickey Rose.▼
I Wonder Who's Kissing Her Now (1947) C-104m. **½ D: Lloyd Bacon. June Haver, Mark Stevens, Martha Stewart, Reginald Gardiner, Lenore Aubert, William Frawley. Innocuous recreation of life and loves of 1890s songwriter, Joseph E. Howard. As usual, music is better than script. Gene Nelson makes his film debut.
Izzy and Moe (1985) C-100m. TVM D: Jackie Cooper. Jackie Gleason, Art Carney, Cynthia Harris, Zohra Lampert, Dick Latessa, Drew Snyder. Gleason and Carney shuck their Ralph Kramden–Ed Norton guises to play two real-life ex-vaudevillians who became N.Y. Prohibition agents. Colorful though episodic and only marginally amusing, despite the chemistry of the pair. Gleason even wrote the music for this one. Average.▼

Jabberwocky (1977-British) C-100m. **½ D: Terry Gilliam. Michael Palin, Max Wall, Deborah Fallender, John Le Mesurier, Annette Badland. Gilliam and Palin of MONTY PYTHON AND THE HOLY GRAIL fame give us another satire of medieval times, but the humor is even more spotty than its predecessor's. For fans.▼
J'Accuse (1937-French) C-95m. *** D: Abel Gance. Victor Francen, Jean Max, Delaitre, Renee Devillers. Very good—but not great—antiwar film, focusing on exploited war veteran Francen; in a vivid sequence, he calls on war casualties to rise from their graves. Previously filmed by Gance in 1918.▼
Jackals, The (1967) C-105m. ** D: Robert D. Webb. Vincent Price, Diana Ivarson, Robert Gunner, Bob Courtney, Patrick Mynhardt. William Wellman's striking YELLOW SKY reset in the South African Transvaal, with six bandits terrorizing a grizzled old miner (Price) and his granddaughter into surrendering their gold cache.
Jackals (1986) C-92m. ** D: Gary Grillo.

Jack Lucarelli, Gerald McRaney, Wilford Brimley, Jameson Parker, Jeannie Wilson. Predictable, forgettable action drama starring TV's *Simon & Simon* duo with ex-cop Lucarelli taking on evil McRaney, a white slave trader. You've seen this one a hundred times before. Also known as AMERICAN JUSTICE.▼

Jack and the Beanstalk (1952) **C/B&W-87m.** **½ D: Jean Yarbrough. Bud Abbott, Lou Costello, Dorothy Ford, Barbara Brown, Buddy Baer. A&C version of fairy tale OK for kids, but not as funny as their earlier films. Begins in b&w, switches to color.▼

√ **Jackass Mail** (1942) **80m.** ** D: Norman Z. McLeod. Wallace Beery, Marjorie Main, J. Carrol Naish, Darryl Hickman, William Haade, Dick Curtis. Easygoing Beery vehicle about fugitive who accidentally becomes a hero. Take it or leave it; no harm done either way.

Jackie Chan's Police Story SEE: **Police Story** (1985)▼

Jackie Robinson Story, The (1950) **76m.** *** D: Alfred E. Green. Jackie Robinson, Ruby Dee, Minor Watson, Louise Beavers, Richard Lane, Harry Shannon, Ben Lessy, Joel Fluellen. Straightforward bio of Robinson, the first black man to play major-league baseball. Fascinating as a social history; pointed in its presentation of the racial issues involved. Interestingly, Robinson's Negro League ball club is called the Black Panthers!▼

Jack Johnson (1971) **90m.** *** D: William Cayton. Narrated by Brock Peters. Documentary on world-famous heavyweight champion. Features excellent jazz score by Miles Davis.

Jack London (1943) **94m.** *½ D: Alfred Santell. Michael O'Shea, Susan Hayward, Osa Massen, Harry Davenport, Frank Craven, Virginia Mayo. Hokey, episodic "biography" of famed writer spends too much time maligning Japanese—which was supposed to give topical slant to this period drama in 1943. Also known as THE ADVENTURES OF JACK LONDON and THE LIFE OF JACK LONDON.▼

Jack London's Klondike Fever SEE: **Klondike Fever**

Jack McCall, Desperado (1953) **C-76m.** ** D: Sidney Salkow. George Montgomery, Angela Stevens, Jay Silverheels, Douglas Kennedy. Civil War yarn of Southerner Montgomery capturing man who framed him as spy.

Jacknife (1989) **C-102m.** *** D: David Jones. Robert De Niro, Ed Harris, Kathy Baker, Charles Dutton, Loudon Wainwright III. Simple and involving story of a Vietnam vet (De Niro) who looks up an old Army buddy (Harris) and tries to get him to face up to his repressed memories of Nam, and their mutual best friend who died there.

Meanwhile, a romance blossoms between De Niro and Harris' wallflower sister, with whom he lives. Three terrific performances make this a must. Stephen Metcalfe adapted the script from his play *Strange Snow*.▼

Jack of Diamonds (1967-U.S.-German) **C-105m.** *½ D: Don Taylor. George Hamilton, Joseph Cotten, Marie Laforet, Maurice Evans, Carroll Baker, Zsa Zsa Gabor, Lilli Palmer. Hamilton plays a cat burglar who robs jewels from Baker, Gabor, and Palmer, who are "special guests" in this film. Skip this one and wait for TO CATCH A THIEF to be shown.

Jackpot, The (1950) **87m.** **½ D: Walter Lang. James Stewart, Barbara Hale, James Gleason, Fred Clark, Natalie Wood. Dated, minor comedy, uplifted by stars; Stewart is winner of radio contest but can't pay taxes on winnings.

Jack's Back (1988) **C-97m.** *½ D: Rowdy Herrington. James Spader, Cynthia Gibb, Rod Loomis, Rex Ryon, Robert Picardo, Chris Mulkey, Danitza Kingsley. Umpteenth retelling of the JACK THE RIPPER saga is updated to contemporary L.A. where young doctor Spader is the #1 suspect when prostitutes are killed in grisly fashion 100 years to the day after Bloody Jack's legendary crimes. Plot twist halfway through is preposterous; Spader is earnest but miscast.▼

Jack Slade (1953) **90m.** ** D: Harold Schuster. Mark Stevens, Dorothy Malone, Barton MacLane, John Litel. Oater programmer of Stevens turning criminal with tragic results; Malone is wasted.

Jackson County Jail (1976) **C-89m.** **½ D: Michael Miller. Yvette Mimieux, Tommy Lee Jones, Robert Carradine, Frederic Cook, Severn Darden, Howard Hesseman, Mary Woronov. Prisoner Yvette, dumped on by everyone she meets, goes on the lam with fellow inmate in yet another chase pic. Livelier than most, this one has developed a cult reputation. Miller later remade it for TV as OUTSIDE CHANCE.▼

Jack the Giant Killer (1962) **C-94m.** *** √ D: Nathan Juran. Kerwin Mathews, Judi Meredith, Torin Thatcher, Walter Burke. Marvelous special effects make this costume adventure yarn (in the SINBAD tradition) a lot of fun. Beware reissue version, which was dubbed into an ersatz musical!

Jack the Ripper (1960-British) **88m.** ** D: Robert Baker, Monty Berman. Lee Patterson, Eddie Byrne, George Rose, Betty McDowall. Middling retelling of notorious knife-wielder, with alternating scenes of Scotland Yard and fiend at work in London. Sometimes hits the mark with gory sensationalism.▼

Jack the Ripper (1988) **C-200m.** TVM D: David Wickes. Michael Caine, Armand Assante, Ray McAnally, Susan George,

Jane Seymour, Lewis Collins, Ken Bones. Taut, evocative drama about the infamous 1888 East End London serial killer, with Caine as Scotland Yard Detective Inspector Frederick Abberline, who conducted the original investigation. In this fictionalized account, he unmasks the real murderer (based on director-cowriter Wickes' contemporary research). Originally broadcast in two parts. Above average.▼

Jacobo Timerman: Prisoner Without a Name, Cell Without a Number (1983) C-100m. TVM D: Linda Yellen. Roy Scheider, Liv Ullmann, Sam Robards, David Cryer, Michael Pearlman, Zach Galligan. Disappointing dramatization of the real-life experiences of activist Argentine newspaper publisher who was unjustly imprisoned and then tortured for several years. Given story and talent involved, this should have been a powerhouse, but lead actors were miscast, and script was apparently changed in mid-production (writer Budd Schulberg removed his name from credits in favor of pseudonym). Results are surprisingly boring. Below average. Retitled: PRISONER WITHOUT A NAME, CELL WITHOUT A NUMBER.

Jacob the Liar (1977-East German) C-95m. *** D: Frank Beyer. Vlastimil Brodsky, Erwin Geschonneck, Manuela Simon, Henry Hubchen, Blanche Kommerell. Touching, sometimes comic tale of Polish Jew Brodsky, whose false tales to fellow ghetto dwellers give some hope against their Nazi captors. Brodsky won a Best Actor Award at the Berlin Film Festival, film was an Oscar nominee here.

Jacob Two-Two Meets the Hooded Fang (1977-Canadian) C-80m. **½ D: Theodore J. Flicker. Stephen Rosenberg, Alex Karras, Guy L'Ecuyer, Joy Coghill, Earl Pennington, Claude Gail. Engaging fantasy for kids written by Mordecai Richler, about a boy who dreams he's sent to children's prison. Low-budget production values are unfortunate detriment.▼

Jacqueline (1956-British) C-92m. *** D: Roy Baker. John Gregson, Kathleen Ryan, Jacqueline Ryan, Noel Purcell, Cyril Cusack. Captivating drama of lovable little Irish girl and how she helps her tippler father find work. Lots of warmth.

Jacqueline Bouvier Kennedy (1981) C-150m. TVM D: Stephen Gethers. Jaclyn Smith, James Franciscus, Rod Taylor, Stephen Elliott, Claudette Nevins, Donald Moffat. Writer-director Gethers' lengthy valentine to Jackie O. from age five through finishing school and newspaper work to JFK's assassination. Taylor's flamboyant Blackjack Bouvier portrayal is a welcome break in the tedium. Average.▼

Jacqueline Susann's Once Is Not Enough (1975) C-121m. BOMB D: Guy Green. Kirk Douglas, Alexis Smith, David Janssen, Deborah Raffin, George Hamilton, Melina Mercouri, Brenda Vaccaro. Trashy film based on Susann's trashy novel of jet-set intrigue, and a blossoming young woman (Raffin) with a father-fixation. Incurably stupid, and surprisingly dull. Vaccaro offers brightest moments as unabashed man-chaser.▼

Jacqueline Susann's Valley of the Dolls (1981) C-240m. TVM D: Walter Grauman. Catherine Hicks, Lisa Hartman, Veronica Hamel, David Birney, Jean Simmons, James Coburn, Gary Collins, Bert Convy, Britt Ekland, Carol Lawrence, Camilla Sparv, Denise Nicholas Hill, Steve Inwood. Updating of the bestseller, "with characters and material created by Miss Susann which she omitted from the published novel." Slickly made romantic drama is empty-headedly entertaining, and thus superior to the 1967 theatrical version. Originally shown in two parts. Average.

Jacques Brel Is Alive and Well and Living in Paris (1975) C-98m. ** D: Denis Heroux. Elly Stone, Mort Shuman, Joe Masiell, Jacques Brel. Musical revue featuring 26 bittersweet songs on life, love, war and death by Belgian balladeer Jacques Brel. No plot, no dialogue. Based on 1968 stage show. An American Film Theater Production.

Jade Mask, The (1945) 66m. D: Phil Rosen. Sidney Toler, Mantan Moreland, Edwin Luke, Janet Warren, Edith Evanson, Alan Bridge, Ralph Lewis. SEE: **Charlie Chan** series.

Jagged Edge (1985) C-108m. **½ D: Richard Marquand. Jeff Bridges, Glenn Close, Peter Coyote, Robert Loggia, John Dehner, Leigh Taylor-Young, Karen Austin, Lance Henriksen, James Karen. Wealthy publishing magnate is accused of murdering his wife; hotshot lawyer Close will defend him only if she believes he's innocent. Not only is she convinced—she immediately falls in love with him! Credibility goes out the window in this otherwise well-made, often gripping combination of thriller and courtroom drama. How could such a "smart" movie allow so many silly loopholes? Loggia is terrific as usual as Close's street-smart leg man.▼

Jaguar (1956) 66m. *½ D: George Blair. Sabu, Chiquita, Barton MacLane, Jonathan Hale, Mike Connors. Presence of former elephant-boy Sabu is only virtue of ridiculous programmer about mysterious murders on an oilfield.

Jaguar Lives! (1979) C-90m. *½ D: Ernest Pintoff. Joe Lewis, Christopher Lee, Donald Pleasence, Barbara Bach, Capucine, Joseph Wiseman, Woody Strode, John Huston. Karate champ Lewis is featured in this predictable action cheapie as a special agent sent to dispatch narcotics biggies in various world capitals. Top cast, but don't be fooled.▼

Jail Bait (1954) **70m.** *½ D: Edward D. Wood, Jr. Timothy Farrell, Lyle Talbot, Steve Reeves, Herbert Rawlinson, Dolores Fuller, Clancey Malone, Theodora Thurman, Mona McKinnon. Farrell leads young Malone into life of crime; when the law closes in, he forces Malone's plastic surgeon father to change his face. Misleadingly titled thriller is less inept than Wood's "classics," and thus less funny, but inspired teaming of Talbot and Reeves (in his first speaking part) as cops is good for a few giggles.▼

Jailbreakers, The (1960) **64m.** *½ D: Alexander Grasshoff. Robert Hutton, Mary Castle, Michael O'Connell, Gabe Delutri, Anton Van Stralen. Escaped prisoners harass a young couple in a deserted town. Tepid programmer.

Jail Busters (1955) **61m.** D: William Beaudine. Leo Gorcey, Huntz Hall, Percy Helton, Lyle Talbot, Fritz Feld, Barton MacLane. SEE: **Bowery Boys** series.

Jailhouse Rock (1957) **96m.** *** D: Richard Thorpe. Elvis Presley, Judy Tyler, Vaughn Taylor, Dean Jones, Mickey Shaughnessy. Elvis learns to pick a guitar in the Big House, later becomes a surly rock star. Presley's best film captures the legend in all his nostril-flaring, pre-Army glory. Great Leiber-Stoller score, including "Treat Me Nice," "Don't Leave Me Now," and terrific title song (with a dance number choreographed by Elvis). Also shown in computer-colored version.▼

Jake Spanner, Private Eye (1989) **C-100m. TVM** D: Lee H. Katzin. Robert Mitchum, Ernest Borgnine, John Mitchum, Jim Mitchum, Richard Yniguez, Laurie Latham, Dick Van Patten, Edie Adams, Kareem Abdul-Jabbar, Terry Moore, Sheree North, Clive Revill, Stella Stevens, Nita Talbot, Edy Williams. Mitchum plays "The Old Dick" (the name of the L.A. Morse book that's the source of this lighthearted mystery), an over-the-hill private eye coaxed out of retirement to find the kidnapped daughter of an old Mob pal. Lots of in-jokes, with clips from OUT OF THE PAST and a host of cameo players, but results are disappointing—to say the least. Below average.

Jake Speed (1986) **C-104m. BOMB** D: Andrew Lane. Wayne Crawford, Dennis Christopher, Karen Kopins, John Hurt, Leon Ames, Roy London, Donna Pescow, Barry Primus, Monte Markham. Utter waste of time about a paperback hero who turns up in real life to help a damsel in distress. Crawford, who has all the star appeal of a can of tuna, presumably got the lead role because he also cowrote and coproduced the film.▼

Jalopy (1953) **62m.** D: William Beaudine.

Leo Gorcey, Huntz Hall, Bernard Gorcey, Robert Lowery, Murray Alper. SEE: **Bowery Boys** series.

Jamaica Inn (1939-British) **98m.** ** D: Alfred Hitchcock. Charles Laughton, Maureen O'Hara, Leslie Banks, Robert Newton, Emlyn Williams, Mervyn Johns. Stodgy Victorian costumer of cutthroat band headed by nobleman Laughton; O'Hara is lovely, but plodding Hitchcock film is disappointing. Based on Daphne du Maurier novel; Hitch had far more success a year later with du Maurier's *Rebecca*. Remade for British TV in 1985.▼

Jamaica Inn (1985-British) **C-200m. TVM** D: Lawrence Gordon Clark. Jane Seymour, Patrick McGoohan, Trevor Eve, John McEnery, Billie Whitelaw, Vivien Pickles, Peter Vaughan. Moody, atmospheric remake of the old Hitchcock movie, with Seymour as the spunky damsel-in-constant-distress and McGoohan as her nasty Uncle Joss. Apparently it was lavishly filmed, but it's hard to tell from all that fog on the moors. Derek Marlowe provided the adaptation of Daphne du Maurier's book. Originally shown in two parts. Average.▼

Jamaica Run (1953) **C-92m.** ** D: Lewis R. Foster. Ray Milland, Arlene Dahl, Wendell Corey, Patric Knowles. Ray goes salvage-diving in the Caribbean for Dahl's nutty family. Unexciting production.

Jamboree (1957) **71m.** ** D: Roy Lockwood. Kay Medford, Robert Pastine, Paul Carr, Freda Halloway, Slim Whitman, Jodie Sands, Frankie Avalon, Fats Domino, Jerry Lee Lewis, Carl Perkins, Lewis Lymon and the Teen Chords, Buddy Knox, Count Basie, Joe Williams. Slight plot—singers Carr and Halloway fall in love, are manipulated by ambitious manager Medford—highlighted by rock, rockabilly, and jazz vignettes. Avalon looks about 12 years old, and Lewis sings "Great Balls of Fire." Also known as DISC JOCKEY JAMBOREE.

James at 15 (1977) **C-100m. TVM** D: Joseph Hardy. Lance Kerwin, Linden Chiles, Lynn Carlin, Melissa Sue Anderson, Kate Jackson, Kim Richards. Comedy-drama about the problems and pain of adolescence, with Kerwin, smitten with a high school cheerleader, faced with moving across the country with his parents. Arch family sitcom with standard plot twists. A series subsequently evolved. Average.

James Dean (1976) **C-100m. TVM** D: Robert Butler. Stephen McHattie, Michael Brandon, Dane Clark, Meg Foster, Candy Clark, Jayne Meadows, Katherine Helmond, Amy Irving, Robert Foxworth, Brooke Adams. Dramatization of the memoirs of William Bast, Dean's roommate, from their meeting as acting students until Dean's death. McHattie is excellent in title role, Brandon is fine as writer Bast. Bast's script, though, is a bore. Average.▼

James Dean Story, The (1957) **82m.** ** D: George W. George, Robert Altman. Narrated by Martin Gabel. Uninspired use of available material makes this a slow-moving documentary on life of 1950s movie star.▼

James Michener's Dynasty (1976) **C-100m. TVM** D: Lee Philips. Sarah Miles, Stacy Keach, Harris Yulin, Granville Van Dusen, Amy Irving, Harrison Ford. Ohio dirt farmers establish a powerful family business in the mid-19th century. Strong performances by Yulin, Miles and Keach as husband, wife and the brother-in-law for whom she abandons her family, but epic qualities are sacrificed to running time and the plot suffers. Average.

Jam Session (1944) **77m.** ** D: Charles Barton. Ann Miller, Jess Barker, Charles Brown, Eddie Kane, Louis Armstrong, Duke Ellington and His Band, Glen Gray and His Band, Teddy Powell and His Band, Charlie Barnet Orchestra, Nan Wynn, Pied Pipers. Mild musical of showgirl Miller trying to crash Hollywood; notable for many musical guests doing enjoyable specialty numbers.

Jane Austen in Manhattan (1980) **C-108m.** *½ D: James Ivory. Robert Powell, Anne Baxter, Michael Wager, Tim Choate, John Guerrasio, Katrina Hodiak, Kurt Johnson, Sean Young. Dreary, confusing oddity about charismatic acting-teacher Powell and his rival Baxter, each trying to produce a newly discovered play written by Jane Austen. Overlong; a disappointment from director Ivory. Hodiak is the daughter of Baxter and John Hodiak.▼

Jane Doe (1983) **C-100m. TVM** D: Ivan Nagy. Karen Valentine, William Devane, Eva Marie Saint, David Huffman, Stephen Miller, Jackson Davies, Anthony Holland. Engaging suspense thriller about an amnesiac found buried alive who is being stalked by a killer trying to finish her off. Above average.▼

Jane Eyre (1934) **67m.** ** D: Christy Cabanne. Virginia Bruce, Colin Clive, Beryl Mercer, Aileen Pringle, David Torrence, Lionel Belmore, Jameson Thomas. Thin version of the oft-filmed Brontë novel, produced by Monogram, of all studios, with Bruce in the title role and Clive as Mr. Rochester. Still, it's not uninteresting as a curio.▼

Jane Eyre (1944) **96m.** *** D: Robert Stevenson. Orson Welles, Joan Fontaine, Margaret O'Brien, Henry Daniell, John Sutton, Agnes Moorehead, Elizabeth Taylor, Peggy Ann Garner, Sara Allgood, Aubrey Mather, Hillary Brooke. Artistically successful if slow-moving version of Charlotte Brontë novel about orphan girl who grows up to become a governess in

mysterious household. One of Elizabeth Taylor's early films.

Jane Eyre (1970-British) **C-110m. TVM** D: Delbert Mann. George C. Scott, Susannah York, Ian Bannen, Jack Hawkins, Rachel Kempson, Jean Marsh, Nyree Dawn Porter. Sumptuous Gothic settings and Scott's great performance highlight this pleasant if somewhat uninspired retelling of the Brontë classic. Above average.

Janie (1944) **106m.** **½ D: Michael Curtiz. Joyce Reynolds, Edward Arnold, Ann Harding, Robert Benchley, Robert Hutton, Alan Hale, Hattie McDaniel. Naive (now) but pleasant comedy about small-town teenage girl falling in love with serviceman despite father's objections to love-hungry soldiers. From the Broadway play by Josephine Bentham and Herschel Williams. Followed by JANIE GETS MARRIED.

Janie Gets Married (1946) **89m.** **½ D: Vincent Sherman. Joan Leslie, Robert Hutton, Edward Arnold, Ann Harding, Robert Benchley, Dorothy Malone. Pleasant follow-up to JANIE, with bright-eyed Leslie helping soldier-hubby Hutton readjust to civilian life.

Janis (1975) **C-96m.** *** D: Howard Alk, Seaton Findlay. Documentary on Janis Joplin was filmed with cooperation of her family, so it ignores the singer's dark side. OK within its limits, with a dozen or so songs performed (including "Piece of My Heart," "Me and Bobby McGee," "Kozmic Blues," "Mercedes Benz").▼

January Man, The (1989) **C-97m.** *½ D: Pat O'Connor. Kevin Kline, Mary Elizabeth Mastrantonio, Susan Sarandon, Harvey Keitel, Danny Aiello, Rod Steiger, Alan Rickman, Faye Grant, Tandy Cronyn. Appallingly wrongheaded mix of cop movie, romantic drama, and offbeat comedy written by John Patrick Shanley, with Kline as a self-styled eccentric whose brother, the police chief of N.Y.C., is forced to hire him to help catch a serial killer. Fine cast founders in this unfunny, illogical mess.▼

Japanese War Bride (1952) **91m.** **½ D: King Vidor. Don Taylor, Shirley Yamaguchi, Cameron Mitchell, Marie Windsor, Philip Ahn. Penetrating study of WW2 veterans who return to life in U.S.A. with Oriental brides.

Jarrett (1973) **C-78m. TVM** D: Barry Shear. Glenn Ford, Anthony Quayle, Forrest Tucker, Laraine Stephens, Yvonne Craig, Richard Anderson. Pedestrian pilot with Ford as an erudite investigator specializing in fine arts cases, here on the trail of rare Biblical scrolls also coveted by urbane villain Quayle. Average.

Jason and the Argonauts (1963-British) **C-104m.** *** D: Don Chaffey. Todd Armstrong, Gary Raymond, Nancy Kovack, Honor Blackman, Nigel Green. Good special effects (by Ray Harryhausen) and colorful backgrounds in fable about Jason's search for golden fleece. Rich score by Bernard Herrmann.▼

Jassy (1947-British) **C-96m.** **½ D: Bernard Knowles. Margaret Lockwood, Patricia Roc, Dennis Price, Dermot Walsh, Basil Sydney, Nora Swinburne. Brooding drama of gypsy girl accused of causing her husband's death; well-mounted 19th century yarn.

Java Head (1934-British) **70m.** *** D: J. Walter Ruben. Anna May Wong, Elizabeth Allan, Edmund Gwenn, John Loder, Ralph Richardson, Herbert Lomas. Perceptive, literate account of sea captain Loder, whose roots are in a puritanical English port city, and his marriage to a Mandarin princess (Wong). Based on the Joseph Hergesheimer best-seller (which was set in Massachusetts).▼

Jaws (1975) **C-124m.** **** D: Steven Spielberg. Roy Scheider, Robert Shaw, Richard Dreyfuss, Lorraine Gary, Murray Hamilton, Jeffrey Kramer, Susan Backlinie, Carl Gottlieb. A rare case of a bubble-gum story (by Peter Benchley) scoring as a terrific movie. The story: New England shore community is terrorized by shark attacks; local cop (Scheider), icthyologist (Dreyfuss) and salty shark expert (Shaw) determine to kill the attacker. Hold on to your seats! Screenplay by Benchley and Gottlieb. Three Oscars include John Williams' now-classic score, Verna Fields' sensational editing. Followed by three sequels. Benchley has cameo as reporter on beach.▼

Jaws 2 (1978) **C-117m.** **½ D: Jeannot Szwarc. Roy Scheider, Lorraine Gary, Murray Hamilton, Joseph Mascolo, Jeffrey Kramer, Collin Wilcox. Just when you thought it was safe to turn on your TV set again, here comes another gratuitous sequel. The shark scenes deliver the goods, but Robert Shaw and Richard Dreyfuss are sorely needed when film is on land.▼

Jaws 3-D (1983) **C-97m.** ** D: Joe Alves. Dennis Quaid, Bess Armstrong, Simon MacCorkindale, Louis Gossett, Jr., John Putch, Lea Thompson. Road-company Irwin Allen-type disaster film, unrelated to first two JAWS except by contrivance; this time a shark's on the loose in Florida's Sea World. (Does this make it an unofficial remake of REVENGE OF THE CREATURE?) Might play on TV, but in theaters its only real assets were excellent 3-D effects. Retitled JAWS III for TV and homevideo.▼

Jaws the Revenge (1987) **C-89m.** ** D: Joseph Sargent. Lorraine Gary, Lance Guest, Mario Van Peebles, Karen Young, Michael Caine, Judith Barsi, Lynn Whitfield. Watchable but mediocre retread of JAWS, the fourth time around, with Gary

as the widow of sheriff Scheider (from the original film) who's convinced that the great white shark is deliberately seeking out and killing off members of her family. Marginal movie is really sunk by its stupid, abrupt finale; Caine is wasted in frivolous supporting role. Set mostly in the Bahamas.▼

Jaws of Death, The SEE: **Mako: The Jaws of Death**

Jaws of Satan (1981) **C-92m.** *½ D: Bob Claver. Frtiz Weaver, Gretchen Corbett, Jon Korkes, Norman Lloyd, Diana Douglas. Ludicrous JAWS ripoff involving a deadly snake who is actually Satan himself! Filmed in 1979 and shelved . . . with good reason.▼

Jayhawkers, The (1959) **C-100m.** **½ D: Melvin Frank. Jeff Chandler, Fess Parker, Nicole Maurey, Henry Silva, Herbert Rudley. Turgid Western set in 1850s, with Chandler and Parker battling for power, Maurey the love interest.

Jayne Mansfield: A Symbol of the '50s SEE: **Jayne Mansfield Story, The**▼

Jayne Mansfield Story, The (1980) **C-100m.** TVM D: Dick Lowry. Loni Anderson, Arnold Schwarzenegger, Raymond Buktenica, Kathleen Lloyd, G. D. Spradlin, Dave Shelley. Stunning Loni is merely OK as Jayne in this factually questionable biopic of the platinum blonde sex queen of the '50s, who according to this version would let nothing stand in her way of becoming the next Marilyn Monroe. With the exception of Mickey Hargitay (played by iron-pumping Schwarzenegger), all characters have fictitious names. Also known as JAYNE MANSFIELD: A SYMBOL OF THE '50s. Average.▼

Jazz Boat (1960-British) **90m.** **½ D: Ken Hughes. Anthony Newley, Anne Aubrey, Lionel Jeffries, David Lodge, Bernie Winters, James Booth. Energetic caper of handyman Newley pretending to be a crook and then having to carry through, with dire results.

Jazz on a Summer's Day (1959) **C-85m.** ***½ D: Bert Stern. Louis Armstrong, Big Maybelle, Chuck Berry, Dinah Washington, Gerry Mulligan, Thelonious Monk, Anita O'Day, Mahalia Jackson, Sonny Stitt, Jack Teagarden. Candid, enjoyable filmed record of the 1958 Newport Jazz Festival. A must for jazz aficionados.▼

Jazz Singer, The (1927) **89m.** **½ D: Alan Crosland. Al Jolson, May McAvoy, Warner Oland, Eugenie Besserer, Otto Lederer, William Demarest, Roscoe Karns. Legendary first talkie is actually silent with several sound musical sequences. Story of Cantor Oland's son (Jolson) going into show business is creaky, but this movie milestone should be seen once. Songs: "My Mammy," "Toot Toot Tootsie Goodbye," "Blue Skies," etc. Look fast for

Myrna Loy as a chorus girl. Remade twice (so far!).▼

Jazz Singer, The (1953) **C-107m.** **½ D: Michael Curtiz. Danny Thomas, Peggy Lee, Mildred Dunnock, Eduard Franz, Tom Tully, Allyn Joslyn. Slick remake benefits from Curtiz' no-nonsense direction and presence of Lee and Dunnock . . . but it's still just *so* schmaltzy.

Jazz Singer, The (1980) **C-115m.** BOMB D: Richard Fleischer. Neil Diamond, Laurence Olivier, Lucie Arnaz, Catlin Adams, Franklyn Ajaye, Paul Nicholas, Sully Boyar, Mike Kellin. Cantor Olivier shouts, "I hef no son!"—one of the highpoints of this mothballed sudser in which Diamond becomes a rock star in about as much time as it takes to get a haircut. This remake may actually contain more clichés than the 1927 version!▼

J. D.'s Revenge (1976) **C-95m.** ** D: Arthur Marks. Glynn Turman, Joan Pringle, Lou Gossett, Carl Crudup, James Louis Watkins, Alice Jubert. Black horror melodrama: possession of innocent man by vengeful spirit. Fairly well executed.

Jealousy (1945) **71m.** ** D: Gustav Machaty. John Loder, Nils Asther, Jane Randolph, Karen Morley. Obvious plot line of renowned writer being murdered and wrong person accused; well served by capable cast.

Jealousy (1984) **C-100m.** TVM D: Jeffrey Bloom. Angie Dickinson, Paul Michael Glaser, David Carradine, Richard Mulligan, Bo Svenson, France Nuyen. Angie gets a workout in three separate stories about the effects of that proverbial green-eyed monster. Best is number two, where she finds herself competing, with unusual results, for her zillionaire husband Mulligan's affections. Number one isn't all that bad either—and two out of three's a good average. Average.

Jean de Florette (1986-French) **C-122m.** ***½ D: Claude Berri. Yves Montand, Gerard Depardieu, Daniel Auteuil, Elisabeth Depardieu, Ernestine Mazurowna, Marcel Champel, Armand Meffre. Proud, cocky French farmer schemes with his simple-minded nephew to acquire some nearby farmland by making sure the new owners never discover an all-important natural spring on the property. Richly textured, emotionally powerful adaptation of Marcel Pagnol novel, exquisitely and meticulously filmed, with galvanizing performances—especially by Depardieu as the doggedly optimistic novice farmer. Story continues in MANON OF THE SPRING.▼

Jeanne Eagels (1957) **109m.** **½ D: George Sidney. Kim Novak, Jeff Chandler, Agnes Moorehead, Gene Lockhart, Virginia Grey. Novak tries but can't rise to demands of portraying famed actress of 1920s. Chandler is her virile love interest.

Jeannie (1941-British) **101m.** *** D: Har-

old French. Michael Redgrave, Barbara Mullen, Wilfrid Lawson, Kay Hammond, Albert Lieven, Edward Chapman, Googie Withers, Rachel Kempson, Ian Fleming. Enjoyable comedy-romance with Scottish lass Mullen vacationing in Vienna and becoming involved with washing machine salesman Redgrave and gigolo Lieven. Anatole de Grunwald was one of the writers. Also known as GIRL IN DISTRESS. Remade as LET'S BE HAPPY.

J. Edgar Hoover (1987) **C-110m.** TVM D: Robert Collins. Treat Williams, Rip Torn, David Ogden Stiers, Andrew Duggan, Robert Harper, Art Hindle, Joe Regalbuto, Louise Fletcher. Treat is a white-washed J. Edgar in this drama about the Director's 55-year government career, 48 of them with the FBI. Torn rips it up as Lyndon Johnson (following his earlier Richard Nixon on television). Director Collins adapted his teleplay from the book *My 30 Years in Hoover's FBI* by William G. Sullivan and William S. Brown. Made for cable. Average.▼

Jekyll & Hyde (1990-U.S.-British) **C-100m.** TVM D: David Wickes. Michael Caine, Cheryl Ladd, Joss Ackland, Ronald Pickup, Kim Thomson, Lionel Jeffries, Kevin McNally, Lee Montague. Caine, reunited with much of the same behind-the-scenes talent from JACK THE RIPPER, has a high old scenery-chewing time playing the famous Robert Louis Stevenson character. Director Wickes wrote the script for this atmospheric but unmemorable remake. Average.

Jekyll & Hyde . . . Together Again (1982) **C-87m.** *½ D: Jerry Belson. Mark Blankfield, Bess Armstrong, Krista Errickson, Tim Thomerson, Michael McGuire, George Chakiris. Nothing here that Jerry Lewis's Nutty Professor didn't do better, as Blankfield exaggerates on his druggist character from *Fridays* TV show in tasteless excursion into cheap sex and drug jokes. A few scattered laughs in disappointing directorial debut by veteran comedy writer Belson.▼

Jennie Gerhardt (1933) **85m.** *** D: Marion Gering. Sylvia Sidney, Donald Cook, Mary Astor, Edward Arnold, Louise Carter, Cora Sue Collins, H. B. Warner. Meticulously produced version of Theodore Dreiser saga of poor-girl Sidney finding kind benefactor Arnold, losing him, and living as Cook's back-street lover. Actors and elaborate production lend credibility to episodic soaper set at turn of the century.

Jennifer (1953) **73m.** **½ D: Joel Newton. Ida Lupino, Howard Duff, Robert Nichols, Mary Shipp. Turgid programmer of Lupino working at eerie old mansion where she discovers a murder.

Jennifer (1978) **C-90m.** ** D: Brice Mack.

Lisa Pelikan, Bert Convy, Nina Foch, Amy Johnston, John Gavin, Jeff Corey, Wesley Eure. Unusually good cast in blatant rip-off of CARRIE, with Pelikan as ostracized high-school girl whose powers include ability to unleash deadly snakes on her victims. Retitled JENNIFER (THE SNAKE GODDESS) for TV.▼

Jennifer: A Woman's Story (1979) C-100m. TVM D: Guy Green. Elizabeth Montgomery, Bradford Dillman, Scott Hylands, James Booth, John Beal, Robin Gammell, Doris Roberts, Kate Mulgrew. Wealthy ship tycoon's widow finds herself locked in battle with boardroom associates who are trying to wrest the business from her. Based on the British TV series *The Foundation.* Average.

Jennifer on My Mind (1971) C-90m. BOMB D: Noel Black. Michael Brandon, Tippy Walker, Lou Gilbert, Steve Vinovich, Peter Bonerz, Renee Taylor, Chuck McCann. Probably the worst of many drug films released in the early 70's; rootless American drifter and rich American girl smoke grass in Venice, advance to hard drugs back home. Awful script is by Erich Segal; of interest mainly for the presence of Robert De Niro, in the small, prophetic role of a gypsy cab driver.

Jennifer (The Snake Goddess) SEE: **Jennifer** (1978)▼

Jenny (1970) C-88m. BOMB D: George Bloomfield. Marlo Thomas, Alan Alda, Marian Hailey, Elizabeth Wilson, Vincent Gardenia, Stephen Strimpell. Sappy soaper about filmmaker who marries pregnant girl in order to avoid the draft. Opening scene includes a clip from A PLACE IN THE SUN, which is best thing in film.▼

Jeopardy (1953) 69m. **½ D: John Sturges. Barbara Stanwyck, Barry Sullivan, Ralph Meeker, Lee Aaker. Taut but superficial account of Stanwyck trying to save husband from drowning.

Jeremiah Johnson (1972) C-107m. *** D: Sydney Pollack. Robert Redford, Will Geer, Stefan Gierasch, Allyn Ann McLerie, Charles Tyner, Josh Albee. Atmospheric chronicle of life of a mountain man, surviving wintry wilderness, Indians, rival trappers. Unfortunately, film doesn't know where to quit, rambling on to inconclusive ending. Geer is delightful as feisty mountain hermit. Script by John Milius and Edward Anhalt.▼

Jeremy (1973) C-90m. *** D: Arthur Barron. Robby Benson, Glynnis O'Connor, Len Bari, Leonard Cimino, Ned Wilson, Chris Bohn. Two shy teen-agers in N.Y.C. meet, fall in love, then separate. Poignant and real; situations, characters, and atmosphere are memorable. Some scenes cut for TV, others added from cutting-room floor to build running time.

Jericho SEE: **Dark Sands**

Jericho Mile, The (1979) C-100m. TVM D: Michael Mann. Peter Strauss, Roger E. Mosley, Brian Dennehy, Billy Green Bush, Ed Lauter, Beverly Todd. Folsom Prison lifer works at becoming the world's fastest runner and aims for a spot on the Olympic team. Offbeat, gritty, and thoughtful. Written by Mann and Patrick J. Nolan. Above average.▼

Jerk, The (1979) C-94m. **½ D: Carl Reiner. Steve Martin, Bernadette Peters, Catlin Adams, Mabel King, Richard Ward, Dick Anthony Williams, Bill Macy, Jackie Mason. Martin's first starring feature is a hit-or-miss comedy about the misadventures of a terminally stupid man. Some very funny moments, but after a while they're spread pretty thin. Martin later produced a TV version, THE JERK, TOO.▼

Jerk, Too, The (1984) C-100m. TVM D: Michael Schultz. Mark Blankfield, Ray Walston, Stacey Nelkin, Thalmus Rasulala, Mabel King, Pat McCormick, Gwen Verdon, Jimmie Walker, Martin Mull, Lainie Kazan. Bumbling Navin Johnson leaves his adoptive parents, black sharecroppers, and goes on a cross-country odyssey to find his true love in producer Steve Martin's redo of his one- or two-joke 1979 movie, a crazy-quilt starring vehicle for stand-up comic Blankfield. Even as a TV pilot, it's a tepid affair. Below average.

Jerrico, The Wonder Clown SEE: **Three Ring Circus**

Jerusalem File, The (1972-U.S.-Israeli) C-96m. ** D: John Flynn. Bruce Davison, Nicol Williamson, Daria Halprin, Donald Pleasence, Ian Hendry, Koya Yair Rubin. Uneasy mixture of political intrigue and straight action as American student Davison gets entangled in Arab-Israeli terrorism following the Six Day War.

Jesse (1988) C-100m. TVM D: Glenn Jordan. Lee Remick, Scott Wilson, Richard Marcus, Priscilla Lopez, Leon Rippy, Albert Salmi, Kevin Conway. A selfless nurse in a Death Valley community with no regular doctor is put on trial for practicing medicine without a license. Remick is let down by James Lee Barrett's pedestrian script, based on a true story. Average.

Jesse James (1939) C-105m. *** D: Henry King. Tyrone Power, Henry Fonda, Nancy Kelly, Randolph Scott, Henry Hull, Brian Donlevy, John Carradine, Jane Darwell. Sprawling, glamorous Western with Power and Fonda as Jesse and Frank James; movie builds for audience acceptance that Jesse was misguided. Sequel: THE RETURN OF FRANK JAMES.▼

Jesse James Meets Frankenstein's Daughter (1966) C-88m. *½ D: William Beaudine. John Lupton, Estelita, Cal Bolder, Steven Geray, Jim Davis. Low-budget nonsense mixture of horror and Western genres, with title character practicing weird experiments—including turning Jesse's pal into new monster—conflicting with noted outlaw.▼

Jesse James vs. the Daltons (1954) **C-65m.** ** D: William Castle. Brett King, Barbara Lawrence, James Griffith, Bill Phipps, John Cliff. Bland shoot-out between alleged son of Jesse James and the other notorious outlaw gang.

Jesse James' Women (1954) **C-83m.** *½ D: Donald Barry. Don Barry, Jack Buetel, Peggie Castle, Lita Baron. Romancing a variety of women leaves James little time for outlaw activities; cute premise doesn't work out.

Jesse Owens Story, The (1984) **C-200m.** TVM D: Richard Irving. Dorian Harewood, Georg Stanford Brown, Debbi Morgan, Tom Bosley, LeVar Burton, Ronny Cox, Greg Morris, Ben Vereen, George Kennedy. Lovingly made biopic of famed black track star who won four gold medals at 1936 Olympics in Berlin. Follows Owens from college days to his post-Olympic period when he was shamefully exploited. Harewood's tour-de-force performance, Harold Gast's incisive script, and Michel Legrand's score make this one of the better sports films. Originally shown in two parts. Above average. ▼

Jessica (1962) **C-112m.** **½ D: Jean Negulesco. Angie Dickinson, Maurice Chevalier, Noel-Noel, Gabriele Ferzetti, Sylva Koscina, Agnes Moorehead. Dickinson is an Italian midwife who has men in her village lusting for her, with Chevalier as the local priest. Malarkey.

Jesus (1979) **C-117m.** **½ D: Peter Sykes, John Krish. Brian Deacon, Rivka Noiman, Yossef Shiloah, Niko Nitai, Gadi Roi, David Goldberg. Narrated by Alexander Scourby. Straightforward but unmemorable retelling of Jesus' life, produced by The Genesis Project and filmed in Israel.▼

√ **Jesus Christ Superstar** (1973) **C-103m.** *** D: Norman Jewison. Ted Neeley, Carl Anderson, Yvonne Elliman, Barry Dennen, Joshua Mostel, Bob Bingham. From record album to Broadway show to motion picture—film retains the Tim Rice–Andrew Lloyd Webber score, adds some interesting settings and visual trappings. It's not everyone's cup of religious experience, but certainly innovative. Watch for ubiquitous porno star Paul Thomas in the chorus.▼

Jesus of Montreal (1989-Canadian-French) **C-119m.** ***½ D: Denys Arcand. Lothaire Bluteau, Catherine Wilkening, Johanne-Marie Tremblay, Remy Girard, Robert Lepage, Gilles Pelletier, Marie-Christine Barrault. A group of actors come together to stage an unconventional production of the Passion Play, and find themselves embroiled in controversy. Writer-director Arcand takes on religious hypocrisy, commercialism, and other social ills in this wise, profoundly moving and sometimes savagely funny film. A real gem. Arcand also appears in the role of the judge.

Jesus Trip, The (1971) **C-84m.** ** D: Russ Mayberry. Tippy Walker, Robert Porter, Billy "Green" Bush, Frank Orsati, Robert Tessier, Allan Gibbs. Motorcycle gang kidnaps attractive young nun in film that isn't as bad as it sounds; cast is good.▼

Jet Attack (1958) **68m.** BOMB D: Edward L. Cahn. John Agar, Audrey Totter, Gregory Walcott, James Dobson. Sloppy Korean War programmer about rescue of U.S. scientist caught behind North Korean lines.

Jet Over the Atlantic (1960) **95m.** ** D: Byron Haskin. Guy Madison, Virginia Mayo, George Raft, Ilona Massey. Capable cast in clichéd situation of plane with bomb on board. Madison's the former air force pilot saving the day; predictable plot line.▼

Jet Pilot (1957) **C-112m.** ** D: Josef von Sternberg. John Wayne, Janet Leigh, Jay C. Flippen, Paul Fix, Richard Rober, Roland Winters, Hans Conried. One of Howard Hughes' movie curios, updating his HELL'S ANGELS interest in aviation with cold war theme, as American pilot Wayne falls in love with Russian jet ace Leigh. Ridiculous, to say the least, though some of its humor seems to have been intentional. Completed in 1950, unreleased for seven years! Incidentally, some of the stunt flying was done by Chuck Yeager.

Jetsons: The Movie (1990) **C-81m.** ** D: William Hanna, Joseph Barbera. Voices of George O'Hanlon, Penny Singleton, Mel Blanc, Tiffany, Don Messick, Patric Zimmerman. Disappointing expansion of the 1960s animated TV sitcom has nothing to offer now-grownup fans of the series, but remains a palatable offering for very young children, with pro-social messages thrown in at the end.

Je Vous Aime (1981-French) **C-105m.** *½ D: Claude Berri. Catherine Deneuve, Jean-Louis Trintignant, Gerard Depardieu, Alain Souchon, Christian Marquand, Serge Gainsbourg. Shallow, solemn tale of liberated career-woman Deneuve, who is unable to remain monogamous. Good cast can do little with material; disappointing.

Jewel of the Nile, The (1985) **C-104m.** ** D: Lewis Teague. Michael Douglas, Kathleen Turner, Danny DeVito, Spiros Focas, Avner Eisenberg, The Flying Karamazov Brothers. Contrived "high adventure" involving an evil potentate and a precious "jewel." Sequel to ROMANCING THE

STONE can't capture charm of original, because the characters are set—and character change (particularly Turner's) is what made the first movie fun. Some good stunts and funny lines, but it all rings hollow.▼

Jewel Robbery (1932) **70m.** *** D: William Dieterle. William Powell, Kay Francis, Hardie Albright, C. Henry Gordon, Helen Vinson, Herman Bing. Lubitsch-like bauble of noblewoman Francis falling in love with debonair burglar Powell during theft. Breathlessly paced, handsome comedy.

Jezebel (1938) **103m.** ***½ D: William Wyler. Bette Davis, Henry Fonda, George Brent, Margaret Lindsay, Donald Crisp, Fay Bainter, Spring Byington, Richard Cromwell, Henry O'Neill. Davis won her second Oscar as tempestuous Southern belle who goes too far to make fiancé Fonda jealous; Bainter also received Oscar as Davis' sympathetic aunt. Fine production, entire cast excellent. John Huston was one of the writers. Also shown in computer-colored version.▼

Jezebels, The SEE: **Switchblade Sisters**▼
Jigsaw (1949) **70m.** ** D: Fletcher Markle. Franchot Tone, Jean Wallace, Myron McCormick, Marc Lawrence, Betty Harper (Doe Avedon). Pedestrian caper of assistant D.A. Tone on the trail of a journalist's killer, uncovering a racist hate group. Sparked by unbilled appearances of Marlene Dietrich, Henry Fonda, John Garfield, Burgess Meredith, Marsha Hunt. Retitled: GUN MOLL.▼

Jigsaw (1968) **C-97m.** **½ D: James Goldstone. Harry Guardino, Bradford Dillman, Hope Lange, Pat Hingle, Diana Hyland, Victor Jory. Fast-paced, utterly confusing yarn about amnesiac Dillman trying to figure out his past and unravel murder caper he was involved in. Frantic editing and music don't help viewer; remake of MIRAGE. Made for TV but shown theatrically first.

Jigsaw (1971) **C-100m. TVM** D: William Graham. James Wainwright, Vera Miles, Richard Kiley, Andrew Duggan, Edmond O'Brien. Cop specializing in missing-persons cases discovers he's been lured into sophisticated cover-up scheme. Occasional tension, but should have been far better. Pilot to short-lived series; later retitled MAN ON THE MOVE. Average.▼

Jigsaw Man, The (1984-British) **C-91m.** ** D: Terence Young. Michael Caine, Laurence Olivier, Susan George, Robert Powell, Charles Gray, Michael Medwin. Caine, an ex-British Secret Service honcho who defected to Russia, comes back to England (following rejuvenating plastic surgery) for one final mission. Will he serve one country, the other, or play both ends against the middle? Unfortunately this

Caine-Olivier pairing is no SLEUTH, so you won't care.▼

Jim Buck SEE: **Portrait of a Hitman**▼
Jimi Hendrix (1973) **C-102m.** **½ D: Joe Boyd, John Head, Gary Weis. Documentary on life of noted black rock guitarist; good segments from various concerts, interviews with those who knew him well. Songs include "Purple Haze," "Wild Thing," "Johnny B. Goode."▼

Jimmy and Sally (1933) **68m.** **½ D: James Tinling. James Dunn, Claire Trevor, Harvey Stephens, Lya Lys, Jed Prouty. Go-getter Dunn lets his ambition cloud his devotion to Trevor in amiable little film of no consequence whatsoever.

Jimmy B. & Andre (1980) **C-105m. TVM** D: Guy Green. Alex Karras, Marge Sinclair, Eddie Barth, Curtis Yates, Susan Clark, Kay Armen. Drama based on the true-life story of Detroit restaurateur Jimmy Butsicaris and a black youngster whom he tried to adopt. Karras and Clark produced it, and she deftly steals it with occasional appearances as a hooker in a Harpo Marx wig. Average.

Jimmy the Gent (1934) **67m.** **½ D: Michael Curtiz. James Cagney, Bette Davis, Alice White, Allen Jenkins, Philip Reed, Mayo Methot. Crooked businessman Cagney pretends to refine himself to impress Davis in this bouncy comedy.

Jimmy the Kid (1983) **C-85m.** *½ D: Gary Nelson. Gary Coleman, Paul LeMat, Walter Olkewicz, Dee Wallace, Ruth Gordon, Don Adams, Cleavon Little, Avery Schreiber. Bored, brilliant son of wealthy husband-and-wife singing team is kidnapped by gang of pathetically incompetent bunglers who teach him how to enjoy being a kid. Coleman returns favor by bringing good cast down to his level of nonacting, consisting of endless mugging and exaggerated eyeball rolling, in this lame comedy. Based on a Donald Westlake novel, with LeMat as the same character played by Robert Redford in THE HOT ROCK.▼

Jim Thorpe—All American (1951) **107m.** **½ D: Michael Curtiz. Burt Lancaster, Charles Bickford, Steve Cochran, Phyllis Thaxter, Dick Wesson. The life of the famed American Indian athlete who was stripped of his Olympic medals for playing professional baseball. Lancaster tries, but the results are only adequate.

Jinxed! (1982) **C-103m.** ** D: Don Siegel. Bette Midler, Ken Wahl, Rip Torn, Val Avery, Jack Elam, Benson Fong. Messy black comedy about a Vegas lounge singer, the lout she lives with, and a young blackjack dealer the lout has managed to jinx at his own table. Though a characteristically ripped Rip provides some amusement, the much-reported lack of rapport between Midler/Wahl and Midler/Siegel comes through on the screen. Screenwriter "Brian Blessed" is actually Frank D. Gilroy.▼

Jinx Money (1948) 61m. D: William Beaudine. Leo Gorcey, Huntz Hall, Billy Benedict, David Gorcey, Bennie Bartlett, Sheldon Leonard, Donald MacBride, Wanda McKay, John Eldredge. SEE: **Bowery Boys** series.

Jitterbugs (1943) 74m. ** D: Mal St. Clair. Stan Laurel, Oliver Hardy, Vivian Blaine, Robert Bailey, Douglas Fowley, Noel Madison. One of the team's better later efforts, with Blaine sharing the spotlight and doing quite nicely. Ollie's scene with Southern belle Lee Patrick is a gem. Previously filmed as ARIZONA TO BROADWAY.

Jivaro (1954) C-91m. ** D: Edward Ludwig. Fernando Lamas, Rhonda Fleming, Brian Keith, Lon Chaney, Richard Denning. Cornball adventure in wild headhunting country, with gold-hungry group seeking valuable ore.

J-Men Forever! (1979) 75m. *** D: Richard Patterson. Philip Proctor, Peter Bergman, voice of M. G. Kelly. Clever stunt that really works—scenes from countless Republic serials are re-edited into new feature, with redubbed soundtrack and a few new scenes. Story (by Firesign Theatre's Proctor and Bergman) has The Lightning Bug ("From the Moon, Baby!") out to conquer Earth by flooding radio airwaves with rock; various heroes try to make the world safe for Lawrence Welk. Amazing job of editing by Gail Werbin; one great gag involves a young Leonard Nimoy.▼

Joanna (1968-British) C-107m. **½ D: Michael Sarne. Genevieve Waite, Christian Doermer, Calvin Lockhart, Donald Sutherland, Glenna Forster-Jones. Flashy story of wide-eyed girl falling in with loose-living London crowd, growing up through heartbreak, conflict. Sutherland steals film in flamboyant role as frail, wealthy young man trying to enjoy life to fullest.

Joan of Arc (1948) C-100m. **½ D: Victor Fleming. Ingrid Bergman, Jose Ferrer, Francis L. Sullivan, J. Carrol Naish, Ward Bond, Shepperd Strudwick, Hurd Hatfield, Gene Lockhart, John Emery, Cecil Kellaway, George Coulouris, John Ireland. Bergman is staunchly sincere in this overlong, faithful adaptation of Maxwell Anderson's play. Not enough spectacle to balance talky sequences. Originally released theatrically at 145m.▼

Joan of Ozark (1942) 80m. ** D: Joseph Santley. Judy Canova, Joe E. Brown, Eddie Foy, Jr., Jerome Cowan, Alexander Granach, Anne Jeffreys. Hillbilly Canova hunts down Nazi underground ring in U.S.

Joan of Paris (1942) 91m. ***½ D: Robert Stevenson. Michele Morgan, Paul Henreid, Thomas Mitchell, Laird Cregar, May Robson, Alexander Granach, Alan Ladd. Excellent WW2 tale of dedicated Morgan giving herself up so Henreid and fellow-pilots can return to Allied lines. U.S. debuts for both Morgan and Henreid.▼

Jocks (1987) C-91m. *½ D: Steve Carver. Scott Strader, Perry Lang, Mariska Hargitay, Richard Roundtree, R. G. Armstrong, Christopher Lee, Stoney Jackson, Adam Mills, Katherine Kelly Lang, Trinidad Silva, Don Gibb. Silly teen comedy of college tennis team's hijinx in Las Vegas during a tournament. Despite oddball roles for vets Lee and Armstrong, picture only comes to life on the tennis court. Filmed in 1984.▼

Joe (1970) C-107m. **½ D: John G. Avildsen. Peter Boyle, Dennis Patrick, K. Callan, Audrey Caire, Susan Sarandon, Patrick McDermott. Sleeper film brought Boyle to prominence as hardhat bigot who practices genteel blackmail on executive Patrick, who's murdered his daughter's hippie boyfriend. Overrated film owes much to Boyle's characterization, not to contrived plot. Sarandon's film debut.▼

J.O.E. and the Colonel (1985) C-100m. TVM D: Ron Satlof. Gary Kasper, William Lucking, Terence Knox, Gail Edwards, Aimee Eccles, Allan Miller, Marie Windsor. J.O.E.'s your TV-standard $12-million man, sent to foil a terrorist plot to short-circuit America's defense systems. Pilot for prospective series. Average.

Joe Butterfly (1957) C-90m. **½ D: Jesse Hibbs. Audie Murphy, Burgess Meredith, George Nader, Keenan Wynn, Fred Clark. Another variation on TEAHOUSE OF THE AUGUST MOON, set in post-WW2 Japan. American soldiers at mercy of wily Jap Meredith to get needed supplies.

Joe Cocker: Mad Dogs and Englishmen (1971-British) C-119m. *** D: Pierre Adidge. Joe Cocker, Leon Russell, Chris Stainton, Carl Radle, John Price, Bobby Keys, Rita Coolidge, Claudia Linnear. Excellent rockumentary of Cocker's '70 American tour, highlighted by Cocker, Russell, and Linnear in performance. Songs include "Feelin' Alright," "With a Little Help from My Friends," "Darlin' Be Home Soon," many others. Also known as MAD DOGS AND ENGLISHMEN.▼

Joe Dancer SEE: **Big Black Pill, The**

Joe Dakota (1957) C-79m. **½ D: Richard Bartlett. Jock Mahoney, Luana Patten, Charles McGraw, Lee Van Cleef. Folksy oater of Mahoney renewing a town's pride in itself.

Joe Hill (1971-Swedish) C-114m. *** D: Bo Widerberg. Thommy Berggren, Ania Schmidt, Kelvin Malave, Everl Anderson, Cathy Smith. Fabricated story of legendary labor leader has usual Widerberg matter-of-taste glossiness, but also some affecting scenes and pleasant performances. Joan Baez sings title song.

Joe Kidd (1972) **C-88m.** ** D: John Sturges. Clint Eastwood, Robert Duvall, John Saxon, Don Stroud, Stella Garcia, James Wainwright. Eastwood is hired to hunt down some Mexican-Americans by land baron Duvall in ordinary Western; nice photography and a rousing scene where Eastwood drives a train through a barroom. Written by Elmore Leonard.▼

Joe Louis Story, The (1953) **88m.** ** D: Robert Gordon. Coley Wallace, Paul Stewart, Hilda Simms, James Edwards, John Marley, Dots Johnson. Biopic of the heavyweight champ is interesting historically but dramatically hokey; Wallace looks the part of Louis, but is no actor.▼

Joe Macbeth (1955-British) **90m.** **½ D: Ken Hughes. Paul Douglas, Ruth Roman, Bonar Colleano, Gregoire Aslan, Sidney James. Occasionally amusing variation on Shakespeare's *Macbeth*, with Douglas a 1930s gangster whose wife (Roman) nags him into murdering his way to the top of his "profession."

Joe Palooka SEE: Palooka▼

Joe Panther (1976) **C-110m.** *** D: Paul Krasny. Brian Keith, Ricardo Montalban, Alan Feinstein, Cliff Osmond, A Martinez, Ray Tracey. Good family film about modern-day Seminole youth (Tracey) striving to make his way in the white man's world.▼

Joe Smith, American (1942) **63m.** ** D: Richard Thorpe. Robert Young, Marsha Hunt, Harvey Stephens, Darryl Hickman. Dated WW2 morale-booster about kidnapped munitions worker Young who refuses to divulge secrets to Nazis. Paul Gallico story remade as THE BIG OPERATOR.

Joe Versus the Volcano (1990) **C-102m.** **½ D: John Patrick Shanley. Tom Hanks, Meg Ryan, Lloyd Bridges, Robert Stack, Dan Hedaya, Abe Vigoda, Ossie Davis, Barry McGovern, Amanda Plummer, Carol Kane. Pleasant if pointless fable about a stressed-out nerd who learns he has six months to live, and accepts an eccentric millionaire's offer to enable him to live like a king—so long as he jumps into a volcano at the end of his "vacation." Unfortunately, the story also takes a dive. Writer Shanley's directorial debut turns out to be a shaggy-dog story that doesn't pay off. However, it *is* fun watching Ryan play three distinctively different women . . . and remember, luggage is everything.▼

Joey (1985) **C-97m.** ** D: Joseph Ellison. Neill Barry, James Quinn, Elisa Heinsohn, Linda Thorson, Ellen Hammill, Dan Grimaldi, Frankie Lanz. Hokey but harmless ode to Oldies and Doo Wop, chronicling the troubled personal life of teen rock musician Barry and his relationship with his dad (Quinn), who used to turn out hit records but now toils in a gas station and drinks away his paycheck. This otherwise minor item does feature cameo appearances by The Limelights (who perform "Daddy's Home"), Silhouettes ("Get a Job"), Ad-Libs ("Boy From New York City"), Elegants ("Little Star"), Screamin' Jay Hawkins ("I Put a Spell on You") and, all too fleetingly, Jimmy Merchant and Herman Santiago, the only surviving Teenagers ("Why Do Fools Fall in Love?").▼

John and Mary (1969) **C-92m.** **½ D: Peter Yates. Dustin Hoffman, Mia Farrow, Michael Tolan, Sunny Griffin, Stanley Beck, Tyne Daly, Alix Elias, Marian Mercer, Olympia Dukakis, Cleavon Little, Kristoffer Tabori. John and Mary meet, make love, but don't know if the relationship should end right there. Innocuous, uncompelling trifle. Hoffman seems to be sleepwalking; audience may join him.

John and Yoko: A Love Story (1985) **C-150m.** TVM D: Sandor Stern. Mark McGann, Kim Miyori, Kenneth Price, Peter Capaldi, Philip Walsh, Richard Morant. Skin-deep portrayal of John Lennon and Yoko Ono, their relationship to each other and, to a lesser extent, the other Beatles, covering the years from 1966 to Lennon's killing in 1980. At least there's actual Beatles recordings (31 of them) to keep interest sparked. Written by director Stern. Average.▼

John F. Kennedy: Years of Lightning, Day of Drums (1966) **C-85m.** **** D: Bruce Herschensohn. Brilliant documentary, originally commissioned by the United States Information Agency, on the life and times of John Kennedy.

John Goldfarb, Please Come Home (1964) **C-96m.** *½ D: J. Lee Thompson. Shirley MacLaine, Peter Ustinov, Richard Crenna, Jim Backus, Fred Clark. Trapped in desert kingdom, two Americans (pilot, woman reporter) conspire to help Arabian chief Ustinov's football team beat Notre Dame. Notre Dame University found this spoof so offensive it sued in court; the viewer has an easier alternative. Screenplay by William Peter Blatty.

John Loves Mary (1949) **96m.** **½ D: David Butler. Ronald Reagan, Jack Carson, Patricia Neal, Wayne Morris, Edward Arnold, Virginia Field. Genial adaptation of Norman Krasna's Broadway hit about a soldier (Reagan) who does his pal a favor by marrying the fellow's British girl friend, so she can come to the U.S.—intending to get divorce upon arrival. Naive fluff was Neal's film debut.

John Meade's Woman (1937) **87m.** ** D: Richard Wallace. Edward Arnold, Gail Patrick, Francine Larrimore, George Bancroft, Aileen Pringle, Sidney Blackmer. Arnold plays another Great American Businessman, marrying one girl to spite another. Idea backfires; so does film.

Johnnie Mae Gibson: FBI (1986) **C-100m.** TVM D: Bill Duke. Howard E. Rollins, Jr., Richard Lawson, William Allan Young, John Lehne, Marta Du Bois, Lynn Whitfield. Pedestrian treatment of a fact-based subject: the determination of a black woman to become an FBI agent. Video title: JOHNNIE GIBSON F.B.I. Average.▼

Johnny Allegro (1949) **81m.** **½ D: Ted Tetzlaff. Nina Foch, George Raft, George Macready, Will Geer. Seamy gangster melodrama of ex-racketeer Raft helping federal agents capture counterfeiting gang. Last half of story imitates THE MOST DANGEROUS GAME.

Johnny Angel (1945) **79m.** *** D: Edwin L. Marin. George Raft, Claire Trevor, Signe Hasso, Lowell Gilmore, Hoagy Carmichael, Marvin Miller, Margaret Wycherly, J. Farrell MacDonald. Tough, well-done melodrama, with Raft cleaning up notorious mob, solving mystery of father's murder. Trevor lends good support.▼

Johnny Apollo (1940) **93m.** *** D: Henry Hathaway. Tyrone Power, Dorothy Lamour, Edward Arnold, Lloyd Nolan, Charles Grapewin, Lionel Atwill, Marc Lawrence. Good-natured Power turns crook, resentful of father Arnold, white-collar thief. Good acting, especially by Lamour as the girlfriend.

Johnny Banco (1967-French-Italian-German) **C-95m.** BOMB D: Yves Allegret. Horst Buchholz, Sylva Koscina, Fee Calderone, Elisabeth Wiener, Michel de Re, Jean Paredes. Idiotic tale of carefree, boyish dreamer-hustler Buchholz, from the Barcelona slums, who robs a gangster of $200,000 and galavants off to Monte Carlo. A bore, and Buchholz is no comedian. Original running time: 98m.

Johnny Be Good (1988) **C-84m.** BOMB D: Bud Smith. Anthony Michael Hall, Robert Downey, Jr., Paul Gleason, Uma Thurman, Steve James, Seymour Cassel, Howard Cosell, Jim McMahon, Robert Downey, Sr., Jennifer Tilly. Offensive, bottom-of-the-barrel comedy about star high-school jock Hall and how various colleges attempt to illegally recruit him. The seriousness of the issue completely eludes the makers of this turkey. R-rated scenes were added for homevideo version.▼

Johnny Belinda (1948) **103m.** ***½ D: Jean Negulesco. Jane Wyman, Lew Ayres, Charles Bickford, Jan Sterling, Agnes Moorehead, Stephen McNally. Sensitively acted, atmospheric drama of young deaf-mute girl (Wyman) and doctor (Ayres) who works with her. Setting of provincial fishing-farming community vividly realized. Wyman won an Oscar for her fine performance.▼

Johnny Belinda (1982) **C-100m.** TVM D: Anthony Harvey. Richard Thomas, Rosanna Arquette, Dennis Quaid, Candy Clark, Roberts Blossom, Fran Ryan. Interesting update of the Elmer Harris play, with some notable changes (there's no trial scene, which was a highlight of the 1948 film), but most notably a terrific performance by Rosanna Arquette. Above average.▼

Johnny Bull (1986) **C-100m.** TVM D: Claudia Weill. Jason Robards, Colleen Dewhurst, Peter MacNicol, Kathy Bates, Suzanna Hamilton. Strong performances elevate this drama about a Cockney girl whose dreams of America are shattered when she and her G.I. husband move into his disgruntled parents' home in a Pennsylvania town where the mine has been played out. Award-winning first script by Kathleen Betsko Yale. Above average.

Johnny Come Lately (1943) **97m.** **½ D: William K. Howard. James Cagney, Grace George, Marjorie Main, Marjorie Lord, Hattie McDaniel, Ed McNamara. Tame but amusing Cagney vehicle, with Jimmy as wandering newspaperman who helps elderly editor George in small-town political battle.▼

Johnny Concho (1956) **84m.** **½ D: Don McGuire. Frank Sinatra, Keenan Wynn, William Conrad, Phyllis Kirk, Wallace Ford, Dorothy Adams. Plodding Western with novelty of Sinatra as cowardly soul who must build courage for inevitable shootout. Adapted from a *Studio One* TV play.

Johnny Cool (1963) **101m.** *** D: William Asher. Henry Silva, Elizabeth Montgomery, Sammy Davis, Jr., Wanda Hendrix, Telly Savalas, Jim Backus, Joey Bishop. Sadistic study of vicious gangster seeking revenge. Brutal account, realistically told.

Johnny Dangerously (1984) **C-90m.** *½ D: Amy Heckerling. Michael Keaton, Joe Piscopo, Marilu Henner, Maureen Stapleton, Peter Boyle, Griffin Dunne, Richard Dimitri, Glynnis O'Connor, Byron Thames, Danny DeVito, Dom DeLuise, Ray Walston, Sudie Bond. Lame comedy about Prohibition-era gangsters; looks like a TV show and plays that way, too, with scattershot jokes (only a few of them funny) instead of a script. ▼

Johnny Dark (1954) **C-85m.** **½ D: George Sherman. Tony Curtis, Piper Laurie, Don Taylor, Paul Kelly, Ilka Chase, Sidney Blackmer. Curtis is energetic as auto designer who enters big race.

Johnny Doesn't Live Here Any More (1944) **77m.** **½ D: Joe May. Simone Simon, James Ellison, Minna Gombell, Alan Dinehart, Robert Mitchum, Grady Sutton. WW2 ancestor of THE APARTMENT, with Simon's flat becoming a madhouse, all ending happily with marriage. Retitled: AND SO THEY WERE MARRIED.

Johnny Eager (1941) **107m.** *** D: Mervyn

LeRoy. Robert Taylor, Lana Turner, Edward Arnold, Van Heflin, Robert Sterling, Patricia Dane, Glenda Farrell, Barry Nelson. Slick MGM melodrama with convoluted plot about sociology student (and daughter of D.A. Arnold) Turner falling in love with unscrupulous racketeer Taylor. Heflin won Best Supporting Actor Oscar for his performance as Taylor's alcoholic friend.

Johnny Got His Gun (1971) C-111m. *** D: Dalton Trumbo. Timothy Bottoms, Kathy Fields, Marsha Hunt, Jason Robards, Donald Sutherland, Diane Varsi, David Soul, Tony Geary. Morbid film version of Trumbo's novel about WWI basket case has moving opening and climax, but everything in the middle is either talky, pretentious, or amateurish.▼

Johnny Guitar (1954) C-110m. ***½ D: Nicholas Ray. Joan Crawford, Sterling Hayden, Scott Brady, Mercedes McCambridge, Ward Bond, Ben Cooper, Ernest Borgnine, Royal Dano, John Carradine, Paul Fix, Frank Ferguson. The screen's great kinky Western, a memorable confrontation between saloonkeeper Crawford and righteous hellion McCambridge, who wants her run out of town and/or hanged. Simply fascinating with symbolism rampant throughout. Script by Philip Yordan.▼

Johnny Hamlet (1972-U.S.-Italian) C-91m. ** D: Enzo G. Castellari. Chip Corman, Gilbert Roland, Horst Frank. Southerner returns home to Texas, gets involved in robbery, murder, and torture in this undistinguished oater with Shakespeare-inspired plot line.

Johnny Handsome (1990) C-94m. ** D: Walter Hill. Mickey Rourke, Ellen Barkin, Elizabeth McGovern, Morgan Freeman, Forest Whitaker, Lance Henriksen, Scott Wilson, Blake Clark. Disfigured Rourke is imprisoned after his abandonment by fellow lowlifes during a heist; a doctor then proposes performing plastic surgery on his features, hoping to lower his recidivism potential. Eccentric, to say the least, and not totally without interest given the cast, but eventually wears out its welcome. Given Rourke's standard appearance, this must be the only skull surgery ever performed without benefit of a shampoo.▼

Johnny Holiday (1949) 92m. *** D: Willis Goldbeck. William Bendix, Allen Martin, Jr., Stanley Clements, Jack Hagen. Remarkably sincere study of juvenile delinquent torn between friends from dishonest past and those trying to help him at reform farm.

Johnny in the Clouds SEE: **Way to the Stars, The**

Johnny Nobody (1961-British) 88m. *** D: Nigel Patrick. Nigel Patrick, Yvonne Mitchell, Aldo Ray, William Bendix, Cyril Cusack. Irish priest suspects murder when drunken author is killed. Unusual plot twists

with religious overtones. Neat, well-made little thriller.▼

Johnny O'Clock (1947) 95m. **½ D: Robert Rossen. Dick Powell, Evelyn Keyes, Lee J. Cobb, Ellen Drew, Nina Foch. Cast and director make script about high-class gambler in trouble with the law seem better than it is; Powell is fine in lead role.

Johnny One Eye (1950) 78m. ** D: Robert Florey. Pat O'Brien, Wayne Morris, Dolores Moran, Gayle Reed. Schmaltzy Damon Runyon yarn of O'Brien, a gangster with a heart of gold, on the lam.

Johnny Reno (1966) C-83m. BOMB D: R.G. Springsteen. Dana Andrews, Jane Russell, Lon Chaney, John Agar, Lyle Bettger, Tom Drake, Richard Arlen, Robert Lowery. Laughably clichéd Western has Marshal Andrews trying to save accused killer from lynching. Only for buffs who want to play "spot the star."

Johnny Rocco (1958) 84m. ** D: Paul Landres. Richard Eyer, Stephen McNally, Coleen Gray, Russ Conway. Gangster's son (Eyer) is focal point of gangland hunt because he witnessed a killing; OK drama.

Johnny Shiloh (1963) C-90m. **½ D: James Neilson. Kevin Corcoran, Brian Keith, Darryl Hickman, Skip Homeier. Young Corcoran loses his family and tags along with Civil War Army led by Keith. Set-bound adventure, but well acted and easy to watch. Originally shown in two parts on the Disney TV show.▼

Johnny Stool Pigeon (1949) 76m. **½ D: William Castle. Howard Duff, Shelley Winters, Dan Duryea, Anthony (Tony) Curtis. Standard drama of convict being sprung from prison so he can lead federal agents to former gang members.

Johnny Tiger (1966) C-102m. **½ D: Paul Wendkos. Robert Taylor, Geraldine Brooks, Chad Everett, Brenda Scott. Set in Florida, tame tale of teacher Taylor, doctor Brooks, and half-breed Seminole Everett trying to come to conclusions about Indians' role in modern world.▼

Johnny Tremain (1957) C-80m. *** D: Robert Stevenson. Hal Stalmaster, Luana Patten, Jeff York, Sebastian Cabot, Dick Beymer, Walter Sande. Excellent Disney film, from Esther Forbes' novel about a young boy who gets involved in the Revolutionary War; sprinkles fiction with fact to bring history to life.▼

Johnny Trouble (1957) 80m. **½ D: John H. Auer. Ethel Barrymore, Cecil Kellaway, Carolyn Jones, Stuart Whitman, Jesse White, Jack Larson. Tender story of elderly Barrymore, convinced that her long-missing son will return and that he wasn't a bad boy. Ethel's final film. Remake of SOMEONE TO REMEMBER.

Johnny, We Hardly Knew Ye (1977) C-100m. TVM D: Gilbert Cates. Paul

Rudd, Kevin Conway, Burgess Meredith, William Prince, Richard Venture, Tom Berenger, Kenneth McMillan, Shirley Rich, Joseph Bova, Brian Dennehy. Well-acted account of John F. Kennedy's first try for public office, based on 1972 best-seller. Rudd tries but lacks JFK's charisma; Meredith's charm makes up for it as "Honey Fitz" Fitzgerald. Average.

Johnny Yuma (1966-Spanish-Italian) **C-99m.** ** D: Romolo Guerrieri. Mark Damon, Lawrence Dobkin, Rosalba Neri, Louis Vanner. Blood-drenched story of man fighting for his inheritance.

John O'Hara's Gibbsville SEE: **Turning Point of Jim Malloy, The**

John Paul Jones (1959) **C-126m.** **½ D: John Farrow. Robert Stack, Marisa Pavan, Charles Coburn, Erin O'Brien, Macdonald Carey, Jean-Pierre Aumont, Peter Cushing, Bruce Cabot, Bette Davis. Empty spectacle of 18th-century American hero, with cameo by Davis as Russian empress.

John Steinbeck's The Winter of Our Discontent SEE: **Winter of Our Discontent, The**

Johnstown Flood, The (1926) **70m.** **½ D: Irving Cummings. George O'Brien, Florence Gilbert, Janet Gaynor, Anders Randall. Silent-era disaster film, and no worse than a lot of newer ones; compactly told, with still-dazzling special effects. Gaynor's first feature-length movie.

Jo Jo Dancer, Your Life Is Calling (1986) **C-97m.** ** D: Richard Pryor. Richard Pryor, Debbie Allen, Art Evans, Fay Hauser, Barbara Williams, Carmen McRae, Paula Kelly, Diahnne Abbott, Scoey Mitchlll, Billy Eckstine, Wings Hauser, E'lon Cox, Virginia Capers, Dennis Farina. Pryor examines his life, with the help of an alter-ego character; largely autobiographical film only sparks when chronicling the comedian's early life and first show-biz encounters. From there it's downhill: jumbled, at arm's-length, and boring. Pryor's directorial debut, if you don't count an earlier concert film (he also coscripted and produced).▼

Joke of Destiny, A (1983-Italian) **C-105m.** *½ D: Lina Wertmuller. Ugo Tognazzi, Piera Degli Esposti, Gastone Moschin, Renzo Montagnani. A high government official is accidentally locked in his computer-controlled limousine, and his dilemma is dealt with as if it's a national crisis. Loud, overwrought satire has a couple of laughs but will either put you to sleep or give you a headache. Full title: A JOKE OF DESTINY, LYING IN WAIT AROUND THE CORNER LIKE A BANDIT.▼

Joker Is Wild, The (1957) **123m.** *** D: Charles Vidor. Frank Sinatra, Mitzi Gaynor, Jeanne Crain, Eddie Albert, Beverly Garland, Jackie Coogan, Sophie Tucker. Sinatra is fine in biography of nightclub performer Joe E. Lewis, with Crain and Gaynor diverting as his two loves. Song "All the Way" won an Oscar; in fact, the film was reissued as ALL THE WAY.

Jokers, The (1966-British) **C-94m.** *** D: Michael Winner. Michael Crawford, Oliver Reed, Gabriella Licudi, Harry Andrews, James Donald, Daniel Massey. Droll satire on the Establishment with Reed and Crawford two brothers from upper classes, putting everyone on and carrying out perfect caper; ironic results.

Jolly Bad Fellow, A (1964-British) **94m.** ** D: Don Chaffey. Leo McKern, Janet Munro, Maxine Audley, Duncan MacRae. Peculiar yarn of college professor who plays God by trying to kill those people whom he feels are evil parasites; strange blend of drama-satire. Retitled: THEY ALL DIED LAUGHING.

Jolson Sings Again (1949) **C-96m.** **½ D: Henry Levin. Larry Parks, Barbara Hale, William Demarest, Ludwig Donath, Tamara Shayne. Attempt to continue THE JOLSON STORY only partially succeeds, and is a curio at best . . . especially when Parks (playing Jolson) meets Parks (playing Parks). Jolson standards ("Baby Face," "Sonny Boy," "Back In Your Own Back Yard," and many others) are still great.▼

Jolson Story, The (1946) **C-128m.** ***½ D: Alfred E. Green. Larry Parks, Evelyn Keyes, William Demarest, Bill Goodwin, Ludwig Donath, Tamara Shayne. Hokey but very entertaining biography of all-time great Al Jolson, with Parks giving his all in story of brash vaudeville performer's rise in the show biz world. Songs: "April Showers," "Avalon," "You Made Me Love You," "My Mammy" plus many others, all dubbed by Jolson; that's the real Jolson in long shot on the runway during the "Swanee" sequence. Morris Stoloff earned an Oscar for his scoring. Sequel: JOLSON SINGS AGAIN.▼

Jonah Who Will Be 25 in the Year 2000 (1976-Swiss) **C-115m.** ***½ D: Alain Tanner. Myriam Boyer, Jean-Luc Bideau, Miou-Miou, Roger Jendly, Jacques Denis. Sensitive, literate, engaging comedy about eight individuals all affected by the political events of the late '60s. Miou-Miou is lovely as a supermarket clerk with no qualms about liberating groceries. A companion to Tanner's later NO MAN'S LAND (1985).

Jonathan Livingston Seagull (1973) **C-120m.** **½ D: Hall Bartlett. Unique film based on Richard Bach's best-seller about an existential seagull. Superb photography allows us to take bird's point of view as he forsakes his flock to explore wonders of flying. Dialogue doesn't work nearly as well, nor does Neil Diamond's overbearing score.▼

Joni (1980) **C-108m.** **½ D: James F.

Collier. Joni Eareckson, Bert Remsen, Katherine De Hetre, Cooper Huckabee, John Milford, Michael Mancini, Richard Lineback. Earnest account of Eareckson's actual struggle to rebuild her life and find religion after breaking her spine in a diving mishap. Based on a book by Eareckson; financed by Billy Graham.▼

Jordan Chance, The (1978) **C-100m.** TVM D: Jules Irving. Raymond Burr, Ted Shackelford, James Canning, Stella Stevens, John McIntire, Peter Haskell, Gerald McRaney, George DiCenzo. Prominent attorney (and one-time con) heads foundation to help those wrongly accused and unjustly convicted in this pilot to another lawyer series for Burr. Average.

Jory (1972) **C-96m.** ** D: Jorge Fons. John Marley, B. J. Thomas, Robby Benson, Brad Dexter, Patricia Aspillaga. Familiar Western about 15-year-old who becomes a man when father and close friends are senselessly murdered. Filmed in Mexico.▼

Joseph and His Brethren (1962) **C-103m.** ** D: Irving Rapper. Marietto, Geoffrey Horne, Belinda Lee, Finlay Currie, Antonio Segurini, Charles Borromel, Carlo Giustini. Juvenile biblical tale, lavishly produced but empty-headed.

Joseph Andrews (1977-British) **C-103m.** ** D: Tony Richardson. Ann-Margret, Peter Firth, Michael Hordern, Beryl Reid, Jim Dale, Natalie Ogle, Peter Bull. Director Richardson returns to Henry Fielding but TOM JONES lightning fails to strike again; well photographed farce based on concealed identities is dull throughout.▼

Josette (1938) **73m.** **½ D: Allan Dwan. Don Ameche, Simone Simon, Robert Young, Bert Lahr, Joan Davis, Tala Birell, Paul Hurst, William Collier, Sr. Above-par musicomedy of mistaken identity, with sturdy cast and such forgettable songs as "May I Drop A Petal In Your Glass of Wine."

Joshua (1976) **C-75m.** *½ D: Larry Spangler. Fred Williamson, Isela Vega, Brenda Venus, Stacy Newton, Kathryn Jackson. Modest Western of Williamson patiently tracking down and killing one by one the bandits who murdered his mother, maid to a frontier family. Embarrassing, cynical script by Williamson insults the audience; Mexican superstar Vega is wasted. Originally titled: THE BLACK RIDER. ▼

Joshua Then and Now (1985-Canadian) **C-127m.** *** D: Ted Kotcheff. James Woods, Gabrielle Lazure, Alan Arkin, Michael Sarrazin, Linda Sorenson, Alan Scarfe, Alexander Knox, Robert Joy. Unorthodox life and times of a Jewish writer in Canada whose father was a small-time gangster and who marries into a politically and socially prominent WASP family. Uneven but entertaining comedy-drama, based on Mordecai Richler's semiautobiographical novel; Woods is fine in rare leading-man role, Arkin terrific as his colorful dad. If story seems abrupt at times, that's because this was filmed as a TV miniseries and cut down to feature length. ▼

Jour De Fete (1949-French) **70m.** ***½ D: Jacques Tati. Jacques Tati, Guy Decomble, Paul Frankeur, Santa Relli, Maine Vallee, Roger Rafal. In this exquisite feature-film directorial debut French comedian/mime Tati plays a postman whose attempts to modernize delivery link up a series of delightful gags built around a small town's Bastille Day celebration. Tati's cleverness and timing make him one of the most accomplished cinematic comedians since Buster Keaton.▼

Journey, The (1959) **C-125m.** *** D: Anatole Litvak. Deborah Kerr, Yul Brynner, Jason Robards, Jr., Robert Morley, E. G. Marshall, Anne Jackson, Ronny Howard, Kurt Kasznar, Anouk Aimee. Heady melodrama set in 1956 Budapest, with assorted types seeking to leave. Offbeat romance between Kerr and Communist officer Brynner. Film debuts of Robards and Howard.

Journey (1972-Canadian) **C-87m.** BOMB D: Paul Almond. Genevieve Bujold, John Vernon, Gale Garnett, George Sperdakos, Elton Hayes. Young woman, saved from drowning by head of wilderness commune, believes that she brings bad luck to everyone with whom she comes in contact. Including the people who made this film. Heavy going.

Journey Back to Oz (1974) **C-90m.** **½ D: Hal Sutherland. Voices of Liza Minnelli, Milton Berle, Margaret Hamilton, Jack E. Leonard, Paul Lynde, Ethel Merman, Mickey Rooney, Rise Stevens, Danny Thomas, Mel Blanc. Long-delayed (made in 1964) animated sequel without the Wizard. Okay for the kids; main interest for grownups is familiar voices, including Minnelli in her late mother's role.▼

Journey for Margaret (1942) **81m.** *** D: W. S. Van Dyke II. Robert Young, Laraine Day, Fay Bainter, Nigel Bruce, Margaret O'Brien, William Severn. Stirring WW2 drama of children left homeless by British bombing. O'Brien is very appealing scene-stealer, Young her adopted father.

Journey from Darkness (1975) **C-100m.** TVM D: James Goldstone. Marc Singer, Kay Lenz, Wendell Burton, William Windom, Joseph Campanella, Jack Warden, Dorothy Tristan. Fact-based drama about blind college student's struggle to get into medical school. Sincere work by the cast keeps this tale of courage on track. Average.

Journey Into Autumn SEE: **Dreams**▼

Journey Into Fear (1942) **69m.** *** D:

Norman Foster. Orson Welles, Joseph Cotten, Dolores Del Rio, Ruth Warrick, Agnes Moorehead, Everett Sloane, Jack Moss, Hans Conried. Often baffling WW2 spy drama started by Welles, taken out of his hands. Much of tale of smuggling munitions into Turkey still exciting. Cotten and Welles scripted this adaptation of the Eric Ambler novel. Remade in 1975.▼

Journey into Fear (1975-Canadian) C-103m. ** D: Daniel Mann. Sam Waterston, Zero Mostel, Yvette Mimieux, Scott Marlowe, Ian McShane, Joseph Wiseman, Shelley Winters, Stanley Holloway, Donald Pleasence, Vincent Price. Muddled remake of 1942 film, shot throughout Europe, with Waterston as research geologist who becomes involved in international intrigue.▼

Journey Into Light (1951) 87m. **½ D: Stuart Heisler. Sterling Hayden, Viveca Lindfors, Thomas Mitchell, H. B. Warner, Ludwig Donath. Thought-provoking theme, poorly paced; Hayden is clergyman who finds his belief in God again with aid of blind Lindfors.

Journey of Natty Gann, The (1985) C-101m. *** D: Jeremy Kagan. Meredith Salenger, John Cusack, Ray Wise, Lainie Kazan, Barry Miller, Scatman Crothers, Verna Bloom, Bruce M. Fischer. Girl travels cross-country during the hardest days of the Depression, in order to be with her father; along the way she acquires an unlikely companion and protector—a wolf. Low-key but entertaining Disney film travels smoothly to expected conclusion. Rich 1930s atmosphere helps a lot, and the wolf (actually played by a dog!) is great. ▼

Journey of Robert F. Kennedy SEE: **Unfinished Journey of Robert F. Kennedy, The**

Journey Through Rosebud (1972) C-93m. **½ D: Tom Gries. Robert Forster, Kristoffer Tabori, Victoria Racimo, Eddie Little Sky, Roy Jenson, Wright King. Sympathetic but dully directed drama about the modern-day Indian's plight. Location footage in South Dakota helps.▼

Journey Through the Past (1972) C-78m. *½ D: Bernard Shakey (Neil Young). Crosby, Stills, Nash and Young, Buffalo Springfield, Carrie Snodgress, Jack Nitzsche. Overblown, phony, pseudo-hip home movie centering on rock superstar Young.

Journey to Freedom (1957) 60m. *½ D: Robert C. Dertano. Jacques Scott, Genevieve Aumont, Morgan Lane, Fred Kohler, Don Marlowe. Lukewarm spy hunt, with Communist agents tracking down pro-American refugee now in the U.S.

Journey Together (1946-British) 80m. ** D: John Boulting. Richard Attenborough, Jack Watling, Edward G. Robinson, Bessie Love. More of a documentary than a feature story, this film retraces lives of U.S. fliers in England during WW2.▼

Journey to Shiloh (1968) C-101m. *½ D: William Hale. James Caan, Michael Sarrazin, Brenda Scott, Don Stroud, Paul Petersen, Harrison Ford. Limp Civil War programmer about young Texans anxious to engage in battle. Veterans Rex Ingram, John Doucette, and Noah Beery are lost in this jumble.

Journey to the Center of the Earth (1959) C-132m. *** D: Henry Levin. James Mason, Pat Boone, Arlene Dahl, Diane Baker, Thayer David, Alan Napier. Entertaining, old-fashioned fantasy-adventure, from Jules Verne's story of daring expedition headed by Mason; long in telling, with silly digressions, but generally fun. Remade as WHERE TIME BEGAN.▼

Journey to the Center of Time (1967) C-82m. *½ D: D. L. Hewitt. Scott Brady, Gigi Perreau, Anthony Eisley, Abraham Sofaer, Poupee Gamin, Lyle Waggoner. Very cheap sci-fi time travel adventure to future and past, using plot elements from earlier THE TIME TRAVELERS.▼

Journey to the Far Side of the Sun (1969-British) C-99m. *** D: Robert Parrish. Roy Thinnes, Lynn Loring, Herbert Lom, Patrick Wymark. Entertaining exploration of a planet that is hidden behind the sun. The ending makes the movie. Originally titled DOPPELGANGER.▼

Journey to the Lost City SEE: **Indian Tomb, The** and **Tiger of Eschnapur**

Journey to the Seventh Planet (1961-Danish) C-83m. *½ D: Sidney Pink. John Agar, Greta Thyssen, Ann Smyrner, Mimi Heinrich, Carl Ottosen. In year 2001, expedition to Uranus discovers hostile alien brain that can turn thoughts into reality. Cheap, clumsy, dull, with just a smidge of imagination.▼

Joy House (1964-French) 98m. **½ D: René Clement. Jane Fonda, Alain Delon, Lola Albright, Sorrell Booke. Living on his looks, a playboy on the run seeks refuge in gloomy French mansion run by two American women. Fate and quicker wits than his control this brooding tale of irony. Also known as THE LOVE CAGE.▼

Joy in the Morning (1965) C-103m. ** D: Alex Segal. Richard Chamberlain, Yvette Mimieux, Arthur Kennedy, Sidney Blackmer. Betty Smith's gentle novel of struggling law student and his marital problems becomes mild vehicle for Chamberlain, who crusades for human dignity amid stereotypes of a college town.

Joyless Street, The (1925-German) 90m. *** D: G.W. Pabst. Asta Nielsen, Greta Garbo, Werner Krauss, Valeska Gert, Jaro Furth, Agnes Esterhazy, Einar Hanson. Fascinating, expressionistic account of economic and moral decay, focusing on the inhabitants of one sorry Viennese street after WW1. Garbo, in her third feature, plays a professor's daughter who attempts to keep her family from starving. Marlene Dietrich is an extra in this. Also known as THE STREET OF SORROW.▼

Joy of Living (1938) 90m. *** D: Tay Garnett. Irene Dunne, Douglas Fairbanks, Jr., Alice Brady, Guy Kibbee, Jean Dixon, Eric Blore, Lucille Ball. Delightful screwball musicomedy with gay-blade Fairbanks wooing singing star Dunne.▼

Joy of Loving SEE: **School for Love**

Joy of Sex (1984) C-93m. BOMB D: Martha Coolidge. Michelle Meyrink, Cameron Dye, Lisa Langlois, Charles Van Eman, Christopher Lloyd, Colleen Camp, Ernie Hudson. Virgin Meyrink, believing she has weeks to live, decides to "do it all" before she dies. Nothing of Alex Comfort's book—including his name—is left (and despite the title, no one seems to be having a good time) in embarrassingly bad high-school comedy.▼

Joy Ride (1958) 60m. *½ D: Edward Bernds. Rad Fulton, Ann Doran, Regis Toomey, Nicholas King, Robert Levin. Minor account of middle-aged man trying to reform hot-rod gang members; occasionally bristling.

Joyride (1977) C-92m. ** D: Joseph Ruben. Desi Arnaz, Jr., Robert Carradine, Melanie Griffith, Anne Lockhart, Tom Ligon, Cliff Lenz. Meandering tale of two young-and-footloose couples on the road to Alaska looking for adventure but drifting into crime. Four show-biz offspring play the leads: the sons of Desi Arnaz and John Carradine, the daughters of Tippi Hedren and June Lockhart.▼

Joysticks (1983) C-88m. BOMB D: Greydon Clark. Joe Don Baker, Leif Green, Jim Greenleaf, Scott McGinnis, Logan Ramsey. Loud, inane ode to video games, with meanie Baker (looking as if he just spent a week on skid row) attempting to shut down video arcade populated by requisite Lolitas, nerds, slobs, punks, etc. Original title: VIDEO MADNESS.▼

J. R. SEE: **Who's That Knocking at My Door?**

Juarez (1939) 132m. *** D: William Dieterle. Paul Muni, Bette Davis, Brian Aherne, Claude Rains, John Garfield, Gale Sondergaard, Donald Crisp, Gilbert Roland, Louis Calhern, Grant Mitchell. Interesting biography of Mexican leader (Muni), with unforgettable performance by Rains as Napoleon III; also notable is Garfield's offbeat casting as Mexican General Diaz. Elaborately done, but never as inspiring as it's intended to be.▼

Jubal (1956) C-101m. *** D: Delmer Daves. Glenn Ford, Ernest Borgnine, Rod Steiger, Valerie French, Felicia Farr, Noah Beery, Jr., Charles Bronson. It's Bard in the Saddle with this Western version of OTHELLO: when jealous rancher Borgnine seeks some lovemaking advice from cowhand Ford, along comes Steiger with hints that Ford's giving Borgnine's wife French a few "lessons" as well. Brooding, intense drama is pretty good on its own terms, more intriguing if you know the original.▼

Jubilee Trail (1954) C-103m. **½ D: Joseph Kane. Vera Ralston, Joan Leslie, Forrest Tucker, John Russell, Ray Middleton, Pat O'Brien. Expansive Republic Western vehicle for Ralston as heart-of-gold chanteuse sorting out rancher's life in old California.▼

Judge, The (1949) 69m. *½ D: Elmer Clifton. Milburn Stone, Katherine DeMille, Paul Guilfoyle, Jonathan Hale, Norman Budd. Cheapie flick vaguely detailing man's moral disintegration from respected attorney to fugitive criminal.▼

Judge and Jake Wyler, The (1972) C-100m. TVM D: David Lowell Rich. Bette Davis, Doug McClure, Eric Braeden, James McEachin, Kent Smith, Joan Van Ark. Tolerable whodunit with sense of humor. Eccentric judge (Davis) takes on parolee as detective partner in new agency investigating suspicious death of businessman. For TV, good banter, convincing situations. Produced and cowritten by Richard Levinson and William Link. Above average.

Judge and the Assassin, The (1975-French) C-130m. ***½ D: Bertrand Tavernier. Philippe Noiret, Michel Galabru, Isabelle Huppert, Jean-Claude Brialy, Renée Faure. In a way, the title tells all in this incisive, expertly directed and acted drama: Judge Noiret must determine whether murderer Galabru is insane or faking. Fascinating from start to finish.▼

Judge Dee and the Monastery Murder (1974) C-100m. TVM D: Jeremy Kagan. Khigh Dhiegh, Mako, Soon-Taik Oh, Miiko Taka, Irene Tsu, James Hong, Keye Luke. Murder mystery with a definite twist: the detective is a seventh century Chinese sleuth. Based on Robert Van Gulick's Judge Dee mysteries; decidedly offbeat and lavishly made. Script by Nicholas Meyer. Above average.

Judge Hardy & Son (1939) 87m. D: George B. Seitz. Lewis Stone, Mickey Rooney, Cecilia Parker, Fay Holden, Sara Haden, Ann Rutherford, June Preisser, Maria Ouspenskaya, Henry Hull, Martha O'Driscoll. SEE: **Andy Hardy** series.

Judge Hardy's Children (1938) 78m. D: George B. Seitz. Lewis Stone, Mickey Rooney, Cecilia Parker, Fay Holden, Betty Ross Clark, Ann Rutherford, Robert Whitney, Ruth Hussey. SEE: **Andy Hardy** series.

Judge Horton and the Scottsboro Boys (1976) C-100m. TVM D: Fielder Cook. Arthur Hill, Vera Miles, Lewis J. Stadlen, Ken Kercheval, Ellen Barber, Susan Lederer, Tom Ligon. Excellent courtroom-based drama detailing 1931 rape trial of nine blacks and the embattled Southern judge who presided over the proceedings. Hill is the backbone of virtue as the courageous judge. Above average.▼

Judge Priest (1934) **80m.** ***½ D: John Ford. Will Rogers, Tom Brown, Anita Louise, Henry B. Walthall, Stepin Fetchit, Hattie McDaniel. Exceptional slice of Americana with Rogers as commonsensical yet controversial judge in small town; full of warm and funny character vignettes. Ford remade it in 1953 as THE SUN SHINES BRIGHT.▼

Judge Steps Out, The (1949) **91m.** **½ D: Boris Ingster. Alexander Knox, Ann Sothern, George Tobias, Sharyn Moffett. Judge Knox runs away from his job and shrewish wife, hides out as a short-order cook, falls in love with Sothern.

Judgment at Nuremberg (1961) **178m.** **** D: Stanley Kramer. Spencer Tracy, Burt Lancaster, Richard Widmark, Marlene Dietrich, Judy Garland, Maximilian Schell, Montgomery Clift, William Shatner. Superior production revolving around U.S. judge Tracy presiding over German war-criminal trials. Schell won Oscar as defense attorney, as did Abby Mann for his screenplay. Fine performances by Dietrich as widow of German officer, Garland as hausfrau, Clift as unbalanced victim of Nazi atrocities.▼

Judgment in Berlin (1988) **C-92m.** ** D: Leo Penn. Martin Sheen, Sam Wanamaker, Sean Penn, Max Gail, Juerger Hemrich, Carl Lumbly, Max Volkert Martens. U.S. judge Sheen, thrown into one of those Spencer Tracy/Nuremberg situations, has to determine if the hijacking of an East German jet into Berlin is justified. Ragged but *just* watchable, with actor Penn (the director's son) turning in one unexpectedly heartfelt cameo during some climactic courtroom testimony. Shown on TV as ESCAPE TO FREEDOM.▼

Judgment in Stone, A (1986-Canadian) **C-102m.** *½ D: Ousama Rawi. Rita Tushingham, Ross Petty, Tom Kneebone, Shelley Peterson, Jessica Stern, Jonathan Crombie, Jackie Burroughs. Tushingham is well cast in this otherwise tiresome, drawn-out chiller as a repressed, illiterate, and psychotic spinster who takes a job as a housemaid with predictably tragic results. Also known as THE HOUSEKEEPER.▼

Judith (1966) **C-109m.** BOMB D: Daniel Mann. Sophia Loren, Peter Finch, Jack Hawkins, Hans Verner, Zharira Charifai. Austrian Jewess Loren survives prison camp with makeup intact, comes to Israel in 1948 to locate Nazi husband who betrayed her. Film is both dull and unbelievable, a bad combination. Video title: CONFLICT.▼

Juggernaut (1974-British) **C-109m.** *** D: Richard Lester. Richard Harris, Omar Sharif, David Hemmings, Anthony Hopkins, Shirley Knight, Ian Holm, Roy Kinnear, Freddie Jones. Surprisingly effective thriller about bomb threat on luxury ocean liner, and demolition experts' attempts to avoid disaster. Harris is first-rate and so is Lester's direction of a formula story.▼

Juggler, The (1953) **86m.** **½ D: Edward Dmytryk. Kirk Douglas, Milly Vitale, Paul Stewart, Alf Kjellin. Sentimental account of Jewish refugee Douglas going to Israel to rebuild his life, overcoming bitterness from life in a concentration camp. Filmed in Israel.

Juke Box Rhythm (1959) **81m.** *½ D: Arthur Dreifuss. Jo Morrow, Jack Jones, Brian Donlevy, George Jessel, Hans Conried, Karin Booth, Marjorie Reynolds, Fritz Feld, Johnny Otis, The Treniers, The Earl Grant Trio. Perfectly awful minor musical focusing on various schemes of clean-cut young singer Jones. However, Otis does sing "Willie and the Hand Jive."

Juke Girl (1942) **90m.** **½ D: Curtis Bernhardt. Ann Sheridan, Ronald Reagan, Richard Whorf, Gene Lockhart, Faye Emerson, George Tobias. Saga of fruit-workers' troubles in Florida never really hits the mark, but Sheridan and Reagan are good as laborers who get involved in murder.

Jules and Jim (1961-French) **104m.** **** D: Francois Truffaut. Jeanne Moreau, Oskar Werner, Henri Serre, Marie Dubois, Vanna Urbino. Truffaut's memorable tale of three people in love, and how the years affect their interrelationships. A film of rare beauty and charm. Americanized by Paul Mazursky in WILLIE AND PHIL.▼

Julia (1977) **C-118m.** **** D: Fred Zinnemann. Jane Fonda, Vanessa Redgrave, Jason Robards, Maximilian Schell, Hal Holbrook, Rosemary Murphy, Meryl Streep, Lisa Pelikan, Cathleen Nesbitt, John Glover. Fonda plays Lillian Hellman in adaptation of author's story in *Pentimento* about her exuberant, unusual friend Julia, and how she drew Hellman into involvement with European resistance movement in 1930s. Fine story-telling in beautifully crafted film; Robards (as Dashiell Hammett), screenwriter Alvin Sargent, and radiant Redgrave won Oscars. Streep's film debut.▼

Julia and Julia (1987-Italian) **C-97m.** **½ D: Peter Del Monte. Kathleen Turner, Gabriel Byrne, Sting, Gabriele Ferzetti, Angela Goodwin. Turner is compelling as a woman whose life splits in two, leaving her caught between a happily married existence with Byrne and a dangerous affair with photographer Sting. Intriguing, well-acted psychological thriller that unfortunately leads nowhere. Handsomely photographed by Guiseppe Rutunno, this theatrical release was actually made on high-definition video, then transferred to film.▼

Julia Misbehaves (1948) **99m.** *** D: Jack Conway. Greer Garson, Walter Pidgeon, Peter Lawford, Elizabeth Taylor, Cesar Romero, Mary Boland, Nigel Bruce. Bouncy account of showgirl Garson returning to dignified husband Pidgeon when daughter Taylor is about to marry; Romero is fun as bragging acrobat. Stars seem right at home with slapstick situations.

Julie (1956) **99m.** ** D: Andrew L. Stone. Doris Day, Louis Jourdan, Barry Sullivan, Frank Lovejoy, Jack Kelly, Ann Robinson, Mae Marsh. Overbaked soaper in which Day contends with jealous, psychopathic spouse Jourdan, who strangled her first husband and now threatens to kill her. Sometimes tense, but too often unintentionally funny.

Julie Darling (1982-Canadian-German) **C-100m.** *½ D: Paul Nicolas, Maurice Smith. Anthony Franciosa, Isabelle Mejias, Sybil Danning, Cindy Girling, Paul Hubbard. Awful thriller, with teenager Mejias plotting to do in stepmom Danning after seeing her own mother raped and murdered.

Juliet of the Spirits (1965-Italian) **C-148m.** *** D: Federico Fellini. Giulietta Masina, Sandra Milo, Mario Pisu, Valentina Cortese, Lou Gilbert, Sylva Koscina. Surrealistic fantasy triggered by wife's fears that her well-to-do husband is cheating on her. A film requiring viewer to delve into woman's psyche via a rash of symbolism; coun terbalanced with rich visual delights.▼

Julietta (1957-French) **96m.** **½ D: Marc Chamarat. Jean Marais, Jeanne Moreau, Dany Robin, Denise Grey. Frilly comedy with sturdy cast. Heroine journeys to marry a prince, misses her train and dallies with handsome lawyer.

Julius Caesar (1953) **120m.** ***½ D: Joseph L. Mankiewicz. Marlon Brando, James Mason, John Gielgud, Louis Calhern, Edmond O'Brien, Greer Garson, Deborah Kerr, George Macready, Michael Pate, Alan Napier, Ian Wolfe, Douglass Dumbrille, Edmund Purdom. Superior adaptation of William Shakespeare's play of political power and honor in ancient Rome. Lavishly produced (by John Houseman), with an excellent cast and Oscar-winning art direction-set decoration. Screenplay by director Mankiewicz.▼

Julius Caesar (1970) **C-117m.** **½ D: Stuart Burge. Charlton Heston, Jason Robards, John Gielgud, Richard Johnson, Robert Vaughn, Richard Chamberlain, Diana Rigg, Jill Bennett, Christopher Lee. Technically ragged, but acceptable version of Shakespeare play, negated somewhat by Robards' zombielike portrayal of Brutus. The 1953 version (also starring Gielgud) is much better.▼

Jumbo SEE: **Billy Rose's Jumbo**▼

Jumping Jacks (1952) **96m.** **½ D: Norman Taurog. Dean Martin, Jerry Lewis, Mona Freeman, Don DeFore, Robert Strauss. Daffy duo has good opportunity for plenty of sight gags when they join military paratroop squad.

Jumpin' Jack Flash (1986) **C-100m.** *½ D: Penny Marshall. Whoopi Goldberg, Stephen Collins, John Wood, Carol Kane, Annie Potts, Peter Michael Goetz, Roscoe Lee Browne, Sara Botsford, Jeroen Krabbe, Jonathan Pryce, Tracy Reiner, Jim Belushi. Computer programmer is pulled into international intrigue when spy who wants in from the cold contacts her on her terminal. Lively but stupid star vehicle for Goldberg, who's infinitely better than the script (or her poorly defined character). Feature directing debut for comedienne Marshall, who cast her producer-director brother Garry as a police detective, and former TV costar Michael McKean in an unbilled cameo as a British party guest. ▼

Jump Into Hell (1955) **93m.** **½ D: David Butler. Jacques Sernas, Kurt Kasznar, Peter Van Eyck, Pat Blake. Neatly paced actioner of paratroopers involved in Indochina war.

June Bride (1948) **97m.** *** D: Bretaigne Windust. Bette Davis, Robert Montgomery, Fay Bainter, Tom Tully, Barbara Bates, Jerome Cowan, Mary Wickes. Flippant comedy of magazine writers Davis and Montgomery inspired by feature story they are doing on June brides. Breezy script by Ranald MacDougall. Don't blink or you'll miss Debbie Reynolds in her film debut.

June Night (1940-Swedish) **86m.** **½ D: Per Lindberg. Ingrid Bergman, Olof Widgren, Gunnar Sjoberg, Carl Strom, Marianne Lofgren, Lill-Tollie Zellman, Alf Kjellen. Generally fine performances compensate for melodramatic nature of this soaper, detailing the plight of small-town girl Bergman after she becomes involved with sailor Sjoberg. Bergman's final Swedish film before coming to Hollywood.▼

Jungle, The (1952) **74m.** *½ D: William Berke. Rod Cameron, Cesar Romero, Marie Windsor, Sulchana. Romantic triangle burdens tale of expedition in India that encounters still living mammoths. Shot on location but still dull and pedestrian.

Jungle Book (1942) **C-109m.** *** D: Zoltan Korda. Sabu, Joseph Calleia, John Qualen, Frank Puglia, Rosemary DeCamp, Noble Johnson. Colorful Kipling fantasy of boy (Sabu) raised by wolves. Exciting family fare, fine Miklos Rozsa score. Remade as an animated Disney feature in 1967.▼

Jungle Captive (1945) **63m.** BOMB D: Harold Young. Otto Kruger, Amelita Ward, Phil Brown, Vicky Lane, Jerome Cowan, Rondo Hatton. Sloppy sequel to JUNGLE WOMAN dealing with yet another mad scientist's attempt to transform ape woman into beautiful girl. Three strikes and you're out.

Jungle Cat (1960) **C-70m.** **½ D: James Algar. Narrated by Winston Hibler. One of Disney's weaker True-Life Adventures suffers from script and presentation, not raw material: wildlife footage of the title character, a jaguar, is excellent.▼

Jungle Cavalcade (1941) **76m.** **½ D: Clyde Elliot, Armand Denis, Frank Buck. A compilation film of Buck capturing and caging a zooful of wild animals, edited from his first three features (BRING 'EM BACK ALIVE, WHITE CARGO, FANG AND CLAW). Buck's narration is laughably hokey and self-serving, and his attitude will not endear him to animal rights activists . . . but there's still plenty of exciting footage. ▼

Jungle Drums of Africa SEE: **U-238 and the Witch Doctor**

Jungle Fighters SEE: **Long and the Short and the Tall, The**

Jungle Gents (1954) **64m.** D: Edward Bernds, Austen Jewell. Leo Gorcey, Huntz Hall, Laurette Luez, Bernard Gorcey, David Condon. SEE: **Bowery Boys** series.

Jungle Girl SEE: **Bomba and the Jungle Girl**

Jungle Goddess (1948) **65m.** *½ D: Lewis D. Collins. Ralph Byrd, George Reeves, Wanda McKay, Armida. Very low-budget swamp saga is good only for laughs.

Jungle Gold (1944) **100m.** ** D: Spencer Bennet, Wallace Grissell. Allan Lane, Linda Stirling, Duncan Renaldo, George J. Lewis. Okay Republic cliffhanger vehicle for the Queen of the Serials. Stirling (Tiger Woman) romps through innumerable adventures to prevent wrong parties from uncovering gold treasure. Reedited from serial THE TIGER WOMAN; reissued under title PERILS OF THE DARKEST JUNGLE.▼

Jungle Heat SEE: **Dance of the Dwarfs**▼

Jungle Jim When athletic Johnny Weissmuller left the Tarzan series after sixteen years in the role, enterprising producer Sam Katzman proposed a new series that would enable the more mature but still rugged star to cavort in familiar surroundings. It was Jungle Jim, presold to an anxious audience via a successful comic strip and radio show. One critic accurately summed it up as "Tarzan with clothes on." The series was sure-fire and performed well at the box office for seven years, despite a conspicuous absence of commendation by the critics. From the first film, JUNGLE JIM, to the last, DEVIL GODDESS, the series was noted for its incredible plots and rousing action scenes, aimed primarily at juvenile audiences. Most efforts had Jungle Jim helping some Columbia Pictures heroine in distress (a lady scientist seeking a rare drug, a WAC captain lost in the jungle, etc.) and getting tangled up with hostile natives, voodoo curses, and nefarious villains (often all three at once). In the last three films of the series (CANNIBAL ATTACK, JUNGLE MOON MEN, DEVIL GODDESS) the name Jungle Jim was dropped and Weissmuller played himself, but the format remained the same, with Johnny's ever-faithful chimpanzee friend Tamba at his side. Perhaps the highlight of the series was CAPTIVE GIRL, an average entry which had the distinction of Buster Crabbe, whose career paralleled Weissmuller's in many ways, as the villain.

Jungle Jim (1948) **73m.** D: William Berke. Johnny Weissmuller, Virginia Grey, George Reeves, Lita Baron.

Jungle Jim in the Forbidden Land (1952) **65m.** D: Lew Landers. Johnny Weissmuller, Angela Greene, Jean Willes, William Fawcett.

Jungle Man-Eaters (1954) **68m.** D: Lee Sholem. Johnny Weissmuller, Karin Booth, Richard Stapley, Bernard Hamilton. SEE: **Jungle Jim** series.

Jungle Manhunt (1951) **66m.** D: Lew Landers. Johnny Weissmuller, Bob Waterfield, Sheila Ryan, Rick Vallin, Lyle Talbot. SEE: **Jungle Jim** series.

Jungle Moon Men (1955) **70m.** D: Charles S. Gould. Johnny Weissmuller, Jean Byron, Helene Stanton, Myron Healey. SEE: **Jungle Jim** series.

Jungle Princess, The (1936) **85m.** *** D: William Thiele. Dorothy Lamour, Ray Milland, Akim Tamiroff, Lynne Overman, Molly Lamont, Mala, Hugh Buckler. Lamour's first sarong film is quite unpretentious and pleasant; Milland is explorer who brings her back to civilization.

Jungle Warriors (1984-German-Mexican) **C-93m.** *½ D: Ernst R. von Theumer. Nina Van Pallandt, Paul L. Smith, John Vernon, Alex Cord, Sybil Danning, Woody Strode, Dana Elcar, Louisa Moritz, Marjoe Gortner. How's this for a plot: fashion models are taken prisoner by South American drug kingpin and tortured by his kinky half-sister (Danning). Credible cast stuck in sub-par action yarn.▼

Jungle Woman (1944) **54m.** *½ D: Reginald LeBorg. Acquanetta, Evelyn Ankers, J. Carrol Naish, Samuel S. Hinds. Psychiatrist fails to cure killer-ape tendencies of Aquanetta in this sorry sequel to CAPTIVE WILD WOMAN. Tries to emulate the style of Val Lewton's classy horror movies, even eliminates ape-woman makeup (until final shot). Followed by JUNGLE CAPTIVE.

Junior Bonner (1972) **C-103m.** ***½ D: Sam Peckinpah. Steve McQueen, Robert Preston, Ida Lupino, Ben Johnson, Joe Don Baker, Barbara Leigh, Mary Murphy. Totally captivating rodeo comedy-drama as an aging McQueen returns to his home and family to take part in a local contest. Peckinpah's most gentle film is full of natural performances, particularly by Preston and Lupino as McQueen's estranged parents. Written by Jeb Rosebrook.▼

Junior Miss (1945) **94m.** **½ D: George Seaton. Peggy Ann Garner, Allyn Joslyn, Michael Dunne, Faye Marlowe, Mona Freeman, Sylvia Field, Barbara Whiting, Mel Torme. Naive but entertaining comedy of teen-ager Garner and harried father Joslyn, based on Broadway play by Jerome Chodorov and Joseph Fields (from Sally Benson's stories).

Junkman (1982) **C-96m.** *½ D: H. B. Halicki. H. B. Halicki, Christopher Stone, Susan Shaw, Lang Jeffries, Hoyt Axton, Lynda Day George. Cars speed, crash, and practically bring each other to orgasm. Oh, yes, there *is* a story . . .▼

Jupiter's Darling (1955) **C-96m.** **½ D: George Sidney. Esther Williams, Howard Keel, George Sanders, Marge and Gower Champion, Norma Varden. Lavish musical of Robert Sherwood's *Road to Rome*, which bogs down in tedium: Williams is temptress who dallies with Hannibal (Keel) to prevent attack on Rome.

Jury Duty: The Comedy (1990) **C-100m.** TVM D: Michael Schultz. Stephen Baldwin, Mark Blankfield, Barbara Bosson, Heather Locklear, Bronson Pinchot, Lynn Redgrave, Tracy Scoggins, Alan Thicke, Reginald VelJohnson. A panel of familiar faces is called on to render a decision in a farcical, headline-making embezzlement trial of a mild-mannered accountant (versatile Pinchot, who plays three roles in all). The verdict: Average.

Jury of One (1974-French-Italian) **C-97m.** ** D: Andre Cayatte. Sophia Loren, Jean Gabin, Henri Garcin, Julien Bertheau, Michel Albertini. Plodding melodrama about a woman who goes to outrageous extremes to protect her son, on trial for murder and rape. Gabin plays the judge. Also known as THE VERDICT.

Just Across the Street (1952) **78m.** ** D: Joseph Pevney. Ann Sheridan, John Lund, Cecil Kellaway, Natalie Schafer, Harvey Lembeck. Mild shenanigans with working-woman Sheridan being mistaken for wealthy estate owner.

Just a Gigolo (1979-West German) **C-105m.** **½ D: David Hemmings. David Bowie, Sydne Rome, Kim Novak, David Hemmings, Maria Schell, Curt Jurgens, Marlene Dietrich. *Very* interesting cast is chief attraction of weird melodrama starring Bowie as Prussian war vet who drifts from job to job in Berlin before finally discovering his true calling. Dietrich, in her last film, only pops in long enough to croak the title song; Rome's spirited performance gives lift to uneven film that possibly made more sense in original 147m. version released in Europe.▼

Just a Little Inconvenience (1977) **C-100m.** TVM D: Theodore J. Flicker. Lee Majors, James Stacy, Barbara Hershey, Charles Cioffi, Jim Davis. Vietnam veteran Majors attempts to rehabilitate his best friend who lost an arm and a leg during the war. Actor Stacy delivers an inspirational portrayal in film close to the heart of producer Majors. But the script, co-written by Flicker, is unmoving. Average.

Just an Old Sweet Song (1976) **C-78m.** TVM D: Robert Ellis Miller. Cicely Tyson, Robert Hooks, Kevin Hooks, Eric Hooks, Beah Richards, Lincoln Kilpatrick, Edward Binns, Minnie Gentry. Melvin Van Peebles' contemporary drama about a black family from Detroit whose two-week vacation in the South changes their lives. Lovingly acted family film. Above average.

Just Another Secret (1989-British) **C-100m.** TVM D: Lawrence Gordon Clark. Beau Bridges, Beatie Edney, Kenneth Cranham, Enn Reitel, Dermot Crowley. CIA agent Bridges, looking for some colleagues who have mysteriously disappeared, uncovers a plot to assassinate Soviet Premier Gorbachev during a secret visit to East Germany. Frederick Forsyth wrote this screen original, but political winds of change dated it even before its TV debut. Average.

Just Around the Corner (1938) **70m.** ** D: Irving Cummings. Shirley Temple, Joan Davis, Charles Farrell, Amanda Duff, Bill Robinson, Bert Lahr, Claude Gillingwater. Simpleminded corn with Shirley single-handedly ending the Depression, manipulating pessimistic tycoon Gillingwater into creating new jobs. But the musical numbers with Robinson are still a delight.▼

Just Ask for Diamond (1988-British) **C-94m.** *** D: Stephen Bayly. Susannah York, Patricia Hodge, Roy Kinnear, Michael Medwin, Peter Eyre, Nickolas Grace, Dursley McLinden, Colin Dale, Bill Paterson, Jimmy Nail, Saeed Jaffrey. Clever, if occasionally cartoonish, detective-film parody, about the kid brother of a dumbbell private eye and the mystery surrounding a box of candy. Best for older children (although they might not get all the references to 1940s Hollywood detective dramas). Screenplay by Anthony Horowitz, from his novel *The Falcon's Malteser*.

Just Before Dawn (1946) **65m.** D: William Castle. Warner Baxter, Adele Roberts, Charles D. Brown, Martin Kosleck, Mona Barrie, Marvin Miller. SEE: **Crime Doctor** series.

Just Between Friends (1986) **C-110m.** **½ D: Allan Burns. Mary Tyler Moore, Ted Danson, Christine Lahti, Sam Waterston, Salome Jens, Jane Greer, James MacKrell. Genteel tearjerker about two women who strike up a friendship, unaware that they share the same man—one as wife, one as lover. Too pat, too neat and clean to really hit home, though the acting is first-rate, and Lahti is terrific as the single career woman. Nice role for Jane Greer, too, as Mary's mom. Directing debut for writer Burns.▼

Just for Fun (1963-British) **85m.** *½ D: Gordon Flemyng. Mark Wynter, Cherry Roland, Richard Vernon, Reginald Beckwith, John Wood, Bobby Vee, The Crickets, Freddie Cannon, Johnny Tillotson, Ketty Lester, The Tremeloes. A wisp of a plot—teens establish their own political party to run a pop election—surrounds this forgettable musical trifle. Among the more recognizable tunes are "The Night Has a Thousand Eyes" (Bobby Vee) and "Keep on Dancin' " (The Tremeloes).

Just for You (1952) **C-104m.** *** D: Elliott Nugent. Bing Crosby, Jane Wyman, Ethel Barrymore, Natalie Wood, Cora Witherspoon. Zesty musical of producer Crosby who can't be bothered with his growing children, till Wyman shows him the way.

Just Imagine (1930) **102m.** *½ D: David Butler. El Brendel, Maureen O'Sullivan, John Garrick, Marjorie White, Frank Albertson, Hobart Bosworth. Famous but utterly disappointing sci-fi musical set in 1980, with Brendel, officially dead since 1930, suddenly revived and unable to get used to phenomenal changes in living. Futuristic sets, gags, costumes made tremendous impression on everyone who saw film in 1930, but alas, it doesn't wear well at all. Songs by DeSylva-Brown-Henderson.

Justin Case (1988) **C-78m. TVM** D: Blake Edwards. George Carlin, Molly Hagan, Douglas Sill, Gordon Jump, Timothy Stack, Paul Sand. Loopy private eye flick involving the dapper ghost of a dead p.i. who joins forces with an aspiring, unemployed actress to find out who bumped him off. This marked Blake Edwards' return to TV after more than two decades. He also wrote the script for the Disney folks, based on a story he and actress daughter Jennifer Edwards concocted. Pilot to a prospective series. Average.

Justine (1969) **C-116m.** *** D: George Cukor. Anouk Aimee, Dirk Bogarde, Robert Forster, Anna Karina, Philippe Noiret, Michael York. Stylish film won't please fans of Lawrence Durrell's *Alexandria Quartet,* but works as exotic kitsch; Cukor's great use of widescreen won't mean much on TV. Filmed in Tunis.▼

Just Me and You (1978) **C-100m. TVM** D: John Erman. Louise Lasser, Charles Grodin, Julie Bovasso, Paul Fix, Michael Aldredge. Comedy-drama about a cross country odyssey shared by a dizzy New York dame and a down-to-earth salesman. Lasser wrote this one, probably after over-dosing on Judy Holliday movies, but it misfires. Average.▼

Just Off Broadway (1942) **66m.** ** D: Herbert I. Leeds. Lloyd Nolan, Marjorie Weaver, Phil Silvers, Janis Carter. Acceptable Michael Shayne caper, with swanky dame on trial for murder; outcome is easy for mystery fans.

Just One of the Guys (1985) **C-100m.** *** D: Lisa Gottlieb. Joyce Hyser, Clayton Rohner, Billy Jacoby, Toni Hudson, William Zabka, Leigh McCloskey. Pretty high school senior, convinced that looks have kept patronizing male teachers from supporting her in citywide journalism competition, dons male disguise and tries again at another school. Engagingly eccentric characterizations take this fast-paced sleeper out of the ordinary; performed with gusto by an unknown cast that's aiming to please.▼

Just Tell Me What You Want (1980) **C-112m.** **½ D: Sidney Lumet. Ali MacGraw, Alan King, Myrna Loy, Keenan Wynn, Tony Roberts, Peter Weller, Judy Kaye, Dina Merrill, Joseph Maher, Michael Gross, Leslie Easterbrook, David Rasche, John Gabriel. Obnoxious tycoon King drives long-time mistress MacGraw into arms of younger man, then does everything he can to get her back. Bitchy upper-class comedy may be too strident for some tastes, but King's flamboyant performance is sensational, as is Loy's quiet one as his long-suffering secretary. Screenplay by Jay Presson Allen, from her novel.▼

Just the Way You Are (1984) **C-94m.** *** D: Edouard Molinaro. Kristy McNichol, Michael Ontkean, Kaki Hunter, Andre Dussolier, Catherine Salviat, Robert Carradine, Lance Guest, Alexandra Paul, Timothy Daly, Patrick Cassidy. Episodic but likable film about crippled musician (McNichol) who goes to French ski resort with her leg in a cast—to see, for once, what it's like when people don't know she's handicapped. Elements of sharp comedy, escapist romance, and travelogue aren't seamlessly connected, but results are extremely pleasant, and McNichol has never been more appealing. Script by Allan Burns.▼

Just This Once (1952) **90m.** **½ D: Don Weis. Janet Leigh, Peter Lawford, Lewis Stone, Marilyn Erskine, Richard Anderson. Cute little comedy of stern Leigh in charge of playboy Lawford's dwindling fortunes, and their inevitable romance.

Just Tony (1922) **58m.** **½ D: Lynn Reynolds. Tom Mix, Claire Adams, J. P. Lockney, Duke Lee, Frank Campeau. Amiable Tom Mix Western sheds spotlight on his beloved horse Tony, tracing his life from mistreated mustang to benevolent protector of cowboy Mix.

Just You and Me, Kid (1979) **C-95m.**
*½ D: Leonard Stern. George Burns, Brooke
Shields, Lorraine Gary, Nicolas Coster,
Burl Ives, Ray Bolger, Leon Ames, Carl
Ballantine, Keye Luke. Burns struggles to
keep awful comedy afloat, but it ain't
easy. Shields plays a runaway who comes
to stay with the ex-vaudevillian. Commercial interruptions might help this one.
J. W. Coop (1972) **C-112m.** ***½ D:
Cliff Robertson. Cliff Robertson, Geraldine Page, Cristina Ferrare, R. G. Armstrong, John Crawford. Vivid character
study of none-too-bright drifter who sets
his sights on becoming No. 1 rodeo star.
Tour de force for director/writer/star Robertson, who scores in all departments.

Kagemusha (1980-Japanese) **C-159m.** ****
D: Akira Kurosawa. Tatsuya Nakadai,
Tsutomo Yamazaki, Kenichi Hagiwara,
Jinpachi Nezu, Shuji Otaki. Sixteenth-
century thief is spared execution if he will
pose as secretly deceased warlord whose
throne is coveted by others. Grand combination of humanism and spectacle from a
great filmmaker in the twilight of his career.
Released outside the U.S. at 179m. Also
known as KAGEMUSHA (THE SHADOW
WARRIOR.)▼
Kaleidoscope (1966) **C-103m.** ** D: Jack
Smight. Warren Beatty, Susannah York,
Clive Revill, Eric Porter, Murray Melvin.
Idea of Beatty-York teaming can't miss,
but does, in bland comedy about American
playboy/card-shark forced to capture narcotics smuggler or go to jail. Flashy but
forgettable. Filmed in England.
Kamikaze '89 (1982-German) **C-106m.**
*** D: Wolf Gremm. Rainer Werner
Fassbinder, Gunther Kaufmann, Boy Go-
bert, Arnold Marquis, Richy Mueller, Bri-
gitte Mira, Frank Ripploh, Franco Nero.
Police lieutenant Fassbinder (in his final
screen role) attempts to foil an alleged
bomb plot, set in a futuristic Germany.
Exciting if sometimes confusing thriller,
based on a Per Wahloo novel.▼
Kamilla (1981-Norwegian) **C-100m.** ***
D: Vibeke Lokkeberg. Nina Knapskog,
Vibeke Lokkeberg, Helge Jordal, Kenneth
Johansen, Karin Zetlitz Haerem. Briskly
paced yet quietly disturbing chronicle of
7-year-old Knapskog and the world around
her: most distressingly, her constantly squabbling parents; most specially, the secret
world she shares with a little boy. Knapskog
is remarkable, and the film can be favorably compared to SMALL CHANGE and
FORBIDDEN GAMES, the celluloid masterpieces about childhood.
Kanal (1956-Polish) **90m.** *** D: Andrzej
Wajda. Teresa Izewska, Tadeusz Janczar,
Wienczylaw Glinski, Wladyslaw (Vladek)
Sheybal. Intense, almost unrelentingly
graphic account of the final days of the

September, 1944, Warsaw uprising in
Nazi-occupied Poland. This is the second
of Wajda's war trilogy, after A GENERA-
TION and before ASHES AND DIA-
MONDS. Also known as THEY LOVED
LIFE.▼
Kandyland (1987) **C-93m.** BOMB D: Rob-
ert Schnitzer. Kim Evenson, Sandahl Berg-
man, Charles Laulette, Bruce Baum, Cole
Stevens, Irwin Keyes. Dumb exploitation
film charts the misadventures of cute
Evenson (a former *Playboy* model) be-
coming a stripper at the Kandyland club,
under the tutelage of old pro Bergman.
Unintentionally silly dialogue sinks this
one.▼
Kangaroo (1952) **C-84m.** ** D: Lewis
Milestone. Maureen O'Hara, Peter Lawford,
Finlay Currie, Richard Boone. Uninspired
blend of romance and adventure, salvaged
by good on-location Australian landscapes
and fetching O'Hara.
Kangaroo (1986-Australian) **C-105m.** **
D: Tim Burstall. Colin Friels, Judy Davis,
John Walton, Julie Nihill, Hugh Keays-
Byrne. Muddled account of controversial
British writer (Friels) who exiles himself
and wife Davis to Australia in the early
1920s, and develops an intellectual attachment to a group of Fascists. Potentially
fascinating, insightful portrait of a man of
letters and his difficulties in dealing with
the real world, but there's little feel for the
characters and their motivations. Adapted
from D. H. Lawrence's autobiographical
novel. Incidentally, Friels and Davis are
real-life husband and wife.▼
Kansan, The (1943) **79m.** **½ D: George
Archainbaud. Richard Dix, Jane Wyatt,
Victor Jory, Albert Dekker, Eugene Pallette, Robert Armstrong. Zippy Western,
with Dix becoming town hero, taming
gangsters, but facing more trouble with
corrupt town official.▼
Kansas (1988) **C-108m.** BOMB D: David
Stevens. Matt Dillon, Andrew McCarthy,
Leslie Hope, Brent Jennings. McCarthy
gets stranded in the Midwest after his car
and possessions blow up on the road,
and takes it on the lam after boxcar acquaintance (and punk) Dillon implicates
him in a bank robbery. Goes into fast
free-fall around the time McCarthy rescues
the governor's daughter from drowning
(!)—and falls for the kind of farmer's
daughter who wears makeup and pearls in
the field. Second only to Toto as the Sunflower State's top movie dog.▼
Kansas City Bomber (1972) **C-99m.** **
D: Jerrold Freedman. Raquel Welch, Kevin
McCarthy, Helena Kallianiotes, Norman
Alden, Jeanne Cooper, Mary Kay Place,
Dick Lane, Jodie Foster. Once you've
seen five minutes, it doesn't pay to stay
through the rest. Raquel stars as good-
hearted roller derby star who has female

colleagues jealous, male employers drooling. Dialogue, situations often unintentionally funny.

Kansas City Confidential (1952) **98m.** *** D: Phil Karlson. John Payne, Coleen Gray, Preston Foster, Neville Brand, Lee Van Cleef, Jack Elam. Tough action drama with ex-con Payne nailed for armored robbery he didn't commit, determined to expose cunning mastermind Foster. Silly wrapup scene is only detraction.▼

Kansas City Kitty (1944) **63m.** ** D: Del Lord. Joan Davis, Bob Crosby, Jane Frazee, Erik Rolf. Programmer sparked by Davis, involved in purchase of song-publishing company on the skids.

Kansas City Massacre, The (1975) **C-100m.** TVM D: Dan Curtis. Dale Robertson, Bo Hopkins, Robert Walden, Scott Brady, Mills Watson, Harris Yulin, Matt Clark, John Karlen, Sally Kirkland. Action-packed period piece, sequel to MELVIN PURVIS, G-MAN, has indomitable Purvis (cigar-chomping Robertson) vying with Pretty Boy Floyd, Baby Face Nelson, John Dillinger, Alvin Karpis and other public enemies. Snappily directed, with a dandy cast and a sense of humor. Above average.▼

Kansas Pacific (1953) **C-73m.** ** D: Ray Nazarro. Sterling Hayden, Eve Miller, Barton MacLane, Reed Hadley, Irving Bacon. Inoffensive account of building of title railway during 1860s, with Reb soldiers trying to prevent its completion.▼

Kansas Raiders (1950) **C-80m.** *½ D: Ray Enright. Audie Murphy, Brian Donlevy, Marguerite Chapman, Tony Curtis, Richard Arlen. Formula Western has Jesse James (Murphy) joining Quantrill's Raiders during the Civil War.

Karate Kid, The (1984) **C-126m.** ***½ D: John G. Avildsen. Ralph Macchio, Noriyuki (Pat) Morita, Elisabeth Shue, Randee Heller, Martin Kove, William Zabka, Chad McQueen, Tony O'Dell, Larry Drake. Teenager is beset by bullies until an unlikely mentor (the Japanese handyman in his apartment house) teaches him about self-confidence—and karate. Unabashedly old-fashioned, manipulative movie that's a real audience-pleaser; from the director of the original ROCKY. Winning performances by Macchio and Morita. If only they'd trimmed it a bit. Followed by two sequels.▼

Karate Kid, Part II, The (1986) **C-113m.** **½ D: John G. Avildsen. Ralph Macchio, Noriyuki (Pat) Morita, Nobu McCarthy, Danny Kamekona, Yuji Okumoto, Tamlyn Tomita, Martin Kove. Purposeless sequel takes main characters from original film to Japan, where they're confronted by Morita's long-ago arch-enemy and his nasty nephew. Corny in the extreme (all that's missing from climax is hounds and ice floes), but made palatable by winning performances of Macchio and Morita. Aimed strictly at kids.▼

Karate Kid III, The (1989) **C-111m.** BOMB D: John G. Avildsen. Ralph Macchio, Noriyuki (Pat) Morita, Robyn Elaine Lively, Thomas Ian Griffith, Martin Kove, Sean Kanan, Jonathan Avildsen. Utterly stupid sequel has the "kid" (27-year-old Macchio) being set up for slaughter by nemesis Kove (in an obligatory appearance). When Morita refuses to train him, Macchio turns instead to Griffith—a sadistic millionaire Vietnam vet (who also turns out to be a buddy of Kove's!). Will Morita save him? Naturally . . . but this film is hopeless.

Karen Carpenter Story, The (1989) **C-100m.** TVM D: Joseph Sargent. Cynthia Gibb, Mitchell Anderson, Peter Michael Goetz, Michael McGuire, Lise Hilboldt, Louise Fletcher. Docudrama about the dark side of the sunny pop singer who worked with her brother as The Carpenters. Traces her rise to fame, her death from bulimia, and his troubles (touched on briefly) with prescription drugs. About a dozen of the duo's hits (well lip-synched) should keep their fans happy. Written by Barry Morrow, who dramatizes real-life stories so well; Richard Carpenter served as executive producer. Above average.

Kashmiri Run (1969-Spanish) **C-101m.** ** D: John Peyser. Pernell Roberts, Alexandra Bastedo, Julian Mateos, Gloria Gamata. Two men and a girl try to stay one step ahead of the Chinese Communists while fleeing Tibet; plodding actioner.▼

Kate Bliss and the Ticker Tape Kid (1978) **C-100m.** TVM D: Burt Kennedy. Suzanne Pleshette, Don Meredith, Tony Randall, Burgess Meredith, Harry Morgan, David Huddleston, Harry Carey, Jr., John Lone. Western comedy involving a lady detective from back east, a stuffy English rancher with a rustling problem, and a dapper bandit who fashions himself as a western Robin Hood. Good cast plays it well. Script by William Bowers and John Zodorow. Above average.

Kate McShane (1975) **C-78m.** TVM D: Marvin Chomsky. Anne Meara, Sean McClory, Charles Haid, Cal Bellini, Christine Belford, Charles Cioffi. Flamboyant lady lawyer teams up with dad, a retired cop, and brother, a priest/university law professor, to defend society woman accused of murder. Routine drama with Meara miscast here and in series that followed. Average.

Kate's Secret (1986) **C-100m.** TVM D: Arthur Allan Seidelman. Meredith Baxter Birney, Edward Asner, Shari Belafonte-Harper, Ben Masters, Tracy Nelson, Mackenzie Phillips, Georgann Johnson. Beautiful Birney turns out to be a closet bulimic in this unappealing "affliction of the week" movie. Below average.

Katherine (1975) **C-100m. TVM** D: Jeremy Kagan. Art Carney, Sissy Spacek, Henry Winkler, Julie Kavner, Jane Wyatt, Hector Elias, Jenny Sullivan. Absorbing drama written by Kagan about one young woman's radical experience, from innocent to activist to terrorist. Spacek is remarkable in title role. Subsequently cut to 78m. Above average.▼

Kathleen (1941) **88m.** ** D: Harold S. Bucquet. Shirley Temple, Herbert Marshall, Laraine Day, Gail Patrick, Felix Bressart. Predictable story of neglected daughter Temple bringing widower father Marshall and Day together.

Kathy O' (1958) **C-99m.** **½ D: Jack Sher. Dan Duryea, Jan Sterling, Patty McCormack, Mary Fickett. Sluggish frolic of temperamental child star McCormack and her desperate public relations agent Duryea.

Katie Did It (1951) **81m.** **½ D: Frederick de Cordova. Ann Blyth, Mark Stevens, Cecil Kellaway, Jesse White. Blyth is perkier than usual as square New England librarian who becomes hep when romanced by swinging New Yorker Stevens.

Katie: Portrait of a Centerfold (1978) **C-100m. TVM** D: Robert Greenwald. Kim Basinger, Glynn Turman, Vivian Blaine, Dorothy Malone, Fabian, Tab Hunter, Don Johnson, Melanie Mayron. Naive beauty queen from Texas grows up fast after going to Hollywood in search of stardom. Below average.

Kavik, the Wolf Dog SEE: **Courage of Kavik, the Wolf Dog, The**▼

Kazablan (1974-Israeli) **C-114m.** *** D: Menahem Golan. Yehoram Gaon, Arie Elias, Efrat Lavie, Joseph Graber. Entertaining musical made in Old Jaffa and Jerusalem, in English, based on a popular show. Gaon repeats his stage role as streetwise war hero out to save his neighborhood from being torn down. Excellent color and location work.

Keefer (1978) **C-74m. TVM** D: Barry Shear. William Conrad, Kate Woodville, Michael O'Hare, Cathy Lee Crosby, Jeremy Kemp, Brioni Farrell. Crack team of WW2 secret agents led by Conrad (in this post-*Cannon* pilot) face predictable risks and formula action behind enemy lines. Average.

Keegans, The (1976) **C-78m. TVM** D: John Badham. Adam Roarke, Spencer Mulligan, Heather Menzies, Tom Clancy, Joan Leslie, Paul Shenar, Judd Hirsch, Janit Baldwin, Penelope Windust. Crime drama concerning investigative reporter's attempts to clear his pro-football brother of murdering their sister's attacker. Average.

Keep, The (1983) **C-96m.** *½ D: Michael Mann. Scott Glenn, Ian McKellen, Alberta Watson, Jurgen Prochnow, Robert Prosky, Gabriel Byrne. German soldiers try to defend a Rumanian mountain pass during WW2 by headquartering in an ancient fortress—ignoring villagers' warnings of a strange presence inside. Outlandish, incoherent, and mostly awful; recommended only for connoisseurs of Strange Cinema.▼

Keep 'em Flying (1941) **86m.** **½ D: Arthur Lubin. Bud Abbott, Lou Costello, Carol Bruce, Martha Raye, William Gargan, Dick Foran. Good A&C mixed in with clichéd plot of stunt-pilot Foran unable to accustom himself to Air Force discipline. Raye is fun playing twins.

Keep 'em Slugging (1943) **60m.** D: Christy Cabanne. Bobby Jordan, Huntz Hall, Gabriel Dell, Norman Abbott, Evelyn Ankers. SEE: **Bowery Boys** series.

Keeper of the Flame (1942) **100m.** *** D: George Cukor. Spencer Tracy, Katharine Hepburn, Richard Whorf, Margaret Wycherly, Forrest Tucker, Frank Craven. Interesting but dated drama of reporter Tracy exposing unsavory background of late American hero; Hepburn is man's widow.

Keeping On (1981) **C-75m. TVM** D: Barbara Kopple. Dick Anthony Williams, Carol Kane, James Broderick, Marcia Rodd, Rosalind Cash, Carl Lee, Danny Glover, Trazana Beverly, Guy Boyd. Good drama of proud preacher-worker Williams trying to unionize mill with assistance of organizer Broderick. Unsubtle, but not unfair, in its pro-union viewpoint; a fictional counterpart of Kopple's documentary, HARLAN COUNTY, U.S.A. Screenplay by Horton Foote. Originally made for PBS' *American Playhouse*. Above average.▼

Keep It Cool SEE: **Let's Rock!**

Keep Your Powder Dry (1945) **93m.** ** D: Edward Buzzell. Lana Turner, Laraine Day, Susan Peters, Agnes Moorehead, Bill Johnson, Natalie Schafer, Lee Patrick. Hackneyed tale of WW2 WACs, glossy on the outside, empty on the inside.

Kelly (1981-Canadian) **C-93m.** ** D: Christopher Chapman. Robert Logan, Twyla-Dawn Vokins, George Clutesi, Elaine Nalee, Doug Lennox. Young Vokins leaves the city to live with her father (Logan) in the wilderness. Static and boring; Logan wrote the screenplay.

Kelly and Me (1957) **C-86m** ** D: Robert Z. Leonard. Van Johnson, Piper Laurie, Martha Hyer, Onslow Stevens. Johnson is unsuccessful hoofer who hits movie big-time with talented dog for partner. Mild musical.

Kelly's Heroes (1970) **C-145m.** **½ D: Brian G. Hutton. Clint Eastwood, Telly Savalas, Don Rickles, Donald Sutherland, Carroll O'Connor, Gavin MacLeod, Stuart Margolin, (Harry) Dean Stanton. Large-scale WW2 film tries for Sergeant Bilko-ish atmosphere with middling results; hippie Sutherland isn't credible in 1940s setting. But actionful aspects of Savalas and Eastwood's far-fetched gold heist behind enemy lines make film worth watching.▼

Kennel Murder Case, The (1933) **73m.** D: Michael Curtiz. William Powell, Mary Astor, Eugene Pallette, Ralph Morgan, Helen Vinson, Jack LaRue, Robert Barrat, Arthur Hohl, Paul Cavanagh. SEE: **Philo Vance** series.▼

Kenner (1969) **C-92m.** ** D: Steve Sekely. Jim Brown, Madlyn Rhue, Robert Coote, Ricky Cordell, Charles Horvath. Small, bittersweet romance of soldier of fortune in Bombay (filmed on location), whose search for partner's murderer involves young native dancer.

Kenny & Co. (1976) **C-90m.** **½ D: Don Coscarelli. Dan McCann, Mike Baldwin, Jeff Roth, Ralph Richmond, Reggie Bannister. Sweet-natured, upbeat look at adolescent life, focusing on one boy's growing pains. Virtually a one-man-show behind the camera by young Coscarelli.

Kenny Rogers as The Gambler (1980) **C-94m.** TVM D: Dick Lowry. Kenny Rogers, Bruce Boxleitner, Christine Belford, Harold Gould, Clu Gulager, Lance LeGault, Lee Purcell. In his first starring role Rogers brings his charisma and credible acting abilities to this Western, which used his hit song as a narrative springboard. Average; also known as THE GAMBLER; followed by two sequels.▼

Kenny Rogers as The Gambler, Part II—The Adventure Continues (1983) **C-200m.** TVM D: Dick Lowry. Kenny Rogers, Bruce Boxleitner, Linda Evans, Johnny Crawford, Cameron Mitchell, Mitchell Ryan, Gregory Sierra, Ken Swofford, Harold Gould. The title, just about sums it up. There's Kenny's charisma, Bruce's charm, and Linda in jeans as the fastest female gun in the West. The original held a record (for a while) as the most-watched TV-movie ever, so why not give the fans twice as much of a good thing? Originally shown in two parts. Average.▼

Kenny Rogers as The Gambler, Part III—The Legend Continues (1987) **C-200m.** TVM D: Dick Lowry. Kenny Rogers, Bruce Boxleitner, Linda Gray, Melanie Chartoff, Matt Clark, George Kennedy, Dean Stockwell, Charles Durning, Jeffrey Jones. Rogers gets even more mileage out of his hit record of the late 1970s, this time getting the fictional gambler involved with such real-life figures as Sitting Bull (George American Horse) and Buffalo Bill (Jones), mediating between the U.S. government and the Sioux nation. Originally shown in two parts. Average.

Kent Chronicles, The SEE: **Bastard, The**

Kent State (1981) **C-150m.** TVM D: James Goldstone. Jane Fleiss, Charley Lang, Talia Balsam, Keith Gordon, Jeff Mc-

Cracken, Michael Higgins, John Getz, Ann Gillespie, Shepperd Strudwick, George Coe, David Marshall Grant, Will Patton, Ellen Barkin. Uncompromising depiction of the four days in 1970 that ended in a tragic confrontation at Kent State University in Ohio with four students dead and nine others wounded. Incisive script by Gerald Green and Richard Kramer and intelligent direction by Goldstone, who won an Emmy as Outstanding Director. Above average.▼

Kentuckian, The (1955) **C-104m.** **½ D: Burt Lancaster. Burt Lancaster, Diana Lynn, Dianne Foster, Walter Matthau, John McIntire, Una Merkel, John Carradine. Minor but spirited frontier adventure set in 1820s with Lancaster (doing double duty as star and director) traveling to Texas with his son, hoping to start new life. Matthau's film debut.▼

Kentucky (1938) **C-95m.** *** D: David Butler. Loretta Young, Richard Greene, Walter Brennan, Douglass Dumbrille, Karen Morley, Moroni Olsen, Russell Hicks. Lushly filmed story of rival horsebreeding families in blue-grass country, with lovers Young and Greene clinching at finale. Brennan won Best Supporting Actor Oscar.▼

Kentucky Fried Movie, The (1977) **C-78m.** *** D: John Landis. Evan Kim, Master Bong Soo Han, Bill Bixby, George Lazenby, Henry Gibson, Donald Sutherland, Tony Dow, Boni Enten. Vulgar, often funny skits strung together. Best: a lengthy Bruce Lee takeoff, a black and white spoof of the old courtroom TV shows. Idea originated with Kentucky Fried Theatre, a Madison, Wisconsin, satirical group whose key members—Jim Abrahams, David Zucker, and Jerry Zucker—went on to do AIRPLANE! Followed a decade later by AMAZON WOMEN ON THE MOON.▼

Kentucky Kernels (1934) **75m.** *** D: George Stevens. Bert Wheeler, Robert Woolsey, Mary Carlisle, Spanky McFarland, Noah Beery, Lucille LaVerne. Wheeler & Woolsey take little Spanky into the deep South to collect inheritance, but find themselves in the midst of a family feud. Good vehicle for the team with great slapstick finale.

Kentucky Moonshine (1938) **85m.** ** D: David Butler. Tony Martin, Marjorie Weaver, Ritz Brothers, Slim Summerville, John Carradine. Slim little vehicle with Ritz Brothers causing chaos amidst feuding hillbillies in Kentucky; Martin and Weaver are the love/musical interest.

Kentucky Woman (1983) **C-100m.** TVM D: Walter Doniger. Cheryl Ladd, Ned Beatty, Peter Weller, Philip Levien, Sandy McPeak, Tess Harper, Lewis Smith, John Randolph. Waitress turns coal miner to support her son and her black lung-afflicted dad. "Charlie's Angel" doesn't cut it greased up and coal dusted. Below average.

Kettles in the Ozarks, The (1956) 81m. D: Charles Lamont. Marjorie Main, Arthur Hunnicutt, Una Merkel, Ted de Corsia, Olive Sturgess. SEE: **Ma and Pa Kettle** series.

Kettles on Old Macdonald's Farm, The (1957) 80m. D: Virgil Vogel. Marjorie Main, Parker Fennelly, Gloria Talbott, John Smith, Claude Akins, Pat Morrow. SEE: **Ma and Pa Kettle** series.

Key, The (1934) 69m. **½ D: Michael Curtiz. William Powell, Edna Best, Colin Clive, Hobart Cavanaugh, Halliwell Hobbes, Phil Regan, Arthur Treacher. Powell is miscast as a soldier of fortune who goes to work for the British in wartorn Dublin, finds his old flame (Best) married to buddy Clive. Good cast makes this watchable.

Key, The (1958-British) 125m. **½ D: Carol Reed. William Holden, Sophia Loren, Trevor Howard, Oscar Homolka. Jan de Hartog novel becomes pointless romance tale. Loren is disillusioned woman passing out key to her room to series of naval captains during WW2, hoping to make their dangerous lives a little happier.▼

Key Exchange (1985) C-90m. *** D: Barnet Kellman. Ben Masters, Brooke Adams, Daniel Stern, Danny Aiello, Nancy Mette, Tony Roberts. Masters plays a neurotic New Yorker who exchanges apartment keys with Adams but can't commit himself to her alone. Amusing adaptation of Kevin Wade's off-Broadway play with fine performances and good use of N.Y.C. locations. ▼

✓ **Key Largo** (1948) 101m. ***½ D: John Huston. Humphrey Bogart, Edward G. Robinson, Lauren Bacall, Lionel Barrymore, Claire Trevor, Thomas Gomez, Jay Silverheels. Dandy cast in adaptation of Maxwell Anderson's play about tough gangster (Robinson) holding people captive in Florida hotel during rough storm. Trevor won Best Supporting Actress Oscar as Robinson's boozy moll. Script by Huston and Richard Brooks. Also shown in computer-colored version.▼

Key Man (1954-British) 78m. **½ D: Montgomery Tully. Angela Lansbury, Keith Andes, Brian Keith. Competent little picture about illicit love affair leading to mysterious accidents involving Lansbury's architect husband. Retitled: A LIFE AT STAKE.

Keys of the Kingdom (1944) 137m. *** D: John M. Stahl. Gregory Peck, Thomas Mitchell, Vincent Price, Edmund Gwenn, Roddy McDowall, Cedric Hardwicke, Peggy Ann Garner. Peck is fine in this long but generally good film about missionary's life (played as boy by McDowall); from A. J. Cronin novel.▼

Key to the City (1950) 101m. **½ D:

George Sidney. Clark Gable, Loretta Young, Frank Morgan, Marilyn Maxwell, Raymond Burr, James Gleason. Bland romance between Gable and Young, two mayors who meet at convention in San Francisco.

Key to Rebecca, The (1985) C-200m. TVM D: David Hemmings. Cliff Robertson, David Soul, Season Hubley, Lina Raymond, Anthony Quayle, David Hemmings, Robert Culp. Ken Follett's bestselling wartime spy thriller—a cat-and-mouse game between a ruthless, chameleonlike Nazi (Soul) and a single-minded British major (Robertson)—goes limp on film. Miscasting, including Culp as General Rommel(!), adds to the woes. Still watchable. Originally shown in two parts. Average.

Key West (1972) C-100m. TVM D: Philip Leacock. Stephen Boyd, Woody Strode, Sheree North, Earl Hindman, Tiffany Bolling, William Prince. Ex-CIA operative and friend, now running boat service in Florida, become involved in chase for incriminating evidence involving U.S. Senator. Good cast, story overcome uninspired directon. Above average.

Key Witness (1960) 82m. **½ D: Phil Karlson. Jeffrey Hunter, Pat Crowley, Dennis Hopper, Joby Baker, Susan Harrison, Johnny Nash, Corey Allen. Overlong but effective narrative of pressures from street gang on Hunter's family to prevent his wife from testifying in criminal case.

Khartoum (1966-British) C-134m. ** D: Basil Dearden. Charlton Heston, Laurence Olivier, Richard Johnson, Ralph Richardson, Alexander Knox, Johnny Sekka. Dull historical spectacle about "Chinese" Gordon and his famous defeat by Arab tribesman in 1833. Olivier is good, Heston better than usual, but film is way too talky for a spectacle.▼

Khyber Patrol (1954) C-71m. ** D: Seymour Friedman. Richard Egan, Dawn Addams, Patric Knowles, Raymond Burr. Cast is above pedestrian film of British officers fighting in India, with usual love conflicts.

Kickboxer (1989) C-105m. *½ D: Mark DiSalle. Jean-Claude Van Damme, Denis Alexio, Dennis Chan, Tong Po, Haskell Anderson, Rochelle Ashana. Dull, dumb martial-arts time killer, with Van Damme seeking revenge against the Thai fighter who crippled his brother. Strictly by the numbers.▼

Kicks (1985) C-100m. TVM D: William Wiard. Anthony Geary, Shelley Hack, Tom Mason, Ian Abercrombie, Susan Ruttan, James Avery, Larry Cedar. Kinky thriller about a wealthy eccentric and a lady professor who become lovers with an obsession for living on the edge and playing life-endangering games. Average.▼

Kid, The (1921) 60m. ***½ D: Charles ✓

Chaplin. Charlie Chaplin, Jack (Jackie) Coogan, Edna Purviance, Chuck Reisner, Lita Grey. Chaplin's first real feature mixes slapstick and sentiment in a winning combination, as the Tramp raises a streetwise orphan. Wonderful film launched Coogan as major child star, and it's easy to see why.▼

Kid Blue (1973) **C-100m.** *½ D: James Frawley. Dennis Hopper, Warren Oates, Ben Johnson, Peter Boyle, Janice Rule, Lee Purcell. Pseudo-hip Western comedy about misfit Hopper's faltering attempts to exist in small Texas town in early 20th century. Laughs, excitement, and interest are at a minimum here in spite of cast; Hopper is too old for his role.

Kid Brother, The (1927) **82m.** **** D: Ted Wilde, J. A. Howe. Harold Lloyd, Jobyna Ralston, Walter James, Leo Willis, Olin Francis. Delightfully winning, beautifully filmed silent comedy with Harold as Cinderella-type kid brother in robust all-male family, who gets to prove his mettle in exciting finale where he subdues beefy villain. One of Lloyd's all-time best.

Kidco (1984) **C-105m.** **½ D: Ronald F. Maxwell. Scott Schwartz, Cinnamon Idles, Tristine Skyler, Elizabeth Gorcey. Okay comedy about the problems of preteen entrepreneur Schwartz and his cohorts, yuppies-in-training all. Ideal fare for the money-obsessed '80s yet barely released theatrically. Based on a true-life story; filmed in 1982.▼

Kid Dynamite (1943) **73m.** D: Wallace Fox. Leo Gorcey, Huntz Hall, Bobby Jordan, Gabriel Dell, Pamela Blake, Bennie Bartlett, Sammy Morrison. SEE: **Bowery Boys** series.▼

Kid for Two Farthings, A (1955-British) **C-91m.** *** D: Carol Reed. Celia Johnson, Diana Dors, David Kossoff, Jonathan Ashmore, Brenda De Banzie, Primo Carnera, Sidney Tafler, Lou Jacobi. Imaginative fable of boy on London's Petticoat Lane who buys a little goat and thinks it is a wish-fulfilling unicorn. This leads to some delightful vignettes of human nature. Story and screenplay by Wolf Mankowitz. Originally 96m.

Kid from Brooklyn, The (1946) **C-113m.** *** D: Norman Z. McLeod. Danny Kaye, Virginia Mayo, Vera-Ellen, Steve Cochran, Eve Arden, Walter Abel, Lionel Stander, Fay Bainter. Comedy of milkman accidentally turned into prizefighter is often overdone but still a funny Kaye vehicle; remake of Harold Lloyd's THE MILKY WAY.▼

Kid from Cleveland, The (1949) **89m.** ** D: Herbert Kline. George Brent, Lynn Bari, Rusty Tamblyn, Tommy Cook, Ann Doran. Brent is a sports reporter involved with a disturbed youth; Cleveland Indians ball team play themselves. A bit sticky at times.

Kid from Kansas, The (1941) **66m.** *½ D: William Nigh. Leo Carrillo, Andy Devine, Dick Foran, Ann Doran. When a fruit buyer offers ridiculously low prices for planters' crops, competitors take drastic measures; low budget, low quality.

Kid from Left Field, The (1953) **80m.** ** D: Harmon Jones. Dan Dailey, Anne Bancroft, Billy Chapin, Lloyd Bridges, Ray Collins, Richard Egan. Homey little film with Dailey as ex-baseball star turned ballpark vendor who uses his son as cover while trying to turn a losing team around. Remade as a TV movie.

Kid from Left Field, The (1979) **C-100m.** TVM D: Adell Aldrich. Gary Coleman, Robert Guillaume, Tab Hunter, Tricia O'Neil, Gary Collins, Ed McMahon. Appealing remake of 1953 baseball movie about a bat boy who guides the San Diego Padres from the cellar to the World Series, using the strategy passed on by his father, a big league has-been reduced to hawking hot dogs in the stands. Above average.▼

Kid From Nowhere, The (1982) **C-100m.** TVM D: Beau Bridges. Beau Bridges, Susan Saint James, Loretta Swit, Ricky Wittman, Lynn Carlin, Rene Auberjonois, Nicholas Pryor, Janet MacLachlan. Sentimental drama about a retarded child's involvement with the Special Olympics. Young Wittman, real-life Downs Syndrome victim, is especially good in his acting debut under the tutelage of actor-turned-director Bridges (who plays the coach at a school for the handicapped). Script is by Judy Farrell. Above average.

Kid from Spain, The (1932) **96m.** *** D: Leo McCarey. Eddie Cantor, Lyda Roberti, Robert Young, Ruth Hall, John Miljan, Stanley Fields. Lavish Cantor musical with Eddie mistaken for famed bullfighter; Roberti is his vivacious leading lady. Striking Busby Berkeley musical numbers; look for Paulette Goddard and Betty Grable in the chorus line.

Kid from Texas, The (1950) **C-78m.** ** D: Kurt Neumann. Audie Murphy, Gale Storm. Albert Dekker, Shepperd Strudwick. Another version of life of Billy the Kid, with Murphy in title role, Storm the romantic interest.

Kid Galahad (1937) **101m.** *** D: Michael Curtiz. Edward G. Robinson, Bette Davis, Humphrey Bogart, Wayne Morris, Jane Bryan, Harry Carey, Veda Ann Borg. Well-paced actioner of promoter Robinson making naive Morris boxing star, losing his girl Davis to him at same time. Remade in 1941 (as THE WAGONS ROLL AT NIGHT) and in 1962. Shown on TV as BATTLING BELLHOP.

Kid Galahad (1962) **C-95m.** **½ D: Phil Karlson. Elvis Presley, Gig Young, Lola Albright, Joan Blackman, Charles Bronson, Ned Glass. This remake lacks wallop of the original. Elvis stars as a boxer who wins championship—and sings six forgettable songs—but prefers quiet life as garage mechanic. ▼

Kid Glove Killer (1942) **74m.** ******* D: Fred Zinnemann. Van Heflin, Lee Bowman, Marsha Hunt, Samuel S. Hinds, Cliff Clark, Eddie Quillan. Solid B film about police chemist Heflin uncovering the killer of a mayor, with taut direction by Zinnemann.

Kid Millions (1934) **90m.** ******* D: Roy Del Ruth. Eddie Cantor, Ethel Merman, Ann Sothern, George Murphy, Warren Hymer. Elaborate Cantor musical about Eddie inheriting a fortune. Musical numbers and comedy set-pieces boost a weak script. Color segment in ice-cream factory a delight. Songs include "When My Ship Comes In." Lucille Ball is one of the Goldwyn Girls in this one. ▼

Kidnap of Mary Lou, The SEE: **Almost Human** ▼

Kidnapped (1938) **90m.** ****½** D: Alfred L. Werker. Warner Baxter, Freddie Bartholomew, Arleen Whelan, C. Aubrey Smith, Reginald Owen, John Carradine, Nigel Bruce. Good adventure yarn of 1750s Scotland and England but not Robert Louis Stevenson; fine cast in generally entertaining script.

Kidnapped (1948) **80m.** ****** D: William Beaudine. Roddy McDowall, Sue England, Dan O'Herlihy, Roland Winters, Jeff Corey. Disappointing low-budget adaptation of Robert Louis Stevenson novel.

Kidnapped (1960) **C-97m.** ****½** D: Robert Stevenson. Peter Finch, James MacArthur, Bernard Lee, Niall MacGinnis, John Laurie, Finlay Currie, Peter O'Toole. Disney feature filmed in England is faithful to Robert Louis Stevenson's classic novel, but surprisingly dull. Good cast and vivid atmosphere are its major assets. ▼

Kidnapped (1971-British) **C-100m.** ****** D: Delbert Mann. Michael Caine, Trevor Howard, Jack Hawkins, Donald Pleasence, Gordon Jackson, Vivien Heilbron. Disappointing version of Stevenson tale is made endurable by Caine's pleasing performance as Alan Breck.

Kidnapping of the President, The (1980-U.S.-Canadian) **C-113m.** ****½** D: George Mendeluk. William Shatner, Hal Holbrook, Van Johnson, Ava Gardner, Miguel Fernandes, Cindy Girling. The title tells all: Third World terrorists kidnap president Holbrook, with Secret Service chief Shatner intervening. OK actioner is certainly topical; based on Charles Templeton's novel. ▼

Kidnap Syndicate (1975-Italian) **C-83m.** ****** D: Fernando Di Leo. James Mason, Valentina Cortese, Luc Merenda, Irina Maleeva, Vittorio Caprioli. Crime drama about the snatching of two youngsters—the son of a multimillionaire and an auto

mechanic's boy—and how the industrialist's rash actions cause all manner of violence and a rampage of vengeance. ▼

Kid Rodelo (1966) **91m.** ***½** D: Richard Carlson. Don Murray, Janet Leigh, Broderick Crawford, Richard Carlson. After jail term, cowboys go off to search for hidden $50,000 in gold. You've seen it all before. Filmed in Spain. Based on a Louis L'Amour novel.

Kids Are Alright, The (1979) **C-108m.** ******* D: Jeff Stein. Overlong and disjointed, yet frequently exhilarating documentary on The Who that manages to capture the anarchic spirit of the group—and of rock 'n' roll. Brief appearances by Steve Martin, Tom Smothers, and Ringo Starr. Songs include "Magic Bus," "Happy Jack," and several numbers from *Tommy*. ▼

Kids Don't Tell (1985) **C-100m. TVM** D: Sam O'Steen. Michael Ontkean, JoBeth Williams, Leo Rossi, John Sanderford, Ari Meyers, Jordan Charney, Robin Gammell. A film documentarian finds his own attitudes—and relationship with his family—changing as he works on a project about sexual abuse of youngsters. Intelligent film about child molestation written by Peter Silverman and Maurice Hurley. Above average.

Kids Like These (1987) **C-100m. TVM** D: Georg Stanford Brown. Tyne Daly, Richard Crenna, Martin Balsam. Well-acted drama about a mother whose young son has Down's Syndrome. She takes up the challenge of rearing him while crusading for public awareness about the affliction. Writer Emily Perl Kingsley based her story on her own experiences. Daly was directed here by her real-life husband, Brown. Above average.

Kid Vengeance (1977) **C-94m.** ***½** D: Joe Manduke. Lee Van Cleef, Jim Brown, John Marley, Leif Garrett, Glynnis O'Connor, Matt Clark. Bloody, gory, obnoxious Western about young Garrett seeking revenge against outlaws who killed his parents and kidnapped his sister. ▼

Kid with the Broken Halo, The (1982) **C-100m. TVM** D: Leslie Martinson. Gary Coleman, Robert Guillaume, June Allyson, Mason Adams, Ray Walston, John Pleshette, Lani O'Grady, Telma Hopkins, Kim Fields, Georg Stanford Brown. Apprentice angel Coleman is out to win his wings by patching up the lives of three families in this prospective pilot, teaming for the third time with Guillaume. Average. ▼

Kid with the 200 I.Q., The (1983) **C-96m.** **TVM** D: Leslie Martinson. Gary Coleman, Robert Guillaume, Dean Butler, Kari Michaelsen, Mel Stewart, Harriet Nelson. Yet another Coleman vehicle; this time he's a thirteen-year-old genius who goes to college and copes with campus life, with expected results. Average. ▼

Kill A Dragon (1967) **C-91m.** *½ D: Michael Moore. Jack Palance, Fernando Lamas, Aldo Ray, Alizia Gur. Complicated, far-fetched tale of feudal baron in modern China and his American adversary.

Kill and Kill Again (1981) **C-100m.** ** D: Ivan Hall. James Ryan, Anneline Kriel, Ken Gampu, Norman Robinson, Michael Meyer. OK chop-socky actioner, with Ryan foiling scientist Meyer's plot to take over the world. Filmed in South Africa.▼

Killbots SEE: **Chopping Mall**▼

Kill Castro SEE: **Cuba Crossing**▼

Killdozer (1974) **C-78m. TVM** D: Jerry London. Clint Walker, Carl Betz, Neville Brand, James Wainwright, James Watson, Jr., Robert Urich. Alien being turns bulldozer against hard-hat crew bossed by Walker. Man-vs.-machine thriller in the shadow of DUEL. Based on the short story by Theodore Sturgeon. Average.

Killer Ape (1953) **68m.** D: Spencer Bennet. Johnny Weissmuller, Carol Thurston, Max Palmer, Nestor Paiva, Nick Stuart. SEE **Jungle Jim** series.

Killer Bait SEE: **Too Late for Tears**▼

Killer Bats SEE: **Devil Bat, The**▼

Killer Bees (1974) **C-78m. TVM** D: Curtis Harrington. Gloria Swanson, Edward Albert, Kate Jackson, Roger Davis, Don McGovern, Craig Stevens. Symbolic drama with Swanson a winegrowing family matriarch with strange power over a colony of bees thriving in the vineyard. Middling thriller with stagey acting and unexplained mittle-European accents. Below average.

Killer By Night (1971) **C-100m. TVM** D: Bernard McEveety. Robert Wagner, Diane Baker, Greg Morris, Theodore Bikel, Robert Lansing, Mercedes McCambridge. Somewhat tame attempt at two-sided approach to mad-killer-on-loose story. Diphtheria outbreak conflicts with police efforts until source for both problems found to be one and same. Only asset good atmosphere. Average.

Killer Elite, The (1975) **C-122m.** ** D: Sam Peckinpah. James Caan, Robert Duvall, Arthur Hill, Bo Hopkins, Mako, Burt Young, Gig Young. Mercenary Duvall double-crosses partner Caan, leading to characteristic but lesser Peckinpah bloodbath involving the CIA. Trashy script slightly redeemed by director's flair for action sequences.▼

Killer Fish (1979-Italian-Brazilian) **C-101m.** ** D: Anthony M. Dawson (Antonio Margheriti). Lee Majors, Karen Black, James Franciscus, Margaux Hemingway, Marisa Berenson, Gary Collins. Pursuit of stolen jewels dumped in lake full of deadly piranha fish forms basis for this predictable outing filmed in Brazil. Same fishy predators were used in much more enjoyable film, PIRANHA. Also known as

DEADLY TREASURE OF THE PIRANHA.▼

Killer Force (1975) **C-101m.** ** D: Val Guest. Peter Fonda, Telly Savalas, Hugh O'Brian, Christopher Lee, Maud Adams, O. J. Simpson, Ian Yule. Dirty doings at diamond syndicate's desert mine in South Africa. Has cast and potential but overly diffuse and complex.▼

Killer Grizzly SEE: **Grizzly**▼

Killer Inside Me, The (1976) **C-99m.** *** D: Burt Kennedy. Stacy Keach, Susan Tyrrell, Keenan Wynn, Tisha Sterling, Don Stroud, Charles McGraw. Bizarre opus about a psychotic deputy sheriff (flashbacks accounting for his present state) about to go off the deep end; saved and made believable by strong performance from Keach.▼

Killer Instinct (1988) **C-100m. TVM** D: Waris Hussein. Melissa Gilbert, Woody Harrelson, Kevin Conroy, Lane Smith, Fernando Lopez, William Marshall. A novice psychiatrist finds herself in peril after deciding to put a dangerous mental patient she feels she's cured back on the streets. Average.

Killer in the Family, A (1983) **C-100m. TVM** D: Richard T. Heffron. Robert Mitchum, James Spader, Lance Kerwin, Eric Stoltz, Salome Jens, Lynn Carlin, Stuart Margolin. Mitchum cons his three teenaged sons into springing him and a psycho pal from prison and then involves them on a murderous spree. Mitchum towers over the material, as usual. Based on a true story. Average.

Killer in the Mirror (1986) **C-100m. TVM** D: Frank De Felitta. Ann Jillian, Len Cariou, Max Gail, Allen Garfield, Christopher Noth, Jessica Walter. Jillian has the old Bette Davis role in this mediocre remake of DEAD RINGER. It's a good/bad twin murder mystery involving mistaken identity and an inordinate amount of coincidence. Average.

Killer Is Loose, The (1956) **73m.** **½ D: Budd Boetticher. Joseph Cotten, Rhonda Fleming, Wendell Corey, Alan Hale, Michael Pate. Fairly tense vengeance tale of ex-con swearing to get even with detective who nabbed him.

Killer Klowns from Outer Space (1988) **C-88m.** BOMB D: Stephen Chiodo. Grant Cramer, Suzanne Snyder, John Allen Nelson, Royal Dano, John Vernon. A small town is invaded by sadistic alien clowns. Strictly tenth-rate.▼

Killer Leopard (1954) **70m.** D: Ford Beebe, Edward Morey, Jr. Johnny Sheffield, Beverly Garland, Barry Bernard, Donald Murphy. SEE: **Bomba, the Jungle Boy** series.

Killer McCoy (1947) **104m.** *** D: Roy Rowland. Mickey Rooney, Brian Donlevy, Ann Blyth, James Dunn, Tom Tully, Sam Levene. Good drama of fighter Rooney accidentally involved in murder, with fine supporting cast of promoters and racketeers. Remake of THE CROWD ROARS (1938).

Killer on Board (1977) C-100m. TVM D: Philip Leacock. Claude Akins, Beatrice Straight, George Hamilton, Patty Duke Astin, Frank Converse, Jane Seymour, William Daniels. So-so drama involving vacationers on a cruise ship who are infected with a deadly virus and must be quarantined. Echoes of THE CASSANDRA CROSSING with a change of locale. Average.▼

Killers, The (1946) 105m. **** D: Robert Siodmak. Burt Lancaster, Ava Gardner, Edmond O'Brien, Albert Dekker, Sam Levene, Virginia Christine, William Conrad, Charles McGraw. Compelling crime drama (based on Hemingway story) of ex-fighter found murdered, subsequent investigation. Film provides fireworks, early success of Lancaster (in film debut) and Gardner. Miklos Rozsa's dynamic score features the familiar dum-da-dum-dum theme later utilized by *Dragnet*. Screenplay by Anthony Veiller (and, uncredited, John Huston). Reworked in 1964.

Killers, The (1964) C-95m. **½ D: Don Siegel. Lee Marvin, John Cassavetes, Angie Dickinson, Ronald Reagan, Clu Gulager, Claude Akins, Norman Fell. Two inquisitive hit men piece together the story of the man they've just murdered, in this free adaptation of Hemingway's short story. Originally shot for TV, it was rejected as "too violent" and released to theaters instead. Some latter-day notoriety derives from Reagan's casting as a brutal crime kingpin; it was his last movie role. Marvin has a great closing line.▼

Killers Are Challenged SEE: **Secret Agent Fireball**

Killer's Carnival (1965) C-95m. **½ D: Albert Cardiff, Robert Lynn, Sheldon Reynolds. Stewart Granger, Lex Barker, Pierre Brice, Karin Dor, Pascal Petit. Three stories of intrigue set in Rome, Vienna, and Brazil; tired cast in OK espionage tales.

Killers from Space (1954) 71m. BOMB D: W. Lee Wilder. Peter Graves, James Seay, Steve Pendleton, Barbara Bestar, Frank Gerstle. Scientist Graves, killed in a plane crash, is brought back to life by aliens from the planet Astron Delta. They're planning to invade Earth and want him to pilfer atomic data. Poor in all departments and too dull to be funny. ▼

Killer Shark (1950) 76m. *½ D: Oscar (Budd) Boetticher, Roddy McDowall, Laurette Luez, Roland Winters, Edward Norris, Douglas Fowley, Dick Moore. Back Bayite McDowall learns new values as skipper of shark-hunting vessel; cheapie film.

Killer Shrews, The (1959) 70m. **½ D: Ray Kellogg. James Best, Ingrid Goude, Ken Curtis, Baruch Lumet, Gordon McLendon. No, this isn't about an attack of nagging wives, it's an inventive but silly sci-fi tale of people isolated on a Texas island, menaced by title creatures created by well-intentioned scientist.▼

Killer's Kiss (1955) 67m. ** D: Stanley Kubrick. Frank Silvera, Jamie Smith, Irene Kane, Jerry Jarret. Meandering account of revenge when boxer's courting of working-girl causes her boss to commit murder. Interesting early Kubrick; the inspiration for the film-within-a-film of STRANGER'S KISS. Leading lady Kane is now TV and newspaper journalist Chris Chase.

Killers of Kilimanjaro (1960-British) C-91m. ** D: Richard Thorpe. Robert Taylor, Anne Aubrey, John Dimech, Gregoire Aslan, Anthony Newley, Martin Boddey. Spotty adventure yarn of railroad-building in East Africa.

Killer Spy (1958-French) 82m. ** D: Georges Lampin. Jean Marais, Nadja Tiller, Andre Luguet, Bernadette Lafont. Capable cast tries to instill life into this spy-and-murder yarn; scenery outshines script.

Killers Three (1968) C-88m. BOMB D: Bruce Kessler. Robert Walker, Diane Varsi, Dick Clark, Norman Alden, Maureen Arthur, Merle Haggard. Take-off on BONNIE AND CLYDE doesn't offer much by way of comparison, unless you find the idea of Dick Clark in wirerims a gas.

Killer That Stalked New York, The (1950) 79m. **½ D: Earl McEvoy. Evelyn Keyes, Charles Korvin, William Bishop, Dorothy Malone. Interesting B film of a diamond-smuggling couple sought by police because they contracted contagious disease while abroad.

Killer Who Wouldn't Die, The (1976) C-100m. TVM D: William Hale. Mike Connors, Samantha Eggar, Patrick O'Neal, Clu Gulager, James Shigeta, Robert Colbert, Robert Hooks, Gregoire Aslan, Mariette Hartley. Detective-turned-charter boat operator takes up search for the killer of his undercover agent friend, and becomes entangled in a network of espionage. Busted pilot with Connors back in the Mannix mold. Average.

Kill Her Gently (1957-British) 73m. ** D: Charles Saunders. Marc Lawrence, Maureen Connell, George Mikell, Griffith Jones, John Gayford. Brutal B film of supposedly cured mental patient hiring two convicts-at-large to kill his wife.

Killing, The (1956) 83m. ***½ D: Stanley Kubrick. Sterling Hayden, Coleen Gray, Vince Edwards, Jay C. Flippen, Marie Windsor, Joe Sawyer, Ted de Corsia, Elisha Cook, Jr., Timothy Carey. Early Kubrick classic about elaborate racetrack robbery.

Unusual structure, Carey's cool killer, Cook's doomed marriage to Windsor among highlights. Major flaw: *Dragnet*-like narration. Kubrick scripted from Lionel White's novel *Clean Break*.▼

Killing Affair, A (1977) **C-100m. TVM** D: Richard Sarafian. Elizabeth Montgomery, O. J. Simpson, Rosalind Cash, Dean Stockwell, Dolph Sweet. Two detectives working on a homicide case become involved in (interracial) love affair. A cop show is a cop show, even if the leads make a handsome couple. Retitled BEHIND THE BADGE. Average.

Killing Affair, A (1988) **C-100m. *½ D:** David Saperstein. Peter Weller, Kathy Baker, John Glover, Bill Smitrovich. Dreary goings on in the Southern backwoods, circa 1943, where Weller kills Baker's hateful husband, and then develops a turbulent relationship with her. Based on Robert Houston's novel *Monday, Tuesday, Wednesday*, this marks writer Saperstein's directing debut. Filmed in 1985.▼

Killing at Hell's Gate (1981) **C-100m. TVM** D: Jerry Jameson. Robert Urich, Deborah Raffin, Lee Purcell, Joel Higgins, George DiCenzo, John Randolph, Mitch Carter, Brion James. River rafters' pleasure trip becomes a whitewater nightmare when snipers begin stalking the group. DELIVERANCE with a couple of girls added. Average.▼

Killing 'em Softly (1985-Canadian) **C-81m. BOMB** D: Max Fischer. George Segal, Irene Cara, Clark Johnson, Nicholas Campbell, Joyce Gordon. Segal kills a rock band manager who owes him money; Cara's boyfriend is charged with the crime. Guess what—Segal and Cara fall in love. Sloppily made and embarrassingly bad. ▼

Killing Fields, The (1984-British) **C-141m. ***½ D:** Roland Joffe. Sam Waterston, Haing S. Ngor, John Malkovich, Julian Sands, Craig T. Nelson, Bill Paterson, Athol Fugard, Spalding Gray. Highly charged drama based on the memoirs of *N.Y. Times* reporter Sidney Schanberg, who remained in Cambodia after American evacuation—putting his native translator and assistant Dith Pran in great jeopardy. Frighteningly realistic depiction of a country torn apart by war and terrorism; an emotional powerhouse. Long but worthwhile. Impressive feature debut for documentary director Joffe; Ngor (who lived through Cambodian turmoil in real life) won Best Supporting Actor Oscar for his acting debut. Oscars also went to cinematographer Chris Menges, editor Jim Clark.▼

Killing Floor, The (1984) **C-117m. TVM** D: William Duke. Damien Leake, Moses Gunn, Alfre Woodard, Clarence Felder, Ernest Rayford. Impressive drama about interracial union organizing during WW1 in the Chicago stockyards, centering on the plight of black sharecropper Leake, who's just arrived from the rural South. Most intriguing are the depictions of slaughterhouse atmosphere and union organizing. A PBS *American Playhouse* presentation. Above average.▼

Killing Game, The (1967-French) **C-94m. **½ D:** Alain Jessua. Jean-Pierre Cassel, Claudine Auger, Michael Duchaussoy, Eleanore Hirt. Mystery comic strip writer comes up with his ultimate puzzler. Not bad.

Killing Heat SEE: **Grass Is Singing, The**▼

Killing Machine (1986-Spanish) **C-97m. ** D:** Anthony Loma (J. Antonio de la Loma). George (Jorge) Rivero, Margaux Hemingway, Lee Van Cleef, Willie Aames, Hugo Stiglitz, Ana Obregon, Richard Jaeckel. Rivero is convincing as an heroic trucker from Spain on one last run to Germany, caught up in European labor wars. Suffers from multinational casting (Obregon is supposed to be all-American boy Aames's sister) that hurts its credibility.▼

Killing of a Chinese Bookie, The (1976) **C-136m. *½ D:** John Cassavetes. Ben Gazzara, Timothy Agoglia Carey, Seymour Cassel, Azizi Johari, Meade Roberts, Alice Friedland. Strange, self-indulgent (even for Cassavetes) home movie centering around the owner of a strip joint, the mob and what used to be called "B-girls." Small cult may take to this; others beware.

Killing of Angel Street, The (1981-Australian) **C-101m. **½ D:** Donald Crombie. Liz Alexander, John Hargreaves, Alexander Archdale, Reg Lye, Gordon McDougall. Fair melodrama about corrupt real estate manipulators harassing homeowners to sell their property. Communist Hargreaves and geologist Alexander take on the villains when her activist father mysteriously dies. Supposedly based on actual events that also inspired HEATWAVE (1983).▼

Killing of Randy Webster, The (1981) **C-100m. TVM** D: Sam Wanamaker. Hal Holbrook, Dixie Carter, James Whitmore, Jr., Jennifer Jason Leigh, Nancy Malone, Sean Penn, Gary McCleery, Anthony Edwards, Anne Ramsey. Holbrook is terrific as a grieving father who wages a tireless investigation into his son's slaying by the Houston police. Based on an actual incident and adapted from a magazine article, "The Throwdown" (police parlance for a weapon planted on a victim after a shooting), by Texas journalist Tom Curtis. Above average.▼

Killing of Sister George, The (1968) **C-138m. **½ D:** Robert Aldrich. Beryl Reid, Susannah York, Coral Browne, Ronald Fraser, Patricia Medina. Overwrought but entertaining drama, with comedy touches, about soap opera actress Reid who fears her character (Sister George) is due to be "killed." Story follows her deteriorating lesbian relationship with dependent, child-like York, who's caught the eye of network executive Browne. Very good performances in this adaptation of Frank Marcus' play. Shot in England.▼

Killing Stone (1978) C-100m. TVM D: Michael Landon. Gil Gerard, J. D. Cannon, Jim Davis, Matthew Laborteaux, Corinne Michaels, Nehemiah Persoff. A writer is freed after ten years in prison, determined to find real murderer of U.S. Senator's son. Pilot for a prospective series, believe it or not. Landon also wrote and produced. Average.▼

Killjoy (1981) C-100m. TVM D: John Llewellyn Moxey. Kim Basinger, Robert Culp, Stephen Macht, Nancy Marchand, John Rubinstein, Ann Dusenberry, Ann Wedgeworth. Crafty thriller about a young woman's untimely murder and the various people who become involved, told with delicious wit and filled with engaging twists until the revelation of whodunit. Written by Sam H. Rolfe. Above average.▼

Kill! Kill! Kill! (1972-French-Spanish-German-Italian) C-90m. *½ D: Romain Gary. Jean Seberg, James Mason, Stephen Boyd, Curt Jurgens, Daniel Emilfork. Interpol agent Mason, on the trail of Italian drug kingpins, gets competition from fellow low agent Boyd, who believes in playing dirty. Hardened violence clashes with writer-director Gary's purple prose. Original title KILL, at 102m.

Kill Me Again (1989) C-94m. **½ D: John Dahl. Val Kilmer, Joanne Whalley-Kilmer, Michael Madsen, Jonathan Gries, Pat Mulligan, Nick Dimitri, Bibi Besch. Femme fatale Whalley-Kilmer makes like Jane Greer in this contemporary *film noir,* sexily scamming her way through the Nevada desert (and a couple of big cities) trying to steal gangland booty. Fans of detective genre will enjoy this mild send-up of crime flicks. Fun, but also inherently derivative.▼

✓ **Kill Me If You Can** (1977) C-100m. TVM D: Buzz Kulik. Alan Alda, Talia Shire, John Hillerman, Walter McGinn, Barnard Hughes, John Randolph, Ben Piazza. Fact-based drama by John Gay about Caryl Chessman, the "red light bandit" who spent twelve years on San Quentin's death row before being executed in 1960. Alda's superb portrayal of Chessman gives this one guts. Takes, naturally, the anti-capital-punishment view. Death-penalty advocates should stick with CELL 2455, DEATH ROW, taken from Chessman's best-seller. Above average.

Kill Me Tomorrow (1957-British) 80m. ** D: Terence Fisher. Pat O'Brien, Lois

Maxwell, George Coulouris, Robert Brown, Tommy Steele. Adequate B film about newspaperman cracking murder case leading to arrest of diamond-smuggling syndicate.

Kill or Be Killed (1950) 67m. *½ D: Max Nosseck. Lawrence Tierney, George Coulouris, Marissa O'Brien, Rudolph Anders. Pedestrian account of man on lam hunted down in jungle by law enforcers.

Kill or Be Killed (1980) C-90m. ** D: Ivan Hall. James Ryan, Norman Combes, Charlotte Michelle, Danie DuPlessis. Karate champions lock limbs as ex-Nazi coach seeks revenge against Japanese counterpart who bested him in a tournament during WW2. A cut above the usual martial arts fodder.▼

Killpoint (1984) C-89m. *½ D: Frank Harris. Leo Fong, Richard Roundtree, Cameron Mitchell, Stack Pierce, Hope Holiday. Dreary, one-dimensional actioner with cop Fong and agent Roundtree on the trail of gunrunners. Sickeningly violent.▼

Kill the Umpire (1950) 78m. **½ D: Lloyd Bacon. William Bendix, Una Merkel, Ray Collins, Gloria Henry, William Frawley, Tom D'Andrea. Lightweight comedy about baseball lover who becomes the sport's most hated man, the umpire. Ends with spectacular slapstick chase. Screenplay by Frank Tashlin.

Kilroy Was Here (1947) 68m. *½ D: Phil Karlson. Jackie Cooper, Jackie Coogan, Wanda McKay, Frank Jenks. Supposedly topical comedy (then) is pretty limp now, with innocent victim of "Kilroy Was Here" joke trying to lead normal life despite his name.

Kim (1950) C-113m. ***½ D: Victor Saville. Errol Flynn, Dean Stockwell, Paul Lukas, Thomas Gomez, Cecil Kellaway. Rousing actioner based on Kipling classic, set in 1880s India, with British soldiers combatting rebellious natives. Flavorful production. Remade for TV.▼

Kim (1984) C-150m. TVM D: John Davies. Peter O'Toole, Bryan Brown, John Rhys-Davies, Ravi Sheth, Julian Glover, Lee Montague. Enthusiastic new version of the Kipling tale about Indian boy recruited by the British for some high adventure. Brown has the old Errol Flynn role, Sheth makes an impressive debut as Kim, and O'Toole has a high old time as an Indian mystic in a bald wig. James Brabazon wrote this flavorful adaptation. Above average.

Kimberley Jim (1965-South African) C-82m. ** D: Emil Nofal. Jim Reeves, Madeleine Usher, Clive Parnell, Arthur Swemmer, Mike Holt. Minor musical of two carefree gamblers who win diamond mine in fixed poker game, and then have a change of heart. Rare screen appearance by late country singer Reeves.

Kind Hearts and Coronets (1949-British) **104m.** ***½ D: Robert Hamer. Dennis Price, Alec Guinness, Valerie Hobson, Joan Greenwood, Miles Malleson, Hugh Griffith, Jeremy Spenser, Arthur Lowe. Peerless black comedy of castoff member of titled family setting out to eliminate them all. Guinness plays all eight victims! Hamer and John Dighton adapted Roy Horniman's novel *Israel Rank*.▼

Kind Lady (1936) **76m.** **½ D: George B. Seitz. Aline MacMahon, Basil Rathbone, Mary Carlisle, Frank Albertson, Dudley Digges, Doris Lloyd, Donald Meek. MacMahon is being blackmailed and held prisoner in her own house by Rathbone and his cronies; fairly entertaining, but not as good as the remake. Adapted from the Edward Chodorov play, which was based on a Hugh Walpole story.

Kind Lady (1951) **78m.** *** D: John Sturges. Ethel Barrymore, Maurice Evans, Angela Lansbury, Betsy Blair, Keenan Wynn, John Williams, Doris Lloyd. Gripping psychological thriller, coscripted by Edward Chodorov and based on his play, with vicious Evans attempting to fleece elderly, wealthy Barrymore. Well-acted, with Evans making a delicious villain. First filmed in 1936.

Kind of Loving, A (1962-British) **112m.** *** D: John Schlesinger. Alan Bates, June Ritchie, Thora Hird, Bert Palmer, Gwen Nelson, Malcolm Patton, Leonard Rossiter, Peter Madden. Intelligent account of young couple forced to marry when girl becomes pregnant, detailing their home life; well acted.▼

Kindred, The (1987) **C-97m.** **½ D: Stephen Carpenter, Jeffrey Obrow. Rod Steiger, Kim Hunter, David Allen Brooks, Amanda Pays, Talia Balsam, Timothy Gibbs, Peter Frechette, Julia Montgomery. Enjoyable horror flick of teens in danger from a scientific experiment that resulted in a grotesque monster. OK special effects in a film marking Steiger's latter-day entry into Donald Pleasence-type horror roles.▼

King: A Filmed Record . . . Montgomery to Memphis (1970) **153m.** ***½ D: Joseph L. Mankiewicz, Sidney Lumet. Superior documentary covering life of Dr. Martin Luther King from 1955 until his death in 1968 is marred only by the pretentious and unnecessary "bridges" featuring such stars as Paul Newman, Joanne Woodward, and James Earl Jones. Otherwise, well-chosen compilation of news footage carries tremendous wallop.▼

King and Country (1964-British) **90m.** ***½ D: Joseph Losey. Dirk Bogarde, Tom Courtenay, Leo McKern, Barry Foster, James Villiers, Peter Copley. Vivid antiwar treatise beautifully acted by strong supporting cast. Bogarde is detached Army captain lawyer assigned to defend deserter private Courtenay during WW1. Score composed by harmonica virtuoso Larry Adler.

King and Four Queens, The (1956) **C-86m.** **½ D: Raoul Walsh. Clark Gable, Eleanor Parker, Jo Van Fleet, Jean Willes, Barbara Nichols, Sara Shane, Jay C. Flippen. Static misfire with Gable on the search for money hidden by husbands of four women he encounters.

King and I, The (1956) **C-133m.** ***½ D: Walter Lang. Deborah Kerr, Yul Brynner, Rita Moreno, Martin Benson, Terry Saunders, Rex Thompson, Alan Mowbray. Excellent film adaptation of Rodgers and Hammerstein Broadway musical, based on ANNA AND THE KING OF SIAM: Kerr is widowed teacher who runs head-on into the stubborn King (Brynner, in an Oscar-winning performance), gradually falling in love with him; beautifully acted. Songs: "Hello Young Lovers," "Getting to Know You," "Shall We Dance," "Something Wonderful." Kerr's singing voice was dubbed by Marni Nixon. Also won Oscars for art direction-set decoration, Irene Sharaff's costumes, and Alfred Newman and Ken Darby's scoring.▼

King and the Chorus Girl, The (1937) **94m.** **½ D: Mervyn LeRoy. Joan Blondell, Fernand Gravet, Edward Everett Horton, Jane Wyman. Gravet is nobleman on a lark, finding true love with beautiful chorine Blondell. Lively production. Written by Norman Krasna and Groucho Marx!

King Crab (1980) **C-105m. TVM** D: Marvin J. Chomsky. Barry Newman, Julie Bovasso, Jeffrey DeMunn, Joel Fabian, Gail Strickland, Harold Gould. Well-acted drama about two brothers who turn the family seafood business into a battleground, where they wage war for their father's love. Strong performances in an original film that revives memories of the kind of drama that was the mainstay of TV's Golden Age. Written by Preston M. Ransome. Above average.

King Creole (1958) **116m.** **½ D: Michael Curtiz. Elvis Presley, Carolyn Jones, Dolores Hart, Dean Jagger, Walter Matthau, Paul Stewart. Elvis is quite good as young New Orleans night-club singer who is eventually dragged into the criminal underworld. Toned-down adaptation of Harold Robbins' *A Stone For Danny Fisher* (which was set in Chicago), coscripted by Michael V. Gazzo. Songs include "Hard Headed Woman," "Trouble," title number.▼

King David (1985) **C-114m.** **½ D: Bruce Beresford. Richard Gere, Edward Woodward, Alice Krige, Denis Quilley, Niall Buggy, Cherie Lunghi, Hurd Hatfield, Jack Klaff. Solid biblical story traces young David's life from boyhood battle with Goliath to uneasy reign as king; only goes awry in second half, where abruptness undermines narrative. Visually striking, with Donald McAlpine's photography, Carl Davis's music strong assets—along with outstanding performance by Woodward as deposed King Saul.▼

Kingdom of the Spiders (1977) **C-94m.** *** D: John (Bud) Cardos. William Shatner, Tiffany Bolling, Woody Strode, Lieux Dressler, Altovise Davis. Unsurprising but well-made chiller about veterinarian Shatner and entomologist Bolling discovering that tarantulas are going on the warpath in Arizona.▼

Kingfisher Caper, The (1975-South African) **C-90m.** **½ D: Dirk DeVilliers. Hayley Mills, David McCallum, Jon Cypher. Typical tale of intrigue, love and passion interwoven with a family feud over the running of a South African diamond empire.▼

King in New York, A (1957-British) **105m.** **½ D: Charles Chaplin. Charles Chaplin, Dawn Addams, Oliver Johnston, Maxine Audley, Harry Green, Michael Chaplin. Unseen in U.S. until 1973, supposedly anti-American film is rather mild satire of 1950s sensibilities, witch hunts, and technology. Chaplin over-indulges himself, and film lacks focus, but there are good moments, and interesting performance by son Michael as young malcontent.▼

King In Shadow (1956-German) **87m.** ** D: Harald Braun. O. W. Fischer, Horst Buchholz, Odile Versois, Gunther Hadank. Buchholz is mentally disturbed young King of Sweden in 1760s; court intrigue encouraged by his domineering mother (Versois) makes only occasionally interesting costume tale.▼

King Kong (1933) **100m.** **** D: Merian C. Cooper, Ernest B. Schoedsack. Fay Wray, Robert Armstrong, Bruce Cabot, Frank Reicher, Sam Hardy, Noble Johnson, James Flavin. Classic version of beauty-and-beast theme is a moviegoing must, with Willis O'Brien's special effects and animation of monster Kong still unsurpassed. Final sequence atop Empire State Building is now folklore; Max Steiner music score also memorable. Non-TV prints with restored footage run 103m. Followed immediately by SON OF KONG; remade in 1976. Also shown in computer-colored version.▼

King Kong (1976) **C-134m.** *½ D: John Guillermin. Jeff Bridges, Charles Grodin, Jessica Lange, John Randolph, Rene Auberjonois, Julius Harris, Jack O'Halloran, Ed Lauter. Addle-brained remake of 1933 classic has great potential but dispels all the mythic, larger-than-life qualities of the original with idiotic characters and campy approach. Highly-touted special effects (which earned a special Oscar) run hot-and-cold; real marvel is Rick Baker in a gorilla suit. Extra footage added for network showing. Lange's film debut; Joe Piscopo has a small role. Followed a decade later by KING KONG LIVES.▼

King Kong Escapes (1968-Japanese) **C-96m.** BOMB D: Inoshiro Honda. Rhodes Reason, Mie Hama, Linda Miller, Akira Takarada. Contrived new plot involving girl who wins ape's heart, battle against would-be world conqueror. Kong never had it so bad.

King Kong Lives (1986) **C-105m.** BOMB D: John Guillermin. Brian Kerwin, Linda Hamilton, John Ashton, Peter Michael Goetz, Frank Maraden, Alan Sader. Dino De Laurentiis sequel gives the ape a mate with everything he loves: She's tall, statuesque, with great mossy teeth. The Army tries to kill them (naturally), but not before a finale that actually rips off the final scene in SPARTACUS. Desperate.▼

King Kong vs. Godzilla (1963-Japanese-U.S.) **C-90m.** **½ D: Thomas Montgomery, Inoshiro Honda. Michael Keith, James Yagi, Tadao Takashima, Mie Hama. All talk, talk, talk until the rousing finale, when the two monsters clash. Special effects are above average.▼

King Lear (1971-British) **137m.** ***½ D: Peter Brook. Paul Scofield, Irene Worth, Jack MacGowran, Alan Webb, Cyril Cusack, Patrick Magee. This version of Shakespeare tragedy could be heavy going for the uninitiated, but often a strong and rewarding experience. Starkly photographed in Denmark.▼

King Lear (1987-U.S.-Swiss) **C-91m.** *½ D: Jean-Luc Godard. Peter Sellars, Burgess Meredith, Molly Ringwald, Jean-Luc Godard, Woody Allen, Norman Mailer, Kate Mailer. Bizarre, garish, contemporary punk-apocalyptic updating of the Shakespeare classic. There's little to be said about this pretentious mess except . . . avoid it.▼

King of Alcatraz (1938) **56m.** **½ D: Robert Florey. J. Carrol Naish, Gail Patrick, Lloyd Nolan, Harry Carey, Robert Preston, Anthony Quinn. Alcatraz escapee Naish takes over passenger ship, encountering rough-and-tumble seamen Nolan and Preston. Film moves like lightning, with outstanding cast making you forget this is just a B picture.

King of America (1982) **C-90m.** TVM D: Dezso Magyar. Michael Welden, Larry Atlas, Andreas Katsulas, Barry Miller. Compelling drama about a Greek sailor (Welden) who jumps ship in 1915 and struggles for survival in America; the idealism versus the gritty reality of the times is effectively presented. Music by Elizabeth Swados. A PBS *American Playhouse* presentation. Above average.▼

King of Burlesque (1935) **83m.** **½ D: Sidney Lanfield. Warner Baxter, Jack Oakie, Alice Faye, Mona Barrie, Dixie Dunbar.

Dumb but enjoyable musical; cliché-ridden story of burlesque producer who risks all on ambitious Broadway show. Faye, Fats Waller (used all too briefly), hit song "I'm Shootin' High" provide highspots.▼

King of Chinatown (1939) **60m.** **½ D: Nick Grinde. Anna May Wong, Sidney Toler, Akim Tamiroff, J. Carrol Naish, Anthony Quinn, Roscoe Karns, Philip Ahn. Interesting little B movie with good cast, about underworld racketeers trying to gain power in Chinatown.

King of Comedy, The (1983) **C-109m.** ***½ D: Martin Scorsese. Robert De Niro, Jerry Lewis, Diahnne Abbott, Sandra Bernhard, Shelley Hack, Tony Randall, Ed Herlihy, Fred de Cordova. Pungent black comedy about a show-business hanger-on and world class loser who idolizes America's top TV comedian/talk-show host and figures out a bizarre scheme to get on the program. The denouement is a wow! Too mordant and "sick" for many viewers' taste, though it's all been done with a minimum of exaggeration . . . and a pair of knock-out performances by De Niro and Lewis. Written by Paul D. Zimmerman. Filmed in 1981.▼

King of Hearts (1966-French-British) **C-102m.** *** D: Philippe De Broca. Alan Bates, Pierre Brasseur, Jean-Claude Brialy, Genevieve Bujold, Francoise Christophe, Adolfo Celi. Scotsman Bates walks into French town in WW1 that has been abandoned by everyone except those in the insane asylum. Stylish film isn't for all tastes, but has become a staple in revival theaters. Offbeat.▼

King of Jazz, The (1930) **C-93m.** *** D: John Murray Anderson. Paul Whiteman and His Orchestra, John Boles, Jeanette Loff, The Rhythm Boys (Bing Crosby, Al Rinker, Harry Barris). Million-dollar musical revue, shot in two-color Technicolor process, is filled with larger-than-life production numbers and wonderful songs. Highlights include Walter Lantz's cartoon sequence, Joe Venuti's swing violin, young Bing Crosby with the Rhythm Boys, and, of course, Gershwin's "Rhapsody in Blue" (which in early Technicolor is more a rhapsody in turquoise). Uneven, to be sure, but a lot of fun. Originally released at 105m.▼

King of Kings, The (1927) **115m.** *** D: Cecil B. DeMille. H. B. Warner, Ernest Torrence, Jacqueline Logan, Joseph Schildkraut, Victor Varconi, Robert Edeson, William Boyd. Lavish silent film holds up rather well, benefits from DeMille's superb storytelling skills and reverence for the subject. The Resurrection sequence is in two-color Technicolor. Remade in 1961.▼

King of Kings (1961) **C-168m.** ***½ D: Nicholas Ray. Jeffrey Hunter, Siobhan McKenna, Robert Ryan, Hurd Hatfield, Viveca Lindfors, Rita Gam, Rip Torn. The life of Christ, intelligently told and beautifully filmed; full of deeply moving moments, such as the Sermon on the Mount. Not without flaws, but well worthwhile; grandly filmed in CinemaScope, bound to lose some of its visual impact on TV. Narrated by Orson Welles.▼

King of Kong Island (1978-Spanish) **C-92m.** BOMB D: Robert Morris. Brad Harris, Esmeralda Barros, Marc Lawrence, Adrianna Alben, Mark Farran. Mercenary Harris on the trail of loony scientist Lawrence, who's been monkeying around with the brains of apes, making them act like robots. Couldn't be any worse; not even good for laughs. Also known as KONG ISLAND.

King of Love, The (1987) **C-100m.** TVM D: Anthony Wilkinson. Nick Mancuso, Sela Ward, Rip Torn, Michael Lerner, Alan Rosenberg, Katy Boyer, Robin Gammell. The rise of a Hugh Hefner/Bob Guccione–type magnate, stirring everything from McCarthyism to the Black Panther movement into this preposterous mix concocted by British playwright Donald Freed. Below average.

King of Marvin Gardens, The (1972) **C-104m.** ***½ D: Bob Rafelson. Jack Nicholson, Bruce Dern, Ellen Burstyn, Julia Anne Robinson, Scatman Crothers. Pretentious but genuinely haunting, original drama about Nicholson's failure to discourage brother Dern's outlandish financial schemes. Burstyn's performance as an aging beauty is chilling in its perfection, and Laszlo Kovacs' photography rates with the best of the decade.

King of the Coral Sea (1956-Australian) **74m.** **½ D: Lee Robinson. Chips Rafferty, Charles Tingwell, Ilma Adey, Rod Taylor, Lloyd Berrell, Reginald Lye. On-location filming in Australia aids this account of wetback smuggling into the mainland.

King of the Grizzlies (1970) **C-93m.** **½ D: Ron Kelly. John Yesno, Chris Wiggins, Hugh Webster, Jack Van Evera; narrated by Winston Hibler. Standard Disney animal-adventure about Indian who was "brother" to bear as a cub, and who now faces the full-grown grizzly in a different light. Filmed in the Canadian Rockies.▼

King of the Gypsies (1978) **C-112m.** **½ D: Frank Pierson. Eric Roberts, Judd Hirsch, Susan Sarandon, Sterling Hayden, Annette O'Toole, Brooke Shields, Shelley Winters, Annie Potts, Michael V. Gazzo, Danielle Brisebois. Loose adaptation of Peter Maas' best seller about three generations of gypsies in N.Y.C. Dying Hayden passes tribe leadership to grandson Roberts (in his film debut), skipping over sleazy son Hirsch, who promptly sets out to kill his offspring. Initially fascinating melodrama eventually turns into conventional chase thriller, but still intriguing, with fine acting, moody Sven Nykvist photography, and infectious score by David Grisman and Stephane Grappelli (who also appear in the film).▼

King of the Jungle (1933) 72m. **½ D: H. Bruce Humberstone, Max Marcin. Buster Crabbe, Frances Dee, Sidney Toler, Nydia Westman, Robert Barrat, Irving Pichel, Douglass Dumbrille. Imitation Tarzan yarn comes off well, with Crabbe being dragged into civilization against his will. Good fun.

King of the Khyber Rifles (1953) C-100m. **½ D: Henry King. Tyrone Power, Terry Moore, Michael Rennie, John Justin. Power is half-caste British officer involved in native skirmishes, Moore the general's daughter he loves. Film lacks finesse or any sense of Kipling reality-fantasy.

King of the Mountain (1981) C-90m. ** D: Noel Nosseck. Harry Hamlin, Joseph Bottoms, Deborah Van Valkenburgh, Richard Cox, Dennis Hopper, Dan Haggerty, Seymour Cassel. Garage mechanic Hamlin and friends guzzle beer and race their cars down L.A.'s treacherous Mulholland Drive. Pretentious, clichéd script and situations, with superficial and obvious finale. Hopper overacts outrageously as a burned-out former king of the Drive. Inspired by David Barry's feature in *New West* magazine.▼

King of the Olympics: The Lives and Loves of Avery Brundage (1988) C-200m. TVM D: Lee Philips. David Selby, Renee Soutendijk, Sybil Maas, Shelagh McLeod, Kristoffer Tabori. There may be an interesting story to be told about the man who championed the modern-day Olympics, but this isn't it. Shown in two parts, yet! Below average.

King of the Roaring 20's—The Story of Arnold Rothstein (1961) 106m. **½ D: Joseph M. Newman. David Janssen, Dianne Foster, Jack Carson, Diana Dors, Mickey Rooney. Slow-paced narrative of famous gambler's rise and fall miscasts lead role (the real Rothstein was short and fat), slightly whitewashes him, and gets most of the facts wrong. Stray gangster-movie elements are unappropriately added.

King of the Rocket Men SEE: **Lost Planet Airmen**▼

King of the Underworld (1939) 69m. ** D: Lewis Seiler. Humphrey Bogart, Kay Francis, James Stephenson, John Eldredge, Jessie Busley. Farfetched story of doctor Francis becoming involved with Bogart's underworld gang; ludicrous finale. Remake of DR. SOCRATES.

King of the Wild Horses (1947) 79m. *½ D: George Archainbaud. Preston Foster, Gail Patrick, Bill Sheffield, Guinn Williams. Youth's companionship with fierce stallion is focus of this mild Western.

King of the Wild Stallions (1959) C-75m. ** D: R. G. Springsteen. George Montgomery, Diane Brewster, Edgar Buchanan, Emile Meyer, Byron Foulger. Horse is the hero of this oater, protecting a widow and her son.

King of the Zombies (1941) 67m. *½ D: Jean Yarbrough. Dick Purcell, Joan Woodbury, Mantan Moreland, Henry Victor, John Archer. Scientist develops corps of zombies to use in WW2; ridiculous chiller saved by Moreland's comedy relief.▼

King, Queen, Knave (1972-British) C-92m. BOMB D: Jerzy Skolimowski. David Niven, Gina Lollobrigida, John Moulder-Brown, Mario Adorf. Coarse, heavy-handed adaptation of Vladimir Nabokov story about a klutzy youth who falls in love with his sexy aunt (Lollobrigida). Never released theatrically in the U.S.▼

King Rat (1965) 133m. *** D: Bryan Forbes. George Segal, Tom Courtenay, James Fox, Patrick O'Neal, Denholm Elliott, James Donald, John Mills, Alan Webb. James Clavell novel of WW2 Japanese POW camp, focusing on effect of captivity on Allied prisoners. Thoughtful presentation rises above clichés; many exciting scenes.▼

King Richard and the Crusaders (1954) C-114m. *½ D: David Butler. Rex Harrison, Virginia Mayo, George Sanders, Laurence Harvey, Robert Douglas. Cardboard costumer of Middle Ages, with laughable script.

Kings and Desperate Men (1983-Canadian) C-118m. *½ D: Alexis Kanner. Patrick McGoohan, Alexis Kanner, Andrea Marcovicci, Margaret Trudeau, Robin Spry, Frank Moore. Abrasive talk-show host McGoohan is held hostage in his studio by amateurish terrorists seeking public forum to debate plight of their comrade, convicted of manslaughter. Interesting premise sabotaged by poor direction, choppy editing. McGoohan overacts shamelessly. Trudeau has limited footage as his wife.▼

Kings Go Forth (1958) 109m. *** D: Delmer Daves. Frank Sinatra, Tony Curtis, Natalie Wood, Leora Dana, Karl Swenson. Soapy but well done three-cornered romance, set in WW2 France. Two GI buddies both fall for same girl, unaware that she is half-black. Script by Merle Miller; several jazz greats, including Red Norvo and Pete Candoli, put in appearances.

Kings of the Road (1976-German) 176m. ***½ D: Wim Wenders. Rudiger Vogler, Hanns Zischler, Lisa Kreuzer, Rudolf Schundler, Marquard Bohm. Deliberately slow, introspective, disarming tale of itinerant cinema mechanic Vogler, traveling with Zischler along the underpopulated, forgotten border regions between East and West Germany—a dying area that serves as a metaphor for the decline of the German film industry. It's also about cars, rock 'n' roll, and the American cultural imperialism of Wenders's homeland.▼

Kings of the Sun (1963) **C-108m.** **½ D: J. Lee Thompson. Yul Brynner, George Chakiris, Shirley Anne Field, Richard Basehart, Brad Dexter. Skin-deep spectacle, badly cast, telling of Mayan leader who comes to America with surviving tribesmen and encounters savage Indians. Filmed in Mexico.

King Solomon's Mines (1937-British) **80m.** *** D: Robert Stevenson. Paul Robeson, Cedric Hardwicke, Roland Young, John Loder, Anna Lee. Robust adventure given full-blooded treatment by fine cast, scouring Africa in search of treasure-filled mines. One of Robeson's best screen roles even allows him to sing. H. Rider Haggard story remade in 1950 and 1985.▼

King Solomon's Mines (1950) **C-102m.** ***½ D: Compton Bennett, Andrew Marton. Deborah Kerr, Stewart Granger, Richard Carlson, Hugo Haas. Remake of H. Rider Haggard story is given polished production, with Granger-Kerr-Carlson trio leading safari in search for famed diamond mines. Scripted by Helen Deutsch. This won Oscars for Cinematography (Robert Surtees) and Editing; excess footage used in WATUSI and other later jungle films. Remade in 1985.▼

King Solomon's Mines (1985) **C-100m.** *½ D: J. Lee Thompson. Richard Chamberlain, Sharon Stone, Herbert Lom, John Rhys-Davies, Ken Gampu. H. Rider Haggard's adventure yarn is updated for the Indiana Jones generation, but the results are unsuccessful. Cartoon characters and outlandish cliffhanger situations abound—but where's the charm? Followed by sequel (shot simultaneously), ALLAN QUATERMAIN AND THE LOST CITY OF GOLD.▼

King Solomon's Treasure (1977-Canadian-British) **C-89m.** *½ D: Alvin Rakoff. David McCallum, John Colicos, Patrick Macnee, Britt Ekland, Yvon Dufour, Ken Gampu, Wilfrid Hyde-White. Silly, low-budget adaptation of H. Rider Haggard's *Allan Quatermain* has miscast trio of Colicos, McCallum (with comedy-relief stutter) and Macnee hunting for African treasure, fighting off dinosaurs and meeting Phoenician queen Ekland. Despite obvious similarities, this is no RAIDERS OF THE LOST ARK.▼

King's Pirate, The (1967) **C-100m.** **½ D: Don Weis. Doug McClure, Jill St. John, Guy Stockwell, Mary Ann Mobley. Cardboard, juvenile swashbuckler set in 18th century, with McClure the nominal hero. Remake of AGAINST ALL FLAGS.

Kings Row (1942) **127m.** ***½ D: Sam Wood. Ann Sheridan, Robert Cummings, Ronald Reagan, Betty Field, Charles Coburn, Claude Rains, Judith Anderson, Maria Ouspenskaya. Forerunner of PEYTON PLACE still retains its sweep of life in pre-WW1 Midwestern town, with the fates of many townsfolk intertwined. Beautiful Erich Wolfgang Korngold music score backs up plush production, fine characterizations. Notable, too, as Reagan's finest performance. Screenplay by Casey Robinson, from Henry Bellamann's bestselling book. Also shown in computer-colored version.▼

King's Story, A (1967-British) **C-100m.** *** D: Harry Booth. With the voices of Orson Welles, Flora Robson, Patrick Wymark, David Warner. Strong documentary focusing on early life of Duke of Windsor and his ultimate abdication from throne of England to marry the woman he loved.

King Steps Out, The (1936) **85m.** *** D: Josef von Sternberg. Grace Moore, Franchot Tone, Walter Connolly, Raymond Walburn, Elizabeth Risdon, Nana Bryant, Victor Jory. Fanciful musical romance with fine cast supporting Moore's lovely voice; direction big asset to otherwise average musical.

King's Thief, The (1955) **C-78m.** *** D: Robert Z. Leonard. David Niven, Ann Blyth, George Sanders, Edmund Purdom, Roger Moore, Alan Mowbray. Ornately produced costumer of 17th-century court intrigue involving England's King Charles II.

Kingston (1976) **C-100m. TVM** D: Robert Day. Raymond Burr, Bradford Dillman, Dina Merrill, James Canning, Biff McGuire, Robert Sampson. Freelance journalist Burr is hired by publishing mogul to investigate strange editorial positions on her papers and uncovers a plot using nuclear power plants to take over the world. Pilot for the series. Also known as KINGSTON: THE POWER PLAY and THE NEWSPAPER GAME. Average.

Kingston: The Power Play SEE: **Kingston**

King's Vacation, The (1933) **60m.** **½ D: John G. Adolfi. George Arliss, Dudley Digges, Dick Powell, Patricia Ellis, Marjorie Gateson, Florence Arliss. Refreshing story of monarch Arliss returning to ex-wife Gateson in search for "the simple life," only to find she's living even better than he is! Typical of Arliss' lighter vehicles.

Kinjite: Forbidden Subjects (1989) **C-97m.** ** D: J. Lee Thompson. Charles Bronson, Juan Fernandez, James Pax, Kumiko Hayakawa, Perry Lopez, Peggy Lipton, Amy Hathaway, Bill McKinney, Sy Richardson, Alex Hyde-White, Richard Egan, Jr. Glum urban thriller pitting supercop Bronson against scummy pimp Fernandez, who specializes in turning teenage girls to prostitution. Also involved is a Japanese businessman, newly come to L.A., whose daughter is kidnapped by the pimp.

Some interesting ideas are dropped in favor of the same old thing, done the same old way.▼

Kipperbang (1982-British) **C-80m.** *½ D: Michael Apted. John Albasiny, Alison Steadman, Gary Cooper, Abigail Cruttenden, Maurice Lee. Annoyingly lightweight comedy detailing the romantic fantasies and predicaments of young teens and their elders—particularly, their English teacher—in 1948 Britain. Originally made for British television, released here theatrically in 1984.▼

Kipps (1941-British) **82m.** *** D: Carol Reed. Michael Redgrave, Diana Wynyard, Arthur Riscoe, Phyllis Calvert, Max Adrian, Helen Haye, Michael Wilding. Meticulous adaptation of H. G. Wells's story about a shopkeeper who inherits money and tries to crash Society. Faithfully scripted by Sidney Gilliat, but a bit stodgy overall. Basis for musical HALF A SIXPENCE. Originally released in U.S. as THE REMARKABLE MR. KIPPS. Original British running time 108m.▼

Kismet (1944) **C-100m.** **½ D: William Dieterle. Ronald Colman, Marlene Dietrich, Edward Arnold, Florence Bates, James Craig, Joy Ann Page, Harry Davenport. Colman tries a change of pace playing the "king of beggars," a wily magician whose daughter is wooed by the handsome young Caliph in this plot-heavy Arabian Nights-type tale. Passably entertaining but nothing special, despite opulent MGM production. Best of all is Dietrich, with tongue in cheek and body painted gold for one famous dance scene. Filmed before in 1920 and 1930; remade in 1955 after the Broadway musical version. Retitled ORIENTAL DREAM.

Kismet (1955) **C-113m.** **½ D: Vincente Minnelli. Howard Keel, Ann Blyth, Dolores Gray, Monty Woolley, Sebastian Cabot, Vic Damone. Handsome but uninspired filming of the Broadway musical of this Arabian Nights-type tale. Robert Wright-George Forrest songs (based on Borodin themes) include "Stranger in Paradise," "Baubles, Bangles, and Beads." ▼

Kiss, The (1988) **C-101m.** ** D: Pen Densham. Joanna Pacula, Meredith Salenger, Mimi Kuzyk, Nicholas Kilbertus, Jan Rubes. Occasionally scary horror film builds up to but downplays the sexual implications of its CAT PEOPLE–style story of a family curse passed down to each generation by a woman-to-woman kiss. Salenger is the unlucky target of beautiful aunt Pacula's evil smooch.▼

Kiss and Kill SEE: **Blood of Fu Manchu**▼

Kiss and Tell (1945) **90m.** **½ D: Richard Wallace. Shirley Temple, Jerome Courtland, Walter Abel, Katherine Alexander, Robert Benchley, Porter Hall. Film of successful Broadway play about wacky teenager Corliss Archer is a bit forced but generally funny; one of Temple's better grown-up roles. Sequel: A KISS FOR CORLISS.

Kiss Before Dying, A (1956) **C-94m.** *** D: Gerd Oswald. Robert Wagner, Virginia Leith, Jeffrey Hunter, Joanne Woodward, Mary Astor, George Macready. Effective chiller with Wagner superb as psychopathic killer and Astor his devoted mother; well paced. Based on an Ira Levin novel.

Kiss Before the Mirror, The (1933) **67m.** **½ D: James Whale. Frank Morgan, Paul Lukas, Nancy Carroll, Jean Dixon, Gloria Stuart, Walter Pidgeon, Donald Cook, Charles Grapewin. While defending Lukas for killing his adulterous wife, attorney Morgan begins to see the entire chain of events recurring in his own home! Strange romantic melodrama is made even stranger by being shot on leftover FRANKENSTEIN sets; good performances and typical Whale stylistics keep one watching. Remade by the director as WIVES UNDER SUSPICION.

Kiss Daddy Good Night (1987) **C-89m.** *½ D: Peter Ily Huemer. Uma Thurman, Paul Dillon, Paul Richards, Steve Buscemi, Annabelle Gurwitch, David Brisbin. Vague, forgettable melodrama-thriller about a young vamp (Thurman, in her screen debut), who seduces and robs men, and her strange relationship with older bohemian Richards.▼

Kisses for My President (1964) **113m.** **½ D: Curtis Bernhardt. Fred MacMurray, Polly Bergen, Arlene Dahl, Edward Andrews, Eli Wallach. Thirties-style comedy of Bergen becoming President of the U.S., with MacMurray her husband caught in unprecedented protocol. Sometimes funny, often witless.

Kiss for Corliss, A (1949) **88m.** ** D: Richard Wallace. Shirley Temple, David Niven, Tom Tully, Virginia Welles. Puffed-up comedy of teenager Temple convincing all that she and playboy Niven are going together; naïve fluff. Limp follow-up to KISS AND TELL with Shirley as Corliss Archer; this was her final film. Retitled ALMOST A BRIDE.

Kiss From Eddie, A SEE: **Arousers, The**▼

Kissin' Cousins (1964) **C-96m.** **½ D: Gene Nelson. Elvis Presley, Arthur O'Connell, Glenda Farrell, Pamela Austin, Yvonne Craig. Elvis has a dual role as military officer trying to convince yokel relative to allow missile site to be built on homestead; good supporting cast, usual amount of singing—mostly forgettable—and dancing.▼

Kissing Bandit, The (1948) **C-102m.** ** D: Laslo Benedek. Frank Sinatra, Kathryn Grayson, Ann Miller, J. Carrol Naish, Ricardo Montalban, Mildred Natwick, Cyd Charisse, Billy Gilbert. Frail Sinatra vehicle about son of Western kissing bandit who picks up where Dad left off; song "Siesta" sums it up.

Kiss In the Dark, A (1949) **87m.** ** D: Delmer Daves. David Niven, Jane Wyman, Victor Moore, Wayne Morris, Broderick Crawford. Drab comedy effort involving pianist Niven, who gets more than he bargained for when he inherits an apartment building.

Kiss Kiss-Bang Bang (1966-Spanish) **C-90m.** **½ D: Duccio Tessari. Giuliano Gemma, George Martin, Antonio Casas, Daniel Vargas. Routine spy yarn of British Secret Service efforts to prevent sale of secret formula to foreign powers.

Kiss Me Deadly (1955) **105m.** ***½ D: Robert Aldrich. Ralph Meeker, Albert Dekker, Paul Stewart, Cloris Leachman, Maxine Cooper, Gaby Rodgers, Jack Elam, Strother Martin, Jack Lambert. Meeker is a perfect Mike Hammer in moody, fast and violent adaptation of Mickey Spillane novel. Years ahead of its time, a major influence on French New Wave directors and one of Aldrich's best films.

KISS Meets the Phantom of the Park (1978) **C-100m. TVM** D: Gordon Hessler. KISS (Peter Criss, Ace Frehley, Gene Simmons, Paul Stanley), Anthony Zerbe, Carmine Caridi, Deborah Ryan, Terry Webster. The famed rock group (in their acting debut) try to thwart a mad scientist's plan to clone the foursome for evil purposes. Already a period piece, but worth catching for those wanting to see Zerbe at his slimiest. Average.▼

Kiss Me Goodbye (1982) **C-101m.** ** D: Robert Mulligan. Sally Field, James Caan, Jeff Bridges, Paul Dooley, Claire Trevor, Mildred Natwick, Dorothy Fielding, William Prince. Strained romantic comedy-fantasy about young woman who's visited by her dead husband just as she's about to remarry. Attractive cast is pretty much wasted in this reworking of the Brazilian film DONA FLOR AND HER TWO HUSBANDS.▼

Kiss Me Kate (1953) **C-109m.** *** D: George Sidney. Kathryn Grayson, Howard Keel, Ann Miller, Bobby Van, Keenan Wynn, James Whitmore, Bob Fosse, Tommy Rall, Kurt Kaszner, Ron Randell. Bright filmization of Cole Porter's Broadway musical, adapted from Shakespeare's *The Taming of the Shrew.* Grayson and Keel are married couple whose off-stage and on-stage lives intertwine. Songs include "So in Love," "Always True to You in My Fashion," "Brush Up Your Shakespeare" (delightfully performed by Wynn and Whitmore); the "From This Moment On" number, highlighting Fosse and Carol Haney, is outstanding. Originally in 3D.▼

Kiss Me . . . Kill Me (1976) **C-126m. TVM** D: Michael O'Herlihy. Stella Stevens, Michael Anderson, Jr., Dabney Coleman, Claude Akins, Bruce Boxleitner, Pat O'Brien, Robert Vaughn, Tisha Sterling. D.A.'s special investigator Stevens goes on trail of young schoolteacher's killer and allows herself to be bait to trap psycho. Strictly in *Police Woman* rut, but nice bit by O'Brien as morgue attendant. Average.

Kiss Me, Stupid (1964) **126m.** ** D: Billy Wilder. Dean Martin, Ray Walston, Kim Novak, Felicia Farr, Cliff Osmond, Barbara Pepper, Doro Merande, Henry Gibson, John Fiedler, Mel Blanc. Martin plays womanizing crooner named "Dino" whose interest in unsuccessful songwriter Walston might increase if he gets a crack at his wife. Lewd farce (by Wilder and I. A. L. Diamond) was condemned as "smut" when first released, and hasn't improved very much—although it does have its defenders. Maybe in another ten years . . .

Kiss of Death (1947) **98m.** *** D: Henry Hathaway. Victor Mature, Brian Donlevy, Coleen Gray, Richard Widmark, Karl Malden, Taylor Holmes, Mildred Dunnock. Famous gangster saga is showing its age, with both the cops and robbers a little too polite—except, of course, for Widmark, in his notorious film debut as giggling, psychopathic killer who shoves a wheel-chair-bound old woman down a flight of stairs! Mature is solid as thief who turns state's evidence. Scripted by Ben Hecht and Charles Lederer; filmed on authentic N.Y.C. locations.

Kiss of Evil SEE: **Kiss of the Vampire**

Kiss of Fire (1955) **C-87m.** **½ D: Joseph M. Newman. Barbara Rush, Jack Palance, Rex Reason, Martha Hyer. Run-of-the-mill costumer. Rush gives up Spanish throne to remain in America with true love.

Kiss of the Spider Woman (1985-U.S.-Brazilian) **C/B&W-119m.** *** D: Hector Babenco. William Hurt, Raul Julia, Sonia Braga, Jose Lewgoy, Nuno Leal Maia, Denise Dumont. Adaptation of Manuel Puig's highly regarded novel actually gets better as it goes along, revealing layers in story of gay man and political activist locked together in South American prison cell. Hurt is superb in Oscar-winning performance as man whose only food for survival is his memory of tacky Hollywood movies. Script by Leonard Schrader.▼

Kiss of the Tarantula (1972) **C-85m.** *½ D: Chris Munger. Suzanne Ling, Eric Mason, Herman Wallner, Patricia Landon, Beverly Eddins. Unstable teenager uses pet tarantulas against her stepmother and other "enemies." Heavy handed.▼

Kiss of the Vampire (1963-British) **C-88m.** **½ D: Don Sharp. Clifford Evans, Edward DeSouza, Noel Willman, Jennifer Daniel. Intelligent treatment of vampire tale, well done in color, with many chilling sequences. Unfortunately, much of film's punch is lost in reedited TV version known as KISS OF EVIL.

Kiss Shot (1989) **C-100m.** **TVM** D: Jerry London. Whoopi Goldberg, Dorian Harewood, Dennis Franz, Tasha Scott, David Marciano, Teddy Wilson. Whoopi's TV-movie debut has her a pool-playing minimum wage single mom looking for some fast money to pay the mortgage. THE HUSTLER it ain't, but Whoopi's impressive bank shots (her own, it appears) and her nice feel for romantic comedy compensate for the white-washing of the dialogue that's her theatrical and cable TV stock in trade. Average.

Kiss the Blood Off My Hands (1948) **80m.** ** D: Norman Foster. Burt Lancaster, Joan Fontaine, Robert Newton, Lewis L. Russell, Aminta Dyne, Jay Novello. London nurse Fontaine shelters sailor Lancaster, on the lam for murder. Good elements—including hammy Newton and terse Miklos Rozsa score—can't salvage tepid thriller.

Kiss the Boys Goodbye (1941) **85m.** **½ D: Victor Schertzinger. Mary Martin, Don Ameche, Oscar Levant, Virginia Dale, Barbara Jo Allen (Vera Vague), Raymond Walburn, Elizabeth Patterson, Connee Boswell. Enjoyable backstage musical of aspiring actress and director, with good support from Levant and bright score.

Kiss the Girls and Make Them Die (1966-Italian) **C-101m.** BOMB D: Henry Levin. Michael Connors, Dorothy Provine, Terry-Thomas, Raf Vallone, Beverly Adams, Oliver McGreevy. Dull spy spoof about power-crazy industrialist who has a satellite capable of sterilizing the world, which is something Bond, Flint, and Matt Helm wouldn't mind. Awful film.

Kiss Them for Me (1957) **C-105m.** **½ D: Stanley Donen. Cary Grant, Jayne Mansfield, Leif Erickson, Suzy Parker, Larry Blyden, Ray Walston. Forced comedy about romantic entanglements of navy officers on shore leave.

Kiss the Other Sheik (1968-Italian-French) **C-85m.** BOMB D: Luciano Salce, Eduardo De Filippo. Marcello Mastroianni, Pamela Tiffin, Virna Lisi, Luciano Salce. Off-color and off-base comedy of crazy man and his sexy wife.

Kiss Tomorrow Goodbye (1950) **102m.** **½ D: Gordon Douglas. James Cagney, Barbara Payton, Luther Adler, Ward Bond, Helena Carter, Steve Brodie, Barton Mac-Lane, Rhys Williams, Frank Reicher, John Litel, William Frawley, Neville Brand, Kenneth Tobey. Violent thriller in the wake of WHITE HEAT, with Cagney as criminal so ruthless he even blackmails crooked cops! Despite impressive cast, Jimmy's practically the whole show; only Adler as shyster lawyer gives him any competition.

Cagney's brother William produced—and also plays his brother.▼

Kit Carson (1940) **97m.** *** D: George B. Seitz. Jon Hall, Lynn Bari, Dana Andrews, Harold Huber, Ward Bond, Renie Riano, Clayton Moore. Sturdy Western with Hall in title role, Andrews as cavalry officer, Bari the woman they fight over; plenty of action in Indian territory.▼

Kitchen Toto, The (1987) **C-96m.** *** D: Harry Hook. Edwin Mahinda, Bob Peck, Phyllis Logan, Robert Urquhart, Kirsten Hughes, Edward Judd. Moving account of Kenya's final break from British rule in the mid-1950s. This complicated and violent struggle for freedom is told through the eyes of a young "kikuyu" boy slowly drawn into these events when he goes to work in the household of the British police chief after his father is murdered by terrorists. Demanding but ultimately rewarding; first-rate debut for director Hook, who grew up in Kenya during the period depicted here.▼

Kitten with a Whip (1964) **83m.** ** D: Douglas Heyes. Ann-Margret, John Forsythe, Patricia Barry, Peter Brown, Ann Doran. Uninspired account of delinquent (Ann Margret) and friends forcing businessman Forsythe to drive them to Mexico.

Kitty (1945) **104m.** *** D: Mitchell Leisen. Paulette Goddard, Ray Milland, Patric Knowles, Reginald Owen, Cecil Kellaway, Constance Collier. Overlong but entertaining costumer of girl's rise from guttersnipe to lady in 18th-century England with help of impoverished rake Milland; one of Goddard's best roles.

Kitty and the Bagman (1982-Australian) **C-95m.** **½ D: Donald Crombie. Liddy Clark, John Stanton, Val Lehman, Gerard McGuire, Collette Mann, Reg Evans. Flavorful period detail is the star of this inconsequential comedy-drama about crooked cop Stanton and young Clark, who becomes Underworld Queen of Sydney during the Roaring Twenties.▼

Kitty Foyle (1940) **107m.** ***½ D: Sam Wood. Ginger Rogers, Dennis Morgan, James Craig, Eduardo Ciannelli, Ernest Cossart, Gladys Cooper. Tender love story won Rogers an Oscar as Christopher Morley's working-girl heroine; Ciannelli memorable as speakeasy waiter.▼

Klansman, The (1974) **C-112m.** BOMB D: Terence Young. Lee Marvin, Richard Burton, Cameron Mitchell, Lola Falana, Luciana Paluzzi, Linda Evans, O. J. Simpson. Thoroughly trashy racial melodrama casts Marvin as a Southern sheriff and Burton as a local landowner who get involved in a hotbed (and hot beds) of racial activity. Original director Sam Fuller (who is still credited as coscripter) wisely took an early hike. Video title: THE BURNING CROSS.▼

Klondike Annie (1936) **80m.** *** D: Raoul Walsh. Mae West, Victor McLaglen, Philip Reed, Harold Huber, Soo Young, Lucile Webster Gleason. West and McLaglen are rugged team, with Mae on the lam from police, going to the Yukon and masquerading as Salvation Army worker. West chants "I'm An Occidental Woman in An Oriental Mood For Love," and other hits.

Klondike Fever (1980) **C-106m.** *½ D: Peter Carter. Rod Steiger, Angie Dickinson, Jeff East, Lorne Greene, Barry Morse. Jack London (East) in Alaska during the Gold Rush. Poorly made adventure yarn. Also known as JACK LONDON'S KLONDIKE FEVER.

Klondike Kate (1943) **64m.** *½ D: William Castle. Ann Savage, Tom Neal, Glenda Farrell, Constance Worth, Sheldon Leonard, Lester Allen. Low-budget humdrum of innocent Neal accused of murder in Alaska, fighting for his life and his girl.

Klute (1971) **C-114m.** ***½ D: Alan J. Pakula. Jane Fonda, Donald Sutherland, Charles Cioffi, Roy Scheider, Dorothy Tristan, Rita Gam, Jean Stapleton. Fine combination detective-thriller/character-study, with Sutherland a private-eye searching for suburban husband last seen in N.Y.C. Fonda won Oscar as call girl who once saw man in question. Beware: Commercial TV print runs 108m. and omits one crucial scene that helps Sutherland solve the mystery!▼

Knack, and How to Get It, The (1965-British) **84m.** ***½ D: Richard Lester. Rita Tushingham, Ray Brooks, Michael Crawford, Donal Donnelly. One of the funniest comedies ever imported from Britain. One man's a whiz with the ladies, and his buddy simply wants to learn his secret. Fast-moving, constantly funny. Jacqueline Bisset may be seen briefly.

Knave of Hearts SEE: Lovers, Happy Lovers

Knickerbocker Holiday (1944) **85m.** ** D: Harry Brown. Nelson Eddy, Charles Coburn, Constance Dowling, Shelley Winters, Percy Kilbride, Chester Conklin. Plodding film of Kurt Weill-Maxwell Anderson musical of New York's early days; score includes "September Song."▼

Knife in the Head (German-1978) **C-113m.** ***½ D: Reinhard Hauff. Bruno Ganz, Angela Winkler, Hans Christian Blech, Hans Honig, Hans Brenner. Ganz is excellent as a biogeneticist who is paralyzed after being shot in the head in a police raid, then used as a pawn by both police and political radicals. Fascinating, disturbing drama.

Knife in the Water (1962-Polish) **94m.** **** D: Roman Polanski. Leon Niemczyk, Jolanta Umecka, Zygmunt Malanowicz. Absorbing drama grows out of the tensions created when a couple off for a sailing weekend pick up a student hitchhiker. Polanski's first feature film is a brilliant piece of cinematic storytelling, and a must-see movie.▼

Knight of the Dragon, The SEE: **Star Knight**

Knightriders (1981) **C-145m.** *** D: George A. Romero. Ed Harris, Gary Lahti, Tom Savini, Amy Ingersoll, Patricia Tallman, Christine Forrest, Warner Shook, Brother Blue. Ambitious, unusual film about a traveling band that stages medieval fairs at which knights joust on motorcycles, and their self-styled King Arthur, who tries to get his followers to live under an old-fashioned code of honor. Finely crafted little change-of-pace for horror master Romero, who also wrote the screenplay; Stephen King has a funny cameo as a beer-guzzling spectator.▼

Knights and Emeralds (1986-British) **C-94m.** **½ D: Ian Emes. Christopher Wild, Beverly Hills, Warren Mitchell, Bill Leadbitter, Rachel Davies, Tracie Bennett. Fair chronicle of young, white, working-class musician Wild, and what happens when he begins associating with his black counterparts. A well-meaning examination of racism and its effects, combined with mostly forgettable musical numbers.▼

Knights of the Round Table (1953) **C-115m.** **½ D: Richard Thorpe. Robert Taylor, Ava Gardner, Mel Ferrer, Stanley Baker, Felix Aylmer. MGM's first widescreen film (made in England) was excuse for this pretty but empty mini-spectacle of King Arthur's Court, revealing famous love triangle.▼

Knight Without Armour (1937-British) **101m.** *** D: Jacques Feyder. Marlene Dietrich, Robert Donat, Irene Vanbrugh, Herbert Lomas, Miles Malleson, David Tree. Secret agent Donat helps countess Dietrich flee Russian revolutionaries. Sumptuous production, charismatic stars.▼

K-9 (1989) **C-102m.** BOMB D: Rod Daniel. James Belushi, Mel Harris, Kevin Tighe, Ed O'Neill, Jerry Lee, James Handy, Cotter Smith. Cop Belushi teams with a German shepherd (Jerry Lee) to crack a drug case. Dubbing this one a dog would be much too kind.▼

Knock on Any Door (1949) **100m.** **½ D: Nicholas Ray. Humphrey Bogart, John Derek, George Macready, Allene Roberts, Susan Perry. More a showcase for young Derek—as a "victim of society" who turns to crime—than a vehicle for Bogart, as conscience-stricken attorney who defends him. Serious but dated drama. Sequel: LET NO MAN WRITE MY EPITAPH.▼

Knock on Wood (1954) **C-103m.** *** D: Norman Panama, Melvin Frank. Danny Kaye, Mai Zetterling, Torin Thatcher, David Burns, Leon Askin, Abner Biberman. Superior Kaye vehicle, with ventriloquist Danny involved with beautiful Zetterling and international spies; good Kaye routines.

Knockout (1941) **73m.** **½ D: William Clemens. Arthur Kennedy, Virginia Field, Anthony Quinn, Olympe Bradna. Slick little programmer of a prizefighter seesawing between fame and folly.

Knock Out Cop, The (1978-Italian-German) **C-113m.** ** D: Steno. Bud Spencer, Werner Pochat, Enzo Cannavale, Joe Stewardson, Bodo, Dagmar Lassander. Silly live-action comic strip with tough, beefy police inspector Spencer on the hunt for drug smugglers. For prepubescent boys only. Originally titled FLATFOOT.▼

√ **Knute Rockne, All American** (1940) **84m.** *** D: Lloyd Bacon. Pat O'Brien, Gale Page, Donald Crisp, Ronald Reagan, Albert Bassermann, John Qualen. Corny but entertaining bio of famed Notre Dame football coach (O'Brien, in a standout performance), with Reagan as his star player, George Gipp. Important note: several scenes, including O'Brien's famous lockerroom pep talk and Reagan's "win just one for the Gipper" speech, are missing from TV prints due to legal complications, so don't blame your local station. You *can* see it all on homevideo where it's been restored to 96m. Also shown in computer-colored version.▼

Kojak and the Marcus-Nelson Murders SEE: **Marcus-Nelson Murders, The**

Kojak: The Belarus File (1985) **C-100m.** TVM D: Robert Markowitz. Telly Savalas, Suzanne Pleshette, Max von Sydow, Herbert Berghof, Dan Frazer, George Savalas. Telly's new "go" at the role of N.Y.C. cop Theo Kojak is handicapped by having him play second fiddle to a convoluted tale about Nazi spies and Russian émigrés in Manhattan, with the Kojak character dropped into a dramatization of John Loftus's spy thriller, *The Belarus Secret*. Average.▼

Kojak: The Price of Justice (1987) **C-100m.** TVM D: Alan Metzger. Telly Savalas, Kate Nelligan, Pat Hingle, Jack Thompson, Brian Murray, John Bedford Lloyd, Jeffrey DeMunn. Theo Kojak, now a police inspector and minus his familiar cop colleagues, gets involved with an enigmatic woman accused of killing her two young sons. Like the previous *Kojak* movie, this one none-too-successfully overlaid the familiar TV character on an existing novel (here it's Dorothy Uhnak's *The Investigation,* dealing vaguely with an Alice Crimmins-like case). Average.▼

Kona Coast (1968) **C-93m.** **½ D: Lamont Johnson. Richard Boone, Vera Miles, Joan Blondell, Steve Ihnat, Chips Rafferty, Kent Smith. Good cast in routine melodrama of fishing boat skipper's fight to get the guys who murdered his daughter. Fifties rock star Duane Eddy has small part. Filmed in Hawaii. From a screen story by John D. MacDonald.

Konga (1961-British) **C-90m.** *½ D: John Lemont. Michael Gough, Margo Johns, Jess Conrad, Claire Gordon. Small monkey grows into huge beast threatening the people of London; silly sci-fi.

Kong Island SEE: **King of Kong Island**

Kongo (1932) **85m.** *** D: William Cowan. Walter Huston, Lupe Velez, Conrad Nagel, Virginia Bruce, C. Henry Gordon. Bizarre, fascinating melodrama of crippled madman Huston ruling African colony, seeking revenge on man who paralyzed him by torturing his daughter (Bruce). Not for the squeamish. Remake of WEST OF ZANZIBAR.

Kon-Tiki (1951) **73m.** *** Narrated by √ Ben Grauer, Thor Heyerdahl. This documentary won an Oscar in 1951; it traces Heyerdahl's raft trip from Peru to Tahiti, substantiating his theory that sailing boats in ancient times crossed the Pacific Ocean.

Koroshi (1967) **C-93m.** TVM D: Peter Yates, Michael Truman. Patrick McGoohan, Yoko Tani, Amanda Barrie, Ronald Howard, George Coulouris. British agent John Drake sent to Japan to combat deadly sect of assassins based on secret offshore island. First half better than second (originally two episodes of the *Secret Agent* series); generally uncontrived, exciting. Average.

Kotch (1971) **C-113m.** ***½ D: Jack Lemmon. Walter Matthau, Deborah Winters, Felicia Farr, Charles Aidman. Heartwarming comedy of elderly man who refuses to be put out to pasture by his children. Matthau superb in Lemmon's first directorial effort.▼

Koyaanisqatsi (1983) **C-87m.** **** D: ⌐ Godfrey Reggio. Spellbinding, senses-staggering nonnarrative film soars across the United States in search of vistas both natural and man-made. Much of the photography is slow-motion or time-lapse (the title is Hopi Indian for "life out of balance"), all of it set to a mesmerizing score by Philip Glass. So rich in beauty and detail that with each viewing it becomes a new and different film. Should be seen in a theatre for maximum impact. Followed by POWAQQATSI.▼

Krakatoa, East of Java (1969) **C-101m.** **½ D: Bernard Kowalski. Maximilian Schell, Diane Baker, Brian Keith, Barbara Werle, John Leyton, Rossano Brazzi, Sal Mineo. Muddled epic-adventure of disparate group sailing for location of treasure-laden sunken ship. Attempt at Jules Verne-ish saga hampered by shallow characterizations, dialogue, but action footage is first-rate, climaxed by volcanic explosion and tidal wave. Shot in Cinerama; heavily cut after premiere, leaving story more jumbled than before. P.S.: Krakatoa is *West* of Java. Retitled VOLCANO. Originally 136m.

Kramer vs. Kramer (1979) **C-104m.** ******** D: Robert Benton. Dustin Hoffman, Meryl Streep, Jane Alexander, Justin Henry, Howard Duff, George Coe, JoBeth Williams. Wife walks out on upwardly mobile husband, leaving him to fend for himself and their young son; an intelligent, beautifully crafted, intensely moving film. Adapted by Benton from Avery Corman's novel and acted to perfection by entire cast. Oscar winner for Best Picture, Actor, Screenplay, Director, Supporting Actress (Streep).▼

Kremlin Letter, The (1970) **C-113m.** *½ D: John Huston. Bibi Andersson, Richard Boone, Max von Sydow, Orson Welles, Patrick O'Neal, Barbara Parkins, Dean Jagger, George Sanders, Raf Vallone. Dull, complicated thriller based on best-seller concerns efforts to retrieve bogus treaty supposedly signed by U.S. and Soviet Union that will pit them against Red China. Good cast is thrown away; film does provide rare opportunity to see Sanders in drag.

Kronos (1957) **78m.** **½ D: Kurt Neumann. Jeff Morrow, Barbara Lawrence, John Emery, George O'Hanlon, Morris Ankrum. Diverting science-fiction with unique monster: an enormous metallic walking machine capable of absorbing the Earth's energy. Occasionally shaky special effects are compensated for by nice touch of mysterioso and convincing performances, especially by Emery as the alien's catspaw.▼

Kronos (1974) SEE: **Captain Kronos: Vampire Hunter**▼

Krull (1983) **C-117m.** ** D: Peter Yates. Ken Marshall, Lysette Anthony, Freddie Jones, Francesca Annis, Alun Armstrong, David Battley. Overly familiar story elements and plodding treatment keep this traditional fantasy quest from going anywhere, despite its elaborate trappings. Marshall is the young hero who must recover a magic ornament to save his damsel, and his kingdom.▼

Krush Groove (1985) **C-97m.** ** D: Michael Schultz. Blair Underwood, Joseph Simmons, Sheila E., Fat Boys, Daryll McDaniels, Kurtis Blow. Yet another rap musical, with a silly (almost nonexistent) story but lots of music, rapping, and street culture artifacts. Aficionados of this kind of music rate the soundtrack very highly.▼

Kung Fu (1972) **C-75m.** **TVM** D: Jerry Thorpe. David Carradine, Barry Sullivan, Keith Carradine, Philip Ahn, Keye Luke, Wayne Maunder, Albert Salmi, Benson Fong, Richard Loo, Victor Sen Yung. Stylish tale of young Carradine, a half-American/half-Chinese Buddhist monk trained in karate, who flees mainland China after he's accused of murder and comes to the American West. Good performances

and offbeat direction that counterpoints the script's moods. Above average; pilot for the series. Carradine reprised the role 14 years later in KUNG FU: THE MOVIE.▼

Kung Fu: The Movie (1986) **C-100m.** **TVM** D: Richard Lang. David Carradine, Kerri Keane, Mako, William Lucking, Luke Askew, Benson Fong, Keye Luke, Martin Landau, Brandon Lee. Carradine reprises his now cult role of Kwai Chang Caine from the original *King Fu* series of the early 1970s, here being stalked by evil warlord Mako, who's mixed up in California's opium trade in the late 1880s. Bruce Lee's son Brandon is "introduced" as a young Manchu assassin who clashes with Carradine, and Keye Luke repeats (in flashback only) his original part as Master Po, Carradine's blind teacher. Average.

Kwaidan (1964-Japanese) **C-164m.** ***½ D: Masaki Kobayashi. Rentaro Mikuni, Michiyo Aratama, Keiko Kishi, Tatsuya Nakadai, Takashi Shimura. Four tales of the supernatural, based on works by Lafcadio Hearn, focusing on samurais, balladeers, monks, spirits. Subtle, moody, well staged; stunning use of color and widescreen.▼

La Balance (1982-French) **C-102m.** *** D: Bob Swaim. Nathalie Baye, Philippe Leotard, Richard Berry, Maurice Ronet, Christophe Malavoy, Jean-Paul Connart. Extremely tough, violent Parisian cop movie (directed and cowritten by an American) about effort to nail criminal kingpin by forcing one-time associate (Leotard) to turn informer. Baye is excellent as prostitute in love with victimized pimp. Winner of many Cesar Awards (France's Oscar) including Best Picture.▼

La Bamba (1987) **C-108m.** *** D: Luis Valdez. Lou Diamond Phillips, Esai Morales, Rosana De Soto, Elizabeth Pena, Danielle von Zerneck, Joe Pantoliano, Rick Dees, Marshall Crenshaw, Brian Setzer. Solid musical biography of Ritchie Valens, a poor Mexican-American who became a rock 'n' roll sensation at the age of 17. Writer-director Valdez can't avoid some of the standard Hollywood bio trappings, but the good-time music and Phillips' commanding, sympathetic performance more than compensate. Morales is also excellent in a flashy role as Ritchie's troubled brother. Valens' music is performed on the soundtrack by Los Lobos—who also appear as the Tijuana band. Original music by Carlos Santana and Miles Goodman.▼

La Boum (1981-French) **C-100m.** **½ D: Claude Pinoteau. Claude Brasseur, Brigitte Fossey, Sophie Marceau, Denise Grey, Bernard Giraudeau. Cliched but harmless chronicle of the life of pretty 13-year-old Marceau, whose parents (Brasseur, Fossey) are having marital difficulties.

A French box-office smash. Sequel: LA BOUM 2.▼

La Boum 2 (1982-French) **C-109m.** **½ D: Claude Pinoteau. Sophie Marceau, Claude Brasseur, Brigitte Fossey, Pierre Cosso, Shiela O'Connor, Denise Grey. Here teenager Marceau is two years older and has a romance with another student. Her parents are still squabbling. A formula film, neither better nor worse than the original.

Labyrinth (1986) **C-101m.** *** D: Jim Henson. David Bowie, Jennifer Connelly, Toby Froud. Teenage girl's baby brother is kidnapped by the King of the Goblins (Bowie); in order to rescue him she must navigate a devilish labyrinth. Entertaining variation on *Alice in Wonderland* written by Monty Python's Terry Jones, executive produced by George Lucas, and filtered through the sensibilities of The Muppets' Jim Henson. A treat for kids and the young at heart (Muppet fans in particular); only weakness is that it does get slow at times.▼

La Cage aux Folles (1978-French-Italian) **C-91m.** *** D: Edouard Molinaro. Ugo Tognazzi, Michel Serrault, Michel Galabru, Claire Maurier, Remy Laurent, Benny Luke. A gay couple tries to act straight for the sake of Tognazzi's son, who's bringing home his fiancée and her parents. Entertaining adaptation of French stage farce, with some hilarious moments and a wonderful performance by Serrault as the more feminine half of the middle-aged twosome—but why this became such a raging success is a mystery. Followed by sequels in 1980 and 1985, as well as a hit Broadway musical.▼

La Cage aux Folles II (1980-French) **C-101m.** **½ D: Edouard Molinaro. Michel Serrault, Ugo Tognazzi, Marcel Bozzuffi, Michel Galabru, Paola Borboni, Benny Luke. St. Tropez nightclub owner (Tognazzi) and his female-impersonator housemate (Serrault) become involved with a spy ring in this mild sequel.▼

La Cage aux Folles 3: The Wedding (1985-French-Italian) **C-87m.** *½ D: Georges Lautner. Michel Serrault, Ugo Tognazzi, Michel Galabru, Benny Luke, Stephane Audran, Antonella Interlenghi. Pointless sequel has drag queen Albin (Serrault) in line for big inheritance—if he marries and produces a son. This farce has been milked dry by now.▼

Lace (1984) **C-240m.** TVM D: Billy Hale. Bess Armstrong, Brooke Adams, Arielle Dombasle, Phoebe Cates, Angela Lansbury, Anthony Higgins, Herbert Lom, Anthony Quayle, Honor Blackman. Glamour-splashed trash about an international sex symbol's single-minded search to find and destroy the mother she never knew—one of three free-spirited school chums who each became fabulously successful. Even a French-accented Lansbury can't pump respectability into this lengthy adaptation of Shirley Conran's best seller. Originally in two parts. Average.

Lace II (1985) **C-200m.** TVM D: Billy Hale. Brooke Adams, Deborah Raffin, Arielle Dombasle, Phoebe Cates, Anthony Higgins, Christopher Cazenove, James Read, Patrick Ryecart, Michael Gough, Francois Guetary. Spurred on by the success of the glitter-trash original, the producers contracted for a sequel, and in this concoction (with Raffin in for Bess Armstrong), our heroine—having found out which "rich bitch" was her mother—goes in search of the "bastard" who is her father. Originally shown in two parts. Below average.

La Chinoise (1967-French) **C-95m.** *** D: Jean-Luc Godard. Anne Wiazemsky, Jean-Pierre Leaud, Michel Semianko, Lex de Bruijn, Juliet Berto. Five young Maoists share an apartment and try to apply their politics to the reality of their lives. Godard aficionados will be fascinated; others may be bored.

La Collectioneuse (1971-French) **C-88m.** *** D: Eric Rohmer. Patrick Bauchau, Haydee Politoff, Daniel Pommerulle, Alain Jouffroy, Mijanou Bardot. No. 3 of Rohmer's "Six Moral Tales" is less compelling than later films, still intriguing for fans of contemplative stories in this series, focusing on young man's gradual attraction to aloof young girl sharing summer villa on the Mediterranean. Made in 1967.

Lacombe, Lucien (1974-French) **C-137m.** **** D: Louis Malle. Pierre Blaise, Aurore Clement, Holger Lowenadler, Therese Giehse. Brilliant, perceptive account of opportunist French peasant Blaise, who joins the Gestapo during the Nazi Occupation—after setting out to join the Resistance—and falls in love with a Jewish tailor's daughter. Subtle, complex tale of guilt, innocence, and the amorality of power; masterfully directed.

Lacy and the Mississippi Queen (1978) **C-74m.** TVM D: Robert Butler. Kathleen Lloyd, Debra Feuer, Edward Andrews, Jack Elam, James Keach, Matt Clark, David Comfort. Gun-toting tomboy joins forces with her long lost sister, a bubble-headed beauty, to avenge their father's killing—with the help of a drunken Indian. Lighthearted western pilot. Average.

Lad: A Dog (1962) **C-98m.** **½ D: Aram Avakian, Leslie H. Martinson. Peter Breck, Peggy McCay, Carroll O'Connor, Angela Cartwright, Maurice Dallimore. Genuine if schmaltzy version of Albert Payson Terhune novel of dog who brings new zest for life to lame child.

L'Addition (1985-French) **C-85m.** ** D: Denis Amar. Richard Berry, Richard Bohringer, Victoria Abril, Farid Chopel.

Drab prison drama of criminal Berry vs. ruthless guard Bohringer. Never finds the spark to catch fire, despite presence of Spanish actress Abril (who resembles Rosanna Arquette).▼

Ladies and Gentlemen, The Fabulous Stains (1981) C-87m. ** D: Lou Adler. Diane Lane, Ray Winstone, Peter Donat, David Clennon, John Lehne, Cynthia Sikes, Laura Dern, John (Fee) Waybill, Christine Lahti. Antisocial teenage girl decides to become a punk rock star and takes to the road. This unreleased major studio film, directed by music industry veteran Adler, has acquired a certain mystique, which evaporates immediately upon trying to watch it. It's strident and unappealing, despite good cast. Lahti shines in her two scenes. Members of Clash and The Sex Pistols appear as a British punk band.

Ladies and Gentlemen, the Rolling Stones (1975) C-90m. **½ D: Rollin Binzer. Disappointing documentary on the rock group's 1972 U.S. tour is unworthy of subject, but fans should take a look. Loss of quadrophonic sound on TV will hurt.

Ladies Club, The (1986) C-90m. ** D: A. K. Allen. Karen Austin, Diana Scarwid, Christine Belford, Bruce Davison, Shera Danese, Beverly Todd. Policewoman and rape victim team up with other angry women to teach rapists a lesson they won't forget. May offer distaff viewers some vicarious pleasure, but it's still not a very good film. Made in 1984.▼

Ladies Courageous (1944) 88m. ** D: John Rawlins. Loretta Young, Geraldine Fitzgerald, Diana Barrymore, Evelyn Ankers, Frank Jenks, Ruth Roman, Anne Gwynne, Philip Terry, Lois Collier, Kane Richmond. Well-meant idea fails because of hackneyed script and situations; saga of the WAFs during WW2 who played a vital part in air warfare.

Ladies in Love (1936) 97m. **½ D: Edward Griffith. Janet Gaynor, Loretta Young, Constance Bennett, Simone Simon, Don Ameche, Paul Lukas, Tyrone Power. Manhunting girls in Budapest stick together to find likely victims; large cast makes it entertaining; young Power seen to good advantage.

Ladies in Retirement (1941) 92m. *** D: Charles Vidor. Ida Lupino, Louis Hayward, Evelyn Keyes, Elsa Lanchester, Edith Barrett, Isobel Elsom, Emma Dunn. Static but well-made gothic melodrama about housekeeper Lupino's attempt to cover up murder in eccentric British household. Not as potent—or as shocking—as it must have been in 1941, but still good. Remade as THE MAD ROOM.

Ladies' Man (1931) 70m. *½ D: Lothar Mendes. William Powell, Kay Francis, Carole Lombard, Gilbert Emery, John Holland. Lifeless story of gigolo Powell becoming involved with society mother (Olive Tell) and daughter (Lombard), trying to find true happiness with Francis. Strange, downbeat film.

Ladies' Man (1947) 91m. ** D: William D. Russell. Eddie Bracken, Cass Daley, Virginia Welles, Spike Jones and His City Slickers. Brassy comedy of hayseed inheriting a fortune, coming to N.Y.C. to paint the town.

Ladies' Man, The (1961) C-106m. *** D: Jerry Lewis. Jerry Lewis, Helen Traubel, Kathleen Freeman, Hope Holiday, Pat Stanley, Jack Kruschen, Doodles Weaver, Harry James and His Band. Pretty funny comedy with Jerry the handyman in a girls' school run by Mrs. Wellenmelon (Traubel). Enormous set is the real star; Buddy Lester and George Raft have amusing cameo appearances.▼

Ladies of Leisure (1930) 98m. **½ D: Frank Capra. Barbara Stanwyck, Ralph Graves, Lowell Sherman, Marie Prevost, Nance O'Neill, George Fawcett. Stanwyck falls in love with playboy-artist Graves, but cannot shake her reputation as gold-digger. Creaky story made worthwhile by Stanwyck's believable performance and Capra's fluent filmmaking technique. Remade as WOMEN OF GLAMOR.

Ladies of the Big House (1931) 76m. **½ D: Marion Gering. Sylvia Sidney, Gene Raymond, Wynne Gibson, Purnell Pratt, Louise Beavers, Jane Darwell, Noel Francis. Sidney is framed and imprisoned; a tearful, well-acted prison drama.

Ladies of the Chorus (1949) 61m. ** D: Phil Karlson. Adele Jergens, Rand Brooks, Marilyn Monroe, Nana Bryant. Cheapie about mother/daughter burlesque chorines, and their differences when daughter Monroe seems headed for same romantic blunder that mom Jergens made. Worth a look for young MM in her first sizable role.

Ladies Should Listen (1934) 62m. ** D: Frank Tuttle. Cary Grant, Frances Drake, Edward Everett Horton, Nydia Westman, Ann Sheridan. Grant's life is manipulated by telephone operator Drake in flimsy comedy, no great shakes.

Ladies They Talk About (1933) 68m. **½ D: Howard Bretherton, William Keighley. Barbara Stanwyck, Preston S. Foster, Lyle Talbot, Dorothy Burgess, Maude Eburne, Lillian Roth, Ruth Donnelly. Stanwyck is terrific as usual in punchy pre-Code women's prison picture. More than a bit silly at times.

Ladies Who Do (1963-British) 85m. **½ D: C. M. Pennington-Richards. Peggy Mount, Robert Morley, Harry H. Corbett, Nigel Davenport, Carol White, Miriam Karlin. When a charwoman discovers that waste paper scraps contain valuable stock market tips, a mild satire on British financial world unfolds.

La Dolce Vita (1960-Italian) 175m. ***½

D: Federico Fellini. Marcello Mastroianni, Anita Ekberg, Anouk Aimée, Yvonne Furneaux, Magali Noel, Alain Cuny, Annibale Ninchi, Walter Santesso, Lex Barker, Jacques Sernas, Nadia Gray. Lengthy trend-setting film, not as ambiguous as other Fellini works—much more entertaining, with strong cast. Mastroianni stars as tabloid reporter who sees his life in shallow Rome society as worthless but can't change. Story and screenplay by Fellini, Ennio Flajano, and Tullio Pinelli, with Brunello Rondi. Piero Gherardi's costumes earned an Academy Award.▼

L'Adolescente (1979-French-German) C-90m. **½ D: Jeanne Moreau. Laetitia Chauveau, Simone Signoret, Edith Clever, Jacques Weber, Francis Huster. One-dimensional tale of anxious, confused Chauveau, just beginning her teen years at the outset of WW2. A heartfelt effort by Moreau that falls flat. Also known as THE ADOLESCENT.

Lady and the Bandit, The (1951) 79m. ** D: Ralph Murphy. Louis Hayward, Patricia Medina, Suzanne Dalbert, Tom Tully. Harmless costumer about career and love of highwayman Dick Turpin.

Lady and the Highwayman, The (1989) C-100m. TVM D: John Hough. Emma Samms, Oliver Reed, Claire Bloom, Christopher Cazenove, Lysette Anthony, Hugh Grant, Michael York, John Mills, Ian Bannen, Robert Morley, Bernard Miles, Gordon Jackson. Sumptuously filmed (and impressively cast) romantic swashbuckler set in 17th-century England, based on Barbara Cartland's bodice-ripper *Cupid Rides Pillion*. Average.

Lady and the Mob, The (1939) 66m. **½ D: Ben Stoloff. Fay Bainter, Lee Bowman, Ida Lupino, Henry Armetta. Bainter gives dignity to this mini-tale of eccentric rich lady involved with gangster mob.

Lady and the Monster, The (1944) 86m. **½ D: George Sherman. Vera Ralston, Erich von Stroheim, Richard Arlen, Sidney Blackmer. Pretty good chiller of mysterious brain taking over man's life. Remade as DONOVAN'S BRAIN.

Lady and the Outlaw, The SEE: Billy Two Hats

✓ **Lady and the Tramp** (1955) C-75m. ***½ D: Hamilton Luske, Clyde Geronimi, Wilfred Jackson. Voices of Peggy Lee, Barbara Luddy, Bill Thompson, Bill Baucon, Stan Freberg, Verna Felton, Alan Reed, George Givot, Dallas McKennon, Lee Millar. One of Walt Disney's most endearing animated features, based on Ward Greene's story about a rakish dog named Tramp who helps pedigreed canine named Lady out of a jam—and into a romance. Elements of adventure and drama are masterfully blended with comedy and music in this stylish film, the Disney studio's first in CinemaScope. Songs by Sonny Burke and Peggy Lee (who's the voice of Peg, Darling, Si and Am, the Siamese cats). ▼

Lady Be Good (1941) 111m. *** D: Norman Z. McLeod. Eleanor Powell, Ann Sothern, Robert Young, Lionel Barrymore, John Carroll, Red Skelton, Virginia O'Brien, Dan Dailey, Jimmy Dorsey and His Orchestra. Spunky musical of married songwriters Sothern and Young, with dancer Powell and comic Skelton along for good measure. Fine score: title tune, "Fascinating Rhythm," "You'll Never Know," Oscar-winning "Last Time I Saw Paris."

Lady Beware (1987) C-108m. **½ D: Karen Arthur. Diane Lane, Michael Woods, Cotter Smith, Viveca Lindfors, Peter Nevargic, Edward Penn, Tyra Ferrell. Lane's mildly kinky store-window displays arouse a married psychotic; he soon graduates from irritating phone calls and mail interception to breaking into her window-barred loft. Imperfect, but compelling, feminist exploitation film builds to a satisfying (and surprisingly nonviolent) conclusion; Lane's performance is uneven, but her rage convincing. Filmed and set in Pittsburgh.▼

Lady Blue (1985) C-100m. TVM D: Gary Nelson. Jamie Rose, Danny Aiello, Katy Jurado, Bibi Besch, Jim Brown, Tony Lo Bianco. This female "Dirty Harry" is one tough titian-haired cookie, a cop out to nail the deadly matriarch of the local cocaine trade. Popular, ultraviolent pilot for subsequent series. Average.

Ladybug Ladybug (1963) 84m. *** D: Frank Perry. Jane Connell, William Daniels, James Frawley, Richard Hamilton, Kathryn Hays, Jane Hoffman, Elena Karam, Judith Lowry, Nancy Marchand, Estelle Parsons, Miles Chapin, Marilyn Rogers, Alice Playten, Christopher Howard. Ambitious and provocative (if a bit too obvious) account of some rural schoolchildren and their reactions when a civil defense system warns of an impending nuclear attack. Screenplay by Eleanor Perry, and a followup of sorts to DAVID AND LISA. Based on an actual incident.

Lady by Choice (1934) 78m. **½ D: David Burton. Carole Lombard, May Robson, Roger Pryor, Walter Connolly, Arthur Hohl. Enjoyable follow-up to LADY FOR A DAY; dancer Lombard takes in scraggly Robson, makes her proper lady.

Lady Caroline Lamb (1972-British) C-118m. BOMB D: Robert Bolt. Sarah Miles, Jon Finch, Richard Chamberlain, John Mills, Margaret Leighton, Ralph Richardson, Laurence Olivier. Wretched filmization of famous story; wife of English politician scandalizes everyone by her open affair with Lord Byron. Bolt's banal script is often unintentionally funny.▼

Lady Chatterley's Lover (1981-French-British) **C-105m.** BOMB D: Just Jaeckin. Sylvia Kristel, Nicholas Clay, Shane Briant, Ann Mitchell, Elizabeth Spriggs, Peter Bennett. Dull, cheap version of the D. H. Lawrence classic, with Kristel as the lady and Clay as the lover. Kristel is beautiful, but still cannot act. From the director of EMMANUELLE. Previously filmed in France in 1955.▼

Lady Confesses, The (1945) **66m.** *½ D: Sam Newfield. Mary Beth Hughes, Hugh Beaumont, Edmund McDonald, Claudia Drake, Emmett Vogan. Quickie independent flick enhanced by Hughes in title role as woman willing to take murder rap to protect boyfriend.▼

Lady Consents, The (1936) **75m.** **½ D: Stephen Roberts. Ann Harding, Herbert Marshall, Margaret Lindsay, Walter Abel. Pat triangle with married Marshall discovering that he still loves his ex-wife.

Lady Dances, The SEE: **Merry Widow, The** (1934)▼

Lady Doctor (1956-Italian) **90m.** **½ D: Camillo Mastrocinque. Abbe Lane, Vittorio De Sica, Toto, Titina De Filippo, German Cobos, Teddy Reno. Pungent nonsense as Toto and De Sica try to con doctor Lane out of a fortune hidden in her house.

Lady Dracula (1973) **C-80m.** BOMB D: Richard Blackburn. Cheryl Smith, Lesley Gilb, William Whitton, Richard Blackburn. Perfectly awful low-budgeter about a lady vampire with lesbian tendencies. Bring back Gloria Holden! Also known as LEGENDARY CURSE OF LEMORA and LEMORA, THE LADY DRACULA.

Lady Eve, The (1941) **94m.** ***½ D: Preston Sturges. Barbara Stanwyck, Henry Fonda, Charles Coburn, Eugene Pallette, William Demarest, Eric Blore, Melville Cooper. Stanwyck is a con artist who sets her eyes on wealthy Fonda—the dolt to end all dolts, to whom "snakes are my life." Sometimes silly and strident, this film grows funnier with each viewing—thanks to Sturges's script, breathless pace, and two incomparable stars. Remade as THE BIRDS AND THE BEES.▼

Lady for a Day (1933) **88m.** **** D: Frank Capra. Warren William, May Robson, Guy Kibbee, Glenda Farrell, Jean Parker, Walter Connolly, Ned Sparks, Nat Pendleton. Wonderful Damon Runyon fable of seedy apple vendor Robson transformed into perfect lady by softhearted racketeer William. Robert Riskin adapted Runyon's story "Madame La Gimp." Sequel: LADY BY CHOICE. Remade by Capra as POCKETFUL OF MIRACLES.

Lady for a Night (1941) **87m.** ** D: Leigh Jason. Joan Blondell, John Wayne, Ray Middleton, Philip Merivale, Blanche Yurka, Edith Barrett. Plodding costume drama of woman gambling-boat owner marrying wealthy man for position, then implicated in murder. Good cast seems out of place.▼

Lady Forgets, The (1989) **C-100m.** TVM D: Bradford May. Donna Mills, Greg Evigan, Andrew Robinson, Roy Dotrice. Mills plays a double amnesia victim accused of a murder she cannot recall in this so-so adaptation of Cornell Woolrich's novel *The Black Curtain*. Average.

Lady Frankenstein (1971-Italian) **C-84m.** BOMB D: Mel Welles. Joseph Cotten, Mickey Hargitay, Sarah Bey, Paul Muller, Paul Whiteman. Poor horror entry with Cotten a tired, ill-fated Baron; his daughter (Bey) takes up where he leaves off in the monster-making department.▼

Lady from Cheyenne (1941) **87m.** **½ D: Frank Lloyd. Loretta Young, Robert Preston, Edward Arnold, Frank Craven, Gladys George. Average fare of schoolteacher Young (in 1869 Wyoming) striking a blow for women's rights about a century too early, as she fights for the opportunity to sit on a jury. Good supporting cast helps.

Lady from Chungking (1942) **66m.** ** D: William Nigh. Anna May Wong, Harold Huber, Mae Clarke, Rick Vallin, Paul Bryar. Middling account of Wong heading band of Chinese partisans against Japanese during WW2.

Lady from Louisiana (1941) **82m.** **½ D: Bernard Vorhaus. John Wayne, Ona Munson, Ray Middleton, Henry Stephenson, Helen Westley, Jack Pennick. Wayne and Munson fall in love, then discover they're on opposite sides of gambling controversy; so-so period-piece.▼

Lady from Shanghai, The (1948) **87m.** *** D: Orson Welles. Rita Hayworth, Orson Welles, Everett Sloane, Glenn Anders, Ted de Corsia, Gus Schilling. The camera's the star of this Welles thriller, with the cast incidental in bizarre murder-mystery plot; hall of mirrors climax is riveting.▼

Lady from Texas, The (1951) **C-77m.** ** D: Joseph Pevney. Howard Duff, Mona Freeman, Josephine Hull, Gene Lockhart, Craig Stevens. Strange minor film of eccentric old lady Hull; Duff and Freeman come to her rescue.

Lady from Yesterday, The (1985) **C-100m.** TVM D: Robert Day. Wayne Rogers, Bonnie Bedelia, Pat Hingle, Barrie Youngfellow, Blue Deckert, Bryan Price, Tina Chen. Young Vietnamese woman turns up—son in tow—and turns the life of a married executive with whom she had a long-ago affair into turmoil. Average.▼

Lady Gambles, The (1949) **99m.** *** D: Michael Gordon. Barbara Stanwyck, Robert Preston, Stephen McNally, Edith Barrett, Anthony (Tony) Curtis. Dynamic acting by Stanwyck as compulsive gambler buoys this bland tale of a woman who almost wrecks her marriage.

Lady Godiva (1955) **C-89m.** ** D: Arthur Lubin. Maureen O'Hara, George Nader, Victor McLaglen, Torin Thatcher, Robert Warwick. Cardboard costumer involving famed lady and her horseback ride set in Middle Ages England . . . and what a dull ride! Look for Clint Eastwood, billed as the "First Saxon."

Lady Godiva Rides Again (1951-British) **90m.** ** D: Frank Launder. Pauline Stroud, Stanley Holloway, Diana Dors, Alastair Sim, George Cole, Dennis Price, John McCallum. Intriguing cast keeps one watching this OK comedy about a simple young lass who wins a beauty contest and is thereafter exposed to the seamy side of glamour. Joan Collins' film debut, as one of the other contestants.

Lady Grey (1980) **C-100m.** BOMB D: Worth Keeter. Ginger Alden, David Allen Coe, Paul Ott, Herman Bloodsworth, Ed Grady, Paula Baldwin. Low-grade drama chronicling the trials of aspiring country singer played by Elvis Presley's last girlfriend. Shot in North Carolina; an Earl Owensby production.▼

Lady Hamilton SEE: **That Hamilton Woman**▼

Lady Has Plans, The (1942) **77m.** ** D: Sidney Lanfield. Paulette Goddard, Ray Milland, Roland Young, Albert Dekker, Margaret Hayes, Cecil Kellaway. Jumbled spy comedy with innocent Goddard suspected of being agent and Milland tailing her in Lisbon.

Ladyhawke (1985) **C-124m.** *** D: Richard Donner. Matthew Broderick, Rutger Hauer, Michelle Pfeiffer, Leo McKern, John Wood, Ken Hutchison, Alfred Molina. Overlong but generally entertaining medieval fantasy adventure about star-crossed lovers caught in an evil spell—and a young thief who becomes their unlikely ally. Hauer and Pfeiffer are perfectly cast as stalwart hero and heroine, but Broderick's manner and dialogue seem better suited to a Woody Allen movie! Thunderous music by Andrew Powell.▼

Lady Ice (1973) **C-93m.** ** D: Tom Gries. Donald Sutherland, Jennifer O'Neill, Robert Duvall, Patrick Magee, Eric Braeden, Jon Cypher. Dull caper film pairs insurance investigator Sutherland and wealthy O'Neill, whose father is a major "fence" for stolen jewels. Good cast wasted.▼

✓ **Lady in a Cage** (1964) **93m.** **½ D: Walter Grauman. Olivia de Havilland, Ann Sothern, Jeff Corey, James Caan, Rafael Campos, Scatman Crothers. Rich widow de Havilland is trapped in her mansion's elevator, then taunted by a trio of hoodlums. Serious, well-acted thriller.▼

Lady in a Jam (1942) **78m.** **½ D: Gregory La Cava. Irene Dunne, Patric Knowles, Ralph Bellamy, Eugene Pallette, Queenie Vassar, Jane Garland. Thirties-type screwball comedy doesn't really hit bull's-eye, with wacky Dunne convincing psychiatrist Knowles to marry her to cure her ills.

Lady in Cement (1968) **C-93m.** ** D: Gordon Douglas. Frank Sinatra, Raquel Welch, Dan Blocker, Richard Conte, Martin Gabel, Lainie Kazan, Richard Deacon, Joe E. Lewis. Sequel to TONY ROME finds Sinatra discovering nude corpse with feet encased in cement. Typical private-eye hokum, with heavy doses of violence, leering sex.▼

Lady in Distress (1939-British) **76m.** *** D: Herbert Mason. Paul Lukas, Sally Gray, Michael Redgrave, Patricia Roc, Hartley Power. Redgrave falls for wife of jealous magician after witnessing what looked like her murder. Originally titled A WINDOW IN LONDON.▼

Lady in Question, The (1940) **81m.** **½ D: Charles Vidor. Brian Aherne, Rita Hayworth, Glenn Ford, Irene Rich, George Coulouris, Lloyd Corrigan. Aherne plays a juror interested in defendant Hayworth. He manages to save her, but later falls prey to jealousy. Varies awkwardly from comedy to drama.▼

Lady in Red, The (1979) **C-93m.** **½ D: Lewis Teague. Pamela Sue Martin, Robert Conrad, Louise Fletcher, Robert Hogan, Laurie Heineman, Glenn Withrow, Christopher Lloyd, Dick Miller. Martin suffers a life on the lam, before and after her period of notoriety as girlfriend of John Dillinger (Conrad). Lurid, low-budget retread of familiar material is handled with surprising verve. A Roger Corman production; screenplay by John Sayles. Robert Forster appears uncredited in key supporting role. Retitled GUNS, SIN AND BATHTUB GIN.▼

Lady in the Car with Glasses and a Gun, The (1970-French) **C-105m.** **½ D: Anatole Litvak. Samantha Eggar, Oliver Reed, John McEnery, Stephane Audran, Billie Dixon. Eggar is best thing about otherwise unexceptional film. Psychological thriller about attempt to drive young woman crazy is only occasionally interesting.

Lady in the Corner (1989) **C-100m.** TVM D: Peter Levin. Loretta Young, Brian Keith, Lindsay Frost, Bruce Davison, Christopher Neame, Roscoe Lee Browne. Young's the sole focus here as the editor of a classy fashion magazine who finds herself in the middle of a takeover bid that'll probably cost her her job. The lady still has charm, flair, and her heyday oomph, but this feature plays like an expansion of the half-hour dramas she did on her '50s and '60s TV series. Average.

Lady in the Dark (1944) **C-100m.** **½ D: Mitchell Leisen. Ginger Rogers, Ray

Milland, Jon Hall, Warner Baxter, Barry Sullivan, Gail Russell, Mischa Auer. Lavish version of Moss Hart show (minus most Kurt Weill-Ira Gershwin songs) about career woman who undergoes psychoanalysis to find root of her problems. Intriguing but ultimately ponderous.

Lady in the Iron Mask (1952) C-78m. ** D: Ralph Murphy. Louis Hayward, Patricia Medina, Alan Hale, John Sutton. Variation of Dumas tale, with Three Musketeers still about; moderate costumer.

Lady in the Lake (1946) 103m. **½ D: Robert Montgomery. Robert Montgomery, Audrey Totter, Lloyd Nolan, Tom Tully, Leon Ames, Jayne Meadows. Raymond Chandler whodunit has novelty of camera taking first-person point of view of detective Philip Marlowe (Montgomery); unfortunately, confusing plot is presented in more prosaic (and dated) manner.

Lady in the Morgue (1938) 67m. ** D: Otis Garrett. Preston Foster, Patricia Ellis, Frank Jenks, Barbara Pepper. When a girl's body is stolen from city morgue, law enforcers set out to solve snowballing mystery; acceptable programmer.

Lady in White (1988) C-112m. *** D: Frank LaLoggia. Lukas Haas, Len Cariou, Alex Rocco, Katherine Helmond, Jason Presson, Jared Rushton, Renata Vanni, Angelo Bertolini. Sleeper film combines 1960s nostalgia with supernatural horror in original fashion. Haas is an inquisitive youngster who becomes involved with ghosts in a mystery story about an unsolved murder and the legendary Lady in White (Helmond) who resides in a spooky house nearby. Villain's identity is a bit too easy to guess, but there are plenty of chills and great period atmosphere along the way.▼

Lady Is Willing, The (1942) 92m. *** D: Mitchell Leisen. Marlene Dietrich, Fred MacMurray, Aline MacMahon, Arline Judge, Stanley Ridges, Roger Clark. Agreeable comedy; glamorous Dietrich wants to adopt a baby, so she marries pediatrician MacMurray. Dramatic segment near the end spoils lively mood.

Lady Jane (1985-British) C-142m. *** D: Trevor Nunn. Helena Bonham Carter, Cary Elwes, John Wood, Michael Hordern, Jill Bennett, Jane Lapotaire, Sara Kestelman, Patrick Stewart, Warren Saire, Joss Ackland, Ian Hogg, Richard Johnson. Absorbing historical drama about the machinations that put a sixteen-year-old girl on the throne of England for just nine days. Exquisite looking, well-acted, just a trifle slow at times. Same story told before in a 1936 film, TUDOR ROSE.▼

Lady Killer (1933) 74m. *** D: Roy Del Ruth. James Cagney, Mae Clarke, Leslie Fenton, Margaret Lindsay, Henry O'Neill, Raymond Hatton, George Chandler. Vintage Cagney, with tangy tale of mobster becoming Hollywood actor, torn between two professions; Cagney repeats his Clarke slapfest.

Ladykillers, The (1955-British) C-90m. ***½ D: Alexander Mackendrick. Alec Guinness, Katie Johnson, Cecil Parker, Herbert Lom, Peter Sellers, Danny Green, Frankie Howerd. Droll black comedy of not-so-bright crooks involved with seemingly harmless old lady. Guinness scores again (even his *teeth* are funny) with topnotch supporting cast in this little Ealing Studios gem, written by William Rose. Original British running time: 97m.▼

Ladykillers (1988) C-100m. TVM D: Robert Lewis. Marilu Henner, Susan Blakely, Lesley-Anne Down, Thomas Calabro, William Lucking. Lady cop hunts down the killer of male strippers at a steamy disco. How's that for turning the tables? Below average.

Lady L (1966-British) C-107m. **½ D: Peter Ustinov. Sophia Loren, Paul Newman, David Niven, Claude Dauphin, Philippe Noiret, Michel Piccoli. Stars and sets are elegant, but this wacky comedy set in early 20th-century London and Paris fizzles, despite Ustinov's writing, directing, and cameo appearance.

Lady Liberty (1972-Italian) C-95m. *½ D: Mario Monicelli. Sophia Loren, William Devane, Luigi Proietti, Beeson Carroll. Dull comedy of immigrant bride-to-be who tries to get an enormous sausage through U.S. customs. Watch for Warhol's Candy Darling in transvestite cameo; originally titled MORTADELLA.

Lady Luck (1946) 97m. *** D: Edwin L. Marin. Robert Young, Barbara Hale, Frank Morgan, James Gleason. Hale marries gambler Young with hopes of reforming him but meets more problems than she bargained for.

Lady Mobster (1988) C-100m. TVM D: John Llewellyn Moxey. Susan Lucci, Michael Nader, Roscoe Born, Thom Brey, Al Ruscio, Joseph Wiseman. A brilliant dish becomes a mouthpiece for the mob, trying to legitimize the business of the aging godfather who has adopted her. An obvious attempt to capitalize on the success of Lucci's 1986 telefilm MAFIA PRINCESS. Below average.

Lady of Burlesque (1943) 91m. *** D: William Wellman. Barbara Stanwyck, Michael O'Shea, J. Edward Bromberg, Iris Adrian, Marion Martin, Pinky Lee, Frank Conroy, Gloria Dickson. Stanwyck attempts to uncover—no pun intended—killer of strippers in this amusing adaptation of Gypsy Rose Lee's *G-String Murders.*▼

Lady of Secrets (1936) 73m. **½ D: Marion Gering. Ruth Chatterton, Otto Kruger, Lionel Atwill, Marian Marsh, Lloyd Nolan, Robert Allen. Smooth but soapy story of woman whose one unhappy love affair has made her live a life of seclusion. Good cast makes standard film worth seeing.

Lady of the House (1978) C-100m. TVM D: Ralph Nelson, Vincent Sherman. Dyan Cannon, Armand Assante, Zohra Lampert, Susan Tyrrell, Colleen Camp, Christopher Norris, Melvin Belli. Cannon gives a colorful performance as Sally Stanford, flamboyant San Francisco madam of the late 30s who rose to power and respectability and became mayor of Sausalito, California, in '76. Script by Ron Koslow. Above average.▼

Lady of the Tropics (1939) 92m. ** D: Jack Conway. Hedy Lamarr, Robert Taylor, Joseph Schildkraut, Frederick Worlock, Natalie Moorhead. Sad love affair between playboy Taylor and halfbreed Lamarr in exotic setting; slow-moving.

Lady of Vengeance (1957-British) 73m. ** D: Burt Balaban. Dennis O'Keefe, Ann Sears, Patrick Barr, Vernon Greeves. Tedious account of man hiring killer to avenge a girl's death, becoming embroiled in further murder.

Lady on a Train (1945) 93m. *** D: Charles David. Deanna Durbin, Ralph Bellamy, Edward Everett Horton, George Coulouris, Allen Jenkins, David Bruce, Patricia Morison, Dan Duryea, William Frawley. Excellent comedy/murder-mystery with Deanna witnessing a murder, then getting involved with nutty family of the deceased tycoon. You'll never guess killer's identity in neatly plotted yarn which even allows Deanna to sing a few tunes. Based on a Leslie Charteris story.

Lady on the Bus (1978-Brazilian) C-102m. *½ D: Neville D'Almeida. Sonia Braga, Nuno Leal Maia, Paulo Cesar Pereio, Jorge Doria, Yara Amaral, Claudio Marzo. Braga, the least likely of all actresses to project frigidity, is unresponsive on her wedding night—but wait! Soon she begins sampling other men, and sampling, and sampling. . . . Follow-up to DONA FLOR AND HER TWO HUSBANDS has even more sex but far less wit and charm. A dull ride.▼

Lady Pays Off, The (1951) 80m. **½ D: Douglas Sirk. Linda Darnell, Stephen McNally, Gigi Perreau, Virginia Field. Fanciful drama of schoolteacher Darnell who must pay off gambling debts in Reno by tutoring casino owner's daughter.

Lady Possessed (1952-British) 87m. ** D: William Spier, Roy Kellino. James Mason, June Havoc, Pamela Kellino, Fay Compton, Odette Myrtil. Bizarre film of ill woman thinking she is controlled by will of Mason's dead wife.

Lady Says No, The (1951) 80m. ** D: Frank Ross. David Niven, Joan Caulfield, Lenore Lonergan, James Robertson Justice. Lightweight comedy of fickle Caulfield, who won't decide if marriage is for her.

Lady Scarface (1941) 69m. ** D: Frank Woodruff. Dennis O'Keefe, Judith Anderson, Frances Neal, Mildred Coles, Eric Blore, Marc Lawrence. Anderson tries to elevate this episodic yarn of police hunting for dangerous gunwoman and her gang.▼

Lady's from Kentucky, The (1939) 67m. **½ D: Alexander Hall. George Raft, Ellen Drew, Hugh Herbert, ZaSu Pitts, Louise Beavers, Stanley Andrews. Regardless of title, Raft's horse takes precedence over his lady in this usual but well-done horse-racing saga.

Lady Sings the Blues (1972) C-144m. **½ D: Sidney J. Furie. Diana Ross, Billy Dee Williams, Richard Pryor, James Callahan, Paul Hampton, Sid Melton. Black version of Hollywood cliché-biography, sparked by superb performance by Ross (in her acting debut) as Billie Holiday, legendary jazz singer whose life was ruined by drug addiction. Valueless as biography, but OK as soap opera, with excellent support from Pryor as "Piano Man."▼

Lady's Morals, A (1930) 75m. ** D: Sidney Franklin. Grace Moore, Reginald Denny, Wallace Beery, Jobyna Howland. First attempt to make star of opera singer Moore doesn't click. She plays Jenny Lind, who learns value of love from devoted Denny.

Lady Surrenders, A SEE: **Love Story** (1944)

Lady Takes a Chance, A (1943) 86m. *** D: William A. Seiter. Jean Arthur, John Wayne, Charles Winninger, Phil Silvers, Mary Field, Don Costello. Wayne and Arthur make fine comedy team as burly rodeo star and wide-eyed city girl who falls for him; Silvers adds zip as bus-tour guide.▼

Lady Takes a Flyer, The (1958) C-94m. **½ D: Jack Arnold. Lana Turner, Jeff Chandler, Richard Denning, Andra Martin. Different-type Turner fare. Lana is lady flier who marries pilot Chandler, each finds it hard to settle down to married life.

Lady Takes a Sailor, The (1949) 99m. ** D: Michael Curtiz. Jane Wyman, Dennis Morgan, Eve Arden, Robert Douglas, Allyn Joslyn. Featherweight comedy fully described by title tag.

Lady Vanishes, The (1938-British) 97m. **** D: Alfred Hitchcock. Margaret Lockwood, Michael Redgrave, Paul Lukas, Dame May Whitty, Googie Withers, Cecil Parker, Linden Travers, Catherine Lacey. An old woman's disappearance during a train ride leads baffled young woman into a dizzying web of intrigue. Delicious mystery-comedy; Hitchcock at his best, with a witty script by Frank Launder and Sidney Gilliat, and wonderful contribution by Naunton Wayne and Basil Radford, who scored such a hit as a pair of twits that they repeated those roles in several other films! Based on Ethel Lina White's novel *The Wheel Spins*. Remade in 1979.▼

Lady Vanishes, The (1979-British) **C-99m.** *½ D: Anthony Page. Elliott Gould, Cybill Shepherd, Angela Lansbury, Herbert Lom, Arthur Lowe, Ian Carmichael. Remake of Hitchcock classic retains basic story but is sabotaged by the obnoxious characterizations of its "screwball" stars, Gould and Shepherd. Screenplay by George Axelrod.▼

Lady Wants Mink, The (1953) **C-92m.** *** D: William A. Seiter. Eve Arden, Ruth Hussey, Dennis O'Keefe, William Demarest, Gene Lockhart. Most diverting little film of wife Hussey breeding mink to get the coat she's always wanted.

Lady with a Dog (1959-Russian) **90m.** **½ D: Josif Heifits. Iya Savvina, Alexei Batalov, Ala Chostakova, N. Alisova. Intelligent tale of adulterous love, sensibly handled, with no contrived ending.

Lady with a Lamp, The (1951-British) **112m.** *** D: Herbert Wilcox. Anna Neagle, Michael Wilding, Felix Aylmer, Maureen Pryor, Gladys Young, Julian D'Albie. Methodical recreation of 19th century nurse-crusader Florence Nightingale, tastefully enacted by Neagle.

Lady Without Passport, A (1950) **72m.** **½ D: Joseph H. Lewis. Hedy Lamarr, John Hodiak, James Craig, George Macready. Turgid melodrama as Lamarr seeks to leave Havana, former romantic and business associations behind her.

Lady with Red Hair, The (1940) **81m.** **½ D: Curtis Bernhardt. Miriam Hopkins, Claude Rains, Richard Ainley, Laura Hope Crews, Helen Westley, John Litel, Victor Jory. Breathless pace, likable cast make up for silliness in story of actress Mrs. Leslie Carter and her colorful mentor David Belasco. Look fast for young Cornel Wilde at boarding house.

Lafayette (1963-French) **C-110m.** ** D: Jean Dreville. Jack Hawkins, Orson Welles, Howard St. John, Edmund Purdom, Vittorio De Sica, Michel Le Royer. Overblown, badly scripted costumer of famed 18th-century Frenchman, resulting in episodic minor spectacle film.

Lafayette Escadrille (1958) **93m.** **½ D: William Wellman. Tab Hunter, Etchika Choureau, Marcel Dalio, David Janssen, Clint Eastwood, Tom Laughlin. Attempted epic of famous French flying legion of WW1 becomes pat actioner with typical romantic interlude, featuring wholesome Hunter.

La Femme Infidele (1969-French-Italian) **C-98m.** ***½ D: Claude Chabrol. Stephane Audran, Michel Bouquet, Maurice Ronet, Stephen Di Napolo, Michel Duchaussoy. Atmospheric drama about wife who acquires more respect for her husband when he murders her lover; Audran and Bouquet are fine in yet another memorable film from director Chabrol. Also known as UNFAITHFUL WIFE.

L'Age d'Or (1930-French) **63m.** **** D: Luis Buñuel. Gaston Modot, Lya Lys, Max Ernst, Pierre Prevert. Bishops turn into skeletons and the cow wanders into the bedroom in Buñuel's first feature, a surrealistic masterpiece coscripted by Salvadore Dali. Right-wing agitators caused a riot at the film's first (and for a long time, only) public screening; its anticlericalism put it into the "banned film" category for decades. Still has the power to delight, if no longer shock.▼

La Grande Bouffe (1973-French-Italian) **C-125m.** **½ D: Marco Ferreri. Marcello Mastroianni, Ugo Tognazzi, Michel Piccoli, Philippe Noiret, Andrea Ferreol. Four bored middle-aged men decide to commit group suicide by eating themselves to death. Outrageous idea, but overbaked—no pun intended—and excessively, graphically gross.

La Grande Bourgeoise (1974-Italian) **C-115m.** **½ D: Mauro Bolognini. Catherine Deneuve, Giancarlo Giannini, Fernando Rey, Tina Aumont, Paolo Bonicelli. Strong cast adds some punch to true story about Giannini's murder of sister Deneuve's loutish husband and the political storm it generates. Stylish but not terribly compelling.▼

La Gran Fiesta (1987-Puerto Rican) **C-101m.** **½ D: Marcos Zurinaga. Daniel Lugo, Miguelangel Suarez, Luis Prendes, Cordelia Gonzalez, Laura Delano, Raul Julia, E.G. Marshall, Julian Pastor. Sometimes low-keyed and other times melodramatic account of intrigue—both personal and political—among the various folk who attend the final grand ball in the Casino at Old San Juan on the eve of its takeover by the U.S. Armed Forces in 1942. Interesting subject but it misses the mark.

La Guerre Est Finie (1966-French-Swedish) **121m.** ***½ D: Alain Resnais. Yves Montand, Ingrid Thulin, Genevieve Bujold, Jean Daste, Michel Piccoli. Aging, tired leftist Montand travels from Spain to Paris, reports to his political associates, and visits mistress Thulin. Complex, emotionally powerful drama, with striking direction, performances.

Laguna Heat (1987) **C-115m.** TVM D: Simon Langton. Harry Hamlin, Jason Robards, Rip Torn, Catherine Hicks, Anne Francis, James Gammon. Atmospheric private-eye drama, cowritten by Pete Hamill, with Hamlin a mercurial detective returning home to Laguna to "find himself," after his partner was bumped off . . . only to discover himself neck-deep in a bizarre series of murders. Based on T. Jefferson Parker's best-selling thriller. Made for cable. Average.▼

Lair of the White Worm, The (1988-British) **C-94m.** **½ D: Ken Russell.

Amanda Donohoe, Hugh Grant, Catherine Oxenberg, Peter Capaldi, Sammi Davis, Stratford Johns, Paul Brooke. Typically outrageous Ken Russell farce, adapted from a novel by Bram Stoker (of *Dracula* fame). Strange doings begin when an archeologist unearths a huge wormlike skull on the grounds of an estate; they get curioser and curioser when it turns out worms are the stuff of legend in that area. Bizarre, campy, and altogether outlandish.▼

Lake Placid Serenade (1944) 85m. ** D: Steve Sekely. Vera Hruba Ralston, Robert Livingston, Vera Vague (Barbara Jo Allen), Eugene Pallette, Stephanie Bachelor, Walter Catlett, John Litel; guest star, Roy Rogers. Flimsy musical romance about an ice skater, played by real-life skating queen Ralston. Supporting cast does its best.

La Lectrice (1988-French) C-98m. *** D: Michel Deville. Miou-Miou, Christian Ruché, Sylvie Laporte, Michel Raskine, Brigitte Catillion, Régis Royer, Maria Casarés, Pierre Dux. Fascinating, multi-textured account of Miou-Miou reading a book aloud to her boyfriend and imagining herself the heroine in the story: a professional reader who becomes involved in the lives of her various clients. Scripted by Deville and his wife, Rosalinde.▼

La Maternelle (1932-French) 86m. *** D: JeanBenoit-Levy. Madeleine Renaud, Alice Tissot, Paulette Elambert, Sylvette Fillacier, Mady Berri, Henri Debain. Insightful, compassionate drama about the plight of slum children in Montmartre day nursery. The focus is on little Elambert's pain, confusion, and attachment to nurse Renaud. Its observations about the perceptions of children have dated not one bit.

Lambada (1990) C-98m. BOMB D: Joel Silberg. J. Eddie Peck, Melora Hardin, Shabba-Doo, Ricky Paull Goldin, Basil Hoffman, Dennis Burkley. By day, Peck teaches math to snots in a posh Beverly Hills high school; by night, he tries to "reach" barrio kids in an East L.A. lambada nightclub. In other words, it's STAND AND DELIVER with better buns; avoid at all costs unless you never miss a Shabba-Doo movie.▼

Lancer Spy (1937) 84m. *** D: Gregory Ratoff. Dolores Del Rio, George Sanders, Peter Lorre, Joseph Schildkraut, Virginia Field, Sig Ruman, Fritz Feld. Sanders disguises himself as German officer to get information in this taut thriller; Del Rio has to choose between love and loyalty to her country.

Land Before Time, The (1988) C-69m. **½ D: Don Bluth. Voices of Pat Hingle, Gabriel Damon, Helen Shaver, Candice Houston, Judith Barsi, Will Ryan, Burke Barnes. A young dinosaur is orphaned and must make his way to a valley green with vegetation where he and his tribe can sur-

vive. Along the way he meets other young friends of different dinosaur species, and they make the trek together. Enjoyable if leisurely paced (and plotted) cartoon feature for younger viewers. Biggest complaint: the muddy look of the colors.▼

Landlord, The (1970) C-113m. ***½ D: Hal Ashby. Beau Bridges, Pearl Bailey, Diana Sands, Louis Gossett, Lee Grant, Susan Anspach, Bob (Robert) Klein. Vibrant comedy-drama with Bridges as aimless rich-kid who buys Brooklyn tenement planning to renovate it for himself, changing plans when he meets tenants. Delightful comic touches combined with perceptive sidelights on black experience. Ashby's first film as director. TV version runs 104m.

Land of Fury SEE: **Seekers, The** (1954)

Land of No Return, The (1978) C-84m. BOMB D: Kent Bateman. Mel Torme, William Shatner, Donald Moffat. The only novelty of this dreary wilderness-survival opus is the (mis)casting of Torme as an animal trainer whose plane crashes in Utah. Filmed in 1975. Also know as SNOWMAN and CHALLENGE TO SURVIVE.

Land of the Minotaur (1976-U.S.-British) C-88m. *½ D: Costa Carayiannis. Donald Pleasence, Luan Peters, Peter Cushing, Nikos Verlekis, Costas Skouras. Tourists are kidnapped by Greek Minoan devil-worship cult, and a local priest tries to save them, in this draggy, uninteresting yarn. Also known as MINOTAUR. Released in England at 94m. as THE DEVIL'S MEN.▼

Land of the Pharaohs (1955) C-106m. **½ D: Howard Hawks. Jack Hawkins, Joan Collins, James Robertson Justice, Dewey Martin, Alexis Minotis, Sydney Chaplin. Talky, fruity spectacle about building of the Great Pyramid, filmed on an epic scale. Hawks claimed that neither he nor his writers (including William Faulkner and Harry Kurnitz) "knew how a pharaoh talked" . . . and it shows. Still worth catching for great surprise ending and now-campy villainy by Collins.

Land Raiders (1970) C-100m. ** D: Nathan Juran. Telly Savalas, George Maharis, Arlene Dahl, Janet Landgard, Jocelyn Lane, George Coulouris, Guy Rolfe. Even if you can accept Savalas and Maharis as brothers, this Western about family feuds amidst Indian attacks has little to offer.

Landru SEE: **Bluebeard** (1962)▼

Land That Time Forgot, The (1975-British) C-90m. **½ D: Kevin Connor. Doug McClure, John McEnery, Susan Penhaligon, Keith Barron, Anthony Ainley. Edgar Rice Burroughs' 1918 sci-fi novel about Germans and Americans in WW1 submarine discovering unknown land in South America is not bad as adventure yarn, but special effects (dinosaurs, volcanic eruption) are not convincing. Sequel: THE PEOPLE THAT TIME FORGOT.▼

Land Unknown, The (1957) 78m. ** D: Virgil Vogel. Jock Mahoney, Shawn Smith, Henry Brandon, Douglas Kennedy. Naval helicopter in Antarctica is forced down in lost valley of prehistoric animals. Monsters are clumsily done but film is OK.

Lanigan's Rabbi (1976) C-100m. TVM D: Lou Antonio. Art Carney, Stuart Margolin, Janet Margolin, Janis Paige, Lorraine Gary, Robert Reed. Mystery-comedy teams small town police chief with local rabbi to solve killing of woman whose body was found on front steps of synagogue. Carney at his best. Based on Harry Kemelman's best-selling *Friday the Rabbi Slept Late,* its subsequent TV title. Above average. Pilot for the TV series.

La Notte (1961-French-Italian) 120m. **½ D: Michelangelo Antonioni. Jeanne Moreau, Marcello Mastroianni, Monica Vitti, Bernhard Wicki. Moreau is bored and troubled by one-dimensional husband Mastroianni in this study of noncommunication. Moody, introverted, abstract—and superficial—filled with "empty, hopeless images." Also known as THE NIGHT.

La Nuit de Varennes (1982-Italian-French) C-133m. *** D: Ettore Scola. Marcello Mastroianni, Jean-Louis Barrault, Hanna Schygulla, Harvey Keitel, Jean-Claude Brialy. Witty historical fable allows such famous figures as Casanova and Thomas Paine to cross paths at the time of the French Revolution. Original French running time 150m.▼

La Parisienne (1958-French) C-85m. **½ D: Michel Boisrond. Brigitte Bardot, Charles Boyer, Henri Vidal, Andre Luguet, Nadia Gray. At times spicy account of plucky Bardot involved with visiting royalty, much to her diplomat father's dismay.

La Passante (1982-French-German) C-106m. *** D: Jacques Rouffio. Romy Schneider, Michel Piccoli, Wendelin Werner, Helmut Griem, Gerard Klein, Dominique Labourier, Mathieu Carriere, Maria Schell. Why does nonviolence advocate Piccoli kill a Paraguayan ambassador, an ex-Nazi living under an assumed name? Interesting drama is ambitious in scope, but could have been better. Schneider, in her final film, plays both Piccoli's wife and the woman who sheltered him as a boy.▼

La Pelle (1981-Italian-French) C-131m. *½ D: Liliana Cavani. Marcello Mastroianni, Burt Lancaster, Claudia Cardinale, Ken Marshall, Alexandra King, Carlo Giuffre. Distastefully bitter panorama of American troops in Naples after the Liberation, based on the memoirs of Curzio Malaparte (played here by Mastroianni). Overlong; poorly directed and scripted (by Cavani and Robert Katz). A disaster.

La Prisonniere (1969-French) 104m. **

D: Henri-Georges Clouzot. Laurent Terzieff, Bernard Fresson, Elsabeth Wiener, Dany Carrel, Dario Moreno, Daniel Riviere. From the director of DIABOLIQUE comes this obscure, confused study of woman obsessed with a photographer of sado-masochism. Strikingly photographed.

La Provinciale SEE: **Girl from Lorraine, The**

Larceny (1948) 89m. **½ D: George Sherman. John Payne, Joan Caulfield, Dan Duryea, Shelley Winters, Dorothy Hart. Slick but ordinary underworld tale, with roguish Payne deciding to help lovely Caulfield; Duryea is slimy villain.

Larceny, Inc. (1942) 95m. ***½ D: Lloyd Bacon. Edward G. Robinson, Jane Wyman, Broderick Crawford, Jack Carson, Anthony Quinn, Edward Brophy. Hilarious little comedy of ex-cons Robinson, Crawford, and Brophy using luggage store as front for shady activities; villain Quinn tries to horn in. Look for Jackie Gleason in a small role as a soda jerk.

L'Argent (1983-French-Swiss) C-90m. ***½ D: Robert Bresson. Christian Patey, Sylvie van den Elsen, Michel Briguet, Caroline Lang, Jeanne Aptekman. How the petty maneuverings of some upperclass boys and shopkeepers result in the ruin of working-man Patey: the rich lie, and get their workers to lie for them, but are aghast when the workers lie to them. Subtle, powerful film, simply and effectively directed by a master filmmaker; based on a Tolstoi short story.

La Ronde (1950-French) 97m. ***½ D: Max Ophuls. Anton Walbrook, Serge Reggiani, Simone Simon, Simone Signoret, Daniel Gelin, Danielle Darrieux, Fernand Gravet, Odette Joyeux, Jean-Louis Barrault, Isa Miranda, Gerard Philipe. Wise, witty account of various people having affairs, forming a chain that eventually comes full circle, all held together by sarcastic Walbrook. A film of style and charm, based on an Arthur Schnitzler play. Remade as CIRCLE OF LOVE.▼

Larry (1974) C-78m. TVM D: William A. Graham. Frederic Forrest, Tyne Daly, Michael McGuire, Robert Walden, Katherine Helmond, Ted Lange. Forrest gives a moving performance in this true story about a man, wrongly confined as a mental patient, released after 26 years to try and reestablish himself in the outside world. Script by David Seltzer. Above average.

Larsen, Wolf of the Seven Seas SEE: **Wolf Larsen** (1975)▼

La Salamandre (1971-Swiss) 125m. *** D: Alain Tanner. Bulle Ogier, Jean-Luc Bideau, Jacques Denis. Simple, funny examination of truth: journalist Bideau and writer Denis research facts behind the case of mysterious Ogier, accused by her uncle of attempted murder. Fine performances by the three leads.

Laserblast (1978) **C-90m.** **½ D: Michael Raye. Kim Milford, Cheryl Smith, Roddy McDowall, Ron Masak, Keenan Wynn, Dennis Burkley. Low-budget sci-fi with teenage Milford finding alien ray gun which enables him to become a creature who can destroy his enemies. David Allen's stop-motion effects are a highlight.▼

Lassie Come Home (1943) **C-88m.** *** D: Fred M. Wilcox. Roddy McDowall, Donald Crisp, Dame May Whitty, Edmund Gwenn, Nigel Bruce, Elsa Lanchester, Elizabeth Taylor. Winning, wonderful film of poor family forced to sell their beloved dog, who undertakes tortuous journey to return to them. Remade as GYPSY COLT and THE MAGIC OF LASSIE.▼

Lassiter (1984) **C-100m.** **½ D: Roger Young. Tom Selleck, Jane Seymour, Lauren Hutton, Bob Hoskins, Joe Regalbuto, Ed Lauter, Warren Clarke. A second-story man is shanghaied into doing espionage work in London on the eve of WW2. Stylish and nicely acted, but too plodding to overcome its basic problem of ordinariness. Selleck's second star vehicle is at least an improvement over his first (HIGH ROAD TO CHINA).▼

Last Adventure, The (1967-French) **C-102m.** **½ D: Robert Enrico. Alain Delon, Lino Ventura, Joanna Shimkus, Hans Meyer. Two adventurers and a beautiful woman go on a very engaging treasure hunt.

Last American Hero, The (1973) **C-100m.** *** D: Lamont Johnson. Jeff Bridges, Valerie Perrine, Geraldine Fitzgerald, Art Lund, Gary Busey, Ed Lauter, Ned Beatty. Unusual, engrossing saga of Junior Jackson, North Carolinan backwoods moonshiner and racing fanatic, pitting his ability against the System. Three-dimensional, believable characters enhance cynical point of view. Retitled HARD DRIVER.▼

Last American Virgin, The (1982) **C-90m.** **½ D: Boaz Davidson. Lawrence Monoson, Diane Franklin, Steve Antin, Joe Rubbo, Louisa Moritz. Formula teen comedy-drama (derived from one of Cannon's Israeli-made LEMON POPSICLE films) works thanks to attractive and talented young cast. Monoson has the title role, with pals Antin and Rubbo trying desperately to find a willing girlfriend. Moritz is very funny as the stereotyped Latin bombshell.▼

Last Angry Man, The (1959) **100m.** *** D: Daniel Mann. Paul Muni, David Wayne, Betsy Palmer, Luther Adler, Joby Baker, Joanna Moore, Godfrey Cambridge, Billy Dee Williams. Sentimental story of an old, dedicated family doctor in Brooklyn whose life is going to be portrayed on TV. Muni (in his last film) makes it worth seeing. Adapted by Gerald Green from his novel. Remade as a TVM in 1974.▼

Last Angry Man, The (1974) **C-78m.** TVM D: Jerrold Freedman. Pat Hingle, Lynn Carlin, Paul Jabara, Tracy Bogart, Sorrell Booke, Penny Santon, Ann Doran, Andrew Duggan. Hingle is irascible and concerned Jewish doctor in Brooklyn of 1936, the role played by Paul Muni in 1959. OK remake was likewise adapted by Gerald Green from his novel. Average.

Last Blitzkrieg, The (1958) **84m.** ** D: Arthur Dreifuss. Van Johnson, Kerwin Mathews, Dick York, Larry Storch. WW2 actioner trying to focus on German point of view.

Last Bridge, The (1957-Austrian) **90m.** ***½ D: Helmut Kautner. Maria Schell, Bernhard Wicki, Barbara Rutting, Carl Mohner. Schell gives well-modulated performance as German doctor captured by Yugoslavian partisans during WW2, first administering medical aid reluctantly, then realizing all people deserve equal attention.

Last Challenge, The (1967) **C-105m.** ** D: Richard Thorpe. Glenn Ford, Angie Dickinson, Chad Everett, Gary Merrill, Jack Elam, Delphi Lawrence, Royal Dano. Punk Everett is out to get Marshal Ford in well-cast but routine Western; Angie plays saloon-keeper, which makes one wonder why the two men don't just settle their problems over a drink.

Last Chance, The (1968-Italian) **C-91m.** ** D: Niny Rosati. Tab Hunter, Michael Rennie, Daniela Bianchi, Liz Barrett. American journalist Hunter is given valuable documents about an international crime syndicate and finds himself a hunted man. Listless thriller.

Last Chase, The (1981-Canadian) **C-101m.** *½ D: Martyn Burke. Lee Majors, Burgess Meredith, Chris Makepeace, Alexandra Stewart, Ben Gordon. Oil shortage causes the demise of auto travel during the 1980s; 20 years later, ex-race-car driver Majors reassembles his Porsche and becomes a "symbol of freedom" as he races across the country. Flimsy drama that reeks of Reaganomics.▼

Last Child, The (1971) **C-73m.** TVM D: John Llewellyn Moxey. Michael Cole, Janet Margolin, Van Heflin, Harry Guardino, Edward Asner, Kent Smith, Barbara Babcock. 1994: U.S. government forbids more than one child per family. The Millers (Cole & Margolin) seek escape from prison by running to Canada, pursued by authorities, finally aided by retired U.S. Senator (Heflin). Accent on drama, softpedaling aspects of totalitarianism, but action and performances (including Heflin's last) more than adequate. Above average.

Last Circus Show, The (1974-Italian) **C-91m.** ** D: Mario Garriazzo. James Whitmore, Lee J. Cobb, Cyril Cusack, Renato Cestie. Family-style tearjerker about a young boy who tries to reunite his parents, then falls deathly ill and begs to see a circus performance. Also known as THE BALLOON VENDOR.

Last Command, The (1928) 88m. **** D: Josef von Sternberg. Emil Jannings, Evelyn Brent, William Powell, Nicholas Soussanin, Michael Visaroff, Jack Raymond, Fritz Feld. Stunning silent drama of refugee Russian general Jannings, who is now reduced to working as a Hollywood extra—and destined to appear in a movie depicting the Russian revolution. A fascinating story laced with keen perceptions of life and work in Hollywood. Lajos Biros' story was based on an actual person; Jannings' gripping performance won him an Oscar (shared for his work in THE WAY OF ALL FLESH).▼

Last Command, The (1955) C-110m. **½ D: Frank Lloyd. Sterling Hayden, Anna Maria Alberghetti, Richard Carlson, Ernest Borgnine, J. Carrol Naish, Virginia Grey, Ben Cooper. Elaborate, sweeping account of the battle of the Alamo, hampered by tedious script.▼

Last Cry for Help, A (1979) C-100m. TVM D: Hal Sitowitz. Linda Purl, Shirley Jones, Tony LoBianco, Murray Hamilton, Grant Goodeve. High school coed withdraws into world of her own, fearing she is not living up to parents' expectations, and attempts suicide. Average.▼

Last Day, The (1975) C-100m. TVM D: Vincent McEveety. Richard Widmark, Christopher Connelly, Robert Conrad, Gene Evans, Richard Jaeckel, Tim Matheson, Barbara Rush, Tom Skerritt, Loretta Swit. Western about retired gunman (Widmark) forced to defend his town when the Dalton gang rides in for its final bank heist. Straightforward hoss-opera gussied up with pseudo-documentary touch and narration by Harry Morgan. Above average.

Last Day of the War, The (1969) C-96m. ** D: Juan Antonio Bardem. George Maharis, Maria Perschy, James Philbrook, Gerard Herter. Germans and Americans race to find noted German scientist during waning days of WW2. Low-grade drama filmed in Spain.▼

Last Days of Dolwyn, The (1949-British) 95m. **½ D: Emlyn Williams. Edith Evans, Emlyn Williams, Richard Burton, Anthony James, Hugh Griffith. A dowager is called upon for help when her Welsh village is slated for extinction as part of a reservoir project; well acted but somewhat aloof. Written by actor-director Williams; Burton's first film. Also known as WOMAN OF DOLWYN.

Last Days of Frank and Jesse James, The (1986) C-100m. TVM D: William A. Graham. Johnny Cash, Kris Kristofferson, Willie Nelson, Ed Bruce, David Allan Coe, Gail Youngs, June Carter Cash. Flavorful good buddy "home movie" version of the oft-told legend with three recording superstars uniting with a number of their pals for this made-in-and-around Nashville Western. Oddly, Johnny Cash's wife, June, plays his and Kristofferson's mother! Willie steals it in what amounts to a cameo as colorful Confederate General Jo Shelby. Average.▼

Last Days of Man on Earth, The (1973-British) C-78m. *½ D: Robert Fuest. Jon Finch, Jenny Runacre, Sterling Hayden, Patrick Magee, Hugh Griffith, Harry Andrews. Muddled sci-fi comedy set in Lapland, London and Turkey as world nears its end. A few scattered laughs. Longer, original British version (called THE FINAL PROGRAMME, running 89m.) has more substance. Based on one of Michael Moorcock's "Jerry Cornelius" stories; film has gained cult reputation.▼

Last Days of Patton, The (1986) C-150m. TVM D: Delbert Mann. George C. Scott, Eva Marie Saint, Richard Dysart, Murray Hamilton, Ed Lauter, Kathryn Leigh Scott. Scott returns to the role of George S. Patton after a 16-year hiatus in this woefully overlong drama chronicling the general's controversial last days following end of WW2. Scott's deathbed scene ranks among the longest in movie history. William Luce's script was based on Ladislas Farago's book of the same name. Average.▼

Last Days of Planet Earth, The (1974-Japanese) C-90m. BOMB. D: Toshio Masuda. Tetsuro Tamba, Toshio Kurosawa, So Yamamura, Kaoru Yumi. The air and sea are polluted, children attend school in gas masks, parents hallucinate—all predictions of Nostradamus. Preachy, laughably staged, atrociously dubbed; presented, perhaps, by the *National Enquirer*. Original title PROPHECIES OF NOSTRADAMUS: CATASTROPHE 1999.

Last Days of Pompeii, The (1935) 96m. *** D: Ernest B. Schoedsack. Preston Foster, Basil Rathbone, Dorothy Wilson, David Holt, Alan Hale, John Wood, Louis Calhern. Blacksmith Foster aspires to wealth and power as gladiator; climactic spectacle scenes are thrilling and expertly done, by the same special effects team responsible for KING KONG. Also shown in computer-colored version.▼

Last Days of Pompeii, The (1960-Italian) C-105m. **½ D: Mario Bonnard. Steve Reeves, Christine Kaufmann, Barbara Carroll, Anne Marie Baumann, Mimmo Palmara. New version of venerable tale focuses on muscleman Reeves and synthetic account of Christian martyrs. Very little spectacle.▼

Last Detail, The (1973) C-105m. ***½ D: Hal Ashby. Jack Nicholson, Otis Young, Randy Quaid, Clifton James, Carol Kane, Michael Moriarty, Nancy Allen. Superior comedy-drama about two career sailors ordered to transport a kleptomaniac prisoner to the brig. Robert Towne's brilliant off-color dialogue contributes to a quintessential Nicholson performance. Based on a Darryl Ponicsan novel. Look quickly for Gilda Radner.▼

Last Dinosaur, The (1977) **C-100m. TVM** D: Alex Grasshoff, Tom Kotani. Richard Boone, Joan Van Ark, Steven Keats, Luther Rackley, Tatsu Nakamura. Fantasy tale, made in Japan, about the world's richest man who invades a newly-discovered prehistoric world to stalk a Tyrannosaurus Rex. Entertaining foolishness out of the "Godzilla" school, originally intended for theaters. Average.

Last Dragon, The (1985) **C-109m.** ** D: Michael Schultz. Taimak, Vanity, Chris Murney, Julius J. Carry 3rd, Faith Prince. Juvenile film about would-be martial arts master who gets involved with glamorous video deejay (Vanity) and some overwrought gangsters. Campy and heavy-handed; strictly kid stuff, except for one gag: the name of the Chinatown warehouse. Released theatrically as BERRY GORDY'S THE LAST DRAGON.▼

Last Embrace (1979) **C-102m.** *** D: Jonathan Demme. Roy Scheider, Janet Margolin, John Glover, Sam Levene, Christopher Walken, Charles Napier. CIA agent Scheider sees wife ambushed, spends rest of the picture believing he's next. One of the better Hitchcock-influenced suspense thrillers offers good performances and a punchy climax at Niagara Falls. Fine Miklos Rozsa score; watch for Mandy Patinkin.▼

Last Emperor, The (1987-Italian-British-Chinese) **C-160m.** ***½ D: Bernardo Bertolucci. John Lone, Joan Chen, Peter O'Toole, Ying Ruocheng, Victor Wong, Dennis Dun, Ryuichui Sakamoto, Maggie Han, Ric Young. Remarkable film inspired by true story of Pu Yi, the last emperor of China, who is crowned at age three and lives a cloistered life in the Forbidden City until he is deposed (as a young man) during the revolution and forced to fend for himself in the outside world for the first time. A magnificent journey to another time and place, hampered by unanswered questions in the narrative and a main character who remains somewhat cold. Nothing can top the spectacle of life in the Forbidden City (where scenes were actually filmed)—or the twists of fate that fill Pu Yi's life. Photographed by Vittorio Storaro; music by Ryuichi Sakamoto, David Byrne, and Cong Su. Reportedly, Bertolucci has prepared a longer version of this for miniseries use on TV. Winner of nine Academy Awards including Best Picture, Director, Adapted Screenplay (Mark Peploe, Bertolucci), Cinematography, Art Direction, Editing, Costume Design, and Original Score. Hong Kong–produced version, based on Pu Yi's autobiography, predates this.▼

Last Escape, The (1970) **C-90m.** *½ D: Walter Grauman. Stuart Whitman, John Collin, Pinkas Braun, Martin Jarvis, Gunther Neutze, Margit Saad. O.S.S. Captain Whitman is ordered to sneak rocket expert out of Germany near the end of WW2 with predictable results.

Last Exit to Brooklyn (1989-W. German) **C-102m.** **½ D: Uli Edel. Stephen Lang, Jennifer Jason Leigh, Burt Young, Peter Dobson, Jerry Orbach, Stephen Baldwin, Ricki Lake, John Costelloe, Alexis Arquette. Gritty, brutal but stylish adaptation of Hubert Selby, Jr.'s notorious slice-of-life novel set on the mean streets of 1952 Brooklyn, where violence—verbal, physical, sexual, and otherwise—rules. Crammed with local color, but all the characters are thoroughly repellent and the film is difficult to like and to take. Selby himself appears as a cab driver.

Last Fight, The (1983) **C-86m.** *½ D: Fred Williamson. Willie Colon, Ruben Blades, Fred Williamson, Joe Spinell, Darlanne Fluegel, Nereida Mercado, Jose "Chegui" Torres, Don King. Poor melodrama with salsa music star Blades a singer-turned-boxer vying for the world championship. Simple-minded direction; doesn't even come up to level of old boxing B movies.▼

Last Flight of Noah's Ark, The (1980) **C-97m.** **½ D: Charles Jarrott. Elliott Gould, Genevieve Bujold, Ricky Schroder, Tammy Lauren, John Fujioka, Yuki Shimoda, Vincent Gardenia. Typical Disney sentimentality, somewhat effective. Pilot Gould, missionary Bujold, stowaway children Schroder and Lauren, and a planeload of animals are forced down in the Pacific, where they unite with two Japanese soldiers, who didn't know the war was over, to convert the plane into an ark. Filmed largely on Waikiki Beach. Story by Ernest K. (THE HIGH AND THE MIGHTY) Gann.▼

Last Fling, The (1987) **C-100m. TVM** D: Corey Allen. John Ritter, Connie Sellecca, Randee Heller, Scott Bakula, Paul Sand, John Bennett Perry, Shannon Tweed. Bride-to-be sets her sights on a lonely yuppie for one final fling before marrying her stuffy fiancé. Average.

Last Frontier, The (1956) **C-98m.** **½ D: Anthony Mann. Victor Mature, Guy Madison, Robert Preston, James Whitmore, Anne Bancroft. Three wilderness scouts see their lives change with the coming of cavalry outpost and military martinet (Preston). Offbeat characterizations in this cavalry drama. Also known as SAVAGE WILDERNESS.

Last Frontier, The (1986) **C-200m. TVM** D: Simon Wincer. Linda Evans, Jack

Thompson, Jason Robards, Judy Morris, Tony Bonner, Meredith Salenger, Peter Billingsley. Gutsy American widow gets involved in a feud with a greedy Australian land baron and falls for his renegade son. The first American TV movie to be filmed primarily in Australia. Originally shown in two parts. Average.

Last Gangster, The (1937) 81m. *** D: Edward Ludwig. Edward G. Robinson, James Stewart, Rosa Stradner, Lionel Stander, Douglas Scott, John Carradine, Sidney Blackmer, Louise Beavers, Edward Brophy, Grant Mitchell. Robinson's dynamic performance, and slick MGM production, elevate this tale of an underworld chief who's sent away for ten years, obsessed by the thought of the son he's never met. Entertaining story by William Wellman and Robert Carson was originally to have been called *Another Public Enemy*.

Last Gentleman, The (1934) 80m. *** D: Sidney Lanfield. George Arliss, Edna May Oliver, Charlotte Henry, Janet Beecher, Ralph Morgan, Edward Ellis, Donald Meek. Delightful comedy with Arliss as dying millionaire whose family descends on him in hopes of carting away a piece of his fortune. Ingenious denouement gives Arliss last laugh.

Last Giraffe, The (1979) C-100m. TVM D: Jack Couffer. Susan Anspach, Simon Ward, Gordon Jackson, Don Warrington, Saeed Jaffrey. American wild-life photographer and safari-guide husband fight to save the endangered Rothschild giraffe of Kenya from poachers in this entertaining Sherman Yellen adaptation of the book *Raising Daisy Rothschild*. Above average.

Last Grenade, The (1970-British) C-94m. **½ D: Gordon Flemyng. Stanley Baker, Alex Cord, Honor Blackman, Richard Attenborough, Rafer Johnson, Andrew Keir. Solid cast in grim, unevenly plotted tale of duel to death between two British mercenaries. Good location shooting can't hide lack of character development, motivation.

Last Hard Men, The (1976) C-103m. *½ D: Andrew V. McLaglen. Charlton Heston, James Coburn, Barbara Hershey, Michael Parks, Jorge Rivero, Larry Wilcox, Thalmus Rasulala, Morgan Paull, Robert Donner, Christopher Mitchum. Outlaw Coburn leads a gang of men on a jailbreak, then sets into motion plan of vengeance on sheriff Heston: kidnapping daughter Hershey and threatening to gang-rape her. Repellently violent and tasteless Western, loosely based on a Brian Garfield novel, saved only by Parks' interesting performance as reform-minded sheriff.

Last Holiday (1950-British) 89m. *** D: Henry Cass. Alec Guinness, Beatrice Campbell, Kay Walsh, Bernard Lee, Wilfrid Hyde-White. Ordinary man is told he is dying and decides to live it up at a swank

resort. A droll, biting script by J. B. Priestley, with sterling performances by all.

Last Horror Film, The (1984) C-87m. BOMB D: David Winters. Caroline Munro, Joe Spinell, Judd Hamilton. Laughably amateurish mishmash about cabbie Spinell obsessed with horror movie star Munro. He follows her to the Cannes Film Festival, where this was partially shot (in 1981).▼

Last Hours Before Morning (1975) C-78m. TVM D: Joseph Hardy. Ed Lauter, Thalmus Rasulala, George Murdock, Sheila Sullivan, Rhonda Fleming, Robert Alda, Kaz Garas, Victoria Principal, Don Porter, Art Lund. Period detective movie about a hot-shot house detective who moonlights by chasing deadbeats and stumbles onto a jewel robbery/homicide. Interesting performance by Lauter in a rare starring role. Average.

Last House on the Left (1972) C-91m. BOMB D: Wes Craven. David Hess, Lucy Grantham, Sandra Cassel, Marc Sheffler, Jeramie Rain, Fred Lincoln, Gaylord St. James. Repugnant film in which sadistic, Manson-type group rapes and tortures two girls to death, only to meet even sterner justice from one girl's parents. Technically inept and really sick. Based on, believe it or not, Bergman's VIRGIN SPRING. Runs 83m. on video.▼

Last Hunt, The (1956) C-108m. **½ D: Richard Brooks. Robert Taylor, Stewart Granger, Lloyd Nolan, Debra Paget, Russ Tamblyn, Constance Ford. Rampaging buffalo herd is primary excitement of Taylor-Granger feuding partnership in 1880s West.

Last Hurrah, The (1958) 121m. ***½ D: John Ford. Spencer Tracy, Jeffrey Hunter, Dianne Foster, Basil Rathbone, Pat O'Brien, Donald Crisp, James Gleason, Ed Brophy, John Carradine, Ricardo Cortez, Frank McHugh, Jane Darwell. Flavorful version of Edwin O'Connor novel of politics, loosely based on life of Boston's Mayor Curley. Top-notch veteran cast makes film sparkle.▼

Last Hurrah, The (1977) C-110m. TVM D: Vincent Sherman. Carroll O'Connor, John Anderson, Dana Andrews, Jack Carter, Mariette Hartley, Burgess Meredith, Patrick O'Neal, Patrick Wayne, Kitty Winn. O'Connor not only plays Mayor Frank Skeffington but also wrote this adaptation of the Edwin O'Connor best seller. Doesn't hold a candle to John Ford's 1958 movie. Average.

Last Innocent Man, The (1987) C-109m. TVM D: Roger Spottiswoode. Ed Harris, Roxanne Hart, David Suchet, Bruce McGill, Darrell Larson, Rose Gregorio, Clarence Williams III. Burned-out attorney (famous for establishing "innocence" of sleazy clients) begins a torrid love affair with the woman whose estranged husband he is defending for murder. Off-beat, well-acted suspense drama adapted by Dan Bronson from real-life defense attorney/author Phillip M. Margolin's novel. Made for cable. Above average.▼

Last Laugh, The (1924-German) 77m. ***½ D: F. W. Murnau. Emil Jannings. Silent-film classic told entirely by camera, without title cards. Jannings plays proud doorman at posh hotel who is suddenly and summarily demoted; film details his utter and grievous humiliation. Brilliantly filmed by pioneer cameraman Karl Freund, with towering performance by Jannings.▼

Last Man on Earth, The (1964-U.S.-Italian) 86m. ** D: Sidney Salkow. Vincent Price, Franca Bettoia, Emma Danieli, Giacomo Rossi-Stuart, Tony Cerevi. Often crude chiller with Price the sole survivor of plague, besieged by victims who arise at night thirsting for his blood; erratic production. Based on Richard Matheson's *I Am Legend*; remade as THE OMEGA MAN.

Last Man to Hang, The (1956-British) 75m. ** D: Terence Fisher. Tom Conway, Elizabeth Sellars, Eunice Gayson, Freda Jackson, Raymond Huntley, Anthony Newley. Forthright courtroom film of man on trial for alleged murder of wife.

Last Married Couple in America, The (1980) C-103m. *½ D: Gilbert Cates. George Segal, Natalie Wood, Richard Benjamin, Valerie Harper, Bob Dishy, Dom DeLuise. Likable cast in stupid sex comedy about happily married couple so upset by breakup of married friends that they begin to question their own relationship. Smutty and ridiculous.▼

Last Metro, The (1980-French) C-133m. **½ D: Francois Truffaut. Catherine Deneuve, Gerard Depardieu, Jean Poiret, Heinz Bennent, Andrea Ferreol, Paulette Dubost. A beautiful actress struggles to keep her "exiled" husband's theater alive during the German occupation of Paris. A film with charm and style but no point—a problem underscored by its abrupt and quizzical finale. Watching the elegant Deneuve provides most of this film's appeal.▼

Last Mile, The (1932) 70m. *** D: Sam Bischoff. Howard Phillips, Preston S. Foster, George E. Stone, Noel Madison, Alan Roscoe, Paul Fix. Stark, atmospheric drama about life on death row, with Killer Mears (Foster) leading a takeover of the cellblock. Based on John Wexley's play. Remade in 1959.▼

Last Mile, The (1959) 81m. **½ D: Howard W. Koch. Mickey Rooney, Clifford David, Harry Millard, Don "Red" Barry, Ford Rainey, Leon Janney. The "big house" oldie dusted off as a dramatic vehicle for Rooney.

Last Millionaire, The (1934-French) 90m. *** D: Rene Clair. Max Dearly, Renee Saint-Cyr, Jose Noguero, Raymond Cordy, Paul Olivier. Light, mildly funny satire about the world's wealthiest man (Dearly), who is asked to govern a bankrupt, mythical kingdom; he is knocked on the head, and his idiotic rulings are interpreted as acts of genius. Not bad, but not up to Clair's best films of the period.

Last Movie, The (1971) C-108m. *½ D: Dennis Hopper. Dennis Hopper, Julie Adams, Peter Fonda, Kris Kristofferson, Sylvia Miles, John Phillip Law, Rod Cameron, Sam Fuller. Hopper's fatally pretentious follow-up to EASY RIDER is interesting only as curio; incomprehensible story of small Peruvian village after a movie company pulls out has lovely photography, good acting by Adams. Otherwise, you've been warned. Among the supporting cast: Dean Stockwell, Russ Tamblyn, Michelle Phillips. Kristofferson's film debut (he also wrote the music). Also known as CHINCHERO.▼

Last Musketeer, The (1954-French) C-95m. ** D: Fernando Cerchio. Georges Marchal, Dawn Addams, Jacques Dumesnil. Another variation on the THREE MUSKETEERS, with Marchal as D'Artagnan combating corruption in Louis XIV's court; adequate swashbuckler. Retitled: THE COUNT OF BRAGELONNE.

Last Night at the Alamo (1983) 80m. *** D: Eagle Pennell. Sonny Davis, Lou Perry, Steve Matilla, Tina Hubbard, Doris Hargrave. The last night at the Alamo, no famous battle site but a small, obscure Houston bar. A fascinating portrayal of the modern-era "cowboy" as henpecked, alcoholic, ultimately pathetic. Independently produced, with a hilariously profane script by Kim Henkel, author of THE TEXAS CHAINSAW MASSACRE.▼

Last Ninja, The (1983) C-100m. TVM D: William A. Graham. Michael Beck, Nancy Kwan, John McMartin, Mako, Richard Lynch, Carolyn Seymour, John Larroquette. American art dealer who also practices the Oriental martial arts as a Ninja is recruited to free a group of scientists from international terrorists. A possible contemporary *Kung Fu* series was the aim of its producer. Average.

Last of Mrs. Cheyney, The (1937) 98m. *** D: Richard Boleslawski. Joan Crawford, William Powell, Robert Montgomery, Frank Morgan, Jessie Ralph, Nigel Bruce. Glossy remake of Norma Shearer's 1929 success, from Frederick Lonsdale's play about a chic American jewel thief in England. Great fun for star watchers (especially since it's been out of circulation for many years), though it was considered a dated dud in 1937. Remade in 1951 as THE LAW AND THE LADY.

Last of Sheila, The (1973) C-120m. ***½ D: Herbert Ross. James Coburn, James Mason, Dyan Cannon, Ian McShane, Joan Hackett, Raquel Welch, Richard Benjamin. Super murder-puzzler about jet-set gamester who devises what turns into a deadly game of whodunit. Many red herrings make it all the more fun. Script by Anthony Perkins and Stephen Sondheim, real-life puzzle fans.▼

Last of the Badmen (1957) **C-79m. ** D:** Paul Landres. George Montgomery, Meg Randall, James Best, Michael Ansara, Keith Larsen. Western about Chicago detectives in 1880s chasing after killers of their fellow-worker.

Last of the Buccaneers (1950) **C-79m.** *½ D: Lew Landers. Paul Henreid, Jack Oakie, Mary Anderson, John Dehner. Quickie costumer tainting the legendary name of Jean Lafitte with plodding account of his post-War of 1812 exploits.

Last of the Comanches (1952) **C-85m.** **½ D: Andre de Toth. Broderick Crawford, Barbara Hale, Lloyd Bridges, Martin Milner, John War Eagle. Capable rehash of cavalrymen fighting off Indian attack. Western remake of SAHARA.

Last of the Cowboys, The SEE: **Great Smokey Roadblock, The**▼

Last of the Fast Guns, The (1958) **C-82m.** ** D: George Sherman. Jock Mahoney, Gilbert Roland, Linda Cristal, Eduard Franz. Adequately told Western of search for missing man, and obstacles the hired gunslinger must overcome.

Last of the Finest, The (1990) **C-106m.** ** D: John Mackenzie. Brian Dennehy, Joe Pantoliano, Jeff Fahey, Bill Paxton, Deborra-Lee Furness, Guy Boyd, Henry Darrow, Lisa Jane Persky. Honest, independent-minded L.A. cop Dennehy and his comrades discover sinister forces at work while attempting to bust drug traffickers. Dennehy's usual solid performance can't overcome occasionally outlandish scenario, with obvious parallels to the Iran-Contra affair.

Last of the Good Guys (1978) **C-100m.** TVM D: Theodore J. Flicker. Robert Culp, Dennis Dugan, Richard Narita, Ji-Tu Cumbuka, Larry Hagman, Marlyn Mason. Comedy-drama pitting a hard-nosed by-the-book police sergeant against a bunch of rookies trying to help a dying veteran cop protect his pension. Average.

Last of the Great Survivors (1984) **C-100m.** TVM D: Jerry Jameson. Pam Dawber, James Naughton, Thom Bray, Michael Callan, Fritz Feld, Nedra Volz. Dodo-dead comedy pitting a perky social worker and a batch of senior citizens against city hall, which wants to condemn their dilapidated building. The plot collapses first. Below average.

Last of the Mobile Hot-Shots (1970) **C-108m.** ** D: Sidney Lumet. James Coburn, Lynn Redgrave, Robert Hooks, Perry Hayes, Reggie King. Ambitious flop from Tennessee Williams' *Seven Descents*

of Myrtle about volatile interracial triangle set in Deep South. ("Mobile" refers to the Alabama town.)

Last of the Mohicans, The (1936) **91m.** *** D: George B. Seitz. Randolph Scott, Binnie Barnes, Heather Angel, Hugh Buckler, Henry Wilcoxon, Bruce Cabot. Big-scale action based on James Fenimore Cooper tale of the French-Indian War in colonial America. Cabot makes good villainous Indian.▼

Last of the Mohicans (1977) **C-100m.** TVM D: James L. Conway. Steve Forrest, Ned Romero, Andrew Prine, Robert Tessier, Don Shanks, Jane Actman. Sturdy new version of the adventure classic, with Forrest fine as the stalwart Hawkeye. Above average.▼

Last of the Red Hot Lovers (1972) **C-98m.** BOMB D: Gene Saks. Alan Arkin, Sally Kellerman, Paula Prentiss, Renee Taylor. Appalling film version of typical Neil Simon play concerns Arkin's unsuccessful attempts to carry on sneaky love affair with three different women (not all at once). Actors scream at each other for more than an hour and a half in shoddy production for which the term "photographed stage play" must have been invented.▼

Last of the Redmen (1947) **C-77m.** **½ D: George Sherman. Jon Hall, Michael O'Shea, Evelyn Ankers, Julie Bishop, Buster Crabbe. OK Western with thoughtful Indian (Hall) facing decision involving group of ambushed white men; loosely based on James Fenimore Cooper's LAST OF THE MOHICANS.

Last of the Secret Agents?, The (1966) **C-90m.** *½ D: Norman Abbott. Marty Allen, Steve Rossi, John Williams, Nancy Sinatra, Lou Jacobi. Tiring spoof on spy movies ends up unintentional self-mockery. Strictly for Allen and Rossi fans. Look for Harvey Korman as a German colonel.

Last of the Ski Bums (1969) **C-86m.** *** D: Dick Barrymore. Ron Funk, Mike Zuetell, Ed Ricks. Made by same team that produced THE ENDLESS SUMMER, film details exploits of three men who win large sum of money, spend it on long ski holiday. Not only will effect diminish on small screen, film includes weak narrative whose point of view conflicts with beauty of visuals.

Last of the Vikings, The (1960-Italian) **C-102m.** ** D: Giacomo Gentilomo. Cameron Mitchell, Edmund Purdom, Isabelle Corey, Helene Remy. Filmed with gusto, elaborate epic deals with Mitchell out to punish the Norse for devastating his homelands; poorly acted.

Last Outlaw, The (1936) **72m.** *** D: Christy Cabanne. Harry Carey, Hoot Gibson, Henry B. Walthall, Tom Tyler, Margaret Callahan. Delightful blend of comedy and Western ingredients with Carey as a once notorious bandit released from prison after twenty-five years, only to find the Old West gone. Carey is wonderful (along with entire cast). There's even a hilarious dig at singing cowboys! John Ford coauthored the story.

Last Outpost, The (1935) 70m. *** D: Louis Gasnier, Charles Barton. Cary Grant, Claude Rains, Gertrude Michael, Kathleen Burke, Colin Tapley, Akim Tamiroff. Exciting action-adventure with British troops in Africa, along lines of LOST PATROL, LIVES OF A BENGAL LANCER, etc.

Last Outpost, The (1951) C-88m. **½ D: Lewis R. Foster. Ronald Reagan, Rhonda Fleming, Bruce Bennett, Bill Williams, Peter Hanson, Noah Beery, Jr. Burst of action saves wornout yarn of two brothers on opposite sides of Civil War, teaming up to fight off Indian attack. This was Reagan's first starring Western.

Last Picture Show, The (1971) 118m. **** D: Peter Bogdanovich. Timothy Bottoms, Jeff Bridges, Ben Johnson, Cloris Leachman, Ellen Burstyn, Cybill Shepherd, Eileen Brennan, Clu Gulager, Sam Bottoms, Randy Quaid. Brilliant study of life in small Texas town during 1950s, and how characters' lives intertwine, from Larry McMurtry's novel (he and director Bogdanovich wrote the script). Oscars went to Johnson and Leachman for sensitive performances, but entire cast works at same level. Beautifully photographed in black & white by Robert Surtees.

Last Plane Out (1983) C-92m. *½ D: David Nelson. Jan-Michael Vincent, Julie Carmen, Mary Crosby, David Huffman, William Windom, Lloyd Battista. Political thriller produced by Jack Cox and based on his real-life experiences as a journalist in the final days of the Somoza regime in Nicaragua suffers from cornball treatment and obvious propaganda slant. Battista as Somoza is Mr. Nice Guy in this version. Low-budget production isn't helped by indifferent direction by Nelson. ▼

Last Porno Flick, The (1974) C-88m. BOMB D: Ray Marsh. Frank Calcanini, Michael Pataki, Marianna Hill, Mike Kellin, Jo Anne Meredith, Robyn Hilton, Tom Signorelli, Carmen Zapata, Antony Carbone. Unfunny spoof of liberated Hollywood filmmakers plays like a dirty episode of *Love, American Style*. Sole point of interest is DEEP THROAT parody; this was distributed by the same company. Originally released as THE MAD, MAD MOVIE MAKERS.

Last Posse, The (1953) 73m.** D: Alfred L. Werker. Broderick Crawford, John Derek, Charles Bickford, Wanda Hendrix, Warner Anderson. Sheriff's men track down robbers, not without surprising results.

Last Precinct, The (1986) C-78m. TVM D: Hy Averback. Jonathan Perpich, Ernie

Hudson, Wings Hauser, Randi Brooks, Keenan Wynn, Adam West. Cartoonish spoof of cop shows that's three notches below the POLICE ACADEMY series, with Adam "Batman" West as the square and oh-so-dumb precinct captain. Pilot to the short-lived series. Average.

La Strada (1954-Italian) 115m. **** D: Federico Fellini. Anthony Quinn, Giulietta Masina, Richard Basehart, Aldo Silvana, Marcella Rovere, Livia Venturini. Deceptively simple tale of brutish strongman Quinn taking simple-minded Masina with him as he tours countryside, where he encounters the gentle acrobat Basehart. Best Foreign Film Oscar winner, with stunning performances, haunting Nino Rota score. ▼

Last Rebel, The (1971) C-89m. BOMB D: Denys McCoy. Joe Namath, Jack Elam, Woody Strode, Ty Hardin, Victoria George. Namath plays Confederate soldier who raises havoc in small Missouri town after the Civil War. Film has obvious camp value, but it's not enough; Joe makes Ty Hardin look like John Gielgud.

Last Remake of Beau Geste, The (1977) C-83m. **½ D: Marty Feldman. Marty Feldman, Ann-Margret, Michael York, Peter Ustinov, James Earl Jones, Trevor Howard, Henry Gibson, Terry-Thomas, Spike Milligan, Roy Kinnear. After uproarious first half, Feldman's Foreign Legion spoof falters and gropes its way to weak conclusion. Enough belly-laughs to make it worthwhile, and sidesplitting performance by butler Milligan. Feldman also cowrote this, his directorial debut. ▼

Last Resort (1986) C-80m. **½ D: Zane Buzby. Charles Grodin, Robin Pearson Rose, John Ashton, Ellen Blake, Megan Mullally, Christopher Ames, Jon Lovitz, Gerrit Graham. Newly unemployed Grodin decides, on impulse, to take his family to a Club Med-type vacation resort, with predictably comic results. Likable but iffy comedy does have some genuine laughs. First-time director Buzby also appears as resort's baby sitter. ▼

Last Reunion, The (1980) C-98m. *½ D: Jay Wertz. Cameron Mitchell, Leo Fong, Chanda Romero, Vic Silayan, Hal Bokar, Philip Baker Hall. Violent drama of WW2 platoon's reunion in the Philippines, where in 1945 they slaughtered a Japanese general and his wife. Now, thirty-three years later, the sole witness is out for revenge. Not very good. ▼

Last Ride, The (1944) 56m. ** D: D. Ross Lederman. Richard Travis, Eleanor Parker, Charles Lang, Jack LaRue. Smooth programmer involving a series of "accidental" deaths and the detective who tracks down the "murderer."

Last Ride of the Dalton Gang, The (1979) C-150m. TVM D: Dan Curtis. Cliff Potts, Randy Quaid, Larry Wilcox, Jack Palance,

Dale Robertson, Bo Hopkins, Sharon Farrell, Harris Yulin. Old-fashioned shoot-em-up recounting (with huge doses of humor) the adventures of the Old West's infamous gang—intimating that the Daltons were inept boobs. The opening and closing, in 1930s Hollywood, is gratuitous. Average.▼

Last Rites (1980) **C-88m.** BOMB D: Domonic Paris. Patricia Lee Hammond, Gerald Fielding, Victor Jorge, Michael Lally, Mimi Weddell. A vampire mortician harasses a family that bears the surname Fonda. The pits. Also known as DRACULA'S LAST RITES.▼

Last Rites (1988) **C-103m.** ** D: Donald P. Bellisario. Tom Berenger, Daphne Zuniga, Chick Vennera, Anne Twomey, Dane Clark, Paul Dooley, Vassili Lambrinos. Routine drama of a priest who uses the auspices of the church to protect a girl on a Mafia hit list. Of course, he falls in love with her. Of course, he also happens to be the son of a Mafia chieftain himself. And of course, the studio sent this one straight to video.▼

Last Roman, The (1968-German-Rumanian) **92m.** ** D: Robert Siodmak. Laurence Harvey, Orson Welles, Sylva Koscina, Honor Blackman, Michael Dunn, Harriet Andersson, Lang Jeffries, Robert Hoffman. Big cast in spears and togas look baffled at what has become of Felix Dann's German bestseller *Kamf um Rom* about the decline of the Roman Empire. Edited down from a two-part spectacular.

Last Run, The (1971) **C-99m.** **½ D: Richard Fleischer. George C. Scott, Tony Musante, Trish Van Devere, Colleen Dewhurst. Mediocre tale of aging gangland driver who has to make one more run for his ego. Great photography by Sven Nykvist. Started by John Huston, majority of film directed by Fleischer.

Last Safari, The (1967-British) **C-110m.** ** D: Henry Hathaway. Kaz Garas, Stewart Granger, Gabriella Licudi, Johnny Sekka, Liam Redmond. Uninteresting action tale with depressed professional hunter (Stewart) coming to terms with himself and rich young couple who hire him. Good cast can't handle script.

Last Shot You Hear, The (1969-British) **87m.** *½ D: Gordon Hessler. Hugh Marlowe, Zena Walker, Patricia Haines, William Dysart, Thorley Walters. Complicated, dull story of marriage counselor Marlowe's understandable problem when his wife takes a lover.

Last Song, The (1980) **C-96m.** TVM D: Alan J. Levi. Lynda Carter, Ronny Cox, Paul Rudd, Nicholas Pryor, Jenny O'Hara, Dale Robinette, Bill Lucking, Don Porter, Louanne, Kene Holliday, Ben Piazza, Charles Aidman. Young woman and daughter become targets of desperate men after accidentally coming across incriminating tapes involving an industrial-waste plant blunder. Average.▼

Last Stagecoach West (1957) **67m.** *½ D: Joseph Kane. Jim Davis, Victor Jory, Mary Castle, Lee Van Cleef. Fair cast cannot save bland Western about stage-driver who loses government contracts and goes out of business.

Last Starfighter, The (1984) **C-100m.** **½ D: Nick Castle. Lance Guest, Robert Preston, Dan O'Herlihy, Catherine Mary Stewart, Barbara Bosson, Norman Snow. Sci-fi fantasy for kids, about a youngster whose video-game prowess makes him a prime recruit to help save real-life planet under attack. Likable but toothless adventure (with an arch-villain who simply disappears from the proceedings) benefits greatly from performances of old pros Preston and O'Herlihy, who's unrecognizable in lizard-like makeup. Preston's last film.▼

Last Summer (1969) **C-97m.** ***½ D: Frank Perry. Richard Thomas, Barbara Hershey, Bruce Davison, Cathy Burns, Ralph Waite, Conrad Bain. Powerful story based on Evan Hunter novel of teenagers playing on the beach in a summer resort. The film follows their games, their sexual awakenings, and how evil manifests itself with calculated determination. Cathy Burns a standout.▼

Last Sunset, The (1961) **C-112m.** *** D: Robert Aldrich. Rock Hudson, Kirk Douglas, Dorothy Malone, Joseph Cotten, Carol Lynley, Neville Brand, Regis Toomey, Jack Elam. Strange on the Range, courtesy Aldrich and scripter Dalton Trumbo; philosophical outlaw Douglas and pursuing sheriff Hudson play cat-and-mouse with each other during lengthy cattle drive. Throws in everything from incest to Indians!

Last Survivors, The (1975) **C-78m.** TVM D: Lee H. Katzin. Martin Sheen, Diane Baker, Tom Bosley, Christopher George, Bruce Davison, Anne Francis, Percy Rodrigues, Anne Seymour, Bethel Leslie. Sea drama with Sheen deciding who stays in the overcrowded lifeboat and who goes overboard. Twice (or more) told harrowing tale done better by Tyrone Power in ABANDON SHIP. Average.

Last Tango in Paris (1973-French-Italian) **C-129m.** ***½ D: Bernardo Bertolucci. Marlon Brando, Maria Schneider, Jean-Pierre Leaud, Darling Legitimus, Catherine Sola, Mauro Marchetti, Dan Diament. Expatriate American in Paris tries purging himself of bad memories after his wife's suicide, enters into a tragic "no questions asked" sexual liaison with a chance acquaintance. The most controversial film of its era is still explicit by today's standards, though it's mellowed somewhat with age. A sterling showcase for Bertolucci's camera mastery; Brando's performance, then as now, is among the best of his career.▼

Last Temptation of Christ, The (1988) **C-164m.** *** D: Martin Scorsese. Willem Dafoe, Harvey Keitel, Barbara Hershey, Harry Dean Stanton, David Bowie, Verna Bloom, Andre Gregory, Juliette Caton, Roberts Blossom, Irvin Kershner, Nehemiah Persoff, Barry Miller. Thought-provoking and deeply felt drama adapted from Nikos Kazantzakis' book which speculates about Jesus' self-doubts when he realizes he has been chosen by God to carry His message. Moments of great power and beauty are diminished somewhat by mundane dialogue and slow stretches; still worthwhile, with a genuine feeling for time and place that help make the story vivid and real. Soundtrack by Peter Gabriel.▼

Last Tenant, The (1978) **C-100m. TVM** D: Jud Taylor. Tony LoBianco, Lee Strasberg, Christine Lahti, Danny Aiello, Jeffrey DeMunn, Julie Bovasso. Acclaimed drama about the effects on a middle-aged bachelor's pending marriage when the family decides he must care for their aging father. George Rubino won an Emmy Award for his original teleplay, lovingly acted by LoBianco and Strasberg. Above average.

Last Ten Days, The (1956-German) **113m.** *** D: G. W. Pabst. Albin Skoda, Oskar Werner, Lotte Tobisch, Willy Krause, Helga Kennedy-Dohrn. Finely etched study of downfall of leader of Third Reich. Retitled: LAST TEN DAYS OF ADOLPH HITLER.

Last Time I Saw Archie, The (1961) **98m.** ** D: Jack Webb. Robert Mitchum, Jack Webb, Martha Hyer, France Nuyen, Louis Nye, Richard Arlen, Don Knotts, Joe Flynn, Robert Strauss. Webb's sole attempt at comedy is less funny than some of his more serious films; a pity, because William Bowers' script—based on his own Army experiences—had real potential, and Mitchum nicely underplays as the titular conman. (By the way, the real Archie Hall sued for invasion of privacy!)

Last Time I Saw Paris, The (1954) **C-116m.** *** D: Richard Brooks. Elizabeth Taylor, Van Johnson, Donna Reed, Walter Pidgeon, Eva Gabor, George Dolenz, Roger Moore. Updated version of F. Scott Fitzgerald story, set in post-WW2 Paris, of ruined marriages and disillusioned people. MGM gloss helps.▼

Last Train from Bombay (1952) **72m.** *½ D: Fred F. Sears. Jon Hall, Christine Larson, Lisa Ferraday, Douglas Kennedy. Hall single-handedly attempts to prevent a train wreck; set in India.

Last Train from Gun Hill (1959) **C-94m.** *** D: John Sturges. Kirk Douglas, Anthony Quinn, Carolyn Jones, Earl Holliman, Brad Dexter, Brian Hutton, Ziva Rodann. Superior Western of staunch sheriff determined to leave Gun Hill with murder suspect, despite necessity for shoot-out.▼

Last Train from Madrid, The (1937) **77m.** *** D: James Hogan. Dorothy Lamour, Lew Ayres, Gilbert Roland, Anthony Quinn, Lee Bowman, Karen Morley, Helen Mack, Evelyn Brent, Robert Cummings, Lionel Atwill, Olympe Bradna. Imitation GRAND HOTEL works out quite well, linking vignettes of various people escaping from wartorn Spain during 1930s. Modest but well-made film, with impressive cast.

Last Tycoon, The (1976) **C-125m.** ***½ D: Elia Kazan. Robert De Niro, Tony Curtis, Robert Mitchum, Jeanne Moreau, Jack Nicholson, Donald Pleasence, Peter Strauss, Ingrid Boulting, Ray Milland, Dana Andrews, Theresa Russell, John Carradine, Anjelica Huston. Low-keyed but effective Harold Pinter adaptation of F. Scott Fitzgerald's final novel benefits immeasurably from De Niro's great, uncharacteristic performance as 1930s movie producer (inspired by Irving Thalberg) who is slowly working himself to death. Along with Joan Micklin Silver's TV film *Bernice Bobs Her Hair*, the best Fitzgerald yet put on the screen.▼

Last Valley, The (1971-British) **C-128m.** ** D: James Clavell. Michael Caine, Omar Sharif, Florinda Bolkan, Nigel Davenport, Per Oscarsson, Arthur O'Connell. Thinking man's adventure epic is an unfortunate misfire; 17th-century story brings warrior Caine and his soldiers to peaceful valley which has remained untouched by the Thirty Years War.▼

Last Victim, The SEE: **Forced Entry**▼

Last Voyage, The (1960) **C-91m.** *** D: Andrew L. Stone. Robert Stack, Dorothy Malone, George Sanders, Edmond O'Brien, Woody Strode. Engrossing drama of luxury ship that goes down at sea, and the ways the crew and passengers are affected. (To heighten the realism of the film, they really sank a ship.) Sanders is ill-fated captain, Stack and Malone a married couple in jeopardy.

Last Wagon, The (1956) **C-99m.** *** D: Delmer Daves. Richard Widmark, Felicia Farr, Susan Kohner, Tommy Rettig, Stephanie Griffin, Ray Stricklyn, Nick Adams. Widmark is condemned killer who saves remnants of wagon train after Indian attack, leading them to safety. Clichéd plot well handled.

Last Waltz, The (1978) **C-117m.** **** D: Martin Scorsese. The Band, Bob Dylan, Neil Young, Joni Mitchell, Van Morrison, Eric Clapton, Neil Diamond, The Staples, Muddy Waters, Emmylou Harris, Paul Butterfield, Dr. John, Ronnie Hawkins, Ringo Starr, Ron Wood. Truly wonderful documentary about The Band's Thanksgiving, 1976, farewell concert, filmed by state-of-the-art Hollywood talent. A pair of studio-shot numbers involving The Staples and Harris are as exciting to watch as listen to, but the whole film is beautifully done.▼

Last Wave, The (1977-Australian) **C-106m.** *** D: Peter Weir. Richard Chamberlain, Olivia Hamnett, (David) Gulpilil, Frederick Parslow, Vivean Gray, Nanjiwarra Amagula. Fascinating chiller about Australian lawyer (Chamberlain) defending aborigine accused of murder. Modern symbolism and ancient tribal rituals make for unusual and absorbing film.▼

Last Will of Dr. Mabuse, The SEE: **Testament of Dr. Mabuse, The**▼

Last Woman, The (1976-French) **C-112m.** ** D: Marco Ferreri. Gerard Depardieu, Ornella Muti, Michel Piccoli, Zouzou, Renato Salvatori, David Biffani, Nathalie Baye. Provocative subject matter is superficially handled in this pointlessly sensationalistic drama about macho, self-absorbed engineer Depardieu, insensitive to women and confused by a world of changing roles and relationships. His final act of self-mutilation is as ridiculous as it is shocking.

Last Woman on Earth, The (1961) **C-71m.** BOMB D: Roger Corman. Antony Carbone, Edward Wain, Betsy Jones-Moreland. Dull three-cornered romance involving last survivors on earth after unexplained disaster. Screenplay by Robert Towne—his first. He also costars, using acting pseudonym Edward Wain.▼

Last Year at Marienbad (1962-French) **93m.** *** D: Alain Resnais. Delphine Seyrig, Giorgio Albertazzi, Sacha Pitoeff, Francoise Bertin, Luce Garcia-Ville. Beautifully photographed but murky, bewildering story of young man attempting to lure a woman to run away with him. An art-house hit in its day, now more of a curiosity.▼

Las Vegas Hillbillys (1966) **C-90m.** *½ D: Arthur C. Pierce. Ferlin Husky, Jayne Mansfield, Mamie Van Doren, Richard Kiel, Sonny James, Del Reeves, Bill Anderson, Connie Smith. How does country hick Husky become a big-time Las Vegas entrepreneur? You really don't want to know. A once-in-a-lifetime cast. Sequel: HILLBILLYS IN A HAUNTED HOUSE.▼

Las Vegas Lady (1976) **C-87m.** BOMB D: Noel Nosseck. Stella Stevens, Stuart Whitman, George DiCenzo, Lynne Moody, Linda Scruggs, Joseph Della Sorte, Jesse White. Substandard heist pic about a security guard who flips for title femme. Even LAS VEGAS HILLBILLYS is better. ▼

Las Vegas Shakedown (1955) **79m.** ** D: Sidney Salkow. Dennis O'Keefe, Coleen Gray, Charles Winninger, Thomas Gomez, Elizabeth Patterson, Robert Armstrong. Improbable yet diverting account of O'Keefe's effort to run an honest gambling house, with on-location filming in Las Vegas.

Las Vegas Story, The (1952) **88m.** ** D: Robert Stevenson. Jane Russell, Victor Mature, Vincent Price, Hoagy Carmichael, Brad Dexter. Synthetic murder yarn supposedly set in gambling capital, sparked by Russell's vitality.

La Symphonie Pastorale (1946-French) **105m.** ***½ D: Jean Delannoy. Pierre Blanchar, Michele Morgan, Jean Desailly, Line Noro, Andree Clement. Quietly powerful classic about pastor Blanchar's all-consuming passion for blind girl Morgan, whom he takes under his wing and educates. This sensitive study of moral and spiritual corruption was coscripted by the director, and based on an Andre Gide novel.▼

L.A. Takedown (1989) **C-100m.** TVM D: Michael Mann. Scott Plank, Alex McArthur, Vincent Guastaffero, Michael Rooker, Ely Pouget. Cop and thief engage in violent cat-and-mouse game following a spectacular heist. Producer-director-writer Mann tried to bring same stylish approach to L.A. locations that he used for *Miami Vice*. Series pilot that didn't make it. Average.

L'Atalante (1934-French) **82m.** **** D: Jean Vigo. Jean Dasté, Dita Parlo, Michel Simon, Gilles Margaritis, Louis Lefévre, Diligent Raya. Naturalism and surrealist fantasy blend beautifully in all-time masterpiece about a young couple who begin their life together sailing down the Seine on a barge. Ultimate in romantic cinema also anticipated neorealist movement by more than a decade; Vigo died at 29, just as film premiered.▼

Late Autumn (1960-Japanese) **C-127m.** *** D: Yasujiro Ozu. Setsuko Hara, Yoko Tsukasa, Mariko Okada, Keiji Sada, Shin Saburi. Widowed Hara seeks a husband for unmarried daughter Tsukasa. Solid Ozu drama, a reworking of the director's LATE SPRING.

Late George Apley, The (1947) **98m.** *** D: Joseph L. Mankiewicz. Ronald Colman, Peggy Cummins, Edna Best, Vanessa Brown, Richard Haydn, Charles Russell. John P. Marquand's gentle satire of Boston bluebloods is smoothly entertaining and perfectly cast.

Late Liz, The (1971) **C-119m.** BOMB D: Dick Ross. Anne Baxter, Steve Forrest, James Gregory, Coleen Gray, Joan Hotchkis, Jack Albertson. Campy drama about Baxter's rejection of alcohol due to religion is well-intentioned, but hardly convincing as presented here; viewers may need a good stiff drink by the time it's over.▼

La Terra Trema (1947-Italian) **160m.** **** D: Luchino Visconti. Narrated by Luchino Visconti, Antonio Pietrangeli. Powerful, lyrical neorealist classic about a poor family in a Sicilian fishing village, and how they're exploited by fish wholesalers and boat owners. Filmed on location, and in Sicilian dialect, with a non-professional cast. Francesco Rosi and Franco Zeffirelli were Visconti's assistant directors. Beware of severely edited versions.▼

Late Show, The (1977) **C-94m.** ***½ D: Robert Benton. Art Carney, Lily Tomlin, Bill Macy, Eugene Roche, Joanna Cassidy, John Considine, Howard Duff. Carney is an aging private eye who tries to solve murder of his ex-partner (Duff), "helped" by flaky, aimless young woman (Tomlin). Echoes of Chandler and Hammett resound in Benton's complex but likable script; chemistry between Carney and Tomlin is perfect. Later a short-lived TV series called *Eye to Eye.*▼

Lathe of Heaven, The (1980) **C-105m.** TVM D: David Loxton, Fred Barzyk. Kevin Conway, Bruce Davison, Margaret Avery. Davison's dreams literally come true; egocentric Dr. Conway tries to manipulate him into eliminating war, racism, and illness. Interesting visual and laser effects do not compensate for lumbering, disconnected scenario. Based on Ursula K. LeGuin's futuristic novel. Average; produced for PBS.

Latin Lovers (1953) **C-104m.** **½ D: Mervyn LeRoy. Lana Turner, Ricardo Montalban, John Lund, Jean Hagen, Louis Calhern. Hokey romance yarn set in South America, with Turner ambling about seeking true love; pointless script.

Latin Lovers (1961-Italian) **80m.** ** D: Lorenza Mazzetti, et al. Maria di Giuseppe, Mariella Zanetti, Jose Creci, Renza Volpi. Eight episodes dealing with love in Italy; most tales superficial and strained.

Latino (1985) **C-105m.** *** D: Haskell Wexler. Robert Beltran, Annette Cardona, Tony Plana, Ricardo Lopez, Luis Torrentes, Juan Carlos Ortiz, Julio Medina, James Karen. Gut-wrenching drama of Vietnam replayed, with Chicano Green Beret Beltran "advising" the U.S.-backed Contras in their war against the Sandanistas in Nicaragua. Unabashedly left-wing; to some it will be propaganda, while to others it will be truth. Striking direction with a fine sense of irony; however, Beltran's relationship with Cardona just doesn't ring true. Filmed in Nicaragua; Wexler's first "fiction" film since MEDIUM COOL in 1969.▼

Latitude Zero (1970-Japanese) **C-99m.** ** D: Inoshiro Honda. Joseph Cotten, Cesar Romero, Richard Jaeckel, Patricia Medina, Linda Haynes, Akira Takarada. Better than average imported cast helps usual wide-eyed sci-fi adventure of underwater civilization of benevolent geniuses fighting legions of Malic (Romero), out to control world. Some good sets, but action and suspense poorly handled.

La Traviata (1982-Italian) **C-112m.** **** D: Franco Zeffirelli. Teresa Stratas, Placido Domingo, Cornell MacNeil, Alan Monk, Axelle Gail. Verdi's opera, adapted from the Alexandre Dumas *Camille* saga, makes a magnificent film. If Domingo looks too old for Alfredo, he still sings beautifully, while Stratas's performance as the tragic Violetta matches her brilliant voice. The cinematography and production design are the equal of anything from the Golden Age of moviemaking in a film that even those who dislike opera will enjoy.▼

La Truite SEE: **Trout, The**▼

Laughing Policeman, The (1974) **C-111m.** **½ D: Stuart Rosenberg. Walter Matthau, Bruce Dern, Lou Gossett, Albert Paulsen, Anthony Zerbe, Anthony Costello, Cathy Lee Crosby, Joanna Cassidy. Reasonably engrossing San Francisco cop drama about search for mass slayer of bus passengers. Matthau and Dern are good as cops with contrasting styles. Based on the Martin Beck novel by Maj Sjowall and Per Wahloo.▼

Laughing Sinners (1931) **72m.** ** D: Harry Beaumont. Joan Crawford, Clark Gable, Neil Hamilton, John Mack Brown, Marjorie Rambeau, Guy Kibbee, Roscoe Karns. Crawford attempts suicide after Hamilton dumps her; Salvation Army preacher Gable (!) stops her. The rest is predictable.

Laughter (1930) **81m.** **½ D: Harry D'Arrast. Nancy Carroll, Fredric March, Frank Morgan, Leonard Carey. Lumpy film with a few bright sequences about Follies girl Carroll marrying millionaire but finding life empty, unhappy.

Laughter in Paradise (1951-British) **95m.** **½ D: Mario Zampi. Alastair Sim, Joyce Grenfell, Hugh Griffith, Fay Compton, John Laurie. Notorious practical joker dies, and leaves hefty sum to four relatives if they will carry out his devilish instructions. Pleasant little comedy. Audrey Hepburn appears fleetingly as cigarette girl. Remade in 1969 as SOME WILL, SOME WON'T.

Laughter in the Dark (1969-British) **C-101m.** ** D: Tony Richardson. Nicol Williamson, Anna Karina, Jean-Claude Drouot, Peter Bowles, Sian Phillips. Excruciating film from Nabokov novel about wealthy married man (Williamson) whose fascination with young girl (Karina) backfires at every turn, eventually ruining his life. Exceedingly unpleasant, and seemingly interminable.

Laura (1944) **85m.** **** D: Otto Preminger. Gene Tierney, Dana Andrews, Clifton Webb, Vincent Price, Judith Anderson, Grant Mitchell, Lane Chandler, Dorothy Adams. Classic mystery with gorgeous Tierney supposedly killed, detective Andrews trying to assemble murder puzzle. Fascinating, witty, classic, with Webb a standout as cynical columnist. Based on the Vera Caspary novel; also features David Raksin's theme. Rouben Mamoulian started directing film, Preminger took over. Screenplay by Jay Dratler, Samuel Hoffenstein, and Betty Reinhardt. Joseph LaShelle's cinematography earned an Oscar. Several minutes have been removed from all existing prints, because of problems with music rights; original version ran 88m.▼

Laura Lansing Slept Here (1988) **C-100m. TVM** D: George Schaefer. Katharine Hepburn, Karen Austin, Joel Higgins, Lee Richardson, Brenda Forbes, Nicolas Surovy, Schuyler Grant. Lightweight comedy vehicle for Hepburn as a famous, flamboyant novelist who accepts her agent's bet that she couldn't survive for one week living with an ordinary, real-life family. Naturally, she takes over the lives of the family whose life she invades, and gets to play Ms. Fix-It. (One of the kids is Hepburn's real-life grandniece, Grant.) Pleasant but unremarkable comedy written especially for Hepburn by James Prideaux. Average.

Laurel and Hardy's Laughing 20's (1965) **90m. ***½** Compiled by Robert Youngson. Stan Laurel, Oliver Hardy, Charley Chase, Edgar Kennedy, James Finlayson, Anita Garvin. Some of L&H's best moments on film are included, with everything from pie-throwing to pants-ripping. Also some excellent sequences of Charley Chase, adding to the fun.

Lavender Hill Mob, The (1951-British) **82m. ***½** D: Charles Crichton. Alec Guinness, Stanley Holloway, Sidney James, Alfie Bass, Marjorie Fielding, John Gregson, Edie Martin. Excellent comedy with droll Guinness a timid bank clerk who has perfect scheme for robbing the safe, with a madcap chase climax. Won an Oscar for Best Story and Screenplay (T. E. B. Clarke); look fast for Audrey Hepburn in final scene.▼

La Venexiana SEE: **Venetian Woman, The**

La Viaccia (1962-Italian) **103m. **½** D: Mauro Bolognini. Jean-Paul Belmondo, Claudia Cardinale, Pietro Germi, Romolo Valli, Gabriella Pallotta, Gina Sammarco. Zesty yarn of country youth finding romance in the city with prostitute. Retitled: THE LOVEMAKERS.

La Vie Continue (1982-French) **C-93m. *½** D: Moshe Mizrahi. Annie Girardot, Jean-Pierre Cassel, Pierre Dux, Giulia Salvatori, Emmanuel Gayet, Rivera Andres. Dreary sudser wastes Girardot as middle-aged woman whose husband suddenly drops dead of a heart attack; she struggles with her new-found widowhood. Loosely remade as MEN DON'T LEAVE.▼

La Vie de Chateau SEE: **Matter of Resistance, A**

La Vie Privée SEE: **Very Private Affair, A**▼

L'Avventura (1960-Italian) **145m. ***½** D: Michelangelo Antonioni. Monica Vitti, Gabriele Ferzetti, Lea Massari, Dominique Blanchar, James Addams. Woman's disappearance prompts examination of relationships among weekend yachting group. Incisive filmmaking, but not for all tastes.▼

Law, The (1974) **C-120m. TVM** D: John Badham. Judd Hirsch, John Beck, Bonnie Franklin, Barbara Baxley, Sam Wanamaker, Allan Arbus, John Hillerman, Gary Busey, Anne Ramsey. Outstanding drama depicting criminal-justice system of a large city as public defender Hirsch pursues case surrounding a football superstar's torture-killing. Brisk and biting, with first-rate performances. Written by Joel Oliansky, from a story he cowrote with producer William Sackheim. Above average.

Law and Disorder (1958-British) **76m. **½** D: Charles Crichton. Michael Redgrave, Robert Morley, Ronald Squire, Elizabeth Sellars. Brisk comedy of con-man who gives up life of crime to avoid embarrassing situation of making up stories to tell prim son.

Law and Disorder (1974) **C-103m. *** D: Ivan Passer. Carroll O'Connor, Ernest Borgnine, Ann Wedgeworth, Anita Dangler, Leslie Ackerman, Karen Black, Jack Kehoe. Intelligent, original comedy-drama of two middle-aged New Yorkers incensed at rising crime who become auxiliary cops. At first they treat it as a lark, but soon it becomes deadly serious. Full of fine perceptions, interesting vignettes.▼

Law and Jake Wade, The (1958) **C-86m. *** D: John Sturges. Robert Taylor, Richard Widmark, Patricia Owens, Robert Middleton. Robust Western of outlaw forcing his cohort-turned-good to lead him to buried loot. Taylor and Widmark make good adversaries.

Law and Order (1932) **70m. ***½** D: Edward L. Cahn. Walter Huston, Harry Carey, Raymond Hatton, Russell Hopton, Ralph Ince, Andy Devine, Walter Brennan. Exceptional Western that takes a familiar story (Wyatt Earp and Doc Holliday vs. the Clantons) and reworks it with style but no flourishes. Huston plays Saint Johnson, gunslinger and lawman. Stark, realistic, with a finale that's a knockout. Coscripted by John Huston. Remade in 1953, with women added to the scenario.

Law and Order (1953) **C-80m. ** D: Nathan Juran. Ronald Reagan, Dorothy Malone, Alex Nicol, Preston Foster, Ruth Hampton, Russell Johnson, Dennis Weaver, Jack Kelly. Lawman Reagan wants to retire to marry Malone, but first must tame bad guy Foster. Standard Western was filmed far more successfully in 1932.

Law and Order (1976) **C-150m. TVM**

D: Marvin Chomsky. Darren McGavin, Keir Dullea, Robert Reed, Suzanne Pleshette, James Olson, Teri Garr, Scott Brady, Will Geer, Jeanette Nolan, Whitney Blake, Biff McGuire. Sprawling TV movie from Dorothy Uhnak's best-seller tells of three generations of Irish-American N.Y.C. cops. Strong performances. Above average.

Law and the Lady, The (1951) **104m.** **½ D: Edwin H. Knopf. Greer Garson, Michael Wilding, Fernando Lamas, Marjorie Main, Hayden Rorke, Margalo Gillmore. Stylish if standard remake of THE LAST OF MRS. CHEYNEY with Garson (gowned by Cecil Beaton) teaming up with Wilding for slick society jewel robberies.

Law Is the Law, The (1959-French) **103m.** **½ D: Christian-Jaque. Fernandel, Toto, Mario Besozzi, René Genin. Two top Continental comedians work well together in yarn of French customs official and his pal who smuggle items over the border.

Lawless, The (1950) **83m.** ** D: Joseph Losey. Gail Russell, Macdonald Carey, Lalo Rios, Lee Patrick, John Sands, Martha Hyer. Vaguely interesting study of Mexican-American fruit-pickers in Southern California, with facets of racial discrimination pointed out.

Lawless Breed, The (1952) **C-83m.** *** D: Raoul Walsh. Rock Hudson, Julia Adams, Hugh O'Brian, Michael Ansara, Dennis Weaver. Moving Western story of John Wesley Hardin (Hudson), who tries to steer his son from outlaw path by recounting story of his life. Well done.

Lawless Eighties, The (1957) **70m.** ** D: Joseph Kane. Buster Crabbe, John Smith, Ted de Corsia, Marilyn Saris. Average oater about a gunfighter who protects a circuit rider harassed by hoodlums.

Lawless Street, A (1955) **C-78m.** **½ D: Joseph H. Lewis. Randolph Scott, Angela Lansbury, Warner Anderson, Jean Parker, Wallace Ford, Ruth Donnelly, Michael Pate. Hard-bitten marshal Scott tries to eliminate evil forces from western town, then confronts his bittersweet past when musical star Lansbury comes to town. Entertaining Western with disappointing resolution.

Lawman (1970) **C-98m.** *** D: Michael Winner. Burt Lancaster, Robert Ryan, Lee J. Cobb, Sheree North, Joseph Wiseman, Robert Duvall, Albert Salmi. Intriguing thought-Western about stoic marshal (Lancaster) who comes into unfamiliar town to bring back wanted men, refusing to sway from duty even though entire town turns against him. Unsatisfactory resolution mars otherwise compelling story; Ryan gives one of his finest performances as timid sheriff.

Law of Desire (1987-Spanish) **C-100m.** *** D: Pedro Almodóvar. Eusebio Poncela, Carmen Maura, Antonio Banderas, Miguel Molina, Bibi Andersson, Manuela Velasco, Nacho Martinez. Surreal, hedonistic, and hilarious comedy focusing on a gay love triangle, with equal doses of passion, sex, fantasy, and tragedy. Maura is a standout as a free-spirited transsexual; Almodóvar is one of the brightest talents to emerge on the international filmmaking scene during the 1980s.▼

Law of the Lawless (1964) **C-88m.** **½ D: William F. Claxton. Dale Robertson, Yvonne De Carlo, William Bendix, Bruce Cabot, Richard Arlen, John Agar, Lon Chaney, Kent Taylor. Veteran cast is chief interest of this programmer, with Robertson an ex-gunman turned judge.

Law of the Tropics (1941) **76m.** ** D: Ray Enright. Constance Bennett, Jeffrey Lynn, Regis Toomey, Mona Maris, Hobart Bosworth. Fair cast in routine drama of man discovering his wife is accused murderess. Remake of OIL FOR THE LAMPS OF CHINA.

Lawrence of Arabia (1962-British) **C-216m.** **** D: David Lean. Peter O'-Toole, Alec Guinness, Anthony Quinn, Jack Hawkins, Claude Rains, Anthony Quayle, Arthur Kennedy, Omar Sharif, Jose Ferrer. Blockbuster biography of enigmatic adventurer T. E. Lawrence is that rarity, an epic film that is also literate. Loses some momentum in the second half, but still a knockout—especially in 1989 reissue version, which restored many cuts made over the years (and made a few judicious trims in the process). Still, the only way to really appreciate this film is on a big screen. Seven Oscars include Best Picture, Director, Cinematography (Freddie Young), Score (Maurice Jarre), Editing, and Art Direction. O'Toole's first leading role made him an instant star. Beware of shorter prints. Originally 222m.▼

Law vs. Billy the Kid, The (1954) **C-73m.** ** D: William Castle. Scott Brady, Betta St. John, James Griffith, Alan Hale, Jr., Paul Cavanagh. Title gives away plot line of unmemorable Western.

Lawyer, The (1970) **C-117m.** **½ D: Sidney J. Furie. Barry Newman, Harold Gould, Diana Muldaur, Robert Colbert, Kathleen Crowley. Lively story loosely based on famous Dr. Sam Sheppard murder case; Newman is stubborn young lawyer defending doctor accused of murdering his wife, battling legal protocol and uncooperative client. Unexceptional but diverting; Newman later revived role in TV series *Petrocelli*.

Lawyer Man (1932) **72m.** **½ D: William Dieterle. William Powell, Joan Blondell, Claire Dodd, Sheila Terry, Alan Dinehart. Lawyer working his way up gets involved with gangsters; Powell and Blondell bring this one up to par.

Lay That Rifle Down (1955) **71m.** *½ D:

Charles Lamont. Judy Canova, Robert Lowery, Jacqueline de Wit, Richard Deacon, Tweeny Canova. Mild Canova musicomedy, with Judy an overworked drudge in Southern town with hopes of being chic.

Lazybones (1925) 79m. *** D: Frank Borzage. Charles "Buck" Jones, Madge Bellamy, Virginia Marshall, Edythe Chapman, Leslie Fenton, ZaSu Pitts. Story of endearing but aimless character, his romances, and the path life takes him down as years go by. Poignant evocation of small-town life from turn of the century into the 1920s. Unusual role for Jones, better known as cowboy hero.

LBJ: The Early Years (1987) C-150m. TVM D: Peter Werner. Randy Quaid, Patti LuPone, Morgan Brittany, Pat Hingle, Kevin McCarthy, Barry Corbin, Charles Frank. Quaid's flamboyant portrayal of LBJ from 1934, as a Texas congressman's ambitious aide, to the Kennedy assassination in 1963 and LuPone's on-target Lady Bird cut wide swaths through this episodic dramatization by Ken Trevey of Johnson's political and personal rise to fame and fortune. Noteworthy are bald-pated Pat Hingle as Sam Rayburn and James F. Kelly's Bobby Kennedy (a role he's played a number of times). Above average.▼

Leadbelly (1976) C-126m. ***½ D: Gordon Parks. Roger E. Mosley, Paul Benjamin, Madge Sinclair, Alan Manson, Albert P. Hall, Art Evans, Loretta Greene. Poignant biography of the legendary folksinger Huddie Ledbetter, master of the 12-string guitar and long-time convict on Texas and Louisiana chain gangs. Stunning musical performances (including "Rock Island Line," "Goodnight Irene" and many more classics), with Mosley effectively restrained in the title role. Superior entertainment.

League of Frightened Men, The (1937) 65m. ** D: Alfred E. Green. Walter Connolly, Lionel Stander, Eduardo Ciannelli, Irene Hervey, Victor Kilian, Walter Kingsford. Second Nero Wolfe film casts relatively amiable Connolly in the role of Rex Stout's sleuth for a none-too-inscrutable mystery about a band of former college chums who are being killed off one by one.

League of Gentlemen, The (1960-British) 114m. ***½ D: Basil Dearden. Jack Hawkins, Nigel Patrick, Roger Livesey, Richard Attenborough, Bryan Forbes, Kieron Moore, Robert Coote, Nanette Newman. Ex-army colonel enlists the aid of former officers (through blackmail) to pull off big bank heist. High-class British humor makes this tale of crime a delight. Forbes also wrote the script. Look for Oliver Reed as a ballet dancer!▼

Lean on Me (1989) C-109m. **½ D: John G. Avildsen. Morgan Freeman, Beverly Todd, Robert Guillaume, Alan North, Lynne Thigpen, Robin Bartlett, Michael Beach, Ethan Phillips. The story of "Crazy Joe" Clark, the real-life baseball bat, bullhorn toting high school principal from New Jersey who whips his students into shape by alternately bolstering and bullying them. Freeman is riveting in the central role, making up for script's shortcomings and Avildsen's all-too-familiar approach.▼

Leap Into the Void (1979-Italian) C-120m. *** D: Marco Bellocchio. Michel Piccoli, Anouk Aimee, Michele Placido, Gisella Burinato, Antonio Piovanelli. A compassionate comedy about a very unusual topic: suicide. Magistrate Piccoli uses Placido to try to induce his mentally ill sister (Aimee) to do herself in. Of course, things do not go as planned.

Leap of Faith (1988) C-100m. TVM D: Stephen Gyllenhaal. Anne Archer, Sam Neill, Frances Lee McCain, Louis Giambalvo, James Tolkan, Elizabeth Ruscio, CCH Pounder, Michael Constantine. Fact-based drama of Deborah Franke Ogg who, with her husband's help, shuns conventional medical techniques in her battle with cancer. Despite earnest performances and a noble story, this can't escape the disease-of-the-week/based-on-a-true-story TV movie feel. Marlo Thomas was coexecutive producer. Average.

Learning Tree, The (1969) C-107m. **½ D: Gordon Parks. Kyle Johnson, Alex Clarke, Estelle Evans, Dana Elcar, Mira Waters. Parks called virtually every shot in brilliantly photographed but surprisingly mild film version of his autobiographical novel about young black growing up in Kansas. Film's appeal lies more in its intentions than in what it actually accomplishes.▼

Lease of Life (1954-British) C-94m. **½ D: Charles Frend. Robert Donat, Kay Walsh, Denholm Elliott, Adrienne Corri, Cyril Raymond. Donat makes anything worth watching, even this mild tale of poor-but-honest country vicar with one year to live, struggling to make ends meet and maintain his integrity.

Leather Boys, The (1963-British) 105m. *** D: Sidney J. Furie. Rita Tushingham, Colin Campbell, Dudley Sutton, Gladys Henson. Uncompromising study of impulsive Tushingham's incompatible marriage to motorcycle-loving mechanic, focusing on their opposing viewpoints and sleazy environment. Released in U.S. in 1966.▼

Leatherface: Texas Chainsaw Massacre III (1990) C-81m. *½ D: Jeff Burr. Kate Hodge, Ken Foree, R. A. Mihailoff, Viggo Mortensen, William Butler, Joe Unger. Mostly a remake of the first film: cannibal clan battles three would-be dinners. Severely damaged by prerelease cuts designed to reduce gore but which only make the film incoherent.▼

Leather Gloves (1948) 75m. ** D: Richard Quine, William Asher. Cameron Mitchell, Virginia Grey, Sam Levene, Jane Nigh, Henry O'Neill, Blake Edwards. Fight flick about on-the-skids boxer Mitchell lacks sufficient punch to push over clichés.

Leather Saint, The (1956) 86m. **½ D: Alvin Ganzer. Paul Douglas, John Derek, Jody Lawrance, Cesar Romero, Ernest Truex. Forthright account of clergyman who becomes a boxer to earn money to help congregation.

Leave All Fair (1985-New Zealand) C-88m. *** D: John Reid. John Gielgud, Jane Birkin, Feodor Atkine, Simon Ward. Intelligent, rewarding account of the elderly John Middleton Murry (Gielgud), husband and editor of Katherine Mansfield, and his manipulative relationship with her. She's portrayed in flashback by Birkin, who also appears as a young woman who reminds Murry of her. Stick with this one.

Leave 'em Laughing (1981) C-100m. TVM D: Jackie Cooper. Mickey Rooney, Anne Jackson, Allen Goorwitz (Garfield), Elisha Cook, William Windom, Red Buttons, Michael Le Clair. Rooney shines as Jack Thum, a true-life Chicago clown, who with his wife cared for dozens of homeless children while struggling to make a living and fight terminal cancer. Above average.▼

Leave Her to Heaven (1945) C-110m. *** D: John M. Stahl. Gene Tierney, Cornel Wilde, Jeanne Crain, Vincent Price, Mary Philips, Ray Collins, Darryl Hickman, Gene Lockhart. Tierney's mother says, "There's nothing wrong with Ellen. She just loves too much." In fact, she loves some people to death! Slick trash, expertly handled all around with Tierney breathtakingly photographed in Technicolor by Oscar-winner Leon Shamroy. And how about those incredible homes in New Mexico and Maine! Remade for TV as TOO GOOD TO BE TRUE.

Leave It To Blondie (1945) 75m. D: Abby Berlin. Penny Singleton, Arthur Lake, Larry Simms, Marjorie Kent, Jonathan Hale, Chick Chandler, Danny Mummert, Arthur Space. SEE: **Blondie** series.

Leave It to Henry (1949) 57m. *½ D: Jean Yarbrough. Raymond Walburn, Walter Catlett, Gary Gray, Mary Stuart. Quickie film has Walburn destroying the town bridge when son is fired as toll-booth collector. Second in a B-picture series, followed by FATHER MAKES GOOD.

Leave Yesterday Behind (1978) C-97m. TVM D: Richard Michaels. John Ritter, Carrie Fisher, Buddy Ebsen, Ed Nelson, Robert Urich, Carmen Zapata. Paralyzed in college polo match, veterinary student falls for young woman who dumps her fiancé for him. Soapy. Average.

Le Bal (1982-Italian-French) C-112m. *** D: Ettore Scola. Christophe Allwright, Marc Berman, Regis Bouquet, Chantal Capron, Nani Noel, Jean-Francois Perrier, Danielle Rochard. Original, stylish panorama of life, love, loneliness, war and peace, from the mid-30s to 80s. Set in a ballroom, with no major characters; the actors play different roles, in different time periods. No dialogue, just music and sound effects. Quite different, to state the obvious, but most definitely worthwhile.▼

Le Beau Mariage (1982-French) C-97m. ***½ D: Eric Rohmer. Beatrice Romand, Andre Dussollier, Feodor Atkine, Hugette Faget, Arielle Dombasle. Headstrong young woman rather arbitrarily decides she will be married (to no one in particular), initiates an embarrassing pursuit of male with other ideas. If you can accept this hard-to-swallow premise, film is a beautifully acted comedy of humiliation. Romand, incidentally, is the now-grown-up adolescent from Rohmer's CLAIRE'S KNEE, made 11 years earlier.▼

Le Bonheur (1965-French) C-87m. **½ D: Agnes Varda. Jean-Claude Drouot, Claire Drouot, Sandrine Drouot, Oliver Drouot, Marie-France Boyer. Happily married carpenter Drouot falls for postal clerk Boyer, feels he can love both her and wife and they will share him. Intriguing, but emotionally uninvolving and unbelievable. Drouot's real wife and children portray his cinematic spouse and offspring. Also known as HAPPINESS.

Le Boucher (1969-French-Italian) C-93m. *** D: Claude Chabrol. Stephane Audran, Jean Yanne, Antonio Passallia, Mario Beccaria, Pasquale Ferone. Another good psychological thriller from Chabrol, focusing on sympathetic murderer and his relationship with beautiful schoolteacher in small French village. Also known as THE BUTCHER.

Le Caviar Rouge (1985-French-Swiss) C-91m. ** D: Robert Hossein. Robert Hossein, Candice Patou, Ivan Desny. Well-photographed but cold and lifeless three-character drama of spies Hossein and Patou (his real-life wife) spending a long night together in Geneva under Russian spy boss Desny's supervision to determine who is a turncoat. A very glum ending doesn't help. Though not a remake, film closely resembles the format of Hossein's 1959 drama NIGHT ENCOUNTER.

Le Crabe Tambour (1977-French) C-120m. ***½ D: Pierre Schoendoerffer. Jean Rochefort, Claude Rich, Jacques Dufilho, Jacques Perrin, Odile Versois, Aurore Clement. Expertly directed, detailed chronicle, mostly told in flashback, of the complex relationship between dying naval captain Rochefort and legendary officer Perrin, a character out of *Soldier of*

Fortune magazine. Both, along with Rich as the doctor and Dufilho as the chief engineer, offer top-notch performances, and Raoul Coutard's cinematography is breathtaking.▼

Leda SEE: **Web of Passion**

Le Dernier Combat (1984-French) **90m.** ** D: Luc Besson. Pierre Jolivet, Jean Bouise, Fritz Wepper, Christiane Kruger. Wildly overpraised science-fiction film is basically another post-apocalypse epic. Jolivet is curious survivor wandering around a devastated landscape having odd, pointless encounters with strange people. Novelty item is without dialogue, in black and white, with stereo sound, but CinemaScope wide screen visuals will be constricted on TV.▼

Leech Woman, The (1960) **77m.** *½ D: Edward Dein. Coleen Gray, Grant Williams, Philip Terry, Gloria Talbott, John Van Dreelen. In Africa, an aging woman obtains power that restores her youth, but requires her to murder—including her rotten husband. Back in L.A. it's more of the same. Gray is very good, but the movie isn't.

Left-Handed Gun, The (1958) **102m.** **½ D: Arthur Penn. Paul Newman, Lita Milan, John Dehner, Hurd Hatfield. Faltering psychological Western dealing with Billy the Kid's career, method-acted by Newman. Director Penn's first feature, based on a 1955 *Philco Playhouse* TV play by Gore Vidal in which Newman starred.▼

Left-Handed Woman, The (1978-German) **C-119m.** ** D: Peter Handke. Edith Clever, Bruno Ganz, Michel Lonsdale, Markus Muhleisen, Angela Winkler, Ines de Longchamps, Bernhard Wicki, Gerard Depardieu. Clever, as The Woman, demands that husband Ganz leave her. He complies. Time passes . . . and the audience falls asleep.

Left Hand of God, The (1955) **C-87m.** *** D: Edward Dmytryk. Humphrey Bogart, Gene Tierney, Lee J. Cobb, Agnes Moorehead, E. G. Marshall, Benson Fong. Bogart manages to be convincing as American caught in post-WW2 China, posing as clergyman with diverting results.▼

Leftovers, The (1986) **C-100m. TVM** D: Paul Schneider. John Denver, Cindy Williams, George Wyner, Pamela Segall, Henry Jones, Anne Seymour. Denver made his TV movie debut as director of a foster facility for hard-to-adopt older children in this amiable Disney outing. Average.

Left Right and Center (1961-British) **95m.** **½ D: Sidney Gilliat. Ian Carmichael, Patricia Bredin, Alastair Sim, Eric Barker. Simple, entertaining comedy about opponents in political campaign falling in love. Sim is hilarious, as always, as Carmichael's conniving uncle.

Legacy (1975) **90m.** **½ D: Karen Arthur. Joan Hotchkis, George McDaniel, Sean Allen, Dixie Lee. Original but flawed character study of pampered, pathetic upper-class woman (Hotchkis) going through the motions of her life. She role-plays, complains, masturbates in her bath, and eventually goes batty. Hotchkis, who wrote the screenplay and play on which it's based, is extraordinary; however, the direction is sometimes static and the finale is anticlimactic.

Legacy, The (1979) **C-100m.** **½ D: Richard Marquand. Katharine Ross, Sam Elliott, John Standing, Ian Hogg, Margaret Tyzack, Charles Gray, Lee Montague, Roger Daltrey. Two Americans find themselves among group of people shanghaied to British mansion where strange deaths and an occult ceremony await. Acceptable fare for fans of this genre. Filmed in England; also known as THE LEGACY OF MAGGIE WALSH.▼

Legacy of Blood SEE: **Blood Legacy**▼

Legacy of Maggie Walsh, The SEE: **Legacy, The**▼

Legal Eagles (1986) **C-114m.** **½ D: Ivan Reitman. Robert Redford, Debra Winger, Daryl Hannah, Brian Dennehy, Terence Stamp, Steven Hill, David Clennon, John McMartin, Jennie Dundas, Roscoe Lee Browne. Underwritten, overproduced romantic comedy about assistant D.A. who becomes involved with flaky lawyer (Winger) and her even flakier client (Hannah). Redford's considerable charisma is at its brightest, which helps make up for lack of spark between him and Winger, and film's other weaknesses. Commerical TV version of this film offers a completely different ending than the original theatrical movie!▼

Legend (1985-British) **C-89m.** ** D: Ridley Scott. Tom Cruise, Mia Sara, Tim Curry, David Bennent, Alice Playten, Billy Barty. Lavishly mounted fantasy, in the Grimm's Fairy Tale mold, about the devil trying to gain control over young girl who represents absolute innocence. Incredibly handsome but story lacks momentum and characters are not well defined. Kids might enjoy it. Released in U.S. in 1986 with Tangerine Dream score; in Europe it runs 20 minutes longer with Jerry Goldsmith music.▼

Legendary Champions, The (1968) **77m.** *** D: Harry Chapin. Narrated by Norman Rose. Excellent documentary on boxing's heavyweight champions from 1882 to 1929.

Legendary Curse of Lemora SEE: **Lady Dracula**

Legend in Leotards SEE: **Return of Captain Invincible**▼

Legend of Billie Jean, The (1985) **C-96m.** ** D: Matthew Robbins. Helen Slater, Keith Gordon, Christian Slater, Richard Bradford, Peter Coyote, Martha Gehman, Dean Stockwell. Texas girl and her brother are implicated in a shooting; unjustly accused of other crimes, they run from police and soon become rebel heroes. Slater is very good, and film is watchable, but its adult characters come out as caricatures and the "message" gets muddy.▼

Legend of Boggy Creek, The (1972) **C-90m.** ** D: Charles B. Pierce. Willie E. Smith, John P. Nixon, John W. Gates, Jeff Crabtree, Buddy Crabtree. Docudrama about sightings of a horrifying swamp monster in an Arkansas community. This modest but well-touted endeavor became a huge success, inspiring many similar films—including RETURN TO BOGGY CREEK and THE BARBARIC BEAST OF BOGGY CREEK PART II (which is actually the third in the series).▼

Legend of Frenchie King, The (1971-French-Spanish-Italian-British) **C-97m.** *½ D: Christian-Jaque, Guy Casaril. Brigitte Bardot, Claudia Cardinale, Michael J. Pollard, Patty Shepard, Micheline Presle. Clumsy attempt at bawdy western in the style of VIVA MARIA, with Bardot and her sisters as female outlaws at a French settlement in New Mexico, circa 1880. Badly dubbed. Also known as PETROLEUM GIRLS.▼

Legend of Hell House, The (1973-British) **C-95m.** *** D: John Hough. Roddy McDowall, Pamela Franklin, Clive Revill, Gayle Hunnicutt, Roland Culver, Peter Bowles. Harrowing story of occult phenomena as four researchers agree to spend one week in house known to be inhabited by spirits. Not the usual ghost story, and certain to curl a few hairs. Michael Gough turns up as a corpse at conclusion. Written by Richard Matheson from his novel *Hell House.*▼

Legend of Lizzie Borden, The (1975) **C-100m.** TVM D: Paul Wendkos. Elizabeth Montgomery, Ed Flanders, Fionnuala Flanagan, Katherine Helmond, Fritz Weaver, Don Porter, John Beal. Realistic drama blending fact and speculation about New England spinster accused of the axe murders of her father and stepmother. Atmospheric as well as graphic with a thoughtful performance by Montgomery. Script by William Bast. Above average.

Legend of Lobo, The (1962) **C-67m.** **½ No director credited. Narrated by Rex Allen, with songs by Sons of the Pioneers. Disney film follows a wolf named Lobo from birth to adulthood, as he learns the ways of life in the West. Well-done, if unmemorable, with bright soundtrack.▼

Legend of Lylah Clare, The (1968) **C-130m.** ** D: Robert Aldrich. Kim Novak, Peter Finch, Ernest Borgnine, Milton Selzer, Valentina Cortese. Has-been Hollywood director fashions young woman into the image of his late wife for screen biography; flamboyantly awful, but some think it's so bad it's good. Judge for yourself. Based on a 1963 *Dupont Show of the Week* TV play by Robert Thom.

Legend of Machine Gun Kelly, The SEE: **Melvin Purvis—G-Man**▼

Legend of Nigger Charley, The (1972) **C-98m.** **½ D: Martin Goldman. Fred Williamson, D'Urville Martin, Don Pedro Colley, Gertrude Jeanette, Marcia McBroom, Alan Gifford. Violent, routine black Western about Virginia slave who becomes a fugitive after killing treacherous overseer; Lloyd Price sings title tune. Sequel: THE SOUL OF NIGGER CHARLEY.

Legend of Sleepy Hollow, The (1980) **C-98m.** TVM D: Henning Schellerup. Jeff Goldblum, Dick Butkus, Paul Sand, Meg Foster, James Griffith, John Sylvester White, Laura Campbell. "Classics Illustrated" version of the Washington Irving classic, a lighthearted treatment by writers Malvin Wald, Jack Jacobs, and Tom Chapman. Emmy Award-nominated as Outstanding Children's Program. Average.▼

Legend of the Bayou SEE: **Eaten Alive!**▼

Legend of the Golden Gun, The (1979) **C-100m.** TVM D: Alan J. Levi. Jeff Osterhage, Hal Holbrook, Keir Dullea, Carl Franklin, Michele Carey. Offbeat western fantasy about a sagebrush golden boy who becomes the protégé of a legendary gunslinger. Not bad, despite Dullea's interpretation of Custer as a sendup of Douglas MacArthur. Pilot to a proposed series. Average.

Legend of the Holy Drinker, The (1988-Italian) **C-125m.** ***½ D: Ermanno Olmi. Rutger Hauer, Anthony Quayle, Sandrine Dumas, Dominique Pinon, Sophie Segalen. Subtle, poetic tale of a down-and-out man (Hauer, in a very uncharacteristic performance), who drinks too much, sleeps under a bridge, and is haunted by his past. The scenario chronicles what happens when he's presented 200 francs by a stranger. As in Olmi's best films, there are often long silences—but those silences are golden.

Legend—of the Lone Ranger, The (1981) **C-98m.** ** D: William A. Fraker. Klinton Spilsbury, Michael Horse, Christopher Lloyd, Jason Robards, Matt Clark, Juanin Clay, Richard Farnsworth, John Bennett Perry, John Hart. A middling effort to tell the origin of the Masked Man, which wavers between seriousness and tongue-in-cheek. Some fine action, great scenery, and a promising storyline, but sabotaged by awkward handling, uncharismatic leads (Spilsbury was dubbed to no great effect), and an absolutely awful "ballad" narration by Merle Haggard. Bring back Clayton Moore and Jay Silverheels.▼

Legend of the Lost (1957) **C-109m.** ** D: Henry Hathaway. John Wayne, Sophia Loren, Rossano Brazzi, Kurt Kasznar, Sonia Moser. Incredibly insipid hodgepodge interesting as curio: Wayne and Brazzi on treasure hunt in Sahara battle over rights to Loren.▼

Legend of the Sea Wolf SEE: **Wolf Larsen** (1975)▼

Legend of the Werewolf (1975-British) C-87m. ** D: Freddie Francis. Peter Cushing, Ron Moody, Hugh Griffith, Roy Castle, David Rintoul, Lynn Dalby. Trite version has handsome Rintoul as the hairy guy, working in French zoo, tracked down by coroner-investigator Cushing. Man-to-Wolf transformation scenes are subpar.▼

Legend of Tom Dooley, The (1959) 79m. ** D: Ted Post. Michael Landon, Jo Morrow, Jack Hogan, Richard Rust, Dee Pollock, Ken Lynch. Landon is pleasing in title role of Rebel soldier who robs a stage for the cause, only to discover war is over and he's now an outlaw. Based on the hit song.

Legend of Valentino, The (1975) C-100m. TVM D: Melville Shavelson. Franco Nero, Suzanne Pleshette, Judd Hirsch, Lesley Warren, Milton Berle, Yvette Mimieux, Harold Stone. Romantic fiction (as it was labeled) based on life and myth of 1920s star. Nero and Pleshette are just fair as Valentino and June Mathis, the screenwriter who discovered him. Place this one about equidistant between Nureyev's Valentino and Anthony Dexter's. Average.▼

Legend of Walks Far Woman, The (1982) C-122m. TVM D: Mel Damski. Raquel Welch, Bradford Dillman, George Clutesi, Nick Mancuso, Eloy Phil Casados, Frank Sotonoma Salsedo, Hortensia Colorado, Nick Ramos. Welch made her TV acting debut as a 19th-century American Indian living through her people's last great stand. Evan Hunter adapted Colin Stuart's novel for Welch, who filmed it as a personal project in 1979, but it sat for three years, and was cut by 25 minutes—leaving the ending (with Raquel as a 102-year-old) incomprehensible. Average.▼

Legion of the Damned SEE: **Battle of the Commandos**▼

Legion of the Doomed (1958) 75m. *½ D: Thor Brooks. Bill Williams, Dawn Richard. Anthony Caruso, Kurt Kreuger. Minor actioner about French Foreign Legion and its perennial battle with the natives.

Legs (1983) C-100m. TVM D: Jerrold Freedman. Gwen Verdon, John Heard, Sheree North, David Marshall Grant, Shanna Reed, Ron Karabatsos, Maureen Teefy, Deborah Geffner. The competition to be a Rockette at Radio City Music Hall in this distant cousin to A CHORUS LINE gets its kick from Verdon (in her TV-movie debut) as choreographer to the legendary group. Average.▼

Le Jouet (1976-French) C-92m. **½ D: Francis Veber. Pierre Richard, Michel Bouquet, Fabrice Greco, Suzy Dyson, Jacques Francois. To show up his cut-

throat father, a rich boy buys a human toy. Sometimes funny, sometimes not . . . but it's miles ahead of the American remake, THE TOY. Veber also scripted.

Le Jour Se Leve (1939-French) 85m. ***½ D: Marcel Carne. Jean Gabin, Jacqueline Laurent, Jules Berry, Arletty, Mady Berry. A staple of French cinema, from the writer-director team that later created CHILDREN OF PARADISE; factory worker Gabin, trapped in a building, flashes back on events that drove him to murder. Generally holds up, while going a long way toward defining Gabin's screen persona. U.S. title: DAYBREAK. Later remade here as THE LONG NIGHT.▼

Le Mans (1971) C-106m. *** D: Lee H. Katzin. Steve McQueen, Siegfried Rauch, Elga Andersen, Ronald Leigh-Hunt. Exciting study of Grand Prix auto racing with exceptionally fine camera work on the track.

Le Million (1931-French) 85m. ***½ D: Rene Clair. Annabella, Rene Lefevre, Vanda Greville, Paul Olivier, Louis Allibert. A chase after a lost lottery ticket propels this charming, whimsical, innovative gem from Clair. The actors sing their dialogue; as much fun today as when first released.▼

Lemonade Joe (1967-Czech) 84m. *** D: Oldrich Lipsky. Carl Fiala, Olga Schoberova, Veta Fialova, Miles Kopeck, Rudy Dale, Joseph Nomaz. Sometimes repetitious but often quite funny spoof of the American Western; title refers to hero, who drinks Kola Loca lemonade instead of booze.

Lemon Drop Kid, The (1934) 71m. ** D: Marshall Neilan. Lee Tracy, Helen Mack, William Frawley, Minna Gombell, Baby LeRoy, Robert McWade, Henry B. Walthall, Kitty Kelly, Eddie Peabody. Racetrack con man Tracy flees to quiet burg, falls in love, and settles down. Drifts from comedy to sentiment to melodrama, killing off best Damon Runyon elements. Frawley is fun as silver-tongued tout called The Professor. Look for Ann Sheridan in bit part at the track. Remade with Bob Hope.

Lemon Drop Kid, The (1951) 91m. *** D: Sidney Lanfield. Bob Hope, Marilyn Maxwell, Lloyd Nolan, Jane Darwell, William Frawley. Hope is hilarious as racetrack tout who owes big money to gangster and must pay or else. Adapted from Damon Runyon story, filmed before in 1934.▼

Lemon Sky (1987) C-90m. TVM D: Jan Egleson. Kevin Bacon, Tom Atkins, Lindsay Crouse, Kyra Sedgwick, Laura White. Well acted but much too theatrical account of young Bacon, and what he finds when he visits his father (Atkins) and new stepmother (Crouse). Scripted by Lanford Wilson. Bacon and costar Sedgwick later married in real life. A PBS *American Playhouse* pre-sentation. Average.

Lemora, The Lady Dracula SEE: **Lady Dracula**

Lena: My 100 Children (1987) C-100m. TVM D: Ed Sherin. Linda Lavin, Leonore Harris, Cynthia Wilde, Torquil Campbell, Sam Malkin, Victoria Wauchope. Lavin is excellent as Lena Kuchler-Silberman, a dedicated Jewish teacher who survived the Holocaust and helped smuggle 100 young-sters out of post-WW2 Poland to Israel. Based on the book by Kuchler-Silberman, who died in mid-1987. Above average.

Lenny (1974) 112m. **** D: Bob Fosse. Dustin Hoffman, Valerie Perrine, Jan Miner, Stanley Beck, Gary Morton. Powerful biography of troubled nightclub comic Lenny Bruce, whose hip humor and scatological dialogue made him a controversial figure in the 1950s. Fine direction, evocative b&w camerawork (by Bruce Surtees) show-case excellent performances by Hoffman and Perrine (as Lenny's wife, stripper Honey Harlowe). Script by Julian Barry, expanded from his Broadway play.▼

Leo and Loree (1980) C-97m. ** D: Jerry Paris. Donny Most, Linda Purl, David Huffman, Jerry Paris, Shannon Farnon, Allan Rich. Uneven romantic comedy, sometimes awkward, sometimes funny, about Most moving to Hollywood and suf-fering typical difficulties of novice actors. He meets and falls in love with Purl, daughter of an Oscar-winning actress, who is trying to make it on her own. Nothing unusual, ambitious, or offensive about it.

Leonard Part 6 (1987) C-85m. BOMB D: Paul Weiland. Bill Cosby, Tom Cour-tenay, Joe Don Baker, Moses Gunn, Pat Colbert, Gloria Foster, Victoria Rowell. With a band of mad animals knocking off the government's top-secret agents, res-taurateur Cos comes out of retirement to avenge his one-time colleagues by foiling the villainess responsible. Even Cosby warned audiences to stay away from this megabomb (for which he receives story and producer credit).▼

Leon Morin, Priest SEE: **Forgiven Sinner, The**

Leonor (1975-French-Spanish-Italian) C-90m. BOMB D: Juan Bunuel. Michel Piccoli, Liv Ullmann, Ornella Muti, Anto-nio Ferrandis, Jorge Rigaud. Medieval mishmash with Lady Liv rising from the dead a decade after husband Piccoli seals her in a tomb. Deadening and idiotic. Directed by the son of Luis Bunuel.▼

Leopard, The (1963-French-Italian) C-205m. **** D: Luchino Visconti. Burt Lancaster, Alain Delon, Claudia Cardinale, Rina Morelli, Paolo Stoppa. Magnificent spectacle, set in 1860 Sicily, about an aristocrat who tries coming to terms with the unification of Italy. Originally released

here in a badly dubbed 165-minute version, film was restored in 1983 to proper form (though Lancaster's voice is still dubbed, as it was in the original *foreign* version). Delon and Cardinale are close to the final word in romantic pairings; the concluding hour-long banquet scene is among the great set pieces in movie history.

Leopard in the Snow (1978-Canadian-British) C-90m. **½ D: Gerry O'Hara. Keir Dullea, Susan Penhaligon, Kenneth More, Billie Whitelaw, Jeremy Kemp, Yvonne Manners. First movie produced by publishers of Harlequin Romance pa-perbacks is predictably tearful love story about English girl who falls for a testy, reclusive American who's afraid to admit his feelings.▼

Leopard Man, The (1943) 59m. **½ D: Jacques Tourneur. Dennis O'Keefe, Margo, Jean Brooks, Isabel Jewell, James Bell, Margaret Landry, Abner Biberman. Intriguing but flawed Val Lewton thriller about series of murders in small New Mex-ico town blamed on escaped leopard. Based on novel *Black Alibi* by Cornell Wool-rich. Originally released at 66m.▼

Leo the Last (1970-British) C-103m. ** D: John Boorman. Marcello Mastroianni, Billie Whitelaw, Calvin Lockhart, Glenna Forster-Jones, Graham Crowden. Oddball film about reticent Mastroianni, last in a line of princes, who gradually emerges from decaying London mansion to become involved with people living on his black ghetto block. Enigmatic, unsatisfying film, with occasional bright touches. Boorman explored some of the same ideas twenty years later in WHERE THE HEART IS.

Lepke (1975) C-110m. **½ D: Menahem Golan. Tony Curtis, Anjanette Comer, Mi-chael Callan, Warren Berlinger, Milton Berle, Vic Tayback. Cut above usual gang-ster film, with Curtis surprisingly convinc-ing as title character, head of '30s Murder, Inc. Berle has serious cameo as Comer's father. Recut to 98m. by Golan for pay-TV release.▼

Le Rouge et le Noir (1954-French-Italian) C-145m. *** D: Claude Autant-Lara. Ger-ard Philipe, Danielle Darrieux, Antonella Lualdi, Jean Martinelli. Solidly acted, hand-somely produced romance based on un-wieldy Stendahl novel about tutor who seduces the boss' wife and eventually be-comes a priest. Released in the U.S. in 1958; European running time 170m.

Les Biches (1968-French-Italian) C-104m. ***½ D: Claude Chabrol. Jean-Louis Trintignant, Jacqueline Sassard, Stephane Audran, Nane Germon. Excellent film of rich, aging lesbian who picks up unformed waif who earns her living drawing on the sidewalks of Paris.

Les Bons Debarras (1978-Canadian) C-115m. **½ D: Francis Mankiewicz. Charlotte Laurier, Marie Tifo, Germain Houde, Louise Marleau, Roger Lebel. Fatherless 13-year-old girl (Laurier) idolizes and romanticizes her mother (Tifo), with tragic results. Cogent but overlong and repetitious drama about growing up, aided by a strong performance from Tifo.

Les Diaboliques SEE: **Diabolique**▼
Le Sex Shop (1973-French) **C-92m.** *** D: Claude Berri. Claude Berri, Juliet Berto, Nathalie Delon, Jean-Pierre Marielle, Beatrice Romand, Catherine Allegret. Amiable spoof of our preoccupation with sex; failing bookstore owner starts selling porno material, becomes increasingly fascinated by it. Clever idea well done; rated X because of its candid (yet unsensational) scenes.▼
Les Girls (1957) **C-114m.** ***½ D: George Cukor. Gene Kelly, Mitzi Gaynor, Kay Kendall, Taina Elg, Jacques Bergerac, Leslie Phillips, Henry Daniell, Patrick Macnee. Charming, sprightly musical involving three show girls who (via flashback) reveal their relationship to hoofer Kelly; chicly handled in all departments, with Cole Porter tunes and Oscar-winning Orry-Kelly costumes. John Patrick adapted Vera Caspary's novel.▼
✓✓ **Les Miserables** (1935) **108m.** ***½ D: Richard Boleslawski. Fredric March, Charles Laughton, Sir Cedric Hardwicke, Rochelle Hudson, Frances Drake, John Beal, Florence Eldridge, Jessie Ralph, Leonid Kinskey. Meticulous production of Victor Hugo's classic tale. Minor thief March tries to bury past and become respectable town mayor, but police inspector Javert (Laughton) won't let him. John Carradine has bit part as student radical. Screenplay by W.P. Lipscomb.▼
Les Miserables (1952) **104m.** *** D: Lewis Milestone. Michael Rennie, Debra Paget, Robert Newton, Sylvia Sidney, Edmund Gwenn, Cameron Mitchell, Elsa Lanchester, Florence Bates. Glossy but thoughtful remake of the venerable Victor Hugo classic.
Les Miserables (1952-Italian) **118m.** *** D: Riccardo Freda. Gino Cervi, Valentina Cortesa, John Hinrich, Aldo Nicodemi, Duccia Giraldi. Intelligent, handsomely mounted version of the oft-filmed Victor Hugo story, with Cervi making a fine Jean Valjean. Mario Monicelli was one of the scripters. Originally 140m. ▼
Les Miserables (1957-French-German) **C-210m.** **½ D: Jean-Paul Le Chanois. Jean Gabin, Daniele Delorme, Bernard Blier, Bourvil, Gianni Esposito, Serge Reggiani. Oft-filmed Victor Hugo tale, with Gabin as Jean Valjean, Blier as Javert. Respectful adaptation, but generally uninspiring. Often shown in two parts.
Les Miserables (1978) **C-150m. TVM** D: Glenn Jordan. Richard Jordan, Anthony Perkins, Cyril Cusack, Claude Dauphin,

John Gielgud, Flora Robson, Celia Johnson, Joyce Redman. Lavish remake of the perennial with a cerebral interpretation of Valjean by Jordan and a determined one of Javert by Perkins. Sparkling cameos by Dauphin (in his last role) and some British stalwarts. Above average.▼
Lesson in Love, A (1954-Swedish) **95m.** *** D: Ingmar Bergman. Gunnar Bjornstrand, Eva Dahlbeck, Yvonne Lombard, Harriet Andersson, Ake Gronberg. Obstetrician Bjornstrand, happily married for 15 years to Dahlbeck, has an affair with a patient; Dahlbeck then returns to *her* former lover—the husband's best friend. Medium Bergman.▼
Less Than Zero (1987) **C-96m.** ** D: Marek Kanievska. Andrew McCarthy, Jami Gertz, Robert Downey, Jr., James Spader, Tony Bill, Nicholas Pryor. Bret Easton Ellis' nihilistic novel about young, disengaged L.A. have-it-alls is sanitized into pointlessness, though a wholly faithful adaptation would have no doubt turned off everyone; try to imagine it with Eddie Bracken, Veronica Lake, and Sonny Tufts. The two leads are awful, but Spader is creepy as a drug-dealing slug, Downey exceptional as a wealthy addict. *Almost good-bad.*▼
Let 'em Have It (1935) **90m.** **½ D: Sam Wood. Richard Arlen, Virginia Bruce, Alice Brady, Bruce Cabot, Harvey Stephens, Eric Linden, Joyce Compton, Gordon Jones. Predictable gangster saga is interesting for depiction of newly formed FBI at work. Some strong action scenes.▼
Let Freedom Ring (1939) **100m.** **½ D: Jack Conway. Nelson Eddy, Virginia Bruce, Victor McLaglen, Lionel Barrymore, Edward Arnold, Guy Kibbee, Raymond Walburn. Hokey but enjoyable pap of crusading Eddy righting wrongs in home town, combating crooked bosses.
Lethal Weapon (1987) **C-110m.** *** D: Richard Donner. Mel Gibson, Danny Glover, Gary Busey, Mitchell Ryan, Tom Atkins, Darlene Love, Traci Wolfe. Undercover cop Gibson, a borderline psychopath who's always on the edge, is partnered with stable family-man Glover, and they prove a good team as they go after a particularly scummy drug ring. Loud, violent, trashy cop movie done to a turn; fast paced and entertaining so long as you don't think about it too much. Followed by a sequel.▼
Lethal Weapon 2 (1989) **C-113m.** *** D: Richard Donner. Mel Gibson, Danny Glover, Joe Pesci, Joss Ackland, Derrick O'Connor, Patsy Kensit, Darlene Love, Traci Wolfe, Steve Kahan. Ultraviolent, superslick sequel is just as cartoonish as the first movie—and possibly even more entertaining. This time around, our heroes tangle with a nefarious smuggling kingpin

who hides behind diplomatic immunity—but doesn't reckon with Gibson's reckless ways. A must for action fans.▼

Let It Be (1970-British) **C-80m.** *** D: Michael Lindsay-Hogg. John Lennon, Paul McCartney, Ringo Starr, George Harrison. Uneven, draggy documentary is rescued and abetted by brilliant, Oscar-winning score by The Beatles. When they perform it becomes magical; when others are thrown in it becomes a bore.▼

Let It Ride (1989) **C-86m.** ** D: Joe Pytka. Richard Dreyfuss, Teri Garr, David Johansen (Buster Poindexter), Jennifer Tilly, Allen Garfield, Ed Walsh, Michelle Phillips, Mary Woronov, Robbie Coltrane, Richard Edson, Cynthia Nixon. Disjointed, only sporadically funny tale of a compulsive gambler who finally hits a winning streak at a Florida racetrack. First-time director Pytka tries for a Damon Runyon flavor and a fast pace, but it doesn't come off; screenwriter Nancy Dowd had her name removed from credits (in favor of a pseudonym).▼

Let No Man Write My Epitaph (1960) **106m.** *** D: Philip Leacock. Burl Ives, Shelley Winters, James Darren, Jean Seberg, Ricardo Montalban, Ella Fitzgerald. Bizarre account of slum life, focusing on Darren and his dope-addicted mother involved with a variety of corrupt individuals. Sequel to KNOCK ON ANY DOOR.

L'Etoile du Nord (1982-French) **C-101m.** *½ D: Pierre Granier-Deferre. Simone Signoret, Philippe Noiret, Fanny Cottencon, Julie Jezequel, Gamil Ratib. Boring tale of down-and-out Noiret murdering wealthy businessman Ratib, and his relationships with golddigger Cottencon and her mother (Signoret). Just talk, flashbacks, and more talk, with insufficient action or character development. Signoret can't save this one. Based on a Georges Simenon novel.▼

Let's Be Happy (1957-British) **C-93m.** **½ D: Henry Levin. Tony Martin, Vera-Ellen, Zena Marshall, Guy Middleton. Featherweight musical of girl going to Scotland to claim a castle she's inherited.

Let's Dance (1950) **C-112m.** **½ D: Norman Z. McLeod. Betty Hutton, Fred Astaire, Roland Young, Ruth Warrick, Shepperd Strudwick, Lucile Watson, Barton MacLane, Gregory Moffett, Melville Cooper. Lesser-known Astaire vehicle is still fun, with war widow Hutton attempting to shield her young son from the clutches of his wealthy, stuffy great-grandmother. Astaire is the man who loves her, and his dancing (particularly in the "Piano Dance" number) is wonderful. Songs by Frank Loesser.▼

Let's Do It Again (1953) **C-95m.** *** D: Alexander Hall. Jane Wyman, Ray Milland, Aldo Ray, Leon Ames, Tom Helmore. Musical remake of THE AWFUL TRUTH with Milland in Cary Grant's role, Wyman in Irene Dunne's, and Ray in Ralph Bellamy's. Songs add to spicy plot, but no classic like original '37 film.

Let's Do It Again (1975) **C-112m.** *** D: Sidney Poitier. Sidney Poitier, Bill Cosby, Jimmie Walker, Calvin Lockhart, John Amos, Denise Nicholas, Lee Chamberlain. Hilarious follow-up to UPTOWN SATURDAY NIGHT; lodge brothers Poitier and Cosby hypnotize Walker into becoming great boxer, figuring they can clean up on bets. Yes, it's an old "Bowery Boys" plot, but still well done. Followed by A PIECE OF THE ACTION.▼

Let's Face It (1943) **76m.** ** D: Sidney Lanfield. Bob Hope, Betty Hutton, ZaSu Pitts, Phyllis Povah, Dave Willock, Eve Arden. Brassy comedy with loud Hutton competing with Hope for laughs in forced wartime comedy of soldiers hired as male companions.

Let's Get Harry (1986) **C-107m.** *½ D: Alan Smithee. Michael Schoeffling, Tom Wilson, Glen Frey, Gary Busey, Robert Duvall, Rick Rossovich, Ben Johnson, Matt Clark, Gregory Sierra, Elpidia Carrillo, Mark Harmon, Jere Burns. Inherently stupid, unbelievable action yarn about a soldier of fortune's attempt to rescue pipeline worker Harmon, who's been kidnapped (along with an ambassador) by an underground group of drug dealers in South America. Busey and Duvall give lively performances, but that's all one can recommend about this turkey. Director Stuart Rosenberg had his name removed from the credits of this film, which barely received theatrical release. ▼

Let's Get Lost (1989) **119m.** *** D: Bruce Weber. Chet Baker, jazz trumpeter and singer from the "cool" school of the 1950s, is the subject of photographer Weber's high-style, black & white documentary. It's a fascinating (and sometimes disquietingly personal) look at the charismatic musician once referred to as the James Dean of jazz, whose long involvement with drugs never seemed to deter him from making beautiful music. Overlong, but worthwhile.▼

Let's Get Tough! (1942) **62m.** D: Wallace Fox. Leo Gorcey, Bobby Jordan, Huntz Hall, Gabriel Dell, Tom Brown, Florence Rice. SEE: **Bowery Boys** series.▼

Let's Go Navy (1951) **68m.** D: William Beaudine. Leo Gorcey, Huntz Hall, Allen Jenkins, Charlita, Dorothy Ford, Tom Neal. SEE: **Bowery Boys** series.

Let's Hope It's a Girl (1985-Italian) **C-114m.** *** D: Mario Monicelli. Liv Ullmann, Philippe Noiret, Catherine Deneuve, Bernard Blier, Giuliana De Sio, Athina Cenci, Stefania Sandrelli. Complex, funny, seriocomic account of what happens when Count Noiret returns to his former wife (Ullmann) and family and attempts to sell part of their estate. The men all have a variety of faults, and the women can very well live without them. Blier is great as the elderly, hilariously senile uncle.

Let's Kill Uncle (1966-British) **C-92m.** ****½** D: William Castle. Nigel Green, Mary Badham, Pat Cardi, Robert Pickering, Linda Lawson, Reff Sanchez, Nestor Paiva. Green's ham is just right for this outrageous tale of 12-year-old who tries to kill his uncle because his uncle is trying to kill him over a $5 million inheritance. Lots of hokey thrills involving sharks, tarantulas and the like. Loosely based on Rohan O'Grady novel.

Let's Live a Little (1948) **85m.** ****½** D: Richard Wallace. Hedy Lamarr, Robert Cummings, Anna Sten, Robert Shayne, Mary Treen. Amusing but unspectacular romantic comedy, with Lamarr and Cummings falling in love.

Let's Make It Legal (1951) **77m.** ****½** D: Richard Sale. Claudette Colbert, Macdonald Carey, Zachary Scott, Robert Wagner, Marilyn Monroe. OK comedy of couple planning divorce but parting as friends. Good cast is main asset.

Let's Make Love (1960) **C-118m.** ******* D: George Cukor. Marilyn Monroe, Yves Montand, Tony Randall, Frankie Vaughan, Wilfrid Hyde-White, David Burns. Millionaire Montand hears of show spoofing him, wants to stop it, then meets cast member Monroe. To join cast, he hires Bing Crosby to teach him to sing, Milton Berle to coach on comedy, Gene Kelly to make him dance. Bubbly cast.▼

Let's Make Music (1940) **85m.** ****½** D: Leslie Goodwins. Bob Crosby, Jean Rogers, Elisabeth Risdon, Joseph Buloff. Nathanael West wrote this entertaining B musical about bandleader Crosby turning prim schoolteacher's football victory song into a hit. Good fun; other songs include "Big Noise from Winnetka."

Let's Make Up (1955-British) **C-94m.** ****** D: Herbert Wilcox. Errol Flynn, Anna Neagle, David Farrar, Kathleen Harrison, Peter Graves. Froth about overimaginative Neagle trying to decide between suitors Flynn and Farrar. Original title: LILACS IN THE SPRING.

Let's Rock! (1958) **79m.** ****** D: Harry Foster. Julius La Rosa, Phyllis Newman, Conrad Janis, Della Reese, Joy Harmon, Royal Teens, Paul Anka, Danny and the Juniors, Roy Hamilton, Wink Martindale. Balladeer La Rosa resists changing his singing style with the popularity of rock 'n' roll. KING LEAR it isn't. Danny and the Juniors sing "At the Hop"; the Royal Teens do "Short Shorts." Also known as KEEP IT COOL.

Let's Scare Jessica to Death (1971) **C-89m.** ****½** D: John Hancock. Zohra Lampert,

Barton Heyman, Kevin O'Connor, Mari-Claire Costello, Gretchen Corbett. Creepy little tale of murder and deception as unstable girl gets full fright-treatment at country home.▼

Let's Spend the Night Together (1982) **C-94m.** ****** D: Hal Ashby. Tired concert film, edited from three separate performances from the Rolling Stones' 1981 tour. Flirts with excitement only when lookers in appropriate garb help Mick Jagger perform "Honky Tonk Woman." This is at least the *third* Stones concert film, and the republic will stand if it's the last.▼

Let's Switch! (1975) **C-78m. TVM** D: Alan Rafkin. Barbara Eden, Barbara Feldon, George Furth, Richard Schaal, Pat Harrington, Barra Grant, Penny Marshall, Joyce Van Patten, Kaye Stevens, Barbara Cason. Fluff concerning a woman's magazine editor and her homemaker chum swapping life styles. Loaded with familiar sitcom performers, who provide no surprises. Average.

Let's Talk About Men (1965-Italian) **93m.** ******* D: Lina Wertmuller. Nino Manfredi, Luciana Paluzzi, Margaret Lee, Milena Vukotic, Patrizia DeClara, Alfredo Baranchini. Amusing episodic film (four stories tied to a fifth): Manfredi competently and comically plays five different men involved with different women and situations. Made right after Ettore Scola's LET'S TALK ABOUT WOMEN, this took 11 years to cross the ocean but was worth the wait.

Let's Talk About Women (1964-Italian-French) **108m.** ****½** D: Ettore Scola. Vittorio Gassman, Maria Fiore, Donatella Mauro, Giovanna Ralli, Antonella Lualdi, Slyva Koscina, Heidi Stroh, Rosanna Ghevardi, Walter Chiari, Eleonora Rossi-Drago, Jean Valerie. Nine-episode comedy with Gassman starring in each, and encountering a variety of women. Some segments better than others; one of the best has Gassman discovering that the prostitute he's hired is married to an old friend of his! Lina Wertmuller's LET'S TALK ABOUT MEN came a year later.

Letter, The (1940) **95m.** *****½** D: William Wyler. Bette Davis, Herbert Marshall, James Stephenson, Frieda Inescort, Gale Sondergaard. Lushly photographed Somerset Maugham drama set in Malaya, tells of murderess (Davis) who tries to cover up her deed by pleading self-defense. Davis quite appealing in her unsympathetic role. Previously filmed in 1929 (also with Herbert Marshall in cast); remade as THE UNFAITHFUL, then again in 1982.▼

Letter, The (1982) **C-100m. TVM** D: John Erman. Lee Remick, Ronald Pickup, Jack Thompson, Ian McShane, Christopher Cazenove, Kieu Chinh, Wilfrid Hyde-White, Sarah Marshall, Soon-Teck Oh. Florid remake of the Bette Davis oldie, although the Maugham tale is laughably dated. Even Max Steiner's original score gets a reworking, interpolated into Emmy Award-nominated Laurence Rosenthal's new one. Average.

Letter for Evie, A (1945) **89m.** ** D: Jules Dassin. Marsha Hunt, John Carroll, Spring Byington, Hume Cronyn, Pamela Britton, Norman Lloyd. Inconsequential romancer; Hunt is torn between pen-pal Cronyn and his buddy Carroll.

Letter from an Unknown Woman (1948) **90m.** *** D: Max Ophuls. Joan Fontaine, Louis Jourdan, Mady Christians, Marcel Journet, Art Smith. Lush romantic flavor of direction and performances obscures clichés and improbabilities in story of Fontaine's lifelong infatuation with musician Jourdan.▼

Letter of Introduction, A (1938) **104m.** **½ D: John M. Stahl. Adolphe Menjou, Andrea Leeds, Edgar Bergen (and Charlie McCarthy), George Murphy, Rita Johnson, Eve Arden, Ann Sheridan. Smoothly done account of aspiring actress Leeds trying to make it without famous father Menjou's help; personality-plus cast.▼

Letters, The (1973) **C-74m.** TVM D: Gene Nelson, Paul Krasny. John Forsythe, Pamela Franklin, Ida Lupino, Dina Merrill, Ben Murphy, Leslie Nielsen, Jane Powell, Barbara Stanwyck, Lesley (Ann) Warren, Henry Jones. Clever three-part drama that uses letter-writing as unifying element in tales of souring and unrequited love. Standard situations milked for all possible melodrama, good performances by excellent cast notwithstanding. Sequel: LETTERS FROM THREE LOVERS. Average.

Letters from Frank (1979) **C-100m.** TVM D: Edward Parone. Art Carney, Maureen Stapleton, Mike Farrell, Lew Ayres, Margaret Hamilton, Gail Strickland, Michael (J.) Fox. Affecting drama about enforced retirement with Carney tops as a newspaper man done out of a job by a computer. Fox's debut. Above average.

Letters from My Windmill (1954-French) **140m.** ***½ D: Marcel Pagnol. Henri Velbert, Daxely, Yvonne Gamy, Rellys, Robert Vattier, Roger Crouzet. A trio of delights from Pagnol: "The Three Low Masses," "The Elixir of Father Gaucher," "The Secret of Master Cornille." The second is best, with monk Rellys leading his monastery into liquor business.▼

Letters from Three Lovers (1973) **C-73m.** TVM D: John Erman. Martin Sheen, Belinda J. Montgomery, Ken Berry, Juliet Mills, June Allyson, Robert Sterling, Barry Sullivan, Henry Jones. Three-part drama zeroes in on couples in situations somehow incomplete without letters delivered. Corny linking device (Jones as mailman) spoils a lot of intended effect. Sequel to THE LETTERS. Average.

Letters to an Unknown Lover (1985-

British-French) **C-101m.** **½ D: Peter Duffell. Cherie Lunghi, Mathilda May, Yves Beneyton, Ralph Bates, Andrea Ferreol. Unconvincing but not uninteresting tale of escaped POW Beneyton and his relationship with sisters Lunghi and May. Neat direction and an intriguing portrait of life in France during the Occupation, but the characterizations just don't hold up. Filmed in both English and French versions; the latter is titled LES LOUVES.▼

Letter to Brezhnev (1985-British) **C-94m.** *** D: Chris Bernard. Peter Firth, Alfred Molina, Alexandra Pigg, Margi Clarke, Neil Cunningham, Ken Campbell, Angela Clarke, Tracy Lea. Bored, unemployed Pigg and zany girlfriend Margi Clarke meet Russian sailors Firth and Molina, who are on leave in dreary Liverpool. There's the potential for love, yet in a few hours they'll be far apart, perhaps forever. Charming, disarming fable about taking risks and dreaming dreams, whose many assets far outweigh its few defects. Very much a product of Liverpool.▼

Letter to Three Wives, A (1949) **103m.** **** D: Joseph L. Mankiewicz. Jeanne Crain, Linda Darnell, Ann Sothern, Kirk Douglas, Paul Douglas, Jeffrey Lynn, Thelma Ritter. Delicious Americana showing reactions of three women who receive a letter from town flirt who has run off with one of their husbands. Celeste Holm provides the voice of the letter's authoress. Mankiewicz won Oscars for his terrific script and direction. Remade as a TVM in 1985.

Letter to Three Wives, A (1985) **C-100m.** TVM D: Larry Elikann. Loni Anderson, Michele Lee, Stephanie Zimbalist, Charles Frank, Michael Gross, Ben Gazzara, Doris Roberts, Ann Sothern. Tepid (and needless) remake of the 1949 classic proves Yogi Berra's adage: "If it ain't broke, don't fix it!" Sole bright spot is Ann Sothern, one of the original wives. Average.

Let the Good Times Roll (1973) **C-98m.** *** D: Sid Levin, Bob Abel. Chuck Berry, Chubby Checker, Bo Diddley, Little Richard, Five Satins, Shirelles, Coasters, Bill Haley and The Comets. Rockumentary with flavor and wit. Study of 1950s told through incredible compilation of film footage, and some fine performances by leading rock 'n' rollers of the period in revival concerts, highlighted by terrific finale with Berry and Diddley dueting on "Johnny B. Goode." Unfortunately, imaginative multi-image widescreen effects are lost on TV.

Letting Go (1985) **C-100m.** TVM D: Jack Bender. John Ritter, Sharon Gless, Max Gail, Joe Cortese, Kit McDonough, Peter Dvorsky. Two witty people, whose lives are shattered when he loses his wife and she's dumped by her lover, discover each other in a self-help group. The two leads give sparkle to this comedy-drama written by Charlotte Brown. Average.▼

Let Us Live (1939) **68m.** **½ D: John Brahm. Maureen O'Sullivan, Henry Fonda, Ralph Bellamy, Alan Baxter, Stanley Ridges. Weepy melodrama about innocent man Fonda convicted of murder and his girl O'Sullivan trying to clear him.

Leviathan (1989) **C-98m.** *½ D: George Pan Cosmatos. Peter Weller, Richard Crenna, Amanda Pays, Daniel Stern, Ernie Hudson, Michael Carmine, Lisa Eilbacher, Hector Elizondo, Meg Foster. Yet one more dreadful ALIEN clone, this one set underwater (like several other 1989 releases), with a team of men and women imperiled as they toil in the depths of the Atlantic. Skip it.▼

Le Voyage en Douce (1980-French) **C-98m.** **½ D: Michel Deville. Dominique Sanda, Geraldine Chaplin. What do women talk about when men aren't around? Friends Sanda and Chaplin travel to the South of France; they gab, flirt, tell each other lies. Sometimes witty, but ultimately disappointing; director Deville asked 15 French writers of both sexes to provide him with sexual anecdotes, which he worked into screenplay.

Levy and Goliath (1987-French) **C-97m.** **½ D: Gerard Oury. Richard Anconina, Michel Boujenah, Jean-Claude Brialy, Saouad Amidou, Sophie Barjac, Maxime Leroux, Robert Hossein. Director Oury returns to the ethnic humor of his hit THE MAD ADVENTURE OF "RABBI" JACOB with this wacky tale of an Hassidic Jew from Antwerp (Anconina) who gets mixed up with drug smugglers in Paris while becoming romantically involved with Arab beauty Amidou. Young cast is excellent and Brialy is a hoot as a narc working undercover in drag.

Lianna (1983) **C-110m.** *** D: John Sayles. Linda Griffiths, Jane Hallaren, Jon DeVries, Jo Henderson, Jessica Wight MacDonald, Jesse Solomon, Maggie Renzi. Young woman, trapped in an unhappy marriage, finds herself attracted to another woman, and tries to come to grips with being gay. Writer-director Sayles hasn't a false note or an unsure line of dialogue, though the film goes on a bit too long. As usual, he's written himself a good role, as Lianna's best friend's husband.▼

Liar's Moon (1981) **C-105m.** **½ D: David Fisher. Matt Dillon, Cindy Fisher, Christopher Connelly, Hoyt Axton, Maggie Blye, Susan Tyrrell, Yvonne DeCarlo, Broderick Crawford, Mark Atkins, Molly McCarthy. Hokey and obvious but still engaging soaper of poor Dillon and wealthy Fisher falling in love, with a "terrible secret" between them. Director Fisher also wrote the screenplay. Filmed with two different endings, both of which were released.▼

Libel (1959) **100m.** **½ D: Anthony

Asquith. Dirk Bogarde, Olivia de Havilland, Robert Morley, Paul Massie, Wilfrid Hyde-White, Anthony Dawson, Richard Wattis, Millicent Martin. Engrossing if uninspired filming of Edward Wooll's vintage play about a baronet (and former prisoner of war) who is challenged in court to prove his identity—which turns out to be unusually difficult.

Libeled Lady (1936) **98m.** **** D: Jack Conway. Jean Harlow, William Powell, Myrna Loy, Spencer Tracy, Walter Connolly, Charley Grapewin, Cora Witherspoon. Wonderful comedy with the four stars working at full steam: conniving newspaper editor Tracy uses his fiancee (Harlow) and ex-employee (Powell) to get the goods on hot-headed heiress Loy—but everything goes wrong. Sit back and enjoy. Screenplay by Maurine Watkins, Howard Emmett Rogers, and George Oppenheimer. Remade as EASY TO WED.▼

Liberace (1988) **C-100m. TVM** D: Billy Hale. Andrew Robinson, John Rubinstein, Maris Valainis, Deborah Goodrich, Louis Giambalvo, Kario Salem, Rue McClanahan. The weaker of two competing Liberace movies, although Robinson is well-cast as "Mr. Showmanship." AIDS is only fleetingly mentioned in this "approved" version that was poorly researched (a saloon chanteuse warbles "The Man That Got Away" to a young Lee *20 years before* it was actually written). Average.

Liberace: Behind the Music (1988) **C-100m. TVM** D: David Greene. Victor Garber, Saul Rubinek, Michael Dolan, Maureen Stapleton, Shawn Levy. The "other" Liberace movie, from the view of his long-time personal manager Seymour Heller. Garber's portrait is more shaded than Andrew Robinson's (though the physical likeness is less pronounced) and the AIDS factor is approached head on in Gavin Lambert's forthright script. Average.

Liberation of L. B. Jones, The (1970) **C-102m.** **½ D: William Wyler. Lee J. Cobb, Anthony Zerbe, Roscoe Lee Browne, Lola Falana, Lee Majors, Barbara Hershey, Yaphet Kotto, Chill Wills. Wyler's final film is militant tale of racism in the South. Some good performances, especially Falana's, but slow pace and many subplots hurt.▼

Liberators, The (1987) **C-100m. TVM** D: Kenneth Johnson. Robert Carradine, Larry B. Scott, Cynthia Dale, Renee Jones, Bumper Robinson, Caryn Ward, James B. Douglas. Fictionalized Disney adventure of John Fairchild, real-life plantation owner who, with his best friend, a runaway slave, became involved with Levi Coffin and the Underground Railroad in the mid-1800s. Average.

Liberty (1986) **C-150m. TVM** D: Richard C. Sarafian. Chris Sarandon, Frank Langella, Carrie Fisher, Claire Bloom, George Kennedy, LeVar Burton, Jean-Pierre Cassel. Ambitious fact-and-fiction mixture about Frederic Auguste Bartholdi's (Langella) endeavors to build the Statue of Liberty as a gift to the U.S. Sad to say, a real snorer. Filmed in Paris and Baltimore with third-rate special effects. Call it average—to be patriotic.

Licence to Kill (1989-British) **C-133m.** *** D: John Glen. Timothy Dalton, Carey Lowell, Robert Davi, Talisa Soto, Anthony Zerbe, Frank McRae, Everett McGill, Wayne Newton, Benicio Del Toro, Desmond Llewlyn, David Hedison, Priscilla Barnes. Tough, mean James Bond adventure, with Dalton pursuing a drug kingpin to avenge an attack on his best friend. Dazzling stunts, high adventure, and a sexy companion for Bond (Lowell) make this one of the best of the series since Sean Connery's departure (if still lacking that old-time panache).▼

Licensed to Kill SEE: **Second Best Secret Agent in the Whole Wide World**▼

License to Drive (1988) **C-88m.** ** D: Greg Beeman. Corey Haim, Corey Feldman, Carol Kane, Richard Masur, Heather Graham, Michael Manasseri, Harvey Miller, Grant Goodeve, Parley Baer. Noisy teen comedy about a 16-year-old who's just flunked his driver's test, and sneaks his grandfather's prized car out for a "dream" date that turns into a nightmare. Appealing performance by Haim, and a terrific one by the underrated Masur, in this otherwise uneven comedy that too often careens out of control—especially in a long, tasteless sequence involving a drunk driver.▼

License to Kill (1964-French) **95m.** ** D: Henri Decoin. Eddie Constantine, Yvonne Monlaur, Daphne Dayle, Paul Frankeur, Vladimir Inkijinoff, Charles Belmont. Constantine is modern-day Nick Carter involved with Oriental spies and superduper guided missile weapon wanted by Allies; elaborate nonsense.

License to Kill (1984) **C-100m.** TVM D: Jud Taylor. James Farentino, Penny Fuller, Don Murray, Millie Perkins, Donald Moffat, Denzel Washington, Ari Meyers. Two families are torn apart when a high school coed is killed by a drunk driver. More or less a companion film to M.A.D.D.: MOTHERS AGAINST DRUNK DRIVERS, this one pulsates with Farentino's and Murray's performances as the girl's father and her killer (the two reportedly swapped roles during the initial filming stages). Written by William A. Schwartz. Above average.▼

Lies (1983) **C-100m.** **½ D: Ken and Jim Wheat. Ann Dusenberry, Bruce Davison, Gail Strickland, Clu Gulager, Terence Knox, Bert Remsen, Dick Miller. Not bad little thriller about young actress who's used as a pawn in elaborate inheritance scam. Well-cast low budgeter piles up a few too many contrivances toward the climax.▼

Lies My Father Told Me (1975-Canadian)

C-102m. ***½ D: Jan Kadar. Yossi Yadin, Len Birman, Marilyn Lightstone, Jeffrey Lynas. Tender film about young boy in Canadian-Jewish ghetto of the 1920s who idolizes his grandfather, a simple, old-fashioned junk collector. Author Ted Allan plays Mr. Baumgarten. Simple and moving drama.▼

Lieutenant Schuster's Wife (1972) **C-73m.** TVM D: David Lowell Rich. Lee Grant, Jack Warden, Paul Burke, Don Galloway, Eartha Kitt, Nehemiah Persoff. Solid performance by Lee Grant in title role as typical N.Y.C. cop's wife trying to vindicate husband's memory and to put herself back together after his murder. Average.

Lieutenant Wore Skirts, The (1956) **C-99m.** **½ D: Frank Tashlin. Tom Ewell, Sheree North, Rita Moreno, Rick Jason, Les Tremayne, Jean Willes, Alice Reinhart. Ewell makes nonsense acceptable as he chases after wife who reenlisted in service thinking he'd been drafted again.

Life and Adventures of Nicholas Nickleby, The SEE: **Nicholas Nickleby**

Life and Assassination of the Kingfish, The (1977) **C-100m.** TVM D: Robert Collins. Edward Asner, Nicholas Pryor, Diane Kagan, Fred Cook, Dorrie Kavanaugh, Gary Allen. Asner stands out in this docudrama of controversial Huey Long, and overcomes Collins' cliched script with his tour-de-force performance. Above average.

Life and Death of Colonel Blimp, The (1943-British) **C-163m.** **** D: Michael Powell, Emeric Pressburger. Roger Livesey, Deborah Kerr, Anton Walbrook, John Laurie, James McKechnie, Neville Mapp. Superb, sentimental story of a staunch British soldier, and the incidents that dovetail in his long, eventful life. Opens in WW2 and flashes back as far as the Boer War. Kerr is charming as three different women in the Colonel's life. (Title character bears no relation to the famous David Low caricature buffoon on whom he's supposedly based.) Heavily cut for various reissues, and often shown in b&w.▼

Life and Nothing But (1989-French) **C-135m.** *** D: Bertrand Tavernier. Philippe Noiret, Sabine Azema, Pascal Vignal, Maurice Barrier, Francois Perrot. A war film with a twist: it's not about battles and bombs but rather the dirty business of cleaning up after war's end. Noiret is officer whose job is to find and identify his country's dead and missing; Azema and Vignal are searching for their lost loves. Some good, emotionally packed scenes, but too many stretches are weighed down by talk. Still, an ambitious, rewarding drama.

Life and Times of Grizzly Adams, The ✓ (1976) **C-93m.** *½ D: Richard Friedenberg. Dan Haggerty, Don Shanks, Lisa Jones,

Marjorie Harper, Bozo. Poorly made, clumsily scripted family/wilderness saga, about fur trapper innocently pursued for crime, who finds peace in the mountains where he befriends a massive bear. Led to subsequent TV series.▼

Life and Times of Judge Roy Bean, The (1972) **C-120m.** *** D: John Huston. Paul Newman, Ava Gardner, Victoria Principal, Jacqueline Bisset, Anthony Perkins, Tab Hunter, John Huston, Stacy Keach, Roddy McDowall, Ned Beatty. Tongue-in-cheek Western saga with surrealistic touches. Newman plays self-appointed "Judge" who rules over barren territory, encountering various colorful characters as town grows and matures. Engaging cameos by Keach, Huston, McDowall, and Gardner as Lily Langtry. Written by John Milius.▼

Life and Times of Rosie the Riveter, The (1980) **C/B&W-60m.** *** D: Connie Field. Wanita Allen, Gladys Belcher, Lyn Childs, Lola Weixel, Margaret Wright. Thoughtful, enlightening documentary about women factory workers during WW2 effectively combines period newsreel footage and interviews with five "Rosies." Alternate title: ROSIE THE RIVETER.▼

Life at Stake, A SEE: **Key Man**

Life at the Top (1965-British) **117m.** **½ D: Ted Kotcheff. Laurence Harvey, Jean Simmons, Honor Blackman, Michael Craig, Donald Wolfit, Robert Morley, Margaret Johnston, Nigel Davenport. Follow-up to ROOM AT THE TOP picks up the account a decade later; film lacks flavor or life—best moments are flashbacks to Signoret-Harvey romance.

Life Begins (1932) **71m.** *** D: James Flood, Elliott Nugent. Loretta Young, Aline MacMahon, Glenda Farrell, Vivienne Osborne, Eric Linden, Preston Foster, Elizabeth Patterson, Dorothy Tree. Offbeat film of maternity ward, with fine Warner Bros. cast depicting nurses, mothers, and others involved in life-giving process. Remade as A CHILD IS BORN.

Life Begins at College SEE: **Life Begins in College**

Life Begins at Eight-Thirty (1942) **85m.** *** D: Irving Pichel. Monty Woolley, Ida Lupino, Cornel Wilde, Sara Allgood, Melville Cooper, J. Edward Bromberg. Drunken washed-up actor Woolley disrupts daughter Lupino's life. Highlight is scene of Woolley as intoxicated Santa Claus. Produced and adapted by Nunnally Johnson from Emlyn Williams's play.

Life Begins at Forty (1935) **85m.** *** D: George Marshall. Will Rogers, Rochelle Hudson, Richard Cromwell, Jane Darwell, Slim Summerville, George Barbier, Thomas Beck, Sterling Holloway. Delightful Americana, with newspaper editor Rogers trying to clear name of Cromwell, who was framed for bank robbery years ago. Rogers' comments on American life remain surprisingly contemporary.

Life Begins at 17 (1958) **75m.** *½ D: Arthur Dreifuss. Mark Damon, Dorothy Johnson, Edd Byrnes, Luana Anders, Ann Doran, Hugh Sanders. Rich punk Damon is dating plain Anders, but is only using her to get to her beauty-queen sister. Demented specimen of producer Sam Katzman's low-budget (albeit successful) 1950s teenpics.

Life Begins for Andy Hardy (1941) **100m.** D: George B. Seitz. Lewis Stone, Mickey Rooney, Judy Garland, Fay Holden, Ann Rutherford, Sara Haden. SEE: **Andy Hardy** series.

Life Begins in College (1937) **94m.** **½ D: William A. Seiter. Joan Davis, Tony Martin, Ritz Brothers, Gloria Stuart, Nat Pendleton, Fred Stone. Sis-boom-bah college nonsense with zany Ritz trio helping the school team win the big game. Pendleton is fun as an Indian who comes to college.

Lifeboat (1944) **96m.** ***½ D: Alfred Hitchcock. Tallulah Bankhead, William Bendix, Walter Slezak, Mary Anderson, John Hodiak, Henry Hull, Heather Angel, Hume Cronyn, Canada Lee. Penetrating revelations about shipwreck survivors adrift in lonely lifeboat during WW2. Bankhead remarkable as spoiled rich girl, Slezak fine as Nazi taken aboard. Only Hitchcock would take on the challenge of such a film—and succeed. Jo Swerling adapted John Steinbeck's original story.▼

Lifeforce (1985) **C-101m.** ** D: Tobe Hooper. Steve Railsback, Peter Firth, Frank Finlay, Mathilda May, Patrick Stewart, Michael Gothard. Completely crazy science-fiction yarn starts as outer space saga, then becomes a vampire movie, then turns into an end-of-the-world story! Ridiculous, to say the least, but so bizarre, it's fascinating: people disintegrate, London is overrun by zombies, and controlling it all is a beautiful nude space vampiress! Don't say we didn't warn you. Based on Colin Wilson's novel *Space Vampires*.▼

Lifeguard (1976) **C-96m.** **½ D: Daniel Petrie. Sam Elliott, Anne Archer, Kathleen Quinlan, Stephen Young, Parker Stevenson, Steve Burns, Sharon Weber. After his 15-year high school reunion, Elliott can't decide whether to chuck the title job to become a salesman. Slight drama resembles made-for-TV movie, but attractive cast and locations make it pleasant enough.▼

Life in the Balance, A (1955) **74m.** ** D: Harry Horner. Ricardo Montalban, Anne Bancroft, Lee Marvin, Jose Perez. Lukewarm narrative set in a Latin American city, about a series of woman-killings; the police hunt for guilty person.

Life in the Pink SEE: **Operation Petticoat** (1977)

Life Is a Bed of Roses (1983-French) **C-111m.** ***½ D: Alain Resnais. Vittorio Gassman, Ruggero Raimondi, Geraldine Chaplin, Fanny Ardant, Pierre Arditi, Sabine Azema. Enchanting, magical, original fable paralleling the stories of wealthy Raimondi building a "temple of happiness" circa WW1, and a conference on alternative education at that site in the present day. Resnais and screenwriter Jean Gruault beautifully illustrate that there are no simple solutions to problems, that those who impose their ideas of perfection on the world are just as dangerous as those who cause disorder.

Life of Brian (1979-British) **C-93m.** *** D: Terry Jones. Graham Chapman, John Cleese, Terry Gilliam, Eric Idle, Terry Jones, Michael Palin. This Monty Python religious parable will probably offend every denomination equally, but it shouldn't. Story of a man whose life parallels Christ is the funniest and most sustained feature yet from Britain's bad boys.▼

Life of Emile Zola, The (1937) **116m.** **** D: William Dieterle. Paul Muni, Gale Sondergaard, Joseph Schildkraut, Gloria Holden, Donald Crisp, Erin O'Brien-Moore, Morris Carnovsky, Louis Calhern, Harry Davenport, Marcia Mae Jones, Dickie Moore, Ralph Morgan. Sincere biography of famed 19th-century French writer who rose to cause of wrongly accused Captain Dreyfus (Schildkraut); detailed production filled with fine vignettes. Won Oscars for Best Picture, Screenplay, Supporting Actor (Schildkraut).▼

Life of Her Own, A (1950) **108m.** **½ D: George Cukor. Lana Turner, Ray Milland, Tom Ewell, Louis Calhern, Ann Dvorak, Margaret Phillips, Jean Hagen, Barry Sullivan, Phyllis Kirk. Turner is at the center of three-cornered romance leading to heartbreak for all. MGM fluff; Dvorak wraps it up with her expert portrayal of an aging model. Bronislau Kaper's musical theme was later reused for his classic INVITATION.

Life of Jimmy Dolan, The (1933) **89m.** *** D: Archie Mayo. Douglas Fairbanks, Jr., Loretta Young, Guy Kibbee, Fifi D'Orsay, Aline MacMahon, Lyle Talbot. Fast-moving account of boxer Fairbanks, on the run after he thinks he killed a reporter, winding up at a home for crippled children. Look for Mickey Rooney as one of the kids, John Wayne in boxing trunks. Remade as THEY MADE ME A CRIMINAL.

Life of Jack London, The SEE: **Jack London**▼

Life of Oharu, The (1952-Japanese) **146m.** **½ D: Kenji Mizoguchi. Kinuyo Tanaka, Toshiro Mifune, Hisako Yamane, Yuriko Hamada, Ichiro Sugai. Clichéd account of beautiful Tanaka, banished for loving a samurai (Mifune, in a small role) below her station, ending up an aged prostitute. Also known as DIARY OF OHARU.

Life of Riley, The (1948) **87m.** **½ D: Irving Brecher. William Bendix, James Gleason, Rosemary DeCamp, Bill Goodwin, Beulah Bondi, Meg Randall, Richard Long, John Brown. Feature-film adaptation of the popular radio comedy series about hard-luck working stiff Chester A. Riley. More bittersweet than the subsequent TV series but enjoyable, with the black comedy of Brown's Digger O'Dell a real novelty.

Life of the Party, The (1937) **77m.** ** D: William Seiter. Gene Raymond, Harriet Hilliard, Ann Miller, Joe Penner, Parkyakarkas, Victor Moore, Billy Gilbert, Helen Broderick, Franklin Pangborn, Margaret Dumont. Young Raymond will forfeit $3 million if he weds Hilliard before he turns 30. Second-rate musical comedy.

Life of the Party: The Story of Beatrice (1982) **C-100m.** TVM D: Lamont Johnson. Carol Burnett, Lloyd Bridges, Marian Mercer, Geoffrey Lewis, Conchata Ferrell, Gail Strickland. Burnett and two of her writing pals from her classic comedy series, Ken and Mitzi Welch, craft a sensitive drama about one-time alcoholic Beatrice O'Reilly, founder of the first L.A. recovery house for female alcoholics. A Burnett tour-de-force, but don't overlook Bridges as her long-suffering husband. Above average.

Life of Vergie Winters, The (1934) **82m.** **½ D: Alfred Santell. Ann Harding, John Boles, Helen Vinson, Betty Furness, Lon Chaney, Jr., Bonita Granville. Successful adaptation of Louis Bromfield weeper chronicling life of Harding, who defies small-town gossip, following her own instincts.

Life Upside Down (1965-French) **93m.** **½ D: Alain Jessua. Charles Denner, Anna Gaylor, Guy Saint-Jean, Nicole Gueden, Jean Yanne. Somber account of Denner, whose retreat from reality becomes so absorbing that he no longer cares about everyday life.

Life with Blondie (1946) **64m.** D: Abby Berlin. Penny Singleton, Arthur Lake, Jonathan Hale, Ernest Truex, Marc Lawrence, Veda Ann Borg, Jack Rice, Larry Simms, Marjorie Kent. SEE: **Blondie** series.

Life with Father (1947) **C-118m.** **** D: Michael Curtiz. Irene Dunne, William Powell, Edmund Gwenn, ZaSu Pitts, Elizabeth Taylor, Jimmy Lydon, Martin Milner. Rich adaptation of long-running Broadway play (by Howard Lindsay and Russel Crouse) based on Clarence Day's story of growing up in turn-of-the-century N.Y.C. with his loving but eccentric father. Utterly delightful, and a handsome production as well. Screenplay by Donald Ogden Stewart.▼

Life with Henry (1941) **80m.** D: Ted Reed. Jackie Cooper, Leila Ernst, Eddie Bracken, Fred Niblo, Hedda Hopper, Kay Stewart, Moroni Olsen, Rod Cameron, Pierre Watkin, Lucien Littlefield, Frank M. Thomas. SEE: **Henry Aldrich** series.

Lift, The (1983-Dutch) **C-95m.** **½ D: Dick Maas. Huub Stapel, Willeke Van Ammelrooy, Josine Van Dalsum, Pret Romer, Gerard Thoolen, Hans Veerman. Sleek horror thriller set in a new highrise, where the elevators are involved in a suspicious number of accidents. Maas is a better director than writer; smoothly made, suspenseful, and witty, but talky, with no satisfactory explanation for the bizarre events.▼

Light Across the Street, The (1957-French) **76m.** **½ D: George Lacombe. Brigitte Bardot, Raymond Pellegrin, Berval, Roger Pigaut. Above-par Bardot fare, involving three-cornered romance leading to murder. Retitled: FEMALE AND THE FLESH.

Light at the Edge of the World, The (1971-Spanish-Liechtensteinian) **C-119m.** *½ D: Kevin Billington. Kirk Douglas, Yul Brynner, Samantha Eggar, Jean-Claude Drouout, Fernando Rey. Amidst their fight for possession of an island, lighthouse keeper Douglas and sea pirate Brynner battle it out for affections of shipwreck victim Eggar. Jules Verne tale has some excitement, but is more often unintentionally funny.▼

Light Fingers (1957-British) **90m.** ** D: Terry Bishop. Guy Rolfe, Eunice Gayson, Roland Culver, Lonnie Donegan, Hy Hazell, Ronald Howard. Miserly husband (Culver) thinks wife is kleptomaniac; hires bodyguard butler who is really a thief. Adequate production.

Lighthorsemen, The (1987-Australian) **C-111m.** **½ D: Simon Wincer. Jon Blake, Peter Phelps, Nick Wateres, Tony Bonner, Bill Kerr, John Walton, Tim McKenzie, Sigrid Thornton. Saga of the Australian Light Horse Brigade, and their involvement in a disastrous desert campaign during WW1. Sweeping widescreen adventure, stunningly filmed, but marred by simplistic characterizations, and overlength (though helped a bit by trimming for U.S. release). Climactic charge on Beersheba is genuinely exciting. Original Australian running time: 128m.▼

Light in the Forest, The (1958) **C-93m.** *** D: Herschel Daugherty. James MacArthur, Carol Lynley, Fess Parker, Wendell Corey, Joanne Dru, Jessica Tandy, Joseph Calleia, John McIntire. Absorbing Disney film for young people, based on Conrad Richter's story of a white boy raised by Indians, who has difficulty readjusting to life with his real parents. MacArthur's second film. Lynley's film debut.▼

Light in the Piazza (1962) **C-101m.** ***½ D: Guy Green. Olivia de Havilland, Rossano Brazzi, Yvette Mimieux, George Hamilton, Barry Sullivan. Splendid soaper that moves smoothly. Mother is anxious to marry off retarded daughter but isn't sure she's being fair to suitor. Beautifully filmed on location in Italy. Screenplay by Julius Epstein, from Elizabeth Spencer's novel.

Lightning Strikes Twice (1951) **91m.** **½ D: King Vidor. Richard Todd, Ruth Roman, Mercedes McCambridge, Zachary Scott. Muddled yet engaging yarn of ex-con returning home to start new life, finding actual killer of his wife.

Lightning Swords of Death (1974-Japanese) **C-83m.** *** D: Kenji Misumi. Tomisaburo Wakayama, Masahiro Tomikawa, Goh Kato. Discredited samurai roams medieval Japan pushing his young son ahead of him in baby cart in this edited entry from *Sword of Vengeance* series. Unending action and beautifully staged fights, with climactic battle rivaling finale of THE WILD BUNCH. Very bloody, though; followed by SHOGUN ASSASSIN.

Lightning, The White Stallion (1986) **C-95m.** *½ D: William A. Levey. Mickey Rooney, Isabel Lorca, Susan George, Billy Wesley. Extremely weak family fare with Rooney a wealthy man whose racehorse is stolen. The Mick can't save it.▼

Light of Day (1987) **C-107m.** ** D: Paul Schrader. Michael J. Fox, Gena Rowlands, Joan Jett, Michael McKean, Thomas G. Waites, Cherry Jones, Michael Dolan, Jason Miller. Family angst movie masquerading as a rock 'n' roll tale. Jett and Fox are sister and brother who perform together in a local Cleveland band that starts to gain some recognition, just as personal problems threaten to tear the family apart. Rowlands, in a gratuitous subplot, plays their dying mother. Real-life rock star Jett steals the movie with her compelling performance, but the film degenerates as it goes along. Occasional sparks can't save Schrader's muddled script.▼

Lightship, The (1985) **C-89m.** ** D: Jerzy Skolimowski. Robert Duvall, Klaus Maria Brandauer, Tom Bower, Robert Costanzo, Badja Djola, William Forsythe, Arliss Howard, Michael Lyndon. Duvall, practically unrecognizable, gives an outrageously inventive performance as a slimy homosexual thug in this otherwise muddled, pretentiously symbolic saga of a trio of criminals who besiege Brandauer's lightship. Narration, spoken by Brandauer's son (Lyndon—real-life son of Skolimowski), is laughably hokey.▼

Light That Failed, The (1939) **97m.** *** D: William Wellman. Ronald Colman, Walter Huston, Ida Lupino, Dudley Digges, Muriel Angelus, Fay Helm, Francis McDonald. Fine cast in Kipling melodrama of

London artist Colman going blind, determined to finish portrait of Lupino, whose florid cockney performance steals film.

Light Touch, The (1951) 110m. **½ D: Richard Brooks. Stewart Granger, Pier Angeli, George Sanders, Kurt Kasznar. On-location shooting in Europe perks up lukewarm drama of art thief Granger and his innocent girlfriend Angeli.

Light Years Away (1981-French-Swiss) C-105m. *** D: Alain Tanner. Trevor Howard, Mick Ford, Bernice Stegers, Henri Vorlogeux. Irritable old Howard, who resides in a deserted, dilapidated gas station, becomes the mentor of drifter Ford. Thoughtful yarn is well acted by its two leads. Filmed in Ireland.

Like a Crow on a June Bug SEE: **Sixteen**▼

Like a Turtle on Its Back (1978-French) C-110m. **½ D: Luc Beraud. Jean-Francois Stevenin, Bernadette Lafont, Virginie Thevenet, Veronique Silver, Claude Miller. Uneven yet absorbing tale of blocked writer Stevenin's efforts to create, offering a hint of the real struggle a writer must make to pound out meaningful sentences on his typewriter.

Like Father, Like Son (1987) C-98m. BOMB D: Rod Daniel. Dudley Moore, Kirk Cameron, Margaret Colin, Catherine Hicks, Patrick O'Neal, Sean Astin. Heart surgeon accidentally sprinkles an ancient Indian potion into his Bloody Mary and presto!—he and his teenage son have somehow switched identities. Moore's mugging talents get a major workout in this Hall of Fame embarrassment, first of four 1987/1988 comedies to utilize an adult-teen switcheroo theme. Later variations worked somewhat better.▼

Likely Story, A (1947) 88m. **½ D: H. C. Potter. Bill Williams, Barbara Hale, Sam Levene, Lanny Rees. OK comedy about veteran mistakenly thinking he's about to die, taking a last fling, finding romance with Hale and misadventures with crooks.

Like Mom, Like Me (1978) C-100m. TVM D: Michael Pressman. Linda Lavin, Kristy McNichol, Patrick O'Neal, Max Gail, Lawrence Pressman. Mother and daughter face new life when dad deserts them, and mom's new relationships with men are mirrored by her teenager. Well acted, thoughtful drama adapted from Sheila Schwartz's novel; produced by former actress Nancy Malone. Above average.

Like Normal People (1979) C-100m. TVM D: Harvey Hart. Shaun Cassidy, Linda Purl, Zalman King, Hope Lange, Michael McGuire, Maureen Arthur, James Keach, Rhea Perlman. Rock idol Shaun Cassidy's dramatic acting debut was in this drama of mentally retarded young adults who decide to marry despite angry resistance from their families. Virtually identical to NO OTHER LOVE. Average.

Li'l Abner (1940) 78m. *½ D: Albert S. Rogell. Granville Owen, Martha O'Driscoll, Mona Ray, Johnnie Morris, Buster Keaton, Kay Sutton. Actors in grotesque makeup bring Al Capp's Dogpatch comic strip characters to life, but despite the presence of many silent comedy veterans (Keaton, Edgar Kennedy, Chester Conklin, Billy Bevan, Al St. John, to name a few) there's nary a laugh in sight. Later musical is much better.▼

Li'l Abner (1959) C-113m. **½ D: Melvin Frank. Peter Palmer, Leslie Parrish, Stubby Kaye, Howard St. John, Julie Newmar, Stella Stevens, Billie Hayes, Robert Strauss. Lively Gene DePaul-Johnny Mercer musical based on Broadway version of Al Capp's comic strip; loud and brassy, with corny comedy, some good songs. Stubby Kaye is fine as Marryin' Sam; other Dogpatch characters vividly enacted.

Lilacs in the Spring SEE: **Let's Make Up**

Lili (1953) C-81m. **** D: Charles Walters. Leslie Caron, Mel Ferrer, Zsa Zsa Gabor, Jean-Pierre Aumont, Amanda Blake, Kurt Kasznar. Enchanting musical with Leslie as French orphan who attaches herself to carnival and self-pitying puppeteer Ferrer. Bronislau Kaper's Oscar-winning score includes "Hi Lili, Hi Lo." Helen Deutsch scripted, from Paul Gallico's story.▼

Lilies of the Field (1963) 93m. *** D: Ralph Nelson. Sidney Poitier, Lilia Skala, Lisa Mann, Isa Crino, Stanley Adams. A "little" film that made good, winning Poitier an Oscar as handyman who helps build chapel for Skala and her German-speaking nuns. Quiet, well acted, enjoyable. Director Nelson followed this with a TV movie, CHRISTMAS LILIES OF THE FIELD.▼

Lili Marleen (1981-German) C-120m. **½ D: Rainer Werner Fassbinder. Hanna Schygulla, Giancarlo Giannini, Mel Ferrer, Karl Heinz von Hassel, Christine Kaufmann, Hark Bohm, Karin Baal, Udo Kier. Second-rate Fassbinder about third-rate cabaret singer Schygulla, whose recording of the title song becomes a hit in Nazi Germany. Intriguing subject matter is pretentiously handled.

Lilith (1964) 114m. **½ D: Robert Rossen. Warren Beatty, Jean Seberg, Peter Fonda, Kim Hunter, Jessica Walter, Anne Meacham, Gene Hackman. Fairly faithful version of controversial J. R. Salamanca novel about a novice therapist who falls in love with a troubled patient. A probing if not altogether satisfying look at the many facets of madness—and love. Director-writer Rossen's last film.▼

Lillian Russell (1940) 127m. ** D: Irving Cummings. Alice Faye, Don Ameche, Henry Fonda, Edward Arnold, Warren William, Leo Carrillo, Nigel Bruce. Strained biog of early 20th-century star; lavish backgrounds and weak plot line diminish Faye's vehicle; Arnold repeats his Diamond Jim Brady role with gusto.

Lilli Marlene (1950-British) **75m.** ** D: Arthur Crabtree. Lisa Daniely, Hugh McDermott, Richard Murdoch, Leslie Dwyer, John Blythe, Stanley Baker. Potentially exciting film is middling fare, with Daniely the girl used by the Nazis to broadcast pessimistic news to British army. Followed by THE WEDDING OF LILLI MARLENE.

Lily in Love (1985-U.S.-Hungarian) **C-103m.** *½ D: Karoly Makk. Christopher Plummer, Maggie Smith, Elke Sommer, Adolph Green, Szabo Sandor. Flat, unfunny (and uncredited) reworking of Molnar's THE GUARDSMAN and THE CHOCOLATE SOLDIER. Egotistical actor Plummer disguises himself as an Italian, and courts wife Smith. Tries to be charming and sophisticated, but fails dismally despite Plummer and Smith's efforts.▼

Lily Tomlin (1986) **C-90m.** *** D: Nicholas Broomfield, Joan Churchill. A revealing peek into the creative process of Lily Tomlin and her writer/collaborator Jane Wagner, as they prepare their hit show *The Search for Signs of Intelligent Life in the Universe*. Straightforward cinema verité allows us to watch Tomlin and Wagner shape their fascinating material.

Limbo (1972) **C-112m.** ** D: Mark Robson. Kathleen Nolan, Kate Jackson, Katherine Justice, Stuart Margolin, Hazel Medina, Russell Wiggins. Emotional melodrama about three women, whose husbands are either missing or captured in Vietnam, who become friends. One of the first major Hollywood productions to examine homefront repercussions of the war, but its intentions are better than its results. Screenplay by Joan (Micklin) Silver and James Bridges. Also known as WOMEN IN LIMBO.

Limehouse Blues (1934) **65m.** ** D: Alexander Hall. George Raft, Jean Parker, Anna May Wong, Kent Taylor, Billy Bevan, Robert Loraine, Eric Blore. Atmospheric but predictable melodrama of race and class differences, set in London's Limehouse district, where brutalized "white girl" Parker is taken in by half-American/half-Chinese saloonkeeper Raft. Watch for Ann Sheridan in a bit. Retitled: EAST END CHANT.

Limelight (1952) **145m.** *** D: Charles Chaplin. Charles Chaplin, Claire Bloom, Nigel Bruce, Buster Keaton, Sydney Chaplin, Norman Lloyd. Sentimental story of aging, washed-up music hall clown (Chaplin) who saves ballerina Bloom from suicide and regains his own confidence while building her up. Overlong, indulgent Chaplin effort still has many moving scenes, historic teaming of Chaplin and Keaton in comedy skit. This won an Oscar for its score in 1972, the year in which it was first eligible for the competition—because it had not been shown in a Los Angeles theater until then!▼

Limit Up (1989) **C-88m.** ** D: Richard Martini. Nancy Allen, Dean Stockwell, Brad Hall, Danitra Vance, Ray Charles, Rance Howard, Luana Anders. Wannabe Chicago Grain Exchange trader Allen makes a deal with an emissary of the Devil—the goddess Nike (Vance)—but the deal turns out differently than she might expect. Slow going, and would have been better without the supernatural elements, but the ending *is* a surprise. Sally Kellerman has a cameo as a nightclub singer.▼

Limping Man, The (1953-British) **76m.** ** D: Charles De Latour. Lloyd Bridges, Moira Lister, Leslie Phillips, Helene Cordet, Alan Wheatley. Bridges is ex-G.I. returning to England to renew romance with Lister, discovering she's involved with racketeers. Nothing special.▼

Linda (1973) **C-73m.** TVM D: Jack Smight. Stella Stevens, Ed Nelson, John Saxon, John McIntire, Ford Rainey, Mary Robin-Redd. Stevens has field-day as title character, scheming wife who murders wife of her lover, makes it look as if her husband (Nelson) was responsible. Only problem is film's hurried pace; otherwise pretty good adaptation of John D. MacDonald's book. Average.

Lindbergh Kidnapping Case, The (1976) **C-150m.** TVM D: Buzz Kulik. Cliff DeYoung, Anthony Hopkins, Joseph Cotten, Denise Alexander, Sian Barbara Allen, Martin Balsam, Peter Donat, John Fink, Dean Jagger, Laurence Luckinbill, Tony Roberts, Kate Woodville, Keenan Wynn, Walter Pidgeon. Quality dramatization of 1932 kidnapping of infant Charles Lindbergh, Jr., and the apprehension, trial, and execution of Bruno Hauptmann. Lindbergh look-alike DeYoung is rather bland, but Hopkins is terrific as Hauptmann, and a firm thumbs-up for JP Miller's incisive screenplay. Above average.▼

Line, The (1980) **C-94m.** *½ D: Robert Siegel. Russ Thacker, Brad Sullivan, Lewis J. Stadlen, Jacqueline Brooks, David Doyle, Kathleen Tolan, Erik Estrada, Gil Rogers. Poorly made anti-military drama, based on an incident in which 27 prisoners staged a sit-down strike at the Presidio, California military stockade. One-third of the film is made up of footage from Siegel's '71 film, PARADES.▼

Lineup, The (1958) **86m.** **½ D: Don Siegel. Warner Anderson, Emile Meyer, Eli Wallach, Richard Jaeckel, Robert Keith. Expanded version of TV series set in San Francisco, focusing on gun-happy hoodlum after a cache of dope. Cult favorite with fans of director Siegel, but on the

[664]

whole, pretty ordinary except for final car-chase stunt.

Link (1986-British) **C-103m.** BOMB D: Richard Franklin. Terence Stamp, Elisabeth Shue, Steven Pinner, Richard Garnett, David O'Hara, Kevin Lloyd. Primatologist Stamp is experimenting on chimps . . . and his activities get predictably out of hand. A horror film that's not horrifying, or suspenseful, or even mildly entertaining.▼

Lion, The (1962) **C-96m.** ** D: Jack Cardiff. William Holden, Trevor Howard, Capucine, Pamela Franklin, Samuel Romboh, Christopher Agunda. Beautiful scenery of Kenya is far better than melodrama about young girl attached to pet lion, with family concerned it is turning her into a savage.

Lion and the Horse, The (1952) **C-83m.** ** D: Louis King. Steve Cochran, Bob Steele, Sherry Jackson, Ray Teal. Warm B film of valiant horse who combats a fierce African lion; geared for children.

Lion Has Wings, The (1939-British) **76m.** **½ D: Michael Powell, Brian Desmond-Hurst, Adrian Brunel. Merle Oberon, Ralph Richardson, June Duprez, Robert Douglas, Anthony Bushell, Derrick de Marney, Brian Worth, Austin Trevor, Ivan Brandt. Dated British WW2 morale-builder, produced by Alexander Korda in a (then) unique "docudrama" style. Top-notch cast and technical credits boost the propagandist elements dramatizing England's entry into the war and the strength of the RAF.

Lionheart (1987) **C-104m.** BOMB D: Franklin J. Schaffner. Eric Stoltz, Gabriel Byrne, Nicola Cowper, Dexter Fletcher, Deborah Barrymore, Nicholas Clay. A weak script does in this spiritless saga of children in search of King Richard I in the 12th century. Intended for kids, but too silly and boring to engage them.▼

Lion Hunters, The (1951) **75m.** D: Ford Beebe. Johnny Sheffield, Morris Ankrum, Ann B. Todd, Douglas Kennedy. SEE: **Bomba, the Jungle Boy** series.

Lion in Winter, The (1968-British) **C-135m.** **** D: Anthony Harvey. Peter O'Toole, Katharine Hepburn, Jane Merrow, Timothy Dalton, Anthony Hopkins, Nigel Terry. Brilliant, fierce, and personal drama (adapted by James Goldman from his play) of Henry II deliberating over a successor on fateful Christmas Eve. Hepburn co-won Best Actress Oscar for her strong performance as Eleanor of Aquitaine. Oscars also went to Goldman and composer John Barry.▼

Lion Is in the Streets, A (1953) **C-88m.** **½ D: Raoul Walsh. James Cagney, Barbara Hale, Anne Francis, Warner Anderson, John McIntire, Jeanne Cagney, Lon Chaney Jr., Frank McHugh. Cagney, in a Huey Long take-off, is lively as a swamp peddler turned politician, but rambling screenplay

prevents film from having much impact. Well photographed by Harry Stradling.

Lion of Africa, The (1987) **C-115m.** TVM D: Kevin Connor. Brian Dennehy, Brooke Adams, Josef Shiloa, Don Warrington, Katherine Schofield. Rough-hewn diamond trader and no-nonsense lady doctor on a truck trek across Kenya. Made for cable. Average.▼

Lion of St. Mark, The (1963-Italian) **C-87m.** ** D: Luigi Capuano. Gordon Scott, Gianna Maria Canale, Rik Battaglia, Alberto Farnese. Canale is pirate girl who wins the love of Scott, heir to the throne of Venice, in this routine period yarn.

Lion of the Desert (1981-Libyan-British) **C-162m.** *** D: Moustapha Akkad. Anthony Quinn, Oliver Reed, Rod Steiger, John Gielgud, Irene Papas, Raf Vallone, Gastone Moschin. Sweeping "David vs. Goliath" spectacle, with Quinn as Omar Mukhtar, guerrilla leader who stymied Italian forays into Libya between 1911 and 1931. Steiger is Benito Mussolini. Filmed in 1979.▼

Lipstick (1976) **C-89m.** BOMB D: Lamont Johnson. Margaux Hemingway, Chris Sarandon, Perry King, Anne Bancroft, Robin Gammell, Mariel Hemingway. Gorgeous model is brutally raped, must ultimately take justice into her own hands. Totally wretched film gives new dimension to term, "exploitation picture." Mariel's film debut.▼

Liquidator, The (1966-British) **C-105m.** **½ D: Jack Cardiff. Rod Taylor, Trevor Howard, Jill St. John, Wilfrid Hyde-White. Nice location photography and adequate acting add up to a rather limp Bondian imitation. Even Taylor can't save this one.

Liquid Sky (1983) **C-112m.** *** D: Slava Tsukerman. Anne Carlisle, Paula E. Sheppard, Susan Doukas, Otto Von Wernherr, Bob Brady. Gleefully nasty original about a lesbian punker whose Manhattan penthouse patio is trespassed by a UFO. A one-joke movie, but a pretty good joke; Carlisle, who also plays a gay male model, is remarkable, and there's some potent imagery despite the minuscule budget. Not for every taste, but you knew that when you read the plot synopsis.▼

Lisa (1962) **C-112m.** **½ D: Philip Dunne. Stephen Boyd, Dolores Hart, Hugh Griffith, Donald Pleasence, Harry Andrews. Jan de Hartog's suspenseful novel of young Jewish girl being pursued by ex-Nazi in post WW2 Europe, is an exciting film despite gaps in story logic. Stylishly photographed on location.

Lisa and the Devil (1975-Italian) **C-93m.** BOMB D: Mario Bava. Telly Savalas, Elke Sommer, Sylva Koscina, Alida Valli, Robert Alda, Gabriele Tinti. Incoherent witch's brew of devil worshipping, exorcism, and perfectly awful acting that has Savalas as a lollipop-popping M.C. in a house of horrors where one of the wax dummies may or may not be a girl possessed by Satan. Also exists in a differently edited version, with additionally shot footage, as THE HOUSE OF EXORCISM.▼

Lisa, Bright and Dark (1973) **C-78m.** TVM D: Jeannot Szwarc. Anne Baxter, John Forsythe, Kay Lenz, Anne Lockhart, Debralee Scott, Jamie Smith-Jackson, Anson Williams, Erin Moran. Teenager's three girlfriends try their own style of group therapy when she has a nervous breakdown. Well acted, especially by Lenz as the troubled girl; adapted by Lionel E. Siegel from John Neufeld's clinical book. Above average.

Lisbon (1956) **C-90m.** **½ D: Ray Milland. Ray Milland, Maureen O'Hara, Claude Rains, Yvonne Furneaux, Francis Lederer, Percy Marmont, Jay Novello. On-location tale of international thief Rains hiring skipper Milland to rescue Maureen's husband from Communist imprisonment. Nice scenery, nothing special.▼

Listen, Darling (1938) **70m.** **½ D: Edwin L. Marin. Judy Garland, Freddie Bartholomew, Mary Astor, Walter Pidgeon, Alan Hale, Scotty Beckett. Judy and Freddie try to land mother (Astor) a husband; Garland sings "Zing Went The Strings Of My Heart."

Listen to Me (1989) **C-107m.** *½ D: Douglas Day Stewart. Kirk Cameron, Jami Gertz, Roy Scheider, Amanda Peterson, Tim Quill, George Wyner, Anthony Zerbe, Christopher Atkins. Slick travesty about a renowned small-college debating squad, set on the kind of party-school campus where Dick Dale and The Del-Tones wouldn't be out of place. Climactic abortion debate—in front of Supreme Court justices, no less—is cheap and hokey in roughly equal measure. Beware of Cameron's shifting Oklahoma accent.▼

Listen To Your Heart (1983) **C-100m.** TVM D: Don Taylor. Kate Jackson, Tim Matheson, Cassie Yates, George Coe, Will Nye, Tony Plana, Ernest Harada. Ho-hum comedy about a couple of co-workers juggling a love affair, with predictable results. Average.▼

List of Adrian Messenger, The (1963) **98m.** *** D: John Huston. George C. Scott, Clive Brook, Dana Wynter, Herbert Marshall, Tony Curtis, Kirk Douglas, Burt Lancaster, Robert Mitchum, Frank Sinatra, John Huston. Good murder mystery has a gimmick: Curtis, Douglas, Lancaster, Mitchum, and Sinatra are all heavily disguised in character roles. All that trouble wasn't necessary; the mystery is good on its own. The director's son Tony (billed as Anthony Walter Huston) plays Wynter's son. Filmed in Ireland.▼

Lisztomania (1975-British) **C-105m.** *½ D: Ken Russell. Roger Daltrey, Sara Kestelman, Paul Nicholas, Fiona Lewis, Ringo Starr. So-called biography of Franz Liszt is, in truth, one of Ken Russell's most outlandish extravaganzas; director's devotees may enjoy this visual, aural (and sexual) assault. Others beware!▼

Little Accident (1939) **65m.** *½ D: Charles Lamont. Hugh Herbert, Baby Sandy, Florence Rice, Richard Carlson, Ernest Truex, Joy Hodges, Edgar Kennedy. Advice-columnist Herbert finds abandoned baby, decides to raise it himself. Forgettable comedy with OK cast. Previously filmed in 1930; remade (as CASANOVA BROWN) in 1944.

Little Annie Rooney (1925) **97m.** ** D: William Beaudine. Mary Pickford, William Haines, Walter James, Gordon Griffith, Carlo Schippa. One of Mary's weaker starring vehicles mixes comedy, sentiment, melodrama, and blarney in uneven doses, as ragamuffin girl and her brother set out to avenge their father's murder.▼

Little Ark, The (1972) **C-100m.** *** D: James B. Clark. Theodore Bikel, Philip Frame, Genevieve Ambas, Max Croiset, Johan De Slaa, Lo Van Hensbergen. Another good children's film from producer Robert Radnitz; this one concerns two Dutch youngsters who try to find their father after being separated from him during a flood.

Little Big Horn (1951) **86m.** **½ D: Charles Marquis Warren. Lloyd Bridges, John Ireland, Marie Windsor, Reed Hadley. Small-budget film manages to generate excitement in its account of Custer's last stand.

Little Big Man (1970) **C-150m.** **** D: Arthur Penn. Dustin Hoffman, Faye Dunaway, Martin Balsam, Richard Mulligan, Chief Dan George, Jeff Corey, Alan Oppenheimer, Aimee Eccles. Sprawling, superb filmization of Thomas Berger's novel about Jack Crabb, 121-year-old man who reminisces about his life and times as young pioneer, adopted Indian, drinking pal of Wild Bill Hickok, medicine-show hustler, and survivor of Custer's Last Stand. Rich humor, colorful characterizations, moving tragedy are among ingredients, and they all click. Screenplay by Calder Willingham.

Little Bit of Heaven, A (1940) **87m.** ** D: Andrew Marton. Gloria Jean, Robert Stack, Hugh Herbert, C. Aubrey Smith, Stuart Erwin, Nan Grey. Jean has vocal outing as 12-year-old singer supporting family; OK vehicle.

Little Boy Lost (1953) **95m.** *** D: George Seaton. Bing Crosby, Claude Dauphin, Nicole Maurey, Gabrielle Dorziat. Synthetic tear-jerker set in post-WW2 France, where newspaperman Crosby is trying to locate his son, not knowing which boy at orphanage is his.▼

Little Caesar (1930) **80m.** ***½ D: Mervyn LeRoy. Edward G. Robinson, Douglas Fairbanks, Jr., Glenda Farrell, Stanley Fields, Sidney Blackmer, Ralph Ince,

George E. Stone. Small-time hood becomes underworld big-shot; Robinson as Caesar Enrico Bandello gives star-making performance in classic gangster film, still exciting. Francis Faragoh and Robert E. Lee adapted W.R. Burnett's novel.▼

Little Cigars (1973) C-92m. *** D: Chris Christenberry. Angel Tompkins, Billy Curtis, Jerry Maren, Frank Delfino, Emory Souza, Felix Silla, Joe De Santis. A different crime-caper comedy, with a midget gang committing the mayhem. Fast and funny, with especially good work from Tompkins, as a former mistress to gangster De Santis, and Curtis, the leader of the tiny troupe. Look for a funny bit by dwarf Angelo Rossitto during a police lineup.

Little Colonel, The (1935) 80m. *** D: David Butler. Shirley Temple, Lionel Barrymore, Evelyn Venable, John Lodge, Sidney Blackmer, Bill Robinson. Even non-fans should like this, one of Shirley's best films, as she mends broken ties between Grandpa Barrymore and Mama Venable in the Reconstruction South . . . and does that famous step dance with Robinson. Final reel was filmed in Technicolor.▼

Little Darlings (1980) C-95m. ** D: Ronald F. Maxwell. Tatum O'Neal, Kristy McNichol, Armand Assante, Matt Dillon, Maggie Blye, Nicolas Coster, Krista Erickson, Alexa Kenin, Cynthia Nixon. Tatum and Kristy wager which one will be the first to lose her virginity at summer camp. Not quite as sleazy as it sounds, but not very inspiring, either. McNichol easily out-acts her costar with a solid performance.▼

Little Dorrit (1988-British) ** D: Christine Edzard. Derek Jacobi, Alec Guinness, Roshan Seth, Sarah Pickering, Miriam Margolyes, Cyril Cusack, Max Wall, Eleanor Bron, Michael Elphick, Joan Greenwood, Patricia Hayes, Robert Morley, Sophie Ward, Bill Fraser. PART ONE: NOBODY'S FAULT (C-177m.) Ambitious adaptation of Charles Dickens' satiric novel concerns upstanding but ineffectual Jacobi, and the young seamstress Little Dorrit (Pickering) who lives with her father (Guinness) in debtors' prison. Low-budget production is painstakingly slow-moving: viewers will either adore this or despise it. PART TWO: LITTLE DORRIT'S STORY (C-183m.) Second half of saga unfortunately insists on recreating almost the entire first half *scene for scene* before moving forward. As in first part, there are several good performances (notably Guinness's) but screenplay is inadequate.▼

Little Dorrit's Story SEE: **Little Dorrit**▼

Little Dragons, The (1980) C-90m. *½ D: Curtis Hanson. Charles Lane, Ann Sothern, Chris Petersen, Pat Petersen, Sally Boyden, Rick Lenz, Sharon Weber, Joe Spinell, Tony Bill. Junior Kung Fu aficio-

nados solve a kidnapping mystery. May appeal to the less discriminating 9-year-old. Lane and particularly Sothern are wasted.▼

Little Drummer Girl, The (1984) C-130m. *** D: George Roy Hill. Diane Keaton, Yorgo Voyagis, Klaus Kinski, Sami Frey, Michael Cristofer, Thorley Walters, Anna Massey. Adaptation of John Le Carré's best-selling spy thriller is long, slow, confusing, not always believable— but still worthwhile, if only for Keaton's strong performance as a mercurial pro-Palestinian actress recruited to perform as Israeli agent. Globe-trotting story about a novice caught in the world of terrorists holds interest throughout, even with its flaws. Kinski is first-rate as Israeli counterintelligence officer.▼

Little Egypt (1951) C-82m. **½ D: Frederick de Cordova. Mark Stevens, Rhonda Fleming, Nancy Guild, Charles Drake. Chicago Fair in the 1890s is setting for tale of entrepreneurs who popularized the later-famous belly dancer.

Little Fauss and Big Halsy (1970) C-97m. **½ D: Sidney J. Furie. Robert Redford, Michael J. Pollard, Lauren Hutton, Noah Beery, Lucille Benson. So-so character study of two motorcycle racers, one timid and gullible (Pollard), the other a self-centered braggart (Redford) who takes advantage of cohort. Beery and Benson outstanding as Pollard's folks; flavorful song score by Johnny Cash.

Little Foxes, The (1941) 116m. ***½ D: William Wyler. Bette Davis, Herbert Marshall, Teresa Wright, Richard Carlson, Patricia Collinge, Dan Duryea, Charles Dingle. Outstanding filmization of Lillian Hellman's play of greed and corruption within a Southern family on the financial outs, headed by majestic Davis as ruthless Regina. Collinge, Duryea, Dingle, Carl Benton Reid, and John Marriott all recreate their Broadway roles, with Collinge, Duryea, Reid, and Teresa Wright making their film debuts. Prequel: ANOTHER PART OF THE FOREST.▼

Little Fugitive, The (1953) 75m. *** D: Ray Ashley, Morris Engel, Ruth Orkin. Richie Andrusco, Rickie Brewster, Winifred Cushing, Will Lee. A young boy who thinks he has killed his brother wanders lost through Coney Island. A lyrical little comedy-drama, produced independently and on a threadbare budget. A minor classic.

Little Game, A (1971) C-73m. TVM D: Paul Wendkos. Ed Nelson, Diane Baker, Katy Jurado, Howard Duff, Mark Gruner. Eleven-year-old son may be responsible for murder; father thinks he might be next victim. Unusual premise rendered ridiculous by wide-eyed script, lackluster direction. Average.

Little Giant, The (1933) **74m.** *** D: Roy Del Ruth. Edward G. Robinson, Mary Astor, Helen Vinson, Kenneth Thomson, Russell Hopton. Just three years after LITTLE CAESAR, Robinson spoofed his own gangster image in this bright comedy about a bootlegger who decides to better himself and crash high society.

Little Giant (1946) **91m.** ** D: William A. Seiter. Bud Abbott, Lou Costello, Brenda Joyce, Jacqueline de Wit, George Cleveland, Elena Verdugo, Mary Gordon, Margaret Dumont. Fair A&C with Lou becoming a vacuum cleaner salesman in series of familiar but amusing routines. Bud and Lou work separately in this one.

Little Girl Lost (1988) **C-100m.** TVM D: Sharron Miller. Tess Harper, Frederic Forrest, Patricia Kalember, Lawrence Pressman, Christopher McDonald, Marie Martin. Somber tale of a couple's struggle to keep their foster child who has been abused by her natural father. Average.

Little Girl Who Lives Down the Lane, The (1976-Canadian) **C-94m.** *** D: Nicolas Gessner. Jodie Foster, Martin Sheen, Scott Jacoby, Mort Shuman, Alexis Smith. Complex, unique mystery with Foster as young girl whose father never seems to be home—and she gets very nervous when anyone goes near the basement. Think you've figured it out? Forget it, Charlie; you haven't even scratched the surface. Engrossing, one-of-a-kind film written by Laird Koenig.▼

Little Gloria . . . Happy At Last (1982) **C-200m.** TVM D: Waris Hussein. Bette Davis, Angela Lansbury, Christopher Plummer, Maureen Stapleton, Martin Balsam, Glynis Johns, Barnard Hughes, Michael Gross, John Hillerman, Lucy Gutteridge, Jennifer Dundas. Glittering, star-laden adaptation (by William Hanley) of Barbara Goldsmith's best seller about the notorious custody trial of 10-year-old Gloria Vanderbilt in 1934. Lansbury, in her TV dramatic debut as Gertrude Vanderbilt Whitney, Gloria's powerful aunt, is especially fine. Originally shown in two parts. Above average.▼

Little House: Bless All the Dear Children (1984) **C-100m.** TVM D: Victor French. Melissa Gilbert, Dean Butler, Victor French, Richard Bull, Alison Arngrim, Pamela Roylance, Lindsay Kennedy, Shannen Doherty. In the second of the three post-series *Little House on the Prairie* movies, Laura Ingalls Wilder's infant daughter is kidnapped during Christmas season by a deranged woman. Average.

Little House on the Prairie (1974) **C-100m.** TVM D: Michael Landon. Michael Landon, Karen Grassle, Melissa Gilbert, Melissa Sue Anderson, Lindsay and Sidney Greenbush, Victor French. Family drama taken from Laura Ingalls Wilder's novel of her ancestors' adventure-filled life on Kansas frontier. Heartwarming pilot to the long-running series. Above average.▼

Little House on the Prairie: Look Back to Yesterday (1983) **C-100m.** TVM D: Victor French. Michael Landon, Melissa Gilbert, Matthew Laborteaux, Dean Butler, Victor French, Richard Bull, Kevin Hagen, Dabbs Greer, Cooper Huckabee. Tragedy unites members of the Ingalls family as it had\so frequently when they had their own weekly series, and they continue facing it optimistically. First of three post-series *Little House* movies. Average.

Little House: The Last Farewell (1984) **C-100m.** TVM D: Michael Landon. Michael Landon, Karen Grassle, Melissa Gilbert, Victor French, Dean Butler, Richard Bull, James Karen. The final hours of Walnut Grove (and of *Little House on the Prairie*) before the town literally goes boom as the citizens vow to stop a land-grabber from taking control. The last of the three post-series films as Landon and company put the long popular show out to pasture. Average.

Little Hut, The (1957-British) **C-90m.** ** D: Mark Robson. Ava Gardner, Stewart Granger, David Niven, Finlay Currie, Walter Chiari. Busy husband Granger takes sexy wife Gardner for granted. Will her friendship with Niven remain platonic when all three are stranded on an island? Static, flat, talky sex farce, from the Andre Roussin play.

Little Kidnappers, The (1953-British) **95m.** ***½ D: Philip Leacock. Jon Whiteley, Vincent Winter, Adrienne Corri, Duncan Macrae, Jean Anderson, Theodore Bikel. Splendid children's story set in Nova Scotia, 1900. Two orphan youngsters "adopt" abandoned baby when strict grandfather forbids them having a dog. Whiteley and Winter won special Oscars for outstanding juvenile performances. British title: THE KIDNAPPERS.

Little Ladies of the Night (1977) **C-100m.** TVM D: Marvin Chomsky. David Soul, Lou Gossett, Linda Purl, Clifton James, Carolyn Jones, Paul Burke, Lana Wood, Kathleen Quinlan, Vic Tayback, Dorothy Malone. Drama about teenaged runaway Purl being drawn into world of pimps and prostitutes. Exploitation masquerading as social significance. Below average.▼

Little Laura & Big John (1973) **C-82m.** **½ D: Luke Moberly, Bob Woodburn. Fabian Forte, Karen Black, Ivy Thayer, Ken Miller, Paul Gleason, Cliff Frates, Evie Karafotias, Phil Philbin, Margaret Fuller. Surprisingly engaging road company BONNIE AND CLYDE set in Everglades country. One-time teen rock 'n' roll idol Fabian made his acting comeback in this one, although Warren Beatty needn't be too concerned about competition.▼

[668]

Little Lord Fauntleroy (1936) 98m. ***
D: John Cromwell. Freddie Bartholomew, C. Aubrey Smith, Guy Kibbee, Dolores Costello, Mickey Rooney, Jessie Ralph. Young New Yorker Bartholomew suddenly finds himself a British lord in this charming film from classic story. Handsome, well-cast production. Also shown in computer-colored version. Remade for TV.▼

Little Lord Fauntleroy (1980) C-100m. TVM D: Jack Gold. Ricky Schroder, Alec Guinness, Eric Porter, Colin Blakely, Connie Booth, Rachel Kempson. Lavish TV adaptation of the classic Frances Hodgson Burnett novel about an impoverished New York youngster who becomes heir to his titled grandfather's British estate. Blanche Hanalis wrote this version, for which Arthur Ibbetson's magnificent photography won an Emmy Award. Above average.▼

Little Malcolm (1974-British) C-112m. ** D: Stuart Cooper. John Hurt, John McEnery, David Warner, Rosalind Ayres, Raymond Platt. Hurt is prototypical angry young man (booted out of art school) who forms neofascist cult and rails out against society in this well-acted adaptation of David Halliwell's play criticizing 1960s protest movements. Warner takes acting honors as Hurt's obsessive verbal adversary. Ex-Beatle George Harrison's first venture into film production.

Little Man, What Now? (1934) 91m. ***½ D: Frank Borzage. Margaret Sullavan, Douglass Montgomery, Alan Hale, Catherine Doucet, Mae Marsh, Alan Mowbray, Hedda Hopper. Impoverished German newlyweds are further strapped when wife becomes pregnant. Splendid romance was also the first Hollywood film to deal even peripherally with conditions that resulted in Hitler's rise to power. Sullavan is luminous in her second screen role. William Anthony McGuire scripted, from the novel by Hans Fallada.

Little Match Girl, The (1987) C-100m. TVM D: Michael Lindsay-Hogg. Keshia Knight Pulliam, William Daniels, John Rhys-Davies, Jim Metzler, William Youmans, Hallie Foote, Maryedith Burrell, Rue McClanahan. Thin, achingly sweet update (to the 1920s) of the 19th-century Hans Christian Andersen parable about a homeless waif who wins the hearts of a wealthy family. A star vehicle for the pint-sized Cosby kid, written by Maryedith Burrell. Average.

Little Men (1940) 84m. ** D: Norman Z. McLeod. Kay Francis, Jack Oakie, George Bancroft, Jimmy Lydon, Ann Gillis, Charles Esmond, William Demarest. Occasionally cute but otherwise slight, predictable adaptation of the Louisa May Alcott novel, focusing on rough adolescent Lydon "learning the ways" at Francis' school. Oakie

easily steals the film as an irrepressible con man.▼

Little Mermaid, The (1989) C-82m. ***
D: John Musker, Ron Clemente. Voices of Jodi Benson, Pat Carroll, Samuel E. Wright, Kenneth Mars, Buddy Hackett, Christopher Daniel Barnes, Rene Auberjonois, Ben Wright. Delightful Disney animated feature loosely based on Hans Christian Andersen story about a young mermaid named Ariel who longs to know what it's like to be human. One could squabble about certain story points, but the film is so enjoyable it's foolish to try. Best moments are the buoyant musical numbers, including "Kiss The Girl," "Part of Your World," and "Under the Sea," sung by a Jamaican crab named Sebastian (and voiced by Samuel E. Wright). Won Oscars for Best Original Score (Alan Menken) and Song ("Under the Sea," by Menken and Howard Ashman).▼

Little Minister, The (1934) 110m. ***½ D: Richard Wallace. Katharine Hepburn, John Beal, Donald Crisp, Andy Clyde, Beryl Mercer. Charming film of James M. Barrie story about Scottish pastor falling in love, with Hepburn radiant in period romance.▼

Little Miss Broadway (1938) 70m. ** D: Irving Cummings. Shirley Temple, George Murphy, Jimmy Durante, Phyllis Brooks, Edna May Oliver, George Barbier. Not bad Temple, with Shirley bringing Oliver's theatrical boarding house to life; Shirley and Durante are good together. Songs: "Be Optimistic," "If All the World Were Paper," "Hop Skip and Jump." Also shown in computer-colored version.▼

Little Miss Marker (1934) 80m. *** D: Alexander Hall. Adolphe Menjou, Shirley Temple, Dorothy Dell, Charles Bickford, Lynne Overman. Winning Damon Runyon tale of bookie Menjou and N.Y.C. gambling colony reformed by adorable little Shirley, left as IOU for a debt. Remade as SORROWFUL JONES and FORTY POUNDS OF TROUBLE, and again in 1980.

Little Miss Marker (1980) C-103m. ** D: Walter Bernstein. Walter Matthau, Julie Andrews, Tony Curtis, Bob Newhart, Sara Stimson, Lee Grant, Brian Dennehy, Kenneth McMillan. Boring remake of the Damon Runyon story, with Matthau as the bookie, Stimson the little girl, Andrews the love interest, Curtis the heavy. Veteran screenwriter Bernstein's first directing credit.

Little Mo (1978) C-150m. TVM D: Daniel Haller. Glynnis O'Connor, Michael Learned, Anne Baxter, Claude Akins, Martin Milner, Anne Francis, Leslie Nielsen. Inspired if slow-moving drama about teenage tennis great Maureen Connolly and her battle with cancer. Average.

Little Monsters (1989) C-100m. *½ D: Richard Alan Greenberg. Fred Savage,

Howie Mandel, Ben Savage, Daniel Stern, Margaret Whitton, Rick Docommun, Amber Barretto, Frank Whaley. BEETLEJUICE-inspired fantasy comedy suffers from clumsy script and obvious postproduction cuts. Boy finds prankish monster (Mandel) under his bed; their friendship leads to various crises, in our world and in the dimly lit land of the monsters. Premise was promising but results are dismal. Cast tries hard.▼

Little Murders (1971) **C-110m.** *** D: Alan Arkin. Elliott Gould, Marcia Rodd, Vincent Gardenia, Elizabeth Wilson, Jon Korkes, Donald Sutherland, Lou Jacobi, Alan Arkin. Jules Feiffer's unblack comedy about life in nightmarish N.Y.C. focuses on aggressive urbanite (Rodd) who lassoes passive photographer Gould into marriage. Superb performance by Gardenia as Rodd's father, hilarious cameo by Arkin as mind-blown detective, but even funniest moments are overshadowed by frighteningly depressing atmosphere.▼

Little Nellie Kelly (1940) **100m.** **½ D: Norman Taurog. Judy Garland, George Murphy, Charles Winninger, Douglas McPhail. Lightweight musical based on George M. Cohan play about Judy patching up differences between father Murphy and grandfather Winninger. Garland sings "It's A Great Day For The Irish," "Singin' In The Rain," others.

Little Night Music, A (1978) **C-124m.** *½ D: Harold Prince. Elizabeth Taylor, Diana Rigg, Len Cariou, Lesley-Anne Down, Hermione Gingold, Lawrence Guittard. Laughably stilted film version of the Stephen Sondheim stage musical, which in turn was based on Ingmar Bergman's sex-at-a-country-estate comedy, SMILES OF A SUMMER NIGHT. Liz's rendition of "Send in the Clowns" is no chart buster. Filmed in Austria.▼

Little Nikita (1988) **C-98m.** ** D: Richard Benjamin. Sidney Poitier, River Phoenix, Richard Jenkins, Caroline Kava, Richard Bradford, Richard Lynch, Loretta Devine, Lucy Deakins. Intriguing premise—young, all-American Phoenix learning that his parents are Soviet agents—fails to catch fire in this sometimes entertaining but ultimately incoherent thriller. Poitier adds a bit of spark as an FBI agent.▼

Little Nuns, The (1965-Italian) **101m.** **½ D: Luciano Salce. Catherine Spaak, Sylva Koscina, Amedeo Nazzari, Didi Perego, Umberto D'Orsi. Innocent little film of nuns trying to persuade airline to reroute their jets, which disturb the convent.

Little Old New York (1940) **100m.** **½ D: Henry King. Alice Faye, Brenda Joyce, Fred MacMurray, Richard Greene, Henry Stephenson. Claims to be story of Robert Fulton and his steamboat; merely serves as framework for standard romance.

Little Prince, The (1974-British) **C-88m.** **½ D: Stanley Donen. Richard Kiley, Steven Warner, Bob Fosse, Gene Wilder, Joss Ackland, Clive Revill, Donna McKechnie, Victor Spinetti. Antoine de St. Exupery's children's book is considered a classic, but this musical fantasy doesn't do it justice. Kiley plays aviator who counsels and guides a young boy who wants to learn about life. Unmemorable score by Lerner and Loewe is just one of this fable's major letdowns.▼

Little Princess, The (1939) **C-91m.** *** D: Walter Lang. Shirley Temple, Richard Greene, Anita Louise, Ian Hunter, Cesar Romero, Arthur Treacher, Marcia Mae Jones. Shirley stars as a Victorian waif who makes good in this lavishly mounted, colorful production.▼

Little Romance, A (1979) **C-108m.** *** D: George Roy Hill. Laurence Olivier, Diane Lane, Thelonious Bernard, Arthur Hill, Sally Kellerman, David Dukes, Broderick Crawford. Engaging film about relationship of young American girl (Lane, in her film debut) living in Paris and running off with a charming French boy (Bernard), chaperoned by wily old con man (Olivier, wonderfully hammy). A throwback to director Hill's WORLD OF HENRY ORIENT in its winning treatment of adolescence, but not quite as good. Crawford has funny cameo as himself. Georges Delerue's music score won a well-deserved Oscar.▼

Little Sex, A (1982) **C-95m.** ** D: Bruce Paltrow. Tim Matheson, Kate Capshaw, Edward Herrmann, John Glover, Joan Copeland, Susanna Dalton, Wendie Malic, Wallace Shawn, Melinda Culea. MTM Enterprises' first theatrical feature is basically an R-rated TV-movie, with Matheson marrying long-time girlfriend Capshaw hoping it will cure him of his womanizing. It doesn't. Tired but watchable comedy-drama has pretty N.Y.C. locations and pleasing performances, particularly by Herrmann as Matheson's wiser older brother. Capshaw's film debut.▼

Little Shepherd of Kingdom Come, The (1961) **C-108m.** **½ D: Andrew V. McLaglen. Jimmie Rodgers, Luana Patten, Chill Wills, Neil Hamilton. Bland family-type film of boy who fought for the North during Civil War and his return to rural life. Based on the 1903 novel by John William Fox.

Little Shop of Horrors, The (1960) **70m.** ***½ D: Roger Corman. Jonathan Haze, Jackie Joseph, Mel Welles, Dick Miller, Myrtle Vail, Jack Nicholson. Classic black comedy about young schnook who develops bloodthirsty plant and is forced to kill in order to feed it. Initially infamous as The Film Shot In Two Days, but now considered one of Corman's best pictures.

Nicholson has hilarious bit as masochist who thrives on dental pain; delightful screenplay by Charles Griffith (who also plays the hold-up man and is the voice of "Audrey, Jr.") was the basis for the later hit stage musical, which itself was filmed in 1986. Also shown in computer-colored version.▼

Little Shop of Horrors (1986) **C-88m.** ****½ D:** Frank Oz. Rick Moranis, Ellen Greene, Vincent Gardenia, Steve Martin, James Belushi, John Candy, Christopher Guest, Bill Murray, voice of Levi Stubbs. Very entertaining black comedy/musical about a nebbish (played to perfection by Moranis) whose "unusual" new plant brings him good fortune—but turns into a Frankenstein. Greene (repeating her stage role) is a delight as his squeaky-voiced heartthrob, Martin hilarious as her macho boyfriend. But when Audrey II, the plant, turns *really* mean and monstrous, with super-duper special effects, the fun drains away. Based on the off-Broadway musical by Howard Ashman and Alan Menken, which in turn was based on Roger Corman's 1960 low-budget black comedy (written by Charles B. Griffith). ▼

Little Sister, The (1984) **C-103m. TVM** D: Jan Egleson. John Savage, Tracy Pollan, Roxanne Hart, Richard Jenkins, Jack Kehoe, Henry Tomaszewski. Sincere but muddled and underplayed drama about idealistic probation officer Savage and his concern for deeply troubled young Pollan. A PBS *American Playhouse* presentation. Also known as THE TENDER AGE. Average.▼

Little Spies (1986) **C-100m. TVM** D: Greg Beeman. Mickey Rooney, Robert Costanzo, Peter Smith, Candace Cameron, Adam Carl, Sean Hall, James Tolkan. The Mick and a gang of gung-ho youngsters raid a puppy kennel to retrieve their dog from kidnappers in this predictable Disney family adventure. Rooney manages to upstage the kids as well as a kennelful of mutts. Average.

Littlest Hobo, The (1958) **77m. **½ D:** Charles Rondeau. Buddy Hart, Wendy Stuart, Carlyle Mitchell, Howard Hoffman. Aimed at child audience, film recounts tale of dog who saves his master's pet lamb from being killed.

Littlest Horse Thieves, The (1977) **C-104m. *** D:** Charles Jarrott. Alastair Sim, Peter Barkworth, Maurice Colbourne, Susan Tebbs, Andrew Harrison, Chloe Franks. Well-made Disney period piece, filmed in England, about three children's efforts to save pit-ponies who work the mines from abuse and death. Set at the turn of the century. Good location photography. Originally titled ESCAPE FROM THE DARK.▼

Littlest Outlaw, The (1955) **C-75m. ***** D: Roberto Gavaldon. Pedro Armendariz,

Joseph Calleia, Rodolfo Acosta, Andres Velasquez, Pepe Ortiz. Unpretentious little Disney film about Mexican boy (Velasquez) who runs away with a horse rather than see it killed for its misdeeds; filmed on location.▼

Littlest Rebel, The (1935) **70m. *** D:** David Butler. Shirley Temple, John Boles, Jack Holt, Karen Morley, Bill Robinson, Stepin Fetchit, Guinn "Big Boy" Williams. One of Shirley's best films, a Civil War saga set in the Old South, with our little heroine managing to wrap Union officer Holt around her little finger and protect her Confederate officer father (Boles). Temple and Robinson do some delightful dancing as well. Also shown in computer-colored version.▼

Littlest Victims, The (1989) **C-100m. TVM** D: Peter Levin. Tim Matheson, Mary-Joan Negro, Maryann Plunkett, Richard Venture, Lewis Arlt. Offbeat biopic of Dr. James Oleske, New Jersey-based pediatrician who works with AIDS children. Earnest but predictable docudrama was the first major network feature shot on High Definition Tape (HDT). Average.

Little Thief, The (1989-French) **C-104m. **½ D:** Claude Miller. Charlotte Gainsbourg, Didier Bezace, Simon de la Brosse, Nathalie Cardone, Raoul Billerey. So-so character portrait of the title lass, an alienated, amoral teen drifting through life in postwar France. If she comes off as a female Antoine Doinel, it's because the original story was cowritten by Francois Truffaut, who was supposedly planning to film this at the time of his death; resulting film lacks the director's inimitable touch. Miller was for ten years Truffaut's assistant; Gainsbourg is the daughter of Jane Birkin.▼

Little Tough Guy (1938) **63m. D:** Harold Young. Billy Halop, Huntz Hall, Gabriel Dell, Bernard Punsley, David Gorcey, Hally Chester, Helen Parrish, Robert Wilcox, Jackie Searl, Marjorie Main. SEE: **Bowery Boys** series.▼

Little Tough Guys in Society (1938) **76m.** ***½ D:** Erle Kenton. Mischa Auer, Mary Boland, Edward Everett Horton, Helen Parrish, Jackie Searl, Peggy Stewart, Harold Huber, David Oliver, Frankie Thomas. Paper-thin tale of title delinquents—junior Dead End Kids—and their escapades. Auer, Boland and Horton can't save it.

Little Treasure (1985) **C-95m. *½ D:** Alan Sharp. Margot Kidder, Ted Danson, Burt Lancaster, Joseph Hacker, Malena Doria, John Pearce. A stripper ventures to Mexico to meet her long-lost father but spends most of her time searching for treasure with a dropout American. Unsatisfying story marked directing debut for writer Sharp. Danson comes off best.▼

Little Vera (1988-Russian) **C-130m. *****

D: Vassili Pitchul. Natalia Negoda, Andrei Sokolov, Yuri Nazarov, Ludmila Zaisova, Alexander Niegreva. Groundbreaking, post-*glasnost* look at life in modern Russia. Negoda offers a fresh performance as an alienated, working-class, rock music-loving young woman; the depiction of her sexual relationship with Sokolov, plus the manner in which Western culture has affected her life, make this unlike any other Soviet film you've ever seen. Not surprisingly, it was a smash hit in its homeland.▼

Little White Lies (1989) **C-100m. TVM** D: Anson Williams. Ann Jillian, Tim Matheson, Suzie Plakson, Marc McClure, Amy Yasbeck, Robert Costanzo. Harmless romantic comedy about a female detective and a medical intern who lie to one another about their jobs when they meet on vacation; soon they're trapped by the truth. A distant cousin to the Martin Short/Annette O'Toole CROSS MY HEART. The writer on this one lost faith and used a pseudonym in the credits. Average.

Little Women (1933) **115m. ****** D: George Cukor. Katharine Hepburn, Joan Bennett, Paul Lukas, Frances Dee, Jean Parker, Edna May Oliver, Douglass Montgomery, Spring Byington. Film offers endless pleasure no matter how many times you've seen it; a faithful, beautiful adaptation of Alcott's book by Victor Heerman and Sarah Y. Mason, who deservedly received Oscars. The cast is uniformly superb.▼

Little Women (1949) **C-121m. **½** D: Mervyn LeRoy. June Allyson, Peter Lawford, Margaret O'Brien, Elizabeth Taylor, Janet Leigh, Mary Astor. Glossy remake of Louisa May Alcott's gentle account of teenage girls finding maturity and romance—patly cast.▼

Little Women (1978) **C-200m. TVM** D: David Lowell Rich. Meredith Baxter Birney, Susan Dey, Ann Dusenberry, Eve Plumb, Dorothy McGuire, Robert Young, Greer Garson, Cliff Potts, William Shatner. Sugarplum refilming of the classic, sparked by McGuire's Marmee and Garson's Aunt March (her TV movie debut). The pallid short-lived series spun off from this adaptation by Suzanne Clauser. Above average.

√ **Little World of Don Camillo, The** (1951-French-Italian) **96m. **½** D: Julien Duvivier. Fernandel, Sylvie, Gino Cervi, Vera Talqui, Franco Interlenghi, Saro Urzi. Fernandel is the whole show in this comic tale of a small-town priest who's outraged when the Communists are elected to local office. Moderately funny satire of religion and politics, coscripted by Duvivier and based on the novel by Giovanni Guareschi. English language version is narrated by Orson Welles. Followed by several sequels.▼

Live Again, Die Again (1974) **C-78m. TVM** D: Richard A. Colla. Cliff Potts, Walter Pidgeon, Donna Mills, Geraldine Page, Vera Miles, Mike Farrell, Lurene Tuttle. Cryogenics thriller of a beautiful woman (Mills) brought back to her family after 34 years in suspended animation, who discovers somebody is trying to kill her. Adapted by Joseph Stefano from David Sale's novel *Come to Mother*. Average.

Live a Little, Love a Little (1968) **C-90m.** ** D: Norman Taurog. Elvis Presley, Michele Carey, Don Porter, Rudy Vallee, Dick Sargent, Sterling Holloway, Eddie Hodges. Elvis manages to land two well-paying photographer's jobs and work them both by hopping back and forth from office to office. Pleasant, if standard, Presley fare.▼

Live a Little, Steal a Lot (1975) **C-101m.** **½ D: Marvin Chomsky. Robert Conrad, Don Stroud, Donna Mills, Robyn Millan, Luther Adler, Burt Young, Paul Stewart. Unremarkable but engrossing tale based on real-life story of two Florida beach bums who engineered "impossible" heist of 564-carat Star of India. Fine TOPKAPI-like caper scenes, plus good speedboat chase. Originally titled MURPH THE SURF and retitled YOU CAN'T STEAL LOVE.▼

Live and Let Die (1973-British) **C-121m.** **½ D: Guy Hamilton. Roger Moore, Yaphet Kotto, Jane Seymour, Clifton James, Geoffrey Holder, Bernard Lee, Lois Maxwell. Barely memorable, overlong James Bond movie seems merely an excuse to film wild chase sequences; superagent goes after master criminal subverting U.S. economy via drugs. Works on level of old-time serial. This was Moore's first appearance as 007; title song by Paul McCartney.▼

Live Fast, Die Young (1958) **82m.** ** D: Paul Henreid. Mary Murphy, Norma Eberhardt, Michael Connors. Turgid B film of runaway girl and her sister who prevents her from starting a life of crime.

Live for Life (1967-French-Italian) **C-130m.** **½ D: Claude Lelouch. Yves Montand, Annie Girardot, Candice Bergen, Irene Tunc, Anouck Ferjac. TV documentary producer Montand leaves wife Girardot for fashion model Bergen in glossy film helped by some good acting; picture was follow-up to Lelouch's A MAN AND A WOMAN.

Live It Up SEE: **Sing and Swing**

Live, Love and Learn (1937) **78m.** **½ D: George Fitzmaurice. Robert Montgomery, Rosalind Russell, Mickey Rooney, Helen Vinson, Monty Woolley, E. E. Clive, Al Shean, Billy Gilbert. Contract stars glide through this formula MGM fluff, with ritzy Russell marrying nonconformist artist Montgomery.

Lively Set, The (1964) **C-95m.** **½ D: Jack Arnold. James Darren, Pamela Tiffin, Doug McClure, Marilyn Maxwell, Charles Drake, Greg Morris. Empty-headed account of cocky Darren, quitting college to become a champion sports car racer.

Several forgettable songs—including The Surfaris' "Boss Barracuda."

Lives of a Bengal Lancer, The (1935) 109m. **** D: Henry Hathaway. Gary Cooper, Franchot Tone, Richard Cromwell, Sir Guy Standing, C. Aubrey Smith, Monte Blue, Kathleen Burke. Delightful Hollywood foray into British Empire; Cooper and Tone are pals in famed British regiment, Cromwell the callow son of commander Standing whom they take under their wing. Top story, action, repartee—and wonderful snake-charming scene. Remade, with obvious changes, as GERONIMO (1939).▼

Lives of Jenny Dolan, The (1975) C-100m. TVM D: Jerry Jameson. Shirley Jones, Lynn Carlin, James Darren, Farley Granger, George Grizzard, David Hedison, Stephen McNally, Ian McShane, Pernell Roberts, Percy Rodrigues, Collin Wilcox, Dana Wynter, Stephen Boyd, Charles Drake, Virginia Grey. Glamorous newspaper reporter, investigating assassination of political figure, finds her own life in danger. Producer Ross Hunter's first TV movie has Jones sleuthing in mink and changing eye-popping wardrobe in every scene. The plot's familiar, too, if you've caught THE PARALLAX VIEW. Below average.

Live Wires (1946) 64m. D: Phil Karlson. Leo Gorcey, Huntz Hall, Bobby Jordan, Billy Benedict, William Frambes, Pamela Blake. SEE: **Bowery Boys** series.

Living Daylights, The (1987-British) C-130m. **½ D: John Glen. Timothy Dalton, Maryam d'Abo, Jeroen Krabbe, Joe Don Baker, John Rhys-Davies, Art Malik, Andreas Wisniewski, Desmond Llewellyn, Robert Brown, Geoffrey Keen, Walter Gotell. Dalton makes an impressive debut as James Bond in this entertaining, globe-trotting spy story about a double-dealing Russian general; it's brimming with great stunts and gimmicks, and eschews the smirking comic attitude of other recent Bond outings. But like some other Bonds, this one goes on far too long. Caroline Bliss debuts as Miss Moneypenny.▼

Living Desert, The (1953) C-73m. *** D: James Algar. Narrated by Winston Hibler. Disney's first True-Life Adventure feature has dazzling footage of the American desert and its inhabitants, but attracted justifiable criticism for its gimmicky treatment of some material like the famous "scorpion dance." Still worthwhile. Academy Award winner.

Living Free (1972-British) C-91m. **½ D: Jack Couffer. Susan Hampshire, Nigel Davenport, Geoffrey Keen. Sequel to BORN FREE detailing further adventures of lioness Elsa and her three cubs. Nice photography but far too leisurely in pace.▼

Living Ghost, The (1942) 61m. BOMB D: William Beaudine. James Dunn, Joan Woodbury, Paul McVey, Norman Willis, J. Farrell MacDonald, Jan Wiley. Dunn hams outrageously as a detective trying to find a murderer in a houseful of suspects. Grade Z comedy-mystery-thriller.

Living in a Big Way (1947) 103m. ** D: Gregory La Cava. Gene Kelly, Marie McDonald, Charles Winninger, Phyllis Thaxter, Spring Byington. Kelly returns from WW2 to get to know his war bride for the first time and clashes with her *nouveau riche* family. A notorious flop in its day, but not all that bad; Kelly does a couple of first-rate dance numbers.

Living It Up (1954) C-95m. *** D: Norman Taurog. Dean Martin, Jerry Lewis, Janet Leigh, Edward Arnold, Fred Clark, Sheree North, Sig Ruman. Bright remake of NOTHING SACRED. Jerry has Carole Lombard's role as supposed radiation victim brought to N.Y.C. as publicity stunt by reporter Leigh; Martin is Jerry's doctor. Scene at Yankee Stadium is a classic.

Living Legend (1980) C-92m. BOMB D: Worth Keeter. Earl Owensby, Ginger Alden, William T. Hicks, Jerry Rushing, Greg Carswell, Toby Wallace, Kristina Reynolds. Owensby is an Elvis Presley-like entertainer; his girlfriend is played by Alden, the real Elvis's final ladyfriend. Crude and phony; your 12-year-old cousin could make a more professional-looking film.

Living on Tokyo Time (1987) C-83m. **½ D: Steven Okazaki. Minako Ohashi, Ken Nakagawa, Mitzie Abe, Bill Bonham, Brenda Aoki. Occasionally amusing but mostly minor account of an Odd Couple: Ohashi, a Japanese who speaks little English; and Nakagawa, a Japanese-American who speaks no Japanese. They're set up in a marriage so that she may remain in the U.S. Filmed independently in San Francisco.▼

Living on Velvet (1935) 80m. ** D: Frank Borzage. Kay Francis, George Brent, Warren William, Russell Hicks, Maude Turner Gordon, Samuel S. Hinds. Romance between Brent, in state of shock, and upper-class Francis, who vanishes when he gains senses. Chic fluff.

Living Proof: The Hank Williams, Jr., Story (1983) C-100m. TVM D: Dick Lowry. Richard Thomas, Clu Gulager, Allyn Ann McLerie, Lenora May, Liane Langland, Merle Kilgore. Thomas again shows his versatility playing the country singer who nearly killed himself, literally, trying to get out of his legendary dad's awesome shadow to become a star in his own right. Script by Stephen Kandel and I. C. Rapoport, from Hank Williams, Jr.'s book. Above average.

Lizzie (1957) 81m. **½ D: Hugo Haas. Eleanor Parker, Richard Boone, Joan Blondell, Hugo Haas, Ric Roman, Marion

[673]

Ross, Johnny Mathis. Interesting, if ultimately pedantic, adaptation of Shirley Jackson's *The Bird's Nest*, with Parker as a mousy woman who turns out to have three distinct personalities. Boone is a psychiatrist who tries to help her. A project of rare distinction for cultish director Haas, though he injects his familiar personality by playing role of kibitzing neighbor. Parker is excellent. Eclipsed by release of similar (and superior) THE THREE FACES OF EVE soon after.

Lloyd's of London (1936) 115m. ***½ D: Henry King. Freddie Bartholomew, Madeleine Carroll, Sir Guy Standing, Tyrone Power, C. Aubrey Smith, Virginia Field, George Sanders. Handsomely mounted fiction of rise of British insurance company; young messenger boy Bartholomew grows up to be Power, who competes with Sanders for affection of Carroll.

Loan Shark (1952) 74m. ** D: Seymour Friedman. George Raft, Dorothy Hart, Paul Stewart, John Hoyt. Raft tries hard to instill life into flabby yarn about ex-convict smashing a loan-shark racket.

Local Boy Makes Good (1931) 67m. **½ D: Mervyn LeRoy. Joe E. Brown, Dorothy Lee, Ruth Hall, Robert Bennett, Edward Woods. Entertaining Brown vehicle, with mousy Joe turning into a track-and-field star.

Local Hero (1983-British) C-111m. *** D: Bill Forsyth. Peter Riegert, Burt Lancaster, Fulton MacKay, Denis Lawson, Norman Chancer, Peter Capaldi, Jenny Seagrove. Enchantingly off-kilter comedy about an oil company rep (Riegert) who's assigned to buy up a Scottish coastal village which is badly needed for a refinery site. Nothing normal or predictable happens from that point on; writer-director Forsyth is more interested in quirkiness than belly-laugh gags, and his film is overflowing with ingenious characters and incidents. A little gem.▼

Locker Sixty-Nine (1962-British) 56m. ** D: Norman Harrison. Eddie Byrne, Paul Daneman, Walter Brown, Penelope Horner. Byrne is the private-eye framed for his boss' murder in this typically gimmicky Edgar Wallace mystery tale.

Locket, The (1946) 86m. ** D: John Brahm. Laraine Day, Brian Aherne, Robert Mitchum, Gene Raymond, Sharyn Moffet, Ricardo Cortez. Another of those post-WW2 psychological dramas, with Day as a woman who makes men fall in love with her—blinding them to her true personality (and problems). Famed for its flashback within a flashback within a flashback . . . but not very good. Look for young brunette Martha Hyer as a party guest, and Ellen Corby as a household servant.

Lock, Stock and Barrel (1970) C-100m. TVM D: Jerry Thorpe. Tim Matheson, Belinda Montgomery, Claude Akins, Jack Albertson, Neville Brand, Burgess Meredith. Displeased father chases after eloping couple (Matheson & Montgomery) in episodic journey towards Oregon. Old West adventure story with supposedly nostalgic, tongue-in-cheek attitude lumbers along, due to so-so script, sloppy direction. Sequel: HITCHED. Average.

Lock Up (1989) C-106m. *½ D: John Flynn. Sylvester Stallone, Donald Sutherland, Darlanne Fleugel, John Amos, Sonny Landham, Tom Sizemore, Frank McRae. With only six months to go on his sentence, convict Stallone gets abducted from his country-club cell and transported to a hellhole run by old Hun-like adversary Sutherland. Unexpectedly missing are Linda Blair, John Vernon, a lesbian guard, and 15 gratuitous showers; in their place you *do* get a body-shop montage backed by Ides of March's "Vehicle." Bottom of the world, ma.▼

Lock Up Your Daughters! (1969-British) C-102m. BOMB D: Peter Coe. Christopher Plummer, Susannah York, Glynis Johns, Ian Bannen, Tom Bell, Elaine Taylor. Film version of Henry Fielding play tries to be another TOM JONES, but tale of mistaken identities in 18th-century England couldn't be more forced.

Locusts (1974) C-78m. TVM D: Richard Heffron. Ben Johnson, Ron Howard, Katherine Helmond, Lisa Gerritsen, Belinda Balaski, Rance Howard. Formula thriller about a swarm of grasshoppers threatening to destroy an entire town's harvest and a local lad, discharged from the Navy as unfit to fly, trying to conquer his personal terror. Average.

Lodger, The (1926-British) 75m. *** D: Alfred Hitchcock. Ivor Novello, Malcolm Keen, June, Marie Ault, Arthur Chesney. The director's first suspense thriller, with a classic Hitchcockian theme: lodger Novello is accused by jealous detective Keen of being a killer. Memorable finale, in which Novello is chased by a bloodthirsty mob. Also known as THE CASE OF JONATHAN DREW. Remade in 1932 (again with Novello), 1944, and in 1954 as MAN IN THE ATTIC.▼

Lodger, The (1944) 84m. *** D: John Brahm. Merle Oberon, George Sanders, Laird Cregar, Sir Cedric Hardwicke, Sara Allgood, Aubrey Mather, Queenie Leonard, Doris Lloyd, Olaf Hytten, Billy Bevan. That new lodger at a turn-of-the-century London boarding house may be Jack the Ripper. Good, atmospheric chiller with fine performances. Remade as MAN IN THE ATTIC.▼

Logan's Run (1976) C-120m. ** D: Michael Anderson. Michael York, Jenny Agutter, Richard Jordan, Peter Ustinov, Farrah Fawcett-Majors, Roscoe Lee Browne.

Dazzling first half—showing life of unending pleasure and extinction at age 30 in the year 2274—is canceled out by dreary second half. This earned a special Oscar for its visual effects. Based on the novel by William F. Nolan and George Clayton Johnson. Later a brief TV series.▼

Log of the Black Pearl, The (1975) C-100m. TVM D: Andrew McLaglen. Ralph Bellamy, Kiel Martin, Jack Kruschen, Glenn Corbett, Anne Archer, Henry Wilcoxon. Modern-day adventure about search for sunken treasure. Average.

Lois Gibbs and the Love Canal (1982) C-100m. TVM D: Glenn Jordan. Marsha Mason, Robert Gunton, Penny Fuller, Roberta Maxwell, Jeremy Licht, Louise Latham. Mason made her TV movie debut as the celebrated housewife-turned-activist who crusaded to force the government to relocate residents of the chemically polluted Love Canal area of Niagara Falls, N.Y., during the late '70s. Michael Zagor's script reduces the entire incident to a matter-of-fact occurrence, and Mason is left with a futile exercise in windmill-tilting. Average.▼

Lola (1969-British-Italian) C-88m. ** D: Richard Donner. Charles Bronson, Susan George, Trevor Howard, Michael Craig, Honor Blackman, Lionel Jeffries, Robert Morley, Jack Hawkins, Orson Bean, Kay Medford, Paul Ford. Sixteen-year-old nymphet initiates relationship with 38-year-old porno book writer; hyperkinetic film misses target, despite good cast and likable performance by Bronson. Released in England as TWINKY, at 98m.▼

Lola (1982-German) C-114m. ***½ D: Rainer Werner Fassbinder. Barbara Sukowa, Armin Mueller-Stahl, Mario Adorf, Mathias Fuchs, Helga Feddersen, Karin Baal, Ivan Desny. Brilliantly directed and edited chronicle of repercussions when cynical, calculating singer-whore Sukowa sets sights on respectable Mueller-Stahl, the new Building Commissioner and only honest politician in town. Striking, unusual use of lighting and color. One-third of Fassbinder's trilogy of life in postwar Germany (with THE MARRIAGE OF MARIA BRAUN and VERONIKA VOSS.)

Lola Montes (1955-French) C-110m. *** D: Max Ophuls. Martine Carol, Peter Ustinov, Anton Walbrook, Oskar Werner, Ivan Desny. Legendary film about beautiful circus performer and her effect on various men nonetheless suffers from Carol's lack of magnetism in title role. Ophuls' superb use of widescreen won't mean much on TV; the celebrated director's last film.▼

Lolita (1962-British) 152m. *** D: Stanley Kubrick. James Mason, Shelley Winters, Peter Sellers, Sue Lyon, Marianne Stone, Diana Decker. Sexually precocious Lyon becomes involved with stolid professor Mason, and bizarre Sellers provides peculiar romance leading to murder and lust. Screenplay for this genuinely strange film is credited to Vladimir Nabokov, who wrote the novel of the same name, but bears little relation to his actual script, which was later published. Winters is outstanding as Lyon's sex-starved mother.▼

Lollipop SEE: **Forever Young, Forever Free**

Lolly Madonna XXX (1973) C-103m. ** D: Richard C. Sarafian. Rod Steiger, Robert Ryan, Jeff Bridges, Scott Wilson, Season Hubley, Katherine Squire, Ed Lauter. Modern-day Hatfield-McCoy feud erupts between two backwoods families, prompted by mistaken identity situation involving innocent girl (Hubley). Histrionics galore, but no point to it at all. Also known as THE LOLLY-MADONNA WAR.

Lolly-Madonna War, The SEE: **Lolly Madonna XXX**

London Belongs to Me SEE: **Dulcimer Street**

Lone Gun, The (1954) C-78m. ** D: Ray Nazarro. George Montgomery, Dorothy Malone, Frank Faylen, Neville Brand. Standard Western of valiant hero shooting it out with outlaws, winning hand of rancher's daughter, nicely played by Malone.

Lone Hand (1953) C-80m. **½ D: George Sherman. Joel McCrea, Barbara Hale, James Arness, Charles Drake. Sturdy McCrea is undercover agent posing as outlaw to get the goods on a gang.

Loneliest Runner, The (1976) C-78m. TVM D: Michael Landon. Lance Kerwin, Michael Landon, Brian Keith, DeAnn Mears, Melissa Sue Anderson, Walter Edminson, Rafer Johnson. Sensitive drama about the misery and humiliation suffered by a teenaged bed-wetter, a talented athlete who subsequently becomes an Olympic star. Producer-director Landon wrote this from personal experience and turns up briefly to play the title character as an adult. Average.▼

Loneliness of the Long Distance Runner, The (1962-British) 103m. **** D: Tony Richardson. Michael Redgrave, Tom Courtenay, Avis Bunnage, Peter Madden, Alec McCowen, James Fox, Julia Foster. Engrossing story of rebellious young man chosen to represent reform school in track race. Superbly acted film confronts society, its mores and institutions. Screenplay by Alan Sillitoe, from his own story. Key British film of 1960s.

Lonely Are the Brave (1962) 107m. *** D: David Miller. Kirk Douglas, Gena Rowlands, Walter Matthau, Michael Kane, Carroll O'Connor, William Schallert, George Kennedy, Bill Bixby. Penetrating study of rebellious cowboy Douglas escaping from jail, pursued by posse utilizing modern means of communications and transportation. Script by Dalton Trumbo, from Edward Abbey's novel, *Brave Cowboy*.▼

Lonely Guy, The (1984) **C-90m.** **½ D: Arthur Hiller. Steve Martin, Charles Grodin, Judith Ivey, Robyn Douglass, Steve Lawrence, Merv Griffin, Dr. Joyce Brothers. Unusually subdued and offbeat vehicle for Martin, who's quite likable as a nerd-ish type who's just been thrown out by his girlfriend . . . only to find he's not alone. Grodin is a delight as a melancholy soulmate who inducts him into the society of Lonely Guys in N.Y.C., but film is too prolonged and uneven to really hit the bullseye. Based on Bruce Jay Friedman's humor book *The Lonely Guy's Book of Life.* Adapted by Neil Simon and scripted by TV veterans Ed. Weinberger and Stan Daniels.▼

Lonelyhearts (1958) **101m.** **½ D: Vincent J. Donehue. Montgomery Clift, Robert Ryan, Myrna Loy, Dolores Hart, Maureen Stapleton, Frank Maxwell, Jackie Coogan, Mike Kellin. Superior cast in interesting adaptation of Nathanael West's *Miss Lonelyhearts.* Clift is would-be reporter assigned to title column and becomes too deeply involved in the problems of his readers. A bit dated by today's standards, but watchable; scripted and produced by Dore Schary. West's book had previously been filmed as ADVICE TO THE LOVELORN; neither version is very faithful to the original story. Film debuts of Stapleton and director Donehue.▼

Lonely Hearts (1981-Australian) **C-95m.** *** D: Paul Cox. Wendy Hughes, Norman Kaye, Jon Finlayson, Julia Blake, Jonathan Hardy. Delightfully quirky romantic comedy about an unlikely match—a middle-aged piano tuner with a flair for theatrics, and a painfully shy office worker. Lovely performances match director Cox's offbeat screenplay.▼

Lonely Lady, The (1983) **C-92m.** BOMB D: Peter Sasdy. Pia Zadora, Lloyd Bochner, Bibi Besch, Joseph Cali, Anthony Holland, Jared Martin. Terrible movie about an aspiring screenwriter who's used and abused while on her way to the Top in Hollywood; adapted from the Harold Robbins novel. Pia does her best, but this is rock-bottom stuff, not even fun on a trash level (although there's campy dialogue to spare). Filmed mostly in Italy.▼

Lonely Man, The (1957) **87m.** *** D: Henry Levin. Anthony Perkins, Jack Palance, Elaine Aiken, Neville Brand, Claude Akins. Solid acting and taut direction remove sting of hackneyed gunslinger-trying-to-reform plot.▼

Lonely Passion of Judith Hearne, The (1987-British) **C-116m.** **½ D: Jack Clayton. Maggie Smith, Bob Hoskins, Wendy Hiller, Marie Kean, Ian McNeice, Alan Devlin, Rudi Davies, Prunella Scales. Smith gives a knockout performance as a lonely,

driven Irish woman whose life takes yet another turn for the worse after moving into a boardinghouse run by snippy Kean. Hoskins is equally fine as a garrulous gentleman with whom she sparks a relationship based on mutual misunderstanding. In fact, all the performances are superb in this long-awaited adaptation of Brian Moore's 1955 novel about a woman's blind faith in the church—and total lack of faith in herself . . . but dramatically the story has a few too many peaks and valleys.▼

Lonely Profession, The (1969) **C-96m.** TVM D: Douglas Heyes. Harry Guardino, Dean Jagger, Barbara McNair, Joseph Cotten, Ina Balin, Dina Merrill, Fernando Lamas. Brave attempt at painting complete no-nonsense view of realistic private-eye with rounded, big-name cast as gumshoe Gordon (Guardino) must establish own innocence and figure out murder of shipping tycoon's mistress. Good results by any medium's standards. Above average.

Lone Ranger, The (1956) **C-86m.** **½ D: Stuart Heisler. Clayton Moore, Jay Silverheels, Lyle Bettger, Bonita Granville, Perry Lopez, Robert J. Wilke. Feature version of popular TV series focuses on Masked Man and Tonto trying to pacify war-minded Indians.▼

Lone Ranger and the Lost City of Gold, The (1958) **C-80m.** ** D: Lesley Selander. Clayton Moore, Jay Silverheels, Douglas Kennedy, Charles Watts. Typical Lone Ranger fiction for younger audiences, involving hooded killers and mysterious clues to a hidden treasure city.▼

Loners, The (1972) **C-79m.** ** D: Sutton Roley. Dean Stockwell, Todd Susman, Scott Brady, Gloria Grahame, Pat Stich, Alex Dreier, Tim Rooney. Standard bike movie with several screen veterans and a plot involving three drop-out cyclists who turn their backs on society and take it on the lam across the Southwest. All too familiar.▼

Lonesome Trail, The (1955) **73m.** ** D: Richard Bartlett. John Agar, Wayne Morris, Edgar Buchanan, Adele Jergens. Offbeat oater with ranch owner fighting off land-grabbers, using bow and arrow instead of conventional six-shooter.

Lone Star (1952) **94m.** **½ D: Vincent Sherman. Clark Gable, Ava Gardner, Lionel Barrymore, Beulah Bondi, Broderick Crawford, Ed Begley. Texas fights for independence, with good guy Gable vs. badman Crawford, Ava the woman in between. OK oater.

Lone Texan (1959) **70m.** *½ D: Paul Landres. Willard Parker, Grant Williams, Audrey Dalton, Douglas Kennedy, June Blair. Oater's potential never realized. Civil War veteran returns home to find brother a corrupt sheriff.

Lone Wolf, The Michael Lanyard, better known as the Lone Wolf, figured as the

leading character in fourteen films from 1935 to 1949. Louis Joseph Vance's character was a jewel thief who would always sacrifice his own ambitions to help a lady in distress; after the first two films he turned to the right side of the law. Melvyn Douglas played the dapper character in 1935's stylish, delightful LONE WOLF RETURNS, with Gail Patrick as leading lady, and Francis Lederer essayed the role in 1938's LONE WOLF IN PARIS with Frances Drake as a rival thief. In 1939 Warren William took over the role and played Lanyard in eight low-budget, fast-moving, enjoyable films which lacked the class of the first two entries but had a certain charm of their own. There was a heavy accent on comedy, and Eric Blore was added to the cast as Lanyard's valet Jamison, who not only served as comic relief but usually got tangled up in the plot as well. William's best effort by far was his first, THE LONE WOLF SPY HUNT, in which he was aided by a delightfully screwball Ida Lupino as his girlfriend, an alluring Rita Hayworth as a slinky spy, Ralph Morgan as the spy leader, and Virginia Weidler as his curious daughter. Unfortunately the other films in the series lacked the same impressive casts, but William carried them quite well, and the plots were harmless enough. After a respite of a few years, Gerald Mohr took up the role for several fairly good efforts like LONE WOLF IN LONDON, which brought back valet Eric Blore. Ron Randell played Lanyard in the final entry, THE LONE WOLF AND HIS LADY. An enjoyable if not compelling series was the LONE WOLF, with THE LONE WOLF SPY HUNT measuring up as an excellent, chic, entertaining film by any standards.
Lone Wolf and His Lady, The (1949) **60m.** D: John Hoffman. Ron Randell, June Vincent, Alan Mowbray, William Frawley.
Lone Wolf in London, The (1947) **68m.** D: Leslie Goodwins. Gerald Mohr, Nancy Saunders, Eric Blore, Evelyn Ankers.
Lone Wolf in Mexico, The (1947) **69m.** D: D. Ross Lederman. Gerald Mohr, Sheila Ryan, Jacqueline de Wit, Eric Blore, Nestor Paiva, John Gallaudet.
Lone Wolf in Paris, The (1938) **66m.** D: Albert S. Rogell. Francis Lederer, Frances Drake, Walter Kingsford, Leona Maricle, Olaf Hytten, Albert Van Dekker.
Lone Wolf Keeps a Date, The (1941) **65m.** D: Sidney Salkow. Warren William, Frances Robinson, Bruce Bennett, Eric Blore, Thurston Hall, Jed Prouty.
Lone Wolf McQuade (1983) **C-107m.** **½ D: Steve Carver. Chuck Norris, David Carradine, Barbara Carrera, Leon Isaac Kennedy, Robert Beltran, L.Q. Jones, R.G. Armstrong, Sharon Farrell. Maverick Texas Ranger Norris takes on gun-running opera-

tion headed by Carradine. Played as a spaghetti Western, providing perfect milieu for Norris' fighting skills. A little long, with a sappy emotional sub-plot, but mostly good action fare.▼
Lone Wolf Meets a Lady, The (1940) **71m.** D: Sidney Salkow. Warren William, Eric Blore, Jean Muir, Warren Hull, Thurston Hall, Victor Jory, Roger Pryor.
Lone Wolf Returns, The (1935) **69m.** D: Roy William Neill. Melvyn Douglas, Gail Patrick, Tala Birell, Arthur Hohl, Thurston Hall.
Lone Wolf Spy Hunt, The (1939) **67m.** D: Peter Godfrey. Warren William, Ida Lupino, Rita Hayworth, Virginia Weidler, Ralph Morgan, Don Beddoe.
Lone Wolf Strikes, The (1940) **57m.** D: Sidney Salkow. Warren William, Joan Perry, Alan Baxter, Astrid Allwyn, Eric Blore, Montagu Love, Robert Wilcox.
Lone Wolf Takes a Chance, The (1941) **76m.** D: Sidney Salkow. Warren William, June Storey, Henry Wilcoxon, Eric Blore, Thurston Hall, Don Beddoe, Evalyn Knapp.
Long Ago Tomorrow (1970-British) **C-100m.** ** D: Bryan Forbes. Malcolm McDowell, Nanette Newman, Georgia Brown, Bernard Lee, Gerald Sim, Michael Flanders. Rather wrong-headed drama of love between paraplegics. Could have been sensitive if script and direction weren't so porous and obvious. Original British title: THE RAGING MOON.▼
Long and the Short and the Tall, The (1961-British) **105m.** *** D: Leslie Norman. Richard Todd, Laurence Harvey, Richard Harris, David McCallum, Ronald Fraser. Well-delineated account of British patrol unit during WW2, focusing on their conflicting personalities and raids on Japanese. Retitled: JUNGLE FIGHTERS.
Long Arm, The SEE: Third Key, The
Longarm (1988) **C-78m.** TVM D: Virgil Vogel. John T. Terlesky, Whitney Kershaw, Deborah Dawn Slaboda, Daphne Ashbrook, Lee de Broux, John Dennis Johnston, John Quade, Shannon Tweed, John Laughlin, Rene Auberjonois. Prospective comedy Western pilot shoots itself in the foot. Veteran Western writer David J. Chisholm based this only occasionally funny oater on the "Longarm" character from Tabor Evans' series of books. Below average.
Long Dark Hall, The (1951-British) **86m.** **½ D: Anthony Bushell, Reginald Beck. Rex Harrison, Lilli Palmer, Tania Held, Henrietta Barry. Sturdy melodrama of man accused of killing girlfriend, with wife remaining loyal to him.▼
Long, Dark Night, The SEE: Pack, The▼
Long Day's Dying, The (1968-British) **C-93m.** *½ D: Peter Collinson. David Hemmings, Tom Bell, Tony Beckley, Alan Dobie. Dull story of three British soldiers

and their German captive during weary trek through European countryside.

Long Day's Journey Into Night (1962) **136m.** **** D: Sidney Lumet. Katharine Hepburn, Ralph Richardson, Jason Robards, Jr., Dean Stockwell, Jeanne Barr. Faithful, stagy adaptation of Eugene O'Neill's detailed study of family in the 1910s. Hepburn is dope-addicted wife, Richardson her pompous actor husband, Stockwell the son dying of TB, and Robards the alcoholic son. Originally 174m.▼

Long Days of Summer, The (1980) **C-105m. TVM** D: Dan Curtis. Dean Jones, Joan Hackett, Ronnie Scribner, Louanne, Donald Moffat, Andrew Duggan, Michael McGuire, Leigh French. Sequel to WHEN EVERY DAY WAS THE FOURTH OF JULY recreates pre-WW2 America as seen through the eyes of a young Jewish boy and shows his lawyer dad's battle against the prejudices of his staid New England town. Average.▼

Long Duel, The (1967-British) **C-115m.** **½ D: Ken Annakin. Yul Brynner, Trevor Howard, Harry Andrews, Andrew Keir. Brynner leads peasant revolt against British raj in 1920s India; routine adventure saga.

Longest Day, The (1962) **180m.** **** D: Ken Annakin, Andrew Marton, Bernhard Wicki. John Wayne, Rod Steiger, Robert Ryan, Peter Lawford, Henry Fonda, Robert Mitchum, Richard Burton, Richard Beymer, Jeffrey Hunter, Sal Mineo, Roddy McDowall, Eddie Albert, Curt Jurgens, Gert Frobe, Sean Connery, Robert Wagner, Red Buttons, Mel Ferrer, many others. One of the last great epic WW2 films. Brilliant retelling of the Allied invasion of Normandy, complete with all-star international cast, recreation of events on a grand scale, and Oscar-winning special effects and cinematography.▼

Longest Hundred Miles, The (1967) **C-93m. TVM** D: Don Weis. Doug McClure, Katharine Ross, Ricardo Montalban. Philippine locations refreshing change of pace from backlot tedium in WW2 actioner involving G.I., Army nurse, native children, and priest fleeing from Japanese invasion. Fair performances, some good situations. Also titled: ESCAPE FROM BATAAN. Average.

Longest Night, The (1972) **C-74m. TVM** D: Jack Smight. David Janssen, James Farentino, Phyllis Thaxter, Sallie Shockley, Skye Aubrey, Mike Farrell. Upper-middle-class daughter (Shockley) abducted by clever duo and hidden in compartment below ground level. Not the slice-of-life documentary it should've been; stuffy, slick, only moderately tense. Even so, above average.

Longest Yard, The (1974) **C-123m.** ***½ D: Robert Aldrich. Burt Reynolds, Eddie Albert, Ed Lauter, Michael Conrad, Jim Hampton, Bernadette Peters, Charles Tyner, Mike Henry, Harry Caesar, Richard Kiel, Robert Tessier, Malcolm Atterbury. Convict Reynolds, a former football pro, quarterbacks a squad of dirty players against warden Albert's hand-picked team. An audience picture if there ever was one; hilarious bone-crunching comedy written by Tracy Keenan Wynn.▼

Long Goodbye, The (1973) **C-112m.** **½ D: Robert Altman. Elliott Gould, Nina Van Pallandt, Sterling Hayden, Henry Gibson, Mark Rydell, Jim Bouton, David Arkin, Warren Berlinger. Strange, almost spoofy updating of Raymond Chandler's novel, with Gould as a shabby Philip Marlowe involved with mysterious Van Pallandt, alcoholic Hayden, evil Gibson, missing pal Bouton, and Jewish gangster Rydell . . . among others. Some nice touches, especially John Williams' jokey score, but Altman's attitude toward the genre borders on contempt. Screenplay by Leigh Brackett, who had earlier co-scripted THE BIG SLEEP. Look for Arnold Schwarzenegger as a muscleman, David Carradine as a prisoner. Beware TV prints, which are minus the original ending!

Long Good Friday, The (1980-British) **C-114m.** ***½ D: John Mackenzie. Bob Hoskins, Helen Mirren, Eddie Constantine, Dave King, Bryan Marshall, George Coulouris, Stephen Davies, Pierce Brosnan. Occasionally confusing but otherwise terrific portrait of hoodlum rivalry in contemporary London; takes its rightful place with the best gangster movies of all time. Hoskins, brilliant as underworld entrepreneur, is matched by Mirren as subtly sexy mistress.▼

Long Gone (1987) **C-110m. TVM** D: Martin Davidson. William L. Petersen, Virginia Madsen, Dermot Mulroney, Larry Riley, Katy Boyer, Henry Gibson, Teller. Engaging baseball comedy about a third-rate minor league team's battle for the championship. Sassy script by Michael Norell, and performances (Petersen as the team's brash manager, and Madsen as a small-town beauty queen). Made for cable. Above average.▼

Long Gray Line, The (1955) **C-138m.** *** D: John Ford. Tyrone Power, Maureen O'Hara, Robert Francis, Ward Bond, Donald Crisp, Betsy Palmer, Phil Carey. Lengthy sentimental melodrama of West Point athletic trainer Power and his many years at the Academy. O'Hara is radiant as his wife.

Long Haul, The (1957-British) **88m.** ** D: Ken Hughes. Victor Mature, Diana Dors, Patrick Allen, Gene Anderson. Mature is truck driver whose turbulent marriage paves way for his becoming involved with crooks. Minor fare.

Long, Hot Summer, The (1958) **C-117m.**

*** D: Martin Ritt. Paul Newman, Joanne Woodward, Anthony Franciosa, Orson Welles, Lee Remick, Angela Lansbury. Well-blended William Faulkner short stories make a flavorful, brooding drama of domineering Southerner (Welles) and a wandering handyman (Newman), who decides to stick around and marry daughter Woodward. Excellent Alex North score, weak finish to strong film; the Newmans' first film together. Remade for TV.▼

Long Hot Summer, The (1985) C-200m. TVM D: Stuart Cooper. Ava Gardner, Judith Ivey, Don Johnson, Jason Robards, William Russ, Cybill Shepherd, Wings Hauser, William Forsythe, Albert Hall. Surprisingly good remake of the Faulkner tale of sex and sin in a small Southern town. Johnson and Ivey stand out in the roles taken in 1958 film by Paul Newman and Joanne Woodward. Rita Mae Brown and Dennis Turner based their screenplay on the earlier one by Irving Ravetch and Harriet Frank, Jr., as much as on Faulkner's story, *The Hamlet.* Originally shown in two parts. Above average.▼

Long John Silver (1954-Australian) C-109m. **½ D: Byron Haskin. Robert Newton, Connie Gilchrist, Kit Taylor, Grant Taylor. Newton reprises title role from TREASURE ISLAND (with same director as the Disney film) and chews the scenery in this loose adaptation of Robert Louis Stevenson. Look for Rod Taylor in a small role.▼

Long Journey Back (1978) C-100m. TVM D: Mel Damski. Mike Connors, Cloris Leachman, Stephanie Zimbalist, Katy Kurtzman. Fact-based drama about a high school teenager's courageous fight after a school bus accident leaves her emotionally and physically handicapped. Average.▼

Long Journey Home, The (1987) C-100m. TVM D; Rod Holcomb. Meredith Baxter Birney, David Birney, Ray Baker, James Sutorius, Daphne Maxwell (Reid), Kevin McCarthy, Mike Preston. Improbable, haphazardly plotted chase drama about a businesswoman who's drawn into a web of international intrigue when her husband (supposedly MIA in Vietnam) suddenly turns up. Then-married stars coproduced this vehicle, their first TV work together since the long-ago sitcom *Bridget Loves Bernie.* Below average.

Long, Long Trailer, The (1954) C-103m. **½ D: Vincente Minnelli. Lucille Ball, Desi Arnaz, Marjorie Main, Keenan Wynn, Gladys Hurlbut. Pleasant vehicle for Lucy and Desi, on honeymoon with cumbersome trailer that creates havoc for the duo. Plenty of slapstick.

Long Lost Father (1934) 63m. **½ D: Ernest B. Schoedsack. John Barrymore, Helen Chandler, Donald Cook, Alan Mowbray, Claude King. Minor Barrymore vehicle casts him as man who deserted daughter Chandler years ago, tries to make up for it when she gets in a jam.

Long Memory, The (1952-British) 91m. *** D: Robert Hamer. John Mills, John McCallum, Elizabeth Sellars, Geoffrey Keen, John Chandos, Vida Hope. Mills is framed for murder by girlfriend Sellars. When released from prison twelve years later, he sets out to prove his innocence. Well done drama.

Long Night, The (1947) 101m. ** D: Anatole Litvak. Henry Fonda, Barbara Bel Geddes, Vincent Price, Ann Dvorak, Queenie Smith. Plodding drama of killer hiding out overnight with girl who tries to get him to confess; pretty tired drama. Remake of Jean Gabin film DAYBREAK.

Long Ride from Hell, A (1970-Italian) C-94m. *½ D: Alex Burks (Camillo Bazzoni). Steve Reeves, Wayde Preston, Dick Palmer, Silvana Venturelli, Lee Burton, Ted Carter. Title is another instance of truth-in-advertising; dreary Western coauthored by Reeves has to do with rancher who tries to clear himself of phony train-robbery charge.

Long Ride Home, The SEE: **Time for Killing, A**

Long Riders, The (1980) C-100m. *** D: Walter Hill. David, Keith and Robert Carradine, Stacy and James Keach, Randy and Dennis Quaid, Nicholas and Christopher Guest, Pamela Reed, Savannah Smith, James Whitmore, Jr., Harry Carey, Jr. *All in the Family* out West. The Carradines, Keaches, Quaids, and Guests portray, respectively, the Younger, James, Miller, and Ford brothers in this stylish but extremely bloody film. Typically meticulous direction by Hill, with David Carradine and Reed igniting sparks as Cole Younger and Belle Starr. Excellent score by Ry Cooder.▼

Long Rope, The (1961) 61m. ** D: William Witney. Hugh Marlowe, Robert Wilke, Alan Hale, John Alonzo. Lumbering minor oater about circuit judge seeking aid of gunslinger to prevent injustice done to Mexican youth on trial for murder.

Long Shadow, The (1961-British) 64m. *½ D: Peter Maxwell. John Crawford, Susan Hampshire, Bill Nagy, Humphrey Lestocq. Flabby espionage caper set in 1950s Vienna, with Crawford an American foreign correspondent caught up in it all.

Long Ships, The (1964-British-Yugoslav) C-125m. ** D: Jack Cardiff. Richard Widmark, Sidney Poitier, Rosanna Schiaffino, Russ Tamblyn, Oscar Homolka, Colin Blakely. Fairly elaborate but comic-book-level costume adventure of Vikings battling Moors for fabled treasure. Good cast deserves better.

Long Shot, The (1976) SEE: **Target of an Assassin**▼

Longshot, The (1986) **C-89m.** BOMB D: Paul Bartel. Tim Conway, Jack Weston, Harvey Korman, Ted Wass, Jonathan Winters, Stella Stevens, Anne Meara, George DiCenzo. Four lower-middle-class losers borrow $5000 from the local break-ya-fingas financier to finance a sure thing at the track, then bet it on the wrong horse. Pathetic comedy is full of toilet gags and can't even coast on the good will established by the cast in better days. Mike Nichols (*Mike Nichols!!!*) executive produced.▼

Longstreet (1970) **C-93m.** TVM D: Joseph Sargent. James Franciscus, Bradford Dillman, John McIntire, Jeanette Nolan, Martine Beswick. New Orleans-based insurance investigator blinded in explosion which kills wife, must regain self-respect, dignity in new world, solve mystery of assailants' identities. OK juggling of suspense and character study by Stirling Silliphant. Pilot for TV series. Above average.

Long Summer of George Adams, The (1982) **C-100m.** TVM D: Stuart Margolin. James Garner, Joan Hackett, Anjanette Comer, Alex Harvey, Juanin Clay, David Graf. Lighthearted homespun period piece, adapted by John Gay from Weldon Hill's book, with Garner as a small-town railroad man who's done out of a job by diesel power. Garner and his *Rockford Files/Maverick* production gang give this one the charm it exudes, along with some lovely bits of Americana. Above average.

Longtime Companion (1990) **C-96m.** *** D: Norman René. Stephen Caffrey, Patrick Cassidy, Brian Cousins, Bruce Davison, John Dossett, Mark Lamos, Dermot Mulroney, Mary-Louise Parker, Michael Schoeffling, Campbell Scott, Robert Joy. Emotional examination of AIDS in the 80s, focusing on a closely knit group of gay men in N.Y.C. Film spans the entire decade, from first reports of a mystery illness to a time when the disease became a tragic part of everyday life. Craig Lucas's script is insightful, heart-wrenching, and funny. Entire cast is excellent, especially Davison; Campbell Scott, who plays Willy, is the son of George C. Scott and Colleen Dewhurst. A PBS *American Playhouse* production.

Long Time Gone (1986) **C-100m.** TVM D: Robert Butler. Paul LeMat, Wil Wheaton, Ann Dusenberry, Ray Girardin, Barbara Stock, Richard Sarafian. Slightly off-center tale of a divorced, down-on-his-luck gumshoe who suddenly has to take care of his young son, whom he hardly knows. Prospective pilot long time on shelf; written by Glenn Gordon Caron, several years before his *Moonlighting* scored a hit. Average.▼

Long Voyage Home, The (1940) **105m.** ***½ D: John Ford. John Wayne, Thomas Mitchell, Ian Hunter, Ward Bond, Barry Fitzgerald, Wilfrid Lawson, Mildred Natwick, John Qualen, Arthur Shields, Joe Sawyer, J. Warren Kerrigan. Evocative look at men who spend their lives at sea, adapted (by Dudley Nichols) from four short plays by Eugene O'Neill. Richly textured drama with many beautiful vignettes; exquisitely photographed by Gregg Toland.▼

Long Wait, The (1954) **93m.** ** D: Victor Saville. Anthony Quinn, Charles Coburn, Gene Evans, Peggie Castle, Dolores Donlan, Mary Ellen Kay. Meandering, actionless account of man with loss of memory discovering he's been framed for several crimes.

Long Way Home, A (1981) **C-100m.** TVM D: Robert Markowitz. Timothy Hutton, Brenda Vaccaro, George Dzundza, Paul Regina, Rosanna Arquette, John Lehne, Lauren Peterson. Poignant drama by Dennis Nemec of a young man's obsession with finding his brother and sister years after the three of them, abandoned by their parents, were separated into different foster homes. A fine performance into Hutton, matched by Vaccaro as a concerned social worker and friend. Above average.▼

Look Back in Anger (1958-British) **99m.** ***½ D: Tony Richardson. Richard Burton, Claire Bloom, Edith Evans, Mary Ure, Gary Raymond, Glen Byam Shaw, Donald Pleasence. John Osborne's trend-setting angry-young-man play, with Burton rebelling against life and wife, realistically filmed and acted; dialogue bristles.▼

Look Down and Die SEE: **Steel**▼

Looker (1981) **C-94m.** BOMB D: Michael Crichton. Albert Finney, James Coburn, Susan Dey, Leigh Taylor-Young, Dorian Harewood, Tim Rossovich, Darryl Hickman. Conglomerate-head Coburn produces the computerized images of gorgeous models to hawk products and political candidates on TV—and also murders his subjects. As he is losing all his clients, Beverly Hills plastic surgeon Finney investigates. Intriguing premise is illogically and boringly handled; even Finney cannot save this turkey. Watch for Vanna White.▼

Look for the Silver Lining (1949) **C-100m.** **½ D: David Butler. June Haver, Ray Bolger, Gordon MacRae, Charles Ruggles, Rosemary DeCamp. Superficial biography of Marilyn Miller's career in show business, with vintage vaudeville numbers bolstering trivial plot line.

Look in Any Window (1961) **87m.** ** D: William Alland. Paul Anka, Ruth Roman, Alex Nicol, Gigi Perreau, Jack Cassidy. Unhappy home life sets Anka on path of crime. Ho-hum.

Looking for Danger (1957) **62m.** D: Austen Jewell. Huntz Hall, Stanley Clements, Eddie LeRoy, Otto Reichow. SEE: **Bowery Boys** series

[680]

Looking for Love (1964) **C-83m.** BOMB D: Don Weis. Connie Francis, Susan Oliver, Jim Hutton, Barbara Nichols, Danny Thomas, Johnny Carson, George Hamilton, Paula Prentiss. They should have looked for a script instead. Plastic show-biz romance with little help from various guest stars, including Carson (who's taken to making HORN BLOWS AT MIDNIGHT-type jokes about this—his only film appearance).

✓ **Looking for Mr. Goodbar** (1977) C-135m. *½ D: Richard Brooks. Diane Keaton, Richard Gere, William Atherton, Tuesday Weld, Richard Kiley, LeVar Burton, Tom Berenger. Sordid rewrite (by director Brooks) of Judith Rossner's novel begins as intelligent study of repressed young girl, then wallows endlessly in her new "liberated" lifestyle. Keaton's performance outclasses this pointless movie. Story recycled in the TVM TRACKDOWN: FINDING THE GOODBAR KILLER.▼

horrible one of worst films ever made

Looking Forward (1933) 82m. **½ D: Clarence Brown. Lionel Barrymore, Lewis Stone, Benita Hume, Elizabeth Allan, Phillips Holmes, Colin Clive, Doris Lloyd. Stone gives one of his best performances as a man trying to keep his London department store (founded by his family two hundred years ago) afloat during the depths of the Depression; Barrymore is a mousy clerk who's been with the store for forty years. Superficial but pleasant drama boasts that its title came from a speech by F.D.R.

Looking Glass War, The (1970-British) C-108m. *½ D: Frank R. Pierson. Christopher Jones, Pia Degermark, Ralph Richardson, Anthony Hopkins, Paul Rogers, Susan George. Dull film version of John Le Carre's best-seller has Jones risking his life to photograph a rocket in East Berlin. Good opportunity to study the leads' bone structure, since they never change facial expressions.▼

Lookin' to Get Out (1982) C-104m. BOMB D: Hal Ashby. Jon Voight, Burt Young, Ann-Margret, Bert Remsen, Jude Farese, Allen Keller, Richard Bradford. Voight coscripted, coproduced, and tries out his Al Pacino impression in this embarrassing, implausible comedy about two losers who con their way into a suite at the MGM Grand with a plan to win big at blackjack. Remsen's performance as a wily old card shark is the only bright spot in this utter catastrophe. Shot in 1980; unfortunately, it recovered.

Looks and Smiles (1981-British) 104m. *** D: Kenneth Loach. Graham Green, Carolyn Nicholson, Tony Pitts, Phil Askham, Cilla Mason. Working-class teenager Green cannot find a job or place for himself in society. Solid, realistic story of alienation, frustration, anger.

Look What's Happened to Rosemary's

Baby (1976) **C-100m. TVM** D: Sam O'Steen. Stephen McHattie, Patty Duke Astin, Broderick Crawford, Ruth Gordon, Lloyd Haynes, David Huffman, Tina Louise, George Maharis, Ray Milland, Donna Mills. Sequel to the 1968 occult blockbuster traces growth to adulthood of the demon child (McHattie). Patty Duke Astin is his distraught mommy; Milland and Gordon (recreating her original role) head the coven of devil worshippers. Uninspired successor to the Polanski classic, retitled, predictably, ROSEMARY'S BABY II. Below average.

Look Who's Laughing (1941) 78m. ** D: Allan Dwan. Edgar Bergen, Jim and Marion Jordan (Fibber McGee and Molly), Lucille Ball, Harold Peary (The Great Gildersleeve), Lee Bonnell. Bergen's plane inadvertently lands in Wistful Vista, where he becomes involved in a municipal squabble with Fibber and Molly. Slim vehicle for radio favorites only comes alive when Charlie McCarthy takes the spotlight.▼

Look Who's Talking (1989) C-90m. *** D: Amy Heckerling. John Travolta, Kirstie Alley, Olympia Dukakis, George Segal, Abe Vigoda, voice of Bruce Willis. Amiable comedy about an unmarried woman who has a baby (by her no-good married boyfriend) and then sets out to find a suitable "daddy" for him. Good showcase for costars Alley and Travolta. Written by director Heckerling. One quibble: though set in N.Y.C., it's all too obvious that it was shot somewhere else (Vancouver, to be precise). Followed by TV series.▼

Looney, Looney, Looney Bugs Bunny Movie, The (1981) C-80m. **½ D: Friz Freleng. Voice of Mel Blanc. Feature-length compilation of classic Warner Bros. cartoons is divided into three parts. In the first, Yosemite Sam must return Bugs Bunny to the Devil in order to save his own soul. Second part has Bugs rescuing Tweety from gangsters Rocky and Muggsy. Third and best segment is a parody of Hollywood award shows featuring Freleng's wonderful 1957 cartoon THE THREE LITTLE BOPS. Also includes Bugs Bunny's Oscar-winning KNIGHTY KNIGHT BUGS (1958). Official billing is FRIZ FRELENG'S LOONEY, LOONEY, LOONEY BUGS BUNNY MOVIE.▼

Loophole (1954) 80m. **½ D: Harold D. Schuster. Barry Sullivan, Charles McGraw, Dorothy Malone, Don Haggerty, Mary Beth Hughes, Don Beddoe. Imaginative handling of oft-told tale of bank employee accused of theft, catching actual crooks.

Loophole (1980-British) C-105m. **½ D: John Quested. Albert Finney, Martin Sheen, Susannah York, Colin Blakely, Jonathan Pryce, Robert Morley, Alfred Lynch, Christopher Guard. Slick but very ordinary caper film about an unemployed architect who's persuaded to participate in an ambitious break-in of "impenetrable" London bank.▼

Loose Cannons (1990) **C-94m.** *½ D: Bob Clark. Gene Hackman, Dan Aykroyd, Dom DeLuise, Ronny Cox, Nancy Travis, Robert Prosky, Paul Koslo, Dick O'Neill, Jan Triska, David Alan Grier. Below-rock-bottom car-chase excuse about two D.C. cops caught between ex-Nazis and Israeli adversaries scuffling over a mysterious Hitler home movie. Unfunny and offensive, film stagnated on the shelf while the studio figured out what to do with it. The career nadir for most of its participants.

Loose in London (1953) **63m.** D: Edward Bernds. Leo Gorcey, Huntz Hall, Bernard Gorcey, Norma Varden, Angela Greene. SEE: **Bowery Boys** series.

Loose Shoes (1980) **C-74m.** **½ D: Ira Miller. Bill Murray, Howard Hesseman, David Landsburg, Ed Lauter, Susan Tyrrell, Avery Schreiber, Misty Rowe, Jaye P. Morgan, Buddy Hackett, Murphy Dunne, Theodore Wilson, David Downing, Lewis Arquette, Danny Dayton, Ira Miller. Very mixed bag of spoofs of coming-attractions previews, some hilarious, some duds. Highlights: "Skateboarders From Hell," "The Yid and the Kid" (Chaplin), "The Sneaker" (Woody Allen), "Welcome to Bacon County," Jewish "Star Wars," and unbearably funny "Darktown After Dark." Dunne also composed score and songs. Filmed mostly in 1977; Bill Murray's first film. Originally titled COMING ATTRACTIONS.▼

Loot (1972-British) **C-101m.** **½ D: Silvio Narizzano. Lee Remick, Richard Attenborough, Roy Holder, Hywel Bennett, Milo O'Shea, Dick Emery, Joe Lynch. Frantic black comedy from Joe Orton's stage hit. Holder and Bennett knock over a bank, hide the swag in the coffin of the former's mother, and then have a spot of trouble retrieving it. Despite Mod trappings, basically an old-fashioned, door-slamming farce; funny for those in the mood.▼

Looters, The (1955) **87m.** **½ D: Abner Biberman. Rory Calhoun, Julie Adams, Ray Danton, Thomas Gomez. OK drama of survivors of plane crash fighting amongst themselves for money aboard wreckage.

Lord Jeff (1938) **78m.** ** D: Sam Wood. Freddie Bartholomew, Mickey Rooney, Charles Coburn, Herbert Mundin, Terry Kilburn, Gale Sondergaard, Peter Lawford. Acceptable family film about good-boy Bartholomew led astray, sent to straighten out at naval school.

Lord Jim (1965) **C-154m.** **½ D: Richard Brooks. Peter O'Toole, James Mason, Curt Jurgens, Eli Wallach, Jack Hawkins, Paul Lukas, Daliah Lavi, Akim Tamiroff. Overlong, uneven adaptation of Joseph Conrad's story about idealistic young man in British Merchant Marine in the 19th-

century who is discredited as a coward and lives with that scar for the rest of his life. Film's great moments provided by outstanding supporting cast.▼

Lord Love a Duck (1966) **104m.** *** D: George Axelrod. Tuesday Weld, Roddy McDowall, Lola Albright, Martin West, Ruth Gordon, Harvey Korman, Martin Gabel, Sarah Marshall, Lynn Carey. Madcap black comedy about progressive Southern California high school where botany is called "plant skills." Film wavers uncomfortably between comedy and drama at times, but really delivers some belly laughs. Terrific performances in movie that was ahead of its time. Directorial debut of cowriter Axelrod.

Lord of the Flies (1963-British) **90m.** *** D: Peter Brook. James Aubrey, Tom Chapin, Hugh Edwards, Roger Elwin, Tom Gaman. Unique story of a group of British schoolboys stranded on remote island. Their gradual degeneration into a savage horde is compelling. Adapted from William Golding's novel. Remade in 1990.▼

Lord of the Flies (1990) **C-90m.** **½ D: Harry Hook. Balthazar Getty, Chris Furrh, Danuel Pipoly, Badgett Dale, Edward and Andrew Taft. Color update of the novel-to-film turns William Golding's savage schoolboys into TV-savvy American kids; it may make the story more immediate (though even that's arguable), but it also purges the original of its poetry. Visceral, and improves as it progresses, but inferior to Peter Brook's 1963 version whose amateur actors, by and large, were superior to this brood.▼

Lord of the Jungle (1955) **69m.** D: Ford Beebe. Johnny Sheffield, Wayne Morris, Nancy Hale, Smoki Whitfield, Paul Picerni. SEE: **Bomba, The Jungle Boy** series.

Lord of the Rings, The (1978) **C-133m.** **½ D: Ralph Bakshi. Voices of Christopher Guard, William Squire, John Hurt, Michael Sholes, Dominic Guard. Ambitious animated version of J. R. R. Tolkien's fantasy saga covers 1½ books of the trilogy (ending rather abruptly). Story of different races in Middle Earth competing for ownership of all-powerful Rings is inspired and exciting, but begins to drag—and confuse—during last hour. Bakshi's technique awkwardly combines animation and live-action tracings.▼

Lords of Discipline, The (1983) **C-102m.** **½ D: Franc Roddam. David Keith, Robert Prosky, G. D. Spradlin, Rick Rossovich, John Lavachielli, Mitchell Lichtenstein, Mark Breland, Michael Biehn, Barbara Babcock, Judge Reinhold, Bill Paxton, Jason Connery, Matt Frewer, Sophie Ward. Familiar but satisfactory military school drama, set in 1964 South Carolina. Keith plays senior asked to keep an eye on first black cadet (Breland) who's being systematically tortured by secret society called

"The Ten." Good performances, especially by Prosky as school's number-two officer; based on the Pat Conroy novel. Unbelievable as it may appear, most of the film was shot in England!▼

Lords of Flatbush, The (1974) **C-88m.** *** D: Stephen F. Verona, Martin Davidson. Perry King, Sylvester Stallone, Henry Winkler, Paul Mace, Susan Blakely, Paul Jabara, Dolph Sweet. Fun story of a Flatbush gang, circa 1957, with original music score. Training ground for two future stars, with Stallone writing some of the dialogue and Winkler trying out his Fonzie character.▼

Lords of the Deep (1989) **C-79m.** BOMB D: Mary Ann Fisher. Bradford Dillman, Priscilla Barnes, Daryl Haney, Melody Ryane, Eb Lottimer, Stephen Davies, Gregory Sobeck. In undersea base of future, menace seems to be manta-shaped aliens, but it's really loony leader Dillman. Clumsy, cheap, and amateurish, this was the fourth and last of 1989's undersea sci-fi thrillers, and the worst by far. Roger Corman appears unbilled (which is just as well).▼

Lorna Doone (1935-British) **89m.** *** D: Basil Dean. John Loder, Margaret Lockwood, Victoria Hopper, Roy Emerson, Edward Rigby, Mary Clare, Roger Livesey. Well-photographed tale of 17th-century love affair between a farmer and the daughter of an outlaw, though she is hiding the secret of her true identity. Lovely locations and fine acting; remade in 1951.

Lorna Doone (1951) **C-88m.** **½ D: Phil Karlson. Barbara Hale, Richard Greene, Carl Benton Reid, William Bishop. Middling screen version of Richard D. Blackmore's novel of 1860s England, with farmers rebelling against oppressive landlords. Done on small budget, but not bad.

Los Amigos SEE: **Deaf Smith and Johnny Ears**

Loser Takes All (1956-British) **C-88m.** ** D: Ken Annakin. Rossano Brazzi, Glynis Johns, Robert Morley, Tony Britton, Geoffrey Keen, Peter Illing. Brazzi and Johns celebrate their honeymoon in Monte Carlo and try out their "perfect system" for winning at roulette, with unusual effect on their marriage. On-location filming helps. Remade in 1990 as STRIKE IT RICH.

Losing Ground (1982) **C-86m.** * D: Kathleen Collins. Seret Scott, Bill Gunn, Duane Jones, Billie Allen, Gary Bolling, Norberto Kerner, Maritza Rivera. Clever script uplifts this comedy of uptight philosophy professor Scott who examines her feelings when artist husband Gunn paints beautiful Rivera. Unique in that the leading characters are middle-class blacks.

Losin' It (1983) **C-104m.** **½ D: Curtis Hanson. Tom Cruise, Jackie Earle Haley, John Stockwell, Shelley Long, John P. Navin, Jr., Henry Darrow, Hector Elias. Pleasant enough but predictable film about three teenagers out for a wild time in Tijuana—with more bluster than experience. Appealing cast gives it extra value.▼

Los Olvidados (1950-Mexican) **88m.** ***½ D: Luis Buñuel. Alfonso Mejia, Roberto Cobo, Estela Inda, Miguel Inclan. Gripping story of juvenile delinquency among slums of Mexico, with surreal dream sequences interspersed. An offbeat winner from Buñuel, also known as THE YOUNG AND THE DAMNED.▼

Loss of Innocence (1961-British) **C-99m.** **½ D: Lewis Gilbert. Kenneth More, Danielle Darrieux, Susannah York, Maurice Denham. York gives poignant performance as teenager who, through love affair, becomes a woman; events leave her and younger sister and brother stranded on the Continent. Original title: THE GREENGAGE SUMMER.

Lost (1955-British) **C-89m.** **½ D: Guy Green. David Farrar, David Knight, Julia Arnall, Anthony Oliver, Marjorie Rhodes. Offbeat account of effects of a child kidnapping on parents, police, press and crooks.

Lost and Found (1979) **C-112m.** ** D: Melvin Frank. George Segal, Glenda Jackson, Maureen Stapleton, Hollis McLaren, John Cunningham, Paul Sorvino, John Candy, Martin Short. Widowed college prof and British divorcee meet in a French ski resort and quickly cool their romance by marrying. Attempt to recapture the success of the overrated A TOUCH OF CLASS is just more old fashioned nonsense posing as hip comedy.▼

Lost Angel (1943) **91m.** **½ D: Roy Rowland. Margaret O'Brien, James Craig, Marsha Hunt, Philip Merivale, Henry O'Neill, Donald Meek, Keenan Wynn. O'Brien is winning as precocious child—trained as a genius by scientists—who learns life's simple pleasures when she moves in with reporter Craig.

Lost Angels (1989) **C-116m.** ** D: Hugh Hudson. Donald Sutherland, Adam Horovitz, Amy Locane, Don Bloomfield, Celia Weston, Graham Beckel, Kevin Tighe, John C. McGinley, Park Overall. Sincere but obvious and compromised drama of teenaged Horovitz, unjustly sent to a mental clinic treating teenagers far more troubled than he. Sutherland is sole sympathetic psychiatrist. Shallow story grows increasingly incoherent and uninvolving. Horovitz, of singing group Beastie Boys, is good in acting debut.▼

Los Tarantos (1964-Spanish) **C-81m.** *** D: Rovira-Beleta. Carmen Amaya, Sara Lezana, Daniel Martin, Antonio Prieto. Sentimental yet touching account of two young people from rival gypsy families falling in love, with tragic results.

Lost Boundaries (1949) **99m.** *** D: Alfred L. Werker. Beatrice Pearson, Mel

Ferrer, Richard Hylton, Carleton Carpenter, Susan Douglas, Canada Lee. Black family passes for white in New England town, till their heritage is discovered. One of the first racially conscious films; now a curio. Ferrer's screen acting debut.

Lost Boys, The (1987) **C-97m.** ** D: Joel Schumacher. Jason Patric, Corey Haim, Dianne Wiest, Barnard Hughes, Edward Herrmann, Kiefer Sutherland, Jami Gertz, Corey Feldman, Jamison Newlander. Family moves to California town where the local teenage gang turns out to be a pack of vampires! Slick movie aimed at juvenile audiences; both the humor and the plotting are pretty obvious. Only real fireworks come at the end during final showdown.▼

Lost Command (1966) **C-130m.** *** D: Mark Robson. Anthony Quinn, Alain Delon, George Segal, Michele Morgan, Maurice Ronet, Claudia Cardinale, Gregoire Aslan, Jean Servais. Taut, well-made story of French-Algerian guerrilla warfare in North Africa, with Quinn as the peasant who has risen to a position of command. Fine international cast, good direction, and some top-notch action sequences blend very well.▼

Lost Continent, The (1951) **86m.** ** D: Samuel Newfield. Cesar Romero, Hillary Brooke, John Hoyt, Acquanetta. Lavish production values are obviously lacking as Romero leads expedition to prehistoric mountaintop to recover missing rocket.

Lost Continent, The (1968-British) **C-89m.** **½ D: Michael Carreras. Eric Porter, Hildegard Knef, Suzanna Leigh, Tony Beckley, Nigel Stock, Neil McCallum. Tramp steamer wanders into uncharted seas, finds isolated freak civilization derived from Spanish monarchy. Good cast handles lopsided script straightfaced; occasional good action.

Lost Flight (1969) **C-105m.** TVM D: Leonard Horn. Lloyd Bridges, Anne Francis, Ralph Meeker, Bobby Van, Billy Dee Williams. Commercial jet crash-lands on Pacific island; survivors must exist by their wits, learn to work together. Foolish subplots, OK performances, much location work, but direction and script totally mismatched. Average.

Lost Honeymoon (1947) **71m.** ** D: Leigh Jason. Franchot Tone, Ann Richards, Frances Rafferty, Una O'Connor, Winston Severn. Trivial comedy of amnesiac Tone discovering he's the father of two children.

Lost Honor of Katharina Blum, The (1975-German) **C-106m.** ***½ D: Volker Schlondorff, Margarethe von Trotta. Angela Winkler, Mario Adorf, Dieter Laser, Heinz Bennent, Jurgen Prochnow. Solid drama about a woman persecuted because she is suspected of aiding terrorists that is also a stinging commentary on individual freedom, political repression, and the dangers of media manipulation. Based on the Henrich Boll novel; remade as a TVM, THE LOST HONOR OF KATHRYN BECK.▼

Lost Honor of Kathryn Beck, The (1984) **C-100m.** TVM D: Simon Langton. Marlo Thomas, Kris Kristofferson, George Dzundza, Edward Winter, David Rasche, Linda Thorson. Thomas seeks to clear her reputation, smeared by the police and press after she spent the night with a man, unaware he was a long-sought terrorist. Uneven Americanization of the 1975 Volker Schlondorff–Margarethe von Trotta film THE LOST HONOR OF KATHARINA BLUM, adapted by Loring Mandel. Noted cinematographer Gordon Willis and British TV director Langton made their American TV movie debuts here. Also known as ACT OF PASSION. Average.▼

Lost Horizon (1937) **132m.** **** D: Frank Capra. Ronald Colman, Jane Wyatt, John Howard, Edward Everett Horton, Margo, Sam Jaffe, H. B. Warner, Isabel Jewell, Thomas Mitchell. James Hilton's classic story about five people stumbling into strange Tibetan land where health, peace, and longevity reign. A rare movie experience, with haunting finale. After being shown in edited reissue prints for years, this classic has been restored to its original length—though several scenes are still missing, and are represented by dialogue only, illustrated with stills. Remade with music in 1973.▼

Lost Horizon (1973) **C-143m.** *½ D: Charles Jarrott. Peter Finch, Liv Ullmann, Sally Kellerman, George Kennedy, Michael York, Olivia Hussey, Bobby Van, James Shigeta, Charles Boyer, John Gielgud. First half-hour copies 1937 film scene-for-scene, and everything's fine; then we get to Shangri-La and awful Burt Bacharach-Hal David songs, and it falls apart. "Lost" is right. Originally released at 150m.

Lost in a Harem (1944) **89m.** **½ D: Charles Riesner. Bud Abbott, Lou Costello, Marilyn Maxwell, John Conte, Douglass Dumbrille, Lottie Harrison, Jimmy Dorsey Orchestra. Slicker-than-usual A&C (made on infrequent trip to MGM), but strictly routine. Some good scenes here and there with sultan Dumbrille; Maxwell is perfect harem girl.

Lost in Alaska (1952) **76m.** *½ D: Jean Yarbrough. Bud Abbott, Lou Costello, Mitzi Green, Tom Ewell, Bruce Cabot. Unremarkable slapstick set in 1890s, with A&C off to the wilds to help a friend but doing more hindering.

Lost in America (1985) **C-91m.** *** D: Albert Brooks. Albert Brooks, Julie Hagerty, Garry Marshall, Art Frankel, Michael Greene. Two yuppies drop out of the rat race and take to the road ("just like EASY RIDER") in this low-key, often hilarious satire of upwardly mobile types. Written by Brooks and Monica Johnson.

And isn't that Albert's voice on the phone as the Mercedes salesman?▼

Lost in London (1985) **C-100m. TVM** D: Robert Lewis. Emmanuel Lewis, Ben Vereen, Lynne Moody, Freddie Jones. Youngster, fleeing his constantly squabbling parents, finds adventure in the streets of London in this allegedly whimsical drama that's simply humdrum. Below average.

Lost in the Stars (1974) **C-114m.** *** D: Daniel Mann. Brock Peters, Melba Moore, Raymond St. Jacques, Clifton Davis, Paula Kelly. Good American Film Theatre version of the Kurt Weill-Maxwell Anderson musical, based on Alan Paton's CRY, THE BELOVED COUNTRY (filmed on its own in 1951). Owes much of its power to Peters' portrayal of the South African minister. Filmed in Jamaica, B.W.I., and Hollywood.

Lost Island of Kioga (1938) **100m.** ** D: William Witney, John English. Bruce Bennett, Mala, Monte Blue, Jill Martin, Noble Johnson. Acceptable Republic cliff-hanger with white native muscleman (Bennett) saving shipwrecked survivors from a variety of near-disasters; better than usual settings. Reedited from serial HAWK OF THE WILDERNESS.

Lost Lagoon (1958) **79m.** *½ D: John Rawlins. Jeffrey Lynn, Peter Donat, Leila Barry, Don Gibson. Bland account of Lynn starting life anew on South Sea island. His sense of responsibility to family spoils idyll.

Lost Legacy See: **Girl Called Hatter Fox, The**▼

Lost Man, The (1969) **C-122m.** **½ D: Robert Alan Aurthur. Sidney Poitier, Joanna Shimkus, Al Freeman, Jr., Michael Tolan, Leon Bibb, Richard Dysart, David Steinberg, Paul Winfield. Uncomfortable updating of ODD MAN OUT from an Irish setting to present-day black underground has some tension, but doesn't really work. Three stars are good.

Lost Missile, The (1958) **70m.** ** D: Lester Berke. Robert Loggia, Ellen Parker, Larry Kerr, Philip Pine. Unexciting narrative of race-against-time to destroy a rocket before it explodes in N.Y.C.

Lost Moment, The (1947) **88m.** *** D: Martin Gabel. Robert Cummings, Susan Hayward, Agnes Moorehead, Joan Lorring, Eduardo Ciannelli. Henry James' *Aspern Papers* becomes offbeat drama. Publisher Cummings in Italy seeking lost love letters of famous writer, comes across neurotic Hayward who claims to have access to them.▼

Lost One, The (1951-German) **97m.** ** D: Peter Lorre. Peter Lorre, Karl John, Renate Mannhardt, Johanna Hofer. Lorre's only film as director is a talky, grim, but not uninteresting drama about the downfall of a German researcher (played by Peter

himself, with appropriate weariness), whose girlfriend is thought to have been passing on his discoveries to the British during WW2. Of interest mostly as a footnote to Lorre's career; based on a true story.▼

Lost Patrol, The (1934) **65m.** **** D: John Ford. Victor McLaglen, Boris Karloff, Wallace Ford, Reginald Denny, Alan Hale, J. M. Kerrigan, Billy Bevan. McLaglen's small British military group lost in Mesopotamian desert, as Arabs repeatedly attack the dwindling unit. Classic actioner filled with slice-of-life stereotypes, headed by religious fanatic Karloff. Fast-moving fun, great Max Steiner score. Scripted by Dudley Nichols, from Philip MacDonald's novel *Patrol*. Previously filmed in 1929, as a British silent starring Victor McLaglen's brother, Cyril, in the lead role; reworked many times (BAD LANDS, SAHARA, BATAAN, etc.). Original running time 74m.▼

Lost Planet Airmen (1949) **65m.** *½ D: Fred Brannon. Tristram Coffin, Mae Clarke, Dale Van Sickel, Tom Steele, Buddy Roosevelt, House Peters, Jr. Feature version of Republic Pictures' twelve-chapter serial KING OF THE ROCKET MEN. This condensation poorly highlights the scheme of mad scientist trying to rule the world. Special effects are main virtue.▼

Lost Squadron, The (1932) **79m.** **½ D: George Archainbaud. Richard Dix, Mary Astor, Erich von Stroheim, Joel McCrea, Dorothy Jordan, Robert Armstrong. WW1 pilots forced to find work as stunt fliers for movies; interesting idea boosted by von Stroheim's overacting as director "Arthur von Furst."▼

Lost Tribe, The (1949) **72m.** D: William Berke. Johnny Weissmuller, Myrna Dell, Elena Verdugo, Joseph Vitale. SEE: **Jungle Jim** series.

Lost Volcano, The (1950) **67m.** D: Ford Beebe. Johnny Sheffield, Donald Woods, Marjorie Lord, John Ridgely, Elena Verdugo. SEE: **Bomba, The Jungle Boy** series.▼

Lost Weekend, The (1945) **101m.** **** D: Billy Wilder. Ray Milland, Jane Wyman, Philip Terry, Howard da Silva, Doris Dowling, Frank Faylen, Mary Young. Unrelenting drama of alcoholism—and a landmark of adult filmmaking in Hollywood. Milland's powerful performance won him an Oscar; there's fine support from bartender da Silva, sanitarium aide Faylen. Won Academy Awards for Best Picture, Director, Actor, Screenplay (Wilder and Charles Brackett).▼

Lost World, The (1925) **60m.** **½ D: Harry Hoyt. Bessie Love, Wallace Beery, Lewis Stone, Lloyd Hughes. Silent film version of A. Conan Doyle adventure yarn is remarkable for special effects recreating prehistoric beasts encountered on scientific trip to deserted island. Interesting as precursor to KING KONG—in story structure and in Willis O'Brien's special effects. Originally 108m.; remade in 1960.▼

Lost World, The (1960) **C-98m.** ** D: Irwin Allen. Michael Rennie, Jill St. John, David Hedison, Claude Rains, Fernando Lamas, Richard Haydn. Despite cinematic advances, this remake of the 1925 film doesn't match original's special effects. OK juvenile entry of an expedition into remote territory hopefully inhabited by prehistoric monsters.

Lots of Luck (1985) **C-90m. TVM** D: Peter Baldwin. Martin Mull, Annette Funicello, Fred Willard, Polly Holliday, Mia Dillon, Tracey Gold, Jeremy Licht. Annette returned to the Disney fold after two decades, playing a housewife who hits the jackpot with a lottery ticket and discovers the endless problems that come with truckloads of money and other goodies. Made for cable by Disney. Average.▼

Lottery Bride, The (1930) **80m.** **½ D: Paul Stein. Jeanette MacDonald, John Garrick, Joe E. Brown, ZaSu Pitts, Robert Chisholm. Delightfully creaky musical with Yukon setting; Jeanette must deny her true love when she becomes lottery bride for his older brother. Impressive sets, forgettable music, enjoyable comic relief from Brown and Pitts.▼

Louisa (1950) **90m.** *** D: Alexander Hall. Ronald Reagan, Charles Coburn, Ruth Hussey, Edmund Gwenn, Spring Byington, Piper Laurie, Scotty Beckett, Martin Milner. Delightful romantic yarn of Byington seeking to become a December bride, undecided between Coburn and Gwenn; most disarming.

Louis Armstrong—Chicago Style (1976) **C-78m. TVM** D: Lee Philips. Ben Vereen, Margaret Avery, Red Buttons, Janet MacLachlan, Ketty Lester, Albert Paulsen. Dramatization of an incident in Satchmo's life when a death threat from Chicago gangsters unexpectedly made him an international figure. Vereen makes valiant stab at playing Louis, but the script is undeserving of the musical giant. Below average.

Louisiana (1984) **C-206m. TVM** D: Philippe de Broca. Margot Kidder, Ian Charleson, Len Cariou, Lloyd Bochner, Andrea Ferreol, Raymond Pellegrin, Victor Lanoux. French- and Canadian-made glitter-trash based on two novels by Maurice Denuziere, covering a period from 1836 to the antebellum era, marking de Broca's first TV work (in the U.S.) and starring his then-wife Kidder doing a Scarlett O'Hara turn. Made for cable and shown in two parts. Average.▼

Louisiana Hayride (1944) **67m.** ** D: Charles Barton. Judy Canova, Ross Hunter, Minerva Urecal, Lloyd Bridges, Russell Hicks. Hillbilly Canova goes Hollywood in this typical cornball vehicle.

Louisiana Purchase (1941) **C-98m.** **½ D: Irving Cummings. Bob Hope, Vera Zorina, Victor Moore, Irene Bordoni, Dona Drake. Brassy Irving Berlin musicomedy, with Hope's comedy very funny, especially famous filibuster scene in Congress. Opening scene of chorus girls singing lines about characters being fictitious is probably a movie first . . . and last.

Louisiana Story (1948) **77m.** **** D: Robert Flaherty. Classic, influential documentary set in the Louisiana bayous, with a young boy observing oil drillers at work. Beautifully made; produced by the Standard Oil Company. Music by Virgil Thomson.▼

Louis L'Amour's The Shadow Riders SEE: **Shadow Riders, The**

Loulou (1980-French) **C-110m.** ***½ D: Maurice Pialat. Isabelle Huppert, Gerard Depardieu, Guy Marchand, Humbert Balsan, Bernard Tronczyk. Huppert leaves stable hubby for topsy-turvy life with loutish Depardieu. Two leads have terrific sexual rapport in dynamic star vehicle.▼

Lovable Cheat, The (1949) **75m.** ** D: Richard Oswald. Charlie Ruggles, Peggy Ann Garner, Richard Ney, Alan Mowbray, Fritz Feld, Ludwig Donath, Buster Keaton, Curt Bois. Interesting more for cast and credits than actual achievement, this rather odd independent production (based on a Balzac play) centers on the comic antics of Ruggles battling against his creditors. Director Oswald's son, Gerd, was assistant director.

Love (1927) **96m.** **½ D: Edmund Goulding. Greta Garbo, John Gilbert, George Fawcett, Emily Fitzroy, Brandon Hurst, Philippe De Lacy. Silent version of *Anna Karenina* in modern setting, as married Garbo falls in love with dashing military guard Gilbert, an affair doomed from start. Lesser entry for famed screen lovers, with Gilbert's eyebrow-raising gestures at their worst. Garbo's 1935 version of ANNA KARENINA is much better.

Love Affair (1932) **68m.** ** D: Thornton Freeland. Dorothy Mackaill, Humphrey Bogart, Jack Kennedy, Barbara Leonard, Astrid Allwyn. Romance between a spoiled heiress and a dedicated aircraft engineer; pretty tired stuff, even with the curiosity value of a clean-cut Bogart as leading man.

Love Affair (1939) **87m.** ***½ D: Leo McCarey. Irene Dunne, Charles Boyer, Maria Ouspenskaya, Lee Bowman, Astrid Allwyn, Maurice Moscovich. Superior comedy-drama about shipboard romance whose continuation on-shore is interrupted by unforseen circumstances. Dunne and Boyer are a marvelous match. Remade by the same director as AN AFFAIR TO REMEMBER. Beware public-domain videocassette version, which has planted an entirely new music score on the soundtrack!▼

Love Affair, A: The Eleanor and Lou Gehrig Story (1978) **C-96m.** TVM D: Fielder Cook. Blythe Danner, Edward Herrmann, Patricia Neal, Jane Wyatt, Gerald S. O'Loughlin, Ramon Bieri, Georgia Engel, David Ogden Stiers, Lainie Kazan. Danner & Herrmann shine as Eleanor & Lou in Blanche Hanalis' loving retelling of the saga—unlike PRIDE OF THE YANKEES, told from her point of view. Above average.▼

Love Among the Ruins (1975) **C-100m.** TVM D: George Cukor. Katharine Hepburn, Laurence Olivier, Colin Blakely, Joan Sims, Richard Pearson, Leigh Lawson. Grand romantic comedy teaming two acting legends for the first time. Aging actress being sued by a young gigolo for breach of promise is defended by a prominent barrister who had been her long-ago lover. Rich and lustrous with Emmy Awards for its two stars, to director Cukor (his TV movie debut) and to writer James Costigan. Bouquets all around. Above average.▼

Love Among Thieves (1987) **C-100m.** TVM D: Roger Young. Audrey Hepburn, Robert Wagner, Jerry Orbach, Samantha Eggar, Patrick Bauchau. Romantic thriller uniting an elegant lady (Hepburn, of course, in her TV movie debut) with a raffish, cigar-chomping stranger, roughing it in the wilds of Mexico after she has pulled a daring jewel heist to bargain for her abducted fiancé's life. Regrettably it's no CHARADE for Audrey. Average.

Love and Anarchy (1973-Italian) **C-108m.** *** D: Lina Wertmuller. Giancarlo Giannini, Mariangela Melato, Lina Polito, Eros Pagni, Pina Cei, Elena Fiore. Italian bumpkin Giannini tries to assassinate Mussolini in 1932, falls for a prostitute in the brothel serving as his base of operation. Uneven but stylish drama helped establish Wertmuller's reputation in the U.S.▼

Love and Betrayal (1989) **C-100m.** TVM D: Richard Michaels. Stefanie Powers, David Birney, Fran Drescher, Amanda Peterson, Martha Scott. Dispassionate, dreary divorce drama that's a distant relative to KRAMER VS. KRAMER, with Stef in the Hoffman role and Birney doing Meryl Streep's. Below average.

Love and Bullets (1979-British) **C-103m.** ** D: Stuart Rosenberg. Charles Bronson, Rod Steiger, Jill Ireland, Strother Martin, Bradford Dillman, Henry Silva, Michael V. Gazzo. Bronson is supposed to nab gangster's moll Ireland for the FBI, but falls in love with her during his pursuit in Switzerland. Routine action yarn . . . for Bronson fans only.▼

Love and Death (1975) **C-82m.** *** D: Woody Allen. Woody Allen, Diane Keaton, Harold Gould, Alfred Lutter, Olga Georges-Picot, Zvee Scooler. One of Woody's most pretentious films won applause for its spoofs of Russian literature and foreign films, but this tale of a devout coward in the Napoleonic wars is more like a remake of Bob Hope's MONSIEUR BEAUCAIRE. Funny but uneven, with music by Prokofiev.▼

Love and Fear (1988-Italian-German-French) **C-114m.** *** D: Margarethe von Trotta. Fanny Ardant, Greta Scacchi, Valeria Golino, Peter Simonischek, Sergio Castellito, Agnes Sorel, Paolo Hendel. Involving if occasionally melodramatic account of the lives and loves of a trio of sisters: the oldest (Ardent) is an intellectual and all too aware of passing time and advancing age; the middle one (Scacchi) has no professional identity and lives by her emotions; the youngest (Golino) is a passionate, idealistic premed student. Crammed with ideas and observations about how life is in constant flux; loosely based on Chekhov's *Three Sisters.*

Love and Kisses (1965) **C-87m.** **½ D: Ozzie Nelson. Rick Nelson, Kristin Nelson, Jack Kelly, Jerry Van Dyke, Pert Kelton, Madelyn Hines. Harmless fare. Rick gets married, disrupting his family's life.

Love and Larceny (1963-Italian) **94m.** **½ D: Dino Risi. Vittorio Gassman, Anna Maria Ferrero, Dorian Gray, Peppino De Filippo. Saucy comedy of exuberant con-man Gassman making no pretense about his carefree life and pleasures.▼

Love and Learn (1947) **83m.** ** D: Frederick de Cordova. Jack Carson, Robert Hutton, Martha Vickers, Janis Paige, Otto Kruger. Overdone idea of songwriters Carson and Hutton waiting for their big break; young girl comes to their aid, but she doesn't save film.

Love and Lies (1990) **C-100m.** TVM D: Roger Young. Mare Winningham, Peter Gallagher, Tom O'Brien, G. W. Bailey, Robert Harper, Caroline Williams, M. Emmet Walsh. In a change-of-pace role, Winningham is real-life Kim Paris, a novice private eye with an aptitude for assuming colorful personalities; her first case is an unsolved double murder. Pilot to a proposed series. Average.

Love and Marriage (1964-Italian) **106m.** **½ D: Gianni Puccini, Mino Guerrini. Sylva Koscina, Philippe Leroy, Amadeo Girard, April Hennessy. Funny film in four segments relating to male-female relationships of an amorous variety.

Love and Money (1982) **C-90m.** ** D: James Toback. Ray Sharkey, Ornella Muti, Klaus Kinski, Armand Assante, King Vidor, Susan Heldfond, William Prince. Convoluted drama about Sharkey's entanglement in international scheme plotted by billionaire businessman Kinski; has its bright spots, but disappoints nonetheless because director Toback distances himself from his material. Sex scenes with Sharkey and Muti were toned down before film's release. Of interest mainly for presence of legendary director Vidor as Sharkey's senile grandfather. Completed in 1980.

Love and Pain (and the Whole Damn Thing) (1972) **C-110m.** *** D: Alan J. Pakula. Maggie Smith, Timothy Bottoms. Charming story of two introverts who miraculously and humorously find each other, fall in love while touring Spain; written by Alvin Sargent.

Love and the Frenchwoman (1961-French) **143m.** *** D: Jean Delannoy, Michel Boisrond, René Clair, Christian-Jaque, Jean-Paul Lechannois. Martine Lambert, Claude Rich, Dany Robin, Jean-Paul Belmondo, Annie Girardot, Martine Carol. Savory account of the seven ages of love in a woman's life, sensitively acted.▼

Love and the Midnight Auto Supply (1978) **C-93m.** *½ D: James Polakof. Michael Parks, Linda Cristal, Scott Jacoby, Colleen Camp, John Ireland, Rory Calhoun, Rod Cameron. Yahoo action-comedy has ringleader of stolen auto-parts gang turning Robin Hood to help farm workers combat corrupt politicians. Retitled MIDNIGHT AUTO SUPPLY.

Love at First Bite (1979) **C-96m.** *** D: Stan Dragoti. George Hamilton, Susan St. James, Richard Benjamin, Dick Shawn, Arte Johnson, Sherman Hemsley, Isabel Sanford, Barry Gordon, Ronnie Schell, Eric Laneuville. Silly but likable comedy about Count Dracula's adventures in New York City, and love affair with fashion model St. James. Hamilton's comic performance is bloody good. Written by Robert Kaufman.▼

Love at Large (1990) **C-97m.** ** D: Alan Rudolph. Tom Berenger, Anne Archer, Elizabeth Perkins, Kate Capshaw, Annette O'Toole, Ted Levine, Ann Magnuson, Kevin J. O'Connor, Ruby Dee, Barry Miller, Neil Young. A challenge to Rudolph cultists everywhere, this coy mess involves rival private detectives (male and female) who keep tripping over each other while following a case that's already plagued by problems of mistaken identity. Made watchable by the director's typically beguiling use of color and decor, plus his penchant for offbeat casting. Rocker Neil Young has a straight part (uh . . . so to speak).

Love at Stake (1987) **C-83m.** **½ D: John Moffitt. Patrick Cassidy, Kelly Preston, Bud Cort, Barbara Carrera, Stuart Pankin, Dave Thomas, Georgia Brown, Annie Golden. Wacky, overlooked comedy spoofs the Salem witch trials in the irreverent Mel Brooks tradition (producer Michael Gruskoff coproduced several Brooks pictures). Ingenues Cassidy and Preston (who plays baker Sarah Lee) are appeal-

ing, but the show is stolen by Carrera as a very sexy witch and Pankin and Thomas as corrupt officials. Dr. Joyce Brothers cameos as a defense witness at the witch trial and is branded a heretic!▼

Love at the Top (1974-French) **C-105m.** ** D: Michel Deville. Jean-Louis Trintignant, Jean-Pierre Cassel, Romy Schneider, Jane Birkin, Florinda Bolkan, Georges Wilson. Slick but superficial, muddled account of club-footed writer Cassel advising Trintignant on how to become rich and sleep with lots of women. Birkin, Bolkan, and Schneider are attractive, but it's all window dressing. Also known as THE FRENCH WAY IS.

Love at Twenty (1962-International) **113m.** **½ D: Francois Truffaut, Renzo Rossellini, Shintaro Ishihara, Marcel Ophuls, Andrzej Wajda. Jean-Pierre Leaud, Eleonora Rossi-Drago, Zbigniew Cybulski, Nami Tamura, Marie-France Pisier, Barbara Lass. Quintet of middling stories produced in France, Germany, Italy, Japan, Poland; variations on theme of love among younger generation. Truffaut's ANTOINE ET COLETTE is a sequel to THE 400 BLOWS (the first of his Antoine Doinel films). Original French running time: 123m.

Love Before Breakfast (1936) **70m.** **½ D: Walter Lang. Carole Lombard, Preston Foster, Cesar Romero, Janet Beecher, Betty Lawford, Douglas Blackley (Robert Kent). Fast-starting comedy slows down to obvious ending, but Lombard (as object of Foster's and Romero's attention) is always worth watching.

Love Boat, The (1976) **C-100m. TVM** D: Richard Kinon, Alan Myerson. Don Adams, Tom Bosley, Florence Henderson, Gabriel Kaplan, Harvey Korman, Cloris Leachman, Hal Linden, Karen Valentine, Ted Hamilton, Dick Van Patten. Seagoing *Love, American Style*, with four interrelated stories of romantic hijinks on pleasure cruise. First of three pilots for seemingly never-ending series is a shade better than those that followed . . . but still pretty leaky. Average.

Love Boat II, The (1977) **C-100m. TVM** D: Hy Averback. Ken Berry, Bert Convy, Celeste Holm, Hope Lange, Kristy McNichol, Robert Reed, Craig Stevens, Marcia Strassman, Lyle Waggoner, Diana Canova, Tracy Brooks Swope, Wesley Addy, Candy Azzara, Fred Grandy, Bernie Kopell, Ted Lange, Quinn Redeker, Diane Stilwell. The popularity of its predecessor prompted another quartet of stories, enacted by a similarly familiar roster of TV names, and this one led to a weekly series. Average.

Love Boat: A Valentine Voyage, The (1990) **C-100m. TVM** D: Ron Satlof. Gavin McLeod, Bernie Kopell, Ted Lange, Jill Whelan, Tom Bosley, Julia Duffy,

Jerry Lacy, Shanna Reed, Joe Regalbuto, Ted Shackelford, "Rowdy" Roddy Piper. The Love Boat casts off on one of its periodic cruises with a gang of klutzy jewel thieves aboard. With this passenger roster, your captain should have stayed at the dock. Below average.

Love Bug, The (1969) **C-107m.** ***½ D: Robert Stevenson. Dean Jones, Michele Lee, Buddy Hackett, David Tomlinson, Joe Flynn, Benson Fong, Iris Adrian. Delightful Disney comedy about a Volkswagen with a mind of its own; subtle it ain't, but the slapstick and stunts are great fun to watch. Followed by three HERBIE sequels.▼

Love Cage, The SEE: **Joy House**▼

Love Child (1982) **C-96m.** ** D: Larry Peerce. Amy Madigan, Beau Bridges, Mackenzie Phillips, Albert Salmi, Joanna Merlin, Rhea Perlman. Trifling melodrama of prisoner Madigan who has baby by Bridges and fights for the right to motherhood. Plays like an R-rated made-for-TV movie; based on a true story.▼

Love Crazy (1941) **99m.** **½ D: Jack Conway. William Powell, Myrna Loy, Gail Patrick, Jack Carson, Florence Bates, Sidney Blackmer, Sig Ruman. One misunderstanding leads to another in this energetic marital farce that loses steam halfway through. Highlighted by Powell's attempts to prove himself insane, and Carson's hilarious characterization as Ward Willoughby.

Loved One, The (1965) **116m.** ***½ D: Tony Richardson. Robert Morse, Jonathan Winters, Anjanette Comer, Rod Steiger, Dana Andrews, Milton Berle, James Coburn, John Gielgud, Tab Hunter, Margaret Leighton, Liberace, Roddy McDowall, Robert Morley, Lionel Stander. Correctly advertised as the picture with something to offend everyone. Britisher Morse attends to uncle's burial in California, encountering bizarre aspects of funeral business. Often howlingly funny, and equally gross. Once seen, Mrs. Joyboy can never be forgotten. Based on the Evelyn Waugh novel, adapted by Terry Southern and Christopher Isherwood.▼

Love Finds Andy Hardy (1938) **90m.** D: George B. Seitz. Mickey Rooney, Lewis Stone, Judy Garland, Cecilia Parker, Fay Holden, Lana Turner, Ann Rutherford, Betty Ross Clark, Marie Blake. SEE: **Andy Hardy** series.

Love for Ransom SEE: **Roger & Harry: The Mitera Target**

Love for Rent (1979) **C-96m.** TVM D: David Miller. Annette O'Toole, Lisa Eilbacher, Rhonda Fleming, Darren McGavin, Eugene Roche, David Selby. Innocuous TV programmer about two sisters who become seduced by big city glamour and wind up as high-priced call girls in an escort service. Below average.

Love from a Stranger (1937-British) **90m.** ** D: Rowland V. Lee. Ann Harding, Basil Rathbone, Binnie Hale, Bruce Seton, Bryan Powley, Jean Cadell. Working girl Harding wins fortune in a lottery, is swept off her feet by suave Rathbone, but after their marriage she begins to suspect he's not quite what he seemed. Stagy but interesting thriller features Rathbone's most unbridled performance, quite a sight to see. From Frank Vosper's play of a story by Agatha Christie. Joan Hickson, later TV's shrewd Miss Marple, plays a scatterbrained maid. Remade in 1947.▼

Love from a Stranger (1947) **81m.** **½ D: Richard Whorf. Sylvia Sidney, John Hodiak, John Howard, Isobel Elsom, Ernest Cossart. Capable cast goes through familiar paces in SUSPICION-like story of woman who learns she's married a killer. Filmed before in 1937; from an Agatha Christie story.▼

Love God?, The (1969) **C-101m.** ** D: Nat Hiken. Don Knotts, Anne Francis, Edmond O'Brien, James Gregory, Maureen Arthur, Maggie Peterson, Jesslyn Fax. Comedy for those who are amused by Knotts playing Hugh Hefner type; film is final work of Nat Hiken, who created Sergeant Bilko in better days.

Love Goddesses, The (1965) **87m.** *** Compiled by Saul J. Turell and Graeme Ferguson. Marilyn Monroe, Mae West, Jean Harlow, Theda Bara, Rita Hayworth, Claudette Colbert, Dorothy Lamour, many others. Compilation covers a lot of ground, featuring many major female stars from silent days to the present. Not always the ideal clips, but well done, with many welcome classic scenes. Some color sequences. Revised for 1972 theatrical reissue.▼

Love Happy (1949) **91m.** **½ D: David Miller. Harpo, Chico, and Groucho Marx, Ilona Massey, Vera-Ellen, Marion Hutton, Raymond Burr, Eric Blore. No NIGHT AT THE OPERA, but even diluted Marx Brothers are better than none. Putting on a musical forms background for Harpo's antics, with Chico in support, Groucho in a few unrelated scenes. Marilyn Monroe has a brief bit. Among the writers were Ben Hecht and Frank Tashlin; produced by Mary Pickford!▼

Love Has Many Faces (1965) **C-105m.** **½ D: Alexander Singer. Lana Turner, Cliff Robertson, Hugh O'Brian, Ruth Roman, Stefanie Powers, Virginia Grey. Timid attempt at lurid soaper; playgirl Turner's costume changes are the highlights. O'Brian and Robertson are gigolos. Filmed in Acapulco.

Love Hate Love (1970) **C-72m.** TVM D: George McCowan. Ryan O'Neal, Lesley (Ann) Warren, Peter Haskell, Henry Jones, Jeff Donnell, Jack Mullaney. Fair twist of triangle drama. Fashion model engaged to engineer (O'Neal) falls in love with jet setter (Haskell) who turns out to be psychotic. Competent performances, fair situations, one genuine moment of suspense. Script by Eric Ambler. Average.

Love, Honor and Goodbye (1945) 87m. ** D: Albert S. Rogell. Virginia Bruce, Nils Asther, Victor McLaglen, Helen Broderick, Veda Ann Borg, Edward Ashley. Bruce is actress in Broadway show, spending more time at rehearsals than with hubby. Mild frou-frou.

Love in a Goldfish Bowl (1961) C-88m. BOMB D: Jack Sher. Tommy Sands, Fabian, Jan Sterling, Edward Andrews. Film is as bad as its title, a worthless, boring trifle about teenagers taking over a beach house. Forget it.

Love in a Taxi (1980) C-90m. ***½ D: Robert Sickinger. Diane Sommerfield, James H. Jacobs, Earl Monroe, Malik Murray, Lisa Jane Persky. Wonderful little film about love blooming between Jewish cabbie Jacobs and black clerk Sommerfield. Made with care and affection; an audience-pleaser, with nice performances all around.

Love in Bloom (1935) 75m. ** D: Elliott Nugent. George Burns, Gracie Allen, Joe Morrison, Dixie Lee, J. C. Nugent, Lee Kohlmar. Burns and Allen are forced to take back seat to sappy romantic story about struggling songwriter and his girlfriend; George and Gracie give this minor film its only value.

Love in Germany, A (1984-German) C-110m. **½ D: Andrzej Wajda. Hanna Schygulla, Marie-Christine Barrault, Armin Mueller-Stahl, Elisabeth Trissenaar, Daniel Olbrychski, Piotr Lysak, Bernhard Wicki. German shopkeeper, her husband off fighting at the front, risks life and reputation by romancing a much younger Polish POW. Wimpy Lysak doesn't look as if he could drive a girl's hopscotch team into sexual delirium, creating severe credibility problems in this subpar Wajda effort. Barrault is effectively cast against type as conniving Nazi sympathizer.▼

Love-Ins, The (1967) C-92m. BOMB D: Arthur Dreifuss. James MacArthur, Susan Oliver, Richard Todd, Mark Goddard, Carol Booth. Professor Timothy Leary—er, Richard Todd—advocates LSD, becomes a hippie messiah. A bad trip.

Love in the Afternoon (1957) 130m. ***½ D: Billy Wilder. Gary Cooper, Audrey Hepburn, Maurice Chevalier, John McGiver. Forget age difference between Cooper and Hepburn and enjoy sparkling romantic comedy, with Chevalier as Audrey's private-eye dad. McGiver lends good support in witty comedy set in Paris. Wilder's first film cowritten with I.A.L. Diamond, and a tribute to his idol, Ernst Lubitsch.▼

Love in the City (1953-Italian) 90m. ** D: Michelangelo Antonioni, Federico Fellini, Dino Risi, Carlo Lizzani, Alberto Lattuada, Francesco Maselli, Cesare Zavattini. Ugo Tognazzi, Maresa Gallo, Caterina Rigoglioso, Silvio Lillo, Angela Pierro. Six-part film using a hidden-camera technique to give production seeming reality as it relates various aspects of romance in Rome.▼

Love Is a Ball (1963) C-111m. **½ D: David Swift. Glenn Ford, Hope Lange, Charles Boyer, Ricardo Montalban, Telly Savalas. Forced froth trying hard to be chic; gold-digging and romance on the Riviera.

Love Is a Dog From Hell (1987-Belgian) C-90m. *** D: Dominique Deruddere. Josse De Pauw, Geert Hunaerts, Florence Beliard, Anne Van Essche, Amid Chakir, Michael Pas, Carmela Locantore. Weird yet fascinating, well-acted three-part fantasy chronicling one person's descent from 12-year-old innocent to grungy barfly—and necrophiliac. Originally 30m. long, then expanded to feature length. Script by Marc Didden and Deruddere, loosely based on Charles Bukowski's *The Copulating Mermaid of Venice, Calif.*

Love Is a Many Splendored Thing (1955) C-102m. *** D: Henry King. Jennifer Jones, William Holden, Isobel Elsom, Jorja Curtright, Virginia Gregg, Torin Thatcher, Richard Loo. Well-mounted soaper set in Hong Kong at time of Korean War. Eurasian doctor Jones falls in love with war correspondent Holden. Trite plot, beautifully executed, with Oscar-winning costumes (Charles LeMaire), scoring (Alfred Newman) and title song (Sammy Fain and Paul Francis Webster).▼

Love Is a Racket (1932) 72m. ** D: William Wellman. Douglas Fairbanks, Jr., Ann Dvorak, Frances Dee, Lee Tracy, Lyle Talbot, Andre Luguet, Warren Hymer. Attractive cast in curiously unappealing story of a Broadway columnist and his private intrigues. Tracy, who portrayed Winchell types so often, here plays the columnist's legman.

Love Is Better than Ever (1952) 81m. **½ D: Stanley Donen. Elizabeth Taylor, Larry Parks, Josephine Hutchinson, Tom Tully, Ann Doran, Elinor Donahue, Kathleen Freeman. Forgettable froth involving talent agent Parks and dance teacher Taylor. Mild MGM musical, but Liz looks terrific. Gene Kelly has an unbilled cameo.

Love Is Forever (1983) C-150m. TVM D: Hall Bartlett. Michael Landon, Priscilla Presley, Moira Chen, Jurgen Prochnow, Edward Woodward. Controversial dramatization of journalist John Everingham's heralded rescue of his Laotian girlfriend following Communist takeover of her country. Behind-the-scenes details of this film's production are more interesting than the film itself, which was aimed for theatrical release as COMEBACK. Produced by Landon, who also reportedly took a hand in directing. Moira Chen is better known as softcore pornography actress Laura Gemser. Revamped and re-edited for later showing at 100m. Average.

Love Is Never Silent (1985) **C-100m. TVM** D: Joseph Sargent. Mare Winningham, Phyllis Frelich, Ed Waterstreet, Fredric Lehne, Cloris Leachman, Sid Caesar. Compelling period drama about a young girl torn between being her deaf parents' link to the hearing world and having a life of her own. Winningham is winning as usual, as are Frelich and Waterstreet, both stars of the National Theatre of the Deaf. Darlene Craviotto's loving script is based on Joanne Greenberg's novel *In This Sign*. Emmy winner for Best Director and Outstanding Drama/Comedy Special. Above average.

Love Is News (1937) **78m.** ** D: Tay Garnett. Tyrone Power, Loretta Young, Don Ameche, Slim Summerville, George Sanders, Jane Darwell, Stepin Fetchit, Pauline Moore, Elisha Cook, Jr., Dudley Digges, Walter Catlett. Heiress Young decides to get even with relentless reporter Power by announcing she's going to marry him—so he'll see what it's like to be in the spotlight for a change. Comedy misfire was remade more successfully as THAT WONDERFUL URGE, with Power repeating his starring role.

Love Is Not Enough (1978) **C-100m. TVM** D: Ivan Dixon. Bernie Casey, Stuart K. Robinson, Renee Brown, Dain Turner, Stu Gilliam, Eddie Singleton. Warm but predictable comedy-drama about a Detroit black family's search for the better life in California. A very brief series called *Harris and Co.* spun off from this pilot. Average.

Love Is on the Air (1937) **61m.** ** D: Nick Grinde. Ronald Reagan, June Travis, Eddie Acuff, Ben Welden, Robert Barrat, Addison Richards. Reagan's first film casts him as a brash headline-making radio personality who goes after corrupt city officials— but is sidetracked by his cautious boss. Passable B picture with meaningless title; one of several remakes of Paul Muni's HI, NELLIE.

Love Laughs at Andy Hardy (1946) **93m.** D: Willis Goldbeck. Mickey Rooney, Lewis Stone, Sara Haden, Bonita Granville, Lina Romay, Fay Holden, Dorothy Ford. SEE: **Andy Hardy** series.▼

Love Leads the Way (1984) **C-110m. TVM** D: Delbert Mann. Timothy Bottoms, Eva Marie Saint, Arthur Hill, Glynnis O'Connor, Susan Dey, Patricia Neal, Ernest Borgnine, Ralph Bellamy. Treacly Disney movie (with a stellar cast and top director) about the first Seeing Eye guide dog. The estimable Henry Denker based his surprisingly pedestrian script on the book *First Lady of the Seeing Eye* by Morris Frank (played woodenly by Bottoms) and Blake Clark. Made for cable. Average.▼

Loveless, The (1983) **C-84m.** **½ D: Kathryn Bigelow, Monty Montgomery. J. Don Ferguson, Willem Dafoe, Marin Kanter, Robert Gordon, Tina L'Hotsky, Liz Gans. A group of bikers stop in a small Southern town while on their way to the races at Daytona. Uneven homage to THE WILD ONE: pretentious and practically plotless, with about five times as much rockabilly music as dialogue; still, visually stunning, like an Edward Hopper painting of the 1950s.▼

Love Letters (1945) **101m.** ** D: William Dieterle. Jennifer Jones, Joseph Cotten, Ann Richards, Anita Louise, Cecil Kellaway, Gladys Cooper, Reginald Denny. Artificial soaper of amnesiac Jones cured by Cotten's love; only real asset is Victor Young's lovely title song. Ayn Rand adapted Chris Massie's book, *Pity My Simplicity.*

Love Letters (1983) **C-98m.** *** D: Amy Jones. Jamie Lee Curtis, James Keach, Amy Madigan, Bud Cort, Matt Clark, Bonnie Bartlett, Sally Kirkland. Moving drama about a young single woman (nicely played by Curtis) who discovers deceased mother's correspondence with lover, then takes up with a married man of her own (Keach). Originally titled MY LOVE LETTERS.▼

Lovelines (1984) **C-93m.** *½ D: Rod Amateau. Greg Bradford, Mary Beth Evans, Michael Winslow, Don Michael Paul, Tammy Taylor. Lamebrained youth comedy with music. No discernible plot . . . and no discernible laughs, either.▼

Love Lives On (1985) **C-100m. TVM** D: Larry Peerce. Christine Lahti, Sam Waterston, Ricky Paull Goldin, Louise Latham, Joe Regalbuto, Mary Stuart Masterson. Even this talented cast is at a loss to save this hand-wringer that manages to weave every known TV-movie "disease of the week" into its soapy plot. Below average.

Love Lottery, The (1953-British) **C-89m.** ** D: Charles Crichton. David Niven, Peggy Cummins, Anne Vernon, Herbert Lom, Hugh McDermott. Niven is famed movie star involved in international lottery; the winner gets him! Vernon is the girl he really loves. Potential satire never comes off. Humphrey Bogart has guest bit in finale.

Lovely To Look At (1952) **C-105m.** **½ D: Mervyn LeRoy. Kathryn Grayson, Red Skelton, Howard Keel, Ann Miller, Marge & Gower Champion, Zsa Zsa Gabor. Second screen version of ROBERTA is a lesser MGM musical, but definitely has its moments as American comic Skelton inherits half-interest in a Paris dress salon run by Grayson and Marge Champion. Miller and the Champions add punch to the musical sequences; Vincente Minnelli directed the fashion show sequence. Songs include "Smoke Gets in Your Eyes," "I Won't Dance," and title tune.

Lovely Way to Die, A (1968) **C-103m.** **½ D: David Lowell Rich. Kirk Douglas, Sylva Koscina, Eli Wallach, Kenneth Haigh, Sharon Farrell, Gordon Peter, Martyn Green. Odd detective suspenser. Douglas is likable cop turned private-eye assigned by D.A. (Wallach) to protect Koscina, awaiting murder trial. Pacing and script offbeat at right moments, otherwise standard. Look for Ali MacGraw in screen debut.

Love Machine, The (1971) **C-108m.** *½ D: Jack Haley, Jr. John Phillip Law, Dyan Cannon, Robert Ryan, Jackie Cooper, David Hemmings, Shecky Greene, Maureen Arthur. Ridiculous screen version of Jacqueline Susann's best-seller about Robin Stone (Law), ruthless TV executive who uses others for self-gain.▼

Lovemakers, The SEE: La Viaccia
Love Maniac, The SEE: Blood of Ghastly Horror▼

Love, Mary (1985) **C-100m. TVM** D: Robert Day. Kristy McNichol, Matt Clark, David Paymer, Piper Laurie, Rachel Ticotin. Kristy shows true grit in this fact-based account of a woman's travels from practically illiterate teenager to reform school inmate to stroke-afflicted mother to award-winning physician. Average.

Love Me Forever (1935) **90m.** **½ D: Victor Schertzinger. Grace Moore, Leo Carrillo, Robert Allen, Spring Byington, Douglass Dumbrille. Entertaining musical of down-and-out singer who miraculously rises to top and becomes star. Good cast helped make Moore become star in real life too.

✓ **Love Me or Leave Me** (1955) **C-122m.** ***½ D: Charles Vidor. Doris Day, James Cagney, Cameron Mitchell, Robert Keith, Tom Tully. Engrossing musical bio (from an Oscar-winning story by Daniel Fuchs) of singer Ruth Etting, whose life and career were dominated by a gangster called the Gimp. Day and Cagney give strong performances. Score includes Doris' hit "I'll Never Stop Loving You," plus oldies like "Ten Cents a Dance," "Shaking the Blues Away."▼

Love Me Tender (1956) **89m.** **½ D: Robert D. Webb. Richard Egan. Debra Paget, Elvis Presley, Robert Middleton, William Campbell, Neville Brand, Mildred Dunnock. Presley's film debut is Civil War yarn of conflicting politics among sons in a Southern family, and their mutual love for Paget. Elvis' singing ("Let Me," "We're Gonna Move (to a Better

Home," "Poor Boy," and the title tune) highlights so-so Western. Elvis's swivel hips *might* not be authentic period detail!
▼
Love Me Tonight (1932) **96m.** **** D: Rouben Mamoulian. Maurice Chevalier, Jeanette MacDonald, Charlie Ruggles, Myrna Loy, C. Aubrey Smith, Charles Butterworth, Robert Greig. One of the best musicals ever made; Chevalier plays a tailor who falls in love with a princess (MacDonald). Along the way they get to sing Rodgers and Hart's "Lover," "Mimi," "Isn't It Romantic?" among others. Mamoulian's ingenious ideas keep this fresh and alive. Originally released at 104m. Screenplay by Samuel Hoffenstein, Waldemar Young, and George Marion, Jr., from a play by Leopold Marchand and Paul Armont.

Love Nest (1951) **84m.** ** D: Joseph M. Newman. June Haver, William Lundigan, Frank Fay, Marilyn Monroe, Jack Paar, Leatrice Joy. Tepid comedy based on premise that wacky goings-on in apartment building can carry a film.

Love on a Pillow (1963-French) **C-102m.** ** D: Roger Vadim. Brigitte Bardot, Robert Hossein, James Robertson Justice, Jean-Marc Bory. Charitable Bardot bestows her pleasures on young man, hoping to divert his intended suicide; saucy little comedy.

Love on the Dole (1941-British) **100m.** *** D: John Baxter. Deborah Kerr, Clifford Evans, Mary Merrall, George Carney, Geoffrey Hibbert, Joyce O'Neill. Serious, well-acted study of struggling London family during Depression. From Walter Greenwood novel.▼

Love on the Ground (1984-French) **C-126m.** *½ D: Jacques Rivette. Geraldine Chaplin, Jane Birkin, Andre Dussollier, Jean-Pierre Kalfon, Facundo Bo, Laszlo Szabo. Boring, confusing, pretentious story of actresses Chaplin and Birkin, hired by Kalfon to rehearse and perform his play—whose ending has not yet been written. For Rivette admirers only.

Love on the Run (1936) **80m.** **½ D: W. S. Van Dyke II. Joan Crawford, Clark Gable, Franchot Tone, Reginald Owen, Mona Barrie, Ivan Lebedeff, Charles Judels. Another film that's all stars and no plot to support them. If you like Gable or Crawford, you'll enjoy this globe-trotting romance involving foreign correspondents and Continental spies.

Love on the Run (1979-French) **C-90m.** *** D: Francois Truffaut. Jean-Pierre Leaud, Marie-France Pisier, Claude Jade, Dani, Dorothee, Rosy Varte, Julien Bertheau, Daniel Mesguich. Further romantic adventures of Truffaut's alter ego, Antoine Doinel (Leaud): Here, he divorces wife Jade and sets out again on his hopeless chase after love. Fine, but not top-notch

Truffaut. Fifth entry in the series, following BED AND BOARD; included are clips of the others, which really don't work here. Leaud's final appearance as Doinel.▼

Love on the Run (1985) **C-100m. TVM** D: Gus Trikonis. Stephanie Zimbalist, Alec Baldwin, Constance McCashin, Howard Duff, Madison Mason, Ernie Hudson. Fictionalization of the not-long-ago case of the lady lawyer who helped her convict client bust out of jail. Real life was better. Average.▼

Love Parade, The (1929) **110m. ***** D: Ernst Lubitsch. Maurice Chevalier, Jeanette MacDonald, Lillian Roth, Lionel Belmore, Lupino Lane, Ben Turpin. Initial teaming of Chevalier and MacDonald is enjoyable operetta with chic Lubitsch touch, about love among the royalty of Sylvania. Acrobatic comedian Lane and personality performer Roth make wonderful second leads. Virginia Bruce is one of Jeanette's ladies-in-waiting. "Dream Lover" is film's best song. Score by Victor Schertzinger (later a film director himself) and Clifford Grey. MacDonald's film debut.

Lover Boy (1954) SEE: **Lovers, Happy Lovers!**

Loverboy (1989) **C-98m. *½** D: Joan Micklin Silver. Patrick Dempsey, Kate Jackson, Robert Ginty, Nancy Valen, Charles Hunter Walsh, Barbara Carrera, Bernie Coulson, Ray Girardin, Robert Camilletti, Vic Tayback, Kim Miyori, Kirstie Alley, Carrie Fisher. Paper-thin comedy of pizza delivery boy Dempsey turning on a bevy of frustrated older women, with resulting predictable complications. Curiously anachronistic, and not even up to sitcom level; a major disappointment from the otherwise dependable Silver.▼

Lover Come Back (1946) **90m. **½** D: William A. Seiter. Lucille Ball, George Brent, Vera Zorina, Carl Esmond, William Wright, Charles Winninger. Bright little comedy of Lucy suing Brent for divorce when she sees his companion during war, photographer Zorina. Retitled WHEN LOVERS MEET.

Lover Come Back (1961) **C-107m. ***½** D: Delbert Mann. Rock Hudson, Doris Day, Tony Randall, Edie Adams, Jack Oakie, Jack Kruschen, Ann B. Davis, Joe Flynn, Jack Albertson, Howard St. John, Donna Douglas. Early Day-Hudson vehicle is one of the best. Funny, fast-moving comedy has ad exec Doris trying to get account away from rival Rock—unaware that the product doesn't exist! Edie Adams stands out in fine supporting cast.▼

Lovers, The (1959-French) **90m. ***** D: Louis Malle. Jeanne Moreau, Alain Cuny, Jose-Luis de Villalonga, Jean-Marc Bory. Sensational, chic love tale of Moreau bored with husband and home, having a most sensual romance with an overnight guest.▼

Lovers and Liars (1979-Italian) **C-96m. **** D: Mario Monicelli. Goldie Hawn, Giancarlo Giannini, Claudine Auger, Aurore Clement, Laura Betti, Andrea Ferreol. Forgettable black comedy centering on complications surrounding romance between American tourist Hawn and Italian bank executive Giannini. Also known as TRAVELS WITH ANITA; original running time: 125m.▼

Lovers and Lollipops (1956) **80m. **½** D: Morris Engel, Ruth Orkin. Lori March, Gerald O'Loughlin, Cathy Dunn, William Ward. Pleasing minor film of romance between widow and professional man, disrupted by her daughter's jealousy of their happiness.

Lovers and Other Strangers (1970) **C-106m. ***½** D: Cy Howard. Gig Young, Bea Arthur, Bonnie Bedelia, Anne Jackson, Harry Guardino, Michael Brandon, Richard Castellano, Bob Dishy, Marian Hailey, Cloris Leachman, Anne Meara. Vividly real, genuinely funny movie about side-effects, reverberations when young couple gets married. Film won fame for Castellano, with catch-line "So what's the story?" just one of many memorable vignettes. Gig Young delightful as perennially cheerful father of the bride. From the play by Renee Taylor and Joseph Bologna; with Oscar-winning song, "For All We Know." Diane Keaton's film debut.▼

Lovers, Happy Lovers! (1954-British) **105m. **½** D: Rene Clement. Gerard Philipe, Valerie Hobson, Joan Greenwood, Margaret Johnston, Natasha Parry. Philipe is footloose playboy in London who finally meets his match and is marriage-bound. Original title: KNAVE OF HEARTS. Retitled: LOVER BOY.

Lovers Like Us (1975-French) **C-103m. **½** D: Jean-Paul Rappeneau. Catherine Deneuve, Yves Montand, Luigi Vanucchi, Tony Roberts, Dana Wynter. Globetrotting screwball comedy has Deneuve and Montand running away from their respective spouses, meeting and falling in love with each other. Nothing special, but easy to take.▼

Lovers of Montparnasse, The (1957-French) **103m. **½** D: Jacques Becker. Gerard Philipe, Lilli Palmer, Anouk Aimee, Lea Padovani, Lino Ventura, Gerald Sety. Fictionalized bio of 1900s painter Modigliani, his romances and escapades; cast is forced into stereotyped performances. Original title: MONTPARNASSE 19.

Lovers of Paris (1957-French) **115m. **½** D: Julien Duvivier. Gerard Philipe, Danielle Darrieux, Dany Carrel. Spirited drama of Philipe coming to Paris bent on success and marriage; Darrieux is his perfect choice. Original title: POT-BOUILLE.

Loves and Times of Scaramouche, The (1975-Italian) **C-95m. *½** D: Enzo G. Castellari. Michael Sarrazin, Ursula Andress, Aldo Maccione, Giancarlo Prete, Michael

Forest. Scaramouche has his way with women, and runs afoul of an oafish Napoleon in this energetic but empty-headed farce. Maccione adds some laughs as Bonaparte. Poorly dubbed. Filmed in Rome and Zagreb.▼

Love's Dark Side (1978) **C-100m. TVM** D: Delbert Mann. Cliff Potts, Carrie Snodgress, Jane Seymour, Granville Van Dusen, Shelly Novack, Tom Sullivan. Tepid fact-based drama about an ad executive who is blinded in a gun accident and falls in love with a nightclub entertainer he has befriended. Average.

Lovesick (1983) **C-95m. ** D: Marshall Brickman. Dudley Moore, Elizabeth McGovern, Alec Guinness, John Huston, Wallace Shawn, Alan King, Renee Taylor, Ron Silver, Gene Saks. "Sick" is right; this romantic comedy (about a psychiatrist who falls in love with his newest patient) needs a shot of adrenalin. Fine cast founders; Guinness's turn as the shade of Sigmund Freud is a waste. Only Silver gets real laughs as a Pacino-like actor.▼

Love Slaves of the Amazon (1957) **C-81m. ** D: Curt Siodmak. Don Taylor, Eduardo Ciannelli, Gianna Segale, Harvey Chalk. Title tag removes all surprises about this programmer.

Loves of a Blonde (1965-Czech) **88m. ***½** D: Milos Forman. Hana Brejchova, Josef Sebanek, Vladimir Pucholt, Jan Vostrell. Thoroughly engaging boy-meets-girl comedy, directed with sensitivity and a remarkable feel for original cinema.▼

Loves of Carmen, The (1948) **C-99m. **½** D: Charles Vidor. Rita Hayworth, Glenn Ford, Ron Randell, Victor Jory, Luther Adler. Hayworth's beauty is all there is in this colorful but routine retelling of the story of a gypsy man-killer, minus Bizet's music.▼

Loves of Edgar Allan Poe, The (1942) **67m. ** D: Harry Lachman. Linda Darnell, John (Shepperd Strudwick) Shepperd, Virginia Gilmore, Jane Darwell, Mary Howard. Plodding biography of 19th-century writer and women who influenced him.

Loves of Isadora, The SEE: Isadora▼

Loves of Salammbo, The (1962-Italian) **C-72m. ** D: Sergio Grieco. Jeanne Valerie, Jacques Sernas, Edmund Purdom, Arnoldo Foa, Riccardo Garrone. Spectacle features Purdom in an uneven tale of Carthaginians battling the Mercenaries. Filmed on location.

Loves of Sunya, The (1927) **80m. *** D: Albert Parker. Gloria Swanson, John Boles, Anders Randolph, Andres de Segurola, Hugh Miller, Pauline Garon. Lavish vehicle for silent-star Swanson has Eastern yogi enabling her to envision her life with each of three suitors. Soap opera deluxe, remake of earlier EYES OF YOUTH.

Loves of Three Queens (1953-Italian)

**C-90m. ** D: Marc Allegret. Hedy Lamarr, Massimo Serato, Cathy O'Donnell, Luigi Tosi, Guido Celano, Robert Beatty. Three-part film involving lives and loves of Genevieve of Brabant, Empress Josephine, and Helen of Troy (Lamarr). Originally three-hour meandering epic, now chopped down; still lacks continuity or interest. Retitled: THE FACE THAT LAUNCHED A THOUSAND SHIPS.

Love Songs (1986-Canadian-French) **C-107m. ** D: Elie Chouraqui. Catherine Deneuve, Richard Anconina, Christopher Lambert, Jacques Perrin, Nick Mancuso, Dayle Haddon, Charlotte Gainsbourg. Lightweight, predictable soap opera about the loves and ambitions of a pair of young rock singers (Anconina, Lambert), focusing mostly on the latter's relationship with an older woman (Deneuve). Attempts to be touching and bittersweet but doesn't ring true. ▼

Lovespell (1979) **C-91m. BOMB** D: Tom Donovan. Richard Burton, Kate Mulgrew, Nicholas Clay, Cyril Cusack, Geraldine Fitzgerald, Niall Toibin, Diana Van Der Vlis, Niall O'Brien. Thoroughly inept retelling of the romantic Tristan and Isolde legend. One-take-only filming on Irish locations has static direction and writing out of a *Classics Illustrated* comic book. Mulgrew is too old for the Isolde role, and her American accent clashes with the rest of the cast. Also known as TRISTAN AND ISOLDE.▼

Love's Savage Fury (1979) **C-100m. TVM** D: Joseph Hardy. Jennifer O'Neill, Perry King, Raymond Burr, Connie Stevens, Robert Reed, Ed Lauter. Petulant southern belle fights to hold onto the family mansion when the Union boys march through in this blatant ripoff of GONE WITH THE WIND—and even the letters of the title sweep across the screen in the opening credits! Below average (and contempt).▼

Love Story (1944-British) **108m. *** D: Leslie Arliss. Margaret Lockwood, Stewart Granger, Patricia Roc, Tom Walls, Reginald Purdell, Moira Lister. No relation to later hit film, this one has dying pianist Lockwood finding true love at summer resort with pilot Granger, whose eyesight is failing. Originally released here as A LADY SURRENDERS.

Love Story (1970) **C-99m. *** D: Arthur Hiller. Ali MacGraw, Ryan O'Neal, Ray Milland, John Marley, Katherine Balfour, Russell Nype, Tom (Tommy) Lee Jones. Just what it says: simple, modern boy-meets-girl story set against New England college backdrop, tinged with tragedy of girl's sudden illness. Straightforward filming of Erich Segal's book can't hold a candle to older Hollywood schmaltz, but on its own terms, pretty good (and a box-office smash). Francis Lai won an Oscar for his score. Followed by OLIVER'S STORY.▼

Love Streams (1984) C-141m. ** D: John Cassavetes. Gena Rowlands, John Cassavetes, Diahnne Abbott, Risa Martha Blewitt, Seymour Cassel, Margaret Abbott. Typical Cassavetes fodder about a brother and sister with a strong emotional bond: for her, love never ends; and for him, love is an abstract undone by the harsh realities of life. Cassavetes aficionados will probably like it; for others, only marginally bearable. Based on a play by Ted Allan, who cowrote screenplay with Cassavetes. ▼

Love Tapes, The (1980) C-105m. TVM D: Allen Reisner. Martin Balsam, Larry Breeding, Michael Constantine, Mariette Hartley, Arte Johnson, Jan Smithers, Loretta Swit, Larry Wilcox. Limp comedy about the misadventures of a videotape dating service's clients, familiar TV faces all. A deservedly busted pilot. Below average.

Love That Brute (1950) 85m. **½ D: Alexander Hall. Paul Douglas, Jean Peters, Cesar Romero, Joan Davis, Arthur Treacher. Douglas comes off well as loud-talking, good-natured prohibition racketeer with a yen for innocent Peters. Remake of TALL, DARK AND HANDSOME.

Love Thy Neighbor (1940) 82m. ** D: Mark Sandrich. Jack Benny, Fred Allen, Mary Martin, Verree Teasdale, Eddie "Rochester" Anderson, Virginia Dale, Theresa Harris. Contrived attempt to capitalize on Benny-Allen radio feud. Martin still good, though, and Rochester has some sprightly scenes, but disappointment for fans of both Benny and Allen.

Love Thy Neighbor (1984) C-100m. TVM D: Tony Bill. John Ritter, Penny Marshall, Bert Convy, Cassie Yates, Contance McCashin. Two squabbling neighbors reluctantly bury the hatchet and drift into romance after his wife runs off with her husband. Brightening this serio-comedy are two of TV's best farceurs, making a good if unlikely team. Average.

Love Trap SEE: **Curse of the Black Widow**▼

Love Under Fire (1937) 75m. **½ D: George Marshall. Loretta Young, Don Ameche, Frances Drake, Walter Catlett, Sig Ruman, John Carradine, Holmes Herbert. Romance and adventure as detective Ameche has to arrest alleged thief Young in Madrid amid Spanish Civil War. Disjointed but enjoyable.

Love War, The (1970) C-74m. TVM D: George McCowan. Lloyd Bridges, Angie Dickinson, Harry Basch, Dan Travanty (Daniel J. Travanti), Byron Foulger, Judy Jordan. Two planets decide to end quarrel over Earth by arranging contest to the death in small town. Victor gets total control.

Typical TV resolution. Foolish drama must be seen to be believed. Below average.

Love with the Proper Stranger (1963) 100m. *** D: Robert Mulligan. Natalie Wood, Steve McQueen, Edie Adams, Herschel Bernardi, Tom Bosley. Nifty, cynical romance tale of working girl Wood and trumpet player McQueen. Much N.Y.C. on-location filming, nice support from Adams. Written by Arnold Schulman. Good bit: the title tune.▼

Lovey: A Circle of Children, Part II (1978) C-100m. TVM D: Jud Taylor. Jane Alexander, Ronny Cox, Kris McKeon, Jeff Lynas, Karen Allen, Helen Shaver, Danny Aiello. Alexander reprises her role from A CIRCLE OF CHILDREN as a teacher of disturbed youngsters—and again is top-notch. Above average.

Loving (1970) C-90m. ***½ D: Irvin Kershner. George Segal, Eva Marie Saint, Sterling Hayden, Keenan Wynn, Nancie Phillips, Janis Young, Roy Scheider, Sherry Lansing. Extremely good drama chronicles Segal's marital and occupational problems. Director Kershner has great feeling for day-to-day detail; film's superb climax involves public lovemaking.

Loving Couples (1980) C-97m. ** D: Jack Smight. Shirley MacLaine, James Coburn, Susan Sarandon, Stephen Collins, Sally Kellerman, Nan Martin. Couples MacLaine/Coburn and Sarandon/Collins switch partners. A titillating title for a predictable comedy.▼

Loving You (1957) C-101m. **½ D: Hal Kanter. Elvis Presley, Lizabeth Scott, Wendell Corey, Dolores Hart, James Gleason. Publicist Liz and country-western musician Corey discover gas station attendant Presley and promote him to stardom. Elvis's second movie is highlighted by his performance of "Teddy Bear" and the title tune.▼

Lovin' Molly (1974) C-98m. ** D: Sidney Lumet. Anthony Perkins, Beau Bridges, Blythe Danner, Edward Binns, Susan Sarandon, Conard Fowkes. Danner is just right in otherwise indifferent filmization of Larry McMurtry's novel *Leaving Cheyenne,* about two friends in Texas and their life-long love for the same woman.

Lower Depths, The (1957-Japanese) 125m. *** D: Akira Kurosawa. Toshiro Mifune, Isuzu Yamada, Ganjiro Nakamura, Kyoko Kagawa. Well-directed and acted but endlessly talky drama of tortured, poverty-stricken souls, with Mifune a thief who becomes involved with Kagawa. Based on a Maxim Gorki play.▼

Loyalties (1986-Canadian) C-98m. **½ D: Anne Wheeler. Kenneth Welsh, Tantoo Cardinal, Susan Wooldridge, Vera Martin, Christopher Barrington-Leigh. Nicely paced but predictable psychological drama about an ever-so-proper British couple

(Welsh, Wooldridge) who've settled in a remote Canadian village, and what happens when they take on half-Indian Cardinal as a housekeeper.▼

L-Shaped Room, The (1963-British) **125m.** *** D: Bryan Forbes. Leslie Caron, Tom Bell, Brock Peters, Avis Bunnage, Emlyn Williams, Cicely Courtneidge, Bernard Lee, Patricia Phoenix, Nanette Newman. French woman crosses the Channel to face pregnancy alone, comes to meet interesting assortment of characters in shabby London boarding house. Caron is superb in the lead.

Lt. Robin Crusoe, USN (1966) **C-110m.** BOMB D: Byron Paul. Dick Van Dyke, Nancy Kwan, Akim Tamiroff, Arthur Malet, Tyler McVey. Labored Disney comedy is unworthy of Van Dyke, who plays modern-day Robinson Crusoe, a navy pilot who drifts onto deserted island, becomes involved with pretty native girl. Film has virtually nothing of merit to recommend.▼

Lucan (1977) **C-78m.** TVM D: David Greene. Kevin Brophy, Stockard Channing, Ned Beatty, William Jordan, Lou Frizzell, George Wyner. Youth who spent his first ten years running wild and raised by wolves strikes out in search of his identity. Of its type, pretty good, and it bred a series. Average.

Lucas (1986) **C-100m.** *** D: David Seltzer. Corey Haim, Kerri Green, Charlie Sheen, Courtney Thorne-Smith, Winona Ryder, Thomas E. Hodges. Thoroughly winning story of a precocious 14-year-old boy who develops a serious crush on the new girl in town—and the various ramifications that follow. One of the few Hollywood films about young people in the 80s that doesn't paint its characters in shades of black and white only. A real sleeper, marking writer Seltzer's directing debut.▼

Lucas Tanner (1974) **C-78m.** TVM D: Richard Donner. David Hartman, Rosemary Murphy, Kathleen Quinlan, Nancy Malone, Ramon Bieri, Michael Baseleon. High school teacher's career is threatened after a student's death when rumor spreads that his negligence killed the boy. Hartman's ingratiating style made this and the later series winners. Above average.

Lucifer Project, The SEE: **Barracuda**▼

Luckiest Man in the World, The (1989) **C-82m.** *** D: Frank D. Gilroy. Philip Bosco, Doris Belack, Joanne Camp, Matthew Gottlieb, Arthur French, Stan Lachow. Scrooge-like businessman Bosco is almost killed in a plane crash, and abruptly decides to change his ways. Gilroy also scripted this unpretentious, well-acted little tale; the "voice" in the bathroom is that of Moses Gunn.

Luck of Ginger Coffey, The (1964-Canadian) **100m.** *** D: Irvin Kershner. Robert Shaw, Mary Ure, Liam Redmond,

Tom Harvey, Libby McClintock. Effective kitchen-sink drama with Shaw in one of his best performances as an out-of-work Irish-born dreamer, approaching middle age, who moves to Montreal with wife Ure and their teenage daughter, hoping to find success. Scripted by Brian Moore, based on his novel.

Luck of the Irish, The (1948) **99m.** **½ D: Henry Koster. Tyrone Power, Anne Baxter, Cecil Kellaway, Lee J. Cobb, Jayne Meadows. Leprechaun Kellaway becomes reporter Power's conscience in this "cute" but unremarkable romance.

Lucky Devils (1932) **64m.** ** D: Ralph Ince. William Boyd, Dorothy Wilson, William Gargan, Bruce Cabot, Creighton Chaney (Lon Chaney, Jr.), Roscoe Ates, William Bakewell, Bob Rose, Julie Haydon, Betty Furness. Stuntman Gargan likes extra Wilson, but she loves stuntman Boyd. Hokey programmer, but great opening scene; Hollywood-on-film buffs will surely want to see it.

Lucky Jim (1957-British) **95m.** **½ D: John Boulting. Ian Carmichael, Terry-Thomas, Hugh Griffith, Sharon Acker, Jean Anderson. Comic misadventures of puckish history professor at provincial British university; amusing adaptation of Kingsley Amis book, though not up to Boulting Brothers standard.▼

Lucky Jordan (1942) **84m.** **½ D: Frank Tuttle. Alan Ladd, Helen Walker, Marie McDonald, Mabel Paige, Sheldon Leonard, Lloyd Corrigan. Far-fetched story of army con-man Ladd involved with Nazi agents with USO worker Walker (her feature-film debut).

Lucky Lady (1975) **C-118m.** ** D: Stanley Donen. Gene Hackman, Liza Minnelli, Burt Reynolds, Geoffrey Lewis, John Hillerman, Robby Benson, Michael Hordern. Star trio make an engaging team, as amateur rum-runners in the 1930s who practice a menage-a-trois after business hours . . . but the script goes astray and drags along to a limp, hastily refilmed conclusion. Unfortunate waste of talent; written by Willard Huyck and Gloria Katz.

Lucky Losers (1950) **69m.** D: William Beaudine. Leo Gorcey, Huntz Hall, Hillary Brooke, Gabriel Dell, Lyle Talbot, Bernard Gorcey, William Benedict, Joseph Turkel, Frank Jenks. SEE: **Bowery Boys** series.

Lucky Luciano (1974-Italian-French-U.S.) **C-110m.** ** D: Francesco Rosi. Gian-Maria Volonte, Rod Steiger, Edmond O'Brien, Vincent Gardenia, Charles Cioffi. Fair international coproduction about the deported crime kingpin, given a good interpretation by Volonte. Former federal narcotics agent Charles Siragusa, Luciano's real-life nemesis, plays himself.▼

Lucky Me (1954) **C-100m.** ** D: Jack

Donohue. Doris Day, Robert Cummings, Phil Silvers, Eddie Foy, Nancy Walker, Martha Hyer. Unemployed chorus girl in Florida finds love instead of work. Lackluster musical with then-widescreen novelty lost to viewers. Angie Dickinson's first film.

Lucky Nick Cain (1951) 87m. **½ D: Joseph M. Newman. George Raft, Coleen Gray, Charles Goldner, Walter Rilla. Acceptable gangster yarn of Raft involved with counterfeiting gang, accused of murder; filmed in Italy.

Lucky Night (1939) 82m. *½ D: Norman Taurog. Myrna Loy, Robert Taylor, Henry O'Neill, Marjorie Main, Irving Bacon. Fizzle with Loy and Taylor as struggling young marrieds.

Lucky Partners (1940) 99m. ** D: Lewis Milestone. Ronald Colman, Ginger Rogers, Jack Carson, Spring Byington, Cecilia Loftus, Harry Davenport. Far-fetched comedy about Colman and Rogers winning sweepstakes together, then taking "imaginary" honeymoon. Stars try to buoy mediocre script.▼

Lucky Star, The (1980-Canadian) C-110m. *** D: Max Fischer. Louise Fletcher, Rod Steiger, Lou Jacobi, Brett Marx, Helen Hughes. Entertaining tale of a young Jewish boy (Marx) whose parents are taken away by the Nazis. He is sheltered on a Rotterdam farm and singlehandedly goes up against German Colonel Steiger. A sleeper.

Lucky Stiff, The (1949) 99m. ** D: Lewis R. Foster. Dorothy Lamour, Brian Donlevy, Claire Trevor, Irene Hervey, Marjorie Rambeau. Sturdy cast in slim vehicle of lawyer setting trap for actual killer after girl suspect has death sentence reprieved! Produced by, of all people, Jack Benny!

Lucky Stiff (1988) C-82m. ** D: Anthony Perkins. Joe Alaskey, Donna Dixon, Jeff Kober, Morgan Sheppard, Barbara Howard, Charles Frank, Fran Ryan, Leigh McCloskey, Bill Quinn. Uneven black comedy about cannibalism improves as it goes along. Fat Alaskey, full of jokes and yearning to be married, is romanced by gorgeous Dixon, but doesn't know that she's selected him as Mr. Christmas Dinner for her inbred family. Awkwardly structured script and odd rhythms of film are helped by Alaskey's ingratiating performance.▼

Lucky 13 SEE: **Running Hot**▼

Lucky to Be a Woman (1958-Italian) 95m. **½ D: Alessandro Blasetti. Charles Boyer, Sophia Loren, Marcello Mastroianni, Nino Besozzi, Titina De Filippo. Boyer is lecherous count who helps make peasant gal Loren a cultured movie star; Mastroianni is her photographer boyfriend; charmingly acted.

Lucy Gallant (1955) C-104m. **½ D: Robert Parrish. Charlton Heston, Jane Wyman, Thelma Ritter, Claire Trevor, William Demarest, Wallace Ford. Spiritless soaper of success-bent Wyman rejecting suitors Heston et al, wanting to get ahead instead; set in Western oil town.

[handwritten marginnote: ✓ Soap opera]

Ludwig (1973-Italian-French-German) C-173m. ** D: Luchino Visconti. Helmut Berger, Romy Schneider, Trevor Howard, Silvana Mangano, Helmut Griem, Gert Frobe. Lavish film about Mad King of Bavaria keeps main character so cold, aloof that one feels no sympathy; after nearly three hours, effect is deadening. Authentic locations are breathtaking. Schneider and Howard excellent, but slow-moving film doesn't work. Incredibly, the original version of this runs 246m.!

Luggage of the Gods! (1983) C-75m. **½ D: David Kendall. Mark Stolzenberg, Gabriel Barre, Gwen Ellison, Martin Haber, Rochelle Robins. A couple of chuckles in this comedy about cavemen and women, and what happens when a jet plane—yes, *jet plane*—drops its cargo over them. Unusual, to say the least.▼

Lullaby of Broadway (1951) C-92m. **½ D: David Butler. Doris Day, Gene Nelson, Gladys George, S. Z. Sakall, Billy de Wolfe, Florence Bates, Anne Triola. Musical comedy star Day returns to N.Y.C., unaware that her singer mother has hit the skids. Warner Bros. musical is decent but no big deal; good cast and lots of great old songs keep it moving.

Lulu Belle (1948) 87m. ** D: Leslie Fenton. Dorothy Lamour, George Montgomery, Albert Dekker, Otto Kruger, Glenda Farrell. Hackneyed drama of singer Lamour stepping on anyone and everyone to achieve fame.

Lumiere (1976-French) C-95m. **½ D: Jeanne Moreau. Jeanne Moreau, Francine Racette, Lucia Bose, Caroline Cartier, Marie Henriau, Keith Carradine, Bruno Ganz, François Simon. Elaborate but not very involving drama about four actresses of different ages and status and their relationships with careers, men, each other. Curio is worth seeing for Moreau's directorial debut.▼

Luna (1979) C-144m. *** D: Bernardo Bertolucci. Jill Clayburgh, Matthew Barry, Veronica Lazar, Renato Salvatori, Fred Gwynne, Alida Valli, Roberto Benigni. Initially dazzling tale of male adolescent's identity crisis becomes ponderous when it turns into a mother-son soap opera with incestuous implications. Cinematically exciting, nonetheless, with a bravura finale.

Lunatics and Lovers (1975-Italian) C-93m. *½ D: Flavio Mogherini. Marcello Mastroianni, Claudia Mori, Lino Morelli, Flora Carabella, Adriano Celentano. Aristocrat Mastroianni has an imaginary wife; an organ grinder convinces prostitute Mori to "impersonate" her. When it's not silly, it's dull.▼

Lunch Wagon (1980) **C-88m.** **½ D: Ernest Pintoff. Pamela Jean Bryant, Rosanne Katon, Candy Moore, Rick Podell, Rose Marie, Chuck McCann, Vic Dunlop, Jimmy Van Patten, Dick Van Patten, George Memmoli. Above average drive-in comedy about trio of young lovelies who set up their lunch truck at a prime construction site, unaware that their competition is really a cover for a planned bank robbery. Fine cast and spirited direction lift this above the norm; Dale Bozzio sings "Mental Hopscotch." Reissued as LUNCH WAGON GIRLS and COME 'N' GET IT.▼

Lunch Wagon Girls SEE: **Lunch Wagon**▼

Lured (1947) **102m.** **½ D: Douglas Sirk. George Sanders, Lucille Ball, Charles Coburn, Alan Mowbray, Cedric Hardwicke, Boris Karloff. Ball turns detective in this melodrama, encounters strange characters and harrowing experiences while tracking murderer; pretty good, with top cast.

Lure of the Sila (1949-Italian) **72m.** **½ D: Duilio Coletti. Silvana Mangano, Amedeo Nazzari, Jacques Sernas, Vittorio Gassman. Steamy, moderately entertaining melodrama about the tragedy that results after young Gassman is falsely accused of murder, and how, years later, his sister (the serenely beautiful, seemingly innocent Mangano) gains revenge. ▼

Lure of the Swamp (1957) **74m.** *½ D: Hubert Cornfield. Marshall Thompson, Willard Parker, Joan Vohs, Jack Elam. Tawdry B film of man's lust for wealth, leading to destruction of group hunting loot in murky swamp.

Lure of the Wilderness (1952) **C-92m.** **½ D: Jean Negulesco. Jeffrey Hunter, Jean Peters, Constance Smith, Walter Brennan, Jack Elam. Remake of SWAMP WATER doesn't match earlier version's atmosphere of Southern swamps where murderer holds young man hostage to keep his whereabouts secret.▼

Lurkers (1988) **C-90m.** BOMB D: Roberta Findlay. Christine Moore, Gary Warner, Marina Taylor, Carissa Channing, Tom Billett. Incomprehensible muddle about a young woman who's spent her whole life experiencing weird phenomena—like this script.▼

Lust for Evil SEE: **Purple Noon**

Lust for Gold (1949) **90m.** **½ D: S. Sylvan Simon. Ida Lupino, Glenn Ford, Gig Young, Jay Silverheels, Eddy Waller. Lupino gets overly dramatic as grasping woman stopping at nothing to obtain riches of gold-laden mine.

Lust for Life (1956) **C-122m.** **** D: Vincente Minnelli. Kirk Douglas, Anthony Quinn, James Donald, Pamela Brown, Everett Sloane, Niall MacGinnis, Noel Purcell, Henry Daniell, Lionel Jeffries, Eric Pohlmann. Brilliant adaptation of Irving Stone's biography of painter Van Gogh, vividly portraying his anguished life. Quinn won well-deserved Oscar for performance as painter-friend Gauguin, in this exquisite color production. Script by Norman Corwin. Produced by John Houseman.▼

Lust in the Dust (1985) **C-85m.** BOMB D: Paul Bartel. Tab Hunter, Divine, Lainie Kazan, Geoffrey Lewis, Henry Silva, Cesar Romero, Gina Gallego, Woody Strode, Pedro Gonzales-Gonzales. Hunter and Divine descend on a New Mexico hellhole—he (like most of the cast) to locate some buried treasure, she (he?) to fulfill a dream of becoming a saloon singer. Dreadful attempt at camp despite an apparently whimsical casting director; what's to say about a movie where Divine's warbling is the comical highlight?▼

Lusty Men, The (1952) **113m.** *** D: Nicholas Ray. Susan Hayward, Robert Mitchum, Arthur Kennedy, Arthur Hunnicutt, Frank Faylen. Intelligent, atmospheric rodeo drama, with ex-champ Mitchum becoming mentor of novice Kennedy—and finding himself attracted to Kennedy's no-nonsense wife (Hayward). Solid going most of the way—until that hokey finale. Well-directed by Ray.▼

Luther (1974-British) **C-112m.** **½ D: Guy Green. Stacy Keach, Patrick Magee, Hugh Griffith, Robert Stephens, Alan Badel. Sincere but placid American Film Theatre re-creation of John Osborne's play about Martin Luther (Keach), founder of a new religion.▼

Luv (1967) **C-95m.** *½ D: Clive Donner. Jack Lemmon, Peter Falk, Elaine May, Eddie Mayehoff, Paul Hartman, Severn Darden. Murray Schisgal's three-character hit play about pseudo-intellectuals was not a natural for the screen anyway, but this version is truly an abomination. The cast tries. Look for a young Harrison Ford.▼

Luxury Liner (1948) **C-98m.** ** D: Richard Whorf. George Brent, Jane Powell, Lauritz Melchior, Frances Gifford, Xavier Cugat. MGM fluff aboard a cruise ship, with Powell singing her heart out.

Lydia (1941) **104m.** *** D: Julien Duvivier. Merle Oberon, Edna May Oliver, Alan Marshal, Joseph Cotten, Hans Yaray, George Reeves. Sentimental tale of elderly woman (Oberon) meeting her former beaux and recalling their courtship. Adapted from famous French film CARNET DE BAL.

Lydia Bailey (1952) **C-89m.** **½ D: Jean Negulesco. Dale Robertson, Anne Francis, Luis Van Rooten, Juanita Moore, William Marshall. Handsome but empty version of Kenneth Roberts actioner of 1800s Haiti and revolt against French rulers.

M (1931-German) **99m.** **** D: Fritz Lang. Peter Lorre, Ellen Widmann, Inge Landgut, Gustav Grundgens. Harrowing melodrama about psychotic child murderer brought to justice by Berlin underworld. Riveting and frighteningly contemporary; cinematically dazzling, especially for an early talkie. Lorre's performance is unforgettable. Originally 118m, though some prints still carry original German ending, a brief courtroom coda that subtly changes film's final message. Remade in 1951.▼

M (1951) **88m.** **½ D: Joseph Losey. David Wayne, Howard da Silva, Luther Adler, Karen Morley, Jorja Curtright, Martin Gabel. Tepid remake of famed Peter Lorre German classic, concerning child-killer hunted down by fellow-criminals not wanting police investigation of underworld.

Ma and Pa Kettle Betty MacDonald's best-selling book *The Egg and I* told of the hardships a city girl faced moving with her husband to a rural chicken farm. Among the problems were the incredible local characters, two of whom, Ma and Pa Kettle, were given prime footage in the screen version of THE EGG AND I. Played by veterans Marjorie Main and Percy Kilbride, the hillbilly duo created a hit and became the stars of their own series, which was extremely popular through the 1950s. Rambunctious Ma and hesitant Pa's adventures were not exactly out of Noel Coward, but they scored a hit and the two stars were naturals for the roles. In fact, the role of Ma was not so different from the stereotyped character Marjorie Main had become associated with in scores of other films. Meg Randall and Lori Nelson took turns playing the eldest daughter in the Kettles' tremendous brood (at least a dozen kids), as the Kettles battled with neighbors and local authorities, visiting Paris, Hawaii, and New York, and engaged in predictable but amusing situations for eight years. In 1955 Percy Kilbride left the series; Arthur Hunnicutt played a "cousin" in THE KETTLES IN THE OZARKS and Parker Fennelly took his turn in THE KETTLES ON OLD MACDONALD'S FARM, but neither one caught on and the series came to an end in 1957. Intellectuals liked to assume that the cornball humor had lost its audience, but then several years later a TV show called *The Beverly Hillbillies* came along to prove them wrong.

✓ **Ma and Pa Kettle** (1949) **75m.** D: Charles Lamont. Marjorie Main, Percy Kilbride, Richard Long, Meg Randall, Patricia Alphin, Esther Dale.

Ma and Pa Kettle at Home (1954) **81m.** D: Charles Lamont. Marjorie Main, Percy Kilbride, Alice Kelley, Brett Halsey, Alan Mowbray, Oliver Blake, Stan Ross.

Ma and Pa Kettle at the Fair (1952) **78m.** D: Charles Barton. Marjorie Main, Percy Kilbride, Lori Nelson, James Best, Esther Dale.

Ma and Pa Kettle at Waikiki (1955) **79m.** D: Lee Sholem. Marjorie Main, Percy Kilbride, Lori Nelson, Lowell Gilmore, Mabel Albertson, Ida Moore.

Ma and Pa Kettle Back on the Farm (1951) **80m.** D: Edward Sedgwick. Marjorie Main, Percy Kilbride, Richard Long, Barbara Brown, Meg Randall.

Ma and Pa Kettle Go to Town (1950) **79m.** D: Charles Lamont. Percy Kilbride, Marjorie Main, Richard Long, Jim Backus, Hal March, Meg Randall.

Ma and Pa Kettle on Vacation (1953) **75m.** D: Charles Lamont. Percy Kilbride, Marjorie Main, Ray Collins, Sig Ruman, Jack Kruschen, Teddy Hart.

Ma Barker's Killer Brood (1960) **82m.** ** D: Bill Karn. Lurene Tuttle, Tris Coffin, Paul Dubov, Nelson Leigh. Energetic performance by Tuttle in lead role and occasional bursts of gunplay hoist this programmer gangster yarn above tedium.

Macabra SEE: **Demonoid, Messenger of Death**▼

Macabre (1958) **73m.** ** D: William Castle. William Prince, Jim Backus, Christine White, Jacqueline Scott. Weird goings-on in small town when doctor's wife and her sister are murdered. Film promises much, delivers little. Famous for gimmick of handing out policies insuring moviegoers against death by fright.

Macahans, The (1976) **C-125m. TVM** D: Bernard McEveety. James Arness, Eva Marie Saint, Bruce Boxleitner, Richard Kiley, Gene Evans, John Crawford. Arness' first post-*Gunsmoke* role as a buckskinclad mountain scout guiding his brother's family on its westward trek from pre-Civil War Virginia. William Conrad narrates this lusty outdoor drama based in part on HOW THE WEST WAS WON; later it became a mini-series (and weekly show) using that title. Above average.

Mac and Me (1988) **C-93m.** *½ D: Stewart Raffill. Christine Ebersole, Jonathan Ward, Katrina Caspary, Lauren Stanley, Jade Calegory. Slight E.T. clone about Mac, an outer space creature, and his plight in suburban L.A. More a TV commercial than a movie: There's a production number set in a McDonald's, and the alien survives by sipping Coca-Cola.▼

Macao (1952) **80m.** ** D: Josef von Sternberg. Robert Mitchum, Jane Russell, William Bendix, Gloria Grahame, Thomas Gomez, Philip Ahn. Flat yarn supposedly set in murky title port, with Russell as a singer and Mitchum the action-seeking man she loves.▼

Macaroni (1985-Italian) **C-104m.** **½ D: Ettore Scola. Jack Lemmon, Marcello Mastroianni, Daria Nicolodi, Isa Danieli, Maria Luisa Saniella. Uptight American businessman goes to Naples and finds some unfinished personal business left over from his last visit—when he was an amorous soldier during WW2. Two of the world's

[699]

most endearing actors try to keep this souffle from falling, and almost succeed.▼

MacArthur (1977) **C-130m.** *** D: Joseph Sargent. Gregory Peck, Dan O'Herlihy, Ed Flanders, Sandy Kenyon, Dick O'Neill, Marj Dusay, Art Fleming. Solid, absorbing saga of flamboyant military chief during WW2 and Korean War. Peck is excellent but film doesn't pack the punch of PATTON. Originally trade-screened at 144m. then cut for release.▼

MacArthur's Children (1985-Japanese) **C-115m.** ***½ D: Masahiro Shinoda. Masako Natsume, Shima Iwashita, Hiromi Go, Takaya Yamauchi, Yoshiyuka Omori, Shiori Sakura. Extremely poignant, proud, loving remembrance of life in a small Japanese fishing village immediately following that nation's defeat in WW2. Most effectively delineated are the Japanese reaction to losing the war, as well as the cultural effects of the American occupation—from styles of dress to baseball. ▼

Macbeth (1948) **89m.** *** D: Orson Welles. Orson Welles, Jeanette Nolan, Dan O'Herlihy, Edgar Barrier, Roddy McDowall, Robert Coote, Erskine Sanford, Alan Napier, John Dierkes. Welles brought the Bard to Republic Pictures with this moody, well-done adaptation, filmed entirely on bizarre interiors (which deliberately emphasize its theatricality). Most revival houses now show Welles' original version, which runs 105m. and has actors speaking with authentic Scot accents.▼

Macbeth (1971-British) **C-140m.** ***½ D: Roman Polanski. Jon Finch, Francesca Annis, Martin Shaw, Nicholas Selby, John Stride, Stephan Chase. Gripping, atmospheric, and extremely violent recreation of Shakespeare tragedy of young Scots nobleman lusting for power, driven onward by crazed wife and prophecies. Great example of film storytelling, thanks to excellent direction.▼

Machine-Gun Kelly (1958) **80m.** **½ D: Roger Corman. Charles Bronson, Susan Cabot, Barboura Morris, Morey Amsterdam, Wally Campo, Jack Lambert, Connie Gilchrist. With typical efficiency, Corman gives this gangster chronicle pacing and more than passing interest. Bronson is fine in title role.

Machine Gun McCain (1970-Italian) **C-94m.** ** D: Giuliano Montaldo. John Cassavetes, Britt Ekland, Peter Falk, Gabriele Ferzetti, Salvo Randone, Gena Rowlands. Junk about just-released gangster who tries to rob Mafia-controlled casino in Las Vegas.

Macho Callahan (1970) **C-99m.** **½ D: Bernard Kowalski. David Janssen, Lee J. Cobb, Jean Seberg, David Carradine, Pedro Armendariz, Jr., James Booth, Richard Anderson. Janssen miscast as Civil War P.O.W.-escapee, out to kill man who got him arrested in first place; will recognize

latter by his yellow shoes. Interesting view of West, but dialogue often unbelievable.▼

Maciste—The Mighty (1960-Italian) **C-87m.** ** D: Carlo Campogalliani. Mark Forest, Chelo Alonso, Angelo Zanolli, Federica Ranchi. Forest in title role tries to instill some animation in wooden tale of old Egypt and the barbaric Persians.

Mack, The (1973) **C-110m.** ** D: Michael Campus. Max Julien, Don Gordon, Richard Pryor, Carol Speed, Roger E. Mosley, William C. Watson. Extremely violent melodrama about a black pimp in Oakland was one of the most popular blaxploitation films; strange, because it's utterly ordinary.▼

Mackenna's Gold (1969) **C-128m.** **½ D: J. Lee Thompson. Gregory Peck, Omar Sharif, Telly Savalas, Camilla Sparv, Keenan Wynn, Julie Newmar, Lee J. Cobb, Raymond Massey, Burgess Meredith, Anthony Quayle, Edward G. Robinson, Eli Wallach, Ted Cassidy, Eduardo Ciannelli. Overblown adventure saga about search for lost canyon of gold, with doublecrosses, conflicts, mysterious clues, etc. Super cast saddled with ludicrous script, made worse by pre-release tampering that cut extremely long film, leaving abrupt denouement, several loose ends. Fine Quincy Jones score; produced by Carl Foreman (who also scripted) and Dimitri Tiomkin. Narrated by Victor Jory.▼

Mackintosh and T.J. (1975) **C-96m.** ** D: Marvin J. Chomsky. Roy Rogers, Clay O'Brien, Billy Green Bush, Andrew Robinson, Joan Hackett. Old-fashioned modern-day Western about an aging ranch hand and a young boy. Those charmed by the idea of a Roy Rogers comeback will want to see it; others beware. Music by Waylon Jennings.

Mackintosh Man, The (1973) **C-105m.** **½ D: John Huston. Paul Newman, Dominique Sanda, James Mason, Harry Andrews, Ian Bannen, Nigel Patrick, Michael Hordern. Well-made espionage thriller has only one problem: it's all been done before. Filmed in Ireland, England, and Malta; screenplay credited to Walter Hill.▼

Mack the Knife (1989) **C-120m.** BOMB D: Menahem Golan. Raul Julia, Richard Harris, Julia Migenes, Roger Daltrey, Julie Walters, Rachel Robertson, Clive Revill. Name cast over-emotes in this ill-conceived, overly stylized version of *The Threepenny Opera*. More a filmed stage revue than anything else, and not a very good one; Golan adapted the script, and completely misses the spirit of the original. This one blots the memory of Brecht and Weill (not to mention Bobby Darin).▼

Macomber Affair, The (1947) **89m.** ***½ D: Zoltan Korda. Gregory Peck, Joan Bennett, Robert Preston, Reginald Denny, Carl Harbord. Penetrating, intelligent filmization of Hemingway story about conflicts that develop when hunter Peck takes married couple (Preston, Bennett) on safari. Bristling performances help make this one of the most vivid screen adaptations of a Hemingway work.

Macon County Line (1974) **C-89m.** **½ D: Richard Compton. Alan Vint, Cheryl Waters, Max Baer, Jr., Jesse Vint, Joan Blackman, Geoffrey Lewis. Bloody thriller based on fact, set in 1954 Georgia; three outsiders are pursued for a murder they didn't commit. Baer produced and wrote it; Bobbie Gentry sings her own theme song. Followed by RETURN TO MACON COUNTY.▼

Macumba Love (1960) **C-86m.** *½ D: Douglas Fowley. Walter Reed, Ziva Rodann, William Wellman, Jr., June Wilkinson. Trivia of author delving into voodoo practices in South America.

Mad About Men (1954-British) **C-90m.** ** D: Ralph Thomas. Glynis Johns, Donald Sinden, Anne Crawford, Margaret Rutherford, Dora Bryan, Noel Purcell. Mermaid and young woman look-alike change places in this pleasant fantasy, and love takes its course. Sequel to MIRANDA.

Mad About Music (1938) **98m.** *** D: Norman Taurog. Deanna Durbin, Herbert Marshall, Gail Patrick, Arthur Treacher, Helen Parrish, Marcia Mae Jones, William Frawley. Excellent Durbin vehicle; busy mother Patrick leaves Deanna in Swiss girls' school, where she pretends Marshall is her father. Holds up better than remake TOY TIGER.

Mad Adventures of "Rabbi" Jacob, The (1974-French) **C-96m.** *** D: Gerard Oury. Louis De Funes, Suzy Delair, Marcel Dalio, Claude Giraud, Claude Pieplu. Broad slapstick comedy about hotheaded, bigoted businessman who—for complicated reasons—is forced to disguise himself as a rabbi. Uneven but often quite funny, with echoes of silent-screen humor.

Madame (1962-French) **C-104m.** **½ D: Christian-Jaque. Sophia Loren, Robert Hossein, Julien Bertheau, Marina Berti. Uninspired remake of MADAME SANS-GENE with Loren, who uses looks and wits to rise from laundress to nobility in Napoleonic France.

✓ **Madame Bovary** (1949) **115m.** ***½ D: Vincente Minnelli. Jennifer Jones, James Mason, Van Heflin, Louis Jourdan, Christopher Kent, Gene Lockhart, Gladys Cooper, George Zucco, Henry (Harry) Morgan. Gustave Flaubert's 19th-century heroine sacrifices her husband and their security for love, meets a horrible end. Once-controversial adaptation looks better every year, despite an odd "framing" device involving Flaubert's morals trial. Justifiably celebrated ball sequence is among the greatest set pieces of Minnelli's—or anyone else's—career.▼

Madame Butterfly (1932) **86m.** **½ D:

Marion Gering. Sylvia Sidney, Cary Grant, Charlie Ruggles, Irving Pichel, Helen Jerome Eddy. Puccini opera (minus music) of Oriental woman in love with American (Grant) is sensitive, tragic romance, dated but well handled.

Madame Curie (1943) **124m.** *** D: Mervyn LeRoy. Greer Garson, Walter Pidgeon, Henry Travers, Albert Basserman, Robert Walker, C. Aubrey Smith. Despite stretches of plodding footage, biography of famed female scientist is generally excellent. Garson and Pidgeon team well, as usual.

Madame Racketeer (1932) **71m.** **½ D: Alexander Hall, Henry Wagstaff Gribble. Alison Skipworth, Richard Bennett, George Raft, Evalyn Knapp, Gertrude Messinger, J. Farrell MacDonald, Robert McWade. Entertaining vehicle for Skipworth as con-woman supreme known as The Countess, who reveals a heart of gold when she encounters her two grown daughters for the first time.

Madame Rosa (1977-French) **C-105m.** **½ D: Moshe Mizrahi. Simone Signoret, Samy Ben Youb, Claude Dauphin, Gabriel Jabbour, Michal Bat-Adam, Costa-Gavras. Signoret's magnetic performance gives substance to this interesting but aimless film about an aging madam who earns her keep by sheltering prostitutes' children. Oscar winner as Best Foreign Film.▼

Madame Sin (1971) **C-73m. TVM** D: David Greene. Robert Wagner, Bette Davis, Roy Kinnear, Paul Maxwell, Denholm Elliott, Gordon Jackson. Evil genius (Davis) uses former C.I.A. agent as pawn for control of Polaris submarine. Elaborate production has Bad beating out Good at end; with Bette in charge, it's well worth seeing. Above average.▼

Madame Sousatzka (1988) **C-122m.** *** D: John Schlesinger. Shirley MacLaine, Navin Chowdhry, Peggy Ashcroft, Twiggy, Shabana Azmi, Leigh Lawson, Geoffrey Bayldon, Lee Montague. Eccentric, reclusive London piano teacher (MacLaine, wearing clanky jewelry and piles of makeup) implores her students to cultivate their artistic spirit and bring passion to their music. She meets her match in her star pupil, a 15-year-old boy of Indian heritage. Beautifully made film succeeds largely due to the strong emotions being played out, and to the superb supporting cast (especially young Chowdhry and mother Azmi—the latter a major star in her native India).▼

Madame X (1929) **90m.** ** D: Lionel Barrymore. Ruth Chatterton, Lewis Stone, Raymond Hackett, Holmes Herbert, Eugenie Besserer, Sidney Toler, Ullrich Haupt. Leaden weeper, filmed previously in 1906, 1916, and 1920, about cold, cruel husband Stone forcing wife Chatterton onto the streets. Their son comes of age believing she's dead . . . and then gets to defend her on a murder charge. A curio at best; the remakes are better. Plays on TV as ABSINTHE.

Madame X (1937) **71m.** **½ D: Sam Wood. Gladys George, John Beal, Warren William, Reginald Owen, William Henry, Henry Daniell, Phillip Reed, Ruth Hussey. Alexandre Bisson's stalwart soap opera gets polished MGM treatment and a fine performance by Gladys George as the woman whose ultimate sacrifice is never detected by her son. Goes astray toward the end (with Beal a bit much), but worth a look.

Madame X (1966) **C-100m.** **½ D: David Lowell Rich. Lana Turner, John Forsythe, Constance Bennett, Ricardo Montalban, Burgess Meredith, Keir Dullea, Virginia Grey. Plush remake of perennial soaper of attorney defending a woman accused of murder, not knowing it's his mother. Fine cast and varied backgrounds bolster Turner's pivotal performance. Constance Bennett's last film.▼

Madame X (1981) **C-100m. TVM** D: Robert Ellis Miller. Tuesday Weld, Len Cariou, Eleanor Parker, Robert Hooks, Jerry Stiller, Jeremy Brett, Martina Deignan, Robin Strand, Tom Tully. Hard to believe this hardy soap opera would show up again, but here it is, updated somewhat by writer Edward Anhalt (who also appears in the film as a judge). Average.

Madam Satan (1930) **105m.** *** D: Cecil B. DeMille. Kay Johnson, Reginald Denny, Roland Young, Lillian Roth, Elsa Peterson, Tyler Brooke. Bizarre semimusical extravaganza with placid Johnson posing as wicked Madam Satan to win back errant husband Denny. Mad party scene on Zeppelin is certainly an eye-popper.

Mad at the World (1955) **72m.** *½ D: Harry Essex. Frank Lovejoy, Keefe Brasselle, Cathy O'Donnell, Karen Sharpe. Pointless study of Brasselle seeking vengeance on teenage slum gang who harmed his baby; Lovejoy is the detective on the case.

Mad Bomber, The (1972) **C-95m.** ** D: Bert I. Gordon. Vince Edwards, Chuck Connors, Neville Brand, Hank Brandt, Cristina Hart. Hardnosed cop Edwards relentlessly dogs paranoid villain Connors who's out to waste those he imagines have wronged him.▼

Mad Bull (1977) **C-100m. TVM** D: Walter Doniger, Len Steckler. Alex Karras, Susan Anspach, Nicholas Colasanto, Elisha Cook, Jr., Mike Mazurki, Christopher DeRose. Hulking wrestler becomes involved with warm, sensitive woman. Off-the-beaten path drama involving ex-football pro Karras in the bizarre world of wrestling. Average.▼

Mad Checkmate SEE: **It's Your Move**

M.A.D.D.: Mothers Against Drunk Drivers (1983) **C-100m. TVM** D: William A. Graham. Mariette Hartley, Paula Prentiss,

Bert Remsen, John Rubinstein, Cliff Potts, David Huddleston, Grace Zabriskie, Elizabeth Huddle, Nicolas Coster. Hartley stands out as Candy Lightner, the California housewife/lobbyist behind the national anti-drunk driving group. Written and produced by Michael Braverman. Above average.▼

Mad Doctor, The (1941) **90m.** ** D: Tim Whelan. Basil Rathbone, Ellen Drew, John Howard, Barbara Jo Allen (Vera Vague), Ralph Morgan, Martin Kosleck. Not a horror film, but a polished B about suave medico who marries women and murders them for their money. Interesting for a while, but misses the mark.

Mad Doctor of Blood Island (1969) **C-85m.** BOMB D: Gerry DeLeon, Eddie Romero. John Ashley, Angelique Pettyjohn, Ronald Peary, Alicia Alonzo. Newcomers to remote tropical island quickly discover why it has a reputation for evil. It's a tossup which is worst: the dialogue, the music, or the hyperactive zoom lens. Filmed in the Philippines. Retitled TOMB OF THE LIVING DEAD and followed by a sequel(!), BEAST OF BLOOD.▼

Mad Doctor of Market Street, The (1942) **61m.** *½ D: Joseph H. Lewis. Lionel Atwill, Una Merkel, Claire Dodd, Nat Pendleton, Anne Nagel. Mini-chiller from Universal Pictures about insane scientist on Pacific isle using natives for strange experiments.

Mad Dog SEE: **Mad Dog Morgan**▼

Mad Dog Coll (1961) **86m.** *½ D: Burt Balaban. John Davis Chandler, Brooke Hayward, Kay Doubleday, Jerry Orbach, Telly Savalas. Minor crime melodrama about the career of Vincent "Mad Dog" Coll, the most vicious killer in all gangland. Hayward is the daughter of Margaret Sullavan, and the author of *Haywire*; that's Vincent Gardenia as Dutch Schultz, Gene Hackman (in his film debut) as a cop.

Mad Dog Morgan (1976-Australian) **C-102m.** *** D: Philippe Mora. Dennis Hopper, Jack Thompson, David Gulpilil, Frank Thring, Michael Pate. Hopper gives lively performance as legendary Australian outlaw of the 1800s in this moody, well-made, but extremely violent film; TV print runs 93m. Retitled: MAD DOG.▼

Mad Dogs and Englishmen SEE: **Joe Cocker: Mad Dogs and Englishmen**▼

Made For Each Other (1939) **93m.** *** D: John Cromwell. Carole Lombard, James Stewart, Charles Coburn, Lucile Watson, Alma Kruger, Esther Dale, Ward Bond, Louise Beavers. First-rate soaper of struggling young marrieds Stewart and Lombard battling illness, lack of money, Stewart's meddling mother Watson. Fine acting makes this all work. Also shown in computer-colored version.▼

Made for Each Other (1971) **C-107m.** *** D: Robert B. Bean. Renee Taylor, Joseph Bologna, Paul Sorvino, Olympia Dukakis. Exceptionally funny tale of two oddball types who meet at encounter session and fall in love. Original screenplay by Taylor and Bologna.

Made in Heaven (1987) **C-103m.** ** D: Alan Rudolph. Timothy Hutton, Kelly McGillis, Maureen Stapleton, Don Murray, Marj Dusay, Ray Gideon, Amanda Plummer, Mare Winningham, Timothy Daly. Young man dies and goes to heaven, where he meets a yet-unborn beauty and falls in love. The Big Question: how long will it take for them to meet, in their new identities on earth, and realize that they were "made for each other"? Potentially sweet fantasy-romance is undermined by too many kinky touches and inside-joke cameos (Debra Winger, in drag, plays Hutton's guardian angel). This is apparently director Rudolph's idea of a mainstream Hollywood movie. Among the other cameos: Neil Young, Tom Petty, Ellen Barkin, Ric Ocasek, David Rasche, Tom Robbins, Gary Larson.▼

Made in Italy (1967-Italian-French) **101m.** **½ D: Nanni Loy. Virna Lisi, Anna Magnani, Sylva Koscina, Walter Chiari, Lea Massari, Alberto Sordi, Jean Sorel, Catherine Spaak. Enjoyable collage of short vignettes about natives, tourists, sophisticates, laborers and all others in Italy. Episodic, of course, but well done.

Made in Paris (1966) **C-101m.** **½ D: Boris Sagal. Ann-Margret, Louis Jourdan, Richard Crenna, Edie Adams, Chad Everett. Witless, unpolished shenanigans of Ann-Margret, fashion designer in France, falling for Jourdan.

Madeleine (1949-British) **101m.** **½ D: David Lean. Ann Todd, Leslie Banks, Elizabeth Sellars, Ivor Barnard. Superior cast improves oft-told drama of woman accused of murdering her lover. A vehicle for Lean's then wife, Ann Todd, and one of the filmmaker's few disappointments. Retitled: STRANGE CASE OF MADELEINE.

Madeleine (1958-German) **86m.** *½ D: Kurt Meisel. Eva Bartok, Sabina Sesselmann, Ilse Steppat, Alexander Kerst. Unsensational study of prostitutes, with a witless plot of Bartok trying to shed her shady past.

Mademoiselle Fifi (1944) **69m.** **½ D: Robert Wise. Simone Simon, John Emery, Kurt Kreuger, Alan Napier, Jason Robards, Sr., Helen Freeman, Norma Varden. A laundress reveals more integrity and patriotic spirit than her condescending fellow passengers on an eventful coach ride during the Franco-Prussian war. Uneven Val Lewton production (with allegorical implications about WW2), adapted from two Guy de Maupassant stories.

Mademoiselle Striptease SEE: **Please! Mr. Balzac**▼

Mad Executioners, The (1963-German) **94m.** ** D: Edwin Zbonek. Wolfgang Preiss, Harry Riebauer, Rudolph Fernau,

Chris Howland. Muddled Edgar Wallace-ish suspenser about Scotland Yard inspector setting up his own court of justice to execute criminals.

Mad Genius, The (1931) **81m.** *** D: Michael Curtiz. John Barrymore, Marian Marsh, Donald Cook, Carmel Myers, Charles Butterworth, Mae Madison, Frankie Darro, Luis Alberni, Boris Karloff. Followup to SVENGALI has Barrymore a deranged entrepreneur who lives vicariously through Cook's dancing career. Bizarre, entertaining film with hilarious Butterworth as Barrymore's crony, Alberni as a dope fiend. Karloff has small role near the beginning.

Mad Ghoul, The (1943) **65m.** **½ D: James Hogan. David Bruce, Evelyn Ankers, George Zucco, Turhan Bey, Charles McGraw, Robert Armstrong, Milburn Stone, Rose Hobart. Strong cast buoys grim story of scientist and his strange life-preserving methods.

Madhouse (1974-British) **C-89m.** *** D: Jim Clark. Vincent Price, Peter Cushing, Robert Quarry, Adrienne Corri, Natasha Payne, Linda Hayden. Price plays horror-film actor making a TV comeback after a long mental breakdown—until he's implicated in a series of grisly homicides. Good, if somewhat unimaginative, adaptation of Angus Hall novel *Devilday.* ▼

Madhouse (1990) **C-90m.** *½ D: Tom Ropelawski. John Larroquette, Kirstie Alley, Alison LaPlaca, John Diehl, Jessica Lundy, Bradley Gregg, Dennis Miller, Robert Ginty. Larroquette and Alley find themselves unable to enjoy their new home when unwanted house guests drop in and *never* leave. The gags are drawn out endlessly, and though Larroquette is a talented farceur, he can't sustain the whole film. The humor here would never pass muster on the two stars' hit TV series.▼

Madhouse Mansion (1974-British) **C-86m.** **½ D: Stephen Weeks. Marianne Faithfull, Leigh Lawson, Anthony Bate, Larry Dann, Sally Grace, Penelope Keith, Vivian Mackerell, Murray Melvin, Barbara Shelley. Bizarre, sometimes effective chiller about affable chap Dann, who with a couple of mysterious college acquaintances spends a holiday in a spooky old house that seems to be caught in a time warp. Originally titled GHOST STORY. ▼

Madigan (1968) **C-101m.** ***½ D: Donald Siegel. Richard Widmark, Henry Fonda, Harry Guardino, Inger Stevens, James Whitmore, Michael Dunn, Steve Ihnat, Sheree North. Excellent, unpretentious film blends day-to-day problems of detective Madigan (Widmark) with endless dilemmas facing police commissioner Fonda. Shot largely on location in N.Y.C., with fine work by Guardino, Whitmore, and supporting cast. Later adapted as TV series.▼

Madigan's Million (1967) **C-86m.** BOMB D: Stanley Prager. Dustin Hoffman, Elsa

Martinelli, Cesar Romero. Pre-GRADUATE Hoffman is caught in amateurish movie released to capitalize on later success; he plays bumbling Treasury agent sent to Italy to recover money stolen by recently murdered gangster Romero. Inept.▼

Madison Avenue (1962) **94m.** **½ D: H. Bruce Humberstone. Dana Andrews, Eleanor Parker, Jeanne Crain, Eddie Albert, Howard St. John, Henry Daniell. Tightly produced programmer centering on machinations in N.Y.C.'s advertising jungle.

Mad Little Island (1957-British) **C-94m.** **½ D: Michael Relph. Jeannie Carson, Donald Sinden, Roland Culver, Noel Purcell, Ian Hunter, Duncan MacRae, Catherine Lacey, Jean Cadell, Gordon Jackson. Sequel to TIGHT LITTLE ISLAND finds that little Scottish isle's tranquility disturbed again, this time by imminent installation of missile base. Not up to its predecessor, but on its own terms, decent enough. Original title: ROCKETS GALORE!

Mad Love (1935) **70m.** *** D: Karl Freund. Peter Lorre, Frances Drake, Colin Clive, Isabel Jewell, Ted Healy, Sara Haden, Edward Brophy, Keye Luke. Famous *Hands of Orlac* story refitted for Lorre as mad doctor in love with married Drake. He agrees to operate on her pianist husband's injured hands, with disastrous results. Stylishly directed by legendary cameraman Freund; only debit is unwelcome comedy relief by Healy.

Mad, Mad Movie Makers, The SEE: Last Porno Flick, The

Mad Magazine Presents Up the Academy SEE: Up the Academy▼

Mad Magician, The (1954) **72m.** **½ D: John Brahm. Vincent Price, Mary Murphy, Eva Gabor, Patrick O'Neal, John Emery. In this imitation of HOUSE OF WAX (filmed in 3-D, like its predecessor) Price plays a demented magic-act inventor who kills famous magicians and then impersonates them.

Madman (1978-Israeli) **C-92m.** *½ D: Dan Cohen. Michael Beck, F. Murray Abraham, Alan Feinstein, Sigourney Weaver, Esther Zevko. Bitterly vengeful Soviet-Jewish mental patient joins the Israeli army, intent on killing Russians. Slow, poorly directed film lacks conviction. Casting of Weaver, in her first leading role, and future Oscar-winner Abraham, gives this film its only distinction.▼

Mad Max (1979-Australian) **C-93m.** ***½ D: George Miller. Mel Gibson, Joanne Samuel, Hugh Keays-Byrne, Steve Bisley, Tim Burns, Roger Ward. In the desolate near-future, the police have their hands full keeping roads safe from suicidally daring drivers and roving gangs. Top cop Gibson tires and quits, but when his wife and child are murdered by vicious cyclists, he embarks on high-speed revenge. Weird atmosphere and characters combine with amazing stunt work in this remarkable action film. Thrown away by its U.S. distributor (which also redubbed it with American voices), later found its audience in the wake of successful sequel.▼

Mad Max 2 (1981-Australian) **C-94m.** ***½ D: George Miller. Mel Gibson, Bruce Spence, Vernon Wells, Mike Preston, Virginia Hey, Emil Minty, Kjell Nilsson. Sequel to the above finds Max, now a loner, reluctantly helping tiny oil-producing community defend itself against band of depraved crazies thirsty for precious fuel. Far less original script-wise, but trend-setting visual design and some of the most unbelievable car stunts ever filmed make this equal to, if not better than, the first one. Retitled THE ROAD WARRIOR for American release; followed by MAD MAX BEYOND THUNDERDOME.▼

Mad Max Beyond Thunderdome (1985-Australian) **C-106m.** **½ D: George Miller, George Ogilvie. Mel Gibson, Tina Turner, Angelo Rossitto, Helen Buday, Rod Zuanic, Frank Thring, Angry Anderson. In the desolate future Mad Max comes upon Turner's cutthroat city of Bartertown, survives a battle-to-the-death in Roman-style Thunderdome arena, and is exiled to the desert, where he's rescued by tribe of wild children. Thunderous film has lots of action and stunts, and even some philosophical moments, but lacks the kinetic energy of MAD MAX 2 (ROAD WARRIOR).▼

Madmen of Mandoras SEE: They Saved Hitler's Brain▼

Mad Miss Manton, The (1938) **80m.** **½ D: Leigh Jason. Barbara Stanwyck, Henry Fonda, Sam Levene, Frances Mercer, Stanley Ridges, Vicki Lester, Whitney Bourne, Hattie McDaniel, Penny Singleton, Grady Sutton. Socialite Stanwyck involves her friends in murder mystery; trivial but enjoyable film, with sleuthing and slapstick combined.▼

Mad Monster, The (1942) **72m.** *½ D: Sam Newfield. Johnny Downs, George Zucco, Anne Nagel, Sarah Padden, Glenn Strange, Gordon DeMain. Dull, low-budget mad-scientist thriller drags heavy feet for unintended laughs. Zucco effortlessly steals show as crazed doctor changing man into beast.▼

Mad Monster Party? (1967) **C-94m.** ** D: Jules Bass. Voices of Phyllis Diller, Boris Karloff, Gale Garnett, Ethel Ennis. Famous monsters are brought together by Frankenstein, who wants to announce his retirement, in this silly animated kiddie feature.▼

Madonna of the Seven Moons (1946-British) **88m.** *** D: Arthur Crabtree. Phyllis Calvert, Stewart Granger, Patricia Roc, Jean Kent, John Stuart, Peter Glenville. Calvert is pushed in two directions because of strange gypsy curse; she is wife, mother, and mistress at same time. Taut melodrama, may be considered camp in some circles.

Madonna's Secret, The (1946) 79m. ** D: William Thiele. Francis Lederer, Gail Patrick, Ann Rutherford, Linda Stirling, John Litel. OK whodunit involving hunt for killer of murdered artist's model.

Madron (1970) C-93m. ** D: Jerry Hopper. Richard Boone, Leslie Caron, Paul Smith, Gabi Amrani, Chaim Banai, Avraham Telya. A nun who survived wagontrain massacre and a scowling gunslinger try to elude Apaches on the warpath in this ho-hum Western shot in Israel's Negev Desert.▼

Mad Room, The (1969) C-92m. ** D: Bernard Girard. Stella Stevens, Shelley Winters, James Ward, Carol Cole, Severn Darden, Beverly Garland, Michael Burns. Mild but unexceptional remake of LADIES IN RETIREMENT concerns the skeletons in Stella's closet. Grisly tale has a few shocking scenes.

Mad Wednesday SEE: **Sin of Harold Diddlebock, The**▼

Madwoman of Chaillot, The (1969) C-132m. ** D: Bryan Forbes. Katharine Hepburn, Charles Boyer, Claude Dauphin, Edith Evans, John Gavin, Paul Henreid, Oscar Homolka, Margaret Leighton, Giulietta Masina, Nanette Newman, Richard Chamberlain, Yul Brynner, Donald Pleasence, Danny Kaye. Unfortunate misfire, with Hepburn as eccentric woman who refuses to believe the world no longer beautiful. Stellar cast wasted in heavy-handed allegory that just doesn't work; adapted from Jean Giradoux' play.

Maedchen in Uniform (1931-German) 90m. ***½ D: Leontine Sagan. Dorothea Wieck, Hertha Thiele, Emilia Unda, Hedwig Schlichter, Ellen Schwannecke. Winning drama about sensitive student Thiele forming lesbian relationship with teacher Wieck in oppressive girls boarding school. Simply, sympathetically handled by Sagan; this highly acclaimed and once-controversial film was also written by a woman, Christa Winsloe. Remade in 1958.▼

Maedchen in Uniform (1958-German) C-91m. **½ D: Geza von Radvanyi. Lilli Palmer, Romy Schneider, Christine Kaufmann, Therese Giehse. Rather talky story of girls' school and one particularly sensitive youngster (Schneider) who is attracted to her teacher (Palmer). Remake of famous 1931 movie is shade above average.

Mae West (1982) C-100m. TVM D: Lee Philips. Ann Jillian, James Brolin, Piper Laurie, Roddy McDowall, Chuck McCann, Louis Giambalvo, Lee-Jones DeBroux. Jillian is quite convincing, sashaying her way through the title role in this unexpectedly zesty biopic of La West. Written by E. Arthur Kean. Above average.▼

Mafia Princess (1986) C-100m. TVM D: Robert Collins. Tony Curtis, Susan Lucci, Kathleen Widdoes, Chuck Shamata, Louie DiBianco. Silver-haired Curtis is terrific as Chicago mob boss Sam Giancana, while Lucci hones her well-established soap opera bitch role as his petulant, self-centered daughter in this adaptation of Antoinette Giancana's best-selling autobiography. Script doesn't quite complement performances, though. Average.▼

Mafu Cage, The (1978) C-102m. *½ D: Karen Arthur. Lee Grant, Carol Kane, Will Geer, James Olson. Grant and Kane are sisters in this offbeat, unfocused melodrama of incest, jealousy, and murder. Mafu is Kane's pet orangutan, with each protagonist in turn assuming the animal's caged, victimized role. Retitled MY SISTER, MY LOVE and THE CAGE.▼

Magee and the Lady (1978-Australian) C-92m. TVM D: Gene Levitt. Tony Lo Bianco, Sally Kellerman, Anne Semler, Rod Mullinar, Kevin Leslie. Elements of THE AFRICAN QUEEN and SWEPT AWAY combine in story of skipper's attempt to stall repossession of his freighter by kidnapping the feisty daughter of the man who's threatening to foreclose on him. Average. Originally titled SHE'LL BE SWEET.▼

Maggie, The SEE: **High and Dry**

Magic (1978) C-106m. ** D: Richard Attenborough. Anthony Hopkins, Ann-Margret, Burgess Meredith, Ed Lauter, Jerry Houser, David Ogden Stiers. Ludicrous thriller about demented ventriloquist Hopkins who's tormented by his dummy—even as he tries to rekindle romance with high-school sweetie Ann-Margret. Wait for a rerun of DEAD OF NIGHT instead. Screenplay by William Goldman, from his novel.▼

Magic Bow, The (1947-British) 105m. **½ D: Bernard Knowles. Stewart Granger, Phyllis Calvert, Jean Kent, Dennis Price, Cecil Parker. As usual, music overshadows weak plot in biography of violinist Paganini.

Magic Box, The (1951-British) C-103m. **** D: John Boulting. Robert Donat, Maria Schell, Margaret Johnston, Robert Beatty; guests Laurence Olivier, Michael Redgrave, Eric Portman, Glynis Johns, Emlyn Williams, Richard Attenborough, Stanley Holloway, Margaret Rutherford, Peter Ustinov, Bessie Love, Cecil Parker, etc. Practically every British star appears in this superb biography of William Friese-Greene, the forgotten inventor of movies. Beautifully done; one scene where Donat perfects the invention, pulling in a cop off the street (Olivier) to see it, is superb.

Magic Carpet, The (1951) C-84m. ** D: Lew Landers. Lucille Ball, John Agar, Patricia Medina, Raymond Burr, George

Tobias. Mild costumer that has virtue of Ball as heroine, and little else.

Magic Carpet (1971) **C-100m. TVM** D: William Graham. Susan Saint James, Robert Pratt, Cliff Potts, Enzo Cerusico, Jim Backus, Wally Cox, Abby Dalton, Nanette Fabray. Easy-going comedy with mystery overtones has fill-in tour guide (Saint James) earning her way through college in Rome, experiencing various problems in connection with odd assortment of bus passengers. Enjoyable, unpretentious dialogue, clever situations. Written and produced by Fabray's husband, Ranald MacDougall. Above average.

Magic Christian, The (1970-British) **C-93m.** *** D: Joseph McGrath. Peter Sellers, Ringo Starr; guest stars Richard Attenborough, Christopher Lee, Raquel Welch, Laurence Harvey, Yul Brynner, Wilfrid Hyde-White, Spike Milligan, Dennis Price, John Cleese, Graham Chapman, Roman Polanski. In series of wacky schemes, world's wealthiest man and his protégé wreak havoc on society by demonstrating how people will do *anything* for money. Fiendishly funny adaptation of Terry Southern's insane novel, scripted by Southern and McGrath, with contributions from Sellers, Cleese, and Chapman. Some prints run 88m.▼

Magic Face, The (1951) **89m.** ** D: Frank Tuttle. Luther Adler, Patricia Knight, William L. Shirer, Ilka Windish. Low-key study of impersonator who murders Hitler and assumes his place; Adler rises above material.

Magic Fire (1956) **C-95m.** ** D: William Dieterle. Yvonne De Carlo, Carlos Thompson, Rita Gam, Valentina Cortese, Alan Badel. Uninspired musical biography of 19th-century German composer Richard Wagner.

Magic Flute, The (1974-Swedish) **C-134m.** ***½ D: Ingmar Bergman. Ulric Cold, Josef Kostlinger, Erik Saeden, Birgit Nordin, Irma Urrila, Hakan Hagegard. Lively, intelligent filmization of Mozart's opera of activities surrounding the kidnapping of Urrila, the Queen's daughter, by sorcerer Cold. Shot for Swedish TV, released as a feature in the U.S.▼

Magic Garden of Stanley Sweetheart, The (1970) **C-117m.** *½ D: Leonard Horn. Don Johnson, Linda Gillin, Michael Greer, Dianne Hull, Holly Near, Victoria Racimo. Vapid film from Robert Westbrook's novel about sexual and drug-oriented experiences of aimless college student trying to put his head together. A yawn, except for Greer, and Stanley's underground film "Headless."

Magician, The (1959-Swedish) **102m.** *** D: Ingmar Bergman. Max von Sydow, Ingrid Thulin, Gunnar Bjornstrand, Naima Wifstrand, Bibi Andersson. Brooding, complex account set in 19th-century Sweden involving mesmerizer and magician who becomes involved in murder and afterlife; revealing parable of life's realities.▼

Magician, The (1973) **C-78m. TVM** D: Marvin J. Chomsky. Bill Bixby, Keene Curtis, Joan Caulfield, Kim Hunter, Elizabeth Ashley, Barry Sullivan, Signe Hasso, Anne Lockhart. Pilot to the semi-successful series dealing with a magician-sleuth, here looking into a possible conspiracy and exposing a staged plane crash. Average.

Magician of Lublin, The (1979) **C-105m.** *½ D: Menahem Golan. Alan Arkin, Louise Fletcher, Valerie Perrine, Shelley Winters, Lou Jacobi, Maia Danziger, Lisa Whelchel. Turn-of-the-century Jewish magician tries for the big time in stilted, poorly acted version of Isaac Bashevis Singer's Polish-based novel. However, you do get to see Winters destroy a jailhouse even more impressively than Sam Jaffe's elephant did in GUNGA DIN.▼

Magic Moments (1989-British) **C-105m. TVM** D: Lawrence Gordon Clarke. John Shea, Jenny Seagrove, Paul Freeman, Debora Weston, Sam Douglas. Suave stage magician from America captures the heart of a comely TV producer in London . . . though it takes her nearly two television years to realize it. Picaresque, by-the-numbers *Harlequin Romance*. Made for cable. Average.

Magic of Lassie, The (1978) **C-100m.** **½ D: Don Chaffey. James Stewart, Lassie, Mickey Rooney, Alice Faye, Stephanie Zimbalist, Pernell Roberts, Michael Sharrett, Mike Mazurki. Stewart is worth watching in this bland remake of LASSIE COME HOME, as grandfather of Zimbalist and Sharrett, who are forced to turn over their beloved Lassie to mean owner Roberts. Songs performed by Pat and Debby Boone, plus Faye and even Stewart.▼

Magic Sword, The (1962) **C-80m.** **½ D: Bert I. Gordon. Basil Rathbone, Estelle Winwood, Gary Lockwood, Anne Helm, Liam Sullivan, Jacques Gallo. Fanciful juvenile costumer with fine special effects, pleasing cast.▼

Magic Town (1947) **103m.** *** D: William Wellman. James Stewart, Jane Wyman, Kent Smith, Regis Toomey, Donald Meek. Intriguing satire of pollster Stewart finding perfect average American town, which ruins itself when people are told his discovery. Doesn't always hit bull's-eye but remains engrossing throughout; written by Frank Capra's frequent scripter, Robert Riskin.▼

Magic World of Topo Gigio, The (1965-Italian) **C-75m.** *½ D: Luca de Rico. Ermanno Roveri, Ignazio Colnaghi, Frederica Milani, Topo Gigio. Unsuccessful attempt to build a feature-film around the little puppet mouse who scored such success on TV's *Ed Sullivan Show* in the 1960s.

Magnet, The (1951-British) 78m. *** D: Charles Frend. William Fox, Kay Walsh, Stephen Murray, Meredith Edwards. Disarming study of fun-loving children at play, told intelligently from their own point of view; no phony psychology thrown in. Young William Fox is known today as James Fox.

Magnetic Monster, The (1953) 76m. **½ D: Curt Siodmak. Richard Carlson, King Donovan, Jean Byron, Byron Foulger. Magnetic isotope is stolen, grows in size and creates havoc; stunning climax features special effects lifted from 1930s German film, GOLD.

Magnificent Ambersons, The (1942) 88m. **** D: Orson Welles. Tim Holt, Joseph Cotten, Dolores Costello, Anne Baxter, Agnes Moorehead, Ray Collins, Richard Bennett, Erskine Sanford. Brilliant drama from Booth Tarkington novel of family unwilling to change its way of life with the times; mother and son conflict over her lover. Welles' follow-up to CITIZEN KANE is equally exciting in its own way, though film was taken out of his hands, recut and reshot by others.▼

Magnificent Brute, The (1936) 80m. ** D: John G. Blystone. Victor McLaglen, Binnie Barnes, William Hall, Jean Dixon. Pertly acted love triangle, with McLaglen the roughneck blast furnace boss, involved in romance and stolen money.

Magnificent Cuckold, The (1966-Italian) 111m. **½ D: Antonio Pietrangeli. Claudia Cardinale, Ugo Tognazzi, Michele Girardon, Bernard Blier. Saucy sex comedy of marital infidelity, with Tognazzi, the businessman husband of Cardinale, outwitted by his curvaceous wife.

Magnificent Doll (1946) 95m. ** D: Frank Borzage. Ginger Rogers, Burgess Meredith, David Niven, Horace (Stephen) McNally, Peggy Wood. Rogers just isn't right as Dolley Madison, and historical drama with Meredith as President Madison and Niven as Aaron Burr falls flat.

Magnificent Dope, The (1942) 83m. *** D: Walter Lang. Henry Fonda, Lynn Bari, Don Ameche, Edward Everett Horton, Hobart Cavanaugh, Pierre Watkin. Entertaining comedy of hopeless hayseed Fonda who shows up sharper Ameche in big city; Bari is the girl between them.▼

Magnificent Fraud, The (1939) 78m. ** D: Robert Florey. Akim Tamiroff, Lloyd Nolan, Mary Boland, Patricia Morison. Spry Paramount B film involving South American republic and its phony dictator.

Magnificent Magnet of Santa Mesa, The (1977) C-78m. TVM D: Hy Averback. Michael Burns, Dick Dlasucci, Jane Connell, Keene Curtis, Susan Blanchard, Harry Morgan, Tom Poston, Susan Sullivan, Conrad Janis, Loni Anderson. Disneyesque farce with young scientist (Burns) invent-ing an energy disk that can solve the world's problems, then trying to protect it from his altruistic bosses. The performances: stereotyped and frantic; the special effects: rock bottom. Below average.

Magnificent Matador, The (1955) C-94m. **½ D: Budd Boetticher. Anthony Quinn, Maureen O'Hara, Manuel Rojas, Thomas Gomez, Richard Denning, Lola Albright. Another of director Boetticher's bullfighting films has Quinn an aging matador who reexamines his commitment to bullfighting, while protecting his young "protege" (Rojas) and being romanced by American O'Hara.▼

Magnificent Obsession (1935) 101m. *** D: John M. Stahl. Irene Dunne, Robert Taylor, Betty Furness, Charles Butterworth, Sara Haden, Ralph Morgan. Dated but sincere adaptation of Lloyd Douglas' story about drunken playboy who mends his ways, becomes respected surgeon in order to restore the eyesight of a woman (Dunne) he blinded in an auto accident. Original running time was 112m.

Magnificent Obsession (1954) C-108m. *** D: Douglas Sirk. Jane Wyman, Rock Hudson, Barbara Rush, Otto Kruger, Agnes Moorehead. Director Sirk pulls out all the stops in this baroque, melodramatic remake of 1935 film which remains faithful to original story.▼

Magnificent Rebel, The (1962) C-95m. **½ D: Georg Tressler. Karl Boehm, Ernst Nadhering, Ivan Desny, Gabriele Porks. Boehm makes an intense Beethoven in this rather serious Disney film, not really for kids at all. Great musical sequences and very good German location photography, though romantic angle of story never really compels attention. Released theatrically in Europe, shown in U.S. as two-part Disney TV show.

Magnificent Roughnecks (1956) 73m. BOMB D: Sherman A. Rose. Jack Carson, Mickey Rooney, Nancy Gates, Jeff Donnell. Allied Artists disaster with two "comics" as partners trying to wildcat oilfields.

Magnificent Seven, The (1960) C-126m. ***½ D: John Sturges. Yul Brynner, Steve McQueen, Eli Wallach, Horst Buchholz, James Coburn, Charles Bronson, Robert Vaughn, Brad Dexter. Enduringly popular Western remake of THE SEVEN SAMURAI, about paid gunslingers who try to rout the bandits who are devastating a small Mexican town. Great cast of stars-to-be; memorable Elmer Bernstein score. Followed by three sequels, starting with RETURN OF THE SEVEN.▼

Magnificent Seven Ride!, The (1972) C-100m. **½ D: George McCowan. Lee Van Cleef, Stefanie Powers, Mariette Hartley, Michael Callan, Luke Askew, Pedro Armendariz, Jr. Newly married gunfighter decides to help his buddy fight bandits after they kidnap his wife. Fourth "ride" for the Seven isn't bad.

Magnificent Sinner (1959-French) **C-97m.** ** D: Robert Siodmak. Romy Schneider, Curt Jurgens, Pierre Blanchar, Monique Melinand. Lackluster proceedings of Schneider as mistress to Russian Czar, involved in court intrigue. Remake of 1938 French film KATIA with Danielle Darrieux.

Magnificent Yankee, The (1950) **80m.** *** D: John Sturges. Louis Calhern, Ann Harding, Eduard Franz, James Lydon, Philip Ober. Calhern as Oliver Wendell Holmes, Supreme Court Justice, and Harding his patient wife, give poignancy to this sensitive biographical study.

Magnum Force (1973) **C-124m.** **½ D: Ted Post. Clint Eastwood, Hal Holbrook, Mitchell Ryan, David Soul, Felton Perry, Robert Urich, Kip Niven, Tim Matheson. Eastwood's second go-round as individualistic San Francisco cop Dirty Harry Callahan. This time he traces a series of mysterious slayings to the police department itself, and finds himself in extra-hot water. Some brutal scenes; not nearly as stylish as the original. Written by John Milius and Michael Cimino. Look for Suzanne Somers at gangster's pool party. Followed by THE ENFORCER.▼

Magus, The (1968-British) **C-117m.** BOMB D: Guy Green. Anthony Quinn, Michael Caine, Candice Bergen, Anna Karina, Paul Stassino, Julian Glover. Pretentious, hopelessly confusing story from John Fowles' novel about a magus, or magician (Quinn), who tries to control destiny of Caine, new arrival on his Greek island. At first mazelike story is fun, but with no relief it grows tiresome.

Mahler (1974-British) **C-115m.** *** D: Ken Russell. Robert Powell, Georgina Hale, Richard Morant, Lee Montague, Rosalie Crutchley. Not for every taste (could it be a Russell film if it were?) but one of the director's best films; a gorgeously shot, set, and costumed bio about the turn-of-the-century composer and his tormented life. If you think this means it's refined, check out the purposely anachronistic Nazi humor. Energetic to a fault.▼

Mahogany (1975) **C-109m.** *½ D: Berry Gordy. Diana Ross, Billy Dee Williams, Anthony Perkins, Jean-Pierre Aumont, Beah Richards, Nina Foch. Silly, contrived affair about fashion designer who becomes world famous, then finds happiness only in arms of unsuccessful boy friend. Wooden performances except for Perkins' extension of PSYCHO role.▼

Maid in America (1982) **C-100m.** TVM D: Paul Aaron. Susan Clark, Alex Karras, Fritz Weaver, Mildred Natwick, Barbara Byrne, David Spielberg, Beverly Hope Atkinson, Colby Chester. Genial romantic comedy about role changing, with hulking Karras signing on as the family maid to crusading lawyer Clark's eccentric family. Written by Peter Feibleman. Above average.

Maid in Paris (1957-French) **84m.** ** D: Gaspard-Hult. Dany Robin, Daniel Gelin, Marie Daems, Tilda Thamar. Bland story of girl going to the big city seeking romance.

Maid of Salem (1937) **86m.** *** D: Frank Lloyd. Claudette Colbert, Fred MacMurray, Louise Dresser, Gale Sondergaard, Beulah Bondi, Bonita Granville, Virginia Weidler, Donald Meek, Harvey Stephens, Edward Ellis, Mme. Sul-te-wan. Colonial witch-burning era is backdrop for fine drama with many similarities to Arthur Miller's The Crucible (minus the philosophy).

Maids, The (1975-British) **C-95m.** ** D: Christopher Miles. Glenda Jackson, Susannah York, Vivien Merchant, Mark Burns. Jean Genet's windy, pointless, exasperating play about two maids who hate their mistress. Excellent acting wasted on tripe. An American Film Theater Production.▼

Maid's Night Out (1938) **64m.** ** D: Ben Holmes. Joan Fontaine, Allan Lane, Hedda Hopper, George Irving, William Brisbane, Billy Gilbert, Cecil Kellaway. Fontaine is one of those heiresses of the 1930s, mistaken for housemaid, in mild low-budget comedy.▼

Maid to Order (1987) **C-96m.** **½ D: Amy Jones. Ally Sheedy, Beverly D'Angelo, Michael Ontkean, Valerie Perrine, Dick Shawn, Tom Skerritt, Merry Clayton, Begona Plaza. Cute fairytale comedy about spoiled rich girl who's robbed of her identity, and forced to work as a maid for a gaudy and self-centered Malibu couple (played to perfection by Perrine and Shawn). D'Angelo is fun as her fairy godmother, and Ontkean is a sweet Prince Charming. Clayton scores as the household cook who belts out two numbers. Film's good-heartedness makes up for its shortcomings.▼

Maigret (1988-British) **C-100m.** TVM D: Paul Lynch. Richard Harris, Patrick O'Neal, Victoria Tennant, Barbara Shelley, Ian Ogilvy, Eric Deacon, Caroline Munro, Andrew McCulloch. Harris does an Anglicized Jean Gabin as rumpled Paris cop Jules Maigret, looking for the killer of his close friend, a French private eye, and playing cat-and-mouse games with crafty American industrialist O'Neal. Laid-back Harris and fellow cast members seem somewhat uneasy doing French characters with decidedly English (or in Harris' case, Irish) accents. Pilot to a prospective syndicated Maigret series. Average.

Mailbag Robbery (1958-British) **70m.** ** D: Compton Bennett. Lee Patterson, Kay Callard, Alan Gifford, Kerry Jordan. Title explains full contents of programmer.

Mail Order Bride (1964) **C-83m.** **½ D: Burt Kennedy. Buddy Ebsen, Keir Dullea,

Lois Nettleton, Warren Oates, Marie Windsor, Barbara Luna. Harmless—and plotless—Western with rambunctious young rancher Dullea marrying widow Nettleton to satisfy his late father's old friend (Ebsen). Climactic shoot-out is virtual duplicate of the one in RIDE THE HIGH COUNTRY.

Main Attraction, The (1962) C-90m. *½ D: Daniel Petrie. Pat Boone, Mai Zetterling, Nancy Kwan, Yvonne Mitchell, Kieron Moore. Boone is fatally out of his depth as a guitar-playing drifter in Europe who causes romantic complications when he falls in with a traveling circus. Filmed in England.

Main Chance, The (1966-British) 60m. **½ D: John Knight. Gregoire Aslan, Tracy Reed, Edward DeSouza, Stanley Meadows. Offbeat account of diamond robbery.

Main Event, The (1979) C-112m. *½ D: Howard Zieff. Barbra Streisand, Ryan O'Neal, Paul Sand, Whitman Mayo, Patti D'Arbanville, Richard Lawson, James Gregory. Tortuous farce about a bankrupt executive who inherits a hapless boxer and goads him into resuming his career. O'Neal comes off slightly better than Streisand, but only because his yelling and screaming isn't as abrasive as hers; D'Arbanville tops them both as a girl with a *really* bad cough. ▼

Main Street After Dark (1944) 57m. **½ D: Edward L. Cahn. Edward Arnold, Audrey Totter, Dan Duryea, Hume Cronyn, Selena Royle. Offbeat drama of family pickpocket gang put out of business by civic clean-up campaign.

Main Street to Broadway (1953) 102m. **½ D: Tay Garnett. Tom Morton, Mary Murphy, Clinton Sundberg, Rosemary De-Camp, guest stars Ethel Barrymore, Lionel Barrymore, Shirley Booth, Rex Harrison, Lilli Palmer, Helen Hayes, Henry Fonda, Tallulah Bankhead, Mary Martin, others. Very slight story of romance, struggle, and success on the Great White Way; chief interest is large cast of Broadway stars in cameo appearances. Rodgers & Hammerstein appear on camera and contribute a song, "There's Music in You." ▼

Maisie Maisie was a middling series of ten MGM features made between 1939 and 1947, starring lively Ann Sothern as a brassy showgirl involved in a progression of topical if trivial situations encompassing the changing role of American women during WW2 America. The series never rose above the B category; all were filmed in black and white and ran about 85 minutes. Production values were too often static, utilizing rear projection and indoor sets to establish the varied locales of the episodes. The Maisie series relied almost exclusively on Miss Sothern's vivacious personality to carry the slight tales of the conventional tough-girl-with-a-heart-of-gold.

Her costars were competent contract players such as Robert Sterling (Sothern's then-husband), Lew Ayres, John Hodiak, and George Murphy. Unlike the Andy Hardy series, few fledgling starlets appeared in these features, although guests like Red Skelton helped out from time to time. In general the series lacked a basic continuity and flavor; and earlier entries such as MAISIE and CONGO MAISIE (a remake of the Gable-Harlow RED DUST), while no classics, had more punch than later efforts such as UNDERCOVER MAISIE.

Maisie (1939) 74m. D: Edwin L. Marin. Ann Sothern, Robert Young, Ruth Hussey, Ian Hunter, George Tobias.

Maisie Gets Her Man (1942) 85m. D: Roy Del Ruth. Ann Sothern, Red Skelton, Leo Gorcey, Pamela Blake, Allen Jenkins, Donald Meek, Walter Catlett, Fritz Feld, Rags Ragland, Frank Jenks.

Maisie Goes to Reno (1944) 90m. D: Harry Beaumont. Ann Sothern, John Hodiak, Tom Drake, Ava Gardner, Donald Meek.

Maisie Was a Lady (1941) 79m. D: Edwin L. Marin. Ann Sothern, Lew Ayres, Maureen O'Sullivan, C. Aubrey Smith, Joan Perry, Paul Cavanagh.

Major and the Minor, The (1942) 100m. ***½ D: Billy Wilder. Ginger Rogers, Ray Milland, Diana Lynn, Rita Johnson, Robert Benchley, Norma Varden. Memorable comedy of working girl Rogers disguised as 12-year-old to save train fare, becoming involved with Milland's military school. Wilder's first directorial effort (written with Charles Brackett) is still amusing. That's Ginger's real-life mom playing her mother near the end of the film. Remade as YOU'RE NEVER TOO YOUNG.

Major Barbara (1941-British) 135m. **** D: Gabriel Pascal. Wendy Hiller, Rex Harrison, Robert Morley, Robert Newton, Emlyn Williams, Sybil Thorndike, Deborah Kerr. Topnotch adaptation of Shaw play about wealthy girl who joins Salvation Army. Excellent cast in intelligent comedy. Kerr's film debut. Also shown at 115m. ▼

Major Dundee (1965) C-124m. **½ D: Sam Peckinpah. Charlton Heston, Richard Harris, Jim Hutton, James Coburn, Michael Anderson, Jr., Senta Berger, Warren Oates, Slim Pickens, Ben Johnson, R.G. Armstrong, L.Q. Jones. Very fine cast and lavish production make up for overlong, confused story of cavalry officer (Heston) who leads assorted misfits against Apaches. Peckinpah disowned the film, which was recut by others. ▼

Majority of One, A (1961) C-153m. **½ D: Mervyn LeRoy. Rosalind Russell, Alec Guinness, Ray Danton, Madlyn Rhue, Mae Questel. Compared to Broadway play, this is overblown, overacted account of Jewish matron Russell falling in love with Japanese widower Guinness. Written by Leonard Spiegelgass.

Major League (1989) **C-107m.** **½ D: David S. Ward. Tom Berenger, Charlie Sheen, Corbin Bernsen, Margaret Whitton, James Gammon, Rene Russo, Wesley Snipes, Charles Cyphers, Bob Uecker. Bitchy baseball team owner Whitton seeks to get out of her Cleveland franchise by organizing a team that's guaranteed to lose games—and fans. Pleasant but completely unremarkable baseball comedy, with no surprises whatsoever.▼

Make a Wish (1937) **76m.** ** D: Kurt Neumann. Basil Rathbone, Bobby Breen, Marion Claire, Ralph Forbes, Henry Armetta, Leon Errol, Donald Meek, Billy Lee. Inconsequential musical about a summer camp for boys where singing prodigy Breen encounters composer Rathbone. Supporting comedians offer most of the film's best moments.▼

Make Haste to Live (1954) **90m.** **½ D: William A. Seiter. Dorothy McGuire, Stephen McNally, Mary Murphy, Edgar Buchanan, John Howard. McGuire gives believable performance as woman faced with criminal husband who's returned to seek vengeance.▼

Make Me an Offer (1955-British) **C-88m.** **½ D: Cyril Frankel. Peter Finch, Adrienne Corri, Rosalie Crutchley, Finlay Currie. Satisfactory highbrow shenanigans in the antique-buying field, with Finch after priceless vase.▼

Make Me an Offer (1980) **C-100m. TVM** D: Jerry Paris. Susan Blakely, Patrick O'Neal, John Rubinstein, Edie Adams, Stella Stevens, Kathleen Lloyd. Sitcom-style romantic pap set against the real estate game in Southern California. Average.▼

Make Mine Laughs (1949) **64m.** *½ D: Richard Fleischer. Frances Langford, Joan Davis, Leon Errol, Ray Bolger, Gil Lamb. RKO mini-musical, no more than uninspired footage lumped together à la vaudeville.

Make Mine Mink (1960-British) **100m.** *** D: Robert Asher. Terry-Thomas, Athene Seyler, Hattie Jacques, Billie Whitelaw, Elspeth Duxbury, Raymond Huntley. Former military man Terry-Thomas organizes unlikely band of fur thieves in this delightful British farce. Beware of shorter version on tape.▼

Make Mine Music (1946) **C-74m.** **½ D: Joe Grant (production supervisor). Voices of Nelson Eddy, Dinah Shore, Jerry Colonna, The Andrews Sisters, Andy Russell, Sterling Holloway, and music by The Benny Goodman Quartet. Ten-part Walt Disney animated feature with such segments as "Peter and the Wolf," "Johnny Fedora and Alice Blue Bonnet," and "Casey at the Bat." At its worst when it

tries to be "arty," and at its best when it offers bright, original pieces like "The Whale Who Wanted to Sing at the Met," and the dazzling Benny Goodman number "After You've Gone." A mixed bag, to be sure.

Make Way For a Lady (1936) **65m.** ** D: David Burton. Herbert Marshall, Anne Shirley, Gertrude Michael, Margot Grahame, Clara Blandick, Frank Coghlan, Jr. Routine comedy of Shirley playing matchmaker for her widowed father Marshall; pleasant enough.

Make Way For Tomorrow (1937) **92m.** ***½ D: Leo McCarey. Victor Moore, Beulah Bondi, Fay Bainter, Thomas Mitchell, Porter Hall, Barbara Read, Louise Beavers. Sensitive film of elderly couple in financial difficulty, shunted aside by their children, unwanted and unloved; shatteringly true, beautifully done.

Make Your Own Bed (1944) **82m.** *½ D: Peter Godfrey. Jack Carson, Jane Wyman, Alan Hale, Irene Manning, George Tobias, Ricardo Cortez. Forced comedy of detective Carson disguised as butler, Wyman as maid, to get lowdown on racketeer.

Making It (1971) **C-97m.** ** D: John Erman. Kristoffer Tabori, Joyce Van Patten, Marlyn Mason, Bob Balaban, Lawrence Pressman, Louise Latham, Dick Van Patten. Uneven, seriocomic "youth picture" with Tabori (impressive in his first starring role) as a 17-year-old with little but sex on his mind—until he shares a traumatic experience with his mother. Filmed in Albuquerque.▼

Making Love (1982) **C-113m.** **½ D: Arthur Hiller. Michael Ontkean, Kate Jackson, Harry Hamlin, Wendy Hiller, Arthur Hill, Nancy Olson, Terry Kiser. Repressed homosexual doctor jeopardizes 8-year marriage by coming out of the closet with sexually carefree novelist. Soaper is easy to take, but that's its problem; script, direction, nonstereotyped performances, lack edge in bland attempt to avoid offending anyone. From the director of LOVE STORY.▼

Making Mr. Right (1987) **C-95m.** **½ D: Susan Seidelman. John Malkovich, Ann Magnuson, Glenne Headly, Ben Masters, Laurie Metcalf, Polly Bergen, Harsh Nayyar, Hart Bochner, Susan Anton. Nerdy scientist Malkovich has created a nearly human android in his own image; public relations whiz Magnuson is hired to sell the concept of Ulysses to the public. Hit-or-miss comedy has good performances and many effective moments, but misses the bullseye. Filmed and set in Miami Beach.▼

Making of a Male Model (1983) **C-100m. TVM** D: Irving J. Moore. Joan Collins, Jon-Erik Hexum, Kevin McCarthy, Roxie Roker, Arte Johnson, Ted McGinley, Jeff Conaway. Slick hokum about a rancher who is plucked from obscurity by agency head Collins and transformed into a commercial "hunk" and centerfold sex object. Below average.

Making the Grade (1984) **C-105m.** *½ D: Dorian Walker. Judd Nelson, Jonna Lee, Carey Scott, Dana Olsen, Gordon Jump, Walter Olkewicz, Ronald Lacey, Scott McGinnis. Spoiled rich kid hires young hustler to take his place at prep school. Better than the average raunchy youth comedies of the 80s, but that's faint praise. Andrew Clay plays a character here named Dice.▼

Mako: The Jaws of Death (1976) **C-93m.** **½ D: William Grefe. Richard Jaeckel, Jennifer Bishop, Harold Sakata, John Chandler, Buffy Dee. Good horror premise has Jaeckel a friend and protector of sharks who goes berserk when both he and his "friends" are exploited. Shown theatrically as THE JAWS OF DEATH.

Malaga (1960-British) **97m.** **½ D: Laslo Benedek. Trevor Howard, Dorothy Dandridge, Edmund Purdom, Michael Hordern. Bizarre casting in routine robbery tale is primary diversion. Originally titled MOMENT OF DANGER.

Malaya (1949) **98m.** **½ D: Richard Thorpe. Spencer Tracy, James Stewart, Valentina Cortese, Sydney Greenstreet. Routine WW2 melodrama set in the Pacific, about Allies' efforts to smuggle out rubber. Good cast let down by so-so script.

Malcolm (1986-Australian) **C-86m.** *** D: Nadia Tass. Colin Friels, John Hargreaves, Lindy Davies, Chris Haywood, Charles "Bud" Tingwell, Beverly Phillips, Judith Stratford. Charming, disarmingly offbeat comedy about a slow-witted young man with a genius for Rube Goldberg-like mechanical devices and his unusual entry into a life of crime. Surefooted directorial debut for actress Tass, whose husband David Parker wrote the screenplay (and designed the Tinkertoys) and whose real-life brother was the inspiration for the character of Malcolm. Infectious music score performed by The Penguin Cafe Orchestra. Australian Film Institute winner for Best Picture and other awards. ▼

Male Animal, The (1942) **101m.** ***½ D: Elliott Nugent. Henry Fonda, Olivia de Havilland, Jack Carson, Joan Leslie, Herbert Anderson, Don DeFore, Hattie McDaniel, Eugene Pallette. Intelligent, entertaining Elliott Nugent-James Thurber comedy of college professor Fonda defending his rights, while losing wife de Havilland to old flame Carson. Excellent performances in this fine, contemporary film, with spoof on typical football rallies a highlight. Remade as SHE'S WORKING HER WAY THROUGH COLLEGE.

Male Hunt (1965-French) **92m.** *** D: Edouard Molinaro. Jean-Paul Belmondo, Jean-Claude Brialy, Catherine Deneuve, Francoise Dorleac, Marie Laforet. Spicy romp about trio of Frenchmen avoiding the clutches of marriage-minded women.

Male of the Century, The (1975-French) **C-90m.** **½ D: Claude Berri. Juliet Berto, Claude Berri, Hubert Deschamps, Laszlo Szabo, Yves Afonso. Writer-director Berri stars in this slight, occasionally perceptive comedy as a jealous chauvinistic husband; his wife is taken hostage during a bank robbery . . . and he's positive that she's becoming sexually involved with her captor.

Malibu (1934) SEE: **Sequoia**

Malibu (1983) **C-200m.** TVM D: E.W. Swackhamer. William Atherton, James Coburn, Susan Dey, Chad Everett, Steve Forrest, George Hamilton, Jenilee Harrison, Ann Jillian, Richard Mulligan, Dyan Cannon, Anthony Newley, Kim Novak, Valerie Perrine, Troy Donahue, Eva Marie Saint. Sun, surf, sand and sex involving the pretty people of Southern California as glitteringly trashed in William Murray's novel. All-star cast makes the flying fun, though the story's forgettable. Originally shown in two parts. Average.

Malibu Beach (1978) **C-94m.** *½ D: Robert J. Rosenthal. Kim Lankford, James Daughton, Susan Player-Jarreau, Stephen Oliver, Michael Luther. BEACH BLANKET BINGO 1970s style—without Frankie and Annette, and with pot instead of booze. If you're desperate . . . ▼

Malibu Express (1985) **C-101m.** ** D: Andy Sidaris. Darby Hinton, Sybil Danning, Art Metrano, Shelley Taylor Morgan, Lori Sutton, Barbara Edwards, Kimberly McArthur, Lynda Wiesmeier. Hinton is a private detective working on a complex espionage and blackmail case, but this film is just an excuse to showcase the charms of numerous *Playboy* centerfold models (accounting for its frequent programming on pay-cable services). A loose remake of Sidaris' 1973 STACEY.▼

Malibu High (1979) **C-92m.** BOMB D: Irv Berwick. Jill Lansing, Stuart Taylor, Katie Johnson, Tammy Taylor, Garth Howard, Phyllis Benson. Sleazy, decidedly unpleasant story of a high-school girl who turns out to be something of a sociopath. Not the innocent youth opus its title might lead you to expect.▼

Malice in Wonderland (1985) **C-100m.** TVM D: Gus Trikonis. Elizabeth Taylor, Jane Alexander, Richard Dysart, Joyce Van Patten, Jon Cypher, Leslie Ackerman, Bonnie Bartlett, Thomas Byrd, Rick Lenz, John Pleshette. Liz and Jane as Louella Parsons and Hedda Hopper give stylish oomph to this atmospheric but historically muddled account of the monumental feud between the legendary Hollywood gossip columnists. Jacqueline Feather and David Seidler based their lighthearted script on George Eels's book, *Hedda and Louella*. Also known as THE RUMOR MILL. Average.▼

Malicious (1973-Italian) **C-97m.** **½ D: Salvatore Samperi. Laura Antonelli, Turi Ferro, Alessandro Momo, Angela Luce, Pino Caruso, Tina Aumont. Seriocomic slice of life about an earthy young woman who comes to work as housekeeper for a widower and his three sons—and tantalizes both the father and one of his teenage boys. Intriguing but often unpleasant look at mores, morals, and hypocrisy, with typically titillating role for Antonelli. Originally titled MALIZIA.▼

Malizia SEE: **Malicious**▼

Mallory: Circumstantial Evidence (1976) **C-100m. TVM** D: Boris Sagal. Raymond Burr, Robert Loggia, Roger Robinson, Mark Hamill, Peter Mark Richman, A Martinez. Burr is celebrated lawyer with a tarnished reputation whose client, a car thief, is charged with committing homicide in jail. A pilot that got Burr out of the wheelchair. Average.

Malone (1987) **C-92m.** *½ D: Harley Cokliss. Burt Reynolds, Cliff Robertson, Kenneth McMillan, Cynthia Gibb, Scott Wilson, Lauren Hutton. Robertson is a megalomaniac plotting to take over America; lucky for us the mountain-town gas station essential to his plans is the same one ex-CIA agent Reynolds stops at for a fill-up. Hybrid of SHANE and a modern-day shoot-em-up turns pretty ludicrous after a passable beginning; note how quickly Burt recovers from a golf ball-size bullet wound.▼

Malta Story, The (1953-British) **98m.** **½ D: Brian Desmond Hurst. Alec Guinness, Jack Hawkins, Anthony Steel, Muriel Pavlow. On-location filming of this WW2 British-air-force-in-action yarn is sparked by underplayed acting.▼

Maltese Bippy, The (1969) **C-88m.** ** D: Norman Panama. Dan Rowan, Dick Martin, Carol Lynley, Julie Newmar, Mildred Natwick, Fritz Weaver, Robert Reed. Werewolves, haunted houses, good cast, but few true laughs in tired horror-movie spoof.

Maltese Falcon, The (1931) **80m.** *** D: Roy Del Ruth. Bebe Daniels, Ricardo Cortez, Dudley Digges, Robert Elliott, Thelma Todd, Una Merkel, Dwight Frye. First film version of Dashiell Hammett story is quite good, with Cortez more of a ladies' man than Bogart; otherwise very similar to later classic. Retitled DANGEROUS FEMALE for TV. Remade in 1936 (as SATAN MET A LADY) and 1941.▼

✓ **Maltese Falcon, The** (1941) **100m.** **** D: John Huston. Humphrey Bogart, Mary Astor, Peter Lorre, Sydney Greenstreet, Ward Bond, Gladys George, Barton MacLane, Elisha Cook, Jr., Lee Patrick, Jerome Cowan. Outstanding detective drama improves with each viewing; Bogey is Dashiell Hammett's "hero" Sam Spade, Astor his client, Lorre the evasive Joel Cairo, Greenstreet (in his talkie film debut) the Fat Man, and Cook the neurotic gunsel Wilmer. Huston's first directorial effort (which he also scripted) moves at lightning pace, with cameo by his father Walter Huston as Captain Jacobi. Previously filmed in 1931 and in 1936 (as SATAN MET A LADY). Also shown in computer-colored version.▼

Mama Dracula (1980-French-Belgian) **C-90m.** BOMB D: Boris Szulzinger. Louise Fletcher, Maria Schneider, Marc-Henri Wajnberg, Alexander Wajnberg, Jess Hahn. Dreadful vampire satire with Fletcher as the title character, an eternity away from the cuckoo's nest.▼

Mama, There's a Man in Your Bed (1989-French) **C-111m.** *** D: Coline Serreau. Daniel Auteuil, Firmine Richard, Pierre Vernier, Maxime Leroux, Gilles Privat, Muriel Combeau, Catherine Salviat. Unlikely romance between the harried CEO of a yogurt company and the financially strapped cleaning woman who will do anything to keep her five children (from five different marriages) from going hungry. Clever, heartwarming story from the director of THREE MEN AND A CRADLE has a lot to say about class and color differences in a world none too tolerant of either. Original French title: ROMUALD ET JULIET.

Mambo (1954-U.S.-Italian) **94m.** **½ D: Robert Rossen. Silvana Mangano, Michael Rennie, Shelley Winters, Vittorio Gassman, Eduardo Ciannelli, Mary Clare, Katherine Dunham. Offbeat romance set in Venice; young saleswoman, her love life complicated by a penniless gambler and a sickly count, becomes a famous dancer. Strong cast keeps it watchable. Original Italian running time 107m.

Mame (1974) **C-131m.** BOMB D: Gene Saks. Lucille Ball, Beatrice Arthur, Robert Preston, Jane Connell, Bruce Davison, Kirby Furlong, John McGiver, Joyce Van Patten. Hopelessly out-of-date musical taken from Jerry Herman's Broadway hit and based on AUNTIE MAME will embarrass even those who love Lucy. Calling Fred and Ethel Mertz.▼

Mammy (1930) **84m.** ** D: Michael Curtiz. Al Jolson, Lois Moran, Louise Dresser, Lowell Sherman, Hobart Bosworth. Story of backstage murder in a minstrel troupe is only tolerable during musical numbers; Jolson sings "Let Me Sing and I'm Happy." Some sequences originally filmed in color.

Mam'zelle Pigalle (1958-French) **C-77m.** **½ D: Michel Boisrond. Brigitte Bardot, Jean Bretonniere, Francoise Fabian, Bernard Lancret. Not as saucy as most BB flicks; here she's a songstress mixed up with counterfeiters. Retitled: NAUGHTY GIRL.▼

Man, The (1972) **C-93m.** ****** D: Joseph Sargent. James Earl Jones, Martin Balsam, Burgess Meredith, Lew Ayres, William Windom, Barbara Rush, Janet MacLachlan. Black Senator Jones becomes President of U.S. after freak disaster kills chief executive in Europe. Originally made for TV but released theatrically; marginally interesting Rod Serling adaptation of Irving Wallace bestseller plus acceptable performances add up to forgettable experience. Cameo appearance by Jack Benny.

Man About the House, A (1947-British) **83m.** ****½** D: Leslie Arliss, Kieron Moore, Margaret Johnston, Dulcie Gray, Guy Middleton. Murky drama of British girls almost outmaneuvered by Italian con-artist.▼

Man About Town (1939) **85m.** ****½** D: Mark Sandrich. Jack Benny, Dorothy Lamour, Edward Arnold, Binnie Barnes, Phil Harris, Betty Grable, Monty Woolley, Eddie "Rochester" Anderson. Jack tries to crash London society while there with his troupe; lively but undistinguished musical.

Man About Town (1947-French) **89m.** ******* D: René Clair. Maurice Chevalier, Francois Perier, Marcelle Derrien, Dany Robin. Chevalier in a quaint musical, doing what he knows best: a boulevardier with an eye for les femmes. American version is actually in French (without subtitles); Chevalier occasionally translates the dialogue on the soundtrack.

Man Afraid (1957) **84m.** ****½** D: Harry Keller. George Nader, Phyllis Thaxter, Tim Hovey, Reta Shaw, Martin Milner. Well-acted story of clergyman Nader protecting family against father of boy he killed in self-defense.

Man Against the Mob (1988) **C-100m. TVM** D: Steven Hilliard Stern. George Peppard, Kathryn Harrold, Max Gail, Barry Corbin, Fredric Lehne, Norman Alden, Stella Stevens. *Noir*-ish detective drama set in 1940s L.A. with no-nonsense Peppard leading what few good cops he can find against the bad guys moving in from Chicago. Prospective series pilot; followed by a sequel. Average.

Man Against the Mob: The Chinatown Murders (1989) **C-100m. TVM** D: Michael Pressman. George Peppard, Richard Bradford, Charles Haid, Ursula Andress, Julia Nickson, Jason Beghe, James Pax. In this atmospheric sequel Peppard and pals go after a mob-run Chinatown prostitution ring in '40s L.A. The feel's right, so's the swinging big band sound track, and Peppard's got the right Chandleresque approach, but the tale is stale. Average.

Man Alive (1945) **70m.** ****½** D: Ray Enright. Pat O'Brien, Adolphe Menjou, Ellen Drew, Rudy Vallee, Fortunio Bona-

nova, Joseph Crehan, Jonathan Hale, Minna Gombell, Jason Robards, Sr. Amusing comedy of O'Brien, supposedly dead, playing ghost to scare away wife's new love interest; moves along at brisk pace.

Man Alone, A (1955) **C-96m.** ****½** D: Ray Milland. Ray Milland, Mary Murphy, Ward Bond, Raymond Burr, Lee Van Cleef. Intelligent oater of fugitive from lynch mob (Milland) hiding with sheriff's daughter (Murphy) in small town. Milland's first directorial attempt isn't bad.▼

Man and a Woman, A (1966-French) **C-102m.** *****½** D: Claude Lelouch. Anouk Aimee, Jean-Louis Trintignant, Pierre Barouh, Valerie Lagrange. Moving romantic drama about young widow and widower who fall in love; one of the 1960s' most popular love stories, thanks to intelligent script, winning performances, innovative direction and camerawork, Francis Lai's music score. Oscar winner for Best Foreign Film, Best Original Screenplay. Remade by co-writer/director Lelouch in 1977 as ANOTHER MAN, ANOTHER CHANCE, and followed by A MAN AND A WOMAN: 20 YEARS LATER.▼

Man and a Woman: 20 Years Later, A (1986) **C-108m.** ***½** D: Claude Lelouch. Anouk Aimee, Jean-Louis Trintignant, Richard Berry, Evelyne Bouix, Robert Hossein, Marie-Sophie Pochat. Badly misconceived sequel to one of the '60s' essential "date" movies finds former script girl Aimee now a film producer, race driver Trintignant involved in a Paris-to-Dakar rally. Silly film-within-a-film pays homage to DIAL M FOR MURDER and—in one desert scene—the opening to HATARI! Someone should have reminded Lelouch that "hatari!" means "danger" in Swahili.▼

Man and Boy (1972) **C-98m.** ****½** D: E. W. Swackhamer. Bill Cosby, Gloria Foster, Leif Erickson, George Spell, Douglas Turner Ward, John Anderson, Yaphet Kotto, Henry Silva, Dub Taylor. Civil War veteran and young son take after the thief who has stolen their horse in a kind of black BICYCLE THIEF. Decent enough family film with Cosby in rare dramatic role.▼

Man at the Carlton Tower (1961-British) **57m.** ****** D: Robert Tronson. Maxine Audley, Lee Montague, Allan Cuthbertson, Terence Alexander. Routine Edgar Wallace thriller churned out against backdrop of plush London hotel involving jewel robbery and murder.

Man at the Top (1975-British) **C-92m.** ******* D: Mike Vardy. Kenneth Haigh, Nanette Newman, Harry Andrews, John Quentin, Mary Maude. Feature spin-off of British TV show which in turn is a spin-off of ROOM AT THE TOP, with Haigh as Joe Compton, now caught in EXECUTIVE SUITE-type business conflicts.

Man, a Woman and a Bank, A (1979-Canadian) **C-100m.** **½ D: Noel Black. Donald Sutherland, Brooke Adams, Paul Mazursky, Allen Magicovsky, Leigh Hamilton. Needless but inoffensive caper movie about a $4 million bank heist, with pleasing performances by the three leads. Magicovsky isn't too appealing as a suicidal whipped cream freak, but how many suicidal whipped cream freaks do you know that *are*?▼

Man Bait (1952-U.S.-British) **78m.** **½ D: Terence Fisher. George Brent, Marguerite Chapman, Diana Dors, Raymond Huntley, Peter Reynolds. British made suspense programmer has Brent a book dealer entangled in blackmail and murder. British title: THE LAST PAGE.

Man Beast (1955) **72m.** BOMB D: Jerry Warren. Rock Madison, Virginia Maynor, George Skaff, Lloyd Nelson, Tom Maruzzi. An expedition goes in search of the abominable snowman but comes up with a turkey instead.▼

Man Behind the Gun, The (1952) **C-82m.** ** D: Felix E. Feist. Randolph Scott, Patrice Wymore, Philip Carey, Dick Wesson, Lina Romay. Army man Scott goes undercover to investigate southern California secessionist movement in 1850s. Formula stuff.

Man Betrayed, A (1941) **83m.** ** D: John H. Auer. John Wayne, Frances Dee, Edward Ellis, Wallace Ford, Ward Bond, Harold Huber, Alexander Granach. Country lawyer crusades against father of girlfriend to prove that he's crooked politician. Minor melodrama with the Duke in one of his oddest roles. Retitled: WHEEL OF FORTUNE.▼

Man Between, The (1953-British) **101m.** *** D: Carol Reed. James Mason, Claire Bloom, Hildegarde Neff, Geoffrey Toone. Hardened black-market dealer falls in love and finds himself torn between East and West. Taut, moody, and well-acted drama set in post-WW2 Berlin.

Man Called Adam, A (1966) **102m.** ** D: Leo Penn. Sammy Davis, Jr., Ossie Davis, Cicely Tyson, Louis Armstrong, Frank Sinatra, Jr., Peter Lawford, Mel Torme, Lola Falana, Gerald O'Loughlin. Pretentious melodrama of trumpet-player Davis trying to find some purpose in life; amateurishly produced.▼

Man Called Dagger, A (1967) **C-86m.** BOMB D: Richard Rush. Terry Moore, Jan Murray, Sue Ane Langdon, Paul Mantee, Eileen O'Neill, Maureen Arthur. Ex-Nazi scientist journeys to L.A. followed by secret agent Richard Dagger to assist former S.S. colonel (Murray!) in world-conquering plan. Embarrassing script, acting.

Man Called Flintstone, The (1966) **C-87m.** **½ D: Joseph Barbera, William Hanna. Voices of Alan Reed, Mel Blanc, Jean Vander Pyl, June Foray. Feature-length cartoon based on TV series of Stone Age characters satirizes superspy films. Mainly for kids.▼

Man Called Gannon, A (1969) **C-105m.** *½ D: James Goldstone. Tony Franciosa, Michael Sarrazin, Judi West, Susan Oliver. Remade version of MAN WITHOUT A STAR is poor substitute. It's ranch-war time again ..

Man Called Horse, A (1970) **C-114m.** **½ D: Elliot Silverstein. Richard Harris, Judith Anderson, Jean Gascon, Manu Tupou, Corinna Tsopei, Dub Taylor. English aristocrat gets captured by Sioux Indians in the Dakotas, undergoes torture to prove his worth. Sometimes gripping, sometimes gory; fine score by Leonard Rosenman. Followed by RETURN OF A MAN CALLED HORSE and TRIUMPHS OF A MAN CALLED HORSE.▼

Man Called Peter, A (1955) **C-119m.** *** D: Henry Koster. Richard Todd, Jean Peters, Marjorie Rambeau, Doris Lloyd, Emmett Lynn. Moving account of Scotsman Peter Marshall who became clergyman and U.S. Senate chaplain; sensitively played by Todd, with fine supporting cast.▼

Man Called Sledge, A (1970-Italian) **C-93m.** ** D: Vic Morrow. James Garner, Dennis Weaver, Claude Akins, John Marley, Laura Antonelli, Wade Preston. Violent Western about a gunman whose gang goes after a cache of gold stored in a prison, and then fights over the loot. Notable mainly for Garner's atypical role as brutal outlaw.

Manchu Eagle Murder Caper Mystery (1973) **C-80m.** **½ D: Dean Hargrove. Gabriel Dell, Will Geer, Joyce Van Patten, Anjanette Comer, Jackie Coogan, Huntz Hall, Barbara Harris. Fairly successful satire of tough private eye melodramas of 1940s. Cast and director on top of their material help make up for cheapness of production; never released theatrically.

Manchurian Candidate, The (1962) **126m.** ***½ D: John Frankenheimer. Frank Sinatra, Laurence Harvey, Janet Leigh, Angela Lansbury, Henry Silva, James Gregory, John McGiver, Leslie Parrish, Khigh Deigh. Tingling political paranoia thriller about strange aftermath of a Korean war hero's decoration and his mother's machinations to promote her Joseph McCarthy-like husband's career. Harrowing presentation of Richard Condon story (adapted by George Axelrod). Music score by David Amram. Rereleased theatrically in 1987.▼

Man Could Get Killed, A (1966) **C-99m.** **½ D: Ronald Neame, Cliff Owen. James Garner, Melina Mercouri, Sandra Dee, Tony Franciosa, Robert Coote, Roland Culver. Businessman Garner is mistaken for international spy in this so-so secret agent spoof with beautiful Rome and Lisbon locations. Bert Kaempfert's score introduces the hit tune "Strangers in the Night."

Mandalay (1934) 65m. *½ D: Michael Curtiz. Kay Francis, Lyle Talbot, Warner Oland, Raffaela Ottiano, Ruth Donnelly. Strange, silly, largely incoherent film set in Rangoon, about a woman with a past who helps a man on the run. Francis abandons convention to become the notorious Spot White (who "should be called Spot Cash," according to one observer). Shirley Temple is supposed to be in this film, but *we* can't find her.

Mandela (1987) C-135m. TVM D: Philip Saville. Danny Glover, Alfre Woodard, John Matshikiza, Warren Clarke, Allan Corduner, Julian Glover. Danny Glover and Woodard are perfectly cast in this literate, poignant (and partisan) social history as Nelson and Winnie Mandela, who lead a lifelong struggle against South African apartheid . . . much of the time with Nelson in hiding, and finally imprisoned. Ronald Harwood's script is simple and effective; filmed on location in Zimbabwe. Made for cable. Above average.▼

Man Detained (1961-British) 59m. **½ D: Robert Tronson. Bernard Archard, Elvi Hale, Paul Stassino, Michael Coles. Trim Edgar Wallace yarn, enhanced by Hale's performance as secretary involved with counterfeiting gang and murder.

Mandingo (1975) C-127m. BOMB D: Richard Fleischer. James Mason, Susan George, Perry King, Richard Ward, Brenda Sykes, Ken Norton, Lillian Hayman, Roy Poole, Ji-Tu Cumbuka, Paul Benedict, Ben Masters. Trashy potboiler will appeal only to the s & m crowd. Mason is a bigoted plantation patriarch, George his oversexed daughter, Norton—what else?—a fighter. Stinko! Based on the Kyle Onstott novel, the first of a long series, although only one more—DRUM—was filmed.▼

Mandrake (1979) C-100m. TVM D: Harry Falk. Anthony Herrera, Simone Griffeth, Ji-Tu Cumbuka, Gretchen Corbett, Peter Haskell, Robert Reed. The long-time comic-strip favorite's TV debut in this pilot has him using his legendary legerdermain to fight an extortionist trying to take a business tycoon for $10-million. Average.

Mandy SEE: **Crash of Silence**

Man-Eater SEE: **Shark!**▼

Maneater (1973) C-78m. TVM D: Vince Edwards. Ben Gazzara, Sheree North, Kip Niven, Laurette Spang, Richard Basehart, Claire Brennan. Four city-bred vacationers vs. two hungry tigers set on them by mad animal trainer Basehart. Interesting thriller written by director Edwards and acted with verve by good cast. Above average.

Man-Eater of Hydra (1967-West German-Spanish) C-88m. ** D: Mel Welles. Cameron Mitchell, Elisa Montes, George Mar-

tin, Kay Fischer, Ralph Naukoff. Remote island with meat-eating plants is setting for predictable, mildly entertaining horror pic. Interesting special effects and atmosphere obscure silly script. Alternate title: ISLAND OF THE DOOMED.

Man-Eater of Kumaon (1948) 79m. **½ D: Byron Haskin. Sabu, Wendell Corey, Joanne Page, Morris Carnovsky, Argentina Brunetti. Good adventure tale of hunter determined to kill deadly tiger on the loose.

Maneaters Are Loose! (1978) C-100m. TVM D: Timothy Galfas. Tom Skerritt, Steve Forrest, G. D. Spradlin, Harry Morgan, Diana Muldaur, Dabney Coleman. Down-and-out animal trainer abandons his tigers near a small California community and lets them fend for themselves. Average.

Man Facing Southeast (1986-Argentine) C-108m. *** D: Eliseo Subiela. Lorenzo Quinteros, Hugo Soto, Ines Vernengo. Intriguing movie about a staff psychiatrist at a large mental hospital who tries to penetrate the enigma of a new patient who claims to be an alien visitor—and who, in fact, does seem to possess unusual powers. Fascinating at first, slow going at times, this is the kind of film that deliberately leaves the viewer to draw his own conclusions . . . and that is a great part of its mystique.▼

Manfish (1956) C-76m. ** D: W. Lee Wilder. John Bromfield, Lon Chaney, Victor Jory, Barbara Nichols. Variation of Edgar Allan Poe's *Gold Bug* story is timid account of treasure hunt in Jamaica.▼

Man for All Seasons, A (1966-British) C-120m. **** D: Fred Zinnemann. Paul Scofield, Wendy Hiller, Leo McKern, Robert Shaw, Orson Welles, Susannah York, John Hurt, Nigel Davenport, Vanessa Redgrave. Splendid film based on Robert Bolt's play about Sir Thomas More's personal conflict when King Henry VIII asks his support in break with Pope and formation of Church of England. Scofield's rich characterization matched by superb cast, vivid atmosphere. Six Oscars include Best Actor, Director, Picture, Screenplay (Robert Bolt), Cinematography (Ted Moore), Costumes. Remade for TV in 1988.▼

Man for All Seasons, A (1988) C-150m. TVM D: Charlton Heston. Charlton Heston, Vanessa Redgrave, John Gielgud, Richard Johnson, Roy Kinnear, Martin Chamberlain. A fine showcase for Heston, who plays Thomas More in Robert Bolt's reworking of his outstanding stage play. Having recently performed the part on stage in London, Heston opted to direct and star in this TV adaptation, with able support from Gielgud and Redgrave (who had a small part in the 1966 movie version). Made for cable. Above average.▼

Man Friday (1976-British) C-115m. *½ D: Jack Gold. Peter O'Toole, Richard

Roundtree, Peter Cellier, Christopher Cabot, Joel Fluellen. Defoe classic rewritten to conform to today's racial standards. Amid gore and confusing flashbacks, Friday revolts against bondage, outwits master Crusoe, and also drives him mad (as shown in Cannes, Crusoe, having failed to "educate" Friday to British standards, and himself refused admission to Friday's tribe, blows his brains out!).▼

Man from Atlantis (1977) **C-100m. TVM** D: Lee H. Katzin. Patrick Duffy, Belinda Montgomery, Art Lund, Dean Santoro, Victor Buono, Lawrence Pressman. Scifier about last surviving citizen of underwater kingdom who teams up with a pretty marine biologist to fight evil on Earth. Duffy is quite good as underwater romantic lead with webbed hands who outswims and outleaps dolphins, and made an unlikely hero for subsequent TV series. Above average.▼

Man from Atlantis: The Death Scouts (1977) **C-100m. TVM** D: Marc Daniels. Patrick Duffy, Belinda Montgomery, Kenneth Tigar, Alan Fudge, Tiffany Bolling, Burr DeBenning, Russell Arms, Annette Cardona. Sci-fi drama in which title humanoid tries to thwart an invasion of earth by water-breathing aliens of another planet. Enjoyable nonsense. Average.

Man from Bitter Ridge, The (1955) **C-80m. **½** D: Jack Arnold. Lex Barker, Mara Corday, Stephen McNally, Trevor Bardette. Peppy oater of Barker tracking down outlaws by tying in with local banker.

Man from Button Willow, The (1965) **C-84m. ** D: David Detiege. Cartoon Western featuring the voices of Dale Robertson, Edgar Buchanan, Howard Keel, Herschel Bernardi, Ross Martin and others is only for small kiddies; story deals with America's first undercover agent in 1869 who prevents crooks from forcing settlers to get rid of their land.▼

Man from Cairo (1953-Italian) **81m. ** D: Ray Enright. George Raft, Gianna Maria Canale, Massimo Serato, Irene Papas. Disappointing mishmash of intrigue set in Africa, with everyone scurrying about for gold.

Man from Colorado, The (1948) **C-99m. *** D: Henry Levin. Glenn Ford, William Holden, Ellen Drew, Ray Collins, Edgar Buchanan. Unusual Western of brutal Ford appointed Federal judge, taking tyrannical hold of the territory.▼

Man from Dakota, The (1940) **75m. **½** D: Leslie Fenton. Wallace Beery, John Howard, Dolores Del Rio, Donald Meek, Robert Barrat. Above-average Beery vehicle set in Civil War times, with glamorous Del Rio helping him and Howard, Union spies, cross Confederate lines.

Man from Del Rio (1956) **82m. ** D: Harry Horner. Anthony Quinn, Katy Jurado,

Peter Whitney, Douglas Fowley, John Larch, Whit Bissell. Dank Western of Mexican gunslinger Quinn saving a town from outlaws.

Man from Down Under, The (1943) **103m. **½** D: Robert Z. Leonard. Charles Laughton, Binnie Barnes, Richard Carlson, Donna Reed, Christopher Severn, Clyde Cook. Well-meaning Laughton claims two orphan waifs as his own children, raising them in Australia. Entertaining, trivial little comedy.

Man From Frisco, The (1944) **91m. **½** D: Robert Florey. Michael O'Shea, Anne Shirley, Dan Duryea, Gene Lockhart, Stephanie Bachelor, Ray Walker. O'Shea is pushy shipbuilding genius who meets resistance from residents of small town where he wants to build a new plant. Fairly entertaining action hokum with a little too much romance.

Man From Galveston, The (1963) **57m. ** D: William Conrad. Jeffrey Hunter, Preston Foster, James Coburn, Joanna Moore, Edward Andrews, Kevin Hagen, Martin West, Ed Nelson. Unsatisfying little Western with lawyer Hunter defending ex-girlfriend Moore on a murder charge in a frontier town.

Man from God's Country (1958) **C-72m. ** D: Paul Landres. George Montgomery, Randy Stuart, Gregg Barton, Kim Charney, Susan Cummings. Quiet oater involving land-hungry ranchers trying to outfox the railroad.

Man from Hong Kong, The (1975-Australian-Chinese) **C-103m. ** D: Brian Trenchard Smith. Jimmy Wang Yu, George Lazenby, Ros Spiers, Hugh Keays-Byrne, Rebecca Gilling. Undemanding action fans should get their fill in this stunt-crazy story of Hong Kong emissary (and Kung Fu expert) called to Sydney to help nail drug kingpin. Originally titled THE DRAGON FLIES; surprisingly triggered a hit song, "Sky High."

Man from Laramie, The (1955) **C-104m. *** D: Anthony Mann. James Stewart, Arthur Kennedy, Donald Crisp, Cathy O'Donnell, Alex Nicol, Aline MacMahon, Wallace Ford. Taut action tale of revenge, with Stewart seeking those who killed his brother.▼

Man from O.R.G.Y. (1970) **C-92m. *½** D: James A. Hill. Robert Walker, Steve Rossi, Slappy White, Louisa Moritz. Banal counterespionage comedy-drama. Who's got the secrets?

Man from Planet X, The (1951) **70m. *½** D: Edgar G. Ulmer. Robert Clarke, Margaret Field, Raymond Bond, William Schallert. Scottish Highlands are visited by alien from wandering planet; at first he is benign, but evil designs of Schallert turn him against human race.

Man from Snowy River, The (1982-Aus-

[716]

tralian) **C-115m.** ***½ D: George Miller. Kirk Douglas, Tom Burlinson, Sigrid Thornton, Jack Thompson, Lorraine Bayly, Tommy Dysart, Bruce Kerr. Grand, old-fashioned Western saga, based on epic Australian poem, about strong-willed young man who goes to work for an empire-building cattleman, and falls in love with his daughter. Hokey, simplistic, but great fun, with eye-filling scenery and incredible action scenes with some wild horses. Douglas has fun in a dual role; Thompson's part is virtually a cameo. Followed by RETURN TO SNOWY RIVER PART II▼

Man from the Alamo, The (1953) **C-79m.** *** D: Budd Boetticher. Glenn Ford, Julia (Julie) Adams, Victor Jory, Hugh O'Brian, Chill Wills, Jeanne Cooper, Neville Brand. Ford escapes from the Alamo to warn others, but is branded a deserter, and forced to prove himself anew in further battles against the Mexicans. Typically offbeat Boetticher Western, well acted and exciting.▼

Man from the Diner's Club, The (1963) **96m.** **½ D: Frank Tashlin. Danny Kaye, Martha Hyer, Cara Williams, Telly Savalas, Everett Sloane, George Kennedy. Silly shenanigans of Diner's Club employee Kaye involved with Damon Runyonish gangsters. Danny has certainly had more inspired antics than these, but okay slapstick. Screenplay by William Peter Blatty. Look for Harry Dean Stanton as a beatnik.

Man from Yesterday, The (1932) **71m.** *** D: Berthold Viertel. Claudette Colbert, Clive Brook, Charles Boyer, Andy Devine, Alan Mowbray. Story of Colbert marrying Boyer thinking husband Brook has died is surprisingly well done, thanks mainly to top performances.

Manganinnie (1980-Australian) **C-90m.** **½ D: John Honey. Mawuyul Yanthalawuy, Anna Ralph, Phillip Hinton, Elaine Mangan. White child Ralph, separated from her family, is watched over by aborigine Yanthalawuy, separated from her tribe. Slow and uninvolving, though the scenery is pretty.

Mango Tree, The (1977-Australian) **C-93m.** **½ D: Kevin Dobson. Christopher Pate, Geraldine Fitzgerald, Robert Helpmann, Diane Craig, Gerald Kennedy, Gloria Dawn. A young man's coming of age in Australia, around the time of WW1; pictorially pleasing, with a warm performance by Fitzgerald as the young man's wise, gentle grandmother, but nothing out of the ordinary. Written and produced by former actor Michael Pate, whose son plays the lead.▼

Manhandled (1949) **97m.** ** D: Lewis R. Foster. Dorothy Lamour, Dan Duryea, Sterling Hayden, Irene Hervey, Philip Reed. Crooked private eye Duryea tries to pin robbery-murder rap on innocent Lamour. Turgid drama that reliable cast can't salvage.

Manhattan (1979) **96m.** ***½ D: Woody Allen. Woody Allen, Diane Keaton, Michael Murphy, Mariel Hemingway, Anne Byrne, Meryl Streep. Bittersweet slice-of-life about a N.Y.C. comedy writer and his cerebral friends; blisteringly accurate and ultimately poignant, a worthy followup to Woody's ANNIE HALL. Magnificently photographed (in b&w and Panavision) by Gordon Willis, with splendid use of Gershwin music on the soundtrack. Wallace Shawn's role is especially funny; that's Mark Linn-Baker as one of the Shakespearean actors. Released in the "letterbox" format on homevideo to preserve widescreen look.▼

Manhattan Melodrama (1934) **93m.** *** D: W. S. Van Dyke II. Clark Gable, William Powell, Myrna Loy, Leo Carrillo, Isabel Jewell, Mickey Rooney, Nat Pendleton. Boyhood pals remain adult friends though one is a gangster and the other a D.A. (a plot device reused many times). What might be unbearably corny is top entertainment, thanks to this star trio and a director with gusto. Arthur Caesar's original story won an Oscar. Footnoted in American history as the film John Dillinger saw before being gunned down at the Biograph Theatre in Chicago.

Manhattan Merry-Go-Round (1938) **80m.** ** D: Charles Riesner. Phil Regan, Ann Dvorak, Leo Carrillo, James Gleason. Gangster Carrillo takes over a record company. Flimsy script, with romantic subplot, is just an excuse for none-too-thrilling specialty numbers by Gene Autry, Cab Calloway, Ted Lewis, Louis Prima, The Kay Thompson Singers, and Joe DiMaggio (!), to name just a few.▼

Manhattan Project, The (1986) **C-117m.** ** D: Marshall Brickman. John Lithgow, Christopher Collet, Cynthia Nixon, Jill Eikenberry, John Mahoney, Sully Boyar. Precocious teenager breaks into top-secret plant, steals some plutonium, and builds his own nuclear reactor, ostensibly to make a point but also to show off. Slick, extremely well-acted film is blatantly irresponsible and has us cheering for the kid as he outwits the dopey grownups and nearly blows up the world!▼

Man Hunt (1941) **105m.** ***½ D: Fritz Lang. Walter Pidgeon, Joan Bennett, George Sanders, John Carradine, Roddy McDowall. Farfetched yet absorbing drama of man attempting to kill Hitler, getting into more trouble than he bargained for. Tense, well-done. Screenplay by Dudley Nichols, from Geoffrey Household's novel. Remade as ROGUE MALE.

Manhunt (1973) SEE: **The Italian Connection**

Manhunt, The (1986-Italian) **C-89m.** ** D: Larry Ludman (Fabrizio De Angelis). John Ethan Wayne, Raymund Harmstorf, Henry Silva, Bo Svenson, Ernest Borgnine. Wayne (son of John Wayne) is a young, would-be horse trainer unjustly arrested as a horse thief. Cast uplifts routine plot in this made-in-U.S.A. Italian production, filmed in 1984. ▼

Manhunter (1974) **C-78m. TVM** D: Walter Grauman. Ken Howard, Gary Lockwood, Tim O'Connor, James Olson, Stefanie Powers, John Anderson, L. Q. Jones. Period action drama pitting ex-marine (WWI) Howard against Bonnie-and-Clyde style bank robbers. Later became a series. Average.▼

Manhunter, The (1976) **C-98m. TVM** D: Don Taylor. Sandra Dee, Roy Thinnes, William Smith, David Brian, Madlyn Rhue, Albert Salmi, Al Hirt. Safari hunter hired by American banker to avenge death of son during small-town bank robbery. Typical premise-gone-awry situation, due to contrived plotting. Made in 1968. Average.

Manhunter (1986) **C-119m.** *** D: Michael Mann. William L. Petersen, Kim Greist, Joan Allen, Brian Cox, Dennis Farina, Stephen Lang, Tom Noonan. Forceful contemporary cops-and-robbers melodrama told with *Miami Vice* stylistics (and hard-pounding music) by that show's creator, writer-director Mann. Petersen plays a troubled former FBI agent who's called back to service to capture a serial killer, which he does by getting himself to think just like the murderer! Gripping all the way and surprisingly nonexploitive, considering subject matter. Don't examine story too carefully or the holes start to show through. Based on Thomas Harris' novel *Red Dragon.* ▼

Manhunt for Claude Dallas (1986) **C-100m. TVM** D: Jerry London. Matt Salinger, Claude Akins, Lois Nettleton, Rip Torn, Pat Hingle, Beau Starr, Fred Coffin. Fact-based drama about a self-styled mountain man whose killings, capture, trial, conviction, and subsequent escape made for headlines. John Gay's slow-moving script was adapted from Jeff Long's book *Outlaw.* Average.

Manhunt in the Jungle (1958) **C-79m.** BOMB D: Tom McGowan. Robin Hughes, Luis Alvarez, James Wilson, Jorge Montoro, John B. Symmes. Hackneyed safari set in Brazil.

Manhunt of Mystery Island SEE: **Captain Mephisto and the Transformation Machine**

Manhunt: Search for the Night Stalker (1989) **C-100m. TVM** D: Bruce Seth Green. Richard Jordan, A Martinez, Lisa Eilbacher, Julie Carmen, Jenny Sullivan. Docudrama focuses on two cops and the routine police work that led to the arrest of serial killer Richard Ramirez, who terrorized Southern California in the spring and summer of 1985 and was sentenced to the gas chamber on the very day that this movie premiered. Average.

Maniac (1934) **67m.** BOMB D: Dwain Esper. Bill Woods, Horace Carpenter, Ted Edwards, Phyllis Diller (not the comedienne), Thea Ramsey, Jennie Dark. Typically delirious Esper schlockfest—filmed mostly in somebody's basement—about a lunatic who murders a mad doctor and assumes his identity. High points include a passionate soliloquy on insanity, pulling out a cat's eye and eating it, and a climactic fight between two women armed with hypodermic needles!▼

Maniac (1962-British) **86m.** **½ D: Michael Carreras. Kerwin Mathews, Nadia Gray, Donald Houston, Justine Lord. One of the better British thrillers made in wake of PSYCHO, with Mathews as vacationing artist in France arousing hatred of girlfriend's sick father. Good plot twists. Written by Jimmy Sangster.▼

Maniac (1977) SEE: **Ransom▼**

Maniac (1980) **C-87m.** BOMB D: William Lustig. Joe Spinell, Caroline Munro, Gail Lawrence (Abigail Clayton), Kelly Piper, Rita Montone, Tom Savini. Unrelenting exercise in nihilistic gore about a cretin who murders women and then scalps them so that he can dress up his mannequins. Although an excellent character actor, coscriptwriter-producer-star Spinell bears most of the blame for this claustrophobic, sickening film.▼

Maniac Cop (1988) **C-85m.** *½ D: William Lustig. Tom Atkins, Bruce Campbell, Laurene Landon, Richard Roundtree, William Smith, Robert Z'dar, Sheree North. Potentially intriguing premise, of a killer on the police force striking terror in the hearts of N.Y.C. residents, is bungled by failed black humor and ham-fisted direction into standard stalk-and-slash fare. Best work is done by North as a crippled, embittered policewoman.▼

Manifesto (1988-U.S.-Yugoslavian) **C-96m.** **½ D: Dusan Makavejev. Camilla Søeberg, Alfred Molina, Simon Callow, Eric Stoltz, Lindsay Duncan, Rade Šerbedžija, Svetozar Svetković, Chris Haywood, Patrick Godfrey, Linda Marlowe, Ronald Lacey. Set in the 1920s, this anarchic dark comedy depicts a small Balkan community that's a hotbed of assassination plots, sexual freedom, and repressive ideas. Loosely derived from a story by Emile Zola, the film is brightly colored and impishly written (by the director), but eventually becomes *too* anarchic for its own good. More notable for what it attempts than what it achieves.▼

Man I Killed, The SEE: **Broken Lullaby**

Manila Calling (1942) 81m. ** D: Herbert I. Leeds. Lloyd Nolan, Carole Landis, Cornel Wilde, James Gleason, Martin Kosleck, Ralph Byrd, Elisha Cook, Jr., Louis Jean Heydt. Pat WW2 film of one guy taking 'em all on with his small but dedicated outfit.

Man I Love, The (1946) 96m. *** D: Raoul Walsh. Ida Lupino, Robert Alda, Bruce Bennett, Andrea King, Dolores Moran, Martha Vickers, Alan Hale. Slick, well-acted melodrama casts Ida as nightclub singer pursued by no-good mobster Alda. Forget logic and just enjoy. This film inspired Scorsese's NEW YORK, NEW YORK.

Man I Married, The (1940) 77m. *** D: Irving Pichel. Joan Bennett, Francis Lederer, Lloyd Nolan, Anna Sten, Otto Kruger. Strong story of German Lederer taken in by Nazi propaganda while American wife Bennett tries to stop him. Taut, exciting script.

Man in a Cocked Hat (1959-British) 88m. *** D: Jeffrey Dell, Roy Boulting. Terry-Thomas, Peter Sellers, Luciana Paluzzi, Thorley Walters, Ian Bannen, John Le Mesurier, Miles Malleson. Screwball farce about Island of Gallardia, a British protectorate forgotten for 50 years; when rediscovered, bumbling Terry-Thomas of the Foreign Office is left in charge. British title: CARLTON-BROWNE OF THE F.O.▼

Man in Grey, The (1943-British) 116m. *** D: Leslie Arliss. Margaret Lockwood, James Mason, Phyllis Calvert, Stewart Granger, Helen Haye, Martita Hunt. Wealthy Calvert befriends impoverished schoolmate Lockwood; years later, Lockwood repays the kindness by trying to steal her husband. Elaborate costume drama, told in flashback, is entertaining, and notable for boosting Mason (as Calvert's hateful husband) to stardom. Originally shown in the U.S. at 93m.▼

Man in Half Moon Street, The (1944) 92m. **½ D: Ralph Murphy. Nils Asther, Helen Walker, Brandon Hurst, Reginald Sheffield. Not-bad horror tale of scientist Asther experimenting with rejuvenation; done on better scale than many of these little epics. Remade as THE MAN WHO COULD CHEAT DEATH.

Man in Hiding (1953-British) 79m. *½ D: Terence Fisher. Paul Henreid, Lois Maxwell, Kieron Moore, Hugh Sinclair. Tame detective-capturing-elusive-killer plot.

Man in Love, A (1987-French-Italian) C-117m. *** D: Diane Kurys. Peter Coyote, Greta Scacchi, Peter Riegert, Claudia Cardinale, Jamie Lee Curtis, John Berry, Vincent Lindon, Jean Pigozzi. Full-blooded romance about a married American actor who falls in love with his leading lady while making a movie in Rome. Coyote and Scacchi are believable (and extremely sexy) in this sensual and intelligent film, written by Israel Horovitz and director Kurys, whose first English language film this is.▼

Man Inside, The (1958-British) 90m. *½ D: John Gilling. Jack Palance, Anita Ekberg, Nigel Patrick, Anthony Newley, Sidney James, Donald Pleasence, Eric Pohlmann. Shoddy robbery caper with private investigator hunting jewel thieves throughout Europe.▼

Man in the Attic (1954) 82m. **½ D: Hugo Fregonese. Jack Palance, Constance Smith, Byron Palmer, Frances Bavier, Rhys Williams, Sean McClory, Isabel Jewell, Leslie Bradley. Flavorful account of notorious Jack the Ripper, with Palance going full-blast. Remake of THE LODGER.

Man in the Dark (1953) 70m. **½ D: Lew Landers. Edmond O'Brien, Audrey Totter, Ruth Warren, Ted de Corsia, Horace McMahon. Convict O'Brien undergoes brain surgery to eliminate criminal bent, and loses memory in the process; his old cohorts only care that he remember where he stashed their stolen loot. Routine remake of THE MAN WHO LIVED TWICE was originally shown in 3-D.

Man in the Dinghy SEE: **Into the Blue**

Man in the Glass Booth, The (1975) C-117m. **½ D: Arthur Hiller. Maximilian Schell, Lois Nettleton, Luther Adler, Lawrence Pressman, Henry Brown, Richard Rasof. American Film Theatre version of Robert Shaw's play about a glib Jewish industrialist brought to trial for Nazi war crimes. Schell is good, but overall effect is contrived. Shaw had his name removed from credits of film.▼

Man in the Gray Flannel Suit, The (1956) C-153m. ***½ D: Nunnally Johnson. Gregory Peck, Jennifer Jones, Fredric March, Marisa Pavan, Lee J. Cobb, Keenan Wynn, Gene Lockhart, Gigi Perreau, Arthur O'Connell, Henry Daniell. Sloan Wilson's slick novel of Madison Avenue executive struggling to get ahead and to find meaning in his home life. Nice cameo by Ann Harding as March's wife. Scripted by the director; music score by Bernard Herrmann.▼

Man in the Iron Mask, The (1939) 110m. *** D: James Whale. Louis Hayward, Joan Bennett, Warren William, Joseph Schildkraut, Alan Hale, Walter Kingsford, Marion Martin. Rousing adventure of twin brothers: one becomes King of France, the other a carefree gay blade raised by D'Artagnan (William) and the 3 Musketeers. Fine swashbuckler, originally filmed with Douglas Fairbanks as THE IRON MASK.▼

Man in the Iron Mask, The (1977) **C-100m. TVM D:** Mike Newell. Richard Chamberlain, Patrick McGoohan, Louis Jourdan, Jenny Agutter, Vivien Merchant, Ian Holm, Ralph Richardson. Stylish romantic adventure in this William Bast adaptation of the Dumas classic acted with panache by a sterling cast. Chamberlain can swashbuckle with the best of them. Grand entertainment. Above average.▼

Man in the Middle (1964-British) **94m.** ** D:** Guy Hamilton. Robert Mitchum, France Nuyen, Barry Sullivan, Keenan Wynn, Alexander Knox, Trevor Howard. Unconvincing, confusing film of Howard Fast novel *The Winston Affair*, about American military officer accused of homicide; static courtroom sequences.

Man in the Moon (1961-British) **98m.** *** D:** Basil Dearden. Kenneth More, Shirley Anne Field, Norman Bird, Michael Hordern, John Phillips. Top comedy satirizing space race. Government recruits man unaffected by cold, heat, speed, etc., to be perfect astronaut.

Man in the Net, The (1959) **97m.** **½ D:** Michael Curtiz. Alan Ladd, Carolyn Jones, Diane Brewster, Charles McGraw, John Lupton, Tom Helmore. Fair drama of Ladd trying to clear himself of murder charge for wife's death.

Man in the Raincoat, The (1957-French-Italian) **97m.** ** D:** Julien Duvivier. Fernandel, John McGiver, Bernard Blier, Claude Sylvain, Jean Rigaux, Rob Murray. Middling comedy-mystery with Fernandel as a bumbling musician who accidentally becomes involved with murder. Tries hard and has its moments but simply doesn't gel. ▼

Man in the Road, The (1957-British) **83m.** *½ D:** Lance Comfort. Derek Farr, Ella Raines, Donald Wolfit, Karel Stepanek. Despite sturdy cast, humdrum telling of Communists trying to get scientist to divulge secret formula.

Man in the Saddle (1951) **C-87m.** ** D:** Andre de Toth. Randolph Scott, Joan Leslie, Ellen Drew, Alexander Knox. Scott is involved in romantic triangle causing death on the range; justice triumphs.

Man in the Santa Claus Suit, The (1978) **C-100m. TVM D:** Corey Allen. Fred Astaire, Gary Burghoff, John Byner, Bert Convy, Nanette Fabray, Harold Gould. Yuletide fantasy of how Astaire (playing seven different characters) affects the lives of various familiar TV faces. He also sings the title song—delightfully. Average.▼

Man in the Shadow (1957) **80m.** **½ D:** Jack Arnold. Orson Welles, Jeff Chandler, Colleen Miller, James Gleason. Welles chomps his way through role of rancher responsible for helper's death. Chandler is the earnest sheriff.

Man in the Shadow (1957-British) SEE: **Violent Stranger**

Man in the Vault (1956) **73m.** *½ D:** Andrew V. McLaglen. William Campbell, Karen Sharpe, Anita Ekberg, Berry Kroeger, Paul Fix. Programmer of drab locksmith involved in robbery; nothing special.

Man in the White Suit, The (1951-British) **84m.** ***½ D:** Alexander Mackendrick. Alec Guinness, Joan Greenwood, Cecil Parker, Michael Gough, Ernest Thesiger, Vida Hope, George Benson, Edie Martin. Guinness is inventor who discovers a fabric that can't wear out or soil; dismayed garment manufacturers set out to bury his formula. Most engaging comedy. Screenplay by Roger Macdougall, John Dighton, and Mackendrick, from Macdougall's play.▼

Man in the Wilderness (1971) **C-105m.** *** D:** Richard C. Sarafian. Richard Harris, John Huston, John Bindon, Ben Carruthers, Prunella Ransome, Henry Wilcoxon. Trapper Harris abandoned in wasteland, must fight for survival, and revenge as well. Well-made, engrossing, but bloody film.

Man Is Armed, The (1956) **70m.** *½ D:** Franklin Adreon. Dane Clark, William Talman, May Wynn, Robert Horton, Barton MacLane. Low-jinks about robbery; competent cast stifled by incompetent production.

Manitou, The (1978) **C-104m.** BOMB **D:** William Girdler. Tony Curtis, Susan Strasberg, Michael Ansara, Ann Sothern, Burgess Meredith, Stella Stevens. Long-dead Indian medicine man gets himself resurrected through a fetus on Strasberg's neck. Veterans Curtis, Sothern, and Meredith look properly embarrassed.▼

Man Killer (1933) **67m.** **½ D:** Michael Curtiz. William Powell, Margaret Lindsay, Ruth Donnelly, Arthur Hohl, Natalie Moorehead, Arthur Byron. Powell accepts job with shady private-detective Hohl and agrees to dupe wealthy Lindsay, but falls in love with her instead. Warner Bros. programmer picks up after a slow start. Originally released as PRIVATE DETECTIVE 62.

Mankillers (1987) **C-88m.** BOMB **D:** David Prior. Edd Byrnes, Gail Fisher, Edy Williams, Lynda Aldon, William Zipp. Made-for-video feature teases the viewer with a tame story of a dozen women enlisted as commandos by the CIA to wipe out renegade agent Zipp south of the border. Return of TV stars Byrnes and Fisher is unexciting, as they're saddled with nothing roles; ditto perennial starlet Williams.▼

Man Made Monster (1941) **59m.** ** D:** George Waggner. Lionel Atwill, Lon Chaney, Jr., Anne Nagel, Frank Albertson, Samuel S. Hinds, William Davidson, Ben Taggart, Connie Bergen. Sci-fi yarn of scientist Atwill making Chaney invulnerable to electricity; fairly well done. Mainly for fans of the genre. Reissued as ATOMIC MONSTER.

Man Named John, A (1968-Italian) **C-94m.** *** D: Ermanno Olmi. Rod Steiger. Excellent documentary on Pope John XXIII, encompassing many facets of his life, work, and beliefs on mankind.

Mannequin (1937) **95m.** **½ D: Frank Borzage. Joan Crawford, Spencer Tracy, Alan Curtis, Ralph Morgan, Leo Gorcey, Elisabeth Risdon. Prototype rags-to-riches soaper, with working-girl Crawford getting ahead via wealthy Tracy. Predictable script, but nice job by stars, usual MGM gloss (even in the tenements!).▼

Mannequin (1987) **C-89m.** BOMB D: Michael Gottlieb. Andrew McCarthy, Kim Cattrall, Estelle Getty, G. W. Bailey, James Spader, Meshach Taylor, Carole Davis. Cattrall is an ancient Egyptian spirit who embodies a department store mannequin; McCarthy is the only one who sees her come to life, and falls in love with her. Attempt to recreate the feeling of old screwball comedies is absolute rock-bottom fare. Dispiriting to anyone who remembers what movie comedy ought to be.▼

Manny's Orphans SEE: **Here Come the Tigers**▼

Man of Aran (1934-British) **77m.** **** D: Robert Flaherty. Colman (Tiger) King, Maggie Dillane. Superb, classic documentary about day-to-day existence, and constant fight for survival, of fisherman in remote Irish coastal community. Scenes at sea are breathtaking.

Man of a Thousand Faces (1957) **122m.** ***½ D: Joseph Pevney. James Cagney, Dorothy Malone, Jane Greer, Marjorie Rambeau, Jim Backus, Snub Pollard, Jeanne Cagney. Surprisingly dedicated, well-acted biography of silent star Lon Chaney. Cagney as Chaney, Malone as disturbed first wife, Greer as wife who brings him happiness, are all fine. Chaney's life and screen career are recreated with taste (if not accuracy). Touching portrayal of movie extra by Rambeau.

Man of Conflict (1953) **72m.** ** D: Hal Makelim. Edward Arnold, John Agar, Susan Morrow, Russell Hicks. Lukewarm drama of generation clash between father Arnold and son Agar over business and philosophy of life.

Man of Conquest (1939) **105m.** **½ D: George Nicholls, Jr. Richard Dix, Gail Patrick, Edward Ellis, Joan Fontaine. Republic Pictures tried to give this biography of Texas' Sam Houston good production values, but script slows down action.

Man of Evil (1944-British) **90m.** ** D: Anthony Asquith. Phyllis Calvert, James Mason, Stewart Granger, Wilfrid Lawson, Jean Kent. Elaborate but ponderous costumer of maniac who tries to run people's lives to

suit his fancy; overdone and not effective. Original title: FANNY BY GASLIGHT.

Man of Flowers, A (1984-Australian) **C-91m.** **½ D: Paul Cox. Norman Kaye, Alyson Best, Chris Haywood, Sarah Walker, Julia Blake, Bob Ellis, Barry Dickins. Kaye, a wealthy flower-loving bachelor with a mother fixation, pays artist's model Best $100 a week to disrobe for him on call. Original but monotonal mix of somberness and silliness; may catch your interest if you're in the right mood. Werner Herzog plays Kaye's father in flashback. ▼

Man of Iron (1956-Italian) **116m.** *** D: Pietro Germi. Pietro Germi, Luisa Della Noce, Sylva Koscina, Carlo Giuffre. Somber account of Germi, railroad engineer, whose life takes a tragic turn, affecting his whole family; realistically presented. Original title: THE RAILROAD MAN.

Man of Iron (1980-Polish) **C-140m.** ***½ D: Andrzej Wajda. Jerzy Radziwilowicz, Krystyna Janda, Marian Opiana. Sequel to MAN OF MARBLE finds documentary filmmaker Janda married to son of the fallen hero whose life she had been researching. Rousing march for Solidarity is not quite up to its predecessor, but two films taken together are as epic in scope as our own GODFATHER sagas. Brief appearance by Lech Walesa as himself.

Man of La Mancha (1972) **C-130m.** BOMB D: Arthur Hiller. Peter O'Toole, Sophia Loren, James Coco, Harry Andrews, John Castle. Plodding, abysmal adaptation of Dale Wasserman's popular musical based on *Don Quixote*, with Joe Darion-Mitch Leigh score. Beautiful source material has been raped, murdered, and buried.▼

Man of Legend (1971-Italian-Spanish) **C-97m.** **½ D: Sergio Grieco. Peter Strauss, Tina Aumont, Luciana Paluzzi, Massimo Serato. WWI German soldier, mistaken for spy and condemned to death, flees to Africa, joins French Foreign Legion, falls in with Moroccan rebels and steals the heart of the chief's daughter. Uninspired sex-and-sand saga.▼

Man of Marble (1977-Polish) **C-160m.** **** D: Andrzej Wajda. Krystyna Janda, Jerzy Radziwilowicz, Tadeusz Lomnicki, Jacek Lomnicki, Krystyna Zachwatowicz. Compelling, controversial, brilliantly directed tale of determined filmmaker Janda retracing the life of Radziwilowicz, naive bricklayer lionized in the 1950s as a worker-hero of the State. Wajda celebrates the role of filmmaker as a speaker of truth; ironically, the film's finale, an explanation of the bricklayer's fate, was excised by the Polish censors. Followed by MAN OF IRON.▼

Man of the West (1958) **C-100m.** *** D: Anthony Mann. Gary Cooper, Julie London, Lee J. Cobb, Arthur O'Connell, Jack Lord, John Dehner, Royal Dano. Dismissed in 1958, this powerful story deserves another look. Cooper plays a reformed outlaw who is forced to rejoin his ex-boss (Cobb) to save himself and other innocent people from the gang's mistreatment. Strong, epic-scale Western, with script by Reginald Rose.

Man of the World (1931) **71m.** ** D: Richard Wallace. William Powell, Carole Lombard, Wynne Gibson, Guy Kibbee, George Chandler. Routine tale of good-girl Lombard in love with con-man Powell. If Carole's performance seems heartfelt it may be due to the fact the two stars married the same year.

Man on a String (1960) **92m.** *** D: Andre de Toth. Ernest Borgnine, Kerwin Mathews, Colleen Dewhurst, Alexander Scourby, Glenn Corbett. Fictionalized account of counterspy Boris Morros, involved in Russian-U.S. Cold War conflict. Taut action sequences.

Man on a String (1971) **C-73m. TVM** D: Joseph Sargent. Christopher George, William Schallert, Joel Grey, Jack Warden, Kitty Winn, Michael Baseleon, Keith Carradine. Undercover government agent maneuvers two Mafia families into confrontation, almost dies when identity is discovered. Predictable. Average.

Man on a Swing (1974) **C-110m.** **½ D: Frank Perry. Cliff Robertson, Joel Grey, Dorothy Tristan, Elizabeth Wilson, George Voskovec. Mysterious clairvoyant (Grey) offers to help a cop (Robertson) solve sex-slaying that's been troubling him, but generates more questions than answers. Intriguing idea sadly misses the mark by building up to an unsatisfying conclusion. Based on a true story.

Man on a Tightrope (1953) **105m.** *** D: Elia Kazan. Fredric March, Gloria Grahame, Terry Moore, Cameron Mitchell, Adolphe Menjou. Atmospheric circus drama of troupe planning to escape from behind the Iron Curtain; sturdy cast.

Man on Fire (1957) **95m.** **½ D: Ranald MacDougall. Bing Crosby, Mary Fickett, Inger Stevens, E.G. Marshall, Malcolm Broderick, Anne Seymour, Richard Eastham. Divorced father (Crosby) refuses to grant his remarried ex-wife partial custody of their son in this modest domestic drama.

Man on Fire (1987-French-Italian) **C-93m.** BOMB D: Elie Chouraqui. Scott Glenn, Jade Malle, Paul Shenar, Brooke Adams, Jonathan Pryce, Joe Pesci, Danny Aiello. International mishmash of pacifist Glenn, hired as young Malle's bodyguard, who turns into a minor league Rambo when she is kidnapped. Good cast wasted.▼

Manon of the Spring (1986-French) **C-113m.** *** D: Claude Berri. Yves Montand, Emmanuelle Beart, Daniel Auteuil, Hippolyte Girardot, Elisabeth Depardieu, Gabriel Bacquier. Conclusion of the story begun in JEAN DE FLORETTE resumes

with Manon, now a beautiful, free-spirited young shepherdess, learning the truth behind her father's death, and plotting her revenge on the pathetic Auteuil and the scheming Montand. Berri spins his story slowly, deliberately, savoring every moment leading to the unexpected conclusion. Only thing missing in this second half is the strong presence of Gerard Depardieu.▼

Man on the Eiffel Tower, The (1949) **C-97m.** *** D: Burgess Meredith. Charles Laughton, Franchot Tone, Burgess Meredith, Robert Hutton, Jean Wallace, Patricia Roc, Wilfrid Hyde-White, Belita. Taut psychological drama filmed in Paris involving cat-and-mouse game between police inspector Maigret (Laughton) and suspected murderer Tone. Based on a Simenon novel. Meredith's first try at directing a feature.▼

Man on the Flying Trapeze, The (1935) **65m.** ***½ D: Clyde Bruckman. W. C. Fields, Mary Brian, Kathleen Howard, Grady Sutton, Vera Lewis, Walter Brennan. Hilarious Fieldsian study in frustration, with able assistance from hardboiled wife Howard, good-for-nothing Sutton. Best sequence has W. C. receiving four traffic tickets in a row!

Man on the Move SEE: **Jigsaw** (1971)▼

Man on the Outside (1975) **C-100m. TVM** D: Boris Sagal. Lorne Greene, James Olson, Lee H. Montgomery, Lorraine Gary, Brooke Bundy. Retired police captain's son is shot down before his eyes and his grandson is kidnapped by a syndicate hit man. Greene is properly strong in the lead; Larry Cohen wrote this pilot to the short-lived series called *Griff.* Average.

Man on the Roof (1977-Swedish) **C-110m.** ***½ D: Bo Widerberg. Gustav Lindstedt, Hakan Serner, Sven Wallter, Thomas Hellberg. A cop killer is the subject of a Stockholm manhunt in this police film with substance and style. Absorbing for its look at police methodology as well as its suspense and action. Based on the Martin Beck novel by Maj Sjowall and Per Wahloo (Walter Matthau played Beck in THE LAUGHING POLICEMAN).

Man or Gun (1958) **79m.** ** D: Albert Gannaway. Macdonald Carey, Audrey Totter, James Craig, James Gleason. Bland Western with Carey cleaning up the town.

Man Outside, The (1968-British) **C-98m.** **½ D: Samuel Gallu. Van Heflin, Heidelinde Weis, Pinkas Braun, Peter Vaughan, Charles Gray, Ronnie Barker. Heflin is fired from CIA job but cannot extricate himself from international tug-of-war over Russian defector; unpretentious spy stuff.▼

Man Outside (1986) **C-109m.** *½ D: Mark Stouffer. Robert Logan, Kathleen Quinlan, Bradford Dillman, Levon Helm, Andrew Barach, Alex Liggett. Why has Logan dropped out and chosen to isolate himself and live off the land in rural Arkansas? Anthropology professor Quinlan decides to find out and promptly falls for him . . . even as he's accused of kidnapping a young boy. Slickly made but obvious, overbaked, and a bore. In addition to Helm, other former members of The Band (Rick Danko, Garth Hudson, Richard Manuel) are in the cast.▼

Manpower (1941) 105m. *** D: Raoul Walsh. Edward G. Robinson, Marlene Dietrich, George Raft, Alan Hale, Walter Catlett, Frank McHugh, Eve Arden. Lively, typical Warner Bros. film, with nightclub "hostess" Dietrich coming between Robinson and Raft. Scene in a diner is worth the price of admission.

Man-Proof (1938) 74m. ** D: Richard Thorpe. Myrna Loy, Franchot Tone, Rosalind Russell, Walter Pidgeon, Nana Bryant, Rita Johnson, Ruth Hussey. Flimsy plot with bright stars: Loy and Russell both love Pidgeon, but Tone is ready to step in any time.

Man's Castle (1933) 66m. ***½ D: Frank Borzage. Spencer Tracy, Loretta Young, Marjorie Rambeau, Arthur Hohl, Walter Connolly, Glenda Farrell, Dickie Moore. Typically lovely Borzage romance; penniless Young moves in with shantytown tough-guy Tracy, hoping to develop a real relationship in spite of his reluctance. Tracy's ultra-macho character is a bit tough to stomach at times, but film's enormous heart conquers all, bolstered by appealing performances. Originally released at 75m.

Man's Favorite Sport? (1964) C-120m. **½ D: Howard Hawks. Rock Hudson, Paula Prentiss, John McGiver, Maria Perschy, Roscoe Karns, Charlene Holt. Amusing, often labored variation on Hawks' own BRINGING UP BABY. Fishing "expert" Hudson, who in reality has never fished, is forced to enter big tournament by pushy Prentiss (in her best performance to date). Loaded with slapstick and sexual innuendo; Norman Alden is hilarious as wisecracking Indian guide.▼

Mansion of the Doomed (1977) C-85m. *½ D: Michael Pataki. Richard Basehart, Gloria Grahame, Trish Stewart, Lance Henriksen, Al Ferrara. Eye surgeon Basehart seeks eyeballs for blinded daughter from hapless victims who pile up in basement. Cheap horror opus.▼

Man They Could Not Hang, The (1939) 72m. **½ D: Nick Grinde. Boris Karloff, Lorna Gray, Robert Wilcox, Roger Pryor, Ann Doran. First of a series of four Karloff vehicles with basically the same plot; hanged man brought back to life seeks revenge on his killers. Good of its type.▼

Man to Man Talk (1958-French) 89m. ** D: Luis Saslavski. Yves Montand, Nicole

Berger, Yves Noel. Trite little tale of father forced to explain facts of life to youngster when mother is having a baby. Retitled: PREMIER MAY.

Man-Trap (1961) 93m. **½ D: Edmond O'Brien. Jeffrey Hunter, David Janssen, Stella Stevens, Hugh Sanders. Capable cast involved in adultery, robbery and disaster; unusual fling at directing by O'Brien.

Manuela SEE: Stowaway Girl

Man Under Suspicion (1984-German) C-126m. **½ D: Norbert Kuckelmann. Maximilian Schell, Lena Stolze, Robert Aldini, Wolfgang Kieling, Kathrin Ackermann, Reinhard Hauff. Lawyer Schell investigates the motives behind a young man's act of violence at a political rally. Provocative subject matter—how the roots of fascism must be destroyed before they are given the opportunity to blossom—but low-keyed to the point of tedium, and much too long, though final twenty minutes are fairly effective.

Man Upstairs, The (1958-British) 88m. *** D: Don Chaffey. Richard Attenborough, Bernard Lee, Donald Houston, Virginia Maskell. Compact study, excellently acted, of Attenborough, a man gone berserk much to everyone's amazement.

Man Who Broke 1,000 Chains, The (1987) C-115m. TVM D: Daniel Mann. Val Kilmer, Charles Durning, Sonia Braga, James Keach, Elisha Cook, William Sanderson, Kyra Sedgewick. The episodic adventures of Robert Elliot Burns, whose life inspired the Paul Muni classic I AM A FUGITIVE FROM A CHAIN GANG, of which this drama is *not* a remake. Made for cable. Average.▼

Man Who Broke the Bank at Monte Carlo, The (1935) 66m. **½ D: Stephen Roberts. Ronald Colman, Joan Bennett, Colin Clive, Nigel Bruce, Montagu Love, Ferdinand Gottschalk. Flimsy film carried by Colman charm, translating famous title song into story of man who calculates to clean out treasury of Riviera gambling establishment.

Man Who Came to Dinner, The (1941) 112m. ***½ D: William Keighley. Bette Davis, Ann Sheridan, Monty Woolley, Billie Burke, Jimmy Durante, Richard Travis, Grant Mitchell, Mary Wickes, Elizabeth Fraser, Reginald Gardiner. Pompous critic Woolley (recreating his Broadway role) is forced to stay with Burke's Midwestern family for the winter, driving them crazy with assorted wacky friends passing through. Delightful adaptation of George S. Kaufman-Moss Hart play. Scripted by the Epstein brothers.▼

Man Who Changed His Mind SEE: **Man Who Lived Again, The**▼

Man Who Cheated Himself, The (1950) 81m. **½ D: Felix E. Feist. Lee J. Cobb,

Jane Wyatt, John Dall, Terry Frost. Good cast uplifts typical murder film.

Man Who Could Cheat Death, The (1959-British) **C-83m.** **½ D: Terence Fisher. Anton Diffring, Hazel Court, Christopher Lee, Arnold Marle, Delphi Lawrence. OK remake of THE MAN IN HALF MOON STREET, about sculptor with somewhat messy method of retarding the aging process; typical Hammer production.

Man Who Could Talk to Kids, The (1973) **C-74m.** TVM D: Donald Wrye. Peter Boyle, Scott Jacoby, Robert Reed, Collin Wilcox-Horne, Tyne Daly, Denise Nickerson, Jack Wade. Parents upset by their withdrawn, rebellious teen-age son, must resort to social worker (Boyle) to reunite family. Documentary approach to direction enhances effect. Above average.

Man Who Could Work Miracles, The (1937-British) **82m.** ***½ D: Lothar Mendes. Roland Young, Ralph Richardson, Joan Gardner, Ernest Thesiger, Wallace Lupino, George Zucco, Bernard Nedell. H. G. Wells' fantasy of timid British department store clerk (Young) endowed with power to do anything he wants. Special effects are marvelous, supported by good cast, in charming film.▼

Man Who Cried Wolf, The (1937) **66m.** **½ D: Lewis R. Foster. Lewis Stone, Tom Brown, Barbara Read, Robert Gleckler, Forrester Harvey. Hammy actor Stone confesses to various murders, convinces cops he's crazy, planning perfect alibi for real killing. Cheaply filmed; Stone is mainstay of film, with Marjorie Main in good supporting role as society woman.

Man Who Dared, The (1933) **75m.** **½ D: Hamilton McFadden. Preston Foster, Zita Johann, Joan Marsh, Frank Sheridan. Modest but engrossing film based on life of Anton Cermak, Polish immigrant who became Chicago mayor and died when hit by bullet intended for FDR. Foster is excellent.

Man Who Died Twice, The (1958) **70m.** ** D: Joseph Kane. Rod Cameron, Vera Ralston, Mike Mazurki, Gerald Milton. Ralston's last film to date is mild account of chanteuse involved in murder.

Man Who Died Twice, The (1970) **C-100m.** TVM D: Joseph Sargent. Stuart Whitman, Brigitte Fossey, Jeremy Slate, Bernard Lee, Severn Darden, Peter Damon. Odd plot features Whitman as aimless drifter and painter in Spain, attracted to depressed French girl, unaware of her love's shady background. Various well-conceived supporting characters make lead character's previous life interesting, but film as whole fails to jell. Average.

Man Who Fell to Earth, The (1976-British) **C-140m.** ***½ D: Nicolas Roeg. David Bowie, Rip Torn, Candy Clark, Buck Henry, Bernie Casey, Jackson D. Kane. Title character ostensibly heads world conglomerate, but is actually here to find water for his planet. Highly original, fabulously photographed adaptation of Walter Tevis' classic fantasy novel is riveting for the first two-thirds, goes downhill toward the end. Still tops of its kind. Originally released in the U.S. at 118m. Remade a decade later as a TV movie.▼

Man Who Fell to Earth, The (1987) **C-100m.** TVM D: Robert J. Roth. Lewis Smith, Beverly D'Angelo, Wil Wheaton, Annie Potts, James Laurenson, Robert Picardo, Bruce McGill. Pilot to a prospective series based on the Nicolas Roeg/David Bowie cult classic but only a fraction as imaginative. Adapted by Richard Kletter from Walter Tevis' sci-fi novel. Average.

Man Who Finally Died, The (1962-British) **100m.** ** D: Quentin Lawrence. Stanley Baker, Peter Cushing, Mai Zetterling, Eric Portman, Niall MacGinnis, Nigel Green, Barbara Everest. Tepid attempt at Hitchcock-like thriller: Baker returns to German home town and tries to discover what happened to his father during WW2.

Man Who Had Power Over Women, The (1970-British) **C-89m.** **½ D: John Krish. Rod Taylor, James Booth, Carol White, Penelope Horner, Charles Korvin, Clive Francis, Magali Noel. Seriocomic satire about an executive with ethics in a London talent agency. Andrew Meredith's script (from the Gordon Williams novel) tends toward overstatement, which a good cast tries to moderate.▼

Man Who Haunted Himself, The (1970-British) **C-94m.** ** D: Basil Dearden. Roger Moore, Hildegard Neil, Alastair Mackenzie, Hugh Mackenzie, Kevork Malikyan. Strange psychological drama about Moore encountering a duplicate of himself in the aftermath of a car crash. Mildly interesting; good location footage of London.▼

Man Who Knew Too Much, The (1934-British) **75m.** *** D: Alfred Hitchcock. Leslie Banks, Edna Best, Peter Lorre, Nova Pilbeam, Frank Vosper, Pierre Fresnay. Film buffs argue which version of exciting story is better. We vote this one, with Hitchcock in fine form weaving dry British humor into a story of heart-pounding suspense; young girl is kidnapped to prevent her parents from revealing what they've learned about assassination plot.▼

Man Who Knew Too Much, The (1956) **C-120m.** **½ D: Alfred Hitchcock. James Stewart, Doris Day, Brenda De Banzie, Bernard Miles, Ralph Truman, Daniel Gelin, Alan Mowbray, Carolyn Jones, Hillary Brooke. Hitchcock's remake of his 1934 film is disappointing. Even famous Albert Hall murder sequence rings flat in tale of American couple accidentally involved in international intrigue. Doris's "Que Sera, Sera" won Jay Livingston and

Ray Evans the Best Song Oscar. That's Bernard Herrmann conducting the orchestra at the climax. ▼

Man Who Lived Again, The (1936-British) **61m.** *** D: Robert Stevenson. Boris Karloff, Anna Lee, John Loder, Frank Cellier, Lyn Harding, Cecil Parker. Mad doctor Karloff has been transferring personalities from one monkey to another. How soon will he be experimenting with human subjects? Solid, above-par chiller. Original British title: THE MAN WHO CHANGED HIS MIND.▼

Man Who Lived at the Ritz, The (1988-British) **C-200m.** TVM D: Desmond Davis. Perry King, Leslie Caron, Cherie Lunghi, David McCallum, David Robb, Patachou, Mylene Demongeot, Sophie Barjac, Joss Ackland. American art student in WW2 Paris tries to shut out the Nazi threat and continue living in opulence at the Ritz Hotel. A not-so-hot version of A. E. Hotchner's novel, with arrogant King hobnobbing with Coco Chanel (Caron), Hermann Goering (Ackland) and Mme. Ritz herself (legendary French chanteuse Patachou). Originally shown in two parts. Average.

Man Who Lived Twice, The (1936) **73m.** **½ D: Harry Lachman. Ralph Bellamy, Marian Marsh, Thurston Hall, Isabel Jewell, Nana Bryant, Ward Bond. Killer (Bellamy) ditches his cohorts, undergoes brain surgery which literally changes him into a new man. Interesting premise should have made for better film. Remade as MAN IN THE DARK.

Man Who Loved Cat Dancing, The (1973) **C-122m.** *** D: Richard C. Sarafian. Burt Reynolds, Sarah Miles, George Hamilton, Lee J. Cobb, Jack Warden, Bo Hopkins, Robert Donner, Jay Silverheels. Western tale of defiant woman who leaves her husband and takes up riding along with a band of outlaws. Sluggish in spots, but enjoyable; script by Eleanor Perry.▼

Man Who Loved Redheads, The (1955-British) **C-103m.** *** D: Harold French. John Justin, Moira Shearer, Roland Culver, Denholm Elliott, Harry Andrews, Patricia Cutts. Delightful British comedy written by Terence Rattigan about a man with lifelong crush on redheads, dating back to boyhood meeting with beautiful Shearer. American print runs 89m.

Man Who Loved Women, The (1977-French) **C-119m.** *** D: Francois Truffaut. Charles Denner, Brigitte Fossey, Nelly Borgeaud, Leslie Caron, Genevieve Fontanel. Charming, sophisticated comedy about a bachelor who is obsessed with women and, it turns out, they with him. To make sense of the fact that he falls in love with almost every woman he meets, he writes his autobiography. Remade in 1983.▼

Man Who Loved Women, The (1983)

C-110m. ** D: Blake Edwards. Burt Reynolds, Julie Andrews, Kim Basinger, Marilu Henner, Barry Corbin, Cynthia Sikes, Jennifer Edwards, Tracy Vaccaro. Lackluster, snail's pace remake of the Francois Truffaut film—minus the climactic revelation that gave the earlier movie its point. Reynolds gives one of his most appealing performances, but spends an eternity discussing his adoration of women with stone-faced psychoanalyst Andrews. Director-writer Edwards gave co-screenplay credit to his own psychiatrist!▼

Man Who Never Was, The (1956-British) **C-103m.** *** D: Ronald Neame. Clifton Webb, Gloria Grahame, Robert Flemyng, Josephine Griffin, Stephen Boyd. Good WW2 spy yarn based on true story of Allies planting elaborate red herring to divert attention from invasion of Sicily.

Man Who Played God, The (1932) **81m.** **½ D: John G. Adolfi. George Arliss, Bette Davis, Violet Heming, Louise Closser Hale, Donald Cook, Ray Milland. Well-acted tale of musician Arliss going deaf, infatuated student Davis sticking by him. Not as stagy as other Arliss films, with Bette getting her first big break and young Milland in a small role. Remade as SINCERELY YOURS.

Man Who Reclaimed His Head, The (1934) **80m.** *** D: Edward Ludwig. Claude Rains, Lionel Atwill, Joan Bennett, Baby Jane, Henry O'Neill, Wallace Ford. Odd drama adapted from Jean Bart stage play, told in flashback. Struggling writer and advocate of world peace used by capitalists (led by Atwill) to their own, selfish ends. Unusual story well acted, especially by Rains, but too slowly paced.

Man Who Shot Liberty Valance, The (1962) **119m.** **** D: John Ford. James Stewart, John Wayne, Vera Miles, Lee Marvin, Edmond O'Brien, Andy Devine, Woody Strode, Jeanette Nolan, Ken Murray, John Qualen, Strother Martin, Lee Van Cleef, John Carradine, Carleton Young. Tenderfoot lawyer Stewart helps civilize the West, but needs help from he-man Wayne to do so. Panned and patronized upon original release, but now regarded as an American classic by virtually every Ford scholar; one of the great Westerns. Producer Willis Goldbeck and James Warner Bellan adapted Dorothy Johnson's story.▼

Man Who Skied Down Everest, The (1976-Japanese) **C-86m.** **½ D: Bruce Nyznik. Irresistible idea for a documentary (Japanese sports figure Yuichiro Miura's 1970 skiing expedition) sabotaged by inane narration on soundtrack of English language version. Oscar winner for Best Documentary.▼

Man Who Talked Too Much, The (1940) **75m.** **½ D: Vincent Sherman. George

Brent, Virginia Bruce, Brenda Marshall, Richard Barthelmess, William Lundigan, George Tobias. Good courtroom drama with D.A. Brent and lawyer Lundigan, brothers fighting same case. Remake of THE MOUTHPIECE, made again as ILLEGAL.

Man Who Turned to Stone, The (1957) 80m. BOMB D: Leslie Kardos. Victor Jory, Ann Doran, Charlotte Austin, William Hudson, Paul Cavanagh, Jean Willes, Victor Varconi. Jory and his followers stay immortal by siphoning off the life forces of others. If they don't get renewed, they petrify. So does the movie.

Man Who Understood Women, The (1959) C-105m. **½ D: Nunnally Johnson. Leslie Caron, Henry Fonda, Cesare Danova, Myron McCormick, Marcel Dalio, Conrad Nagel. Unsatisfactory narrative of movie-maker genius Fonda who hasn't slightest notion of how to treat wife Caron.

Man Who Wagged His Tail, The (1957-Spanish-Italian) 91m. **½ D: Ladislao Vajda. Peter Ustinov, Pablito Calvo, Aroldo Tieri, Silvia Marco. Scrooge-like slumlord Ustinov is transformed into a dog. OK fantasy filmed in Madrid and Brooklyn. Released in the U.S. in 1961.▼

Man Who Wanted to Live Forever, The (1970) C-100m. TVM D: John Trent. Stuart Whitman, Sandy Dennis, Burl Ives. New head of heart research center in Canadian wilderness slowly realizes diabolical purpose of current project. Poor climax, script, and dialogue. Average. Jumbled due to cutting from original length used for foreign release. Alternate title: ONLY WAY OUT IS DEAD.

Man Who Wasn't There, The (1983) C-111m. BOMB D: Bruce Malmuth. Steve Guttenberg, Jeffrey Tambor, Lisa Langlois, Art Hindle, Morgan Hart, Bill Forsythe, Vincent Baggetta. Inept—not to mention inane—invisibility comedy that touted its 3D effects but offered little in *any* dimension. Better writing, directing, and acting can be found at a nursery school pageant.▼

Man Who Watched Trains Go By SEE: **Paris Express, The**▼

Man Who Would Be King, The (1975) C-129m. *** D: John Huston. Sean Connery, Michael Caine, Christopher Plummer, Saeed Jaffrey, Shakira Caine. Old-fashioned adventure and derring-do from Kipling via Huston: two British soldier-pals try to bamboozle high priests of remote Kafiristan into turning over their riches by convincing them that Connery is a god. Caine and Connery are ideal, and film is entertaining, but lacks the buoyancy to make it another GUNGA DIN.▼

Man Who Wouldn't Die, The (1942) 65m. ** D: Herbert I. Leeds. Lloyd Nolan, Marjorie Weaver, Helene Reynolds, Henry Wilcoxon. Nolan is efficient as wisecracking

detective Mike Shayne with a tougher caper than usual.

Man Who Wouldn't Talk, The (1940) 72m. ** D: David Burton. Lloyd Nolan, Jean Rogers, Onslow Stevens, Eric Blore, Mae Marsh. Routine drama with Nolan refusing to defend himself on murder charge; silly ending. Based on one-act play *The Valiant* filmed in 1929 with Paul Muni.

Man Who Wouldn't Talk, The (1958-British) 97m. *½ D: Herbert Wilcox. Anna Neagle, Anthony Quayle, Zsa Zsa Gabor, Katherine Kath, Dora Bryan. Britain's foremost female lawyer (Neagle) defends Quayle on murder charge, even though he cannot speak, for fear of revealing top-secret information. Dreadful.

Man With a Cloak, The (1951) 81m. **½ D: Fletcher Markle. Barbara Stanwyck, Joseph Cotten, Louis Calhern, Leslie Caron, Jim Backus, Margaret Wycherly, Joe DeSantis. Intriguing little mystery, set in 19th-century N.Y.C.; housekeeper Stanwyck plots to kill Calhern for his money and romances Cotten, whose identity is kept secret until the climax. Not bad, with spooky David Raksin score, but having Barbara sing was a mistake.

Man with a Million (1954-British) C-90m. **½ D: Ronald Neame. Gregory Peck, Jane Griffith, Ronald Squire, A. E. Matthews, Wilfrid Hyde-White, Reginald Beckwith. Often tedious telling of Mark Twain story of American Peck given million-pound note, and the havoc it causes. Original title: THE MILLION POUND NOTE.

Man With Bogart's Face, The (1980) C-106m. **½ D: Robert Day. Robert Sacchi, Michelle Phillips, Olivia Hussey, Franco Nero, Misty Rowe, Victor Buono, Herbert Lom, Sybil Danning, Dick Bakalyan, George Raft, Mike Mazurki, Yvonne DeCarlo, Henry Wilcoxon, Victor Sen Yung, Jay Robinson. Offbeat mystery about present-day detective who has plastic surgery to resemble his idol and immediately becomes involved in MALTESE FALCON-esque case. Not really a comedy, although it has its lighter moments; good fun, especially for buffs. Adapted from his own novel and produced by Andrew J. Fenady; ironically, Raft's final film. Also known as SAM MARLOWE, PRIVATE EYE.▼

Man with Connections, The (1970-French) C-93m. **½ D: Claude Berri. Guy Bedos, Yves Robert, Rosy Varte, Georges Geret, Zorica Lozic. Good-natured comedy about young Frenchman who tries to use "pull" to make Army hitch as pleasant as possible. Berri's autobiographical film is, like his others, amiable, quietly entertaining.

Man With My Face, The (1951) 86m. ** D: Edward Montagne. Barry Nelson, Lynn Ainley, John Harvey, Carole Mathews. Good plot idea not handled too well; predicament of businessman who discovers lookalike has taken over his life completely.

Man with Nine Lives, The (1940) 73m. **½ D: Nick Grinde. Boris Karloff, Roger Pryor, Jo Ann Sayers, Stanley Brown, John Dilson, Hal Taliaferro. Scientist Karloff seeks cure for cancer by freezing bodies in suspended animation. Hokey, but fun when Karloff himself thaws out. Also known as BEHIND THE DOOR.

Man With One Red Shoe, The (1985) C-93m. ** D: Stan Dragoti. Tom Hanks, Dabney Coleman, Lori Singer, Charles Durning, Carrie Fisher, Edward Herrmann, Jim Belushi, Irving Metzman, Gerrit Graham, David L. Lander, David Ogden Stiers. Flat remake of THE TALL BLOND MAN WITH ONE BLACK SHOE, about an innocent guy wrongly targeted by CIA types for elimination. Wastes the considerable comic talents of its cast—and doesn't allow leading man Hanks to be funny at all!▼

Man Without a Country, The (1973) C-78m. TVM D: Delbert Mann. Cliff Robertson, Beau Bridges, Peter Strauss, Robert Ryan, Walter Abel, John Cullum, Geoffrey Holder, Shepperd Strudwick, Patricia Elliott. Tour-de-force performance by Robertson as Philip Nolan makes this Sidney Carroll adaptation of the Edward Everett Hale classic shine. Not much action but a magnificent character study. Above average.

Man Without a Star (1955) C-89m. *** D: King Vidor. Kirk Douglas, Jeanne Crain, Claire Trevor, Richard Boone, Jay C. Flippen, William Campbell. Rugged Western with individualist Douglas helping Crain keep her ranch land, dallying with saloon girl Trevor. Remade as A MAN CALLED GANNON.▼

Man with the Balloons, The (1968-Italian-French) 85m. ** D: Marco Ferreri. Marcello Mastroianni, Catherine Spaak. Mastroianni plays successful businessman who loses his girl, eventually goes mad because he becomes obsessed with finding out how much air a balloon needs before it bursts. Offbeat idea, to be sure, but result is just plain silly.

Man With the Golden Arm, The (1955) 119m. *** D: Otto Preminger. Frank Sinatra, Eleanor Parker, Kim Novak, Darren McGavin, Arnold Stang, Doro Merande. Then-daring film of drug addiction is now dated, but still powerful; Sinatra is the junkie, Parker the crippled wife. Memorable Elmer Bernstein jazz score.▼

Man With the Golden Gun, The (1974-British) C-125m. *** D: Guy Hamilton. Roger Moore, Christopher Lee, Britt Ekland, Maud Adams, Herve Villechaize, Clifton James, Richard Loo, Marc Lawrence, Bernard Lee, Lois Maxwell, Desmond Llewelyn. Moore's second shot as super agent James Bond is good, gimmicky fun but the actor had one more film to go (THE SPY WHO LOVED ME) before actually growing into the character; Lee is excellent as assassin Scaramanga. Great car stunts, worldwide locales.▼

Man With the Gun (1955) 83m. **½ D: Richard Wilson. Robert Mitchum, Jan Sterling, Angie Dickinson, Barbara Lawrence, Karen Sharpe, Henry Hull. Mitchum as lawman who brings peace to a Western town is the whole show.

Man With the Power, The (1977) C-100m. TVM D: Nicholas Sgarro. Bob Neill, Persis Khambatta, Tim O'Connor, Vic Morrow, Roger Perry. High school teacher discovers he has inherited superhuman powers from his dad, a native of another planet, and is made an operative of a secret government agency. Entertaining *Six Million Dollar Man* clone. Average.

Man With the Synthetic Brain, The SEE: **Blood of Ghastly Horror**▼

Man With Two Brains, The (1983) C-93m. *** D: Carl Reiner. Steve Martin, Kathleen Turner, David Warner, Paul Benedict, Richard Brestoff, James Cromwell, George Furth, Randi Brooks. While trapped in a loveless marriage with venal Turner, brilliant surgeon Michael Hfuhruhurr (Martin) falls in love with a brain in a jar (voiced by Sissy Spacek) and immediately starts searching for a new "home" for it. As silly as it sounds, but put your brain in neutral and the laughs are there, particularly the decor of Warner's condo and the identity of "The Elevator Killer."▼

Man With Two Faces, The (1934) 72m. **½ D: Archie Mayo. Edward G. Robinson, Mary Astor, Ricardo Cortez, Mae Clarke, Louis Calhern. Minor but entertaining yarn (from a play by Alexander Woollcott and George S. Kaufman) about a ham actor who tries to protect his sister from her sinister husband.

Man, Woman and Child (1983) C-99m. *** D: Dick Richards. Martin Sheen, Blythe Danner, Sebastian Dungan, Arlene McIntyre, Missy Francis, Craig T. Nelson, David Hemmings, Nathalie Nell. Unabashed tearjerker (from Erich Segal's book) about a happily married man, with two children, who learns that a brief affair he had with a Frenchwoman ten years ago produced a son—and that the boy has just been orphaned. Simple, honestly sentimental movie.▼

Manxman, The (1929-British) 90m. **½ D: Alfred Hitchcock. Carl Brisson, Malcolm Keen, Anny Ondra, Randle Ayrton. Fisherman Brisson and lawyer Keen, best friends since childhood, both love Ondra. OK melodrama was Hitchcock's last silent film.▼

Many Happy Returns (1934) 60m. **½ D: Norman McLeod. George Burns, Gracie

[727]

Allen, Joan Marsh, George Barbier, Franklin Pangborn, Ray Milland, William Demarest, Guy Lombardo and His Royal Canadians. Gracie wants to replace father's department store with a bird sanctuary! Typically silly Burns and Allen comedy, with Lombardo providing the music. For Larry Adler's harmonica number, Guy Lombardo's band appears on screen, but the music was performed by Duke Ellington!

Many Happy Returns (1986) **C-100m.** TVM D: Steven Hilliard Stern. George Segal, Ron Leibman, Helen Shaver, Walter Olkewicz, Linda Sorenson, Sean McCann. Sprightly but mean-spirited comedy about an average Joe whose middle-class existence is turned into a nightmare by an IRS audit—until he decides to fight back. Segal and Leibman, as sparring in-laws, make a dandy pair in their third teaming. Average.

Many Rivers to Cross (1955) **C-92m.** **½ D: Roy Rowland. Robert Taylor, Eleanor Parker, Victor McLaglen, James Arness, Josephine Hutchinson, Rosemary DeCamp. Parker shows more vim and vigor than Taylor in this 1800s Western, centering on her yen for him.

Maracaibo (1958) **C-88m.** **½ D: Cornel Wilde. Cornel Wilde, Jean Wallace, Abbe Lane, Francis Lederer, Michael Landon. Wilde is expert firefighter who goes to Venezuela to combat oil blaze, romancing ex-girlfriend between action scenes.

Mara Maru (1952) **98m.** **½ D: Gordon Douglas. Errol Flynn, Ruth Roman, Raymond Burr, Richard Webb, Nestor Paiva. Turgid adventure pits Flynn against Burr as they vie for sunken treasure, with Roman the love interest.

Mara of the Wilderness (1965) **C-90m.** **½ D: Frank McDonald. Adam West, Linda Saunders, Theo Marcuse, Denver Pyle, Sean McClory. Sometimes diverting account of Saunders, who grew up in the wild north country, with West trying to rehabilitate her.▼

Marathon (1980) **C-100m.** TVM D: Jackie Cooper. Bob Newhart, Leigh Taylor-Young, Herb Edelman, Dick Gautier, Anita Gillette, John Hillerman. Flat comedy about a happily married middle-aged stockbroker whose head is turned by a pretty young thing and is encouraged to move from casual jogging to marathon running. Average.▼

Marathon Man (1976) **C-125m.** **½ D: John Schlesinger. Dustin Hoffman, Laurence Olivier, Roy Scheider, William Devane, Marthe Keller, Fritz Weaver. Glossy thriller adapted by William Goldman from his book. Basic premise of graduate student Hoffman propelled into dizzying world of international intrigue spoiled by repellent violence and some gaping story holes. Hoffman and arch-villain Olivier are superb but film doesn't do them justice.▼

Marat/Sade (Persecution and Assassination of Jean-Paul Marat as Performed by the Inmates of the Asylum of Charenton Under the Direction of the Marquis de Sade, The) (1966-British) **C-115m.** **** D: Peter Brook. Patrick Magee, Clifford Rose, Glenda Jackson, Ian Richardson, Brenda Kempner, Ruth Baker, Michael Williams, Freddie Jones. Chilling adaptation of Peter Weiss play about "performance" staged by inmates of French insane asylum, under direction of Marquis de Sade. Lurid atmosphere is so vivid that it seems actors are breathing down your neck; brilliantly directed by Brook. Not for weak stomachs. Screenplay by Adrian Mitchell; Jackson's film debut.▼

Marauders, The (1955) **C-81m.** ** D: Gerald Mayer. Dan Duryea, Jeff Richards, Keenan Wynn, Jarma Lewis. OK story of rancher fighting against greedy cattle ranchers.

March of the Wooden Soldiers SEE: **Babes in Toyland** (1934)▼

March or Die (1977) **C-104m.** ** D: Dick Richards. Gene Hackman, Terence Hill, Max von Sydow, Catherine Deneuve, Ian Holm. Homage to French Foreign Legion adventures of filmdom's past. Good cast wages losing battle with static script and walks downheartedly through action scenes. Disappointing epic-that-might-have-been. Additional footage tacked on for network showing.▼

Marciano (1979) **C-100m.** TVM D: Bernard L. Kowalski. Tony Lo Bianco, Belinda J. Montgomery, Vincent Gardenia, Richard Herd, Dolph Sweet. The story of heavyweight champ Rocky Marciano—the only fighter to retire from the ring undefeated with a perfect record. The focus here is on his less-than-enthralling private life, and the romantic slush sends Rocky down for the long count. Average.▼

Marco (1973) **C-109m.** ** D: Seymour Robbie. Desi Arnaz, Jr., Jack Weston, Zero Mostel. Lavish but lumbering musical, filmed on Oriental locations, with Arnaz as young Marco Polo and Mostel as Kublai Khan. Disappointing.▼

Marco Polo (1962-Italian) **C-90m.** **½ D: Hugo Fregonese. Rory Calhoun, Yoko Tani, Robert Hundar, Camillo Pilotto, Pierre Cressoy, Michael Chow. Unspectacular epic about medieval adventurer and his journey to China. Calhoun and film lack needed vigor.

Marco the Magnificent (1966) **C-100m.** **½ D: Denys De La Patelliere, Noel Howard. Horst Buchholz, Anthony Quinn, Omar Sharif, Elsa Martinelli, Akim Tamiroff, Orson Welles. Laughable mini-epic, extremely choppy, with episodic sequences pretending to recount events in life of medieval adventurer.

Marcus-Nelson Murders, The (1973) **148m.** TVM D: Joseph Sargent. Telly

Savalas, Marjoe Gortner, Jose Ferrer, Ned Beatty, Allen Garfield, Lorraine Gary, Gene Woodbury, Chita Rivera. Top-notch thriller about hard-boiled detective's efforts to keep a ghetto teenager from being wrongly convicted of murder. Based on real life Wylie-Hoffert murders in N.Y. in 1963, it became pilot for long-running *Kojak* series, won Emmys for director Sargent and writer Abby Mann, and stardom for Savalas. Also known as KOJAK AND THE MAR-CUS-NELSON MURDERS; the Kojak character was reprised twelve years later in KOJAK: THE BELARUS FILE. Above average.

Marcus Welby, M.D. (1968) **C-100m.** TVM D: David Lowell Rich. Robert Young, James Brolin, Anne Baxter, Peter Duel, Susan Strasberg, Lew Ayres. When neighborhood doctor, after suffering mild coronary, finally hires assistant to lighten work load, help turns out to be as irascible and stubborn as himself. No different from the subsequent TV series. Retitled A MATTER OF HUMANITIES, and followed years later by THE RETURN OF MARCUS WELBY. Average.

Marcus Welby, M.D.: A Holiday Affair (1988) **C-100m.** TVM D: Steven Gethers. Robert Young, Alexis Smith, Craig Stevens, Delphine Forest, Robert Hardy, Betsy Blair. Retired Marcus Welby finds romance in France with American divorcée Smith, who dumps a suitor (played by her real-life husband Stevens) for him. Not much in common with the Welby TV series, but a decent-enough vehicle for Young. Average.

Mardi Gras (1958) **C-107m.** **½ D: Edmund Goulding. Pat Boone, Christine Carere, Tommy Sands, Sheree North, Gary Crosby. Perky, unpretentious musical with energetic cast. Boone wins military school raffle date with movie star Carere.

Margaret Bourke-White (1989) **C-105m.** TVM D: Lawrence Schiller. Farrah Fawcett, Frederic Forrest, Mitchell Ryan, David Huddleston, Jay Patterson, Ken Marshall. Languid, picturesque biopic of the ambitious camera bug who pursued her dream of becoming a professional photographer, and made a name for herself shooting pictures for *Life* magazine in the 1930s and '40s . . . while juggling an affair with writer Erskine Caldwell. Fawcett is more believable in her romantic scenes with Forrest than she is setting up tripods and determining F-stops in this adaptation of Vicki Goldberg's biography. Made for cable. Average.▼

Margie (1946) **C-94m.** *** D: Henry King. Jeanne Crain, Glenn Langan, Lynn Bari, Esther Dale, Hobart Cavanaugh, Alan Young, Barbara Lawrence, Conrad Janis. Colorful, entertaining nostalgia about teen-

agers in the Roaring Twenties, with lots of good songs.

Margin for Error (1943) **74m.** ** D: Otto Preminger. Joan Bennett, Milton Berle, Otto Preminger, Carl Esmond, Howard Freeman, Ed McNamara. Dated, awkward "comedy" of Jewish cop Berle assigned to guard German consul in N.Y.C. during WW2. Director Preminger should have told actor Preminger to stop overacting.

Margin for Murder SEE: **Mickey Spillane's Margin for Murder**

Marianne (1929) **112m.** *** D: Robert Z. Leonard. Marion Davies, George Baxter, Lawrence Gray, Cliff Edwards, Benny Rubin. Davies' first talkie also one of her best; fine vehicle for her charm and comic talent as French girl pursued by two American soldiers during WW1.

Marianne and Juliane (1982-German) **C-106m.** ***½ D: Margarethe von Trotta. Jutta Lampe, Barbara Sukowa, Rudiger Vogler, Doris Schade, Franz Rudnick. Profound, multileveled, and memorable chronicle of the relationship between two sisters, alike in some ways yet so very different in others. Juliane (Lampe) is a feminist editor working within the system; Marianne (Sukowa) is a radical political terrorist. Superbly acted, a must-see.

Marian Rose White (1982) **C-100m.** TVM D: Robert Day. Nancy Cartwright, Valerie Perrine, Katharine Ross, Charles Aidman, Frances Lee McCain, Louis Giambalvo, John Considine, Anne Ramsey. True story of a normal teenager who was dumped into a home for the feebleminded by her widowed mother and spent the next 30 years there (condensed to just four in this movie). Cartwright is excellent as the teenaged Marian but hampered by Garry Rusoff's weak script. Average.

Maria's Lovers (1984) **C-100m.** ** D: Andrei Konchalovsky. Nastassia Kinski, John Savage, Robert Mitchum, Keith Carradine, Anita Morris, Bud Cort, Tracy Nelson, Vincent Spano. Young soldier returns home from WW2, after suffering nervous breakdown, and finds himself unable to consummate his love with new bride. Richly atmospheric film, set in Pennsylvania mining town, has fine performances and other attributes, but is unrelievedly ponderous. Opening sequence cleverly integrates footage from John Huston's famous documentary LET THERE BE LIGHT with newly shot material of Savage.▼

Marie (1985) **C-112m.** *** D: Roger Donaldson. Sissy Spacek, Jeff Daniels, Keith Szarabajka, Morgan Freeman, Fred Thompson, Don Hood, John Cullum. Solid drama about divorcée and mother of three who takes a job in Tennessee state government, then blows the whistle on corruption and finds herself in very hot water. Might be hard to believe if it wasn't true (though knowing the outcome of the case will certainly remove a lot of the suspense). Based on Peter Maas' book; defense attorney Fred Thompson plays himself.▼

Marie Antoinette (1938) **149m. **½ D:** W. S. Van Dyke II. Norma Shearer, Tyrone Power, John Barrymore, Robert Morley, Gladys George, Anita Louise, Joseph Schildkraut. Opulent MGM production of life of 18th-century French queen lacks pace but has good acting, with great performance by Morley as Louis XVI. Shearer captures essence of title role as costumer retells her life from Austrian princess to doomed queen of crumbling empire.▼

Marie Antoinette (1955-French) **C-108m. **½ D:** Jean Delannoy. Michele Morgan, Richard Todd, Jean Morel. Epic on life of famed 18th-century French queen has marvelous Morgan in title role but lacks perspective and scope.

"Marihuana" (1936) **58m.** BOMB D: Dwain Esper. Harley Wood, Hugh McArthur, Pat Carlyle, Paul Ellis, Dorothy Dehn, Richard Erskine. Some naive, fun-loving kids puff on the title weed, offered them by a man you know is evil incarnate because he has a mustache, and the result is nude swimming, a drowning . . . and worse! This exploitation fare is a real scream, almost mind-boggling in its dopiness. And don't forget that it was researched "with the help of federal, state and police narcotic officers." A companion piece to REEFER MADNESS. Originally titled "MARIJUANA"—THE DEVIL'S WEED.▼

Marilyn (1963) **83m. **½ Narrated by Rock Hudson. Standard, often patronizing documentary on Marilyn Monroe built around clips from most of her movies, including the unfinished SOMETHING'S GOT TO GIVE.▼

Marilyn: The Untold Story (1980) **C-150m.** TVM D: John Flynn, Jack Arnold, Lawrence Schiller. Catherine Hicks, Richard Basehart, Frank Converse, John Ireland, Viveca Lindfors, Jason Miller, Sheree North, Bill Vint, Anne Ramsey. The second—and far superior—Marilyn Monroe movie, with a sterling MM portrayal by Hicks (Emmy Award-nominated). Dalene Young's script was based on Norman Mailer's Monroe biography. This one gets a special mention as the only TV film crediting three directors! Above average.▼

Marine Issue SEE: **Instant Justice**▼

Marine Raiders (1944) **91m. ** D: Harold D. Schuster. Pat O'Brien, Robert Ryan, Ruth Hussey, Frank McHugh, Barton MacLane. Typical RKO WW2 film, this time focusing on marines training for warfare.▼

Marines, Let's Go (1961) **C-104m.** *½ D: Raoul Walsh. Tom Tryon, David Hedison, Barbara Stuart, William Tyler. Tedium about four soldiers, their comic adventures on leave in Tokyo, and their dramatic encounters on the battlefield in Korea.

Mario Puzo's "The Fortunate Pilgrim" (1988) **C-250m.** TVM D: Stuart Cooper. Sophia Loren, Edward James Olmos, Hal Holbrook, John Turturro, Anna Strasberg, Yorgo Voyagis, Roxann Biggs, Ed Wiley, Mirjana Karanovic, Ron Marquette. Atmospheric adaptation of the novel Puzo wrote prior to The Godfather paced by Loren's strong performance as turn-of-the-century Italian immigrant who brings her family to N.Y.C. (Belgrade, Yugoslavia, stands in for the Big Apple) and spends the next three decades searching for the American dream. Writer John McGreevey kept the saga sprawling, and Reginald Morris's cinematography is impressive. The composers, unfortunately, thought they were scoring grand opera—perhaps because producers Carlo Ponti and son Alex were able to enlist Pavarotti to sing Caruso-style on the soundtrack. Originally shown in two parts. Above average.

Marius (1931-French) **125m. *** D:** Alexander Korda. Raimu, Pierre Fresnay, Charpin, Alida Rouffe, Orane Demazis. Amusing, flavorful if a bit too theatrical satire of provincial life, centering on the love of Marius (Fresnay) for Fanny (Demazis). Raimu is wonderful as Cesar, cafe owner and father of Marius. Screenplay by Marcel Pagnol; first of a trilogy, followed by FANNY and CESAR. All three were the basis of the play and movie FANNY (1961).▼

Marjoe (1972) **C-88m. **½ D:** Howard Smith, Sarah Kernochan. Oscar-winning documentary about life of fake evangelist Marjoe Gortner is certainly interesting, but is a little too pleased with itself, a little too pat to be totally convincing. Marjoe himself is likable enough.▼

Marjorie Morningstar (1958) **C-123m. **½ D:** Irving Rapper. Gene Kelly, Natalie Wood, Claire Trevor, Ed Wynn, Everett Sloane, Carolyn Jones, Martin Milner, Martin Balsam, Ruta Lee. Wood is only adequate as Herman Wouk's heroine in tale of N.Y.C. girl aspiring to greatness but ending up a suburban housewife, with Kelly her summer romance.▼

Mark, The (1961-British) **127m. ***½ D:** Guy Green. Stuart Whitman, Maria Schell, Rod Steiger, Brenda De Banzie, Maurice Denham, Donald Wolfit, Paul Rogers, Donald Houston. Whitman received Oscar nomination for portrayal of emotionally broken sex criminal who has served time, now wants to make new start. Thoughtful, well-acted adult drama written by Sidney Buchman and Stanley Mann.▼

Marked Woman (1937) **99m. *** D:**

Lloyd Bacon. Bette Davis, Humphrey Bogart, Lola Lane, Isabel Jewell, Jane Bryan, Eduardo Ciannelli, Allen Jenkins, Mayo Methot. Bristling gangster drama of D.A. Bogart convincing Bette and four girlfriends to testify against their boss, underworld king Ciannelli.▼

Mark, I Love You (1980) **C-96m. TVM** D: Gunnar Hellstrom. Kevin Dobson, James Whitmore, Cassie Yates, Dana Elcar, Peggy McCay, Molly Cheek. Widower and his dead wife's parents engage in bitter custody battle over his small son. Adapted by Sue Grafton from Hal W. Painter's book, with Dobson playing Painter. Average.

Mark of the Gorilla (1950) **68m.** D: William Berke. Johnny Weissmuller, Trudy Marshall, Onslow Stevens, Selmer Jackson. SEE: **Jungle Jim** series.

Mark of the Hawk, The (1957-British) **C-83m.** *** D: Michael Audley. Eartha Kitt, Sidney Poitier, Juano Hernandez, John McIntire. Unusual tale intelligently acted, set in contemporary Africa, with peaceful vs. violent means for racial equality the main theme. Originally titled ACCUSED.▼

Mark of the Renegade (1951) **C-81m.** **½ D: Hugo Fregonese. Ricardo Montalban, Cyd Charisse, J. Carrol Naish, Gilbert Roland. Peculiar Western tale of 1820s, with Montalban an outlaw who romances Charisse.

Mark of the Vampire (1935) **61m.** *** D: Tod Browning. Lionel Barrymore, Elizabeth Allan, Bela Lugosi, Lionel Atwill, Carol Borland, Jean Hersholt, Donald Meek. Delightful, intriguing tale of vampires terrorizing rural village; inspector Atwill, vampire expert Barrymore investigate. Beautifully done, with an incredible ending. Remake of Browning's silent LONDON AFTER MIDNIGHT.▼

Mark of the Vampire (1957) SEE: **Vampire, The**

Mark of the Whistler, The (1944) **61m.** D: William Castle. Richard Dix, Janis Carter, Porter Hall, Paul Guilfoyle, John Calvert. SEE: **The Whistler** series.

Mark of Zorro, The (1920) **90m.** ***½ D: Fred Niblo. Douglas Fairbanks Sr., Marguerite De La Motte, Noah Beery, Robert McKim, Charles Mailes. Silent classic with Fairbanks as the hero of old California; perhaps Doug's best film. Nonstop fun.▼

Mark of Zorro, The (1940) **93m.** ***½ D: Rouben Mamoulian. Tyrone Power, Linda Darnell, Basil Rathbone, Gale Sondergaard, Eugene Pallette, J. Edward Bromberg. Lavish swashbuckler with Power as foppish son of California aristocrat in 1800s, masquerading as dashing avenger of evil: climactic duel with Rathbone a cinematic gem. Great score by Alfred Newman.

Mark of Zorro, The (1974) **C-78m. TVM**

D: Don McDougall. Frank Langella, Ricardo Montalban, Gilbert Roland, Yvonne de Carlo, Louise Sorel, Anne Archer, Robert Middleton. Langella buckles and swashes in this tepid remake. Montalban is properly villainous, Roland surprisingly spry at wall-scaling. Best of all: unforgettable Alfred Newman musical score from the 1940 film, interpolated here. Average.

Marksman, The (1953) **62m.** *½ D: Lewis D. Collins. Wayne Morris, Elena Verdugo, Frank Ferguson, Rick Vallin. Flabby little tale of Morris, a law enforcer with a telescopic gun, chasing after outlaws.

Marlene (1984-German) **C/B&W-96m.** *** D: Maximilian Schell. Utterly, unexpectedly fascinating look at Marlene Dietrich, built on unusual foundation of a tape-recorded interview with Schell that she refused to allow to be filmed! How Schell turns this liability into an asset for the film—just one of its layers—and how Dietrich reveals so much about herself even in her stubborn rejection of basic interview questions, is all part of the film's mystique (and Marlene's). Includes most of her finest moments on screen.▼

Marlowe (1969) **C-95m.** *** D: Paul Bogart. James Garner, Gayle Hunnicutt, Carroll O'Connor, Rita Moreno, Sharon Farrell, William Daniels, Jackie Coogan, Bruce Lee. Slick updating of Raymond Chandler's *The Little Sister* with Garner as Philip Marlowe, hired by girl to find missing brother. Really belongs in 1940s, but works fairly well; Moreno memorable as stripper who helps solve case in exciting finale, plus hilarious scene where Lee reduces Marlowe's office to rubble.

Marnie (1964) **C-129m.** *** D: Alfred Hitchcock. Sean Connery, Tippi Hedren, Diane Baker, Martin Gabel, Louise Latham, Alan Napier. This story of a habitual thief (Hedren) whose employer (Connery) is determined to understand her illness was considered a misfire in 1964 . . . but there's more than meets the eye, especially for Hitchcock buffs. Script by Jay Presson Allen. Look for Bruce Dern and Mariette Hartley in small roles.▼

Maroc 7 (1967-British) **C-91m.** ** D: Gerry O'Hara. Gene Barry, Elsa Martinelli, Cyd Charisse, Leslie Phillips. Slow robbery-murder tale of secret agent out to catch split-personality thief.

Marooned (1969) **C-134m.** ** D: John Sturges. Gregory Peck, Richard Crenna, James Franciscus, David Janssen, Gene Hackman, Lee Grant, Nancy Kovack, Mariette Hartley. Glossy but disappointing story of astronauts unable to return to earth, while space agency head Peck tries to keep lid from blowing off. Alternately boring and excruciating; climactic scenes in space produce agony, not excitement. Oscar-winning special effects are chief asset.▼

Marquise of O, The (1976-French-German) **C-102m.** *** D: Eric Rohmer. Edith Clever, Bruno Ganz, Peter Luhr, Edda Seippel, Otto Sander. Delicate, disarmingly simple story set in 18th century Italy; a young widow saved from rape by a Russian soldier during Franco-Prussian war finds herself pregnant some months later, and doesn't understand how. Beautiful period flavor, but film's charm is very low-key.

Marriage Circle, The (1924) **90m.** *** D: Ernst Lubitsch. Florence Vidor, Monte Blue, Marie Prevost, Creighton Hale, Adolphe Menjou, Harry Myers, Dale Fuller, Esther Ralston. Classic, influential silent comedy about the flirtations and infidelities of several well-to-do characters in Vienna, the "city of laughter and romance." Lubitsch's initial American comedy of manners, inspired by Chaplin's A WOMAN OF PARIS. Remade by Lubitsch and George Cukor as the musical ONE HOUR WITH YOU. ▼

Marriage-Go-Round, The (1960) **C-98m.** **½ D: Walter Lang. Susan Hayward, James Mason, Julie Newmar, Robert Paige, June Clayworth. Film version of Leslie Stevens' saucy play about marriage: Mason is professor attracted to free-love-oriented Newmar. Amusing, but lacks real bite.

Marriage Is Alive and Well (1980) **C-100m. TVM** D: Russ Mayberry. Joe Namath, Jack Albertson, Melinda Dillon, Judd Hirsch, Susan Sullivan, Fred McCarren, Nicholas Pryor, Swoosie Kurtz. Standard sitcom view of marriage with Namath playing a freelance wedding photographer tying together several occasionally humorous vignettes. Average.▼

Marriage Is a Private Affair (1944) **116m.** ** D: Robert Z. Leonard. Lana Turner, James Craig, John Hodiak, Frances Gifford, Hugh Marlowe, Keenan Wynn. Somewhat dated, glossy MGM yarn of manchasing Turner, not about to be stopped just because she's married.

Marriage Italian-Style (1964-Italian) **C-102m.** *** D: Vittorio De Sica. Sophia Loren, Marcello Mastroianni, Aldo Puglisi, Pia Lindstrom, Vito Moriconi. Spicy account of Loren's efforts to get long-time lover Mastroianni to marry her and stay her husband. Based on Eduardo De Filippo's 1946 play *Filumena*.

Marriage of a Young Stockbroker, The (1971) **C-95m.** **½ D: Lawrence Turman. Richard Benjamin, Joanna Shimkus, Elizabeth Ashley, Adam West, Patricia Barry, Tiffany Bolling. Humorous and sad depiction of marital breakdown; husband indulges in voyeurism, wife has own problems. Good cast working with script that seems uncertain as to what point it wants to drive across. Director Turman, who'd produced THE GRADUATE, hoped lightning would strike twice with this adaptation of novel by same author, Charles Webb.▼

Marriage of Maria Braun, The (1978-German) **C-120m.** ***½ D: Rainer Werner Fassbinder. Hanna Schygulla, Ivan Desny, Gottfried John, Klaus Lowitsch, Gisela Uhlen. Schygulla shines in the Joan Crawfordesque role of a penniless soldier's wife who builds an industrial empire after the end of WW2. Riveting; the first of Fassbinder's three parables of postwar Germany, followed by LOLA and VERONIKA VOSS.▼

Marriage on the Rocks (1965) **C-109m.** **½ D: Jack Donohue. Frank Sinatra, Deborah Kerr, Dean Martin, Cesar Romero, Hermione Baddeley, Tony Bill, Nancy Sinatra, John McGiver, Trini Lopez. Frank and Deborah have marital spat, get quickie Mexican divorce, she ends up married to his best pal, Dino. A waste of real talent.

Marriage: Year One (1971) **C-100m. TVM** D: William Graham. Sally Field, Robert Pratt, Cicely Tyson, William Windom, Agnes Moorehead, Neville Brand. Tedious love story, with modern city important backdrop as two newlyweds try to make it through first tough year. Great supporting cast only asset. Average.

Married Man, A (1984-British) **C-200m. TVM** D: John Davies. Anthony Hopkins, Ciaran Madden, Lise Hilboldt, Yvonne Coulette, John LeMesurier, Sophie Ashton. Veddy-British domestic drama about a bored barrister, his proper wife and his paramour. Mixed in with the suds and lather is a murder, but despite another of Hopkins' always interesting performances, this is a lethargic exercise that easily could have been halved. Originally shown in two parts. Average.▼

Married to the Mob (1988) **C-103m.** *** D: Jonathan Demme. Michelle Pfeiffer, Matthew Modine, Dean Stockwell, Mercedes Ruehl, Alec Baldwin, Joan Cusack, Trey Wilson, Charles Napier, Tracey Walter, Al Lewis. A woman tries to escape from the Mafia after the death of her hitman husband, only to find that the local boss has the hots for her. Amiable, entertaining farce with right-on performances by Pfeiffer and Stockwell (in a neat comic turn as the mafioso). Only director Demme could make a mob movie with likable characters in it! Score by David Byrne.▼

Married Woman, A (1965-French) **94m.** **½ D: Jean-Luc Godard. Macha Meril, Philippe Leroy, Bernard Noel. Turgid three-cornered romance, with Meril involved with husband and lover; pretentious.▼

Marrying Kind, The (1952) **93m.** *** D: George Cukor. Judy Holliday, Aldo Ray,

Madge Kennedy, Mickey Shaughnessy, Griff Barnett. Bittersweet drama of young couple on verge of divorce recalling their life together via flashbacks; sensitive performers outshine soapy script.

Marry Me Again (1953) **73m.** ** D: Frank Tashlin. Robert Cummings, Marie Wilson, Mary Costa, Jess Barker. Mild shenanigans of aviator Cummings and beauty contest winner Wilson's on-again, off-again romance.

Marry Me, Marry Me (1969-French) **C-87m.** *** D: Claude Berri. Elisabeth Wiener, Regine, Claude Berri, Luisa Colpeyn. Delightful story of love and (what else?) marriage, Berri-style.

Marseilles Contract, The SEE: **Destructors, The**▼

Marshal's Daughter, The (1953) **71m.** *½ D: William Berke. Ken Murray, Laurie Anders, Preston Foster, Hoot Gibson. Cornpone oater with Murray and Anders ridding their town of outlaws; Tex Ritter even sings a song, with veteran Gibson in supporting role.▼

Mars Invades Puerto Rico SEE: **Frankenstein Meets the Space Monster**▼

Mars Needs Women (1968) **C-80m.** *½ D: Larry Buchanan. Tommy Kirk, Yvonne Craig, Byron Lord, Roger Ready, Warren Hammack, Anthony Houston. Just as the title suggests, Martians Kirk and four pals, hoping to increase birthrate on their planet, arrive here to capture live women. Strangely sincere but extremely silly and distended. Texas-made film written by the director. Most important revelation: Mars abandoned neckties 50 years ago.▼

Marsupials, The: The Howling III SEE: **Howling III**▼

Martians Go Home (1990) **C-89m.** *½ D: David Odell. Randy Quaid, Margaret Colin, Anita Morris, Barry Sobel, Vic Dunlop, John Philbin, Gerrit Graham, Ronny Cox, Harry Basil. TV songwriter Quaid accidentally summons a billion green wisecracking Martians to Earth; chaos (limited by the film's low budget) ensues. Fredric Brown's classic sci-fi humor novel misfires on the screen, partly because the pesky Martians are all played by mediocre standup comics.▼

Martin (1978) **C-95m.** *** D: George A. Romero. John Amplas, Lincoln Maazel, Christine Forrest, Elayne Nadeau, Tom Savini, Sarah Venable, George A. Romero. Typical Romero mix of social satire and stomach-churning gore: 17-year-old Amplas thinks he's a vampire (lacking fangs, he must resort to razor blades); thanks to his frequent calls to a late-night radio show, he's also something of a local celebrity! Intriguing little shocker is worth seeing, but not right after dinner.▼

Martin's Day (1984-Canadian) **C-98m.** ** D: Alan Gibson. Richard Harris, Lind-

say Wagner, James Coburn, Justin Henry, Karen Black, John Ireland. Creditable cast in utterly ordinary "family film" about escaped prisoner who kidnaps (and ultimately befriends) young boy. Bland and unconvincing.▼

Marty (1955) **91m.** ***½ D: Delbert Mann. Ernest Borgnine, Betsy Blair, Joe Mantell, Joe De Santis, Esther Minciotti, Augusta Ciolli, Karen Steele, Jerry Paris, Frank Sutton. Oscar for Borgnine as Bronx butcher who doesn't hope to find love, but does, in this moving Paddy Chayefsky script, originally a TV play; also won Oscars for Chayefsky, Mann, and Best Picture.▼

Marva Collins Story, The (1981) **C-100m.** TVM D: Peter Levin. Cicely Tyson, Morgan Freeman, Roderick Wimberly, Mashaune Hardy, Brett Bouldin, Samuel Muhammad, Jr., Edward Asner (narrator). Moving drama about the Chicago schoolteacher who gained national recognition for her stunning achievements with ghetto "unteachables" after she and they had abandoned the traditional school system. Glorious performance by Tyson (in a rare contemporary role). Script by Clifford Campion. Above average.

Marvin and Tige (1983) **C-104m.** **½ D: Eric Weston. John Cassavetes, Gibran Brown, Billy Dee Williams, Denise Nicholas Hill, Fay Hauser. Tearjerker about a loser (Cassavetes) who takes in an aimless eleven-year-old (Brown) who tried to kill himself. Well acted, and well intentioned, but pretty standard stuff.▼

Marx Brothers at the Circus SEE: **At the Circus**▼

Marx Brothers Go West SEE: **Go West**▼

Mary and Joseph: A Story of Faith (1979) **C-100m.** TVM D: Eric Till. Blanche Baker, Jeff East, Colleen Dewhurst, Stephen McHattie, Lloyd Bochner, Paul Hecht. Pedestrian what-might-have-been depiction of Biblical events focusing on Christ's parents as a struggling young couple and the early days of their marriage. The leads play it as a pair of American youngsters plunked down in Biblical Nazareth. Below average.▼

Mary Burns, Fugitive (1935) **84m.** *** D: William K. Howard. Sylvia Sidney, Melvyn Douglas, Pert Kelton, Alan Baxter, Wallace Ford, Brian Donlevy. Fine gangster melodrama. Sidney is dragged into underworld, valiantly tries to escape her gangster lover (Baxter).

Maryjane (1968) **C-104m.** *½ D: Maury Dexter. Fabian, Diane McBain, Michael Margotta, Kevin Coughlin, Patty McCormack, Terri (Teri) Garr. 1960s version of REEFER MADNESS casts Fabian as high school art teacher who tries to keep his students from smoking grass; film is terrible, but may play better if you're stoned.

Mary Jane Harper Cried Last Night (1977) **C-100m. TVM** D: Allen Reisner. Susan Dey, Bernie Casey, Tricia O'Neil, John Vernon, Kevin McCarthy, Natasha Ryan, Rhea Perlman. Drama about child abuse benefits from a sensitive Joanna Lee script and sincere performances by all involved. Average.

Maryland (1940) **C-92m.** **½ D: Henry King. Walter Brennan, Fay Bainter, Brenda Joyce, John Payne, Charles Ruggles, Marjorie Weaver. Predictable story given elaborate treatment. Bainter refuses to let son Payne ride horses since his father was killed that way. Beautiful color scenery.

Mary, Mary (1963) **C-126m.** **½ D: Mervyn LeRoy. Debbie Reynolds, Barry Nelson, Michael Rennie, Diane McBain, Hiram Sherman. Unremarkable, stagy adaptation of Jean Kerr's sex comedy about divorced couple trying to screw up each other's new romances. Stick with THE AWFUL TRUTH.

Mary of Scotland (1936) **123m.** ***½ D: John Ford. Katharine Hepburn, Fredric March, Florence Eldridge, Douglas Walton, John Carradine, Robert Barrat. Lavish, excellent historical drama, with Hepburn playing Scottish queen sentenced to death by jealous English rival Elizabeth.▼

Mary Poppins (1964) **C-140m.** **** D: Robert Stevenson. Julie Andrews, Dick Van Dyke, David Tomlinson, Glynis Johns, Ed Wynn, Hermione Baddeley, Karen Dotrice, Matthew Garber, Arthur Treacher, Reginald Owen. There's charm, wit, and movie magic to spare in Walt Disney's adaptation of P.L. Travers's book about a "practically perfect" nanny who brings profound change to the Banks family of London, circa 1910. Oscars went to Richard and Robert Sherman for their tuneful score, the song "Chim-Chim-Cheree," the formidable Visual Effects team, Cotton Warburton for his editing, and Andrews, in her film debut (though Van Dyke is equally good as Bert, the whimsical jack of all trades). That's Jane Darwell, in her last screen appearance, as the bird lady. A wonderful movie.▼

Mary, Queen of Scots (1971) **C-128m.** *** D: Charles Jarrott. Vanessa Redgrave, Glenda Jackson, Patrick McGoohan, Timothy Dalton, Nigel Davenport, Trevor Howard, Daniel Massey, Ian Holm. Inaccurate history lesson but good costume drama, with strong performances from Redgrave as Mary, Jackson as Queen Elizabeth, rivals for power in Tudor England.

Mary White (1977) **C-100m. TVM** D: Jud Taylor. Ed Flanders, Kathleen Beller, Fionnula Flanagan, Tim Matheson, Donald Moffat. Moving drama, told poetically, based on the writings of Pulitzer Prize-winning newsman William Allen White after the tragic death of his teenaged daughter in 1921. Leisurely-paced, not for every taste, but class tells and so does Ed Flanders, who is superb. Script by Caryl Ledner. Above average.▼

Masculine-Feminine (1966-French-Swedish) **103m.** *** D: Jean-Luc Godard. Jean-Pierre Leaud, Chantal Goya, Marlene Jobert, Michel Debord, Catherine-Isabelle Duport, Eva-Britt Strandberg, Brigitte Bardot. Engaging, original concoction mixes politics, sex, comedy, nostalgia with standard boy-meets-girl theme. Interviewer/journalist Leaud has affair with would-be rock star Goya in 1960s Paris.▼

M*A*S*H (1970) **C-116m.** **** D: Robert Altman. Donald Sutherland, Elliott Gould, Tom Skerritt, Sally Kellerman, Robert Duvall, Jo Ann Pflug, Rene Auberjonois, Roger Bowen, Gary Burghoff, Fred Williamson, John Schuck, Bud Cort, G. Wood. Altman's first major success gave new meaning to the word "irreverence," set new style for contemporary filmmaking; follows black-comedy exploits of wild and woolly medical unit during Korean War in hilarious, episodic fashion. Oscar-winning screenplay by Ring Lardner, Jr.; reissued in 1973 at 112m., with new title music by Ahmad Jamal. Later a hit TV series.▼

Mask, The (1961) SEE: **Eyes of Hell**▼

Mask (1985) **C-120m.** ***½ D: Peter Bogdanovich. Cher, Sam Elliott, Eric Stoltz, Estelle Getty, Richard Dysart, Laura Dern, Harry Carey, Jr., Lawrence Monoson, Marsha Warfield, Barry Tubb, Andrew Robinson. Irresistible film based on true story of Rocky Dennis, teenage boy whose face has been terribly disfigured by a rare disease, and his mother Rusty, who's instilled a sense of confidence and love in her son, though her own defenses are easily broken down. Anna Hamilton Phelan's script dodges cliché, while Cher and Stoltz make their characters warm and real. A winner.▼

Mask, The (1988-Italian) **C-90m.** *½ D: Fiorella Infascelli. Helena Bonham Carter, Michael Maloney, Feodor Chaliapin, Roberto Herlitzka. Trivial, dull account of self-centered count's son Maloney, who becomes obsessed with pretty young actress Carter. She's put off by him, so he commences to woo her by donning various masks and changing his identity. Extremely slow-moving.

Masked Marvel, The SEE: **Sakima and the Masked Marvel**▼

Mask of Diljon, The (1946) **73m.** ** D: Lewis Landers. Erich von Stroheim, Jeanne Bates, Denise Vernac, William Wright, Edward Van Sloan. Stroheim is hypnotist who has delusions of grandeur, and schemes in murder attempts; exciting finish.

Mask of Dimitrios, The (1944) 95m. *** D: Jean Negulesco. Peter Lorre, Sydney Greenstreet, Zachary Scott, Faye Emerson, Victor Francen, George Tobias, Steve Geray, Eduardo Ciannelli, Florence Bates. Fine, offbeat melodrama with mild-mannered mystery writer Lorre reviewing life of notorious scoundrel Scott (in his first film). Eric Ambler's novel, *A Coffin for Dimitrios,* was adapted by Frank Gruber. As always, Lorre and Greenstreet make a marvelous team.

Mask of Fu Manchu, The (1932) 72m. **½ D: Charles Brabin. Boris Karloff, Lewis Stone, Karen Morley, Myrna Loy, Charles Starrett, Jean Hersholt. Elaborate chiller of Chinese madman Karloff menacing expedition in tomb of Ghengis Khan. Adaptation of Sax Rohmer novel is ornate and hokey, but fun; Loy is terrific as Fu's deliciously evil daughter.

Mask of Marcella SEE: **Cool Million**

Mask of Sheba, The (1969) C-100m. TVM D: David Lowell Rich. Walter Pidgeon, Inger Stevens, Eric Braeden, William Marshall, Stephen Young. Typical jungle drama mixes search for missing safari members, gold statue coveted by natives, treacherous territory, angry tribesmen, intrigue within rescue party. Cast tries hard but script stacked against them. Also known as QUEST: MASK OF SHEBA. Below average.

Mask of the Avenger (1951) C-83m. ** D: Phil Karlson. John Derek, Anthony Quinn, Jody Lawrance, Arnold Moss. Not up to snuff; man posing as count of Monte Cristo is involved in swordplay.

Masque of the Red Death, The (1964) C-86m. ***½ D: Roger Corman. Vincent Price, Hazel Court, Jane Asher, David Weston, Patrick Magee, Skip Martin, Nigel Green, John Westbrook. The most Bergmanlike of Corman's films, an ultra-stylish adaptation of the Poe tale (with another, *Hop Frog,* worked in as a subplot), starring Price as evil Prince Prospero, living it up in eerie, timeless castle while Plague ravages the countryside. Beautifully photographed in England by Nicolas Roeg; a must in color. Remade in 1989.▼

Masque of the Red Death (1989) C-83m. ** D: Larry Brand. Adrian Paul, Clare Hoak, Jeff Osterhage, Patrick Macnee, Tracy Reiner. Roger Corman produced this remake of one of his best films. Poe's Prince Prospero (Paul) is still dissipated, but this time more thoughtful and troubled. Despite an interesting approach to the figure of the Red Death and a literate (if talky) script, overall cheapness and very slow pace cripple this medieval melodrama.▼

Masquerade (1965-British) C-101m. **½ D: Basil Dearden. Cliff Robertson, Jack Hawkins, Marisa Mell, Michel Piccoli, Bill Fraser, John LeMesurier. Above-average spy satire highlighted by Robertson's portrayal of recruited agent. Good support casting with good location shooting to give Arabic atmosphere.

Masquerade (1988) C-91m. **½ D: Bob Swaim. Rob Lowe, Meg Tilly, Kim Cattrall, Doug Savant, John Glover, Dana Delany, Erik Holland. Lowe essentially has the ambiguous Cary Grant SUSPICION role: Does he really love delicate (and in this case, filthy rich) spouse Tilly—or is he planning to murder her at the first opportunity? Romantic suspense thriller has its moments, and might have had more with a better leading man. Merely OK, with Tilly, Glover, Delany and lovely Hamptons scenery offering compensation.▼

Masquerade in Mexico (1945) 96m. ** D: Mitchell Leisen. Dorothy Lamour, Arturo de Cordova, Patric Knowles, Ann Dvorak, George Rigaud, Natalie Schafer, Billy Daniels. Frivolous plot, forgettable songs combine in this limp musicomedy of bullfighters, romance, and Mexican intrigue. Remake of MIDNIGHT (1939) by the same director.

Masquerader, The (1933) 78m. **½ D: Richard Wallace. Ronald Colman, Elissa Landi, Halliwell Hobbes, Helen Jerome Eddy. Dated but enjoyable film goes on theory that two Colmans are better than one; journalist pretends he is his drug addict cousin, a member of Parliament. Hobbes is splendid as loyal and long-suffering butler.

Massacre (1934) 70m. **½ D: Alan Crosland. Richard Barthelmess, Ann Dvorak, Dudley Digges, Claire Dodd, Henry O'Neill, Robert Barrat. Unusual story about college-educated Sioux (Barthelmess) who tries to fight injustice and discrimination against his people back on the reservation. Interesting attempt to show an enlightened view of contemporary Indians, in the context of typical Warner Bros. melodramatic fodder.

Massacre (1956) C-76m. ** D: Louis King. Dane Clark, James Craig, Marta Roth, Miguel Torruco, Jaime Fernandez. Uninspired account of greedy Indian gunsellers.

Massacre at Central High (1976) C-85m. *** D: Renee Daalder. Derrel Maury, Andrew Stevens, Kimberly Beck, Robert Carradine, Roy Underwood, Steve Bond. Newcomer to California high school doesn't like the way students are being terrorized by a gang, so he decides to eliminate them, in ultra-violent fashion . . . but that's not the end of the story. Seemingly typical blend of teen and revenge formulas given offbeat twists by writer-director Daalder.▼

Massacre at Fort Holman SEE: **Reason to Live, A Reason to Die, A**▼

Massacre in Rome (1973-French-Italian) **C-103m.** *** D: George Pan Cosmatos. Richard Burton, Marcello Mastroianni, Leo McKern, John Steiner, Anthony Steel. Good drama has priest Mastroianni opposed to idealistic German Colonel Burton, who must execute 330 Roman hostages in retaliation for the deaths of 33 Nazi soldiers.▼

Massacre River (1949) **75m.** *½ D: John Rawlins. Guy Madison, Rory Calhoun, Johnny Sands, Carole Mathews, Cathy Downs. Minor Western, with trio of soldiers fighting over women.

Mass Appeal (1984) **C-100m.** *** D: Glenn Jordan. Jack Lemmon. Zeljko Ivanek, Charles Durning, Louise Latham, Lois de Banzie, James Ray, Talia Balsam, Gloria Stuart. Feisty young seminarian rattles the complacency of a popular parish priest in this entertaining filmization of Bill C. Davis' glib Broadway play. Lemmon is first-rate as usual, and though film belies its stage origins it still works fine.▼

Massarati and the Brain (1982) **C-100m.** TVM D: Harvey Hart. Peter Billingsley, Christopher Hewett, Markie Post, Ann Turkel, Camilla Sparv, Christopher Lee. Soldier of fortune teams up with genius twelve-year-old nephew to thwart neo-Nazi terrorists' grab for sunken treasure. TV pilot aimed at the Saturday morning crowd. Average.

Master Gunfighter, The (1975) **C-121m.** BOMB D: Frank Laughlin. Tom Laughlin, Ron O'Neal, Lincoln Kilpatrick, Geo Anne Sosa, Barbara Carrera, Victor Campos. BILLY JACK'S creator-star is an intense gunfighter who hates to kill but does it just the same. Lots of rhetoric. Remake of a 1969 Japanese samurai film, GOYOKIN.

Mastermind (1976) **C-131m.** *** D: Alex March. Zero Mostel, Bradford Dillman, Keiko Kishi, Gawn Grainger, Herbert Berghof, Jules Munshin, Sorrell Booke. Enjoyable spoof of Charlie Chan films with Mostel as Inspector Hoku, who tries to protect robot-like invention sought by international interests. Some good slapstick, rousing car chase. Received limited release after sitting on shelf since 1969.▼

Master Minds (1949) **64m.** D: Jean Yarbrough. Leo Gorcey, Huntz Hall, Glenn Strange, Gabriel Dell, Alan Napier, Jane Adams, Billy Benedict, Bernard Gorcey, Bennie Bartlett, David Gorcey. SEE: **Bowery Boys** series.

Master of Ballantrae, The (1953) **C-89m.** **½ D: William Keighley. Errol Flynn, Roger Livesey, Anthony Steel, Yvonne Furneaux. Robert Louis Stevenson's historical yarn. Flynn involved in plot to make Bonnie Prince Charles king of England; on-location filming in Great Britain adds scope to costumer. Remade for TV.

Master of Ballantrae, The (1984) **C-150m.** TVM D: Douglas Hickox. Richard Thomas, Michael York, John Gielgud, Brian Blessed, Timothy Dalton, Nicholas Grace, Finola Hughes, Ian Richardson. Lavish swashbuckler with York in the old Errol Flynn part and Thomas as the brother with whom he battles for the old family homestead and the honor of joining Bonnie Prince Charlie's cause. R. L. Stevenson done to a TV T. Above average.

Master of the World (1961) **C-104m.** *** D: William Witney. Vincent Price, Charles Bronson, Mary Webster, Henry Hull, Richard Harrison. Sci-fi adventure adapted from two Jules Verne novels about a 19th-century genius (Price) seeking to stop war from his ingenious flying machine, a cross between a zeppelin and a helicopter. Bronson (oddly cast) admires his ends, deplores his methods, and sets out to stop him. Very well done. Screenplay by Richard Matheson.▼

Masterpiece of Murder, A (1986) **C-100m.** TVM D: Charles S. Dubin. Bob Hope, Don Ameche, Jayne Meadows Allen, Yvonne De Carlo, Anne Lloyd Francis, Frank Gorshin, Kevin McCarthy, Clive Revill, Stella Stevens, Jamie Farr. Over-the-hill gumshoe Hope (in his first TV movie) reluctantly teams with worldly retired master thief Ameche to solve a string of art thefts and murders. A tired walkthrough by Hope, who used to toss off this kind of vehicle with relish in years gone by. Below average.

Master Race, The (1944) **96m.** *** D: Herbert J. Biberman. George Coulouris, Stanley Ridges, Osa Massen, Nancy Gates, Lloyd Bridges. Engrossing account of German officer who escapes when Nazi empire is destroyed, continuing to plot even afterward.▼

Masters of the Universe (1987) **C-106m.** ** D: Gary Goddard. Dolph Lundgren, Frank Langella, Courteney Cox, James Tolkan, Meg Foster, Christina Pickles, Billy Barty, Jon Cypher. He-Man (Lundgren) comes to Earth seeking a key that controls the power of the universe, stolen by cosmic crud Skeletor (unrecognizable Langella); somehow two teen puppy-lovers get involved. Elaborate comic book nonsense (which has had another life in kiddie animation) is dumb but inoffensive.▼

Masterson of Kansas (1954) **C-73m.** ** D: William Castle. George Montgomery, Nancy Gates, James Griffith, Jean Willes, Benny Rubin. Despite presence of trio of famed gunmen—Doc Holliday, Wyatt Earp and Bat Masterson—film is just standard.

Master Spy (1964-British) **71m.** **½ D: Montgomery Tully. Stephen Murray, June Thorburn, Alan Wheatley, John Carson.

OK drama of Allied counteragent escaping from Communist prison.

Master Touch, The (1973-Italian-German) **C-96m.** ** D: Michele Lupo. Kirk Douglas, Florinda Bolkan, Giuliano Gemma, Rene Koldehoff. Safecracker Douglas, just out of jail, attempts to trip up a foolproof alarm and rip off a safe for $1 million. Deadening.▼

Matador (1986-Spanish) **C-102m.** *** D: Pedro Almodóvar. Assumpta Serna, Antonio Banderas, Nacho Martinez, Carmen Maura, Eva Cobo, Julieta Serrano, Chus Lampreave. Dazzling black comedy chronicling the plight of retired matador Martinez, who passes his time by appearing in snuff films—and his young, troubled protégé (Banderas). The opening sequence is a real stunner.▼

Mata Hari (1932) **90m.** *** D: George Fitzmaurice. Greta Garbo, Ramon Novarro, Lionel Barrymore, Lewis Stone, C. Henry Gordon, Karen Morley. Garbo is the alluring spy of WW1, beguiling everyone from Novarro to Barrymore. Highlights: Garbo's exotic dance sequence, Morley stalked by gang executioner.

Mata Hari (1985) **C-108m.** *½ D: Curtis Harrington. Sylvia Kristel, Christopher Cazenove, Oliver Tobias, Gaye Brown, Gottfried Iohn. The famous femme fatale of WW1 *must* have been more interesting than this! Kristel's frequent nudity is only possible attraction.▼

Mata Hari's Daughter (1954-Italian) **C-102m.** ** D: Renzo Meruis. Frank Latimore, Ludmilla Tcherina, Erno Crisa. Humdrum account of alleged daughter of famed WW1 spy in 1940 Java involved in espionage; sterile dubbing. Retitled: DAUGHTER OF MATA HARI.

Match King, The (1932) **80m.** **½ D: Howard Bretherton, William Keighley. Warren William, Lili Damita, Glenda Farrell, Harold Huber, John Wray, Hardie Albright. Clever, ambitious young man will stop at nothing to succeed, becomes a multimillionaire buying exclusive rights to manufacture matches around the world! Interesting if uneven, story is doubly compelling because it's mostly true, based on life of Ivar Kreuger.

Matchless (1967-Italian) **C-104m.** ** D: Alberto Lattuada. Patrick O'Neal, Ira Furstenberg, Donald Pleasence, Henry Silva. Dashing, romantic 007-like journalist is pursued for his knowledge of a chemical formula and his magical ring, which makes him invisible. Usual imitation James Bond potboiler.

Matchmaker, The (1958) **101m.** *** D: Joseph Anthony. Shirley Booth, Anthony Perkins, Shirley MacLaine, Paul Ford, Robert Morse, Wallace Ford. Endearing Thornton Wilder comedy about middle-aged widower deciding to rewed . . . but the matchmaker he consults has plans of her own. Solid performances, fine period detail; later musicalized as HELLO, DOLLY!

Matewan (1987) **C-130m.** ***½ D: John Sayles. Chris Cooper, Will Oldham, Mary McDonnell, Bob Gunton, James Earl Jones, Kevin Tighe, Gordon Clapp, Josh Mostel, Joe Grifasi, Maggie Renzi, David Strathairn. Compelling and compassionate drama about labor troubles in the heart of coalmining country, Matewan, West Virginia, in the 1920s. As usual, writer-director Sayles (who appears briefly as a preacher) makes every note ring true in this meticulous period piece; he even cowrote some phony labor songs! Beautifully photographed by Haskell Wexler.▼

Matilda (1978) **C-103m.** BOMB D: Daniel Mann. Elliott Gould, Robert Mitchum, Harry Guardino, Clive Revill, Karen Carlson, Lionel Stander, Larry Pennell, Art Metrano. Good cast wasted in awful kiddie pic about a boxing kangaroo, played by a man in a suit (Gary Morgan). Paul Gallico's novel loses everything in translation.▼

Mating Game, The (1959) **C-96m.** *** D: George Marshall. Debbie Reynolds, Tony Randall, Paul Douglas, Fred Clark, Una Merkel, Philip Ober, Charles Lane. Zippy comedy romp of tax agent Randall falling in love with farm girl Reynolds, with Douglas rambunctious as Debbie's father.

Mating of Millie, The (1948) **87m.** **½ D: Henry Levin. Glenn Ford, Evelyn Keyes, Ron Randell, Willard Parker, Virginia Hunter. Ford tries to help Keyes trap a husband so she can adopt a child, but falls in love with her himself. Predictable but pleasant.

Mating Season, The (1951) **101m.** ***½ D: Mitchell Leisen. Gene Tierney, John Lund, Miriam Hopkins, Thelma Ritter, Jan Sterling, Larry Keating, James Lorimer. Excellent, underrated comedy with cynical undertones about the American dream. Hardworking Lund marries socialite Tierney, suffers embarrassment when his plain-talking mother (Ritter) comes to town and is mistaken for servant. Ritter is simply superb. Written by Walter Reisch, Richard Breen, and producer Charles Brackett.

Mating Season, The (1980) **C-100m. TVM** D: John Llewellyn Moxey. Lucie Arnaz, Laurence Luckinbill, Swoosie Kurtz, Diane Stilwell, Joel Brooks, Bob Herman. Whimsical tale of an uptight lady lawyer who finds love and aggravation with a good-natured small businessman at a birdwatching retreat. Average.▼

Mattei Affair, The (1973-Italian) **C-118m.** **½ D: Francesco Rosi. Gian Maria Volonte, Luigi Squarizina, Peter Baldwin. Semi-documentary study of rise of Italian industrialist and his mysterious death.

Matter of Humanities, A SEE: **Marcus Welby, M.D.**

Matter of Innocence, A (1967-British) C-102m. **½ D: Guy Green. Hayley Mills, Trevor Howard, Sashi Kapoor, Brenda De Banzie. Plain Jane (Mills) travels to Singapore with aunt, has an affair with Eurasian Kapoor and becomes woman. Trite soaper with unusual role for suave Howard; from Noel Coward story "Pretty Polly."

Matter of Life and Death, A (1946) SEE: **Stairway to Heaven**

Matter of Life and Death, A (1981) C-98m. TVM D: Russ Mayberry. Linda Lavin, Salome Jens, Gail Strickland, Ramon Bieri, Tyne Daly, Larry Breeding, John Bennett Perry, Gerald S. O'Loughlin. The true-life story of Joy Ufema, a nurse dedicated to treating the terminally ill. Writer Lane Slate based his teleplay on Ufema's career after she gained national recognition on *60 Minutes*. Average.▼

Matter of Resistance, A (1966-French) 92m. **½ D: Jean-Paul Rappeneau. Catherine Deneuve, Philippe Noiret, Pierre Brasseur, Mary Marquet, Henri Garcin, Carlos Thompson. Pleasant French comedy of bored housewife (Deneuve) who welcomes arrival of soldiers to her village prior to Normandy invasion. Originally titled LA VIE DE CHATEAU.

Matter of Sex, A (1984) C-100m. TVM D: Lee Grant. Jean Stapleton, Dinah Manoff, Judge Reinhold, Pamela Putch, Gillian Farrell, Diana Reis, Nancy Beatty. The saga of the Willmar 8—eight women bank employees in Minnesota who waged a two-year struggle walking a picket line seeking pay equality with their male co-workers. A concerned effort by all, but nowhere near the acclaimed PBS documentary on the same subject that Grant produced. Manoff is Grant's daughter; Putch is Stapleton's. Average.

Matter of Time, A (1976) C-99m. BOMB D: Vincente Minnelli. Liza Minnelli, Ingrid Bergman, Charles Boyer, Spiros Andros, Tina Aumont, Anna Proclemer. Depressing schmaltz about a chambermaid in pre-WW1 Europe taught to love life by a batty contessa. Director Minnelli's worst film, though, for his part, he denounced this version as edited. Final film for both Boyer and the director. Bergman's daughter, Isabella Rossellini, makes her screen debut as a nun.▼

Matter of WHO, A (1962-British) 90m. *** D: Don Chaffey. Terry-Thomas, Alex Nicol, Sonja Ziemann, Guy Deghy, Richard Briers, Carol White, Honor Blackman. Thomas goes through madcap antics involving World Health Organization's tracking down of disease-carrier.

Matter of Wife . . . and Death, A (1975) C-78m. TVM D: Marvin Chomsky. Rod Taylor, Joe Santos, Luke Askew, Tom Drake, John Colicos, Anita Gillette, Anne Archer, Lynda Carter, Cesare Danova. Freewheeling private eye Taylor goes after the killers of friend, a small-time hood, and gets involved in big-time gambling operation. Taylor plays Shamus, the unorthodox detective done on the big screen by Burt Reynolds. Average.

Matt Helm (1975) C-78m. TVM D: Buzz Kulik. Tony Franciosa, Ann Turkel, Gene Evans, Patrick Macnee, Hari Rhodes, James Shigeta, Laraine Stephens, John Vernon, Catherine Bach. Private eye Helm finds himself neck deep in international black market arms operation while trying to protect a movie star whose life is threatened. When ol' Dino played Helm in four movies, he was a crack secret agent. Pilot to the short-lived series. Average.

Maurice (1987-British) C-140m. *** D: James Ivory. James Wilby, Hugh Grant, Rupert Graves, Denholm Elliott, Simon Callow, Billie Whitelaw, Ben Kingsley, Judy Parfitt, Phoebe Nicholls, Barry Foster. Typically meticulous Merchant-Ivory production of a literary work (by E.M. Forster) about a young Britisher's coming of age in the 1910s, and coming to terms with his homosexuality. Beautifully realized and extremely well acted all around . . . but overlong. Helena Bonham Carter (the star of Ivory's previous hit, A ROOM WITH A VIEW) makes a cameo appearance.▼

Maurie (1973) C-113m. ** D: Daniel Mann. Bernie Casey, Bo Svenson, Janet MacLachlan, Stephanie Edwards, Paulene Myers, Bill Walker. Well-meaning but downbeat tearjerker based on true story of basketball star Maurice Stokes (Casey). His sudden paralysis spurs teammate Jack Twyman (Svenson) to devote himself to Maurie's rehabilitation. Too similar to other sports-tragedy films to stand out. Shown on TV as BIG MO.▼

Maverick Queen, The (1956) C-92m. **½ D: Joseph Kane. Barbara Stanwyck, Barry Sullivan, Scott Brady, Mary Murphy, Wallace Ford. Stanwyck is peppy as outlaw who's willing to go straight for lawman Sullivan.▼

Max and Helen (1990-U.S.-British) C-100m. TVM D: Philip Saville. Treat Williams, Alice Krige, Martin Landau, Jonathan Phillips, Adam Kotz, Jodhi May. Plodding adaptation of Simon Wiesenthal's book about a pair of lovers, separated during the war in a German labor camp, who manage to find one another two decades later. Williams' miscasting as a blank-faced German Jew who becomes a Paris doctor is counterbalanced by Landau's thoughtful, soft-spoken turn as Wiesenthal. Made for cable. Average.

Max Dugan Returns (1983) C-98m. *** D: Herbert Ross. Marsha Mason, Jason

Robards, Donald Sutherland, Matthew, Broderick, Dody Goodman, Sal Viscuso, David Morse, Kiefer Sutherland, Charlie Lau. Sweet, simple Neil Simon comedy about a long-lost father who tries to make amends to his daughter (a struggling schoolteacher and single parent) by showering her with presents—using money he's obtained by slightly shady means. Acted with verve and sincerity by a perfect cast. Broderick's film debut.▼

Max Havelaar (1976-Dutch-Indonesian) **C-167m.** ** D: Fons Rademakers. Peter Faber, Sacha Bulthuis, Elang Mohanad, Adenan Soesilanigrat. Uneven chronicle of colonial exploitation in 19th century Dutch East Indies (now Indonesia), with Faber an officer struggling to change the rules. Tries hard, but predictable and unexciting most of the way.

Maxie (1985) **C-90m.** ** D: Paul Aaron. Glenn Close, Mandy Patinkin, Ruth Gordon, Barnard Hughes, Valerie Curtin, Googy Gress, Harry Hamlin. Roaring twenties flapper inhabits the body of hardworking eighties woman, and titillates her husband to boot! *Very* old-fashioned screwball comedy-fantasy just doesn't come off, despite good intentions. Incidentally, the actress playing Maxie in authentic silent movie footage is Carole Lombard.▼

Maxime (1958-French) **93m.** **½ D: Henri Verneuil. Michele Morgan, Charles Boyer, Arletty, Felix Marten. Morgan is good match for Parisian scoundrel Boyer in this love tale set in 1910s.

Maximum Overdrive (1986) **C-97m.** BOMB D: Stephen King. Emilio Estevez, Pat Hingle, Laura Harrington, Yeardley Smith, John Short, J. C. Quinn. Customers and employees of interstate truck stop are terrorized by the trucks themselves, which have come to demonic life. Novelist King, making his directing debut, said he set out to create a junk movie, nothing more . . . but he made it stupid and boring. ▼

Maya (1966) **C-91m.** ** D: John Berry. Clint Walker, Jay North, I. S. Johar, Sajid Kahn, Jairaj, Sonia Sahni. Silly juvenile jungle tale has young North temporarily losing respect for his big-game hunter father Walker, who has lost his nerve.

Maybe Baby (1988) **C-100m.** TVM D: Tom Moore. Dabney Coleman, Jane Curtin, Julia Duffy, Florence Stanley, David Doyle, Peter Michael Goetz. A happily married, career-minded couple comes to a crossroads when, fairly late in the game, she decides to have a baby. Average.

Maybe I'll Come Home in the Spring (1970) **C-74m.** TVM D: Joseph Sargent. Sally Field, Jackie Cooper, Eleanor Parker, Lane Bradbury, David Carradine, Harry Lauter. Year in the life of Miller family: Denise (Field) can't take home life, splits for commune existence, returns after disillusionment and drug experiences take toll. Experiences after she returns make film worthwhile, refusing to pull punches. Game attempt by Bruce Feldman at scripting without set lines of dialogue. Linda Ronstadt performs the songs. Above average.

Mayday at 40,000 Feet! (1976) **C-100m.** TVM D: Robert Butler. David Janssen, Don Meredith, Christopher George, Ray Milland, Lynda Day George, Marjoe Gortner, Broderick Crawford, Jane Powell. All-star cast aloft with Janssen at the controls, a ruthless killer in first-class, the 747 disabled and the airport snowed in. Just what you'd expect from the title. Average.

Mayerling (1936-French) **89m.** *** D: Anatole Litvak. Charles Boyer, Danielle Darrieux, Suzy Prim, Jean Dax, Vladimir Sokoloff. Touching, well-made romantic tragedy based on true story of Austrian Crown Prince Rudolph, who dared to fall in love with a commoner. Good performances spark international hit; miles ahead of 1969 remake.▼

Mayerling (1969-British) **C-140m.** **½ D: Terence Young. Omar Sharif, Catherine Deneuve, James Mason, Ava Gardner, James Robertson Justice, Genevieve Page. Remake of 1936 classic casts Sharif as Austrian prince who defies convention, and his father (Mason), by falling in love with commoner Deneuve. Old-fashioned tragic romance is pleasant but uncompelling. Justice steals film as spirited Prince of Wales.

Mayflower Madam (1987) **C-100m.** TVM D: Lou Antonio. Candice Bergen, Chris Sarandon, Caitlin Clarke, Jim Antonio, Chita Rivera, Sydney Biddle Barrows. Drama (un)inspired by the life of Sydney Biddle Barrows, onetime debutante and Mayflower descendant who became the proprietor of a high-class N.Y.C. escort service supplying expensive "fantasy girls." Bergen tries hard to look interested as Barrows, and Barrows herself turns up as a pal. Interesting only for a rare TV appearance by Chita Rivera as Barrows' lawyer. Below average.▼

Mayflower: The Pilgrims' Adventure (1979) **C-100m.** TVM D: George Schaeffer. Anthony Hopkins, Richard Crenna, Jenny Agutter, Trish Van Devere, John Heffernan, David Dukes, Michael Beck. Lavish production, earnest performances, period costumes—but it's reduced to soap opera circa 1620. Stick with Spencer Tracy & friends in PLYMOUTH ADVENTURE. Average.

Mayor of Hell, The (1933) **80m.** *** D: Archie Mayo. James Cagney, Madge Evans, Allen Jenkins, Dudley Digges, Arthur Byron, Frankie Darro, Allen "Farina" Hoskins. Fascinating, somewhat strange melodrama with political-machine appointee

Cagney taking a genuine interest in the way kids are being mistreated at reform school run by slimy Digges. Climax is both unexpected and bizarre. Remade as CRIME SCHOOL and HELL'S KITCHEN.

Maytime (1937) **132m.** *** D: Robert Z. Leonard. Jeanette MacDonald, Nelson Eddy, John Barrymore, Herman Bing, Rafaela Ottiano, Paul Porcasi, Sig Ruman. One of singing duo's best films, despite occasional heavy-handedness and piercing operatic sequence near the end. Exquisite filming of simple story: opera star and penniless singer fall in love in Paris, but her husband/mentor (Barrymore) interferes. Songs include "Will You Remember," "Sweetheart."▼

Maytime in Mayfair (1949-British) **94m.** **½ D: Herbert Wilcox. Anna Neagle, Michael Wilding, Peter Graves, Nicholas Phipps. Guided tour through chic London with its society folks, enhanced by Neagle and Wilding.

Maze, The (1953) **81m.** ** D: William Cameron Menzies. Richard Carlson, Veronica Hurst, Hillary Brooke, Michael Pate, Katherine Emery. Mysterious doings at a Scottish castle; a low-budgeter with a ludicrous (and unsatisfying) payoff. Stylishly composed as a 3D movie by designer-director Menzies.

Mazes and Monsters (1982-Canadian) **C-100m.** TVM D: Steven H. Stern. Tom Hanks, Wendy Crewson, David Wallace, Chris Makepeace, Lloyd Bochner, Peter Donat, Anne Francis, Murray Hamilton, Vera Miles, Louise Sorel, Susan Strasberg. Four college students become involved in the medieval fantasy world of game-playing. Tom Lazarus's intriguing "Dungeons and Dragons" script from Rona Jaffe's book makes this an engrossing suspenser. Above average.▼

McCabe and Mrs. Miller (1971) **C-121m.** ***½ D: Robert Altman. Warren Beatty, Julie Christie, Rene Auberjonois, John Schuck, Bert Remsen, Keith Carradine, William Devane, Shelley Duvall, Michael Murphy, Hugh Millais, Jack Riley. Richly textured mood piece about an ambitious small-timer who opens a bordello in turn-of-the-century boom town. Altman deglamorizes Hollywood image of the period with his realistic visions, and Beatty is first-rate as the two-bit braggart McCabe. Edmund Naughton's novel *McCabe* was adapted by Brian McKay and Altman.▼

McCloud: Who Killed Miss U.S.A.? (1969) **C-100m.** TVM D: Richard Colla. Dennis Weaver, Craig Stevens, Diana Muldaur, Mark Richman, Terry Carter, Raul Julia, Shelly Novack, Julie Newmar. U.S. deputy marshal assigned to transport valuable witness from New Mexico to N.Y.C. must prove worth to Eastern superiors when he loses witness soon after he disembarks from plane. Good location work

in pilot for long-running series, inspired by movie COOGAN'S BLUFF. Above average. Retitled PORTRAIT OF A DEAD GIRL.

McConnell Story, The (1955) **C-107m.** *** D: Gordon Douglas. Alan Ladd, June Allyson, James Whitmore, Frank Faylen. Weepy yet effective fictional biography of jet test pilot, with Allyson as his understanding wife.

McCullochs, The SEE: **Wild McCullochs, The**

McGuffin, The (1985-British) **C-95m.** ** D: Colin Bucksey. Charles Dance, Ritza Brown, Francis Matthews, Brian Glover, Phyllis Logan, Jerry Stiller, Anna Massey, Ann Todd, Bill Shine. Meandering, confusing thriller about film critic Dance, whose curiosity about a couple of his neighbors leads to his involvement in murder and mayhem. Starts off nicely but goes downhill all too quickly. An homage to Hitchcock in general, REAR WINDOW in particular.▼

McGuire, Go Home! (1966-British) **C-101m.** **½ D: Ralph Thomas. Dirk Bogarde, George Chakiris, Susan Strasberg, Denholm Elliott. Set in 1954 Cyprus; peppy account of terrorist campaign against British occupation, with side-plot of officer Bogarde in love with American girl Strasberg.▼

McHale's Navy (1964) **C-93m.** **½ D: Edward J. Montagne. Ernest Borgnine, Joe Flynn, Tim Conway, George Kennedy, Claudine Longet, Bob Hastings, Carl Ballantine, Billy Sands, Gavin MacLeod, Jean Willes. Theatrical feature inspired by popular TV series finds the PT-73 crew doing everything possible to try and raise money to pay off gambling debts. Usual blend of slapstick and snappy dialogue; entertaining for fans.

McHale's Navy Joins the Air Force (1965) **C-90m.** **½ D: Edward J. Montagne. Tim Conway, Joe Flynn, Bob Hastings, Ted Bessell, Susan Silo, Henry Beckman, Billy Sands, Gavin MacLeod, Tom Tully, Jacques Aubuchon. Rather unusual comedy with little relation to either the first feature or the TV series (including no Borgnine). Ensign Parker (Conway) is mistaken for an Air Force hot-shot, and the more he screws up, the higher he's promoted! John Fenton Murray's intricate script adds some mild satire to normal quota of slapstick; a genuine curio.

McKenzie Break, The (1970) **C-106m.** *** D: Lamont Johnson. Brian Keith, Helmut Griem, Ian Hendry, Jack Watson, Patrick O'Connell. Daring escape from a P.O.W. camp for Germans in Scotland makes for engrossing movie fare.

McLintock! (1963) **C-122m.** *** D: Andrew V. McLaglen. John Wayne, Maureen O'Hara, Patrick Wayne, Stefanie Powers, Yvonne De Carlo, Chill Wills, Bruce

Cabot, Jack Kruschen, Jerry Van Dyke. Rowdy, lively Western-comedy with Wayne encountering his refined wife O'Hara, who wants a divorce, and his grown-up daughter Powers, caught between father and mother. Plenty of slapstick to keep things moving.

McMasters, The (1970) C-89/97m. **½ D: Alf Kjellin. Burl Ives, Brock Peters, David Carradine, Nancy Kwan, Jack Palance, John Carradine. Pretty grim drama of bigotry and violence gone crazy as black Union soldier (Peters) returns to ranch of former master (Ives), eventually made co-owner of land. Dual running times indicates two different endings: bad guys (led hy Palance) win out or good guys emerge victorious. Both versions were released to theaters.▼

McNaughton's Daughter (1976) C-100m. TVM D: Jerry London. Susan Clark, Ricardo Montalban, James Callahan, John Elerick, Vera Miles, Ralph Bellamy, Mike Farrell. Deputy D.A. (Clark) prosecutes saintlike missionary Miles on homicide charges in this pilot for a short-lived series. Average.

McQ (1974) C-116m. ** D: John Sturges. John Wayne, Eddie Albert, Diana Muldaur, Colleen Dewhurst, Clu Gulager, David Huddleston, Al Lettieri, Julie Adams. An aging Duke tries to be Clint Eastwood as a Camaro-driving cop out to get the gangster who murdered his partner. Good action, but that's about all.▼

McVicar (1980-British) C-111m. *** D: Tom Clegg. Roger Daltrey, Adam Faith, Cheryl Campbell, Brian Hall, Steven Berkoff, Jeremy Blake, Ian Hendry. Impressive drama about John McVicar (Daltrey), England's Public Enemy Number 1, and his escape from prison. Screenplay by McVicar, who adapted his book; Daltrey is surprisingly good, with Faith and Campbell fine as his prison buddy/fellow escapee and his common-law wife.▼

Meal, The (1975) C-90m. ** D: R. John Hugh. Dina Merrill, Carl Betz, Leon Ames, Susan Logan, Vicki Powers, Steve Potter. Symbolic but brutal film about a wealthy woman who invites a group of the rich and powerful to a banquet, lets them devour the feast as they expose and devour each other's lives. Video title: DEADLY ENCOUNTER.▼

Me and My Gal (1932) 78m. *** D: Raoul Walsh. Spencer Tracy, Joan Bennett, Marion Burns, George Walsh, J. Farrell MacDonald, Noel Madison. Wholly entertaining film blending comedy, romance, melodrama in one neat package; cop Tracy falls in love with waitress Bennett, whose sister and father become involved with a gangster. Stars at their most charming, with bottomless reserve of snappy dialogue.

Mean Dog Blues (1978) C-108m. **½ D: Mel Stuart. George Kennedy, Gregg Henry,

Kay Lenz, Scatman Crothers, Tina Louise, Felton Perry, Gregory Sierra, James Wainwright, William Windom. Henry is railroaded onto prison farm run by Kennedy and a team of bloodthirsty Dobermans; unsurprising but well-made action film.▼

Me and the Colonel (1958) 109m. **½ D: Peter Glenville. Danny Kaye, Curt Jurgens, Nicole Maurey, Francoise Rosay. Franz Werfel's *Jacobowsky and the Colonel* is source for spotty satire; Jacobowsky is played by Kaye, and Jurgens is the anti-Semitic military officer, both brought together during crisis in WW2. Filmed in France.

Meanest Man in the World, The (1943) 57m. *** D: Sidney Lanfield. Jack Benny, Priscilla Lane, Eddie "Rochester" Anderson, Edmund Gwenn, Matt Briggs, Anne Revere. Snappy yarn of good-natured lawyer Benny discovering that he can only succeed in business by being nasty. Benny-Rochester repartee is hilarious; film is a must for Benny devotees. That's cult figure Tor Johnson as a wrestler.

Mean Frank and Crazy Tony (1975-Italian) C-85m. ** D: Michele Lupo. Lee Van Cleef, Tony Lo Bianco, Jean Rochefort, Jess Hahn. Cute Italian gangster film closely resembles the buddy-format of a Western, with Lo Bianco the young groupie who attaches himself to his hero Van Cleef. U.S. version of this 1973 Dino De Laurentiis production was prepared by film doctor Simon Nuchtern.▼

Mean Johnny Barrows (1976) C-85m. ** D: Fred Williamson. Fred Williamson, Jenny Sherman, Aaron Banks, Anthony Caruso, Luther Adler, Stuart Whitman, Roddy McDowall, Elliott Gould. Mean but dull; Vietnam vet gets involved with the Mafia. Williamson made directorial debut with this slow-paced film, notable for unlikely cast and Gould's incongruous comedy relief.▼

Means and Ends (1985) C-105m. ** D: Gerald Michenaud. William Windom, Cyril O'Reilly, Reed Birney, Ken Michelman, Lori Lethin, Doyle Baker, John Randolph, Jack Fletcher, Michael Greene. Static direction and a meandering script do in this potentially incisive drama about ethics, values, responsibility: several novice Hollywood filmmakers, planning to film a sex movie in a small town, attempt to deceive the community into thinking they are shooting a screwball comedy.

Mean Season, The (1985) C-103m. **½ D: Phillip Borsos. Kurt Russell, Mariel Hemingway, Richard Jordan, Richard Masur, Joe Pantoliano, Andy Garcia. Miami newspaper reporter (Russell, in a very credible performance) becomes sole contact for crazed killer, but as the headlines (and murders) continue, it becomes a question of who is "using" whom. Intriguing and initially believable idea goes awry in latter half of this mean movie.▼

Mean Streets (1973) **C-110m.** **** D: Martin Scorsese. Robert De Niro, Harvey Keitel, David Proval, Amy Robinson, Richard Romanus, Cesare Danova, George Memmoli, Robert Carradine, David Carradine. Masterpiece about small-time hood Keitel, irresponsible friend De Niro and their knockabout cronies in N.Y.C.'s Little Italy. Technically dazzling film put director Scorsese on the map and deservedly so.▼

Meantime (1983-British) **C-104m.** **½ D: Mike Leigh. Marion Bailey, Phil Daniels, Tim Roth, Pam Ferris, Jeff Robert, Alfred Molina, Gary Oldman. Downbeat kitchen-sink drama about the problems of a working-class London family; no one captures this milieu quite like director Leigh, though it can be pretty bleak. Molina and Oldman later costarred in PRICK UP YOUR EARS.

Meatballs (1979-Canadian) **C-92m.** *½ D: Ivan Reitman. Bill Murray, Harvey Atkin, Kate Lynch, Russ Banham, Kristine DeBell, Sarah Torgov. Alternately cruel and sloppily sentimental comedy about summer camp will no doubt wow fifth graders of all ages, though myopic screen characters named "Spaz" aren't really all that funny. Pretty desperate. Followed by two sequels.▼

Meatballs Part II (1984) **C-87m.** ** D: Ken Wiederhorn. Richard Mulligan, John Mengatti, Hamilton Camp, Kim Richards, Tammy Taylor, John Larroquette, Archie Hahn, Misty Rowe, Paul Reubens (Pee-wee Herman), Vic Dunlop, Felix Silla, Elayne Boosler. In-name-only sequel throws in everything from Jewish aliens to FROM HERE TO ETERNITY take-off, as the fate of Camp Sasquatch rides on a boxing match against nearby Camp Patton ("Where Outdoor Living Molds Killers"). Slightly better than its predecessor (which isn't saying much). Followed by MEATBALLS III.▼

Meatballs III (1987) **C-94m.** *½ D: George Mendeluk. Sally Kellerman, Patrick Dempsey, Al Waxman, Isabelle Mejias, Shannon Tweed, Ian Taylor, George Buza. What do you say about a movie dealing with a dead porno star who coaches a teen-age nerd on how to lose his virginity at summer camp? As little as possible.▼

Mechanic, The (1972) **C-100m.** **½ D: Michael Winner. Charles Bronson, Keenan Wynn, Jan-Michael Vincent, Jill Ireland. Detailed study of James Bond-type assassin and youth he trains to take his place. Worth watching for the double-twist ending; terse script by Lewis John Carlino.▼

Medal for Benny, A (1945) **77m.** ***½ D: Irving Pichel. Dorothy Lamour, Arturo de Cordova, J. Carrol Naish, Mikhail Rasumny, Fernando Alvarado, Charles Dingle, Frank McHugh. Small town hypocritically honors one of its war dead. Excellent comedy-drama scripted by Frank Butler from a story by John Steinbeck and Jack Wagner.

Medical Story (1975) **C-100m. TVM** D: Gary Nelson. Beau Bridges, Jose Ferrer, Claude Akins, Wendell Burton, Shirley Knight, Carl Reiner, Martha Scott, Sidney Chaplin. Idealistic intern Bridges clashes with noted gynecologist Ferrer over unnecessary surgery. Intelligent drama by Abby Mann that led the way to the subsequent hospital anthology series. Average.

Medicine Ball Caravan (1971) **C-90m.** **½ D: Francois Reichenbach. B. B. King, Alice Cooper, Delaney and Bonnie, Doug Kershaw, David Peel. The Caravan is a 150-member troupe that traveled the U.S. during the summer of '70 to spread peace, love, music—and make a movie. Superficially arty direction; Martin Scorsese was associate producer and supervising editor.

Medicine Man, The (1930) **66m.** *½ D: Scott Pembroke. Jack Benny, Betty Bronson, Eva Novak, E. Alyn Warren, Billy Butts, Adolph Milar, George E. Stone, Tommy Dugan. Smooth-talking carny medicine man comes to the aid of Bronson and her brother, who live with the most abusive father in screen history! Dull melodrama would be worthless if not for the curiosity value of Benny in the lead.▼

Medium, The (1951) **84m.** **½ D: Gian-Carlo Menotti. Marie Powers, Anna Maria Alberghetti, Leo Coleman, Belva Kibler. Murky filmization of Gian-Carlo Menotti opera about eccentric spiritualist, the girl living in her seedy apartment, the outcast mute boy in love with girl.▼

Medium Cool (1969) **C-110m.** **** D: Haskell Wexler. Robert Forster, Verna Bloom, Peter Bonerz, Marianna Hill, Harold Blankenship, Peter Boyle. Arresting, unique film of TV cameraman who remains detached though surrounded by events that demand his involvement. Director/writer/cameraman Wexler used real footage of his actors at 1968 Democratic convention in Chicago, and subsequent riots, as basis for ultrarealistic film. Music score by Mike Bloomfield; Paul Butterfield and The Mothers of Invention are among the artists on the soundtrack.▼

Medusa Touch, The (1978-British) **C-110m.** ** D: Jack Gold. Richard Burton, Lino Ventura, Lee Remick, Harry Andrews, Alan Badel, Marie-Christine Barrault, Jeremy Brett, Michael Hordern, Gordon Jackson, Derek Jacobi. Burton has spent his whole life willing people's deaths, and now he's completely out of control; Remick is his psychiatrist in this derivative, unappealing film.▼

Meet Boston Blackie (1941) **61m.** D: Robert Florey. Chester Morris, Rochelle Hudson, Richard Lane, Charles Wagenheim,

Constance Worth. SEE: **Boston Blackie** series.

Meet Danny Wilson (1952) 86m. **½ D: Joseph Pevney. Frank Sinatra, Shelley Winters, Alex Nicol, Raymond Burr. Sinatra gives solid performance as entertainer involved with racketeers; script wavers.

Meet Dr. Christian (1939) 63m. ** D: Bernard Vorhaus. Jean Hersholt, Dorothy Lovett, Robert Baldwin, Enid Bennett, Paul Harvey, Marcia Mae Jones, Jackie Moran. Overly folksy entry in film series of small-town doctor who solves everyone's difficulties.▼

Meeting at Midnight SEE: **Black Magic** (1944)▼

Meet John Doe (1941) 132m. *** D: Frank Capra. Gary Cooper, Barbara Stanwyck, Edward Arnold, Walter Brennan, Spring Byington, James Gleason, Gene Lockhart. Overlong but interesting social commentary, with naive Cooper hired to spearhead national goodwill drive benefitting corrupt politician Arnold. Wordy idealism can't bury good characterizations, usual Capra touches. Many existing prints (from reissue) run 123m. Also shown in computer-colored version.▼

Meet Me After the Show (1951) C-86m. **½ D: Richard Sale. Betty Grable, Macdonald Carey, Rory Calhoun, Eddie Albert, Lois Andrews, Irene Ryan. Undistinguished Grable musical lacking bounce of her other vehicles, with usual show biz storyline.

Meet Me at the Fair (1952) C-87m. **½ D: Douglas Sirk. Dan Dailey, Diana Lynn, Hugh O'Brian, Carole Mathews, Rhys Williams, Chet Allen, Scatman Crothers. Dailey is good as a sideshow medicine man who helps a young orphan and courts Lynn; pleasant musical.

Meet Me in Las Vegas (1956) C-112m. **½ D: Roy Rowland. Dan Dailey, Cyd Charisse, Agnes Moorehead, Lili Darvas, Jim Backus; guest stars Jerry Colonna, Paul Henreid, Lena Horne, Frankie Laine, Mitsuko Sawamura. Charisse's dancing is highlight of mild musical involving rancher Dailey and ballet star Cyd in gambling capital. Cameos by many top stars add to the flavor.

Meet Me in St. Louis (1944) C-113m. **** D: Vincente Minnelli. Judy Garland, Margaret O'Brien, Lucille Bremer, Tom Drake, Mary Astor, Leon Ames, Marjorie Main, June Lockhart, Harry Davenport, Joan Carroll, Hugh Marlowe. Captivating musical based on Sally Benson's slice of Americana about a family's experiences during the year of the St. Louis World's Fair, 1903. Judy sings wonderful Ralph Blane–Hugh Martin songs "The Boy Next Door," "Have Yourself a Merry Little Christmas," "The Trolley Song," while Margaret O'Brien steals every scene she's

in as little sister Tootie. (In fact, she won a special Oscar, as the year's best child actress.) Screenplay by Irving Brecher and Fred F. Finkelhoffe.▼

Meet Me Tonight SEE: **Tonight at 8:30**

Meet Mr. Lucifer (1953-British) 83m. ** D: Anthony Pelissier. Stanley Holloway, Peggy Cummins, Jack Watling, Barbara Murray, Joseph Tomelty, Gordon Jackson, Jean Cadell, Kay Kendall, Ian Carmichael. Meek little satire on the evils of television, with Holloway in dual role as Devil and his earthly helper.

Meet Nero Wolfe (1936) 73m. **½ D: Herbert Biberman. Edward Arnold, Lionel Stander, Joan Perry, Victor Jory, Nana Bryant, Dennie Moore. Rex Stout's corpulent detective makes his screen debut, with Arnold faithfully playing him as demanding and difficult—in short, none too endearing; Stander is his legman, Archie. The mystery itself (with two seemingly unrelated murders) is not bad. Bonus: a young and beautiful Rita Cansino (later Hayworth) in a minor role.

Meet the Baron (1933) 65m. **½ D: Walter Lang. Jack Pearl, Jimmy Durante, ZaSu Pitts, Ted Healy and his Stooges, Edna May Oliver. Comic hodgepodge was an attempt to fashion a movie vehicle for radio comedian Pearl, in character as the tale-spinning, malaprop-laden Baron Munchausen. Supporting comics steal the show, especially Healy and his (Three) Stooges. There's also out of left field—a Busby Berkeleyish musical number with nearly nude coeds singing "Clean as a Whistle" while taking a shower!

Meet the Chump (1941) 60m. ** D: Edward Cline. Hugh Herbert, Lewis Howard, Jeanne Kelly (Brooks), Anne Nagel, Kathryn Adams, Shemp Howard, Richard Lane. Wacky Hugh plays inept trustee of estate due young Howard, desperate to find a way to cover the fact that he's dissipated $10 million. Mildly amusing, but generally routine.

Meet the People (1944) 100m. **½ D: Charles Riesner. Lucille Ball, Dick Powell, Virginia O'Brien, Bert Lahr, Rags Ragland, June Allyson, Mata and Hari. OK musicomedy of ex-stage star Ball trying to revive career; so-so score, many guests (Spike Jones, Vaughn Monroe, etc.).

Meet the Stewarts (1942) 73m. **½ D: Alfred E. Green. William Holden, Frances Dee, Grant Mitchell, Anne Revere, Mary Gordon, Marjorie Gateson, Margaret Hamilton, Don Beddoe. Wealthy girl marries hard-working Holden, can't adjust to new financial arrangement; not earthshaking, but enjoyable.

Megaforce (1982) C-99m. BOMB D: Hal Needham. Barry Bostwick, Persis Khambatta, Michael Beck, Edward Mulhare, George Furth, Henry Silva. Atrocious bubble-gum movie about an ultra-modern fighting force headed by one Ace Hunter (Bostwick, badly miscast). Embarrassing performances, clunky hardware, uninspired action scenes.▼

Mein Kampf (1961-Swedish) **117m.** *** D: Erwin Leiser. Narrated by Claude Stephenson. Technically smooth, impressive documentary chronicle of the horrors of Nazi Germany. The restrained narration allows the visuals to speak for themselves.▼

Melba (1953-British) **C-113m.** **½ D: Lewis Milestone. Patrice Munsel, Robert Morley, Sybil Thorndike, Martita Hunt, John McCallum. Occasionally interesting biography of Australian opera star Nellie Melba.

Melinda (1972) **C-109m.** *½ D: Hugh A. Robertson. Calvin Lockhart, Rosalind Cash, Vonetta McGee, Paul Stevens, Rockne Tarkington. Black disc jockey goes after his girlfriend's killers in violent melodrama; typical of the films that helped kill the blaxploitation genre.

Mélo (1986-French) **C-110m.** *** D: Alain Resnais. Sabine Azéma, Pierre Arditi, Andre Dussollier, Fanny Ardant, Jacques Dacqmine, Catherine Arditi. A different sort of film experiment from innovator Resnais, rigorously adapting Henry Bernstein's 1929 play about a tragic love triangle. Top-notch acting and direction make this one a winner, but static nature of the (intentionally) stagy production makes it not for all tastes.

Melody (1971-British) **C-103m.** *** D: Waris Hussein. Jack Wild, Mark Lester, Tracy Hyde, Sheila Steafel, Kate Williams, Roy Kinnear. Adolescent view of life, disarmingly played by Lester and Wild (from OLIVER!) as friends who rebel against adult establishment, particularly when Lester and girlfriend Hyde decide they want to get married. Music by The Bee Gees.▼

Melody Cruise (1933) **76m.** **½ D: Mark Sandrich. Charlie Ruggles, Phil Harris, Helen Mack, Greta Nissen, Chick Chandler, June Brewster. Sexy (pre-Production Code) musical comedy with Harris romancing Mack and Ruggles providing the laughs. Notable mainly for its imaginative use of photography and optical effects, which virtually steal the show. Director Sandrich went on to do the Astaire-Rogers musicals. Look for Betty Grable in an unbilled bit.▼

Melody for Three (1941) **67m.** ** D: Erle C. Kenton. Jean Hersholt, Fay Wray, Walter Woolf King, Astrid Allwyn, Schuyler Standish, Maude Eburne, Irene Ryan. Wray's presence uplifts this otherwise adequate entry in Hersholt's *Dr. Christian* series; she's the music-teacher mother of violin prodigy Standish, and is divorced from orchestra conductor King. You can

be sure that, by the final reel, the kindly doctor will reunite them.▼

Melvin and Howard (1980) **C-95m.** ***½ D: Jonathan Demme. Paul LeMat, Jason Robards, Mary Steenburgen, Jack Kehoe, Pamela Reed, Dabney Coleman, Michael J. Pollard, Gloria Grahame, Elizabeth Cheshire, Martine Beswicke, Charles Napier, Kathleen Sullivan, John Glover. Wonderful slice-of-life comedy based on the story of Melvin Dummar, who once gave a lift to a grizzled Howard Hughes and later produced a will naming himself as heir to the Hughes fortune. An endearing, bittersweet American fable, with Oscar-winner Steenburgen providing most of the comic highlights, including a memorable TV talent contest. Bo Goldman's script also won an Academy Award. (That's the real Melvin Dummar behind a bus station lunch counter, by the way.)▼

Melvin Purvis—G-Man (1974) **C-78m.** TVM D: Dan Curtis. Dale Robertson, Harris Yulin, Margaret Blye, Matt Clark, Elliott Street, John Karlen, David Canary, Dick Sargent. Robertson flamboyantly portrays lawman Purvis in this breezy fictional account (by John Milius) of his pursuit of Machine Gun Kelly (Yulin) through the midwest of the early '30s. A wonderful send-up of the type of gangster movie they don't make anymore. Above average. Retitled THE LEGEND OF MACHINE GUN KELLY. Sequel: THE KANSAS CITY MASSACRE.▼

Member of the Wedding, The (1952) **91m.** *** D: Fred Zinnemann. Ethel Waters, Julie Harris, Brandon de Wilde, Arthur Franz, Nancy Gates, James Edwards. Carson McCullers' sensitive account of child Harris prodded into growing up by her brother's forthcoming marriage. Waters, Harris and de Wilde movingly recreate their Broadway roles, the latter two making their film debuts. Slow but worthwhile.▼

Memed My Hawk (1987-British) **C-101m.** ** D: Peter Ustinov. Peter Ustinov, Herbert Lom, Denis Quilley, Michael Elphick, Simon Dutton, Leonie Mellinger, Barry Dennen, Siobhan McKenna, T.P. McKenna, Michael Gough. Disappointing drama with Ustinov cast as Abdi Aga, slimy, self-centered dictator of a Turkish village. Boring, despite the cast. Scripted by Ustinov, from the Yashar Kemal novel.

Memoirs of a Survivor (1981-British) **C-117m.** *½ D: David Gladwell. Julie Christie, Christopher Guard, Leonie Mellinger, Debbie Hutchings, Nigel Hawthorne, Pat Keen. Christie's presence cannot save this dismal, badly directed fantasy about a woman and a teenager (Mellinger) surviving in a decayed urban civilization. Good idea—film is based on a Doris Lessing novel—but poorly realized.

Memorial Day (1983) **C-100m. TVM** D: Joseph Sargent. Mike Farrell, Shelley Fabares, Keith Mitchell, Bonnie Bedelia, Robert Walden, Edward Herrmann, Bert Remsen. Successful lawyer's unplanned reunion with some Vietnam war buddies triggers memories he had struggled to put behind him. Powerful performances by Farrell and Walden give this one—an original by Michael Bortman—guts. Above average.▼

Memories Never Die (1982) **C-100m. TVM** D: Sandor Stern. Lindsay Wagner, Gerald McRaney, Melissa Michaelsen, Peter Billingsley, Barbara Babcock, Barbara Cason, Richard McKenzie, Richard Yniguez, Jay Robinson. Psychological drama about a woman who returns home after six years in a mental hospital only to find the same hostile environment she left behind. Based on Zoe Sherbourne's *A Stranger in the House.* Average.

Memories of Me (1988) **C-105m.** ** D: Henry Winkler. Billy Crystal, Alan King, JoBeth Williams, Janet Carroll, David Ackroyd, Phil Fondacaro, Robert Pastorelli, Sidney Miller. A heart surgeon, who recently suffered a heart attack himself, seeks out his father, from whom he's been estranged, hoping to put his life in order. Contrived comedy-drama combines comic shtick with mawkish emotional scenes and never quite manages to be convincing. Crystal cowrote the screenplay and coproduced with King.▼

Memory of Eva Ryker, The (1980) **C-144m. TVM** D: Walter Grauman. Natalie Wood, Robert Foxworth, Ralph Bellamy, Roddy McDowall, Bradford Dillman, Jean-Pierre Aumont, Peter Graves, Mel Ferrer, Morgan Fairchild. Stellar Irwin Allen disaster movie, with Wood, in a mother/daughter dual role, haunted by her experience in the wartime torpedoing of a luxury liner, which decades later still has a fascination for a number of people. Average.

Memory of Justice, The (1976-German-U.S.) **C-278m.** **** D: Marcel Ophuls. Outstanding documentary from the director of THE SORROW AND THE PITY questions how one country can pass judgment on the atrocities of others by examining the Nuremberg trials and their aftermath, the French performance in Algeria and the American intervention in Vietnam. Always riveting in spite of its mammoth length.▼

Memory of Us (1974) **C-93m.** **½ D: H. Kaye Dyal. Ellen Geer, Jon Cypher, Barbara Colby, Peter Brown, Robert Hogan, Rose Marie, Will Geer. Modest, interesting contemporary drama about a happily married woman who begins to question her role as wife and mother; script by star Ellen Geer, whose father Will makes brief appearance.▼

Men, The (1950) **85m.** ***½ D: Fred

Zinnemann. Marlon Brando, Teresa Wright, Jack Webb, Everett Sloane, Howard St. John. Brando excels in film debut as ex-GI trying to readjust to life after wartime injury; low-keyed acting is most effective. Retitled: BATTLE STRIPE.▼

Men . . . (1985-German) **C-99m.** ***½ D: Doris Dörrie. Heiner Lauterbach, Uwe Ochsenknecht, Ulrike Kriener, Janna Marangosoff. Ingenious comedy-satire about an uptight adman who becomes haplessly jealous when he learns that his wife's having an affair. He promptly befriends her lover and becomes his roommate, with hilarious results. ▼

Menace, The (1932) **64m.** ** D: Roy William Neill. H. B. Warner, Bette Davis, Walter Byron, Natalie Moorhead, William B. Davidson, Crauford Kent. Man seeks revenge on his stepmother and her cohorts, who framed him for his father's murder. Based on an Edgar Wallace story; handsome, but stodgy, and pretty obvious. Davis plays a demure British ingenue.

Menace in the Night (1958-British) **78m.** *½ D: Lance Comfort. Griffith Jones, Lisa Gastoni, Vincent Ball, Eddie Byrne. Tired tale of witness to murder being pressured by gang not to testify.

Men Against the Sky (1940) **75m.** *½ D: Leslie Goodwins. Richard Dix, Wendy Barrie, Kent Taylor, Edmund Lowe, Granville Bates, Grant Withers. Veteran cast in RKO programmer about personnel at aircraft-building plant.

Menage (1986-French) **C-84m.** *** D: Bertrand Blier. Gerard Depardieu, Michel Blanc, Miou-Miou, Bruno Cremer, Jean-Pierre Marielle. Outrageous, fast-paced farce about a roguish, gay crook (Depardieu), who thoroughly disrupts the lives of an impoverished couple (Blanc and Miou-Miou)—sexually and otherwise. Peters out at the end but still worth a look.

Men Are Not Gods (1937-British) **90m.** **½ D: Walter Reisch. Miriam Hopkins, Gertrude Lawrence, Sebastian Shaw, Rex Harrison, A.E. Matthews. Talky predecessor to A DOUBLE LIFE, with Harrison et al. almost making their play-acting *Othello* come true.

Me, Natalie (1969) **C-111m.** **½ D: Fred Coe. Patty Duke, James Farentino, Martin Balsam, Elsa Lanchester, Salome Jens, Nancy Marchand, Deborah Winters, Al Pacino. Soap opera-ish tale about unattractive N.Y.C. girl struggling to find herself gets tremendous boost by Duke's great performance; otherwise, film wavers uncomfortably between comedy and drama. Pacino's feature debut.

Men Don't Leave (1990) **C-115m.** *** D: Paul Brickman. Jessica Lange, Arliss Howard, Joan Cusack, Chris O'Donnell, Charlie Korsmo, Kathy Bates, Tom Mason, Jim Haynie. Widowed Lange, left broke with two sons, relocates from small-town Maryland to a downtown Baltimore high rise. Erratic but well-performed comedy-drama is compromised by introduction of movie-predictable (if, in this case, welcomely eccentric) Mr. Right. Good moments abound, though, particularly between Lange and flaky nurse Cusack. And ultimately, film offers a good cry. Brickman's second directorial credit, following a seven-year layoff after RISKY BUSINESS. Remake of French film LA VIE CONTINUE.▼

Men in Her Diary (1945) 73m. **½ D: Charles Barton. Peggy Ryan, Jon Hall, Louise Allbritton, Ernest Truex, Virginia Grey, William Terry, Alan Mowbray, Eric Blore, Maxie Rosenbloom. Zesty comedy of jealous wife, helpless husband, and knockout secretary; vivacious Allbritton, who never really got her due in films, is seen to good advantage here.

Men in Her Life, The (1941) 90m. **½ D: Gregory Ratoff. Loretta Young, Conrad Veidt, Dean Jagger, Eugenie Leontovich, John Shepperd (Shepperd Strudwick), Otto Kruger. Ballerina Young marries her dancing teacher but recalls many suitors she's known in the past. Fairly interesting love-life saga.

Men in War (1957) 104m. **½ D: Anthony Mann. Robert Ryan, Aldo Ray, Robert Keith, Vic Morrow, James Edwards, Scott Marlowe, Victor Sen Yung. Standard war film set in Korea in 1950s, with good action scenes distinguishing usual story.▼

Men in White (1934) 80m. **½ D: Richard Boleslawski. Clark Gable, Myrna Loy, Jean Hersholt, Elizabeth Allan, Otto Kruger, Wallace Ford, Henry B. Walthall, Samuel S. Hinds. Sterling cast in sterile filming of Sidney Kingsley's play; Gable is doctor torn between study with Hersholt and marriage to society girl Loy.

Men of Boys Town (1941) 106m. **½ D: Norman Taurog. Spencer Tracy, Mickey Rooney, Bobs Watson, Larry Nunn, Darryl Hickman, Henry O'Neill, Lee J. Cobb. If you liked BOYS TOWN . . .

Men of Brazil (1960-Brazilian) C-68m. ** D: Nelson Marcellino de Carvalho, Otto Lopes Barbosa, Carlos Anselmo. Damasio Cardoso, Nair Cardoso, Nelson Marcellino de Carvalho, Odette de Carvalho. Strained diatribe on labor unions, mixed with far-fetched human-interest dramatics.

Men of Sherwood Forest (1954-British) C-77m. ** D: Val Guest. Don Taylor, Reginald Beckwith, Eileen Moore, David King Wood. Yet another Robin Hood yarn, with Taylor properly sword-wielding and cavalier.

Men of Steel SEE: Steel▼

Men of the Dragon (1974) C-78m. TVM D: Harry Falk. Jared Martin, Katie Saylor,

Robert Ito, Lee Tit War, David Chow, Joseph Wiseman. Chopsocky action, a TV-movie rarity, with a team of kung fu experts thwarting a gang of modern-day white slavers. The pits. Below average.

Men of the Fighting Lady (1954) C-80m. *** D: Andrew Marton. Van Johnson, Walter Pidgeon, Louis Calhern, Dewey Martin, Keenan Wynn, Frank Lovejoy, Robert Horton, Bert Freed. Above-par Korean War actioner, focusing on lives of men on U. S. aircraft carrier.

Men of Two Worlds (1946-British) C-107m. ** D: Thorold Dickinson. Phyllis Calvert, Eric Portman, Robert Adams, Cathleen Nesbitt, Orlando Martins, Cyril Raymond. Unhappy conglomeration of clichés about well-meaning British officials trying to protect natives in Africa. Retitled WITCH DOCTOR.

Men's Club, The (1986) C-100m. BOMB D: Peter Medak. David Dukes, Richard Jordan, Harvey Keitel, Frank Langella, Roy Scheider, Craig Wasson, Treat Williams, Stockard Channing, Cindy Pickett, Gwen Welles, Ann Dusenberry, Jennifer Jason Leigh, Ann Wedgeworth. Jumbled, barely released expansion of Leonard Michaels' novel (scripted by the author) about seven males who try starting an encounter group in Jordan's home. Undistinguished performances despite that interesting cast; only noteworthy aspect is the elegant brothel for high-rollers, "The House of Affection." Ridiculous finale. ▼

Men Without Souls (1940) 62m. ** D: Nick Grinde. Barton MacLane, John Litel, Rochelle Hudson, Glenn Ford, Don Beddoe, Cy Kendall. Strictly standard prison film, with young Ford caught up in prison scandal. MacLane repeats role from dozens of other bighouse epics.

Men With Wings (1938) C-105m. **½ D: William A. Wellman. Fred MacMurray, Louise Campbell, Ray Milland, Andy Devine, Walter Abel, Virginia Weidler. Fictional tale of the epic of flight, with usual love triangle. After good start, it drags on. Donald O'Connor is one of the kids in the opening scenes.

Mephisto (1981-Hungarian) C-135m. *** D: Istvan Szabo. Klaus Maria Brandauer, Krystyna Janda, Ildiko Bansagi, Karin Boyd, Rolf Hoppe, Christine Harbot. Brandauer is magnetic as a vain, brilliant German actor who sells himself to gain prestige when the Nazis come to power. Engrossing drama is handsomely produced if a bit uneven. Based on a novel by Klaus Mann, son of Thomas, who committed suicide allegedly because he could not get the book published. Academy Award winner as Best Foreign Film. First of a trilogy, followed by COLONEL REDL and HANUSSEN.▼

Mephisto Waltz, The (1971) C-108m.

*** D: Paul Wendkos. Alan Alda, Jacqueline Bisset, Barbara Parkins, Curt Jurgens, Brad Dillman, William Windom, Kathleen Widdoes. Chiller about young journalist who falls prey to Satanic cult after meeting dying concert pianist Jurgens; good occult story with some truly frightening moments. Adapted by Ben Maddow from the Fred Mustard Stewart novel.▼

Mercenaries, The SEE: Cuba Crossing▼

Mercenary, The (1970-Italian) **C-105m.** ****½ D:** Sergio Corbucci. Franco Nero, Tony Musante, Jack Palance, Giovanna Ralli. Better-than-average Italian pasta Western with loads of action and violence and a welcome serving of humor. At odds with one another: a stalwart mercenary (Nero), his sadistic rival (Palance), a patriotic revolutionary (Musante), a lusty peasant girl and a greedy mineowner.

Merchant of Four Seasons, The (1971-German) **C-88m.** ***** D:** Rainer Werner Fassbinder. Hans Hirschmuller, Irm Hermann, Hanna Schygulla, Andrea Schober, Gusti Kreissl. Fruit peddler trapped in unhappy marriage and frustrated with his life disintegrates mentally and emotionally in this surprisingly rich and poignant meditation on mundane existence and failed dreams.▼

Mercy or Murder? (1987) **C-100m.** TVM D: Steve Gethers. Robert Young, Frances Reid, Michael Learned, Marshall Colt, Eddie Albert. Docudrama about highly publicized case of Roswell Gilbert, a Florida senior citizen who took the life of his beloved wife after she contracted Alzheimer's disease. Young effectively portrays the man who went to prison largely because he refused to show remorse for what he had done. It's interesting to compare this with the much earlier movie AN ACT OF MURDER with Fredric March and Florence Eldridge. Average.

Merrill's Marauders (1962) **C-98m.** ****½ D:** Samuel Fuller. Jeff Chandler, Ty Hardin, Peter Brown, Andrew Duggan, Will Hutchins, Claude Akins. Rugged action scenes spark this typical Fuller actioner set in Burma during WW2.

Merrily We Go to Hell (1932) **78m.** ***½ D:** Dorothy Arzner. Fredric March, Sylvia Sidney, Adrienne Allen, Skeets Gallagher, Kent Taylor, Cary Grant. Plodding story (despite intriguing title) of heiress Sidney marrying reporter March on whim, discovering that he's a problem-drinker. Starts well but sinks fast.

Merrily We Live (1938) **90m.** ***** D:** Norman Z. McLeod. Constance Bennett, Brian Aherne, Alan Mowbray, Billie Burke, Bonita Granville, Tom Brown, Ann Dvorak, Patsy Kelly. It's all been done before, but fluttery Burke hiring suave Aherne as butler who tames spoiled Bennett is still engaging fun.

Merry Andrew (1958) **C-103m.** ****½ D:** Michael Kidd. Danny Kaye, Pier Angeli, Baccaloni, Robert Coote. Danny is a British teacher-archeologist with a yen for the circus and one of its performers (Angeli) in this bright musicomedy. Not as wacky as earlier Kaye efforts, but good.

Merry Christmas, Mr. Lawrence (1983-British-Japanese) **C-122m.** ***** D:** Nagisa Oshima. Tom Conti, David Bowie, Ryuichi Sakamoto, Takeshi, Jack Thompson. Oshima's first film in English (for the most part) is strange, haunting drama set in Japanese POW camp, centering on test of wills between martinet commander Sakamoto and British major Bowie. Quite rewarding for those willing to stick with it, but it does take some effort; splendid performances all around, especially Takeshi as tough sergeant and Conti as title character, camp's only bilingual prisoner. Japanese music superstar Sakamoto also composed the score.▼

Merry Go Round of 1938 (1937) **87m.** ****½ D:** Irving Cummings. Bert Lahr, Jimmy Savo, Billy House, Mischa Auer, Alice Brady, Joy Hodges, Louise Fazenda. Disappointing backstage story with sentimental overtones as comedy foursome adopts little girl. Good specialty acts, great cast make tired tale endurable.

Merry Monahans, The (1944) **91m.** ****½ D:** Charles Lamont. Donald O'Connor, Peggy Ryan, Jack Oakie, Ann Blyth, Rosemary De Camp, John Miljan. Spirited cast does its best with bland, utterly predictable vaudeville saga, filled with period tunes like "When You Wore a Tulip."

Merry Widow, The (1934) **99m.** ***** D:** Ernst Lubitsch. Maurice Chevalier, Jeanette MacDonald, Una Merkel, Edward Everett Horton, George Barbier, Herman Bing. Lavish, delightful filming of Lehar operetta, with usual Lubitsch charm and hand-picked cast. Infectious score is still first-rate. Retitled: THE LADY DANCES.▼

Merry Widow, The (1952) **C-105m.** ****½ D:** Curtis Bernhardt. Lana Turner, Fernando Lamas, Una Merkel, Richard Haydn. Franz Lehar's operetta seems dated and trite in plush but unenthusiastic remake.

Merton of the Movies (1947) **82m.** **** D:** Robert Alton. Red Skelton, Virginia O'Brien, Gloria Grahame, Leon Ames, Alan Mowbray, Hugo Haas. Lifeless remake of George S. Kaufman–Marc Connelly play (filmed before in 1924 and 1932) about movie-struck simpleton's adventures in Hollywood. A real disappointment. Choreographer Alton's directing debut.

Mesmerized (1986-British-Australian-New Zealand) **C-97m.** ***½ D:** Michael Laughlin. Jodie Foster, John Lithgow, Michael Murphy, Harry Andrews, Dan Shor, Reg Evans, Philip Holder. Weird, ultimately silly drama about innocent orphan Foster, who weds a stern, older man (Lithgow) in late 19th century New Zealand. Laughlin wrote the screenplay, from an original treatment by Jerzy Skolimowski.▼

Message, The SEE: **Mohammad, Messenger of God**▼

Message from Space (1978-Japanese) **C-105m.** **½ D: Kinji Fukasaku. Vic Morrow, Sonny Chiba, Philip Casnoff, Peggy Lee Brennan, Sue Shiomi, Tetsuro Tamba. Embattled planet sends SOS, and intergalactic team comes to its rescue. Cardboard performances take back seat to special effects and "cute" robot, both obviously patterned after STAR WARS.

Message to Garcia, A (1936) **77m.** *** D: George Marshall. Wallace Beery, Barbara Stanwyck, John Boles, Alan Hale, Mona Barrie, Herbert Mundin. Historical fiction about agent Boles trying to reach General Garcia during Spanish-American war, with dubious help of roguish Beery and well-bred Stanwyck. Very entertaining.

Message to My Daughter (1973) **C-78m. TVM.** D: Robert Michael Lewis. Martin Sheen, Bonnie Bedelia, Kitty Winn, Neva Patterson, Mark Slade, Lucille Benson. Poignant melodrama about confused teenager (Winn) who finds emotional strength from tapes recorded years earlier by her long-deceased mother (Bedelia). Quality casting makes the difference on this weeper, not unlike SUNSHINE. Average.

Messenger of Death (1988) **C-91m.** *½ D: J. Lee Thompson. Charles Bronson, Trish Van Devere, Laurence Luckinbill, Jeff Corey, Marilyn Hassett, John Ireland, Daniel Benzali. Boring Bronson vehicle casts him as a reporter determined to get to the bottom of an odd murder case involving two warring Mormon sects led by Corey and Ireland. By-the-numbers filmmaking wastes a potentially interesting look at a different culture.▼

Metalstorm: The Destruction of Jared-Syn (1983) **C-84m.** BOMB D: Charles Band. Jeffrey Byron, Tim Thomerson, Kelly Preston, Mike Preston, Richard Moll. Derivative sci-fi film set in the future, with an intrepid hunter searching out megalomaniac who wants to rule the planet. Even 3D couldn't do much to help this amateurish—and seemingly interminable—outing.▼

Meteor (1979) **C-103m.** *½ D: Ronald Neame. Sean Connery, Natalie Wood, Karl Malden, Brian Keith, Henry Fonda, Martin Landau, Trevor Howard, Richard Dysart. Switzerland, Hong Kong, and Manhattan all get a big piece of the rock when a giant meteor comes crashing to Earth. Late entry in Hollywood's disaster cycle wastes fine cast with dull script, shoddy effects.▼

Metropolis (1926-German) **120m.** **** D: Fritz Lang. Brigitte Helm, Alfred Abel, Gustav Froelich, Rudolf Klein-Rogge, Fritz Rasp. Classic silent-film fantasy of futuristic city and its mechanized society, with upper-class young man abandoning his life of luxury to join oppressed workers in a revolt. Heavy going at times, but startling set design and special effects command attention throughout. Many shorter prints exist; reissued in 1984 at 87m. with color-tints and score by Giorgio Moroder.▼

Metropolitan (1935) **75m.** **½ D: Richard Boleslawski. Lawrence Tibbett, Virginia Bruce, Alice Brady, Cesar Romero, Thurston Hall, Luis Alberni, Ruth Donnelly, George Marion, Sr., Jane Darwell. Enjoyable if predictable musical with Tibbett ideally cast as a talented but struggling opera singer who yearns for stardom. Tibbett's many songs include "Road to Mandalay" and "Figaro," which he performs most impressively.

Mexican Hayride (1948) **77m.** ** D: Charles Barton. Bud Abbott, Lou Costello, Virginia Grey, Luba Malina, John Hubbard, Pedro de Cordoba, Fritz Feld. Lackluster A&C vehicle, with the boys on a wild goose chase with a mine deed in Mexico. Based on a Cole Porter Broadway musical, but without the songs!

Mexican Manhunt (1953) **71m.** *½ D: Rex Bailey. George Brent, Hillary Brooke, Morris Ankrum, Karen Sharpe. Actors walk through thin script about solving of old crime.

MGM's Big Parade of Comedy (1964) **100m.** **½ Compiled by Robert Youngson. Fifty of the greatest stars of all time appear in this compilation, but too briefly. Harlow's scenes are seconds long; you can miss others if you blink. Still worthwhile for many priceless sequences with Garbo, Laurel and Hardy, Keaton, Gable, Robert Benchley, Marion Davies, Marx Brothers, et al.

Miami Blues (1990) **C-99m.** ** D: George Armitage. Fred Ward, Alec Baldwin, Jennifer Jason Leigh, Nora Dunn, Charles Napier, Jose Perez, Paul Gleason, Obba Babatunde, Martine Beswicke. Psychopathic thief and murderer (Baldwin) arrives in Miami, hooks up with a naive young woman who's blind to his problems, and sets a world-weary cop on his trail by stealing the detective's badge and I.D. Three dynamic performances and some hip, high-style filmmaking command your attention—but the rampant amorality and violence leave a bad taste. Jonathan Demme and costar Ward were among the producers.

Miami Expose (1956) **73m.** *½ D: Fred F. Sears. Lee J. Cobb, Patricia Medina, Edward Arnold, Michael Granger. Boring round-up of criminal syndicate in Sunshine State.

Miami Story, The (1954) **75m.** ** D: Fred F. Sears. Barry Sullivan, Luther Adler, John Baer, Adele Jergens, Beverly Garland. Stern ex-con Sullivan redeems himself in Florida resort city.

Michael Shayne, Private Detective (1940) 77m. **½ D: Eugene Forde. Lloyd Nolan, Marjorie Weaver, Joan Valerie, Walter Abel, Elizabeth Patterson, Donald MacBride. Nolan gives vivid portrayal of detective Shayne, keeping an eye on heavy gambler Weaver in average private-eye thriller. First of a brief series.

Michael Strogoff SEE: **Soldier and the Lady, The**

Michigan Kid (1947) C-69m. ** D: Ray Taylor. Jon Hall, Victor McLaglen, Rita Johnson, Andy Devine, Byron Foulger. Colorful but routine refilming of Rex Beach story of female ranch owner Johnson falling victim to corrupt town government.

Mickey (1948) C-87m. ** D: Ralph Murphy. Lois Butler, Bill Goodwin, Irene Hervey, Hattie McDaniel, John Sutton, Rose Hobart. Naive yarn about rambunctious teen-ager (Butler) who turns matchmaker for father (Goodwin).

Mickey One (1965) 93m. *** D: Arthur Penn. Warren Beatty, Hurd Hatfield, Alexandra Stewart, Teddy Hart, Jeff Corey, Franchot Tone. Beatty stars as confused nightclub comedian looking for new life and some worthwhile values. Will put off some because of hero's offbeat character. Highly underrated, quite good.

Mickey Spillane's Margin for Murder (1981) C-100m. TVM D: Daniel Haller. Kevin Dobson, Charles Hallahan, Cindy Pickett, Donna Dixon, Asher Brauner, Floyd Levine, Aarika Wells, John Considine. Fictional gumshoe Mike Hammer returns to track down the killer of his best friend; this pilot to a new series about the toughguy detective didn't sell, but a subsequent one, 'MURDER ME, MURDER YOU,' with Stacy Keach, did. Average.

Mickey Spillane's Mike Hammer 'Murder Me, Murder You' SEE: **'Murder Me, Murder You'**

Mickey Spillane's Mike Hammer: Murder Takes All (1989) C-100m. TVM D: John Nicolella. Stacy Keach, Lynda Carter, Lindsay Bloom, Don Stroud, Lyle Alzado, Ed Winter, Michelle Phillips. Hammer works his way through Vegas glitz and double dealing after becoming prime suspect in the murder of a club singer during a nationwide telethon. Average.

Micki & Maude (1984) C-118m. **½ D: Blake Edwards. Dudley Moore, Amy Irving, Ann Reinking, Richard Mulligan, George Gaynes, Wallace Shawn, Lu Leonard, Priscilla Pointer. Dudley has a wife and a girlfriend—and they're both pregnant! Surprisingly warmhearted comedy that turns into old-fashioned farce. Runs out of steam somewhere along the line but benefits from winning performances by all three leads.▼

Midas Run (1969) C-106m. **½ D: Alf Kjellin. Fred Astaire, Richard Crenna, Anne Heywood, Ralph Richardson, Roddy McDowell, Cesar Romero. British secret serviceman plots a daring gold heist in this routine caper film, enlivened by Astaire's peerless presence in the lead. Fred Astaire, Jr. appears briefly as copilot of plane.

Midas Valley (1985) C-100m. TVM D: Gus Trikonis. Jean Simmons, Robert Stack, George Grizzard, Brett Cullen, Joseph Hacker, France Nuyen, Linda Purl, James Read, Shanna Reed, Catherine Mary Stewart. *Knots Landing/Falcon Crest* clone set in silicon valley of Northern California. Busted series pilot. Average.

Middle Age Crazy (1980-Canadian) C-95m. *½ D: John Trent. Bruce Dern, Ann-Margret, Graham Jarvis, Eric Christmas, Deborah Wakeham. Title tells all: 40-year-old Dern buys a Porsche, some new threads, and leaves wife Ann-Margret for pro-football cheerleader Wakeham. Nothing new; inspired by the hit song.▼

Middle of the Night (1959) 118m. **½ D: Delbert Mann. Kim Novak, Fredric March, Glenda Farrell, Jan Norris, Lee Grant, Effie Afton, Martin Balsam, Joan Copeland. Slow-moving screen version of Paddy Chayefsky play, with March a middle-aged man about to marry much younger Novak.

Middle of the World, The (1974-French-Swiss) C-115m. *** D: Alain Tanner. Olimpia Carlisi, Philippe Leotard, Juliet Berto, Jacques Denis, Roger Jendly. Intelligent, quietly effective tale of married engineer Leotard, running for political office, who has scandalous affair with waitress Carlisi.

Midnight (1934) 80m. **½ D: Chester Erskine. Sidney Fox, O. P. Heggie, Henry Hull, Margaret Wycherly, Lynne Overman, Richard Whorf, Humphrey Bogart. Jury foreman is persecuted by the press—and even his family—after sending woman to the electric chair. Dated but interesting theatrical piece, reissued as CALL IT MURDER to capitalize on Bogart's later stardom.▼

Midnight (1939) 94m. ***½ D: Mitchell Leisen. Claudette Colbert, Don Ameche, John Barrymore, Francis Lederer, Mary Astor, Hedda Hopper, Monty Woolley. Penniless Colbert masquerades as Hungarian countess in chic Parisian marital mixup; near-classic comedy written by Billy Wilder and Charles Brackett. Barrymore's antics are especially memorable. Remade as MASQUERADE IN MEXICO.

Midnight (1981) C-94m. **½ D: John Russo. Lawrence Tierney, Melanie Verliin, John Amplas, John Hall, Charles Jackson, Doris Hackney. Low-budget horror, shot in Pennsylvania, isn't bad. Unfortunate teenager Verliin, driven out of her home by a

[749]

lecherous policeman stepfather (Tierney), meets two young thieves and then a family of cultists who sacrifice young women. Russo adapted his own novel. Also known as BACKWOODS MASSACRE.▼

Midnight (1989) **C-86m.** *½ D: Norman Thaddeus Vane. Lynn Redgrave, Tony Curtis, Steven Parrish, Frank Gorshin, Wolfman Jack, Gustav Vintas, Karen Witter. Tiresome story of TV horror-movie hostess who finds people around her mysteriously dying. Always-watchable Redgrave does her best, but meager, slow-moving script does her in. A longer "director's cut" of the film had theatrical showings following its video release.▼

Midnight Auto Supply SEE: Love and the Midnight Auto Supply

Midnight Cop (1989-West German) **C-96m.** **½ D: Peter Patzak. Armin Mueller-Stahl, Michael York, Morgan Fairchild, Frank Stallone, Julia Kent, Monica Bleibtreu, Allegra Curtis, Henry Friedman. Slow but interesting murder mystery pitting quirky Berlin cop against both a serial killer and a blackmailer. Overdone tenor sax jazz score and murky plot developments hamper things, but Mueller-Stahl is very good.▼

Midnight Cowboy (1969) **C-113m.** **** D: John Schlesinger. Dustin Hoffman, Jon Voight, Sylvia Miles, John McGiver, Brenda Vaccaro, Barnard Hughes, Ruth White, Jennifer Salt, Bob Balaban. Emotionally shattering dramatization of James Leo Herlihy's novel was rated X in 1969, but it's essentially an old-fashioned story with some unusual modern twists: hayseed Voight comes to N.Y.C., becomes a stud, and develops unusual and deep friendship with seedy Ratso Rizzo (Hoffman). Seamiest side of N.Y.C. is backdrop for compelling, keen-eyed character study that if anything looks better today than it did when it first came out. Oscar winner for Best Picture, Director, Screenplay (Waldo Salt). But please don't watch it on commercial TV: the most lenient prints run 104m. and are ludicrously dubbed to remove foul language. ▼

Midnight Crossing (1988) **C-104m.** *½ D: Roger Holzberg. Faye Dunaway, Daniel J. Travanti, Kim Cattrall, Ned Beatty, John Laughlin. Hokey, boring, needlessly violent soaper-adventure, with insurance agent Travanti intent on recovering some booty he and his late pal buried years before. Dunaway is thanklessly cast as his wife, who is blind.▼

Midnight Express (1978) **C-121m.** ***½ D: Alan Parker. Brad Davis, Irene Miracle, Bo Hopkins, Randy Quaid, John Hurt, Mike Kellin, Paul Smith. Riveting, harshly violent story of young American Billy Hayes (Davis), who faces physical and emotional brutalization in Turkish prison after being caught drug-smuggling. Great moviemaking,

though not as faithful to Hayes' true story as filmmakers would have us believe. Oscar winner for Oliver Stone's script and Giorgio Moroder's score.▼

Midnight Hour, The (1985) **C-100m.** TVM D: Jack Bender. Shari Belafonte-Harper, LeVar Burton, Lee Montgomery, Dick Van Patten, Kevin McCarthy, Jonelle Allen, Dedee Pfeiffer, Mark Blankfield. Bland concoction of teen comedies, music videos, horror spoofs, and monster mashes involving a gang of high-school pranksters whose invocation of an ancient curse has ghouls and goblins descending on their town. Below average.▼

Midnight Lace (1960) **C-108m.** *** D: David Miller. Doris Day, Rex Harrison, John Gavin, Myrna Loy, Roddy McDowall, Herbert Marshall, Natasha Parry. Shrill murder mystery; unbelievable plot line, but star cast and decor smooth over rough spots. Set in London; redone as a TVM.▼

Midnight Lace (1980) **C-100m.** TVM D: Ivan Nagy. Mary Crosby, Gary Frank, Celeste Holm, Carolyn Jones, Shecky Greene, Robin Clarke, Susan Tyrrell. Trite road-company update of the old Doris Day thriller providing Bing Crosby's daughter, Mary, with her first starring role. Based on Janet Green's novel, *Matilda Shouted Fire*. Below average.

Midnight Madness (1980) **C-110m.** BOMB D: David Wechter, Michael Nankin. David Naughton, Debra Clinger, Eddie Deezen, Brad Wilkin, Maggie Roswell, Stephen Furst. Idiotic comedy about college students participating in an all-night scavenger hunt. Nothing to stay up for (unless you want to see Michael J. Fox in his feature film debut). First PG-rated Disney film (although the name "Disney" is nowhere in evidence on the credits).▼

Midnight Man, The (1974) **C-117m.** **½ ✓ D: Roland Kibbee, Burt Lancaster. Burt Lancaster, Susan Clark, Cameron Mitchell, Morgan Woodward, Joan Lorring, Ed Lauter, Catherine Bach, Linda Kelsey. Involved, overlong mystery with Lancaster as college security officer looking into a coed's murder. Lancaster and Kibbee also co-wrote and co-produced.

Midnight Mary (1933) **74m.** *** D: William A. Wellman. Loretta Young, Ricardo Cortez, Franchot Tone, Andy Devine, Una Merkel, Frank Conroy, Warren Hymer, Ivan Simpson, Harold Huber. Visually arresting story, told in flashback, of hard luck Young, orphaned at nine, seduced at sixteen, sent to prison. Loaded with Wellman flourishes, and Loretta is mesmerizingly beautiful. Story by Anita Loos.

Midnight Offerings (1981) **C-100m.** TVM D: Rod Holcomb. Melissa Sue Anderson, Mary McDonough, Patrick Cassidy, Marion Ross, Gordon Jump, Cathryn Damon.

Teenage witchcraft results in a contest between good and evil. Below average.

Midnight Run (1988) C-122m. ***½ D: Martin Brest. Robert De Niro, Charles Grodin, Yaphet Kotto, John Ashton, Dennis Farina, Joe Pantoliano, Wendy Phillips, Richard Foronjy. Socko action-comedy with bounty hunter (and ex-cop) De Niro determined to bring bail-jumper Grodin, an embezzling accountant, from N.Y. to L.A. What De Niro *doesn't* know is that the Mob is also on Grodin's trail—with orders to kill. Sensational byplay between the stars is matched by first-rate action and a sharply written script by George Gallo. Director Brest handles the blend of violence and comedy as well as he did in BEVERLY HILLS COP. Dynamic music score by Danny Elfman.▼

Midnight Story, The (1957) 89m. **½ D: Joseph Pevney. Tony Curtis, Marisa Pavan, Gilbert Roland, Ted de Corsia, Kathleen Freeman. Atmospheric murder yarn with Curtis an ex-cop seeking the culprit who killed neighborhood priest.

Midsummer Night's Dream, A (1935) 117m. *** D: Max Reinhardt, William Dieterle. James Cagney, Dick Powell, Joe E. Brown, Jean Muir, Hugh Herbert, Olivia de Havilland, Ian Hunter, Frank McHugh, Victor Jory, Ross Alexander, Verree Teasdale, Anita Louise, Mickey Rooney, Arthur Treacher, Billy Barty. Hollywood-Shakespeare has good and bad points; Cagney as Bottom and the Mendelssohn music are among good parts; Hugh Herbert and other incongruous cast members make up the latter. After a while Rooney (as Puck) gets to be a bit too much. Hal Mohr's glistening cinematography won an Oscar—the only one ever awarded on a write-in. This was the only sound film of esteemed European stage director Reinhardt. Film debut of Olivia de Havilland (who had appeared in Reinhardt's Hollywood Bowl production of the play a year earlier). Originally 132m.▼

Midsummer Night's Dream, A (1966) C-93m. **½ D: Dan Eriksen. Suzanne Farrell, Edward Villella, Arthur Mitchell, Mimi Paul, Nicholas Magallanes. Filmed record of New York City Ballet's presentation of Shakespeare's comedy is mostly for dance buffs; film makes some attempt to be cinematic, but not enough.

Midsummer Night's Dream, A (1968-British) C-124m. **½ D: Peter Hall. Diana Rigg, David Warner, Michael Jayston, Ian Richardson, Judi Dench, Ian Holm, Bill Travers. Fine cast of England's Royal Shakespeare Co. in middling performance of the Shakespeare classic.▼

Midsummer Night's Sex Comedy, A (1982) C-88m. *** D: Woody Allen. Woody Allen, Mia Farrow, Jose Ferrer, Mary Steenburgen, Tony Roberts, Julie

Hagerty. SMILES OF A SUMMER NIGHT, Woody Allen-style; a quirky, entertaining diversion about sexual byplay among three couples on a summer weekend in the country, circa 1900. Appealing cast (including Farrow, in her first film with Woody), exquisite Gordon Willis photography.▼

Midway (1976) C-132m. ** D: Jack Smight. Charlton Heston, Henry Fonda, James Coburn, Glenn Ford, Hal Holbrook, Robert Mitchum, Cliff Robertson, Toshiro Mifune, Robert Wagner, Robert Webber, Christopher George, Kevin Dobson. Close to being a rip-off as prominent cast acts to cans of stock shots from THIRTY SECONDS OVER TOKYO, antique Japanese war films, and actual wartime footage. Silly soap opera (Heston's ensign son in love with Japanese girl) doesn't help. The wonder is that some of the drama and impact of the great naval battle still comes through. Tom Selleck has a bit.▼

Mighty Barnum, The (1934) 87m. *** D: Walter Lang. Wallace Beery, Adolphe Menjou, Virginia Bruce, Rochelle Hudson, Janet Beecher, Herman Bing. Fanciful biography of world-famous showman, with Menjou as his reluctant partner Bailey. More Beery than Barnum.

Mighty Crusaders, The (1957-Italian) C-87m. ** D: Carlo Ludovico Bragaglia. Francisco Rabal, Sylva Koscina, Gianna Maria Canale, Rik Battaglia. Sloppy picturization of Tasso's epic poem, with contrived love tale between Saracen and Christian backdrop to siege of Jerusalem; amateurish production values.

Mighty Joe Young (1949) 94m. *** D: Ernest B. Schoedsack. Terry Moore, Ben Johnson, Robert Armstrong, Mr. Joseph Young, Frank McHugh. Updating of KING KONG theme has comparable (and Oscar-winning) special effects by Willis O'Brien and Ray Harryhausen, but no matching story line, and Moore is no Fay Wray. Mr. Young is good, though. Last sequence was originally shown with color tints, which have been restored for laserdisc. Also shown in computer-colored version.▼

Mighty McGurk, The (1946) 85m. *½ D: John Waters. Wallace Beery, Dean Stockwell, Dorothy Patrick, Edward Arnold, Aline MacMahon, Cameron Mitchell. Formula Beery vehicle with the star a punchy prizefighter and Stockwell as adorable boy he adopts.

Mighty Quinn, The (1989) C-98m. **½ D: Carl Schenkel. Denzel Washington, Robert Townsend, James Fox, Mimi Rogers, M. Emmet Walsh, Sheryl Lee Ralph, Art Evans, Esther Rolle, Norman Beaton, Keye Luke. Washington plays the independent-minded police chief of a Caribbean island who's determined to get to the bottom of a murder, even though it apparently involves political sensitivities—and his boyhood pal, a now-notorious character played by Townsend. Colorful locale spices this ordinary tale and makes it a pleasant time-filler.▼

Mighty Ursus, The (1962-Italian) **C-92m.** ** D: Carlo Campogalliani. Ed Fury, Christina Gajoni, Maria Orfei, Mario Scaccia, Mary Marlon, Luis Prendez. In title role Fury goes through expected gymnastics, rescuing his woman from marauding natives.

Migrants, The (1974) **C-78m. TVM** D: Tom Gries. Cloris Leachman, Ron Howard, Sissy Spacek, Cindy Williams, Ed Lauter, Lisa Lucas, Mills Watson, Claudia McNeil, Dolph Sweet. Acclaimed Tennessee Williams drama, adapted for TV by Lanford Wilson, using one fictional family's plight as a microcosm for the migratory worker's "harvest of shame" that Edward R. Morrow graphically documented years earlier. Produced on tape. Above average.

Mikado, The (1939) **C-90m.** *** D: Victor Schertzinger. Kenny Baker, John Barclay, Martyn Green, Jean Colin, Constance Wills. Baker may not be the ideal Nanki-Poo, but this color film of Gilbert and Sullivan's operetta is still worthwhile, with the marvelous G&S songs intact.

Mike's Murder (1984) **C-97m.** *½ D: James Bridges. Debra Winger, Mark Keyloun, Darrell Larson, Paul Winfield, Brooke Alderson, William Ostrander, Dan Shor. One of the worst movies ever made by a filmmaker of Bridges' stature; after an acquaintance is butchered in a drug deal, Winger decides to investigate for herself. Filmed in 1982, followed by years at the editing table to no avail; Winfield provides only life as jaded record exec. Escapes BOMB rating only because several critics thought highly of it.▼

Mikey and Nicky (1976) **C-116m.** **½ D: Elaine May. Peter Falk, John Cassavetes, Ned Beatty, Rose Arrick, Carol Grace, Joyce Van Patten. Ragged film (in the editing room for several years) improves as it goes along, examining relationship between small-time hoods who were childhood pals, one of whom may be fingering the other for hit-man Beatty. Superb performances by Falk and Cassavetes.▼

Milagro Beanfield War, The (1988) **C-117m.** ***½ D: Robert Redford. Ruben Blades, Richard Bradford, Sonia Braga, Julie Carmen, James Gammon, Melanie Griffith, John Heard, Carlos Riquelme, Daniel Stern, Chick Vennera, Christopher Walken, Freddy Fender, Robert Carricart, M. Emmet Walsh, Trinidad Silva. Spirited, fanciful tale of a rugged individualist (dirt-poor, hard-luck Vennera) who decides to stand up to the big, brash developers who plan to milk his (and his neighbors') New Mexico land for all it's worth. Distilled from John Nichols' sprawling novel by Nichols and David Ward, this film

takes a whimsical tone that's positively infectious . . . aided by a top ensemble cast, beautiful scenery, and Dave Grusin's lyrical, Oscar-winning score.▼

Mildred Pierce (1945) **109m.** ***½ D: Michael Curtiz. Joan Crawford, Jack Carson, Zachary Scott, Eve Arden, Bruce Bennett, Ann Blyth. Crawford won an Oscar as housewife-turned-waitress who finds success in business but loses control of ungrateful daughter Blyth—especially when she finds they're competing for the love of the same man. Solid adaptation (scripted by Ranald MacDougall) of James M. Cain's novel with top supporting cast.▼

Miles from Home (1988) **C-114m.** *½ D: Gary Sinise. Richard Gere, Kevin Anderson, Penelope Ann Miller, Laurie Metcalf, John Malkovich, Brian Dennehy, Judith Ivey, Helen Hunt, Terry Kinney. The "Farm of the Year" from 1959 goes bankrupt in 1988; heir Gere burns it down rather than see it taken over by the bank, then takes off on a Midwest spree accompanied by acquiescent brother Anderson. Gere's actions (and his performance) are so off-putting that you begin to wonder if he doesn't deserve his fate, which can hardly be the point. Miller and Metcalf both put a spin on marginal roles.▼

Miles to Go (1986) **C-100m. TVM** D: David Greene. Jill Clayburgh, Tom Skerritt, Mimi Kuzyk, Rosemary Dunsmore, Cyndy Preston, Andrew Bednarski. Woman's struggle with cancer leads to her quiet, occasionally humorous mission to find a potential replacement for herself in her family's life. Clayburgh overcomes tepid script. Average.▼

Miles to Go Before I Sleep (1975) **C-78m. TVM** D: Fielder Cook. Martin Balsam, Mackenzie Phillips, Kitty Winn, Pamelyn Ferdin, Elizabeth Wilson, Florida Friebus, James Keach, Lillian Randolph. Lonely old man and teenaged delinquent develop a mutual bond in the type of quiet drama that was a staple of live TV in an earlier day; director Cook, who did so many of them so well, should know the territory. Average.

Milkman, The (1950) **87m.** ** D: Charles Barton. Donald O'Connor, Jimmy Durante, Joyce Holden, Piper Laurie, Henry O'Neill. Trivia of O'Connor working for dairy company, with Durante doing his best to liven up the proceedings.

Milky Way, The (1936) **89m.** *** D: Leo McCarey. Harold Lloyd, Adolphe Menjou, Verree Teasdale, Helen Mack, William Gargan, George Barbier, Dorothy Wilson, Lionel Stander. Milquetoasty milkman is recruited by scheming fight promoter Menjou after inadvertently knocking out the middleweight champion! Bland but entertaining film is one of Lloyd's best talkies. Remade, almost scene for scene, as THE KID FROM BROOKLYN, with Danny Kaye, but they couldn't top the hilarious ducking scene with Lloyd and matron Marjorie Gateson. Some prints run 83m.▼

Milky Way, The (1970-French) **C-102m.** **** D: Luis Buñuel. Paul Frankeur, Laurent Terzieff, Alain Cuny, Bernard Verley, Michel Piccoli, Pierre Clementi, Georges Marchal, Delphine Seyrig. Two men making religious pilgrimage through France form basis for string of Buñuel "jokes," parables, surrealistic visions. Heretical, funny, haunting, thoroughly enjoyable.▼

Millennium (1989) **C-108m.** ** D: Michael Anderson. Kris Kristofferson, Cheryl Ladd, Robert Joy, Daniel J. Travanti, Brent Carver, Maury Chaykin, David McIlwraith, Al Waxman, Lloyd Bochner. Intriguing premise features time travelers from the future kidnapping doomed passengers from crashing airliners; suspicious crash investigator Kristofferson becomes involved with Ladd, one of the time travelers. Story slowly falls apart, decaying into sheer corn. Highly regarded sci-fi writer John Varley adapted his own short story "Air Raid," but someone didn't trust the audience's intelligence.

Millerson Case, The (1947) **72m.** D: George Archainbaud. Warner Baxter, Nancy Saunders, Barbara Pepper, Clem Bevans, Griff Barnett, Paul Guilfoyle. SEE: **Crime Doctor** series.

Millionaire, The (1931) **80m.** **½ D: John Adolfi. George Arliss, Evalyn Knapp, David Manners, Noah Beery, Florence Arliss, J. Farrell MacDonald, James Cagney. One of Arliss' audience-proof formula films, about a Henry Ford-like industrialist who's forced to retire—but can't stay idle for long. Pleasant fluff, with Cagney memorable in a one-scene appearance as a go-getting insurance salesman. Based on a story by Earl Derr Biggers—with dialogue by Booth Tarkington! Remade as THAT WAY WITH WOMEN.

Millionaire, The (1978) **C-100m. TVM** D: Don Weis. Martin Balsam, Edward Albert, The Hudson Bros., Pat Crowley, Ralph Bellamy, Jane Wyatt, John Ireland, William Demarest, Robert Quarry. Updated version of 1950s TV series with eccentric (and never seen) John Beresford Tipton doling out million-dollar cashier checks through his discreet right-hand man, Michael Anthony (played here by Quarry). Familiar faces, familiar situations. Average.

Millionaire for Christy, A (1951) **91m.** *** D: George Marshall. Fred MacMurray, Eleanor Parker, Richard Carlson, Una Merkel. 1930s-type screwball comedy; fast, unpretentious, very funny, with winning performances by Parker and MacMurray

in tale of gold-digging girl out to snare rich husband.

Millionairess, The (1960-British) **C-90m.** **½ D: Anthony Asquith. Sophia Loren, Peter Sellers, Alastair Sim, Vittorio De Sica, Dennis Price. Loren is an heiress who thinks money can buy anything, until she meets Indian doctor Sellers, who won't sell his principles, or his love. Sophia is stunning, but this adaptation of G. B. Shaw's play is heavy-handed comedy.▼

Million Dollar Baby (1941) **102m.** **½ D: Curtis Bernhardt. Priscilla Lane, Jeffrey Lynn, Ronald Reagan, May Robson, Lee Patrick, Helen Westley. The sudden acquisition of a million dollars causes strain between wide-eyed Lane and her boyfriend (Reagan), a poor but proud pianist. Innocuous comedy sparked by Robson's patented performance as gruff but good-hearted millionairess.

Million Dollar Face, The (1981) **C-97m. TVM** D: Michael O'Herlihy. Tony Curtis, David Huffman, Herschel Bernardi, Gayle Hunnicutt, Lee Grant, Polly Bergen, William Daniels, Sylvia Kristel, Roddy McDowall, Murray Matheson. Busted pilot for Curtis, who plays the ruthless head of a cosmetics firm locked in fierce competition with a firm run by his ex-lover Grant. Based on Lois Wyse's novel, *Kiss, Inc.* Average.

Million Dollar Infield (1982) **C-100m. TVM** D: Hal Cooper. Rob Reiner, Bonnie Bedelia, Bob Costanza, Christopher Guest, Bruno Kirby, Candy Azzara, Gretchen Corbett, Elizabeth Wilson. Four affluent Long Islanders devote themselves to their softball team at the expense of their crumbling personal lives. Bittersweet comedy cowritten (with pal Phil Mishkin) and coproduced (with Peter Katz) by Reiner. Average.

Million Dollar Kid (1944) **65m.** D: Wallace Fox. Leo Gorcey, Huntz Hall, Gabriel Dell, Louise Currie, Noah Beery, Sr., Iris Adrian, Mary Gordon. SEE: **Bowery Boys** series.▼

Million Dollar Legs (1932) **64m.** ***½ D: Edward Cline. W. C. Fields, Jack Oakie, Susan Fleming, Lyda Roberti, Andy Clyde, Ben Turpin, Dickie Moore, Billy Gilbert, Hugh Herbert. Wacky nonsense with Fields as President of Klopstokia, a nutty country entering the Olympics. Oakie is a young American pursuing W. C.'s daughter (Fleming). Joseph Mankiewicz was one of the writers of this little gem.

Million Dollar Legs (1939) **65m.** **½ D: Nick Grinde. Betty Grable, Jackie Coogan, Donald O'Connor, Buster Crabbe, Peter Lind Hayes, Richard Denning. Title supposedly refers to winning horse, but Grable is star so draw your own conclusions. Pleasant college comedy of school trying to keep on its feet has nothing to do with W. C. Fields film of same name. Look fast for William Holden.

Million Dollar Manhunt (1956-British) **79m.** BOMB D: Maclean Rogers. Richard Denning, Carole Mathews, Ronald Adam, Danny Green, Brian Worth, Hugh Moxey. Drab account of American agent Denning on the tail of counterfeiters and £12 million printed in Nazi Germany. Also known as ASSIGNMENT REDHEAD.

Million Dollar Mermaid (1952) C-**115m.** **½ D: Mervyn LeRoy. Esther Williams, Victor Mature, Walter Pidgeon, David Brian, Jesse White. Williams does OK as real-life aquatic star Annette Kellerman, alternating her swimming with romancing Mature. Some typically elaborate production numbers by Busby Berkeley.▼

Million Dollar Mystery (1987) C-**95m.** ** D: Richard Fleischer. Eddie Deezen, Penny Baker, Tom Bosley, Rich Hall, Wendy Sherman, Rick Overton, Mona Lyden. Bosley, in his dying breath, informs customers at a roadside diner that $4 million is hidden nearby—giving them just enough clues to send the rabid group scrambling in the same direction. Shameless rip-off of IT'S A MAD MAD MAD MAD WORLD is directed with more gusto than you'd expect from Fleischer. See how many plugs for Glad Bags (cosponsor, along with De Laurentiis Entertainment Group, of a real-life promotional million-dollar treasure hunt) you can spot.▼

Million Dollar Rip-Off, The (1976) C-**78m.** TVM D: Alexander Singer. Freddie Prinze, Allen Garfield, Linda Scruggs Bogart, Joanna de Varona, Christine Belford, Brooke Mills. Heist movie; ex-con electronics wizard Prinze (in his only film) and four female accomplices knock over Chicago subway system, to the annoyance of ulcer-ridden detective Garfield. Below average.

Million Dollar Weekend (1948) **72m.** ** D: Gene Raymond. Gene Raymond, Francis Lederer, Stephanie Paull (Osa Massen), Robert Warwick, James Craven. Average mystery yarn with veteran cast. Stockbroker steals firm's money and heads for Hawaii, where complications snowball.

Million Eyes of Su-Muru, The (1967) C-**95m.** ** D: Lindsay Shonteff. Frankie Avalon, George Nader, Shirley Eaton, Wilfrid Hyde-White, Klaus Kinski. Tongue-in-cheek tale of murder and women's organization bent on enslaving all of mankind. From a Sax Rohmer story.

Million Pound Note, The SEE: **Man with a Million**

Millions Like Us (1943-British) **103m.** *** D: Frank Launder, Sidney Gilliat. Eric Portman, Patricia Roc, Gordon Jackson, Anne Crawford, Megs Jenkins, Basil Radford, Naunton Wayne, Irene Handl, Brenda Bruce. Memorable depiction of ordinary people coping with war. Roc is an airplane-factory worker during WW2, rooming in nearby hostel with women from varied social classes. Boasts realistic approach sorely missing from SWING SHIFT forty years later.

Million to One, A (1937) **60m.** *½ D: Lynn Shores. Herman Brix (Bruce Bennett), Joan Fontaine, Monte Blue, Kenneth Harlan, Suzanne Kaaren, Reed Howes. Static account of athlete preparing for the Olympic decathlon; a showcase for Brix's abilities—in fact, he competed in the 1932 games as a shot-putter. Fontaine is the society girl who falls for him.▼

Mill on the Floss, The (1937-British) **94m.** ** D: Tim Whelan. Frank Lawton, Victoria Hopper, Fay Compton, Geraldine Fitzgerald, Griffith Jones, Mary Clare, James Mason. Disappointing, dramatically uneven adaptation of George Eliot novel about a feud between a mill owner and solicitor; the latter's crippled son (Lawton) falls for the former's daughter (Fitzgerald), and various complications and tragedies ensue.▼

Mimi (1935-British) **98m.** *½ D: Paul Stein. Gertrude Lawrence, Douglas Fairbanks, Jr., Diana Napier, Harold Warrender, Carol Goodner, Austin Trevor. Lawrence is badly miscast as the tragic heroine in this straight adaptation of *La Boheme,* set in Paris' Latin Quarter, though she does get to perform one song. Incredibly sluggish, even in current 62m. prints.▼

Min and Bill (1930) **70m.** **½ D: George Hill. Marie Dressler, Wallace Beery, Dorothy Jordan, Marjorie Rambeau, Frank McGlynn. Sentimental early talkie with unforgettable team of Beery and Dressler as waterfront characters trying to protect Marie's daughter (Jordan) from being taken to "proper" home. Dressler won an Academy Award for her performance.▼

Mind Benders, The (1963-British) **101m.** *** D: Basil Dearden. Dirk Bogarde, Mary Ure, John Clements, Michael Bryant, Wendy Craig. Top cast in slow-moving but compelling account of experiments in sensory deprivation, with espionage theme worked into plot.

Mind of Mr. Soames, The (1970-British) C-**95m.** ***½ D: Alan Cooke. Terence Stamp, Robert Vaughn, Nigel Davenport, Christian Roberts. Exceptionally fine sci-fi tale of man who has been in a coma since birth; finally revived, he must be taught thirty years' worth of knowledge in brief span of time.

Mind Over Murder (1979) C-**100m.** TVM D: Ivan Nagy. Deborah Raffin, David Ackroyd, Bruce Davison, Andrew Prine, Christopher Carey. Model with precognition senses she's being stalked by a killer in this tepid thriller. Average.

Mind Snatchers, The SEE: **Happiness Cage, The**▼

Mindwarp: An Infinity of Terror SEE: **Galaxy of Terror**▼
Mine Own Executioner (1947-British) **108m.** *** D: Anthony Kimmins. Burgess Meredith, Dulcie Gray, Kieron Moore, Christine Norden, Barbara White, John Laurie, Michael Shepley. Engrossing drama about a brilliant, dedicated psychoanalyst (Meredith), who can't seem to sort out his own problems, and his efforts to help a schizophrenic ex-POW (Moore). Perceptive screenplay by Nigel Balchin, from his novel; solid performances all around, and some arresting visual highlights.▼
Miniskirt Mob, The (1968) **C-82m.** *½ D: Maury Dexter. Jeremy Slate, Diane McBain, Sherry Jackson, Patty McCormack, Ross Hagen, Harry Dean Stanton, Ronnie Rondell. McBain plays leader of female motorcycle gang, even though she looks as if she'd be more comfortable on a Tournament of Roses float. Those who like the title will probably like the film.
Ministry of Fear (1944) **85m.** *** D: Fritz Lang. Ray Milland, Marjorie Reynolds, Carl Esmond, Dan Duryea, Hillary Brooke, Alan Napier, Percy Waram. Atmospheric thriller of wartime London, with Milland framed in complicated espionage plot; good cast, fine touches by director Lang. From the Graham Greene novel.
Miniver Story, The (1950) **104m.** **½ D: H. C. Potter. Greer Garson, Walter Pidgeon, John Hodiak, Leo Genn, Cathy O'Donnell, Henry Wilcoxon, Reginald Owen, Peter Finch. Sequel to MRS. MINIVER (filmed this time in England) doesn't work as well, but Garson and Pidgeon have some poignant scenes as family reunited in post-WW2 England.
Minnesota Clay (1965-French-Italian-Spanish) **C-95m.** ** D: Sergio Corbucci. Cameron Mitchell, Georges Riviere, Ethel Rojo, Diana Martin, Anthony Ross. Standard European oater, with Mitchell giving a good performance as gunslinger who escapes prison to find the man who can clear him. He's going blind and faces his enemies aided by a heightened sense of hearing.
Minnie and Moskowitz (1971) **C-114m.** *** D: John Cassavetes. Gena Rowlands, Seymour Cassel, Val Avery, Timothy Carey, Katherine Cassavetes, Elsie Ames. One of Cassavetes' most likable films chronicles manic romance between lonely museum curator (Rowlands) and crazy parking-lot attendant (Cassel). Touching, amusing, and most enjoyable.
Minotaur (1976) SEE: **Land of the Minotaur**▼
Minotaur, The (1961-Italian) **C-92m.** *½ D: Silvio Amadio. Bob Mathias, Rosanna Schiaffino, Alberto Lupo, Rik Battaglia. Occasional atmosphere and Schiaffino's appearance still cannot elevate story of

mythological hero thwarting attempt of evil queen to subjugate city-dwellers with hideous monster.
Minstrel Man (1977) **C-100m. TVM** D: William A. Graham. Glynn Turman, Ted Ross, Stanley Clay, Saundra Sharp, Art Evans, Gene Bell. Engrossing drama tracing the era of black minstrelsy and the evolution of ragtime at the turn of the century. Rich performances by Turman as ambitious song-and-dance man, Clay as a dedicated musician racked by racial consciousness, Ross as rascally impresario. Written by Richard and Esther Shapiro (*Dynasty*). Outstanding.
Minute to Pray, a Second to Die, A (1967-Italian) **C-97m.** *** D: Franco Giraldi. Alex Cord, Arthur Kennedy, Robert Ryan, Nicoletta Machiavelli, Mario Brega. Outlaw seeks refuge in Escondido from outlaws, bounty hunters, territorial lawmen, and anyone out to take advantage of his occasional paralytic seizures. Outstanding color photography adds to great atmosphere.▼
Miracle, The (1959) **C-121m.** **½ D: Irving Rapper. Carroll Baker, Roger Moore, Walter Slezak, Vittorio Gassman, Katina Paxinou, Dennis King, Isobel Elsom. Claptrap vehicle resurrected as glossy, empty spectacle of 1810s Spain, with Baker the would-be nun unsure of her decision, Moore the soldier she romances.
Miracle at Beekman's Place (1988) **C-100m. TVM** D: Bernard L. Kowalski. Scoey Mitchill, Theresa Merritt, Liz Torres, Robert Costanzo, Brian Matthews, Jane Sibbett. Idealist doctor dumps high-paying job as hospital chief of staff to open walk-in inner city clinic. Pedestrian doctor show created by comedian turned actor/producer Mitchill as prospective series pilot. Below average.
Miracle in Milan (1951-Italian) **95m.** ***½ D: Vittorio de Sica. Francesco Golisano, Paolo Stoppa, Emma Gramatica, Guglielmo Barnabo. Toto the Good (Golisano) brings cheer to a dreary village of poor people, aided by the old lady who raised him, who is now in heaven. Bitingly comic condemnation of the manner in which displaced Europeans were treated after WW2.
Miracle in the Rain (1956) **107m.** **½ D: Rudolph Maté. Jane Wyman, Van Johnson, Peggie Castle, Fred Clark, Eileen Heckart, Josephine Hutchinson, Barbara Nichols, William Gargan, Alan King, Arte Johnson. Above-par soaper of two lost souls, Wyman and Johnson, falling in love in N.Y.C. during WW2.
Miracle Landing (1990) **C-100m. TVM** D: Dick Lowry. Wayne Rogers, Connie Sellecca, Ana-Alicia, Nancy Kwan, James Cromwell. Yet another real-life plane disaster movie, this one recounting the plight of passengers and crew when the top skin

of the fuselage peeled away during a 1988 flight to Honolulu. Average.

Miracle Mile (1989) **C-87m.** *½ D: Steve DeJarnatt. Anthony Edwards, Mare Winningham, John Agar, Lou Hancock, Mykel T. Williamson, Kelly Minter, Kurt Fuller, Denise Crosby, Robert Doqui, Danny De La Paz. Good-natured musician who's just gotten to first base with a coffee shop waitress picks up a ringing pay phone and learns that the U.S. has fired a nuclear warhead—which means that the end of the world is about an hour away. Artificial and overwrought from the word go, the film loses all hope of credibility in its final half-hour when illogic really takes over. Credible costars Edwards and Winningham can't do anything with this material.

Miracle of Fatima SEE: **Miracle of Our Lady of Fatima, The**▼

Miracle of Kathy Miller, The (1981) **C-100m. TVM** D: Robert Lewis. Sharon Gless, Frank Converse, Helen Hunt, Bill Beyers, John deLancie, Michael Greene. Dramatization of the true story of an Arizona teenager who overcame massive brain and other physical damage after being run over by a speeding auto and became a world-famed athlete. Script by Mel and Ethel Brez. Above average.

√ **Miracle of Morgan's Creek, The** (1944) **99m.** **** D: Preston Sturges. Eddie Bracken, Betty Hutton, William Demarest, Diana Lynn, Brian Donlevy, Akim Tamiroff, Porter Hall, Almira Sessions, Jimmy Conlin. Frantic, hilarious comedy of Betty attending all-night party, getting pregnant and forgetting who's the father. Bracken and Demarest have never been better than in this daring wartime farce. Filmed in 1942; sort of remade as ROCK-A-BYE BABY.▼

Miracle of Our Lady of Fatima, The (1952) **C-102m.** *** D: John Brahm. Gilbert Roland, Angela Clarke, Frank Silvera, Jay Novello, Sherry Jackson. Thoughtful account of religious miracle witnessed by farm children in 1910s; intelligent script. Retitled: MIRACLE OF FATIMA.▼

Miracle of the Bells, The (1948) **120m.** *½ D: Irving Pichel. Fred MacMurray, Valli, Frank Sinatra, Lee J. Cobb, Charles Meredith. Contrived story of miracle occurring when movie star is laid to rest in coal-mining home town; often ludicrous, despite sincere cast. Screenplay by Ben Hecht and Quentin Reynolds. Also shown in computer-colored version.▼

Miracle of the Heart: A Boys Town Story (1986) **C-100m. TVM** D: Georg Stanford Brown. Art Carney, Casey Siemaszko, Jack Bannon, Anne Pitoniak, Darrell Larson, Reginald T. Dorsey. Inoffensive update of the old Spencer Tracy/Mickey Rooney chestnut, with Carney as a kindly priest (one of Father Flanagan's successors) fighting being put out to pasture by the Church, and Siemaszko as the latest juvenile delinquent to be taken under his wing. Carney, as usual, makes all the right acting moves. Average.▼

Miracle of the Hills (1959) **73m.** *½ D: Paul Landres. Rex Reason, Theona Bryant, Jay North, Gilbert Smith, Tracy Stratford, Gene Roth. Timid little Western of town-running gal who bucks new clergyman.

Miracle of the White Stallions (1963) **C-117m.** *½ D: Arthur Hiller. Robert Taylor, Lilli Palmer, Curt Jurgens, Eddie Albert, James Franciscus, John Larch. Long, talky, confusing drama about evacuation of prized Lippizan horses from Vienna during WW2. A most un-Disneylike Disney film.▼

Miracle on Ice (1981) **C-150m. TVM** D: Steven Hilliard Stern. Karl Malden, Andrew Stevens, Steven Guttenberg, Jerry Houser, Jessica Walter, Robert F. Lyons, Robert Peirce, Eugene Roche, Peter Horton. The story of the U.S. hockey team's gold medal triumph at the 1980 Olympics at Lake Placid. Malden is exhilarating as Coach Herb Brooks; so is the skating. The story, written by Lionel Chetwynd, is otherwise pedestrian. Average.

Miracle on Main Street (1939) **68m.** ** D: Steve Sekely. Margo, Walter Abel, Jane Darwell, Lyle Talbot, William Collier, Sr. Limp drama about depressed carnival dancer Margo, and what happens after she finds an abandoned baby on Christmas Eve. Artistically ambitious B movie that doesn't work.

Miracle on 34th Street (1947) **96m.** **** ✓ D: George Seaton. Maureen O'Hara, John Payne, Edmund Gwenn, Gene Lockhart, Natalie Wood, Porter Hall, William Frawley. Classic Valentine Davies fable of Kris Kringle (Gwenn) working in Macy's, encountering an unbelieving child (Wood), and going on trial to prove he's Santa. Delightful comedy-fantasy won Oscars for Gwenn, Davies, and screenwriter Seaton. It also marked Thelma Ritter's auspicious screen debut and gave an amusing bit to young Jack Albertson, as a postal employee. Remade for TV. Also shown in computer-colored version.▼

Miracle on 34th Street (1973) **C-100m. TVM** D: Fielder Cook. Jane Alexander, David Hartman, Roddy McDowall, Sebastian Cabot, Suzanne Davidson, Jim Backus, Tom Bosley, David Doyle, James Gregory, Roland Winters. Heartwarming humor and old-fashioned whimsy in this TV adaptation of the 1947 Christmas classic. Good cast, but the plot's awfully dated now. Average.

Miracles (1986) **C-86m.** *½ D: Jim Kouf. Tom Conti, Teri Garr, Paul Rodriguez, Christopher Lloyd, Adalberto Martinez, Jorge Russek. Conti and Garr, recently divorced, are whisked away to South American hellhole by jewel thief Rodriguez in this clone of ROMANCING THE STONE. The stars do their best, but we've seen it all before, and better. Written by first-time director Kouf.▼

Miracles Still Happen (1974-U.S.-Italian) C-93m. *½ D: Giuseppe Scotese. Susan Penhaligon, Paul Muller, Graziella Galvani, Clyde Peters. Teenager Penhaligon treks through the Amazon alone after surviving a plane crash. Inferior, poorly made programmer, based on a true story. Original running time: 97m.

Miracle Woman, The (1931) 90m. *** D: Frank Capra. Barbara Stanwyck, David Manners, Sam Hardy, Beryl Mercer, Russell Hopton. Stanwyck plays an evangelist (patterned after Aimee Semple McPherson) whose splashy sermons become big business. Manners is a blind man who falls in love with her. Story contrivances overcome by fine performances, direction, and camerawork (by Joseph Walker).

Miracle Worker, The (1962) 107m. ***½ D: Arthur Penn. Anne Bancroft, Patty Duke, Victor Jory, Inga Swenson, Andrew Prine, Beah Richards, Kathleen Comegys. Moving adaptation of William Gibson's play about blind, deaf Helen Keller and her remarkable teacher, Anne Sullivan. Few changes were made from the play, and as onstage, the fight-for-authority sequence is a high point. Bancroft and Duke both won Oscars recreating their Broadway roles. Originally staged as a 1957 *Playhouse 90* on TV, also directed by Penn. Remade for TV with Duke taking on the role of Sullivan.▼

Miracle Worker, The (1979) C-100m. TVM D: Paul Aaron. Patty Duke Astin, Melissa Gilbert, Diana Muldaur, Charles Siebert, Anne Seymour, Stanley Wells. Powerful refilming of the William Gibson classic about young Helen Keller's first encounters with Anne Sullivan, who would be her teacher and life-long companion. Having Patty Duke Astin—who won an Oscar as Keller in 1962—play Sullivan was more a novelty than an inspired piece of casting, making this one just a notch below its predecessor. Above average.▼

Miraculous Journey (1948) C-83m. *½ D: Peter Stewart (Sam Newfield). Rory Calhoun, Andrew Long, Virginia Grey, George Cleveland. Substandard psychological study of victims of plane crash in jungle.

Mirage (1965) 109m. *** D: Edward Dmytryk. Gregory Peck, Diane Baker, Walter Matthau, Kevin McCarthy, Jack Weston, Leif Erickson, Walter Abel, George Kennedy. Fine Hitchcock-like thriller, with Peck the victim of amnesia, and everyone else out to get him. Matthau steals film as easygoing private-eye; interesting on-location footage in N.Y.C. Remade as JIGSAW (1968).▼

Miranda (1948-British) 80m. **½ D: Ken Annakin. Googie Withers, Glynis Johns, Griffith Jones, John McCallum, David Tomlinson, Margaret Rutherford, Maurice Denham. Droll frou-frou of mermaid preferring sophisticated land-life to the sea; capably played by all. Johns is a very fetching mermaid. Sequel: MAD ABOUT MEN.

Mirror, The (1976-Russian) C-106m. ***½ D: Andrei Tarkovsky. Margarita Terekhova, Philip Yankovsky, Ignat Daniltsev, Oleg Yankovsky. Extremely personal, moving tale of life in Russia during WW2. Superbly directed; overall, it works most effectively as an homage to childhood innocence.▼

Mirror Crack'd, The (1980-British) C-105m. **½ D: Guy Hamilton. Angela Lansbury, Elizabeth Taylor, Rock Hudson, Kim Novak, Tony Curtis, Edward Fox, Geraldine Chaplin, Wendy Morgan, Charles Gray, Pierce Brosnan. A mild Agatha Christie whodunit made enjoyable by its quartet of 1950s stars, particularly Taylor and Novak, who are fun as catty rival movie stars. Lansbury is a crisp Miss Marple. Rather flat in theaters, this ought to play better on TV. A highlight: the black-and-white movie-in-a-movie "Murder at Midnight."▼

Mirror Has Two Faces, The (1959-French) 98m. **½ D: André Cayatte. Michele Morgan, Bourvil, Gerald Oury, Ivan Desny, Elizabeth Manet, Sylvie, Sandra Milo. Morgan is quite good as woman who begins life anew after plastic surgery.

Mirror, Mirror (1979) C-100m. TVM D: Joanna Lee. Janet Leigh, Lee Meriwether, Loretta Swit, Robert Vaughn, Peter Bonerz, Christopher Lemmon, Robin Mattson. Three women's efforts to reshape their lives through cosmetic surgery. Earnest but less than uplifting. Average.

Mirrors (1985) C-100m. TVM D: Harry Winer. Marguerite Hickey, Antony Hamilton, Timothy Daly, Keenan Wynn, Patricia Morison, Signe Hasso, Shanna Reed, Ron Field. Young hopeful from the Midwest comes to the Big Apple to become a Broadway musical "gypsy" in this road-company A CHORUS LINE. Average.

Misadventures of Merlin Jones, The (1964) C-88m. *½ D: Robert Stevenson. Tommy Kirk, Annette Funicello, Leon Ames, Stuart Erwin, Alan Hewitt, Connie Gilchrist. Skimpy Disney comedy about college brain (Kirk) and his misadventures with mind-reading and hypnotism. Sequel: THE MONKEY'S UNCLE.▼

Misadventures of Mr. Wilt, The (1989-British) C-92m. **½ D: Michael Tuchner. Griff Rhys-Jones, Mel Smith, Alison Steadman, Diana Quick, Jeremy Clyde, Roger Allam. Two stars of the hit British TV series *Alias Smith and Jones* are featured in this silly farce about college lecturer Henry Wilt (Rhys-Jones), who hates his bitchy wife—and becomes the prime suspect when the police think she's been murdered. Smith is the twit of an inspector assigned to the case. Funny—if it hits you in the right mood. Based on Tom Sharpe's best-seller. Original British title: WILT.

Mischief (1985) **C-93m.** ** D: Mel Damski. Doug McKeon, Catherine Mary Stewart, Kelly Preston, Chris Nash, D. W. Brown, Jami Gertz. Amiable but leaden-paced teen movie set in 1950s. Likable cast and vivid period atmosphere are chief assets—but any film that shows a clip from REBEL WITHOUT A CAUSE and then tries to duplicate the scene is asking for trouble.▼

✓ **Misfits, The** (1961) **124m.** *** D: John Huston. Clark Gable, Marilyn Monroe, Montgomery Clift, Thelma Ritter, Eli Wallach, James Barton, Estelle Winwood. Unsatisfying but engrossing parable authored by Arthur Miller, involving disillusioned divorcee Monroe and her brooding cowboy friends. Both Monroe's and Gable's last film.▼

Mishima (1985) **C/B&W-120m.** *** D: Paul Schrader. Ken Ogata. Narration read by Roy Scheider. Ambitious, highly stylized drama about Japan's most controversial post-WW2 author, playwright, actor, director, and militarist, Yukio Mishima, whose passion to merge life and art led to his ritualistic suicide in 1970. Scenes of Mishima's life (shot in black & white) are contrasted with vivid dramatizations (in opulent color) of key fictional works that grappled with his emotional crises. Long, difficult, not always successful, but fascinating. Beautifully photographed by Donald Bailey, swept along by stunning Philip Glass score.▼

Miss All-American Beauty (1982) **C-96m.** TVM D: Gus Trikonis. Diane Lane, Cloris Leachman, David Dukes, Jayne Meadows, Alice Hirson, Brian Kerwin. A toothless SMILE lacking the bite as well as Michael Ritchie's satirical touch, though Meadows's nasty pageant director gives it a near shot. Below average.▼

Miss Annie Rooney (1942) **84m.** ** D: Edwin L. Marin. Shirley Temple, William Gargan, Guy Kibbee, Dickie Moore, Peggy Ryan, Gloria Holden, Selmer Jackson, June Lockhart, Virginia Sale. Moore gives Shirley her first screen kiss in slight tale of girl from wrong side of tracks in love with rich boy. Also shown in computer-colored version.▼

Miss Europe SEE: **Prix de Beauté**▼

Miss Firecracker (1989) **C-102m.** *** D: Thomas Schlamme. Holly Hunter, Mary Steenburgen, Tim Robbins, Alfre Woodard, Scott Glenn, Ann Wedgeworth, Trey Wilson, Amy Wright, Bert Remsen. Beth Henley's Off-Broadway play, *The Miss Firecracker Contest,* becomes a most enjoyable movie, with a peerless Hunter recreating her stage role. In a Mississippi hamlet, lonely, pitiful (and hilarious) Hunter yearns for love and self-esteem. Cast is first-rate in this sweet-natured comedy-drama, scripted by Henley; reminiscent of 1930s screwball films. Director Schlamme's feature debut; that's his real-life wife, Christine Lahti, as a neighbor (holding their own newborn baby!).▼

Miss Grant Takes Richmond (1949) **87m.** **½ D: Lloyd Bacon. Lucille Ball, William Holden, Janis Carter, James Gleason, Frank McHugh. Ball is wacky secretary innocently involved with crooks; she's the whole show.

Missile Base at Taniak (1953) **100m.** *½ D: Franklin Adreon. William Henry, Susan Morrow, Arthur Space, Dale Van Sickel. Uninspired Republic cliff-hanger concerning Canadian mounties' efforts to track down foreign agents setting up rocket centers to launch projectiles and destroy key American cities. Reedited from serial CANADIAN MOUNTIES VS. ATOMIC INVADERS.

Missile Monsters (1958) **75m.** *½ D: Fred C. Brannon. Walter Reed, Lois Collier, Gregory Gay, James Craven. Tedious sci-fi about Martian attempt to take over the earth via guided missiles. Re-edited from 1951 Republic serial FLYING DISC MAN FROM MARS.

Missiles From Hell (1958-British) **72m.** ** D: Vernon Sewell. Michael Rennie, Patricia Medina, Milly Vitale, David Knight, Christopher Lee. British work with Polish partisans during WW2 to obtain projectile weapon held by Nazis; choppy editing.

Missile to the Moon (1959) **78m.** *½ D: Richard Cunha. Richard Travis, Cathy Downs, K.T. Stevens, Tommy Cook. Preposterous low-budget sci-fi about lunar expedition finding sinister female presiding over race of moon-women. Lots of laughs, for all the wrong reasons. Remake of CAT WOMEN OF THE MOON (ROCKET TO THE MOON).▼

Missing (1982) **C-122m.** ***½ D: Constantin Costa-Gavras. Jack Lemmon, Sissy Spacek, Melanie Mayron, John Shea, Charles Cioffi, David Clennon, Joe Regalbuto, Richard Venture, Janice Rule. A carefully manipulated drama that works, because of Costa-Gavras' convincing direction, and Lemmon's emphatic performance as a stiff-backed father who comes to a politically volatile Latin American country in search of his missing son—unable and unwilling to believe that American representatives there might not be telling him the truth. Based on the true experiences of Ed Horman; Costa-Gavras and Donald Stewart earned Oscars for their screenplay adaptation.▼

Missing Are Deadly, The (1974) **C-78m.** TVM D: Don McDougall. Ed Nelson, Jose Ferrer, Leonard Nimoy, George O'Hanlon, Jr., Marjorie Lord, Kathleen Quinlan. Suspense tale about the panic caused when disturbed teenager takes a rat infected with a deadly virus from his father's lab. Average.

Missing Children: A Mother's Story (1982) **C-100m. TVM** D: Dick Lowry. Mare Winningham, Polly Holliday, John Anderson, Jane Wyatt, Kate Capshaw, Scatman Crothers, Richard Dysart, Peter Scolari, Soleil Moon Frye. Abused and penniless young mother loses her children to an adoption agency posing as a childcare center. Winningham rises above the drama's predictability. Average.

Missing Corpse, The (1945) **62m.** *½ D: Albert Herman. J. Edward Bromberg, Eric Sinclair, Frank Jenks, Isabel Randolph, Paul Guilfoyle, John Shay, Lorell Sheldon. Cheaply made chiller of harried newspaperman Bromberg involved in murder mystery.▼

Missing Guest, The (1938) **68m.** *½ D: John Rawlins. Paul Kelly, Constance Moore, William Lundigan, Edwin Stanley, Selmer Jackson, Billy Wayne. As in many 1930s B melodramas, a newspaper reporter (named "Scoop," no less) is on hand when murders are being committed, this time in a haunted house. Routine. Filmed before as SECRET OF THE BLUE ROOM, later as MURDER IN THE BLUE ROOM.

Missing in Action (1984) **C-101m.** ** D: Joseph Zito. Chuck Norris, M. Emmet Walsh, David Tress, Lenore Kasdorf, James Hong. Colonel Norris, an ex-POW in Vietnam, returns to Asia to liberate American prisoners. A simplistic, revisionist fantasy-actioner, in the mold of UNCOMMON VALOR and RAMBO: FIRST BLOOD PART 2. Followed by a prequel.▼

Missing in Action 2—The Beginning (1985) **C-96m.** *½ D: Lance Hool. Chuck Norris, Soon-Teck Oh, Steven Williams, Bennett Ohta, Cosie Costa. In this limp prequel to you-know-what, Col. Norris escapes from a POW camp in Vietnam. For Norris lovers only. Followed by BRADDOCK: MISSING IN ACTION III.▼

Missing Juror, The (1944) **66m.** *** D: Oscar (Budd) Boetticher. Jim Bannon, Janis Carter, George Macready, Jean Stevens, Joseph Crehan, Carole Mathews. Brisk, engrossing drama of unknown killer taking revenge on jury that sent innocent man to his death; low budget, but quite good.

Missing Pieces (1983) **C-96m. TVM** D: Mike Hodges. Elizabeth Montgomery, Louanne, John Reilly, Ron Karabatsos, Robin Gammell, Julius Harris. Montgomery turns private eye to track down the killers of her reporter husband in this engaging thriller which director Hodges adapted from Karl Alexander's novel *A Private Investigation*. Karabatsos nearly steals the film from her as the world-weary detective for whom she goes to work. Above average.▼

Mission, The (1986-British) **C-125m.** **½ D: Roland Joffe. Robert De Niro, Jeremy Irons, Ray McAnally, Aidan Quinn, Cherie Lunghi, Ronald Pickup, Chuck Low, Liam Neeson, Daniel Berrigan. Productive (and profitable) Jesuit mission in the jungles of Brazil is threatened by greedy merchants and by political factions within the church itself, in the late 18th century. Magnificent-looking film (Chris Menges' cinematography won an Oscar), rich in imagery, that goes on so long—to such an inevitable conclusion—that its dramatic power is drained. Literate, high-minded screenplay by Robert Bolt; fine performances by Irons and De Niro.▼

Missionary, The (1982-British) **C-90m.** ** D: Richard Loncraine. Michael Palin, Maggie Smith, Phoebe Nicholls, Trevor Howard, Denholm Elliott, Michael Hordern, Graham Crowden. Fans of Monty Python's Palin may be surprised by this mild comedy, which he also wrote and coproduced. Returning from Africa, young man of the cloth is recruited to run a home for fallen women ("Women who've tripped?") and quickly finds himself the recipient of, uh, fringe benefits. Great supporting cast, gorgeous locations and beautiful cinematography (by Peter Hannan) overwhelm this modest picture.▼

Mission Batangas (1969) **C-100m.** *½ D: Keith Larsen. Dennis Weaver, Vera Miles, Keith Larsen, Vic Diaz. Callous American flyer in early WW2 eventually becomes a hero; poor excuse for a war movie.▼

Mission Hill (1982) **C-90m.** ***½ D: Robert Jones. Brian Burke, Alice Barrett, Barbara Orson, Robert Kerman, Daniel Silver, Nan Mulleneaux, John Mahoney. Solid, uncompromising drama of working-class dreams and disappointments, centering on aspiring singer Barrett and her troublesome teenage brother (Burke). Sensitively directed; filmed in Boston.

Mission Mars (1968) **C-95m.** *½ D: Nick Webster. Darren McGavin, Nick Adams, George DeVries, Heather Hewitt, Michael DeBeausset, Shirley Parker. Typical astronaut drama has three U.S. space men battling unseen forces while on a mission.▼

Mission Over Korea (1953) **85m.** *½ D: Fred F. Sears. John Hodiak, John Derek, Maureen O'Sullivan, Audrey Totter. Substandard Korean War tale.

Mission Stardust (1968-Italian) **C-95m.** *½ D: Primo Zeglio. Essy Persson, Lang Jeffries, John Karelsen, Pinkas Braun, Luis Davila. Space expedition from Earth lands on Moon and encounters alien space ship whose beings are suffering from a mysterious disease. Based on first of internationally popular *Perry Rhodan* series of novels, but worthless nonetheless.▼

Mission to Moscow (1943) **123m.** ***½ D: Michael Curtiz. Walter Huston, Ann Harding, Oscar Homolka, George Tobias, Gene Lockhart, Frieda Inescort, Eleanor

Parker, Richard Travis. Fascinating propaganda of real-life ambassador Joseph Davies (played by Huston) in then-peaceful Russia. Well-done, giving interesting insights to American concepts of USSR at the time. Davies himself introduces the film.

Mississippi (1935) 73m. ***½ D: A. Edward Sutherland. Bing Crosby, W. C. Fields, Joan Bennett, Queenie Smith, Gail Patrick, Claude Gillingwater. Fine cast in musicomedy of riverboat captain Fields and singer Crosby, with Rodgers-Hart score including "It's Easy To Remember But So Hard to Forget." Unforgettable poker game with W. C. Look quickly for Ann Sheridan.

Mississippi Blues (1983) C-96m. *** D: Bertrand Tavernier, Robert Parrish. Easygoing documentary from American Parrish and Frenchman Tavernier about the American South—its country folk, its landscape, its customs and, most wonderfully, its music.

Mississippi Burning (1988) C-125m. *** D: Alan Parker. Gene Hackman, Willem Dafoe, Frances McDormand, Brad Dourif, R. Lee Ermey, Gailard Sartain, Stephen Tobolowsky, Michael Rooker, Pruitt Taylor Vince, Park Overall. Two FBI agents—one a tight-jawed, by-the-book type, the other an experienced Southern lawman who knows how to handle people—head the government investigation into the disappearance of three civil rights workers in Mississippi during the summer of 1964. Vivid recreation of the period and setting helps carry a less-than-perfect script (inspired by real-life events); the real ace here is Hackman, in a dynamic performance as the former small-town sheriff who figures out how to crack the case. Peter Biziou's cinematography won an Oscar.▼

Mississippi Gambler (1953) C-98m. **½ D. Rudolph Maté. Tyrone Power, Piper Laurie, Julia Adams, John McIntire, Dennis Weaver. Power is title figure with ambitions of establishing a gambling business in New Orleans.

Mississippi Mermaid (1969-French-Italian) C-110m. *** D: Francois Truffaut. Jean-Paul Belmondo, Catherine Deneuve, Michel Bouquet, Nelly Borgeaud. One of the director's few flops, but any film with Belmondo-Deneuve-Truffaut combo is of interest; story concerns tobacco planter whose mail-order bride turns out to be Deneuve. Always buy brand names. Originally ran 123m.

Miss Mary (1986-Argentine) C-100m. **½ D: Maria Luisa Bemberg. Julie Christie, Nacha Guevara, Luisina Brando, Iris Marga, Eduardo Pavlovsky, Gerardo Romano. Proper, prim British governness Christie arrives in Argentina in 1938, to look after the children in a proper, prim, upper-class family. A few nice touches but mostly forgettable tale of unreleased passion and emerging sexuality. An offbeat role for Christie.▼

Missouri Breaks, The (1976) C-126m. BOMB D: Arthur Penn. Marlon Brando, Jack Nicholson, Kathleen Lloyd, Randy Quaid, Frederic Forrest, Harry Dean Stanton. Dynamite star combo in hired gun vs. horse thief confrontation—all for naught. Jumbled, excessively violent pseudo-event; a great director's worst film and one of the worst "big" movies ever made.▼

Missouri Traveler, The (1958) C-104m. **½ D: Jerry Hopper. Brandon de Wilde, Lee Marvin, Gary Merrill, Mary Hosford, Paul Ford. Folksy, minor account of orphaned youth (de Wilde) finding new roots in Southern country town in 1910s; earnest but predictable.▼

Miss Pinkerton (1932) 66m. ** D: Lloyd Bacon. Joan Blondell, George Brent, John Wray, Ruth Hall, C. Henry Gordon, Elizabeth Patterson, Holmes Herbert. Nurse Blondell has sixth sense for mysteries, decides to go after one in easy-to-take story.

Miss Robin Crusoe (1954) C-75m. *½ D: Eugene Frenke. Amanda Blake, George Nader, Rosalind Hayes. Female version of Robinson Crusoe; nothing added, a lot to be desired.

Miss Robin Hood (1952-British) 78m. ** D: John Guillermin. Margaret Rutherford, Richard Hearne, Edward Lexy, Frances Rowe. OK mixture of fantasy and farce, with Rutherford an elderly nut seeking retrieval of family whiskey formula; Hearne is meek girl's-magazine writer who aids her.

Miss Sadie Thompson (1953) C-91m. *** D: Curtis Bernhardt. Rita Hayworth, Jose Ferrer, Aldo Ray, Russell Collins, Charles Bronson. Rita gives a provocative performance in musical remake of Somerset Maugham's RAIN, also previously made as SADIE THOMPSON and DIRTY GERTIE FROM HARLEM. Originally in 3D.▼

Miss Susie Slagle's (1945) 88m. **½ D: John Berry. Veronica Lake, Sonny Tufts, Joan Caulfield, Lillian Gish, Ray Collins, Billy DeWolfe, Lloyd Bridges. Mild tale of turn-of-the-century boarding house for aspiring doctors and nurses.

Miss Tatlock's Millions (1948) 101m. **½ D: Richard Haydn. John Lund, Wanda Hendrix, Monty Woolley, Robert Stack, Ilka Chase, Dorothy Stickney. Original comedy of Hollywood stunt man who must masquerade as a nitwit to help young heiress; offbeat, to say the least.

Mister Buddwing (1966) 100m. **½ D: Delbert Mann. James Garner, Jean Simmons, Suzanne Pleshette, Angela Lansbury, Katharine Ross, Raymond St. Jacques, Nichelle Nichols. Misfire; over-familiar amnesia plot with Garner trying to fill in his past, meeting assorted women who might have been part of his prior life.

Mister Cory (1957) C-92m. **½ D: Blake

Edwards. Tony Curtis, Charles Bickford, Martha Hyer, Kathryn Grant (Crosby). Curtis does OK as poor-boy-turned-rich-gambler who returns to home town to show off his wealth.

Mister Drake's Duck (1950-British) **76m.** *** D: Val Guest. Douglas Fairbanks, Jr., Yolande Donlan, Howard Marion-Crawford, Reginald Beckwith. Droll comedy of Fairbanks on honeymoon getting more publicity than he bargained for when pet duck lays radioactive eggs.

Mister 880 (1950) **90m.** *** D: Edmund Goulding. Dorothy McGuire, Burt Lancaster, Edmund Gwenn, Millard Mitchell, Minor Watson. Easygoing comedy, with Gwenn an elderly N.Y.C. counterfeiter tracked down by federal agent Lancaster. Script by Robert Riskin.

Mister Jerico (1969) **C-85m.** **TVM** D: Sidney Hayers. Patrick Macnee, Marty Allen, Connie Stevens, Herbert Lom, Leonardo Pieroni, Peter Yapp. Con-man Jerico (Macnee) and assistant go after famed Gemini diamond owned by corrupt millionaire (Lom) on Malta, but who has real one? Enjoyable caper concocted by many of *The Avengers* production team, reunited here with their star, Macnee. There's a memorable chase involving great location work, too. Above average.

Mister Moses (1965-British) **C-113m.** **½ D: Ronald Neame. Robert Mitchum, Carroll Baker, Ian Bannen, Alexander Knox, Raymond St. Jacques, Reginald Beckwith. Malarkey of rugged Mitchum and virtuous Baker leading African native tribe to their new homeland.

Mister Roberts (1955) **C-123m.** **** D: John Ford, Mervyn LeRoy. Henry Fonda, James Cagney, William Powell, Jack Lemmon, Betsy Palmer, Ward Bond, Nick Adams, Philip Carey, Harry Carey, Jr., Ken Curtis. Superb comedy-drama with Fonda recreating his favorite stage role as restless officer on WW2 cargo ship who yearns for combat action but has to contend with an irascible and eccentric captain (Cagney) instead. Fonda, Cagney, Powell (in his last screen appearance) as a philosophical doctor, and Lemmon (in an Oscar-winning performance) as the irrepressible Ensign Pulver, are all terrific. Thomas Heggen and Joshua Logan's Broadway hit was adapted for film by Logan and Frank Nugent. LeRoy replaced Ford as director sometime during production . . . but it certainly doesn't show. Sequel: ENSIGN PULVER.▼

Mister Scoutmaster (1953) **87m.** *** D: Henry Levin. Clifton Webb, Edmund Gwenn, George Winslow, Frances Dee, Veda Ann Borg. Child-hater Webb becomes scoutmaster in this airy film which will appeal mainly to kids.

Mister Superinvisible (1973-Italian-German-Spanish) **C-91m.** **½ D: Anthony M. Dawson (Antonio Margheriti). Dean Jones, Ingeborg Schoener, Gastone Moschin, Peter Carsten. Engaging comedy made in Geneva has American researcher Jones becoming invisible as he seeks a cure for the common cold. Good for kids, okay for grownups.▼

Mister V SEE: **Pimpernel Smith**▼

Mistress (1987) **C-100m.** TVM D: Michael Tuchner. Victoria Principal, Don Murray, Kerrie Keane, Joanna Kerns, Alan Rachins, Guy Boyd, Grace Zabriskie. Wealthy contractor's mistress is at loose ends with few marketable talents when he suddenly dies. Tedious woman's drama. Below average.▼

Mistress of Paradise (1981) **C-100m.** TVM D: Peter Medak. Genevieve Bujold, Chad Everett, Anthony Andrews, Olivia Cole, John McLiam, Lelia Goldoni, Carolyn Seymour. Gothic-style pap that wastes Bujold, in her TV movie debut, as a beauty from up North who marries a worldly Southern plantation owner and gets involved in voodoo. Below average.

Misty (1961) **C-92m.** *** D: James B. Clark. David Ladd, Pam Smith, Arthur O'Connell, Anne Seymour. Marguerite Henry's popular children's book is nicely realized, with Ladd and Smith as children on island off Virginia coast who fall in love with a wild horse.

Misunderstood (1984) **C-91m.** **½ D: Jerry Schatzberg. Gene Hackman, Henry Thomas, Rip Torn, Huckleberry Fox, Maureen Kerwin, Susan Anspach. Boy cries out for the love of his father, who's too busy (and too consumed by the loss of his wife) to understand how much the boy needs his attention—and affection. Extremely well acted but emotionally uneven drama. Filmed in Tunisia in 1982.▼

Mitchell (1975) **C-96m.** **½ D: Andrew V. McLaglen. Joe Don Baker, Martin Balsam, Linda Evans, John Saxon, Merlin Olsen, Morgan Paull. Baker plays tough cop whose singleminded pursuit of drug ring leads to expected action and violence; slick handling of typical action fodder.

Mixed Blood (1985-French) **C-97m.** *½ D: Paul Morrissey. Marilia Pera, Richard Ulacia, Linda Kerridge, Geraldine Smith. Wildly overrated black comedy set in the "alphabet city" district of East Greenwich Village where Brazilian crime matriarch Pera has run-in with rival gang's young punks. Leading man Ulacia's acting is embarrassing, while director Morrissey's tongue-in-cheek violence is strictly amateur night. ▼

Mixed Company (1974) **C-109m.** **½ D: Melville Shavelson. Barbara Harris, Joseph Bologna, Tom Bosley, Lisa Gerritsen, Dorothy Shay. Less than heartwarming but still entertaining comedy of losing basketball coach Bologna coping with wife Harris' adopting orphans of mixed ethnic backgrounds.

Mix Me a Person (1962-British) 116m. *½ D: Leslie Norman. Anne Baxter, Donald Sinden, Adam Faith, Jack MacGowran, Topsy Jane, Walter Brown. Unexceptional drama of psychiatrist Baxter proving teenager Faith innocent of murdering a policeman.

Moana (1925) 85m. ***½ D: Robert Flaherty. Ta'avale, Fa'amgase, Tu'ugaita, Moana, Pe'a. Flaherty's follow-up to NANOOK OF THE NORTH is at once a realistic yet poetic look at life in the South Seas, focusing on a young Polynesian (Moana) and his family. Filmed over a two-year period on the island of Savai'i, in the Somoas. A classic, influential film (although not as highly regarded as NANOOK or LOUISIANA STORY).▼

Mob, The (1951) 87m. ** D: Robert Parrish. Broderick Crawford, Betty Buehler, Richard Kiley, Otto Hulett, Neville Brand, Ernest Borgnine, Charles Bronson. Study of lawman cracking waterfront gang syndicate; Crawford is good but script is second-rate. Interesting cast, however.

Mobile Two (1975) C-78m. TVM D: David Moessinger. Jackie Cooper, Julie Gregg, Mark Wheeler, Edd Byrnes, Jack Hogan, Joe E. Tata. Jack Webb-produced story about investigative TV reporter's various assignments (in proven tradition of Webb's *Adam-12* and *Emergency*). Standard TV fodder that led to a brief series, *Mobile One* (accounting, presumably, for a lower budget). Average.

Mob Town (1941) 70m. D: William Nigh. Billy Halop, Huntz Hall, Gabriel Dell, Bernard Punsley, Dick Foran, Anne Gwynne, Samuel S. Hinds. SEE: **Bowery Boys** series.

Moby Dick (1930) 75m. **½ D: Lloyd Bacon. John Barrymore, Joan Bennett, Walter Long, Nigel de Brulier, Noble Johnson, Virginia Sale. Barrymore is a vivid Captain Ahab, though film is more Hollywood than Melville. Pointless love story added to original narrative, as in Barrymore's earlier silent-film version, THE SEA BEAST. Remade in 1956.

Moby Dick (1956) C-116m. *** D: John Huston. Gregory Peck, Richard Basehart, Friedrich Ledebur, Leo Genn, Orson Welles, James Robertson Justice, Harry Andrews, Bernard Miles. Moody version of Herman Melville sea classic, with Peck miscast as Captain Ahab. Some fine scenes scattered about. Screenplay by Huston and Ray Bradbury.▼

Model and the Marriage Broker, The (1951) 103m. *** D: George Cukor. Jeanne Crain, Scott Brady, Thelma Ritter, Zero Mostel, Michael O'Shea, Frank Fontaine, Nancy Kulp. Poignant, perceptive little comedy-drama chronicling the affairs of marriage broker Ritter, who plays Cupid for model Crain and X-ray technician Brady. However, most of her clients don't have

pretty faces: they're shy, lonely, desperate for companionship. A winner.

Model For Murder (1958-British) 75m. ** D: Terry Bishop. Keith Andes, Hazel Court, Jean Aubrey, Michael Gough. Andes is American in England seeking late brother's girlfriend, becoming involved in jewel robbery. Adequate yarn.

Model Shop, The (1969-French) C-95m. *** D: Jacques Demy. Anouk Aimee, Gary Lockwood, Alexandra Hay, Carole Cole, Severn Darden, Tom Fielding. Twenty-four hours in life of disenchanted young architect (Lockwood), his affair with recently abandoned fashion model (Aimee). Director Demy's eye for L.A. (film's setting) is striking, but overall feel to story is ambiguous.

Model Wife (1941) 78m. **½ D: Leigh Jason. Joan Blondell, Dick Powell, Lee Bowman, Charlie Ruggles, Lucile Watson, Ruth Donnelly, Billy Gilbert. Joan's boss won't let her get married, but she does, to Powell, and has to keep it a secret. Fairly amusing comedy.

Modern Girls (1986) C-84m. BOMB D: Jerry Kramer. Daphne Zuniga, Virginia Madsen, Cynthia Gibb, Clayton Rohner, Chris Nash, Steve Shellen. Three femme free spirits club-hop raucous L.A. punk spots in the course of a single early a.m.; a spiritual odyssey it's not. Trashy, barely released bomb degrades young performers who've made much stronger impressions in other films; low point is Madsen's near gang rape on a pool table.▼

Modern Problems (1981) C-91m. *½ D: Ken Shapiro. Chevy Chase, Patti D'Arbanville, Mary Kay Place, Nell Carter, Brian Doyle-Murray, Dabney Coleman, Mitch Kreindel. Air-traffic controller Chase acquires telekinetic powers. A couple of funny bits, but mostly flat and boring.▼

Modern Romance (1981) C-93m. **½ D: Albert Brooks. Albert Brooks, Kathryn Harrold, Bruno Kirby, Jane Hallaren, James L. Brooks, George Kennedy. Writer-director Brooks plays a world-class neurotic who's obsessively devoted to Harrold but unable to maintain a normal relationship with her. Alternately obnoxious and hilarious, with wonderful in-jokes about moviemaking (Brooks plays a film editor) and a nice cameo in which Brooks's brother Bob Einstein plays a sporting-goods salesman. Real-life writer-director James L. Brooks plays a director here; he returned the favor to Albert by writing him that plum role in BROADCAST NEWS several years later.▼

Moderns, The (1988) C-128m. **½ D: Alan Rudolph. Keith Carradine, Linda Fiorentino, John Lone, Genevieve Bujold, Geraldine Chaplin, Wallace Shawn, Kevin J. O'Connor. Beautifully mounted but dramatically flawed period piece about a community of "artistes" in 1926 Paris. Bland Carradine is a major liability as an art forger, and portraits of Hemingway and Gertrude Stein are less than half baked. Lone and Fiorentino are standouts as a menacing U.S rubber baron and his wife, the latter a lost love of Carradine's. Worthy but iffy.▼

Modern Times (1936) 89m. **** D: Charlie Chaplin. Charlie Chaplin, Paulette Goddard, Henry Bergman, Chester Conklin, Stanley "Tiny" Sandford. Charlie attacks the machine age in inimitable fashion, with sharp pokes at other social ills and the struggle of modern-day survival. Goddard is the gamin who becomes his partner in life. Chaplin's last silent film (with his own music—including "Smile"—sound effects and gibberish song) is consistently hilarious, and unforgettable. Final shot is among Chaplin's most famous, and most poignant. One of Goddard's sisters in early scenes is young Gloria DeHaven (daughter of Chaplin's assistant director).▼

Modesty Blaise (1966-British) C-119m. ** D: Joseph Losey, Monica Vitti, Dirk Bogarde, Terence Stamp, Harry Andrews, Michael Craig, Scilla Gabel, Tina Marquand, Clive Revill, Alexander Knox. Director Losey ate watermelon, pickles, and ice cream, went to sleep, woke up, and made this adaptation of the comic strip about a sexy female spy. Filmed at the height of the pop-art craze, it tries to be a spoof at times, doesn't know what it's supposed to be at other moments.

Mogambo (1953) C-115m. ***½ D: John Ford, Clark Gable, Ava Gardner, Grace Kelly, Donald Sinden, Philip Stainton, Eric Pohlmann, Laurence Naismith, Denis O'Dea. Lusty remake of RED DUST. Gable repeats his role, Ava replaces Harlow, Kelly has Mary Astor's part. John Lee Mahin reworked his 1932 screenplay. Romantic triangle in Africa combines love and action; beautifully filmed in color (by Robert Surtees and Freddie Young).▼

Mohammad, Messenger of God (1977-Arabic) C-180m. *** D: Moustapha Akkad. Anthony Quinn, Irene Papas, Michael Ansara, Johnny Sekka, Michael Forest, Neville Jason. Spectacle of the beginnings of Moslem religion is sincere effort, more impressive with action than religious angles. In accordance with the religion, Mohammad is never shown. Also known as THE MESSAGE.▼

Mohawk (1956) C-79m. **½ D: Kurt Neumann. Scott Brady, Rita Gam, Neville Brand, Lori Nelson, Allison Hayes, John Hoyt, Vera Vague (Barbara Jo Allen), Mae Clarke, Ted de Corsia. Unintentionally hilarious hokum of devil-may-care painter Brady attempting to thwart Iroquois uprising while tangling with squaw Gam, among other femmes. There's plenty of heavy breathing, 1950's-style, here.▼

Mokey (1942) 88m. ** D: Wells Root. Dan Dailey, Donna Reed, Bobby (Robert) Blake, William "Buckwheat" Thomas, Cordell Hickman, Matt Moore, Etta McDaniel. Reed has problems with her stepson, who almost winds up in reform school. Typical of genre.

Mole People, The (1956) 78m. ** D: Virgil Vogel. John Agar, Cynthia Patrick, Hugh Beaumont, Alan Napier. Agar and others find lost underground civilization of albino Sumerians, who have half-human creatures of the title as their slaves. Probably the worst of Universal-International's '50s sci-fi movies.

Molly SEE: **Goldbergs, The**

Molly and Lawless John (1972) C-97m. ** D: Gary Nelson. Vera Miles, Clu Gulager, Sam Elliott, John Anderson. Young criminal dupes sheriff's wife into running away with him; OK Western with Miles' capable performance.▼

Molly and Me (1945) 76m. *** D: Lewis Seiler. Gracie Fields, Monty Woolley, Roddy McDowall, Reginald Gardiner, Natalie Schafer, Edith Barrett, Clifford Brooke. Entertaining little comedy of Fields becoming Woolley's housekeeper, taking over his life as well. Well played by fine cast.

Molly Maguires, The (1970) C-123m. **½ D: Martin Ritt. Sean Connery, Richard Harris, Samantha Eggar, Frank Finlay, Art Lund, Anthony Costello. Well-crafted film about secret society of Irish mineworkers in Pennsylvania, circa 1876, led by Connery; newcomer Harris is working as informer. Vivid atmosphere, good performances, but downbeat film lacks appeal, and is hurt by inconclusive ending.▼

Mom and Dad (1947) 97m. **½ D: William Beaudine. Hardie Albright, Lois Austin, George Eldredge, June Carlson, Jimmy Clarke. The saga of pretty, innocent Joan Blake, whose repressive mother neglects to inform her about the birds and bees; she does "it," and finds herself "in trouble." Even though this notorious film opens with the National Anthem, and is a "vital educational production, appealing to all true-Americans," it was banned as obscene in some communities. Today, it's pretty tame—and a fascinating curio.▼

Moment by Moment (1978) C-102m. BOMB D: Jane Wagner. Lily Tomlin, John Travolta, Andra Akers, Bert Kramer, Shelley R. Bonus. A role-reversal romance with Travolta as the sex object and Tomlin as bored Malibu resident that gives new dimension to the word "dreary."

Moment of Danger SEE: **Malaga**

Moment of Truth, The (1952-French) 90m. ** D: Jean Delannoy. Michele Morgan, Jean Gabin, Daniel Gelin, Simone Paris. Effective playing of trite yarn of married couple realizing how little they know each other.

Moment to Moment (1966) C-108m. **½ D: Mervyn LeRoy. Jean Seberg, Honor Blackman, Sean Garrison, Arthur Hill.

Unconvincing, confused murder mystery set on the Riviera, but filmed largely on Universal's sound stage.

Mommie Dearest (1981) **C-129m.** **½ D: Frank Perry. Faye Dunaway, Diana Scarwid, Steve Forrest, Howard da Silva, Mara Hobel, Rutanya Alda, Harry Goz. Vivid, well-crafted filmization of Christina Crawford's book about growing up the adopted and abused daughter of movie queen Joan Crawford (brilliantly played by Dunaway). Knowing that the story is (allegedly) real makes watching this film a strange, creepy experience, something akin to voyeurism . . . though now it's being hailed on another level entirely, as a camp classic!▼

Mom, the Wolfman and Me (1980) **C-100m. TVM** D: Edmond Levy. Patty Duke Astin, David Birney, Danielle Brisebois, Keenan Wynn, Viveca Lindfors, John Lithgow. Amiable comedy about the efforts of an eleven-year old to get her free-spirited fashion photographer mother to make a romantic commitment. Director Levy adapted the screenplay from Norma Klein's novel. Average.

Mona Lisa (1986-British) **C-104m.** *** D: Neil Jordan. Bob Hoskins. Cathy Tyson, Michael Caine, Robbie Coltrane, Clarke Peters, Kate Hardie, Zoe Nathenson, Sammi Davis. Absorbing adult drama about a small-time hood who's given a job driving around a high-priced callgirl but remains naive about the life she leads, and about the degree of depravity his underworld chums have sunk to. Director Jordan (who cowrote screenplay with David Leland) leads us into this nether world along with Hoskins, allowing us to discover things at the same time. Hoskins and newcomer Tyson are terrific; Caine is wonderfully slimy in support.▼

√ **Mondo Cane** (1963-Italian) **C-105m.** **½ Producer: Gualtiero Jacopetti. First and best of Italian shockumentaries, with dubbed American narration; focuses on peculiarities of man in various parts of the world. Features song "More."▼

Money From Home (1953) **C-100m.** **½ D: George Marshall. Dean Martin, Jerry Lewis, Pat Crowley, Robert Strauss, Jack Kruschen. Average hijinks of duo involved with gangsters, steeplechase racing, Arab ruler and his harem. Originally in 3D.

Money Jungle, The (1968) **C-95m.** ** D: Francis D. Lyon. John Ericson, Lola Albright, Leslie Parrish, Nehemiah Persoff, Charles Drake, Kent Smith, Don Rickles. Geologists involved in oil-rights bidding are being knocked off, but Ericson is there to stop them; good cast wasted.

Money Money Money (1973-French) **C-113m.** *** D: Claude Lelouch. Lino Ventura, Jacques Brel, Charles Denner, Aldo Maccione, Charles Gerard. Gang of successful thieves decide that changing times demand their switch to political crimes, which pay more handsomely. Clever, funny spoof of our heated political era as seen through eyes of men whose only belief is in money.

Money on the Side (1982) **C-100m. TVM** D: Robert Collins. Karen Valentine, Jamie Lee Curtis, Linda Purl, Christopher Lloyd, Richard Masur, Gary Graham, Edward Edwards, Susan Flannery. Suburban housewives become afternoon hookers to bring in extra cash. Who says TV-movies are exploitive? Average.

Money Pit, The (1986) **C-91m.** ** D: Richard Benjamin. Tom Hanks, Shelley Long, Alexander Godunov, Maureen Stapleton, Joe Mantegna, Philip Bosco, Josh Mostel. A young couple's slapstick misadventures trying to repair and remodel a lemon of a house. Hanks and Long are very likable, but this yuppie update of MR. BLANDINGS BUILDS HIS DREAM HOUSE loses all contact with reality (and humor). Starts out funny but just gets worse and worse. Produced by Steven Spielberg and company.▼

Money, Power, Murder (1989) **C-100m. TVM** D: Lee Philips. Kevin Dobson, Blythe Danner, Josef Sommer, John Cullum, Paul McCrane. Dobson's tough as a wisecracking investigative TV reporter delving into the disappearance of a star anchorwoman and stumbling onto hanky-panky involving a charismatic televangelist. Based on Mike Lupica's *Dead Air.* Average.

Money to Burn (1973) **C-73m. TVM** D: Robert Michael Lewis. E. G. Marshall, Mildred Natwick, Alejandro Rey, Cleavon Little, David Doyle, Charles McGraw, Ronald Feinberg, Lou Frizzell. Marshall's the standout in tale of fairly clever scheme to make use of counterfeit currency printed up in federal penitentiary. Average.▼

Money Trap, The (1966) **92m.** **½ D: Burt Kennedy. Glenn Ford, Rita Hayworth, Elke Sommer, Joseph Cotten, Ricardo Montalban. Ford is detective turned crook in pedestrian murder yarn. Hayworth most convincing as middle-aged woman no longer self-sufficient. Rare non-Western from Kennedy; adapted by Walter Bernstein from Lionel White's novel.

Money, Women and Guns (1958) **C-80m.** ** D: Richard Bartlett. Jock Mahoney, Kim Hunter, Tim Hovey, Gene Evans. Modest Western about lawman sent to track down killers and to find heirs to victim's will.

√ **Mongols, The** (1960-Italian) **C-102m.** ** D: Andre de Toth, Leopoldo Savona. Jack Palance, Anita Ekberg, Antonella Lualdi, Franco Silva. Unimaginative spectacle set in 13th century, with Palance the son of Genghis Khan on the rampage in Europe, Ekberg his girl.

Mongo's Back in Town (1971) **C-73m.**

[764]

TVM D: Marvin Chomsky. Joe Don Baker, Telly Savalas, Sally Field, Anne Francis, Charles Cioffi, Martin Sheen. Ultragrim, deliberately slow-moving crime drama has recently released con (Baker) returning to home town, hired by brother to kill rival. Adaptation of story by actual convict strong on atmosphere but uncertain about point of view. Above average.

Monika SEE: **Summer With Monika**▼

Monitors, The (1969) **C-92m.** ** D: Jack Shea. Guy Stockwell, Susan Oliver, Avery Schreiber, Larry Storch, Ed Begley, Keenan Wynn, Alan Arkin, Xavier Cugat, Stubby Kaye, Jackie Vernon, Everett Dirksen. Great cast wasted in this failed attempt at science fiction satire filmed in Chicago by Second City company. Alien Monitors control Earth and keep everything peaceful, but rebels plot against them. From novel by popular sci-fi writer Kenneth Laumer.

Monk, The (1969) **C-73m.** TVM D: George McCowan. George Maharis, Janet Leigh, Jack Albertson, Carl Betz, Jack Soo, Raymond St. Jacques, Rick Jason, Joe Besser, Edward G. Robinson, Jr., Linda Marsh. Stereotyped modern-day private-eye Gus Monk (Maharis) framed into embarrassing situation when man who gave him envelope for safekeeping is found murdered. Embarrassing dialogue, predictable resolution, unbelievable villains. Blake Edwards created the characters for this busted pilot. Below average.

Monkey Business (1931) **77m.** ***½ D: Norman Z. McLeod. Groucho, Harpo, Chico, Zeppo Marx, Thelma Todd, Ruth Hall, Harry Woods. Four brothers stow away on luxury liner; Groucho goes after Thelma, all four pretend to be Maurice Chevalier to get off ship. Full quota of sight gags and puns in typically wacky comedy, co-scripted by S.J. Perelman; their first film written directly for the screen.▼

Monkey Business (1952) **97m.** *** D: Howard Hawks. Ginger Rogers, Cary Grant, Charles Coburn, Marilyn Monroe, Hugh Marlowe. Grant discovers rejuvenation serum, which affects him, wife Rogers, boss Coburn, and secretary Monroe in this zany comedy. Coburn's classic line to MM: "Find someone to type this." Written by Ben Hecht, Charles Lederer, and I.A.L. Diamond; that's Hawks' voice during the opening credits.▼

Monkey Grip (1982-Australian) **C-101m.** **½ D: Ken Cameron. Noni Hazlehurst, Colin Friels, Alice Garner, Harold Hopkins, Candy Raymond. Unmemorable drama detailing the trials of singleminded single mother Hazlehurst, particularly her relationship with obnoxious drug addict boyfriend Friels. Nice performance by Hazlehurst, but ultimately just a superficial soap opera.▼

Monkey Hustle (1977) **C-90m.** *½ D: Arthur Marks. Yaphet Kotto, Rosalind Cash,

Rudy Ray Moore, Kirk Calloway, Randy Brooks. Appealing cast is only saving grace of dumb comedy actioner designed for black audiences, shot in Chicago. Kotto is a black Fagin; ghetto neighborhood's impending demise for an expressway forms a bit of plot.

Monkey Mission, The (1981) **C-96m.** TVM D: Burt Brinckerhoff. Robert Blake, Keenan Wynn, Mitchell Ryan, Clive Revill, John Fiedler, Pepe Serna, Sondra Blake, Logan Ramsey, Alan Napier. Hard-boiled private eye plots the ingenious theft of an art treasure on behalf of a wealthy client with the help of a monkey. The second of Blake's *Joe Dancer* movies that he hoped would sell as a series; followed by MURDER 1, DANCER 0. Average.

Monkey on My Back (1957) **93m.** **½ D: Andre de Toth. Cameron Mitchell, Paul Richards, Dianne Foster, Jack Albertson, Kathy Garver. Mitchell as fighter Barney Ross, who became a dope addict, turns in sincere performance. Well-meant, engrossing little film.

Monkeys, Go Home! (1967) **C-101m.** ** D: Andrew V. McLaglen. Maurice Chevalier, Dean Jones, Yvette Mimieux, Bernard Woringer, Clement Harari, Yvonne Constant. Disney trivia about a man who inherits French olive farm and trains monkeys to pick his crop. Gossamer-thin, for kids only. Chevalier's final film appearance.▼

Monkey Shines: An Experiment in Fear (1988) **C-115m.** ** D: George Romero. Jason Beghe, John Pankow, Melanie Parker, Joyce Van Patten, Christine Forrest, Stephen Root. A cute monkey (injected with human brain cells) is enlisted to help a quadraplegic get on with his life. From that premise writer-director Romero tries to build horror and suspense, but it only works in spurts, and taxes our credibility (and our patience) far too often.▼

Monkey's Uncle, The (1965) **C-87m.** ** D: Robert Stevenson. Tommy Kirk, Annette Funicello, Leon Ames, Frank Faylen, Arthur O'Connell, Norman Grabowski. Juvenile Disney comedy has Kirk again as Merlin Jones, college whiz-kid who first tries sleep-learning method on monkey, then sets himself up in makeshift flying machine. Flight sequences provide brightest moments. Unforgettable title song warbled by Annette and The Beach Boys. Sequel to THE MISADVENTURES OF MERLIN JONES.▼

Monolith Monsters, The (1957) **77m.** ** D: John Sherwood. Lola Albright, Grant Williams, Les Tremayne, Trevor Bardette. Engrossing sci-fi mystery set in desert town. When exposed to water, fragments of shattered meteorites grow and reproduce—wreaking havoc on innocent bystanders. Story by sci-fi director Jack Arnold.

Mon Oncle (1958-French) **C-126m.** ****

D: Jacques Tati. Jacques Tati, Jean-Pierre Zola, Adrienne Servantie, Alain Bercourt. Tati's first color film is a masterpiece. M. Hulot's simple, uncluttered life is sharply contrasted to that of his sister and brother-in-law, who live in an ultramodern, gadget-laden home reminiscent of those in Buster Keaton's silent classics. Continuous flow of sight gags (including the funniest fountain you'll ever see) makes this easygoing, nearly dialogue-less comedy a total delight. Oscar winner as Best Foreign Film; also known as MY UNCLE and MY UNCLE, MR. HULOT. Original U.S. release ran 110m.▼

Mon Oncle d'Amerique (1980-French) C-123m. ***½ D: Alain Resnais. Gerard Depardieu, Nicole Garcia, Roger Pierre, Marie Dubois, Nelly Bourgeaud, Henri Laborit. Intensely directed, acted, and written (by Jean Gruault) film illustrating research scientist Laborit's theories on human conduct. The focus is on the intertwined lives of a plant manager (Depardieu), actress (Garcia), and media executive (Pierre). Intelligent, thought-provoking.▼

Monsieur Beaucaire (1946) 93m. *** D: George Marshall. Bob Hope, Joan Caulfield, Patric Knowles, Marjorie Reynolds, Cecil Kellaway, Joseph Schildkraut, Reginald Owen, Constance Collier. Pleasing Hope vehicle with Bob in costume as barber sent on mission as dead duck sure to be murdered. Plush settings, funny gags.

Monsieur Hire (1989-French) C-88m. ***½ D: Patrice Leconte. Michel Blanc, Sandrine Bonnaire, Luc Thuillier, Eric Berenger. Bald, middle-aged Peeping Tom falls in love with the object of his obsession— a young woman, peripherally involved in a murder, who lives across the courtyard. Cold, but involving and terrifically acted version of a Georges Simenon novel; the short running time helps. Previously filmed in 1946 as PANIQUE.

Monsieur Verdoux (1947) 123m. ***½ D: Charles Chaplin. Charles Chaplin, Martha Raye, Isobel Elsom, Marilyn Nash, Irving Bacon, William Frawley. Chaplin's controversial black comedy about a Parisian Bluebeard who murders wives for their money was years ahead of its time; its wry humor and pacifist sentiments make it quite contemporary when seen today. Broad comic sequence with Raye is particular highlight.▼

Monsignor (1982) C-122m. ** D: Frank Perry. Christopher Reeve, Genevieve Bujold, Fernando Rey, Jason Miller, Joe Cortese, Adolfo Celi, Leonardo Cimino, Tomas Milian, Robert J. Prosky. Saga of ambitious priest who commits every heresy imaginable (including having an affair with a nun!) while operating as the Vatican's business manager. Grows more ridiculous as it goes along—with unintentional comedy on a grand scale—culminating in an astonishing final shot involving the Pope. Another camp classic from the producer and director of MOMMIE DEAREST.▼

Monsoon (1943) SEE: **Isle of Forgotten Sins**▼

Monsoon (1953) C-79m. *½ D: Rodney Amateau. Ursula Thiess, Diana Douglas, George Nader, Ellen Corby. Trite drama of several people destroyed by their passions; set in India.

Monster, The (1925) 86m. ** D: Roland West. Lon Chaney, Gertrude Olmstead, Hallam Cooley, Johnny Arthur, Charles Sellon. Overdose of comedy relief hampers moody Chaney mad-doctor doings; still OK, though, as whole film has tongue-in-cheek. From Crane Wilbur's play.

Monster and the Girl, The (1941) 65m. **½ D: Stuart Heisler. Ellen Drew, Robert Paige, Paul Lukas, Joseph Calleia, George Zucco, Rod Cameron. Unusual B-film starts off with story of gangsters dragging Drew into life of prostitution, then veers off into horror as Zucco transfers her dead brother's brain into body of a gorilla! White slavery angle more original than the mad-scientist stuff.

Monster Club, The (1980-British) C-97m. *½ D: Roy Ward Baker. Vincent Price, John Carradine, Donald Pleasence, Stuart Whitman, Warren Saire, Richard Johnson, Britt Ekland, Simon Ward, Anthony Steel, Patrick Magee. A trio of horror stories, all told by vampire Price. Disappointing and unimaginative, with only the barest of shudders; never released theatrically in the U.S. The club, by the way, is a disco patronized by Transylvanians.▼

Monster From Green Hell (1957) 71m. *½ D: Kenneth Crane. Jim Davis, Robert E. Griffin, Barbara Turner, Joel Fluellen, Vladimir Sokoloff, Eduardo Ciannelli. Laboratory wasps are sent into orbit, crash-land in Africa as giant mutations. Standard 1950s sci-fi formula stuff, with lots of talk, little action. Uses ample stock footage from STANLEY AND LIVINGSTONE.▼

Monster from the Ocean Floor, The (1954) 64m. BOMB D: Wyott Ordung. Anne Kimball, Stuart Wade, Wyott Ordung. Producer Roger Corman's first effort is a dreadful film about a squid-like creature pursued by a minisubmarine; 20,000 yawns under the sea.

Monster in the Closet (1986) C-87m. *** D: Bob Dahlin. Donald Grant, Denise DuBarry, Claude Akins, Howard Duff, Henry Gibson, Donald Moffat, Paul Dooley, John Carradine, Jesse White, Stella Stevens. Perceptive and funny homage to 1950s sci-fi flicks. Clark Kent–type reporter Grant and scientist DuBarry team up to track down and destroy California monsters who pop out of closets and kill people. A must for buffs. Filmed in 1983.▼

Monster Island (1981-U.S.-Spanish) **C-100m.** *½ D: Juan Piquer Simon. Terence Stamp, Peter Cushing, Ian Serra, David Hatton, Blanca Estrada. Humdrum actioner, with Serra and Hatton shipwrecked on an island loaded with gold and strange creatures. Based on a story by Jules Verne.

Monster Maker, The (1944) **62m.** ** D: Sam Newfield. J. Carrol Naish, Ralph Morgan, Wanda McKay, Terry Frost. Peculiarly distasteful horror yarn with mad scientist Naish infecting his enemies with acromegaly "germs," causing hideous deformities.▼

Monster of Piedras Blancas, The (1958) **71m.** *½ D: Irvin Berwick. Les Tremayne, Forrest Lewis, John Harmon, Frank Arvidson. Sluggish chiller with humanoid sea monster thirsting for blood on a deserted seacoast; obvious and amateurish.▼

Monster on the Campus (1958) **76m.** **½ D: Jack Arnold. Arthur Franz, Joanna Moore, Judson Pratt, Nancy Walters, Troy Donahue. Above-par chiller involving discovery of prehistoric fish whose blood turns a college professor into rampaging beast.

Monster Squad, The (1987) **C-81m.** **½ D: Fred Dekker. Andre Gower, Robby Kiger, Stephen Macht, Duncan Regehr, Tom Noonan, Brent Chalem, Ryan Lambert, Ashley Bank. Young friends belong to a club that's devoted to monsters, but they unexpectedly encounter the horror heavies in real life when Dracula (accompanied by the Frankenstein monster, the Mummy, the Wolf Man, and the Gill Man) comes to their town in search of an amulet vital to his continued existence. Affectionate homage to classic horror films and their monster stars is ultimately too bland and unbelievable (even for a kiddie horror film). Climactic showdown boasts Richard Edlund's super-duper special effects.▼

Monster That Challenged the World, The (1957) **83m.** **½ D: Arnold Laven. Tim Holt, Audrey Dalton, Hans Conried, Casey Adams. Above-average giant-bug-on-the-loose film is set in the Salton Sea, where colossal crustaeceans (like big catepillars in snail shells) menace mankind. Intelligent, low-key, with good monsters.

Monster Walks, The (1932) **63m.** **½ D: Frank Strayer. Rex Lease, Vera Reynolds, Mischa Auer, Sheldon Lewis, Sleep 'N' Eat (Willie Best). Campy old-house thriller, good for some fun. Heiress Reynolds is marked for death by paralyzed uncle Lewis, who wants moronic Auer to kill her and blame it on an ape that's kept in the cellar for scientific experiments. Willie bests Mischa for laughs, but it's a close race.▼

Monster Zero (1966-Japanese) *½ D: Inoshiro Honda. Nick Adams, Akira Takarada. Godzilla and Rodan are swiped from Earth to battle Ghidrah on an alien planet.

The title may refer to Ghidrah, but it's anyone's guess. Lesser monster movie from the Toho Studio. Video title: GODZILLA VS. MONSTER ZERO.▼

Monstrosity (1964) **72m.** *½ D: Joseph Mascelli. Frank Gerstle, Erika Peters, Judy Bamber, Frank Fowler, Marjorie Eaton. Eaton is wealthy matron who hires doctor (Gerstle) to perform brain transplant on her; lumbering mess. Retitled: THE ATOMIC BRAIN.▼

Montana (1950) **C-76m.** **½ D: Ray Enright. Errol Flynn, Alexis Smith, S. Z. Sakall, Monte Blue, Douglas Kennedy. Slick yet unexciting Western with formula Warner Bros. plot line and type casting; minor Flynn vehicle.

Montana (1990) **C-100m. TVM** D: William A. Graham. Gena Rowlands, Richard Crenna, Lea Thompson, Justin Deas, Elizabeth Berridge, Darren Dalton, Scott Coffey. In this contemporary Larry McMurtry Western, Rowlands and Crenna (doing a Gabby Hayes turn!) are a brawling couple caught in changing times: she wants to hold onto the family ranch, he wants to sell it to a power company for oil drilling. Colorful but talkative tale about values. Made for cable. Average.

Montana Belle (1952) **C-81m.** ** D: Allan Dwan. Jane Russell, George Brent, Scott Brady, Andy Devine, Forrest Tucker. Mildly interesting Western with Russell as Belle Starr, involved with fellow-outlaws, the Dalton Brothers.

Montana Mike SEE: **Heaven Only Knows**

Montana Moon (1930) **89m.** ** D: Mal St. Clair. Joan Crawford, John Mack Brown, Dorothy Sebastian, Ricardo Cortez, Benny Rubin, Cliff Edwards, Karl Dane. OUR DANCING DAUGHTERS goes west, with hot jazz baby Joan marrying down-to-earth cowboy Brown. Dated, and stiff as a board.

Montana Territory (1952) **C-64m.** ** D: Ray Nazarro. Lon McCallister, Wanda Hendrix, Preston Foster, Jack Elam, Clayton Moore. McCallister is deputized cowboy who's out to bring in the outlaws.

Monte Carlo (1930) **90m.** **½ D: Ernst Lubitsch. Jeanette MacDonald, Jack Buchanan, ZaSu Pitts, Claude Allister, Tyler Brooke. Dated but enjoyable musical froth with Jeanette an impoverished countess wooed by royal Buchanan, who's incognito, of course. Lubitsch's methods of integrating songs into the film were innovations in 1930; most memorable is "Beyond the Blue Horizon."

Monte Carlo (1986) **C-200m. TVM** D: Anthony Page. Joan Collins, George Hamilton, Lisa Eilbacher, Lauren Hutton, Robert Carradine, Malcolm McDowell. Collins is a Russian-born chanteuse spying for the allies on the eve of WW2 in this splashy

[767]

but wonderfully tacky contemporized B movie. Joan deserves a rightful place next to Eleanor Powell power-tapping Morse Code messages about the Nazis in SHIP AHOY four decades earlier. Originally shown in two parts. Average.▼

Monte Carlo or Bust SEE: **Those Daring Young Men in Their Jaunty Jalopies**

Monte Carlo Story, The (1957-Italian) **C-99m.** ** D: Samuel Taylor. Marlene Dietrich, Vittorio De Sica, Arthur O'Connell, Natalie Trundy, Mischa Auer. Charming stars try to support thin story of troubled romance between two compulsive gamblers; filmed on location.

Montenegro (1981-Swedish-British) **C-98m.** *** D: Dusan Makavejev. Susan Anspach, Erland Josephson, Per Oscarsson, John Zacharias, Svetozar Cvetkovic, Patricia Gelin. Bored middle-class housewife Anspach becomes sexually liberated when she accidentally falls in with Yugoslav workers who frequent a boisterous bar. Funny and entertaining; also known as MONTENEGRO—OR PIGS AND PEARLS.▼

Monterey Pop (1969) **C-88m.** ***½ D: James Desmond, Barry Feinstein, D.A. Pennebaker, Albert Maysles, Roger Murphy, Richard Leacock, Nick Proferes. Otis Redding. Mamas and Papas, Jimi Hendrix, The Who, Janis Joplin, Animals, Jefferson Airplane. First major rock concert film, shot at 1967 Monterey Pop Festival, is still one of the best ever, with Joplin's "Ball and Chain" and Hendrix's pyrotechnic performance of "Wild Thing" among the highlights. ▼

Monte Walsh (1970) **C-106m.** *** D: William Fraker. Lee Marvin, Jeanne Moreau, Jack Palance, Mitch Ryan, Jim Davis, Allyn Ann McLerie. Melancholy Western with Marvin a veteran cowboy who finds himself part of a dying West. Sensitive filming of novel by Jack Schaefer (who wrote SHANE). Fine performance by Palance in atypical good-guy role. Directorial debut for noted cinematographer Fraker.▼

Month in the Country, A (1987-British) **C-96m.** *** D: Pat O'Connor. Colin Firth, Kenneth Branagh, Natasha Richardson, Patrick Malahide, Tony Haygarth, Jim Carter. Occasionally slow but still thoughtful, rewarding drama about shellshocked WW1 vet Firth, and his experiences while uncovering a medieval painting on a church wall in a remote Yorkshire town. Screenplay by Simon Gray, from a novel by J.R. Carr. Stick with this one.▼

Monty Python and the Holy Grail (1974-British) **C-90m.** **½ D: Terry Gilliam, Terry Jones. Graham Chapman, John Cleese, Terry Gilliam, Eric Idle, Terry Jones, Michael Palin. The Python troupe's second feature is wildly uneven, starting

out well and then getting lost—in the "story" of a medieval crusade. Some inspired lunacy, and a lot of dry stretches; awfully bloody, too. Recommended for fans only.▼

Monty Python Live at the Hollywood Bowl (1982-British) **C-77m.** *** D: Terry Hughes, "Monty Python." Graham Chapman, John Cleese, Terry Gilliam, Eric Idle, Terry Jones, Michael Palin, Neil Innes, Carol Cleveland. Britain's bad boys invade Los Angeles with this madcap series of sketches and routines, including many old favorites. A must for Python aficionados. Videotaped, then transferred to film.▼

Monty Python's Life of Brian SEE: **Life of Brian**▼

Monty Python's The Meaning of Life (1983-British) **C-103m.** *** D: Terry Jones. Graham Chapman, John Cleese, Terry Gilliam, Eric Idle, Terry Jones, Michael Palin, Carol Cleveland, Simon Jones. Original, outrageous comedy exploring various facets of life and death—from procreation to the Grim Reaper himself—with typical Python irreverence. Highlights include the world's most obese man (an unforgettable scene, like it or not) and a cheerful, elaborate production number about sperm! A barrel of bellylaughs for Python fans; others beware.▼

Moochie of the Little League (1959) **90m.** *** D: William Beaudine. Kevin Corcoran, Frances Rafferty, James Brown, Reginald Owen, Stuart Erwin. Funny, homespun, sometimes satirical piece of Americana takes a Disney-ized look at Little League baseball as young Corcoran attempts to organize a team with help of British gentleman Owen. Originally shown as two-part Disney TV show, released as a feature in Europe. Sequel: MOOCHIE OF POP WARNER FOOTBALL.

Moon and Sixpence, The (1942) **89m.** *** D: Albert Lewin. George Sanders, Herbert Marshall, Doris Dudley, Eric Blore, Elena Verdugo, Florence Bates, Albert Basserman, Heather Thatcher. Faithful film of Maugham's tale of man who decides to fulfill lifelong ambition to paint, moving to Tahitian island. Superb acting by Sanders in lead, Marshall as the author. Paintings in film are shown in color.▼

Moonfire (1970) **C-107m.** BOMB D: Michael Parkhurst. Richard Egan, Charles Napier, Sonny Liston, Dayton Lummis, Joaquin Martinez. Trucker Napier unknowingly becomes involved in blackmail plot. Atrociously scripted and directed; though toplined, Egan has about eight lines; Boxer Liston, as "The Farmer," proved himself no actor.

Moonfleet (1955) **C-89m.** **½ D: Fritz Lang. Stewart Granger, Jon Whiteley, George Sanders, Viveca Lindfors, Joan

Greenwood, Ian Wolfe. Tepid 18th-century story of Britisher Granger becoming a buccaneer.▼

Moon in the Gutter, The (1983-French) **C-126m.** *½ D: Jean-Jacques Beineix. Nastassia Kinski, Gerard Depardieu, Victoria Abril, Vittorio Mezzogiorno, Dominique Pinon. Overbaked, pompously surreal tale of dockworker Depardieu, seeking his sister's rapist, and his involvement with wealthy, beautiful Kinski. Both stars couldn't be worse. From the director of DIVA.▼

Moon Is Blue, The (1953) 95m. **½ D: Otto Preminger. William Holden, David Niven, Maggie McNamara, Tom Tully, Dawn Addams. Once-saucy sex comedy about a young woman who flaunts her virginity now seems tame, too much a filmed stage play, with most innuendoes lacking punch. Adapted by F. Hugh Herbert from his stage hit.▼

Moon Is Down, The (1943) 90m. *** D: Irving Pichel. Cedric Hardwicke, Henry Travers, Lee J. Cobb, Dorris Bowden, Margaret Wycherly, Peter Van Eyck, William Post, Jr. Fine drama from Steinbeck novel of Norway's invasion by Nazis, tracing local effect and reactions.

Moonlight (1982) **C-78m. TVM** D: Alan Smithee. Robert Desiderio, Michelle Phillips, William Prince, Antony Ponzini, Benson Fong, Rosalind Chao. Fast-food delivery man stumbles upon an international terrorist's assassination plot. Pilot to a busted series. Familiar pseudonym covers two real directors—Jackie Cooper and Rod Holcomb. Average.

Moonlight and Cactus (1944) 60m. *½ D: Edward Cline. Andrews Sisters, Elyse Knox, Leo Carrillo, Eddie Quillan, Shemp Howard, Minerva Urecal. Singing trio find themselves out West running a ranch and chasing romance. Lightweight production.

Moonlighter, The (1953) 75m. ** D: Roy Rowland. Barbara Stanwyck, Fred MacMurray, Ward Bond, William Ching, John Dierkes, Jack Elam. Dull Western with its 3-D virtue lost to TV viewers; MacMurray is a rustler and Stanwyck his ex-girlfriend.

Moonlighting (1982-British) **C-97m.** **** D: Jerzy Skolimowski. Jeremy Irons, Eugene Lipinski, Jiri Stanislav, Eugeniusz Haczkiewicz. Slow-paced but mesmerizing allegory about a Polish man sent to London with a trio of workmen to renovate a wealthy man's apartment. The supervisor (Irons) must keep their job a secret, since they have no work permits; the pressure increases when he learns that Poland has imposed martial law. Fascinating study of loneliness and desperation, full of irony and bittersweet humor, with an outstanding performance by Irons. Written and directed by Polish emigre Skolimowski.▼

Moonlight Sonata (1938-British) **80m.** **½ D: Lothar Mendes. Ignace Jan Paderewski, Charles Farrell, Marie Tempest, Barbara Greene, Eric Portman. Well-made but stodgy romance, set in household of Swedish baroness, is excuse for screen appearance by famous concert pianist.▼

Moon of the Wolf (1972) **C-73m. TVM** D: Daniel Petrie. David Janssen, Barbara Rush, Bradford Dillman, John Beradino, Geoffrey Lewis, Royal Dano. Muddy motivation major liability in somewhat likable modern day thriller involving werewolf in Louisiana. Resolution is offbeat but forgettable. Average.▼

Moon Over Burma (1940) **76m.** ** D: Louis King. Dorothy Lamour, Preston Foster, Robert Preston, Doris Nolan, Albert Basserman, Frederick Worlock. Island setting tries to cover up for same old triangle with Foster and Preston fighting over Lamour.

Moon Over Miami (1941) **C-91m.** *** D: Walter Lang. Don Ameche, Betty Grable, Robert Cummings, Carole Landis, Charlotte Greenwood, Jack Haley. Grable, sister Landis, and Greenwood go fortune-hunting in Miami, come up with more than they bargained for in smoothly entertaining musical romance, especially nice in color. Tuneful songs include title number, "You Started Something." Remake of THREE BLIND MICE, also remade as THREE LITTLE GIRLS IN BLUE.▼

Moon Over Parador (1988) **C-105m.** **½ D: Paul Mazursky. Richard Dreyfuss, Raul Julia, Sonia Braga, Jonathan Winters, Michael Greene, Polly Holliday, Charo, Marianne Sägebrecht, Sammy Davis, Jr., Dick Cavett, Ed Asner, Ike Pappas. Amiable comedy about an American actor who's shanghaied into portraying a recently deceased Latin American dictator; reluctant at first, he soon finds he enjoys the charade (and the despot's sexy companion). Entertaining enough, but never quite hits the bull's-eye. Cowriter/director Mazursky has a hilarious cameo in drag.▼

Moon Pilot (1962) **C-98m.** *** D: James Neilson. Tom Tryon, Brian Keith, Edmond O'Brien, Dany Saval, Tommy Kirk, Bob Sweeney, Kent Smith. Dated but enjoyable Disney comedy about astronaut Tryon who meets mysterious girl from another planet (Saval) just before his mission.▼

Moonraker, The (1958-British) **C-82m.** *** D: David MacDonald. George Baker, Sylvia Syms, Peter Arne, Marius Goring. Well-mounted costumer set in 1650s England, involving followers of Charles Stuart.

Moonraker (1979) **C-126m.** ** D: Lewis Gilbert. Roger Moore, Lois Chiles, Michael Lonsdale, Richard Kiel, Corinne Clery, Bernard Lee, Desmond Llewelyn, Lois Maxwell. James Bond no longer resembles Ian Fleming's creation; now he's a tired punster pursuing an intergalactic madman. Overblown comic-strip adventure is strictly for the bubble-gum set . . . but tune in for eye-popping free-fall opening, the best part of this movie. Lee's last appearance as "M."▼

Moonrise (1948) **90m.** **½ D: Frank Borzage. Dane Clark, Gail Russell, Ethel Barrymore, Allyn Joslyn, Henry (Harry) Morgan, Lloyd Bridges, Selena Royle, Rex Ingram, Harry Carey, Jr. Uneven script does in this psychological melodrama of angry, alienated Clark and his plight after accidentally killing the banker's son who's been taunting him for years. However, it's beautifully directed; check out that stunning opening shot, and opening sequence.▼

Moonrunners (1974) **C-102m.** ** D: Gy Waldron. James Mitchum, Kiel Martin, Arthur Hunnicutt, Joan Blackman, Waylon Jennings, Chris Forbes. Action-comedy about modern day bootleggers sputters because of Mitchum's lethargic acting and the script's lack of credibility. Later developed into the *Dukes of Hazzard* TV series.

Moonshine County Express (1977) C-95m. **½ D: Gus Trikonis. John Saxon, Susan Howard, William Conrad, Morgan Woodward, Claudia Jennings, Jeff Corey, Dub Taylor, Maureen McCormick. Murdered moonshiner's three sexy daughters decide to compete with local biggie (Conrad) whom they believe caused their father's death. Strong cast buoys good action programmer.▼

Moonshine War, The (1970) **C-100m.** ** D: Richard Quine. Richard Widmark, Alan Alda, Patrick McGoohan, Melodie Johnson, Will Geer, Joe Williams, Lee Hazlewood. Tediously plotted mixture of comedy and drama during late Prohibition era enlivened by unusual cast and honest attempt to evoke country atmosphere. Script by Elmore Leonard, from his novel. Look for Teri Garr as the tourist's wife.

Moon's Our Home, The (1936) **76m.** ** D: William A. Seiter. Margaret Sullavan, Henry Fonda, Charles Butterworth, Beulah Bondi, Walter Brennan. Flyweight comedy about turbulent courtship and marriage of movie star and N.Y. novelist; too silly to matter, though stars do their best. (Footnote: Fonda and Sullavan had already been married and divorced when this film was made.)▼

Moon-Spinners, The (1964) C-118m. **½ D: James Neilson. Hayley Mills, Eli Wallach, Pola Negri, Peter McEnery, Joan Greenwood, Irene Papas. Disney's attempt at Hitchcock-like intrigue with a light touch has Hayley a vacationer in Crete who becomes involved with jewelry-smuggling ring. Too long and muddled to hit bullseye, but still entertaining, with Negri (off-screen since 1943) an enjoyable villainess.▼

Moonstruck (1987) C-102m. **** D: Norman Jewison. Cher, Nicolas Cage, Vincent Gardenia, Olympia Dukakis, Danny Aiello, Julie Bovasso, John Mahoney, Louis Guss, Feodor Chaliapin, Anita Gillette. A gem of a movie that unfolds like a good play, without ever seeming static or stagy. Cher plays an independent young widow who agrees to marry an older man (Aiello) —and then finds herself inexorably drawn to his misfit younger brother (Cage). John Patrick Shanley's script is brimming with wonderful vignettes and acute observations about Italian-American families. Cher, Dukakis (terrific as the mother), and Shanley won Academy Awards for their work.▼

Moontide (1942) **94m.** **½ D: Archie Mayo. Jean Gabin, Ida Lupino, Thomas Mitchell, Claude Rains, Jerome Cowan, Helene Reynolds, Ralph Byrd, (Victor) Sen Yung, Tully Marshall. Jean Gabin's portrayal of rough seaman who cares for potential suicide (Lupino) saves an otherwise average "realistic" movie.

Moon Zero Two (1970-British) C-100m. *½ D: Roy Ward Baker. James Olson, Catherina Von Schell (Catherine Schell), Warren Mitchell, Adrienne Corri, Ori Levy, Dudley Foster. Sci-fi adventure is almost like a Western, with people making mining claims on the moon and having to fight for their rights. You've seen it before without the craters.

More American Graffiti (1979) C-111m. *½ D: B. W. L. Norton. Candy Clark, Bo Hopkins, Ron Howard, Paul Le Mat, Mackenzie Phillips, Charles Martin Smith, Cindy Williams, Anna Bjorn, Scott Glenn, Mary Kay Place, Rosanna Arquette. More is less, in this sequel to 1973 hit, placing that film's likable characters in a quartet of pointless vignettes.

More Dead Than Alive (1969) C-101m. ** D: Robert Sparr. Clint Walker, Vincent Price, Anne Francis, Paul Hampton. Modest Western about a gunslinger traveling in a side show as sharpshooter. Not a horror film, despite title and presence of Price.

More Than a Miracle (1967-Italian-French) C-105m. ** D: Francesco Rosi. Sophia Loren, Omar Sharif, Dolores Del Rio, Georges Wilson, Leslie French, Marina Malfatti. Sophia has never looked better but this absurd fairy tale about a prince and a peasant girl is just a waste of time.

More Than a Secretary (1936) **77m.** ** D: Alfred E. Green. Jean Arthur, George Brent, Lionel Stander, Ruth Donnelly, Reginald Denny, Dorothea Kent. Arthur's charm gives distinction to routine comedy of secretary in love with handsome boss Brent.

More Than Friends (1979) C-100m. TVM D: Jim Burrows. Penny Marshall, Rob Reiner, Kay Medford, Claudette Nevins, Howard Hesseman, Dabney Coleman. Occasionally hilarious romantic comedy by Reiner loosely based on his early courtship of then real-life wife Marshall. Above average.

More the Merrier, The (1943) **104m.** *** D: George Stevens. Jean Arthur, Joel McCrea, Charles Coburn, Richard Gaines, Bruce Bennett, Ann Savage, Ann Doran, Frank Sully, Grady Sutton. Working-girl Arthur finds herself sharing small apartment in WW2 Washington with McCrea and Coburn (who won an Oscar for this). Later remade as WALK DON'T RUN, but peerless Arthur can't be beat.▼

More Wild Wild West (1980) **C-100m.** TVM D: Burt Kennedy. Robert Conrad, Ross Martin, Jonathan Winters, Harry Morgan, Rene Auberjonois, Liz Torres, Victor Buono, Dr. Joyce Brothers, Jack LaLanne, Randi Brough, Candi Brough. The further adventures of secret service agents James T. West and Artemus Gordon in this sequel to THE WILD, WILD WEST REVISITED and the classic series of a decade earlier. Here the intrepid twosome engage in a battle of wits with a daffy megalomaniac (Winters). Average.▼

Morgan! (1966-British) **97m.** ***½ D: Karel Reisz. Vanessa Redgrave, David Warner, Robert Stephens, Irene Handl. Decidedly offbeat gem. Artist Warner verges on insanity, keyed off by wife Redgrave's divorcing him, and goes on eccentric escapades. Script by David Mercer, from his play. Complete title is MORGAN—A SUITABLE CASE FOR TREATMENT.▼

Morgan Stewart's Coming Home (1987) **C-96m.** *½ D: Alan Smithee. Jon Cryer, Lynn Redgrave, Nicholas Pryor, Viveka Davis, Paul Gleason. Inane comedy from the notorious, and pseudonymous, director Smithee (in this case Paul Aaron) about a teenager who returns home from boarding school and tries to change the ways of his obnoxious, politically ambitious parents. It all plays like an unsold sitcom pilot. Redgrave is wasted, and even Cryer's considerable screen charm can't turn this into anything worth coming home to see.▼

Morgan the Pirate (1961-Italian) **C-95m.** ** D: Andre de Toth. Steve Reeves, Valerie Lagrange, Lydia Alfonsi, Chelo Alonso. Considering cast and Reeves' career, fairly likely and interesting swashbuckler based on life of illustrious pirate. Original Italian running time: 105m.▼

Morituri SEE: **Saboteur: Code Name Morituri**▼

Morning After, The (1974) **C-78m.** TVM D: Richard T. Heffron. Dick Van Dyke, Lynn Carlin, Don Porter, Linda Lavin, Richard Derr, Robert Hover. Forceful movie written by Richard Matheson and based on Jack Wiener's book, with Van Dyke making an auspicious dramatic debut in his portrait of a corporate executive turned alcoholic. Above average.

Morning After, The (1986) **C-103m.** ** D: Sidney Lumet. Jane Fonda, Jeff Bridges, Raul Julia, Diane Salinger, Richard Foronjy, Geoffrey Scott, James (Gypsy) Haake. So-called thriller about an alcoholic actress who wakes up in bed with a dead man and doesn't know how it happened. Tiresome story and ill-defined characters send this one down the tubes, despite that promising star combo. ▼

Morning Glory (1933) **74m.** *** D: Lowell Sherman. Katharine Hepburn, Adolphe Menjou, Douglas Fairbanks, Jr., C. Aubrey Smith, Mary Duncan. Dated but lovely film from Zoe Akins' play about stagestruck young girl called Eva Lovelace who tries to succeed in N.Y.C. Good cast, sharp script, but it's magically compelling Hepburn who makes this memorable; she won first Oscar for her work. Remade in 1958 as STAGE STRUCK.▼

Morocco (1930) **92m.** *** D: Josef von Sternberg. Gary Cooper, Marlene Dietrich, Adolphe Menjou, Francis McDonald, Eve Southern, Paul Porcasi. Dietrich is alluring and exotic in her first Hollywood film, as a cabaret singer (improbably stuck in Morocco) who must choose between wealthy Menjou and Foreign Legionnaire Cooper. A treat. Marlene sings three numbers, including "What Am I Bid."▼

Morons From Outer Space (1985-British) **C-87m.** **½ D: Mike Hodges. Griff Rhys Jones, Mel Smith, James B. Sikking, Dinsdale Landen, Jimmy Nail, Joanne Pearce, Paul Brown. Chaos reigns supreme in this inventive, uneven, but sometimes hilarious comedy about some very human aliens with British accents—who also happen to be brainless twits—and what happens when their spaceship crash-lands on Earth. Sight gags galore.▼

Mortadella SEE: **Lady Liberty**

Mortal Storm, The (1940) **100m.** ***½ D: Frank Borzage. Margaret Sullavan, James Stewart, Robert Young, Frank Morgan, Robert Stack, Bonita Granville, Irene Rich, Maria Ouspenskaya. Nazi takeover in Germany splits family, ruins life of father, professor Morgan; Stewart tries to leave country with professor's daughter (Sullavan). Sincere filming of Phyllis Bottome's novel is beautifully acted, with one of Morgan's finest performances. Film debut of Dan Dailey (billed as Dan Dailey, Jr.); look sharp in second classroom scene for Tom Drake.

Moscow Does Not Believe in Tears (1980-Russian) **C-152m.** *** D: Vladimir Menshov. Vera Alentova, Irina Muravyova, Raisa Ryazonova, Natalia Vavilova, Alexei Batalov. A trio of young women come to Moscow during the late '50s to seek love and work. Enjoyable if slow-moving; closer in spirit to THE BEST OF EVERYTHING than WAR AND PEACE. Oscar winner as Best Foreign Film.▼

Moscow Nights SEE: **I Stand Condemned**▼

Moscow on the Hudson (1984) **C-115m.** ***½ D: Paul Mazursky. Robin Williams, Maria Conchita Alonso, Cleavant Derricks, Alejandro Rey, Savely Kramarov, Elya Baskin. Fine original comedy-drama by Mazursky and Leon Capetanos about a Russian musician who defects during a trip to N.Y.C. —in Bloomingdale's, no less—and tries to come to grips with his new life in a new land. Full of endearing performances, perceptive and bittersweet moments—but a few too many false endings. Williams is superb in the lead.▼

Moses (1975-British-Italian) **C-141m. TVM** D: Gianfranco DeBosio. Burt Lancaster, Anthony Quayle, Ingrid Thulin, Irene Papas, William Lancaster, Mariangela Melato, Laurent Terzieff. Theatrical version of the six-hour *Moses—the Lawgiver* is not very impressive, with so-so special effects and a solid cast wasted. Screenplay by Anthony Burgess and Vittorio Bonicelli, but you're better off reading the book. Below average.▼

Mosquito Coast, The (1986) **C-117m.** ***½ D: Peter Weir. Harrison Ford, Helen Mirren, River Phoenix, Jadrien Steele, Hilary Gordon, Rebecca Gordon, Conrad Roberts, Andre Gregory, Dick O'Neill, Martha Plimpton, Butterfly McQueen. Utterly compelling, novelistic saga of iconoclastic inventor and idealist (Ford, in a knockout performance) who moves his family to remote village in Central America where he creates an incredible utopia . . . and proceeds to play God. Not for all tastes, since Ford's character is unsympathetic (though he was even worse in Paul Theroux's novel!). Beautifully crafted, with fine screenplay by Paul Schrader. A serious and emotionally gripping film. ▼

Mosquito Squadron (1969-British) **C-90m.** **½ D: Boris Sagal. David McCallum, Suzanne Neve, David Buck, David Dundas, Dinsdale Landen, Charles Gray. Good ensemble performances in tired story of Canadian-born RAF pilot (McCallum)'s crucial behind-the-lines mission to destroy Germany's ultimate weapon project.

Moss Rose (1947) **82m.** **½ D: Gregory Ratoff. Peggy Cummins, Victor Mature, Ethel Barrymore, Vincent Price, Margo Woode. OK period-piece of ambitious chorus girl who blackmails her way into high society; scheme nearly backfires on her.

Most Beautiful, The (1944-Japanese) **85m.** ** D: Akira Kurosawa. Takashi Shimura, Ichiro Sugai, Soji Kiyokawa, Takako Irie, Yoko Yaguchi. One of Kurosawa's earliest features includes considerable WW2 propaganda; young women factory workers are exhorted by foreman Shimura (star

of Kurosawa's IKIRU and SEVEN SAMURAI) to become production warriors by increasing output of optical weaponry. Tearful young girl Yaguchi later married Kurosawa. Not released in America until 1987.

Most Dangerous Game, The (1932) **63m.** *** D: Ernest B. Shoedsack, Irving Pichel. Joel McCrea, Fay Wray, Leslie Banks, Robert Armstrong, Noble Johnson. Vivid telling of Richard Connell's famous, oft-filmed story about a megalomaniac named Count Zaroff who hunts human beings on his remote island. Banks is a florid, sometimes campy villain. Made at the same time as KING KONG by many of the same people. Remade as GAME OF DEATH and RUN FOR THE SUN, and ripped off many other times.▼

Most Dangerous Man Alive (1961) **82m.** ** D: Allan Dwan. Ron Randell, Debra Paget, Elaine Stewart, Anthony Caruso, Gregg Palmer. Inventive premise adequately handled; escaped convict involved in chemical explosion is transformed into "iron man" and seeks revenge on enemies.

Most Dangerous Sin, The SEE: **Crime and Punishment** (1958)

Most Wanted (1976) **C-78m. TVM** D: Walter Grauman. Robert Stack, Shelly Novack, Leslie Charleson, Tom Selleck, Kitty Winn, Sheree North, Stephen McNally. Stack heads special police unit in search of a nun killer and winds up with another TV series. Average.▼

Most Wanted Man SEE: **Most Wanted Man in the World, The**

Most Wanted Man in the World, The (1953-French) **85m.** ** D: Henri Verneuil. Fernandel, Zsa Zsa Gabor, Nicole Maurey, Alfred Adam. Fernandel vehicle is heavy-handed buffoonery, with bucolic comic mistaken for arch-criminal. Retitled: THE MOST WANTED MAN.

Most Wonderful Moment, The (1959-Italian) **94m.** ** D: Luciano Emmer. Marcello Mastroianni, Giovanna Ralli, Marisa Merlini, Ernesto Calindri. Lackluster account of doctor Mastroianni and nurse Ralli, involved in new method of childbirth.

Motel Hell (1980) **C-92m.** *½ D: Kevin Connor. Rory Calhoun, Paul Linke, Nancy Parsons, Nina Axelrod, Wolfman Jack, Elaine Joyce, Dick Curtis. Just *what* are Calhoun and his rotund sister putting in their smoked sausage out there in the boondocks? Good to see Rory and Wolfman sharing screen credit, but scattered laughs and a lively finish fail to distinguish this gory horror comedy.▼

Mother and Daughter: The Loving War (1980) **C-100m. TVM.** D: Burt Brinckerhoff. Tuesday Weld, Frances Sternhagen, Kathleen Beller, Jeanne Lang, Ed Winter. A young woman turns to her mother for help when her teenage daughter begins to rebel—just as *she* did twenty years earlier. Harry Chapin appears as himself (performing songs cowritten with wife Sandy Chapin). Teleplay by Rose Leiman Goldemberg. Above average.▼

Mother Carey's Chickens (1938) 82m. ** D: Rowland V. Lee. Fay Bainter, Anne Shirley, Ruby Keeler, James Ellison, Walter Brennan, Frank Albertson, Virginia Weidler, Ralph Morgan. Bainter is mother, Keeler and Shirley her "chickens" in ordinary tear-jerker romance based on Kate Douglas Wiggin's novel.

Mother Didn't Tell Me (1950) 88m. **½ D: Claude Binyon. Dorothy McGuire, William Lundigan, June Havoc, Gary Merrill, Jessie Royce Landis. Naive young woman marries a doctor, not contemplating demands of being a professional man's wife. McGuire brightens this lightweight comedy.

Mother Is a Freshman (1949) C-81m. **½ D: Lloyd Bacon. Loretta Young, Van Johnson, Rudy Vallee, Barbara Lawrence, Robert Arthur, Betty Lynn. Refreshing, wholesome confection; Young and daughter Lynn both attend college, vying for Van's affection.

Mother, Jugs & Speed (1976) C-95m. *** D: Peter Yates. Bill Cosby, Raquel Welch, Harvey Keitel, Allen Garfield, Larry Hagman, Bruce Davison, Dick Butkus, L.Q. Jones, Toni Basil. Hilarious black comedy about a rundown ambulance service more interested in number of patients serviced than their welfare. Hagman especially good as oversexed driver.▼

Mother Lode (1982) C-101m. ** D: Charlton Heston. Charlton Heston, Nick Mancuso, Kim Basinger, John Marley. Heston's a meanie here—in twin brother roles—playing a Scottish miner who'll stop at nothing to get his sullied hands on a mother lode of gold in the mountains of British Columbia. Lackluster script was written by his son, Fraser Clarke Heston, who also produced the film. Reissued as SEARCH FOR THE MOTHER LODE: THE LAST GREAT TREASURE.▼

Mother's Courage: The Mary Thomas Story, A (1989) C-100m. TVM D: John Patterson. Alfre Woodard, A. J. Johnson, Leon, Garland Spencer, Chick Vennera, Larry O. Williams, Jr., Jamey Sheridan. The story of basketball great Isiah Thomas and how his dedicated mom kept him on the straight and narrow—as filtered through the Disney vision. Average.

Mothers, Daughters and Lovers (1989) C-78m. TVM D: Matthew Robbins. Helen Shaver, David McIlwraith, Perrey Reeves, Marcianne Warman, Claude Akins. Single working mom, who runs a truck-stop diner and motel in a whistle-stop town, tries to cope with two daughters: one a studious type, the other a rebel who's burning to get away. Pilot to prospective series. Average.

Mother's Day (1980) C-98m. *½ D: Charles Kaufman. Tiana Pierce, Nancy Hendrickson, Deborah Luce, Rose Ross, Holden McGuire, Billy Ray McQuade. Just about the final word in the horror-misogyny genre. Three college chums are victimized by, then turn the tables on, a hillbilly mother and her two sons. No MURDER, HE SAYS, but Drano/electric carving-knife finale does boast showmanship.▼

Mother's Day (1989) C-105m. TVM D: Susan Rohrer. Denise Nicholas, Bernie Casey, Melba Moore, Jose Ferrer, Malcolm-Jamal Warner, Joseph Lambie, Art Hindle, Gregory Salata, Grant Goodeve. A resourceful mother sets out to clear her son of a drug-related murder while the cops sit on their hands. Made for cable. Average.

Mother's Day on Waltons Mountain (1982) C-100m. TVM D: Gwen Arner. Ralph Waite, Michael Learned, Jon Walmsley, Judy Norton-Taylor, Mary Beth McDonough, Eric Scott, David W. Harper, Kami Cotler, Joe Conley, Ronnie Claire Edwards, Kip Niven, Richard Gilliland, John Considine. The second *Waltons* TV movie drama following the series' demise involving the family in the days just after WW2. Average.

Mother Wore Tights (1947) C-107m. *** D: Walter Lang. Betty Grable, Dan Dailey, Mona Freeman, Connie Marshall, Vanessa Brown, Veda Ann Borg. One of Grable's most popular films, about a vaudeville family. Colorful production, costumes, nostalgic songs and an Oscar-winning Alfred Newman score, plus specialty act by the great Señor Wences. Narrated by Anne Baxter.

Mothra (1962-Japanese) C-100m. **½ D: Inoshiro Honda, Lee Kresel. Franky Sakai, Hiroshi Koizumi, Kyoko Kagawa, Emi Itoh, Yumi Itoh, Jelly Itoh, Ken Uehara. Colorful Japanese monster movie about a giant caterpillar who invades Tokyo to rescue tiny twin girls, who are guiding it with their supernatural powers. Caterpillar then turns into a giant moth (natch), which carries on the destruction. Mothra (or its descendants) turned up in later films too.▼

Motorcycle Gang (1957) 78m. *½ D: Edward L. Cahn. Anne Neyland. John Ashley, Carl (Alfalfa) Switzer, Raymond Hatton, Edmund Cobb. Cheap production dealing with crackdown on rampaging cycle gang.

Moulin Rouge (1952) C-123m. ***½ D: John Huston. Jose Ferrer, Zsa Zsa Gabor, Suzanne Flon, Eric Pohlmann, Colette Marchand, Christopher Lee, Michael Balfour, Peter Cushing. Rich, colorful film based on life of Henri de Toulouse-Lautrec, the 19th century Parisian artist whose growth was stunted by childhood accident. Huston brilliantly captures the flavor of Montmartre, its characters, and Lautrec's sadly distorted view of life. Excellent cast; memorable theme song by Georges Auric. Oscar winner for its stunning art direction-set decoration and costumes. If you can't catch this in color, skip it.▼

Mountain, The (1956) **C-105m.** **½ D: Edward Dmytryk. Spencer Tracy, Robert Wagner, Claire Trevor, William Demarest, Richard Arlen, E. G. Marshall. Turgid tale of brothers Tracy and Wagner climbing peak to reach wreckage, for different reasons.▼

Mountain Family Robinson (1979) C-100m. **½ D: John Cotter. Robert F. Logan, Susan Damante Shaw, William Bryant, Heather Rattray, Ham Larsen, George (Buck) Flower. Kids may not understand "déjà vu," but they'll feel it if they watch this clone of earlier Wilderness Family pictures. Not bad, but so similar to others it hardly seems worth the effort.▼

Mountain Men, The (1980) C-102m. BOMB D: Richard Lang. Charlton Heston, Brian Keith, Victoria Racimo, Stephen Macht, John Glover, Seymour Cassel, David Ackroyd, Victor Jory. Heston and Keith star as fur trappers in this unnecessarily bloody, crude, tiresome good-guys-vs.-Indians epic. Screenplay by Fraser Clarke Heston, the star's son.▼

Mountain Road, The (1960) 102m. **½ D: Daniel Mann. James Stewart, Lisa Lu, Glenn Corbett, Henry (Harry) Morgan, Frank Silvera, James Best. Stewart is always worth watching, but this saga of American squadron working in China during waning days of WW2 is pretty flat.

Mountains of the Moon (1990) **C-135m.** ***½ D: Bob Rafelson. Patrick Bergin, Iain Glen, Richard E. Grant, Fiona Shaw, John Savident, James Villiers, Adrian Rawlins, Delroy Lindo, Paul Onsongo, Bernard Hill, Roshan Seth, Anna Massey, Leslie Phillips. Captivating saga of explorer Sir Richard Burton and his search for the source of the Nile River in the late 1800s. Bergin is a charismatic lead, with Glen as John Hanning Speke, the dilettante who accompanies (and later tries to overtake) him. Vivid, stimulating, and satisfying; manages to embrace the sweep of an epic film along with a compellingly personal story. Screenplay by Rafelson and William Harrison, based on the latter's biographical novel *Burton and Speke* and on actual journals of the two explorers.▼

Mourning Becomes Electra (1947) 173m. **½ D: Dudley Nichols. Rosalind Russell, Michael Redgrave, Raymond Massey, Katina Paxinou, Nancy Coleman, Leo Genn, Kirk Douglas. Eugene O'Neill's play set in New England and adapted from the Greek tragedy *Oresteia*. Civil War general is killed by wife and their children seek revenge. Heavy, talky drama, even in 105m. version shown on TV.

Mouse and His Child, The (1977) **C-83m.** BOMB D: Fred Wolf, Chuck Swenson. Voices of Peter Ustinov, Alan Barzman, Marcy Swenson, Cloris Leachman, Andy Devine, Sally Kellerman. Boring animated film about a toy mouse and his child, and their adventures in the real world. Talk, talk, talk and no action.▼

Mouse on the Moon, The (1963-British) **C-82m.** ***½ D: Richard Lester. Margaret Rutherford, Bernard Cribbins, Ron Moody, Terry-Thomas, Michael Crawford. Hilarious sequel to THE MOUSE THAT ROARED, about Duchy of Grand Fenwick. Tiny country enters space race, with little help from its befuddled Grand Duchess, Margaret Rutherford.

Mouse That Roared, The (1959-British) **C-83m.** ***½ D: Jack Arnold. Peter Sellers, Jean Seberg, David Kossoff, William Hartnell, Monty Landis, Leo McKern. Hilarious satire about the Duchy of Grand Fenwick declaring war on the U. S. Sellers stars in three roles, equally amusing. Gag before opening titles is a masterpiece. Roger Macdougall and Stanley Mann adapted Leonard Wibberley's novel. Sequel: THE MOUSE ON THE MOON. ▼

Mousey (1974) **C-78m.** TVM D: Daniel Petrie. Kirk Douglas, Jean Seberg, John Vernon, Bessie Love, Suzanne Lloyd, Sam Wanamaker, James Bradford. Thriller about a milquetoast teacher (Douglas) who stops at nothing to take vengeance on his ex-wife. Tightly made, and Kirk's wonderfully sinister. Released theatrically overseas as CAT AND MOUSE. Above average.

Mouthpiece, The (1932) 90m. ***½ D: Elliott Nugent, James Flood. Warren William, Sidney Fox, Mae Madison, Aline MacMahon, John Wray. Solid story based on life of flamboyant attorney William Fallon; up-and-coming prosecutor in D.A.'s office turns to defending people instead, becomes slick and successful, leaving morals behind. First-rate all the way. Remade as THE MAN WHO TALKED TOO MUCH and ILLEGAL.

Mouth to Mouth (1978-Australian) **C-95m.** ***½ D: John Duigan. Kim Krejus, Sonia Peat, Ian Gilmour, Sergio Frazetto, Walter Pym. A pair of unemployed, aimless teenage couples steal and hustle to survive. Fascinating, funny, sad, with lively direction by Duigan.

Move (1970) **C-90m.** BOMB D: Stuart Rosenberg. Elliott Gould, Paula Prentiss, Genevieve Waite, John Larch, Joe Silver, Ron O'Neal. One of those comedies that helped to kill Gould's career within a year; porn-writer/dog-walker has problems when he moves from one apartment to another, but not as many as viewers will have trying to make sense out of the film.

Move Over, Darling (1963) **C-103m.** **½ D: Michael Gordon. Doris Day, James

[774]

Garner, Polly Bergen, Chuck Connors, Thelma Ritter, Fred Clark, Don Knotts, Elliott Reid, John Astin, Pat Harrington, Jr. Day, Garner, and Bergen redo the Irene Dunne, Cary Grant, and Gail Patrick roles from MY FAVORITE WIFE in this slick and amusing film. Edgar Buchanan stands out as a judge confused by the wife-brought-back-to-life situation. This started production as SOMETHING'S GOT TO GIVE with Marilyn Monroe.

Movers and Shakers (1985) **C-79m.** *½ D: William Asher. Walter Matthau, Charles Grodin, Vincent Gardenia, Tyne Daly, Bill Macy, Gilda Radner. Satiric look at movie-making in the 80s, written and coproduced by Grodin, who spent years trying to get it made. Talented cast (including cameos by Steve Martin and Penny Marshall) largely wasted in this unfunny comedy sprinkled with just an occasional insight or laugh. Too bad . . . *Love in Sex* had great possibilities.▼

Movie Crazy (1932) **84m.** *** D: Clyde Bruckman. Harold Lloyd, Constance Cummings, Kenneth Thomson, Sydney Jarvis, Eddie Fetherstone. Lloyd's best talkie recaptures the spirit of his silent-comedy hits, telling story of small-town boy who goes to Hollywood with stars in his eyes, gets rude awakening but finally makes good. Includes his famous magician's coat scene. Cummings is a charming leading lady.

Movie Maker, The (1967) **C-91m. TVM** D: Josef Leytes. Rod Steiger, Robert Culp, Anna Lee, James Dunn, Sally Kellerman. Strong performances by Steiger and Culp in drama detailing rivalry for control of movie studio. Stagy enactment of Rod Serling script. Originally a two-part *Chrysler Theatre* of 1965 titled "A Slow Fade to Black." Above average.

Movie Maker, The (1986) SEE: **Smart Alec** ▼

Movie Movie (1978) **C/B&W-107m.** *** D: Stanley Donen. George C. Scott, Trish Van Devere, Eli Wallach, Red Buttons, Barbara Harris, Barry Bostwick, Harry Hamlin, Art Carney, Rebecca York, Ann Reinking, Kathleen Beller. Affectionate parody of 1930s double feature: "Dynamite Hands" is b&w boxing saga with Hamlin in the John Garfield-ish role; "Baxter's Beauties of 1933" is Busby Berkeley-type musical, with numbers staged by Michael Kidd (who plays Hamlin's father in first story). There's even a Coming Attractions prevue! Introduced by George Burns.▼

Movie Murderer, The (1970) **C-99m. TVM** D: Boris Sagal. Arthur Kennedy, Robert Webber, Warren Oates, Tom Selleck, Norma Crane, Nita Talbot, Russell Johnson, Elisha Cook. Arsonist specializing in destroying jet liners inadvertently

filmed, searches for negatives, becomes quarry of insurance investigator and detective. Passable hunter-versus-hunted story with good performances, novelty value of many vintage film clips. Average.

Movie Struck SEE: **Pick a Star**▼

Moving (1988) **C-89m.** *½ D: Alan Metter. Richard Pryor, Beverly Todd, Randy Quaid, Dave Thomas, Dana Carvey, Stacey Dash. Mass transit engineer Pryor falls into a dream job following his unexpected and unceremonious firing—only hitch: he and the family must relocate from New Jersey to Boise, Idaho. Wallows in the predictable (kids rebel, the movers are psychos), with a modest chuckle every half-hour or so. Pryor seems uncomfortable as Ozzie Nelson.▼

Moving Target (1967-Italian) **C-92m.** *½ D: Sergio Corbucci. Ty Hardin, Michael Rennie, Grazielle Granata, Paola Pitagora, Vittorio Caprioli. Incredibly plotted spy/counterspy stuff set in Athens, marred even further by sadistic, explicitly violent action.

Moving Target (1988) **C-100m. TVM** D: Chris Thomson. Jason Bateman, John Glover, Jack Wagner, Chynna Phillips, Richard Dysart, Tom Skerritt. Teen returns from summer camp to find his family gone (moved out, dog and all) and killers on his trail. Good premise, indifferently acted. Star vehicle for Batman of TV's *The Hogan Family*; his leading lady is the daughter of John and Michelle Phillips of The Mamas and the Papas. Average.▼

Moving Violation (1976) **C-91m.** ** D: Charles S. Dubin. Stephen McHattie, Kay Lenz, Eddie Albert, Lonny Chapman, Will Geer, Jack Murdock, John S. Ragin. Redneck sheriff goes after young couple, leading to usual car chases. So what else is new?▼

Moving Violations (1985) **C-90m.** *½ D: Neal Israel. John Murray, Jennifer Tilly, James Keach, Brian Backer, Sally Kellerman, Fred Willard, Lisa Hart Carroll, Wendie Jo Sperber, Clara Peller, Nedra Volz, Ned Eisenberg. Threadbare comedy of adventures in traffic violations school; more potholes than laughs. Incidentally, wiseacre star Murray is Bill M.'s brother.▼

Movin' On SEE: **In Tandem**

Moviola SEE: **Scarlett O'Hara War, The**

Moviola SEE: **Silent Lovers, The**

Moviola SEE: **This Year's Blonde**

Mozambique (1965-British) **C-98m.** *½ D: Robert Lynn. Steve Cochran, Hildegarde Neff, Vivi Bach, Paul Hubschmid, Martin Benson. Tiresome programmer with world-weary pilot Cochran unknowingly becoming immersed in drug smuggling and white slavery.

Mr. Ace (1946) **84m.** **½ D: Edwin L. Marin. George Raft, Sylvia Sidney, Stanley Ridges, Sara Haden, Jerome Cowan. Ordinary dirty-politics drama of office-seeking Sidney using Raft to achieve her goals.▼

Mr. and Mrs. Bo Jo Jones (1971) **C-73m.** TVM D: Robert Day. Desi Arnaz, Jr., Christopher Norris, Dan Dailey, Dina Merrill, Susan Strasberg, Tom Bosley, Jessie Royce Landis. Young couple in small town undergo parental and neighborhood pressures. Despite OK performances, mediocre script makes film forgettable. Average.

Mr. and Mrs. North (1941) **67m.** **½ D: Robert B. Sinclair. Gracie Allen, William Post, Jr., Paul Kelly, Rose Hobart, Virginia Grey, Tom Conway. Radio characters come to screen in comedy involving dead bodies being discovered; sometimes funny, sometimes forced, though it's interesting to see Gracie without George. Later a TV series.

Mr. and Mrs. Smith (1941) **95m.** *** D: Alfred Hitchcock. Carole Lombard, Robert Montgomery, Gene Raymond, Jack Carson, Philip Merivale, Betty Compson, Lucile Watson. Madcap comedy of Lombard and Montgomery discovering their marriage wasn't legal. One of Hitchcock's least typical films, but bouncy nonetheless; written by Norman Krasna.▼

Mr. Arkadin (1955-British) **99m.** **½ D: Orson Welles. Orson Welles, Michael Redgrave, Patricia Medina, Akim Tamiroff, Mischa Auer. Brooding, rambling drama about oddball financier. Retitled: CONFIDENTIAL REPORT.▼

Mr. Belvedere Goes to College (1949) **83m.** ** D: Elliott Nugent. Clifton Webb, Shirley Temple, Tom Drake, Alan Young, Jessie Royce Landis. The sharp-tongued character from SITTING PRETTY enrolls in college, with predictable results. Nothing special.

Mr. Belvedere Rings the Bell (1951) **87m.** **½ D: Henry Koster. Clifton Webb, Joanne Dru, Hugh Marlowe, Zero Mostel, Doro Merande, Billy Lynn. Another followup to SITTING PRETTY isn't as witty. Webb enters old folks' home to prove his theory that age has nothing to do with leading a full life.

Mr. Billion (1977) **C-93m.** ** D: Jonathan Kaplan. Terence Hill, Valerie Perrine, Jackie Gleason, Slim Pickens, Chill Wills, William Redfield. Uninspired comedy about a lowly Italian mechanic (Hill, in his American debut) on a mad, cross-country scramble to claim a billion dollar legacy, and the attempts of scoundrels to swindle him out of it.▼

Mr. Blandings Builds His Dream House (1948) **94m.** *** D: H. C. Potter. Cary Grant, Myrna Loy, Melvyn Douglas, Reginald Denny, Sharyn Moffett, Connie Marshall, Louise Beavers, Ian Wolfe, Lurene Tuttle, Lex Barker. Slick comedy of city couple attempting to build a house in the country; expertly handled, with Cary at his peak. And no one ever described room colors better than Loy! Norman Panama

and Melvin Frank scripted, from Eric Hodgins' novel.▼

Mr. Bug Goes to Town SEE: **Hoppity Goes to Town**▼

Mr. Deeds Goes to Town (1936) **115m.** **** D: Frank Capra. Gary Cooper, Jean Arthur, George Bancroft, Lionel Stander, Douglass Dumbrille, Mayo Methot, Raymond Walburn, Walter Catlett, H. B. Warner. Cooper is Longfellow Deeds, who inherits 20 million dollars and wants to give it all away to needy people. Arthur is appealing as the hard-boiled big-city reporter who tries to figure out what makes him tick. Capra won his second Oscar for this irresistible film, written by Robert Riskin. Later a short-lived TV series.▼

Mr. Denning Drives North (1953-British) **93m.** **½ D: Anthony Kimmins. John Mills, Phyllis Calvert, Eileen Moore, Sam Wanamaker. Cast's sincerity makes this murder yarn palatable, the biggest hunt being for the corpus delicti.

Mr. Forbush and the Penguins SEE: **Cry of the Penguins**

Mr. Hex (1946) **63m.** D: William Beaudine. Leo Gorcey, Huntz Hall, Bobby Jordan, Gabriel Dell, Gale Robbins, Billy Benedict, David Gorcey, Ian Keith. SEE: **Bowery Boys** series.

Mr. Hobbs Takes a Vacation (1962) **C-116m.** **½ D: Henry Koster. James Stewart, Maureen O'Hara, Fabian, John Saxon, Marie Wilson, Reginald Gardiner, Lauri Peters. Ultra-wholesome family fare. Stewart and O'Hara, taking brood to seaside summer house, try to meet family problems.▼

Mr. Horn (1979) **C-200m.** TVM D: Jack Starrett. David Carradine, Richard Widmark, Karen Black, Jeremy Slate, Enrique Lucero, Jack Starrett. Rambling, episodic Western by William Goldman about legendary frontier folk hero beat Steve McQueen's TOM HORN to the punch. Average.▼

Mr. Hulot's Holiday (1953-French) **86m.** ***½ D: Jacques Tati. Jacques Tati, Nathalie Pascaud, Michelle Rolla, Valentine Camax, Louis Perrault. Tati introduced his delightful Hulot character in this amusing excursion to a French resort town; a fond throwback to the days of silent-screen comedy. French version runs 114m.▼

Mr. Imperium (1951) **C-87m.** **½ D: Don Hartman. Lana Turner, Ezio Pinza, Marjorie Main, Barry Sullivan, Cedric Hardwicke, Debbie Reynolds. Threadbare romance between Turner and Pinza, now a monarch; colorful but paper-thin.

Mr. Inside/Mr. Outside (1973) **C-74m.** TVM D: William Graham. Hal Linden, Tony Lo Bianco, Phil Bruns, Paul Benjamin, Stefan Schnabel, Arnold Soboloff. Tough, atmospheric crime drama with two N.Y.C. cops working to foil diamond smugglers. Excellent action compensates for OK scripting in this busted pilot. Average.▼

Mr. Kingstreet's War (1973) **C-92m.** **½ D: Percival Rubens. John Saxon, Tippi Hedren, Rossano Brazzi, Brian O'Shaughnessy. Loner and his wife find idyllic life at African game preserve disrupted by WW2 and set out to do something about it. Interesting and unusual.

Mr. Klein (1977-French) **C-122m.** **½ D: Joseph Losey. Alain Delon, Jeanne Moreau, Michael Lonsdale, Juliet Berto, Suzanne Flon. French-Catholic art dealer exploits Jews desperately in need of money during WW2, then has the tables turned on him when he's mistaken for a Jew with the same name. Intriguing premise only partially fulfilled due to overlength and occasionally self-conscious direction. A curiosity.▼

Mr. Love (1985-British) **C-98m.** *** D: Roy Battersby. Barry Jackson, Maurice Denham, Christina Collier, Helen Cotterill, Julia Deakin, Linda Marlowe, Margaret Tyzack. Gentle, winning tale of quiet, reserved gardener Jackson, in a loveless marriage for almost 30 years and whom most everybody thinks is a joke—so why do all those women appear at his funeral? The *Casablanca* scene is a gem.▼

Mr. Lucky (1943) **100m.** *** D: H. C. Potter. Cary Grant, Laraine Day, Charles Bickford, Gladys Cooper, Alan Carney, Henry Stephenson, Paul Stewart, Kay Johnson, Florence Bates. Gambling-ship-owner Grant intends to fleece virtuous Day, instead falls in love and goes straight. Basis for later TV series has spirited cast, engaging script. Love that rhyming slang!▼

Mr. Majestyk (1974) **C-103m.** **½ D: Richard Fleischer. Charles Bronson, Al Lettieri, Linda Cristal, Lee Purcell, Paul Koslo, Alejandro Rey. Above average Bronson thriller, casting him as Colorado watermelon farmer (!) marked for destruction by syndicate hit man Lettieri; surprisingly tongue-in-cheek script by Elmore Leonard.▼

Mr. Mom (1983) **C-91m.** **½ D: Stan Dragoti. Michael Keaton, Teri Garr, Martin Mull, Ann Jillian, Christopher Lloyd, Frederick Koehler, Taliesin Jaffe, Graham Jarvis, Jeffrey Tambor. Pleasant enough rehash of age-old sitcom premise: Mom gets a job when dad gets fired, leaving him to learn the perils of running a household. Likable stars make it palatable, but you've seen it all before.▼

Mr. Moto With the Charlie Chan films going strong, John P. Marquand's character of a seemingly timid but cunning and intelligent sleuth named Mr. Moto seemed a natural for the movies. Twentieth Century-Fox, the same studio that was making the Chans, inaugurated the series in 1937 with THINK FAST, MR. MOTO, with the offbeat casting of Peter Lorre in the lead.

Lorre fell into the role of the crafty, lighthearted Moto quite well, and played the character in all eight Moto films, through 1939. The series was entertaining, but somehow lacked the heart of the Chan films. Fortunately, they were endowed with slick productions and fine casts of character actors, which tended to overshadow the films' shortcomings. Moto globe-trotted from country to country, solving various mysteries with and without the help of police authorities, and confronted such formidable villains as Sig Ruman, Sidney Blackmer, John Carradine, Leon Ames, Ricardo Cortez, Jean Hersholt and Lionel Atwill. Needless to say, the diminutive Lorre was victorious in every encounter, with the negligible help of such "assistants" as dim-witted Warren Hymer in MR. MOTO IN DANGER ISLAND. Many consider THANK YOU MR. MOTO (1938) the best of the series, with our hero hunting for a valuable map leading to an ancient treasure. In 1965 Fox decided to revive the long-dormant Moto character in a very low-budget second feature called, appropriately enough, THE RETURN OF MR. MOTO. Movie villain Henry Silva starred as Moto, but the film was cheaply done and completely unfaithful to the original conception of the character. Hopefully, future movie historians will ignore it and realize that for everyone Peter Lorre was *the* Mr. Moto.

Mr. Moto in Danger Island (1939) **63m.** D: Herbert I. Leeds. Peter Lorre, Jean Hersholt, Amanda Duff, Warren Hymer, Richard Lane, Leon Ames, Douglass Dumbrille, Robert Lowery. Also known as DANGER ISLAND.

Mr. Moto's Gamble (1938) **71m.** D: James Tinling. Peter Lorre, Keye Luke, Dick Baldwin, Lynn Bari, Douglas Fowley, Jayne Regan, Harold Huber, Maxie Rosenbloom.

Mr. Moto's Last Warning (1939) **71m.** D: Norman Foster. Peter Lorre, Ricardo Cortez, Virginia Field, John Carradine, George Sanders, Robert Coote, John Davidson.▼

Mr. Moto Takes a Chance (1938) **63m.** D: Norman Foster. Peter Lorre, Rochelle Hudson, Robert Kent, J. Edward Bromberg, Chick Chandler, George Regas, Fredrik Vogeding.

Mr. Moto Takes a Vacation (1939) **61m.** D: Norman Foster. Peter Lorre, Joseph Schildkraut, Lionel Atwill, Virginia Field, Iva Stewart, Victor Varconi, John Davidson.

Mr. Muggs Rides Again (1945) **63m.** D: Wallace Fox. Leo Gorcey, Huntz Hall, Billy Benedict, Nancy Brinckman, George Meeker, Pierre Watkin, Bernard Thomas. SEE: **Bowery Boys** series.

Mr. Music (1950) **113m.** **½ D: Richard Haydn. Bing Crosby, Nancy Olson, Charles Coburn, Ruth Hussey, Marge and Gower

Champion, Peggy Lee, Groucho Marx. Easygoing vehicle for crooner Crosby as Broadway songwriter who wants to live the easy life. Remake of ACCENT ON YOUTH.

Mr. North (1988) **C-92m.** **½ D: Danny Huston. Anthony Edwards, Robert Mitchum, Lauren Bacall, Harry Dean Stanton, Anjelica Huston, Mary Stuart Masterson, Virginia Madsen, Tammy Grimes, David Warner, Hunter Carson, Christopher Durang, Mark Metcalf, Katharine Houghton. Bright but penniless young man makes a major impact on Newport high society in the 1920s by being forthright, ingenious, and possessing an unusual amount of electricity in his body! Agreeable fable based on Thornton Wilder's *Theophilus North* has many assets (fine cast, beautiful locations) as well as some liabilities (uneven performances, shifts of tone). Coscripted by John Huston, who also executive produced just before his death; this marks his son's theatrical feature debut as director.▼

Mr. Patman (1980-Canadian) **C-105m.** *½ D: John Guillermin. James Coburn, Kate Nelligan, Fionnula Flanagan, Les Carlson, Candy Kane, Michael Kirby. Coburn is well cast in this convoluted, poorly made tale of a charming but slightly mad psycho-ward orderly and his shenanigans. Disappointing.

Mr. Peabody and the Mermaid (1948) **89m.** **½ D: Irving Pichel. William Powell, Ann Blyth, Irene Hervey, Andrea King, Clinton Sundberg. Mild comedy-fantasy from Nunnally Johnson has its moments, with unsuspecting Powell coming across a lovely mermaid while fishing. Powell makes anything look good.▼

Mr. Perrin and Mr. Traill (1948-British) **90m.** ** D: Lawrence Huntington. Marius Goring, David Farrar, Greta Gynt, Raymond Huntley. Lukewarm study of progressive vs. conservative schoolteaching.

Mr. Quilp (1975-British) **C-118m.** *** D: Michael Tuchner. Anthony Newley, David Hemmings, David Warner, Michael Hordern, Jill Bennett, Sarah Jane Varley. Entertaining musical version of Dickens' *The Old Curiosity Shop* with songs by Newley and musical score by Elmer Bernstein. Light-hearted until last reel when it goes serious in the Dickens vein. Retitled THE OLD CURIOSITY SHOP.▼

Mr. Ricco (1975) **C-98m.** ** D: Paul Bogart. Dean Martin, Eugene Roche, Thalmus Rasulala, Geraldine Brooks, Denise Nicholas, Cindy Williams, Philip Michael Thomas. Martin in offbeat casting as criminal lawyer involved with racist killings, sex and assorted violence, but looks too tired to care. Good mystery angle.

Mr. Robinson Crusoe (1932) **76m.** *** D: Edward Sutherland. Douglas Fairbanks Sr., William Farnum, Earle Browne, Maria Alba. An aging but agile Doug is up to his old tricks, betting that he can survive on a South Sea island à la Robinson Crusoe. Great fun; lovely score by Alfred Newman. Also released in silent version.▼

Mr. Rock and Roll (1957) **86m.** ** D: Charles Dubin. Alan Freed, Little Richard, Clyde McPhatter, Frankie Lymon and the Teenagers, Teddy Randazzo, Chuck Berry, Rocky Graziano, Lois O'Brien, Lionel Hampton, Ferlin Husky, The Moonglows, Brook Benton, LaVern Baker. The saga of how Alan Freed "discovered" rock 'n' roll. In AMERICAN HOT WAX, Berry played opposite Tim McIntire portraying Freed; here, he acts with the real McCoy. Vintage footage of McPhatter, Lymon, Little Richard; Rocky Graziano is along for comic relief.

Mr. Sardonicus (1961) **89m.** ** D: William Castle. Ronald Lewis, Audrey Dalton, Guy Rolfe, Oscar Homolka. Recluse count with face frozen in hideous grin lures wife's boyfriend/doctor to castle to cure him. Minor fare despite good ending; Castle gave the theatrical audiences the option of voting "thumbs up" or "thumbs down" (but only one conclusion was filmed). Screenplay by Ray Russell from his novella *Sardonicus*.

Mrs. Brown, You've Got a Lovely Daughter (1968-British) **C-110m.** ** D: Saul Swimmer. Herman's Hermits, Stanley Holloway, Mona Washbourne, Sara Caldwell, Lance Percival. A silly excuse for a movie, with Herman and his Hermits heading for London to enter their greyhound in a race. In between the suspense they sing "There's a Kind of Hush All Over the World" and the title tune. ▼

Mrs. Delafield Wants to Marry (1986) **C-100m.** TVM D: George Schaefer. Katharine Hepburn, Harold Gould, Denholm Elliott, David Ogden Stiers, Charles Frank, Kathryn Walker, Bibi Besch, Brenda Forbes, John Pleshette. Sunny romantic comedy created especially for Kate by Broadway playwright James Prideaux, a December/December relationship between a high society WASP and her kindly Jewish doctor. Above average.

Mr. Sebastian SEE: Sebastian▼

Mr. Skeffington (1944) **127m.** *** D: Vincent Sherman. Bette Davis, Claude Rains, Walter Abel, Richard Waring, Jerome Cowan, Charles Drake, Gigi Perreau. Grand soap opera spanning several decades of N.Y.C. life from 1914 onward. Davis is vain society woman who marries stockbroker Rains for convenience, discovering his true love for her only after many years. Lavish settings, bravura Davis performance. Restored to original 146m. release for homevideo.▼

Mr. Skitch (1933) **70m.** **½ D: James Cruze. Will Rogers, ZaSu Pitts, Rochelle Hudson, Charles Starrett, Eugene Pallette,

Harry Green. Airy Rogers vehicle following family's adventures traveling by car to California. Pure fluff, highlighted by British entertainer Florence Desmond's comic impressions of costar Pitts, and Greta Garbo.

Mrs. Mike (1949) **99m.** **½ D: Louis King. Dick Powell, Evelyn Keyes, J. M. Kerrigan, Angela Clarke. Powell and Keyes are pleasing duo, as Canadian mountie indoctrinates his urban wife to rural life.

Mrs. Miniver (1942) **134m.** ***½ D: William Wyler. Greer Garson, Walter Pidgeon, Dame May Whitty, Teresa Wright, Reginald Owen, Henry Travers, Richard Ney, Henry Wilcoxon. Moving drama about middle-class English family learning to cope with war. Winner of seven Academy Awards—for Garson, Wright, director Wyler, and Best Picture, among others—this film did much to rally American support for our British allies during WW2, though its depiction of English life was decidedly Hollywoodized. Sequel: THE MINIVER STORY.▼

Mr. Smith Goes to Washington (1939) **129m.** **** D: Frank Capra. James Stewart, Jean Arthur, Claude Rains, Edward Arnold, Guy Kibbee, Thomas Mitchell, Eugene Pallette, Beulah Bondi, Harry Carey, H. B. Warner, Charles Lane, Porter Hall, Jack Carson. Stewart is young idealist who finds nothing but corruption in U.S. Senate. Fine Capra Americana, with Stewart's top performance bolstered by Arthur as hard-boiled dame won over by earnest Mr. Smith, and a stellar supporting cast; Carey is magnificent as the Vice President. Brilliant script by Sidney Buchman; however, Lewis R. Foster's Original Story received the Oscar. Remade as BILLY JACK GOES TO WASHINGTON.▼

Mr. Soft Touch (1949) **93m.** ** D: Henry Levin, Gordon Douglas. Glenn Ford, Evelyn Keyes, John Ireland, Beulah Bondi, Percy Kilbride, Ted de Corsia. Ford and Keyes are mild romantic duo in unimportant story of ex-G.I. involved with social worker and gangster-run nightclub.

Mrs. O'Malley and Mr. Malone (1950) **69m.** ** D: Norman Taurog. Marjorie Main, James Whitmore, Ann Dvorak, Fred Clark, Dorothy Malone, Phyllis Kirk. Main is rambunctious but can't elevate film about small-towner winning prize contest, involved with murder on a N.Y.C-bound train. Whitmore is most enjoyable.

Mrs. Parkington (1944) **124m.** *** D: Tay Garnett. Greer Garson, Walter Pidgeon, Edward Arnold, Gladys Cooper, Agnes Moorehead, Peter Lawford, Dan Duryea, Lee Patrick. Determined Garson has lofty ambitions, marries wealthy but homespun Pidgeon, and pushes her way into society; overlong, well-mounted soaper.

Mrs. Pollifax—Spy (1971) **C-110m.** *½ D: Leslie Martinson. Rosalind Russell, Darren McGavin, Nehemiah Persoff, Harold Gould, Albert Paulsen, John Beck. A bored widow volunteers as a CIA agent—and gets accepted—in this lame comedy spy caper. Russell's last theatrical film (for which she did the screenplay, under pseudonym) is also one of her worst.

Mrs. R.—Death Among Friends SEE: **Death Among Friends**

Mrs. R's Daughter (1979) **C-100m. TVM** D: Dan Curtis. Cloris Leachman, Season Hubley, Donald Moffat, John McIntire, Stephen Elliott, Ron Rifkin. The frustrating battle of a determined mother to bring her daughter's rapist to trial. Hell hath no fury like an angry Leachman, as seen in this none-too-encouraging glimpse at our contemporary court system. Average.▼

Mrs. Soffel (1984) **C-110m.** ** D: Gillian Armstrong. Diane Keaton, Mel Gibson, Matthew Modine, Edward Herrmann, Trini Alvarado, Jennie Dundas, Danny Corkill. Interesting but gloomy, emotionally aloof rendering of true story, set in 1901, when wife of Pittsburgh prison warden falls in love with convicted murderer Gibson. Well made, but a pall hangs over entire film. ▼

Mrs. Sundance (1974) **C-78m. TVM** D: Marvin Chomsky. Elizabeth Montgomery, Robert Foxworth, L. Q. Jones, Arthur Hunnicutt, Lurene Tuttle, Claudette Nevins. Further adventures of Etta Place, widow of The Sundance Kid (of BUTCH CASSIDY AND . . . fame), who leads a fugitive's existence brightened by the memory of her late husband. Lighthearted Western by Christopher Knopf tries vainly to recapture the charm of its blockbuster predecessor. Average; character later played by Katharine Ross, who originated the role, in WANTED: THE SUNDANCE WOMAN.

Mrs. Sundance Rides Again SEE: **Wanted: The Sundance Woman**

Mrs. Wiggs of the Cabbage Patch (1934) **80m.** *** D: Norman Taurog. W. C. Fields, Pauline Lord, ZaSu Pitts, Evelyn Venable, Kent Taylor, Donald Meek, Virginia Weidler. More story than Fields in this one, a melodrama of poor woman about to be evicted; the domestic scenes with W. C. and Pitts are priceless.▼

Mrs. Wiggs of the Cabbage Patch (1942) **80m.** **½ D: Ralph Murphy. Fay Bainter, Hugh Herbert, Vera Vague, Barbara Britton, Carolyn Lee, Billy Lee, Carl Switzer, Moroni Olsen. Abandoned wife with large family waits patiently for husband to return. A notch above average.

Mr. Sycamore (1974) **C-88m.** *½ D: Pancho Kohner. Jason Robards, Sandy Dennis, Jean Simmons, Robert Easton, Mark Miller. A milquetoasty mailman with a nagging wife (and a crush on local librarian) decides to escape rat race by turning into a tree! A definite curio, sadly defeated by heavy-handed treatment of material.▼

Mr. Universe (1951) **79m.** *½ D: Joseph Lerner. Jack Carson, Janis Paige, Vincent Edwards, Bert Lahr, Robert Alda. Quickie comedy with good cast wasted on bad material; young Edwards plays wrestler promoted by Carson.

Mr. Universe (1988-Hungarian) **C-96m.** *½ D: Gyorgy Szomjas. Mickey Hargitay, Laszlo Szabo, George Pinter, Mariska Hargitay. Tedious film mixes fact and fancy as a Hungarian dreamer comes to America to make a movie about Hungarian-born Mickey Hargitay, husband of Jayne Mansfield and a former Mr. Universe. Could have been an intriguing look at the American dream, as seen through a foreigner's eyes, but turns out pretentious and boring.

Mr. Winkle Goes to War (1944) **80m.** **½ D: Alfred E. Green. Edward G. Robinson, Ruth Warrick, Ted Donaldson, Robert Armstrong, Ann Shoemaker. Minor yarn of aging henpecked man accidentally drafted during WW2, who becomes military hero. Spirited Robinson is enjoyable.▼

Mr. Wise Guy (1942) **70m.** D: William Nigh. Leo Gorcey, Huntz Hall, Bobby Jordan, Guinn Williams, Billy Gilbert, Benny Rubin, Douglas Fowley, Ann Doran, Jack Mulhall, Warren Hymer, David Gorcey. SEE: **Bowery Boys** series.

Mr. Wong, Detective (1938) **69m.** ** D: William Nigh. Boris Karloff, Grant Withers, Maxine Jennings, Evelyn Brent, Lucien Prival, William Gould. First and best of six films in which Karloff portrays Hugh Wiley's Chinese detective Mr. Wong. The murder is neatly carried out—and the murderer's identity is a real surprise. Monogram Pictures' attempt to emulate the success of the Charlie Chan and Mr. Moto series.▼

Mr. Wong in Chinatown (1939) **70m.** *½ D: William Nigh. Boris Karloff, Grant Withers, William Royle, Marjorie Reynolds, Peter George Lynn, Lotus Long, Richard Loo. Blah Mr. Wong mystery, third in the series, with the sleuth becoming involved in the case of a Chinese princess' murder.▼

Mr. Wrong SEE: **Dark of the Night**

Ms. Don Juan (1973-French) **C-87m.** *½ D: Roger Vadim. Brigitte Bardot, Maurice Ronet, Robert Hossein, Mathieu Carriere, Jane Birkin, Michele Sand. Bardot, in title role, seduces and/or humiliates everyone in her sight: a priest (who's also her cousin), a politician, a businessman. Glossy but limp; may be good for some unintended laughs.▼

Ms. 45 (1981) **C-84m.** **½ D: Abel Ferrara. Zoe Tamerlis, Steve Singer, Jack Thibeau, Peter Yellen, Darlene Stuto. Tamerlis is raped twice, gets her "revenge" by murdering every male in sight. Well-made, violent role-reversal formula film with echoes of PSYCHO, REPULSION,

CARRIE, etc., which won some strong reviews and a cult reputation. Also known as ANGEL OF VENGEANCE.▼

M Station: Hawaii (1980) **C-105m. TVM** D: Jack Lord. Jared Martin, Jo Ann Harris, Andrew Duggan, Dana Wynter, Lyle Bettger, Andrew Prine. Cloak-and-dagger suspenser involving a Soviet sub missing off the coast of Hawaii. Hawaii-based crime-show pilot produced by Lord after retiring his *Hawaii Five-O* team. Average.

Muddy River (1982-Japanese) **105m.** ***½ D: Kohei Oguri. Nobutaka Asahara, Takahiro Tamura, Yumiko Fujita, Minoru Sakurai, Makiko Shibato. Life in postwar Japan, as perceived by two young boys. Stunning, memorable Ozu-like tale, with lovely black-and-white photography. Independently produced, and an Academy Award nominee.

Mudlark, The (1950) **99m.** *** D: Jean Negulesco. Irene Dunne, Alec Guinness, Finlay Currie, Anthony Steel, Andrew Ray, Beatrice Campbell, Wilfrid Hyde-White. Offbeat drama of Queen Victoria (Dunne), a recluse since her husband's death, coming back to reality after meeting waif who stole into her castle. Dunne does quite well as Queen, with Guinness a joy as Disraeli. Filmed in England.

Muggable Mary, Street Cop (1982) **C-100m. TVM** D: Sandor Stern. Karen Valentine, John Getz, Anne DeSalvo, Robert Christian, Michael Pearlman, Vincent Gardenia. Single parent becomes an undercover cop in this dramatization of the true story of Mary Glatzle. Director Stern based his screenplay on her book, *Muggable Mary.* Average.

Mug Town (1943) **60m.** D: Ray Taylor. Billy Halop, Huntz Hall, Bernard Punsley, Gabriel Dell, Tommy Kelly, Grace McDonald, Edward Norris. SEE: **Bowery Boys** series.

Mulligan's Stew (1977) **C-78m. TVM** D: Noel Black. Lawrence Pressman, Elinor Donahue, Johnny Whitaker, Alex Karras, K. C. Martel, Julie Haddock. Sentimental comedy about high school coach with wife and three kids who takes four orphans into his house. The innumerable complications have been similarly explored in MIXED COMPANY as well as TV's *Fish* but they developed a series from this one regardless. Average.

Mummy, The (1932) **72m.** ***½ D: Karl Freund. Boris Karloff, Zita Johann, David Manners, Arthur Byron, Edward Van Sloan, Bramwell Fletcher, Noble Johnson. Horror classic stars Karloff as Egyptian mummy, revived after thousands of years, believing Johann is reincarnation of ancient mate. Remarkable makeup and atmosphere make it chills ahead of many follow-ups.▼

Mummy, The (1959-British) **C-88m.** **½

[780]

D: Terence Fisher. Peter Cushing, Christopher Lee, Yvonne Furneaux, Eddie Byrne, Felix Aylmer, Raymond Huntley. Against warnings of severe consequences, archaeologists desecrate ancient tomb of Egyptian Princess Ananka. They return to England and those consequences. Stylish Hammer horror film.▼

Mummy's Curse, The (1944) 62m. **
D: Leslie Goodwins. Lon Chaney, Jr., Peter Coe, Virginia Christine, Kay Harding, Dennis Moore, Martin Kosleck, Kurt Katch. Last of the series finds Kharis and Ananka dug up in a Louisiana bayou; usual havoc ensues. Novelty of the setting boosts this one a little; silent screen star William Farnum has a bit part as a caretaker.

Mummy's Ghost, The (1944) 60m. ** D: Reginald LeBorg. Lon Chaney, Jr., John Carradine, Ramsay Ames, Robert Lowery, Barton MacLane, George Zucco. Sequel to THE MUMMY'S TOMB finds seemingly unkillable Kharis and his mentor (Carradine) on the trail of a woman who is the reincarnation of Princess Ananka. Least interesting of the series, with nothing new or different to offer. Followed by THE MUMMY'S CURSE.

Mummy's Hand, The (1940) 67m. ***
D: Christy Cabanne. Dick Foran, Wallace Ford, Peggy Moran, Cecil Kellaway, George Zucco, Tom Tyler, Eduardo Ciannelli, Charles Trowbridge. Archeologists seeking lost tomb of Egyptian princess get more than they bargained for when they find it guarded by a living—and very deadly—mummy. First of the "Kharis" series is entertaining blend of chills and comedy, with good cast, flavorful music and atmosphere. Not a sequel to THE MUMMY (1932), although it does utilize flashback footage; itself followed by three sequels.

Mummy's Shroud, The (1967-British) C-90m. BOMB D: John Gilling. Andre Morell, John Phillips, David Buck, Elizabeth Sellars, Maggie Kimberley, Michael Ripper. British expedition takes mummy of child pharaoh back to Cairo; boy's guardian, also a mummy, murders those responsible. One of the least of the Hammer horrors.

Mummy's Tomb, The (1942) 61m. ** D: Harold Young. Lon Chaney, Jr., Elyse Knox, John Hubbard, Turhan Bey, Dick Foran, Wallace Ford, George Zucco, Mary Gordon. Sequel to THE MUMMY'S HAND finds Kharis (now played by Chaney) transported to America to kill off surviving members of the expedition. Weak script and too much stock footage are the real villains.

Mumsy, Nanny, Sonny and Girly (1970-British) C-101m. BOMB D: Freddie Francis. Vanessa Howard, Michael Bryant, Ursula Howells, Pat Heywood, Howard

Trevor. Rock-bottom murder tale of eccentric family where children's "gameplaying" has lethal overtones. Stupid. Also known as GIRLY.▼

Munster, Go Home (1966) C-96m. **½ D: Earl Bellamy. Fred Gwynne, Yvonne De Carlo, Terry-Thomas, Hermione Gingold, John Carradine, Debby Watson, Butch Patrick. Monster family goes to England to claim a castle they've inherited; juvenile production based on the popular TV sitcom.

Munsters' Revenge, The (1981) C-100m. TVM D: Don Weis. Fred Gwynne, Yvonne De Carlo, Al Lewis, Jo McDonnell, K. C. Martel, Sid Caesar, Howard Morris, Ezra Stone, Bob Hastings. A visit 15 years after the original series to that gothic mansion at 1313 Mockingbird Lane; the Munsters become involved with a demented scientist who has created robot look-alikes for Herman, Lily, and Grampa. Average.▼

Muppet Movie, The (1979) C-94m. *** D: James Frawley. Kermit the Frog, Miss Piggy, Fozzie Bear, and the Muppets (Jim Henson, Frank Oz, Jerry Nelson, Richard Hunt, Dave Goelz), Charles Durning, Austin Pendleton; 15 guest stars. Enjoyable showcase for Jim Henson's irresistible characters, charting Kermit's odyssey from a Georgia swamp to Hollywood. Unnecessary movie-star cameos and pedestrian music score can't dim Muppets' appeal in their first feature film. Trimmed from 97m. after initial release.▼

Muppets Take Manhattan, The (1984) C-94m. *** D: Frank Oz. Kermit the Frog, Miss Piggy, Fozzie Bear, Gonzo, et al. (Jim Henson, Frank Oz, Jerry Nelson, Richard Hunt, Dave Goelz, Steve Whitmire), Dabney Coleman, Art Carney, James Coco, Joan Rivers, Gregory Hines, Linda Lavin, surprise guest stars. The Muppets try to crash Broadway with their college show, but Kermit soon discovers there's a broken heart for every light . . . Enjoyable outing with bouncy songs, nice use of N.Y.C. locations.▼

Murder! (1930-British) 108m. *** D: Alfred Hitchcock. Herbert Marshall, Norah Baring, Phyllis Konstam, Edward Chapman. Good early Hitchcock casts Marshall as actor who serves on jury at murder trial and believes accused woman innocent.▼

Murder Ahoy (1964-British) 93m. ***½ D: George Pollock. Margaret Rutherford, Lionel Jeffries, Charles Tingwell, William Mervyn, Joan Benham, Stringer Davis, Miles Malleson. This time out, Miss Marple investigates murder on a naval cadet training-ship. Original screenplay based on wonderful Agatha Christie character.

Murder at 45 R.P.M. (1960-French) 105m. **½ D: Etienne Perier. Danielle Darrieux, Michel Auclair, Jean Servais, Henri Guisol. Darrieux is an engaging songstress, whose husband seemingly returns from the grave to haunt her and lover (Auclair); neat plot twists, but slow-moving.

Murder at the Gallop (1963-British) **81m. ***½** D: George Pollock. Margaret Rutherford, Robert Morley, Flora Robson, Charles Tingwell, Duncan Lamont, Stringer Davis, James Villiers, Robert Urquhart. Amateur sleuth Miss Marple suspects foul play when wealthy old recluse dies. Based on Agatha Christie's *After the Funeral.*

Murder at the Mardi Gras (1978) **C-100m. TVM** D: Ken Annakin. Didi Conn, Bill Daily, David Groh, David Wayne, Harry Morgan, Joyce Van Patten, Barbi Benton. Featherbrained thriller about a bubble-headed girl (Conn) who witnesses title crime, then is stalked by the killer. How did a director like Annakin get involved with this? Below average.

Murder at the Vanities (1934) **89m. **½** D: Mitchell Leisen. Jack Oakie, Kitty Carlisle, Carl Brisson, Victor McLaglen, Donald Meek, Gail Patrick, Toby Wing, Gertrude Michael, Jessie Ralph, Dorothy Stickney, Duke Ellington. Offbeat murder mystery set backstage at Earl Carroll's Vanities, with detective McLaglen holding everyone under suspicion, including show's stars (Carlisle, Brisson). Songs include "Cocktails for Two," bizarre "Sweet Marijuana" number; look for Ann Sheridan as chorus girl.▼

Murder at the World Series (1977) **C-100m. TVM** D: Andrew V. McLaglen. Lynda Day George, Murray Hamilton, Karen Valentine, Michael Parks, Janet Leigh, Hugh O'Brian, Nancy Kelly, Joseph Wiseman, Tamara Dobson, Gerald S. O'Loughlin, Bruce Boxleitner. Psycho plots bizarre kidnapping during the World Series at Houston Astrodome. Predictable, second-rate thriller with the usual all-star cast of stereotypes. Below average.

Murder by Contract (1958) **81m. **** D: Irving Lerner. Vince Edwards, Philip Pine, Herschel Bernardi, Caprice Toriel. Intriguing little film about a hired killer and what makes him tick; ultimately sabotaged by pretentious dialogue and posturing.

Murder by Death (1976) **C-94m. *** D: Robert Moore. Peter Sellers, Peter Falk, David Niven, Maggie Smith, James Coco, Alec Guinness, Elsa Lanchester, Eileen Brennan, Nancy Walker, Estelle Winwood, Truman Capote. Capote invites world's greatest detectives to his home and involves them in a baffling whodunit. Neil Simon spoofs such characters as Charlie Chan, Miss Marple, and Sam Spade in this enjoyable all-star comedy, with marvelous sets by Stephen Grimes. Simon followed this with THE CHEAP DETECTIVE.▼

Murder by Decree (1979-Canadian-British) **C-121m. *** D: Bob Clark. Christopher Plummer, James Mason, Donald Sutherland, Genevieve Bujold, Susan Clark, David Hemmings, Frank Finlay, John Gielgud, Anthony Quayle. Sherlock Holmes investigates slayings of prostitutes by Jack the Ripper, with surprising results. Involved, often lurid story doesn't sustain through conclusion, but flaws overshadowed by warm interpretations of Holmes and Watson by Plummer and Mason. For another version of Holmes vs. the Ripper, see A STUDY IN TERROR.▼

Murder by Moonlight (1989) **C-100m. TVM** D: Michael Lindsay-Hogg. Brigitte Nielsen, Julian Sands, Brian Cox, Jane Lapotaire, Gerald McRaney. El cheapo production plays like a bad Saturday matinée item, with Nielsen as a NASA space cop joining her Russian counterpart (Sands) in a joint investigation of murder on an international moon colony in the year 2015. What first-class talent like actress Lapotaire and director Lindsay-Hogg are doing on a project like this is anybody's guess. Below average.

Murder by Natural Causes (1979) **C-100m. TVM** D: Robert Day. Hal Holbrook, Katharine Ross, Richard Anderson, Barry Bostwick, Bill Fiore, Jeff Donnell. Outstanding thinking man's thriller that has the unfaithful wife of a famed mentalist trying to do him in by literally scaring him to death. Well acted and written—and don't blink for the last reel or you'll miss countless clever twists. One of the best from the writing/producing team of Richard Levinson and William Link. Above average.▼

Murder by Night (1989) **C-100m. TVM** D: Paul Lynch. Robert Urich, Kay Lenz, Jim Metzler, Michael Ironside, Michael Williams. Amnesia victim Urich learns he's the sole witness to a murder by a serial killer and begins to suspect he may be the next victim, in this ho-hum whodunit. Made for cable. Average.▼

Murder by Phone (1980-Canadian) **C-79m. *** D: Michael Anderson. Richard Chamberlain, John Houseman, Sara Botsford, Robin Gammell, Gary Reineke, Barry Morse. Talented cast and director go slumming in this hoary horror exercise involving a crazed killer who literally phones in his murders, doing in his victims by ingenious long distance device. Filmed as BELLS.▼

Murder by Proxy SEE: Blackout (1954)

Murder: By Reason of Insanity (1985) **C-100m. TVM** D: Anthony Page. Candice Bergen, Jurgen Prochnow, Hector Elizondo, Eli Wallach. Fact-based drama involving a battered woman who fears for her life when her mentally unstable husband walks out of the hospital where he is confined to carry out a death threat. Prochnow is chilling as the husband on the brink of insanity. Written by Scott Swanton. Above average.

Murder by Television (1935) **60m.** *½
D: Clifford Sandforth. Bela Lugosi, June
Collyer, Huntley Gordon, George Meeker, Claire McDowell. A professor who
perfects the technology of television is
murdered; Lugosi, his assistant, is a prime
suspect. Grade Z production holds some
interest as a curio.▼

Murder by the Book (1987) **C-100m.**
TVM D: Mel Damski. Robert Hays,
Catherine Mary Stewart, Celeste Holm,
Fred Gwynne, Christopher Murney. Amiable caper flick about a mild-mannered
mystery writer who teams with his alter
ego, a hard-boiled fictional private eye, to
help a damsel in distress and solve a case
of forged antiquities. Filmed as *Alter Ego*
(after the novel by Mel Arrighi, from which
it was adapted), it sat gathering dust for
nearly a year and a half before premiering.
Average.

Murder by the Clock (1931) **76m.** **½ D:
Edward Sloman. William "Stage" Boyd,
Lilyan Tashman, Irving Pichel, Regis
Toomey, Blanche Frederici, Sally O'Neil,
Lester Vail. Creepy, creaky mystery designed and played like a horror film. Complicated plot involves elderly woman who
installs a horn in her crypt in case she's
buried alive, a mysterious reincarnation
drug, and drooling half-wit Pichel. Plenty
of atmosphere if not much sense.

Murder Can Hurt You (1980) **C-105m.**
TVM D: Roger Duchowny. Victor Buono,
John Byner, Tony Danza, Jamie Farr, Gavin
MacLeod, Buck Owens, Connie Stevens,
Jimmie Walker, Burt Young, Marty Allen,
Richard Deacon, Liz Torres, Don Adams
(narrator). TV's answer to MURDER BY
DEATH, with eight comic super-sleuths
forming an uneasy alliance against a common foe, the evil Man in White. It's silly
season. Average.

Murder Clinic (1966-Italian-French) **C-87m.** *½ D: William Hamilton (Elio
Scardamaglia). William Berger, Francoise
Prevost, Mary Young, Barbara Wilson,
Delphia Maurin. Period thriller of isolated
clinic peopled with eccentric patients,
terrorized by monster which roams in
corridors and woods outside. Slow going.

Murder, Czech Style (1968-Czech) **90m.**
**½ D: Jiri Weiss. Rudolf Hrusinsky,
Kyeta Fialova, Vaclav Voska, Vladimir
Mensik. Clever, gentle spoof of romantic
triangle melodramas, with pudgy middleaged clerk (Hrusinsky) marrying beautiful
woman, realizing she's been cheating
on him, planning revenge, via dream
sequences.

Murderers Among Us: The Simon Wiesenthal Story (1989-U.S.-British-Hungarian) **C-175m.** TVM D: Brian Gibson.
Ben Kingsley, Renee Soutendijk, Craig T.
Nelson, Louisa Haigh, Jack Shepherd, Paul
Freeman. Moving but overlong drama with

a mesmerizing Kingsley as the Holocaust
survivor who dedicated the rest of his life
to hunting down the war's Nazi bigwigs.
Abby Mann's thoughtful script, written
with Robin Vote and Ron Hutchinson, has
been criticized for its historical selectivity
(giving, for instance, Wiesenthal's stillcontroversial role in the capture of Eichmann a scant five minutes), but the exceptionally strong death camp scenes rank
alongside those of TV's WAR AND REMEMBRANCE in impact. Made for cable. Above average.

Murderers' Row (1967) **C-108m.** BOMB
D: Henry Levin. Dean Martin, AnnMargret, Karl Malden, Camilla Sparv,
James Gregory, Beverly Adams. Malden
kidnaps A-M's father, threatens to melt
Washington, D.C. with a "helio beam";
only Matt Helm can save both. (What if
he'd had to make a choice?) Second Helm
caper—after THE SILENCERS—offers
one funny jibe at Frank Sinatra, absolutely nothing else. Sequel: THE AMBUSHERS.▼

Murder Game, The (1966-British) **75m.**
*½ D: Sidney Salkow. Ken Scott, Marla
Landi, Trader Faulkner, Conrad Phillips,
Gerald Sim, Duncan Lamont. Routine
murder-blackmail drama about woman who
skips out on her husband, changes her
name, then marries again.

Murder, He Says (1945) **93m.** *** D:
George Marshall. Fred MacMurray, Helen
Walker, Marjorie Main, Jean Heather, Porter Hall, Peter Whitney, Barbara Pepper,
Mabel Paige. Zany slapstick of pollster
MacMurray encountering Main's family
of hayseed murderers. Too strident at
times, but generally funny; clever script
by Lou Breslow.

Murder In Black and White (1990)
C-100m. TVM D: Robert Iscove. Richard
Crenna, Diahann Carroll, Cliff Gorman,
Philip Bosco, Joan Copeland, Fred Gwynne.
Crenna and Gorman reprise their roles
from DOUBLETAKE and INTERNAL AFFAIRS to track down the killer of a newly
appointed black N.Y.C. police commissioner,
with an interracial Crenna-Carroll dalliance tossed into the mix. Average.

Murder, Inc. (1960) **103m.** *** D: Burt
Balaban, Stuart Rosenberg. Stuart Whitman, May Britt, Henry Morgan, Peter
Falk, David J. Stewart, Simon Oakland,
Morey Amsterdam. Solid little fact-based
chronicle of the title crime organization,
with Falk in particular scoring as Abe
Reles, the syndicate's ill-fated numberone killer. Lots of familiar faces (Vincent
Gardenia, Sylvia Miles, Seymour Cassel)
in supporting roles.

Murder in Coweta County (1983) **C-100m.** TVM D: Gary Nelson. Johnny
Cash, Andy Griffith, Earl Hindman, June
Carter Cash, Cindi Knight, Ed Van Nuys.

No-nonsense county sheriff Cash stops at nothing—including his legal jurisdiction—to track down local bigwig Griffith, who thinks he's gotten away with murder. Dennis Nemac wrote the straightforward script from Margaret Anne Barnes's book about an actual 1948 Georgia murder. Average.▼

Murder in Greenwich Village (1937) 68m. ** D: Albert S. Rogell. Richard Arlen, Fay Wray, Raymond Walburn, Wyn Cahoon, Scott Colton, Thurston Hall. Dated romantic mystery comedy with heiress Wray using photographer Arlen as alibi for whereabouts when murder took place. Mystery is secondary, solved only as an afterthought.

Murder in Mississippi (1990) C-200m. TVM D: Roger Young. Tom Hulce, Blair Underwood, Josh Charles, Jennifer Grey, CCH Pounder, Andre Braugher, John Dennis Johnson. Riveting drama about Mickey Schwerner, James Chaney, and Andrew Goodman, three young civil rights workers whose killing in the summer of 1964 became one of the landmarks in the movement. This drama, written by Stanley Weiser, is the flip side of the theatrical (and largely fictional) MISSISSIPPI BURNING. Originally shown in two parts. Above average.

Murder in Music City (1979) C-100m. TVM D: Leo Penn. Sonny Bono, Lee Purcell, Claude Akins, Belinda Montgomery, Harry Bellaver. The cherished memory of Nick and Nora Charles is tarnished with this tacky (rather than wacky) whodunit pilot that sends a brash songwriter-turned-detective and his photographer's model bride on the trail of a killer in Nashville. Also known as THE COUNTRY MUSIC MURDERS. Below average.

Murder in Paradise (1990) C-100m. TVM D: Fred Walton. Keven Kilner, Maggie Han, Barbara Carrera, Mako, James Sutorious, John Pleshette, Yuji Okumoto, Manu Tupou. Burned-out cop from the Big Apple goes to Hawaii to drink away memories of a serial killer he couldn't stop, only to find the murders have followed him—and he's the prime suspect. Pilot to a prospective series. Average.

Murder in Peyton Place (1977) C-100m. TVM D: Bruce Kessler. Christopher Connelly, Dorothy Malone, Ed Nelson, Stella Stevens, Janet Margolin, David Hedison, Tim O'Connor, Linda Gray, Catherine Bach. Mystery-drama reuniting members of the old TV series following strange deaths of Allison MacKenzie and Rodney Harrington (whom everyone remembers as Mia Farrow and Ryan O'Neal before they became stars). Everything's the same in town—with ten years of gossip and intrigue added. Followed by PEYTON PLACE: THE NEXT GENERATION. Average.

Murder in Space (1985) C-89m. TVM D: Steven Hilliard Stern. Wilford Brimley, Arthur Hill, Martin Balsam, Michael Ironside, Damir Andrei, Tom Butler, Peter Dvorsky, Cathie Shirriff, Alberta Watson. Flaccid whodunnit about several murders aboard a multinational space flight returning from Mars. Made for cable. Below average.▼

Murder in Texas (1981) C-200m. TVM D: Billy Hale. Katharine Ross, Sam Elliott, Farrah Fawcett, Andy Griffith, Craig T. Nelson, Dimitra Arliss, Barry Corbin, Pamela Meyers, Bill Dana. Dramatization of the murder case revolving around Houston plastic surgeon Dr. John Hill, who was accused of killing his socially prominent first wife. John McGreevey based his script on the book *Prescription: Murder*, written by Hill's second wife, Ann Kurth (played by Ross). Andy Griffith won an Emmy Award nomination for his performance as Hill's father-in-law, wealthy oilman Ash Robinson. Above average.▼

Murder in the Air (1940) 55m. ** D: Lewis Seiler. Ronald Reagan, John Litel, James Stephenson, Eddie Foy, Jr., Lya Lys. The fourth and final Ronald Reagan Brass Bancroft film, with the Secret Service agent assigned to stop enemy spies from stealing government plans.

Murder in the Blue Room (1944) 61m. ** D: Leslie Goodwins. Anne Gwynne, Donald Cook, John Litel, Grace McDonald, Betty Kean, June Preisser, Regis Toomey. Film has distinction of being an Old Dark House musical, but otherwise has nothing to recommend it. Typical brassy songs against OK whodunit background; filmed before as THE MISSING GUEST and SECRET OF THE BLUE ROOM.

Murder in the Music Hall (1946) 84m. ** D: John English. Vera Hruba Ralston, William Marshall, Helen Walker, Nancy Kelly, William Gargan, Ann Rutherford, Julie Bishop. Not-bad whodunit, a backstage murder with above-average cast for Republic Pictures.

Murder Is Easy (1982) C-100m. TVM D: Claude Whatham. Bill Bixby, Lesley-Anne Down, Olivia de Havilland, Helen Hayes, Timothy West, Patrick Allen, Shane Briant. Atmospheric but routine adaptation (by Carmen Culver) of Agatha Christie's murder mystery about the death of seven residents of a quiet English village. Making the amateur detective an American hardly helps. Average.

Murder Is My Beat (1955) 77m. ** D: Edgar G. Ulmer. Paul Langton, Barbara Payton, Robert Shayne, Selena Royle. Standard B treatment of alleged killer Payton discovering actual criminal.

Murder Is My Business (1946) **64m.** **
D: Sam Newfield. Hugh Beaumont, Cheryl
Walker, Lyle Talbot, George Meeker, Pierre
Watkin. Programmer Mike Shayne caper,
with Beaumont a tame shamus on prowl
for killer.
Murder Man, The (1935) **70m.** *** D:
Tim Whelan. Spencer Tracy, Virginia Bruce,
Lionel Atwill, Harvey Stephens, Robert
Barrat, James Stewart. Tracy is good as
usual playing a hard-drinking newspaper
reporter who specializes in covering murders.
Snappy little film also offers Stewart in
his first feature appearance (playing a fellow
reporter named Shorty).
Murder Mansion, The (1970-Spanish)
C-90m. ** D: F. Lara Polop. Analia Gade,
Evelyn Stewart (Ida Galli), Andres Resino.
Travelers are lost in a fog, find themselves
stranded in eerie old house with strange
mistress and ghosts. A couple of good
scares.▼
'Murder Me, Murder You' (1983) **C-
100m.** **TVM** D: Gary Nelson. Stacy Keach,
Tanya Roberts, Don Stroud, Delta Burke,
Tom Atkins, Lisa Blount, Michelle Phillips.
Keach is aces as private eye Mike Hammer
going in search of the daughter he never
knew in this pilot to the second TV series
about Mickey Spillane's hard-hitting shamus.
(The 1950s version starred Darren Mc-
Gavin.) This one was scripted by Bill
Stratton. Above average.
Murder Most Foul (1965-British) **90m.**
*** D: George Pollock. Margaret Ruther-
ford, Ron Moody, Charles Tingwell, An-
drew Cruickshank, Stringer Davis, Frances-
ca Annis, Dennis Price, James Bolam.
When Miss Marple is lone jury member
who believes defendant is innocent, she
sets out to prove it. Based on Agatha
Christie's *Mrs. McGinty's Dead.*
Murder, My Sweet (1944) **95m.** ***½ D:
Edward Dmytryk. Dick Powell, Claire
Trevor, Anne Shirley, Otto Kruger, Mike
Mazurki, Miles Mander. Adaptation of
Raymond Chandler's book *Farewell My
Lovely* gave Powell new image as hard-
boiled detective Philip Marlowe, involved
in homicide and blackmail. Still packs a
wallop. Scripted by John Paxton. Story
previously used for THE FALCON TAKES
OVER; remade again as FAREWELL, MY
LOVELY in 1975.▼
Murder of Mary Phagan, The (1988)
C-250m. TVM D: Billy Hale. Jack Lem-
mon, Peter Gallagher, Richard Jordan, Rob-
ert Prosky, Paul Dooley, Rebecca Miller,
Kathryn Walker, Charles Dutton, Kevin
Spacey, Wendy J. Cooke. Leisurely, atmospheric retelling of the controversial 1913
Leo Frank murder case in which a Jewish
factory manager in Atlanta was convicted
of killing a young female employee and
sentenced to hang. Lemmon excels as then-
Governor John M. Slaton, who put his

political career on the line by reexamining
the case and questioning the verdict. Rebecca Miller, daughter of playwright Arthur Miller, makes her acting debut as the
accused man's steadfast wife. Fictionalized version of the incident was filmed in
1937 as THEY WON'T FORGET. Larry
McMurtry's story was adapted by George
Stevens, Jr., and Jeffrey Lane, whose
script easily might have been shortened.
Originally shown in two parts. Above
average.
Murder on Approval (1956-British) **90m.**
** D: Bernard Knowles. Tom Conway,
Delphi Lawrence, Brian Worth, Michael
Balfour. Veteran detective-player Conway
can't save humdrum treasure-hunt caper.
Retitled: BARBADOS QUEST.
Murder Once Removed (1971) **C-74m.**
TVM D: Charles Dubin. John Forsythe,
Richard Kiley, Barbara Bain, Joseph Cam-
panella, Wendell Burton. "Perfect crime"
attempted by respectable doctor. Cast pro-
vides ensemble quality to plot, atmosphere
convincing, but film is carbon copy of 100
you've seen before. Average.▼
Murder One (1969) SEE: **D.A.: Murder
One**▼
Murder One, Dancer O (1983) **C-100m.**
TVM D: Reza Badiyi. Robert Blake, Ken-
neth McMillan, William Prince, Jane Daly,
Royal Dano, Sydney Lassick, Sondra Blake,
Robin Dearden. The third of Blake's *Joe
Dancer* movies has the shamus out to clear
himself of trumped-up manslaughter charges
while investigating a Hollywood scandal.
Blake gave this personal project three
good shots, but it was no go as a series.
Average.
Murder on Flight 502 (1975) **C-100m.**
TVM D: George McCowan. Ralph Bel-
lamy, Polly Bergen, Theodore Bikel, Sonny
Bono, Dane Clark, Laraine Day, Fernando
Lamas, George Maharis, Farrah Fawcett-
Majors, Hugh O'Brian, Molly Picon, Wal-
ter Pidgeon, Robert Stack, Rosemarie Stack.
All-star cast is terrorized by a maniac on a
transatlantic jumbo jet piloted by Stack.
Seems we've heard that story before.
Average.▼
Murder on Monday SEE: **Home at Seven**
Murder on the Orient Express (1974-
British) **C-127m.** *** D: Sidney Lumet.
Albert Finney, Lauren Bacall, Martin Bal-
sam, Ingrid Bergman, Jacqueline Bisset,
Jean-Pierre Cassel, Sean Connery, John
Gielgud, Wendy Hiller, Anthony Perkins,
Vanessa Redgrave, Rachel Roberts, Rich-
ard Widmark, Michael York, Colin Blakely,
George Coulouris. Elegant all-star produc-
tion of Agatha Christie's whodunit set in
the 1930s, with unrecognizable Finney as
super-sleuth Hercule Poirot, and all his
suspects on the same railroad train. Colorful entertainment, but awfully sluggish;
sharp viewers will be able to guess the

denoument, as well. Bergman won Best Supporting Actress Oscar. First of several lavish Christie adaptations; followed by DEATH ON THE NILE.▼

Murder Ordained (1987) **C-200m. TVM** D: Mike Robe. Keith Carradine, JoBeth Williams, Terry Kinney, Guy Boyd, Terence Knox, Darrell Larson, M. Emmet Walsh. Well-crafted drama based on events surrounding a pair of real-life murders in Kansas involving a Lutheran minister, his married lover, and their respective spouses. Writers Robe and James Sadwith based their script on newspaper accounts by a pair of women reporters who are depicted in the film. Originally shown in two parts. Above average.

Murder or Mercy (1974) **C-78m. TVM** D: Harvey Hart, Bradford Dillman, Melvyn Douglas, David Birney, Mildred Dunnock, Denver Pyle, Robert Webber, Kent Smith. Courtroom drama about mercy killing, with noted doctor Douglas on trial for the death of his terminally ill wife. Douglas and Dunnock are wonderful as always, but the plot too closely resembles AN ACT OF MURDER. Average.▼

Murder Over New York (1940) **65m.** D: Harry Lachman. Sidney Toler, Marjorie Weaver, Robert Lowery, Ricardo Cortez, Donald MacBride, Melville Cooper, Sen Yung. SEE: **Charlie Chan** series.▼

Murder, She Said (1962-British) **87m.** *** D: George Pollock. Margaret Rutherford, Arthur Kennedy, Muriel Pavlow, James Robertson Justice, Charles Tingwell, Thorley Walters. Miss Marple takes a job as a domestic in order to solve a murder she witnessed. Based on Agatha Christie's *4:50 From Paddington*; first of four films starring Rutherford as Marple.

Murders in the Rue Morgue (1932) **75m.** **½ D: Robert Florey. Bela Lugosi, Sidney Fox, Leon Ames, Brandon Hurst, Arlene Francis. Expressionistic horror film based on Poe story, with Lugosi as fiendish Dr. Mirakle, with eyes on lovely Fox as the bride of his pet ape. Considered strong stuff back then, but pretty mild now. John Huston was one of the writers. Remade as PHANTOM OF THE RUE MORGUE, and twice more under original title.

Murders in the Rue Morgue (1971) **C-87m.** *½ D: Gordon Hessler. Jason Robards, Herbert Lom, Christine Kaufmann, Lilli Palmer, Adolfo Celi, Maria Perschy, Michael Dunn. Sensationalistic reworking of Poe story; players at Grand Guignol-type theater suddenly become victims of real-life murders, gory goings-on. Set in Paris, but filmed in Spain.▼

Murders in the Rue Morgue, The (1986) **C-100m. TVM** D: Jeannot Szwarc. George C. Scott, Rebecca de Mornay, Ian McShane, Neil Dickson, Val Kilmer. An-

other tour-de-force for George C. Scott, in this fifth film version of the Poe tale of a hideous double murder in 19th-century Paris. David Epstein's script and Bruno de Keyzer's atmospheric location photography add to the panache. One quibble: why are the store signs in English, the street designations in French? Above average.

Murders in the Zoo (1933) **64m.** *** D: A. Edward Sutherland. Lionel Atwill, Charles Ruggles, Randolph Scott, Gail Patrick, John Lodge, Kathleen Burke. Astonishingly grisly horror film about an insanely jealous zoologist and sportsman (Atwill) who dispatches his wife's suitors (genuine and otherwise) with the help of various animals. Pretty potent stuff, right from the opening scene of Atwill sewing a victim's mouth shut!

Murder That Wouldn't Die, The (1980) **C-105m. TVM** D: Ron Satlof. William Conrad, Marj Dusay, Robin Mattson, Jose Ferrer, Sharon Acker, Mike Kellin, John Hillerman. Retired L.A. cop turned security chief at Hawaii State can't shake the old life and becomes involved in the investigation of a 40-year-old homicide. Busted pilot for post-*Cannon* and pre-*Nero Wolfe* series for Conrad. Average.

Murder Will Out (1952-British) **83m.** *** D: John Gilling. Valerie Hobson, Edward Underdown, James Robertson Justice, Henry Kendall. Underplayed suspenser with creditable red herrings to engage the viewer. Retitled: THE VOICE OF MERRILL.

Murder With Mirrors (1985) **C-100m. TVM** D: Dick Lowry. Helen Hayes, Bette Davis, John Mills, Leo McKern, Liane Langland, Dorothy Tutin. Miss Marple tries to unmask the villain who'd stoop to murder to steal her dear old friend's ancestral home. Hayes and Davis act together for the first time in this amiable version of Agatha Christie's mystery, adapted by George Eckstein. Average.

Murdock's Gang (1973) **C-74m. TVM** D: Charles S. Dubin. Alex Dreier, Janet Leigh, Murray Hamilton, William Daniels, Harold Gould, Don Knight. Embezzling bookkeeper is object of search by disbarred attorney (Dreier) and group of ex-cons. Colorful cast and amusing situations in inconsequential but diverting tale by Edmund H. North. Average.

Muriel (1963-French-Italian) **C-115m.** **½ D: Alain Resnais. Delphine Seyrig, Jean-Pierre Kerien, Nita Klein, Claude Sainval. Confusing/depressing/brilliant film (take your choice). Not for all tastes, this French film of people who lead empty lives isn't an evening of fun. Cinema students may find interest in Resnais' direction.

Murmur of the Heart (1971-French-German-Italian) **C-118m.** ***½ D: Louis

Malle. Lea Massari, Benoit Ferreux, Daniel Gelin, Marc Winocourt, Michel Lonsdale. Fresh, intelligent, affectionately comic tale of bourgeois, sensuous Massari and her precocious 14-year-old son (Ferreux), which builds to a thoroughly delightful resolution. Wonderful performances.▼

Murph the Surf SEE: **Live a Little, Steal a Lot**▼

Murphy's Law (1986) C-100m. *½ D: J. Lee Thompson. Charles Bronson, Kathleen Wilhoite, Carrie Snodgress, Robert F. Lyons, Richard Romanus, Angel Tompkins, Bill Henderson, James Luisi, Janet MacLachlan, Lawrence Tierney. All-too-typical Bronson vehicle about a cop framed for murders by psychopathic ex-con he originally sent to prison; only novelty is that the psycho is a woman (Snodgress). Strictly formula; violent and unpleasant.▼

Murphy's Romance (1985) C-107m. *** D: Martin Ritt. Sally Field, James Garner, Brian Kerwin, Corey Haim, Dennis Burkley, Georgann Johnson, Charles Lane. Young divorcée (with 12-year-old son) makes fresh start in small Arizona community, where she's attracted to older, laid-back, widowed pharmacist—and vice versa. Charming, easygoing comedy written by Irving Ravetch and Harriet Frank, Jr. (from Max Schott's novella), with Garner in a standout performance as Murphy, the last of the rugged individualists. In fact, this earned him his first Oscar nomination. ▼

Murphy's War (1971-British) C-108m. *** D: Peter Yates. Peter O'Toole, Sian Phillips, Philippe Noiret, Horst Janson, John Hallam, Ingo Morgendorf. Well-staged, gripping action sequences combine with psychological study of British seaman (O'Toole) only survivor of German massacre, out to get revenge. Good idea, but nonaction sequences tend to bog film down; script by Stirling Silliphant.▼

Murrow (1986) C-110m. TVM D: Jack Gold. Daniel J. Travanti, Dabney Coleman, Edward Herrmann, David Suchet, John McMartin, Robert Vaughn, Kathryn Leigh Scott. Plodding made-for-cable biopic of Edward R. Murrow, which was pilloried by his contemporaries, many of whom are portrayed (Coleman as CBS founder and board chairman William S. Paley, Herrmann as Murrow's longtime producer and associate Fred Friendly, McMartin as former CBS president Frank Stanton, Bob Sherman as *60 Minutes* producer Don Hewitt, etc.). A glum Travanti, though, does an admirable job in the lead. Written by Ernest Kinoy. Average. ▼

Muscle Beach Party (1964) C-94m. **½ D: William Asher. Frankie Avalon, Annette Funicello, Buddy Hackett, Luciana Paluzzi, Don Rickles, John Ashley, Jody McCrea, Morey Amsterdam, Peter Lupus, Candy Johnson, Dan Haggerty. Followup to BEACH PARTY picks up the pace as the gang finds the beach has been invaded by Rickles and his stable of bodybuilders. Usual blend of surf, sand, and corn; Rickles' first series appearance and the screen debut of "Little" Stevie Wonder. Sequel: BIKINI BEACH.▼

MUSE Concert: No Nukes, The SEE: **No Nukes**▼

Music for Millions (1944) 120m. **½ D: Henry Koster. Margaret O'Brien, Jimmy Durante, June Allyson, Marsha Hunt, Hugh Herbert, Jose Iturbi, Connie Gilchrist, Harry Davenport, Marie Wilson, Larry Adler, Ethel Griffies. Teary tale of sisters joining the great Iturbi's orchestra is overly long; Durante steals film with "Umbriago."

Music in Darkness SEE: **Night Is My Future**▼

Music in My Heart (1940) 70m. ** D: Joseph Santley. Tony Martin, Rita Hayworth, Edith Fellows, Alan Mowbray, Eric Blore, George Tobias. Routine musical of Continental Martin cast in show where he meets lovely Hayworth. One good song, "It's a Blue World."

Music in the Air (1934) 85m. *** D: Joe May. Gloria Swanson, John Boles, Douglass Montgomery, June Lang, Reginald Owen, Al Shean. Predictable plot given chic treatment; leading-lady Swanson and lyricist Boles constantly quarreling, trying jealousy ploy when naive young couple come on the scene. Good Jerome Kern-Oscar Hammerstein score enhances bright production.

Music Is Magic (1935) 65m. ** D: George Marshall. Alice Faye, Ray Walker, Bebe Daniels, Frank Mitchell, Jack Durant. Limp musical of fading star Daniels and rising Faye, with no great songs and not much else, either.

Music Lovers, The (1971-British) C-122m. **½ D: Ken Russell. Glenda Jackson, Richard Chamberlain, Max Adrian, Christopher Gable, Kenneth Colley. Occasionally striking but self-indulgent and factually dubious account of Tchaikovsky (Chamberlain), who marries and abandons the whorish Nina (Jackson). Overacted, over-directed.

Music Man, The (1962) C-151m. ***½ D: Morton Da Costa. Robert Preston, Shirley Jones, Buddy Hackett, Hermione Gingold, Paul Ford, Pert Kelton, Ronny Howard. Peerless Preston reprises his Broadway performance as super salesman/con man Prof. Harold Hill, who mesmerizes Iowa town with visions of uniformed marching band. Faithful filmization of Meredith Willson's affectionate slice of Americana. Score includes "76 Trombones," "Till There Was You," and showstopping "Trouble."▼

Music Teacher, The (1988-Belgian) C-95m. **½ D: Gerard Corbiau. Jose Van

Dam, Anne Roussel, Philippe Volter, Sylvie Fennec, Patrick Bauchau, Johan Leyson. A familiar plot and stale script sink this musical drama detailing what happens when opera star Van Dam retires at the pinnacle of his fame to train fetching young Roussel and petty thief Volter. The charisma and magnificent singing voice of Van Dam, the Belgian bass-baritone, almost (but not quite) redeem this.▼

Musketeers of the Sea (1960-Italian) **C-116m.** ** D: Massimo Patrizi. Robert Alda, Pier Angeli, Aldo Ray. Anonymous sea yarn, standard in all departments, involving search for gold in Maracaibo.

Mussolini: The Decline and Fall of Il Duce (1985) **C-192m. TVM** D: Alberto Negrin. Susan Sarandon, Anthony Hopkins, Bob Hoskins, Annie Girardot, Barbara De Rossi, Fabio Testi, Kurt Raab. The focus, despite the title (and Hoskins's shadowy portrayal of Benito), is on Il Duce's crafty son-in-law, Count Galeazzo Ciano (Hopkins). Muddled drama as viewed through the eyes of Mussolini's daughter, Edda (Sarandon). (This Mussolini "exposé" predated the George C. Scott miniseries by several months.) Originally shown in two parts and made for cable. Average.▼

Mustang Country (1976) **C-79m.** *** D: John Champion. Joel McCrea, Robert Fuller, Patrick Wayne, Nika Mina. Excellent Western set along Montana-Canadian border in 1925. 70-year-old McCrea most convincing as ex-rancher and rodeo star who shares adventures with runaway Indian boy while hunting a wild stallion.

Mutant SEE: **Forbidden World**▼

Mutations, The (1973-British) **C-92m.** ** D: Jack Cardiff. Donald Pleasence, Tom Baker, Brad Harris, Julie Ege, Michael Dunn, Jill Haworth. Scientist Pleasence is crossbreeding humans with plants—and his unsuspecting university students are being abducted as guinea pigs. Predictable story with truly grotesque elements—and characters. Not recommended for dinnertime viewing. Video title: THE FREAK-MAKER.▼

Mutineers, The (1949) **60m.** *½ D: Jean Yarbrough. Jon Hall, Adele Jergens, George Reeves, Noel Cravat. Hastily-thrown-together flick of Hall and mates combating rebellion aboard ship. Retitled: PIRATE SHIP.

Mutiny (1952) **77m.** *½ D: Edward Dmytryk. Mark Stevens. Angela Lansbury, Patric Knowles, Gene Evans. Mediocre tale of Stevens et al trying to capture gold to help cause against British during War of 1812.

Mutiny in Outer Space (1965) **81m.** *½ D: Hugo Grimaldi. William Leslie, Dolores Faith, Pamela Curran, Richard Gar-

land, Harold Lloyd, Jr., James Dobson, Glenn Langan. Creeping fungus starts killing astronauts on the way back from trip to the moon in mediocre sci-fi meller.

Mutiny on the Bounty (1935) **132m.** **** D: Frank Lloyd. Charles Laughton, Clark Gable, Franchot Tone, Herbert Mundin, Eddie Quillan, Dudley Digges, Donald Crisp, Movita, Henry Stephenson, Spring Byington. Storytelling at its best, in this engrossing adaptation of the Nordhoff-Hall book about mutiny against tyrannical Captain Bligh (Laughton) on voyage to the South Seas. Whole cast is good, but Laughton is unforgettable. Oscar winner for Best Picture; knots ahead of its 1962 remake, and the 1985 film THE BOUNTY. Also shown in computer-colored version.▼

Mutiny on the Bounty (1962) **C-179m.** **½ D: Lewis Milestone. Marlon Brando, Trevor Howard, Richard Harris, Hugh Griffith, Richard Haydn, Tim Seely, Percy Herbert, Tarita, Gordon Jackson. Lavish remake of the 1935 classic can't come near it, although it's visually beautiful; Howard is good as Captain Bligh, but Brando is all wrong as Fletcher Christian.▼

My American Cousin (1985-Canadian) **C-95m.** *** D: Sandy Wilson. Margaret Langrick, John Wildman, Richard Donat, Jane Mortifee. Well-acted, nostalgic coming-of-age story set in British Columbia in the summer of 1959, about a young girl's infatuation with her James Dean-like California cousin. Winner of six Genie awards (Canada's Oscar) including Best Picture. Donat, who plays the father, is Robert Donat's son.▼

My Beautiful Laundrette (1985-British) **C-98m.** ***½ D: Stephen Frears. Saeed Jaffrey, Roshan Seth, Daniel Day-Lewis, Gordon Warnecke, Derrick Branche, Shirley Anne Field. Extremely entertaining, perceptive examination of both race relations and the economic state in Britain, centering on a pair of young friends, Omar (Warnecke) and Johnny (Day-Lewis) and what happens when they take over a beat-up laundrette. On-target script by Hanif Kureishi, a Pakistani playwright who resides in England. Originally made for British TV.▼

My Best Friend Is a Vampire (1988) **C-90m.** *½ D: Jimmy Huston. Robert Sean Leonard, Evan Mirand, Cheryl Pollak, René Auberjonois, Cecilia Peck, Fannie Flagg, Kenneth Kimmins, David Warner, Paul Wilson. One-joke comedy, in the wake of TEEN WOLF, has a high-school kid transformed into a vampire and trying to cope with it as a fact of life. Solid supporting cast does what it can to help.▼

My Best Friend's Girl (1983-French) **C-99m.** **½ D: Bertrand Blier. Coluche,

Isabelle Huppert, Thierry Lhermitte, Daniel Colas, Francois Perrot. Medium sex comedy with Lhermitte bringing home pick-up Huppert; she moves in, and his best friend (Coluche) falls for her. A familiar Blier theme (the sexual relationship between one woman and two men) is indifferently handled.▼

My Bill (1938) **64m.** **½ D: John Farrow. Kay Francis, Bonita Granville, Anita Louise, Bobby Jordan, Dickie Moore. Francis is poverty-stricken widow with four children, involved in scandal; OK soaper.

My Blood Runs Cold (1965) **104m.** **½ D: William Conrad. Troy Donahue, Joey Heatherton, Barry Sullivan, Jeanette Nolan. Young man thinks girl is long-dead ancestor, and recalls love affair from generations before. Not all that bad, but not worth missing *I Love Lucy* for, either.

My Bloody Valentine (1981-Canadian) **C-91m.** *½ D: George Mihalka. Paul Kelman, Lori Hallier, Neil Affleck, Keith Knight, Alf Humphreys, Cynthia Dale. Another gory HALLOWEEN/FRIDAY THE 13TH clone. Coalminer axes various victims (male as well as female) in the friendly little town of Valentine Bluffs. Ecch.▼

My Blue Heaven (1950) **C-96m.** **½ D: Henry Koster. Betty Grable, Dan Dailey, David Wayne, Jane Wyatt, Mitzi Gaynor, Una Merkel. Pleasing musicomedy with Grable and Dailey as radio stars who try to adopt a child.

My Bodyguard (1980) **C-96m.** **½ D: Tony Bill. Chris Makepeace, Adam Baldwin, Martin Mull, Ruth Gordon, Matt Dillon, John Houseman, Joan Cusack, Craig Richard Nelson. Pleasant little film about high-school boy who hires a behemoth classmate to protect him from toughs at school. Totally likable but ultimately simplistic comedy-drama. Filmed in and around Chicago; look for Tim Kazurinsky, George Wendt. Bill's directorial debut.▼

My Body, My Child (1982) **C-100m.** TVM D: Marvin J. Chomsky. Vanessa Redgrave, Joseph Campanella, Stephen Elliott, James Naughton, Gail Strickland, Jack Albertson. A woman's choice: having an abortion or giving birth to a deformed child. Redgrave gives it stature, and Albertson, as her invalid father, turns in an Emmy-nominated performance in his final role. Written by Louisa Burns-Bisogno. Above average.

My Boyfriend's Back (1989) **C-100m.** TVM D: Paul Schneider. Sandy Duncan, Judith Light, Jill Eikenberry, Stephen Macht, Alan Feinstein, John Sanderford. A '60s teen singing group's reluctant reunion 25 years later for a TV special

triggers suppressed emotions and recriminations among the three women. Nice attitudes, much insight, in this unexpectedly delightful comedy-drama written by Lindsay Harrison. Look for vintage rockers Gary Lewis, Mary Wells, Peggy March, Gary Puckett, The Penguins. Above average.

My Boys Are Good Boys (1978) **C-90m.** *½ D: Bethel Buckalew. Ralph Meeker, Ida Lupino, Lloyd Nolan, David F. Doyle, Sean T. Roche. Odd little film mixes 1940s approach to juvenile delinquency with far-fetched story of teenagers robbing armored car. Produced by Meeker and his wife.▼

My Brilliant Career (1979-Australian) **C-101m.** ***½ D: Gillian Armstrong. Judy Davis, Sam Neill, Wendy Hughes, Robert Grubb, Max Cullen, Pat Kennedy. Excellent portrait of a headstrong young woman determined to live a life of independent and intelligent pursuits in turn-of-the-century Australia. Armstrong's eye for detail and Davis's performance dominate this fine import, based on a true story.▼

My Brother's Keeper (1949-British) **96m.** ** D: Alfred Roome. Jack Warner, Jane Hylton, George Cole, Bill Owen, David Tomlinson, Christopher Lee. Hunt-the-escaped convicts film has gimmick of the two escaped prisoners being handcuffed together.

My Brother's Wife (1989) **C-100m.** TVM D: Jack Bender. John Ritter, Mel Harris, Polly Bergen, Dakin Matthews, Lee Weaver. Quirky comedy-drama about an irresponsible cutup who spends two decades pursuing the woman of his dreams, who happens to be his sister-in-law. Flat adaptation by Percy Granger of A. R. Gurney's play *The Middle Ages*. Average.

My Brother Talks to Horses (1946) **93m.** ** D: Fred Zinnemann. "Butch" Jenkins, Peter Lawford, Beverly Tyler, Edward Arnold, Charlie Ruggles, Spring Byington. Gimmick comedy that's fun at the start but drags to slow finish.

My Chauffeur (1986) **C-97m.** ** D: Daniel Beaird. Deborah Foreman, Sam Jones, E.G. Marshall, Sean McClory, Howard Hesseman. Heavily male chauvinist chauffeur service has to contend not only with Foreman's hiring, but her emergence as the most popular employee on the staff. Strange mix of 30s screwball with today's cruder comedies doesn't really come off, yet is enough of a curiosity to keep you watching.▼

My Cousin Rachel (1952) **98m.** *** D: Henry Koster. Olivia de Havilland, Richard Burton, Audrey Dalton, John Sutton, Ronald Squire. Successful filmization of Daphne du Maurier mystery, with Burton trying to discover if de Havilland is guilty or innocent of murder and intrigue.

✓ **My Darling Clementine** (1946) **97m.** **** D: John Ford. Henry Fonda, Linda Darnell, Victor Mature, Walter Brennan, Cathy Downs, Tim Holt, Ward Bond, Alan Mowbray, John Ireland, Jane Darwell. Beautifully directed, low-key Western about Wyatt Earp (Fonda) and Doc Holliday (Mature), leading to inevitable gunfight at O.K. Corral. Full of wonderful details and vignettes; exquisitely photographed by Joseph P. MacDonald. One of director Ford's finest films, and an American classic. Screenplay by Samuel G. Engel and Winston Miller, from a story by Sam Hellman. Based on a book by Stuart N. Lake. Remake of FRONTIER MARSHAL (1939).▼

My Darling Daughters' Anniversary (1973) **C-74m.** TVM D: Joseph Pevney. Robert Young, Ruth Hussey, Darleen Carr, Raymond Massey, Darrell Larson, Judy Strangis, Jerry Fogel, Sharon Gless, Colby Chester. Now that Judge Raleigh has married off his daughters, what's to become of his widower status? Amusing sequel to ALL MY DARLING DAUGHTERS has a couple of decent situations, adequate performances. Script by John Gay. Average.

My Darling Shiksa SEE: **Over the Brooklyn Bridge**▼

My Daughter Joy SEE: **Operation X**

My Dear Secretary (1948) **94m.** **½ D: Charles Martin. Laraine Day, Kirk Douglas, Keenan Wynn, Helen Walker, Rudy Vallee, Florence Bates, Alan Mowbray. Bright, trivial comedy of writer Douglas and best-seller authoress Day; Wynn steals the show. Douglas is a bit too earnest at times.▼

My Demon Lover (1987) **C-86m.** ** D: Charles Loventhal. Scott Valentine, Michelle Little, Arnold Johnson, Gina Gallego, Robert Trebor. Trendy horror comedy has Valentine turning into a variety of monsters whenever he becomes sexually aroused, with Little the modern girl who tries to save him. Cast, including knockout beauty Gallego, is far better than the special effects-oriented material would indicate.▼

My Dinner With Andre (1981) **C-110m.** **½ D: Louis Malle. Andre Gregory, Wallace Shawn. Playwright-actor Shawn has dinner with his old friend, theater director Gregory, who's been having a series of strange life-experiences; they talk about them and their philosophies for nearly two hours. A daring and unique film, written by its two principals, with moments of insight, drama, and hilarity—but not enough to sustain a feature-length film.▼

My Dream Is Yours (1949) **C-101m.** **½ D: Michael Curtiz. Jack Carson, Doris Day, Lee Bowman, Adolphe Menjou, Eve Arden. Carson makes Day a radio star in standard musicomedy; highlights are Bugs Bunny dream sequence, Edgar Kennedy's performance as Day's uncle. Remake of TWENTY MILLION SWEETHEARTS, with Doris stepping into Dick Powell's role (and reprising the 1934 hit "I'll String Along With You").

My Enemy, The Sea SEE: **Alone on the Pacific**▼

My Fair Lady (1964) **C-170m.** ***½ D: George Cukor. Rex Harrison, Audrey Hepburn, Stanley Holloway, Wilfrid Hyde-White, Gladys Cooper, Jeremy Brett, Theodore Bikel, Henry Daniell, Mona Washbourne, Isobel Elsom. Ultrasmooth filmization of Lerner and Loewe's enchanting musical from Shaw's PYGMALION, with Prof. Henry Higgins (Harrison) transforming guttersnipe Hepburn into regal lady, to win a bet. Sumptuously filmed, with "The Rain in Spain," fantasy "Just You Wait," Harrison's soliloquys among highlights. Eight Oscars include Picture, Actor, Director, Cinematography (Harry Stradling), Costumes (Cecil Beaton), Score Adaptation (Andre Previn), Art Direction (Beaton and Gene Allen).▼

My Father, My Son (1988) **C-100m.** TVM D: Jeff Bleckner. Keith Carradine, Karl Malden, Michael Horton, Dirk Blocker, Jenny Lewis, Billy Sullivan, Grace Zabriskie. Poignant but passionless dramatization of the book by Admiral Elmo Zumwalt and son Elmo III about the latter's problems with cancer as the result of being sprayed by Agent Orange in Vietnam—which his dad (as Secretary of the Navy) had ordered. (Elmo III died several months after the film premiered.) Average.

My Father's House (1975) **C-100m.** TVM D: Alex Segal. Cliff Robertson, Robert Preston, Eileen Brennan, Rosemary Forsyth, Michael-James Wixted, Brad Savage, Ruth McDevitt. Contemporary drama, slowed by repetitious flashbacks, about heart attack patient (Robertson) whose fond memories of his father (Preston) and his childhood in simpler times make him question the life he has created for his own family. Good cast does its best. Average.▼

My Favorite Blonde (1942) **78m.** ** D: Sidney Lanfield. Bob Hope, Madeleine Carroll, Gale Sondergaard, George Zucco, Victor Varconi. Bob and his trained penguin become sitting ducks when spy Madeleine uses them to help deliver secret orders; very funny Hope vehicle.

✓ **My Favorite Brunette** (1947) **87m.** *** D: Elliott Nugent. Bob Hope, Dorothy Lamour, Peter Lorre, Lon Chaney, John Hoyt, Reginald Denny. Better-than-usual Hope nonsense with Bob as a photographer mixed up with mobsters; Lorre and Chaney add authenticity. Two very funny surprise cameos at beginning and end of film. Also shown in computer-colored version.▼

My Favorite Spy (1942) 86m. ** D: Tay Garnett. Kay Kyser, Ellen Drew, Jane Wyman, Robert Armstrong, William Demarest, Una O'Connor, Helen Westley, George Cleveland, Ish Kabibble. How did we win WW2 with bandleader Kyser as spy? Nonsensical musicomedy tries to explain.

My Favorite Spy (1951) 93m. *** D: Norman Z. McLeod. Bob Hope, Hedy Lamarr, Francis L. Sullivan, Mike Mazurki, John Archer, Iris Adrian, Arnold Moss. Bob resembles murdered spy, finds himself thrust into international intrigue. Fast-moving fun, with glamorous Hedy aiding Bob on all counts.

My Favorite Wife (1940) 88m. *** D: Garson Kanin. Cary Grant, Irene Dunne, Gail Patrick, Randolph Scott, Ann Shoemaker, Scotty Beckett, Donald MacBride. Dunne, supposedly dead, returns to U.S. to find hubby Grant remarried to Patrick, in familiar but witty marital mixup, remade as MOVE OVER, DARLING. Produced and co-written (with Sam and Bella Spewack) by Leo McCarey. Also shown in computer-colored version.▼

My Favorite Year (1982) C-92m. *** D: Richard Benjamin. Peter O'Toole, Mark Linn-Baker, Jessica Harper, Joseph Bologna, Bill Macy, Lainie Kazan, Anne DeSalvo, Lou Jacobi, Adolph Green, George Wyner, Selma Diamond, Cameron Mitchell. Enjoyable comedy about a young writer on TV's top comedy show in 1954 who's given the job of chaperoning that week's guest star, screen swashbuckler and off-screen carouser Alan Swann (O'Toole, in a tailor-made role). Shifts gears, and focus, a bit too often, but has many good moments, and likable performances (including Bologna as Sid Caesar-ish TV star). The woman O'Toole dances with in night club is 1930s leading lady Gloria Stuart.▼

My First Love (1988) C-100m. TVM D: Gilbert Cates. Beatrice Arthur, Richard Kiley, Joan Van Ark, Anne Francis, Richard Herd, Barbara Barrie. Pleasant comedy about a widow, challenged by her friends to take another chance at love, who seeks out the one-time high school sweetheart she hasn't seen in years. Average.

My First Wife (1984-Australian) C-95m. **½ D: Paul Cox. John Hargreaves, Wendy Hughes, Lucy Angwin, Anna Jemison, David Cameron. Painful, provocative drama about self-centered man who literally goes crazy when his wife leaves him after ten years. Achingly real, superbly acted, but slow and talky at times. Cox (who coscripted with Bob Ellis) based film on his own experiences.▼

My Foolish Heart (1949) 98m. *** D: Mark Robson. Dana Andrews, Susan Hayward, Kent Smith, Lois Wheeler, Jessie Royce Landis, Robert Keith, Gigi Perreau. Deftly handled sentimental WW2 romance tale between soldier Andrews and Hayward; Victor Young's lovely theme helps. Based on J.D. Salinger's story "Uncle Wiggily in Connecticut," the only one of the author's works ever adapted to film.

My Forbidden Past (1951) 81m. **½ D: Robert Stevenson. Robert Mitchum, Ava Gardner, Melvyn Douglas, Janis Carter. Silly tripe about Gardner, who's got a skeleton in her family closet, seeking revenge on Mitchum for jilting her. Fast-moving, watchable nonsense set in antebellum New Orleans.▼

My Friend Flicka (1943) C-89m. *** D: Harold Schuster. Roddy McDowall, Preston Foster, Rita Johnson, Jeff Corey, James Bell. Sentimental story of boy who loves rebellious horse; nicely done, beautifully filmed in color. Followed by sequel THUNDERHEAD, SON OF FLICKA and a TV series.

My Friend Irma (1949) 103m. ** D: George Marshall. Marie Wilson, John Lund, Diana Lynn, Don DeFore, Dean Martin, Jerry Lewis, Hans Conried. Based on radio series, movie concerns Wilson in title role as dumb blonde, Lynn as her level-headed pal, encountering wacky Martin and Lewis in their film debut. Followed by a sequel.

My Friend Irma Goes West (1950) 90m. **½ D: Hal Walker. Marie Wilson, Diana Lynn, Dean Martin, Jerry Lewis, Corinne Calvet, John Lund. Daffy Irma (Wilson) and pals join Martin and Lewis on their trek to Hollywood.

My Gal Sal (1942) C-103m. *** D: Irving Cummings. Rita Hayworth, Victor Mature, John Sutton, Carole Landis, James Gleason, Phil Silvers, Mona Maris, Walter Catlett. Nostalgic Gay 90s musical about songwriter Paul Dresser (Mature) in love with beautiful singer Hayworth. Includes Dresser's songs, such as title tune and other old-time numbers. The two stars (and knockout Technicolor) really put this one across. That's co-choreographer Hermes Pan featured with Rita in the "Gay White Way" number. Based on the book *My Brother Paul* by Theodore Dreiser.

My Geisha (1962) C-120m. **½ D: Jack Cardiff. Shirley MacLaine, Yves Montand, Edward G. Robinson, Robert Cummings, Yoko Tani. Occasionally amusing comedy. MacLaine is movie star who tries the hard way to convince husband-director Montand that she's right for his movie. Filmed in Japan.

My Girlfriend's Boyfriend SEE: **Boyfriends and Girlfriends**▼

My Girl Tisa (1948) 95m. **½ D: Elliott Nugent. Lilli Palmer, Sam Wanamaker, Akim Tamiroff, Alan Hale, Hugo Haas, Gale Robbins, Stella Adler. Sincere but uninspiring tale of devoted immigrant girl

Palmer working to bring her father to the U. S. Palmer is fine as usual in lead.▼

My Gun Is Quick (1957) 88m. *½ D: George White, Phil Victor. Robert Bray, Whitney Blake, Pamela Duncan, Donald Randolph. Drab Mickey Spillane yarn about detective Mike Hammer tracking down a murderer.

My Husband Is Missing (1978) C-100m. TVM D: Richard Michaels. Sally Struthers, Tony Musante, Martine Beswick, James Hong, Jeff David, Nam Loc. Sincere but somber odyssey of a Vietnam war widow who goes to Hanoi seeking word of her MIA husband. Average.

My Kidnapper, My Love (1980) C-100m. TVM D: Sam Wanamaker. James Stacy, Glynnis O'Connor, Mickey Rooney, Jan Sterling, J. D. Cannon, Richard Venture, Ellen Geer. Wealthy, emotionally disturbed girl falls in love with the crippled newsvendor who has kidnapped her (in a plot with his smalltime crook brother) to extort money from her parents. Written by Louie Elias from Oscar Saul's novel *The Dark Side of Love*. Average.

My Left Foot (1989-Irish) C-103m. ***½ D: Jim Sheridan. Daniel Day-Lewis, Brenda Fricker, Ray McAnally, Hugh O'Conor, Fiona Shaw, Cyril Cusack, Adrian Dunbar, Ruth McCabe, Alison Whelan. Exhilarating film with Day-Lewis in a tour de force as Christy Brown, feisty Irish artist-writer who was born with cerebral palsy. This is no disease-of-the-week weeper; it's an intensely moving story with just the right touches of humor, warmth, and poignancy. Fricker and McAnally are ideal as Christy's parents, and O'Conor is absolutely remarkable as the young Christy. Sheridan coscripted (with Shane Connaughton) from Brown's autobiography. Lovely score by Elmer Bernstein. Both Day-Lewis and Fricker won Oscars for their performances.▼

My Life as a Dog (1985-Swedish) C-101m. *** D: Lasse Hallström. Anton Glanzelius, Tomas von Brömssen, Anki Liden, Melinda Kinnaman, Kicki Rundgren, Ing-mari Carlsson. Warm-hearted look at the tumultuous life of an irrepressibly mischievous 12-year-old boy who's shipped off to live with relatives in a rural village in 1950s Sweden. Both comedic and poignant, this is ultimately an honest depiction of the often confusing nature of childhood. Glanzelius is excellent in the lead; based on an autobiographical novel by Reidar Jönsson.▼

My Life With Caroline (1941) 81m. **½ D: Lewis Milestone. Ronald Colman, Anna Lee, Charles Winninger, Reginald Gardiner, Gilbert Roland. Colman's charm sustains this frothy comedy of man suspecting his wife of having a lover.

My Little Chickadee (1940) 83m. **½ D: Edward Cline. Mae West, W. C. Fields,

Joseph Calleia, Dick Foran, Ruth Donnelly, Margaret Hamilton, Donald Meek. Team of West and Fields out West is good, but should have been funnier; W. C.'s saloon scenes are notable. The two stars also wrote screenplay.▼

My Little Girl (1986) C-113m. *** D: Connie Kaiserman. Mary Stuart Masterson, James Earl Jones, Geraldine Page, Pamela Payton Wright, Anne Meara, Peter Gallagher, Page Hannah, Erika Alexander, Traci Lin, Jordan Charney. Subtle, perceptive account of affluent, romantic, naive young Masterson, who volunteers to work one summer in a children's detention center. Extremely well played by all, with a special nod to Alexander and Lin (as a pair of troubled, abused girls with whom Masterson becomes involved).▼

My Little Pony (1986) C-89m. ** D: Michael Joens. Voices of Danny DeVito, Madeline Kahn, Tony Randall, Cloris Leachman, Rhea Pearlman. Animated fantasy pits the good Little Ponies against an evil witch. Highlight is an encounter with the Smooze, an evergrowing mass of living lava—a good idea hampered by bad animation. Too "cute" for anyone over the age of 7. Followed by a TV series.▼

My Love Came Back (1940) 81m. **½ D: Curtis Bernhardt. Olivia de Havilland, Jeffrey Lynn, Eddie Albert, Jane Wyman, Charles Winninger, Spring Byington, Grant Mitchell. Entertaining little romance of violinist de Havilland looking for husband.

My Love for Yours SEE: **Honeymoon in Bali**▼

My Love Letters SEE: **Love Letters** (1983)▼

My Lucky Star (1938) 84m. **½ D: Roy Del Ruth. Sonja Henie, Richard Greene, Cesar Romero, Buddy Ebsen, Joan Davis, Arthur Treacher, Billy Gilbert, Louise Hovick (Gypsy Rose Lee), George Barbier. Typical Henie vehicle with the skating star becoming the belle of a college campus—and helping department-store heir Romero score a hit with his dad. Finale is an imaginative "Alice in Wonderland" ice ballet.

My Main Man from Stony Island SEE: **Stony Island**

My Man Adam (1985) C-84m. ** D: Roger L. Simon. Raphael Sbarge, Page Hannah, Veronica Cartwright, Larry B. Scott, Dave Thomas, Charlie Barnett, Austin Pendleton. Yet another youth wish-fulfillment comedy, done as a teen version of UP THE SANDBOX. Sbarge is a pizza delivery boy who fantasizes about dreamgirl Hannah (Daryl's redheaded sister, in her first starring role) and becomes involved in a real-life murder adventure. Barely released film is pleasant but uneventful.▼

My Man and I (1952) 99m. **½ D: William Wellman. Shelley Winters, Ricardo Montalban, Wendell Corey, Claire Trevor.

Trials and tribulations of kindly Mexican worker Montalban; good cast helps OK script.

My Man Godfrey (1936) 95m. ***½ D: Gregory La Cava. William Powell, Carole Lombard, Gail Patrick, Alice Brady, Eugene Pallette, Alan Mowbray, Mischa Auer, Franklin Pangborn. Delightful romp with Lombard and crazy household hiring Powell as butler thinking he's a tramp who needs a job; he teaches them that money isn't everything. Mischa Auer is impressive as starving artist, sheltered by patroness Brady. But Pallette—as harried head of household—has some of the best lines. Screenplay by Morrie Ryskind and Eric Hatch, from Hatch's novel. Jane Wyman is an extra in the party scene. Classic screwball comedy; remade in 1957.▼

My Man Godfrey (1957) C-92m. **½ D: Henry Koster. June Allyson, David Niven, Martha Hyer, Eva Gabor, Jeff Donnell. Shallow compared to original, but on its own a harmless comedy of rich girl Allyson finding life's truths from butler Niven.

My Mother's Secret Life (1984) C-100m. TVM D: Robert Markowitz. Loni Anderson, Paul Sorvino, Amanda Wyss, James Sutorius, Sandy McPeak. She's a high-priced hooker, so her long-forgotten daughter who suddenly turns up on her doorstep discovers. Cold and passionless. Below average.

My Name Is Bill W. (1989) C-100m. TVM D: Daniel Petrie. James Woods, James Garner, JoBeth Williams, Fritz Weaver, Robert Harper, Gary Sinise, George Coe. Woods gives another flamboyant acting lesson as Bill Wilson, a fall-down drunk who sees the light, and joins a fellow boozer, Dr. Robert Smith (Garner), to found Alcoholics Anonymous. Strong script by William G. Borchert. Above average.

My Name Is Ivan (1963-Russian) 94m. *** D: Andrei Tarkovsky. Kolya Burlaiev, Valentin Zubkov, Ye Zharikov. Taut account of Russian youth sent as spy into Nazi territory. Retitled: THE YOUNGEST SPY.

My Name is Julia Ross (1945) 65m. *** D: Joseph H. Lewis. Nina Foch, Dame May Whitty, George Macready, Roland Varno, Anita Bolster, Doris Lloyd. An unsuspecting young woman answers newspaper ad for a job and winds up the prisoner of a crazy family. Often cited as a model B movie, it does go a long way on a low budget, though it's a bit more obvious now than it must have been in 1945. Foch's performance is still a standout. Later the inspiration for DEAD OF WINTER.

My Name Is Nobody (1974-Italian-French-German) C-115m. *** D: Tonino Valerii. Henry Fonda, Terence Hill, Leo Gordon, Geoffrey Lewis, R. G. Armstrong. Underrated, enjoyable if overlong Western spoof with Hill as an easygoing gunman who worships aging Fonda, a gunfighter

who wants to retire. Filmed in the U.S. and Spain; produced by Sergio Leone. Released in Italy at 130m.▼

My Night at Maud's (1969-French) 105m. *** D: Eric Rohmer. Jean-Louis Trintignant, Francoise Fabian, Marie-Christine Barrault, Antoine Vitez. No. 3 of Rohmer's "Six Moral Tales" is most intellectual, with Trintignant as moral Catholic man infatuated with woman completely unlike himself. Talky, fascinating, more specialized in appeal than later entries in series. Barrault's first film.▼

My Old Man (1979) C-100m. TVM D: John Erman. Kristy McNichol, Warren Oates, Eileen Brennan, Mark Arnold, David Margulies, Howard E. Rollins, Jr. The saga of a spunky teenage girl and her down-and-out horse trainer dad, from a Hemingway short story. Sound familiar? Try Wallace Beery and Jackie Cooper four decades removed. Filmed before as UNDER MY SKIN. Average.▼

My Old Man's Place (1972) C-93m. **½ D: Edwin Sherin. Mitchell Ryan, Arthur Kennedy, William Devane, Michael Moriarty, Topo Swope. Moriarty (in his first film) returns home from war with two soldier pals; inevitable tensions lead to rape and murder. Not profound, but moody and interesting. Original title: GLORY BOY.▼

My Outlaw Brother (1951) 82m. ** D: Elliott Nugent. Mickey Rooney, Wanda Hendrix, Robert Preston, Robert Stack, Jose Torvay. Texas Ranger Preston takes on villainous Stack, the brother of dude Rooney. Strictly conventional south-of-the-border oater.▼

My Own True Love (1948) 84m. ** D: Compton Bennett. Melvyn Douglas, Phyllis Calvert, Wanda Hendrix, Philip Friend, Binnie Barnes. Calvert is placed in the awkward position of choosing between two suitors, a father and son; drama lacks ring of truth.

My Pal Gus (1952) 83m. **½ D: Robert Parrish. Richard Widmark, Joanne Dru, Audrey Totter, George Winslow, Regis Toomey. Wholesome film of Widmark coming to realize importance of son Winslow, finding romance with teacher Dru.

My Palikari (1982) C-90m. TVM D: Charles Dubin. Telly Savalas, Keith Gordon, Dora Volonaki, Michael Constantine. Savalas is surprisingly effective as Pete Panakos, a proud Greek-American who returns to his homeland with teenaged, American-born son Gordon. An honest, touching drama with a fine script by George Kirgo, based on a story by Leon Capetanos. A PBS *American Playhouse* presentation. Above average.

My Pleasure Is My Business (1974-Canadian) C-85m. BOMB D: Al Waxman. Xaviera Hollander, Henry Ramer, Colin Fox, Kenneth Lynch, Jayne Eastwood. "The Happy Hooker" makes her own

[793]

attempt at acting in this witless comedy which purports to tell her true story (albeit just as cleaned-up as THE HAPPY HOOKER itself). Hollander is so expressionless she can't even play herself well.

Myra Breckinridge (1970) **C-94m.** BOMB D: Michael Sarne. Mae West, John Huston, Raquel Welch, Rex Reed, Roger Herren, Farrah Fawcett, Jim Backus, John Carradine, Andy Devine, Grady Sutton. Gore Vidal's loosely structured comic novel about sex-change operation was probably unfilmable, but this version doesn't even give book a chance; as bad as any movie ever made, it taste-lessly exploits many old Hollywood favorites through film clips. That's Tom Selleck— minus mustache—as one of Mae's "studs."▼

My Reputation (1946) **94m.** *** D: Curtis Bernhardt. Barbara Stanwyck, George Brent, Warner Anderson, Lucile Watson, John Ridgely, Eve Arden. Well-mounted Warner Bros. soaper; widow Stanwyck is center of scandal when she dates Brent soon after her husband's death.

Myrt and Marge (1934) **62m.** ** D: Al Boasberg. Myrtle Vail, Donna Damerel, Eddie Foy, Jr., Grace Hayes, Ted Healy, Howard, Fine, and Howard (The 3 Stooges), Bonnie Bonnell. Lackluster backstage musical, based on popular radio show of the same name. Mainly a curio for fans of the Stooges, who get to sing as well as clown.

My Science Project (1985) **C-94m.** BOMB D: Jonathan Beteul. John Stockwell, Danielle Von Zerneck, Fisher Stevens, Raphael Sbarge, Dennis Hopper, Barry Corbin, Ann Wedgeworth, Richard Masur. Laughless, often tasteless comedy about high school kids who unearth an other-worldly device that can create time and space warps. Lost in the quagmire is Hopper in funny role as a latter-day hippie science teacher.▼

My Seven Little Sins (1954-French) **C-98m.** ** D: Jean Boyer. Maurice Chevalier, Collette Ripert, Paolo Stoppa, Delia Scala. Pleasant, inconsequential musicomedy, with Chevalier an old roué "adopting" group of Riviera chorines. Retitled: I HAVE SEVEN DAUGHTERS.

My Side of the Mountain (1969) **C-100m.** **½ D: James B. Clark. Ted Eccles, Theodore Bikel, Tudi Wiggins, Frank Perry, Peggi Loder. Children should enjoy this tale about 13-year-old Canadian boy who runs away from home to get closer to nature.▼

My Sister Eileen (1942) **96m.** **½ D: Alexander Hall. Rosalind Russell, Brian Aherne, Janet Blair, George Tobias, Allyn Joslyn, Elizabeth Patterson, June Havoc. Amusing tale of two Ohio girls trying to survive in Greenwich Village apartment; strained at times. Belongs mainly to Russell as older sister of knockout Blair. Ruth McKinney, Joseph Fields, and Jerome Chodorov adapted their Broadway hit (based

on McKinney's autobiographical book). Remade as a musical in 1955 (and musicalized on Broadway as *Wonderful Town*).

My Sister Eileen (1955) **C-108m.** ***½ D: Richard Quine. Betty Garrett, Janet Leigh, Jack Lemmon, Kurt Kasznar, Dick York, Horace McMahon, Bob Fosse, Tommy Rall. Delightful, unpretentious musical version of 1942 comedy of Ohio girls seeking success while living in nutty Greenwich Village apartment. Lemmon even sings in this one.

My Sister, My Love SEE: **Mafu Cage, The**▼

My Six Convicts (1952) **104m.** *** D: Hugo Fregonese. Millard Mitchell, Gilbert Roland, John Beal, Marshall Thompson, Regis Toomey, Harry Morgan. Unusual comedy of prison life centering on title group who manage to make jail routine tolerable, egged on by prison psychiatrist.

My Six Loves (1963) **C-101m.** **½ D: Gower Champion. Debbie Reynolds, Cliff Robertson, David Janssen, Eileen Heckart, Hans Conried, Alice Pearce, Jim Backus. Syrupy fluff of theater star Reynolds "adopting" six waifs.

My Son John (1952) **122m.** **½ D: Leo McCarey. Helen Hayes, Robert Walker, Dean Jagger, Van Heflin, Frank McHugh, Richard Jaeckel. Archetypal apple-pie parents (Hayes, Jagger) suspect their son (Walker) of being a Communist in this reactionary period piece. Dramatically overwrought, but fascinating as social history. Walker (who's superb) died before film was finished; most shots of him in final reel are cribbed from STRANGERS ON A TRAIN.

My Son, My Son (1940) **115m.** ** D: Charles Vidor. Madeleine Carroll, Brian Aherne, Louis Hayward, Laraine Day, Henry Hull, Josephine Hutchinson, Scotty Beckett. Drawn-out, unconvincing tale of rags-to-riches Aherne who spoils his son, and lives to regret it. Some good performances wasted on banal script.

My Son, The Hero (1963-Italian) **C-111m.** ** D: Duccio Tessari. Pedro Armendariz, Jacqueline Sassard, Antonella Lualdi, Tanya Lopert. Italian spectacle with good twist. Instead of typical, ludicrous dialogue, U.S. firm dubbed Jewish accents onto the track.

My Stepmother Is an Alien (1988) **C-108m.** *½ D: Richard Benjamin. Dan Aykroyd, Kim Basinger, Jon Lovitz, Alyson Hannigan, Joseph Maher, Ann Prentiss (voice of purse), Seth Green, Wesley Mann, Harry Shearer (voice of Carl Sagan). Luscious Basinger, who knows nothing of romance or sex, marries widowed scientist (Aykroyd); he wants to settle into domesticity, while her mind is only on saving her planet from destruction. Somehow, Jimmy Durante imitations get worked into this new low in "high-concept" comedy.▼

Mysterians, The (1959-Japanese) **C-85m.**

**½ D: Inoshiro Honda. Kenji Sahara, Yumi Shirakawa, Momoko Kochi, Akihiko Hirata. Centuries after the destruction of their planet, the title aliens land on Earth, install an impregnable dome by a lake, and demand women. The world does not take this well. Colorful special effects and fast pace make this one of the better Japanese sci-fis.▼

Mysterious Doctor, The (1943) 57m. **½ D: Ben Stoloff. John Loder, Eleanor Parker, Bruce Lester, Lester Matthews, Forrester Harvey. Average story of a doctor who murders people to keep secret of his being Nazi. Moor locations interesting; cast adequate.

Mysterious Dr. Satan SEE: **Doctor Satan's Robot**▼

Mysterious Intruder, The (1946) 61m. D: William Castle. Richard Dix, Nina Vale, Regis Toomey, Pamela Blake, Charles Lane, Helen Mowery, Mike Mazurki. SEE: **The Whistler** series.

Mysterious Island (1961-British) C-101m. *** D: Cy Endfield. Michael Craig, Joan Greenwood, Michael Callan, Gary Merrill, Herbert Lom. Deliberately paced fantasy adventure based on two-part Jules Verne novel, a sequel to his *20,000 Leagues Under the Sea.* Confederate prison escapees, blown off course, find uncharted island with gigantic animals. Great special effects by Ray Harryhausen; rousing Bernard Herrmann score. Filmed before in 1929.▼

Mysterious Island of Beautiful Women (1979) C-100m. TVM D: Joseph Pevney. Steven Keats, Peter Lawford, Clint Walker, Jamie Lyn Bauer, Jayne Kennedy, Kathryn Davis, Rosalind Chao. Six men fight for survival on a South Sea island populated by a tribe of hostile, bikini-clad lovelies. Unfortunately, nobody plays this one for laughs. Below average.▼

Mysterious Island of Captain Nemo, The (1974-French-Italian) C-96m. ** D: Juan Antonio Bardem, Henri Colpi. Omar Sharif, Philippe Nicaud, Gerard Tichy, Jess Hahn, Rafael Bardem, Ambrose M'Bia. Jules Verne's Nemo (Sharif) again sees service in juvenile-level action piece, a bit less acceptable than others in this vein.

Mysterious Lady (1928) 96m. **½ D: Fred Niblo. Greta Garbo, Conrad Nagel, Gustav von Seyffertitz, Albert Pollet, Edward Connelly. Austrian military officer (Nagel) falls in love with Garbo, unaware that she's a Russian spy. Another contrived plot made worthwhile by Garbo herself.

Mysterious Magician, The (1965-German) 95m. **½ D: Alfred Vohrer. Joachim Fuchsberger, Eddi Arent, Sophie Hardy, Karl John, Heinz Drache. Mysterious murderwave in London causes Scotland Yard to suspect that the "Wizard," archfiend, is still alive; enjoyable suspenser from Edgar Wallace story.

Mysterious Mr. Moto (1938) 62m. D:

Norman Foster. Peter Lorre, Henry Wilcoxon, Mary Maguire, Erik Rhodes, Harold Huber, Leon Ames, Forrester Harvey. SEE: **Mr. Moto** series.

Mysterious Two (1982) C-100m. TVM D: Gary Sherman. John Forsythe, James Stephens, Priscilla Pointer, Robert Pine, Karen Werner, Noah Beery, Vic Tayback. Extraterrestrial twosome comes to Earth on a recruiting mission. This busted sci-fi pilot was called FOLLOW ME IF YOU DARE from its filming several years earlier until the very eve of its first showing. Average.▼

Mystery in Mexico (1948) 66m. ** D: Robert Wise. William Lundigan, Jacqueline White, Ricardo Cortez, Tony Barrett, Jacqueline Dalya, Walter Reed. Competent but overly familiar second-feature mystery about insurance investigator Lundigan who goes to Mexico City to find out what happened to White's brother.

Mystery Liner (1934) 62m. ** D: William Nigh. Noah Beery, Astrid Allyn (Allwyn), Cornelius Keefe, Gustav von Steyffertitz, Edwin Maxwell, Ralph Lewis, Zeffie Tilbury. A mysterious secret radio-control weapon being developed aboard a cruise ship is sought after by various parties in this intriguing but slowly paced B-picture. That's a clean-shaven Gabby Hayes as the crew member named Wathman! Based on an Edgar Wallace novel.

Mystery of Edwin Drood, The (1935) 87m. *** D: Stuart Walker. Claude Rains, Douglass Montgomery, Heather Angel, David Manners, E. E. Clive, Valerie Hobson. Seemingly respectable Rains is responsible for series of horrible murders. Fine thriller adapted from Dickens' unfinished novel, which inspired a hit Broadway musical in the 1980s.

Mystery of Kaspar Hauser, The SEE: **Every Man for Himself and God Against All**▼

Mystery of Marie Roget, The (1942) 91m. **½ D: Phil Rosen. Maria Montez, Maria Ouspenskaya, John Litel, Patric Knowles, Charles Middleton. Poe story provides basis for fairly good murder mystery. Detective tries to unravel mystery of actress' strange disappearance.

Mystery of Mr. Wong (1939) 67m. *½ D: William Nigh. Boris Karloff, Grant Withers, Dorothy Tree, Lotus Long, Morgan Wallace, Holmes Herbert. Modest Mr. Wong mystery, second entry in the series, has Oriental sleuth becoming embroiled in mystery surrounding a rare gem and a suspiciously changed will.▼

Mystery of Picasso, The (1955-French) C-85m. **½ D: Henri-Georges Clouzot. Pablo Picasso actually creates a work of art right on camera—through the means of a translucent "canvas." A unique piece of film, but past its novelty value, it doesn't really reveal much of the man or the artist.▼

Mystery of the Black Jungle (1955-German) **72m.** *½ D: Ralph Murphy. Lex Barker, Jane Maxwell, Luigi Tosi, Paul Muller. Embarrassing lowjinks set in India involving idol-worshiping natives. Retitled: THE BLACK DEVILS OF KALI.

Mystery of the Golden Eye SEE: **Golden Eye, The**

Mystery of the Mary Celeste SEE: **Phantom Ship**▼

Mystery of the Wax Museum (1933) **C-77m,** **½ D: Michael Curtiz. Lionel Atwill, Fay Wray, Glenda Farrell, Allen Vincent, Frank McHugh, Arthur Edmund Carewe. Long-lost horror film disappoints somewhat in overabundant "comic relief" and contrivances, but basic plot line of madman Atwill encasing victims in wax, with Wray next on his list, is still exciting. Filmed in early two-color Technicolor; noteworthy as first horror film with contemporary urban setting. Remade as HOUSE OF WAX.▼

Mystery of the White Room (1939) **58m.** *** D: Otis Garrett. Bruce Cabot, Helen Mack, Constance Worth, Joan Woodbury, Mabel Todd, Tom Dugan. Very good *Crime Club* mystery of murders in an operating room; modest, nicely done.

Mystery of Thug Island, The (1964-Italian-West German) **C-96m.** *½ D: Luigi Capuano. Guy Madison, Peter Van Eyck, Giacomo Rossi Stuart, Ivan Desny, Inge Schoener. Below-average formula drama with the daughter of a British Army captain abducted in India, becoming member of a sect. Bulk of the film takes place 15 years later.

Mystery Street (1950) **93m.** **½ D: John Sturges. Ricardo Montalban, Sally Forrest, Bruce Bennett, Elsa Lanchester, Marshall Thompson, Jan Sterling. Trim murder caper set in Boston; nicely done, with fine cast.

Mystery Submarine (1950) **78m.** **½ D: Douglas Sirk. Macdonald Carey, Marta Toren, Carl Esmond, Ludwig Donath. Involved plot of military officer Carey being instrumental in destruction of Nazi sub in South America.

Mystery Submarine (1963-British) **90m.** *½ D: C. M. Pennington-Richards. Edward Judd, James Robertson Justice, Laurence Payne, Arthur O'Sullivan, Albert Lieven. A tame WW2 espionage tale of German submarine manned by British crew, only to be recaptured by English fleet. Alternate title: DECOY.

Mystery Train (1989) **C-113m.** *** D: Jim Jarmusch. Masatoshi Nagase, Youki Kudoh, Screamin' Jay Hawkins, Cinque Lee, Nicoletta Braschi, Elizabeth Bracco, Joe Strummer, Rick Aviles, Steve Buscemi, Tom Noonan, Rockets Redglare, Rufus Thomas, voice of Tom Waits. Typically

quirky slice-of-life from Jarmusch, a trio of stories depicting foreigners' stays in a sleazy Memphis hotel. Jarmusch's minimalist style results in some slow stretches, but there are enough genuinely funny moments to make this worth seeing.

Mystic Pizza (1988) **C-104m.** ** D: Donald Petrie. Julia Roberts, Annabeth Gish, Lili Taylor, Vincent D'Onofrio, William R. Moses, Adam Storke, Conchata Ferrell, Joanna Merlin. The amorous adventures of three young women who work at a pizzeria in Mystic, Connecticut. Superficial in the extreme but geared to appeal to a young female audience. A "nice little film" that isn't all that good.▼

Mystic Warrior, The (1984) **C-240m.** TVM D: Richard T. Heffron. Robert Beltran, Devon Erickson, Victoria Racimo, Nick Ramus, Ned Romero, Will Sampson, Rion Hunter, Ron Soble. This long-incoming adaptation of Ruth Beebe Hill's novel *Hanta Yo*, about a proud band of Sioux Indians and the brave who becomes his people's savior, fell victim to a firestorm of controversy as well as various pressure groups who belatedly questioned the book's authenticity and its Caucasian author's credentials as an authority on Indian culture. Besides, the film is "mystic" to tedium. Originally presented in two parts. Average.

Mystique SEE: **Circle of Power**▼

My Sweet Charlie (1970) **C-97m.** TVM D: Lamont Johnson. Patty Duke, Al Freeman Jr., Ford Rainey, William Hardy, Chris Wilson, Noble Willingham. White unwed mother and black N.Y.C lawyer are thrown together in abandoned house in rural Texas. Good adaptation of David Westheimer novel, with excellent performances; believable and moving. A television landmark by Richard Levinson and William Link; this earned theatrical showings after debut on TV. Above average.▼

My Tutor (1983) **C-97m.** ** D: George Bowers. Matt Lattanzi, Caren Kaye, Kevin McCarthy, Arlene Golonka, Clark Brandon, Bruce Bauer, Crispin Glover. Rich, hunky (but still virginal) Lattanzi won't graduate high school unless he passes French, so his folks hire beautiful Kaye to spend the summer tutoring him—guess what happens next. Earns points for sincerity, but credulity is low, other characters embarrassing, and Kaye's considerable comic talents are wasted.▼

My Two Loves (1986) **C-100m.** TVM D: Noel Black. Mariette Hartley, Lynn Redgrave, Barry Newman, Sada Thompson, Sarah Inglis, Robert L. Leonard, Eve Roberts. Bisexual widow and mother is torn between her latest male lover and a woman coworker at her new job. Cowritten by veteran television writer Reginald Rose and earnestly but unbelievably played by a bunch of pros. Below average.

My Uncle SEE: **Mon Oncle▼**

My Uncle Antoine (1971-Canadian) C-110m. **½ D: Claude Jutra. Jean Duceppe, Olivette Thibault, Claude Jutra, Jacques Gagnon, Helene Louselle. Fifteen-year-old Gagnon observes those around him while growing up in a small mining town during the 1940s. Not bad, but nothing special.

My Uncle, Mr. Hulot SEE: **Mon Oncle▼**

My Undercover Years With the KKK SEE: **Undercover With the KKK**

My Wicked, Wicked Ways . . . The Legend of Errol Flynn (1985) C-100m. TVM D: Don Taylor. Duncan Regehr, Barbara Hershey, Darren McGavin, Lee Purcell, Barrie Ingham, George Coe, Michael C. Gwynne, Hal Linden, Michael Callan. A devil-be-damned dramatization of the famed film swashbuckler's Hollywood life (through 1943), entertainingly essayed by a game cast; cowritten and produced by Flynn's goddaughter, Doris Keating, from Errol's autobiography. Middling results. Average.▼

My Wife's Best Friend (1952) 87m. ** D: Richard Sale. Anne Baxter, Macdonald Carey, Cecil Kellaway, Leif Erickson, Frances Bavier. Unexceptional film of married couple Baxter-Carey confessing their past indiscretions when their plane seems about to crash.

My Wild Irish Rose (1947) C-101m. ** D: David Butler. Dennis Morgan, Andrea King, Arlene Dahl, Alan Hale, George Tobias. Irish songs galore support limp biography of songwriter Chauncey Olcott.

Nabonga (1944) 75m. *½ D: Sam Newfield. Buster Crabbe, Julie London, Fifi D'Orsay, Barton MacLane, Bryant Washburn. Incredible cheapie of plane-crash survivor (London) making friends with local gorilla. Good for laughs, anyway. Retitled: GORILLA.▼

Nadia (1984) C-100m. TVM D: Alan Cooke. Talia Balsam, Jonathan Banks, Joe Bennett, Simone Blue, Johann Carlo, Conchata Ferrell, Carrie Snodgress. Nadia Comaneci, the young Romanian athlete whose gymnastic feats during the 1976 Olympics enthralled the world, gets a curiously flat retelling of her story, with all of the lead actors either British or American (some working with Mittle-European accents) and the rest of the cast fleshed out with Yugoslavians. Gymnastic gyrations remain wondrous as performed by contemporary Olympic class performers. Average.▼

Nadine (1987) C-82m. *** Robert Benton. Jeff Bridges, Kim Basinger, Rip Torn, Gwen Verdon, Glenne Headly, Jerry Stiller, Jay Patterson. Lightweight but pleasing comedy set in 1954 Austin, about a pregnant but nearly divorced hairdresser who accidentally witnesses a murder while trying to retrieve some nude "art studies"

she posed for in a weak moment. Very well cast, with Basinger a surprising standout; catchy credit tune is performed by Sweethearts of the Rodeo.▼

Nairobi Affair (1984) C-100m. TVM D: Marvin J. Chomsky. Charlton Heston, John Savage, Maud Adams, John Rhys-Davies, Connie Booth, Shane Rimmer. Limp rehash of countless safari movies of yesteryear involving the big white hunter, poachers, familial conflicts, forbidden love, ad nauseum. Even the casting of Heston promotes a feeling of déjà vu. Below average.▼

Naked Alibi (1954) 86m. **½ D: Jerry Hopper. Sterling Hayden, Gloria Grahame, Gene Barry, Marcia Henderson, Casey Adams, Chuck Connors. Dismissed from force because of "police brutality," ex-cop Hayden continues to stalk cop-killer suspect Barry.

Naked and the Dead, The (1958) C-131m. *** D: Raoul Walsh. Aldo Ray, Cliff Robertson, Raymond Massey, William Campbell, Richard Jaeckel, James Best, Joey Bishop, L. Q. Jones, Robert Gist, Lili St. Cyr, Barbara Nichols. Norman Mailer's intensive novel about WW2 soldiers in the Pacific gets superficial but rugged filmization. Ray is the tough sergeant, Robertson the rich-kid lieutenant, Bishop the comic Jew, Jones the hick, Gist the loner, etc.▼

Naked Ape, The (1973) C-85m. *½ D: Donald Driver. Johnny Crawford, Victoria Principal, Dennis Oliveri, Diana Darrin. Tongue-in-cheek *Playboy* production loosely based on the pop anthropology of Desmond Morris's nonfiction best-seller. Snickering sex jokes and mediocre animation (by Charles Swenson) add nothing to this episodic summary of 10 million years of Man's evolution. Musical score by Jimmy Webb.

Naked Brigade, The (1965) 99m. ** D: Maury Dexter. Shirley Eaton, Ken Scott, Mary Chronopoulou, John Holland, Sonia Zoidou. Mild WW2 actioner of Eaton hiding from Nazi invasion of Crete.

Naked Cage, The (1986) C-97m. ** D: Paul Nicholas. Shari Shattuck, Angel Tompkins, Lucinda Crosby, Faith Minton, Christina Whitaker, John Terlesky. Standard women's prison drama as innocent Shattuck is framed for a bank robbery and ends up in the slammer. Shattuck shows promise in otherwise cornball exercise.▼

Naked City, The (1948) 96m. ***½ D: Jules Dassin. Barry Fitzgerald, Howard Duff, Dorothy Hart, Don Taylor, Ted de Corsia. Realistic, trendsetting drama, shot on actual locations throughout N.Y.C., detailing the based-on-fact story of a young girl who is brutally murdered and the subsequent manhunt for her killer. The Williamsburg Bridge finale is truly memorable; William Daniels and Paul Weatherwax earned Oscars for their cinematography and editing. Later a TV series.

Naked Dawn, The (1955) **C-82m.** **½ D: Edgar G. Ulmer. Arthur Kennedy, Betta St. John, Roy Engel, Eugene Iglesias, Charita. Acceptable robbery caper of initial act snowballing into series of crimes.

Naked Earth (1958-British) **96m.** *½ D: Vincent Sherman. Juliette Greco, Richard Todd, John Kitzmiller, Finlay Currie. Misguided soap opera set in 1890s Africa, trying to build up aspiring star Greco.

Naked Edge, The (1961) **99m.** **½ D: Michael Anderson. Gary Cooper, Deborah Kerr, Eric Portman, Diane Cilento, Hermione Gingold, Michael Wilding. Uneven suspenser of Kerr thinking husband Cooper is guilty of murder. Cooper's last film, made in London.

Naked Face, The (1985) **C-103m.** **½ D: Bryan Forbes. Roger Moore, Rod Steiger, Elliott Gould, Anne Archer, David Hedison, Art Carney. Change of pace for Moore, portraying a psychiatrist suspected by cops Steiger and Gould of murdering one of his patients. Low-budget adaptation of Sidney Sheldon's novel crudely injects clues and red herrings; female cast is very weak. ▼

Naked Gun: From the Files of Police Squad, The (1988) **C-85m.** *** D: David Zucker. Leslie Nielsen, George Kennedy, Priscilla Presley, Ricardo Montalban, O.J. Simpson, Nancy Marchand. A failed (but loyally supported) TV sitcom, *Police Squad,* is reincarnated as a hilarious feature film, with a deadpan, dead-perfect Nielsen as Lt. Frank Drebin, the stupidest law officer since Inspector Clouseau. Writers David and Jerry Zucker, Jim Abrahams, and Pat Proft can't keep their momentum from slowing a bit during the baseball game finale, but they provide solid, silly laughs from start to finish. ▼

Naked Heart, The (1949-Canadian) **96m.** ** D: Marc Allegret. Michele Morgan, Kieron Moore, Francoise Rosay, Jack Watling. Little of consequence happens in this sad story based on book *Maria Chapdelaine* by Louis Hémon. Filmed before in 1935 (in France) and 1983 (in Canada).

Naked Hills, The (1956) **C-73m.** *½ D: Josef Shaftel. David Wayne, Keenan Wynn, James Barton, Marcia Henderson, Jim Backus. Raggedy account of Wayne who has gold fever and spends life searching for ore, ignoring wife and family. ▼

Naked in the Sun (1957) **C-79m.** ** D: R. John Hugh. James Craig, Lita Milan, Barton MacLane, Tony Hunter. Somewhat sluggish account of Indian tribes involved with slave traders. ▼

✓ **Naked Jungle, The** (1954) **C-95m.** *** D: Byron Haskin. Eleanor Parker, Charlton Heston, Abraham Sofaer, William Con-

rad. High-class South American jungle adventure, with Heston and wife Parker surrounded on their plantation by advancing army of red ants. Produced by George Pal. ▼

Naked Kiss, The (1964) **93m.** **½ D: Samuel Fuller. Constance Towers, Anthony Eisley, Virginia Grey, Betty Bronson, Patsy Kelly, Michael Dante. Girl arrested for murder reveals her shady past; lurid but provocative melodrama. ▼

Naked Lie (1989) **C-100m. TVM** D: Richard A. Colla. Victoria Principal, James Farentino, Glenn Withrow, William Lucking, Dakin Matthews. Lady D.A.'s hot 'n' heavy affair with a judge gets dicey when she's assigned to a politically explosive blackmail/murder case he's presiding over. Average.

Naked Maja, The (1959) **C-111m.** ** D: Henry Koster. Ava Gardner, Anthony Franciosa, Amedeo Nazzari, Gino Cervi, Massimo Serato, Lea Padovani, Carlo Rizzo. Mishmash involving 18th-century Spanish painter Goya and famed model for title painting.

Naked Night, The SEE: **Sawdust and Tinsel**▼

Naked Paradise (1957) **C-68m.** BOMB D: Roger Corman. Richard Denning, Beverly Garland, Lisa Montell, Richard (Dick) Miller, Leslie Bradley. On-location filming in Hawaii can't salvage this balderdash about crooks using cruise boat to rob local plantations. Retitled: THUNDER OVER HAWAII. Remade as BEAST FROM HAUNTED CAVE and CREATURE FROM THE HAUNTED SEA.

Naked Prey, The (1966) **C-94m.** *** D: ✓ Cornel Wilde. Cornel Wilde, Gert Van Den Bergh, Ken Gampu. Harrowing, well-done safari movie. African natives give prisoner Wilde headstart before they close in on him for kill, forcing Wilde to combat them with savage tactics; memorable brutal sequences. ▼

Naked Runner, The (1967-British) **C-104m.** *½ D: Sidney J. Furie. Frank Sinatra, Peter Vaughan, Toby Robins, Edward Fox. ✓ Dull spy melodrama focusing on American (Sinatra) who is pawn in bizarre plot to get him to assassinate enemy agent. Farfetched, too heavily plotted.

Naked Spur, The (1953) **C-91m.** ***½ ✓ D: Anthony Mann. James Stewart, Janet Leigh, Ralph Meeker, Robert Ryan, Millard Mitchell. One of the best Westerns ever made: a tough, hard little film about self-styled bounty hunter Stewart trying to capture Ryan, who stirs tension among Stewart's newly-acquired "partners." Strikingly directed and photographed (by William Mellor) on location in the Rockies. Written by Sam Rolfe and Harold Jack Bloom.▼

Naked Street, The (1955) **84m.** ** D: Maxwell Shane. Farley Granger, Anthony

Quinn, Anne Bancroft, Peter Graves, Jerry Paris, Jeanne Cooper. Capable cast wasted in bland yarn of reporter exposing crime syndicate.

Naked Truth, The SEE: **Your Past Is Showing▼**

Naked Under Leather SEE: **Girl on a Motorcycle▼**

Naked Weekend, The SEE: **Circle of Power▼**

Naked Youth (1959) **69m.** BOMB D: John F. Schreyer. Carol Ohmart, Robert Hutton, Steve Rowland, Jan Brooks, Robert Arthur, John Goddard. Awful potboiler about drug smuggling, murder and some youths who escape from the "State Boys Honor Farm." That "Switch"—short for switchblade—is a real peach. Plenty of blasting saxophones and bongo drums on the soundtrack. Also known as WILD YOUTH.▼

Nakia (1974) **C-78m.** TVM D: Leonard Horn. Robert Forster, Arthur Kennedy, Linda Evans, Chief George Clutesi, Stephen McNally, Christopher Stone. American Indian deputy sheriff torn between his heritage and his job, with strong overtones of BILLY JACK. Forster is granite-like and no-nonsense in the lead, Kennedy provides the nuances as his boss. Both were in TV series which later spun off. Average.

Name of the Game Is Kill, The (1968) **C-88m.** ** D: Gunnar Hellstrom. Jack Lord, Susan Strasberg, Collin Wilcox, Tisha Sterling, T. C. Jones. Crazy melodrama concerns refugee Lord's problems in Arizona when he gets mixed up with a trio of sisters and their mother. Retitled THE FEMALE TRAP.

Name of the Rose, The (1986-Italian-German-French) **C-130m.** ** D: Jean-Jacques Annaud. Sean Connery, F. Murray Abraham, Christian Slater, Elya Baskin, Feodor Chaliapin, Jr., William Hickey, Michael Lonsdale, Ron Perlman, narrated by Dwight Weist. Unusual film (to say the least) based on Umberto Eco's best-seller, which places a Sherlock Holmesian monk (Connery) in the midst of a mysterious Italian abbey during the inquisition of the 13th century. Too provocative to dismiss, too lumbering to thoroughly enjoy, buoyed considerably by Connery's charismatic performance. ▼

Namu, the Killer Whale (1966) **C-88m.** **½ D: Laslo Benedek. Robert Lansing, John Anderson, Lee Meriwether, Richard Erdman, Robin Mattson. Intriguing tale, based on true story of naturalist Lansing capturing and training a killer whale. Nicely done, good family fare.

Nana (1934) **89m.** **½ D: Dorothy Arzner. Anna Sten, Phillips Holmes, Lionel Atwill, Muriel Kirkland, Richard Bennett, Mae Clarke. Initially interesting adaptation of Emile Zola story of luxury-loving woman in tragic love affair runs out of steam towards the middle. Producer Samuel Goldwyn's first attempt to make a new Garbo out of exotic but wooden Sten.

Nancy Drew and the Hidden Staircase (1939) **60m.** *½ D: William Clemens. Bonita Granville, Frankie Thomas, John Litel, Frank Orth, Vera Lewis. Formula happenings as Granville et al. aid elderly spinsters being victimized by crooks.

Nancy Drew, Detective (1938) **66m.** *½ D: William Clemens. Bonita Granville, John Litel, James Stephenson, Frankie Thomas. Timid entry in girl-detective series, as amateur sleuth tries to help rich woman involved with gangsters.

Nancy Drew—Reporter (1939) **68m.** *½ D: William Clemens. Bonita Granville, John Litel, Frankie Thomas. Granville comes to rescue of another elderly victim of crooked schemes.

Nancy Drew—Trouble Shooter (1939) **69m.** *½ D: William Clemens. Bonita Granville, John Litel, Frankie Thomas, Aldrich Bowker, Renie Riano. Warner Bros. mystery programmer loosely based on famed girls' story heroine, with Granville tracking down crooks.

Nancy Goes to Rio (1950) **C-99m.** **½ D: Robert Z. Leonard. Ann Sothern, Jane Powell, Barry Sullivan, Carmen Miranda, Louis Calhern, Fortunio Bonanova, Hans Conried. Agreeable if artificial MGM musical (remake of Deanna Durbin's IT'S A DATE), with Sothern and Powell as mother and daughter who compete for a plum acting role and, through misunderstanding, the same man.

Nancy Steel Is Missing (1937) **85m.** **½ D: George Marshall. Victor McLaglen, Walter Connolly, Peter Lorre, June Lang, Jane Darwell, John Carradine. Story of ex-con McLaglen passing off Lang as long-ago kidnapped child is pat but smooth-going.

Nanny, The (1965-British) **93m.** *** D: Seth Holt. Bette Davis, Wendy Craig, Jill Bennett, James Villiers, Pamela Franklin, William Dix, Maurice Denham. Twisting, scary plot plus fine direction reap results. Suspects of child murder narrowed to governess Davis and disturbed youngster Dix. Unusual Hammer production, written by Jimmy Sangster. From the novel by Evelyn Piper.

Nanook of the North (1922) **55m.** ***½ D: Robert Flaherty. Pioneer documentary of Eskimos' daily life withstands the test of time quite well, remains as absorbing saga, well filmed. Set the standard for many documentaries to follow. Soundtrack added in 1939. Recently restored to full 65m.▼

Napoleon (1927-French) **235m.** **** D: Abel Gance. Albert Dieudonné, Antonin Artaud, Pierre Batcheff, Armand Bernard, Harry Krimer, Albert Bras, Abel Gance.

[799]

Hard to put into words the impact of this monumental silent epic. Dieudonné mesmerizingly plays the famed emperor; notable sequences include snowball fight, the Reign of Terror, and eye-popping three-screen Polyvision finale. Recut and shortened many times over the years (often by Gance himself), finally painstakingly pieced together by historian Kevin Brownlow and reissued in 1981 with a serviceable music score by Carmine Coppola. Not the kind of film one can really appreciate on TV.▼

Napoleon and Samantha (1972) **C-92m.** **½ D: Bernard McEveety. Michael Douglas, Jodie Foster, Johnny Whitaker, Will Geer, Arch Johnson, Henry Jones. Disney tale of two kids who run away with pet lion is OK family fare.▼

Narrow Corner, The (1933) **71m.** *** D: Alfred E. Green. Douglas Fairbanks, Jr., Patricia Ellis, Ralph Bellamy, Dudley Digges, William V. Mong, Sidney Toler, Henry Kolker, Willie Fung. Fairbanks is on the lam, and winds up on an East Indies island where he finds friendship—and illicit romance. Remarkably adult adaptation of W. Somerset Maugham novel (made in the pre-Production Code era), with only minor flaws. Remade as ISLE OF FURY.

Narrow Margin, The (1952) **70m.** ***½ D: Richard Fleischer. Charles McGraw, Marie Windsor, Jacqueline White, Queenie Leonard. Hard-boiled cop, transporting a gangster's widow against his will to the trial in which she'll testify, must dodge hit-men aboard their train who are trying to silence her. One of the best B's ever made—fast-paced, well-acted, impressively shot in claustrophobic setting.▼

Nashville (1975) **C-159m.** **** D: Robert Altman. Henry Gibson, Karen Black, Ronee Blakley, Keith Carradine, Geraldine Chaplin, Lily Tomlin, Michael Murphy, Barbara Harris, Allen Garfield, Ned Beatty, Barbara Baxley, Shelley Duvall, Keenan Wynn, Scott Glenn, Jeff Goldblum, Gwen Welles, Bert Remsen, Robert Doqui. Altman's brilliant mosaic of American life as seen through 24 characters involved in Nashville political rally. Full of cogent character studies, comic and poignant vignettes, done in seemingly free-form style. Carradine's song "I'm Easy" won an Oscar; Elliott Gould and Julie Christie appear as themselves. Screenplay by Joan Tewkesbury.▼

Nashville Girl (1976) **C-93m.** ** D: Gus Trikonis. Monica Gayle, Glenn Corbett, Roger Davis, Johnny Rodriguez, Jesse White. OK low-budgeter about small-town girl who wants to make it big as a singer and falls in with typical no-good types in the music biz. Country superstar Rodriguez makes his movie debut. Reissued as COUNTRY MUSIC DAUGHTER.▼

Nashville Grab (1981) **C-100m. TVM** D: James L. Conway. Jeff Conaway, Cristina Raines, Gary Sandy, Slim Pickens, Henry Gibson, Dianne Kay, Mari Gorman, Betty Thomas. Madcap chases and bumbling cops dominate this down-home romp about the kidnapping of an egotistical country singer by a couple of female convicts as their passport to freedom. From the folks who brought you the "Classics Illustrated" adventure movies. Below average.

Nasty Boys (1989) **C-100m. TVM** D: Rick Rosenthal. Benjamin Bratt, Don Franklin, Craig Hurley, Jeff Kaahe, James Pax, William Russ, Nia Peeples. An elite, masked, ninja-clad Vegas police undercover narcotics unit (the real-life North Las Vegas Nasty Boys, as they are known) take on local drug lords in this by-the-numbers action pilot for the series. Average.

Nasty Habits (1977) **C-96m.** *½ D: Michael Lindsay-Hogg. Glenda Jackson, Melina Mercouri, Geraldine Page, Sandy Dennis, Anne Jackson, Anne Meara, Susan Penhaligon, Edith Evans, Rip Torn, Eli Wallach, Jerry Stiller. Labored comedy sets allegory of Nixon and Watergate scandal in Philadelphia convent, with Jackson as conniving Mother Superior, Dennis a dead ringer for John Dean. A one-joke film.▼

Nasty Rabbit, The (1964) **C-85m.** ** D: James Landis. Arch Hall, Jr., Micha Terr, Melissa Morgan, John Akana. Weak spoof with serious overtones involving Russian attempt to set loose a disease-infected rabbit in the U. S. Retitled: SPIES A GO GO.▼

Nate and Hayes (1983-U.S.-New Zealand) **C-100m.** ** D: Ferdinand Fairfax. Tommy Lee Jones, Michael O'Keefe, Max Phipps, Jenny Seagrove, Grant Tilly, Peter Rowley. An adventure movie for people who've never seen a *real* adventure movie: watchable enough but pretty pale. Seagoing rogue "Bully" Hayes (Jones) helps a young missionary rescue his fiancee, who's been kidnapped by a scurrilous pirate. Lots of serial-type action, but the leading characters lack charisma.▼

National Lampoon Goes to the Movies (1981) **C-89m.** BOMB D: Henry Jaglom, Bob Giraldi. Peter Riegert, Diane Lane, Candy Clark, Teresa Ganzel, Ann Dusenberry, Robert Culp, Bobby DiCicco, Fred Willard, Joe Spinell, Mary Woronov, Dick Miller, Robby Benson, Richard Widmark, Christopher Lloyd, Elisha Cook, Julie Kavner, Henny Youngman. Incredibly idiotic parody of the movies, presented in three excrutiating parts, each one worse than the next. "Personal growth" films, Harold Robbins/Sidney Sheldon soap operas and police movies are spoofed; a fourth segment, parodying disaster films and featuring Allen Goorwitz (Garfield), Marcia Strassman and Kenneth Mars, was excised. It's easy to see why this never received theatrical release. Also known as NATIONAL LAMPOON'S MOVIE MADNESS.

National Lampoon's Animal House (1978) **C-109m.** ** D: John Landis. John Belushi, Tim Matheson, John Vernon, Verna Bloom, Thomas Hulce, Cesare Danova, Peter Riegert, Stephen Furst, Donald Sutherland, Karen Allen, Sarah Holcomb, Bruce McGill, Martha Smith, Mary Louise Weller, James Daughton, Kevin Bacon, Mark Metcalf, James Widdoes. Spoof of early 1960s college life is only sporadically funny, depends largely on Belushi's mugging as frat-house animal. Not nearly as roisterous or amusing as any issue of the *Lampoon*, but it became a tremendous hit—and spawned a number of truly terrible imitations—as well as a short-lived TV series, *Delta House.*▼

National Lampoon's Christmas Vacation (1989) **C-97m.** *** D: Jeremiah S. Chechik. Chevy Chase, Beverly D'Angelo, Randy Quaid, Diane Ladd, John Randolph, E. G. Marshall, Doris Roberts, Julia Louis-Dreyfuss, Mae Questel, William Hickey, Brian Doyle-Murray, Juliette Lewis, Johnny Galecki, Nicholas Guest, Miriam Flynn. Funny (if typically spotty, sometimes tasteless) saga of the Griswold family's disaster-filled holiday season, with Chase as the terminally stupid head of the household. Sprinkles some believably poignant moments into its slapstick brew with surprising deftness. Third in the VACATION series. Written by John Hughes.▼

National Lampoon's Class Reunion (1982) **C-84m.** BOMB D: Michael Miller. Gerrit Graham, Michael Lerner, Fred McCarren, Miriam Flynn, Stephen Furst, Marya Small, Shelley Smith, Zane Buzby, Anne Ramsey. Spectacularly unfunny comedy about a high-school reunion that's shaken by a mad killer on the prowl. If you went to high school with people like this, no jury in the world would convict you for turning homicidal, either.▼

National Lampoon's European Vacation (1985) **C-94m.** *½ D: Amy Heckerling. Chevy Chase, Beverly D'Angelo, Jason Lively, Dana Hill, Eric Idle, Victor Lanoux, John Astin. Pretty sorry sequel to VACATION, with idiotic Chase and his family stumbling through Europe. Misfire gags right and left, and surprising sexism in a film directed by a woman. Script by John Hughes and Robert Klane. Followed by NATIONAL LAMPOON'S CHRISTMAS VACATION.▼

National Lampoon's Movie Madness SEE: National Lampoon Goes to the Movies

National Lampoon's Vacation (1983) **C-98m.** *** D: Harold Ramis. Chevy Chase, Beverly D'Angelo, Anthony Michael Hall, Imogene Coca, Randy Quaid, Dana Barron, Christie Brinkley, John Candy, Eddie Bracken, Brian Doyle-Murray, Eugene Levy. Enjoyable lightweight comedy about a sappy middle-class family's cross-country trip by car. Given the obvious premise, there are a surprising number of genuine laughs—including the ultimate fate of Aunt Edna. Written by John Hughes. Followed by two sequels.▼

National Velvet (1944) **C-125m.** **** D: Clarence Brown. Mickey Rooney, Elizabeth Taylor, Donald Crisp, Anne Revere, Angela Lansbury, Reginald Owen, Norma Varden, Jackie "Butch" Jenkins, Terry Kilburn. Outstanding family film about a girl who determines to enter her horse in the famed Grand National Steeplechase. Taylor is irresistible, Rooney was never better, and they're surrounded by a perfect supporting cast. Revere won a Best Supporting Actress Oscar as Taylor's mother. Screenplay by Theodore Reeves and Helen Deutsch, from Enid Bagnold's novel. Followed years later by a sequel, INTERNATIONAL VELVET.▼

Native Son (1950) **91m.** **½ D: Pierre Chenal. Richard Wright, Jean Wallace, Gloria Madison, Nicholas Joy, Charles Cane, George Rigaud. Well-meaning but superficial, ultimately disappointing filming of Richard Wright's milestone novel and play, with the author himself starring as Bigger Thomas, frightened black chauffeur who unintentionally kills a white woman. Defeated by its low budget, but still a curio. Remade in 1986.▼

Native Son (1986) **C-112m.** **½ D: Jerrold Freedman. Victor Love, Matt Dillon, Elizabeth McGovern, Geraldine Page, Oprah Winfrey, Akosua Busia, Carroll Baker, John McMartin, Art Evans, John Karlen, Willard E. Pugh, David Rasche. Second, star-studded filming of Richard Wright's landmark 1940 novel. Nineteen-year-old Bigger Thomas (played by newcomer Love) is a poor black in 1930s Chicago whose life takes a tragic turn. Capable cast and serviceable script cannot overcome film's deliberate alterations and softening of some of the novel's key plot points and themes. Still, for those unfamiliar with the book, an OK melodrama. A co-production of PBS's *American Playhouse.*▼

Nativity, The (1978) **C-100m.** TVM D: Bernard L. Kowalski. Madeleine Stowe, John Shea, Jane Wyatt, Paul Stewart, Audrey Totter, Leo McKern. Reverent Biblical retelling of the Joseph and Mary story hampered by pedestrian performances by the two leads and so-so direction by Kowalski. Average.▼

Natural, The (1984) **C-134m.** **½ D: Barry Levinson. Robert Redford, Robert Duvall, Glenn Close, Kim Basinger, Wilford Brimley, Richard Farnsworth, Barbara Hershey, Robert Prosky, Darren McGavin, Joe Don Baker. Serpentine saga of a young man with a gift for baseball, whose life takes more than a few surprising turns. Freely adapted from Bernard Malamud's offbeat novel, with heavy doses of sentiment and larger-than-life imagery (courtesy of cinematographer Caleb Deschanel). Some effective moments, with a fine cast, but too long and inconsistent. Best of all: Randy Newman's music score.▼

Natural Enemies (1979) **C-100m.** *½ D: Jeff Kanew. Hal Holbrook, Louise Fletcher, Peter Armstrong, Beth Berridge, Steve Austin, Jose Ferrer, Viveca Lindfors. Successful publisher Holbrook wakes up one day with the urge to kill his family. Cold, uninvolving, and (needless to say) strange little film, written, directed and edited by Kanew.▼

Nature's Mistakes SEE: **Freaks**▼

Naughty Arlette SEE: **Romantic Age, The**

Naughty But Nice (1939) **90m.** **½ D: Ray Enright. Dick Powell, Ann Sheridan, Gale Page, Helen Broderick, Ronald Reagan, Allen Jenkins, ZaSu Pitts, Jerry Colonna. Stuffy music professor Powell unwittingly writes popular song hit, leading to various complications and gradual personality change. Silly but fun; songs adapted from Wagner, Liszt, Mozart, Bach.

Naughty Girl SEE: **Mam'zelle Pigalle**▼

Naughty Marietta (1935) **106m.** **½ D: W. S. Van Dyke II. Jeanette MacDonald, Nelson Eddy, Frank Morgan, Elsa Lanchester, Douglass Dumbrille, Cecilia Parker. First teaming of Eddy and MacDonald has her a French princess running off to America, falling in love with Indian scout Eddy. Agreeable operetta with Victor Herbert score, including "The Italian Street Song," "Tramp, Tramp, Tramp," and "Ah, Sweet Mystery of Life."▼

Naughty Nineties, The (1945) **76m.** ** D: Jean Yarbrough. Bud Abbott, Lou Costello, Alan Curtis, Rita Johnson, Henry Travers, Lois Collier, Joe Sawyer, Joe Kirk. Ordinary A&C comedy of riverboat gamblers, sparked by duo's verbal exchanges (including "Who's on First?") and slapstick finale.▼

Naughty Wives (1974-British) **C-84m.** BOMB D: Wolf Rilla. Brendan Price, Graham Stark, Chic Murray, Felicity Devonshire, Sue Longhurst. Silly sex farce about Price's misadventures as a door-to-door salesman. Quite a comedown for Rilla, who made the classic VILLAGE OF THE DAMNED. Opens with a highlights-of-the-action montage edited for U.S. release by Jonathan Demme.▼

Navajo Joe (1966-Italian-Spanish) **C-89m.** *½ D: Sergio Corbucci. Burt Reynolds, Aldo Sanbrell, Tanya Lopert, Fernando Rey. Sole survivor of massacre swears revenge on his enemies in this tepid

Western, of interest only for Reynolds' presence.▼

Navigator, The: A Medieval Odyssey (1988-New Zealand) **C/B&W-92m.** *** D: Vincent Ward. Hamish McFarlane, Bruce Lyons, Chris Haywood, Marshall Napier, Noel Appleby, Paul Livingston, Sarah Pierse. Engrossing, very imaginative tale of psychic boy in tiny medieval English village who, to protect villagers from the plague, leads a tunneling expedition—which emerges in a modern city in 1988. Directed and written with great clarity, the film has much of the feel of a genuine medieval fable. Beautifully produced on a low budget.▼

Navy Blue and Gold (1937) **94m.** **½ D: Sam Wood. Robert Young, James Stewart, Florence Rice, Billie Burke, Lionel Barrymore, Tom Brown, Samuel S. Hinds, Paul Kelly. Hackneyed but entertaining saga of three pals (one rich and innocent, one a cynic, and one mysterious "with a past") going to Annapolis. Predictable football game climax is fun. That's Dennis Morgan (billed under his real name, Stanley Morner) dancing with Billie Burke.

Navy Blues (1941) **108m.** *** D: Lloyd Bacon. Ann Sheridan, Jack Oakie, Martha Raye, Jack Haley, Herbert Anderson, Jack Carson. Brassy musical with fine cast (including young Jackie Gleason), with Raye stealing most of the film.

Navy Comes Through, The (1942) **82m.** ** D: A. Edward Sutherland. Pat O'Brien, George Murphy, Jane Wyatt, Jackie Cooper, Carl Esmond, Max Baer, Desi Arnaz. RKO programmer dealing with merchant marines in action during WW2.

Navy SEALS (1990) **C-113m.** ** D: Lewis Teague. Charlie Sheen, Michael Biehn, Joanne Whalley-Kilmer, Rick Rossovich, Cyril O'Reilly, Bill Paxton, Dennis Haysbert, Paul Sanchez. Middle Eastern terrorists are mere putty in the hands of the U.S. Navy's elite commando unit (SEa, Air, Land); "inspired" by the actual team formed under J.F.K.'s administration. G.I. Joe-level action is the name of the game here. Sheen's character operates at the maturity level of Dennis the Menace. Climactic invasion of a besieged Beirut is exciting, but how about putting off the sequel until J.F.K., Jr.'s oath of office?

Navy vs. the Night Monsters, The (1966) **C-90m.** BOMB D: Michael Hoey. Mamie Van Doren, Anthony Eisley, Pamela Mason, Bill Gray, Bobby Van, Walter Sande, Edward Faulkner, Phillip Terry. 1) Look at the title. 2) Examine the cast. 3) Be aware that the plot involves omniverous trees. 4) Don't say you weren't warned.

Navy Wife (1956) **83m.** *½ D: Edward Bernds. Joan Bennett, Gary Merrill, Shirley Yamaguchi, Maurice Manson, Judy Nugent. Trivial tale of Japanese women revolting to obtain equal treatment from their men as they observe American military and their wives.

Nazarin (1961-Spanish) **92m.** **½ D: Luis Buñuel. Francisco Rabal, Rita Macedo, Marga Lopez Tarso, Ofelia Guilmain. Relentlessly grim drama of saintly priest Rabal and hypocritical peasants who shun him. Filmed in Mexico.▼

Nazi Agent (1942) **83m.** ** D: Jules Dassin. Conrad Veidt, Anne Ayars, Dorothy Tree, Frank Reicher, Sidney Blackmer, Martin Kosleck, Marc Lawrence, William Tannen. Veidt plays twin brothers: one a peaceful American; the other a Nazi official. When the latter blackmails the former into being a spy, the good Veidt kills the bad Veidt and impersonates him. Slow-moving, rather arid tale that could have been much better. Dassin's first feature; good photography by Harry Stradling.

Nazi Hunter: The Beate Klarsfeld Story (1986) **C-100m. TVM** D: Michael Lindsay-Hogg. Farrah Fawcett, Tom Conti, Geraldine Page, Catherine Allegret. Fawcett does a creditable job as real-life German housewife whose unrelenting campaign to bring Nazi war criminals to justice helped snare Klaus Barbie. Conti is a quiet tower of strength as her dedicated Jewish husband, and Page is standout as a concentration camp survivor. Frederic Hunter's no-frills script is another plus. Above average.

Neanderthal Man, The (1953) **78m.** *½ D: E. A. Dupont. Robert Shayne, Richard Crane, Robert Long, Doris Merrick. Shayne turns a tiger into a sabertooth and himself into a murderous caveman in this below-par 50s entry. Colorless and cheap; director Du Pont was a long way from his German classic VARIETY.

Near Dark (1987) **C-95m.** **½ D: Kathryn Bigelow. Adrian Pasdar, Jenny Wright, Lance Henriksen, Bill Paxton, Jenette Goldstein, Tim Thomerson. Better-than-average vampire yarn actually plays more like a werewolf film. Cowboy Pasdar is literally bitten by Wright and joins a band of hillbilly bloodsuckers who roam the West in a van. Stylishly directed horror film reunites three cast members from ALIENS: Henriksen, Paxton and Goldstein.▼

Nearly a Nasty Accident (1962-British) **86m.** ** D: Don Chaffey. Jimmy Edwards, Kenneth Connor, Shirley Eaton, Richard Wattis, Ronnie Stevens, Jon Pertwee, Eric Barker. Minor comedy of mechanic who innocently puts the touch of disaster on everyone.

'Neath Brooklyn Bridge (1942) **61m.** D: Wallace Fox. Leo Gorcey, Huntz Hall, Bobby Jordan, Gabriel Dell, Noah Beery, Jr., Sunshine Sammy Morrison, Jack Mulhall, Dave O'Brien, Anne Gillis. SEE: Bowery Boys series.

Nebraskan, The (1953) **C-68m.** ** D: Fred F. Sears. Phil Carey, Roberta Haynes, Wallace Ford, Richard Webb, Lee Van Cleef, Jay Silverheels. Tame Western of white man justice preventing Indian uprising.

Necessity (1988) **C-100m. TVM** D: Michael Miller. Loni Anderson, John Heard, James Naughton, Harris Laskawy. High fashion model discovers hubby to be a Mafia biggie, flees his armed compound to create a new identity for herself, and then attempts to snatch the baby she left behind. Adapted from Brian Garfield's novel, which reads much better than it plays. Average.

Necromancy (1972) **C-83m.** *½ D: Bert I. Gordon. Orson Welles, Pamela Franklin, Michael Ontkean, Lee Purcell, Harvey Jason. High priest Welles tries to manipulate Franklin into becoming a witch. Mindless, poorly crafted thriller was originally released without its nude coven scenes, if anybody cares. Some prints run 75m. Also known as THE WITCHING.▼

Ned Kelly (1970-British) **C-100m.** **½ D: Tony Richardson. Mick Jagger, Clarissa Kaye, Mark McManus, Frank Thring. Rambling film of Australian cowboy. Worth watching if you like Jagger, otherwise, stay away. Retitled NED KELLY, OUTLAW.

Negatives (1968-British) **C-90m.** ** D: Peter Medak. Peter McEnery, Diane Cilento, Glenda Jackson, Maurice Denham, Steven Lewis, Norman Rossington. Strange movie about unmarried couple who dress up like famed Dr. Crippen and his wife for kicks; he later switches his characterization to Baron von Richtofen. Jackson is good, but direction is too mannered.▼

Neighborhood, The (1982) **C-78m. TVM** D: Lee H. Katzin. Christine Belford, Ron Masak, Ben Masters, Howard Rollins, Jr., Mary Joan Negro, Carol Potter, Michael Gross, Sheryl Lee Ralph, Thomas Quinn, Olympia Dukakis. Several black families move into a white working-class urban area and stir up the residents in this unsold pilot based on a concept by syndicated columnist Jimmy Breslin. Average.

Neighbors (1981) **C-94m.** BOMB D: John G. Avildsen. John Belushi, Dan Aykroyd, Cathy Moriarty, Kathryn Walker, Lauren-Marie Taylor, Tim Kazurinsky. Appallingly unfunny and tiresome "comedy" based on Thomas Berger's novel about a middle-class milquetoast whose suburban existence is shaken by the arrival of bizarre and destructive neighbors. Screenplay credited to Larry Gelbart. Pointless; sadly, Belushi's last film.▼

Nelson Affair, The (1973-British) **C-118m.** **½ D: James Cellan Jones. Glenda Jackson, Peter Finch, Michael Jayston, Anthony Quayle, Margaret Leighton, Dominic Guard, Nigel Stock, Barbara Leigh-Hunt. Handsome retelling of Lord Nelson-Lady Hamilton affair, making the "Lady" a slut; interesting but claustrophobic—even climactic sea battle was shot indoors! British title: A BEQUEST TO THE NATION.

Neon Ceiling, The (1970) **C-100m. TVM** D: Frank R. Pierson. Lee Grant, Gig Young, Denise Nickerson, Herb Edelman, William Smithers. Woman and daughter, finding refuge from bad marriage in desert cafegas station, meet up with stranger who eventually becomes part of new start. Good cast deserves far better material. Average.

Neptune Disaster, The SEE: **Neptune Factor, The▼**

Neptune Factor, The (1973-Canadian) **C-98m. **** D: Daniel Petrie. Ben Gazzara, Yvette Mimieux, Walter Pidgeon, Ernest Borgnine. Deep-sea-diving sub races to save three men trapped by an earthquake in ocean floor laboratory. Soggy underwater yarn lifts its plot almost in toto from MAROONED. Also known as AN UNDERWATER ODYSSEY and THE NEPTUNE DISASTER.▼

Neptune's Daughter (1949) **C-93m. **** D: Edward Buzzell. Esther Williams, Red Skelton, Keenan Wynn, Betty Garrett, Ricardo Montalban, Mel Blanc. Musical romance with Esther a bathing-suit designer, Skelton a no-account mistaken for polo star by Garrett. Bubbly fun, with Academy Award-winning song: "Baby It's Cold Outside."▼

Nero Wolfe (1977) **C-97m. TVM** D: Frank D. Gilroy. Thayer David, Anne Baxter, Tom Mason, Brooke Adams, John Randolph, Biff McGuire, David Hurst, John Hoyt. Series pilot built on fine Gilroy adaptation of Rex Stout's *The Doorbell Rang.* David is ideally cast as the corpulent armchair sleuth, but his untimely death delayed a series for four years until a suitable replacement (William Conrad) could be found. Well worth watching, especially for mystery fans. Above average.

Nest, The (1980-Spanish) **C-109m. **** D: Jaime De Arminan. Hector Alterio, Ana Torrent, Luis Politti, Agustin Gonzalez, Patricia Adriani. Diverting but predictable drama detailing the relationship between wealthy, aging widower Alterio and alienated 13-year-old Torrent. Helped immeasurably by Arminan's precise script and direction.▼

Nest, The (1988) **C-88m. **** D: Terence H. Winkless. Robert Lansing, Lisa Langlois, Franc Luz, Terri Treas, Stephen Davies, Diana Bellamy, Nancy Morgan. Trifling, ever so familiar chronicle of a failed scientific experiment resulting in the creation of large, hungry cockroaches. Neither the best nor the worst of its type.▼

Nesting, The (1981) **C-104m. **** D: Armand Weston. Robin Groves, Christopher Loomis, Michael David Lally, John Carradine, Gloria Grahame, Bill Rowley. Gothic novelist moves into eerie Victorian man-

sion to which she's been mysteriously drawn. Starts off interestingly but wanders and drags on, to unsatisfying finish. ▼

Network (1976) **C-121m. **** D: Sidney Lumet. William Holden, Faye Dunaway, Peter Finch, Robert Duvall, Ned Beatty, Beatrice Straight, Wesley Addy, William Prince, Marlene Warfield. Paddy Chayefsky's outrageous satire on television looks less and less like fantasy as the years pass; uninhibited tale chronicles fourth-place network that will air anything for a rating, including a patently insane, profanity-shouting "mad prophet of the airwaves" (Finch). Entire cast explodes, particularly Dunaway as ruthless programmer, Holden as conscientious newsman, Duvall as shark-like v.p., and Beatty as evangelistical board chairman. Well-deserved Oscars went to Finch (posthumously), Dunaway, Straight, and Chayefsky.▼

Nevada (1944) **62m. **** D: Edward Killy. Robert Mitchum, Anne Jeffreys, Guinn "Big Boy" Williams, Nancy Gates, Harry Woods. Standard Zane Grey Western of good-guy Mitchum mopping up gang of outlaws. Filmed before in 1935.

Nevadan, The (1950) **C-81m. **** D: Gordon Douglas. Randolph Scott, Dorothy Malone, Forrest Tucker, George Macready, Jock Mahoney. Stern Scott is the lawman who tracks down crooks, still finding time to court Malone. Shown on TV in b&w.

Nevada Smith (1966) **C-135m. *** D: Henry Hathaway. Steve McQueen, Karl Malden, Brian Keith, Arthur Kennedy, Suzanne Pleshette, Raf Vallone, Pat Hingle, Howard da Silva, Martin Landau. Good Western story. Smith swears revenge for senseless murder of his parents at the hands of outlaw gang. Based on character from THE CARPETBAGGERS. Remade as a TVM in 1975.▼

Nevada Smith (1975) **C-78m. TVM** D: Gordon Douglas. Cliff Potts, Lorne Greene, Adam West, Warren Vanders, Jorge Luke, Jerry Gatlin. Western drama inspired by Steve McQueen movie and characters from Harold Robbins' THE CARPETBAGGERS, with half-breed (Potts) joining his former mentor (Greene) to escort a shipment of explosives across Utah Territory. Standard fare. Average.

Never a Dull Moment (1943) **60m. **½ D: Edward Lilley. Ritz Brothers, Frances Langford, Stuart Crawford, Elisabeth Risdon, Mary Beth Hughes, George Zucco, Jack LaRue, Franklin Pangborn. Pretty good comedy with the Ritzes getting involved with gang of hoods; fast-paced, with LaRue enjoyable as semicomic heavy.

Never a Dull Moment (1950) **89m. **½ D: George Marshall. Irene Dunne, Fred MacMurray, William Demarest, Natalie Wood, Andy Devine, Ann Doran, Gigi

Perreau. Middling froth of chic Dunne marrying rancher MacMurray, adjusting to country life and his two daughters.

Never a Dull Moment (1968) **C-100m.** ** D: Jerry Paris. Dick Van Dyke, Edward G. Robinson, Dorothy Provine, Henry Silva, Joanna Moore, Tony Bill. Tired Disney comedy belies title, as TV performer Van Dyke gets involved with gangsters; even Robinson's performance is lifeless.▼

Never Cry Wolf (1983) **C-105m.** *** D: Carroll Ballard. Charles Martin Smith, Brian Dennehy, Zachary Ittimangnaq, Samson Jorah. Smith plays real-life Canadian author Farley Mowat who braved the Arctic, alone, to study behavior of wolves . . . and wound up learning as much about himself. Uneven, but filled with striking moments and passages, plus a wonderful performance by Smith. There's also the irony of a Walt Disney Production in which the leading character takes to eating mice!▼

NeverEnding Story, The (1984-West German-British) **C-92m.** *** D: Wolfgang Petersen. Noah Hathaway, Barrett Oliver, Tami Stronach, Moses Gunn, Patricia Hayes, Sydney Bromley, Gerald Mac-Rancy, voice of Alan Oppenheimer. Petersen's first English-language film is magical, timeless fantasy built around young Oliver visualizing what he's reading from a mystical book: boy warrior Hathaway is the only hope of saving the empire of Fantasia from being swallowed up by The Nothing. Amazing, unique effects, characters, and visual design (and a not-so-subtle message that Reading Is Good).▼

Never Fear (1950) **82m.** ** D: Ida Lupino. Sally Forrest, Keefe Brasselle, Hugh O'Brian, Eve Miller, Larry Dobkin. Forrest overcomes polio and its disastrous effect on her dancing career. Earnest low-budget production.

Never Give a Inch SEE: **Sometimes a Great Notion**▼

Never Give a Sucker an Even Break (1941) **71m.** ***½ D: Edward Cline. W. C. Fields, Gloria Jean, Leon Errol, Susan Miller, Franklin Pangborn, Margaret Dumont. Completely insane comedy with Fields (in his last starring film) playing himself; no coherent plot, many loose ends, and a lot of funny scenes. Dumont plays "Mrs. Hemoglobin." Climactic chase is a classic, reused by Abbott and Costello in IN SOCIETY. Story by "Otis Criblecoblis."▼

Never Let Go (1963-British) **90m.** ** D: John Guillermin. Richard Todd, Peter Sellers, Elizabeth Sellars, Carol White, Mervyn Johns. Sellers gives heavy-handed performance as ruthless and sadistic racketeer in weak story about car thievery. Billed as his first dramatic role, it was a poor choice.▼

Never Let Me Go (1953) **94m.** **½ D: Delmer Daves. Clark Gable, Gene Tierney, Bernard Miles, Richard Haydn, Kenneth More, Belita, Theodore Bikel. Unconvincing yet smooth account of Gable trying to smuggle ballerina-wife Tierney out of Russia.

Never Love a Stranger (1958) **91m.** ** D: Robert Stevens. John Drew Barrymore, Lita Milan, Peg Murray, Robert Bray, Steve McQueen. Chronicle of a racketeer, from Harold Robbins' novel; predictable all the way.▼

Never Never Land (1980-British) **C-86m.** *** D: Paul Annett. Petula Clark, Cathleen Nesbitt, John Castle, Anne Seymour, Evelyn Laye, Roland Culver, Heather Miller. Nice little film about lonely child (Miller), her fascination with Peter Pan and connection with elderly Nesbitt. Best for the kids.

Never on Sunday (1960-Greek) **91m.** ***½ D: Jules Dassin. Melina Mercouri, Jules Dassin, Georges Foundas, Titos Vandis, Mitsos Liguisos, Despo Diamantidou. Charming idyll of intellectual boob coming to Greece, trying to make earthy prostitute Mercouri cultured. Grand entertainment, with Oscar-winning title song by Manos Hadjidakis. Later a Broadway musical, *Illya Darling*.▼

Never Put It in Writing (1964) **93m.** *½ D: Andrew Stone. Pat Boone, Milo O'Shea, Fidelma Murphy, Reginald Beckwith, Harry Brogan. Grade-B comedy, set in London, with Pat trying to retrieve a letter that will get him fired from his job if the boss sees it. Not much.

Never Say Die (1939) **80m.** *** D: Elliott Nugent. Martha Raye, Bob Hope, Andy Devine, Gale Sondergaard, Sig Ruman, Alan Mowbray, Monty Woolley. Bob marries Martha at Swiss spa of Bad Gaswasser, thinking he has only two weeks to live. Good cast in lively, trivial romp. Cowritten by Preston Sturges.

Never Say Goodbye (1946) **97m.** **½ D: James V. Kern. Errol Flynn, Eleanor Parker, Lucile Watson, S. Z. Sakall, Hattie McDaniel, Forrest Tucker, Donald Woods. Flynn tries hard in routine comedy of husband rewinning his divorce-bound wife.

Never Say Goodbye (1956) **C-96m.** **½ D: Jerry Hopper. Rock Hudson, Cornell Borchers, George Sanders, Ray Collins, David Janssen, Shelley Fabares. Spotty tear-jerker of Hudson and Borchers, long separated, discovering one another again and creating fit home for their child. Remake of THIS LOVE OF OURS. Clint Eastwood is cast as Rock's lab assistant.

Never Say Never Again (1983) **C-137m.** **½ D: Irvin Kershner. Sean Connery, Klaus Maria Brandauer, Max von Sydow, Barbara Carrera, Kim Basinger, Bernie Casey, Alec McCowen, Edward Fox.

Connery's stylish performance and self-deprecating humor make his return performance as James Bond (after twelve years) a real treat—but the film, a remake of THUNDERBALL, is uneven and overlong. Brandauer is a smooth villain, and Carrera a memorably sexy villainess, Fatima Blush.▼

Never So Few (1959) **C-124m.** **½ D: John Sturges. Frank Sinatra, Gina Lollobrigida, Peter Lawford, Steve McQueen, Richard Johnson, Paul Henreid, Brian Donlevy, Dean Jones, Charles Bronson. WW2 action and romance tale filled with salty performances which make one forget the clichés and improbabilities.▼

Never Steal Anything Small (1959) **C-94m.** **½ D: Charles Lederer. James Cagney, Shirley Jones, Roger Smith, Cara Williams, Nehemiah Persoff, Royal Dano, Horace McMahon. Odd musical comedy-drama, with Cagney a waterfront union racketeer who'll do anything to win union election. From Maxwell Anderson-Rouben Mamoulian play *The Devil's Hornpipe*.▼

Never Steal Anything Wet SEE: **Catalina Caper**

Never the Twain Shall Meet (1931) **79m.** *½ D: W. S. Van Dyke. Leslie Howard, Conchita Montenegro, C. Aubrey Smith, Karen Morley, Mitchell Lewis, Clyde Cook, Hale Hamilton. Rich, proper Howard loves rich, proper Morley . . . and then he becomes the guardian of beautiful, uninhibited Montenegro. Wooden soaper of clashing cultures.

Never to Love SEE: **Bill of Divorcement, A** (1940)

Never Too Late (1965) **C-105m.** **½ D: Bud Yorkin. Paul Ford, Connie Stevens, Maureen O'Sullivan, Jim Hutton, Jane Wyatt, Henry Jones, Lloyd Nolan. Occasionally amusing film version of hit Broadway play about impending parenthood of middle-agers Ford and O'Sullivan. Older performers are funny; Hutton, Stevens, script, and direction are not.

Never Too Young To Die (1986) **C-92m.** *½ D: Gil Bettman. John Stamos, Vanity, Gene Simmons, George Lazenby, Peter Kwong, Ed Brock, John Anderson, Robert Englund. Stamos, son of a spy, takes up with Vanity, one of his father's associates, to find out who murdered his dad. Pretty awful, though Simmons scores a few points for outrageousness in his portrayal of a power-crazed hermaphrodite.▼

Never Trust a Gambler (1951) **79m.** *½ D: Ralph Murphy. Dane Clark, Cathy O'Donnell, Tom Drake, Jeff Corey, Myrna Dell. Hackneyed account of man on the run, seeking shelter from ex-wife who has fallen in love with detective seeking him.

Never Wave at a WAC (1952) **87m.** **½ D: Norman Z. McLeod. Rosalind Russell, Marie Wilson, Paul Douglas, Arleen Whelan, Hillary Brooke, Louise Beavers, Frieda Inescort. Expanded from a TV play, this farce involves socialite Russell joining the WACs, forced to buckle down to hard work; Wilson as dumb comrade-at-arms is most diverting.

New Adventures of Heidi, The (1978) **C-100m. TVM** D: Ralph Senensky. Katy Kurtzman, Burl Ives, John Gavin, Marlyn Mason, Sean Marshall. The Johanna Spyri perennial given an unfortunate contemporary setting (The Big Apple!) and an unmemorable musicalization. Heidi go home. Average.

New Adventures of Pippi Longstocking, The (1988) **C-100m.** ** D: Ken Annakin. Tami Erin, Eileen Brennan, Dennis Dugan, Dianne Hull, George DiCenzo, John Schuck, Dick Van Patten. Dreary Americanization of Astrid Lindgren's popular books about a plucky young girl—here, transformed into a tiresome troublemaker. May entertain undiscriminating children; adults should avoid at all costs.▼

New Adventures of Tarzan, The (1935) **75m.** D: Edward Kull. Herman Brix (Bruce Bennett), Ula Holt, Don Castello, Frank Baker, Lewis Sargent, Dale Walsh. Feature version of serial. Retitled TARZAN'S NEW ADVENTURE. SEE: **Tarzan** series.▼

New Centurions, The (1972) **C-103m.** *** D: Richard Fleischer. George C. Scott, Stacy Keach, Jane Alexander, Rosalind Cash, Scott Wilson, Erik Estrada, Clifton James, Isabel Sanford, James B. Sikking, Ed Lauter, William Atherton, Roger E. Mosley. Fine, episodic adaptation by Stirling Silliphant of Joseph Wambaugh novel of rookie cops on modern-day L.A. police force, ultimately pessimistic in outlook. Great casting, performances; good storytelling.▼

New Daughters of Joshua Cabe, The (1976) **C-78m. TVM** D: Bruce Bilson. John McIntire, Jeanette Nolan, Liberty Williams, Renne Jarrett, Lezlie Dalton, Jack Elam, John Dehner, Geoffrey Lewis. Third time around for rascally Joshua with the three gals he's passed off as his daughters coming to his rescue after he's framed for murder. Cabe and the girls have been different in all three films, which is more than can be said of the plot. Below average.

New Faces (1954) **C-99m.** **½ D: Harry Horner. Ronny Graham, Robert Clary, Eartha Kitt, Alice Ghostley, Paul Lynde, Carol Lawrence. Vaudeville hodgepodge of variety numbers, based on Leonard Sillman's popular Broadway revue, which was springboard for much new talent. One of the writers was Mel Brooks.▼

New Faces of 1937 (1937) **100m.** ** D: Leigh Jason. Joe Penner, Milton Berle, Parkyakarkus, Harriet Hilliard (Nelson), Jerome Cowan. Silly movie with same initial premise as THE PRODUCERS, as Berle is patsy left as owner of unwatchable Broadway show. Comic highlight is Berle's stockbroker skit with Richard Lane; Ann Miller featured in finale as one of the New Faces.

New Interns, The (1964) 123m. **½ D: John Rich. Michael Callan, Dean Jones, Telly Savalas, Inger Stevens, George Segal, Greg Morris, Stefanie Powers, Lee Patrick, Barbara Eden. Follow-up to THE INTERNS contains unusual hospital soap opera with better than average cast and a nifty party sequence.

New Invisible Man, The (1957-Mexican) 89m. ** D: Alfredo Crevena. Arturo de Cordova, Ana Luisa Peluffo, Augusto Benedico, Raul Meraz. OK Mexican update of the classic H. G. Wells story. Also known as 'H. G. WELLS' NEW INVISIBLE MAN.▼

New Kids, The (1985) C-90m. ** D: Sean Cunningham. Shannon Presby, Lori Loughlin, James Spader, John Philbin, Eric Stoltz. Unexciting thriller about a brother and sister (Presby, Loughlin), two nice kids who are harassed by meanie Spader and his cronies. There's no gratuitous gore, but there are also no real chills.▼

New Kind of Love, A (1963) C-110m. **½ D: Melville Shavelson. Paul Newman, Joanne Woodward, Thelma Ritter, Eva Gabor, Maurice Chevalier, George Tobias. Newman as reporter and Woodward as fashion buyer on the loose in Paris fall in love; lacks oomph to make fluff worthwhile.

New Land, The (1972-Swedish) C-161m. *** ½ D: Jan Troell. Max von Sydow, Liv Ullmann, Eddie Axberg, Hans Alfredson, Monica Zetterlund, Per Oscarsson. Sequel to THE EMIGRANTS follows same characters as they settle in Minnesota, up to the ends of their lives. Fine epic contains superior performances, photography, many stirring scenes. A real winner; both films have been edited together for TV, dubbed in English, and presented as THE EMIGRANT SAGA.

New Leaf, A (1971) C-102m. **½ D: Elaine May. Walter Matthau, Elaine May, Jack Weston, George Rose, William Redfield, James Coco. Amusing comedy of destitute playboy Matthau planning to marry and murder klutzy May in order to inherit her fortune. Many funny moments, highlighted by May's performance, but topped by curious resolution, lack of strong overall impact. Director/writer/star May disavowed finished film, which was reedited by others.▼

New Life, A (1979) SEE: **Suicide's Wife, The**

New Life, A (1988) C-104m. **½ D: Alan Alda. Alan Alda, Ann-Margret, Hal Linden, Veronica Hamel, John Shea, Mary Kay Place, Beatrice Alda. Pleasant but pat comedy about a middle-aged couple's trials and tribulations after divorcing. Alda (sporting a beard and curly hair) also wrote the script.▼

Newman's Law (1974) C-98m. *½ D: Richard Heffron. George Peppard, Roger Robinson, Eugene Roche, Gordon Pinsent, Louis Zorich, Abe Vigoda. Honest cop Peppard, bounced from the force for alleged corruption, investigates the case on his own. Dreary and predictable.▼

New Maverick, The (1978) C-100m. TVM D: Hy Averback. Charles Frank, Susan Blanchard, James Garner, Jack Kelly, Susan Sullivan, Eugene Roche, George Loros. Stars of well-remembered *Maverick* show (Garner and Kelly) appear in this new series pilot to introduce their equally crafty Harvard-dropout nephew (Frank), who pursues his own freewheeling Western adventures. Good fun. Above average.

New Mexico (1951) C-76m. **½ D: Irving Reis. Lew Ayres, Marilyn Maxwell, Robert Hutton, Andy Devine, Raymond Burr. Moderately exciting Western of cavalry vs. Indians.

New Moon (1940) 105m. **½ D: Robert Z. Leonard. Jeanette MacDonald, Nelson Eddy, Mary Boland, George Zucco, H. B. Warner, Grant Mitchell, Stanley Fields. Nelson and Jeanette in old Louisiana, falling in love, singing "One Kiss," "Softly as in a Morning Sunrise," "Lover Come Back to Me," "Stout-Hearted Men." Oscar Hammerstein-Sigmund Romberg score sung before in 1930 filming with Lawrence Tibbett and Grace Moore.▼

New, Original Wonder Woman, The (1975) C-78m. TVM D: Leonard Horn. Lynda Carter, Lyle Waggoner, John Randolph, Red Buttons, Stella Stevens, Cloris Leachman, Eric Braeden, Henry Gibson, Fannie Flagg. The 1940s comic book heroine performs proverbial incredible exploits anew. Later a TV series. Silly but tolerable. Average.

New Orleans (1947) 89m. **½ D: Arthur Lubin. Arturo de Cordova, Dorothy Patrick, Billie Holiday, Louis Armstrong, Woody Herman & Band, Meade Lux Lewis, other jazz stars. Hackneyed fictionalization of the birth of jazz, spanning 40 years, but there's plenty of good music. Holiday (cast as a maid!) does "Do You Know What it Means to Miss New Orleans" with Armstrong and all-star band, and it's sublime. Shelley Winters appears briefly as de Cordova's secretary.

New Orleans After Dark (1958) 69m. *½ D: John Sledge. Stacy Harris, Louis Sirgo, Ellen Moore, Tommy Pelle. Programmer about capture of dope smugglers.

New Orleans Uncensored (1955) 76m.

½ D: William Castle. Arthur Franz, Beverly Garland, Helene Stanton, Michael Ansara. Weak exposé account of racketeer-busting in Louisiana, with competent cast trying to overcome script.

News at Eleven (1986) **C-100m. TVM** D: Mike Robe. Martin Sheen, Peter Riegert, Barbara Babcock, Sheree J. Wilson, Sydney Penny, David S. Sheiner, Christopher Allport. Local TV news anchorman, on his way down from the big time, clashes with his ambitious young boss and wrestles with his own integrity after stumbling across a story involving a high school coed and the teacher she accuses of rape. Average.

Newsfront (1978-Australian) **C-110m.** *** D: Phillip Noyce. Bill Hunter, Gerard Kennedy, Angela Punch, Wendy Hughes, Chris Haywood, John Ewart, Bryan Brown. Enjoyable, well-crafted tale of newsreel filmmakers—centering on dedicated cameraman Hunter—is a valentine to the movie newsreel industry. Among highlights are actual late 1940s and 1950s newsreel footage, nicely integrated into scenario. ▼

News Hounds (1947) **68m.** D: William Beaudine. Leo Gorcey, Huntz Hall, Bobby Jordan, Christine McIntyre, Gabriel Dell, Billy Benedict. SEE: **Bowery Boys** series.

Newspaper Game, The SEE: **Kingston**

New Year's Evil (1981) **C-90m.** BOMB D: Emmett Alston. Roz Kelly, Kip Niven, Chris Wallace, Grant Cramer, Louisa Moritz. Atrocious thriller revolving around disc jockey Kelly and killer Niven. Another HALLOWEEN ripoff.▼

New York Confidential (1955) **87m.** **½ D: Russell Rouse. Broderick Crawford, Richard Conte, Marilyn Maxwell, Anne Bancroft, J. Carrol Naish. Energetic cast perks up formula exposé of racketeer narrative.

New York, New York (1977) **C-164m.** **½ D: Martin Scorsese. Robert De Niro, Liza Minnelli, Lionel Stander, Georgie Auld, Mary Kay Place, George Memmoli, Barry Primus, Dick Miller, Diahnne Abbott. Elaborate but off-putting musical drama loosely based on THE MAN I LOVE; saxophonist De Niro and vocalist Minnelli love and fight with each other right through the Big Band era. Some people consider this film extraordinary, but we're not among them; kudos, though, to production designer Boris Leven, music arranger Ralph Burns, and the Kander-Ebb title song. Initially released at 153m., then cut to 137m., and finally reissued in 1981 at current length with splashy "Happy Endings" number (featuring Larry Kert) added.▼

New York Stories (1989) **C-123m.** **½ D: Martin Scorsese, Francis Coppola, Woody Allen. Nick Nolte, Rosanna Arquette, Steve Buscemi, Peter Gabriel, Deborah Harry, Heather McComb, Talia Shire, Giancarlo Giannini, Don Novello, Chris Elliott, Carole Bouquet, Woody Allen, Mia Farrow, Mae Questel, Julie Kavner, Mayor Edward I. Koch. Three-part anthology film: Scorsese's is an obvious, heavy-handed tale of a macho artist (Nolte) and his assistant/lover (Arquette) who wants to fly the coop. Coppola's is a cute but pointless variation on the old children's book *Eloise* about a little rich girl who lives in a N.Y.C. hotel while her parents globetrot. Finally, we get to the good stuff with Allen's comedy segment, in which a man is literally haunted by his nagging mother; Woody is in great form on-camera as the hapless victim, and Questel is a howl as his mom. All told, a waste of time until the concluding sequence.▼

New York Town (1941) **76m.** **½ D: Charles Vidor. Fred MacMurray, Mary Martin, Robert Preston, Akim Tamiroff, Lynne Overman, Eric Blore, Fuzzy Knight. Bright little comedy of wide-eyed Martin manhunting in N.Y.C., assisted by photographer MacMurray. Songs include "Love In Bloom."

Next Man, The (1976) **C-108m.** *** D: Richard C. Sarafian. Sean Connery, Cornelia Sharpe, Albert Paulsen, Adolfo Celi, Charles Cioffi. Good melodrama in which scenery (N.Y.C., Bavaria, London, Morocco, etc.) and violence are blended to tell of international hitlady Sharpe fall-ing in love with Saudi Arabian ambassador Connery as he tries to arrange peace with Palestine. Video title: DOUBLE HIT.▼

Next of Kin (1989) **C-108m.** *½ D: John Irvin. Patrick Swayze, Liam Neeson, Adam Baldwin, Helen Hunt, Andreas Katsulas, Bill Paxton, Ben Stiller, Michael J. Pollard. Chicago cop Swayze, of Appalachian descent, takes on Mr. Mob with the help of backwoods brother Neeson. Kitchen-sink scripting also has Swayze's wife, Lisa Niemi, a classical violinist. High-concept, low-rent star vehicle. Would *you* stay in a hotel managed by Pollard?▼

Next One, The (1984) **C-105m.** ** D: Nico Mastorakis. Keir Dullea, Adrienne Barbeau, Jeremy Licht, Peter Hobbs. Dullea is title character, a Christ-like visitor from the future who washes up on a Greek island where widow Barbeau, living with her young son, Licht, falls in love with him. Mediocre sci-fi strains for significance. Filmed in 1981. ▼

Next Stop, Greenwich Village (1976) **C-109m.** *** D: Paul Mazursky. Lenny Baker, Shelley Winters, Ellen Greene, Christopher Walken, Lou Jacobi, Mike Kellin, Lois Smith, Dori Brenner, Antonio Fargas, Jeff Goldblum. Comic and poignant film about Brooklyn boy Baker who moves to Greenwich Village in 1953 hoping to become an actor. Wonderful period atmosphere and characterizations; Winters is

excellent as Baker's domineering mother. Semiautobiographical script by Mazursky.
Next Time We Love (1936) **87m.** ******* D: Edward H. Griffith. Margaret Sullavan, James Stewart, Ray Milland, Grant Mitchell, Robert McWade, Anna Demetrio. Trim romantic soaper with Milland in love with actress Sullavan, who is married to struggling reporter Stewart.
Next to No Time (1958-British) **C-93m.** ******* D: Henry Cornelius. Kenneth More, Betsy Drake, Bessie Love, Harry Green, Patrick Barr, Roland Culver. Whimsical comedy from Paul Gallico story, about mild-mannered engineer (More) who loses inhibitions on ocean voyage where he's trying to put over important business deal.
Next Voice You Hear, The (1950) **83m.** ****½** D: William Wellman. James Whitmore, Nancy Davis (Reagan), Lillian Bronson, Jeff Corey. The voice of God is heard on the radio and has a profound impact on Anytown, U.S.A. Ambitious if not terribly successful message film produced by Dore Schary.
Niagara (1953) **C-89m.** ******* D: Henry Hathaway. Marilyn Monroe, Joseph Cotten, Jean Peters, Casey Adams, Don Wilson, Richard Allan. Black murder tale of honeymoon couple staying at Niagara Falls, the wife planning to kill husband. Produced and co-written by Charles Brackett; good location work.▼
Nice Girl? (1941) **95m.** ******* D: William A. Seiter. Deanna Durbin, Franchot Tone, Walter Brennan, Robert Stack, Robert Benchley. Little Deanna grows up in this cute comedy, with Tone and Stack developing amorous ideas about her. Songs: "Love At Last," "Thank You America."
Nice Girl Like Me, A (1969-British) **C-91m.** ****** D: Desmond Davis. Barbara Ferris, Harry Andrews, Gladys Cooper, Bill Hinnant, James Villiers. Orphaned Ferris accidentally becomes impregnated twice by different men, is looked after by caretaker Andrews, whom she really loves. Appealing, though silly and predictable.▼
Nice Girls Don't Explode (1987) **C-92m.** ****** D: Chuck Martinez. Barbara Harris, Michelle Meyrink, William O'Leary, Wallace Shawn, James Nardini. Silly comedy (with a memorable title) about a girl who causes things to explode, especially when she gets amorous. Harris and Meyrink, as mother and daughter who share this curse, give it their best, but the sparks don't ignite.▼
Nice Little Bank that Should be Robbed, A (1958) **87m.** ****** D: Henry Levin. Tom Ewell, Mickey Rooney, Mickey Shaughnessy, Dina Merrill. Cast is game, but story is pure cornball about goofy crooks using their gains to buy a racehorse.
Nicholas and Alexandra (1971-British) **C-183m.** ****½** D: Franklin Schaffner. Michael Jayston, Janet Suzman, Tom Baker, Harry Andrews, Jack Hawkins, Laurence Olivier, Michael Redgrave, Alexander Knox, Curt Jurgens. Lavishly filmed (with Oscar-winning art direction-set decoration and costumes), well-acted chronicle of Russian leaders, and revolution that turned their world upside down. Sure and steady, but eventually tedious, despite cameos by Olivier et al.▼
Nicholas Nickleby (1947-British) **108m.** ******* D: Alberto Cavalcanti. Derek Bond, Cedric Hardwicke, Alfred Drayton, Bernard Miles, Sally Ann Howes, Mary Merrall, Sybil Thorndike, Cathleen Nesbitt. Dickens's classic tale of young man's struggle to protect his family from scheming uncle and a cruel world is vividly brought to life. Can't compare with the Royal Shakespeare Company's 8½ hour version—but still quite good. Some American prints run 95m.▼
Nick and Nora (1975) **C-78m. TVM** D: Seymour Burns. Craig Stevens, Jo Ann Pflug, Jack Kruschen, Charles Macaulay, Denny Miller, Whit Bissell. The two leads desecrate the memories of William Powell and Myrna Loy in this dreadful update of THE THIN MAN. Below average.
Nick Carter in Prague SEE: **Dinner for Adele**
Nick Carter—Master Detective (1939) **60m.** ****** D: Jacques Tourneur. Walter Pidgeon, Rita Johnson, Henry Hull, Donald Meek, Milburn Stone, Addison Richards, Sterling Holloway. Pidgeon is good, tracking down industrial spy in slickly done detective film. Starts out very snappy and fast-paced, then slows to a crawl and loses its way. Memorable for some striking aerial shots.
Nickel Mountain (1985) **C-88m.** ****½** D: Drew Denbaum. Michael Cole, Heather Langenkamp, Patrick Cassidy, Brian Kerwin, Grace Zabriskie, Don Beddoe, Ed Lauter. Warm drama of unwed teenage mother growing up in rural America, befriended by pathetic older man. Winning performance by Langenkamp. Adapted from John Gardner's novel; filmed in 1983.▼
Nickelodeon (1976) **C-121m.** ******* D: Peter Bogdanovich. Ryan O'Neal, Burt Reynolds, Tatum O'Neal, Brian Keith, Stella Stevens, John Ritter, Jane Hitchcock, Harry Carey, Jr. Heartfelt valentine to early days of moviemaking, with O'Neal literally stumbling into his job as director, Reynolds an overnight screen hero. Based on actual reminiscences of such veterans as Raoul Walsh and Allan Dwan, film unfortunately loses steam halfway through . . . remains entertaining on the whole, sparked by fine cast; script by Bogdanovich and W.D. Richter.
Nickel Ride, The (1975) **C-99m.** ****** D:

Robert Mulligan. Jason Miller, Linda Haynes, Victor French, John Hillerman, Bo Hopkins. Uneven and generally obscure little drama about a syndicate contact man (Miller) who keeps keys to L.A. warehouses used by dealers in stolen goods. Originally ran 106m. when it debuted at the 1974 Cannes Film Festival.

Nick Knight (1989) **C-100m. TVM** D: Farhad Mann. Rick Springfield, John Kapelos, Robert Harper, Richard Fancy, Laura Johnson, Michael Nader. A vampire moonlights as a homicide detective so he can be near his blood supply but struggles to keep his true identity from the brass. Offbeat (but failed) pilot for pop singer Springfield. Below average.

Nicky's World (1974) **C-78m. TVM** D: Paul Stanley. Mark Shera, Charles Cioffi, George Voskovec, Despo, Olympia Dukakis, Emily Bindiger. Teenager in closeknit Greek-American family searches for the culprit who put the torch to his parents' bakery. Family drama in *The Waltons* tradition. Average.

Night, The SEE: La Notte

Night After Night (1932) **70m. ** D: Archie Mayo. George Raft, Mae West, Constance Cummings, Wynne Gibson, Roscoe Karns, Louis Calhern, Alison Skipworth. Story of nightclub owner Raft's infatuation with "classy" Cummings is a crashing bore, but when Mae West comes on the screen lights up. It's her film debut, and she's in rare form.

Night Ambush (1957-British) **93m. *** D: Michael Powell, Emeric Pressburger. Dirk Bogarde, Marius Goring, David Oxley, Cyril Cusack, Christopher Lee. Taut WW2 actioner set in Crete, with fine British cast. Originally released in England as ILL MET BY MOONLIGHT at 104m.▼

Night and Day (1946) **C-128m. ** D: Michael Curtiz. Cary Grant, Alexis Smith, Monty Woolley, Ginny Simms, Jane Wyman, Eve Arden, Mary Martin, Victor Francen, Alan Hale, Dorothy Malone. Music only worthy aspect of fabricated biography of songwriter Cole Porter, stiffly played by Grant, who even sings "You're The Top." Martin recreates "My Heart Belongs To Daddy" in film's highlight.▼

Night and the City (1950) **95m. **½ D: Jules Dassin. Richard Widmark, Gene Tierney, Googie Withers, Hugh Marlowe, Francis L. Sullivan, Herbert Lom, Mike Mazurki. Interesting *film noir* portrait of assorted losers in the nether world of London, focusing on a young hustler (Widmark) who's desperate to succeed. Marvelous showcase for Sullivan as an oily nightclub owner. Filmed in England.

Night at the Opera, A (1935) **92m. ****** D: Sam Wood. Groucho, Chico, Harpo Marx, Kitty Carlisle, Allan Jones, Walter Woolf King, Margaret Dumont, Sig Ruman. The Marx Brothers invade the world of opera with devastating results. Arguably their finest film (a close race with DUCK SOUP), with tuneful music and appealing romance neatly interwoven. One priceless comedy bit follows another: the stateroom scene, the Party of the First Part contract, etc. This is as good as it gets.▼

Night Before, The (1988) **C-85m. ** D: Thom Eberhardt. Keanu Reeves, Lori Loughlin, Theresa Saldana, Trinidad Silva, Suzanne Snyder, Morgan Lofting, Gwil Richards, Michael Greene. Mild (and alltoo-familiar) comic misadventures, as a high-school nerd tries to remember what happened to him the previous night on the way to the prom.▼

Nightbreaker (1989) **C-100m. TVM** D: Peter Markle. Martin Sheen, Emilio Estevez, Lea Thompson, Melinda Dillon, Joe Pantoliano, Nicholas Pryor. A naive doctor witnesses the U.S. Government's use of the military as guinea pigs in 1950s atomic tests in Nevada. Sheen and real-life son Estevez play the same character, in the '50s and '80s respectively. T.S. Cook's emotional script is based on Howard Rosenberg's novel *Atomic Soldiers*. Made for cable. Above average.▼

Night Caller (1975-French-Italian) **C-91m. ** D: Henri Verneuil. Jean-Paul Belmondo, Charles Denner, Adalberto-Maria Meril, Lea Massari, Rosy Varte. Detective Belmondo tackles both a bank robbery case and an obscene phone caller who murders women at the end of the line. Action but little else.

Night Caller from Outer Space (1965-British) **84m. **½ D: John Gilling. John Saxon, Maurice Denham, Patricia Haines, Alfred Burke, Jack Watson, Aubrey Morris. Well done, sci-fi thriller of alien mutant kidnapping humans to take back to his troubled planet.▼

Night Call Nurses (1972) **C-85m. ** D: Jonathan Kaplan. Patti Byrne, Alana Collins, Mittie Lawrence, Dick Miller, Dennis Dugan, Stack Pierce. Kaplan's feature debut is typical drive-in sex comedy; lighthearted and fast-paced, with good comic performances by Dugan and the ubiquitous Miller. Third in Roger Corman-produced series; followed by THE YOUNG NURSES.▼

Night Chase (1970) **C-100m. TVM** D: Jack Starrett. David Janssen, Yaphet Kotto, Victoria Vetri, Elisha Cook, Jr., Joe De Santis. Wealthy businessman, believing he has killed his wife's lover, is forced to hire out cab to drive to Mexico. Great on-the-road drama; suspense falls apart at resolution. Above average.

Night Club Scandal (1937) **70m. **½ D: Ralph Murphy. John Barrymore, Lynne Overman, Louise Campbell, Charles Bickford, Evelyn Brent, Elizabeth Patterson, J.

Carrol Naish. Enjoyable B mystery with detectives seeking murderer who tried to frame innocent man. Remake of 1932 film GUILTY AS HELL.

Nightcomers, The (1972-British) **C-96m.** ** D: Michael Winner. Marlon Brando, Stephanie Beacham, Thora Hird, Harry Andrews, Verna Harvey, Christopher Ellis, Anna Palk. Poor direction hurts attempt to chronicle what happened to the children in Henry James' *Turn of the Screw* before original story began.▼

Night Court (1932) **90m.** ** D: W.S. Van Dyke. Phillips Holmes, Walter Huston, Anita Page, Lewis Stone, Mary Carlisle, John Miljan, Jean Hersholt. Slimy, crooked night court judge Huston will stop at nothing to avoid being pinned by city watchdog Stone; that includes framing an innocent young couple. Watchable but far from subtle, or surprising, until final twist.

Night Creature (1978) **C-83m.** BOMB D: Lee Madden. Donald Pleasence, Nancy Kwan, Ross Hagen, Lesly Fine, Jennifer Rhodes. Macho writer Pleasence lives on Xanadu-like island retreat near Thailand, but a prowling leopard is giving him the jitters. A low-grade thriller, minus the thrills. Also known as OUT OF THE DARKNESS.▼

Night Creatures (1962-British) **C-81m.** **½ D: Peter Graham Scott. Peter Cushing, Yvonne Romain, Patrick Allen, Oliver Reed, Michael Ripper, Martin Benson, David Lodge. In 18th century England, country parson is also the notorious "dead" pirate leader of smugglers who pose as ghosts. Good fun with some scary moments. Remake of DR. SYN. Original British title: CAPTAIN CLEGG.

Night Cries (1978) **C-100m.** TVM D: Richard Lang. Susan Saint James, Michael Parks, Jamie Smith Jackson, William Conrad, Dolores Dorn, Cathleen Nesbitt. Young mother is haunted by dreams that her dead child is alive and in danger. Middling suspense tale. Average.▼

Night Crossing (1981-British) **C-106m.** **½ D: Delbert Mann. John Hurt, Jane Alexander, Glynnis O'Connor, Doug McKeon, Beau Bridges, Ian Bannen, Klaus Lowitsch, Kay Walsh. Unexceptional though well-cast and not unexciting tale of two families' escape from East Berlin via hot-air balloon. A Walt Disney production, based on a true story.▼

Night Digger, The (1971-British) **C-100m.** *** D: Alastair Reid. Patricia Neal, Pamela Brown, Nicholas Clay, Jean Anderson, Graham Crowden, Yootha Joyce. Odd, usually effective psychological thriller adapted from Joy Cowley novel by Roald Dahl. With the unexpected arrival of young handyman, sad relationship between two country women takes turn for the better, until they discover what he does on off-

hours. Excellent performances, fine Bernard Herrmann score.

Night Editor (1946) **68m.** ** D: Henry Levin. William Gargan, Janis Carter, Jeff Donnell, Coulter Irwin. Minor yarn about Gargan, a law enforcer gone wrong, trying to redeem himself.

Night Evelyn Came Out of the Grave, The (1971-Italian) **C-90m.** *½ D: Emilio Miraglia. Anthony Steffen, Marina Malfatti, Rod Murdock, Giacomo Rossi-Stuart, Umberto Raho. Dreadful horror whodunit about British lord, released from psychiatric clinic following his wife's death, who begins to suspect that she is still alive when her crypt is discovered empty.

Nightfall (1956) **78m.** *** D: Jacques Tourneur. Aldo Ray, Brian Keith, Anne Bancroft, Jocelyn Brando, James Gregory, Frank Albertson. Fast-moving, well-made story of innocent man wanted by police for killing of friend, chased by actual killers for stolen money he found.

Nightfall (1988) **C-82m.** BOMB D: Paul Mayersberg. David Birney, Sarah Douglas, Alexis Kanner, Andra Millian, Charles Hayward, Susie Lindeman, Starr Andreeff. Hopelessly muddled adaptation of Isaac Asimov's classic short story about an alien world in a three-star solar system whose inhabitants face the coming darkness of nightfall (occurring only once every 1000 years) with abject terror. Birney is miscast in this cheesy production.▼

Night Fighters (1960-British) **85m.** **½ D: Tay Garnett. Robert Mitchum, Anne Heywood, Dan O'Herlihy, Cyril Cusack, Richard Harris, Marianne Benet. Sporadically actionful tale of Irish Revolution, with Mitchum joining the cause against his will. Original title: A TERRIBLE BEAUTY.

Night Flight From Moscow (1973-French-Italian-West German) **C-113m.** **½ D: Henri Verneuil. Yul Brynner, Henry Fonda, Dirk Bogarde, Philippe Noiret, Virna Lisi, Farley Granger, Robert Alda, Marie Dubois, Elga Andersen. Espionage thriller about the defection of Russian diplomat Brynner is compromised by the middling screenplay adapted from Pierre Nord's cloak-and-dagger novel *Le 13e Suicide*. Originally titled THE SERPENT.▼

Nightflyers (1987) **C-89m.** *½ D: T.C. Blake (Robert Collector). Catherine Mary Stewart, Michael Praed, John Standing, Lisa Blount, Glenn Withrow. Dreary, derivative sci-fi about a dangerous and harmful force wreaking havoc among scientists aboard a spaceship. Director Collector had his name removed from the credits. Based on a novella by George R. R. Martin.▼

Nightforce (1987) **C-82m.** *½ D: Lawrence D. Foldes. Linda Blair, James Van Patten, Richard Lynch, Chad McQueen, Dean R. Miller, James Marcel, Claudia

Udy, Bruce Fisher, Cameron Mitchell. Cornball action film has Blair and fellow youngsters organizing a commando mission to Central America to free a kidnapped daughter of a U. S. senator. OK stunt work and Udy's beauty are redeeming features.▼

Night Freight (1955) **79m.** ****½ D:** Jean Yarbrough. Forrest Tucker, Barbara Britton, Keith Larsen, Thomas Gomez. Straightforward tale about railroad competing with trucking line for survival.

Night Full of Rain, A (1978-Italian) **C-104m.** **** D:** Lina Wertmuller. Giancarlo Giannini, Candice Bergen, Allison Tucker, Jill Eikenberry, Anne Byrne. Wertmuller's first English language effort (shot in Rome and San Francisco) is unsatisfying fantasy drama about relationship between journalist Giannini and feminist wife Bergen, who's quite good. Full title: THE END OF THE WORLD IN OUR USUAL BED IN A NIGHT FULL OF RAIN.

Night Gallery (1969) **C-98m. TVM D:** Boris Sagal, Steven Spielberg, Barry Shear. Roddy McDowall, Ossie Davis, Barry Sullivan, Tom Bosley, George Macready, Joan Crawford, Richard Kiley, Sam Jaffe. Three-story anthology, each part revolving around lessons learned (via Rod Serling) from paintings: despicable nephew speeds up death of wealthy old man, art collector arranges for eye transplant, death camp fugitive in South American country. Effective mixture of melodrama, morality, and supernatural spawned popular series; middle tale was Spielberg's maiden directorial effort. Above average.▼

Night Game (1989) **C-95m.** ***½ D:** Peter Masterson. Roy Scheider, Karen Young, Richard Bradford, Paul Gleason, Carlin Glynn. Texas police detective goes after a serial killer. What a shame to find good actors and a talented director wasting their time with such third-rate material.

Night Games (1974) **C-78m. TVM D:** Don Taylor. Barry Newman, Susan Howard, Albert Salmi, Luke Askew, JoAnna Cameron, Anjanette Comer, Ralph Meeker, Stefanie Powers. Newman reprises the role he first did in THE LAWYER in 1970, this time establishing himself in a small Arizona town and defending socialite Powers accused of murdering her husband. *Petrocelli* TV series spun off from this film. Average.

Night Games (1980) **C-100m.** ***½ D:** Roger Vadim. Cindy Pickett, Joanna Cassidy, Barry Primus, Paul Jenkins, Gene Davis. Frigid housewife will make it only with guy who shows up at night in a bird suit. Vadim may be kidding, but it's tough to tell.▼

Night Has a Thousand Eyes (1948) **80m.** ****½ D:** John Farrow. Edward G. Robinson, Gail Russell, John Lund, Virginia Bruce, William Demarest. Intriguing story of magician who has uncanny power to predict the future; script is corny at times. Based on a story by Cornell Woolrich.

Night Has Eyes, The (1942-British) **79m.** ****½ D:** Leslie Arliss. James Mason, Joyce Howard, Mary Clare, Wilfrid Lawson, Tucker McGuire. OK mystery of schoolteacher Howard discovering why a friend disappeared in the Yorkshire Moors; Mason is a shellshocked composer she loves. Also known as TERROR HOUSE.

Nighthawks (1981) **C-99m.** ***** D:** Bruce Malmuth. Sylvester Stallone, Billy Dee Williams, Lindsay Wagner, Persis Khambatta, Nigel Davenport, Rutger Hauer, Joe Spinell, Catherine Mary Stewart. Exciting story of two N.Y.C. street cops reassigned to special unit that's tracking a ruthless international terrorist (Hauer). On target from the first scene to the fade-out, with plenty of hair-raising moments along the way.▼

Night Heaven Fell, The (1958-French) **C-90m.** ****½ D:** Roger Vadim. Brigitte Bardot, Alida Valli, Stephen Boyd, Pepe Nieto. Turgid drama of Bardot dallying with Boyd, who's planning to kill her uncle.

Night Holds Terror, The (1955) **86m.** **** D:** Andrew L. Stone. Jack Kelly, Hildy Parks, Vince Edwards, John Cassavetes, Jack Kruschen, Joel Marston, Jonathan Hale. Somber little film of family being held captive for ransom.

Night in Casablanca, A (1946) **85m.** ***** D:** Archie Mayo. Groucho, Harpo, Chico Marx, Lisette Verea, Charles Drake, Lois Collier, Dan Seymour, Sig Ruman. No classic, but many funny sequences in latter-day Marx outing, ferreting out Nazi spies in Casablanca hotel.▼

Nightingales (1988) **C-100m. TVM D:** Mimi Leder. Mimi Kuzyk, Susan Walters, Britta Phillips, Chelsea Field, Kristy Swanson, Neith Hunter, Galyn Gorg. The lives and loves of student nurses in a coed dorm. Ho-hum pilot to a subsequent, short-lived TV series which starred Suzanne Pleshette. Later shown at 78m. Average.

Nightingale Sang in Berkeley Square, A (1979) **C-102m.** ****½ D:** Ralph Thomas. Richard Jordan, David Niven, Oliver Tobias, Elke Sommer, Gloria Grahame, Hugh Griffith, Richard Johnson. American ex-con Jordan, released from a British prison, is coerced into taking part in an elaborate bank heist masterminded by Niven. Grahame, seen briefly as Jordan's brassy mom, is a joy to watch in one of her last roles.

Night in Heaven, A (1983) **C-80m.** **** D:** John G. Avildsen. Lesley Ann Warren, Christopher Atkins, Robert Logan, Carrie Snodgress, Deborah Rush, Sandra Beall, Alix Elias, Denny Terrio. Teacher Warren lets her friends drag her to a male strip joint, where the star attraction (Atkins) is a student she's flunking. Off-beat romantic drama penned by Joan Tewkesbury had real possibilities, but many of them were apparently left on the cutting room floor (note brief running time). Still worth a peek for fine performance by Warren.▼

Night in New Orleans, A (1942) 75m. *½ D: William Clemens. Preston Foster, Patricia Morison, Albert Dekker, Charles Butterworth, Dooley Wilson, Cecil Kellaway. Thin yarn of Morison trying to clear husband Foster of murder charge.

Night in Paradise, A (1946) C-84m. ** D: Arthur Lubin. Merle Oberon, Turhan Bey, Thomas Gomez, Gale Sondergaard, Ray Collins, Ernest Truex. Tongue-in-cheek costumer of Aesop wooing lovely princess Oberon in ancient times; colorful, pleasant at best.

Night in the Life of Jimmy Reardon, A (1988) C-90m. **½ D: William Richert. River Phoenix, Ann Magnuson, Meredith Salenger, Ione Skye, Louanne, Matthew L. Perry. Richert's film of his own youthful novel (*Aren't You Even Gonna Kiss Me Goodbye?*) doesn't work overall . . . but it has something. Phoenix is a high school Romeo preparing for a fall from grace when his more affluent friends prepare to leave for ritzier colleges; Magnuson's cameo (as an amorous family friend) is a standout, but other performances fall short. Handsomely photographed by John Connor.▼

Night Into Morning (1951) 86m. *** D: Fletcher Markle. Ray Milland, John Hodiak, Nancy Davis (Reagan), Lewis Stone, Jean Hagen, Rosemary DeCamp. Small-town professor loses family in fire, almost ruins own life through drink and self-pity. Realistic settings in modest production, with fine performance by Milland.

Night Is My Future (1947-Swedish) 87m. **½ D: Ingmar Bergman. Mai Zetterling, Birger Malmsten, Olof Winnerstrand, Naima Wifstrand, Hilda Borgstrom. Somber, brooding tale of young Malmsten, blinded while in military service; he struggles for self-respect, and is befriended by housemaid Zetterling. Early, minor Bergman; also known as MUSIC IN DARKNESS.▼

Night Key (1937) 67m. ** D: Lloyd Corrigan. Boris Karloff, Warren Hull, Jean Rogers, Hobart Cavanaugh. Middling yarn about crooks forcing elderly inventor to help them with their crimes.

Nightkill (1980-W. German) C-97m. **½ D: Ted Post. Jaclyn Smith, Mike Connors, James Franciscus, Robert Mitchum, Fritz Weaver, Sybil Danning. Confused suspense drama involving a love triangle that ends in murder and a cat-and-mouse game between a wealthy widow and a mysteri-

ous investigator. Filmed on location in Arizona by a German company, with (except for cast and director) a German crew.▼

Nightlife (1989) C-100m. TVM D: Daniel Taplitz. Ben Cross, Maryam D'Abo, Keith Szarabajka, Jessie Cortie, Camille Saviola, Oliver Clark, Glenn Shadix. Tongue-in-fang comedy about a vampiress in modern-day Mexico City who's being pursued by her ancient lover and wooed by a Jewish doctor, a hematologist who runs the blood clinic that she's begun haunting. One-joke concept that runs itself into the ground mighty quickly. Made for cable. Average.▼

Nightmare (1942) 81m. **½ D: Tim Whelan. Diana Barrymore, Brian Donlevy, Gavin Muir, Henry Daniell, Hans Conried, Arthur Shields. Occasionally flavorful mystery with gambler Donlevy breaking into Barrymore's home on the night husband Daniell is murdered, and their subsequent flight from both the police and Nazi spies.

Nightmare (1956) 89m. **½ D: Maxwell Shane. Edward G. Robinson, Kevin McCarthy, Connie Russell, Virginia Christine. McCarthy is musician involved in bizarre murder set in New Orleans; OK mystery, with Robinson sparking proceedings. Remake of FEAR IN THE NIGHT.

Nightmare (1964-British) 82m. *** D: Freddie Francis. David Knight, Moira Redmond, Brenda Bruce, John Welsh. Well-directed thriller with enough subplots to keep any viewer busy. Girl is blackmailed into committing murder by scheming gardener.

Nightmare (1974) C-78m. TVM D: William Hale. Richard Crenna, Patty Duke Astin, Vic Morrow, Peter Bromilow, Arch Johnson, Richard Schaal. Witness to a killing realizes he may be the sniper's next target. Bread and butter TV thriller. Look fast for Henry Winkler as an auditioning actor. Average.

Nightmare (1976) SEE: **Nightmare in Badham County**▼

Nightmare (1981) C-97m. BOMB D: Romano Scavolini. C. J. Cooke, Mik Cribben, Kathleen Ferguson. Psycho who had a traumatic childhood murders, murders, and murders again. Rated D for disgusting.▼

Nightmare Alley (1947) 111m. ***½ D: Edmund Goulding. Tyrone Power, Joan Blondell, Coleen Gray, Helen Walker, Taylor Holmes, Mike Mazurki, Ian Keith, Julia Dean. Morbid story of carnival heel Power entangled with mind-reading Blondell, blackmailing psychiatrist Walker, other assorted weirdos in original, fascinating melodrama. Jules Furthman scripted, from William Lindsay Gresham's novel.

Nightmare at Bitter Creek (1988) C-100m. TVM D: Tim Burstall. Lindsay Wagner,

Tom Skerritt, Constance McCashin, Joanna Cassidy, Janne Mortil. Four women, roughing it in high-mountain country with an alcoholic guide, find themselves being stalked by trigger-happy extremists on the run. A tepid female version of DELIVERANCE, marking the American TV debut of Australian director Burstall. Average.

Nightmare Castle (1966-Italian) **90m.** ** D: Allan Grunewald (Mario Caiano). Barbara Steele, Paul Mueller, Helga Line, Lawrence Clift. Typically atmospheric European horror film about doctor experimenting in regeneration of human blood through electrical impulses. Good photography.▼

Nightmare City SEE: **City of the Walking Dead**▼

Nightmare Honeymoon (1973) **C-115m.** ** D: Elliot Silverstein. Dack Rambo, Rebecca Dianna Smith, Pat Hingle, Bob Steele, David Huddleston, John Beck, Jeanette Nolan. Young couple suffers at the hands of rural killers and rapists; routine and unpleasant.

Nightmare Hotel (1970-Spanish) **C-95m.** ** D: Eugenio Martin. Judy Geeson, Aurora Bautista, Esperanza Roy, Victor Alcazar, Lone Fleming. Geeson goes to small Spanish inn looking for relative who has disappeared, and confronts two mad sisters who run establishment; several murders follow. Passable thriller.

Nightmare in Badham County (1976) **C-100m. TVM** D: John Llewellyn Moxey. Deborah Raffin, Lynne Moody, Ralph Bellamy, Chuck Connors, Tina Louise, Robert Reed, Della Reese, Lana Wood, Fionnuala Flanagan. Exploitation drama about two comely hitchhikers tossed into a rural prison farm after spurning the advances of lecherous sheriff Connors. Stereotype acting; ditto for dialogue. Below average; also known as NIGHTMARE.▼

Nightmare in Blood (1976) **C-89m.** **½ D: John Stanley. Jerry Walter, Dan Caldwell, Barrie Youngfellow, Kathleen Quinlan, Kerwin Mathews. Horror film actor visiting fan convention turns out to be a real vampire after all; low-budget spoof made in San Francisco will appeal particularly to horror buffs for its many in-jokes.▼

Nightmare in Chicago (1964) **C-80m. TVM** D: Robert Altman. Philip Abbott, Robert Ridgley, Ted Knight, Charles McGraw, John Alonzo, Barbara Turner. Psychotic killer, known to tri-state police via newspapers as Georgie Porgie, terrorizes Chicago area for 72 hours in mad murder spree. Totally location-shot, film does resemble nightmare. Interesting early credit for director Altman; expanded from a one-hour 1964 episode of *Kraft Suspense Theater*. Above average.

Nightmare in the Sun (1965) **C-80m.** *½

D: Marc Lawrence. John Derek, Aldo Ray, Arthur O'Connell, Ursula Andress, Sammy Davis, Jr., Allyn Joslyn, Keenan Wynn. Turgid account of what happens when sexy Andress picks up hitchhiker Derek. Look for Richard Jaeckel and Robert Duvall as motorcylists.

Nightmare in Wax (1969) **C-91m.** ** D: Bud Townsend. Cameron Mitchell, Anne Helm, Scott Brady, Berry Kroeger, Victoria Carroll. Paraphrase of HOUSE OF WAX has Mitchell as former movie makeup man whose wax museum is full of actors "missing" from the studio.▼

Nightmare on Elm Street, A (1984) **C-92m.** *½ D: Wes Craven. John Saxon, Ronee Blakley, Heather Langenkamp, Amanda Wyss, Nick Corri, Johnny Depp, Charles Fleischer. High-school pals, all plagued by the same terrifying dream, are systematically murdered by the nightmare's lead character. Standard teen slaughter movie inexplicably caught on with dropouts, leading to NIGHTMARE ON ELM STREET 2, 3 . . . Even Craven has done better than this.▼

Nightmare on Elm Street 2, A: Freddy's Revenge (1985) **C-84m.** ** D: Jack Sholder. Mark Patton, Kim Myers, Robert Rusler, Clu Gulager, Hope Lange, Marshall Bell, Sydney Walsh, Robert Englund. Reworking of first film's story (set five years later) has teenage boy plagued by dreams of demonic Freddy, who is intent on taking over his mind *and* body . . . so he can kill all the neighborhood teens. Gruesome special effects dominate this slasher saga, which, like the first, was a box-office hit.▼

Nightmare on Elm Street 3, A: Dream Warriors (1987) **C-96m.** *½ D: Chuck Russell. Heather Langenkamp, Patricia Arquette, Larry Fishburne, Priscilla Pointer, Craig Wasson, Robert Englund, Brooke Bundy, Rodney Eastman, John Saxon, Dick Cavett, Zsa Zsa Gabor. Third go-round for teen-murderer Freddy (Englund) has the best cast (though many are *mis*-cast), the most cluttered story line (set in a psycho ward where the traumatized teens are committed), and the most flamboyant (often repellent) special effects.▼

Nightmare on Elm Street 4, A: The Dream Master (1988) **C-92m.** **½ D: Renny Harlin. Robert Englund, Rodney Eastman, Danny Hassel, Andras Jones, Tuesday Knight, Toy Newkirk, Ken Sagoes, Brooke Theiss, Lisa Wilcox, Brooke Bundy. Fast-paced entry in the hit horror series benefits from greater emphasis on Englund as wisecracking monster Freddy Krueger, now preying on the friends of the young victims from previous films. Outstanding special effects make this the best of the NIGHTMARE films. The TV series followed.▼

Nightmare on Elm Street, A: The Dream

Child (1989) **C-89m.** *½ D: Stephen Hopkins. Robert Englund, Lisa Wilcox, Kelly Jo Minter, Erika Anderson, Whitby Hertford, Danny Hassel. Fifth and least in the NIGHTMARE series, with everyone except Englund just going through the paces. Here, scarred, dream-haunting Freddy Krueger (Englund) uses the unborn child of Wilcox to strike at her friends. As usual, special effects are a highlight but don't save the film from being a bore.▼

Nightmares (1983) **C-99m.** ** D: Joseph Sargent. Cristina Raines, Timothy James, William Sanderson, Emilio Estevez, Moon Zappa, Lance Henriksen, Robin Gammell, Richard Masur, Veronica Cartwright, Bridgette Andersen, Albert Hague. Four-part film (originally made for TV) with *Twilight Zone* aspirations but uninspired writing, and mostly predictable outcomes. Hasn't anyone read O. Henry lately? Themes range from a knife-wielding loony on the loose to a kid who becomes obsessed with beating a video arcade game.▼

Night Monster (1942) **80m.** **½ D: Ford Beebe. Irene Hervey, Don Porter, Nils Asther, Lionel Atwill, Leif Erickson, Bela Lugosi, Ralph Morgan. Intriguing grade-B thriller about creepy figure stalking country estate, murdering doctors who are treating crippled Morgan.

'night, Mother (1986) **C-96m.** ** D: Tom Moore. Sissy Spacek, Anne Bancroft. Unhappy young woman who lives with her mother decides to commit suicide; her mother spends the night trying to talk her out of it. Well acted, directed, and edited, but still just a photographed stage drama, missing the electricity of a live performance . . . and without the element of doubt about its conclusion that marked Marsha Norman's Pulitzer Prize-winning play.▼

Night Moves (1975) **C-95m.** ***½ D: Arthur Penn. Gene Hackman, Jennifer Warren, Susan Clark, Edward Binns, Harris Yulin, Melanie Griffith, James Woods. L.A. detective Hackman puts aside his marital woes to track nymphet Griffith to Florida Keys. Complicated but underrated psychological suspenser by Alan Sharp leads to stunning climax.▼

Night Must Fall (1937) **117m.** *** D: Richard Thorpe. Robert Montgomery, Rosalind Russell, Dame May Whitty, Alan Marshal, Kathleen Harrison, E. E. Clive, Beryl Mercer. Famous film of Emlyn Williams' suspenseful play. Young woman (Russell) slowly learns identity of mysterious brutal killer terrorizing the countryside. Montgomery has showy role in sometimes stagy but generally effective film, with outstanding aid from Russell and Whitty. Screenplay by playwright John Van Druten. Remade in 1964.

Night Must Fall (1964-British) **105m.** **½

D: Karel Reisz. Albert Finney, Susan Hampshire, Mona Washbourne, Sheila Hancock, Michael Medwin, Joe Gladwin, Martin Wyldeck. Cerebral attempt to match flair of original, this remake is too obvious and theatrical for any credibility. Reisz and Finney produced.

Night My Number Came Up, The (1955-British) **94m.** **** D: Leslie Norman. Michael Redgrave, Sheila Sim, Alexander Knox, Denholm Elliott, Ursula Jeans, Michael Hordern, George Rose, Alfie Bass. First-rate suspense film will have you holding your breath as it recounts tale of routine military flight, the fate of which may or may not depend on a prophetic dream. Screenplay by R. C. Sherriff, from an article by Victor Goddard.

Night Nurse (1931) **72m.** *** D: William Wellman. Barbara Stanwyck, Ben Lyon, Joan Blondell, Clark Gable, Charlotte Merriam, Charles Winninger. Excellent, hard-bitten tale of nurse (Stanwyck) who can't ignore strange goings-on in home where she works. Blondell adds zingy support; one of Gable's most impressive early appearances. Still potent today.

Night of Adventure, A (1944) **65m.** **½ D: Gordon Douglas. Tom Conway, Audrey Long, Nancy Gates, Emory Parnell, Jean Brooks, Louis Borell, Edward Brophy, Addison Richards. Entertaining little drama with lawyer Conway attempting to exonerate bored wife Long's suitor on a murder rap, all the while avoiding scandal. A remake of HAT, COAT AND GLOVE.

Night of Courage (1987) **C-100m. TVM** D: Elliot Silverstein. Barnard Hughes, Geraldine Fitzgerald, Daniel Hugh Kelly, David Hernandez, Holly Fulger. An old man and his bedridden wife refuse refuge to a young Hispanic who is running for his life from a gang of thugs, and watch him being beaten to death on their doorstep. Dramatization by Brian Williams of his acclaimed play *In This Fallen City*. Average.

Night of Dark Shadows (1971) **C-97m.** BOMB D: Dan Curtis. David Selby, Lara Parker, Kate Jackson, Grayson Hall, John Karlen, Nancy Barrett. Ripoff exploitation film bears little resemblance to popular TV serial in predictable yawner about ghosts and reincarnation in New England. Follow-up to HOUSE OF DARK SHADOWS lacks everything that made first one so good.

Night of January 16th, The (1941) **79m.** *½ D: William Clemens. Robert Preston, Ellen Drew, Nils Asther, Donald Douglas, Rod Cameron, Alice White, Cecil Kellaway. Hit Broadway play receives lackluster screen treatment; a talky and uninspired whodunit.

Night of Mystery (1937) **66m.** D: E.A. Dupont. Grant Richards, Roscoe Karns,

Helen Burgess, Ruth Coleman, Elizabeth Patterson, Harvey Stephens, June Martel, Terry Ray, Purnell Pratt. SEE: **Philo Vance** series.

Night of Terror (1933) **60m.** BOMB D: Ben Stoloff. Sally Blane, Wallace Ford, Tully Marshall, Bela Lugosi, George Meeker, Edwin Maxwell, Bryant Washburn. Empty, inept "B" chiller about ugly homicidal madman prowling the grounds of swanky estate. Top-billed Lugosi is wasted in nothing part as Hindu servant; Ford plays mandatory wise-cracking reporter. Almost worth sitting through for really unbelievable ending.

Night of Terror (1972) **C-73m.** TVM D: Jeannot Szwarc. Donna Mills, Martin Balsam, Chuck Connors, Catherine Burns, Eddie Egan, Agnes Moorehead. Violent, paranoid thriller hinging on unremembered clues, vulnerable woman, syndicate runner with nothing to lose. OK performances but plot built around pileup of crazy situations. Average.

Night of the Big Heat SEE: **Island of the Burning Doomed**▼

Night of the Blood Beast (1958) **65m.** *½ D: Bernard Kowalski. Michael Emmet, Angela Greene, John Baer, Ed Nelson, Tyler McVey. Astronaut returns from space apparently dead; when he awakens, he's found to have alien embryos within him—a pregnant man! The alien also turns up murderously. Well-directed but too low-budget to succeed.▼

Night of the Blood Monster (1972-British) **C-84m.** ** D: Jess Franco. Christopher Lee, Maria Schell, Leo Genn, Maria Rohm, Margaret Lee. Witch-hunts and mayhem in the time of King Henry V.

Night of the Claw SEE: **Island Claws**▼

Night of the Comet (1984) **C-94m.** **½ D: Thom Eberhardt. Catherine Mary Stewart, Kelli Maroney, Robert Beltran, Geoffrey Lewis, Mary Woronov, Sharon Farrell, Michael Bowen. World comes to an end, leaving only a couple of California valley girls behind! Smart satire, with clever and occasionally chilling moments, but plays all its cards too soon.▼

Night of the Demons (1987) **C-89m.** *½ D: Kevin S. Tenney. Cathy Podewell, Alvin Alexis, William Gallo, Mimi Kinkade, Linnea Quigley, Lance Fenton. On Halloween night, wouldn't you know it, some Typical Teenagers pick the wrong possessed mortuary to party in. Everything about this amateurish movie is gratuitous, including the movie itself. Good makeup, though.▼

Night of the Eagle SEE: **Burn, Witch, Burn!**

Night of the Following Day, The (1969) **C-93m.** **½ D: Hubert Cornfield. Marlon Brando, Richard Boone, Rita Moreno, Pamela Franklin, Jess Hahn, Gerard Buhr.

Good cast makes this sordid tale of young girl's kidnapping somewhat more interesting than it should be; pretty rough in spots. Filmed in France.

Night of the Generals (1967-British) **C-148m.** ** D: Anatole Litvak. Peter O'Toole, Omar Sharif, Tom Courtenay, Donald Pleasence, Joanna Pettet, Christopher Plummer, John Gregson, Philippe Noiret. Essentially a WW2 whodunit, film has potential but gets lost in murky script, lifeless performances. A dud.▼

Night of the Ghouls SEE: **Revenge of the Dead**

Night of the Grizzly, The (1966) **C-102m.** **½ D: Joseph Pevney. Clint Walker, Martha Hyer, Keenan Wynn, Nancy Kulp, Ron Ely, Regis Toomey, Jack Elam. Acceptable Western of rancher Walker overcoming all obstacles, even a persistent vicious bear, to Western life.▼

Night of the Hunter, The (1955) **93m.** ***½ D: Charles Laughton. Robert Mitchum, Shelley Winters, Lillian Gish, Evelyn Varden, Peter Graves, James Gleason, Billy Chapin, Sally Jane Bruce. Atmospheric allegory of innocence, evil and hypocrisy, with psychotic religious fanatic Mitchum chasing homeless children for money stolen by their father. Mitchum is marvelously menacing, matched by Gish as wise matron who takes in the kids. Starkly directed by Laughton; his only film behind the camera. Screenplay by James Agee, from the Davis Grubb novel.▼

Night of the Iguana, The (1964) **118m.** *** D: John Huston. Richard Burton, Deborah Kerr, Ava Gardner, Sue Lyon, Skip Ward, Grayson Hall, Cyril Delevanti. More interesting for its cast than for plodding tale based on Tennessee Williams play; alcoholic former clergyman Burton, a bus-tour guide in Mexico, is involved with Kerr, Gardner, and Lyon. Dorothy Jeakins won an Oscar for her costumes.▼

Night of the Juggler (1980) **C-101m.** *½ D: Robert Butler. James Brolin, Cliff Gorman, Richard Castellano, Abby Bluestone, Linda G. Miller, Julie Carmen, Barton Heyman, Mandy Patinkin. A sickie mistakenly kidnaps the daughter of an ex-cop (Brolin), who then leads a city-wide rampage to get her back. Fast-paced but wildly implausible movie paints a notably ugly portrait of N.Y.C. and its people.▼

Night of the Laughing Dead SEE: **Crazy House** (1975)▼

Night of the Lepus (1972) **C-88m.** *½ D: William F. Claxton. Stuart Whitman, Janet Leigh, Rory Calhoun, DeForest Kelley, Paul Fix, Melanie Fullerton. Rabbits weighing 150 pounds and standing four feet high terrorize the countryside; National Guard, not Elmer Fudd, comes to the rescue.

Night of the Living Dead (1968) **96m.** ***½ D: George A. Romero. Duane Jones,

[816]

Judith O'Dea, Russell Streiner, Karl Hardman, Keith Wayne. Romero's first feature is the touchstone modern horror film: seven people barricade themselves inside a farmhouse while an army of flesh-eating zombies roams the countryside. Once considered the *ne plus ultra* of gore, film is less stomach-churning by today's standards, yet its essential power to chill remains undiminished despite scores of imitations. Shoestring production values merely add to authentic feel. Don't watch this alone! Sequel: DAWN OF THE DEAD. Also shown in computer-colored version.▼

Night of the Quarter Moon (1959) **96m.** *½ D: Hugo Haas. Julie London, John Drew Barrymore, Nat King Cole, Dean Jones, James Edwards, Anna Kashfi, Agnes Moorehead, Jackie Coogan. Trite handling of miscegenation theme; good cast wasted. Retitled: FLESH AND FLAME.

Night of the Shooting Stars, The (1982-Italian) **C-106m.** ***½ D: Paolo and Vittorio Taviani. Omero Antonutti, Margarita Lozano, Claudio Bigagil, Massimo Bonetti, Norma Martel. Extraordinarily touching, involving, richly textured drama of a group of Tuscan villagers during WW2, in final days before liberation by Americans. With simple, lyrical images, the filmmakers unravel this life-affirming story of war's absurdities— and hope, survival.▼

Night Partners (1983) **C-100m. TVM** D: Noel Nosseck. Yvette Mimieux, Diana Canova, Arlen Dean Snyder, M. Emmet Walsh, Patricia McCormack, Patricia Davis, Larry Linville, Dick Anthony Williams. Busted pilot has suburban housewives Mimieux and Canova volunteer to aid crime victims and pretend to be Cagney and Lacey, tooling around nights in an unmarked police car and righting wrongs without guns. Average.▼

Night Passage (1957) **C-90m.** *** D: James Neilson. James Stewart, Audie Murphy, Dan Duryea, Brandon de Wilde, Dianne Foster. Soundly handled Western of Stewart working for railroad and brother Murphy belonging to gang planning to rob train payroll; exciting climactic shoot-out.

Night Patrol (1985) **C-82m. BOMB** D: Jackie Kong. Linda Blair, Pat Paulsen, Jaye P. Morgan, Jack Riley, Billy Barty, Murray Langston, Pat Morita, Andrew (Dice) Clay. Threadbare rip-off of PO-LICE ACADEMY—can you actually imagine any film being *influenced* by POLICE ACADEMY?—combines Barty's flatulence with crude one-liners you simply won't believe. If you must watch, see if you can figure out why the opening sequence has subtitles.▼

Night People (1954) **C-93m.** *** D: Nunnally Johnson. Gregory Peck, Broderick Crawford, Anita Bjork, Rita Gam, Walter Abel, Buddy Ebsen. Sensibly told, intertwining plots of Cold War espionage; filmed on location in Berlin.

Night Plane From Chungking (1943) **69m.** **½ D: Ralph Murphy. Ellen Drew, Robert Preston, Otto Kruger, Steven Geray, (Victor) Sen Yung, Tamara Geva, Soo Yong. Adequate adventure yarn about a plane shot down in the jungle, with captain Preston falling for Drew while going up against the Japanese.

Night Porter, The (1974-Italian) **C-115m.** ** D: Liliana Cavani. Dirk Bogarde, Charlotte Rampling, Philippe Leroy, Gabriele Ferzetti, Isa Miranda. Bizarre drama, set in 1957, about a sado-masochistic relationship between an ex-Nazi and the woman he used to abuse sexually in a concentration camp. Strictly for students of the sleazy.▼

Night Rider, The (1979) **C-78m. TVM** D: Hy Averback. David Selby, Percy Rodrigues, Kim Cattrall, George Grizzard, Anthony Herrera, Pernell Roberts, Anna Lee, Harris Yulin. So-So *Zorro* variant with a New Orleans dandy-by-day donning mask and cape after dark to right wrongs and avenge his family's murder. Swashbuckler pilot without panache. Average.

Night Runner, The (1957) **79m.** ** D: Abner Biberman. Ray Danton, Colleen Miller, Merry Anders, Eddy Waller. Violent B film of insane Danton on killing spree, about to gun down his girlfriend.

Night School (1981) **C-88m. BOMB** D: Ken Hughes. Leonard Mann, Rachel Ward, Drew Snyder, Joseph R. Sicari. Female students attending title place of learning are being decapitated. Not as graphically bloody as others of its genre, but still pretty bad. Ward's feature debut.▼

Night Shadows (1984) **C-99m.** ** D: John (Bud) Cardos. Wings Hauser, Bo Hopkins, Lee Montgomery, Jennifer Warren, Jody Medford, Cary Guffey. Yet another tale of toxic waste creating monsters that terrorize small Southern town. Same old stuff, with inferior special effects and makeup.

Night Shift (1982) **C-105m.** *** D: Ron Howard. Henry Winkler, Michael Keaton, Shelley Long, Gina Hecht, Pat Corley, Bobby DiCicco, Nita Talbot, Richard Belzer, Charles Fleischer, Kevin Costner. A nebbish takes a night job at the city morgue, seeking peace and quiet, but his new assistant draws him into wild scheme to start a prostitution business! Delightful, good-natured comedy (despite seamy subject matter) sharply directed by Howard, written with verve by Lowell Ganz and Babaloo Mandel. (Soundtrack also features Rod Stewart introducing "That's What Friends Are For," years before it became a hit.) Winkler has never been better; Keaton's smash debut performance made him an instant star. Is this a great country or what?▼

Nightside (1980) **C-78m.** TVM D: Bernard Kowalski. Doug McClure, Michael Cornelison, John DeLancie, Roy Jenson, Jason Kincaid, Melinda Naud. Predictable cop show pilot that McClure plays with a rather nice light touch. Average.

Night Slaves (1970) **C-73m.** TVM D: Ted Post. James Franciscus, Lee Grant, Scott Marlowe, Andrew Prine, Tisha Sterling, Leslie Nielsen. Aliens hypnotize town residents into helping repair spacecraft. Story built up as a mystery, from point of view of vacationing couple (Franciscus & Grant). Good story, reminiscent of IT CAME FROM OUTER SPACE, is hurt by indifferent script and direction. Average.

Nights of Cabiria (1957-Italian) **110m.** **** D: Federico Fellini. Giulietta Masina, Francois Perier, Amedeo Nazzari, Franca Marzi, Dorian Gray. Masina is a joy as waifish prostitute dreaming of rich, wonderful life but always finding sorrow. Basis for Broadway musical and film SWEET CHARITY. One of Fellini's best, and a most deserving Oscar-winner as Best Foreign Film.▼

Nights of Rasputin (1960-Italian) **C-95m.** ** D: Pierre Chenal. Edmund Purdom, Gianna Maria Canale, John Drew Barrymore, Jany Clair. Purdom is miscast as Rasputin in this plodding retelling of the conniving quack who gained power in Czarina Alexandra's court.

Night Song (1947) **101m.** ** D: John Cromwell. Dana Andrews, Merle Oberon, Ethel Barrymore, Hoagy Carmichael, Jacqueline White. Overlong, soapy drama of socialite Oberon falling in love with blind pianist Andrews. Barrymore is very good in the unusual role of comic relief. Arthur Rubenstein and conductor Eugene Ormandy appear in the climactic concert sequence, playing the concerto composed especially for the film by Leith Stevens.

Nightsongs (1984) **C-113m.** TVM D: Marva Nabili. Mabel Kwong, David Lee, Victor Wong, Ida F. O. Chung, Rose Lee, Roger Chang. Ambitious, sometimes moving chronicle of a Chinese immigrant family's struggle for survival in N.Y.C.'s Chinatown, as observed through the eyes of relative Kwong. Filmed mostly in Chinese, with English subtitles. Screenplay by director Nabili, who is herself an immigrant—from Iran. A PBS *American Playhouse* presentation. Average.

Night Stalker, The (1971) **C-73m.** TVM D: John Llewellyn Moxey. Darren McGavin, Carol Lynley, Simon Oakland, Ralph Meeker, Claude Akins, Kent Smith, Barry Atwater. Wise-guy reporter assigned to series of strange murders in Las Vegas. Near-brilliant mixture of double-edged horror, comedy; well-constructed script by

Richard Matheson. Kudos to flawless cast. Sequel: THE NIGHT STRANGLER. Later a TV series. Above average.▼

Night Stalker, The (1987) **C-89m.** ** D: Max Kleven. Charles Napier, Michelle Reese, Katherine Kelly Lang, Robert Viharo, Robert Zdar, Joey Gian, Leila Carlin, Gary Crosby, James Louis Watkins, Ola Ray, Tally Chanel, Joan Chen. Napier steps out impressively from supporting roles to star as a down and out L.A. cop who goes after a serial killer preying on prostitutes. Standard B-movie was made in 1985.▼

Night Star Goddess of Electra SEE: **War of the Zombies**

Night Strangler, The (1972) **C-74m.** TVM D: Dan Curtis. Darren McGavin, Simon Oakland, Jo Ann Pflug, Richard Anderson, John Carradine, Margaret Hamilton, Wally Cox. Sequel to THE NIGHT STALKER finds McGavin eking out living in Seattle; he latches onto series of murders involving blood drainage by syringe, discovers secret underground city and lone "resident." Great cast, but script has problems. Above average.

Night Terror (1977) **C-78m.** TVM D: E. W. Swackhamer. Valerie Harper, Richard Romanus, Nicholas Pryor, John Quade, Michael Tolan, Beatrice Manley, Quinn Cummings. Housewife Harper vs. psychopath Romanus whom she had seen shooting a highway patrolman. Another relentless pursuit suspense story that's resolved predictably by the fadeout. Average.▼

Night That Panicked America, The (1975) **C-100m.** TVM D: Joseph Sargent. Vic Morrow, Cliff De Young, Michael Constantine, Walter McGinn, Eileen Brennan, Meredith Baxter, Tom Bosley, Will Geer, Paul Shenar, John Ritter. Intriguing recreation of Orson Welles' famed "War of the Worlds" broadcast on Halloween night, 1938, intermixed with various real-life minidramas. Shenar offers an interesting Welles, but author Nicholas Meyer could have side-stepped the soap opera stuff. Later cut to 78m. Above average.

Night the Bridge Fell Down, The (1983) **C-150m.** TVM D: Georg Fenady. James MacArthur, Desi Arnaz, Jr., Char Fontane, Richard Gilliland, Leslie Nielsen, Eve Plumb, Barbara Rush, Gregory Sierra. Bank robber on the lam (Arnaz) is trapped with eight others on a collapsing bridge. Yet another Irwin Allen formula disaster film, though this was shelved for three years and (mercifully) trimmed by one hour before making its debut. Below average.

Night the City Screamed, The (1980) **C-100m.** TVM D: Harry Falk. Raymond Burr, Georg Stanford Brown, Robert Culp, David Cassidy, Linda Purl, Don Meredith, Clifton Davis, George DiCenzo, Gary Frank, Vic Tayback, Dick Anthony Williams,

Shelley Smith. A big blackout and its effect on the lives of a diverse group of citizens. Average.

Night the Lights Went Out in Georgia, The (1981) **C-120m.** **½ D: Ronald F. Maxwell. Kristy McNichol, Mark Hamill, Dennis Quaid, Sunny Johnson, Don Stroud, Arlen Dean Snyder. Kristy, the more ambitious half of brother-sister country music duo, tries in vain to keep sibling Quaid out of romantic scrapes. Poor beginning and conclusion somewhat redeemed by rather appealing middle. Inspired by title-named hit record of years past.▼

Night the World Exploded, The (1957) **94m.** ** D: Fred F. Sears. Kathryn Grant, William Leslie, Tris Coffin, Raymond Greenleaf, Marshall Reed. Scientists discover a strange, exploding mineral that threatens to bring about title catastrophe and rush to prevent it. OK idea hampered by low budget.

Night They Raided Minsky's, The (1968) **C-99m.** *** D: William Friedkin. Jason Robards, Britt Ekland, Norman Wisdom, Forrest Tucker, Harry Andrews, Joseph Wiseman, Denholm Elliott, Elliott Gould, Jack Burns, Bert Lahr, narrated by Rudy Vallee. Flavorful period piece about Amish girl who comes to N.Y.C., gets involved with burlesque comic Robards. Many nice backstage and onstage moments. Abruptness of Lahr's role is due to his death during filming. Produced and cowritten by Norman Lear.▼

Night They Saved Christmas, The (1984) **C-100m.** TVM D: Jackie Cooper. Jaclyn Smith, Art Carney, Paul LeMat, Mason Adams, June Lockhart, Paul Williams, Scott Grimes. Amiable yuletide fantasy involving three youngsters' efforts to save Santa's toy factory from destruction by nearby oil drilling station. Carney's delightful as old Saint Nick, and Williams is fun as one of his elves. Written by James C. Moloney and David Niven, Jr. Above average.▼

Night They Took Miss Beautiful, The (1977) **C-100m.** TVM D: Robert Michael Lewis. Chuck Connors, Gary Collins, Henry Gibson, Peter Haskell, Sheree North, Phil Silvers, Stella Stevens. Skyjack drama involving a terrorist group headed by North, five beauty pageant finalists who are abducted, and deadly mutant germs for conducting bacterial warfare. Routine thriller with a planeload of familiar TV personalities. Average.

Night Tide (1963) **84m.** **½ D: Curtis Harrington. Dennis Hopper, Linda Lawson, Gavin Muir, Luana Anders, Marjorie Eaton, Tom Dillon, H. E. West, Cameron. Lonely sailor Hopper falls for Lawson, who works as a mermaid at the Santa Monica pier, but learns she may be a killer—

and a descendant of the sirens. Odd, dreamy little drama is strangely compelling, though not a horror film, as often promoted. Written by the director.▼

Night to Remember, A (1943) **91m.** ***½ D: Richard Wallace. Loretta Young, Brian Aherne, Jeff Donnell, William Wright, Sidney Toler, Gale Sondergaard, Donald MacBride, Blanche Yurka. Sparkling comedy-mystery of whodunit author Aherne and wife Young trying to solve murder.▼

Night to Remember, A (1958-British) **123m.** **** D: Roy (Ward) Baker. Kenneth More, David McCallum, Jill Dixon, Laurence Naismith, Frank Lawton, Honor Blackman, Alec McCowen, George Rose. Meticulously produced documentary-style account of sinking of the passenger liner Titanic. Far superior to Hollywood's TITANIC. Vivid adaptation by Eric Ambler of Walter Lord's book.▼

Night Train (1940) SEE: **Night Train to Munich**

Night Train (1959-Polish) **90m.** ** D: Jerzy Kawalerowicz. Lucyna Winnicka, Leon Niemczyk, Teresa Szmigielowna, Zbigniew Cybulski. Murky account of young woman on a train, forced to share compartment with a doctor; their lack of communication and presence of killer on train are film's focal points.

Night Train to Kathmandu, The (1988) **C-105m.** TVM D: Robert Wiemer. Pernell Roberts, Eddie Castrodad, Milla Jovovitch, Kavi Raz, Tim Eyster, Robert Stoeckle. Unimaginative family adventure mixes dollops of BRIGADOON and LOST HORIZON into its trite tale of teens from two different cultures running afoul of a gruff archeologist who's doing research in the Himalayas. Made for cable. Below average.▼

Night Train to Munich (1940-British) **93m.** *** D: Carol Reed. Rex Harrison, Margaret Lockwood, Paul Von Hernried (Henreid), Basil Radford, Naunton Wayne, Felix Aylmer, Roland Culver. Expert Hitchcockian thriller about British intelligence agent Harrison trying to rescue Czech scientist who escaped from the Nazis to London only to be kidnapped back to Berlin. Stylishly photographed (by Otto Kanturek), sharply scripted by Frank Launder and Sidney Gilliat, who also wrote Hitchcock's THE LADY VANISHES (which introduced the comic characters reprised here by Radford and Wayne). Based on Gordon Wellesley's novel *Report on a Fugitive*. Originally released in U.S. as NIGHT TRAIN.

Night unto Night (1949) **85m.** ** D: Don Siegel. Ronald Reagan, Viveca Lindfors, Broderick Crawford, Rosemary DeCamp, Osa Massen, Art Baker, Craig Stevens. Somber, unconvincing film about relationship of dying scientist and mentally disturbed widow. Finished in 1947 and shelved for two years; it's not hard to see why. Reagan's performance isn't bad, but script is against him.

Night Visitor, The (1970) **C-106m.** **½ D: Laslo Benedek. Max von Sydow, Liv Ullmann, Trevor Howard, Per Oscarsson, Rupert Davies, Andrew Keir. An inmate plots to escape from an asylum for the criminally insane for one night, to avenge himself on people who put him away. Ponderous, heavy in detail, but interesting. Filmed in Denmark and Sweden.▼

Night Visitor (1990) **C-94m.** ** D: Rupert Hitzig. Derek Rydall, Allen Garfield, Teresa Vander Woude, Elliott Gould, Michael J. Pollard, Brooke Bundy, Richard Roundtree, Shannon Tweed. Teenage Rydall discovers his most hated schoolteacher (Garfield) is a Satanist and serial killer of prostitutes; when no one believes him, he turns to retired cop Gould for help. Silly, unconvincing blend of teenage comedy and thriller, helped by good performances.▼

Night Walk (1989) **C-100m. TVM** D: Jerrold Freedman. Robert Urich, Lesley-Anne Down, Mark Joy, Ryan Urich, Bert Remsen. Down spots a killing on a deserted stretch of beach but is unable to convince the cops, since the body's disappeared. Now *she's* the target of professional hit men who know she witnessed the crime. Average.

Night Walker, The (1964) **86m.** *** D: William Castle. Barbara Stanwyck, Robert Taylor, Lloyd Bochner, Rochelle Hudson, Judi Meredith, Hayden Rorke. One of the better Castle horror films has Stanwyck as wealthy widow discovering cause of recurring dreams about lost husband. Effective psychological thriller with good cast, unusual script by Robert Bloch.

Night Warning (1982) **C-94m.** **½ D: William Asher. Jimmy McNichol, Susan Tyrrell, Bo Svenson, Marcia Lewis, Julia Duffy. Explosive, tour-de-force acting by Tyrrell distinguishes this formula horror film. She's a sexually repressed aunt, overly protective of her nephew McNichol, who finally turns to murder. Svenson as the cop on the case is typed as an exaggerated, gay-baiting extension of his earlier Buford Pusser role.▼

Night Watch (1973-British) **C-105m.** **½ D: Brian G. Hutton. Elizabeth Taylor, Laurence Harvey, Billie Whitelaw, Robert Lang, Tony Britton. Woman (Taylor) believes she has witnessed a murder, but cannot prove it. Tired plot based on Lucille Fletcher play.▼

Nightwing (1979) **C-105m.** *½ D: Arthur Hiller. Nick Mancuso, David Warner, Kathryn Harrold, Stephen Macht, Strother Martin. Warner is an oddball who comes to Arizona to kill vampire bats in their caves.

Well, it's a living. From a Martin Cruz Smith novel.▼

Night Without Sleep (1952) **77m.** ** D: Roy Baker. Linda Darnell, Gary Merrill, Hildegarde Neff, Hugh Beaumont, Mae Marsh. Pat treatment of man thinking he's committed murder.

Night Without Stars (1951-British) **86m.** **½ D: Anthony Pelissier. David Farrar, Nadia Gray, Maurice Teynac, June Clyde, Gerard Landry. Adequate mystery with partially blind lawyer Farrar becoming involved with Gray, and a murder.

Night World (1932) **56m.** *** D: Hobart Henley. Lew Ayres, Mae Clarke, Boris Karloff, Dorothy Revier, Russell Hopton, Clarence Muse, Hedda Hopper, Bert Roach, George Raft. Outrageous little pre-Code item about the various goings on in a Prohibition-era nightclub. Karloff is its corrupt owner; Ayres a troubled young man whose mother has murdered his father; Clarke a wiscracking chorus girl; Muse a philosophical doorman; Raft (in a small role) a Broadway tinhorn. Add to this some vintage Busby Berkeley choreography . . . and the result is a real curio, a must for 1930s film buffs.

Night Zoo (1987-Canadian) **C-115m.** ** D: Jean-Claude Lauzon. Roger Le Bel, Gilles Maheu, Lyne Brass, Lorne Brass, Germain Houde. French-Canadian melodrama, wildly overrated on its home turf, unconvincingly mixes a moving story of love between ex-con Le Bel and his father with a brutal tale of sex and drugs unfolding in Montreal. Title refers to a ludicrous climax at the local zoo. Graphic sex scenes almost reduce this one to exploitation film level.▼

Nijinsky (1980-British) **C-125m.** **½ D: Herbert Ross. Alan Bates, George de la Pena, Leslie Browne, Ronald Pickup, Alan Badel, Colin Blakely, Ronald Lacey, Carla Fracci, Jeremy Irons, Janet Suzman, Sian Phillips. Handsome but disappointing chronicle of the homosexual relationship between the legendary dancer Nijinsky (de la Pena) and Ballet Russe impresario Sergei Diaghilev (Bates). Worthy subject matter defeated by soap-opera scenario, allegedly inauthentic characterizations. Fine performance by Bates, superb one by Badel as a wealthy patron.▼

Nikki, Wild Dog of the North (1961) **C-74m.** *** D: Jack Couffer, Don Haldane. Jean Coutu, Emile Genest, Uriel Luft, Robert Rivard. Wolfdog Nikki is separated from his master, a Canadian trapper, and fends for himself in a variety of adventures. Exciting Disney film.▼

9½ Weeks (1986) **C-113m.** *½ D: Adrian Lyne. Mickey Rourke, Kim Basinger, Margaret Whitton, David Margulies, Christine Baranski, Dwight Weist, Roderick Cook. Saga of an obsessive sexual relationship;

uninvolving and unerotic, not to mention degrading. Promises sexual fireworks, but all it delivers is a big tease (some explicit material was cut prior to release). As to the characters, who cares? Videocassette version is more explicit, though not so much as European release version.▼

Nine Girls (1944) **78m.** **½ D: Leigh Jason. Ann Harding, Evelyn Keyes, Jinx Falkenburg, Anita Louise, Jeff Donnell, Nina Foch, Marcia Mae Jones, Leslie Brooks, Lynn Merrick, Shirley Mills, William Demarest. Wisecrack-laden comedy mystery about murder at a sorority house.

Nine Hours to Rama (1963) **C-125m.** **½ D: Mark Robson. Horst Buchholz, Jose Ferrer, Robert Morley, Diane Baker, Harry Andrews. Ambitious attempt to make meaningful story of events leading up to assassination of Mahatma Gandhi; bogs down in trite script. Filmed on location in India.

Nine Lives Are Not Enough (1941) **63m.** **½ D: A. Edward Sutherland. Ronald Reagan, Joan Perry, James Gleason, Peter Whitney, Faye Emerson, Howard da Silva, Edward Brophy, Charles Drake. Reagan is an aggressive newspaperman who solves a murder case. Enjoyable, fast-paced Warner Bros. B entry.

976-Evil (1988) **C-89m.** **½ D: Robert Englund. Stephen Geoffreys, Patrick O'Bryan, Sandy Dennis, Jim Metzler, Maria Rubell, Robert Picardo, Lezlie Deane, J.J. Cohen, Darren Burrows. Snappy CARRIE-like outsider's-revenge horror flick. Introverted teenager Geoffreys calls 976 number that provides him with satanic powers. Story is confusing, and script too jokey, but as often as not, it delivers the goods. Director Englund is Freddy Krueger in the NIGHTMARE ON ELM ST. series.▼

1918 (1984) **C-94m.** **½ D: Ken Harrison. William Converse-Roberts, Hallie Foote, Matthew Broderick. Rochelle Oliver, Michael Higgins, Jeannie McCarthy, Bill McGhee, Horton Foote, Jr. Stagy, PBSy Horton Foote drama concerns the catastrophic late teens influenza epidemic that hit America—and its tragic effect on a small Texas town. Will probably be seen to best advantage on the small screen; Hallie Foote (the playwright's daughter) is excellent as a woman (based on her own real-life grandmother) whose husband and infant are both stricken. Produced for *American Playhouse*; followed by prequel ON VALENTINE'S DAY. Both were telecast as STORY OF A MARRIAGE.▼

1984 (1956-British) **91m.** *** D: Michael Anderson. Edmond O'Brien, Michael Redgrave, Jan Sterling, David Kossoff, Mervyn Johns, Donald Pleasence. Thought-provoking version of George Orwell's futuristic novel. Lovers O'Brien and Sterling are trapped in all-powerful state, try val-iantly to rebel against "Big Brother." Remade in 1984.

1984 (1984-British) **C-115m.** *** D: Michael Radford. John Hurt, Richard Burton, Suzanna Hamilton, Cyril Cusack, Gregor Fisher, James Walker, Phyllis Logan, Bob Flag. Appropriately grim, well-cast version of the Orwell classic, with Hurt as the government functionary who illegally falls in love, Hamilton as his bedmate, and Burton—excellent in his final feature—as the party official who somehow seems human even when feeding his victims' faces to the rats. Superior to the 1956 version, though the oppressive gloominess of the second half does wear you down. Seedily impressive production design.▼

1941 (1979) **C-118m.** **½ D: Steven Spielberg. Dan Aykroyd, Ned Beatty, John Belushi, Treat Williams, Nancy Allen, Robert Stack, Tim Matheson, Toshiro Mifune, Christopher Lee, Warren Oates, Bobby DiCicco, Dianne Kay, Murray Hamilton, Lorraine Gary, Slim Pickens, Eddie Deezen, John Candy, many others. Gargantuan comedy from the bigger-is-funnier school of filmmaking. Some excellent vignettes and dazzling special effects in freewheeling story of war panic in L.A. following Pearl Harbor attack, but on the whole film suffers from overkill. Written by Bob Gale and Robert Zemeckis. The network version included 26m. of outtakes.▼

1900 (1977-Italian-French-German) **C-243m.** ***½ D: Bernardo Bertolucci. Robert De Niro, Gerard Depardieu, Donald Sutherland, Burt Lancaster, Dominique Sanda, Stefania Sandrelli, Sterling Hayden. Sweeping chronicle of 20th-century Italy focusing on two contrasting families; ambitious, powerful film full of potent, beautiful images. Continuity problems caused, no doubt, by trimming from six-hour original; beware further cutting.▼

19/19 (1985-British) **C/B&W-99m.** ** D: Hugh Brody. Paul Scofield, Maria Schell, Frank Finlay, Diana Quick, Clare Higgins, Colin Firth. Scofield and Schell are two former patients of Sigmund Freud, who come together many years later to reminisce and remember. Slow and boring, wasting talents of a fine cast.

1990: The Bronx Warriors (1983-Italian) **C-84m.** BOMB D: Enzo G. Castellari. Vic Morrow, Christopher Connelly, Fred Williamson, Mark Gregory, Stefania Girolami. Bronx gang leaders vs. nasty corporation agent Morrow. Gregory plays a character named Trash, which is the best way to describe this movie. Filmed in the Bronx and Rome. Sequel: ESCAPE FROM THE BRONX.▼

1969 (1988) **C-93m.** ** D: Ernest Thompson. Robert Downey, Jr., Kiefer Sutherland, Bruce Dern, Mariette Hartley, Joanna

Cassidy, Winona Ryder. Sutherland is terrific as a sensitive antiwar youth, and Hartley fine as his understanding mother, in this story of troubled times and troubled lives. Playwright Thompson makes an earnest effort in his directorial debut, but the result is disconnected and ultimately disappointing. Has a can't-miss soundtrack, but could have missed the clichés.▼

9 to 5 (1980) **C-110m.** **½ D: Colin Higgins. Jane Fonda, Lily Tomlin, Dolly Parton, Dabney Coleman, Sterling Hayden, Elizabeth Wilson, Henry Jones, Lawrence Pressman, Marian Mercer. Three savvy secretaries have to contend with a doltish boss—and inadvertently find their chance to take revenge. The first half of this comedy is dynamite, culminating in Tomlin's Disneyesque fantasy of murdering the slavedriver, but the film then takes a disastrous turn, losing its bearings and topical momentum. Appealing performances by the star trio help make up for the ultimate silliness. Later a TV series.▼

Ninety Degrees in the Shade (1964-Czech) **90m.** **½ D: Jiri Weiss. Anne Heywood, James Booth, Donald Wolfit, Ann Todd. Turgid account of Heywood, who works in food store, accused of theft; intertwined with passionate love episodes. Czech-made, with British stars.

99 and 44/100% Dead (1974) **C-98m.** BOMB D: John Frankenheimer. Richard Harris, Chuck Connors, Edmond O'Brien, Bradford Dillman, Ann Turkel. Idiotic, poorly made gangster melodrama with satirical overtones: hit-man Harris is hired by mobster O'Brien to knock off rival Dillman. The pits.▼

99 River Street (1953) **83m.** *** D: Phil Karlson. John Payne, Evelyn Keyes, Brad Dexter, Peggie Castle, Ian Wolfe, Frank Faylen. Rugged crime caper with Payne caught up in tawdry surroundings, trying to prove himself innocent of murder charge. Unpretentious film really packs a punch.

99 Women (1969-Spanish-German-British-Italian) **C-90m.** *½ D: Jess Franco. Maria Schell, Luciana Paluzzi, Mercedes McCambridge, Herbert Lom. Absurd drama about lesbianism in women's prison may have some scenes cut for TV, unless film puts the censors to sleep. Also known as ISLE OF LOST WOMEN.▼

92 in the Shade (1975) **C-93m.** *** D: Thomas McGuane. Peter Fonda, Warren Oates, Margot Kidder, Burgess Meredith, Harry Dean Stanton, Sylvia Miles, Elizabeth Ashley. National Book Award-nominated novel about rival fishing boat captains in Florida Keys; directed by the author. Wildly uneven but well cast and frequently hilarious.▼

Ninja III—The Domination (1984) **C-95m.** **½ D: Sam Firstenberg. Lucinda

Dickey, Jordan Bennett, Sho Kosugi, David Chung. Follow-up to REVENGE OF THE NINJA about an evil Ninja, "killed" by the police, who forces his spirit on innocent Dickey. Lots of action; good of its type.▼

Ninotchka (1939) **110m.** ***½ D: Ernst Lubitsch. Greta Garbo, Melvyn Douglas, Ina Claire, Bela Lugosi, Sig Ruman, Felix Bressart, Alexander Granach, Richard Carle. Amid much outdated sociological banter, a lighthearted Garbo still shines. Lubitsch's comedy pegged on tale of cold Russian agent Garbo coming to Paris, falling in love with gay-blade Douglas. Supporting cast shows fine comedy flair. Script by Billy Wilder, Charles Brackett, and Walter Reisch was basis for Broadway musical and film SILK STOCKINGS.▼

Ninth Configuration, The (1980) **C-118m.** ***½ D: William Peter Blatty. Stacy Keach, Scott Wilson, Jason Miller, Ed Flanders, Neville Brand, Moses Gunn, George Di Cenzo, Robert Loggia, Tom Atkins, Alejandro Rey, Joe Spinell, Steve Sandor, Richard Lynch. In old castle used by U.S. government as asylum, new head shrink Keach quickly proves to be nuttier than any of the patients. Hilarious yet thought-provoking, with endlessly quotable dialogue and an amazing barroom fight scene. Blatty also produced and adapted his novel *Twinkle, Twinkle, Killer Kane* (this film's title at one point). Myriad versions run anywhere from 99m. to 140m.; above time is Blatty's cut, and rating applies to this version only.▼

Nitti (1988) **C-100m. TVM** D: Michael Switzer. Anthony LaPaglia, Vincent Guastaferro, Trini Alvarado, Michael Moriarty, Michael Russo, Louis Guss, Bruno Kirby. The life and times of Capone's Chicago "enforcer" Frank Nitti, played chameleon-like by LaPaglia, who seems to have overdosed on Robert De Niro movies. A large cast of relative unknowns (save Moriarty as prosecutor Hugh Kelly, who makes assorted disparaging references to rival Elliot Ness) helps keep the atmospheric and quite bloody (fictional) biography on track. Average.

Nitwits, The (1935) **81m.** *** D: George Stevens. Bert Wheeler, Robert Woolsey, Betty Grable, Hale Hamilton, Evelyn Brent, Erik Rhodes. Enjoyable Wheeler & Woolsey vehicle mixes their nonsense comedy with murder mystery in an office building; smashing slapstick climax.

Noah's Ark (1929) **100m.** **½ D: Michael Curtiz. Dolores Costello, George O'Brien, Noah Beery, Louise Fazenda, Gwynne (Guinn) Williams, Paul McAllister, Myrna Loy. Hokey and derivative story (by Darryl F. Zanuck) has devil-may-care O'Brien, gallivanting through Europe, falling in love with German girl Costello on the eve of WW1, and finally realizing his duty and enlisting in the U.S. Army. Somehow all this is paralleled to the days of Noah in a lengthy flashback sequence. Biblical segment is dazzlingly elaborate and full of great special effects. Silent film with somewhat awkward talking sequences; originally shown at 135m., then cut to 104m. after premiere. Restored in 1989; beware of 1957 reissue prints running 75m.

Nob Hill (1945) **C-95m.** **½ D: Henry Hathaway. George Raft, Joan Bennett, Vivian Blaine, Peggy Ann Garner, Alan Reed, B. S. Pully, Emil Coleman. Gold Coast saloon owner Raft has his head turned when socialite Bennett shows an interest in him. Predictable formula musical given first-class treatment and handsome Technicolor production.

No Big Deal (1983) **C-86m.** **½ D: Robert Charlton. Kevin Dillon, Christopher Gartin, Mary Joan Negro, Jane Krakowski, Tammy Grimes, Sylvia Miles. Fair drama about troubled, alienated, streetwise teen Dillon and his attempt to fit in with his peers. A decent effort at portraying adolescent problems and pressures, but the result is a bit too pat. Interestingly, Miles is cast as a strict, bureaucratic school principal.

No Blade of Grass (1970) **C-97m.** *½ D: Cornel Wilde. Nigel Davenport, Jean Wallace, John Hamill, Lynne Frederick, Patrick Holt, Anthony May. Sober-sided film trying to drive home ecology message is just an update of films like PANIC IN YEAR ZERO, with family fleeing virus-stricken London for Scottish countryside, facing panic and attack along the way. Based on John Christopher's popular novel.

Nobody Lives Forever (1946) **100m.** *** D: Jean Negulesco. John Garfield, Geraldine Fitzgerald, Walter Brennan, Faye Emerson, George Coulouris, George Tobias. Well-done but familiar yarn of con-man Garfield fleecing rich widow Fitzgerald, then falling in love for real.

Nobody Runs Forever SEE: **High Commissioner, The**

Nobody's Child (1986) **C-100m.** **TVM** D: Lee Grant. Marlo Thomas, Ray Baker, Blanche Baker, Caroline Kava, Kathy Baker, Anna Maria Horsford, Madeleine Sherwood. Marlo won an Emmy playing real-life Marie Balter, who survived twenty years in a mental institution, confounding physicians who considered her incapable of leading a normal life. (Today she's a mental health administrator!) Famed cinematographer Sven Nykvist made his American television debut here. Written by Mary Gallagher and Ara Watson. Average.

Nobody's Fault SEE: **Little Dorrit▼**

Nobody's Fool (1986) **C-107m.** **½ D: Evelyn Purcell. Rosanna Arquette, Eric Roberts, Mare Winningham, Jim Youngs, Louise Fletcher, Gwen Welles, Stephen

Tobolowsky, Charlie Barnett, Lewis Arquette. Innocuous romantic comedy by Beth Henley about a flaky waitress in a small Southwestern town who's become an outcast (after having a baby out of wedlock), and only begins to find herself when she meets Roberts, who's passing through town. Very modest film that benefits from a relaxed and unmannered performance by Roberts.▼

Nobody's Perfect (1968) **C-103m.** **½ D: Alan Rafkin. Doug McClure, Nancy Kwan, James Whitmore, David Hartman, Gary Vinson. Witless military service comedy involving pat shenanigans of U.S. submarine based in Japan, with every predictable gimmick thrown in.

Nobody's Perfect (1989-Swiss-U.S.) **C-91m.** **½ D: Robert Kaylor. Chad Lowe, Gail O'Grady, Patrick Breen, Kim Flowers, Eric Bruskotter, Carmen Moré, Robert Vaughn. Shy guy at a new college wants to make friends with an attractive girl, but is too tongue-tied, so at a friend's urging, disguises himself as a girl and ends up his target's roommate. Little comedy based on the last line of SOME LIKE IT HOT is pleasant throughout, predictable but entertaining.▼

Nobody's Perfekt (1981) **C-95m.** BOMB D: Peter Bonerz. Gabe Kaplan, Alex Karras, Robert Klein, Susan Clark, Paul Stewart, Alex Rocco, Peter Bonerz. Entirely unfunny comedy, made in Miami, about three misfits who decide to fight City Hall when their car is totalled in a pothole and—because of a loophole—they can't sue. Klein, who can be funny, does awful imitations of James Cagney and Bette Davis. An inauspicious theatrical directing debut for Bonerz.▼

Nobody Waved Goodbye (1965-Canadian) **80m.** *** D: Don Owen. Peter Kastner, Julie Biggs, Claude Rae, Toby Tarnow, Charmion King, Ron Taylor. Straightforward, perceptive account of alienated teenager Kastner, and his problems and frustrations. A sequel, UNFINISHED BUSINESS, is set 20 years later, and details the plight of Kastner and Biggs's own teen offspring.

Nocturna (1978) **C-83m.** BOMB D: Harry Tampa (Harry Hurwitz). Yvonne de Carlo, John Carradine, Nai Bonet, Brother Theodore. Grade-Z sleaze with a tired Carradine phoning in his performance as Dracula. The Count, in trouble with the taxman, turns his castle into a disco!▼

Nocturne (1946) **88m.** *** D: Edwin L. Marin. George Raft, Lynn Bari, Virginia Huston, Joseph Pevney, Myrna Dell. Detective Raft is convinced supposed suicide was murder; police force suspends him, but he continues investigations on his own; taut private-eye thriller.

No Deposit, No Return (1976) **C-112m.**

**½ D: Norman Tokar. David Niven, Darren McGavin, Don Knotts, Herschel Bernardi, Barbara Feldon, Brad Savage, Kim Richards. Two neglected kids stage their own bogus kidnapping to stir up attention and enable them to join their mother in Hong Kong. OK Disney comedy with so-so material enlivened by good cast.▼

No Down Payment (1957) **105m.** *** D: Martin Ritt. Joanne Woodward, Jeffrey Hunter, Sheree North, Tony Randall, Cameron Mitchell, Patricia Owens, Barbara Rush, Pat Hingle. Turgid suburban soaper of intertwining problems of several young married couples; very capable cast.

No Drums, No Bugles (1971) **C-85m.** **½ D: Clyde Ware. Martin Sheen. Nicely done drama, based on West Virginia legend about conscientious objector during Civil War who spends three years in a cave rather than fight. Good acting by Sheen, who's the only one on screen for most of film.▼

No Escape (1943) SEE: **I Escaped from the Gestapo**

No Escape (1953) **76m.** *½ D: Charles Bennett. Lew Ayres, Marjorie Steele, Sonny Tufts, Gertrude Michael. Modest narrative about couple seeking actual killer to clear themselves of homicide charge. Retitled: CITY ON A HUNT.

No Highway in the Sky (1951-British) **98m.** *** D: Henry Koster. James Stewart, Marlene Dietrich, Glynis Johns, Jack Hawkins, Elizabeth Allan, Kenneth More. Excellent drama of Stewart's discovery of metal fatigue causing plane crashes; Dietrich a glamorous passenger on crash-bound plane; Johns a girl in love with Stewart.

No Holds Barred (1952) **65m.** D: William Beaudine. Leo Gorcey, Huntz Hall, Marjorie Reynolds, Bernard Gorcey, Tim Ryan, Leonard Penn. SEE: **Bowery Boys** series.

No Holds Barred (1989) **C-91m.** ** D: Thomas J. Wright. Hulk Hogan, Joan Severance, Kurt Fuller, Tiny Lister, Mark Pellegrino, Jesse (The Body) Ventura, Bill Henderson. For those who can't get enough of wrestling star Hulk Hogan, he appears in this vehicle as a TV wrestling star who must defend himself after refusing a greedy businessman's offer to switch networks. Aimed squarely at the legion of Hulkster fans, who presumably won't mind how predictable the whole thing is.▼

No Leave, No Love (1946) **119m.** ** D: Charles Martin. Van Johnson, Keenan Wynn, Pat Kirkwood, Guy Lombardo, Edward Arnold, Marie Wilson. No script, no laughs; Johnson and Wynn are sailors on the town in this overlong romantic comedy.

No Love for Johnnie (1961-British) **110m.** *** D: Ralph Thomas. Peter Finch, Stanley Holloway, Mary Peach, Mervyn Johns,

Donald Pleasence, Dennis Price, Oliver Reed. Civilized study of politician who cares only about winning the election.▼

Nomads (1986) **C-95m.** *½ D: John McTiernan. Lesley-Anne Down, Pierce Brosnan, Adam Ant, Anna-Maria Monticelli, Hector Mercado, Mary Woronov. Doctor (Down) treats an apparent madman, then undergoes a hallucinatory rerun of his recent experiences: he's a French anthropologist who's come to L.A. and has been drawn to a band of strange street people. Potentially interesting idea for a half-hour *Twilight Zone* but pretty deadly as a feature. Unpleasant, too.▼

No Man Is an Island (1962) **C-114m.** **½ D: John Monks, Jr., Richard Goldstone. Jeffrey Hunter, Marshall Thompson, Barbara Perez, Ronald Remy, Paul Edwards, Jr., Rolf Bayer, Vicente Liwanag. Spotty production values mar true story of serviceman Hunter trapped on Guam during the three years Japanese controlled area.

No Man of Her Own (1932) **85m.** **½ D: Wesley Ruggles. Clark Gable, Carole Lombard, Dorothy Mackaill, Grant Mitchell, Elizabeth Patterson, Lillian Harmer, George Barbier, J. Farrell MacDonald, Charley Grapewin. Snappy story of heel reformed by good girl, noteworthy for only co-starring of Gable and Lombard (then not married).▼

No Man of Her Own (1950) **98m.** **½ D: Mitchell Leisen. Barbara Stanwyck, John Lund, Jane Cowl, Phyllis Thaxter, Richard Denning, Milburn Stone. Turgid drama based on Cornell Woolrich tale of Stanwyck assuming another's identity, later being blackmailed by ex-boyfriend. Remade as I MARRIED A SHADOW.

No Man's Land (1984) **C-100m.** TVM D: Rod Holcomb. Stella Stevens, Terri Garber, Melissa Michaelsen, Donna Dixon, Estelle Getty, Janis Paige, Robert Webber, Sam Jones, John Rhys-Davies. Female sheriff and three winsome daughters vs. Old West desperado and foreign revolutionaries. Light-hearted sagebrush TV pilot. Average.

No Man's Land (1985-French-Swiss) **C-110m.** *** D: Alain Tanner. Hugues Quester, Myriam Mezieres, Jean-Philippe Ecoffey, Betty Berr, Marie-Luce Felber. Sober, provocative account of several characters involved with smuggling contraband across the French-Swiss border, focusing on their motivations and disillusionment. May be effectively contrasted to Tanner's earlier JONAH WHO WILL BE 25 IN THE YEAR 2000.

No Man's Land (1987) **C-106m.** ** D: Peter Werner. Charlie Sheen, D.B. Sweeney, Lara Harris, Randy Quaid, Bill Duke, R.D. Call, M. Emmet Walsh. Rookie cop goes undercover to trap a wealthy young auto buff who operates a hot car ring, finds he

[824]

likes his target, the target's sister, *and* stealing Porsches. Good premise largely botched; casting two low-key actors as adversaries was probably a mistake. Passable.▼

No Man's Woman (1955) **70m.** ** D: Franklin Adreon. Marie Windsor, John Archer, Patric Knowles, Nancy Gates, Louis Jean Heydt. OK whodunit about finding murderer of strong-willed woman.

No Mercy (1986) **C-105m.** *½ D: Richard Pearce. Richard Gere, Kim Basinger, Jeroen Krabbe, George Dzundza, Gary Basaraba, William Atherton, Ray Sharkey. Chicago cop Gere storms into Louisiana Bayou country seeking the killer of his partner, falls for Cajun beauty Basinger—who's been "sold" to the kingpin perpetrator of the murder. Even mindless melodramas have to make sense, at least on their own terms; this one's pretty ridiculous, especially in a climactic shoot-out inside a burning building. The two sexy stars don't really click.▼

No Mercy Man, The SEE: **Trained to Kill**

No Minor Vices (1948) **96m.** ** D: Lewis Milestone. Dana Andrews, Lilli Palmer, Louis Jourdan, Jane Wyatt, Norman Lloyd. Comedy of mooching house guest Jourdan winning over Andrews' wife Palmer; starts out well but bogs down.

No More Ladies (1935) **81m.** **½ D: Edward H. Griffith. Joan Crawford, Robert Montgomery, Charlie Ruggles, Franchot Tone, Edna May Oliver, Gail Patrick. Crawford marries playboy Montgomery, tries to settle him down by making him jealous over her attention to Tone. Airy comedy. Joan Burfield (Fontaine) made her film debut here.

No More Women (1934) **77m.** **½ D: Albert Rogell. Victor McLaglen, Edmund Lowe, Sally Blane, Minna Gombell, Alphonse Ethier, Tom Dugan. Typically lusty vehicle for the two stars, as rival deep-sea divers who swear off brawling over "Dames"—until the new owner of their ship turns out to be gorgeous Blane! Good action and underwater sequences, amusing script by Delmer Daves and Lou Breslow.

No My Darling Daughter (1961-British) **97m.** **½ D: Ralph Thomas. Michael Redgrave, Michael Craig, Juliet Mills, Roger Livesey, Rad Fulton, Renee Houston. Generally funny film with Mills, rich industrialist's daughter, torn between two suitors, playboy and hard-working businessman.

No Name on the Bullet (1959) **C-77m.** *** D: Jack Arnold. Audie Murphy, Charles Drake, Joan Evans, Virginia Grey, Warren Stevens, Edgar Stehli, R. G. Armstrong, Willis Bouchey, Karl Swenson, Charles Watts, Jerry Paris, Whit Bissell. A quiet, cultured gunman (Murphy, in a fine performance) rides into a small town to kill someone, though no one but him knows who his target is. Guilt and paranoia create their own victims. Slow, philosophical, and intelligent, this is the best of sci-fi director Arnold's several Westerns.

None But the Brave (1965) **C-105m.** **½ D: Frank Sinatra. Frank Sinatra, Clint Walker, Tommy Sands, Tony Bill, Brad Dexter. Taut war drama focusing on crew of cracked-up plane and Japanese army patrol who make peace on a remote island during WW2.

None But the Lonely Heart (1944) **113m.** **½ D: Clifford Odets. Cary Grant, Ethel Barrymore, Barry Fitzgerald, Jane Wyatt, Dan Duryea, George Coulouris, June Duprez. Odets' moody drama of a Cockney drifter features one of Grant's most ambitious performances, and some fine moments, but suffers from censorship restrictions of the time, and misplaced WW2 rhetoric. Barrymore won Supporting Actress Oscar as Grant's dying mother.▼

None Shall Escape (1944) **85m.** *** D: Andre de Toth. Marsha Hunt, Alexander Knox, Henry Travers, Richard Crane, Dorothy Morris, Trevor Bardette. Trial of Nazi officer reviews his savage career, in taut drama that retains quite a punch. Released before, but set after, the end of WWII.

Non-Stop New York (1937-British) **71m.** *** D: Robert Stevenson. John Loder, Anna Lee, Francis L. Sullivan, Frank Cellier, Desmond Tester. Fast-paced, tongue-in-cheek Hitchcock-like yarn about a woman who can provide alibi for innocent man accused of murder—but no one will believe her. Love that luxury airplane!▼

No Nukes (1980) **C-103m.** *** D: Julian Schlossberg, Danny Goldberg, Anthony Potenza. Jackson Browne, Crosby, Stills & Nash, The Doobie Brothers, John Hall, Gil Scott-Heron, Bonnie Raitt, Carly Simon, Bruce Springsteen, James Taylor, Jesse Colin Young. Super-Springsteen joins several appealing, if long in the tooth, fellow rock stars to protest nuclear power. Pleasant, if not very magnetic, concert film-documentary does boast chillingly hilarious clip from pro-nuke "Big Picture" episode from early '50s. Also known as THE MUSE CONCERT: NO NUKES.▼

No One Man (1932) **73m.** ** D: Lloyd Corrigan. Carole Lombard, Ricardo Cortez, Paul Lukas, George Barbier. Another tired love triangle, with spoiled rich-girl Lombard caught between suave but heartless Cortez and earnest doctor Lukas. Becomes laughable before long.

Noon Wine (1985) **C-81m. TVM** D: Michael Fields. Fred Ward, Lise Hilboldt, Stellan Skarsgard, Pat Hingle, Enrique Brown. Unsettling, haunting adaptation of the Katherine Anne Porter story, about a hard-working turn-of-the-century Texas family whose lives are irrevocably altered

[825]

by the arrival of stranger Skarsgard. A PBS *American Playhouse* presentation; the executive producers are James Ivory and Ismail Merchant. Above average.▼

Noose Hangs High, The (1948) **77m.** **½ D: Charles Barton. Bud Abbott, Lou Costello, Joseph Calleia, Leon Errol, Cathy Downs, Mike Mazurki, Fritz Feld. Mistaken identity leads to complications with the boys robbed of a large sum of money; typical A&C, bolstered by presence of Errol. Highlight: "Mudder and Fodder."

No Other Love (1979) **C-100m. TVM** D: Richard Pearce. Richard Thomas, Julie Kavner, Elizabeth Allen, Rogert Loggia, Scott Jacoby, Frances Lee McCain. Sensitive drama focusing on love affair of two mentally retarded young people. Thomas and Kavner's acting gives this one the edge over the similar LIKE NORMAL PEOPLE. Above average.

No Place for Jennifer (1951-British) **89m.** ** D: Henry Cass. Leo Genn, Rosamund John, Beatrice Campbell, Guy Middleton. Low-key sob story of little girl with bleak future when parents divorce.

No Place Like Home (1989) **C-100m. TVM** D: Lee Grant. Christine Lahti, Jeff Daniels, Scott Marlowe, Kathy Bates, CCH Pounder. Hard-hitting drama about a working-class family in Pittsburgh who find themselves out on the street and in the world of the homeless. Lahti shows why there are few better actresses around. Written by Ara Watson and Sam Blackwell, based on incidents in director Grant's documentary HOMELESS. Above average.

No Place Like Homicide! (1962-British) **87m.** ** D: Pat Jackson. Kenneth Connor, Sidney James, Shirley Eaton, Donald Pleasence, Dennis Price, Michael Gough. At times strained satire about group of people gathered at haunted house for the reading of a will. Remake of THE GHOUL. British title: WHAT A CARVE UP!▼

No Place to Hide (1956) **C-71m.** **½ D: Josef Shaftel. David Brian, Marsha Hunt, Hugh Corcoran, Ike Jariega, Jr., Celia Flor. Tense account of search for two children who accidentally have disease-spreading pellets in their possession; filmed in Philippines.

No Place to Hide (1981) **C-100m. TVM** D: John Llewellyn Moxey. Mariette Hartley, Keir Dullea, Kathleen Beller, Arlen Dean Snyder, Gary Graham, Sandy McPeak. Psychological suspense thriller about a young woman who, for unknown reasons, is stalked by a man who threatens to kill her. Script by Jimmy Sangster. Average.▼

No Place to Land (1958) **78m.** *½ D: Albert Gannaway. John Ireland, Mari Blanchard, Gail Russell, Jackie Coogan. Sleazy little film of three-cornered romance, leading nowhere.

No Place to Run (1972) **C-73m. TVM** D:

Delbert Mann. Herschel Bernardi, Stefanie Powers, Larry Hagman, Scott Jacoby, Neville Brand, Tom Bosley. Old shopkeeper (Bernardi) decides to take adopted grandson and flee to Canada when authorities decide failing health and retirement not right for boy (Jacoby). Fair dialogue and performances, but script's point of view questionable. Average.▼

No Questions Asked (1951) **81m.** **½ D: Harold F. Kress. Barry Sullivan, Arlene Dahl, Jean Hagen, George Murphy, William Reynolds, Mari Blanchard. Snappy little film of Sullivan seeking easy road to success via crime rackets.

Nora Prentiss (1947) **111m.** **½ D: Vincent Sherman. Ann Sheridan, Kent Smith, Robert Alda, Bruce Bennett, Rosemary DeCamp. Chanteuse Sheridan ruins doctor Smith's life; contrived but glossy melodrama.

Norliss Tapes, The (1973) **C-98m. TVM** D: Dan Curtis. Roy Thinnes, Angie Dickinson, Claude Akins, Michele Carey, Vonetta McGee, Hurd Hatfield, Don Porter. Unsuccessful pilot by William F. Nolan about writer who investigates the supernatural, hot on the trail of a vampire killer loose in Monterey, California. Above average.

Norman . . . Is That You? (1976) **C-91m.** ** D: George Schlatter. Redd Foxx, Pearl Bailey, Dennis Dugan, Michael Warren, Tamara Dobson, Vernee Watson, Jayne Meadows. Leering comedy based on flop Broadway show and revamped with black stars: Foxx is distraught when he discovers his son is gay, and determines to "straighten him out." Shot on videotape and transferred to film.

Norman Loves Rose (1982-Australian) **C-98m.** **½ D: Henri Safran. Carol Kane, Tony Owen, Warren Mitchell, Myra de Groot, David Downer. OK comedy of teenager Owen enamored with sister-in-law Kane. She becomes pregnant, and who is the father?▼

Norman Rockwell's Breaking Home Ties (1987) **C-100m. TVM** D: John Wilder. Jason Robards, Eva Marie Saint, Doug McKeon, Erin Gray, Claire Trevor. Nostalgic drama about a college student's coming of age in the 1950s, inspired by the famous Rockwell illustration. Trevor is a delight as the teacher who guided the boy through his high school years. Lovingly written by director/executive producer Wilder, beautifully photographed by Hector Figueroa, dedicated to the memory of veteran TV producer Quinn Martin. Above average.

Norma Rae (1979) **C-113m.** *** D: Martin Ritt. Sally Field, Ron Leibman, Beau Bridges, Pat Hingle, Barbara Baxley, Gail Strickland, Lonny Chapman, Noble Willingham, Grace Zabriskie. Field is excellent in Oscar-winning performance as real-life poor Southern textile worker gradually won over toward unionization by N.Y.C. labor organizer. Entertaining, though not entirely believable; haunting theme "It Goes Like it Goes" sung by Jennifer Warnes, also won an Oscar.▼

No Road Back (1957-British) **83m.** ** D: Montgomery Tully. Sean Connery, Skip Homeier, Paul Carpenter, Patricia Dainton, Norman Wooland, Margaret Rawlings. Blind and deaf woman sacrifices everything for her son, and becomes involved with criminals—who then try to pin robbery on the innocent son. Plodding melodrama; Connery's feature debut.

No Room for the Groom (1952) **82m.** **½ D: Douglas Sirk. Tony Curtis, Piper Laurie, Spring Byington, Don DeFore, Jack Kelly. Harmless shenanigans of ex-G.I. Curtis returning home to find it filled with in-laws.

No Room to Run (1978-Australian) **C-97m.** TVM D: Robert Michael Lewis. Richard Benjamin, Paula Prentiss, Barry Sullivan, Noel Ferrier, Ray Barrett. Boring thriller with lawyer Benjamin swallowed up by high-level intrigue on a business trip to Australia. Below average.▼

Norseman, The (1978) **C-90m.** *½ D: Charles B. Pierce. Lee Majors, Cornel Wilde, Mel Ferrer, Jack Elam, Chris Connelly, Kathleen Freeman, Susie Coelho (Bono), Denny Miller. Stodgy period adventure casts Majors as 11th-century Viking prince who sails to North America in search of his father, a norse King abducted by Indians. Majors' first starring movie is definitely minor league.▼

North Avenue Irregulars, The (1979) **C-99m.** **½ D: Bruce Bilson. Edward Herrmann, Barbara Harris, Susan Clark, Karen Valentine, Michael Constantine, Cloris Leachman, Patsy Kelly, Virginia Capers. Young priest (Herrmann) enlists churchgoing ladies for crime-fighting brigade; innocuous Disney comedy starts well but reverts to formula, including obligatory car pile-up finale. Fine actresses like Harris, Clark, and Leachman wasted.▼

North Beach and Rawhide (1985) **C-100m.** TVM D: Harry Falk. William Shatner, Tate Donovan, James Olson, Ron O'Neal, Lori Loughlin, Conchata Ferrell, Gretchen Corbett, Christopher Penn, Leo Penn. Ex-con who now runs a dude ranch takes on delinquent city teens to teach them responsibility. This one's a thinly disguised BOYS TOWN update with Shatner as Spencer Tracy and nearly everyone else as Mickey Rooney. Average.

North by Northwest (1959) **C-136m.** **** D: Alfred Hitchcock. Cary Grant, Eva Marie Saint, James Mason, Leo G. Carroll, Martin Landau, Jessie Royce Landis, Philip Ober, Adam Williams, Josephine Hutchinson, Edward Platt. Quintes-

sential Hitchcock comedy-thriller, with bewildered ad-man Grant chased cross country by both spies (who think he's a double agent) and the police (who think he's an assassin). One memorable scene after another, including now-legendary crop-dusting and Mount Rushmore sequences; one of the all-time great entertainments. Witty script by Ernest Lehman, exciting score by Bernard Herrmann.▼

North Dallas Forty (1979) **C-119m.** ***½ D: Ted Kotcheff. Nick Nolte, Mac Davis, Charles Durning, Dayle Haddon, G. D. Spradlin, Bo Svenson, Steve Forrest, John Matuszak, Dabney Coleman. Seriocomic version of Peter Gent's best-seller about labor abuse in the National Football League is the best gridiron film ever made and one of the best on any sport. Boasts Super Bowl-level performances for the most part. Scripted by its producer (Frank Yablans), director, and author.▼

Northern Lights (1979) **90m.** ***½ D: John Hanson, Rob Nilsson. Robert Behling, Susan Lynch, Joe Spano, Henry Martinson, Marianne Astrom-DeFina, Ray Ness, Helen Ness. Incisive, unforgettable Americana about the struggles of farmers in pre-WW1 North Dakota, with Behling attempting to organize populist Nonpartisan League. Fine first feature for Hanson and Nilsson, independently produced.▼

Northern Pursuit (1943) **94m.** **½ D: Raoul Walsh. Errol Flynn, Julie Bishop, Helmut Dantine, John Ridgely, Gene Lockhart, Tom Tully. Mountie Flynn tracks his man, a downed Nazi pilot, throughout Canada in this standard but slickly done drama.▼

North Sea Hijack SEE: **ffolkes**

North Shore (1987) **C-96m.** ** D: William Phelps. Matt Adler, Nia Peeples, John Philbin, Gerry Lopez, Cristina Raines, Gregory Harrison. The top young surfer in Arizona (think about it) pits himself against the famed title Oahu waves, as well as the family of the native Hawaiian local he loves. Exceptional surfing photography carries a generally dippy script only so far.▼

North Star, The (1943) **105m.** **½ D: Lewis Milestone. Anne Baxter, Dana Andrews, Walter Huston, Ann Harding, Erich von Stroheim, Jane Withers, Farley Granger, Walter Brennan. Dramatic battle sequences in WW2 Russia marred by uninteresting stretches until German von Stroheim matches wits with village leader Huston. Good performances all around; script by Lillian Hellman. Later edited to 82m. to deemphasize the good Russians and retitled ARMORED ATTACK. Also shown in computer-colored version.▼

Northstar (1986) **C-78m.** TVM D: Peter Levin. Greg Evigan, Deborah Wakeham, Mitchell Ryan, Mason Adams, David Hayward. Pedestrian sci-fier about an astronaut with superpowers (thanks to a freak accident in space) who becomes the target for a mysterious killer with a grudge against NASA. Below average.

North to Alaska (1960) **C-122m.** *** D: Henry Hathaway. John Wayne, Stewart Granger, Ernie Kovacs, Fabian, Capucine, Mickey Shaughnessy, Joe Sawyer, John Qualen. Fast-moving actioner with delightful tongue-in-cheek approach; prospectors Wayne and Granger have their hands full dealing with latter's kid brother Fabian, con artist Kovacs, and gold-digging (in the other sense) Capucine.▼

Northwest Mounted Police (1940) **C-125m.** **½ D: Cecil B. DeMille. Gary Cooper, Madeleine Carroll, Preston Foster, Paulette Goddard, Robert Preston, George Bancroft, Akim Tamiroff, Lon Chaney, Jr., Robert Ryan. DeMille at his most ridiculous, with Cooper as Dusty Rivers, Goddard a fiery half-breed in love with Preston, Lynne Overman as Scottish philosopher in superficial tale of Texas Ranger searching for fugitive in Canada. Much of outdoor action filmed on obviously indoor sets.

Northwest Outpost (1947) **91m.** *½ D: Allan Dwan. Nelson Eddy, Ilona Massey, Hugo Haas, Elsa Lanchester, Lenore Ulric. Rudolf Friml operetta of California calvarymen lumbers along pretty lamely.▼

Northwest Passage (Book I-Rogers' Rangers) (1940) **C-125m.** ***½ D: King Vidor. Spencer Tracy, Robert Young, Walter Brennan, Ruth Hussey, Nat Pendleton, Robert Barrat, Addison Richards. Gritty, evocative filming of Kenneth Roberts' book about Rogers' Rangers and their stoic leader (Tracy), enduring hardships and frustrations while opening up new territory in Colonial America. Young and Brennan are greenhorns who learn hard knocks under taskmaster Tracy.

Northwest Stampede (1948) **C-79m.** **½ D: Albert S. Rogell. Joan Leslie, James Craig, Jack Oakie, Chill Wills, Victor Kilian, Stanley Andrews. Lightweight oater about lady rancher Leslie competing with cowboy Craig for prize horses.

Norwood (1970) **C-96m.** ** D: Jack Haley, Jr. Glen Campbell, Kim Darby, Joe Namath, Carol Lynley, Pat Hingle, Tisha Sterling, Dom DeLuise. Ex-Marine Campbell hits the road for series of unrelated adventures with service buddy Namath, a midget (Billy Curtis), a Greenwich Village girl (Sterling), a shiftless brother-in-law (DeLuise), a dancing chicken, and a young girl (Darby) with whom he falls in love. Easy to take, but pointless.

No Sad Songs for Me (1950) **89m.** *** D: Rudolph Maté. Margaret Sullavan, Wendell Corey, Viveca Lindfors, Natalie Wood, Ann Doran. Moving account of dying mother Sullavan preparing her family to go on without her. Ironically, Sullavan's last film.

Nosferatu (1922-German) **63m.** ***½ D: F. W. Murnau. Max Schreck, Alexander Granach, Gustav von Wangenheim, Greta Schroeder. Early film version of *Dracula* is brilliantly eerie, full of imaginative touches that none of the later films quite recaptured. Schreck's vampire is also the ugliest in film history. Remade in 1979.▼

Nosferatu the Vampyre (1979-West German) **C-107m.** ***½ D: Werner Herzog. Klaus Kinski, Isabelle Adjani, Bruno Ganz, Roland Topor. Spooky, funny, reverent remake of F. W. Murnau's vampire masterpiece should please Dracula fans of all persuasions. Kinski is magnificent as the good Count, and Adjani's classic beauty is utilized to the hilt. English-language version, which runs 96m., also exists; even though the German version is dubbed, it's still preferable.

No Small Affair (1984) **C-102m.** ** D: Jerry Schatzberg. Jon Cryer, Demi Moore, George Wendt, Peter Frechette, Elizabeth Daily, Ann Wedgeworth, Jeffrey Tambor, Tim Robbins, Jennifer Tilly, Rick Ducommun. Self-possessed, smartassy, but virginal teenager becomes obsessed with an "older woman"—struggling rock singer Moore—and will do just about anything to make her like him. Some good moments here and there, but basically unappealing characters torpedo this film's chances.▼

No Surrender (1985-British) **C-100m.** **½ D: Peter K. Smith. Michael Angelis, Ray McAnally, Avis Bunnage, James Ellis, Bernard Hill, Mark Mulholland, Joanne Whalley, Michael Ripper, Elvis Costello. Interesting parable of modern British society and its problems, set in a remote nightclub where two warring sets of old folks come into conflict, paralleling the troubles in Northern Ireland. Ambitious script by Alan Bleasdale tries to cover too much ground, but McAnally's strong performance as a ruthless IRA gunman stands out. ▼

Not as a Stranger (1955) **135m.** *** D: Stanley Kramer. Olivia de Havilland, Frank Sinatra, Robert Mitchum, Charles Bickford, Gloria Grahame, Broderick Crawford, Lee Marvin, Lon Chaney, Henry (Harry) Morgan, Virginia Christine. Morton Thompson novel of Mitchum marrying nurse de Havilland who supports him through medical school despite oft-strained relationship. Glossy tribute to medical profession contains excellent performances by all. Producer Stanley Kramer's directorial debut.

Not for Publication (1984-U.S.-British) **C-88m.** ** D: Paul Bartel. Nancy Allen, David Naughton, Laurence Luckinbill, Alice Ghostley, Richard Paul, Barry Dennen, Cork Hubbert, Paul Bartel. Unsuccessful attempt to replicate an old-fashioned screwball comedy. Allen leads double life as the star reporter of a sleazy N.Y.C. tabloid and a worker in the reelection campaign of oddball mayor Luckinbill. Along the way shy photographer Naughton falls for her.▼

Nothing But a Man (1964) 92m. *** D: Michael Roemer. Ivan Dixon, Abbey Lincoln, Gloria Foster, Julius Harris, Martin Priest, Yaphet Kotto. Sincere study of black worker Dixon deciding that his family should not suffer from his frustrations over racial inequality.

Nothing But the Best (1964-British) C-99m. ***½ D: Clive Donner. Alan Bates, Denholm Elliott, Harry Andrews, Millicent Martin, Pauline Delany. Biting look at social-climbing playboy Bates who commits murder to get ahead in the world. Written by Frederic Raphael.

Nothing But the Night (1972-British) C-90m. *½ D: Peter Sasdy. Christopher Lee, Peter Cushing, Diana Dors, Georgia Brown, Keith Barron, Fulton Mackay, Gwyneth Strong. Uninvolving supernatural thriller about a cult that attempts immortality by projecting their personalities into the bodies of children. Filmed by Lee's production banner in a failed attempt to encourage more serious genre films. Also known as: THE DEVIL'S UNDEAD and THE RESURRECTION SYNDICATE.▼

Nothing But the Truth (1941) 90m. *** D: Elliott Nugent. Bob Hope, Paulette Goddard, Edward Arnold, Leif Erickson, Helen Vinson, Willie Best. Entertaining comedy based on sure-fire idea: Bashful stockbroker Hope wagers that he can tell the absolute truth for 24 hours. Good fun all the way. Filmed before in 1920 (with Taylor Holmes) and 1929 (with Richard Dix).

Nothing But Trouble (1944) 69m. ** D: Sam Taylor. Stan Laurel, Oliver Hardy, Mary Boland, Philip Merivale, David Leland, Henry O'Neill. Lesser L&H vehicle with duo hired as servants, meeting young boy king whose life is in danger. Boland is amusing as usual.

Nothing in Common (1986) C-118m. ** D: Garry Marshall. Tom Hanks, Jackie Gleason, Eva Marie Saint, Hector Elizondo, Barry Corbin, Bess Armstrong, Sela Ward, John Kapelos. Interminably long, highly uneven comedy-drama about a perpetual adolescent who's forced to deal with his aging, unloving father when his mom leaves him flat. Some poignant, relevant conclusions about love and responsibility (and some funny shots at the advertising business) are undermined by overlength and meandering nature of film. Hanks is excellent; Gleason is abrasive (in his last film appearance). Later a TV series.▼

Nothing Lasts Forever (1984) C/B&W-82m. **½ D: Tom Schiller. Zach Galligan, Apollonia van Ravenstein, Lauren Tom, Dan Aykroyd, Imogene Coca, Eddie Fisher, Sam Jaffe, Paul Rogers, Mort Sahl, Bill Murray, Anita Ellis. Strange, occasionally

entertaining comedy of aspiring artist Galligan's experiences in a N.Y.C. of the future—and also on a trip to the moon. A most unusual cast; much better seen than described. Written by first-time director Schiller, produced by Lorne Michaels, both of TV's *Saturday Night Live.*

Nothing Personal (1980-U.S.-Canadian) C-97m. *½ D: George Bloomfield. Donald Sutherland, Suzanne Somers, Lawrence Dane, Roscoe Lee Browne, Dabney Coleman, Saul Rubinek, John Dehner. Sutherland is a professor attempting to stop a corporation from slaughtering baby seals, Somers (in her first starring movie) a lawyer who helps him. Inane romantic comedy, from Robert Kaufman's script. Look for appearances by Craig Russell, Tony Rosato, Joe Flaherty, and Eugene Levy.▼

Nothing Sacred (1937) C-75m. ***½ D: William Wellman. Carole Lombard, Fredric March, Walter Connolly, Charles Winninger, Sig Ruman, Frank Fay. Classic comedy about hotshot reporter (March) who exploits Vermont girl's "imminent" death for headline value in N.Y.C. Ben Hecht's cynical script vividly enacted by March and Lombard (at her best). Gershwinesque music score by Oscar Levant. Remade as LIVING IT UP.▼

No Time for Comedy (1940) 98m. **½ D: William Keighley. James Stewart, Rosalind Russell, Genevieve Tobin, Charles Ruggles, Allyn Joslyn, Louise Beavers. Slick but dated adaptation of S. N. Behrman play about actress who tries to keep her playwright-husband from taking himself too seriously. Smoothly done but artificial. Also known as GUY WITH A GRIN.

No Time for Flowers (1952) 83m. ** D: Don Siegel. Viveca Lindfors, Paul Christian, Ludwig Stossel, Manfred Ingor. Lowgrade version of NINOTCHKA set in Prague; a pale shadow of its ancestor.

No Time for Love (1943) 83m. *** D: Mitchell Leisen. Claudette Colbert, Fred MacMurray, Ilka Chase, Richard Haydn, Paul McGrath, June Havoc. Sophisticated romance between photographer Colbert and illiterate MacMurray, who becomes her un-chic assistant, in good form here.

No Time for Sergeants (1958) 111m. ***½ D: Mervyn LeRoy. Andy Griffith, Myron McCormick, Nick Adams, Murray Hamilton, Don Knotts. Funny army comedy based on Ira Levin's Broadway play (which got its start as a 1955 *U.S. Steel Hour* TV play). Griffith and McCormick repeat roles as hayseed inducted into service and his harried sergeant. Griffith's best comedy, with good support from Adams, and, in a small role, Don Knotts. Script by John Lee Mahin. Followed years later by a TV series.▼

No Time to Be Young (1957) 82m. ** D: David Lowell Rich. Robert Vaughn, Roger

Smith, Merry Anders, Kathy Nolan. Programmer of supermarket robbery and repercussions thereafter to those involved. Early effort of four cast members who fared better on TV.

Not in Front of the Children (1982) **C-100m. TVM** D: Joseph Hardy. Linda Gray, John Getz, John Lithgow, Stephen Elliott, Carol Rossen, Cathryn Damon, George Grizzard. Divorcée fights to keep custody of her children after moving in with a younger man. Average.

Not Just Another Affair (1982) **C-100m. TVM** D: Steven Hilliard Stern. Victoria Principal, Gil Gerard, Robert Webber, Barbara Barrie, Richard Kline, Markie Post, Albert Hague, Ed Begley, Jr. Just another romantic comedy involving a chaste marine biologist and the woman-chasing lawyer who falls for her. Average.

Not My Kid (1985) **C-100m. TVM** D: Michael Tuchner. George Segal, Stockard Channing, Andrew Robinson, Gary Bayer, Nancy Cartwright, Tate Donovan, Viveka Davis. Drug abuse by a teenage daughter shatters a family in this emotionally charged dramatization of the book by producer Beth Polson and Dr. Miller Newton. Christopher Knopf's incisive script helps make this one of the best films on the subject. Above average.▼

Not of This Earth (1957) **67m. **½ D: Roger Corman. Paul Birch, Beverly Garland, Morgan Jones, William Roerick. Above par low-budget entry from Roger Corman with blank-eyed Birch as an alien vampire here to get blood for his atom war-ravaged home world. Good supporting cast; great bit by Dick Miller. Remade in 1988.

Not of This Earth (1988) **C-80m. ** D: Jim Wynorski. Traci Lords, Arthur Roberts, Lenny Juliano, Ace Mask, Roger Lodge. Strictly standard remake of the Roger Corman quickie, in which Roberts comes to earth in search of blood to replenish his dying planet's population. Film's chief interest is the casting of ex-porn queen Lords as a nurse.▼

Notorious (1946) **101m. ***½ D: Alfred Hitchcock. Cary Grant, Ingrid Bergman, Claude Rains, Louis Calhern, Leopoldine Konstantin, Reinhold Schunzel, Moroni Olsen. Top-notch espionage tale by Ben Hecht, set in post-WW2 South America, with Ingrid marrying spy Rains to aid U.S. and agent Grant. Frank, tense, well acted, with amazingly suspenseful climax (and one memorably passionate love scene).▼

Notorious Gentleman (1945-British) **123m. *** D: Sidney Gilliat. Rex Harrison, Lilli Palmer, Godfrey Tearle, Griffith Jones, Margaret Johnston, Guy Middleton, Jean Kent. Philandering life of irresponsible playboy is told with wit and style in this handsome production. British title: THE RAKE'S PROGRESS.

Notorious Landlady, The (1962) **123m. **½ D: Richard Quine. Kim Novak, Jack Lemmon, Fred Astaire, Lionel Jeffries, Estelle Winwood, Maxwell Reed. Lemmon entranced by houseowner Novak, decides to find out if she really did kill her husband; set in London. Offbeat comedy-mystery written by Quine and Larry Gelbart.

Notorious Lone Wolf, The (1946) **64m.** D: D. Ross Lederman. Gerald Mohr, Janis Carter, Eric Blore, John Abbott, William B. Davidson, Don Beddoe, Adele Roberts. SEE: Lone Wolf series.

Notorious Mr. Monks, The (1958) **70m. ** D: Joseph Kane. Vera Ralston, Don Kelly, Paul Fix, Leo Gordon. Tame Ralston vehicle involving a hitchhiker and murder.

Notorious Sophie Lang (1934) **64m. **½ D: Ralph Murphy. Gertrude Michael, Paul Cavanagh, Alison Skipworth, Leon Errol, Arthur Hoyt. Tightly knit yarn of police using title character (Michael) to lead them to international crime ring.

Not Quite Human (1987) **C-97m. TVM** D: Steven Hilliard Stern. Alan Thicke, Joseph Bologna, Jay Underwood, Robyn Lively, Robert Harper. Inventor creates an android son as the brother his teenage daughter always wanted, but a ruthless toy tycoon sees dollar signs instead. PINOCCHIO it ain't, though it was made for cable by Disney. Followed by a sequel. Average.

Not Quite Human II (1989) **C-105m. TVM** D: Eric Luke. Alan Thicke, Jay Underwood, Robin Lively, Greg Mullavey, Katie Barberi, Mark Arnott. Further adventures of Chip the Android as he (it?) goes to college in this sequel to the Disney Channel's surprisingly popular 1987 feature. Made for cable. Average.

Not Quite Jerusalem SEE: **Not Quite Paradise** ▼

Not Quite Paradise (1986-British) **C-105m. **½ D: Lewis Gilbert. Joanna Pacula, Sam Robards, Todd Graff, Kevin McNally, Selina Cadell, Kate Ingram, Libby Morris. Love on a kibbutz; pleasant, low-key story of volunteers from the U.S., England, and other nations adjusting to the hard life on an Israeli farm, where Yank Robards falls in love with sabra Pacula. Not much oomph but an OK, old-fashioned romance. Originally titled: NOT QUITE JERUSALEM. ▼

No Trees in the Street (1958-British) **108m. ** D: J. Lee Thompson. Sylvia Syms, Stanley Holloway, Herbert Lom, Ronald Howard, Joan Miller. Lower-class British life examined for its strengths and weaknesses; too sterile a human document.

Not Wanted (1949) **94m. **½ D: Elmer Clifton. Sally Forrest, Keefe Brasselle, Leo Penn, Dorothy Adams. Well-intentioned account of unwed mother seeking affection and understanding; produced and co-scripted by Ida Lupino. ▼

[830]

Not With My Wife You Don't! (1966) C-118m. **½ D: Norman Panama. Tony Curtis, Virna Lisi, George C. Scott, Carroll O'Connor, Richard Eastham. Trivial fluff about air force officer Curtis and bored wife Lisi; pointless and aimless, but attractive to the eye.

Novel Affair, A (1957-British) C-83m. *** D: Muriel Box. Ralph Richardson, Margaret Leighton, Patricia Dainton, Carlo Justini, Marjorie Rhodes, Megs Jenkins. Amusing tale of Leighton who writes a sexy novel, finding the fantasy come true. Nearly everyone plays dual roles, in real life and scenes from the novel! Original British title: THE PASSIONATE STRANGER.

Now About All These Women SEE: **All These Women**

Now and Forever (1934) 81m. **½ D: Henry Hathaway. Gary Cooper, Carole Lombard, Shirley Temple, Sir Guy Standing, Charlotte Granville. Standard jewel-thief-going-straight yarn; Lombard overshadowed by Cooper and Temple.

Now and Forever (1983-Australian) C-93m. ** D: Adrian Carr. Cheryl Ladd, Robert Coleby, Carmen Duncan, Christine Amor, Aileen Britton. Chic Ladd's husband is unfaithful, then is falsely accused of rape and sent to jail. This puts quite a strain on their marriage. Based on Danielle Steel's novel. If you like Harlequin romances . . .▼

No Way Out (1950) 106m. *** D: Joseph L. Mankiewicz. Richard Widmark, Linda Darnell, Stephen McNally, Sidney Poitier, Ruby Dee, Ossie Davis, Bill Walker. Violent tale of racial hatred involving bigot Widmark, who has gangster pals avenge his brother's death by creating race riots. Once-provocative film is still engrossing but seems a bit artificial at times. Poitier's film debut.

No Way Out (1972-Italian) C-100m. *½ D: Duccio Tessari. Alain Delon, Richard Conte, Carla Gravina, Roger Hanin, Nicoletta Machiavelli. Boring Mafia movie about a hit-man (Delon) who turns on his bosses, four crime kingpins, when they kill his wife and child to dissuade him from hanging up his guns. Also called BIG GUNS.

No Way Out (1987) C-116m. *** D: Roger Donaldson. Kevin Costner, Gene Hackman, Sean Young, Will Patton, Howard Duff, George Dzundza, Jason Bernard, Iman, Fred Dalton Thompson. Taut melodramatic thriller about a murder and cover-up within the inner circles of the federal government. Young is tantalizingly sexy as the woman involved with both CIA liaison Costner and Secretary of Defense Hackman. Hard to tell at first that this is a remake of THE BIG CLOCK, but it is—except for a ludicrous (and totally unnecessary) "twist" ending. Script by Robert Garland, who also produced.▼

No Way to Treat a Lady (1968) C-108m. ***½ D: Jack Smight. Rod Steiger, Lee Remick, George Segal, Eileen Heckart, Murray Hamilton, Michael Dunn, Barbara Baxley, Ruth White, Doris Roberts, David Doyle. Delicious blend of romantic comedy and murder, with Steiger as flamboyant ladykiller, Segal as "Mo Brummel," cop on his trail, Remick as Segal's new lady-friend who could be next victim. Script by John Gay from the William Goldman novel.▼

Nowhere to Go (1958-British) 97m. *** D: Seth Holt. George Nader, Maggie Smith, Bernard Lee, Geoffrey Keen, Bessie Love. Unsung, beautifully realized *film noir* stars Nader as a smooth Canadian burglar in England who hides out with Smith while on the run. Brilliant deep-focus photography by Paul Beeson and a moody score by jazz trumpeter Dizzy Reece stand out. Smith's film debut.

Nowhere to Hide (1977) C-78m. TVM D: Jack Starrett. Lee Van Cleef, Tony Musante, Charles Robinson, Lelia Goldoni, Noel Fournier, Russell Johnson, Edward Anhalt. U.S. Marshal Van Cleef protects former syndicate hit man Musante who is to testify against his ex-boss. The stuff B-movies did so well. Written by the usually reliable Edward Anhalt. Below average.▼

Nowhere to Hide (1987-Canadian) C-90m. ** D: Mario Azzopardi. Amy Madigan, Daniel Hugh Kelly, Robin MacEachern, Michael Ironside, John Colicos. Obvious thriller with Madigan cast as the wife of Marine Kelly. He's killed while investigating suspicious helicopter crashes . . . and she becomes a target. Madigan is much better than the material.▼

Nowhere to Run (1978) C-100m. TVM D: Richard Lang. David Janssen, Stefanie Powers, Allen Garfield, Linda Evans, Neva Patterson, John Randolph. Good yarn of Janssen's elaborate scheme to get his money-grabbing wife and the gumshoe she's hired off his back. Adapted by Jim Byrnes from Charles Eisenstein's novel *The Blackjack Hijack*. Above average.

Now, Voyager (1942) 117m. ***½ D: Irving Rapper. Bette Davis, Paul Henreid, Claude Rains, Gladys Cooper, Bonita Granville, John Loder, Ilka Chase, Lee Patrick, Mary Wickes, Janis Wilson. Vintage, first-class soaper with Bette as sheltered spinster brought out of her shell by psychiatrist Rains, falling in love with suave Henreid, helping shy girl Wilson. All this set to beautiful, Oscar-winning Max Steiner music makes for top entertainment of this kind. Olive Higgins Prouty's bestseller was adapted by Casey Robinson.▼

Now You See Him, Now You Don't (1972) C-88m. **½ D: Robert Butler. Kurt Russell, Cesar Romero, Joe Flynn, Jim Backus, William Windom, Michael McGreevy, Ed Begley, Jr. Follow-up to THE COM-

PUTER WORE TENNIS SHOES has student Russell inventing an invisible spray, which of course is coveted by a gang of crooks. Some good special effects in this so-so Disney comedy.▼
Now You See It, Now You Don't (1967) C-100m. TVM D: Don Weis. Jonathan Winters, Luciana Paluzzi, Jack Weston, Steve Allen, Jayne Meadows. Mild-mannered, bumbling art expert hired by insurance company, responsible for security of Rembrandt painting on loan from Louvre. Couple of good gags in middling comedy. Average.
Nuclear Terror SEE: **Golden Rendezvous**▼
Nude Bomb, The (1980) C-94m. **½ D: Clive Donner. Don Adams, Andrea Howard, Vittorio Gassman, Dana Elcar, Pamela Hensley, Sylvia Kristel, Robert Karvelas, Norman Lloyd, Rhonda Fleming, Joey Forman. Secret Agent 86 from 1960s *Get Smart* sitcom returns in feature-length spoof about a madman whose bombs will destroy the world's clothing; co-scripter Bill Dana has a funny bit as fashion designer Jonathan Levinson Siegel. Agreeable time-filler. Shown on TV as THE RETURN OF MAXWELL SMART. Followed by the TV movie GET SMART, AGAIN!
Nude In a White Car (1960-French) 87m. **½ D: Robert Hossein. Marina Vlady, Robert Hossein, Odile Versois, Helena Manson, Henri Cremieux. Hossein's only clue to a crime is title person; suspenser set on French Riviera. Retitled: BLONDE IN A WHITE CAR.
Nudo di Donna (1981-Italian-French) C-105m. *** D: Nino Manfredi. Nino Manfredi, Eleonora Giorgi, Jean-Pierre Cassel, Georges Wilson. Suffering marital problems with wife of 16 years (Giorgi), Manfredi becomes infatuated with a nude rearview photo and takes up with its model, who looks just like his wife! Stunning location photography in Venice and a solid cast highlight this social comedy.▼
Number One (1969) C-105m. *½ D: Tom Gries. Charlton Heston, Jessica Walter, Bruce Dern, John Randolph, Diana Muldaur. Heston turns in his loincloth for a jockstrap in this ludicrous drama about a New Orleans Saints quarterback who's fighting advancing age; interesting subject matter deserves better treatment.
Number One With a Bullet (1987) C-101m. **½ D: Jack Smight. Robert Carradine, Billy Dee Williams, Valerie Bertinelli, Peter Graves, Doris Roberts, Bobby Di Cicco. Carradine and Williams do well in this otherwise standard actioner, cast as a pair of "odd couple" detectives out to dethrone a drug kingpin.▼
Number Seventeen (1932-British) 83m. *** D: Alfred Hitchcock. Leon M. Lion, Anne Grey, John Stuart, Donald Calthrop, Barry Jones, Garry Marsh. Entertaining

comedy-thriller has tramp Lion stumbling upon a jewel thieves' hideout. Exciting chase sequence involves a train and bus (though the "special effects" are pretty obvious). Screenplay by Hitchcock.▼
Number Six (1962-British) 59m. ** D: Robert Tronson. Nadja Regin, Ivan Desny, Brian Bedford, Michael Goodliffe. Regin is heiress mixed up in espionage and murder; OK Edgar Wallace suspenser.
Numero Deux (1975-French) C-88m. **½ D: Jean-Luc Godard. Sandrine Battistella, Pierre Oudry, Alexandre Rignault, Rachel Stefanopoli. Fascinating but self-conscious and confusing aural and visual smorgasbord detailing the effects of capitalism on a modern family. Shot on videotape, then transferred to 35mm.
Nun and the Sergeant, The (1962) 73m. ** D: Franklin Adreon. Robert Webber, Anna Sten, Leo Gordon. Hari Rhodes, Robert Easton, Dale Ishimoto, Linda Wong. Set in Korea during the war; title tells rest.
Nuns on the Run (1990-British) C-90m. **½ D: Jonathan Lynn. Eric Idle, Robbie Coltrane, Camille Coduri, Janet Suzman, Doris Hare, Lila Kaye, Robert Patterson. Genial farce about two career henchmen, fed up with their violent young boss, who try to make a score for themselves and skip the country—but bungle the job and hide out in a convent, disguised as nuns. Idle and Coltrane are great, and the film is genuinely funny at times—enough to forgive its periodic lulls. Written by director Lynn.
Nun's Story, The (1959) C-149m. ***½ D: Fred Zinnemann. Audrey Hepburn, Peter Finch, Edith Evans, Peggy Ashcroft, Dean Jagger, Mildred Dunnock. Tasteful filming of Kathryn Hulme book, with Hepburn the nun who serves in Belgian Congo and later leaves convent. Colleen Dewhurst, as a homicidal patient, is electrifying.▼
Nunzio (1978) C-87m. **½ D: Paul Williams. David Proval, James Andronica, Tovah Feldshuh, Morgana King, Vincent Russo, Theresa Saldana, Monica Lewis. Retarded Brooklyn grocery delivery boy Proval imagines he's Superman, falls in love with bakery assistant Feldshuh. Mild story enhanced by Proval's fine performance; script by Andronica, who plays his tough but loving brother.
Nurse (1980) C-105m. TVM D: David Lowell Rich. Michael Learned, Robert Reed, Tom Aldredge, Hattie Winston, Antonio Fargas, Leora Dana. Strong portrait of a widow who has shipped her son off to college and decides to resume her career as head nurse of a metropolitan hospital. Later a weekly series. Based on Peggy Anderson's book. Above average.▼
Nurse Edith Cavell (1939) 108m. *** D: Herbert Wilcox. Anna Neagle, Edna May Oliver, George Sanders, ZaSu Pitts, May

[832]

Robson, H. B. Warner, Robert Coote. Neagle is fine as dedicated WW1 nurse who worked with the Brussels underground to aid wounded soldiers. Sturdy production.▼

Nurse on Wheels (1963-British) **86m.** *** D: Gerald Thomas. Juliet Mills, Ronald Lewis, Joan Sims, Noel Purcell, Raymond Huntley, Jim Dale. The trials of nurse Mills, who settles down to practice in a rural community. Entertaining, sometimes even touching.

Nurse Sherri SEE: **Beyond the Living**
Nutcracker (1982-British) **C-101m.** *½ D: Anwar Kawadri. Joan Collins, Carol White, Paul Nicholas, Finola Hughes, William Franklyn, Leslie Ash, Murray Melvin. Silly soaper about a Russian dancer who defects and joins the ballet company of a powerful, rich bitch (who else but Collins, in a role she can play in her sleep—and does).

Nutcracker, The Motion Picture (1986) **C-89m.** **½ D: Carroll Ballard. Hugh Bigney, Vanessa Sharp, Patricia Barker, Wade Walthall, Russell Burnett, voice of Julie Harris. Much of this version of *The Nutcracker,* performed by the Pacific Northwest Ballet, is like a music video: quick cutting and close-ups of legs, faces, and elbows. Very annoying. But the Tchaikovsky music is, of course, wonderful, as are Maurice Sendak's sets and costumes.▼

Nuts (1987) **C-116m.** *** D: Martin Ritt. Barbra Streisand, Richard Dreyfuss, Maureen Stapleton, Eli Wallach, Robert Webber, James Whitmore, Karl Malden, Leslie Nielsen, William Prince, Dakin Matthews, Hayley Taylor Block. Compelling drama about a belligerent woman assigned a Legal Aid lawyer who must fight for her right to stand trial for manslaughter, when both the state and her own parents insist that she's not in her right mind. Peerless cast of pros, and nimble staging by Ritt, manage to make you forget that this is an adaptation of a stage play, until the climax, when Streisand delivers a lengthy monologue—in loving close-up (she also produced the picture). Tom Topor adapted his play along with Darryl Ponicsan and Alvin Sargent. Streisand also composed the score.▼

Nutty, Naughty Chateau (1964-French) **C-100m.** **½ D: Roger Vadim. Monica Vitti, Curt Jurgens, Jean-Claude Brialy, Sylvie, Jean-Louis Trintignant, Francoise Hardy. Bizarre minor comedy involving the strange inhabitants of a castle romping about in 1750s styles; most diverting cast. Based on a Francoise Sagan play.

Nutty Professor, The (1963) **C-107m.** *** D: Jerry Lewis. Jerry Lewis, Stella Stevens, Del Moore, Kathleen Freeman, Med Flory, Howard Morris, Elvia Allman, Henry Gibson. Jerry's wildest (and most narcissistic) comedy casts him as chipmunk-faced college professor who does Jekyll-and-Hyde transformation into swaggering Buddy Love (whom some have interpreted as a Dean Martin caricature). More interesting than funny, although "Alaskan Polar Bear Heater" routine with Buddy Lester is a riot; Lewis buffs regard this as his masterpiece.▼

Nyoka and the Lost Secrets of Hippocrates (1942) **100m.** **½ D: William Witney. Kay Aldridge, Clayton Moore, William Benedict, Lorna Gray, Charles Middleton. Enjoyable, campy cliff-hanger set in Africa with Kay Aldridge (Nyoka) pitted against Lorna Gray (Vultura) in search for mystical tablets. Reedited from Republic serial PERILS OF NYOKA. Reissued as NYOKA AND THE TIGERMEN.▼

Nyoka and the Tigermen SEE: **Nyoka and the Lost Secrets of Hippocrates**▼

Oasis (1955-French) **C-84m.** ** D: Yves Allegret. Michele Morgan, Pierre Brasseur, Cornell Borchers, Carl Raddatz. Morgan's radiance brightens this oft-told story of gold-smuggling in Africa.

Oasis, The (1984) **C-90m.** **½ D: Sparky Greene. Chris Makepeace, Scott Hylands, Richard Cox, Dori Brenner, Rick Podell, Mark Metcalf, Ben Slack, Anne Lockhart. Unrelentingly grim, harrowing (and bloody) account of interaction among plane crash survivors in Mexican desert. At times compelling, and opening sequence is a stunner, but overall, too unpleasant.

Objective, Burma! (1945) **142m.** ***½ D: Raoul Walsh. Errol Flynn, William Prince, James Brown, George Tobias, Henry Hull, Warner Anderson. Zestful WW2 action film with Flynn and company as paratroopers invading Burma to wipe out important Japanese post; top excitement. Later reworked as DISTANT DRUMS, also directed by Walsh. Some prints cut to 127m. Also shown in computer-colored version.

Obliging Young Lady (1941) **80m.** **½ D: Richard Wallace. Eve Arden, Edmond O'Brien, Ruth Warrick, Joan Carroll, Franklin Pangborn, George Cleveland. Agreeable comedy about youngster, center of custody fight, finding herself the focal point at a country resort.

Oblomov (1980-Russian) **C-146m.** ***½ D: Nikita Mikhalkov. Oleg Tabakov, Yuri Bogatryev, Elena Soloyei, Andrei Popov. Thirtyish civil servant and absentee landlord, nicely played by Tabakov, retires to a listless existence in bed. Lyrical adaptation of Ivan Goncharov's 1858 novel; flashback sequences of Oblomov as a boy in his mother's arms are wonderful. Outstanding cinematography. Alternate title: A FEW DAYS IN THE LIFE OF I. I. OBLOMOV.▼

Oblong Box, The (1969-British) **C-91m.** ** D: Gordon Hessler. Vincent Price, Christopher Lee, Alastair Williamson, Hillary

Dwyer, Peter Arne, Maxwell Shaw, Sally Geeson. Boring treatment of halfway interesting situation: Price plays British aristocrat tormented by disfigured brother who's kept in tower room; periodically, he escapes and goes on the town. Hammy performances, long drawn-out narrative, lackluster direction (some of it by Michael Reeves).▼

Obsessed, The (1951-British) **77m.** ** D: Maurice Elvey. David Farrar, Geraldine Fitzgerald, Roland Culver, Jean Cadell. Lackluster story of Farrar suspected of homicide.▼

Obsessed With a Married Woman (1985) **C-100m. TVM** D: Richard Lang. Jane Seymour, Tim Matheson, Richard Masur, Dori Brenner, Donna Pescow, David Spielberg. Role-reversal drama, with married Seymour taking on a male "mistress" (Matheson), who happens to be one of her employees. Below average.

Obsession (1949) SEE: **Hidden Room, The**
Obsession (1976) **C-98m.** **½ D: Brian DePalma. Cliff Robertson, Genevieve Bujold, John Lithgow, Sylvia Kuumba Williams, Wanda Blackman. Viewers who don't remember Hitchcock's VERTIGO might enjoy this rehash by DePalma and writer Paul Schrader. Robertson loses his wife and child to kidnappers, then miraculously finds wife "reborn" in another woman. Holds up until denouement. Superb Bernard Herrmann score.▼

Obsessive Love (1984) **C-100m. TVM** D: Steven Hilliard Stern. Yvette Mimieux, Simon MacCorkindale, Constance McCashin, Kin Shriner, Allan Miller, Lainie Kazan. Sleek and svelte Mimieux (who co-produced and co-wrote the story) has an obsession for younger men and sinks her beautiful claws into an increasingly reluctant MacCorkindale. The ultimate in the older woman/younger man TV movie cycle of the '80s. Average.

Ocean's Eleven (1960) **C-127m.** **½ D: Lewis Milestone. Frank Sinatra, Dean Martin, Sammy Davis, Jr., Peter Lawford, Angie Dickinson, Richard Conte, Cesar Romero, Patrice Wymore, Joey Bishop, Akim Tamiroff. Fanciful crime comedy about eleven-man team headed by Danny Ocean (Sinatra) attempting to rob five Vegas casinos simultaneously. Everyone's in it, but no one does much, including some surprise guests. There is a clever twist ending, though.▼

Oceans of Fire (1986) **C-100m. TVM** D: Steve Carver. Gregory Harrison, Billy Dee Williams, David Carradine, Cynthia Sikes, Ken Norton, Ray "Boom Boom" Mancini, Lyle Alzado, Tony Burton, Ramon Bieri. The old tension-among-oil-drillers-aboard an-offshore-rig plot, sans Richard Arlen and Chester Morris, is dusted off for another go. Average.▼

O.C. & Stiggs (1985) **C-109m.** ** D: Robert Altman. Daniel H. Jenkins, Neill Barry, Paul Dooley, Jane Curtin, Jon Cryer, Ray Walston, Louis Nye, Tina Louise, Martin Mull, Dennis Hopper, Melvin Van Peebles, King Sunny Ade and His African Beats. Quirky (even by Altman standards) film recounts title teens' summer adventures, which consist mainly of making life miserable for the Schwab family and the cutthroat insurance agent father (Dooley) who cut off Stiggs' grandfather's old-age policy. Not without its moments and Altman weirdos—including Hopper as a drug and gun dealing vet, Louise as the sexy school nurse, and Curtin as the drunken Schwab matriarch—but ultimately incoherent. This sat on the shelf for several years.▼

Octagon, The (1980) **C-103m.** ** D: Eric Karson. Chuck Norris, Karen Carlson, Lee Van Cleef, Art Hindle, Jack Carter. OK Kung Fu drama with Norris taking on all comers when hired by Carlson for protection from Ninja assassins. Fair of its kind, with above-average production values.▼

Octaman (1971) **C-90m.** BOMB D: Harry Essex. Kerwin Mathews, Pier Angeli, Jeff Morrow, Jerry Guardino, Norman Fields. Rick Baker's "octopus" creation almost— but not quite—makes this dreadful thriller about the title monster discovered on an expedition to Mexico tolerable. Angeli died during shooting.▼

October (1928-Russian) **103m.** *** D: Sergei Eisenstein, Grigori Alexandrov. Nikandrov, N. Popov, Boris Livanov. Brilliant reconstruction of the Russian Revolution contains some of Eisenstein's most striking use of montage, though most impressive sequences—such as the masterful massacre around the bridges of St. Petersburg—are heavily weighted in the film's first half. Based on John (REDS) Reed's TEN DAYS THAT SHOOK THE WORLD, the other title by which this film is equally well known.▼

October Man, The (1947-British) **98m.** *** D: Roy (Ward) Baker. John Mills, Joan Greenwood, Edward Chapman, Joyce Carey, Kay Walsh, Felix Aylmer, Juliet Mills. Stranger with history of mental disorders is suspected of murder and must prove innocence, even to himself. Strong character study and good local atmosphere enhance suspenseful mystery written by Eric Ambler. British running time at 110m.

October Moth (1959-British) **54m.** *½ D: John Kruse. Lee Patterson, Lana Morris, Peter Dyneley, Robert Crawdon. Turgid melodrama set on lonely farm, with Morris trying to cope with dim-witted brother (Patterson) who has injured a passerby.

Octopussy (1983-British) **C-130m.** ***½ D: John Glen. Roger Moore, Maud Adams, Louis Jourdan, Kristina Wayborn, Kabir Bedi, Steven Berkoff, Desmond Llewelyn,

[834]

Vijay Amritraj, Lois Maxwell. Grand escapist fare as Moore, growing nicely into the role of James Bond, matches wits with a handful of nemeses, including title-named character (Adams), whose motives—and modus operandi—are more than a bit vague. Film throws in everything but the kitchen sink for the sake of an entertaining show. This is the thirteenth Bond outing (not counting CASINO ROYALE).▼

Odd Angry Shot, The (1979-Australian) **½ D: Tom Jeffrey. John Hargreaves, Graham Kennedy, Bryan Brown, John Jarratt. Interesting film about a group of Australian professional soldiers stationed in Vietnam. Personal drama emphasized more than combat in sometimes poignant, sometimes broadly comic work about soldiers dealing with a war they don't think is really theirs.▼

Odd Birds (1985) C-90m. **½ D: Jeanne Collachia. Michael Moriarty, Donna Lai Ming Lew, Nancy Lee, Bruce Gray, Karen Maruyama, Scott Crawford. Awkward direction and uneven performances defeat this sensitive drama about Lew, a dreamy teenager with braces who yearns for a career as an actress, and her friendship with compassionate but disillusioned brother-teacher Moriarty. However, there's a nice feel for the way real teen girls acted back in 1965, when the story is set, and for the pain of being fifteen and shy.

Odd Couple, The (1968) C-105m. *** D: Gene Saks. Jack Lemmon, Walter Matthau, John Fiedler, Herb Edelman, Monica Evans, Carole Shelley. Film version of Neil Simon stage hit about two divorced men living together, sloppy Oscar (Matthau) and fussy Felix (Lemmon). Lemmon's realistic performance makes character melancholy instead of funny; other surefire comic sequences remain intact. Later developed into two TV series.▼

Odd Job, The (1978-British) C-86m. **½ D: Peter Medak. Graham Chapman, David Jason, Diana Quick, Simon Williams, Edward Hardwicke. British update of timeworn premise (used as early as 1916 by Douglas Fairbanks in FLIRTING WITH FATE): an unhappy man, jilted by his wife, hires a hit man to murder her, then has a change of heart . . . but convincing the hired killer is a formidable challenge! Coscripted by Bernard McKenna and Chapman, of Monty Python fame.▼

Odd Jobs (1984) C-88m. ** D: Mark Story. Paul Reiser, Robert Townsend, Scott McGinnis, Paul Provenza, Julianne Phillips, Leon Askin. Lame vehicle about five college students working for a moving company for the summer. Top young comedy talent is wasted. Radio personality Don Imus has a cameo.▼

Odd Man Out (1947-British) 115m. **** D: Carol Reed. James Mason, Robert Newton, Kathleen Ryan, Robert Beatty, Cyril

Cusack, F.J. McCormick, William Hartnell, Fay Compton, Denis O'Dea, Dan O'Herlihy. Incredibly suspenseful tale of Irish rebel leader hunted by police after daring robbery. Watch this one! Scripted by R.C. Sherriff and F.L. Green, from the latter's novel. Remade as THE LOST MAN.▼

Odd Obsession (1959-Japanese) C-96m. **½ D: Kon Ichikawa. Machiko Kyo, Ganjiro Nakamura, Tatsuya Nakadai, Junko Kano. Elderly, vain Nakamura tempts beautiful wife (Kyo) into an affair with his young doctor (Nakadai). Uneven soap opera; a few bright moments, but disappointing overall. Original running-time 107m. Remade in Italy in 1984 as THE KEY, which is also this film's alternative title (a literal translation of the Japanese title, KAGI).▼

Odds Against Tomorrow (1959) 95m. *** D: Robert Wise. Harry Belafonte, Robert Ryan, Shelley Winters, Ed Begley, Gloria Grahame. Brutal robbery story with entire cast pulling out all stops; taut, exciting drama. Jazz score by John Lewis. Film debut of Wayne Rogers.

Odessa File, The (1974-British) C-128m. **½ D: Ronald Neame. Jon Voight, Maximilian Schell, Maria Schell, Mary Tamm, Derek Jacobi, Klaus Lowitsch. Voight carries this plodding adaptation of the Frederick Forsyth best-seller, set in 1963, about a German journalist who tracks down former Nazis. OK time killer, no more.▼

Ode to Billy Joe (1976) C-108m. ** D: Max Baer. Robby Benson, Glynnis O'Connor, Joan Hotchkis, Sandy McPeak, James Best, Terence Goodman. Bobbie Gentry's 1967 song hit provides basis for standard rural romance that grows progressively ridiculous. Benson and O'Connor, reunited after JEREMY, still have appeal.▼

Odette (1951-British) 100m. *** D: Herbert Wilcox. Anna Neagle, Trevor Howard, Marius Goring, Peter Ustinov, Bernard Lee. Neagle is excellent in true story of Odette Churchill, undercover British agent imprisoned by Nazis during WW2.

Odongo (1956-British) C-85m. BOMB D: John Gilling. Rhonda Fleming, Macdonald Carey, Juma, Eleanor Summerfield, Francis De Wolff. Juvenile jungle flick about search for missing native boy.

Odyssey of the Pacific (1981-Canadian-French) C-100m.** D: Fernando Arrabal. Mickey Rooney, Monique Mercure, Jean-Louis Roux, Guy Hoffman. Slight tale of Rooney, a retired train engineer living near an abandoned railway station, befriending a trio of homeless youngsters. Originally titled THE EMPEROR OF PERU.▼

Oedipus Rex (1957-Canadian) C-87m. **½ D: Tyrone Guthrie. Douglas Rain, Douglas Campbell, Eric House, Eleanor Stuart. Restrained, professional rendering of Sophocles' Greek tragedy.▼

Oedipus Rex (1967-Italian) C-110m. **½

D: Pier Paolo Pasolini. Franco Citti, Silvana Mangano, Alida Valli, Carmelo Bene, Julian Beck. Pictorially arresting but dull, disappointing adaptation of Sophocles' *Oedipus Rex* and *Oedipus at Colonus*, with Citti, as Oedipus, murdering his father and marrying his mother. Presented in both contemporary and historical settings; that's Pasolini himself as the High Priest.▼

Oedipus the King (1967-British) **C-97m.** **½ D: Philip Saville. Christopher Plummer, Orson Welles, Lilli Palmer, Richard Johnson, Cyril Cusack, Roger Livesey, Donald Sutherland. Film version of Sophocles' play is OK for students who have a test on it the next day, but others won't appreciate this version. Pretty static, despite that cast.

Off Beat (1986) **C-92m.** ** D: Michael Dinner. Judge Reinhold, Meg Tilly, Cleavant Derricks, Joe Mantegna, Jacques D'Amboise, James Tolkan, Amy Wright, John Turturro, Anthony Zerbe, Julie Bovasso, Fred Gwynne, Harvey Keitel, Austin Pendleton, Penn Jillette. Library worker Reinhold, filling in for policeman friend at rehearsal for a dance recital, falls in love with female cop. Modest comedy works hard to live up to its name but comes up short. Reinhold and Tilly are so low-key, they almost disappear! Great supporting cast can't save it. Written by playwright Mark Medoff. ▼

Offence, The (1973-British) **C-112m.** *** D: Sidney Lumet. Sean Connery, Trevor Howard, Vivien Merchant, Ian Bannen, Derek Newark. Intense drama about how London detective Connery's frustrations cause him to beat a suspect to death; a fine performance by Connery.

Officer and a Gentleman, An (1982) **C-125m.** **½ D: Taylor Hackford. Richard Gere, Debra Winger, David Keith, Louis Gossett, Jr., Robert Loggia, Lisa Blount, Lisa Eilbacher. Two misfits seek direction in their dead-end lives—he by enrolling in Naval Officer Candidate School, she by trying to snag him as a husband. Four-letter words and steamy sex scenes can't camouflage a well-worn Hollywood formula script—with virtually every plot point telegraphed ahead of time! Made agreeable by an appealing cast, though even Gossett's Oscar-winning performance as a drill instructor is just a reprise of earlier work like Jack Webb's in THE D.I. Film's love song, ''Up Where We Belong,'' also won an Oscar.▼

Official Story, The (1985-Argentina) **C-110m.** **** D: Luis Puenzo. Norma Aleandro, Hector Alterio, Analia Castro, Chunchuna Villafane. Aleandro is exceptional as woman who lives the good life, sheltered from political turmoil that surrounds her in Argentina . . . until she begins to suspect that her adopted daughter may have been the offspring of a political

prisoner. One of those rare films that manages to make a strong political statement in the midst of a crackling good story. Hard to believe it was director Puenzo's first feature film (he also scripted with Aida Bortnik). Oscar winner as Best Foreign Language Film. A knockout.▼

Of Flesh and Blood (1962-French) **C-92m.** **½ D: Christian Marquand, Robert Hossein, Renato Salvatori, Anouk Aimee, André Bervil, Jean Lefebvre. Murky account of passerby Salvatori having an affair with Aimee, involved with card-cheat-turned-murderer Hossein.

Off Limits (1953) **89m.** *** D: George Marshall. Bob Hope, Mickey Rooney, Marilyn Maxwell, Marvin Miller. Peppy shenanigans with Hope and Rooney in the Army, Maxwell a nightclub singer.▼

Off Limits (1988) **C-102m.** *½ D: Christopher Crowe. Willem Dafoe, Gregory Hines, Fred Ward, Amanda Pays, Scott Glenn, Kay Tong Lim, David Alan Grier, Keith David, Raymond O'Connor, Richard Brooks. Sluggish, predictable, unusually sordid melodrama about two pros in the U.S. Army's Criminal Investigation Detachment (CID) who track down the ghoul murdering Vietnamese hookers in 1968 Saigon. Dafoe's goo-goo eyes at nun Pays are good for a few unintentional chuckles; if you can't guess the murderer, get a new hobby.▼

Off Sides (1984) **100m. TVM** D: Dick Lowry. Tony Randall, Eugene Roche, Grant Goodeve, Adam Baldwin, Penny Peyser, Brian Dennehy, Gloria DeHaven, William Windom, Elisha Cook, Jr., Stephen Furst, Patrick Swayze. Outdated ''hippie'' flick (which sat on the shelf for nearly four years) about a football game between the local j.d.s—coached by bearded guru Randall—and the town fuzz. Based by Jack Epps, Jr., on his award-winning 1970 American Film Institute short PIGS VS. FREAKS, which is also this film's theatrical title. Average.

Off the Minnesota Strip (1980) **C-105m. TVM** D: Lamont Johnson. Mare Winningham, Hal Holbrook, Michael Learned, Ben Marley, James Murtaugh, Leon Isaac Kennedy. Teenage runaway returns to her midwest home after being a prostitute in N.Y.C. and tries to regain her innocence but cannot break through to her parents. Sordid tale brightened by Winningham's performance. Script by David Chase. Above average.

Off the Wall (1983) **C-85m.** BOMB D: Rick Friedberg. Paul Sorvino, Rosanna Arquette, Patrick Cassidy, Billy Hufsey, Ralph Wilcox, Dick Chudnow, Monte Markham, Brianne Leary, Mickey Gilley, Lewis Arquette. Phony comedy set in a Tennessee prison. Rosanna Arquette is wasted as daughter of state governor (Markham).▼

Of Human Bondage (1934) **83m.** *** D: John Cromwell. Leslie Howard, Bette Davis, Frances Dee, Kay Johnson, Reginald Denny, Alan Hale, Reginald Owen. Smoothly filmed, well-acted version of W. Somerset Maugham's story of doctor Howard's strange infatuation with a vulgar waitress (Davis). Many find Davis' performance overdone, but by any standards it's powerfully impressive, and put her on the map in Hollywood. Howard, lovely Johnson, others are superb. Remade in 1946 (with Eleanor Parker) and 1964. Also shown in computer-colored version.▼

Of Human Bondage (1964-British) **98m.** **½ D: Ken Hughes. Kim Novak, Laurence Harvey, Siobhan McKenna, Robert Morley, Roger Livesey, Nanette Newman, Brenda Fricker. Third and least successful filming of Maugham novel of doctor's passion for lowbrow waitress, marred by miscasting and general superficiality.▼

Of Human Hearts (1938) **100m.** **½ D: Clarence Brown. Walter Huston, James Stewart, Gene Reynolds, Beulah Bondi, Guy Kibbee, Charles Coburn, John Carradine, Ann Rutherford. Odd blend of potent 19th-century Americana and mile-high corn, in tale of dedicated preacher Huston who never established rapport with his son. When Abraham Lincoln (Carradine) lectures Stewart about neglecting his mother, it gets to be a bit much.

Of Life and Love (1957-Italian) **103m.** **½ D: Aldo Fabrizi, Luchino Visconti, Mario Soldati, Giorgio Pastina. Anna Magnani, Walter Chiari, Natale Cirino, Turi Pandolfini, Myriam Bru, Lucia Bose. Four satisfactory episodes, three of which are based on Pirandello tales; fourth is actual event in Magnani's life (THE LAP-DOG). Actually distilled from two Italian episodic features from 1953 and 1954.

Of Love and Desire (1963) **C-97m.** *½ D: Richard Rush. Merle Oberon, Steve Cochran, Curt Jurgens, John Agar, Steve Brodie. Beautiful settings (including Oberon's lavish Mexican home) offset overwrought sexual drama of neurotic woman who plays with the affection of several men—including her own stepbrother.

✓ **Of Mice and Men** (1939) **107m.** **** D: Lewis Milestone. Lon Chaney, Jr., Burgess Meredith, Betty Field, Charles Bickford, Bob Steele, Noah Beery, Jr. Chaney gives best performance of his career as feeble-brained Lenny who, with migrant-worker Meredith, tries to live peacefully on ranch. John Steinbeck's morality tale remains intact in sensitive screen version. Script by Eugene Solow. Music by Aaron Copland. Remade as a TVM.▼

Of Mice and Men (1981) **C-125m. TVM** D: Reza Badiyi. Robert Blake, Randy Quaid, Lew Ayres, Pat Hingle, Mitchell Ryan, Cassie Yates, Ted Neeley, Whitman Mayo.

Fulfilling a long-time dream, producer-star Blake turns out a sturdy remake of the Steinbeck classic with his *Baretta* and *Joe Dancer* production buddies. Above average.▼

Of Pure Blood (1986) **C-100m. TVM** D: Joseph Sargent. Lee Remick, Patrick McGoohan, Gottfried John, Edith Schneider, Richard Munch, Katharina Bohm. N.Y.C. casting director, in Germany to look into her son's violent death, stumbles onto a mystery leading back to the SS *Lebensborn* human breeding program designed by the Nazis. Remick is superb in an engrossing melodrama that has a few too many stock characterizations. "Suggested" by the book by Marc Hillel and Clarissa Henry. Average.

Of Unknown Origin (1983-Canadian) **C-88m.** ** D: George Pan Cosmatos. Peter Weller, Jennifer Dale, Lawrence Dane, Kenneth Welsh, Louis Del Grande, Shannon Tweed. N.Y.C. businessman, bacheloring it temporarily, is driven to distraction by a giant rodent on the loose in his apartment. Slightly better than simultaneously released DEADLY EYES.▼

Oh, Alfie SEE: **Alfie, Darling**▼

O Happy Day SEE: **Seventeen and Anxious**

O'Hara's Wife (1982) **C-87m.** **½ D: William S. Bartman. Edward Asner, Mariette Hartley, Jodie Foster, Perry Lang, Tom Bosley, Ray Walston, Allen Williams, Mary Jo Catlett, Richard Schaal, Nehemiah Persoff. Only Asner is aware of the presence of wife Hartley, who's a ghost. Earnest but forgettable; paging TOPPER.▼

O'Hara: U.S. Treasury (1971) **C-100m.** ✓ **TVM** D: Jack Webb. David Janssen, William Conrad, Lana Wood. Jerome Thor, Gary Crosby, Charles McGraw. Standard, unimaginative Jack Webb production portraying efficiency of government agents cracking down on narcotics smuggling ring. Adequate performances, fair action every second. Average; pilot for TV series.

Oh Dad, Poor Dad, Mama's Hung You in the Closet and I'm Feeling So Sad (1967) **C-86m.** **½ D: Richard Quine. Rosalind Russell, Robert Morse, Barbara Harris, Hugh Griffith, Jonathan Winters, Lionel Jeffries, Cyril Delevanti. Impressive cast tries to sustain black comedy about overpossessive widow (Russell) and weirdo son (Morse) taking vacation on tropical island accompanied by coffin of her late husband. From the Arthur Kopit play.▼

O. Henry's Full House (1952) **117m.** ✓ **½ D: Henry Hathaway, Howard Hawks, Henry King, Henry Koster, Jean Negulesco. Fred Allen, Anne Baxter, Charles Laughton, Marilyn Monroe, Gregory Ratoff, Jeanne Crain, Oscar Levant, Jean Peters, Richard

Widmark, Farley Granger. Five varying stories by O. Henry; cast better than script. "The Clarion Call," "Last Leaf," "Ransom of Red Chief," "Gift of the Magi," and "Cop and the Anthem."

Oh, God! (1977) C-104m. *** D: Carl Reiner. George Burns, John Denver, Teri Garr, Paul Sorvino, George Furth, Ralph Bellamy, Barnard Hughes, David Ogden Stiers. God appears in person of Burns to summon Denver as his messenger, to tell the world that he's alive and well. Film eschews cheap jokes to build a credible story with warm performances and upbeat message. Followed by a pair of sequels.▼

Oh God! Book II (1980) C-94m. *½ D: Gilbert Cates. George Burns, Suzanne Pleshette, David Birney, Louanne, Howard Duff, Hans Conried, Wilfrid Hyde-White, Conrad Janis. Burns returns as title character; here, he enlists a child (Louanne) to remind the world that God is not dead. Contrived sequel with just a trickle of laughs; Pleshette, as usual, is wasted.▼

Oh, God! You Devil (1984) C-96m. ** D: Paul Bogart. George Burns, Ted Wass, Ron Silver, Roxanne Hart, Eugene Roche, Robert Desiderio. Third go-round for Burns gives him dual role of God *and* the Devil, with Wass as struggling songwriter and performer who sells his soul for success. Good cast and good-natured attitude can't overcome blandness and predictability of this comedy. Written by Andrew Bergman.▼

Oh, Heavenly Dog! (1980) C-103m. **½ D: Joe Camp. Chevy Chase, Benji, Jane Seymour, Omar Sharif, Donnelly Rhodes, Robert Morley, Alan Sues. Private eye Chase returns to earth in the form of a dog to solve his own murder. Benji (in his third film) is as adorable as ever as Chase's alter ego; Seymour is lovely as—what else? —the love interest. Filmed in England; a reverse rip-off of YOU NEVER CAN TELL. Followed by BENJI THE HUNTED.▼

Oh, Men! Oh, Women! (1957) C-90m. **½ D: Nunnally Johnson. Ginger Rogers, David Niven, Dan Dailey, Barbara Rush, Tony Randall. Often bouncy sex farce revolving around psychiatrist and his assorted patients. Randall's feature debut.

OHMS (1980) C-100m. TVM D: Dick Lowry. Ralph Waite, David Birney, Talia Balsam, Dixie Carter, Cameron Mitchell, Leslie Nielsen, Paul Hecht. Farmer Waite and activist Birney battle a power company planning to run a million volt line across local farmlands. Sincere ecology awareness drama becomes too pat and cops out at the end. Average.

Oh, Susanna (1951) C-90m. ** D: Joseph Kane. Rod Cameron, Forrest Tucker, Adrian Booth, Chill Wills. Too much feuding between cavalry officers and too little real action mar this Western.

Oh! Those Most Secret Agents (1966-Italian) C-83m. *½ D: Lucio Fulci. Franco Franchi, Ciccio Ingrassia, Ingrid Schoeller, Arnoldo Tieri. Pathetic superspy spoof. Retitled: WORST SECRET AGENTS.

Oh! What a Lovely War (1969-British) C-139m. **½ D: Richard Attenborough. Laurence Olivier, John Gielgud, Ralph Richardson, Michael Redgrave, John Mills, Vanessa Redgrave, Dirk Bogarde, Susannah York, Maggie Smith, Jack Hawkins, Kenneth More, Corin Redgrave, Jane Seymour. Actor Attenborough's directing debut; impressive but cumbersome series of vignettes on WW1, ranging from colorful musical numbers to poignant human sidelights. Adapted from stage show. Beautifully designed, wildly cinematic, but too drawn-out to make maximum antiwar impact.

Oh, You Beautiful Doll (1949) C-93m. **½ D: John M. Stahl. June Haver, Mark Stevens, S. Z. Sakall, Charlotte Greenwood, Gale Robbins, Jay C. Flippen. Chipper period musical about song plugger who turns serious composer's works into popular songs. Based on true story of Fred Fisher. Songs include title tune, "Peg o' My Heart," "Dardanella."

Oil (1977-Italian) C-95m. BOMB D: Mircea Dragan. Stuart Whitman, Woody Strode, Ray Milland, George Dinica, William Berger, Tony Kendall. A Sahara oilfield ablaze. After the twenty-eighth shot of the fire, you'll be ready to douse your TV set.▼

Oil for the Lamps of China (1935) 110m. *** D: Mervyn LeRoy. Pat O'Brien, Josephine Hutchinson, Jean Muir, Lyle Talbot, Arthur Byron, John Eldredge, Henry O'Neill, Donald Crisp, Keye Luke. Dated but absorbing saga (from best-selling book by Alice Tisdale Hobart) about a man who dedicates his life to working for big oil company, which shows little regard for him in return; set mostly in China. Hutchinson's role, as his dedicated wife, is particularly interesting today in light of her comments about a woman's place in a man's life . . . while the film's foreword (and *deus ex machina* ending) indicates an uneasiness about attacking powerful oil companies too harshly!

Okinawa (1952) 67m. ** D: Leigh Jason. Pat O'Brien, Cameron Mitchell, James Dobson, Richard Denning, Richard Benedict, Alvy Moore. Adequate programmer about men on a warship during the Pacific campaign of WW2.

Oklahoma! (1955) C-145m. ***½ D: Fred Zinnemann. Gordon MacRae, Shirley Jones, Charlotte Greenwood, Rod Steiger, Gloria Grahame, Eddie Albert, James Whitmore, Gene Nelson, Barbara Lawrence, Jay C.

Flippen. Expansive film version of Rodgers and Hammerstein's landmark 1943 Broadway musical, filled with timeless songs (and the beautiful voices of MacRae and Jones to sing them) . . . plus a fine supporting cast led by incomparable Grahame as Ado Annie. Enough fine ingredients to make up for overlength of film. Songs include "The Surrey with the Fringe on Top," "Oh, What a Beautiful Mornin'," "People Will Say We're in Love."▼

Oklahoma Annie (1952) **C-90m.** *½ D: R. G. Springsteen. Judy Canova, John Russell, Grant Withers, Allen Jenkins, Almira Sessions, Minerva Urecal. Rambunctious Canova is involved with mopping up corruption in her Western town.▼

Oklahoma City Dolls, The (1981) **C-100m.** TVM D: E. W. Swackhamer. Susan Blakely, Ronee Blakley, Eddie Albert, Sarah Cunningham, Judyann Elder, Jack Ging, Joan Goodfellow, Robert Hooks, Art Lund, David Huddleston, Lynne Moody, Waylon Jennings. Female factory workers battle for their rights by forming a football team, with Blakely leading the rebellion and Albert as the girls' down-on-his-luck coach. Average.

Oklahoma Crude (1973) **C-108m.** *** D: Stanley Kramer. George C. Scott, Faye Dunaway, John Mills, Jack Palance, Harvey Jason, Woodrow Parfrey. Old-fashioned, nonthink entertainment. Strong-willed, man-hating Dunaway determined to defend lone oil well from pressures of Palance, who represents big oil trust, hires drifter Scott to help her. Scott gives brilliant comic performance in mildly enjoyable film.▼

Oklahoma Kid, The (1939) **85m.** *** D: Lloyd Bacon. James Cagney, Humphrey Bogart, Rosemary Lane, Donald Crisp, Harvey Stephens, Charles Middleton, Ward Bond. Cagney's the hero, Bogey's the villain in this sturdy Western about a cowboy seeking redress for the lynching of his father. Classic scene has Cagney singing "I Don't Want to Play in Your Yard."▼

Oklahoman, The (1957) **C-80m.** **½ D: Francis D. Lyon. Joel McCrea, Barbara Hale, Brad Dexter, Gloria Talbott, Verna Felton, Douglas Dick, Michael Pate. Town doc McCrea tries to keep Indian Pate from getting rooked out of his land. Pretty routine, though Talbott cultists may want to see her play an Indian maiden the same year she had the title role in DAUGHTER OF DR. JEKYLL. Laundry note: Hale wears the same outfit in a disturbingly high number of scenes.▼

Oklahoma Territory (1960) **67m.** ** D: Edward L. Cahn. Bill Williams, Gloria Talbott, Ted de Corsia, Grant Richards, Walter Sande. Western concentrating on Williams' effort to find actual killer of local Indian agent.

Oklahoma Woman, The (1956) **72m.** BOMB D: Roger Corman. Richard Denning, Peggie Castle, Cathy Downs, Touch (Mike) Connors, Tudor Owen, Richard (Dick) Miller. Grade Z Corman quickie Western about ex-con Denning attempting to stay clean but tangling instead with the title character, who is "queen of the outlaws."

Old Acquaintance (1943) **110m.** *** D: Vincent Sherman. Bette Davis, Miriam Hopkins, Gig Young, John Loder, Dolores Moran, Phillip Reed, Roscoe Karns, Anne Revere. Well-matched stars of THE OLD MAID are reunited as childhood friends who evolve personal and professional rivalry that lasts 20 years. Davis is noble and Hopkins is bitchy in this entertaining film. John Van Druten and Lenore Coffee scripted, from the former's play. Remade as RICH AND FAMOUS.

Old Boyfriends (1979) **C-103m.** BOMB D: Joan Tewkesbury. Talia Shire, Richard Jordan, Keith Carradine, John Belushi, John Houseman, Buck Henry. Distressing botch of an intriguing idea about woman who seeks out her former lovers in an attempt to analyze her past. Shire is too lightweight to carry the acting load, and Belushi is totally wasted. Written by Paul and Leonard Schrader.▼

Old Curiosity Shop, The SEE: **Mr. Quilp**

Old Dark House, The (1932) **71m.** ***½ D: James Whale. Boris Karloff, Melvyn Douglas, Charles Laughton, Gloria Stuart, Lilian Bond, Ernest Thesiger, Raymond Massey, Eva Moore. Outstanding melodrama (with tongue-in-cheek) gathers stranded travelers in mysterious household, where brutish butler Karloff is just one of many strange characters. A real gem, based on J.B. Priestley's *Benighted*; remade in 1963.

Old Dark House, The (1963-British) **C-86m.** **½ D: William Castle. Tom Poston, Robert Morley, Peter Bull, Joyce Grenfell, Janette Scott. Uneven blend of comedy and chiller, with Poston at loose ends in eerie mansion. Released theatrically in b&w.

Old Dracula (1974-British) **C-89m.** *½ D: Clive Donner. David Niven, Teresa Graves, Peter Bayliss, Jennie Linden, Linda Hayden, Bernard Bresslaw. Niven somehow maintains his dignity in this one-joke Dracula spoof that has him extracting samples from the necks of various Playboy Bunnies in search of correct blood type to resurrect his departed wife. British title: VAMPIRA.

Old Enough (1984) **C-91m.** **½ D: Marisa Silver. Sarah Boyd, Rainbow Harvest, Neill Barry, Danny Aiello, Susan Kingsley, Roxanne Hart, Fran Brill. Two adolescent girls from wildly diverse socioeconomic backgrounds forge a tenuous friendship, then try to keep it going through thick and thin. Boyd (the rich one) has infinitely more screen appeal than counterpart Harvest, which further undercuts an already too-mild comedy. Funny subplot about sexy hairdresser who lives in Harvest's building. Written by first-time director Silver, produced by her sister Dina.▼

Oldest Profession, The (1967-French-German-Italian) **C-97m.** *½ D: Franco Indovina, Mauro Bolognini, Philippe De Broca, Michel Pfleghar, Claude Autant-Lara, Jean-Luc Godard. Elsa Martinelli, Jeanne Moreau, Raquel Welch, Anna Karina, France Anglade, Jean-Pierre Leaud. Totally unfunny six-part story of prostitution through the ages. Original French running time: 115m.▼

Old-Fashioned Way, The (1934) **74m.** ***½ D: William Beaudine. W. C. Fields, Judith Allen, Joe Morrison, Baby LeRoy, Jack Mulhall, Oscar Apfel. Fields is in fine form managing troupe of old-time melodrama *The Drunkard,* encountering various troubles as they travel from town to town. Baby LeRoy has memorable scene throwing W. C.'s watch into a jar of molasses; also contains Fields' classic juggling routine.

Old Gringo (1989) **C-119m.** *** D: Luis Puenzo. Jane Fonda, Gregory Peck, Jimmy Smits, Patricio Contreras, Jenny Gago, Jim Metzler, Gabriela Rosi, Anne Pitoniak, Pedro Armendariz, Jr. A youngish spinster, a fiery young Mexican general, and an aging American writer, Ambrose Bierce, cross paths amid the tumult of Pancho Villa's revolution in 1913. Intense, epic-scale drama has its share of flaws, but its rich atmosphere and superlative star performances make it well worth seeing. Director Puenzo and Aida Bortnik wrote the screenplay, from Carlos Fuentes' novel.▼

Old Heidelberg SEE: **Student Prince in Old Heidelberg, The**

Old Hutch (1936) **80m.** ** D: J. Walter Ruben. Wallace Beery, Eric Linden, Cecilia Parker, Elizabeth Patterson, Robert McWade. Cute story of shiftless bum discovering $100,000, trying to use it without arousing suspicion. Filmed before in 1920 with Will Rogers as HONEST HUTCH.

Old Ironsides (1926) **111m.** *** D: James Cruze. Charles Farrell, Esther Ralston, Wallace Beery, George Bancroft, Charles Hill Mailes, Johnnie Walker, Eddie Fetherston, George Godfrey. Elaborate, expansive hokum based on the American merchant marine's run-ins with Mediterranean pirates in the early 19th century. Full of rollicking, boisterous seamen—and in their midst, a prim leading lady and leading man. Subtle it ain't, but certainly entertaining, especially with Gaylord Carter's

rousing organ score on the homevideo release. Boris Karloff has small role as a Saracen sailor.▼

Old Maid, The (1939) **95m.** ***½ D: Edmund Goulding. Bette Davis, Miriam Hopkins, George Brent, Jane Bryan, Donald Crisp, Louise Fazenda, Jerome Cowan. Soap opera par excellence based on Zoe Akins play about unwed mother (Davis), whose unsuspecting daughter Bryan grows up ignoring her, loving Bette's scheming cousin Hopkins. The two female stars create fireworks as they enact this chronicle of love and hate in the 1860s.▼

Old Man and the Sea, The (1958) **C-86m.** *** D: John Sturges. Spencer Tracy, Felipe Pazos, Harry Bellaver. Well-intentioned but uneven parable of aging fisherman's daily battle with the elements. Tracy is the whole film, making the most of Hemingway's un-filmic story; Dimitri Tiomkin's expressive score won an Oscar. Remade as a TVM.

Old Man and the Sea, The (1990) **C-100m.** TVM D: Jud Taylor. Anthony Quinn, Gary Cole, Patricia Clarkson, Valentina Quinn, Francesco Quinn, Alexis Cruz. Quinn is terrific as Hemingway's famed fisherman in this colorful remake, but noted TV dramatist Roger O. Hirson has added too much story and too many extraneous characters. Average.

Old Man Rhythm (1935) **75m.** **½ D: Edward Ludwig. Charles "Buddy" Rogers, George Barbier, Barbara Kent, Grace Bradley, Betty Grable, Eric Blore. Business tycoon Barbier goes back to college to keep an eye on his playboy son (Rogers) in this light, fluffy musical; songwriter Johnny Mercer appears as one of the students.

Old Man Who Cried Wolf, The (1970) **C-73m.** TVM D: Walter Grauman. Edward G. Robinson, Martin Balsam, Diane Baker, Percy Rodrigues, Ruth Roman, Sam Jaffe, Edward Asner. Emile Pulska (Robinson) can't even convince own family that good friend Stillman (Jaffe) died of wounds from assault, not from natural causes. Unconvincing drama, despite good performances. Average.

Old Spanish Custom, An (1936-British) **61m.** BOMB D: Adrian Brunel. Buster Keaton, Lupita Tovar, Esme Percy, Lyn Harding, Hilda Moreno. Depressing, bottom-of-the-barrel comedy, with Buster a wealthy yachtsman who docks in Spain and is duped by temptress Tovar. Only for terminally curious Keaton fans. Original title: THE INVADER.▼

Old Yeller (1957) **C-83m.** *** D: Robert Stevenson. Dorothy McGuire, Fess Parker, Tommy Kirk, Kevin Corcoran, Jeff York, Beverly Washburn, Chuck Connors. Disney's first film about a boy and his dog, from Fred Gipson's popular novel, is still one of the best. Atmospheric recreation of farm life in 1859 Texas, where Kirk becomes attached to a yellow hunting dog. Sequel: SAVAGE SAM.▼

Oliver! (1968-British) **C-153m.** **** D: Carol Reed. Ron Moody, Oliver Reed, Shani Wallis, Mark Lester, Jack Wild, Harry Secombe, Hugh Griffith, Sheila White. Superb musical by Lionel Bart from Dickens' *Oliver Twist* about young boy (Lester) swept into gang of youthful thieves led by scurrilous Fagin (Moody). Fine settings, atmosphere complement rousing score including "Consider Yourself," "As Long as He Needs Me." Six Oscars including Best Picture, Director, Art Direction, Scoring (John Green), and a special prize to Onna White for her spirited choreography.▼

Oliver's Story (1978) **C-92m.** *½ D: John Korty. Ryan O'Neal, Candice Bergen, Nicola Pagett, Edward Binns, Ray Milland, Swoosie Kurtz. Sequel to LOVE STORY pits money against money this time around, as O'Neal romances heiress to Bonwit Teller fortune. Tough to see how anyone could care by now, and judging from the film's box office performance, not many did.▼

Oliver Twist (1922) **77m.** *** D: Frank Lloyd. Jackie Coogan, Lon Chaney, Gladys Brockwell, George Siegmann, Esther Ralston. Entertaining silent version of the Charles Dickens classic, geared as a vehicle for Coogan, who was then at the height of his juvenile stardom. Chaney, that master of makeup, is ideally cast as Fagin. ▼

Oliver Twist (1933) **77m.** ** D: William Cowen. Dickie Moore, Irving Pichel, William "Stage" Boyd, Doris Lloyd, Barbara Kent. Superficial, low-budget version of Dickens's story is mediocre by any standards, but pales particularly in comparison to the later British classic.▼

✓**Oliver Twist** (1948-British) **105m.** **** D: David Lean. Alec Guinness, Robert Newton, John Howard Davies, Kay Walsh, Francis L. Sullivan, Anthony Newley, Henry Stephenson. Superlative realization of Dickens tale of ill-treated London waif involved with arch-fiend Fagin (Guinness) and his youthful gang, headed by the Artful Dodger (Newley). Later musicalized as OLIVER! Original British running time: 116m.▼

Oliver Twist (1982) **C-100m. TVM** D: Clive Donner. George C. Scott, Tim Curry, Michael Hordern, Timothy West, Eileen Atkins, Cherie Lunghi, Richard Charles, Lysette Anthony. Full-bodied Fagin by George C. paces this umpteenth version of the Dickens classic, from James Goldman's script. Above average.▼

Olly, Olly, Oxen Free (1978) **C-83m.** ** D: Richard A. Colla. Katharine Hepburn, Kevin McKenzie, Dennis Dimster, Peter Kilman. Hepburn plays a colorful junk dealer who befriends two young boys and helps them realize their dream of hot-air ballooning. Kate's always worth watching, but except for airborne scenes, this film is nothing special. Also known as THE GREAT BALLOON ADVENTURE.▼

O Lucky Man! (1973-British) **C-173m.** **** D: Lindsay Anderson. Malcolm McDowell, Rachel Roberts, Arthur Lowe, Ralph Richardson, Alan Price, Lindsay Anderson, Helen Mirren, Mona Washbourne. Mammoth allegory with surrealistic flavor about young coffee salesman who pushes his way to the top only to fall and rise again. Brilliant performances (several actors have multiple roles) throughout, incredible score by Alan Price, make this a memorable screen experience.▼

Olympia (1936-German) **220m.** **** D: Leni Riefenstahl. Two-part record of the 1936 Berlin Olympics, highlighted by truly eyepopping cinematography, camera movement and editing. Of course, it's all supposed to be a glorification of the Nazi state. Various edited versions exist (some of which omit all footage of Hitler, who appears throughout the original print).▼

Omar Khayyam (1957) **C-101m.** **½ D: William Dieterle. Cornel Wilde, Debra Paget, John Derek, Raymond Massey, Michael Rennie, Yma Sumac, Sebastian Cabot. Childish but spirited costumer set in medieval Persia; cast defeated by juvenile script.

Omega Man, The (1971) **C-98m.** **½ D: Boris Sagal. Charlton Heston, Rosalind Cash, Anthony Zerbe, Paul Koslo, Lincoln Kilpatrick, Eric Laneuville. Visually striking but unsatisfying second filming of Richard Matheson's sci-fi thriller *I Am Legend* involving frenzy of a man immune to germs that are decimating Earth's population after the ultimate war. Heston is superior to Vincent Price (who had role in THE LAST MAN ON EARTH).▼

Omega Syndrome (1987) **C-88m.** ** D: Joseph Manduke. Ken Wahl, George DiCenzo, Doug McClure, Nicole Eggert. Standard-issue tale of down-and-out reporter Wahl who whips into action (with Army buddy DiCenzo) when his teenage daughter (Eggert) is kidnapped by right-wing terrorists.▼

Omen, The (1976) **C-111m.** **½ D: Richard Donner. Gregory Peck, Lee Remick, Billie Whitelaw, David Warner, Harvey Stephens, Patrick Troughton, Leo McKern. Effective but sensationalistic horror piece on the coming of the "antiChrist," personified in young son of Peck and Remick, Americans living in England. Plenty of gore and a now-famous decapitation, for those who like that kind of thing. Jerry Goldsmith's score won an Oscar. Sequels:

DAMIEN—OMEN II and THE FINAL CONFLICT.▼

On a Clear Day You Can See Forever (1970) **C-129m.** **½ D: Vincente Minnelli. Barbra Streisand, Yves Montand, Bob Newhart, Larry Blyden, Simon Oakland, Jack Nicholson. Colorful entertainment from Alan Jay Lerner-Burton Lane show about girl (Streisand) whose psychiatrist (Montand) discovers that she lived a former life, in 19th-century England. Sumptuous flashback scenes outclass fragmented modern-day plot, much of it apparently left on cutting-room floor. Glossy but never involving.▼

On an Island With You (1948) **C-107m.** **½ D: Richard Thorpe. Esther Williams, Peter Lawford, Ricardo Montalban, Jimmy Durante, Cyd Charisse, Xavier Cugat, Leon Ames. Splashy, colorful Williams vehicle of movie star who finds off-screen romance on location in Hawaii.

On Any Sunday (1971) **C-91m.** *** D: Bruce Brown. Steve McQueen, Mert Lawwill, Malcolm Smith. Fine documentary on many aspects of motorcycling by Bruce Brown of ENDLESS SUMMER fame. Followed by a sequel.▼

On Any Sunday II (1981) **C-90m.** ** D: Ed Forsyth, Don Shoemaker. Undistinguished sequel to ON ANY SUNDAY, documenting the exploits of championship motorcyclists. For cycle fans only.▼

On Approval (1943-British) **80m.** *** D: Clive Brook. Beatrice Lillie, Clive Brook, Googie Withers, Roland Culver. Minor British gem showcasing the hilarious Bea Lillie as woman who exchanges boyfriends with her companion. Drawing-room comedy par excellence. Leading-man Brook also directed, produced, and cowrote script (from Frederick Lonsdale's play)—the only time he ever worked behind the camera!▼

Onassis: The Richest Man in the World (1988) **C-200m. TVM** D: Waris Hussein. Raul Julia, Jane Seymour, Anthony Quinn, Francesca Annis, Anthony Zerbe, Lorenzo Quinn. Julia's and Annis' miscasting as Aristotle Onassis and Jackie Kennedy is offset by Emmy winner Jane Seymour's performance as fiery Maria Callas, and Quinn in a tailor-made part as Ari's larger-than-life father Socrates (Quinn played a fictionalized Aristotle years earlier in THE GREEK TYCOON). Overlong adaptation of Peter Evans' book. Originally shown in two parts. Average.

On Borrowed Time (1939) **99m.** *** D: Harold S. Bucquet. Lionel Barrymore, Cedric Hardwicke, Beulah Bondi, Una Merkel, Ian Wolfe, Philip Terry, Eily Malyon. Engrossing fable of Death, Mr. Brink (Hardwicke), coming for grandpa Barrymore, finding himself trapped in tree by Lionel and grandson Bobs Watson.

Once Again (1986) **C-105m.** ** D: Amin Q. Chaudhri. Richard Cox, Jessica Harper,

Martin Balsam, Frances Sternhagen, Harley Cross. Overage rock musician Cox and cynical stewardess Harper have long been estranged when their respective parents (Balsam, Sternhagen) announce their plans to marry. Tries to be charming, touching, and cute, but the script just isn't there.

Once a Thief (1950) **88m.** ** D: W. Lee Wilder. June Havoc, Cesar Romero, Marie McDonald, Lon Chaney, Iris Adrian. OK little film of shoplifter Havoc and her tawdry romance with Romero.

Once a Thief (1965-U.S.-French) **107m.** ** D: Ralph Nelson. Ann-Margret, Alain Delon, Van Heflin, Jack Palance, John David Chandler. When young ex-con tries to go straight, he finds himself the pawn in another crime. Not at all interesting.

Once Before I Die (1965) **C-97m.** **½ D: John Derek. Ursula Andress, John Derek, Rod Lauren, Richard Jaeckel, Ron Ely. Brutal, offbeat story of band of American soldiers in Philippines during WW2, trying to survive Japanese attack. Andress is only woman in group, and you can guess the rest.▼

Once Bitten (1985) **C-93m.** BOMB D: Howard Storm. Lauren Hutton, Jim Carrey, Karen Kopins, Cleavon Little, Thomas Ballatore, Skip Lackey. Inept comedy about vampiress (Hutton) who intrudes on amorous pursuits of some teenagers because she needs the blood of a virgin to maintain her youthful glow. Pretty anemic. ▼

Once In a Lifetime (1932) **75m.** *** D: Russell Mack. Jack Oakie, Sidney Fox, Aline MacMahon, Russell Hopton, ZaSu Pitts, Louise Fazenda, Onslow Stevens, Gregory Ratoff. Stagebound but still hilarious adaptation of Kaufman-Hart play about a trio of connivers who take advantage of Hollywood's state of panic when talkies arrive by pretending to be vocal coaches.

Once in Paris . . . (1978) **C-100m.** *** D: Frank D. Gilroy. Wayne Rogers, Gayle Hunnicutt, Jack Lenoir, Clement Harari, Tanya Lopert, Doris Roberts. Gilroy produced, directed, and wrote this charming tale of Hollywood screenwriter who goes to Paris to work on script, falls in love instead. Lovely location filming; Lenoir steals the film as Rogers' all-knowing chauffeur (which he actually was prior to this picture).▼

Once Is Not Enough SEE: **Jacqueline Susann's Once Is Not Enough▼**

Once More My Darling (1949) **94m.** **½ D: Robert Montgomery. Robert Montgomery, Ann Blyth, Jane Cowl, Taylor Holmes, Charles McGraw. Satisfying comedy of young girl infatuated with middle-aged movie star.

Once More, With Feeling (1960-British) **C-92m.** **½ D: Stanley Donen. Yul Brynner, Kay Kendall, Maxwell Shaw, Mervyn Johns. Despite sparkling Kendall (her last film) as musical conductor Brynner's dissatisfied wife, this marital sex comedy fizzles.

Once Upon a Dead Man (1971) C-100m. TVM D: Leonard Stern. Rock Hudson, Susan Saint James, Jack Albertson, Rene Auberjonois, Kurt Kasznar, Jonathan Harris. Stolen sarcophagus precipitates San Francisco police commissioner's involvement in case. Standard, homespun police comedy drama. Average; pilot for *McMillan and Wife* TV series.

Once Upon a Family (1980) C-100m. TVM D: Richard Michaels. Barry Bostwick, Maureen Anderman, Lee Chamberlin, Nancy Marchand, Lara Parker, John Pleshette, Marcia Strassman, Elizabeth Wilson. When Mommy walks, Daddy struggles to succeed as a single parent in this TV carbon of KRAMER VS. KRAMER, plagued by pedestrian acting and writing. Average.

Once Upon a Honeymoon (1942) 117m. **½ D: Leo McCarey. Ginger Rogers, Cary Grant, Walter Slezak, Albert Dekker, Albert Basserman, Ferike Boros, Harry Shannon, Hans Conried. Strange but intriguing curio with status-seeking ex-burlesque queen Rogers marrying secret Nazi bigwig Slezak . . . and radio commentator Grant coming to her rescue. Some boring stretches do it in; however, the scenes in which the star duo are mistaken for Jews and almost sent to a concentration camp are fascinating.▼

Once Upon a Horse (1958) 85m. **½ D: Hal Kanter. Dan Rowan, Dick Martin, Martha Hyer, Leif Erickson, Nita Talbot, John McGiver, David Burns, James Gleason. Oddball Western spoof runs hot and cold, with some nutty gags and enough spark to make it worth watching. Old-time Western stars Bob Steele, Kermit Maynard, Tom Keene, Bob Livingston appear briefly as themselves.

Once Upon A Scoundrel (1973) C-90m. **½ D: George Schaefer. Zero Mostel, Katy Jurado, Tito Vandis. Priscilla Garcia. A Martinez. Minor but enjoyable comedy about selfish Mexican land baron Mostel, who schemes to frame the fiancé of the young girl he craves, and how he is hoodwinked into "dying" by Jurado. ▼

Once Upon a Spy (1980) C-100m. TVM D: Ivan Nagy. Ted Danson, Mary Louise Weller, Christopher Lee, Eleanor Parker, Leonard Stone, Terry Lester. Parker's a secret agent who lures reluctant computer genius Danson into superspydom. Jimmy Sangster's script is entertaining enough, as is villainous Lee's army of gorgeous blonde killers. Average.

Once Upon a Texas Train (1988) C-100m. TVM D: Burt Kennedy. Willie Nelson, Richard Widmark, Angie Dickinson, Stuart Whitman, Shaun Cassidy, Chuck Connors,

Kevin McCarthy, Ken Curtis, Gene Evans, Jack Elam, Royal Dano, Harry Carey, Jr., Dub Taylor. Entertainingly lighthearted Western with a stellar cast of veterans—and Shaun Cassidy as a young turk out to scotch the train robbery plans that have pitted aging ex-con Nelson and his gang of old codgers against longtime adversary lawman Widmark and his over-the-hill posse. Old Western hand Kennedy also wrote and produced. Average.

Once Upon a Time (1944) 89m. **½ D: Alexander Hall. Cary Grant, Janet Blair, James Gleason, Ted Donaldson, Art Baker. Amusing comedy-fantasy of entrepreneur Grant promoting a dancing caterpillar; trivial fun. Based on a Norman Corwin radio play, from Lucille Fletcher short story.

Once Upon a Time in America (1984) C-139m. *** D: Sergio Leone. Robert De Niro, James Woods, Elizabeth McGovern, Tuesday Weld, Larry Rapp, William Forsythe, James Hayden, Treat Williams, Darlanne Fleugel, Burt Young, Joe Pesci, Danny Aiello, Jennifer Connelly. Long, engrossing homage to the gangster film, following the rise and fall of Jewish childhood pals on N.Y.C.'s Lower East Side. Shorn of 88m. for U.S. release, story ceases to make sense at several points, and characters appear and disappear with amazing suddenness. Even so, Leone's feel for this genre, compelling performances by De Niro and Woods, and stunning art direction makes this well worth watching. Complete 227m. version is quite a different film—and not without flaws of its own. (Even this long version is minus several minutes of violent footage—notably from a key rape sequence—which exist in European prints.)▼

Once Upon a Time in the West (1969-U.S.-Italian) C-165m. ***½ D: Sergio Leone. Charles Bronson, Henry Fonda, Claudia Cardinale, Jason Robards, Gabriele Ferzetti, Paolo Stoppa, Frank Wolff, Jack Elam, Woody Strode, Lionel Stander, Keenan Wynn. Leone's follow-up to his "Dollars" trilogy is languid, operatic masterpiece. Plot, admittedly lifted from JOHNNY GUITAR, has landowner Cardinale waiting for the railroad to come through, unaware she's been targeted by hired killer Fonda (brilliantly cast as one of the coldest villains in screen history). Exciting, funny, and reverent, with now-classic score by Ennio Morricone; not to be missed. Story by Leone, Bernardo Bertolucci, and Dario Argento. Beware chopped-up 140m. version.▼

Once You Kiss a Stranger (1969) C-106m. BOMB D: Robert Sparr. Paul Burke, Carol Lynley, Martha Hyer, Peter Lind Hayes, Philip Carey, Stephen McNally, Whit Bissell. Thinly disguised remake of STRANGERS ON A TRAIN, with Lynley as nut who pulls golfer Burke into bizarre "reciprocal murder" scheme. Slick but empty-headed, laughable.

On Dangerous Ground (1951) **82m.** ******* D: Nicholas Ray. Robert Ryan, Ida Lupino, Ward Bond, Ed Begley, Cleo Moore, Charles Kemper. Effective mood-piece with hardened city cop Ryan softened by blind-girl Lupino, whose brother is involved in rural manhunt. Bernard Herrmann's score was reportedly his favorite work.▼

On Dress Parade (1939) **62m.** D: William Clemens. Billy Halop, Bobby Jordan, Huntz Hall, Gabriel Dell, Leo Gorcey, Selmer Jackson, John Litel, Bernard Punsley. SEE: **Bowery Boys** series.

One and Only, The (1978) **C-98m.** ****½** D: Carl Reiner. Henry Winkler, Kim Darby, Gene Saks, Herve Villechaize, Harold Gould, William Daniels, Polly Holliday. Winkler is a brash college kid determined to make it in show biz, but winds up a flamboyant wrestler. Some truly funny moments build to gradual disenchantment with his basically obnoxious character. Written by Steve Gordon.▼

One and Only, Genuine, Original Family Band, The (1968) **C-117m.** ****½** D: Michael O'Herlihy. Walter Brennan, Buddy Ebsen, Lesley Ann Warren, John Davidson, Janet Blair, Kurt Russell. Musical family becomes involved in 1888 Presidential campaign; innocuous Disney entertainment with forgettable songs by the Sherman Brothers. Goldie (billed as Goldie Jeanne) Hawn debuts in tiny part as giggling dancer.▼

One Big Affair (1952) **80m.** ****** D: Peter Godfrey. Evelyn Keyes, Dennis O'Keefe, Mary Anderson, Connie Gilchrist. On-location filming in Mexico highlights this lightweight romance yarn of Keyes and O'Keefe.

One Body Too Many (1944) **75m.** ****** D: Frank McDonald. Bela Lugosi, Jack Haley, Jean Parker, Blanche Yurka, Lyle Talbot, Douglas Fowley. Detective comedy-spoof with Lugosi tossed in for good measure; Haley is carefree salesman mistaken for private eye, forced to solve caper.▼

One Cooks, the Other Doesn't (1983) **C-100m.** TVM D: Richard Michaels. Suzanne Pleshette, Joseph Bologna, Rosanna Arquette, Oliver Clark, Evan Richards, Carl Franklin. Cutesy comedy revolving around a financially strapped realtor, his ex-wife and son, and his child-bride, all of whom are forced to share the same house. Average.▼

One Crazy Summer (1986) **C-93m.** ****** D: Savage Steve Holland. John Cusack, Demi Moore, Joel Murray, Curtis Armstrong, Bobcat Goldthwait, Tom Villard, William Hickey, Joe Flaherty. Holland's followup to BETTER OFF DEAD is another loosely connected comedy (styled like a cartoon) about a teenage misfit spending summer on Nantucket Island in New England. Some good sight gags and bright moments but no story or real characterizations to hang on to.▼

One Dangerous Night (1943) **77m.** D: Michael Gordon. Warren William, Marguerite Chapman, Eric Blore, Mona Barrie, Tala Birell, Margaret Hayes, Ann Savage. SEE: **Lone Wolf** series.

One Dark Night (1983) **C-89m.** ***½** D: Tom McLoughlin. Meg Tilly, Robin Evans, Leslie Speights, Elizabeth Daily, Adam West. Teenagers spend the night in a mausoleum. You've seen it all before, and you don't want to see it again.▼

One Day in the Life of Ivan Denisovich (1971-British-Norwegian) **C-100m.** ****½** D: Caspar Wrede. Tom Courtenay, Espen Skjonberg, James Maxwell, Alfred Burke, Eric Thompson. Another instance where a novel was just too difficult to film; Alexander Solzhenitsyn's story of a prisoner in Siberian labor camp only occasionally works on the screen. Good photography by Sven Nykvist; script by Ronald Harwood.▼

One Deadly Summer (1983-French) **C-133m.** ******* D: Jean Becker. Isabelle Adjani, Alain Souchon, Francois Cluzet, Manuel Gelin, Jenny Cleve, Suzanne Flon, Michel Galabru, Maria Machado. Overlong but engrossing drama with astonishing performance by Adjani as young sexpot whose disturbed behavior masks elaborate revenge plan. Extremely well acted, especially by Souchon as her likable beau and Flon as his deaf aunt, but Adjani's character is just too obnoxious to warrant much sympathy. Sebastien Japrisot's screenplay (from his novel) retains unusual device of having several characters take turns narrating.▼

One Desire (1955) **C-94m.** ****½** D: Jerry Hopper. Anne Baxter, Rock Hudson, Julie Adams, Natalie Wood, Betty Garde. Baxter's strong performance as woman in love with gambler Hudson elevates standard soaper.

One-Eyed Jacks (1961) **C-141m.** ******* D: Marlon Brando. Marlon Brando, Karl Malden, Pina Pellicer, Katy Jurado, Ben Johnson, Slim Pickens, Timothy Carey, Elisha Cook, Jr. Fascinating but flawed psychological western with outlaw Brando seeking revenge on former friend Malden, now a sheriff. Visually striking, and a rich character study, but overlong.▼

One Eyed Soldiers (1966-U.S.-British-Yugoslavian) **C-80m.** ***½** D: Jean Christophe. Dale Robertson, Luciana Paluzzi, Guy Deghy, Andrew Faulds, Mila Avramovic. Dying man leaves his daughter a clue to whereabouts of money in Swiss bank, leading to international scramble for the loot. If you're hoping for a fresh approach, forget it.

One Fatal Hour SEE: **Two Against the World**

One Flew Over the Cuckoo's Nest (1975) **C-133m.** **** D: Milos Forman. Jack Nicholson, Louise Fletcher, Brad Dourif, William Redfield, Michael Berryman, Peter Brocco, Will Sampson, Danny DeVito, Christopher Lloyd, Scatman Crothers, Vincent Schiavelli, Louisa Moritz. Ken Kesey's story is a triumph of the human spirit; a feisty misfit (Nicholson) enters an insane asylum and inspires his fellow patients to assert themselves, to the chagrin of strong-willed head nurse (Fletcher). The first film since IT HAPPENED ONE NIGHT to win all five top Oscars: Best Picture, Actor, Actress, Director, Screenplay (Lawrence Hauben, Bo Goldman).▼

One Foot in Heaven (1941) **108m.** ***½ D: Irving Rapper. Fredric March, Martha Scott, Beulah Bondi, Gene Lockhart, Elisabeth Fraser, Harry Davenport, Laura Hope Crews, Grant Mitchell. Superior acting in honest, appealing story of minister and wife facing various problems as church life and 20th century America clash. Very entertaining, with memorable scene of minister March going to his first movie (a William S. Hart silent).

One Foot in Hell (1960) **C-90m.** **½ D: James B. Clark, Alan Ladd, Don Murray, Dan O'Herlihy, Dolores Michaels, Barry Coe, Larry Gates, Karl Swenson. Ambitious but peculiar production of sheriff seeking retribution against small town for negligent death of his wife; co-written by Aaron Spelling.

One for the Book SEE: **Voice of the Turtle**

One Frightened Night (1935) **65m.** **½ D: Christy Cabanne. Charley Grapewin, Mary Carlisle, Arthur Hohl, Wallace Ford, Lucien Littlefield, Regis Toomey, Hedda Hopper, Evalyn Knapp, Rafaela Ottiano. Fast-moving, intricately plotted little chiller about crusty old millionaire Grapewin, who wishes to give away his fortune so as to avoid a new inheritance tax.▼

One from the Heart (1982) **C-100m.** ** D: Francis Coppola. Frederic Forrest, Teri Garr, Raul Julia, Nastassia Kinski, Lainie Kazan, Harry Dean Stanton, Allen Goorwitz (Garfield), Luana Anders. Lavishly produced but practically plotless romantic comedy about couple (Forrest, Garr) who quarrel, then seek out other partners (Kinski, Julia). Dean Tavoularis's stylized Las Vegas set and the cinematography by Vittorio Storaro and Ronald V. Garcia are astonishing! Unfortunately, pretty images do not a film make. Tom Waits songs fill the soundtrack while the actors play out one of Coppola's most surreal entertainments. A must for the curious—others beware. Look sharp for Rebecca De Mornay as a restaurant patron.▼

One Girl's Confession (1953) **74m.** ** D: Hugo Haas. Cleo Moore, Hugo Haas, Glenn Langan, Russ Conway. Cleo steals from her loutish guardian, then serves jail sentence knowing the loot is waiting for her. Typical Hugo Haas production, with intriguing premise but flimsy development. Moore is presented as (unbelievably) chaste—but our first look at her is in an alluring low-cut bathing suit. Thanks, Hugo.

One Good Turn (1954-British) **78m.** ** D: John Paddy Carstairs. Norman Wisdom, Joan Rice, Shirley Abicair, William Russell, Thora Hird. Minor musical vehicle for man-on-the-street comedian Wisdom, putting forth such homey tunes as "Take a Step in the Right Direction."

One Heavenly Night (1931) **82m.** ** D: George Fitzmaurice. Evelyn Laye, John Boles, Leon Errol, Lilyan Tashman, Hugh Cameron, Marian Lord. Lesser Goldwyn musical features Laye as a Budapest flower girl posing as a famous singer in order to trap Count Boles. OK for fanciers of old-fashioned romantic nonsense. Elegant photography by Gregg Toland and George Barnes.

One Horse Town SEE: **Small Town Girl** (1936)

One Hour with You (1932) **80m.** ***½ D: Ernst Lubitsch, George Cukor. Maurice Chevalier, Jeanette MacDonald, Genevieve Tobin, Roland Young, Charlie Ruggles. Chic romance of happily married couple upset by arrival of flirtatious Tobin. Remake of Lubitsch's 1924 THE MARRIAGE CIRCLE; started by Cukor, completed by Lubitsch with Cukor as his assistant. Songs include title tune, "What Would You Do?"

One Hundred Men and a Girl (1937) **84m.** ***½ D: Henry Koster. Deanna Durbin, Leopold Stokowski, Adolphe Menjou, Alice Brady, Eugene Pallette, Mischa Auer, Frank Jenks, Billy Gilbert. Superior blend of music and comedy as Deanna pesters conductor Stokowski to give work to her unemployed father and musician friends. Brimming with charm—and beautiful music, with Charles Previn's score earning an Oscar.

100 Rifles (1969) **C-110m.** ** D: Tom Gries. Jim Brown, Raquel Welch, Burt Reynolds, Fernando Lamas, Dan O'Herlihy. Overripe Western saga has deputy Brown going after Reynolds, fleeing with shipment of guns into Mexico, but meeting and falling for guerrilla leader Welch. Reynolds easily steals film.▼

One in a Million (1936) **95m.** *** D: Sidney Lanfield. Sonja Henie, Adolphe Menjou, Don Ameche, Ned Sparks, Jean Hersholt, The Ritz Brothers, Arline Judge, Borrah Minevich and his Harmonica Rascals. Debut film vehicle for skating star

Henie was built around then-timely Winter Olympics. Still fun; fine supporting cast.

One in a Million: The Ron LeFlore Story (1978) **C-100m.** TVM D: William A. Graham. LeVar Burton, Madge Sinclair, Paul Benjamin, James Luisi, Billy Martin, Zakes Mokae. Well-acted, inspiring story of the major league baseball player, from his days as a street-corner punk to his conviction for armed robbery and his one-in-a-million chance to make good on the outside. Adapted by Stanford Whitmore from LeFlore's autobiography, *Breakout.* Above average.▼

One Is a Lonely Number (1972) **C-97m.** *** D: Mel Stuart. Trish Van Devere, Monte Markham, Janet Leigh, Melvyn Douglas, Jane Elliott, Jonathan Lippe. Sympathetic performance by Van Devere helps this better-than-usual soaper about life of an attractive divorcee; good supporting work by Douglas and Leigh.

One Last Fling (1949) **74m.** ** D: Peter Godfrey. Alexis Smith, Zachary Scott, Douglas Kennedy, Ann Doran, Veda Ann Borg, Helen Westcott. Limp tale of overly suspicious wife checking up on her husband by going to work for him.

One Little Indian (1973) **C-90m.** **½ D: Bernard McEveety. James Garner, Vera Miles, Clay O'Brien, Pat Hingle, Andrew Prine, Jodie Foster. Garner is AWOL cavalry corporal escaping through desert with young Indian boy and a camel. Unusual Disney comedy-drama.▼

One Magic Christmas (1985) **C-88m.** *** D: Phillip Borsos. Mary Steenburgen, Gary Basaraba, Harry Dean Stanton, Arthur Hill, Elizabeth Harnois, Robbie Magwood, Michelle Meyrink. Wife and mom enduring hard times has lost the Christmas spirit, but Santa Claus and guardian angel conspire with her daughter to show her the light. Entertaining Disney family fare, though pretty serious at times . . . and Stanton is the unlikeliest guardian angel in movie history! Made in Canada.▼

One Man Force (1989) **C-89m.** ** D: Dale Trevillion. John Matuszak, Ronny Cox, Charles Napier, Sharon Farrell, Sam Jones, Richard Lynch, Stacey Q. Formula action vehicle for former football star Matuszak, who plays an L.A. cop who goes off the deep end when drug dealers murder his partner. Other cast members play roles they've done before in other, similar films. Matuszak died suddenly before this film's release.▼

One Man Jury (1978) **C-104m.** *½ D: Charles Martin. Jack Palance, Christopher Mitchum, Pamela Shoop, Angel Tompkins, Joe Spinell, Cara Williams. DIRTY HARRY rip-off with Palance as vigilante cop who administers his own brand of violent justice on some particularly repulsive felons.▼

One Man's Way (1964) **105m.** *** D: Denis Sanders. Don Murray, Diana Hyland, Veronica Cartwright, Ian Wolfe, Virginia Christine, Carol Ohmart, William Windom. Tasteful fictionalized biography of Norman Vincent Peale, his religious convictions and preaching; Murray is earnest in lead role.

One Million B.C. (1940) **80m.** **½ D: Hal Roach, Hal Roach, Jr. Victor Mature, Carole Landis, Lon Chaney, Jr., John Hubbard, Mamo Clark, Jean Porter. Bizarre caveman saga told in flashback is real curio, part of it allegedly directed by D. W. Griffith. Excellent special effects, which have turned up as stock footage in countless other cheapies. Remade in 1966.▼

$1,000,000 Duck (1971) **C-92m.** **½ D: Vincent McEveety. Dean Jones, Sandy Duncan, Joe Flynn, Tony Roberts, James Gregory, Lee H. Montgomery. A duck who lays golden eggs spurs predictable twists and turns in this standard Disney comedy.

One Million Years B.C. (1966-British) **C-100m.** **½ D: Don Chaffey. Raquel Welch, John Richardson, Percy Herbert, Robert Brown, Martine Beswick. Hammer remake of 1940 adventure boosted fur-bikinied Welch to stardom; watchable prehistoric saga with spectacular Ray Harryhausen dinosaurs and percussive score by Mario Nascimbene.

One Minute to Zero (1952) **105m.** **½ D: Tay Garnett. Robert Mitchum, Ann Blyth, William Talman, Richard Egan, Charles McGraw. Mitchum adds guts to generally bloodless tale about Korean War.▼

One More River (1934) **90m.** *** D: James Whale. Diana Wynyard, Colin Clive, Frank Lawton, Mrs. Patrick Campbell, Jane Wyatt, Reginald Denny, C. Aubrey Smith, Henry Stephenson, Lionel Atwill, Alan Mowbray. Heartfelt, nicely acted but dated drama chronicling a divorce: ruthless husband Clive accuses wife Wynyard of indiscretion with young Lawton. From John Galsworthy's last novel.

One More Saturday Night (1986) **C-95m.** BOMB D: Dennis Klein. Tom Davis, Al Franken, Moira Harris, Frank Howard, Bess Meyer, Dave Reynolds. Unfunny comedy written by and starring the nerdy duo from TV's *Saturday Night Live.* Unlike one of their TV skits, this feature, about various goings-on during a Saturday evening in Minnesota, runs an hour and a half. Forget it. ▼

One More Time (1970) **C-93m.** *½ D: Jerry Lewis. Peter Lawford, Sammy Davis, Jr., Esther Anderson, Maggie Wright. Sequel to SALT AND PEPPER is far worse. They still own nightclub, still can't keep their noses out of trouble. Of marginal interest as the only film Lewis directed that he hasn't starred in.

One More Tomorrow (1946) **88m.** ****** D: Peter Godfrey. Ann Sheridan, Dennis Morgan, Jack Carson, Alexis Smith, John Loder, Jane Wyman, Reginald Gardiner. Light-comedy players flounder in reworking of Philip Barry's THE ANIMAL KINGDOM, about a wealthy playboy (Morgan) and a radical magazine editor (Sheridan) who fall in love but *don't* get married—to their eventual regret.

One More Train to Rob (1971) **C-108m.** ****½** D: Andrew V. McLaglen. George Peppard, Diana Muldaur, John Vernon, France Nuyen, Steve Sandor. Peppard seeks revenge on former robbery partner who sent him to jail. Unremarkable Western has some flavor, nice supporting cast of familiar faces.

One Mysterious Night (1944) **61m.** D: Oscar (Budd) Boetticher. Chester Morris, Janis Carter, Richard Lane, William Wright, George E. Stone, Dorothy Malone, Joseph Crehan. SEE: **Boston Blackie** series.

One Night in Lisbon (1941) **97m.** ****½** D: Edward H. Griffith. Fred MacMurray, Madeleine Carroll, Patricia Morison, Billie Burke, John Loder. Mild screwball comedy with gorgeous Carroll falling in love with flier MacMurray despite interference from his ex (Morison).

One Night in the Tropics (1940) **82m.** ****½** D: A. Edward Sutherland. Allan Jones, Nancy Kelly, Bud Abbott, Lou Costello, Robert Cummings, Leo Carrillo, Mary Boland. Ambitious but unmemorable musical with songs by Jerome Kern, Oscar Hammerstein and Dorothy Fields, from Earl Derr Biggers' gimmicky story *Love Insurance* (filmed before in 1919 and 1924). Abbott and Costello, in film debut, have secondary roles to Jones-Kelly-Cummings love triangle, but get to do a portion of their "Who's on First?" routine.

One Night of Love (1934) **80m.** *****½** D: Victor Schertzinger. Grace Moore, Tullio Carminati, Lyle Talbot, Mona Barrie, Luis Alberni, Jessie Ralph. Classic musical, with an Oscar-winning Louis Silvers score, of aspiring opera star Moore and her demanding teacher Carminati. A delight from start to finish, and a must for music lovers; remains remarkably fresh and entertaining. Unquestionably Moore's best film.▼

One Night With You (1948-British) **90m.** ****** D: Terence Young. Nino Martini, Patricia Roc, Bonar Colleano, Guy Middleton, Stanley Holloway, Miles Malleson, Christopher Lee. Diluted musical with socialite Roc intrigued by singer Martini.

One of My Wives Is Missing (1976) **C-100m. TVM** D: Glenn Jordan. Jack Klugman, Elizabeth Ashley, James Franciscus, Joel Fabiani, Ruth McDevitt, Milton Seltzer. Small-town cop faces baffling case when rich vacationer's wife disappears and later turns up, only to be claimed an imposter. Good suspense drama and good Klugman, as usual. Above average.▼

One of Our Aircraft Is Missing (1942-British) **106m.** *****½** D: Michael Powell and Emeric Pressburger. Godfrey Tearle, Eric Portman, Hugh Williams, Bernard Miles, Hugh Burden, Emrys Jones, Googie Withers, Joyce Redman, Pamela Brown, Peter Ustinov, Hay Petrie, Roland Culver, Robert Helpmann, John Longden. Thoughtful study of RAF pilots who crash-land in the Netherlands and seek to return to England. Powell and Pressburger scripted, from the latter's story. Powell makes an appearance as a dispatcher. Some U.S. prints run 82m.▼

One of Our Dinosaurs Is Missing (1976) **C-93m. BOMB** D: Robert Stevenson. Peter Ustinov, Helen Hayes, Clive Revill, Derek Nimmo, Joan Sims. The Disney studio's answer to insomnia, a boring film about spy with secret formula hidden in dinosaur bone, and a group of nannies determined to retrieve stolen skeleton. Filmed in England.▼

One of Our Own (1975) **C-100m. TVM** D: Richard Sarafian. George Peppard, William Daniels, Louise Sorel, Strother Martin, Oscar Homolka, Zohra Lampert. Chief neurosurgeon Peppard faces a familiar series of crises as hospital administrator and predictably resolves all outstanding situations. He later continued his character in the brief *Doctors' Hospital* series. Average.

One on One (1977) **C-98m.** ******* D: Lamont Johnson. Robby Benson, Annette O'Toole, G. D. Spradlin, Gail Strickland, Melanie Griffith. Benson co-wrote this sincere, upbeat film about naive basketball player who tries to buck corrupt world of college athletics, and sadistic coach Spradlin. Director Johnson plays Benson's alumni big-brother.▼

One Plus One SEE: **Sympathy for the Devil**▼

One Police Plaza (1986) **C-100m. TVM** D: Jerry Jameson. Robert Conrad, Anthony Zerbe, George Dzundza, James Olson, Jamey Sheridan, Larry Riley, Lisa Banes. Cop thriller about a routine murder case that escalates into a scandal involving the top brass. So-so adaptation of William J. Caunitz's best-seller. Average.

One Potato, Two Potato (1964) **92m.** *****½** D: Larry Peerce. Barbara Barrie, Bernie Hamilton, Richard Mulligan, Robert Earl Jones, Harry Bellaver, Faith Burwell, Tom Ligon. Frank study of interracial marriage, beautifully acted by Barrie and Hamilton. Perceptive script by Raphael Hayes and Orville H. Hampton.

One Rainy Afternoon (1936) **79m.** ****½**

D: Rowland V. Lee. Francis Lederer, Ida Lupino, Roland Young, Hugh Herbert, Erik Rhodes, Mischa Auer. Silly but likable piece of froth about a charming, impetuous young man who causes a stir by kissing a young woman in a movie theater.▼

One Romantic Night (1930) 71m. *½ D: Paul L. Stein. Lillian Gish, Rod La Rocque, Conrad Nagel, Marie Dressler, O. P. Heggie, Albert Conti. Static, wooden version of Molnar's *The Swan*, with princess Gish (in her talkie debut) half-heartedly pursued by playboy prince La Rocque while adored by commoner Nagel. Dressler comes off best, as Gish's dowager mother. Filmed previously in 1925 and again in 1956 (with Grace Kelly) as THE SWAN.

One Russian Summer (1973-Italian-British) **C-112m.** BOMB D: Antonio Calenda. Oliver Reed, John McEnery, Carol Andre, Raymond Lovelock, Zova Velcova, Claudia Cardinale. Cripple McEnery, with a score to settle, stirs up trouble for sadistic, temperamental landowner Reed, who laughs like a hyena and chews up the scenery. Fancy camerawork, one-dimensional characterizations; a mess. From M. Lermontov's novel *Vadim*.▼

One Shoe Makes It Murder (1982) **C-100m.** TVM D: William Hale. Robert Mitchum, Angie Dickinson, Mel Ferrer, Jose Perez, John Harkins, Howard Hesseman, Cathee Shirriff, Asher Brauner. Mitchum made his belated TV acting debut as a has-been private eye who becomes enmeshed in the disappearance of gambling czar Ferrer's roving wife. Felix Culver adapted the script from Eric Bercovici's novel *So Little Cause for Caroline*, but failed to give it that extra edge for Mitchum to hone. Average.▼

One Sings, The Other Doesn't (1977-French) **C-105m.** ** D: Agnes Varda. Therese Liotard, Valerie Mairesse, Ali Raffi, Robert Dadies, Francis Lemaire. Simplistic, sugar-coated feminist story paralleling the lives of two women from the early '60s to 1976. An honest attempt to examine the meaning of womanhood, but awfully superficial.▼

One Spy Too Many (1966) **C-102m.** ** D: Joseph Sargent. Robert Vaughn, David McCallum, Rip Torn, Dorothy Provine, Leo G. Carroll. Torn tries to take over the world, with Vaughn and McCallum to the rescue. Forgettable feature, edited from *The Man from U.N.C.L.E.* TV series.

One Step to Eternity (1955-French) **94m.** ** D: Henri Decoin. Danielle Darrieux, Michel Auclair, Corinne Calvet, Gil Delamare. Capable cast led astray by meandering production about unknown persons trying to kill four women.

One Step to Hell (1967) **C-90m.** ** D: Sandy Howard. Ty Hardin, Pier Angeli,

George Sanders, Rossano Brazzi, Helga Line, Jorge Rigaud. Crude period melodrama in turn-of-the-century African bush. Lawman Hardin pursues gang of vicious killers.▼

One Summer Love (1976) **C-98m.** ** D: Gilbert Cates. Beau Bridges, Susan Sarandon, Mildred Dunnock, Ann Wedgeworth, Michael B. Miller, Linda Miller. Ambitious but muddled drama of Bridges, just out of a mental hospital, attempting to trace his family; Sarandon, who sells candy in a movie theater, takes a liking to him. Screenplay by N. Richard Nash; originally released as DRAGONFLY.

One Sunday Afternoon (1948) **C-90m.** **½ D: Raoul Walsh. Dennis Morgan, Janis Paige, Don DeFore, Dorothy Malone, Ben Blue. Musical remake of the 1932 Gary Cooper feature (and 1941's THE STRAWBERRY BLONDE) set in 1910, about a dentist who wonders if he married the right girl; pleasant but nothing more, with attractive cast and unmemorable songs.

One Terrific Guy (1986) **C-100m.** TVM D: Lou Antonio. Mariette Hartley, Wayne Rogers, Laurence Luckinbill, Brian Robbins, Susan Rinnell, Jim Antonio. Popular high school coach manipulates coeds into bogus sex research for his "dissertation." Provides Wayne Rogers with a change of pace from his well-established good guy image. Average.

One That Got Away, The (1958-British) **106m.** *** D: Roy (Ward) Baker. Hardy Kruger, Colin Gordon, Michael Goodliffe, Terence Alexander. Kruger gives sincere performance as Nazi prisoner in England who believes it is his duty to escape and get back to Germany. Many exciting moments.▼

One Third of a Nation (1939) 79m. **½ D: Dudley Murphy. Sylvia Sidney, Leif Erickson, Myron McCormick, Hiram Sherman, Sidney Lumet, Iris Adrian, Byron Russell. Sidney is a poor girl yearning to escape from the N.Y.C. tenements; young Lumet is her troubled brother, Erickson an unknowing slumlord who falls for her. Still timely social document.▼

1001 Arabian Nights (1959) **C-75m.** **½ D: Jack Kinney. Voices of Jim Backus, Kathryn Grant (Crosby), Dwayne Hickman, Hans Conried, Herschel Bernardi, Alan Reed. Elaborate updating of Arabian Nights tales featuring nearsighted Mr. Magoo has a nice score, pleasing animation, especially in color.▼

One Touch of Venus (1948) **81m.** **½ D: William A. Seiter. Ava Gardner, Robert Walker, Dick Haymes, Eve Arden, Olga San Juan, Tom Conway. Broadway success of young man in love with store-window statue of Venus which suddenly comes to life; not great, but amusing with good cast. Lovely Kurt Weill-Ogden Nash score includes "Speak Low."▼

One Trick Pony (1980) **C-98m.** ** D: Robert M. Young. Paul Simon, Blair Brown, Rip Torn, Joan Hackett, Mare Winningham, Allen Goorwitz (Garfield), Lou Reed, The B-52's, Harry Shearer, The Lovin' Spoonful, Sam and Dave, Tiny Tim. Aging rock star tries to salvage marriage while trying to weather changes in audience tastes. Good premise, impressive supporting cast undermined by haphazard construction, lack of Simon's appeal as a leading man. Scripted and scored by Simon; one of those Hare Krishnas is Daniel Stern.▼

One, Two, Three (1961) **108m.** **** D: Billy Wilder. James Cagney, Arlene Francis, Horst Buchholz, Pamela Tiffin, Lilo Pulver, Howard St. John, Hans Lothar, Leon Askin, Red Buttons. Hilarious Wilder comedy about Coke executive in contemporary West Berlin freaking out when the boss's visiting daughter secretly weds a Communist. Cagney is a marvel to watch in this machine-gun-paced comedy, his last film appearance until 1981's RAGTIME. Andre Previn's score makes inspired use of Khachaturian's "Sabre Dance." The script, by Wilder and I.A.L. Diamond, was inspired by a Ferenc Molnar one-act play.▼

One Way Passage (1932) **69m.** ***½ D: Tay Garnett. Kay Francis, William Powell, Aline MacMahon, Warren Hymer, Frank McHugh, Herbert Mundin. Tender shipboard romance of con-man Powell and fatally ill Francis, splendidly acted, with good support by MacMahon and McHugh as two other con-artists playing Cupid. Robert Lord won an Oscar for his original story. Remade as TILL WE MEET AGAIN.

One-Way Street (1950) **79m.** **½ D: Hugo Fregonese. James Mason, Marta Toren, Dan Duryea, William Conrad, Jack Elam, King Donovan. Turgid crime drama chronicling what happens after doctor Mason strips hood Duryea of $200,000—and his moll (Toren). Look for Rock Hudson as a truck driver.

One Way to Love (1945) **83m.** ** D: Ray Enright. Chester Morris, Janis Carter, Marguerite Chapman, Willard Parker. Pleasant programmer about two radio writers finding romance and new program ideas on cross-country train trip.

One Wild Moment (1977-French) **C-88m.** ** D: Claude Berri. Jean-Pierre Marielle, Victor Lanoux, Agnes Soral, Christine Dejoux, Martine Sarcey. Lightweight, unsatisfying sex farce about two middle-aged buddies (Marielle, Lanoux) who vacation with their sexy teen daughters (Soral, Dejoux). Not nearly as clever as other

Berri comedies. Remade as BLAME IT ON RIO.▼

One Woman or Two (1985-French) **C-97m.** *½ D: Daniel Vigne. Gerard Depardieu, Sigourney Weaver, Dr. Ruth Westheimer, Michel Aumont, Zabou. Paleontologist Depardieu discovers the fossil remains of the first Frenchwoman; crass ad exec Weaver is intent on exploiting this to hype perfume. An utterly silly BRINGING UP BABY derivation, with its two stars wasted. Dr. Ruth makes her film debut, cast as a philanthropist but essentially playing herself.▼

One Woman's Story SEE: **Passionate Friends.**

On Fire (1987) **C-100m. TVM** D: Robert Greenwald. John Forsythe, Carroll Baker, Gordon Jump, Woody Strode, Alan Feinstein, Sandy Ward, Michael Bowen, Brian McNamara. The topic of mandatory retirement gets a sympathetic if ultimately melodramatic examination, with the film's executive producer Forsythe as the man trying to recapture his self-worth after being kicked off the force as Chief Arson Inspector because of age. Average.

On Golden Pond (1981) **C-109m.** *** D: Mark Rydell. Katharine Hepburn, Henry Fonda, Jane Fonda, Doug McKeon, Dabney Coleman, William Lanteau. Fonda, in his last feature, is no less than brilliant as crochety retired professor Norman Thayer, Jr., angry at being 80 years old and scared of losing his faculties. Hepburn fine as his devoted, all-knowing wife who shares his summers at Maine lakefront home; Jane is his alienated daughter. Sometimes simplistic comedy-drama, scripted by Ernest Thompson from his play, gets a heavy dose of Star Quality. Fonda, Hepburn, and writer Thompson all won Academy Awards for their work.▼

On Her Majesty's Secret Service (1969-British) **C-140m.** ***½ D: Peter R. Hunt. George Lazenby, Diana Rigg, Gabriele Ferzetti, Telly Savalas, Bernard Lee, Lois Maxwell, Desmond Llewellyn. Usual globe-hopping Bond vs. Blofeld plot with novel twist: agent Bond ends up marrying Spanish contessa (Rigg)! Lazenby, first non-Connery Bond, is OK, but incredible action sequences take first chair; some 007 fans consider this the best of the series.▼

Onion Field, The (1979) **C-122m.** *** D: Harold Becker. John Savage, James Woods, Franklyn Seales, Ted Danson, Ronny Cox, Dianne Hull, Christopher Lloyd. Heart-wrenching true story about a cop who cracks up after witnessing his partner's murder and fleeing; adapted by author Joseph Wambaugh without any studio interference. Well-acted and impassioned, but never quite peaks.▼

Onionhead (1958) **110m.** **½ D: Norman Taurog. Andy Griffith, Felicia Farr,

[849]

Walter Matthau, Erin O'Brien, Joey Bishop. Film tries to capture flavor of NO TIME FOR SERGEANTS, with Griffith in the Coast Guard this time.

Only Angels Have Wings (1939) **121m.** ***½ D: Howard Hawks. Cary Grant, Jean Arthur, Richard Barthelmess, Rita Hayworth, Thomas Mitchell, Sig Ruman, John Carroll, Allyn Joslyn, Noah Beery, Jr. Quintessential Howard Hawks movie, full of idealized men and women (and what men and women!) in this look at relationships among mail pilots stationed in South America—and how things heat up when a showgirl (Arthur) is tossed into the stew. An important star-boosting showcase for Hayworth, too. Jules Furthman scripted, from a story by Hawks.▼

Only Game in Town, The (1970) **C-113m.** *** D: George Stevens. Elizabeth Taylor, Warren Beatty, Charles Braswell, Hank Henry, Olga Valery. Romance of chorus girl and gambler takes place in Las Vegas, but was shot in Paris and suffers for it; restriction of action to indoor scenes slows pace of this pleasant adaptation of Frank D. Gilroy's play. Beatty is excellent. Stevens' final film.▼

Only One Day Left Before Tomorrow SEE: **How to Steal an Airplane**

Only the Best SEE: **I Can Get It for You Wholesale**

Only the French Can (1955-French) **C-93m.** *** D: Jean Renoir. Jean Gabin, Francoise Arnoul, Maria Felix, Edith Piaf. Not top-drawer Renoir, but still an impressive, enjoyable fiction about beginnings of the Moulin Rouge and impresario Gabin's creation of the cancan. Originally released in the U.S. in 1956; a brilliantly beautiful restored version, with approximately 10m. of additional footage, opened theatrically in 1985. Originally released in France as FRENCH CAN CAN at 102m.▼

Only the Valiant (1951) **105m.** ** D: Gordon Douglas. Gregory Peck, Barbara Payton, Ward Bond, Gig Young, Lon Chaney, Neville Brand, Jeff Corey. Unmemorable oater of army officer Peck showing his courage by holding off the rampaging Indians.▼

Only Two Can Play (1962-British) **106m.** *** D: Sidney Gilliat. Peter Sellers, Mai Zetterling, Virginia Maskell, Richard Attenborough, Kenneth Griffith. Well-intentioned filming of Kingsley Amis novel, striving for quick laughs rather than satire. Sellers is librarian flirting with society woman Zetterling.▼

Only Way Out Is Dead SEE: **Man Who Wanted to Live Forever, The**

Only When I Larf (1968-British) **C-104m.** **½ D: Basil Dearden. Richard Attenborough, David Hemmings, Alexandra Stewart, Nicholas Pennell. Fun con-game film finds three confidence men scheming to sell militant African diplomat scrap metal in ammunition cases.

Only When I Laugh (1981) **C-120m.** *** D: Glenn Jordan. Marsha Mason, Kristy McNichol, James Coco, Joan Hackett, David Dukes, John Bennett Perry, Kevin Bacon. Bittersweet Neil Simon comedy about alcoholic actress Mason struggling to stay off the bottle and her relationship with teenaged daughter McNichol. Fine performances by the leads, superior ones by Coco as a gay failed actor and Hackett as an aging Park Avenue beauty. Screenplay by Simon, loosely based on his play The Gingerbread Lady.▼

Only with Married Men (1974) **C-78m.** TVM D: Jerry Paris. David Birney, Michele Lee, John Astin, Judy Carne, Dom DeLuise, Gavin MacLeod. Romantic fluff involving a sexy girl who avoids commitment by dating only married men and a bachelor who pretends he's wed to woo and win her. Consider the possibilities and guess the outcome. Average.▼

Only Yesterday (1933) **105m.** *** D: John M. Stahl. Margaret Sullavan, John Boles, Billie Burke, Reginald Denny, Edna May Oliver, Benita Hume. Though Boles is a drag, Sullavan's performance in her screen debut is still luminous enough to carry this familiar, flashbacked unwed mother saga spanning from the end of WW1 to the Depression. Opening scenes, depicting effect of the stock market crash on a group of partying high-rollers, are extremely evocative but tend to overshadow the rest of the film.

On Moonlight Bay (1951) **C-95m.** **½ D: Roy Del Ruth. Doris Day, Gordon MacRae, Billy Gray, Mary Wickes, Leon Ames, Rosemary DeCamp. Turn-of-the-century, folksy musical based on Booth Tarkington's Penrod stories with tomboy (Day) and next door neighbor (MacRae) the wholesome young lovers. Sequel: BY THE LIGHT OF THE SILVERY MOON.

On My Way to the Crusades, I Met a Girl Who . . . (1969-Italian) **C-93m.** BOMB D: Pasquale Festa Campanile. Tony Curtis, Monica Vitti, Hugh Griffith, John Richardson, Ivo Garrani, Nino Castelnuovo. Weak comedy, if that's the word, about Vitti's chastity belt was held back from release for a long time, and no wonder. Also known as THE CHASTITY BELT.

On Our Merry Way (1948) **107m.** **½ D: King Vidor, Leslie Fenton. Burgess Meredith, Paulette Goddard, Fred MacMurray, Hugh Herbert, James Stewart, Henry Fonda, Dorothy Lamour, Victor Moore. Episodic film has good Stewart-Fonda segment (written by John O'Hara, directed by George Stevens), but flock of stars can't overcome mediocre stretches as reporter Meredith asks various people about their relationship to children.

On Stage Everybody (1945) 65m. ** D: Jean Yarbrough. Jack Oakie, Peggy Ryan, Otto Kruger, Julie London, Wallace Ford, King Sisters. Run-of-the-mill Universal musical, with frantic Oakie helping to put on the big radio variety program.

On the Air Live With Captain Midnight (1979) C-93m. ** D: Ferd and Beverly Sebastian. Tracy Sebastian, John Ireland, Dena Dietrich, Ted Gehring, Mia Kovacs. A young loser finds his niche in life as a rebel disc jockey broadcasting illegally from his converted van. Also known as CAPTAIN MIDNIGHT.▼

On the Avenue (1937) 89m. *** D: Roy Del Ruth. Dick Powell, Madeleine Carroll, Alice Faye, Ritz Brothers, Alan Mowbray, Billy Gilbert, Cora Witherspoon, Joan Davis, Sig Ruman. Tasteful, intelligent musical of socialite Carroll getting involved with stage star Powell. One good Irving Berlin song after another: "I've Got My Love To Keep Me Warm," "This Year's Kisses," "Let's Go Slumming," "The Girl on the Police Gazette."

On the Beach (1959) 133m. **** D: Stanley Kramer. Gregory Peck, Ava Gardner, Fred Astaire, Anthony Perkins, Donna Anderson, John Tate, Guy Doleman. Thoughtful version of Nevil Shute's novel about Australians awaiting effects of nuclear fallout from explosion that has destroyed the rest of the world. Good performances by all, including Astaire in his first dramatic role. Screenplay by John Paxton.▼

On the Beat (1962-British) 105m. **½ D: Robert Asher. Norman Wisdom, Jennifer Jayne, Raymond Huntley, David Lodge. Overly cute comedy with Wisdom a dumbbunny helping Scotland Yard round up a criminal gang; too many pat routines and stereotyped performances.

On the Double (1961) C-92m. *** D: Melville Shavelson. Danny Kaye, Dana Wynter, Wilfrid Hyde-White, Margaret Rutherford, Diana Dors. Danny's resemblance to English general makes him valuable as a WW2 spy. At one point he does a Dietrich imitation! Repeats dual-identity gimmick from Kaye's earlier ON THE RIVIERA with equally entertaining results.

On the Edge (1985) C-92m. ** D: Rob Nilsson. Bruce Dern, Pam Grier, Bill Bailey, Jim Haynie, John Marley. Well-meaning but predictable, ultimately disappointing tale of middle-aged Dern, who attempts to redeem his life by competing in a grueling footrace.▼

On the Fiddle SEE: Operation Snafu

On the Isle of Samoa (1950) 65m. *½ D: William Berke. Jon Hall, Susan Cabot, Raymond Greenleaf, Henry Marco. Sloppy little story of Hall finding love with native girl, inspiring him to clear up his shady past.

On the Loose (1951) 78m. *½ D: Charles Lederer. Joan Evans, Melvyn Douglas, Lynn Bari, Robert Arthur, Hugh O'Brian. Lukewarm drama of overindulgent parents and their wayward daughter.

On the Nickel (1980) C-96m. **½ D: Ralph Waite. Donald Moffat, Ralph Waite, Penelope Allen, Hal Williams, Jack Kehoe. Odd, sentimental film about bums Moffat and Waite and their experiences on L.A.'s skid row. Directed, scripted, and produced by Waite, light years away from *The Waltons.*▼

On the Right Track (1981) C-98m. **½ D: Lee Philips. Gary Coleman, Lisa Eilbacher, Michael Lembeck, Norman Fell, Maureen Stapleton, Bill Russell, Herb Edelman. Coleman is a lovable 10-year-old shoeshine boy who lives out of a train station locker and predicts horserace winners like the hero of THREE MEN ON A HORSE; Stapleton is on hand as a bag lady. Coleman's theatrical starring debut is hardly feature-film material.▼

On the Riviera (1951) C-90m. *** D: Walter Lang. Danny Kaye, Gene Tierney, Corinne Calvet, Marcel Dalio, Jean Murat. Bouncy musicomedy with Danny in dual role as entertainer and French military hero. "Ballin' the Jack," other songs in lively film. Gwen Verdon is one of chorus girls. Remake of Maurice Chevalier's FOLIES BERGERE.

On the Road Again SEE: Honeysuckle Rose▼

On the Threshold of Space (1956) C-98m. **½ D: Robert D. Webb. Guy Madison, Virginia Leith, John Hodiak, Dean Jagger, Warren Stevens. Capable cast merely bridges the span between sequences of astronaut endurance tests and other space-flight maneuvers.

On the Town (1949) C-98m. **** D: Gene Kelly, Stanley Donen. Gene Kelly, Frank Sinatra, Vera-Ellen, Betty Garrett, Ann Miller, Jules Munshin, Alice Pearce, Florence Bates. Jubilant Betty Comden-Adolph Green-Leonard Bernstein musical (inspired by Jerome Robbins' ballet *Fancy Free*) about three sailors on leave for one day in N.Y.C. "New York, New York" tops a bright, inventive score, with Roger Edens and Lennie Hayton earning Oscars for their arrangements. This was Kelly and Donen's first full directing assignment—and (rare for an MGM movie) they actually shot on location in New York.▼

On the Waterfront (1954) 108m. **** D: Elia Kazan. Marlon Brando, Karl Malden, Lee J. Cobb, Rod Steiger, Pat Henning, Eva Marie Saint, Leif Erickson, Tony Galento, John Hamilton, Nehemiah Persoff. Budd Schulberg's unflinching account of N.Y.C. harbor unions (suggested by articles by Malcolm Johnson), with Brando unforgettable as misfit, Steiger his crafty brother, Cobb his waterfront boss, and Saint the girl he loves. That classic scene in the back of a taxicab is just as moving as ever. Winner of eight Oscars: Best Picture, Director, Actor (Brando), Supporting Actress (Saint), Story & Screenplay, Cinematography (Boris Kaufman), Art Direction-Set Decoration (Richard Day), and Editing (Gene Milford). Leonard Bernstein's music is another major asset. Film debuts of Saint, Martin Balsam, Fred Gwynne, and Pat Hingle.▼

On the Yard (1979) **C-102m.** ** D: Raphael D. Silver. John Heard, Thomas D. Waites, Mike Kellin, Richard Bright, Joe Grifasi, Lane Smith. Convict Heard makes a fatal mistake by mixing it up with jailhouse kingpin Waites. So-so prison picture seems hardly worth the effort, though Kellin is memorable as an aging loser trying to get paroled; produced by Joan Micklin Silver.▼

On Trial (1953-French) **70m.** ** D: Julien Duvivier. Madeleine Robinson, Daniel Gelin, Eleonora Rossi-Drago, Charles Vanel, Anton Walbrook, Jacques Chabassol. Chabassol, son of D.A. Vanel, investigates conviction of Gelin, discovering disparity between justice and truth; well-intentioned film gone astray.

On Valentine's Day (1986) **C-106m.** **½ D: Ken Harrison. William Converse-Roberts, Hallie Foote, Michael Higgins, Steven Hill, Rochelle Oliver, Richard Jenkins, Carol Goodheart, Horton Foote, Jr., Matthew Broderick. Literate but unmemorable account of the various goings-on in a small Texas town in 1917. Interesting characterizations, good performances all around, but it doesn't add up to much. Semiautobiographical screenplay by Horton Foote, and a prequel to **1918**. Produced for PBS's *American Playhouse*, where it was telecast (along with **1918**) as STORY OF A MARRIAGE.▼

On Wings of Eagles (1986) **C-250m. TVM** D: Andrew V. McLaglen. Burt Lancaster, Richard Crenna, Paul LeMat, Jim Metzler, James Sutorius, Lawrence Pressman, Constance Towers, Karen Carlson, Cyril O'Reilly. Mediocre action adventure based on Ken Follett's best-seller about millionaire H. Ross Perot's attempts to rescue two of his executives from Iranian prisons following the Ayatollah's takeover. Lancaster, as the retired general recruited to lead the mission, is his usual tower of strength and nearly as energetic as he was when swashbuckling thirty-five years ago. Originally shown in two parts. Average.

On Your Toes (1939) **94m.** **½ D: Ray Enright. Vera Zorina, Eddie Albert, Frank McHugh, Alan Hale, James Gleason, Donald O'Connor. Long-winded backstage story about jealousy and attempted murder has little to do with George Abbott's Broadway

hit; even the Rodgers and Hart songs are gone, relegated to background music! Fortunately, Zorina's dancing of "Slaughter on Tenth Avenue" remains, with choreography by George Balanchine.

Open Admissions (1988) **C-100m. TVM** D: Gus Trikonis. Jane Alexander, Dennis Farina, Estelle Parsons, Michael Beach. A black teenager who has gained entrance to a college through its open-admissions policy—but reads only at a fourth-grade level—clashes with a speech professor whose fire to teach has gone out. A tepid adaptation by Shirley Lauro of her original one-act play and later full-length Broadway drama. Average.

Open City (1946-Italian) **105m.** **** D: Roberto Rossellini. Aldo Fabrizi, Anna Magnani, Marcello Pagliero, Maria Michi, Vito Annicchiarico, Nando Bruno, Harry Feist. Classic Rossellini account of Italian underground movement during Nazi occupation of Rome; powerful moviemaking gem.▼

Opening Night (1978) **C-144m.** *** D: John Cassavetes. Gena Rowlands, John Cassavetes, Ben Gazzara, Joan Blondell, Paul Stewart, Zohra Lampert. Fascinating if you appreciate Cassavetes' style (he also wrote it); interminable if you don't. Rowlands is an actress facing a midlife crisis triggered by the death of an adoring fan on the opening night of her new play. Blondell fine as the sympathetic authoress, Cassavetes himself no less interesting as Rowlands' costar.

Open Season (1974-Spanish) **C-103m.** BOMB D: Peter Collinson. Peter Fonda, John Phillip Law, Richard Lynch, William Holden, Cornelia Sharpe. Sordid mixture of violence and sex as three Vietnam War buddies hunt humans.

Open the Door and See All the People (1964) **82m.** **½ D: Jerome Hill. Maybelle Nash, Alec Wilder, Charles Rydell, Ellen Martin. Weird little comedy of elderly twin sisters, their contrasting personalities and rivalry.

Operation, The (1990) **C-100m. TVM** D: Thomas J. Wright. Joe Penny, Lisa Hartman, Jason Beghe, Kathleen Quinlan, Dori Brenner. Successful doctor, in the midst of a complicated divorce from his wife, becomes involved in a medical malpractice suit that leads to murder. Twisty suspense drama written by Douglas Stefen Borghi that plays better than it sounds. Above average.

Operation Amsterdam (1960-British) **105m.** **½ D: Michael McCarthy. Peter Finch, Eva Bartok, Tony Britton, Alexander Knox, Malcolm Keen. Standard wartime suspense fare as British expedition tries to sneak a cache of diamonds out of Holland before Nazis can get to them.▼

Operation Bikini (1963) **83m.** ** D: Anthony Carras. Tab Hunter, Frankie Avalon, Eva Six, Scott Brady, Gary Crosby, Jim Backus. Occasionally perky cast livens tame WW2 narrative of attempt to destroy sunken treasure before enemy grabs it. Some color sequences.

Operation Bottleneck (1961) 78m. *½ D: Edward L. Cahn. Ron Foster, Miiko Taka, Norman Alden, John Clarke. Miniactioner of WW2 Burma; not much to offer.

Operation C.I.A. (1965) 90m. **½ D: Christian Nyby. Burt Reynolds, Kieu Chinh, Danielle Aubry, John Hoyt, Cyril Collack. Burt attempts to thwart an assassination in Saigon. Neat little actioner, and an intriguing look at a Vietnam of politics and spies, where innocent old men and children die.▼

Operation Conspiracy (1957-British) 69m. *½ D: Joseph Sterling. Philip Friend, Mary Mackenzie, Leslie Dwyer, Allan Cuthbertson. Timid little espionage film. Retitled: CLOAK WITHOUT DAGGER.

✓ **Operation Crossbow** (1965) C-116m. ***½ D: Michael Anderson. George Peppard, Sophia Loren, Trevor Howard, Tom Courtenay, Anthony Quayle, John Mills, Sylvia Syms, Richard Todd, Lilli Palmer. Fine "impossible mission" tale of small band of commandos out to destroy Nazi secret missile stronghold during WW2. Sensational ending, and the pyrotechnics are dazzling. Scripted by Robert Imrie (Emeric Pressburger), Derry Quinn, and Ray Rigby. Retitled THE GREAT SPY MISSION.

Operation Cross Eagles (1969) C-90m. *½ D: Richard Conte. Richard Conte, Rory Calhoun, Aili King, Phil Brown. Undistinguished war film about a WW2 mission in Yugoslavia to rescue captured American officer.▼

Operation Daybreak (1976) C-102m. **½ D: Lewis Gilbert. Timothy Bottoms, Martin Shaw, Joss Ackland, Nicola Pagett, Anthony Andrews, Anton Diffring. Well-made but uninspiring account of Czech underground's attempt to assassinate Reinhard "Hangman" Heydrich, Hitler's right-hand man, during WW2. Retitled PRICE OF FREEDOM.

Operation Disaster (1951-British) 102m. *** D: Roy (Ward) Baker. John Mills, Helen Cherry, Richard Attenborough, Lana Morris, Nigel Patrick. Vivid actioner of submarine warfare during WW2, tautly presented. Originally titled MORNING DEPARTURE.

Operation Eichmann (1961) 93m. **½ D: R. G. Springsteen. Werner Klemperer, Ruta Lee, Donald Buke, Barbara Turner, John Banner. Fairly intriguing account of the Nazi leader's postwar life and his capture by Israelis.

Operation Haylift (1950) 75m. ** D:

William Berke. Bill Williams, Ann Rutherford, Jane Nigh, Tom Brown. Minor account of air force assisting farmers to save stranded cattle during snowstorm.

Operation Heartbeat SEE: **U.M.C.**

Operation Kid Brother (1967-Italian) C-104m. *½ D: Alberto De Martino. Neil Connery, Daniela Bianchi, Adolfo Celi, Bernard Lee, Anthony Dawson, Lois Maxwell. Screen debut of Sean Connery's brother in James Bond spinoff is a disaster, in tale of master criminal (Celi)'s plan to blackmail Allied governments into controlling half of world's gold supply.

Operation M SEE: **Hell's Bloody Devils**

Operation Mad Ball (1957) 105m. ** D: Richard Quine. Jack Lemmon, Kathryn Grant (Crosby), Mickey Rooney, Ernie Kovacs, Arthur O'Connell, James Darren, Roger Smith. Weak service comedy about crafty soldiers planning wild party off base. Dull stretches, few gags. O'Connell comes off better than supposed comedians in film. Blake Edwards and Jed Harris were among the writers.

Operation Mermaid SEE: **Bay of Saint Michel**

Operation Pacific (1951) 111m. *** D: George Waggner. John Wayne, Patricia Neal, Ward Bond, Scott Forbes. Overzealous Wayne is ultradedicated to his navy command; the few WW2 action scenes are taut, and Neal makes a believable love interest.

Operation Petticoat (1959) C-124m. ***½ ✓ D: Blake Edwards. Cary Grant, Tony Curtis, Dina Merrill, Gene Evans, Arthur O'Connell, Richard Sargent, Virginia Gregg, Robert F. Simon, Gavin McLeod, Madlyn Rhue, Marion Ross, Nicky Blair. Hilarious comedy about submarine captain Grant who's determined to make his injured ship seaworthy again, and con-artist Curtis who wheels and deals to reach that goal. Some truly memorable gags; Grant and Curtis are a dynamite team in this happy film. Remade for TV in 1977.▼

Operation Petticoat (1977) C-100m. TVM D: John Astin. John Astin, Richard Gilliland, Jackie Cooper, Yvonne Wilder, Richard Bresthoff, Jamie Lee Curtis, Jim Varney. Here's that pink sub and the WW2 nurses reluctantly aboard in a silly rehash of the fondly remembered Cary Grant-Tony Curtis movie. Of single interest: one of the friendly nurses is Curtis' daughter Jamie Lee in her pre-HALLOWEEN days. Pilot for the TV series. Average. Retitled LIFE IN THE PINK.

Operation St. Peter's (1968-Italian) C-100m. ** D: Lucio Fulci. Edward G. Robinson, Lando Buzzanca, Jean-Claude Brialy. Heist film with a twist: attempt to steal Michelangelo's Pietà from Vatican, which is tough to fence. Average.

Operation Secret (1952) 108m. ** D:

Lewis Seiler. Cornel Wilde, Steve Cochran, Phyllis Thaxter, Karl Malden, Dan O'Herlihy Tame WW2 actioner involving a traitor in midst of Allied division.

Operation Snafu (1961-British) **97m. **½** D: Cyril Frankel. Alfred Lynch, Sean Connery, Cecil Parker, Stanley Holloway, Alan King, Wilfrid Hyde-White, Eric Barker, Kathleen Harrison. Sluggish WW2 account of two buddies becoming heroes unintentionally; most capable cast. Retitled: OPERATION WARHEAD. Originally titled ON THE FIDDLE.

Operation Snafu (1970-Italian-Yugoslavian) **C-97m.** BOMB D: Nanni Loy. Peter Falk, Jason Robards, Martin Landau, Nino Manfredi, Scott Hylands, Slim Pickens, Frank Latimore, Anthony Dawson. Aggressively unfunny comedy about a group of Algeria-based soldiers led by Falk on special mission to Sicily during WW2. Actual title on film is SITUATION NORMAL ALL FOULED UP.

Operation Snatch (1962-British) **83m.** ** D: Robert Day. Terry-Thomas, George Sanders, Lionel Jeffries, Jackie Lane, Lee Montague, Michael Trubshawe. Fitfully funny satire involving British attempt to keep "their flag flying" on Gibraltar during WW2.

Operation Thunderbolt (1977) **C-125m.** *** D: Menahem Golan. Yehoram Gaon, Klaus Kinski, Assaf Dayan, Shai K. Ophir, Sybil Danning. Stunning retelling of the famed raid by Israeli commandos on July 4, 1976 to rescue 104 hijacked passengers from a plane at Entebbe in Uganda. The stamp of official Israeli approval given this film, along with government cooperation, and dedicated performances by a basically Israeli cast make this one outshine both star-laden American-made dramatizations, RAID ON ENTEBBE and VICTORY AT ENTEBBE.▼

Operation Warhead SEE: **Operation Snafu**

Operation X (1951-British) **79m.** ** D: Gregory Ratoff. Edward G. Robinson, Peggy Cummins, Richard Greene, Nora Swinburne. Heady yarn with Robinson overly ambitious businessman forgetting his scruples. Original title: MY DAUGHTER JOY.

Operator 13 (1934) **86m.** **½ D: Richard Boleslavsky. Marion Davies, Gary Cooper, Katharine Alexander, Jean Parker, Ted Healy, Russell Hardie, The Four Mills Brothers, Sidney Toler. Davies plays an actress who's recruited as a Union spy during the Civil War; she spends the first half of the film in blackface disguise, the second half falling in love with Confederate officer Cooper. Patently absurd but still somehow entertaining; fast-moving and handsomely shot.

Opportunity Knocks (1990) **C-105m.** **½

D: Donald Petrie. Dana Carvey, Robert Loggia, Todd Graff, Julia Campbell, Milo O'Shea, James Tolkan, Doris Belack, Sally Gracie, Del Close. Innocuous comedy about a con artist who assumes someone else's identity and falls into a plum job with a bathroom-fixture tycoon, who happens to have a cute daughter. First starring showcase for *Saturday Night Live* comic Carvey lets him do his dialect shticks (and even his impression of George Bush), but never catches fire. At least it's pleasant.▼

Opposing Force (1986) **C-97m.** ** D: Eric Karson. Tom Skerritt, Lisa Eichhorn, Anthony Zerbe, Richard Roundtree, Robert Wightman, John Considine. Eichhorn, only female in a military experiment designed to simulate p.o.w.-torture conditions, falls victim to madman commander Zerbe—who justifies his rape of her as a training technique. Barely released action film builds some modest suspense, then fizzles out with an exceedingly flat conclusion. Also known as HELLCAMP.▼

Opposite Sex, The (1956) **C-117m.** *** D: David Miller. June Allyson, Joan Collins, Dolores Gray, Ann Sheridan, Joan Blondell, Ann Miller, Agnes Moorehead, Carolyn Jones, Charlotte Greenwood. Well-heeled musical remake of Clare Boothe Luce's THE WOMEN has stellar cast, but still pales next to brittle original (Shearer, Crawford, Russell, etc.). Major difference: music and men appear in this expanded version.

Optimists, The (1973-British) **C-110m.** *** D: Anthony Simmons. Peter Sellers, Donna Mullane, John Chaffey, David Daker. Entertaining comedy-drama of London busker (street entertainer) Sellers and the two tough little kids he takes in hand. Songs by Lionel Bart include effective "Sometimes." Alternate TV version runs 94m.

Orca (1977) **C-92m.** ** D: Michael Anderson. Richard Harris, Charlotte Rampling, Will Sampson, Peter Hooten, Bo Derek, Keenan Wynn, Robert Carradine. Killer whale revenges himself on bounty hunter Harris and crew for killing pregnant mate. For undiscriminating action fans whose idea of entertainment is watching Bo getting her leg bitten off.▼

Orchestra Conductor, The (1980-Polish) **C-101m.** ** D: Andrzej Wajda. John Gielgud, Krystyna Janda, Andrzej Seweryn, Jan Ciercierski. Uneven drama about aged Polish conductor Gielgud returning to his hometown. Excellent cast is defeated by a superficially philosophical script.

Orchestra Rehearsal (1979-Italian) **C-72m.** **½ D: Federico Fellini. Baldwin Baas, Clara Colosimo, Elizabeth Lubi, Ronoldo Bonacchi, Ferdinand Villella. Heavy-handed allegory that examines an orchestra as microcosm of troubled world; occasional moments of wit and insight, but overall a disappointment. Made for Italian television. Music by Nino Rota.

Orchestra Wives (1942) **98m. **½** D: Archie Mayo. George Montgomery, Glenn Miller, Lynn Bari, Carole Landis, Cesar Romero, Ann Rutherford, Virginia Gilmore, Mary Beth Hughes, Jackie Gleason, The Nicholas Brothers, Henry (Harry) Morgan. Story woven around Glenn Miller's band and the musicians' neglected wives. Not bad, with vintage music: "I've Got a Gal in Kalamazoo," "At Last," "Serenade in Blue."▼

Ordeal (1973) **C-74m. TVM** D: Lee H. Katzin. Arthur Hill, Diana Muldaur, James Stacy, Macdonald Carey, Michael Ansara. Mojave Desert location shooting enhances morality tale of scheming wife (Muldaur) abandoning broken-legged husband (Hill) in wilderness. Remake of INFERNO. Average.

Ordeal by Innocence (1984) **C-87m. *½** D: Desmond Davis. Donald Sutherland, Faye Dunaway, Christopher Plummer, Sarah Miles, Ian McShane, Diana Quick, Annette Crosbie. Agatha Christie mystery has American Sutherland as amateur sleuth in 1950s English hamlet. Cast wasted, logic absent in utterly pointless film. Score by Dave Brubeck. Made in England.▼

Ordeal of Bill Carney, The (1981) **C-100m. TVM** Jerry London. Ray Sharkey, Richard Crenna, Betty Buckley, Ana Alicia, Jeremy Licht, Vincent Baggetta, Martin Milner, Tony Dow, Robert Prosky. Handicapped crusading lawyer Crenna and quadraplegic Sharkey wage a landmark court battle for the custody of the latter's children. Average.

Ordeal of Dr. Mudd, The (1980) **C-143m. TVM** D: Paul Wendkos. Dennis Weaver, Susan Sullivan, Richard Dysart, Michael McGuire, Nigel Davenport, Arthur Hill. Overlong drama about Dr. Samuel Mudd, who unwittingly aided John Wilkes Booth after Lincoln's assassination and was sent to prison for conspiracy (a story filmed before as PRISONER OF SHARK ISLAND and HELLGATE). Weaver's earnest, carefully shaded performance as Mudd makes the viewing worthwhile. Above average.▼

Ordeal of Patty Hearst, The (1979) **C-150m. TVM** D: Paul Wendkos. Dennis Weaver, Lisa Eilbacher, David Haskell, Stephen Elliott, Felton Perry, Rosanna Arquette. Self-named headline story is recreated through the eyes of an FBI agent who turned this bizarre kidnap case into his eve-of-retirement crusade. A feature film version of the story called PATTY HEARST followed in 1988. Average.

Ordered to Love (1960-German) **82m. **½** D: Werner Klinger. Maria Perschy, Marisa Mell, Rosemarie Kirstein, Birgitt Bergen. Potentially explosive film gets tame

treatment; account of Nazi "breeding" camps for new generation of master race soldiers.

Order of Death SEE: Corrupt▼

Orders Are Orders (1954-British) **78m. **** D: David Paltenghi. Margot Grahame, Maureen Swanson, Peter Sellers, Tony Hancock, Sidney James. Hancock as befuddled lieutenant is best item in this slapstick yarn of movie company using an Army barracks for headquarters. Based on a 1932 play, filmed once before.

Orders to Kill (1958-British) **93m. **½** D: Anthony Asquith. Eddie Albert, Paul Massie, Lillian Gish, James Robertson Justice. Low-key account of American agent sent into France to kill a traitor.

Ordet (1955-Danish) **125m. ****** D: Carl Dreyer. Henrik Malberg, Emil Hass, Christensen Preben, Lerdorff Rye. Two rural families, at odds with each other over religious differences, are forced to come to grips with their children's love for each other. Arguably Dreyer's greatest film, but certainly the movies' final word on the struggle between conventional Christianity and more personalized religious faith. Truly awe-inspiring, with a never-to-be-forgotten climactic scene. Based on a play by Kaj Munk, which was filmed before in 1943.▼

Ordinary People (1980) **C-123m. ****** D: Robert Redford. Donald Sutherland, Mary Tyler Moore, Judd Hirsch, Timothy Hutton, M. Emmet Walsh, Elizabeth McGovern, Dinah Manoff, James B. Sikking. Superb adaptation of Judith Guest's novel about a well-to-do family's deterioration after the death of the eldest son, told mostly from the point of view of his guilt-ridden younger brother. Intelligent, meticulously crafted film, an impressive directorial debut for Redford, who won an Academy Award, and young Hutton, who took the Best Supporting Actor prize. Other Oscars for screenwriter Alvin Sargent and for Best Picture of the Year.▼

Oregon Passage (1957) **C-82m. *½** D: Paul Landres. John Ericson, Lola Albright, Edward Platt, Jon Shepodd. Bland fare about army officer trying to do good, but interfering with Indian way of life.

Oregon Trail, The (1959) **C-86m. **** D: Gene Fowler, Jr. Fred MacMurray, William Bishop, Nina Shipman, Gloria Talbott, Henry Hull, John Carradine. Uneventful Western with MacMurray a reporter investigating Indian attacks on settlers; set in 19th-century Oregon.

Oregon Trail, The (1976) **C-110m. TVM** D: Boris Sagal. Rod Taylor, Blair Brown, David Huddleston, Linda Purl, Andrew Stevens, G. D. Spradlin, Douglas V. Fowley, Wilford Brimley. Pioneer family pulls up stakes and heads West for a new life. Solid outdoor drama blessed with usual strong performance by Taylor, who also starred in the subsequent series. Average.

Organization, The (1971) **C-107m.** ******* D: Don Medford. Sidney Poitier, Barbara McNair, Sheree North, Gerald S. O'Loughlin, Raul Julia, Fred Beir, Allen Garfield, Ron O'Neal, Dan Travanty (Daniel J. Travanti). Poitier, in his third and final appearance as Virgil Tibbs, tries to bust open a major dope-smuggling operation. Exciting chase sequences, realistic ending.▼

Organizer, The (1964-Italian) **126m.** ******* D: Mario Monicelli. Marcello Mastroianni, Annie Girardot, Renato Salvatori, Bernard Blier. Serious look at labor union efforts in Italy, with Mastroianni giving low-keyed performance in title role.

Orgasmo SEE: **Paranoia** (1968)▼
Oriental Dream SEE: **Kismet** (1944)

Original Sin (1989) **C-100m. TVM** D: Ron Satlof. Ann Jillian, Charlton Heston, Robert Desiderio, Lou Liberatore, Louis Guss, Marshall Teague. Jillian's a happily married woman who comes to discover that father-in-law Heston is an underworld kingpin—and might be behind the kidnapping of her young son. Average.

Orphans (1987) **C-120m.** ****½** D: Alan J. Pakula. Albert Finney, Matthew Modine, Kevin Anderson. Young punk brings a well-heeled drunk home one night, planning to fleece him, but soon learns that his "victim" is no dummy; in fact, he quickly takes over the lives of the hot-tempered mugger and his slow-witted younger brother. Lyle Kessler's script (from his own play) fails to adapt its stage conventions to the new medium . . . but the three lead performances are so powerful, and the basic material so emotional, that it's still worthwhile. Besides, Finney can do no wrong.▼

Orphans of the Storm (1922) **125m.** ******* D: D. W. Griffith. Lillian Gish, Dorothy Gish, Joseph Schildkraut, Morgan Wallace, Lucille LaVerne, Sheldon Lewis, Frank Puglia, Creighton Hale, Monte Blue, Louis Wolheim. Griffith's epic film about sisters cruelly separated, one blind and raised by thieves, one innocent and plundered by lecherous aristocrats. Implausible plot segues into French Revolution, with lavish settings and race-to-the-rescue climax. For all its creaky situations, and extreme length, still a dazzling film. Based on a 19th-century French play, *The Two Orphans*, which was filmed before in 1915 and again in 1933 and 1955.▼

√ **Orphan Train** (1979) **C-150m. TVM** D: William A. Graham. Jill Eikenberry, Kevin Dobson, Linda Manz, Graham Fletcher-Cook, Melissa Michaelsen, Glenn Close, Morgan Farley, Severn Darden. Historical drama taken from Dorothea G. Petrie's novel dealing with a dedicated young social worker, a newspaper photographer, and a group of slum kids on their mid-19th-century railroad odyssey from Manhattan to new lives out West. Scripted by Millard Lampell. Above average.▼

Orpheus (1949-French) **95m.** ******* D: Jean Cocteau. Jean Marais, Francois Perier, Maria Casares, Marie Dea, Juliette Greco, Roger Blin. Compelling cinematic allegory set in modern times with poet Marais encountering Princess of Death, exploring their mutual fascination. Heavy-handed at times, but still quite special. Remade by Jacques Demy as PARKING. Original French running time: 112m.▼

Oscar, The (1966) **C-119m.** ****½** D: Russell Rouse. Stephen Boyd, Elke Sommer, Eleanor Parker, Milton Berle, Joseph Cotten, Jill St. John, Ernest Borgnine, Edie Adams, Tony Bennett, Jean Hale. Shiny tinsel view of Hollywood and those competing for Academy Awards; Parker as love-hungry talent agent comes off best. Loosely based on Richard Sale novel, with many guest stars thrown in. Some of the dialogue is so bad it's laughable.▼

Oscar Wilde (1960-British) **96m.** ******* D: Gregory Ratoff. Robert Morley, Phyllis Calvert, John Neville, Ralph Richardson, Dennis Price, Alexander Knox. Morley is ideally cast as famed 19th century playwright and wit, in film that focuses on his traumatic trials and eventual conviction for sodomy. Released at the same time as THE TRIALS OF OSCAR WILDE with Peter Finch.

O'Shaughnessy's Boy (1935) **88m.** ****½** D: Richard Boleslawski. Wallace Beery, Jackie Cooper, Spanky McFarland, Henry Stephenson, Leona Maricle, Sara Haden. Sentimental tale of Beery searching for his son, taken from him by cruel wife.

O.S.S. (1946) **107m.** ******* D: Irving Pichel. Alan Ladd, Geraldine Fitzgerald, Patric Knowles, Richard Benedict, Richard Webb, Don Beddoe, Onslow Stevens. Brisk WW2 espionage film with Ladd and company on important mission in France unaware that D-Day is rapidly approaching.

Ossessione (1942-Italian) **140m.** *****½** D: Luchino Visconti. Massimo Girotti, Clara Calamai, Juan deLanda, Elio Marcuzzo. Visconti's first feature triggered the great era of Italian neorealism, transplanting James Cain's *The Postman Always Rings Twice* quite successfully to Fascist Italy; however, as an unauthorized version of the book, it was not permitted to be shown in the U.S. until 1975. Heavy going at times, but fascinating nonetheless. Filmed earlier in France, twice later in the U.S.▼

O.S.S. 117 Double Agent (1967-French-Italian) **C-90m.** ***½** D: Andre Hunebelle. John Gavin, Curt Jurgens, Margaret Lee, Luciana Paluzzi. Gavin is a poor man's James Bond in this plodding thriller about a spy who takes on an assassination bureau.

O. S. S. 117—Mission for a Killer

[856]

(1966-French) **C-84m.** **½ D: Andre Hunebelle. Frederick Stafford, Mylene Demongeot, Raymond Pellegrin. At times interesting malarkey about super spy trying to combat a world-hungry political organization.

Osterman Weekend, The (1983) **C-102m.** **½ D: Sam Peckinpah. Rutger Hauer, John Hurt, Craig T. Nelson, Dennis Hopper, Chris Sarandon, Meg Foster, Helen Shaver, Cassie Yates, Burt Lancaster. Intriguing, sometimes confusing adaptation of Robert Ludlum thriller about a controversial talk-show host who's recruited by the CIA to expose some friends who are supposedly Soviet agents. Consistently interesting but aloof and cold, despite a top-notch cast. Peckinpah's final film.▼

✓ **Otello** (1986-Italian) **C-120m.** ***½ D: Franco Zeffirelli. Placido Domingo, Katia Ricciarelli, Justino Diaz, Petra Malakova, Urbano Barberini. Beautifully filmed version of the Verdi opera, with Domingo in fine voice in the title role; he is more than ably assisted by Ricciarelli as wife Desdemona and Diaz as the evil, manipulative Iago. Nearly flawless in all respects; a must for opera buffs.▼

Othello (1952-Italian) **92m.** ***½ D: Orson Welles. Orson Welles, Micheal MacLiammoir, Suzanne Cloutier, Robert Coote, Michael Lawrence, Fay Compton, Doris Dowling. Riveting, strikingly directed version of the Shakespeare play with Welles in the title role, lied to by Iago (MacLiammoir) into thinking that wife Desdemona (Cloutier) has been unfaithful. Shot, incredibly, between 1949 and 1952, because of budget difficulties; one of the most fascinating (and underrated) attempts at Shakespeare ever filmed. Joseph Cotten appears as a Senator, Joan Fontaine as a Page.

Othello (1965-British) **C-166m.** **** D: Stuart Burge. Laurence Olivier, Frank Finlay, Maggie Smith, Joyce Redman, Derek Jacobi. Brilliant transferral to the screen of Shakespeare's immortal story of the Moor of Venice. Burge directed the filming, Olivier staged the production.

Other, The (1972) **C-100m.** *** D: Robert Mulligan. Uta Hagen, Diana Muldaur, Chris Udvarnoky, Martin Udvarnoky, Norma Connolly, Victor French, Portia Nelson, John Ritter. Eerie tale of supernatural, with twin brothers representing good and evil. Stark, chilling mood tale adapted by Thomas Tryon from his novel.▼

Other Love, The (1947) **95m.** **½ D: Andre de Toth. Barbara Stanwyck, David Niven, Richard Conte, Maria Palmer, Joan Lorring, Gilbert Roland, Richard Hale, Lenore Aubert. Dying Stanwyck decides to live wild life with gambler Conte, unaware that doctor Niven loves her. Not convincing, but enjoyable.

Other Lover, The (1985) **C-100m. TVM** D: Robert Ellis Miller. Lindsay Wagner, Jack Scalia, Max Gail, Millie Perkins, John Bennett Perry, Shannen Doherty. Married publishing exec Wagner has an affair with one of her authors in this predictable hand-wringing romantic drama. Average.

Other Man, The (1970) **C-99m. TVM** D: Richard Colla. Joan Hackett, Roy Thinnes, Tammy Grimes, Arthur Hill, Virginia Gregg, Rodolfo Hoyos. Husband's disinterest propels wife into clandestine affair with stranger, attempted murder the outcome. Fairly tense situation at film's climax, but overindulgent direction and script detract. Average.

Other Men's Women (1931) **70m.** **½ D: William A. Wellman. Grant Withers, Mary Astor, Regis Toomey, James Cagney, Joan Blondell. Love triangle set in the world of railroad men; interesting melodrama, dated in some ways, but vivid in its atmosphere, with great action finale. Cagney and Blondell have supporting roles.

Other Side of Hell, The (1978) **C-150m. TVM** D: Jan Kadar. Alan Arkin, Roger E. Mosley, Morgan Woodward, Seamon Glass. Harrowing tale of a man's fight to get out of a mental institution, made even more depressing by Arkin's overly intense acting style. Average.

Other Side of Midnight, The (1977) **C-165m.** BOMB D: Charles Jarrott. Marie-France Pisier, John Beck, Susan Sarandon, Raf Vallone, Clu Gulager, Christian Marquand, Michael Lerner. Trashy Sidney Sheldon novel gets the treatment it deserves in ponderous story, set from 1939-1947, about a woman who parlays her body into film stardom. Dull, as opposed to lively, drek.▼

Other Side of Paradise, The SEE: Foxtrot▼

Other Side of the Mountain, The (1975) **C-101m.** **½ D: Larry Peerce. Marilyn Hassett, Beau Bridges, Belinda J. Montgomery, Nan Martin, William Bryant, Dabney Coleman. Pleasantly performed but undistinguished true-life tragedy about skier Jill Kinmont, once a shoo-in for the Olympics until a sporting accident left her paralyzed from the shoulders down. Followed by 1978 sequel.▼

Other Side of the Mountain Part 2, The (1978) **C-100m.** **½ D: Larry Peerce. Marilyn Hassett, Timothy Bottoms, Nan Martin, Belinda J. Montgomery, Gretchen Corbett, William Bryant. Smooth continuation of story of crippled skier Jill Kinmont (Hassett), who finds true love with trucker Bottoms. Timothy's real-life father James plays his dad in this film.▼

Other Victim, The (1981) **C-96m. TVM** D: Noel Black. William Devane, Jennifer O'Neill, James Blendick, Charles Hallahan, Todd Susman, Mary McDonough, John

Crawford, Bruce Kirby, Sr., Janet Mac-Lachlan. Construction foreman's life and feelings are profoundly altered after his wife's rape at knife-point. Highlighted by another of Devane's patented performances of rage. Script by Richard Deroy. Above average.

Other Woman, The (1954) 81m. BOMB D: Hugo Haas. Hugo Haas, Cleo Moore, Lance Fuller, Lucille Barkley, Jack Macy, John Qualen. Typical Hugo Haas fare involving a girl's plot for revenge on her former boss.

Other Woman, The (1983) C-100m. TVM D: Melville Shavelson. Hal Linden, Anne Meara, Jerry Stiller, Madolyn Smith, Warren Berlinger, Janis Paige, Joe Regalbuto, Nita Talbot, Alley Mills. In this real sparkler written by Anne Meara and producer Lila Garrett, widower Linden marries a girl half his age whom he met at his wife's funeral, and then falls for Meara, an ebullient grandmother of his own generation. Above average.

Otley (1969-British) C-90m. ** D: Dick Clement. Tom Courtenay, Romy Schneider, Alan Badel, James Villiers, Leonard Rossiter, Fiona Lewis. Static spy spoof about petty thief and beautiful secret agent is helped a bit by Courtenay and Schneider, but otherwise has little to recommend it.

Our Betters (1933) 83m. **½ D: George Cukor. Constance Bennett, Gilbert Roland, Charles Starrett, Anita Louise, Alan Mowbray, Minor Watson, Violet Kemble Cooper. Dated but enjoyable film of Somerset Maugham drawing-room comedy about British lord marrying rich American girl.

Our Blushing Brides (1930) 74m. **½ D: Harry Beaumont. Joan Crawford, Anita Page, Dorothy Sebastian, Robert Montgomery, Raymond Hackett, John Miljan, Hedda Hopper, Edward Brophy, Albert Conti. Level-headed department-store worker Crawford and flighty roommates Page and Sebastian try to nab rich husbands. Crawford shines in this otherwise unconvincing drama.

Our Daily Bread (1934) 74m. **½ D: King Vidor. Karen Morley, Tom Keene, John Qualen, Barbara Pepper, Addison Richards, Harry Holman. Hailed as a classic, this Depression drama is intriguing in its communal back-to-the-soil message, but spoiled by terrible performance by leading-man Keene. Final irrigation sequence is memorable, however.▼

Our Dancing Daughters (1928) 97m. *** D: Harry Beaumont. Joan Crawford, Johnny Mack Brown, Dorothy Sebastian, Nils Asther, Anita Page, Kathlyn Williams, Edward Nugent. One of the best Jazz Age silents, with absurdly melodramatic story: flapper Joan loses Johnny to Anita Page, who's been pushed into marriage against her will. Crystallization of the Roaring 20s. Silent film with synchronized music track (and even an occasional bit of off-screen dialogue).

Our Family Business (1981) C-74m. TVM D: Robert Collins. Sam Wanamaker, Vera Miles, Ray Milland, Ted Danson, Deborah Carney, Ayn Ruyman, Chip Mayer, James Luisi. A real off-the-wall pilot for proposed series dealing with the Mafia and the difficulties of staying alive within the Syndicate. The big question, undetermined by Lane Slate's teleplay, remains: Where would this one go after an episode or two? One asset in addition to the acting of the veteran leads (including Milland, curiously cast as a capo) is Reynaldo Villalobos' camerawork, several notches above TV standards. Average.▼

Our Girl Friday SEE: **Adventures of Sadie, The**

Our Hearts Were Growing Up (1946) 83m. **½ D: William D. Russell. Gail Russell, Diana Lynn, Brian Donlevy, James Brown, Bill Edwards, William Demarest. Follow-up to OUR HEARTS WERE YOUNG AND GAY doesn't match it, with girls on their own at Princeton.

Our Hearts Were Young and Gay (1944) 81m. *** D: Lewis Allen. Gail Russell, Diana Lynn, Charlie Ruggles, Dorothy Gish, James Brown, Bill Edwards, Beulah Bondi, Alma Kruger. Extremely pleasant bit of fluff from Cornelia Otis Skinner's memory of traveling to Europe during 1920s with her girlfriend Emily Kimbrough. Sequel: OUR HEARTS WERE GROWING UP.

Our Hitler (1980-German) C-420m. ** D: Hans-Jurgen Syberberg. Heinz Schubert, Peter Kern, Hellmut Lange, Rainer von Artenfels, Martin Sperr. Frightfully pretentious, stage-influenced 7-hour rationalization of Hitler's rise to power would probably play better if shown in four parts, as it was on German TV. A stimulating intellectual exercise for some, a laxative for most; distributed in the U.S. by Francis Ford Coppola.

Our Hospitality (1923) 74m. **** D: Buster Keaton, Jack Blystone. Buster Keaton, Natalie Talmadge, Joe Keaton, Buster Keaton, Jr., Kitty Bradbury, Joe Roberts. Buster goes to the South to claim a family inheritance, and falls in love with the daughter of a longtime rival clan. Sublime silent comedy, one of Buster's best, with a genuinely hair-raising finale. Incidentally, Buster married his leading lady in real life.▼

Our Little Girl (1935) 63m. **½ D: John Robertson. Shirley Temple, Rosemary Ames, Joel McCrea, Lyle Talbot, Erin O'Brien-Moore. Usual Temple plot of Shirley bringing separated parents McCrea and Ames together again. Also shown in computer-colored version.▼

Our Man Flint (1966) C-107m. **½ D:

Daniel Mann. James Coburn, Lee J. Cobb, Gila Golan, Edward Mulhare, Benson Fong, Gianna Serra. One of the countless James Bond spoofs, this saga of the man from Z.O.W.I.E. starts briskly, becomes forced after a while. Coburn makes a zesty hero, Golan an attractive decoration. Followed by a sequel (IN LIKE FLINT) and a TV movie.

Our Man Flint: Dead on Target (1976) C-78m. TVM D: Joseph L. Scanlon. Ray Danton, Sharon Acker, Lawrence Dane, Donnelly Rhodes, Linda Sorenson, Susan Sullivan. Tired action film has super agent Derek Flint assigned to the rescue of a kidnapped oil executive. Another unsuccessful pilot. Below average.

Our Man in Havana (1960-British) 107m. **½ D: Carol Reed. Alec Guinness, Burl Ives, Maureen O'Hara, Ernie Kovacs, Noel Coward, Ralph Richardson, Jo Morrow. Weak satirical spy spoof, adapted by Graham Greene from his novel. Guinness is vacuum cleaner salesman who becomes British agent.

Our Men in Bagdad (1967-Italian) C-100m. *½ D: Paolo Bianchini. Rory Calhoun, Roger Hanin, Evi Marandi, Ralph Baldwin, Jean Gaven, Lea Padovani. Unsurprising espionage caper set in the Middle East.

Our Miss Brooks (1956) 85m. **½ D: Al Lewis. Eve Arden, Gale Gordon, Nick Adams, Robert Rockwell, Richard Crenna, Don Porter, Jane Morgan. Fairly amusing feature based on beloved TV series has Arden's Brooks trying to snag Rockwell's Mr. Boynton and interest Adams in journalism. Crenna's screeching serenade, "It's Magic," is a high point.▼

Our Mother's House (1967-British) C-105m. *** D: Jack Clayton. Dirk Bogarde, Margaret Brooks, Louis Sheldon-Williams, John Gugolka, Pamela Franklin, Mark Lester. Children's scheme to carry on normally when their mother dies works well until their worthless father shows up. Director Clayton gets fine performances from all in offbeat film.

Our Relations (1936) 74m. *** D: Harry Lachman. Stan Laurel, Oliver Hardy, Alan Hale, Sidney Toler, Daphne Pollard, Betty Healy, James Finlayson, Arthur Housman, Iris Adrian, Lona Andre. Stan and Ollie get into snowballing comedy of errors with their long-lost twins; best scenes in Hale's beer garden.▼

Our Time (1974) C-88m. **½ D: Peter Hyams. Pamela Sue Martin, Parker Stevenson, Betsy Slade, George O'Hanlon, Jr., Karen Balkin. Nice nostalgic tale of young love, set in a Massachusetts girls' school in 1955. Bad color photography mars otherwise effective comedic and dramatic elements. Shown on network TV as DEATH OF HER INNOCENCE.

Our Town (1940) 90m. ***½ D: Sam Wood. William Holden, Martha Scott, Frank Craven, Fay Bainter, Beulah Bondi, Thomas Mitchell, Guy Kibbee, Stuart Erwin. Sensitive adaptation of Thornton Wilder's Pulitzer Prize-winning play about small New England town with human drama and conflict in every family. Splendid score by Aaron Copland and production design by William Cameron Menzies. Screenplay by Wilder, Harry Chandlee, and Frank Craven. Craven, Doro Merande, Arthur Allen, and Scott (in her film debut) recreate their Broadway roles.▼

Our Very Own (1950) 93m. **½ D: David Miller. Ann Blyth, Farley Granger, Jane Wyatt, Donald Cook, Ann Dvorak, Natalie Wood, Martin Milner. Melodramatic account of Blyth's shock upon discovering she's an adopted child.

Our Vines Have Tender Grapes (1945) 105m. ***½ D: Roy Rowland. Edward G. Robinson, Margaret O'Brien, James Craig, Frances Gifford, Agnes Moorehead, Morris Carnovsky. Excellent view of American life in Wisconsin town with uncharacteristic Robinson as O'Brien's kind, understanding Norwegian father.

Our Wife (1941) 95m. **½ D: John M. Stahl. Melvyn Douglas, Ruth Hussey, Ellen Drew, Charles Coburn, John Hubbard. Douglas adds dignity to this OK marital comedy involving musician seeking divorce to marry another.

Our Winning Season (1978) C-92m. ** D: Joseph Ruben. Scott Jacoby, Deborah Benson, Dennis Quaid, Randy Herman, Joe Penny, Jan Smithers, P. J. Soles. Yet another 1960s high school film focuses mostly on growing pains of aspiring track star Jacoby; not bad, but awfully familiar.

Out (1982) C-83m. **½ D: Eli Hollander. Peter Coyote, O-Lan Sheperd, Jim Haynie, Danny Glover, Scott Beach. Medium road movie of existential revolutionary Coyote and his odyssey through America from the 1960s to 1980s. Sometimes imaginative, thanks to Hollander and Ronald Sukenick's clever script, but often boring as well. Filmed independently; a bigger budget might have helped.▼

Out All Night (1933) 68m. ** D: Sam Taylor. ZaSu Pitts, Slim Summerville, Laura Hope Crews, Shirley Grey, Alexander Carr. OK film from long-run teaming of Pitts and Summerville; this time, he's a mother-dominated young man who marries ZaSu against Mama's wishes.

Outback (1971-U.S.-Australian) C-99m. *** D: Ted Kotcheff. Gary Bond, Donald Pleasence, Chips Rafferty, Sylvia Kay, Jack Thompson. Intriguing film about sensitive schoolteacher whose personality disintegrates after interaction with rough, primitive men in Australian outback. Toned down for TV from original 114m. version;

still unlikely to be endorsed by Australian tourist commission. Original title: WAKE IN FRIGHT.

Outback Bound (1988) **C-100m. TVM** D: John Llewellyn Moxey. Donna Mills, Andrew Clarke, John Meillon, Collette Mann, Robert Harper, Nina Foch, John Schneider. Down-on-her-luck Beverly Hills princess roughs it in the Australian Outback looking for her deceased dad's played-out opal mine. Average.

Outcast, The (1954) **C-90m.** **½ D: William Witney. John Derek, Joan Evans, Jim Davis, Catherine McLeod, Ben Cooper. Simply told Western of Derek battling to win his rightful inheritance.▼

Outcast, The (1962-Japanese) **118m.** ***½ D: Kon Ichikawa. Raizo Ichikawa, Shiho Fujimura, Hiroyuki Nagato, Rentaro Mikuni. Schoolteacher Ichikawa hides his identity as member of an outcast class until a writer he greatly respects is murdered. Intense drama is well made, fascinating.

Outcast of the Islands (1951-British) **102m.** *** D: Carol Reed. Ralph Richardson, Trevor Howard, Robert Morley, Wendy Hiller, Kerima, George Coulouris, Wilfrid Hyde-White. Compelling adaptation of Joseph Conrad story set on Malayan island, where a desperate, misguided man turns to crime and soon becomes the object of massive manhunt. Screenplay by William Fairchild. Good job all around. Some TV prints run 94m.

Outcasts of Poker Flat, The (1952) **81m.** **½ D: Joseph M. Newman. Anne Baxter, Miriam Hopkins, Dale Robertson, Cameron Mitchell, John Ridgely. Obvious, uninspired version of Bret Harte tale of social rejects trapped together in cabin during snowstorm. Filmed before in 1937.

Outcasts of the City (1958) **61m.** *½ D: Boris Petroff. Osa Massen, Robert Hutton, Maria Palmer, Nestor Paiva, George Neise. Junky flick of pilot Hutton involved with German woman (Palmer).

Outcry, The (1957-Italian) **115m.** **½ D: Michelangelo Antonioni. Steve Cochran, Alida Valli, Dorian Gray, Betsy Blair, Lyn Shaw. Leisurely paced yet compelling study of Cochran's mental disintegration due to lack of communication with those he loves; Cochran is quite good. Original title: IL GRIDO.

Outfit, The (1974) **C-103m.** **½ D: John Flynn. Robert Duvall, Karen Black, Joe Don Baker, Robert Ryan, Timothy Carey, Richard Jaeckel, Sheree North, Jane Greer, Elisha Cook, Jr., Marie Windsor. Engagingly trashy mob melodrama, with ex-con Duvall tackling the syndicate responsible for his brother's death. Solid supporting cast helps. Based on a novel by Donald E. Westlake (writing as Richard Stark).

Outland (1981) **C-109m.** **½ D: Peter Hyams. Sean Connery, Peter Boyle, Frances Sternhagen, James B. Sikking, Kika Markham, Clarke Peters, John Ratzenberger. HIGH NOON on Jupiter's Moon, as 21st-century marshal Connery discovers that this outer-space mining planet is riddled with corruption—and he's the only one willing to do anything about it. Slickly made, but predictable and generally unpleasant in tone. Script by director Hyams.▼

Outlaw, The (1943) **115m.** *** D: Howard Hughes. Jane Russell, Jack Buetel, Walter Huston, Thomas Mitchell, Mimi Aguglia, Joe Sawyer. Notorious "sex western" (and Russell's ballyhooed screen debut) is actually compelling—if offbeat—story of Billy the Kid, with principal honors going to Huston as Doc Holliday. Filmed in 1941 and directed mostly by Howard Hawks, though Hughes' interest in Russell's bosom is more than evident. Some prints run 95m. and 103m., but no one seems to have uncensored 117m. version.▼

Outlaw Blues (1977) **C-100m.** *** D: Richard T. Heffron. Peter Fonda, Susan Saint James, John Crawford, James Callahan, Michael Lerner. Ex-convict Fonda is promoted into a country star by back-up singer Saint James, to the consternation of star Callahan, who had stolen Fonda's song. Saint James is good in her first major movie role; the picture is fun when it isn't too silly.▼

Outlaw-Josey Wales, The (1976) **C-135m.** **½ D: Clint Eastwood. Clint Eastwood, Chief Dan George, Sondra Locke, Bill McKinney, John Vernon, Paula Trueman, Sam Bottoms. Long, violent Western set in post-Civil War era; Eastwood is a peaceful farmer who turns vigilante when Union soldiers murder his family. He in turn has a price on his head, propelling cat-and-mouse chase odyssey. Clint took over direction from Philip Kaufman, who also co-wrote the screenplay. Followed by THE RETURN OF JOSEY WALES—without Eastwood.▼

Outlaw of Gor (1989) **C-89m.** *½ D: John "Bud" Cardos. Urbano Barberini, Jack Palance, Rebecca Ferrati, Donna Denton, Nigel Chipps, Russel Savadier, Alex Heyns, Tulio Monetta, Larry Taylor, Michelle Clarke. Worthless sequel to GOR (which wasn't any good in the first place). Earthman hero is magically transported back to the barbaric planet Gor, where he's soon branded an assassin by evil priest Palance and wicked queen Denton. Lots of swords, no sorcery; dull and predictable besides. Based on the John Norman novel. Filmed in 1987.▼

Outlaws, The (1984) **C-78m. TVM** D: James Frawley. Christopher Lemmon, Charles Rocket, Joan Sweeny, Charles Napier, Robert Mandan, Dub Taylor, Mel Stewart, M. Emmet Walsh, Joe Mantegna. Fitfully amusing sitcom-style adventure about two pals—a strait-laced junior executive (Lemmon) and his flaky inventor friend (Rocket) who bungle their way into a get-rich-quick scheme, get slapped in the clink, and spend the rest of this prospective pilot breaking out and staying ahead of the law. Average.

Outlaw's Daughter, The (1954) **C-75m.** *½ D: Wesley Barry. Bill Williams, Kelly Ryan, Jim Davis, George Cleveland, Elisha Cook. Weak oater of stagecoach robbery and girl implicated because her elderly father used to be an outlaw.

Outlaws Is Coming, The (1965) **89m.** **½ D: Norman Maurer. The Three Stooges, Adam West, Nancy Kovack, Mort Mills, Don Lamond, Emil Sitka, Joe Bolton, Henry Gibson. The Stooges' last feature is one of their best, with some sharp satire and good Western atmosphere as the boys, their cowardly friend (West), and Annie Oakley (Kovack) combat an army of gunslingers and a genteel crook. Local TV kiddie-show hosts cast as outlaws, Gibson as a hip Indian.

Outlaw's Son (1957) **89m.** ** D: Lesley Selander. Dane Clark, Ben Cooper, Lori Nelson, Ellen Drew, Eddie Foy III. Clark is most earnest in modest Western about outlaw and the son he deserted years before.

Outlaw Stallion, The (1954) **C-64m.** *½ D: Fred F. Sears. Phil Carey, Dorothy Patrick, Billy Gray, Roy Roberts, Gordon Jones. Programmer of horse thieves conning ranch woman and her son to get their herd.

Outlaw Territory (1953) **C-79m.** **½ D: John Ireland, Lee Garmes. Macdonald Carey, Joanne Dru, John Ireland, Don Haggerty, Peter Ireland, Frank Ferguson. Carey is hired killer who runs afoul of marshal Ireland, and arouses the interest of cafe-owner Dru, against her better judgment. Routine Western shot in 3-D; original title: HANNAH LEE.

Out of Africa (1985) **C-161m.** ***½ D: Sydney Pollack. Meryl Streep, Robert Redford, Klaus Maria Brandauer, Michael Kitchen, Mallick Bowens, Joseph Thiaka, Stephen Kinyanjui, Michael Gough, Suzanna Hamilton, Rachel Kempson, Graham Crowden. Exquisite, intelligent romantic drama based on life of Karen Blixen, who married for convenience, moved from Denmark to Nairobi, and fell in love with a British adventurer and idealist (before gaining latter-day fame as author Isak Dinessen). Pollack's film brilliantly captures time and place, with superb performances by Streep and Brandauer, sumptuous photography by David Watkin, and a rich score by John Barry. Film's only fault is overlength—and biggest challenge is asking us to accept Redford as an Englishman. Oscars include Best Picture, Director, Screenplay (Kurt Luedtke, who synthesized four books

into one seamless script), Cinematography, and Music Score.▼

Out of Bounds (1986) **C-93m.** *½ D: Richard Tuggle. Anthony Michael Hall, Jenny Wright, Jeff Kober, Glynn Turman, Raymond J. Barry, Pepe Serna, Meat Loaf. Iowa farm kid goes to L.A. and within twenty-four hours is hunted by the police (for murders he didn't commit) and a scuzzy drug dealer (whose stash he mistakenly took from the airport). Outlandishly unbelievable teen thriller might be retitled OUT OF BRAINS.▼

Out of Control (1985) **C-78m.** BOMB D: Allan Holzman. Martin Hewitt, Betsy Russell, Claudia Udy, Andrew J. Lederer, Cindi Dietrich, Richard Kantor, Sherilyn Fenn, Jim Youngs. Embarrassing teen-exploitation film has eight kids surviving a plane crash on small island where they play sex games, get drunk, and get in trouble with local drug runners. Mishmash wastes a catchy title song performed by the Brothers Johnson. ▼

Out of It (1969) **95m.** **½ D: Paul Williams. Barry Gordon, Jon Voight, Lada Edmund, Jr., Gretchen Corbett, Peter Grad. Generally amusing film about high school intellectual (Gordon) bucking high school athlete (Voight). A throwback to the days when life was one big Archie comic book.

Out of Season (1975-British) **C-90m.** ** D: Alan Bridges. Vanessa Redgrave, Cliff Robertson, Susan George, Edward Evans, Frank Jarvis. Mood-triangle affair: dark stranger returns to English seaside resort twenty years after affair with woman who now has grown daughter. Hints of incest and unresolved ending. Formerly titled WINTER RATES, played Berlin Festival, had limited release in this country.▼

Out of Sight (1966) **C-87m.** *½ D: Lennie Weinrib. Jonathan Daly, Karen Jensen, Robert Pine, Carole Shelayne, Gary Lewis and The Playboys, The Turtles, Freddie and The Dreamers, Dobie Gray. A butler and a blonde band together to halt a spy organization's conspiracy against rock groups. Idiotic combination beach party–spy movie that fails in both departments.

Out of the Blue (1947) **84m.** **½ D: Leigh Jason. Virginia Mayo, George Brent, Turhan Bey, Ann Dvorak, Carole Landis, Hadda Brooks. Naive Brent is in trouble when far from innocent young woman is discovered unconscious in his apartment; fluffy fun. Dvorak is a delight in an offbeat role.▼

Out of the Blue (1980) **C-94m.** **½ D: Dennis Hopper. Linda Manz, Sharon Farrell, Dennis Hopper, Raymond Burr, Don Gordon. Manz, daughter of ex-biker Hopper and junkie Farrell, cannot cope with the problems of her elders, with tragic results. Taut, low-key drama; could be retitled "Child of Easy Rider."▼

[861]

Out of the Clouds (1957-British) **C-88m.** ** D: Michael Relph, Basil Dearden. Anthony Steel, James Robertson Justice, Gordon Harker, Bernard Lee, Megs Jenkins. Work and play among commercial pilots; nothing special.

Out of the Dark (1988) **C-89m.** **½ D: Michael Schroeder. Cameron Dye, Lynn Danielson, Tracey Walter, Silvana Gallardo, Karen Black, Bud Cort, Starr Andreeff, Geoffrey Lewis, Paul Bartel, Divine, Lainie Kazan, Tab Hunter. A clown-masked killer murders the employees of an L.A. telephone sex-talk service, one by one. Good cast and sense of humor relieve heavy-handed visual approach to the material.▼

Out of the Darkness (1978) SEE: **Night Creature**▼

Out of the Darkness (1985) **C-100m.** TVM D: Jud Taylor. Martin Sheen, Hector Elizondo, Matt Clark, Jennifer Salt, Eddie Egan, Robert Trebor. Sheen gives a shining performance as Eddie Zigo, the N.Y.C. cop who broke the Son of Sam case in the late '70s. Refreshingly, this one focuses on the cop rather than the criminal. T. S. Cook's suspenseful script is a model of its type. Above average.▼

Out of the Fog (1941) **93m.** *** D: Anatole Litvak. Ida Lupino, John Garfield, Thomas Mitchell, Eddie Albert, George Tobias, Leo Gorcey, John Qualen, Aline MacMahon. Fine filmization of Irwin Shaw play *The Gentle People*, with racketeer Garfield terrorizing Brooklyn fishermen Qualen and Mitchell—and falling in love with the latter's daughter (Lupino). Scripted by Robert Rossen, Jerry Wald, and Richard Macauley.

Out of the Frying Pan SEE: **Young and Willing**▼

Out of the Past (1947) **97m.** ***½ D: Jacques Tourneur. Robert Mitchum, Jane Greer, Kirk Douglas, Richard Webb, Rhonda Fleming, Dickie Moore, Steve Brodie. Mitchum finds he can't escape former life when one-time employer (gangster Douglas) and lover (Greer) entangle him in web of murder and double-dealings. Classic example of 1940s *film noir*, with dialogue a particular standout. Script by Geoffrey Homes (Daniel Mainwaring), from his novel *Build My Gallows High*. Remade as AGAINST ALL ODDS. Also shown in computer-colored version.▼

Out of the Shadows (1988-British) **C-105m.** TVM D: Willi Patterson. Charles Dance, Alexandra Paul, Michael J. Shannon, David De Keyser. Romantic mystery (from the *Harlequin Romance* series) about an American woman who becomes innocently involved in an international smuggling ring in Athens. Average.

Out of this World (1945) **96m.** **½ D: Hal Walker. Eddie Bracken, Veronica Lake, Diana Lynn, Cass Daley, Parkyakarkus, Donald MacBride, Florence Bates, Gary, Philip, Dennis and Lindsay Crosby. Bracken becomes pop crooner (with a very familiar-sounding voice); a cute idea mercilessly padded with loud musical specialties by Daley, Lynn, and guest stars.

Out of Time (1988) **C-100m.** TVM D: Robert Butler. Bruce Abbott, Bill Maher, Adam Ant, Rebecca Schaeffer, Kristian Alfonso. Harmless comedy/drama about a maverick cop from the 21st century who pursues a dangerous criminal back to 1988 and meets his great-grandfather, who will soon become a legendary criminologist. Pilot to a prospective series. Average.

Out-of-Towners, The (1970) **C-97m.** *½ D: Arthur Hiller. Jack Lemmon, Sandy Dennis, Sandy Baron, Anne Meara, Ann Prentiss, Graham Jarvis, Ron Carey, Phil Bruns, Carlos Montalban, Billy Dee Williams, Paul Dooley, Dolph Sweet, Robert Walden, Richard Libertini. Excruciating Neil Simon script about stupidly stubborn Lemmon and wife Dennis having everything imaginable go wrong on trip to N.Y.C. More harrowing than funny, with curiously unsympathetic leading characters.▼

Out on a Limb (1987) **C-200m.** TVM D: Robert Butler. Shirley MacLaine, Charles Dance, John Heard, Anne Jackson, Jerry Orbach. MacLaine stars as herself in this lumbering film of her best-selling book about her passionate love affair with an unnamed British politician (played by Dance) and her spiritual trek that gave her the chance to look at herself as an "outer being." Jackson plays Bella Abzug as a sounding board for Shirley, who cowrote the teleplay with Colin Higgins. Originally shown in two tiresome parts. Average.

Out on Probation SEE: **Daddy-O**

Out on the Edge (1989) **C-100m.** TVM D: John Pasquin. Rick Schroder, Mary Kay Place, Richard Jenkins, Natalia Mogulich, Dakin Matthews, Maya Lebenzon. OK drama about a troubled teen who is committed to a behavior-treatment center against his will. Similar plotwise to the theatrical LOST ANGELS, which was released around the same time. It may be better remembered for Ricky Schroder's emergence as simply Rick. Average.

Outpost in Malaya (1952-British) **88m.** **½ D: Ken Annakin. Claudette Colbert, Jack Hawkins, Anthony Steel, Jeremy Spencer. Mostly about marital disharmony on a rubber plantation. Original title: PLANTER'S WIFE.

Outpost in Morocco (1949) **92m.** ** D: Robert Florey. George Raft, Marie Windsor, Akim Tamiroff, John Litel, Eduard Franz. Cardboard adventure saga of good-guy Raft battling desert foes while romancing enemy-girl Windsor.▼

Outrage, The (1964) **97m.** **½ D: Martin Ritt. Paul Newman, Edward G. Robin-

[862]

son, Claire Bloom, Laurence Harvey, William Shatner, Albert Salmi. Western remake of RASHOMON is pretentious fizzle, with Newman hamming it as Mexican bandit who allegedly rapes Bloom while husband Harvey stands by. Robinson as philosophical narrator is best thing about film.

Outrage (1973) **C-78m. TVM** D: Richard T. Heffron. Robert Culp, Marlyn Mason, Beah Richards, Jacqueline Scott, Ramon Bieri, Thomas Leopold. Local doctor (Culp) turns vigilante to deal with teen gang terrorizing his upper-middle-class neighbors. Or your-average-outraged-citizen plot. Average.

Outrage! (1986) **C-100m. TVM** D: Walter Grauman. Robert Preston, Beau Bridges, Burgess Meredith, Linda Purl, Anthony Newley, William Allen Young, Mel Ferrer. Preston is a man who admits killing his daughter's rapist/murderer and insists on his day in court; Bridges is a young attorney who takes on his defense and turns the trial into an attack on our judicial system. Written by lawyer-turned-novelist Henry Denker (*A Case of Libel*), based on his best-seller. Above average.

Outrageous! (1977-Canadian) **C-100m.** *** D: Richard Benner. Craig Russell, Hollis McLaren, Richert Easley, Allan Moyle, Helen Shaver. Excellent comedy-drama about a very odd couple: gay hairdresser and a pregnant mental patient. McLaren's effective emoting is outshone by female impersonator Russell's flamboyant playing and imitations of Garland, Davis, Bankhead, etc. Followed ten years later by TOO OUTRAGEOUS.▼

Outrageous Fortune (1987) **C-100m.** *** D: Arthur Hiller. Bette Midler, Shelley Long, Peter Coyote, Robert Prosky, John Schuck, George Carlin, Anthony Heald, Ji-Tu Cumbuka. Raucously funny tale of a female odd couple who learn they were both having a fling with the same man, after he apparently dies in a mysterious explosion . . . then things *really* get going! Bright script by Leslie Dixon is a perfect showcase for Midler and Long.▼

Outriders, The (1950) **C-93m.** ** D: Roy Rowland. Joel McCrea, Arlene Dahl, Barry Sullivan, Claude Jarman, Jr., Ramon Novarro. Standard account of Reb soldiers trying to capture gold shipment for Confederate cause.

Outside Chance (1978) **C-100m. TVM** D: Michael Miller. Yvette Mimieux, Royce D. Applegate, Dick Armstrong, Beverly Atkinson, Susan Batson, Howard Hesseman, Betty Thomas. Unusual misfire begins as a precis-rehash of same director's JACKSON COUNTY JAIL (also starring Mimieux)—then goes off in new directions, getting as "lurid" as TV standards will allow. Below average.▼

Outside Chance of Maximilian Glick, The (1988-Canadian) **C-96m.** *** D: Allan A. Goldstein. Saul Rubinek, Jan Rubes, Noam Zylberman, Susan Douglas Rubes, Fairuza Balk, Nigel Bennet, Sharon Corder, Aaron Schwartz. Pleasing tale of bright 12-year-old Zylberman, growing up in a small Canadian town in the early 1960s, who's caught between his own dreams and desires and his family's traditional Jewish values. Despite its cop-out ending, this intelligent little comedy-drama is perfect fare for preteens.▼

Outside In (1972) **C-90m.** ** D: Allen Baron. Darrell Larson, Heather Menzies, Dennis Olivieri, Peggy Feury, Logan Ramsey, John Bill. Long-haired draft-dodger returns home for father's funeral, immediately splits when Feds show up. Unintentionally funny "youth" movie filmed mostly on location in and around L.A. area. Beware cuts.

Outside Man, The (1973) **C-104m.** *** D: Jacques Deray. Jean-Louis Trintignant, Ann-Margret, Angie Dickinson, Roy Scheider, Michel Constantin, Georgia Engel. Okay French-American actioner, made in L.A., as interesting for its cast as its offbeat quality. Hired killer Trintignant kills gang boss Ted de Corsia, then must elude Scheider, who's out to eliminate him. Ann-Margret's plunging neckline and a shootout around de Corsia's bier (he's embalmed in a sitting position) are worth looking at, also Engel's dumb housewife.

Outsider, The (1961) **108m.** *** D: Delbert Mann. Tony Curtis, James Franciscus, Bruce Bennett, Gregory Walcott, Vivian Nathan. Thoughtful biopic with Curtis giving one of his best performances as a reluctant American hero: Ira Hamilton Hayes, the Pima Indian who was one of the marines to raise the U.S. flag at Iwo Jima.

Outsider, The (1967) **C-98m. TVM** D: Michael Ritchie. Darren McGavin, Anna Hagan, Edmond O'Brien, Sean Garrison, Shirley Knight, Nancy Malone, Ann Sothern, Audrey Totter, Ossie Davis, Joseph Wiseman. Unusual private eye whodunit with McGavin featured as David Ross, ex-con, hired by theatrical manager who suspects one of his employees of embezzlement. Good performances. Average; pilot for the series.

Outsider, The (1979) **C-128m.** *** D: Tony Luraschi. Craig Wasson, Patricia Quinn, Sterling Hayden, Niall Toibin, Elizabeth Begley, T. P. McKenna, Frank Grimes. A young American raised on his grandfather's stories of fighting "the Tans" in Ireland goes there to join the IRA—and is used for political and public-relations purposes. No-frills narrative, authentic and interesting, filmed on location. Script by director Luraschi.

Outsiders, The (1983) **C-91m.** **½ D: Francis Coppola. C. Thomas Howell, Matt Dillon, Ralph Macchio, Patrick Swayze, Rob Lowe, Diane Lane, Emilio Estevez, Tom Cruise, Leif Garrett, Tom Waits. Florid, highly stylized treatment of S. E. Hinton's best-selling book about troubled teenagers in 60s Oklahoma, as seen through the eyes of a boy (Howell) who likes poetry and *Gone With the Wind*. Ambitious film evokes GWTW and 50s melodramas (right down to overstated music score by Carmine Coppola), but never quite connects, despite some powerful moments. Hinton makes a cameo appearance as a nurse. Followed by another Coppola-Hinton project, RUMBLE FISH. Later a TV series.▼

Outside the Law (1956) **81m.** *½ D: Jack Arnold. Ray Danton, Leigh Snowden, Grant Williams, Onslow Stevens. Half-baked yarn of Danton proving his worth by snaring counterfeiters.

Outside the Wall (1950) **80m.** **½ D: Crane Wilbur. Richard Basehart, Dorothy Hart, Marilyn Maxwell, Signe Hasso, Harry Morgan. Excellent cast carries off this tale of former convict snafuing a robbery syndicate.

Outside Woman, The (1989) **C-100m. TVM** D: Lou Antonio. Sharon Gless, Scott Glenn, Max Gail, Kyle Secor, Ken Jenkins, Peter Michael Goetz. Southern mill worker trades her humdrum life for romance and adventure when she's sweet-talked by a likable convict into hijacking a helicopter, and helping him and a couple of inmate pals to escape from Louisiana State Penitentiary. Well-written by William Blinn, and based on a true story. Above average.

Outward Bound (1930) **84m.** *** D: Robert Milton. Leslie Howard, Douglas Fairbanks, Jr., Helen Chandler, Beryl Mercer, Alec B. Francis, Alison Skipworth, Montagu Love. Illicit lovers Fairbanks and Chandler, "half-way" persons who have attempted suicide, find themselves aboard a mysterious ocean liner. Well-acted allegory, from Sutton Vane's play. Remade as BETWEEN TWO WORLDS.

Out West with the Hardys (1938) **90m.** D: George B. Seitz. Lewis Stone, Mickey Rooney, Cecilia Parker, Fay Holden, Ann Rutherford, Sara Haden, Don Castle, Virginia Weidler, Gordon Jones, Ralph Morgan. SEE: **Andy Hardy** series.

Overboard (1978) **C-100m. TVM** D: John Newland. Angie Dickinson, Cliff Robertson, Andrew Duggan, Stephen Elliott, Skip Homeier, Lewis VanBergen, Michael Strong. Bored wife falls overboard while sailboating off Tahiti with disinterested husband, and bobs around for nearly two hours reliving their marriage in flashback. Average.

Overboard (1987) **C-112m.** *** D: Garry Marshall. Goldie Hawn, Kurt Russell, Edward Herrmann, Katherine Helmond, Michael Hagerty, Roddy McDowall. Cute comedy about a spoiled heiress who falls off her yacht, suffers amnesia, and is "claimed" at the hospital by her supposed husband, a rough-hewn carpenter with a pack of unruly kids. Lightweight and good-natured, with appealing performances by the star duo (who are a couple off-screen as well). McDowall also served as executive producer; director Marshall has a cameo as a drummer, and Hector Elizondo (who's been in all of his films) does an unbilled bit as skipper of a garbage scow.▼

Overcoat, The (1959-Russian) **73m.** **** D: Alexei Batalov. Roland Bykov, Y. Tolubeyev. Charming, fully realized rendition of Gogol's oft-filmed story about lowly clerk and the effect a new overcoat has on his life. Runs full gamut of emotions in simple, moving style; not shown here until 1965.▼

Over-Exposed (1956) **80m.** *½ D: Lewis Seiler. Cleo Moore, Richard Crenna, Isobel Elsom, Raymond Greenleaf, Shirley Thomas. Flabby study of blackmail, with Cleo Moore vacationing from Hugo Haas spectacles . . . some vacation!

Overexposed (1990) **C-80m.** ** D: Larry Brand. Catherine Oxenberg, David Naughton, Jennifer Edwards, William Bumiller, John Patrick Reger, Gretchen Eichholz, Karen Black, Larry Brand, George Derby. Soap opera star Oxenberg is apparently being stalked by an angry fan, but she also has recurring and horrifying memories of a burning child at a birthday party. Well made on a tight budget, but the clueless story develops too slowly, and the ending is weirdly protracted.

Over Forty (1982-Canadian) **C-105m.** ***½ D: Anne Claire Poirier. Roger Blay, Monique Mercure, Pierre Theriault, Patricia Nolin, Jacques Godin, Luce Guilbeaut. The Gang, a group of men and women who grew up together, reunite after 30 years to sing, then reminisce, then reveal. THE BIG CHILL for the 1940s generation but with far more depth; a magical gem of a movie about the essence of friendship, the passage of time, the capacity of innocence. Also known as BEYOND FORTY.

Overlanders, The (1946-Australian-British) **91m.** ***½ D: Harry Watt. Chips Rafferty, Daphne Campbell, John Fernside, Jean Blue. Riveting account (based on fact) of Australian cattle drovers, headed by Rafferty, bringing their herds across the continent during WW2. Beautiful scenery.▼

Overland Pacific (1954) **C-73m.** ** D: Fred F. Sears. Jock Mahoney, Peggie Castle, Adele Jergens, William Bishop. Mahoney is staunch railroad investigator trying to get at crux of Indian attacks on the trains.

Over My Dead Body (1942) **68m.** **½ D: Malcolm St. Clair. Milton Berle, Mary Beth Hughes, Reginald Denny, Frank Orth, William Davidson. Berle gives peppery performance in farfetched yarn about amateur sleuth who accidentally frames himself for murder.

Overnight (1986-Canadian) **C-96m.** **½ D: Jack Darcus. Gale Garnett, Victor Ertmanis, Alan Scarfe, Duncan Fraser, Ian White, Barbara Gordon. Fair film industry satire about a serious but unemployed actor (Ertmanis), who takes a job in a porn movie about a vampire nymphomaniac. A few bright lines but too much silliness.

Over the Brooklyn Bridge (1984) **C-106m.** ** D: Menahem Golan. Elliott Gould, Margaux Hemingway, Sid Caesar, Burt Young, Shelley Winters, Carol Kane. Brooklyn Jewish restaurant owner Gould wants to borrow money from uncle Caesar to open a fancy Manhattan eatery, but the family objects to his Catholic girlfriend (Hemingway). Some good supporting players (especially Caesar) cannot save this stupid comedy. One of the in-production titles was MY DARLING SHIKSA.▼

Over the Edge (1979) **C-95m.** ***½ D: Jonathan Kaplan. Michael Kramer, Pamela Ludwig, Matt Dillon, Vincent Spano, Tom Fergus, Andy Romano, Ellen Geer, Lane Smith, Harry Northrup. Powerful, disturbing chronicle of alienated youth in a suburban planned community; 14-year-old rebels without causes who play with guns, deal and abuse drugs, taunt cops, chug whiskey till they're blotto. Perceptive script by Charlie Haas and Tim Hunter; stunning music score by Sol Kaplan; taut direction. A winner. Dillon's film debut.▼

Over-the-Hill Gang, The (1969) **C-73m.** TVM D: Jean Yarbrough. Walter Brennan, Pat O'Brien, Edgar Buchanan, Andy Devine, Jack Elam, Gypsy Rose Lee, Kris Nelson, Rick Nelson. Fair Western comedy detailing attempts of retired Texas Rangers to clean up corrupt town, first by using old skills, then "strategy." Fun mainly for veteran cast. Average.

Over the Hill Gang Rides Again, The (1970) **C-73m.** TVM D: George McCowan. Walter Brennan, Fred Astaire, Edgar Buchanan, Andy Devine, Chill Wills, Lana Wood. Coming to aid old-time friend turned-drunk, retired Texas Rangers find they've been made deputies of Waco. Standout performance by Astaire in otherwise mediocre comedy-Western. Average.

Over the Moon (1937-British) **C-78m.** *½ D: Thornton Freeland, William K. Howard. Merle Oberon, Rex Harrison, Ursula Jeans, Robert Douglas, Louis Borell, Zena Dare, David Tree, Elisabeth Welch, Wilfrid Hyde-White, Evelyn Ankers. Dis-

appointingly bad comedy of country girl squandering inherited fortune. Interesting cast cannot save clinker. Beware black-and-white prints.

Over the Top (1987) **C-93m.** BOMB D: Menahem Golan. Sylvester Stallone, Robert Loggia, Susan Blakely, Rick Zumwalt, David Mendenhall, Chris McCarty, Terry Funk. Mawkish is a kind way to describe this heavy-handed variation on THE CHAMP, with Stallone competing with his fat-cat father-in-law for the custody (and affection) of his son. It all climaxes, logically enough, at an arm-wrestling championship in Las Vegas. Stallone tries to underplay (speaking so quietly that you often can't hear what he's saying), and essays a much "softer" character than usual—but when push comes to shove, he *will* drive his truck through a living room!▼

Over 21 (1945) **102m.** *** D: Charles Vidor. Irene Dunne, Alexander Knox, Charles Coburn, Jeff Donnell, Lee Patrick, Phil Brown, Cora Witherspoon. Zesty comedy of middle-aged Knox trying to survive in officer's training for WW2 service, with help of wife Dunne; from Ruth Gordon's play.

Owen Marshall, Counsellor at Law (1971) **C-100m.** TVM D: Buzz Kulik. Arthur Hill, Vera Miles, Joseph Campanella, Dana Wynter, William Shatner, Bruce Davison. Hippie accused of murdering socialite wife; case becomes crucial to recently widowed lawyer (Hill) as hate campaign simmers in background. One-dimensional characters fill this boring pilot that nevertheless spawned the hit series. Below average. Retitled A PATTERN OF MORALITY.

Owl and the Pussycat, The (1970) **C-95m.** *** D: Herbert Ross. Barbra Streisand, George Segal, Robert Klein, Allen Garfield, Roz Kelly. Hit Broadway comedy about semi-illiterate prostitute and stuffy intellectual sometimes substitutes bombast for wit, but the laughs are there. The Streisand-Segal pairing really works; adapted by Buck Henry from Bill Manoff's play. Originally released at 98m.▼

Ox-Bow Incident, The (1943) **75m.** **** D: William Wellman. Henry Fonda, Dana Andrews, Mary Beth Hughes, Anthony Quinn, William Eythe, Henry (Harry) Morgan, Jane Darwell, Frank Conroy, Harry Davenport. The irony and terror of mob rule are vividly depicted in this unforgettable drama about a lynch mob taking the law into its own hands, despite protests of some level-headed onlookers. Based on Walter Van Tilburg Clark's book; superb script by Dudley Nichols.▼

Oxford Blues (1984) **C-97m.** **½ D: Robert Boris. Rob Lowe, Ally Sheedy, Julian Sands, Amanda Pays, Michael Gough, Aubrey Morris, Gail Strickland, Alan Howard. Lightweight remake of A

YANK AT OXFORD, with rough-edged Lowe pursuing titled beauty Pays while building "character" on the rowing team. Boris' wildly inconsistent script is salvaged by engaging performances.▼

Pacific Destiny (1956-British) **C-97m.** ** D: Wolf Rilla. Denholm Elliott, Susan Stephen, Michael Hordern, Gordon Jackson, Inia Te Wiata. Boring (but true) story of Arthur Grimble, who serves in South Seas for British Colonial service circa 1912, and tries to quell native disputes.

Pacific Liner (1939) **75m.** ** D: Lew Landers. Chester Morris, Wendy Barrie, Victor McLaglen, Barry Fitzgerald. Formula programmer focusing on breakout of epidemic and mutiny aboard a ship; cast is better than the material.

Pacific Vibrations (1971) **C-92m.** **½ D: John Severson. Jock Sutherland, Rolf Aurness, Corky Carroll, Tom Stone, Mike Tabeling. Colorful surfing documentary.

Pack, The (1977) **C-99m.** **½ D: Robert Clouse. Joe Don Baker, Hope Alexander-Willis, Richard B. Shull, R. G. Armstrong, Ned Wertimer, Bibi Besch. Predictable but well-made story of resort islanders terrorized by abandoned dogs who have become a bloodthirsty pack. Also known as THE LONG, DARK NIGHT.▼

Package, The (1989) **C-108m.** ** D: Andrew Davis. Gene Hackman, Joanna Cassidy, Tommy Lee Jones, John Heard, Dennis Franz, Pam Grier, Kevin Crowley, Reni Santoni, Ike Pappas, Thalmus Rasulala. Slack political paranoia thriller with Hackman as a career Army sergeant who learns he's been used as a pawn in a conspiracy plot engineered by Russian and American military dissidents. Hackman is always worth watching, but the story loses ground (and credibility) just when it ought to be peaking.▼

Packin' It In (1983) **C-100m. TVM** D: Jud Taylor. Richard Benjamin, Paula Prentiss, Tony Roberts, Andrea Marcovicci, Molly Ringwald, Mari Gorman, Kenneth McMillan, Susan Ruttan. Benjamin and Prentiss's first TV-movie together is a routine comedy about an urban couple who pack themselves and their children off to the boondocks for the simpler, safer life . . . with predictable results. Average.▼

Pack of Lies (1987) **C-100m. TVM** D: Anthony Page. Ellen Burstyn, Teri Garr, Alan Bates, Sammi Davis, Ronald Hines, Clive Swift, Daniel Benzali. Top-notch filming of Hugh Whitemore's play about a suburban London couple whose friendship with the neighbors across the street is torn apart when they allow British Intelligence to use their house to spy on their best pals. Ralph Gallup's adaptation and Burstyn's

performance earned Emmy nominations. Above average.

Pack Up Your Troubles (1932) **68m.** **½ D: George Marshall, Ray McCarey. Stan Laurel, Oliver Hardy, Mary Carr, James Finlayson, Charles Middleton, Grady Sutton, Billy Gilbert. Daffy duo are drafted during WW1; after some Army shenanigans they try to locate relatives of late pal's daughter. Good fun.

Pack Up Your Troubles (1939) **75m.** ** D: H. Bruce Humberstone. Ritz Brothers, Jane Withers, Lynn Bari, Joseph Schildkraut, Stanley Fields, Leon Ames. Watch the Ritz Brothers' opening routine, then forget the rest of this WW1 hodgepodge, especially when Jane is focus of the film.

Paco (1976) **C-97m.** *½ D: Robert Vincent O'Neil. Jose Ferrer, Panchito Gomez, Allen Garfield, Pernell Roberts. South American urchin Gomez visits uncle Ferrer in the big city, finds him to be a Fagin-like leader of a band of juvenile thieves. Obvious and slow-moving; producer-writer Andre Marquis cast himself in vanity role as a great actor. Some prints may run 87m.▼

Pad and How to Use It, The (1966) **C-86m.** **½ D: Brian Hutton. Brian Bedford, Julie Sommars, James Farentino, Edy Williams. Peter Shaffer play *The Private Ear* is basis for sex romp involving Bedford's attempt to become Sommars' lover.

Paddy (1970-Irish) **C-97m.** ** D: Daniel Haller. Milo O'Shea, Des Cave, Dearbhla Molloy, Judy Cornwell, Donal LeBlanc. Irish lover Cave tries to juggle varied sexual encounters with uninspired home life in ordinary comedy-drama.▼

Padre Padrone (1977-Italian) **C-114m.** ** D: Vittorio and Paolo Taviani. Omero Antonutti, Saverio Marioni, Marcella Michelangeli, Fabrizio Forte. Sad, illiterate Sardinian boy, brutalized by his peasant father, still grows up to master Greek and Latin and graduate college. Even sadder still, uninvolving and curiously forgettable. Based on an autobiographical book by Gavino Ledda.▼

Pagan Love Song (1950) **C-76m.** ** D: Robert Alton. Esther Williams, Howard Keel, Minna Gombell, Rita Moreno. Stale MGM musical; Keel goes to Tahiti, romances Williams.

Pagans, The (1958-Italian) **80m.** *½ D: Ferrucio Cereo. Pierre Cressoy, Helen Remy, Vittorio Sanipoli, Luigi Tosi, Franco Fabrizi. Uninspired costumer set in Rome, with the Spanish invaders ramming the city walls.

Page Miss Glory (1935) **90m.** **½ D: Mervyn LeRoy. Marion Davies, Pat O'Brien, Dick Powell, Mary Astor, Frank McHugh, Lyle Talbot, Patsy Kelly, Allen Jenkins, Barton MacLane. Fine cast overshadows Davies in this amiable spoof of publicity stunts, with con-man O'Brien winning beauty contest with composite photograph of nonexistent girl.

Paid (1931) **80m.** **½ D: Sam Wood. Joan Crawford, Kent Douglass (Douglass Montgomery), Robert Armstrong, Marie Prevost, John Miljan, Polly Moran. Notbad early Crawford. Innocent girl sent to prison; she hardens and seeks revenge. Remade as WITHIN THE LAW.

Paid in Full (1950) **105m.** **½ D: William Dieterle. Robert Cummings, Lizabeth Scott, Diana Lynn, Eve Arden, Ray Collins, Stanley Ridges, John Bromfield, Frank McHugh. Turgid soaper involving sisters Scott and Lynn both in love with Cummings. Film debut of Carol Channing.

Paid to Kill (1954-British) **70m.** ** D: Montgomery Tully. Dane Clark, Paul Carpenter, Thea Gregory, Anthony Forwood. Oft-told premise of man who hires hood to kill him for insurance and changes his mind.

Pain in the A——, A (1974-French-Italian) **C-90m.** *** D: Edouard Molinaro. Lino Ventura, Jacques Brel, Caroline Cellier, Nino Castelnuovo, Jean-Pierre Darras. Very funny black comedy about the chance meeting of a hit man trying to make good on a contract and a pathetic would-be suicide who's likely to mess up the job. Wonderful performances by Ventura and Brel in adaptation of Francis Veber's stage hit, later Americanized as BUDDY BUDDY.▼

Painted Desert, The (1931) **75m.** **½ D: Howard Higgin. William Boyd, Helen Twelvetrees, William Farnum, J. Farrell MacDonald, Clark Gable. Conflict and romance between the son and daughter of two long-feuding Westerners. More than a bit stiff, though the scenery is beautiful; notable mainly for Gable's talkie debut as the bad guy. Remade in 1938.▼

Painted Hills, The (1951) **C-65m.** **½ D: Harold F. Kress. Paul Kelly, Bruce Cowling, Gary Gray, Art Smith, Ann Doran. Nicely photographed Lassie tale set in 1870s West.▼

Painted Veil, The (1934) **83m.** **½ D: Richard Boleslawsky. Greta Garbo, Herbert Marshall, George Brent, Warner Oland, Jean Hersholt, Keye Luke. Set in mysterious Orient, film tells Maugham's story of unfaithful wife mending her ways. Mundane script uplifted by Garbo's personality, supported by Marshall as her husband, Brent as her lover. Remade as THE SEVENTH SIN.

Painting the Clouds with Sunshine (1951) **C-87m.** ** D: David Butler. Dennis Morgan, Virginia Mayo, Gene Nelson, Lucille Norman, Virginia Gibson, Tom Conway. Lukewarm musical of trio of gold-diggers in Las Vegas searching for rich husbands, a mild reworking of an old musical formula.

Paint Your Wagon (1969) **C-166m.** ***

D: Joshua Logan. Lee Marvin, Clint Eastwood, Jean Seberg, Harve Presnell, Ray Walston, Tom Ligon, Alan Dexter. Splashy, expensive musical from Lerner-Loewe play about gold-rush days in No-Name City, California, where prospectors Marvin and Eastwood share one wife (Seberg) whom they bought at auction. Pure entertainment; witty, often risque script (by Paddy Chayefsky!). Presnell outshines cast of nonsingers with "They Call the Wind Maria." Beware of shorter prints.▼

Pair of Aces (1990) **C-100m.** TVM D: Aaron Lipstadt. Willie Nelson, Kris Kristofferson, Rip Torn, Helen Shaver, Jane Cameron, Michael Marich, Emily Warfield. Amiable modern-day Western that teams a reluctant Texas Ranger (Kris) and a footloose safecracker (Willie) in pursuit of a serial killer. Average.

Paisan (1946-Italian) **90m.** ***½ D: Roberto Rossellini. Carmela Sazio, Gar Moore, Bill Tubbs, Harriet White, Maria Michi, Robert van Loon, Dale Edmonds, Carla Pisacane, Dots Johnson. Early Rossellini classic, largely improvised by a mostly non-professional cast. Six vignettes depict life in Italy during WW2; best has American nurse White searching for her lover in battle-torn Florence. Written by Rossellini and Federico Fellini; Giulietta Masina, the latter's wife and frequent star, has a bit role. Italian running time 115m.▼

Pajama Game, The (1957) **C-101m.** ***½ D: George Abbott, Stanley Donen. Doris Day, John Raitt, Carol Haney, Eddie Foy, Jr., Barbara Nichols, Reta Shaw. Rousing movie version of Broadway musical, with Day a joy as the head of factory grievance committee and Raitt the foreman. Richard Adler and Jerry Ross's songs include "Hernando's Hideaway, "Hey, There" and "There Once Was a Man"; Haney shines in her "Steam Heat" number. Choreography by Bob Fosse.▼

Pajama Party (1964) **C-85m.** ** D: Don Weis. Tommy Kirk, Annette Funicello, Dorothy Lamour, Elsa Lanchester, Harvey Lembeck, Jody McCrea, Buster Keaton, Susan Hart, Donna Loren, Candy Johnson. Fourth BEACH PARTY movie moves indoors, changes director and star (although Frankie Avalon and Don Rickles do have cameos). Kirk plays Martian teenager who drops in on the shenanigans and is understandably perplexed. Just fair, though it's always nice to see Keaton at work. Teri Garr is one of the dancers buried in the sand. Went back outside for BEACH BLANKET BINGO.▼

Paleface, The (1948) **C-91m.** *** D: Norman Z. McLeod. Bob Hope, Jane Russell, Robert Armstrong, Iris Adrian, Robert Watson, Jack Searle. Enjoyable comedy-Western, a spoof of THE VIRGINIAN, has timid Bob backed up by sharpshooting

Russell in gunfighting encounters; Oscar-winning song "Buttons and Bows." Remade as THE SHAKIEST GUN IN THE WEST. Sequel: SON OF PALEFACE.▼

Pale Rider (1985) **C-113m.** ** D: Clint Eastwood. Clint Eastwood, Michael Moriarty, Carrie Snodgress, Christopher Penn, Richard Dysart, Sydney Penny, Richard Kiel, Doug McGrath, John Russell. Eastwood's first Western since THE OUTLAW-JOSEY WALES starts out just fine, the saga of a Good Stranger coming to the aid of some struggling miners, but winds up draggy, pretentious, and dull—with so much cloning of SHANE as to be preposterous. Well crafted, but attempts to be mythical come off as heavy-handed and ridiculous.▼

Pal Joey (1957) **C-111m.** *** D: George Sidney. Rita Hayworth, Frank Sinatra, Kim Novak, Barbara Nichols, Elizabeth Patterson, Bobby Sherwood. Heel-hero of John O'Hara/Rodgers & Hart musical becomes a flippant nice guy who seeks to build a sleek nightclub in San Francisco. Hayworth and Novak battle over Frank with diverting results. Songs: "Bewitched, Bothered, and Bewildered" (with sanitized lyrics), "Small Hotel," "My Funny Valentine," "The Lady Is a Tramp," etc.▼

Palm Beach Story, The (1942) **90m.** ***½ D: Preston Sturges. Claudette Colbert, Joel McCrea, Rudy Vallee, Mary Astor, Sig Arno, Robert Dudley, William Demarest, Jack Norton, Franklin Pangborn, Jimmy Conlin. Hilarious screwball comedy with Claudette running away from hubby McCrea, landing in Palm Beach with nutty millionairess Astor and her bumbling brother Vallee; overflowing with Sturges madness—from the mystifying title sequence to the arrival of the Ale & Quail Club (not to mention the Wienie King!).▼

Palm Springs Weekend (1963) **C-100m.** **½ D: Norman Taurog. Troy Donahue, Connie Stevens, Stefanie Powers, Robert Conrad, Ty Hardin, Jack Weston, Andrew Duggan. Cast tries to play teen-agers; yarn of group on a spree in resort town is mostly predictable.▼

Palmy Days (1931) **77m.** **½ D: A. Edward Sutherland. Eddie Cantor, Charlotte Greenwood, Charles Middleton, George Raft, Walter Catlett. Elaborate early musical. Cantor romps through story of patsy for shady fortune-telling gang.

Palooka (1934) **86m.** *** D: Benjamin Stoloff. Jimmy Durante, Stu Erwin, Lupe Velez, Marjorie Rambeau, Robert Armstrong, Mary Carlisle, William Cagney, Thelma Todd. Not much relation to Ham Fisher's comic strip, but delightful entertainment with Erwin as naive young man brought into fight game by flashy promoter Knobby Walsh (Durante). Fine cast includes James Cagney's lookalike brother William, and has Schnozzola in top form. Also known as JOE PALOOKA.▼

Pals (1987) **C-100m. TVM** D: Lou Antonio. George C. Scott, Don Ameche, Sylvia Sidney, Susan Rinell, James Green. Engaging comedy in which two retired Army buddies, living in a trailer park, find that wealth's not all it's cracked up to be after stumbling on a fortune in drug-related cash. Average.

Panache (1976) **C-78m. TVM** D: Gary Nelson. Rene Auberjonois, David Healy, Charles Frank, Charles Siebert, Amy Irving, John Doucette, Joseph Ruskin, Michael O'Keefe. Lavishly-produced swashbuckler send-up, mixing romance, sword-play, political treachery and pratfalls in 17th century France. The title serves as the name of the hero and the spirit of the movie. An unheralded dandy, written by producer E. Duke Vincent. Above average.

Panama Hattie (1942) **79m.** **½ D: Norman Z. McLeod. Ann Sothern, Red Skelton, Rags Ragland, Ben Blue, Marsha Hunt, Virginia O'Brien, Alan Mowbray, Lena Horne, Dan Dailey, Carl Esmond. Cole Porter's Broadway musical (which starred Ethel Merman) about nightclub owner in Panama, falls flat on screen. Porter's score mostly absent, but Lena sings "Just One of Those Things," and sprightly Sothern sings "I've Still Got My Health."

Panama Sal (1957) **70m.** BOMB D: William Witney. Elena Verdugo, Carlos Rivas, Joe Flynn, Edward Kemmer. Lowjinks blend of poor comedy and flat songs.

Pan Americana (1945) **84m.** ** D: John H. Auer. Philip Terry, Eve Arden, Robert Benchley, Audrey Long, Jane Greer. Another 40s gesture toward Latin-American goodwill. Romantic trivia of magazine writers visiting South American country.

Pancho Barnes (1988) **C-150m. TVM** D: Richard T. Heffron. Valerie Bertinelli, Ted Wass, James Stephens, Cynthia Harris, Geoffrey Lewis, Sam Robards. Disappointing biopic about the pioneer American aviatrix, from bored debutante to barnstormer, female movie stunt pilot, and confidante of space age figures. Just for starters, there's Bertinelli's gross miscasting—and she's in every scene! The script, by the estimable John Michael Hayes, just plods along except when the action's airborne. Average.

Pancho Villa (1972-Spanish) **C-92m.** ** D: Eugenio Martin. Telly Savalas, Clint Walker, Anne Francis, Chuck Connors, Angel del Pozo, Luis Davila. Noisy but dull period piece has Savalas chewing up scenery in title role, Walker playing gunrunner on his payroll, and Connors as polo-playing military martinet. Hang on, though, for smashing climax as two trains collide head-on.▼

Pandemonium (1982) **C-82m.** ** D: Al-

[868]

fred Sole. Tom Smothers, Carol Kane, Miles Chapin, Debralee Scott, Candy Azzara, Marc McClure, Judge Reinhold, Paul Reubens (Pee-wee Herman); guest stars, Tab Hunter, Donald O'Connor, Eve Arden, Eileen Brennan. Sporadically funny spoof of slasher films, set in a school for cheerleaders. Some clever ideas (in keeping with Canadian origin of many of those films, hero Smothers is a Mountie), but too often just forced. Filmed as THURSDAY THE 12TH, changed to avoid confusion with SATURDAY THE 14TH; that alone is funnier than anything in the picture!▼

Pandora and the Flying Dutchman (1951-British) C-123m. **½ D: Albert Lewin. James Mason, Ava Gardner, Nigel Patrick, Sheila Sim, Harold Warrender. Slowly paced fantasy romance with Gardner encountering mysterious Mason who seems to have no future, just an endless past.

Pandora's Box (1928) 110m. **** D: G. W. Pabst. Louise Brooks, Fritz Kortner, Franz (Francis) Lederer, Carl Goetz. Hypnotic silent film stars legendary Brooks as flower girl who becomes protégée—then wife of newspaper editor, with bizarre and unexpected consequences. Striking sexuality and drama, with Brooks an unforgettable Lulu. Scripters Pabst and Laszlo Wajda adapted two plays by Franz Wedekind. Many shorter versions have been around for decades; full version was restored in 1983.▼

Panic at Lakewood Manor SEE: It Happened at Lakewood Manor

Panic Button (1964) 90m. BOMB D: George Sherman. Maurice Chevalier, Eleanor Parker, Jayne Mansfield, Michael Connors, Akim Tamiroff. Good cast is wasted in this amateurish, pathetically unfunny production involving the making of a TV pilot in Italy that's supposed to flop so gangster producers will have legitimate tax loss. Wait for a rerun of THE PRODUCERS.▼

Panic in Echo Park (1977) C-78m. TVM D: John Llewellyn Moxey. Dorian Harewood, Robin Gammell, Catlin Adams, Ramon Bieri, Movita, Tamu. Determined physician Harewood fights hospital authority and city government to trace cause of apparent epidemic. He's street-wise, the film's predictable. Average.▼

Panic in Needle Park, The (1971) C-110m. ***½ D: Jerry Schatzberg. Al Pacino, Kitty Winn, Alan Vint, Richard Bright, Kiel Martin, Michael McClanathan, Warren Finnerty, Marcia Jean Kurtz, Raul Julia, Gil Rogers, Paul Sorvino. Easily the best of many drug-abuse films made in the early 1970s. Spunky small-time crook and decent young girl get hooked on heroin and go straight downhill. Pacino and Winn are tremendous.▼

Panic in the City (1967) C-97m. ** D: Eddie Davis. Howard Duff, Linda Cristal, Stephen McNally, Nehemiah Persoff. Attempt by subversives to start World War 3 by detonating a bomb in L.A. has the aging Duff in a dizzy attempt to stop it.

Panic in the Parlor (1957-British) 81m. **½ D: Gordon Parry. Peggy Mount, Shirley Eaton, Gordon Jackson, Ronald Lewis. Broad but diverting humor about a sailor coming home to get married, and the chaos it causes all concerned. Originally titled SAILOR BEWARE!

Panic in the Streets (1950) 93m. ***½ D: Elia Kazan. Richard Widmark, Paul Douglas, Barbara Bel Geddes, (Walter) Jack Palance, Zero Mostel. Taut drama involving gun-happy gangsters, one of whom is a carrier of disease, and the manhunt to find him. Makes fine use of New Orleans locale; Edward and Edna Anhalt won an Oscar for their story.

Panic in Year Zero (1962) 95m. **½ D: Ray Milland. Ray Milland, Jean Hagen, Frankie Avalon, Mary Mitchel, Joan Freeman, Richard Garland. Intriguing film about family that escapes atomic bomb explosion to find a situation of every-man-for-himself. Milland doubles as actor-director. Good cast, but loud, tinny music spoils much of film's effects.

Panic on the 5:22 (1974) C-78m. TVM D: Harvey Hart. Ina Balin, Bernie Casey, Andrew Duggan, Dana Elcar, Eduard Franz, Lynda Day George, Laurence Luckinbill, Reni Santoni. Passengers on a commuters' club car are terrorized by three toughs. Echoes of THE INCIDENT, done earlier and better. Average.▼

Panic on the Trans-Siberian Express SEE: Horror Express▼

Pantaloons (1957-French) C-93m. **½ D: John Berry. Fernandel, Carmen Sevilla, Christine Carrere, Fernando Rey. Fernandel is peppy in this brisk little period-piece as a phony gay-blade intent on female conquests.▼

Panther Girl of the Kongo SEE: Claw Monsters, The

Panther Island SEE: Bomba on Panther Island

Papa, Mama, the Maid and I (1956-French) 94m. **½ D: Jean-Paul Le Chanois. Fernand Ledoux, Gaby Morlay, Nicole Courcel, Robert Lamoureux. Sometimes saucy sex comedy, fully explained by title.

Papa's Delicate Condition (1963) C-98m. **½ D: George Marshall. Jackie Gleason, Glynis Johns, Charlie Ruggles, Laurel Goodwin, Charles Lane, Elisha Cook, Juanita Moore, Murray Hamilton. Amusing nostalgia of Corinne Griffith's childhood; Gleason dominates everything as tipsy railroad inspector father; set in 1900s. Oscarwinning song, "Call Me Irresponsible."▼

Paperback Hero (1973-Canadian) C-94m.

**½ D: Peter Pearson. Keir Dullea, Elizabeth Ashley, John Beck, Dayle Haddon. Local hockey hero and womanizer leads fantasy life as town gunslinger. Interesting and well-acted, but ultimately a misfire.▼

Paper Chase, The (1973) **C-111m.** ***½ D: James Bridges. Timothy Bottoms, Lindsay Wagner, John Houseman, Graham Beckel, Edward Herrmann, Craig Richard Nelson, James Naughton, Bob Lydiard. Near-classic comedy-drama about pressures of freshman year at Harvard Law School; Bottoms' obsession with tyrannical professor Kingsfield (Houseman) becomes even more complicated when he discovers his girl friend is Kingsfield's daughter! Splendidly adapted by Bridges from the John Jay Osborn, Jr., novel, with wonderful Gordon Willis photography and peerless acting, led by Houseman's Oscar-winning performance in the role that made him a "star" (and which he continued in the subsequent TV series).▼

Paper Dolls (1982) **C-100m. TVM** D: Edward Zwick. Joan Hackett, Jennifer Warren, Joan Collins, Daryl Hannah, Alexandra Paul, Marc Singer, Barry Primus, Craig T. Nelson, Antonio Fargas, Eric Stoltz. Behind the scenes in the glamorous—and competitive—world of teenage models. The older women—Hackett, Warren, and Collins—are the ones to watch here. Later a series. Average.

Paperhouse (1988-British) **C-94m.** *** D: Bernard Rose. Charlotte Burke, Elliott Spiers, Glenne Headly, Ben Cross, Gemma Jones, Sarah Newbold. Insightful fantasy drama of girl on the verge of puberty who has vivid dreams that both reflect her own life and seem to be affecting the life of a boy she has never met—while awake. Tense, even frightening, psychologically valid and well-acted . . . but not to every taste. Feature debut of music-video director Rose.

Paper Lion (1968) **C-107m.** *** D: Alex March. Alan Alda, Lauren Hutton, Alex Karras, David Doyle, Ann Turkel, John Gordy, Roger Brown, Sugar Ray Robinson. Funny film, loosely based on George Plimpton's book, about that writer's experiences when he becomes honorary member of Detroit Lions football team. Even non-football fans should enjoy this one, especially scenes with Karras (then a member of the team). Look for Roy Scheider in small role.▼

√ **Paper Man** (1971) **C-73m. TVM** D: Walter Grauman. Dean Stockwell, Stefanie Powers, James Stacy, Tina Chen. College computer workers find themselves in eerie situation that began innocuously with credit card scheme. Excellent idea gone awry, thanks to rotten script, indifferent acting. Average.

Paper Moon (1973) **102m.** **** D: Peter

Bogdanovich. Ryan O'Neal, Tatum O'Neal, Madeline Kahn, John Hillerman, P. J. Johnson, Burton Gilliam, Randy Quaid. Unbeatable entertainment, harking back to Damon Runyonesque 1930s, as con man O'Neal unwillingly latches onto young girl (his real-life daughter) who's pretty sharp herself. Tatum made her film debut here, and won an Oscar for her scene-stealing work; Kahn is fun, too, as Trixie Delight. Script by Alvin Sargent from Joe David Brown's *Addie Pray*. Later a TV series.▼

Paper Tiger (1976-British) **C-99m.** ** D: Ken Annakin. David Niven, Toshiro Mifune, Hardy Kruger, Ando, Ivan Desny, Ronald Fraser. Lackluster tale of a plucky kidnapped lad (Ando) and his English tutor (Niven). Since the boy is the son of Japanese ambassador Mifune, Niven sees the chance to act out his many tales of heroism that have impressed the youngster. Tepid action involving political terrorism and Disney-style cuteness muck up the proceedings entirely.▼

Papillon (1973) **C-150m.** *** D: Franklin J. Schaffner. Steve McQueen, Dustin Hoffman, Victor Jory, Don Gordon, Anthony Zerbe, George Coulouris, Robert Deman. Henri Charrière—"the butterfly"—(McQueen) is determined to escape from Devil's Island, despite the odds, in this exciting adventure yarn. Extreme length and graphic realism work against its total success. Script by Dalton Trumbo and Lorenzo Semple, Jr., from Charrière's bestselling book; that's Trumbo cast as the Commandant. Music by Jerry Goldsmith.▼

Parachute Battalion (1941) **75m.** ** D: Leslie Goodwins. Edmond O'Brien, Nancy Kelly, Robert Preston, Harry Carey, Buddy Ebsen, Paul Kelly. Efficient WW2 programmer which gets a bit sticky with flag-waving.

Parachute Jumper (1933) **65m.** **½ D: Alfred E. Green. Douglas Fairbanks, Jr., Leo Carrillo, Bette Davis, Frank McHugh, Claire Dodd. Former flyers Fairbanks and McHugh strike up fast friendship with Davis, but all three are victimized by involvement with gangster Carrillo. Fast-moving, enjoyable Warner Bros. programmer.

Parade, The (1984) **C-100m. TVM** D: Peter H. Hunt. Michael Learned, Frederic Forrest, Rosanna Arquette, Maxwell Caulfield, James Olson, Geraldine Page. Three generations of women find their lives in turmoil when the husband of one comes home seeking revenge after seven years in prison, as the town prepares for its July 4th parade. N. Richard Nash's compact story and teleplay revive pleasant memories of his writings during TV's Golden Age. Above average.

Paradine Case, The (1948) **116m.** **½ √ D: Alfred Hitchcock. Gregory Peck, (Alida) Valli, Ann Todd, Charles Laughton, Charles

Coburn, Ethel Barrymore, Louis Jourdan, Leo G. Carroll, John Williams. Talk, Talk, Talk in complicated, stagy courtroom drama, set in England. Below par for Hitchcock; producer David O. Selznick also wrote the script. Originally 132m., then cut to 125m. and finally 116m.▼

Paradise (1982) **C-100m.** *½ D: Stuart Gillard. Willie Aames, Phoebe Cates, Tuvia Tavi, Richard Curnock, Neil Vipond, Aviva Marks. Silly BLUE LAGOON rip-off, with Aames and Cates discovering sex while stranded in the desert. Both, however, do look good sans clothes.▼

Paradise Alley (1961) **85m.** *½ D: Hugo Haas. Marie Windsor, Hugo Haas, Billy Gilbert, Carol Morris, Chester Conklin, Margaret Hamilton, Corrine Griffith. Grade-D mishmash about elderly moviemaker involved in amateur film production. Interesting only for veteran cast. Original title: STARS IN THE BACK YARD.

Paradise Alley (1978) **C-109m.** *½ D: Sylvester Stallone. Sylvester Stallone, Lee Canalito, Armand Assante, Frank McRae, Anne Archer, Kevin Conway, Joyce Ingalls. Sly made his directorial debut with this Damon Runyonesque story of three none-too-bright brothers from the N.Y.C. tenements, one of whom hopes to make it big as a wrestler. Some nice moments lost in comic-book-level dramatics. Director Stallone clearly admires his star (he also croons the title song!).▼

Paradise Connection, The (1979) **C-100m.** TVM D: Michael Preece. Buddy Ebsen, Bonnie Ebsen, John Colicos, Marj Dusay, Brian Kerwin. In this pilot to a post-*Barnaby Jones* project, Ebsen (who also produced it) is a Chicago lawyer who goes to Hawaii in search of his estranged son who, he learns, is involved in drug smuggling. Average.

Paradise for Three (1938) **75m.** ** D: Edward Buzzell. Frank Morgan, Robert Young, Mary Astor, Edna May Oliver, Florence Rice, Reginald Owen, Henry Hull. Strange story of American businessman trying to mingle with German people to discover how they live. Good cast helps fair script.

Paradise, Hawaiian Style (1966) **C-91m.** **½ D: Michael Moore. Elvis Presley, Suzanna Leigh, James Shigeta, Donna Butterworth, Marianna Hill, Irene Tsu, Julie Parrish, Philip Ahn, Mary Treen. Rehash of Presley's earlier BLUE HAWAII, with Elvis a pilot who runs a charter service while romancing local dolls. Attractive fluff.▼

Paradise Lagoon SEE: **Admirable Crichton, The**

Parallax View, The (1974) **C-102m.** ***½ D: Alan J. Pakula. Warren Beatty, Paula Prentiss, William Daniels, Walter McGinn, Hume Cronyn, Kenneth Mars. Director-photographer-production designer team later responsible for ALL THE PRESIDENT'S MEN gives this political thriller a brilliant "look" as reporter Beatty investigates a senator's assassination. Frightening story unfolds with each piece of evidence he uncovers. Gripping to the very end.▼

Paramount on Parade (1930) **77m.** **½ D: Dorothy Arzner, Otto Brower, Edmund Goulding, Victor Heerman, Edwin Knopf, Rowland V. Lee, Ernst Lubitsch, Lothar Mendes, Victor Schertzinger, A. Edward Sutherland, Frank Tuttle. Jean Arthur, Clara Bow, Maurice Chevalier, Gary Cooper, Nancy Carroll, Leon Errol, Stuart Erwin, Kay Francis, Fredric March, Helen Kane, Jack Oakie, William Powell, Buddy Rogers, many others. Early-talkie variety revue designed to show off Paramount's roster of stars. Some amusing songs and skits, but a lot of dry spots in between. Highlights include Nancy Carroll's "Dancing to Save Your Sole" and Chevalier's two numbers. Film originally ran 102m. with several sequences in color; current prints feature director Edmund Goulding and such stars as Gary Cooper and Jean Arthur "introducing" a sequence that never comes!

Paranoia (1968) **C-91m.** BOMB D: Umberto Lenzi. Carroll Baker, Lou Castel, Colette Descombes, Tino Carraro. Trash about sultry widow involved in various sexual encounters. Also shown as ORGASMO.▼

Paranoia (1969) SEE: **Quiet Place to Kill, A**▼

Paranoiac (1963-British) **80m.** **½ D: Freddie Francis. Janette Scott, Oliver Reed, Liliane Brousse, Alexander Davion, Sheila Burrell, Maurice Denham. Murder, impersonation, insanity all part of thriller set in large English country estate.

Parasite (1982) **C-85m.** BOMB D: Charles Band. Robert Glaudini, Demi Moore, Luca Bercovici, James Davidson, Al Fann, Cherie Currie, Vivian Blaine. In repressive near-future, scientist who's developed voracious parasites flees with one inside him and (surprise, surprise) it gets loose. Set in the California desert, with several revolting sequences copied from ALIEN. Filmed in 3D, with blood and parasites thrust at the viewer.▼

Parasite Murders, The SEE: **They Came From Within**▼

Paratrooper, The (1954-British) **C-87m.** ** D: Terence Young. Alan Ladd, Leo Genn, Susan Stephen, Harry Andrews. Minor Ladd vehicle involving special tactical forces and Ladd's guilt-ridden past. Original title: THE RED BERET.

Pardners (1956) **C-90m.** **½ D: Norman Taurog. Dean Martin, Jerry Lewis, Lori Nelson, Jackie Loughery, John Baragrey, Agnes Moorehead, Jeff Morrow, Lon Chaney, Jr. Ironically titled M&L vehicle (they were already on the road to their breakup) is pleasant remake of RHYTHM ON THE RANGE, with Jerry as Manhattan millionaire who cleans up Western town in his own inimitable fashion. Written by Sidney Sheldon.

Pardon Mon Affaire (1977-French) **C-105m.** *** D: Yves Robert. Jean Rochefort, Claude Brasseur, Guy Bedos, Victor Lanoux, Daniele Delorme, Anny Duperey. Sprightly comedy about efforts of happily married Rochefort to meet and court a dazzling model he spots in a parking garage. Another enjoyable French farce from director Robert. Sequel: WE WILL ALL MEET IN PARADISE. Later Americanized as THE WOMAN IN RED.▼

Pardon Mon Affaire, Too SEE: **We Will All Meet in Paradise**▼

Pardon My French (1951-U.S.-French) **81m.** **½ D: Bernard Vorhaus. Paul Henreid, Merle Oberon, Paul Bonifas, Maximilliene, Jim Gerald. Fluff of Oberon inheriting a mansion in France occupied by charming composer Henreid.

Pardon My Past (1945) **88m.** *** D: Leslie Fenton. Fred MacMurray, Marguerite Chapman, Akim Tamiroff, William Demarest, Rita Johnson, Harry Davenport. Excellent tale of unsuspecting MacMurray, look-alike for famous playboy, incurring his debts and many enemies; fine comedy-drama.

Pardon My Rhythm (1944) **62m.** ** D: Felix E. Feist. Gloria Jean, Evelyn Ankers, Patric Knowles, Bob Crosby. Naive minor musical set in ultra-wholesome high school, with Gloria the singing belle of the ball.

Pardon My Sarong (1942) **84m.** *** D: Erle C. Kenton. Lou Costello, Bud Abbott, Lionel Atwill, Virginia Bruce, Robert Paige, William Demarest, Leif Erickson, Samuel S. Hinds, Nan Wynn, Four Ink Spots, Tip, Tap, Toe. A&C in good form as bus drivers who end up on tropical island, getting involved with notorious jewel thieves.

Pardon My Trunk SEE: **Hello Elephant**▼

Pardon Us (1931) **55m.** **½ D: James Parrott. Stan Laurel, Oliver Hardy, Wilfred Lucas, Walter Long, James Finlayson, June Marlowe. L&H's first starring feature film is amusing spoof of THE BIG HOUSE and prison films in general; slow pacing is its major debit, but many funny bits make it a must for fans of Stan and Ollie.▼

Parenthood (1989) **C-124m.** ***½ D: Ron Howard. Steve Martin, Mary Steenburgen, Dianne Wiest, Jason Robards, Rick Moranis, Tom Hulce, Martha Plimpton, Keanu Reeves, Harley Kozak, Dennis Dugan, Leaf Phoenix, Paul Linke. Insightful multi-character comedy about the trials and tribulations of parenthood, as seen from several points of view within the same large family. Warm, winning, and truthful; Martin is ideal in the lead, and surrounded by a perfect ensemble. Screenplay by Lowell Ganz and Babaloo Mandel (from a story they concocted with fellow parent Ron Howard). Followed by a TV series.▼

Parents (1989) **C-82m.** ** D: Bob Balaban. Randy Quaid, Mary Beth Hurt, Sandy Dennis, Bryan Madorsky, Juno Mills-Cockell, Kathryn Grody, Deborah Rush, Graham Jarvis. Coal-black horror comedy set in the 1950s centers on a young boy who worries about where his highly conformist parents get all that meat they eat . . . and what goes on down in the basement. Well acted but thinly plotted; a good sense of visual style and amusing production design can't keep it afloat. Feature directing debut for actor Balaban.▼

Parent Trap, The (1961) **C-124m.** *** D: David Swift. Hayley Mills, Maureen O'Hara, Brian Keith, Charlie Ruggles, Una Merkel, Leo G. Carroll, Joanna Barnes. Hayley plays twins who've never met until their divorced parents send them to the same summer camp; after initial rivalry they join forces to reunite their mom and dad. Attempt to mix slapstick and sophistication doesn't work, but overall it's fun. Erich Kastner's story filmed before as 1953 British film TWICE UPON A TIME. Followed by several TV sequels twenty-five years later.▼

Parent Trap II (1986) **C-95m.** TVM D: Ronald F. Maxwell. Hayley Mills, Tom Skerritt, Carrie Kei Heim, Bridgette Andersen, Alex Harvey. Belated sequel reuniting Hayley with the Disney studio has the erstwhile hellion twins now in romantic adult mix-ups of their own as parents. Pleasant diversion. Made for cable. Followed by PARENT TRAP III. Average.

Parent Trap III (1989) **C-100m.** TVM D: Mollie Miller. Hayley Mills, Barry Bostwick, Ray Baker, Patricia Richardson, Joy Creel, Leanna Creel, Monica Creel. Hayley Mills and Hayley Mills return in this second sequel as adult twins who vie for widower Bostwick—father of triplets! Followed by PARENT TRAP HAWAIIAN HONEYMOON. Average.

Parent Trap Hawaiian Honeymoon (1989) **C-100m.** TVM D: Mollie Miller. Hayley Mills, Barry Bostwick, John M. Jackson, Leanna Creel, Monica Creel, Joy Creel, Jayne Meadows. Technically this is PARENT TRAP IV, from the Disney studio, with Mills again playing the twins grown up—in circumstances fully described by the title. Average.

Paris After Dark (1943) **85m.** ** D: Leonide Moguy. George Sanders, Philip Dorn, Brenda Marshall, Madeleine LeBeau, Marcel Dalio. Tame anti-Nazi film with husband and wife on opposite sides of fence.

Paris Blues (1961) **98m.** *** D: Martin Ritt. Paul Newman, Joanne Woodward, Diahann Carroll, Sidney Poitier, Louis Armstrong, Serge Reggiani. Film improves with each viewing; offbeat account of musicians Newman and Poitier in Left Bank Paris, romancing tourists Woodward and Carroll. Great Duke Ellington score, including explosive "Battle Royal" number; a must for jazz fans.

Paris Calling (1941) **95m.** *** D: Edwin L. Marin. Elisabeth Bergner, Randolph Scott, Basil Rathbone, Gale Sondergaard, Eduardo Ciannelli, Lee J. Cobb. Exciting story of underground movement in Paris to destroy Nazis occupying France, with top-notch cast.

Paris Does Strange Things (1956-French) **C-98m.** ** D: Jean Renoir. Ingrid Bergman, Jean Marais, Mel Ferrer, Jean Richard, Magali Noel, Juliette Greco, Pierre Bertin. Claude Renoir's exquisite cinematography highlights this otherwise so-so account of impoverished Polish princess Bergman's romantic intrigues with Marais and Ferrer. Overrated by some; far from Renoir's (or Bergman's) best. French-language version, called ELENA AND HER MEN, is better, and runs 95m.▼

Paris Express, The (1953-British) **C-80m.** **½ D: Harold French. Claude Rains, Marta Toren, Marius Goring, Anouk Aimee, Herbert Lom, Lucie Mannheim, Felix Aylmer, Ferdy Mayne, Eric Pohlmann. A clerk embezzles money, hoping to use it for travel, but gets into more of an adventure than he bargained for. Middling crime yarn based on a George Simenon novel. Original British title: THE MAN WHO WATCHED TRAINS GO BY.▼

Paris Follies of 1956 SEE: Fresh From Paris

Paris Holiday (1958) **C-100m.** **½ D: Gerd Oswald. Bob Hope, Fernandel, Anita Ekberg, Martha Hyer, Preston Sturges. Mixture of French and American farce humor makes for uneven entertainment, with Hope in France to buy a new screenplay. Features writer-director Sturges in a small acting role.▼

Paris Honeymoon (1939) **92m.** **½ D: Frank Tuttle. Bing Crosby, Shirley Ross, Edward Everett Horton, Akim Tamiroff, Ben Blue, Rafaela Ottiano, Raymond Hatton. Texan Crosby visits France planning to marry Ross, but meets native Franciska Gaal and falls in love with her.

Paris Model (1953) **81m.** *½ D: Alfred E. Green. Eva Gabor, Tom Conway, Paulette Goddard, Marilyn Maxwell, Cecil Kellaway, Barbara Lawrence, Florence Bates. Lackluster vehicle for veteran actors, revolving around a dress and four women who purchase copies of same.

Paris Playboys (1954) **62m.** D: William Beaudine. Leo Gorcey, Huntz Hall, Bernard Gorcey, Veola Vonn, Steven Geray. SEE: **Bowery Boys** series.

Paris, Texas (1984) **C-150m.** **½ D: Wim Wenders. Harry Dean Stanton, Nastassia Kinski, Dean Stockwell, Aurore Clement, Hunter Carson, Bernhard Wicki. Man who's been lost four years tries to put his life back together—and win back his wife and son. Oblique, self-satisfied, and slow, like all of Sam Shepard's writing, but distinguished by fine performances and rich Southwestern atmosphere by Wenders and cinematographer Robby Muller. This won raves from many critics, so it may be a matter of personal taste.▼

Paris Underground (1945) **97m.** **½ D: Gregory Ratoff. Constance Bennett, Gracie Fields, George Rigaud, Kurt Kreuger, Leslie Vincent, Charles Andre. Well-acted story of American Bennett and Britisher Fields working in underground movement even while imprisoned in Nazi POW camp.

Paris Was Made for Lovers SEE: **Time for Loving, A**

Paris—When It Sizzles (1964) **C-110m.** *½ D: Richard Quine. William Holden, Audrey Hepburn, Noel Coward, Gregoire Aslan. Labored, unfunny comedy defeats a game cast, in story of screenwriter and secretary who act out movie fantasies in order to finish script. Paris locations, cameos by Marlene Dietrich and other stars don't help.▼

Park Is Mine, The (1985) **C-105m. TVM** D: Steven Hilliard Stern. Tommy Lee Jones, Helen Shaver, Yaphet Kotto, Eric Peterson, Lawrence Dane. Incomprehensible drama about a confused Vietnam vet who forcefully takes over Central Park in N.Y.C. (except that the entire thing was shot in Toronto!). Made for cable. Below average. ▼

Park Row (1952) **83m.** *** D: Samuel Fuller. Gene Evans, Mary Welch, Herbert Heyes, Tina Rome, Forrest Taylor. Good, tough little film with newsman Evans starting his own paper, rivaling newspaper magnate Welch in 1880s N.Y.C.

Parlor, Bedroom and Bath (1931) **75m.** ** D: Edward Sedgwick. Buster Keaton, Charlotte Greenwood, Reginald Denny, Cliff Edwards, Dorothy Christy, Joan Peers, Sally Eilers, Natalie Moorhead, Edward Brophy. Great moments with Buster are few and far between in this contrived vehicle, but at least he's surrounded by compatible costars.▼

Parnell (1937) **119m.** *½ D: John Stahl. Clark Gable, Myrna Loy, Edna May Oliver, Edmund Gwenn, Alan Marshal, Donald Crisp, Billie Burke, Donald Meek. Biography of popular and powerful Irish nationalist leader of the late 1800s whose career was destroyed by the exposure of his adulterous affair with Katie O'Shea. Plodding film fails to realize great story potential; this was (understandably) a notorious flop in 1937.

Parole (1982) **C-100m. TVM** D: Michael Tuchner. James Naughton, Lori Cardille, Mark Soper, Ted Ross, Barbara Meek, Brent Jennings, Ellen Barkin, Patricia Wettig. Dedicated Boston parole officer and his young charges populate this conventional pilot. Edward Hume's script nearly gets it over the hurdle, but one must settle instead for Sting singing Bob Dylan's "I Shall Be Released" at crucial points in the plot. Filmed in 1980. Average.

Parole, Inc. (1949) **71m. ** D: Alfred Zeisler. Michael O'Shea, Evelyn Ankers, Turhan Bey, Lyle Talbot. Turgid independent cheapie with low-budget class, about crackdown on gangster infiltration of parole system.▼

Parrish (1961) **C-140m. *½** D: Delmer Daves. Claudette Colbert, Troy Donahue, Karl Malden, Dean Jagger, Connie Stevens, Diane McBain, Sharon Hugueny, Madeleine Sherwood. Slurpy soaper is so bad that at times it's funny; emotionless Donahue lives with his mother (Colbert) on Jagger's tobacco plantation and falls in love with three girls there. Malden overplays tyrannical tobacco czar to the nth degree.

Parson and the Outlaw, The (1957) **C-71m. *½** D: Oliver Drake. Anthony Dexter, Sonny Tufts, Marie Windsor, Buddy Rogers, Jean Parker, Bob Steele. Minor version of life and times of Billy the Kid.

Parson of Panamint, The (1941) **84m. **½** D: William McGann. Charlie Ruggles, Ellen Drew, Phillip Terry, Joseph Schildkraut, Porter Hall. Minor offbeat Western with Terry as preacher in mining town, involved in murder while reforming the community.

Parting Glances (1986) **C-90m. **½** D: Bill Sherwood. John Bolger, Richard Ganoung, Steve Buscemi, Adam Nathan, Patrick Tull. Two longtime gay roommates spend their final 24 hours together before one leaves New York on a job transfer. Earnest, intelligent drama is OK within its modest framework; subsidiary characters—one of them dying of AIDS—are more compelling than the two protagonists. This was Sherwood's only feature; he died of AIDS in 1990.▼

Partners (1982) **C-98m. BOMB** D: James Burrows. Ryan O'Neal, John Hurt, Kenneth McMillan, Robyn Douglass, Jay Robinson, Denise Galik, Rick Jason. Foolish, offensive parody of CRUISING, with straight cop O'Neal impersonating homosexual while investigating gay murder. Hurt is wasted as O'Neal's partner, who really is gay. Screenplay by Francis (LA

CAGE AUX FOLLES) Veber. Undistinguished feature debut for TV comedy director Burrows.▼

Partners in Crime (1973) **C-78m. TVM** D: Jack Smight. Lee Grant, Lou Antonio, Bob Cummings, Harry Guardino, Richard Jaeckel, Charles Drake, Richard Anderson, John Randolph, William Schallert, Lorraine Gary, Gary Crosby, Vic Tayback. Lady judge-turned-detective and her ex-con associate seek stolen loot in this reworking of the earlier Bette Davis pilot THE JUDGE AND JAKE WYLER that producers Richard Levinson and William Link failed for a second time to develop into a series. Average.

Parts: The Clonus Horror (1978) **C-90m. ** D: Robert S. Fiveson. Tim Donnelly, Dick Sargent, Peter Graves, Paulette Breen, David Hooks, Keenan Wynn. Cleanly made programmer about an insidious government plan to start cloning the population. Watchable but uninspired. Also known as THE CLONUS HORROR.▼

Part-Time Wife (1961-British) **70m. *½** D: Max Varnel. Anton Rodgers, Nyree Dawn Porter, Kenneth J. Warren, Henry McCarthy. Lumbering account of Rodgers loaning wife Porter to scoundrel friend Warren, who wants to make an impression; wooden farce.

Part 2, Sounder (1976) **C-98m. ***½** D: William A. Graham. Harold Sylvester, Ebony Wright, Taj Mahal, Annazette Chase, Darryl Young. Excellent follow-up to SOUNDER, retaining the dignity and human values in the continuing tale of a proud family of Depression-era Southern sharecroppers.

Part 2, Walking Tall (1975) **C-109m. ** D: Earl Bellamy. Bo Svenson, Luke Askew, Robert DoQui, Bruce Glover, Richard Jaeckel, Noah Beery, Jr. Tepid follow-up to ultraviolent movie about club-swinging Tennessee Sheriff Buford Pusser. Svenson now takes the role of the one-man crusader against organized crime, but makes him come off like a standard TV hero rather than a real-life character. Sequel: FINAL CHAPTER—WALKING TALL.▼

Party, The (1968) **C-99m. *** D: Blake Edwards. Peter Sellers, Claudine Longet, Marge Champion, Denny Miller, Gavin MacLeod. Side-splitting gags highlight loosely structured film about chic Hollywood party attended by bumbling Indian actor (Sellers). Doesn't hold up to the very end, but has some memorable setpieces.▼

Party Crashers, The (1958) **78m. *½** D: Bernard Girard. Mark Damon, Bobby Driscoll, Connie Stevens, Frances Farmer. Sleazy goings-on of teen-age gangs who become involved in reckless mayhem. Both Driscoll's and Farmer's last film.

Party Girl (1958) **C-99m. *** D: Nicho-

las Ray. Robert Taylor, Cyd Charisse, Lee J. Cobb, John Ireland, Kent Smith. Crooked lawyer (Taylor) and showgirl (Charisse) try to break free from Chicago mob life. Charisse has a couple of torrid dance numbers; Ray's stylish treatment has won this film a cult following.
Party Line (1988) **C-91m.** BOMB D: William Webb. Richard Hatch, Shawn Weatherly, Leif Garrett, Greta Blackburn, Richard Roundtree, James O'Sullivan, Terrence McGovern. Sleazy, amateurish story capitalizing on the party-line fad in which young swingers call a special phone number to get a date—in this case, with murder. You'll want to hang up on this one long before the final credits.▼
Party's Over, The (1966-British) **94m.** ** D: Guy Hamilton. Oliver Reed, Ann Lynn, Clifford David, Louise Sorel, Eddie Albert. Sordid drama of wealthy American girl becoming involved with group of aimless London youths, with tragic results.
Party Wire (1935) **72m.** *** D: Erle C. Kenton. Jean Arthur, Victor Jory, Helen Lowell, Robert Allen, Charley Grapewin, Matt McHugh. Arthur is delightful as smalltown girl wooed by prosperous prodigal son Jory, only to have their courtship maliciously distorted by local gossips via communal telephone party line. Insightful look at provincial mores employs a healthy dose of generic Capra-style humor.
Pascali's Island (1988-British) **C-104m.** **½ D: James Dearden. Ben Kingsley, Charles Dance, Helen Mirren, George Murcell, Sheila Allen, Nadim Sawalha. A largely ignored Turkish spy for the collapsing Ottoman Empire forms a duplicitous alliance with a mysterious Brit to rob the Greek island Nisi of an archeological treasure. Well-acted drama isn't wholly successful, but it certainly holds your interest. Scripted by the director.▼
Passage, The (1979-British) **C-99m.** *½ D: J. Lee Thompson. Anthony Quinn, James Mason, Malcolm McDowell, Patricia Neal, Kay Lenz, Christopher Lee, Paul Clemens, Michael Lonsdale, Marcel Bozzuffi. Trashy WW2 story of Basque guide Quinn helping chemist Mason and his family escape over the Pyrenees with Nazi fanatic McDowell in hot pursuit. McDowell's campy performance must be seen to be disbelieved.
Passage to India, A (1984-British) **C-163m.** *** D: David Lean. Judy Davis, Victor Banerjee, Peggy Ashcroft, James Fox, Alec Guinness, Nigel Havers, Richard Wilson, Antonia Pemberton, Michael Culver, Art Malik, Saeed Jaffrey. Meticulous adaptation of E.M. Forster novel set in the late 1920s, about an East/West culture clash, as a young, headstrong British woman goes to India for the first time, accompanied by the mother of her fiancé. Not a

great movie, but so rich in flavor, nuance, and the sheer expressiveness of *film* that it offers great satisfaction, despite its shortcomings (and extreme length). Ashcroft won Best Supporting Actress Oscar for her fine performance as Mrs. Moore. Maurice Jarre also got an Oscar for his anachronistic score.▼
Passage to Marseille (1944) **110m.** **½ D: Michael Curtiz. Humphrey Bogart, Claude Rains, Michele Morgan, Philip Dorn, Sydney Greenstreet, Peter Lorre, George Tobias, Helmut Dantine, John Loder, Victor Francen, Vladimir Sokoloff, Edward (Eduardo) Ciannelli, Hans Conried. WW2 Devil's Island escape film marred by flashback-within-flashback confusion. Not a bad war film, just too talky; a disappointment considering the top-notch cast.▼
Passage West (1951) **C-80m.** *½ D: Lewis R. Foster. John Payne, Dennis O'Keefe, Arleen Whelan, Mary Beth Hughes, Frank Faylen, Dooley Wilson. Outlaws join up with wagon train with predictable results.
Passenger, The (1975-Italian) **C-119m.** **½ D: Michelangelo Antonioni. Jack Nicholson, Maria Schneider, Jenny Runacre, Ian Hendry, Steven Berkoff, Ambrose Bia. Enigmatic narrative about dissatisfied TV reporter on assignment in Africa who exchanges identities with an Englishman who has died suddenly in a hotel room. Some found this brilliant; judge for yourself.▼
Passion (1954) **C-84m.** **½ D: Allan Dwan. Cornel Wilde, Yvonne De Carlo, Raymond Burr, Lon Chaney, John Qualen. Picturesque tale of old California, with Wilde the outlaw seeking revenge for wrongs done to his family.▼
Passion (1982-French-Swiss) **C-87m.** **½ D: Jean-Luc Godard. Isabelle Huppert, Hanna Schygulla, Michel Piccoli, Jerzy Radziwilowicz, Laszlo Szabo. Characters named Isabelle, Hanna, Michel, Jerzy and Laszlo are connected with the making of a film called PASSION, which seems to be more the visualization of a Rembrandt or Delacroix than an actual movie. Meanwhile, the extras are treated like cattle, and the moviemaking art is tainted by commerce. Truffaut's DAY FOR NIGHT celebrates the joy of filmmaking; this is, in its own way, an anti-movie.
Passion and Paradise (1989) **C-200m.** TVM D: Harvey Hart. Armand Assante, Catherine Mary Stewart, Mariette Hartley, Rod Steiger, Kevin McCarthy, Michael Sarrazin, Wayne Rogers, Andrew Ray. Adroit mixture of fact and fiction, sex and romance, and the still-unsolved real-life murder of British millionaire Sir Harry Oakes (Steiger) in the Bahamas during WW2. Assante, as his playboy son-in-law Alfred de Marigny, is the prime suspect;

Rogers is a low-key, fictitious Columbo-like detective. (Before this could air on British TV, the producers were obliged to shoot new footage, altering the way Oakes' socialite pals the Duke and Duchess of Windsor were portrayed.) Originally shown in two parts. Average.

Passionate Friends, The (1949-British) **95m. **½ D:** David Lean. Ann Todd, Trevor Howard, Claude Rains, Betty Ann Davies, Isabel Dean, Wilfrid Hyde-White. Predictable love triangle among the upper classes, enhanced by strong cast and Lean's craftsmanship. Based on H. G. Wells novel. Originally released in U.S. as ONE WOMAN'S STORY.

Passionate Plumber, The (1932) **73m. ** D:** Edward Sedgwick. Buster Keaton, Jimmy Durante, Irene Purcell, Polly Moran, Gilbert Roland, Mona Maris. Stilted adaptation of HER CARDBOARD LOVER as vehicle for Keaton, hired by Parisienne Purcell to make lover Roland jealous. Truly funny moments are few and far between.

Passionate Sentry, The (1952-British) **84m. ** D:** Anthony Kimmins. Nigel Patrick, Peggy Cummins, Valerie Hobson, George Cole, A. E. Matthews, Anthony Bushell. Wispy romantic comedy about madcap gal who falls in love with a guard at Buckingham Palace. Retitled: WHO GOES THERE?

Passionate Stranger, The SEE: **Novel Affair, A**

Passionate Thief, The (1960-Italian) **105m. **½ D:** Mario Monicelli. Anna Magnani, Toto, Ben Gazzara, Fred Clark, Edy Vessel. Offbeat serio-comedy with Magnani a film extra, Gazzara a pickpocket, Toto an unemployed actor—all meshed together in a minor tale of love and larceny.▼

Passion d'Amore (1981-Italian-French) **C-118m. **½ D:** Ettore Scola. Bernard Giraudeau, Laura Antonelli, Valerie D' Obici, Jean-Louis Trintignant, Massimo Girotti, Bernard Blier. Hideous D'Obici pursues handsome cavalry officer Giraudeau, who's in love with gorgeous Antonelli. Intriguing Beauty and the Beast story is not completely convincing—and far from Scola's best work. Video release is titled PASSION OF LOVE.▼

Passion Flower (1986) **C-100m. TVM** D: Joseph Sargent. Bruce Boxleitner, Barbara Hershey, Nicol Williamson, John Waters, Dick O'Neill, Peggy Williamson. Sinister doings in exotic Singapore among the monied class in this homage to B movies of the late '30s. Except that George Brent, Ann Sheridan, and Claude Rains did it so much better. Average.

Passion Flower Hotel, The SEE: **Boarding School**▼

Passion of Anna, The (1969-Swedish) **C-101m. ***½ D:** Ingmar Bergman. Liv Ullmann, Bibi Andersson, Max von Sydow, Erland Josephson, Erik Hell. Stark drama,

beautifully acted, about von Sydow, living alone on a barely populated island, and relationship with widow Ullmann, architect Josephson, and wife Andersson. Superior cinematography by Sven Nykvist. Original title was simply—and more accurately—A PASSION.

Passion of Beatrice, The SEE: **Beatrice**▼

Passion of Joan of Arc, The (1928-French) **77m. **** D:** Carl Theodor Dreyer. Maria Falconetti, Eugene Sylvain, Maurice Schutz. Joan of Arc's inquisition, trial, and burning at the stake; the scenario is based on transcript of historical trial. Masterfully directed, with groundbreaking use of close-ups; Falconetti glows in the title role. Photographed by Rudolph Maté.▼

Passion of Love SEE: **Passion d'Amore**▼

Passions (1984) **C-100m. TVM** D: Sandor Stern. Lindsay Wagner, Joanne Woodward, Richard Crenna, Mason Adams, Heather Langenkamp, John Considine, Albert Hague, Viveca Lindfors. High-gloss soaper elevated by Woodward's portrayal of loving wife who finds herself pitted against her wealthy hubby's mistress after he suddenly dies and she discovers that he has another family. Average.

Passport to Adventure SEE: **Passport to Destiny**

Passport to China (1961-British) **C-75m. ** D:** Michael Carreras. Richard Basehart, Alan Gifford, Athene Seyler, Burt Kwouk, Eric Pohlmann. Uninspired help-the-refugee-out-of-Red-China caper.

Passport to Destiny (1944) **64m. ** D:** Ray McCarey. Elsa Lanchester, Gordon Oliver, Lloyd Corrigan, Gavin Muir, Lenore Aubert, Fritz Feld. Tidy programmer with Elsa a patriotic scrubwoman determined to eliminate the Fuehrer. Retitled: PASSPORT TO ADVENTURE.

Passport to Pimlico (1949-British) **85m. ***½ D:** Henry Cornelius. Stanley Holloway, Margaret Rutherford, Betty Warren, Hermione Baddeley, Barbara Murray, Basil Radford, Naunton Wayne, Paul Dupuis, Michael Hordern. Salty farce of ancient treaty enabling small group of people to form their own bounded territory in the middle of London. Screenplay by Cornelius and T.E.B. Clarke.▼

Passport to Suez (1943) **71m.** D: Andre de Toth. Warren William, Ann Savage, Eric Blore, Robert Stanford, Sheldon Leonard, Lloyd Bridges, Gavin Muir. SEE: **Lone Wolf** series.

Passport to Treason (1955-British) **70m. *½ D:** Robert S. Baker. Rod Cameron, Lois Maxwell, Clifford Evans. Minor drama, with Cameron trying to solve homicide case for sake of friend.

Pass the Ammo (1988) **C-97m. BOMB** D: David Beaird. Bill Paxton, Linda Kozlowski, Tim Curry, Annie Potts, Dennis Burkley, Glenn Withrow, Anthony

Geary, Richard Paul. Shrill, heavy-handed spoof of televangelists that blunts its satiric edge by making its "heroes" (a young couple out to rob the church) so thoroughly disreputable. This subject cries for a better comedy.▼

Password Is Courage, The (1963-British) **116m.** *** D: Andrew L. Stone. Dirk Bogarde, Maria Perschy, Alfred Lynch, Nigel Stock, Reginald Beckwith, Richard Marner. Bogarde tops a fine cast in droll account of British soldier's plot to escape from WW2 prison camp.

Past Caring (1985-British) **C-77m.** ** D: Richard Eyre. Denholm Elliott, Emlyn Williams, Connie Booth, Joan Greenwood, Dave Atkins. Tepid, disappointing tale of roguish Elliott, approaching old age, who finds himself incarcerated in a home for senile senior citizens. Williams scores as an elderly homosexual bent on reliving his youth.

Pat and Mike (1952) **95m.** *** D: George Cukor. Spencer Tracy, Katharine Hepburn, Aldo Ray, William Ching, Jim Backus, Carl ("Alfalfa") Switzer, Charles Buchinski (Bronson), William Self, Chuck Connors. Hepburn is Pat, top female athlete; Tracy is Mike, her manager, in pleasing comedy, not up to duo's other films. Ray is good as thick-witted sports star. Written by Ruth Gordon and Garson Kanin; many sports notables appear briefly as themselves.▼

Patch of Blue, A (1965) **105m.** *** D: Guy Green. Sidney Poitier, Elizabeth Hartman, Shelley Winters, Wallace Ford, Ivan Dixon, John Qualen, Elisabeth Fraser. Sensitive drama of blind girl (Hartman) falling in love with black man (Poitier); well acted, not too sticky. Winters won Oscar as Hartman's harridan mother.▼

Paternity (1981) **C-94m.** *½ D: David Steinberg. Burt Reynolds, Beverly D'Angelo, Norman Fell, Paul Dooley, Elizabeth Ashley, Lauren Hutton, Juanita Moore, Mike Kellin. Bachelor Burt, the manager of Madison Square Garden, yearns to be a papa, so he hires waitress-music student D'Angelo as surrogate mother. Predictable comedy with lethargic performances. Actor-comic Steinberg's directorial debut.▼

Pat Garrett and Billy the Kid (1973) **C-122m.** ** D: Sam Peckinpah. James Coburn, Kris Kristofferson, Richard Jaeckel, Katy Jurado, Chill Wills, Jason Robards, Bob Dylan, Rita Coolidge, Jack Elam, R. G. Armstrong, Slim Pickens, Harry Dean Stanton, L. Q. Jones, Barry Sullivan, Elisha Cook, Jr. Revisionist look at Sheriff Garrett (Coburn) and his pursuit of ex-crony Billy the Kid (Kristofferson) is interesting but far from grade-A Peckinpah; for one thing, there isn't enough contrast in the two low-key lead performances. The director's version, which was never released

to theaters, now appears on homevideo and cable, and is a definite improvement over the badly paced 103m. that opened in 1973. Dylan's role is insignificant, but his score does include the hit "Knockin' on Heaven's Door." Yet another version of the film, minus much violence, was released to commercial TV in the 1970s.▼

Pather Panchali (1955-Indian) **112m.** ***½ D: Satyajit Ray. Kanu Banerji, Karuna Banerji, Subir Banerji, Runki Banerji, Uma Das Gupta, Chunibala Devi. Unrelenting study of a poverty-stricken Indian family in Bengal. Grippingly realistic, with Karuna and Subir Banerji outstanding as the mother and her young son Apu. Ray's feature debut, and the first of his "Apu" trilogy. Music by Ravi Shankar.▼

Pathfinder, The (1952) **C-78m.** *½ D: Sidney Salkow. George Montgomery, Helena Carter, Jay Silverheels, Elena Verdugo, Chief Yowlachie. Low-budget version of James Fenimore Cooper tale of 1750s Great Lakes area, with Indian and French attacks on Americans.

Paths of Glory (1957) **86m.** **** D: Stanley Kubrick. Kirk Douglas, Ralph Meeker, Adolphe Menjou, George Macready, Wayne Morris, Richard Anderson, Timothy Carey, Suzanne Christian, Bert Freed. During WW1, French general Macready orders his men on a futile mission; when they fail, he picks three soldiers to be tried and executed for cowardice. Shattering study of the insanity of war has grown even more profound with the years; stunningly acted and directed. Calder Willingham, Jim Thompson, and Kubrick adapted Humphrey Cobb's novel—based on fact.▼

Patricia Neal Story, The (1981) **C-100m.** TVM D: Anthony Harvey, Anthony Page. Glenda Jackson, Dirk Bogarde, Mildred Dunnock, Ken Kercheval, Jane Merrow, John Reilly. Splendid performances by the two leads in their American TV-movie debuts and Dunnock playing herself give added distinction to this dramatized account of Neal's recovery from a near-fatal stroke with the aid of author husband Roald Dahl. Sensitively adapted by playwright Robert Anderson from Barry Farrell's book *Pat and Roald*. Above average.

Patrick (1978-Australian) **C-96m.** *½ D: Richard Franklin. Susan Penhaligon, Robert Helpmann, Robert Thompson, Rod Mullinar, Bruce Barry, Julia Blake. Patrick's in a comatose state after violently murdering his mum, but his psychokinetic powers are still intact, as the hospital staff soon discovers in this tacky thriller.▼

Patriot, The (1986) **C-88m.** *½ D: Frank Harris. Gregg Henry, Simone Griffeth,

Michael J. Pollard, Jeff Conaway, Leslie Nielsen, Stack Pierce, Glenn Withrow. Underwater action dominates this low-key action film. Dishonorably discharged Henry is recruited to retrieve a stolen nuclear warhead and redeem himself.▼

Patsy, The (1964) **C-101m.** ** D: Jerry Lewis. Jerry Lewis, Ina Balin, Everett Sloane, Keenan Wynn, Peter Lorre, John Carradine, Neil Hamilton, Nancy Kulp. When a top comedian is killed in a plane crash, his sycophants try to groom a bellhop (guess who?) into taking his place. Forced, unfunny combination of humor and pathos, much inferior to somewhat similar ERRAND BOY; even first-rate supporting cast can't bail itself out. Lorre's last film.▼

Pattern of Morality, A SEE: **Owen Marshall, Counsellor at Law**

Patterns (1956) **83m.** ***½ D: Fielder Cook. Van Heflin, Everett Sloane, Ed Begley, Beatrice Straight, Elizabeth Wilson. Trenchant Rod Serling drama of company power struggle, with bravura performance by Begley. Executive psychology of mid-50s is dated, but much better than similar EXECUTIVE SUITE. Based on Serling's 1955 *Kraft TV Theatre* play, which also starred Sloane and Begley.▼

Patti Rocks (1988) **C-86m.** ** D: David Burton Morris. Chris Mulkey, John Jenkins, Karen Landry, David L. Turk, Stephen Yoakum. Married male chauvinist engages an estranged male pal to accompany him on a marathon drive to visit the woman he's impregnated; she turns out to be a self-assured, no-nonsense type—the very opposite of how she's been portrayed. Low budget film has a compelling idea, but doesn't play nearly as well as it should. Same characters previously seen in Victoria Wozniak's LOOSE ENDS (1975).▼

Patton (1970) **C-169m.** **** D: Franklin Schaffner. George C. Scott, Karl Malden, Stephen Young, Michael Strong, Frank Latimore, James Edwards, Lawrence Dobkin, Michael Bates, Tim Considine. Milestone in screen biographies; Scott unforgettable as eccentric, brilliant General George Patton, whose temper often interferes with command during WW2. Malden equally impressive as General Omar Bradley in intelligently written, finely wrought biographical war drama. Winner of seven Oscars, including Best Picture, Actor, Director, Screenplay (Francis Ford Coppola and Edmund H. North). Scott reprised the role 16 years later in the TVM, THE LAST DAYS OF PATTON.▼

Patty Hearst (1988) **C-108m.** *½ D: Paul Schrader. Natasha Richardson, William Forsythe, Ving Rhamer, Dana Delany, Frances Fisher, Jodi Long, Olivia Barash, Scott Kraft, Ermal Washington, Gerald Gordon. Stillborn dramatization of the newspaper heiress's kidnapping and subsequent brainwashing by the Symbionese Liberation Army. Film never recovers from a deadly opening half hour that attempts to convey, from victim's point of view, the effects of highly orchestrated psychological torture. Richardson manages to make a strong impression, despite having almost nothing to work with. Screenplay by Nicholas Kazan.▼

Paula (1952) **80m.** **½ D: Rudolph Mate. Loretta Young, Kent Smith, Alexander Knox, Tommy Rettig. Young gives credibility to role of woman who repents for hit-and-run accident by helping injured child regain his speech.

Paul and Michelle (1974-British) **C-103m.** BOMB D: Lewis Gilbert. Sean Bury, Anicee Alvina, Keir Dullea, Catherine Allegret, Ronald Lewis. Why anyone would even *want* a sequel to FRIENDS requires an investigation we must take up one of these days; further antics of those lovable teeny-boppers have about as much bearing on real life as anything Dullea encountered while going through the 2001 space-warp.

Pauline at the Beach (1983-French) **C-94m.** *** D: Eric Rohmer. Amanda Langlet, Arielle Dombasle, Pascal Greggory, Feodor Atkine, Simon de la Brosse, Rosette. Witty, entertaining comedy of morals and manners that contrasts the hypocrisy of adult relationships and the straightforwardness of young people, as seen when a teenage girl (Langlet) spends the summer with her sexy, self-possessed older cousin (Dombasle). The third of Rohmer's "Comedies and Proverbs" series.▼

Pawnbroker, The (1965) **116m.** **** D: Sidney Lumet. Rod Steiger, Geraldine Fitzgerald, Brock Peters, Jaime Sanchez, Thelma Oliver, Juano Hernandez, Raymond St. Jacques. Important, engrossing film shot on location in N.Y.C. Steiger is excellent as Sol Nazerman, a Jewish pawnbroker in Harlem who lives in a sheltered world with haunting memories of Nazi prison camps. Notable editing by Ralph Rosenblum and music by Quincy Jones. Edward Lewis Wallant's novel was adapted by David Friedkin and Morton Fine.▼

Pawnee (1957) **C-80m.** ** D: George Waggner. George Montgomery, Bill Williams, Lola Albright, Francis J. McDonald, Raymond Hatton. Pat Western about Indian-raised white man with conflicting loyalties.

Payday (1973) **C-103m.** ***½ D: Daryl Duke. Rip Torn, Ahna Capri, Elayne Heilveil, Cliff Emmich, Michael C. Gwynne. Solidly acted, finely scripted (by Don Carpenter) tale of life on the road with country singer Torn. Engrossing and very well done: a sleeper.▼

Payment Deferred (1932) **81m.** *** D:

[878]

Lothar Mendes. Charles Laughton, Maureen O'Sullivan, Dorothy Peterson, Verree Teasdale, Ray Milland, Billy Bevan. Very theatrical yet engrossing little film about a milquetoast who finds himself tangled up in murder. Laughton is at his most idiosyncratic, with all manner of facial grimaces and gestures.

Payment on Demand (1951) **90m.** *** D: Curtis Bernhardt. Bette Davis, Barry Sullivan, Peggie Castle, Jane Cowl, Kent Taylor, Betty Lynn, John Sutton, Frances Dee, Otto Kruger. Well-handled chronicle of Davis-Sullivan marriage, highlighting events which lead to divorce.

Pay or Die (1960) **110m.** **½ D: Richard Wilson. Ernest Borgnine, Zohra Lampert, Al Austin, John Duke, Robert Ellenstein, Franco Corsaro, Mario Siletti. Above-par, flavorful account of Mafia activities in 1910s N.Y.C.; sturdy performances.▼

Payroll (1961-British) **94m.** **½ D: Sidney Hayers. Michael Craig, Francoise Prevost, Billie Whitelaw, William Lucas, Kenneth Griffith, Tom Bell. Well-handled account involving widow of payroll guard tracking down culprits.

Peace Killers, The (1971) **C-88m.** *½ D: Douglas Schwartz. Clint Ritchie, Jesse Walton, Paul Prokop, Darlene Duralia. Motorcycle hoods ravage peaceful commune like Attila the Hun. Sick, Sick, Sick.▼

Peacemaker, The (1956) **82m.** ** D: Ted Post. James Mitchell, Rosemarie Bowe, Robert Armstrong, Jan Merlin, Dorothy Patrick, Jess Barker, Hugh Sanders. Exgunslinger, now clergyman, tries to clean up the town.

Peacemaker (1990) **C-90m.** ** D: Kevin S. Tenney. Robert Forster, Lance Edwards, Hilary Shepard, Robert Davi, Bert Remsen. Yet another alien cop after alien villain movie, pitting Forster against Edwards, with novel twist: both claim to be the cop, causing Earthwoman Shepard any number of problems. Lots of stunts and action, but also lots of absolutely awful wisecracks. Written by the director.▼

Pearl, The (1948) **77m.** *** D: Emilio Fernandez. Pedro Armendariz, Maria Elena Marques. Mexican-filmed John Steinbeck tale of poor fisherman whose life is unhappily altered by finding valuable pearl; a bit heavy-handed. Beautifully photographed by Gabriel Figueroa.▼

Pearl of Death, The (1944) **69m.** D: Roy William Neill. Basil Rathbone, Nigel Bruce, Evelyn Ankers, Miles Mander, Dennis Hoey, Rondo Hatton, Richard Nugent, Mary Gordon, Holmes Herbert. SEE: **Sherlock Holmes** series.▼

Pearl of the South Pacific (1955) **C-86m.** *½ D: Allan Dwan. Virginia Mayo, Dennis Morgan, David Farrar, Murvyn Vye. Dud of a film trying to be exotic, intriguing; just a boring murder tale.▼

Peck's Bad Boy (1921) **51m.** *** D: Sam Wood. Jackie Coogan, Wheeler Oakman, Doris May, Raymond Hatton, Lillian Leighton. Still-fresh and enjoyable vehicle for child-star Coogan as young mischief-maker; clever card-titles written by humorist Irvin S. Cobb.▼

Peck's Bad Boy (1934) **70m.** **½ D: Edward Cline. Jackie Cooper, Thomas Meighan, Jackie Searle, O. P. Heggie. Cooper is ideally cast in familiar tale of troublesome brat causing his parents endless problems.

Peck's Bad Boy With the Circus (1938) **78m.** ** D: Edward Cline. Tommy Kelly, Ann Gillis, Edgar Kennedy, Billy Gilbert, Benita Hume, Spanky MacFarland, Grant Mitchell. Standard circus story slanted for kiddies. Kennedy and Gilbert wrap this one up.▼

Pedestrian, The (1974-German) **C-97m.** ***½ D: Maximilian Schell. Gustav Rudolf Sellner, Peter Hall, Maximilian Schell, Gila von Weitershausen. Excellent award-winner examines death and guilt, when successful industrialist Sellner is revealed to have been a Nazi officer who participated in the slaughter of a Greek village. Veteran actresses Elisabeth Bergner, Francoise Rosay, Lil Dagover and Peggy Ashcroft appear in one scene.▼

Peeper (1975) **C-87m.** *½ D: Peter Hyams. Michael Caine, Natalie Wood, Kitty Winn, Thayer David, Liam Dunn, Dorothy Adams. Tepid take-off of 40s detective dramas with Caine becoming involved with a weird family while trying to locate the long-lost daughter of his client. Best bit: the opening credits, recited by Bogart impersonator Jerry Lacy. Also known as FAT CHANCE!

Peeping Tom (1960-British) **109m.** *** D: Michael Powell. Carl Boehm, Moira Shearer, Anna Massey, Maxine Audley, Brenda Bruce, Martin Miller. Sensational film—denounced in 1960—has developed a fervent following in recent years; personal feelings will dictate your reaction to story of psychopathic murderer who photographs his victims at the moment of death. Originally released in the U.S. at 101m.; full version restored in 1979.▼

Pee-wee's Big Adventure (1985) **C-90m.** **½ D: Tim Burton. Pee-wee Herman (Paul Reubens), Elizabeth Daily, Mark Holton, Diane Salinger, Tony Bill, Cassandra Peterson, James Brolin, Morgan Fairchild. A live-action cartoon (directed by former animator Burton) featuring the cartoonish Pee-wee, a nine-year-old boy in a grown-up's body. Some real laughs and clever ideas as Pee-wee searches for his stolen bicycle, but not enough to sustain a feature-length film. Best sequence: the tour of the Alamo. Wonderful music by Danny Elfman.▼

Peg o' My Heart (1933) **89m.** *** D:

Robert Z. Leonard. Marion Davies, Onslow Stevens, J. Farrell MacDonald, Irene Browne, Juliette Compton, Alan Mowbray. Sweet, old-fashioned vehicle for Davies as spunky Irish lass who's separated from her father and brought to ritzy English manor, to fulfill terms of inheritance. Corny but fun. Filmed before in 1922 with Laurette Taylor.

Peggy (1950) **C-77m.** **½ D: Frederick de Cordova. Diana Lynn, Charles Coburn, Charlotte Greenwood, Rock Hudson, Jerome Cowan, Barbara Lawrence. Lightweight comedy of sisters Lynn and Lawrence entered in Rose Bowl Parade beauty contest.

Peggy Sue Got Married (1986) **C-104m.** **½ D: Francis Coppola. Kathleen Turner, Nicolas Cage, Barry Miller, Catherine Hicks, Joan Allen, Kevin J. O'Connor, Barbara Harris, Don Murray, Maureen O'Sullivan, Leon Ames, Helen Hunt, John Carradine. 43-year-old woman, on the verge of divorce, magically travels back in time to her senior year in high school and has to deal with (among other things) her boyfriend and future husband. Turner's radiant star-power bolsters this pleasant, often wistful film, whose script leaves far too many plot threads dangling. Cage's annoying performance as the boyfriend is another debit. ▼

Peking Blonde (1968-French) **C-80m.** *½ D: Nicolas Gessner. Mirielle Darc, Claudio Brook, Edward G. Robinson, Pascale Roberts, Francoise Brion. Obscure melodrama with Chinese, Russian and American spies searching for missile information and a pearl. Robinson looks bored in a small role as a CIA agent. Also known as THE BLONDE FROM PEKING.

Peking Express (1951) **95m.** **½ D: William Dieterle. Joseph Cotten, Corinne Calvet, Edmund Gwenn, Marvin Miller, Benson Fong. Remake of SHANGHAI EXPRESS lacks flavor or distinction. Cotten is the doctor and Calvet the shady lady he encounters on train.

Pelle the Conqueror (1988-Danish-Swedish) **C-150m.** ***½ D: Bille August. Max von Sydow, Pelle Hvenegaard, Erik Paaske, Kristina Törnqvist, Morten Jorgensen. Wonderful 19th-century drama about a humble old widower (von Sydow) and his young son Pelle (Hvenegaard), Swedish immigrants in Denmark. They are simple folk with simple, modest dreams, yet they must valiantly struggle for survival in a world rife with everyday cruelties and injustices. The life-sustaining closeness between father and son is especially poignant. Martin Andersen Nexo's four-volume novel (only a fraction of which is depicted here) was adapted by the director. Oscar winner as Best Foreign Film.▼

Penalty, The (1941) **81m.** ** D: Harold S. Bucquet. Edward Arnold, Lionel Barrymore, Marsha Hunt, Robert Sterling, Gene Reynolds, Emma Dunn, Veda Ann Borg. Unengrossing mystery-drama of F.B.I. agent's scheme to catch gangster by using his son for bait. Good cast in dull script.

Penalty Phase (1986) **C-100m. TVM** D: Tony Richardson. Peter Strauss, Melissa Gilbert, Jonelle Allen, Karen Austin, Jane Badler, Millie Perkins, Mitchell Ryan. Well-turned drama of a respected judge who jeopardizes his career by letting a vicious killer, whose rights may have been violated, walk. A rare television sojourn by noted British director Richardson, working from a splendid script by lawyer-turned-writer Gale Patrick Hickman. Above average.▼

Pendulum (1969) **C-106m.** **½ D: George Schaefer. George Peppard, Jean Seberg, Richard Kiley, Charles McGraw, Madeleine Sherwood, Robert F. Lyons, Marj Dusay. Half baked whodunit has intriguing aspects but leaves too many loose ends, as police captain Peppard is suddenly accused of murder. Smoothly done, with flashy role for Sherwood as mother of young criminal, good score by Walter Scharf, but no great shakes.▼

Penelope (1966) **C-97m.** *½ D: Arthur Hiller. Natalie Wood, Ian Bannen, Dick Shawn, Peter Falk, Jonathan Winters, Lila Kedrova, Lou Jacobi, Jerome Cowan. Neglected Nat robs her husband's bank of $60,000 in this quite unfunny comedy; Winters' bit lasts only three minutes.

Penguin Pool Murder (1932) **70m.** *** D: George Archainbaud. Edna May Oliver, James Gleason, Mae Clarke, Robert Armstrong, Donald Cook. Cop Gleason and schoolteacher Oliver team up to solve unusual murder in entertaining film that launched short-lived series.

Penitent, The (1988) **C-94m.** **½ D: Cliff Osmond. Raul Julia, Armand Assante, Rona Freed, Julie Carmen, Lucy Reina. Odd, ironic little fable bites off more than it can chew, with ex-con Assante seducing pal Julia's young wife. Set in a remote town whose villagers each year reenact Christ's crucifixion—which, of course, plays a major part in the proceedings. Actor Osmond's directing debut. Filmed in 1986.▼

Penitentiary (1979) **C-99m.** **½ D: Jamaa Fanaka. Leon Isaac Kennedy, Thommy Pollard, Hazel Spears, Badja Djola, Gloria Delaney, Chuck Mitchell. Predictable but impassioned prison film, produced, directed and written by Fanaka, about a young black man (Kennedy) wrongly accused and imprisoned who improves his lot by boxing. Hard-hitting look at corruption, violence and homosexuality of daily prison life. Followed by several sequels.▼

Penitentiary II (1982) **C-103m.** BOMB D: Jamaa Fanaka. Leon Isaac Kennedy, Ernie Hudson, Mr. T., Glynn Turman, Peggy Blow, Malik Carter, Cephaus Jaxon, Marvin Jones. Atrocious, disappointing sequel, with Kennedy back in prison and the ring. Leon Isaac plays "Too Sweet," the villain's name is "Half Dead," the viewer is "Ripped Off."▼

Penitentiary III (1987) **C-91m.** *½ D: Jamaa Fanaka. Leon Isaac Kennedy, Anthony Geary, Steve Antin, Ric Mancini, Kessler Raymond, Jim Bailey. Latest in the series is an improvement over number II—but that's not saying very much. Here, Kennedy is back in jail, where both warden and mob kingpin want him for their boxing teams. Silly and mindless time killer.▼

Penn & Teller Get Killed (1989) **C-90m.** ** D: Arthur Penn. Penn Jillette, Teller, Caitlin Clarke, David Patrick Kelly, Jon Cryer, Christopher Durang, Leonardo Cimino, Celia McGuire. The bad boys of magic, guesting on a nationally televised talk show, touch off gore galore when partner Penn speculates how much fun life might be if some viewer would attempt to kill him. Barely released effort does have the courage of some sicko comic convictions. Definite cult possibilities; others beware.▼

Pennies From Heaven (1936) **81m.** **½ D: Norman Z. McLeod. Bing Crosby, Edith Fellows, Madge Evans, Donald Meek, Louis Armstrong. Minor but pleasant Crosby vehicle about a self-styled troubadour and drifter who befriends orphaned girl (Fellows) and her grandfather (Meek). Bing's rendition of title tune is particularly pretty.

Pennies From Heaven (1981) **C-107m.** *** D: Herbert Ross. Steve Martin, Bernadette Peters, Christopher Walken, Jessica Harper, Vernel Bagneris, John McMartin, Jay Garner, Tommy Rall. A unique, remarkable film, parts of which are greater than the whole. Based on Dennis Potter's British TV mini-series about a sheet-music salesman during the Depression whose restless, unhappy life is sharply contrasted with cheery songs of the day. Stunning 1930s-style musical numbers (set to original recordings) clash with bleak, Edward Hopper-esque vision of the period. The mixture is intellectually provocative, but troubling as entertainment. Beautifully photographed by Gordon Willis and designed by Ken Adam.▼

Penn of Pennsylvania SEE: **Courageous Mr. Penn**.

Penny Princess (1951-British) **C-91m.** *** D: Val Guest. Dirk Bogarde, Yolande Donlan, Fletcher Lightfoot, Kynaston Reeves. Charming frou-frou of American Donlan going to Europe to collect inheritance of small principality, and Bogarde who courts her.

Penny Serenade (1941) **125m.** ***½ D: George Stevens. Irene Dunne, Cary Grant, Beulah Bondi, Edgar Buchanan, Ann Doran, Eva Lee Kuney. Quintessential soap opera, with Dunne and Grant as couple who adopt baby after their unborn baby dies. A wonderful tearjerker, written by Morrie Ryskind.▼

Penrod and His Twin Brother (1938) **63m.** ** D: William McGann. Billy Mauch, Bobby Mauch, Frank Craven, Spring Byington, Charles Halton, Claudia Coleman. Penrod gets blamed for something he didn't do; answer is his lookalike who's really guilty. Vaguely captures 1900s Midwest America.

Penrod and Sam (1937) **64m.** **½ D: William McGann. Billy Mauch, Frank Craven, Spring Byington, Craig Reynolds, Bernice Pilot. Based on Booth Tarkington characters, family-style film relates tale of Mauch getting involved with bank robbers.

Penrod's Double Trouble (1938) **61m.** ** D: Lewis Seiler. Billy Mauch, Bobby Mauch, Dick Purcell, Gene Lockhart, Kathleen Lockhart, Hugh O'Connell. There's a reward up for Penrod's return, but a lookalike is turned in instead. Satisfactory for younger audiences; based on Booth Tarkington characters.

Penthouse (1933) **90m.** ***½ D: W. S. Van Dyke. Warner Baxter, Myrna Loy, Charles Butterworth, Mae Clarke, C. Henry Gordon. Terrific comedy-melodrama, with Baxter as criminal lawyer who enlists the help of sprightly call-girl Loy to nail a crime kingpin. A neglected gem. Remade as SOCIETY LAWYER.

Penthouse, The (1967-British) **C-96m.** *½ D: Peter Collinson. Suzy Kendall, Terence Morgan, Tony Beckley, Martine Beswick. Lurid thriller of adulterous couple whose "love nest" is invaded by two thugs who, by torture, bring out true nature of the pair.

Penthouse, The (1989) **C-100m.** TVM D: David Greene. Robin Givens, Robert Guillaume, David Hewlett, Cedric Smith, Donnelly Rhodes. Givens stars as a pampered young woman held prisoner in her lavish penthouse by a wacko. Average.

People, The (1971) **C-74m.** TVM D: John Korty. Kim Darby, Dan O'Herlihy, Diane Varsi, William Shatner, Laurie Walters. Young teacher taking job in desolate area discovers she's got out-of-the-ordinary kids for students. Adaptation of Zenna Henderson novel leaves lots to be desired, but performances, script's uneven qualities and atmosphere still worthwhile. Above average sci-fi.▼

People Across the Lake, The (1988) **C-100m.** TVM D: Arthur Allan Seidelman. Valerie Harper, Gerald McRaney, Barry

Corbin, Tammy Lauren, Dorothy Lyman, Daryl Anderson, Jeff Kizer. A couple abandons big-city life for a lakeside community, only to find that they haven't left crime behind; bodies start popping up in their basement! Leisurely paced, straight-faced thriller that's shot full of holes. Average.

People Against O'Hara, The (1951) **102m.** **½ D: John Sturges. Spencer Tracy, Pat O'Brien, Diana Lynn, John Hodiak, Eduardo Ciannelli, Jay C. Flippen, James Arness, Arthur Shields, William Campbell. Middling drama, with Tracy a noted criminal lawyer who repents for unethical behavior during a case. Look fast for Charles Bronson as one of Campbell's brothers.

People Next Door, The (1970) **C-93m.** ** D: David Greene. Deborah Winters, Eli Wallach, Julie Harris, Stephen McHattie, Hal Holbrook, Cloris Leachman, Nehemiah Persoff. JP Miller's adaptation of his TV play has dated pretty badly; Wallach and Harris' hand-wringing concern over their junkie teenage daughter now seems stiff, and Winters' overacting just the opposite. Good cast and intentions, but there are many other, better films on the topic.▼

People's Enemy SEE: **Prison Train** ▼
People That Time Forgot, The (1977-British) **C-90m.** **½ D: Kevin Connor. Patrick Wayne, Doug McClure, Sarah Douglas, Dana Gillespie, Thorley Walters, Shane Rimmer. OK sequel to THE LAND THAT TIME FORGOT. Wayne leads a party back to mysterious island in 1919 to find friend McClure, lost three years before. Based on Edgar Rice Burroughs' book, film has some effective monsters, though special effects are erratic.▼

People Toys SEE: **Devil Times Five**▼
People vs. Dr. Kildare, The (1941) **78m.** D: Harold S. Bucquet. Lew Ayres, Lionel Barrymore, Laraine Day, Bonita Granville, Alma Kruger, Red Skelton, Paul Stanton, Diana Lewis. SEE: **Dr. Kildare** series.

People vs. Jean Harris, The (1981) **C-150m.** TVM D: George Schaefer. Ellen Burstyn, Martin Balsam, Richard Dysart, Peter Coyote, Priscilla Morrill, Sarah Marshall, Millie Slavin (narrator). The murder trial of private-school headmistress Jean Harris, convicted of the slaying of her lover, *Scarsdale Diet* author Dr. Herman Tarnower, was recreated in record time for a movie (TV or otherwise), premiering five weeks after the fact. Burstyn won an Emmy Award nomination as Best Actress. Shot on videotape. Above average.▼

People Will Talk (1935) **67m.** **½ D: Alfred Santell. Mary Boland, Charles Ruggles, Leila Hyams, Dean Jagger, Ruthelma Stevens, Hans Steinke. Slim comedy about married couple pretending to fight to teach daughter a lesson. Boland and Ruggles could read a newspaper and make it funny.

People Will Talk (1951) **110m.** ***½ D: Joseph L. Mankiewicz. Cary Grant, Jeanne Crain, Finlay Currie, Walter Slezak, Hume Cronyn, Sidney Blackmer. Genuinely offbeat, absorbing comedy-drama of philosophical doctor Grant and patient Crain who becomes his wife. Fine cast in talky but most worthwhile film.

Pepe (1960) **C-157m.** BOMB D: George Sidney. Cantinflas, Dan Dailey, Shirley Jones, 35 guest stars. Incredibly long, pointless film wastes talents of Cantinflas and many, many others (Edward G. Robinson, Maurice Chevalier, etc.). This one's only if you're desperate. Originally released at 195m.

Pepe Le Moko (1937-French) **86m.** **** D: Julien Duvivier. Jean Gabin, Mireille Balin, Gabriel Gabrio, Lucas Gridoux. Gabin is magnetic (in role that brought him international prominence) as gangster who eludes capture in Casbah section of Algiers, until he is lured out of hiding by a beautiful woman. Exquisitely photographed and directed; faithfully remade the following year as ALGIERS, later musicalized as CASBAH.▼

Peppermint Soda (1977-French) **C-97m.** *** D: Diane Kurys. Eleanore Klarwein, Odile Michel, Coralie Clement, Marie-Veronique Maurin. Sensitive, keenly realized autobiographical (by Kurys, who also scripted) examination of early adolescence, complete with disciplinarian teacher, parents' divorce, menstrual cramps, first love. Followed by COCKTAIL MOLOTOV.▼

Percy (1971-British) **C-100m.** *½ D: Ralph Thomas. Hywel Bennett, Denholm Elliott, Elke Sommer, Britt Ekland, Cyd Hayman, Janet Key. Bennett receives the world's first penis transplant and, curious, sets out to learn about its previous owner. Some interesting points could've been made, but Thomas apparently thought he was making a *Carry On* film; too bad. Followed by PERCY'S PROGRESS.

Percy's Progress SEE: **It's Not the Size That Counts**▼

Perfect (1985) **C-120m.** *½ D: James Bridges. John Travolta, Jamie Lee Curtis, Jann Wenner, Anne De Salvo, Stefan Gierasch, Laraine Newman, Marilu Henner. *Rolling Stone* reporter Travolta (who keeps his computer running all night in case he gets a sudden inspiration) is writing an exposé of L.A. health clubs but finds himself attracted to aerobics instructor Curtis, whom he's about to trash in print. A smug, overlong, misguided, miscast movie, with hints of intelligent intentions; written by Bridges and reporter Aaron Latham. Real-life *Rolling Stone* editor Wenner plays himself. Wait till you hear John and Jamie Lee expound on Emersonian values!▼

Perfect Couple, A (1979) **C-110m.** ***
D: Robert Altman. Paul Dooley, Marta
Heflin, Titos Vandis, Belita Moreno, Henry
Gibson, Dimitra Arliss, Alan Nicholls,
Ted Neeley. Offbeat but endearing roman-
tic comedy about unlikely match-up (by
computer dating) of straitlaced Dooley,
under the thumb of his overbearing father,
and singer Heflin, whose life is wrapped
up with her familial rock group. Enjoyable
music by Neeley's *ad hoc* group Keepin'
'em Off the Streets.
Perfect Friday (1970-British) **94m.** ***
D: Peter Hall. Stanley Baker, Ursula
Andress, David Warner, Patience Collier,
T.P. McKenna. Staid bank employee
Baker decides to break loose, and plans
daring heist, with beautiful Andress and
her oddball husband Warner in cahoots.
Entertaining caper movie with some delicious twists.
Perfect Furlough, The (1958) **C-93m.**
**½ D: Blake Edwards. Tony Curtis,
Janet Leigh, Keenan Wynn, Linda Cristal,
Elaine Stritch, Troy Donahue. Diverting
comedy of soldier Curtis winning trip
to France, romancing military psychiatrist
Leigh.▼
Perfect Gentlemen (1978) **C-100m. TVM**
D: Jackie Cooper. Lauren Bacall, Ruth
Gordon, Sandy Dennis, Lisa Pelikan, Rob-
ert Alda, Stephen Pearlman. Engaging bank
heist tale by Nora Ephron involving three
prison widows and a safe-cracking old
lady. Bacall's TV movie debut. Above
average.
Perfect Marriage, The (1946) **87m.**
** D: Lewis Allen. Loretta Young, David
Niven, Eddie Albert, Charles Ruggles,
Virginia Field, Rita Johnson, ZaSu Pitts.
Niven's tired of wife Young; Young's
tired of husband Niven; tired comedy-
drama.
Perfect Match, A (1980) **C-100m. TVM**
D: Mel Damski. Linda Kelsey, Michael
Brandon, Charles Durning, Colleen Dew-
hurst, Lisa Lucas, Bonnie Bartlett. John
Sayles wrote this drama about a mother
stricken with a mysterious illness who must
locate the daughter she gave up for adop-
tion as a teenager. Average.
Perfect Match, The (1987) **C-92m.** **½
D: Mark Deimel. Marc McClure, Jennifer
Edwards, Diane Stilwell, Rob Paulsen,
Wayne Woodsen, Karen Witter, Jeane Byron. Likable leads in a modest romantic
comedy about two singles who meet through
the newspaper's personal ads.▼
Perfect People (1988) **C-100m. TVM** D:
Bruce Seth Green. Lauren Hutton, Perry
King, Priscilla Barnes, Karen Valentine,
June Lockhart, David Leisure. Amusing
look at a long-married couple that opts to
trade in their out-of-shape couch-potato
selves for a new lifestyle of diet, exercise,
and plastic surgery. The fun is seeing

"perfect" people Lauren and Perry as
middle-aged schlumps in this teleplay by
Greg Goodell. Above average.
Perfect Specimen, The (1937) **97m.** **½
D: Michael Curtiz. Errol Flynn, Joan
Blondell, Hugh Herbert, Edward Everett
Horton, Dick Foran, May Robson, Bev-
erly Roberts, Allen Jenkins. Fairly amus-
ing whimsy about super-rich Flynn, who's
kept locked up and sheltered by grand-
mother Robson until vivacious Blondell
comes crashing through his fence and they
go off on a whirlwind courtship.
Perfect Strangers (1945) SEE: **Vacation
From Marriage**
Perfect Strangers (1950) **88m.** **½ D:
Bretaigne Windust. Ginger Rogers, Dennis Morgan, Thelma Ritter, Margalo Gillmore, Paul Ford, Alan Reed. Rogers and
Morgan are jury members who fall in love;
engaging romance story.
Perfect Strangers (1984) **C-91m.** ** D:
Larry Cohen. Anne Carlisle, Brad Rijn,
John Woehrle, Matthew Stockley, Stephen
Lack, Ann Magnuson. Three-year-old
Stockley witnesses Rijn carrying out gang-
land slaying . . . then Rijn strikes up a
romance with Stockley's mom (Carlisle)
in this listlessly acted will-he-or-won't-he
suspense yarn. Carlisle was seen to much
better effect as the star of LIQUID SKY.
Also known as BLIND ALLEY.▼
Perfect Witness (1989) **C-105m. TVM**
D: Robert Mandel. Brian Dennehy, Stockard
Channing, Aidan Quinn, Laura Harring-
ton, Joe Grifasi. Big-city restaurant owner
Quinn witnesses a gangland killing but is
too terrified to testify before a grand jury,
resisting all pressures from determined U.S.
Attorney Dennehy, who is investigating
the case. Some interesting character studies, although most come on too strong.
Coproduced by actor Wayne Rogers and
stunningly photographed by Lajos Koltai.
Made for cable. Average.▼
Perfect Woman, The (1949-British) **89m.**
**½ D: Bernard Knowles. Patricia Roc,
Stanley Holloway, Miles Malleson, Nigel
Patrick, Irene Handl, Patti Morgan. Screwy
scientist tries to improve on nature by
making a "perfect" robot woman, mod-
eled on his niece. Naturally mix-ups fol-
low in this OK British comedy.
Performance (1970-British) **C-105m.** ***
D: Donald Cammell, Nicolas Roeg. James
Fox, Mick Jagger, Anita Pallenberg, Mi-
chele Breton, Ann Sidney, John Burdon.
Psychological melodrama about criminal
on the lam hiding out with rock performer,
and how their lives intertwine. Not for
all tastes, but a bizarre and unique film;
Jagger's performance of "Memo from
Turner" a highlight.▼
Perfumed Nightmare, The (1977-Filipino)
C-93m. ***½ D: Kidlat Tahimik. Kidlat
Tahimik, Dolores Santamaria, Georgette

Baudry, Katrin Muller, Harmut Lerch. Surreal, whimsical, thoroughly original fable of an idealistic young Filipino (played by the director), fascinated by American culture and technology, and his awakening to the disadvantages of "progress" while in Paris. Crammed with striking images and a dazzling soundtrack.▼

Perilous Holiday (1946) **89m. ***** D: Edward H. Griffith. Pat O'Brien, Ruth Warrick, Alan Hale, Edgar Buchanan, Audrey Long. Another good O'Brien vehicle, with troubleshooter encountering dangerous counterfeiting gang south of the border.

Perilous Journey, A (1953) **90m. **** D: R. G. Springsteen. Vera Ralston, David Brian, Scott Brady, Virginia Grey, Charles Winninger, Ben Cooper, Hope Emerson, Veda Ann Borg, Leif Erickson. Predictable but diverting Western of a ship manned by women who are heading to California to find husbands.

Perilous Voyage (1976) **C-97m. TVM** D: William Graham. Michael Parks, William Shatner, Michael Tolan, Louise Sorel, Victor Jory, Charles McGraw, Stuart Margolin. Boat and passengers held hostage by revolutionary. Stereotyped characters, nothing in script to make situation novel. Filmed in 1968. Below average.

Perils from the Planet Mongo (1940) **91m. **½** D: Ford Beebe, Ray Taylor. Buster Crabbe, Carol Hughes, Charles Middleton, Frank Shannon, Anne Gwynne, Roland Drew. Truncated version of FLASH GORDON CONQUERS THE UNIVERSE serial. On Mongo, Flash, Dale Arden, and Dr. Zarkov contend with the planet's civilizations, eventually restore Prince Barin as rightful ruler and return to Earth. Uninspired handling of footage from this great serial.

Perils of Gwendoline in the Land of the Yik Yak, The (1984-French) **C-88m.** BOMB D: Just Jaeckin. Tawny Kitaen, Brent Huff, Zabou, Bernadette Lafont, Jean Rougerie. Idiotic adaptation of erotic French comic strip, seemingly a RAIDERS OF THE LOST ARK spoof, with virginal, amply breasted Kitaen searching for her long-lost dad. Lots of nudity, little else.▼

Perils of Nyoka SEE: **Nyoka and the Lost Secrets of Hippocrates**▼

Perils of Pauline, The (1947) **C-96m. ***** D: George Marshall. Betty Hutton, John Lund, Constance Collier, Billy de Wolfe, William Demarest. Lively, entertaining musical-comedy purports to be biography of silent-screen heroine Pearl White, but isn't; energetic Hutton, good Frank Loesser songs, colorful atmosphere, and presence of silent-film veterans make up for it . . . until sappy denouement.▼

Perils of Pauline, The (1967) **C-99m. **** D: Herbert Leonard, Joshua Shelley. Pat Boone, Terry-Thomas, Pamela Austin, Edward Everett Horton, Hamilton Camp. Cutesy expanded TV pilot, with Boone traveling around the globe seeking childhood sweetheart Austin; overlong, mainly for kids.

Perils of P.K., The (1986) **C-92m.** BOMB D: Joseph Green. Naura Hayden, Dick Shawn, Larry Storch, Kaye Ballard, Sheila MacRae, Louise Lasser, Prof. Irwin Corey, Sandy Baron, Sammy Davis, Jr., Anne Meara, Jackie Mason, Virginia Graham, Al Nuti, Rockets Redglare, Sammy Cahn, Capt. Haggerty. Amateurish vanity production by Hayden has her on psychiatrist Shawn's couch telling how her film star career degenerated into working in dives as a stripper; tons of guest stars filter in and out of the office doing hoary burlesque gag routines. Built around flashback footage filmed in Buenos Aires over a decade earlier for an unfinished film.

Perils of the Darkest Jungle SEE: **Jungle Gold**▼

Period of Adjustment (1962) **112m. ***** D: George Roy Hill. Tony Franciosa, Jane Fonda, Jim Hutton, Lois Nettleton, John McGiver, Jack Albertson. Newlyweds (Fonda and Hutton) try to help troubled marriage of Nettleton and Franciosa, in this heartwarming comedy based on a Tennessee Williams play. Engaging performers make the most of both comic and tender moments.

Permanent Record (1988) **C-91m. ***** D: Marisa Silver. Alan Boyce, Keanu Reeves, Michelle Meyrink, Jennifer Rubin, Pamela Gidley, Michael Elgart, Richard Bradford, Barry Corbin, Kathy Baker. Teen drama packs a wallop in tale of model student Boyce whose unexpected suicide throws high school classmates and officials into turmoil: if he went that route, who's safe? Subtle treatment by Silver of a pressing social problem, aided by excellent cast, especially Reeves as Boyce's underachieving pal.▼

Permission to Kill (1975-British) **C-96m. ***** D: Cyril Frankel. Dirk Bogarde, Ava Gardner, Bekim Fehmiu, Timothy Dalton, Frederic Forrest. Fascinating expose of spying as dirty business. Bogarde, spy chief of "Western Intelligence Liaison," tries to prevent Fehmiu, head of "National Freedom Party" from returning to his dictator-controlled country. Beautiful, exciting production.▼

Perri (1957) **C-75m. ***** D: N. Paul Kenworthy, Jr., Ralph Wright. Narrated by Winston Hibler. Unusual Disney film combines elements of BAMBI with True-Life nature photography, in a romanticized look at a squirrel through the cycle of four seasons in the forest. Based on Felix Salten's book.

Perry Mason Returns (1985) **C-100m. TVM** D: Ron Satlof. Raymond Burr, Barbara Hale, William Katt, Patrick O'Neal, Richard Anderson, Cassie Yates, Al Freeman, Jr. Burr and Hale play their most notable roles again after a 19-year hiatus, with Perry Mason stepping down from a judgeship to defend his onetime girl Friday, Della Street, against charges of doing in her wealthy (subsequent) employer for his money. Hale's real-life son, William Katt, plays Paul Drake, Jr. Writer Dean Hargrove's script is given the time and space to evoke the real Erle Stanley Gardner. Followed by a series of successful TV movies. Above average.▼

Perry Mason: The Case of the All-Star Assassin (1989) C-100m. TVM D: Christian I. Nyby II. Raymond Burr, Barbara Hale, Alexandra Paul, William R. Moses, Shari Belafonte, Deidre Hall, Pernell Roberts, Bruce Greenwood, Jason Beghe. Perry and cohorts defend an injured pro hockey star accused of murdering his sports mogul boss. Average.

Perry Mason: The Case of the Avenging Ace (1988) C-100m. TVM D: Christian I. Nyby II. Raymond Burr, Barbara Hale, William Katt, Patty Duke, Erin Gray, Larry Wilcox, Charles Siebert, James Sutorius, James McEachin, Richard Sanders, David Ogden Stiers. Perry defends an army officer he sent to prison years ago, after finding a witness who can testify to the man's innocence. Average.

Perry Mason: The Case of the Desperate Deception (1990) C-100m. TVM D: Christian I. Nyby II. Raymond Burr, Barbara Hale, William R. Moses, Ian Bannen, Ian McShane, Yvette Mimieux, Terry O'Quinn, Marcy Walker, Teresa Wright, Paul Freeman, Mickey Knox. Perry's in Paris to defend a U.S. Marine accused of killing the Nazi war criminal responsible for the long-ago torturing of his mother. A strong entry in the series with a suspense-packed screenplay by George Eckstein. Above average.

Perry Mason: The Case of the Lady in the Lake (1988) C-100m. TVM D: Ron Satlof. Raymond Burr, Barbara Hale, William Katt, David Ogden Stiers, David Hasselhoff, John Beck, Doran Clark, John Ireland, Liane Langland, Audra Lindley. Perry investigates the lakeside disappearance of a young heiress and uncovers a kidnapping-murder conspiracy. Average.

Perry Mason: The Case of the Lethal Lesson (1989) C-100m. TVM D: Christian I. Nyby II. Raymond Burr, Barbara Hale, Alexandra Paul, William R. Moses, Brian Keith, Leslie Ackerman, Richard Allen, Karen Kopins. A young law student is defended in a murder case by Mason, whose longtime friend is the victim's father. Paul and Moses join the Perry Mason company, replacing the departed William Katt. Average.

Perry Mason: The Case of the Lost Love (1987) C-100m. TVM D: Ron Satlof. Raymond Burr, Barbara Hale, William Katt, Jean Simmons, Gene Barry, Robert Walden, Stephen Elliott, Robert Mandan, David Ogden Stiers. Perry finds himself defending the husband of an old flame he hadn't seen in 30 years, who is now on the verge of a Senate appointment. Average.

Perry Mason: The Case of the Murdered Madam (1987) C-100m. TVM D: Ron Satlof. Raymond Burr, Barbara Hale, William Katt, David Ogden Stiers, Ann Jillian, Anthony Geary, Daphne Ashbrook, John Rhys-Davies, Bill Macy, Vincent Baggetta. Perry unravels the murder of an ex-madam turned PR specialist and uncovers a multimillion-dollar banking fraud. Average.

Perry Mason: The Case of the Musical Murder (1989) C-100m. TVM D: Christian I. Nyby II. Raymond Burr, Barbara Hale, Alexandra Paul, William R. Moses, Debbie Reynolds, Jerry Orbach, Dwight Schultz, Mary Cadorette, Raymond Singer. Perry goes after the murderer of a tyrannical Broadway director. Reynolds plays the star of the Broadway-bound musical production in progress, based on the life of Polly Adler (she even has a song that sounds suspiciously like it might be called "Hello, Polly!"). Average.

Perry Mason: The Case of the Notorious Nun (1986) C-100m. TVM D: Ron Satlof. Raymond Burr, Barbara Hale, William Katt, Timothy Bottoms, Jon Cypher, Michele Greene, Barbara Parkins, David Ogden Stiers, James McEachin, Gerald S. O'Loughlin, Arthur Hill, Tom Bosley. The second of the Mason "reunion" movies has him defending a young nun accused of murdering a priest with whom, supposedly, she was romantically involved. Above average.

Perry Mason: The Case of the Poisoned Pen (1990) C-100m. TVM D: Christian I. Nyby II. Raymond Burr, Barbara Hale, William R. Moses, Cindy Williams, Tony LoBianco, Barbara Babcock, Kiel Martin, David Warner. An angry author is accused of murdering her scheming ex-husband at a mystery writers' convention, and Perry Mason must sort things out. Average.

Perry Mason: The Case of the Scandalous Scoundrel (1987) C-100m. TVM D: Christian I. Nyby II. Raymond Burr, Barbara Hale, William Katt, David Ogden Stiers, Robert Guillaume, Morgan Brittany, Rene Enriquez, George Grizzard, Wings Hauser, Yaphet Kotto. Perry investigates the murder of a sleazy tabloid publisher. Average.

Perry Mason: The Case of the Shooting Star (1986) C-100m. TVM D: Ron Satlof. Raymond Burr, Barbara Hale, William

Katt, Jennifer O'Neill, David Ogden Stiers, Joe Penny, Alan Thicke, Ivan Dixon. Perry defends a noted movie star accused of murdering a famous talk show host in full view of millions of viewers. Thicke is puckishly cast as the TV talker in this Mason TV movie. Average.

Perry Mason: The Case of the Sinister Spirit (1987) **C-100m. TVM** D: Richard Lang. Raymond Burr, Barbara Hale, William Katt, Robert Stack, Dwight Schultz, Kim Delaney, Leigh-Taylor Young, David Ogden Stiers, Percy Rodrigues. A peg-down Mason whodunit involving him in the haunted house (or, in this case, hotel) murder of a successful horror novelist. Average.

Persecution (1974-British) **C-92m.** *½ D: Don Chaffey. Lana Turner, Trevor Howard, Ralph Bates, Olga Georges-Picot, Suzan Farmer. Overwrought, disjointed thriller with Lana as monstrous cat-loving mother of Bates, whom she torments his entire life. Slow, unpleasant, and unintentionally hilarious. Also known as THE TERROR OF SHEBA.▼

Persona (1966-Swedish) **81m.** ***½ D: Ingmar Bergman. Bibi Andersson, Liv Ullmann, Gunnar Bjornstrand, Margaretha Krook. Actress Ullmann withdraws and becomes mute, is cared for by nurse Andersson; their minds and personalities switch. Haunting, poetic, for discerning viewers; also shown at 85m. and 90m.▼

Personal Affair (1954-British) **82m.** ** D: Anthony Pelissier. Gene Tierney, Leo Genn, Glynis Johns, Walter Fitzgerald, Pamela Brown. Timid murder story involving suspected schoolteacher.

Personal Best (1982) **C-124m.** ***½ D: Robert Towne. Mariel Hemingway, Scott Glenn, Patrice Donnelly, Kenny Moore, Jim Moody, Larry Pennell. Athletes Hemingway and Donnelly have lesbian relationship while training for the 1980 Olympics. Annoying direction—too many close-ups of feet—but scores touchdowns galore when dealing with feelings, and women's relationship to manipulative coach Glenn. Perceptive, sensitive performance by Hemingway. Directing debut for top screenwriter Towne.▼

Personal Foul (1987) **C-92m.** *** D: Ted Lichtenfeld. David Morse, Adam Arkin, Susan Wheeler Duff, F. William Parker. Honest, heartfelt tale of drifter/ex-con Morse and teacher Arkin, who meet, become pals, and then rivals for Duff (who lights up the screen in her every scene). Sometimes lags but still sweet and ingratiating.

Personal Property (1937) **84m.** **½ D: W. S. Van Dyke II. Jean Harlow, Robert Taylor, Una O'Connor, Reginald Owen, Cora Witherspoon. Taylor stiffly maneuvers through a series of masquerades, and finally courts Harlow in this MGM fluff.

Remake of 1931 film THE MAN IN POSSESSION.

Personal Services (1987-British) **C-105m.** **½ D: Terry Jones. Julie Walters, Alec McCowen, Danny Schiller, Shirley Stelfox, Victoria Hardcastle, Tim Woodward, Dave Atkins. Naive working woman stumbles into a career as a madam, and becomes bolder as her business prospers. Bittersweet comedy, based on the real experiences of Cynthia Payne, is unabashedly adult, but uneven in tone. Benefits from a terrific performance by Walters as the woman who learns that sex is good business. Written by David Leland. Payne's earlier years are dramatized in WISH YOU WERE HERE.▼

Personals, The (1981) **C-88m.** *** D: Peter Markle. Bill Schoppert, Karen Landry, Paul Eiding, Michael Laskin, Vickie Dakil. Sweet, lovable—but also honest, realistic—little comedy about what happens when recently divorced, slightly balding Schoppert places a personal ad. Perhaps a bit too much extraneous footage, but still it works nicely, and "Shelly" is a riot. Filmed independently, in Minneapolis. ▼

Personals (1990) **C-100m. TVM** D: Steven Hilliard Stern. Jennifer O'Neill, Stephanie Zimbalist, Robin Thomas, Gina Gallego, Rosemary Dunsmore. Mousey librarian by day, femme fatale by night, O'Neill is a psycho who meets men through the personal ads, then kills them . . . until the wife of one victim decides to investigate. Interesting thriller that ultimately goes over the top. Average.

Persuader, The (1957) **72m.** ** D: Dick Ross. William Talman, James Craig, Kristine Miller, Darryl Hickman. Another Western involved with clergyman taking up arms to combat outlaws.

Pete Kelly's Blues (1955) **C-95m.** **½ D: Jack Webb. Jack Webb, Janet Leigh, Edmond O'Brien, Peggy Lee, Andy Devine, Lee Marvin, Jayne Mansfield, Ella Fitzgerald, Martin Milner. Realistic to the point of tedium, this film recreates the jazz age of the 1920's and musicians involved. Cast perks goings-on, despite Webb. Peggy Lee, in a rare dramatic role, was nominated for an Academy Award.▼

Pete 'n' Tillie (1972) **C-100m.** **½ D: Martin Ritt. Walter Matthau, Carol Burnett, Geraldine Page, Barry Nelson, Rene Auberjonois, Lee H. Montgomery, Henry Jones, Kent Smith. Slick comedy-drama has its moments as wry bachelor Matthau laconically woos and marries Burnett. Later turn to melodrama doesn't work, however, and supporting characters Page and Auberjonois simply don't make sense. Enough good points for innocuous entertainment; adapted by Julius J. Epstein from Peter de Vries' *Witch's Milk*.▼

Peter and Paul (1981) **C-200m. TVM** D: Robert Day. Anthony Hopkins, Robert

Foxworth, Eddie Albert, Raymond Burr, Jose Ferrer, Jon Finch, David Gwillim, Herbert Lom, Jean Peters. Ambitious but lackluster Biblical drama chronicling the saga of Peter (Foxworth) and Paul (Hopkins) from the Crucifixion to their deaths in Rome, A.D.64. Written by Christopher Knopf. Average.▼

Peter Gunn (1989) **C-100m. TVM** D: Blake Edwards. Peter Strauss, Barbara Williams, Jennifer Edwards, Charles Cioffi, Pearl Bailey, Peter Jurasik, David Rappaport. Here's a novelty: a 1950s TV series "reunion" movie with none of the original cast! Strauss is bemused as the suave private eye who finds himself caught between feuding mobsters and rogue cops. Pearl Bailey makes a rare acting appearance as Mother, who runs the bar and lounge where Gunn relaxes, and Williams, Jurasik, and Rappaport do the parts played way back when by Lola Albright, Herschel Bernardi, and Billy Barty. Writer-director Edwards' daughter Jennifer is on hand as Gunn's bubble-headed temporary secretary. Henry Mancini's memorable music sets the tone. Average.

Peter Ibbetson (1935) **88m. ***** D: Henry Hathaway. Gary Cooper, Ann Harding, John Halliday, Ida Lupino, Douglass Dumbrille, Virginia Weidler, Dickie Moore, Doris Lloyd. Most unusual fantasy-romance, based on George du Maurier novel about sweethearts who are separated in childhood but whose destinies draw them together years later, and for all eternity. Someone more ethereal than Harding might have put this over better, but it's still a moving and strikingly artistic endeavor. Beautifully photographed by Charles Lang.

Peter Lundy and the Medicine Hat Stallion (1977) **C-100m. TVM** D: Michael O'Herlihy. Leif Garrett, Milo O'Shea, Mitch Ryan, Bibi Besch, Charles Tyner, John Anderson, John Quade. Teenaged frontier lad becomes a rider for the Pony Express in the mid-1800s in this Disney-like adventure tale. Good family entertainment. Above average.▼

Peter Pan (1953) **C-77m. *** ** D: Hamilton Luske, Clyde Geronimi, Wilfred Jackson. Voices of Bobby Driscoll, Kathryn Beaumont, Hans Conried, Bill Thompson, Heather Angel, Paul Collins, Tommy Luske, Candy Candido, Tom Conway. Delightful Walt Disney cartoon feature of the classic James M. Barrie story, with Peter leading Wendy, Michael, and John Darling to Neverland, where they do battle with Captain Hook and his band of pirates. Musical highlight: "You Can Fly," as the children sail over the city of London.▼

Peter Rabbit and Tales of Beatrix Potter (1971-British) **C-90m. ***½** D: Reginald Mills. Beautiful ballet film with Royal Ballet Company, which tells of the adventures of several creatures that live by the pond; interesting version of Beatrix Potter tales. British title: TALES OF BEATRIX POTTER.▼

Pete's Dragon (1977) **C-134m. **** D: Don Chaffey. Helen Reddy, Jim Dale, Mickey Rooney, Red Buttons, Shelley Winters, Sean Marshall, Jane Kean, Jim Backus, Jeff Conaway, voice of Charlie Callas. Heavy-handed Disney musical about orphaned boy and his only friend, a protective dragon. Endearing animated "monster" almost makes up for the live actors' tiresome mugging. Another try for MARY POPPINS magic that doesn't come close. Some prints run 121m.; the 1984 reissue was further cut to 104m.▼

Petrified Forest, The (1936) **83m. ***½** D: Archie Mayo. Leslie Howard, Bette Davis, Dick Foran, Humphrey Bogart, Genevieve Tobin, Charley Grapewin, Porter Hall. Solid adaptation of Robert Sherwood play, focusing on ironic survival of the physically fit in civilized world. Bogart is Duke Mantee, escaped gangster, who holds writer Howard, dreamer Davis, and others hostage at roadside restaurant in Arizona. Stagy, but extremely well acted and surprisingly fresh. Howard and Bogart recreate their Broadway roles. Scripted by Charles Kenyon and Delmer Daves. Remade as ESCAPE IN THE DESERT.▼

Petroleum Girls SEE: **The Legend of Frenchie King**

Pet Sematary (1989) **C-102m. BOMB** D: Mary Lambert. Dale Midkiff, Fred Gwynne, Denise Crosby, Brad Greenquist, Michael Lombard, Blaze Berdahl, Miko Hughes. Couple is shocked to discover that danger lurks for their kids just outside a newly purchased rural home; aside from a spooked adjacent pet cemetery, they somehow failed to notice that semis roar down their frontyard highway every 90 seconds or so. A box-office hit whose contempt for its audience was sensed even by undiscriminating moviegoers. Stephen King scripted from his own best-seller.▼

Petticoat Fever (1936) **81m. **½** D: George Fitzmaurice. Robert Montgomery, Myrna Loy, Reginald Owen, Irving Bacon. Professionally handled comedy with lonely Montgomery (working for U.S. in northlands) romancing pilot Loy, whose plane crashes nearby.

Petty Girl, The (1950) **C-87m. **½** D: Henry Levin. Robert Cummings, Joan Caulfield, Elsa Lanchester, Melville Cooper, Mary Wickes, Tippi Hedren. Mild comedy of pin-up artist George Petty (Cummings) falling for prudish Caulfield, with Lanchester stealing every scene she's in.

Petulia (1968) **C-105m. **** ** D: Richard Lester. Julie Christie, George C. Scott, Richard Chamberlain, Shirley Knight, Arthur Hill, Joseph Cotten, Pippa Scott, Kathleen Widdoes. Brilliant film, set against mid-

60s San Francisco scene, about recently divorced doctor and his relationship with unhappily married kook. Terrific acting, especially by Scott and Knight, in one of decade's top films; script by Lawrence B. Marcus.▼

Peyton Place (1957) **C-157m.** ***½ D: Mark Robson. Lana Turner, Hope Lange, Arthur Kennedy, Lloyd Nolan, Lee Philips, Terry Moore, Russ Tamblyn, Betty Field, David Nelson, Mildred Dunnock, Diane Varsi, Barry Coe, Leon Ames, Lorne Greene. Grace Metalious's once-notorious novel receives Grade A filming. Soap opera of life behind closed doors in a small New England town boasts strong cast, fine Franz Waxman score. Original running time: 162m. Sequel: RETURN TO PEYTON PLACE. Later a TV series.

Peyton Place: The Next Generation (1985) **C-100m.** TVM D: Larry Elikann. Christopher Connelly, James Douglas, Dorothy Malone, Pat Morrow, Ed Nelson, Tim O'Connor, Barbara Parkins, Evelyn Scott, Ruth Warrick. A visit to Peyton Place twenty years after the disappearance of Allison MacKenzie (Mia Farrow in the original series), with the arrival in town of her long-lost daughter. Less a sequel to MURDER IN PEYTON PLACE than a re-gearing-up of the long-ago series. Average.

Phaedra (1962-U.S.-French-Greek) 115m. *** D: Jules Dassin. Melina Mercouri, Anthony Perkins, Raf Vallone, Elizabeth Ercy. Mercouri, wife of shipping magnate Vallone, has an affair with stepson Perkins. Well-acted and directed; inspired by Euripides' *Hippolytus*.

Phantasm (1979) **C-87m.** *½ D: Don Coscarelli. Michael Baldwin, Bill Thornbury, Reggie Bannister, Kathy Lester, Angus Scrimm. Two not very interesting brothers take on a flying object that punctures skulls, as well as a creepy cemetery worker whose ties are so thin he should be playing "Louie, Louie" at a 1963 prom. Followed by a sequel.▼

Phantasm II (1988) **C-90m.** *½ D: Don Coscarelli. James Le Gros, Reggie Bannister, Angus Scrimm, Paula Irvine, Samantha Phillips, Kenneth Tigar. Bigger-budgeted sequel to the 1979 cult success follows similar path, with psychic teenagers experiencing recurring nightmarish visions of The Tall Man (Scrimm) . . . only this time the gore is more graphic and unrelenting.▼

Phantom Express, The (1932) 66m. ** D: Emory Johnson. William Collier, Jr., Sally Blane, J. Farrell MacDonald, Hobart Bosworth, Axel Axelson, Lina Basquette, Eddie Phillips, Claire McDowell. Melodramatic, ever-so-obvious account of some villains attempting to sabotage a railroad . . . and it's the company president's son (Collier) to the rescue. Notice those

violins after engineer Smokey North is sacked from his job!▼

Phantom from Space (1953) 72m. *½ D: W. Lee Wilder. Ted Cooper, Rudolph Anders, Noreen Nash, Harry Landers. Dull sci-fi horror opus about invisible alien stranded on Earth.▼

Phantom Lady (1944) 87m. ***½ D: Robert Siodmak. Ella Raines, Franchot Tone, Alan Curtis, Thomas Gomez, Elisha Cook, Jr., Fay Helm, Andrew Tombes, Regis Toomey. First-rate suspense yarn of innocent man (Curtis) framed for murder of his wife. Secretary Raines seeks real killer with help of Curtis' best friend (Tone) and detective (Gomez). Drumming scene with Cook is simply astonishing. Based on a Cornell Woolrich novel.

Phantom of Chinatown (1940) 61m. BOMB D: Phil Rosen. Keye Luke, Lotus Long, Grant Withers, Paul McVey, Charles Miller. Sixth and final mystery in the Mr. Wong series is bottom-of-the-barrel fare, with Luke replacing Boris Karloff as a younger version of the Oriental sleuth. He's on the trail of a killer out to obtain an ancient scroll and locate an oil deposit.▼

Phantom of Crestwood, The (1932) 77m. *** D: J. Walter Ruben. Ricardo Cortez, Karen Morley, Anita Louise, Pauline Frederick, H. B. Warner, Sam Hardy, Skeets Gallagher. First-rate whodunit with crafty Morley calling together the men in her life for mass-blackmail scheme, resulting in murder. Eye-riveting flashback technique highlights solid mystery.

Phantom of Hollywood, The (1974) **C-78m.** TVM D: Gene Levitt. Skye Aubrey, Jack Cassidy, Jackie Coogan, Broderick Crawford, Peter Haskell, John Ireland, Peter Lawford, Kent Taylor, Corinne Calvet, Bill Williams. A movie buff's dream: a masked monster goes on a rampage against those selling his home—the MGM back lot. Silly but watchable. Average.

Phantom of Liberty, The (1974-French) **C-104m.** ***½ D: Luis Buñuel. Jean-Claude Brialy, Adolfo Celi, Michel Piccoli, Monica Vitti. A dreamlike comedy of irony, composed of surreal, randomly connected anecdotes. Highlighted is a dinner party, in which the openness of eating and the privacy of defecating are reversed, and a sequence in which adults fret over a young girl's disappearance—even though she remains present all along.▼

Phantom of Paris, The (1931) 73m. ** D: John S. Robertson. John Gilbert, Leila Hyams, Lewis Stone, Jean Hersholt, C. Aubrey Smith, Natalie Moorhead, Ian Keith. Gilbert elevates this otherwise static, talky melodrama as a dapper magician-illusionist accused of murdering the father of the woman he loves—with an ironic twist. Police detective Stone is his coldhearted nemesis. Based on a novel by Gaston (*The Phantom of the Opera*) LeRoux.

Phantom of Terror, The SEE: **Bird With the Crystal Plumage, The**▼

Phantom of the Opera, The (1925) 79m. ***½ D: Rupert Julian. Lon Chaney, Mary Philbin, Norman Kerry, Snitz Edwards, Gibson Gowland. Not so much a horror film as great melodrama, with Chaney as vengeful composer who lives in catacombs of the Paris Opera, kidnapping young Philbin as new protege. Famed unmasking scene still packs a jolt; several scenes originally filmed in color. One of Chaney's finest hours.▼

Phantom of the Opera (1943) C-92m. *** D: Arthur Lubin. Claude Rains, Susanna Foster, Nelson Eddy, Edgar Barrier, Jane Farrar, Miles Mander, J. Edward Bromberg, Hume Cronyn, Fritz Leiber, Leo Carrillo. First talkie version of venerable melodrama often has more opera than Phantom, but Rains gives fine, sympathetic performance as disfigured composer worshipping young soprano Foster. Oscar winner for Cinematography (Hal Mohr and W. Howard Greene) and Art Direction; a must in color.▼

Phantom of the Opera, The (1962-British) C-84m. ** D: Terence Fisher. Herbert Lom, Heather Sears, Thorley Walters, Edward DeSouza, Michael Gough, Miles Malleson. Third version of horror classic is generally plodding, with only occasional moments of terror. Made worse by expansion to 90m. for TV, with added subplot of detectives investigating the elusive murderer.

Phantom of the Opera, The (1983) C-100m. TVM D: Robert Markowitz. Maximilian Schell, Jane Seymour, Michael York, Jeremy Kemp, Diana Quick. Sumptuous 80s version of the grand guignol classic is highlighted by Schell's scenery-chewing portrait of the deranged Hungarian voice teacher who's not just another pretty face. Sherman Yellen's adaptation and Stan Winston's "Phantom" makeup aren't to be overlooked either, though this version goes far astray from the original Gaston Leroux novel—it isn't even set in Paris! Above average.

Phantom of the Opera, The (1989) C-90m. *½ D: Dwight H. Little. Robert Englund, Jill Schoelen, Alex Hyde-White, Billy Nighy, Stephanie Lawrence, Terence Harvey. Good-looking but gory, slow-moving remake, shot in Budapest but set in London. Closer to original novel than other versions. Its changes are no improvements; instead of a mask, the Phantom stitches dead flesh onto his scarred face and has made a deal with the devil. He's still killing people to advance the career of a chosen singer. No chandelier, either. Englund ("Freddy Krueger") ranges from effective to hammy as the Phantom.▼

Phantom of the Opera, The (1990-U.S.-British) C-200m. TVM D: Tony Richard-

son. Burt Lancaster, Charles Dance, Teri Polo, Ian Richardson, Andrea Ferreol, Adam Storke, Jean-Pierre Cassel. Handsome but almost high-camp remake of the venerable story, closest in spirit to the Claude Rains version, with Dance making a romantic Phantom; Lancaster is his resigned but protective father, while Polo plays Christine as if she's Cinderella. The operatic interludes are atrociously dubbed. Adapted by the estimable Arthur Kopit from his 1982 play. Originally shown in two parts. Average.

Phantom of the Paradise (1974) C-92m. *** D: Brian DePalma. Paul Williams, William Finley, Jessica Harper, George Memmoli, Gerrit Graham. Effective rock version of . . . OPERA, with Finley out for revenge against Faustian producer (Williams, miscast but not bad) who stole his songs. A flop in its time—because it was sold as a spoof—but now finding a cult; ironically, many of the film's "weird" rock performers (including Graham as "Beef") seem pretty tame alongside some of today's artists. Williams also composed the score, and Sissy Spacek was the set decorator!▼

Phantom of the Rue Morgue (1954) C-84m. ** D: Roy Del Ruth. Karl Malden, Claude Dauphin, Patricia Medina, Steve Forrest, Allyn Ann McLerie, Erin O'Brien-Moore. Remake of MURDERS IN THE RUE MORGUE suffers from Malden's hamminess in the Lugosi role, plus little real atmosphere. On the other hand, there *is* Merv Griffin as a college student! Originally in 3-D.

Phantom Planet, The (1961) 82m. *½ D: William Marshall. Dean Fredericks, Coleen Gray, Tony Dexter, Dolores Faith, Francis X. Bushman. Astronaut crash-lands on an invisible asteroid, is shrunken to the tiny size of its inhabitants, and becomes involved in their war with silly-looking aliens. Bushman plays tiny folks' leader Sesom, but he's no Moses, backward or forward. Fascinatingly terrible movie.▼

Phantom President, The (1932) 80m. ** D: Norman Taurog. George M. Cohan, Claudette Colbert, Jimmy Durante, Sidney Toler. Musical antique about presidential candidate, with lookalike entertainer (Cohan) falling in love with former's girl (Colbert). Interesting only as a curio, with forgettable Rodgers-Hart score.

Phantom Raiders (1942) 70m. **½ D: Jacques Tourneur. Walter Pidgeon, Donald Meek, Joseph Schildkraut, Florence Rice, Nat Pendleton, John Carroll. Slick, fast-paced Nick Carter detective entry has our hero investigating sabotage in the Panama Canal after Allied ships are sunk.

Phantom Ship (1935-British) 80m. ** D: Denison Clift. Bela Lugosi, Shirley Grey, Arthur Margetson, Edmund Willard, Dennis Hoey, Ben Welden, Gibson Gowland.

Slow-paced "explanation" of one of the great unsolved maritime mysteries, the disappearance of the crew of the *Mary Celeste*, in late 1872. Routine but holds interest. Lugosi is broad but entertaining as superstitious one-armed seaman. All exteriors filmed on a real ship. Original title: MYSTERY OF THE MARY CELESTE.▼

Phantom Stagecoach, The (1957) **69m.** *½ D: Ray Nazarro. William Bishop, Kathleen Crowley, Richard Webb, Frank Ferguson. Programmer Western about clashing stagecoach lines competing for business.

Phantom Thief, The (1946) **65m.** D: D. Ross Lederman. Chester Morris, Jeff Donnell, Richard Lane, Dusty Anderson, George E. Stone, Marvin Miller, Murray Alper. SEE: **Boston Blackie** series.

Phantom Tollbooth, The (1969) **C-90m.** *** D: Chuck Jones, Abe Levitow (animation); David Monahan (live-action). Butch Patrick, and voices of Hans Conried, Mel Blanc, Candy Candido, June Foray, Les Tremayne, Daws Butler. Unusual animated feature (the first for both Jones and MGM), based on Norton Juster's book about bored little boy who enters strange world where letters and numbers are at war. A bit sophisticated for the Saturday matinee crowd, and the songs are pretty icky, but still quite worthwhile, especially for Jones fans.▼

Pharaoh's Curse (1957) **66m.** ** D: Lee Sholem. Mark Dana, Ziva Rodann, Diane Brewster. Standard story of Egyptian expedition finding centuries-old monster guarding tomb.

Pharaoh's Woman, The (1960-Italian) **C-87m.** ** D: Giorgio Rivalta. Linda Cristal, Pierre Brice, Armando Francioli, John Drew Barrymore. Senseless epic set in Egypt with Francioli combating Barrymore, pretender to the throne; ornate settings.

Phar Lap (1983-Australian) **C-108m.** *** D: Simon Wincer. Tom Burlinson, Martin Vaughan, Judy Morris, Ron Leibman, Celia de Burgh, Vincent Ball. Entertaining chronicle of champion Australian racehorse Phar Lap, who suddenly and mysteriously died in 1932 in America. Nicely directed and acted; Down Under, the story of Phar Lap is now legend. Reedited for U.S. release from original 118m.▼

Phase IV (1974) **C-86m.** **½ D: Saul Bass. Nigel Davenport, Lynne Frederick, Michael Murphy, Alan Gifford, Helen Horton, Robert Henderson. Feature directing debut of famed title-maker Bass is visually stunning but rather incomprehensible science fiction about colony of superintelligent ants (normal-sized, for a change) running rampant at a lonely scientific outpost. Difficult, but not without its rewards.▼

Phenix City Story, The (1955) **100m.** *** D: Phil Karlson. John McIntire, Richard Kiley, Kathryn Grant, Edward Andrews. Fast-paced exposé film, compactly told,

with realistic production, fine performances as lawyer returns to corrupt home town, tries to do something about it. Sometimes shown without 13-minute prologue.

Phffft! (1954) **91m.** *** D: Mark Robson. Judy Holliday, Jack Lemmon, Jack Carson, Kim Novak, Donald Curtis. Saucy sex romp by George Axelrod, with Holliday and Lemmon discovering that they were better off before they divorced.

Philadelphia Experiment, The (1984) **C-102m.** **½ D: Stewart Raffill. Michael Paré, Nancy Allen, Eric Christmas, Bobby Di Cicco, Kene Holliday. Sailor on WWII ship falls through a hole in time and winds up in 1984. Just entertaining enough to cover production flaws and some gaping story holes.▼

Philadelphia, Here I Come (1975) **C-95m.** **½ D: John Quested. Donal McCann, Des Cave, Siobhan McKenna, Eamon Kelly, Fidelma Murphy, Liam Redmond. Brian Friel adapted his own stage play about a young man and his alter ego who debate whether or not he should leave his dreary Irish home town and join an aunt in Philadelphia, U.S.A. Filmed on location with fine performances.

Philadelphia Story, The (1940) **112m.** **** D: George Cukor. Cary Grant, Katharine Hepburn, James Stewart, Ruth Hussey, John Howard, Roland Young, John Halliday, Virginia Weidler, Mary Nash, Henry Daniell, Hillary Brooke. Talky but brilliant adaptation of Philip Barry's hit Broadway comedy about society girl who yearns for down-to-earth romance; Grant is her ex-husband, Stewart a fast-talking (!) reporter who falls in love with her. Entire cast is excellent, but Stewart really shines in his offbeat, Academy Award-winning role. Donald Ogden Stewart's script also earned an Oscar. Later musicalized as HIGH SOCIETY.▼

Philo Vance Debonair detective Philo Vance, created by master novelist S. S. Van Dine (real name Willard Wright) enjoyed a long and varied screen career, in the guise of many different actors, in films made over a span of some twenty years by several different studios. The man most closely identified with the role was William Powell, who starred in the first three mysteries for Paramount: THE CANARY MURDER CASE, THE GREENE MURDER CASE, and THE BENSON MURDER CASE. While these very early talkies are somewhat stilted (particularly CANARY, which was completed as a silent film, then hastily adapted for sound) the whodunit angles are first-rate, as urbane Powell solves the bizarre N.Y.C.-based murders. Eugene Pallette was a fine foil as skeptical Sergeant Heath of the homicide squad, with E. H. Calvert as the N.Y.C. D.A. MGM interrupted this series with one of its own, THE BISHOP MURDER CASE, casting Basil Rathbone as Vance; though a clever whodunit, with the villain matching his crimes to Mother Goose rhymes, the film was all but done in by a snail-like pacing. Powell's last appearance as Vance was in Warner Brothers' THE KENNEL MURDER CASE, probably the best film in the series, brilliantly directed by Michael Curtiz, and also one of the most complex cases of all. None of the later Vance outings reached this peak of ingenuity and sophisticated filmmaking, although Warren William did well in THE DRAGON MURDER CASE at Warners. MGM's next duo cast Paul Lukas in THE CASINO MURDER CASE, and Edmund Lowe in THE GARDEN MURDER CASE; slickly done, they suffered from formula scripting, acting, and direction. Wilfrid Hyde-White starred in a British production of THE SCARAB MURDER CASE in 1936, but this one never found its way to America. Meanwhile, Paramount remade THE GREENE MURDER CASE as NIGHT OF MYSTERY, a routine "B" with Grant Richards, and Warren William returned for THE GRACIE ALLEN MURDER CASE, with Vance taking back seat to the comedienne, whose stupidity became a bit overpowering in this story written for her by Van Dine. Warners then redid THE KENNEL MURDER CASE as CALLING PHILO VANCE, another forgettable "B" with James Stephenson in the role. Philo Vance went into retirement until 1947, when cheapie company PRC brought him back for three final outings, all surprisingly good little whodunits: William Wright starred in PHILO VANCE RETURNS, and Alan Curtis was a deadpan hero in PHILO VANCE'S GAMBLE, and the best of all, PHILO VANCE'S SECRET MISSION, with perky Sheila Ryan as his sleuthing girlfriend. The character of Philo Vance, sophisticated and aloof, did not really fit the hard-boiled detective image of the 1940s and 1950s, so the character never appeared again onscreen, but his better outings, from the beginning and end of his film career, remain first-rate murder mysteries today.

Philo Vance Returns (1947) 64m. D: William Beaudine. William Wright, Terry Austin, Leon Belasco, Clara Blandick, Iris Adrian, Frank Wilcox.

Philo Vance's Gamble (1947) 62m. D: Basil Wrangell. Alan Curtis, Terry Austin, Frank Jenks, Tala Birell, Gavin Gordon.

Philo Vance's Secret Mission (1947) 58m. D: Reginald Le Borg. Alan Curtis, Sheila Ryan, Tala Birell, Frank Jenks, James Bell.

Phobia (1980-Canadian) C-90m. BOMB D: John Huston. Paul Michael Glaser, Susan Hogan, John Colicos, David Bolt, Patricia Collins, David Eisner. Absolutely

terrible film about psychiatrist whose patients, all suffering from various phobias, are being murdered one by one. Relentlessly stupid, illogical, and unpleasant.▼

Phoenix, The (1981) C-74m. TVM D: Douglas Hickox. Judson Scott, E.G. Marshall, Fernando Allende, Shelley Smith, Darryl Anderson, Hersha Parady. Banal pilot for the short-lived series about a godlike being with extraordinary powers, discovered in an ancient sarcophagus and brought back to life, who must learn to cope with today's society. Below average.

Phone Call from a Stranger (1952) 96m. *** D: Jean Negulesco. Bette Davis, Shelley Winters, Gary Merrill, Michael Rennie, Keenan Wynn, Evelyn Varden, Warren Stevens, Beatrice Straight, Craig Stevens. Engrossing narrative of Merrill, survivor of a plane crash, visiting families of various victims.

Phony American, The (1962-German) 72m. **½ D: Akos Rathony. William Bendix, Christine Kaufmann, Michael Hinz, Ron Randell. Strange casting is more interesting than tale of a German WW2 orphan, now grown up, wishing to become an American, and a U.S. air force pilot.

Photo Finish (1957-French) 110m. ** D: Norbert Carbonnaux. Fernand Gravet, Jean Richard, Micheline, Louis de Funes. Strained comedy about con-men at work at the racetrack.

Phynx, The (1970) C-92m. BOMB D: Lee H. Katzin. A. Michael Miller, Ray Chippeway, Dennis Larden, Lonny Stevens, Lou Antonio, Mike Kellin, Joan Blondell, George Tobias, Richard Pryor. A way-off-base satire about a rock group (Miller, Chippeway, Larden, Stevens) recruited to spy behind Iron Curtain and the kidnapping of America's pop-culture heroes (in cameos, Leo Gorcey, Huntz Hall, Guy Lombardo, Joe Louis, Johnny Weissmuller, Col. Sanders, Ruby Keeler, Xavier Cugat, Dick Clark, George Jessel, and many others). Diehards may want to see some of these stars, but it's hardly worth it.

Physical Evidence (1989) C-99m. *½ D: Michael Crichton. Burt Reynolds, Theresa Russell, Ned Beatty, Kay Lenz, Ted McGinley, Tom O'Brien. Boring drama with Reynolds going through the paces as a tough cop who's been suspended from the force, and is now the prime suspect in a murder case. Russell is badly miscast as a public defender who takes up his cause.▼

Piaf—The Early Years (1974-U.S.-French) C-104m. **½ D: Guy Casaril. Brigitte Ariel, Pascale Christophe, Guy Trejan, Pierre Vernier, Jacques Duby, Anouk Ferjac. Maddeningly uneven depiction of the early life and career of the legendary singer. Fascinating subject matter, good Ariel performance and great music, but melodramatic and sloppily directed. Based on the best-selling book by Simone Berteaut, Piaf's half-sister (played here by Christophe). Unreleased in America until 1982.

Piano for Mrs. Cimino, A (1982) **C-100m.** TVM D: George Schaefer. Bette Davis, Penny Fuller, Keenan Wynn, Alexa Kenin, George Hearn, Christopher Guest, Graham Jarvis. A widow, diagnosed as senile by her doctor and declared incompetent by the courts, fights to regain control of her estate and her life, with Bette Davis giving another postgraduate acting course (sometimes a smidge too obviously) to her army of students and fans. John Gay wrote the sensitive script. Above average.▼

Picasso Summer, The (1969) **C-90m.** *½ D: Serge Bourguignon. Albert Finney, Yvette Mimieux. Boring, rambling tale of young couple so enamored by paintings that they take European vacation to find Picasso himself, wind up breaking up. Animated sequence midway can stand on its own without surrounding plot. Based on the Ray Bradbury story.

Picasso Trigger (1989) **C-99m.** ** D: Andy Sidaris. Steve Bond, Dona Spier, John Aprea, Hope Marie Carlton, Harold Diamond, Roberta Vasquez, Guich Koock, Bruce Penhall. Harmless, low-budget James Bond-like thriller with U.S. agent Bond tracking assassin Aprea, who uses fish (from a painting he admires) as his emblem. Sequel to HARD TICKET TO HAWAII and MALIBU EXPRESS has usual mix of action and t&a, with uneven performances—and some peculiar gadgets (a killer crutch?).▼

Piccadilly Incident (1946-British) **88m.** *** D: Herbert Wilcox. Anna Neagle, Michael Wilding, Michael Laurence, Reginald Owen, Frances Mercer. Familiar Enoch Arden theme of supposedly dead wife appearing after husband has remarried. Good British cast gives life to oft-filmed plot.

Piccadilly Jim (1936) **100m.** **½ D: Robert Z. Leonard. Robert Montgomery, Madge Evans, Frank Morgan, Eric Blore, Billie Burke. Fine light-comedy players in P. G. Wodehouse story of father and son's romantic pursuits; ultimately defeated by overlength.

Pick a Star (1937) **70m.** **½ D: Edward Sedgwick. Jack Haley, Rosina Lawrence, Patsy Kelly, Mischa Auer, Tom Dugan, Stan Laurel, Oliver Hardy. Mistaken as L&H vehicle, actually a Hal Roach production about small-town girl (Lawrence) hoping for stardom in Hollywood. Sappy story, bizarre musical production numbers, but guest stars Stan and Ollie have two very funny scenes. Retitled: MOVIE STRUCK.▼

Picking Up the Pieces (1985) **C-100m.** TVM D: Paul Wendkos. Margot Kidder, David Ackroyd, Ari Meyers, James Farentino, Joyce Van Patten, Herbert Edelman, Robin Gammell. Abused wife, vindictive

husband, supportive widower are the elements of this so-so drama about a woman's new quest for self-esteem. Average.

Pick-up (1933) **80m.** **½ D: Marion Gering. Sylvia Sidney, George Raft, Lillian Bond, William Harrigan, Clarence Wilson, Brooks Benedict, Robert McWade, Louise Beavers. Occasionally entertaining little drama about ex-con Sidney, who's down on her luck; she conceals her identity, and becomes involved with cabdriver Raft.

Pickup (1951) **78m.** *½ D: Hugo Haas. Beverly Michaels, Hugo Haas, Allan Nixon, Howland Chamberlin, Jo Carroll Dennison. First of writer-producer-director-actor Haas' tawdry low-budget melodramas is a kind of poor man's THE POSTMAN ALWAYS RINGS TWICE, with gold-digger Michaels marrying aging railroad inspector thinking he's got lots of dough. Not as enjoyably bad as Hugo's later efforts.

Pickup Alley (1957-British) **92m.** *½ D: John Gilling. Victor Mature, Anita Ekberg, Trevor Howard, Eric Pohlmann. Lackluster account of federal agent's tracking down of dope-smuggling syndicate.

Pick-up Artist, The (1987) **C-81m.** *½ D: James Toback. Molly Ringwald, Robert Downey (Jr.), Dennis Hopper, Danny Aiello, Mildred Dunnock, Harvey Keitel, Brian Hamill, Vanessa Williams, Victoria Jackson, Polly Draper, Robert Towne, Lorraine Bracco, Bob Gunton. Womanizing youth meets his match when he falls for the daughter of a boozy gambler in hock to the mob. Standard Toback lowlifes integrated into a conventionally romantic framework. Dismal, dour and deadeningly dull.▼

Pickup on 101 (1972) **C-93m.** ** D: John Florea. Jack Albertson, Lesley Ann Warren, Martin Sheen, Michael Ontkean, Hal Baylor, George Chandler. Coed who wants to be liberated hits the road with rock musician and friendly hobo in this inoffensive melodrama.

Pickup on South Street (1953) **80m.** ***½ D: Samuel Fuller. Richard Widmark, Jean Peters, Thelma Ritter, Richard Kiley, Murvyn Vye. Pickpocket Widmark inadvertently acquires top-secret microfilm, and becomes target for espionage agents. Tough, brutal, well-made film, with superb performance by Ritter as street peddler who also sells information. Remade as THE CAPE TOWN AFFAIR.

Pick-Up Summer (1981-Canadian) **C-92m.** BOMB D: George Mihalka. Michael Zelniker, Carl Marotte, Karen Stephen, Helene Udy. Boys and girls prepare for pinball and beauty contests, with motorcycle rowdies thrown in for good measure. Less rewarding than an average *Archie* comic book. Also known as PINBALL SUMMER and PINBALL PICK-UP.▼

Pickwick Papers (1954-British) **109m.** ***

D: Noel Langley. James Hayter, James Donald, Hermione Baddeley, Kathleen Harrison, Hermione Gingold, Joyce Grenfell, Alexander Gauge, Lionel Murton, Nigel Patrick. Flavorful, episodic version of Dickens' classic of sly actor whose underhanded enterprises pay off.▼

Picnic (1955) **C-115m.** ***½ D: Joshua Logan. William Holden, Rosalind Russell, Kim Novak, Betty Field, Cliff Robertson, Arthur O'Connell, Verna Felton, Susan Strasberg, Nick Adams, Phyllis Newman. Excellent film of William Inge play about drifter (Holden) who stops over in Kansas, stealing alluring Novak from his old buddy Robertson (making his film debut). Russell and O'Connell almost steal film in second leads, and supporting roles are expertly filled; script by Daniel Taradash.▼

Picnic at Hanging Rock (1975-Australian) **C-110m.** *** D: Peter Weir. Rachel Roberts, Dominic Guard, Helen Morse, Jacki Weaver, Vivean Gray, Margaret Nelson, Anne (Louise) Lambert. Moody, atmospheric film set in 1900 about three school-girls and their teacher who mysteriously disappear during an outing one sunny day. Eerie and richly textured by director Weir; based on a novel by Joan Lindsay.▼

Picture Mommy Dead (1966) **C-88m.** **½ D: Bert I. Gordon. Don Ameche, Martha Hyer, Zsa Zsa Gabor, Signe Hasso, Susan Gordon. Hokey melodrama with Hyer newly married to Ameche, battling stepdaughter Gordon, possessed by late mother's spirit.▼

Picture of Dorian Gray, The (1945) **110m.** ***½ D: Albert Lewin. George Sanders, Hurd Hatfield, Donna Reed, Angela Lansbury, Peter Lawford, Lowell Gilmore. Haunting Oscar Wilde story of man whose painting ages while he retains youth. Young Lansbury is poignant, singing "Little Yellow Bird" (keep an eye out for Lansbury's real-life mother Moyna MacGill as the Duchess). Sanders leaves indelible impression as elegant heavy. Several color inserts throughout the film . . . though not in some TV prints. Harry Stradling's cinematography won an Oscar. Narrated by Cedric Hardwicke. Remade in 1970 as DORIAN GRAY.▼

Picture Show Man, The (1977-Australian) **C-99m.** ***½ D: John Power. Rod Taylor, John Meillon, John Ewart, Harold Hopkins, Patrick Cargill, Judy Morris. Funny, moving account of the beginnings of the movie business in Australia, with showman Meillon bringing the flicks to the bush and outback. A must for buffs; based on an autobiography by Lyle Penn.▼

Picture Snatcher (1933) **77m.** *** D: Lloyd Bacon. James Cagney, Ralph Bellamy, Alice White, Patricia Ellis, Ralf Harolde. Fast, funny, exciting little film based on true story of daring photographer who got taboo photo of woman in electric chair. Remade as ESCAPE FROM CRIME.

Piece of the Action, A (1977) **C-135m.** **½ D: Sidney Poitier. Sidney Poitier, Bill Cosby, James Earl Jones, Denise Nicholas, Hope Clark, Tracy Reed, Titos Vandis, Ja'net DuBois. Third Poitier-Cosby teaming casts them as con men obliged to help social worker set ghetto kids on the right track. Typical comic crime material offset by serious, sometimes preachy moments.▼

Pieces (1983-Italian-Spanish) **C-85m.** BOMB D: Juan Piquer Simon. Christopher George, Edmund Purdom, Lynda Day George, Paul Smith, Frank Brana, Ian Sera. Repulsive and nauseating do not describe this gorefest about a sickie who slices up coeds to create a life-sized jigsaw puzzle. View at your own risk.▼

Pied Piper, The (1942) **86m.** *** D: Irving Pichel. Monty Woolley, Roddy McDowall, Otto Preminger, Anne Baxter, Peggy Ann Garner. Woolley, not very fond of children, finds himself leading a swarm of them on chase from the Nazis. Entertaining wartime film scripted by Nunnally Johnson from a Nevil Shute novel. Remade for TV as CROSSING TO FREEDOM.

Pied Piper, The (1972-British) **C-90m.** ***½ D: Jacques Demy. Donovan, Donald Pleasence, Michael Hordern, Jack Wild, Diana Dors, John Hurt. Chilling story of piper who rids evil hamlet of rats. While originally conceived as children's tale, director Demy succeeds in weaving grimy portrait of the Middle Ages.

Pied Piper of Hamelin (1957) **C-87m.** TVM D: Bretaigne Windust. Van Johnson, Kay Starr, Claude Rains, Jim Backus, Doodles Weaver. TV special of famed children's tale, musicalized, with Johnson in title role; uses haunting Edvard Grieg music for effective results. Average.▼

Pierrot le Fou (1965-French-Italian) **C-110m.** *** D: Jean-Luc Godard. Jean-Paul Belmondo, Anna Karina, Dirk Sanders, Raymond Devus, Samuel Fuller, Jean-Pierre Leaud. Belmondo and Karina run away together to the South of France; he is leaving his rich wife, she is escaping her involvement with gangsters. Complex, confusing, but engrossing drama, which exudes an intriguing sense of spontaneity. Allegedly shot without a script; also shown at 90m. and 95m.▼

Pier 13 (1940) **66m.** *½ D: Eugene Forde. Lynn Bari, Lloyd Nolan, Joan Valerie, Douglas Fowley. Nolan is cop trailing waterfront crooks in this 20th Century-Fox programmer.

Pigeon, The (1969) **C-74m.** TVM D: Earl Bellamy. Sammy Davis, Jr., Dorothy Malone, Pat Boone, Ricardo Montalban, Victoria Vetri. Private-eye driven by events to help old flame and daughter to retrieve diary and protect them from gang of criminals. Despite efforts of cast, singularly uninvolving drama. Average.

Pigeons (1971) **C-87m.** *½ D: John Dexter. Jordan Christopher, Jill O'Hara, Robert Walden, Kate Reid, William Redfield, Lois Nettleton, Elaine Stritch, Melba Moore. Smug film about 24-year-old Princeton graduate who drives a taxi in Manhattan. The character is unattractive and film looks as if it were designed for stage, not screen. Also known as THE SIDELONG GLANCES OF A PIGEON KICKER.

Pigeon That Took Rome, The (1962) **101m.** **½ D: Melville Shavelson. Charlton Heston, Elsa Martinelli, Harry Guardino, Baccaloni, Marietto, Gabriella Pallotta, Debbie Price, Brian Donlevy. Sometimes amusing WW2 comedy of Heston, behind enemy lines, using pigeons to send message to Allies, romancing local girl in whose home he is based.

Pigskin Parade (1936) **93m.** *** D: David Butler. Stuart Erwin, Judy Garland, Patsy Kelly, Jack Haley, Johnny Downs, Betty Grable. Entertaining football musicomedy with fine cast; songs include: "It's Love I'm After," "You Say the Darndest Things." Garland's first feature film.

Pigs vs. Freaks SEE: **Off Sides**

Pilgrimage (1933) **95m.** **½ D: John Ford. Henrietta Crosman, Heather Angel, Norman Foster, Marian Nixon, Lucille La Verne, Hedda Hopper, Charles Grapewin. Unusual film, beautifully directed by Ford, about old woman who breaks up son's romance by sending him off to war (WW1), living to regret it, but finding solace on visit to France. Delicately sentimental, it works up to a point, then goes overboard, but still has some memorable sequences.

Pilgrim, Farewell (1982) **C-119m. TVM** D: Michael Roemer. Elizabeth Huddle, Christopher Lloyd, Laurie Prange, Lesley Paxton, Shelley Wyant, Elizabeth Franz, Robert Brown. Thoughtful drama about a woman, dying of cancer, who must come to terms with her lover—and her bitter teen-aged daughter, whom she abandoned years before. Script by Roemer; a PBS *American Playhouse* presentation. Average.

Pillars of the Sky (1956) **C-95m.** **½ D: George Marshall. Jeff Chandler, Dorothy Malone, Ward Bond, Keith Andes, Lee Marvin, Sydney Chaplin. Chandler is apt as swaggering army officer fighting Indians, courting Malone.

Pillow of Death (1945) **66m.** ** D: Wallace Fox. Lon Chaney, Brenda Joyce, J. Edward Bromberg, Rosalind Ivan, Clara Blandick. Another Chaney *Inner Sanctum* vehicle about lawyer turning to murder to clear the way for his true love.

Pillow Talk (1959) **C-105m.** ***½ D: Michael Gordon. Doris Day, Rock Hudson, Tony Randall, Thelma Ritter, Nick Adams, Julia Meade, Allen Jenkins, Lee Patrick, William Schallert. Rock pursues Doris, with interference from Randall and sideline witticisms from Ritter. Imaginative sex comedy has two stars sharing a party line without knowing each other's identity. Fast-moving; plush sets, gorgeous fashions. Oscar-winning story and screenplay by Stanley Shapiro, Russell Rouse, Clarence Greene, and Maurice Richlin.▼

Pillow to Post (1945) **92m.** ** D: Vincent Sherman. Ida Lupino, Sydney Greenstreet, William Prince, Stuart Erwin, Ruth Donnelly, Barbara Brown. Obvious WW2 comedy of salesgirl Lupino having soldier Prince pose as her husband so she can get a room; good cast saddled with predictable script.

Pilot, The (1979) **C-99m.** ** D: Cliff Robertson. Cliff Robertson, Diane Baker, Frank Converse, Dana Andrews, Milo O'Shea, Ed Binns, Gordon MacRae. Airline pilot who flies at the end of a bottle discovers that his world is collapsing. Predictable drama given a boost by Walter Lassally's spectacular aerial photography and John Addison's soaring (and seemingly misplaced) score.▼

Pilot No. 5 (1943) **70m.** ** D: George Sidney. Franchot Tone, Marsha Hunt, Gene Kelly, Van Johnson, Alan Baxter, Dick Simmons. Sad waste of fine cast, as Tone takes on suicide mission and others recall his jumbled life.

Pimpernel Smith (1941-British) **122m.** *** D: Leslie Howard. Leslie Howard, Mary Morris, Francis L. Sullivan, Hugh McDermott. Zesty updating of THE SCARLET PIMPERNEL to WW2, with Howard replaying the role of the savior of Nazi-hounded individuals. Retitled: MISTER V.▼

Pinball Pick-Up SEE: **Pick-Up Summer**▼

Pinball Summer SEE: **Pick-Up Summer**▼

Pine Canyon Is Burning (1977) **C-78m. TVM** D: Chris Nyby II. Kent McCord, Diana Muldaur, Andrew Duggan, Richard Bakalyan, Megan McCord, Shane Sinutko. Family adventure film has McCord as a widowered fireman raising his two small children while operating a one-man fire-rescue station. Below average.

Pink Cadillac (1989) **C-122m.** ** D: Clint Eastwood. Clint Eastwood, Bernadette Peters, Timothy Carhart, Tiffany Gail Robinson, Angela Louise Robinson, John Dennis Johnston, Geoffrey Lewis, William Hickey. Harmless but off-the-cuff throwaway comedy about a bail-bond bounty hunter who helps the wife of his latest target rescue her kidnapped baby from the neo-Nazi associates of her weakling husband. No Edsel, but at two hours, seriously in need of a tuneup. Eastwood's uncharacteristically broad performance does more for the film than the film does for him.▼

Pink Floyd—The Wall (1982-British) C-99m. **½ D: Alan Parker. Bob Geldof, Christine Hargreaves, James Laurenson, Eleanor David, Bob Hoskins. Visualization of Pink Floyd's somber best-selling album, about a rock star's mental breakdown, is perhaps the longest rock video to date, and certainly the most depressing. Many of the images are hypnotic, but the air of self-indulgence, and relentlessly downbeat theme, erode one's interest after a while. Striking animated sequences by political cartoonist Gerald Scarfe.▼

Pink Jungle, The (1968) C-104m. **½ D: Delbert Mann. James Garner, Eva Renzi, George Kennedy, Nigel Green, Michael Ansara, George Rose. Offbeat blend of comedy and adventure with photographer Garner and model Renzi involved in diamond smuggling while on-location in South America. Film shifts gears too often, but provides lighthearted entertainment.

Pink Motel (1983) C-88m. BOMB D: Mike MacFarland. Phyllis Diller, Slim Pickens, Terri Berland, Brad Cowgill, Cathryn Hartt, Andrea Howard, Tony Longo. Diller and Pickens run a hot-sheets motel in this R-rated movie version of TV's *Love— American Style*. Corny dialogue, listless direction. ▼

Pink Nights (1985) C-84m. ** D: Philip Koch. Shaun Allen, Kevin Anderson, Peri Kaczmarek, Larry King, Jonathan Jancovic Michaels, Jessica Vitkus. Inconsequential teen comedy about Anderson, who does not seem to have much luck with the opposite sex, and how he comes to live with a trio of girls. Attempt to satirize punk life-style is only moderately successful.▼

Pink Panther, The (1964) C-113m. ***½ D: Blake Edwards. Peter Sellers, David Niven, Capucine, Robert Wagner, Claudia Cardinale, Brenda DeBanzie, John LeMesurier, Fran Jeffries. Delightful caper comedy introduced bumbling Inspector Clouseau to the world (as well as the cartoon character featured in the opening titles), so obsessed with catching notorious jewel thief "The Phantom" that he isn't even aware his quarry is also his wife's lover! Loaded with great slapstick and especially clever chase sequence; beautiful European locations, memorable score by Henry Mancini. Immediately followed by A SHOT IN THE DARK.▼

Pink Panther Strikes Again, The (1976-British) C-103m. ***½ D: Blake Edwards. Peter Sellers, Herbert Lom, Colin Blakely, Leonard Rossiter, Lesley-Anne Down, Burt Kwouk, Andre Maranne. Fifth PINK PANTHER is one of the funniest. Sellers' former boss (Lom) goes crazy, threatens to destroy the world with a ray-gun he has commandeered. Sellers' hilarious Inspector Clouseau is backed up by better-than-usual gags—with the usual number of pain-and-destruction jokes thrown in for good measure. Sequel: REVENGE OF THE PINK PANTHER.▼

Pinky (1949) 102m. *** D: Elia Kazan. Jeanne Crain, Ethel Barrymore, Ethel Waters, Nina Mae McKinney, William Lundigan. Pioneer racial drama of black girl passing for white, returning to Southern home; still has impact, with fine support from Mmes. Waters and Barrymore.▼

Pinocchio (1940) C-88m. **** D: Ben Sharpsteen, Hamilton Luske. Voices of Dickie Jones, Christian Rub, Cliff Edwards, Evelyn Venable, Walter Catlett, Frankie Darro. Walt Disney's brilliant, timeless animated cartoon feature, based on the Collodi story about an inquisitive, tale-spinning wooden puppet who wants more than anything else to become a real boy. Technically dazzling, emotionally rich, with unforgettable characters and some of the scariest scenes ever put on film (Lampwick's transformation into a jackass, the chase with Monstro the whale). A joy, no matter how many times you see it. Songs are the icing on the cake, including Oscar-winning "When You Wish Upon a Star."▼

Pinocchio and the Emperor of the Night (1987) C-87m. ** D: Hal Sutherland. Voices of Edward Asner, Tom Bosley, Lana Beeson, Linda Gary, Jonathan Harris, James Earl Jones, Ricky Lee Jones, Don Knotts, William Windom. Uninspired continuation of the Pinocchio story: now a real boy, Pinocchio is guided by "Gee Whillikers," a wooden bug come to life, and they enjoy many adventures which parallel the Disney classic. Fully animated by Filmation Studios, but an embarrassment next to the 1940 gem.▼

Pinocchio in Outer Space (1964-U.S.-French) C-90m. ** D: Ray Goosens. Voices of Arnold Stang, Jess Cain. Watchable cartoon adventure for kids, with unmemorable songs.▼

Pin-Up Girl (1944) C-83m. **½ D: H. Bruce Humberstone. Betty Grable, Martha Raye, John Harvey, Joe E. Brown, Eugene Pallette, Mantan Moreland, Charlie Spivak Orchestra. One of Grable's weaker vehicles, despite support from Raye and Brown; songs are nil, so is plot.▼

Pioneer Builders SEE: **Conquerors, The**

Pioneer Woman (1973) C-78m. TVM D: Buzz Kulik. Joanna Pettet, William Shatner, David Janssen, Lance LeGault, Helen Hunt, Russell Baer. Frontier drama about joys and hardships of homesteading in Wyoming circa 1867. The Old West from the woman's viewpoint. Average.▼

Pipe Dreams (1976) C-89m. **½ D: Stephen Verona. Gladys Knight, Barry Hankerson, Bruce French, Sherry Bain, Wayne

[895]

Tippit, Altovise Davis, Sally Kirkland. Singing star Knight makes acting debut in highly dramatic story set against Alaskan pipeline. Excellent location shooting. Soundtrack filled with songs by Knight and her group, the Pips.▼

Piranha (1978) **C-92m.** ******* D: Joe Dante. Bradford Dillman, Heather Menzies, Kevin McCarthy, Keenan Wynn, Dick Miller, Barbara Steele, Belinda Balaski, Bruce Gordon, Paul Bartel. Fast-paced, funny spoof of JAWS and countless 1950s sci-fi films; in-jokes and campy supporting cast will make it particular fun for film buffs. Written by John Sayles. Followed by a sequel.▼

Piranha II: The Spawning (1981-Italian-U.S.) **C-95m.** ***½** D: James Cameron. Tricia O'Neil, Steve Marachuk, Lance Henriksen, Ricky G. Paul, Ted Richert, Leslie Graves. A sequel to PIRANHA in name only, this silly horror film is set at a Club Med-type resort where human mating rituals are interrupted by the spawning ritual of mutated flying fish (grunions), which are oversize, deadly killers. You'd have to be psychic to have spotted any talent from director Cameron in this debut picture; he made THE TERMINATOR next and hit the big time. ▼

Pirate, The (1948) **C-102m.** ******* D: Vincente Minnelli. Judy Garland, Gene Kelly, Walter Slezak, Gladys Cooper, Reginald Owen, George Zucco, The Nicholas Brothers. Judy thinks circus clown Kelly is really Caribbean pirate; lavish costuming, dancing and Cole Porter songs (including "Be a Clown") bolster stagy plot. Kelly's dances are exhilarating, as usual. Based on S.N. Behrman play.▼

Pirate, The (1978) SEE: **Harold Robbins' The Pirate**

Pirate and the Slave Girl (1961-Italian) **C-87m.** ****** D: Piero Pierotti. Lex Barker, Massimo Serato, Chelo Alonso, Michele Malaspina, Enzo Maggio. Formula costumer with Barker the hero who sees the light of the true cause, helping benevolent pirates vs. wicked governor.

Pirate Movie, The (1982-Australian) **C-99m.** BOMB D: Ken Annakin. Kristy McNichol, Christopher Atkins, Ted Hamilton, Bill Kerr, Maggie Kirkpatrick, Garry McDonald. Appalling "update" of Gilbert & Sillivan's *The Pirates of Penzance* not only trashes the original but fails on its own paltry terms—as a teenybopper comedy with bubblegum music. Parodies (and steals from) so many other films it should have been called THE RIP-OFF MOVIE.▼

Pirates (1986-French-Tunisian) **C-124m.** ****½** D: Roman Polanski. Walter Matthau, Damien Thomas, Richard Pearson, Cris Campion, Charlotte Lewis, Olu Jacobs, Roy Kinnear, Ferdy Mayne. Rich-looking, robust pirate comedy, filmed on a grand scale (in widescreen, which will be lost on a TV set), with plenty of broad comedy, a delightful performance by Matthau, a rousing score by Philippe Sarde . . . and a certain lack of story. It's still fun.▼

Pirate Ship SEE: **Mutineers, The**

Pirates of Blood River, The (1962-British) **C-87m.** ****** D: John Gilling. Kerwin Mathews, Glenn Corbett, Christopher Lee, Marla Landi, Oliver Reed, Andrew Keir, Peter Arne. Earnest but hackneyed account of Huguenots fighting off buccaneers.

Pirates of Capri, The (1949) **94m.** ****** D: Edgar G. Ulmer. Louis Hayward, Binnie Barnes, Alan Curtis, Rudolph (Massimo) Serato. Below-average adventure film has Neapolitan natives revolting against tyrant. Lots of action but not much else. Filmed in Italy. Retitled: CAPTAIN SIROCCO.

Pirates of Monterey (1947) **C-77m.** ****** D: Alfred L. Werker. Maria Montez, Rod Cameron, Mikhail Rasumny, Philip Reed, Gilbert Roland, Gale Sondergaard. Dull film of exciting period in history, the fight against Mexican control of California in the 1800s. 1840s

Pirates of Penzance, The (1983) **C-112m.** ******* D: Wilford Leach. Kevin Kline, Angela Lansbury, Linda Ronstadt, George Rose, Rex Smith, Tony Azito. Joseph Papp's hit stage revival of the Gilbert and Sullivan perennial is transferred to film with the original cast (plus Lansbury) and director—who decided to make no bones about its theatricality! Not for G&S purists, perhaps, but fun. Splendid production design by Elliot Scott.▼

Pirates of Tortuga (1961) **C-97m.** ****** D: Robert D. Webb. Ken Scott, John Richardson, Letitia Roman, Dave King, Rafer Johnson. Lumbering costumer involving buccaneer Sir Henry Morgan.

Pirates of Tripoli (1955) **C-72m.** ****** D: Felix E. Feist. Paul Henreid, Patricia Medina, Paul Newland, John Miljan, William Fawcett. Veteran cast tries to be lively in tired costumer, with colorful scenery the only virtue.

Pistol for Ringo, A (1966-Italian) **C-97m.** ****½** D: Duccio Tessari. Montgomery Wood, Fernando Sancho, Hally Hammond, Nieves Navarro. Wood is the gun-shooting hero in Texas where he combats maurauding Mexicans hiding out at a ranch.

Pit and the Pendulum, The (1961) **C-80m.** *****½** D: Roger Corman. Vincent Price, John Kerr, Barbara Steele, Luana Anders, Antony Carbone. Slick horror tale set right after Spanish Inquisition. Price thinks he is his late father, the most vicious torturer during bloody inquisition. Beautifully staged; watch out for that incredible pendulum . . . and bear with slow first half. The second of Corman's Poe adaptations, scripted by Richard Matheson.▼

Pitfall, The (1948) **84m.** *** D: Andre de Toth. Dick Powell, Lizabeth Scott, Jane Wyatt, Raymond Burr, John Litel, Byron Barr. Married man's brief extramarital fling may cost him his job and marriage. Intriguing *film noir* look at the American dream gone sour, typefied by Powell's character, who's got a house, a little boy, and a perfect wife—but feels bored and stifled.

Pit Stop (1969) **92m.** BOMB D: Jack Hill. Brian Donlevy, Richard Davalos, Ellen McRae (Burstyn), Sid Haig, Beverly Washburn, George Washburn. Donlevy runs racing organization that will stop at nothing to win, in extremely low-budget action pic.

Pittsburgh (1942) **90m.** ** D: Lewis Seiler. Marlene Dietrich, John Wayne, Randolph Scott, Frank Craven, Louise Allbritton, Thomas Gomez, Shemp Howard. Big John loves the coal and steel business more than he does Marlene, which leaves field open for rival Scott. Slow-moving despite cast.

Pixote (1981-Brazilian) **C-127m.** **** D: Hector Babenco. Fernando Ramos da Silva, Marilia Pera, Jorge Juliano, Gilberto Moura, Jose Nilson dos Santos, Edilson Lino. Chilling drama about an abandoned 10-year-old street criminal who pimps, sniffs glue, and murders three people before the finale. Haunting performance by the baby-faced da Silva; Pera equally superb as a prostitute. Extraordinarily graphic film is not for the squeamish.▼

Pizza Triangle, The (1970-Italian) **C-99m.** **½ D: Ettore Scola. Marcello Mastroianni, Monica Vitti, Giancarlo Giannini. Scene-stealing stars compete in this flamboyant black comedy of two guys both in love with flower seller Vitti. Colorful photography by Carlo Di Palma (adopted 15 years later as Woody Allen's cameraman). Also known as A DRAMA OF JEALOUSY.

P.J. (1968) **C-109m.** ** D: John Guillermin. George Peppard, Raymond Burr, Gayle Hunnicutt, Brock Peters, Wilfrid Hyde-White, Coleen Gray, Susan Saint James. Private-eye takes job bodyguarding the mistress of a tycoon. OK for those who'll sit through any film of this genre, but no big deal; TV print runs 101m., and cuts out much violence—including memorable subway death.

P.K. and the Kid (1982) **C-89m.** ** D: Lou Lombardo. Paul Le Mat, Molly Ringwald, Alex Rocco, Fionnula Flanagan, Charles Hallahan, Bert Remsen, Esther Rolle, Leigh Hamilton. Stillborn tale of arm wrestling (made several years before the Sylvester Stallone classic OVER THE TOP, but released afterward) teams strong-wristed Le Mat with runaway teen Ringwald on the road to nowhere. With that cast and a mood resembling Le Mat's MEL-VIN AND HOWARD, this should have been more interesting.▼

Place Called Glory, A (1966-German) **C-92m.** ** D: Ralph Gideon. Lex Barker, Pierre Brice, Marianne Koch, Jorge Rigaud. German-made Western with Karl May's recurring characters Winnetou and Old Satterhand. Plot killed by dubbing.

Place Called Today, A (1972) **C-103m.** BOMB D: Don Schain. Cheri Caffaro, J. Herbert Kerr, Lana Wood, Richard Smedley, Tim Brown. Ugly, lurid drive-in sex-and-violence ragout (originally rated X) masquerading as important statement about political campaigning. Made by the GINGER people, in a classic case of over-reaching.▼

Place for Lovers, A (1969-Italian-French) **C-90m.** BOMB D: Vittorio De Sica. Faye Dunaway, Marcello Mastroianni, Caroline Mortimer, Karin Engh. One well-known critic called this "the most godawful piece of pseudo romantic slop I've ever seen!" Love story about American fashion designer and Italian engineer marks career low points for Dunaway, Mastroianni, De Sica.

Place in the Sun, A (1951) **122m.** *** D: George Stevens. Montgomery Clift, Elizabeth Taylor, Shelley Winters, Keefe Brasselle, Raymond Burr, Anne Revere. Ambitious film seems curiously dated; remake of Dreiser's AN AMERICAN TRAGEDY derives most of its power from Clift's brilliant performance, almost matched by Winters as plain girl who loses him to alluring Taylor. Depiction of the idle rich, and American morals, seems outdated, and Burr's scenes as fiery D.A. are downright absurd. Everyone gets A for effort; six Oscars included Best Direction, Screenplay (Michael Wilson, Harry Brown), Score (Franz Waxman), Cinematography (William C. Mellor), Film Editing, and Costume Design.▼

Place of One's Own, A (1945-British) **92m.** **½ D: Bernard Knowles. James Mason, Margaret Lockwood, Barbara Mullen, Dennis Price, Helen Haye, Ernest Thesiger. Well-made film about couple who buy "haunted" house, and young woman who becomes possessed by spirit of former owner. Weakened by low-key presentation, but kept going by good performances. Mason plays unusual role of older, retired man.

Places in the Heart (1984) **C-102m.** *** D: Robert Benton. Sally Field, Lindsay Crouse, Ed Harris, Amy Madigan, John Malkovich, Danny Glover. Writer-director Benton's affectionate look at life in his hometown, Waxahachie, Texas, during the Depression 1930s. A bit too calculated and predictable, but Field is so good (as a young widow determined to survive as a cotton farmer), and film is so well made (beautifully shot by Nestor Almendros), it's hard not to like. Field won Best Actress Oscar for her performance as did Benton for his original screenplay.▼

Place to Call Home, A (1987) **C-100m.** TVM D: Russ Mayberry. Linda Lavin, Lane Smith, Lori Loughlin, Robert Macnaughton, Paul Cronin, Maggie Fitzgibbon. Houston housewife moves to the Australian Outback with eleven children to run a sheep ranch with her husband—who never shows up. Average.

Plague (1978-Canadian) **C-88m.** BOMB D: Ed Hunt. Daniel Pilon, Kate Reid, Celine Lomez, Michael J. Reynolds, Brenda Donohue, Barbara Gordon. Deadly bacterium is on the loose. Phony and stultifyingly boring. Orginally titled M3: THE GEMINI STRAIN.

Plague Dogs, The (1982) **C-86m.** *** D: Martin Rosen. Voices of John Hurt, James Bolam, Christopher Benjamin, Judy Geeson, Barbara Leigh-Hunt. Unusual animated adventure, adapted from Richard Adams's novel about a pair of dogs who escape from animal experimentation lab and are hunted down like criminals. A bit slow-moving but beautifully animated and most worthwhile; a poignant plea for animal rights. For adults and older children only. A follow-up to WATERSHIP DOWN from same producer-director.▼

Plague of the Zombies, The (1966-British) **C-90m.** **½ D: John Gilling. Andre Morell, Diane Clare, Brook Williams, Jacqueline Pearce. Beautiful low-key photography and direction in fairly tense story of voodoo cult in Cornish village.

Plainsman, The (1936) **113m.** *** D: Cecil B. DeMille. Gary Cooper, Jean Arthur, James Ellison, Charles Bickford, Porter Hall, Victor Varconi, Helen Burgess, John Miljan, Gabby Hayes. Typical DeMille hokum, a big, outlandish Western which somehow manages to involve Wild Bill Hickok, Calamity Jane, Buffalo Bill, George Custer and Abraham Lincoln in adventure of evil Bickford selling guns to the Indians. About as authentic as BLAZING SADDLES, but who cares? Look for Anthony Quinn as a Cheyenne warrior. Remade in 1966.▼

Plainsman, The (1966) **C-92m.** *½ D: David Lowell Rich. Don Murray, Guy Stockwell, Abby Dalton, Bradford Dillman, Leslie Nielsen. Static remake of the Cooper-Arthur vehicle that is dull even on its own.

Plainsman and the Lady, The (1946) **87m.** ** D: Joseph Kane. William Elliott, Vera Ralston, Gail Patrick, Joseph Schildkraut, Andy Clyde. Wild Bill Elliott is tame in uninspiring saga of pony express pioneer battling slimy villains and winning lovely Ralston.

Plainsong (1982) **C/B&W-78m.** ***½ D: Ed Stabile. Jessica Nelson, Teresanne Joseph, Lyn Traverse, Steve Geiger, Sandon McCall, Howard Harris. Extremely moving, starkly realistic yet poetic drama of life and death in pioneer Nebraska, focusing on experiences of three young women settlers. Wonderfully directed; filmed, incredibly, in New Jersey.

Planes, Trains & Automobiles (1987) **C-93m.** **½ D: John Hughes. Steve Martin, John Candy, Laila Robbins, Michael McKean, Kevin Bacon, Dylan Baker, William Windom, Edie McClurg. Bittersweet farce about a businessman trying to get home for Thanksgiving who encounters disaster at every turn and has to share most of it with a lout who becomes his steadfast companion. Martin mostly plays straight to the overbearing Candy, but writer-director Hughes refuses to make either one a caricature—which keeps this amiable film teetering between slapstick shenanigans and compassionate comedy. Five demerits, however, for that awful music score.▼

Planet Earth (1974) **C-78m.** TVM D: Marc Daniels. John Saxon, Janet Margolin, Ted Cassidy, Diana Muldaur, Johana DeWinter, Christopher Gary. Sci-fi fun as future race of humans finds itself in combat with a sadistic matriarchy. Reworking of Gene Roddenberry's GENESIS II, though not as elaborate. Average.

Planet of Blood (1966) **C-81m.** **½ D: Curtis Harrington. John Saxon, Basil Rathbone, Judi Meredith, Dennis Hopper, Florence Marly. Eerie space opera (utilizing effects footage cribbed from a big-budget Russian film) about a space vampire brought to Earth. Best thing is the bizarre climax, if you can wait that long. Originally titled QUEEN OF BLOOD.▼

Planet of Horrors SEE: Galaxy of Terror▼

Planet of the Apes (1968) **C-112m.** ***½ D: Franklin J. Schaffner. Charlton Heston, Roddy McDowall, Kim Hunter, Maurice Evans, James Whitmore, James Daly, Linda Harrison. Modern near-classic sci-fi. Heston leads a group of surviving astronauts in shocking future world where apes are masters, humans slaves. Only liabilities: somewhat familiar plot, self-conscious humor; otherwise, a must-see. Michael Wilson and Rod Serling scripted from Pierre Boulle's novel, spawning four sequels and two TV series. Won a special Oscar for make-up created by John Chambers.▼

Planet of the Vampires (1965-Italian) **C-86m.** **½ D: Mario Bava. Barry Sullivan, Norma Bengell, Angel Aranda, Evi Marandi, Fernando Villena. Eerily photographed, atmospheric science-fantasy of spaceship looking for missing comrades on misty planet where strange power controls their minds. Shown on TV as THE DEMON PLANET.▼

Planet on the Prowl SEE: **War Between the Planets**▼

Planets Against Us (1961-Italian-French) **85m.** *½ D: Romano Ferara. Michel Lemoine, Maria Pia Luzi, Jany Clair, Marco Guglielmi, Otello Toso. Human-like aliens come to earth and destroy everyone they touch. Pretty bad.▼

Plan 9 From Outer Space (1959) **79m.** BOMB D: Edward D. Wood, Jr. Gregory Walcott, Tom Keene, Duke Moore, Mona McKinnon, Dudley Manlove, Joanna Lee, Tor Johnson, Lyle Talbot, Bela Lugosi, Vampira, Criswell. Hailed as the worst movie ever made; certainly one of the funniest. Pompous aliens believe they can conquer Earth by resurrecting corpses from a San Fernando Valley cemetery. Lugosi died after two days' shooting in 1956; his remaining scenes were played by a taller, younger man holding a cape over his face! So mesmerizingly awful it actually improves (so to speak) with each viewing. And remember: it's all based on sworn testimony! Also known as GRAVE ROBBERS FROM OUTER SPACE; followed by REVENGE OF THE DEAD.▼

Planter's Wife SEE: **Outpost in Malaya**

Platinum Blonde (1931) **90m.** *** D: Frank Capra. Jean Harlow, Loretta Young, Robert Williams, Louise Closser Hale, Donald Dillaway, Walter Catlett. Snappy comedy about wisecracking reporter who marries wealthy girl (Harlow) but can't stand confinement of life among high society. Despite engaging presence of Harlow and Young, it's Williams' show all the way.

Platinum High School (1960) **93m.** ** D: Charles Haas. Mickey Rooney, Terry Moore, Dan Duryea, Yvette Mimieux, Conway Twitty, Jimmy Boyd. Limp attempt at sensationalism, with Rooney a father discovering that his son's death at school wasn't accidental. Retitled: TROUBLE AT 16.

Platoon (1986) **C-120m.** ***½ D: Oliver Stone. Tom Berenger, Willem Dafoe, Charlie Sheen, Forest Whitaker, Francesco Quinn, John C. McGinley, Richard Edson, Kevin Dillon, Reggie Johnson, Keith David, Johnny Depp. Penetrating first-person account of life on the line as a young soldier in the Vietnam War. Harrowingly realistic and completely convincing, though the motives and reactions of its main character (played by Sheen, based on writer-director Stone) are hard to relate to—leaving this otherwise excellent film with a certain degree of aloofness. Academy Award winner for Best Picture, Director, Film Editing (Claire Simpson), and Sound.▼

Platoon Leader (1988) **C-100m.** BOMB D: Aaron Norris. Michael Dudikoff, Robert F. Lyons, Michael De Lorenzo, Rick Fitts, Jesse Dabson. Obnoxious, bloody PLATOON rip-off, about a group of American GIs battling the commies in Southeast Asia. Director Norris is the brother of Chuck.▼

Playboy of the Western World, The (1962-Irish) **C-100m.** *** D: Brian Desmond Hurst. Gary Raymond, Siobhan McKenna, Elspeth March, Michael O'Brien, Liam Redmond, Niall MacGinnis. Simple and eloquent, if a bit stagy, version of J. M. Synge's classic satire. Boyish, boastful Christy Mahon (Raymond) charms a small Irish village with his tale of how he did in his dad.▼

Play Dirty (1969-British) **C-117m.** *** D: Andre de Toth. Michael Caine, Nigel Davenport, Nigel Green, Harry Andrews, Aly Ben Ayed. British army captain leads group of ex-cons into the North African campaign in WW2; film invites comparison with THE DIRTY DOZEN and holds its own quite well.

Players (1979) **C-120m.** BOMB D: Anthony Harvey. Ali MacGraw, Dean-Paul Martin, Maximilian Schell, Pancho Gonzalez, Steve Guttenberg, Melissa Prophet. Aspiring tennis pro has to choose between forehand and foreplay when he falls for a "kept" woman. There's something wrong with any movie where Pancho Gonzalez gives the best performance.▼

Players (1980) SEE: **Club, The**

Play Girl (1940) **75m.** **½ D: Frank Woodruff. Kay Francis, Nigel Bruce, James Ellison, Margaret Hamilton, Mildred Coles. Francis is hip gold-digger who teaches younger women how to fleece clients; offbeat programmer.

Playgirl (1954) **85m.** **½ D: Joseph Pevney. Shelley Winters, Barry Sullivan, Gregg Palmer, Richard Long, Kent Taylor. Winters is most comfortable in drama about girl involved with gangsters.

Playgirl After Dark SEE: **Too Hot to Handle** (1959)

Playgirl Gang SEE: **Switchblade Sisters**▼

Playgirl Killer, The SEE: **Decoy for Terror**▼

Playing for Time (1980) **C-150m.** TVM D: Daniel Mann. Vanessa Redgrave, Jane Alexander, Maud Adams, Viveca Lindfors, Shirley Knight, Melanie Mayron, Marisa Berenson, Verna Bloom, Martha Schlamme, Marta Heflin. Outstanding drama about Fania Fenelon, who survived Auschwitz by performing in a bizarre orchestra "playing for time" while other inmates are marched to their death. Redgrave, as Fenelon, and Alexander, as the orchestra's leader, won Emmy Awards for their performances (Knight also received a nomination). Arthur Miller's stunning teleplay earned him an Emmy, and the film itself won as Outstanding Drama Special. Above average.▼

Playing with Fire (1985) **C-100m. TVM**
D: Ivan Nagy. Gary Coleman, Cicely
Tyson, Yaphet Kotto, Ron O'Neal, Salome
Jens, Tammy Lauren. Young Gary's dramatic debut has him playing a disturbed
teenaged arsonist while a good supporting
cast goes through its paces. He caps simplistic plot turns by stepping out of character at the end to lecture the audience on
arson. Below average.

Play It Again, Sam (1972) **C-87m. ***½**
D: Herbert Ross. Woody Allen, Diane
Keaton, Tony Roberts, Jerry Lacy, Susan
Anspach, Jennifer Salt, Joy Bang, Viva.
Delightful adaptation of Woody's own play
about film buff coached by the ghost of
Bogart in fumbling attempts to meet a girl
after his wife divorces him. More "con-
ventional" than other early Allen films,
but just as funny.▼

Play It As It Lays (1972) **C-99m. **½ D:**
Frank Perry. Tuesday Weld, Anthony Perkins, Tammy Grimes, Adam Roarke, Ruth
Ford, Eddie Firestone. Film version of
Joan Didion's best seller about neglected
wife of self-centered film director is helped
by Weld-Perkins casting. Story is believable enough, but rambles inconclusively.
Look for Tyne Daly as a journalist.

Play It Cool (1962-British) **82m. *½ D:**
Michael Winner. Billy Fury, Michael Anderson, Jr., Dennis Price, Richard Wattis,
Anna Palk, Keith Hamshere, Ray Brooks.
Mild rock 'n' roll entry, with thin plot
line of groovy group preventing a rich girl
from going wrong.

Playmates (1941) **94m. *½ D:** David Butler. Kay Kyser, Lupe Velez, John Barrymore, May Robson, Patsy Kelly, Peter
Lind Hayes. Poor musical "comedy" of
Shakespearean actor teaming up with
bandleader to pay back taxes. Film is unbelievably bad at times, only worth seeing
for poor John Barrymore in his last
film.▼

Playmates (1972) **C-73m. TVM** D: Theodore J. Flicker. Alan Alda, Connie
Stevens, Doug McClure, Barbara Feldon,
Eileen Brennan, Tiger Williams, Severn
Darden. Chance meeting of divorced men
(Alda and McClure) slowly precipitates
plan to check up on ex-wives. Fairly intelligent complications; cast seems to be enjoying themselves. Above average.▼

Play Misty for Me (1971) **C-102m. ***
D: Clint Eastwood. Clint Eastwood, Jessica Walter, Donna Mills, John Larch,
Irene Hervey, Jack Ging, Johnny Otis,
Cannonball Adderley Quintet. Well-done
shocker of late night radio D.J. stalked by
homicidal ex-fan Walter. Eastwood's first
film as director; his frequent director, Don
Siegel, plays Murphy the bartender.▼

Playtime (1967-French) **C-108m. **** D:**
Jacques Tati. Jacques Tati, Barbara Dennek,
Jacqueline Lecomte, Valerie Camille, Leon

Doyen. Tati's famous character, M. Hulot,
wanders through an unrecognizable modern Paris of steel and glass skyscrapers.
Sight and sound gags abound in this superbly constructed film, the various episodes of which are linked by Hulot's trying
to keep an appointment. Art Buchwald
provided dialogue for English-speaking
scenes. Cut from original 155m. French
version.▼

Plaza Suite (1971) **C-115m. *** D:** Arthur
Hiller. Walter Matthau, Maureen Stapleton,
Barbara Harris, Lee Grant, Louise Sorel.
One of Neil Simon's funniest plays well-
adapted to screen. Three separate stories
about people staying in certain room at
famed N.Y.C. hotel, with Matthau in
all three vignettes. Best one is the last,
with Matthau as flustered father of a reluctant bride.▼

Please Believe Me (1950) **87m. **½ D:**
Norman Taurog. Deborah Kerr, Robert
Walker, James Whitmore, Peter Lawford,
Mark Stevens, Spring Byington. Pleasant
fluff of Britisher Kerr aboard liner headed
for America, wooed by assorted bachelors
aboard, who think she's an heiress.

Please Don't Eat the Daisies (1960)
C-111m. * D:** Charles Walters. Doris
Day, David Niven, Janis Paige, Spring
Byington, Richard Haydn, Patsy Kelly,
Jack Weston, Margaret Lindsay. Bright
film based on Jean Kerr's play about a
drama critic and his family. Doris sings
title song; her kids are very amusing, as
are Byington (the mother-in-law), Kelly
(housekeeper), and especially Paige as a
temperamental star. Later a TV series.

Please! Mr. Balzac (1957-French) **99m.**
*** D: Marc Allegret. Daniel Gelin, Brigitte Bardot, Robert Hirsch, Darry Cowl.
Engaging BB romp of girl involved in
theft of rare book and her shenanigans to
become disinvolved. Retitled: MADEMOI-
SELLE STRIPTEASE.▼

Please Murder Me (1956) **78m. **½ D:**
Peter Godfrey. Angela Lansbury, Raymond
Burr, Dick Foran, John Dehner, Lamont
Johnson. Lansbury and Burr's energetic
performances elevate this homicide yarn.

Please Turn Over (1960-British) **86m.**
**½ D: Gerald Thomas. Ted Ray, Jean
Kent, Leslie Phillips, Joan Sims, Julia
Lockwood, Tim Seely. OK froth about
teen daughter's lurid novel-writing and the
repercussions it causes.

Pleasure Cove (1979) **C-100m. TVM**
D: Bruce Bilson. Tom Jones, Constance
Forslund, Melody Anderson, Joan Hackett,
Harry Guardino, Shelley Fabares, Jerry
Lacy. Busted pilot taking the *Love Boat*
multiplot premise and relocating it to a
posh resort. Jones' acting debut. Average.

Pleasure Cruise (1933) **72m. **½ D:**
Frank Tuttle. Roland Young, Genevieve
Tobin, Ralph Forbes, Una O'Connor, Her-

[900]

bert Mundin, Minna Gombell. Husband and wife take "separate vacations," but he jealously follows her on board ocean liner. Chic Lubitsch-like comedy runs out of steam halfway through.

Pleasure Garden, The (1925-British) **75m.** ** D: Alfred Hitchcock. Virginia Valli, Carmelita Geraghty, Miles Mander, John Stuart, George Snell. Hitchcock's first feature, shot in Munich; uneven account of a pair of chorus girls, one (Valli) sweet and knowing, the other (Geraghty) a waif who becomes a glamorous bitch. Forgettable silent melodrama served as an apprenticeship for its director.

Pleasure of His Company, The (1961) **C-115m.** ***½ D: George Seaton. Fred Astaire, Lilli Palmer, Debbie Reynolds, Tab Hunter, Charlie Ruggles. Delightful piece of fluff, from Samuel Taylor and Cornelia Otis Skinner's play about charming ex-husband who comes to visit, enchanting his daughter and hounding his wife's new husband. Entire cast in rare form.

Pleasure Palace (1980) **C-100m.** TVM D: Walter Grauman. Omar Sharif, Victoria Principal, J. D. Cannon, Gerald S. O'Loughlin, Jose Ferrer, Hope Lange, Alan King. High-rolling lothario finds his reputation at stake when he comes to the aid of a lady casino owner in distress; predictable teleplay by Blanche Hanalis. Average.▼

Pleasures (1986) **C-100m.** TVM D: Sharron Miller. Joanna Cassidy, Linda Purl, Tracy Nelson, Barry Bostwick, Rick Moses, Pamela Segall, David Paymer. Three ladies with lust in their eyes live out their fantasies with the men of their dreams one sensual summer. Smarmy romance-novel type drama written by, directed by, and starring women. Average.

Pleasure Seekers, The (1964) **C-107m.** **½ D: Jean Negulesco. Ann-Margret, Tony Franciosa, Carol Lynley, Gene Tierney, Brian Keith, Gardner McKay, Isobel Elsom. Glossy semi-musical remake of THREE COINS IN THE FOUNTAIN about three girls seeking fun and romance in Spain.

Plenty (1985) **C-124m.** **½ D: Fred Schepisi. Meryl Streep, Charles Dance, Tracey Ullman, John Gielgud, Sting, Ian McKellen, Sam Neill, Burt Kwouk. Filmization of David Hare's play about a British woman who (like Britain itself) experiences her finest hours during WW2, working for the underground . . . and never finds fulfillment or satisfaction the rest of her life. Superlative performances (Gielgud is a particular delight as aging career diplomat) and isolated moments of insight and wit can't overcome the fact that central character played by Streep is so tedious. Schepisi makes excellent use of

wide-screen frame (which unfortunately won't carry over to TV screen). ▼

Plot Against Harry, The (1989) **80m.** *** D: Michael Roemer. Martin Priest, Ben Lang, Maxine Woods, Henry Nemo, Jacques Taylor, Jean Leslie, Ellen Herbert, Sandra Kazan. Amusing, perceptive slice of N.Y.C. life about an aging racketeer, just sprung from prison, who finds the old order changing, and his life coming apart at the seams. Sad-faced Priest is perfectly cast in this modest, location-filmed production, which was filmed in 1969 but never released—until film-festival showings in 1989 won critical acclaim and a distributor.

Plot Thickens, The (1936) **69m.** **½ D: Ben Holmes. James Gleason, ZaSu Pitts, Oscar Apfel, Owen Davis, Jr., Louise Latimer. OK Entry in Hildegarde Withers mystery-comedy series with Pitts the schoolmarm who helps solve robbery and murder with inspector Gleason.

Plot to Kill Hitler, The (1990) **C-100m.** TVM D: Lawrence Schiller. Brad Davis, Madolyn Smith, Ian Richardson, Mike Gwilym, Helmut Griem, Jonathan Hyde, Kenneth Colley. Period rehash of how a group of disillusioned German officers (headed by a woefully miscast, eye-patched Davis) attempted to do away with Der Fuehrer in 1944. Needless to say, the outcome holds no suspense. Below average.

Plough and the Stars, The (1936) **78m.** ** D: John Ford. Barbara Stanwyck, Preston Foster, Barry Fitzgerald, Una O'Connor, J. M. Kerrigan, Bonita Granville, Arthur Shields. Dreary, theatrical filmization of Sean O'Casey's play with Foster as Irish revolutionary leader and Stanwyck as long-suffering wife who fears for his life; script by Dudley Nichols.

Ploughman's Lunch, The (1983-British) **C-100m.** *** D: Richard Eyre. Jonathan Pryce, Tim Curry, Rosemary Harris, Frank Finlay, Charlie Dore. Complex, cynical condemnation of British manners, morals and politics, centering on the activities of thoroughly self-centered radio reporter Pryce and others during the Falklands war. Quite perceptive, within the confines of its viewpoint.▼

Plumber, The (1980-Australian) **C-76m.** *** D: Peter Weir. Judy Morris, Ivar Kants, Robert Coleby, Candy Raymond. Obnoxious plumber tears apart bathroom of unwilling tenants; film's single joke is stretched no further than it will go in slight but amusing black comedy made for Australian television.▼

Plunderers, The (1948) **C-87m.** ** D: Joseph Kane. Rod Cameron, Ilona Massey, Adrian Booth, Forrest Tucker. OK Republic Western involving outlaws and Army joining forces against rampaging redskins: clichés are there.

Plunderers, The (1960) **93m.** **½ D: Joseph Pevney. Jeff Chandler, John Saxon, Dolores Hart, Marsha Hunt, Jay C. Flippen, Ray Stricklyn, James Westerfield. Above-par study of outlaws interacting with honest townsfolk.

Plunderers of Painted Flats (1959) **77m.** *½ D: Albert C. Gannaway. Corinne Calvet, John Carroll, Skip Homeier, George Macready, Edmund Lowe, Bea Benaderet, Madge Kennedy, Joe Besser. Flabby Western of cowpoke seeking his father's killer.

Plunder of the Sun (1953) **81m.** **½ D: John Farrow. Glenn Ford, Diana Lynn, Patricia Medina, Francis L. Sullivan. Competent cast in above-average goings-on. Ford is involved with treasure hunt and murder in Mexico.

Plunder Road (1957) **71m.** **½ D: Hubert Cornfield. Gene Raymond, Jeanne Cooper, Wayne Morris, Elisha Cook, Jr., Stafford Repp. A little sleeper about robbery caper, with competent cast giving life to intriguing story.▼

Plutonium Incident, The (1980) **C-100m. TVM** D: Richard Michaels. Janet Margolin, Bo Hopkins, Joseph Campanella, Powers Boothe, Bibi Besch, Nicholas Pryor. Suspense tale about nuclear power plant accident, with Margolin, as an activist trying to stir employee awareness, becoming the target of company harassment. Inspired, no doubt, by the Karen Silkwood story. Average.

Plymouth Adventure (1952) **C-105m.** **½ D: Clarence Brown. Spencer Tracy, Gene Tierney, Van Johnson, Leo Genn, Dawn Addams, Lloyd Bridges, Barry Jones. Superficial soap opera, glossily done, of the cynical captain of the *Mayflower* (Tracy) and the settlers who sailed from England to New England in the 17th century. This won an Oscar for its special effects.

Poacher's Daughter, The (1960-Irish) **74m.** **½ D: George Pollock. Julie Harris, Harry Brogan, Tim Seeley, Marie Keen, Brid Lynch, Noel Magee, Paul Farrell. Harris lends authenticity in title role as simple girl who straightens out her philandering boyfriend. Originally titled SALLY'S IRISH ROGUE.

Pocketful of Miracles (1961) **C-136m.** **½ D: Frank Capra. Bette Davis, Glenn Ford, Hope Lange, Thomas Mitchell, Peter Falk, Edward Everett Horton, Ann-Margret, Mickey Shaughnessy, David Brian, Sheldon Leonard, Barton MacLane, John Litel, Jerome Cowan, Fritz Feld, Jack Elam, Ellen Corby. Capra's final film, a remake of his 1933 LADY FOR A DAY, is just as sentimental, but doesn't work as well. Bette is Apple Annie, a Damon Runyon character; Ford is Dave the Dude, the racketeer who turns her into a lady. Ann-Margret is appealing in her first film.▼

Pocket Money (1972) **C-102m.** **½ D: Stuart Rosenberg. Paul Newman, Lee Marvin, Strother Martin, Christine Belford, Kelly Jean Peters, Fred Graham, Wayne Rogers. Debt-ridden cowboy and shifty pal get mixed up with crooked cattleman in modern-day Western. Strangely tepid comedy is helped by good Laszlo Kovacs photography, nice bit by Peters. Marvin's car is the damnedest thing you'll ever see.

Point, The (1971) **C-73m. TVM** D: Fred Wolf. Engaging children's cartoon about boy banished from homeland because his head is rounded, not pointed like everybody else's. Charming score by Harry Nilsson. First network airing narrated by Dustin Hoffman; his voice was replaced by Alan Thicke's for later showings. Ringo Starr narrates the video version. Above average.▼

Point Blank (1967) **C-92m.** ***½ D: John Boorman. Lee Marvin, Angie Dickinson, Keenan Wynn, Carroll O'Connor, Lloyd Bochner, Michael Strong, John Vernon. Marvin, shot and left for dead by unfaithful wife and mobster boyfriend, gets revenge two years later. Taut thriller, ignored in 1967, but now regarded as a top film of the mid-60s. Based on a novel by Donald E. Westlake (writing as Richard Stark).▼

Poison Ivy (1953-French) **90m.** ** D: Bernard Borderie. Eddie Constantine, Dominique Wilms, Howard Vernon, Dario Moreno, Gaston Modot. Constantine is again FBI agent Lemmy Caution, involved in stolen gold shipment in North Africa: grade-B actioner.

Poison Ivy (1985) **C-100m. TVM** D: Larry Elikann. Michael J. Fox, Nancy McKeon, Caren Kaye, Robert Klein, Adam Baldwin, Cary Guffey. Your typical made-for-TV tale of teenage hijinks with a boys' summer camp as the setting, Klein as the bumbling camp director, Kaye his oversexed wife, and Fox the college-age counselor and camp lothario. Average.▼

Poker Alice (1987) **C-100m. TVM** D: Arthur Allan Seidelman. Elizabeth Taylor, George Hamilton, Tom Skerritt, Richard Mulligan, David Wayne, Susan Tyrrell, Pat Corley. Lighthearted Western with Elizabeth winning a brothel at the poker table, pal George helping her run it, bounty-hunting Tom falling for her. Highlight is a DESTRY RIDES AGAIN cat fight between Liz and Susan. Written by old Western hand James Lee Barrett. Average.▼

Police (1984-French) **C-113m.** **½ D: Maurice Pialat. Gerard Depardieu, Sophie Marceau, Richard Anconina, Pascale Rocard, Sandrine Bonnaire. Taut but repetitive drama about the thin line separating cop and criminal. Depardieu is a brutal, sex-obsessed, love-starved policeman attempting to break up a drug ring; he becomes involved with tough young Marceau, one of the dealers.

Police Academy (1984) **C-95m.** **½ D: Hugh Wilson. Steve Guttenberg, G. W. Bailey, George Gaynes, Kim Cattrall, Bubba Smith, Michael Winslow, Andrew Rubin, David Graf, Bruce Mahler, Leslie Easterbrook, Georgina Spelvin. Generally good-natured comedy (with typical 80's doses of sexism and tastelessness) about a group of weirdos and misfits who enroll in big-city police academy. Winslow's comic sound effects are perfect antidote for slow spots in script. Followed by five sequels.▼

Police Academy 2: Their First Assignment (1985) **C-87m.** BOMB D: Jerry Paris. Steve Guttenberg, Bubba Smith, David Graf, Michael Winslow, Bruce Mahler, Marion Ramsey, Colleen Camp, Howard Hesseman, Art Metrano, George Gaynes, Ed Herlihy. Dreadful follow-up to 1984 hit (with different writers and director responsible). There are *Dragnet* episodes with more laughs than this movie.▼

Police Academy 3: Back in Training (1986) **C-82m.** *½ D: Jerry Paris. Steve Guttenberg, Bubba Smith, David Graf, Michael Winslow, Marion Ramsey, Leslie Easterbrook, Art Metrano, Tim Kazurinsky, Bobcat Goldthwait, George Gaynes, Shawn Weatherly. An improvement over #2, but that's not saying much: just another collection of pea-brained gags and amateurish performances.▼

Police Academy 4: Citizens on Patrol (1987) **C-87m.** BOMB D: Jim Drake. Steve Guttenberg, Bubba Smith, Michael Winslow, David Graf, Tim Kazurinsky, Sharon Stone, Leslie Easterbrook, Marion Ramsey, Lance Kinsey, G. W. Bailey, Bobcat Goldthwait, George Gaynes, Billie Bird. More of the same, only worse.▼

Police Academy 5: Assignment Miami Beach (1988) **C-90m.** BOMB D: Alan Myerson. Bubba Smith, George Gaynes, G.W. Bailey, David Graf, Michael Winslow, Leslie Easterbrook, Marion Ramsey, Janet Jones, Matt McCoy. Gaynes is in Miami to receive an award before his mandatory retirement; arch-rival Bailey comes along to gum up the works. Fourth attempt to improve on imperfection is no charm; what can you say about a sequel that Steve Guttenberg won't even appear in?▼

Police Academy 6: City Under Siege (1989) **C-83m.** BOMB D: Peter Bonerz. Bubba Smith, David Graf, Michael Winslow, Leslie Easterbrook, Marion Ramsey, Lance Kinsey, Matt McCoy, Bruce Mahler, G.W. Bailey, George Gaynes, Kenneth Mars, Gerrit Graham. Those wacky cops are back to solve a crime wave perpetrated by a trio that makes The Three Stooges look like Nobel laureates. This latest series entry is only—repeat *only*—

for those who thought POLICE ACADEMY 5 was robbed at Oscar time.▼

Police Force SEE: **Police Story** (1985)▼

Police Story, The (1973) **C-100m.** TVM D: William Graham. Vic Morrow, Chuck Connors, Diane Baker, Edward Asner, Harry Guardino, Ralph Meeker, Ina Balin, Dianne Hull, Barbara Rhoades. Long-sought criminal vows defiance, cop La Frieda (Morrow) vows capture. Joseph Wambaugh-based script includes interesting station atmosphere, department hassles. Clever direction, with Morrow solid as usual. The hit series followed. Above average.

Police Story (1985-Hong Kong) **C-89m.** *** D: Jackie Chan. Jackie Chan, Bridget Lin, Maggie Cheung, Cho Yuen, Bill Tung, Kenneth Tong. Lightning-paced kung fu comedy about cop Chan, a one-man police force attempting to get the goods on some thugs. Crammed with incredible stuntwork; a real popcorn movie that's perfect for fans of the genre. Also known as JACKIE CHAN'S POLICE STORY and POLICE FORCE.▼

Police Story: The Freeway Killings (1987) **C-150m.** TVM D: William A. Graham. Richard Crenna, Angie Dickinson, Tony LoBianco, Don Meredith, Ben Gazzara. Cops versus a serial killer in this OK "reunion" movie serving as a pilot to a possible new *Police Story* series with several members of the old anthology drama, along with much of the same behind-the-camera crew on hand. Average.

Policewoman Centerfold (1983) **C-100m.** TVM D: Reza Badiyi. Melody Anderson, Ed Marinaro, Donna Pescow, Bert Remsen, David Spielberg, Michael LeClair, Greg Monaghan. Lady cop does nude layout for girlie magazine and finds her job on the line and her personal life in turmoil. Exploitive trash based on a true story of Springfield, Ohio, cop who appeared in *Playboy*. Below average.▼

Policewomen (1974) **C-99m.** *½ D: Lee Frost. Sondra Currie, Tony Young, Phil Hoover, Jeanne Bell, Laurie Rose, William Smith, Wes Bishop. Unexceptional, violent actioner saved by talented Currie as karate-expert cop.▼

Polly (1989) **C-100m.** TVM D: Debbie Allen. Keshia Knight Pulliam, Phylicia Rashad, Celeste Holm, Brock Peters, Dorian Harewood, Butterfly McQueen, Larry Riley, Ken Page. Sunshiny Disney musical remake of the studio's 1960 POLLYANNA, turned into a showcase for young Pulliam and her *Cosby* series mom. Splashy choreography by director Allen (Rashad's sister) and hand-clapping original score by Joel McNeely. William Blinn wrote this all-black adaptation (save for Holm), setting it in a small Alabama town in the 1950s. Above average.

Pollyanna (1960) **C-134m.** ***½ D: David Swift. Hayley Mills, Jane Wyman,

Richard Egan, Karl Malden, Nancy Olson, Adolphe Menjou, Donald Crisp, Agnes Moorehead. Disney's treatment of Eleanor Porter story (filmed before with Mary Pickford) is first-rate, as "the glad girl" spreads cheer to misanthropes of a New England town, including her own Aunt Polly (Wyman). Fine direction and script by Swift, excellent performances all around. Mills was awarded a special Oscar for Outstanding Juvenile Performance. First filmed in 1920 with Mary Pickford. Remade for TV in 1989 as POLLY.▼

Polly of the Circus (1932) 69m. ** D: Alfred Santell. Clark Gable, Marion Davies, Raymond Hatton, C. Aubrey Smith, David Landau, Maude Eburne. Ill-conceived vehicle for Davies as sexy trapeze artist who falls in love with minister Gable. Ray Milland has bit part as church usher.

Polo Joe (1936) 62m. ** D: William McGann. Joe E. Brown, Carol Hughes, Skeets Gallagher, Joseph King, Gordon (Bill) Elliott, George E. Stone. Typical Brown comedy in which Joe's got to learn polo fast to impress his girl.

Poltergeist (1982) C-114m. ***½ D: Tobe Hooper. Craig T. Nelson, JoBeth Williams, Beatrice Straight, Dominique Dunne, Oliver Robins, Heather O'Rourke, Zelda Rubinstein, James Karen. A young family finds its home invaded by unfriendly spirits, who "kidnap" their 5-year-old girl! Sensationally scary ghost story co-written and co-produced by Steven Spielberg. Paced like a roller-coaster ride, with dazzling special effects—and a refreshing sense of humor. Followed by two sequels.▼

Poltergeist II (1986) C-91m. **½ D: Brian Gibson. JoBeth Williams, Craig T. Nelson, Heather O'Rourke, Oliver Robins, Zelda Rubinstein, Will Sampson, Julian Beck, Geraldine Fitzgerald. The Freeling family finds itself terrorized again by otherworld creatures. Another pointless sequel made palatable by some jolting state-of-the-art special effects, and more importantly, a still-very-likable family. Be warned, however, that an actor receives billing as The Vomit Creature. Followed by yet another sequel.▼

Poltergeist III (1988) C-97m. ** D: Gary Sherman. Tom Skerritt, Nancy Allen, Heather O'Rourke, Zelda Rubinstein, Lara Flynn Boyle, Kip Wentz, Richard Fire. O'Rourke moves in with uncle Skerritt and aunt Allen—and is still pursued by strange, evil forces. Undistinguished and occasionally plodding; eerily, young O'Rourke died four months before the film's release.▼

Polyester (1981) C-86m. **½ D: John Waters. Divine (Harris Glenn Milstead), Tab Hunter, Edith Massey, Mary Garlington, Ken King, David Samson, Mink Stole, Stiv Bators. Waters' first mainstream feature is wacky middle-class satire; housewife Francine Fishpaw (Divine), driven to

the brink by nightmarish husband, children, and mother, is "rescued" by handsome drive-in owner Todd Tomorrow (Hunter). Less offensive than Waters' underground films, but still not for all tastes; Vincent Peranio's sets are hilariously hideous. Released in "Odorama"—with audience members given scratch-and-sniff cards.▼

Pom-Pom Girls, The (1976) C-90m. ** D: Joseph Ruben. Robert Carradine, Jennifer Ashley, Lisa Reeves, Michael Mullins, Bill Adler. Comedy about spoiled suburban teenagers who celebrate their senior year having food fights, making love in the back of vans, and stealing a fire truck. Routinely good-natured mayhem.▼

Pontius Pilate (1966-Italian-French) C-100m. ** D: Irving Rapper. Jean Marais, Jeanne Crain, Basil Rathbone, John Drew Barrymore, Massimo Serato, Leticia Roman. Adequate retelling of events before and after Christ's crucifixion from viewpoint of Roman procurator. Dubbing and confused script hamper good intentions. Barrymore plays Christ and Judas.

Pony Express (1953) C-101m. *** D: Jerry Hopper. Charlton Heston, Rhonda Fleming, Jan Sterling, Forrest Tucker. Exuberant action Western (set in 1860s) of the founding of mail routes westward, involving historical figures Buffalo Bill and Wild Bill Hickok.▼

Pony Express Rider (1976) C-100m. *** D: Robert Totten. Stewart Peterson, Henry Wilcoxon, Buck Taylor, Maureen McCormick, Joan Caulfield, Ken Curtis, Slim Pickens, Dub Taylor, Jack Elam. Good family outing with Peterson joining Pony Express in 1860 to help find the man whom he believes has killed his father.▼

Pony Soldier (1952) C-82m. **½ D: Joseph M. Newman. Tyrone Power, Cameron Mitchell, Robert Horton, Thomas Gomez, Penny Edwards. Power is sturdy in actioner about Canadian mounties and their efforts to stave off Indian war.

Poor Cow (1967-British) C-104m. **½ D: Kenneth Loach. Carol White, Terence Stamp, John Bindon, Kate Williams, Queenie Watts. OK drama about working-class loners, centering on promiscuous White's relationship with husband (Bindon), a thief, and his best friend (Stamp), whom she really loves.

Poor Devil (1972) C-100m. TVM D: Robert Scheerer. Sammy Davis, Jr., Jack Klugman, Christopher Lee, Gino Conforti, Adam West, Madlyn Rhue. Silly mixture of farce and low-I.Q. drama as lowly assistant in Hell dreams of chance to earn stripes on Earth. Crazy cast, with Lee alternately playing straight and for laughs as Lucifer. Average.

Poor Little Rich Girl (1936) 72m. ***½ D: Irving Cummings. Shirley Temple,

Alice Faye, Jack Haley, Gloria Stuart, Michael Whalen, Jane Darwell, Claude Gillingwater, Henry Armetta. One of Shirley's best films, a top musical on any terms, with Temple running away from home, joining vaudeville team of Haley and Faye, winning over crusty Gillingwater, eventually joining her father (Whalen) and lovely Stuart. Best of all is closing "Military Man" number. Also shown in computer-colored version.▼

Poor Little Rich Girl: The Barbara Hutton Story (1987) C-250m. TVM D: Charles Jarrott. Farrah Fawcett, James Read, Kevin McCarthy, Burl Ives, Anne Francis, Bruce Davison, David Ackroyd, Stephane Audran, Amadeus August, Tony Peck, Zoe Wanamaker. Superficial biodrama of the famed Woolworth heiress and her extravagant lifestyle, from age five to her death in 1979; based on C. David Heymann's book. James Read is surprisingly good as Cary Grant, Hutton's third husband. Tony Peck, Gregory's son, is on hand late in the proceedings as one of Hutton's younger "companions." Originally shown in two parts. Average.

Pop Always Pays (1940) 67m. **½ D: Leslie Goodwins. Leon Errol, Dennis O'Keefe, Walter Catlett, Adele Pearce, Marjorie Gateson, Tom Kennedy. Sometimes funny comedy with Errol, much to his regret, promising to allow daughter Pearce to wed O'Keefe if the latter can save $1,000—which he also promises to match.▼

Popcorn (1970) C-85m. *½ D: Peter Clifton. Mick Jagger, Jimi Hendrix, Rolling Stones, Otis Redding, Bee Gees, Joe Cocker. Don't be misled by the talent assembled; most of them seem to have been captured during their worst performances for this concert film.

Pope Joan (1972-British) C-132m. BOMB D: Michael Anderson. Liv Ullmann, Keir Dullea, Robert Beatty, Jeremy Kemp, Olivia de Havilland, Patrick Magee, Maximilian Schell, Trevor Howard, Franco Nero. Dim story of woman who, disguised as man, works her way up to the papacy, only to be destroyed when revealed. Performers seem to be embarrassed, as well they should; screenplay by John Briley. Reissued as THE DEVIL'S IMPOSTER, with much material cut.

Pope John Paul II (1984) C-150m. TVM D: Herbert Wise. Albert Finney, Michael Crompton, Jonathan Newth, Nigel Hawthorne, Brian Cox, Caroline Bliss, John McEnery, Ronald Pickup, Lee Montague. Finney's American TV acting debut allows him to add another memorable portrait to his diverse gallery of colorful, full-bodied portrayals. His charismatic Karol Wojtyla is a reverential tour-de-force, covering the Pontiff's adult life from an adver-

sary of Nazism and Communism in Poland to his installation as Pope in 1978. Script by Christopher Knopf. Above average.▼

Pope of Greenwich Village, The (1984) C-120m. *** D: Stuart Rosenberg. Eric Roberts, Mickey Rourke, Daryl Hannah, Geraldine Page, Kenneth McMillan, Tony Musante, M. Emmet Walsh, Burt Young, Jack Kehoe, Philip Bosco, Val Avery, Joe Grifasi. Richly textured, sharply observant film about a young hustler in N.Y.C.'s Little Italy and his inability to separate himself from a cousin (Roberts) who's a perpetual screw-up. Not so much a story as a collection of character studies; Page stands out in great supporting cast, as harridan mother of crooked cop. Based on Vincent Patrick's novel.▼

Popeye (1980) C-114m. BOMB D: Robert Altman. Robin Williams, Shelley Duvall, Ray Walston, Paul Smith, Paul Dooley, Richard Libertini, Wesley Ivan Hurt, Linda Hunt. The beloved sailorman boards a sinking ship in this astonishingly boring movie. A game cast does its best with Jules Feiffer's unfunny script, Altman's cluttered staging, and some alleged songs by Harry Nilsson. For entertainment, tune in an old Max Fleischer cartoon instead; you'll be much better off.▼

Popeye Doyle (1986) C-100m. TVM D: Peter Levin. Ed O'Neill, Matthew Laurance, James Handy, Candy Clark, George de la Pena, Audrey Landers. Fast-paced cop flick revolving around the no-nonsense detective of THE FRENCH CONNECTION (played then by Oscar-winner Gene Hackman), out after the killer of a beautiful model and becoming enmeshed in a worldwide drug operation. Written by Richard Dilello. Pilot to a prospective series. Average.

Popi (1969) C-115m. *** D: Arthur Hiller. Alan Arkin, Rita Moreno, Miguel Alejandro, Ruben Figueroa. Charming story of poverty in the ghetto, focusing on one man's often zany antics in securing better life for his children. Odd ending for farfetched story.▼

Poppy (1936) 75m. **½ D: A. Edward Sutherland. W. C. Fields, Rochelle Hudson, Richard Cromwell, Catherine Doucet, Lynne Overman. Mild Fields, re-creating his stage role as Hudson's ever-conniving dad. Too much romantic subplot, not enough of W. C.'s antics. The Great Man also starred in a silent version, SALLY OF THE SAWDUST.

Poppy Is Also a Flower, The (1966) C-100m. BOMB D: Terence Young. Senta Berger, Stephen Boyd, E. G. Marshall, Trevor Howard, Eli Wallach, Marcello Mastroianni, Angie Dickinson, Rita Hayworth, Yul Brynner, Trini Lopez, Gilbert Roland, Bessie Love. Incredibly bad anti-drug feature from story by Ian Fleming,

[905]

originally produced as United Nations project for TV. Acting is downright poor at times. Though never referred to that way, title actually appears on screen as POPPIES ARE ALSO FLOWERS.▼

Popsy Pop SEE: **Butterfly Affair, The**

Porgy and Bess (1959) **C-138m. **½** D: Otto Preminger. Sidney Poitier, Dorothy Dandridge, Pearl Bailey, Sammy Davis, Jr., Brock Peters, Diahann Carroll, Ivan Dixon, Clarence Muse. Classic Gershwin folk opera about love, dreams, and jealousy among poor folk of Catfish Row; a bit stiff, but full of incredible music: "Summertime," "It Ain't Necessarily So," "I Got Plenty Of Nothin." Davis shines as Sportin' Life. Music arrangers Andre Previn and Ken Darby won Oscars. Final film of producer Samuel Goldwyn.

Pork Chop Hill (1959) **97m. ***** D: Lewis Milestone. Gregory Peck, Harry Guardino, Rip Torn, George Peppard, James Edwards, Bob Steele, Woody Strode, Robert Blake. Grim Korean War actioner with top-notch cast; rugged and believable.▼

Porky's (1981-Canadian) **C-94m. **½** D: Bob Clark. Dan Monahan, Mark Herrier, Wyatt Knight, Roger Wilson, Kim Cattrall, Scott Colomby, Kaki Hunter, Nancy Parsons, Alex Karras, Susan Clark. Endless recycling of AMERICAN GRAFFITI theme continues, this time set in South Florida circa 1954. A lusty, fun-loving bunch of high school guys discover that sex is great, revenge is sweet, and Jews are OK after all. Some belly laughs. This raunchy, low-budget comedy made a fortune and spawned two sequels—so far.▼

Porky's II: The Next Day (1983-Canadian) **C-95m. *½** D: Bob Clark. Dan Monahan, Wyatt Knight, Mark Herrier, Roger Wilson, Kaki Hunter, Scott Colomby, Nancy Parsons, Edward Winter. In-name-only sequel has same cast of kids in new (and tamer) set of escapades in Florida high school—with no coherency, and not even the raunchiness that made the first film so popular. Sequel: PORKY'S REVENGE.▼

Porky's Revenge (1985) **C-91m.** BOMB D: James Komack. Dan Monahan, Wyatt Knight, Tony Ganios, Kaki Hunter, Mark Herrier, Scott Colomby. Will the gang throw the big high school basketball game or won't they? Beware of high-school seniors with post-collegiate hairlines; these guys are starting to look older than the mid-'50s Bowery Boys. This *Revenge* is preferable to Montezuma's—but not by much.▼

Porridge SEE: **Doing Time**

Port Afrique (1956-British) **C-92m. **** D: Rudolph Maté. Pier Angeli, Phil Carey, Eugene Deckers, James Hayter, Rachel Gurney, Anthony Newley, Christopher Lee. Bernard Dyer's picaresque actioner gets middling screen version; adulterous wife's

past comes to light when husband investigates her death.

Portnoy's Complaint (1972) **C-101m.** BOMB D: Ernest Lehman. Richard Benjamin, Karen Black, Lee Grant, Jack Somack, Jeannie Berlin, Jill Clayburgh. Karen Black's excellent portrayal of "The Monkey" is buried in otherwise incredibly inept filmization of Philip Roth's novel about a not exactly warm relationship between Jewish boy and his mother. Terrible directorial debut by famed screenwriter Lehman.▼

Port of Call (1948-Swedish) **95m. **** D: Ingmar Bergman. Nine-Christine Jonsson, Bengt Eklund, Erik Hell, Berta Hall, Mimi Nelson. Slim, minor early Bergman drama about troubled young outcast Jonsson and her relationship with seaman Eklund. Setting is a grim harbor slum, and film's ultimately hopeful, upbeat tone just doesn't ring true.▼

Port of Hell (1954) **80m. **** D: Harold Schuster. Wayne Morris, Dane Clark, Carole Mathews, Otto Waldis, Marshall Thompson, Marjorie Lord, Tom Hubbard. Poor production values detract from tense situation of skipper et al trying to take an A-bomb out to sea before it explodes.

Port of New York (1949) **86m. **** D: Laslo Benedek. Scott Brady, Richard Rober, K. T. Stevens, Yul Brynner. Gloomy tale of customs agents cracking down on narcotics smuggling; Brynner's film debut . . . with hair!▼

Port of Seven Seas (1938) **81m. **** D: James Whale. Wallace Beery, Frank Morgan, Maureen O'Sullivan, John Beal, Jessie Ralph, Cora Witherspoon. Marcel Pagnol's FANNY isn't quite suitable Beery material, but he and good cast try their best as O'Sullivan falls in love with adventuresome sailor in Marseilles. Script by Preston Sturges.

Portrait in Black (1960) **C-112m. **½** D: Michael Gordon. Lana Turner, Anthony Quinn, Sandra Dee, John Saxon, Richard Basehart, Lloyd Nolan, Ray Walston, Anna May Wong. Average murder/blackmail mystery filled with gaping holes that producer Ross Hunter tried to hide with glamorous decor and offbeat casting.

Portrait of a Dead Girl SEE: **McCloud: Who Killed Miss U.S.A.?**

Portrait of a Hitman (1977) **C-86m.** BOMB D: Allan A. Buckhantz. Jack Palance, Richard Roundtree, Rod Steiger, Bo Svenson, Ann Turkel, Philip Ahn. Gangster Steiger hires "sensitive" hitman Palance to kill Svenson, but there are complications: Svenson is a pal who once saved Palance's life, and both of them are in love with Turkel. B-movie has ragged structure that makes it seem like an unfinished feature. Originally titled JIM BUCK.▼

Portrait of a Mobster (1961) **108m. **½**

D: Joseph Pevney. Vic Morrow, Leslie Parrish, Peter Breck, Ray Danton, Norman Alden, Ken Lynch. Pretty good gangster movie following the career of Dutch Schultz (Morrow), centering on his relationship with a woman who marries a crooked cop. Danton reprises his role as Legs Diamond from an earlier film.

Portrait of an Escort (1980) **C-100m.** TVM D: Steven Hilliard Stern. Susan Anspach, Tony Bill, Cyd Charisse, Kevin McCarthy, Edie Adams, Mary Frann, Gretchen Wyler, Todd Susman. Divorcée takes a night job with a professional dating service to make ends meet and causes tongues to wag. Average.

Portrait of a Rebel: The Remarkable Mrs. Sanger (1980) **C-96m.** TVM D: Virgil W. Vogel. Bonnie Franklin, David Dukes, Richard Johnson, Frances Lee McCain, Milo O'Shea, Albert Salmi, William Windom, Yvonne Wilder. Unremarkable biopic about the controversial WW1-era women's rights crusader, who pioneered the country's first birth-control clinic. Script by Blanche Hanalis. Average.

Portrait of a Showgirl (1982) **C-100m.** TVM D: Steven H. Stern. Lesley Ann Warren, Rita Moreno, Dianne Kay, Tony Curtis, Barry Primus, Kenneth Gilman, Howard Morris. The predictable life and times of a Vegas dancer. Moreno glitters as a world-weary chorus line gypsy. Average.▼

Portrait of a Sinner (1959-British) **96m.** **½ D: Robert Siodmak. William Bendix, Nadja Tiller, Tony Britton, Donald Wolfit, Adrienne Corri, Joyce Carey. Tiller is effective in leading role as corrupting female who taints all in her path. Based on Robin Maugham story. Original British title: THE ROUGH AND THE SMOOTH.

Portrait of a Stripper (1979) **C-100m.** TVM D: John A. Alonzo. Lesley Ann Warren, Edward Herrmann, Vic Tayback, Sheree North, Allan Miller, K. C. Martel. A young widow supports her son by stripping in local nightclub, while fighting custody battle with the boy's grandfather. Pure sleaze. Below average.▼

Portrait of Clare (1951-British) **94m.** ** D: Lance Comfort. Margaret Johnston, Richard Todd, Robin Bailey, Ronald Howard. Unpretentious little film, pegged on gimmick of woman telling granddaughter about her past romances.

Portrait of Jennie (1948) **86m.** *** D: William Dieterle. Jennifer Jones, Joseph Cotten, Ethel Barrymore, Lillian Gish, David Wayne, Henry Hull. Strange otherworldly girl Jones inspires penniless artist Cotten. David O. Selznick craftsmanship and a fine cast work wonders with foolish story based on the Robert Nathan novella. Originally released with last reel tinted green and final shot in Technicolor;

the special effects earned an Academy Award.▼

Poseidon Adventure, The (1972) **C-117m.** *** D: Ronald Neame. Gene Hackman, Ernest Borgnine, Red Buttons, Carol Lynley, Roddy McDowall, Stella Stevens, Shelley Winters, Jack Albertson, Leslie Nielsen, Pamela Sue Martin, Arthur O'Connell, Eric Shea. Mindless but engrossing, highly charged entertainment. Luxury cruise ship capsized by tidal wave, leaving small band of survivors to make way to top (bottom) of ship and hopefully escape. Introductory sequences are laughably bad, but one soon gets caught up in the story and ignores script's weaknesses. Oscar-winning song: "The Morning After"; also earned a special Oscar for special effects. Sequel: BEYOND THE POSEIDON ADVENTURE.▼

Positive I.D. (1987) **C-95m.** ** D: Andy Anderson. Stephanie Rascoe, John Davies, Steve Fromholtz, Laura Lane, Gail Cronauer, Matthew Sacks. Independently made feature about a married woman unable to put her life back together after a violent rape, who decides instead to adopt a new identity and live a secret life away from her family. Intriguing story always seems to be leading somewhere but never does, until the final sequence. Well made on a minuscule budget in Texas by writer-producer-director Anderson.▼

Posse (1975) **C-94m.** *** D: Kirk Douglas. Kirk Douglas, Bruce Dern, Bo Hopkins, James Stacy, Luke Askew, David Canary. Offbeat but solid Western about a cynical lawman who tries to fulfill political ambitions by capturing an escaped robber, only to find the people are siding with the outlaw! Well photographed (by Fred Koenekamp) and performed.▼

Posse From Hell (1961) **C-89m.** ** D: Herbert Coleman. Audie Murphy, John Saxon, Zohra Lampert, Vic Morrow, Lee Van Cleef. Murphy is tight-lipped gunslinger hunting outlaws who killed his sheriff pal. The usual.

Possessed (1931) **76m.** *** D: Clarence Brown. Joan Crawford, Clark Gable, Wallace Ford, Skeets Gallagher, John Miljan. Factory girl Crawford becomes the mistress of Park Avenue lawyer Gable. Fascinating feminist drama, crammed with symbolism and featuring a radiant Crawford. Outrageous pre-Code script by Lenore Coffee.▼

Possessed (1947) **108m.** *** D: Curtis Bernhardt. Joan Crawford, Van Heflin, Raymond Massey, Geraldine Brooks, Stanley Ridges. Crawford gives fine performance in intelligent study of woman whose subtle mental problems ruin her life. Heflin and Massey are the men in her life; Brooks, as Massey's daughter, is radiant in her film debut.

Possessed, The (1977) **C-78m. TVM** D: Jerry Thorpe. James Farentino, Joan Hackett, Claudette Nevins, Eugene Roche, Harrison Ford, Ann Dusenberry, Diana Scarwid, Dinah Manoff. Supernatural drama with Farentino, a defrocked priest, called upon to do an exorcism at Hackett's exclusive girls' school. She keeps it from going off the deep end. Average.

Possession (1981 French-West German) **C-127m.** *½ D: Andrzej Zulawski. Isabelle Adjani, Sam Neill, Heinz Bennent, Margit Carstensen, Michael Hogben. Adjani "creates" a monster, to the consternation of husband Neill, lover Bennent—and the viewer. Confusing drama of murder, horror, intrigue, though it's all attractively directed. Filmed in English; hacked down to 81m. for American release.▼

Possession of Joel Delaney, The (1972) **C-105m.** *** D: Waris Hussein. Shirley MacLaine, Perry King, Lisa Kohane, David Elliott, Michael Hordern, Miriam Colon, Lovelady Powell. Uneven but satisfying mix of horror and social commentary with unsympathetic, affluent Manhattanite MacLaine threatened by mysterious transformations of her brother Joel (King). Offbeat throughout.

Possessors, The (1958-French) **94m.** **½ D: Denys De La Patelliere. Jean Gabin, Jean Desailly, Pierre Brasseur, Emmanuele Riva, Bernard Blier. Diffuse yet forceful study of patriarch Gabin forcing issues to make his family self-sufficient.

Postal Inspector (1936) **58m.** ** D: Otto Brower. Ricardo Cortez, Patricia Ellis, Michael Loring, Bela Lugosi, David Oliver, Wallis Clark. A real-life postal inspector's life could never be this unusual: a novel romantic tale, a big robbery, and a major flood are all worked into this routine B picture. Lugosi plays a nightclub owner forced into crime by gambling debts. Oh, yes, there's also a song titled "Let's Have Bluebirds On All Our Wallpaper."▼

√ **Postman Always Rings Twice, The** (1946) **113m.** **** D: Tay Garnett. Lana Turner, John Garfield, Cecil Kellaway, Hume Cronyn, Audrey Totter, Leon Ames, Alan Reed. Garfield and Turner ignite the screen in this bristling drama of lovers whose problems just begin when they do away with her husband (Kellaway). Despite complaints of changes in James M. Cain's original story (mostly for censorship purposes), the film packs a real punch and outshines the more explicit 1981 remake. Harry Ruskin and Niven Busch scripted (from Cain's novel). Filmed twice before, in France and Italy.▼

Postman Always Rings Twice, The (1981) **C-123m.** *½ D: Bob Rafelson. Jack Nicholson, Jessica Lange, John Colicos, Michael Lerner, Christopher Lloyd, John P. Ryan, Anjelica Huston. Exceedingly unpleasant adaptation of James M. Cain's Depression-era novel about a drifter and a sensual young woman who conspire to free her from her loveless marriage. David Mamet's screenplay may be more faithful to Cain than the 1946 version, but who cares? Despite its much-touted sex scenes (more violent than erotic), it's dreary and forgettable. Moodily photographed by Sven Nykvist.▼

Postman's Knock (1962-British) **87m.** ** D: Robert Lynn. Spike Milligan, Barbara Shelley, John Wood, Miles Malleson, Ronald Adam, Wilfrid Lawson. Milligan is an overly efficient postal worker who upsets the equilibrium of the London post office—and some ambitious thieves. Scattered laughs in this generally heavy-handed comedy.

Postmark for Danger (1955-British) **84m.** *½ D: Guy Green. Terry Moore, Robert Beatty, William Sylvester, Geoffrey Keen, Josephine Griffin, Allan Cuthbertson. Hokey, overbaked murder mystery about what happens when an artist's journalist brother is "accidentally" killed in a car crash, and the actress who supposedly died with him mysteriously appears. As the latter, Moore gives an embarrassingly bad performance.▼

Potemkin (1925-Russian) **65m.** **** D: Sergei Eisenstein. Alexander Antonov, Vladimir Barsky, Grigori Alexandrov, Mikhail Goronorov. Landmark film about 1905 Revolution goes beyond status of mere classic; unlike many staples of film history classes, this one has the power to grip any audience. Odessa Steps sequence is possibly the most famous movie scene of all time.▼

Pot o' Gold (1941) **86m.** ** D: George Marshall. James Stewart, Paulette Goddard, Horace Heidt, Charles Winninger, Mary Gordon, Jed Prouty. Very minor item about harmonica-playing, music-mad Stewart, and his experiences with a band of struggling musicians. Stewart calls this his worst movie! Look briefly for Art Carney as a radio announcer.▼

Pound Puppies and the Legend of Big Paw (1988) **C-76m.** *½ D: Pierre DeCelles. Voices of George Rose, B. J. Ward, Ruth Buzzi, Brennan Howard. Yet another TV-style cartoon based on merchandising characters, with the Pound Puppies trying to retrieve a magical bone that's been stolen from a museum. Yawn. Upbeat 50's music helps a bit.

Pourquoi Pas! SEE: **Why Not!**

Powaqqatsi (1988) **C-97m.** **½ D: Godfrey Reggio. Follow-up to KOYAANISQATSI is a visual collage in which scenes of various cultures around the world are edited together to show how Third World societies have been exploited. Beautifully photographed and crammed with stunning images, but the result is somehow shallow—much like a coffee-table picture book—and not nearly as impressive as its predecessor. Music is again by Philip Glass; part two of a scheduled trilogy.▼

Powderkeg (1970) **C-100m.** TVM D: Douglas Heyes. Rod Taylor, Dennis Cole, Michael Ansara, Fernando Lamas, Luciana Paluzzi, Tisha Sterling. Tongue-in-cheek adventure set in 1914; two trouble-shooters are hired to retrieve hijacked train. Great action ruined by sloppy direction. Average; pilot for TV series THE BEARCATS.▼

Powder River (1953) **C-78m.** ** D: Louis King. Rory Calhoun, Corrine Calvet, Cameron Mitchell, Carl Betz. Straightforward minor Western, with Calhoun becoming town sheriff and clearing up a friend's murder.

Power, The (1968) **C-109m.** *** D: Byron Haskin. George Hamilton, Suzanne Pleshette, Richard Carlson, Yvonne De Carlo, Earl Holliman, Gary Merrill, Ken Murray, Barbara Nichols, Arthur O'Connell, Nehemiah Persoff, Aldo Ray, Michael Rennie. Research team discovers one of their number is an evil super-genius with powerful ESP abilities who starts killing the others one by one. Can Hamilton identify the man with the power before the villain kills him too? Could you ever doubt George Hamilton? Good, underrated George Pal production.

Power (1980) **C-200m.** TVM D: Barry Shear and Virgil Vogel. Joe Don Baker, Karen Black, Howard da Silva, Ralph Bellamy, Red Buttons, Brian Keith, Jo Van Fleet, Victor Jory, Paul Stewart, Scott Brady. An influential labor leader's rise to power from the docks of Chicago during the Depression. Big cast populates this sprawling saga written by Ernest Tidyman that's actually the thinly disguised story of Jimmy Hoffa. Codirector Shear died in 1979, during production. Above average.

Power (1986) **C-111m.** *½ D: Sidney Lumet. Richard Gere, Julie Christie, Gene Hackman, Kate Capshaw, Denzel Washington, E. G. Marshall, Beatrice Straight, Fritz Weaver, Michael Learned, J. T. Walsh, E. Katherine Kerr, Polly Rowles, Matt Salinger. Slick, sanctimonious story of ruthless political media manipulator (Gere) who, it turns out, isn't as smart as he thinks he is. Subject isn't headline news anymore, but this movie treats it that way—and then asks us to go along with some pretty silly story points. Downright embarrassing at times. ▼

Power and the Glory, The (1933) **76m.** *** D: William K. Howard. Spencer Tracy, Colleen Moore, Ralph Morgan, Helen Vinson. Considered by many a precursor to CITIZEN KANE, Preston Sturges' script tells rags-to-riches story of callous indus-

trialist (Tracy) in flashback. Silent-star Moore gives sensitive performance as Tracy's wife.

Power and the Prize, The (1956) **98m.** **½ D: Henry Koster. Robert Taylor, Elisabeth Mueller, Burl Ives, Charles Coburn, Cedric Hardwicke, Mary Astor. Sporadically effective study of big men in corporation and their private lives.

Power of the Whistler, The (1945) **66m.** D: Lew Landers. Richard Dix, Janis Carter, Jeff Donnell, Loren Tindall, Tala Birell, John Abbott. SEE: Whistler series.

Power Play (1978-Canadian-British) **C-102m.** *½ D: Martyn Burke. Peter O'Toole, David Hemmings, Donald Pleasence, Barry Morse, Jon Granik, Marcella Saint-Amant. Story of a military coup in a country that looks vaguely European but where everybody sounds British or Canadian. That's just one problem in this flat, unsuspenseful drama.▼

Powers Girl, The (1942) **93m.** ** D: Norman Z. McLeod. George Murphy, Anne Shirley, Dennis Day, Benny Goodman, Carole Landis. Trifling plot revolving about Shirley's attempt to become member of famed modeling school, with musical numbers tossed in.

Power Within, The (1979) **C-78m.** TVM D: John Llewellyn Moxey. Art Hindle, Edward Binns, Eric Braeden, Susan Howard, David Hedison, Richard Sargent. Barnstorming pilot is struck by lightning, acquires mysterious powers, and is menaced by enemy agents who want his secret. Silly attempt to grab *The Incredible Hulk's* audience. Below average.▼

P.O.W. The Escape (1986) **C-90m.** *½ D: Gideon Amir. David Carradine, Charles R. Floyd, Mako, Steve James, Phil Brock. Mindless, one-dimensional RAMBO variation, about some American P.O.W.s, headed by Col. Carradine, who battle their way to freedom as Saigon falls to the Commies. Formerly titled BEHIND ENEMY LINES.▼

Powwow Highway (1989) **C-90m.** *** D: Jonathan Wacks. Gary Farmer, A Martinez, Amanda Wyss, Joanelle Romero, Sam Vlahos, Wayne Waterman, Margo Kane. Big, amiable Cheyenne, on a "medicine" journey to New Mexico in a beat-up Buick, gives a lift to a lifelong friend, an Indian activist. Not a totally successful film, but unusual and satisfying, with a standout performance by Farmer, an immensely likable actor who makes his character both endearing and ennobling.▼

Practically Yours (1944) **90m.** ** D: Mitchell Leisen. Claudette Colbert, Fred MacMurray, Gil Lamb, Robert Benchley, Rosemary DeCamp, Cecil Kellaway. Stars' expertise redeems contrived story of girl intercepting pilot's message to his dog.

Practice Makes Perfect (1978-French)

C-104m. *** D: Philippe de Broca. Jean Rochefort, Nicole Garcia, Annie Girardot, Danielle Darrieux, Catherine Alric, Lila Kedrova, Jean Desailly. Funny, knowing comedy about bored, self-centered concert pianist, supposedly living ideal life, eventually receiving his retribution. Rochefort is perfectly cast as engaging womanizer.▼

Prayer for the Dying, A (1987-British) **C-107m.** *½ D: Mike Hodges. Mickey Rourke, Bob Hoskins, Alan Bates, Sammi Davis, Christopher Fulford, Liam Neeson, Alison Doody. Ponderous adaptation of Jack Higgins' novel about an IRA hit man (Rourke, with a dubious Irish accent) who can't escape his chosen calling, even when he tries to. Hoskins is badly miscast as a priest who becomes entangled with Rourke, while Bates chews it up as a flamboyant racketeer who doubles as a mortician. Heavy going all the way.▼

Pray for the Wildcats (1974) **C-100m.** TVM D: Robert Michael Lewis. Andy Griffith, William Shatner, Angie Dickinson, Janet Margolin, Robert Reed, Marjoe Gortner, Lorraine Gary. Mildly diverting "macho" flick about three advertising executives who are forced to join their sadistic client (Griffith) on a desert motorcycle trip. Average.▼

Pray TV (1982) **C-100m.** TVM D: Robert Markowitz. John Ritter, Ned Beatty, Richard Kiley, Madolyn Smith, Louise Latham, Jonathan Prince, Michael Currie, Lois Areno. Newly ordained idealistic minister Ritter becomes involved with dynamic TV evangelist Beatty. Lane Slate's potentially incisive look at the power born of TV celebrity appears to have been tempered (and tampered with?) by the network before film's initial airing. Average.▼

Predator (1987) **C-107m.** *** D: John McTiernan. Arnold Schwarzenegger, Carl Weathers, Elpidia Carrillo, Bill Duke, Jesse Ventura, Sonny Landham, Richard Chaves, R.G. Armstrong, Shane Black, Kevin Peter Hall. Schwarzenegger and his super-SWAT-team-for-hire are assigned by the U.S. to a delicate rescue mission in South American jungle . . . but Arnold and his men soon find themselves battling a faceless, ferocious enemy that's picking them off one by one. Solid, suspenseful action film takes time getting started, but emerges a grabber.▼

Prehistoric Women (1950) **C-74m.** BOMB D: Gregg Tallas. Laurette Luez, Allan Nixon, Joan Shawlee, Judy Landon. Ludicrous account of cavewomen hunting for their mates, only good for laughs.▼

Prehistoric Women (1967-British) **C-91m.** *½ D: Michael Carreras. Michael Latimer, Martine Beswick, Edina Ronay, Carol White, John Raglan, Stephanie Randall, Stephen Berkoff. Idiotic Hammer adventure in which Great White Hunter stumbles into lost Amazon civilization where blondes have been enslaved by brunettes. Honest! Nevertheless, this does have a cult following, due to Beswick's commanding, sensual performance as the tribe's leader. Released in Britain as SLAVE GIRLS, at 74m.▼

Prehistoric World SEE: **Teenage Caveman**

Premature Burial, The (1962) **C-81m.** ** D: Roger Corman. Ray Milland, Hazel Court, Richard Ney, Heather Angel, Alan Napier, John Dierkes. Title tells the story in another of Corman's Poe adaptations, with a 1962 Milland unconvincingly cast as medical student. Lavish (for this series), but not one of director's best.▼

Premier May SEE: **Man to Man Talk**

Premonition, The (1976) **C-94m.** ** D: Robert Allen Schnitzer. Sharon Farrell, Richard Lynch, Jeff Corey, Ellen Barber, Edward Bell. Muddled script works against eerie atmosphere in this supernatural tale that stresses parapsychology as clue to young girl's disappearance. Mediocre results. Filmed in Mississippi.▼

Preppie Murder, The (1989) **C-100m.** TVM D: John Herzfeld. William Baldwin, Lara Flynn Boyle, Danny Aiello, Joanna Kerns, Dorothy Fielding, James Handy, William Devane. Exploitive dramatization of the Jennifer Levin killing in N.Y.C.'s Central Park in 1987, and the Robert Chambers murder trial that followed amid sensational headlines. Average.

Prescription: Murder (1967) **C-99m.** TVM D: Richard Irving. Peter Falk, Gene Barry, Katherine Justice, William Windom, Nina Foch, Anthony James, Virginia Gregg. Doc Fleming (Barry) thinks he's committed fool-proof murder of wife, so at first he humors efforts of seemingly slow-witted police lieutenant (Falk) to check alibi. Interesting debut of Falk's Columbo character with excellent cast, subplots. Adapted by Richard Levinson and William Link from their Broadway play (with Thomas Mitchell as Columbo). Above average. Followed by RANSOM FOR A DEAD MAN.▼

Presenting Lily Mars (1943) **104m.** ** D: Norman Taurog. Judy Garland, Van Heflin, Fay Bainter, Richard Carlson, Spring Byington, Marta Eggerth, Marilyn Maxwell, Ray McDonald, Leonid Kinskey, Connie Gilchrist, Bob Crosby, Tommy Dorsey. Well, there she is, and there lies the script. Stale story of determined girl getting big chance on Broadway only comes alive when Judy sings. From a Booth Tarkington novel.▼

President's Analyst, The (1967) **C-104m.** **** D: Theodore J. Flicker. James Coburn, Godfrey Cambridge, Severn Darden, Joan Delaney, Pat Harrington, Will Geer, William Daniels. Totally nutty, brilliantly maneuvered satire of many sacred cows, as Coburn is pursued by half the government when he quits title job. The ending is a beauty. Screenplay by the director.▼

President's Lady, The (1953) **96m.** ******* D: Henry Levin. Charlton Heston, Susan Hayward, John McIntire, Fay Bainter, Carl Betz. Heston as Andrew Jackson and Hayward the lady with a past he marries work well together in this fictional history of 1800s America, based on the Irving Stone novel.▼

President's Mistress, The (1978) **C-100m.** TVM D: John Llewellyn Moxey. Beau Bridges, Susan Blanchard, Karen Grassle, Larry Hagman, Joel Fabiani, Don Porter. Government courier is caught in a conspiracy after learning his murdered sister was the President's mistress as well as a Soviet spy. Average.▼

President's Plane Is Missing, The (1971) **C-100m.** TVM D: Daryl Duke. Buddy Ebsen, Peter Graves, Arthur Kennedy, Rip Torn, Louise Sorel, Raymond Massey, James Wainwright, Mercedes McCambridge, Dabney Coleman, Joseph Campanella. Adaptation of Robert Serling novel depicts second-by-second crisis concerning plot to overthrow U.S. government. Impressive cast cannot obscure faulty narrative and direction. Average.▼

Presidio, The (1988) **C-97m.** ****½** D: Peter Hyams. Sean Connery, Mark Harmon, Meg Ryan, Jack Warden, Mark Blum, Dana Gladstone, Jenette Goldstein, Don Calfa. San Francisco cop Harmon investigates a murder that took place on local military base, and clashes with an old nemesis, the presidio's chief provost Connery—whose daughter he's attracted to. Strictly formula stuff, though slickly done, with some good S.F. chase scenes. A waste of time for Connery in particular.▼

Press for Time (1966-British) **C-102m.** ****** D: Robert Asher. Norman Wisdom, Angela Browne, Derek Bond, Derek Francis. Bumbling son of a commoner is sent by his government minister granddad to work as a reporter on a provincial newspaper. Wisdom has fun doing three roles; film benefits from infectious musical score by Mike Vickers.

Pressure Point (1962) **91m.** ******* D: Hubert Cornfield. Sidney Poitier, Bobby Darin, Peter Falk, Carl Benton Reid, Mary Munday, Barry Gordon, Howard Caine. Intelligent drama, with Poitier the prison psychiatrist trying to ferret out the problems of his Nazi patient (Darin).

Prestige (1932) **71m.** ****½** D: Tay Garnett. Ann Harding, Melvyn Douglas, Adolphe Menjou, Clarence Muse, Ian MacLaren. Flamboyant direction and solid performances elevate hackneyed melodrama about life at British Army outpost in the Far East where White Supremacy—and Douglas' sanity—are threatened.

Presumed Innocent (1990) **C-127m.** ******* D: Alan J. Pakula. Harrison Ford, Brian Dennehy, Raul Julia, Bonnie Bedelia, Paul Winfield, Greta Scacchi, John Spencer, Joe Grifasi, Tom Mardirosian, Anna Maria Horsford, Sab Shimono, Christine Estabrook, Michael Tolan. Solid, well-cast screen version of Scott Turow's crackling best-seller about a prosecutor assigned to investigate the murder of a sexy assistant prosecutor with whom he'd had an affair. Soon, he's charged with the murder himself! Slow going at times, film misses its potential for greatness but still delivers many powerful moments. Screenplay by Pakula and Frank Pierson.

Pretender, The (1947) **69m.** ****½** D: W. Lee Wilder. Albert Dekker, Catherine Craig, Linda Stirling, Charles Drake, Charles Middleton, Alan Carney. Dekker gives sharply etched performance as N.Y.C. financier trying to do in a competitor, discovering he may be the victim instead.

Pretty Baby (1950) **92m.** ****** D: Bretaigne Windust. Dennis Morgan, Betsy Drake, Zachary Scott, Edmund Gwenn, Barbara Billingsley. Coy minor comedy involving working-girl Drake, who snowballs a gimmick to a get a subway sent on the morning train into a good job and romance.

Pretty Baby (1978) **C-109m.** ****½** D: Louis Malle. Keith Carradine, Susan Sarandon, Brooke Shields, Antonio Fargas, Frances Faye, Gerrit Graham, Mae Mercer, Diana Scarwid, Barbara Steele. Malle's first American film is beautifully mounted but distressingly low-keyed story of marriage between a 12-year-old New Orleans prostitute and an older photographer, set around time of WW1. Shields is striking in title role, but Carradine is his lifeless self. Designed and co-written (with Malle) by Polly Platt; photographed by Sven Nykvist.▼

Pretty Boy Floyd (1960) **96m.** ****** D: Herbert J. Leder. John Ericson, Barry Newman, Joan Harvey, Herb (Jason) Evers, Carl York, Peter Falk, Roy Fant, Shirley Smith. Average chronicle of infamous 1930s gangster, played energetically by Ericson.

Pretty Boy Floyd (1974) SEE: **Story of Pretty Boy Floyd, The**

Pretty in Pink (1986) **C-96m.** ******* D: Howard Deutch. Molly Ringwald, Jon Cryer, Andrew McCarthy, Harry Dean Stanton, Annie Potts, James Spader, Alexa Kenin, Andrew "Dice" Clay, Margaret Colin, Gina Gershon, Dweezil Zappa. A high school have-not finds herself in a quandary when one of the "richies" asks her out; her fellow outcast and fanatical devotee (Cryer) isn't too happy, either. Another credible look at growing pains by writer-producer John Hughes (THE BREAKFAST CLUB), nicely acted, if a bit slow and self-serious. Stanton, playing Molly's dad, has never been so tender on screen!▼

Prettykill (1987) **C-95m.** BOMB D: George Kaczender. David Birney, Season

Hubley, Susannah York, Yaphet Kotto, Suzanne Snyder, Germaine Houde. Noxious exploitation film about down on his luck cop Birney and his girlfriend/hooker Hubley enmeshed in a case of a slasher who preys on prostitutes. Snyder gives an overwrought, laughable performance as a sweet young thing with a dual personality (she lapses into her southern fried incestuous father's voice at times!).▼

Pretty Maids All in a Row (1971) **C-92m.** *** D: Roger Vadim. Rock Hudson, Angie Dickinson, Telly Savalas, John David Carson, Roddy McDowall, James Doohan, Keenan Wynn, Amy (Aimee) Eccles, Barbara Leigh. Silly but enjoyable black comedy; high school guidance-counselor/coach Hudson advises frustrated Carson in sexual matters, while school is plagued with murders of pretty female students. Written and produced by Gene Roddenberry.

Pretty Poison (1968) **C-89m.** *** D: Noel Black. Anthony Perkins, Tuesday Weld, Beverly Garland, John Randolph, Dick O'Neill. Oddball arsonist Perkins enlists aid of sexy high-schooler Weld for scheme he's hatching, but soon discovers that she's got stranger notions than he does! Bright, original screenplay by Lorenzo Semple, Jr., sparked by Weld's vivid performance.▼

Pretty Woman (1990) **C-117m.** *** D: Garry Marshall. Richard Gere, Julia Roberts, Ralph Bellamy, Jason Alexander, Laura San Giacomo, Hector Elizondo, Alex Hyde-White, Elinor Donahue, Larry Miller. Surprisingly successful variation on an old formula: wealthy, cold-blooded business tycoon Gere chances to meet Hollywood Boulevard hooker Roberts. He hires her to be his companion for a week, spruces her up, and—well, you can figure out the rest. Light, charming, and thoroughly entertaining, with Roberts a particular delight.▼

Price of Fear, The (1956) **79m.** **½ D: Abner Biberman. Merle Oberon, Lex Barker, Charles Drake, Gia Scala, Warren Stevens. Middling account of Oberon involved in hit-and-run accident which snowballs her life into disaster.

Price of Freedom, The SEE: **Operation Daybreak**

Prick Up Your Ears (1987-British) **C-108m.** *** D: Stephen Frears. Gary Oldman, Alfred Molina, Vanessa Redgrave, Wallace Shawn, Julie Walters, James Grant, Frances Barber, Lindsay Duncan, Janet Dale, Dave Atkins. Chillingly realistic and evocative look at young British playwright Joe Orton, who was murdered by his longtime lover Kenneth Halliwell in 1967. Stunning performances by Oldman (as Orton), Molina (as the tormented Halliwell) and Redgrave (as Orton's agent) make up for some lags in Alan Bennett's script. Unflinching look at homosexuality in England during the 1950s and 60s (when it

was a criminal act), but the film offers no insight into Orton's great theatrical success.▼

Pride and Extreme Prejudice (1990-British) **C-100m.** TVM D: Ian Sharp. Brian Dennehy, Simon Cadell, Lisa Eichhorn, Leonie Mellinger, Alan Howard. Frederick Forsyth's written-for-TV spy thriller has Dennehy as a CIA agent who recovers from a nervous breakdown while on a mission in East Germany, only to find both the KGB and "The Company" on his tail. Yet another Cold War spy film rendered largely passé in light of political upheaval in Eastern Europe at the turn of the decade. Made for cable. Average.

Pride and Prejudice (1940) **118m.** **** ✓ D: Robert Z. Leonard. Greer Garson, Laurence Olivier, Edna May Oliver, Edmund Gwenn, Mary Boland, Maureen O'Sullivan, Karen Morley, Melville Cooper, E. E. Clive, Ann Rutherford, Marsha Hunt. Outstanding adaptation of Jane Austen's novel about five husband-hunting sisters in 19th-century England. Excellent cast, fine period flavor in classic comedy of manners; Aldous Huxley was one of the screenwriters. Cedric Gibbons and Paul Groesse's art direction deservedly earned an Oscar.▼

Pride and the Passion, The (1957) **C-132m.** **½ D: Stanley Kramer. Cary Grant, Frank Sinatra, Sophia Loren, Theodore Bikel, John Wengraf. Miscast actioner involving capture of huge cannon by British naval officer (Grant) in 19th century Spain. Spectacle scenes—filmed on location—are impressive; but most of the film is ridiculous. From the C.S. Forester novel.▼

Pride of Jesse Hallam, The (1981) **C-100m.** TVM D: Gary Nelson. Johnny Cash, Brenda Vaccaro, Ben Marley, Eli Wallach, Guy Boyd, Chrystal Smith. Cash plays a man who is forced to battle with his illiteracy. Suzanne Clauser wrote the story, and Cash the music, which he and wife June Carter Cash sing. Dennis Weaver later covered similar ground in BLUFFING IT. Average.▼

Pride of St. Louis, The (1952) **93m.** **½ D: Harmon Jones. Dan Dailey, Joanne Dru, Richard Crenna, Hugh Sanders. Pleasing if fanciful biography of baseball pitcher Dizzy Dean.

Pride of the Blue Grass (1954) **C-71m.** ** D: William Beaudine. Lloyd Bridges, Vera Miles, Margaret Sheridan, Arthur Shields. Familiar racetrack story; competent production.

Pride of the Bowery (1940) **63m.** D: Joseph H. Lewis. Leo Gorcey, Bobby Jordan, Donald Haines, Carleton Young, Kenneth Howell, David Gorcey. SEE: **Bowery Boys** series.▼

Pride of the Marines (1945) **119m.** ***½ D: Delmer Daves. John Garfield, Eleanor Parker, Dane Clark, John Ridgely, Rosemary DeCamp, Ann Doran, Ann Todd, Warren Douglas. Ensemble acting by Warner Bros. stock company enhances true account of Marine blinded during Japanese attack, with Garfield as injured Al Schmid, Clark as sympathetic buddy. Screenplay by Albert Maltz.

Pride of the Yankees, The (1942) **127m.** **** D: Sam Wood. Gary Cooper, Teresa Wright, Babe Ruth, Walter Brennan, Dan Duryea, Ludwig Stossel, Addison Richards, Hardie Albright. Superb biography of baseball star Lou Gehrig, with Cooper giving excellent performance; fine support from Wright as devoted wife. Truly memorable final sequence. Script by Jo Swerling and Herman J. Mankiewicz, with Oscar-winning editing by Daniel Mandell.▼

Priest Killer, The (1971) **C-100m. TVM** D: Richard A. Colla. Raymond Burr, George Kennedy, Don Galloway, Don Mitchell, Louise Latham, Anthony Zerbe, Peter Brocco. Sleuthing priest Kennedy and police chief Ironside combine forces in search for motive for series of murders of Catholic priests. Second pilot for Kennedy's short-lived *Sarge* series. Average.

Priest of Love (1981-British) **C-125m.** *** D: Christopher Miles. Ian McKellen, Janet Suzman, Ava Gardner, Penelope Keith, Jorge Rivero, John Gielgud, Sarah Miles. Literate account of the last years of D. H. Lawrence (McKellen)—"the one who writes the dirty books"—highlighted by his relationship with his wife (Suzman) and the publication of *Lady Chatterley's Lover*. Slow-moving but rewarding; 11 years earlier, Miles directed the screen version of Lawrence's THE VIRGIN AND THE GYPSY.▼

Priest's Wife, The (1971-Italian-French) **C-106m.** *½ D: Dino Risi. Sophia Loren, Marcello Mastroianni, Venantino Venantini, Jacques Stany, Pippo Starnazza, Augusto Mastrantoni. Barely entertaining mixture of drama and humor with Loren as disillusioned singer who thinks she can convince priest (Mastroianni) to obtain release from his vow of celibacy and marry her. Weightier handling of subject matter can be heard on radio talk shows; film seems designed merely as vehicle for two stars.

Prime Cut (1972) **C-86m.** *** D: Michael Ritchie. Lee Marvin, Gene Hackman, Angel Tompkins, Gregory Walcott, Sissy Spacek, Janit Baldwin. Mob hijinks at a Kansas City slaughterhouse inspire well-cast, fast-moving, tongue-in-cheek trash that fans of sleazy crime melodramas should love. Spacek's first film.▼

Prime of Miss Jean Brodie, The (1969) **C-116m.** ***½ D: Ronald Neame. Maggie Smith, Robert Stephens, Pamela Franklin, Gordon Jackson, Celia Johnson, Jane Carr. Oscar-winning showcase for Smith as eccentric teacher in Edinburgh school who wields a spellbinding influence on her "girls." Remarkable character study, adapted by Jay Presson Allen from stage version of Muriel Spark's novel; filmed on location. Smith and Stephens were then real-life husband and wife. Later remade as a TV mini-series.▼

Prime Suspect (1982) **C-100m. TVM** D: Noel Black. Mike Farrell, Teri Garr, Veronica Cartwright, Lane Smith, Barry Corbin, James Sloyan, Charles Aidman. Following a TV investigative reporter's overzealousness, a law-abiding citizen becomes prime suspect in a young girl's murder. The closeness to ABSENCE OF MALICE seems more than coincidental. Average.▼

Prime Target (1989) **C-100m. TVM** D: Robert Collins. Angie Dickinson, Joseph Bologna, David Soul, Yaphet Kotto, Joe Regalbuto, Dennis Lipscomb, Mills Watson, Charles Durning. Routine cop movie with Dickinson a detective assigned to track down the killer of other policewomen. No, this is not an extension of her old TV series. Average.

Primrose Path, The (1940) **93m.** **½ D: Gregory La Cava. Ginger Rogers, Joel McCrea, Marjorie Rambeau, Miles Mander, Henry Travers. Girl from wrong side of the tracks falls in love with ambitious young McCrea; starts engagingly, drifts into dreary soap opera and melodramatics. Rambeau is excellent as Ginger's prostitute mother.▼

Prince and the Pauper, The (1937) **120m.** ***½ D: William Keighley. Errol Flynn, Billy and Bobby Mauch, Claude Rains, Alan Hale, Montagu Love, Henry Stephenson, Barton MacLane. Rousing filmization of Mark Twain's story of young look-alikes, one a mistreated urchin, the other a prince, exchanging places. Great music score by Erich Wolfgang Korngold. Remade as CROSSED SWORDS. Also available in computer-colored version; beware of edited print prepared for two-hour time slots.▼

Prince and the Pauper, The (1978) SEE: **Crossed Swords**

Prince and the Showgirl, The (1957) **C-117m.** **½ D: Laurence Olivier. Marilyn Monroe, Laurence Olivier, Sybil Thorndike. Jeremy Spenser, Richard Wattis. Thoughtful but slow-moving comedy of saucy American showgirl Monroe being romanced by Prince Regent of Carpathia (Olivier) during the 1911 coronation of George V. Filmed in England, with delightful performances by Monroe and Olivier. Script by Terence Rattigan from his play *The Sleeping Prince*.▼

Prince Jack (1984) **C-100m.** ** D: Bert Lovitt. Robert Hogan, James F. Kelly, Kenneth Mars, Lloyd Nolan, Cameron Mitchell, Robert Guillaume, Theodore

Bikel, Jim Backus, Dana Andrews. Yet another chronicle of life among the Kennedys, here focusing mainly on the men and their personalities. Superficial at best.▼

Prince of Bel Air (1986) **C-100m. TVM** D: Charles Braverman. Mark Harmon, Kirstie Alley, Robert Vaughn, Patrick Laborteaux, Bartley Braverman, Deborah Harmon, Katherine Moffat, Michael Horton. Glitter trash about a swinging Southern California bachelor who services Bel Air swimming pools as well as restless wives and nubile bimbos. Created for Mark Harmon to cash in on his image as "the sexiest man in America." Average.▼

Prince of Central Park, The (1977) **C-76m. TVM** D: Harvey Hart. Ruth Gordon, T. J. Hargrave, Lisa Richard, Brooke Shields, Marc Vahanian, Dan Hedaya. Engaging tale of a pair of orphans living in a tree in Central Park and the lonely old lady who befriends them. Jeb Rosebrook scripted, from Evan H. Rhodes' ingratiating novel (which a decade later was adapted for Broadway). Above average.▼

Prince of Darkness (1987) **C-110m.** BOMB D: John Carpenter. Donald Pleasence, Lisa Blount, Jameson Parker, Victor Wong, Dennis Dun, Susan Blanchard, Anne Howard, Alice Cooper. The anti-God entombs wayward son Satan in a cannister of glop in an abandoned L.A. church; it's up to priest Pleasence and the grad students of prof Wong to clean up the mess. Not for nothing is the religious sect involved called "Brotherhood of Death"; anyone who survives this snoozer will feel initiated into a select fraternity.▼

Prince of Foxes (1949) **107m. **½ D: Henry King. Tyrone Power, Wanda Hendrix, Orson Welles, Marina Berti, Everett Sloane, Katina Paxinou. Lavish, incredibly handsome costume epic of medieval Italy (filmed on location), with adventurer Power defying all-powerful Cesare Borgia. Story elements don't match visual impact of film; sumptuous photography by Leon Shamroy.

Prince of Pennsylvania, The (1988) **C-87m. **½ D: Ron Nyswaner. Fred Ward, Keanu Reeves, Bonnie Bedelia, Amy Madigan, Jeff Hayenga, Tracey Ellis. Extremely quirky character comedy of free spirit Reeves (whose strange half-Mohawk hairdo will put off many viewers) "finding" himself while battling with his equally wacko dad (Ward, in a marvelous performance). Madigan is excellent as the older woman whom Reeves romances; in-joke has her dressing up in a Freddy Krueger mask for a fake kidnapping. Writer Nyswaner (SMITHEREENS) turns director with many striking individual scenes that unfortunately fail to grip as a whole.▼

Prince of Pirates (1953) **C-80m. **½ D:

Sidney Salkow. John Derek, Barbara Rush, Whitfield Connor, Edgar Barrier. Enjoyable little costumer involving French-Spanish wars.

Prince of Players (1955) **C-102m. **½ D: Philip Dunne. Richard Burton, Maggie McNamara, Raymond Massey, Charles Bickford, John Derek, Eva Le Gallienne, Mae Marsh, Sarah Padden. Burton is 19th-century actor Edwin Booth, embroiled in more offstage drama than on. Shakespearean excerpts thrown in; well performed by earnest cast. Script by Moss Hart.

Prince of the City (1981) **C-167m.** *** D: Sidney Lumet. Treat Williams, Jerry Orbach, Richard Foronjy, Don Billett, Kenny Marino, Carmine Caridi, Bob Balaban, James Tolkan, Lindsay Crouse. Emotionally powerful story (which unfortunately is true) about a cop in a N.Y.C. special investigations unit who blows the whistle on department corruption but finds himself more a victim than a hero. Standout performances by Williams, fellow cop Orbach, weasely prosecutor Tolkan, but film's extreme length hurts overall impact; there are more details than really necessary to tell the story. Script by Lumet and Jay Presson Allen.▼

Prince of Thieves, The (1948) **C-72m.** ** D: Howard Bretherton. Jon Hall, Patricia Morison, Adele Jergens, Alan Mowbray, Michael Duane. Colorful swashbuckler of Robin Hood and Maid Marian, aimed at juvenile audiences.▼

Princess Academy, The (1987-U.S.-French-Yugoslav) **C-90m.** BOMB D: Bruce Block. Eva Gabor, Lar Park Lincoln, Lu Leonard, Richard Paul, Carole Davis, Badar Howar. Allegedly titillating comedy about young women at a Swiss school who compare notes on losing virginity and snaring rich husbands. In any language, it stinks.▼

Princess and the Cabbie, The (1981) **C-100m. TVM** D: Glenn Jordan. Valerie Bertinelli, Robert Desiderio, Cynthia Harris, Peter Donat, Shelley Long, Ellen Geer. Rich young girl encounters feisty, self-taught cab driver, and love blossoms. Below average.

Princess and the Pirate, The (1944) **C-94m.** *** D: David Butler. Bob Hope, Virginia Mayo, Walter Brennan, Walter Slezak, Victor McLaglen. One of Bob's wackiest; he and glamorous Virginia are on the lam from pirate McLaglen, trapped by potentate Slezak. Brennan is hilarious in truly offbeat pirate role; great closing gag, too.▼

Princess Bride, The (1987) **C-98m. **½ D: Rob Reiner. Cary Elwes, Mandy Patinkin, Chris Sarandon, Christopher Guest, Wallace Shawn, Andre the Giant, Fred Savage, Robin Wright, Peter Falk, Peter Cook, Carol Kane, Billy Crystal, Mel

Smith. Revisionist fairy tale/adventure about a beautiful young woman and her one true love, who must find and rescue her after a long separation. Some wonderful scenes and character vignettes are periodically undermined by a tendency toward comic shtick (as in Crystal's cameo appearance) and occasional incoherency (as in the opening scenes with Castilian-tongued Patinkin and marble-mouthed Andre the Giant). Best of all: the swashbuckling sequences. Bonus for old-movie buffs: watching Guest, as Count Rugen, imitate Henry Daniell (from THE SEA HAWK). Screenplay by William Goldman, from his novel.▼

Princess Comes Across, The (1936) **76m.** *** D: William K. Howard. Carole Lombard, Fred MacMurray, Douglass Dumbrille, Alison Skipworth, William Frawley, Porter Hall, Sig Ruman, Mischa Auer. Lombard, posing as royalty on ocean voyage, meets romantic MacMurray; together they are involved in whodunit. And Fred sings "My Concertina." Delightful blend of comedy and mystery.

Princess Daisy (1983) **C-200m. TVM** D: Waris Hussein. Merete Van Kamp, Lindsay Wagner, Paul Michael Glaser, Robert Urich, Claudia Cardinale, Rupert Everett, Sada Thompson, Ringo Starr, Barbara Bach, Stacy Keach. Judith Krantz's best-selling poor little-rich-girl novel in all its trashy glory, bolstered by Keach, dashing as her Russian Prince dad, and Cardinale, sleek as her cultured French companion (and father's mistress). Originally shown in two parts. Average.▼

Princess of the Nile (1954) **C-71m.** **½ D: Harmon Jones. Debra Paget, Jeffrey Hunter, Michael Rennie, Dona Drake, Wally Cassell, Jack Elam, Lee Van Cleef. Hokey script diverts any potential this costumer may have had.

Princess O'Rourke (1943) **94m.** **½ D: Norman Krasna. Olivia de Havilland, Robert Cummings, Charles Coburn, Jack Carson, Jane Wyman, Harry Davenport, Gladys Cooper. Very dated comedy starts charmingly with pilot Cummings falling in love with Princess de Havilland, bogs down in no longer timely situations, unbearably coy finale involving (supposedly) F.D.R. himself. Krasna won Best Screenplay Oscar.

Princess Tam-Tam (1935-French) **77m.** *** D: Edmond T. Greville. Josephine Baker, Albert Prejean, Germaine Aussey, Viviane Romance. Baker lives up to her legend in this disarming reworking of *Pygmalion*: a poor, beautiful, wild African lass is polished and educated by writer Prejean, then passed off as an Indian princess—much to the consternation of his snobbish, two-timing wife. Charming story (by Pepito Abatino, then Baker's husband), lavish Busby Berkeley-ish musical numbers. Partially filmed in Tunisia.▼

Princess Yang Kwei Fei (1955-Japanese) **C-91m.** **** D: Kenji Mizoguchi. Machiko Kyo, Masayuki Mori, So Yamamura, Eitaro Shindo, Sakae Ozawa. Emperor Mori takes country girl Kyo as his concubine. He is forced out of power by his greedy family: she is killed, and he worships her statue. Breathtakingly beautiful, poetic love story/fable/tragedy.

Prince Valiant (1954) **C-100m.** **½ D: Henry Hathaway. James Mason, Janet Leigh, Robert Wagner, Debra Paget, Sterling Hayden, Victor McLaglen, Donald Crisp, Brian Aherne. Hal Foster's famed comic-strip character is the hero of this cardboard costumer decked out in 20th Century-Fox splendor, battling and loving in Middle Ages England. Script by Dudley Nichols.

Prince Who Was a Thief, The (1951) **C-88m.** **½ D: Rudolph Maté. Tony Curtis, Piper Laurie, Everett Sloane, Jeff Corey, Betty Garde. Juvenile costumer with Curtis fighting to regain his rightful seat on the throne; sparked by enthusiastic performances.

Principal, The (1987) **C-109m.** ** D: Christopher Cain. James Belushi, Louis Gossett, Jr., Rae Dawn Chong, Michael Wright, J.J. Cohen, Esai Morales, Troy Winbush. Following some drunken vandalism on his estranged spouse's car, schoolteacher Belushi is "promoted" to top job at the district's most crime-ridden school. Unlikely mix of comedy and drama benefits from likable performances and a reasonably tense HIGH NOON finale between Belushi and the school's leading thug.▼

Prison (1988) **C-102m.** ** D: Renny Harlin. Lane Smith, Viggo Mortensen, Chelsea Field, Andre De Shields, Lincoln Kilpatrick, Ivan Kane. The spirit of a prisoner who was executed twenty years ago seeks revenge on his one-time guard—who's now the warden (Smith). OK special effects and location atmosphere are strongest assets of this clichéd horror film, shot at an actual Wyoming state pen.▼

Prisoner, The (1955-British) **91m.** *** D: Peter Glenville. Alec Guinness, Jack Hawkins, Raymond Huntley, Wilfrid Lawson. Grim account of cardinal in iron curtain country undergoing grueling interrogation. Guinness-Hawkins interplay is superb.▼

Prisoner of Second Avenue, The (1975) **C-105m.** ***½ D: Melvin Frank. Jack Lemmon, Anne Bancroft, Gene Saks, Elizabeth Wilson, Florence Stanley, M. Emmet Walsh. Neil Simon walks a tightrope between comedy and melancholia, and never falls, thanks to warm performances by Lemmon, as suddenly unemployed executive who has a nervous breakdown, and Bancroft, as his understanding wife. Look for Sylvester Stallone as an alleged pickpocket, F. Murray Abraham as a cabbie.▼

Prisoner of Shark Island, The (1936)

95m. ***½ D: John Ford. Warner Baxter, Gloria Stuart, Claude Gillingwater, John Carradine, Harry Carey, Arthur Byron, Ernest Whitman. Excellent film based on true story of Dr. Samuel Mudd, who innocently treated John Wilkes Booth's leg after Lincoln assassination, and was sentenced to life imprisonment. Gripping story; Baxter superb, Carradine memorable as villainous sergeant, Whitman fine as Baxter's black comrade. Scripted by Nunnally Johnson. Remade as HELLGATE and the TV movie THE ORDEAL OF DR. MUDD.

Prisoner of the Iron Mask, The (1962-Italian) **C-80m. **½** D: Francesco De Feo. Michael Lemoine, Wandisa Guida, Andrea Bosic, Jany Clair, Giovanni Materassi. Usual costume shenanigans: an evil count imprisons a man who has proof of the nobleman's treachery. Based not on the expected Alexandre Dumas novel, but on his *Ten Years After*. D'Artagnan and The Three Musketeers do not appear.

Prisoner of the Volga (1960-Yugoslavian) **C-102m. **** D: W. Tourjansky. John Derek, Elsa Martinelli, Dawn Addams, Wolfgang Preiss, Gert Frobe. Well-mounted but ordinary costume drama of soldier who suffers when he seeks revenge on general who impregnated his wife.

Prisoner of War (1954) **80m. **** D: Andrew Marton. Ronald Reagan, Steve Forrest, Dewey Martin, Oscar Homolka, Robert Horton, Paul Stewart, Harry Morgan, Stephen Bekassy. Sincere but two-dimensional drama exposing mistreatment of American P.O.W.s during Korean War.

Prisoner of Zenda, The (1937) **101m. ***½** D: John Cromwell. Ronald Colman, Madeleine Carroll, Douglas Fairbanks, Jr., C. Aubrey Smith, Raymond Massey, Mary Astor, David Niven, Montagu Love, Alexander D'Arcy. Lavish costumer with excellent casting; Colman is forced to substitute for lookalike cousin, King of Ruritanian country, but commoner Colman falls in love with regal Carroll. Fairbanks is outstanding as Rupert of Hentzau. Screenplay by John L. Balderston, from Anthony Hope's novel. Previously filmed in 1913 and 1922, then again in 1952 and 1979.

Prisoner of Zenda, The (1952) **C-101m. **½** D: Richard Thorpe. Stewart Granger, Deborah Kerr, Jane Greer, Louis Calhern, Lewis Stone, James Mason, Robert Douglas, Robert Coote. Plush but uninspired remake of the Anthony Hope novel, chronicling the swashbuckling adventures of Granger, a dead ringer for a small European country's king. Stick with the Ronald Colman version; this one copies it scene for scene.▼

Prisoner of Zenda, The (1979) **C-108m.** BOMB D: Richard Quine. Peter Sellers, Lynne Frederick, Lionel Jeffries, Elke Sommer, Gregory Sierra, Jeremy Kemp, Catherine Schell. Famous swashbuckler is played for laughs, but there aren't any. A return to the kind of picture that helped to destroy Sellers' career until the second series of Clouseau comedies rescued it.▼

Prisoners of the Casbah (1953) **C-78m. *½** D: Richard Bare. Gloria Grahame, Turhan Bey, Cesar Romero, Nestor Paiva. Low-budget costumer with diverting cast in stale plot of princess and her lover fleeing killers in title locale.

Prisoners of the Lost Universe (1983) **C-90m.** TVM D: Terry Marcel. Richard Hatch, Kay Lenz, John Saxon, Dawn Abraham, Peter O'Farrell, Ray Charleson. Sadistic warlord on a hostile planet keeps two space travelers, accidentally hurled into the future, on their toes. Made for cable. Average.▼

Prisoner Without a Name, Cell Without a Number SEE: **Jacobo Timerman: Prisoner Without a Name, Cell Without a Number**

Prison for Children (1987) **C-100m.** TVM D: Larry Peerce. Raphael Sbarge, Kenny Ransom, Jonathan Chapin, Josh Brolin, John Ritter, Betty Thomas. Teenage roustabout gets sucked into juvenile prison system, run by a sympathetic warden (Ritter, in a relatively minor role) who's preoccupied with fighting bureaucrats for better conditions. Average.

Prison Train (1938) **84m. **½** D: Gordon Wiles. Fred Keating, Linda Winters (Dorothy Comingore), Clarence Muse, Faith Bacon, Alexander Leftwich, Nestor Paiva, Franklyn Farnum. Stylized, atmospheric little chronicle of racketeer Keating, who's convicted of murder and is traveling crosscountry to begin doing time at Alcatraz. Hampered by its ultra-low budget but still a nice surprise. Also known as PEOPLE'S ENEMY.▼

Private Affairs (1988-Italian) **C-104m.** BOMB D: Francesco Massaro. Kate Capshaw, David Naughton, Giuliana de Sio, Michele Placido, Luca Barbareschi. Various romantic complications among the boring people, mostly connected with the Roman fashion industry. Characters are as dull as the thin, diffuse plot; as near to unwatchable as a movie can be.▼

Private Affairs of Bel Ami, The (1947) **112m. ***½** D: Albert Lewin. George Sanders, Angela Lansbury, Ann Dvorak, Frances Dee, Albert Basserman, Warren William, John Carradine. Delicious, literate adaptation of Guy de Maupassant's "story of a rogue." Sanders, who gets ahead by using his charm on prominent women, denies himself the real love of Lansbury. Fine gallery of performances; beautifully photographed by Russell Metty.

Private Battle, A (1980) **C-100m.** TVM D: Robert Lewis. Jack Warden, Anne Jackson, David Stockton, Rachel Kelly, Walter Cronkite, Rebecca Schull. John Gay's affecting drama, lovingly played by Warden and Jackson, based on the story of writer Cornelius (THE LONGEST DAY) Ryan's struggle against cancer. Above average.

Private Benjamin (1980) **C-100m.** *** D: Howard Zieff. Goldie Hawn, Eileen Brennan, Armand Assante, Robert Webber, Sam Wanamaker, Barbara Barrie, Mary Kay Place, Harry Dean Stanton, Albert Brooks, Hal Williams, P. J. Soles, Sally Kirkland. A bubbleheaded Jewish American Princess enlists in the Army, and after a disastrous initiation finds direction and self-esteem for the first time in her life. Entertaining comedy with more substance than one might expect; Goldie is terrific in this tailor-made vehicle (which she produced). Later a TV series.▼

Private Buckaroo (1942) **68m.** ** D: Edward Cline. The Andrews Sisters, Dick Foran, Joe E. Lewis, Donald O'Connor, Peggy Ryan, Jennifer Holt. Mini-musical from Universal Pictures is vehicle for 1940s favorite sister trio, accompanied by Harry James, et al in Army camp show.▼

Private Contentment (1982) **C-90m.** TVM D: Vivian Matalon. Trini Alvarado, Peter Gallagher, John McMartin, Kathryn Walker, Beatrice Winde, Mark Zimmerman. Intelligent but sometimes overbaked soaper about WW2 soldier Gallagher, his reunion with his family, and the various skeletons that come creeping out of the closet. Screenplay by Reynolds Price. A PBS *American Playhouse* presentation. Average.

Private Detective 62 SEE: **Man Killer**

Private Duty Nurses (1971) **C-80m.** BOMB D: George Armitage. Kathy Cannon, Joyce Williams, Pegi Boucher, Joseph Kaufmann, Herbert Jefferson, Jr., Paul Hampton, Paul Gleason. Second of Roger Corman's five "nurse" pictures is the worst. Glum and humorless, it spends more time on then-new waterbeds than in the hospital; dull cast doesn't help. Followed by NIGHT CALL NURSES.▼

Private Eyes (1953) **64m.** D: Edward Bernds. Leo Gorcey, Huntz Hall, Bernard Gorcey, Chick Chandler, Myron Healey, Tim Ryan. SEE: **Bowery Boys** series.

Private Eyes, The (1980) **C-91m.** **½ D: Lang Elliott. Tim Conway, Don Knotts, Trisha Noble, Bernard Fox, John Fujioka, Fred Stuthman, Mary Nell Santacroce. Conway and Knotts are bumbling Scotland Yard sleuths—and Abbott and Costello incarnate—in this silly, well-mounted murder-in-an-old-dark-house mystery. One of the better Conway-Knotts comedies.▼

Private Files of J. Edgar Hoover, The (1977) **C-112m.** **½ D: Larry Cohen. Broderick Crawford, Dan Dailey, Jose Ferrer, Rip Torn, Michael Parks, Raymond St. Jacques, Ronee Blakley, Celeste Holm, Howard da Silva, June Havoc, John Marley, Andrew Duggan, Lloyd Nolan. Sleazy bio of former FBI chief makes for great camp with its all-star lineup of true-life political personalities—not to mention that cast! The New-Heights-in-Screen-Surrealism Award goes to the Miklos Rozsa-scored scene in which John Edgar gets drunk listening to sex tapes of a government official.▼

Private Function, A (1985-British) **C-93m.** **½ D: Malcolm Mowbray. Michael Palin, Maggie Smith, Liz Smith, Denholm Elliott, Richard Griffiths, John Normington, Bill Paterson. Droll, very British comedy by Alan Bennett set in post-WW2 England, where food rationing is still in force and a contraband pig becomes the center of attention. Often funny, but also cynical and cruel. Smith is hilarious as the social-climbing wife of milquetoasty podiatrist Palin.▼

Private Hell 36 (1954) **81m.** **½ D: Don Siegel. Ida Lupino, Steve Cochran, Howard Duff, Dean Jagger, Dorothy Malone. Well-balanced account of guilt overcoming two cops who retrieve stolen money but keep some for themselves. Lupino also wrote and produced the film with Collier Young.▼

Private Lessons (1981) **C-87m.** *½ D: Alan Myerson. Sylvia Kristel, Howard Hesseman, Eric Brown, Pamela Bryant, Ed Begley, Jr., Crispin Glover. Male adolescent from wealthy family finds sexual delight with the maid, unaware that she has other plans for him. Surprise box-office hit is pretty mild piece of sleaze. Written by humorist Dan Greenburg (who also appears as a desk clerk).▼

Private Life of Don Juan, The (1934-British) **80m.** ** D: Alexander Korda. Douglas Fairbanks, Merle Oberon, Binnie Barnes, Joan Gardner, Benita Hume, Athene Seyler, Melville Cooper. Lifeless costumer with aging Fairbanks in title role, pursuing a bevy of beauties. This was his final film.▼

Private Life of Henry VIII, The (1933-British) **97m.** **** D: Alexander Korda. Charles Laughton, Binnie Barnes, Robert Donat, Elsa Lanchester, Merle Oberon, Miles Mander, Wendy Barrie, John Loder. Sweeping historical chronicle of 16th-century British monarch, magnificently captured by Oscar-winning Laughton in a multifaceted performance. Lanchester fine as Anne of Cleves, with top supporting cast. Also shown in computer-colored version.▼

Private Life of Sherlock Holmes, The (1970) **C-125m.** ***½ D: Billy Wilder. Robert Stephens, Colin Blakely, Genevieve Page, Irene Handl, Stanley Holloway, Christopher Lee, Clive Revill. Atypical but extremely personal Wilder film takes melancholy look at famed sleuth. Acting, photography and score are tops in neglected film whose reputation should soar in future years. Intended as a 3½-hour film; full-length version may yet be released. Made in England.▼

Private Lives (1931) **84m.** ******* D: Sidney Franklin. Norma Shearer, Robert Montgomery, Una Merkel, Reginald Denny, Jean Hersholt. Sparkling adaptation of Noel Coward comedy about bickering couple; a stylish treat all the way.

Private Lives of Adam and Eve, The (1960) **C/B&W-87m.** BOMB D: Albert Zugsmith, Mickey Rooney. Mickey Rooney, Mamie Van Doren, Fay Spain, Mel Torme, Martin Milner, Tuesday Weld, Cecil Kellaway, Paul Anka, Ziva Rodann. Perfectly awful fantasy about a stranded Nevada couple, Ad (Milner) and Evie (Van Doren), who dream that they are back in the Garden of Eden. Rooney chews the scenery as the Devil.

Private Lives of Elizabeth and Essex, The (1939) **C-106m.** *****½** D: Michael Curtiz. Bette Davis, Errol Flynn, Olivia de Havilland, Donald Crisp, Alan Hale, Vincent Price, Henry Stephenson, Henry Daniell, James Stephenson, Ralph Forbes, Robert Warwick, Leo G. Carroll. Colorful, elaborate costume drama with outstanding performance by Davis as queen whose love for dashing Flynn is thwarted. Not authentic history, but good drama. Norman Reilly Raine and Aeneas MacKenzie adapted Maxwell Anderson's play *Elizabeth the Queen*. Adult film debut of Nanette Fabray (billed as Fabares). Also known as ELIZABETH THE QUEEN.▼

Private Navy of Sgt. O'Farrell, The (1968) **C-92m.** BOMB D: Frank Tashlin. Bob Hope, Phyllis Diller, Jeffrey Hunter, Gina Lollobrigida, Mylene Demongeot, John Myhers, Mako. O'Farrell tries to import some beautiful nurses to improve his men's morale, gets Diller instead. Of the many terrible Hope comedies of the 1960s, this may be the worst. Unfunny and offensive.

Private Number (1936) **80m.** ****** D: Roy Del Ruth. Robert Taylor, Loretta Young, Patsy Kelly, Basil Rathbone, Marjorie Gateson, Paul Harvey, Joe E. Lewis. Not to disgrace family, wealthy Taylor must keep marriage to family housemaid Young a secret. Tearful soaper is OK.

Private Parts (1972) **C-86m.** ******* D: Paul Bartel. Ann Ruymen, Lucille Benson, Laurie Main, John Ventantonio. Truly perverse black-comedic suspense film about runaway teenage girl staying at her aunt's strange hotel where occupants are extremely weird. There's a series of murders but the focus is more on sexual eccentricities including voyeurism, narcissism and transvestism. If Andy Warhol's CHELSEA

GIRLS had been co-directed by Alfred Hitchcock and John Waters it would come close to this directorial debut by Bartel. Clearly not for every taste.

Private Resort (1985) **C-85m.** BOMB D: George Bowers. Rob Morrow, Johnny Depp, Hector Elizondo, Dody Goodman, Tony Azito, Emily Longstreth, Karyn O'Bryan, Hilary Shapiro, Michael Bowen, Andrew (Dice) Clay. Imbecilic sex comedy about a couple of young fellows on the make at a resort hotel. Good supporting cast is pitifully wasted.▼

Private's Affair, A (1959) **C-92m.** ****½** D: Raoul Walsh. Sal Mineo, Christine Carere, Barry Coe, Barbara Eden, Gary Crosby, Terry Moore, Jim Backus, Jessie Royce Landis. Energetic young cast involved in putting on the "big Army show" on TV.

Private School (1983) **C-97m.** BOMB D: Noel Black. Phoebe Cates, Betsy Russell, Matthew Modine, Michael Zorek, Fran Ryan, Julie Payne, Ray Walston, Sylvia Kristel. Raunchy teenage hijinks at a girls' school, with ample nudity but no brains in sight. Even voyeurs might have a hard time sloshing through this heavyhanded, amateurish "comedy."▼

Private Sessions (1985) **C-100m.** TVM D: Michael Pressman. Mike Farrell, Maureen Stapleton, Kelly McGillis, Hope Lange, Tom Bosley, Kim Hunter, Kathryn Walker, Greg Evigan, Victor Garber, Robert Vaughn. Uninspired pilot to a prospective series about a psychologist/therapist who violates the first rule of his profession—getting involved in the lives of his patients. Awfully good cast but no go. McGillis' TV movie debut. Below average.

Privates on Parade (1982-British) **C-100m.** ****½** D: Michael Blakemore. John Cleese, Denis Quilley, Nicola Pagett, Patrick Pearson, Michael Elphick, Joe Melia. Uneven adaptation of Peter Nichols' British play about SADUSEA (Song And Dance Unit, South East Asia), based in Singapore in the late 40s. Quilley is an aging queen who directs and stars in their camp shows, Cleese his thickwitted commander. Some funny musical numbers mix awkwardly with satire—and unexpected drama.▼

Private's Progress (1956-British) **99m.** ******* D: John Boulting. Richard Attenborough, Jill Adams, Dennis Price, Terry-Thomas, Ian Carmichael, Peter Jones. Prize collection of funny men, splendidly played by cast, involved in Army shenanigans.

Private War of Major Benson, The (1955) **C-100m.** ****½** D: Jerry Hopper. Charlton Heston, Julie Adams, William Demarest, Tim Hovey, Sal Mineo, David Janssen, Tim Considine, Milburn Stone. Hovey is the little boy at military school who charms rugged commander Heston into sympathetic person; Adams is the love interest.

Private Worlds (1935) **84m.** **½ D: Gregory La Cava. Claudette Colbert, Charles Boyer, Joan Bennett, Joel McCrea, Helen Vinson, Esther Dale, Jean Rouverol. Dated but engrossing tale of mental institution, with doctors Boyer and Colbert giving restrained performances; noteworthy support by Bennett.

Privilege (1967-British) **C-101m.** *** D: Peter Watkins. Paul Jones, Jean Shrimpton, Marc London, Max Bacon, Jeremy Child. Overambitious yet effective account of 1970s England where all-powerful welfare state manipulates masses through such media as pop singers. Jones is good as disillusioned teen-age idol.

Prix de Beauté (1930-French) **78m.** **½ D: Augusto Genina. Louise Brooks, Jean Bradin, Georges Charlia, Gaston Jacquet, A. Nicolle. Brooks is the whole show in this, her first sound film (and last major screen role). The story may be clichéd—a melodrama in which she's cast as a typist who becomes a beauty queen and finds tragedy—but Brooks is as lovely and sensuous as ever. Rene Clair, originally scheduled to direct, had a hand in the script. Also known as MISS EUROPE.▼

Prize, The (1963) **C-136m.** *** D: Mark Robson. Paul Newman, Edward G. Robinson, Elke Sommer, Diane Baker, Micheline Presle, Leo G. Carroll. Irving Wallace novel is mere stepping stone for glossy spy yarn set in Stockholm, involving participants in Nobel Prize ceremony. Newman and Sommer make handsome leads; Robinson has dual role. Fast-moving fun; script by Ernest Lehman.

Prize Fighter, The (1979) **C-99m.** ** D: Michael Preece. Tim Conway, Don Knotts, David Wayne, Robin Clarke, Cisse Cameron, Mary Ellen O'Neill, Michael LaGuardia. If you like Knotts and Conway, you'll probably get through this lame, kiddie-oriented comedy about a dumb boxer and his smart-aleck manager, set in the 1930s.▼

Prizefighter and the Lady, The (1933) **102m.** *** D: W. S. Van Dyke. Myrna Loy, Max Baer, Otto Kruger, Walter Huston, Jack Dempsey, Primo Carnera, Jess Willard, James J. Jeffries. Entertaining film breathes life into potential clichés; Baer falls for high-class gangster's moll Loy. Exciting prize-fight finale.

Prize of Arms, A (1961-British) **105m.** **½ D: Cliff Owen. Stanley Baker, Tom Bell, Helmut Schmid, John Phillips. Effective yarn is hindered by heavy British accents ruining much dialogue. Tale unfolds methodical plan for big heist of Army funds.

Prize of Gold, A (1955-British) **C-98m.** *** D: Mark Robson. Richard Widmark,

Mai Zetterling, Nigel Patrick, Donald Wolfit, Eric Pohlmann. Taut caper in post-WW2 Berlin involving a planned heist of gold from the air lift circuit.

Prizzi's Honor (1985) **C-129m.** ***½ D: John Huston. Jack Nicholson, Kathleen Turner, Anjelica Huston, Robert Loggia, William Hickey, John Randolph, Lee Richardson, Michael Lombard, Lawrence Tierney, Joseph Ruskin. Delicious, very off-beat black comedy about a slow-witted hit man from a close-knit Mafia family who gets more than he bargained for when he falls in love with Turner. Nicholson is a joy to watch, matched by a superlative cast (Randolph is a treat as his father). Huston wrings every drop from Richard Condon and Janet Roach's wry screenplay (based on Condon's novel). Beautifully photographed by Andrzej Bartkowiak. Anjelica Huston won Best Supporting Actress Oscar for her sly performance, directed by her father.▼

Probe (1972) **C-97m. TVM** D: Russ Mayberry. Hugh O'Brian, Elke Sommer, John Gielgud, Burgess Meredith, Angel Tompkins, Lilia Skala, Kent Smith, Byron Chung. Good Leslie Stevens thriller about theft of fabulous jewel collection has nifty gimmick: detective O'Brian has tiny bug implanted in him, allowing what he sees and hears to be sent back to control center (and letting them transmit helpful advice). Look quickly for Jaclyn Smith. Pilot for the series *Search* (this film's subsequent title). Average.

Problem Child (1990) **C-81m.** *½ D: Dennis Dugan. John Ritter, Michael Oliver, Jack Warden, Amy Yasbeck, Gilbert Gottfried, Michael Richards. Botched comic twist on THE BAD SEED has Ritter as an unlucky father who adopts devil-child Oliver. A promising opening leads nowhere as bad performances and crude jokes prevail.

Prodigal, The (1955) **C-114m.** **½ D: Richard Thorpe. Lana Turner, Edmund Purdom, James Mitchell, Louis Calhern, Audrey Dalton, Neville Brand, Taina Elg, Cecil Kellaway, Henry Daniell, Walter Hampden, Joseph Wiseman. Juvenile biblical semi-spectacle, with Turner the evil goddess of love corrupting Purdom; glossy MGM production.

Producers, The (1968) **C-88m.** ***½ D: Mel Brooks. Zero Mostel, Gene Wilder, Kenneth Mars, Dick Shawn, Lee Meredith, Christopher Hewett, Andreas Voustinas, Estelle Winwood, Renee Taylor, Bill Hickey. Classic piece of insanity stars incomparable Mostel as hard-luck Broadway producer Max Bialystock, who cons meek accountant Wilder into helping him with outrageous scheme: selling 25,000% of a play that's certain to flop, then heading to

Rio with the excess cash. One of those rare films that gets funnier with each viewing, highlighted by legendary "Springtime for Hitler" production number. Brooks' first feature earned him an Oscar for his screenplay. Listen for his voice dubbed into "Springtime For Hitler."▼

Profane Comedy, The SEE: **Set This Town on Fire**

Professionals, The (1966) C-117m. *** D: Richard Brooks. Burt Lancaster, Lee Marvin, Robert Ryan, Jack Palance, Claudia Cardinale, Woody Strode, Ralph Bellamy. Bellamy employs four soldiers-of-fortune to rescue his wife from Mexican varmint Palance. Far-fetched story, but real action, taut excitement throughout; beautifully photographed by Conrad Hall.▼

Professional Soldier (1936) 78m. **½ D: Tay Garnett. Victor McLaglen, Freddie Bartholomew, Gloria Stuart, Constance Collier, Michael Whalen. McLaglen is hired to kidnap young king Bartholomew, but mutual friendship gets in the way. Good teaming supports average script, based on a Damon Runyon story.

Professional Sweetheart (1933) 68m. ** D: William A. Seiter. Ginger Rogers, ZaSu Pitts, Norman Foster, Frank McHugh, Edgar Kennedy, Betty Furness, Gregory Ratoff, Sterling Holloway, Franklin Pangborn. Good cast can't put over weak radio spoof, with Rogers as airwaves star who becomes engaged to hick Foster in publicity stunt.

Professor Beware (1938) 87m. **½ D: Elliott Nugent. Harold Lloyd, Phyllis Welch, William Frawley, Etienne Girardot, Raymond Walburn, Lionel Stander, Thurston Hall, Cora Witherspoon. One of Lloyd's last vehicles has good moments, but tale of archeologist searching for rare tablet is thin.

Profile of Terror SEE: **Sadist, The**▼

Projected Man, The (1967-British) C-77m. ** D: Ian Curteis. Bryant Halliday, Mary Peach, Norman Wooland, Ronald Allen, Derek Farr. Using a teleportation machine something like that in all the FLY movies, scientist accidentally disfigures himself and gains the touch of death. Not bad but unoriginal.

Projectionist, The (1971) C-85m. **½ D: Harry Hurwitz. Chuck McCann, Ina Balin, Rodney Dangerfield, Jara Kohout, Harry Hurwitz, Robert Staats. Independently made film has ups and downs, but many pearly moments in story of daydreaming projectionist McCann who envisions himself a superhero, Captain Flash. Many film clips imaginatively used: best of all is coming-attractions trailer for the end of the world.▼

Project X (1968) C-97m. **½ D: William Castle. Christopher George, Greta Baldwin, Henry Jones, Monte Markham, Phillip Pine,

Harold Gould. Offbeat but ultimately unconvincing mixture of time travel, biological warfare, and psychology in tale of future Earth civilization searching for secret germ formula. Their amnesiac secret agent has it; how to get it?

Project X (1987) C-108m. **½ D: Jonathan Kaplan. Matthew Broderick, Helen Hunt, Bill Sadler, Johnny Ray McGhee, Jonathan Stark, Robin Gammell, Stephen Lang, Jean Smart, Dick Miller. Young military foul-up is assigned to top secret lab where he works with chimps—and soon becomes enraged at the tests they're being subjected to. Watchable but patently predictable story, with a finale vaguely reminiscent of a 1960s Disney comedy. The chimps (especially Willie, in the role of Virgil) are great, however.▼

Promise, The (1979) C-98m. BOMB D: Gilbert Cates. Kathleen Quinlan, Stephen Collins, Beatrice Straight, Laurence Luckinbill, William Prince. Boy loves girl. Girl loses face in car accident. Boy thinks girl dead. Girl gets new face from plastic surgeon. Boy falls for old girl's new face. Viewer runs screaming from room.

Promise (1986) C-100m. TVM D: Glenn Jordan. James Garner, James Woods, Piper Laurie, Peter Michael Goetz, Michael Alldredge, Alan Rosenberg. Footloose bachelor Garner finds he must honor a long-ago promise made to his recently deceased mother to care for his schizophrenic brother in this beautifully written (by Richard Friedenberg) drama of love and responsibility. Garner coproduced this one. Emmy winner for Woods, Laurie, writing, directing, and Outstanding Special. Above average.

Promise at Dawn (1970-U.S.-French) C-101m. **½ D: Jules Dassin. Melina Mercouri, Assaf Dayan, Francois Raffoul, Despo, Fernand Gravey, Perlo Vita (Jules Dassin). Seventh teaming of Mercouri and husband Dassin, who produced, directed, wrote, and also does a bit role as Russian silent-film star Ivan Mousjoukine. It's mostly Mercouri's show, an uneven but well-acted chronicle of the life of writer Romain Gary and his resourceful actress mother. Dayan is good as the young adult Gary.

Promised a Miracle (1988) C-100m. TVM D: Stephen Gyllenhaal. Rosanna Arquette, Judge Reinhold, Tom Bower, Vonni Ribisi, Gary Bayer, Maria O'Brien. Moving drama of a deeply religious couple accused of manslaughter in 1974 following the death of their diabetic son, whom they sought to heal through spiritual rather than medical means. Based on the true story told in Larry Parker's book, *We Let Our Son Die*. Arquette and Reinhold beautifully interpret David Hill's script. Above average.

Promised Land (1988) **C-101m.** **½ D: Michael Hoffman. Jason Gedrick, Kiefer Sutherland, Meg Ryan, Tracy Pollan, Googy Gress, Deborah Richter, Oscar Rowland, Sondra Seacat. Uneven but moody little sleeper, set in the rural Northwest, about two casual high school acquaintances whose lives intersect tragically a couple of years after graduation. Ryan is a standout as a tattooed, rod-packing high school hellcat. Film was developed and produced at Robert Redford's Sundance Institute.▼

Promise Her Anything (1966) **C-98m.** **½ D: Arthur Hiller. Warren Beatty, Leslie Caron, Bob Cummings, Hermione Gingold, Lionel Stander, Keenan Wynn. Limp premise of blue-moviemaker (Beatty) taking care of neighbor Caron's baby. Filmed in England but supposed to be Greenwich Village; screenplay by William Peter Blatty. Look for Bessie Love as a petshop customer, Donald Sutherland as a baby's father.

Promise Him Anything (1974) **C-78m.** TVM D: Edward Parone. Eddie Albert, Frederic Forrest, Meg Foster, William Schallert, Tom Ewell, Aldo Ray, Steven Keats. Comedy tracing the tangled romantic web of a young man who sues his computer date for breach of promise. Sprightly performed fluff. Average.

Promise of Love, The (1980) **C-96m.** TVM D: Don Taylor. Valerie Bertinelli, Jameson Parker, Andy Romano, Joanna Miles, David James Carroll, Craig T. Nelson, Shelley Long. Undistinguished melodrama about a young bride who tries to rebuild her life when her Marine husband is killed in Vietnam. Below average.

Promises in the Dark (1979) **C-115m.** **½ D: Jerome Hellman. Marsha Mason, Ned Beatty, Susan Clark, Michael Brandon, Kathleen Beller, Paul Clemens, Donald Moffat. Unrelievedly depressing (though well-made) film about young girl (Beller) dying of cancer, and her compassionate doctor (Mason). Directorial debut of producer Hellman.▼

Promises to Keep (1985) **C-100m.** TVM D: Noel Black. Robert Mitchum, Christopher Mitchum, Bentley C. Mitchum, Tess Harper, Claire Bloom. Dreary vehicle about a footloose man's visit to the family he abandoned thirty years earlier, giving Mitchum the opportunity to act with his son Chris as well as his grandson (the latter in his debut, narrating and demonstrating only the bare outlines of acting talent). Below average.

Prom Night (1980-Canadian) **C-91m.** ** D: Paul Lynch. Leslie Nielsen, Jamie Lee Curtis, Casey Stevens, Antoinette Bower, Pita Oliver, Robert Silverman. Killer menaces teens who were responsible for the death of a little girl six years earlier. Not

the worst of its type, but that's nothing to brag about. Followed by HELLO MARY LOU: PROM NIGHT II.▼

Promoter, The (1952-British) **88m.** *** D: Ronald Neame. Alec Guinness, Glynis Johns, Valerie Hobson, Petula Clark, Edward Chapman. Charming comedy about a likable but penniless young man who sees how to get ahead in the world—and seizes his opportunity. Script by Eric Ambler from Arnold Bennett's story *The Card,* also its title in England.▼

Prophecy (1979) **C-95m.** *½ D: John Frankenheimer. Talia Shire, Robert Foxworth, Armand Assante, Richard Dysart, Victoria Racimo. Classical musician and her doctor husband fight off what appears to be a giant salami in upstate Maine after mercury poisoning turns animals into huge mutants and worse. Ridiculous horror film is good for a few laughs.▼

Protocol (1984) **C-96m.** ** D: Herbert Ross. Goldie Hawn, Chris Sarandon, Richard Romanus, Andre Gregory, Gail Strickland, Cliff De Young, Keith Szarabajka, Ed Begley, Jr., James Staley, Kenneth Mars, Kenneth McMillan. Or, Goldie Goes to Washington: a contrived comedy vehicle for Hawn as inadvertent heroine (and overnight celebrity) who's rewarded with do-nothing government job . . . but soon becomes a pawn for dealing with Middle Eastern potentate. Some funny moments give way to obvious satire and a hard-to-swallow finish in which Goldie makes like Capra's Mr. Smith. Goldie's enduring likability is really put to the test this time. ▼

Prototype (1983) **C-100m.** TVM D: David Greene. Christopher Plummer, David Morse, Frances Sternhagen, James Sutorius, Stephen Elliott, Arthur Hill. Richard Levinson and William Link's ingenious updating of the Frankenstein legend has Nobel Prize-winning scientist Plummer developing the first android, then stealing him from the Pentagon's clutches, fearing they plan on reprogramming "it" for a destructive mission. Above average.▼

Proud and Profane, The (1956) **111m.** **½ D: George Seaton. William Holden, Deborah Kerr, Thelma Ritter, Dewey Martin, William Redfield, Ross Bagdasarian, Marion Ross. Spotty WW2 romance story has many parallels to FROM HERE TO ETERNITY, but Kerr-Holden romance is never believable.

Proud and the Beautiful, The (1953-French-Mexican) **94m.** *** D: Yves Allegret. Michele Morgan, Gerard Philipe, Victor Manuel Mendoza, Michele Cordoue. Morgan and Philipe interact beautifully as widow in Mexico whose love for down-and-out doctor helps him regain sense of values.

Proud and the Damned, The (1973) **C-94m.** ** D: Ferde Grofe, Jr. Chuck

[921]

Connors, Jose Greco, Cesar Romero, Aron Kincaid, Anita Quinn. Uneven performances and script in formula story of Civil War veterans and mercenaries drifting through Latin America, caught up in local revolution.▼

Proud Men (1987) **C-100m. TVM** D: William A. Graham. Charlton Heston, Peter Strauss, Belinda Belaski, Alan Autry, Nan Martin, Maria Mayenzet. Heston and Strauss' strong characterizations as a cattle rancher and his expatriate son, who are bitterly estranged, can't make up for a pedestrian script. Average.

Proud Ones, The (1956) **C-94m. **½** D: Robert D. Webb. Robert Ryan, Virginia Mayo, Jeffrey Hunter, Robert Middleton, Walter Brennan. Staunch acting involving the inevitable showdown between disabled sheriff and outlaws perks up this Western.

Proud Rebel, The (1958) **C-103m. ***** D: Michael Curtiz, Alan Ladd, Olivia de Havilland, Dean Jagger, David Ladd, Cecil Kellaway, Henry Hull, John Carradine, (Harry) Dean Stanton. Well-presented study of two-fisted Ladd seeking medical help for mute son (played by Ladd's real-life son); de Havilland is the woman who tames him.▼

Proud Valley (1940-British) **77m. **½** D: Pen Tennyson. Paul Robeson, Edward Chapman, Simon Lack, Rachel Thomas, Edward Rigby. Mild drama of Welsh coalmining village beset by mine shutdown; uplifted only by Robeson's commanding presence and fine voice.

Providence (1977-British) **C-104m. **** D: Alain Resnais. Dirk Bogarde, John Gielgud, Ellen Burstyn, David Warner, Elaine Stritch. Odd fantasy marked director Resnais' English-language debut. Writer Gielgud tries to complete his last novel, juxtaposes imagined thoughts about his family with real-life encounters. Muddled drama by David Mercer; interesting Miklos Rozsa score.▼

Prowler, The (1951) **92m. **½** D: Joseph Losey. Van Heflin, Evelyn Keyes, John Maxwell, Katharine Warren. Fairly good thriller about sector car cop Heflin, who complains he's had one too many "lousy breaks." He becomes obsessed with, and seduces, married Keyes . . . and plots to do in her husband.

Prowler, The (1981) **C-88m. *½** D: Joseph Zito. Vicki Dawson, Christopher Goutman, Cindy Weintraub, Farley Granger, John Seitz. WW2 veteran kills ex-girlfriend and her new amour with a pitchfork, then suddenly resumes his murderous ways 35 years later. Illogically plotted, with gruesome special effects by Tom Savini.▼

Prudence and the Pill (1968-British) **C-98m. **½** D: Fielder Cook, Ronald Neame. Deborah Kerr, David Niven, Robert Coote, Irina Demick, Joyce Redman,

Judy Geeson, Keith Michell. Labored comedy treatment of modern sexual mores. Niven thinks he can patch up his in-name-only marriage by substituting aspirin for his wife's birth control pills. Good cast and performances, but weak script.

Psyche '59 (1964-British) **94m. **½** D: Alexander Singer. Patricia Neal, Curt Jurgens, Samantha Eggar, Ian Bannen, Elspeth March. Turgid melodrama involving infidelity, with good cast doing their best.

Psychiatrist: God Bless the Children, The (1970) **C-100m. TVM** D: Daryl Duke. Roy Thinnes, Peter Duel, Luther Adler, John Rubinstein, Joy Bang, Norman Alden, Barry Brown. Entertaining drama showcases new group therapy techniques applied to young patients; stagy dialogue, fiery performances. Teleplay by Jerrold Freedman. Pilot for a short-lived series. Retitled: CHILDREN OF THE LOTUS EATER. Above average.

Psychic, The (1978-Italian) **C-89m.** BOMB D: Lucio Fulci. Jennifer O'Neill, Gabriele Ferzetti, Marc Porel, Gianni Garko, Evelyn Stewart. O'Neill has frightening premonitions of deaths in this low-grade thriller.▼

Psychic Killer (1975) **C-90m.** BOMB D: Raymond Danton. Jim Hutton, Julie Adams, Paul Burke, Aldo Ray, Neville Brand, Whit Bissell. Ugly, violent shocker of mental institute patient who acquires psychic powers to revenge himself on those who wronged him. Lots of cameos: Rod Cameron, Nehemiah Persoff, Della Reese, others.▼

Psycho (1960) **109m. ****** D: Alfred Hitchcock. Anthony Perkins, Janet Leigh, Vera Miles, John Gavin, Martin Balsam, John McIntire, Simon Oakland, John Anderson, Frank Albertson, Patricia Hitchcock. The Master's most notorious film, a jet-black comedy set in the desolate Bates Motel (12 cabins, 12 vacancies . . . and 12 showers), run by peculiar young man and his crotchety old "mother." Despite decades of parody and imitation, this picture has lost none of its power to manipulate audiences' emotions; pure filmmaking at its finest. Bernard Herrmann's legendary (and much imitated) score adds to the excitement. Script by Joseph Stefano from the Robert Bloch novel. Followed by two sequels and a TV movie (BATES MOTEL) years later!▼

Psycho II (1983) **C-113m. **½** D: Richard Franklin. Anthony Perkins, Vera Miles, Meg Tilly, Robert Loggia, Dennis Franz, Hugh Gillin. Surprisingly good sequel, with Perkins in a wonderfully canny reprise of his role as Norman Bates—now being released from asylum, supposedly rehabilitated, returning to his mother's creaky old mansion. Director Franklin builds some terrific suspense scenes, without that trendy 80s gore, but finally goes for graphic violence toward the end, and tacks on a silly conclusion, undermining an otherwise first-rate shocker. Followed by another sequel.▼

Psycho III (1986) C-96m. *½ D: Anthony Perkins. Anthony Perkins, Diana Scarwid, Jeff Fahey, Roberta Maxwell, Hugh Gillin, Lee Garlington, Robert Alan Browne. Pointless sequel plays Norman Bates strictly for laughs, but maintains a slasher-film mentality. No suspense, just some gratuitous blood and unpleasantness. Perkins' directorial debut. Good night, Norman.▼

Psycho a Go-Go! SEE: **Blood of Ghastly Horror**▼

Psycho-Circus (1967-British-West German) C-65m. **½ D: John Moxey. Christopher Lee, Heinz Drache, Margaret Lee, Suzy Kendall, Leo Genn. Confused (due to distributor cuts) Edgar Wallace-based story of murderer stalking odd assortment of characters in big top. Is it hooded Gregor the knife thrower? Short running time gives film old-style serial-type pacing. Original title: CIRCUS OF FEAR.▼

Psychomania (1963) 93m. *½ D: Richard Hilliard. Lee Philips, Shepperd Strudwick, Jean Hale, Lorraine Rogers, Margot Hartman, Kaye Elhardt, James Farentino, Dick Van Patten, Sylvia Miles. War hero turned painter, suspected of murdering two beautiful young women, undertakes his own investigation. Exploitive independent production filmed in Connecticut. Originally titled VIOLENT MIDNIGHT.▼

Psychomania (1971-British) C-95m. **½ D: Don Sharp. George Sanders, Nicky Henson, Mary Larkin, Patrick Holt, Beryl Reid. Pact with Devil brings British motorcycle gang back from the grave. Lots of weird violence as undead bikers blaze a kamikaze trail of destruction across prepunk England. Screenplay by Julian Halevy.▼

Psychopath, The (1966-British) 83m. *** D: Freddie Francis. Patrick Wymark, Margaret Johnston, John Standing, Judy Huxtable. A demented killer leaves dolls as his calling card at the scene of the murders; well-made thriller from Robert Bloch script.

Psycho Sisters SEE: **So Evil, My Sister**▼

Psych-Out (1968) C-82m. **½ D: Richard Rush. Susan Strasberg, Jack Nicholson, Adam Roarke, Dean Stockwell, Max Julien, Bruce Dern, Henry Jaglom, The Strawberry Alarm Clock, The Seeds. Deaf runaway Strasberg comes to Haight-Ashbury looking for missing brother Dern, falls in with rock band led by ponytailed Nicholson. Any serious intentions have long since vanished; gloriously goofy dialogue ("C'mon! Warren's freakin' out at the gallery!'') and psychedelic Laszlo Kovacs camerawork

make this—depending on your age and sensibilities—either amusing nostalgia or a campy embarrassment. Produced by Dick Clark!▼

PT 109 (1963) C-140m. ** D: Leslie Martinson. Cliff Robertson, Robert Culp, Ty Hardin, James Gregory, Robert Blake, Grant Williams. Standard action film based on true story of PT-boat commander John F. Kennedy; neither here nor there; for younger audiences.▼

PT Raiders SEE: **Ship That Died of Shame, The**

Puberty Blues (1981-Australian) C-86m. **½ D: Bruce Beresford. Neil Schofield, Jad Capelja, Geoff Rhoe, Tony Hughes, Sandy Paul. Teenage growing pains, told (refreshingly) from the girls' point of view; simple and honest, but still somewhat familiar. Based on a best-selling Australian book by two former surfing groupies.▼

Public Enemy (1931) 84m. ***½ D: William Wellman. James Cagney, Jean Harlow, Eddie Woods, Beryl Mercer, Donald Cook, Joan Blondell, Mae Clarke. Prohibition gangster's rise and fall put Cagney on the map, and deservedly so; he makes up for film's occasional flaws and dated notions. Still pretty powerful, this is the one where he smashes a grapefruit in Clarke's face. Originally released at 96m.▼

Public Enemy's Wife (1936) 69m. **½ D: Nick Grinde. Pat O'Brien, Margaret Lindsay, Robert Armstrong, Cesar Romero, Dick Foran. Romero is good as mobster serving life whose insane jealousy over wife (Lindsay) makes her a perfect pawn for G-Man O'Brien. Not-bad Warner Bros. B.

Public Eye, The (1972-British) C-95m. **½ D: Carol Reed. Mia Farrow, Topol, Michael Jayston, Margaret Rawlings, Annette Crosbie, Dudley Foster. Stuffy husband hires private-eye to watch his wife, but the sleuth falls for her. Fair expansion of Peter Shaffer's play, *The Public Eye;* Farrow is good, but Topol's grin is flashed once too often.

Public Hero No. 1 (1935) 91m. **½ D: J. Walter Ruben. Lionel Barrymore, Jean Arthur, Chester Morris, Joseph Calleia, Paul Kelly, Lewis Stone. Highly uneven hybrid of gangster yarn with light comedy and romance. Interesting ingredients don't mix, though it's always a pleasure to watch Arthur. Remade in 1941 as THE GETAWAY.

Public Pigeon No. One (1957) C-79m. ** D: Norman Z. McLeod. Red Skelton, Vivian Blaine, Janet Blair, Allyn Joslyn, Jay C. Flippen. Bland Skelton vehicle with Red accidentally exposing gang of crooks; typical slapstick. Based on a *Climax* TV episode of 1955 in which Skelton starred.

Pudd'nhead Wilson (1984) C-90m. TVM D: Alan Bridges. Ken Howard, Lise

Hilboldt, Stephen Weber, Preston Maybank. Fine adaptation of Mark Twain's classic comic story of a mulatto slave woman (Hilboldt), and what happens when she exchanges her baby for that of her white master. Adapted from the Mark Twain novel by Philip Reisman, Jr. Filmed at Harper's Ferry, West Virginia; a PBS *American Playhouse* presentation. Above average.▼

Pufnstuf (1970) **C-98m.** **½ D: Hollingsworth Morse. Jack Wild, Billie Hayes, Martha Raye, "Mama" Cass Elliott, Billy Barty, Angelo Rossitto, Johnny Silver. OK theatrical feature based on Sid and Marty Krofft's TV series *H.R. Pufnstuf*, with Wild as young boy brought by a magic flute to Oz-like kingdom ruled by bumbling witches. Fine for kids, tolerable for grown-ups; Hayes is fun as "Witchie-poo."

Pulp (1972) **C-95m.** *** D: Michael Hodges. Michael Caine, Mickey Rooney, Lionel Stander, Lizabeth Scott, Nadia Cassini, Al Lettieri, Dennis Price. Rooney, a retired expatriate Hollywood actor, hires paperback writer Caine to ghost his autobiography. Uneven, but good fun and well acted, especially by Rooney.▼

Pulse (1988) **C-91m.** **½ D: Paul Golding. Joey Lawrence, Cliff De Young, Roxanne Hart, Charles Tyner, Myron Healey. What's got into the appliances in the home of Lawrence and his family? Scary, tense film, written by the director, a cut above the usual sci-fi/horror thriller but seriously damaged by a lack of any explanation for its outrageous premise (a living, evil short circuit). Excellent special effects.▼

Pumping Iron (1977) **C-85m.** *** D: George Butler, Robert Fiore. Arnold Schwarzenegger, Louis Ferrigno, Matty and Victoria Ferrigno, Mike Katz. Fascinating documentary about men's bodybuilding, centering on Schwarzenegger and his pursuit of yet another Mr. Olympia title. Schwarzenegger exudes charm and registers strong screen presence; his main rival is Ferrigno, pre-*Incredible Hulk*. Followed by PUMPING IRON II: THE WOMEN.▼

Pumping Iron II: The Women (1985) **C-107 min.** *** D: George Butler. Poutylipped sexpot Rachel McLish, manlike Australian Bev Francis, and two dozen more female bodybuilders compete in a Vegas non-event where winners are offered a choice of "cash, check, or chips." Funny, if suspiciously stagy look at the profession buoyed by some hilariously incompetent judges and an "in it for the money" emcee job by smiling George Plimpton.▼

Pumpkin Eater, The (1964-British) **110m.** *** D: Jack Clayton. Anne Bancroft, Peter Finch, James Mason, Cedric Hardwicke,

Alan Webb, Richard Johnson, Maggie Smith, Eric Porter. Intelligent if overlong drama chronicling the plight of Bancroft, the mother of eight children, who discovers third husband Finch has been unfaithful. Fine performances all around, with Bancroft a standout. Script by Harold Pinter, from the Penelope Mortimer novel.

Pumpkinhead (1988) **C-86m.** **½ D: Stan Winston. Lance Henriksen, Jeff East, John DiAquino, Kimberly Ross, Joel Hoffman, Cynthia Bain, Kerry Remsen, Florence Schauffler, Buck Flower, Tom Woodruff, Jr. Makeup expert Winston made his directorial debut with this interesting horror film set in the backwoods. When his young son is accidentally killed by "city folk," a storekeeper unleashes a powerful, fiendish demon on the interlopers, but when he changes his mind, finds he has no more control over the monstrous killer. Slides into the routine at times, but a nice try.▼

Punch and Jody (1974) **C-78m. TVM** D: Barry Shear. Glenn Ford, Ruth Roman, Pam Griffin, Kathleen Widdoes, Susan Brown, Parley Baer, Donald Barry. Circus grifter Ford suddenly finds himself with custody of teen-aged daughter he never knew. Sawdust, tears and Gibraltar-like Ford for those who like these ingredients. Average.

Punchline (1988) **C-128m.** *** D: David Seltzer. Sally Field, Tom Hanks, John Goodman, Mark Rydell, Kim Greist, Pam Matteson, Taylor Negron, Barry Neikrug, Mae Robbins, Max Alexander, Paul Kozlowski, Barry Sobel. Well-written, well-cast movie about aspiring stand-up comics, focusing on brash young Hanks, who's got real talent but also a knack for pushing people away, and Field, a housewife and mom who feels driven to become a comedienne. Seltzer's serious script is compassionate and believable and manages to avoid clichés and easy answers. Field and (especially) Hanks are first-rate; actor-turned-director Rydell is perfect as the unctious nightclub owner/entrepreneur. Director Paul Mazursky also appears in the opening scene.▼

Puppet on a Chain (1970-British) **C-98m.** *½ D: Geoffrey Reeve. Sven-Bertil Taube, Barbara Parkins, Alexander Knox, Patrick Allen, Vladek Sheybal. Half-baked version of Alistair MacLean's best-seller about international drug trafficking; only an exciting speedboat chase (directed by Don Sharp) keeps this film from total disaster.▼

Puppetoon Movie, The (1987) **C-80m.** **½ No director credited. Arnold Leibovit compiled this collage of George Pal's animated short subjects from the 1930s and '40s. Some of them (JOHN HENRY AND THE INKI POO, TUBBY THE TUBA,

JASPER IN A JAM) are terrific, but like so many shorts, they're better seen one or two at a time than put together into a feature format. Still, there's some delightful entertainment here.▼

Pure Hell of St. Trinian's, The (1961-British) **94m.** ** D: Frank Launder. Cecil Parker, Joyce Grenfell, George Cole, Thorley Walters. Absence of Alastair Sim from series lessens glow; outrageous girls' school is visited by sheik seeking harem.

Purlie Victorious SEE: **Gone Are The Days**▼

Purple Death from Outer Space (1940) **87m.** **½ D: Ford Beebe, Ray Taylor. Buster Crabbe, Carol Hughes, Charles Middleton, Frank Shannon, Anne Gwynne, Roland Drew. Edited version of FLASH GORDON CONQUERS THE UNIVERSE serial has Flash, Dale Arden, and Dr. Zarkov discovering Ming's new plan to control Earth, join forces with Arboria, Prince Barin, and Aura to counteract threat. Uninspired handling of original footage.▼

Purple Gang, The (1960) **85m.** ** D: Frank McDonald. Barry Sullivan, Robert Blake, Elaine Edwards, Marc Cavell, Jody Lawrance, Suzy Marquette, Joseph Turkel. Capable cast, limp police-vs.-gangster yarn.

Purple Haze (1982) **C-104m.** *** D: David Burton Morris. Peter Nelson, Chuck McQuary, Bernard Baldan, Susanne Lack, Bob Breuler, Joanne Bauman, Katy Horsch. Overlong yet involving chronicle of alienated youth Nelson, just expelled from college, and his experiences during the summer of 1968. McQuary is excellent as his comical, "chemically dependent" friend. Effective use of period music.

Purple Heart, The (1944) **99m.** *** D: Lewis Milestone. Dana Andrews, Farley Granger, Sam Levene, Richard Conte, Tala Birell, Nestor Paiva, Benson Fong, Marshall Thompson, Richard Loo. Absorbing tale of U.S. air force crew shot down during Tokyo raid receives strong performances by good cast. Produced and co-written by Darryl F. Zanuck.▼

Purple Hearts (1984) **C-115m.** ** D: Sidney J. Furie. Cheryl Ladd, Ken Wahl, Stephen Lee, David Harris, Lane Smith, Annie McEnroe, Paul McCrane, James Whitmore, Jr., Lee Ermey. Navy medic falls in love with feisty nurse in Vietnam. What starts out as good bread-and-butter story gets worse as it goes along toward silly conclusion. Overlong, to boot.▼

Purple Hills, The (1961) **C-60m.** *½ D: Maury Dexter. Gene Nelson, Joanna Barnes, Kent Taylor, Russ Bender. Cheapie oater, with ex-dancer Nelson unconvincing as cowpoke on the run from rampaging Indians.

Purple Mask, The (1955) **C-82m.** **½ D: H. Bruce Humberstone. Tony Curtis, Gene Barry, Angela Lansbury, Colleen Miller, Dan O'Herlihy. Set in early 19th-century France; Curtis is sword-wielding nobleman out to champion the cause of justice.

Purple Monster Strikes, The SEE: **D-Day on Mars**▼

Purple Noon (1961-French) **C-115m.** *** D: Rene Clement. Alain Delon, Marie Laforet, Maurice Ronet, Frank Latimore, Ave Ninchi. Marvelously photographed, tautly edited study of playboy Delon who commits murder and thinks he has gotten away with it. Retitled LUST FOR EVIL.

Purple People Eater (1988) **C-87m.** *½ D: Linda Shayne. Ned Beatty, Shelley Winters, Neil (Patrick) Harris, Peggy Lipton, Chubby Checker, Little Richard, James Houghton, Thora Birch, Molly Cheek. Corny, unimaginative (if harmless) children's picture based on the famous novelty song hit of 1959, with the title character (looking more like a kid in a Halloween costume) coming to Earth to form a rock band with some neighborhood teens. The song's original writer-performer Sheb Wooley appears as a trapeze teacher.▼

Purple Plain, The (1955-British) **C-100m.** *** D: Robert Parrish. Gregory Peck, Bernard Lee, Win Min Than, Maurice Denham, Brenda De Banzie. Eric Ambler thriller set in WW2 Burma; Peck is neurotic pilot whose plane crashes, forcing him to fight his way to freedom and new sense of values.

Purple Rain (1984) **C-111m.** **½ D: Albert Magnoli. Prince, Apollonia Kotero, Morris Day, Olga Karlatos, Clarence Williams III, Jerome Benton, Billy Sparks, The Revolution, The Time. Prince's film debut is about a young Minneapolis black who struggles to gain acceptance for his own brand of futuristic (and sexy) rock music . . . but it's *not* autobiographical. Right. Dynamic concert sequences are undercut by soppy storyline and sexist, unappealing characters—especially Prince's. Oscar-winning song score includes title tune, "When Doves Cry."▼

Purple Rose of Cairo, The (1985) **C-82m.** ***½ D: Woody Allen. Mia Farrow, Jeff Daniels, Danny Aiello, Dianne Wiest, Van Johnson, Zoe Caldwell, John Wood, Milo O'Shea, Edward Herrmann, Karen Akers, Deborah Rush, Michael Tucker, Glenne Headly. Bittersweet comedy-fantasy about a Depression-era movie fan whose latest idol walks right off the screen and into her life! Farrow and Daniels's wonderful performances help offset the cold cleverness of Allen's script. The finale is a heartbreaker.▼

Purple Taxi, The (1977-French-Italian-Irish) **C-107m.** *½ D: Yves Boisset. Charlotte Rampling, Philippe Noiret, Agostina Belli, Peter Ustinov, Fred Astaire, Edward Albert. Confusing, overblown drama about expatriates in Ireland, with Astaire miscast as eccentric doctor who drives title vehicle. Based on Michel Deon's bestselling novel. Originally 120m.▼

Pursued (1947) **101m.** *** D: Raoul Walsh. Teresa Wright, Robert Mitchum, Judith Anderson, Dean Jagger, Alan Hale, Harry Carey, Jr., John Rodney. Grim Western of determined Mitchum out to find father's killers; very well acted, suspenseful.▼

Pursuers, The (1961-British) **63m.** ** D: Godfrey Grayson. Cyril Shaps, Francis Matthews, Susan Denny, Sheldon Lawrence. Trim programmer with Matthews tracking down Nazi war criminal Shaps in England; conventionally told.

Pursuit (1972) **C-73m. TVM** D: Michael Crichton. Ben Gazzara, E. G. Marshall, William Windom, Joseph Wiseman, Jim McMullan, Martin Sheen. Extremist aching for confrontation in convention city threatens mass destruction with deadly government nerve gas. Fair tension and OK dialogue as agent Gazzara must outwit adversary at his own game. Based on novel by John Lange (Michael Crichton). Above average.▼

Pursuit of D. B. Cooper, The (1981) **C-100m.** ** D: Roger Spottiswoode. Robert Duvall, Treat Williams, Kathryn Harrold, Ed Flanders, Paul Gleason, R. G. Armstrong. What may have happened to the "legendary" D. B. Cooper (Williams, in a disappointing performance), who hijacked a plane in 1971 and bailed out with $200,000, never to be heard from again. Who cares? Lackluster comedy-chase story, with Duvall wasted as one of Cooper's pursuers. Film was plagued with production problems, multiple directors, hastily refilmed ending—and it shows in finished product.▼

Pursuit of Happiness, The (1971) **C-98m.** *** D: Robert Mulligan. Michael Sarrazin, Barbara Hershey, Robert Klein, Sada Thompson, Arthur Hill, E. G. Marshall, Barnard Hughes, Rue McClanahan. Director Mulligan has made lots of overrated films, but never got enough credit for this sympathetic tale of young man sent to jail more for his attitude in court than any particular offense. Good performances. Watch for William Devane, Charles Durning.▼

Pursuit of The Graf Spee (1957-British) **C-119m.** **½ D: Michael Powell, Emeric Pressburger. John Gregson, Anthony Quayle, Peter Finch, Ian Hunter, Bernard Lee, Patrick Macnee, Christopher Lee. Taut documentary-style account of WW2 chase of German warship by British forces. Original title: THE BATTLE OF THE RIVER PLATE.▼

Pursuit to Algiers (1945) **65m.** D: Roy William Neill. Basil Rathbone, Nigel Bruce, Marjorie Riordan, Rosalind Ivan, Martin Kosleck, John Abbott, Frederick K. Worlock. SEE: **Sherlock Holmes** series.▼

Pushover (1954) **88m.** **½ D: Richard Quine. Fred MacMurray, Kim Novak, Phil Carey, Dorothy Malone, E. G. Marshall. MacMurray is cop who falls in love with gangster moll Novak; good cast covers familiar ground.

Putney Swope (1969) **C/B&W-88m.** *** D: Robert Downey. Arnold Johnson, Pepi Hermine, Ruth Hermine, Allen Garfield, Antonio Fargas, Mel Brooks. Hilarious, but dated, story of blacks taking over Madison Avenue ad agency, instituting considerable changes. Best bit: series of commercial spoofs. Fargas, as The Arab, steals the film.▼

Puttin' on the Ritz (1930) **88m.** ** D: Edward Sloman. Harry Richman, Joan Bennett, James Gleason, Aileen Pringle, Lilyan Tashman, Purnell Pratt, Richard Tucker, Eddie Kane. Famed nightclub entertainer Richman made his film debut in this primitive early talkie about vaudevillian who can't handle success and turns to drink. You may do the same after watching Richman's performance—though he does introduce the title song by Irving Berlin. Partially redeemed by a few production numbers orignally filmed in Technicolor, including a charming "Alice in Wonderland." Sets by William Cameron Menzies.

Puzzle (1978-Australian) **C-90m. TVM** D: Gordon Hessler. James Franciscus, Wendy Hughes, Sir Robert Helpmann, Peter Gwynne, Gerald Kennedy, Kerry McGuire. Muddled melodrama involving a faded tennis ace, his ex-wife who is seeking his help in finding a cache of gold bars her recently departed second husband had embezzled, and a probable murder. Average.▼

Puzzle of a Downfall Child (1970) **C-104m.** ** D: Jerry Schatzberg. Faye Dunaway, Barry Primus, Viveca Lindfors, Barry Morse, Roy Scheider. Puzzling is the word for this confusing story of fashion model trying to put together the pieces of her unhappy life.

Puzzle of the Red Orchid, The (1962-German) **94m.** ** D: Helmut Ashley. Christopher Lee, Marisa Mell, Klaus Kinski, Fritz Rasp, Adrian Hoven. Moderate Edgar Wallace entry; Scotland Yard and F.B.I. track down international crime syndicate. Retitled: THE SECRET OF THE RED ORCHID.

Pygmalion (1938-British) **95m.** **** D: Anthony Asquith, Leslie Howard. Leslie Howard, Wendy Hiller, Wilfrid Lawson, Marie Lohr, David Tree. Superlative filmization of the witty G. B. Shaw play which became MY FAIR LADY. Howard excels as the professor, with Hiller his Cockney pupil. Shaws's screenplay won an Oscar, as did its adaptation by Ian Dalrymple, Cecil Lewis, and W.P. Lipscomb.▼

Pygmy Island (1950) **69m.** D: William Berke. Johnny Weissmuller, Ann Savage, David Bruce, Tristram Coffin, Steven Geray. SEE: **Jungle Jim** series.

Pyro (1964-Spanish) **C-99m.** **½ D: Julio Coll. Barry Sullivan, Martha Hyer, Sherry Moreland, Soledad Miranda. Strange chiller of man burned in fire seeking revenge on ex-girlfriend who started it.

Python Wolf SEE: **C.A.T. Squad: Python Wolf**▼

Pyx, The (1973-Canadian) **C-111m.** ***½ D: Harvey Hart. Karen Black, Christopher Plummer, Donald Pilon, Lee Broker, Yvette Brind'Amour. Ignored in this country, this Montreal-made suspenser is an excellent blend of horror, science-fiction and detective thriller with a mystical theme. Police Sergeant Plummer investigates prostitute Black's death, finds a devil cult, numerous decadent suspects and a new twist on Catholic guilt.▼

Q (1982) **C-93m.** *** D: Larry Cohen. David Carradine, Michael Moriarty, Richard Roundtree, Candy Clark, John Capodice, James Dixon, Malachy McCourt. Through plot tissue that discourages elaboration, a prehistoric Aztec deity finds itself flying out of its nest atop a Manhattan skyscraper to rip the heads off rooftop sunbathers and other assorted victims; somehow, all this is integrated into a standard N.Y.C. cop story. Spirited, occasionally hilarious trash sparked by Moriarty's eccentric performance as the loser who knows where the beast resides and intends to cash in on it. Also known as THE WINGED SERPENT.▼

Q & A (1990) **C-132m.** ** D: Sidney Lumet. Nick Nolte, Timothy Hutton, Armand Assante, Patrick O'Neal, Lee Richardson, Luis Guzman, Charles Dutton, Jenny Lumet, Paul Calderon, Leonard Cimino. Wet-behind-the-ears Assistant D.A. (Hutton) is assigned to investigate an incident in which veteran street cop Nolte killed a Puerto Rican druggie . . . and soon finds himself waist-deep in departmental corruption and collusion. Gritty, graphic, well-acted story gets slower as it goes along, dragging toward an increasingly predictable conclusion. Lumet scripted from Edwin Torres's novel. Ruben Blades' "Don't Double-Cross The Ones You Love" bids fair to become the worst movie song of the 90s.▼

Q Planes (1939-British) **78m.** *** D: Tim Whelan. Laurence Olivier, Ralph Richardson, Valerie Hobson, George Curzon, David Tree, George Merritt, Gus McNaughton. Delightful tongue-in-cheek espionage tale, with masterminds stealing British aircraft secrets. Richardson is a joy as lighthearted inspector who cracks the case. Retitled: CLOUDS OVER EUROPE.

Quackser Fortune Has A Cousin in the Bronx (1970-Irish) **C-90m.** ***½ D: Waris Hussein. Gene Wilder, Margot Kidder, Eileen Colgen, Seamus Ford. Delightfully offbeat love story. Quackser Fortune follows the horses around Dublin selling their manure for gardening. The day the horses are replaced by cars he falls in love with an American coed. Original in every way. Reissued as FUN LOVING.▼

Quadrophenia (1979-British) **C-115m.** ***½ D: Franc Roddam. Phil Daniels, Mark Wingett, Philip Davis, Leslie Ash, Garry Cooper, Sting. Superior mixture of early '60s "Angry Young Man" drama and rock movie tells of teenage gang battles between Mods and Rockers on the English seaside. A real sleeper. Inspired by The Who's record album. Sting makes an impressive acting debut.▼

Quality Street (1937) **84m.** *** D: George Stevens. Katharine Hepburn, Franchot Tone, Fay Bainter, Eric Blore, Cora Witherspoon, Estelle Winwood. Hepburn is radiant in delicate adaptation of James Barrie's whimsical play: "old maid" masquerades as her own niece in order to win back the love of a man who hasn't seen her in ten years. Filmed before in 1927, with Marion Davies.

Quantez (1957) **C-80m.** **½ D: Harry Keller. Fred MacMurray, Dorothy Malone, Sydney Chaplin, John Gavin, John Larch, Michael Ansara. Above-par Western involving robbery gang heading for Mexico border, encountering stiff opposition along the way.

Quantrill's Raiders (1958) **C-68m.** ** D: Edward Bernds. Steve Cochran, Diane Brewster, Leo Gordon, Gale Robbins. Predictable Civil War account of the outlaw's planned attack on a Kansas arsenal.

Quarantined (1970) **C-74m.** TVM D: Leo Penn. John Dehner, Gary Collins, Sharon Farrell, Wally Cox, Sam Jaffe, Susan Howard, Dan Ferrone. Daily tribulations of family-run medical clinic. complicated by problems of rebellious son, uncooperative movie star, and cholera epidemic. Average.

Quare Fellow, The (1962-Irish) **85m.** ***½ D: Arthur Dreifuss. Patrick McGoohan, Sylvia Syms, Walter Macken, Dermot Kelly, Jack Cunningham, Hilton Edwards. Irish-made adaptation of Brendan Behan play deals with new prison guard, well-played by McGoohan, who changes mind about capital punishment. Finely acted; excellent script by director Dreifuss.

Quarterback Princess (1983) **C-100m.** TVM D: Noel Black. Helen Hunt, Don Murray, Barbara Babcock, Dana Elcar, John Stockwell, Daphne Zuniga. High school girl goes out for varsity football team and becomes one of "the boys"—as well as homecoming queen. Based on the real-life story of Tami Maida but pedestrian in its telling. Average.▼

Quartet (1949-British) **120m.** ******** D: Ken Annakin, Arthur Crabtree, Harold French, Ralph Smart. Basil Radford, Naunton Wayne, Mai Zetterling, Ian Fleming, Jack Raine, Dirk Bogarde. Superb movie with Somerset Maugham introducing four of his tales, each with different casts and moods. Its success prompted a sequel, TRIO.▼

Quartet (1981-British-French) **C-101m.** ******* D: James Ivory. Alan Bates, Maggie Smith, Isabelle Adjani, Anthony Higgins, Pierre Clementi, Daniel Mesguich, Virginie Thevenet, Suzanne Flon. Adjani is taken in by Bohemian Bates and victimized wife Smith when her husband (Higgins) is imprisoned; Bates seduces her into becoming his lover. Expertly acted drama of decadence and change; based on a book by Jean Rhys.▼

Quatermass and the Pit SEE: **Five Million Years to Earth**

Quatermass Conclusion (1980-British) **C-107m.** ****½** D: Piers Haggard. John Mills, Simon MacCorkindale, Barbara Kellerman, Margaret Tyzack, Brewster Mason. Mills is fine as heroic Professor Bernard Quatermass (of earlier screen and British television adventures) in this entertaining though poorly produced sci-fi adventure. He comes to the rescue when a death beam from outer space evaporates the world's young. Made for British TV.▼

Quatermass Experiment, The SEE: **Creeping Unknown, The**▼

Quatermass II SEE: **Enemy From Space**▼

Quebec (1951) **C-85m.** ****** D: George Templeton. John Barrymore, Jr., Corinne Calvet, Barbara Rush, Patric Knowles. Historical nonsense set in 1830s Canada during revolt against England. Filmed on location.▼

Queen Bee (1955) **95m.** ******* D: Ranald MacDougall. Joan Crawford, Barry Sullivan, Betsy Palmer, John Ireland, Fay Wray, Tim Hovey. Crawford in title role has field-day maneuvering the lives of all in her Southern mansion, with husband Sullivan providing the final ironic twist.

Queen Christina (1933) **97m.** ******** D: Rouben Mamoulian. Greta Garbo, John Gilbert, Ian Keith, Lewis Stone, C. Aubrey Smith, Gustav von Seyffertitz, Reginald Owen, Elizabeth Young. Probably Garbo's best film, with a haunting performance by the radiant star as 17th-century Swedish queen who relinquishes her throne for her lover, Gilbert. Garbo and Gilbert's love scenes together are truly memorable, as is the famous final shot. Don't miss this one.▼

Queenie (1987) **C-200m.** **TVM** D: Larry Peerce. Mia Sara, Kirk Douglas, Martin Balsam, Claire Bloom, Topol, Joel Grey, Sarah Miles, Joss Ackland. Lavishly produced but unenthralling adaptation of Mi-

chael Korda's best-seller tracing the rise of an exotic young girl from Calcutta's slums to the brink of Hollywood stardom. Queenie's character is based on Merle Oberon, while Douglas plays a thinly disguised Alexander Korda, the author's late movie-mogul uncle. Stellar cast is of little help to the unseasoned Sara, miscast in the title role. Originally shown in two parts. Average.▼

Queen Kelly (1929) **96m.** *****½** D: Erich von Stroheim. Gloria Swanson, Seena Owen, Walter Byron, Tully Marshall, Madame Sul Te Wan. A convent girl is swept off her feet by a roguish prince—then sent to live in East Africa where her aunt runs a brothel! Fascinating, extravagantly decadent von Stroheim melodrama that was never completed; this restored version wraps up story with stills and subtitles. A must for film buffs; exquisitely photographed, with scene-stealing performance by Owen as the mad queen. The European-release version, in which the girl meets with an entirely different fate, is also available.▼

Queen of Babylon, The (1956-Italian) **C-98m.** ***½** D: Carlo Bragaglia. Rhonda Fleming, Ricardo Montalban, Roldano Lupi, Carlo Ninchi. American stars can't elevate elephantine study of ancient Babylonia.

Queen of Blood SEE: **Planet of Blood**▼

Queen of Burlesque (1946) **70m.** ***½** D: Sam Newfield. Evelyn Ankers, Carleton G. Young, Marion Martin, Rose La Rose, Alice Fleming, Craig Reynolds. Low-budget suspenser unstrung backstage at burlesque theater.

Queen of Destiny SEE: **Sixty Glorious Years**

Queen of Hearts (1989-British) **C-112m.** *****½** D: Jon Amiel. Vittorio Duse, Joseph Long, Anita Zagaria, Eileen Way, Vittorio Amandola, Ian Hawkes, Tat Whalley. Extraordinary and unusual film, better seen than described, about an Italian couple who lead a pleasantly quixotic life in England running a family café. Tony Grisoni's original screenplay embraces elements of romance, humor, melodrama, mysticism, and fantasy in a heady mix. Remarkable first feature for director Amiel, who did *The Singing Detective* for British TV.▼

Queen of Outer Space (1958) **C-80m.** ***½** D: Edward Bernds. Zsa Zsa Gabor, Eric Fleming, Laurie Mitchell, Paul Birch. Inane sci-fi about expedition that crashlands on Venus, where planet is ruled entirely by women. At least some of the laughs are intentional.

Queen of Spades, The (1949-British) **95m.** ******* D: Thorold Dickinson. Anton Walbrook, Edith Evans, Ronald Howard, Mary Jerrold, Yvonne Mitchell, Anthony Dawson. Unusual, macabre fantasy from Alexander Pushkin story about Russian officer obsessed with learning the secret of winning

[928]

at cards. Well-mounted production, set in 1806.▼

Queen of Spades (1960-Russian) **C-100m.** **½ D: Roman Tikhomirov. Oleg Strizhenov, Zurab Anzhaparidze, Olga Krasina, Tamara Milashkina. Stark version of Tchaikovsky opera *Pikovaya Dama*, performed by Bolshoi Theater company; deals with young man consumed by gambling urge, leading to his and girlfriend's destruction.

Queen of the Jungle (1935) **87m. BOMB** D: Robert Hill. Mary Kornman, Reed Howes, Dickie Jones, Marilyn Spinner, Lafe McKee. Hilariously awful feature adapted from cheapie serial that rivals anything ever made by Edward Wood. A little girl is accidentally cast off in a balloon; she lands in the middle of the African jungle and grows up to become the title monarch. Incredibly stilted dialogue and acting . . . a laugh riot. ▼

Queen of the Nile (1961-Italian) **C-85m.** ** D: Fernando Cerchio. Jeanne Crain, Vincent Price, Edmund Purdom, Amedeo Nazzari. Dull account of court life in 2000 B.C. Egypt. Not even campy.

Queen of the Pirates (1960-Italian) **C-79m.** ** D: Mario Costa. Gianna Maria Canale, Massimo Serato, Scilla Gabel, Paul Muller. Vivid setting can't salvage wooden account of Canale in title role overcoming tyrannical Duke of Doruzzo (Muller). Sequel: TIGER OF THE SEVEN SEAS.

Queen of the Stardust Ballroom (1975) **C-100m. TVM** D: Sam O'Steen. Maureen Stapleton, Charles Durning, Michael Brandon, Michael Strong, Charlotte Rae. Beautifully realized love story between a widowed grandmother and a married mailman who meet at a local dance hall. A filmed song of joy by Jerome Kass, with sensitive performances by the two leads. Later a Broadway musical, *Ballroom*. Above average.▼

Queen's Guards, The (1960-British) **C-110m.** ** D: Michael Powell. Daniel Massey, Robert Stephens, Raymond Massey, Ursula Jeans. Tedious, patriotic chronicle of young Massey distinguishing himself in service, saving family name; humdrum film.

Queimada! SEE: **Burn!**▼

Quentin Durward (1955) **C-101m.** **½ D: Richard Thorpe. Robert Taylor, Kay Kendall, Robert Morley, George Cole, Alec Clunes, Duncan Lamont, Marius Goring. Taylor plays Sir Walter Scott's dashing Scots hero in this handsome but static costumer about Louis XI's reign in 15th-century France.

Querelle (1982-German) **C-120m. BOMB.** D: Rainer Werner Fassbinder. Brad Davis, Franco Nero, Jeanne Moreau, Gunther Kaufmann, Hanno Poschl. Might have been called "A Guy in Every Port." Davis is the French sailor whose venture into an infamous whorehouse in Brest permits him to discover his true homosexual nature. Fassbinder's final film was rejected even by his admirers; gamy but slickly produced adaptation of Jean Genet novel manages to induce boredom and giggles in equal measure.▼

Quest, The (1976) **C-100m. TVM** D: Lee H. Katzin. Tim Matheson, Kurt Russell, Brian Keith, Keenan Wynn, Will Hutchins, Cameron Mitchell, Neville Brand, Morgan Woodward, Art Lund. Two brothers search the Old West for their sister, captured years earlier by Indians. Evokes memories of John Ford's THE SEARCHERS but worth seeing for colorful performances of veteran actors Keith, Wynn and Mitchell, and for refreshing touches like a horse-camel race. Script by Tracy Keenan Wynn. Later evolved into a series. Average.

Quest, The (1986-Australian) **C-93m.** *½ D: Brian Trenchard-Smith. Henry Thomas, Tony Barry, Rachel Friend, Tamsin West, Dennis Miller, Katya Manning. Abortive Australian attempt to capitalize on young Thomas' success as the star of E.T.; here he plays a precocious child who, along with a couple of pals, visits an aboriginal burial ground where a Loch Ness-style monster lives. Competently made but uninteresting. ▼

Quest for Fire (1981-French-Canadian) **C-97m.** ***½ D: Jean-Jacques Annaud. Everett McGill, Rae Dawn Chong, Ron Perlman, Nameer El Kadi. Peaceful tribe living 80,000 years ago is attacked by apes and wolves and loses its fire, essential for survival. They don't know how to make fire, so three of their own trek off to find it again. Not the epic intended, but still funny, tense, touching—and fascinating, with the creation of fire the equivalent of our landing astronauts on the moon. Special languages devised by Anthony Burgess, and body languages and gestures by Desmond Morris; the costumes earned an Academy Award. Filmed in Kenya, Scotland, Iceland, and Canada.▼

Quest for Love (1971-British) **C-90m.** *** D: Ralph Thomas. Tom Bell, Joan Collins, Denholm Elliott, Laurence Naismith, Lyn Ashley, Juliet Harmer, Neil McCallum, Simon Ward. Intriguing sci-fi story of man who accidentally passes into another dimension on Earth almost identical to ours, with some strange differences. Based on a short story by John Wyndham.▼

Question of Adultery, A (1959-British) **86m.** **½ D: Don Chaffey. Julie London, Anthony Steel, Basil Sydney, Donald Houston, Anton Diffring, Andrew Cruickshank. Tepid drama involving pros and cons of artificial insemination. Retitled: THE CASE OF MRS. LORING.

Question of Guilt, A (1978) **C-100m. TVM** D: Robert Butler. Tuesday Weld,

Ron Leibman, Peter Masterson, Alex Rocco, Viveca Lindfors, Lana Wood. Flashy, fun-loving divorcee is accused of murdering her child in this drama obviously inspired by the headline-making Alice Crimmins case in N.Y.C. Leibman's character is named Martin Kazinsky, but this has no relation to his later *Kaz* series. Average.▼

Question of Honor, A (1982) **C-150m.** TVM D: Jud Taylor. Ben Gazzara, Paul Sorvino, Robert Vaughn, Tony Roberts, Danny Aiello, Carol Rossen, Steve Inwood, Anthony Zerbe. TV's answer to PRINCE OF THE CITY, with Gazzara as an honest cop caught in a trap set by ruthless fed Vaughn. Budd Schulberg wrote the script from Sonny Grosso and Philip Rosenberg's book, *Point Blank.* Average.▼

Question of Love, A (1978) **C-100m.** TVM D: Jerry Thorpe. Gena Rowlands, Jane Alexander, Ned Beatty, Clu Gulager, Bonnie Bedelia, James Sutorius, Jocelyn Brando. Top-notch cast enriches this sensitive fact-based drama by William Blinn about two lesbians and the custody battle one has with her ex-husband over their young son. Above average.▼

Quest: Mask of Sheba SEE: **Mask of Sheba, The**

Questor Tapes, The (1974) **C-100m.** TVM D: Richard A. Colla. Robert Foxworth, Mike Farrell, John Vernon, Lew Ayres, James Shigeta, Robert Douglas, Dana Wynter. Busted Gene Roddenberry pilot about sophisticated android (Foxworth) looking for his identity, using his computerized brain to locate his missing creator. Despite the twist of having a robot as the lead, only mild diversion. Average.

Quick and the Dead, The (1987) **C-93m.** TVM D: Robert Day. Sam Elliott, Kate Capshaw, Tom Conti, Kenny Morrison, Matt Clark. Lean Louis L'Amour Western out of the SHANE school involving a homesteading couple, their young son, and a mysterious stranger who rides into their lives when they come under attack by a ruthless gang. James Lee Barrett's script recaptures the flavor of the old movie West, and British cinematographer Dick Bush puts it craftily on film. Made for cable. Above average.▼

Quick Before It Melts (1964) **C-98m.** **½ D: Delbert Mann. George Maharis, Robert Morse, Anjanette Comer, James Gregory, Yvonne Craig, Doodles Weaver, Howard St. John, Michael Constantine. Trivia involving Maharis and Morse in the Antarctic; they have bright idea of bringing in a planeload of girls, with predictable results.

Quick Change (1990) **C-88m.** *** D: Howard Franklin, Bill Murray. Bill Murray, Geena Davis, Randy Quaid, Jason Robards, Bob Elliott, Philip Bosco, Phil Hartman, Kurtwood Smith, Jamie Sheridan, Kath-ryn Grody. Very low-key but funny outing for Murray as a malcontent who stages a clever bank robbery—disguised as a clown—but can't seem to get out of New York City with his accomplices, Davis and Quaid. It's possible that only New Yorkers will truly appreciate the anti-City sentiments (and often hilarious vignettes) that permeate the film. Jay Conley's novel was previously filmed in France in 1985 as HOLD-UP, with Jean-Paul Belmondo.

Quick Gun, The (1964) **C-87m.** ** D: Sidney Salkow. Audie Murphy, Merry Anders, James Best, Ted de Corsia, Frank Ferguson, Raymond Hatton. Formula Murphy Western, with Audie redeeming himself by combating town outlaws.

Quick, Let's Get Married (1964) **C-96m.** BOMB D: William Dieterle. Ginger Rogers, Ray Milland, Barbara Eden, Michael Ansara, Walter Abel, Elliott Gould. Easy to see why this dud sat on the shelf so long; bordello madam Rogers and adventurer Milland perpetrate "miracle" hoax on gullible prostitute (Eden). Gould makes inauspicious film debut as deaf mute. Also known as SEVEN DIFFERENT WAYS. Released in 1971.

Quick Millions (1931) **72m.** **½ D: Rowland Brown. Spencer Tracy, Marguerite Churchill, Sally Eilers, Robert Burns, John Wray, George Raft. OK gangster film with Tracy as ambitious truck driver who climbs to top of the rackets. Nothing special, except to see dynamic early Tracy.

Quicksand (1950) **79m.** **½ D: Irving Pichel. Mickey Rooney, Jeanne Cagney, Barbara Bates, Peter Lorre, Taylor Holmes, Wally Cassell. Atmospheric programmer about auto mechanic Rooney, who is hot for trampy Cagney, and what happens when he "borrows" $20 from his boss's cash register. Lorre is wonderfully menacing as a sleazy penny arcade owner.▼

Quicksilver (1986) **C-106m.** *½ D: Tom Donnelly. Kevin Bacon, Jami Gertz, Paul Rodriguez, Rudy Ramos, Andrew Smith, Gerald S. O'Loughlin, Larry Fishburne, Louis Anderson. The lives of big-city bicycle messengers (confusingly shot in three *different* cities), and one white-collar dropout in particular. Low-gear all the way.▼

Quiet American, The (1958) **120m.** **½ D: Joseph L. Mankiewicz. Audie Murphy, Michael Redgrave, Claude Dauphin, Giorgia Moll, Bruce Cabot. Sanitized version of the Graham Greene novel, with the book's "un-American" feeling eliminated; naive American Murphy arrives in Saigon with his own plan to settle country's conflicts. More a murder mystery than the political thriller intended.

Quiet Earth, The (1985-New Zealand) **C-100m.** **½ D: Geoff Murphy. Bruno Lawrence, Alison Routledge, Peter Smith. Intriguing (and extremely good-looking) end-of-the-world saga; not entirely successful but well worth a look.▼

Quiet Man, The (1952) **C-129m.** **** D: John Ford. John Wayne, Maureen O'Hara, Barry Fitzgerald, Victor McLaglen, Mildred Natwick, Arthur Shields, Ward Bond, Jack MacGowran. American boxer Wayne returns to native Ireland, wins over townsfolk, and tames strong-willed O'Hara. Boisterous blarney, with beautiful scenery and equally beautiful music by Victor Young. Maurice Walsh's story was scripted by Frank Nugent. Oscar winner for director Ford and Cinematography by Winton Hoch and Archie Stout.▼

Quiet Place to Kill, A (1969-Italian-Spanish) **C-88m.** BOMB D: Umberto Lenzi. Carroll Baker, Jean Sorel, Marina Coffa, Anna Proclemer, Alberto Dalbes. Dreary drama of Baker and ex-husband Sorel covering up the latter's accidental murder of his new wife. Cut to 77m., and also known as PARANOIA; not to be confused with Lenzi's not dissimilar ORGASMO (1968), starring Baker, which was also shown as PARANOIA.▼

Quiet Please, Murder (1942) **70m.** **½ D: John Larkin. George Sanders, Gail Patrick, Richard Denning, Sidney Blackmer, Lynne Roberts, Kurt Katch, Minerva Urecal, Theodore von Eltz. Offbeat, intriguing yarn of master forger Sanders stealing priceless Shakespeare volume, passing off his copies as the original. Murder and romance expertly woven into story.

Quiet Victory: The Charlie Wedemeyer Story (1988) **C-100m.** TVM D: Roy Campanella II. Pam Dawber, Michael Nouri, Bess Meyer, Peter Berg, James Handy, Dan Lauria, Gracie Harrison. Inspiring drama about the one-time football all-star who developed Lou Gehrig's disease in 1977 at age 30 and went on to become a victorious high school coach—and was still coaching in 1988, although wheelchair-bound and unable to speak. Written by Barry Morrow and directed by the son of another disabled sports figure. Above average.

Quiller Memorandum, The (1966-British) **C-105m.** *** D: Michael Anderson. George Segal, Alec Guinness, Max von Sydow, Senta Berger, George Sanders, Robert Helpmann. Good Harold Pinter script about American secret agent who investigates neo-Nazi movement in modern-day Berlin. Film is a relief from most spy films of the 60s.▼

Quincannon, Frontier Scout (1956) **C-83m.** *½ D: Lesley Selander. Tony Martin, Peggie Castle, John Bromfield, John Smith, Ron Randell. Martin is miscast in title role of programmer.

Quinns, The (1977) **C-78m.** TVM D: Daniel Petrie. Barry Bostwick, Blair Brown, Susan Browning, Geraldine Fitzgerald, Peter Masterson, Virginia Vestoff. Soap opera by Sidney Carroll focusing on three generations of Irish-American N.Y.C. firefighters. Average.

Quintet (1979) **C-110m.** ** D: Robert Altman. Paul Newman, Bibi Andersson, Fernando Rey, Vittorio Gassman, Nina Van Pallandt, Brigitte Fossey, David Langton. Pretentious, unappealing story about cutthroat game of survival in a frozen city of the future. Not as puzzling as it is ponderous.▼

Quo Vadis? (1951) **C-171m.** *** D: Mervyn LeRoy. Robert Taylor, Deborah Kerr, Peter Ustinov, Leo Genn, Patricia Laffan, Finlay Currie, Abraham Sofaer, Buddy Baer. Gargantuan MGM adaptation of Henryk Sienkiewicz' novel set during the reign of Nero; Roman soldier Taylor has to figure out how to romance Christian Kerr without both of them ending up as lunch for the lions. Meticulous production includes fine location shooting and Miklos Rozsa score based on music of the era. Remade for Italian TV.▼

Quo Vadis? (1985-Italian) **C-200m.** TVM D: Franco Rossi. Klaus Maria Brandauer, Frederic Forrest, Cristina Raines, Barbara DeRossi, Francesco Quinn, Marie-Theres Relin, Gabriele Ferzetti, Massimo Girotti, Leopoldo Trieste, Max von Sydow. Bloated, slow-moving adaptation of the Henryk Sienkiewicz saga, notable solely for Brandauer's extravagant Nero. That's Anthony Quinn's son Francesco (in his first important role) in the old Robert Taylor part. Made for Italian television, first shown in the U.S. on cable TV. Average.▼

Rabbit, Run (1970) **C-94m.** ** D: Jack Smight. James Caan, Carrie Snodgress, Anjanette Comer, Jack Albertson, Melodie Johnson, Henry Jones, Carmen Matthews. Brilliant cast, brilliant book (by John Updike), but dull film centering around former high school athlete who suddenly finds that life is tougher than being on the playing field.

Rabbit Test (1978) **C-86m.** **½ D: Joan Rivers. Billy Crystal, Alex Rocco, Joan Prather, Doris Roberts, George Gobel, Imogene Coca, Paul Lynde. Rivers' first film is like low-budget Mel Brooks: wacky comedy surrounding slim plot about first pregnant man. Some wild ideas, mostly in bad taste. Many guest-star cameos (including Rivers as a nurse).▼

Rabbit Trap, The (1959) **72m.** **½ D: Philip Leacock. Ernest Borgnine, David Brian, Bethel Leslie, Kevin Corcoran, June Blair, Jeanette Nolan, Don Rickles. Intelligent if slow-moving study of motivational factors behind Borgnine's compulsive work life and ignoring of his family. Script by JP Miller, from his TV play.

Rabid (1977-Canadian) **C-90m.** **½ D: David Cronenberg. Marilyn Chambers,

Frank Moore, Joe Silver, Patricia Gage, Susan Roman. Motorcyclist Chambers has plastic surgery after an accident, develops an insatiable hankering for human blood. Good of its type; well directed by cult favorite Cronenberg. Porn star Chambers removes her clothes—but nothing more.▼

Race for Life (1954-British) **68m.** *½ D: Terence Fisher. Richard Conte, Mari Aldon, George Coulouris, Peter Illing, Alec Mango, Meredith Edwards. Formula programmer with Conte as an American racing his way around some of Europe's fastest tracks against wishes of wife Aldon. Competent stock-car footage in this pre-horror Hammer production.

Race for Your Life, Charlie Brown (1977) **C-75m.** **½ D: Bill Melendez. Voices of Duncan Watson, Greg Felton, Stuart Brotman, Gail Davis, Liam Martin. Third animated feature based on Charles Schulz's *Peanuts* comic strip is set in summer camp, highlighted by treacherous raft race. Mildly entertaining, but lacks punch.▼

Racers, The (1955) **C-112m.** **½ D: Henry Hathaway. Kirk Douglas, Bella Darvi, Gilbert Roland, Lee J. Cobb, Cesar Romero, Katy Jurado. Hackneyed sports-car racing yarn, not salvaged by Douglas' dynamics or European location shooting.

Race Street (1948) **79m.** ** D: Edwin L. Marin. George Raft, William Bendix, Marilyn Maxwell, Frank Faylen, Henry (Harry) Morgan, Gale Robbins. San Francisco bookie is up against extortion ring in this well-acted but ordinary crime story.

Race to the Yankee Zephyr (1981-Australian-New Zealand) **C-108m.** ** D: David Hemmings. Ken Wahl, Lesley Ann Warren, Donald Pleasence, George Peppard, Bruno Lawrence, Grant Tilly. Addle-brained drama about good guys Wahl and Pleasence and nemesis Peppard attempting to recover $50 million in gold from DC-3 wrecked during WW2. Retitled TREASURE OF THE YANKEE ZEPHYR for 1984 American release.

Race with the Devil (1975) **C-88m.** *½ D: Jack Starrett. Peter Fonda, Warren Oates, Loretta Swit, Lara Parker, R. G. Armstrong. Two vacationing couples are pursued by local satanic witches after witnessing a human sacrifice. It takes quite a human sacrifice to sit through this hybrid car-chase/horror film.▼

Rachel and the Stranger (1948) **79m.** *** D: Norman Foster. Loretta Young, William Holden, Robert Mitchum, Tom Tully, Sara Haden. Star trio is fine in this Western of man whose love for his wife is first aroused when stranger Mitchum visits their home. Originally 93m.▼

Rachel, Rachel (1968) **C-101m.** ***½ D: Paul Newman. Joanne Woodward, James Olson, Kate Harrington, Estelle Parsons, Donald Moffat, Terry Kiser. Beautifully

sensitive, mature film about spinster schoolteacher trying to come out of her shell. Woodward is superb; husband Newman's directorial debut. Screenplay by Stewart Stern, from a novel by Margaret Laurence.▼

Rachel River (1987) **C-90m.** **½ D: Sandy Smolan. Zeljko Ivanek, Pamela Reed, Craig T. Nelson, James Olson, Alan North, Viveca Lindfors, Jo Henderson, Jon De Vries. Occasionally contrived but mostly intelligent chronicle of Reed, a rural Minnesota mother and radio journalist, and the various people who inhabit her town. Thoughtful performances overcome the occasional insipidness. Screenplay by Judith Guest; a PBS *American Playhouse* theatrical production.

Racing Fever (1964) **C-80m.** BOMB D: William Grefe. Joe Morrison, Charles Martin, Maxine Carroll, Barbara Biggart. Torrid trash of speedboat racing, an accidental killing, and revenge.

Racing With the Moon (1984) **C-108m.** *** D: Richard Benjamin. Sean Penn, Elizabeth McGovern, Nicolas Cage, John Karlen, Rutanya Alda, Carol Kane, Crispin Glover. Teenage romance set in small California town just as the young man is about to go off to fight in WW2. Appealing stars and loving eye for 1940s detail make up for slow pace. That bowling alley is a gem!▼

Rack, The (1956) **100m.** *** D: Arnold Laven. Paul Newman, Wendell Corey, Walter Pidgeon, Edmond O'Brien, Anne Francis, Lee Marvin. Newman is pensively convincing as Korean War veteran on trial for treason, with Pidgeon as his father and Francis his friend. Slick production adapted from Rod Serling teleplay.

Racket, The (1951) **88m.** *** D: John Cromwell. Robert Mitchum, Robert Ryan, Lizabeth Scott, Ray Collins, William Talman, Robert Hutton, William Conrad, Don Porter. Police officer Mitchum and gangster Ryan spend almost as much time fighting their corrupt superiors as they do each other. Unusual *film noir* with strong performances (especially Ryan's) and bizarre ending; based on play previously filmed by producer Howard Hughes in 1928. Coscripted by W.R. Burnett; some scenes were directed by Nicholas Ray.▼

Racket Busters (1938) **71m.** ** D: Lloyd Bacon. George Brent, Humphrey Bogart, Gloria Dickson, Allen Jenkins, Walter Abel, Henry O'Neill, Penny Singleton. Mobster Bogie's going to take over the trucking business, but Brent doesn't want to cooperate. Standard programmer moves along well; co-written by Robert Rossen.

Racquet (1979) **C-89m.** *½ D: David Winters. Bert Convy, Edie Adams, Lynda Day George, Phil Silvers, Bobby Riggs, Susan Tyrrell, Bruce Kimmel, Bjorn Borg. Pea-brained SHAMPOO clone with Convy as Beverly Hills tennis pro who uses his sex appeal to raise money for a court of his own.▼

Rad (1986) **C-91m.** BOMB D: Hal Needham. Bart Connor, Lori Laughlin, Talia Shire, Jack Weston, Ray Walston. Connor is supposed to take his SATs, but wouldn't you know it, there's a big BMX race on the same Saturday? "Rad" is short for *radical*—as in "Radical, man"—which this trash definitely is not: Didn't we see this same plot in late '50s hot-rod and late '70s roller-disco movies?▼

Radar Men From the Moon SEE: **Retik, The Moon Menace▼**

Radioactive Dreams (1986) **C-98m.** ** D: Albert Pyun. John Stockwell, Michael Dudikoff, Lisa Blount, George Kennedy, Don Murray, Michele Little. So-so post-apocalypse drama about Stockwell and Dudikoff, who've come to maturity in a bomb shelter. They've read all of Raymond Chandler's Philip Marlowe books and have taken on the private eye's personality. Nicely filmed, but it doesn't hold up.▼

Radio Days (1987) **C-85m.** *** D: Woody Allen. Mia Farrow, Seth Green, Julie Kavner, Josh Mostel, Michael Tucker, Dianne Wiest, Wallace Shawn, Tito Puente, Danny Aiello, Jeff Daniels, Tony Roberts, Diane Keaton, Kitty Carlisle Hart, Kenneth Mars. Richly nostalgic reminiscence (narrated by Woody) about growing up in 1940s Queens, mixing family vignettes with incidents about radio performers from that medium's golden age. The narrative never really gels, though it's always enjoyable to watch . . . especially with Allen's eye for detail and ear for dialogue. Beautifully photographed by Carlo Di Palma and designed by Santo Loquasto; filled with wonderful vintage music.▼

Radio On (1979-British) **101m.** **½ D: Chris Petit. David Beames, Lisa Kreuzer, Sting. Downbeat, rambling story of disc jockey who travels across Britain because of the mysterious circumstances of his brother's recent death. Written and directed by Petit, disciple of German director Wim Wenders (film's associate producer); plot is only hinted at in this meditation on the bleakness of modern life. Snatches of music by such rock acts as David Bowie, Lene Lovich, Devo, and Kraftwerk.

Radium City (1987) **C/B&W-110m.** *** D: Carole Langer. Solid documentary about the young women of Ottawa, Ill., who in the 1920s were hired to paint radium on clock dials . . . and how they paid for their labor with their lives. A poignant, touching human drama.

Ra Expeditions, The (1971-Norwegian) **C-93m.** *** D: Lennart Ehrenborg. Narrated by Thor Heyerdahl and Roscoe Lee Browne. Exciting documentary about modern adventurer Heyerdahl's determination to cross the Atlantic in a papyrus boat, to prove theory that such a voyage was made thousands of years ago. Fine follow-up to KON-TIKI.

Rafferty and the Gold Dust Twins (1975) **C-92m.** **½ D: Dick Richards. Alan Arkin, Sally Kellerman, Mackenzie Phillips, Alex Rocco, Charlie Martin Smith, Harry Dean Stanton. Appealing but aimless film about a pair of women who force nebbish Arkin to drive them to New Orleans from L.A. Retitled RAFFERTY AND THE HIGHWAY HUSTLERS for TV.▼

Raffles (1930) **72m.** *** D: Harry D'Arrast, George Fitzmaurice. Ronald Colman, Kay Francis, Bramwell Fletcher, Frances Dade, David Torrence, Alison Skipworth. Colman is his usual charming self in a breezy tale of gentleman thief who constantly eludes Scotland Yard. Good fun all the way. Screenplay by Sidney Howard, based on E.W. Hornung's novel *The Amateur Cracksman*, filmed before in 1917 with John Barrymore, in 1925 with House Peters, and remade in 1940 with David Niven.

Raffles (1940) **72m.** **½ D: Sam Wood. David Niven, Olivia de Havilland, Dudley Digges, Dame May Whitty, Douglas Walton, Lionel Pape. Niven is good but can't match Ronald Colman in this nearly scene-for-scene remake of the 1930 film about a gentleman thief (with a notably different finale). Medium-grade fluff.

Rage (1966-U.S.-Mexican) **C-103m.** *½ D: Gilberto Gazcon. Glenn Ford, Stella Stevens, David Reynoso, Armando Silvestre, Ariadna Welter. Overstated drama of misanthropic doctor Ford who contracts rabies and races clock across Mexican desert to get help.

Rage (1972) **C-104m.** ** D: George C. Scott. George C. Scott, Richard Basehart, Martin Sheen, Barnard Hughes, Nicolas Beauvy, Paul Stevens. When peaceful rancher Scott's young son is killed by chemical testing, he seeks revenge on those responsible for accident. Good photography, but Scott's transition from nice-guy to killer isn't convincing. Scott's directorial debut.▼

Rage (1980) **C-100m.** TVM D: William A. Graham. David Soul, James Whitmore, Yaphet Kotto, Caroline McWilliams, Vic Tayback, Sharon Farrell, Craig T. Nelson, Garry Walberg, John Durren, Darleen Carr, Leo Gordon. Harrowing drama of a convicted rapist who undergoes intensive therapy. Well-acted by good cast. Script by George Rubino. Above average.▼

Rage at Dawn (1955) **C-87m.** ** D: Tim Whelan. Randolph Scott, Forrest Tucker, Mala Powers, J. Carrol Naish, Edgar Buchanan. Routine Scott Western entry, with Randy et al involved in hunting down outlaw gang.▼

Rage in Heaven (1941) **83m.** ** D: W. S. Van Dyke II. Robert Montgomery, Ingrid Bergman, George Sanders, Lucile Watson, Oscar Homolka, Philip Merivale, Matthew Boulton. Disappointing adaptation of James Hilton novel about mentally disturbed steel mill owner who plots unusual murder-revenge scheme; set in England.

Rage of Angels (1983) **C-200m. TVM** D: Buzz Kulik. Jaclyn Smith, Ken Howard, Armand Assante, Ron Hunter, Kevin Conway, George Coe, Joseph Wiseman, Deborah May, Joseph Warren, Wesley Addy. Ambitious lady lawyer on way to the top juggles affairs with two powerful men on opposite sides of the law. Glamour abounds, though acting suffers, in this adaptation of Sidney Sheldon's trashy bestseller. Originally shown in two parts. Followed by a sequel. Average.▼

Rage of Angels: The Story Continues (1986) **C-200m. TVM** D: Paul Wendkos. Jaclyn Smith, Ken Howard, Michael Nouri, Susan Sullivan, Brad Dourif, Angela Lansbury, Mason Adams. Flashily designed sequel to the initial two-parter from Sidney Sheldon's romantic potboiler rapidly decelerates and sputters out of the fast lane; charged intermittently by guest star Lansbury's forays onto the scene as a boozy Italian marchesa. Originally shown in two parts. Average.

Rage of Paris, The (1938) **75m.** *** D: Henry Koster. Danielle Darrieux, Douglas Fairbanks, Jr., Mischa Auer, Louis Hayward, Helen Broderick. Fast-talkers team up to use lovely Darrieux to snare rich husband; fast-paced comedy is fun all the way, with Darrieux a delight. Same team that Hollywoodized neophyte Deanna Durbin concocted this winsome image for the French actress. Look quickly for Mary Martin.▼

Rage of the Buccaneers, The (1961-Italian) **C-88m.** ** D: Mario Costa. Ricardo Montalban, Vincent Price, Giulia Rubini, Liana Orfei. Juvenile but bouncy yarn which is set more on land than at sea, with pirate Montalban vs. Price, villainous governor's secretary.

Rage to Live, A (1965) **101m.** ** D: Walter Grauman. Suzanne Pleshette, Bradford Dillman, Ben Gazzara, Peter Graves, Bethel Leslie, James Gregory. Poor version of John O'Hara novel of free-swinging girl who tries marriage only to discover she still needs to have affairs with men.

Raggedy Ann and Andy (1977) **C-85m.** *½ D: Richard Williams. Voices of Didi Conn, Mark Baker, Fred Stuthman, Joe Silver. Slow-moving, uninvolving children's cartoon with endless songs by Joe Raposo that stop action dead in its tracks. Appealing characters with nowhere to go; only highlight is Camel with Wrinkled Knees singing "Song Blue."▼

Raggedy Man (1981) **C-94m.** *** D: Jack Fisk. Sissy Spacek, Eric Roberts, William Sanderson, Tracey Walter, Sam Shepard, Henry Thomas, Carey Hollis, Jr. A young divorced woman with two children tries to forge a life for herself and her family in a small Texas town during WW2. Absorbing slice-of-life Americana with a misconceived melodramatic finale. Directorial debut for art director Fisk, who's Spacek's husband.▼

Raging Bull (1980) **128m.** **** D: Martin Scorsese. Robert De Niro, Cathy Moriarty, Joe Pesci, Frank Vincent, Nicholas Colasanto, Theresa Saldana. Extraordinarily compelling look at prizefighter Jake LaMotta, whose leading opponent outside the ring was always himself. That such an unappealing man could inspire so vivid a portrait is a tribute to the collaboration of Scorsese, De Niro, and writers Paul Schrader and Mardik Martin. There's not a false note in characterization or period detail. De Niro and editor Thelma Schoonmaker won richly deserved Academy Awards.▼

Raging Moon SEE: **Long Ago, Tomorrow**▼

Raging Tide, The (1951) **93m.** **½ D: George Sherman. Richard Conte, Shelley Winters, Stephen McNally, Charles Bickford. Stereotyped script and typecast acting make this murderer-on-the-run yarn tame. Adapted by Ernest K. Gann from his novel.

Ragman's Daughter, The (1972-British) **C-94m.** *** D: Harold Becker. Simon Rouse, Victoria Tennant, Patrick O'Connell, Leslie Sands. Stylishly filmed but generally overlooked kitchen-sink drama written by Alan Sillitoe. Rouse is a young thief who falls in love with awesomely beautiful Tennant. Gem was released (barely) in the U.S. in 1974; Becker's first feature.

Ragtime (1981) **C-155m.** *** D: Milos Forman. James Cagney, Elizabeth McGovern, Howard E. Rollins, Jr., Mary Steenburgen, James Olson, Brad Dourif, Kenneth McMillan, Mandy Patinkin, Donald O'Connor, Pat O'Brien, Debbie Allen, Moses Gunn, Norman Mailer, Jeff Daniels. E. L. Doctorow's semi-fictional mosaic of 1906 America is glorious until Michael Weller's script narrows its focus to just one story thread: a black man's fanatical pursuit of justice. While the initial momentum is lost, there's still much to enjoy: fine performances (including Cagney's last in a theatrical film, after a 20-year hiatus), and Randy Newman's delightful score.▼

Raid, The (1954) **C-83m.** *** D: Hugo Fregonese. Van Heflin, Anne Bancroft, Richard Boone, Lee Marvin, Tommy Rettig, James Best, Peter Graves, Claude

Akins. Well-handled story of Confederate prisoners escaping from jail in upper New England, with Bancroft and Rettig trying to snafu their marauding.

Raiders, The (1952) C-80m. **½ D: Lesley Selander. Richard Conte, Viveca Lindfors, Barbara Britton, Hugh O'Brian, Richard Martin, William Reynolds. Sometimes with-it oater about judge during California gold rush days, leading a land-grabbing gang. Retitled: RIDERS OF VENGEANCE.

Raiders, The (1963) C-75m. **½ D: Herschel Daugherty. Robert Culp, Brian Keith, Judi Meredith, James McMullan, Alfred Ryder, Simon Oakland. Enthusiastic cast helps this story of cattle drives and the railroad expansion westward.

Raiders of Leyte Gulf, The (1963) 80m. **½ D: Eddie Romero. Michael Parsons, Leopold Salcedo, Jennings Sturgeon, Liza Moreno, Efren Reyes. Gritty account of WW2 against Japanese forces, filmed in the Philippines.

Raiders of Old California (1957) 72m. BOMB D: Albert Gannaway. Jim Davis, Arleen Whelan, Lee Van Cleef, Louis Jean Heydt. Minor Western set in the 1850s.

Raiders of the Lost Ark (1981) C-115m. **** D: Steven Spielberg. Harrison Ford, Karen Allen, Wolf Kahler, Paul Freeman, Ronald Lacey, John Rhys-Davies, Denholm Elliott. A roller-coaster ride of a movie, rekindling the spirit of Saturday matinee serials but outdoing them for genuine thrills and chills. Ford plays Indiana Jones, an archeologist-adventurer who goes globe-trotting in search of a unique religious artifact and runs into bloodcurdling danger every step of the way. Perhaps a bit too much at times, but why carp? Conceived by Spielberg and George Lucas, with Philip Kaufman; scripted by Lawrence Kasdan. Visual effects, editing, sound effects editing, and art direction-set decoration all earned Oscars. Followed by two INDIANA JONES films.▼

Raiders of the Seven Seas (1953) C-88m. **½ D: Sidney Salkow. John Payne, Donna Reed, Gerald Mohr, Lon Chaney. Pirate Barbarossa saves countess from marriage to cutthroat, eventually falls in love.

Raid on Entebbe (1977) C-150m. TVM D: Irvin Kershner. Peter Finch, Charles Bronson, Horst Buchholz, Martin Balsam, John Saxon, Jack Warden, Sylvia Sidney, Yaphet Kotto, Robert Loggia, James Woods, Dinah Manoff. Intelligent drama about Israeli commando rescue of hijacked hostages at Entebbe, Uganda, on July 4, 1976. Finch's last film garnered him an Emmy nomination. Covers same ground as VICTORY AT ENTEBBE and OPERATION THUNDERBOLT. Above average.▼

Raid on Rommel (1971) C-99m. *½ D: Henry Hathaway. Richard Burton, John Colicos, Clinton Greyn, Wolfgang Preiss. Poor excuse to utilize old desert footage (mostly from TOBRUK) and new faces in worn-out WW2 actioner.▼

Railroaded (1947) 71m. *** D: Anthony Mann. John Ireland, Sheila Ryan, Hugh Beaumont, Ed Kelly, Jane Randolph, Keefe Brasselle. Another tight, well-made, low-budget film noir by Anthony Mann. This time Ireland is a ruthless gangster after Ryan; Beaumont is the cop trying to save her. ▼

Railroad Man, The SEE: **Man of Iron** (1956)

Rails Into Laramie (1954) C-81m. ** D: Jesse Hibbs. John Payne, Mari Blanchard, Dan Duryea, Joyce MacKenzie, Barton MacLane, Lee Van Cleef. Pat movie of Payne's efforts to clean up title town and keep railroad construction moving westward.

Railway Children, The (1972-British) C-102m. *** D: Lionel Jeffries. Dinah Sheridan, Bernard Cribbins, William Mervyn, Iain Cuthbertson, Jenny Agutter, Gary Warren. Charming story of youthful trio whose one goal is to clear their father of false espionage prison sentence. Lovely Yorkshire locales add to overall effectiveness. From the novel by E. Nesbit.▼

Rain (1932) 93m. **½ D: Lewis Milestone. Joan Crawford, Walter Huston, William Gargan, Guy Kibbee, Walter Catlett, Beulah Bondi. Considered a flop in 1932, this version of Maugham's story looks better today. Crawford is good as South Seas island trollop confronted by fire-and-brimstone preacher Huston. Director Milestone does gymnastics with camera during stagier scenes; an interesting antique. Previously filmed in 1928 with Gloria Swanson as SADIE THOMPSON, then again as DIRTY GERTIE FROM HARLEM, and MISS SADIE THOMPSON. Some prints run 77m.▼

Rainbow (1978) C-100m. TVM D: Jackie Cooper. Andrea McArdle, Don Murray, Piper Laurie, Martin Balsam, Michael Parks, Jack Carter, Donna Pescow. Young Judy Garland's rise from struggling vaudeville performer to THE WIZARD OF OZ, with the star of Broadway's *Annie* completely miscast in the lead. Story is seemingly accurate and given a touch of authenticity by director Jackie Cooper, one-time Garland beau in his youth. Average.▼

Rainbow, The (1989-British) C-104m. **½ D: Ken Russell. Sammi Davis, Amanda Donohoe, Paul McGann, Christopher Gable, David Hemmings, Glenda Jackson, Ken Colley. Director Russell's most restrained film in years (a relative term) is in fact a prequel to his hit adaptation of D.H. Lawrence's *Women in Love*, with Davis as a sheltered young schoolteacher who's taken under the wing (sexually and otherwise) of worldly Donohoe. Many beautiful and striking moments don't quite gel, but the film is still worth watching. Jackson appears as the mother of the character she played in WOMEN IN LOVE.▼

Rainbow Island (1944) **C-97m.** **½ D: Ralph Murphy. Dorothy Lamour, Eddie Bracken, Gil Lamb, Barry Sullivan, Anne Revere, Olga San Juan, Elena Verdugo, Yvonne De Carlo, Reed Hadley, Marc Lawrence. Good cast main asset in musical comedy of merchant marines stranded on island with beautiful natives. Lamour, in her umpteenth sarong, wisely keeps her tongue in her cheek.

Rainbow Jacket, The (1954-British) **C-99m.** ** D: Basil Dearden. Kay Walsh, Bill Owen, Fella Edmonds, Robert Morley, Wilfrid Hyde-White, Honor Blackman. Colorful racetrack sequences spark this predictable study of Owen, veteran jockey gone wrong, who teaches Edmonds how to race properly.

Rainbow 'Round My Shoulder (1952) **C-78m.** ** D: Richard Quine. Frankie Laine, Billy Daniels, Charlotte Austin, Ida Moore, Arthur Franz, Barbara Whiting, Lloyd Corrigan. Young girl wants to be a movie star, her socialite grandma forbids it, and no surprises ensue. Blah musical written by Quine and Blake Edwards; songs include "Bye, Bye, Blackbird" and "Wrap Your Troubles In Dreams."

Rainbow Trail, The (1925) **58m.** *** D: Lynn Reynolds. Tom Mix, Anne Cornwall, George Bancroft, Lucien Littlefield, Mark Hamilton, Vivien Oakland. Sequel to RIDERS OF THE PURPLE SAGE, another robust Zane Grey tale about man who determines to penetrate isolated Paradise Valley, where his uncle trapped himself with a young woman. Handsome production of oft-filmed story.

Rainmaker, The (1956) **C-121m.** *** D: Joseph Anthony. Burt Lancaster, Katharine Hepburn, Wendell Corey, Lloyd Bridges, Earl Holliman, Cameron Prud'homme, Wallace Ford. Lancaster is in top form as a charismatic con man who offers hope to a Southwestern town beset by drought, and a woman whose life is at a crossroads. Hepburn is wonderful. N. Richard Nash play was later musicalized on Broadway as *110 in the Shade.*▼

Rain Man (1988) **C-140m.** *** D: Barry Levinson. Dustin Hoffman, Tom Cruise, Valeria Golino, Jerry Molden, Jack Murdock, Michael D. Roberts. Young, self-centered hotshot goes home to the Midwest for his father's funeral, and learns not only that he's been cut out of his inheritance, but that he has a grown brother who's autistic, and who's been kept in an institution for most of his life. The balance of the film details the growing relationship between the two men. Top-drawer performances from Hoffman, as the idiot savant,

and Cruise, as his selfish sibling, make this a must-see, even though the story meanders and falls into a predictable pattern. That's director Levinson as the examining psychiatrist at the end of the film. Winner of Oscars for Best Picture, Director, Actor (Hoffman), and Screenplay (Ronald Bass and Barry Morrow).▼

Rain or Shine (1930) **92m.** **½ D: Frank Capra. Joe Cook, Louise Fazenda, Joan Peers, Dave Chasen, William Collier, Jr., Tom Howard. Curious little circus film spotlights puckish Broadway clown Cook (and his stooges Chasen and Howard) in a storyline so thin it's hardly there. Personality and Capra's early talkie technique make this worth seeing for film buffs.

Rain People, The (1969) **C-102m.** *** D: Francis Ford Coppola. James Caan, Shirley Knight, Robert Duvall, Marya Zimmet, Tom Aldredge, Laurie Crewes. Pregnant Long Island housewife, unable to take married life, flees husband and picks up simple-minded football player on the road. Strong acting and direction triumph over weak script in film whose subject matter was years ahead of its time.▼

Rains Came, The (1939) **104m.** **½ D: Clarence Brown. Myrna Loy, Tyrone Power, George Brent, Brenda Joyce, Nigel Bruce, Maria Ouspenskaya, Joseph Schildkraut, Laura Hope Crews. Louis Bromfield novel reduced to Hollywood terms. Indian Power loves socialite Loy. Good earthquake scenes; in fact, the special effects earned an Academy Award. Remade as THE RAINS OF RANCHIPUR.

Rains of Ranchipur, The (1955) **C-104m.** **½ D: Jean Negulesco. Lana Turner, Richard Burton, Fred MacMurray, Joan Caulfield, Michael Rennie, Eugenie Leontovich. Superficial remake of THE RAINS CAME; story of wife of Englishman having affair with Hindu doctor. Attractive in color.

Raintree County (1957) **C-168m.** *** D: Edward Dmytryk. Elizabeth Taylor, Montgomery Clift, Eva Marie Saint, Lee Marvin, Nigel Patrick, Rod Taylor, Agnes Moorehead, Walter Abel. Humongous MGM attempt to outdo GWTW, with Taylor as spoiled Civil War-era belle who discovers marriage isn't all it's cracked up to be. Solid acting and memorable Johnny Green score help compensate for rambling, overlong script; Clift was disfigured in near-fatal car accident during production, and his performance understandably suffers for it.▼

Raise the Titanic! (1980-British) **C-112m.** *½ D: Jerry Jameson. Jason Robards, Richard Jordan, David Selby, Anne Archer, Alec Guinness, J. D. Cannon. Long, dull adaptation of Clive Cussler's best-seller about intrigue leading to the biggest salvage job of all time. Silly plotting and laughable dialogue undermine excitement of climactic ship-raising. Cut from 122m. just prior to release.▼

Raising a Riot (1955-British) **C-90m.** ** D: Wendy Toye. Kenneth More, Ronald Squire, Mandy Miller, Shelagh Fraser, Bill Shine. Predictable situation comedy of More, on vacation in countryside, trying to cope with his rambunctious children.

Raising Arizona (1987) **C-92m.** ***½ D: Joel Coen. Nicolas Cage, Holly Hunter, Trey Wilson, John Goodman, William Forsythe, Sam McMurray, Frances McDormand, Randall (Tex) Cobb. Formidably flaky comedy about an odd couple (chronic convenience-store robber Cage and former law-enforcement officer Hunter) who decide to kidnap one of a set of quintuplets, since they can't have a child of their own. Aggressively wacked-out sense of humor may not be for all tastes, but if you're attuned to it, it's a scream—a heady mix of irony and slapstick. Look out for those chase scenes! Written by Ethan and Joel Coen; spry cinematography by Barry Sonnenfeld and music by Carter Burwell.▼

Raising the Wind (1961-British) **C-91m.** **½ D: Gerald Thomas. James Robertson Justice, Leslie Phillips, Sidney James, Paul Massie, Kenneth Williams. Zany shenanigans of eccentric group of students at a London school of music; well paced.

✓ **Raisin in the Sun, A** (1961) **128m.** **** D: Daniel Petrie. Sidney Poitier, Claudia McNeil, Ruby Dee, Diana Sands, Ivan Dixon, John Fiedler, Louis Gossett. Lorraine Hansberry play receives perceptive handling by outstanding cast in drama of black Chicago family's attempts to find sense in their constrained existence.▼

Rake's Progress, The SEE: **Notorious Gentleman**

Rally 'Round the Flag, Boys! (1958) **C-106m.** **½ D: Leo McCarey. Paul Newman, Joanne Woodward, Joan Collins, Jack Carson, Dwayne Hickman, Tuesday Weld, Gale Gordon. Disappointing film of Max Shulman's book about small community in uproar over projected missile base. Wit is noticeably lacking.

Ramblin' Man SEE: **Concrete Cowboy**

Rambo: First Blood Part II (1985) **C-95m.** ** D: George P. Cosmatos. Sylvester Stallone, Richard Crenna, Charles Napier, Julia Nickson, Steven Berkoff, Martin Kove. Comic-book action saga of one-man army who goes to Cambodia in search of American MIAs and finds he's been duped by Uncle Sam. Never boring but incredibly dumb; if one were to take it seriously, it would also be offensive, as it exploits real-life frustrations of MIA families and Vietnam vets. Followed by RAMBO III.▼

Rambo III (1988) **C-101m.** **½ D: Peter Macdonald. Sylvester Stallone, Richard Crenna, Marc de Jonge, Kurtwood Smith, Spiros Focas, Sasson Gabai, Doudi Shoua, Randy Raney. A definite improvement over RAMBO: FIRST BLOOD PART II, this one remains firmly footed in the genre of Idiot Action Movies, as our brawny hero goes behind Russian-dominated battle lines in Afghanistan to rescue his friend and former superior (Crenna) from a prison fortress. More explosions than any film in recent memory, to keep things lively—and some (unintentionally?) hilarious dialogue too.▼

Ramona (1936) **C-90m.** ** D: Henry King. Loretta Young, Don Ameche, Kent Taylor, Pauline Frederick, Jane Darwell, Katherine DeMille. Oft-told tale doesn't wear well, with aristocratic Spanish girl Young and outcast Indian Ameche in love and shunned by society. Settings are picturesque.

Rampage (1963) **C-98m.** **½ D: Phil Karlson. Robert Mitchum, Elsa Martinelli, Jack Hawkins, Sabu, Cely Carillo, Emile Genest. German gamehunter (Hawkins), his mistress (Martinelli), and hunting guide (Mitchum) form love triangle, with men battling for Elsa. Elmer Bernstein's score is memorable.

Rampage at Apache Wells (1966-German) **C-90m.** ** D: Harold Philipps. Stewart Granger, Pierre Brice, Macha Meril, Harold Leipnitz. Granger stars as Old Shatterhand, who fights for rights of Indians taken in by crooked white men. Adequate acting cannot compete with atrocious dubbing.

Ramparts of Clay (1971-French-Algerian) **C-85m.** *** D: Jean-Louis Bertucelli. Leila Schenna. Intriguing film about Tunisian woman, disillusioned with her way of life, who becomes involved with strike between a wealthy company and poor villagers. Very strong for patient, critical viewers; for others, boredom.▼

Ramrod (1947) **94m.** **½ D: Andre de Toth. Veronica Lake, Joel McCrea, Arleen Whelan, Don DeFore, Preston Foster, Charles Ruggles, Donald Crisp, Lloyd Bridges. Fairly good Western of territorial dispute between ranch-owner Lake and her father (Ruggles). Good supporting cast.▼

Ran (1985-Japanese-French) **C-161m.** ***½ D: Akira Kurosawa. Tatsuya Nakadai, Satoshi Terao, Jinpachi Nezu, Daisuke Ryu, Mieko Harada, Peter, Hisashi Igawa. Beautifully filmed adaptation of Shakespeare's *King Lear*, with Nakadai as a warlord who turns over his domain to his eldest son, inducing a power struggle by his two younger sons. Slowly paced and overly expository at the start, epic picks up with two superb battle scenes. Harada is excellent in supporting role as the most evil of women, getting her just desserts in violent fashion.▼

Rancho Deluxe (1975) **C-93m.** ***½ D:

Frank Perry. Jeff Bridges, Sam Waterston, Elizabeth Ashley, Charlene Dallas, Clifton James, Slim Pickens, Harry Dean Stanton, Richard Bright, Patti D'Arbanville. Off-beat present-day comedy centers on two casual cattle rustlers; cult favorite written by Thomas McGuane (92 IN THE SHADE), with music by Jimmy Buffett (who also appears in the film). TV version runs 95m.

Rancho Notorious (1952) **C-89m.** *** D: Fritz Lang. Marlene Dietrich, Arthur Kennedy, Mel Ferrer, Lloyd Gough, Gloria Henry, William Frawley, Jack Elam, George Reeves. Entertaining, unusual Western with Kennedy looking for murderer of his sweetheart, ending up at Marlene's bandit hideout. Colorful characters spice up routine story by Daniel Taradash.▼

Random Harvest (1942) **124m.** ***½ D: Mervyn LeRoy. Ronald Colman, Greer Garson, Philip Dorn, Susan Peters, Henry Travers, Reginald Owen, Bramwell Fletcher, Margaret Wycherly, Ann Richards. Colman is left an amnesiac after WW1, and saved from life in a mental institution by vivacious music-hall entertainer Garson. Supremely entertaining James Hilton story given top MGM treatment, with Colman and Garson at their best. Screenplay by Claudine West, George Froeschel, Arthur Wimperis, and Hilton.▼

Rangers, The (1974) **C-78m. TVM** D: Chris Nyby II. James G. Richardson, Colby Chester, Jim B. Smith, Laurette Spang, Laraine Stephens, Michael Conrad, Roger Bowen. The rescue operations of U.S. Park Rangers as saluted by Jack Webb. Pilot to the short-lived *Sierra* series. Average.

Rangers of Fortune (1940) **80m.** **½ D: Sam Wood. Fred MacMurray, Albert Dekker, Gilbert Roland, Patricia Morison, Dick Foran, Joseph Schildkraut. Smartly-whipped-together yarn of trio fleeing Mexicans, stopping off in Southwestern town to offer assistance.

Ransom (1956) **109m.** **½ D: Alex Segal. Glenn Ford, Donna Reed, Leslie Nielsen, Juano Hernandez, Alexander Scourby, Juanita Moore, Robert Keith. Brooding narrative of Ford's efforts to rescue his son who's been kidnapped.

Ransom (1977) **C-90m.** **½ D: Richard Compton. Oliver Reed, Deborah Raffin, Stuart Whitman, Jim Mitchum, John Ireland, Paul Koslo. Pretty good programmer about a town's efforts to catch a killer. Originally titled ASSAULT ON PARADISE, then MANIAC.▼

Ransom for a Dead Man (1971) **C-100m. TVM** D: Richard Irving. Lee Grant, Peter Falk, John Fink, Harold Gould, Patricia Mattick, Paul Carr. Lawyer Williams (Grant) murders husband but is foiled in escape plan by deceptively simple-minded

police lieutenant (Falk). Good script, performances by entire cast. Second pilot for the *Columbo* series; the first was PRESCRIPTION: MURDER. Above average.

Ransom for Alice (1977) **C-78m. TVM** D: David Lowell Rich. Gil Gerard, Yvette Mimieux, Charles Napier, Gene Barry, Harris Yulin, Laurie Prange, Barnard Hughes, Gavin MacLeod. Cop show set in 1890s Seattle with Gerard and Mimieux as deputy marshals turned undercover agents to crack a white slavery ring. Average.

Rape and Marriage: The Rideout Case (1980) **C-96m. TVM** D: Peter Levin. Mickey Rourke, Linda Hamilton, Rip Torn, Eugene Roche, Conchata Ferrell, Gail Strickland, Bonnie Bartlett, Alley Mills, Gerald McRaney, Rita Taggert. A shrill, torn-from-the-headlines treatment of a unique marital dispute, based on landmark 1978 Oregon case about a housewife who brought a rape charge against her husband. Average.▼

Rape of Love (1977-French) **C-117m.** ** D: Yannick Bellon. Nathalie Nell, Alain Foures, Michele Simonnet, Pierre Arditi, Daniel Anteuil, Bernard Granger. Nurse Nell is raped by four drunken jerks, but that's not the end of her ordeal. Not ineffective as a consciousness-raising tool, but still overly preachy; director Bellon has a tendency to depict all her male characters as insensitive chauvinists.▼

Rape of Malaya SEE: **Town Like Alice, A**

Rape of Richard Beck, The (1985) **C-100m. TVM** D: Karen Arthur. Richard Crenna, Meredith Baxter Birney, Pat Hingle, Frances Lee McCain, Cotter Smith, George Dzundza, Joanna Kerns. Crenna won an Emmy for his portrayal of a macho cop whose own humiliation by a pair of cop-haters radically changes his chauvinistic view of sexually assaulted women. Taut script by James G. Hirsch augments Crenna's strong performance. Above average.▼

Rape Squad (1974) **C-90m.** **½ D: Bob Kelljan. Jo Ann Harris, Peter Brown, Jennifer Lee, Steve Kanaly, Lada Edmund, Jr. Well-told vigilante tale has raped women banding together to avenge themselves on sadistic Brown, who gets off by forcing women to sing "Jingle Bells" as he assaults them. Also known as ACT OF VENGEANCE.▼

Rappin' (1985) **C-92m.** ** D: Joel Silberg. Mario Van Peebles, Tasia Valenza, Charles Flohe, Leo O'Brien, Eriq La Salle, Richie Abanes, Kadeem Hardison, Harry Goz. Just what the world needs, another break-dancing–rap music musical. This one chronicles the plight of breakdancer/ex-con Van Peebles and his conflicts with street gangster Flohe and contractor Goz.▼

Rapture (1965-French) **104m.** *** D: John Guillermin. Melvyn Douglas, Dean Stockwell, Patricia Gozzi, Gunnel Lindblom, Leslie Sands. Intensive, sensitive account of Gozzi's tragic romance with Stockwell, a man on the run.

Rare-Book Murder, The SEE: **Fast Company** (1938)

Rare Breed, The (1966) C-108m. **½ D: Andrew V. McLaglen. James Stewart, Maureen O'Hara, Brian Keith, Juliet Mills, Jack Elam, Ben Johnson. Wholesome oater, with fetching O'Hara as woman who brings Hereford bull to U.S. to be bred, and can't decide whether to marry ranch owner Keith or former associate Stewart.▼

Rare Breed, A (1981) C-94m. *½ D: David Nelson. George Kennedy, Forrest Tucker, Tracy Vaccaro, Tom Hallick, Don DeFore. Old-fashioned story of a girl and her horse, with unconvincing depiction of the real-life incident of racehorse Carnauba kidnapped in Italy for ransom. Cute, squeaky-clean tomboy Vaccaro became a *Playboy* magazine Playmate two years after filming this family picture, whose director is the former actor offspring of Ozzie and Harriet. ▼

Rascal (1969) C-85m. **½ D: Norman Tokar. Steve Forrest, Bill Mumy, Pamela Toll, Bettye Ackerman, Elsa Lanchester, Henry Jones. Disney adaptation of Sterling North's well-regarded autobiographical novel about his boyhood friendship with raccoon; reworked to Disney formula, with pleasant but predictable results.

Rascals and Robbers—The Secret Adventures of Tom Sawyer and Huck Finn (1982) C-100m. TVM D: Dick Lowry. Patrick Creadon, Anthony Michael Hall, Anthony Zerbe, Anthony James, Allyn Ann McLerie, Ed Begley, Jr., Cynthia Nixon. Tom and Huck join a ragtag circus while playing a cat and mouse game with a bunco artist in these new, non-Twain "further adventures." Average.▼

Rashomon (1951-Japanese) 88m. **** D: Akira Kurosawa. Toshiro Mifune, Machiko Kyo, Masayuki Mori, Takashi Shimura. Kurosawa's first huge international success is superlative study of truth and human nature; four people involved in a rape-murder tell varying accounts of what happened. The film's very title has become part of our language. Oscar winner as Best Foreign Film. Remade as THE OUTRAGE.▼

Rasputin and the Empress (1932) 123m. *** D: Richard Boleslavsky. John, Ethel and Lionel Barrymore, Ralph Morgan, Diana Wynyard, Tad Alexander, C. Henry Gordon, Edward Arnold, Jean Parker. Good drama that should have been great, with all three Barrymores in colorful roles, unfolding story of mad monk's plotting against Russia. (Contrary to expectations, it is Lionel and not John who plays Rasputin.) The three Barrymores' only film together,

and Ethel's talkie debut. Wynyard's first film.

Rasputin—the Mad Monk (1966-British) C-92m. ** D: Don Sharp. Christopher Lee, Barbara Shelley, Richard Pasco, Francis Matthews. Confused historical drama of "monk" who actually controlled Russia before Revolution. Script uncommonly bad; Lee's performance manages to redeem film.

Ratboy (1986) C-105m. *½ D: Sondra Locke. Sondra Locke, Robert Townsend, Christopher Hewett, Larry Hankin, Gerrit Graham, Louie Anderson. Window dresser Locke stumbles across a half-man, half-rat—then tries to parlay him into show-biz success by becoming his manager. Locke's directorial debut is technically competent (much of then-friend Clint Eastwood's standard crew helped out), but film plays like an E.T./ELEPHANT MAN derivation that's no longer fresh. Barely released.▼

Ratings Game, The (1984) C-102m. TVM D: Danny DeVito. Danny DeVito, Rhea Pearlman, Gerrit Graham, Kevin McCarthy, Jayne Meadows, Steve Allen, George Wendt, Ronny Graham, Huntz Hall, Barry Corbin. Rollicking send-up of the television business and its incessant quest for ratings. Danny's a third-rate producer turned fawned-over power broker when his truly awful idea becomes the biggest hit since the invention of the wheel. Written by Jim Mulholland and Michael Barric. Made for cable. Above average.▼

Rationing (1944) 93m. **½ D: Willis Goldbeck. Wallace Beery, Marjorie Main, Donald Meek, Gloria Dickson, Henry O'Neill, Connie Gilchrist. Butcher in small town is main character in story of problems during WW2; typical Beery vehicle.

Raton Pass (1951) 84m. **½ D: Edwin L. Marin. Dennis Morgan, Patricia Neal, Steve Cochran, Scott Forbes, Dorothy Hart. Middling Warner Bros. Western, with Morgan and Neal married couple fighting each other for cattle empire.

Rat Race, The (1960) C-105m. *** D: Robert Mulligan. Tony Curtis, Debbie Reynolds, Jack Oakie, Kay Medford, Don Rickles, Joe Bushkin. Comedy-drama of would-be musician (Curtis) and dancer (Reynolds) coming to N.Y.C., platonically sharing an apartment, and falling in love. Nice comic cameos by Oakie and Medford. Script by Garson Kanin, from his play.

Rats, The SEE: **Deadly Eyes**▼

Rattle of a Simple Man (1964-British) 96m. *** D: Muriel Box. Harry H. Corbett, Diane Cilento, Thora Hird, Michael Medwin. Pleasant saucy sex comedy of timid soul Corbett spending the night with Cilento to win a bet; set in London.▼

Ravagers, The (1965) 79m. *½ D: Eddie Romero. John Saxon, Fernando Poe, Jr., Bronwyn Fitzsimmons, Mike Parsons,

Kristina Scott. Uninspired account of Allied fight against Japanese in WW2 Philippines; filmed on location. Fitzsimmons, incidentally, is Maureen O'Hara's daughter.

Ravagers (1979) **C-91m.** BOMB D: Richard Compton. Richard Harris, Ann Turkel, Ernest Borgnine, Art Carney, Anthony James, Woody Strode, Alana Hamilton. Instant tax loss finds Harris searching for civilization in 1991 after most human life has been wiped out. Instead, he finds Borgnine.

Raven, The (1935) **62m.** *** D: Louis Friedlander (Lew Landers). Boris Karloff, Bela Lugosi, Irene Ware, Lester Matthews, Samuel S. Hinds. Momentous teaming of horror greats with Lugosi as doctor with Poe-obsession, Karloff a victim of his wicked schemes. Hinds is subjected to torture from *Pit and the Pendulum* in film's climax. Great fun throughout.▼

Raven, The (1963) **C-86m.** *** D: Roger Corman. Vincent Price, Boris Karloff, Peter Lorre, Hazel Court, Jack Nicholson, Olive Sturgess. Funny horror satire finds magicians Price and Lorre challenging power-hungry colleague Karloff. Climactic sorcerer's duel is a highlight. Screenplay by Richard Matheson, "inspired" by the Poe poem.▼

Ravine, The (1969-Italian-Yugoslavian) **C-97m.** ** Paolo Cavara. David McCallum, Nicoletta Machiavelli, John Crawford, Lars Loch, Demeter Bietnc. Tepid story of German soldier (McCallum) who falls in love with sniper he is supposed to kill during WW2.

Ravishing Idiot (1965-French) **110m.** ** D: Edouard Molinaro. Anthony Perkins, Brigitte Bardot. Bungler used to help steal file on NATO ship maneuvers. Supposedly it's funny, but don't you believe it.▼

Raw Courage SEE: Courage (1984)▼

Raw Deal (1948) **79m.** *** D: Anthony Mann. Dennis O'Keefe, Claire Trevor, Marsha Hunt, Raymond Burr, John Ireland. Beautifully made, hard-boiled story of O'Keefe escaping from jail to take out revenge on slimy Burr, who framed him; what's more, he gets caught between love of two women. Tough and convincing, with Burr a sadistic heavy.

Raw Deal (1986) **C-97m.** *½ D: John Irvin. Arnold Schwarzenegger, Kathryn Harrold, Darren McGavin, Sam Wanamaker, Paul Shenar, Steven Hill, Joe Regalbuto, Robert Davi, Ed Lauter, Blanche Baker. Stupid action movie about brawny ex-Fed who helps an old pal clean some dirty laundry—and bust a major crime ring. Has a sense of humor, which helps . . . but not enough.▼

Raw Edge (1956) **C-76m.** **½ D: John Sherwood. Rory Calhoun, Yvonne De Carlo, Mara Corday, Rex Reason, Neville Brand. Bizarre premise routinely told; rancher's

workers plan to kill him, with his widow to be the prize stake.

Raw Force (1982) **C-86m.** BOMB D: Edward Murphy. Cameron Mitchell, Geoff Binney, Jillian Kesner, John Dresden, Jennifer Holmes. Incredibly dumb, amateurish chop-socky epic: The Burbank Karate Club, vacationing in the Orient, meets up with baddies who eat barbecued women! Too repulsive to be funny.▼

Rawhide (1951) **86m.** **½ D: Henry Hathaway. Tyrone Power, Susan Hayward, Hugh Marlowe, Dean Jagger, Edgar Buchanan, Jack Elam, George Tobias, Jeff Corey. Climactic shoot-out sparks this Western of outlaws holding group of people captive at stagecoach station. Script by Dudley Nichols. Remake of 1935 gangster film SHOW THEM NO MERCY. Retitled: DESPERATE SIEGE.▼

Rawhide Trail, The (1958) **67m.** *½ D: Robert Gordan. Rex Reason, Nancy Gates, Richard Erdman, Ann Doran. Humdrum tale of duo proving their innocence of helping the Indians attack settlers.

Rawhide Years, The (1956) **C-85m.** ** D: Rudolph Maté. Tony Curtis, Colleen Miller, Arthur Kennedy, William Demarest, William Gargan. Youthful Curtis perks this routine fare of gambler trying to clear himself of murder charge.

Raw Meat (1973-British) **C-87m.** **½ D: Gary Sherman. Donald Pleasence, David Ladd, Sharon Gurney, Christopher Lee, Norman Rossington, Clive Swift. Entertaining though overdone horror tale of descendants of people trapped in an abandoned underground tunnel preying as cannibals on modern-day London travelers. Good atmosphere; filmed on location at the Russell Square station. Originally titled DEATH-LINE.

Raw Wind in Eden (1958) **C-89m.** **½ D: Richard Wilson. Esther Williams, Jeff Chandler, Rossana Podesta, Carlos Thompson, Rik Battaglia. Plane carrying rich couple on way to yachting party crashes on isolated island. Entertaining adventure yarn is mixed with romance and jealousy. Filmed in Italy.

Raymie (1960) **72m.** ** D: Frank McDonald. David Ladd, Julie Adams, John Agar, Charles Winninger, Richard Arlen, Frank Ferguson, Ray Kellogg. Quiet little film about youngster (Ladd) whose greatest ambition is to catch the big fish that always eludes him.

Razorback (1984-Australian) **C-95m.** BOMB D: Russell Mulcahy. Gregory Harrison, Arkie Whiteley, Bill Kerr, Chris Haywood. Ludicrous horror film about a giant pig terrorizing the Australian countryside. Inauspicious feature film debut by music video director Mulcahy. ▼

Razor's Edge, The (1946) **146m.** ***½ D: Edmund Goulding. Tyrone Power, Gene

Tierney, John Payne. Anne Baxter, Clifton Webb, Herbert Marshall, Lucile Watson, Frank Latimore. Slick adaptation of Maugham's philosophical novel, with Marshall as the author, Power as hero seeking goodness in life, Baxter in Oscar-winning role as a dipsomaniac, Elsa Lanchester sparkling in bit as social secretary. Screenplay by Lamar Trotti. Long but engrossing; remade in 1984.▼

Razor's Edge, The (1984) C-128m. **½ D: John Byrum. Bill Murray, Theresa Russell, Catherine Hicks, Denholm Elliott, James Keach, Peter Vaughan, Brian Doyle-Murray, Saeed Jaffrey. Ambitious, if anachronistic, remake of 1946 film with enough plot for *five* movies. Young American survives WW1 and begins to question meaning of his life—while his closest friends go through personal crises of their own. It's hard to read much spiritual thought on Murray's deadpan face, but he gives it a good try (and cowrote script with director Byrum). Russell comes off best in the showy role previously played by Anne Baxter. Warts and all, it's still an interesting film.▼

R.C.M.P. and the Treasure of Genghis Khan (1948) 100m. *½ D: Fred Brannon, Yakima Canutt. Jim Bannon, Virginia Belmont, Anthony Warde, Dorothy Granger. Spotty actioner with too few real cliffhangers, dealing with Canadian mounties' efforts to combat criminal syndicate searching for fabled Oriental buried treasure. Reedited from Republic serial DANGERS OF THE CANADIAN MOUNTED.

Reach for Glory (1963-British) 89m. **½ D: Philip Leacock. Harry Andrews, Kay Walsh, Oliver Grimm, Michael Anderson, Jr., Martin Tomlinson, Alexis Kanner. Sensitive, if minor tale about WW2 England, involving youths and their special code of ethics, leading to one member's death.

Reach for the Sky (1956-British) 123m. **½ D: Lewis Gilbert. Kenneth More, Muriel Pavlow, Alexander Knox, Sydney Tafler, Nigel Green. Sensibly told account of British pilot who overcame leg injury to continue his flying career. British running time: 135m.

Reaching for the Moon (1931) 62m. **½ D: Edmund Goulding. Douglas Fairbanks, Sr., Bebe Daniels, Edward Everett Horton, Jack Mulhall, Helen Jerome Eddy, Bing Crosby. Enjoyable Depression comedy depicting effect of booze on financier Fairbanks, with Horton as his valet, Bebe the girl, and Crosby singing one Irving Berlin song. Originally 91m.▼

Reaching for the Sun (1941) 90m. **½ D: William Wellman. Joel McCrea, Ellen Drew, Eddie Bracken, Albert Dekker, Billy Gilbert, George Chandler. OK comedy of North Woods clam-digger who journeys to Detroit to earn money for outboard motor by working on auto assembly line.

Ready, Willing and Able (1937) 95m. ** D: Ray Enright. Ruby Keeler, Lee Dixon, Allen Jenkins, Louise Fazenda, Carol Hughes, Ross Alexander, Winifred Shaw, Teddy Hart. Undistinguished Warner Bros. musical about college girl who impersonates British star in order to land Broadway role. Notable only for introduction of "Too Marvelous for Words," with a production number featuring a giant typewriter!

Real American Hero, A (1978) C-100m. TVM D: Lou Antonio. Brian Dennehy, Forrest Tucker, Brian Kerwin, Ken Howard, Sheree North, Lane Bradbury. Buford Pusser, the club-wielding law-and-order sheriff of Selmer, Tennessee, whose career inspired three ultra-violent movies beginning with WALKING TALL, is the American "hero." This time he's battling a dapper local moonshiner. Average.▼

Real Genius (1985) C-104m. **½ D: Martha Coolidge. Val Kilmer, Gabe Jarret, Michelle Meyrink, William Atherton, Jonathan Gries, Patti D'Arbanville. Idealistic whiz-kid is recruited by self-styled genius (Atherton) to join his college think tank — only to find that its members are being exploited, co-opted, and generally burned out. Potentially clever satire turns into just another youth/revenge comedy with caricatures instead of characters.▼

Real Glory, The (1939) 95m. *** D: Henry Hathaway. Gary Cooper, David Niven, Andrea Leeds, Reginald Owen, Kay Johnson, Broderick Crawford, Vladimir Sokoloff, Henry Kolker. Cooper's fine as Army medic who solves all of Philippines' medical and military problems almost single-handedly after destructive Spanish-American War. Excellent action scenes.

Real Life (1979) C-99m. **½ D: Albert Brooks. Albert Brooks, Charles Grodin, Frances Lee McCain, J. A. Preston, Matthew Tobin. Writer-director-comedian Brooks' first feature doesn't sustain its comic premise as well as his hilarious short subjects, but still presents the world's greatest put-on artist in a compatible vehicle, as a shifty opportunist who sets out to make a filmed record of a typical American family.▼

Real Men (1987) C-96m. *½ D: Dennis Feldman. James Belushi, John Ritter, Barbara Barrie, Bill Morey, Iva Andersen, Mark Herrier. Unfunny spy film satire with CIA agent Belushi recruiting reluctant Ritter as a courier. Barely released to theaters, and with good reason.▼

Re-Animator (1985) C-86m. *** D: Stuart Gordon. Jeffrey Combs, Bruce Abbott, Barbara Crampton, Robert Sampson, David Gale. Knockout horror thriller and black comedy about H. P. Lovecraft's character Herbert West (Combs), an uppity young medical student who develops a serum to bring the dead back to life. Debut film director Gordon goes entertainingly over the line, especially in an off-color scene involving heroine Crampton and a lustful severed head. Major defect: Richard Band's music score, which is a little too reminiscent of Bernard Herrmann's classic PSYCHO sound track. *Lengthened* (and toned down) by Gordon for homevideo: this review refers to original version.▼

Reap the Wild Wind (1942) C-124m. *** D: Cecil B. DeMille. Ray Milland, John Wayne, Paulette Goddard, Raymond Massey, Robert Preston, Susan Hayward, Charles Bickford, Hedda Hopper, Louise Beavers, Martha O'Driscoll, Lynne Overman. Brawling DeMille hokum of 19th-century salvagers in Georgia, with Goddard as fiery Southern belle, Milland and Wayne fighting for her, Massey as odious villain. Exciting underwater scenes, with the special effects earning an Oscar. Milland good in off-beat characterization.▼

Rearview Mirror (1984) C-100m. TVM D: Lou Antonio. Lee Remick, Tony Musante, Michael Beck, Jim Antonio, Don Galloway, Ned Bridges. Crazed ex-con and terrorized lady motorist are pursued through the swamps of South Carolina. Acceptable thriller based on Caroline B. Crosney's novel. Average.

Rear Window (1954) C-112m. **** D: Alfred Hitchcock. James Stewart, Grace Kelly, Wendell Corey, Thelma Ritter, Raymond Burr, Judith Evelyn. One of Hitchcock's most stylish thrillers has photographer Stewart confined to wheelchair in his apartment, using binoculars to spy on courtyard neighbors, and discovering a possible murder. Inventive Cornell Woolrich story adapted by John Michael Hayes. Stewart, society girlfriend Kelly, and no-nonsense nurse Ritter make a wonderful trio.▼

Reason to Live, A (1985) C-100m. TVM D: Peter Levin. Ricky Schroder, Peter Fonda, Deidre Hall, Tracey Gold, Carrie Snodgress, Bruce Weitz. Teenager fights to save his dad from committing suicide. Average.

Reason to Live, a Reason to Die, A (1974-Italian-French-German-Spanish) C-92m. ** D: Tonino Valerii. James Coburn, Telly Savalas, Bud Spencer, Robert Burton. Union Colonel Coburn and seven condemned men attempt to recapture a Missouri fort from brutal Confederate Major Savalas. So-so Western, retitled MASSACRE AT FORT HOLMAN.▼

Rebecca (1940) 130m. **** D: Alfred Hitchcock. Laurence Olivier, Joan Fontaine, George Sanders, Judith Anderson, Nigel Bruce, Reginald Denny, C. Aubrey Smith, Gladys Cooper, Florence Bates, Leo G. Carroll, Melville Cooper. Hitchcock's first American film is sumptuous David O. Selznick production of Daphne du Maurier novel of girl who marries British nobleman but lives in shadow of former wife. Stunning performances by Fontaine and Anderson; haunting score by Franz Waxman. Screenplay by Robert E. Sherwood and Joan Harrison. Academy Award winner for Best Picture and Cinematography (George Barnes).▼

Rebecca of Sunnybrook Farm (1938) 80m. **½ D: Allan Dwan. Shirley Temple, Randolph Scott, Jack Haley, Gloria Stuart, Phyllis Brooks, Helen Westley, Slim Summerville, William Demarest. Contrived but entertaining Temple vehicle with surefire elements from earlier movies tossed into simple story of Scott trying to make Shirley a radio star. Has nothing to do with Kate Douglas Wiggin's famous story. Also shown in computer-colored version.▼

Rebel (1985-Australian) C-91m. ** D: Michael Jenkins. Matt Dillon, Debbie Byrne, Bryan Brown, Bill Hunter, Ray Barrett, Julie Nihill, Kim Deacon. Odd mixture of drama and music in this tale of traumatized AWOL American GI Dillon, who attaches himself to Sydney cabaret performer Byrne during WW2. Plenty of flash and style, but there's little substance . . . and Dillon is fatally miscast.▼

Rebel in Town (1956) 78m. ** D: Alfred L. Werker. John Payne, Ruth Roman, J. Carrol Naish, Ben Cooper, John Smith. Sensitive minor Western; renegade is present when his brother accidentally kills a child. Ironic events bring him into contact with boy's father.

Rebel Love (1984) C-90m. *½ D: Milton Bagby, Jr. Jamie Rose, Terence Knox, Fran Ryan, Carl Spurlock. Awkward drama chronicling relationship between actor-turned-Confederate spy Knox and Yankee widow Rose during the Civil War. Attempts to be poetic and allegorical. ▼

Rebel of the Road SEE: **Hot Rod**▼

Rebel Rousers (1967) C-78m. **½ D: Martin B. Cohen. Cameron Mitchell, Jack Nicholson, Bruce Dern, Diane Ladd, (Harry) Dean Stanton. Architect Mitchell isn't pleased when Dern holds drag-race to see who will "win" Mitchell's pregnant girlfriend. Nicholson, decked out in outrageous striped pants, steals the show in this amusing time-capsule.▼

Rebels, The (1979) C-200m. TVM D: Russ Mayberry. Andrew Stevens, Don Johnson, Doug McClure, Richard Basehart, Joan Blondell, Jim Backus, Tom Bosley, Rory Calhoun, Macdonald Carey, Kim Cattrall, William Daniels, Anne Francis, Peter Graves, Pamela Hensley, Forrest Tucker, Robert Vaughn, William Conrad (narrator). In this sequel to THE BASTARD, author John Jakes's fictional Philip Kent fights in the American Revolution and hobnobs with the Founding Fathers. One more Philip Kent adventure, THE SEEKERS, followed. Originally shown in two parts. Average.

Rebel Set, The (1959) 72m. *½ D: Gene Fowler, Jr. Gregg Palmer, Kathleen Crowley, Edward Platt, Ned Glass, John Lupton. Minor crime caper involving youths used by gangster to help carry out a robbery.

Rebel Son, The (1939-British) 88m. ** D: Alexis Granowsky, Adrian Brunel, Albert de Courville. Harry Baur, Anthony Bushell, Roger Livesey, Patricia Roc, Joan Gardner, Frederick Culley, Joseph Cunningham. Ineffectual English-language version of 1936 French film TARASS BOULBA (which also starred the legendary Baur) makes liberal use of action footage from the original, highlighting tale of 16th-century battle between Cossacks and Poles. Remade as TARAS BULBA. (Absurdly) retitled THE BARBARIAN AND THE LADY, and cut to 70m.

Rebel Without a Cause (1955) C-111m. **** D: Nicholas Ray. James Dean, Natalie Wood, Sal Mineo, Jim Backus, Ann Doran, William Hopper, Rochelle Hudson, Corey Allen, Edward Platt, Dennis Hopper, Nick Adams. This portrait of youthful alienation spoke to a whole generation and remains wrenchingly powerful, despite some dated elements. The yearning for self-esteem, the barrier to communication with parents, the comfort found in friendships, all beautifully realized by director Ray, screenwriter Stewart Stern, and a fine cast (far too many of whom met early ends). This was Dean's seminal performance and an equally impressive showcase for young Mineo.▼

Reckless (1935) 96m. ** D: Victor Fleming. Jean Harlow, William Powell, Franchot Tone, May Robson, Ted Healy, Nat Pendleton, Rosalind Russell, Henry Stephenson, Leon Waycoff (Ames), Allan Jones, Mickey Rooney, Farina (Allen Hoskins). Big cast, big production, musical numbers—all can't save script of chorus girl tangling up several people's lives. Tired and phony.

Reckless (1984) C-90m. **½ D: James Foley. Aidan Quinn, Daryl Hannah, Kenneth McMillan, Cliff DeYoung, Lois Smith, Adam Baldwin, Dan Hedaya. Rebellious teenager from wrong side of tracks takes up with straight-arrow coed, who finds in him a sense of danger and excitement missing from her comfortable existence. Nothing here we haven't seen in 1950s films about alienated youth—except for some very contemporary sex scenes—but it's done with sincerity and a pulsing rock soundtrack.▼

Reckless Disregard (1985) C-95m. TVM D: Harvey Hart. Tess Harper, Leslie Nielsen, Ronny Cox, Kate Lynch, Henry Ramer, Sean McCann. Inspired (or uninspired) by Dan Rather's well-publicized *60 Minutes* story that caused him to be sued by a doctor for defamation of character, this flat drama has an arrogant TV newscaster being prosecuted by an inexperienced lady lawyer after her doctor client was accused of turning his clinic into a pill factory. Made for cable. Average.▼

Reckless Moment, The (1949) 82m. ***½ D: Max Ophuls. James Mason, Joan Bennett, Geraldine Brooks, Henry O'Neill, Shepperd Strudwick, Roy Roberts. Bennett becomes a murderer, pursued by blackmailer Mason. First-rate suspenser. Henry Garson and R.W. Soderborg adapted Elizabeth Sanxay Holding's novel *The Blank Wall.*

Reckoning, The (1969-British) C-111m. **½ D: Jack Gold. Nicol Williamson, Rachel Roberts, Paul Rogers, Zena Walker, Ann Bell. Contrived, latter day "angry young man" film, with Williamson (excellent as usual) as brooding businessman incapable of living in harmony with society, and out to avenge long-ago slight to his father.

Record City (1977) C-90m. *½ D: Dennis Steinmetz. Leonard Barr, Ed Begley, Jr., Sorrell Booke, Dennis Bowen, Jack Carter, Ruth Buzzi, Michael Callan, Alice Ghostley, Frank Gorshin, Kinky Friedman. CAR WASH-type youth comedy with music, set in a record store. Nothing much. Shot on videotape, then transferred to film.

Red Alert (1977) C-100m. TVM D: William Hale. William Devane, Michael Brandon, Adrienne Barbeau, Ralph Waite, David Hayward, M. Emmet Walsh. Taut suspense thriller about an accident at a nuclear power plant. Interesting science-fact with Devane and Waite as antagonists. Based on the novel *Paradigm Red* by Harold King. Average.▼

Red Badge of Courage, The (1951) 69m. ***½ D: John Huston. Audie Murphy, Bill Mauldin, John Dierkes, Royal Dano, Arthur Hunnicutt, Andy Devine, Douglas Dick. Stephen Crane's human focus on Civil War, not treated as spectacle, resulting in realistic drama with natural performances. Film's troubled production was recounted in a classic book, Lillian Ross' *Picture.* Remade for TV in 1974.▼

Red Badge of Courage, The (1974) C-78m. TVM D: Lee Philips. Richard Thomas, Michael Brandon, Wendell Burton, Charles Aidman, Warren Berlinger, Lee DeBroux. TV remake of Stephen Crane classic, telling of the youth who runs away from his first Civil War battle but returns to be a soldier. Thomas is fine in the lead. Adaptation by John Gay. Above average.

Red Ball Express (1952) 83m. *** D: Budd Boetticher. Jeff Chandler, Alex Nicol, Judith Braun, Hugh O'Brian, Jack Kelly, Sidney Poitier, Jack Warden. Energetic cast and fast-paced action blend well in this account of supply unit working behind the German lines. Script by John Michael Hayes.

Red Beard (1965-Japanese) **185m.** ****½** D: Akira Kurosawa. Toshiro Mifune, Yuzo Kayama, Yoshio Tsuchiya, Reiko Dan, Kyoko Kagawa, Terumi Niki. Tough but kind doctor Mifune takes intern Kayama under his wing in charity clinic. Unoriginal drama is also way overlong.▼

Red Beret, The SEE: **Paratrooper, The**

Red Canyon (1949) **C-82m.** ** D: George Sherman. Ann Blyth, Howard Duff, George Brent, Edgar Buchanan, Chill Wills, Jane Darwell, Lloyd Bridges. Routine Zane Grey Western of wild horses being tamed.

Red Circle, The (1960-German) **94m.** ****½** D: Jurgen Roland. Fritz Rasp, Karl Saebisch, Renate Ewert, Klaus-Jurgen Wussow. Scotland Yard investigates series of murders with each victim having telltale circle mark on his neck; slickly paced.

Red Dance, The (1928) **103m.** ****½** D: Raoul Walsh. Charles Farrell, Dolores Del Rio, Ivan Linow, Boris Charsky, Dorothy Revier. Opulent production makes up for silly story of romance and intrigue during the Russian revolution.

Red Danube, The (1949) **119m.** ****½** D: George Sidney. Walter Pidgeon, Ethel Barrymore, Peter Lawford, Angela Lansbury, Janet Leigh. Louis Calhern, Francis L. Sullivan. Meandering drama of ballerina Leigh pursued by Russian agents, aided by amorous Lawford; heavy-handed at times.

Red Dawn (1984) **C-114m.** *½ D: John Milius. Patrick Swayze, C. Thomas Howell, Lea Thompson, Charlie Sheen, Powers Boothe, Ben Johnson, Harry Dean Stanton, Jennifer Grey. Small-town teens become guerrilla fighters when Commies invade U.S. Good premise gunned down by purple prose and posturing—not to mention violence. Swayze and Grey were later paired in DIRTY DANCING.▼

Red Desert (1964-French-Italian) **C-116m.** ** D: Michelangelo Antonioni. Monica Vitti, Richard Harris, Rita Renoir, Carlo Chionetti. Vague, boring, monotonous tale of Vitti alienated from her surroundings and on the verge of madness. Antonioni's first color film does have its followers, though.▼

Red Dragon, The (1945) **64m.** D: Phil Rosen. Sidney Toler, Fortunio Bonanova, Benson Fong, Robert Emmett Keane, Willie Best, Carol Hughes. SEE: **Charlie Chan** series.

Red Dragon (1967-German) **C-88m.** ****½** D: Ernst Hofbauer. Stewart Granger, Rosanna Schiaffino, Horst Frank, Suzanne Roquette. Granger is F.B.I. agent in Hong Kong chasing smuggling gang, Schiaffino another agent. Well paced, but predictable script.

Red Dust (1932) **83m.** *****½** D: Victor Fleming. Clark Gable, Jean Harlow, Mary Astor, Donald Crisp, Gene Raymond, Tully Marshall, Willie Fung. Robust romance of Indochina rubber worker Gable, his floozie gal Harlow, and visiting Astor, who is married to Raymond, but falls for Gable. Harlow has fine comic touch. Tart script by John Lee Mahin. Remade as CONGO MAISIE and MOGAMBO.▼

Red Earth, White Earth (1989) **C-100m.** TVM D: David Greene. Genevieve Bujold, Timothy Daly, Richard Farnsworth, Ralph Waite, Alberta Watson, Billy Merasty. Contemporary drama involving a three-generation farm family caught up in personal problems, trouble on the land, and political turmoil with local Indian factions. Trenchant script by Michael De Guzman adapted from Will Weaver's novel. Above average.

Red Flag: The Ultimate Game (1981) **C-100m.** TVM D: Don Taylor. Barry Bostwick, William Devane, Joan Van Ark, Fred McCarren, Debra Feuer, George Coe, Linden Chiles, Arlen Dean Snyder. Two pilots involved in war games rekindle an old rivalry that leads to tragedy. Despite a plot reminiscent of an old Richard Arlen-Chester Morris B movie, this one has quite a bit of bite, thanks to an intelligent script by T.S. Cook and the realism of contemporary fighter-pilot training under simulated combat conditions. Above average.▼

Red Garters (1954) **C-91m.** ****½** D: George Marshall. Rosemary Clooney, Jack Carson, Guy Mitchell, Pat Crowley, Gene Barry, Cass Daley, Frank Faylen, Reginald Owen. Musical western spoof gets A for effort—with strikingly stylized color sets, offbeat casting—but falls short of target.

Redhead and the Cowboy, The (1950) **82m.** ****½** D: Leslie Fenton. Glenn Ford, Rhonda Fleming, Edmond O'Brien, Morris Ankrum. Effective Western set in Civil War times, with Fleming a Reb spy trying to get message across Union lines.

Red-Headed Stranger (1986) **C-105m.** *½ D: William Wittliff. Willie Nelson, Morgan Fairchild, Katharine Ross, Royal Dano, Sonny Carl Davi.. Limp drama, screenwriter Wittliff's directorial debut, about a preacher (Nelson), his wayward wife (Fairchild, in an awful performance), a "good woman" (Ross), and some hooligans that have overridden his town. Adapted from Willie's 1975 album . . . and proof that hit records don't necessarily make hit (or even good) movies. Completed in 1984.▼

Red-Headed Woman (1932) **79m.** ******* D: Jack Conway. Jean Harlow, Chester Morris, Una Merkel, Lewis Stone, May Robson, Leila Hyams, Charles Boyer. Harlow has never been sexier than in this precensorship story (by Anita Loos) of a gold-digging secretary who sets out to corral her married boss (Morris).

Redhead From Wyoming, The (1952) **C-80m.** **½ D: Lee Sholem. Maureen O'Hara, Alexander Scourby, Alex Nicol, Jack Kelly, William Bishop, Dennis Weaver. Saucy Western pepped up by exuberant O'Hara as girl who falls in love with sheriff while protecting local cattle rustler.

Red Heat (1988) **C-106m.** *½ D: Walter Hill. Arnold Schwarzenegger, James Belushi, Peter Boyle, Ed O'Ross, Larry Fishburne, Gina Gershon, Richard Bright, Oleg Vidov. Grim-faced Soviet cop (played by Guess Who?) tracks a scummy Russian drug dealer to Chicago, where he's partnered with belligerent Belushi from the Chicago P.D. Cheerless, foul-mouthed action film with two of the least appealing characters imaginable as the good guys. This film had the distinction of being the first American production allowed to shoot scenes in Moscow's Red Square (. . . but *why*?).▼

Red, Hot and Blue (1949) 84m. **½ D: John Farrow. Betty Hutton, Victor Mature, William Demarest, June Havoc, Frank Loesser, Raymond Walburn. Noisy Hutton vehicle of ambitious girl trying to make it big in show biz, mixed up with gangsters.

Red House, The (1947) 100m. *** D: Delmer Daves. Edward G. Robinson, Lon McCallister, Allene Roberts, Judith Anderson, Rory Calhoun, Julie London. Ona Munson. Title refers to strange old house containing many mysteries, providing constant fear for farmer Robinson. Exciting melodrama with fine cast.▼

Red Inn, The (1954-French) 100m. **½ D: Claude Autant-Lara. Fernandel, Francoise Rosay, Carette, Marie-Claire Olivia, Lud Germain. Bizarre black comedy about stagecoach passengers who stop at wayside inn run by woman who robs and murders guests.

Red Kiss (1986-French) **C-112m.** *** D: Vera Belmont. Charlotte Valandrey, Lambert Wilson, Marthe Keller, Gunter Lamprecht, Laurent Terzieff. Sincere, thoughtful drama about the coming of age of teen Valandrey in early 1950s Paris. She's a committed Stalinist, as are her parents, but she also is fascinated by American culture— and falls in love with photographer Wilson. Original title: ROUGE BAISER.

Red Light (1949) 83m. ** D: Roy Del Ruth. George Raft, Virginia Mayo, Gene Lockhart, Barton MacLane, Henry (Harry) Morgan, Raymond Burr. Turgid drama of innocent Raft seeking revenge when freed from prison, hunting brother's killer.

Red-Light Sting, The (1984) **C-100m.** TVM D: Rod Holcomb. Farrah Fawcett, Beau Bridges, Harold Gould, Paul Burke, Conrad Janis, Lawrence Pressman, Kathe-

rine Cannon. Classy call girl is recruited to front for a government-run brothel set up to nab a crime czar. Average.▼

Red Line 7000 (1965) **C-110m.** **½ D: Howard Hawks. James Caan, Laura Devon, Gail Hire, Charlene Holt, John Robert Crawford, Marianna Hill, James Ward, Norman Alden, George Takei. Attempt by director Hawks to do same kind of expert adventure pic he'd done for 40 years is sabotaged by overly complex script and indifferent acting, but is a faster and less pretentious racing-car drama than GRAND PRIX.

Red Menace, The (1949) 87m. *½ D: R. G. Springsteen. Robert Rockwell, Hanne Axman, Betty Lou Gerson, Barbara Fuller. War vet Rockwell is duped by the Commies! McCarthyesque propaganda is now an unintentionally funny antique.

Red Mountain (1951) **C-84m.** **½ D: William Dieterle. Alan Ladd, Lizabeth Scott, John Ireland, Arthur Kennedy. Generally actionful Western dealing with the career of Quantrill, Yankee renegade officer during Civil War.

Redneck (1972-Italian-British) **C-89m.** BOMB D: Silvio Narizzano. Franco Nero, Telly Savalas, Mark Lester, Ely Galleani, Duilio Del Prete, Maria Michi. Tawdry, sadistic crime drama about two inept (and unappealing) robbers on the lam who inadvertently "kidnap" a young boy. Unpleasant and unbelievable.▼

Red Planet Mars (1952) 87m. **½ D: Harry Horner. Peter Graves, Andrea King, Marvin Miller, Herbert Berghof, House Peters, Vince Barnett. Outrageous sci-fi of scientist deciphering messages from Mars which turn out to be from God! Hilariously ludicrous anti-Communist propaganda (*Red* Planet Mars, get it?).

Red Pony, The (1949) **C-89m.** *** D: Lewis Milestone. Myrna Loy, Robert Mitchum, Peter Miles, Louis Calhern, Shepperd Strudwick, Margaret Hamilton. Tasteful version of John Steinbeck book about boy attached to horse, seeking escape from bickering family; leisurely pacing, fine Aaron Copland score. Remade for TV in 1973.▼

Red Pony, The (1973) **C-100m.** TVM D: Robert Totten. Henry Fonda, Maureen O'Hara, Ben Johnson, Jack Elam, Clint Howard, Richard Jaeckel, Julian Rivero, Victor Sen Yung. Beautifully realized remake of the Steinbeck novella, minus the Billy Buck character played by Mitchum in the original. Fonda is especially good as the gruff father who loves his son in his own distant way. Winner of the Peabody Award as Outstanding Drama Special; adapted by Robert Totten and Ron Bishop. Above average.

Red River (1948) 133m. **** D: Howard Hawks. John Wayne, Montgomery Clift,

Walter Brennan, Joanne Dru, John Ireland, Noah Beery, Jr., Paul Fix, Coleen Gray, Harry Carey, Jr., Harry Carey, Sr., Chief Yowlatchie, Hank Worden. One of the greatest American adventures is really a Western MUTINY ON THE BOUNTY: Clift (in his first film) rebels against tyrannical guardian Wayne (brilliant in an unsympathetic role) during crucial cattle drive. Spellbinding photography by Russell Harlan, rousing Dmitri Tiomkin score; an absolute must. Many TV stations still show mutilated 125m. version (with Brennan's narration in place of diary pages). Screenplay by Borden Chase and Charles Schnee, from Chase's *Saturday Evening Post* story. Remade for TV.▼

Red River (1988) **C-100m. TVM** D: Richard Michaels. James Arness, Bruce Boxleitner, Gregory Harrison, Ray Walston, Laura Johnson, Stan Shaw, Ty Hardin, Robert Horton, John Lupton, Guy Madison. The next time somebody says "They don't make 'em like they used to," this perfectly ordinary redo of the forty-year-old Howard Hawks classic will serve as the definitive example. The only thing going for it is the well-cast Arness, Duke Wayne's long-ago protege, in the Wayne role—but then he's off-screen for the latter half of the cattle drive! Richard Fielder, who wrote the script for the much-praised mini-series on George Washington, adapted Borden Chase and Charles Schnee's original screenplay. Average.

Reds (1981) **C-200m.** *** D: Warren Beatty. Warren Beatty, Diane Keaton, Edward Herrmann, Jerzy Kosinski, Jack Nicholson, Paul Sorvino, Maureen Stapleton, Nicolas Coster, Gene Hackman, William Daniels, Max Wright, M. Emmet Walsh, Ian Wolfe, Bessie Love, George Plimpton, Dolph Sweet, Josef Sommer. Sprawling, ambitious film about American idealist/journalist John Reed's involvement with Communism, the Russian Revolution, and a willful, free-thinking woman named Louise Bryant. Provocative political saga is diffused, and overcome at times, by surprisingly conventional, often sappy approach to the love story (climaxed by Bryant's Little Eva-like journey to Russia over the ice floes). Interesting but wildly overpraised film won Oscars for Beatty as Best Director (he also produced and co-scripted), Stapleton as Best Supporting Actress, Vittorio Storaro for Best Cinematography.▼

Red Salute (1935) **78m.** **½ D: Sidney Lanfield. Barbara Stanwyck, Robert Young, Hardie Albright, Cliff Edwards, Ruth Donnelly, Gordon Jones. Runaway screwball Stanwyck meets no-nonsense soldier Young in this imitation IT HAPPENED ONE NIGHT with wild sociopolitical wrinkle: Barbara's boyfriend (Albright) is a student radical who makes Communist speeches! A real oddity. Also known as HER ENLISTED MAN and RUNAWAY DAUGHTER.

Red Scorpion (1989) **C-102m.** BOMB D: Joseph Zito. Dolph Lundgren, M. Emmet Walsh, Al White, T.P. McKenna, Carmen Argenziano, Brion James, Regopstann. Bottom-of-the-barrel actioner with Lundgren a Soviet officer sent to Africa to murder a rebel leader. The direction is dull, the performances even worse.▼

Red Shoes, The (1948-British) **C-133m.** **** D: Michael Powell, Emeric Pressburger. Anton Walbrook, Marius Goring, Moira Shearer, Robert Helpmann, Leonide Massine, Albert Basserman, Ludmilla Tcherina, Esmond Knight. A superb, stylized fairy tale. Young ballerina is torn between two creative, possessive men, one a struggling composer, the other an autocratic dance impresario. Landmark film for its integration of dance in storytelling, and a perennial favorite of balletomanes. Brian Easdale's score and Hein Heckroth and Arthur Lawson's art direction-set decoration won Oscars, and Jack Cardiff's cinematography *should* have. Shearer is exquisite in movie debut.▼

Red Skies of Montana (1952) **C-89m.** **½ D: Joseph M. Newman. Richard Widmark, Jeffrey Hunter, Constance Smith, Richard Boone, Richard Crenna. Trite account of forest-fire fighters, salvaged by spectacular fire sequences.

Red Sky at Morning (1970) **C-112m.** *** D: James Goldstone. Richard Thomas, Catherine Burns, Desi Arnaz, Jr., Richard Crenna, Claire Bloom, John Colicos, Harry Guardino, Strother Martin, Nehemiah Persoff. Unspectacular but pleasing adaptation of Richard Bradford's novel about adolescence in New Mexico during WW2. Comparable to SUMMER OF '42, and in many ways better; Thomas is superb.

Red Sonja (1985) **C-89m.** *½ D: Richard Fleischer. Brigitte Nielsen, Arnold Schwarzenegger, Sandahl Bergman, Paul Smith, Ernie Reyes, Jr., Ronald Lacey, Pat Roach. Spectacularly silly sword-and-sorcery saga with female lead, based on pulp writings of Robert E. Howard (of CONAN fame). Might amuse juvenile viewers, but only point of interest for adults is deciding who gives the worse performance, Nielsen or villainess Bergman.▼

Red Spider, The (1988) **C-100m. TVM** D: Jerry Jameson. James Farentino, Jennifer O'Neill, Amy Steel, Philip Casnoff, Soon-Teck Oh, Stephen Joyce, Ed Hindman. Dogged N.Y.C. cop stumbles across bizarre murders linked to Vietnam in this follow-up to ONE POLICE PLAZA, with a different cast stepping into the earlier roles. Average.

Red Stallion, The (1947) **C-82m.** *½ D:

Lesley Selander. Robert Paige, Noreen Nash, Ted Donaldson, Jane Darwell, Daisy. Weak little film of ranch boy and his pet horse.▼

Red Stallion in the Rockies (1949) **C-85m.** ** D: Ralph Murphy. Arthur Franz, Wallace Ford, Ray Collins, Jean Heather, Leatrice Joy. OK outdoor drama of two men rounding up herd of wild horses.

Red Sun (1972-Italian-French-Spanish) **C-112m.** ** D: Terence Young. Charles Bronson, Ursula Andress, Toshiro Mifune, Alain Delon, Capucine. East meets West in this odd story of samurai warrior pursuing valuable Japanese sword stolen from train crossing American West. Intriguing elements, and refreshingly tongue-in-cheek, but a misfire.▼

Red Sundown (1956) **C-81m.** **½ D: Jack Arnold. Rory Calhoun, Martha Hyer, Dean Jagger, Robert Middleton, James Millican. Virile cast adds zest to standard yarn of bad-guy-gone-good (Calhoun), squeezing out the criminal elements in town.

Red Tent, The (1971-Italian-Russian) **C-121m.** *** D: Mikhail K. Kalatozov. Sean Connery, Claudia Cardinale, Hardy Kruger, Peter Finch, Massimo Girotti. Top-notch adventure saga for kids and adults alike, based on true story of explorer General Nobile (Finch) whose 1928 Arctic expedition turns into disaster. Exciting scenes of survival against elements, dramatic rescue, marred by awkward flashback framework.▼

Red Tomahawk (1967) **C-82m.** *½ D: R. G. Springsteen. Howard Keel, Joan Caulfield, Broderick Crawford, Scott Brady, Wendell Corey, Richard Arlen, Tom Drake, Ben Cooper, Donald Barry. Captain Keel saves town from Sioux in routine Western with many likable performers in the cast.

Reefer Madness (1936) **67m.** BOMB D: Louis Gasnier. Dave O'Brien, Dorothy Short, Warren McCollum, Lillian Miles, Carleton Young, Thelma White. The granddaddy of all "Worst" movies; one of that era's many low-budget "Warning!" films depicts (in now-hilarious fashion) how one puff of pot can lead clean-cut teenagers down the road to insanity and death. Miles' frenzied piano solo is a highlight, but in this more enlightened age, overall effect is a little sad. Originally titled THE BURNING QUESTION, then TELL YOUR CHILDREN; beware shorter prints.▼

Reflection of Fear, A (1973) **C-102m.** **½ D: William A. Fraker. Robert Shaw, Mary Ure, Sally Kellerman, Sondra Locke, Signe Hasso. Muddled story of beautiful girl who becomes the crucial link in chain of violence and murder.▼

Reflections in a Golden Eye (1967) **C-108m.** **½ D: John Huston. Elizabeth Taylor, Marlon Brando, Brian Keith, Julie Harris, Robert Forster, Zorro David. Kinky version of Carson McCullers' novel about homosexual army officer in the South. Not really very good, but cast, subject matter, and Huston's pretentious handling make it fascinating on a minor level.▼

Reflections of Murder (1974) **C-100m.** TVM D: John Badham. Tuesday Weld, Joan Hackett, Sam Waterston, Lucille Benson, Michael Lerner, R. G. Armstrong. Lance Kerwin. Wife and mistress conspire to kill a tyrannical schoolteacher who then returns to haunt them. First-class performances make this new version of French classic DIABOLIQUE a superior thriller. Script by Carol Sobieski. Above average.▼

Reformer and the Redhead, The (1950) **90m.** **½ D: Norman Panama, Melvin Frank. June Allyson. Dick Powell, David Wayne, Cecil Kellaway, Ray Collins. Sassy shenanigans with Allyson, a zoo-keeper's daughter, courted by lawyer Powell.

Reform School Girl (1957) **71m.** BOMB D: Edward Bernds. Gloria Castillo, Ross Ford, Edward Byrnes, Ralph Reed, Jack Kruschen, Sally Kellerman. Cheapie production about girl involved with hit-and-run murder.

Reform School Girls (1986) **C-94m.** *½ D: Tom DeSimone. Linda Carol, Wendy O. Williams, Pat Ast, Sybil Danning, Charlotte McGinnis, Sherri Stoner, Denise Gordy, Tiffany Schwartz. Comic strip-styled spoof of women's prison films offers some knowing winks (director DeSimone also made the successful THE CONCRETE JUNGLE) for fans of the genre, but the level of exaggeration is a turnoff, such as imagining veteran rock singer Williams as a teenager. Carol is the innocent young girl learning the ropes in prison, while chubby Ast, an Andy Warhol film graduate, was born to play a prison matron—yet even her campy acting becomes monotonous. ▼

Refuge (1984) **C-90m.** TVM D: Huck Fairman. Anne Twomey, James Congdon, Alexandra O'Karma, Will Jeffries. Dreary, minor soap opera about a quartet of people and their various entanglements while together on a remote island. A PBS *American Playhouse* presentation. Below average.

Reggae Sunsplash (1980-German-Jamaican) **C-107m.** **½ D: Stefan Paul. Bob Marley, Peter Tosh, Third World, Burning Spear. OK documentary, filmed at the '79 Sunsplash II Festival in Montego Bay, benefits from commanding presences of Marley and company.▼

Reg'lar Fellers (1941) **66m.** ** D: Arthur Dreifuss. Billy Lee, Carl "Alfalfa" Switzer, Buddy Boles, Janet Dempsey, Sarah Padden, Roscoe Ates. Extremely dated comedy, based on Gene Byrnes' popular comic strip, chronicling the escapades of some typically all-American youngsters who help soften miserable, kid-hating Padden. "Alfalfa" fans will not be disappointed.▼

Rehearsal for Murder (1982) **C-100m.** TVM D: David Greene. Robert Preston, Lynn Redgrave, Patrick Macnee, Lawrence Pressman, Madolyn Smith, Jeff Goldblum, William Daniels, William Russ. Engrossing Richard Levinson-William Link mystery about death of a famous movie star on the night of her Broadway debut. Preston and pals, as N.Y.C. stage folk, guide the viewer challengingly through countless twists and turns. Above average.▼

Reign of Terror (1949) **89m. *** D:** Anthony Mann. Robert Cummings, Arlene Dahl, Richard Hart, Richard Basehart, Arnold Moss, Beulah Bondi. Vivid costume drama set during French Revolution, with valuable diary eluding both sides of battle; retitled: BLACK BOOK.

Reincarnation of Peter Proud, The (1975) **C-104m. **½ D:** J. Lee Thompson. Michael Sarrazin, Jennifer O'Neill, Margot Kidder, Cornelia Sharpe, Paul Hecht, Tony Stephano. The soul of a man murdered years before roosts inside Sarrazin, in moderately gripping version of Max Ehrlich's book, adapted by the author.▼

Reivers, The (1969) **C-107m. ***½ D:** Mark Rydell. Steve McQueen, Sharon Farrell, Will Geer, Michael Constantine, Rupert Crosse, Mitch Vogel, Lonny Chapman, Juano Hernandez, Clifton James. Picaresque film from Faulkner novel about young boy (Vogel) in 1905 Mississippi who takes off for adventurous automobile trip with devil-may-care McQueen and buddy Crosse. Completely winning Americana, full of colorful episodes, equally colorful characters.▼

Relentless (1948) **C-93m. **½ D:** George Sherman. Robert Young, Marguerite Chapman, Willard Parker, Akim Tamiroff. Satisfactory Western about cowpoke and his gal trying to prove him innocent of murder charge.

Relentless (1977) **C-100m. TVM D:** Lee H. Katzin. Will Sampson, Monte Markham, John Hillerman, Mariana Hill, Larry Wilcox, John Lawlor. Stark chase movie that has American Indian state trooper pursuing a band of bank robbers and their hostage through the Arizona mountains. Sampson makes an imposing if offbeat hero. Average.

Relentless (1989) **C-93m. *½ D:** William Lustig. Judd Nelson, Robert Loggia, Leo Rossi, Meg Foster, Patrick O'Bryan, Ken Lerner, Mindy Seeger, Angel Tompkins. Nelson gives his one memorable performance to date, as a serial killer. Otherwise thoroughly routine, and that goes double for the finale.▼

Reluctant Astronaut, The (1967) **C-101m.** ** D: Edward Montagne. Don Knotts, Leslie Nielsen, Joan Freeman, Arthur

O'Connell, Jesse White. Featherweight comedy dealing with hicksville alumnus Knotts becoming title figure; predictable and often not even childishly humorous. For kids only.

Reluctant Debutante, The (1958) **C-94m.** **½ D: Vincente Minnelli. Rex Harrison, Kay Kendall, John Saxon, Sandra Dee, Angela Lansbury. Bright drawing-room comedy which Harrison, Kendall, and Lansbury make worthwhile: British parents must present their Americanized daughter to society.

Reluctant Dragon, The (1941) **C/B&W-72m. *** D:** Alfred L. Werker (live-action). Robert Benchley gets a tour of the Walt Disney studio in this pleasant feature that incorporates a number of first-rate cartoon sequences (*Baby Weems, The Reluctant Dragon*), offers some interesting glimpses of studio at work. Clarence "Ducky" Nash and Florence Gill do cartoon voices, Ward Kimball animates Goofy, Frances Gifford shows Benchley around, and young Alan Ladd appears as one of the story men. Opens in black and white, turns to beautiful Technicolor hues.▼

Reluctant Heroes, The (1971) **C-73m.** TVM D: Robert Day. Ken Berry, Jim Hutton, Trini Lopez, Don Marshall, Ralph Meeker, Cameron Mitchell, Warren Oates. Odd assortment of soldiers collected to take pivotal Hill 656 under command of Army historian with no combat experience. Excellent performances work well with dialogue which would've been ruined in other hands. Above average.

Reluctant Saint, The (1962-U.S.-Italian) **105m. **½ D:** Edward Dmytryk. Maximilian Schell, Ricardo Montalban, Lea Padovani, Akim Tamiroff, Harold Goldblatt, Mark Damon. Loosely biographical account of St. Joseph of Cupertino, a 17th-century Franciscan whose modest upbringing and simple intellect would never have foretold the religious life he would lead (or the great number of miracles he would perform). Unusual fare; worth a look.

Reluctant Spy, The (1963-French) **93m.** **½ D: Jean-Charles Dudrumet. Jean Marais, Genevieve Page, Maurice Teynac, Jean Gallar. Marais properly spoofs James Bond spy thrillers as secret agent chasing around the Continent.

Reluctant Widow, The (1951-British) **86m.** *½ D: Bernard Knowles. Jean Kent, Guy Rolfe, Kathleen Byron, Paul Dupuis. Mild drama set in late 18th century, of governess Kent marrying rogue Rolfe.

Remains to Be Seen (1953) **89m. *** D:** Don Weis. Van Johnson, June Allyson, Angela Lansbury, Louis Calhern, Dorothy Dandridge. Disarming comedy based on Howard Lindsay-Russel Crouse play, with Allyson a singer and Johnson the apartment-house manager involved in swank East

Side N.Y.C. murder; script by Sidney Sheldon.

Remarkable Andrew, The (1942) **80m.** **½ D: Stuart Heisler. William Holden, Ellen Drew, Brian Donlevy, Rod Cameron, Porter Hall, Nydia Westman, Montagu Love, Jimmy Conlin. Donlevy is the ghost of Andrew Jackson, who comes back to help crusading Holden in small town. Farfetched fantasy, well played; written by Dalton Trumbo.

Remarkable Mr. Pennypacker, The (1959) **C-87m.** **½ D: Henry Levin. Clifton Webb, Dorothy McGuire, Charles Coburn, Ray Stricklyn, Jill St. John, Ron Ely, David Nelson. Prodded along by Webb's brittle manner, period tale unfolds of Pennsylvania businessman who leads dual life, with two families (seventeen kids in all).

Rembrandt (1936-British) **84m.** ***½ D: Alexander Korda. Charles Laughton, Elsa Lanchester, Gertrude Lawrence, Edward Chapman, Roger Livesey, Raymond Huntley, John Clements, Marius Goring, Abraham Sofaer. Handsome Korda bio of Dutch painter, full of visual tableaux and sparked by Laughton's excellent performance. One of Gertrude Lawrence's rare film appearances.▼

Remedy for Riches (1940) **60m.** ** D: Erle C. Kenton. Jean Hersholt, Dorothy Lovett, Edgar Kennedy, Jed Prouty, Walter Catlett, Maude Eburne, Robert Baldwin, Warren Hull. There's more comedy than drama in this moderately entertaining *Dr. Christian* series entry. A swindler "uncovers" oil in dear old River's End, and the townsfolk line up to invest their hard-earned savings.▼

Remember? (1939) **83m.** ** D: Norman Z. McLeod. Robert Taylor, Greer Garson, Lew Ayres, Billie Burke, Reginald Owen, Laura Hope Crews, Henry Travers, Sig Ruman. Blah comedy about bickering couple taking potion which gives them amnesia—whereupon they fall in love all over again. Nice try, but no cigar.

Remember Last Night? (1935) **81m.** **½ D: James Whale. Edward Arnold, Constance Cummings, Robert Young, Sally Eilers, Robert Armstrong, Reginald Denny, Monroe Owsley, Gustav von Seyffertitz, Arthur Treacher. Freewheeling, perpetually tipsy couple find themselves—and their society friends—involved with multiple murders; detective Arnold tries to get them to take matters seriously enough to solve the mystery. Lightheaded comedy-whodunit is more shrill than funny, though stellar cast of character actors and Whale's trademarked stylistics make it worth watching.

Remember My Name (1978) **C-96m.** *** D: Alan Rudolph. Geraldine Chaplin, Anthony Perkins, Moses Gunn, Berry Berenson, Jeff Goldblum, Timothy Thomerson,

Alfre Woodard. Dream-like film presents fragmented story of woman returning from prison, determined to disrupt her ex-husband's new life. Moody, provocative film definitely not for all tastes; striking blues vocals on soundtrack by Alberta Hunter. Produced by Robert Altman.

Remember the Day (1941) **85m.** *** D: Henry King. Claudette Colbert, John Payne, John Shepperd (Shepperd Strudwick), Ann B. Todd, Douglas Croft, Jane Seymour, Anne Revere. Sentimental flashback story of pre-WW1 America, with fine performances by Colbert and Payne as schoolteachers who fall in love.

Remember the Night (1940) **94m.** *** D: Mitchell Leisen. Barbara Stanwyck, Fred MacMurray, Beulah Bondi, Elizabeth Patterson, Sterling Holloway. Beautifully made, sentimental story of prosecutor MacMurray falling in love with shoplifter Stanwyck during Christmas court recess; builds masterfully as it creates a very special mood. Script by Preston Sturges.

Remember When (1974) **C-100m. TVM** D: Buzz Kulik. Jack Warden, Robby Benson, Jamie Smith-Jackson, William Schallert, Tim Matheson, Nan Martin, Robert Middleton. Nostalgic drama centering around a suburban family with four boys in combat in WW2. Warden is tops as the live-in uncle filled with memories. Written by Herman Raucher, author of SUMMER OF '42. Above average.

Remembrance of Love (1982) **C-100m. TVM** D: Jack Smight. Kirk Douglas, Pam Dawber, Chana Eden, Robert Clary, Yoram Gall, Michael Goodwin, Eric Douglas. Widower has an emotional reunion with a woman he had loved as a teenager in the Warsaw Ghetto forty years earlier. Melodramatically written by Harold Jack Bloom. Average.▼

Remo Williams: The Adventure Begins . . . (1985) **C-121m.** **½ D: Guy Hamilton. Fred Ward, Joel Grey, Wilford Brimley, J. A. Preston, George Coe, Charles Cioffi, Kate Mulgrew, Michael Pataki, William Hickey. Bubble-gum action-adventure yarn based on the popular *Destroyer* books by Richard Sapir and Warren Murphy, with Ward a N.Y.C. cop recruited by secret society out to avenge society's wrongs (motto: "Thou shalt not get away with it") . . . then he's trained for job by inscrutable Korean Sinanju master (Grey). Comes frustratingly close to scoring bulls-eye but misfires too many times—and goes on too long. ▼

Renaldo and Clara (1978) **C-292m.** BOMB. D: Bob Dylan. Bob Dylan, Sara Dylan, Sam Shepard, Ronee Blakley, Ronnie Hawkins, Joni Mitchell, Harry Dean Stanton, Arlo Guthrie, Bob Neuwirth, Joan Baez, Allen Ginsberg, Mick Ronson, Roberta Flack. Self-important, poorly made fictionalized account of Dylan's *Rolling Thunder Revue*. Dylan plays Renaldo; his wife Sara is Clara; Hawkins is Bob Dylan; Blakley is Mrs. Dylan; Neuwirth is The Masked Tortilla. Pretentious and obnoxious. Dylan later cut it to 122m.; what's left is mostly concert footage, but it doesn't help much. Sam Shepard's first film.

Rendezvous (1935) **91m.** ** D: William K. Howard. William Powell, Rosalind Russell, Binnie Barnes, Lionel Atwill, Cesar Romero. OK WW1 intrigue, with Powell assigned to office work instead of combat during war, running into notorious spy ring. Russell's "comedy" character is only obtrusive here.

Rendez-vous (1985-French) **C-82m.** *** D: André Téchiné. Juliette Binoche, Lambert Wilson, Wadeck Stanczak, Jean-Louis Trintignant, Olimpia Carlisi, Dominique Lavanant, Anne Wiazemsky. Stylish melodrama perceptively investigates the borderline between play-acting and real life as stage actress (Binoche) becomes involved with obsessive live-sex show star Wilson and his mentor, a renowned director (Trintignant). Morbid mood and extreme sex scenes may repel some audiences; stunning widescreen photography will suffer on TV.▼

Rendezvous at Midnight (1935) **64m.** ** D: Christy Cabanne. Ralph Bellamy, Valerie Hobson, Catherine Doucet, Irene Ware, Helen Jerome Eddy. Fair whodunit of city commissioner being murdered just as his replacement (Bellamy) begins to investigate his corrupt administration.

Rendezvous Hotel (1979) **C-100m. TVM** D: Peter H. Hunt. Bill Daily, Jeff Redford, Teddy Wilson, Edward Winter, Bruce French, Sean Garrison, Jeff Donnell. Formula smile-inducer about life in a breezy California resort hotel. A beached version of *Love Boat* is what this prospective series pilot adds up to. Average.

Rendezvous with Annie (1946) **89m.** **½ D: Allan Dwan. Eddie Albert, Faye Marlowe, Gail Patrick, Phillip Reed, C. Aubrey Smith, Raymond Walburn, William Frawley. Frantic comedy concerning G.I. Albert stationed in England who goes AWOL for a few days to see wife back in the States; engaging cast and some funny moments.

Renegade Girls SEE: **Caged Heat**▼

Renegades (1930) **84m.** ** D: Victor Fleming. Warner Baxter, Myrna Loy, Noah Beery, Gregory Gaye, George Cooper, C. Henry Gordon, Bela Lugosi. Stodgy story of renegades from Foreign Legion posted in Morocco, one of whom (Baxter) has been betrayed by seductive spy Loy. Complex story builds to offbeat, and downbeat, ending.

Renegades, The (1982) **C-100m. TVM** D: Roger Spottiswoode. Philip Casnoff, Patrick Swayze, Randy Brooks, Cheryl Tracy, Paul Mones, Angel Granados, Jr., Peter Kwong, Kurtwood Smith. Move *The Mod Squad* to the 80s, add a couple of ethnically balanced members, send the gang out to uncover a gun-running operation, and you've got this pilot to the subsequent short-lived series. Average.

Renegades (1989) **C-106m.** ** D: Jack Sholder. Kiefer Sutherland, Lou Diamond Phillips, Jami Gertz, Rob Knepper, Bill Smitrovich, Floyd Westerman. An undercover cop and a Lakota Indian put aside their differences to team up and chase down a criminal who's done them both wrong. Yet another buddy/cop movie which is just an excuse to keep stuntmen gainfully employed . . . though it does give Sutherland and Phillips a chance to use the gunslinging technique they learned in YOUNG GUNS. Maybe next time they'll even get a script!▼

Rent-a-Cop (1988) **C-96m.** BOMB D: Jerry London. Burt Reynolds, Liza Minnelli, James Remar, Richard Masur, Dionne Warwick, Bernie Casey, Robby Benson. Chicago dick Reynolds is suspended after his botched hotel drug bust leaves half a dozen dead; Minnelli's eyewitness hooker helps him track down the bullet-happy killer responsible. Burt seems fatigued but is at least easier to take than his costar's lounge-act prostie. Didn't the stars learn their lesson after LUCKY LADY?▼

Rentadick (1972-British) **C-94m.** ** D: Jim Clark. James Booth, Julie Ege, Ronald Fraser, Donald Sinden, Michael Bentine, Richard Briers, Spike Milligan. Out of the nether-land between *The Goon Show* and *Monty Python* comes this romp written by Python pals John Cleese and Graham Chapman, spoofing formula private-eye flicks. An experimental nerve gas that paralyzes from the waist down has been stolen and Rentadick, Inc. is hired to track down the culprits. The humor occasionally aims for the inspired heights later to be approached by the Python gang, and therein lies the interest.▼

Repeat Performance (1947) **93m.** *** D: Alfred L. Werker. Louis Hayward, Joan Leslie, Tom Conway, Benay Venuta, Richard Basehart, Virginia Field. On New Year's Eve, woman gets chance to relive the past year, leading up to the moment she murdered her husband. Fine premise smoothly executed in this B production; Basehart's first film. Remade for TV in 1989 as TURN BACK THE CLOCK.

Repentance (1987-Russian) **C-155m.** ** D: Tengiz Abuladze. Avtandil Makharadze, Zeinab Botsvadze, Ketevan Abuladze, Edisher Giorgobiani, Kakhi Kavsadze. A beloved city father dies, but why is his body mysteriously—and continuously—

exhumed? This allegory about small town smallmindedness and political repression offers a critical look at the Stalin era, and has been screened widely as a result of Mikhail Gorbachev's glasnost . . . but the result bogs down into a talkfest, and is much too obvious and boring. Completed in 1984; the final part of a trilogy, following THE PLEA (1968) and THE WISHING TREE (1977).▼

Replica of a Crime SEE: **Amuck**

Repo Man (1984) **C-92m.** **½ D: Alex Cox. Emilio Estevez, Harry Dean Stanton, Vonetta McGee, Olivia Barash, Sy Richardson, Tracey Walter, Susan Barnes, Fox Harris, The Circle Jerks. Instant cult-movie about a new-wave punk who takes a job repossessing cars. Mixes social satire and science-fiction with engaging results, though a little of this film goes a long way. Stanton is perfect as a career repo man who shows Estevez the ropes. Michael Nesmith was executive producer.▼

Report to the Commissioner (1975) **C-112m.** **½ D: Milton Katselas. Michael Moriarty, Yaphet Kotto, Susan Blakely, Hector Elizondo, Tony King, Michael McGuire, Dana Elcar, Robert Balaban, William Devane, Stephen Elliott, Richard Gere, Vic Tayback, Sonny Grosso. Rookie cop Moriarty accidentally kills undercover cop Blakely and becomes embroiled in department-wide cover-up. Brutal melodrama ranges from realistic to overblown; taut but not always convincing. Script by Abby Mann and Ernest Tidyman. Gere's film debut.▼

Reprieve SEE: **Convicts Four**▼

Reprisal! (1956) **C-74m.** **½ D: George Sherman. Guy Madison, Felicia Farr, Kathryn Grant, Michael Pate, Edward Platt. Madison has to clear himself of murder charge when a powerful rancher is killed. Decent cast in ordinary grade-B Western drama.

Reptile, The (1966-British) **C-90m.** *** D: John Gilling. Noel Willman, Jennifer Daniels, Ray Barrett, Jacqueline Pearce. Hammer chiller about village girl with strange power to change into snake receives excellent direction and sympathetic characterizations.

Reptilicus (1962) **C-90m.** ** D: Sidney Pink. Carl Ottosen, Ann Smyrner, Mimi Heinrich, Asbjorn Andersen, Marla Behrens. The tail of a prehistoric monster—recently discovered—spawns the full-sized beast. Good for laughs as script hits every conceivable monster-movie cliché, right to the final shot. Filmed in Denmark.

Repulsion (1965-British) **105m.** **** D: Roman Polanski. Catherine Deneuve, Ian Hendry, John Fraser, Patrick Wymark, Yvonne Furneaux, James Villiers. Polanski's first English-language film is excellent psychological shocker depicting mental deterioration of sexually repressed girl left alone in her sister's apartment for several days. Hasn't lost a bit of its impact; will leave you feeling uneasy for days afterward. Screenplay by Polanski and Gerald Brach.▼

Requiem for a Gunfighter (1965) **C-91m.** *½ D: Spencer G. Bennet. Rod Cameron, Stephen McNally, Mike Mazurki, Olive Sturgess, Tim McCoy, John Mack Brown, Bob Steele, Lane Chandler, Raymond Hatton. Veteran cast is sole virtue of low-budget Western. Cameron impersonates a judge to insure that justice is done at murder trial.

Requiem for a Heavyweight (1962) **100m.** *** D: Ralph Nelson. Anthony Quinn, Jackie Gleason, Mickey Rooney, Julie Harris, Nancy Cushman, Madame Spivy, Cassius Clay (Muhammad Ali). Grim account of fighter whose ring career is over, forcing him into corruption and degradation. Rooney as pathetic cohort and Harris as unrealistic social worker are fine. Adapted by Rod Serling from his great teleplay; footage added to 87m. theatrical release for television.

Requiem for a Secret Agent (1965-Italian) **C-105m.** *½ D: Sergio Sollima. Stewart Granger, Daniela Bianchi, Giorgia Moll, Peter Van Eyck. English adventurer called upon by U.S. secret service to fight enemy spy network. Requiescat in pace.

Rescue, The (1988) **C-98m.** BOMB D: Ferdinand Fairfax. Kevin Dillon, Christina Harnos, Marc Price, Ned Vaughan, Ian Giatti, Charles Haid, Edward Albert. Dumb, obnoxious actioner featuring the exploits of a group of teens as they attempt to liberate their POW dads—and really do Rambo proud in the process. A sick movie aimed at less discriminating 13-year-old boys.▼

Rescue From Gilligan's Island (1978) **C-107m.** TVM D: Les Martinson. Bob Denver, Alan Hale, Jim Backus, Natalie Schaefer, Russell Johnson, Dawn Wells, Judith Baldwin. The hapless TV castaways (with Baldwin replacing Tina Louise) return 14 years after washing ashore on their uncharted desert isle in the first of three pilots to a prospective new silly-time series. Below average.

Resting Place (1986) **C-100m.** TVM D: John Korty. John Lithgow, Richard Bradford, Morgan Freeman, CCH Pounder, G. D. Spradlin, Frances Sternhagen, M. Emmet Walsh. Army officer encounters racial tension while trying to secure the burial of a black Vietnam War hero in an all-white Georgia cemetery in the 1970s. Beautiful script by Walter Halsey Davis, well performed by all. Above average.

Rest Is Silence, The (1960-German) **106m.** *** D: Helmut Kautner, Hardy Kruger, Peter Van Eyck, Ingrid Andree, Adelheid

Seeck, Rudolf Forster, Boy Gobert. Updating of Hamlet, with young man trying to prove uncle killed his father.
Restless Breed, The (1957) **C-81m. ****
D: Allan Dwan. Scott Brady, Anne Bancroft, Jim Davis, Scott Marlowe, Evelyn Rudie. Usual Western fare of Brady out to get his father's killer.
Restless Years, The (1958) **86m. **½ D:**
Helmut Kautner. John Saxon, Sandra Dee, Margaret Lindsay, Teresa Wright, James Whitmore. Capable cast in overblown melodramatics involving small-town life, the generation gap, skeletons in family closets, etc.
Resurrection (1980) **C-103m. ***½ D:**
Daniel Petrie. Ellen Burstyn, Sam Shepard, Richard Farnsworth, Roberts Blossom, Clifford David, Pamela Payton-Wright, Eva LeGallienne. Beautifully realized story (by Lewis John Carlino) about a woman who returns to life from the brink of death with amazing healing powers. Burstyn's moving performance is the centerpiece of a wonderful and underrated film.▼
Resurrection of Zachary Wheeler, The (1971) **C-100m. ***** D: Bob Wynn. Angie Dickinson, Bradford Dillman, James Daly, Leslie Nielsen, Jack Carter. Offbeat mixture of sci-fi and action. U.S. Senator brought to mysterious clinic in Alamogordo, New Mexico after car crash, is accidentally recognized by TV reporter. Only unconvincing aspect: fadeout explanation by clinic director. Shot on video, then transferred to film.▼
Resurrection Syndicate, The SEE: **Nothing But The Night**▼
Retik, the Moon Menace (1952) **100m. *½ D:** Fred C. Brannon. George Wallace, Aline Towne, Roy Barcroft, William Bakewell, Clayton Moore. Ludicrous low-grade cliffer from Republic, introducing Commando Cody, who zooms through space with his jet pack, combating alien lunar powers trying to conquer Earth. Reedited from serial RADAR MEN FROM THE MOON.▼
Retreat, Hell! (1952) **95m. **½ D:** Joseph H. Lewis. Frank Lovejoy, Richard Carlson, Russ Tamblyn, Anita Louise. Grim drama chronicling the Marine withdrawal from Korea's Changjin Reservoir in the wake of a massive Chinese offensive.▼
Retribution (1988) **C-107m.** BOMB D: Guy Magar. Dennis Lipscomb, Leslie Wing, Suzanne Snyder, Jeff Pomerantz, George Murdock, Pamela Dunlap, Hoyt Axton. Hokey, derivative supernatural horror film in which Lipscomb is possessed by a dead man's spirit that forces him to seek out the guy's murderers for vengeance sake. Hyped-up special effects and musical score, plus miserable acting, make this one a chore to watch.▼
Return, The (1980) **C-91m.** BOMB D:

Greydon Clark. Jan-Michael Vincent, Cybill Shepherd, Martin Landau, Raymond Burr, Neville Brand, Brad Rearden, Vincent Schiavelli. Deadeningly dull story of a "close encounter" and how it affects two children and an old man in a small New Mexico town. Inept from start to finish. Retitled THE ALIEN'S RETURN.▼
Return (1985) **C-82m. **** D: Andrew Silver. Karlene Crockett, John Walcutt, Lisa Richards, Frederic Forrest, Anne Lloyd Francis. Hokey, superficial tale of Crockett attempting to understand and unravel the mystery of her grandfather's death. Her investigation leads her to his birthplace and a series of bizarre secrets. Interesting premise, disappointing result.▼
Return from the Ashes (1965-British) **105m. ***** D: J. Lee Thompson. Maximilian Schell, Samantha Eggar, Ingrid Thulin, Herbert Lom, Talitha Pol. Engrossing melodrama of a philandering husband taking up with his stepdaughter when his wife is supposedly killed. Trio of stars lend credibility to the far-fetched proceedings.
Return from the Past (1967) **C-84m.** BOMB D: David L. Hewitt. Lon Chaney, John Carradine, Rochelle Hudson, Roger Gentry. Veteran stars wasted in utter monstrosity; five tales of supernatural told here are five too many. Original titles: DR. TERROR'S GALLERY OF HORRORS, THE BLOOD SUCKERS.▼
Return from the Sea (1954) **80m. **** D: Lesley Selander. Jan Sterling, Neville Brand, John Doucette, Paul Langton, John Pickard. Tepid story of Brand-Sterling romance, set in San Diego.
Return from Witch Mountain (1978) **C-95m. ***** D: John Hough. Bette Davis, Christopher Lee, Kim Richards, Ike Eisenman, Denver Pyle, Jack Soo, Dick Bakalyan. Sequel to ESCAPE TO WITCH MOUNTAIN has Davis and Lee kidnapping Eisenman, hoping to put his special powers to evil use. Good fun from Disney.▼
Returning Home (1975) **C-78m.** TVM D: Daniel Petrie. Dabney Coleman, Tom Selleck, James R. Miller, Whitney Blake, Joan Goodfellow, Sherry Jackson, Laurie Walters. Remake of the 1946 classic THE BEST YEARS OF OUR LIVES, with three returning WW2 vets facing the challenge of adjusting to civilian life. Or the pitfalls of telescoping a memorable film to 78 minutes. Average.
Return of a Man Called Horse, The (1976) **C-129m. ***** D: Irvin Kershner. Richard Harris, Gale Sondergaard, Geoffrey Lewis, Bill Lucking, Jorge Luke, Enrique Lucero. Excellent sequel has Harris returning from England to right wrongs done the Yellow Hand Sioux by whites. Sun Vow ceremony now performed by dozen braves. Magnificent score by Lau-

rence Rosenthal; followed by TRIUMPHS OF A MAN CALLED HORSE.▼

Return of a Stranger (1961-British) **63m.** **½ D: Max Varnel. John Ireland, Susan Stephen, Cyril Shaps, Timothy Beaton. Taut thriller of psychopath Shaps released from prison, terrorizing former victim Stephen and husband Ireland.

Return of Ben Casey, The (1988) **C-100m. TVM** D: Joseph L. Scanlan. Vince Edwards, Al Waxman, Gwynyth Walsh, Lynda Mason Green, Harry Landers. The fabled TV doctor returns (with Edwards as immobile as ever)—but this retread of the 1960s series pales next to newer medical shows like *St. Elsewhere*. Made in Canada with an all-Canadian cast. Average.

Return of Captain Invincible, The (1983-Australian-U.S) **C-90m.** **½ D: Philippe Mora. Alan Arkin, Christopher Lee, Kate Fitzpatrick, Michael Pate. Bizarre, campy, ambitious comedy about drunken, derelict ex-superhero persuaded to come out of retirement because of current predicament of world; sounds better than it works. Oddly placed musical numbers seem to aim for ROCKY HORROR ambiance but film is too badly paced for them to succeed. Also known as LEGEND IN LEOTARDS.▼

Return of Charlie Chan, The (1971) **C-97m. TVM** D: Leslie Martinson. Ross Martin, Leslie Nielsen, Louise Sorel, Richard Haydn, Don Gordon. Stale attempt at camping up the venerable detective series, with Charlie brought out of retirement to solve murders aboard a luxury yacht. Understandably, this sat on the studio shelf until 1979. Filmed as HAPPINESS IS A WARM CLUE. Below average.

Return of Count Yorga (1971) **C-97m.** **½ D: Bob Kelljan. Robert Quarry, Mariette Hartley, Roger Perry, Yvonne Wilder. The Count goes out for more blood, wreaking havoc on neighboring orphanage.

Return of Desperado, The (1988) **C-100m. TVM** D: E. W. Swackhamer. Alex McArthur, Robert Foxworth, Billy Dee Williams, Marcy Walker, Victor Love. Roving saddletramp comes to the aid of black homesteaders. Sequel to DESPERADO, which had turned out to be a surprise hit. Followed by DESPERADO: AVALANCHE AT DEVIL'S RIDGE. Average.

Return of Don Camillo, The (1965-Italian) **115m.** **½ D: Julien Duvivier. Fernandel, Gino Cervi, Charles Vissieres, Edouard Delmont. Fernandel is again the irresponsible smalltown Italian priest involved in more projects of goodwill.

Return of Dracula, The (1958) **77m.** ** D: Paul Landres. Francis Lederer, Norma Eberhardt, Ray Stricklyn, Jimmie Baird. Low-budget flick about the Count (Lederer) killing a man, taking his papers, and coming to U.S. Lederer thwarted by medium script. TV title: THE CURSE OF DRACULA.

Return of Dr. X, The (1939) **62m.** ** D: Vincent Sherman. Humphrey Bogart, Rosemary Lane, Dennis Morgan, John Litel, Huntz Hall, Wayne Morris. Only Bogart as a zombie makes this low-grade sci-fi yarn worth viewing. Despite the title, not a sequel to DR. X.

Return of Frank Cannon, The (1980) **C-96m. TVM** D: Corey Allen. William Conrad, Allison Argo, Arthur Hill, Burr DeBenning, Taylor Lacher, Diana Muldaur, Ed Nelson, Joanna Pettet, William Smithers, Rafael Campos. In the growing tradition of trying to revive former hit series, Cannon is brought out of semi-retirement to investigate the questionable suicide of an old friend and Army Intelligence colleague. Average.▼

Return of Frank James, The (1940) **C-92m.** *** D: Fritz Lang. Henry Fonda, Gene Tierney, Jackie Cooper, Henry Hull, John Carradine, J. Edward Bromberg, Donald Meek. Fonda reprises role from 1939 JESSE JAMES in story of attempt to avenge his brother's death; colorful production was Tierney's film debut.▼

Return of Jack Slade, The (1955) **79m.** ** D: Harold Schuster. John Ericson, Mari Blanchard, Neville Brand, Angie Dickinson. To redeem his father's wrongdoings, Ericson joins the law to fight outlaws; adequate Western.

Return of Jesse James, The (1950) **75m.** **½ D: Arthur Hilton. John Ireland, Ann Dvorak, Henry Hull, Hugh O'Brian, Reed Hadley. Compact budget Western dealing with rumors that lookalike for outlaw is notorious gunslinger.

Return of Joe Forrester, The SEE: Cop on the Beat

Return of Josey Wales, The (1986) **C-90m.** BOMB D: Michael Parks. Michael Parks, Rafael Campos, Bob Magruder, Paco Vela, Everett Sifuentes, Charlie McCoy. Incomprehensible sequel to OUTLAW . . . , minus Clint Eastwood,(!) with director-star Parks taking over the title role—and that's certainly no improvement. Here, Wales takes on, and repeatedly embarrasses, a determined but ineffectual lawman.▼

Return of Marcus Welby, M.D., The (1984) **C-100m. TVM** D: Alexander Singer. Robert Young, Darren McGavin, Morgan Stevens, Elena Verdugo, Jessica Walter, Cristina Raines, Dennis Haysbert. The kindly old family practitioner comes out of TV retirement only to learn that the hospital in which he works part-time is trying to strip him of his accreditation in favor of younger, more productive doctors. Pilot to a proposed new *Marcus Welby* series;

followed by MARCUS WELBY, M.D.: A HOLIDAY AFFAIR. Average.

Return of Martin Guerre, The (1982-French) **C-111m.** ***** D: Daniel Vigne. Gerard Depardieu, Nathalie Baye, Roger Planchon, Maurice Jacquemont, Bernard Pierre Donnadieu. Blockbuster art house hit, based on fact, about a sixteenth-century peasant who returns to his wife and family a much better person than the misfit he was seven years earlier; could it be that he's really an impostor? No artistic groundbreaker, but a solid romance and history lesson, well acted by the two leads.▼

Return of Maxwell Smart, The SEE: **Nude Bomb, The**

Return of Mickey Spillane's Mike Hammer, The (1986) **C-100m.** TVM D: Ray Danton. Stacy Keach, Lindsay Bloom, Don Stroud, Kent Williams, Lauren Hutton, Mickey Rooney, Vince Edwards, Leo Penn, Mike Preston, Dabney Coleman, Bruce Boxleitner, Dionne Warwick. Hammer chases a gang of renegade Vietnam vets whose racket is stealing and selling children in Hollywood. Rooney deftly pilfers it in a cameo as a gabby movie agent. Basically a pilot for the "new" Mike Hammer TV series following Keach's drug bust in England. Average.

Return of Monte Cristo, The (1946) **91m.** ** D: Henry Levin. Louis Hayward, Barbara Britton, George Macready, Una O'Connor, Henry Stephenson. Rather ordinary swashbuckler of original count's young descendant, thwarted in attempt to claim inheritance by dastardly villain.

Return of Mr. Moto, The (1965-British) **71m.** D: Ernest Morris. Henry Silva, Terence Longdon, Suzanne Lloyd, Marne Maitland, Martin Wyldeck. SEE: **Mr. Moto** series.

Return of October, The (1948) **C-98m.** ** D: Joseph H. Lewis. Glenn Ford, Terry Moore, Albert Sharpe, James Gleason, Steve Dunne. Moore is wholesome girl who thinks her horse (October) is a reincarnation of her favorite uncle, much to her relatives' consternation. Weird comedy written by Norman Panama and Melvin Frank.

Return of Peter Grimm, The (1935) **82m.** **½ D: George Nicholls, Jr. Lionel Barrymore, Helen Mack, Edward Ellis, Donald Meek, Allen Vincent. Patriarch of a close-knit family returns from the dead to make amends for all he did wrong in his lifetime. Hoary old David Belasco play gets full-blooded treatment from Barrymore and a cast of pros.

Return of Rin Tin Tin, The (1947) **C-65m.** *½ D: Max Nosseck. Bobby (Robert) Blake, Donald Woods, Rin Tin Tin (III), Claudia Drake, Gaylord Pendleton, Earl Hodgins. Easy-to-take low-budget tale of young boy who comes out of his shell

whenever he's with Rin Tin Tin, but bad man takes the dog away. Not too bad of this kind, but filmed in ultracheap Vitacolor process.

Return of Sabata, The (1972-Italian-Spanish) **C-106m.** *½ D: Frank Kramer (Gianfranco Parolini). Lee Van Cleef, Reiner Schone, Annabelle Incontrera, Jacqueline Alexandre, Pedro Sanchez (Ignazio Spalla). Last of the spaghetti Western series—and not a moment too soon—finds Van Cleef chasing down some baddies who bilked him out of $5,000.

Return of Sam McCloud, The (1989) **C-100m.** TVM D: Alan J. Levi. Dennis Weaver, J. D. Cannon, Terry Carter, Patrick Macnee, Kerrie Keane, Roger Rees, Melissa Anderson, David McCallum. *McCloud* reunion movie, set in England, has him now a U.S. senator involved in international intrigue, on the trail of a greedy pharmaceutical entrepreneur. Pilot to prospective revival series. Average.

Return of Sherlock Holmes, The (1987) **C-100m.** TVM D: Kevin Connor. Margaret Colin, Michael Pennington, Lila Kaye, Connie Booth, Nicholas Guest. Dr. Watson's modern-day great-granddaughter, a private eye from Boston, stumbles upon Sherlock Holmes' body in frozen suspension and restores the inimitable Victorian Era sleuth to life in the 1980s. Lighthearted fluff introducing Shakespearean actor Pennington to American audiences; this original bit of Holmesiana is not to be confused with the similarly titled British series with Jeremy Brett shown on PBS. Average.

Return of Sophie Lang, The (1936) **65m.** **½ D: George Archainbaud. Gertrude Michael, Sir Guy Standing, Ray Milland, Elizabeth Patterson, Colin Tapley, Paul Harvey. Jewel-thief-gone-straight Michael seeks Milland's help in staying out of public eye. OK low-budgeter.

Return of Swamp Thing, The (1989) **C-88m.** *½ D: Jim Wynorski. Dick Durock, Heather Locklear, Louis Jourdan, Sarah Douglas, Daniel Taylor, Ronreaco Lee, Ace Mask, Joey Sagal. It's back to the swamp in this sequel to SWAMP THING, as the vegetable man superhero learns that mad scientist Jourdan, who's been blending people with animals, has similar designs on his chirpy stepdaughter Locklear. Oafish spoof sequel to straight original can't find a style, and wastes time with two unfunny little boys. The comic books are much better.▼

Return of the Ape Man (1944) **60m.** ** D: Philip Rosen. Bela Lugosi, John Carradine, George Zucco, Judith Gibson, Michael Ames (Tod Andrews), Frank Moran, Mary Currier. Scientist Lugosi transplants Carradine's brain into body of recently discovered

Missing Link (Zucco!). Typical Monogram fare; no relation to THE APE MAN.

Return of the Bad Men (1948) **90m.** ****½** D: Ray Enright. Randolph Scott, Robert Ryan, Anne Jeffreys, George "Gabby" Hayes, Jacqueline White, Steve Brodie, Lex Barker. Newly settled Oklahoman Scott gets one female outlaw (Jeffreys) to go straight, but has a tougher time dealing with Billy the Kid, The Dalton Gang, The Younger Brothers, and a particularly nasty Sundance Kid (Ryan) in this routine Western. Also shown in computer-colored version.▼

Return of the Beverly Hillbillies (1981) **C-100m. TVM** D: Robert Leeds. Buddy Ebsen, Donna Douglas, Nancy Kulp, Linda Henning, Ray Young, Imogene Coca, Werner Klemperer, King Donovan, Lurene Tuttle, Earl Scruggs. The Clampetts are dragged out of comfortable retirement in TV heaven to help solve the country's energy crisis. Below average.

Return of the Dragon (1973-Hong Kong) **C-91m.** ****½** D: Bruce Lee. Bruce Lee, Chuck Norris, Nora Miao. Country hick Lee visits relatives who run Chinese restaurant in Italy and helps fight off gangsters trying to take over. Many fine comic and action sequences, including final battle with Chuck Norris in Roman Colosseum.▼

Return of the Fly, The (1959) **80m.** ****½** D: Edward L. Bernds. Vincent Price, Brett Halsey, David Frankham, John Sutton, Dan Seymour, Danielle De Metz. Adequate sequel to THE FLY proves "like father, like son." Youth attempts to reconstruct his late father's teleportation machine and likewise gets scrambled with an insect. Followed six years later by CURSE OF THE FLY.▼

Return of the Frontiersman (1950) **C-74m.** ****** D: Richard Bare. Gordon MacRae, Rory Calhoun, Julie London, Jack Holt, Fred Clark. Easygoing yarn of sheriff's son falsely accused of murder.

Return of the Gunfighter (1967) **C-100m. TVM** D: James Neilson. Robert Taylor, Chad Everett, Ana Martin, Mort Mills, Lyle Bettger. Likable Western, thanks mainly to excellent Taylor performance, as he comes to aid of accused killer and Mexican girl avenging death of her parents. Above average.▼

Return of the Hulk, The (1977) **C-100m. TVM** D: Alan Levi. Bill Bixby, Laurie Prange, Dorothy Tristan, William Daniels, Jack Colvin, Lou Ferrigno. Further adventures of the Marvel Comics favorite with Banner still searching for a cure for his growth affliction that uncontrollably transforms him into a raging beast. The hit series followed. Followed a decade later by THE INCREDIBLE HULK RETURNS. Average.

Return of the Jedi (1983) **C-133m.** *****½**

D: Richard Marquand. Mark Hamill, Harrison Ford, Carrie Fisher, Billy Dee Williams, Anthony Daniels, Peter Mayhew, Sebastian Shaw, Ian McDiarmid, David Prowse, Alec Guinness, Frank Oz, Kenny Baker, Denis Lawson, Warwick Davis, voices of James Earl Jones, Frank Oz. Third installment in the STAR WARS saga is a sheer delight, following the destiny of Luke Skywalker as his comrades reunite to combat a powerful Deathstar. Some lazy performances are compensated for by ingenious new characters and Oscar-winning special effects. More sentimental and episodic than its predecessors (and probably incomprehensible if you haven't seen them both) —but carried out in the best tradition of Saturday matinee serials, from which it draws its inspiration. Followed by two Ewok adventures for TV.▼

Return of the Killer Tomatoes! (1988) **C-99m.** ***½** D: John De Bello. Anthony Starke, George Clooney, Karen Mistal, Steve Lundquist, Charlie Jones, John Astin. Sequel to the cult item ATTACK OF THE KILLER TOMATOES!, this is an improvement, but still nothing much. In a tomato-fearing world, mad scientist Astin is turning tomatoes into people and vice-versa; our hero falls for an attractive one-time tomato. Too long, too silly, but has its moments.▼

Return of the Living Dead, The (1985) **C-90m.** ****** D: Dan O'Bannon. Clu Gulager, James Karen, Don Calfa, Thom Mathews, Beverly Randolph, John Philbin. What starts out as a spoof of George Romero's zombie films (with wonderful comic performance by Karen as supervisor of medical warehouse) loses its footing when the tone, and the violence, turn serious. Directing debut for sci-fi screenwriter O'Bannon. Followed by a sequel.▼

Return of the Living Dead Part II (1988) **C-89m.** ****** D: Ken Wiederhorn. James Karen, Thom Mathews, Michael Kenworthy, Marsha Dietlein, Dana Ashbrook, Suzanne Snyder. Awkward title identifies this as a sequel not to the George Romero zombie classics but rather the 1985 comedy offshoot. Inquisitive kids release deadly gas from a misplaced military canister, causing corpses from a nearby cemetery to rise and wreak havoc. OK effects.▼

Return of the Man from U.N.C.L.E., The (1983) **C-100m. TVM** D: Ray Austin. Robert Vaughn, David McCallum, Patrick Macnee, Tom Mason, Gayle Hunnicutt, Geoffrey Lewis, Anthony Zerbe, Keenan Wynn, George Lazenby. Great fun as Napoleon Solo and Illya Kuryakin return from the good life after fifteen years' retirement from the weekly TV grind and do battle once more with THRUSH's nefarious Justin Sepheran (Zerbe). Old chemistry between the stars is still there . . . and look for one-time James Bond Lazenby in an amusing cameo. Above average.▼

Return of the Mod Squad, The (1979) **C-100m. TVM** D: George McCowan. Michael Cole, Clarence Williams III, Peggy Lipton, Tige Andrews, Tom Bosley, Ross Martin, Victor Buono, Tom Ewell. The three former cops of the "flower child" generation come out of TV-rerun retirement, looking decidedly long of tooth, in search of new adventure and a possible new series to equal the success of their 1968-73 hit. Average.

Return of the Pink Panther, The (1975-British) **C-113m. **½** D: Blake Edwards. Peter Sellers, Christopher Plummer, Catherine Schell, Herbert Lom, Burt Kwouk, Peter Arne, Gregoire Aslan, Andre Maranne, Victor Spinetti. Fourth PANTHER film, and first with Sellers since A SHOT IN THE DARK. Inspector Clouseau is a superb comedy character, but director-writer Edwards thinks big, violent gags are funny. Best part of this diamond-heist farce is the opening title, animated by Richard Williams and Ken Harris. Immediate sequel—THE PINK PANTHER STRIKES AGAIN!—is much better.▼

Return of the Rebels (1981) **C-100m. TVM** D: Noel Nosseck. Barbara Eden, Don Murray, Christopher Connelly, Michael Baseleon, Patrick Swayze, Robert Mandan, Jamie Farr, DeAnna Robbins. Lighthearted drama about the reunion of a motorcycle gang 25 years later. Dig Ms. Eden as a biking mama. Average.▼

Return of the Scarlet Pimpernel, The (1938-British) **88m. **** D: Hans Schwartz. Barry K. Barnes, Sophie Stewart, Margaretta Scott, James Mason, Francis Lister, Anthony Bushell. Far below stunning original, with lower production values and less-than-stellar cast in costumer set in 1790s London and Paris. Original British running time: 94m.

Return of the Secaucus 7 (1980) **C-100m. *** D: John Sayles. Mark Arnott, Gordon Clapp, Maggie Cousineau, Adam Lefevre, Bruce MacDonald, Jean Passanante, Maggie Renzi, David Strathairn. A simple low-budget film about a weekend reunion of good friends who shared the 60s radical college life and have since gone in different directions. Credible, winning performances (including one by director-writer Sayles, as Howie) enhance a script that seems to tell the story of an entire generation. Filmed with unknown actors for a reported budget of $60,000! An interesting precursor to THE BIG CHILL.▼

Return of the Seven (1966) **C-96m. **** D: Burt Kennedy. Yul Brynner, Robert Fuller, Warren Oates, Jordan Christopher, Claude Akins, Emilio Fernandez. The gang has reformed for more protection in this drab sequel to THE MAGNIFICENT SEVEN; it was a lot more fun when Eli Wallach was the heavy. Followed by GUNS OF THE MAGNIFICENT SEVEN.▼

Return of the Shaggy Dog, The (1987) **C-100m. TVM** D: Stuart Gillard. Gary Kroeger, Todd Waring, Michelle Little, Cindy Morgan, Jane Carr, Gavin Reed, K Callan. Uninspired Disney sequel to the hit 1959 fantasy (that simply ignores the existence of the other theatrical follow-up, THE SHAGGY D.A.). Average.

Return of the Six-Million-Dollar Man and the Bionic Woman, The (1987) **C-100m. TVM** D: Ray Austin. Lee Majors, Lindsay Wagner, Richard Anderson, Martin Landau, Gary Lockwood, Tom Schanley, Lee Majors II. Reunion show for the characters of two hit series of the 1970s finds the bionically rebuilt son of Steve Austin (Majors) following in his dad's footsteps with the help of the Bionic Woman. Schanley plays Majors' son, while Majors' real-life son is the brash new assistant of Oscar Goldman (Anderson). Pilot for a "new" series which never materialized—though they tried again with BIONIC SHOWDOWN: THE SIX MILLION DOLLAR MAN AND THE BIONIC WOMAN. Average.

Return of the Soldier, The (1981-British) **C-101m. **** D: Alan Bridges. Alan Bates, Julie Christie, Glenda Jackson, Ann-Margret, Ian Holm, Frank Finlay. A shell-shocked soldier comes home from WW1 with no memory of the last twenty years, but feels a vague dissatisfaction with his life, as personified by wife Christie. Fine cast in this adaptation of Rebecca West's first novel, but it's slow going, and ultimately not that interesting.▼

Return of the Tall Blond Man With One Black Shoe, The (1974-French) **C-84m. **½** D: Yves Robert. Pierre Richard, Mireille Darc, Michel Duchaussoy, Jean Rochefort, Jean Carmet. Sequel to the 1972 hit reunites the principals for a lesser if still entertaining sendup of the spy game. Spy chief Rochefort wants violinist Richard killed, but the tall blond avoids danger without even realizing what's happening. Nice shots of Rio and a fairly deft James Bond takeoff help offset slow buildup.▼

Return of the Texan (1952) **88m. ** D: Delmer Daves. Dale Robertson, Joanne Dru, Walter Brennan, Richard Boone, Robert Horton. Flabby Western about Robertson et al fighting to save his ranch.

Return of the Vampire, The (1943) **69m. **** D: Lew Landers, Kurt Neumann. Bela Lugosi, Frieda Inescort, Nina Foch, Roland Varno, Miles Mander, Matt Willis. Lugosi plays a vampire in wartorn London (with a werewolf assistant!) in limp attempt to capitalize on previous success as Dracula. Final scene is memorable, though.▼

Return of the Whistler, The (1948) **63m.**

D: D. Ross Lederman. Michael Duane, Lenore Aubert, Richard Lane, James Cardwell, Ann Doran. SEE: **Whistler** series.

Return of the World's Greatest Detective, The (1976) **C-78m. TVM** D: Dean Hargrove. Larry Hagman, Jenny O'Hara, Nicholas Colasanto, Woodrow Parfrey, Helen Verbit, Ivor Francis. Bumbling motorcycle cop believes he actually is Sherlock Holmes and is aided in this delusion by psychiatric social worker named Doc Watson. Enjoyable comedy/drama, mixing slapstick with elements of THEY MIGHT BE GIANTS. Average.

Return to Boggy Creek (1977) **C-87m.** ** D: Tom Moore. Dawn Wells, Dana Plato. More sightings of monsters in this sequel to THE LEGEND OF BOGGY CREEK, but this time two children are involved. G-rated nonsense may intrigue young viewers. Followed by THE BARBARIC BEAST OF BOGGY CREEK PART II, which is actually the third Boggy Creek film.▼

Return to Earth (1976) **C-78m. TVM** D: Jud Taylor. Cliff Robertson, Ralph Bellamy, Shirley Knight, Charles Cioffi, Stefanie Powers. Robertson is A-OK in real-life drama of the breakdown of astronaut Buzz Aldrin after his 1969 moonwalk. Adapted by George Malko from the book Aldrin wrote with Wayne Warga. Above average.▼

Return to Fantasy Island (1977) **C-100m. TVM** D: George McCowan. Ricardo Montalban, Adrienne Barbeau, Joseph Campanella, Joseph Cotten, Laraine Day, Cameron Mitchell, Karen Valentine, George Chakiris, George Maharis, France Nuyen, Horst Buchholz, Herve Villechaize. Dapper Mr. Roarke and his diminutive pal Tattoo host the regular complement of guest stars seeking dream fulfillment in this second pilot to the hit series. Average.▼

Return to Macon County (1975) **C-90m.** *½ D: Richard Compton. Don Johnson, Nick Nolte, Robin Mattson, Robert Viharo, Eugene Daniels, Matt Greene. Unworthy follow-up to MACON COUNTY LINE, as youngsters get mixed up in drag races, sex, the law, violence and murder, in about that order. Nolte's first film.▼

Return to Mayberry (1986) **C-100m. TVM** D: Bob Sweeney. Andy Griffith, Ron Howard, Don Knotts, Jim Nabors, Aneta Corsaut, Jack Dodson, George Lindsay, Betty Lynn. Wonderfully nostalgic update of *The Andy Griffith Show* with Andy Taylor returning to Mayberry after nearly 20 years to seek his old job as sheriff again, only to find that former deputy Barney Fife is running for it and on the verge of finally marrying Thelma Lou. Sixteen of the original actors reunited along with most of the original production crew (producers, director, writers, etc.) for this hugely successful TV movie recreating a happy slice of television Americana. Above average.▼

Return to Oz (1985) **C-110m.** ** D: Walter Murch. Nicol Williamson, Jean Marsh, Fairuza Balk, Piper Laurie, Matt Clark. Distressingly downbeat sequel to THE WIZARD OF OZ, with Dorothy fleeing a spooky sanitarium in Kansas to return to her beloved land—only to find evil rulers now in charge. Many colorful characters, but few engender any warmth or feeling. Best moments involve Will Vinton's Claymation effects, where rock faces come to life. Best sequence: final showdown with the Nome King. Inauspicious directing debut for celebrated sound technician Murch (who cowrote script). ▼

Return to Paradise (1953) **C-100m.** ** D: Mark Robson. Gary Cooper, Roberta Haynes, Barry Jones, Moira MacDonald. Lackluster South Sea tale of beach bum Cooper in love with native girl; loosely based on James Michener's story. Filmed in Samoa.

Return to Peyton Place (1961) **C-122m.** ** D: Jose Ferrer. Carol Lynley, Jeff Chandler, Eleanor Parker, Mary Astor, Robert Sterling, Luciana Paluzzi, Brett Halsey, Gunnar Hellstrom, Tuesday Weld, Bob Crane. Muddled follow-up to PEYTON PLACE suffers from faulty direction, and, save for stalwarts Astor and Parker, miscasting. Followed by TV movie MURDER IN PEYTON PLACE.

Return to Salem's Lot, A (1987) **C-96m.** ** D: Larry Cohen. Michael Moriarty, Ricky Addison Reed, Samuel Fuller, Andrew Duggan, Evelyn Keyes, Jill Gatsby, June Havoc, Ronee Blakely, James Dixon, David Holbrook. Anthropologist Moriarty, trying to befriend his estranged son, is lured to a small Maine town where the populace—almost all vampires—want him to write their history. Typically cheap, oddball Cohen film, which he cowrote, has little to do with Stephen King's novel or the TV miniseries based on it.▼

Return to Sender (1963-British) **63m.** ** D: Gordon Hales. Nigel Davenport, Yvonne Romain, Geoffrey Keen, William Russell, John Horsley. Programmer action tale of revenge, based on Edgar Wallace yarn of industrialist's plot to ruin career and life of a D.A.

Return to Snowy River (1988-Australian) **C-97m.** **½ D: Geoff Burrowes. Tom Burlinson, Sigrid Thornton, Brian Dennehy, Nicholas Eadie, Bryan Marshall. Follow-up to THE MAN FROM SNOWY RIVER is not nearly as good. Young Burlinson must again prove his worth as he battles villainous Eadie, who's become engaged to his beloved (Thornton). All those shots of galloping horses, however, are still eye-popping.▼

Return to the Edge of the World (1978-

British) **C/B&W-85m.** *** D: Michael Powell. Michael Powell, John Laurie, Hamish Sutherland. In the mid-1930s Powell directed a drama about the depopulation of an island, THE EDGE OF THE WORLD, shot on location on Foula in the North Sea. Forty years later and the cast and crew still living—most poignantly, the actor John Laurie—returned for a reunion. This fascinating film includes footage of this trip, plus the original feature.

Return to Treasure Island (1954) **C-75m.** *½ D: E. A. Dupont, Tab Hunter, Dawn Addams, Porter Hall, James Seay, Harry Lauter. Poor updating of Stevenson novel, with student Hunter vying with crooks for buried treasure.

Return to Warbow (1958) **C-67m.** *½ D: Ray Nazarro. Phil Carey, Catherine McLeod, Andrew Duggan, William Leslie. Pedestrian narrative of outlaws backtracking to site of crime to collect loot left behind.

Reuben, Reuben (1983) **C-101m.** *** D: Robert Ellis Miller. Tom Conti, Kelly McGillis, Roberts Blossom, Cynthia Harris, E. Katherine Kerr, Joel Fabiani, Kara Wilson, Lois Smith. Boozy Scottish poet (an amalgam of Dylan Thomas and Brendan Behan) sponges off hospitable women in New England college town—then falls in love with beautiful young student McGillis (in her film debut). Deliciously witty script by Julius J. Epstein (adapted from writings of Peter DeVries) and fine performances help offset general feeling of anachronism about the film . . . and a curious finale.▼

Reunion (1980) **C-100m.** TVM D: Russ Mayberry. Kevin Dobson, Joanna Cassidy, Linda Hamilton, Lew Ayres, George DiCenzo, Conchata Ferrell, Rick Lenz, Nicholas Pryor, Nick Cassavetes. A 20th high school reunion sets the scene for a married man to meet his old sweetheart and become attracted to her teenaged daughter. Average.

Reunion at Fairborough (1985) **C-110m.** TVM D: Herbert Wise. Robert Mitchum, Deborah Kerr, Red Buttons, Judi Trott, Barry Morse. And a disappointing, overly talky reunion it is for Mitchum and Kerr (together for the fourth time—after 25 years) as a former American flyer and the British girl he seduced and abandoned during WW2. Written by Albert Ruben; co-produced by Alan King. Made for cable. Average.

Reunion in France (1942) **104m.** ** D: Jules Dassin. Joan Crawford, John Wayne, Philip Dorn, Reginald Owen, Albert Bassermann, John Carradine, Henry Daniell. Glossy romance, with Crawford and Wayne trying to flee Nazi-occupied France; propaganda elements date badly.▼

Reunion in Reno (1951) **79m.** **½ D: Kurt Neumann. Mark Stevens, Peggy Dow, Gigi Perreau, Frances Dee, Leif Erickson. Diverting comedy of Perreau deciding to divorce her parents so she won't be in the way.

Reunion in Vienna (1933) **98m.** *** D: Sidney Franklin. John Barrymore, Diana Wynyard, Frank Morgan, May Robson, Eduardo Ciannelli, Una Merkel, Henry Travers. Too-literal adaptation of Robert Sherwood's dated stage play depends on its stars' considerable charm to come across. Barrymore (who seems to have wandered in from another movie) provides most of the film's life with hilarious performance as exiled nobleman who returns to Vienna and tries to rekindle romance with Wynyard under the nose of her tolerant husband (Morgan).

Reveille with Beverly (1943) **78m.** ** D: Charles Barton. Ann Miller, William Wright, Dick Purcell, Franklin Pangborn, Larry Parks. Columbia Pictures mini-musical, with Miller a versatile disk jockey throwing ''big show'' for servicemen. Jazz fans will shoot that rating higher, since guest stars include Frank Sinatra, Mills Brothers, Bob Crosby, Count Basie, and Duke Ellington.

Revenge (1971-British) SEE: **Inn of the Frightened People**▼

Revenge (1971) **C-78m.** TVM D: Jud Taylor. Shelley Winters, Stuart Whitman, Bradford Dillman, Carol Rossen, Roger Perry, Gary Clarke. Winters plots to avenge her daughter's rape by imprisoning the man she suspects of the deed in a cage in her basement. Shelley tears it up in Joseph Stefano's adaptation of Elizabeth Davis' novel, and John A. Alonzo's striking photography doesn't hurt one bit. Above average.

Revenge (1979) SEE: **Blood Feud**▼

Revenge (1986) **C-100m.** BOMB D: Christopher Lewis. Patrick Wayne, John Carradine, Bennie Lee McGowan. Boring, filmed sequel to the videotaped horror opus BLOOD CULT details the further goings-on of a Tulsa, Oklahoma, devil-worship cult led this time by (who else?) Carradine, that preys on students for human sacrifices. Strictly for fans of mindless violence; never released theatrically. Director Lewis is (gulp!) Loretta Young's son.▼

Revenge (1990) **C-124m.** *½ D: Tony Scott. Kevin Costner, Anthony Quinn, Madeleine Stowe, Sally Kirkland, Tomas Milian, Joaquin Martinez, James Gammon, Miguel Ferrer, Joe Santos. Navy pilot Costner (yes, Tony—we *know* you directed TOP GUN) visits power-broker pal Quinn at the latter's posh Mexican estate; soon he and Stowe (Quinn's young Mrs.) are enjoying a closet quickie, in both senses of the term. Ponderous mix of the slick and the sordid died at the box office despite Kevin's clout; the second half—source of the film's title—is especially tough to endure.▼

Revenge for a Rape (1976) **C-100m. TVM** D: Timothy Galfas. Mike Connors, Tracy Brooks Swope, Robert Reed, Deanna Lund, Larry Watson. Predictable drama of a lone vigilante (Connors) who relentlessly tracks the three men who raped his wife. Average.

Revenge Is My Destiny (1971) **C-95m.** *½ D: Joseph Adler. Sidney Blackmer, Chris Robinson, Elisa Ingram, Joe E. Ross. Vietnam vet (Robinson) returns to Miami only to find wife missing and stumbles upon sordid maze of events that lead to her death. Script has too many loopholes and does not use locations effectively.

Revenge of Al Capone, The (1989) **C-100m. TVM** D: Michael Pressman. Ray Sharkey, Keith Carradine, Debrah Farentino, Charles Haid, Scott Paulin, Jayne Atkinson, Charles Hallahan. Good old-fashioned gangster flick sparked by Sharkey's flamboyant Capone—conducting business behind bars—and Carradine as the Fed who put him there, upstaging an incensed Eliot Ness. Written with verve by Tracy Keenan Wynn. Above average.

Revenge of Frankenstein (1958-British) **C-91m.** *** D: Terence Fisher. Peter Cushing, Francis Matthews, Eunice Gayson, Michael Gwynn, Lionel Jeffries, John Welsh. Sequel to THE CURSE OF FRANKENSTEIN is quite effective with the good doctor still making a new body from others, ably assisted by hunchback dwarf and young medical student. Thought-provoking script has fine atmosphere, especially in color. Followed by THE EVIL OF FRANKENSTEIN.

Revenge of the Creature (1955) **82m.** ** D: Jack Arnold. John Agar, Lori Nelson, John Bromfield, Nestor Paiva, Robert B. Williams. OK sequel to THE CREATURE FROM THE BLACK LAGOON destroys much of that film's mystery and terror by removing gill-man from Amazonian home and placing him in Florida aquarium. Originally in 3D. Clint Eastwood has his first screen role as lab technician; sort of remade as JAWS 3-D.

Revenge of the Dead (1960) **69m. BOMB** D: Edward D. Wood, Jr. Duke Moore, Kenne Duncan, Paul Marco, Tor Johnson, John Carpenter, Valda Hansen, Jeannie Stevens, Criswell. Long-lost sequel to BRIDE OF THE MONSTER (and to a lesser extent, PLAN 9 FROM OUTER SPACE) doesn't reach the same heights of lunacy, but is still dreadful enough to tickle any bad-movie fan. "Ghosts" have been sighted in East L.A., so cops Moore and Marco are once more shoved into action; the trail leads to phony mystic Dr. Acula (Duncan, who really looks like he's in a trance). Criswell again narrates the proceedings, this time from a coffin. Sat unreleased for *23 years* because Wood couldn't pay the lab bill! Retitled NIGHT OF THE GHOULS.▼

Revenge of the Gladiators (1965-Italian) **C-100m.** *½ D: Michele Lupo. Roger Browne, Scilla Gabel, Giacomo Rossi Stuart, Daniele Vargas, Gordon Mitchell. Badly directed story of gladiator rescuing princess from barbarians.

Revenge of the Nerds (1984) **C-90m.** ** D: Jeff Kanew. Robert Carradine, Anthony Edwards, Julie Montgomery, Curtis Armstrong, Ted McGinley, Michelle Meyrink, Bernie Casey, James Cromwell. Geeky college freshmen, tired of being humiliated by the campus jocks and coed cuties, form their own fraternity, leading to all-out war. As raunchy teen comedies go, not bad, helped immeasurably by two leads' likable performances. Followed by a sequel.▼

Revenge of the Nerds, II: Nerds in Paradise (1987) **C-92m.** *½ D: Joe Roth. Robert Carradine, Curtis Armstrong, Larry B. Scott, Timothy Busfield, Courtney Thorne-Smith, Andrew Cassese, Donald Gibb, Ed Lauter, Anthony Edwards. Sequel, set at a fraternity gathering in Ft. Lauderdale, is strictly by-the-numbers; once again the geeky "heroes" manage to triumph over their beefier (but not brainier) college counterparts . . . but this predictable comedy is a lot less fun than the original. Edwards, Carradine's costar in the first picture, makes a token appearance.▼

Revenge of the Ninja (1983) **C-88m.** ** D: Sam Firstenberg. Sho Kosugi, Keith Vitali, Virgil Frye, Arthur Roberts, Mario Gallo. Good ninja Kosugi takes on evil ninja Roberts, a heroin smuggler/kidnapper/killer. Kung fu aficionados should enjoy it, otherwise beware. A follow-up to ENTER THE NINJA, followed by NINJA III—THE DOMINATION.▼

Revenge of the Pink Panther (1978) **C-99m.** ** D: Blake Edwards. Peter Sellers, Herbert Lom, Robert Webber, Dyan Cannon, Burt Kwouk, Robert Loggia, Paul Stewart, Andre Maranne, Graham Stark, Ferdy Mayne. Sellers' final go-round as bumbling Inspector Clouseau is one of the dullest, until a bright wrap-up in Hong Kong with some good sight gags and plenty of spark from Cannon. The "plot" has Clouseau supposedly murdered, allowing him to find "killer" incognito. Followed by TRAIL OF THE PINK PANTHER.▼

Revenge of the Pirates (1951-Italian) **95m.** ** D: Primo Zeglio. Maria Montez, Milly Vitale, Jean-Pierre Aumont, Saro Urzi, Paul Muller, Robert Risso. Aumont and Montez (offscreen husband and wife) try to spark this trite swashbuckler of wicked governor hoarding stolen gold, with Robin Hood of the seas coming to rescue.

Revenge of the Stepford Wives (1980) **C-100m. TVM** D: Robert Fuest. Sharon Gless, Julie Kavner, Audra Lindley, Don Johnson, Mason Adams, Arthur Hill, Ellen Weston, Millie Slavin. Mediocre sequel to 1975 theatrical feature finds an eager-beaver lady journalist coming to town and stumbling onto the sinister secret behind the robotlike behavior of all the women (a different secret than the original film revealed). If the women's movement failed to endorse the original, it'll find less to cheer about here. Followed by another TVM, THE STEPFORD CHILDREN. Average.▼

Revenge of the Zombies (1943) **61m.** *½ D: Steve Sekely. John Carradine, Robert Lowery, Gale Storm, Veda Ann Borg, Mantan Moreland, Mauritz Hugo. Low-budget mad doctor saga, with Carradine experimenting on human guinea pigs. Moreland's comic relief saves the day, as usual.

Revenge of Ukeno-Jo, The SEE: **Actor's Revenge, An**

Revengers, The (1972) **C-112m.** BOMB D: Daniel Mann. William Holden, Ernest Borgnine, Susan Hayward, Woody Strode, Roger Hanin, Rene Koldehoff. Rancher goes after those who massacred his family. Holden and Borgnine are reunited, but WILD BUNCH magic isn't there. Hayward (in her final theatrical feature) is the only good thing about this terrible Western.

Revenge Squad SEE: **Hit and Run** (1982)▼

Revolt at Fort Laramie (1957) **C-73m.** ** D: Lesley Selander. John Dehner, Frances Helm, Gregg Palmer, Don Gordon, Robert Keys. Grade-B Western of internal rivalries of North-South soldiers at government fort during Civil War. Look for Harry Dean Stanton in his film debut.

Revolt in the Big House (1958) **79m.** **½ D: R. G. Springsteen. Gene Evans, Robert Blake, Timothy Carey, John Qualen. Taut little programmer about convict life.

Revolt of Job, The (1983-Hungarian-German) **C-97m.** ***½ D: Imre Gyongyossy, Barna Kabay. Ferenc Zenthe, Hedi Temessy, Gabor Feher, Peter Rudolf, Leticia Caro. Beautiful tale of a Jewish couple in WW2 Hungary who adopt a non-Jewish boy; their relationship, as he begins to perceive of them as family while the Holocaust hangs over them, is quite touching.▼

Revolt of Mamie Stover, The (1956) **C-92m.** **½ D: Raoul Walsh. Jane Russell, Richard Egan, Joan Leslie, Agnes Moorehead, Jorja Curtright, Jean Willes, Michael Pate. Gorgeous Jane, in glorious color, is Honolulu-based "saloon singer" in 1941. Weak plot; Jane sings "Keep Your Eyes On the Hands."

Revolt of the Zombies (1936) **65m.** *½ D: Victor Halperin. Dorothy Stone, Dean Jagger, Roy D'Arcy, Robert Noland, George Cleveland. Jagger brings dead Cambodian soldiers back to life to do his evil bidding. Should have stayed dead.▼

Revolution (1969) **C-90m.** **½ D: Jack O'Connell. Today Malone. Documentary of late-60s hippie life, mostly in San Francisco, has some interesting footage, but directorial technique is sometimes too flashy. Music by Country Joe & the Fish, Quicksilver Messenger Service, Steve Miller Band, Mother Earth.▼

Revolution (1985) **C-123m.** BOMB D: Hugh Hudson. Al Pacino, Donald Sutherland, Nastassja Kinski, Joan Plowright, Dave King, Annie Lennox. Only a half-dozen or so movies have dealt more than superficially with the Revolutionary War; thanks to this megabomb, it'll be 2776 until we get another one. Pacino, two centuries too contemporary to be convincing, is the trapper whose boat and son are conscripted by the Continental Army; Kinski is the headstrong rebel from a family of Tories. Ludicrous script and acting sink some splendid production values.▼

Revolutionary, The (1970) **C-100m.** *** D: Paul Williams. Jon Voight, Jennifer Salt, Seymour Cassel, Robert Duvall. Tight, well-written study of a college youth who slowly gets drawn into role of political revolutionary with near-tragic results.▼

Reward, The (1965) **C-92m.** **½ D: Serge Bourguignon. Max von Sydow, Yvette Mimieux, Efrem Zimbalist, Jr., Gilbert Roland, Emilio Fernandez, Henry Silva, Rodolfo Acosta. Promising premise and good cast led astray in static Western: group of bounty hunters turn on each other, as greed for larger share of reward money goads them into conflict.

Reward (1980) **C-105m. TVM** D: E. W. Swackhamer. Michael Parks, Richard Jaeckel, Louis Giambalvo, Malachy McCourt, Annie McEnroe, Andrew Robinson, Lance LeGault. Unsold pilot written by Jason Miller about a disenchanted San Francisco cop who quits the force and sets out to solve the murder of a colleague with the help of a young co-ed. Average.

Rhapsody (1954) **C-115m.** **½ D: Charles Vidor. Elizabeth Taylor, Vittorio Gassman, John Ericson, Louis Calhern, Michael Chekhov. Three-cornered romance among rich Taylor, violinist Gassman, and pianist Ericson: melodic interludes bolster soaper. Script by Fay and Michael Kanin.

Rhapsody in Blue (1945) **139m.** *** D: Irving Rapper. Robert Alda, Joan Leslie, Alexis Smith, Oscar Levant, Charles Coburn, Julie Bishop, Albert Basserman, Morris Carnovsky, Herbert Rudley, Rosemary DeCamp, Paul Whiteman, Hazel Scott. Hollywood biography of George

Gershwin is largely pulp fiction, but comes off more credibly and interestingly than most other composer biopics, capturing Gershwin's enthusiasm for his work, and some of the inner conflicts he faced. Highlight is virtually complete performance of title work.

Rhinestone (1984) **C-111m.** *½ D: Bob Clark. Sylvester Stallone, Dolly Parton, Richard Farnsworth, Ron Leibman, Tim Thomerson. Parton bets that she can turn anyone into a country singer—even N.Y.C. cabdriver Stallone. Contrived, cornball comedy with acres of unfunny dialogue.▼

Rhino! (1964) **C-91m.** **½ D: Ivan Tors. Robert Culp, Harry Guardino, Shirley Eaton, Harry Mekela. Diverting African gamehunting nonsense, with an enthusiastic cast, good action scenes.

Rhinoceros (1974) **C-101m.** BOMB D: Tom O'Horgan. Zero Mostel, Gene Wilder, Karen Black, Robert Weil, Joe Silver, Marilyn Chris, Robert Fields. Eugene Ionesco entry in "Theater of the Absurd" makes sorry transition from stage to screen as clerk Wilder refuses to conform by turning into a pachyderm. The performers try. An American Film Theater Production.

Rhode Island Murders, The SEE: **Demon Murder Case, The**

Rhodes (1936 British) **91m.** ** D: Berthold Viertel. Walter Huston, Oscar Homolka, Basil Sydney, Frank Cellier, Peggy Ashcroft, Renne De Vaux, Percy Parsons, Bernard Lee, Ndanisa Kumalo. Biography of Cecil Rhodes (Huston), who founded Rhodesia and opened up the Transvaal to British exploitation. Huston's performance is big, romantic, and hammy, but the movie is a justification for Rhodes' rape of Africa and the Boer War. Homolka's dour, crafty Kruger is more interesting than Huston's Rhodes. Also known as RHODES OF AFRICA▼

Rhodes of Africa SEE: **Rhodes**

Rhubarb (1951) **95m.** *** D: Arthur Lubin. Ray Milland, Jan Sterling, Gene Lockhart, William Frawley, Elsie Holmes, Leonard Nimoy. Frisky comedy of baseball team inherited by a cat, from famous story by H. Allen Smith.

Rhythm on the Range (1936) **85m.** **½ D: Norman Taurog. Bing Crosby, Frances Farmer, Bob Burns, Martha Raye, Lucile Watson, Samuel S. Hinds. Film noteworthy as Raye's feature-film debut and pleasant excuse for musical nonsense songs include "I'm an Old Cowhand (from the Rio Grande)". Remade as PARDNERS.

Rhythm on the River (1940) **92m.** *** D: Victor Schertzinger. Bing Crosby, Mary Martin, Basil Rathbone, Oscar Levant, Oscar Shaw, Charley Grapewin, William Frawley. Lots of fun, with Crosby and Martin ghost-writing songs for phony

Rathbone, trying to break loose on their own. Billy Wilder was one of the writers.

Rhythm Romance SEE: **Some Like It Hot** (1939)

Rice Girl (1963-Italian) **C-90m.** **½ D: Raffaello Matarazzo. Elsa Martinelli, Folco Lulli, Michel Auclair, Rik Battaglia, Susanne Levesy, Liliana Gerace. Atmospheric account of seamy rice workers and Martinelli's past life catching up with her.

Rich and Famous (1981) **C-117m.** ** D: George Cukor. Jacqueline Bisset, Candice Bergen, David Selby, Hart Bochner, Steven Hill, Meg Ryan, Matt Lattanzi, Michael Brandon. Muddled, misguided remake of OLD ACQUAINTANCE, with Bisset and Bergen as women who maintain a stormy friendship for more than 20 years, despite rivalries in love and career. Idiotic dialogue and Bisset's sexual ruminations weaken what should have been a strong contemporary version of John Van Druten's story. Bisset's company produced. Among guests at Malibu party are Marsha Hunt, Christopher Isherwood, and Roger Vadim; later party offers glimpses of Ray Bradbury, Nina Foch, and Frances Bergen (Candice's mother). Cukor's last film.▼

Rich and Strange (1932-British) **92m.** *** D: Alfred Hitchcock. Henry Kendall, Joan Barry, Betty Amann, Percy Marmont, Elsie Randolph. Kendall and Barry, married and bored, inherit money and travel around the world. Each has an affair; eventually they are shipwrecked. A well-made message film: money does not bring happiness. Screenplay by Alma Reville (Mrs. H.) and Val Valentine. Originally released in America as EAST OF SHANGHAI.▼

Richard Pryor Here and Now (1983) **C-83m.** *½ D: Richard Pryor. The comedian's fourth concert film is his least satisfying to date, though hecklers in the audience are as much to blame as any defects in Pryor's material. Some amusing bits on drunks and dopeheads, plus some biting digs at the Reagan White House. Filmed on Bourbon Street in New Orleans.▼

Richard Pryor Is Back Live in Concert (1979) **C-78m.** ** D: Jeff Margolis. Pryor's still funny, but much of the material is ripped off from RICHARD PRYOR—LIVE IN CONCERT, released earlier that year.

Richard Pryor—Live in Concert (1979) **C-78m.** *** D: Jeff Margolis. Pryor on race, sex, machismo, death, filmed in performance in Long Beach, California. The comedian, uncensored, is at his raunchy best.▼

Richard Pryor Live on the Sunset Strip (1982) **C-82m.** **½ D: Joe Layton. Pryor on Africa, sex, lawyers, his wife, sex, Italian mobsters, more sex, and—inevitably—freebasing. Some of it's funny, some isn't, but the audience is always shown doubled over with laughter.▼

Richard's Things (1980-British) **C-104m.** ** D: Anthony Harvey. Liv Ullmann, Amanda Redman, Tim Pigott-Smith, Elizabeth Spriggs, David Markham. Widow Ullmann is seduced by her late husband's girlfriend. Dreary drama, with a catatonic performance by Liv. Screenplay by Frederic Raphael, based on his novel. Made for British TV.▼

Richard III (1956-British) **C-155m.** ***½ D: Laurence Olivier. Laurence Olivier, John Gielgud, Ralph Richardson, Claire Bloom, Alec Clunes, Cedric Hardwicke, Stanley Baker, Pamela Brown, Michael Gough. Elaborate if stagy verson of Shakespeare's chronicle of insane 15th-century British king and his court intrigues. Some prints run 139m.▼

Rich Are Always With Us, The (1932) **73m.** ** D: Alfred E. Green. Ruth Chatterton, Adrienne Dore, George Brent, Bette Davis, John Miljan, Robert Warwick, Berton Churchill. Wealthy woman (Chatterton) cannot fall out of love with irresponsible husband (Miljan), even after bitter divorce and new romance with Brent. Silly script.

Richest Cat in the World, The (1986) **C-100m. TVM** D: Gregg Beeman. Ramon Bieri, Steve Kampmann, Caroline McWilliams, Steve Vinovich, George Wyner, Brandon Call. Disney comedy about a talking cat who has inherited $5 million and is catnapped by its deceased master's money-grubbing relatives. Humorist Marshall Efron was one of the platoon of writers. Average.

Richest Girl in the World, The (1934) **76m.** *** D: William A. Seiter. Miriam Hopkins, Joel McCrea, Fay Wray, Reginald Denny, Henry Stephenson. Entertaining romantic comedy by Norman Krasna about millionairess wanting to make sure her next boyfriend loves her for herself, not for her money. Remade as BRIDE BY MISTAKE.

Richest Girl in the World, The (1960-Danish) **C-78m.** *½ D: Lau Lauritzen. Nina, Frederik, Poul Reichhardt, Birgitte Bruun. Syrupy musical fluff with Nina out to marry singer Frederick; overly cute.

Richie SEE: **Death of Richie, The**

Richie Brockelman: The Missing 24 Hours (1976) **C-78m. TVM** D: Hy Averback. Dennis Dugan, Suzanne Pleshette, Norman Fell, Lloyd Bochner, William Windom, Sharon Gless. Private eye caper involving a neophyte gumshoe and his amnesiac client. Plodding pilot to the short-lived series with a cast desperately trying to inject the needed spark. Title character was originally seen in a two-part episode of *The Rockford Files*. Below average.

Rich Kids (1979) **C-101m.** *** D: Robert M. Young. Trini Alvarado, Jeremy Levy,

John Lithgow, Kathryn Walker, David Selby, Terry Kiser, Paul Dooley, Olympia Dukakis, Jill Eikenberry. Alvarado and Levy are upper class N.Y.C. kids who become best friends as her parents are dissolving their marriage. Effect of divorce is focal point for this fine acting showcase, which also makes good use of N.Y.C. locations. Produced by Robert Altman.▼

Rich Man, Poor Girl (1938) **65m.** ** D: Reinhold Schunzel. Robert Young, Lew Ayres, Ruth Hussey, Lana Turner, Rita Johnson, Don Castle, Guy Kibbee. Good cast, fair film. Title tells story; only noteworthy item is radiant young Turner.

Rich Men, Single Women (1990) **C-100m. TVM** D: Elliot Silverstein. Suzanne Somers, Heather Locklear, Deborah Adair, Larry Wilcox, Douglas Barr, John Allen Nelson, Joel Higgins. A glance at the title and cast of this TV movie should tell you what to expect: an update of HOW TO MARRY A MILLIONAIRE with three sexy gold diggers out to snare themselves some tycoons. Average.

Rich, Young and Pretty (1951) **C-95m.** **½ D: Norman Taurog. Jane Powell, Danielle Darrieux, Wendell Corey, Vic Damone, Fernando Lamas, Marcel Dalio, Una Merkel, Richard Anderson. Frivolous MGM musical with Powell in Paris, sightseeing and romancing, meeting mother Darrieux. Cowritten by Sidney Sheldon.

Ricochet Romance (1954) **80m.** **½ D: Charles Lamont. Marjorie Main, Chill Wills, Pedro Gonzalez-Gonzalez, Rudy Vallee, Ruth Hampton. Another Main frolic, with the rambunctious gal hired as ranch cook but putting her two cents' worth into everything.

Ricochets (1986-Israeli) **C-90m.** *** D: Eli Cohen. Roni Pincovich, Shaul Mizrahi, Alon Aboutboul, Dudu Ben-Ze'ev, Boaz Ofri. Gritty, uncompromising look at a group of Israeli soldiers living and dying in occupied Lebanon, focusing on the experiences of one young officer. Made as an Israeli Army training film and shot on location; nevertheless, an eloquent anti-war drama.

Riddle of the Sands, The (1979-British) **C-102m.** ** D: Tony Maylam. Simon MacCorkindale, Michael York, Jenny Agutter, Alan Badel, Jurgen Andersen, Olga Lowe, Wolf Kahler. Sailing off the coast of Germany in 1901, yachtsman MacCorkindale stumbles onto what seems to be a plan to invade England, and summons old chum York to help him out. Erskine Childers' novel is considered the prototype of the modern spy thriller, but this adaptation is just too slow and stiff to be really effective. Good to look at, though. Released in the U.S. in 1984.▼

Ride a Crooked Trail (1958) **C-87m.**

**½ D: Jesse Hibbs. Audie Murphy, Gia Scala, Walter Matthau, Henry Silva. Trim Western with Murphy involved in bank robbery.

Ride a Violent Mile (1957) 80m. *½ D: Charles Marquis Warren. John Agar, Penny Edwards, John Pickard, Sheb Wooley, Eva Novak. Trivial Western set in Civil War times about Southern blockade runners.

Ride a Wild Pony (1976 Australian) C-91m. *** D: Don Chaffey. Michael Craig, John Meillon, Robert Bettles, Eva Griffith, Graham Rouse. Genial, atmospheric Disney story about an irresistible pony and the two children—son of poor farm family and crippled rich girl—who vie for its love and ownership. Sentimental tale adapted from James Aldridge's *A Sporting Proposition*.▼

Ride Back, The (1957) 79m. *** D: Allen H. Miner. Anthony Quinn, Lita Milan, William Conrad, Ellen Hope Monroe, Louis Towers. Well-handled account of sheriff and prisoner who find they need each other's help to survive elements and Indian attacks.

Ride Beyond Vengeance (1966) C-100m. **½ D: Bernard McEveety. Chuck Connors, Michael Rennie, Kathryn Hays, Joan Blondell, Gloria Grahame, Gary Merrill, Bill Bixby, James MacArthur, Claude Akins, Paul Fix, Ruth Warrick, Arthur O'Connell, Frank Gorshin. Good supporting cast makes the most of stereotyped roles in flashback account of Connors' sundry encounters with outlaws.

Ride Clear of Diablo (1954) C-80m. **½ D: Jesse Hibbs. Audie Murphy, Dan Duryea, Susan Cabot, Abbe Lane, Russell Johnson, Jack Elam. Above-par Murphy oater, with Audie swearing revenge for family's murder.

Ride 'Em Cowboy (1942) 86m. **½ D: Arthur Lubin. Bud Abbott, Lou Costello, Dick Foran, Anne Gwynne, Johnny Mack Brown, Ella Fitzgerald, Douglass Dumbrille. Good combination of Western, comedy, and musical in A&C vehicle, with Ella and the Merry Macs singing tunes including "A Tisket A Tasket," Foran crooning "I'll Remember April."

Ride in the Whirlwind (1965) C-83m. **½ D: Monte Hellman. Cameron Mitchell, Jack Nicholson, Tom Filer, Millie Perkins, Katherine Squire, Rupert Crosse, Harry Dean Stanton. Nicholson co-produced and wrote the screenplay for this offbeat Western about three cowboys who find themselves wrongly pursued as outlaws. Neither as arty nor as intriguing as THE SHOOTING, which was filmed simultaneously.▼

Ride Lonesome (1959) C-73m. *** D: Budd Boetticher. Randolph Scott, Karen Steele, Pernell Roberts, James Best, Lee Van Cleef, James Coburn. Tightly woven Burt Kennedy script has Scott bringing in

wanted outlaw as bait to flush out his brother, only to find several others tagging along for their own purposes. Typically terse Boetticher Western; Coburn's film debut.

Ride Out for Revenge (1957) 79m. *½ D: Bernard Girard. Rory Calhoun, Gloria Grahame, Lloyd Bridges, Vince Edwards. Tiresome account of gold-hungry men trying to dispossess Indians from their lands.

Rider on a Dead Horse (1962) 72m. *½ D: Herbert L. Strock. John Vivyan, Bruce Gordon, Kevin Hagen, Lisa Lu, Charles Lampkin. Seedy account of trio of gold prospectors trying to do each other in.

Rider on the Rain (1970-French) C-115m. ***½ D: René Clement. Charles Bronson, Marlene Jobert, Jill Ireland, Annie Cordy. Chilling suspense piece about mysterious man who winds up using Jobert as accomplice when she discovers what he is up to. Best sequence: long, rainy prologue.▼

Riders of the Purple Sage (1925) 56m. *** D: Lynn Reynolds. Tom Mix, Beatrice Burnham, Arthur Morrison, Warner Oland, Fred Kohler, Harold Goodwin, Marion Nixon. Engrossing Zane Grey story filmed on beautiful locations, with Mix a Texas Ranger seeking scoundrel (Oland) who abducted his sister (Burnham). Fascinating twists in this tale, first filmed in 1918, again in 1931, 1941. Mix also filmed sequel, THE RAINBOW TRAIL, as done in 1918 and 1932.

Riders of the Storm (1986-British) C-92m. *½ D: Maurice Phillips. Dennis Hopper, Michael J. Pollard, Eugene Lipinski, James Aubrey, Nigel Pegram. Unsatisfactory chronicle of Vietnam vets who run a pirate television station and jam right-wing broadcasts; they attempt to sabotage the campaign of a female presidential candidate who is not to their liking. Bright premise, thoroughly stale result. Originally titled THE AMERICAN WAY, at 105m.▼

Riders of Vengeance SEE: **Raiders, The**

Riders to the Stars (1954) C-81m. **½ D: Richard Carlson. William Lundigan, Herbert Marshall, Richard Carlson, Dawn Addams, Martha Hyer. Labored programmer about early days of space missiles, quite outdated now.

Ride the High Country (1962) C-94m. ✓ **** D: Sam Peckinpah. Randolph Scott, Joel McCrea, Mariette Hartley, Ronald Starr, Edgar Buchanan, R. G. Armstrong, Warren Oates, John Anderson, L. Q. Jones, James Drury. Literate, magnificent Western about two aged gunfighter pals who reflect on the paths their lives have taken while guarding gold shipment. Considered by some to be Peckinpah's finest film; breathtaking widescreen photography (by Lucien Ballard) and scenery, and flawless performances, with Buchanan notable as a drunken judge. Hartley's first film, Scott's last.▼

Ride the High Iron (1956) **74m.** *½ D: Don Weis. Don Taylor, Sally Forrest, Raymond Burr, Lisa Golm, Otto Waldis, Nestor Paiva, Mae Clarke. Korean veteran Taylor works for slick P.R. man Burr who makes his living keeping people's indiscretions out of the paper. Taylor tries to latch on to rich girl whose family Burr works for. Originally made for TV but shown theatrically.

Ride the Man Down (1952) **C-90m.** ** D: Joseph Kane. Brian Donlevy, Rod Cameron, Ella Raines, Barbara Britton, Chill Wills, Jack LaRue, J. Carrol Naish, Jim Davis. Lumbering account of ranchland feuding in old West.▼

Ride the Pink Horse (1947) **101m.** ***½ D: Robert Montgomery. Robert Montgomery, Wanda Hendrix, Thomas Gomez, Andrea King, Fred Clark, Art Smith, Rita Conde, Grandon Rhodes. Strong *film noir* of Montgomery coming to small New Mexican town during fiesta to blackmail gangster Clark, but romantic Hendrix and FBI agent Smith keep getting in his way. Taut script by Ben Hecht and Charles Lederer; super performance by Gomez as friendly carny. Remade for TV as THE HANGED MAN. (1964).

Ride the Wild Surf (1964) **C-101m.** **½ D: Don Taylor. Fabian, Tab Hunter, Barbara Eden, Anthony Hayes, James Mitchum, Shelley Fabares. Formula beach boys tale, set in Hawaii; Jan and Dean sing the title song. It's not Shakespeare, but it *is* a cut above the usual BEACH PARTY shenanigans, and the surfing footage is great.

Ride to Hangman's Tree, The (1967) **C-90m.** **½ D: Al Rafkin. Jack Lord, James Farentino, Don Galloway, Melodie Johnson, Richard Anderson, Robert Yuro. Formula Universal backlot Western, of outlaws in old West.

Ride, Vaquero (1953) **C-90m.** **½ D: John Farrow. Robert Taylor, Ava Gardner, Howard Keel, Anthony Quinn, Charlita. Oddball casting perks brooding Western set on Mexican border, with sultry Gardner responsible for most of the action.

Riding High (1943) **C-89m.** *½ D: George Marshall. Dorothy Lamour, Dick Powell, Victor Moore, Gil Lamb, Cass Daley, Milt Britton and Band, Rod Cameron. Unmemorable songs, flat script, fair performances add up to dubious entertainment; Powell is obsessed with silver mine, while wooing Lamour.

Riding High (1950) **112m.** **½ D: Frank Capra. Bing Crosby, Coleen Gray, Charles Bickford, Margaret Hamilton, Frances Gifford, James Gleason, Raymond Walburn, William Demarest, Ward Bond, Clarence Muse, Percy Kilbride, Gene Lockhart, Douglass Dumbrille. Musical remake of

BROADWAY BILL follows it so closely that stock footage is included from 1934 film. Crosby is racehorse owner whose nag has yet to come through. OK songs, Capra touch make this pleasing if unmemorable entertainment. Oliver Hardy is fun in rare solo appearance.

Riding on Air (1937) **71m.** ** D: Edward Sedgwick. Joe E. Brown, Guy Kibbee, Florence Rice, Vinton Haworth, Anthony Nace, Harlan Briggs. Average Brown vehicle has him mixed up with smugglers and a wacky invention of a radio beam to control airplanes.▼

Riding Shotgun (1954) **C-74m.** ** D: Andre de Toth. Randolph Scott, Wayne Morris, Joan Weldon, Joe Sawyer, James Millican. Typical, undemanding Scott Western of man seeking to clear his reputation.

Riding Tall (1972) **C-92m.** ** D: Patrick J. Murphy. Andrew Prine, Gilmer McCormick, Harriet Medin, Jack Mather, William Wentersole. Rodeo rider-drifter Prine and Vassar dropout McCormick meet and become involved. Harmless drama, with a nice performance by Prine, is ultimately defeated by its low budget. Originally titled SQUARES.

Riffraff (1935) **89m.** **½ D: J. Walter Ruben. Jean Harlow, Spencer Tracy, Una Merkel, Joseph Calleia, Victor Kilian, Mickey Rooney. Comedy-drama doesn't always work, but worth viewing for stars playing married couple in fishing business who end up on wrong side of law.

Riffraff (1947) **80m.** *** D: Ted Tetzlaff. Pat O'Brien, Anne Jeffreys, Walter Slezak, Percy Kilbride, Jerome Cowan, George Givot, Jason Robards. Fast-paced story of O'Brien foiling villains' attempts to take over oilfield in Panama.▼

Riff Raff Girls (1962-French) **97m.** **½ D: Alex Joffe. Nadja Tiller, Robert Hossein, Silvia Monfort, Roger Hanin, Pierre Blanchar. Tiller is quite convincing as club owner whose aim is to be self-sufficient; set on Brussels waterfront.

Rififi (1954-French) **115m.** **** D: Jules Dassin. Jean Servais, Carl Mohner, Magali Noel, Robert Manuel, Perlo Vita (Jules Dassin). The granddaddy of all caper/heist movies, centering on quartet of French jewel thieves who find each other more dangerous than the cops. The burglary sequence itself is famous for being in complete silence.▼

Rififi in Tokyo (1963-French) **89m.** ** D: Jacques Deray. Karl Boehm, Michel Vitold, Charles Vanel, Eiji Okada, Keiko Kishi, Barbara Lass, Yanagi. Aging European gangster recruits men for bank heist. Cast is so-so; strictly standard plot line.

Right Approach, The (1961) **92m.** **½ D: David Butler. Frankie Vaughan, Martha Hyer, Juliet Prowse, Gary Crosby, Jane Withers. Plucky minor film of Vaughan, a good-for-nothing who uses anything to get ahead. Adapted by Fay and Michael Kanin from a play by his brother Garson.

Right Cross (1950) **90m.** ****½** D: John Sturges. June Allyson, Dick Powell, Lionel Barrymore, Ricardo Montalban. Fairly compact account of boxing world, with sports-writer Powell and fighter Montalban in love with Allyson. One of Marilyn Monroe's early films.

Right Hand Man, The (1987-Australian) **C-100m.** ****½** D: Di Drew. Rupert Everett, Hugo Weaving, Catherine McClements, Arthur Dignam, Jennifer Claire. Well-made but only occasionally involving drama about the various troubles of aristocrat Everett, and what happens when he hires stagecoach driver Weaving. Has its moments, but ultimately peters out.▼

Right of the People, The (1986) **C-100m.** TVM D: Jeffrey Bloom. Michael Ontkean, Jane Kaczmarek, Billy Dee Williams, John Randolph, M. Emmet Walsh, Jamie Smith Jackson, Joanne Linville. Exasperating drama revolving around the Second Amendment of the Constitution and the right-to-bear-arms issue, with a whole town voting to let every citizen strap on a gun. Provocative script by director Bloom is muddled in execution. Average.

Right of Way (1983) **C-106m.** TVM D: George Schaefer. Bette Davis, James Stewart, Melinda Dillon, Priscilla Morrill, John Harkins. An aging couple decide to end their lives together. This pedestrian tale has the dubious distinction of making two Hollywood legends (in their first co-starring effort) seem dreary. An abrupt resolution, apparently changed by the producers at the last minute, doesn't help. Made for cable. Average.▼

Right Stuff, The (1983) **C-193m.** ******* D: Philip Kaufman. Sam Shepard, Scott Glenn, Ed Harris, Dennis Quaid, Fred Ward, Barbara Hershey, Kim Stanley, Veronica Cartwright, Kathy Baker, Pamela Reed, Donald Moffat, Levon Helm, Scott Wilson, David Clennon, William Russ, Jeff Goldblum, Harry Shearer. Offbeat look at the birth of America's space program and the first astronauts, adapted from Tom Wolfe's best-selling book, and tethered to the story of icono-clastic test pilot Chuck Yeager. Writer-director Kaufman draws all his characters as cartoons (including Lyndon Johnson) except for the pilots—and puts thrillingly realistic recreations of space flights against broadly caricatured scenes on Earth. A real curio of a film, with some astonishing performances, exhilarating moments, but a curious overall air of detachment. Yet even at more than three hours, it's never boring. Oscarwinning score by Bill Conti. The real Chuck Yeager has a cameo role as a bartender.▼

Right to Die (1987) **C-100m.** TVM D: Paul Wendkos. Raquel Welch, Michael Gross, Bonnie Bartlett, Peter Michael Goetz, Joanna Miles, Ed O'Neill. Maudlin drama about a woman's battle against Lou Gehrig's Disease, watchable solely for Welch's cast-against-type performance. Average.

Right to Kill? (1985) **C-100m.** TVM D: John Erman. Frederic Forrest, Christopher Collet, Karmin Murcelo, Justine Bateman, Ann Wedgeworth. Well-crafted dramatization of a true story about teenager who shot his father to spare himself, his sister, and their mother further physical and emotional assaults. Forrest excels as the nearly psychopathic father. Written by Joyce Eliason. Above average.

Rikki and Pete (1988-Australian) **C-107m.** ****½** D: Nadia Tass. Stephen Kearney, Nina Landis, Tetchie Agbayani, Bill Hunter, Bruno Lawrence, Bruce Spence, Dorothy Allison, Don Reid, Lewis Fitz-gerald. Pete is a misfit with a penchant for gimmicky inventions, Rikki is his sister who's still trying to find herself; together they flee to a remote mining village where their lives take some unexpected turns. Follow-up to the delightful MALCOLM by the same writing-directing team (Tass and writer/cinematographer David Parker) hasn't the same sweetness or consistency, but it's admirably quirky, and Parker's Rube Goldberg-ish devices are a lot of fun.▼

Ring, The (1952) **79m.** ******* D: Kurt Neumann. Gerald Mohr, Rita Moreno, Lalo Rios, Robert Arthur, Art Aragon, Jack Elam. Neat little boxing yarn with a conscience: under the tutelage of fight manager Mohr, poor Chicano Rios tries his hand in the ring. Film offers a refreshingly nonstereotypical portrait of Mexican-Americans, plus a perceptive view of the fight racket. Scripted by Irving Shulman, based on his novel.▼

Ring-a-Ding Rhythm (1962-British) **78m.** ****** D: Richard Lester. Helen Shapiro, Craig Douglas, Felix Felton, Arthur Mullard, John Leyton, Chubby Checker, Del Shannon, Gary "U.S." Bonds, Gene Vincent, Gene McDaniels, Acker Bilk, The Temperance Seven. Shapiro and Douglas—whose characters are called Helen and Craig—organize a rock 'n' roll and Dixieland jazz show. Of interest only for the appearances of Bonds, Vincent, and company—although there's not one memorable song performed—and the fact that it's director Lester's first feature. British title: IT'S TRAD, DAD!

Ringer, The (1952-British) **78m.** ******* D: Guy Hamilton. Herbert Lom, Mai Zetterling, Donald Wolfit, Greta Gynt, William Hartnell, Norman Wooland. Entertaining mystery from Edgar Wallace novel and play: The Ringer, an arch criminal, gets on the case of an unscrupulous lawyer involved in his sister's death. Filmed previously in 1931, and in 1938 as THE GAUNT STRANGER.

Ring of Bright Water (1969-British) C-107m. *** D: Jack Couffer. Bill Travers, Virginia McKenna, Peter Jeffrey, Jameson Clark, Helena Gloag. Fine children's film should be a treat for adults, too; modest story of man's love for his pet otter is intelligently and believably told. Nice acting and photography.▼

Ring of Fear (1954) C-93m. ** D: James Edward Grant. Clyde Beatty, Pat O'Brien, Mickey Spillane, Sean McClory, Marian Carr, John Bromfield. Offbeat murder-mystery set in a circus; interesting for acting appearance by Spillane, although, curiously, he is *not* one of the credited writers!

Ring of Fire (1961) C-91m. **½ D: Andrew L. Stone. David Janssen, Joyce Taylor, Frank Gorshin, Joel Marston, Doodles Weaver. Assistant sheriff is held hostage by trio of young hoods. Highlight of film is climactic forest holocaust.

Ring of Passion (1978) C-100m. TVM D: Robert Michael Lewis. Bernie Casey, Stephen Macht, Britt Ekland, Denise Nicholas, Allen Garfield, Joseph Campanella, Beah Richards. Fact-based drama about the two Louis-Schmeling heavyweight fights, set against the politics of the pre-WW2 era. Long on ideology, short on fisticuffs, and decidedly offbeat. Average.

Ring of Terror (1962) 72m. BOMB D: Clark Paylow. George Mather, Esther Furst, Austin Green, Joseph Conway. A medical student must confront a corpse as a fraternity initiation prank in this low-budget loser.▼

Ring of Treason (1963-British) 90m. *** D: Robert Tronson. Bernard Lee, William Sylvester, Margaret Tyzack, David Kossoff. Solid spy thriller based on true story of ex-Navy man Lee blackmailed into helping Russian agents. Builds truly exciting atmosphere. British title: RING OF SPIES.

Rings Around the World (1967) C-79m. **½ D: Gilbert Cates. Don Ameche. Ameche introduces world-famous circus acts. OK for those who care; similar to Ameche's TV series, *International Showtime*.▼

Ringside Maisie (1941) 96m. D: Edwin L. Marin. Ann Sothern, George Murphy, Robert Sterling, Virginia O'Brien, Natalie Thompson. SEE: **Maisie** series.

Rings on Her Fingers (1942) 85m. **½ D: Rouben Mamoulian. Henry Fonda, Gene Tierney, Laird Cregar, Spring Byington, Marjorie Gateson, Iris Adrian, Clara Blandick, Mary Treen. Con-artist Tierney falls for Fonda instead of fleecing him; standard

romance with good cast hoping to repeat success of Fonda's THE LADY EVE.

Rio (1939) 75m. ** D: John Brahm. Basil Rathbone, Victor McLaglen, Sigrid Gurie, Robert Cummings, Leo Carrillo, Billy Gilbert. Rathbone, serving ten-year prison term, suspects his wife (Gurie) is being unfaithful. His performance is sole virtue of this slick potboiler.

Rio Bravo (1959) C-141m. ***½ D: Howard Hawks. John Wayne, Dean Martin, Ricky Nelson, Angie Dickinson, Walter Brennan, Ward Bond, John Russell, Claude Akins, Bob Steele. Sheriff Wayne tries to prevent a killer with connections from escaping from the town jail, with only a drunken Dino, leggy Angie, gimpy Brennan and lockjawed Ricky to help him. Quintessential Hawks Western, patronized by reviewers at the time of its release, is now regarded as an American classic; overlong, but great fun. Written by Leigh Brackett and Jules Furthman. Followed by EL DORADO; sort of remade as ASSAULT ON PRECINCT 13.▼

Rio Conchos (1964) C-107m. *** D: Gordon Douglas. Richard Boone, Stuart Whitman, Tony Franciosa, Edmond O'Brien, Jim Brown. Post–Civil War Texas is the setting for this action-filled Western centering around a shipment of stolen rifles, and Boone taking on Franciosa. Brown is notable in his film debut, and there's a zesty performance by O'Brien.▼

Rio Grande (1950) 105m. *** D: John Ford. John Wayne, Maureen O'Hara, Ben Johnson, Harry Carey, Jr., Victor McLaglen, Claude Jarman, Jr., Chill Wills, J. Carrol Naish. The last of director Ford's Cavalry trilogy (following FORT APACHE and SHE WORE A YELLOW RIBBON), and the most underrated: a vivid look at the gentlemanly spirit of the Cavalry during post-Civil War days . . . and the difficult relationship between an estranged father (commander Wayne) and his son (new recruit Jarman). Beautifully shot by Bert Glennon and Archie Stout, with lovely theme by Victor Young, songs by Sons of the Pioneers (including Ken Curtis). ▼

Rio Lobo (1970) C-114m. *** D: Howard Hawks. John Wayne, Jorge Rivero, Jennifer O'Neill, Jack Elam, Chris Mitchum, Mike Henry, Susana Dosamantes, Victor French, Sherry Lansing, Bill Williams, David Huddleston, Jim Davis, Robert Donner. Hawks' final film is a lighthearted Western in the RIO BRAVO mold, with the Duke as ex-Union colonel out to settle some old scores. Youthful co-stars are weak, but stays on track thanks to snappy dialogue, crisp action, and riotous performance by Elam as shotgun toting old looney. Future studio head Lansing's last film as an actress; George Plimpton has a one-line bit that served as the basis of a TV special.▼

Rio Rita (1942) **91m.** **½ D: S. Sylvan Simon. Bud Abbott, Lou Costello, Kathryn Grayson, John Carroll, Tom Conway, Barry Nelson. Vintage Broadway musical brought up to date, with Nazis invading Western ranch where Bud and Lou work; some good music helps this one. Previously filmed in 1929 with Wheeler and Woolsey.

Riot (1969) **C-97m.** **½ D: Buzz Kulik. Jim Brown, Gene Hackman, Ben Carruthers, Mike Kellin, Gerald O'Loughlin. Unsurprising but extremely violent prison film; Hackman in stereotyped characterization. Produced by William Castle.

Riot in Cell Block 11 (1954) **80m.** *** D: Don Siegel. Neville Brand, Emile Meyer, Frank Faylen, Leo Gordon, Robert Osterloh. Realistic, powerful prison drama still packs a punch. Among the contemporary themes in this 1954 film is "media manipulation," with prisoners trying to use press for leverage.▼

Riot in Juvenile Prison (1959) **71m.** BOMB D: Edward L. Cahn. Jerome Thor, Marcia Henderson, Scott Marlowe, John Hoyt, Dick Tyler, Dorothy Provine, Ann Doran. Programmer fully explained by title.

Riot on Sunset Strip (1967) **C-85m.** *½ D: Arthur Dreifuss. Aldo Ray, Mimsy Farmer, Michael Evans, Laurie Mock, Tim Rooney, Bill Baldwin. Weak exploitation of real-life mid-60s riots on the Strip concerns cop Ray's enraged response when his daughter gets involved with drugs and hippies.

Ripped Off (1971-Italian) **C-83m.** **½ D: Franco Prosperi. Robert Blake, Ernest Borgnine, Gabriele Ferzetti, Catherine Spaak, Tomas Milian. Boxer Blake, framed for the murder of his corrupt manager, is hounded by detective Borgnine and protected by victim's daughter (Spaak). OK of its type; also known as THE BOXER.▼

Ripper, The (1985) **C-104m.** *½ D: Christopher Lewis. Tom Schreier, Wade Tower, Mona Van Pernis, Andrea Adams, Tom Savini. Extremely gory murders punctuate horror tale of college professor possessed by the evil in Jack the Ripper's ring. Intelligently written, but ultra-cheap and heavily padded. Shot on videotape and released directly to home video.▼

Riptide (1934) **90m.** *** D: Edmund Goulding. Norma Shearer, Robert Montgomery, Herbert Marshall, Mrs. Patrick Campbell, Skeets Gallagher, Ralph Forbes, Lilyan Tashman, Helen Jerome Eddy. Silly but entertaining story of vivacious Shearer marrying stodgy British Lord (Marshall), then becoming involved in scandal with Montgomery. Don't miss opening scene where stars are dressed as giant insects for costume party! That's Walter Brennan as a chauffer; Bruce Bennett is an extra at the bar at Cannes.

Rise and Fall of Legs Diamond, The (1960) **101m.** *** D: Budd Boetticher. Ray Danton, Karen Steele, Elaine Stewart, Jesse White, Simon Oakland, Robert Lowery, Warren Oates. Snappy chronicle of Depression-days gangster, well balanced between action gun battles and Danton's romancing flashy dolls (like young Dyan Cannon). Outstanding photography by Lucien Ballard.

Rise and Shine (1941) **93m.** **½ D: Allan Dwan. Jack Oakie, Linda Darnell, George Murphy, Walter Brennan, Sheldon Leonard, Donald Meek, Ruth Donnelly, Milton Berle, Donald MacBride, Raymond Walburn. Oakie has field day as dumb football player abducted by crooks so team won't win big game. Film is often unconsciously funny. Adapted by Herman J. Mankiewicz from James Thurber's *My Life and Hard Times*.

Rising of the Moon, The (1957-Irish) **81m.** **½ D: John Ford. Introduced by Tyrone Power. Cyril Cusack, Maureen Connell, Noel Purcell, Frank Lawton, Jimmy O'Dea. Trio of flavorful stories about Irish life: "Majesty of the Law," "A Minute's Wait," "1921," as performed by the renowned Abbey Players.

Rise of Catherine the Great, The SEE: **Catherine the Great**▼

Rise of Louis XIV, The (1966-French) **C-100m.** *** D: Roberto Rossellini. Jean-Marie Patte, Raymond Jourdan, Silvagni, Katharina Renn, Dominique Vincent, Pierre Barrat. Attractive, but somewhat pedantic effort to show color-filled court of not-quite straitlaced Louis XIV. Very objective, almost documentary-like, but final effect is noninvolving. Made for French TV.▼

Risk, The (1961-British) **81m.** *** D: Roy and John Boulting. Tony Britton, Peter Cushing, Ian Bannen, Virginia Maskell, Donald Pleasence. Tense drama of spies chasing scientist who has secret formula to combat plague. Good direction and cast.

Risky Business (1983) **C-96m.** *** D: Paul Brickman. Tom Cruise, Rebecca De Mornay, Curtis Armstrong, Bronson Pinchot, Raphael Sbarge, Joe Pantoliano, Nicholas Pryor, Janet Carroll, Nicholas Masur, Kevin Anderson. Piquant, original comedy about a reticent teenager who goes a bit wild while his parents are out of town, and becomes involved—in more ways than one—with a prostitute. Brickman's darkly satiric script is balanced by Cruise's utterly likable (and believable) performance in the lead.▼

Rita Hayworth: The Love Goddess (1983) **C-100m.** TVM D: James Goldstone. Lynda Carter, Michael Lerner, John

Considine, Alejandro Ray, Sharon Ipale, Edward Edwards, Dave Shelley. Limp addition to the TV portrait gallery of moviestar dramatizations; alluring Lynda's superficial drawing of Hayworth proves again there is only one Rita. Based on John Kobal's book. Average.▼

Rita, Sue and Bob Too (1986-British) **C-95m.** *** D: Alan Clarke. Siobhan Finneran, Michelle Holmes, George Costigan, Lesley Sharp, Willie Ross, Patti Nicholls, Kulvinder Ghir. Rita and Sue, two plain-looking, slightly overweight working class teens, babysit for Bob and his frigid wife . . . and soon, Rita, Sue and Bob are making three-way whoopee. A shamelessly funny, profane, well-acted sleeper that's definitely not for all tastes. Some of the sex scenes—particularly those in Bob's car—are a riot.▼

Ritual of Evil (1969) **C-100m. TVM** D: Robert Day. Louis Jourdan, Anne Baxter, Diana Hyland, John McMartin, Wilfrid Hyde-White, Belinda Montgomery. Curious mixture of wide-eyed paranoia and serious black magic explorations as psychiatrist Sorrell (Jourdan) investigates contributing factors of patient's suicide. Desperately in need of polished dialogue, film succeeds in spite of itself. Sequel to FEAR NO EVIL. Average.

Rituals (1978-Canadian) **C-100m.** *½ D: Peter Carter. Hal Holbrook, Lawrence Dane, Robin Gammell, Ken James, Gary Reineke. Ripoff of DELIVERANCE with Holbrook and four fellow M.D.s terrorized during wilderness vacation. Unpleasant, to say the least. Reissued as THE CREEPER.▼

Ritz, The (1976) **C-91m.** **½ D: Richard Lester. Jack Weston, Rita Moreno, Jerry Stiller, Kaye Ballard, F. Murray Abraham, Treat Williams, Paul Price, George Coulouris, Bessie Love. Brisk filming of Terence McNally's farce about a schnook fleeing his murderous brother-in-law by hiding in gay baths suffers from feeling that it's all a photographed stage performance. Moreno is memorable re-creating her Tony-winning role as no-talent entertainer Googie Gomez. Filmed in England.▼

Rivals (1972) **C-103m.** **½ D: Krishna Shah. Robert Klein, Joan Hackett, Scott Jacoby. A remarriage forces young child to try and murder the new rival for his mother's affections. Offbeat, to say the least.▼

River, The (1951-Indian) **C-99m.** **** D: Jean Renoir. Patricia Walters, Nora Swinburne, Arthur Shields, Radha, Adrienne Corri, Esmond Knight, narrated by June Hillman, Immensely moving, lyrical adaptation of Rumer Godden novel about English children growing up in Bengal. One of the great color films, a total triumph for cinematographer Claude and director

Jean Renoir. Scripted by Godden and Renoir.▼

River, The (1984) **C-122m.** **½ D: Mark Rydell. Sissy Spacek, Mel Gibson, Shane Bailey, Becky Jo Lynch, Scott Glenn, Don Hood, Billy Green Bush, James Tolkan. Close-knit family struggles to make good on their farm, which is constantly threatened by river that flows alongside. Spacek's a perfect farm woman (and mother) but Gibson's character is so coldly stubborn that it's hard to empathize. Beautifully shot by Vilmos Zsigmond. ▼

River Lady (1948) **C-78m.** ** D: George Sherman. Yvonne De Carlo, Dan Duryea, Rod Cameron, Helena Carter, Lloyd Gough, Florence Bates. Typical De Carlo vehicle about riverboat queen trying to buy her man when she can't win him with love; colorful and empty.

River Niger, The (1976) **C-105m.** *** D: Krishna Shah. James Earl Jones, Cicely Tyson, Glynn Turman, Lou Gossett, Roger E. Mosley, Jonelle Allen. Intelligent, moving story (based on 1972 Tony Award-winning play) of black family trying to come to terms with the world and themselves. Touching and convincing.▼

River of Death (1989) **C-111m.** * ½ D: Steve Carver. Michael Dudikoff, Donald Pleasence, Herbert Lom, Cynthia Erland, Robert Vaughn, L. Q. Jones, Sarah Maur Thorp. Complicated jungle yarn involving a lost city, mad Nazi scientist Vaughn, vengeful Nazi war criminal Pleasence, hero Dudikoff, and the usual hangers-on. Absurd adventure from Alistair MacLean's novel.▼

River of Gold (1970) **C-72m. TVM** D: David Friedkin. Dack Rambo, Roger Davis, Ray Milland, Suzanne Pleshette, Melissa Newman. Various groups wheel and deal, threaten each other in search for key to sunken treasure off Mexican coast. Fair attempt at giving subordinate characters some depth, but resolution strictly for laughs. Average.

River of Mystery (1969) **C-96m. TVM** D: Paul Stanley. Vic Morrow, Claude Akins, Niall MacGinnis, Louise Sorel, Nico Minardos, Edmond O'Brien. Two explosives experts find themselves sought after by diamond hunter and revolutionary leader in South America. Fair location work, lame script. Morrow and Akins perform well together but deserve far better material. Below average.

River of No Return (1954) **C-91m.** **½ D: Otto Preminger. Robert Mitchum, Marilyn Monroe, Rory Calhoun, Tommy Rettig, Murvyn Vye, Douglas Spencer. Mitchum rescues Calhoun and Monroe from leaky raft; Calhoun returns the favor by stealing his horse and abandoning them (and Mitchum's young son) to hostile Indians. Script isn't much, but fine cast and thrilling raft-ing sequences make this worth catching; gorgeous locations and splendid use of CinemaScope will be lost on the tube.▼

River Rat, The (1984) **C-93m.** **½ D: Tom Rickman. Tommy Lee Jones, Nancy Lea Owen, Brian Dennehy, Martha Plimpton. Occasionally perceptive drama about ex-con Jones, falsely imprisoned for murder, and his arrival home after 13 years in the slammer. Works best when focusing on his relationship with his 12-year-old daughter (Plimpton), but spins out of control when dealing with a search for hidden money. Directorial debut for screenwriter Rickman (COAL MINER'S DAUGHTER).▼

Riverrun (1970) **C-87m.** ** D: John Korty. John McLiam, Louise Ober, Mark Jenkins, Josephine Nichols. Unmarried couple expecting a baby has its happiness intruded upon by disagreeable visit from her sea-captain father. Mild drama has lovely photography (by Korty), but the leads are bland, story not that interesting.

River's Edge, The (1957) **C-87m.** *** D: Allan Dwan. Ray Milland, Anthony Quinn, Debra Paget, Byron Foulger. Melodrama about heel (Milland), his ex-girlfriend (Paget), and her husband (Quinn) trying to cross Mexican border with suitcase of money. Ray has never been nastier.

River's Edge (1986) **C-99m.** *** D: Tim Hunter. Crispin Glover, Keanu Reaves, Ione Skye Leitch, Roxana Zal, Daniel Roebuck, Tom Bower, Constance Forslund, Leo Rossi, Jim Metzler, Dennis Hopper. Gripping story of teenagers who don't know how to react when one of their friends murders a girl from their clique and leaves her body along the riverbank. Absorbing, if not perfect, study of contemporary kids and their feelings of alienation from grown-ups, from society, and from responsibility . . . with a wild performance by Glover as their self-styled ringleader. Best of all is Hopper, perfectly cast as a leftover biker and druggie who can't relate to the kids' lack of values. Disturbing and thought-provoking—all the more so when you learn that the story was based on a real-life incident!▼

Rivkin: Bounty Hunter (1981) **C-100m.** TVM D: Harry Harris. Ron Leibman, Harry Morgan, Harold Gary, Verna Bloom, George DiCenzo, Glenn Scarpelli, John Getz, Harry Bellaver. Energetic pilot movie about a nickel-and-dime bounty hunter who makes his living chasing and capturing bail jumpers. Average.

Road Back, The (1937) **97m.** ** D: James Whale. Richard Cromwell, John King, Slim Summerville, Andy Devine, Barbara Read, Louise Fazenda, Noah Beery, Jr., Lionel Atwill. The German soldiers from ALL QUIET ON THE WESTERN FRONT find postwar life at home full of frustra-tions. Heavy-handed sequel to the Erich Maria Remarque classic; interesting to watch but unsatisfying. Summerville repeats his role from the 1930 original.

Roadblock (1951) **73m.** **½ D: Harold Daniels. Charles McGraw, Joan Dixon, Lowell Gilmore, Louis Jean Heydt, Milburn Stone. Insurance investigator's growing attachment to a money-hungry woman leads him to crime. Typical *film noir* formula, smoothly executed.

Road Games (1981-Australian) **C-100m.** **½ D: Richard Franklin. Stacy Keach, Jamie Lee Curtis, Marion Edward, Grant Page, Bill Stacey. Adequate thriller about truckdriver Keach pursuing a murderer. Curtis is a hitchhiker he picks up. Not bad. Director Franklin, an avowed Hitchcock disciple, went on to make PSYCHO II.▼

Road House (1948) **95m.** *** D: Jean Negulesco. Ida Lupino, Cornel Wilde, Celeste Holm, Richard Widmark, O. Z. Whitehead, Robert Karnes. Lupino comes between bitter enemies, roadhouse owner Widmark and parolee Wilde; Ida even sings (introducing the standard "Again") in this engrossing melodrama.

Road House (1989) **C-114m.** *½ D: Rowdy Herrington. Patrick Swayze, Kelly Lynch, Sam Elliott, Ben Gazzara, Marshall Teague, Kevin Tighe, Kathleen Wilhoite, The Jeff Healey Band. Bouncer Swayze—an N.Y.U. philosophy major, no less—is hired to clean house at a hellhole Midwest saloon, and tangles with local kingpin Gazzara, who regards the burg as his own. One broken limb won't suffice when twenty-seven more will do; brain-dead yahoo fare is fun for a while, until it goes way overboard with violence.▼

Roadhouse 66 (1984) **C-96m.** *½ D: John Mark Robinson. Willem Dafoe, Judge Reinhold, Kaaren Lee, Kate Vernon, Stephen Elliot, Alan Autry. Predictable, paper-thin nonsense about upper-class Reinhold and hitchhiker Dafoe and their troubles in a small Arizona town after their car breaks down. Pretty boring stuff.▼

Roadie (1980) **C-105m.** *½ D: Alan Rudolph. Meat Loaf, Kaki Hunter, Art Carney, Gailard Sartain, Alice Cooper, Blondie, Roy Orbison, Hank Williams, Jr., Ramblin' Jack Elliot. Fat roadie (Loaf) and skinny aspiring groupie (Hunter) spend nearly two hours of screen time trying to meet Cooper. Talented director Rudolph turns into a Hal Needham clone with loud, excruciatingly dopey comedy, which does have a handful of defenders.▼

Road Raiders, The (1989) **C-100m.** TVM D: Richard Lang. Bruce Boxleitner, J. D. Cannon, Mark Blankfield, Susan Diol, Reed McCants, Noble Willingham, Clyde Kusatsu, Tia Carrere. Cartoonish action adventure about a band of WW2 misfits and oddballs battling the Japanese in the

South Pacific. These guys seemingly flunked out of *The A-Team* 101. Average.

Road Show (1941) **87m.** **½ D: Hal Roach, Gordon Douglas, Hal Roach, Jr. Adolphe Menjou, Carole Landis, John Hubbard, Charles Butterworth, Patsy Kelly, George E. Stone. Offbeat comedy of young man, wrongfully committed to an insane asylum, escaping and joining up with traveling carnival; some bright moments in inconsequential film. Cowritten by Harry Langdon.

Road to Bali (1952) **C-90m.** *** D: Hal Walker. Bob Hope, Dorothy Lamour, Bing Crosby, Murvyn Vye, Ralph Moody. Only color ROAD film has lush trappings, many guest stars and good laughs, as Bob and Bing save Dorothy from evil princess and jungle perils. Carolyn Jones makes her film debut in a brief bit.▼

Road to Denver, The (1955) **C-90m.** **½ D: Joseph Kane. John Payne, Lee J. Cobb, Skip Homeier, Mona Freeman, Ray Middleton, Lee Van Cleef, Andy Clyde, Glenn Strange. Fast pacing aids this narrative of Payne and brother Homeier on opposite sides of the law, involved in shoot-out.

Road to Glory, The (1936) **95m.** *** D: Howard Hawks. Fredric March, Warner Baxter, Lionel Barrymore, June Lang, Gregory Ratoff, Victor Kilian. Solid production, direction, and acting make more of script (cowritten by William Faulkner) than is really there. Hardened officer Baxter finds his father (Barrymore) serving in his unit in WW1 France. Romantic subplot involves officer March and nurse Lang. Unrelated to same-titled film directed by Hawks in 1926.

Road to Hong Kong, The (1962) **91m.** **½ D: Norman Panama. Bob Hope, Bing Crosby, Joan Collins, Dorothy Lamour, Robert Morley, Walter Gotell, Peter Sellers. Final ROAD picture was the first in a decade, and while it's fun it lacks the carefree spirit of its predecessors; Bob and Bing are con men who become involved in international intrigue—and space travel! Sellers has a hilarious cameo; Lamour appears briefly as herself. Filmed in England.

Road to Morocco (1942) **83m.** *** D: David Butler. Bing Crosby, Dorothy Lamour, Bob Hope, Dona Drake, Anthony Quinn, Vladimir Sokoloff, Monte Blue, Yvonne De Carlo. Typically funny ROAD picture, with Bing selling Bob to slave-trader in mysterious Morocco, both going after princess Lamour. Songs include "Moonlight Becomes You."

Road to Nashville (1967) **C-110m.** *½ D: Robert Patrick. Marty Robbins, Doodles Weaver, Connie Smith, Richard Arlen. Inept promoter tries to line up talent for

Country-Western jamboree. The music's not bad when the plot gets out of the way.

Road to Rio (1947) **100m.** *** D: Norman Z. McLeod. Bing Crosby, Bob Hope, Dorothy Lamour, Gale Sondergaard, Frank Faylen, The Wiere Brothers. Bob and Bing are musicians trying to wrest Dorothy from sinister aunt Sondergaard. Very funny outing in series. Songs: "But Beautiful," "You Don't Have To Know The Language," sung with guests, Andrews Sisters.▼

Road to Salina (1971-French-Italian) **C-96m.** **½ D: Georges Lautner. Mimsy Farmer, Robert Walker, Rita Hayworth, Ed Begley, Bruce Pecheur. Enjoyably trashy tale about wanderer who returns to his mother's diner, and spends much time making love with a girl who might be his sister. And if that isn't kinky enough for you, Rita does the frug with Ed Begley!▼

Road to Singapore (1940) **84m.** **½ D: Victor Schertzinger. Bing Crosby, Dorothy Lamour, Bob Hope, Charles Coburn, Judith Barrett, Anthony Quinn. Bing and Bob swear off women, hiding out in Singapore; then they meet saronged Lamour. First ROAD film is not the best, but still fun.

Road to Utopia (1945) **90m.** *** D: Hal Walker. Bing Crosby, Bob Hope, Dorothy Lamour, Hillary Brooke, Douglass Dumbrille, Jack LaRue. Bob and Bing in the Klondike with usual quota of gags, supplemented by talking animals, Dorothy's song "Personality," Robert Benchley's dry commentary.▼

Road to Yesterday, The (1925) **110m.** *** D: Cecil B. DeMille. Joseph Schildkraut, Jetta Goudal, Vera Reynolds, William Boyd, Julia Faye. Criss-crossed couples in romantic tangle are contrasted with 17th century ancestors, who play out similar story against colorful period setting. DeMille at his best: lavish, hokey, always entertaining.▼

Road to Zanzibar (1941) **92m.** **½ D: Victor Schertzinger. Bing Crosby, Bob Hope, Dorothy Lamour, Una Merkel, Eric Blore. Weaker ROAD series entry, still amusing, with Bob and Bing circus performers traveling through jungle with Lamour and Merkel, looking for diamond mine.

Road Warrior, The SEE: Mad Max 2▼

Roanoak (1986) **C-180m.** TVM D: Jan Egleson. Victor Garber, Will Sampson, Joseph Runningfox, Tino Juarez, Adrian Sparks, Patrick Kilpatrick, Hallie Foote. This account of the initial attempt to establish an English colony in the Carolinas during the 16th century—and the village's fate—works most of the way. A bit overlong but worth staying with. Originally presented over several evenings on PBS' *American Playhouse*. Average.

Roar (1981) **C-102m.** ** D: Noel Marshall. Tippi Hedren, Noel Marshall, John

Marshall, Melanie Griffith, Jerry Marshall, Kyalo Mativo. Accident-ridden production that took 11 years and $17 million for Hedren and husband Marshall to finish. Comedy-adventure about wife and children visiting eccentric scientist husband in jungle after being separated for years is also pro-preservation-of-African-wildlife statement. Nice try, but no cigar. Of additional interest today for early appearance of Hedren's daughter Griffith.

Roaring Timber SEE: **Come and Get It▼**

Roaring Twenties, The (1939) **104m.** *** D: Raoul Walsh. James Cagney, Priscilla Lane, Humphrey Bogart, Gladys George, Jeffrey Lynn, Frank McHugh, Joe Sawyer. Army buddies Cagney, Bogart, and Lynn find their lives intertwining dramatically after WW1 ends. Cagney becomes big-time prohibition racketeer in largely hackneyed script punched across by fine cast, vivid direction. Also shown in computer-colored version.▼

Roar of the Crowd (1953) **C-71m.** *½ D: William Beaudine. Howard Duff, Helene Stanley, Louise Arthur, Harry Shannon, Minor Watson, Don Haggerty. Hackneyed auto-racing tale done on low budget.

Robbers of the Sacred Mountain SEE: **Falcon's Gold▼**

Robber's Roost (1955) **C-82m.** ** D: Sidney Salkow, George Montgomery, Richard Boone, Bruce Bennett, Warren Stevens, Peter Graves, Sylvia Findley. Rugged cast gives zip to this Zane Grey Western of outlaw gangs fighting for control of ranchland. Previously filmed in 1933.

Robbery (1967-British) **C-114m.** *** D: Peter Yates. Stanley Baker, Joanna Pettet, James Booth, Frank Finlay, Barry Foster, William Marlowe. Another study of the British Royal Mail robbery; few surprises, but generally exciting, well-handled.▼

Robbery Under Arms (1957-British) **C-83m.** ** D: Jack Lee. Peter Finch, Ronald Lewis, Laurence Naismith, Maureen Swanson, David McCallum. Quiet account of romance and robbery set in 19th-century Australia.▼

Robe, The (1953) **C-135m.** **½ D: Henry Koster. Richard Burton, Jean Simmons, Victor Mature, Michael Rennie, Richard Boone, Jay Robinson, Dawn Addams, Dean Jagger, Jeff Morrow, Ernest Thesiger. Earnest but episodic costume drama from Lloyd C. Douglas novel about Roman centurion who presides over Christ's crucifixion. Burton's Oscar-nominated performance seems stiff and superficial today, while Mature (as his slave Demetrius) comes off quite well! Famed as first movie in CinemaScope, though it was simultaneously shot "flat," and that's what's shown on TV. Sequel: DEMETRIUS AND THE GLADIATORS. ▼

Roberta (1935) **85m.** *** D: William A.

Seiter. Irene Dunne, Fred Astaire, Ginger Rogers, Randolph Scott, Helen Westley, Claire Dodd, Victor Varconi. The story of this famous Jerome Kern-Otto Harbach musical creaks and groans, but "supporting" characters Astaire and Rogers make up for it in their exuberant dance numbers. You can try counting how many times Scott says "swell," or try to spot young Lucille Ball in fashion-show sequence to get through the rest. Songs include "I Won't Dance," "Smoke Gets In Your Eyes." Based on the Alice Duer Miller novel *Gowns By Roberta*. Remade as LOVELY TO LOOK AT.▼

Robert et Robert (1978-French) **C-105m.** *** D: Claude Lelouch. Charles Denner, Jacques Villeret, Jean-Claude Brialy, Macha Meril, Germaine Montero, Regine. Winning comedy about a friendship between two lonely bachelors named Robert, one an eccentric, impatient cab driver, the other a shy, indecisive apprentice traffic cop. Villeret really scores as the latter.▼

Robin and Marian (1976-British) **C-112m.** **½ D: Richard Lester. Sean Connery, Audrey Hepburn, Robert Shaw, Richard Harris, Nicol Williamson, Denholm Elliott, Kenneth Haigh, Ian Holm, Ronnie Barker. Middle-aged Robin Hood returns to Sherwood Forest after years in exile, rekindles romance with Maid Marian and faces final challenge against arch-enemy Sheriff of Nottingham. Arid, uninvolving film strips beloved characters of all their magic. "Revisionist" script by James Goldman.▼

Robin and the Seven Hoods (1964) **C-103m.** *** D: Gordon Douglas. Frank Sinatra, Dean Martin, Sammy Davis, Jr., Bing Crosby, Peter Falk, Barbara Rush, Victor Buono, Sig Ruman, Allen Jenkins, Hans Conried, Jack LaRue, Edward G. Robinson. Rat Pack's final fling is amusing transposition of the legend to 1928 Chicago, with gangleader Sinatra surprised to find he's something of a local hero. No classic, but good-looking and easy to take; Crosby is adroit as gang's elder statesman. Cahn-Van Heusen songs include "My Kind of Town," "Style," "Mr. Booze."▼

Robin Hood (1973) **C-83m.** **½ D: Wolfgang Reitherman. Voices of Brian Bedford, Phil Harris, Monica Evans, Peter Ustinov, Terry-Thomas, Andy Devine, Roger Miller, Pat Buttram, George Lindsey, Carole Shelley. Undistinguished Disney cartoon feature is pleasant enough for kids, but lacks story strength (and heart). Animals fill traditional Robin Hood roles, with Phil Harris' Little John a virtual reprise of his Baloo the Bear from THE JUNGLE BOOK. Disney's live-action STORY OF ROBIN HOOD was much better. ▼

Robin Hood of El Dorado, The (1936) **86m.** **½ D: William Wellman. Warner

Baxter, Ann Loring, Margo, Bruce Cabot, J. Carrol Naish. Pseudobiography of Mexican bandit Joaquin Murietta, who turns to crime to avenge his wife's murder. Well made, on beautiful locations, but fools around too much for its dramatic moments to be truly effective.

Robinson Crusoe SEE: **Adventures of Robinson Crusoe**

Robinson Crusoe of Clipper Island SEE: **Robinson Crusoe of Mystery Island**▼

Robinson Crusoe of Mystery Island (1936) **100m.** ** D: Mack V. Wright, Ray Taylor. Mala, Rex, Buck, Mamo Clark, Herbert Rawlinson. Overly simple plot is salvaged by spotty action in this cliff-hanger set on a South Sea island; federal agents hunt down foreign powers causing chaos. Reedited from Republic serial ROBINSON CRUSOE OF CLIPPER ISLAND.▼

Robinson Crusoe on Mars (1964) **C-109m.** **½ D: Byron Haskin. Paul Mantee, Vic Lundin, Adam West. Surprisingly agreeable reworking of the classic Defoe story, with Mantee as stranded astronaut, at first accompanied only by a monkey, "Friday" turns out to be a similarly trapped alien. Beautifully shot in Death Valley by Winton C. Hoch; film's intimate nature helps it play better on TV than most space films.

Robocop (1987) **C-103m.** *** D: Paul Verhoeven. Peter Weller, Nancy Allen, Daniel O'Herlihy, Ronny Cox, Kurtwood Smith, Miguel Ferrer, Robert DoQui, Ray Wise, Felton Perry, Paul McCrane, Del Zamora. The setting: Detroit, in the near future. A cop who dies in the line of duty is transformed into an ultrasophisticated cyborg by the corporation which now runs the police department. Only hitch: this "perfect" cop still seeks revenge on the sadistic creeps who killed him. Sharp, slick, slam-bang action entertainment, with fantastic stop-motion animation supervised by Phil Tippet (ED 209 is a wow!) . . . but its view of life in the future is unremittingly bleak and ugly. Followed by a sequel.▼

Robocop 2 (1990) **C-118m.** *½ D: Irvin Kershner. Peter Weller, Nancy Allen, Daniel O'Herlihy, Belinda Bauer, Tom Noonan, Gabriel Damon, Felton Perry, Robert Do'Qui, Willard Pugh, Patricia Charbonneau. Appallingly (and unnecessarily) mean, ugly sequel in which coldblooded corporation czar O'Herlihy and drug kingpin Noonan threaten to end Robo's existence—while the laboratory whizzes cook up a bigger, "better" cyborg cop to take his place. Offensively violent, and doesn't even have the saving grace of humor. Phil Tippet's stop-motion animation is the film's only asset.

Robot Monster (1953) **63m.** BOMB D: Phil Tucker. George Nader, Gregory Moffett, Claudia Barrett, Selena Royle, John Mylong. Gorilla in diving helmet wipes out entire Earth population save one family, then spends most of film's running time lumbering around Bronson Canyon trying to find them. One of the genuine legends of Hollywood: embarrassingly, hilariously awful . . . and dig that bubble machine with the TV antenna! Originally in 3-D (except for the dinosaur stock footage from ONE MILLION B.C.).▼

Rob Roy, the Highland Rogue (1954) **C-85m.** *½ D: Harold French. Richard Todd, Glynis Johns, James Robertson Justice, Michael Gough, Finlay Currie, Jean Taylor-Smith. Disney's dreariest British film casts Todd as leader of Scottish clan planning uprising against England's King George in 18th century. Turgid and unrewarding.▼

Rocambole (1962-French) **C-106m.** **½ D: Bernard Borderie. Channing Pollock, Hedy Vessel, Nadia Gray, Guy Delorme, Lilla Brignone. Further adventures of Ponson du Terrail's carefree rogue, played tongue-in-cheek by Pollock, involved in Parisian nightlife.

Rocco and His Brothers (1960-Italian) **155m.** ***½ D: Luchino Visconti. Alain Delon, Renato Salvatori, Annie Girardot, Katina Paxinou, Claudia Cardinale, Roger Hanin. Long, absorbing study of poor farm woman who moves to Milan with her four sons in search of better life; Visconti's powerful emotional landscape makes this a modern classic. Beware 95m. edited version.▼

Rockabye (1933) **67m.** *½ D: George Cukor. Constance Bennett, Joel McCrea, Paul Lukas, Jobyna Howland, Walter Pidgeon, Sterling Holloway. Other than offering a memorable shot of Bennett immersed in balloons, soaper about a morally ambiguous actress's love for her toddler is painful going. A curio for film buffs, but a minor credit for both star and director.

Rockabye (1986) **C-100m.** TVM D: Richard Michaels. Valerie Bertinelli, Rachel Ticotin, Jason Alexander, Ray Baker, Roderick Cook, Jo Henderson. Plucky out-of-towner pursues her young son, snatched from her as she steps off a bus in Manhattan. The cops are apathetic, but a streetwise lady reporter smells a good story and offers help. Our heroine even manages to come up with a dime after being mugged and finds a working phone on the first try in the middle of the bombed-out South Bronx! Below average.

Rock-a-Bye Baby (1958) **C-103m.** *** D: Frank Tashlin. Jerry Lewis, Marilyn Maxwell, Connie Stevens, Baccaloni, Reginald Gardiner, James Gleason, Hans Conried. Good-natured schnook Jerry becomes full-time baby-sitter for movie sex-siren Maxwell, who doesn't want her public to know she's had triplets. Loose remake of Preston Sturges's THE MIRACLE OF MORGAN'S CREEK, with many funny moments. That's Lewis's son Gary playing Jerry as a boy in the musical flashback sequence.

Rock All Night (1957) **63m.** ** D: Roger Corman. Dick Miller, Russell Johnson, Jonathan Haze, Abby Dalton, The Platters, Robin Morse. AIP quickie about a pair of killers taking refuge in a bar and terrorizing captive customers. OK Corman potboiler with better-than-average performances, and dig this—Johnson's one of the bad guys and Miller's the hero!

Rock & Rule (1983) **C-85m.** **½ D: Clive A. Smith. Voices of Don Francks, Paul Le Mat, Susan Roman, Sam Langevin, Catherine O'Hara. Animated rock fable, with innovative, often dazzling visuals and a solid score (featuring Lou Reed, Debbie Harry, Cheap Trick, Earth, Wind and Fire, Iggy Pop, and others) . . . but story leaves something to be desired. A triumph of technique for Canada's Nelvana animation studio, and certainly worth a look.▼

Rock Around the Clock (1956) **77m.** ** D: Fred F. Sears. Bill Haley and His Comets, The Platters, Tony Martinez and His Band, Freddie Bell and His Bellboys, Alan Freed, Johnny Johnston. Premise is slim (unknown band brought to N.Y.C. where they become famous) but picture is now a time-capsule look at an American phenomenon: the emergence of rock 'n' roll. Bill Haley and the Comets perform "See You Later Alligator," "Razzle Dazzle" and the title song; the Platters chip in with "Only You" and "The Great Pretender." Remade as TWIST AROUND THE CLOCK.▼

Rock Around the World (1957-British) **71m.** *½ D: Gerard Bryant. Tommy Steele, Patrick Westwood, Dennis Price, Tom Littlewood. Humdrum account of Tommy Steele's rise in the singing profession. Originally titled THE TOMMY STEELE STORY.

Rock Baby, Rock It (1957) **84m.** *½ D: Murray Douglas Sporup. Johnny Carroll and His Hot Rocks, Rosco Gordon and The Red Tops, The Five Stars, The Belew Twins, Don Coats and The Bon-Aires, Preacher Smith and The Deacons, The Cell Block Seven, Kay Wheeler. Teens vs. syndicate bookies in this silly period piece that's become a minor cult item, mostly because it was shot in Dallas and highlights performances by regional rock acts. For diehard fans of the genre only.▼

Rockers (1978-Jamaican) **C-100m.** *** D: Theodoros Bafaloukos. Leroy Wallace. Richard Hall, Monica Craig, Marjorie Norman, Jacob Miller. Winningly funky though predictable comedy/drama about Rastafarian drummer Wallace's efforts to earn money and crack open the music establishment. Superior reggae score fea-

turing Peter Tosh, Bunny Wailer, Burning Spear, Third World and Gregory Isaacs.

Rocket Attack, U.S.A. (1959) **71m.** BOMB D: Barry Mahon. Monica Davis, John McKay, Daniel Kern, Edward Czerniuk, Arthur Metrano. Spy attempts to uncover Russian missile plans; meanwhile, the dastardly Commies are planning to nuke N.Y.C. Perfectly awful Cold War melodrama with hilarious dialogue, atrocious performances, lots of stock footage.▼

Rocket Gibraltar (1988) **C-100m.** *** D: Daniel Petrie. Burt Lancaster, Suzy Amis, Patricia Clarkson, Frances Conroy, Sinead Cusack, John Glover, Bill Pullman, Kevin Spacey, Macaulay Culkin. A family gathers to celebrate patriarch Lancaster's 77th birthday; his grown-up children love him but don't really understand what he's going through, while his grandchildren make a more emotional connection to the old man . . . and vow to carry out his unusual final wish. Lancaster's presence gives the film authority, and a talented ensemble lends credibility to Amos Poe's script. Culkin is wonderful as Lancaster's canny five-year-old grandson. Filmed at beautiful locations on Long Island.▼

Rocket Man, The (1954) **79m.** ** D: Oscar Rudolph. Charles Coburn, Spring Byington, Anne Francis, John Agar, George Winslow. OK fantasy of Winslow possessing a space gun that turns crooked people honest. Believe it or not, the principal writer of this kid-oriented film was Lenny Bruce!

Rockets Galore SEE: **Mad Little Island**

Rocket Ship X-M (1950) **77m.** **½ D: Kurt Neumann. Lloyd Bridges, Osa Massen, Hugh O'Brian, John Emery. Slightly better than average production of spaceship to moon that is blown off-course to Mars. Nice photography, good acting. Videocassette version contains new special effects shot in 1976.▼

Rocket to the Moon SEE: **Cat Women of the Moon**▼

Rockford Files, The (1974) **C-78m.** TVM D: Richard T. Heffron. James Garner, Lindsay Wagner, William Smith, Nita Talbot, Joe Santos, Stuart Margolin. Ex-con private eye looks into a skid row bum's murder at the urging of the dead man's daughter. Garner, the reluctant hero, at what he does best. The hit series followed. Written and produced by Stephen J. Cannell; Robert Donley plays Rockford, Sr., the role inherited by Noah Beery in the weekly show. Above average.

Rock Hudson (1990) **C-100m.** TVM D: John Nicolella. Thomas Ian Griffith, Daphne Ashbrook, William R. Moses, Andrew Robinson, Don Galloway, Diane Ladd. Episodic, why-bother docudrama about the star's life and death, with unknown Griffith trying to impersonate Rock. Robinson is his mentor and manager Henry Willson, Galloway is director John Frankenheimer, and Ashbrook is Phyllis Gates, Hudson's onetime wife whose book was the partial basis for this humdrum film. Average.

Rocking Horse Winner, The (1950-British) **91m.** ***½ D: Anthony Pelissier. Valerie Hobson, John Howard Davies, John Mills, Ronald Squire. Truly unique, fascinating drama based on D. H. Lawrence story; small boy has knack for picking racetrack winners, but complications set in before long. Beautifully done.

Rockin' the Blues (1955) **66m.** ** D: Arthur Rosenblum. Mantan Moreland, F. E. Miller, Connie Carroll, The Wanderers, The Harptones, The Hurricanes, The Five Miller Sisters, Pearl Woods, Linda Hopkins, Hal Jackson. Grade-Z production values hamper this intriguing curio, an all-black rhythm-and-blues show emceed by Jackson, with Moreland along for comic relief. Dance routines are generally awful, but much of the music is priceless; The Hurricanes' army-life number is a real showstopper.▼

Rock 'n' Roll High School (1979) **C-93m.** *** D: Allan Arkush. P. J. Soles, Vincent Van Patten, Clint Howard, Dey Young, The Ramones, Mary Woronov, Paul Bartel, Alix Elias. A 1950's movie gone berserk. A rock-crazy teenager marshals her fellow students to rebel against the repression of new principal Miss Togar. An irresistible, high-energy comedy set to a nonstop soundtrack of Ramones music (and a few oldies). Soles is wonderful as the group's number one fan, Riff Randell. The songs include "Teenage Lobotomy," "Blitzkrieg Bop," "I Wanna Be Sedated," and "Sheena Is a Punk Rocker."▼

Rock 'n' Roll Mom (1988) **C-100m. TVM** D: Michael Schultz. Dyan Cannon, Michael Brandon, Telma Hopkins, Heather Locklear, Nancy Lenehan, Alex Rocco, Nina Blackwood. Amiable Disney comedy about a suburban housewife with teenage kids who becomes an overnight hit as a pop music star. Average.

Rock, Pretty Baby (1956) **89m.** ** D: Richard Bartlett. Sal Mineo, John Saxon, Luana Patten, Edward C. Platt, Fay Wray, Rod McKuen. Prototype of rock 'n' roll entries of 1950s revolving around high school rock group's effort to win big-time musical contest.▼

Rock, Rock, Rock! (1956) **83m.** ** D: Will Price. Tuesday Weld, Teddy Randazzo, Alan Freed, Frankie Lymon and the Teenagers, The Moonglows, Chuck Berry, The Flamingos, Johnny Burnette Trio, LaVern Baker, Cirino and the Bowties. Weld, in her film debut and barely out of her training bra, must raise $30 to buy a strapless evening dress for a prom! Filmed on a budget of $6.95—and it shows. But the rock 'n' rollers, particularly Chuck Berry, are lively. Lymon and the Teenagers sing "I'm Not a Juvenile Delinquent." Weld's singing voice was dubbed by Connie Francis. One of the teens is young Valerie Harper.▼

Rockshow (1980-British) **C-105m.** **½ No director credited. Paul McCartney, Linda McCartney, Jimmy McCulloch, Joe English, Denny Laine. Adequate concert film of Paul McCartney and Wings on tour. Effect of Dolby sound recording will be lost on the small screen.

Rockula (1990) **C-87m.** *½ D: Luca Bercovici. Dean Cameron, Tawny Fere, Susan Tyrrell, Bo Diddley, Thomas Dolby, Toni Basil. Teen vampire Cameron is unable to lose his virginity because of a centuries-old curse. Pretty stale stuff; of interest only for—but not redeemed by—the presence of Diddley.▼

Rocky (1976) **C-119m.** ***½ D: John G. Avildsen. Sylvester Stallone, Talia Shire, Burt Young, Carl Weathers, Burgess Meredith, Thayer David. This story of a two-bit fighter who gets his "million-to-one shot" for fame, and self-respect, in a championship bout is impossible to dislike, even though it's just an old B-movie brought up to date. Knowing that the film was a similar do-or-die project for writer-star Stallone added to its good vibes. Oscar winner for Best Picture, Director, Editing (Richard Halsey, Scott Conrad). Followed by three sequels.▼

Rocky II (1979) **C-119m.** *** D: Sylvester Stallone. Sylvester Stallone, Talia Shire, Burt Young, Carl Weathers, Burgess Meredith. Officially a sequel, this slightly silly film is more of a rehash, but the climactic bout (and buildup to it) hits home.▼

Rocky III (1982) **C-99m.** **½ D: Sylvester Stallone. Sylvester Stallone, Talia Shire, Burt Young, Burgess Meredith, Carl Weathers, Mr. T. Here, the Italian Stallion (Stallone) is trained by Apollo Creed (Weathers) after being dethroned by obnoxious Clubber Lang (Mr. T). Stallone's got a winning formula, but enough already.▼

Rocky IV (1985) **C-91m.** **½ D: Sylvester Stallone. Sylvester Stallone, Dolph Lundgren, Carl Weathers, Talia Shire, Burt Young, Brigitte Nielsen, Michael Pataki, James Brown. Totally artificial (and unnecessary) sequel has Rocky doin' what a man's gotta do—avenging a friend's demise and fighting for the U.S.A. (and world peace) against a superhuman Russian champ. Still in all, Stallone knows how to milk a formula and press all the right buttons, especially in a great training montage.▼

Rocky Horror Picture Show, The (1975-British) **C-95m.** *** D: Jim Sharman. Tim Curry, Susan Sarandon, Barry Bostwick, Richard O'Brien, Jonathan Adams, Meatloaf, Little Nell (Campbell), Charles Gray, Patricia Quinn. Outrageously kinky horror movie spoof, spiced with sex, transvestism, and rock music, about a straight couple, Janet and Brad (Sarandon, Bostwick), stranded in an old dark house full of weirdos from Transylvania. Music and lyrics by O'Brien; songs include "Time Warp," "Dammit Janet," and "Wild and Untamed Thing." British running time: 100m. Followed by SHOCK TREATMENT.

Rocky Mountain (1950) **83m.** ****½** D: William Keighley. Errol Flynn, Patrice Wymore, Scott Forbes, Slim Pickens, Sheb Wooley, Yakima Canutt. Lumbering Flynn vehicle set in Civil War times, with Rebs and Yankees fighting off an Indian attack.

Rodan (1957-Japanese) **C-70m.** ****** D: Inoshiro Honda. Kenji Sawara, Yumi Shirakawa, Akihiko Hirata, Akio Kobori. Colossal pterodactyl hatches in mine, later goes on destructive rampage in Tokyo. Colorful comic book stuff, all too typical of Toho Studios' monster formula.▼

Rodeo (1952) **C-70m.** ***½** D: William Beaudine. Jane Nigh, John Archer, Wallace Ford, Frances Rafferty. Tame little account of girl managing a roping show.

Rodeo Girl (1980) **C-100m.** TVM D: Jackie Cooper. Katharine Ross, Bo Hopkins, Candy Clark, Jacqueline Brookes, Wilford Brimley, Parley Baer. Bronco buster's bored wife joins an all-girl rodeo circuit in this agreeable adaptation by Kathryn Micaelian Powers of the true story of world champion rodeo star Sue Pirtle. Average.▼

Roe vs. Wade (1989) **C-100m.** TVM D: Gregory Hoblit. Holly Hunter, Amy Madigan, Terry O'Quinn, Kathy Bates, James Gammon, Annabella Price. Provocative attempt to take the middle road in the abortion issue, dramatizing the landmark '70s case in which the U.S. Supreme Court upheld the right of a woman to have an abortion (a decision being reexamined by the Court as this film premiered). Hunter plays Roe as a spunky, unmarried Texas woman; Madigan is the recent law school graduate who argues her case. Alison Cross' script manages a high-wire balancing act to inflame neither side in this emotional issue. Average.▼

Roger & Harry: The Mitera Target (1977) **C-78m.** TVM D: Jack Starrett. John Davidson, Barry Primus, Carole Mallory, Anne Randall Stewart, Richard Lynch, Susan Sullivan, Harris Yulin, Biff McGuire. Contemporary swashbuckler featuring a pair of professional retrievers of people and jewelry, attempting to recover a kidnapped heiress. A live-action cartoon. Below average. Retitled LOVE FOR RANSOM.

Roger and Me (1989) **C-87m.** *****½** D:

Michael Moore. Inspired, darkly ironic documentary-style film about one man's attempts to track down General Motors chairman Roger Smith, to show him what his factory closing did to the town of Flint, Michigan, where 40,000 jobs were lost. Filmmaker/narrator Moore creates an irresistible blend of documentary and humorous essay in this unique piece of Americana.▼

Roger Touhy, Gangster (1944) **65m.** ****½** D: Robert Florey. Preston Foster, Victor McLaglen, Lois Andrews, Anthony Quinn, Kent Taylor, Henry (Harry) Morgan, Trudy Marshall, Kane Richmond. Supposed biographical film of famous murderer is just another gangster film.

Rogue Cop (1954) **92m.** ******* D: Roy Rowland. Robert Taylor, Janet Leigh, George Raft, Steven Forrest, Anne Francis, Vince Edwards. Dynamic account of policeman Taylor on the underworld payroll, tracking down his brother's killer.

Rogue Male (1976-British) **C-100m.** TVM D: Clive Donner. Peter O'Toole, John Standing, Alastair Sim, Cyd Hayman, Harold Pinter, Hugh Manning. Remake of MAN HUNT with O'Toole as British aristocrat who tries to assassinate Hitler in the 1930s and then is hounded by the Gestapo. First-class BBC production with Frederic Raphael script (from the Geoffrey Household novel). Above average.

Rogue River (1950) **C-81m.** ****** D: John Rawlins. Rory Calhoun, Peter Graves, Frank Fenton, Ralph Sanford. Talky study of family relationships; not much on Western action.

Rogues' Gallery (1968) **C-88m.** ****** D: Leonard Horn. Roger Smith, Greta Baldwin, Dennis Morgan, Farley Granger, Edgar Bergen, Brian Donlevy, Mala Powers. Private eye comes to aid of beautiful woman attempting suicide, eventually seduced into frameup scheme. Forgettable mystery drama with uneven performances, unbelievable dialogue. Never released theatrically.

Rogue's March (1952) **84m.** ****** D: Allan Davis. Peter Lawford, Richard Greene, Janice Rule, Leo G. Carroll. Programmer-costumer set in India (via stock footage and rear projection scenes), with Lawford trying to redeem himself with regiment.

Rogues of Sherwood Forest (1950) **C-80m.** ****** D: Gordon Douglas. John Derek, Diana Lynn, George Macready, Alan Hale. Despite good production and fair cast, pretty limp; Robin Hood's son (Derek) fights to get the Magna Carta signed.

Rogue's Regiment (1948) **86m.** ****** D: Robert Florey. Dick Powell, Marta Toren, Vincent Price, Stephen McNally, Edgar Barrier, Henry Rowland. Contrived actioner about American agent Powell, who joins the French Foreign Legion in Indochina to hunt down Nazi bigwig McNally.

Rollerball (1975) **C-128m.** **½ D: Norman Jewison. James Caan, John Houseman, Maud Adams, John Beck, Moses Gunn, Ralph Richardson. Great-looking but disappointing drama of the 21st century; Caan is the champ at a violent sport in a society where violence has been outlawed. Filmed in Munich and London, adapted by William Harrison from his story *Roller Ball Murders.*▼

Roller Boogie (1979) **C-103m.** BOMB D: Mark L. Lester. Linda Blair, Jim Bray, Beverly Garland, Roger Perry, Mark Goddard, Sean McClory. Blair, Bray, and friends join forces to thwart evil Goddard from closing local roller skating rink. Made to cash in on roller-disco fad, but amateurish script and performances should roll this into oblivion.

Rollercoaster (1977) **C-119m.** ** D: James Goldstone. George Segal, Richard Widmark, Timothy Bottoms, Henry Fonda, Harry Guardino, Susan Strasberg. Silly disaster-type film almost redeemed by Segal's winning performance as civic inspector who tries to nail extortionist (Bottoms) before he sabotages another amusement park. Overlong, but at least TV audiences won't have to watch it in "Sensurround."▼

Roll, Freddy, Roll (1974) **C-78m.** TVM D: Bill Persky. Tim Conway, Jan Murray, Scott Brady, Henry Jones, Ruta Lee, Moosie Drier, Robert Hogan. Overblown TV sitcom has divorced computer programmer Conway, desperate to compete for his son's attention by out-doing the boy's flamboyant new stepdad, determined to win a place in the Guinness Book of World Records as a nonstop rollerskater. Average.

Rolling Man (1972) **C-73m.** TVM D: Peter Hyams. Dennis Weaver, Don Stroud, Donna Mills, Slim Pickens, Jimmy Dean, Agnes Moorehead, Sheree North. Vivid atmosphere of small-town existence excellent counterpoint to saga of Lonnie McAfee (Weaver) barely making headway through one raw deal after another: wife's desertion, murder, prison term, searching for children . . . Some characters verge on stereotypes but film's point of view, direction, and plot line make up for it; written by Stephen and Elinor Knarpf. Above average.

Rolling Thunder (1977) **C-99m.** ** D: John Flynn. William Devane, Tommy Lee Jones, Linda Haynes, James Best, Dabney Coleman, Lisa Richards, Luke Askew. Devane comes home after eight years as P.O.W. in Vietnam, sees his family murdered, and cold-bloodedly goes for revenge. Intriguing aspects of story (by Paul Schrader) and main characters thrown off-course by graphic violence and vigilante melodramatics.▼

Roll of Thunder, Hear My Cry (1978) **C-150m.** TVM D: Jack Smight. Claudia McNeil, Janet MacLachlan, Robert Chris-tian, Larry Scott, Roy Poole, Rockne Tarkington, John Cullum, Morgan Freeman, Lark Ruffin. Simple, predictably uplifting chronicle of a close-knit black family, struggling along in Depression-era Mississippi, seen through the eyes of an 11-year-old girl (Ruffin). Adapted from the novels of Mildred D. Taylor. Average.▼

Rollover (1981) **C-118m.** *½ D: Alan J. Pakula. Jane Fonda, Kris Kristofferson, Hume Cronyn, Josef Sommer, Bob Gunton. Laughably pretentious, barely comprehensible drama about petrochemical heiress (and former film star) Fonda, banker-troubleshooter Kristofferson, and their high-financial dealings. Cronyn excels as a cunning banker. One of the few examples of financial science fiction.▼

Romance (1930) **76m.** ** D: Clarence Brown. Greta Garbo, Lewis Stone, Gavin Gordon, Elliott Nugent, Florence Lake, Clara Blandick. Garbo is miscast in this static, hokey early talkie about an Italian opera star who philosophizes about love and has a relationship with an inexperienced young priest (limply played by Gordon).

Romance and Riches SEE: **Amazing Adventure**▼

Romance in Manhattan (1934) **78m.** *** D: Stephen Roberts. Ginger Rogers, Francis Lederer, J. Farrell MacDonald, Arthur Hohl, Sidney Toler. Chorus girl Rogers helps illegal alien Lederer, and romance blossoms, in this most enjoyable Capraesque comedy.

Romance in the Dark (1938) **80m.** ** D: H. C. Potter. Gladys Swarthout, John Barrymore, John Boles, Claire Dodd, Curt Bois. A womanizing tenor uses a naive young singer (Swarthout) in a scheme to distract his rival, but his plans backfire when he falls in love with her. Stylish treatment of trite material; more a showcase for funny Fritz Feld (as Boles's valet) than for opera star Swarthout.

Romance of a Horsethief (1971-U.S.-Yugoslav) **C-100m.** *½ D: Abraham Polonsky. Yul Brynner, Eli Wallach, Jane Birkin, Oliver Tobias, Lainie Kazan, David Opatoshu. Wily Jewish horsetraders scheme to outwit Cossack captain Brynner and his men, in a Polish village circa 1904. A heartfelt endeavor for director Polonsky and actor-screenwriter Opatoshu that just doesn't come off.▼

Romance of Rosy Ridge, The (1947) **105m.** *** D: Roy Rowland. Van Johnson, Thomas Mitchell, Janet Leigh, Marshall Thompson. Selena Royle. Set in post-Civil War days, Missouri farmer Mitchell casts suspicious eye on young Johnson, who is courting his daughter, Leigh (in her film debut).

Romance on the High Seas (1948) **C-99m.** *** D: Michael Curtiz. Jack Carson, Janis

Paige, Don Defore, Doris Day, Oscar Levant, S. Z. Sakall, Fortunio Bonanova, Eric Blore, Franklin Pangborn. Sparkling, trivial romantic musical set on an ocean voyage, with Doris' film debut, singing "It's Magic," "Put 'em in a Box." Easygoing fun.

Romance on the Orient Express (1985) **C-100m. TVM** D: Lawrence Gordon Clark. Cheryl Ladd, Stuart Wilson, Renee Asherson, Ralph Michael, John Gielgud, Julian Sands. Magazine editor Ladd and old English flame Wilson rekindle a romance on the train from Venice to Paris. Lushly filmed with a Gielgud performance that's pure panache (and the sole reason for those not hooked on romance novels to watch). Average.

Romancing the Stone (1984) **C-105m.** *** D: Robert Zemeckis. Kathleen Turner, Michael Douglas, Danny DeVito, Zack Norman, Alfonso Arau, Manuel Ojeda. Very likable high-adventure hokum about mousy writer of romantic fiction who finds herself up to her neck in trouble in Colombia, with only a feisty American soldier-of-fortune as her ally. Silly story never stops moving—with some terrific action and stunts—but it's Turner's enormously appealing performance that really makes the film worthwhile. Sequel: THE JEWEL OF THE NILE.▼

Roman Holiday (1953) **119m.** ***½ D: William Wyler. Audrey Hepburn, Gregory Peck, Eddie Albert, Tullio Carminati. Hepburn got first break and an Oscar as princess, yearning for normal life, who runs away from palace, has romance with reporter Peck. Screenplay by John Dighton and Ian McLellan Hunter, from Hunter's Oscar-winning story. Utterly charming. Remade as a TV movie.▼

Roman Holiday (1987) **C-100m. TVM** D: Noel Nosseck. Catherine Oxenberg, Tom Conti, Ed Begley, Jr., Eileen Atkins. Contemporary remake of the William Wyler classic without the magic of Hepburn, the panache of Peck, the charm of Eddie Albert as, respectively, the runaway princess, the brash newspaperman, and his crafty photographer buddy. Falls neatly into the "if it ain't broke, don't fix it" category of moviemaking. Average.

Romanoff and Juliet (1961) **C-103m.** *** D: Peter Ustinov. Peter Ustinov, Sandra Dee, John Gavin, Akim Tamiroff, Rik Von Nutter. Ustinov wrote, directed and stars in this cold war satire with offspring of U.S. and Russian ambassadors falling in love. Italian locations substitute for mythical country which Ustinov rules.

Roman Scandals (1933) **92m.** *** D: Frank Tuttle. Eddie Cantor, Ruth Etting, Gloria Stuart, David Manners, Verree Teasdale, Alan Mowbray, Edward Arnold. Old-fashioned, enjoyable musical vehicle for Cantor to romp through as dreamer who is transported back to ancient Rome. Full of funny gags and delightful songs. Big Busby Berkeley production numbers include young Lucille Ball.▼

Roman Spring of Mrs. Stone, The (1961) **C-104m.** *** D: Jose Quintero. Vivien Leigh, Warren Beatty, Lotte Lenya, Jill St. John, Jeremy Spenser, Coral Browne, Cleo Laine, Bessie Love. Middle-aged actress retreats to Rome, buying a fling at romance from gigolo Beatty. Lenya, as Leigh's waspish friend, comes off best. Adapted from Tennessee Williams novella.▼

Romantic Age, The (1949-British) **86m.** ** D: Edmond T. Greville. Mai Zetterling, Hugh Williams, Margot Grahame, Petula Clark, Carol Marsh, Adrienne Corri. Art teacher Williams falls for flirtatious French schoolgirl Zetterling. Trifling; also known as NAUGHTY ARLETTE.

Romantic Comedy (1983) **C-103m.** *½ D: Arthur Hiller. Dudley Moore, Mary Steenburgen, Frances Sternhagen, Janet Eilber, Robyn Douglass, Ron Leibman. Faithful adaptation of Bernard Slade's paper-thin play looks even worse on screen than it did on stage, despite a perfect cast. Moore is a playwright who tries to stifle his feelings for his female writing partner over many years' time. Title sounds suspiciously like a generic product—like Canned Peas or Toilet Tissue. Hold out for brand names.

Romantic Englishwoman, The (1975-British) **C-115m.** ***½ D: Joseph Losey. Michael Caine, Glenda Jackson, Helmut Berger, Beatrice Romand, Kate Nelligan, Nathalie Delon, Michel Lonsdale. Caine, a successful novelist married to Jackson, invites Berger into their home to generate material for a screenplay he's writing. Underrated comedy-drama by Tom Stoppard and Thomas Wiseman; stylish and believable.▼

Rome Adventure (1962) **C-119m.** *** D: Delmer Daves. Troy Donahue, Angie Dickinson, Rossano Brazzi, Suzanne Pleshette, Constance Ford, Chad Everett, Al Hirt, Hampton Fancher. Plush soaper with Pleshette as schoolteacher on Roman fling to find romance, torn between roué (Brazzi) and architect (Donahue). As Troy's mistress, Dickinson has some rare repartee. Lush Max Steiner score. Donahue and Pleshette married two years later.

Rome Express (1932-British) **94m.** *** D: Walter Forde. Conrad Veidt, Esther Ralston, Harold Huth, Gordon Harker, Donald Calthrop, Joan Barry, Cedric Hardwicke, Frank Vosper, Hugh Williams. Seminal mystery-thriller that spawned many imitations, including THE LADY VANISHES and NIGHT TRAIN TO MUNICH, among others. Entertaining, if slightly talky, tale of assorted group of passengers caught up in criminal activities aboard train. Remade as SLEEPING CAR TO TRIESTE.

Romeo and Juliet (1936) **126m.** ***½ D: George Cukor. Norma Shearer, Leslie Howard, John Barrymore, Edna May Oliver, Basil Rathbone, C. Aubrey Smith, Andy Devine, Reginald Denny, Ralph Forbes. Well-acted, lavish production of Shakespeare's play about ill-fated lovers. Howard and Shearer are so good that one can forget they are too old for the roles. Not the great film it might have been, but a very good one.

Romeo and Juliet (1954-British) **C-140m.** *** D: Renato Castellani. Laurence Harvey, Susan Shentall, Flora Robson, Mervyn Johns, Bill Travers, Sebastian Cabot; introduced by John Gielgud. Sumptuously photographed in Italy, this pleasing version of Shakespeare's tragedy has the virtue of good casting.▼

Romeo and Juliet (1966-British) **C-126m.** **½ D: Paul Czinner. Margot Fonteyn, Rudolf Nureyev, David Blair, Desmond Doyle, Julia Farron, Michael Somes. Anyone interested in dance will want to see this filmed record of the Royal Ballet production, but actually, it doesn't adapt very well to film; zoom lens is poor substitute for immediacy of live performance.▼

Romeo and Juliet (1968-British-Italian) **C-138m.** ***½ D: Franco Zeffirelli. Leonard Whiting, Olivia Hussey, Milo O'Shea, Michael York, John McEnery, Pat Heywood, Robert Stephens. One of the best cinematic versions of Shakespeare's immortal tale of two young lovers kept apart by their families. Unique for its casting leads who were only 17 and 15, respectively, this exquisitely photographed film (by Pasquale de Santis, who won an Oscar) has a hauntingly beautiful musical score by Nino Rota and Oscar-winning costumes by Danilo Donati.▼

Romero (1989) **C-102m.** *** D: John Duigan. Raul Julia, Richard Jordan, Ana Alicia, Eddie Velez, Alejandro Bracho, Tony Plana, Lucy Reina, Harold Gould, Al Ruscio, Robert Viharo. Absorbing biography of El Salvador's Archbishop Oscar Romero, chronicling his transformation from passive cleric to eloquent defender of his church and people. Thoughtfully directed with a good script by John Sacret Young and a quietly powerful performance by Julia. The initial feature film financed by officials of the United States Roman Catholic Church.▼

Rona Jaffe's Mazes and Monsters SEE: **Mazes and Monsters**▼

Roof, The (1956-Italian) **98m.** **½ D: Vittorio De Sica. Gabriella Pallotta, Giorgio Listuzzi, Gastone Renzelli, Maria Di Rollo. Realistic if unexciting account of young couple trying to find a home in crowded postwar Rome; they find technicality in law to solve their problem.▼

Rooftops (1989) **C-95m.** *½ D: Robert Wise. Jason Gedrick, Troy Beyer, Eddie Velez, Tisha Campbell, Alexis Cruz, Allen Payne. Routine urban B musical about a teenage white male, his forbidden Hispanic girlfriend, drug pushers, and a form of "combat dancing"—the last employing martial-arts footwork, but without the bone crushing. Sole distinction: that it was directed by veteran Wise, who won an Oscar for the thematically similar WEST SIDE STORY.▼

Rookie, The (1959) **86m.** BOMB D: George O'Hanlon. Tommy Noonan, Pete Marshall, Julie Newmar, Jerry Lester, Joe Besser, Vince Barnett, Peter Leeds. Feeble Army comedy of draftee, tough sergeant, movie starlet, and other stereotypes set during 1940s.

Rookies, The (1971) **C-73m.** TVM D: Jud Taylor. Darren McGavin, Paul Burke, Cameron Mitchell, Robert F. Lyons, Georg Stanford Brown, Sam Melville. Rigorous training period, indoctrination, and first weeks of active duty in lives of several specially recruited young men of L.A. police force. Lots of action, but film tries to bite off more than it can chew. Average; pilot for TV series, but better than subsequent episodes.

Room at the Top (1959-British) **118m.** **** D: Jack Clayton. Laurence Harvey, Simone Signoret, Heather Sears, Hermione Baddeley, Donald Wolfit, Ambrosine Philpotts, Donald Houston. Brilliant drama of Harvey sacrificing Signoret's love to get ahead by marrying factory boss' daughter. Trenchant and powerful adaptation of John Braine novel won Oscars for Signoret and screenwriter Neil Paterson. Followed by LIFE AT THE TOP and MAN AT THE TOP.▼

Room for One More (1952) **98m.** *** D: Norman Taurog. Cary Grant, Betsy Drake, Lurene Tuttle, George Winslow, John Ridgely. Grant and Drake are softhearted couple who can't resist adopting needy kids. Sentimental comedy retitled THE EASY WAY; basis for later TV series.

Roommate, The (1984) **C-96m.** TVM D: Nell Cox. Lance Guest, Barry Miller, Elaine Wilkes, Melissa Ford, David Bachman. Funny, intelligent comedy-drama about a very odd couple, ultrastraight Guest and politically conscious Miller, who find themselves sharing a dorm at Northwestern University in 1952. Perceptively scripted—despite some loose ends about Miller's character—and the era is nicely evoked. It's also refreshing to see a movie about students who actually study. Based on a story by John Updike; a PBS *American Playhouse* presentation. Above average. ▼

Room Service (1938) 78m. *** D: William A. Seiter. Groucho, Chico and Harpo Marx, Lucille Ball, Ann Miller, Frank Albertson, Donald MacBride. Broadway farce about destitute producers trying to keep their play afloat—and avoid being evicted from their hotel room—is transformed by scenarist Morrie Ryskind into a vehicle for the Marx Bros. More conventional than their earlier outings, but still has a lot of funny material (and, thankfully, no intrusive songs). Remade as a musical, STEP LIVELY.▼

Room Upstairs, The (1987) C-100m. TVM D: Stuart Margolin. Stockard Channing, Sam Waterston, Linda Hunt, Sarah Jessica Parker, James Handy. A lonely teacher is brought romantically alive by the gentle cellist who has taken a room in her boardinghouse. Offbeat comedy-drama adapted by Steve Lawson from Norma Levinson's novel. Average.

Room with a View, A (1985-British) C-115m. *** D: James Ivory. Maggie Smith, Helena Bonham Carter, Denholm Elliott, Julian Sands, Daniel Day-Lewis, Simon Callow, Judi Dench, Rosemary Leach, Rupert Graves. Elegant and witty adaptation of E. M. Forster novel about British manners and mores, and a young woman's awakening experiences during a trip (chaperoned, of course) to Florence. Splendid performances, fine attention to detail; only fault is its deliberate pace, which allows interest level to lag from time to time. Won Oscars for screenplay adaptation (Ruth Prawer Jhabvala), art direction, and costume design.▼

Rooney (1958-British) 88m. *** D: George Pollock. John Gregson, Muriel Pavlow, Barry Fitzgerald, June Thorburn. Sprightly tale of Irish sanitation worker Gregson with an eye for the girls, trying to avoid marriage; Fitzgerald is bedridden geezer whom Rooney helps.

Rooster (1982) C-100m. TVM D: Russ Mayberry. Paul Williams, Pat McCormick, J. D. Cannon, Ed Lauter, Jill St. John, Katherine Baumann, Delta Burke, Charlie Callas, Pamela Hensley, William Daniels, John Saxon, Eddie Albert, Henry Darrow, Marie Osmond. Williams and McCormick go the Laurel and Hardy route as a pair of mismatched investigators hot on the trail of a band of arsonists in this pilot inspired by their comic teaming in SMOKEY AND THE BANDIT et. al. Average.

Rooster Cogburn (1975) C-107m. ** D: Stuart Millar. John Wayne, Katharine Hepburn, Richard Zerbe, Strother Martin, Richard Jordan, John McIntire. Reprising Wayne's character from TRUE GRIT and teaming him with Hepburn was an obvious attempt to spark an AFRICAN QUEEN-type hit, but starpower is all this film has going for it. Dull story of unlikely duo

going after men who murdered her father may play better on TV.▼

Roots of Heaven, The (1958) C-131m. **½ D: John Huston. Errol Flynn, Juliette Greco, Trevor Howard, Eddie Albert, Orson Welles, Herbert Lom, Paul Lukas. Turgid melodramatics set in Africa, with conglomerate cast philosophizing over sanctity of elephants; loosely based on Romain Gary novel.

Roots: The Gift (1988) C-100m. TVM D: Kevin Hooks. Louis Gossett, Jr., LeVar Burton, Michael Learned, Avery Brooks, Kate Mulgrew, Shaun Cassidy, John McMartin. Gossett and Burton reprise their roles as Fiddler and Kunta Kinte in this story of a secret plot to lead fellow slaves to freedom one Christmas Eve on the Underground Railroad. After two epic ROOTS miniseries, this seems like an afterthought—and a pointless contrivance. Average.

Rope (1948) C-80m. *** D: Alfred Hitchcock. James Stewart, John Dall, Farley Granger, Cedric Hardwicke, Joan Chandler, Constance Collier, Douglas Dick. Two young men kill prep-school friend, just for the thrill of it, and challenge themselves by inviting friends and family to their apartment afterward—with the body hidden on the premises. Hitchcock's first color film was shot in ten-minute takes to provide a seamless flow of movement, but it remains today what it was then: an interesting, highly theatrical experiment. Inspired by the real-life Leopold-Loeb murder case. Patrick Hamilton's play was adapted by Hume Cronyn and scripted by Arthur Laurents.▼

Rope of Sand (1949) 104m. *** D: William Dieterle. Burt Lancaster, Paul Henreid, Corinne Calvet, Claude Rains, Peter Lorre, Sam Jaffe, John Bromfield, Mike Mazurki. Sturdy cast in adventure tale of smooth thief trying to regain treasure he hid away, with various parties interfering.

Rosalie (1937) 122m. ** D: W. S. Van Dyke. Eleanor Powell, Nelson Eddy, Frank Morgan, Edna May Oliver, Ray Bolger, Ilona Massey, Billy Gilbert. Elephantine MGM musical about romance between West Point cadet and mythical-kingdom princess. Living proof that money alone can't make a good movie. Cole Porter score includes "In the Still of the Night."▼

Rosalie Goes Shopping (1989-German) C-94m. *** D: Percy Adlon. Marianne Sägebrecht, Brad Davis, Judge Reinhold, William Harlander, Erika Blumberger, Patricia Zehentmayr. Bavarian-born Sägebrecht has settled with American husband Davis in Stuttgart, Arkansas, and they have more children than you can count; she's become obsessed with spending money and having possessions, and devises an ingenious plan to beat the bill collector. Delightfully loopy comedy is also a laced-in-acid satire of consumerism American-style.▼

Rosa Luxemburg (1986-German) **C-122m.** ***½ D: Margarethe von Trotta. Barbara Sukowa, Daniel Olbrychski, Otto Sander, Adelheid Arndt, Jurgen Holtz, Doris Schade. Sukowa offers a towering performance in this compelling, multileveled biography of the dedicated, idealistic democratic socialist/pacifist/humanist who played a prominent role in German politics in the early years of the century. Extremely provocative and well directed.

Rosary Murders, The (1987) **C-101m.** ** D: Fred Walton. Donald Sutherland, Charles Durning, Belinda Bauer, Josef Sommer, James Murtaugh, John Danelle, Addison Powell, Kathleen Tolan. Mass killer of Motown priests and nuns confesses to Sutherland, who obviously can't inform the cops. Despite an Elmore Leonard script, Sutherland's performance is the sole reward. Starts promisingly but soon fizzles. Filmed on location in Detroit. See I CONFESS instead.▼

Rose, The (1979) **C-134m.** ** D: Mark Rydell. Bette Midler, Alan Bates, Frederic Forrest, Harry Dean Stanton, Barry Primus, David Keith. Spin-off of the Janis Joplin saga equates show biz with hell, then concentrates on giving the audience too much of the latter. Midler (in her starring debut) and Forrest deliver dynamic performances, but film leaves a lot to be desired. Impressive photography by Vilmos Zsigmond.▼

Roseanna McCoy (1949) **100m.** ** D: Irving Reis. Farley Granger, Joan Evans, Charles Bickford, Raymond Massey, Richard Basehart, Aline MacMahon. Witless drama of Hatfield-McCoy feud, with young lovers from opposite sides of the fence rekindling old wounds.

Rose Bowl Story, The (1952) **C-73m.** ** D: William Beaudine. Marshall Thompson, Vera Miles, Natalie Wood, Ann Doran, Jim Backus. Clichéd hogwash about football players, their work and home life.

Rosebud (1975) **C-126m.** BOMB D: Otto Preminger. Peter O'Toole, Richard Attenborough, Cliff Gorman, Claude Dauphin, John V. Lindsay, Peter Lawford, Raf Vallone, Isabelle Huppert, Kim Cattrall. Nadir for director Preminger and usually competent performers. Arab terrorists kill crew of yacht "Rosebud" and kidnap five wealthy young ladies aboard. O'Toole and Attenborough (to say nothing of former N.Y.C. Mayor Lindsay) are embarrassingly bad.

Rosebud Beach Hotel, The (1984) **C-87m.** *½ D: Harry Hurwitz. Colleen Camp, Peter Scolari, Christopher Lee, Fran Drescher, Monique Gabrielle, Eddie Deezen,

Chuck McCann. Thoroughly idiotic, fifth-rate comedy about buffoon Scolari, who with girlfriend Camp operates a resort hotel and hires happy hookers as bellgirls. Camp's bright presence raises the rating of this from BOMB. Originally titled THE BIG LOBBY. ▼

Rose for Everyone, A (1965-Italian) **C-107m.** ** D: Franco Rossi. Claudia Cardinale, Nino Manfredi, Mario Adorf, Akim Tamiroff. Brazilian locale with NEVER ON SUNDAY plot. Girl brings happiness to many men and takes active interest in their private lives as well as their sexual lives. Nice locales, banal story.

Rose Garden, The (1989-U.S.-West German) **C-111m.** **½ D: Fons Rademakers. Liv Ullmann, Maximilian Schell, Peter Fonda, Jan Niklas, Kurt Hubner. Attorney Ullmann defends Schell on charges of attacking an elderly man whom he recognized as the commandant of a Nazi concentration camp in which his family was killed. Story is earnest and compassionate but uninspired; benefits from fine performances by Ullmann and an almost unrecognizable Schell.▼

Roseland (1977) **C-103m.** *** D: James Ivory. Teresa Wright, Lou Jacobi, Geraldine Chaplin, Helen Gallagher, Joan Copeland, Christopher Walken, Lilia Skala, David Thomas. Trilogy set in N.Y.C.'s venerable Roseland Ballroom examines bittersweet lives of people who gravitate there. First story is weakest, but other two are absorbing and beautifully performed, with Copeland and Skala as standouts.▼

Rose Marie (1936) **110m.** *** D: W. S. Van Dyke II. Jeanette MacDonald, Nelson Eddy, Reginald Owen, Allan Jones, James Stewart, Alan Mowbray, Gilda Gray. Don't expect the original operetta: story has opera star Jeanette searching for fugitive brother Stewart, as mountie Nelson pursues the same man. The two fall in love, sing "Indian Love Call," among others. David Niven appears briefly as Jeanette's unsuccessful suitor. Retitled INDIAN LOVE CALL; previously filmed in 1928, then again in 1954.▼

Rose Marie (1954) **C-115m.** **½ D: Mervyn LeRoy. Ann Blyth, Howard Keel, Fernando Lamas, Bert Lahr, Marjorie Main, Joan Taylor, Ray Collins. More faithful to original operetta than 1936 version, but not as much fun. Mountie Keel tries to "civilize" tomboy Blyth, but falls in love with her instead. Adventurer Lamas completes the triangle. Lahr sings "I'm the Mountie Who Never Got His Man" in comic highlight.

Rosemary (1958-German) **99m.** **½ D: Rolf Thiele. Nadja Tiller, Peter Van Eyck, Gert Frobe, Mario Adorf, Carl Raddatz. Convincing study of famed post-WW2

Frankfurt prostitute (Tiller) who blackmailed industrialist; satirically sensational.

Rosemary's Baby (1968) **C-136m.** **** D: Roman Polanski. Mia Farrow, John Cassavetes, Ruth Gordon, Sidney Blackmer, Maurice Evans, Ralph Bellamy, Elisha Cook, Jr., Patsy Kelly, Charles Grodin. Classic modern-day thriller by Ira Levin, perfectly realized by writer-director Polanski: Farrow is unsuspecting young wife whose husband becomes involved with witches' coven and their diabolical plans. Gordon won Best Supporting Actress Oscar. Produced by William Castle; followed by a made-for-TV sequel.▼

Rosemary's Baby II SEE: **Look What's Happened to Rosemary's Baby**

Rose of Washington Square (1939) **86m.** **½ D: Gregory Ratoff. Tyrone Power, Alice Faye, Al Jolson, William Frawley, Horace McMahon, Moroni Olsen. Pleasant musical of thinly disguised Fanny Brice, with Alice singing her heart out as heelhusband Power hits the skids.

Roses Are for the Rich (1987) **C-200m. TVM** D: Michael Miller. Lisa Hartman, Bruce Dern, Joe Penny, Richard Masur, Howard Duff, Morgan Stevens, Jim Youngs, Betty Buckley, Kate Mulgrew. Soapy tale of a social-climbing miner's daughter out for deadly revenge against the coal magnate responsible for destroying her family. A trash wallower's holiday. Based on Jonell Lawson's novel. Originally shown in two parts. Average.

Rose Tattoo, The (1955) **117m.** ***½ D: Daniel Mann. Anna Magnani, Burt Lancaster, Marisa Pavan, Ben Cooper, Virginia Grey, Jo Van Fleet. Magnani shines in Oscar-winning role as earthy widow in Gulf Coast city who puts aside her husband's memory when rambunctious truck driver Lancaster romances her. Flavorful adaptation of Tennessee Williams play; cinematographer James Wong Howe also won an Oscar.

Rosetti and Ryan: Men Who Love Women (1977) **C-100m. TVM** D: John Astin. Tony Roberts, Squire Fridell, Patty Duke Astin, Jane Elliot, Susan Anspach, Dick O'Neill, Bill Dana, William Marshall. Free-wheeling criminal lawyers with a way with women vs. hardnosed judge at the trial of their client Duke, charged with slaying her husband. Pilot for the shortlived series. Average.

Rosie! (1968) **C-98m.** *** D: David Lowell Rich. Rosalind Russell, Sandra Dee, Brian Aherne, Audrey Meadows, James Farentino, Vanessa Brown, Leslie Nielsen, Margaret Hamilton. One of Russell's best late-career performances as mad-cap grandmother, whose children want her money now. Veteran supporting cast outshine young leads. Based on a play by Ruth Gordon.

Rosie the Riveter SEE: **Life and Times of Rosie the Riveter, The**▼

Rosie: The Rosemary Clooney Story (1982) **C-100m. TVM** D: Jackie Cooper. Sondra Locke, Tony Orlando, Penelope Milford, Katherine Helmond, Kevin McCarthy, John Karlen, Cheryl Anderson, Robert Ridgely, Joey Travolta. Locke does the acting but Rosie does the singing in this straightforward filming of the Clooney autobiography *This for Remembrance*, tracing her career from a sister act on Cincinnati radio to her stardom, mental breakdown and journey back to the limelight. Orlando's Jose Ferrer, however, is gross miscasting. Above average.▼

Rothko Conspiracy, The (1983-British) **C-90m. TVM** D: Paul Watson. Larry Hoodekoff, Ronald Lacey, Barry Morse, Douglas Lambert, Andrea Levine, Pat Starr. Detailed, absorbing, but unevenly produced chronicle of the legal battle between the executors of the estate of famed abstract expressionist painter Mark Rothko and his daughter, Kate (Levine). A high-stakes drama of conflict of interest, fraud, and N.Y.C. art world shenanigans that have nothing to do with art as a creative endeavor. A PBS *American Playhouse* presentation. Average.

Rotten to the Core (1965-British) **90m.** *** D: John Boulting. Anton Rodgers, Eric Sykes, Charlotte Rampling, Ian Bannen, Avis Bunnage, Victor Maddern. Wellhandled caper of ex-con trio joining forces with crook to carry off large-scale robbery.

Rouge Baiser SEE: **Red Kiss**

Rough Cut (1980) **C-112m.** **½ D: Donald Siegel. Burt Reynolds, Lesley-Anne Down, David Niven, Timothy West, Patrick Magee, Al Matthews. Handsome but uneven romantic caper uses its stars' charm and chemistry to offset weaknesses in script. World-class jewel thief Reynolds falls in love with beautiful woman who's been set up to snag him for Scotland Yard. Filmed in England and Holland. Troubled David Merrick production went through four directors, and scripter Larry Gelbart used a pseudonym; hastily refilmed ending is chief giveaway.▼

Roughly Speaking (1945) **117m.** *** D: Michael Curtiz. Rosalind Russell, Jack Carson, Robert Hutton, Jean Sullivan, Alan Hale, Donald Woods. Generally good but long comedy-drama of Russell raising a family while hubby Carson embarks on wild moneymaking schemes; two stars are tops.

Roughnecks (1980) **C-200m. TVM** D: Bernard McEveety. Steve Forrest, Sam Melville, Ana Alicia, Cathy Lee Crosby, Stephen McHattie, Vera Miles, Harry Morgan, Wilford Brimley, Andrew Rubin, Sarah Rush, Timothy Scott. Oil wildcatters find time for romance while seeking black gold. Originally shown in two parts. Average.▼

✓ **Rough Night in Jericho** (1967) **C-97m.** ** D: Arnold Laven. Dean Martin, George Peppard, Jean Simmons, John McIntire, Slim Pickens, Don Galloway. Gory Western casts Martin as total villain who owns the town. Attractive cast can't fight clichés.

Roughshod (1949) **88m.** **½ D: Mark Robson. Robert Sterling, Claude Jarman, Jr., Gloria Grahame, Jeff Donnell, John Ireland, Myrna Dell, Martha Hyer. Intriguing drama of three fugitives out West and the disturbed farmer who fears they are seeking revenge against him.

Rough Shoot SEE: **Shoot First**

✓ **Rounders, The** (1965) **C-85m.** **½ D: Burt Kennedy. Glenn Ford, Henry Fonda, Sue Ane Langdon, Hope Holiday, Chill Wills, Edgar Buchanan, Kathleen Freeman. Agreeable comedy-Western about two cowboys and an ornery horse was one of the sleepers of its year; nothing much happens, but cast and scenery make it a pleasant way to kill an hour-and-a-half.

Round Midnight (1986-U.S.-French) **C-131m.** ***½ D: Bertrand Tavernier. Dexter Gordon, Francois Cluzet, Gabrielle Haker, Sandra Reaves-Phillips, Lonette McKee, Herbie Hancock, Bobby Hutcherson, Wayne Shorter, John Berry, Martin Scorsese, Philippe Noiret. A boozy American jazzman working in 1950s Paris is virtually adopted by a fan, and their unusual relationship causes them both to thrive and prosper. A loving homage to jazz musicians and their world (inspired by the lives of Bud Powell and Lester Young), with a once-in-a-lifetime performance by real-life tenor-sax great Gordon. Music director—and Oscar winner—Herbie Hancock and his colleagues not only create great jazz right on-screen but also help establish a perfect ambiance. Written by Tavernier and David Rayfiel; designed by premier art director Alexandre Trauner.▼

✓ **Roustabout** (1964) **C-101m.** **½ D: John Rich. Elvis Presley, Barbara Stanwyck, Leif Erickson, Joan Freeman, Sue Ane Langdon. Elvis is a free-wheeling singer who joins Stanwyck's carnival, learns the meaning of hard work and true love. Stanwyck and supporting cast make this a pleasing Presley songer, with "Little Egypt" his one outstanding tune. Raquel Welch has a bit.▼

Rover, The (1967) **C-103m.** *½ D: Terence Young. Anthony Quinn, Rosanna Schiaffino, Rita Hayworth, Richard Johnson, Ivo Garrani, Mino Doro. Quinn stars as 18th-century pirate whose escape from French authorities is sidetracked by relationship with innocent, feeble-minded girl (Schiaffino). Plodding film from Joseph Conrad story; made in Italy, barely released here.

Rowdyman, The (1971-Canadian) **C-95m.** **½ D: Peter Carter. Gordon Pinsent, Frank Converse, Will Geer, Linda Gorenson, Ted Henley. Pinsent is the whole show in this occasionally intriguing but ultimately superficial drama about a hard-living womanizer and his fate after accidentally causing the death of a childhood pal. Filmed in Newfoundland; Pinsent also scripted.

Roxanne (1987) **C-107m.** **½ D: Fred Schepisi. Steve Martin, Daryl Hannah, Rick Rossovich, Shelley Duvall, John Kapelos, Fred Willard, Max Alexander, Michael J. Pollard. Martin fashioned this update of *Cyrano de Bergerac* as a vehicle for himself, with Hannah as the object of his affection and Rossovich as the empty-headed hunk for whom he "fronts." Extremely likable and sweet-natured romantic comedy set in a sleepy ski town. Peters out somewhere along the line, unfortunately.▼

Roxanne: The Prize Pulitzer (1989) **C-100m. TVM** D: Richard A. Colla. Perry King, Chynna Phillips, Courteney Cox, Betsy Russell, Sondra Blake, Caitlin Brown. Muddled recounting of the headline-making 1980s divorce proceedings and custody battle between Herbert "Pete" Pulitzer, the publishing heir, and his much younger wife. This sanitized version of her Palm Beach life was adapted by Elizabeth Gill from Roxanne Pulitzer's best-selling book. Average.

Roxie Hart (1942) **75m.** **½ D: William Wellman. Ginger Rogers, Adolphe Menjou, George Montgomery, Lynne Overman, Nigel Bruce, Phil Silvers, Spring Byington, Iris Adrian, George Chandler. Fast-moving spoof of Roaring 20s, with Ginger as publicity-seeking woman on trial for murder, Menjou her overdramatic lawyer. Hilarious antics make up for dry spells; scripted and produced by Nunnally Johnson. Previously filmed in 1927 as CHICAGO, also the title of the subsequent Broadway musical.

Royal Affairs in Versailles (1954-French) **C-152m.** **½ D: Sacha Guitry. Claudette Colbert, Orson Welles, Jean-Pierre Aumont, Edith Piaf, Gérard Philipe, Jean Marais, Sacha Guitry. Overambitious, episodic approach to French history, with varying performances by host of guest stars. Retitled: AFFAIRS IN VERSAILLES.

Royal African Rifles, The (1953) **C-75m.** ** D: Lesley Selander. Louis Hayward, Veronica Hurst, Michael Pate, Angela Greene. Adequate actioner set in Africa in 1910, with Hayward the British officer leading mission to recover cache of arms.

Royal Family of Broadway, The (1930) **82m.** ***½ D: George Cukor, Cyril Gardner. Fredric March, Ina Claire, Mary Brian, Henrietta Crosman, Charles Starrett,

Arnold Korff, Frank Conroy, Delightful screen version of Edna Ferber-George S. Kaufman play about Barrymore-like theatrical family torn by conflict of show business tradition vs. "normal" private life. March is wickedly funny in his John Barrymore portrayal.

Royal Flash (1975-British) **C-98m.** *** D: Richard Lester. Malcolm McDowell, Alan Bates, Florinda Bolkan, Oliver Reed, Britt Ekland, Lionel Jeffries, Tom Bell, Alastair Sim, Michael Hordern, Joss Ackland, Christopher Cazenove, Bob Hoskins. Comic swashbuckler with McDowell forced to impersonate a Prussian nobleman and marry Ekland. Zippy Lester entry with a fine cast; script by George MacDonald Fraser, from his novel.▼

Royal Hunt of the Sun (1969-British) **C-118m.** *** D: Irving Lerner. Robert Shaw, Christopher Plummer, Nigel Davenport, Michael Craig, Leonard Whiting, James Donald. Colorful tale of Spanish explorer Pizarro and his quest for gold in South America; from acclaimed stage play by Peter Shaffer, adapted by Philip Yordan.

Royal Romance of Charles and Diana, The (1982) **C-100m. TVM** D: Peter Levin. Catherine Oxenberg, Christopher Baines, Ray Milland, Dana Wynter, Stewart Granger, Olivia de Havilland. This version of the Prince Charles–Lady Diana Spencer story is the one to look for, based solely on the casting of Wynter as Queen Elizabeth, Granger as Prince Philip, and de Havilland as the Queen Mother. Premiered almost simultaneously with CHARLES AND DIANA: A ROYAL LOVE STORY. Average.

Royal Scandal, A (1945) **94m.** **½ D: Ernst Lubitsch, Otto Preminger. Tallulah Bankhead, Charles Coburn, Anne Baxter, William Eythe, Vincent Price, Mischa Auer. Comedy of manners about Catherine the Great of Russia promoting favored soldier Eythe to high rank; started by Lubitsch, "finished" by Preminger. Remake of Lubitsch's 1924 FORBIDDEN PARADISE.

Royal Wedding (1951) **C-93m.** *** D: Stanley Donen. Fred Astaire, Jane Powell, Peter Lawford, Sarah Churchill, Keenan Wynn. Astaire's dancing overcomes bland plot line of he and sister Powell performing in London at time of Queen Elizabeth II's marriage; each finds true love. Highlights: Fred dances on the ceiling and with a coat rack, Powell sings "Too Late Now." Songs by Alan Jay Lerner (who also scripted) and Burton Lane. Donen's first solo directing credit.▼

R.P.M. (1970) **C-97m.** *½ D: Stanley Kramer. Anthony Quinn, Ann-Margret, Gary Lockwood, Paul Winfield, Graham Jarvis, Alan Hewitt. Old-fashioned liberal Quinn becomes head of university, then authorizes a police bust of radicals to save

institution. (*Revolutions* Per Minute, get it?). Ideal match of inept Erich Segal script with equally bad Kramer direction gives film certain camp value, but otherwise, look out.▼

Ruby (1977) **C-84m.** **½ D: Curtis Harrington. Piper Laurie, Stuart Whitman, Roger Davis, Janit Baldwin, Crystin Sinclaire, Paul Kent. Complex plot has long-dead gangster's spirit possessing deaf-mute girl, sending her on a killing spree at drive-in theater (which specializes in horror movies) run by ex-gang members. A few moments, comic and horrific, stand out in generally uneven supernatural thriller. Some prints run 85m, with a hastily added epilogue designed to add a final CARRIE-like shock. That version is credited to pseudonymous director Allen Smithee.▼

Ruby and Oswald (1978) **C-133m. TVM** D: Mel Stuart, Michael Lerner, Frederic Forrest, Doris Roberts, Lou Frizzell, Lanna Saunders, Brian Dennehy. Dramatic recreation of the days just preceding and following the Kennedy assassination unfortunately pales beside the real events so graphically covered live in those days. Retitled FOUR DAYS IN DALLAS. Average.

Ruby Gentry (1952) **82m.** **½ D: King Vidor. Jennifer Jones, Charlton Heston, Karl Malden, Josephine Hutchinson. Turgid, meandering account of easy-virtue Southerner Jones marrying wealthy Malden to spite Heston, the man she loves.▼

Ruckus (1982) **C-91m.**** D: Max Kleven. Dirk Benedict, Linda Blair, Ben Johnson, Matt Clark, Richard Farnsworth. Slick but ordinary drive-in fare about a shell-shocked Vietnam vet who becomes object of massive manhunt in sleepy Alabama town. Same basic story as later FIRST BLOOD, but less pretentious.▼

Rude Awakening (1989) **C-100m.** *½ D: Aaron Russo, David Greenwalt. Cheech Marin, Eric Roberts, Julie Hagerty, Robert Carradine, Buck Henry, Louise Lasser, Cindy Williams, Andrea Martin, Cliff DeYoung. "Cheech and Roberts" lacks zing as a comedy-team concept; so does hippie-dippy political farce about a pair of long-haired '60s burnouts who return to N.Y.C. after twenty years in a Central American commune. Henry scrapes up a few chuckles in his only scene.

Rude Boy (1980-British) **C-133m.** *** D: Jack Hazan, David Mingay. The Clash, Ray Gange, John Green, Barry Baker, Terry McQuade, Caroline Coon. Angry young rebel Gange is hired by the punk rock group The Clash as a roadie. Gritty, realistic, documentary-like character study; excellent concert footage. Punk rock fans will not be disappointed: others, beware. Most U.S. prints run 120m.▼

Ruggles of Red Gap (1935) **92m.** **** D: Leo McCarey. Charles Laughton, Mary

Boland, Charlie Ruggles, ZaSu Pitts, Roland Young, Leila Hyams. Laughton is marvelous as butler won in poker game by uncouth Westerner Ruggles and socially ambitious wife Boland; Pitts is spinster he falls in love with. A completely winning movie. Harry Leon Wilson's story was filmed before in 1918 and 1923, then remade as FANCY PANTS.▼

Rulers of the Sea (1939) **96m.** **½ D: Frank Lloyd. Douglas Fairbanks, Jr., Will Fyffe, Margaret Lockwood, George Bancroft, Montagu Love, Alan Ladd, Mary Gordon, Neil Fitzgerald. Well-made drama of problems surrounding first steamship voyage across Atlantic.

Rules of Marriage, The (1982) **C-200m. TVM** D: Milton Katselas. Elizabeth Montgomery, Elliott Gould, Michael Murphy, Kenneth Mars, Neva Patterson, William Windom. Affluent suburban couple decide to split after fifteen years in this overlong contemporary drama written by Reginald Rose. Originally shown in two parts. Average.

Rules of the Game (1939-French) **105m.** **** D: Jean Renoir. Marcel Dalio, Nora Gregor, Mila Parely, Jean Renoir, Gaston Modot. Sublime comedy-drama contrasting affairs d'amour of aristocrats and working class on weekend outing in the country. Poignant, funny, endlessly imitated; perhaps Renoir's best film.▼

Ruling Class, The (1972-British) **C-154m.** **** D: Peter Medak. Peter O'Toole, Alastair Sim, Arthur Lowe, Harry Andrews, Coral Browne, Michael Bryant, Carolyn Seymour, Nigel Green, William Mervyn, James Villiers. Hilarious, irreverent black comedy by Peter Barnes about heir to British lordship (O'Toole) who thinks he's Jesus Christ. Overflowing with crazy ideas, people bursting into song, boisterously funny characterizations, and one-and-only Sim as befuddled bishop. Some prints run 130m; the "uncut" version released in 1983 runs 141m.▼

Ruling Voice, The (1931) **71m.** *** D: Rowland V. Lee. Walter Huston, Loretta Young, Doris Kenyon, David Manners, John Halliday, Dudley Digges, Gilbert Emery, Willard Robertson. Gangster Huston rules the nation's underworld, but starts to go soft when his innocent daughter returns from school abroad. Slows down in Loretta's scenes, but when Huston is on screen it really hums.

Rumba (1935) **77m.** ** D: Marion Gering. George Raft, Carole Lombard, Margo, Lynne Overman, Gail Patrick, Akim Tamiroff, Iris Adrian. Weak follow-up to BOLERO, with Raft and Lombard in and out of love in silly, contrived story; most of their "dancing" actually done by Veloz and Yolanda.

Rumble Fish (1983) **94m.** ** D: Francis Coppola. Matt Dillon, Mickey Rourke, Diane Lane, Dennis Hopper, Diana Scarwid, Vincent Spano, Nicolas Cage, Christopher Penn, Tom Waits. Ambitious mood piece from S. E. Hinton's young-adult novel about alienated teenager who lives in the shadow of his older brother. Emotionally intense but muddled and aloof; highly stylized, in looks (filmed mostly in black & white) and sounds (with impressionistic music score by Stewart Copeland). Dillon's third Hinton film, Coppola's second (following THE OUTSIDERS).▼

Rumble on the Docks (1956) **82m.** ** D: Fred F. Sears. James Darren, Laurie Carroll, Michael Granger, Jerry Janger, Robert Blake, Edgar Barrier. Low-key waterfront corruption tale, with Darren the street-gang leader aiding racketeers.

Rumor Mill, The SEE: **Malice in Wonderland**▼

Rumor of War, A (1980) **C-200m. TVM** D: Richard T. Heffron. Brad Davis, Keith Carradine, Michael O'Keefe, Richard Bradford, Brian Dennehy, John Friedrich, Perry Lang, Christopher Mitchum, Steve Forrest, Stacy Keach, Jeff Daniels. The first of the major TV films set in Vietnam, adapted from Philip Caputo's best-seller by John Sacret Young. Davis gives an intense performance as Caputo, following him through his transformation from idealistic college student to enthusiastic Marine to embittered veteran charged at court-martial for murder in Vietnamese village. Originally shown in two parts. Above average.▼

Rumpelstiltskin (1987) **C-84m.** ** D: David Irving. Amy Irving, Billy Barty, Clive Revill, Priscilla Pointer, John Moulder-Brown, Robert Symonds. Threadbare musical adaptation of the Grimms' fairy tale, with Irving and Barty well cast in the leads. Likely to bore even the small-fry. Filmed in Israel, this was a family affair: writer-director Irving is Amy's brother, and Pointer (who plays the Queen) is her mother. For the record, this was the first of Cannon's Films' fairy-tale features. ▼

Run a Crooked Mile (1969) **C-100m. TVM** D: Gene Levitt. Louis Jourdan, Mary Tyler Moore, Alexander Knox, Wilfrid Hyde-White, Laurence Naismith, Terence Alexander. Highway mishap precipitates math teacher's involvement in plot to change European gold standard. Good, intricate amnesia-gimmicked plot and fine British cast on hand in serviceable suspenser. Above average.

Runaround, The (1946) **86m.** ** D: Charles Lamont. Rod Cameron, Broderick Crawford, Ella Raines, Samuel S. Hinds. Raines is heiress whom detectives Cameron and Crawford must return to Gotham; tepid comedy programmer.

Runaway (1971) SEE: **Runaway, Runaway**

Runaway! (1973) **C-73m. TVM** D: David Lowell Rich. Ben Johnson, Ben Murphy, Vera Miles, Ed Nelson, Darleen Carr, Martin Milner, Lee H. Montgomery, Ray Danton. Train careening down mountain passage without brakes, the lives of various stereotyped characters sway with Fate's whim. Some moments of suspense, but overall, film recks of formula. Average.

Runaway (1984) **C-100m. ** D: Michael Crichton. Tom Selleck, Cynthia Rhodes, Gene Simmons, Kirstie Alley, Stan Shaw, Joey Cramer, G. W. Bailey. Futuristic comic-book nonsense that actually takes itself seriously. Selleck plays a cop who specializes in tracking down robots that have gone "bad." Simmons (from rock group KISS) is ultra-bad-guy who uses robots and other high-tech devices to carry out his evil deeds. Special effects are good, but characters are cold and story is for the birds.▼

Runaway Barge, The (1975) **C-78m. TVM** D: Boris Sagal. Bo Hopkins, Tim Matheson, Jim Davis, Nick Nolte, Devon Ericson, Christina Hart, James Best. Adventures of three men trying to earn a living on a modern day riverboat. Typical TV action movie including a trio of two-fisted scalawags. Average.▼

Runaway, Runaway (1971) **C-85m. *** D: Bickford Otis Webber. William Smith, Gilda Texter, Rita Murray, Tom Baker, Beach Dickerson. Unsung little gem has young Texter running away from home, taking up with older businessman. Unusually sympathetic role for tough guy Smith, plus a standout performance by Murray as Texter's lesbian roommate. Retitled RUNAWAY.

Runaways, The (1975) **C-78m. TVM** D: Harry Harris. Dorothy McGuire, Van Williams, John Randolph, Neva Patterson, Josh Albee, Lenka Peterson. Poignant family drama about unhappy teenaged orphan and an escaped leopard from wild-animal compound. Well-acted filming of Victor Canning's sentimental novel. Above average.▼

Runaway Train (1985) **C-111m. *** D: Andrei Konchalovsky. Jon Voight, Eric Roberts, Rebecca DeMornay, Kyle Heffner, John P. Ryan, T. K. Carter, Kenneth McMillan, Stacey Pickren. A rare bird, this film: an existential action movie! Hardened criminal and young accomplice escape from prison and hide out on a train that's barreling through Alaska without an engineer. Tough, violent, with hair-raising action footage and a superb characterization by Voight in his most atypical role to date. Based on a screenplay by Akira Kurosawa.▼

Run for Cover (1955) **C-93m. **½ D: Nicholas Ray. James Cagney, Viveca Lindfors, John Derek, Jean Hersholt, Ernest Borgnine. Offbeat Western has excon Cagney becoming sheriff, while his embittered young companion (Derek) grows restive and antagonistic. Interesting touches cannot overcome familiar storyline.

Run for the Roses (1978) **C-93m. ** D: Henry Levin. Vera Miles, Stuart Whitman, Sam Groom, Panchito Gomez, Theodore Wilson, Lisa Eilbacher. Formula family film about Puerto Rican boy living with his stepfather in Kentucky, raising a lame colt to run in the Kentucky Derby. Uninspired stuff for undemanding audiences. Originally titled THOROUGHBRED.▼

Run for the Sun (1956) **C-99m. *** D: Roy Boulting. Richard Widmark, Jane Greer, Trevor Howard, Peter Van Eyck, Carlos Henning. Third version of THE MOST DANGEROUS GAME has author Widmark and magazine writer Greer stumbling onto strange plantation run by mysterious Howard and Van Eyck. Engrossing, extremely well-made film.

Run for Your Money, A (1949-British) **83m. *** D: Charles Frend. Donald Houston, Meredith Edwards, Moira Lister, Alec Guinness, Hugh Griffith, Joyce Grenfell. Way-above-par comic study of two Welsh miners having a spree in London.

Run Like A Thief (1967-Spanish) **C-92m. ** D: Harry Spalding. Kieron Moore, Ina Balin, Keenan Wynn, Fernando Rey. Soldier of fortune goes after diamond hijackers with a mobster chief who foils him every step of the way.

Runner Stumbles, The (1979) **C-99m. *½** D: Stanley Kramer. Dick Van Dyke, Kathleen Quinlan, Maureen Stapleton, Ray Bolger, Tammy Grimes, Beau Bridges. Sober adaptation of Milan Stitt's Broadway play, based on true story of small-town priest accused of murdering young nun for whom he'd shown unusual affection. Aloof and unconvincing, with Van Dyke unbearably stiff as the clergyman.▼

Running (1979-Canadian) **C-103m. *½** D: Steven Hilliard Stern. Michael Douglas, Susan Anspach, Lawrence Dane, Eugene Levy, Charles Shamata. Douglas—32, out of work and father of two daughters—wants to run in the Olympics. A few yocks in this absurdly melodramatic jock drama, but not enough of them.

Running Brave (1983-Canadian) **C-105m. **½ D: D. S. Everett (Donald Shebib). Robby Benson, Pat Hingle, Claudia Cron, Jeff McCracken, August Schellenberg. Story of real-life Olympic champion Billy Mills, who left the Sioux reservation to find his destiny as a runner—and win a gold medal at the 1964 Tokyo Olympics. Modestly entertaining, but too corny and simplistic to really score.▼

Running From the Guns (1987-Australian)

C-87m. **½ D: John Dixon. Jon Blake, Mark Hembrow, Nikki Coghill, Terence Donovan, Bill Kerr, Peter Whitford, Warwick Sims. Adequate timekiller about pals Blake and Hembrow accidently coming upon laundered money—which some thugs wish to retrieve. Action yarn fizzles out at the finale, but it's entertaining most of the way.

Running Hot (1984) **C-95m.** ** D: Mark Griffiths. Monica Carrico, Eric Stoltz, Stuart Margolin, Virgil Frye, Richard Bradford, Sorrells Pickard. Downbeat road movie (with nihilistic finish) has teenager Stoltz on the run from the cops, hooking up with older woman Carrico, who's also in deep trouble after her lover Bradford dies in mysterious circumstances.▼

Running Man, The (1963-British) **C-103m.** *** D: Carol Reed. Laurence Harvey, Lee Remick, Alan Bates, Felix Aylmer, Eleanor Summerfield, Allan Cuthbertson. Harvey fakes his death to collect insurance money, but pursuing insurance investigator Bates forces him and wife Remick to go on the lam in Spain. Entertaining but not suspenseful enough.

Running Man, The (1987) **C-100m.** **½ D: Paul Michael Glaser. Arnold Schwarzenegger, Maria Conchita Alonso, Yaphet Kotto, Jim Brown, Richard Dawson, Jesse Ventura, Mick Fleetwood, Dweezil Zappa. It's 2019, and the U.S. is a totalitarian state; framed mass murderer Arnie is ordered to take part in a *Most Dangerous Game*-type TV show where convicted felons get their one chance for freedom. Relentlessly trashy big-bucks exploitation picture gets big boost from Dawson's sleazy portrayal of the game-show host. Based on a novel by Richard Bachman (Stephen King).▼

Running on Empty (1988) **C-116m.** ***½ D: Sidney Lumet. Christine Lahti, River Phoenix, Judd Hirsch, Martha Plimpton, Jonas Arby, Ed Crowley, L.M. Kit Carson, Steven Hill, Augusta Dabney. Intense, moving story of onetime student radicals who are still on the run from the FBI after seventeen years—now with two kids in tow, whose lives are stifled for the sake of sheer survival. Quiet and believable throughout, with superior performances by all. Written by coexecutive producer Naomi Foner.▼

Running Out (1983) **C-100m.** TVM D: Robert Day. Deborah Raffin, Tony Bill, Toni Kalem, Ari Meyers, Paul Hecht, Joseph Buloff, Anthony Michael Hall. Raffin happily breathes new life into this now-worn KRAMER VS. KRAMER situation, playing a woman trying to reenter the lives of the husband and daughter she abandoned years earlier. Teleplay by Elissa Haden Guest. Above average.

Running Scared (1986) **C-106m.** **½ D:

Peter Hyams. Gregory Hines, Billy Crystal, Steven Bauer, Darlanne Fluegel, Joe Pantoliano, Dan Hedaya, Jonathan Gruies, Tracy Reed, Jimmy Smits. Two longtime Chicago street cops (who act more like Dead End Kids) decide maybe it's time to retire—but there's one more scuzzbag to track down first. Crystal lights up the screen, and there's a great car chase on the Chicago El tracks, but otherwise this is pretty blah.▼

Running Target (1956) **C-83m.** ** D: Marvin Weinstein. Doris Dowling, Arthur Franz, Richard Reeves, Myron Healey, James Parnell. Minor film of modern-day sheriff leading chase for escaped convicts.

Running Wild (1927) **68m.** **½ D: Gregory La Cava. W.C. Fields, Mary Brian, Claude Buchanan, Marie Shotwell, Barney Raskle, Tom Madden, Frederick Burton. Fields (sporting his silent-film mustache) plays the ultimate milquetoast who undergoes a galvanizing change of personality when he chances to encounter a hypnotist. Fast, funny outing with the surefire satisfaction of seeing the worm turn.▼

Running Wild (1955) **81m.** **½ D: Abner Biberman. William Campbell, Mamie Van Doren, Keenan Wynn, Walter Coy. Tawdry, actionful account of young police officer getting the goods on car thief gangs.

Running Wild (1973) **C-103m.** *** D: Robert McCahon. Lloyd Bridges, Dina Merrill, Pat Hingle, Morgan Woodward, Gilbert Roland, Lonny Chapman, R. G. Armstrong. Good family-oriented drama about a news photographer (Merrill) who protests treatment of wild horses while doing a story in Colorado. Beautiful scenery complements solid script.▼

Run of the Arrow (1957) **C-86m.** **½ D: Samuel Fuller. Rod Steiger, Sarita Montiel, Brian Keith, Ralph Meeker, Jay C. Flippen, Charles Bronson, Tim McCoy. Confederate soldier (played by Steiger with a broad Irish brogue!) cannot accept surrender to the North, aligns himself instead with Sioux Indians after submitting to a grueling test of endurance. Quite violent for its time; Angie Dickinson reportedly dubbed Montiel's voice. Video title: HOT LEAD.▼

Run Silent, Run Deep (1958) **93m.** *** D: Robert Wise. Clark Gable, Burt Lancaster, Jack Warden, Brad Dexter, Nick Cravat, Mary LaRoche, Don Rickles, Eddie Foy III. Battle of wits between officers Gable and Lancaster on WW2 submarine is basis for interesting drama; little action, though. Script by John Gay, from a novel by Commander Edward L. Beach.▼

Run, Simon, Run (1970) **C-73m.** TVM D: George McCowan. Burt Reynolds, Inger Stevens, Royal Dano, James Best, Rodolfo Acosta, Don Dubbins, Ken Lynch. Unpretentious, straightforward tale (by Lionel E. Siegel) of Papago Indian returning to tribe after prison term, swearing tribal vengeance on man who really murdered his brother. Excellent, tense atmosphere; great use of locations; convincing performances (including Stevens' last). Above average.

Run, Stranger, Run SEE: **Happy Mother's Day, Love, George**▼

Run Till You Fall (1988) C-78m. TVM D: Mike Farrell. Jamie Farr, Fred Savage, Shelley Fabares, CCH Pounder, Beatrice Straight. Struggling gumshoe with nickel-and-dime cases tries to win back his estranged wife and their crippled son in this warm-hearted but mundane drama. Below average.

Run Wild, Run Free (1969-British) C-100m. **½ D: Richard C. Sarafian. John Mills, Mark Lester, Sylvia Syms, Gordon Jackson, Bernard Miles, Fiona Fullerton. Good cast helps leisurely, but better-than-usual children's film about young mute and his love for a white colt; nice subdued photography by Wilkie Cooper.

Russian Roulette (1975) C-93m. **½ D: Lou Lombardo. George Segal, Cristina Raines, Bo Brundin, Denholm Elliott, Gordon Jackson, Peter Donat, Louise Fletcher, Val Avery. Assassins threaten to kill Soviet premier Kosygin during his trip to Vancouver; Segal is assigned to capture elusive troublemaker thought to be the hit-man in this violent, unsatisfying thriller. Filmed in Canada.▼

Russians Are Coming! The Russians Are Coming! The (1966) C-120m. **½ D: Norman Jewison. Carl Reiner, Eva Marie Saint, Alan Arkin, Brian Keith, Jonathan Winters, Paul Ford, Theodore Bikel, Tessie O'Shea, John Phillip Law, Ben Blue, Andrea Dromm, Dick Schaal, Parker Fennelly, Doro Merande, Johnnie Whitaker. Popular comedy about Russian submarine that lands off New England coast was incredibly overrated in 1966; now it's merely a TV sitcom saved by pretty photography and good comic bits by Arkin and Winters. Script by William Rose from Nathaniel Benchley's novel *The Off-Islanders*. Alan Arkin's starring film debut.▼

Russkies (1987) C-99m. *½ D: Rick Rosenthal. Whip Hubley, Leaf Phoenix, Peter Billingsley, Stefan DeSalle, Susan Walters, Patrick Kilpatrick, Vic Polizos, Charles Frank, Susan Blanchard, Carole King, Summer Phoenix. Feeble reworking of THE RUSSIANS ARE COMING! THE RUSSIANS ARE COMING! about Soviet sailor Hubley, washed ashore in Florida, and the trio of youngsters who befriend him. Well-meaning in its message of fellowship, but slight and uninspired.▼

Rustlers' Rhapsody (1985) C-88m. ** D: Hugh Wilson. Tom Berenger, G. W. Bailey, Marilu Henner, Andy Griffith, Fernando Rey, Sela Ward, Patrick Wayne. Good-natured but only sporadically funny send-up of Saturday matinee Westerns. If the old cowboy movies were as dull as this film, they never would have survived.▼

Rust Never Sleeps (1979) C-103m. *** D: Bernard Shakey (Neil Young). Ragged-out but rousing record of Neil Young in concert, with 16 well-performed tunes by rockdom's most lovable downer. My My, Hey, Hey.▼

Ruthless (1948) 104m. *** D: Edgar G. Ulmer. Zachary Scott, Louis Hayward, Diana Lynn, Sydney Greenstreet, Lucille Bremer, Martha Vickers, Raymond Burr. Scott steps on everyone to become big shot in this engrossing drama. Greenstreet is especially good as Southern tycoon.

Ruthless Four, The (1968-Italian-German) C-96m. *** D: Giorgio Capitani. Van Heflin, Gilbert Roland, George Hilton, Klaus Kinski, Sarah Ross. Good Western explores the complicated relationships of four dubious partners in a Nevada gold mine. Apart from the action, it's a pleasure just to watch Heflin and Roland. Also known as EVERY MAN FOR HIMSELF, EACH ONE FOR HIMSELF, and SAM COOPER'S GOLD.▼

Ruthless People (1986) C-93m. **½ D: Jim Abrahams, David Zucker, Jerry Zucker. Danny DeVito, Bette Midler, Judge Reinhold, Helen Slater, Anita Morris, Bill Pullman, William G. Schilling, Art Evans. Wealthy DeVito plans to murder his obnoxious wife—unaware that at that moment she's being kidnapped, and equally unaware that his paramour plans to take *him* for his dough. Clever farce written by Dale Launer has lots of laughs, bright performances, but turns sour: these really *are* unpleasant people!▼

RX Murder (1958-British) 85m. ** D: Derek Twist. Rick Jason, Marius Goring, Lisa Gastoni, Mary Merrall. Jason stars as American physician settling in British village to find strange murder. Fair mystery.

Ryan's Daughter (1970-British) C-176m. **½ D: David Lean. Robert Mitchum, Trevor Howard, Sarah Miles, Christopher Jones, John Mills, Leo McKern, Barry Foster. Simple love story blown up to gargantuan proportions in Northern Ireland, where young girl (Miles) marries simple, plodding schoolteacher (Mitchum) and has affair with British soldier (Jones) stationed in town. Elephantine production overpowers Robert Bolt's thin story, admittedly beautiful scenes dwarfing what plot there is. Story moves along briskly, maintains interest, but never becomes classic film its creators were attempting. Mills won Oscar in supporting role as hunchback, as did—most deservedly—cinematographer Freddie Young. Re-edited by director Lean after film's debut; original running time 206m.▼

Ryan White Story, The (1989) C-100m.

TVM D: John Herzfeld. Judith Light, Lukas Haas, George C. Scott, Michael Bowen, George Dzundza, Valerie Landsburg, Sarah Jessica Parker, Mitchell Ryan, Peter Scolari, Grace Zabriskie. The emotional based-on-fact story of a teenage hemophiliac and his mom who campaign to allow him to attend public school after he is diagnosed as having AIDS. Average.

Saadia (1953) **C-82m.** *½ D: Albert Lewin. Cornel Wilde, Mel Ferrer, Rita Gam, Cyril Cusack, Richard Johnson. Misfire; intellectual story of modernistic Moroccan ruler and doctor vying for love of superstitious native dancing girl.

Sabaka (1955) **C-81m.** ** D: Frank Ferrin. Boris Karloff, Reginald Denny, Victor Jory, Lisa Howard, Jeanne Bates, Jay Novello, June Foray. Splashy trivia enhanced by veteran cast, about spooky religious cult in exotic India.▼

Sabata (1970-Italian-Spanish) **C-107m.** ** D: Frank Kramer (Gianfranco Parolini). Lee Van Cleef, William Berger, Franco Ressel, Linda Veras, Pedro Sanchez (Ignazio Spalla). First of three spaghetti Westerns is the best, though that isn't saying much. Van Cleef plays a gambler hired by a trio of nasty businessmen to steal $100,000. Needless to say, the transaction becomes trickier than they expected. Sequel: ADIOS, SABATA.

√ **Sabotage** (1936-British) **76m.** *** D: Alfred Hitchcock. Sylvia Sidney, Oscar Homolka, John Loder, Desmond Tester, Joyce Barbour. Elaborately detailed thriller about woman who suspects that her kindly husband (Homolka), a movie theater manager, is keeping something from her. Full of intriguing Hitchcock touches. Based on Joseph Conrad's *Secret Agent*, originally retitled A WOMAN ALONE for the U.S.▼

Saboteur (1942) **108m.** *** D: Alfred Hitchcock. Robert Cummings, Priscilla Lane, Norman Lloyd, Otto Kruger, Alan Baxter, Alma Kruger, Dorothy Peterson, Vaughan Glaser. Extremely offbeat wartime Hitchcock yarn about a munitions worker who's falsely accused of sabotage and forced to take it on the lam. Full of quirky touches, unusual supporting characters, and some outstanding set-pieces, including famous Statue of Liberty finale . . . though actual story resolution is unfortunately abrupt. Screenplay by Peter Viertel, Joan Harrison and Dorothy Parker.▼

Saboteur, Code Name Morituri, The (1965) **123m.** **½ D: Bernhard Wicki. Marlon Brando, Yul Brynner, Janet Margolin, Trevor Howard, Wally Cox, William Redfield, Carl Esmond. Brando highlights great cast in study of anti-Nazi German who helps British capture cargo ship. Cast and Conrad Hall's photography are only assets; script degenerates. Originally released as MORITURI.▼

Sabra (1970-French-Italian) **C-98m.** ** D: Denys de la Patalliere. Akim Tamiroff, Assaf Dayan, Jean Claudio. Simplistic, contrived story of an Arab police inspector who "befriends" a young Israeli spy, in order to gain his confidence. Reissued as DEATH OF A JEW.

Sabre Jet (1953) **C-96m.** **½ D: Louis King. Robert Stack, Coleen Gray, Richard Arlen, Julie Bishop. Routine Korean War story of lonely wives and fighting husbands.

Sabrina (1954) **113m.** ***½ D: Billy Wilder. Humphrey Bogart, Audrey Hepburn, William Holden, John Williams, Francis X. Bushman, Martha Hyer, Nancy Kulp. Samuel Taylor's play *Sabrina Fair* is good vehicle for Hepburn as chauffeur's daughter romanced by aging tycoon Bogart to keep her from his playboy brother (Holden). Offbeat casting works in this fun film. Screenplay by Ernest Lehman, Billy Wilder, and Taylor.▼

Sabu and the Magic Ring (1957) **C-61m.** *½ D: George Blair. Sabu, Daria Massey, Vladimir Sokoloff, Robin Moore. Low-budget backlot Arabian Nights nonsense, with Sabu chasing thieves to regain stolen girl and priceless gem. Originally shot as two separate TV pilots.

Sacco and Vanzetti (1971-French-Italian) **C-120m.** *½ D: Giuliano Montaldo. Gian Maria Volonte, Riccardo Cucciolla, Milo O'Shea, Cyril Cusack, Rosanna Fratello, Geoffrey Keen. Classic tale of American miscarriage of justice cries for cinematic treatment, but this version makes South Braintree, Massachusetts, look like a town in a Clint Eastwood spaghetti Western. Joan Baez sings title song.▼

Sacketts, The (1979) **C-200m. TVM** D: Robert Totten. Sam Elliott, Tom Selleck, Jeff Osterhage, Glenn Ford, Ben Johnson, Gilbert Roland, Ruth Roman, Jack Elam, Mercedes McCambridge. Rambling sagebrush saga taken from two Louis L'Amour novels following the fortunes of the three Sackett Brothers in the post-Civil War west. Average. Followed by THE SHADOW RIDERS.▼

Sacred Ground (1983) **C-100m.** **½ D: Charles B. Pierce. Tim McIntire, Jack Elam, Serene Hedin, Mindi Miller, Eloy Phil Casados, L. Q. Jones. Fair drama of turmoil resulting when mountain man McIntire, his Apache wife and baby settle on holy Paiute burial ground.▼

Sacred Hearts (1985-British) **C-95m.** **½ D: Barbara Rennie. Anna Massey, Katrin Cartlidge, Oona Kirsch, Fiona Shaw, Anne Dyson, Gerard Murphy, Murray Melvin. Repressive, tyrannical Sister Thomas (Massey) ignores the questions, feelings, and fears of her young charges in a convent as the bombs explode around them in WW2 Britain. Sometimes quietly stimulating but also slow and predictable; occasional bits of humor help.

Sacrifice, The (1986-Swedish-French) **C-145m.** **½ D: Andrei Tarkovsky. Erland Josephson, Susan Fleetwood, Valerie Mairesse, Allan Edwall, Gundun Gisladottir. A cataclysmic event occurs during the birthday festivities of intellectual Josephson, who as a result becomes compelled to perform an act of faith. Slow, overly intense, but beautifully filmed (by Sven Nykvist) examination of the need for, and lack of, spirituality in modern society. Decidedly not for all tastes. Tarkovsky's final film.▼

Sadat (1983) **C-200m. TVM** D: Richard Michaels. Louis Gossett, Jr., Madolyn Smith, John Rhys-Davies, Jeremy Kemp, Anne Heywood, Paul L. Smith, Jeffrey Tambor, Barry Morse, Nehemiah Persoff. Imaginatively cast Gossett gives a curiously subdued performance, and Lionel Chetwynd's script merely skims Anwar Sadat's career in this skin-deep portrait of the Egyptian leader. Originally shown in two parts. Average.

Saddle the Wind (1958) **C-84m. *** D: Robert Parrish. Robert Taylor, Julie London, John Cassavetes, Donald Crisp, Charles McGraw, Royal Dano. Well-acted Western of turned-good rancher (Taylor) fated to shoot it out with brother (Cassavetes). If you've ever wondered what a Western written by Rod Serling would be like, here's your chance.

Saddle Tramp (1950) **C-77m. **½ D: Hugo Fregonese. Joel McCrea, Wanda Hendrix, John McIntire, John Russell, Ed Begley, Jeanette Nolan, Antonio Moreno. Homey Western with McCrea in title role, "adopting" four kids and fighting the good cause.

Sad Horse, The (1959) **C-78m. ** D: James B. Clark. David Ladd, Chill Wills, Rex Reason, Patrice Wymore. Tender, undemanding tale of a racehorse and a lonely boy (Ladd).

Sadie and Son (1987) **C-100m. TVM** D: John Llewellyn Moxey. Debbie Reynolds, Brian McNamara, Sam Wanamaker, Cynthia Dale, David Ferry. Mother-and-son cop team in the Big Apple—if you can accept a Jewish Debbie with a badge collaring "perps." Below average.

Sadie McKee (1934) **90m. *** D: Clarence Brown. Joan Crawford, Franchot Tone, Gene Raymond, Edward Arnold, Esther Ralston, Leo G. Carroll, Akim Tamiroff, Gene Austin. Solidly entertaining film follows serpentine story of working-girl Crawford and the three men in her life: smooth-talking Raymond, tipsy millionaire Arnold, earnest employer Tone. Beautifully paced, handsomely filmed. Song: "All I Do Is Dream of You," plus amusing rendition of "After You've Gone" by Austin, Candy Candido.

Sadie Thompson (1928) **97m. *** D: Raoul Walsh. Gloria Swanson, Lionel Barrymore, Raoul Walsh, Blanche Frederici, Charles Lane, James Marcus. Fascinating, frequently high-powered version of W. Somerset Maugham's *Rain,* about a lusty, fun-loving prostitute (Swanson) who arrives in Pago Pago and tangles with stuffy, hypocritical reformer Barrymore while Marine Sgt. Walsh falls for her. Swanson, and especially Barrymore, are well cast. Unseen (except in archival showings) for many years, because the final reel decomposed years ago. Now the footage (about eight minutes) has been recreated, using stills and the original title cards. Remade as RAIN, DIRTY GERTIE FROM HARLEM, and MISS SADIE THOMPSON.▼

Sadist, The (1963) **81m. **½ D: James Landis. Arch Hall, Jr., Helen Hovey, Richard Alden, Marilyn Manning, Don Russell. Taut little B-picture about a psychotic punk who terrorizes three innocent people who've stopped at a roadside gas station. Hall is distressingly believable as the psycho. Imaginatively shot by Vilmos (billed as William) Zsigmond. Retitled PROFILE OF TERROR.▼

Sad Sack, The (1957) **98m. ** D: George Marshall. Jerry Lewis, Phyllis Kirk, David Wayne, Peter Lorre, Gene Evans, Mary Treen. Disjointed comedy vaguely based on George Baker comic strip of Army misfit. Not enough funny sequences to succeed. Lorre appears as Arab in last part of film.▼

Safari (1940) **80m. ** D: Edward H. Griffith. Douglas Fairbanks, Jr., Madeleine Carroll, Tullio Carminati, Lynne Overman, Muriel Angelus, Billy Gilbert. Standard jungle expedition story, with attractive stars.

Safari (1956-British) **C-91m. **½ D: Terence Young. Victor Mature, Janet Leigh, John Justin, Roland Culver, Liam Redmond. Fierce jungle drama has Mature leading expedition against Mau Maus. Cast gives good performances.

Safari Drums (1953) **71m.** D: Ford Beebe. Johnny Sheffield, Douglas Kennedy, Barbara Bestar, Emory Parnell, Smoki Whitfield. SEE: **Bomba, the Jungle Boy** series.

Safari 3000 (1982) **C-91m. *½** D: Harry Hurwitz. David Carradine, Stockard Channing, Christopher Lee, Hamilton Camp, Ian Yule. Ex-Hollywood stuntman is pitted against various adversaries in an international race; third-rate action yarn whose tongue-in-cheek attitude doesn't help. ▼

Safe at Home! (1962) **83m. **½ D: Walter Doniger. Mickey Mantle, Roger Maris, William Frawley, Patricia Barry, Don Collier, Bryan Russell. Kid is pressured into lying to Little League pals about friendship with M&M. The stoic poetry of Jack Webb's acting pales beside that of Maris' in this kiddie time-capsule; leads, cameos by Whitey Ford and Ralph Houk make it a must for Yankee fans . . . if no one else.

Safecracker, The (1958-British) **96m.** ** D: Ray Milland. Ray Milland, Barry Jones, Jeannette Sterke, Ernest Clark, Melissa Stribling, Victor Maddern. Contrived story of burglar who almost goes straight, later forced to use his talents for war effort.

Safe Place, A (1971) **C-94m.** ** D: Henry Jaglom. Tuesday Weld, Jack Nicholson, Orson Welles, Philip Proctor, Gwen Welles. Spaced-out, water-logged fantasy of weird girl who lives in dream world where she can never grow up.

Safety Last (1923) **78m.** *** D: Fred Newmeyer, Sam Taylor. Harold Lloyd, Mildred Davis, Bill Strothers, Noah Young. Crackerjack silent comedy about go-getter Harold determined to make good in the big city includes his justly famous building-climbing sequence—still hair-raising after all these years. Edited for TV and paired with hilarious excerpt from 1924 feature HOT WATER.▼

Saga of Hemp Brown, The (1958) **C-80m.** ** D: Richard Carlson. Rory Calhoun, Beverly Garland, John Larch, Russell Johnson. Calhoun is bounced from Army, and seeks to find real crooks in just another Western.

✓ **Sahara** (1943) **97m.** ***½ D: Zoltan Korda. Humphrey Bogart, Bruce Bennett, J. Carrol Naish, Lloyd Bridges, Rex Ingram, Richard Nugent, Dan Duryea. Excellent actioner of British-American unit stranded in Sahara desert; Bogie's the chief, of course, with fine support by Naish and Ingram. Remade as Western LAST OF THE CO-MANCHES, and imitated many other times.▼

Sahara (1984) **C-104m.** *½ D: Andrew V. McLaglen. Brooke Shields, Lambert Wilson, Horst Buchholz, John Rhys-Davies, Ronald Lacey, John Mills, Steve Forrest, Perry Lang, Cliff Potts. Tacky modern variation on THE PERILS OF PAULINE with Brooke filling in for her late father in free-for-all auto race across North African desert in the 1920s, being kidnapped by handsome desert sheik. Any resemblance to a good movie is just a mirage.▼

Saigon (1948) **94m.** ** D: Leslie Fenton. Alan Ladd, Veronica Lake, Luther Adler, Douglas Dick, Wally Cassell, Morris Carnovsky. Glossy Paramount caper about airmen stationed in Vietnam involved in robbery; only fair.

Sail a Crooked Ship (1961) **88m.** **½ D: Irving S. Brecher. Robert Wagner, Ernie Kovacs, Dolores Hart, Carolyn Jones, Frankie Avalon, Frank Gorshin, Harvey Lembeck. Bungled crime-caper comedy has

hilarious moments, but not enough to make it a winner. Based on a Nathaniel Benchley novel.

Sail into Danger (1957-British) **72m.** ** D: Kenneth Hume. Dennis O'Keefe, Kathleen Ryan, James Hayter, Pedro de Cordoba, John Bull, Felix de Pommes. O'Keefe is ensnared into helping Ryan in smuggling plot; set in Barcelona. Meek actioner.

Sailor Beware (1951) **108m.** *** D: Hal Walker. Dean Martin, Jerry Lewis, Corinne Calvet, Marion Marshall, Robert Strauss; guest, Betty Hutton. Hilarious adventures of Martin & Lewis in the Navy. Induction scenes, boxing sequence are highlights in one of the team's funniest outings. James Dean can be glimpsed in the boxing scene. Remake of THE FLEET'S IN.

Sailor Beware! (1957) SEE: **Panic in the Parlor**

Sailor from Gibraltar, The (1967-British) **89m.** ** D: Tony Richardson. Jeanne Moreau, Ian Bannen, Vanessa Redgrave, Zia Mohyeddin, Hugh Griffith, Orson Welles, Umberto Orsini, Eleanor Bron, John Hurt. Uneven adaptation of Marguerite Duras' novel has Moreau (who even gets to warble a song) as the mythical nymphomaniac wandering the seas in search of reunion with her dream sailor. Boasts an intriguing cast, but Richardson's handheld camera and other 1960s techniques have badly dated.

Sailor of the King (1953-U.S.-British) **83m.** *** D: Roy Boulting. Jeffrey Hunter, Michael Rennie, Wendy Hiller, Bernard Lee, Peter Van Eyck. Solid WW2 naval action story, based on C. S. Forester novel *Brown on Resolution*, with Hunter rising to challenge when opportunity arises to attack German raider. British title: SINGLE HANDED. Filmed before in 1935.

Sailor's Lady (1940) **66m.** ** D: Allan Dwan. Nancy Kelly, Jon Hall, Joan Davis, Dana Andrews, Mary Nash, Larry "Buster" Crabbe, Katherine (Kay) Aldridge. Witless comedy of Kelly pretending to have baby to see if sailor-fiance Hall will still marry her.

Sailor's Luck (1933) **78m.** *** D: Raoul Walsh. James Dunn, Sally Eilers, Sammy Cohen, Victor Jory, Frank Moran, Esther Muir. Funny, offbeat film of sailors on leave; Dunn and Eilers carry boy-meets-girl plot while crazy comedy touches surround them, including Jory as oily Baron DeBartolo, landlord who runs dance marathon!

Sailor Takes a Wife, The (1945) **91m.** ** D: Richard Whorf. Robert Walker, June Allyson, Hume Cronyn, Audrey Totter, Eddie "Rochester" Anderson, Reginald Owen. Mild little comedy is summed up by title.

Sailor Who Fell From Grace With the Sea, The (1976-British) **C-104m.** *** D:

Lewis John Carlino. Sarah Miles, Kris Kristofferson, Jonathan Kahn, Margo Cunningham, Earl Rhodes. A troubled, impressionable boy tries to deal with his widowed mother's love affair with an amiable sailor, and falls under the influence of a morbid young friend. Passionate love scenes, and a bizarre ending, highlight this unusual film, beautifully shot by Douglas Slocombe on English seacoast locations. Based on a novel by Yukio Mishima.▼

Saint, The Leslie Charteris' literate, debonair detective has been the subject of an extremely popular British television show. But he never quite made it in the movies. From 1938 to 1942, RKO tried no less than three actors in the leading role, finding moderate success but nothing earthshaking. Louis Hayward seemed at home in the role in THE SAINT IN NEW YORK, a smooth underworld saga with a bland leading lady (Kay Sutton) and a fine supporting cast (Sig Rumann as a ganglord, Jack Carson as a thug, etc.). Nevertheless, he didn't repeat the role; it went instead to suave George Sanders, who portrayed the Saint, usually with Wendy Barrie as leading lady, in four quickly made, entertaining mysteries taking him from Palm Springs to London. The scripts were competent, but it was Sanders' usual offhand manner that kept them alive. In 1942 stage star Hugh Sinclair took a fling in THE SAINT MEETS THE TIGER but gave up after a second effort. Sanders left the series only to begin another, The Falcon, at the same studio, although without the main titles to inform viewers which series it was, one could hardly have told the difference. The Falcon continued through the 1940s, while the Saint came to a premature end in 1942. There was one revival attempt with Louis Hayward made in England in 1953, THE SAINT'S GIRL FRIDAY, which was average but no improvement over the original series. It took British television and an actor named Roger Moore to give life to The Saint at last in the 1960s.

Sainted Sisters, The (1948) 89m. **½ D: William Russell. Veronica Lake, Joan Caulfield, Barry Fitzgerald, William Demarest, George Reeves, Beulah Bondi. Fitzgerald's blarney is a bit overdone in this tale of two bad girls who go straight under his guidance.

Saint in London, The (1939-British) 72m. D: John Paddy Carstairs. George Sanders, David Burns, Sally Gray, Henry Oscar, Ralph Truman, Norah Howard, Carl Jaffe. SEE: **The Saint** series.▼

Saint in New York, The (1938) 71m. D: Ben Holmes. Louis Hayward, Kay Sutton, Sig Ruman, Jonathan Hale, Frederick Burton, Jack Carson. SEE: **The Saint** series.▼

Saint in Palm Springs, The (1941) 65m. D: Jack Hively. George Sanders, Wendy Barrie, Paul Guilfoyle, Jonathan Hale, Linda Hayes, Ferris Taylor. SEE: **The Saint** series.

Saint Jack (1979) C-112m. *** D: Peter Bogdanovich. Ben Gazzara, Denholm Elliott, James Villiers, Joss Ackland, Rodney Bewes, George Lazenby, Lisa Lu, Peter Bogdanovich. Absorbing character study of an amiable, ambitious pimp who thrives in Singapore during early 1970s. Fine performances from Gazzara and Elliott, excellent use of location milieu. From a Paul Theroux novel.▼

Saint Joan (1957) 110m. ** D: Otto Preminger. Jean Seberg, Richard Widmark, Richard Todd, Anton Walbrook, John Gielgud, Felix Aylmer, Harry Andrews, Barry Jones, Finlay Currie, Bernard Miles, Margot Grahame. Big-scale filming of Shaw's play sounded large thud when released; some good acting, but Seberg (who won her first film role after a nationwide search) not suited to film's tempo, throws production askew. Script by Graham Greene. Also shown in computer-colored version.▼

Saint Meets the Tiger, The (1943-British) 70m. D: Paul Stein. Hugh Sinclair, Jean Gillie, Clifford Evans, Wylie Watson, Dennis Arundell. SEE: **The Saint** series.

Saint's Double Trouble, The (1940) 68m. D: Jack Hively. George Sanders, Helene Whitney, Jonathan Hale, Bela Lugosi, Donald MacBride, John F. Hamilton. SEE: **The Saint** series.▼

Saint's Girl Friday, The (1954-British) 68m. D: Seymour Friedman. Louis Hayward, Naomi Chance, Sydney Tafler, Charles Victor. SEE: **The Saint** series.

Saint Strikes Back, The (1939) 67m. D: John Farrow. George Sanders, Wendy Barrie, Jonathan Hale, Jerome Cowan, Neil Hamilton, Barry Fitzgerald, Edward Gargan, Robert Strange. SEE: **The Saint** series.▼

Saint's Vacation, The (1941-British) 60m. D: Leslie Fenton. Hugh Sinclair, Sally Gray, Arthur Macrae, Cecil Parker, Leueen McGrath, Gordon McLeod. SEE: **The Saint** series.▼

Saint Takes Over, The (1940) 69m. D: Jack Hively. George Sanders, Jonathan Hale, Wendy Barrie, Paul Guilfoyle, Morgan Conway, Robert Emmett Keane, Cyrus W. Kendall. SEE: **The Saint** series.▼

Sakima and the Masked Marvel (1943) 100m. **½ D: Spencer Bennet. Tom Steele, William Forrest, Louise Currie, Johnny Arthur, Rod Bacon, Richard Clarke. Abovepar Republic actioner set during WW2, with Japanese espionage in the U.S. combatted by heroic mysterious Masked Marvel. Reedited from serial THE MASKED MARVEL.

Salaam Bombay! (1988-Indian-British) C-113m. *** D: Mira Nair. Shafiq Syed, Sarfuddin Quarrassi, Raju Barnad, Raghubir Yadav, Aneeta Kanwar. Gut-wrenching chronicle of young country boy Syed and his various experiences among the street hustlers, drug peddlers, and prostitutes of Bombay. Unravels as a novel, with a gallery of vividly drawn supporting characters. Fine feature debut for director Nair.▼

Salamander, The (1981-U.S.-British-Italian) **C-101m.** *½ D: Peter Zinner. Franco Nero, Anthony Quinn, Martin Balsam, Sybil Danning, Christopher Lee, Cleavon Little, Paul Smith, Claudia Cardinale, Eli Wallach. Colonel Nero attempts to prevent a fascist coup d'etat in Italy. A cornball script sinks this potentially intriguing drama, from a Morris West novel.▼

Salem's Lot (1979) **C-200m. TVM** D: Tobe Hooper. David Soul, James Mason, Lance Kerwin, Bonnie Bedelia, Lew Ayres, Reggie Nalder, Ed Flanders, Elisha Cook, Marie Windsor, Clarissa Kaye, Fred Willard, James Gallery, Kenneth McMillan. Well-made hair-raiser based on Stephen King's bestseller about vampirism running rampant in small New England town. Mason is great as sinister antique dealer, and Nalder's vampire is terrifying, but Soul is only so-so as successful writer returning home to strange goings-on. Later cut to 150m.; the 112m. version shown on cassettes and cable-TV as SALEM'S LOT: THE MOVIE is the overseas theatrical version and contains more explicit violence. Followed by A RETURN TO SALEM'S LOT. Above average.▼

Sallah (1965-Israeli) **C-105m.** *** D: Ephraim Kishon. Haym Topol, Geula Noni, Gila Almagor, Arik Einstein, Shraga Friedman, Esther Greenberg. Topol is amusing as an Oriental Jew who emigrates to Israel with his wife and seven children and who is forever scheming to improve his lot. A modest, lighthearted, thoroughly enjoyable satire.▼

Sally and Saint Anne (1952) **90m.** **½ D: Rudolph Maté. Ann Blyth, Edmund Gwenn, Hugh O'Brian, Jack Kelly, King Donovan. Cutesy and a bit tasteless; Blyth is daughter in screwball family who believes St. Anne will help them in times of need.

Sally, Irene and Mary (1938) **72m.** **½ D: William A. Seiter. Alice Faye, Tony Martin, Fred Allen, Joan Davis, Marjorie Weaver, Gregory Ratoff, Jimmy Durante, Louise Hovick (Gypsy Rose Lee). Predictable story of three stage-struck girls trying to break into show business, with good comedy spots by Davis, pleasant songs from Faye and Martin: "I Could Use a Dream," "This Is Where I Came In."

Sally of the Sawdust (1925) **91m.** **½ D: D. W. Griffith. W. C. Fields, Carol Dempster, Alfred Lunt, Erville Alderson, Effie Shannon. Pleasant yarn of sideshow con-man Fields who tries to restore his ward (Dempster) to her rightful place in society, knowing identity of her wealthy grandparents. Interesting to see W. C. in a silent film, particularly since one can compare this to its remake, POPPY.▼

Sally's Irish Rogue SEE: **Poacher's Daughter, The**

Salo, or The 120 Days of Sodom (1975-Italian) **C-117m.** BOMB D: Pier Paolo Pasolini. Paolo Bonacelli, Giorgio Cataldi, Umberto P. Quinavalle, Aldo Valletti, Caterina Boratto. Controversial, disturbing adaptation of de Sade's novel, set during WW2 in Italy, where Fascist rulers brutalize and degrade adolescents. Sadism, scatology, and debauchery galore; Pasolini, whose last film this is, wallows in his own sensationalism.▼

Salome (1953) **C-103m.** **½ D: William Dieterle. Rita Hayworth, Stewart Granger, Charles Laughton, Judith Anderson, Cedric Hardwicke, Maurice Schwartz. Great cast struggles with unintentionally funny script in biblical drama of illustrious dancer who offers herself to spare John the Baptist. Filmed before with Nazimova in 1923.▼

Salome's Last Dance (1988-British) **C-90m.** **½ D: Ken Russell. Glenda Jackson, Stratford Johns, Nickolas Grace, Imogen Millais-Scott, Douglas Hodge. As Oscar Wilde lounges in a brothel (the same one where his subsequent arrest would lead to his downfall), the proprietor stages a production of the playwright's title work, with Salome, Herod, John the Baptist and Co. all strutting their stuff. Typical Russell litmus test for one's tolerance of the outrageous, but wittier and less oppressive than some of the director's other historical pageants. Grace's weak Wilde aside, the actors do remarkably well under the circumstances.▼

Salome, Where She Danced (1945) **C-90m.** BOMB D: Charles Lamont. Yvonne De Carlo, Rod Cameron, David Bruce, Walter Slezak, Albert Dekker, Marjorie Rambeau, J. Edward Bromberg. Ludicrous film provides some laughs while trying to spin tale of exotic dancer becoming Mata Hari-type spy. Nevertheless, this boosted De Carlo to stardom.▼

Salsa (1988) **C-97m.** ** D: Boaz Davidson. Robby Rosa, Rodney Harvey, Magali Alvarado, Miranda Garrison, Moon Orona, Angela Alvarado, Celia Cruz, Tito Puente. All flash and no substance in this DIRTY DANCING-inspired feature-length music video with a Latin beat. Rosa (of the pop group Menudo) stars as a young auto repairman who'd much rather be shaking his body to salsa. Main problem: Where's the script?▼

Salt and Pepper (1968-British) **C-101m.** **½ D: Richard Donner. Sammy Davis, Jr., Peter Lawford, Michael Bates, Ilona Rodgers, John LeMesurier. Soho nightclub owners find trouble when two baddies turn up at their club. Contrived, broad comedy. Sequel: ONE MORE TIME.

Salt of the Earth (1953) **94m.** ***½ D: Herbert Biberman. Juan Chacon, Rosoura Revueltas, Will Geer, Mervin Williams, Frank Talavera, Clinton Jencks, Virginia Jencks. Taut drama about striking New Mexico mineworkers, with a refreshingly pro-feminist viewpoint. Director Biberman, actor Geer, producer Paul Jarrico, and screenwriter Michael Wilson were all blacklisted when the film was made.▼

Salty (1973) **C-92m.** ** D: Ricou Browning. Mark Slade, Clint Howard, Nina Foch, Julius W. Harris, Linda Scruggs. Two orphaned brothers adopt a mischievous sea lion in this predictable kiddie film made in Florida.▼

Salty O'Rourke (1945) **99m.** *** D: Raoul Walsh. Alan Ladd, Gail Russell, William Demarest, Stanley Clements, Bruce Cabot, Spring Byington. Lively tale of smooth conman Ladd aiming to clean up with jockey Clements, who turns out to be a large headache. Schoolteacher Russell steps in to foil Ladd's plans.

Salute to the Marines (1943) **C-101m.** **½ D: S. Sylvan Simon. Wallace Beery, Fay Bainter, Reginald Owen, Keye Luke, Ray Collins, Marilyn Maxwell. OK Beery vehicle of Marine veteran who reluctantly retires, finds himself caught in surprise attack on Philippines.

Salut l'Artiste (1974-French) **C-102m.** *** D: Yves Robert. Marcello Mastroianni, Jean Rochefort, Francoise Fabian, Carla Gravina. Light comedy about second-rate actors Mastroianni and Rochefort; the former scampers about while going nowhere; the latter opts out for an ad executive job. Amusing, with first-rate cast and performances.▼

Salvador (1986) **C-123m.** **½ D: Oliver Stone. James Woods, James Belushi, Michael Murphy, John Savage, Elpedia Carrillo, Tony Plana, Colby Chester, Cindy (Cynthia) Gibb, John Doe. Uneven but compelling drama based on real experiences of journalist Richard Boyle in strife-ridden El Salvador in 1980–81. Effective propaganda, often potent drama; it takes time to grab hold because lead characters Woods and Belushi are such incredible sleazeballs. Woods's dynamic performance makes up for a lot; his first visit to confession in thirty-two years is a memorably funny scene.▼

Salvage (1979) **C-100m. TVM** D: Lee Philips. Andy Griffith, Joel Higgins, Trish Stewart, J. Jay Saunders, Richard Jaeckel. Amiable pilot to the short-lived series in which a hotshot junkman goes into the moonshot business for himself with two young companions to recover a fortune in space junk. Average.

Salvation! (1987) **C-80m.** *½ D: Beth B. Stephen McHattie, Dominique Davalos, Exene Cervenka, Viggo Mortensen, Rockets Redglare, Billy Bastani. This project seemingly couldn't miss: a satire of false TV evangelist (McHattie) who gets involved in a sex incident, picture was released right after the Jim & Tammy Bakker scandal. Unfortunately, underground film-maker Beth B directs in the manner of an incoherent music video, swamping McHattie's convincing central performance (resembling a young John Carradine). Interesting cast of newcomers.▼

Salzburg Connection, The (1972) **C-92m.** *½ D: Lee H. Katzin. Barry Newman, Anna Karina, Klaus-Maria Brandauer, Karen Jensen, Joe Maross, Wolfgang Preiss. Terrible film version of Helen MacInnes' bestseller about American lawyer on vacation in Salzburg who gets mixed up with spies; irritating use of slow-motion and freeze-frame gimmicks.▼

Samar (1962) **C-89m.** ** D: George Montgomery. George Montgomery, Gilbert Roland, Ziva Rodann, Joan O'Brien, Nico Minardos, Mario Barri. Average actioner has Montgomery as head of prison compound on a Philippine island who rejects inhumane treatment of prisoners and leads them on escape route.▼

Samaritan: The Mitch Snyder Story (1986) **C-100m. TVM** D: Richard T. Heffron. Martin Sheen, Cicely Tyson, Roxanne Hart, Joe Seneca, Stan Shaw, James Avery, Conchata Ferrell. Social drama about the real-life Vietnam vet who champions the cause of America's homeless by staging well-publicized hunger strikes in the shadow of the White House. Written by Clifford Campian. Above average.

Same Time, Next Year (1978) **C-117m.** *** D: Robert Mulligan. Ellen Burstyn, Alan Alda. Bernard Slade's two-character Broadway play makes pleasing film, with Alda and Burstyn as adulterous couple who share one weekend a year for 26 years; warm, human comedy-drama reflects changes in American life and attitudes since early '50s in likable fashion.▼

Sam Hill: Who Killed Mr. Foster? (1971) **C-100m. TVM** D: Fielder Cook. Ernest Borgnine, Sam Jaffe, J. D. Cannon, Judy Geeson, Will Geer, Bruce Dern, Slim Pickens, John McGiver, Jay C. Flippen. Pending town election jeopardizes security of cynical Western marshal. Uneventful situations, boring dialogue; even somewhat unusual casting doesn't enliven proceedings. A rare misfire from the producing/writing team of Richard Levinson and William Link. Below average. Also known as WHO KILLED THE MYSTERIOUS MR. FOSTER?

Sam Marlowe, Private Eye SEE: **Man with Bogart's Face, The**▼
Sammy and Rosie Get Laid (1987-British) **C-100m.** ** D: Stephen Frears. Shashi Kapoor, Claire Bloom, Ayub Khan Din, Frances Barber, Roland Gift, Wendy Gazelle, Suzette Llewellyn. The curious lives of a couple with an open sexual relationship are thrown into disarray by the arrival of his father, a powerful reactionary political figure from India who cannot understand their lifestyle—or what has happened to the traditional British way of life he used to enjoy. Disturbing but monotonous look at social and sexual anarchy in England, written by Hanif Kureishi, who previously collaborated with director Frears on MY BEAUTIFUL LAUNDRETTE.▼
Sammy Going South SEE: **Boy Ten Feet Tall, A**
Sammy Stops the World (1979) **C-104m.** BOMB D: Mel Shapiro. Sammy Davis, Jr., Marian Mercer, Dennis Daniels, Donna Lowe. Pathetic update of *Stop the World, I Want to Get Off* combines nail-your-camera-to-the-ground direction with a stage production that couldn't get by at Three Mile Island Dinner Theatre.
Sammy the Way Out Seal (1962) **C-90m.** **½ D: Norman Tokar. Robert Culp, Jack Carson, Billy Mumy, Patricia Barry. Pretty funny sitcom for the kids about a seal who becomes Mumy's pet and wreaks havoc upon Culp and family. Shown as a feature in Europe, originally made as a two-part Disney TV show.▼
Samson and Delilah (1949) **C-128m.** *** D: Cecil B. DeMille. Victor Mature, Hedy Lamarr, George Sanders, Angela Lansbury, Henry Wilcoxon, Olive Deering, Fay Holden. With expected DeMille touches, this remains a tremendously entertaining film. Mature is surprisingly good as Samson, though his famous fight with lion is hopelessly phony; also difficult to swallow idea of Lansbury being Lamarr's *older* sister. Sanders supplies biggest surprise by underplaying his role as the Saran. This won Oscars for its Art Direction-Set Decoration and Costumes. Remade as a TVM.▼
Samson and Delilah (1984) **C-100m. TVM** D: Lee Philips. Antony Hamilton, Belinda Bauer, Max von Sydow, Stephen Macht, Maria Schell, Jose Ferrer, Victor Mature. New rendition of the original man of steel and the woman who gave him a clipping; offbeat touch here is having original Samson, Mature (in his TV acting debut), playing Samson's father. Average.▼
Samson and the Slave Queen (1963-Italian) **C-92m.** *½ D: Umberto Lenzi. Pierre Brice, Alan Steel, Moira Orfei, Maria Grazia Spina. Juvenile muscleman epic that is ludicrous in its approach to adventure.
Sam's Son (1984) **C-104m.** ** D: Michael Landon. Eli Wallach, Anne Jackson, Timothy Patrick Murphy, Hallie Todd, Alan Hayes, Jonna Lee, Michael Landon. Landon wrote, directed, and appears briefly in this autobiographical saga about an underdog kid, who's a champion javelin thrower, and his loving but frustrated father, who never got to pursue his dreams. Wallach's performance as the father is major asset of this sometimes syrupy film.▼
Sam's Song (1969) **C-92m.** *½ D: Jordan Leondopoulos (John Shade, John C. Broderick). Robert De Niro, Jennifer Warren, Jered Mickey, Martin Kelley, Viva. Dreary film about film editor's weekend with friends on Long Island, interesting only for early De Niro performance. Extensive reshooting includes new characters played by Lisa Blount and Sybil Danning; film was reissued in 1979 as THE SWAP.▼
Samurai (1979) **C-78m. TVM** D: Lee H. Katzin. Joe Penny, Dana Elcar, Beulah Quo, James Shigeta, Charles Cioffi, Geoffrey Lewis. Incredible series hopeful about an eager beaver San Francisco assistant DA who moonlights as a samurai swordsman to uphold justice! Must be seen to be disbelieved, or better yet, forget it. Below average.
Sam Whiskey (1969) **C-96m.** ** D: Arnold Laven. Burt Reynolds, Clint Walker, Ossie Davis, Angie Dickinson, Rick Davis, William Schallert, Woodrow Parfrey. Modestly mounted, uninteresting Western wasting talents of good cast. Schemer Whiskey coerced into organizing heist of golden bell. For Western aficionados and Reynolds addicts only.
San Antone (1953) **90m.** **½ D: Joseph Kane. Rod Cameron, Arleen Whelan, Forrest Tucker, Katy Jurado, Rodolfo Acosta, Bob Steele, Harry Carey, Jr. Offbeat Western tends to ramble, but story of Cameron and friends being victimized by despicable Tucker and bitchy Southern belle Whelan is intriguing.
San Antonio (1945) **C-111m.** *** D: David Butler. Errol Flynn, Alexis Smith, S. Z. Sakall, Victor Francen, Florence Bates, John Litel, Paul Kelly. Elaborate Western has predictable plot but good production as dance-hall girl Smith, working for villain Francen, falls for good-guy Flynn.▼
Sanctuary (1961) **100m.** ** D: Tony Richardson. Lee Remick, Yves Montand, Bradford Dillman, Odetta, Reta Shaw, Howard St. John, Strother Martin. Faulkner's novel of Southern degradation, rape, and murder, filmed before as THE STORY OF TEMPLE DRAKE; much more explicit here.
Sanctuary of Fear (1979) **C-100m. TVM** D: John Llewellyn Moxey. Barnard Hughes, Kay Lenz, Michael McGuire, Fred Gwynne, Elizabeth Wilson, George Hearn. Disappointing pilot to proposed series based on G. K. Chesterton's *Father Brown*, the English parish priest (here transplanted to

N.Y.C.) and amateur sleuth, played so wonderfully by Alec Guinness in the 1954 movie. Average. Retitled GIRL IN THE PARK.▼

Sand (1949) **C-78m.** ** D: Louis King. Mark Stevens, Rory Calhoun, Coleen Gray, Charley Grapewin. Visually picturesque but dull account of show horse who turns wild. Retitled: WILL JAMES' SAND.

Sand Castle, The (1960) **C-67m.** **½ D: Jerome Hill. Barry Cardwell, Laurie Cardwell, George Dunham, Alec Wilder. Imaginative little film of small boy building mud castles on the beach, dreaming of people living in his creation.

Sandcastles (1972) **C-74m.** TVM D: Ted Post. Herschel Bernardi, Jan-Michael Vincent, Bonnie Bedelia, Mariette Hartley, Gary Crosby. Love story of young female musician and spirit of young man returning to clear his name. Thanks to somber mood and offbeat point of view, not as unbearable as expected. Movie shot on video tape. Average.

Sanders (1963-British) **C-83m.** ** D: Lawrence Huntington. Richard Todd, Marianne Koch, Albert Lieven, Vivi Bach, Jeremy Lloyd. Loose adaptation of Edgar Wallace novel *Sanders of the River* follows police inspector's investigation of murder in an African hospital and discovery of hidden silver mine. British title DEATH DRUMS ALONG THE RIVER. Todd repeated role of Harry Sanders in 1964 COAST OF SKELETONS.

Sanders of the River (1935-British) **98m.** *** D: Zoltan Korda. Paul Robeson, Leslie Banks, Nina Mae McKinney, Robert Cochran, Martin Walker. Dated adventure story (by Edgar Wallace) about river patrol officer maintains interest today, particularly for Robeson's strong presence and African location shooting. A fascinating relic of the sun-never-sets school of British imperialism. Sanders character revived in 1960s' SANDERS (DEATH DRUMS ALONG THE RIVER) and COAST OF SKELETONS.▼

San Diego, I Love You (1944) **83m.** *** D: Reginald LeBorg. Jon Hall, Louise Allbritton, Edward Everett Horton, Eric Blore, Buster Keaton, Irene Ryan. Whimsical comedy of unconventional family trying to promote father Horton's inventions in San Diego. Allbritton is perky, Keaton memorable in delightful sequence as bored bus driver.

Sandokan Against The Leopard of Sarawak (1964-Italian) **C-94m.** ** D: Luigi Capuano. Ray Danton, Guy Madison, Franca Bettoja, Mario Petri. Danton vs. Madison in this papier mâché, run-of-the-mill epic.

Sandokan Fights Back (1964-Italian) **C-96m.** ** D: Luigi Capuano. Ray Danton, Guy Madison, Franca Bettoja, Mino

Doro. Unconvincing, juvenile narrative of princely ruler fighting to regain his throne.

Sandokan the Great (1965-Italian) **C-105m.** ** D: Umberto Lenzi. Steve Reeves, Genevieve Grad, Rik Battaglia, Maurice Poli. Reeves actioner in which he rebels against the invading forces of Queen Victoria. At least the time period is different.

Sand Pebbles, The (1966) **C-179m.** *** D: Robert Wise. Steve McQueen, Richard Attenborough, Richard Crenna, Candice Bergen, Mako, Marayat Andriane, Simon Oakland, Larry Gates, Gavin MacLeod. McQueen gives one of his finest performances as cynical sailor on U.S. gunboat cruising China's Yangtze River in 1926. Long but generally compelling drama mixes traditional action and romance with some pointed notions about American imperialism (and a few parallels to Vietnam). Splendidly photographed by Joseph MacDonald.▼

Sandpiper, The (1965) **C-116m.** **½ D: Vincente Minnelli. Elizabeth Taylor, Richard Burton, Eva Marie Saint, Charles Bronson, Robert Webber, Torin Thatcher, Morgan Mason, Tom Drake. Ordinary triangle love affair, Beatnik Taylor in love with Burton, who is married to Saint. Nothing new, but beautiful California Big Sur settings help; so does Oscar-winning theme, "The Shadow Of Your Smile." Written by Dalton Trumbo and Michael Wilson.▼

Sandpit Generals, The SEE: **Wild Pack, The**

Sands of Beersheba (1966) **90m.** **½ D: Alexander Ramati. Diane Baker, David Opatoshu, Tom Bell, Paul Stassino. Pretentious retelling of Absalom (Bell) and David (Opatoshu) conflict, filmed in Israel, dabbling in philosophy on the Arab-vs.-Jew animosity.

Sands of Iwo Jima (1949) **110m.** *** D: Allan Dwan. John Wayne, John Agar, Adele Mara, Forrest Tucker, Arthur Franz, Julie Bishop, Richard Jaeckel. Enormously popular WW2 saga, with Wayne in one of his best roles, as a tough Marine topsergeant. The story and characters are pretty two-dimensional, and a bit worn from having been copied so many times since, but it's still good entertainment, and the use of authentic combat footage is striking. Wayne's first Oscar-nominated performance. Also shown in computer-colored version.▼

Sands of the Desert (1960-British) **C-92m.** ** D: John Paddy Carstairs. Charlie Drake, Peter Arne, Sarah Branch, Rebecca Dignam. Heavy-handed comedy set in Arabia, with Drake trying to uncover sabotage attempts at holiday camp.

Sands of the Kalahari (1965-British) **C-119m.** *** D: Cy Endfield. Stuart Whitman, Stanley Baker, Susannah York, Harry

Andrews, Theodore Bikel, Nigel Davenport. Well-done story of plane crash survivors struggling through desert and battling simian inhabitants (and each other).

Sandy Gets Her Man (1940) 74m. *½ D: Otis Garrett, Paul Smith. Stuart Erwin, Una Merkel, Baby Sandy, Edgar Kennedy, William Frawley. Precocious Baby Sandy is final arbiter of mama's courters; naive little film kept alive by character actors in cast.

Sandy Is a Lady (1940) 65m. *½ D: Charles Lamont. Nan Grey, Baby Sandy, Eugene Pallette, Tom Brown, Mischa Auer, Billy Gilbert, Edgar Kennedy, Anne Gwynne. Simplicity-saturated comedy as precocious child helps her family get ahead.

✓ **San Francisco** (1936) 115m. ***½ D: W. S. Van Dyke II. Clark Gable, Jeanette MacDonald, Spencer Tracy, Jack Holt, Jessie Ralph, Ted Healy, Shirley Ross, Al Shean. Top-grade entertainment with extremely lavish production. Jeanette overdoes it a bit as the belle of San Francisco, but the music, Tracy's performance, and earthquake climax are still fine. Originally had footage of Golden Gate Bridge under construction, other rhythmically edited shots of S.F. were changed for later reissue. Script by Anita Loos. Also shown in computer-colored version.▼

San Francisco International (1970) C-100m. TVM D: John Llewellyn Moxey. Van Johnson, Pernell Roberts, Clu Gulager, Beth Brickell, Tab Hunter, Nancy Malone, David Hartman, Jill Donahue. Fair suspense in otherwise typical day-in-the-life portrayal of major transportation center, centering around manager and security chief. Uneven characterizations and dialogue, but pace holds interest. Lloyd Bridges replaced Roberts in the subsequent series. Average.

San Francisco Story, The (1952) 80m. ** D: Robert Parrish. Joel McCrea, Yvonne De Carlo, Sidney Blackmer, Florence Bates. Tame Western actioner set in gold-rush days, with cleanup of city's criminal elements.

Sangaree (1953) C-94m. **½ D: Edward Ludwig. Fernando Lamas, Arlene Dahl, Patricia Medina, Francis L. Sullivan. Frank Slaughter's historical novel set in 1780s becomes an empty, handsome costumer about a slave who inherits a plantation owner's fortune. Filmed in 3-D.

Sanjuro (1962-Japanese) 96m. *** D: Akira Kurosawa. Toshiro Mifune, Tatsuya Nakadai, Takashi Shimura, Yuzo Kayama, Reiko Dan. Sequel to YOJIMBO has shabby, wandering samurai Mifune aiding nine bumbling younger warriors in exposing corruption among the elders of their clan. Satirical comic-book actioner features a typically deadpan Mifune performance.▼

San Pedro Bums, The (1977) C-78m. TVM D: Barry Shear. Christopher Murney, Jeff Druce, John Mark Robinson, Stuart Pankin, Darryl McCullough, Bill Lucking. Comedy adventure of five knockabouts, living on an old fishing boat, who try to collar a gang of waterfront toughs. A real bummer that somehow became a series. Below average.

San Quentin (1937) 70m. **½ D: Lloyd Bácon. Pat O'Brien, Humphrey Bogart, Ann Sheridan, Veda Ann Borg, Barton MacLane. Warner Bros. formula prison film; convict Bogart's sister (Sheridan) loves O'Brien, who's captain of the guards. MacLane is memorable as tough prison guard.

San Quentin (1946) 66m. **½ D: Gordon Douglas. Lawrence Tierney, Barton MacLane, Marian Carr, Harry Shannon, Carol Forman, Richard Powers (Tom Keene). Prison drama with different plot for a change, of organization for ex-cons not having intended results. Raymond Burr's first film.

Sansho the Bailiff (1954-Japanese) 125m. **** D: Kenji Mizoguchi. Kinuyo Tanaka, Kisho Hanayagi, Kyoko Kagawa, Eitaro Shindo, Ichiro Sugai. Epic, poetic drama of 11th-century Japan, focusing on the tribulations of a family. Kindly father, a provincial governor, is exiled; children (Hanayagi, Kagawa) become slaves; mother (Tanaka) is sold as a prostitute. Haunting, with stunning direction and cinematography (by Kazuo Miyagawa). Original running-time: 130m. Also known as THE BAILIFF.▼

Santa Claus (1985) C-112m. **½ D: Jeannot Szwarc. Dudley Moore, John Lithgow, David Huddleston, Burgess Meredith, Judy Cornwell, Jeffrey Kramer, Christian Fitzpatrick, Carrie Kei Heim. Story of how Santa came to be starts out so wonderfully—with eye-filling looks at his North Pole toy factory, reindeer, and sleigh—that it's too bad the rest of the film (with contemporary tale of humbug kid and greedy toy magnate) can't measure up. Still entertaining, just a bit less magical than it should have been. Referred to as SANTA CLAUS: THE MOVIE everywhere but in the main titles on screen!▼

Santa Claus Conquers the Martians (1964) C-80m. BOMB D: Nicholas Webster. John Call, Leonard Hicks, Vincent Beck, Donna Conforti. Absurd low-budget fantasy (with a Milton Delugg score!) about Santa and two Earth children being abducted to Mars to help solve some of their domestic problems—like kids watching too much TV. One of the Martian tykes is none other than Pia Zadora.▼

Santa Fe (1951) C-89m. ** D: Irving Pichel. Randolph Scott, Janis Carter, Jerome Courtland, Peter Thompson, John Archer, Warner Anderson, Roy Roberts,

Jock Mahoney. Routine account of brothers in post-Civil War days, on opposite sides of the law.

Santa Fe Passage (1955) **C-70m.** ** D: William Witney. John Payne, Faith Domergue, Rod Cameron, Slim Pickens. Routine wagon train westward; Indian attacks, love among the pioneers, etc.

Santa Fe Satan SEE: **Catch My Soul**

Santa Fe Trail (1940) **110m.** ** D: Michael Curtiz. Errol Flynn, Olivia de Havilland, Raymond Massey, Ronald Reagan, Alan Hale, Guinn Williams, William Lundigan, Ward Bond, Van Heflin, Gene Reynolds. Lopsided picture can't make up its mind about anything: what side it's taking, what it wants to focus on, etc. Worthless as history, but amid the rubble are some good action scenes as Jeb Stuart (Flynn) and cohorts go after John Brown (Massey). Reagan plays Flynn's West Point classmate and romantic rival, George Armstrong Custer (!). Also shown in computer-colored version.▼

Santa Sangre (1989 Italian-Mexican) **C-118m.** ** D: Alejandro Jodorowsky. Axel Jodorowsky, Blanca Guerra, Sabrina Dennison, Guy Stockwell, Thelma Tixou, Adan Jodorowsky, Faviola Elenka Tapia. Grotesque story about an entertainer whose act consists of performing as the arms for his armless mother; he's also an unwilling murderer. Made in luxurious color with dreamy art direction, this lacks the intellectual charge of Jodorowsky's earlier films. Filmed in English.

Santee (1973) **C-93m.** ** D: Gary Nelson. Glenn Ford, Michael Burns, Dana Wynter, Jay Silverheels, Harry Townes, John Larch, Robert Wilke, Robert Donner. Bounty hunter Ford, whose boy has been murdered, adopts son of outlaw he has just killed. OK Western.▼

Santiago (1956) **C-93m.** **½ D: Gordon Douglas. Alan Ladd, Rossana Podesta, Lloyd Nolan, Chill Wills, Paul Fix, L.Q. Jones, Frank DeKova. Ladd and Nolan are involved in gun-running to Cuba during fight with Spain. Ladd becomes humane when he encounters partisan Podesta.

Sapphire (1959-British) **C-92m.** *** D: Basil Dearden. Nigel Patrick, Yvonne Mitchell, Michael Craig, Paul Massie, Bernard Miles, Rupert Davies, Yvonne Buckingham. When music student is murdered, it is discovered she was passing as white. Considered daring in its day, still absorbing today—both as entertainment and social comment. Fine performances.▼

Saps At Sea (1940) **57m.** *** D: Gordon Douglas. Stan Laurel, Oliver Hardy, James Finlayson, Ben Turpin, Richard Cramer, Harry Bernard. L&H comedy is short and sweet: Ollie has breakdown working in horn factory, tries to relax on a small boat

with Stan . . . and that's impossible. Cramer is a memorable heavy. Harry Langdon was one of the writers.▼

Saraband (1948-British) **C-95m.** *** D: Basil Dearden. Stewart Granger, Joan Greenwood, Flora Robson, Françoise Rosay, Peter Bull, Anthony Quayle, Michael Gough, Christopher Lee. Lavish, tearful romance with Greenwood torn between royal responsibility and love for young rogue. British title: SARABAND FOR DEAD LOVERS.

Saracen Blade, The (1954) **C-76m.** *½ D: William Castle. Ricardo Montalban, Betta St. John, Rick Jason, Carolyn Jones, Whitfield Connor. Pretty bad 13th-century stuff, with young man avenging death of father. Unbelievable script traps cast.

Sarah and Son (1930) **76m.** ** D: Dorothy Arzner. Ruth Chatterton, Fredric March, Doris Lloyd, Philippe de Lacy. Chatterton, obsessed with finding the son taken from her years ago, enlists aid of lawyer March.

Sarah T.—Portrait of a Teenage Alcoholic (1975) **C-100m.** TVM D: Richard Donner. Linda Blair, Verna Bloom, Larry Hagman, William Daniels, Mark Hamill, Laurette Spang. Young girl turns to liquor to escape family problems; Blair shows competence with another of the meaty roles that made her the most put-upon screen teenager of the 1970s. Average.

Saratoga (1937) **94m.** **½ D: Jack Conway. Clark Gable, Jean Harlow, Lionel Barrymore, Frank Morgan, Walter Pidgeon, Una Merkel, Cliff Edwards, George Zucco, Hattie MacDaniel, Margaret Hamilton. Harlow's last film has stand-in Mary Dees doing many scenes, but comes off pretty well, with Jean as granddaughter of horse-breeder Barrymore, Gable an influential bookie.

Saratoga Trunk (1945) **135m.** *½ D: Sam Wood. Gary Cooper, Ingrid Bergman, Flora Robson, Jerry Austin, John Warburton, Florence Bates. Elaborate but miscast, overlong version of Edna Ferber's novel of New Orleans vixen Bergman and cowboy Cooper. Unbearable at times. Made in 1943.

Sarge (1970) **C-100m.** TVM D: Richard Colla. George Kennedy, Diane Baker, Ricardo Montalban, Nico Minardos, Harold Sakata, Henry Wilcoxon. Detective on police department decides he can do more as priest, works same district as he did as cop. Melodramatic to the hilt, Kennedy saves film with excellent performance. Average; pilot for the series. Alternate titles: SARGE: THE BADGE OR THE CROSS, THE BADGE OR THE CROSS.

Saskatchewan (1954) **C-87m.** **½ D: Raoul Walsh. Alan Ladd, Shelley Winters, J. Carrol Naish, Hugh O'Brian, Robert Douglas, Richard Long, Jay Silverheels.

Cotton-candy Western about Ladd and fellow Canadian mounties trying to prevent Indian uprisings.

Sasquatch (1978) **C-102m.** *½ D: Ed Ragozzini. George Lauris, Steve Boergadine, Jim Bradford, Ken Kenzie. Semidocumentary about expedition that goes in search of Bigfoot, including "authentic" if blurry footage of the monster.

Satan Bug, The (1965) **C-114m.** ***½ D: John Sturges. George Maharis, Richard Basehart, Anne Francis, Dana Andrews, Edward Asner, Frank Sutton, John Larkin, Henry Beckman. Overlooked little suspense gem, loosely based on Alistair MacLean novel, detailing nerve-racking chase after lunatic who's stolen flasks containing horribly lethal virus from government lab. Taut script (by Edward Anhalt and James Clavell) and direction, stunning photography by Robert Surtees.

Satanic (1969-Spanish-Italian) **C-85m.** BOMB D: Piero Vivarelli. Magda Konopka, Julio Pena, Armando Calva, Umi Raho, Lugi Montini. A stolen elixir turns an ugly old woman into a young beauty, but propels her into a life of terror, and forces her to star in this awful movie.▼

Satanic Rites of Dracula, The SEE: **Count Dracula and His Vampire Bride**▼

Satan Met a Lady (1936) **75m.** ** D: William Dieterle. Bette Davis, Warren William, Alison Skipworth, Arthur Treacher, Winifred Shaw, Marie Wilson, Porter Hall. Dashiell Hammett's MALTESE FALCON incognito; far below 1941 remake. William is private eye, Davis the mysterious client, Skipworth the strange woman searching for priceless artifact (here, a ram's horn).

Satan Never Sleeps (1962) **C-126m.** ** D: Leo McCarey. William Holden, Clifton Webb, France Nuyen, Athene Seyler, Martin Benson, Edith Sharpe. Dreary goings-on of two priests holding fast when Communist China invades their territory. McCarey's last film.

Satan's Cheerleaders (1977) **C-92m.** ** D: Greydon Clark. Kerry Sherman, John Ireland, Yvonne DeCarlo, Jacqueline Cole, Jack Kruschen, John Carradine, Sydney Chaplin. Amusing drive-in fodder about a busload of high school cheerleaders who fall into clutches of a demonic cult and have to muster all their considerable wits to escape. Humor and a cast full of old pros help, but this film (surprisingly PG-rated) is too tame to be really effective.▼

Satan's Claw SEE: **Blood on Satan's Claw**▼

Satan's Harvest (1970) **C-104m.** ** D: George Montgomery (credited on TV to Douglas K. Stone). George Montgomery, Tippi Hedren, Matt Monro, Davy Kaye, Brian O'Shaughnessy, Tromp Terreblanche, Melody O'Brian. American detective Mont-

gomery inherits South African ranch and discovers it to be headquarters for a drug smuggling operation. Colorful scenery, tepid story.▼

Satan's Sadists.(1970) **C-88m.** BOMB D: Al Adamson. Russ Tamblyn, Scott Brady, Kent Taylor, John Cardos. Renegade cyclists on the loose down the highway. Change the channel.▼

Satan's Satellites (1958) **70m.** *½ D: Fred Brannon. Judd Holdren, Aline Towne, Wilson Wood, Lane Bradford. Condensation of 1952 Republic serial ZOMBIES OF THE STRATOSPHERE is pretty juvenile sci-fi, but has added trivia interest today since Leonard Nimoy plays a Martian who helps save the Earth from destruction!

Satan's School for Girls (1973) **C-74m.** TVM D: David Lowell Rich. Pamela Franklin, Kate Jackson, Jo Van Fleet, Roy Thinnes, Jamie Smith Jackson, Lloyd Bochner, Cheryl Jean Stoppelmoor (Ladd). What's behind spate of suicides at fashionable girls' school? Hard-nosed but vulnerable young woman (Franklin) passes herself off as student to get answer in this wide-eyed, inconsequential thriller. Below average.▼

Satan's Skin SEE: **Blood on Satan's Claw**▼

Satan's Triangle (1974) **C-78m.** TVM D: Sutton Roley. Kim Novak, Doug McClure, Alejandro Rey, Jim Davis, Ed Lauter, Michael Conrad. Novak, lone survivor of a shipwreck, and her two would-be survivors have a devilish time after trespassing in the Bermuda Triangle. Below average.

Satellite in the Sky (1956-British) **C-85m.** **½ D: Paul Dickson. Kieron Moore, Lois Maxwell, Donald Wolfit, Bryan Forbes, Jimmy Hanley. Spunky female reporter stows away aboard first British satellite rocket. Complications arise when bomb to be tested sticks to the side of the satellite and ticks away the moments to doom. Elaborate but unexciting.

Satisfaction (1988) **C-92m.** BOMB D: Joan Freeman. Justine Bateman, Liam Neeson, Trini Alvarado, Britta Phillips, Julia Roberts, Scott Coffey. Bubble-gum theatrical release about a four-girl/one-guy garage band that gets its first break rocking in a wealthy summer resort town. With the entire band shacked up in a single room, figure out where sole male member Coffey sleeps—or *how* he sleeps. Duds like this were more fun in the 1950s.▼

Saturday Morning (1971) **C-82m.** **½ D: Kent Mackenzie. Cinema-verité documentary chronicling the gripes of contemporary adolescents may interest those teen-agers who don't mind an hour and a half of young people saying "ya know" at least once in every sentence.

Saturday Night and Sunday Morning

(1960-British) **90m.** ***½ D: Karel Reisz. Albert Finney, Shirley Anne Field, Rachel Roberts, Norman Rossington. Grim yet refreshing look at angry young man, who in a burst of nonconformity alters the lives of girlfriends Field and Roberts. Superbly enacted. Script by Alan Sillitoe, from his novel. One of the first and best of Britain's "angry young men" dramas of the 60s.

Saturday Night Fever (1977) **C-119m.** *** D: John Badham. John Travolta, Karen Lynn Gorney, Barry Miller, Joseph Cali, Paul Pape, Donna Pescow, Julie Bovasso. Travolta's first starring film is thoughtful study of Brooklyn youth who finds only meaning in his life when dancing at local disco. Film pulses to dynamic Bee Gees music score. Plethora of street language may offend some, but not in "alternate" 108m. PG-rated version, where dialogue and certain scenes have been changed or dropped entirely. Sequel: STAYING ALIVE.▼

Saturday's Children (1940) **101m.** **½ D: Vincent Sherman. John Garfield, Anne Shirley, Claude Rains, Lee Patrick, George Tobias, Roscoe Karns, Dennis Moore, Elisabeth Risdon. N.Y.C. based story of poor, hardworking Shirley, her dreamer-boyfriend Garfield, and what happens when they marry. Rains steals film as Shirley's sacrificing father. Based on Maxwell Anderson play previously filmed in 1929 and (as MAYBE IT'S LOVE) in 1935.

Saturday's Hero (1951) **111m.** **½ D: David Miller. John Derek, Donna Reed, Sidney Blackmer, Alexander Knox. Football player Derek wins a college scholarship, then discovers he isn't expected to spend much time in class. Pretty good attack on collegiate sports remains fairly timely; Reed is fine as love interest. Look quickly for Aldo Ray.

Saturday's Heroes (1937) **60m.** **½ D: Edward Killy. Van Heflin, Marian Marsh, Richard Lane, Alan Bruce, Minor Watson, Frank Jenks, Al St. John. Zippy little programmer about outspoken college football star Heflin, and his crusade against the hypocrites and bureaucrats who exploit amateur athletes. Biting indictment of the business of college football remains relevant today.

Saturday's Island SEE: **Island of Desire**▼

Saturday the 14th (1981) **C-75m.** *½ D: Howard R. Cohen. Richard Benjamin, Paula Prentiss, Severn Darden, Jeffrey Tambor, Kari Michaelsen, Kevin Brando, Rosemary DeCamp. Limp horror film parody, with Benjamin and Prentiss moving into a weird house and dealing with an assortment of menacing types. Followed by a sequel.▼

Saturday the 14th Strikes Back (1988) **C-78m.** BOMB D: Howard R. Cohen. Jason Presson, Ray Walston, Avery Schreiber, Patty McCormack, Julianne McNamara,

Rhonda Aldrich, Leo V. Gordon. Follow-up to 1981 turkey is even worse, if that seems imaginable: a schlocky, amateurish spoof of horror films with a bevy of monsters attacking Presson on his birthday.▼

Saturn 3 (1980-British) **C-88m.** ** D: Stanley Donen. Farrah Fawcett, Kirk Douglas, Harvey Keitel, Douglas Lambert. Flashy but empty-headed outer-space opus, with Douglas and Fawcett menaced by Keitel and his sex-starved robot Hector; good-looking package with nothing inside.▼

Savage, The (1952) **C-95m.** **½ D: George Marshall. Charlton Heston, Susan Morrow, Peter Hanson, Joan Taylor, Ted de Corsia. Heston is sincere and energetic as white man raised by the Indians and forced to choose sides when skirmishes break out.

Savage (1973) **C-74m. TVM** D: Steven Spielberg. Martin Landau, Barbara Bain, Will Geer, Paul Richards, Michele Carey, Barry Sullivan, Susan Howard, Dabney Coleman, Pat Harrington. Investigative reporters find a skeleton in the closet of a Supreme Court nominee. Pilot for a prospective Landau-Bain series, and, notably, Spielberg's last TV-movie. Average.▼

Savage Attraction SEE: **Hostage** (1983)▼

Savage Bees, The (1976) **C-99m. TVM** D: Bruce Geller. Ben Johnson, Michael Parks, Horst Buchholz, Gretchen Corbett, Paul Hecht, James Best. Thriller involving a plague of African killer bees descending on New Orleans at Mardi Gras. Neat little neo-cultist chiller written by Guerdon Trueblood. Above average. Sequel: TERROR OUT OF THE SKY.▼

Savage Drums (1951) **73m.** ** D: William Berke. Sabu, Lita Baron, H. B. Warner, Sid Melton, Steve Geray. U. S.-educated Sabu returns to the islands to put down local warfare; fair low-budgeter.

Savage Eye, The (1960) **68m.** *** D: Ben Maddow, Sidney Meyers, Joseph Strick. Barbara Baxley, Herschel Bernardi, Gary Merrill, Jean Hidey. Documentary-style drama of divorcee Baxley trying to start life anew in L.A.; contrived but intriguing.

Savage Harvest (1981) **C-87m.** *½ D: Robert Collins. Tom Skerritt, Michelle Phillips, Shawn Stevens, Anne-Marie Martin, Derek Partridge. Lions prey on Skerritt, Phillips, and children in Kenya. Scary but pointless; enough to turn you into a vegetarian.

Savage Hordes, The (1961-Italian) **C-82m.** ** D: Remigio Del Grosso. Ettore Manni, Yoko, Akim Tamiroff, Joe Robinson, Roland Lesaffre. Routine adventure yarn set in 17th-century Poland under siege by Tartars.

Savage Innocents, The (1959-Italian-French-British) **C-110m.** **½ D: Nicholas Ray. Anthony Quinn, Yoko Tani, Peter O'Toole, Marie Yang, Anna May Wong. Striking but uneven film about conflict of civilization vs. simple ways of Eskimo people. Quinn gives remarkable performance as native Eskimo; beautiful documentary-type location photography combined with studio work. O'Toole's voice is dubbed.

Savage Island (1985-U.S.-Italian-Spanish) **C-74m.** *½ D: Edward Muller, Nicholas Beardsley. Linda Blair, Anthony Steffen, Ajita Wilson, Christina Lai, Leon Askin. Awful exploitation fare (about tropical women's prison) made even more exploitive by audacity of promoting Blair as film's "star" when in fact she's only in it for a few minutes, in tacky American footage that sandwiches original European film, which is *also* released on video as ESCAPE FROM HELL. ▼

Savage Is Loose, The (1974) **C-114m.** BOMB D: George C. Scott. George C. Scott, Trish Van Devere, John David Carson, Lee H. Montgomery. Scott produced, directed, starred in and even distributed this farrago about the eventual incest between mother and son after they, along with dad, have been stranded on an island for years. Not very stimulating. ▼

Savage Messiah (1972-British) **C-100m.** *** D: Ken Russell. Dorothy Tutin, Scott Antony, Helen Mirren, Lindsay Kemp, Peter Vaughan. Thoughtful, if intense chronicle of the platonic affair between sculptor Henri Gaudier-Brzeska (Antony), who died in WW1 at age 24, and Sophie Brzeska (Tutin). A convincing, impressive "portrait of an artist as a young man."

Savage Mutiny (1953) **73m.** D: Spencer Bennet. Johnny Weissmuller, Angela Stevens, Lester Matthews, Paul Marion. SEE: **Jungle Jim** series.

✓ **Savage Pampas** (1966-Spanish) **C-100m.** ** D: Hugo Fregonese. Robert Taylor, Ron Randell, Ty Hardin, Rosenda Monteros. Remake of 1946 Argentinian film PAMPA BARBARA. Taylor is rugged army captain combating outlaw Randell whose gang is made up of army deserters. Adequate actioner.

Savages (1974) **C-78m. TVM** D: Lee H. Katzin. Andy Griffith, Sam Bottoms, Noah Beery, James Best, Randy Boone, Jim Antonio. Cat-and-mouse thriller with Griffith as sadistic hunter relentlessly pursuing his defenseless young guide in the desert. *The Most Dangerous Game* played out among the cacti, but still intriguing. Above average. ▼

Savage Sam (1963) **C-103m.** **½ D: Norman Tokar. Brian Keith, Tommy Kirk, Kevin Corcoran, Dewey Martin, Jeff York, Royal Dano, Marta Kristen. Sequel to Disney's OLD YELLER has Keith and country neighbors trying to rescue children who've been kidnapped by Indians. Colorful but uneven. ▼

Savage Seven, The (1968) **C-96m.** *½ D:

Richard Rush. Robert Walker, Larry Bishop, Adam Roarke, Max Julien, Duane Eddy. Below-par motorcycle melodrama that lives up to its title but nothing else.

Savage Streets (1984) **C-93m.** ** D: Danny Steinmann. Linda Blair, John Vernon, Robert Dryer, Johnny Venocur, Sal Landi. Blair, hilariously miscast as a "nice girl," pits her mild-mannered high school gang against a pack of sadistic tramps. Fairly transcendent trash with a hilariously arty bathtub scene, bravura human torch finale . . . but also features an obscene, gratuitously prolonged rape scene. ▼

Savage Wilderness SEE: **Last Frontier, The** (1956)

Savannah Smiles (1982) **C-107m.** **½ D: Pierre DeMoro. Mark Miller, Donovan Scott, Bridgette Andersen, Peter Graves, Chris Robinson, Michael Parks. A rich little girl (Andersen) runs away from home and reforms criminals. Fair morality tale for kids, written by leading actor Miller. ▼

Save the Children (1973) **123m.** ***½ D: Stan Lathan. Isaac Hayes, Jackson Five, Sammy Davis, Jr., Nancy Wilson, Roberta Flack, Wilson Pickett, Marvin Gaye, The Temptations, Gladys Knight and The Pips, Bill Withers, many others. All-star music documentary filmed at 1972 exposition in Chicago held by Jesse Jackson's Operation PUSH. Fabulous in-concert performances, including Gaye's "What's Going On," The Temptations' "Papa Was a Rolling Stone," and Withers's "Lean On Me."

Save the Dog! (1988) **C-95m. TVM** D: Paul Aaron. Cindy Williams, Tony Randall, Katherine Helmond, Tom Poston, Charlotte Rae, Billie Bird, Al Lewis. Spirited Disney comedy about a beleaguered aspiring actress' frantic attempts to save her beloved pooch—her meal ticket via dog food commercial residuals—who has overindulged in canine junk food. Good cast brings home the blue ribbon. Made for cable. Above average.

Save the Tiger (1973) **C-101m.** ** D: John G. Avildsen. Jack Lemmon, Jack Gilford, Laurie Heineman, Normann Burton, Patricia Smith, Thayer David, Lara Parker. Pretentious Steve Shagan script about dress manufacturer trying to reconcile hero-worship of his childhood with degradations he submits himself to in business world. Film purports to be totally honest, but phoniness comes through; David has best scenes as professional arsonist. Lemmon won Best Actor Oscar. ▼

Saving Grace (1986) **C-112m.** *½ D: Robert M. Young. Tom Conti, Fernando Rey, Erland Josephson, Giancarlo Giannini, Donald Hewlett, Edward James Olmos, Patricia Mauceri. Youthful Pope Conti, overwhelmed by meaningless duties and a general feeling of uselessness, sneaks incognito out of the Vatican and into a small Italian village that has lost its spirit. If you're going to spin a whopper like this, don't pace it so slowly that the audience has too much time to ponder the improbabilities. Well-intentioned, but dull.▼

Sawdust and Tinsel (1953-Swedish) **92m.** **** D: Ingmar Bergman. Harriet Andersson, Ake Gronberg, Anders Ek, Gudrun Brost. Beautiful film about human relationships set as an allegory in a small-time circus. Also known as THE NAKED NIGHT.▼

Saxon Charm, The (1948) **88m.** *** D: Claude Binyon. Robert Montgomery, Susan Hayward, John Payne, Audrey Totter, Harry Morgan, Cara Williams, Harry Von Zell, Heather Angel. Well-acted but unconvincing study of ruthless producer, with Montgomery miscast in lead role. Still interesting, with fine work from playwright Payne, wife Hayward, and chanteuse Totter.

Say Amen, Somebody (1982) **C-100m.** **** D: George T. Nierenberg. Willie Mae Ford Smith, Thomas A. Dorsey, Sallie Martin, The Barrett Sisters, The O'Neal Brothers. Wonderful documentary about gospel music and two of its shining stars, "Mother" Willie Mae Ford Smith and "Professor" Thomas Dorsey, that brings us into their lives as well as their careers and demonstrates the power of music sung from the heart. A genuine treat.▼

Say Anything . . . (1989) **C-100m.** *** D: Cameron Crowe. John Cusack, Ione Skye, John Mahoney, Lili Taylor, Amy Brooks, Pamela Segall, Jason Gould, Joan Cusack, Eric Stoltz. Satisfying teenage comedy-drama about a self-assured loner who goes after the Class Brain, and finds her surprisingly human. Amusing, endearing, and refreshingly original; written by first-time director Crowe. Cusack's reallife sister Joan plays his sister here, and Lois Chiles does an unbilled cameo as Skye's mother.▼

Say Goodbye, Maggie Cole (1972) **C-73m. TVM** D: Jud Taylor. Susan Hayward, Darren McGavin, Michael Constantine, Michele Nichols, Dane Clark, Beverly Garland. After husband's death, research doctor returns to general practice in Chicago slum area. Impressive performances by Hayward (in her last role) and McGavin in touching, realistic drama by Sandor Stern. Above average.▼

Say Hello to Yesterday (1971-British) **C-91m.** *½ D: Alvin Rakoff. Jean Simmons, Leonard Whiting, Evelyn Laye, John Lee, Jack Woolgar, Constance Chapman. Ridiculous plot concerning 40-year-old Simmons' affair with 22-year-old Whiting. Symbolic touches by director Rakoff further shroud purpose of film.▼

Say It in French (1938) **70m.** ** D: Andrew L. Stone. Ray Milland, Olympe Bradna, Irene Hervey, Janet Beecher, Mary Carlisle, Holmes Herbert, Walter Kingsford. Milland goes to great extremes with wife Bradna and ex-fiancee Hervey to pull father out of the red.

Sayonara (1957) **C-147m.** ***½ D: Joshua Logan. Marlon Brando, Ricardo Montalban, Miiko Taka, Miyoshi Umeki, Red Buttons, Martha Scott, James Garner. Romantic James Michener tale of Korean War pilot Brando falling in love with Japanese entertainer Taka; extremely well acted, with Oscar-winning support from Buttons and Umeki, and statuettes also going to the art direction-set decoration. Theme song by Irving Berlin. Paul Osborn wrote the screenplay.▼

Say One for Me (1959) **C-119m.** *½ D: Frank Tashlin. Debbie Reynolds, Bing Crosby, Robert Wagner, Ray Walston, Les Tremayne, Connie Gilchrist, Stella Stevens, Frank McHugh, Joe Besser, Sebastian Cabot. Bing plays a Broadway priest who gets mixed up with a chorus girl (Debbie) and a TV charity show. Terribly contrived; no memorable music.

Say Yes (1986) **C-91m.** ** D: Larry Yust. Lissa Layng, Art Hindle, Jonathan Winters, Logan Ramsey, Laurie Prange, Anne Ramsey, David Leisure. Spoiled rich kid Hindle has 24 hours to get married or he'll lose out on a vast inheritance. Corny situation comedy is only slightly enlivened by Winters' presence as the family patriarch and refreshingly unglamorous heroine Layng. Filmed in 1982. ▼

Scalawag (1973) **C-93m.** *½ D: Kirk Douglas. Kirk Douglas, Mark Lester, Don Stroud, Neville Brand, Lesley-Anne Down. TREASURE ISLAND goes West in this weak adaptation, with a hammy Kirk as one-legged cutthroat; songs turn up when you least expect them. Filmed in Yugoslavia.

Scalpel (1976) **C-96m.** *½ D: John Grissmer. Robert Lansing, Judith Chapman, Arlen Dean Snyder, David Scarroll, Sandy Martin. Plastic surgeon transforms young woman into image of his long-missing daughter, in order to dupe family out of large inheritance. Lurid, violent drama. Originally released as FALSE FACE.▼

Scalphunters, The (1968) **C-102m.** **½ D: Sydney Pollack. Burt Lancaster, Shelley Winters, Ossie Davis, Telly Savalas, Armando Silvestre, Nick Cravat, Dabney Coleman. Western comedy about a fur trapper and his highly educated slave has its moments, but isn't funny enough, nor exciting enough, nor pointed enough to qualify as all-out success. Cast helps.▼

Scalplock (1966) **C-100m. TVM** D: James Goldstone. Dale Robertson, Diana Hyland, Lloyd Bochner, Robert Random, Sandra Smith. Tired Western features Robertson as gambler who wins ownership of railroad. Usual complications, stereotyped characters; even production looks rushed. Below average. Pilot for *Iron Horse* TV series.

Scandal (1989) **C-106m.** *** D: Michael Caton-Jones. John Hurt, Joanne Whalley-Kilmer, Bridget Fonda, Ian McKellen, Leslie Phillips, Britt Ekland, Daniel Massey, Roland Gift, Jeroen Krabbe. Absorbing look at the people behind Britain's incredible government-sex scandal of the early '60s, with Whalley-Kilmer just right as impressionable showgirl Christine Keeler, and Hurt outstanding as Stephen Ward, the social gadfly and sexual provocateur who introduces Keeler to Cabinet Minister John Profumo (whose wife, incidentally, was a former film star, Valerie Hobson). Fascinating and credible; a good job by first-time director Michael Caton-Jones. Screenplay by Michael Thomas. Original 114m. British version was trimmed to avoid an X-rating in the U.S. Both versions are available on video.▼

Scandal at Scourie (1953) **C-90m.** **½ D: Jean Negulesco. Greer Garson, Walter Pidgeon, Donna Corcoran, Agnes Moorehead, Arthur Shields. Tepid Garson-Pidgeon entry set in Canada, involving Protestant couple who shock community when they plan to adopt a Catholic child.

Scandal in a Small Town (1988) **C-100m. TVM** D: Anthony Page. Raquel Welch, Christa Denton, Frances Lee McCain, Peter Van Norden, Robin Gammell, Ronny Cox. Small-town cocktail waitress with a dubious past takes on the establishment when she learns her teenage daughter's teacher is espousing anti-Semitism in his classes. Almost the same plot as the earlier EVIL IN CLEAR RIVER with a dose of HARPER VALLEY P.T.A. tossed in. And what attorney would allow client Welch to turn up in court wearing a leather micromini? Below average.

Scandal, Inc. (1956) **79m.** *½ D: Edward Mann. Robert Hutton, Patricia Wright, Paul Richards, Robert Knapp. Sensational-style account of scandal magazines.

Scandal in Paris SEE: **Thieves' Holiday**

Scandal in Sorrento (1957-Italian) **C-92m.** *½ D: Dino Risi. Vittorio De Sica, Sophia Loren, Antonio Cifariello, Tina Pica. Listless sex romp of Loren romancing De Sica to make lover jealous.

Scandalous (1984) **C-94m.** ** D: Rob Cohen. Robert Hays, John Gielgud, Pamela Stephenson, Jim Dale, M. Emmet Walsh, Bow Wow Wow. Featherbrained farce about investigative TV reporter who runs afoul of team of con artists as he tries to extricate himself from murder charge. Alternately stupid and obnoxious, with Gielgud presumably having fun as a disguise-happy sharpster.▼

Scandal Sheet (1931) **77m.** **½ D: John Cromwell. George Bancroft, Kay Francis, Clive Brook, Lucien Littlefield, Jackie Searl.

Usual triangle with good twist. Editor Bancroft has goods on Brook, the man his wife Francis plans to run off with.

Scandal Sheet (1952) **82m.** *** D: Phil Karlson. Broderick Crawford, Donna Reed, John Derek, Rosemary DeCamp, Henry O'Neill, Henry (Harry) Morgan. Engrossing melodrama about an ambitious editor who accidentally kills his ex-wife, then finds his ace reporters investigating the story. Based on a Samuel Fuller novel.

Scandal Sheet (1985) **C-100m. TVM** D: David Lowell Rich. Burt Lancaster, Pamela Reed, Robert Urich, Lauren Hutton, Bobby DiCicco, Max Wright. Unscrupulous publisher Lancaster stops at nothing to increase circulation on his glossy, supermarket checkout-counter tabloid. Could this be what happened to J. J. Hunsecker after all these years? Average.

Scandal Street (1938) **62m.** **½ D: James Hogan. Louise Campbell, Roscoe Karns, Porter Hall, Lew Ayres, Edgar Kennedy, Virginia Weidler, Elizabeth Patterson, Cecil Cunningham, Lucien Littlefield, Carl "Alfalfa" Switzer, Louise Beavers. Strange B-movie, a combination soap opera/slapstick comedy/murder mystery centering around librarian Campbell's arrival in "nice, small town." Elements don't mesh too well, but it's fun to watch the attempt. Based on a Vera Caspary story.

Scanners (1981-Canadian) **C-102m.** **½ D: David Cronenberg. Jennifer O'Neill, Stephen Lack, Patrick McGoohan, Lawrence Dane, Charles Shamata. Title refers to superbrains who can read minds and cause others' heads to explode; here, a "good" scanner helps doctors track down a bad one. Rather plodding treatment of interesting idea, aided somewhat by great (if yucky) special effects.▼

Scapegoat, The (1959-British) **92m.** **½ D: Robert Hamer. Alec Guinness, Bette Davis, Nicole Maurey, Irene Worth, Peter Bull, Pamela Brown, Geoffrey Keen. Decent acting rescues a fuzzy script. French gentleman murders his wife, tries to involve his British lookalike in scheme. Davis has small but impressive role as the guilty Guinness' dope-ridden mother. Adapted by Hamer and Gore Vidal from a Daphne du Maurier novel.

Scar, The SEE: **Hollow Triumph**

Scarab Murder Case, The (1936-British) **68m.** D: Michael Hankinson. Wilfrid Hyde-White, Kathleen Kelly, John Robinson, Wally Patch, Wallace Geoffrey. SEE: **Philo Vance** series.

Scaramouche (1952) **C-118m.** ***½ D: George Sidney. Stewart Granger, Eleanor Parker, Janet Leigh, Mel Ferrer, Henry Wilcoxon, Lewis Stone, Nina Foch, Richard Anderson, Robert Coote. Excellent cast in roaring adaptation of Sabatini novel of illustrious cynic who sets out to avenge brother's death, set in 18th-century France. Impeccably done. Highlight is climactic sword duel—the longest in swashbuckling history. Screenplay by Ronald Millar and George Froeschel. Filmed before in 1923.▼

Scarecrow (1973) C-115m. *** D: Jerry Schatzberg. Gene Hackman, Al Pacino, Dorothy Tristan, Eileen Brennan, Ann Wedgeworth, Richard Lynch. Drifter Hackman, who wants to start car-wash business, meets drifter Pacino, who has abandoned his wife. Moody, not altogether successful tale benefits from top performances and photography (by Vilmos Zsigmond), plus good use of locations.▼

Scarecrow, The (1982-New Zealand) C-87m. **½ D: Sam Pillsbury. Jonathan Smith, Daniel McLaren, John Carradine, Tracy Mann, Anne Flannery, Des Kelly. Adequate thriller about a small-town New Zealand teen who must deal with both a rival bully and a crazed killer. Adapted from Ronald Hugh Morrieson's novel.

Scared Stiff (1945) 65m. *½ D: Frank McDonald. Jack Haley, Barton MacLane, Ann Savage, Veda Ann Borg, Arthur Aylesworth, George E. Stone. Stiff Haley vehicle with few laughs. He plays a reporter caught in a haunted house on the trail of some jade chess pieces. TV title: TREASURE OF FEAR ▼

Scared Stiff (1953) 108m. **½ D: George Marshall. Dean Martin, Jerry Lewis, Lizabeth Scott, Carmen Miranda, Dorothy Malone. Usual Martin and Lewis hijinks with duo on spooky Caribbean island inherited by Scott; Jerry and Carmen make a wild team. Remake of Bob Hope's GHOST BREAKERS.▼

Scared Straight: Another Story (1980) C-100m. TVM D: Richard Michaels. Cliff DeYoung, Stan Shaw, Terri Nunn, Randy Brooks, Tony Burton, Linden Chiles, Eric Laneuville. Fictional story based on the explosive TV documentary about the use of prison encounter groups to curb crimes among youths. Harsh, realistic, and quite frank, with adult language. Above average.▼

Scared to Death (1947) C-65m. *½ D: Christy Cabanne. Bela Lugosi, Douglas Fowley, Joyce Compton, George Zucco, Nat Pendleton, Angelo Rossitto, Molly Lamont. Cheaply made chiller, loosely revolving around effects of those who confront a murderess with her crime. Oddly, Lugosi's only color film.▼

Scarf, The (1951) 93m. **½ D: E. A. Dupont. John Ireland, Mercedes McCambridge, Emlyn Williams, James Barton. Capably handled drama of Ireland trying to prove his innocence of murder charge.

Scarface (1932) 90m. ***½ D: Howard Hawks. Paul Muni, Ann Dvorak, George Raft, Boris Karloff, Karen Morley, Vince Barnett, Osgood Perkins, C. Henry Gordon.

Powerful gangster film is the most potent of the 1930s, with Muni delivering emotionally charged performance as Caponelike mobster with more than just a soft spot for his sister (Dvorak). Raw, harsh, and brimming with unsubtle symbolism; five writers include Ben Hecht and W.R. Burnett. Filmed in 1931, release delayed by censors. The full title is SCARFACE, THE SHAME OF THE NATION. Remade in 1983.▼

Scarface (1983) C-170m. *½ D: Brian De Palma. Al Pacino, Steven Bauer, Michelle Pfeiffer, Mary Elizabeth Mastrantonio, Robert Loggia, Miriam Colon, F. Murray Abraham, Paul Shenar, Harris Yulin. 1932 gangster movie updated by making lead character a Cuban refugee in Miami, and changing profession from bootlegging to drug-dealing . . . but this film wallows in excess and unpleasantness for nearly *three hours,* and offers no new insights except that crime doesn't pay. At least the 1932 movie *moved.*▼

Scarface Mob, The (1962) 102m. **½ D: Phil Karlson. Robert Stack, Keenan Wynn, Barbara Nichols, Pat Crowley, Neville Brand, Bruce Gordon. Feature version of a two-part *Desilu Playhouse* from 1959 that led to the hugely popular *Untouchables* TV series with Stack as racket-buster Eliot Ness, who sets out to break Chicago's underworld kingpin Al Capone. Still pretty potent (especially by TV standards) and blessed with the inimitable staccato narration of Walter Winchell.▼

Scarlet and the Black, The (1983) C-155m. TVM D: Jerry London. Gregory Peck, Christopher Plummer, John Gielgud, Raf Vallone, Barbara Bouchet, Olga Karlatos, Bill Berger, Edmund Purdom. Peck (in his first dramatic starring role on TV) and Plummer play a real-life cat-and-mouse game as, respectively, a Vatican official who clandestinely harbored allied POW escapees throughout German-occupied Rome and the Nazi officer trying to catch him red-handed. Gielgud is Pope Pius XII in this well-made thriller, adapted by David Butler from J. P. Gallagher's book *The Scarlet Pimpernel of the Vatican.* Above average.▼

Scarlet Angel (1952) C-80m. **½ D: Sidney Salkow. Yvonne De Carlo, Rock Hudson, Richard Denning, Amanda Blake. Neat little drama set in 1860 New Orleans, with De Carlo the dance-hall girl who assumes a dead woman's identity and goes West to stay with wealthy in-laws.

Scarlet Blade, The SEE: **Crimson Blade, The**

Scarlet Claw, The (1944) 74m. D: Roy William Neill. Basil Rathbone, Nigel Bruce, Gerald Hamer, Arthur Hohl, Miles Mander, Ian Wolfe, Paul Cavanagh, Kay Harding. SEE: **Sherlock Holmes** series.

Scarlet Clue, The (1945) 65m. D: Phil Rosen. Sidney Toler, Mantan Moreland,

Ben Carter, Benson Fong, Virginia Brissac, Robert Homans, Jack Norton, Janet Shaw. SEE: **Charlie Chan** series.

Scarlet Coat, The (1955) **C-101m.** **½ D: John Sturges. Cornel Wilde, Michael Wilding, George Sanders, Anne Francis, Bobby Driscoll. Plucky costumer livened by cast and bright photography; set in colonial America, dealing with Benedict Arnold spy caper.

Scarlet Empress, The (1934) **110m.** *** D: Josef von Sternberg. Marlene Dietrich, John Lodge, Louise Dresser, Sam Jaffe, C. Aubrey Smith, Edward Van Sloan. Von Sternberg tells the story of Catherine the Great and her rise to power in uniquely ornate fashion, with stunning lighting and camerawork and fiery Russian music. It's a visual orgy, dramatically uneven, but cinematically fascinating.

Scarlet Hour, The (1956) **95m.** ** D: Michael Curtiz. Carol Ohmart, Tom Tryon, Jody Lawrance, James Gregory, Elaine Stritch, E. G. Marshall, Edward Binns. Sluggish study of marital discord leading to murder.

Scarlet Letter, The (1926) **80m.** *** D: Victor Seastrom. Lillian Gish, Lars Hanson, Henry B. Walthall, Karl Dane, William H. Tooker, Marcelle Corday. Excellent, straightforward adaptation of Hawthorne classic about Hester Prynne (Gish) who bears scar of adultery in Salem, having had clandestine affair with minister Hanson. Filmed several times in the silent era; talkie versions in 1934 and (for TV) 1979.

Scarlet Letter, The (1934) **70m.** ** D: Robert G. Vignola. Colleen Moore, Hardie Albright, Henry B. Walthall, Cora Sue Collins, Alan Hale, Virginia Howell, William Farnum, Betty Blythe. Slow, poorly directed, though not uninteresting version of the Nathaniel Hawthorne novel. Moore is miscast as Hester Prynne; Walthall repeats his role from the 1926 version as Roger Prynne. A real curio. ▼

Scarlet Pimpernel, The (1935-British) **95m.** ***½ D: Harold Young. Leslie Howard, Merle Oberon, Raymond Massey, Nigel Bruce, Bramwell Fletcher, Anthony Bushell, Joan Gardner, Melville Cooper. Excellent costumer with Howard leading double life, aiding innocent victims of French revolution while posing as foppish member of British society. Baroness Orczy's novel was scripted by Robert E. Sherwood, Sam Berman, Arthur Wimperis, and Lajos Biro; produced by Alexander Korda. Also shown in computer-colored version. Remade for TV.▼

Scarlet Pimpernel, The (1982) **C-150m.** TVM D: Clive Donner. Anthony Andrews, Jane Seymour, Ian McKellen, James Villiers, Eleanor David, Malcolm Jamieson. Lavish filming (the seventh) of Baroness Orczy's historical adventure classic, reeks

with class, derring-do and intrigue, as well as spirited performances by all involved. William Bast's entertaining adaptation of two of the Baroness's novels, *The Scarlet Pimpernel* and *Eldorado*, deserves special mention. Above average.▼

Scarlet Spear, The (1954) **C-78m.** BOMB D: George Breakston, Ray Stahl. John Bentley, Martha Hyer, Morasi. Programmer nonsense of African tribe with sacrifice ceremony.▼

Scarlet Street (1945) **103m.** *** D: Fritz Lang. Edward G. Robinson, Joan Bennett, Dan Duryea, Margaret Lindsay, Rosalind Ivan. Meek, henpecked Robinson is pulled into world of crime and deception by seductive Bennett and her manipulative boyfriend Duryea. Stars and director of WOMAN IN THE WINDOW keep it interesting, but don't match earlier film. Dudley Nichols adapted this story, filmed before by Jean Renoir as LA CHIENNE. Also shown in computer-colored version.▼

Scarlett O'Hara War, The (1980) **C-105m.** TVM D: John Erman. Tony Curtis, Sharon Gless, Harold Gould, Bill Macy, George Furth, Edward Winter, Barrie Youngfellow, Clive Revill, Carrie Nye, Morgan Brittany. Curtis jauntily plays David O. Selznick in his epic search for a Scarlett O'Hara for GONE WITH THE WIND. Taken from Garson Kanin's *Moviola*, it's packed with portrayals of film personalities of the '30s—and fun to boot. Above average.

Scars of Dracula (1971-British) **C-94m.** *** D: Roy Ward Baker. Christopher Lee, Dennis Waterman, Jenny Hanley, Christopher Matthews, Wendy Hamilton. Good fang work as young couple tangles with Dracula in search of the young man's missing brother. A doozy of a demise, we might add. Last of Hammer's period Draculas; followed by DRACULA A.D. 1972.▼

Scavenger Hunt (1979) **C-117m.** BOMB D: Michael Schultz. Richard Benjamin, James Coco, Scatman Crothers, Ruth Gordon, Cloris Leachman, Cleavon Little, Roddy McDowall, Robert Morley, Richard Mulligan, Tony Randall, Dirk Benedict, Willie Aames, Stephanie Faracy, Meat Loaf, Carol Wayne. Vincent Price dies, and his relatives and servants are practically forced to kill each other for his inheritance by collecting commodes, wild animals, etc. in an allotted time. Hard to believe a comedy with so much talent could misfire so greatly, but it does; only Mulligan manages to get some laughs.▼

Scavengers (1988) **C-94m.** BOMB D: Duncan McLachlan. Kenneth Gilman, Brenda Bakke, Crispin De Nys. Bottom-of-the-barrel thriller with Gilman and Bakke becoming involved with spy plot. This one's only if you're desperate.▼

Scene of the Crime (1949) **94m.** ** D: Roy Rowland. Van Johnson, Arlene Dahl,

Gloria DeHaven, Tom Drake, Leon Ames. Bland detective whodunit, with Johnson a cop trying to solve police murder.

Scene of the Crime (1986-French) **C-90m.** *** D: Andre Techine. Catherine Deneuve, Danielle Darrieux, Wadeck Stanczak, Nicholas Giraudi, Victor Lanoux, Jean Bousquet, Claire Nebout. Stylish, Chabrol–like drama about an unhappy young boy (Giraudi), his equally unhappy mother (Deneuve), and what results when escaped convict Stanczak invades their lives. Entertaining, perceptive, if occasionally uneven examination of repression and desperation.▼

Scenes from a Marriage (1973-Swedish) **C-168m.** **** D: Ingmar Bergman. Liv Ullmann, Erland Josephson, Bibi Andersson, Jan Malmsjo, Anita Wall. Passionate, probing and honest look at a marriage, its disintegration, and the relationship that follows. Ullmann and Jacobson are remarkable throughout this intimate and often painful portrait, originally made as six TV episodes and edited into feature-length by writer-director Bergman.▼

Scenes from a Murder (1972-Italian) **C-90m.** ** D: Alberto DeMartino. Telly Savalas, Anne Heywood, Giorgio Piazza, Osvaldo Ruggeri, Rossella Falk. Murder and mayhem in the theater world with Savalas stalking an actress (Heywood) whose lover he has killed. Limp thriller.▼

Scenes from the Class Struggle in Beverly Hills (1989) **C-102m.** *½ D: Paul Bartel. Jacqueline Bisset, Ray Sharkey, Mary Woronov, Robert Beltran, Ed Begley, Jr., Wallace Shawn, Arnetia Walker, Paul Bartel, Paul Mazursky, Rebecca Schaeffer. Bizarre, scattershot sex romp with various characters of various classes playing musical beds in Beverly Hills. Tries to be outrageous and irreverent while satirizing L.A. types and lifestyles, but too often succeeds only in being inane, veering uncomfortably between drama and farce. The best thing about this is its title.▼

Schizoid (1980) **C-91m.** BOMB D: David Paulsen. Klaus Kinski, Marianna Hill, Craig Wasson, Donna Wilkes, Richard Herd, Christopher Lloyd. Kinski's group therapy patients are mysteriously being knocked off. Lurid shocker.▼

Schlock (1971) **C-80m.** **½ D: John Landis. Saul Kahan, Joseph Piantadosi, Eliza Garrett, John Landis. Landis' first film is enjoyable spoof of B-horror flicks; director (in gorilla suit by Rick Baker) plays missing link on the loose in small town. Many in-jokes for film buffs. Retitled: THE BANANA MONSTER.▼

School Daze (1988) **C-114m.** **½ D: Spike Lee. Larry Fishburne, Giancarlo Esposito, Tisha Campbell, Kyme, Joe Seneca, Art Evans, Ellen Holly, Ossie Davis, Spike Lee, Branford Marsalis. Comedy-cum-fantasy about life on a black college campus in the South, where one self-serious student activist fights a lonely battle not only against the administration, but the pervasive mindlessness of his fellow students, most of whom are wrapped up in fraternity and sorority nonsense. Writer-director-costar Lee (who plays Half-Pint) offers much entertainment and some provocative ideas, though he doesn't follow up on his initial premise until the anticlimactic final scene.▼

School for Love (1955-French) **72m.** ** D: Yves Allegret. Jean Marais, Brigitte Bardot, Isabelle Pia. Occasionally sensual flick with Bardot and Pia competing for Marais' affection. Retitled: JOY OF LOVING.

School for Scoundrels (1960-British) **94m.** *** D: Robert Hamer. Alastair Sim, Terry-Thomas, Ian Carmichael, Janette Scott, Dennis Price. Entertaining comedy barb about training school for one-upmanship, giving the viewer complete course in coming out tops in any situation.

School For Unclaimed Girls (1969-British) **C-95m.** ** D: Robert Hartford-Davis. Madeline Hinde, Renee Asherson, Dennis Waterman, Maureen Lipman, Lesley-Anne Down. Hinde is sent to reform school after killing her mom's boyfriend. Unusual British entry in the cycle of women's prison films features a moving performance by Lipman as a fellow prisoner. U.S. release in 1973. Originally titled THE SMASHING BIRD I USED TO KNOW; also known as HOUSE OF UNCLAIMED WOMEN.

School Spirit (1985) **C-90m.** BOMB D: Alan Holleb. Tom Nolan, Elizabeth Foxx, Roberta Collins, John Finnegan, Larry Linville. Forgettable entry in the briefly popular teen fantasy-comedy sweepstakes, film has Nolan returned to Earth (after dying in a car crash) to have one more day in order to score with women. Emphasis is on slapstick in this cheapie.▼

Scorchy (1976) **C-99m.** *½ D: Hikmet Avedis. Connie Stevens, Cesare Danova, William Smith, Marlene Schmidt, Normann Burton, Joyce Jameson. Tawdry action film with Stevens as undercover cop in Seattle who sets out to bust high-level drug ring. Plenty of action and gore.▼

Scorned and Swindled (1984) **C-100m.** TVM D: Paul Wendkos. Tuesday Weld, Keith Carradine, Peter Coyote, Fionnula Flanagan, Sheree North, Susan Ruttan, Pat Corley. Weld finds herself in title situation and has the gumption to go after the man who makes his living by marrying women and taking them for all they have. Weld is wonderfully gritty; Coyote's perfectly unctuous as the swindler. Script by Jerome Kass and Karol Ann Hoeffner. Above average.

Scorpio (1973) **C-114m.** **½ D: Michael Winner. Burt Lancaster, Alain Delon, Gayle Hunnicutt, Paul Scofield, John Colicos, J.

D. Cannon, Joanne Linville. Tough espionage film of CIA agent in trouble, and hired killer who wants to go straight but finds himself caught in the system. Good action, dialogue amid familiar trappings.

Scorpio Letters, The (1967) **C-98m. TVM** D: Richard Thorpe. Alex Cord, Shirley Eaton, Laurence Naismith, Oscar Beregi, Lester Matthews. American hired by British government and beautiful spy work together to track down mysterious head of blackmail ring, known only by code name. Excellent suspense in above-average spy-thriller from Victor Canning's novel.

Scotland Yard Inspector (1952-British) **73m.** ** D: Sam Newfield. Cesar Romero, Lois Maxwell, Bernadette O'Farrell, Geoffrey Keen, Alistair Hunter, Peter Swanwick. Run-of-the-mill actioner with Romero assisting Maxwell in capturing her brother's killer.

Scotland Yard Investigator (1945) **68m.** ** D: George Blair. C. Aubrey Smith, Erich von Stroheim, Stephanie Bachelor, Forrester Harvey, Doris Lloyd, Eva Moore. Low-budget mystery wastes two leading players in routine art-theft tale.

Scott Free (1976) **C-78m. TVM** D: William Wiard. Michael Brandon, Susan Saint James, Stephen Nathan, Robert Loggia, Ken Swofford, Michael Lerner. Glib hustler Brandon gets involved with Indians, the Mafia and the Feds over a piece of land he won in a poker game. Offbeat pilot for a series that never was. Average.

✓ **Scott Joplin** (1977) **C-96m.** **½ D: Jeremy Paul Kagan. Billy Dee Williams, Clifton Davis, Godfrey Cambridge, Art Carney, Seymour Cassel, Eubie Blake, Margaret Avery, Sam Fuller. Well-made, colorful but down-beat life story of famed ragtime composer. Made for TV, then given fitful theatrical release. Best sequence: the barrelhouse piano "duel."

Scott of the Antarctic (1948-British) **C-110m.** **½ D: Charles Frend. John Mills, Derek Bond, James Robertson Justice, Kenneth More, Christopher Lee. Unrelenting drama of dynamic British 20th-century explorer who led expedition to frigid subcontinent.▼

Scoundrel, The (1935) **78m.** *** D: Ben Hecht, Charles MacArthur. Noel Coward, Julie Haydon, Stanley Ridges, Martha Sleeper, Ernest Cossart, Eduardo Ciannelli, Alexander Woollcott, Lionel Stander. Fascinating Hecht-MacArthur original about a cynical, self-centered N.Y.C. publisher who toys with other people's lives—until his own existence is put on the line. Bizarre, sophisticated, indulgent—and unique. Coward, in his first starring film, puts over a challenging and unusual role. Famed critic/curmudgeon Woollcott plays one of the hangers-on, while Hecht and MacArthur can be seen in a funny flop-house cameo.

Academy Award winner for Best Original Story.

Scoundrel in White SEE: **High Heels▼**

Scout's Honor (1980) **C-96m. TVM** D: Henry Levin. Gary Coleman, Katherine Helmond, Wilfrid Hyde-White, Harry Morgan, Pat O'Brien, Joanna Moore, Meeno Peluce, Angela Cartwright, Lauren Chapin, Jay North, Paul Petersen. Orphan dreams of becoming a cub scout in this final film by veteran director Henry Levin, who died on the last day of production. Cutesy Coleman holds his own among the film veterans and now-grown former child stars. Average.▼

Scream (1983) **C-81m.** BOMB D: Byron Quisenberry. Pepper Martin, Hank Worden, Alvy Moore, (John) Ethan Wayne, Julie Marine, Gregg Palmer, Woody Strode, Bobby Diamond. Interesting cast cannot save this boring tale of a group of people hiking through a western ghost town, each of whom is killed off. Poor in all departments. Wayne is the son of John. Filmed in 1981. ▼

Scream and Scream Again (1970-British) **C-95m.** **½ D: Gordon Hessler. Vincent Price, Christopher Lee, Peter Cushing, Judy Huxtable, Alfred Marks, Peter Sallis. Distinguished cast does their darnedest to enliven (no pun intended) tired, confusing plot concerning mad scientist's organ/limbs experiments and race of emotionless beings he creates.▼

Scream, Blacula, Scream! (1973) **C-95m.** ** D: Bob Kelljan. William Marshall, Don Mitchell, Pam Grier, Michael Conrad, Richard Lawson. Poor sequel to BLACULA finds black vampire recalled from eternal rest and forced to go out and nibble again in contemporary black U.S.

Screaming Eagles (1956) **81m.** ** D: Charles Haas. Tom Tryon, Jan Merlin, Alvy Moore, Martin Milner, Jacqueline Beer. Routine WW2 film focusing on D-Day.

Screaming Mimi (1958) **79m.** ** D: Gerd Oswald. Anita Ekberg, Phil Carey, Harry Townes, Gypsy Rose Lee, Romney Brent, Red Norvo. Lurid low-budget melodrama about a woman who cracks up after being assaulted, takes a job as exotic dancer in Lee's nightclub but remains under the influence of a possessive psychiatrist. Strange, kinky film that sounds more interesting than it really is. Based on the novel by Frederic Brown.

Screaming Woman, The (1972) **C-73m. TVM** D: Jack Smight. Olivia de Havilland, Ed Nelson, Joseph Cotten, Walter Pidgeon, Laraine Stephens, Alexandra Hay. Wide-eyed thriller has recently institutionalized woman trying to convince family and neighbors that she hears voice coming from the ground. Script can't maintain credibility. Based on a Ray Bradbury story. Below average.

Scream of Fear (1961-British) **81m.** ***
D: Seth Holt. Susan Strasberg. Christopher Lee, Ann Todd, Ronald Lewis. Only wheelchair-bound Strasberg sees her father's corpse—while stepmom Todd insists he's on a trip. Good Hammer thriller written by Jimmy Sangster. Original British title: TASTE OF FEAR.▼

Scream of the Wolf (1974) **C-78m. TVM**
D: Dan Curtis. Peter Graves, Clint Walker, Jo Ann Pflug, Philip Carey, Don Megowan, Brian Richards. Predictable excercise in terror by Richard Matheson that has adventure writer Graves stalking a murderous creature that may or may not be human. Average.

Scream, Pretty Peggy (1973) **C-78m. TVM** D: Gordon Hessler. Bette Davis, Ted Bessell, Sian Barbara Allen, Charles Drake, Allan Arbus, Tovah Feldshuh, Jessica Rains. Thriller about a college coed who takes a housekeeper job in the mansion a deranged sculptor and his strange mother supposedly share with his insane sister. Horror tale with a touch or two of PSYCHO and Bette having a fine old time. Average.

Screwballs (1983) **C-80m.** BOMB D: Rafal Zielinski. Peter Keleghan, Linda Speciale, Alan Daveau, Linda Shayne, Kent Deuters. Yet another embarrassingly bad teenage sex comedy, this one about some high school boys intent on leering at the breasts of a girl named Purity Bush. Made by morons, for morons.▼

Scrooge (1935-British) **78m.** **½ D: Henry Edwards. Sir Seymour Hicks, Donald Calthrop, Robert Cochran, Mary Glynne, Oscar Asche, Maurice Evans. Faithful adaptation of A CHRISTMAS CAROL, with an impressive Sir Seymour (who also co-wrote the script) as Scrooge. Dickens's era brought colorfully to life.▼

Scrooge (1970-British) **C-118m.** *** D: Ronald Neame. Albert Finney, Alec Guinness, Edith Evans, Kenneth More, Lawrence Naismith, Michael Medwin, David Collings, Gordon Jackson, Roy Kinnear, Kay Walsh. Handsome musicalization of Dickens' A CHRISTMAS CAROL, with Finney genially hamming it up in the title role and Guinness a surprisingly fey Marley's Ghost. Leslie Bricusse's score is pretty forgettable, save effervescent "Thank You Very Much," lovely sets by Terry Marsh and evocative title design by Ronald Searle.▼

Scrooged (1988) **C-101m.** ** D: Richard Donner. Bill Murray, Karen Allen, John Forsythe, John Glover, Bobcat Goldthwait, David Johansen, Carol Kane, Robert Mitchum, Nicholas Phillips, Michael J. Pollard, Alfre Woodard, Mabel King, John Murray, Jamie Farr, Robert Goulet, Buddy Hackett, John Houseman, Lee Majors, Pat McCormick, Brian Doyle Murray, Mary

Lou Retton. Ostensibly a hip, funny rereading of Dickens' A Christmas Carol, with Murray as a venal TV executive. The laughs are mild and widely scattered, and toward the end the film seems to want us to take its brotherhood message seriously. Or does it? A variety of "guest stars" appear in cameo roles.▼

Scrubbers (1982-British) **C-90m.** ** D: Mai Zetterling. Chrissie Cotterill, Amanda York, Elizabeth Edmonds, Kate Ingram, Kathy Burke. Life in a teenage girls' borstal (reform school), complete with heartbreak, cruelty, lesbianism, suicide. Harrowing but repetitious, and the hows and whys of the girls' anger is never explored.▼

Scruples (1981) **C-100m. TVM** D: Robert Day. Shelley Smith, Priscilla Barnes, Dirk Benedict, James Darren, Vonetta McGee, Laraine Stephens, Robert Peirce, Roy Thinnes, Jessica Walter, Brett Halsey. Lust, greed, and glitter surround a woman plunged (in Judith Krantz' best-seller as well as in the miniseries previously made from the book) into a life of corporate intrigue after inheriting a vast conglomerate. Slick soap opera. Average.

Scudda Hoo! Scudda Hay! (1948) **C-95m.** ** D: F. Hugh Herbert. June Haver, Lon McCallister, Walter Brennan, Anne Revere, Natalie Wood. Any film with a title like that can't be all good, and it isn't; McCallister's life is devoted to two mules. Marilyn Monroe can be glimpsed in a canoe.

Scum (1980-British) **C-98m.** **½ D: Alan Clarke. Ray Winstone, Mick Ford, John Judd, Phil Daniels, John Blundell, Ray Burdis, Julian Firth, Alrick Riley. The horrors of a borstal (British reform school). Harrowing but familiar; the accents are almost unintelligible. An earlier TV version was commissioned, then banned by the BBC.▼

Sea Around Us, The (1953) **C-61m.** ***
Produced by Irwin Allen. Narrated by Don Forbes. Academy Award-winning documentary based on Rachel Carson's study of the history of the ocean, its fauna and life.▼

Sea Chase, The (1955) **C-117m.** **½ D: John Farrow. John Wayne, Lana Turner, Tab Hunter, David Farrar, Lyle Bettger, James Arness, Claude Akins. Strange WW2 film, with Wayne as German (!) captain of fugitive ship with unusual cargo, assorted crew, plus passenger/girlfriend Turner.▼

Sea Devils (1937) **88m.** ** D: Ben Stoloff. Victor McLaglen, Preston Foster, Ida Lupino, Donald Woods, Helen Flint, Gordon Jones. One of those brawling-can-be-fun formula films, with McLaglen and Foster as Coast Guard rivals and McLaglen's daughter (Lupino) a focal point of further conflict. Filmed and acted with zest, but script's stupidities all but sink it.

Sea Devils (1953-British) **C-91m.** ** D:

Raoul Walsh. Yvonne De Carlo, Rock Hudson, Maxwell Reed, Denis O'Dea, Michael Goodliffe, Bryan Forbes. Smuggler Hudson becomes involved in the activities of British spy De Carlo in this unmemorable programmer set in the Napoleonic era. Filmed on and around the Channel Islands.▼

Sea Fury (1958-British) 72m. ** D: C. Raker Endfield. Stanley Baker, Victor McLaglen, Luciana Paluzzi, Gregoire Aslan, Francis de Wolff, Percy Herbert, Rupert Davies, Robert Shaw. Tug captain McLaglen is set to wed Paluzzi; however, she is attracted to first mate Baker. Routine romantic adventure. Original running time: 97m.

Sea Gull, The (1968-British) C-141m. **½ D: Sidney Lumet. James Mason, Vanessa Redgrave, Simone Signoret, David Warner, Harry Andrews, Eileen Herlie, Denholm Elliott. Tasteful but reverentially slow-moving transcription of Chekhov play. Signoret's accent becomes rather disconcerting among British players, all trying to be 19th-century Russians.

Sea Gypsies, The (1978) C-101m. *** D: Stewart Raffill. Robert Logan, Heather Rattray, Mikki Jamison-Olsen, Shannon Saylor, Cjon Damitri Patterson. Nice family adventure has Logan sailing round the world with daughters, journalist Jamison-Olsen and little stowaway Patterson, learning to survive when shipwrecked in Alaska. Fine location filming.▼

√ **Sea Hawk, The** (1940) 127m. **** D: Michael Curtiz. Errol Flynn, Brenda Marshall, Claude Rains, Donald Crisp, Flora Robson, Alan Hale, Henry Daniell, Una O'Connor, Gilbert Roland. Top-notch combination of classy Warner Bros. costumer and Flynn at his dashing best in adventure on the high seas; lively balance of piracy, romance, and swordplay, handsomely photographed and staged, with rousing Erich Wolfgang Korngold score. Has nothing to do with the Sabatini novel, which was filmed faithfully in 1924. Beware of shorter prints in circulation. Restored for home-video, with additional scene intended for British audiences, in which Queen Elizabeth I offers morale-building wartime message. Also available in computer-colored version.▼

Sea Hornet, The (1951) 84m. *½ D: Joseph Kane. Rod Cameron, Adele Mara, Adrian Booth, Chill Wills. Lowjinks about deep-water divers and their women.

Sea Killer SEE: **Beyond the Reef**

Sealed Cargo (1951) 90m. **½ D: Alfred L. Werker. Dana Andrews, Carla Balenda, Claude Rains, Philip Dorn. Taut melodrama of Nazi submarines in coastal waters off Newfoundland.

Sealed Verdict (1948) 83m. ** D: Lewis Allen. Ray Milland, Florence Marly,

Broderick Crawford, John Hoyt, John Ridgely. Far-fetched drama of army lawyer who falls in love with traitorous woman he is supposed to prosecute in court; pretty dismal.

Séance on a Wet Afternoon (1964-British) 115m. **** D: Bryan Forbes. Kim Stanley, Richard Attenborough, Patrick Magee, Nanette Newman, Judith Donner, Gerald Sim, Maria Kazan, Margaret Lacey. Gripping drama of crazed medium Stanley involving husband Attenborough in shady project. Brilliant acting, direction in this must-see film. Forbes adapted Mark Mc-Shane's novel and coproduced the film with Attenborough.▼

Sea of Grass, The (1947) 131m. **½ D: Elia Kazan. Katharine Hepburn, Spencer Tracy, Melvyn Douglas, Phyllis Thaxter, Robert Walker, Edgar Buchanan, Harry Carey. Plodding drama from Conrad Richter story of farmer-rancher feud over New Mexico grasslands. Walker stands out in hardworking but unsuccessful cast.

Sea of Lost Ships (1953) 85m. ** D: Joseph Kane. John Derek, Wanda Hendrix, Walter Brennan, Richard Jaeckel. Standard fare of two Coast Guard men fighting over Hendrix.

Sea of Love (1989) C-112m. ***½ D: Harold Becker. Al Pacino, Ellen Barkin, John Goodman, Michael Rooker, William Hickey, Richard Jenkins, Christine Estabrook, Barbara Baxley, Patricia Barry, Jacqueline Brookes. Streetwise cop, going through mid-life crisis, falls in love with a suspect while investigating a serial murder case. Tough, smart, sexy urban thriller with a dynamite script by Richard Price, a perfect role for Pacino, and a steamy showcase for Barkin as the woman who turns him on.▼

Sea of Sand SEE: **Desert Patrol**

Sea Pirate, The (1967-Italian) C-85m. **½ D: Roy Rowland. Gerald Barray, Antonella Lualdi, Genevieve Casile, Terence Morgan. Not-bad pirate tale with Barray setting off to amass a fortune so he can marry Lualdi. Colorful escapism.

Search, The (1948) 105m. **** D: Fred Zinnemann. Montgomery Clift, Ivan Jandl, Aline MacMahon, Jarmila Novotna, Wendell Corey. Poignant drama of American soldier Clift caring for concentration camp survivor Jandl in postwar Berlin, while the boy's mother desperately searches all Displaced Person's Camps for him. Beautifully acted and directed; won a Best Story Academy Award for Richard Schweitzer and David Wechsler and a special prize for Jandl for outstanding juvenile performance.

Search (1972) SEE: **Probe**

Search and Destroy (1981) C-93m. ** D: William Fruet. Perry King, Tisa Farrow, Don Stroud, Park Jong Soo, Geroge Kennedy. Undistinguished actioner about former South Vietnamese official Soo seeking revenge against American G.I.s King and Stroud. Filmed in 1978.▼

Searchers, The (1956) **C-119m.** **** D: John Ford. John Wayne, Jeffrey Hunter, Vera Miles, Ward Bond, Natalie Wood, John Qualen, Harry Carey, Jr., Olive Carey, Antonio Moreno, Henry Brandon, Hank Worden, Lana Wood, Dorothy Jordan, Pat Wayne. Superb Western saga of Wayne's relentless search for niece (Wood) kidnapped by Indians, spanning many years. Color, scenery, photography all splendid, with moving, insightful Frank Nugent script to match. And who could ever forget that final shot? Remade and imitated many times since (CARAVANS, WINTERHAWK, GREYEAGLE, etc.).▼

Search for Bridey Murphy, The (1956) **84m.** **½ D: Noel Langley. Teresa Wright, Louis Hayward, Nancy Gates, Kenneth Tobey, Richard Anderson. Strange account of woman under hypnosis with recollection of prior life; low-key telling to obtain realism makes it sluggish going. Based on a supposedly true (and then-topical) story.

Search for Danger (1949) **62m.** D: Jack Bernhard. John Calvert, Albert Dekker, Myrna Dell, Douglas Fowley, Ben Welden. SEE: **The Falcon** series.

Search for the Gods (1975) **C-100m.** TVM D: Jud Taylor. Kurt Russell, Stephen McHattie, Ralph Bellamy, Victoria Racimo, Raymond St. Jacques. Adventure drama involving an archeological dig in Pueblo territory and the discovery of a priceless medallion. Standard TV fare. Average.

Search for the Mother Lode: The Last Great Treasure SEE: **Mother Lode**▼

Searching Wind, The (1946) **108m.** **½ D: William Dieterle. Robert Young, Sylvia Sidney, Ann Richards, Dudley Digges, Douglas Dick, Albert Basserman. Lillian Hellman's play about overdiplomatic diplomat Young about to forsake family when tragedy makes him realize mistake; talky drama adapted by the author.

Sea Serpent, The (1986-Spanish) **C-92m.** *½ D: Gregory Greens. Timothy Bottoms, Taryn Power, Jared Martin, Ray Milland, Gerard Tichy, Carole James. In order to clear his name, discredited captain Bottoms searches for sea monster that has been roused from the deep by A-bomb tests. Childish sci-fi with a monster depicted by puppets! Notable only as Milland's final feature film. Shot in 1984.▼

Sea Shall Not Have Them, The (1954-British) **91m.** ** D: Lewis Gilbert. Michael Redgrave, Dirk Bogarde, Anthony Steel, Nigel Patrick, Nigel Green, Rachel Kempson. British bomber plane is forced down in the ocean during WW2; a rescue attempt is made.▼

Seaside Swingers (1965-British) **C-94m.** *½ D: James Hill. John Leyton, Mike Sarne, Freddie and The Dreamers, Ron Moody, Liz Fraser. Group of teen-agers working at seaside resort prepare for major talent contest which is to be the highlight of the summer season. Should have given them all the hook.▼

Season of Dreams SEE: **Stacking**▼

Season of Passion (1961-Australian) **93m.** **½ D: Leslie Norman. Anne Baxter, John Mills, Angela Lansbury, Ernest Borgnine, Janette Craig. Tasteful study of human relationships; Mills and Borgnine are country workers who each year come to the city for their fling with Baxter and Lansbury. Based on Ray Lawlor's play, *Summer of the 17th Doll.*

Sea Tiger (1952) **75m.** *½ D: Frank McDonald. John Archer, Mara Corday, Marguerite Chapman, Lyle Talbot. Heavyhanded mini-actioner, with Archer entangled with homicide; set in New Guinea.

Sea Wall, The SEE: **This Angry Age**

Sea Wife (1957-British) **C-82m.** *** D: Bob McNaught. Richard Burton, Joan Collins, Basil Sydney, Ronald Squire, Cy Grant. Disarming yarn of Burton and Collins surviving from a torpedoed ship. He falls in love with her, not knowing she's a nun. Set during WW2.▼

Sea Wolf, The (1941) **90m.** ***½ D: Michael Curtiz. Edward G. Robinson, John Garfield, Ida Lupino, Alexander Knox, Gene Lockhart, Barry Fitzgerald, Stanley Ridges. Bristling Jack London tale of brutal but educated sea captain (Robinson) battling wits with accidental passenger Knox, as brash seaman Garfield and fugitive Lupino try to escape. Script by Robert Rossen. Originally released at 100m. Remade many times (BARRICADE, WOLF LARSEN, etc.), as well as several silent versions.

Sea Wolves, The (1980-British-U.S.) **C-120m.** *** D: Andrew V. McLaglen. Gregory Peck, Roger Moore, David Niven, Trevor Howard, Barbara Kellerman, Patrick Macnee. You may have to be over 30 to like this true story of a retired British cavalry unit undertaking an espionage operation in WW2, but it's both action-filled and funny. The target: a German radio transmitter on a ship in an Indian port. Moore can't shake his Bond image, and Peck struggles with his British accent, so nothing is to be taken very seriously. Script by Reginald Rose.▼

Sebastian (1968-British) **C-100m.** **½ D: David Greene. Dirk Bogarde, Susannah York, Lilli Palmer, John Gielgud, Margaret Johnston, Nigel Davenport. Flashy but cluttered espionage film of counterintelligence agent Bogarde, who deciphers codes for England, becoming enmeshed in international battle of wits. Intriguing, colorful, but a bit trying; look for Donald Sutherland in a small role.▼

Second Best Secret Agent in the Whole Wide World (1965-British) **C-96m.** **½ D: Lindsay Shonteff. Tom Adams, Veronica Hurst, Peter Bull, Karel Stepanek, John Arnatt. Snappy James Bondish entry, with virtue of satirical performance by Adams; he prevents the Russians from stealing scientist Stepaneck's anti-gravity invention. Original British title: LICENSED TO KILL.▼

Second Chance (1953) **C-81m.** **½ D: Rudolph Maté. Robert Mitchum, Linda Darnell, Jack Palance, Reginald Sheffield, Roy Roberts, Dan Seymour, Fortunio Bonanova, Milburn Stone. Two runaways—gambler's girlfriend Darnell and tainted prizefighter Mitchum—fall in love in Mexico. Complications arise when Palance arrives with orders to kill Darnell. OK melodrama, made in 3D.▼

Second Chance (1971) **C-74m. TVM** D: Peter Tewksbury. Brian Keith, Elizabeth Ashley, Juliet Prowse, Roosevelt Grier, Pat Carroll, William Windom. Stockbroker drops out, buys ghost town in Nevada, converts it into haven for people who never had chance in life. Passable mixture of comedy and drama; cast far better than material. Average.

Second Chorus (1940) **83m.** ** D: H. C. Potter. Fred Astaire, Paulette Goddard, Artie Shaw and Orchestra, Charles Butterworth, Burgess Meredith. Routine musical of Astaire and Meredith, both musicians with designs on Goddard. Easy to take, but nothing special.▼

Second Face, The (1950) **77m.** **½ D: Jack Bernhard. Ella Raines, Bruce Bennett, Rita Johnson, Jane Darwell, John Sutton. Concise study of the effects of plastic surgery on Raines, whose face has been scarred.

Second Fiddle (1939) **86m.** **½ D: Sidney Lanfield. Sonja Henie, Tyrone Power, Rudy Vallee, Edna May Oliver, Lyle Talbot, Brian Sisters. Contrived Henie musical of Power promoting Hollywood romance for Henie, falling in love himself. Irving Berlin score.

Second Greatest Sex, The (1955) **C-87m.** *½ D: George Marshall. Jeanne Crain, George Nader, Bert Lahr, Mamie Van Doren, Kitty Kallen, Keith Andes, Tommy Rall, Paul Gilbert, Jimmy Boyd. Second-rate musical up-dating of *Lysistrata,* about women out West protesting men's violence by going on sex strike.

Second-Hand Hearts (1981) **C-102m.** BOMB D: Hal Ashby. Robert Blake, Barbara Harris, Collin Boone, Amber Rose Gold, Bert Remsen, Shirley Stoler. Blake, beer-bellied and jowly, is Loyal Muke (rhymes with Puke), middle-aged drifter, who married Dinette Dusty (Harris) while

in a drunken stupor. Pointless, confusing, overblown, a comedy that is embarrassingly unfunny. Even the usually reliable Harris can't salvage this mess. Filmed in 1979 as THE HAMSTER OF HAPPINESS.

Second Honeymoon (1937) **79m.** **½ D: Walter Lang. Tyrone Power, Loretta Young, Stuart Erwin, Claire Trevor, Lyle Talbot. Power tries to win back ex-wife Young in pat marital farce with attractive cast.

Seconds (1966) **106m.** ***½ D: John Frankenheimer. Rock Hudson, Salome Jens, John Randolph, Will Geer, Jeff Corey, Murray Hamilton, Wesley Addy. Frustrated middle-aged businessman is transformed into new identity (Hudson) but finds himself at odds with old and new life conflicts. Fascinating from start to finish, with good performances, striking camerawork by James Wong Howe; script by Lewis John Carlino.

Second Serve (1986) **C-100m. TVM** D: Anthony Page. Vanessa Redgrave, Martin Balsam, William Russ, Alice Krige, Kerrie Keane, Reni Santoni, Louise Fletcher, Nina Van Pallandt, Jeff Corey. The story of transsexual Renee Richards, the male surgeon turned female tennis luminary. A single-handed triumph for Redgrave as both Richard Raskins (here called Radley) and Renee Richards. Stephanie Liss and Gavin Lambert wrote the absorbing script based on Richards' autobiography. Above average.

Second Sight (1989) **C-84m.** BOMB D: Joel Zwick. John Larroquette, Bronson Pinchot, Bess Armstrong, Stuart Pankin, John Schuck, James Tolkan, William Prince, Christine Estabrook, Cornelia Guest. Superpsychic Pinchot and an otherworldly entity assist ex-cop Larroquette's Second Sight Detective Agency; if that's not enough, there's a cute-'n'-perky nun as love interest! No psychic was needed to gauge how long this one would last in theaters.▼

Second Sight: A Love Story (1984) **C-100m. TVM** D: John Korty. Elizabeth Montgomery, Barry Newman, Nicholas Pryor, Michael Horton, Ben Marley, Richard Romanus, Susan Ruttan. Actually, two love stories—one of a blind woman and her dog, the other with the man who breaks down her resistance to emotional involvements. Another in Montgomery's gallery of very special portraits. Script by Dennis Turner from Susan Miller's adaptation of Sheila Hocken's *Emma and I* (Emma's the dog). Above average.

Second Thoughts (1983) **C-98m.** BOMB D: Lawrence Turman. Lucie Arnaz, Craig Wasson, Ken Howard, Anne Schedeen, Arthur Rosenberg, Peggy McCay. Dreary, laughably unrealistic account of lawyer Arnaz divorcing banker Howard and, to her regret, taking up with idealistic Wasson, who is still living in the 1960s.▼

Second Time Around, The (1961) **C-99m.** **½ D: Vincent Sherman. Debbie Reynolds, Andy Griffith, Steve Forrest, Juliet Prowse, Thelma Ritter, Isobel Elsom. Mild comic Western with widow Debbie moving to Arizona, becoming sheriff, tangling with suitors Griffith and Forrest.

Second Woman, The (1951) **91m.** **½ D: James V. Kern. Robert Young, Betsy Drake, John Sutton, Henry O'Neill, Florence Bates. Brooding drama of architect Young who feels responsible for girlfriend's accidental death.▼

Secret Admirer (1985) **C-98m.** **½ D: David Greenwalt. C. Thomas Howell, Lori Laughlin, Kelly Preston, Dee Wallace Stone, Cliff De Young, Leigh Taylor-Young, Fred Ward, Casey Siemaszko, Corey Haim. Comedy of errors about an unsigned love letter that causes chain of confusion among some teenagers *and* their parents. Cute farce with some appealing performers, but surrenders to the obvious too often. Nice score by Jan Hammer.▼

Secret Agent (1936-British) **86m.** **½ D: Alfred Hitchcock. John Gielgud, Madeleine Carroll, Robert Young, Peter Lorre, Percy Marmont, Lilli Palmer. Strange blend of comedy and thriller elements which don't quite mesh; Carroll and Gielgud are secret agents who pose as man and wife while on assignment in Switzerland to kill enemy spy. One of Hitchcock's oddest films.▼

Secret Agent Fireball (1966-Italian) **C-89m.** ** D: Martin Donan (Mario Donen). Richard Harrison, Dominique Boschero, Wandisa Guida. Harrison is American superspy substituted for U.S. scientist in gambit to protect coalition between U.S.-Germany-Russia on new petroleum mechanism project; standard treatment. Retitled: KILLERS ARE CHALLENGED.

Secret Agent of Japan (1942) **72m.** ** D: Irving Pichel. Preston Foster, Lynn Bari, Noel Madison, Janis Carter, Sen Yung, Addison Richards, Frank Puglia, Ian Wolfe. Dated espionage film of soldier-of-fortune Foster working in the Pacific for England before Pearl Harbor.

Secret Agent Super Dragon (1966-French-Italian-W. German) **C-95m.** *½ D: Calvin Jackson Padget (Giorgio Ferroni). Ray Danton, Marisa Mell, Margaret Lee, Jess Hahn. Sloppy foreign spy meller has fair cast but sometimes silly script and atrocious dubbing. Danton repeats role from CODE NAME: JAGUAR.

Secret Beyond the Door (1948) **98m.** ** D: Fritz Lang. Joan Bennett, Michael Redgrave, Anne Revere, Barbara O'Neil, Natalie Schafer. Tedious Lang misfire along lines of Hitchcock's SUSPICION, with Bennett believing her husband is a demented murderer.▼

Secret Bride, The (1935) **64m.** **½ D: William Dieterle. Barbara Stanwyck, Warren William, Glenda Farrell, Grant Mitchell, Arthur Byron. D.A. William is trying to expose governor Byron while he's secretly married to his daughter Stanwyck.

Secret Ceremony (1968-British) **C-109m.** ***½ D: Joseph Losey. Elizabeth Taylor, Mia Farrow, Robert Mitchum, Pamela Brown, Peggy Ashcroft. Farrow resembles Taylor's dead daughter, Taylor resembles Farrow's dead mother, and their meeting has strange results. Originally an excellent psychological drama, but then Universal cut footage and shot extra scenes to make film more "acceptable" for TV, at 101m. This rating applies only to original version.▼

Secret Command (1944) **82m.** *** D: A. Edward Sutherland. Pat O'Brien, Carole Landis, Chester Morris, Ruth Warrick, Wallace Ford. No-nonsense O'Brien tries to find source of sabotage in California shipyard during WW2. Good, fast moving espionage story. O'Brien also produced this film.

Secret Diary of Sigmund Freud, The (1984) **C-90m.** *½ D: Danford B. Greene. Bud Cort, Carol Kane, Klaus Kinski, Marisa Berenson, Carroll Baker, Dick Shawn, Ferdinand Mayne. Dreary comedy about the early life of Freud (Cort), with Baker his mother, Kinski a doctor she becomes involved with, and Kane a nurse with a lisp. Pretty boring, even annoying at times.▼

Secret Door, The (1964-British) **72m.** *½ D: Gilbert Kay. Robert Hutton, Sandra Dorne, Peter Illing, George Pastell. Uneven direction mars otherwise OK plot of U.S. safecrackers out to steal Japanese code secrets in Lisbon.

Secret File: Hollywood (1962) **85m.** BOMB D: Ralph Cushman. Robert Clarke, Francine York, Syd Mason, Maralou Gray, John Warburton. A Crown International classic; Clarke is a detective hired for a scandal magazine to investigate shady doings in Tinseltown. A film so inept that you can see the lights, the boom, and just about everything else on the ceiling in almost every shot!

Secret Fury, The (1950) **86m.** *** D: Mel Ferrer. Claudette Colbert, Robert Ryan, Jane Cowl, Paul Kelly, Vivian Vance, Philip Ober. Unknown person tries to drive Claudette crazy to prevent her marriage to Ryan. Exciting whodunit with twist ending.

Secret Garden, The (1949) **92m.** *** D: Fred M. Wilcox. Margaret O'Brien, Herbert Marshall, Dean Stockwell, Gladys Cooper, Elsa Lanchester. Young girl who comes to live at run-down Victorian estate finds abandoned garden, devotes herself to it and eventually changes the lives of everyone living there. Vividly atmospheric film with some color sequences. Remade as a TV movie.

Secret Garden, The (1987) C-100m. TVM D: Alan Grint. Gennie James, Barret Oliver, Jadrien Steele, Michael Hordern, Billie Whitelaw, Derek Jacobi, Lucy Gutteridge. Sumptuous but lifeless version of Frances Hodgson Burnett's children's favorite (adapted by Blanche Hanalis), with Jacobi's performance as lord of the manor more than compensating for the less than appealing youngsters who star. This one's a perfect reason for bringing back the seldom seen 1949 version. Average.

Secret Heart, The (1946) 97m. **½ D: Robert Z. Leonard. Claudette Colbert, Walter Pidgeon, June Allyson, Lionel Barrymore, Robert Sterling, Patricia Medina, Marshall Thompson. This is Allyson's film, as young girl obsessed with dead father, unable to accept stepmother Colbert. Film creates eerie mood, and acting is good, but it's offbeat and not for all tastes.

Secret Honor (1984) C-90m. ***½ D: Robert Altman. Philip Baker Hall. Richard Nixon, with a Chivas Regal assist, paces around his study in a near-psychotic rail against Hiss, Castro, Ike, Kissinger, and anyone named Kennedy. Hall's one-man stage show is fluidly filmed and outrageously conceived—a titillating one-of-a-kind for anyone who rooted for Khrushchev in the Kitchen Debates.▼

Secret Invasion, The (1964) C-95m. *** D: Roger Corman. Stewart Granger, Mickey Rooney, Raf Vallone, Henry Silva, Edd Byrnes, Mia Massini. Good action, location photography, and direction in story of British Intelligence using criminals to work behind enemy lines in WW2 Yugoslavia.

Secret Land, The (1948) C-71m. *** Produced by Orville O. Dull. Narrated by Van Heflin, Robert Montgomery, Robert Taylor. Glossy but penetrating documentary study of Admiral Richard Byrd's exploratory missions to Antarctic.

Secret Life of an American Wife, The (1968) C-92m. ** D: George Axelrod. Walter Matthau, Anne Jackson, Patrick O'Neal, Edy Williams, Richard Bull, Paul Napier. Talky, generally unfunny farce about neglected wife who decides to pose as a call girl with one of her husband's clients—a screen lover (Matthau). Disappointing next to the writer-director's hilarious LORD LOVE A DUCK.▼

Secret Life of Ian Fleming, The (1990-British) C-100m. TVM D: Ferdinand Fairfax. Jason Connery, Kristin Scott Thomas, Joss Ackland, Patricia Hodge, David Warner, Colin Welland, Fiona Fullerton, Richard Johnson. Fictionalized, episodic tale about the writer's colorful pre-James Bond adventures of derring-do, packed with 007 in-jokes starting with the lead, Sean's ac-

tor son. Made for cable. Video version, titled SPYMAKER, is the foreign theatrical release. Average.▼

Secret Life of John Chapman, The (1976) C-78m. TVM D: David Lowell Rich. Ralph Waite, Susan Anspach, Pat Hingle, Elaine Heilveil, Brad Davis, Maury Cooper. Contemporary drama of college president who takes a sabbatical to become a ditch-digger and short-order cook. Earnest adaptation of John Chapman's book, *Blue Collar Journal,* with Waite wonderful as Chapman. Above average.

Secret Life of Kathy McCormick, The (1988) C-100m. TVM D: Robert Lewis. Barbara Eden, Josh Taylor, Jenny O'Hara, Robert Costanzo, Judith-Marie Bergan, Judy Geeson, Dick O'Neill. Romantic Cinderella comedy about a grocery-store checker who gets involved in high society, falls for an elegant playboy who's unaware of her identity, and . . . Harmless, and brightly played by Eden (who also produced) et al. Average.

Secret Life of Walter Mitty, The (1947) C-105m. **½ D: Norman Z. McLeod. Danny Kaye, Virginia Mayo, Boris Karloff, Fay Bainter, Ann Rutherford, Florence Bates, Thurston Hall. Formula comedy casts Danny as milquetoast who dreams of manly glory. Not much Thurber here, but daydream sequences are lots of fun, and so is Kaye's famous "Anatole of Paris" patter number.▼

Secret Man, The (1958-British) 68m. BOMB D: Ronald Kinnoch. Marshall Thompson, John Loder, Anne Aubrey, John Stuart, Magda Miller. Unremittingly dull crime meller of an American missile expert who tries to find a spy among members of an experimental lab.

Secret Mark of D'Artagnan, The (1962-Italian) C-91m. **½ D: Siro Marcellini. George Nader, Mario Petri, Magali Noel, Georges Marchal. Loosely based on Dumas' characters-Nader is D'Artagnan fighting for Louis XIII and Richelieu; plot is silly but moves along.

Secret Mission (1942-British) 82m. **½ D: Harold French. Hugh Williams, James Mason, Roland Culver, Carla Lehmann, Michael Wilding, Herbert Lom, Stewart Granger. Well-paced WW2 actioner of Anglo mission in occupied France.

Secret Night Caller, The (1975) C-78m. TVM D: Jerry Jameson. Robert Reed, Hope Lange, Sylvia Sidney, Michael Constantine, Robin Mattson, Elaine Giftos. Reed is an IRS agent with a compulsion to make obscene phone calls, to the distress of his wife and family. Competent actors trapped in tawdry drama. Below average.

Secret of Blood Island, The (1965-British) C-84m. **½ D: Quentin Lawrence. Barbara Shelley, Jack Hedley, Charles Tingwell,

Patrick Wymark. Woman agent parachutes into Malayan prison behind enemy lines.

Secret of Convict Lake, The (1951) **83m.** **½ D: Michael Gordon. Glenn Ford, Gene Tierney, Ethel Barrymore, Zachary Scott, Ann Dvorak, Jeanette Nolan, Ruth Donnelly. Set in 1870s California, escaped prisoners hide out at settlement comprised largely of women; fine cast makes the most of script.

Secret of Dorian Gray, The SEE: **Dorian Gray▼**

Secret of Dr. Kildare (1939) **84m.** D: Harold S. Bucquet. Lew Ayres, Lionel Barrymore, Lionel Atwill, Helen Gilbert, Laraine Day, Sara Haden, Samuel S. Hinds, Emma Dunn, Grant Mitchell, Martha O'Driscoll, Alma Kruger. SEE: **Dr. Kildare** series.

Secret of Dr. Mabuse, The SEE: **Thousand Eyes of Dr. Mabuse, The▼**

Secret Of Madame Blanche, The (1933) **83m.** **½ D: Charles Brabin. Irene Dunne, Lionel Atwill, Phillips Holmes, Douglas Walton, Una Merkel, C. Henry Gordon, Jean Parker. Another MGM tearjerker in the MADAME X vein; Dunne is quite effective as a music-hall singer who loses her son to callous father-in-law Atwill when husband Holmes kills himself. Twenty years later, mother and son meet by accident and are involved in a murder. Contrived but well-made soaper.

Secret of My Success, The (1965-British) **C-112m.** *½ D: Andrew L. Stone. James Booth, Shirley Jones, Stella Stevens, Honor Blackman, Amy Dalby, Lionel Jeffries. Film certainly doesn't succeed. Naive boy is taken in by several crafty females on his road to maturity. Picturesque settings, variety of characterizations by Jeffries.

Secret of My Success, The (1987) **C-110m.** **½ D: Herbert Ross. Michael J. Fox, Helen Slater, Richard Jordan, Margaret Whitton, John Pankow, Fred Gwynne, Elizabeth Franz, Christopher Durang. Naive but bright, ambitious young man from the sticks hustles his way into the corporate world of N.Y.C., deftly juggling the various complications he encounters. Likable comedy goes on too long, gets most of its juice from Fox's energetic and appealing performance.▼

Secret of NIMH, The (1982) **C-82m.** **½ D: Don Bluth. Voices of Elizabeth Hartman, Derek Jacobi, Dom DeLuise, John Carradine, Peter Strauss. When her family homestead is threatened, a young widowed mouse seeks help, and comes upon a secret society of superintelligent rats. Well-animated adaptation of Robert C. O'Brien's prize-winning children's book, but not as involving, or as well paced, as it ought to be. First feature from Don Bluth Productions, the studio founded by a group of former Disney artists.▼

Secret of Santa Vittoria, The (1969)

C-140m. **½ D: Stanley Kramer. Anthony Quinn, Anna Magnani, Virna Lisi, Hardy Kruger, Sergio Franchi, Renato Rascel, Eduardo Ciannelli, Giancarlo Giannini, Valentina Cortese. Entertaining comedy from Robert Crichton's novel of Italian town which hides a million bottles of wine from occupying Germans in WW2. Story wanders, however, with needless subplots that make it overlong. Kruger excellent as civilized German officer.

Secret of the Black Trunk, The (1962-German) **96m.** **½ D: Werner Klingler. Joachim Hansen, Senta Berger, Hans Reiser, Leonard Steckel, Peter Carsten. Filmed in England, this Edgar Wallace-esque yarn involves a series of murders at a famed hotel; predictable but engaging.

Secret of the Blue Room (1933) **66m.** **½ D: Kurt Neumann. Lionel Atwill, Gloria Stuart, Paul Lukas, Edward Arnold, Onslow Stevens, William Janney. Atmospheric whodunit set in eerie European castle where Stuart's three suitors accept challenge to sleep in room where several murders took place. Cast makes this one worthwhile; remade as THE MISSING GUEST and MURDER IN THE BLUE ROOM.

Secret of the Incas (1954) **C-101m.** **½ D: Jerry Hopper. Charlton Heston, Robert Young, Nicole Maurey, Thomas Mitchell, Glenda Farrell, Yma Sumac. Good adventure of explorer searching for location of fabled treasure. Adequate direction, good performances.

Secret of the Purple Reef, The (1960) **C-80m.** ** D: William Witney. Jeff Richards, Margia Dean, Peter Falk, Richard Chamberlain, Robert Earle, Terence DeMarney. Programmer whose capable cast bounces the story along; brothers seek clues to their father's killing in the Caribbean.

Secret of the Red Orchid, The SEE: **Puzzle of the Red Orchid, The**

Secret of the Whistler (1946) **65m.** D: George Sherman. Richard Dix, Leslie Brooks, Mary Currier, Michael Duane, Mona Barrie, Ray Walker. SEE **Whistler** series.

Secret of Treasure Mountain (1956) **68m.** *½ D: Seymour Friedman. Valerie French, Raymond Burr, William Prince, Lance Fuller, Susan Cummings. Junky trivia about hunt for buried wealth in Indian country.

Secret Partner, The (1961-British) **91m.** *** D: Basil Dearden. Stewart Granger, Haya Harareet, Bernard Lee, Conrad Phillips. Fast-paced, atmospheric mystery about man trying to pull off ingenious scheme whereby he is accused of robbery.

Secret People, The (1951-British) **87m.** ** D: Thorold Dickinson. Valentina Cortese, Serge Reggiani, Audrey Hepburn, Megs Jenkins, Irene Worth, Sydney Tafler. Capable cast invigorates this standard tale of intrigue set in pre-WW2 London.

[1013]

Secret Places (1985-British) **C-96m.** **½ D: Zelda Barron. Marie-Theres Relin, Tara MacGowran, Claudine Auger, Jenny Agutter, Cassie Stuart, Ann-Marie Gwatkin. Two schoolgirls from very different backgrounds form a friendship that leads to heartbreak on the eve of WW2; set in small English village. Warm, often moving film that somehow still falls short. Lead roles are well played by Relin (daughter of Maria Schell) and MacGowran (daughter of Jack MacGowran).▼

Secret Policeman's Other Ball, The (1982-British) **C-91m.** *** D: Julian Temple, Roger Graef. John Cleese, Peter Cook, Michael Palin, Graham Chapman, Terry Jones, Pete Townshend, Sting, Phil Collins, Eric Clapton, Jeff Beck, Eleanor Bron, Pamela Stephenson, Alexei Sayle. Poorly photographed but entertaining distillation of two concerts (in 1979 and 1981) organized as fund-raisers for Amnesty International. Almost as much music as comedy, but several funny bits by Cook and the Python boys stand out, including hilarious "Cheese Shop" routine.▼

Secrets (1971) **C-86m.** *½ D: Philip Saville. Jacqueline Bisset, Per Oscarsson, Shirley Knight Hopkins, Robert Powell, Tarka Kings, Martin C. Thurley. A husband, wife, and daughter all have sexual experiences during the course of a day, which must remain secrets. Dull, somewhat pretentious film notable only for nude Bisset in passionate lovemaking scene. Released in 1978.▼

Secrets (1977) **C-100m. TVM** D: Paul Wendkos. Susan Blakely, Roy Thinnes, Joanne Linville, John Randolph, Melody Thomas, Anthony Eisley, Andrew Stevens. Silly drama about unhappily married young woman who, following the death of her repressive mother, becomes a nymphomaniac while looking for the bluebird of happiness. Below average.▼

Secret Service in Darkest Africa SEE: **Baron's African War, The**

Secret Service of the Air (1939) **61m.** ** D: Noel Smith. Ronald Reagan, John Litel, Ila Rhodes, James Stephenson, Eddie Foy, Jr., Rosella Towne. Reagan stars as Lt. Brass Bancroft, a pilot who joins the Secret Service and exposes a smuggling ring. Fast-paced Warner Bros. B entry, the first of a series of four.

Secret Seven, The (1966-Italian) **C-94m.** BOMB D: Alberto de Martino. Tony Russel, Helga Line, Massimo Serato, Gerard Tichy. Adventurer enlists aid of six illustrious heroes to restore rightful queen to throne. Typically poor Italian "spectacle."

Secret Six, The (1931) **83m.** **½ D: George Hill. Wallace Beery, Lewis Stone, Clark Gable, Jean Harlow, Johnny Mack Brown, Ralph Bellamy, Marjorie Rambeau, John Miljan. Admirably hard-boiled gang-

ster saga with powerhouse cast; sluggish at times, but worth seeing for milk-drinking racketeer Beery, aristocratic crime-lord Stone, moll-with-a-heart-of-gold Harlow, et al.

Secrets of a Married Man (1984) **C-100m. TVM** D: William A. Graham. William Shatner, Michelle Phillips, Cybill Shepherd, Glynn Turman. Awards to all involved for keeping straight faces while plodding through this drama in which happily married Shatner finds himself with a compulsive need for hookers, even one looking like Shepherd. Below average.▼

Secrets of a Mother and Daughter (1983) **C-100m. TVM** D: Gabrielle Beaumont. Katharine Ross, Linda Hamilton, Michael Nouri, Bibi Besch, Joanna Barnes, Mary Beth Evans. The primary secret is that they're both bedding the same hunk. Another is that they're trying to elevate this to a standard afternoon soap's level. Below average.

Secrets of an Actress (1938) **71m.** ** D: William Keighley. Kay Francis, George Brent, Ian Hunter, Gloria Dickson, Isabel Jeans, Penny Singleton, Dennie Moore. Run-of-the-mill romantic melodrama with actress Francis attracting distraught Brent, an unhappily married architect.

Secrets of a Secretary (1931) **71m.** ** D: George Abbott. Claudette Colbert, Herbert Marshall, George Metaxa, Mary Boland, Berton Churchill. Stiff drawing-room stuff, with Colbert finding ex-hubby Marshall blackmailing her new boss.

Secrets of Life (1956) **C-75m.** *** D: James Algar. Narrated by Winston Hibler. Disney True-Life Adventure features closeup looks at plant life, insect life, sea creatures, and natural wonders like volcanoes. Wonderful footage includes time-lapse photography of plants set to a rousing bolero on the soundtrack.▼

Secrets of the Lone Wolf (1941) **67m.** D: Edward Dmytryk. Warren William, Ruth Ford, Roger Clark, Victor Jory, Eric Blore, Thurston Hall, Fred Kelsey. SEE: **Lone Wolf** series.

Secrets of the Red Bedroom SEE: **Secret Weapons**▼

Secrets of Three Hungry Wives (1978) **C-97m. TVM** D: Gordon Hessler. Jessica Walter, Gretchen Corbett, Eve Plumb, Heather MacRae, James Franciscus, Craig Stevens. Sleazy melodrama that asks the nagging question: Who killed handsome zillionaire Franciscus (who's been having affairs with three bored socialites)? Who cares? Below average.▼

Secrets of Women (1952-Swedish) **114m.** *** D: Ingmar Bergman. Anita Bjork, Karl Arne Homsten, Jarl Kulle, Maj-Britt Nilsson, Birger Malmsten, Eva Dahlbeck, Gunnar Bjornstrand. Episodic early Bergman drama about several women in a summer house who confide about their relationships with their men. Final sequence, with Dahlbeck and Bjornstrand trapped in an elevator, is most fascinating.▼

Secret War of Harry Frigg, The (1968) **C-110m.** ** D: Jack Smight. Paul Newman, Sylva Koscina, Andrew Duggan, Tom Bosley, John Williams, Vito Scotti, James Gregory. Noncom soldier selected to free five generals held captive during WW2 in this slick but inane comedy, one of Newman's few real losers.▼

Secret War of Jackie's Girls, The (1980) **C-100m.** **TVM** D: Gordon Hessler. Mariette Hartley, Lee Purcell, Ann Dusenberry, Tracy Brooks Swope, Dee Wallace, Caroline Smith, John Reilly, Sheila MacRae, Ben Murphy. Routine pilot about a group of female fliers in WW2 who perform secret missions behind enemy lines. Average.

Secret Ways, The (1961) **112m.** **½ D: Phil Karlson. Richard Widmark, Sonja Ziemann, Senta Berger, Charles Regnier. Much on-location shooting helps strengthen caper with Widmark as grim American sent into Communist Hungary to plan escape of pro-West refugee; from an Alistair MacLean novel.

Secret Weapon (1942) SEE: **Sherlock Holmes and The Secret Weapon**▼

Secret Weapon (1990-U.S.-Australian) **C-100m.** **TVM** D: Ian Sharp. Griffin Dunne, Karen Allen, Jeroen Krabbe, Stuart Wilson, Brian Cox, John Rhys-Davies, Iain Mitchell. Dunne is Mordecai Vanunu, the Israeli technician who fled the country with atomic secrets, not to sell them but to make a statement. Allen is a Mossad agent sent to seduce him so he can be returned and tried for violating his country's secrets act. Languid, somewhat fictionalized telling vitiates the suspense. Made for cable. Average.

Secret Weapons (1985) **C-100m.** **TVM** D: Don Taylor. Linda Hamilton, Sally Kellerman, Hunt Block, Viveca Lindfors, Christopher Atkins, Geena Davis, James Franciscus. Barrel scrapings about young Russian beauties trained by Kellerman for the KGB as seductresses, spies, and blackmailers of U.S. officials. Not even up to being camp. Retitled SECRETS OF THE RED BEDROOM. Below average.▼

Secret Witness (1988) **C-78m.** **TVM** D: Eric Laneuville. David Rasche, Paul LeMat, Leif Phoenix, Kellie Martin, Barry Corbin. Two mischievous 12-year-olds' game of Peeping Tom draws them into a murder case during their summer vacation. Average.

Secret World (1969-French) **C-94m.** ** D: Robert Freeman. Jacqueline Bisset, Giselle Pascal, Pierre Zimmer, Marc Porel, Jean-Francois Maurin. Bisset's presence gives slight boost to pretentiously directed film about young boy's infatuation with his uncle's mistress.

Security Risk (1954) **69m.** ** D: Harold Schuster. John Ireland, Dorothy Malone, Keith Larsen, John Craven, Joe Bassett. Routine F.B.I.-vs-Communist-agent; even Malone isn't diverting in this B thriller.

Seduced (1985) **C-100m.** **TVM** D: Jerrold Freedman. Gregory Harrison, Cybill Shepherd, Jose Ferrer, Mel Ferrer, Adrienne Barbeau, Michael C. Gwynne, Karmin Murcelo, Paul Stewart. Ambitious politician gets involved with the wife of a wealthy industrialist who turns up murdered, leaving him to track down the killer himself. Average.▼

Seduced and Abandoned (1964-Italian) **118m.** ***½ D: Pietro Germi. Stefania Sandrelli, Saro Urzi, Lando Buzzanca, Leopoldo Trieste. Richly flavorful bedroom romp involving a sex-loving man who plays and runs, till his activities catch up with him.▼

Seducers, The SEE: **Death Game**

Seduction, The (1982) **C-104m.** BOMB D: David Schmoeller. Morgan Fairchild, Michael Sarrazin, Vince Edwards, Andrew Stevens, Colleen Camp, Wendy Smith Howard. A flashy L.A. TV newswoman is terrorized by a persistent fan. Preposterous, derivative film is neither suspenseful nor titillating, despite its title and sexy star (in her first movie vehicle).▼

Seduction of Gina, The (1984) **C-100m.** **TVM** D: Jerrold Freedman. Valerie Bertinelli, Michael Brandon, Frederic Lehne, Ed Lauter, John Harkins, Dinah Manoff. Wealthy young bride, bored by medical intern hubby's lack of attention, becomes a compulsive gambler. That's the "seduction" of the exploitive title. Average.

Seduction of Joe Tynan, The (1979) **C-107m.** **½ D: Jerry Schatzberg. Alan Alda, Barbara Harris, Meryl Streep, Rip Torn, Charles Kimbrough, Melvyn Douglas. Earnest but shallow drama (written by Alda) about young senator who faces moral dilemmas while climbing political ladder in Washington. Ludicrous resolution really hurts film as a whole.▼

Seduction of Mimi, The (1974-Italian) **C-89m.** *** D: Lina Wertmuller. Giancarlo Giannini, Mariangela Melato, Agostina Belli, Elena Fiore. Mimi is actually a man (Giannini) whose stubbornness and stupidity get him into trouble politically and sexually. Climactic scene where he tries to make love to an impossibly obese woman is unforgettable. Entertaining film was later Americanized as WHICH WAY IS UP?▼

Seduction of Miss Leona, The (1980) **C-100m.** **TVM** D: Joseph Hardy. Lynn Redgrave, Anthony Zerbe, Conchata Ferrell, Elizabeth Cheshire, Brian Dennehy, Garn Stephens. Intelligent romantic drama about the involvement between a reclusive college teacher and a married maintenance man who has been repairing her house.

Author Dan Wakefield adapted Elizabeth Gundy's novel *Bliss*. Above average.

Seeding of Sarah Burns, The (1979) **C-100m. TVM** D: Sandor Stern. Kay Lenz, Martin Balsam, Cliff DeYoung, Cassie Yates, Charles Siebert. So-so drama of a young woman who acts as a baby factory and then has second thoughts about giving up the child to the couple who paid her. Average.

Seed of Innocence (1980) **C-91m.** *½ D: Boaz Davidson. Tim Wead, Mary Cannon, T. K. Carter, Vincent Schiavelli, Azizi Johari, Shirley Stoler. Runaway teenaged couple (she's pregnant) try to survive on their own in big, bad N.Y.C. Sophomoric emotional drama.

Seeds of Evil (1974) **C-97m.** *½ D: James H. Kay III. Katharine Houghton, Joe Dallesandro, Rita Gam, James Congdon. Odd little horror film, spoiled by unnecessary exposition. Mysterious gardener Dallesandro has the power to make plants grow and to turn himself into a tree. See why this was one of Houghton's few films after GUESS WHO'S COMING TO DINNER? Filmed in Puerto Rico. Former title: THE GARDENER.▼

✓ **See Here, Private Hargrove** (1944) **100m.** *** D: Wesley Ruggles. Robert Walker, Donna Reed, Keenan Wynn, Robert Benchley, Bob Crosby, Grant Mitchell. Marion Hargrove's anecdotes of army life make an amusing, episodic film; Benchley hilarious as Reed's garrulous dad. Sequel: WHAT NEXT, CORPORAL HARGROVE?

See How She Runs (1978) **C-100m. TVM** D: Richard T. Heffron. Joanne Woodward, John Considine, Lissy Newman, Mary Beth Manning, Barnard Hughes. Breath-of-fresh-air drama about a middle-aged housewife's decision to express herself by entering the grueling 26-mile Boston Marathon. Woodward won an Emmy for her performance (and her run). One of her daughters is played by real-life daughter Lissy Newman in her acting debut. Above average.▼

See How They Run (1964) **C-100m. TVM** D: David Lowell Rich. John Forsythe, Senta Berger, Jane Wyatt, Franchot Tone, Leslie Nielsen, Pamela Franklin, George Kennedy. Pretty fair chase-drama involving three orphans journeying to America, not knowing they carry crucial evidence exposing international organization and that murderers of their father pursue them. Good performances and action, obscuring inadequate motivation and believability. Based on Michael Blankfort's novel *The Widow Makers*. Earns a historical footnote as the first made-for-TV movie. Average.

Seeing Red: Stories of American Communists (1983) **C/B&W-100m.** *** D: Julia Reichert, James Klein. Informative, perceptive documentary about the generation of American humanists and radicals who reached maturity during the Depression and embraced the Communist party. Most effectively evoked are the essence of their idealism, problems during McCarthyism, and eventual disillusionment with Stalinism.

Seekers, The (1954-British) **C-90m.** **½ D: Ken Annakin. Jack Hawkins, Glynis Johns, Noel Purcell, Laya Raki, Tony Erstich. Sincere but clichéd account of British colonization of New Zealand in 1820s, with Hawkins and Johns a married couple emigrating there. Originally released in U.S. as LAND OF FURY.

Seekers, The (1979) **C-200m. TVM** D: Sidney Hayers. Randolph Mantooth, Edie Adams, Neville Brand, Delta Burke, John Carradine, Rosey Grier, George Hamilton, Brian Keith, Ross Martin, Gary Merrill, Martin Milner, Vic Morrow, Robert Reed, Barbara Rush, Stuart Whitman, Hugh O'Brian, Ed Harris. The third installment of the Kent family saga (following THE BASTARD and THE REBELS) from John Jakes' popular historical novels about the American Revolution. This one follows Philip Kent and his two sons as they explore the Northwest Territory. Originally shown in two parts. Average.

Seems Like Old Times (1980) **C-121m.** *** D: Jay Sandrich. Goldie Hawn, Chevy Chase, Charles Grodin, Robert Guillaume, Harold Gould, George Grizzard, Yvonne Wilder, T. K. Carter. Neil Simon's homage to 1930s screwball farces is quite enjoyable, with Goldie as a good-hearted lawyer whose ex-husband (Chase) disrupts her life and threatens the career of her new spouse (Grodin). Funny lines and situations all the way up to pointless finale. Feature debut of TV comedy director Sandrich.▼

See My Lawyer (1945) **67m.** ** D: Edward F. Cline. Ole Olsen, Chic Johnson, Alan Curtis, Grace McDonald, Noah Beery, Jr., Franklin Pangborn, Edward S. Brophy, Richard Benedict. Last and least of Olsen and Johnson's movie vehicles, with the daffy duo at war with nightclub owner Pangborn—and aiding a trio of struggling lawyers. Tissue-thin plot serves only as framework for a variety of specialty acts, including Carmen Amaya and the (Nat) King Cole Trio.

See No Evil (1971-British) **C-89m.** *** D: Richard Fleischer. Mia Farrow, Dorothy Alison, Robin Bailey, Diane Grayson, Lila Kaye. Terrifying chiller by Brian Clemens; blind girl slowly discovers that her uncle's entire family has been murdered and that the killer is silently stalking her. Watch out for the boots. British title: BLIND TERROR.▼

See No Evil, Hear No Evil (1989) **C-103m.** ** D: Arthur Hiller. Richard Pryor, Gene Wilder, Joan Severance, Kevin Spacey,

Kirsten Childs, Alan North, Anthony Zerbe. Wilder and Pryor are reteamed in this stupid comedy about a deaf man and a blind man who inadvertently become murder suspects and take it on the lam, hoping to catch the real killers. Five writers (including Wilder) are credited for this labored, foul-mouthed comedy; two such talented stars deserve a better vehicle.▼

See the Man Run (1971) **C-73m.** TVM D: Corey Allen. Robert Culp, Angie Dickinson, Eddie Albert, June Allyson, Charles Cioffi, Robert Lipton. Down-and-out actor and wife devise foolproof extortion scheme, instead find themselves in middle of two-way chase. Fair performances, but dialogue reeks and direction far too sloppy. Average.

See You in the Morning (1989) **C-119m.** ** D: Alan J. Pakula. Jeff Bridges, Alice Krige, Farrah Fawcett, Linda Lavin, Drew Barrymore, Lukas Haas, David Dukes, Frances Sternhagen, Theodore Bikel. Bridges and Krige follow a bumpy road to a second marriage (for both of them), trying to erase bad memories and lingering problems . . . and having to win over each other's children. Overall intelligence, warmth, and gentility cannot overcome a certain patness (and forced cuteness) in director Pakula's script—or the greater problem of not knowing when to wrap things up.▼

Seguin (1982) **C-90m.** TVM D: Jesus Salvador Trevino. Henry Darrow, Danny De La Paz, A Martinez, Rose Portillo, Pepe Serna, Robert Viharo, Edward James Olmos. Well-meaning and occasionally interesting but ultimately unconvincing drama about Juan Nepomuceno Seguin (Martinez), controversial Mexican-American war hero, San Antonio mayor, and Texas senator, who ended his life in exile. Screenplay by Trevino; a PBS *American Playhouse* presentation. Average.

Seize the Day (1986) **C-93m.** ***½ D: Fielder Cook. Robin Williams, Joseph Wiseman, Jerry Stiller, Glenne Headly. Williams is outstanding as Tommy Wilhelm, pushing 40 and a failure by society's standards, who's broke, much abused, and desperate for love. Wiseman and Stiller offer fine support as his coldhearted father and a con man he naively trusts. A small masterpiece, like the Saul Bellow novel on which it's based, with a faithful screenplay by Ronald Ribman. Plenty of familiar faces in small roles: Tony Roberts, Richard Shull, John Fiedler, Jo Van Fleet, William Hickey, Eileen Heckart, many others.▼

Seizure (1974-Canadian) **C-93m.** ** D: Oliver Stone. Jonathan Frid, Martine Beswick, Christina Pickles, Joe Sirola, Herve Villechaize, Mary Woronov, Troy Donahue. Stone's directorial debut is stylish but incoherent shocker in which novelist Frid, his family and friends are forced to play games of death by trio of evil weirdos who may or may not be his nightmares come to life. Certainly bizarre, but that's about it; has a handful of admirers, due mainly to the cast.▼

Seizure: The Story of Kathy Morris (1980) **C-103m.** TVM D: Gerald I. Isenberg. Leonard Nimoy, Penelope Milford, Christopher Allport, Fredric Lehne, Linda G. Miller. Pedestrian dramatic recounting of real-life singer's struggle to recover from a coma after undergoing brain surgery. Average.

Sellout, The (1952) **83m.** **½ D: Gerald Mayer. Walter Pidgeon, John Hodiak, Audrey Totter, Paula Raymond, Cameron Mitchell, Karl Malden, Everett Sloane, Thomas Gomez. Small town newspaper editor Pidgeon finds himself in over his head when he tries to get the goods on corrupt sheriff Gomez. OK exposé drama.

Seminole (1953) **C-87m.** **½ D: Budd Boetticher. Rock Hudson, Barbara Hale, Anthony Quinn, Richard Carlson, Hugh O'Brian, Russell Johnson, Lee Marvin, James Best. Capable cast in unusual Boetticher drama about earnest cavalry lieutenant Hudson trying to help Indian tribe's efforts to remain free of white man law.

Seminole Uprising (1955) **C-74m.** *½ D: Earl Bellamy. George Montgomery, Karin Booth, John Pickard, Ed Hinton. Trite handling of Indians vs. cavalry; too little action.

Semi-Tough (1977) **C-108m.** *** D: Michael Ritchie. Burt Reynolds, Kris Kristofferson, Jill Clayburgh, Robert Preston, Bert Convy, Lotte Lenya, Roger Mosley, Richard Masur, Carl Weathers, Brian Dennehy. Easygoing comedy about two football stars and their mutual girlfriend wanders too much to hit any major targets but has some funny moments. Reynolds' charm makes up for film's other deficiencies. Adapted from Dan Jenkins' novel by Ring Lardner, Jr. (who took his name off the credits) and Walter Bernstein. Later a brief TV series.▼

Senator Was Indiscreet, The (1947) **81m.** *** D: George S. Kaufman. William Powell, Ella Raines, Peter Lind Hayes, Arleen Whelan, Hans Conried. Wit-playwright Kaufman's only directorial fling turns out quite well, with Powell as Senator whose diary causes embarrassment. Entertaining satire.▼

Sender, The (1982-British) **C-91m.** *** D: Roger Christian. Kathryn Harrold, Zcljko Ivanek, Shirley Knight, Paul Freeman, Sean Hewitt, Harry Ditson. Solid thriller about telepathic, suicidal Ivanek, unable to control his powers, who transfers his nightmares to psychiatrist Harrold and causes havoc in a hospital. Very good of its type.▼

Send Me No Flowers (1964) **C-100m.**

*** D: Norman Jewison. Rock Hudson, Doris Day, Tony Randall, Clint Walker, Paul Lynde, Hal March, Edward Andrews, Patricia Barry. Hypochondriac Rock, convinced he has a short time to live, has Randall find new husband for wife Doris. Funny script by Julius J. Epstein; Lynde is a riot as aggressive cemetery plot salesman.▼

Senechal the Magnificent (1958-French) **78m.** **½ D: Jacques Boyer. Fernandel, Nadia Gray, Georges Chamarat, Jeanne Aubert, Armontel, Robert Pizani. Fernandel is well cast as buffoon actor who, through mistaken identities and an ability to mimic, becomes a Parisian hit.

Senior Prom (1959) **82m.** *½ D: David Lowell Rich. Jill Corey, Paul Hampton, Tom Laughlin, Barbara Bostock, Jimmy Komack. The title tells all in this flimsy, mostly boring musical. The "guest stars" include Louis Prima, Keely Smith, Mitch Miller, Ed Sullivan, Connee Boswell, Bob Crosby, Les Elgart, and Freddy Martin.

Seniors, The (1978) **C-87m.** ** D: Rod Amateau. Jeffrey Byron, Gary Imhof, Dennis Quaid, Lou Richards, Priscilla Barnes, Alan Reed, Edward Andrews, Robert Emhardt, Alan Hewitt. Four collegians open a bogus sex clinic, which mushrooms into a multimillion-dollar business. Alternately silly and satirical, with some innocuous nudity thrown in. Veteran character actors help a great deal. Written by Stanley (PILLOW TALK) Shapiro.▼

Senior Trip (1981) **C-100m. TVM** D: Kenneth Johnson. Scott Baio, Fay Grant, Randy Brooks, Peter Coffield, Jane Hoffman, Jeffrey Marcus, Vincent Spano, Robert Townsend. A spirited class of highschoolers come out of the Midwest to celebrate their graduation with a trip to the Big Apple, where they find adventure, romance, and Mickey Rooney (playing himself). Average.▼

Senior Year (1974) **C-78m. TVM** D: Richard Donner. Gary Frank, Glynnis O'Connor, Barry Livingston, Debralee Scott, Scott Colomby, Lionel Johnston, Dana Elcar. Blend of nostalgia and drama, tracing lives of several high school seniors in the '50s. A straight version of *Happy Days* earnestly acted. Became short-lived series *Sons and Daughters*. Average.

Sensations (1944) **86m.** **½ D: Andrew L. Stone. Eleanor Powell, Dennis O'Keefe. C. Aubrey Smith, Eugene Pallette, W. C. Fields, Cab Calloway, Sophie Tucker. Publicity-wise Powell shows press-agent O'Keefe how to attract attention in this campy musical; one incredible number has her tap-dancing inside giant pinball machine! Fields' skit (his last appearance on film) is only fair, other specialty numbers are fun. Originally titled SENSATIONS OF 1945.▼

Sensitive, Passionate Man, A (1977) **C-100m. TVM** D: John Newland. Angie Dickinson, David Janssen, Mariclare Costello, Richard Venture, Rhodes Reason. Sacked aerospace engineer turns into psychotic, self-destructive drunk. Pretentious weeper in which the stars try valiantly to make something out of dumb dialogue. Below average.

Senso (1954-Italian) **C-104m.** **½ D: Luchino Visconti. Alida Valli, Farley Granger, Massimo Girotti, Heinz Moog. Carefully paced study of human emotions, lingering on each twisted impact in relationship between aristrocrat Valli and earthy, materialistic Granger. Retitled: WANTON CONTESSA. Released in Italy at 115m.▼

Sensualita (1954-Italian) **72m.** ** D: Clemente Fracassi. Eleonora Rossi-Drago, Amadeo Nazzari, Marcello Mastroianni, Francesco Liddi, Corrado Nardi. At-times spicy account of two men fighting over sensual Rossi-Drago. Retitled: BAREFOOT SAVAGE.

Sensuous Nurse, The (1976-Italian) **C-78m.** *½ D: Nello Rossati. Ursula Andress, Jack Palance, Duilio Del Prete, Luciana Paluzzi, Lino Toffolo, Mario Pisu. Voluptuous Ursula hires on to help hasten the demise of a wealthy vintner with a heart condition by keeping his pulse racing in this smarmy sex comedy. Ursula does look great in the nude, however.▼

Sentimental Journey (1946) **94m.** ** D: Walter Lang. John Payne, Maureen O'Hara, William Bendix, Cedric Hardwicke, Glenn Langan, Mischa Auer, Connie Marshall. Maudlin yarn of dying actress O'Hara adopting little girl to give husband Payne a companion when she is gone; no holds barred here. Remade as THE GIFT OF LOVE (1958) and as a TV movie.

Sentimental Journey (1984) **C-100m. TVM** D: James Goldstone. Jaclyn Smith, David Dukes, Maureen Stapleton, Jessica Rene Carroll. Man whose wife may be unable to bear children takes in an orphan he meets in Central Park. Contemporary version of 1946 weeper (remade before as THE GIFT OF LOVE). Ho-hum all the way. Below average.

Sentinel, The (1977) **C-93m.** ** D: Michael Winner. Cristina Raines, Ava Gardner, Chris Sarandon, Burgess Meredith, Sylvia Miles, Jose Ferrer, Arthur Kennedy, John Carradine, Christopher Walken, Eli Wallach, Jerry Orbach, Jeff Goldblum, Beverly D'Angelo, Martin Balsam, William Hickey, Tom Berenger. Slick but empty-headed shocker about N.Y.C. fashion model who rents Brooklyn Heights brownstone, finds it's full of demons and she's to be the next sentinel guarding the gateway to Hell. Good cast makes it somewhat endurable, but climax is awfully yucky.

Freely based on Jeffrey Konvitz' best-seller.▼

Senza Pieta SEE: **Without Pity**

Separate Peace, A (1972) **C-104m.** BOMB D: Larry Peerce. John Heyl, Parker Stevenson, William Roerick, Peter Brush, Victor Bevine, Scott Bradbury. Supposedly sensitive story of two roommates in a 1940s prep school, taken from John Knowles' overrated novel, is enough to make anyone gag. Story is morbid, acting incredibly amateurish, and direction has no feeling at all for the period. A total bummer.▼

Separate Tables (1958) **99m.** ******** D: Delbert Mann. Burt Lancaster, Rita Hayworth, David Niven, Deborah Kerr, Wendy Hiller, Gladys Cooper, Cathleen Nesbitt, Rod Taylor, Felix Aylmer. Terence Rattigan's pair of romantic playlets set at English seaside resort are reworked here into superb drama in the GRAND HOTEL vein; Lancaster and Hayworth are divorced couple trying to make another go of it, Hiller is his timid mistress, Niven a supposed war hero, Kerr a lonely spinster dominated by mother Cooper. Bouquets all around, especially to Oscar winners Niven and Hiller. Screenplay by Rattigan and John Gay.▼

Separate Vacations (1986) **C-91m.** *½ D: Michael Anderson. David Naughton, Jennifer Dale, Mark Keyloun, Lally Cadeau, Blanca Guerra. Married architect takes off for Mexico looking for fleeting sex, leaving his bewildered wife to solo it with kids and baby-sitter at a ski resort; guess which one ends up having a fling? As tired as you might expect, though Dale's performance is a little more three-dimensional than anything you normally see in a comedy this minor. ▼

Separate Ways (1981) **C-92m.** ** D: Howard Avedis. Karen Black, Tony LoBianco, Arlene Golonka, David Naughton, Jack Carter, Sharon Farrell, William Windom, Robert Fuller, Noah Hathaway, Sybil Danning. Low-budget U.S. answer to A MAN AND A WOMAN has former racecar driver LoBianco suffering marital problems with wife Black, exacerbated by her one-night stand with younger man Naughton. Good cast is wasted. ▼

September (1987) **C-82m.** ** D: Woody Allen. Denholm Elliott, Mia Farrow, Elaine Stritch, Sam Waterston, Jack Warden, Dianne Wiest. Six people vent their angst during a weekend in the country. Intelligent and well acted, but after a while it dawns on you that there's no earthly reason to be interested in these people and their whining. Stritch is a standout as Mia's flamboyant mom, and it's hard to completely dislike a film that plugs jazz pianist Art Tatum so vigorously. Set in Vermont but filmed completely on a soundstage.

Writer-director Allen fared better with his earlier drama, INTERIORS.▼

September Affair (1950) **104m.** **½ D: William Dieterle. Joseph Cotten, Joan Fontaine, Francoise Rosay, Jessica Tandy, Robert Arthur, Fortunio Bonanova, Jimmy Lydon. Trim romance tale of married man Cotten and pianist Fontaine who find that they're listed as dead in plane crash and now have chance to continue their affair. Makes effective use of classical music and Walter Huston's recording of "September Song" (which once again became a hit).▼

September Gun (1983) **C-94m.** TVM D: Don Taylor. Robert Preston, Patty Duke Astin, Geoffrey Lewis, Sally Kellerman, David Knell, Jacques Aubuchon, Christopher Lloyd. This distant cousin to LILIES OF THE FIELD, relocated to Old West, finds an aging gunfighter hired to help a dedicated nun care for a brood of abandoned Apache kids. Preston's a joy, as usual, as the salty old cowpoke. Average.▼

September Storm (1960) **99m.** BOMB D: Byron Haskin. Joanne Dru, Mark Stevens, Robert Strauss, Asher Dann, M. Jean-Pierre Kerien, Vera Valmont. Scheming fashion model joins a group of adventurers searching for buried treasure off the coast of Majorca. Film's only novelty is that it was shot in 3-D Cinema-Scope.

September 30, 1955 (1978) **C-101m.** **½ D: James Bridges. Richard Thomas, Susan Tyrrell, Deborah Benson, Lisa Blount. Thomas Hulce, Dennis Quaid, Dennis Christopher, Collin Wilcox. Arkansas undergrad, well played by Thomas, goes off his nut when James Dean dies, with tragic results for a girl friend. Original, if excessively uneven drama, is worth consideration for being one of the few films to deal at all seriously with the movie star mystique. Quaid's film debut. Original title: 9/30/55; shown on TV as 24 HOURS OF THE REBEL.

Sequoia (1934) **73m.** **½ D: Chester Franklin. Jean Parker, Russell Hardie, Samuel S. Hinds, Paul Hurst. Girl living near national forest raises orphaned deer and mountain lion to be friends. Fascinating animal footage burdened by simplistic, often heavy-handed story. Reissued as MALIBU, also the name of book on which it's based.

Serena (1962-British) **62m.** **½ D: Peter Maxwell. Patrick Holt, Emrys Jones, Honor Blackman, Bruce Beeby. Neat mystery programmer with Holt the detective inspector ferreting out the killer of artist Jones' wife.

Serenade (1956) **C-121m.** **½ D: Anthony Mann. Mario Lanza, Joan Fontaine, Sarita Montiel, Vincent Price, Joseph Calleia, Vince Edwards. James M. Cain novel becomes surface soaper of Lanza, the protégé of swank Fontaine, manipulated by manager Price and loved by earthy Montiel; spotty musical interludes.

Sergeant, The (1968) **C-107m.** ** D: John Flynn. Rod Steiger, John Phillip Law, Ludmila Mikael, Frank Latimore, Elliott Sullivan. Predictable drama, set in France, about homosexual Army sergeant Steiger and his desire for handsome private Law. Director Flynn has nice eye for detail, but overall, film doesn't make much of an impression.

Sergeant Deadhead (1965) **C-89m.** *½ D: Norman Taurog. Frankie Avalon, Deborah Walley, Eve Arden, Cesar Romero, Fred Clark, Buster Keaton, Gale Gordon, Harvey Lembeck. Bungling Army sergeant goes into space with a chimpanzee and undergoes personality change. Oh, that poor monkey. Also known as SERGEANT DEADHEAD, THE ASTRONUT.

Sergeant Madden (1939) **82m.** ** D: Josef von Sternberg. Wallace Beery, Tom Brown, Alan Curtis, Laraine Day, Fay Holden, David Gorcey, Etta McDaniel, Horace McMahon. Director von Sternberg out of his element with standard Beery vehicle of policeman whose son alienates him, marries orphan girl he raised.

Sergeant Matlovich Vs. the U.S. Air Force (1978) **C-100m. TVM** D: Paul Leaf. Brad Dourif, Marc Singer, Frank Converse, William Daniels, Stephen Elliott, David Spielberg, Rue McClanahan, Mitchell Ryan, David Ogden Stiers. Fact-based drama about homosexual serviceman's battle to stay in uniform. Strong adult stuff. Above average.▼

Sergeant Murphy (1938) **57m.** ** D: B. Reeves Eason. Ronald Reagan, Mary Maguire, Donald Crisp, Ben Hendricks, William Davidson. Reagan stars in this forgettable programmer as a soldier who loves a talented horse. The sergeant of the title is the animal; Ronnie is a lowly private.

Sergeant Rutledge (1960) **C-118m.** *** D: John Ford. Jeffrey Hunter, Woody Strode, Constance Towers, Billie Burke, Carleton Young, Juano Hernandez, Willis Bouchey, Mae Marsh. Unusual story of black cavalry officer (Strode) on trial for rape and murder; during court-martial his story is recounted in flashback. Interesting material in the hands of a master, John Ford.

Sergeant Ryker (1968) **C-85m.** **½ D: Buzz Kulik. Lee Marvin, Bradford Dillman, Vera Miles, Peter Graves, Lloyd Nolan, Murray Hamilton. Adapted from TV film *The Case Against Sergeant Ryker,* story concerns court-martial of Marvin in title role, an Army sergeant during Korean War suspected of being a traitor; Miles is his wife and Dillman the dynamic defense attorney.▼

Sergeant Steiner SEE: **Breakthrough** (1978)▼

Sergeants 3 (1962) **C-112m.** **½ D: John Sturges. Frank Sinatra, Dean Martin, Sammy Davis, Jr., Peter Lawford, Joey Bishop, Ruta Lee, Henry Silva. Second reworking of GUNGA DIN is amusing, but not up to 1939 original. This time it's out West with the Rat Pack as cavalry sergeants. Davis can't eclipse Sam Jaffe as Gunga Din.

Sergeant York (1941) **134m.** ***½ D: Howard Hawks. Gary Cooper, Walter Brennan, Joan Leslie, George Tobias, Stanley Ridges, Margaret Wycherly, Ward Bond, Noah Beery, Jr., June Lockhart. Excellent story of pacifist York (Cooper) drafted during WW1, realizing purpose of fighting and becoming hero. Oscar-winning performance by Cooper in fine, intelligent film, balancing segments of rural America with battle scenes. John Huston was one of the writers. Also available in computer-colored version.▼

Serial (1980) **C-86m.** *** D: Bill Persky. Martin Mull, Tuesday Weld, Sally Kellerman, Bill Macy, Tom Smothers, Christopher Lee, Peter Bonerz, Jennifer McAlister, Nita Talbot, Stacey Nelkin, Barbara Rhoades, Pamela Bellwood. Trenchant satire on Marin County, Cal., and its residents' obsession with various freakish fads, sexual trends, and psychological mumbo-jumbo, with a Frank Capra-esque finale. Mull (in his first starring role) plays the only sane one in the bunch. Adapted from Cyra McFadden's column and book.▼

Serpent, The SEE: **Night Flight From Moscow**▼

Serpent and the Rainbow, The (1988) **C-98m.** ** D: Wes Craven. Bill Pullman, Cathy Tyson, Zakes Mokae, Paul Winfield, Brent Jennings, Theresa Merritt, Michael Gough. Ambitious (by Craven standards) but gratuitous chiller about a real-life anthropologist's experiences with black magic and voodoo in Haiti. Well done, but wallows in its atmosphere and special effects; however, Craven fans will boost the rating by a star. Based on the book by Wade Davis.▼

Serpent of the Nile (1953) **C-81m.** *½ D: William Castle. Rhonda Fleming, William Lundigan, Raymond Burr, Michael Ansara, Julie Newmar. Antony and Cleopatra, B-movie style; good for a few laughs, anyway. Producer Sam Katzman used all the sets left over from Rita Hayworth's SALOME.

Serpent's Egg, The (1978-German-U.S.) **C-120m.** *½ D: Ingmar Bergman. Liv Ullmann, David Carradine, Gert Frobe, Heinz Bennent, Glynn Turman, James Whitmore. Smorgasbord of depravities makes story of Jewish trapeze artist in pre-WW2 Germany an overwhelmingly

[1020]

unpleasant movie experience. Sven Nykvist's camerawork is brilliant as usual, but Carradine is fatally miscast.▼

Serpico (1973) **C-129m.** ***½ D: Sidney Lumet. Al Pacino, John Randolph, Jack Kehoe, Biff McGuire, Barbara Eda-Young, Cornelia Sharpe, Tony Roberts, James Tolkan, Lewis J. Stadlen, M. Emmet Walsh, F. Murray Abraham, Kenneth McMillan. Tough, exciting filmization of Peter Maas book based on true-life accounts of N.Y.C. undercover cop whose nonconformism—and exposure of department corruption—isolate him from the force. Screenplay by Waldo Salt and Norman Wexler. Followed by a TV movie and short-lived series.▼

Serpico: The Deadly Game (1976) **C-100m. TVM** D: Robert Collins. David Birney, Allen Garfield, Burt Young, Lane Bradbury, Walter McGinn, Tom Atkins. Birney takes over Al Pacino's role for this TV movie about N.Y.C. undercover cop Frank Serpico, and his battle against corruption in and out of the department. Subsequent series also starred Birney. Retitled THE DEADLY GAME. Average.

Servant, The (1963-British) **115m.** ***½ D: Joseph Losey. Dirk Bogarde, James Fox, Sarah Miles, Wendy Craig, Catherine Lacey, Patrick Magee. Insidious study of moral degradation as corrupt manservant Bogarde becomes master of employer Fox; superb study of brooding decadence. Scripted by Harold Pinter.▼

Service De Luxe (1938) **85m.** ** D: Rowland V. Lee. Constance Bennett, Vincent Price, Charles Ruggles, Mischa Auer, Joy Hodges, Helen Broderick. Easy-to-take but empty-headed froth about a woman who runs a service company that does just about anything its customers require. Price makes his film debut as man who finally breaks through Bennett's "strictly business" facade.

Sesame Street Presents Follow That Bird (1985) **C-88m.** **½ D: Ken Kwapis. Carroll Spinney, Jim Henson, Frank Oz, Paul Bartel, Sandra Bernhard, John Candy, Chevy Chase, Joe Flaherty, Waylon Jennings, Dave Thomas. Sweet, simple film about Sesame Street's beloved Big Bird, who's placed in foster home but tries to hitchhike back to Sesame Street. Aimed solely at young children, who should enjoy it—though for adults nothing can top Oscar the Grouch's opening anthem. Cute songs throughout by Van Dyke Parks and Lennie Niehaus.▼

Sessions (1983) **C-100m. TVM** D: Richard Pearce. Veronica Hamel, Jeffrey DeMunn, Jill Eikenberry, David Marshall Grant, Deborah Hedwall, George Coe, Henderson Forsythe, Tracy Pollan. High-priced call girl begins to question the many facets of her life. If you can't identify with that, stunning Hamel, in her first starring role

after *Hill Street Blues* prominence, should hold your attention. Average.▼

Session With the Committee, A (1969) **C-90m.** **½ D: Del Jack. Peter Bonerz, Barbara Bosson, Garry Goodrow, Carl Gottlieb, Jessica Myerson, Christopher Ross, Melvin Stewart, Don Sturdy (Howard Hesseman). Filmed collection of live skits by L.A. comic troupe isn't exactly "pure" cinema, but has the same appeal as a good comedy record album. Plenty of laughs.▼

Set This Town on Fire (1973) **C-100m. TVM** D: David Lowell Rich. Carl Betz, Chuck Connors, Charles Robinson, Lynda Day, James Westerfield, Jeff Corey, Paul Fix, Nancy Malone. Connors has served time on manslaughter conviction—but now he's back in town running for mayor, as local drunk has confessed to original crime. Good drama with nice small-town atmosphere, interesting subplots. Filmed in 1969. Above average. Retitled THE PROFANE COMEDY.

Settle the Score (1989) **C-100m. TVM** D: Edwin Sherin. Jaclyn Smith, Jeffrey DeMunn, Louise Latham, Howard Duff, Amy Wright, Richard Masur. Woman returns to her hometown, with bitter memories of being raped years ago by an unknown assailant, and finds that similar assaults are still being committed. Average.

Set-Up, The (1949) **72m.** ***½ D: Robert Wise. Robert Ryan, Audrey Totter, George Tobias, Alan Baxter, James Edwards, Wallace Ford. Gutsy account of washed-up fighter refusing to give up or go crooked; Ryan has never been better. Art Cohn's pungent screenplay was inspired by a narrative poem(!) by Joseph Moncure March. Photographed by Milton Krasner. Played out in real time—as you'll see by the clock shown in opening and closing shots.▼

Seven (1979) **C-100m.** ** D: Andy Sidaris. William Smith, Barbara Leigh, Guich Koock, Art Metrano, Martin Kove, Richard Le Pore, Susan Kiger. Brawny Smith is hired by U.S. intelligence to destroy Hawaiian crime syndicate, which he does with enthusiastic team of "specialists." Violent, sexy, tongue-in-cheek action yarn includes the "shooting the swordsman" gag later immortalized in RAIDERS OF THE LOST ARK.▼

Seven Alone (1975) **C-96m.** **½ D: Earl Bellamy. Dewey Martin, Aldo Ray, Anne Collins, Dean Smith, Stewart Peterson. OK family-wilderness picture on true story of seven children who make perilous 2,000 mile trek West during the 1800s after their parents die en route.▼

Seven Angry Men (1955) **90m.** *** D: Charles Marquis Warren. Raymond Massey, Debra Paget, Jeffrey Hunter, James Best, Dennis Weaver, Dabbs Greer, Ann Tyrrell. Good historical drama of John

Brown (Massey) and family fighting to free slaves during 1800s. Massey is fine in lead role, which he previously played in SANTA FE TRAIL.

Seven Beauties (1976-Italian) **C-115m.** **** D: Lina Wertmuller. Giancarlo Giannini, Fernando Rey, Shirley Stoler, Elena Fiore, Enzo Vitale. Director-writer Wertmuller's masterpiece follows a small-time casanova through the horrors of WW2 battle and imprisonment in a concentration camp, where he learns to survive—at any cost. Giannini is superb in this harrowing, unforgettable film.▼

Seven Brides for Seven Brothers (1954) **C-103m.** **** D: Stanley Donen. Howard Keel, Jane Powell, Jeff Richards, Russ Tamblyn, Tommy Rall, Virginia Gibson, Julie Newmeyer (Newmar), Ruta Kilmonis (Lee), Matt Mattox. Rollicking musical perfectly integrates song, dance, and story: Keel's decision to get himself a wife (Powell) inspires his rowdy brothers to follow suit. Tuneful Johnny Mercer-Gene DePaul score (with Oscar-winning musical direction by Adolph Deutsch and Saul Chaplin), but it's Michael Kidd's energetic dance numbers that really stand out, with rare screen work by dancers Jacques D'Amboise and Marc Platt. The barn-raising sequence is an absolute knockout. Screenplay by Albert Hackett, Frances Goodrich, and Dorothy Kingsley, from a Stephen Vincent Benet story. Later a TV series and a Broadway musical.▼

Seven Brothers Meet Dracula, The (1974-British-Hong Kong) **C-72m.** ** D: Roy Ward Baker. Peter Cushing, David Chiang, Julie Ege, Robin Stewart, Shih Szu, John Forbes-Robertson. Vampire hunter Van Helsing (Cushing) is in China in the late 19th century to vanquish Dracula with the help of some karate-chopping assistants. Odd blend of Kung Fu action, supernatural, and Dracula themes reportedly worked better in original 89m. version called LEGEND OF THE SEVEN GOLDEN VAMPIRES.▼

7 Capital Sins (1961-French) **113m.** ** D: Jean-Luc Godard, Roger Vadim, Sylvaine Dhomme, Edouard Molinaro, Philippe De Broca, Claude Chabrol, Jacques Demy. Marie-Jose Nat, Dominique Paturel, Jean-Marc Tennberg, Perrette Pradier. Potpourri of directors and talents play out modern parables concerning anger, envy, gluttony, greed, laziness, lust, and pride.

Seven Cities of Gold (1955) **C-103m.** **½ D: Robert D. Webb. Richard Egan, Anthony Quinn, Jeffrey Hunter, Rita Moreno, Michael Rennie. Average spectacle adventure has good cast and fair direction. "Roughneck" learns ways of God in search for fabled Indian treasure in Western U.S.▼

Seven Daring Girls (1960-German) **62m.**

*½ D: Otto Meyer. Jan Hendricks, Adrian Hoven, Ann Smyrner, Dorothee Glocklen. Poorly executed yarn of seven girls from Swiss finishing school marooned on isle inhabited by crooks seeking gold there.

Seven Days in May (1964) **118m.** *** D: John Frankenheimer. Burt Lancaster, Kirk Douglas, Fredric March, Ava Gardner, Edmond O'Brien, Martin Balsam, George Macready, Whit Bissell, Hugh Marlowe. Absorbing story of military scheme to overthrow the government. Fine cast includes Lancaster and Douglas as military officials, March as U.S. President; intelligent suspense in Rod Serling screenplay. John Houseman made his screen acting debut in small but crucial role.▼

Seven Days' Leave (1942) **87m.** **½ D: Tim Whelan. Lucille Ball, Victor Mature, Harold Peary, Ginny Simms, Peter Lind Hayes, Arnold Stang, Ralph Edwards. Mature is an army private who will inherit $100,000 if he can marry heiress Ball. Sprightly musical comedy, featuring Freddy Martin and Les Brown's bands.▼

Seven Days to Noon (1950-British) **93m.** **** D: John Boulting. Barry Jones, Olive Sloane, Andre Morell, Sheila Manahan, Hugh Cross, Joan Hickson. Superbly paced thriller (from Paul Dehn and James Bernard's Oscar-winning story) about scientist threatening to explode bomb in London if his demands are not met. Screenplay by Roy Boulting and Frank Harvey.

Seven Deadly Sins (1952) **120m.** **½ D: Eduardo De Filippo, Jean Dreville, Yves Allegret, Roberto Rossellini, Carlo Rim, Claude Autant-Lara. Michele Morgan, Françoise Rosay, Gerard Philipe, Isabelle Miranda, Eduardo De Filippo. Episodic potpourri illustrating seven major vices; lack of internal continuity mars total effort.

Seven Different Ways SEE: **Quick, Let's Get Married**

711 Ocean Drive (1950) **102m.** **½ D: Joseph M. Newman. Edmond O'Brien, Joanne Dru, Otto Kruger, Bert Freed. Tidy racketeer yarn of the bookie syndicate in the U.S. with exciting climax at Hoover Dam.

7 Faces of Dr. Lao (1964) **C-100m.** *** D: George Pal. Tony Randall, Barbara Eden, Arthur O'Connell, John Ericson, Kevin Tate, Argentina Brunetti, Noah Beery, Jr., Minerva Urecal, John Qualen, Lee Patrick. Engaging fantasy of Western town brought to its senses by parables performed by mysterious traveling circus; tour de force for Randall, who plays six roles. William Tuttle won special Oscar for makeup creations. Based on Charles G. Finney's novel *The Circus of Dr. Lao.*▼

Seven Golden Men (1965-Italian) **C-87m.** **½ D: Marco Vicario. Philippe Leroy, Rossana Podesta, Gastone Moschin, Gabriele Tinti, Jose Suarez. Standard but diverting heist film, with Leroy as mastermind who plans to steal seven tons of gold from Swiss bank. Clumsy dubbing, brassy music track. Released here in 1969. Followed by a sequel.

Seven Golden Men Strike Again (1966-Italian) **C-102m.** ** D: Marco Vicario. Philippe Leroy, Rossana Podesta, Gastone Moschin, Giampiero Albertini, Gabriele Tinti, Maurice Poli. Espionage expert Leroy is hired under pressure from American agents to spy on Latin American general, but he and Podesta have their eye on gold instead. Complicated cat-and-mouse plot.

Seven Graves for Rogan SEE: **Time to Die, A▼**

Seven Guns for the MacGregors (1968-Italian-Spanish) **C-97m.** *½ D: Frank Garfield (Franco Giraldi). Robert Wood, Manny Zarzo, Nick Anderson, Paul Carter. Standard spaghetti Western about seven brothers unjustly put in jail who escape and go after the crooked sheriff. Sequel: UP THE MAC GREGORS.

Seven Hills of Rome, The (1958) **C-104m.** **½ D: Roy Rowland. Mario Lanza, Peggie Castle, Marisa Allasio, Renato Rascel, Rosella Como. Formula vehicle for Lanza, as a television star who retreats to Rome and falls in love, mellower than usual, with nice scenery and supporting cast.

Seven Hours to Judgment (1988) **C-89m.** ** D: Beau Bridges. Beau Bridges, Ron Leibman, Julianne Phillips, Reggie Johnson, Al Freeman, Jr. Bridges directs himself in an earnest but farfetched revenge saga as the hapless judge whom nut case Leibman feels had been too lenient with the minority punks who killed Leibman's wife; Ron retaliates by kidnapping Beau's beautiful spouse (Phillips) and setting Bridges on a survival quest in a tough part of town.▼

Seven in Darkness (1969) **C-75m. TVM** D: Michael Caffey. Dina Merrill, Barry Nelson, Sean Garrison, Milton Berle, Arthur O'Connell, Alejandro Rey, Lesley Ann Warren. Commercial flight carrying group on way to convention for the blind crashes on mountain; they must find their way down to nearest village. Standard melodrama with barely interesting assortment of stereotyped characters, adequate performances, dull direction. Average.

Seven Keys to Baldpate, (1947) **66m.** **½ D: Lew Landers. Philip Terry, Jacqueline White, Eduardo Ciannelli, Margaret Lindsay, Arthur Shields. Mystery writer finds plenty of real-life mystery at the Baldpate Inn, in this fifth go-round for the hardy George M. Cohan stage comedy (based on Earl Derr Biggers' book). Remade as HOUSE OF THE LONG SHADOWS.

Seven Little Foys, The (1955) **C-95m.** *** D: Melville Shavelson. Bob Hope, Milly Vitale, George Tobias, Billy Gray, James Cagney. Pleasant biography of vaudevillian Eddie Foy and his performing family. Hope lively in lead role, Cagney guests as George M. Cohan; their dance duet is the movie's high point.▼

Seven Men From Now (1956) **C-78m.** *** D: Budd Boetticher. Randolph Scott, Gail Russell, Lee Marvin, Walter Reed, John Larch, Donald Barry. Scott tracks down seven bandits who held up Wells Fargo station and killed his wife. Solid Western, first of seven from the Scott-Boetticher team, with a script by Burt Kennedy.

Seven Miles from Alcatraz (1942) **62m.** **½ D: Edward Dmytryk. James Craig, Bonita Granville, Frank Jenks, Cliff Edwards, George Cleveland, Tala Birell, John Banner. Craig and Jenks break out of the "Rock" and hide out at a nearby lighthouse which is being used by Nazi spies. Which, then, is more important: America's freedom, or their own? Medium-grade Hollywood propaganda in this OK B picture.▼

Seven Minutes, The (1971) **C-116m.** **½ D: Russ Meyer. Wayne Maunder, Marianne McAndrew, Philip Carey, Yvonne De Carlo, Jay C. Flippen, Edy Williams, John Carradine, Harold J. Stone. Host of fine character actors fail to save laughable adaptation of Irving Wallace's best-seller about pornography trial; interesting mainly as Meyer's only "straight" film. TV prints are cut to 102m. Look for Tom Selleck as a publisher.

Seven Percent Solution, The (1976) **C-113m.** *** D: Herbert Ross. Nicol Williamson, Alan Arkin, Vanessa Redgrave, Robert Duvall, Laurence Olivier, Joel Grey, Samantha Eggar, Jeremy Kemp, Charles Gray, Regine. Sherlock Holmes meets Sigmund Freud in this handsome, entertaining film adapted from his novel by Nicholas Meyer. Shifts gears from serious drama to tongue-in-cheek adventure, but stays on target all the way. Nice score by John Addison.▼

Seven Samurai, The (1954-Japanese) **141m.** **** D: Akira Kurosawa. Toshiro Mifune, Takashi Shimura, Yoshio Inaba, Ko Kimura, Seiji Miyaguchi, Minoru Chiaki. Classic film about 16th-century Japanese village which hires professional warriors to fend off bandits. Kurosawa's "eastern Western" has served as model for many films since, including American remake THE MAGNIFICENT SEVEN (a title once given this film for U.S. release). The complete 208m. version is available on video, and it's even *more* impressive for its humanity as well as its powerful action sequences.▼

Seven Seas to Calais (1962-Italian) **C-102m.** **½ D: Rudolph Maté, Primo Zeglio. Rod Taylor, Keith Michell, Irene Worth, Anthony Dawson, Basil Dignam. Minor but entertaining swashbuckler with Taylor as Sir Francis Drake.

Seven Sinners (1940) 87m. *** D: Tay Garnett. Marlene Dietrich, John Wayne, Albert Dekker, Broderick Crawford, Anna Lee, Mischa Auer, Billy Gilbert. Alluring Dietrich makes Wayne forget about the Navy for a while in this engaging action-love story with excellent supporting cast. Remade as SOUTH SEA SINNER.▼

Seven Slaves Against the World (1965-Italian) C-96m. BOMB D: Michele Lupo. Roger Browne, Gordon Mitchell, Scilla Gabel, Germano Longo, Alfredo Rizzo. Terrible spectacle with nonexistent plot of swordsman freeing ancient city from tyrant.

Seven Surprizes (1963-Canadian) C-77m. *** Unusual program of shorts from National Film Board of Canada including delightful animated work by Norman McLaren and Evelyn Lambart. Offbeat, entertaining.

Seven Sweethearts (1942) 98m. **½ D: Frank Borzage. Kathryn Grayson, Van Heflin, Marsha Hunt, S. Z. Sakall, Cecilia Parker, Peggy Moran, Diana Lewis, Isobel Elsom, Donald Meek, Louise Beavers. Schmaltz about Sakall's brood of daughters, none of whom can marry until the eldest does. Song: "You and the Waltz and I."

Seventeen (1940) 78m. **½ D: Louis King. Jackie Cooper, Betty Field, Otto Kruger, Richard Denning, Peter Lind Hayes, Betty Moran, Ann Shoemaker, Norma Nelson. Cooper is delightful as teen-ager facing adolescent problems, in adaptation of Booth Tarkington story.

Seventeen and Anxious (1970-German) C-86m. **½ D: Zbynek Brynych. Anne Koster, Nadja Tiller, Karl Michael Vogler, Peter Kern, Siegfried Rauch. Thoughtful coming-of-age film with excellent Continental supporting cast. Originally titled O HAPPY DAY, making extensive use of the original hit gospel recording of that name.

1776 (1972) C-141m. *** D: Peter H. Hunt. William Daniels, Howard da Silva, Ken Howard, Donald Madden, Ron Holgate, David Ford, Blythe Danner, Roy Poole, Virginia Vestoff, John Cullum. America's first Congress in struggle for independence from Britain provides framework for this unique musical by Sherman Adams and Peter Stone. Almost all of the original Broadway cast remain, with Daniels as John Adams and da Silva as Benjamin Franklin leading the pack.▼

Seventh Cavalry (1956) C-75m. **½ D: Joseph H. Lewis. Randolph Scott, Barbara Hale, Jay C. Flippen, Jeanette Nolan, Frank Faylen. Scott plays an officer who must prove that he didn't desert Custer at the Little Bighorn battle.

Seventh Cross, The (1944) 110m. *** D:

Fred Zinnemann. Spencer Tracy, Signe Hasso, Hume Cronyn, Agnes Moorehead, Jessica Tandy, George Macready, Kaaren Verne, George Zucco, Felix Bressart. Seven men escape from Nazi concentration camp and are pursued by the Gestapo. Exciting film makes strong statement about a cynic who regains hope when others risk their lives to save him. An early winner for Zinnemann.

7th Dawn, The (1964-British) C-123m. *½ D: Lewis Gilbert. William Holden, Susannah York, Capucine, Tetsuro Tamba, Michael Goodliffe. Dreary tale of personal and political conflict among WW2 allies—now adversaries—in postwar Malaya.

Seventh Heaven (1927) 119m. **½ D: Frank Borzage. Janet Gaynor, Charles Farrell, Ben Bard, David Butler, Marie Mosquini, Albert Gran. One of the most famous screen romances of all time does not hold up as perfectly as one would like; Gaynor won first Academy Award as Diane, mistreated Paris waif redeemed and revived by cocky sewer-worker Chico (Farrell). His performance weakens film, as does terrible war subplot and finale. Still interesting, though; beautifully filmed, with lovely theme "Diane." Gaynor's Oscar was shared for her performances in SUNRISE and STREET ANGEL. Also won Oscars for Screenplay (Benjamin Glazer) and Director. Remade in 1937.

Seventh Heaven (1937) 102m. ** D: Henry King. Simone Simon, James Stewart, Jean Hersholt, Gregory Ratoff, Gale Sondergaard, J. Edward Bromberg, John Qualen. Famous silent film of poignant lovers in France doesn't do as well this time, with Gallic Stewart and soggy script.

Seven Thieves (1960) 102m. ***½ D: Henry Hathaway. Edward G. Robinson, Rod Steiger, Joan Collins, Eli Wallach, Alexander Scourby, Michael Dante, Berry Kroeger, Sebastian Cabot. Taut caper of well-planned Monte Carlo heist, with excellent cast giving credibility to far-fetched premise.

Seventh Seal, The (1956-Sweden) 96m. ✓ **** D: Ingmar Bergman. Max von Sydow, Gunnar Bjornstrand, Nils Poppe, Bibi Andersson, Bengt Ekerot. Sydow, a disillusioned knight on his way back from the Crusades, tries to solve the mysteries of life while playing chess game with Death, who has offered him a short reprieve. Spellbinding, one-of-a-kind masterpiece helped gain Bergman international acclaim.▼

Seventh Sign, The (1988) C-98m. *½ D: Carl Schultz. Demi Moore, Michael Biehn, Jurgen Prochnow, Peter Friedman, Manny Jacobs, John Taylor, Lee Garlington, Akosua Busia, John Heard, Ian Buchanan. Pregnant Moore is convinced it's apocalypse now and that boarder Prochnow wants her baby for his end-of-the-world machinations. Could be; look out for dead ocean life, icy deserts and rivers running with blood. Supernatural grab bag is directed with all the zeal one brings to a documentary on stock portfolios; result has an extraordinarily high "oh, come on" quotient.▼

Seventh Sin, The (1957) 94m. **½ D: Ronald Neame. Eleanor Parker, Bill Travers, Françoise Rosay, George Sanders, Jean-Pierre Aumont, Ellen Corby. Remake of Maugham's THE PAINTED VEIL has virtue of Parker's earnest performance as adulterous wife of a doctor who redeems herself during an epidemic; set in Hong Kong and inner China.

Seventh Sword (1962-Italian) **C-84m.** ** D: Riccardo Freda. Brett Halsey, Beatrice Altariba, Giulio Bosetti, Gabriele Antonini. Wooden costumer with Halsey trying to stamp out plot to overthrow Philip III of Spain.

Seventh Veil, The (1945-British) **95m.** ***½ D: Compton Bennett. James Mason, Ann Todd, Herbert Lom, Hugh McDermott, Albert Lieven. Superb psychological drama of pianist Todd, left as ward to her neurotic cousin Mason. Psychiatrist Lom uses hypnosis to enable Todd to regain her professional and personal sanity. All three stars are first-rate in one of the key British films of the forties. Muriel and Sydney Box's screenplay won an Oscar.▼

Seventh Victim, The (1943) 71m. *** D: Mark Robson. Tom Conway, Kim Hunter, Jean Brooks, Evelyn Brent, Elizabeth Russell, Hugh Beaumont, Erford Gage, Isabel Jewell, Barbara Hale. Offbeat Val Lewton chiller of innocent Hunter stumbling onto N.Y.C. group of devil-worshipers. Genuinely eerie.▼

7th Voyage of Sinbad, The (1958) **C-87m.** ***½ D: Nathan Juran. Kerwin Mathews, Kathryn Grant (Crosby), Richard Eyer, Torin Thatcher. Top-notch adventure/fantasy pits hero Sinbad against unscrupulous magician (Thatcher) who has reduced Princess Grant to miniature size. Good pacing, eye-popping special effects by Ray Harryhausen (including famed duel with skeleton), music score by Bernard Herrmann a winner all the way.▼

Seven Times Seven (1969-Italian) **C-92m.** ** D: Michele Lupo. Terry-Thomas, Lionel Stander, Gastone Moschin, Gordon Mitchell, Adolfo Celi. Middling cops & robbers farce that has a gang of convicts go over the wall, rob the Royal Mint, and then break back into prison.

Seven-Ups, The (1973) **C-103m.** **½ D: Philip D'Antoni. Roy Scheider, Tony LoBianco, Bill Hickman, Richard Lynch, Victor Arnold. THE FRENCH CONNECTION producer directed this unofficial sequel, with Scheider scoring as a tough cop. Action outweighs plot and car chase

is one of the best yet filmed. Shot in N.Y.C.▼

Seven Waves Away SEE: **Abandon Ship!**

Seven Ways From Sundown (1960) **C-87m.** **½ D: Harry Keller. Audie Murphy, Barry Sullivan, Venetia Stevenson, John McIntire, Kenneth Tobey, Mary Field. Murphy is Texas ranger assigned to bring in seasoned killer Sullivan, with usual results.

7 Women (1966) **C-87m.** ** D: John Ford. Anne Bancroft, Sue Lyon, Margaret Leighton, Flora Robson, Mildred Dunnock, Anna Lee, Betty Field, Eddie Albert, Mike Mazurki, Woody Strode. Flat soaper of dedicated missionaries in China in 1935, menaced by warrior cutthroats. Despite cast and director, a dull film. Ford's last feature.

Seven Women From Hell (1961) **88m.** ** D: Robert D. Webb. Patricia Owens, Denise Darcel, Cesar Romero, John Kerr, Yvonne Craig. Able cast wasted on trite account of female prisoners in Japanese prison, set in WW2 New Guinea.

Seven Year Itch, The (1955) **C-105m.** *** D: Billy Wilder. Marilyn Monroe, Tom Ewell, Evelyn Keyes, Sonny Tufts, Victor Moore, Oscar Homolka, Carolyn Jones, Doro Merande. Ewell's wife summer vacations, Marilyn moves in upstairs, in this George Axelrod comedy set in N.Y.C. MM delightful as dumb blonde with more obvious assets than brains.▼

Severed Head, A (1971-British) **C-96m.** *** D: Dick Clement. Ian Holm, Lee Remick, Richard Attenborough, Claire Bloom, Clive Revill, Jennie Linden. Sophisticated sex comedy-drama seemed out of step with the youthful 70s, looks better today; vintner Holm is expected to keep a stiff upper lip while wife Remick has an open affair with her shrink (Attenborough). Sharp performances, thoughtful adaptation of the Iris Murdoch novel by Frederic Raphael.

Sex and the Married Woman (1977) **C-100m.** TVM D: Jack Arnold. Barry Newman, Joanna Pettet, Keenan Wynn, Dick Gautier, Jayne Meadows, Nita Talbot, Chuck McCann, F. Murray Abraham. Listless comedy of how success can ruin a good marriage, with a free-spirited husband becoming jealous of his wife's sudden fame after she writes a book on the sex habits of her friends. Kooky cameos spark it minimally. Below average.

Sex and the Single Girl (1964) **C-114m.** **½ D: Richard Quine. Natalie Wood, Tony Curtis, Lauren Bacall, Henry Fonda, Mel Ferrer, Fran Jeffries, Edward Everett Horton, Larry Storch, Stubby Kaye, Count Basie and Orchestra. Helen Gurley Brown's book shoved aside, title used to exploit fairly amusing tale of smut-magazine editor Curtis wooing notorious female psychologist Wood. Bacall and Fonda wrap it up as a battling married couple. Coscripted by Joseph Heller.

Sex and the Single Parent (1979) **C-96m.** TVM D: Jackie Cooper. Susan Saint James, Mike Farrell, Dori Brenner, Warren Berlinger, Julie Sommars, Barbara Rhoades. Sitcom approach to the plight of two divorcees whose newly realized independence and burgeoning social life is complicated by their respective children. Average.

Sex Kittens Go to College (1960) **94m.** BOMB D: Albert Zugsmith. Mamie Van Doren, Tuesday Weld, Mijanou Bardot (Brigitte's sister), Louis Nye, Martin Milner, Mickey Shaughnessy, Pamela Mason, (Norman) "Woo Woo" Grabowski, Jackie Coogan, John Carradine. Priceless title and cast fail to deliver in shockingly unfunny comedy; new head of college science department (Mamie, working very hard to convince us she's a genius) turns out to be an ex-stripper. Finding a movie with worse direction would be almost as impossible as finding another movie with a night club jazz combo fronted by *Conway Twitty!* Don't say you weren't warned. Also known as THE BEAUTY AND THE ROBOT.

sex, lies, and videotape (1989) **C-100m.** *** D: Steven Soderbergh. James Spader, Andie MacDowell, Peter Gallagher, Laura San Giacomo. A selfish, successful lawyer—whose wife has turned frigid and whose sister-in-law has become his lover—welcomes an old college friend for a visit, little dreaming the effect he'll have on all of them. This intriguing, exceptionally well-acted first feature for writer-director Soderbergh took top prize at the Cannes Film Festival; its deliberate pace and talky nature are reminiscent of an Eric Rohmer film—and like one of his, it's not to everyone's taste.▼

Sex Play SEE: **Bunny Caper, The**

Sex Symbol, The (1974) **C-74m. TVM** D: David Lowell Rich. Connie Stevens, Shelley Winters, Don Murray, Jack Carter, James Olson, Nehemiah Persoff, William Castle. Alvah Bessie adapted his 1966 novel, *The Symbol,* about a fictitious movie queen of the '40s and '50s, but images of Marilyn Monroe come through in every frame. Initially, real or imagined libel suits threatened to keep this from ever being shown, and what got on the air after severe editing was only a fraction of the exploitive, nudity-spiced film eventually shown theatrically overseas. Average.

Sextette (1978) **C-91m.** BOMB D: Ken Hughes. Mae West, Tony Curtis, Ringo Starr, Dom DeLuise, Timothy Dalton, George Hamilton, Alice Cooper, Keith Moon, Rona Barrett, Walter Pidgeon, George Raft. Astonishing is the only word for this comedy about a Hollywood glamor queen whose many ex-husbands keep popping up during her latest honeymoon. Naturally there's curiosity value in seeing octogenarian Mae still strutting her stuff, but it wears out pretty fast. Her last movie, based on her play.▼

Sex Through a Window SEE: **Extreme Close-Up**▼

Sex With a Smile (1976-Italian) **C-100m.** *½ D: Sergio Martino. Marty Feldman, Edwige Fenech, Sydne Rome, Barbara Bouchet, Dayle Haddon, Enrico Monterrano, Giovanni Ralli. Five episodes that promise a lot in terms of sex and laughter, then (outside of Feldman segment) fail to deliver. Heavy on slapstick, and heavy reliance on knowledge of Italian affairs.▼

Sgt. Pepper's Lonely Hearts Club Band (1978) **C-111m.** *½ D: Michael Schultz. Peter Frampton, The Bee Gees, George Burns, Frankie Howerd, Donald Pleasence, Sandy Farina, Dianne Steinberg, Billy Preston, Steve Martin, Earth, Wind & Fire. Attempt to link songs from The Beatles' classic album into some sort of storyline just doesn't work; sequences range from tolerable to embarrassing. As to The Bee Gees' acting talent, if you can't say something nice . . .▼

Shack Out on 101 (1955) **80m.** *** D: Edward Dein. Terry Moore, Frank Lovejoy, Lee Marvin, Keenan Wynn, Whit Bissell. Lee Marvin *is* Slob in this trash classic about the efforts of hash slinger Moore to combat Communism while juggling the lecherous advances of nearly all her co-stars. Absolutely one of a kind, with most of the action taking place on a single shabby set (Wynn's beanery).▼

Shadey (1985-British) **C-106m.** **½ D: Philip Saville. Antony Sher, Billie Whitelaw, Patrick Macnee, Lesley Ash, Larry Lamb, Bernard Hepton, Katherine Helmond. Occasionally funny but mostly uninvolving comedy-fantasy-thriller about the title character (Sher), who is able to transmit to film visions from his mind. He wants to use his ability only for peaceful purposes—yet he also needs money for a sex-change operation. Helmond's role is best, that of a hilariously unpredictable, loony Lady.▼

Shadow Box, The (1980) **C-100m. TVM** D: Paul Newman. Joanne Woodward, Christopher Plummer, Valerie Harper, James Broderick, Sylvia Sidney, Melinda Dillon, Ben Masters, Curtiss Marlowe, John Considine. Playwright Michael Cristofer adapted his Pulitzer Prize-and Tony Award-winning play about three terminally ill patients and their families during one day at an experimental rustic retreat in California. A powerful and insightful story, well served by this stellar cast. Above average.▼

Shadow in the Sky (1951) **78m.** **½ D: Fred M. Wilcox. Ralph Meeker, Nancy Davis (Reagan), James Whitmore, Jean Hagen, Gladys Hurlbut. Meeker is quite believable as shellshocked ex-G.I. trying to regain his sanity.

Shadow in the Streets, A (1975) **C-78m.** TVM D: Richard Donner. Tony LoBianco, Sheree North, Dana Andrews, Ed Lauter, Jesse Welles, Dick Balduzzi. Paroled excon becomes a parole officer in attempt at rehabilitation. LoBianco's gutsy acting style and offbeat premise make this one. Written by John D. F. Black. Above average.

Shadowlands (1985-British) **C-90m.** *** D: Norman Stone. Joss Ackland, Claire Bloom, David Waller, Rupert Baderman, Rhys Hopkins. Poignant, wise, quietly rewarding drama about British writer C. S. Lewis (Ackland), a confirmed bachelor, and how he is changed when he falls in love with American divorcée Bloom. Lovely performances by the stars; exceptional awardcaliber script by William Nicholson. Video title: C.S. LEWIS: THROUGH THE SHADOWLANDS.▼

Shadow Man, The (1953-British) **75m.** ** D: Richard Vernon. Cesar Romero, Kay Kendall, Victor Maddern. Standard action-programmer with Romero a casino owner in love with Kendall, involved with homicide.

Shadow of a Doubt (1943) **108m.** ***½ D: Alfred Hitchcock. Teresa Wright, Joseph Cotten, Macdonald Carey, Patricia Collinge, Henry Travers, Wallace Ford, Hume Cronyn. Perceptive Americana intertwined with story of young girl who slowly comes to realize her beloved Uncle Charley is really the Merry Widow murderer; Cronyn steals film as nosy pulp-story fan. Co-written by Thornton Wilder. Remade as STEP DOWN TO TERROR.▼

Shadow of Evil (1964-French-Italian) **C-92m.** *½ D: Andre Hunebelle. Kerwin Mathews, Pier Angeli, Robert Hossein, Stuart Nesbitt. Evil doctor plans control of the world by unleashing a virus to contaminate the inferior inhabitants. Too bad they don't have the serum perfected for movies yet.

Shadow of Fear (1956-British) **76m.** ** D: Albert S. Rogell. Mona Freeman, Jean Kent, Maxwell Reed, Hugh Miller, Gretchen Franklin. Flabby suspenser of Freeman realizing that her stepmother is planning to murder her as she did hubby; set in England. Original title: BEFORE I WAKE.

Shadow of the Cat (1961-British) **79m.** ** D: John Gilling. Barbara Shelley, Andre Morell, William Lucas, Richard Warner, Freda Jackson. Engaging horror yarn about feline who avenges her mistress's murder.

Shadow of the Hawk (1976-Canadian) **C-92m.** *½ D: George McCowan. Jan-Michael Vincent, Marilyn Hassett, Chief Dan George, Pea Shandel, Marianne Jones. Formula action meller has Vincent battling supernatural Indian spirits.

Shadow of the Thin Man (1941) **97m.** D: W. S. Van Dyke II. William Powell, Myrna Loy, Barry Nelson, Donna Reed, Sam Levene, Alan Baxter. SEE: **Thin Man** series.▼

Shadow of Zorro, The (1962-Italian) **C-84m.** *½ D: Joaquin Romero Marchent. Frank Latimore, Maria Luz Galicia, Mario Felciani, Marco Tulli. Clumsy film unaided by Latimore in title role of Don Jose who combats outlaws masked as Zorro.

Shadow on the Land (1968) **C-97m.** TVM D: Richard C. Sarafian. Jackie Cooper, John Forsythe, Gene Hackman, Carol Lynley, Marc Strange, Janice Rule. America is under the rule of ruthless dictator; two men lead an underground group hoping to restore democracy. Given the obvious limits of TV, this intriguing situation doesn't get very far; cast is more interesting than Nedrick Young's script. Below average.

Shadow on the Sun (1988) **C-200m.** TVM D: Tony Richardson. Stefanie Powers, Claire Bloom, Peter Bowles, Brian Cox, Niamh Cusack, Trevor Eve, Frederic Forrest, James Fox, John Rubinstein, Jack Thompson. Boring, overlong dramatization of the life and loves of Beryl Markham, pioneer '30s aviatrix, African bush pilot, horse trainer, and adventuress. TV's weak response to OUT OF AFRICA, based on interviews by James Fox (not the actor who stars in the film as her wealthy husband). Originally shown in two parts. Below average.▼

Shadow on the Wall (1950) **84m.** *** D: Patrick Jackson. Ann Sothern, Zachary Scott, Nancy Davis (Reagan), Gigi Perreau, Barbara Billingsley, Kristine Miller. Slick mystery of Perreau going into shock when she sees mother murdered, and the eventual trapping of killer.

Shadow on the Window (1957) **73m.** ** D: William Asher. Phil Carey, Betty Garrett, John Barrymore, Jr., Corey Allen, Jerry Mathers. Fair programmer; Garrett is held hostage by robber-killers.

Shadow Over Elveron (1968) **C-100m.** TVM D: James Goldstone. James Franciscus, Shirley Knight, Leslie Nielsen, Franchot Tone, James Dunn, Don Ameche. Small-town corruption disgusts young physician who wants to set up practice there; whitewash murder trial becomes final straw. Most of dialogue and situations OK, performances ditto, but film as whole too insistent. Average.

Shadow Play (1986) **C-95m.** *½ D: Susan Shadburne. Dee Wallace Stone, Cloris Leachman, Ron Kuhlman, Barry Laws, Al Strobel. Tepid chiller about playwright Stone, and the psychological problems she's been facing since her lover's demise. Very minor fare.▼

Shadow Riders, The (1982) **C-100m.** TVM D: Andrew V. McLaglen. Tom

Selleck, Sam Elliott, Ben Johnson, Katharine Ross, Geoffrey Lewis, Jeffrey Osterhage, Gene Evans, Harry Carey, Jr., Jane Greer, Dominique Dunne. Engrossing Louis L'Amour Western about two brothers' post-Civil War search for their family, kidnapped by Rebel guerrillas during the war. Most of the same players had previously appeared in L'Amour's THE SACKETTS. Above average. Also known as LOUIS L'AMOUR'S THE SHADOW RIDERS.

Shadows (1960) 87m. *** D: John Cassavetes. Hugh Hurd, Lelia Goldoni, Ben Carruthers, Anthony Ray, Rupert Crosse. Cassavetes' first film as director, an improvisational, groundbreaking, independently made effort about a light-skinned black girl (Goldoni) living in Manhattan with her two brothers. White Ray becomes involved with her, then rejects her after discovering her race. Formless, crude, but strikingly realistic.

Shadows in the Night (1944) 67m. D: Eugene Forde. Warner Baxter, Nina Foch, George Zucco, Minor Watson, Ben Welden, Edward Norris, Charles Halton, Jeanne Bates. SEE: **Crime Doctor** series.

Shadows of the Peacock SEE: **Echoes of Paradise**▼

Shadows Over Chinatown (1946) 61m. D: Terry Morse. Sidney Toler, Mantan Moreland, Victor Sen Yung, Tanis Chandler, Bruce Kellogg, John Gallaudet. SEE: **Charlie Chan** series.

Shadows Run Black (1981) C-89m. *½ D: Howard Heard. William J. Kulzer, Elizabeth Trosper, Shea Porter, George J. Engelson, Dianne Hinkler, Terry Congie. Routine slasher film about cop Kulzer tracking down supposed vigilante killer who is preying on a high school ring dealing in drugs and prostitution. An early role for future star Kevin Costner. Filmed in 1981.▼

Shady Lady (1945) 94m. ** D: George Waggner. Charles Coburn, Robert Paige, Ginny Simms, Alan Curtis, Martha O'-Driscoll, Kathleen Howard. Shaky mixture of music and drama in crime tale with genial Coburn saving the day for all in the end.

Shaft (1971) C-100m. *** D: Gordon Parks. Richard Roundtree, Moses Gunn, Charles Cioffi, Christopher St. John, Drew Bundini Brown, Gwenn Mitchell, Lawrence Pressman, Antonio Fargas. Slick, upbeat entertainment has Ernest Tidyman's black private-eye John Shaft hired to find kidnapped daughter of Harlem ganglord. Heavy doses of sex and violence professionally packaged by director Parks. Isaac Hayes' theme won Oscar. Followed by two sequels and a TV series.▼

Shaft in Africa (1973) C-112m. *** D: John Guillermin. Richard Roundtree, Frank Finlay, Vonetta McGee, Neda Arneric, Cy Grant, Jacques Marin. Strong action vehicle for Roundtree finds detective Shaft forced into helping African nation stop latter-day slave trading. Extremely tough and violent. Script by Stirling Silliphant.

Shaft's Big Score! (1972) C-104m. *** D: Gordon Parks. Richard Roundtree, Moses Gunn, Drew Bundini Brown, Joseph Mascolo, Kathy Imrie, Wally Taylor, Joe Santos. Dynamic sequel to SHAFT (reteaming director Parks and writer Ernest Tidyman) has private eye Roundtree running afoul of the underworld as he investigates a friend's murder. Sexy, violent, with hair-raising chase finale; Parks also did the music.

Shag (1989) C-98m. **½ D: Zelda Barron. Phoebe Cates, Scott Coffey, Bridget Fonda, Annabeth Gish, Page Hannah, Robert Rusler, Tyrone Power, Jr., Jeff Yagher, Carrie Hamilton, Shirley Anne Field. Southern belle high-school grad Cates is about to get married, so her three girlfriends decide to take her on a "last fling" weekend to Myrtle Beach. Pleasant outing set in 1963 with an unusually appealing and talented young cast. Released in 1988 outside the U.S.

Shaggy D.A., The (1976) C-91m. *** D: Robert Stevenson. Dean Jones, Suzanne Pleshette, Tim Conway, Keenan Wynn, Jo Anne Worley, Dick Van Patten. Sequel to Disney's SHAGGY DOG is winning slapstick romp, with Jones as helpless victim of transformations. Cast is peppered with a score of movie veterans in supporting and bit parts. Followed by THE RETURN OF THE SHAGGY DOG.▼

Shaggy Dog, The (1959) 104m. **½ D: Charles Barton. Fred MacMurray, Jean Hagen, Tommy Kirk, Annette Funicello, Tim Considine, Kevin Corcoran, Cecil Kellaway, Alexander Scourby. Disney's first slapstick comedy has fine fantasy premise (a boy who turns into a sheepdog through ancient spell) but sluggish script. Some good gags, but not up to later Disney standard. Jack Albertson has bit part as reporter. Also shown in computer-colored version. Sequels: THE SHAGGY D.A. and THE RETURN OF THE SHAGGY DOG.▼

Shakedown (1950) 80m. **½ D: Joseph Pevney. Howard Duff, Peggy Dow, Brian Donlevy, Bruce Bennett, Peggie Castle, Anne Vernon, Lawrence Tierney. Fast-paced but familiar chronicle of ambitious photographer Duff, who uses any and all means—starting with blackmail—to get ahead. Look for Rock Hudson as a doorman.

Shakedown, The (1959-British) 92m. *½ D: John Lemont. Terence Morgan, Hazel Court, Donald Pleasence, Bill Owen. Lackluster account of shakedown racket involving a photography school of nudes; good cast but no script.

Shakedown (1988) **C-90m.** *** D: James Glickenhaus. Peter Weller, Sam Elliott, Patricia Charbonneau, Blanche Baker, Antonio Fargas, Richard Brooks, Tom Waits, Kathryn Rossetter. Entertaining actioner with public defender Weller and undercover cop Elliott combining forces to rid N.Y.C. of drugs and corruption. Good of its kind, with oodles of sensational stuntwork to compensate for the dearth of originality.▼

Shakedown on the Sunset Strip (1988) **C-100m. TVM** D: Walter Grauman. Perry King, Season Hubley, Joan Van Ark, Vincent Baggetta, Michael McGuire, David Graf, Charles Siebert. Ambitious L.A. vice cop pursues a notorious madam in the late 1940s and finds himself bucking the system, with incongruous dollops of humor which give the finished product a kind of identity crisis. Average.

Shake Hands with the Devil (1959) **110m.** ***½ D: Michael Anderson. James Cagney, Don Murray, Dana Wynter, Glynis Johns, Michael Redgrave, Cyril Cusack, Sybil Thorndike, Richard Harris. Gripping drama of war-torn Ireland in 1920s, with American student trying to stay aloof, but, drawn by circumstances, he joins rebel army led by iron-willed Cagney. Strikingly filmed on location.

Shake, Rattle and Rock (1956) **72m.** ** D: Edward L. Cahn. Touch (Mike) Connors, Lisa Gaye, Sterling Holloway, Fats Domino, Joe Turner, Tommy Charles, Margaret Dumont, Raymond Hatton. Sub-par 1950s rock film with standard plot about adults trying to put the lid on kids' music, benefitting from presences of Domino, Turner, and veteran character actors.

Shaker Run (1985-New Zealand) **C-90m.** ** D: Bruce Morrison. Cliff Robertson, Leif Garrett, Lisa Harrow, Shane Briant, Ian Mune, Peter Rowell, Peter Hayden, Bruce Phillips. Robertson adds character to this otherwise predictable (and implausible) car chase drama. He's a crusty American stunt driver, touring in New Zealand, who unknowingly becomes involved in a plot to transport a stolen virus. ▼

Shakespeare Wallah (1965-Indian) **115m.** *** D: James Ivory. Shashi Kapoor, Felicity Kendal, Geoffrey Kendal, Laura Liddell, Madhur Jaffrey, Uptal Dutt. Playboy Kapoor, who has an actress-mistress, romances Felicity Kendal, a member of a two-bit English theatrical company touring Shakespeare in India. Simple, poignant drama.▼

Shakiest Gun in the West, The (1968) **C-101m.** **½ D: Alan Rafkin. Don Knotts, Barbara Rhoades, Jackie Coogan, Donald Barry, Ruth McDevitt, Frank McGrath. Remake of Bob Hope's THE PALEFACE provides Knotts with one of his better vehicles, as Philadelphia dentist who finds himself out West, tangled up with gunslingers and beautiful Rhoades.▼

Shalako (1968-British) **C-113m.** *½ D: Edward Dmytryk. Sean Connery, Brigitte Bardot, Stephen Boyd, Jack Hawkins, Peter Van Eyck, Honor Blackman, Woody Strode, Alexander Knox, Valerie French. European aristocrats on hunting tour of New Mexico during 1880s are menaced by Apaches. Supposed potent casting of Connery and Bardot can't revive slow-moving Western, based on a Louis L'Amour novel.▼

Shalimar (1978-Indian) **C-85m.** *½ D: Krishna Shah. Rex Harrison, Sylvia Miles, John Saxon, Dharmendra, Zenat Aman, Shammi Kapoor. Wily Harrison invites the world's greatest thieves to try and steal the world's most valuable ruby from his custody—at the risk of their lives. This was filmed in both English and Hindi-language versions, but the results were so dull that the English print never made it to theaters. Video title: DEADLY THIEF.▼

Shall We Dance (1937) **116m.** ***½ D: Mark Sandrich. Fred Astaire, Ginger Rogers, Eric Blore, Edward Everett Horton, Ann Shoemaker, Jerome Cowan, Harriet Hoctor. Lesser Astaire-Rogers is still top musical, with Gershwin's "Let's Call The Whole Thing Off," "They All Laughed," and "They Can't Take That Away From Me" holding together flimsy plot about dance team pretending to be wed.▼

Shame (1961) SEE: **Intruder, The**▼

Shame (1968-Swedish) **103m.** **** D: Ingmar Bergman. Liv Ullmann, Max von Sydow, Gunnar Bjornstrand, Sigge Furst, Birgitta Valberg, Hans Alfredson. Powerful, brilliantly acted drama examines how married concert violinists are morally challenged by a civil war that rages across their island. One of Bergman's best.

Shame (1988-Australian) **C-90m.** ** D: Steve Jodrell. Deborra-Lee Furness, Tony Barry, Simone Buchanan, Gillian Jones, Peter Aanensen, Margaret Ford. Unusual, watchable, but not terribly successful feminist revenge piece, as femme motorcyclist/lawyer takes on a village of goons who look the other way when a gang of teen boys rapes a 16-year-old girl. Strange mix of genres—biker movie, neo-Western, and more—but no MAD MAX. Has definite cult possibilities.▼

Shameless Old Lady, The (1965-French) **94m.** *** D: Rene Allio. Sylvie, Malka Ribovska, Victor Lanoux, Etienne Bierry. Bertolt Brecht story charmingly brought to the screen. Sylvie is terrific as old woman who lives alone and follows a drab and uneventful routine until there is a strange turnabout in her relationships with others.

Shame of the Jungle (1975-French-Belgian) **C-73m.** *½ D: Picha, Boris Szulzinger. Voices of Johnny Weissmuller, Jr., John Belushi, Bill Murray, Brian Doyle-Murray,

[1029]

Christopher Guest, Andrew Duncan. R-rated cartoon spoof of Tarzan films, created by Belgian cartoonist Picha, then Americanized for U.S. release in 1979 by *Saturday Night Live* writers Anne Beatts and Michael O'Donoghue, with stars of that show providing voices. Crass, unfunny, and unattractive, despite a promising start. Original French-language version ran 85m.

Shampoo (1975) **C-109m.** **½ D: Hal Ashby. Warren Beatty, Julie Christie, Goldie Hawn, Lee Grant, Jack Warden, Tony Bill, Carrie Fisher, Howard Hesseman. Muddy satire of morals and mores in Southern California, centered around restless hairdresser and his demanding female customers. Some bright moments lost in dreary comedy-drama by Beatty and Robert Towne. Fisher's film debut; Grant won Best Supporting Actress Oscar.▼

Shamus (1973) **C-106m.** *** D: Buzz Kulik. Burt Reynolds, Dyan Cannon, Giorgio Tozzi, John Ryan, Joe Santos. Exciting but mindless story of offbeat private-eye trying to crack bizarre case while recovering from numerous beatings, jumpings, and other heroic exploits.▼

Shane (1953) **C-118m.** **** D: George Stevens. Alan Ladd, Jean Arthur, Van Heflin, (Walter) Jack Palance, Brandon de Wilde, Ben Johnson, Edgar Buchanan, Emile Meyer, Elisha Cook, Jr. Former gunfighter comes to defense of homesteaders and is idolized by their son. Classic Western is splendid in every way. Breathtaking cinematography by Loyal Griggs won an Oscar. Screenplay by A.B. Guthrie, Jr. from the Jack Schaefer novel.▼

Shanghai (1935) **75m.** *½ D: James Flood. Loretta Young, Charles Boyer, Warner Oland, Fred Keating, Charles Grapewin, Alison Skipworth. Dreary drama of American girl falling in love with mysterious Boyer, who turns out to be (gasp!) Eurasian. Two good stars can't save this turgid outing.

Shanghai Chest, The (1948) **56m.** D: William Beaudine. Roland Winters, Mantan Moreland, Deannie Best, John Alvin, Victor Sen Yung. SEE: **Charlie Chan** series.

Shanghai Cobra, The (1945) **64m.** D: Phil Karlson. Sidney Toler. Benson Fong, Mantan Moreland, Joan Barclay, James Flavin, Addison Richards. SEE: **Charlie Chan** series.

Shanghai Express (1932) **80m.** *** D: Josef von Sternberg. Marlene Dietrich, Anna May Wong, Warner Oland, Clive Brook, Eugene Pallette, Louise Closser Hale. Dated but prime Dietrich vehicle, grandly photographed by Lee Garmes (who won an Oscar). Marlene is Shanghai Lily, Brook her old flame, Oland a cruel war lord, Wong a spunky partisan, in Jules Furthman-scripted yarn of train ride through China during civil warfare. Remade as PEKING EXPRESS.

Shanghai Gesture, The (1941) **98m.** ** D: Josef von Sternberg. Gene Tierney, Walter Huston, Victor Mature, Ona Munson, Maria Ouspenskaya, Phyllis Brooks, Albert Bassermann, Eric Blore, Mike Mazurki. Slow, overblown drama of Huston discovering daughter Tierney in Oriental gambling setup. Intriguing direction somehow never makes it.▼

Shanghai Story, The (1954) **99m.** ** D: Frank Lloyd. Ruth Roman, Edmond O'Brien, Richard Jaeckel, Barry Kelley, Whit Bissell. Tawdry yet intriguing little film about Americans trapped by Red Chinese.

Shanghai Surprise (1986) **C-97m.** BOMB D: Jim Goddard. Sean Penn, Madonna, Paul Freeman, Richard Griffiths, Philip Sayer, Clyde Kusatsu, Kay Tong Lim. Missionary Madonna hires adventurer Penn (her then real-life husband) to capture a cache of stolen opium (for medicinal purposes only) in 1937 China. It's all stupefyingly dull. As one critic noted, it's tough for Penn to succeed in the grand adventure movie tradition when the screen legend he most reminds you of here is Ratso Rizzo. Coexecutive producer George Harrison, who appears briefly as a nightclub singer, wrote the songs.▼

Shanks (1974) **C-93m.** *** D: William Castle. Marcel Marceau, Tsilla Chelton, Philippe Clay, Cindy Eilbacher, Helena Kallianiotes, Larry Bishop. One of the strangest movies ever made: mute puppeteer Marceau is given device by dying inventor (also Marceau) which can animate dead bodies. Relatively little dialogue in this bizarre horror-fantasy; alternately amusing and disturbing, with unique performances by three top mimes. A real curio from Castle; his final film as director.

Shannon's Deal (1989) **C-100m.** TVM D: Lewis Teague. Jamey Sheridan, Elizabeth Pena, Martin Ferrero, Jenny Lewis, Alberta Watson, Miguel Ferrer. Tangy dialogue and sharp characterizations energize this slick thriller about a disillusioned Philadelphia lawyer turned private investigator who becomes embroiled in an international drug-smuggling case. Written with grit by John Sayles; scored by Wynton Marsalis. Pilot to the TV series. Above average.

Shape of Things to Come, The (1979-Canadian) **C-95m.** *½ D: George McCowan. Jack Palance, Carol Lynley, John Ireland, Barry Morse, Nicholas Campbell, Eddie Benton. Lackluster, low-budget remake of H. G. Wells story has nothing in common with 1936 THINGS TO COME, as few survivors of Earth's destruction are now living in peril on the moon. Diehard sci-fi fans may want to take a look, but it's hardly worth the trouble.

Sharad of Atlantis (1936) **100m.** *½ D:

B. Reeves Eason, Joseph Kane. Ray "Crash" Corrigan, Lois Wilde, Monte Blue, William Farnum, Boothe Howard, Lon Chaney, Jr. Mediocre actioner involving finding of underwater kingdom; uninspired special effects don't help. Reedited from Republic serial UNDERSEA KINGDOM.▼

Share Out, The (1962-British) 62m. **½ D: Gerard Glaister. Bernard Lee, Patrick Cargill, Alexander Knox, Moira Redmond. Another Edgar Wallace actioner with Lee the Scotland Yard investigator determined to crack a blackmail ring.

Sharing Richard (1988) C-100m. TVM D: Peter Bonerz. Ed Marinaro, Eileen Davidson, Nancy Frangione, Hillary Bailey Smith, Janet Carroll, Lisa Jane Persky. Three unmarried bosom buddies decide the doctor of their dreams is worth sharing among them and devise a plan to alternate nights with him. Amiable romp that raised an eyebrow or two, given the new sexual mores in the era of AIDS. Average.

Shark! (1969-U.S.-Mexican) C-92m. ** D: Samuel Fuller. Burt Reynolds, Barry Sullivan, Arthur Kennedy, Silvia Pinal, Enrique Lucero, Charles Berriochoa. Tired drama of adventurers diving for shark-guarded treasure earned some infamy when a stunt diver was killed by one of the beasts. Fuller disowned this production, which was taken out of his hands and re-edited. Reissued as MANEATER.▼

Shark Boy of Bora Bora SEE: **Beyond the Reef**

Sharkfighters, The (1956) C-73m. *½ D: Jerry Hopper. Victor Mature, Karen Steele, James Olson, Philip Coolidge, Claude Akins. Bland account of Mature et al seeking some way to repel the man-killing fish.

Shark Kill (1976) C-78m. TVM D: William A. Graham. Richard Yniguez, Phillip Clark, David Huddleston, Jennifer Warren, Elizabeth Gill, Victor Campos. Thriller in the JAWS school pits two men, motivated by vengeance and a $10,000 bounty, against a great white shark. Great underwater but not-so-hot on land. Average.

Sharks' Treasure (1975) C-95m. ** D: Cornel Wilde. Cornel Wilde, Yaphet Kotto, John Nellson, Cliff Osmond, David Canary, David Gilliam. Old-fashioned adventure yarn about diving for sunken treasure in the Caribbean is peppered with physical-fitness messages from director-writer-star Wilde.▼

Sharky's Machine (1981) C-119m. ** D: Burt Reynolds. Burt Reynolds, Rachel Ward, Vittorio Gassman, Brian Keith, Charles Durning, Bernie Casey, Henry Silva, Earl Holliman, Richard Libertini, John Fiedler, Darryl Hickman, Hari Rhodes. Jarring, loud, and extremely bloody actioner; vice cop Reynolds' vendetta against under-world honcho Gassman intensifies after he falls for one of his $1000-a-night hookers (Ward). Action scenes are competently staged, but you'll eventually become numbed by all the sleaze; film's weirdest aspect is its mainstream jazz score. Based on the William Diehl novel, but won't fool anyone who's ever seen LAURA.▼

Sharon: Portrait of a Mistress (1977) C-100m. TVM D: Robert Greenwald. Trish Van Devere, Patrick O'Neal, Janet Margolin, Gloria De Haven, Mel Ferrer, Sam Groom, Salome Jens, Gower Champion. Drama of a woman's series of affairs with married men. Boring soap opera, though earnestly performed. Average.

Shatter SEE: **Call Him Mr. Shatter**▼

Shattered SEE: **Something to Hide**▼

Shattered Innocence (1988) C-100m. TVM D: Sandor Stern. Jonna Lee, Melinda Dillon, John Pleshette, Kris Kamm, Ben Frank, Dennis Howard, Richard Cox. Small-town cheerleader's dream of Hollywood stardom turns to nightmare as she becomes a porno star. Fictionalized version of the life and suicide of real-life porno queen Shauna Grant, which previously was the subject of top-notch PBS documentary, *Death of a Porn Queen*. Average.

Shattered Silence SEE: **When Michael Calls**

Shattered Spirits (1986) C-100m. TVM D: Robert Greenwald. Martin Sheen, Melinda Dillon, Matthew Laborteaux, Lukas Haas, Roxana Zal, Jill Schoelen. An abusive drunk tears his family apart. Powerful performances by Sheen and Dillon; strong script by Gregory Goodell. Look for Sheen's daughter Rene Estevez in a small part as a telephoning teenager. Above average.

Shattered Vows (1984) C-100m. TVM D: Jack Bender. Valerie Bertinelli, David Morse, Caroline McWilliams, Patricia Neal, Millie Perkins, Leslie Ackerman, Lisa Jane Persky. Young nun is caught between her calling and her unspoken love for a priest. Based on the life of nun-turned-clinical psychologist Dr. Mary Gilligan Wong as described in her *Nun: A Memoir*. Average.

She (1935) 95m. *** D: Irving Pichel and Lansing C. Holden. Helen Gahagan, Randolph Scott, Helen Mack, Nigel Bruce, Gustav von Seyffertitz. Escapist adventure on a grand scale, from H. Rider Haggard's story of expedition seeking Flame of Eternal Life, which has been given to one all-powerful woman. Gahagan's cold personality is major drawback, but film is still fun, with outstanding Max Steiner score. Most TV prints run 89m. Previously filmed in 1917 and 1926, remade several times.

She (1965-British) C-106m. **½ D: Robert Day. Ursula Andress, John Richardson, Peter Cushing, Bernard Cribbins, Christopher Lee, Andre Morell. Effective refilm-

[1031]

ing of H. Rider Haggard's fantasy of love-starved eternal queen, seeking the reincarnation of her long-dead lover. There's Andress for the men, Richardson for the women. Followed by THE VENGEANCE OF SHE.

S*H*E (1980) **C-100m. TVM.** D: Robert Lewis. Omar Sharif, Cornelia Sharpe, Anita Ekberg, Robert Lansing, Fabio Testi, Isabella Rye. James Bondish derring-do involving a woman superspy who crosses swords with suave playboy head of an international crime ring. (S*H*E stands for Security Hazards Expert.) Script by Bond veteran Richard Maibaum. Average.▼

She (1985-Italian) **C-106m. BOMB** D: Avi Nesher. Sandahl Bergman, David Goss, Quin Kessler, Harrison Muller, Elena Wiedermann, Gordon Mitchell. Bottom-of-the-barrel remake, loosely based on the H. Rider Haggard novel, chronicling the various adventures of the title character (Bergman). Shot in 1982. ▼

Sheba Baby (1975) **C-90m. **** D: William Girdler. Pam Grier, Austin Stoker, D'Urville Martin, Rudy Challenger, Dick Merrifield. Fair-to-middling black action-melodrama with Grier as female private eye trying to help father and friend save their loan business. Less sex and violence than usual, but weak script and amateurish acting.▼

She-Beast, The (1966-Italian-Yugoslavian) **C-74m. *½** D: Michael Reeves. Barbara Steele, John Karlsen, Ian Ogilvy, Mel Welles, Jay Riley, Richard Watson. A witch killed by Transylvanian villagers in 18th century comes back to life as modern, attractive English girl on her honeymoon. Really tacky, though it has some laughs.▼

She Couldn't Say No (1954) **89m. *½** D: Lloyd Bacon. Robert Mitchum, Jean Simmons, Arthur Hunnicutt, Edgar Buchanan, Wallace Ford, Raymond Walburn, Pinky Tomlin. Silly fluff about wealthy, misguided young Simmons, who shows up in Progress, Arkansas, with a scheme to shower its citizens with free money; Mitchum is out of his element as the town doctor. A real dud. ▼

She Couldn't Take It (1935) **75m. ***** D: Tay Garnett. George Raft, Joan Bennett, Billie Burke, Walter Connolly, Lloyd Nolan, Franklin Pangborn, Alan Mowbray, Donald Meek, Wallace Ford. Fast-paced social comedy of bootlegger Raft impressing his henpecked cell mate Connolly (in stir on an income-tax-evasion rap). Upon release, Connolly appoints Raft his family guardian, causing rivalry with his madcap daughter Bennett.

She Creature, The (1957) **77m. **** D: Edward L. Cahn. Marla English, Tom Conway, Chester Morris, Ron Randell, Frieda Inescort, Cathy Downs, El Brendel, Jack Mulhall, Frank Jenks. Bizarre blend of CREATURE FROM THE BLACK LA-

GOON and THE SEARCH FOR BRIDEY MURPHY. Evil hypnotist uses mesmerized assistant to call back the murderous ghost of the sea creature of which she is a reincarnation. Slow and preposterous but effectively moody, with one of Paul Blaisdell's more memorable monsters, which he also plays. Really odd cast. Remade as CREATURE OF DESTRUCTION.

She Cried Murder (1973) **C-73m. TVM** D: Herschel Daugherty. Telly Savalas, Lynda Day George, Mike Farrell, Kate Reid, Jeff Toner, Stu Gillard. Young model witnesses subway murder, finds herself in a bind when she recognizes one of the two police inspectors answering her phone call as the murderer. Nonexistent as psychological drama; forgettable as a chase thriller. Below average.

She Dances Alone (1981-U.S.-Austrian) **C-87m. ***** D: Robert Dornhelm. Kyra Nijinsky, Bud Cort, Patrick Dupond, Sauncey Le Sueur, Max von Sydow. Engrossing blend of reality and fiction, with Cort a director attempting to make a documentary about the late, legendary dancer Vaslav Nijinsky, starring Nijinsky's plump, aging, single-minded daughter Kyra. Her overwhelming presence dominates this strikingly unusual film. Von Sydow appears as himself, and that's his voice reading Nijinsky's diary.

She Demons (1958) **80m. BOMB** D: Richard E. Cunha. Irish McCalla, Tod Griffin, Victor Sen Yung, Rudolph Anders, Gene Roth. Three men and sexy, spoiled McCalla are stranded on an island inhabited by Nazi criminals, a mad scientist, and the title creatures. Too boring to be funny; even McCalla's request to "give me some privacy while I undress" doesn't help.▼

She Devil (1957) **77m. BOMB** D: Kurt Neumann. Mari Blanchard, Jack Kelly, Albert Dekker, John Archer. Blanchard is injected with fruit fly serum in effort to cure her of TB; already rotten, she can now physically adapt to almost anything. Based on a story by Stanley G. Weinbaum.

She-Devil (1989) **C-99m. **** D: Susan Seidelman. Meryl Streep, Roseanne Barr, Ed Begley, Jr., Linda Hunt, Sylvia Miles, Elizabeth Peters, Bryan Larkin, A Martinez. When her slimeball husband walks out on her, unliberated housewife Barr sets out to methodically destroy his life—while creating one for herself. Extremely disappointing comedy offers no surprises and no irony; what it has is a magnificent comedic performance by Streep as the glamorous, self-absorbed romance novelist who lures Roseanne's husband away. She alone makes the film worth watching. Based on Fay Weldon's novel *The Life and Loves of a She-Devil*, which spawned a British miniseries.▼

She Done Him Wrong (1933) **66m. ******

D: Lowell Sherman. Mae West, Cary Grant, Gilbert Roland, Noah Beery, Rochelle Hudson, Rafaela Ottiano, Louise Beavers. West repeats her stage role of Diamond Lil in Gay 90s spoof. Grant is invited by Mae to come up and see her sometime—he does, fireworks result. Mae sings "Frankie and Johnny" and "Easy Rider" in her best film, which she coscripted from her Broadway hit.▼

Sheena (1984) **C-117m.** BOMB D: John Guillermin. Tanya Roberts, Ted Wass, Donovan Scott, Elizabeth of Toro. Tanya looks great as the queen of jungle jiggle, but Mother Nature forgot to endow her with a script. Supposed to be campy, but it's just plain awful.▼

Sheep Has Five Legs, The (1954-French) **95m.** *** D: Henri Verneuil. Fernandel, Delmont, Françoise Arnoul, Paulette Dubost. Fernandel's tour de force, playing an old wine-grower and each of his five sons who have gathered together for a family reunion.▼

Sheepman, The (1958) **C-85m.** *** D: George Marshall. Glenn Ford, Shirley MacLaine, Leslie Nielsen, Mickey Shaughnessy, Edgar Buchanan. Modest, entertaining comedy-Western with Ford battling Nielsen for sheep herds and MacLaine, though not always in that order. Shaughnessy is typically amusing. Written by genre vets William Bowers and James Edward Grant.

She Gets Her Man (1945) **65m.** *** D: Erle C. Kenton. Joan Davis, Leon Errol, William Gargan, Vivian Austin, Russell Hicks, Donald MacBride. Hilarious slapstick whodunit with daughter of legendary female police chief hired to stop crime wave in city. Davis and Errol make marvelous duo in this fast-moving farce.

She Gods of Shark Reef (1956) **C-63m.** BOMB D: Roger Corman. Bill Cord, Don Durant, Lisa Montell, Carol Lindsay, Jeanne Gerson. Location filming in Hawaii does nothing for this confusing tale of brothers Cord and Durant shipwrecked on an isolated isle inhabited only by women.▼

✓ **Sheik, The** (1921) **80m.** *** D: George Melford. Rudolph Valentino, Agnes Ayres, Adolphe Menjou, Walter Long, Lucien Littlefield, George Waggner. Ayres, a "civilized" woman, falls completely under the spell of desert chieftain Valentino. The silent film that helped create the Valentino legend is hokey and campy, but still entertaining . . . and it's easy to see why women went crazy for the Latin star. Racist/imperialist angle of the story is equally fascinating. Followed by SON OF THE SHEIK.

Sheila Levine Is Dead and Living in New York (1975) **C-113m.** BOMB D: Sidney J. Furie. Jeannie Berlin, Roy Scheider, Rebecca Dianna Smith, Janet Brandt, Sid Melton. Dead is right. Gail

Parent's sardonically funny novel about a Jewish American Princess trying to make good in N.Y.C. becomes an unbelievably bad movie, that just goes on and on.

She Knows Too Much (1989) **C-100m. TVM** D: Paul Lynch. Meredith Baxter Birney, Robert Urich, John Bennett Perry, Erik Estrada, Lawrence Pressman. Lady cat burglar comes out of prison to help a bungling undercover agent investigate a number of Washington murders. Pilot to a prospective series. Average.

She Learned About Sailors (1934) **76m.** *½ D: George Marshall. Lew Ayres, Alice Faye, Harry Green, Frank Mitchell, Jack Durant. Silly romantic comedy with complications delaying inevitable final clinch between sailor Ayres and cabaret singer Faye. Much footage devoted to the violent comedy of Mitchell and Durant.

She Lives! (1973) **C-74m. TVM** D: Stuart Hagmann. Desi Arnaz, Jr., Season Hubley, Anthony Zerbe, Michael Margotta, Jack Soo. Young college couple coping with news that she's contracted terminal disease; inspirational love affair ensues. Too-obvious spinoff of LOVE STORY. Average.

She'll Be Sweet SEE: **Magee and the Lady**

Shell Game (1975) **C-78m. TVM** D: Glenn Jordan, John Davidson, Tommy Atkins, Marie O'Brien, Robert Sampson, Signe Hasso, Jack Kehoe. Cross breed the old Robin Hood story with THE STING and you get a saga of a resourceful ex-con out to fleece the crooked head of a charity fund. Below average.

She'll Have to Go (1962-British) **90m.** **½ D: Robert Asher. Bob Monkhouse, Alfred Marks, Hattie Jacques, Anna Karina, Dennis Lotis. Broad farce about two brothers who compete to win the family inheritance left to attractive Corsican cousin (Karina).

Shell Seekers, The (1989-U.S.-British) **C-100m. TVM** D: Waris Hussein. Angela Lansbury, Sam Wanamaker, Christopher Bowen, Michael Gough, Patricia Hodge, Sophie Ward, Denis Quilley, Irene Worth. Lansbury plays a starchy widow battling for independence from her grown-up children following a heart attack in this sudsy adaptation (by playwright John Pielmeier) of Rosamunde Pilcher's novel. Shorn up by a sturdy cast of Britons. Average.

She Loves Me Not (1934) **83m.** *** D: Elliott Nugent. Bing Crosby, Miriam Hopkins, Kitty Carlisle, Lynne Overman, Henry Stephenson, George Barbier, Warren Hymer. Hopkins is ebullient (and hilarious) as a nightclub performer running from murder scene who hides out with college man Crosby in his Princeton dorm. Gets funnier as it goes along, and introduces "Love in Bloom" to boot. Based on Howard Lindsay's play. Remade as TRUE TO

THE ARMY and HOW TO BE VERY, VERY POPULAR.

She Married Her Boss (1935) 90m. **½ D: Gregory La Cava. Claudette Colbert, Melvyn Douglas, Edith Fellows, Michael Bartlett, Raymond Walburn, Jean Dixon. That's what she did, and nothing much happens until tipsy butler Walburn staggers in. Good stars with fair script by usually reliable Sidney Buchman.

✓ **Shenandoah** (1965) C-105m. *** D: Andrew V. McLaglen. James Stewart, Doug McClure, Glenn Corbett, Patrick Wayne, Rosemary Forsyth, Katharine Ross, Tim McIntire, Paul Fix, Denver Pyle, George Kennedy, James Best, Harry Carey, Jr., Dabbs Greer, Strother Martin. Rousing, well-acted saga of Virginia widower indifferent to War between the States until his family is involved. Sentimental drama captures heartbreak of America's Civil War. Basis for later Broadway musical. Ross's film debut.▼

Shenanigans SEE: **Great Bank Hoax, The**▼

Shepherd of the Hills (1941) C-98m. **½ D: Henry Hathaway. John Wayne, Betty Field, Harry Carey, Beulah Bondi, James Barton, Samuel S. Hinds, Marjorie Main, Ward Bond. Uneven film adaptation of Harold Bell Wright story of emotional flare-up between Ozark natives and outsiders trying to buy land. Good performances, beautifully filmed in Technicolor by Charles Lang.

She Played With Fire (1958-British) 95m. ** D: Sidney Gilliat. Jack Hawkins, Arlene Dahl, Dennis Price, Violet Farebrother, Ian Hunter, Christopher Lee. OK drama of Hawkins, insurance investigator, becoming involved with Dahl, an arsonist.

Sheriff, The (1971) C-73m. TVM D: David Lowell Rich. Ossie Davis, Kaz Garas, Kyle Johnson, Ruby Dee, Moses Gunn, Brenda Sykes, Lynda Day (George), John Marley, Ross Martin. Unimaginative title obscures solid drama dealing with controversial rape case that tears California town apart. Strong performances, uneven script by Arnold Perl; story's resolution only major liability. Average.

Sheriff of Fractured Jaw, The (1959-British) C-103m. **½ D: Raoul Walsh. Kenneth More, Jayne Mansfield, Henry Hull, William Campbell, Bruce Cabot, Robert Morley. Innocuous Western spoof with Englishman More handed job of sheriff in war-torn town, which he handles surprisingly well.▼

Sherlock Holmes In 1939, by some genius of casting, Basil Rathbone and Nigel Bruce were signed to play Sherlock Holmes and Dr. Watson in an adaptation of Sir Arthur Conan Doyle's HOUND OF THE BASKERVILLES; its immediate success prompted a follow-up, THE ADVEN-TURES OF SHERLOCK HOLMES, that same year. These were beautiful, atmospheric productions, faithful to Doyle's stories. Three years later, the series resumed with SHERLOCK HOLMES AND THE VOICE OF TERROR, updating the Doyle tales to have Holmes battling the Nazis. The twelve "modern" films never captured the flavor of the initial two (THE SCARLET CLAW came closest), but they were always worth seeing for the performances of the two stars: Rathbone—smooth, cunning, seldom caught by surprise; and Bruce—talkative, bumbling, never close to understanding the situation at hand. Mary Gordon made token appearances as Holmes' landlady Mrs. Hudson, and Dennis Hoey appeared in several films as Scotland Yard Inspector Lestrade, who always managed to get in the way. Holmes was at his best battling wits with Pofessor Moriarty, played in various episodes by George Zucco and Henry Daniell. Every episode ended with a stirring ode by Holmes to the glory of England, America, Canada, or some comparable topic, in keeping with the wartime flag-waving nature of Hollywood films. Seldom faithful to Doyle, later episodes like DRESSED TO KILL wearing thin, dialogue often awkward (S. H. IN WASHINGTON, for example), the Sherlock Holmes series relied on Rathbone and Bruce for enjoyment, and they never failed. Since that time there have been numerous Sherlock Holmes films—a plethora of them in recent years—but no attempts to launch another continuing series. The one earlier series, in 1930s England with Arthur Wontner, was never widely seen in the U.S.

Sherlock Holmes (1932) 68m. **½ D: William K. Howard. Clive Brook, Ernest Torrence, Miriam Jordan, Alan Mowbray, Herbert Mundin, Reginald Owen. Genteel, stylish approach to Holmes, set in modern-day London. Yields pleasing but subdued results. Torrence is a most enjoyable Moriarty.

Sherlock Holmes and the Masks of Death (1984-British) C-75m. TVM D: Roy Ward Baker. Peter Cushing, John Mills, Gordon Jackson, Anton Diffring, Ray Milland, Anne Baxter, Susan Penhaligon, Jenny Laird. This adventure of Holmes (Cushing) and Watson (Mills) in 1913 involves mysterious deaths in London and the kidnapping of a German prince. Cushing is one of the all-time greatest Sherlocks, though the film is a little flat. Longer version runs 90m. Original title: THE MASKS OF DEATH. Above average.

Sherlock Holmes and the Secret Weap- ✓ **on** (1942) 68m. D: Roy William Neill. Basil Rathbone, Nigel Bruce, Lionel Atwill, Kaaren Verne, William Post, Jr., Dennis

Hoey, Mary Gordon, Holmes Herbert. Also available in computer-colored version.▼

Sherlock Holmes and the Spider Woman (1944) 62m. D: Roy William Neill. Basil Rathbone, Nigel Bruce, Gale Sondergaard, Dennis Hoey, Mary Gordon, Arthur Hohl, Alec Craig. Also known as SPIDER WOMAN▼

Sherlock Holmes and the Voice of Terror (1942) 65m. D: John Rawlins. Basil Rathbone, Nigel Bruce, Evelyn Ankers, Reginald Denny, Thomas Gomez, Henry Daniell, Montagu Love.▼

Sherlock Holmes and the Woman in Green SEE: **Woman in Green, The**▼

Sherlock Holmes Faces Death (1943) 68m. D: Roy William Neill. Basil Rathbone, Nigel Bruce, Hillary Brooke, Milburn Stone, Arthur Margetson, Halliwell Hobbes, Dennis Hoey.▼

Sherlock Holmes in New York (1976) C-100m. TVM D: Boris Sagal. Roger Moore, John Huston, Patrick Macnee, Gig Young, Charlotte Rampling, David Huddleston, Signe Hasso, Leon Ames, Jackie Coogan. Stylish Holmes original by Alvin Sapinsley that has the sleuth rushing to America after learning that Moriarty has imperiled the world's gold supply and is threatening Holmes' long-time love, Irene Adler. Period valentine for the Baker Street Irregulars and others who seek just plain entertainment. Above average.

Sherlock Holmes in Washington (1943) 71m. D: Roy William Neill. Basil Rathbone, Nigel Bruce, Marjorie Lord, Henry Daniell, George Zucco, John Archer, Gavin Muir.▼

Sherlock, Jr. (1924) 45m. **** D: Buster Keaton. Buster Keaton, Kathryn McGuire, Ward Crane, Joseph Keaton, Erwin Connolly, Horace Morgan. Keaton reached his technical and artistic pinnacle with this brilliant and hilarious story of a hapless projectionist who walks right into the screen and takes part in the imaginary detective drama unfolding. Sublime study of film and fantasy; five reels of unadulterated joy which has undoubtedly influenced countless filmmakers such as Woody Allen, Jacques Rivette, even Bunuel.

Sherman's March (1986) C-155m. **** D: Ross McElwee. Totally unique documentary odyssey, as romantic sadsack McElwee retraces the title Civil War trek while simultaneously examining the mystique of Southern womanhood. Overlong by a half hour, but the flesh-and-blood subjects end up getting to you the way people in real life do; CRIMES OF THE HEART suffers terribly by comparison. Hilarious subplot involving Burt Reynolds.▼

She's a Soldier Too (1944) 67m. ** D: William Castle. Beulah Bondi, Lloyd Bridges, Nina Foch, Percy Kilbride, Shelley Winters, Ida Moore. OK little B film with cab-driver Bondi helping out soldier Bridges.

She's a Sweetheart (1944) 69m. *½ D: Del Lord. Larry Parks, Jane Frazee, Jane Darwell, Nina Foch, Ross Hunter, Carole Mathews. Musical programmer with G.I. Parks doubting the quality of vocalist Frazee's affection for him.

She's Back on Broadway (1953) C-95m. **½ D: Gordon Douglas. Virginia Mayo, Steve Cochran, Gene Nelson, Frank Lovejoy, Patrice Wymore. Fading Hollywood star returns to Broadway, finds dealing with director Cochran her biggest challenge. Good cast in slick but predictable musical drama.

She's Dressed to Kill (1979) C-100m. TVM D: Gus Trikonis. Eleanor Parker, Jessica Walter, John Rubinstein, Connie Sellecca, Jim McMullen, Clive Revill, Corinne Calvet, Joanna Cassidy, Peter Horton. Who's bumping off the high-fashion models who've gathered to help a once-renowned designer stage a gala comeback in her isolated mountaintop retreat? Notable, if at all, for the wonderfully outré Parker send-up of Tallulah Bankhead. Retitled SOMEONE'S KILLING THE WORLD'S GREATEST MODELS. Average.▼

She's Gotta Have It (1986) C/B&W-84m. *** D: Spike Lee. Tracy Camilla Johns, Tommy Redmond Hicks, John Canada Terrell, Spike Lee, Raye Dowell, Bill Lee. Breezy, funky film about a sexy, independent black woman and the three "macho" men who compete for her undivided attention. The acting is far from smooth, but the film's streetwise charm compensates. Writer-director Lee also appears as the iconoclastic Mars; his father Bill Lee wrote the music score. One charming sequence is filmed in color. ▼

She's Having a Baby (1988) C-106m. **½ D: John Hughes. Kevin Bacon, Elizabeth McGovern, Alec Baldwin, Isabel Lorca, William Windom, Cathryn Damon, Holland Taylor, James Ray, Dennis Dugan, John Ashton, Edie McClurg, Paul Gleason. Trials and tribulations of a young couple as they embark on marriage, domestic life, and impending parenthood, as told by the young husband, who feels trapped from the start and questions the meaning of it all. Likable enough comedy-drama grows monotonous after a while; the stars are very appealing, however.▼

She's in the Army Now (1981) C-100m. TVM D: Hy Averback. Kathleen Quinlan, Jamie Lee Curtis, Susan Blanchard, Melanie Griffith, Julie Carmen, Janet MacLachlan, Dale Robinette, Robert Peirce, Damita Jo Freeman. Pilot in the PRIVATE BENJAMIN mold about the comic rigors and romantic run-ins of five young women recruits during basic training. Average.▼

She's Out of Control (1989) **C-95m.** *½ D: Stan Dragoti. Tony Danza, Catherine Hicks, Wallace Shawn, Dick O'Neill, Ami Dolenz, Laura Mooney, Derek McGrath, Dana Ashbrook. Superficial expanded sitcom with Danza offering a one-note performance as a widower suffering anxiety pangs over the budding sexuality of daughter Dolenz (whose real-life dad is ex-Monkee Micky). This one seems as if it was spit out of a computer.▼

She's Working Her Way Through College (1952) **C-101m.** **½ D: H. Bruce Humberstone. Virginia Mayo, Ronald Reagan, Gene Nelson, Don Defore, Phyllis Thaxter, Patrice Wymore, Roland Winters. Reworking of THE MALE ANIMAL diminishes the role of the professor (played by Reagan), showcasing Mayo instead, as a burlesque star who tries to bury her past and pursue a college education. Pleasant but minor musical.

She Waits (1971) **C-74m. TVM** D: Delbert Mann. Patty Duke, David McCallum, Lew Ayres, Beulah Bondi, Dorothy McGuire, James Callahan, Nelson Olmstead. Straightforward but ultimately boring thriller featuring Duke as unbalanced young bride possessed by spirit of husband's first wife. Game attempt at hypo-ing story via direction, but you've seen this one before. Average.▼

She Was Marked for Murder (1988) **C-100m. TVM** D: Charles Thomson. Stefanie Powers, Lloyd Bridges, Hunt Block, Debrah Farentino, Polly Bergen. High-powered, recently widowed publisher impulsively marries a younger man after a whirlwind courtship—and discovers he's too good to be true, in this tepid suspense drama. Average.

She Went to the Races (1945) **86m.** ** D: Willis Goldbeck. James Craig, Frances Gifford, Ava Gardner, Edmund Gwenn, Sig Ruman, Reginald Owen. Gifford has developed scientific system for beating the horses, but falls in love with horsetrainer; mild comedy.

She-Wolf of London (1946) **61m.** ** D: Jean Yarbrough. Don Porter, June Lockhart, Sara Haden, Jan Wiley, Lloyd Corrigan. Low-grade thriller with nary a werewolf in sight, though killer tries to convince confused Lockhart she is one.

She Wore a Yellow Ribbon (1949) **C-103m.** ***½ D: John Ford. John Wayne, Joanne Dru, John Agar, Ben Johnson, Harry Carey, Jr., Victor McLaglen, Mildred Natwick, George O'Brien. Director Ford's stock company in fine form. Wayne excellent as cavalry officer about to retire, unwilling to walk out on impending war with Indians. Beautifully filmed in color by Oscar-winning Winton C. Hoch, but a bit top-heavy with climaxes. Second of

Ford's cavalry trilogy; followed by RIO GRANDE.▼

She Wouldn't Say Yes (1945) **87m.** **½ D: Alexander Hall. Rosalind Russell, Lee Bowman, Adele Jergens, Charles Winninger, Harry Davenport, Sara Haden, Percy Kilbride. Psychiatrist Russell tests theories on Bowman but finds herself involved with him romantically, too; predictable but amusing comedy.

She Wrote the Book (1946) **72m.** ** D: Charles Lamont. Joan Davis, Jack Oakie, Mischa Auer, Kirby Grant, John Litel, Jacqueline de Wit, Gloria Stuart. OK comedy about prim professor Davis posing as author of torrid best-seller. Fun for Davis fans, but not one of her best vehicles.

Shield for Murder (1954) **80m.** **½ D: Edmond O'Brien, Howard Koch. Edmond O'Brien, John Agar, Mara English, Carolyn Jones. Tidy, tough yarn of crooked detective involved in theft-murder, trying to keep his loot and avoid capture.

Shillingbury Blowers, The (1980-British) **C-82m.** *½ D: Val Guest. Trevor Howard, Robin Nedwell, Diane Keen, Jack Douglas, Sam Kydd, John LeMesurier. Dated trifle about cantankerous Howard and cronies resisting attempts by young Nedwell to improve the band in an Olde English village.

Shimmering Light (1978-Australian) **C-85m. TVM** D: Don Chaffey. Beau Bridges, Lloyd Bridges, Victoria Shaw, John Meillon, Ingrid Mason, Wendy Playfair. American dropout chucks a job with his business tycoon father to pursue his passion for surfing and find the perfect wave Down Under. Average.

shinbone alley (1971) **C-86m.** **½ D: John D. Wilson, David Detiege. Voices of Eddie Bracken, Carol Channing, John Carradine, Alan Reed, Sr. Animated tale of archy and mehitabel is second-rate but tuneful, from Joe Darion musical based on Don Marquis characters.▼

Shine On, Harvest Moon (1944) **112m.** **½ D: David Butler. Ann Sheridan, Jack Carson, Dennis Morgan, Irene Manning, S. Z. Sakall, Marie Wilson, Step Brothers and Jack Norworth merely provide starting point for fairly entertaining musical. Finale filmed in color.

Shining, The (1980) **C-142m.** ** D: Stanley Kubrick. Jack Nicholson, Shelley Duvall, Danny Lloyd, Scatman Crothers, Barry Nelson, Joe Turkel, Anne Jackson. Intriguing but ineffectual adaptation of Stephen King's thriller about a man who becomes off-season caretaker at isolated resort hotel—and almost immediately begins to lose his mind. Nicholson goes off the wall so quickly there's no time to get involved in his plight. Some eerie scenes, to be sure, but the film goes on forever. Cut by Kubrick after premiering at 146m.▼

Shining Hour, The (1938) 80m. **½ D: Frank Borzage. Joan Crawford, Margaret Sullavan, Robert Young, Melvyn Douglas, Fay Bainter, Allyn Joslyn. Raging fire burns out all hatred and problems from tangled family in intelligent soap opera. Crawford and Sullavan are a most interesting contrast.

Shining Season, A (1979) C-100m. TVM D: Stuart Margolin. Timothy Bottoms, Allyn Ann McLerie, Rip Torn, Connie Forslund, Mason Adams. Inspired stricken-athlete story based on that of college track star John Baker who, despite a terminal illness, devoted his final year of life leading an underdog girl's track team to the championship. Above average.▼

Shining Star (1975) C-100m. *½ D: Sig Shore. Harvey Keitel, Ed Nelson, Cynthia Bostick, Bert Parks, Jimmy Boyd, Michael Dante. Low key yarn about mob-dominated recording company. Poor sound and photography. Saved—barely—by intriguing look behind the scenes of music business. Music by Earth, Wind and Fire. Originally titled THAT'S THE WAY OF THE WORLD.▼

Shining Victory (1941) 80m. **½ D: Irving Rapper. James Stephenson, Geraldine Fitzgerald, Donald Crisp, Barbara O'Neil, Montagu Love, Sig Ruman. Handsome production of A. J. Cronin play about ultradedicated research psychologist who can't even see that his new assistant is in love with him. Very watchable but not terribly inspiring. Publicity from the time insists that Bette Davis makes a walk-on appearance as a nurse; just try to find her!

Ship Ahoy (1942) 95m. **½ D: Edward Buzzell. Eleanor Powell, Red Skelton, Virginia O'Brien, Bert Lahr, John Emery, Tommy Dorsey Orch. with Frank Sinatra and Jo Stafford. Nonsensical plot of Skelton thinking U.S. agent is working for Axis; shipboard yarn has some salty dancing and singing, good Dorsey numbers featuring drummer Buddy Rich.

Shipmates Forever (1935) 124m. **½ D: Frank Borzage. Dick Powell, Ruby Keeler, Lewis Stone, Ross Alexander, Eddie Acuff, Dick Foran, John Arledge. Cocky Powell takes navy lightly until pressed into action. Usual plot, with songs and dances with Keeler. Reissued at 108m.

Ship of Fools (1965) 149m. **** D: Stanley Kramer. Vivien Leigh, Oskar Werner, Simone Signoret, Jose Ferrer, Lee Marvin, Jose Greco, George Segal, Elizabeth Ashley, Michael Dunn, Charles Korvin, Lilia Skala. GRAND HOTEL at sea in pre-WW2 days. Superb cast including Leigh, in her last film, as disillusioned divorcée, Werner and Signoret as illicit lovers, Marvin as punchy baseball player. Penetrating drama, when not a soaper. Script by Abby Mann from Katherine Anne Porter's novel; won Oscars for Cinematography (Ernest Laszlo) and Art Direction.▼

Ships With Wings (1942-British) 89m. *** D: Sergei Nolbandov. John Clements, Ann Todd, Leslie Banks, Hugh Williams, Michael Wilding, Michael Rennie, Cecil Parker. Sterling, patriotic WW2 movie showing British soldiers at their finest, despite momentary lapses of discipline.

Ship That Died of Shame, The (1955-British) 91m. *** D: Basil Dearden. Richard Attenborough, George Baker, Bill Owen, Virginia McKenna, Roland Culver, Bernard Lee, Ralph Truman. Crew of British gunboat reteam after WW2 and use the same vessel for smuggling purposes, until "it" begins to rebel at their increasingly grimy exploits. Fine cast in offbeat drama. Retitled PT RAIDERS and cut to 78m.

Ship Was Loaded, The (1957-British) 81m. ** D: Val Guest. David Tomlinson, Peggy Cummins, Alfie Bass, Ronald Shiner. Inconsequential zaniness involving impersonations and shenanigans in Her Majesty's Navy. Retitled: CARRY ON ADMIRAL.

Shiralee, The (1957-British) 99m. **½ D: Leslie Norman. Peter Finch, Elizabeth Sellars, Dana Wilson, Rosemary Harrys, Tessie O'Shea, Sidney James, George Rose. Rough-hewn Australian swagman takes daughter away from unfaithful wife to accompany him on his wanderings. Moving portrayal of their relationship compensates for diffuse, episodic nature of film. On-location scenery helps, too. Remade as a TV miniseries.

Shirley Valentine (1989-U.S.-British) C-108m. *** D: Lewis Gilbert. Pauline Collins, Tom Conti, Alison Steadman, Julia McKenzie, Joanna Lumley, Bernard Hill, Sylvia Syms. Collins repeats her London and Broadway stage triumphs in the role of a saucy, middle-aged, married woman who feels that life has passed her by—until she gets the opportunity to travel to Greece, sans husband. Collins' endearing performance (much of it talking directly to the audience) makes this a must, smoothing over lulls in Willy Russell's adaptation of his own stage play. The same team made EDUCATING RITA.▼

Shirts/Skins (1973) C-74m. TVM D: William Graham. Bill Bixby, Doug McClure, Leonard Frey, Rene Auberjonois, McLean Stevenson, Robert Walden, Loretta Swit, Audrey Christie. Six young professionals cook up contest to settle basketball argument which snowballs, due to day-to-day pressure and group's own inter-rivalries, into near-tragic situation. Excellent performances by well-picked cast make film believable. Above average.

Shivers SEE: **They Came From Within▼**
Shoah (1985-French) **C-503m.** **** D: Claude Lanzmann. Remarkable documentary, shown in two parts, each lasting about four and a half hours, chronicling the memories of those who lived through the Holocaust—both victims and oppressors. Lanzmann's persistent interview approach hammers away at details in order to intensify our cumulative response . . . and we begin to see exactly how the unthinkable became a reality. A unique and eloquent film. ▼
Shock (1946) **70m.** *½ D: Alfred L. Werker. Vincent Price, Lynn Bari, Frank Latimore, Anabel Shaw, Michael Dunne, Reed Hadley. Killers plan elaborate method of silencing girl who witnessed one of their hits. Eh.▼
Shock (1979) SEE: **Beyond the Door II▼**
Shock Corridor (1963) **101m.** *** D: Samuel Fuller. Peter Breck, Constance Towers, Gene Evans, James Best, Hari Rhodes. Journalist Breck gets admitted to mental institution to unmask murderer, but soon goes crazy himself. Powerful melodrama with raw, emotional impact. Fuller also produced and wrote the script; imaginative photography by Stanley Cortez. Original theatrical prints had one dream sequence in color.▼
Shocking Miss Pilgrim, The (1947) **C-85m.** ** D: George Seaton. Betty Grable, Dick Haymes, Anne Revere, Allyn Joslyn, Gene Lockhart, Elizabeth Patterson. Labored story of 1870s Boston woman in business world. Fair Gershwin score includes "For You, For Me, For Evermore."
Shockproof (1949) **79m.** *** D: Douglas Sirk. Cornel Wilde, Patricia Knight, John Baragrey, Esther Minciotti, Howard St. John. Parole officer Wilde is lured into love affair with parolee Knight which threatens to destroy him. Stylish *film noir*, cowritten by Samuel Fuller, which unfortunately cops out at the end.
Shock to the System, A (1990) **C-91m.** **½ D: Jan Egleson. Michael Caine, Elizabeth McGovern, Peter Riegert, Swoosie Kurtz, Will Patton, Jenny Wright, John McMartin, Barbara Baxley. Caine adds luster to this so-so black comedy as a harried ad executive who discovers how easy it is to kill anyone in his way after he's passed over for a promotion. Has its moments as a topical look at greed, corporate-style, but could have been far more pointed and involving.▼
Shocktrauma (1982-Canadian) **C-100m.** TVM D: Eric Till. William Conrad, Scott Hylands, Linda Sorensen, Lawrence Dane, Kerrie Keane, Beau Starr, Ken Pogue, Chris Wiggins. Standard medical drama, hidden in the story of Baltimore's Dr. R. Adams Cowley, shocktrauma pioneer. Average.

Shock Treatment (1964) **94m.** ** D: Denis Sanders. Stuart Whitman, Carol Lynley, Roddy McDowall, Lauren Bacall, Olive Deering, Ossie Davis, Donald Buka, Bert Freed, Douglass Dumbrille. Out-of-work actor (Whitman) goes undercover at state mental asylum to discover whereabouts of murderer McDowall's supposed million-dollar stash. Odd, unsatisfying melodrama.
Shock Treatment (1981) **C-94m.** *½ D: Jim Sharman. Jessica Harper, Cliff De Young, Richard O'Brien, Patricia Quinn, Charles Gray, Ruby Wax, Nell Campbell. Dreary, disappointing spin-off from THE ROCKY HORROR PICTURE SHOW, with same director and many cast members. Brad and Janet (played here by De Young and Harper) find themselves contestants (or more appropriately, prisoners) on a TV game show—spoofed far more successfully in MELVIN AND HOWARD.▼
Shock Waves (1977) **C-86m.** ** D: Ken Wiederhorn. Peter Cushing, Brooke Adams, John Carradine, Fred Buch, Jack Davidson, Luke Halpin. Former SS officer and scientist Cushing has created undrownable Nazi androids to operate the Third Reich's submarines. Oddball low-budgeter, also known as DEATH CORPS.▼
Shoeshine (1946-Italian) **93m.** **** D: Vittorio De Sica. Rinaldo Smerdoni, Franco Interlenghi, Anniello Mele, Bruno Ortensi, Pacifico Astrologo. A brilliant, haunting neorealist drama about two youngsters struggling to survive in war-scarred Italy; they become involved with black marketeering and are sent to reform school. This deservedly won a special Oscar—before Best Foreign Film prizes were awarded.▼
Shoes of the Fisherman, The (1968) **C-157m.** ** D: Michael Anderson. Anthony Quinn, Laurence Olivier, Oskar Werner, David Janssen, Vittorio De Sica, Leo McKern, John Gielgud, Barbara Jefford. Pope Quinn, a Russian who spent twenty years as a political prisoner in Siberia, tries to fend off atomic war plus starvation in Red China for half a film while correspondent Janssen tries to patch up his petty marital problems the rest of the time. Fine cast is wasted in slap-dash film version of Morris L. West's best-seller, dully directed by Anderson.▼
Shogun (1981) **C-125m.** TVM D: Jerry London. Richard Chamberlain, Toshiro Mifune, Yoko Shimada, Frankie Sakai, Yuri Meguro, John Rhys-Davies, Michael Hordern. Orson Welles (narrator). Colorful, Emmy-winning saga from James Clavell's best-seller about shipwrecked British sailor in feudal Japan, taken under wing of powerful warlord to become the first Western samurai warrior. The flavor of the 10-hour miniseries from which this was chopped down (at least five subplots bit the dust

and subtitles were added) remains intact, although it often plays like a movie trailer. (This version, with graphic violence and nudity added, initially was edited specifically for homevideo.) Above average.▼

Shogun Assassin (1981-Japanese-U.S.) **C-86m.** ***½ D: Kenji Misumi, Robert Houston. Tomisaburo Wakayama, Masahiro Tomikawa, voices of Lamont Johnson, Marshall Efron. Coherent film brilliantly edited out of two different features in Japanese *Sword of Vengeance* series about samurai warrior who travels across countryside pushing his young son in a baby cart, stopping only to get involved in inordinate amounts of combat. Americanized version, narrated by child, is absolutely stunning visual ballet of violence and bloodletting. Sort of a sequel to LIGHTNING SWORDS OF DEATH, in that it was edited from its sequel.▼

Shoot (1976-Canadian) **C-98m.** BOMB D: Harvey Hart. Cliff Robertson, Ernest Borgnine, Henry Silva, James Blendick, Larry Reynolds, Les Carlson, Kate Reid, Helen Shaver. There's a faint echo of DELIVERANCE in this ludicrous tale of gun-happy pals who allow the shooting of one hunter to escalate into warfare. Supposedly anti-gun, the film is also apparently anti-entertainment.▼

Shootdown (1988) **C-100m.** TVM D: Michael Pressman. Angela Lansbury, George Coe, Kyle Secor, Molly Hagan, Jennifer Savidge, John Cullum. After the infamous downing of Korean Air Lines flight 007 in 1983, the mother of one of the victims determines to learn the truth surrounding the event. Lansbury is good as always. Same incident was later dramatized in another TV movie, TAILSPIN, which took an entirely different perspective. Average.

Shooter (1988) **C-100m.** TVM D: Gary Nelson. Jeffrey Nordling, Alan Ruck, Noble Willingham, Carol Huston, Rosalind Chao, Helen Hunt, Steven Ford, Nick Cassavetes, Grace Zabriskie. This look at combat photographers in Vietnam is all talk, no action, even though it was created by real-life Pulitzer Prize-winning Vietnam cameraman David Hume Kennerly. A busted series pilot. Average.

Shoot First (1953-British) **88m.** **½ D: Robert Parrish. Joel McCrea, Evelyn Keyes, Herbert Lom, Marius Goring. Capable cast helps this routine espionage tale. Originally titled ROUGH SHOOT.

Shooting, The (1967) **C-82m.** *** D: Monte Hellman. Millie Perkins, Jack Nicholson, Will Hutchins, Warren Oates. Cryptic, unconventional Western with deceptively familiar revenge "story." Ultimately powerful film, with offbeat performance by Nicholson as a hired gun . . . and an incredible, unexpected finale. Filmed simultaneously with RIDE IN THE WHIRLWIND.▼

Shooting High (1940) **65m.** *½ D: Alfred E. Green. Jane Withers, Gene Autry, Marjorie Weaver, Robert Lowery, Jack Carson. Overhelpful Withers, aided by cowboy Autry, tries to restore peaceful times to her rambunctious family.

Shooting Party, The (1984-British) **C-108m.** ***½ D: Alan Bridges. James Mason, Dorothy Tutin, Edward Fox, Cheryl Campbell, John Gielgud, Gordon Jackson, Aharon Ipale, Rupert Frazer, Robert Hardy, Judi Bowker. Rewarding film about varied personalities, intrigues, and conflicts that crisscross during weekend shooting party in 1913. Mason, the weekend's host, presides over all with grace, wit, and understanding. A telling look at class structure and class consciousness; screenplay by Julian Bond from a novel by Isabel Colegate.

▼

Shooting Stars (1983) **C-100m.** TVM D: Richard Lang. Billy Dee Williams, Parker Stevenson, Robert Webber, Efrem Zimbalist, Jr., Edie Adams, Herb Edelman, Kathleen Lloyd, Denny Miller. Amiable pilot to a prospective series about a pair of TV private eyes who, after being fired from their show by a jealous costar, set up their own real-life P.I. shop. Average.

Shootist, The (1976) **C-99m.** ***½ D: Don Siegel. John Wayne, Lauren Bacall, Ron Howard, James Stewart, Richard Boone, Hugh O'Brian, Harry Morgan, Rick Lenz, John Carradine, Sheree North, Scatman Crothers. Intelligent story about a legendary gunfighter who learns he has cancer and tries to die in peace, but cannot escape his reputation. A fitting (and poignant) valedictory to Wayne's career. Miles Hood Swarthout and Scott Hale adapted Glendon Swarthout's novel.▼

Shoot Loud, Louder . . . I Don't Understand (1966-Italian) **C-100m.** ** D: Eduardo De Filippo. Marcello Mastroianni, Raquel Welch, Guido Alberti, Leopoldo Trieste. Surrealistic but flat film in which Mastroianni plays antique dealer whose life suddenly becomes very complex.▼

Shootout (1971) **C-95m.** ** D: Henry Hathaway. Gregory Peck, Pat Quinn, Robert F. Lyons, Susan Tyrrell, Jeff Corey, James Gregory, Rita Gam, Dawn Lyn. Same producer, director and screenwriter of TRUE GRIT in another Western about cowboy and little girl. Formula doesn't work; in spite of title, film has too much talk and not enough action.

Shoot Out at Medicine Bend (1957) **87m.** ** D: Richard L. Bare. Randolph Scott, James Craig, Angie Dickinson, Dani Crayne, James Garner, Gordon Jones. Fair studio Western features Scott as leader of group avenging death of brother at hands of Sioux

Indians and men who supplied faulty guns and ammunition.

Shootout in a One-Dog Town (1974) **C-78m. TVM** D: Burt Kennedy. Richard Crenna, Richard Egan, Stefanie Powers, Jack Elam, Arthur O'Connell, Michael Ansara, Michael Anderson Jr., Dub Taylor. Frontier banker Crenna is pitted against gangleader Egan and his boys out to steal $200,000 in the vault. Despite title and director, not a comedy; written by Larry Cohen. Average.

Shoot the Moon (1982) **C-123m. *** D:** Alan Parker. Albert Finney, Diane Keaton, Karen Allen, Peter Weller, Dana Hill, Viveka Davis, Tracey Gold, Tina Yothers, Leora Dana. Highly charged, emotional drama about the breakup of a marriage. The insights and emotional touchstones of Bo Goldman's script—and superlative acting—help make up for strange gaps of logic and credibility. We learn precious little about what makes the central characters tick; director Parker gives us picture-postcard views of Marin County, California instead.▼

Shoot the Piano Player (1962-French) **85m. **** D:** François Truffaut. Charles Aznavour, Marie Dubois, Nicole Berger, Michele Mercier. Aznavour is marvelous as antihero playing rundown Parisian cafe, pushed by ambitious girlfriend to resume once-prominent concert career but getting involved with gangsters instead.▼

Shoot the Sun Down (1981) **C-93m. *½** D: David Leeds. Margot Kidder, Geoffrey Lewis, Bo Brundin, A Martinez, Christopher Walken, Sacheen Littlefeather. Fine cast wasted in slow-moving, amateurish Western about strange group of people (including scalp hunter, gunslinging loner, indentured female servant, retired sea captain) thrown together in quest for gold. Filmed in 1976.▼

Shoot to Kill (1947) **64m. **½ D:** William Berke. Russell Wade, Edmund MacDonald, Vince Barnett, Susan Walters, Douglas Blackley, Nestor Paiva. Low-budget *film noir* thriller about a brilliant but crooked government prosecutor (MacDonald), his not-so-innocent secretary (Walters), an aggressive newspaperman (Wade), and a ruthless escaped convict (Blackley). Not bad of its type. ▼

Shoot to Kill (1988) **C-110m. **½ D:** Roger Spottiswoode. Sidney Poitier, Tom Berenger, Kirstie Alley, Clancy Brown, Richard Masur, Andrew Robinson, Kevin Scannell, Frederick Coffin. Big-city cop (Poitier) is forced to team up with stubborn mountain guide (Berenger) to go into the wilds of the Pacific Northwest in search of a hunting party being led by the guide's girlfriend (Alley)—and infiltrated by a ruthless killer whom Poitier is determined to capture. Slick but highly improbable tale strains credibility throughout, but keeps its grip thanks mostly to a riveting Poitier (his first starring role in ten years).▼

Shop Angel (1932) **66m. ** D:** E. Mason Hopper. Marion Shilling, Holmes Herbert, Anthony Bushell, Walter Byron, Dorothy Christy, Creighton Hale, Hank Mann. Static drama about pretty young department store buyer Shilling, whose ambitions expose her to lust, blackmail, and other assorted histrionics. ▼

Shop Around the Corner, The (1940) **97m. ***½ D:** Ernst Lubitsch. Margaret Sullavan, James Stewart, Frank Morgan, Joseph Schildkraut, Sara Haden, Felix Bressart. The ultimate in sheer charm, a graceful period comedy about coworkers in a Budapest notions shop who don't realize that they are lonelyhearts penpals. Later musicalized as IN THE GOOD OLD SUMMERTIME, then brought to Broadway as *She Loves Me.*▼

Shop on Main Street, The (1965-Czech) **128m. **** D:** Jan Kadar, Elmar Klos. Josef Kroner, Ida Kaminska, Han Slivkova, Frantisek Holly, Martin Gregor. Potent, poignant drama set in WW2 Czechoslovakia, where an old Jewish woman loses her small button shop, and depends on man who takes it over to shield her from further persecution. Oscar winner as Best Foreign Film. Originally titled THE SHOP ON HIGH STREET.▼

Shopworn (1932) **72m. ** D:** Nick Grinde. Barbara Stanwyck, Regis Toomey, ZaSu Pitts, Lucien Littlefield, Clara Blandick. Standard Depression soaper with Toomey's rich family rejecting working girl Stanwyck, who shows 'em all and becomes famous star.

Shopworn Angel, The (1938) **85m. *** D:** H. C. Potter. Margaret Sullavan, James Stewart, Walter Pidgeon, Hattie McDaniel, Sam Levene, Nat Pendleton. Stewart and Sullavan are always a fine pair, even in this fairly routine soaper. Naive soldier falls in love with loose-moraled actress, who gradually softens under his influence. Beautifully done, including Slavko Vorkapich's masterful opening WW1 montage. Remake of 1929 film with Gary Cooper and Nancy Carroll; filmed again as THAT KIND OF WOMAN.

Shore Leave (1925) **74m. **½ D:** John S. Robertson. Richard Barthelmess, Dorothy Mackaill, Ted McNamara, Nick Long, Marie Shotwell, Arthur Metcalf, Warren Cooke, Samuel Hinds. Appealing if sometimes slow-moving romantic comedy with Barthelmess at his best as reluctant seaman Bilge Smith; Mackaill is a dressmaker, approaching old-maidhood, who's out to make him captain of her schooner. Later musicalized as HIT THE DECK and FOLLOW THE FLEET.▼

Short Circuit (1986) **C-98m. **½ D:**

John Badham. Ally Sheedy, Steve Guttenberg, Fisher Stevens, G. W. Bailey, Austin Pendleton, Brian McNamara, voice of Tim Blaney. State-of-the-art robot develops a mind of its own and decides that it doesn't want to go "home" to weapons company from which it escaped. Sheedy is cute as the animal-lover who becomes protective of "No. 5," the equally cute robot. E. T. clone is good fodder for kids but too formula-bound for our taste. Followed by a sequel.▼

Short Circuit 2 (1988) **C-110m. ** D:** Kenneth Johnson. Fisher Stevens, Michael McKean, Cynthia Gibb, Jack Weston, Dee McCaffrey, David Hemblen, voice of Tim Blaney. Innocuous (but overlong) sequel has malaprop-prone Stevens and No. 5 (now called Johnny Five) out on their own, falling in with would-be toymaker McKean and bad-guy Weston. Okay for kids, with some chuckles for adults here and there.▼

Short Cut to Hell (1957) 87m. **½ D: James Cagney. Robert Ivers, Georgann Johnson, William Bishop, Murvyn Vye, Yvette Vickers, Roscoe Ates. Generally taut, if uninspired remake of Graham Greene's THIS GUN FOR HIRE, about killer reevaluating his situation. Unusual fling at directing by Cagney.

Short Eyes (1977) C-104m. ***½ D: Robert M. Young. Bruce Davison, Jose Perez, Nathan George, Don Blakely, Shawn Elliott, Curtis Mayfield, Freddy Fender. Raw, uncompromisingly powerful story of men in prison, from Miguel Pinero's highly acclaimed play. Utterly realistic film was shot at N.Y.C.'s now-shuttered Men's House of Detention, known as The Tombs. Title is prison slang for child molester (played by Davison). Scripted by Pinero, who also appears as GoGo. Retitled: SLAMMER.▼

Short Fuse SEE: **Good to Go**▼

Short Walk to Daylight (1972) **C-73m.** TVM D: Barry Shear. James Brolin, Don Mitchell, James McEachin, Abbey Lincoln, Brooke Bundy, Lazaro Perez. Violent earthquake derails early morning subway in Manhattan; passengers must grope their way to safety, experience every conceivable hardship. Script piles situation upon situation, strives too hard for documentary effects; otherwise, performances OK. Average.

Shotgun (1955) **C-81m. ** D: Lesley Selander. Sterling Hayden, Zachary Scott, Yvonne De Carlo, Guy Prescott, Angela Greene. Unremarkable Western with sheriff Hayden vs. culprit Scott; De Carlo is the half-breed girl they love.▼

Shot in the Dark, A (1964) **C-101m.** **** D: Blake Edwards. Peter Sellers, Elke Sommer, George Sanders, Herbert Lom, Tracy Reed, Burt Kwouk, Graham Stark, Andre Maranne, Turk Thrust (Bryan

Forbes). Second Inspector Clouseau comedy is far and away the funniest, with the great detective convinced gorgeous Sommer is innocent of murder despite all evidence to the contrary. Gaspingly hilarious farce never slows down for a second, with memorable scene in a nudist colony. Script by Edwards and William Peter Blatty; fine Henry Mancini score. Series debuts of Lom, Kwouk, Stark, and Maranne; last Clouseau film (excluding 1968's INSPECTOR CLOUSEAU, made by other hands) until THE RETURN OF THE PINK PANTHER in 1975.▼

Shout, The (1979-British) **C-87m.** **½ D: Jerzy Skolimowski. Alan Bates, Susannah York, John Hurt, Robert Stephens, Tim Curry. Well-filmed but obscure yarn about an off-his-nut wanderer who dominates the household of a young married couple. Title refers to his aboriginal ability to kill by *shouting*. Worth a look on a slow evening.▼

Shout at the Devil (1976-British) **C-119m.** **½ D: Peter R. Hunt. Lee Marvin, Roger Moore, Barbara Parkins, Ian Holm, Rene Kolldehoff. Plot-heavy action nonsense, set in Mozambique, about a poacher, his daughter and an expatriate Englishman who eventually set out to blow up a German battle cruiser at the outset of WW1. Occasionally fun but overlong. Original British running-time: 144m.▼

Show Boat (1936) 113m. *** D: James Whale. Irene Dunne, Allan Jones, Helen Morgan, Paul Robeson, Charles Winninger, Hattie McDaniel. Entertaining treatment of Jerome Kern-Oscar Hammerstein musical (filmed before in 1929) mixes music, sentiment, and melodrama, with enough great moments to make up for the rest: Robeson doing "Old Man River," Morgan singing her unforgettable "Bill," etc. Originally an Edna Ferber novel; Hammerstein also wrote the screenplay. Filmed again in 1951.▼

Show Boat (1951) C-107m. **½ D: George Sidney. Kathryn Grayson, Ava Gardner, Howard Keel, Joe E. Brown, Marge and Gower Champion, Agnes Moorehead, Robert Sterling, William Warfield. Colorful but empty remake of the Kern-Hammerstein musical of life on the Mississippi in 1900s. Songs: "Bill," "Can't Help Loving That Man," "Old Man River," "Make Believe."▼

Show Business (1944) 92m. **½ D: Edwin L. Marin. Eddie Cantor, Joan Davis, George Murphy, Nancy Kelly, Constance Moore. If you like Cantor or Davis you'll enjoy this vaudeville musical entirely supported by them; songs include "It Had To Be You." Followed by IF YOU KNEW SUSIE.▼

Showdown (1963) 79m. ** D: R. G. Springsteen. Audie Murphy, Kathleen

Crowley, Charles Drake, Harold Stone, Skip Homeier, Strother Martin, L.Q. Jones. Unremarkable Western with Murphy and Drake escaped convicts involved in a holdup.
Showdown (1973) **C-99m.** **½ D: George Seaton. Rock Hudson, Dean Martin, Susan Clark, Donald Moffat, John McLiam. Two friends in love with the same woman go their separate ways, until Hudson (now a sheriff) is forced to hunt down Martin (now a robber). Agreeable but unexceptional Western yarn was Seaton's final film.
Showdown at Abilene (1956) **C-80m.** ** D: Charles Haas. Jock Mahoney, Martha Hyer, Lyle Bettger, David Janssen, Grant Williams. Standard Western fare. Mahoney as sheriff returns from Civil War sick of bloodshed.
Showdown at Boot Hill (1958) **72m.** ** D: Gene Fowler, Jr. Charles Bronson, Fintan Meyler, Robert Hutton, John Carradine, Carole Mathews. Unpretentious Western of bounty killer Bronson trying to collect reward money.▼
Show of Force, A (1990) **C-93m.** ** D: Bruno Barretto. Amy Irving, Robert Duvall, Andy Garcia, Lou Diamond Phillips, Kevin Spacey, Joe Campanella, Erik Estrada, Priscilla Pointer, Hattie Winston. Oddly stagnant political thriller about Puerto Rico's 1978 version of Watergate. Irving plays a local TV reporter convinced that the F.B.I. set up and killed two political radicals to earn voting support for the current governor. Garcia's role is a glorified cameo; Phillips is surprisingly effective as a flamboyant villain.
Show People (1928) **82m.** ***½ D: King Vidor. Marion Davies, William Haines, Del Henderson, Paul Ralli, Harry Gribbon, Polly Moran. Delightful silent comedy about a girl from the sticks who tries to crash Hollywood—and succeeds, but not as she expected to. Davies' best movie vehicle confirms her comic talent, and offers a lively glimpse behind the scenes of moviemaking. Some amusing guest-star cameos include director Vidor, who plays himself in the closing scene.▼
Show Them No Mercy (1935) **76m.** *** D: George Marshall. Rochelle Hudson, Cesar Romero, Bruce Cabot, Edward Norris, Edward Brophy, Warren Hymer. Thugs kidnap a young couple and their baby, but don't count on the resourcefulness of the FBI. Solid gangster saga from the G-Man era, well cast, with an unforgettable burst of violence at the finish. Remade in a Western setting as RAWHIDE.
Shriek in the Night, A (1933) **66m.** **½ D: Albert Ray. Ginger Rogers, Lyle Talbot, Arthur Hoyt, Purnell Pratt, Harvey Clark. Ultra-cheap but interesting B-picture whodunit, reuniting Ginger and Lyle from THE THIRTEENTH GUEST as rival reporters

on a murderer's trail; starts with a bang and then simmers down.▼
Shriek of the Mutilated (1974) **C-92m.** BOMB D: Michael Findlay. Alan Brock, Jennifer Stock, Michael Harris, Tawn Ellis, Darcy Brown. Students hunt abominable snowman, but so-called monster turns out to be a decoy, covering up more grisly activities on remote island. Low-budget junk.▼
Shrike, The (1955) **88m.** **½ D: Jose Ferrer. June Allyson, Jose Ferrer, Joy Page, Ed Platt, Mary Bell. Allyson almost succeeds in change of pace title role, playing ultranag who has driven her theater director husband (Ferrer) into a nervous breakdown. Based on Joseph Kramm's play.
Shut My Big Mouth (1942) **71m.** ** D: Charles Barton. Joe E. Brown, Adele Mara, Victor Jory, Fritz Feld, Lloyd Bridges, Forrest Tucker, Pedro de Cordoba. Meek Joe goes West and innocently gets mixed up with gang of outlaws.
Shuttered Room, The (1966-British) **C-99m.** **½ D: David Greene. Gig Young, Carol Lynley, Oliver Reed, Flora Robson. Young couple inherit old house in New England, threatened by local toughs and unseen presence. Good cast deserves better material; even revelation is tame. Based on an H.P. Lovecraft story.
Shy People (1987) **C-118m.** **½ D: Andrei Konchalovsky. Jill Clayburgh, Barbara Hershey, Martha Plimpton, Mare Winningham, Merritt Butrick, John Philbin, Don Swayze, Pruitt Taylor Vince. N.Y.C. photojournalist Clayburgh ventures into the Louisiana bayous (dragging along rebellious daughter Plimpton and a totally inappropriate wardrobe) to research a *Cosmopolitan* article on a *very* distant branch of her family. Hodgepodge of a film is equal parts implausible, melodramatic, ridiculous—and fascinating. Recommended chiefly for Barbara Hershey's riveting performance (as the head of the backwoods clan), and for cinematographer Chris Menges' remarkable opening shot of Manhattan. ▼
Sicilian, The (1987) **C-115m.** BOMB D: Michael Cimino. Christopher Lambert, Terence Stamp, Barbara Sukowa, Giulia Boschi, Joss Ackland, John Turturro, Richard Bauer, Barry Miller, Aldo Ray. Militantly lugubrious bio of Salvatore Giuliano, who took on Church, State, and Mafia in an attempt to promote Sicily's secession from Italy in the late 1940s. Gore Vidal contributed to the screenplay, credited to Steve Shagan. The 146-minute director's cut (**) is available on cassette and actually seems shorter, thanks to more coherency and Sukowa's strengthened role. Neither version, though, can overcome two chief liabilities: Cimino's missing sense of humor and Lambert's laughably stone-faced performance. Title figure was previously the

[1042]

subject of Francesco Rosi's 1962 SALVA-
TORE GIULIANO.▼
Sicilian Clan, The (1969-French) **C-121m.**
*** D: Henri Verneuil. Jean Gabin, Alain
Delon, Lino Ventura, Irina Demick, Amedeo Nazzari, Sydney Chaplin. Gangland
family's plans for major jewel heist grow
increasingly complex; crime caper on grandiose scale, totally implausible but great
fun. Gabin is smooth head of clan, Delon a
young ambitious thief hired for the occasion.
Sid and Nancy (1986) **C-111m.** *** D:
Alex Cox. Gary Oldman, Chloe Webb,
Drew Schofield, David Hayman, Debby
Bishop, Tony London, Perry Benson, Gloria LeRoy. Harrowing look at the bizarre,
self-destructive, and curiously compelling
relationship between British punk rock
singer Sid Vicious (of The Sex Pistols) and
American groupie Nancy Spungen in the
1970s. Director Cox achieves a masterful
level of docu-realism, then laces it with
allegorical dream images, with striking
results. At the core of the film are two
remarkable performances, by Oldman and
Webb, who don't seem to be performing at
all: they *are* Sid and Nancy. A downer, to
be sure, but fascinating.▼
Siddhartha (1973) **C-95m.** **½ D: Conrad Rooks. Shashi Kapoor, Simi Garewal,
Romesh Shama, Pinchoo Kapoor, Zul
Vellani, Amrik Singh. Uneven version of
famous Hermann Hesse novel follows Indian as he leaves family to find more
exciting life. Too arty, but on-location
photography by Sven Nykvist (Ingmar Bergman's cinematographer) is often dazzling.
Side by Side (1988) **C-100m.** **TVM** D:
Jack Bender. Milton Berle, Sid Caesar,
Danny Thomas, Morey Amsterdam, Marjorie Lord, Georgann Johnson, Michael
Lembeck. Inspired teaming of three veteran comedians sparks this feel-good story
about a trio of senior citizens who, instead
of being put out to pasture, decide to pool
their resources and launch a clothing company run by (and for) people their age.
Schmaltzy but entertaining. Average.
**Side By Side: The True Story of the
Osmond Family** (1982) **C-100m. TVM**
D: Russ Mayberry. Marie Osmond, Jo-
seph Bottoms, Shane Chournos, David
Eaves, Todd Dutson, Vinc Massa, Shane
Wallace. A mom-and-pop movie, literally,
about Mom and Pop Osmond and their
brood, produced by the Osmonds, and
starring Marie as her mother. Average.
Sidecar Racers (1975-Australian) **C-100m.**
** D: Earl Bellamy. Ben Murphy, Wendy
Hughes, John Clayton, Peter Graves, John
Meillon, John Derum. Murphy becomes a
champion sidecar racer; the usual.
Sidekicks (1974) **C-78m. TVM** D: Burt
Kennedy. Larry Hagman, Lou Gossett,
Blythe Danner, Jack Elam, Harry Morgan,
Gene Evans, Noah Beery, Denver Pyle.

Western satire about two inept con men
on the sagebrush trail trying to collect an
outlaw bounty. Busted pilot loosely adapted
from SKIN GAME with Gossett reprising
his role of college graduate posing as a
Civil War slave and Hagman as pal who
continually "sells" him. Average.
Sidelong Glances of a Pigeon-Kicker SEE:
Pigeons
Side Out (1990) **C-100m.** *½ D: Peter
Israelson. C. Thomas Howell, Peter Horton,
Courtney Thorne-Smith, Harley Jane Kozak,
Christopher Rydell, Terry Kiser, Randy
Stoklos, Sinjin Smith, Kathy Ireland. College kid comes to Southern California for a
summer job evicting tenants for his sleazy
uncle but instead winds up joining with
one of his intended victims for the ultimate
beach volleyball match. Sand, surf, and
sun are the sole highlights of this no-
brainer which purports to be the first major
studio film about volleyball. What's next?
Badminton?
Side Show (1981) **C-100m. TVM** D: William Conrad. Lance Kerwin, Connie Stevens, Tony Franciosa, William Windom,
Red Buttons, Barbara Rhoades, Calvin
Levels, Albert Paulsen, Jerry Maren, Patty
Maloney. Kerwin is a 16-year-old big top
puppeteer who has joined the circus and
lost his innocence. The milieu is well
captured, but the characters are stock and
the teleplay contrived. The songs were
written by director Conrad, who also provides
the voice of the ringmaster. Average.▼
Side Street (1949) **83m.** *** D: Anthony
Mann. Farley Granger, Cathy O'Donnell,
James Craig, Paul Kelly, Jean Hagen, Paul
Harvey. Grim drama of poor clerk Granger
whose minor theft snowballs, affecting his
whole life.
Sidewalks of London (1938-British) **84m.**
*** D: Tim Whelan. Charles Laughton,
Vivien Leigh, Rex Harrison, Tyrone Guthrie, Larry Adler. Laughton is superb as a
busker (street entertainer), with Leigh almost matching him as his protegée, who
uses and abuses all in her quest for success
as a stage star (a character not unlike
Scarlett O'Hara!). Top entertainment . . .
until that ill-conceived final sequence. Original British title: ST. MARTIN'S LANE.▼
Sidewalks of New York (1931) **70m.** **
D: Jules White, Zion Myers. Buster Keaton,
Anita Page, Cliff Edwards, Frank Rowan,
Norman Phillips, Jr. Nowhere near Keaton's
silent-film classics, but this talkie vehicle
has some funny moments as witless young
millionaire tries to reform tough street gang.
Sidewalk Stories (1989) **97m.** *** D:
Charles Lane. Charles Lane, Nicole Alysia,
Sandye Wilson, Darnell Williams, Trula
Hoosier. Charming, Chaplinesque fantasy
that, in its own modest way, boldly com-
ments on the plight of the homeless in
America. Lane stars as a homeless man

struggling for survival on the streets of Greenwich Village who finds himself caring for a cute toddler whose father has been stabbed by muggers. There's almost no dialogue; Marc Marder's evocative score adds immeasurably to the film's mood. Don't miss this sweet, gentle sleeper.
Sidewinder 1 (1977) **C-97m.** *½ D: Earl Bellamy. Marjoe Gortner, Michael Parks, Susan Howard, Alex Cord, Charlotte Rae, Bill Vint. Low-grade actioner about motocross (motorcycle) racing; some exciting scenes, lots of nonacting.▼
Sidney Sheldon's Bloodline SEE: **Bloodline**▼
Sidney Sheldon's Rage of Angels SEE: **Rage of Angels**▼
Sidney Sheldon's Windmills of the Gods SEE: **Windmills of the Gods**
Sidney Shorr: A Girl's Best Friend (1981) **C-100m. TVM** D: Russ Mayberry. Tony Randall, Lorna Patterson, David Huffman, Kaleena Kiff, Ann Weldon, John Lupton. Bittersweet comedy about a middle-aged N.Y.C. bachelor who takes in a young actress, who then has a child out of wedlock. Honest script by Oliver Hailey raised a tempest in a teapot over the homosexuality of the lead character. Notably superior to subsequent *Love, Sidney* series (where the gay angle was whitewashed). Above average.
Siege (1978) **C-100m. TVM** D: Richard Pearce. Martin Balsam, Sylvia Sidney, Dorian Harewood, James Sutorius. Tough senior citizen takes a stand against the gang that's been terrorizing the community. Balsam towers as the one-man vigilante army in this well-written drama by Conrad Bromberg. Above average.
Siege at Red River, The (1954) **C-81m.** **½ D: Rudolph Mate. Van Johnson, Joanne Dru, Richard Boone, Milburn Stone, Jeff Morrow. Predictable Western set during Civil War days with an Indian attack finale.
Siege of Pinchgut SEE: **Four Desperate Men**
Siege of Sidney Street, The (1960-British) **94m.** ** D: Robert Baker, Monty Berman. Donald Sinden, Nicole Berger, Kieron Moore, Peter Wyngarde. Based on real incident, this film traces account of anarchists in 1910 London, with climactic confrontation between hundreds of cops and battling criminals.
Siege of Syracuse (1962-Italian) **C-97m.** *½ D: Pietro Francisci. Rossano Brazzi, Tina Louise, Enrico Maria Salerno, Gino Cervi. No less than Archimedes defends Syracuse from invading armada by use of giant mirrors that make ships burst into flames. Despite that, it's routine.
Siege of the Saxons (1963-British) **C-85m.** **½ D: Nathan Juran. Janette Scott, Ronald Lewis, Ronald Howard, John Laurie, Mark Dignam. Colorful escapism about King Arthur's daughter trying to protect her kingdom, and her right to marry the

knight she chooses, from takeover by nefarious Edmund of Cornwall.
Sierra (1950) **C-83m.** **½ D: Alfred E. Green. Audie Murphy, Wanda Hendrix, Dean Jagger, Burl Ives, Sara Allgood, James Arness, Anthony (Tony) Curtis. Capable cast elevates story of son and father on the lam from the law, trying to prove dad's innocence of crime. Remake of 1938 film FORBIDDEN VALLEY.
Sierra Baron (1958) **C-80m.** ** D: James B. Clark. Brian Keith, Rick Jason, Rita Gam, Mala Powers, Steve Brodie. Western set in 19th century California and Mexico has virtue of pleasing scenery, marred by usual land-grabbing shoot-out plot.
Sierra Passage (1951) **81m.** *½ D: Frank McDonald. Wayne Morris, Lola Albright, Alan Hale, Jr., Roland Winters. Quickie oater with Morris on manhunt for father's murderer.
Sierra Stranger (1957) **74m.** *½ D: Lee Sholem. Howard Duff, Dick Foran, Barton MacLane, Gloria McGhee. Tame dust-raiser of Duff intervening in a lynching, romancing McGhee.
Siesta (1987) **C-97m.** *½ D: Mary Lambert. Ellen Barkin, Gabriel Byrne, Jodie Foster, Martin Sheen, Grace Jones, Julian Sands, Isabella Rossellini, Alexi Sayle. Sky diver Barkin ends up dissheveled and semi-nude in Spain (by way of Death Valley); her subsequent odyssey has something to do with murder (which may actually be a fantasy) and a taxi driver with rusty teeth who keeps trying to rape her. So-called experimental film is a throwback to some of the more incomprehensible efforts of the 1960s; a few more unintentional laughs would help. Music score by Miles Davis. Barkin and Byrne married in real life in 1988.▼
Signal 7 (1983) **C-92m.** **½ D: Rob Nilsson. Bill Ackridge, Dan Leegant, Bob Elross, Hagit Farber, John Tidwell, Herb Mills. Touching and revealing but ultimately rambling stream-of-consciousness tale of middle-aged cabdrivers Ackridge and Leegant—their camaraderie, illusions, desperation. Ambitious but uneven; dedicated, appropriately, to John Cassavetes.
Sign of Four, The (1983-British) **C-103m. TVM** D: Desmond Davis. Ian Richardson, David Healy, Cherie Lunghi, Terence Rigby, Thorley Walters, John Pedrick, Joe Melia, Clive Merrison. Fine Sherlock Holmes adventure based closely on Conan Doyle's most colorful novel, pitting the great detective against a vengeful one-legged man and a homicidal dwarf. Richardson is an excellent Holmes, delighting in his own brilliance; it's too bad that he made only this and the equally good HOUND OF THE BASKERVILLES (1983). Above average.
Sign of the Cross, The (1932) **118m.** **½ D: Cecil B. DeMille. Fredric March, Elissa

Landi, Charles Laughton, Claudette Colbert, Ian Keith, Vivian Tobin, Nat Pendleton, Joe Bonomo. Well-meaning but heavy-handed account of Christians seeking religious freedom in Rome under Emperor Nero. Very slow going, despite fine work by March as Marcus Superbus, Laughton as Nero, and especially Colbert as alluring Poppaea. Originally 124m.; reissued in 1944 with many cuts of sexy and sadistic scenes, and a nine-minute WW2 prologue added. Unfortunately, it's the 1944 version that's usually shown today.

Sign of the Gladiator (1959-Italian) **C-84m.** *½ D: Vittorio Musy Glori. Anita Ekberg, Georges Marchal, Folco Lulli, Chelo Alonso, Jacques Sernas. Gladiator allows himself to be captured by queen of Syria so he can win her confidence. Not so hot.

Sign of the Pagan (1954) **C-92m.** **½ D: Douglas Sirk. Jeff Chandler, Jack Palance, Ludmilla Tcherina, Rita Gam, Jeff Morrow, Alexander Scourby. Uneven script hampers story of Attila the Hun threatening Rome; Sirk's stylish direction helps somewhat.

Sign of the Ram (1948) **84m.** **½ D: John Sturges. Susan Peters, Alexander Knox, Peggy Ann Garner, Dame May Whitty, Phyllis Thaxter, Ron Randell. Well-wrought drama of crippled wife using ailment to hamstring husband and children.

Sign of Zorro, The (1960) **91m.** *½ D: Norman Foster, Lewis R. Foster. Guy Williams, Henry Calvin, Gene Sheldon, Britt Lomond, George J. Lewis, Lisa Gaye. Several episodes of Disney's *Zorro* TV show pasted together; clumsy continuity undermines what charm the series had to offer.▼

Sign O' the Times (1987) **C-85m.** *** D: Prince. Prince, Sheila E., Sheena Easton, Dr. Fink, Miko Weaver, Levi Seacer, Jr., Wally Safford, Gregory Allen Brooks, Boni Boyer, Eric Leads, Atlanta Bliss. Mostly punchy Prince concert film, shot in Rotterdam and Minnesota, features 13 numbers, some overhead photography and lots of bump and grind from both sexes. Stolen to some degree by star drummer Sheila E.; otherwise "live" film features Sheena Easton's rock video "U Got the Look."▼

Signpost to Murder (1965) **74m.** **½ D: George Englund. Stuart Whitman, Joanne Woodward, Edward Mulhare, Alan Napier, Joyce Worsley, Murray Matheson. Escapee from prison for criminally insane seeks shelter in home of woman whose husband is away. Contrived plot mars thriller but strong performances help.

Signs of Life (1989) **C-91m.** **½ D: John David Coles. Arthur Kennedy, Kevin J. O'Connor, Vincent Philip D'Onofrio, Michael Lewis, Beau Bridges, Kate Reid, Mary-Louise Parker, Georgia Engel. A generations-old boat-building business in Maine closes its doors, and the people, young and old, who've spent their lives working there try to figure out what to do next. An ideal showcase for Kennedy (in his first film in ten years) and a talented cast, but superlative acting cannot completely make up for an air of familiarity in Mark Malone's script. A PBS *American Playhouse* production.▼

Silas Marner (1985-British) **C-92m.** ***½ D: Giles Foster. Ben Kingsley, Jenny Agutter, Patrick Ryecart, Jonathan Coy, Freddie Jones, Frederick Treves, Angela Pleasence. Solid, marvelously detailed version of the George Eliot novel with Kingsley quite moving as the title character, a weaver who becomes a recluse after he's falsely accused of thievery and sent into exile.▼

Silence, The (1963-Swedish) **95m.** ***½ D: Ingmar Bergman. Ingrid Thulin, Gunnel Lindblom, Hakan Jahnberb, Birger Malmsten. Stark, forceful symbolic narrative of two sisters who stop at a hotel in a North European city. One sister (Thulin) is a frustrated lesbian with no future, the other (Lindblom) a free-loving mother of a 10-year-old boy. The last in Bergman's trilogy on faith, following THROUGH A GLASS DARKLY and WINTER LIGHT.▼

Silence (1974) **C-88m.** **½ D: John Korty. Will Geer, Ellen Geer, Richard Kelton, Ian Geer Flanders, Craig Kelly. Outdoor drama of autistic boy Flanders lost in the wilderness is a Geer family affair, interestingly done. Also known as CRAZY JACK AND THE BOY.▼

Silence, The (1975) **C-78m. TVM** D: Joseph Hardy. Richard Thomas, Cliff Gorman, George Hearn, Percy Granger, James Mitchell, John Kellogg. West Point cadet James Pelosi (Thomas) relives for writer Stanley Greenberg (Gorman) his true-life experiences of being subjected to total exile when accused of cheating. Mechanical performances by Thomas and Gorman (everyone else is reduced to a walk-on) make this one a bore. Average.

Silence of the Heart (1984) **C-100m. TVM** D: Richard Michaels. Mariette Hartley, Dana Hill, Howard Hesseman, Chad Lowe, Silvana Gallardo, Charlie Sheen, Lynnette Mettey. Hartley is a tower of strength as mother of teenager Lowe, a suicide after deciding he can't cope. Phil Penningroth's penetrating script is well acted by all concerned. Above average.

Silence of the North (1981-Canadian) **C-94m.** ** D: Allan Winton King. Ellen Burstyn, Tom Skerritt, Gordon Pinsent, Jennifer McKinney, Donna Dobrijevic, Colin Fox. OK drama of independent-minded Burstyn surviving in the Canadian wilderness. Beautiful scenery; based on a true story.▼

Silencers, The (1966) **C-102m.** **½ D: Phil Karlson. Dean Martin, Stella Stevens, Dahlia Lavi, Victor Buono, Robert Webber, James Gregory, Arthur O'Connell, Cyd

Charisse, Roger C. Carmel, Nancy Kovack. Donald Hamilton's secret agent Matt Helm is pulled out of "retirement" to combat Buono's efforts to destroy a U.S. atomic testing site. First of four theatrical Helms is far and away the best, with Stevens just wonderful as well-meaning klutz. Sequel: MURDERER'S ROW.

Silent Assassins (1988) **C-92m.** **½ D: Lee Doo-yong, Scott Thomas. Sam J. Jones, Linda Blair, Jun Chong, Phillip Rhee, Bill Erwin, Gustav Vintas, Mako, Rebecca Ferratti, Stuart Damon. Well-made actioner has commando Jones whip into action when a scientist is kidnapped by baddies for his secret biological-warfare formula. His helpers, Chong and Rhee, doubled as film's producers and fight choreographers; in real life they run a martial-arts school.▼

Silent Call, The (1961) 63m. BOMB D: John Bushelman. Gail Russell, Roger Mobley. Very mild yarn of a dog traveling cross-country to find his master in L.A.

Silent Death SEE: **Voodoo Island**

Silent Enemy, The (1958-British) **92m.** **½ D: William Fairchild. Laurence Harvey, Dawn Addams, John Clements, Michael Craig. British Naval frogmen, headed by Harvey, are assigned to combat enemy counterpart during WW2; underwater sequences well handled, with some pre-THUNDERBALL gimmicks.▼

Silent Gun, The (1969) **C-75m. TVM** D: Michael Caffey. Lloyd Bridges, John Beck, Ed Begley, Edd Byrnes, Pernell Roberts, Susan Howard. After vowing never to use gun again, famed shooter puts himself to test and rides into town war between Boss Banner (Roberts) and pioneer settler Cole (Begley). Sad waste of talent via ludicrous script, boring direction. Average.

Silent Lovers, The (1980) **C-105m. TVM** D: John Erman. Kristina Wayborn, Barry Bostwick, Brian Keith, Harold Gould, John Rubinstein, James Olson, Mackenzie Phillips, Audra Lindley, Cecilia Hart. Somber drama of the ill-fated romance between Greta Garbo and John Gilbert. Brian Keith's portrayal of director Mauritz Stiller, Garbo's early mentor and lover, is the thing to watch in this adaptation from Garson Kanin's *Moviola*. Average.

Silent Movie (1976) **C-86m.** **½ D: Mel Brooks. Mel Brooks, Marty Feldman, Dom DeLuise, Bernadette Peters, Sid Caesar, Harold Gould, Ron Carey, guests Burt Reynolds, James Caan, Liza Minnelli, Paul Newman, Anne Bancroft, Marcel Marceau, Harry Ritz. Disappointing attempt to revive silent comedy, with Brooks as movie producer hoping for comeback. Blackout gags range from very funny to misfire. Results are only mild instead of the knock-out they should have been.▼

Silent Night, Bloody Night (1973) C-

87m. ** D: Theodore Gershuny. Patrick O'Neal, James Patterson, Mary Woronov, Astrid Heeren, John Carradine, Walter Abel. Uneven low-budgeter about escaped killer from insane asylum terrorizing small New England town, and inhabitants of mysterious old mansion that's up for sale.▼

Silent Night, Deadly Night (1984) **C-79m.** BOMB D: Charles E. Sellier, Jr. Lilyan Chauvan, Gilmer McCormick, Toni Nero, Robert Brian Wilson, Britt Leach. Controversial—and worthless—splatter movie about a psychotic (Wilson), dressed in a Santa suit, who commits brutal ax-murders. Theaters that played this film were picketed; what next—the Easter Bunny as a child molester? Followed by two sequels!▼

Silent Night, Deadly Night Part II (1987) **C-88m.** BOMB D: Lee Harry. Eric Freeman, James L. Newman, Elizabeth Kaitan. Embarrassing (and unnecessary) follow-up to the Santa Claus-killer film has hero's younger brother continuing the psychotic carnage. About half the footage here is lifted from the original film (including a memorable scene featuring Linnea Quigley); new scenes are perfunctory.▼

Silent Night, Deadly Night III—Better Watch Out! (1989) **C-91m.** ** D: Monte Hellman. Samantha Scully, Bill Moseley, Richard Beymer, Robert Culp, Eric Da Re, Laura Herring. Shrewdly made sequel pits now grown killer from Part II against young blind woman linked to him by ESP. Well made, with touches of black comedy, but still only a slasher movie, less gruesome than most. Santa Claus is not the heavy this time—he's a victim.▼

Silent Night, Evil Night SEE: **Black Christmas**▼

Silent Night, Lonely Night (1969) **C-98m.** TVM D: Daniel Petrie. Lloyd Bridges, Shirley Jones, Carrie Snodgress, Robert Lipton, Lynn Carlin, Cloris Leachman, Jeff Bridges. New England resort setting for chance meeting that turns to romance for two tired, lonely middle-agers (Bridges and Jones). Script—not so-so direction—culprit here in that melodrama stops far short of credibility. Based on the Robert Anderson play. Average.▼

Silent Partner, The (1978-Canadian) **C-103m.** *** D: Daryl Duke. Elliott Gould, Christopher Plummer, Susannah York, Celine Lomez, Michael Kirby, Ken Pogue, John Candy. Offbeat film about crafty bank teller Gould playing cat-and-mouse with psychotic robber Plummer. Well-directed, with fine eye for detail, but bursts of graphic violence are jarring. Nice score by Oscar Peterson. Screenplay by Curtis Hanson.▼

Silent Rage (1982) **C-105m.** *½ D: Michael Miller. Chuck Norris, Ron Silver, Steven Keats, Toni Kalem, William Finley,

Brian Libby, Stephen Furst. Small-town Texas sheriff Norris versus sickie killer Libby, a Frankenstein-like creation of science. Ho-hum.▼

Silent Running (1971) **C-89m.** *** D: Douglas Trumbull. Bruce Dern, Cliff Potts, Ron Rifkin, Jesse Vint. Space-age ecology tale of botanist's fight on space station to keep Earth's final vegetation samples from being destroyed. Interesting film marked directorial debut of special effects whiz Trumbull (2001, CLOSE ENCOUNTERS). Script by Deric Washburn, Michael Cimino, and Steven Bochco; unusual score by Peter Schickele.▼

Silent Scream (1980) **C-87m.** *½ D: Denny Harris. Rebecca Balding, Cameron Mitchell, Avery Schreiber, Barbara Steele, Yvonne De Carlo. Another illogical, obvious kids-caught-in-eerie-old-house melodrama. Some scares, but who cares?▼

Silent Victory: The Kitty O'Neil Story (1979) **C-100m.** TVM D: Lou Antonio. Stockard Channing, James Farentino, Colleen Dewhurst, Edward Albert, Brian Dennehy. The real-life account of a deaf girl's victory over her handicap to become a top stuntwoman in Hollywood. Script by Steven Gethers. Above average.▼

Silent Witness (1932) **73m.** ** D: Marcel Varnel, R. L. Hough. Lionel Atwill, Greta Nissen, Weldon Heyburn, Helen Mack, Bramwell Fletcher. Stagy but pretty interesting courtroom drama with Atwill trying to protect his son from murder charge by taking blame himself.

Silent Witness (1985) **C-100m.** TVM D: Michael Miller. Valerie Bertinelli, John Savage, Chris Nash, Melissa Leo, Pat Corley, Steven Williams, Jacqueline Brookes. Working girl and hubby stumble onto a barroom rape involving his brother, and she is torn between stepping forward as a witness and keeping the secret within the close-knit family. Average.▼

Silent World, The (1956-French) **C-86m.** *** D: Jacques-Yves Cousteau. Frederic Duman, Albert Falco, Jacques-Yves Cousteau. Academy Award-winning documentary account of an expedition above and—most memorably—below the sea's surface by Captain Cousteau and his divers and crew. Beautifully photographed; Louis Malle worked with Cousteau on this.

Silken Affair, The (1957-British) **96m.** **½ D: Roy Kellino. David Niven, Genevieve Page, Ronald Squire, Wilfrid Hyde-White, Beatrice Straight. Droll little comedy of meek accountant Niven sparked by saucy Page into some fast bookkeeping manipulations.

Silk Stockings (1957) **C-117m.** *** D: Rouben Mamoulian. Fred Astaire, Cyd Charisse, Janis Paige, Peter Lorre, George Tobias, Jules Munshin, Joseph Buloff, Barrie Chase. Words, music, dance blend perfectly in stylish remake of Garbo's NINOTCHKA. This time Charisse is cold Russian on Paris mission, Astaire the movie producer man-about-town who warms her up. Score by Cole Porter includes "All of You" and "Stereophonic Sound"; Mamoulian's final film.▼

Silkwood (1983) **C-128m.** *** D: Mike Nichols. Meryl Streep, Kurt Russell, Cher, Craig T. Nelson, Diana Scarwid, Fred Ward, Ron Silver, Charles Hallahan, Josef Sommer, Sudie Bond, Henderson Forsythe, E. Katherine Kerr, Bruce McGill. Superb performances, and vivid dramatization of workaday life in an Oklahoma nuclear-parts factory, give strength to a flawed film. Streep is outstanding as real-life Karen Silkwood, but anyone who followed news story knows how this film will end, and that places a special burden on such a long, slowly paced film. Script by Nora Ephron and Alice Arlen.▼

Silverado (1985) **C-132m.** *** D: Lawrence Kasdan. Kevin Kline, Scott Glenn, Kevin Costner, Danny Glover, John Cleese, Rosanna Arquette, Brian Dennehy, Linda Hunt, Jeff Goldblum. Sprawling, well-made Western about four unlikely comrades who join forces against some very bad guys. First major Hollywood Western in a long time is no classic but offers ample entertainment by throwing in everything but the kitchen sink—and making sure it never stops moving. Just don't think about it too hard. Script by Mark and Lawrence Kasdan, fine score by Bruce Broughton.▼

Silver Bears (1978) **C-113m.** *** D: Ivan Passer. Michael Caine, Cybill Shepherd, Louis Jourdan, Martin Balsam, Stephane Audran, Tommy Smothers, David Warner, Charles Gray, Jay Leno. Entertaining comedy better suited to TV than theater screens; fine cast in story of high-level chicanery in world silver market. Adapted from Paul Erdman's novel by Peter Stone; filmed in Switzerland and Morocco.▼

Silver Bullet (1985) **C-95m.** ** D: Daniel Attias. Corey Haim, Gary Busey, Megan Follows, Everett McGill, Terry O'Quinn, Robin Groves, Leon Russom. What can it be that's terrorizing a small town by the light of the full moon? The answer is a werewolf, but it takes the folks in this movie a long time to figure that out. Well acted but often stupid and unbelievable horror tale from Stephen King's novelette, *Cycle of the Werewolf*.▼

Silver Chalice, The (1954) **C-144m.** ** D: Victor Saville. Virginia Mayo, Pier Angeli, Jack Palance, Paul Newman, Walter Hampden, Joseph Wiseman, Alexander Scourby, Lorne Greene, E. G. Marshall, Natalie Wood. Newman's screen debut is undistinguished in story of Greek who designs framework for cup used at Last Supper. This is the film Newman once apologized for in a famous Hollywood trade ad. From the Thomas Costain novel; Greene's first film, too.▼

Silver City (1951) **C-90m.** ** D: Byron Haskin. Edmond O'Brien, Yvonne De Carlo, Richard Arlen, Gladys George, Barry Fitzgerald. Capable cast is above this mishmash set in the mining area of the West, with usual rivalry over gals and ore.

Silver City (1984-Australian) **C-110m.** **½ D: Sophie Turkiewicz. Gosia Dobrowolska, Ivar Kants, Anna Jemison, Steve Bisley, Debra Lawrence. Fair soaper about love affair between Polish immigrants Dobrowolska and Kants in 1940s Australia. The catch: He is married to her close friend.▼

Silver Cord, The (1933) **74m.** **½ D: John Cromwell. Irene Dunne, Joel McCrea, Laura Hope Crews, Frances Dee, Eric Linden. Very much a photographed stage play (by Sidney Howard), but interesting for its look at a self-absorbed woman (Crews) who attempts to dominate her sons' lives completely—not counting on the strength of her new daughter-in-law (Dunne), a career woman with a mind of her own. Both Dunne and Dee are first-rate.

Silver Dollar (1932) **84m.** **½ D: Alfred E. Green. Edward G. Robinson, Bebe Daniels, Aline MacMahon, Robert Warwick, Jobyna Howland. True story (though names are changed) of self-made silver tycoon H. A. W. Tabor, who helped build Denver from mining camp to a thriving city. One of America's great sagas, hampered by unimaginative presentation.

Silver Dream Racer (1980-British) **C-111m.** *½ D: David Wickes. David Essex, Beau Bridges, Cristina Raines, Clarke Peters, Harry H. Corbett, Diane Keen, Lee Montague, Sheila White. Hackneyed drama chronicling the trials of garage-mechanic-turned-motorcyclist Essex as he strives to win the Big Race. Essex wrote and performed music score as well.▼

Silver Lode (1954) **C-80m.** **½ D: Allan Dwan. John Payne, Lizabeth Scott, Dan Duryea, Dolores Moran. Dynamic cast boosts this story of man trying to clear himself of murder charge.▼

Silver Queen (1942) **80m.** ** D: Lloyd Bacon. George Brent, Priscilla Lane, Bruce Cabot, Lynne Overman, Eugene Pallette, Guinn Williams. Post-Civil War tinsel of devoted girl raising money for father; hubby throws it away on "worthless" silver mine.▼

Silver River (1948) **110m.** *½ D: Raoul Walsh. Errol Flynn, Ann Sheridan, Thomas Mitchell, Bruce Bennett, Tom D'Andrea, Barton MacLane, Monte Blue. Mediocre Flynn vehicle: Ann and Errol marry out West, he becomes corrupt.

Silver Streak, The (1934) **72m.** *½ D: Thomas Atkins. Sally Blane, Charles Starrett, Hardie Albright, William Farnum, Irving Pichel, Arthur Lake. High-speed train journey is undertaken to deliver iron lungs to epidemic-stricken Nevada town. Derailed by wooden performances and leaden pace; no relation to 1976 film.▼

Silver Streak (1976) **C-113m.** *** D: Arthur Hiller. Gene Wilder, Jill Clayburgh, Richard Pryor, Patrick McGoohan, Ned Beatty, Ray Walston, Scatman Crothers, Clifton James, Richard Kiel, Fred Willard. Nutty blend of comedy, romance, action and suspense as mild-mannered editor Wilder becomes involved in murder plot on cross-country train ride. Switch from comedy to violence is sometimes jarring, but on the whole a highly entertaining picture. Imitation Hitchcock written by Colin Higgins.▼

Silver Whip, The (1953) **73m.** **½ D: Harmon Jones. Dale Robertson, Rory Calhoun, Robert Wagner, Kathleen Crowley, Lola Albright. Occasionally actionful Western of outlaws vs. stage line.

Simba (1955-British) **C-99m.** ***½ D: Brian Desmond Hurst. Dirk Bogarde, Virginia McKenna, Basil Sydney, Donald Sinden. Fine cast in story of young man arriving in Kenya only to find brother killed by Mau Maus. Some grisly scenes.▼

Simon (1980) **C-97m.** **½ D: Marshall Brickman. Alan Arkin, Madeline Kahn, Austin Pendleton, Judy Graubart, William Finley, Fred Gwynne, Adolph Green. Uneven comedy about psychology professor (Arkin) who's brainwashed by group of think-tank weirdos to believe he's come from another planet. There's a cruel edge to the humor, and signs of a serious film trying to break out, in screenwriter Brickman's directorial debut.▼

Simon and Laura (1956-British) **C-91m.** **½ D: Muriel Box. Peter Finch, Kay Kendall, Muriel Pavlow, Ian Carmichael, Maurice Denham. Spunky farce involving Finch and Kendall, a married acting couple whose TV image contradicts their violent offscreen battles.

Simon of the Desert (1965-Mexican) **45m.** **** D: Luis Buñuel. Claudio Brook, Silvia Pinal, Hortensia Santovena, Enrique Alvarez Felix. Hilarious parable about a bearded ascetic who plops himself atop a pillar to communicate with God better. Could only have been made by one filmmaker; even by Buñuel's standard, the ending of this one is pretty wild.▼

Simple Story, A (1978-French) **C-110m.** *** D: Claude Sautet. Romy Schneider, Bruno Cremer, Claude Brasseur, Arlette Bonnard. Fortyish laborer examines her life after aborting a child and dropping her lover. Schneider gives one of her best performances in this graceful drama.▼

Sin, The SEE: **Good Luck, Miss Wyckoff**▼

Sinbad and the Eye of the Tiger (1977-British) **C-113m.** *½ D: Sam Wanamaker. Patrick Wayne, Jane Seymour, Taryn Power, Margaret Whiting, Patrick Troughton. Dreary followup to GOLDEN VOYAGE OF SINBAD has unusually hackneyed script (even for this kind of film), disappointing Ray Harryhausen effects, and goes on forever. For patient kids only. Taryn is Tyrone Power's daughter.▼

Sinbad the Sailor (1947) **C-117m.** *** D: Richard Wallace. Douglas Fairbanks Jr., Maureen O'Hara, Anthony Quinn, Walter Slezak, George Tobias, Jane Greer, Mike Mazurki, Sheldon Leonard. Tongue-in-cheek swashbuckler, with lavish color production. Great fun.▼

Sincerely Yours (1955) **C-115m.** BOMB D: Gordon Douglas. Liberace, Joanne Dru, Dorothy Malone, William Demarest, Richard Eyer, Lurene Tuttle. Remake of George Arliss' MAN WHO PLAYED GOD becomes a ludicrous vehicle for Liberace. Camp classic written by Irving Wallace, with the star's brother George serving as musical adviser.▼

Since You Went Away (1944) **172m.** ***½ D: John Cromwell. Claudette Colbert, Jennifer Jones, Joseph Cotten, Shirley Temple, Monty Woolley, Hattie McDaniel, Agnes Moorehead, Craig Stevens, Keenan Wynn, Nazimova, Robert Walker, Lionel Barrymore. Tear-jerker supreme with Colbert at her valiant best. Story of family suffering through WW2 with many tragedies and complications dates a bit, but still is very smooth film. Producer David O. Selznick wrote the screenplay, from Margaret Buell Wilder's book. Beautifully photographed by Lee Garmes and Stanley Cortez. Max Steiner's score won an Oscar. Film debuts of Guy Madison (then an actual sailor, in the role of sailor Harold Smith) and John Derek (an extra).▼

Sinful Davey (1969-British) **C-95m.** **½ D: John Huston. John Hurt, Pamela Franklin, Nigel Davenport, Ronald Fraser, Robert Morley, Fidelma Murphy, Maxine Audley, Anjelica Huston, Brenda Fricker. Tale of 19th-century Scottish highwayman and his love for a "nice" girl is rather ordinary, but does have pleasant performance by Franklin. Based on a true story.

Sinful Life, A (1989) **C-90m.** ** D: William Schreiner. Anita Morris, Rick Overton, Dennis Christopher, Mark Rolston, Cynthia Szigeti, Blair Tefkin, Cynthia Songe. Very offbeat comedy (filmed on a low, low budget) about a former Sonny and Cher dancer named Claire Vin Blanc who fights to keep her rather *unusual* child, Baby, from being removed to a more "respectable" environment. Not for every-

one, but it does give Morris a great vehicle for her comedic talent. Based on the play *Just Like the Pom Pom Girls*, originally presented by L.A.'s Groundlings comedy troupe.▼

Sing (1989) **C-97m.** BOMB D: Richard Baskin. Lorraine Bracco, Peter Dobson, Jessica Steen, Louise Lasser, George DiCenzo, Patti La Belle. Title refers to a true-life, decades-old tradition—a songdance competition (or "Sing") between seniors and underclassmen in Brooklyn high schools. Script (by Dean Pitchford) is decades old, too: B-movie clichés about a rebel, a "nice" girl, an understanding teacher, and jelly-spined administrators all locking horns during pageant rehearsals. Threatens to go over the brink throughout . . . and eventually does.▼

Sing and Swing (1963-British) **75m.** ** D: Lance Comfort. David Hemmings, Veronica Hurst, Jennifer Moss, John Pike. Virtue of modest musical is Hemmings in lead role of messenger boy who joins pals in combo; they record a song, and find their musical career in full sway. Originally titled LIVE IT UP.

Singapore (1947) **79m.** ** D: John Brahm. Fred MacMurray, Ava Gardner, Roland Culver, Richard Haydn, Spring Byington. Weak drama of amnesiac Gardner forgetting her true love MacMurray. Remade as ISTANBUL.

Singapore, Singapore (1968-French) **C-103m.** ** D: Bernard Toublanc Michel. Sean Flynn, Marika Green, Terry Downes, Marc Michel, Peter Gayford, Denis Berry. So-so espionage tale interesting primarily for Flynn (Errol's son) playing a CIA agent looking into the disappearance of a number of Marines in Singapore. Based on Jean Bruce's novel. Also called FIVE ASHORE IN SINGAPORE.

Singapore Woman (1941) **64m.** ** D: Jean Negulesco. Brenda Marshall, David Bruce, Virginia Field, Jerome Cowan, Rose Hobart, Heather Angel. Sluggish account of young rubber planter set upon helping to remove oriental curse from Marshall. Remake of DANGEROUS.

Sing, Baby, Sing (1936) **87m.** *** D: Sidney Lanfield. Alice Faye, Adolphe Menjou, Gregory Ratoff, Ted Healy, Patsy Kelly, Tony Martin. Pleasant musicomedy stolen by Menjou as John Barrymore prototype involved with publicity-seeking Faye. Songs: "When Did You Leave Heaven?" "You Turned The Tables On Me," title tune. The Ritz Brothers are quite good in their feature-film debut.

Sing, Boy, Sing (1958) **90m.** ** D: Henry Ephron. Tommy Sands, Lili Gentle, Edmond O'Brien, John McIntire, Nick Adams. Expanded TV drama of the trials and tribulations of rock 'n' roll star.

Singer Not the Song, The (1961-British)

C-129m. **½ D: Roy (Ward) Baker. Dirk Bogarde, John Mills, Mylene Demongeot, Eric Pohlmann. Offbeat, sluggish yarn set in Mexico involving conflict of Catholic priest and local bandit to control the town, with Demongeot in love with the clergyman.▼

Singing Guns (1950) **C-91m.** *½ D: R. G. Springsteen. Vaughn Monroe, Ella Raines, Walter Brennan, Ward Bond, Billy Gray. Minor happenings in the old West with singer Monroe in straight role.

Singing Kid, The (1936) **85m.** ** D: William Keighley. Al Jolson, Sybil Jason, Edward Everett Horton, Lyle Talbot, Allen Jenkins, Beverly Roberts, Claire Dodd. Formula musical with E. Y. Harburg-Harold Arlen score is for Jolson fans only, as he plays himself (more or less) in silly plot about thickwitted star's romances. Musical appearances by Cab Calloway, Wini Shaw, The Yacht Club Boys. Highlight: "I Love to Singa."

Singing Nun, The (1966) **C-98m.** ** D: Henry Koster. Debbie Reynolds, Ricardo Montalban, Greer Garson, Agnes Moorehead, Chad Everett, Katharine Ross, Ed Sullivan. Syrupy comic-book stuff based on real-life Belgian nun whose devotion is split between religious work and making hit records.

Singin' in the Rain (1952) **C-102m.** **** D: Gene Kelly, Stanley Donen. Gene Kelly, Debbie Reynolds, Donald O'Connor, Jean Hagen, Cyd Charisse, Millard Mitchell, Douglas Fowley, Madge Blake, Rita Moreno. Perhaps the greatest movie musical of all time, fashioned by Betty Comden and Adolph Green from a catalogue of Arthur Freed-Nacio Herb Brown songs. The setting is Hollywood during the transition to talkies, with Hagen giving the performance of a lifetime as Kelly's silent screen costar, whose voice could shatter glass. Kelly's title number, O'Connor's "Make 'Em Laugh," are just two highlights in a film packed with gems. Later a Broadway musical.▼

Single Bars, Single Women (1984) **C-100m. TVM** D: Harry Winer. Tony Danza, Paul Michael Glaser, Keith Gordon, Shelley Hack, Christine Lahti, Frances Lee McCain, Kathleen Wilhoite, Mare Winningham. Dolly Parton's song was the inspiration for this by-the-numbers comedy-drama of people pursuing neon-lit fantasies in a local pickup joint. Average.▼

Single Girls, The (1973) **C-85m.** ** D: Ferd and Beverly Sebastian. Claudia Jennings, Jean Marie Ingels, Joan Prather, Cheri Howell, Greg Mullavey, Albert Popwell, Robyn Hilton. Attractive B-movie cast in not bad drive-in thriller about psycho killer on the loose at a Caribbean resort. More sex and comedy than violence, fortunately.

Single Handed SEE: **Sailor of the King**

Single Room Furnished (1968) **C-93m.** *½ D: Matteo Ottaviano (Matt Cimber). Jayne

Mansfield, Dorothy Keller, Fabian Dean, Billy M. Greene, Terri Messina, Martin Horsey, Walter Gregg. Pathetic woman, twice impregnated and thrice deserted, decides to become prostitute. Mansfield's last film, released after her death, opens with Walter Winchell tribute and degenerates as she attempts to display serious acting talent.▼

Single Standard, The (1929) **73m.** ** D: John S. Robertson. Greta Garbo, Nils Asther, John Mack Brown, Dorothy Sebastian, Lane Chandler. Greta is a San Francisco debutante, a free soul who breaks convention and has an affair with artist Asther. Pretty silly stuff, but Garbo is as beautiful as ever. From an Adela Rogers St. Johns novel.

Single Women, Married Men (1989) **C-100m. TVM** D: Nick Havings. Michele Lee, Lee Horsley, Alan Rachins, Carrie Hamilton, Jeanetta Arnette, Mary Frann, Julie Harris. Another of television's perfectly titled movies that saves any suspense about plot—not that there's much of one to describe in this case. It is, however "based on a true story" about a female family counselor who started a support group for women involved with married men. Average.

Sing Your Way Home (1945) **72m.** *½ D: Anthony Mann. Jack Haley, Anne Jeffreys, Marcy McGuire, Glenn Vernon. RKO Pictures minimusical set on the high seas with youthful entertainers providing modicum of singing talent.

Sing Your Worries Away (1942) **71m.** ** D: A. Edward Sutherland. June Havoc, Bert Lahr, Buddy Ebsen, Patsy Kelly, Sam Levene, Margaret Dumont, King Sisters, Alvino Rey. Mild musical comedy as the theatrical world and racketeers clash.▼

Sing, You Sinners (1938) **88m.** *** D: Wesley Ruggles. Bing Crosby, Fred MacMurray, Donald O'Connor, Elizabeth Patterson, Ellen Drew, John Gallaudet. Gambling gay-blade Crosby can't face responsibility, despite prodding of brother MacMurray. Fine film with "I've Got A Pocketful Of Dreams" and memorable "Small Fry" number featuring young O'Connor.

Sinister Invasion (1971-Mexican-U.S.) **C-90m.** BOMB D: Jack Hill and Juan Ibanez. Boris Karloff, Enrique Guzman, Christa Linder, Mauri Monti, Yerye Beirute, Sergio Kleiner. 19th-century scientist Karloff's experiments accidentally summon aliens who dominate a local Ripper-like killer. Cheap, flaccid, ugly film, one of four Karloff worked on simultaneously in 1968; unfortunately this was his last film work. Also known as INCREDIBLE INVASION.▼

Sinister Urge, The (1961) **75m.** BOMB D: Edward D. Wood, Jr. Kenne Duncan, Duke Moore, Carl Anthony, Jean Fontaine, Dino Fantini, Jeanne Willardson. Dedicated cops Duncan and Moore set out to smash the "smut picture racket," which is run by a brassy blonde who writes with a four-foot quill pen. One of Wood's least-known works demonstrates with complete conviction how photos of plump women in their underwear are the principal cause of juvenile deliquency. Also known as THE YOUNG AND THE IMMORAL.

Sink the Bismarck! (1960-British) 97m. *** D: Lewis Gilbert. Kenneth More, Dana Wynter, Carl Mohner, Laurence Naismith, Geoffrey Keen, Karel Stepanek, Michael Hordern. Good war film based on fact. Exciting sea battles as British navy starts deadly hunt for famed German war vessel. Script by Edmund H. North.▼

Sinner, The SEE: **Desert Desperadoes**

Sinner's Holiday (1930) 60m. **½ D: John G. Adolfi. Grant Withers, Evalyn Knapp, James Cagney, Joan Blondell, Lucille LaVerne, Noel Madison. Predictable melodrama is interesting to watch, as period piece (with good Coney Island atmosphere) and as film debuts for Cagney and Blondell, recreating stage roles in support of stars Withers and Knapp. Story involves romance, murder, and overprotective mother who runs penny arcade.

Sinner's Holiday (1947) SEE: **Christmas Eve**

Sinners in Paradise (1938) 65m. ** D: James Whale. John Boles, Madge Evans, Bruce Cabot, Marion Martin, Gene Lockhart, Nana Bryant, Milburn Stone, Donald Barry. Plane crash survivors are stranded on tropic island where mysterious Boles lives as a recluse. Starts great, but peters out.

Sinners in the Sun (1932) 70m. ** D: Alexander Hall. Carole Lombard, Chester Morris, Adrienne Ames, Cary Grant, Walter Byron, Alison Skipworth, Rita La Roy, Ida Lewis. Lovely Lombard learns that money isn't all in this slick, typical triangle; Grant has a bit role.

Sin of Adam and Eve, The (1972-Mexican) C-72m. *½ D: Michael Zachary (Miguel Zacarias). Candy Wilson, George Rivers (Jorge Rivero). Virtually silent film (with narration) about Adam and Eve's expulsion from Paradise and their subsequent attempts to find each other again. Attractive two-person cast in this curio.▼

Sin of Harold Diddlebock, The (1947) 90m. **½ D: Preston Sturges. Harold Lloyd, Frances Ramsden, Jimmy Conlin, Raymond Walburn, Edgar Kennedy, Arline Judge, Lionel Stander, Rudy Vallee. Fascinating idea of updating Lloyd's 1920s character to show what's happened to that go-getter doesn't fulfill its promise. Aimless comedy can't top opening sequence from THE FRESHMAN (1925), despite enthusiasm of fine cast. Reedited to 79m. and reissued in 1950 as MAD WEDNESDAY.▼

Sin of Innocence (1986) C-100m. TVM D: Arthur Allan Seidelman. Bill Bixby, Dee Wallace Stone, Megan Follows, Dermot Mulroney, James Naughton. Exploitively titled domestic drama about a widower and a divorcee who marry, while his teenage son falls in love with her teenage daughter. Average.

Sin of Madelon Claudet, The (1931) *** 73m. D: Edgar Selwyn. Helen Hayes, Lewis Stone, Neil Hamilton, Robert Young, Cliff Edwards, Jean Hersholt, Marie Prevost, Karen Morley, Charles Winninger, Alan Hale. First-rate, fast-moving soaper in the MADAME X vein, about a woman who sacrifices everything so her illegitimate son will have a good life. Hayes won an Oscar portraying woman who goes from bumpkin to Parisian sophisticate to suffering mother to haggard streetwalker—and she's terrific.

Sins of Dorian Gray, The (1983) C-100m. TVM D: Tony Maylam. Anthony Perkins, Joseph Bottoms, Belinda Bauer, Olga Karlatos, Michael Ironside, Caroline Yeager. Dorian's in skirts this time, watching her portrait age in this '80s update of Oscar Wilde's macabre tale. One of the infrequent live-action films from the Rankin/Bass cartoon people. Below average.▼

Sins of Jezebel (1953) C-74m. *½ D: Reginald Le Borg. Paulette Goddard, George Nader, John Hoyt, Eduard Franz. Embarrassing low-budget costumer with Goddard miscast in title role.

Sins of Rachel Cade, The (1961) C-124m. **½ D: Gordon Douglas. Angie Dickinson, Peter Finch, Roger Moore, Woody Strode, Rafer Johnson, Juano Hernandez. Turgid melodrama set in Belgian Congo with Dickinson a missionary nurse involved in romance and native conflicts.

Sins of Rome (1954-Italian) 75m. ** D: Riccardo Freda. Ludmilla Tcherina, Massimo Girotti, Gianna Maria Canale, Yves Vincent. Rebel slave Spartacus incites fellow prisoners to fight Roman republic. Early Italian spectacle doesn't have cheaper look of later grinds.▼

Sins of the Father (1985) C-100m. TVM D: Peter Werner. James Coburn, Ted Wass, Glynnis O'Connor, Marion Ross, Joan Prather, Kathleen Lloyd. Triangle drama involving a dashing attorney having an affair with his ex-partner's daughter, who falls in love with his scientist son. Average.

Sins of the Fathers (1986-German) C-200m. TVM D: Bernhard Sinkel. Burt Lancaster, Julie Christie, Bruno Ganz, Dieter Laser, Tina Engel, Martin Benrath, Cyrielle Claire, Katharina Thalbach, Christian Doermer. Deadly multigenerational German drama about a fictional family of pre-WW2 industrialists who would be caught up in Hitler's war. Lancaster (as the patriarch) and Christie (as his wayward daughter-in-law) are both miscast. Premiered on American cable in two parts, two years after its completion. Below average.

Sins of the Past (1984) **C-100m. TVM** D: Peter H. Hunt. Barbara Carrera, Kim Cattrall, Debby Boone, Tracy Reed, Kirstie Alley, Anthony Geary. A group of call girls who had gotten out of the profession fifteen years earlier (following the murder of one of their cohorts) are reunited when the killer is sprung and vows further vengeance. Single element of surprise here is Boone as a hooker. Below average.

Sin Town (1942) **75m.** **½ D: Ray Enright. Constance Bennett, Broderick Crawford, Anne Gwynne, Ward Bond, Andy Devine, Leo Carrillo, Patric Knowles, Hobart Bosworth. Fast-moving actioner of town in uproar after newspaper editor is killed; good cast in above-average film. Richard Brooks was one of the writers.

Siren of Atlantis (1948) **75m. BOMB** D: Gregg Tallas. Maria Montez, Jean-Pierre Aumont, Dennis O'Keefe, Henry Daniell, Morris Carnovsky. Ridiculous hokum of soldiers Aumont and O'Keefe stumbling upon famed Lost Continent; Montez is the sultry queen. Based on *L'Atlantide*, first filmed in 1921. Despite the title, film takes place in the desert.

Siren of Bagdad (1953) **C-77m.** **½ D: Richard Quine. Paul Henreid, Patricia Medina, Hans Conried, Charlie Lung. Comedy-adventure of magician and friend trying to save dancing girls in slave market. Conried provides film's best moments.

Sir Henry at Rawlinson End (1980-British) **72m.** **½ D: Steve Roberts. Trevor Howard, Patrick Magee, Denise Coffey, J. G. Devlin, Sheila Reid, Harry Fowler. Howard is fine as an eccentric, alcoholic aristocrat who attempts to exorcise a family spirit from his domain. Strange but entertaining, and veddy British.

Sirocco (1951) **98m.** **½ D: Curtis Bernhardt. Humphrey Bogart, Marta Toren, Lee J. Cobb, Everett Sloane, Zero Mostel. Rugged Bogart perks this yarn of gunrunning set in 1920s Syria.▼

Sis Hopkins (1941) **98m.** **½ D: Joseph Santley. Judy Canova, Bob Crosby, Charles Butterworth, Jerry Colonna, Susan Hayward, Katharine Alexander. Fairly amusing comedy of country girl who comes to live with social uncle and attends girls' school. Even Canova is restrained!

Sister-In-Law, The (1974) **C-85m.** ** D: Joseph Ruben. John Savage, W. G. McMillan, Anne Saxon, Meredith Baer, Jon Oppenheim, Tom Mahoney. Interesting curio has Savage becoming involved with destructive title character as his brother's dupe in drug-smuggling. Hurt by needlessly negative finale. Savage also composed the score and sings several folk ballads pleasantly.▼

Sister Kenny (1946) **116m.** ***½ D: Dudley Nichols. Rosalind Russell, Alexander Knox, Dean Jagger, Philip Merivale, Beulah Bondi, Dorothy Peterson. Russell shines in title role, as Australian nurse who initiated treatment for polio. Engrossing drama is among the better Hollywood biopics. Scripted by Nichols, Knox, and Mary McCarthy, from Mary Kenny's autobiography *And They Shall Walk*.▼

Sister Margaret and the Saturday Night Ladies (1987) **C-100m. TVM** D: Paul Wendkos. Bonnie Franklin, Rosemary Clooney, Jeanetta Arnette, Trazana Beverley, Lydia Nicole Commissiong, Jon Chardiet, Sheryl Lee Ralph, Maria O'Brien. A nun starts a halfway house for women prison parolees. Clooney here made her TV-movie acting debut; O'Brien is the daughter of Edmond O'Brien and Olga San Juan. Both play ex-cons to no avail in this dreary drama. Below average.

Sisters, The (1938) **98m.** *** D: Anatole Litvak. Errol Flynn, Bette Davis, Anita Louise, Ian Hunter, Donald Crisp, Beulah Bondi, Jane Bryan, Lee Patrick, Mayo Methot, Laura Hope Crews, Dick Foran, Henry Travers, Patrick Knowles, Alan Hale. Davis, Louise, and Bryan are sisters whose marital problems are traced in this lavish film; Bette's got the most trouble, of course, with unreliable husband Flynn in San Francisco, 1905.

Sisters (1973) **C-93m.** *** D: Brian DePalma. Margot Kidder, Jennifer Salt, Charles Durning, Barnard Hughes, William Finley, Mary Davenport, Lisle Wilson. DePalma's first venture into Hitchcock territory, about separated Siamese twins (Kidder), one of whom is a homicidal maniac, and the reporter (Salt) who—shades of REAR WINDOW—thinks she witnessed one of the slayings. Eerie, gory, tremendously suspenseful, with one of Bernard Herrmann's most chilling scores.▼

Sister, Sister (1982) **C-100m. TVM** D: John Berry. Diahann Carroll, Rosalind Cash, Irene Cara, Paul Winfield, Dick Anthony Williams, Robert Hooks, Christopher St. John, Diana Douglas, Albert Powell. Rewarding drama, written by Maya Angelou, about the uneasy reunion of three sisters that opens up old family wounds. Filmed several years before its initial network showing. Above average.

Sister, Sister (1987) **C-91m.** *½ D: Bill Condon. Eric Stoltz, Jennifer Jason Leigh, Judith Ivey, Dennis Lipscomb, Anne Pitoniak, Benjamin Moulton. Leigh and Ivey are title siblings, two women with myriad problems and repressions. They've converted their parents' mansion into a dreary guest house . . . one which you will not want to visit. Thoroughly unappealing.▼

Sisters of Nishijin (1952-Japanese) **110m.**

[1052]

***½ D: Kozaburo Yoshimura. Yumiko Miyagino, Mitsuko Miura, Yuko Tsumura, Chieko Higashiyama. Family of Kyóto silkweavers cannot adapt to industrialization; the father-patriarch kills himself, and his widow, daughters, and assistants try to carry on. Excellent tale of greed and courage.

Sisters, Or the Balance of Happiness (1979-German) **C-95m.** **½ D: Margarethe von Trotta. Jutta Lampe, Gudrun Gabriel, Jessica Fruh, Rainer Delventhal, Konstantin Wecker. Slow but not unrewarding psychological study of the complex relationship between two sisters; one, a successful executive secretary, is supporting the other, a graduate student in biology.

Sitting Bull (1954) **C-105m.** ** D: Sidney Salkow. Dale Robertson, Mary Murphy, J. Carrol Naish, Iron Eyes Cody, John Litel. Sluggish nonsense about army officer Robertson's efforts to prove he wasn't being overly helpful to the Indians.

Sitting Ducks (1980) **C-90m.** *** D: Henry Jaglom. Michael Emil, Zack Norman, Patrice Townsend, Irene Forrest, Richard Romanus, Henry Jaglom. Energetic, funny sleeper about timid Syndicate accountant Emil and womanizing pal Norman, who take a day's collections and rip off the Mob. Emil and Norman have comedy team potential as the bickering buddies, Townsend (then Mrs. Jaglom) is luscious as a woman they pick up. Lots of belly laughs ▼

Sitting Pretty (1933) **85m.** **½ D: Harry Joe Brown. Ginger Rogers, Jack Oakie, Jack Haley, Thelma Todd, Gregory Ratoff, Lew Cody. First half is bouncy yarn of songwriters Oakie and Haley going Hollywood, meeting homespun Rogers, vamp Todd; remainder bogs down, rescued by finale "Did You Ever See a Dream Walking."

Sitting Pretty (1948) **84m.** ***½ D: Walter Lang. Robert Young, Maureen O'Hara, Clifton Webb, Richard Haydn, Louise Allbritton, Ed Begley. Webb is perfect as self-centered genius who accepts job as full-time babysitter in gossip-laden suburban town. Highly entertaining, followed by the MR. BELVEDERE comedies.

Sitting Target (1972-British) **C-93m.** *½ D: Douglas Hickox. Oliver Reed, Jill St. John, Ian McShane, Edward Woodward, Frank Finlay, Freddie Jones. Reed breaks out of prison to settle two scores—one of them with his cheating wife (St. John). Violent, generally unpleasant film.

Situation Hopeless—But Not Serious (1965) **97m.** ** D: Gottfried Reinhardt. Alec Guinness, Michael Connors, Robert Redford, Anita Hoefer, Mady Rahl, Paul Dahlke. Odd little comedy, from a Robert Shaw novel, about German clerk Guinness holding two American (Redford, Connors) prisoners for years after WW2 has ended.

Interesting characterization by Guinness, but a flat film.

Six Against the Rock (1987) **C-100m.** TVM D: Paul Wendkos. David Carradine, Howard Hesseman, David Morse, Charles Haid, Jan-Michael Vincent, Richard Dysart, Dennis Farina. Standard prison-break tale based on the real-life 1946 escape attempt at Alcatraz. Virile television cast; OK John Gay script with predictable results. Average.

Six Black Horses (1962) **C-80m.** ** D: Harry Keller. Audie Murphy, Dan Duryea, Joan O'Brien, George Wallace. O'Brien pays two men to take her across Indian lands, intending to murder gunman of duo who killed her husband. Mediocre Western with a Burt Kennedy script apparently left over from the Randolph Scott-Budd Boetticher series.

Six Bridges to Cross (1955) **96m.** **½ D: Joseph Pevney. Tony Curtis, Julia (Julie) Adams, George Nader, Sal Mineo, Jay C. Flippen. Entertaining account of Brink's robbery, tracing events leading up to famous heist; on-location filming in Boston. Mineo's film debut.

Six Day Bike Rider (1934) **69m.** **½ D: Lloyd Bacon. Joe E. Brown, Maxine Doyle, Frank McHugh, Lottie Williams. Intriguing gimmick has Brown trying to impress girlfriend by entering marathon race; good little comedy.

Six Hours to Live (1932) **78m.** ** D: William Dieterle. Warner Baxter, Miriam Jordan, John Boles, George Marion, Beryl Mercer, Irene Ware. Unusual story of diplomat Baxter whose stubbornness at international trade conference leads to his murder; scientist brings him back to life for six hours. Stodgy production spoils interesting idea.

Six Lessons from Madame La Zonga (1941) **62m.** ** D: John Rawlins. Lupe Velez, Leon Errol, Helen Parrish, Charles Lang, William Frawley, Eddie Quillan, Shemp Howard. Good cast of professional laugh-getters in typical, silly outing; Leon goes Latin, and Lupe goes gold-digging after him in shipboard comedy. Title derived from popular song of the day.

Six Million Dollar Man, The (1973) **C-73m.** TVM D: Richard Irving. Lee Majors, Darren McGavin, Martin Balsam, Barbara Anderson, Charles Knox Robinson. Test pilot crash-lands, goverment steps in and has him confined to hospital where new techniques enable body to be rebuilt. Result: superhuman strength, whereupon government convinces pilot to undertake secret mission. Pilot for the hit series, followed years later by THE RETURN OF THE SIX-MILLION-DOLLAR MAN AND THE BIONIC WOMAN. Average.

Six of a Kind (1934) **62m.** *** D: Leo McCarey. W. C. Fields, George Burns,

[1053]

Gracie Allen, Charlie Ruggles, Mary Boland, Alison Skipworth. George and Gracie drive Mary and Charlie crazy traveling westward on vacation; Fields as pool-playing sheriff adds to confusion. Zany, wonderful nonsense.

Six Pack (1982) **C-110m.** ** D: Daniel Petrie. Kenny Rogers, Diane Lane, Erin Gray, Barry Corbin, Terry Kiser, Bob Hannah, Anthony Michael Hall. Stock car driver more or less inherits six orphans whose idea of good clean fun is stripping down someone else's auto. Not as bad as it sounds, but it won't make your day, either; Rogers' theatrical debut.▼

Six-Pack Annie (1975) **C-88m.** *** D: Graydon F. David. Lindsay Bloom, Jana Bellan, Ray Danton, Joe Higgins, Stubby Kaye, Louisa Moritz, Richard Kennedy, Doodles Weaver, Bruce Boxleitner, Pedro Gonzalez-Gonzalez, Sid Melton. Minor drive-in classic has busty Bloom as a young girl who goes to Miami to become a hooker to raise money to save her mom's failing diner. Includes a very funny bit by Kennedy as a drunk Texan.

Sixteen (1972) **C-84m.** ** D: Lawrence Dobkin. Mercedes McCambridge, Simone Griffeth, Ford Rainey, Beverly Powers, Parley Baer, Maidie Norman. Sympathetic study of backwoods girl (Griffeth) coming of age in the Deep South. Originally titled LIKE A CROW ON A JUNE BUG.▼

Sixteen Candles (1984) **C-93m.** ** D: John Hughes. Molly Ringwald, Anthony Michael Hall, Michael Schoeffling, Paul Dooley, Justin Henry, Gedde Watanabe, Blanche Baker, Carlin Glynn, Edward Andrews, Billie Bird, Carole Cook, Max Showalter, John Cusack, Joan Cusack, Jami Gertz, Beth Ringwald. A girl turns 16 and dreams of finding Mr. Right—little dreaming that he's already got his eye on her. Observant, potentially winning comedy cluttered up with cheap jokes and offensive material. Redeemed somewhat by Ringwald's charming performance, and Hall's engaging portrayal of a would-be hustler.▼

16 Days of Glory (1986) **C-145m.** *** D: Bud Greenspan. Narrated by David Perry. Expansive look at the 1984 Los Angeles Olympic Games, with enough natural excitement and irresistible moments to make up for overwritten narration and overbearing score. ▼

Sixteen Fathoms Deep (1934) **57m.** **½ D: Armand Schaefer. Creighton Chaney (Lon Chaney, Jr.), Sally O'Neil, George Regas, Maurice Black, Russell Simpson. Some nicely done underwater cinematography helps this otherwise undistinguished account of sponge fisherman Chaney and loyal girlfriend O'Neil going up against greedy moneylender Regas. Remade in 1948, also with Chaney.▼

16 Fathoms Deep (1948) **C-82m.** ** D: Irving Allen. Lon Chaney, Jr., Lloyd Bridges, Arthur Lake, Eric Feldary, Tanis Chandler, John Qualen, Dickie Moore. Harmless story of sponge fishing in Florida, with a pre-*Sea Hunt* Bridges appropriately cast as a diver. Chaney is the heavy here. In the 1934 version he's the hero.

633 Squadron (1964-British) **C-101m.** **½ D: Walter Grauman. Cliff Robertson, George Chakiris, Maria Perschy, Harry Andrews. Pretentious WW2 aviation film about the group's air mission to bomb German-run factory in Norway. Robertson and Chakiris are stiff-lipped throughout; script by James Clavell and Howard Koch.

'68 (1988) **C-97m.** *½ D: Steven Kovacks. Eric Larson, Robert Locke, Neil Young, Sandor Tecsi, Anna Dukasz, Mirlan Kwun, Terra Vandergaw, Shony Alex Braun, Donna Pecora. Gruff Hungarian immigrant struggles to start something called the Budapest Cafe in the Golden Protest era of San Francisco, and butts heads with his two sons (one politically active, the other gay) as the city goes crazy around them. Cheapie qualifies as "personal" filmmaking, but that doesn't make it any better. Rocker Young turns up as a cycle shop owner named "Westy."▼

Sixty Glorious Years (1938-British) **C-95m.** *** D: Herbert Wilcox. Anna Neagle, Anton Walbrook, C. Aubrey Smith, Walter Rilla, Charles Carson. Neagle's follow-up to VICTORIA THE GREAT is a repeat of her fine performance as England's legendary queen; good production values. U.S. title: QUEEN OF DESTINY.

Six Weeks (1982) **C-107m.** ** D: Tony Bill. Dudley Moore, Mary Tyler Moore, Katherine Healy, Shannon Wilcox, Bill Calvert, Joe Regalbuto. Curiously unmoving tearjerker about a politician who meets a precocious young girl who's dying of leukemia, and becomes involved with her mother. Genteel, well acted (Dudley is absolutely charming) but hollow; the characters just don't ring true. Healy, in real life, is an award-winning ballerina.▼

Sizzle (1981) **C-100m. TVM** D: Don Medford. Loni Anderson, John Forsythe, Michael Goodwin, Leslie Uggams, Roy Thinnes, Richard Lynch, Phyllis Davis. Small-town tootsie goes to Prohibition Era Chicago and gets mixed up with mobsters. Roaring '20s melodrama is slick but doesn't live up to its title. Average.▼

Sizzle Beach, U.S.A. (1986) **C-93m.** BOMB D: Richard Brander. Terry Congie, Leslie Brander, Roselyn Royce, Kevin Costner. Ultra-low-budget beach-bimbo junk, of interest solely as the first film appearance of Costner. Made in 1974.▼

Skag (1980) **C-150m. TVM** D: Frank Perry. Karl Malden, Piper Laurie, Craig Wasson, Peter Gallagher, Leslie Ackerman,

Kathryn Holcomb, George Voskovec. Malden's powerhouse performance as a veteran steelworker felled by a serious stroke carries this blue-collar drama (written by Abby Mann) that spun off a series. Above average.▼

Skateboard (1977) **C-97m.** ** D: George Gage. Allen Garfield, Kathleen Lloyd, Leif Garrett, Richard Van Der Wyk, Tony Alva, Antony Carbone. In trouble with his bookie, Garfield organizes local skateboarders into moneymaking team. Good premise given lackluster treatment.▼

Skatetown, U.S.A. (1979) **C-98m.** *½ D: William A. Levey. Scott Baio, Flip Wilson, Ron Palillo, Ruth Buzzi, Dave Mason, Greg Bradford, Kelly Lang, Billy Barty, Dorothy Stratten. Comedy-fantasy for the light of heart and slow of brain, with occasionally amusing comedy bits spicing plotless look at the ultimate roller-disco palace. Film's only real distinction is that it's better than ROLLER BOOGIE. Film debut of Patrick Swayze.

Skeezer (1982) **C-100m.** TVM D: Peter Hunt. Karen Valentine, Dee Wallace, Tom Atkins, Mariclare Costello, Leighton Greer, Justin Lord, Jeremy Licht. Karen works with a therapeutic dog in a home for emotionally disturbed children. Surprisingly good family show that manages to rise above its pat premise, adapted by Robert Hamilton from Elizabeth Yates book *Skeezer, Dog with a Mission.* Above average.▼

Ski Bum, The (1971) **C-136m.** BOMB D: Bruce Clark. Zalman King, Charlotte Rampling, Joseph Mell, Dimitra Arliss, Anna Karen, Tedd King. Deservedly obscure film version of Romain Gary's novel about a ski bum who goes establishment, winds up a pawn in a shady business deal.▼

Skidoo (1969) **C-98m.** **½ D: Otto Preminger. Jackie Gleason, Carol Channing, Frankie Avalon, Fred Clark, Michael Constantine, Frank Gorshin, John Phillip Law, Peter Lawford, Burgess Meredith, George Raft, Cesar Romero, Mickey Rooney, Groucho Marx, Austin Pendleton. Avalon plays an up-and-coming gangster, Groucho a mob kingpin named "God," and every single credit to the film is sung. Consequently, about one in a thousand will have the temperament to like this; everyone else will sit there dumbstruck. Music score by Harry Nilsson. Groucho's final film.

Ski Fever (1969) **C-98m.** *½ D: Curt Siodmak. Martin Milner, Claudia Martin, Vivi Bach, Dietmar Schoenherr, Toni Sailor, Dorit Dom. American ski instructor giving lessons in Austria to finance his education is unpleasantly surprised to learn his duties include entertaining guests after hours. Why complain when most of them are good-looking girls? Claudia is Dean Martin's daughter.

Ski Lift to Death (1978) **C-100m.** TVM D: William Wiard. Deborah Raffin, Charles Frank, Howard Duff, Don Galloway, Don Johnson, Clu Gulager, Gail Strickland, Veronica Hamel. Formula suspense thriller set in a ski resort—and even skiing star Suzy Chaffee is dragged in to give it some dazzle. Average.

Skin Deep (1978-New Zealand) **C-103m.** ***½ D: Geoff Steven. Deryn Cooper, Ken Blackburn, Grant Tilly, Alan Jervis, Glenis Leverstam. Small-town civic leaders import a professional masseuse from the big city—all in the name of progress. Subtle, perceptive, well-made examination of hypocrisy and exploitation.

Skin Deep (1989) **C-101m.** **½ D: Blake Edwards. John Ritter, Vincent Gardenia, Alyson Reed, Joel Brooks, Julianne Phillips, Chelsea Field, Nina Foch, Denise Crosby, Michael Kidd, Bryan Genesse, Sheryl Lee Ralph. Successful L.A. writer (Ritter) can't keep his hedonistic life on track—not with diversions around like wine (he's an alcoholic), women (he's insatiable), and song (Cole Porter's a favorite). Spotty, often obvious comedy from writer-director Edwards does have some real laughs—and some unforgettable condoms.▼

Skin Game, The (1931-British) **86m.** ** D: Alfred Hitchcock. Edmund Gwenn, Jill Esmond, John Longden, C. V. France, Helen Haye, Phyllis Konstam. Gwenn adds the only spark of life to this dull adaptation of the Galsworthy play about rivalry between neighboring landowners. Hitchcock claims he didn't make it by choice, and one can believe it considering the many long, static dialogue scenes; very atypical of the Master.▼

Skin Game (1971) **C-102m.** ***½ D: Paul Bogart. James Garner, Louis Gossett, Susan Clark, Brenda Sykes, Edward Asner, Andrew Duggan. Exceptional comedy about Garner and Gossett running con-game posing as master and slave in post-Civil War era. Serious undertones enhance this offbeat, entertaining film; Clark delightful as female con-artist who joins duo. Scripter "Pierre Marton" is Peter Stone. Remade by original director Burt Kennedy as SIDEKICKS, a TVM.▼

Ski Party (1965) **C-90m.** ** D: Alan Rafkin. Frankie Avalon, Dwayne Hickman, Deborah Walley, Yvonne Craig, Robert Q. Lewis, Bobbi Shaw, Aron Kincaid. BEACH PARTY gang puts on some clothes in this one, but the shenanigans are the same. Guest star Lesley Gore sings "Sunshine, Lollipops and Rainbows."

Ski Patrol (1990) **C-91m.** *½ D: Richard Correll. Roger Rose, T. K. Carter, Paul Feig, Martin Mull, Ray Walston, Yvette Nipar, Tess, Corby Timbrook. From the producer of the POLICE ACADEMY series comes POLICE ACADEMY ON SKIS—and it's just as brain-dead. Only the names have been changed, so don't let them snow you—unless you're in the mood to check out the fine hotdogging stunts on the slopes.▼

Skipper Surprised His Wife, The (1950) 85m. *½ D: Elliott Nugent. Robert Walker, Joan Leslie, Edward Arnold, Spring Byington, Jan Sterling. Unsurprising comedy; weak material about sailor Walker running home like ship. Good cast wasted.

Skippy (1931) 85m. *** D: Norman Taurog. Jackie Cooper, Robert Coogan, Mitzi Green, Jackie Searl, Willard Robertson, Enid Bennett, Donald Haines. Classic children's film from Percy Crosby's popular comic strip, following the misadventures of Cooper, the local health inspector's son, and Coogan, the poor ragamuffin from Shantytown, as they try to scrape up three dollars for a dog license. Simple and dated, but with a timeless innocent charm. Taurog won the Best Director Oscar for this. Followed by a sequel, SOOKY.

Skirts Ahoy! (1952) C-109m. **½ D: Sidney Lanfield. Esther Williams, Joan Evans, Vivian Blaine, Barry Sullivan, Keefe Brasselle, Debbie Reynolds, Bobby Van, Billy Eckstine. Chipper cast can't buoy this wornout story of three WAVES and their boyfriends.

Ski Troop Attack (1960) 63m. ** D: Roger Corman. Michael Forest, Frank Wolff, Wally Campo, Richard Sinatra, James Hoffman, Sheila Carol, Roger Corman. Wintry WW2 adventure with five U.S. soldiers on skis behind enemy lines in Germany. OK Corman low-budgeter.▼

Skokie (1981) C-125m. TVM D: Herbert Wise. Danny Kaye, John Rubinstein, Carl Reiner, Kim Hunter, Eli Wallach, Lee Strasberg, Brian Dennehy, Ed Flanders, George Dzundza, James Sutorius, Ruth Nelson. Powerful dramatization by Ernest Kinoy depicting how citizens of Skokie, Ill., became embroiled in a bitter controversy while trying to prevent street demonstrations by neo-Nazis in 1977. Danny Kaye gives a searing performance as a concentration camp survivor in his TV dramatic debut. Above average.

Skull, The (1965-British) C-83m. **½ D: Freddie Francis. Peter Cushing, Patrick Wymark, Christopher Lee, Nigel Green, Jill Bennett, Michael Gough, George Coulouris, Patrick Magee. Good cast lends needed support to questionable script (based on a Robert Bloch story) of skull of Marquis de Sade that has mysterious powers.

Skullduggery (1970) C-105m. *½ D: Gordon Douglas. Burt Reynolds, Susan Clark, Roger C. Carmel, Chips Rafferty, Edward Fox, Wilfrid Hyde-White, Pat Suzuki, Rhys Williams. In New Guinea, Reynolds and Clark find gentle ape people called the Tropi; their humanity has to be proved in court to keep them from being slaughtered by developers. Unusual but

unsuccessful story whose author had his name removed from the credits.▼

Sky Above, The Mud Below, The (1961-French) C-90m. *** D: Pierre-Dominique Gaisseau. Narrated by William Peacock. Academy Award-winning documentary showing variety of primitive life found within confines of Dutch New Guinea.▼

Sky Bandits (1986-British) C-92m. BOMB D: Zoran Perisic. Scott McGinnis, Jeff Osterhage, Ronald Lacey. McGinnis and Osterhage are a poor man's BUTCH CASSIDY AND THE SUNDANCE KID in this dreary adventure of two Western buddies' aerial exploits during WWI. Touted as the most expensive ($18 million) independent British production ever, film is poorly cast and has nothing to offer but high-flying special effects, designed by director Perisic (who made Chris Reeve "fly" in SUPERMAN).

Sky Commando (1953) 69m. *½ D: Fred F. Sears. Dan Duryea, Frances Gifford, Michael Connors, Michael Fox. Limping account of the responsibilities of being an Air Force officer, with usual rash of hackneyed situations.

Sky Devils (1932) 89m. ** D: A. Edward Sutherland. Spencer Tracy, William "Stage" Boyd, Ann Dvorak, George Cooper, Billy Bevan, Yola D'Avril. Two dumbbells try to avoid WW1 service in this disjointed, low-grade comedy; Dvorak is beautiful, leftover flying scenes from producer Howard Hughes' HELL'S ANGELS are impressive, but stupidity reigns overall.

Sky Dragon (1949) 64m. D: Lesley Selander. Roland Winters, Keye Luke, Mantan Moreland, Tim Ryan, Milburn Stone, Joel Marston, Noel Neill, Iris Adrian, Elena Verdugo, Lyle Talbot. SEE: **Charlie Chan** series.

Sky Full of Moon (1952) 73m. ** D: Norman Foster. Carleton Carpenter, Jan Sterling, Keenan Wynn, Elaine Stewart. Unassuming comedy of naive cowpoke falling in love with a not-so-innocent in Las Vegas.

Sky Heist (1975) C-100m. TVM D: Lee H. Katzin. Don Meredith, Joseph Campanella, Stefanie Powers, Frank Gorshin, Shelley Fabares, Larry Wilcox. Police helicopter is hijacked as part of a scheme to make off with $10 million in gold bullion. Meredith heads team of air-borne cops in pursuit of the perpetrators. Average.

Sky High (1922) 51m. *** D: Lynn Reynolds. Tom Mix, J. Farrell MacDonald, Eva Novak, Sid Jordan, William Buckley. Tom Mix eschews cowboy garb to play immigration officer out to crack alien-smuggling ring on Mexican border; action packed entertainment.

Skyjacked (1972) C-100m. **½ D: John Guillermin. Charlton Heston, Yvette Mimieux, James Brolin, Claude Akins, Jeanne Crain, Susan Dey, Roosevelt Grier, Mariette

Hartley, Walter Pidgeon. Commercial flight hijacked to Russia. Entertaining for first half, even exciting; second half deteriorates. Good cast will distract some from tedium elsewhere. Retitled: SKY TERROR.

Skylark (1941) **94m.** ***½ D: Mark Sandrich. Claudette Colbert, Ray Milland, Brian Aherne, Binnie Barnes, Walter Abel, Ernest Cossart, Grant Mitchell. Sophisticated romance with Aherne trying to take Claudette away from business-minded husband Milland. Stars are at their peak in this smooth adaptation of Samson Raphaelson play.

Sky Murder (1940) **72m.** ** D: George B. Seitz. Walter Pidgeon, Donald Meek, Kaaren Verne, Edward Ashley, Joyce Compton, Tom Conway. Pidgeon as detective Nick Carter decides to help refugee Verne in above-average private-eye yarn.

Sky Pirates (1986-Australian) **C-86m.** *½ D: Colin Eggleston. John Hargreaves, Meredith Phillips, Max Phipps, Bill Hunter, Simon Chilvers, Alex Scott. Yet another RAIDERS–INDIANA JONES variation, about an aircraft that crashes through a time warp, a search for a special stone, and other assorted nonsense. Boring and confusing, but Hargreaves earns an A for effort.▼

Sky Riders (1976) **C-93m.** *** D: Douglas Hickox. James Coburn, Susannah York, Robert Culp, Charles Aznavour, Harry Andrews, John Beck. Lively thriller about a political kidnapping, highlighted by spectacular sequences of hang-gliding. The aerial derring-do and the magnificent Greek scenery make this one worth sitting through.▼

Skyscraper Souls (1932) **99m.** *** D: Edgar Selwyn. Warren William, Maureen O'Sullivan, Gregory Ratoff, Anita Page, Verree Teasdale, Norman Foster, Jean Hersholt, Wallace Ford, Hedda Hopper, Helen Coburn, Ed Brophy. Entertaining comedy-drama in the GRAND HOTEL mode (released four months earlier, also by MGM) about a ruthless empire-builder (well played by William) who manipulates stock prices and double-crosses lovers in his quest to control a 100-story office building. Potent pre-Code entertainment, much of it still pretty risqué.

Skyscraper Wilderness SEE: **Big City, The** (1937)

Sky's No Limit, The (1984) **C-100m.** TVM D: David Lowell Rich. Sharon Gless, Dee Wallace, Anne Archer, David Ackroyd, Barnard Hughes. The lives and loves of three women astronauts, each striving to be the first in space, written, the producers swear, before Sally Ride rode. Average.

Sky's the Limit, The (1943) **89m.** *** D: Edward H. Griffith. Fred Astaire, Joan Leslie, Robert Benchley, Robert Ryan, Elizabeth Patterson, Marjorie Gateson.

Fred's a flier on leave who meets photographer Leslie; Benchley's dinner speech, Astaire's "One For My Baby" and "My Shining Hour" make this worthwhile.▼

Sky Terror SEE: **Skyjacked**

Skyward (1980) **C-100m.** TVM D: Ron Howard. Bette Davis, Howard Hesseman, Suzy Gilstrap, Ben Marley, Clu Gulager, Marion Ross, Lisa Whelchel, Jana Hall. Inspiring story (written by director Ron Howard's *Happy Days* pal and production partner Anson Williams, with a teleplay by Nancy Sackett) about how former stunt pilot Davis and airport watchman Hesseman help a teenaged paraplegic (real-life wheelchair-bound Gilstrap) learn to fly a plane. Above average.

Skyway to Death (1974) **C-78m.** TVM D: Gordon Hessler. Ross Martin, Stefanie Powers, Bobby Sherman, Nancy Malone, John Astin, Joseph Campanella, Tige Andrews. Group of vacationers trapped in a cable car 8000 feet up between mountain peaks; rescue attempt is hindered by an approaching windstorm. Written to formula, and acted that way as well. Average.

Sky West and Crooked SEE: **Gypsy Girl**

Slamdance (1987) **C-100m.** BOMB D: Wayne Wang. Tom Hulce, Mary Elizabeth Mastrantonio, Virginia Madsen, Harry Dean Stanton, Millie Perkins, Don Opper, Adam Ant, John Doe. Underground cartoonist/painter Hulce, devoted to his ex-wife and young child, is framed—apparently by the entire population of L.A.—for the murder of party girl Madsen. Weird, without compensating originality. Lifeless melodrama deals only peripherally with the "club" scene; there is as much slamdancing in PYGMALION.▼

Slammer SEE: **Short Eyes**▼

Slams, The (1973) **C-97m.** ** D: Jonathan Kaplan. Jim Brown, Judy Pace, Roland "Bob" Harris, Frank de Kova, Ted Cassidy. Mindless actioner has Brown in L.A. prison after stashing away a heroin cache and $1.5 million. Halfway through, comedy takes over for a fast pickup.

Slander (1956) **81m.** **½ D: Roy Rowland. Van Johnson, Ann Blyth, Steve Cochran, Marjorie Rambeau, Richard Eyer. Slick, superficial "inside study" of the smut magazines, focusing on their exclusive on a TV personality.

Slap Shot (1977) **C-122m.** *** D: George Roy Hill. Paul Newman, Michael Ontkean, Lindsay Crouse, Jennifer Warren, Melinda Dillon, Strother Martin, Jerry Houser, Swoosie Kurtz. Newman is star of bush-league hockey team that's going nowhere until they decide to play dirty. Uneven but raucously funny at times, with very satisfying wrapup. Andrew Duncan is hilarious as local sports broadcaster; barbed (and very profane) script by Nancy Dowd.▼

Slapstick (Of Another Kind) (1984)

C-82m. *½ D: Steven Paul. Jerry Lewis, Madeline Kahn, Marty Feldman, Jim Backus, John Abbott, Pat Morita, Samuel Fuller, Merv Griffin, Steven Paul, voice of Orson Welles. Lewis and Kahn give birth to enormous, deformed twins (also Lewis and Kahn) who are in reality alien messengers capable of solving the world's problems—as long as they're not separated. Given that cast and a Kurt Vonnegut novel as source material, you'd think there'd be no way to screw it up, but writer/producer/director/costar Paul manages; some funny things do survive (Fuller and the elder Lewis come off best), but overall, pretty appalling. Filmed in 1982.▼

Slate, Wyn & Me (1987-Australian) C-90m. ** D: Don McLennan. Sigrid Thornton, Simon Burke, Martin Sacks, Tommy Lewis, Lesley Baker. Meandering drama of brothers Burke and Sacks, who rob a bank, kill a cop . . . and kidnap Thornton, who witnesses their crime. Potentially intriguing tale falls flat after twenty minutes.▼

Slattery's Hurricane (1949) **83m.** **½ D: Andre de Toth. Richard Widmark, Linda Darnell, Veronica Lake, John Russell, Gary Merrill. Weather-pilot Widmark, in midst of storm, thinks back on his life; Darnell and Lake are his two loves. Interesting idea; coscripted by Herman Wouk, who later expanded it into a novel.

Slaughter (1972) **C-92m.** ** D: Jack Starrett. Jim Brown, Stella Stevens, Rip Torn, Don Gordon, Cameron Mitchell, Marlene Clark, Robert Phillips. Stevens and Torn are far too good for this violent tripe about ex-Green Beret Brown who goes after syndicate after it kills his parents. Sequel: SLAUGHTER'S BIG RIP-OFF.▼

Slaughterhouse Five (1972) **C-104m.** *** D: George Roy Hill. Michael Sacks, Ron Leibman, Eugene Roche, Sharon Gans, Valerie Perrine, John Dehner, Holly Near, Perry King. Sometimes draggy, sometimes on-target, sprawling view of life through eyes of one Billy Pilgrim, professional nobody who becomes "unstuck" in time. Big-budget adaptation of Kurt Vonnegut's bizarre fantasy novel is hard going for those unfamiliar with author's point of view, gains through repeat viewings.▼

Slaughter in San Francisco (1981-Hong Kong) **C-87m.** BOMB D: William Lowe. Don Wong, Chuck Norris, Sylvia Channing, Robert Jones, Dan Ivan. Former cop Wong seeks vengeance on murderer of his partner; Norris, in a supporting role, is the bad guy. Shoddy production will disappoint chop-socky genre buffs. Filmed in 1973; released to take advantage of Norris's subsequent popularity.▼

Slaughter of the Vampires (1961-Italian) **C-72m.** BOMB D: Roberto Mauri. Dieter Eppler, Walter Brandi (Brandt), Graziella Granata, Paolo Solvay. Vampire Eppler

hankers for the new occupants of an Austrian castle. Pretty bad. Original running time: 84m. Also known as CURSE OF THE BLOOD-GHOULS.▼

Slaughter on Tenth Avenue (1957) **103m.** *** D: Arnold Laven. Richard Egan, Jan Sterling, Dan Duryea, Julie Adams, Walter Matthau, Sam Levene, Charles McGraw, Mickey Shaughnessy. Well-handled waterfront racketeer expose, set in N.Y.C. with good supporting cast.

Slaughter's Big Rip-Off (1973) **C-93m.** *½ D: Gordon Douglas. Jim Brown, Ed McMahon, Brock Peters, Don Stroud, Gloria Hendry, Dick Anthony Williams, Art Metrano. Slaughter's still playing cat and mouse with the Mob in this dreary actioner; McMahon gives his role as the Syndicate head better than it deserves.▼

Slaughter Trail (1951) **C-78m.** ** D: Irving Allen. Brian Donlevy, Gig Young, Virginia Grey, Andy Devine. Routine narrative of outlaws killing Indians and cavalry men to get what they want.

Slave, The (1963-Italian) **C-102m.** *½ D: Sergio Corbucci. Steve Reeves, Jacques Sernas, Gianna Maria Canale, Claudio Gora. Interminable Italian spectacle. Son of Spartacus learns story of father, vows vengeance. Good photography only asset. Also titled SON OF SPARTACUS.

Slave Girl (1947) **C-80m.** **½ D: Charles Lamont. Yvonne De Carlo, George Brent, Broderick Crawford, Albert Dekker, Lois Collier, Andy Devine, Arthur Treacher. Tale of adventure with evil potentate holding Americans prisoner; not to be taken seriously (there's even a talking camel), enjoyable on that scale.

Slave Girls SEE: **Prehistoric Women**▼

Slave of the Cannibal God (1978-Italian) **C-86m.** *½ D: Sergio Martino. Ursula Andress, Stacy Keach, Claudio Cassinelli, Antonio Marsina, Franco Fantasia. Too-glamorous Andress captured by natives and painted in preparation for sacrifice in a scene virtually identical to that directed by ex-husband John Derek for current wife Bo years later in TARZAN, THE APE MAN.▼

Slavers (1978-German) **C-102m.** ** D: Jurgen Goslar. Trevor Howard, Ron Ely, Britt Ekland, Jurgen Goslar, Ray Milland, Ken Gampu, Cameron Mitchell. Pulp-fiction stuff about slave trading in Africa during the 19th century. Good cast saddled with second-rate script.▼

Slaves (1969) **C-110m.** *½ D: Herbert J. Biberman. Stephen Boyd, Dionne Warwick, Ossie Davis, Marilyn Clark, Gale Sondergaard, Shepperd Strudwick, Nancy Coleman, Julius Harris, David Huddleston. Strange cast in revisionist drama about Kentucky slave Davis standing up for his rights; might have meant something in the 60s, but now it's just laughable, with Boyd properly embarrassed as Simon Legree-type "Massa." Notable only as Sondergaard's first film after 20-year blacklist, courtesy director-cowriter (and husband) Biberman.

Slave Ship (1937) 92m. *** D: Tay Garnett. Warner Baxter, Wallace Beery, Elizabeth Allan, Mickey Rooney, George Sanders, Jane Darwell, Joseph Schildkraut. Rousing drama of slave ship rebellion with fine atmosphere, good Beery-Rooney teaming, plenty of action.

Slaves of Babylon (1953) C-82m. ** D: William Castle. Richard Conte, Linda Christian, Maurice Schwartz, Michael Ansara, Julie Newmar. Jumbled biblical adventure mixed with romance. Nebuchadnezzar faces army of Israelites led by shepherd.

Slaves of New York (1989) C-125m. *½ D: James Ivory. Bernadette Peters, Adam Coleman Howard, Chris Sarandon, Mary Beth Hurt, Nick Corri, Madeleine Potter, Mercedes Ruehl, Betty Comden, Steve Buscemi, Michael Schoeffling, Tammy Grimes, Charles McCaughan. Misguided filming of Tama Janowitz's bestselling collection of stories, set among the too-hip-for-words denizens of N.Y.C.'s downtown art world. As the central character, the talented Peters seems all wrong: too intelligent to spend most of the film being humiliated by her boyfriend (Howard). Overlong and unfocused. Janowitz (who plays Abby) scripted.▼

Slaves of the Invisible Monster (1950) 100m. BOMB D: Fred Brannon. Richard Webb, Aline Towne, Lane Bradford, Stanley Price, John Crawford, George Meeker. With the aid of secret formula arch-criminal makes himself transparent and carries out master plan; blah actioner. Reedited from Republic serial THE INVISIBLE MONSTER.

Slayground (1984-British) C-89m. *½ D: Terry Bedford. Peter Coyote, Billie Whitelaw, Philip Sayer, Bill Luhr, Mel Smith. Dreary actioner about robber Coyote on the lam from a hired killer. Whitelaw in particular is wasted as an amusement park owner. Based on a novel by Donald E. Westlake, writing as Richard Stark.▼

Sleeper (1973) C-88m. ***½ D: Woody Allen. Woody Allen, Diane Keaton, John Beck, Mary Gregory, Don Keefer, John McLiam. Woody turns to slapstick in this engagingly silly tale of a man who's frozen in 1973 and awakened 200 years later. Typical Allen combination of great jokes and duds, with more sight-gags than usual and energetic score by the Preservation Hall Jazz Band.▼

Sleeping Beauty (1959) C-75m. *** D: Clyde Geronimi. Voices of Mary Costa, Bill Shirley, Eleanor Audley, Verna Felton, Barbara Jo Allen (Vera Vague), Barbara Luddy. Walt Disney's most expensive and elaborate animated feature (at the time) is actually a simple, straightforward telling of the classic fairy tale, with music adapted from Tchaikovsky, and such memorable characters as Flora, Fauna, and Merryweather (the three good fairies) and the evil witch Malefecent. Highlight: the final, fiery confrontation between Malefecent and Prince Phillip. Bound to lose something on TV, since it was filmed in (and designed for) a wide-screen process.▼

Sleeping Car, The (1990) C-87m. ** D: Douglas Curtis. David Naughton, Judie Aronson, Kevin McCarthy, Jeff Conaway, Ernestine Mercer, John Carl Buechler, Dani Minnick. Good-looking but heavily overstated horror film pitting Naughton and friends against a vicious ghost haunting an old railway sleeping car, now used as an apartment.▼

Sleeping Car Murder, The (1965-French) 90m. *** D: Costa-Gavras. Simone Signoret, Yves Montand, Pierre Mondy, Jean-Louis Trintignant, Jacques Perrin, Michel Piccoli, Catherine Allegret, Charles Denner. Quick-paced, atmospheric police-chasing-mad-killer movie. Nice photography by Jean Tournier; original action good but dubbing hurts. Based on a Sebastien Japrisot novel.

Sleeping Car to Trieste (1948-British) 95m. *** D: John Paddy Carstairs. Jean Kent, Albert Lieven, Derrick de Marney, Paul Dupuis, Rona Anderson, David Tomlinson. The Orient Express is the setting for fine cat-and-mouse story of espionage agents competing for possession of "hot" political diary. Remake of ROME EXPRESS.

Sleeping City, The (1950) 85m. **½ D: George Sherman. Richard Conte, Coleen Gray, Alex Nicol, Peggy Dow. OK mystery of private eye who seeks to uncover clues to homicide and dope smuggling at a large hospital.

Sleeping Dogs (1977-New Zealand) C-107m. ** D: Roger Donaldson. Sam Neill, Ian Mune, Warren Oates, Nevan Rowe, Donna Akersten, Ian Watkin, Bill Julliff, Clyde Scott. Muddled thriller about apolitical loner Neill unable to remain aloof from repressive government and revolutionaries during workers' strike. Fascinating concept defeated by confusing direction, illogical plot development, insufficiently defined characters, Michael Seresin's topnotch cinematography helps. The first New Zealand film ever to open in the U.S.▼

Sleeping Tiger, The (1954-British) 89m. *** D: Terence Hanbury (Joseph Losey). Alexis Smith, Alexander Knox, Dirk Bogarde, Hugh Griffith, Patricia McCarron, Billie Whitelaw. Tense triangular love tale of Smith, her psychiatrist husband Knox, and Bogarde, a crook on parole to Knox.▼

Sleep My Love (1948) **97m.** *** D: Douglas Sirk. Claudette Colbert, Robert Cummings, Don Ameche, Hazél Brooks, Rita Johnson, George Coulouris, Keye Luke, Raymond Burr, Ralph Morgan. Familiar territory covered by excellent cast as Ameche tries to drive wife Claudette crazy; Cummings saves her. From a Leo Rosten novel.

Slender Thread, The (1965) **98m.** **½ D: Sydney Pollack. Sidney Poitier, Anne Bancroft, Telly Savalas, Steven Hill, Edward Asner, Dabney Coleman. Interchange between stars is the whole film in an interesting idea that doesn't fulfill potential. Bancroft takes overdose of sleeping pills and calls crisis clinic for help; college student volunteer Poitier tries to keep her on phone while rescue is organized. Filmed on location in Seattle; written by Stirling Silliphant, music by Quincy Jones. Pollack's directorial debut.

Sleuth (1972) **C-138m.** **** D: Joseph L. Mankiewicz. Laurence Olivier, Michael Caine. Lighthearted mystery tour de force for two stars, adapted by Anthony Shaffer from his hit play about games-playing mystery writer Olivier leading his wife's lover (Caine) into diabolical trap. But who gets the last laugh on whom? Delicious from start to finish; remarkable production design by Ken Adam. Mankiewicz's last film to date.▼

Slight Case of Larceny, A (1953) **71m.** ** D: Don Weis. Mickey Rooney, Eddie Bracken, Elaine Stewart, Marilyn Erskine. Low hijinks from Rooney and Bracken as two buddies who open a gas station, siphoning supplies from oil company's pipelines.

Slight Case of Murder, A (1938) **85m.** ***½ D: Lloyd Bacon. Edward G. Robinson, Jane Bryan, Allen Jenkins, Ruth Donnelly, Willard Parker, John Litel, Edward Brophy, Harold Huber. Robinson's in peak comedy form as gangster who goes straight when Prohibition ends. This hilarious adaptation of a play by Damon Runyon and Howard Lindsay has brewer Robinson going bankrupt in a rented summer house filled with characters and corpses. Remade as STOP, YOU'RE KILLING ME.

Slightly Dangerous (1943) **94m.** ** D: Wesley Ruggles. Lana Turner, Robert Young, Walter Brennan, Dame May Whitty, Eugene Pallette, Florence Bates, Alan Mowbray, Bobby (Robert) Blake. Slightly ridiculous comedy of waitress Turner who claims to be daughter of wealthy industrialist. Good cast in trivial piece of fluff.

Slightly French (1949) **81m.** **½ D: Douglas Sirk. Dorothy Lamour, Don Ameche,

Janis Carter, Willard Parker, Adele Jergens. Sassy musical of con-artist director Ameche passing off Lamour as French star.

Slightly Honorable (1940) **83m.** **½ D: Tay Garnett. Pat O'Brien, Edward Arnold, Broderick Crawford, Ruth Terry, Alan Dinehart, Eve Arden, Claire Dodd, Evelyn Keyes, Phyllis Brooks, Janet Beecher. Adequate mystery with lawyers O'Brien and Crawford involved in strange murders with corrupt politician Arnold.▼

Slightly Scarlet (1956) **C-99m.** **½ D: Allan Dwan. John Payne, Arlene Dahl, Rhonda Fleming, Kent Taylor, Ted de Corsia, Lance Fuller. Effective study (from a James M. Cain novel) of corruption within city officialdom; Payne involved with dynamic sister duo (Fleming, Dahl). Arlene steals the show as tipsy ex-con sister.▼

Slightly Terrific (1944) **61m.** ** D: Edward F. Cline. Leon Errol, Anne Rooney, Eddie Quillan, Betty Kean, Lorraine Kreuger, Richard Lane. Errol fans may enjoy his antics as twin brothers involved in backing Broadway musical, but between his comic scenes you've got to endure a parade of variety acts ranging from Donald Novis to the Maritza Dancers.

Slim (1937) **80m.** **½ D: Ray Enright. Pat O'Brien, Henry Fonda, Stuart Erwin, Margaret Lindsay, Dick Purcell, John Litel, Jane Wyman. Interesting little story of men who string high-voltage wire, with Lindsay the girl who comes between tough veteran O'Brien and novice Fonda. Good performances all around. A semi-remake of TIGER SHARK; remade as MANPOWER.

Slim Carter (1957) **C-82m.** ** D: Richard Bartlett. Jock Mahoney, Julie Adams, Tim Hovey, William Hopper, Barbara Hale. Mild goings-on of Mahoney becoming popular Western star, aided by Adams, who loves him, and Hovey, an orphan who enters their lives.

Slime People, The (1962) **76m.** BOMB D: Robert Hutton. Robert Hutton, Les Tremayne, Susan Hart, Robert Burton. Lumpy, lizardy people from beneath the Earth wall off Los Angeles with curtain of fog. Movie talks itself to death, with no slimy globs in sight.▼

Slipper and the Rose, The (1976-British) **C-128m.** *** D: Bryan Forbes. Richard Chamberlain, Gemma Craven, Annette Crosbie, Michael Hordern, Margaret Lockwood, Christopher Gable, Kenneth More, Edith Evans. Bright musical version of Cinderella in which everyone (including veteran British actors) sings and dances; Craven is delightful as Cindy. Songs by the Sherman Brothers. Good fun. British running time: 146m.

Slipstream (1989-British) **C-92m.** ** D: Steven M. Lisberger. Bill Paxton, Bob

Peck, Mark Hamill, Kitty Aldridge, Eleanor David, F. Murray Abraham, Ben Kingsley, Robbie Coltrane. In the future, nature has rebelled, sending people scurrying to live in valleys away from the high-speed slipstream that dominates the planet. Unfortunately this unusual setting has little to do with standard story of adventurer Paxton, who swipes a captive from tough bounty hunter Hamill (delivering a top-notch performance). Just as story should be building to a peak, it lurches into clumsy satire. This big-scale production never made it to theaters in the U.S.▼

Slither (1973) **C-97m.** *** D: Howard Zieff. James Caan, Peter Boyle, Sally Kellerman, Louise Lasser, Allen Garfield, Richard B. Shull. Engaging film is essentially a massive shaggy dog joke; colorful gallery of characters engaged in hunt for elusive cache of money. Perhaps a bit too airy, but perfect TV fare.

Slow Burn (1986) **C-88m. TVM** D: Matthew Chapman. Eric Roberts, Beverly D'Angelo, Dennis Lipscomb, Henry Gibson, Dan Hedaya, Anne Schedeen. Plodding, semi-coherent thriller about newspaperman-turned-detective Jacob Asch, who's hired to track down the son a Palm Springs artist long ago abandoned. Based on Arthur Lyons' novel *Castles Burning.* Made for cable. Below average.▼

Slow Dancing in the Big City (1978) **C-101m.** *½ D: John G. Avildsen. Paul Sorvino, Anne Ditchburn, Nicolas Coster, Anita Dangler, Hector Jaime Mercado. Straight-faced romantic absurdity about Jimmy Breslin-like columnist who falls for ailing ballerina who has been told she should no longer dance; he also befriends a little Hispanic orphan/junkie. Shameless climax will fry your brain cells with its bathos.

Slugger's Wife, The (1985) **C-105m.** *½ D: Hal Ashby. Michael O'Keefe, Rebecca DeMornay, Martin Ritt, Randy Quaid, Cleavant Derricks, Lisa Langlois, Loudon Wainwright III. Remarkably unappealing Neil Simon original about a boorish baseball star who falls in love with a singer. Dull and disjointed, full of mediocre music—in short, a mess! Director Ritt plays baseball manager.

Slumber Party '57 (1977) **C-89m.** BOMB D: William A. Levey. Noelle North, Bridget Hollman, Debra Winger, Mary Ann Appleseth, Rainbeaux Smith, Rafael Campos, Will Hutchins, Joyce Jillson, Joe E. Ross. Smutty, sloppily made schlock about a group of girls who swap tales about their sexual initiations, which are recreated in flashback. Of interest only for the appearance of Winger, in her film debut.▼

Slumber Party Massacre (1982) **C-78m.** *½ D: Amy Jones. Michele Michaels, Robin Stille, Michael Villela, Andre Honore, Debra Deliso, Gina Mari. Girls have overnight party, boys clown around, crazed killer does them all in. The screenplay, incredibly, is by Rita Mae Brown. If it's supposed to be a parody, it's about as clever as *Hogan's Heroes.* Followed by a sequel.▼

Slumber Party Massacre II (1987) **C-75m.** BOMB D: Deborah Brock. Crystal Bernard, Kimberly McArthur, Juliette Cummins, Patrick Lowe. Gory, bottom-of-the-barrel sequel, with yet another driller killer doing in the cast one by one. Yecch.▼

Small Back Room, The (1949-British) **106m.** ***½ D: Michael Powell, Emeric Pressburger. David Farrar, Jack Hawkins, Kathleen Byron, Anthony Bushell, Michael Gough, Leslie Banks, Robert Morley, Cyril Cusack, Renee Asherson. Mature, powerful story of crippled munitions expert Farrar, who's frustrated by his infirmity and mindless government bureaucracy during WW2. Beware of edited versions. Original U.S. title: HOUR OF GLORY.▼

Small Change (1976-French) **C-104m.** **** D: Francois Truffaut. Geory Desmouceaux, Philippe Goldman, Claudio Deluca, Frank Deluca, Richard Golfier, Laurent Devlaeminck. Thoroughly charming, intelligent film examines the lives of young children—their joys, sorrows, frustrations, adventures—in a small French village. Wise, perceptive, and witty.▼

Small Circle of Friends, A (1980) **C-112m.** BOMB D: Rob Cohen. Brad Davis, Karen Allen, Jameson Parker, Shelley Long, John Friedrich, Gary Springer. Cloyingly cute by-the-numbers treatment of '60s campus turmoil as an apparently moronic *ménage à trois* tries to make it through Harvard. Almost makes one long for R.P.M.▼

Smallest Show on Earth, The (1957-British) **80m.** *** D: Basil Dearden. Bill Travers, Virginia McKenna, Margaret Rutherford, Peter Sellers, Bernard Miles, Leslie Phillips. Charming, often hilarious comedy about a couple who inherit a run-down movie house and its three equally run-down attendants (Sellers, Rutherford, Miles). Lovely scene in which the three veterans express their love for silent films.▼

Small Killing, A (1981) **C-100m. TVM** D: Steven Hilliard Stern. Edward Asner, Jean Simmons, Sylvia Sidney, Andrew Prine, J. Pat O'Malley, Mary Jackson, Anne Ramsey. Undercover cop posing as a wino teams up with a woman college professor masquerading as a bag lady, they trail a drug kingpin's hit man and end up falling in love. Based on Richard Barth's book *The Rag Bag Clan.* Average.▼

Small Miracle, The (1973) **C-74m. TVM** D: Jeannot Szwarc. Vittorio De Sica, Raf Vallone, Marco Della Cava, Guidarini Guidi, Jan Larsson. Moving story of young boy who believes St. Francis of Assisi will cure his lame donkey; shot in Assisi and Rome. Paul Gallico's story was filmed before, in 1952, as NEVER TAKE NO FOR AN ANSWER. Average.

Small Sacrifices (1989) **C-200m. TVM** D: David Greene. Farrah Fawcett, Ryan O'Neal, John Shea, Gordon Clapp, Emily Perkins. Fawcett delivers a flamboyant performance as real-life Diane Downs, an Oregon mother accused of shooting her three children. A compelling and emotional story that's very tough to watch; Joyce Eliason based her top-notch script on Ann Rule's bestselling book. Originally shown in two parts. Above average.

Small Town Girl (1936) **108m. *** D: William Wellman. Janet Gaynor, Robert Taylor, Binnie Barnes, Lewis Stone, Andy Devine, James Stewart. Breezy romance about Gaynor trapping Taylor into marriage while he's drunk, then working to win him over when he's sober. Retitled ONE HORSE TOWN.

Small Town Girl (1953) **C-93m. **½ D: Leslie Kardos. Jane Powell, Farley Granger, Ann Miller, S. Z. Sakall, Billie Burke, Bobby Van, Robert Keith, Nat King Cole. Bland MGM musical pairing playboy Granger and apple-pie Powell, who meet when he's thrown in jail by her father for speeding through town. Van's human pogo-stick number and Miller's "I've Gotta Hear That Beat," with Busby Berkeley's disembodied orchestra, are highlights.▼

Small Town in Texas, A (1976) **C-95m. ** D: Jack Starrett. Timothy Bottoms, Susan George, Bo Hopkins, Art Hindle, Morgan Woodward, John Karlen. Bottoms seeks revenge against heinous sheriff Hopkins, who framed him on a drug charge and has stolen his wife (George). Not bad, but you know what to expect.▼

Smart Alec (1986) **C-88m. ** D: Jim Wilson. Ben Glass, Natasha Kautsky, Antony Alda, Lucinda Crosby, Kerry Remsen, Orson Bean, David Hedison, Bill Henderson, Zsa Zsa Gabor. Dull, silly (but not inaccurate) account of pint-sized eccentric Glass, an aspiring filmmaker, and his repeated frustrations as he attempts to finance his movie. Kautsky is most attractive as the model he covets as his leading lady. Also known as THE MOVIE MAKER.▼

Smart Alecks (1942) **88m.** D: Wallace Fox. Leo Gorcey, Huntz Hall, Bobby Jordan, Gabriel Dell, Maxie Rosenbloom, Gale Storm, Walter Woolf King, David Gorcey, Sunshine Sammy Morrison, Roger Pryor. SEE: **Bowery Boys** series.

Smartest Girl in Town (1936) **58m. **½ D: Joseph Santley. Gene Raymond, Ann Sothern, Helen Broderick, Eric Blore, Erik Rhodes. Ann mistakes wealthy Gene for a lowly male model, avoids him as she sets her sights on a rich husband. No surprises, but short and pleasant.▼

Smart Girls Don't Talk (1948) **81m. ** D: Richard Bare. Virginia Mayo, Bruce Bennett, Helen Westcott, Robert Hutton, Tom D'Andrea. Dull drama of socialite Mayo forced to join up with racketeer.

Smart Money (1931) **90m. **½ D: Alfred E. Green. Edward G. Robinson, James Cagney, Margaret Livingstone, Evalyn Knapp, Noel Francis. Known as Cagney and Robinson's only costarring film, but Robinson really stars, as lucky barber who becomes big-time gambler. Cagney is fine as Robinson's crony; watch for Boris Karloff in a bit as hustler.

Smart Woman (1948) **93m. *** D: Edward A. Blatt. Brian Aherne, Constance Bennett, Barry Sullivan, Michael O'Shea, James Gleason, Otto Kruger, Iris Adrian, Isobel Elsom, Selena Royle. Lawyer Bennett doesn't let love interfere with her determined attempt to prosecute crooked D.A. and other officials. Pretty big budget for a Monogram film; Alvah Bessie was one of the writers.

Smashing Bird I Used to Know, The SEE: **School for Unclaimed Girls**

Smashing the Crime Syndicate SEE: **Hell's Bloody Devils**

Smashing the Money Ring (1939) **57m. ** D: Terry Morse. Ronald Reagan, Margot Stevenson, Eddie Foy, Jr., Joe Downing, Charles D. Brown. Reagan, as Lt. Brass Bancroft, again cracks a gang of counterfeiters, as he did in CODE OF THE SECRET SERVICE. Passable programmer.

Smashing Time (1967-British) **96m. **½ D: Desmond Davis. Rita Tushingham, Lynn Redgrave, Michael York, Anna Quayle, Ian Carmichael. Two girls come to London to crash big-time. Spoof of trendy fashion/show biz world tries to turn Redgrave and Tushingham into Laurel and Hardy, with middling results. Slapstick scenes only mildly funny.

Smash Palace (1981-New Zealand) **C-100m. *** D: Roger Donaldson. Bruno Lawrence, Anna Jemison, Greer Robson, Keith Aberdein, Desmond Kelly. Lawrence is more interested in his cars than wife Jemison, who craves attention and affection. Sometimes confusing and overly melodramatic, but still worthwhile—particularly when focusing on their 7-year-old daughter (Robson).▼

Smash-Up Alley (1972) **C-83m. ** D: Edward J. Lakso. Darren McGavin, Richard Petty, Kathie Browne, Noah Beery, Jr., Pierre Jalbert, L. Q. Jones. Stock-car racer Petty plays himself, McGavin is his father, Lee, in this forgettable chronicle of their careers. Aficionados of the sport may enjoy it, however. Also known as 43: THE PETTY STORY.

Smash-Up on Interstate 5 (1976) C-100m. TVM D: John Llewellyn Moxey. Robert Conrad, Sian Barbara Allen, Buddy Ebsen, David Groh, Scott Jacoby, Sue Lyon, Vera Miles, Donna Mills, Terry Moore, Harriet Nelson, David Nelson, Tommy Lee Jones. Familiar multi-character drama with a twist. They're involved in spectacular 39-car crash on a California freeway. Performances understandably pale beside graphic smash-up scenes which—surprise!—turn up at the beginning of the movie. Average.

Smash-Up, the Story of a Woman (1947) 103m. *** D: Stuart Heisler. Susan Hayward, Lee Bowman, Marsha Hunt, Eddie Albert, Carl Esmond, Carleton Young. Hayward is excellent as an insecure nightclub singer who gives up her career when she weds soon to-be radio star Bowman . . . and finds herself helplessly mired in alcoholism. This was Hayward's breakthrough role after a decade in Hollywood, and it deservedly earned her her first Oscar nomination. Taut script by John Howard Lawson, from an original story by Dorothy Parker and Frank Cavett.▼

Smile (1975) C-113m. ***½ D: Michael Ritchie. Bruce Dern, Barbara Feldon, Michael Kidd, Geoffrey Lewis, Nicholas Pryor, Colleen Camp, Joan Prather, Annette O'Toole, Melanie Griffith. Hilarious, perceptive satire centering around the behind-the-scenes activity at a California beauty pageant, presented as a symbol for the emptiness of American middle-class existence. One of the unsung films of the 1970s, written by Jerry Belson; Kidd is terrific as the contest's career-slumped choreographer.▼

Smile, Jenny, You're Dead (1974) C-100m. TVM D: Jerry Thorpe. David Janssen, John Anderson, Howard da Silva, Martin Gabel, Clu Gulager, Zalman King, Jodie Foster, Andrea Marcovicci. Well-plotted mystery in which private eye Janssen looks into the murder of a friend's son-in-law and gets emotionally involved with his daughter, the prime suspect. Pilot for Janssen's *Harry O* series. Above average.

Smile Orange (1976-Jamaican) C-89m. *** D: Trevor Rhone. Carl Bradshaw, Glen Morrison, Vaughn Croskill, Stanley Irons. Crudely made but funny comedy about hustling Montego Bay resort-hotel waiter Bradshaw, playing the same role he created in THE HARDER THEY COME. Originally a stage play.

Smiles of a Summer Night (1955-Swedish) 108m. **** D: Ingmar Bergman. Ulla Jacobsson, Eva Dahlbeck, Margit Carlquist, Harriet Andersson, Gunnar Bjornstrand, Jarl Kulle. One of the finest romantic comedies ever made, a witty treatise on manners, mores, and sex during a weekend at a country estate in the late 19th century.

Inspired the Broadway musical and subsequent film A LITTLE NIGHT MUSIC (as well as Woody Allen's A MIDSUMMER NIGHT'S SEX COMEDY).▼

Smile When You Say "I Do" (1973) C-74m. TVM D: Allen Funt. Extension of *Candid Camera* series, with creator Funt examining battle of the sexes. Average.

Smiley (1957-Australian) C-97m. **½ D: Anthony Kimmins. Ralph Richardson, John McCallum, Chips Rafferty, Reg Lye. Softtreading narrative of young boy who wants a bicycle, becoming entangled with drug-smugglers. Sequel: SMILEY GETS A GUN.

Smiley Gets a Gun (1959-Australian) C-89m. ** D: Anthony Kimmins. Sybil Thorndike, Keith Calvert, Bruce Archer, Chips Rafferty, Margaret Christensen. Easy-going account of young boy trying to win the right to have a gun.

Smilin' Through (1932) 97m. *** D: Sidney Franklin. Norma Shearer, Fredric March, Leslie Howard, O. P. Heggie, Ralph Forbes. Sentimental romantic tale (with fantasy elements) about an embittered old man who lost his love on their wedding day but finds new reason to live when he must raise his orphaned niece (who looks exactly like his long-ago fiancée). Polished MGM production gets a bit pokey midway through but follows through to satisfying finale. Director Franklin originally filmed this with Norma Talmadge in 1922; it was remade in 1941.

Smilin' Through (1941) C-100m. **½ D: Frank Borzage. Jeanette MacDonald, Gene Raymond, Brian Aherne, Ian Hunter, Francis Robinson, Patrick O'Moore. Glossy remake of sentimental story about romance and rivalry spreading over two generations; lacks conviction of 1932 version, though MacDonald and Raymond are a good match (they married in real life). ▼

Smith! (1969) C-112m. *** D: Michael O'Herlihy. Glenn Ford, Nancy Olson, Dean Jagger, Keenan Wynn, Warren Oates, Chief Dan George. Offbeat Disney drama of stubborn, pro-Indian farmer Ford who steps forward to help Indian accused of murder. Well done, with good characterizations, but low-key qualities soften impact.▼

Smithereens (1982) C-90m. ***½ D: Susan Seidelman. Susan Berman, Brad Rinn (Rijn), Richard Hell, Roger Jett, Nada Despotovitch, Kitty Summerall. Gritty little character study of selfish, self-assured, rootless hustler Berman, and her vague dreams of success as a punk-rock band manager. Solid characterizations and simple, fluid direction; the sequence with the hooker and her chicken salad sandwich is memorable.▼

Smoke Signal (1955) C-88m. **½ D: Jerry Hopper. Dana Andrews, Piper Laurie, Rex Reason, Milburn Stone, William Talman. At-times zesty Western involving

Indian massacre and survivors' trek downstream to escape.

Smokey and the Bandit (1977) **C-96m.** ***** D:** Hal Needham. Burt Reynolds, Sally Field, Jackie Gleason, Jerry Reed, Mike Henry, Paul Williams, Pat McCormick. Box-office smash is one long comedy chase, as bootlegger Reynolds outraces Sheriff Gleason for nearly the entire film. Directorial debut of ace stuntman Needham is (expectedly) brimming with stunts. About as subtle as The Three Stooges, but a classic compared to the sequels and countless rip-offs which have followed.▼

Smokey and the Bandit II (1980) **C-104m.** ***½ D:** Hal Needham. Burt Reynolds, Jackie Gleason, Jerry Reed, Dom DeLuise, Sally Field, Paul Williams, Pat McCormick, John Anderson. Strange sequel to 1977 hit has Bandit and friends agreeing to truck a pregnant elephant to Texas. Unfortunately, film has hardly any action, and its main character is portrayed as an embittered egomaniac. Some laughs, but not enough to overcome these obstacles.▼

Smokey and the Bandit 3 (1983) **C-88m.** BOMB **D:** Dick Lowry. Jackie Gleason, Jerry Reed, Colleen Camp, Paul Williams, Pat McCormick, Mike Henry, Burt Reynolds. Desperate attempt to ring more laughs from this formula, with Gleason as a flustered red-neck sheriff and Reed as his latest nemesis. Originally filmed as SMOKEY IS THE BANDIT, with Gleason playing *both* roles; when preview audiences were confused, the film was reshot with Reed replacing the "second" Gleason. ▼

Smokey Bites the Dust (1981) **C-85m.** BOMB **D:** Charles B. Griffith. Jimmy McNichol, Janet Julian, Walter Barnes, Patrick Campbell, Kari Lizer, John Blyth Barrymore. Young McNichol kidnaps homecoming queen, much to the consternation of her sheriff father. Poor excuse for a movie, with all its car-chase action bodily lifted from such earlier films as EAT MY DUST, GRAND THEFT AUTO, THUNDER AND LIGHTNING, and MOVING VIOLATION.▼

Smoky (1946) **C-87m.** ***** D:** Louis King. Fred MacMurray, Anne Baxter, Burl Ives, Bruce Cabot, Esther Dale, Roy Roberts. First-rate family film from Will James story of man's devotion to his horse. Previously filmed in 1933, then again in 1966.

Smoky (1966) **C-103m.** **** D:** George Sherman. Fess Parker, Diana Hyland, Katy Jurado, Hoyt Axton, Chuck Roberson. Third version of the horse opera about especially independent horse named Smoky who knows what he wants.

Smoky Mountain Christmas, A (1986) **C-100m.** TVM **D:** Henry Winkler. Dolly Parton, Lee Majors, Bo Hopkins, Dan Hedaya, Anita Morris, Gennie James, David Aykroyd, Rene Auberjonois. Contemporary musical fairy tale based on *Snow White and the Seven Dwarfs* with Dolly in her TV acting debut and Henry debuting as a TV-movie director. It's innocuous holiday fare, especially for Parton fans. Look for John Ritter as the judge who must decide the fate of Dolly's seven little orphans. Dolly also cowrote the story (with William Bleich) and the six songs she sings. Average.▼

Smooth Talk (1985) **C-92m.** ****½ D:** Joyce Chopra. Treat Williams, Laura Dern, Mary Kay Place, Levon Helm, Elizabeth Berridge. Disarmingly realistic depiction of teenage girl's growing pains and family relations takes sharp left turn when Williams enters as mysterious (and alluring) stranger . . . and all but deadens rest of the film. Worth seeing if only for Dern's fine performance. Impressive feature debut for documentary director Chopra; script by Tom Cole from a Joyce Carol Oates short story. Originally made for PBS' *American Playhouse.*▼

Smorgasbord SEE: **Cracking Up**▼

Smugglers, The (1968) **C-97m.** TVM **D:** Norman Lloyd. Shirley Booth, Carol Lynley, Gayle Hunnicutt, Michael J. Pollard, Kurt Kasznar, David Opatoshu. Uneven mixture of wry humor and suspense in prettily packaged story of American tourists used in smuggling scheme. Entertaining cast, good location work, but abrupt resolution hurts film. Average.

Smugglers' Cove (1948) **66m. D:** William Beaudine. Leo Gorcey, Huntz Hall, Gabriel Dell, Billy Benedict, David Gorcey, Martin Kosleck, Paul Harvey, Amelita Ward. SEE: **Bowery Boys** series.▼

Smuggler's Gold (1951) **64m.** **** D:** William Berke. Cameron Mitchell, Amanda Blake, Carl Benton Reid, Peter Thompson. Adequate drama about deep-sea diver Mitchell coping with girlfriend's (Blake's) father who's in the smuggling game.

Smuggler's Island (1951) **C-75m.** **** D:** Edward Ludwig. Jeff Chandler, Evelyn Keyes, Philip Friend, Marvin Miller. Undemanding adventure story of diver Chandler involved with Keyes and search for sunken gold.

Snafu (1945) **82m.** **** D:** Jack Moss. Robert Benchley, Vera Vague (Barbara Jo Allen), Conrad Janis, Nanette Parks, Janis Wilson, Marcia Mae Jones, Kathleen Howard, Jimmy Lloyd, Enid Markey, Eva Puig. Young Conrad Janis is sent home by army because of his age, but he can't get used to civilian life again; mild comedy with Benchley fine as perplexed father.

Snake People (1970-Mexican-U.S.) **C-90m.** BOMB **D:** Jhon Ibanez (Juan Ibanez and Jack Hill). Boris Karloff, Juliassa, Charles (Carlos) East, Ralph Bertrand, Tongolele. Police captain tries to investigate an island where voodoo, LSD, and snake-worshipers run rampant. Ludicrous horror film wastes Karloff's talent. One of the last four films Karloff made; he shot his scenes in 1968. Original title: ISLE OF THE SNAKE PEOPLE.▼

Snake Pit, The (1948) **108m.** ***½ D: Anatole Litvak. Olivia de Havilland, Mark Stevens, Leo Genn, Celeste Holm, Glenn Langan, Helen Craig, Leif Erickson, Beulah Bondi, Lee Patrick, Natalie Schafer, Ruth Donnelly, Frank Conroy, Minna Gombell, Ann Doran, Betsy Blair, Isabel Jewell. One of the first films to deal intelligently with mental breakdowns and the painstakingly slow recovery process. Gripping film set in mental institution lacks original shock value but still packs a good punch, with de Havilland superb. Screenplay by Frank Partos and Millen Brand, from the Mary Jane Ward novel.

Snatched (1973) **C-73m. TVM** D: Sutton Roley. Howard Duff, Leslie Nielsen, Sheree North, Barbara Parkins, Robert Reed, John Saxon, Tisha Sterling. Usual kidnapping plot complicated by one of three husbands refusing to pay ransom and race against time to resupply one wife with insulin. Good cast walks through threadbare characters effortlessly; otherwise stale action. Average.▼

Sniper, The (1952) **87m.** *** D: Edward Dmytryk. Adolphe Menjou, Arthur Franz, Marie Windsor, Richard Kiley, Mabel Paige. Excellent, realistically filmed drama of mentally deranged sniper (Franz) who can't help himself from killing unsuspecting women. Fine performances by all.

Sniper's Ridge (1961) **61m.** ** D: John Bushelman. Jack Ging, Stanley Clements, John Goddard, Douglas Henderson. Standard Korean War battle actioner.

Sno-Line (1984) **C-94m.** BOMB D: Douglas F. O'Neons. Vincent Edwards, Paul Smith, June Wilkinson, Phil Foster, Louis Guss, Carey Clark. Tedious, mindless melodrama about ambitious hood Edwards and his attempt to corner the Texas cocaine market. Unbelievably wooden performances; when it's not confusing, it's just plain dull.▼

Snoop Sisters, The (1972) **C-100m. TVM** D: Leonard Stern. Helen Hayes, Mildred Natwick, Charlie Callas, Jill Clayburgh, Art Carney, Paulette Goddard, Ed Flanders, Fritz Weaver, Craig Stevens, Kurt Kasznar, Kent Smith, Bill Dana. Good comedy features two mystery writers turned private eyes investigating murder of movie star (Goddard), foiling nephew's attempts to retire them. Teleplay by Leonard B. Stern, Hugh Wheeler. Enjoyable pilot for later series. Clayburgh, Carney, and Goddard make their TV movie debuts. Retitled FEMALE INSTINCT. Above average.

Snoopy, Come Home (1972) **C-70m.** ***

D: Bill Melendez. Voices of Chad Webber, David Carey, Stephen Shea, Bill Melendez. Charming *Peanuts* feature (the second) centering around Snoopy, the world's most independent pooch.▼

Snorkel, The (1958-British) **92m.** **½ D: Guy Green. Peter Van Eyck, Betta St. John, Mandy Miller, Gregoire Aslan. Van Eyck ingeniously murders wife and plots to do away with stepdaughter, when she discovers his gimmick.

Snowball (1960-British) **69m.** ** D: Pat Jackson. Gordon Jackson, Zena Walker, Kenneth Griffith, Daphne Anderson. At times intriguing B film involving small boy's lie which led to the death of a villager.

Snowball Express (1972) **C-99m.** ** D: Norman Tokar. Dean Jones, Nancy Olson, Harry Morgan, Keenan Wynn, Johnny Whitaker, Michael McGreevey. Jones plays N.Y. accountant who inherits battered hotel in Rockies and tries to convert it into ski lodge. Slapstick ski chase is highlight of formula Disney comedy.▼

Snowbeast (1977) **C-100m. TVM** D: Herb Wallerstein. Bo Svenson, Yvette Mimieux, Robert Logan, Clint Walker, Sylvia Sidney. Killer beast terrorizes ski resort during winter carnival. Dumb mystery with slaloming creature and several straight faced actors. Another JAWS ripoff. Below average.▼

Snow Creature, The (1954) **70m.** *½ D: W. Lee Wilder. Paul Langton, Leslie Denison, Teru Shimada, Rollin Moriyama. Yeti brought back from Himalayas languishes in customs while officials wrangle over whether it is cargo or a passenger. Dull film at least has virtue of being made for adults, though only kids may like it now.▼

Snow Demons (1965-Italian) **C-92m.** BOMB D: Anthony Dawson (Antonio Margheriti). Jack Stuart (Giacomo Rossi-Stuarti), Amber Collins (Ombretta Colli), Peter Martell, Halina Zalewska. International expedition discovers snowmen who are really aliens with sinister motives. Incredibly dull, sloppily made film. Also known as SNOW DEVILS.

Snow Devils SEE: **Snow Demons**

Snow Job (1972) **C-90m.** *½ D: George Englund. Jean-Claude Killy, Danielle Gaubert, Cliff Potts, Vittorio De Sica. Heist film involving the taking of $250,000 in loot. Although Killy is appropriate star for film set against the Alps, he can't act; neither can the beautiful Gaubert.

Snow Queen, The (1959) **C-70m.** ** D: Phil Patton. Art Linkletter, Tammy Marihugh, Jennie Lynn. Voices of Sandra Dee, Tommy Kirk, Patty McCormack, Paul Frees, June Foray. American live-action footage frames a lavish, stately Soviet animated feature from 1955 (directed by Lev Atamanov) based on the Hans Christian

Andersen fairy tale about an icy snow queen whose heart is melted by the presence of true love.

Snows of Kilimanjaro, The (1952) C-117m. *** D: Henry King. Gregory Peck, Susan Hayward, Ava Gardner, Hildegarde Neff, Leo G. Carroll. Peck finds his forte as renowned writer coming to the end of his life in Africa, trying to decide if he found any meaning to his past; based on Hemingway story. ▼

Snow White and the Three Stooges (1961) C-107m. BOMB D: Walter Lang. Three Stooges, Patricia Medina, Carol Heiss, Buddy Baer, Guy Rolfe, Edgar Barrier. Big mistake with skating star Heiss as Snow White, Three Stooges as . . . the Three Stooges. Comics aren't given much to do, despite title; rest of film is rather stodgy. Even kids won't be thrilled with it. ▼

Soak the Rich (1936) 87m. BOMB D: Ben Hecht, Charles MacArthur. Walter Connolly, Mary Taylor, John Howard, Alice Duer Miller, Ilka Chase, Lionel Stander. Tycoon's daughter goes to college, falls for the militant anti-capitalist who kidnaps her. Hard to believe that a Hecht-MacArthur collaboration about campus radicals could be thoroughly unwatchable, but it's true. Miller, writer of *The White Cliffs of Dover* and co-member with H&M of the Algonquin Round Table, appears here as Miss Beasely.

S.O.B. (1981) C-121m. **½ D: Blake Edwards. Julie Andrews, William Holden, Richard Mulligan, Robert Preston, Robert Vaughn, Loretta Swit, Larry Hagman, Marisa Berenson, Robert Webber, Stuart Margolin, Craig Stevens, Shelley Winters, Rosanna Arquette, Jennifer Edwards, Robert Loggia, John Pleshette, Larry Storch, Gene Nelson, Joe Penny, Corbin Bernsen. A producer hatches a scheme to turn his latest turkey into a hit: juice it up with pornography and have his wife-star (Andrews) bare her breasts. A glib satire on modern-day Movieland (and writer-director Edwards's revenge for Hollywood's treatment of him in the early '70s) throws in everything from black humor to slapstick, with wildly uneven results. Holden's last film. ▼

So Big (1953) 101m. *** D: Robert Wise. Jane Wyman, Sterling Hayden, Nancy Olson, Steve Forrest, Martha Hyer, Tommy Rettig. Superficial but engrossing soaper about teacher who brings up son to be self-sufficient. Filmed before in 1925 and 1932.

Society Doctor (1935) 63m. ** D: George B. Seitz. Chester Morris, Robert Taylor, Virginia Bruce, Billie Burke, Raymond Walburn, Henry Kolker, Donald Meek. Talky, hokey soaper of the various interactions among doctors, nurses, and patients in a hospital. Morris is the spirited, principled head intern (who even gets to direct his own operation!); Bruce is his nurse-girlfriend, who's loved by intern Taylor; Burke is a pampered patient.

So Dark the Night (1946) 71m. **½ D: Joseph H. Lewis. Steven Geray, Micheline Cheirel, Eugene Borden, Ann Codee, Egon Brecher, Helen Freeman. Famous Parisian detective is put to work during his holiday in the French countryside. Impressively made B movie, something of a sleeper in its time, suffers only for lack of charisma on the part of its (mostly unknown) cast.

So Dear to My Heart (1948) C-84m. ***½ D: Harold Schuster. Burl Ives, Beulah Bondi, Bobby Driscoll, Luana Patten, Harry Carey. Warm, nostalgic Disney film about young boy's determination to tame a black sheep and bring him to State Fair competition. Brimming with period charm and atmosphere; several animated sequences, too. ▼

Sodom and Gomorrah (1963-Italian) C-154m. **½ D: Robert Aldrich. Stewart Granger, Pier Angeli, Stanley Baker, Anouk Aimee, Rossana Podesta. Lavish retelling of life in biblical twin cities of sin. Strong cast, vivid scenes of vice, gore, and God's wrath, make this overly long tale of ancient Hebrews fairly entertaining. ▼

So Ends Our Night (1941) 117m. ***½ D: John Cromwell. Fredric March, Margaret Sullavan, Frances Dee, Glenn Ford, Anna Sten, Erich von Stroheim, Allan Brett. Superior filmization of Erich Maria Remarque novel of German (March) rejecting Nazi reign, fleeing his country with hot pursuit by Axis agents. ▼

So Evil My Love (1948) 109m. *** D: Lewis Allen. Ray Milland, Ann Todd, Geraldine Fitzgerald, Leo G. Carroll, Raymond Huntley, Martita Hunt, Hugh Griffith. Excellent study of corruption; scoundrel Milland drags innocent Todd into larceny at expense of Fitzgerald.

So Evil, My Sister (1972) C-76m. ** D: Reginald LeBorg. Susan Strasberg, Faith Domergue, Sydney Chaplin, Charles Knox Robinson, Steve Mitchell, Kathleen Freeman, John Howard. Gothic B-movie thriller with veteran cast has Strasberg and Domergue as sisters playing cat-and-mouse with the police who are investigating the mysterious death of Strasberg's husband. Several clever twists in the final reel are worth waiting for. Retitled PSYCHO SISTERS. ▼

Sofia (1948) C-82m. ** D: John Reinhardt. Gene Raymond, Sigrid Gurie, Patricia Morison, Mischa Auer. Acceptable programmer with Raymond helping nuclear scientists escape grip of Russians in Turkey.

So Fine (1981) **C-91m.** *** D: Andrew Bergman. Ryan O'Neal, Jack Warden, Mariangela Melato, Richard Kiel, Fred Gwynne, Mike Kellin, David Rounds. Wacky comedy about professor-son of a N.Y.C. garment manufacturer who is dragooned into the business and inadvertently succeeds with an idea for see-through jeans. Film goes off in unexpected directions—some of them surprisingly silly—but remains funny most of the time. After editing for network TV, additional footage was added (from the cutting-room floor) to extend running time to 96m. Writer Bergman's directorial debut.▼

Soft Beds and Hard Battles SEE: **Undercovers Hero**

Soft Boiled (1923) **78m.** **½ D: J. G. Blystone. Tom Mix, Joseph Girard, Billie Dove, L. D. Shumway, Tom Wilson, Frank Beal. Tom Mix tries comedy, as young man with challenge to spend 30 days without losing his temper; enjoyable fluff, with typical Mix action finale.

Soft Skin, The (1964-French) **120m.** *** D: François Truffaut. Françoise Dorleac, Jean Desailly, Nelly Benedetti. Moody tale of married businessman drawn into tragic affair with beautiful airline stewardess; smooth direction uplifts basic plot.▼

So Goes My Love (1946) **88m.** **½ D: Frank Ryan. Myrna Loy, Don Ameche, Rhys Williams, Bobby Driscoll, Richard Gaines, Molly Lamont. Amusing period comedy of fortune-hunting Loy marrying oddball inventor Ameche.

Solarbubbles (1986) **C-94m.** BOMB D: Alan Johnson. Richard Jordan, Jami Gertz, Jason Patric, Lukas Haas, Charles Durning. Futuristic teen junk has Gertz and her mostly male cohorts imprisoned by Nazi-like Jordan inside a fortress; the group plots an escape with the help of "Bohdi" —an ancient mystical force. Appallingly bad stinker from (Mel) Brooksfilm that barely got released; the '80s teen jargon doesn't really capture the futuristic mood.▼

Soldier, The (1982) **C-96m.** *½ D: James Glickenhaus. Ken Wahl, Klaus Kinski, William Prince, Alberta Watson, Jeremiah Sullivan. CIA superagent Wahl takes on Russian terrorists who have planted a plutonium bomb in a Saudi Arabian oil field. Cliched, violent drama.▼

Soldier and the Lady, The (1937) **85m.** **½ D: George Nicholls, Jr. Anton Walbrook, Elizabeth Allan, Margot Grahame, Akim Tamiroff, Fay Bainter, Eric Blore, Edward Brophy. Hollywoodized version of Jules Verne's oft-filmed tale of a Czarist courier sent to deliver critical plans to the army in Siberia. Visually impressive, with sweeping battle scenes, though most exteriors were lifted from previous European version of the film, which also starred

Walbrook. Also known as MICHAEL STROGOFF.

Soldier Blue (1970) **C-112m.** *½ D: Ralph Nelson. Candice Bergen, Peter Strauss, Donald Pleasence, John Anderson, Jorge Rivero, Dana Elcar, James Hampton. Well-meant attempt to dramatize U.S. mistreatment of the Indians (and perhaps equate it with Vietnam) wasn't very good then and hasn't improved; bulk of the film is still cutesy romance between two survivors of Indian attack, climaxed by cavalry's slaughter of entire village in sequence that remains almost unwatchable.▼

Soldier Girls (1981) **C-87m.** ***½ D: Nicholas Broomfield, Joan Churchill. Hilarious, sometimes maddening and sobering documentary about young women Army recruits in basic training at Fort Gordon, Georgia. Definitely no recruiting poster: accurately advertised as the reality behind PRIVATE BENJAMIN.

Soldier in Skirts SEE: **Triple Echo**▼

Soldier in the Rain (1963) **88m.** *** D: Ralph Nelson. Jackie Gleason, Steve McQueen, Tuesday Weld, Tony Bill, Tom Poston. Strange film wavers from sentimental drama to high comedy. Gleason is swinging sergeant, McQueen his fervent admirer. Script by Blake Edwards and Maurice Richlin from William Goldman's novel.▼

Soldier of Fortune (1955) **C-96m.** *** D: Edward Dmytryk. Clark Gable, Susan Hayward, Michael Rennie, Gene Barry, Tom Tully, Alex D'Arcy, Anna Sten. Gable is hired to find Susan's husband (Barry) held captive in Hong Kong. Rennie is good as police chief. Scripted by Ernest K. Gann, from his novel.▼

Soldier of Love SEE: **Fan Fan the Tulip**

Soldier of Orange (1979-Dutch) **C-165m.** ***½ D: Paul Verhoeven. Rutger Hauer, Jeroen Krabbe, Peter Faber, Derek De Lint, Eddy Habbema, Susan Penhaligon, Edward Fox. The lives of six wealthy, carefree Dutch university students are irrevocably altered when the Germans occupy their homeland in 1940. Superior drama, with Hauer coming into his own as a handsome aristocrat who becomes involved in the Resistance. Based on autobiographical novel by Erik Hazelhoff.▼

Soldier's Story, A (1984) **C-101m.** ***½ D: Norman Jewison. Howard E. Rollins, Jr., Adolph Caesar, Dennis Lipscomb, Art Evans, Denzel Washington, Larry Riley, David Alan Grier, Robert Townsend, Patti LaBelle, Wings Hauser, Trey Wilson. Electrifying drama by Charles Fuller from his Pulitzer Prize-winning play (featuring most of original Negro Ensemble Company cast) about murder of a black officer at Southern military post in the 1940s. A solid whodunit plus a probing look at racism within black ranks. It was inspired by Herman

Melville's *Billy Budd*. Can't completely escape its stage origins but still a riveting film.▼

Soldiers Three (1951) **87m.** ******* D: Tay Garnett. Stewart Granger, Walter Pidgeon, David Niven, Robert Newton, Cyril Cusack, Greta Gynt, Robert Coote, Dan O'Herlihy. Boisterous action-adventure with light touch; GUNGA DINesque story has three soldiering comrades in and out of spats with each other as they battle in 19th-century India.

Sole Survivor (1969) **C-100m. TVM** D: Paul Stanley. Vince Edwards, Richard Basehart, William Shatner, Lou Antonio, Larry Casey, Patrick Wayne, Brad Davis, Dennis Cooney, Alan Caillou, Timur Bashtu. Title refers to central character, only person to walk away from suddenly discovered B-25 crash in Libyan desert. Odd drama by Guerdon Trueblood, with Edwards' performance hands-down winner. Above average.

Solid Gold Cadillac, The (1956) **99m.** ******* D: Richard Quine. Judy Holliday, Paul Douglas, Fred Clark, John Williams, Arthur O'Connell, Hiram Sherman, Neva Patterson, Ray Collins; narrated by George Burns. Dazzling Judy in entertaining comedy of small stockholder in large company becoming corporate heroine by trying to oust crooked board of directors. George S. Kaufman-Howard Teichman play adapted by Abe Burrows. Jean Louis earned an Oscar for the costumes. Last scene originally in color.

Solitary Man, The (1979) **C-100m. TVM** D: John Llewellyn Moxey. Earl Holliman, Carrie Snodgress, Nicolas Coster, Lara Parker, Dorrie Kavanaugh. Well-intentioned but somber study of the breakup of a family—from the man's point of view. Predated by several months the more solid KRAMER VS. KRAMER. Average.

Sol Madrid (1968) **C-90m.** ****½** D: Brian G. Hutton. David McCallum, Stella Stevens, Telly Savalas, Ricardo Montalban, Rip Torn, Pat Hingle, Paul Lukas, Michael Ansara. Old-fashioned but solid thriller about police, Mafia, and running heroin from Mexico.

Solomon and Sheba (1959) **C-120m.** ******* D: King Vidor. Yul Brynner, Gina Lollobrigida, George Sanders, Marisa Pavan, John Crawford, Alejandro Rey, Harry Andrews. Splashy spectacle with alluring Gina and stoic Brynner frolicking in biblical days. Tyrone Power died during filming in Spain, was replaced by Brynner who refilmed his early scenes. Vidor's final film as director.▼

Solomon Northrup's Odyssey (1984) **C-113m. TVM** D: Gordon Parks. Avery Brooks, Petronia Paley, Rhetta Greene, John Saxon, Mason Adams, Janet League, Lee Bryant, Joe Seneca, Michael Tolan.

Compelling drama about a Northern-born black man (Brooks), a talented fiddler and carpenter, who's kidnapped into slavery during the 1840s. Made with care and conviction and based on a true story. A PBS *American Playhouse* presentation. Retitled HALF-SLAVE, HALF-FREE. Above average.▼

So Long at the Fair (1950-British) **90m.** ******* D: Terence Fisher, Anthony Darnborough. Jean Simmons, Dirk Bogarde, David Tomlinson, Honor Blackman, Cathleen Nesbitt, Felix Aylmer, Andre Morell, Betty Warren. Atmospheric drama set during 1889 Paris Exposition with English woman searching for brother who's mysteriously vanished. Worth a look for fans of the offbeat.

Sombra, the Spider Woman (1947) **100m.** ****** D: Spencer Bennet, Fred Brannon. Bruce Edwards, Virginia Lindley, Carol Forman, Anthony Warde, (Brother) Theodore Gottlieb, Ramsay Ames. Unremarkable cliffhanger turned feature, with title figure, daughter of Oriental archfiend, seeking to conquer the world. Reedited from Republic serial THE BLACK WIDOW.

Sombrero (1953) **C-103m.** ***½** D: Norman Foster. Ricardo Montalban, Pier Angeli, Vittorio Gassman, Yvonne De Carlo, Nina Foch, Cyd Charisse, Jose Greco, Walter Hampden, Kurt Kasznar, Rick Jason. Strange, overwrought MGM melodrama with music intertwining three love stories in small Mexican village. One good dance number with Charisse.

Somebody Killed Her Husband (1978) **C-97m.** ***½** D: Lamont Johnson. Farrah Fawcett-Majors, Jeff Bridges, John Wood, Tammy Grimes, John Glover, Patricia Elliott. First starring feature for the ex-Charlie's Angel was redubbed "Somebody Killed Her Career" by industry wags, but in any case, this tepid comedy-mystery-romance written by Reginald Rose has little to recommend it. Filmed in Manhattan.

Somebody Loves Me (1952) **C-97m.** ****** D: Irving S. Brecher. Betty Hutton, Ralph Meeker, Adele Jergens, Robert Keith. Schmaltzy vaudeville biography of troupers Blossom Seeley and Benny Fields with no originality and not much entertainment, either.

Somebody Up There Likes Me (1956) **113m.** *****½** D: Robert Wise. Paul Newman, Pier Angeli, Everett Sloane, Eileen Heckart, Sal Mineo, Robert Loggia, Steve McQueen. Top biography of boxer Rocky Graziano's rise from N.Y.C. sidewalks to arena success with fine performance by Newman. Script by Ernest Lehman; cinematographer Joseph Ruttenberg won an Oscar. Film debuts of McQueen and Loggia.▼

Some Call It Loving (1973) **C-103m.** BOMB D: James B. Harris. Zalman King, Carol White, Tisa Farrow, Richard Pryor.

Slow, pretentious fantasy transplanting the story of Sleeping Beauty (played by Farrow, Mia's younger sister) to modern California. As her Prince Charming, King gives a sleepwalking nonperformance. Pryor's vulgar turn as a pathetic graffiti artist/wino clashes with the rest of the picture. ▼

Some Came Running (1958) **C-136m.** *** D: Vincente Minnelli. Frank Sinatra, Dean Martin, Shirley MacLaine, Martha Hyer, Arthur Kennedy, Nancy Gates. Slick adaptation of James Jones's novel about disillusionment in a small midwestern town in the late 1940s; more character study than narrative. MacLaine is especially good as luckless floozie who's stuck on Sinatra; Elmer Bernstein's music score also a standout.▼

Some Girls (1989) **C-94m.** ** D: Michael Hoffman. Patrick Dempsey, Jennifer Connelly, Sheila Kelly, Andre Gregory, Florinda Bolkan, Lila Kedrova. Odd little comedy about American college student Dempsey and the various complications when he spends Christmas in Quebec City with girlfriend Connelly's family. Gregory rises above the material as Connelly's eccentric father.▼

Some Girls Do (1969-British) **C-93m.** **½ D: Ralph Thomas. Richard Johnson, Daliah Lavi, Beba Loncar, Robert Morley, Sydne Rome, James Villiers. Brisk thriller involving Bulldog Drummond (played with a lack of dash by Johnson) vs. long-time archenemy Carl Peterson (Villiers), who is trying to sabotage Britain's supersonic plane plans. Morley is a delight in a cameo as an eccentric teacher of high cuisine. Sequel to DEADLIER THAN THE MALE (1967).

Some Kind of a Nut (1969) **C-89m.** BOMB D: Garson Kanin. Dick Van Dyke, Angie Dickinson, Rosemary Forsyth, Zohra Lampert, Elliott Reid, Pippa Scott. Banker Van Dyke loses his job when he grows a beard. Pathetic "contemporary" comedy dates more than Kanin's films of the '30s and '40s.

Some Kind of Hero (1982) **C-97m.** ** D: Michael Pressman. Richard Pryor, Margot Kidder, Ray Sharkey, Ronny Cox, Lynne Moody, Olivia Cole, Paul Benjamin. Pryor rises above uneven, poorly directed comedy-drama about Vietnam veteran who's in for a few surprises when he returns home after six years as a POW. Based on a James Kirkwood novel.▼

Some Kind of Miracle (1979) **C-100m.** TVM D: Jerrold Freedman. David Dukes, Andrea Marcovicci, Michael C. Gwynne, Art Hindle, Dick Anthony Williams, Nancy Marchand, Stephen Elliott. The trials and tribulations (mostly sexual) of a happy couple after one is permanently paralyzed in a surfing accident. Average.

Some Kind of Wonderful (1987) **C-93m.** **½ D: Howard Deutch. Eric Stoltz, Lea Thompson, Mary Stuart Masterson, Craig Sheffer, John Ashton, Elias Koteas, Molly Hagan. Adorable tomboy Masterson loves Stoltz, but it takes him the entire film to realize she is better for him than the flashier Thompson. Deutch and producer John Hughes have, in effect, done a sex-switch remake of their own PRETTY IN PINK; the OK result has strong performances by both female leads, and surprises by not making Thompson a snooty bitch.▼

Some Like It Hot (1939) **64m.** **½ D: George Archainbaud. Bob Hope, Shirley Ross, Una Merkel, Gene Krupa, Richard Denning. Sideshow owner Hope takes advantage of Ross to raise money for show. Airy comedy includes song "The Lady's In Love With You." Retitled RHYTHM ROMANCE; based on a play previously filmed (in 1934) as SHOOT THE WORKS.

Some Like It Hot (1959) **119m.** **** D: Billy Wilder. Jack Lemmon, Tony Curtis, Marilyn Monroe, Joe E. Brown, George Raft, Pat O'Brien, Nehemiah Persoff, Joan Shawlee, Mike Mazurki. Legendary comedy by Wilder and I.A.L. Diamond about two musicians who witness the St. Valentine's Day Massacre and try to elude their pursuers by joining an all-girl band heading for Miami. Sensational from start to finish, with dazzling performances by Lemmon and Curtis, a memorably comic turn by Monroe as Sugar Kane, and Oscar-winning costumes by Orry-Kelly. Brown has film's now-classic closing line. Basis for hit Broadway musical *Sugar*.▼

Some May Live (1967) **105m.** ** D: Vernon Sewell. Joseph Cotten, Martha Hyer, Peter Cushing, John Ronane. Unexciting suspenser made for TV set in contemporary Saigon with Cotten a U.S. Intelligence officer setting a trap for the espionage agent within his department. Retitled: IN SAIGON, SOME MAY LIVE.

Someone at the Top of the Stairs (1973-British) **C-74m.** TVM D: John Sichel. Donna Mills, Judy Carne, Francis Wallis, Alethea Charlton, Scott Forbes. Two American girls get the creeps when they move into strange Victorian boarding house in London. Familiar stuff, passably done. Average.

Someone Behind the Door (1971-French) **C-97m.** ** D: Nicolas Gessner. Charles Bronson, Anthony Perkins, Jill Ireland, Henri Garcin, Adriano Magestretti. Neuropsychiatrist (Perkins) turns an amnesiac murderer (Bronson) into his tool for revenge on his philandering wife; farfetched melodrama.▼

Someone I Touched (1975) **C-78m.** TVM D: Lou Antonio. Cloris Leachman, James Olson, Glynnis O'Connor, Andy Robinson, Allyn Ann McLerie, Kenneth Mars. Unbelievable melodrama about an architect, his pregnant wife, and a nubile young teen-ager who learn they have VD and try to figure out who gave it to whom. Cloris even sings the romantic title song! Below average.▼

Someone's Killing the World's Greatest Models SEE: **She's Dressed to Kill**▼

Someone's Watching Me! (1978) C-100m. TVM D: John Carpenter. Lauren Hutton, David Birney, Adrienne Barbeau, Charles Cyphers. Dandy thriller about a career woman who takes things into her own hands after being rebuffed by the police when someone begins stalking her. Carpenter also wrote the script; his first TVM (and first film with Barbeau). Above average.

Someone to Love (1987) C-111m. **½ D: Henry Jaglom. Henry Jaglom, Andrea Marcovicci, Sally Kellerman, Orson Welles, Michael Emil, Oja Kodar, Dave Frishberg, Stephen Bishop, Ronee Blakley, Kathryn Harrold, Monte Hellman, Jeremy Kagan, Miles Kreuger. Jaglom is Danny, a filmmaker who's seeking "someone to love." He throws a Valentine's Day party where he questions various friends on the subject . . . and films their responses. Welles, in his last screen appearance, is on hand to offer various insights and profundities, and they're the best thing in this alternately boring and interesting experiment.▼

Someone to Watch Over Me (1987) C-106m. *** D: Ridley Scott. Tom Berenger, Mimi Rogers, Lorraine Bracco, Jerry Orbach, John Rubinstein, Andreas Katsulas, Tony DiBenedetto, James Moriarty. Happily married N.Y.C. cop becomes infatuated with the wealthy and beautiful woman he's assigned to protect from a death threat. Solid romantic thriller, compassionately and believably told; director Scott's warmest film to date (and just as stylish as ever).▼

Something About Amelia (1984) C-100m. TVM D: Randa Haines. Ted Danson, Roxana Zal, Glenn Close, Olivia Cole, Kevin Conway, Lane Smith, Jane Kaczmarek. Teenager reveals her father forced her to have sex with him, which throws the family into turmoil. Sensitively handled film about incest, written by William Hanley, received great notoriety and became one of the most watched television movies ever. Zal won an Emmy. Above average.

something big (1971) C-108m. BOMB D: Andrew V. McLaglen. Dean Martin, Brian Keith, Honor Blackman, Carol White, Ben Johnson, Albert Salmi, Paul Fix, Denver Pyle. Repellent "comedy"-Western detailing long-running feud between outlaw Martin and cavalry colonel Keith; "happy ending" consists of Dino robbing a stagecoach and mowing down hundreds of Mexicans with a gatling gun—all to a peppy Marvin Hamlisch score. Blecch.

Something Evil (1972) C-73m. TVM D: Steven Spielberg. Sandy Dennis, Darren McGavin, Ralph Bellamy, Jeff Corey, John-

nie Whitaker, John Rubinstein. Worden family buys old house in Pennsylvania, unaware of lurking evil presence. Horror aspect handled matter-of-factly, excellent performances. Above average.

Something for a Lonely Man (1968) C-98m. TVM D: Don Taylor. Dan Blocker, Susan Clark, John Dehner, Warren Oates, Paul Peterson, Don Stroud. Blacksmith outcast of Arcana (Blocker) believes he finally has opportunity to bring industry to town when locomotive derails nearby, is aided by one woman who believes in him. Good character study salvages backlot Western. Above average.

Something for Everyone (1970) C-112m. **½ D: Harold Prince. Angela Lansbury, Michael York, Anthony Corlan, Heidelinde Weis, Eva-Maria Meineke, Jane Carr. Very black comedy about amoral, bisexual young man (York) who manipulates staff and family of impoverished Countess (Lansbury) to his advantage. Intriguing but needlessly protracted story; Broadway director Prince's first film, shot on location in Bavaria.▼

Something for Joey (1977) C-100m. TVM D: Lou Antonio. Geraldine Page, Gerald S. O'Loughlin, Marc Singer, Jeff Lynas, Linda Kelsey, Steven Guttenberg, Paul Picerni. True-life story of the relationship between Heisman Trophy winner John Cappelletti and his younger brother, Joey, stricken with leukemia. Sensitive tearjerker that never gets maudlin. Above average.

Something for the Birds (1952) 81m. **½ D: Robert Wise. Patricia Neal, Victor Mature, Edmund Gwenn, Larry Keating. Mild romantic froth, with Mature and Neal on opposite sides of issue in lobbying for bird sanctuary protection.

Something for the Boys (1944) C-85m. **½ D: Lewis Seiler. Carmen Miranda, Michael O'Shea, Vivian Blaine, Phil Silvers, Sheila Ryan, Perry Como, Glenn Langan, Cara Williams, Thurston Hall. Pleasant 20th Century-Fox musical with diverting Cole Porter score, set in heiress Blaine's Southern plantation, which has been recruited as a home for soldiers' wives. Look for Judy Holliday as a defense-plant welder.

Something in Common (1986) C-100m. TVM D: Glenn Jordan. Ellen Burstyn, Tuesday Weld, Patrick Cassidy, Don Murray, Eli Wallach, Amanda Wyss. Breezy romantic comedy about a widowed career woman (Burstyn) whose son falls for a divorcée twice his age—hers. Burstyn and Weld shine in Susan Rice's savvy script. Above average.▼

Something in the Wind (1947) 89m. **½ D: Irving Pichel. Deanna Durbin, Donald O'Connor, Charles Winninger, Helena Carter. Mild comedy of errors with Durbin as female disk jockey who sings, too. Easy to take, amusing.

Something Is Out There (1977) SEE: Day of the Animals▼
Something Is Out There (1988) C-200m. TVM D: Richard A. Colla. Joe Cortese, Maryam D'Abo, George Dzundza, Kim Delaney, Gregory Sierra, John Putch, Robert Webber. Street-smart L.A. undercover cop joins forces with a gorgeous intergalactic woman to track down an unearthly monster killer and thwart an alien takeover of Earth. Only real assets are Rick Baker's extraterrestrial creations and John Dykstra's special effects. Overlong pilot to the short-lived series. Originally shown in two parts. Average.
Something of Value (1957) 113m. *** D: Richard Brooks. Rock Hudson, Dana Wynter, Sidney Poitier, Wendy Hiller, Frederick O'Neal. Robert Ruark's novel transformed to screen, sharply detailing brutal Mau Mau warfare in Kenya. Hudson and Poitier are fine as British colonial farmer and his childhood friend; Hiller memorable as widow struggling to retain dignity and spirit.▼
Something Short of Paradise (1979) C-91m. ** D: David Helpern, Jr. Susan Sarandon, David Steinberg, Jean-Pierre Aumont, Marilyn Sokol, Joe Grifasi, Robert Hitt. Aptly titled romantic comedy pairs movie theater manager Steinberg and magazine writer Sarandon, but offers little; Steinberg's character is particularly obnoxious in this blatant ANNIE HALL rip-off. Film buffs, however, will enjoy main-title sequence comprised of old movie ads.▼
Something So Right (1982) C-100m. TVM D: Lou Antonio. Ricky Schroder, Patty Duke Astin, James Farentino, Fred Dryer, Neva Patterson, Annie Potts, Carole Cook, Dick Anthony Williams. Heartwarmer about a divorcee who finds a Big Brother for her troubled son and gets more than she bargained for. The pleasant surprise here is a change-of-image Farentino, as a paunchy, balding, middle-aged Joe. Written by Shelley List and Jonathan Estrin. Above average.
Something Special (1986) C-93m. *** D: Paul Schneider. Pamela Segall, Patty Duke, Eric Gurry, John Glover, Mary Tanner, Seth Green, Jeb Ellis-Brown. Cute, original, generally pleasing little comedy-drama-fantasy about a 14-year-old girl (Segall, in a spunky performance) who wants to become a male—and has her wish granted. Bogs down when the adults are around, but it's still perfect fare for older kids. A shorter version, with tamer language, runs 86m. Original title: WILLY MILLY. Also known as I WAS A TEENAGE BOY.▼
Something to Hide (1972-British) C-100m. *½ D: Alastair Reid. Peter Finch, Shelley Winters, Colin Blakely, Linda Hayden, John Stride. All-out marital fighting match between memorably overwrought Winters

and Finch deteriorates into unconvincing melodrama concerning pregnant trollop Hayden and Finch's eventual mental breakdown. Unpleasant. Retitled: SHATTERED.▼
Something to Live For (1952) 89m. **½ D: George Stevens. Joan Fontaine, Ray Milland, Teresa Wright, Douglas Dick, Rudy Lee. Turgid melodrama trying to be another LOST WEEKEND. Fontaine is alcoholic in love with Milland, but he's married.
Something to Shout About (1943) 93m. ** D: Gregory Ratoff. Don Ameche, Janet Blair, Jack Oakie, Cobina Wright, Jr., William Gaxton, Veda Ann Borg. Hackneyed backstage Broadway musical with good Cole Porter score (including "You'd Be So Nice to Come Home To"), specialty numbers by Hazel Scott, Teddy Wilson and His Orchestra. Look for Cyd Charisse (billed as Lily Norwood) in her feature debut.
Something to Sing About (1937) 93m. ** D: Victor Schertzinger. James Cagney, Evelyn Daw, William Frawley, Mona Barrie, Gene Lockhart. Low-budget musical doesn't live up to its title, with Cagney the only real asset in this lightweight story of a N.Y. bandleader who goes to Hollywood. Forgettable songs. Reissued at 82m. as BATTLING HOOFER. Also shown in computer-colored version.▼
Something Wicked This Way Comes (1983) C-94m. **½ D: Jack Clayton. Jason Robards, Jonathan Pryce, Diane Ladd, Pam Grier, Royal Dano, Shawn Carson, Vidal Peterson, Mary Grace Canfield, James Stacy, narrated by Arthur Hill. A mysterious carnival pitches its tent outside an idyllic American town in the early part of the century and fulfills the dreams of its citizens—for a heavy price. Told from a young boy's point of view, film has affecting moments, but never really hits its stride, with the ultimate "revelation" about Mr. Dark and his carnival no surprise at all. Disappointing Disney production of Ray Bradbury's story, scripted by the author.▼
Something Wild (1961) 112m. **½ D: Jack Garfein. Carroll Baker, Ralph Meeker, Mildred Dunnock, Martin Kosleck, Jean Stapleton. Bizarre study of rape-victim Baker falling in love with would-be attacker Meeker, coming to rational understanding with mother Dunnock. N.Y.C. location scenes perk melodramatic soaper.
Something Wild (1986) C-113m. ** D: Jonathan Demme. Jeff Daniels, Melanie Griffith, Ray Liotta, Margaret Colin, Tracey Walter, Dana Preu, Jack Gilpin. Straight-arrow businessman Daniels goes for a joyride with a flaky, sexy girl he chances to meet, and in the course of a couple of days she turns his life inside out. Many surprising twists and turns as this film veers from kooky comedy to violent melodrama, but

end result isn't satisfying, especially with tacked-on happy ending. Filmmakers John Waters and John Sayles have amusing cameos as a used-car salesman and a motorcycle cop, respectively.▼

Sometimes a Great Notion (1971) C-114m. ** D: Paul Newman. Paul Newman, Henry Fonda, Lee Remick, Michael Sarrazin, Richard Jaeckel, Linda Lawson. Disappointing film version of Ken Kesey's mammoth novel about modern-day loggers in Oregon. Jaeckel's performance is outstanding and movie has one great scene involving a drowning, but otherwise film is a letdown. Retitled NEVER GIVE A INCH (the family's motto) for TV.▼

Somewhere I'll Find You (1942) 108m. **½ D: Wesley Ruggles. Lana Turner, Clark Gable, Robert Sterling, Reginald Owen, Lee Patrick, Rags Ragland, Patricia Dane. Turner and Gable are improbable as WW2 war correspondents, but their love scenes between battles are most convincing. Film debut of Keenan Wynn.

Somewhere in the Night (1946) 108m. **½ D: Joseph L. Mankiewicz. John Hodiak, Nancy Guild, Lloyd Nolan, Richard Conte, Josephine Hutchinson, Fritz Kortner, Sheldon Leonard, Whit Bissell, Jeff Corey, Henry (Harry) Morgan. Satisfactory drama of amnesiac Hodiak trying to discover his true identity; not up to later Mankiewicz efforts.

Somewhere in Time (1980) C-103m. *½ D: Jeannot Szwarc. Christopher Reeve, Jane Seymour, Christopher Plummer, Teresa Wright, Bill Erwin, George Voskovec, George Wendt, Tim Kazurinsky. Superficial tearjerker about unhappy playwright Reeve who falls in love with a 70-year-old painting of an actress (Seymour), then wills himself back in time to meet her. Stilted dialogue, corny situations, pretty scenery (on Mackinac Island). Script by Richard Matheson from his novel *Bid Time Return*.▼

Somewhere Tomorrow (1983) C-87m. *** D: Robert Wiemer. Sarah Jessica Parker, Nancy Addison, Tom Shea, Rick Weber, Paul Bates, James Congdon. Offbeat drama about fatherless teen Parker who, after seeing TOPPER on TV and bumping her head, meets the ghost of a boy (Shea) who's been killed in a plane crash. Not without flaws, but still charming and moving.▼

Son-Daughter, The (1932) 79m. *½ D: Clarence Brown. Helen Hayes, Ramon Novarro, Lewis Stone, Ralph Morgan, Warner Oland. Designed as a tender love story with tragic overtones set in San Francisco's Chinatown, this film plays more like farce, with dialogue that sounds like Chinese Damon Runyon. One of Hayes's most embarrassing performances.

Song for Miss Julie, A (1945) 69m. *½

D: William Rowland. Shirley Ross, Barton Hepburn, Jane Farrar, Roger Clark, Cheryl Walker, Elisabeth Risdon. Low-budget tale of woman who exposes family's past, then tries to cover it up again.

Song Is Born, A (1948) C-113m. **½ D: Howard Hawks. Danny Kaye, Virginia Mayo, Hugh Herbert, Steve Cochran, Felix Bressart; guest stars Benny Goodman, Louis Armstrong, Charlie Barnet, Lionel Hampton, Tommy Dorsey. Below par musical remake of Hawks' BALL OF FIRE has Kaye and Mayo supported by big-band greats in mild comedy of professors researching the evolution of jazz.

Song of Bernadette, The (1943) 156m. **** D: Henry King. Jennifer Jones, William Eythe, Charles Bickford, Vincent Price, Lee J. Cobb, Anne Revere, Gladys Cooper. Overlong but excellent story of religious French girl in 1800s who sees great vision, incurs local wrath because of it. George Seaton adapted Franz Werfel's best-selling novel. Four Oscars include Best Actress, Cinematography (Arthur Miller), Score (Alfred Newman). That's Linda Darnell, unbilled, as the Virgin Mary.▼

Song of Freedom (1936-British) 80m. **½ D: J. Elder Wills. Paul Robeson, Elizabeth Welch, George Mozart, Esme Percy, Arthur Williams, Robert Adams. Robeson plays stevedore-turned-concert-singer who journeys to Africa in search of his roots. Promising idea doesn't quite work, but Robeson is always worth watching.▼

Song of India (1949) 77m. ** D: Albert S. Rogell. Sabu, Gail Russell, Turhan Bey, Anthony Caruso, Aminta Dyne. Well-meaning Sabu releases jungle animals callously trapped by royal family; typical jungle escapist adventure.

Song of Love (1947) 119m. **½ D: Clarence Brown. Katharine Hepburn, Paul Henreid, Robert Walker, Henry Daniell, Leo G. Carroll, Gigi Perreau, Tala Birell, Henry Stephenson, Else Janssen. Classy production but slow-moving story of Clara Schuman (Hepburn), her composer husband (Henreid) and good friend Brahms (Walker).

Song of Norway (1970) C-142m. BOMB D: Andrew L. Stone. Florence Henderson, Toralv Maurstad, Christina Schollin, Frank Porretta, Edward G. Robinson, Harry Secombe, Robert Morley, Oscar Homolka. A poor biography of composer Edvard Grieg, with weak and abridged versions of his best music. Beautiful to look at in Super Panavision, but not likely to impress on TV.▼

Song of Russia (1943) 107m. **½ D: Gregory Ratoff. Robert Taylor, Susan Peters, John Hodiak, Robert Benchley, Felix Bressart, Joan Lorring, Darryl Hickman. MGM's war-time attempt to do for Russia what MRS. MINIVER did for England;

hokey but effective story of American conductor Taylor falling in love with Russian musician Peters. Then-topical attitude toward U.S.S.R. makes this an interesting period piece.

Song of Scheherazade (1947) **C-106m.** ** D: Walter Reisch. Yvonne De Carlo, Brian Donlevy, Jean-Pierre Aumont, Eve Arden, Philip Reed. Colorful tripe about Rimsky-Korsakov's true inspiration, a dancing girl (De Carlo).

Song of Songs (1933) **90m.** **½ D: Rouben Mamoulian. Marlene Dietrich, Brian Aherne, Lionel Atwill, Alison Skipworth, Hardie Albright, Helen Freeman. Naïve country girl Dietrich falls in love with sculptor Aherne, for whom she poses in the nude . . . but Atwill, a wealthy reprobate, manages to marry her. Humdrum story made worthwhile by good performances, especially Dietrich, who's luminous in her first Hollywood film *not* directed by Josef von Sternberg.

Song of Surrender (1949) **93m.** ** D: Mitchell Leisen. Wanda Hendrix, Claude Rains, Macdonald Carey, Andrea King, Henry O'Neill, Elizabeth Patterson. Mild turn-of-the-century tale of young woman (Hendrix) and older husband Rains.

Song of the Islands (1942) **C-75m.** **½ D: Walter Lang. Betty Grable, Victor Mature, Jack Oakie, Thomas Mitchell, Hilo Hattie, Billy Gilbert. Mature is new arrival to Pacific isle, Grable local girl he feuds with and romances. Slick musical fluff.▼

Song of the Open Road (1944) **93m.** **½ D.S. Sylvan Simon. Edgar Bergen, W. C. Fields, Jane Powell, Bonita Granville, Reginald Denny, Rose Hobart, Sammy Kaye Orchestra. Young Powell's film debut and showcase for her vocal talents is fairly good, with token appearances by Fields and nemesis Charlie McCarthy.

Song of the Sarong (1945) **65m.** ** D: Harold Young. William Gargan, Nancy Kelly, Eddie Quillan. Gargan is involved in pearl-snatching from island natives; moderate production values.

Song of the South (1946) **C-94m.** ***½ D: Wilfred Jackson (animation), Harve Foster (live-action). Ruth Warrick, James Baskett, Bobby Driscoll, Luana Patten, Lucile Watson, Hattie McDaniel, Glenn Leedy. Lonely, misunderstood little boy, living on a plantation in the Old South, finds his only happiness in the tales spun by Uncle Remus. Some may find story cloying, but it serves as framework for three terrific Disney cartoon sequences featuring Brer Rabbit, Brer Fox, and Brer Bear (based on writings of Joel Chandler Harris). Superb blend of live-action and animation, sincere performances (Baskett earned a special Academy Award for his), and tuneful songs including Oscar-winning "Zip a Dee Doo Dah" make this a treat.

Song of the Thin Man (1947) **86m.** D: Edward Buzzell. William Powell, Myrna Loy, Keenan Wynn, Dean Stockwell, Gloria Grahame, Patricia Morison. SEE: **Thin Man** series.▼

Song Remains the Same, The (1976) **C-136m.** ** D: Peter Clifton, Joe Massot. Amateurish mixture of fantasy sequences and documentary footage from Led Zeppelin's 1973 tour is for fans only. Even without the stereo sound, film will still clean out all eight sinus cavities.▼

Song to Remember, A (1945) **C-113m.** **½ D: Charles Vidor. Cornel Wilde, Paul Muni, Merle Oberon, Stephen Bekassy, Nina Foch, George Coulouris, Sig Arno. Colorful but superficial biography of Chopin (Wilde) with exaggerated Muni as his mentor, lovely Oberon as George Sand; good music, frail plot.▼

Song Without End (1960) **C-141m.** **½ D: Charles Vidor, George Cukor. Dirk Bogarde, Capucine, Genevieve Page, Patricia Morison, Ivan Desny, Martita Hunt, Lou Jacobi. Beautiful music (scoring won an Oscar) submerged by dramatics of composer Franz Liszt's life. Bogarde tries; settings are lavish. Vidor died during filming, Cukor completed film.

Songwriter (1984) **C-94m.** **½ D: Alan Rudolph. Willie Nelson, Kris Kristofferson, Melinda Dillon, Rip Torn, Lesley Ann Warren, Mickey Raphael, Rhonda Dotson, Richard C. Sarafian. Loose, friendly, rambling film about a couple of country singers—one of whom (Nelson) has become an entrepreneur but calls on his old partner Kris to help him outwit a greedy backer (played by film director Sarafian). Doesn't add up to much but certainly pleasant to watch, with top supporting cast and lots of music.▼

Sonny and Jed (1973-Italian) **C-98m.** ** D: Sergio Corbucci. Tomas Milian, Telly Savalas, Susan George, Rosanna Janni, Laura Betti. Lighthearted spaghetti Western that teams escaped convict, pillaging his way across Mexico, with free-spirited gal who wants to become an outlaw, while shiny-domed Telly is determined lawman dogging their every move.▼

Son of a Gunfighter (1966-Spanish) **C-92m.** *½ D: Paul Landres. Russ Tamblyn, Kieron Moore, James Philbrook, Fernando Rey. Title tells all in oater peppered with Anglo-Saxon actors and bits of the Old West.

Son of Ali Baba (1952) **C-75m.** ** D: Kurt Neumann. Tony Curtis, Piper Laurie, Susan Cabot, Victor Jory, Hugh O'Brian. Caliph uses princess Laurie to obtain treasure of Ali Baba. After father is captured, son appears and wins hand of princess. Good sets, fair acting.

Son of a Sailor (1933) 73m. *** D: Lloyd Bacon. Joe E. Brown, Jean Muir, Thelma Todd, Frank McHugh, Johnny Mack Brown, Sheila Terry. Joe blunders into espionage and recovers stolen Navy plans; always-vivacious Todd lends fine support in this entertaining comedy.

Son of Belle Starr (1953) C-70m. ** D: Frank McDonald. Keith Larsen, Dona Drake, Peggie Castle, Regis Toomey. Fictional Western history is excuse for another shootout tale.

Son of Blob SEE: **Beware! The Blob**▼

Son of Captain Blood, The (1962-U.S.-Italian-Spanish) C-88m. *½ D: Tulio Demicheli. Sean Flynn, Ann Todd, Alessandra Panaro, Jose Nieto, John Kitzmiller. Interesting only in that Errol Flynn's 23-year-old son plays the son of the character Errol did in CAPTAIN BLOOD. Ann Todd sparkles as the lad's mother (Olivia de Havilland's character in the original). Otherwise, routine. Filmed in Spain, from a screenplay by Casey Robinson.▼

Son of Dracula (1943) 78m. *** D: Robert Siodmak. Lon Chaney, Jr., Robert Paige, Louise Allbritton, Evelyn Ankers, Frank Craven, J. Edward Bromberg, Samuel S. Hinds. Mysterious gentleman named Alucard turns up in the Deep South to sample the local cuisine. Dumb title (it's the Count himself, not his son) masks one of Universal's most atmospheric chillers, with crisp acting, fine effects . . . and an unexpected finale.▼

Son of Dracula (1974-British) C-90m. *½ D: Freddie Francis. Harry Nilsson, Ringo Starr, Rosanna Lee, Freddie Jones, Dennis Price, Skip Martin. Offbeat but uninspired rock horror pic with seven tunes by Nilsson, who plays the title character. Ringo produced. Retitled: YOUNG DRACULA.

Son of Dr. Jekyll, The (1951) 77m. *½ D: Seymour Friedman. Louis Hayward, Jody Lawrance, Alexander Knox, Lester Matthews. Jekyll's son tries to discover and improve upon his father's formula; he never turns into Hyde! Poorly scripted, produced; cast manages to save film from complete ruin.▼

Son of Flubber (1963) 100m. **½ D: Robert Stevenson. Fred MacMurray, Nancy Olson, Keenan Wynn, Tommy Kirk, Elliott Reid, Joanna Moore, Leon Ames, Ed Wynn, Charlie Ruggles, Paul Lynde. Silly, disjointed sequel to THE ABSENT MINDED PROFESSOR has new inventions—flubbergas, dry rain—and appropriate slapstick highlights, to compensate for uneven script. Helped, too, by cast full of old pros, especially Lynde as smug sportscaster.▼

Son of Frankenstein (1939) 99m. *** D: Rowland V. Lee. Basil Rathbone, Boris Karloff, Bela Lugosi, Lionel Atwill, Josephine Hutchinson, Edgar Norton, Donnie Dunagan. Third in the series (after BRIDE) finds late doctor's son attempting to clear family name by making the Monster "good." He should live so long. Lavishly made shocker is gripping and eerie, if a bit talky, with wonderfully bizarre sets by Jack Otterson and Lugosi's finest performance as evil, broken-necked shepherd Ygor. Karloff's last appearance as the Monster. Sequel: GHOST OF FRANKENSTEIN.▼

Son of Fury (1942) 98m. *** D: John Cromwell. Tyrone Power, Gene Tierney, George Sanders, Frances Farmer, Roddy McDowall, Kay Johnson, John Carradine, Elsa Lanchester, Harry Davenport, Dudley Digges, Ethel Griffies. Good costumer about aristocratic Sanders shunning nephew Power, who flees to desert isle to plan revenge; Tierney's on the island, too. Remade as TREASURE OF THE GOLDEN CONDOR.

Son of Godzilla (1967-Japanese) C-86m. *½ D: Jun Fukuda. Tadao Takashima, Akira Kubo, Bibari Maeda, Akihiko Hirata, Kenji Sahara. Godzilla and son are threatened by giant mantises and a huge spider in this good-natured monster rally, but where's Mrs. Godzilla when you really need her? Some of the same footage later seen in GODZILLA'S REVENGE.▼

Son of Kong, The (1933) 70m. **½ D: Ernest B. Schoedsack. Robert Armstrong, Helen Mack, Victor Wong, John Marston, Frank Reicher, Lee Kohlmar. Disappointing sequel to KING KONG, hurriedly put together—and it shows. Armstrong is back as Carl Denham, who returns to Skull Island and discovers Kong's cute li'l offspring. Mostly comedic film has some good moments, and Willis O'Brien's effects are still superb.▼

Son of Lassie (1945) C-102m. **½ D: S. Sylvan Simon. Peter Lawford, Donald Crisp, June Lockhart, Nigel Bruce, William Severn, Leon Ames, Fay Helm, Donald Curtis, Nils Asther, Helen Koford (Terry Moore). Fairly good follow-up to LASSIE COME HOME unfortunately gets the collie mixed up in war episodes.

Son of Monte Cristo, The (1940) 102m. *** D: Rowland V. Lee. Louis Hayward, Joan Bennett, George Sanders, Florence Bates, Lionel Royce, Montagu Love. Nothing new in big-scale swashbuckler, but very well done with Hayward battling Sanders and vying for Bennett's hand.

Son of Paleface (1952) C-95m. ***½ D: Frank Tashlin. Bob Hope, Jane Russell, Roy Rogers, Douglass Dumbrille, Bill Williams, Harry Von Zell, Iron Eyes Cody. One of Hope's best; same basic set-up as THE PALEFACE, but the presence of Rogers gives this one a satirical punch the original doesn't have. Full of director-cowriter Tashlin's cartoon-like gags; the scene where Hope and Trigger share the same bed is an unheralded comedy classic.▼

Son of Robin Hood, The (1959-British) **C-81m.** ** D: George Sherman. David Hedison, June Laverick, David Farrar, Marius Goring, George Coulouris. Bland forest tale continuing the legend of merry men led by Robin's descendant.

Son of Sinbad (1955) **C-88m.** *½ D: Ted Tetzlaff. Dale Robertson, Sally Forrest, Lili St. Cyr, Vincent Price. Limp Arabian Nights adventure has Sinbad, captured by caliph, forced to perform wonders to win freedom and save Baghdad from evil Tamerlane. Look fast for Kim Novak as one of the ladies garbed in full-length hooded capes.▼

Son of Spartacus SEE: **Slave, The**

Son of the Gods (1930) **82m.** ** D: Frank Lloyd. Richard Barthelmess, Constance Bennett, Dorothy Matthews, Dickie Moore. Harmless drama. Barthelmess journeys to Europe for college education but finds it no better than home. Fair cast trapped in hokey material.

Son of the Sheik (1926) **72m.** *** D: George Fitzmaurice. Rudolph Valentino, Vilma Banky, Agnes Ayres, Karl Dane, Bull Montana. Sequel to THE SHEIK contains flavorful account of desert leader who falls in love with dancing-girl Banky. Handsomely mounted silent film is first-rate adventure/romance, with tongue slightly in cheek. Valentino plays a dual role in this, his last film.▼

Son-Rise: A Miracle of Love (1979) **C-96m. TVM** D: Glenn Jordan. James Farentino, Kathryn Harrold, Stephen Elliott, Henry Olek, Michael and Casey Adams. Poignant true story of a couple who refuse to believe gloomy prognoses about their autistic son and devote their lives to treating him. The boy is played, quite remarkably, by veteran director King Vidor's 3½-year-old twin great-grandsons. Above average.

Sons and Lovers (1960-British) **103m.** ***½ D: Jack Cardiff. Trevor Howard, Dean Stockwell, Wendy Hiller, Mary Ure, Heather Sears, William Lucas, Donald Pleasence, Ernest Thesiger. Grim D. H. Lawrence story of sensitive youth Stockwell egged on by mother to make something of his life, away from coalmining town and drunken father Howard. Script by Gavin Lambert and T.E.B. Clarke. Freddie Francis' rich cinematography won an Oscar.

Sons of Katie Elder, The (1965) **C-122m.** *** D: Henry Hathaway. John Wayne, Dean Martin, Martha Hyer, Michael Anderson, Jr., Earl Holliman, Jeremy Slate, James Gregory, George Kennedy, Paul Fix, Dennis Hopper, John Litel, Strother Martin. Typical Western with Duke, Holliman, Anderson, and Martin the rowdy sons of frontier woman Katie Elder, who set out to avenge her death. Lively fun.▼

Sons of the Desert (1933) **69m.** ***½ D: William A. Seiter. Stan Laurel, Oliver Hardy, Charley Chase, Mae Busch, Dorothy Christy, Lucien Littlefield. L&H's best feature film; duo sneaks off to fraternal convention without telling the wives; then the fun begins, with Chase as hilariously obnoxious conventioneer.▼

Sons O' Guns (1936) **82m.** ** D: Lloyd Bacon. Joe E. Brown, Joan Blondell, Eric Blore, Winifred Shaw, Robert Barrat, Beverly Roberts, Craig Reynolds. Stars spark strained comedy of Brown joining the Army, sent to France where Blondell saves him from being shot as spy.

Son's Promise, A (1990) **C-100m. TVM** D: John Korty. Rick Schroeder, David Andrews, Veronica Cartwright, Stephen Dorff, Boyd Gaines, Andrew Lowry, Donald Moffat. Heart-tugger about a teenager who promises his dying mom he'll keep the surviving family of seven brothers together at all costs. Average.

Sooky (1931) **85m.** **½ D: Norman Taurog. Jackie Cooper, Robert Coogan, Jackie Searl, Enid Bennett, Helen Jerome Eddy, Willard Robertson. Middling sequel to SKIPPY with Cooper as Percy Crosby's comic-strip kid and scene-stealing Coogan as his best friend. Lightly comic, with some extra-sentimental scenes.

Sooner or Later (1978) **C-100m. TVM** D: Bruce Hart. Denise Miller, Rex Smith, Barbara Feldon, Judd Hirsch, Lilia Skala, Morey Amsterdam, Vivian Blaine, Lynn Redgrave. Teenybopper falls for rock idol and tries to decide whether or not to "go all the way." Go all the way to the set and change the channel. Below average.▼

Sophia Loren: Her Own Story (1980) **C-150m. TVM** D: Mel Stuart. Sophia Loren, John Gavin, Rip Torn, Armand Assante, Theresa Saldana, R. Cucciolla, Edmund Purdom. Sophia's life from girlhood in Naples to international film stardom and finally motherhood. Unique in its casting of the star not only as herself but as her mother (she's better in the latter role!) and the bizarre miscasting of Gavin as Cary Grant, Torn as Carlo Ponti, Purdom as Vittorio De Sica. Joanna Crawford wrote the teleplay from the A. E. Hotchner biography, but made it far too long for a less-than-compelling life. Average.▼

Sophie's Choice (1982) **C-157m.** **½ D: Alan J. Pakula. Meryl Streep, Kevin Kline, Peter MacNicol, Rita Karin, Stephen D. Newman, Josh Mostel, narrated by Josef Sommer. Streep's Oscar-winning performance is the centerpiece (and raison d'etre) for this slavishly faithful, but deadeningly slow-moving, adaptation of William Styron's book about a Polish woman's attempt to justify her existence in America after surviving a living hell during WW2. Nestor Almendros' camera is in love with Streep, but her stunning characterization can't carry the film alone.▼

Sophie's Place SEE: **Crooks and Coronets**▼

Sophisticated Gents, The (1981) **C-200m.** TVM D: Harry Falk. Bernie Casey, Rosey Grier, Robert Hooks, Ron O'Neal, Thalmus Rasulala, Raymond St. Jacques, Melvin Van Peebles, Dick Anthony Williams, Paul Winfield, Albert Hall, Beah Richards, Janet MacLachlan, Joanna Miles, Denise Nicholas, Marlene Warfield, Harry Guardino, Alfre Woodard. Terrific if overlong multi-character drama focusing on events at the reunion of nine members of a black athletic-social club. Van Peebles wrote the teleplay from John A. Williams' book *The Junior Bachelor Society* and included a pivotal role for himself as a pimp wanted for murder. Above average.

So Proudly We Hail! (1943) **126m.** *** D: Mark Sandrich. Claudette Colbert, Paulette Goddard, Veronica Lake, George Reeves, Sonny Tufts, Barbara Britton, Walter Abel. Flag-waving soaper of nurses in WW2 Pacific, headed by Colbert. Versatile cast, action scenes and teary romancing combine well in this woman's service story. Dated but still entertaining.

So Proudly We Hail (1990) **C-100m.** TVM D: Lionel Chetwynd. David Soul, Edward Herrmann, Chad Lowe, David Lowe, Gloria Carlin, Raphael Sbarge, Kevin Conroy, Harley Jane Kozak. White-supremacist group headed by Soul uses naïve university professor Herrmann to further its neo-Nazi causes. Written by director Chetwynd. Average.

Sorcerer (1977) **C-122m.** **½ D: William Friedkin. Roy Scheider, Bruno Cremer, Francisco Rabal, Amidou, Ramon Bieri, Peter Capell. Four fugitives in seedy Latin American town try to buy freedom by driving trucks of nitroglycerine over bumpy roads to help put out oil fire. Expensive remake of THE WAGES OF FEAR never really catches hold in spite of a few astounding scenes. Strange electronic score by Tangerine Dream.▼

Sorcerers, The (1967-British) **C-87m.** **½ D: Michael Reeves. Boris Karloff, Catherine Lacey, Ian Ogilvy, Elizabeth Ercy, Susan George. Interesting but flawed low-budgeter. Husband-and-wife scientist team attempt to perfect domination-of-will techniques, persuade young man (Ogilvy) to join experiments. Downhill from there.▼

Sorcerers, The (1955-French) **97m.** **½ D: Andre Michel. Maurice Ronet, Marina Vlady, Nicole Courcel, Michel Etcheverry. Bizarre yarn of femme fatale Vlady and her beguiling alliance with Ronet.

So Red the Rose (1935) **82m.** **½ D:

King Vidor. Margaret Sullavan, Walter Connolly, Randolph Scott, Elizabeth Patterson, Janet Beecher, Robert Cummings, Dickie Moore. Story of Sullavan patiently waiting for Scott to return from Civil War battlefield lacks punch, but is well acted and generally enjoyable; Maxwell Anderson was one of the writers.

Sorority Babes in the Slimeball Bowl-O-Rama (1988) **C-78m.** ** D: David DeCoteau. Linnea Quigley, Michelle Bauer, Andras Jones, Robin Rochelle, Brinke Stevens, Kathi Obrecht, Buck Flower. Wacky fantasy shlocker has sorority girls teaming up with nerds at a shopping mall to do battle with a demonic imp released from a bowling trophy. Good-looking young women in various states of undress are the film's drawing card.▼

Sorority Girl (1957) **60m.** *½ D: Roger Corman. Susan Cabot, Dick Miller, Barbara Crane, Fay Baker, June Kenney. Tawdry account of coed Cabot's attempt to dominate everyone in her sorority. A female version of Calder Willingham's *End as a Man*, filmed that same year as THE STRANGE ONE.

Sorority House Massacre (1986) **C-74m.** BOMB D: Carol Frank. Angela O'Neill, Wendy Martel, Pamela Ross, Nicole Rio. With most of her snobbish "sisters" away for a holiday weekend, a less privileged sorority member falls prey to a young psychotic who used to live in the house. Ever notice how these things never take place in fraternities?▼

Sorrow and the Pity, The (1970-Swiss) **260m.** **** D: Marcel Ophuls. Incredibly ambitious documentary about France's performance during WW2 is a total success. Film never becomes dull, in spite of four-and-a-half-hour length, even though bulk of footage is devoted to interviews with those who lived through the Nazi threat. A truly great film.▼

Sorrowful Jones (1949) **88m.** **½ D: Sidney Lanfield. Bob Hope, Lucille Ball, William Demarest, Mary Jane Saunders, Bruce Cabot, Thomas Gomez. Average racetrack comedy, actually a remake of LITTLE MISS MARKER and hardly as good.▼

Sorry, Wrong Number (1948) **89m.** *** D: Anatole Litvak. Barbara Stanwyck, Burt Lancaster, Ann Richards, Wendell Corey, Ed Begley, Leif Erickson, William Conrad. Not up to original radio thriller, movie adaptation is still tense study of woman overhearing murder plan on telephone, discovering she's to be the victim. Stanwyck won an Oscar nomination for her bravura performance; adapted—or rather, expanded—by Lucille Fletcher, from her radio drama (which starred Agnes Moorehead). Remade for cable TV.▼

Sorry, Wrong Number (1989) **C-100m.**

TVM D: Tony Wharmby. Loni Anderson, Carl Weintraub, Patrick Macnee, Hal Holbrook. Loni is a remarkably healthy-looking invalid who overhears a plot to murder somebody and then realizes it's she. Follows original Lucille Fletcher story but inserts some wild tale of drug dealing as an hour-long filler. Loni remade A LETTER TO THREE WIVES and LEAVE HER TO HEAVEN, but should start looking for original material. Made for cable. Average.▼

S.O.S. Pacific (1960-British) **92m.** **½ D: Guy Green. Eddie Constantine, Pier Angeli, Richard Attenborough, John Gregson, Eva Bartok, Jean Anderson. Middling study of human nature when passengers on plane crash-land on nuclear-test island.

S.O.S. Titanic (1979) **C-105m. TVM** D: William Hale. David Janssen, Cloris Leachman, Susan St. James, David Warner, Ian Holm, Helen Mirren, Harry Andrews. Stylish docu-drama about the oft-told sea disaster, mirroring the fictional elements of the 1953 movie TITANIC and the meticulously detailed facts of the 1958 A NIGHT TO REMEMBER, faithfully recreated here through James Costigan's multicharactered teleplay. Above average.▼

So This Is Love (1953) **C-101m.** ** D: Gordon Douglas. Kathryn Grayson, Merv Griffin, Walter Abel, Rosemary DeCamp, Jeff Donnell. Glossy, empty biography of opera star Grace Moore, antiseptically played by Grayson.

So This Is New York (1948) **79m.** *** D: Richard Fleischer. Henry Morgan, Rudy Vallee, Bill Goodwin, Hugh Herbert, Leo Gorcey, Virginia Grey, Dona Drake. Cheaply filmed but hilarious adaptation of Ring Lardner's *The Big Town,* with small-towner Morgan inheriting money and encountering strange ways of N.Y.C. Ingenious, offbeat script; radio/TV star Morgan fares well in screen debut, helped by top supporting cast.

So This Is Paris (1926) **68m.** *** D: Ernst Lubitsch. Monte Blue, Patsy Ruth Miller, Lilyan Tashman, Andre Beranger, Myrna Loy, Sidney D'Albrook. Frothy Lubitsch silent; sophisticated romantic comedy of dancers Tashman and Berenger flirting with Dr. Blue and wife Miller. Entertaining, fast-moving, and funny.

So This Is Paris (1954) **C-96m.** **½ D: Richard Quine. Tony Curtis, Gloria DeHaven, Gene Nelson, Corinne Calvet, Paul Gilbert, Allison Hayes, Mara Corday. Perky stars enliven this unmemorable musical of gobs on leave in France. Nelson also served as co-choreographer.

Sotto, Sotto (1984-Italian) **C-105m.** **½ D: Lina Wertmuller. Enrico Montesano, Veronica Lario, Luisa de Santis, Massimo Wertmuller. Obvious, but not unentertaining, tale of Lario, who finds herself attracted to longtime best friend de Santis; her husband (Montesano), a sexist animal with a fragile ego, then goes comically berserk. Incidentally, actor Wertmuller is the director's nephew. ▼

Soul Man (1986) **C-101m.** ** D: Steve Miner. C. Thomas Howell, Arye Gross, Rae Dawn Chong, James Earl Jones, Melora Hardin, Leslie Nielsen, James B. Sikking, Max Wright, Jeff Altman, Julia Louis Dreyfus, Ron Reagan. Young man desperate to go to Harvard Law School masquerades as a black in order to get minority scholarship. Slick but distressingly superficial; if this is the 1980s version of social satire, we're all in trouble.▼

Soul of a Monster, The (1944) **61m.** BOMB D: Will Jason. Rose Hobart, George Macready, Jim Bannon, Jeanne Bates. Other-worldly Hobart has strange control over doctor Macready.

Soul of Nigger Charley, The (1973) **C-104m.** *½ D: Larry Spangler. Fred Williamson, D'Urville Martin, Denise Nicholas, Pedro Armendariz, Jr. Weak sequel to LEGEND OF NIGGER CHARLEY finds Charley trying to free slaves held captive by former Confederate Army officer in Mexico.

Souls at Sea (1937) **92m.** *** D: Henry Hathaway. Gary Cooper, George Raft, Frances Dee, Olympe Bradna, Henry Wilcoxon, Harry Carey, Robert Cummings, Joseph Schildkraut, George Zucco, Virginia Weidler. Fine actioner with Cooper and Raft struggling to save lives during ship tragedy; Cooper wrongly accused of irresponsibility. The stars make good team in entertaining tale.

Souls for Sale SEE: **Confessions of an Opium Eater**

Soul Soldier (1972) **84m.** BOMB D: John Cardos. Rafer Johnson, Robert DoQui, Lincoln Kilpatrick, Issac Fields, Janee Michelle, Cesar Romero. Awful movie about black troops of the 10th Cavalry and soldier who seduces the wife of his buddy.

Soul to Soul (1971) **C-95m.** *** D: Denis Sanders. Wilson Pickett, Ike and Tina Turner, Santana, Roberta Flack, Les McCann, Willie Bobo, Eddie Harris, The Staple Singers. Good documentary of American soul, jazz and gospel performers in a concert commemorating the 14th anniversary of Ghanaian independence. Pickett is in top form singing "Funky Broadway" and "Land of 1,000 Dances."▼

Sound and the Fury, The (1959) **C-115m.** **½ D: Martin Ritt. Yul Brynner, Joanne Woodward, Margaret Leighton, Stuart Whitman, Ethel Waters, Jack Warden, Albert Dekker. Strange adaptation of William Faulkner novel becomes plodding tale of girl seeking independence from strict family rule in the South.

Sound Barrier, The SEE: **Breaking the Sound Barrier**

Sounder (1972) **C-105m.** **** D: Martin Ritt. Cicely Tyson, Paul Winfield, Kevin Hooks, Carmen Mathews, Taj Mahal, James Best, Janet MacLachlan. Beautiful film, romanticizing in a positive sense experiences of black sharecropper family in 1930s —and the maturation of young Hooks. Full of fine performances that make characters utterly real. Mahal also composed the score. Screenplay by Lonnie Elder III from William Armstrong's novel. Sequel: PART 2, SOUNDER.▼

Sounder, Part Two SEE: **Part 2, Sounder**

Sound of Anger, The (1968) **C-100m.** TVM D: Michael Ritchie. James Farentino, Guy Stockwell, Burl Ives, David Macklin, Lynda Day, Charles Aidman, Collin Wilcox. Brother lawyers drawn into murder case; sister of one of accused reveals that high-priced lawyer Nichols (Ives) hired to defend only one defendant. Uneven performances, lame script; only interesting character is Ives. Pilot to *The Lawyers* segment of *The Bold Ones*. Below average.

Sound Off (1952) **C-83m.** ** D: Richard Quine. Mickey Rooney, Anne James, John Archer, Sammy White. Too-often unimaginative Army comedy with Rooney a performer who's drafted and can't stop showing off. Written by Quine and Blake Edwards.

Sound of Fury, The (1951) **85m.** **½ D: Cyril Endfield. Frank Lovejoy, Lloyd Bridges, Richard Carlson, Katherine Locke, Adele Jergens, Irene Vernon. Taut suspenser as manhunt closes in on kidnapper who killed his victim. Retitled: TRY AND GET ME.▼

Sound of Horror, The (1964-Spanish) **89m.** ** D: Jose Antonio Nieves Conde. Arturo Fernandez, Soledad Miranda, Antonio Casas, James Philbrook, Ingrid Pitt, Jose Badalo. Archeological expedition is terrorized by recently hatched prehistoric creature; it's invisible but noisy.

Sound of Music, The (1965) **C-174m.** ***½ D: Robert Wise. Julie Andrews, Christopher Plummer, Eleanor Parker, Peggy Wood, Richard Haydn. Call it corn if you like, but blockbuster Rodgers-Hammerstein musical based on Austria's real-life Von Trapp family, who fled their homeland in 1938 to escape from Nazi rule, pleased more people than practically any other film in history. Fine music, beautiful scenery help offset coy aspects of script. Five Oscars include Best Picture, Director, Score Adaptation (Irwin Kostal), Editing (William Reynolds). Songs include "Do Re Mi," "My Favorite Things," title tune. Usually cut for TV to 145m.▼

Soupcon (1979-French) **C-93m.** **½ D: Jean-Charles Tacchella. Jean Carmet, Marie Dubois, Alain Doutey, Rachel Jenevein, Jose Laccioni. Middle-aged couple (Carmet, Dubois) decide to separate after a quarter-century of marriage. Spirited and attractively played, but still forgettable; a disappointment from the director of COUSIN, COUSINE.

Soup for One (1982) **C-87m.** **½ D: Jonathan Kaufer. Saul Rubinek, Marcia Strassman, Gerrit Graham, Teddy Pendergrass, Richard Libertini, Andrea Martin, Lewis J. Stadlen. Sometimes winning but uneven account of single New Yorker Rubinek searching for his dream girl. The cast is game; 26-year-old director Kaufer is a talent to watch.▼

Southern Comfort (1981) **C-106m.** ** D: Walter Hill. Keith Carradine, Powers Boothe, Fred Ward, Franklyn Seales, T. K. Carter, Lewis Smith, Les Lannom, Peter Coyote, Brion James. Macho National Guardsmen patronize Cajuns in the Louisiana swamp, much to their regret. Survival-of-the-fittest yarn is an intellectually muddled, Grade B DELIVERANCE, despite its crisp direction.▼

Southerner, The (1945) **91m.** **** D: Jean Renoir. Zachary Scott, Betty Field, Beulah Bondi, J. Carrol Naish, Norman Lloyd, Bunny Sunshine, Jay Gilpin, Estelle Taylor, Percy Kilbride, Blanche Yurka. Superb drama of family struggling to make farmland self-supporting against serious odds. Renoir adapted George Sessions Perry's novel *Hold Autumn in Your Hand*.▼

Southern Star, The (1969-British-French-U.S.) **C-102m.** **½ D: Sidney Hayers. George Segal, Ursula Andress, Orson Welles, Ian Hendry, Harry Andrews, Michel Constantin. Uneven combination comedy-adventure detailing multiparty chase for possession of unusually large diamond boasts beautiful locations in Senegal, Africa, but not much else. Based on a Jules Verne novel.

Southern Yankee, A (1948) **90m.** *** D: Edward Sedgwick. Red Skelton, Brian Donlevy, Arlene Dahl, George Coulouris, Lloyd Gough, John Ireland, Charles Dingle, Joyce Compton. Hilarious Skelton comedy set during Civil War with Red a bumbling Yankee spy down South. Reminiscent of silent comedies, since Buster Keaton devised many of the film's gags.

South of Pago Pago (1940) **98m.** ** D: Alfred E. Green. Victor McLaglen, Jon Hall, Frances Farmer, Olympe Bradna, Gene Lockhart. Juvenile actioner of pirates stealing natives' supply of pearls, encountering local hostility.▼

South of Reno (1987) **C-94m.** **½ D: Mark Rezyka. Jeffrey Osterhage, Lisa Blount, Joe Phelan, Lewis Van Bergen, Julia Montgomery. Desert hermit Osterhage discovers that wife Blount has been unfaithful. Well made and visually arresting but convoluted plot-wise; still, an impressive first feature from Rezyka, who also coscripted.▼

South of St. Louis (1949) **C-88m.** **½

D: Ray Enright. Joel McCrea, Alexis Smith, Zachary Scott, Dorothy Malone, Douglas Kennedy. Alan Hale, Victor Jory. Three ranching partners (McCrea, Scott, Kennedy) fall into dispute over land, money, Civil War gun-running, and women. Unmemorable Western has good cast, fast pacing, and Technicolor on its side.▼

South Pacific (1958) **C-151m.** **½ D: Joshua Logan. Rossano Brazzi, Mitzi Gaynor, John Kerr, Ray Walston, Juanita Hall, France Nuyen, Tom Laughlin, voice of Giorgio Tozzi. Disappointing filmization of great Rodgers & Hammerstein show; adaptation of James Michener's moving vignettes about WW2 life on Pacific island needs dynamic personalities to make it catch fire, and they aren't here. Even location filming is lackluster. Adequate but hardly memorable. Songs include "Some Enchanted Evening," "Bali H'ai," "There Is Nothing Like a Dame," "Happy Talk," "You've Got to Be Taught," etc. Among the sailors and servicemen you'll spot John Gabriel, Ron Ely, Doug McClure, and James Stacy. Originally shown at 171m.▼

South Riding (1938-British) **84m.** *** D: Victor Saville. Ralph Richardson, Edna Best, Edmund Gwenn, Ann Todd, John Clements, Marie Lohr, Milton Rosmer, Glynis Johns. Enjoyable drama from Winifred Holtby's popular novel about political and personal problems among a group of characters living in Yorkshire. Smoothly made and superbly acted by a flawless cast. Original British running time: 90m.

South Sea Sinner (1950) **88m.** ** D: H. Bruce Humberstone. Macdonald Carey, Shelley Winters, Luther Adler, Frank Lovejoy, Liberace. Muddled melodrama involving fugitive from justice being intimidated by those on island who knew his past; Winters is blowsy cafe singer. Remake of 1940 SEVEN SINNERS.

South Sea Woman (1953) **99m.** **½ D: Arthur Lubin. Burt Lancaster, Virginia Mayo, Chuck Connors, Arthur Shields, Paul Burke. Murky tropical isle story of love and deceit with soldier Lancaster sparking with Mayo.

Southside 1-1000 (1950) **73m.** **½ D: Boris Ingster. Don Defore, Andrea King, George Tobias, Barry Kelley. Straightforward narrative of federal agent capturing counterfeiters.

Southwest Passage (1954) **C-82m.** ** D: Ray Nazarro. Joanne Dru, Rod Cameron, John Ireland, John Dehner, Guinn Williams, Mark Hanna. Familiar tale of bank robber and gal joining up with settlers heading West, staving off Indian attack.

So Well Remembered (1947-British) **114m.** *** D: Edward Dmytryk. John Mills, Martha Scott, Trevor Howard, Patricia Roc, Richard Carlson, Ivor Barnard. Author James Hilton narrates saga (adapted by John Paxton) of earnest newspaper editor (Mills) determined to improve living conditions in factory town, sidetracked by marriage to blindly ambitious woman (Scott). Very young Juliet Mills has bit part.

Soylent Green (1973) **C-100m.** ** D: Richard Fleischer. Charlton Heston, Edward G. Robinson, Leigh Taylor-Young, Chuck Connors, Joseph Cotten, Brock Peters, Paula Kelly, Whit Bissell, Mike Henry, Dick Van Patten. Well-intentioned but cardboard adaptation of Harry Harrison's science-fiction classic *Make Room! Make Room!* In the year 2022, Manhattan has become an overcrowded hellhole; cop Heston, investigating murder of bigwig, stumbles onto explosive government secret (which you'll figure out long before he does). Robinson is splendid in his final film; title refers to a precious foodstuff made of soybeans and lentils.▼

So Young, So Bad (1950) **91m.** **½ D: Bernard Vorhaus. Paul Henreid, Catherine McLeod, Grace Coppin, Cecil Clovelly, Anne Francis, Rosita (Rita) Moreno, Anne Jackson, Enid Pulver. Humane psychiatrist Henreid takes on superintendent Clovelly and sadistic head matron Coppin at a correctional home for girls. Effective study of female juvenile delinquency.

So You Won't Talk (1940) **69m.** ** D: Edward Sedgwick. Joe E. Brown, Frances Robinson, Vivienne Osborne, Bernard Nedell, Tom Dugan. Good, typical mistaken identity comedy with bookworm Brown, a dead ringer for notorious mobster.

Spaceballs (1987) **C-96m.** **½ D: Mel Brooks. Mel Brooks, John Candy, Rick Moranis, Bill Pullman, Daphne Zuniga, Dick Van Patten, George Wyner, Michael Winslow, Lorene Yarnell, John Hurt, Ronny Graham, voices of Joan Rivers, Dom DeLuise. Likably silly parody of STAR WARS (some years after the fact) is basically a collection of jokes, both verbal and visual. Enough of them are funny to make for pleasant, if not hilarious, fare. Surprisingly innocuous for Brooks and Co., with Mel tackling two roles, including the diminutive Yogurt.▼

SpaceCamp (1986) **C-107m.** ** D: Harry Winer. Kate Capshaw, Lea Thompson, Kelly Preston, Larry B. Scott, Leaf Phoenix, Tate Donovan, Tom Skerritt, Barry Primus, Terry O'Quinn. Or, BRATS IN SPACE, the story of some kids who wouldn't rate at McDonald's College of Hamburger Knowledge, but somehow get chosen to train at NASA summer camp—and accidentally get launched into space. There's a cute robot, but surprisingly, other special effects are way below par.▼

Space Children, The (1958) **69m.** ** D: Jack Arnold. Michel Ray, Peggy Webber, Adam Williams, Jackie Coogan, Johnny Washbrook. Strange force brainwashes chil-

dren into performing sabotage at Pacific nuclear test site. Anti-war film isn't up to Arnold's other 50s science-fiction classics, but is sufficiently offbeat to warrant a peek.
Spaced Invaders (1990) **C-102m.** *½ D: Patrick Read Johnson. Douglas Barr, Royal Dano, Ariana Richards, J. J. Anderson, Gregg Berger, Kevin Thompson, Jimmy Briscoe, Tony Cox, Debbie Lee Carrington, Tommy Madden. Martians, out to "kick some Earthling butt," fly into a Mayberry-type burg after mistaking a Halloween rebroadcast of Orson Welles' *War of the Worlds* for legitimate invasion orders. Have you ever noticed that Welles couldn't get financing for decades, but movies like this keep getting made? Criminally overlong.
Spaced Out (1981-British) **C-84m.** BOMB D: Norman J. Warren. Barry Stokes, Tony Maiden, Glory Annen, Michael Rowlatt, Ava Cadell, Kate Ferguson, Lynne Ross. Sexy ladies from outer space "imprison" earthlings. Moronic comedy is poorly directed and produced; originally released in 1979 as OUTER TOUCH, without smutty jokes cracked by a computer.▼
Spaceflight IC-1 (1965-British) **65m.** *½ D: Bernard Knowles. Bill Williams, Norma West, John Cairney, Linda Marlowe, Jeremy Longhurst. Dreary, talky film with no space thrills and little action, set aboard a spaceship between planets.
Spacehunter: Adventures in the Forbidden Zone (1983-Canadian) **C-90m.** *½ D: Lamont Johnson. Peter Strauss, Molly Ringwald, Ernie Hudson, Andrea Marcovicci. Title character roams a planet's barren wasteland in order to rescue three damsels in distress, who are being held captive by a vicious mutant called Overdog. Boring and obnoxious, even in 3D.▼
Space Master X-7 (1958) **70m.** ** D: Edward Bernds. Bill Williams, Lyn Thomas, Robert Ellis, Paul Frees. OK sci-fi: space missile returning to earth carries hidden cargo highly toxic.
Space Rage (1985) **C-77m.** BOMB D: Conrad Palmisano. Richard Farnsworth, Michael Paré, John Laughlin, Lee Purcell, Lewis Van Bergen, William Windom. Meek space Western is set on a prison planet. Farnsworth is ex-cop who straps on his laser beam six-shooter to teach Paré and the other outlaws a lesson; he should've turned the laser on this bomb instead!▼
Space Raiders (1983) **C-82m.** ** D: Howard R. Cohen. Vince Edwards, David Mendenhall, Patsy Pease, Thom Christopher, Luca Bercovici. This toothless adventure is another Roger Corman-produced space opera using special effects footage and music from BATTLE BEYOND THE STARS. Acceptable genre fare for the undemanding viewer.▼

Spaceship SEE: **Creature Wasn't Nice, The**▼
Spaceship to the Unknown (1936) **97m.** **½ D: Frederick Stephani. Buster Crabbe, Jean Rogers, Frank Shannon, Charles Middleton, Priscilla Lawson, John Lipson. Condensed version of FLASH GORDON serial covering first half of original story. With planet Mongo heading toward collision with Earth, Flash, Dale Arden, and Dr. Zarkov fly rocketship to remedy impending disaster. Uninspired handling of footage from this famous serial.▼
Spaceways (1953-British) **76m.** *½ D: Terence Fisher. Howard Duff, Eva Bartok, Andrew Osborn, Alan Wheatley. To prove he hasn't murdered her husband and stuffed him into a just-launched satellite, Duff and Bartok go up to look on the next rocket, but that happens only at the very end of this slow movie. From a novel and radio play by Charles Eric Maine.
Spanish Affair (1958-Spanish) **C-95m.** ** D: Don Siegel. Richard Kiley, Carmen Sevilla, Jose Guardiola, Jesus Tordesillas. Virtually a travelogue pegged on slight plot of Kiley, American architect, traveling in Iberia, falling in love with local girl; nice scenery, but hardly typical Siegel fare.
Spanish Gardener, The (1956-British) **C-95m.** *** D: Philip Leacock. Dirk Bogarde, Maureen Swanson, Jon Whiteley, Cyril Cusack, Bernard Lee, Michael Hordern. When gardener befriends employer's young son, diplomat father becomes jealous. Intelligent and beautifully filmed adaptation of A. J. Cronin novel.
Spanish Main, The (1945) **C-100m.** **½ D: Frank Borzage. Paul Henreid, Maureen O'Hara, Walter Slezak, Binnie Barnes, John Emery, Barton MacLane. Colorful escapism with swashbuckling pirate Henreid foiling villain Slezak, winning O'Hara.▼
Spare The Rod (1961-British) **93m.** **½ D: Leslie Norman. Max Bygraves, Donald Pleasence, Jean Anderson, Betty McDowall, Peter Reynolds, Geoffrey Keen. Bygraves is idealistic teacher in tough London school trying to communicate with pupils and cope with the system; OK drama.
Sparkle (1976) **C-100m.** **½ D: Sam O'Steen. Philip M. (Michael) Thomas, Irene Cara, Lonette McKee, Dwan Smith, Mary Alice, Dorian Harewood, Tony King. Rise of singing group not unlike The Supremes suffers from cliché overdose, but benefits from slick filmmaking, good musical numbers (by Curtis Mayfield), vivid performance by McKee. Worth comparing to later (and similar) Broadway musical *Dreamgirls*.▼
Sparkling Cyanide (1983) **C-100m.** TVM D: Robert Lewis. Anthony Andrews, Deborah Raffin, Harry Morgan, Pamela Bellwood, Nancy Marchand, Josef Sommer, David Huffman. Deadly brew loses some of its Agatha Christie zing in this Americani-

[1080]

zation of her whodunit about an Englishman (Andrews, in modern threads for a change) stumbling onto a murder among the upper crust of Pasadena. Filmed back-to-back with A CARIBBEAN MYSTERY by the same production team. Average.

Sparks: The Price of Passion (1990) **C-100m. TVM** D: Richard Colla. Victoria Principal, Ted Wass, Hector Elizondo, William Lucking, Elaine Stritch, Ralph Waite. Principal is the outspoken mayor of Albuquerque, but her political career is threatened by a smear following a night of indiscretion and a threat to her life by a serial killer. Average.

Sparrows (1926) **84m. *** D: William Beaudine. Mary Pickford, Gustav von Seyffertitz, Roy Stewart, Mary Louise Miller, Charlotte Mineau, Spec O'Donnell. One of Mary's best silent pictures is a fullblooded melodrama about intrepid girl who struggles to protect band of younger orphans from their wicked captor. ▼

Spartacus (1960) **C-184m. ***½** D: Stanley Kubrick. Kirk Douglas, Laurence Olivier, Jean Simmons, Tony Curtis, Charles Laughton, Peter Ustinov, John Gavin, Nina Foch, Herbert Lom, John Ireland, Charles McGraw, Woody Strode. Great spectacle based on historical fact. Douglas heads huge cast as leader of slaves rebelling against Republican Rome. Beautiful Alex North score; trenchant script by Dalton Trumbo from Howard Fast's book. Four Oscars include Best Supporting Actor (Ustinov) and Cinematography (Russell Metty). Beware of shorter prints. Originally released at 196m.▼

Spasms (1983-Canadian) **C-87m.** BOMB D: William Fruet. Peter Fonda, Oliver Reed, Kerrie Keane, Al Waxman, Marilyn Lightstone, George Bloomfield. Reed has a telepathic—or, should we say, telepathic—connection with a deadly serpent. Grade Z junk; filmed in 1981.▼

Spawn of the North (1938) **110m. *** D: Henry Hathaway. George Raft, Henry Fonda, Dorothy Lamour, Louise Platt, John Barrymore, Akim Tamiroff, Lynne Overman. Action-packed film of Canadian fisheries with good cast; Lamour surprisingly good. Barrymore amusing as talky newspaperman. The special photographic and sound effects earned a special Academy Award. Remade as ALASKA SEAS.

Speak Easily (1932) **82m. *** D: Edward Sedgwick. Buster Keaton, Jimmy Durante, Ruth Selwyn, Thelma Todd, Hedda Hopper, Sidney Toler. Dimwitted professor Keaton gets involved with show troupe en route to Broadway. One of Keaton's best talkies, with Durante in good form, Todd a wonderful vamp, Toler an amusing stage manager.

Speaking of Murder (1959-French) **80m. **½** D: Gilles Grangier. Jean Gabin, Annie Girardot, Paul Frankeur, Lino Ventura.

Sensibly handled drama of brothers involved with life of crime.

Speaking Parts (1989-Canadian) **C-93m. *** D: Atom Egoyan. Michael McManus, Arsinée Khanjian, Gabrielle Rose, Tony Nardi, David Hemblen, Patricia Collins, Gerard Parkes. Fascinating account of VCR-obsessed laundry worker Khanjian and her fixation on aspiring actor McManus, who in turn commences a most unusual relationship with Rose. A perceptive look at how technology has pervaded modern life; the result is occasionally just a bit too slick. The director also scripted.

Special Agent (1935) **78m. **½** D: William Keighley. Bette Davis, George Brent, Ricardo Cortez, Jack LaRue, Henry O'Neill. Programmer about Brent using Davis to get low-down on racketeer Cortez.

Special Bulletin (1983) **C-105m. TVM** D: Edward Zwick. Ed Flanders, Kathryn Walker, Roxanne Hart, Christopher Allport, Rosalind Cash, David Clennon, David Rasche. Shattering TV experience, presented on tape as a simulated television newscast, about the threatened nuclear destruction of Charleston, S.C. by quintet of war protesters who demand the dismantling of America's arsenal of warheads; interesting subplot examines how the media react in the face of such incidents. Multi-Emmy winner written by Zwick and Marshall Herskovitz. Way above average.▼

Special Day, A (1977-Italian-Canadian) **C-106m. **½** D: Ettore Scola. Sophia Loren, Marcello Mastroianni, John Vernon, Françoise Berd, Nicole Magny. Two lonely people chance to meet on an eventful day in 1938; Loren is frumpy housewife, Mastroianni a troubled homosexual. Fine performances bolster this pleasant but trifling film.▼

Special Delivery (1955) **86m. *** D: John Brahm. Joseph Cotten, Eva Bartok, Niall MacGinnis, Rene Deltgen. Mild froth with Cotten on U.S. diplomatic staff posted in Iron Curtain country, dealing with an abandoned baby and curvaceous refugee Bartok.

Special Delivery (1976) **C-99m. *** D: Paul Wendkos. Bo Svenson, Cybill Shepherd, Michael Gwynne, Tom Atkins, Sorrell Booke, Jeff Goldblum, Vic Tayback, Deidre Hall, Gerrit Graham. Diverting comedy-action caper has Vietnam vets led by Svenson robbing a bank. When only Svenson escapes, he has to contend with nutty artist Shepherd (who's quite good) and killers after he stuffs the loot into a mailbox.▼

Special Effects (1984) **C-93m. **½** D: Larry Cohen. Zoe Tamerlis, Eric Bogosian, Brad Rijn, Kevin O'Connor, Bill Oland. Intriguing but uneven tale of a down-on-his-luck director who films the murder of a young actress, and commences making a movie about his deed. He even finds someone to star in his epic who resembles his victim; both are played by Tamerlis.▼

[1081]

Special Friendship, A (1987) **C-100m.** TVM D: Fielder Cook. Tracy Pollan, Akosua Busia, LeVar Burton, Josef Sommer, Adam Storke, Tom Aldredge, Patricia Elliott. Civil War drama about two women: a wealthy plantation owner's daughter (who goes on to become a spy for the Union Army) and her black slave since childhood. There's more than a passing similarity to Disney's earlier THE LIBERATORS, with a change of gender. Average.

Specialist, The (1975) **C-93m.** ** D: Hikmet Avedis. Ahna Capri, John Anderson, Adam West, Alvy Moore, Christiane Schmidtmer, Marlene Schmidt. Campy exploitation film has Capri well cast as a zaftig female version of usual macho killer-for-hire. Writer-producer Schmidt (director Avedis' wife) plays West's wife. ▼

Specialists, The (1975) **C-78m.** TVM D: Richard Quine. Robert York, Maureen Reagan, Jack Hogan, Jed Allen, Alfred Ryder, Harry Townes. Drama based on the doings of the U.S. Public Health Department, with two dogged dog-and-cat-team doctors trying to thwart possible epidemics. Familiar hospital-style plot complications in this pilot for unsold series called *Vector*. Reagan is daughter of Ronald Reagan and Jane Wyman. Average.

Special Kind of Love, A SEE: **Special Olympics**

Special Olympics (1978) **C-100m.** TVM D: Lee Philips. Charles Durning, Philip Brown, George Parry, Irene Tedrow, Mare Winningham, Herb Edelman, Debra Winger. Heartwarmer by John Sacret Young about a widower's struggle to hold together his family of three teenagers, one mentally retarded, finding self-fulfillment in his love of sports. Above average. Also known as A SPECIAL KIND OF LOVE.

Special People (1984) **C-100m.** TVM D: Marc Daniels. Brooke Adams, Susan Roman, Sandra Ciccone, Lesleh Donaldson, Benny D'Onofrio. Well-played drama about Canada's Famous People Players, a puppet troupe of mentally handicapped young adults (many of whom appear as themselves). Adams plays Diane Dupuy, the troupe's founder. Written by Corey Blechman, best known for BILL. Above average.

Special Section (1975-French) **C-110m.** ** D: Costa-Gavras. Louis Seigner, Michel Lonsdale, Jacques Perrin, Bruno Cremer, Pierre Dux, Henri Serre. Overlong, excessively wordy drama of true happening in occupied Paris in 1941. Four expendables are tried and ceremonially condemned for the murder of a young German naval cadet. Some interest.

Special Treatment (1980-Yugoslavian) **C-94m.** *** D: Goran Paskaljevic. Ljuba Tadic, Dusica Zegarac, Danilo Stojkovic, Milena Dravic, Petar Kralj. Fanatical doctor Tadic brings a group of alcoholics he's been treating to a brewery to show off his skills as a healer; of course, his charges don't remain sober for long. Strange, deadpan comedy is occasionally slow but mostly funny.

Speckled Band, The (1931-British) **90m.** *½ D: Jack Raymond. Lyn Harding, Raymond Massey, Angela Baddeley, Nancy Price, Athole Stewart. Slow-as-molasses version of the Conan Doyle story, with Sherlock Holmes coming to the aid of a frightened girl (Baddeley), whose sister has been murdered. Interesting to see Massey cast as the sleuth, but this film is really boring. ▼

Spectre of the Rose (1946) **90m.** *** D: Ben Hecht. Judith Anderson, Michael Chekhov, Ivan Kirov, Viola Essen, Lionel Stander. Uniquely individual melodrama by Hecht set in the world of ballet, with an unusual cast, including dancers, non-actors, and scene-stealing Chekhov. Fascinating (some might even say strange), though definitely not for all tastes. ▼

Spectre (1977) **C-100m.** TVM D: Clive Donner. Robert Culp, Gig Young, John Hurt, Gordon Jackson, Ann Bell, James Villiers, Majel Barrett. Classy demonology exercise by Gene Roddenberry involving flamboyant criminologist and his associate, an alcoholic doctor, who investigate devilish doings in *Playboy*-type English abbey. Unusually lavish production helps hurdle the foolishness. Average.

Speed (1936) **70m.** ** D: Edwin L. Marin. James Stewart, Wendy Barrie, Una Merkel, Ted Healy, Weldon Heyburn, Ralph Morgan, Patricia Wilder. Stewart enhances this star-building quickie (one of eight features he made in 1936) as a test-car driver who's developed a high-speed carburetor. Most of the racing action consists of blatant rear-projection and stock footage.

Speed Crazy (1959) **75m.** BOMB D: William Hole, Jr. Brett Halsey, Yvonne Lime, Charles Willcox, Slick Slavin, Jacqueline Ravell, Baynes Barron, Jackie Joseph. Trashy, campy bottom-of-the-barrel programmer about a psychotic drifter who's "an accident looking for a place to happen." He's obsessed with fast cars, and keeps complaining that "everybody keeps crowding me." This one really lives up to its title. ▼

Speed to Spare (1948) **57m.** ** D: William Berke. Richard Arlen, Jean Rogers, Richard Travis, Roscoe Karns, Nanette Parks. Arlen is OK as a stunt-car driver who decides to take it easy and become a driver for his friend's trucking company, only to find himself in more trouble. Acceptable programmer from the Paramount "B" factory of Pine-Thomas.

Speedtrap (1977) **C-98m.** ** D: Earl Bellamy. Joe Don Baker, Tyne Daly, Richard Jaeckel, Robert Loggia, Morgan Woodward, Timothy Carey. Private eye Baker is called in by the cops to trap an elusive car thief, and teamed with policewoman Daly. Good cast and predictable screeching tires can't save muddled script.▼

Speedway (1968) **C-94m.** ** D: Norman Taurog. Elvis Presley, Nancy Sinatra, Bill Bixby, Gale Gordon. Routine Presley tuner with Elvis starring as a bighearted stockcar racer and Sinatra along for the ride as a tax inspector. Richard Petty, Cale Yarborough and other real-life auto racers are featured.▼

Speedy (1928) **71m.** *** D: Ted Wilde. Harold Lloyd, Ann Christy, Bert Woodruff, Brooks Benedict. Contrived but enjoyable comedy has Harold trying to save N.Y.C.'s last horse-drawn trolley, run by his girlfriend's grandfather, from extinction. Vivid N.Y.C. location work includes hair-raising chase scene, and appealing cameo by Babe Ruth as himself.

Speed Zone! (1989) **C-95m.** *½ D: Jim Drake. Peter Boyle, Donna Dixon, John Candy, Eugene Levy, Tim Matheson, The Smothers Brothers, Matt Frewer, Joe Flaherty, Shari Belafonte, Art Hindle, John Schneider, Jamie Farr, Lee Van Cleef, Michael Spinks, Brooke Shields, Alyssa Milano, Carl Lewis. Yet another variation on the CANNONBALL RUN cross-country road race, with Boyle as a sheriff who's determined to stop the race before it begins. Pointless, derivative, and unfunny, a particular waste of such talents as Candy, Levy, and Flaherty. You know you're in trouble when Brooke Shields gives the funniest performance in the film!▼

Spell, The (1977) **C-78m.** TVM D: Lee Philips. Lee Grant, James Olson, Susan Myers, Lelia Goldoni, Helen Hunt, Jack Colvin, Barbara Bostock. Occult thriller has an unloved teenager turning her supernatural powers on her tormentors. Merely a sanitized-for-TV CARRIE and a poor substitute. Below average.▼

Spellbinder (1988) **C-99m.** ** D: Janet Greek. Timothy Daly, Kelly Preston, Rick Rossovich, Diana Bellamy, Audra Lindley, Cary-Hiroyuki Tagawa, Anthony Crivello, Roderick Cook, Stefan Gierasch. L.A. lawyer falls for a mysterious beauty, slowly learns she's a witch, a member of a coven that wants her back as a sacrifice. A whybother? occult thriller: slick, empty, and extremely predictable.▼

Spellbound (1945) **111m.** ***½ D: Alfred Hitchcock. Ingrid Bergman, Gregory Peck, Leo G. Carroll, John Emery, Michael Chekhov, Wallace Ford, Rhonda Fleming, Bill Goodwin, Regis Toomey. Absorbing tale of psychiatrist Bergman trying to uncover Peck's hangups; Dali dream sequences, innovative (and Oscarwinning) Miklos Rozsa score help Hitchcock create another unique film. In original theatrical prints, a key gunshot was shown in color.▼

Spencer's Mountain (1963) **C-119m.** ** D: Delmer Daves. Henry Fonda, Maureen O'Hara, James MacArthur, Donald Crisp, Wally Cox. Mawkish sudser about Wyoming landowner Fonda who keeps promising to build another family house. Good cast stuck with inferior script. Based on the Earl Hamner, Jr. novel; later developed into *The Waltons*.

Spetters (1980-Dutch) **C-115m.** *** D: Paul Verhoeven. Hans van Tongeren, Toon Agterberg, Renee Soutendijk, Maarten Spanjer, Marianne Boyer, Rutger Hauer. Adolescent shenanigans and dreams in Holland; teenagers sleep around and race their motorcycles while idolizing race champ Hauer. Graphically sexual, with crisp direction by Verhoeven; luscious Soutendijk scores as an ambitious hash-slinger.▼

Sphinx, The (1933) **63m.** ** D: Phil Rosen. Lionel Atwill, Sheila Terry, Theodore Newton, Paul Hurst, Luis Alberni, Robert Ellis. Atwill plays a dual role as a murderer and his deaf-mute twin, who serves as his perfect alibi, in this passable low-budgeter. Remade in 1942 as THE PHANTOM KILLER.▼

Sphinx (1981) **C-117m.** *½ D: Franklin J. Schaffner. Lesley-Anne Down, Frank Langella, Maurice Ronet, John Gielgud, Martin Benson, John Rhys-Davies. Harried Egyptologist Down continuously eludes death as she searches for a mystery tomb. Awful script, mummy-like performances, impressive Egyptian scenery. Adapted by John Byrum from Robin Cook novel.▼

Spider, The (1945) **62m.** ** D: Robert D. Webb. Richard Conte, Faye Marlowe, Kurt Kreuger, John Harvey, Ann Savage, Cara Williams, Martin Kosleck. Programmer mystery yarn from 20th Century-Fox, not allowing Conte to be his violent best.

Spider and the Fly, The (1949-British) **87m.** **½ D: Robert Hamer. Guy Rolfe, Nadia Gray, Eric Portman, Maurice Denham, James Hayter, Arthur Lowe. Effective drama of Gallic law enforcer and British crook teaming up to retrieve government document; good interplay between cast members.

Spider Baby (1964) **80m.** **½ D: Jack Hill. Lon Chaney, Jr., Sid Haig, Jill Banner, Mantan Moreland, Beverly Washburn, Carol Ohmart. Not bad little chiller about the antics of a very unusual—and very sick—family. At its best it's both scary and funny. Chaney is the clan's chauffeur and sings the title song! The full title is SPIDER BABY, OR THE MADDEST STORY EVER TOLD. Also known as THE LIVER EATERS.▼

Spider-Man (1977) **C-94m.** TVM D: E. W. Swackhamer. Nicholas Hammond, David White, Michael Pataki, Hilly Hicks, Lisa Eilbacher, Thayer David, Jeff Donnell. So-so adaptation of the famed Marvel

Comics character; grad student Hammond is bitten by radio-active spider, transformed into superhero who climbs walls and thwarts $50 million extortion plot. OK special effects; the kids may not mind the illogical plot. The once-in-a-while series followed. Average.▼

Spiders (1919-German) **137m.** *** D: Fritz Lang. Carl de Vogt, Ressel Orla, Lil Dagover, Georg John, Bruno Lettinger. Intrepid explorer/adventurer de Vogt—an early cross between Indiana Jones and James Bond—vies with evil Spider cult for mystic Incan diamond. First two chapters (The Golden Lake and The Diamond Ship) of an unfinished four-part serial abound with lost civilizations, human sacrifice, pirate treasure, and too many perils to count. Lang's obsession with a diabolical underworld foreshadows his DR. MABUSE films. An exciting curio; the earliest of Lang's films to survive. Restored version has original color-tinted scenes and a Gaylord Carter organ score. German title: DIE SPINNEN.▼

Spider's Stratagem, The (1970-Italian) **C-100m.** *** D: Bernardo Bertolucci. Giulio Brogi, Alida Valli, Tino Scotti, Pippo Campanini, Franco Giovanelli. Young man visits the provincial town where his anti-Fascist father was assassinated 30 years earlier, is rejected by the populace at every turn. Exceedingly atmospheric puzzler, from a Jorge Luis Borges short story, boasts some of the most beautiful color cinematography (by Vittorio Storaro) in memory.

Spider Woman SEE: **Sherlock Holmes and the Spider Woman**▼

Spider Woman Strikes Back, The (1946) **59m.** *½ D: Arthur Lubin. Brenda Joyce, Gale Sondergaard, Kirby Grant, Rondo Hatton, Milburn Stone, Hobart Cavanaugh. Pitiful waste of fine actress Sondergaard in campy thriller with little relation to earlier Sherlock Holmes feature.

Spies (1928-German) **90m.** ***½ D: Fritz Lang. Rudolph Klein-Rogge, Gerda Maurus, Willy Fritsch, Lupu Pick, Fritz Rasp. Silent spy-thriller still packs a wallop as government agent Fritsch determines to capture master-fiend Haighi, who runs international espionage organization. One of Lang's early masterpieces, also known as SPIONE.▼

Spies A Go Go SEE: **Nasty Rabbit, The**
Spies Lies & Naked Thighs (1988) **C-100m.** TVM D: James Frawley. Harry Anderson, Ed Begley, Jr., Linda Purl, Wendy Crewson, Rachel Ticotin. Wacky action comedy (with a terrific title) about a bizarre house guest who drags his hosts into a complex mystery involving a killer who's doing obscene things with a cookie cutter. Anderson is wonderfully goofy. Written with appropriate loopiness by Ed Self. Above average.

Spies Like Us (1985) **C-109m.** *** D:

John Landis. Chevy Chase, Dan Aykroyd, Steve Forrest, Donna Dixon, Bruce Davison, William Prince, Bernie Casey, Tom Hatten. Chase and Aykroyd want to be government spies and get the job—never dreaming that they've been set up as decoys. Engagingly silly comedy patterned after the Hope-Crosby ROAD pictures, with at least one pertinent cameo appearance and minor roles filled by a number of film directors (Michael Apted, Constantin Costa-Gavras, Joel Coen, Martin Brest, Bob Swaim, Terry Gilliam, Ray Harryhausen). Written by Aykroyd, Lowell Ganz, and Babaloo Mandel, from a story by Aykroyd and Dave Thomas. ▼

Spike of Bensonhurst (1988) **C-91m.** ** D: Paul Morrissey. Sasha Mitchell, Ernest Borgnine, Anne DeSalvo, Sylvia Miles, Geraldine Smith, Maria Patillo, Talisa Soto, Rick Aviles, Antonia Rey. Blah Mafia comedy with Mitchell as an ambitious Brooklyn street kid who dreams of becoming a boxing champ—and finds himself in trouble when he courts the daughter of the local mob boss (Borgnine). Ethnic stereotypes abound.▼

Spikes Gang, The (1974) **C-96m.** *½ D: Richard Fleischer. Lee Marvin, Ron Howard, Charlie Martin Smith, Arthur Hunnicutt, Noah Beery. Veteran gunfighter turns a trio of runaway boys into bank robbers; old-hat storyline has humor, but not much else.

Spin A Dark Web (1956-British) **76m.** *½ D: Vernon Sewell. Faith Domergue, Lee Patterson, Rona Anderson, Martin Benson. Feeble sensationalism with Domergue queen of the racketeers.

Spinout (1966) **C-90m.** **½ D: Norman Taurog. Elvis Presley, Shelley Fabares, Diane McBain, Deborah Walley, Cecil Kellaway, Una Merkel, Warren Berlinger, Carl Betz. Typical Presley vehicle finds the singer racing autos and wooing the girls. Elvis's songs ("Beach Shack," "Adam and Evil," "Smorgasbord") are far from his best.▼

Spiral Road, The (1962) **C-145m.** *½ D: Robert Mulligan. Rock Hudson, Burl Ives, Gena Rowlands, Geoffrey Keen, Will Kuluva, Neva Patterson. Jan de Hartog's novel about love, leprosy, and lunacy in Java makes for an interminable moviegoing experience. Hudson at his most wooden, Mulligan's direction at its most impersonal.

Spiral Staircase, The (1946) **83m.** ***½ D: Robert Siodmak. Dorothy McGuire, George Brent, Ethel Barrymore, Kent Smith, Rhonda Fleming, Gordon Oliver, Elsa Lanchester, Sara Allgood. Superb Hitchcock-like thriller with unforgettable performance by McGuire as mute servant in eerie household which is harboring a killer. Remade in 1975.▼

Spiral Staircase, The (1975-British) C-

89m. ** D: Peter Collinson. Jacqueline Bisset, Christopher Plummer, Sam Wanamaker, Mildred Dunnock, Gayle Hunnicutt, John Phillip Law, Elaine Stritch. Stellar cast gives Ethel Lina White's mystery novel *Some Must Watch* another go in a somewhat mechanical fashion that can't touch the 1946 version.▼

Spirit, The (1987) **C-78m.** TVM D: Michael Schultz. Sam Jones, Nana Visitor, Bumper Robinson, Garry Walberg, Les Lannom, McKinlay Robinson. Limp adaptation of Will Eisner's comic strip about a small-town cop who becomes a masked crime fighter. And you wondered how Lois Lane never fingered Clark Kent as Superman. A busted series pilot. Below average.

Spirit Is Willing, The (1967) **C-100m.** *½ D: William Castle. Sid Caesar, Vera Miles, Barry Gordon, John McGiver, Cass Daley, Mary Wickes, Jesse White, Harvey Lembeck, Jay C. Flippen, Jill Townsend, John Astin, Doodles Weaver. Some good comedy performers are thrown away in stupid comedy about Caesar and family's summer house that happens to be haunted; based on Nathaniel Benchley's *The Visitors*.

Spirit of Culver (1939) **89m.** ** D: Joseph Santley. Jackie Cooper, Freddie Bartholomew, Tim Holt, Andy Devine, Gene Reynolds, Jackie Moran. All the usual prep-academy clichés adapted for military school setting with Cooper and Bartholomew predictable. Remake of 1932 film TOM BROWN OF CULVER.

Spirit of St. Louis, The (1957) **C-138m.** *** D: Billy Wilder. James Stewart, Patricia Smith, Murray Hamilton, Marc Connelly. Long but inventive presentation of Lindbergh's flight across the Atlantic is mainly a tour de force by Stewart, backed by good Franz Waxman music score.▼

Spirit of the Beehive (1973-Spanish) **C-95m.** ***½ D: Victor Erice. Fernando Fernan Gomez, Teresa Gimpera, Ana Torrent, Isabel Telleria. Torrent is unforgettable as a lonely little village girl who sees Boris Karloff's FRANKENSTEIN in the town hall and becomes entranced by the monster. Her sister convinces her the monster is still alive, and she treks off into the countryside to find him.▼

Spirit of West Point, The (1947) **77m.** **½ D: Ralph Murphy. Felix "Doc" Blanchard, Glenn Davis, Tom Harmon, Robert Shayne, Anne Nagel, Alan Hale, Jr. Good saga of West Point's football heroes, played by themselves; realistically done.▼

Spirits of the Dead (1968-French-Italian) **C-117m.** ***½ D: Roger Vadim, Louis Malle, Federico Fellini. Brigitte Bardot, Alain Delon, Jane Fonda, Terence Stamp, Peter Fonda, James Robertson Justice. Three separate Poe tales, impossible to describe, delightful to watch, done with skill and flair by three top directors.

Spiritualist, The SEE: **Amazing Mr. X, The**▼

Spitfire (1934) **88m.** *** D: John Cromwell. Katharine Hepburn, Robert Young, Ralph Bellamy, Martha Sleeper, Sara Haden, Sidney Toler. Hepburn is effective as backwoods girl in love with married Young. Bellamy in the background again.

Spitfire (1942-British) **117m.** *** D: Leslie Howard. Leslie Howard, David Niven, Rosamund John, Roland Culver, Anne Firth, David Horne, J. H. Roberts, Derrick de Marney, Bernard Miles, Patricia Medina. Howard plays R.J. Mitchell, who developed the ace fighting-plane Spitfire which later became one of the Allies' most valuable WW2 assets. Good biographical drama. Leslie Howard's last screen appearance. Original title: THE FIRST OF THE FEW. U.S. version cut to 90m.▼

Splash (1984) **C-111m.** *** D: Ron Howard. Daryl Hannah, Tom Hanks, John Candy, Eugene Levy, Dody Goodman, Richard B. Shull, Shecky Greene, Howard Morris. Entertaining comedy about a man who falls in love with a mermaid, who's played to perfection by Hannah. Buoyant cast, winning gags make this a lot of fun, despite a tendency toward overlength. Script by Lowell Ganz, Babaloo Mandel, and Bruce Jay Friedman. Followed by the Disney TV movie SPLASH, TOO.▼

Splash, Too (1988) **C-100m.** TVM D: Greg Antonacci. Todd Waring, Amy Yasbeck, Donovan Scott, Rita Taggart, Noble Willingham, Dody Goodman, Mark Blankfield. Disney's TV sitcom follow-up to the theatrical smash, with a Manhattan yuppie and his mermaid wife settling into Big Apple domesticity. Suffers by having a touring company cast and crew taking over for Howard, Hanks, Hannah, et al. Average.

Splendor (1935) **77m.** **½ D: Elliott Nugent. Miriam Hopkins, Joel McCrea, Paul Cavanagh, Helen Westley, Billie Burke, Katharine Alexander, David Niven. Familiar story of McCrea's family upset when he loves poor-girl Hopkins instead of upper-class young lady; script by Rachel Crothers, from her play.

Splendor in the Grass (1961) **C-124m.** *** D: Elia Kazan. Natalie Wood, Warren Beatty, Pat Hingle, Audrey Christie, Sean Garrison, Sandy Dennis, Phyllis Diller, Barbara Loden, Zohra Lampert, Gary Lockwood. Sentimental sudser by William Inge (who won an Oscar) about emotionally broken girl (Wood) rebuilding her life, set in late 1920s Midwest. Film debuts of Beatty, Dennis, and Diller; look for Inge as the minister. Remade for TV.▼

Splendor in the Grass (1981) **C-100m.** TVM D: Richard Sarafian. Melissa Gilbert, Cyril O'Reilly, Ned Beatty, Eva Marie

[1085]

Saint, Michelle Pfeiffer, Jim Youngs, Nicholas Pryor, David-James Carroll, Ally Sheedy, K. Callan, Graham Jarvis. Scene-for-scene remake of the theatrical version, sorely missing the talents of Elia Kazan, Warren Beatty and Natalie Wood. Average.

Split, The (1968) **C-91m.** *½ D: Gordon Flemyng. Jim Brown, Diahann Carroll, Julie Harris, Ernest Borgnine, Gene Hackman, Jack Klugman, Warren Oates, James Whitmore, Donald Sutherland. Cast is good, but it's no match for routine, clichéd story of plot to rob L.A. Coliseum during a Rams game. Only for those who love caper movies.

Split Decisions (1988) **C-95m.** ** D: David Drury. Gene Hackman, Craig Sheffer, Jeff Fahey, Jennifer Beals, John McLiam, Eddie Velez, Carmine Caridi, James Tolkan. Violent family drama set amidst the world of boxing and three generations of prize-fighters. Basically just another ROCKY ripoff, but Hackman, in a supporting role, stands out as usual.▼

Split Image (1982) **C-111m.** *** D: Ted Kotcheff. Michael O'Keefe, Karen Allen, Peter Fonda, James Woods, Elizabeth Ashley, Brian Dennehy, Ronnie Schribner, Pamela Ludwig, Michael Sacks. Solid drama of nice middle-class boy (superbly played by O'Keefe) who falls for Allen and is brainwashed into joining a cult headed by Fonda. Top performances by Dennehy as O'Keefe's father, Woods as a deprogrammer.▼

Split Second (1953) **85m.** **½ D: Dick Powell. Stephen McNally, Alexis Smith, Jan Sterling, Keith Andes, Arthur Hunnicutt, Paul Kelly, Robert Paige, Richard Egan. Capable cast in odd suspenser about escaped convict (McNally) holding several people hostage in Nevada ghost town—though well aware it's a nuclear test site! Script by William Bowers and Irving Wallace. Powell's directorial debut.▼

Spoilers, The (1942) **87m.** **½ D: Ray Enright. Marlene Dietrich, Randolph Scott, John Wayne, Margaret Lindsay, Harry Carey, Richard Barthelmess. Retelling of famous Yukon tale has good cast but thuds out as average Western, with Dietrich as stereotyped saloon gal. Previously filmed in 1914, 1923 and 1930, then again in 1955.▼

Spoilers, The (1955) **C-84m.** **½ D: Jesse Hibbs. Anne Baxter, Jeff Chandler, Rory Calhoun, Barbara Britton, Raymond Walburn. Fifth filming of Rex Beach's Klondike actioner; elaborate fight scene intact.

Spoilers of the Forest (1957) **C-68m.** ** D: Joseph Kane. Rod Cameron, Vera Ralston, Ray Collins, Hillary Brooke, Edgar Buchanan. Another timberland Western, with Cameron as a tree-cutting foreman, romancing Ralston.

Spontaneous Combustion (1990) **C-108m.** *½ D: Tobe Hooper. Brad Dourif, Cynthia Bain, Jon Cypher, William Prince, Dey Young, Melinda Dillon, Dick Butkus, John Landis. Dourif plays an unfortunate soul whose parents were blasted to kingdom come in an atomic explosion; now his arm turns into a flamethrower without warning. Ridiculous from the word go, but it takes itself quite seriously indeed.▼

Spook Busters (1946) **68m.** D: William Beaudine. Leo Gorcey, Huntz Hall, Douglass Dumbrille, Tanis Chandler, Bobby Jordan, Gabriel Dell, Billy Benedict. SEE: **Bowery Boys** series.

Spook Chasers (1957) **62m.** D: George Blair. Huntz Hall, Stanley Clements, Percy Helton, Darlene Fields, Bill Henry, Pierre Watkin. SEE: **Bowery Boys** series.

Spooks Run Wild (1941) **69m.** D: Phil Rosen. Bela Lugosi, Huntz Hall, Leo Gorcey, Bobby Jordan, Sunshine Sammy Morrison, David O'Brien, Dennis Moore. SEE: **Bowery Boys** series.▼

Spook Who Sat By the Door, The (1973) **C-102m.** *½ D: Ivan Dixon. Lawrence Cook, Paula Kelly, Janet League, J. A. Preston, Paul Butler. Cook, token black in the CIA, uses his knowledge to organize bands of teenaged guerrillas to bring whitey to his knees. Offbeat but offensive, and way too talky for cheap action fare.▼

Spooner (1989) **C-100m. TVM** D: George Miller. Robert Urich, Jane Kaczmarek, Paul Gleason, Keith Coogan, Barry Corbin, Rick Lenz. Escaped con, who was in for forgery, lies his way into a teaching job, becomes a winning wrestling coach, and turns around a bunch of going-nowhere teens. Amiable Disney fare. Made for cable. Average.

Sporting Blood (1931) **82m.** **½ D: Charles Brabin. Clark Gable, Ernest Torrence, Madge Evans, Lew Cody, Marie Prevost, J. Farrell MacDonald. Minor but likable film about a thoroughbred horse and its various owners; Gable is a tough-guy gambler (''C'mere, woman,'' he says to Evans, grabbing her for a clinch). Beautifully photographed by Harold Rosson.

Sporting Club, The (1971) **C-105m.** BOMB D: Larry Peerce. Robert Fields, Nicolas Coster, Maggie Blye, Jack Warden, Richard Dysart, William Roerick. Badly directed dud about violence and promiscuity among some beautiful people in Northern Michigan has enough gore and ineptitude to offend everyone.▼

Spot SEE: **Dogpound Shuffle**

Spraggue (1984) **C-78m. TVM** D: Larry Elikann. Michael Nouri, Glynis Johns, James Cromwell, Mark Herrier, Patrick O'Neal, Andrea Marcovicci. Sleuthing Boston professor and his ditsy Back Bay aunt set out to trap a murderous doctor in this pedestrian series pilot. Average.▼

Spree (1967) **C-84m.** *½ D: Mitchell Leisen, Walon Green. Vic Damone, Juliet Prowse, Jayne Mansfield, Mickey Hargitay. Dull documentary on Las Vegas cabaret acts.

Spring and Port Wine (1970-British) **C-101m.** *** D: Peter Hammond. James Mason, Susan George, Diana Coupland, Marjorie Rhodes, Arthur Lowe. Unpretentious little gem about the generation gap in a lower-middle-class English family. Mason has one of his better later roles as the strict patriarch.

Spring Break (1983) **C-101m.** BOMB D: Sean S. Cunningham. David Knell, Steve Bassett, Perry Lang, Paul Land, Richard B. Shull, Corinne Alphen. Life among the party-animals who trek to Fort Lauderdale during Easter vacation. Where are Frankie and Annette when you really need them?▼

Spring Fever (1983-Canadian) **C-100m.** BOMB D: Joseph L. Scanlan. Susan Anton, Frank Converse, Jessica Walter, Stephen Young, Carling Bassett. Young Bassett struggles to be a tennis champ in this bland, feeble tale that is most definitely not the adolescent sex comedy the title implies.▼

Springfield Rifle (1952) **C-93m.** **½ D: Andre de Toth. Gary Cooper, Phyllis Thaxter, David Brian, Lon Chaney, Paul Kelly, Phil Carey, Guinn Williams. Unmemorable Cooper fare, with Gary joining up with outlaws to determine who's stealing government arms.

Spring in Park Lane (1948-British) **100m.** **½ D: Herbert Wilcox. Anna Neagle, Michael Wilding, Tom Wallis, Marjorie Fielding, Nicholas Phipps, Josephine Fitzgerald. Stylish romance story of Wilding courting Neagle, his employer's niece. This was one of Britain's most popular films of all time.

Spring Madness (1938) **80m.** **½ D: S. Sylvan Simon. Maureen O'Sullivan, Lew Ayres, Ruth Hussey, Burgess Meredith, Ann Morriss, Joyce Compton, Jacqueline Wells (Julie Bishop), Frank Albertson. Collegiate romance between O'Sullivan and brainy Ayres, elevated by strong cast. Enjoyable fluff.

Spring Parade (1940) **89m.** *** D: Henry Koster. Deanna Durbin, Robert Cummings, Mischa Auer, Henry Stephenson, Butch and Buddy, Anne Gwynne. Delightful Austrian fluff with Durbin romancing Cummings, working for baker S. Z. Sakall, dancing with wacky Auer, and singing, of course.

Spring Reunion (1957) **79m.** ** D: Robert Pirosh. Betty Hutton, Dana Andrews, Jean Hagen, James Gleason, Laura LaPlante, George Chandler, Irene Ryan. Potentially good soaper marred by low-budget production: Andrews and Hutton revive old memories at high school reunion and try to plan new future together; Hagen has some fine comic moments. Silent star LaPlante plays Hutton's mother.

Springtime in the Rockies (1942) **C-91m.** *** D: Irving Cummings. Betty Grable, John Payne, Carmen Miranda, Cesar Romero, Charlotte Greenwood, Edward Everett Horton, Jackie Gleason. Near-definitive 1940s Fox musical: Grable at her prettiest, Miranda at her silliest (doing a Brazilian "Chattanooga Choo Choo"), Technicolor at its lushest, and Harry James and his Band at their best, with Helen Forrest introducing "I Had the Craziest Dream." The "plot"—about a bickering Broadway duo—is neither too tiresome nor too intrusive. Good fun all the way.▼

Sputnik (1958-French) **85m.** ** D: Jean Dreville. Noel-Noel, Denise Gray, Noel Roquevert, Mischa Auer. Mild Cold War spoof involving Russian missile experiment which has backfired and naive Frenchman caught in the Red trap. Retitled: A DOG, A MOUSE AND A SPUTNIK.▼

Spy (1989) **C-100m.** TVM D: Philip F. Messina. Bruce Greenwood, Jameson Parker, Catherine Hicks, Michael Tucker, Ned Beatty. Former CIA agent who knows too much becomes the quarry of a renegade group within the Agency. Not-bad entry by director Messina in the not-what-one-seems-to-be corner of the espionage game. Made for cable. Average.

Spy Chasers (1955) **61m.** D: Edward Bernds. Leo Gorcey, Huntz Hall, Bernard Gorcey, Leon Askin, Sig Ruman, Veola Vonn, Bennie Bartlett, Richard Benedict. SEE: Bowery Boys series.

Spy Hunt (1950) **75m.** **½ D: George Sherman. Howard Duff, Marta Toren, Robert Douglas, Philip Dorn, Walter Slezak. Diverting yarn of espionage agent planting micro-film secrets in panthers' collars; when they escape captivity various sides of the law seek the animals. Based on a Victor Canning novel.

Spy in Black, The (1939-British) **82m.** *** D: Michael Powell. Conrad Veidt, Sebastian Shaw, Valerie Hobson, Marius Goring, June Duprez, Helen Haye, Cyril Raymond, Hay Petrie. Intriguing espionage melodrama set in WW1 Scotland with Veidt as German naval officer/spy and Hobson a charming double agent. Nice surprise twists in story, with bittersweet romance worked in. That's Bernard Miles as the desk clerk in the opening scene. Scripted by Emeric Pressburger and Roland Pertwee from a novel by J. Storer Clouston. Notable as the first collaboration of Powell and Pressburger (who reteamed with Veidt and Hobson the following year for CONTRABAND). Original U.S. title: U-BOAT 29.▼

Spy in Your Eye (1966-Italian) **C-88m.**

** D: Vittorio Sala. Brett Halsey, Dana Andrews, Pier Angeli, Gastone Moschin. Hokum has Andrews as scientist with telecamera implanted in eye, Halsey as U.S. agent trying to rescue Andrews' daughter (Angeli) captured by the Russians.

Spy Killer, The (1969-British) **C-74m.** TVM D: Roy (Ward) Baker. Robert Horton, Sebastian Cabot, Jill St. John, Barbara Shelley, Lee Montague, Kenneth Warren. Former wife of spy-turned-private-eye part of plan to force agent back into service. His objective: little black book with list of agents. Overly confused drama, seemingly cynical of government secret services, but overall point of view hazy and dialogue sometimes awful. Sequel: FOREIGN EXCHANGE. Average.

Spymaker SEE: **Secret Life of Ian Fleming, The**▼

S*P*Y*S (1974) **C-87m.** BOMB D: Irvin Kershner. Donald Sutherland, Elliott Gould, Zouzou, Joss Ackland, Shane Rimmer, Vladek Sheybal. Sutherland-Gould teaming fails to regenerate M*A*S*H electricity in a good director's worst film. Laughless CIA spoof about the defection of a Russian dancer is unworthy of anyone's time.

Spy Smasher SEE: **Spy Smasher Returns**▼

Spy Smasher Returns (1942) **100m.** **½ D: William Witney. Kane Richmond, Sam Flint, Marguerite Chapman, Hans Schumm, Tristram Coffin. Above par actioner from Republic Pictures based on the comic book about famed crusader for good causes fighting for Allies in France during WW2, aided by newly-added twin brother. Re-edited from serial SPY SMASHER.▼

Spy Who Came In from the Cold, The (1965) **112m.** ***½ D: Martin Ritt. Richard Burton, Claire Bloom, Oskar Werner, Peter Van Eyck, George Voskovec, Sam Wanamaker, Cyril Cusack, Michael Hordern, Bernard Lee. John LeCarre's potent account of a Cold War spy's existence—minus glamorous trappings of movie cliché. Burton is excellent as embittered agent at the end of his career.▼

Spy Who Loved Me, The (1977) **C-125m.** ***½ D: Lewis Gilbert. Roger Moore, Barbara Bach, Curt Jurgens, Richard Kiel, Caroline Munro, Bernard Lee, Lois Maxwell, Desmond Llewelyn. Rousing, lavishly produced James Bond adventure with wily 007 joining forces with a seductive Russian agent to quash arch-villain Stromberg's (Jurgens) plans for world destruction. At his best doing battle with a persistent steel-toothed goon, menacingly played by seven-foot-two-inch Kiel. Grand fun for one and all; Carly Simon sings Marvin Hamlisch's theme, "Nobody Does It Better."▼

Spy with a Cold Nose, The (1966-British)

C-93m. ** D: Daniel Petrie. Laurence Harvey, Daliah Lavi, Lionel Jeffries, Eric Portman, Denholm Elliott, Colin Blakely, Paul Ford. Spoof on secret agent movies. British agents plant bug in bulldog Disraeli, gift to Russian ambassador. Cast tries to keep story afloat.▼

Spy With My Face, The (1966) **C-88m.** **½ D: John Newland. Robert Vaughn, Senta Berger, David McCallum, Leo G. Carroll. Another expanded *Man From U.N.C.L.E.* TV series entry, with Vaughn matching wits with his double (working for foreign powers); Berger is the enemy femme fatale.

Squad Car (1960) **60m.** BOMB D: Ed Leftwich. Vici Raaf, Paul Bryar, Don Marlowe, Lyn Moore. Grade-C narrative of police investigating homicide and counterfeiting.

Square Dance (1987) **C-112m.** **½ D: Daniel Petrie. Jason Robards, Jane Alexander, Winona Ryder, Rob Lowe, Deborah Richter, Guich Koock, Elbert Lewis. Top-notch performances bolster this much too leisurely look at a Texas teenage girl's coming of age, as she leaves her dour grandfather's farm to be with her feisty mom in Fort Worth. Alexander (who coproduced with fellow actor Charles Haid) is a standout as the mother; Lowe effects a real change of pace playing a retarded man befriended by Ryder. Shown on TV as HOME IS WHERE THE HEART IS.▼

Square Jungle, The (1955) **86m.** ** D: Jerry Hopper. Tony Curtis, Pat Crowley, Ernest Borgnine, Paul Kelly, Jim Backus. Overly-familiar boxing yarn with Curtis the fighter on the way up—Crowley his girl.

Square Ring, The (1955-British) **73m.** ** D: Michael Relph, Basil Dearden. Jack Warner, Kay Kendall, Joan Collins, Robert Beatty, Bill Owen, Maxwell Reed. Uninspired intertwining of events in lives of people involved in the fight game.

Squares SEE: **Riding Tall**

Squaw Man, The (1931) **105m.** *** D: Cecil B. DeMille. Warner Baxter, Lupe Velez, Eleanor Boardman, Charles Bickford, Roland Young, Paul Cavanagh, Raymond Hatton, DeWitt Jennings, Dickie Moore, J. Farrell MacDonald. DeMille's talkie version of the story he filmed before in 1913 and 1918 is slow to start, but picks up steam after English aristocrat Baxter flees to America and marries Indian Velez. Surprisingly restrained and unsentimental, with a moving finale.

Squeaker, The (1937-British) **77m.** *** D: William K. Howard. Edmund Lowe, Sebastian Shaw, Ann Todd, Tamara Desni, Robert Newton, Alastair Sim. Classy cast in first-rate Edgar Wallace mystery about disgraced inspector Lowe trying to reform and catch infamous jewelry fence known as 'the Squeaker.' Good, compact Alexander Korda production.

Squeaker, The (1965-German) **95m.** **½ D: Alfred Vohrer. Heinz Drache, Eddi Arent, Klaus Kinski, Barbara Rutting. Overly complex actioner with a variety of plots spinning from action of underworld selling off proceeds of diamond robbery. From an Edgar Wallace novel previously filmed in 1930 and 1937.▼

Squeeze, The (1980-Italian) **C-100m.** *½ D: Anthony M. Dawson (Antonio Margheriti). Lee Van Cleef, Karen Black, Edward Albert, Lionel Stander, Robert Alda, Angelo Infanti. Good cast wasted in humdrum caper film about a retired thief (Van Cleef) breaking open one last safe. Filmed in N.Y.C.

Squeeze, The (1987) **C-101m.** BOMB D: Roger Young. Michael Keaton, Rae Dawn Chong, Liane Langland, Leslie Bevis, John Davidson, Meat Loaf, Ronald Guttman. Dreadful comedy, almost completely devoid of laughs, with Keaton as a con man who gets involved in murder and mayhem. Davidson plays a slick but corrupt TV lottery host.▼

Squeeze Play (1980) **C-92m.** *½ D: Samuel Weil. Jim Harris, Jenni Hetrick, Rick Gitlin, Helen Campitelli, Al Corley. Homemovie level feature about male-female competition in a suburban town where softball is king; most of the jokes deal with the human anatomy and various body functions.▼

Squirm (1976) **C-92m.** *** D: Jeff Lieberman. Don Scardino, Patricia Pearcy, R. A. Dow, Jean Sullivan, Peter MacLean, Fran Higgins. Above-average horror outing builds to good shock sequences: when power line falls to the ground on rainy Georgia night, it drives large, slimy sandworms from the ground, which terrorize small town.▼

Squizzy Taylor (1982-Australian) **C-89m.** *** D: Kevin Dobson. David Atkins, Jacki Weaver, Alan Cassell, Michael Long, Kim Lewis, Steve Bisley. Atkins shines as the title character, a famous gangster in 1920s Melbourne. Enjoyable, with the era colorfully re-created.▼

SSSSSSS (1973) **C-99m.** *** D: Bernard L. Kowalski. Strother Martin, Dirk Benedict, Heather Menzies, Richard B. Shull, Tim O'Connor, Jack Ging. Well-done horror tale of doctor who finds a way of transforming man into King Cobra. Exceptional job by makeup master John Chambers.

SST—Death Flight (1977) **C-93m.** TVM D: David Lowell Rich. Barbara Anderson, Bert Convy, Peter Graves, Lorne Greene, Season Hubley, Tina Louise, George Maharis, Burgess Meredith, Doug McClure, Martin Milner, Brock Peters, Robert Reed, Susan Strasberg, Billy Crystal. Terror aloft with traditional celebrity-studded passenger list. Sabotage aboard the inaugural flight of America's first SST turns it into a nightmare. Sounds familiar—and looks it. Average. Retitled SST—DISASTER IN THE SKY.

Stablemates (1938) **89m.** ** D: Sam Wood. Wallace Beery, Mickey Rooney, Arthur Hohl, Margaret Hamilton, Minor Watson, Marjorie Gateson. Sticky story of jockey Rooney and racetrack mentor Beery. All the stops out during the syrupy scenes.

Stacey (1973) **C-79m.** *½ D: Andy Sidaris. Anne Randall, Alan Landers, James Westmoreland, Cristina Raines, Anitra Ford, Marjorie Bennett. Voluptuous former Playmate Randall stars as near-superwoman private eye on absurdly complex case involving murder, blackmail, and a Moonie-like cult. Very sexy and violent, but not very good, with grating, obnoxious score by jazz veteran Don Randi. Also known as STACEY AND HER GANGBUSTERS.▼

Stacey and Her Gangbusters SEE: **Stacey**▼

Stacking (1987) **C-109m.** ** D: Martin Rosen. Christine Lahti, Frederic Forrest, Megan Follows, Jason Gedrick, Ray Baker, Peter Coyote, James Gammon, Kaiulani Lee, Jacqueline Brookes, Irene Daily. Some fine performers (and performances) are wasted in this boring, ever so obvious account of the various experiences and troubles of a young teen (Follows), growing up in the rural West in the early 1950s. More or less a clone of the far superior DESERT BLOOM. Originally titled SEASON OF DREAMS.▼

Stacy's Knights (1983) **C-95m.** **½ D: Jim Wilson. Andra Millian, Kevin Costner, Eve Lilith, Mike Reynolds, Garth Howard, Ed Semenza. Millian is Plain Jane struck with blackjack gambling fever who recruits a squad of sharpies to break a casino after her young mentor (Costner) is killed by the casino's goons. Unexciting B-movie offers insight into the world of professional gambling and features a flavorful performance by Costner in his first leading role. ▼

Stagecoach (1939) **96m.** **** D: John Ford. Claire Trevor, John Wayne, Andy Devine, John Carradine, Thomas Mitchell, Louise Platt, George Bancroft, Donald Meek, Berton Churchill, Tim Holt, Tom Tyler, Chris-pin Martin. One of the great American films, and a landmark in the maturing of the Western, balancing character study (as disparate passengers travel together on the same stagecoach) and peerless action (in a lengthy Indian attack, featuring Yakima Canutt's famous stuntwork). Also the film that propelled John Wayne to genuine stardom. Mitchell won an Oscar as the drunken doctor, as did the music score. Script by Dudley Nichols, from Ernest Haycox's story "Stage to Lordsburg" (whose plot is reminiscent of Guy de Maupassant's *Boule de Suif*). Filmed in Ford's beloved Monument Valley on the Arizona-Utah border. Remade in 1966 and as a TVM in 1986.▼

Stagecoach (1966) **C-115m.** **½ D: Gordon Douglas. Ann-Margret, Alex Cord, Red Buttons, Michael Connors, Bing Crosby, Bob Cummings, Van Heflin, Slim Pickens, Stefanie Powers, Keenan Wynn. Colorful, star-studded Western is OK, but can't hold a candle to the 1939 masterpiece. Overlong, with only occasional action scenes to liven it up. Wayne Newton sings the title song!

Stagecoach (1986) **C-100m. TVM** D: Ted Post. Willie Nelson, Kris Kristofferson, Johnny Cash, Waylon Jennings, John Schneider, Elizabeth Ashley, Tony Franciosa, Anthony Newley, Mary Crosby, June Carter Cash, Jessi Colter, David Allen Coe, Lash Larue. Country music's self-styled "outlaws" team up with wives and pals for a third go at the Ernest Lee Haycox story about a bumpy stagecoach trip through Indian country to Lordsburg, Arizona. The stars made no secret of their disdain for the simple-minded script. Average.▼

Stagecoach to Dancers' Rock (1962) **72m.** ** D: Earl Bellamy. Warren Stevens, Martin Landau, Jody Lawrance, Judy Dan. Modest production involves stage passengers left stranded in wastelands when driver discovers one of them has smallpox.

Stagecoach to Fury (1956) **76m.** *½ D: William Claxton. Forrest Tucker, Mari Blanchard, Wallace Ford, Margia Dean. Flat outlaw holdup oater.

Stage Door (1937) **92m.** **** D: Gregory La Cava. Katharine Hepburn, Ginger Rogers, Adolphe Menjou, Andrea Leeds, Gail Patrick, Constance Collier, Lucille Ball, Eve Arden, Ann Miller, Ralph Forbes, Franklin Pangborn, Jack Carson. Theatrical boarding house is setting for wonderful film, from Edna Ferber-George S. Kaufman play. Dynamite cast includes Hepburn as rich girl trying to succeed on her own, Menjou as propositioning producer, Leeds as hypersensitive actress, and several stars-to-be: Lucille Ball, Ann Miller, and Eve Arden. Scripted by Morrie Ryskind and Anthony Veiller.▼

Stage Door Canteen (1943) **132m.** **½ D: Frank Borzage. Cheryl Walker, William Terry, Marjorie Riordan, Lon McCallister, Margaret Early, Michael Harrison (Sunset Carson). Wartime story of romance between soldier and hostess at N.Y.C.'s fabled canteen is filled with cameos, walk-ons, speeches, and musical numbers by an incredible battery of stars, including Katharine Hepburn, Harpo Marx, Paul Muni, Helen Hayes, Benny Good-

man, Count Basie, Edgar Bergen. Many prints run 93m.▼

Stage Fright (1950) **110m.** **½ D: Alfred Hitchcock. Marlene Dietrich, Jane Wyman, Michael Wilding, Richard Todd, Kay Walsh, Alastair Sim, Joyce Grenfell, Sybil Thorndike. Drama student is suspected when actress' husband is murdered; some exciting moments, but the Master misses on this one. Filmed in London with delightful British cast; Marlene sings "The Laziest Gal in Town."▼

Stage Mother (1933) **87m.** **½ D: Charles Brabin. Alice Brady, Maureen O'Sullivan, Ted Healy, Franchot Tone, Phillips Holmes. Widowed vaudevillian stakes everything on making her daughter a star. Brady is wonderful, and so is seedy backstage atmosphere. Songs include "Beautiful Girl," later immortalized in SINGIN' IN THE RAIN.

Stage Struck (1936) **86m.** **½ D: Busby Berkeley. Dick Powell, Joan Blondell, Warren William, Frank McHugh, Jeanne Madden. Throwaway film with stale plot kept barely alive by energetic cast; backstage musical has no real production numbers. Highlight is The Yacht Club Boys' insane "The Body Beautiful." Leading lady Madden remained obscure after this one.

Stage Struck (1958) **C-95m.** **½ D: Sidney Lumet. Henry Fonda, Susan Strasberg, Joan Greenwood, Christopher Plummer, Herbert Marshall. Faded remake of MORNING GLORY retelling the ascent of Broadway-bound actress. Supporting cast hampered by unconvincing Strasberg in lead role and by unreal theater world atmosphere.▼

Stage to Thunder Rock (1964) **C-82m.** ** D: William F. Claxton. Barry Sullivan, Marilyn Maxwell, Lon Chaney, Scott Brady, John Agar, Keenan Wynn, Allan Jones. One of producer A. C. Lyles' humdrum Westerns with veteran stars; this one has Sullivan as a sheriff who's put in the position of having to arrest the outlaw family that raised him.

Staircase (1969-British) **C-100m.** ** D: Stanley Donen. Richard Burton, Rex Harrison, Cathleen Nesbitt, Beatrix Lehmann. Shock value of Burton and Harrison as a gay couple was all this film had going for it in 1969, and nothing has changed since then, except heightened sophistication of audiences. A curio, to be sure. Dudley Moore composed the score.

Stairway to Heaven (1946-British) **C-104m.** **** D: Michael Powell, Emeric Pressburger. David Niven, Kim Hunter, Raymond Massey, Roger Livesey, Robert Coote, Marius Goring, Richard Attenborough. Powell and Pressburger manage to straddle reality and fantasy in a most disarming manner in this unusual story of a pilot during WW2 who claims he was accidentally chosen to die, and must now plead for his life in a Heavenly court. Like most films by this writer-director team, an absolute original—and a gem, too. Original British title: A MATTER OF LIFE AND DEATH.

Stakeout (1987) **C-115m.** *** D: John Badham. Richard Dreyfuss, Emilio Estevez, Aidan Quinn, Madeleine Stowe, Dan Lauria, Forest Whitaker, Ian Tracey, Earl Billings, Jackson Davies. While working with his partner on a stakeout, cop Dreyfuss falls in love with the woman he's supposed to be watching. Wildly improbable, and ultimately downright silly, but entertaining throughout, thanks to sharp dialogue and performances, and some big laughs. Dreyfuss and Estevez make a great team. Written by Jim Kouf.▼

Stakeout on Dope Street (1958) **83m.** *½ D: Irvin Kershner. Yale Wexler, Jonathan Haze, Morris Miller, Abby Dalton, Herschel Bernardi. Trio of youths discover cache of heroin, believing their futures will now be uncomplicated; good premise poorly executed.

Stalag 17 (1953) **120m.** **** D: Billy Wilder. William Holden, Don Taylor, Otto Preminger, Robert Strauss, Harvey Lembeck, Richard Erdman, Peter Graves, Neville Brand, Sig Ruman. Granddaddy of all WW2 POW films. Holden (in Oscar-winning performance) is pessimistic sergeant suspected of being German spy. Wilder brilliantly blends drama with comedy to show monotonous, anxiety-ridden life of POWs. Wonderful comic relief by Strauss and Lembeck (repeating their Broadway roles), plus superb turn by Preminger as Nazi camp commander.▼

Stalker (1979-Russian) **C/B&W-160m.** *** D: Andrei Tarkovsky. Alexander Kaidanovsky, Nikolai Grinko, Anatoli Solonitsin, Alice Friendlich. Stark, eerie, cerebral story of title character (Kaidanovsky), who guides intellectuals Grinko and Solonitsin through the "Zone," a mysterious, forbidden wasteland. Very slow but well-acted and rewarding. A must in color.▼

Stalking Moon, The (1969) **C-109m.** ** D: Robert Mulligan. Gregory Peck, Eva Marie Saint, Robert Forster, Noland Clay, Russell Thorson, Frank Silvera. Army scout helps white woman who has lived with the Apaches to escape with her young half-breed son, while boy's father comes after them. Potentially interesting Western is both slick and dull; nice photography by Charles Lang.▼

Stalk the Wild Child (1976) **C-78m. TVM** D: William Hale. David Janssen, Trish Van Devere, Benjamin Bottoms, Joseph Bottoms, Jamie Smith Jackson, Allan Arbus, Rhea Perlman. Behavioral psychologist Janssen attempts to civilize a youth raised by wild dogs. Well-intentioned but plodding Americanization of Truffaut's THE WILD CHILD which spun off a brief series, *Lucan*. Below average.▼

Stallion Road (1947) **91m.** ** D: James V. Kern. Ronald Reagan, Alexis Smith, Zachary Scott, Peggy Knudsen, Patti Brady, Harry Davenport. Dedicated veterinarian Reagan and novelist friend Scott vie for the affection of horse rancher Smith; lowkey drama written by Stephen Longstreet.

Stamboul Quest (1934) **88m.** **½ D: Sam Wood. Myrna Loy, George Brent, Lionel Atwill, C. Henry Gordon, Mischa Auer. Exotic combination of romance and intrigue with German spy Loy falling in love with American student Brent in WW1 Turkey. Herman Mankiewicz's script based on true story also filmed as FRAULEIN DOKTOR.

Stampede (1949) **78m.** **½ D: Lesley Selander. Rod Cameron, Gale Storm, Johnny Mack Brown, Don Castle, John Miljan. Good Western of range war between cattle ranchers.

Stand Alone (1985) **C-90m.** ** D: Alan Beattie. Charles Durning, Pam Grier, James Keach, Bert Remsen, Barbara Sammeth, Lu Leonard, Luis Contreras. Vigilante opus has miscast Durning as a war vet who goes after Latino thugs who are preying on his neighborhood, Grier is wasted in a goody-two-shoes role. Spectacle of overweight Durning running around in action scenes is unintentionally funny.▼

Stand and Deliver (1987) **C-105m.** ***½ D: Ramon Menendez. Edward James Olmos, Lou Diamond Phillips, Rosana de Soto, Andy Garcia, Will Gotay, Ingrid Oliu, Virginia Paris, Mark Eliot. Olmos gives a tour-de-force performance in this outstanding drama as a tough, demanding teacher who inspires his East L.A. barrio students to pass an Advanced Placement Calculus Test . . . and that's only the beginning of the story. Based on fact, with a screenplay by director Menendez and Tom Musca. This *American Playhouse* feature is a triumph for all concerned.▼

Stand at Apache River, The (1953) **C-77m.** ** D: Lee Sholem. Stephen McNally, Julia (Julie) Adams, Hugh Marlowe, Jack Kelly, Hugh O'Brian. Title tells all.

Stand by for Action (1942) **109m.** **½ D: Robert Z. Leonard. Robert Taylor, Brian Donlevy, Charles Laughton, Walter Brennan, Marilyn Maxwell, Henry O'Neill. We're still waiting. Good cast in standard WW2 Navy saga.

Stand by Me (1986) **C-87m.** *** D: Rob Reiner. Wil Wheaton, River Phoenix, Corey Feldman, Jerry O'Connell, Kiefer Sutherland, Casey Siemaszko, John Cusack, Richard Dreyfuss. Affectionate Americana looking back at boyhood friendship and adventures in the 1950s (and narrated by Dreyfuss, representing author Stephen King, whose novella "The Body" is the basis for this film). Irresistible and wholly believable performances from all four youthful leads. Only complaint: the high volume of four-letter words, decidedly not characteristic of the 1950s.▼

Stand by Your Man (1981) **C-100m.** TVM D: Jerry Jameson. Annette O'Toole, Tim McIntire, Cooper Huckabee, James Hampton, Helen Page Camp. The TV-movie answer to COAL MINER'S DAUGHTER, dramatizing the career of country singer Tammy Wynette from impoverished childhood to stardom and her relationship to singing partner and occasional husband George Jones. Lackluster script by the prolific John Gay, based on Wynette's autobiography. Average.

Stand-In (1937) **91m.** *** D: Tay Garnett. Leslie Howard, Humphrey Bogart, Joan Blondell, Alan Mowbray, Marla Shelton, C. Henry Gordon, Jack Carson. Enjoyable spoof of Hollywood, with stuffy banker Howard sent to assess dwindling fortunes of Colossal Pictures, becoming involved with perky stand-in Blondell and mercurial producer Bogart to save company from ruin. Sags in second half.▼

Standing Room Only (1944) **83m.** ** D: Sidney Lanfield. Fred MacMurray, Paulette Goddard, Edward Arnold, Hillary Brooke, Roland Young, Anne Revere. Topical wartime comedy is now dated. MacMurray and Goddard can't find rooms, so they work as servants.

Standing Tall (1978) **C-100m.** TVM D: Harvey Hart. Robert Forster, Linda Evans, Will Sampson, L. Q. Jones, Chuck Connors, Robert Donner. Depression-era Western pitting a small-time half-breed cattle rancher against a ruthless land baron. The time period might change, but the formula remains the same. Average.▼

Stand Up and Be Counted (1972) **C-99m.** *½ D: Jackie Cooper. Jacqueline Bisset, Stella Stevens, Steve Lawrence, Gary Lockwood, Lee Purcell, Loretta Swit, Hector Elizondo. Touted as first film about Women's Lib; writer Bisset returns to home town, first becomes aware of abuses women must endure. Cardboard all the way; only standout is Stevens' comic performance. Script by Bernard Slade.

Stand Up and Cheer (1934) **69m.** ** D: Hamilton MacFadden. Warner Baxter, Madge Evans, James Dunn, Sylvia Froos, John Boles, Shirley Temple, Ralph Morgan, Aunt Jemima, Mitchell and Durant, Nick (Dick) Foran, Nigel Bruce, Stepin Fetchit. Dismal musical fantasy about bigtime show producer Baxter being named Secretary of Amusement by the President, to chase the country's Depression blues. Tough sledding until Shirley Temple shows up with Dunn to perform "Baby Take a Bow" (which helped make her a star).

Originally released at 80m. Also shown in computer-colored version.▼

Stand Up and Fight (1939) **97m.** ** D: W. S. Van Dyke II. Wallace Beery, Robert Taylor, Florence Rice, Charles Bickford, Charley Grapewin, Selmer Jackson. OK Western with railroading pioneer Taylor meeting crisis after crisis, battling stubborn stage-rider Beery. James M. Cain was one of the writers.

Stanley (1972) **C-106m.** ** D: William Grefe. Chris Robinson, Alex Rocco, Susan Carroll, Steve Alaimo, Mark Harris, Paul Avery. Classic depiction of the Vietnam veteran as a one-dimensional psycho: Robinson cannot relate to any other human being; his only friends are poisonous snakes, which he uses to gain revenge on anyone who mistreats him. WILLARD with snakes instead of rats.▼

Stanley & Iris (1990) **C-104m.** **½ D: Martin Ritt. Jane Fonda, Robert De Niro, Swoosie Kurtz, Martha Plimpton, Harley Cross, Jamey Sheridan, Feodor Chaliapin, Zohra Lampert, Loretta Devine, Julie Garfield. Beleaguered working-class Fonda, still grieving over the loss of her husband eight months before, chances to meet De Niro, a loner who harbors a terrible secret— he can't read. She winds up tutoring him, and they circle each other warily before deciding if they're in love. Story is flat and underdeveloped, but the screen presence and charm of two great stars makes it worth watching.

Stanley & Livingstone (1939) **101m.** *** D: Henry King. Spencer Tracy, Cedric Hardwicke, Richard Greene, Nancy Kelly, Walter Brennan, Charles Coburn, Henry Hull, Henry Travers, Miles Mander. Elaborate production with Tracy as determined reporter who searches Africa for missing missionary (Hardwicke) at turn of century. Entertaining drama with beautifully understated performance by Tracy.▼

Star, The (1952) **89m.** ***½ D: Stuart Heisler. Bette Davis, Sterling Hayden, Natalie Wood, Warner Anderson. Incisive study of Oscar-winning actress (Davis) trying to make a comeback, but finding love instead; film is filled with many true Hollywoodisms.

Star! (1968) **C-175m.** **½ D: Robert Wise. Julie Andrews, Richard Crenna, Michael Craig, Daniel Massey, Robert Reed, Bruce Forsyth, Beryl Reid, Jenny Agutter. Razzle-dazzle biography of stage star Gertrude Lawrence never rings true, but does have mammoth production numbers worth seeing (especially in color). Julie tries, but never comes across; Massey is amusing if affected as Noel Coward. After box office flop, film was trimmed to 120 minutes and retitled THOSE WERE THE HAPPY TIMES.

Star Chamber, The (1983) **C-109m.** **½

[1092]

D: Peter Hyams. Michael Douglas, Hal Holbrook, Yaphet Kotto, Sharon Gless, James B. Sikking, Joe Regalbuto, Don Calfa, DeWayne Jessie, Jack Kehoe. Young judge, frustrated by having to turn rapists and murderers free because of legal technicalities, is drawn into a secret judicial society. Well done, but too predictable, and ultimately too unbelievable, to really score. Written by Roderick Taylor and director Hyams.▼

Starcrash (1979-Italian) **C-92m.** *½ D: Lewis Coates (Luigi Cozzi). Marjoe Gortner, Caroline Munro, Christopher Plummer, David Hasselhoff, Robert Tessier, Joe Spinell, voice of Hamilton Camp. Grinning Gortner and sexy Munro are recruited to save the universe from destruction by bad-guy Spinell. Moronic sci-fi movie with variable special effects; unless you're a Munro fan, it's only good for a few laughs, nothing more.▼

Starcrossed (1985) **C-100m. TVM** D: Jeffrey Bloom. James Spader, Belinda Bauer, Peter Kowanko, Clark Johnson, Jacqueline Brookes. Take STARMAN, switch sexes, mix with a music video, and this is what you get. Average

Star Dust (1940) **85m.** **½ D: Walter Lang. Linda Darnell, John Payne, Roland Young, Charlotte Greenwood, William Gargan, Mary Beth Hughes, Mary Healy, Donald Meek. Hokey, entertaining yarn about talent scout Young (from Amalgamated Studios) discovering star-struck Darnell and football player Payne, bringing them to Hollywood.

Stardust (1975-British) **C-97m.** ***½ D: Michael Apted. David Essex, Adam Faith, Larry Hagman, Keith Moon, Dave Edmunds, Ines Des Longchamps, Edd Byrnes. Powerful sequel to THAT'LL BE THE DAY follows amazing rise and fall of Beatles-like rock group and its lead singer (Essex). Candid, provocative, and utterly believable.

Stardust Memories (1980) **91m.** *** D: Woody Allen. Woody Allen, Charlotte Rampling, Jessica Harper, Marie-Christine Barrault, Tony Roberts, Daniel Stern, Amy Wright. Woody plays a character not unlike himself who's persuaded to attend a film-seminar weekend, at which he's hounded by fans, favor-seekers, groupies, studio executives, relatives, and lovers. Pointed, seriocomic look at fame and success—though many viewers found it simply narcissistic. Louise Lasser and Laraine Newman appear unbilled.▼

Star 80 (1983) **C-102m.** *½ D: Bob Fosse. Mariel Hemingway, Eric Roberts, Cliff Robertson, Carroll Baker, Roger Rees, David Clennon, Josh Mostel, Sidney Miller, Jordan Christopher, Keenen Ivory Wayans, Stuart Damon, Ernest Thompson. Straightforward telling of a lurid tale: innocent Dorothy Stratten's mental seduction by small-time hustler Paul Snider, who promoted her career as a *Playboy* centerfold and movie starlet, then murdered her in a rage of jealousy. Extremely well-crafted, well-acted movie that leaves viewer with nothing but a feeling of voyeurism—and no redeeming insights into a tragic true story. Fosse's final film; before his death, he reedited this for network TV. See also TV movie version DEATH OF A CENTERFOLD.▼

Starflight: The Plane That Couldn't Land (1983) **C-155m. TVM** D: Jerry Jameson. Lee Majors, Hal Linden, Lauren Hutton, Ray Milland, Gail Strickland, George Di Cenzo, Tess Harper, Terry Kiser, Michael Sacks, Robert Webber. White-knuckles time as futuristic airliner is accidentally hurled into outer space on its maiden flight. Even the special effects of John Dykstra can't mask a pedestrian and overlong B-movie plot. Also called STARFLIGHT ONE. Average.▼

Starhops (1978) **C-92m.** ** D: Barbara Peeters. Dorothy Buhrman, Sterling Frazier, Jillian Kesner, Peter Paul Liapis, Paul Ryan, Anthony Mannino, Dick Miller. Ultra-low-budget formula film about three car hops who try to salvage a failing drive-in. Not bad of its type; screenplay by Stephanie Rothman.▼

Star in the Dust (1956) **C-80m.** ** D: Charles Haas. John Agar, Mamie Van Doren, Richard Boone, Leif Erickson, Coleen Gray, James Gleason. Intriguing cast is wasted in this trite tale of sheriff Agar forced to fight his townfolk to retain law and order. Look for Clint Eastwood as a ranch hand.

Star Is Born, A (1937) **C-111m.** ***½ D: William Wellman. Fredric March, Janet Gaynor, Adolphe Menjou, May Robson, Andy Devine, Lionel Stander, Franklin Pangborn. Two remakes haven't dimmed the glow of this drama about a self-destructive actor and the young movie hopeful he marries. March and Gaynor are at their best and 1930s flavor (captured in early Technicolor) is a plus; screenplay by Dorothy Parker, Alan Campbell, and Robert Carson was inspired in part by 1932 film WHAT PRICE HOLLYWOOD? Oscar-winner for original story (by Carson and director Wellman) and W. Howard Greene's cinematography.▼

Star Is Born, A (1954) **C-154m.** ***½ D: George Cukor. Judy Garland, James Mason, Charles Bickford, Jack Carson, Tom Noonan. Powerful semi-musical remake of the 1937 classic, with Garland and Mason at their peaks as doomed Hollywood star couple, she on the way up, he down. Incisive script by Moss Hart; great Harold Arlen-Ira Gershwin songs include spellbinding "The Man That Got Away."

Butchered after premiere engagements of 181m.; the "restored" version pieced together in 1983 runs 170m. and merits four stars. (Some of these prints are preceded by an alternate take of ". . . Got Away.")▼

Star Is Born, A (1976) **C-140m.** **½ D: Frank Pierson. Barbra Streisand, Kris Kristofferson, Gary Busey, Oliver Clark, Paul Mazursky, Marta Heflin, M.G. Kelly, Sally Kirkland. By-now familiar story is given an unconvincing treatment, with change of setting to the world of rock music. Only comes to life during Streisand's vibrant numbers, which transcend script and surrounding drama; she and Paul Williams won an Oscar for song "Evergreen."▼

Stark (1985) **C-100m. TVM** D: Rod Holcomb. Marilu Henner, Nicolas Surovy, Pat Corley, Seth Jaffe, Arthur Rosenberg, Dennis Hopper. Tough cop from Wichita takes on the Vegas mob in this unsuccessful pilot. This vehicle for Surovy (opera diva Rise Stevens's son) was the last script written by Ernest Tidyman. Followed by a sequel. Average.▼

Stark: Mirror Image (1986) **C-100m. TVM** D: Noel Nosseck. Nicolas Surovy, Kirstie Alley, Pat Corley, Ben Murphy, Michelle Phillips, David Ackroyd, Barry Gordon, Belinda Montgomery, Dennis Hopper. Evan Stark (Surovy), the no-nonsense police detective from Wichita, returns to Las Vegas to search the Strip for his partner's killer in this sequel to STARK—still looking for a series. Average.

Star Knight (1986-Spanish) **C-90m.** *½ D: Fernando Colomo. Klaus Kinski, Harvey Keitel, Fernando Rey, Maria Lamor, Miguel Bosè. Infantile fantasy about a spaceship that lands in a Spanish lake in medieval times and is thought to be a dragon. Keitel (Bronx accent intact) is the only cast member who isn't dubbed. OK special effects. Originally titled: THE KNIGHT OF THE DRAGON.

Starlift (1951) **103m.** ** D: Roy Del Ruth. Janice Rule, Dick Wesson, Ron Hagerthy, Richard Webb. Flimsy account of GI romancing an actress, allowing for scenes of movie stars entertaining troops. Cameos by Warner Bros. people like Cagney, Virginia Mayo, Ruth Roman, Doris Day, Gordon MacRae, etc.

Starlight Hotel (1987-New Zealand) **C-93m.** *** D: Sam Pillsbury. Peter Phelps, Greer Robson, Marshall Napier, The Wizard, Alice Fraser, Patrick Smyth. Nice little film about the exploits of troubled teen Robson and psychologically scarred WW1 vet Phelps. A friendly film about a most unlikely friendship. Warrick Attewell's cinematography is a standout.▼

Starlight Slaughter SEE: **Eaten Alive!**▼

Star Maker, The (1939) **94m.** **½ D: Roy Del Ruth. Bing Crosby, Louise Campbell, Laura Hope Crews, Ned Sparks, Ethel Griffies, Billy Gilbert. Crosby plays Gus Edwards, vaudeville impresario who turned talented youngsters into stars. Pleasant musical doesn't always stick to facts.

Star Maker, The (1981) **C-200m. TVM** D: Lou Antonio. Rock Hudson, Suzanne Pleshette, Melanie Griffith, Teri Copley, April Clough, Cathie Shirriff, Brenda Vaccaro, Ed McMahon, Titos Vandis. Bigtime movie director and his succession of starlet discoveries. Pedestrian treatment of a slickly made "casting couch" drama written by William Bast. Average.

Starman (1984) **C-115m.** **½ D: John Carpenter. Jeff Bridges, Karen Allen, Charles Martin Smith, Richard Jaeckel. Extremely pleasant, genteel sci-fi about alien who lands on earth, abducts young widow to help him travel cross-country so he can rendezvous with spaceship. Her toughest problem: he's made himself look just like her late husband, and she finds herself attracted to him. Familiar, derivative story line is given solid boost by two lead performances. Later a TV series.▼

Star of India (1954-British) **C-84m.** **½ D: Arthur Lubin. Cornel Wilde, Jean Wallace, Herbert Lom. So-so costumer, overly earnest. Wilde is Gallic nobleman trying to reestablish his rightful inheritance.

Star of Midnight (1935) **90m.** ** D: Stephen Roberts. William Powell, Ginger Rogers, Paul Kelly, Gene Lockhart, Ralph Morgan, Leslie Fenton, J. Farrell MacDonald. Flip, but not terribly funny, comedy-mystery in the THIN MAN vein, with a convoluted story that doesn't offer much involvement. Powell plays a lawyer who enjoys solving cases more than trying them in court.▼

Stars and Bars (1988) **C-94m.** BOMB D: Pat O'Connor. Daniel Day-Lewis, Harry Dean Stanton, Martha Plimpton, Matthew Cowles, Joan Cusack, Maury Chaykin, Dierdre O'Connell, Will Patton, Steven Wright, Keith David, Laurie Metcalf, Glenne Headly, Spalding Gray, Rockets Redglare. A complete misfire, with Day Lewis thoroughly wasted as a British art expert who treks to America to purchase a Renoir, and instead tangles with hick Stanton and other assorted eccentrics. Overbaked, unfunny, and embarrassing.▼

Stars and Stripes Forever (1952) **C-89m.** **½ D: Henry Koster. Clifton Webb, Robert Wagner, Ruth Hussey, Debra Paget, Finlay Currie. Diverting, fictionalized biography of John Philip Sousa, well-played by Webb, with standard march tunes worked into plot nicely.

Stars Are Singing, The (1953) **C-99m.** **½ D: Norman Taurog. Rosemary Clooney, Anna Maria Alberghetti, Lauritz Melchoir, Fred Clark. Frothy musical with ridiculous plot-line of immigration authorities tracking down Alberghetti as contestant on TV talent show.

Starship Invasions (1977-Canadian) C-87m. *½ D: Ed Hunt. Robert Vaughn, Christopher Lee, Daniel Pilon, Helen Shaver, Henry Ramer, Victoria Johnson. Abducted by good aliens to help battle bad aliens who are trying to take over earth, UFO expert Vaughn helps save the day with his pocket calculator. Good cast wasted in film boasting the worst special effects since PLAN 9 FROM OUTER SPACE.

Stars in My Crown (1950) 89m. ***½ D: Jacques Tourneur. Joel McCrea, Ellen Drew, Dean Stockwell, Alan Hale, Lewis Stone, Ed Begley, Amanda Blake, James Arness. Gentle, moving story of a quiet but persuasive minister in rural 19th-century America; episodic film creates warm feeling for characters and setting. Prime Americana from Joe David Brown's popular novel. Also interesting for pre-*Gunsmoke* casting of Arness and Blake.

Starsky and Hutch (1974) C-78m. TVM D: Barry Shear. David Soul, Paul Michael Glaser, Antonio Fargas, Michael Lerner, Richard Ward, Gilbert Green, Michael Conrad. Tough pair of undercover cops investigate a double homicide and discover they are the intended victims. OK pilot to hit TV series. Average.

Stars Look Down, The (1939-British) 110m. **** D: Carol Reed. Michael Redgrave, Margaret Lockwood, Edward Rigby, Emlyn Williams, Nancy Price, Cecil Parker, Linden Travers. Classic adaptation of A.J. Cronin's novel (coscripted by the author) about Welsh coal miners struggling against dangerous working conditions, and Redgrave as a collier's son who intends to run for office. Gripping all the way.▼

Star Spangled Girl (1971) C-92m. *½ D: Jerry Paris. Sandy Duncan, Tony Roberts, Todd Susman, Elizabeth Allen. Very unfunny Neil Simon comedy about the saccharine-sweet girl-next-door who falls in with two ultraradical campus newspaper editors.

Star Spangled Rhythm (1942) 99m. *** D: George Marshall. Bing Crosby, Ray Milland, Bob Hope, Veronica Lake, Dorothy Lamour, Susan Hayward, Dick Powell, Mary Martin, Alan Ladd, Paulette Goddard, Cecil B. DeMille, Arthur Treacher, Eddie Anderson, William Bendix, many others. Paramount's silly but agreeable star-packed WW2 extravaganza, filled with songs and sketches, no plot. Better numbers include "That Old Black Magic," "Time To Hit The Road To Dreamland."

Starstruck (1982-Australian) C-95m. *** D: Gillian Armstrong. Jo Kennedy, Ross O'Donovan, Pat Evison, Margo Lee, Max Cullen, John O'May. Bright little musical comedy about a teenage boy who's determined to promote his cousin to singing stardom as a new-wave rocker . . . no matter what it takes. Amiable tongue-in-cheek outing pokes fun at Hollywood musicals and media hype. Original Australian running time 102m.▼

Start Cheering (1938) 78m. *** D: Albert S. Rogell. Jimmy Durante, Walter Connolly, Joan Perry, Charles Starrett, Gertrude Niesen, Hal LeRoy, The Three Stooges, Broderick Crawford, Louis Prima. Snappy collegiate musical about rugged movie-star Starrett going back to school, with cohorts Connolly and Durante tagging along. Modest, enjoyable film with plenty of specialty numbers, guest stars, songs.

Starting Over (1979) C-106m. *** D: Alan J. Pakula. Burt Reynolds, Jill Clayburgh, Candice Bergen, Charles Durning, Frances Sternhagen, Austin Pendleton, Mary Kay Place, Wallace Shawn, Daniel Stern, Anne De Salvo, Charles Kimbrough. Likable comedy about divorced man who falls in love but can't erase feelings for his ex-wife; top performances but unfortunately, story goes awry toward conclusion for a lackluster turn of events and denouement. Scripted by James L. Brooks, from the Dan Wakefield novel. Look quickly for Kevin Bacon.▼

Star Trek—The Motion Picture (1979) C-132m. **½ D: Robert Wise. William Shatner, Leonard Nimoy, DeForest Kelley, Stephen Collins, Persis Khambatta, James Doohan, Nichelle Nichols, Walter Koenig, George Takei, Majel Barrett, Grace Lee Whitney, Mark Lenard. The crew of the *Enterprise* is reunited to combat a lethal force field headed toward Earth. Slow, talky, and derivative, somewhat redeemed by terrific special effects and majestic Jerry Goldsmith score; still, mainly for purists. Network and videocassette version—generally considered an improvement—runs 143m. Followed by four sequels—and a new TV series!▼

Star Trek II: The Wrath of Khan (1982) C-113m. *** D: Nicholas Meyer. William Shatner, Leonard Nimoy, DeForest Kelley, Ricardo Montalban, James Doohan, Walter Koenig, George Takei, Nichelle Nichols, Kirstie Alley, Bibi Besch, Merritt Butrick, Paul Winfield. Kirk and the *Enterprise* crew must do battle with the nefarious villain of 1967's "Space Seed" episode. A bit hokey and pretentious at times, but a likable adventure overall, with nice touches of warmth and humor. Footage added for network showings. Originally released without the "II" in its title.▼

Star Trek III: The Search for Spock (1984) C-105m. *** D: Leonard Nimoy. William Shatner, DeForest Kelley, James Doohan, George Takei, Walter Koenig, Nichelle Nichols, Christopher Lloyd, Robin Curtis, Merritt Butrick, Mark Lenard, Dame

Judith Anderson, James B. Sikking, John Larroquette, Robert Hooks, Leonard Nimoy. Picking up where #2 left off, Kirk reassembles his crew and shanghais the *Enterprise* to try and rescue Spock—in whatever form he may still be alive—while both he and the rapidly destructing Genesis Planet are endangered by a Klingon warship (led by Lloyd, in an ineffectual performance). Subdued sci-fi outing very much in keeping with tone of the original TV series . . . and therefore, recommended most heartily to *Star Trek* fans.▼

Star Trek IV: The Voyage Home (1986) **C-119m.** ***½ D: Leonard Nimoy. William Shatner, Leonard Nimoy, DeForest Kelley, James Doohan, George Takei, Walter Koenig, Nichelle Nichols, Jane Wyatt, Catherine Hicks, Mark Lenard, Robin Curtis, Robert Ellenstein, John Schuck, Brock Peters. The Enterprise crew takes a sharp left turn toward comedy in this uncharacteristic—and very entertaining—movie. Story has the familiar characters time-traveling back to the 20th century in order to save the Earth of the future, with the help of some humpback whales. Sheer novelty of the comic tone excuses some forays into the obvious; it's all in fun.▼

Star Trek V: The Final Frontier (1989) **C-106m.** ** D: William Shatner. William Shatner, Leonard Nimoy, DeForest Kelley, James Doohan, Walter Koenig, Nichelle Nichols, George Takei, David Warner, Laurence Luckinbill, Charles Cooper. The Enterprise crew takes off on an emergency mission when an apparent madman takes over a distant planet and holds its interstellar ambassadors hostage; his motives, however, turn out to be anything but terroristic. Dramatically shaky trek starts off with a case of the cutes, and gets worse before it (finally) gets better. A weak entry in the series. Shatner's feature-film directing debut; he also shares story credit.▼

Start the Revolution Without Me (1970) **C-91m.** *** D: Bud Yorkin. Gene Wilder, Donald Sutherland, Hugh Griffith, Jack MacGowran, Billie Whitelaw, Victor Spinetti, Ewa Aulin, Orson Welles. Madcap comedy involving two sets of mismatched twins who meet just before French Revolution. Somewhat ignored in 1970, film now has a deserved cult following; the cast, especially Wilder, is hilarious.▼

Star Wars (1977) **C-121m.** ***½ D: George Lucas. Mark Hamill, Harrison Ford, Carrie Fisher, Peter Cushing, Alec Guinness, Anthony Daniels, Kenny Baker, voice of James Earl Jones (as Darth Vader). Elaborate, imaginative update of Flash Gordon incredibly became one of the most popular films of all time. It's a hip homage to B-movie ethics and heroism in the space age, as a callow youth (Hamill) becomes an interplanetary hero with the help of

some human and robot friends. R2D2 and C-3P0 steal the show. Won seven Oscars for various technical achievements and John Williams' rousing score. Followed by THE EMPIRE STRIKES BACK and RETURN OF THE JEDI.▼

Star Witness (1931) **68m.** *** D: William Wellman. Walter Huston, Sally Blane, Chic Sale, Frances Starr, Grant Mitchell, Edward Nugent, Ralph Ince, Dickie Moore. Gritty, no-nonsense account of a family who witnesses a gangland battle and is terrorized to prevent them from testifying in court. Huston is the idealistic district attorney; Sale steals the film as the crotchety but resourceful grandfather.

State Department—File 649 (1948) **C-87m.** ** D: Peter Stewart (Sam Newfield). Virginia Bruce, William Lundigan, Raymond Bond, Nana Bryant. Minor espionage story of American agent involved in Oriental intrigue with a demonic warlord.▼

State Fair (1933) **96m.** *** D: Henry King. Janet Gaynor, Will Rogers, Lew Ayres, Sally Eilers, Norman Foster, Louise Dresser, Victor Jory, Frank Craven. Not just a Rogers vehicle, but slice of life 30s-style as country farm family gets ready for annual outing to state fair: Mom's entering bake-off contest, Dad the pig contest, son and daughter looking for first love. reat atmosphere, good performances. Phil Stong's novel has been remade twice (so far!).

State Fair (1945) **C-100m.** *** D: Walter Lang. Jeanne Crain, Dana Andrews, Dick Haymes, Vivian Blaine, Charles Winninger, Fay Bainter, Donald Meek, Frank McHugh. Remake of the 1933 film is bright, engaging musical of family's adventures at Iowa State Fair; colorful, with fine Rodgers and Hammerstein songs (their only film score): "Grand Night for Singing," Oscar-winning "It Might As Well Be Spring." Retitled IT HAPPENED ONE SUMMER for TV.

State Fair (1962) **C-118m.** BOMB D: Jose Ferrer. Pat Boone, Bobby Darin, Pamela Tiffin, Ann-Margret, Alice Faye, Tom Ewell, Wally Cox. Remake of sprightly 1945 musical is pretty bad. Faye came out of retirement to play Tiffin's mother— a bad mistake. Ewell even sings to a pig! Third-rate Americana.▼

Stateline Motel (1975-Italian) **C-86m.** *½ D: Maurizio Lucidi. Fabio Testi, Ursula Andress, Eli Wallach, Massimo Girotti, Howard Ross, Barbara Bach. Lurid crime tale (filmed in Canada) has virile Testi stealing away sexy Andress from her "Motel Last Chance" owner husband Girotti (who played the young male lead in the similar OSSESSIONE).▼

State of Siege (1973-French) **C-120m.** *** D: Costa-Gavras. Yves Montand, Renato Salvatori, O. E. Hasse, Jacques Weber, Jean-Luc Bideau, Evangeline Peterson. Highly controversial film, based on fact, about political assassination in Uruguay; interesting, but way too one-sided to be truly effective.▼

State of the Union (1948) **124m.** ***½ D: Frank Capra. Spencer Tracy, Katharine Hepburn, Angela Lansbury, Van Johnson, Adolphe Menjou, Lewis Stone, Raymond Walburn, Carl (Alfalfa) Switzer. Howard Lindsay-Russel Crouse play becomes literate comedy-drama with Presidential candidate (Tracy) battling for integrity with his wife (Hepburn); good support from Lansbury as millionairess backing campaign, Johnson as campaign manager.▼

State of Things, The (1982-German) **120m.** *** D: Wim Wenders. Allen Goorwitz (Garfield), Samuel Fuller, Paul Getty III, Roger Corman, Patrick Bauchau. Fascinating if uneven mystery from Wenders, centering on what happens as a film crew attempts to complete a remake of Corman's THE DAY THE WORLD ENDED on location in Portugal. Interesting as a peek behind the scenes at the filmmaking process, and as an homage to Corman.▼

State Penitentiary (1950) **66m.** ** D: Lew Landers. Warner Baxter, Karin Booth, Robert Shayne, Richard Benedict. Programmer with Baxter a prisoner seeking to escape.

State's Attorney (1932) **79m.** *** D: George Archainbaud. John Barrymore, Helen Twelvetrees, William "Stage" Boyd, Ralph Ince, Jill Esmond. Good Barrymore vehicle casts him as flamboyant courtroom attorney with higher ambitions; barely credible but great fun to watch. Coscripted by Gene Fowler.▼

Static (1985) **C-93m.** **½ D: Mark Romanek. Keith Gordon, Amanda Plummer, Bob Gunton, Barton Heyman, Lily Knight, Jane Hoffman. Annoyingly uneven comedy-drama about a strange young man (Gordon) and his rather unusual invention, a TV which can supposedly tune in to heaven. Sometimes genuinely touching and funny, but long stretches are deadening and dull. Gunton steals the film with his expert performance as a hilariously paranoid street evangelist. Written by leading actor Gordon and director Romanek.▼

State Secret SEE: **Great Manhunt, The**

Stationmaster's Wife, The (1977-German) **C-111m.** **½ D: Rainer Werner Fassbinder. Kurt Raab, Elisabeth Trissenaar, Gustal Bayrhammer, Bernhard Helfrich, Udo Kier, Volker Spengler. Studied, stylized look at a beautiful woman's affairs and manipulation of her husband in pre-Hitler Germany. Some telling moments, and fine performances, but awfully slow going. Made for German television at 200m. Released theatrically in U.S. in 1983.

Station Six-Sahara (1964-British) **99m.** *½ D: Seth Holt. Carroll Baker, Peter Van Eyck, Ian Bannen, Denholm Elliott, Biff McGuire. Dreary yarn of five love-starved men who find something new to fight over when sexpot Baker and her estranged husband crash land at their desert oasis. Written by Bryan Forbes and Brian Clemens.

Station West (1948) **92m.** *** D: Sidney Lanfield. Dick Powell, Jane Greer, Tom Powers, Steve Brodie, Gordon Oliver, Raymond Burr, Agnes Moorehead, Burl Ives, Guinn Williams, Regis Toomey. Entertaining adaptation of Luke Short story about undercover military intelligence officer Powell stirring up trouble in Western town to find who's behind series of gold robberies. Script (by Frank Fenton and Winston Miller) has sharp dialogue throughout. Also shown in computer-colored version.▼

Statue, The (1971-British) **C-84m.** BOMB D: Rod Amateau. David Niven, Virna Lisi, Robert Vaughn, Ann Bell, John Cleese, David Mills. Poor comedy concerning 20-foot statue (replica of Niven) with enormous male organ.▼

Stavisky (1974-French) **C-117m.** ***½ D: Alain Resnais. Jean-Paul Belmondo, Anny Duperey, Charles Boyer, Francois Perier. Stylish bio of French swindler of the early 1930s; pleasant cast, lavish photography, fine Stephen Sondheim score.

Stay As You Are (1978-French) **C-95m.** *½ D: Alberto Lattuada. Marcello Mastroianni, Nastassia Kinski, Francisco Rabal, Monica Randal, Giuliana Calandra. Yawner with a twist: Kinski, the teenaged romance of middle-aged Mastroianni, may be his illegitimate daughter. For those who want to see Kinski during her nymphet stage; others beware.▼

Stay Away, Joe (1968) **C-102m.** *½ D: Peter Tewksbury. Elvis Presley, Burgess Meredith, Joan Blondell, Katy Jurado, Thomas Gomez, Henry Jones, L. Q. Jones. Bad film, even for Presley, about contemporary Indians. In addition to reinforcing stereotypes, movie fails as entertainment.▼

Stay Hungry (1976) **C-103m.** *** D: Bob Rafelson. Jeff Bridges, Sally Field, Arnold Schwarzenegger, R. G. Armstrong, Robert Englund, Helena Kallianiotes, Roger Mosley, Scatman Crothers, Fannie Flagg, Joanna Cassidy, Richard Gilliland, Ed Begley, Jr., John David Carson, Joe Spinell. Charles Gaines novel about body-building in the "New South" is eccentric mixture of comedy and drama, but many fine scenes; happy performances from Field and Schwarzenegger make it worthwhile.▼

Staying Alive (1983) **C-96m.** ** D: Sylvester Stallone. John Travolta, Cynthia Rhodes, Finola Hughes, Steve Inwood, Julie Bovasso, Frank Stallone. Sequel to SATURDAY NIGHT FEVER is fashioned by director/co-writer Stallone into a ROCKY-type vehicle for Travolta, who juggles two women in his life while trying to score as a dancer on Broadway. Broadway show finale, *Satan's Alley* (billed, with amazing accuracy, as a musical trip through Hell) may become a camp classic, but neither the script nor the music (mostly by Sly's brother Frank) are in a class with the original 1977 film.▼

Staying Together (1989) **C-91m.** **½ D: Lee Grant. Sean Astin, Stockard Channing, Melinda Dillon, Jim Haynie, Levon Helm, Dinah Manoff, Dermot Mulroney, Tim Quill, Keith Szarabajka, Daphne Zuniga. Close-knit small-town family, with three boys on the verge of manhood, gets pulled in all directions. Pat comedy-drama has one too many subplots, though entire cast is good.▼

St. Benny the Dip (1951) **80m.** **½ D: Edgar G. Ulmer. Dick Haymes, Nina Foch, Roland Young, Lionel Stander, Freddie Bartholomew. Offbeat account of con-men posing as clergymen who predictably become reformed; filmed in N.Y.C.▼

Steagle, The (1971) **C-90m.** ** D: Paul Sylbert. Richard Benjamin, Chill Wills, Cloris Leachman, Jean Allison, Susan Tyrrell. Missile crisis causes professor to go berserk and try living in lifestyles that previously were mental fantasies. Farfetched.▼

Stealing Heaven (1988-British-Yugoslavian) **C-115m.** *** D: Clive Donner. Kim Thompson, Derek De Lint, Denholm Elliott, Mark Jax, Bernard Hepton, Kenneth Cranham, Angela Pleasence, Rachel Kempson. Beautifully photographed (if somewhat anachronistic) period piece about the real-life 12th-century lovers Abelard and Héloise. Intelligent treatment even incorporates discussions of theology in the context of this passionate romance. Threatened with an X rating, film was trimmed to 108m. for U.S. release; both versions available on video.▼

Stealing Home (1988) **C-98m.** **½ D: Steven Kampmann, Will Aldis. Mark Harmon, Jodie Foster, William McNamara, Blair Brown, Harold Ramis, Jonathan Silverman, Richard Jenkins, John Shea, Ted Ross, Helen Hunt, Thatcher Goodwin, Yvette Croskey. Has-been baseball player is summoned home to take care of the ashes of an old friend, who killed herself. Story flashes back to his relationship with her at several ages. Earnest but pat, semi-autobiographical script (by the directors) is helped immeasurably by Foster's wise, outstanding performance as the late friend, a troubled free spirit.▼

Steal the Sky (1988) **C-108m. TVM** D: John Hancock. Mariel Hemingway, Ben Cross, Sasson Gabai, Mark Rolston, Nicolas Surovy, Ronald Guttman, Sam Gray. American spy Hemingway is recruited by the Mossad to seduce Iraqi pilot Cross to defect (with his MIG fighter) to Israel. The plot's farfetched but the flying sequences are aces high. Made for cable. Average.▼

Steamboat Bill, Jr. (1928) **71m.** *** D:

Charles F. Riesner. Buster Keaton, Ernest Torrence, Marion Byron, Tom Lewis, Tom McGuire. Buster plays a milquetoast who must prove his manhood to steamboat captain father (Torrence). Not one of Keaton's best silents, but there are great moments, and classic, eye-popping cyclone finale.▼

Steamboat 'Round the Bend (1935) **96m.** *** D: John Ford. Will Rogers, Anne Shirley, Irvin S. Cobb, Eugene Pallette, John McGuire, Stepin Fetchit. Enjoyable period-piece. Shirley is particularly good as swamp-girl taken in by steamboat captain Rogers.

Steaming (1985-British) **C-95m.** **½ D: Joseph Losey. Vanessa Redgrave, Sarah Miles, Diana Dors, Patti Love, Brenda Bruce, Felicity Dean, Sally Sagoe. Disappointing adaptation of the Nell Dunn play, about the interactions of a group of women in a run-down London steam bath. Not all that bad, really, with collectively above-average performances, but sorely lacks the humor that made it work so well on stage. Director Losey's last film, and Dors's as well.▼

Steel (1980) **C-99m.** **½ D: Steve Carver. Lee Majors, Jennifer O'Neill, Art Carney, George Kennedy, Harris Yulin, Terry Kiser, Richard Lynch, Roger Mosley, Albert Salmi, R. G. Armstrong. Fast-moving, entertaining time-killer about construction workers struggling to complete a skyscraper on schedule. Filmed in Lexington, Ky. Also known as LOOK DOWN AND DIE and MEN OF STEEL.▼

Steel Against the Sky (1941) **68m.** ** D: A. Edward Sutherland. Lloyd Nolan, Alexis Smith, Craig Stevens, Gene Lockhart. Routine tale of brothers Nolan and Stevens, steel workers, both interested in Smith.

Steel Bayonet (1958-British) **84m.** ** D: Michael Carreras. Leo Genn, Kieron Moore, Michael Medwin, Robert Brown. Military unit is ordered to defend deserted farmhouse/lookout base at all costs; tame WW2 film set in Africa.

Steel Cage, The (1954) **80m.** ** D: Walter Doniger. Paul Kelly, Maureen O'Sullivan, Walter Slezak, John Ireland, Lawrence Tierney, Alan Mowbray, George E. Stone, Lyle Talbot. Pedestrian telling of life at San Quentin, despite good cast. Sequel to DUFFY OF SAN QUENTIN.

Steel Claw, The (1961) **C-96m.** **½ D: George Montgomery. George Montgomery, Charito Luna, Mario Barri, Paul Sorensen. Montgomery turns partisan leader when he loses hand in WW2, forcing his marine discharge; on-location filming in Philippines and sufficient combat action spark story along.▼

Steel Cowboy (1978) **C-100m. TVM** D: Harvey Laidman. James Brolin, Rip Torn, Strother Martin, Jennifer Warren, Melanie Griffith, Julie Cobb. Good-old-buddy adventure flick about an independent trucker who puts his marriage on the line to save his rig by hauling stolen cattle. Average.▼

Steel Dawn (1987) **C-100m.** ** D: Lance Hool. Patrick Swayze, Lisa Niemi, Christopher Neame, Brion James, Anthony Zerbe, John Fujioka, Brett Hool. Futuristic rehash of SHANE has Swayze as the mysterious warrior who ends up protecting pretty farmer Niemi (his real-life wife) and her cute son against evil Zerbe and his henchmen. Filmed on attractive desert locations in southern Africa, this failed to extend Swayze's meteoric success in DIRTY DANCING.▼

Steele Justice (1987) **C-95m.** ** D: Robert Boris. Martin Kove, Sela Ward, Ronny Cox, Bernie Casey, Joseph Campanella, Soon-Teck Oh, Jan Gan Boyd, Robert Kim, Peter Kwong, Shannon Tweed, Sarah Douglas, Astrid Plane. Howlingly absurd action-revenge yarn with beefy Vietnam vet Kove investigating the murder of a Vietnamese friend and his family in L.A., and going after former Viet general who's now a druglord in America. Nagging doubts persist—do the filmmakers intend this to be so funny?—but Kove's impromptu wound-cauterizing scene makes it all worthwhile.▼

Steel Fist, The (1952) **73m.** *½ D: Wesley Barry. Roddy McDowall, Kristine Miller, Harry Lauter, Rand Brooks. Quickie flick with McDowall involved in escape from Iron Curtain country; low production values.

Steel Helmet, The (1951) **84m.** ***½ D: Samuel Fuller. Gene Evans, Robert Hutton, Steve Brodie, James Edwards, Richard Loo, Sid Melton. Evans is a gutsy American ser geant caught in dizzying turn of events in early days of Korean war; solid melodrama written by Fuller, with surprisingly contemporary view of war itself.▼

Steel Jungle, The (1956) **86m.** *½ D: Walter Doniger. Perry Lopez, Beverly Garland, Allison Hayes, Walter Abel, Ted de Corsia, Kenneth Tobey. Lukewarm account of prison life.

Steel Key, The (1953-British) **74m.** **½ D: Robert Baker. Terence Morgan, Joan Rice, Raymond Lovell, Dianne Foster, Esmond Knight. Espionage and homicide abound in this fast-clipping caper about stolen formulas for processing hardened steel.

Steel Lady, The (1953) **84m.** **½ D: E. A. Dupont. Rod Cameron, Tab Hunter, John Dehner, Anthony Caruso. Fair adventure of four trapped men in desert who find old German tank.

Steel Magnolias (1989) **C-118m.** *** D: Herbert Ross. Sally Field, Dolly Parton, Shirley MacLaine, Daryl Hannah, Olympia Dukakis, Julia Roberts, Tom Skerritt, Sam Shepard, Dylan McDermott, Kevin J. O'Connor, Bill McCutcheon. Slick comedy-drama about several years in the lives of the women who congregate at Parton's beauty parlor in a small Louisiana town. Ranges from sassy comedy to tear-jerking

drama; unfairly compared to TERMS OF ENDEARMENT, this hasn't anywhere near the depth or resonance, but it does provide solid entertainment. Written by Richard Harling, who expanded his own one-set play for the screen.▼

Steel Town (1952) **C-85m.** ** D: George Sherman. Ann Sheridan, John Lund, Howard Duff, James Best, Nancy Kulp. Uninspired story of steelmaking and the personal problems of nephew of steel plant owner; Sheridan tries, but can't perk up this programmer.

Steel Trap, The (1952) **85m.** **½ D: Andrew. Stone. Joseph Cotten, Teresa Wright, Jonathan Hale, Walter Sande. Trim caper of Cotten who steals money from his bank and over the weekend tries to replace it.

Steelyard Blues (1973) **C-93m.** *** D: Alan Myerson. Jane Fonda, Donald Sutherland, Peter Boyle, Garry Goodrow, Howard Hesseman, John Savage. Entertaining comic concoction by David S. Ward about band of misfits who become involved in nutty project of rejuvenating abandoned airplane. Amiably antiestablishment film highlights Boyle as an ingenious fantasist named Eagle. Retitled THE FINAL CRASH for network TV.▼

Stella (1950) **83m.** **½ D: Claude Binyon. Ann Sheridan, Victor Mature, David Wayne, Frank Fontaine. Screwball comedy and murder don't blend well in tale of nutty family trying to hide a corpse.

Stella (1990) **C-109m.** ** D: John Erman. Bette Midler, John Goodman, Trini Alvarado, Stephen Collins, Marsha Mason, Eileen Brennan, Linda Hart, Ben Stiller, William McNamara. Update of the perennial soaper STELLA DALLAS goes with the times on only one plot element: in this version, Stella *doesn't* marry the father of her child. Tolerable for a while, before fidelity to the original becomes an issue; the rest is hopelessly anachronistic.▼

Stella Dallas (1937) **106m.** *** D: King Vidor. Barbara Stanwyck, John Boles, Anne Shirley, Barbara O'Neil, Alan Hale, Tim Holt, Marjorie Main. Definitive soap opera (from Olive Higgins Prouty's novel) of woman who sacrifices everything for her daughter; Stanwyck gives one of her finest performances. Filmed before in 1925; remade in 1990 as STELLA.▼

St. Elmo's Fire (1985) **C-108m.** **½ D: Joel Schumacher. Rob Lowe, Demi Moore, Andrew McCarthy, Judd Nelson, Ally Sheedy, Emilio Estevez, Mare Winningham, Martin Balsam, Jon Cutler, Joyce Van Patten, Andie MacDowell, Blake Clark, Matthew Laurance, Anna Maria Horsford. Slick vehicle for some charismatic young actors, as recent college grads having a hard time coping with Real Life. Invites comparison to THE BREAKFAST

CLUB and THE BIG CHILL, but these "young adults" are pretty immature, and so is the film, written by director Schumacher.▼

Step by Step (1946) 62m. ** D: Phil Rosen. Lawrence Tierney, Anne Jeffreys, Lowell Gilmore, George Cleveland. Patriotic programmer with Tierney a WW2 veteran uncovering Fascist agents in America.

Step Down to Terror (1958) 75m. ** D: Harry Keller. Colleen Miller, Charles Drake, Rod Taylor, Josephine Hutchinson, Jocelyn Brando. Washed-out remake of Hitchcock's SHADOW OF A DOUBT, retells account of psycho-murderer returning to home town after long absence.

Stepfather, The (1987) C-98m. *** D: Joseph Ruben. Terry O'Quinn, Jill Schoelen, Shelley Hack, Stephen Shellen, Charles Lanyer. Engrossing thriller has well-cast O'Quinn as a meek-looking guy desperately seeking to have the perfect little family. He turns out to be a psycho who marries widows and eventually erupts into violence. Thoughtful screenplay by Donald Westlake and taut direction by Ruben highlight this sleeper. Followed by a sequel.▼

Stepfather II (1989) C-86m. *½ D: Jeff Burr. Terry O'Quinn, Meg Foster, Jonathan Brandis, Caroline Williams, Mitchell Laurance, Henry Brown, Leon Martell, Renata Scott. Mad family killer O'Quinn escapes from the booby hatch, sets himself up in suburbia as a marriage counselor, and starts courting a potential new wife (Foster). Inferior sequel is completely devoid of suspense and looks cheap, but O'Quinn still manages to deliver a good performance.▼

Stepford Children, The (1987) C-100m. TVM D: Alan J. Levi. Barbara Eden, Don Murray, Tammy Lauren, Ken Swofford, Pat Corley, Richard Anderson, Sharon Spelman, Dick Butkus, James Coco, Randal Batnikoff. Murray moves his family back to his hometown of Stepford, where he insists they adapt to the very strange ways of their new neighbors. Yet another rehash of the premise introduced in Ira Levin's *The Stepford Wives* about a town full of curiously contented people. Coco's performance as a high school cooking teacher gives it a brief lift. Below average.

Stepford Wives, The (1975) C-115m. *** D: Bryan Forbes. Katharine Ross, Paula Prentiss, Peter Masterson, Nanette Newman, Patrick O'Neal, Tina Louise, Dee Wallace, William Prince. Effective chiller finds suburban housewives Ross and Prentiss trying to understand perpetually blissful state of the women of Stepford, Connecticut. Script by William Goldman from Ira Levin's best-seller. Seven-year-old Mary Stuart Masterson makes her film debut (playing the daughter of real-life dad Peter Master-son). Followed by two TV sequels: REVENGE OF THE STEPFORD WIVES and THE STEPFORD CHILDREN.▼

Stephen King's Silver Bullet SEE: Silver Bullet▼

Step Lively (1944) 88m. *** D: Tim Whelan. Frank Sinatra, George Murphy, Adolphe Menjou, Gloria DeHaven, Eugene Pallette, Anne Jeffreys, Walter Slezak. Brisk musical remake of ROOM SERVICE with producer Murphy wheeling and dealing to get his show produced. Engagingly frantic, with sharp dialogue, funny contribution by Slezak as the hotel manager.▼

Stepmother, The (1971) C-94m. *½ D: Hikmet Avedis. Alejandro Rey, John Anderson, Katherine Justice, John D. Garfield, Marlene Schmidt, Claudia Jennings, Duncan McLeod. Rey is okay as anti-hero of this cheapie murder-suspenser in the Hitchcock mold. John Garfield's son is unimpressive in support.▼

Step Out of Line, A (1970) C-100m. TVM D: Bernard McEveety. Vic Morrow, Peter Falk, Peter Lawford, Jo Ann Pflug, Tom Bosley, Lynn Carlin. Korean War vets, all in financial straits, decide at reunion party to pull a bank robbery. Good performances enliven otherwise standard script, predictable outcome. Average.

Steppenwolf (1974) C-105m. **½ D: Fred Haines. Max von Sydow, Dominique Sanda, Pierre Clementi, Carla Romanelli, Alfred Bailloux. Literal adaptation of Herman Hesse's unfilmable novel about a misanthropic writer and an enigmatic young woman. Visually jazzy, rarely boring, but a dead end.▼

Steppin' In Society (1945) 72m. *½ D: Alexander Esway. Edward Everett Horton, Ruth Terry, Gladys George, Jack LaRue, Lola Lane, Iris Adrian, Isabel Jewell. Minor flick with vacationing judge Horton involved with rehabilitating jailbirds.

Sterile Cuckoo, The (1969) C-107m. *** D: Alan J. Pakula. Liza Minnelli, Wendell Burton, Tim McIntire. Lonely Pookie Adams (Minnelli) forces herself on shy freshman Burton, who's impelled to pay attention. Winning look at young love and sensitive feelings gives Liza a stand-out role, with Burton equally fine as naive boy who eventually outgrows her. Dory Previn's song "Come Saturday Morning" is featured. Producer Pakula's directorial debut. Based on a novel by John Nichols.▼

Stevie (1978-British) C-102m. *** D: Robert Enders. Glenda Jackson, Mona Washbourne, Alec McCowen, Trevor Howard. Film version of Hugh Whitemore's London stage play about British poetess Stevie Smith (Jackson), who lives with her maiden aunt (Washbourne). Finely wrought character study, with excellent performances.▼

Stewardess School (1987) C-93m. BOMB D: Ken Blancato. Brett Cullen, Mary

Cadorette, Donald Most, Sandahl Bergman, Vicki Frederick, Judy Landers, Wendie Jo Sperber, Vito Scotti. A major studio financed this lowbrow comedy, then kept it on the shelf for almost a year. It should've stayed there.▼

St. Helens (1981) **C-90m.** **½ D: Ernest Pintoff. Art Carney, David Huffman, Cassie Yates, Ron O'Neal, Bill McKinney, Albert Salmi. Mount St. Helens is about to erupt, and old codger Carney (named Harry Truman!) refuses to leave his home. Not too bad, with a fine Carney performance; based on a true story.▼

Stick (1985) **C-109m.** *½ D: Burt Reynolds. Burt Reynolds, Candice Bergen, George Segal, Charles Durning, Jose Perez, Richard Lawson, Alex Rocco, Tricia Leigh Fisher, Dar Robinson. Incredibly boring underworld melodrama about an ex-con who sets out to avenge the death of an old buddy and finds himself knee-deep in ugly drug dealers. Originally set for release in 1984, then pulled back for some reshooting, which apparently didn't help. Based on an Elmore Leonard novel.▼

Stickin' Together (1978) **C-78m.** TVM D: Jerry Thorpe. Clu Gulager, Sean Roche, Sean Marshall, Lori Walsh, Randi Kiger, Keith Mitchell. Cutesy family tale of a bunch of orphans who find a surrogate uncle in a Hawaiian beach bum. This was the pilot to the short-run series *The Mackenzies of Paradise Cove*. Average.

Sticky Fingers (1988) **C-97m.** ** D: Catlin Adams. Helen Slater, Melanie Mayron, Danitra Vance, Eileen Brennan, Carol Kane, Loretta Devine, Stephen McHattie, Christopher Guest, Gwen Welles, Shirley Stoler. Dippy roommates find themselves the custodians of a suitcase full of drug money, which they proceed to "borrow" and spend. Earnest attempt at wacky, female-slanted comedy goes completely askew, substituting abrasiveness for humor and losing all semblance of credibility. Likable stars and a high energy level can't keep it afloat. Scripted by director Adams and costar Mayron.▼

Stigma (1972) **C-93m.** BOMB D: David E. Durston. Philip M. Thomas, Harlan Cary Poe, Josie Johnson, Peter H. Clune, William Magerman, Connie Van Ess. Title refers to venereal disease; assorted orgies catch up with some young people in absurd melodrama. Leading man Thomas restored his middle name (Michael) years later and became a star on TV's *Miami Vice*.▼

Stiletto (1969) **C-98m.** *½ D: Bernard Kowalski. Alex Cord, Britt Ekland, Patrick O'Neal, Joseph Wiseman, Barbara McNair, Roy Scheider, Charles Durning, M. Emmett Walsh. Weak Mafia melodrama about handsome killer who lives like a playboy, kills for money. Repercus-

sions abound when he decides to quit his job. From the Harold Robbins novel. Look fast for Raul Julia in a party scene.▼

Still Crazy Like a Fox (1987) **C-100m.** TVM D: Paul Krasny. Jack Warden, John Rubinstein, Penny Peyser, Robbie Kiger, Graham Chapman, James Faulkner, Michael Jayston, Catherine Oxenberg. One-shot reprise of the *Crazy Like a Fox* TV series (intended to possibly relaunch the show), with the detective father and lawyer son getting involved in a mystery caper in England, where this was filmed. It's a bit of a stretch at feature length, but still fun; at its best when Warden and Monty Python's Chapman are crossing verbal swords. Average.

Still of the Night (1982) **C-91m.** ** D: Robert Benton. Roy Scheider, Meryl Streep, Jessica Tandy, Joe Grifasi, Sara Botsford, Josef Sommer, Irving Metzman. Yet another disappointing homage to Hitchcock in this tale of a psychiatrist attracted to a woman who may or may not have murdered one of his patients. A cold film with more plot holes than one would care to count.▼

Still Smokin' (1983) **C-91m.** BOMB D: Thomas Chong. Cheech Marin, Thomas Chong, Hansman In't Veld, Carol Van Herwijnen, Shireen Stroker, Susan Hahn. Rock bottom. Not even the most forgiving C & C fans can justify this nonmovie that climaxes a scant plot involving an Amsterdam film festival with twenty minutes of laughless concert footage. An unreleaseable film that somehow made it to theaters—for five-day runs.▼

Still the Beaver (1983) **C-100m.** TVM D: Steven Hilliard Stern. Barbara Billingsley, Tony Dow, Jerry Mathers, Ken Osmond, Richard Deacon, Ed Begley, Jr., Joanna Gleason, Diane Brewster. TV's legendary Cleaver family minus the late Hugh Beaumont returns after two decades, reuniting Wally and Beaver with their pals, now grown up, in a so-so pilot which resurrected (albeit on cable) the fondly recalled series *Leave it to Beaver*. Average.

Stillwatch (1987) **C-100m.** TVM D: Rod Holcomb. Lynda Carter, Angie Dickinson, Don Murray, Stuart Whitman, Barry Primus, Louise Latham, Bibi Osterwald. TV reporter Carter plunges into an occult mystery while trying to profile a prominent senator (Dickinson) in Washington. Pedestrian adaptation of the Mary Higgins Clark best-selling novel. Average.

Sting, The (1973) **C-129m.** ***½ D: George Roy Hill. Paul Newman, Robert Redford, Robert Shaw, Charles Durning, Ray Walston, Eileen Brennan, Harold Gould, Dana Elcar, Jack Kehoe, Dimitra Arliss, Charles Dierkop. Two small-time Chicago con-men try to put "the sting" on a bigwig from N.Y.C. (Shaw) after he has one of their pals killed. This long but entertaining film won seven Oscars, including Best Picture, Director, and Screenplay (David S. Ward), and sparked national revival of Scott Joplin's ragtime music (arranged here by Oscar-winner Marvin Hamlisch). Sequel: THE STING II.▼

Sting II, The (1983) C-102m. *½ D: Jeremy Paul Kagan. Jackie Gleason, Mac Davis, Teri Garr, Karl Malden, Oliver Reed, Bert Remsen. Even as recent sequels go, this tardy follow-up to the Oscar winner is pretty limp. Gleason and Davis (in Newman's and Redford's roles!) rig a boxing match designed to shaft Malden, with Reed (in Shaw's role) as an unknowing cog in the scheme. Despite the male milieu, only Garr delivers a lively performance. Oddly, David S. Ward wrote this one, too.▼

Stingray (1978) C-100m. *½ D: Richard Taylor. Sherry Jackson, Christopher Mitchum, Bill Watson, Les Lannom, Sondra Theodore, Bert Hinchman. Low-grade mix of action, blood, and comedy as Mitchum and Lannom buy a Stingray, unaware that it's filled with stolen loot and dope, prompting pursuit by murderous Jackson. Filmed in and around St. Louis.▼

Stingray (1985) C-100m. TVM D: Richard Colla. Nick Mancuso, Susan Blakely, Robyn Douglass, Gregory Sierra, Michael Fairman, Wendell Wright, Lee Richardson. Resourceful mystery man (known only by the car he drives) is recruited to uncover the secret behind the kidnapping and brainwashing of several prominent people. Pilot for the slam-bang series from the man who brought the world *The A-Team* and *Hunter*, Stephen J. Cannell. Average.

Stir (1980-Australian) C-100m. ***½ D: Stephen Wallace. Bryan Brown, Max Phipps, Dennis Miller, Michael Gow, Phil Motherwell, Gary Waddell. Harrowing tale of life in prison, focusing on the jailors' brutality and culminating in riots and destruction. Excellent performances by all, particularly Brown; a memorable first feature for Wallace. Screenplay by Ben Jewson, based on first-hand experience.

Stir Crazy (1980) C-111m. *** D: Sidney Poitier. Gene Wilder, Richard Pryor, Georg Stanford Brown, JoBeth Williams, Miguelangel Suarez, Craig T. Nelson, Barry Corbin, Erland van Lidth de Jeude, Lee Purcell. Broadly funny film about two yoyos who bungle their way into prison. No great shakes in terms of script or direction; just a lot of good laughs. Screenplay by Bruce Jay Friedman; lively score by Tom Scott. Later a brief TV series.▼

Stitches (1985) C-89m. BOMB D: Alan Smithee (Rod Holcomb). Parker Stevenson, Geoffrey Lewis, Brian Tochi, Robin Dearden, Eddie Albert. Derivative comedy about medical students' hijinks is not

titillating or funny enough to be diverting. Director Holcomb had his name removed from the credits after film was doctored during postproduction. ▼

St. Ives (1976) C-93m. ** D: J. Lee Thompson. Charles Bronson, John Houseman, Jacqueline Bisset, Harry Guardino, Maximilian Schell, Harris Yulin, Dana Elcar, Elisha Cook, Michael Lerner, Daniel J. Travanti. Muddled yarn about would-be writer Bronson who becomes a pawn for wealthy conniver Houseman and his beautiful associate (Bisset) and finds himself involved in murder. Glossy but stupid.▼

St. Louis Blues (1939) 87m. *** D: Raoul Walsh. Dorothy Lamour, Lloyd Nolan, Tito Guizar, Jerome Cowan, Jessie Ralph, William Frawley. Showgirl Lamour deserts the Great White Way and her manager to appear incognito on a riverboat. Amusing and entertaining Paramount musical-comedy. TV title: BEST OF THE BLUES.

St. Louis Blues (1958) 93m. ** D: Allen Reisner. Nat "King" Cole, Eartha Kitt, Ruby Dee, Pearl Bailey, Cab Calloway, Ella Fitzgerald, Mahalia Jackson. Treacly dramatics interspersed with outstanding musical performances in this so-called biography of W. C. Handy, who composed the title tune.

St. Louis Kid (1934) 67m. **½ D: Ray Enright. James Cagney, Patricia Ellis, Allen Jenkins, Robert Barrat, Addison Richards. Breezy Cagney vehicle casts him and Jenkins as truckdriving buddies who have a knack for getting into trouble—and wind up in the middle of a war between a dairy trust and angry farmers.

St. Martin's Lane SEE: **Sidewalks of London**▼

Stolen Face, A (1952-British) 72m. **½ D: Terence Fisher. Lizabeth Scott, Paul Henreid, Andre Morell, Susan Stephen, Mary Mackenzie, John Wood. Interesting but far-fetched drama of plastic surgeon Henreid trying to transform female convict into replica of the woman he loves but cannot have.

Stolen Heaven (1938) 88m. **½ D: Andrew L. Stone. Gene Raymond, Olympe Bradna, Glenda Farrell, Lewis Stone, Porter Hall, Douglass Dumbrille, Joe Sawyer. Offbeat story of jewel thieves posing as musicians, on the lam but having change of heart when they meet kindly maestro Stone.

Stolen Hours, The (1963) C-100m. **½ D: Daniel Petrie. Susan Hayward, Michael Craig, Diane Baker, Edward Judd, Paul Rogers. Hayward takes Bette Davis' DARK VICTORY, transplants it to contemporary England, in tale of woman with fatal illness trying to get as much out of life as she can. Original is far superior in all departments.

Stolen Kisses (1968-French) C-90m. ****

D: François Truffaut. Jean-Pierre Leaud, Delphine Seyrig, Michel Lonsdale, Claude Jade, Harry Max, Daniel Ceccaldi. This alternately touching and hilarious film about an inept but likable jerk-of-all-trades is possibly Truffaut's best movie and one of the best treatments of young love ever put on the screen. Third in his Antoine Doinel series, followed by BED AND BOARD.▼

Stolen Life, A (1946) 107m. **½ D: Curtis Bernhardt. Bette Davis, Glenn Ford, Dane Clark, Walter Brennan, Charlie Ruggles, Bruce Bennett, Peggy Knudsen. A twin takes her sister's place as wife of the man they both love in this slick but far-fetched soaper with Bette in dual role; remake of 1939 film with Elisabeth Bergner.▼

Stolen: One Husband (1990) C-100m. TVM D: Catlin Adams. Valerie Harper, Elliott Gould, Brenda Vaccaro, Brenda Baake, Bruce Davison, Valentina Quinn. Limp comedy about a woman whose husband hits the big 5-0 and decides to stray—except she has no intention of letting him get away with it. With such unpleasant characters, this one's played best as a cartoon. Below average.

Stone (1979) C-100m. TVM D: Corey Allen. Dennis Weaver, Pat Hingle, Roy Thinnes, Vic Morrow, Mariette Hartley, Joby Baker, Joey Forman, Kim Hamilton, Steve Allen. Literate cop show pitting a veteran detective-moonlighting-as-novelist (a thinly disguised Joseph Wambaugh) against his hard-nosed superior who's trying to get him off the force. Pilot to the brief series. Above average.

Stone Boy, The (1984) C-93m. ***½ D: Chris Cain. Robert Duvall, Jason Presson, Glenn Close, Frederic Forrest, Wilford Brimley, Gail Youngs, Cindy Fisher, Linda Hamilton. Tragedy sends a simple farming family into shock, and leaves the youngest boy to sort out his problems on his own. Perceptive and poignant look at the way people react to serious situations in real life, with a gallery of outstanding performances. May be too slow and introspective for some viewers' taste.▼

Stone Cold Dead (1980-Canadian) C-97m. **½ D: George Mendeluk. Richard Crenna, Paul Williams, Linda Sorenson, Belinda J. Montgomery, Charles Shamata, George Chuvalo. Cop Crenna versus mobster Williams. Compact little drama.▼

Stone Fox (1987) C-96m. TVM D: Harvey Hart. Buddy Ebsen, Joey Cramer, Belinda Montgomery, Gordon Tootoosis, O.J. the Dog. Good boy-and-his-dog family adventure that pits the youngster against a burly Indian in an exciting dog-sled race. Writer Walter Halsey Davis adapted John Reynolds Gardiner's popular children's book (inspired by a Rocky Mountain folk tale). Above average.

Stone Killer, The (1973) C-95m. **½ D: Michael Winner. Charles Bronson, Martin Balsam, David Sheiner, Norman Fell, Ralph Waite. Good action in thriller about hardheaded cop trying to unravel chain of mystery that leads to elaborate plan using Vietnam vets to stage underworld massacre. Well-made but pretty violent.▼

Stone Pillow (1985) C-100m. TVM D: George Schaefer. Lucille Ball, Daphne Zuniga, William Converse Roberts, Susan Batson, Stephen Lang, Anna Maria Horsford. Despite initial anticipation of Lucille Ball's first dramatic acting in several decades, tackling an important social matter—the homeless street people in big-city America—what emerges is merely Lucy in a fright wig with no laugh track. A major disappointment from the writer of THE BURNING BED, Rose Leiman Goldemberg. Average.

Stones for Ibarra (1988) C-100m. TVM D: Jack Gold. Glenn Close, Keith Carradine, Alfonso Arau, Jorge Cervera, Jr., Trinidad Silva, Angie Porres. Thoughtful, intelligently acted adaptation by veteran Ernest Kinoy of Harriett Doerr's prizewinning novel about an American couple living in a small Mexican village. Aside from the two leads (both hitting all the right chords) the entire cast is Latino. Above average.

Stonestreet: Who Killed the Centerfold Model? (1977) C-78m. TVM D: Russ Mayberry. Barbara Eden, Joseph Mascolo, Joan Hackett, Richard Basehart, Louise Latham, Sally Kirkland. Private eye Eden on a missing-person case that involves blackmail, homicide and the porno rackets. Competent pilot movie for a *Police Woman*-style series. Average.

Stoning in Fulham County, A (1988) C-100m. TVM D: Larry Elikann. Ken Olin, Jill Eikenberry, Ron Perlman, Gregg Henry, Theodore Bikel, Nicholas Pryor, Peter Michael Goetz, Maureen Mueller. An Amish family, whose infant is killed by local teenagers in a harrassing incident, refuses as a matter of conscience to bring the case to trial. Intelligent script by Jud Kinberg and Jackson Gillis, and a solid performance by Perlman, raise this a notch or two above the norm. Above average.

Stony Island (1978) C-97m. *** D: Andrew Davis. Richard Davis, Edward Stony Robinson, Ronnie Barron, George Englund, Gene Barge, Susanna Hoffs. Independent feature, filmed in Chicago, about an integrated group of youthful rhythm and blues performers and the death of an older black musician, nicely played by Barge. Fine music sequences and use of urban locations make up for lack of character and story development. Also known as MY MAIN MAN FROM STONY ISLAND.

Stooge, The (1952) 100m. **½ D: Norman Taurog. Dean Martin, Jerry Lewis, Polly Bergen, Eddie Mayehoff, Marion Marshall. Egocentric singer (Martin) learns the hard way just how important his stooge (Lewis) is to his success. Martin & Lewis go dramatic with middling results.

Stoogemania (1985) **C-83m.** *½ D: Chuck Workman. Josh Mostel, Melanie Chartoff, Sid Caesar, Josh Miner, Thom Sharp. Well-meaning but completely unfunny tale of one Howard F. Howard, whose passion for The Three Stooges has overtaken his life. Incorporates real footage of the Stooges, and while most of it is far from their best, it's still vastly superior to the new material in this feature. For those who care, some of the Stooge footage is computer-colored.▼

Stoolie, The (1974) **C-90m.** **½ D: John G. Avildsen. Jackie Mason, Dan Frazer, Marcia Jean Kurtz, Anne Marie. A slice of low life is portrayed in this flawed but interesting little film, with Mason as a paid police informer who absconds to Miami with $7,500 in a misguided attempt to "retire."

Stop! Look! and Laugh! (1960) **78m.** **½ D: Jules White. The Three Stooges, Paul Winchell, Jerry Mahoney, Knucklehead Smiff, The Marquis Chimps, Officer Joe Bolton. Original Stooges' funniest sequences strung together by Paul Winchell and dummies is aimed at children. Much of it is familiar, but still amusing.

Stop Making Sense (1984) **C-88m.** **** D: Jonathan Demme. Brilliantly conceived, shot, edited, and performed Talking Heads concert film benefits from the presence of a major filmmaker behind the camera, as well as the imagination of lead singer/mastermind David Byrne. One of the greatest rock movies ever made; videocassette version runs 99m. and contains three extra tunes.▼

Stop Me Before I Kill! (1961-British) **109m.** ** D: Val Guest. Claude Dauphin, Diane Cilento, Roland Lewis, Françoise Rosay. Turgid dramatics: mentally unhinged man's new marriage is threatened by his illness and his psychiatrist's yen for his wife. Originally titled THE FULL TREATMENT.

Stopover Tokyo (1957) **C-100m.** **½ D: Richard L. Breen. Robert Wagner, Joan Collins, Edmond O'Brien, Ken Scott. Lumbering spy tale, loosely based on John P. Marquand novel. On location filming in Japan makes a pretty background, but flat characters remain.▼

Stop the World—I Want to Get Off (1966-British) **C-98m.** **½ D: Philip Saville. Tony Tanner, Millicent Martin, Leila Croft, Valerie Croft. One of producer Bill Sargent's photographed stage presentations, this one preserves Anthony Newley and Leslie Bricusse's allegorical musical about an everyman named Littlechap

and his bouts with life and success. A bit heavy-handed, though the score includes "What Kind Of Fool Am I?" Opens in black and white, then changes to color. Remade as SAMMY STOPS THE WORLD.

Stop Train 349 (1964-German-French) **95m.** ** D: Rolf Haedrich. Jose Ferrer, Sean Flynn, Nicole Courcel, Jess Hahn. Average thriller of Communist manhunt for East German refugee hidden aboard U.S. military train heading from Berlin to west zone.

Stop, You're Killing Me (1952) **C-86m.** ** D: Roy Del Ruth. Broderick Crawford, Claire Trevor, Virginia Gibson, Sheldon Leonard, Margaret Dumont. Mild froth based on Damon Runyon story of racketeer Crawford going legitimate. Remake of A SLIGHT CASE OF MURDER.

Stork Club, The (1945) **98m.** **½ D: Hal Walker. Betty Hutton, Barry Fitzgerald, Don Defore, Andy Russell, Iris Adrian, Robert Benchley. Hat-check girl Hutton mysteriously becomes wealthy in fanciful musicomedy, mainly for Betty's fans. She sings "Doctor, Lawyer, Indian Chief."▼

Stork Talk (1961-British) **97m.** ** D: Michael Forlong. Tony Britton, Anne Heywood, John Turner, Nicole Perroult. Harmless sex comedy involving married couples' indiscretions and the pat resolution of their problems.

Storm, The (1938) **75m.** **½ D: Harold Young. Charles Bickford, Barton MacLane, Preston Foster, Tom Brown, Nan Grey, Andy Devine. Not-bad yarn of brothers Bickford and MacLane constantly arguing, mostly over women, reconciled during climactic storm.

Storm (1987-Canadian) **C-99m.** BOMB D: David Winning. David Palfy, Stan Kane, Harry Freedman, Lawrence Elion, Tom Schioler. Incoherent, interminable psychological drama about two students, one a jerk and the other a prankster, and their fate while on a camping trip. If you make it beyond the first two minutes of this turkey, you deserve a medal.▼

Storm at Daybreak (1933) **80m.** **½ D: Richard Boleslawski. Kay Francis, Nils Asther, Jean Parker, Walter Huston, Phillips Holmes, Eugene Pallette. Lavishly mounted soaper set in Serbia. Francis is wife of mayor Huston, and having affair with convalescing soldier Asther.

Storm Center (1956) **85m.** *½ D: Daniel Taradash. Bette Davis, Brian Keith, Kim Hunter, Paul Kelly. Librarian becomes center of controversy over censorship and Communism. Not even Davis can uplift clichés. An inauspicious directorial debut by veteran screenwriter Taradash.

Storm Fear (1955) **88m.** ** D: Cornel Wilde. Cornel Wilde, Jean Wallace, Dan Duryea, Lee Grant. Good cast elevates this yarn of wounded bank robber hiding out at brother's home, intimidating everyone. Script by Horton Foote.

Storm in a Teacup (1937-British) 87m. *** D: Victor Saville, Ian Dalrymple. Vivien Leigh, Rex Harrison, Cecil Parker, Sara Allgood, Arthur Wontner, Ivor Barnard. Witty social comedy with Leigh and Harrison barbing over words, loves and politics in case of old lady who refuses to pay for a license for her dog.▼

Stormin' Home (1985) C-100m. TVM D: Jerry Jameson. Gil Gerard, Lisa Blount, Pat Corley, John Pleshette, Geoffrey Lewis, Emily Moultrie, Joanna Kerns. Footloose, aging biker gears up for one last race in search of the championship. Average.

Storm Over Lisbon (1944) 86m. ** D: George Sherman. Vera Ralston, Richard Arlen, Erich von Stroheim, Otto Kruger, Eduardo Ciannelli, Mona Barrie. WW2 intrigue in Lisbon with nightclub performer Ralston siding with von Stroheim to get goods on American Arlen; only for those who wonder what CASABLANCA would've been like if it'd been made by Republic.

Storm Over the Nile (1956-British) C-113m. **½ D: Zoltan Korda, Terence Young. Anthony Steel, Laurence Harvey, James Robertson Justice, Mary Ure, Christopher Lee. Remake of THE FOUR FEATHERS (by the same director, with stock footage from the original) lacks class and flair, but story is still good; script by R.C. Sherriff.

Storm Over Tibet (1952) 87m. ** D: Andrew Marton. Rex Reason, Diana Douglas, Myron Healey, Robert Karnes, Strother Martin, Harold Fong. Reason is an ex-WW2 pilot who journeys to Tibet and gets in plenty of hot water when he purloins a holy mask from a temple. German documentary footage of the Himalayas is used extensively in this Ivan Tors production.

Storm Rider, The (1957) 70m. *½ D: Edward Bernds. Scott Brady, Mala Powers, Bill Williams, John Goddard. Sagebrush lowjinks of cattle owners vs. ranchers.

Storm Warning (1951) 93m. **½ D: Stuart Heisler. Ginger Rogers, Ronald Reagan, Doris Day, Steve Cochran, Hugh Sanders, Lloyd Gough, Ned Glass. Feverish but engrossing story of a woman who discovers that her sister (Day) has married a loutish Ku Klux Klansman. Good cast, with Reagan in one of his better roles as a crusading D.A.; cowritten by Richard Brooks.

Stormy Monday (1988-British) C-93m. *** D: Mike Figgis. Melanie Griffith, Tommy Lee Jones, Sting, Sean Bean, James Cosmo, Mark Long, Brian Lewis. Extremely stylish *film noir* about the convergence of four characters in the economically depressed city of Newcastle, where Sting runs a jazz club, and a ruthless American businessman (Jones) hopes to make a kill-

ing in redevelopment. More atmosphere than story here, and told at a very deliberate pace, but strong performances by all four leads and striking visual ideas by writer-director Figgis (and cinematographer Roger Deakins) definitely compensate. Figgis is also credited with the music score.▼

Stormy Weather (1943) 77m. **½ D: Andrew L. Stone. Lena Horne, Bill Robinson, Cab Calloway and his Band, Katherine Dunham, Fats Waller, Dooley Wilson, Nicholas Brothers. Delightful musical numbers strung together by silly show biz script which tries to pair Bojangles and Horne as romantic duo. Waller does "Ain't Misbehavin'," Lena sings title number.▼

Story of Adele H, The (1975-French) C-97m. **½ D: Francois Truffaut. Isabelle Adjani, Bruce Robinson, Sylvia Marriott, Reubin Dorey, Joseph Blatchley, M. White. Understated drama of young woman (the daughter of author Victor Hugo) obsessed with a soldier who does not return her love. Adjani's performance is excellent, but film is curiously unmoving. Shot in simultaneous English and French-language versions.▼

Story of Alexander Graham Bell, The (1939) 97m. *** D: Irving Cummings. Don Ameche, Loretta Young, Henry Fonda, Charles Coburn, Spring Byington, Gene Lockhart, Polly Ann Young. Ameche overacts at times in his famous title role, but entertaining version of inventor is given plush 20th Century-Fox presentation.

Story of a Love Story (1973-French) C-110m. **½ D: John Frankenheimer. Alan Bates, Dominique Sanda, Evans Evans, Lea Massari, Michel Auclair, Laurence De Monaghan. Writer Bates has an extramarital affair with Sanda—or is it his imagination? Interesting premise, middling result. Originally titled IMPOSSIBLE OBJECT; never released theatrically.▼

Story of a Marriage, The SEE: On Valentine's Day and 1918

Story of a Three Day Pass, The (1967-French) 87m. *** D: Melvin Van Peebles. Harry Baird, Nicole Berger, Christian Marin, Pierre Doris. Flawed but impressive film about affair between black American soldier and white French girl.▼

Story of a Woman (1970) C-90m. *½ D: Leonardo Bercovici. Bibi Andersson, Robert Stack, James Farentino, Annie Girardot, Didi Perego, Mario Nascimbene. Turgid tale of pianist who tries to remain faithful to her husband, even though she's still hung up on old flame; Bibi is wasted.

Story of David, The (1976) C-250m. TVM D: Alex Segal, David Lowell Rich. Timothy Bottoms, Anthony Quayle, Keith Mitchell, Jane Seymour, Susan Hampshire. Vivid Biblical drama, scripted by Ernest Kinoy, with two hours devoted to the Old

Testament shepherd boy who slew Goliath, and two given over to the now-King David's involvement with Bathsheba. Told with reverence, acted with sincerity, produced with authenticity. Originally shown in two parts. Above average.

Story of Dr. Wassell, The (1944) **C-140m. **½ D: Cecil B. DeMille. Gary Cooper, Laraine Day, Signe Hasso, Dennis O'Keefe, Paul Kelly, Philip Ahn, Barbara Britton. Far from top-grade Cooper or DeMille is this story of real-life dedicated Navy doctor who saved fighting men in Java during WW2; slow-moving adaptation of the James Hilton book.

Story of Esther Costello, The (1957-British) **103m. **½ D: David Miller. Joan Crawford, Rossano Brazzi, Heather Sears, Lee Patterson, Fay Compton, Bessie Love, Ron Randell. Socialite rehabilitates impoverished blind and deaf girl and promotes charity fund in her name. Interesting look at charity huckstering but melodrama is overwrought and often unintentionally funny.

Story of G. I. Joe, The (1945) **109m. ***½ D: William Wellman. Burgess Meredith, Robert Mitchum, Freddie Steele, Wally Cassell, Jimmy Lloyd. Meredith is superb as war correspondent Ernie Pyle living with Yank soldiers on front lines to report their stories; Mitchum's first outstanding film role as soldier.

Story of Gilbert and Sullivan, The SEE: **Great Gilbert and Sullivan, The**

Story of Jacob and Joseph, The (1974) **C-100m. TVM** D: Michael Cacoyannis. Keith Michell, Tony LoBianco, Colleen Dewhurst, Herschel Bernardi, Harry Andrews, Julian Glover. Two-part Biblical movie. First, the tale of Jacob (Michell) and Esau (Glover) and the fight over their birthright. Second, adventures of Joseph (LoBianco) and his brothers who sold him into slavery. Alan Bates narrates these impressively acted stories, written by Ernest Kinoy and reverently approached by director Cacoyannis. Above average.

Story of Louis Pasteur, The (1936) **85m. ***½ D: William Dieterle. Paul Muni, Josephine Hutchinson, Anita Louise, Donald Woods, Fritz Leiber, Porter Hall, Akim Tamiroff. The achievements of the famous French scientist are chronicled in this engrossing film. Muni gives Oscar-winning performance; writers Sheridan Gibney and Pierre Collings also won.

Story of Mankind, The (1957) **C-100m. ** D: Irwin Allen. Ronald Colman, Cedric Hardwicke, Vincent Price; guest stars Hedy Lamarr, Groucho, Harpo, Chico Marx, Virginia Mayo, Agnes Moorehead, Francis X. Bushman, Charles Coburn, Marie Windsor, John Carradine. Ambitious in concept, laughable in juvenile results. Henrik Van Loon book of highlights of man's history becomes string of clichéd costume episodes, badly cast and poorly handled; the Marxes—in their last theatrical film as a "team"—don't even appear together!

Story of Molly X, The (1949) **82m. **½ D: Crane Wilbur. June Havoc, John Russell, Dorothy Hart, Charles McGraw. Havoc is earnest as gangster's widow who goes out to find her husband's killer.

Story of Piera, The (1983-Italian-French) **C-105m. ** D: Marco Ferreri. Isabelle Huppert, Hanna Schygulla, Marcello Mastroianni, Bettina Gruhn, Tanya Lopert. Odd chronicle of the lifelong relationship between nutty, sensuous Schygulla and her daughter (Gruhn as a pre-teen, then Huppert). Ferreri presents a liberated alternative for relating as a wife, mother, daughter, woman; however, the result is mostly rambling, boring.

Story of Pretty Boy Floyd, The (1974) **C-78m. TVM** D: Clyde Ware. Martin Sheen, Kim Darby, Michael Parks, Ellen Corby, Joseph Estevez, Bill Vint, Abe Vigoda, Steven Keats, Ford Rainey. Sheen gives nicely-shaded portrait of the Depression-era farmboy who became infamous bank robber and killer. Picturesque, violent, and surprisingly literate. Scripted by Ware. Above average; also known as PRETTY BOY FLOYD.

Story of Robin Hood and His Merrie Men, The (1952) **C-83m. *** D: Ken Annakin. Richard Todd, Joan Rice, Peter Finch, James Hayter, James Robertson Justice, Martita Hunt, Hubert Gregg, Michael Hordern. Zesty, colorful retelling of the familiar story, filmed in England by Walt Disney with excellent cast. Not as personality-oriented as other versions, but just as good in its own way.▼

Story of Ruth, The (1960) **C-132m. **½ D: Henry Koster. Elana Eden, Stuart Whitman, Tom Tryon, Peggy Wood, Viveca Lindfors, Jeff Morrow. Static biblical nonepic retelling story of woman renouncing her "gods" when she discovers true faith.▼

Story of Seabiscuit, The (1949) **C-93m. **½ D: David Butler. Shirley Temple, Barry Fitzgerald, Lon McCallister, Rosemary DeCamp. Standard horseracing saga with Fitzgerald supporting most of the film as a dedicated trainer.

Story of Three Loves, The (1953) **C-122m. *** D: Vincente Minnelli, Gottfried Reinhardt. Pier Angeli, Ethel Barrymore, Kirk Douglas, Farley Granger, Leslie Caron, James Mason, Agnes Moorehead, Zsa Zsa Gabor. Bittersweet trio of love stories, told as flashbacks involving passengers on ocean liner.

Story of Vernon & Irene Castle, The (1939) **93m. *** D: H. C. Potter. Fred Astaire, Ginger Rogers, Edna May Oliver, Walter Brennan, Lew Fields. Usual Astaire-

Rogers breeziness suffers from slow handling of events in lives of famous early 20th-century dancing duo. Still good, with many fine period dance and song numbers; the last of Fred and Ginger's series of RKO classics.▼

Story of Will Rogers, The (1952) **C-109m.** *** D: Michael Curtiz. Will Rogers, Jr., Jane Wyman, Carl Benton Reid, James Gleason, Mary Wickes, Eddie Cantor. One of few show biz biographies that rings true, with Rogers Jr. faithfully portraying his father, rodeo star turned humorist; Wyman is his loving wife, Cantor appears as himself.

Story of Women, The (1988-French) **C-110m.** *** D: Claude Chabrol. Isabelle Huppert, Francois Cluzet, Marie Trintignant, Nils Tavernier, Louis Ducreux. Huppert gives one of her best performances as a woman who builds a thriving career as an abortionist in Vichy France—and becomes the last of her sex to be guillotined in her country. Ironic, fact-based story provides Chabrol with one of his best subjects; the director is in top form here.

Story on Page One, The (1959) **123m.** *** D: Clifford Odets. Rita Hayworth, Anthony Franciosa, Gig Young, Mildred Dunnock, Hugh Griffith, Sanford Meisner, Robert Burton. Lovers Hayworth and Young dispose of Rita's husband, hire Franciosa to represent them in court. Odets' stark film has high tension and sincere performances, although Dunnock's Mama portrayal is a bit much.

Storyteller, The (1977) **C-100m. TVM** D: Robert Markowitz. Martin Balsam, Patty Duke Astin, James Daly, Doris Roberts, David Spielberg, Rose Gregorio. Veteran writer is troubled by charges his TV play motivated a teen-ager to set his school on fire and die in the blaze. Balsam's fine performance fails to save this disappointing study of the effect of TV violence on children. Written by Richard Levinson and William Link. Average.

Stowaway (1936) **86m.** **½ D: William A. Seiter. Robert Young, Alice Faye, Shirley Temple, Eugene Palette, Helen Westley, Arthur Treacher. Predictable yet engaging shipboard story with Faye and Young romancing, Temple the incurably curious child. Shirley even sings in Chinese! Also shown in computer-colored version.▼

Stowaway Girl (1957-British) **87m.** **½ D: Guy Hamilton. Trevor Howard, Elsa Martinelli, Pedro Armendariz, Donald Pleasence, Warren Mitchell. Trim, sensible romancer of middle-aged captain Howard's infatuation with Martinelli, who hid aboard his ship. Originally titled MANUELA.

Stowaway to the Moon (1975) **C-100m. TVM** D: Andrew V. McLaglen. Lloyd Bridges, Michael Link, Jeremy Slate, Morgan Paull, James McMullan, John Carradine, Keene Curtis. Delightful family-oriented tale about an 11-year-old rocket enthusiast (Link) who fulfills his life's dream by sneaking aboard a space capsule about to blast off. Above average.

Straight on Till Morning (1972-British) **C-96m.** ** D: Peter Collinson. Rita Tushingham, Shane Briant, Tom Bell, Annie Ross, Claire Kelly. Offbeat thriller, but not terribly effective. Naive Tushingham journeys from Liverpool to London to find a willing male to impregnate her, meets ladykiller Briant. The title, if you don't know, is derived from *Peter Pan.*

Straight Through the Heart (1983-German) **C-91m.** *** D: Doris Dörrie. Beate Jensen, Sepp Bierbichler, Gabriele Litty, Nuran Filiz. Highly original, sharply observed tale of a rather peculiar young girl (nicely played by Jensen) and her relationship with divorced, lonely, middle-aged dentist Bierbichler. An impressive initial feature from Dörrie (the director of MEN . . .).

Straight Time (1978) **C-114m.** *** D: Ulu Grosbard. Dustin Hoffman, Theresa Russell, Gary Busey, Harry Dean Stanton, M. Emmet Walsh, Rita Taggart. Hoffman knocks heads with slimy parole officer Walsh following his release from prison and begins a downward slide. Engrossing if not particularly distinguished melodrama gets a real shot in the arm from terrific supporting performances. Hoffman started directing the film himself, then turned it over to Grosbard. Based on Edward Bunker's novel, *No Beast So Fierce.*▼

Straight to Hell (1987) **C-86m.** BOMB D: Alex Cox. Sy Richardson, Joe Strummer, Dick Rude, Courtney Love, Dennis Hopper, Elvis Costello, Grace Jones, Jim Jarmusch, The Pogues. "Self-indulgent" is an understated way of describing this spaghetti Western spoof, written by cult director Cox and costar Rude. Has the insistent air of a hip in-joke, except that it isn't funny. In fact, it's *awful.*▼

Strait-Jacket (1964) **89m.** **½ D: William Castle. Joan Crawford, Diane Baker, Leif Erickson, Anthony Hayes, Howard St. John, Rochelle Hudson. Crawford served twenty years for axe murders; now, living peacefully with daughter Baker, murders start again and she's suspected. Crawford's strong portrayal makes this one of best in the BABY JANE genre of older-star shockers; script by Robert Bloch.▼

Stranded (1935) **76m.** ** D: Frank Borzage. Kay Francis, George Brent, Patricia Ellis, Donald Woods, Robert Barrat, Barton MacLane. Francis is a travelers' aid worker solving everybody's problems, tangling with band of racketeers.

Stranded (1986) **C-100m. TVM** D: Rod Daniel. Loni Anderson, Perry King, Elaine

Stritch, Joel Brooks, William Hickey. Love-hate relationship between feuding advertising executives Loni and Perry, who find themselves stranded on a deserted island in Tahiti. Loni gets periodically dunked in the Pacific and has an amazingly complete collection of sarongs in her overnight case! Average.

Stranded (1987) **C-80m.** ** D: Tex Fuller. Ione Skye, Joe Morton, Maureen O'Sullivan, Susan Barnes, Cameron Dye, Michael Greene, Brendan Hughes. A couple of effective moments cannot uplift this slight, unrewarding sci-fi entry about aliens who come to earth, taking teen Skye and grandmother O'Sullivan hostage.▼

Strange Adventure, A (1956) **70m.** *½ D: William Witney. Joan Evans, Ben Cooper, Marla English, Jan Merlin, Nick Adams. Murky little drama of speed-demon youths involved in hold-up.

Strange Affair, The (1968-British) **C-106m.** **½ D: David Greene. Michael York, Jeremy Kemp, Susan George, Jack Watson, Nigel Davenport, George A. Cooper, Barry Fantoni. Pretty good police melodrama about young recruit York's dallying with sexy hippie and superior Kemp's failure to get needed conviction; George steals the show in one of her first film appearances.

Strange Affair of Uncle Harry, The (1945) **80m.** *** D: Robert Siodmak. George Sanders, Geraldine Fitzgerald, Ella Raines, Sara Allgood, Moyna MacGill, Samuel S. Hinds. Engrossing melodrama about mild-mannered Sanders falling in love, but unable to break from grip of domineering sister (Fitzgerald). Vivid, if not always believable, with unfortunate ending demanded by 1940s censorship. Produced by longtime Hitchcock associate Joan Harrison. Originally titled UNCLE HARRY.

Strange Affection (1957-British) **84m.** ** D: Wolf Rilla. Richard Attenborough, Colin Petersen, Jill Adams, Terence Morgan. A teacher decides to take in a boy who's been accused of murdering his drunkard father. Decent British drama. Original British title: THE SCAMP.

Strange and Deadly Occurrence, The (1974) **C-78m. TVM** D: John Llewellyn Moxey. Robert Stack, Vera Miles, L. Q. Jones, Herb Edelman, Dena Dietrich, Margaret Willock. Family is terrorized by mysterious force in their newly purchased country home. Occult tale with standard thrills at predictable intervals. Average.▼

Strange Awakening (1958-British) **75m.** *½ D: Montgomery Tully. Lex Barker, Carole Mathews, Nora Swinburne, Richard Molinos, Peter Dyneley. Barker is tourist in France involved in snowballing case of fraud; muddled drama.▼

Strange Bargain (1949) **68m.** **½ D: Will Price. Martha Scott, Jeffrey Lynn, Henry (Harry) Morgan, Katherine Emery, Richard Gaines, Henry O'Neill, Walter Sande. Adequate mystery yarn about a bookkeeper (Lynn), who's framed for murder; Scott is his devoted wife, Morgan the police lieutenant on the case. This star trio reprised their roles 38 years later for a sequel, *Strangest of Bargains*, which aired as an episode of the *Murder, She Wrote* TV series.▼

Strange Bedfellows (1964) **C-98m.** **½ D: Melvin Frank. Rock Hudson, Gina Lollobrigida, Gig Young, Terry-Thomas, Nancy Kulp. Hudson ambles through another marital mix-up comedy, this one with fiery Gina and lots of slapstick. Mild entertainment; filmed in London.

Strange Behavior (1981-New Zealand) **C-98m.** ** D: Michael Laughlin. Michael Murphy, Louise Fletcher, Dan Shor, Fiona Lewis, Arthur Dignam, Scott Brady, Charles Lane, Elizabeth Cheshire. This shocker about grisly murders in a small Midwestern town (shot in New Zealand!) got inexplicably good reviews in many quarters. You may rightly wonder what all the shouting was about. Originally titled DEAD KIDS.▼

Strange Brew (1983) **C-90m.** **½ D: Dave Thomas, Rick Moranis. Dave Thomas, Rick Moranis, Max von Sydow, Paul Dooley, Lynne Griffin, voice of Mel Blanc. Uneven but likably goofy film about Bob and Doug, the beer-guzzling McKenzie Brothers introduced on the *SCTV* show. Lags at times, but keeps coming up with funny scenes, especially when playing with the conventions of moviemaking. The stars also directed and co-wrote the film, the first in Hoserama.▼

Strange Cargo (1940) **105m.** *** D: Frank Borzage. Joan Crawford, Clark Gable, Ian Hunter, Peter Lorre, Albert Dekker, Paul Lukas, Eduardo Ciannelli. Intriguing allegorical film of prisoners escaping from Devil's Island with Christ-like presence of Hunter. Not for all tastes, but there are fine, realistic performances and flavorful Franz Waxman score.▼

Strange Case of Dr. Rx, The (1942) **66m.** ** D: William Nigh. Lionel Atwill, Patric Knowles, Anne Gwynne, Mona Barrie, Shemp Howard, Samuel S. Hinds, Paul Cavanagh, Mantan Moreland. Typical Universal Atwill vehicle, a fast-paced whodunit about hunt for mysterious title character, who murders criminals gotten off by unscrupulous attorney. Not particularly puzzling, but good cast helps.

Strange Case of Madeleine SEE: **Madeleine** (1949)

Strange Confession SEE: **Imposter, The** (1944)

Strange Conquest (1946) **65m.** ** D: John Rawlins. Jane Wyatt, Lowell Gilmore, Julie Bishop, Samuel S. Hinds, Abner Biberman. Inauspicious programmer set in the deep jungles where dedicated men try to conquer native diseases. Remake of THE CRIME OF DR. HALLET.

Strange Countess, The (1961-German) **96m.** ** D: Josef Von Baky. Joachim Fuchsberger, Lil Dagover, Marianne Hoppe, Brigitte Grothum. Dagover is in the title role, involved with fortune-hunting killers; from Edgar Wallace yarn.

Strange Death of Adolf Hitler, The (1943) **72m.** ** D: James Hogan. Ludwig Donath, Fritz Kortner, Gale Sondergaard, George Dolenz, Fred Giermann, William Trenk, Merrill Rodin. Hitler's double helps set trap for his demise. Dated, forgettable melodrama.

Strange Door, The (1951) **81m.** *½ D: Joseph Pevney. Charles Laughton, Boris Karloff, Sally Forrest, Richard Stapley, Alan Napier. Pretty bad adaptation of Stevenson story. Laughton overacts as cruel tyrant who gets back at dead sweetheart by imprisoning members of family. Intended horror film may seem comic.

Strange Fascination (1952) **80m.** ** D: Hugo Haas. Hugo Haas, Cleo Moore, Mona Barrie, Rick Vallin, Karen Sharpe. A concert pianist's career—and luck—fall apart because of his obsessive love for a young blonde. Starts interestingly but descends into hollow melodrama. Produced, directed, and written by Haas.

Strange Holiday (1942) **62m.** ** D: Arch Oboler. Claude Rains, Bobbie Stebbins, Barbara Bates, Paul Hilton, Tommy Cook, Martin Kosleck. Adaptation of Oboler's radio play about businessman who returns from vacation to find U.S. democracy overthrown. Unreleased until 1946. This was originally sponsored by General Motors and intended to be shown only to its employees!

Strange Homecoming (1974) **C-78m.** TVM D: Lee H. Katzin. Robert Culp, Glen Campbell, Barbara Anderson, Whitney Blake, John Crawford, Leif Garrett, Tara Talboy, Gerrit Graham. Murderer-on-the-lam Culp returns home after 18 years and moves in with family of his small-town sheriff brother (Campbell, in his TV-movie debut). Culp injects what life he can into limp story. Below average.

Strange Illusion (1945) **80m.** ** D: Edgar G. Ulmer. James Lydon, Sally Eilers, Warren William, Regis Toomey. Intriguing but unconvincing melodrama, a B-movie update of *Hamlet*, with teenaged Lydon having doubts about smooth-talker (William) who's wooing his widowed mother (Eilers). Typically bizarre Ulmer touches in this low-budget quickie.

Strange Impersonation (1946) **68m.** *** D: Anthony Mann. Brenda Marshall, William Gargan, Hillary Brooke, George Chandler, Ruth Ford, H. B. Warner, Lyle Talbot. Marshall is a chemical research scientist

who experiments with her own anesthetic. Ultra-cheap film with almost nonexistent production values is turned into a tour-de-force of expressionistic direction and *noir* lighting in the best Mann style.

Strange Interlude (1932) **110m.** *** D: Robert Z. Leonard. Norma Shearer, Clark Gable, May Robson, Maureen O'Sullivan, Robert Young, Ralph Morgan, Henry B. Walthall, Mary Alden. Eugene O'Neill talky play becomes marathon of inner thoughts revealed only to audience in chronicle of Gable, Shearer, et al growing old without resolving their problems. Engrossing film, with Shearer at her radiant best.

Strange Intruder (1956) **82m.** ** D: Irving Rapper. Edmund Purdom, Ida Lupino, Ann Harding, Jacques Bergerac. Purdom promises dying Korean War buddy that he'll visit the man's family; he does, with strange results.

Strange Invaders (1983) **C-94m.** **½ D: Michael Laughlin. Paul LeMat, Nancy Allen, Diana Scarwid, Michael Lerner, Louise Fletcher, Wallace Shawn, Fiona Lewis, Kenneth Tobey, June Lockhart. Affectionate spoof of 50s sci-fi films (with a touch of 80s New Wave), about a midwestern town overtaken by aliens. Has a wonderful feel to it but suffers from weak writing and lethargic pacing. Evocative score by John Addison.▼

Strange Journey (1946) **65m.** *½ D: James Tinling. Paul Kelly, Osa Massen, Hillary Brooke, Bruce Lester. Low-budget adventure story with group of people on desert isle fighting over treasure map.

Strange Lady in Town (1955) **C-112m.** **½ D: Mervyn LeRoy. Greer Garson, Dana Andrews, Cameron Mitchell, Lois Smith, Walter Hampden. Unsuccessful grand-scale soaper-Western. Set in 1880s Texas, Garson is the doctor coming to Santa Fe, involved with Andrews, perplexed by outlaw brother Mitchell.

Strange Love of Martha Ivers, The (1946) **117m.** *** D: Lewis Milestone. Barbara Stanwyck, Kirk Douglas, Lizabeth Scott, Van Heflin, Judith Anderson, Darryl Hickman. Gripping melodrama, with Stanwyck bound to her husband by crime she committed long ago. Douglas' film debut.▼

Strange Mr. Gregory, The (1946) **63m.** ** D: Phil Rosen. Edmund Lowe, Jean Rogers, Don Douglas, Marjorie Hoshelle, Robert Emmett Keane. Low-budget drama of magician who goes to any length to win love of married woman.

Strange New World (1975) **C-78m.** TVM D: Robert Butler. John Saxon, Kathleen Miller, Keene Curtis. Martine Beswick, James Olson, Ford Rainey, Catherine Bach, Richard Farnsworth. Sci-fi adventure with three astronauts returning to Earth after 180 years in suspended animation to find that scientists have developed eternal life

[1109]

by cloning. Warner Bros.' third attempt in as many years to launch a sci-fi series (following GENESIS II and PLANET EARTH). Below average.

Strange One, The (1957) 100m. *** D: Jack Garfein. Ben Gazzara, George Peppard, Pat Hingle, Mark Richman, Geoffrey Horne, James Olson. Bizarre military school account of far-out Gazzara's peculiar hold over various underclassmen. Remarkably frank version of Calder Willingham's *End as a Man*, scripted by the author; also filmed as SORORITY GIRL. Film debuts of Gazzara and Peppard.

Strange Possession of Mrs. Oliver, The (1977) C-78m. TVM D: Gordon Hessler. Karen Black, George Hamilton, Robert F. Lyons, Lucille Benson, Jean Allison, Gloria LeRoy. Pretentious split-personality study by Richard Matheson of a bored housewife who assumes a seductive blonde's identity, unaware that the girl she pretends to be really exists. Black chews the scenery, all kept in dreamy soft focus by director Hessler. Below average.

Stranger, The (1946) 95m. *** D: Orson Welles. Orson Welles, Loretta Young, Edward G. Robinson, Richard Long, Martha Wentworth. Fine study of escaped Nazi war criminal Welles sedately living in small Connecticut town, about to marry unsuspecting Young. Robinson nicely understates role as federal agent out to get him. Also shown in computer-colored version.▼

Stranger, The (1967-Italian-French) C-105m. ***½ D: Luchino Visconti. Marcello Mastroianni, Anna Karina, Bernard Blier, Georges Wilson, Bruno Cremer. Excellent adaptation of Albert Camus' existential novel about a man who feels completely isolated from society. Mastroianni is perfectly cast in lead.

Stranger, The (1973) C-100m. TVM D: Lee H. Katzin. Glenn Corbett, Cameron Mitchell, Sharon Acker, Lew Ayres, George Coulouris, Dean Jagger, Tim O'Connor. Unsatisfying sci-fi thriller of the "doppelganger" school. Astronaut Corbett crashes on Earth's twin planet and frantically tries to find his way "home" when his hosts try to exterminate him. Average.▼

Stranger, The (1987-U.S.-Argentine) C-88m. **½ D: Adolfo Aristarain. Bonnie Bedelia, Peter Riegert, Barry Primus, David Spielberg, Marcos Woinski. Clever if occasionally shallow thriller about Bedelia, who observes killings . . . and gets amnesia while the culprits are out to get her. Fairly entertaining most of the way, but could have been much better. Filmed in Buenos Aires.▼

Stranger and the Gunfighter, The (1976-Italian-Hong Kong) C-107m. **½ D: Anthony Dawson (Antonio Margheriti). Lee Van Cleef, Lo Lieh, Patty Shepard, Julian Ugarte, Karen Yeh. Lively, low-grade tongue-in-cheek actioner has hard-drinking cowboy joining forces with kung fu expert to recover missing fortune, with portions of the map tattooed on the posteriors of assorted lovelies. Amusing mix of spaghetti Western and karate thriller.▼

Stranger at Jefferson High (1981) C-100m. TVM D: Lyman Dayton. Stewart Peterson, Philip Brown, Dana Kimmell, Jeff Chamberlain, Lachelle Price, Shannon Farnon. Fatherless teenager becomes household breadwinner, moves family from Wyoming farm to L.A., and enters world of drag racing, teen pranks, and young love. Written by sometime director Kieth Merrill, this originally was to have been a theatrical movie called RIVALS. Average.

Stranger at My Door (1956) 85m. **½ D: William Witney. Macdonald Carey, Patricia Medina, Skip Homeier, Louis Jean Heydt, Stephen Wootton, Slim Pickens. Offbeat Western about clergyman jeopardizing his family's safety when he tries to reform an outlaw.

Stranger Came Home, A SEE: **Unholy Four**

Stranger in Between, The (1952-British) 84m. *** D: Charles Crichton. Dirk Bogarde, Elizabeth Sellars, Kay Walsh, Jon Whiteley, Geoffrey Keen. Odd but very entertaining film about orphan boy who grows to understand murderer as both flee police in England. Warm, compassionate performances. Original British title: HUNTED.

Stranger in My Arms (1959) 88m. **½ D: Helmut Kautner. June Allyson, Jeff Chandler, Sandra Dee, Charles Coburn, Mary Astor, Peter Graves, Conrad Nagel. Undemanding old-fashioned weeper, based on Robert Wilder novel. Chandler falls in love with Allyson, wife of Air Force buddy killed in Korean War. Astor is the domineering mother-in-law. Typical Ross Hunter sudser.

Stranger in My Bed (1986) C-100m. TVM D: Larry Elikann. Lindsay Wagner, Armand Assante, Doug Sheehan, Gabriel Damon, Allyn Ann McLerie, Clayton Corzatte. By-the-numbers story of amnesiac struggling to relearn the past, this time based on the book by real-life amnesiac Beverly Slater. Average.

Stranger in Our House (1978) C-100m. TVM D: Wes Craven. Linda Blair, Lee Purcell, Jeremy Slate, Carol Lawrence, Macdonald Carey, Jeff McCracken, Jeff East. Teenage witchcraft thriller with always put-upon Linda Blair in constant peril. Based on Lois Duncan's novel *Summer of Fear*. Average.▼

Stranger in the House SEE: **Black Christmas**▼

Stranger in Town, A (1966-Italian-U.S.) C-86m. *½ D: Vance Lewis (Luigi Vanza). Tony Anthony, Frank Wolff, Yolanda

Modio, Gia Sandri. Poor imitation of Sergio Leone Western finds Anthony blood-bathing a murderous bandit into submission. Sequel: THE STRANGER RETURNS.

Stranger Is Watching, A (1982) **C-92m.** ** D: Sean S. Cunningham. Kate Mulgrew, Rip Torn, James Naughton, Shawn Von Schreiber, Barbara Baxley, Stephen Joyce. Psychopath Torn kidnaps TV newscaster Mulgrew and young Von Schreiber, holding them hostage in catacombs beneath Grand Central Station. Convoluted thriller from the director of FRIDAY THE 13TH.▼

Stranger on Horseback (1955) **C-66m.** ** D: Jacques Tourneur. Joel McCrea, Kevin McCarthy, Jaclynne Greene, Miroslava, Nancy Gates, John Carradine. McCrea is tight-lipped judge who's forced to kill in order to set justice straight and bring a murderer to trial.

Stranger on My Land (1988) **C-100m.** TVM D: Larry Elikann. Tommy Lee Jones, Dee Wallace Stone, Ben Johnson, Pat Hingle, Terry O'Quinn, Richard Anderson, Ned Romero, Barry Corbin. Vietnam vet fights the Feds, who want his ranch for a missile base. Similar to the earlier FIRE ON THE MOUNTAIN, among others. Average.

Stranger on the Prowl (1953-Italian) **82m.** **½ D: Joseph Losey. Paul Muni, Vittorio Manunta, Joan Lorring, Aldo Silvani. Murky drama of Muni a fugitive on the run who tries to set a young would-be-crook straight.

Stranger on the Run (1967) **C-97m. TVM** D: Don Siegel. Henry Fonda, Michael Parks, Anne Baxter, Dan Duryea, Sal Mineo, Lloyd Bochner, Michael Burns, Tom Reese, Bernie Hamilton, Zalman King. Solidly conceived, well-executed chase thriller features Fonda, in his TV movie debut, as drifter in Banner, New Mexico, trying to deliver message to sister of prison friend, accused of murder, chased by railroad police into desert. Great entertainment with something to say; written by Reginald Rose. Above average.

✓ **Stranger on the Third Floor, The** (1940) **64m.** *** D: Boris Ingster. Peter Lorre, John McGuire, Margaret Tallichet, Charles Waldron, Elisha Cook, Jr. Reporter's testimony has convicted Cook in brutal murder case, but the newspaperman has second thoughts. Excellent sleeper, with one nightmare montage that's a knockout.▼

Stranger Returns, The (1968-U.S.-Italian) **C-90m.** BOMB D: Vance Lewis (Luigi Vanza). Tony Anthony, Dan Vadis, Daniele Vargas, Marco Guglielmi, Jill Banner. Sequel to A STRANGER IN TOWN has Anthony chasing solid gold stagecoach full of thieves. Western is worthless, even if local TV stations don't cut the gore.

Strangers (1953-Italian) **97m.** *½ D: Roberto Rossellini. Ingrid Bergman, George Sanders, Paul Muller, Maria Mauban, Natalia Ray. Tedious hokum of married couple Bergman and Sanders trying to reconcile their faltering relationship while on Italian holiday.

Strangers (1979) SEE: **Strangers: The Story of a Mother and Daughter**▼

Strangers at Sunrise (1969) **C-99m.** **½ D: Percival Rubens. George Montgomery, Deana Martin, Brian O'Shaughnessy, Tromp Terreblanche. Turn of the century South African Western with American mining engineer (Montgomery), attracted by the gold rush, trying to clear his name when the British accuse him of spying for the Boers.

Stranger's Hand, The (1954-British) **86m.** *** D: Mario Soldati. Trevor Howard, Alida Valli, Richard Basehart, Eduardo Ciannelli, Richard O'Sullivan, Stephen Murray. British espionage officer, going to Venice to meet schoolboy son, disappears. Intriguing suspense yarn, based on Graham Greene story, with topnotch performances. Filmed in Italy.

Strangers in Love (1932) **76m.** ** D: Lothar Mendes. Kay Francis, Fredric March, Stuart Erwin, Juliette Compton, Sidney Toler, George Barbier, Lucien Littlefield. Mild comedy; Francis is secretary who loves March, weakling playboy forced to impersonate twin brother to expose family fraud.

Strangers in 7A (1972) **C-73m. TVM** D: Paul Wendkos. Andy Griffith, Ida Lupino, Michael Brandon, James Watson, Jr., Suzanne Hildur, Tim McIntire. Bar-girl is used as a lure to get use of middle-aged superintendent's apartment for robbery. Good tension toward end, plus unusual script sympathetic to victim's point of view. Above average.

Strangers Kiss (1984) **C-94m.** **½ D: Matthew Chapman. Peter Coyote, Victoria Tennant, Blaine Novak, Dan Shor, Richard Romanus, Linda Kerridge. Interesting, offbeat little film about the making of a low-budget movie, circa 1955, and the off-camera relationship between lead actors Novak and Tennant. Novak also cowrote screenplay with director Chapman, inspired by Stanley Kubrick's KILLER'S KISS.▼

Strangers May Kiss (1931) **85m.** ** D: George Fitzmaurice. Norma Shearer, Robert Montgomery, Neil Hamilton, Marjorie Rambeau, Jed Prouty, Henry Armetta, Irene Rich. Polished but ridiculous soaper of Shearer in love with—and fooling herself into trusting—unreliable hypocrite Hamilton. Film's conclusion is not to be believed. Montgomery is fine as Shearer's pal; young Ray Milland has a couple of lines as one of her admirers.

Strangers on a Train (1951) **101m.** **** D: Alfred Hitchcock. Farley Granger, Robert Walker, Ruth Roman, Leo G. Carroll,

Patricia Hitchcock, Marion Lorne. Walker gives his finest performance as psychopath involved with tennis star Granger in "exchange murders." Lorne is unforgettable as doting mother; so is merry-go-round climax. First-class Hitchcock, based on a Patricia Highsmith novel and coscripted by Raymond Chandler. Remade as ONCE YOU KISS A STRANGER and the inspiration for THROW MOMMA FROM THE TRAIN.▼

Stranger's Return, The (1933) 89m. ***½ D: King Vidor. Lionel Barrymore, Miriam Hopkins, Franchot Tone, Stuart Erwin, Irene Hervey, Beulah Bondi. A young woman, recently separated from her husband, leaves the city to stay at her grandfather's farm. Here she finds her roots, as well as a kindred spirit in neighboring farmer Tone, a college graduate. Why this rich, mature, beautifully made film isn't better known is a mystery. Phil Stong helped adapt his own novel for director Vidor.

Strangers: The Story of a Mother and Daughter (1979) C-100m. TVM D: Milton Katselas. Bette Davis, Gena Rowlands, Ford Rainey, Donald Moffat, Royal Dano. Davis at her latter-day best (winning an Emmy Award) and matched scene for scene by Rowlands in this drama about a lonely widow's resentment over her estranged daughter's unexpected homecoming after twenty years. Written by Michael DeGuzman. Also known simply as STRANGERS. Above average.▼

Strangers When We Meet (1960) C-117m. **½ D: Richard Quine. Kirk Douglas, Kim Novak, Ernie Kovacs, Barbara Rush, Walter Matthau, Virginia Bruce, Kent Smith. Expensive soaper with attractive stars; both are married, but fall in love with each other. Script by Evan Hunter, from his novel.▼

Stranger Than Paradise (1984) 90m. *** D: Jim Jarmusch. John Lurie, Eszter Balint, Richard Edson, Cecilia Stark. Simple story of a nondescript young man, his doltish best friend, and his 16-year-old female cousin who comes to America from Hungary. Critically acclaimed comedy-road movie is, at its worst, a bit slow; at its best, original, ingratiating, and extremely funny. Independently filmed and developed from a 30m. short. Screenplay by Jarmusch, music by Lurie.▼

Stranger Waits, A (1987) C-100m. TVM D: Robert Lewis. Suzanne Pleshette, Tom Atkins, Paul Benjamin, Justin Deas, Ann Wedgeworth. Fabulously wealthy widow gets involved with mysterious younger man in this tepid suspense drama written by the estimable Durrell Royce Crays, from a story by Bruce Lansbury. Average.

Stranger Who Looks Like Me, The (1974) C-78m. TVM D: Larry Peerce. Beau Bridges, Meredith Baxter, Whitney Blake, Walter Brooke, Neva Patterson, Mary Murphy, Ford Rainey. Adoptees Bridges and Baxter pursue frustrating searches for their natural parents. OK examination of a growing contemporary phenomenon. Baxter and real mother Blake have a few nice scenes together. Script by Gerald DiPego. Patrick Duffy is one of the adoptees. Above average.

Stranger Within, The (1974) C-78m. TVM D: Lee Philips. Barbara Eden, George Grizzard, Joyce Van Patten, David Doyle, Nehemiah Persoff. Melodrama about a woman whose unborn baby begins to control her mind and body. Suspiciously reminiscent of ROSEMARY'S BABY with offbeat touches added by writer Richard Matheson. Average.▼

Stranger Wore a Gun, The (1953) C-83m. ** D: Andre de Toth. Randolph Scott, Claire Trevor, Joan Weldon, George Macready, Lee Marvin, Ernest Borgnine, Alfonso Bedoya. Oddball plot in this Scott Western; Randy is befriended by bandit and becomes involved in a holdup before he can return to normal living. Originally in 3-D.

Strange Shadows in An Empty Room (1977) C-99m. *½ D: Martin Herbert (Alberto DeMartino). Stuart Whitman, John Saxon, Martin Landau, Tisa Farrow, Gayle Hunnicutt, Carole Laure. Far-fetched, violent film has police detective Whitman searching for his sister's murderer. Tawdry stuff; filmed in Montreal as BLAZING MAGNUMS (a far more appropriate title).▼

Strange Skirts SEE: **When Ladies Meet** (1941)

Strange Triangle (1946) 65m. ** D: Ray McCarey. Preston Foster, Signe Hasso, John Shepperd (Shepperd Strudwick), Roy Roberts. OK drama with Hasso as the maneuvering dame who inspires murder and robbery.

Strange Vengeance of Rosalie, The (1972) C-107m. ** D: Jack Starrett. Bonnie Bedelia, Ken Howard, Anthony Zerbe. Offbeat story of Indian girl who holds man captive in rambling house. Far-fetched tale goes way off-base.

Strange Voices (1987) C-100m. TVM D: Arthur Allan Seidelman. Nancy McKeon, Valerie Harper, Stephen Macht, Tricia Leigh Fisher, Millie Perkins, Robert Krantz, Jack Blessing. Well-adjusted teenager McKeon suddenly begins hearing strange voices and sends her family into turmoil when she's judged schizophrenic. Not up to the earlier PROMISE by a long shot. Average.

Strange Woman, The (1946) 100m. ** D: Edgar G. Ulmer. Hedy Lamarr, George Sanders, Louis Hayward, Gene Lockhart, Hillary Brooke, June Storey. Lamarr's a legendary man-killer in this tedious costumer.▼

Strange World of Planet X, The SEE: **Cosmic Monster, The**

Strangler, The (1964) 89m. *** D: Burt Topper. Victor Buono, David McLean, Ellen Corby, Jeanne Bates, Wally Campo. Buono gives fine performance as mother-dominated mad killer who strangles women and pitches Boston into frenzy.▼

Strangler's Morgue SEE: **Crimes of Stephen Hawke, The**

Stranglers of Bombay, The (1960-British) 81m. **½ D: Terence Fisher. Andrew Cruickshank, Marne Maitland, Guy Rolfe, Paul Stassino, Jan Holden, Tutte Lemkow. Grisly story of fanatical Indian cult attempting to drive British from trading station. Good cast helped by tense direction.

Strapless (1989-British) C-103m. **½ D: David Hare. Blair Brown, Bruno Ganz, Bridget Fonda, Hugh Laurie, Alan Howard, Billy Roch, Camille Coduri, Alexandra Pigg, Michael Gough, Gary O'Brien. American doctor Brown, living and working in London, hits 40 and finds herself at a crossroads, just as her 25-year-old sister arrives for an extended vacation. Brown is fine, and Fonda completely winning in this studied, sometimes ponderous story of the need to face emotions head-on, no matter where they may lead.

Strategic Air Command (1955) C-114m. **½ D: Anthony Mann. June Allyson, James Stewart, Frank Lovejoy, Barry Sullivan, Bruce Bennett, Rosemary DeCamp. Film only gets off the ground when Stewart does, as baseball player recalled to air force duty; Allyson is his sugary wife.▼

Stratton Story, The (1949) 106m. ***½ D: Sam Wood. James Stewart, June Allyson, Frank Morgan, Agnes Moorehead, Bill Williams. Stewart is fine as Monty Stratton, baseball player whose loss of one leg did not mark an end to his career; well-played by good cast, Oscar-winner for story (Douglas Morrow). Also shown in computer-colored version.

Strawberry Blonde, The (1941) 97m. *** D: Raoul Walsh. James Cagney, Olivia de Havilland, Rita Hayworth, Alan Hale, Jack Carson, George Tobias, Una O'Connor, George Reeves. Cagney's dynamic in entertaining turn-of-the century story of dentist infatuated with gold-digger Hayworth, and his subsequent marriage to de Havilland. Remade as ONE SUNDAY AFTERNOON, the title of the 1933 Gary Cooper film of which this is a remake.▼

Strawberry Statement, The (1970) C-103m. ** D: Stuart Hagmann. Bruce Davison, Kim Darby, Bob Balaban, James Kunen, Jeannie Berlin, Bud Cort. Cluttered adaptation of James Kunen's book about Columbia University's riots tries to be too many things at once—comedy, social commentary, musical. Good performances. Script by Israel Horovitz.▼

Straw Dogs (1971) C-113m. ***½ D: Sam Peckinpah. Dustin Hoffman, Susan George, Peter Vaughan, T. P. McKenna, Peter Arne, David Warner. One of the most controversial violence-themed films of its day. Hoffman portrays American mathematician whose pacifism is put to supreme test when he and British wife George move to isolated village. Filmed in England. Original running time: 118m.▼

Stray Dog (1949-Japanese) 122m. **** D: Akira Kurosawa. Toshiro Mifune, Takashi Shimura, Keiko Awaji, Ko Kimura. Classic Japanese *film noir*, most effective as a look at life in post-WW2 Tokyo. Mifune does well as a detective whose gun is stolen; he sets out on an odyssey to reclaim his weapon, and to seek out a killer. Although not as well-known as RASHOMON, this film is just as important to the career of Kurosawa and the growth of Japanese cinema.▼

Streamers (1983) C-118m. *** D: Robert Altman. Matthew Modine, Michael Wright, Mitchell Lichtenstein, David Alan Grier, Guy Boyd, George Dzundza. A couple of days in an army barracks at the dawn of America's involvement in Vietman becomes a parable about manhood, death and relationships between the races. Overlong and depressing but still worthwhile, with fine performances in meaty roles. Screenplay by David Rabe, from his play.▼

Street Angel (1928) 102m. *** D: Frank Borzage. Janet Gaynor, Charles Farrell, Alberto Rabagliati, Gino Conti, Guido Trento, Henry Armetta. Italian girl fleeing from police joins traveling circus, meets and falls in love with young painter who finds her an inspiration. Follow-up to success of SEVENTH HEAVEN is actually much better; a delicate, beautifully photographed silent film. Gaynor won a Best Actress Oscar (shared for her performances in SEVENTH HEAVEN and SUNRISE).

Streetcar Named Desire, A (1951) 122m. **** D: Elia Kazan. Marlon Brando, Vivien Leigh, Kim Hunter, Karl Malden. Stunning production of Tennessee Williams' play, with Brando as the animalistic Stanley Kowalski and Leigh as his wistful, neurotic sister-in-law, Blanche Dubois, pressed together in a grim New Orleans tenement. Oscars went to Leigh, Hunter, and Malden for their flawless performances, as well as for the art direction-set decoration—but it's Brando who left an indelible mark on audiences. Highly influential jazz score by Alex North. Remade for TV.▼

Streetcar Named Desire, A (1984) C-124m. TVM D: John Erman. Ann-Margret, Treat Williams, Beverly D'Angelo, Randy Quaid, Rafael Campos, Erica Yohn. Terrific performance by Ann-Margret as

Blanche makes this version stand proudly beside its classic predecessor. Above average.

Street Gang SEE: **Vigilante**▼

Street Justice (1989) C-94m. *½ D: Richard S. Sarafian. Michael Ontkean, Joanna Kerns, Catherine Bach, J.D. Cannon, Jeanette Nolan, Richard Cox, William Windom, Sandra Currie, Dave B. Nichols. Standard Western plot transposed to modern city setting: loner hero cleans up corrupt town dominated by ruthless, wealthy family. Slow, unconvincing, and instantly forgettable, despite good cast.▼

Street Killing (1976) C-78m. TVM D: Harvey Hart. Andy Griffith, Bradford Dillman, Harry Guardino, Robert Loggia, Don Gordon, Adam Wade. Crime drama has Griffith as N.Y. prosecuting attorney seeking to prove that a mugging-murder was ordered by the Mafia. Run-of-the-mill pilot for Griffith. Average.

Street Music (1981) C-92m. **½ D: Jenny Bowen. Elizabeth Daily, Larry Breeding, Ned Glass, Marjorie Eaton, W. F. Walker, Miriam Phillips, D'Alan Moss. Trifling yet occasionally touching tale of ambitious singer Daily, her irresponsible boyfriend Breeding, and elderly residents of a dilapidated hotel who fight the bureaucracy to save their home. Bouncy lead performances; filmed independently, in San Francisco's Tenderloin.▼

Street of Chance (1942) 74m. **½ D: Jack Hively. Burgess Meredith, Claire Trevor, Sheldon Leonard, Frieda Inescort. Effective Paramount B mystery with Meredith an amnesia victim seeking clues to his past; from a Cornell Woolrich story.

Street of Dreams (1988) C-100m. TVM D: William A. Graham. Ben Masters, Morgan Fairchild, John Hillerman, Diane Salinger, Michael Cavanaugh, Alan Autry, David Marciano. Masters is an L.A. beach bum/private eye who is drawn into a seamy Hollywood murder by a down-and-out blonde. Amiable version of novelist Timothy Harris' *Good Night and Good Bye,* with a breezy Bill Stratton script. Average.

Street of Shame (1956-Japanese) 96m. ***½ D: Kenji Mizoguchi. Machiko Kyo, Ayako Wakao, Aiko Mimasu, Michiyo Kogure. The stories of various prostitutes in Dreamland, a Tokyo brothel, are sensitively handled in Mizoguchi's last completed film. Kyo is particularly memorable as a tough, cynical lady of the night; her scene with her father is a highlight.▼

Street of Sorrow, The SEE: **Joyless Street, The**▼

Street People (1976-Italian) C-92m. *½ D: Maurizio Lucidi. Roger Moore, Stacy Keach, Ivo Garrani, Fausto Tozzi, Ettore Manni. Insipid though energetic gangster flick punctuated by several car chases. San Francisco mafioso dispatches nephew Moore

(would you believe him as a Sicilian?) and his Grand Prix driving buddy Keach to find out which rival Don hid a million dollar cache of pure heroin in the cross he imported from Italy as a gift for his church.▼

Street Scene (1931) 80m. ***½ D: King Vidor. Sylvia Sidney, William Collier, Jr., David Landau, Estelle Taylor, Walter Miller, Beulah Bondi. Heartbreakingly realistic account of life in N.Y. tenements, and younger generation's desperation to get out. Elmer Rice's Pulitzer Prize-winning play (adapted by him) enhanced by fine performances, George Barnes' striking camerawork, Alfred Newman's classic music score.▼

Street Smart (1987) C-97m. **½ D: Jerry Schatzberg. Christopher Reeve, Kathy Baker, Mimi Rogers, Morgan Freeman, Jay Patterson, Andre Gregory. Out-of-favor writer for a slick Manhattan magazine pitches a high-profile study of N.Y.C pimpdom; unable to find a cooperative subject, he fakes the story, which boomerangs when the D.A. concludes the story is about a real-life murder suspect. Intriguing idea, based on screenwriter David Freeman's own experience at *New York* magazine, but just misses; powerhouse performances by pimp Freeman and hooker Baker make up for Reeve's blandness in the lead.▼

Streets of Fire (1984) C-93m. *** D: Walter Hill. Michael Paré, Diane Lane, Rick Moranis, Amy Madigan, Willem Dafoe, Deborah Van Valkenburgh, Elizabeth Daily, Lee Ving, Marine Jahan, Ed Begley, Jr., The Blasters. Female rock star is kidnapped by sadistic bikers, and her embittered ex-boyfriend agrees to bring her back—for a price. This "rock 'n' roll fable" is actually a 1950s B movie brought up to date with pulsating rock score (principally by Ry Cooder), state-of-the-art visuals, and a refusal to take itself too seriously. Unfortunately, near the climax the glitter gives out and we're left with the story—which can't carry film to a really satisfying conclusion. Stunningly photographed (mostly on a soundstage, believe it or not) by Andrew Laszlo.▼

Streets of Gold (1986) C-95m. **½ D: Joe Roth. Klaus Maria Brandauer, Adrian Pasdar, Wesley Snipes, Angela Molina, Elya Baskin, Rainbow Harvest. Former Russian boxing champ, now a dishwasher in Brooklyn, trains two street kids for U.S. boxing team—hoping to beat his former Russian coach. Well-meaning "feel-good" movie along ROCKY lines; utterly ordinary but for Brandauer's performance.▼

Streets of Justice (1985) C-100m. TVM D: Christopher Crowe. John Laughlin, Robert Loggia, Lance Henriksen, Jack Thibeau, John Hancock, Douglas Dirkson, Cristina Raines, Robin Gammell. Blue-collar worker wreaks vigilante vengeance on a pack of bikers who wiped out his family. Laughlin does a very pale Charles Bronson imitation in this excessively brutal (by TV standards) DEATH WISH ripoff that was concocted as a prospective series pilot. Below average.

Streets of L.A., The (1979) C-100m. TVM D: Jerrold Freedman. Joanne Woodward, Robert Webber, Michael C. Gwynne, Fernando Allende, Isela Vega. The strength is Joanne Woodward in this contemporary drama about a tenacious woman who goes alone into the L.A. barrio in pursuit of teenaged hoods who slashed her tires. Without her, the whole idea would be just plain silly. Average.▼

Streets of Laredo (1949) C-92m. **½ D: Leslie Fenton. Macdonald Carey, William Holden, William Bendix, Mona Freeman. Standard Western, remake of THE TEXAS RANGERS, but not as good. Three pals out West split when two turn to law and another becomes lawbreaker.

Streets of New York (1939) 73m. **½ D: William Nigh. Jackie Cooper, Martin Spellman, Marjorie Reynolds, Dick Purcell, George Cleveland, George Irving. Good programmer of an upright young man (Cooper) who admires Abraham Lincoln and must overcome much adversity on the streets of N.Y.C.'s Hell's Kitchen. Also known as THE ABE LINCOLN OF NINTH AVENUE.▼

Streets of San Francisco, The (1972) C-98m. TVM D: Walter Grauman. Karl Malden, Michael Douglas, Robert Wagner, Kim Darby, Andrew Duggan, John Rubinstein, Tom Bosley, Edward Andrews, Mako. Moody atmosphere reminiscent of *Peter Gunn* in sinister police whodunit as Detectives Stone and Keller (Malden and Douglas) piece together last days in life of young woman. Explanation, both devious and acceptable, real tour de force. Adapted by Ed Hume from Carolyn Weston's *Poor, Poor Ophelia*. Pilot for the hit series. Above average.

Street Trash (1987) C-91m. BOMB D: Jim Muro. Bill Chepil, Mike Lackey, Vic Noto, Mark Sferrazza, Jane Arakawa, Nicole Potter, Tony Darrow. Thoroughly repellent account of life among some moronic street bums in the bowels of Brooklyn. No discernible plot, just gratuitous gore and violence. Supposedly based on Kurosawa's DODES'KA-DEN.▼

Streetwalkin' (1984) C-85m. BOMB D: Joan Freeman. Melissa Leo, Dale Midkiff, Antonio Fargas, Julie Newmar, Leon Robinson, Annie Golden. Ultra-slick, sleazy, hopelessly predictable trash about hooker-with-a-heart-of-gold and her sadistic, unbelievably stupid pimp.▼

Streetwise (1984) C-92m. ***½ D: Martin Bell. Sad, gut-wrenching documentary about teen vagrants living—and, in one case, dying—on the mean streets of Seattle. This powerful record of young, lost souls would make a telling double bill with any one of a dozen idiotic adolescent comedies of the 1980s.▼

Street With No Name, The (1948) 91m. *** D: William Keighley. Mark Stevens, Richard Widmark, Lloyd Nolan, Barbara Lawrence, Ed Begley, Donald Buka. Fine movie based on actual F.B.I. case of agent uncovering head of city mob. Suspense well handled. Remade as HOUSE OF BAMBOO.

Strictly Dishonorable (1951) 86m. ** D: Melvin Frank, Norman Panama. Ezio Pinza, Janet Leigh, Millard Mitchell, Gale Robbins. Tame shenanigans of opera star Pinza marrying Leigh to save her reputation. Based on the Preston Sturges play, previously filmed in 1931.

Strike (1924-Russian) 73m. ***½ D: Sergei Eisenstein. Grigori Alexandrov, Maxim Strauch, Mikhail Gomarov, Alexander Antonov, Judith Glizer. Eisenstein's debut feature is a still-powerful, vivid account of a 1912 factory workers strike in Czarist Russia and its violent suppression. An appropriate prelude to POTEMKIN; some prints run 82m.▼

Strikebound (1983 Australian) C-100m. *** D: Richard Lowenstein. Chris Haywood, Carol Burns, Hugh Keays-Byrne, Rob Steele, Nik Forster. Documentarylike chronicle, based on actual incidents, of a miners' strike in the Australian coal fields during the 1930s, culminating with the workers—many of them Communist Party members—barricading themselves in their mine. Seems a bit romanticized but still taut, perceptive, and extremely well made.

Strike Force (1975) C-78m. TVM D: Barry Shear. Cliff Gorman, Donald Blakely, Richard Gere, Edward Grover, Joe Spinell. N.Y.C. detective, Federal agent, and state trooper team up to crack a narcotics ring. Mildly interesting for early appearance by Gere; otherwise, just another busted cop show pilot (but unrelated to later same-titled series with Robert Stack). Average.▼

Strike It Rich (1990-British) C-87m. *½ D: James Scott. Robert Lindsay, Molly Ringwald, John Gielgud, Max Wall, Simon de la Brosse, Margi Clarke, Vladek Sheybal, Michel Blanc, Frances De La Tour. Second film version of Graham Greene novella *Loser Takes All,* about an obscure conglomerate accountant talked into honeymooning beyond his means in Monte Carlo following a chance encounter with the firm's Grand Old Man. The leads in DRIVING MISS DAISY have more sexual chemistry than postnuptial Lindsay and Ringwald; sole compensations are Gielgud and some decent '50s production design.▼

Strike Me Pink (1936) 100m. *½ D: Norman Taurog. Eddie Cantor, Ethel Merman, Sally Eilers, Parkyakarkus, William Frawley, Brian Donlevy. One of Cantor's worst films, built around his run-in with racketeers at amusement park which he manages. Good slapstick chase finale, forgettable music numbers.

Strike Up the Band (1940) 120m. **½ D: Busby Berkeley. Mickey Rooney, Judy Garland, Paul Whiteman, June Preisser, William Tracy, Larry Nunn. Rooney is leader of high school band competing in Whiteman's nationwide radio contest. Garland sings "Our Love Affair," "Nell of New Rochelle," "Do The Conga."▼

Strip, The (1951) 85m. ** D: Leslie Kardos. Mickey Rooney, Sally Forrest, William Demarest, James Craig. Rooney gives sincere, energetic performance as former drummer involved with gangsters, trying to help Forrest get a movie break. Routine film enlivened by great music of Louis Armstrong, Earl Hines, Jack Teagarden and all-star group.

Stripes (1981) C-105m. **½ D: Ivan Reitman. Bill Murray, Harold Ramis, Warren Oates, P. J. Soles, Sean Young, John Candy, John Larroquette, Judge Reinhold, Timothy Busfield. Loser Murray joins the Army in this predictable service comedy, which somehow pulled in millions at the box office. Sometimes funny, but eminently forgettable. Ramis, who plays Murray's buddy, also coscripted. Brief appearances by Joe Flaherty and Dave Thomas.▼

Stripped to Kill (1987) C-88m. **½ D: Katt Shea Ruben. Kay Lenz, Greg Evigan, Norman Fell, Pia Kamakahi, Tracey Crowder, Debby Nassar. Who's killing the classy strippers of L.A.? It's up to policewoman Lenz to find out, by posing as a stripper herself. Stylish, inventive Roger Corman B production hampered by too many strip numbers. Followed by STRIPPED TO KILL II.▼

Stripped to Kill II (1989) C-83m. *½ D: Katt Shea Ruben. Maria Ford, Eb Lottimer, Karen Mayo Chandler, Marjean Holden, Birke Tan, Debra Lamb. More strippers, more murders, and a heroine with slight ESP powers—she dreams of murders as they occur. Followup to STRIPPED TO KILL is inferior in every way—despite same director.▼

Stripper, The (1963) 95m. **½ D: Franklin Schaffner. Joanne Woodward, Richard Beymer, Claire Trevor, Carol Lynley, Robert Webber, Gypsy Rose Lee, Louis Nye, Michael J. Pollard. Aging stripper falls in love with teen-age boy in this OK filmization of William Inge's play *A Loss of Roses*. Director Schaffner's first movie.▼

Stroker Ace (1983) C-96m. BOMB D: Hal Needham. Burt Reynolds, Ned Beatty, Jim Nabors, Loni Anderson, Parker Stevenson, Bubba Smith, John Byner, Frank O. Hill. One of Burt's worst has him as champion race-car driver and pea-brain who delights in tormenting his sponsor (Beatty) and leering at buxom Anderson. Lame "good old boy" hijinks, punctuated with TV stock footage of race-car crackups! Note: Jim Nabors sings, too.▼

Stromboli (1950-Italian) 81m. *½ D: Roberto Rossellini. Ingrid Bergman, Mario Vitale, Renzo Cesana, Mario Sponza. Rambling dreariness with Bergman marrying a fisherman; even erupting volcano doesn't jar this plodding film, which reportedly looks better in its original Italian 107m. version.▼

Stronger Than the Sun (1980-British) C-101m. *** D: Michael Apted. Francesca Annis, Tom Bell. Annis is excellent as a nuclear power plant worker who attempts to expose a radioactive leak. Timely drama bears a striking resemblance to the Karen Silkwood story.

Strongest Man in the World, The (1975) C-92m. ** D: Vincent McEveety. Kurt Russell, Joe Flynn, Eve Arden, Cesar Romero, Phil Silvers, Dick Van Patten, Harold Gould, James Gregory. Third of Disney's cookie-cutter student comedies with Russell and pals again discovering a magic formula—this one for super-strength—and battling crooks who want to get their hands on it. Good opening and closing, but even kids may find it draggy midway through.

Stronghold (1951) 82m. *½ D: Steve Sekely. Veronica Lake, Zachary Scott, Arturo de Cordova, Rita Macedo. Pedestrian costumer set in 1860s, with Lake fleeing U.S. and becoming embroiled in Mexican revolution.

Strong Medicine (1979) C-84m. **½ D: Richard Foreman. Kate Mannheim, Scotty Snyder, Bill Raymond, Harry Roskolenko, Ron Vawter, David Warrilow, Ruth Maleczech, Carol Kane, Raul Julia, Buck Henry, Wallace Shawn. Alternately fascinating, boring, surreal chronicle of the various activities and adventures of a mad, manic, eccentric woman. Foreman is an innovative theater director; ultimately, this film is an acquired taste.

Strong Medicine (1986) C-200m. TVM D: Guy Green. Ben Cross, Patrick Duffy, Douglas Fairbanks, Jr., Gayle Hunnicutt, Pamela Sue Martin, Sam Neill, Annette O'Toole, Dick Van Dyke, Kristoffer Tabori. Dramatization of the Arthur Hailey novel about the pharmaceutical business and one woman's determined rise up the ranks of an international drug cartel. Stylish but insubstantial gloss for the romance novel crowd. Originally shown in two parts. Average.

Stroszek (1977-German) C-108m. *** D: Werner Herzog. Bruno S., Eva Mattes, Clemens Scheitz. Berlin street singer and former mental patient Bruno S. joins with whore (Mattes) and aging eccentric (Scheitz) to travel to midwestern U.S. in pursuit of

American dream. Surprisingly positive, tragicomic, poetic narrative.

Stryker (1983-Filipino) **C-84m.** BOMB D: Cirio H. Santiago. Steve Sandor, Andria Savio, William Ostrander, Michael Lane, Julie Gray. Poor MAD MAX clone, with various good and bad characters battling each other for water in a post-nuclear war setting. Sloppy direction; a real downer.▼

Stuck With Each Other (1989) **C-100m.** TVM D: Georg Stanford Brown. Tyne Daly, Richard Crenna, Roscoe Lee Browne, Eileen Heckart, Michael J. Pollard, Bubba Smith. Engaging caper movie about an unlikely duo who team up to split a million bucks they've stumbled on and then live it up while dodging a pair of mob thugs. Rare foray into comedy for the two leads (although that's where Crenna started). Pleasant, untaxing script by Harold Jack Bloom and Howard Albrecht. Above average.

Stud, The (1978-British) **C-95m.** BOMB D: Quentin Masters. Joan Collins, Oliver Tobias, Sue Lloyd, Mark Burns, Walter Gottell, Emma Jacobs. A waiter works his way up in the world (so to speak) by sleeping with the boss' wife. Idiotic softcore porn written by Jackie Collins (Joan's sister). Followed by THE BITCH.▼

Student Bodies (1981) **C-86m.** *½ D: Mickey Rose. Kristen Riter, Matthew Goldsby, Richard Brando, Joe Flood, Joe Talarowski. Spoof of HALLOWEEN-type pictures has a promising start, then simply falls apart; ending is particularly bad. Plagued by production problems, as indicated by producing credit for the ubiquitous and nonexistent Allen Smithee (Michael Ritchie here).▼

Student Confidential (1987) **C-95m.** *½ D: Richard Horian. Eric Douglas, Marlon Jackson, Susan Scott, Richard Horian, Elizabeth Singer, Ronee Blakley. Boring dud about the problems of various students . . . one of whom is a former Playboy bunny. Douglas is the brother of Michael and son of Kirk; Jackson is the brother of Michael.▼

Student Connection, The (1975-Spanish) **C-92m.** *½ D: Rafael Romero Merchent. Ray Milland, Sylva Koscina, Ramon Oliveros, Maria Silva, Franco Ciacobini. Flat melodrama about a headmaster at a boys' school whose initial crime of passion (killing his mistress' husband) leads to a succession of murders when he learns that one of his students was an eyewitness.

Student Exchange (1987) **C-100m.** TVM D: Mollie Miller. Viveka Davis, Todd Field, Mitchell Anderson, Heather Graham, Maura Tierney, Gavin MacLeod, Moon Zappa. Usual Disney romp with a couple of high schoolers masquerading as ultrachic exchange students to fulfill their dreams of popularity. Lindsay Wagner,

Lisa Hartman, and O.J. Simpson do cameo bits. Average.

Student Nurses, The (1970) **C-89m.** **½ D: Stephanie Rothman. Elaine Giftos, Karen Carlson, Brioni Farrell, Barbara Leigh, Reni Santoni, Richard Rust. First of five "nurse" movies produced by Roger Corman (and, in fact, the first film made by his New World Pictures) is easily the best, with good cast, comparatively thoughtful script (cowritten by Rothman), along with expected sex and action; most interesting subplot concerns guilt by young activist nurse after she accidentally shoots a cop. Followed by PRIVATE DUTY NURSES.▼

Student Prince in Old Heidelberg, The (1927) **105m.** **** D: Ernst Lubitsch. Ramon Novarro, Norma Shearer, Jean Hersholt, Gustav von Seyffertitz, Philippe de Lacy, Edgar Norton, George K. Arthur, Edythe Chapman. Silent version of Sigmund Romberg's famed operetta has youthful prince Novarro breaking out of his cloistered life—for the first time—and attending Heidelberg University, where he falls in love with a commoner, pretty barmaid Shearer. This is Lubitsch at his best, an absolute delight from start to finish, and truly the kind of charmer "they just don't make anymore." Also known as OLD HEIDELBERG. Previously filmed in 1919; remade (with music) in 1954.

Student Prince, The (1954) **C-107m.** ** D: Richard Thorpe. Ann Blyth, Edmund Purdom, John Ericson, Louis Calhern, Edmund Gwenn. Romberg music, dubbed voice of Mario Lanza chief assets in venerable operetta about heir to throne sent to Heidelberg for one last fling, where he falls in love with barmaid Blyth. Filmed before (sans music) in 1919 and 1927.

Student Teachers, The (1973) **C-79m.** **½ D: Jonathan Kaplan. Susan Damante, Brooke Mills, Bob Harris, John Cramer, Dick Miller, Don Steele, Robert Phillips, Charles Dierkop. Antics at Valley High School, with both feminist and "alternate learning center" concepts mixed into the usual sexploitation package. Freewheeling direction by Kaplan; followed by SUMMER SCHOOL TEACHERS.▼

Student Tour (1934) **87m.** *½ D: Charles F. Reisner. Jimmy Durante, Charles Butterworth, Maxine Doyle, Phil Regan, Florine McKinney, Betty Grable, Herman Brix (Bruce Bennett). Deservedly obscure MGM musical about college students on world tour with an incredibly clunky leading lady. Pretty bad, though it's fun to see young Grable, and the sight of coeds swimming in front of the Taj Mahal is nothing to sneeze at. Guest star Nelson Eddy sings silly Bolero-type number "The Carlo."

Studs Lonigan (1960) **95m.** **½ D: Irving Lerner. Christopher Knight, Frank Gorshin, Venetia Stevenson, Carolyn Craig,

Jack Nicholson, Dick Foran. Interesting if not altogether successful adaptation of James T. Farrell's "notorious" novel about a restless, sexually active young man in 1920s Chicago. Good period atmosphere, but script makes unfortunate compromises with 1960 taste and censorship. Nicholson is one of Studs' cronies; Foran is impressive as Studs' father. Scripted and produced by Philip Yordan. Basis for a 1979 TV miniseries.▼

Study in Scarlet, A (1933) 70m. **½ D: Edward L. Marin. Reginald Owen, Anna May Wong, June Clyde, Alan Dinehart, John Warburton, Alan Mowbray, Warburton Gamble. Not-bad low-budget Sherlock Holmes outing (for which Owen wrote much of the dialogue), though it has virtually nothing to do with Conan Doyle story of the same name! Owen played Dr. Watson one year earlier in SHERLOCK HOLMES, while Mowbray, who's Inspector LeStrade here, turned up as villainous Col. Moran in the 1946 TERROR BY NIGHT.▼

Study in Terror, A (1965-British) **C-94m.** *** D: James Hill. John Neville, Donald Houston, Georgia Brown, John Fraser, Anthony Quayle, Barbara Windsor, Robert Morley, Cecil Parker, Frank Finlay, Kay Walsh. Compact little thriller pits Sherlock Holmes against Jack the Ripper; violent, well-paced, and well-cast. For another version of Holmes vs. the Ripper, see MURDER BY DECREE.▼

Stuff, The (1985) **C-93m.** **½ D: Larry Cohen. Michael Moriarty, Andrea Marcovicci, Garrett Morris, Paul Sorvino, Scott Bloom, Danny Aiello, James Dixon, Alexander Scourby, Russell Nype, Brian Bloom, Rutanya Alda. The new dessert sensation that's sweeping the country turns out to be deadly stuff indeed. Typically slapdash Larry Cohen production has some engaging performances, and the spirit of silly '50s science-fiction films, but doesn't always come off—as horror *or* comedy. It *does* have its moments, however—and a bunch of familiar "Commercial Spokespersons."▼

Stunt Man, The (1980) **C-129m.** **** D: Richard Rush. Peter O'Toole, Steve Railsback, Barbara Hershey, Chuck Bail, Allen Goorwitz (Garfield), Adam Roarke, Alex Rocco, Sharon Farrell, Philip Bruns. An outrageous black comedy in which reality and make-believe blur. Fugitive Railsback stumbles onto a movie set, where he accidentally causes the death of their ace stunt man; director O'Toole offers to hide him from the police—if he'll replace the stunt man. Crammed with first-rate action and sly wit, plus a mesmerizing performance by O'Toole as the Christ-like Eli Cross. Attention must be paid, but the rewards are more than ample. Dazzlingly scripted (by Lawrence Marcus) and directed; amus-

ing score by Dominic Frontiere. Filmed in 1978.▼

Stunt Pilot (1939) 62m. ** D: George Waggner. John Trent, Marjorie Reynolds, Milburn Stone, Jason Robards, Sr., Pat O'Malley. Not-bad "Tailspin Tommy" tale has him joining a movie studio as a flyer, encountering danger and murder.▼

Stunts (1977) **C-89m.** **½ D: Mark L. Lester. Robert Forster, Fiona Lewis, Joanna Cassidy, Darrell Fetty, Bruce Glover, James Luisi. When a stunt man dies while making a film, his brother (Forster) takes his place in order to probe the "accident." Engaging B movie with terrific action scenes and a wild helicopter-and-car finale. Retitled WHO IS KILLING THE STUNTMEN?▼

Stunt Seven (1979) **C-100m.** TVM D: John Peyser. Christopher Connelly, Christopher Lloyd, Bill Macy, Peter Haskell, Elke Sommer, Patrick Macnee. Pilot film to a never-made-it series about an intrepid team of stunt experts who battle for law and order. Average.

Stunts Unlimited (1980) **C-78m.** TVM D: Hal Needham. Glenn Corbett, Susanna Dalton, Sam Jones, Chip (Christopher) Mayer, Alejandro Rey. Former US intelligence agent Corbett recruits three Hollywood stunt performers to help recover a stolen laser gun in this formula pilot to a prospective series. Skimpy storyline provides padding between stuntman-turned-director Needham's bag of tricks. Average.

St. Valentine's Day Massacre, The (1967) **C-100m.** **½ D: Roger Corman. Jason Robards, Jr., George Segal, Ralph Meeker, Jean Hale, Clint Ritchie, Frank Silvera, Joseph Campanella, Bruce Dern. This had the makings of a good film, but they blew it, with Robards (as Al Capone) and Segal (doing a Jimmy Cagney imitation) overacting as they've never done before. So much shooting throughout film that final massacre seems tame by comparison. Many familiar faces appear throughout: Harold Stone, Kurt Krueger, Milton Frome, Mickey Deems, John Agar, Reed Hadley, Alex D'Arcy, etc. Pay close attention and you'll see Jack Nicholson, too!▼

Sub-A-Dub-Dub SEE: **Hello Down There**

Subject Was Roses, The (1968) **C-107m.** *** D: Ulu Grosbard. Patricia Neal, Jack Albertson, Martin Sheen, Don Saxon, Elaine Williams, Grant Gordon. Frank D. Gilroy's Pulitzer Prize-winning play about young veteran's strained relationship with his parents makes a generally good film. This was Neal's first film after her near fatal stroke. Sheen and Oscar-winner Albertson recreated their Broadway roles. Gilroy adapted his own play for the screen.

Submarine Alert (1943) 67m. ** D: Frank McDonald. Richard Arlen, Wendy Barrie, Nils Asther, Roger Pryor, Abner Biberman,

Marc Lawrence, Dwight Frye. The old yarn about the fed who's made to look like he is banished by the force so that he can join the gang as a spy. If this is a little better than most of Arlen's quickies, it's because the cast is more interesting than usual, and the plot borrows heavily from THE 39 STEPS.

Submarine Command (1951) 87m. **½ D: John Farrow. William Holden, Nancy Olson, William Bendix, Don Taylor. Predictable but acceptable post-WW2 account of naval military life; Olson is wholesome love interest.

Submarine D-1 (1937) 98m. **½ D: Lloyd Bacon. Pat O'Brien, George Brent, Wayne Morris, Frank McHugh, Doris Weston, Henry O'Neill, Regis Toomey, Broderick Crawford. Medium-grade Warner Bros. action hokum about loving and fighting among the crew of a new submarine. Well-made documentary-like scenes mix with the contrived plot. Incidentally, Ronald Reagan was originally in the film's cast but wound up on the cutting room floor.

Submarine Patrol (1938) 95m. **½ D: John Ford. Richard Greene, Nancy Kelly, Preston Foster, George Bancroft, Slim Summerville, John Carradine. Routine actioner with tough captain Greene revitalizing beat-up Splinter Fleet ship and demoralized crew for duty in WW1.

Submarine X-1 (1968-British) C-89m. **½ D: William Graham. James Caan, Rupert Davies, David Summer, William Dysart, Norman Bowler. After losing submarine in battle with German ship, naval officer Caan gets second chance in daring raid with midget subs. Standard WW2 fare.

Subterfuge (1969-British) C-92m. ** D: Peter Graham Scott. Gene Barry, Joan Collins, Richard Todd, Suzanna Leigh, Michael Rennie. American agent Barry is forced into helping British Intelligence in this routine espionage drama.▼

Subterraneans, The (1960) C-89m. **½ D: Ranald MacDougall. Leslie Caron, George Peppard, Janice Rule, Roddy McDowall, Anne Seymour, Jim Hutton, Scott Marlowe. Glossy, superficial study of life and love among the beatniks, with pure cornball stereotype performances; MGM was not the studio for this one. Script by Robert Thom, from the Jack Kerouac novel. Music by Andre Previn, who also appears on screen along with such jazz artists as Gerry Mulligan, Carmen McRae, Art Pepper, Art Farmer, Shelly Manne.

Suburbia SEE: **Wild Side, The**▼

Subway (1985-French) C-104m. ** D: Luc Besson. Isabelle Adjani, Christopher Lambert, Richard Bohringer, Michel Galabru, Jean-Hugues Anglade. Dripping in new wave style and attitude, this (literally) underground fable, set in the Paris métro,

where various lives intertwine, is utterly aimless and pointless. Intrigues and amuses at first, and then just runs out of steam. ▼

Subway in the Sky (1959-German) 85m. *½ D: Muriel Box. Van Johnson, Hildegarde Neff, Katherine Kath, Cec Linder, Albert Lieven, Edward Judd. Flabby caper of soldier Johnson in post-WW2 Berlin, involved in the black market; terrible waste of Neff's talents.

Subway to the Stars (1987-Brazilian) C-103m. **½ D: Carlos Diegues. Guilherme Fontes, Milton Goncalves, Taumaturgo Ferreira, Ze Trindade, Ana Beatriz Wiltgen. Gritty, grim account of young sax player Fontes and his experiences as he roams the back streets of Rio in search of his missing girlfriend. Has its moments of insight, but overall too meandering.▼

Success, The (1963-Italian) 103m. *** D: Dino Risi. Vittorio Gassman, Anouk Aimee, Jean-Louis Trintignant. Intelligent delineation by Gassman as businessman overwhelmed by success urge makes this drama worthy.

Success (1979) SEE: **American Success Company, The**

Success at Any Price (1934) 75m. *** D: J. Walter Ruben. Douglas Fairbanks, Jr., Genevieve Tobin, Frank Morgan, Colleen Moore, Edward Everett Horton, Allen Vincent. Interesting moral tract tracing the rise and fall of ruthless businessman Fairbanks as he crushes everyone who gets in his way—and loses sight of the one woman who loves him. Surprisingly contemporary, and still potent, though it reveals its stage origins.

Successful Calamity, A (1932) 72m. **½ D: John G. Adolfi. George Arliss, Mary Astor, Evalyn Knapp, Grant Mitchell, David Torrence, William Janney, Hardie Albright, Randolph Scott, Leon Waycoff (Ames). Wealthy world figure returns home after almost a year of traveling, anxious to spend time with his family—only to find them all too concerned with themselves to give him more than a passing nod. Ever-so-slight Arliss comedy hews strictly to formula, but it's a formula that works, and Arliss is charming as always.

Success Is the Best Revenge (1984-British) C-90m. **½ D: Jerzy Skolimowski. Michael York, Joanna Szerbic, Michael Lyndon, George Skolimowski, Michel Piccoli, Anouk Aimee, John Hurt. Intriguing if uneven yarn about a Polish director (York) in exile in London and his rebellious teen son (Lyndon), who is anxious to explore his heritage. Skolimowski—himself an exile—explores the meaning of living in a country other than one's own, but he fared better with previous film, MOONLIGHTING.▼

Such a Gorgeous Kid Like Me (1973-French) C-98m. ***½ D: François Truffaut.

[1119]

Bernadette Lafont, Claude Brasseur, Charles Denner, Guy Marchand, Philippe Leotard. Delightful black comedy of female murderer who relates her sordid past to criminology student, gradually entices him just as she did her former "victims." Lafont ideal in leading role.

Such Good Friends (1971) C-100m. *** D: Otto Preminger. Dyan Cannon, James Coco, Jennifer O'Neill, Ken Howard, Nina Foch, Laurence Luckinbill, Louise Lasser, Burgess Meredith, Sam Levene. Tart black comedy about man going to hospital, prompting wife (Cannon) to reexamine their relationship and learn about his romantic sideline activities. Fine ensemble acting buoys acidly funny script (by Elaine May, who used a pseudonym); from the Lois Gould novel.

Sucker Money (1933) 62m. *½ D: Dorothy Reid, Melville Shyer. Mischa Auer, Phyllis Barrington, Earl McCarty, Ralph Lewis, Mae Busch. The title is the best thing about this dull crime drama, with Auer cast as a phony swami who bilks unsuspecting rich folk out of their money.▼

Sudan (1945) C-76m. ** D: John Rawlins. Maria Montez, Jon Hall, Turhan Bey, Andy Devine, George Zucco, Robert Warwick. Queen Montez escapes evil prime minister Zucco with help of Hall and Bey in colorful but empty adventure-romance. Montez and Hall's last film together.

Sudden Danger (1955) 85m. *½ D: Hubert Cornfield. Bill Elliott, Tom Drake, Beverly Garland, Lucien Littlefield, Minerva Urecal, Lyle Talbot, Frank Jenks. Bland hunt-the-murderer-tale.

Sudden Fear (1952) 110m. *** D: David Miller. Joan Crawford, Jack Palance, Gloria Grahame, Bruce Bennett, Touch (Mike) Connors, Virginia Huston. Wealthy playwright Crawford discovers new husband Palance (an actor whom she once fired) is planning to kill her; she uses her writing skills to concoct a scheme to make him trip himself up. Solid suspense thriller with many neat twists.

Sudden Impact (1983) C-117m. **½ D: Clint Eastwood. Clint Eastwood, Sondra Locke, Pat Hingle, Bradford Dillman, Paul Drake, Jack Thibeau, Albert Popwell. Fourth DIRTY HARRY vehicle relies on durable formula, as maverick cop gives us vicarious pleasure of doing in society's scum, but this entry is longer, and sillier, than need be. Locke plays a woman taking out murderous revenge on men (and one lesbian!) who raped her and her sister years ago. Followed by THE DEAD POOL.▼

Suddenly (1954) 77m. ***½ D: Lewis Allen. Frank Sinatra, Sterling Hayden, James Gleason, Nancy Gates, Willis Bouchey, Kim Charney, Paul Frees, Christopher Dark, Charles Smith. Sinatra leads trio of paid assassins who take over house in small town where the President will pass on his way to a fishing trip. White-knuckle thriller, written by Richard Sale, with Sinatra excellent in thoroughly detestable role; rest of cast equally fine. "Suddenly," incidentally, is the name of the town. Also shown in computer-colored version.▼

Suddenly, It's Spring (1947) 87m. ** D: Mitchell Leisen. Paulette Goddard, Fred MacMurray, Macdonald Carey, Arleen Whelan, Lillian Fontaine. Strained comedy about married couple Goddard and MacMurray refusing to divorce each other.

Suddenly, Last Summer (1959) 114m. ***½ D: Joseph L. Mankiewicz. Elizabeth Taylor, Katharine Hepburn, Montgomery Clift, Mercedes McCambridge, Albert Dekker. Fascinating if talky Tennessee Williams yarn about wealthy Southern matriarch (Hepburn), her supposedly mad niece (Taylor) and a neurosurgeon (Clift); grandly acted. Adaptation by Gore Vidal.▼

Suddenly, Love (1978) C-100m. TVM D: Stuart Margolin. Cindy Williams, Paul Shenar, Linwood Boomer, Eileen Heckart, Joan Bennett, Lew Ayres, Kurt Kasznar. Glossy Ross Hunter-produced soap opera involving the unlikely relationship of a plain girl from the ghetto and a socially prominent attorney. It's all updated *Helen Trent*. Average.

Suddenly Single (1971) C-73m. TVM D: Jud Taylor. Hal Holbrook, Barbara Rush, Margot Kidder, Agnes Moorehead, Michael Constantine, Harvey Korman, Cloris Leachman. Fair mix of comedy and drama, marred by a questionable finale: young-ish pharmacist Holbrook, divorced by his wife, tries to make it in the singles world. Average.

Sudden Terror (1970-British) C-95m. ** D: John Hough. Mark Lester, Lionel Jeffries, Susan George, Tony Bonner, Jeremy Kemp. Adequate variation on boy-who-cried-wolf theme: prankish youngster (Lester) witnesses murder of visiting black dignitary, but can't convince others. Almost ruined by self-conscious direction. Good cast, though. Originally titled EYEWITNESS.▼

Suez (1938) 104m. *** D: Allan Dwan. Tyrone Power, Loretta Young, Annabella, Henry Stephenson, Maurice Moscovich, Joseph Schildkraut, Sidney Blackmer, J. Edward Bromberg, Sig Ruman, Nigel Bruce, Miles Mander, George Zucco, Leon Ames. Power is 19th-century French architect (and dreamer) Ferdinand de Lesseps, who pursues a single-minded goal of building the Suez Canal; his real problem is choosing between aristocratic Loretta and down-to-earth Annabella. Entertaining and elaborate hokum which apparently bears no resemblance to history.

Sugarbaby (1985-German) C-87m. **½

D: Percy Adlon. Marianne Sägebrecht, Eisi Gulp. It's love at first sight for chubby mortuary attendant Sägebrecht and subway-train driver Gulp in this droll romantic satire. Players and story are offbeat, but the avant-garde lighting effects and camera movements by cinematographer Johanna Heer become annoying. Remade as BABYCAKES for American TV.▼

Sugar Cane Alley (1984-French) **C-107m.** ***½ D: Euzhan Palcy. Darling Legitimus, Garry Cadenat, Routa Seck, Joby Bernabe, Francisco Charles. Beautifully made, heartfelt drama about an 11-year-old boy and his all-sacrificing grandmother, surviving in a Martinique shantytown during the 1930s. Rich, memorable characterizations; a humanist drama of the highest order.▼

Sugarfoot (1951) **C-80m.** **½ D: Edwin L. Marin. Randolph Scott, Adele Jergens, Raymond Massey, S. Z. Sakall, Arthur Hunnicutt. Above-par Scott Western. Randy is ex-Rebel officer who encounters his old adversary in Arizona. Retitled: SWIRL OF GLORY.

Sugar Hill (1974) **C-91m.** ** D: Paul Maslansky. Marki Bey, Robert Quarry, Don Pedro Colley, Richard Lawson, Betty Anne Rees, Zara Cully. Bey stars as "Sugar" Hill, who avenges the mob's rubout of her fiance, conjuring up black zombies from the grave. Outlandish blend of blaxploitation, revenge, and voodoo/horror elements. Cut to 83m. for TV and retitled THE ZOMBIES OF SUGAR HILL.

Sugarland Express, The (1974) **C-109m.** ***½ D: Steven Spielberg. Goldie Hawn, Ben Johnson, Michael Sacks, William Atherton. Perfect entertainment, based on fact, about a young fugitive couple fleeing with their child (whom they refuse to give up for adoption), and the cops who pursue them throughout Texas. Spielberg's first theatrical feature, written by Hal Barwood and Matthew Robbins.▼

Suicide Battalion (1958) **79m.** BOMB D: Edward L. Cahn. Michael Connors, John Ashley, Jewell Lain, Russ Bender. Static WW2 non-actioner. Army duo goes on mission to destroy government records hidden in building basement at Pearl Harbor.

Suicide Commando (1969-Italian) **C-94m.** *½ D: Camillo Bazzoni. Aldo Ray, Pamela Tudor, Gaetano Cimarosa, Luis Davila, Manuel Zarzo. Familiar war heroics with beefy Ray leading five man team in wreaking wholesale havoc on German airfield, paving way for D-Day landing.

Suicide Mission (1956-Norwegian) **70m.** ** D: Michael Forlong. Leif Larsen. Michael Aldridge, Atle Larsen, Per Christensen. Standard WW2 actioner, set in Norway.

Suicide Run SEE: **Too Late the Hero**▼
Suicide Squadron SEE: **Dangerous Moonlight**

Suicide's Wife, The (1979) **C-100m. TVM** D: John Newland. Angie Dickinson, Gordon Pinsent, Zohra Lampert, Todd Lookinland, Peter Donat. Undemanding drama about a woman's struggle to rebuild her life after her professor husband takes his. Also known as A NEW LIFE. Average.

Sullivans, The (1944) **111m.** *** D: Lloyd Bacon. Anne Baxter, Thomas Mitchell, Selena Royle, Ward Bond, Bobby Driscoll, Addison Richards. Patriotic drama from true story of five brothers serving during WW2 whose devotion to each other took precedence over all else. They are played by Edward Ryan, John Campbell, James Cardwell, John Alvin, and George Offerman, Jr. Well-acted film is unrelentingly sad. Also titled THE FIGHTING SULLIVANS.

Sullivan's Empire (1967) **C-91m.** **½ D: Harvey Hart, Thomas Carr. Martin Milner, Clu Gulager, Karen Jensen, Linden Chiles, Don Quine, Arch Johnson. Unconvincing adventure yarn of rich landowner's trio of sons searching for father, whose plane crashed in South American jungle.

Sullivan's Travels (1941) **91m.** **** D: Preston Sturges. Joel McCrea, Veronica Lake, Robert Warwick, William Demarest, Eric Blore, Robert Greig, Jimmy Conlin, Al Bridge, Franklin Pangborn, Porter Hall. Tired of making fluff, movie director McCrea decides to do a "serious" film; to research it, he sets out with 10¢ in his pocket to experience life in "the real world." Slapstick and sorrow blend seamlessly in this landmark Hollywood satire, which grows more pertinent with each passing year. A unique achievement for writer-director Sturges.▼

Summer (1986-French) **96m.** ***½ D: Eric Rohmer. Marie Riviere, Lisa Heredia, Vincent Gauthier, Beatrice Romand, Carita. Sensitive but whiny Riviere, abandoned by friends on the eve of a group vacation, goes it alone with initially lonely results. Seemingly more improvised than the other Rohmers, this demands viewer patience and some tolerance of Riviere's "difficult" personality, but patience is rewarded. Finale is quite moving, in what emerges as one of the director's better efforts, from his series "Comedies and Proverbs."▼

Summer and Smoke (1961) **C-118m.** ***½ D: Peter Glenville. Geraldine Page, Laurence Harvey, Una Merkel, John McIntire, Pamela Tiffin, Rita Moreno, Thomas Gomez, Earl Holliman, Casey Adams, Lee Patrick. Spinster Page is in love with young doctor Harvey, but he's understandably not interested; vivid adaptation of Tennessee Williams play, set in 1916 in small Mississippi town, with torrid performances making up for frequent staginess. Atmospheric score by Elmer Bernstein.

[1121]

Summer Camp Nightmare (1987) **C-87m.** *½ D: Bert L. Dragin. Chuck Connors, Charles Stratton, Adam Carl, Harold Pruett, Melissa Brennan, Tom Fridley, Nancy Calabrese. Synthetic update of LORD OF THE FLIES has young Fascist Stratton staging a small-scale revolution by having kids take over two adjoining summer camps, imprisoning the adults. Stratton is good in a difficult role, but plot gimmicks fail to convince, especially the kids' quickie descent into barbarism. Based on William Butler's novel *The Butterfly Revolution.* ▼

Summer City (1976-Australian) **C-83m.** ** D: Christopher Fraser. John Jarratt, Mel Gibson, Phil Avalon, Steve Bisley, James Elliot, Debbie Forman. Slight, low-budget rock 'n roll road movie detailing the escapades of four buddies who head out of Sydney for a surfing weekend. The shy, quiet one is played by Mel Gibson—it's his screen debut. ▼

Summer Fantasy (1984) **C-100m. TVM** D: Noel Nosseck. Julianne Phillips, Ted Shackelford, Michael Gross, Dorothy Lyman, Paul Keenan, Danielle von Zerneck. Curvy teenage coed decides to pass up medical school for fun in the California sun as the first female lifeguard on a beach where all the hunks are. A dumb sun-and-sand flick for bikini watchers. Below average. ▼

Summer Girl (1983) **C-100m. TVM** D: Robert Michael Lewis. Barry Bostwick, Kim Darby, Martha Scott, Murray Hamilton, Millie Slavin, Diane Franklin. Live-in baby-sitter alienates the kids from mommy and then goes about seducing daddy. Suspense drama is done in by ho-hum acting and so-so script written by A. J. Crothers from Caroline Crane's novel. Produced by one-time actress Roberta Haynes (RETURN TO PARADISE). Below average.

Summer Heat (1987) **C-90m.** ** D: Michie Gleason. Lori Singer, Anthony Edwards, Bruce Abbott, Kathy Bates, Clu Gulager. How soon will sultry farm wife Singer, neglected by husband Edwards, succumb to the charms of hired hand Abbott? Not long enough for you to want to sit through this bore. Summer Heat, indeed . . . ▼

Summer Holiday (1948) **C-92m.** **½ D: Rouben Mamoulian. Mickey Rooney, Walter Huston, Frank Morgan, Agnes Moorehead, Butch Jenkins, Selena Royle, Marilyn Maxwell, Gloria De Haven, Anne Francis. Lavish musical remake of AH, WILDERNESS! with Rooney (who played the younger brother in 1935) as the young man coming of age. Extremely good-looking film, with exquisite use of Technicolor, but dramatically unexceptional—and not nearly as good as the earlier film.

Summer Holiday (1963-British) **C-107m.** *½ D: Peter Yates. Cliff Richard, Lauri Peters, David Kossoff, Ron Moody, The Shadows, Melvyn Hayes, Una Stubbs, Teddy Green, Jeremy Bulloch. Richard, Hayes, Green, and Bulloch travel through Europe on a bus in this silly musical; inauspicious directorial debut by Yates.

Summer Interlude SEE: **Illicit Interlude**▼

Summer Love (1958) **85m.** ** D: Charles Haas. John Saxon, Molly Bee, Rod McKuen, Judi Meredith, Jill St. John. Sequel to ROCK, PRETTY BABY has Saxon, et al hired to perform at summer resort camp; perky performances.

Summer Lovers (1982) **C-98m.** ** D: Randal Kleiser. Peter Gallagher, Daryl Hannah, Valerie Quennessen, Barbara Rush, Carole Cook. This one's a matter of tolerance: Any movie that makes you think seriously about having a *menage a trois* on a Greek island can't be all bad, but here's a film that's on an even lower intellectual level than you'd *expect* from the director of GREASE and THE BLUE LAGOON. Bouncy rock soundtrack. ▼

Summer Magic (1963) **C-100m.** **½ D: James Neilson. Hayley Mills, Burl Ives, Dorothy McGuire, Deborah Walley, Eddie Hodges, Darren McGavin, Una Merkel. Disney's rehash of MOTHER CAREY'S CHICKENS has McGuire as widow who raises family on a shoestring in rambling Maine house. Pleasant but forgettable. ▼

Summer Night, with Greek Profile, Almond Eyes and Scent of Basil (1987-Italian) **C-94m.** *½ D: Lina Wertmuller. Mariangela Melato, Michele Placido, Roberto Herlipzka, Massimo Wertmuller. Melato's presence, in a sexual cat-and-mouse tale, might lead one to expect another SWEPT AWAY, but this is light years removed: a relentlessly heavy-handed comedy about a rich, sexy Italian capitalist who abducts a notorious terrorist and tries to give him a taste of his own medicine . . . until she finds herself attracted to him. This "night" seems like it will never end!▼

Summer of Fear SEE: **Stranger in Our House**▼

Summer of '42 (1971) **C-102m.** *** D: Robert Mulligan, Jennifer O'Neill, Gary Grimes, Jerry Houser, Oliver Conant, Katherine Allentuck, Christopher Norris, Lou Frizell. Enticing if unprofound nostalgia by Herman Raucher about teenager Grimes with crush on young war bride O'Neill. Captures 1940s flavor, adolescent boyhood, quite nicely. Michel Legrand won an Oscar for his popular score. Followed by CLASS OF '44.▼

Summer of Innocence SEE: **Big Wednesday**▼

Summer of My German Soldier (1978) **C-100m. TVM** D: Michael Tuchner. Kristy McNichol, Bruce Davison, Esther Rolle, Michael Constantine, Barbara Barrie. Bittersweet romance of a Jewish teenager and an escaped Nazi POW in a small Georgia town during WW2. Loving if occasionally oversentimental, with an Emmy Award-winning performance by Esther Rolle as the family housekeeper. Jane-Howard Hammerstein adapted Bette Greene's novel. Above average.▼

Summer of '64 SEE: **Girls on the Beach, The**

Summer Place, A (1959) **C-130m.** *** D: Delmer Daves. Richard Egan, Dorothy McGuire, Sandra Dee, Arthur Kennedy, Troy Donahue, Constance Ford, Beulah Bondi. Lushly photographed (by Harry Stradling) soaper of adultery and teenage love at resort house on Maine coast. Excellent Max Steiner score (the theme was a big hit); based on the Sloan Wilson novel.▼

Summerplay SEE: **Illicit Interlude**▼

Summer Rental (1985) **C-88m.** **½ D: Carl Reiner. John Candy, Karen Austin, Richard Crenna, Rip Torn, John Larroquette, Richard Herd, Lois Hamilton, Carmine Caridi. Breezy, low-key comedy about a working stiff's refusal to let some arrogant fat cats spoil his family's vacation in Florida. Candy proves he can be endearing in a realistic characterization—and still be funny.▼

Summer School (1987) **C-98m.** **½ D: Carl Reiner. Mark Harmon, Kirstie Alley, Robin Thomas, Dean Cameron, Gary Riley, Shawnee Smith, Courtney Thorne-Smith. Harmon is delinquent high school teacher forced to spend his vacation trying to educate group of delinquent students. Not bad as these films go: decent acting, OK pacing, some good laughs . . . with extra chuckles for fans of TEXAS CHAINSAW MASSACRE and those movie-critic TV shows. Director Reiner has a cameo as Harmon's predecessor.▼

Summer School Teachers (1975) **C-87m.** ** D: Barbara Peeters. Candice Rialson, Pat Anderson, Rhonda Leigh-Hopkins, Dick Miller. Well-paced, episodic film of three girls' romantic adventures while teaching high school. A followup to THE STUDENT TEACHERS.▼

Summer Stock (1950) **C-109m.** *** D: Charles Walters, Judy Garland, Gene Kelly, Eddie Bracken, Marjorie Main, Gloria De Haven, Phil Silvers, Hans Conried. Kelly's theater troupe takes over Judy's farm, she gets show biz bug. Thin plot, breezy Judy, frantic Silvers, chipper De Haven. Judy sings "Get Happy," Kelly dances on newspapers.▼

Summer Storm (1944) **106m.** *** D: Douglas Sirk. George Sanders, Linda Darnell, Edward Everett Horton, Sig Ruman, Anna Lee, Sarah Padden, Frank Orth. Darnell has one of her best roles as beautiful woman who brings tragedy to all involved with her, including herself; from Chekhov's story *The Shooting Party*.

Summer Story, A (1988-British) **C-95m.** *** D: Piers Haggard. Imogen Stubbs, James Wilby, Ken Colley, Sophie Ward, Susannah York, Jerome Flynn. Beautifully made romantic drama, circa 1902, set and filmed entirely in rural southwestern England. Young London lawyer Wilby and farm girl Stubbs fall deeply in love; he soon must make decisions of the mind and heart that could change their lives forever. The two leads are superb. Penelope Mortimer adapted John Galsworthy's story "The Apple Tree."▼

Summertime (1955) **C-99m.** ***½ D: David Lean. Katharine Hepburn, Rossano Brazzi, Isa Miranda, Darren McGavin, Mari Aldon, Andre Morell. Lilting film of spinster vacationing in Venice, falling in love with married man. Hepburn's sensitive portrayal is one of her best. Screenplay by Lean and H.E. Bates, from Arthur Laurents' play *The Time of the Cuckoo*. Beautifully filmed on location by Jack Hildyard.▼

Summertime Killer (1973-French-Italian-Spanish) **C-109m.** ** D: Antonio Isasi. Karl Malden, Christopher Mitchum, Raf Vallone, Claudine Auger, Olivia Hussey. Varied cast in OK revenge meller about a man pursuing his father's murderers. Lots of action, if not much continuity.

Summer to Remember, A (1985) **C-100m.** TVM D: Robert Lewis. James Farentino, Tess Harper, Louise Fletcher, Burt Young, Molly Cheek, Bridgette Anderson, Sean Justin Gerlis. Warmhearted comedy-drama about a deaf child and his friendship with an orangutan with which he has established a relationship through sign language. Young actor Gerlis has been deaf since birth. Average.▼

Summertree (1971) **C-88m.** ** D: Anthony Newley. Michael Douglas, Jack Warden, Brenda Vaccaro, Barbara Bel Geddes, Kirk Callaway, Bill Vint. Highly acclaimed (if overrated) off-Broadway play by Ron Cowen fails as a film; Douglas plays a young music student who clashes with parents over Vietnam War.▼

Summer Wishes, Winter Dreams (1973) **C-93m.** *** D: Gilbert Cates. Joanne Woodward, Martin Balsam, Sylvia Sidney, Dori Brenner, Ron Rickards. Sensitive character study of frigid woman (Woodward) obsessed by her childhood, upset by her own aloofness towards others; Balsam equally good as understanding husband.▼

Summer with Monika (1952-Swedish) **96m.** ***½ D: Ingmar Bergman. Harriet Andersson, Lars Ekborg, John Harryson, Georg Skarstedt, Dagmar Ebbesen, Ake Gronberg. A brief affair between two working-class youngsters, aggressive Andersson and boyish Ekborg, results in the birth of their baby and marriage. Simple storyline has been filmed before and since, but rarely with such sensitivity. Also known as MONIKA.▼

Summer Without Boys, A (1973) C-74m. TVM D: Jeannot Szwarc. Barbara Bain, Kay Lenz, Michael Moriarty. Entertaining melodrama about WW2 era triangle affair, from daughter's (Lenz) point of view; she and her mother are competing for same young man. Good performances. Average.

Sun Also Rises, The (1957) C-129m. *** D: Henry King. Tyrone Power, Ava Gardner, Errol Flynn, Mel Ferrer, Gregory Ratoff, Robert Evans, Juliette Greco, Eddie Albert. Hemingway story of expatriates in Parisian 1920s has slow stretches; worthwhile for outstanding cast, especially Flynn as a souse. Mexico City locations add flavor to tale of search for self-identity. Remade (poorly) for TV.

Sun Also Rises, The (1984) C-200m. TVM D: James Goldstone. Jane Seymour, Hart Bochner, Robert Carradine, Zeljko Ivanek, Ian Charleson, Leonard Nimoy, Stephane Audran. Flashy but flat remake of Hemingway tale, audaciously augmented (Nimoy's character is new, among others) by producer Robert L. Joseph, who claimed that this is the way Papa would have wanted it written for television! Best is French cinematographer Jacques Robin's loving explorations of France, Spain, and Jane Seymour. Originally shown in two parts. Below average.

Sun and the Moon, The (1987) C-97m. *½ D: Kevin Conway. Mila Burnette, Joaquim de Almeida, Maria Norman, Kevin Conway, Jose Ferrer. Chic Manhattanite Burnette, fed up with her lifestyle (and cheating husband), moves in with relatives in the South Bronx (described as "the capital of Puerto Rico"), where she organizes tenants and becomes involved with de Almeida. There's the germ of a serious film here, but the result is slight, silly, frustrating. Originally titled THE VIOLINS CAME WITH THE AMERICANS.

Sunbonnet Sue (1945) 89m. ** D: Ralph Murphy. Gale Storm, Phil Regan, George Cleveland, Minna Gombell, Edna Holland, Raymond Hatton. Programmer musical of the Gay 90s enhanced by bouncy Storm in title role, as songstress in father's lower N.Y.C. saloon.

Sunburn (1979) C-94m. **½ D: Richard C. Sarafian. Farrah Fawcett-Majors, Charles Grodin, Art Carney, Joan Collins, Alejandro Rey, William Daniels. Insurance investigator Grodin has Farrah pose as his wife in order to crack a murder/suicide case in Acapulco. Sloppily made film benefits from appealing performances. Eleanor Parker, Keenan Wynn, and John Hillerman get costarring billing but barely appear at all.▼

Sun Comes Up, The (1949) C-93m. ** D: Richard Thorpe. Jeanette MacDonald, Lloyd Nolan, Claude Jarman, Jr., Lewis Stone, Dwayne Hickman. Colorful but overly sentimental story of young orphan and embittered widow who blames her son's dog, Lassie, for his death. MacDonald's last film.

Sunday, Bloody Sunday (1971-British) C-110m. *** D: John Schlesinger. Glenda Jackson, Peter Finch, Murray Head, Peggy Ashcroft, Tony Britton, Maurice Denham, Bessie Love. Glenda loves Murray, but Peter loves Murray, too. Murray loves both, in very good, adult script by Penelope Gilliatt. Schlesinger's direction less forceful than usual, also less effective. Head's bland portrayal offsets brilliant work by Jackson and Finch. A mixed bag. Look for Daniel Day-Lewis as a young vandal.▼

Sunday Dinner for a Soldier (1944) 86m. *** D: Lloyd Bacon. Anne Baxter, John Hodiak, Charles Winninger, Anne Revere, Chill Wills, Bobby Driscoll, Jane Darwell. Winning film of family that invites soldier to dinner; they are repaid for their kindness; enjoyable comedy-drama.

Sunday Drive (1986) C-100m. TVM D: Mark Cullingham. Tony Randall, Carrie Fisher, Ted Wass, Audra Lindley, Hillary Wolf, Raffi DiBlasio, Norman Alden. Disney comedy involving six people and a rambunctious canine in a mix-up brought about by identical autos. Bring back Fred MacMurray and Flubber! Average.

Sunday in New York (1963) C-105m. *** D: Peter Tewksbury. Cliff Robertson, Jane Fonda, Rod Taylor, Robert Culp, Jim Backus. Entire cast bubbles in this Norman Krasna sex romp of virginal Fonda discovering N.Y.C. and love. Peter Nero's score is perky.

Sunday in the Country, A (1984-French) C-94m. ***½ D: Bertrand Tavernier. Louis Ducreux, Sabine Azema, Michel Aumont, Genevieve Mnich, Monique Chaumette, Claude Winter. An elderly widowed French impressionist who never quite made the grade indulges in title gathering with offspring who never quite fulfilled his expectations. Painterly, lovingly acted drama owes not a little to Jean Renoir's A DAY IN THE COUNTRY and is no less affecting for that. Among the best imports of the mid-1980s.▼

Sunday Lovers (1980) C-127m. *½ D: Bryan Forbes, Edouard Molinaro, Dino Risi, Gene Wilder. Roger Moore, Lynn Redgrave, Priscilla Barnes, Lino Ventura, Robert Webber, Ugo Tognazzi, Sylva Koscina, Gene Wilder, Kathleen Quinlan. Love and sex in four countries. British segment, with Moore, is old-hat farce. French vignette, with Ventura, is intriguing but doesn't go anywhere. Italian skit is broadly funny at times. American con-

tribution, written by, directed by, and starring Wilder, is a pretentious fable of a sanitarium patient, and embarrassingly bad.
Sundays and Cybele (1962-French) **110m.** ***½ D: Serge Bourguignon. Hardy Kruger, Nicole Courcel, Patricia Gozzi, Daniel Ivernel. Intelligently told account of shell-shocked Kruger finding source of communication with the world via orphaned waif Gozzi, with tragic results. Splendidly realized, Oscar winner as Best Foreign Language Film.▼
Sunday Too Far Away (1975-Australian) **C-95m.** *** D: Ken Hannam. Jack Thompson, John Ewart, Reg Lyle. The rivalries and problems of macho sheep shearers, focusing on gutsy Thompson, a champion of his trade. Simple and solid.▼
Sunday Woman, The (1976-Italian) **C-110m.** *** D: Luigi Comencini. Marcello Mastroianni, Jacqueline Bisset, Jean-Louis Trintignant, Aldo Reggiani, Pino Caruso. Detective Mastroianni investigates murder among idle rich in Torino, falls in love with wealthy Bisset. Good whodunit makes interesting observation about social structure.
Sundown (1941) **90m.** **½ D: Henry Hathaway. Gene Tierney, Bruce Cabot, George Sanders, Harry Carey, Joseph Calleia, Dorothy Dandridge, Reginald Gardiner. Tierney is surprisingly cast as native girl who assists British troops in Africa during WW2; fairly interesting, lushly photographed by Charles Lang, but it never scores. Also shown in computer-colored version.▼
Sundowners, The (1950) **C-83m.** **½ D: George Templeton. Robert Preston, Cathy Downs, Robert Sterling, John Barrymore, Jr., Jack Elam. Tightly edited Western about brothers fighting on opposite sides of the law.▼
Sundowners, The (1960) **C-113m.** **** D: Fred Zinnemann. Deborah Kerr, Robert Mitchum, Peter Ustinov, Glynis Johns, Dina Merrill, Chips Rafferty, Michael Anderson, Jr., Lola Brooks, Wylie Watson, Mervyn Johns. First-rate film of Australian family whose lives are devoted to sheepherding. Entire cast excellent, Kerr especially fine. Isobel Lennart adapted Jon Cleary's novel. Wonderfully filmed on location by Jack Hildyard.▼
Sunflower (1970-Italian) **C-101m.** ** D: Vittorio De Sica. Sophia Loren, Marcello Mastroianni, Ludmilla Savelyeva, Anna Carena. Weak love story of woman who searches for her lost lover. Sophia is wasted in this soppy tale.
Sun Never Sets, The (1939) **98m.** **½ D: Rowland V. Lee. Douglas Fairbanks, Jr., Basil Rathbone, Barbara O'Neil, Lionel Atwill, Virginia Field, C. Aubrey Smith. Enjoyable patriotic drama of British brothers trying to prevent outbreak of war in Africa. Well done, with top-notch cast.

Sunny (1941) **98m.** **½ D: Herbert Wilcox. Anna Neagle, Ray Bolger, John Carroll, Edward Everett Horton, Paul & Grace Hartman, Helen Westley. New Orleans society scion Carroll falls in love with circus performer Neagle; pleasant enough musical but nothing special. Bolger's dancing is the real treat. Jerome Kern/Oscar Hammerstein/Otto Harbach score includes "Who?" Filmed before in 1930 with Marilyn Miller.
Sunnyside (1979) **C-100m.** *½ D: Timothy Galfas. Joey Travolta, John Lansing, Stacey Pickren, Andrew Rubin, Michael Tucci, Talia Balsam, Joan Darling. John Travolta's brother made bid for stardom in this cliché-ridden picture about a street kid who wants to end local gang warfare and leave that life behind. Sorry, Joey.▼
Sunny Side of the Street (1951) **C-71m.** *½ D: Richard Quine. Frankie Laine, Terry Moore, Jerome Courtland, Audrey Long. Moore has fickle notions over aspiring Laine in this low-grade musical, with guest stars such as Billy Daniels, Toni Arden.
Sunny Side Up (1929) **115m.** *** D: David Butler. Janet Gaynor, Charles Farrell, El Brendel, Marjorie White, Joe Brown, Frank Richardson, Jackie Cooper. Charming antique, quite impressive for early-talkie musical. Fluffy story of tenement girl Gaynor falling in love with wealthy Farrell sufficient excuse for DeSylva-Brown-Henderson songs: "I'm a Dreamer," "If I Had a Talking Picture of You," title tune, and bizarre production number to "Turn on the Heat."▼
Sunrise (1927) **110m.** **** D: F. W. Murnau. George O'Brien, Janet Gaynor, Bodil Rosing, Margaret Livingston, J. Farrell MacDonald. Exquisite silent film is just as powerful today as when it was made, telling simple story of farmer who plans to murder his wife, led on by another woman. Triumph of direction, camerawork, art direction, and performances, all hauntingly beautiful. Screenplay by Carl Mayer, from Hermann Suderman's story. Cinematographers Karl Struss and Charles Rosher won Oscars, as did the film for "artistic quality of production," Gaynor also won Best Actress Oscar (shared for her performances in SEVENTH HEAVEN and STREET ANGEL). Remade in Germany as THE JOURNEY TO TILSIT.▼
Sunrise at Campobello (1960) **C-143m.** *** D: Vincent J. Donehue. Ralph Bellamy, Greer Garson, Hume Cronyn, Jean Hagen, Ann Shoemaker, Alan Bunce, Tim Considine, Zina Bethune, Frank Ferguson, Lyle Talbot. Sincere story of President Franklin Delano Roosevelt, his battle in politics and valiant struggle against polio. Well acted; Bellamy (in his Tony-winning stage role) and Garson ARE Mr. and Mrs.

Roosevelt. Script by Dore Schary, from his hit play.▼

Sunset (1988) **C-107m.** *½ D: Blake Edwards. Bruce Willis, James Garner, Malcolm McDowell, Mariel Hemingway, Jennifer Edwards, Kathleen Quinlan, Patricia Hodge, Richard Bradford, M. Emmet Walsh, Joe Dallesandro. Cowboy star Tom Mix (Willis) joins forces with legendary marshal Wyatt Earp (Garner) to solve a serpentine whodunit involving the seamier side of Tinseltown. Appallingly abysmal murder-mystery set in late 1920s Hollywood; unpleasant and unbelievable from the word go. Willis registers zero playing one of movie's most magnetic stars, while Garner saves this piece of junk from being a total BOMB with his effortless charisma.▼

Sunset Boulevard (1950) **110m.** **** D: Billy Wilder. Gloria Swanson, William Holden, Erich von Stroheim, Fred Clark, Jack Webb, Hedda Hopper, Buster Keaton, Cecil B. DeMille, Anna Q. Nilsson, Nancy Olson. Legendary Hollywood black comedy about faded silent-film star Norma Desmond (Swanson), living in the past with butler (von Stroheim), who shelters hack screenwriter (Holden) as boyfriend. Bitter, funny, fascinating; Gloria's tour de force. Three Oscars include Best Screenplay (Wilder, Charles Brackett, D.M. Marshman, Jr.) and Score (Franz Waxman).▼

Sunset Cove (1978) **C-87m.** *½ D: Al Adamson. Jay B. Larson, Karen Fredrik, John Carradine, John Durren, Burr Schmidt. Condominium developers want to build on a strip of beach now inhabited by the usual teen crowd—who decide to fight for their rights in court. Bubbleheaded fare for bikini watchers.

Sunset Limousine (1983) **C-100m. TVM** D: Terry Hughes. John Ritter, Susan Dey, Lainie Kazan, Martin Mull, Paul Reiser, George Kirby, Louise Sorel, Martin Short. Breezy comedy about an aspiring stand-up comic who moonlights as a limo driver and finds himself in dutch with a couple of hired killers. Ritter's charm keeps things bubbling nicely. Scripted by Dick Clement and Ian LaFrenais. Above average.▼

Sunshine (1973) **C-130m. TVM** D: Joseph Sargent. Cristina Raines, Cliff De-Young, Brenda Vaccaro, Meg Foster, Bill Mumy, Lindsay Greenbush. Penetrating character studies of non-Establishment couple and the woman's doctor in story of terminal cancer case. Deliberately slow pacing, flashback approach hampers lead performances. Songs by John Denver. Sequel: SUNSHINE CHRISTMAS. Average.

Sunshine Boys, The (1975) **C-111m.** *** D: Herbert Ross. Walter Matthau, George Burns, Richard Benjamin, Lee Meredith, Carol Arthur, Howard Hesseman, Ron Rifkin, Fritz Feld, Jack Bernardi, F. Murray Abraham. Two cranky ex-vaudevillians are persuaded to reteam for a TV special in this popular Neil Simon comedy, from his Broadway play. Some of the "humor" is abrasive, but Matthau and Oscar-winning Burns are masters at work. This was George's first starring film role since HONOLULU in 1939.▼

Sunshine Christmas (1977) **C-100m. TVM** D: Glenn Jordan. Cliff DeYoung, Barbara Hershey, Pat Hingle, Eileen Heckart, Elizabeth Cheshire, Meg Foster. Well-made sequel to SUNSHINE and the subsequent short-lived TV series. Charming, sincerely acted tale of how long-widowed DeYoung takes his adopted daughter Cheshire to meet his parents for Christmas and then falls in love with his childhood sweetheart. Above average.

Sunshine Patriot, The (1968) **C-98m. TVM** D: Joseph Sargent. Cliff Robertson, Dina Merrill, Luther Adler, Wilfrid Hyde-White, Antoinette Bower, Lilia Skala. Identity switch only way master spy can get out of sticky situation behind Iron Curtain and bring crucial microfilm to superiors. Fair suspense in gimmicky spy tale, but film doesn't take advantage of basic premise. Look for Donald Sutherland in his first TV movie. Average.

Sun Shines Bright, The (1953) **92m.** *** D: John Ford. Charles Winninger, Arleen Whelan, John Russell, Stepin Fetchit, Milburn Stone, Russell Simpson. This was director Ford's favorite film, a picaresque remake of JUDGE PRIEST with Winninger involved in political contest in small Southern town. Fine array of Ford regulars in character roles.▼

Sun Valley Serenade (1941) **86m.** *** D: H. Bruce Humberstone. Sonja Henie, John Payne, Glenn Miller, Milton Berle, Lynn Bari, Joan Davis, Dorothy Dandridge, The Nicholas Brothers. Light musicomedy with Henie a war refugee, Payne her foster parent, traveling with the Miller band and manager Berle to Sun Valley. Songs: "It Happened In Sun Valley," "Chattanooga Choo-Choo."

Superchick (1973) **C-94m.** ** D: Ed Forsyth. Joyce Jillson, Louis Quinn, Thomas Reardon, Tony Young, John Carradine, Uschi Digard, Mary Gavin (Candy Samples). Silly but harmless drive-in fodder has Jillson (better known as an astrologer) as blonde, free-loving stewardess (juggling boy friends in several cities) who's so desirable she adopts a mousey brunette disguise to get her work done.▼

Super Cops, The (1974) **C-94m.** ***½ D: Gordon Parks. Ron Leibman, David Selby, Sheila Frazier, Pat Hingle, Dan Frazer. Fast, funny, tough telling of the exploits of the Batman and Robin team of David Greenberg (Leibman) and Robert

Hantz (Selby) who used unorthodox methods to stop the drug market in Brooklyn's black Bedford-Stuyvesant area. Filmed on location, with Greenberg and Hantz in bits.

Superdad (1974) **C-96m.** BOMB D: Vincent McEveety. Bob Crane, Kurt Russell, Barbara Rush, Joe Flynn, Kathleen Cody, Dick Van Patten. Disney generation gap comedy is superbad. Crane competes with daughter's fiancé in effort to prove future son-in-law worthy.▼

Superdome (1978) **C-100m.** TVM D: Jerry Jameson. David Janssen, Edie Adams, Ken Howard, Van Johnson, Donna Mills, Jane Wyatt, Peter Haskell, Clifton Davis, Tom Selleck, Bubba Smith, Dick Butkus. Flyweight thriller that looks like a road-company TWO-MINUTE WARNING as a silent killer stalks New Orleans at Super Bowl time, terrifying a stellar TV roster. Average.

Super Dude SEE: **Hangup**

Superfly (1972) **C-96m.** *** D: Gordon Parks Jr. Ron O'Neal, Carl Lee, Sheila Frazier, Julius W. Harris, Charles Mc-Gregor. Morally dubious but undeniably exciting tale of Harlem drug dealer out for the last killing before he quits the business. Film was accused of glorifying drug pushers. Benefits from excellent Curtis Mayfield score. Sequel: SUPERFLY T.N.T.▼

Superfly T.N.T. (1973) **C 87m.** BOMB D: Ron O'Neal. Ron O'Neal, Roscoe Lee Browne, Sheila Frazier, Jacques Sernas, William Berger, Roy Bosier. Confused, sloppily constructed and executed B film about black ex-drug pusher, dissatisfied with idyllic existence in Europe, deciding to aid official from African country (Browne). Followed years later by THE RETURN OF SUPERFLY.

Super Fuzz (1981-U.S.-Italian) **C-94m.** *½ D: Sergio Corbucci. Terence Hill, Ernest Borgnine, Joanne Dru, Marc Lawrence, Julie Gordon, Lee Sandman. Rookie Miami cop Hill is exposed to radiation, gains superpowers and takes on mobster Lawrence. Pretty poor, including the special effects. Also known as SUPER-SNOOPER. Originally 106m.▼

Supergirl (1984-British) **C-114m.** *½ D: Jeannot Szwarc. Faye Dunaway, Helen Slater, Peter O'Toole, Peter Cook, Brenda Vaccaro, Mia Farrow, Simon Ward, Marc McClure, Hart Bochner, Maureen Teefy. This comic-book movie is a superdrag: long, dull, heavy-handed. Slater is cute but bland in title role; Dunaway is a predictably campy villainess.▼

Supergrass, The (1985-British) **C-105m.** ** D: Peter Richardson. Adrian Edmondson, Jennifer Saunders, Peter Richardson, Dawn French, Keith Allen, Nigel Planer, Robbie Coltrane. To impress a girl, Edmondson innocently brags that he's a big-time drug dealer—much to his regret. Inoffensive comedy.▼

Superman (1978) **C-143m.** ***½ D: Richard Donner. Christopher Reeve, Margot Kidder, Marlon Brando, Gene Hackman, Ned Beatty, Jackie Cooper, Marc McClure, Glenn Ford, Valerie Perrine, Phyllis Thaxter, Jeff East, Trevor Howard, Susannah York. Dynamic, grandly entertaining saga of the Man of Steel, tracing his life from Krypton to Smallville to Metropolis, mixing equal parts sincerity, special effects (which earned a special Oscar), and send-up. Great fun. The network TV version added 49m. of outtakes—including cameos by Noel Neill and Kirk Alyn as Lois Lane's parents. Followed by three sequels.▼

Superman II (1980) **C-127m.** *** D: Richard Lester. Christopher Reeve, Margot Kidder, Gene Hackman, Ned Beatty, Jackie Cooper, Valerie Perrine, Susannah York, Clifton James, E. G. Marshall, Marc McClure, Terence Stamp, Sarah Douglas, Jack O'Halloran. Screw the Superman legend, forget logic, and full speed ahead: that's the attitude of this flashy sequel, wherein three villains from Krypton, with powers just like Superman's, threaten the Earth—while Lois Lane and the Man of Steel fall in love. Full of great effects and entertainingly played, but lacking the sense of awe and wonder of the original film, adding cruelty and violence instead. Unreleased in U.S. until 1981.▼

Superman III (1983) **C-123m.** *½ D: Richard Lester. Christopher Reeve, Richard Pryor, Annette O'Toole, Jackie Cooper, Marc McClure, Annie Ross, Pamela Stephenson, Robert Vaughn, Margot Kidder. Appalling sequel trashes everything that Superman is all about for the sake of cheap laughs and a costarring role for Pryor, as computer operator who unwittingly gives villainous Vaughn a chance to conquer the Man of Steel. Director Lester's opening slapstick ballet is a funny setpiece, but doesn't belong in this movie. Network TV added 19m. of footage for its first showing.▼

Superman IV: The Quest for Peace (1987) **C-90m.** ** D: Sidney J. Furie. Christopher Reeve, Gene Hackman, Jackie Cooper, Marc McClure, Jon Cryer, Sam Wanamaker, Mark Pillow, Mariel Hemingway, Margot Kidder. Superman does his bit for world peace by ridding the globe of nuclear weapons—which inspires Lex Luthor to become a black-market arms profiteer. He also challenges Superman by creating Nuclear Man. Disappointing fantasy adventure is an improvement over III but still pretty ordinary, with second-rate special effects. Sincere performances help a lot. Reeve receives co-story credit on this one (along with 2nd unit directing).▼

Superman and the Mole Men (1951)

58m. ** D: Lee Sholem. George Reeves, Phyllis Coates, Jeff Corey, Walter Reed, J. Farrell MacDonald, Stanley Andrews. Reporters Clark Kent and Lois Lane go to small town to see the world's deepest oil well; instead, they discover that "mole men" have climbed out of the well, from their home at the center of the earth. This very low-budget feature served as a pilot for the long-running TV series, but it's more serious (and less fun) than the subsequent show—and we don't even get to see Superman fly! But it's still great to see Reeves as the Man of Steel.▼

Supernatural (1933) **60m. **½ D:** Victor Halperin. Carole Lombard, Randolph Scott, Vivienne Osborne, H. B. Warner, Beryl Mercer, William Farnum. Eerie tale of spirits taking over innocent people is farfetched; Lombard is film's highlight.

Supernaturals, The (1986) **C-85m.** BOMB D: Armand Mastroianni. Maxwell Caulfield, Talia Balsam, Bradford Bancroft, LeVar Burton, Bobby DiCicco, Scott Jacoby, Margaret Shendal, Nichelle Nichols. Ludicrous fantasy has butch drill sergeant Nichols (better known as Lt. Uhura on *Star Trek*) leading young troops on maneuvers, accidentally stumbling on Rebel ghosts from the Civil War who are seeking revenge. Boring tale has the production values of a home movie; never released theatrically.▼

Super Sleuth (1937) **70m. *** D:** Ben Stoloff. Jack Oakie, Ann Sothern, Edgar Kennedy, Eduardo Ciannelli, Joan Woodbury, Bradley Page. Inconsequential but very funny outing with Oakie as egocentric detective-movie star who tries to solve real-life mystery. Kennedy has plum supporting role as police detective. Remade as GENIUS AT WORK.

Supersnooper SEE: **Super Fuzz**▼

Support Your Local Gunfighter (1971) **C-92m. *** D:** Burt Kennedy. James Garner, Suzanne Pleshette, Jack Elam, Harry Morgan, John Dehner, Joan Blondell, Dub Taylor, Ellen Corby, Henry Jones, Marie Windsor, Dick Curtis, Chuck Connors, Grady Sutton. Engaging comedy-Western, not a sequel to SHERIFF despite director and cast. Con artist Garner tries to profit from mining dispute by passing off bumbling Elam as notorious gunslinger. Seemingly endless list of character actors adds sparkle, with Elam giving his most side-splitting performance as "Swifty" Morgan; his final line is a gem.

Support Your Local Sheriff! (1969) **C-93m. ***½ D:** Burt Kennedy. James Garner, Joan Hackett, Walter Brennan, Harry Morgan, Jack Elam, Bruce Dern, Henry Jones, Gene Evans, Dick Peabody. Delightful Western parody in which no-fisted Garner tames lawless town by using his wits, breaking all the rules—and kick-

ing virtually every Western cliché in the pants. Brennan is wonderful spoofing his Old Man Clanton character from MY DARLING CLEMENTINE, but Hackett's wealthy klutz, Elam's inept deputy, and Dern's bratty killer are also fine. Written and produced by William Bowers.▼

Suppose They Gave a War And Nobody Came? (1970) **C-113m. **½ D:** Hy Averback. Tony Curtis, Brian Keith, Ernest Borgnine, Suzanne Pleshette, Ivan Dixon, Bradford Dillman, Tom Ewell, Don Ameche, Arthur O'Connell, John Fiedler. Awful title obscures surprisingly strong satire about strained relations between redneck town and nearby Army base eventually reaching the breaking point. No real "good guys" in this unusual film; not without flaws, but certainly worth a look. Later ripped off by TANK. Retitled WAR GAMES for network TV.▼

Sure Thing, The (1985) **C-94m. **½ D:** Rob Reiner. John Cusack, Daphne Zuniga, Anthony Edwards, Boyd Gaines, Tim Robbins, Lisa Jane Persky, Viveca Lindfors, Nicollette Sheridan. Amusing film updates IT HAPPENED ONE NIGHT as two college students who don't get along find themselves traveling cross-country together. Utterly predictable, but cute.▼

Surf Party (1964) **68m.** BOMB D: Maury Dexter. Bobby Vinton, Jackie De Shannon, Patricia Morrow, Kenny Miller. Teenagers meet and mate in Malibu. Waterlogged.▼

Surf II (1984) **C-91m. *½ D:** Randall Badat. Eddie Deezen, Linda Kerridge, Cleavon Little, Peter Isaacksen, Lyle Waggoner, Eric Stoltz, Morgan Paull, Ruth Buzzi, Carol Wayne, Terry Kiser. Creditable cast washes ashore in 80s spoof of 70s gore films and 60s surfer films (with appropriate oldies on the soundtrack). Deezen's always good for a few laughs, but the film's best joke is its title: there never was a SURF I.▼

Surgeon's Knife, The (1957-British) **75m. ** D:** Gordon Parry. Donald Houston, Adrienne Corri, Lyndon Brook. Tepid drama of doctor Houston implicated in criminal negligence, becoming involved in murder.

Surprise Package (1960-British) **100m. **½ D:** Stanley Donen. Yul Brynner, Mitzi Gaynor, Barry Foster, Eric Pohlmann, Noel Coward, George Coulouris. Versatile Brynner tries screwball comedy, not doing too badly as devil-may-care gambler planning big-time robbery; Gaynor is sprightly leading lady. Script by Harry Kurnitz, from the Art Buchwald novel.

Surrender (1950) **90m. **½ D:** Allan Dwan. Vera Ralston, John Carroll, Walter Brennan, Francis Lederer, Jane Darwell, Jeff York. Ralston is exotic if overdramatic playing everyone against each other; Republic Pictures' nicely mounted costumer.

Surrender (1987) **C-95m.** ** D: Jerry Belson. Sally Field, Michael Caine, Steve Guttenberg, Peter Boyle, Jackie Cooper, Julie Kavner, Louise Lasser, Iman. Attractive cast injects little energy into this tired, familiar comedy about confused Field, oft-married Caine, and their complicated courtship. Even Caine's charm cannot save it. Scripted by the director.▼

Surrender—Hell! (1959) **85m.** ** D: John Barnwell. Keith Andes, Susan Cabot, Paraluman, Nestor de Villa. Predictable account of Andes rallying partisan forces to combat Japanese control of Philippines.

Surrogate, The (1984-Canadian) **C-95m.** **½ D: Don Carmody. Art Hindle, Carole Laure, Shannon Tweed, Michael Ironside, Jim Bailey, Marilyn Lightstone, Jackie Burroughs. Clever whodunit has handsome couple (Tweed and Hindle) reluctantly turning to sex surrogate Laure to help with their marital problems. Solid Canadian cast punches home contrived script in which nearly every character (including top female impersonator Bailey, as Tweed's best friend) appears to be a psychotic suspect.▼

Survival (1976) **C-85m.** ** D: Michael Campus. Barry Sullivan, Anne Francis, Sheree North, Chuck McCann, Otis Young. Intriguing psychodrama that talks itself to death. Elaborate dinner party evolves into parlor games where each guest must justify his existence, and all but two will be permanently eliminated by the vote of the others.

Survival Game (1987) **C-91m.** BOMB D: Herb Freed. Mike Norris, Deborah Goodrich, Seymour Cassel, Ed Bernard, Arlene Golonka. It's Norris (son of Chuck) to the rescue when his girlfriend and her dad are kidnapped. Pretty lame.▼

Survival of Dana (1979) **C-100m.** TVM D: Jack Starrett. Melissa Sue Anderson, Robert Carradine, Marion Ross, Talia Balsam, Judge Reinhold. Pretty high school coed moves to new town, falls in with wrong crowd; you've seen it all before. Video title: ON THE EDGE. Average.▼

Survival Run (1980) **C-90m.** *½ D: Larry Spiegel. Peter Graves, Ray Milland, Vincent Van Patten, Pedro Armendariz, Jr., Alan Conrad. Graves, Milland, and company stalk teenagers stranded in the desert. The object is murder; the film is dreadful.▼

Survive! (1976-Mexican) **C-86m.** *½ D: Rene Cardona, Jr. Pablo Ferrel, Hugo Stiglitz, Luz Maria Aguilar, Fernando Larranga, Norma Lazareno. Survivors of a South American plane crash are forced to cannibalize each other in order to stay alive. Based on a true incident, but do you really care?

Surviving (1985) **C-150m.** TVM D: Waris Hussein. Ellen Burstyn, Len Cariou, Zach Galligan, Marsha Mason, Molly Ringwald,

Paul Sorvino, River Phoenix, Heather O'Rourke, William Windom. Wrenching look at a teenage couple's suicide pact and its effect on their families. Well written by Joyce Eliason and well acted, though often on the edge of hysteria. Above average.

Survivors, The (1983) **C-102m.** ** D: Michael Ritchie. Walter Matthau, Robin Williams, Jerry Reed, James Wainwright, Kristen Vigard. Two disparate men lose their jobs and find their lives intertwined when they identify a robber and are told that they'll be "fixed." One (Williams) decides to arm himself to the teeth in this combination black comedy and social satire. Likable stars do their best with scattershot script credited to Michael Leeson.▼

Susana (1951-Mexican) **82m.** **½ D: Luis Buñuel. Rosita Quintana, Fernando Soler, Victor Manuel Mendoza, Matilde Palou. A voluptuous orphan of the storm, engagingly played by Quintana, undermines the loving fabric of the family that rescues her. Well-handled and staged by Buñuel, until the cop-out finale.▼

Susan and God (1940) **115m.** **½ D: George Cukor. Joan Crawford, Fredric March, Ruth Hussey, John Carroll, Rita Hayworth, Nigel Bruce, Bruce Cabot, Rose Hobart, Rita Quigley, Marjorie Main, Gloria De Haven. Crawford is satisfying as woman whose religious devotion loses her the love of her family. Gertrude Lawrence fared better on stage. Screenplay by Anita Loos, based on Rachel Crothers' play.

Susan Lenox: Her Fall and Rise (1931) **76m.** **½ D: Robert Z. Leonard. Greta Garbo, Clark Gable, Jean Hersholt, John Miljan, Alan Hale. A young woman flees from her loutish father—who wants to marry her off—and finds refuge with Gable, but circumstances keep them apart until the final clinch. Contrived melodrama made compelling by the ever-mesmerizing Garbo.

Susannah of the Mounties (1939) **78m.** **½ D: William A. Seiter. Shirley Temple, Randolph Scott, Margaret Lockwood, J. Farrell MacDonald, Moroni Olsen, Victor Jory. Mountie Scott raises orphan Shirley in this predictable but entertaining Temple vehicle. Also shown in computer-colored version.▼

Susan Slade (1961) **C-116m.** **½ D: Delmer Daves. Troy Donahue, Dorothy McGuire, Connie Stevens, Lloyd Nolan, Brian Aherne, Bert Convy, Kent Smith. Slick soaper, beautifully photographed by Lucien Ballard. McGuire pretends to be mother of daughter's (Stevens) illegitimate child. Donahue is Connie's true love.

Susan Slept Here (1954) **C-98m.** **½ D: Frank Tashlin. Dick Powell, Debbie Reynolds, Anne Francis, Glenda Farrell, Alvy Moore. Cutesy sex comedy filled with innuendoes, but little action; screenwriter

Powell agrees to keep an eye on high-spirited (to put it mildly) Reynolds.▼

Suspect, The (1944) **85m.** *****½** D: Robert Siodmak. Charles Laughton, Ella Raines, Dean Harens, Molly Lamont, Henry Daniell, Rosalind Ivan. Superb, Hitchcock-like thriller of henpecked Laughton planning to get his wife out of the way so he can pursue lovely Raines.

Suspect (1987) **C-121m.** ******* D: Peter Yates. Cher, Dennis Quaid, Liam Neeson, John Mahoney, Joe Mantegna, Philip Bosco, E. Katherine Kerr. Dedicated public defender (Cher) battles a nearly hopeless case, representing a deaf derelict accused of murder, with the unexpected help of one of her jurors (Quaid). Entertaining film manages to override its many implausibilities, with Cher turning in a fine and utterly believable performance.▼

Suspected Alibi SEE: **Suspended Alibi**▼

Suspended Alibi (1956-British) **64m.** ***½** D: Alfred Shaughnessy. Patrick Holt, Honor Blackman, Andrew Keir, Valentine Dyall. Holt becomes involved in homicide via circumstantial evidence in this coincidenceladen drama. Retitled: SUSPECTED ALIBI.▼

Suspense (1946) **101m.** ****** D: Frank Tuttle. Barry Sullivan, Belita, Albert Dekker, Bonita Granville, Eugene Pallette. Completely unsuspenseful story of ambitious heel (Sullivan) who makes time with married ice-skating star Belita. Some nice visual touches, but leaden pacing, *film noir* clichés, and such musical highlights as "Ice Cuba" make this heavy going. Opening shot is the best thing in the movie! Script by Philip Yordan.

Suspicion (1941) **99m.** *****½** D: Alfred Hitchcock. Cary Grant, Joan Fontaine, Cedric Hardwicke, Nigel Bruce, Dame May Whitty, Isabel Jeans, Heather Angel, Leo G. Carroll. Fontaine won Oscar for portraying wife who believes husband Grant is trying to kill her. Suspenser is helped by Bruce as Cary's pal, but finale (imposed by the Production Code) leaves viewer flat. Remade as a TVM. Also shown in computer-colored version.▼

Suspicion (1987-British) **C-90m.** TVM D: Andrew Greieve. Anthony Andrews, Jane Curtin, Jonathan Lynn, Michael Hordern, Betsy Blair. Disappointing scene-for-scene update of the classic Hitchcock thriller, with Curtin uncomfortably miscast. Below average.▼

Suspiria (1977-Italian) **C-92m.** ******* D: Dario Argento. Jessica Harper, Stefania Casini, Joan Bennett, Alida Valli, Flavio Bucci, Udo Kier. Terrifying tale of American student (Harper) attending European ballet school that turns out to be a witches' coven. Often dumb plot is enriched and overcome by brilliant camerawork, atmosphere, music score and performance (by Argento and rock group Goblin). May lose some of its chilling effectiveness on TV. Also available in uncut version.▼

Sutter's Gold (1936) **94m.** ****½** D: James Cruze. Edward Arnold, Lee Tracy, Binnie Barnes, Katharine Alexander, Addison Richards, Montagu Love, Harry Carey. Biography of Johan Sutter starts off well, bogs down midway through story. Arnold is always good, but he's fighting a mediocre script here. Look for Billy Gilbert as a Spanish general taken hostage.

Suzy (1936) **99m.** ****** D: George Fitzmaurice. Jean Harlow, Franchot Tone, Cary Grant, Lewis Stone, Benita Hume. Fine cast sinks in this soapy romantic spy drama set in WW1, with Grant as French flier who falls in love with Harlow. Brightest moment has Cary crooning "Did I Remember?"

Svengali (1931) **81m.** ******* D: Archie Mayo. John Barrymore, Marian Marsh, Donald Crisp, Carmel Myers, Bramwell Fletcher, Luis Alberni. Absorbing tale of artist's obsession with young girl, Trilby, who becomes singing artist under his hypnotic spell. Prime Barrymore in interesting production with bizarre sets by Anton Grot, memorable visual effects. Followed by THE MAD GENIUS.▼

Svengali (1955-British) **C-82.** ****½** D: Noel Langley. Hildegarde Neff, Donald Wolfit, Terence Morgan, Noel Purcell, Alfie Bass. Lacks flair of earlier version of du Maurier's novel about mesmerizing teacher and his beautiful actress-pupil Trilby.

Svengali (1983) **C-100m.** TVM D: Anthony Harvey. Peter O'Toole, Jodie Foster, Elizabeth Ashley, Larry Joshua, Pamela Blair, Barbara Byrne, Holly Hunter. O'Toole's outré performance as a faded musical star who takes young rock singer Foster under his wing makes this new version of the hoary tale watchable. Updated by Frank Cucci from George du Maurier's nearly one-hundred-year-old *Trilby*. Average.▼

Swamp Diamonds SEE: **Swamp Women**▼

Swamp Fire (1946) **69m.** ****** D: William Pine. Johnny Weissmuller, Virginia Grey, Buster Crabbe, Carol Thurston, Pedro DeCordoba, Marcelle Corday. Ex-navy man Weissmuller has lost his nerve; friends try to help him out.

Swamp Thing (1982) **C-91m.** ****½** D: Wes Craven. Louis Jourdan, Adrienne Barbeau, Ray Wise, David Hess, Nicholas Worth. Research scientist continues to love Barbeau from afar even after a chemical turns him into walking vegetation. This was better as a DC comic, though Jourdan's villainous camping in this sweet-natured monster pic is almost on a level with Vincent Price's standard routine. Followed by RETURN OF SWAMP THING and a TV series.▼

Swamp Water (1941) **90m.** ****½** D: Jean

Renoir. Dana Andrews, Walter Brennan, Anne Baxter, Walter Huston, Virginia Gilmore, John Carradine, Ward Bond, Guinn Williams, Eugene Pallette, Joe Sawyer, Mary Howard. Renoir's first American film is moody but erratic thriller set in the Okefenokee. Trapper Andrews finds fugitive Brennan hiding in the swamp, tries to clear him of murder rap without letting on that he knows the man's whereabouts. Powerhouse cast, handsome production, weakened by cornball dialogue and bizarre miscasting of Brennan. Remade as LURE OF THE WILDERNESS.

Swamp Women (1955) **C-73m.** *½ D: Roger Corman. Michael Connors, Marie Windsor, Beverly Garland, Carole Matthews, Susan Cummings. Heavy-handed nonsense of four female convicts escaping jail, chasing after buried loot. Retitled: SWAMP DIAMONDS; CRUEL SWAMP.▼

Swan, The (1956) **C-112m.** *** D: Charles Vidor. Grace Kelly, Alec Guinness, Louis Jourdan, Agnes Moorehead, Jessie Royce Landis, Brian Aherne, Leo G. Carroll, Estelle Winwood. Mild Molnar comedy of manners has attractive cast but not much sparkle. Jourdan good as Kelly's suitor, but she's promised to prince Guinness. Filmed before in 1925 and (as ONE ROMANTIC NIGHT) in 1930.

Swanee River (1939) **C-84m.** **½ D: Sidney Lanfield. Don Ameche, Al Jolson, Andrea Leeds, Felix Bressart, Russell Hicks. Bio of Stephen Foster where every song he writes is cued by a line of dialogue; clichés fill the movie, but it's fun on that level. Jolson is terrific as E.P. Christy; and the minstrel numbers are exceptionally well done.

Swann in Love (1984-French) **C-110m.** **½ D: Volker Schlondorff. Jeremy Irons, Ornella Muti, Alain Delon, Fanny Ardant, Marie-Christine Barrault, Nathalie Juvet. Lavish but lifeless telescoping of Proust's *Remembrance of Things Past* with Irons surprisingly stiff as French aristocrat obsessed with scandalous, lower-class Muti in 1885 Paris. Redeemed somewhat by the latter and Delon (as a homosexual baron), a sexy under-the-covers love scene, and Sven Nykvist photography.▼

Swan Song (1980) **C-105m. TVM** D: Jerry London. David Soul, Bo Brundin, Jill Eikenberry, Murray Hamilton, Leonard Mann, Slim Pickens, John van Dreelen. Once-promising downhill ski-racer aims at a comeback to shake stigma of being branded as a loser. Predictable drama boosted by breathtaking ski footage. Average.

Swap, The SEE: **Sam's Song**▼

Swarm, The (1978) **C-116m.** BOMB D: Irwin Allen. Michael Caine, Katharine Ross, Richard Widmark, Henry Fonda, Richard Chamberlain, Olivia de Havilland, Fred MacMurray, Ben Johnson, Lee Grant, Jose Ferrer, Patty Duke Astin, Slim Pickens, Bradford Dillman. This formula disaster film from Irwin Allen has no sting at all, succeeds only in wasting a lot of talented actors.▼

Swashbuckler (1976) **C-101m.** BOMB D: James Goldstone. Robert Shaw, James Earl Jones, Peter Boyle, Genevieve Bujold, Beau Bridges, Geoffrey Holder, Avery Schreiber, Anjelica Huston. Poorly constructed, bubble-headed picture—laced with kinky sex scenes—would make Errol Flynn turn over in his grave. Incredible waste of talent.

Swastika Savages SEE: **Hell's Bloody Devils**

Swedenhielms (1935-Swedish) **88m.** **½ D: Gustaf Molander. Gosta Ekman, Bjorn Berglund, Hakan Westergren, Tutta Rolf, Ingrid Bergman. Slow-moving but not uninteresting tale of poor but honorable scientist Rolf Swedenhielm (well acted by Ekman), who's up for the Nobel Prize, and his careless, childish offspring. Bergman, in her third feature, plays the wealthy fiancee of Swedenhielm's youngest son—and her star appeal is obvious.▼

Sweeney Todd, The Demon Barber of Fleet Street (1936-British) **68m.** ** D: George King. Tod Slaughter, Bruce Seton, Stella Rho, Eve Lister, Ben Soutten, D.J. Williams. Not many chills in this adaptation of the George Dibdin-Pitt play (later one of the sources for a Broadway musical *Sweeney Todd* by Stephen Sondheim), but it does contain a quintessential eye-rolling performance by Britain's master of grand guignol, Tod Slaughter, playing the sadistic barber who dumps his customers into the cellar and turns them into meat pies. Photographed by Ronald Neame. Not released in the U.S. until 1939.▼

Sweepings (1933) **80m.** ***½ D: John Cromwell. Lionel Barrymore, William Gargan, Gloria Stuart, George Meeker, Eric Linden, Gregory Ratoff. Compelling Edna Ferberish saga of self-made man who devotes his life to building giant department store, hoping that his four children will carry on his work. Fine acting, inventive direction and camerawork—plus montages by Slavko Vorkapich—make this something special. Remade as THREE SONS in 1939.

Sweet Adeline (1935) **87m.** **½ D: Mervyn LeRoy. Irene Dunne, Donald Woods, Hugh Herbert, Ned Sparks, Joseph Cawthorn, Louis Calhern, Winifred Shaw. Combination of spy chase and operetta isn't always smooth, but Kern-Hammerstein songs like "Why Was I Born" and Dunne's know-how make this enjoyable.

Sweet and Lowdown (1944) **75m.** ** D: Archie Mayo. Linda Darnell, Jack Oakie,

Lynn Bari, James Cardwell Allyn Joslyn, Dickie Moore. Thin story-line of Benny Goodman giving poor musician the big break, causing a rift with girlfriend Darnell.
Sweet Bird of Youth (1962) **C-120m.** ***½ D: Richard Brooks. Paul Newman, Geraldine Page, Shirley Knight, Ed Begley, Rip Torn, Mildred Dunnock, Madeleine Sherwood, Philip Abbott, Corey Allen. Tennessee Williams' play, cleaned up for the movies, still is powerful drama. Newman returns to Southern town with dissipated young queen Page, causing corrupt town "boss" Begley (who won an Oscar) to have him fixed proper. Glossy production with cast on top of material. Scripted by Brooks. Remade for TV.▼
Sweet Bird of Youth (1989) **C-100m.** TVM D: Nicolas Roeg. Elizabeth Taylor, Mark Harmon, Rip Torn, Valerie Perrine, Ruta Lee, Kevin Geer, Michael Wilding (Jr.). So-so version of Tennessee Williams' play about a faded movie star and her ambitious young lover, rewritten by Gavin Lambert (and reportedly based on Williams' own rethinking of the material). Earnest and watchable but lacks fire. Wilding, Taylor's son, has one long phone conversation with her but no face-to-face scenes. Average.
Sweet Body of Deborah, The (1969-Italian-French) **C-105m.** BOMB D: Romolo Guerrieri. Carroll Baker, Jean Sorel, Evelyn Stewart, Luigi Pistilli, Michel Bardinet. Convoluted soaper about murder, suicide, blackmail, and other sordid goings-on. This "body" really sags.
Sweet Charity (1969) **C-133m.** *** D: Bob Fosse. Shirley MacLaine, John McMartin, Ricardo Montalban, Sammy Davis, Jr., Chita Rivera, Paula Kelly, Stubby Kaye, Ben Vereen, Lee Roy Reams. Fine, overlooked adaptation of the Broadway musical written by Neil Simon, and based on Fellini's NIGHTS OF CABIRIA, about prostitute-with-heart-of-gold who falls in love with naive young man who doesn't know about her "work." Cy Coleman-Dorothy Fields score includes "Big Spender," "If They Could See Me Now," rousing "Rhythm of Life." Script by Peter Stone. Fosse's debut as film director. Home video version runs 20 minutes longer.▼
Sweet Country (1986) **C-150m.** BOMB D: Michael Cacoyannis. Jane Alexander, Franco Nero, Carole Laure, Joanna Pettet, Irene Papas, Randy Quaid, Jean-Pierre Aumont. Grueling, heavy-handed drama of a family's reactions to the 1973 Chilean revolution. Notable for idiotic miscasting (Laure and Pettet as Papas' daughters; Quaid as a lip-smacking, lecherous soldier named Raoul). Quite a comedown for ZORBA THE GREEK director Cacoyannis, who

includes tasteless sexploitation footage for good measure. Filmed in Greece.▼
Sweet Dreams (1985) **C-115m.** **½ D: Karel Reisz. Jessica Lange, Ed Harris, Ann Wedgeworth, David Clennon, James Staley, Gary Basaraba, P.J. Soles. Flavorful look at 1950s country singing star Patsy Cline can't escape déjà vu from so many other show-biz biopics. Focuses mainly on Cline's marriage to ne-er-do-well Harris, which also has a too-familiar ring. Made worthwhile by truly fine performances (including Wedgeworth as Patsy's mother) and a lot of wonderful music (Lange lip-syncs to Cline's original recordings).▼
Sweet Ecstasy (1962-French) **75m.** *½ D: Max Pecas. Elke Sommer, Pierre Brice, Christian Pezy, Claire Maurier. Silly soaper about life among the wealthy, beautiful, decadent, selfish young on the Riviera. Sommer is a cynical sexpot with an endless supply of false eyelashes.▼
Sweetheart of the Campus (1941) **67m.** **½ D: Edward Dmytryk. Ruby Keeler, Ozzie Nelson, Harriet Hilliard, Gordon Oliver, Don Beddoe, The Four Spirits of Rhythm, Kathleen Howard. Dancer Keeler and bandleader Ozzie start a nightclub on a college campus. Modest musical-comedy, nothing to write home about, but consistently peppy and surprisingly enjoyable.
Sweethearts (1938) **C-114m.** **½ D: W. S. Van Dyke II. Jeanette MacDonald, Nelson Eddy, Frank Morgan, Florence Rice, Ray Bolger, Mischa Auer. Enjoyable but overlong; Nelson and Jeanette are stage stars of Victor Herbert operetta who are manipulated by their producer (Morgan) into having a marital spat. Handsome color production filled with Herbert melodies. Cinematographer Oliver Marsh won an Oscar.▼
Sweet Heart's Dance (1988) **C-101m.** **½ D: Robert Greenwald. Don Johnson, Susan Sarandon, Jeff Daniels, Elizabeth Perkins, Kate Reid, Justin Henry, Holly Marie Combs, Heather Coleman. Comedy-drama, set in a small Vermont town, about the breakup of a marriage between two high-school sweethearts—just as their longtime friend is embarking on a serious relationship. Engaging cast, led by Johnson in a very appealing performance, but after a while you wish the two lead characters would just get on with it. Written by Ernest Thompson.▼
Sweet Hostage (1975) **C-93m.** TVM D: Lee Philips. Linda Blair, Martin Sheen, Jeanne Cooper, Lee DeBroux, Dehl Berti, Bert Remsen. Drama about an escaped psychopath and the illiterate farm girl he drags to a deserted cabin to become her teacher, friend and lover. Performances of Sheen and Blair almost make this talky

adaptation of Nathaniel Benchley's *Welcome to Xanadu* worthwhile. Average.▼

Sweetie (1989-Australian) **C-97m.** **½ D: Jane Campion. Genevieve Lemon, Karen Colston, Tom Lycos, Jon Darling, Dorothy Barry. New Zealander Campion's first feature is the offbeat account of an unbalanced, demanding young woman (Lemon), and her relationship with her weak, obsessive sister (Colston) and her parents. Some brilliant directorial touches, but too many sequences simply don't work. Unsettling, occasionally depressing, and decidedly not for all tastes.▼

Sweet Kill SEE: **Arousers, The**▼

Sweet Liberty (1986) **C-107m.** ** D: Alan Alda. Alan Alda, Michael Caine, Michelle Pfeiffer, Bob Hoskins, Lise Hilboldt, Lillian Gish, Saul Rubinek, Lois Chiles. Amiable but aimless comedy of college professor who becomes involved with a movie troupe as his historical novel is filmed. Ingratiating cast maintains some level of interest, with funny turns by Caine as a cocky leading man, and Hoskins as an eager-to-please screenwriter. But deep down inside, it's really shallow.▼

Sweet Lies (1986) **C-96m.** *½ D: Nathalie Delon. Treat Williams, Joanna Pacula, Julianne Phillips, Laura Manszky, Norbert Weisser, Bernard Fresson. Boring romantic comedy with Williams sorely miscast as an insurance-company detective involved in sexual shenanigans with a trio of women while on assignment in Paris.▼

Sweet Lorraine (1987) **C-91m.** *** D: Steve Gomer. Maureen Stapleton, Trini Alvarado, Lee Richardson, John Bedford Lloyd, Giancarlo Esposito, Edith Falco, Todd Graff, Evan Handler, Freddie Roman. The Lorraine is a cozy little Catskill hotel that's way past its prime; Stapleton is its proprietress, Alvarado her granddaughter who spends a summer working in its kitchen. There's a wealth of atmosphere and some sturdy characterizations in this warm, friendly, very personal slice-of-life sleeper.▼

Sweet Love, Bitter (1967) **92m.** *** D: Herbert Danska. Dick Gregory, Don Murray, Diane Varsi, Robert Hooks. Loosely based on Charlie "Bird" Parker, the legendary jazz musician, film is sometimes touching story of men on the skids.

Sweet Music (1935) **100m.** **½ D: Alfred E. Green. Rudy Vallee, Ann Dvorak, Helen Morgan, Ned Sparks, Alice White, Allen Jenkins. Minor but satisfactory Warners musical offers Vallee as a bandleader romancing singer Dvorak in an attempt to sign her to a contract. Good songs and an excellent supporting cast.

Sweet November (1968) **C-114m.** **½ D: Robert Ellis Miller. Sandy Dennis, Anthony Newley, Theodore Bikel, Burr DeBenning, Sandy Baron, Marj Dusay,

Martin West. Kooky Dennis takes a new lover every month, helping insecure men find confidence, then sending them away; her plans go awry when one of them (Newley) insists on marrying her. Some touching moments in this likable (if implausible) comedy-drama by Herman Raucher.

Sweet Revenge (1977) **C-90m.** BOMB D: Jerry Schatzberg. Stockard Channing, Sam Waterston, Franklin Ajaye, Richard Doughty. Public defender Waterston falls in love with a car thief (Channing) in this turkey, originally called DANDY, THE ALL-AMERICAN GIRL.

Sweet Revenge (1984) **C-100m.** TVM D: David Greene. Kevin Dobson, Kelly McGillis, Alec Baldwin, Savannah Smith, Wings Hauser, Alfre Woodard, Helen Hunt, Dana Elcar. Well acted but far-fetched psychological drama about a woman's vengeance on cold-blooded army officer who done her soldier brother and her wrong when she was a young girl. Average.

Sweet Revenge (1987) **C-78m.** *½ D: Mark Sobel. Nancy Allen, Ted Shackelford, Martin Landau, Sal Landi, Michele Little. Limp programmer with TV journalist Allen kidnapped by a white slavery ring. Plays like a bad TV show.▼

Sweet Ride, The (1968) **C-110m.** *½ D: Harvey Hart. Tony Franciosa, Michael Sarrazin, Jacqueline Bisset, Bob Denver, Michael Wilding, Michele Carey, Warren Stevens. Absurd claptrap about a tennis bum, a surfer and a beautiful girl; some of the Malibu scenery is nice.

Sweet Rosie O'Grady (1943) **C-74m.** **½ D: Irving Cummings. Betty Grable, Robert Young, Adolphe Menjou, Reginald Gardiner, Virginia Grey, Phil Regan. Pleasant musical of ex-burlesque star and exposé reporter. Menjou steals film as editor of Police Gazette. Previously filmed as LOVE IS NEWS; remade again as THAT WONDERFUL URGE.

Sweet 16 (1981) **C-90m.** ** D: Jim Sotos. Bo Hopkins, Susan Strasberg, Don Stroud, Dana Kimmell, Aleisa Shirley, Don Shanks, Steve Antin, Logan Clarke, Patrick Macnee, Michael Pataki, Larry Storch, Henry Wilcoxon, Sharon Farrell. Standard terror film (with good cast) set in Texas about a rash of murders occurring as Shirley's 16th birthday approaches. Identity of the vengeful murderer is quite predictable; integration of a racial prejudice (persecuting Indians) subplot doesn't work. Hopkins plays his slightly slow-witted Southern sheriff role for the umpteenth time.▼

Sweet Smell of Success (1957) **96m.** ***½ D: Alexander Mackendrick. Burt Lancaster, Tony Curtis, Marty Milner, Sam Levene, Barbara Nichols, Susan Harrison, Chico Hamilton. Searing Clifford Odets–Ernest

Lehman script about ruthless, all-powerful columnist J. J. Hunsecker (Lancaster) and a smarmy press agent (Curtis) who'll do anything to curry his favor. Vivid performances, fine jazz score by Elmer Bernstein, outstanding camerawork by James Wong Howe that perfectly captures N.Y.C. nightlife.▼

Sweet Sugar (1972) **C-90m.** **½ D: Michel Levesque. Phyllis Elizabeth Davis, Ella Edwards, Pamela Collins, Cliff Osmond, Timothy Brown. Entertaining women's prison film spotlights statuesque Davis slogging away in the sugar cane fields until the inevitable breakout. Reissued as CHAINGANG GIRLS.▼

Sweet Sweetback's Baadasssss Song (1971) **C-97m.** *** D: Melvin Van Peebles. Melvin Van Peebles, Rhetta Hughes, Simon Chuckster, John Amos. Van Peebles produced, directed, financed, wrote, scored, and stars in this angry, violent, reverse-racist blaxploitation drama as a superstud who runs, runs, runs from the police. Visually exciting, surprisingly effective. Controversial (and X-rated) when first released.▼

Sweet, Sweet Rachel (1971) **C-73m. TVM** D: Sutton Roley. Alex Dreier, Stefanie Powers, Pat Hingle, Louise Latham, Brenda Scott, Steve Ihnat, John Hillerman. Wide-eyed, out-of-breath "thriller" pits ESP expert against unseen presence trying to drive beautiful women crazy. Sloppy direction all but ruins fascinating premise. Pilot for *The Sixth Sense* series. Average.

Sweet Violent Tony SEE: **Cuba Crossing** ▼

Sweet William (1980-British) **C-92m.** **½ D: Claude Whatham. Sam Waterston, Jenny Agutter, Anna Massey, Geraldine James, Daphne Oxenford, Rachel Bell, Arthur Lowe, Tim Pigott-Smith. Waterston is charming as an erratic ALFIE-like bigamist who seduces Agutter in this OK entertainment.▼

Swept Away . . . by an unusual destiny in the blue sea of August (1975-Italian) **C-116m.** **** D: Lina Wertmuller. Giancarlo Giannini, Mariangela Melato. A slovenly sailor is cast adrift on an island with his employer, a rich, selfish woman. Cut off from society, he reverses their roles, stripping her of pride and vanity, and controlling her completely. This fascinating and provocative adult film put writer-director Wertmuller on the map in this country.▼

Swimmer, The (1968) **C-94m.** ***½ D: Frank Perry. Burt Lancaster, Janet Landgard, Janice Rule, Tony Bickley, Marge Champion, Bill Fiore, Kim Hunter, Joan Rivers. Middle-aged man swims from pool to pool on journey home during hot afternoon; each pool evokes past moments and events. Fascinating, vastly underrated film adapted from John Cheever short story; Lancaster is superb, and location filming in Connect-

icut perfectly captures mood. Script by Eleanor Perry.▼

Swimming to Cambodia (1987) **C-87m.** *** D: Jonathan Demme. Spalding Gray talks for nearly an hour and a half—about life in general, and about his experiences in Cambodia, where he spent some time while appearing in a minor role in THE KILLING FIELDS. There is no reason why a lengthy monologue should become such a fascinating film—but it does, thanks to Gray's storytelling skills, and Demme's artful (and subtle) direction. An unusual and rewarding experience.▼

Swimsuit (1989) **C-100m. TVM** D: Chris Thomson. William Katt, Catherine Oxenberg, Cyd Charisse, Nia Peeples, Tom Villard, Billy Warlock, Jack Wagner. Painless romp that has a fledgling ad executive searching for the perfect model to represent a foundering swimsuit company. With a title like this, you know what to expect. Average.

Swim Team (1979) **C-92m** *½ D: James Polakoff. James Daughton, Stephen Furst, Richard Young, Jenny Neumann, guest star Buster Crabbe. Can the Whalers reverse their seven-year losing streak as a swim team? Can you sit through this terrible movie to find out?▼

Swindle, The (1955-Italian) **92m.** ** D: Federico Fellini. Broderick Crawford, Giulietta Masina, Richard Basehart, Franco Fabrizi. Minor Fellini, with cast far better than story: a trio of crooks fleece people in Rome, each planning for a better life. Original title: IL BIDONE.▼

Swinger, The (1966) **C-81m.** ** D: George Sidney. Ann-Margret, Tony Franciosa, Robert Coote, Horace McMahon, Nydia Westman. Brassy, artificial yarn of good-girl Ann-Margret posing as swinger to impress girlie magazine editor Franciosa.

Swing Fever (1944) **80m.** *½ D: Tim Whelan. Kay Kyser, Marilyn Maxwell, William Gargan, Lena Horne. Most uneven blend of music, boxing, and romance pegged on personality of Kyser.

Swing High, Swing Low (1937) **95m.** ** D: Mitchell Leisen. Carole Lombard, Fred MacMurray, Charles Butterworth, Jean Dixon, Dorothy Lamour, Harvey Stephens, Anthony Quinn. Musical drama with cornball plot of musician MacMurray's rise and fall. Redeemed somewhat by good cast, glossy production. From the stage play *Burlesque*, made before as THE DANCE OF LIFE and remade as WHEN MY BABY SMILES AT ME.▼

Swingin' Affair, A (1963) **85m.** BOMB D: Jay O. Lawrence. William Wellman, Jr., Arline Judge, Sandra Gale Bettin, Dick Dale and The Deltones. Young Wellman boxes to subsidize his university vacation. Awful drama with surf music. Also known as A SWINGING AFFAIR.

Swingin' Along (1962) **C-74m.** BOMB D: Charles Barton. Tommy Noonan, Peter Marshall, Barbara Eden, Ray Charles, Roger Williams, Bobby Vee, Connie Gilchrist. The witless shenanigans of aspiring composer Noonan and manager Marshall—with musical "guest stars" to relieve the tedium. Also known as DOUBLE TROUBLE.

Swinging Barmaids, The (1975) **C-84m.** **½ D: Gus Trikonis. Bruce Watson, Laura Hippe, Katie Saylor, William Smith, Dyanne Thorne, John Alderman. Stylish, engaging psycho-thriller, written by Charles Griffith, has cop Smith tracking down nut who preys on B-girls. Reissued as EAGER BEAVERS.

Swingin' Summer, A (1965) **C-80m.** *½ D: Robert Sparr. James Stacy, William Wellman, Jr., Quinn O'Hara, Martin West, Allan Jones, Raquel Welch. The Righteous Brothers, The Rip Chords, Gary Lewis and The Playboys, Jody Miller. Typically thin storyline (about three guys who open a dance hall) as an excuse for music numbers by various guest stars.▼

Swing Parade of 1946 (1946) **74m.** *½ D: Phil Karlson. Gale Storm, Phil Regan, The Three Stooges, Ed Brophy, Will Osborne and his Orchestra, Connee Boswell. Dreary Grade-B musical with enough plot for a 10-minute short. The Stooges add some life, as does Louis Jordan performing "Caledonia," but it's not enough. Auteurists take note: Nicholas Ray is credited with "additional dialogue."

Swing Shift (1984) **C-100m.** ** D: Jonathan Demme. Goldie Hawn, Kurt Russell, Christine Lahti, Ed Harris, Fred Ward, Sudie Bond, Holly Hunter, Patty Maloney, Roger Corman, Belinda Carlisle. Misfired attempt to fashion fictional story around real-life situation of housewives who became factory workers during WW2. All the women are interesting (especially Lahti, in a wonderful performance), but the men are shallow and poorly-defined—and consequently, so is the film. Pseudonymous screenplay credit for "Rob Morton" masks several top writers, with half-an-hour reportedly shot by another director at producer Hawn's insistence.▼

Swing Shift Maisie (1943) **87m.** D: Norman Z. McLeod. Ann Sothern, James Craig, Jean Rogers, Connie Gilchrist, John Qualen, Kay Medford. SEE: **Maisie** series.

Swing Time (1936) **103m.** **** D: George Stevens. Fred Astaire, Ginger Rogers, Victor Moore, Helen Broderick, Eric Blore, Betty Furness. One of the best Astaire-Rogers films, with stars as dance team whose romance is hampered by Fred's engagement to girl back home (Furness). Fine support by Moore and Broderick, unforgettable Jerome Kern-Dorothy Fields songs "A Fine Romance," "Pick Yourself Up." Oscar-winning "The Way You Look Tonight." Astaire's Bojangles production number is a screen classic.▼

Swingtime Johnny (1944) **61m.** *½ D: Edward Cline. Andrews Sisters, Harriet Hilliard, Peter Cookson, Tim Ryan. Show biz performers desert the theater for work in munitions factory; lowbrow entertainment.

Swing Your Lady (1938) **77m.** *½ D: Ray Enright. Humphrey Bogart, Frank McHugh, Louise Fazenda, Nat Pendleton, Penny Singleton, Allen Jenkins, Ronald Reagan. Bogart promotes wrestler Pendleton; embarrassing comedy is easily his worst starring effort. Reagan appears briefly as a sportswriter.

Swirl of Glory SEE: **Sugarfoot**

Swiss Conspiracy, The (1975-U.S.-German) **C-88m.** ** D: Jack Arnold. David Janssen, Senta Berger, John Ireland, John Saxon, Elke Sommer, Ray Milland, Anton Diffring. Confusing cat-and-mouse intrigue set in Switzerland, where Janssen is hired to protect valued bank customers with large secret accounts.▼

Swiss Family Robinson (1940) **93m.** *** D: Edward Ludwig. Thomas Mitchell, Edna Best, Freddie Bartholomew, Tim Holt, Terry Kilburn. Mitchell leads family to remote island where they live idyllic existence. Fine adaptation of Johann Wyss book. Narrated by Orson Welles. Remade in 1960 and 1975.

Swiss Family Robinson (1960) **C-128m.** ***½ D: Ken Annakin. John Mills, Dorothy McGuire, James MacArthur, Janet Munro, Sessue Hayakawa, Tommy Kirk, Kevin Corcoran. Rollicking entertainment Disney-style, with shipwrecked family building island paradise, neatly dispatching Hayakawa and his pirate band. Pure escapism, larger than life.▼

Swiss Family Robinson, The (1975) **C-100m.** TVM D: Harry Harris. Martin Milner, Pat Delany, Cameron Mitchell, Michael-James Wixted, Eric Olson, John Vernon. Adventure classic distilled by Irwin Allen, the disaster master of the movies. It's still worthy of family viewing and somehow had enough thrills to spare for a brief subsequent series. Average.

Swiss Miss (1938) **72m.** ** D: John Blystone. Stan Laurel, Oliver Hardy, Della Lind, Walter Woolf King, Eric Blore, Adia Kuznetzof, Charles Judels. Contrived romantic story with music tries hard to submerge L&H, but Stan and Ollie's scenes save film, especially when Ollie serenades his true love with Stan playing tuba.▼

Switch (1975) **C-78m.** TVM D: Robert Day. Robert Wagner, Eddie Albert, Charles Durning, Sharon Gless, Ken Swofford, Charlie Callas, Jaclyn Smith. Ex-con man Wagner teams up with ex-cop Albert in private eye agency to prove that a cop rather than a con pulled off a diamond heist. TV's best STING rip-off, owing much to the charm of its two leads, went on to become the hit series. Above average.

Switchblade Sisters (1975) **C-91m.** ** D: Jack Hill. Robbie Lee, Joanne Nail, Monica Gayle, Kitty Bruce, Marlene Clark, Michael Miller. Pretty good cheapie about a female gang, although feminism clearly takes a back seat to action. Predates the cycle of gang films by four years; Bruce is Lenny's daughter. Originally released as THE JEZEBELS (the gang's name); reissued as PLAYGIRL GANG. ▼

Switching Channels (1988) **C-105m.** *** D: Ted Kotcheff. Kathleen Turner, Burt Reynolds, Christopher Reeve, Ned Beatty, Henry Gibson, George Newbern, Al Waxman, Ken James, Joe Silver, Tony Rosato. TV reporter Turner tries to quit her job to marry wealthy Reeve, but her boss (and ex-husband) Reynolds isn't going to give her up so easily. Surprisingly good remake of THE FRONT PAGE/HIS GIRL FRIDAY updated to the satellite-television era, but less effective in its use of satire and occasional melodrama than its classic predecessors. All three stars are terrific. ▼

Sword and the Rose, The (1953) **C-93m.** ***½ D: Ken Annakin. Richard Todd, Glynis Johns, James Robertson Justice, Michael Gough, Jane Barrett. Colorful filming of *When Knighthood Was in Flower,* with Johns as Mary Tudor, who uses wiles and power to kindle romance with Todd— but runs afoul of villainous Duke (Gough). Rich period flavor, fine performance by Justice as King Henry VIII. Filmed in England by Walt Disney. ▼

Sword and the Sorcerer, The (1982) **C-100m.** ** D: Albert Pyun. Lee Horsley, Kathleen Beller, Simon MacCorkindale, George Maharis, Richard Lynch, Richard Moll, Robert Tessier, Nina Van Pallandt, Anna Bjorn, Jeff Corey. Aided by resurrected warlock Maharis, nasty Lynch enslaves the kingdom, and it's up to swordswinging Horsley to save the day. Strictly second-rate in scripting, acting, and production, with just enough bloodletting to please undemanding fans of this kind of stuff. ▼

Sword in the Desert (1949) **100m.** **½ D: George Sherman. Dana Andrews, Marta Toren, Stephen McNally, Jeff Chandler, Philip Friend. Interesting account of underground trail of European refugees during WW2; fairly good suspenser.

Sword in the Stone, The (1963) **C-75m.** **½ D: Wolfgang Reitherman. Voices of Ricky Sorenson, Sebastian Cabot, Karl Swenson, Junius Matthews. One of Disney's weakest animated features follows a young boy named Wart, who is destined to become King Arthur—with the considerable help of Merlin the Magician. Mildly entertaining and fast-moving, but dialogue-heavy, and full of "modern" references

that remove much of the magic and wonder from T. H. White's story. Highlight: wizard's duel between Merlin and Madame Mim. ▼

Sword of Ali Baba, The (1965) **C-81m.** ** D: Virgil Vogel. Peter Mann, Jocelyn Lane, Peter Whitney, Gavin MacLeod, Frank Puglia. Outrageous remake of ALI BABA AND THE FORTY THIEVES, using a great deal of footage from the 1944 film. Puglia repeats his role as Prince Cassim from '44 version to link old and new footage.

Sword of El Cid, The (1962-Spanish) **C-85m.** ** D: Miguel Iglesias. Roland Carey, Sandro Moretti, Chantal Deberg, Daniela Bianchi. Sparse plot ruins this potentially good costumer with Moretti et al battling corrupt ruler of Catalonia.

Sword of Gideon (1986-British-Canadian) **C-148m. TVM** D: Michael Anderson. Steven Bauer, Michael York, Rod Steiger, Colleen Dewhurst, Robert Joy, Laurent Malet, Lino Ventura, Leslie Hope. An intelligent and suspenseful thriller with commando Bauer handpicked to head antiterrorist team and avenge Munich Olympic massacre of Israeli athletes. Dewhurst plays Golda Meir. Adapted by Chris Bryant from George Jonas' book *Vengeance.* Made for cable. Above average. ▼

Sword of Lancelot (1963-British) **C-116m.** **½ D: Cornel Wilde. Cornel Wilde, Jean Wallace, Brian Aherne, George Baker. Camelot comes alive, minus music, with profuse action and splendid scenery. Some may find Wilde's approach too juvenile, overly sincere, and Aherne a bit too cavalier. Originally titled LANCELOT AND GUINEVERE. ▼

Sword of Monte Cristo, The (1951) **C-80m.** ** D: Maurice Geraghty. George Montgomery, Paula Corday, Berry Kroeger, William Conrad, Steve Brodie. Uninspired adventure of woman who finds legendary sword of Count with key to treasure inscribed on it. Army officer joins her in fight against evil prime minister.

Sword of Sherwood Forest (1960-British) **C-80m.** **½ D: Terence Fisher. Richard Greene, Peter Cushing, Niall MacGinnis, Richard Pasco, Jack Gwillim, Sarah Branch, Nigel Green, Oliver Reed. Fair continuation of Robin Hood saga as Earl of Newark plots murder of Archbishop of Canterbury. ▼

Sword of the Conqueror (1961-Italian) **C-85m.** *½ D: Carlo Campogalliani. Jack Palance, Eleonora Rossi-Drago, Guy Madison, Carlo D'Angelo. Flabby epic not livened by cast or sets; set in 6th-century Byzantine empire days.

Sword of The Valiant (1982-British) **C-101m.** ** D: Stephen Weeks. Miles O'Keeffe, Cyrielle Claire, Leigh Lawson, Sean Connery, Trevor Howard, Peter Cushing, Ronald Lacey, Lila Kedrova, John Rhys-Davies. Old pro Connery (as the Green Knight) may only be on screen for a few scenes, but he adds zest to this lumbering account of a chivalrous young squire (woodenly acted by O'Keeffe) who must solve a riddle in one year or die. Remake of GAWAIN AND THE GREEN KNIGHT by the same filmmakers . . . and not much of an improvement! ▼

Swordsman, The (1948) C-81m. ** D: Joseph H. Lewis. Larry Parks, Ellen Drew, George Macready, Edgar Buchanan. Parks and Drew have Romeo-Juliet relationship in 18th-century Scotland; OK costumer.

Swordsman of Siena, The (1961-Italian) C-97m. ** D: Etienne Perier. Stewart Granger, Sylva Koscina, Christine Kaufmann, Tullio Carminati, Gabriele Ferzetti. Predictable swashbuckler about 16th-century adventurer with mixed loyalties who becomes involved in Spanish underground movement. Good cast saddled with tired script.

Sworn to Silence (1987) C-100m. TVM D: Peter Levin. Peter Coyote, Dabney Coleman, Caroline McWilliams, Ed Nelson, David Spielberg, Liam Neeson. A lawyer's privileged information versus the public's right to know is explored in this provocative but flawed drama, with Coyote as a troubled defense attorney and Coleman, in an Emmy-winning performance, as his burned-out, boozing colleague. Based by Robert L. Joseph on the book *Privileged Information* by Tom Alibrandi with Frank H. Armani. Average.

Sybil (1976) C-198m. TVM D: Daniel Petrie. Joanne Woodward, Sally Field, Brad Davis, Martine Bartlett, Jane Hoffman, William Prince. Emmy-winning psychological study of a young woman who, disturbed by childhood experiences, has developed seventeen separate personalities. Field is remarkable in title role and Woodward, making a nice turnaround from THE THREE FACES OF EVE, brings special glow to the role of psychiatrist. Fascinating but deeply disturbing drama. Above average. ▼

Sylvester (1985) C-102m. ** D: Tim Hunter. Richard Farnsworth, Melissa Gilbert, Michael Schoeffling, Constance Towers, Pete Kowanko. Seemingly surefire story of a girl and her horse can't clear the hurdles because lead character isn't terribly likable. Some nice riding sequences but uneven narrative (by Carol Sobieski) weighs it down. ▼

Sylvia (1965) 115m. **½ D: Gordon Douglas. Carroll Baker, George Maharis, Joanne Dru, Peter Lawford, Viveca Lindfors, Edmond O'Brien, Aldo Ray, Ann Sothern. Baker's prelude to HARLOW is much better, despite overuse of flashbacks and rambling episodes; she plays a bad girl

turned good with melodrama unfolding as detective Maharis investigates her life.

Sylvia (1985-New Zealand) C-98m. *** D: Michael Firth. Eleanor David, Nigel Terry, Tom Wilkinson, Mary Regan, Joseph George, Eileen Glover. David gives a strong performance as famed educator Sylvia Ashton-Warner, who struggled in the early 1940s to buck New Zealand's educational establishment with innovative reading methods for Maori children. Adapted from her works *Teacher* and *I Passed This Way*. Shirley MacLaine's otherwise unbearable TWO LOVES, based on an Ashton-Warner semiautobiographical story, makes an interesting cross reference. ▼

Sylvia Scarlett (1935) 94m. *** D: George Cukor. Katharine Hepburn, Cary Grant, Brian Aherne, Edmund Gwenn, Natalie Paley, Dennie Moore. Offbeat, charming comedy-drama; Hepburn and ne'er-do-well father Gwenn take to the road when he gets in trouble. She disguises as a boy as they travel with cockney Grant in touring show. Most unusual film made interesting by performances of Hepburn and Grant in their first film together. ▼

Sympathy for the Devil (1970-French) C-92m. ** D: Jean-Luc Godard. Muddled documentary which utilizes the Rolling Stones as a catchall for interspersed study of revolution. Godard's cut, titled ONE PLUS ONE and running somewhat longer, is still extant. ▼

Symphony of Six Million (1932) 94m. **½ D: Gregory La Cava. Irene Dunne, Ricardo Cortez, Anna Appel, Gregory Ratoff, Lita Chevret. Predictable but well-made Fannie Hurst soap opera has young doctor Cortez abandoning his Jewish-ghetto neighborhood, family, friends—and crippled sweetheart Dunne—to join Park Avenue set and make big money.

Synanon (1965) 107m. **½ D: Richard Quine. Chuck Connors, Stella Stevens, Alex Cord, Richard Conte, Eartha Kitt, Edmond O'Brien, Chanin Hale, Alejandro Rey. Potentially powerful study of dope-addiction treatment via the Synanon House methods bogs down in pat romantic tale with stereotyped performances.

Syncopation (1942) 88m. ** D: William Dieterle. Adolphe Menjou, Jackie Cooper, Bonita Granville, Todd Duncan, Connee Boswell, Hall Johnson Choir. Uneven story traces history of Jazz from 1906, with Cooper as young struggling trumpeter (dubbed by Bunny Berrigan). Film redeemed somewhat by terrific jam session featuring Benny Goodman, Harry James, Charlie Barnet, Gene Krupa, and other musical greats.

System, The (1953) 90m. ** D: Lewis Seiler. Frank Lovejoy, Joan Weldon, Bob Arthur, Jerome Cowan. Uneven scripting spoils this potentially good study of gambling syndicate in large metropolitan city.

System, The (1966) SEE: **Girl-Getters, The**

Table for Five (1983) **C-122m.** *** D: Robert Lieberman. Jon Voight, Richard Crenna, Marie-Christine Barrault, Millie Perkins, Roxana Zal, Robby Kiger, Son Hoang Bui, Kevin Costner. Solid (and unabashed) tearjerker with Voight as a divorced man who tries to make up for being an absentee father by taking his three children on a cruise to Europe—little dreaming how tough an experience it will turn out to be. Curl up and have a good cry.▼

Tabu (1931) **82m.** ***½ D: F.W. Murnau. Anna Chevalier, Matahi, Hitu, Jean, Jules, Kong Ah. Fascinating melding of ethnographic documentary and narrative, about pearl fisherman Matahi and his ill-fated love for young Chevalier, who's been deemed by the gods as taboo to all men. Shot in Tahiti in 1929, produced and scripted by Murnau and Robert Flaherty; the latter left the project in mid-production because of differences in opinion with Murnau—who died in a car accident just prior to the film's premiere. Floyd Crosby's cinematography won an Academy Award.▼

Taffin (1988-British) **C-96m.** ** D: Francis Megahy. Pierce Brosnan, Ray McAnally, Alison Doody, Jeremy Child. Dull thriller about a bill collector (an uncharismatic Brosnan) and his exploits as he takes on some shady businessmen attempting to build a chemical plant in an Irish village.▼

Taffy and the Jungle Hunter (1965) **C-87m.** ** D: Terry O. Morse. Jacques Bergerac, Manuel Padilla, Shary Marshall, Hari Rhodes. Unassuming tale of son of big game hunter who takes off for jungle adventures with pet elephant and chimp.

Tag: The Assassination Game (1982) **C-92m.** ** D: Nick Castle. Robert Carradine, Linda Hamilton, Kristine De Bell, Bruce Abbott, Michael Winslow, Frazer Smith. A role-playing game, played by college students with toy guns, turns deadly when one player (Abbott) becomes unhinged and substitutes real bullets. Short on sense and suspense, with some unintended laughs along the way.▼

Taggart (1964) **C-85m.** **½ D: R. G. Springsteen. Tony Young, Dan Duryea, Peter Duryea, David Carradine, Jean Hale, Harry Carey, Jr., Bob Steele. Neat little action Western based on a Louis L'Amour novel with Young on a revenge hunt, pursued by gunslingers in Indian territory.

Tail Gunner Joe (1977) **C-144m.** TVM D: Jud Taylor. Peter Boyle, John Forsythe, Heather Menzies, Burgess Meredith, Patricia Neal, Jean Stapleton, Ned Beatty, John Carradine. The rise and fall of Senator Joseph McCarthy, with a stunning per-formance by Boyle. Gripping drama woven with author Lane Slate's bias. Above average.

Tailor's Maid, The (1959-Italian) **C-92m.** **½ D: Mario Monicelli. Vittorio De Sica, Marcello Mastroianni, Marisa Merlini, Fiorella Mari, Memmo Carotenuto, Raffaele Pisu. Saucy, inconsequential comedy about an amorous tailor.

Tail Spin (1939) **84m.** ** D: Roy Del Ruth. Alice Faye, Constance Bennett, Nancy Kelly, Joan Davis, Charles Farrell, Jane Wyman, Kane Richmond, Wally Vernon. Hackneyed saga of female flyers, with Faye (in a change-of-pace role) in charge of worrier Kelly, funny-girl Davis, etc.; written by Frank "Spig" Wead.

Tailspin: Behind the Korean Airliner Tragedy (1989-U.S.-British) **C-85m.** TVM D: David Darlow. Michael Moriarty, Michael Murphy, Chris Sarandon, Harris Yulin, Ed O'Ross. Intriguing docudrama about downing of Korean airliner that strayed into Soviet airspace in 1983, and the politics and interagency rivalry that superseded the tragedy. Same incident was dramatized in the earlier TV movie SHOOT-DOWN from a totally different perspective. Made for cable. Above average.

Tai-Pan (1986) **C-127m.** *½ D: Daryl Duke. Bryan Brown, Joan Chen, John Stanton, Tim Guinee, Bill Leadbitter, Russell Wong, Kyra Sedgwick, Bert Remsen. Spectacularly silly adventure yarn based on James Clavell's sprawling novel about 19th-century trade baron who establishes his headquarters in Hong Kong. So much story is telescoped, so many characters come and go, and so many accents are poor and plot points handled with sledge-hammer subtlety that there's nothing left to do but treat the whole thing as a goof—or skip it altogether. Actually filmed in China, if that matters.▼

Take, The (1974) **C-93m.** ** D: Robert Hartford-Davis. Billy Dee Williams, Eddie Albert, Vic Morrow, Frankie Avalon, Albert Salmi. Tepid action pic concerns police lieutenant Williams' efforts to stop syndicate chief Morrow while accepting bribe money on the side. Surprisingly neat cameo by Avalon as a cheap crook.

Take, The (1990) **C-100m.** TVM D: Leon Ichaso. Ray Sharkey, Lisa Hartman, Larry Manetti, R. Lee Ermey, Joe Lala, Julio Mechoso. Ex-con cop comes out of stir and falls in with Cuban drug cartel. Dreary *Miami Vice* carbon that has even usually wired Sharkey just going through the drill. Made for cable. Below average.

Take a Chance (1933) **84m.** *½ D: Laurence Schwab, Monte Brice. James Dunn, Cliff Edwards, June Knight, Charles "Buddy" Rogers, Lillian Roth, Dorothy Lee. Awful adaptation of Broadway musical about carnival hucksters aiming for the big time, redeemed somewhat by fine score and campy number with "Ukulele Ike" Edwards.

Take a Giant Step (1959) **100m.** **½ D: Philip Leacock. Johnny Nash, Estelle Hemsley, Ruby Dee, Frederick O'Neal, Ellen Holly, Beah Richards. Earnest but only partly successful account of black teen Nash's problems in a white world. Stagy adaptation of Louis S. Peterson's play benefits from good performances.

Take a Girl Like You (1970-U.S.-British) **C-101m.** **½ D: Jonathan Miller. Hayley Mills, Oliver Reed, Noel Harrison, Sheila Hancock, John Bird, Aimi MacDonald, Ronald Lacey, Penelope Keith. Hayley's a young schoolteacher intent on staying virginal until her wedding day. Reed and Harrison are intent on proving otherwise. Pleasant fare with good cast. Based on a Kingsley Amis novel.

Take a Hard Ride (1975) **C-109m.** ** D: Anthony Dawson (Antonio Margheriti). Jim Brown, Lee Van Cleef, Fred Williamson, Catherine Spaak, Jim Kelly, Dana Andrews, Barry Sullivan, Harry Carey, Jr. Oddball Western filmed in Canary Islands. Brown must carry large bankroll across Mexican border, attracts a colorful band of "comrades" for his journey, runs afoul of bandit Van Cleef. Good personalities wasted in blah script ▼

Take a Letter, Darling (1942) **93m.** *** D: Mitchell Leisen. Rosalind Russell, Fred MacMurray, Constance Moore, Robert Benchley, Macdonald Carey, Dooley Wilson, Cecil Kellaway. Witty repartee as advertising exec Roz hires MacMurray as secretary, but relationship doesn't end there. Benchley is wry as Russell's game-playing business partner.

Take Care of My Little Girl (1951) **C-93m.** ** D: Jean Negulesco. Jeanne Crain, Dale Robertson, Mitzi Gaynor, Jean Peters, Jeffrey Hunter, George Nader, Helen Westcott. Overdramatic story of sorority life at college.

Take Down (1978) **C-107m.** *** D: Kieth Merrill. Edward Herrmann, Kathleen Lloyd, Lorenzo Lamas, Maureen McCormick, Nick Beauvy, Kevin Hooks, Stephen Furst. Seriocomic look at high school wrestling, focusing on rebellious student Lamas and reluctant coach Herrmann. Well done.▼

Take Her, She's Mine (1963) **C-98m.** ** D: Henry Koster. James Stewart, Sandra Dee, Audrey Meadows, Robert Morley, Philippe Forquet, John McGiver. Obvious family comedy with Stewart the harried father of wild teen-age daughter Dee. Predictable gags don't help. Script by Nunnally Johnson, from the Broadway hit by Phoebe and Henry Ephron; later ripped-off by THE IMPOSSIBLE YEARS.

Take It or Leave It (1944) **70m.** *½ D: Benjamin Stoloff. Phil Baker, Phil Silvers,

Edward Ryan, Marjorie Massow, Stanley Prager, Roy Gordon. Claptrap hinged on lives of contestants on popular quiz show; film uses clips from older pictures to liven proceedings.

Take Me Out to the Ball Game (1949) **C-93m.** *** D: Busby Berkeley. Frank Sinatra, Esther Williams, Gene Kelly, Betty Garrett, Edward Arnold, Jules Munshin, Richard Lane, Tom Dugan. Contrived but colorful turn-of-the-century musical, with Williams taking over Sinatra and Kelly's baseball team. "O'Brien to Ryan to Goldberg" and Kelly's "The Hat My Father Wore on St. Patrick's Day" are musical highlights.▼

Take Me to Town (1953) **C-81m.** **½ D: Douglas Sirk. Ann Sheridan, Sterling Hayden, Philip Reed, Lee Patrick, Lane Chandler. Unpretentious Americana of saloon singer Sheridan on the lam, finding love with widowed preacher Hayden and his three children.

Take My Daughters, Please (1988) **C-100m.** TVM D: Larry Elikann. Rue McClanahan, Kim Delaney, Deidre Hall, Stepfanie Kramer, Susan Ruttan, Audra Lindley, Charles Frank. Slight comedy about a widow who launches a campaign to get her four independent daughters to the altar. Average.

Taken Away (1989) **C-100m.** TVM D: John Patterson. Valerie Bertinelli, Kevin Dunn, Juliet Sorcey, Nada Despotovich, Joshua Maurer, Anna Maria Horsford. Single mother fights the system for the return of the child taken from her in a red-tape snarl. Average.

Take One False Step (1949) **94m.** **½ D: Chester Erskine. William Powell, Shelley Winters, James Gleason, Marsha Hunt, Dorothy Hart, Sheldon Leonard. OK mystery-drama with innocent Powell hunted by police as he tries to clear himself of murder charge. Adapted by Erskine and Irwin Shaw from the novel by Shaw and his brother David.

Take the High Ground (1953) **C-101m.** *** D: Richard Brooks. Richard Widmark, Karl Malden, Elaine Stewart, Steve Forrest, Carleton Carpenter. Taut account of infantry basic training with on-location filming at Fort Bliss, Texas helping.

Take the Money and Run (1969) **C-85m.** *** D: Woody Allen. Woody Allen, Janet Margolin, Marcel Hillaire, Jacquelyn Hyde; narrator, Jackson Beck. Woody's first film as director/writer/star is full of funny ideas, telling documentary-style, life story of compulsive thief. Nonstop parade of jokes; some work, some don't, but the ones that *do* are a riot! Louise Lasser seen briefly.▼

Take This Job and Shove It (1981) **C-100m.** **½ D: Gus Trikonis. Robert Hays, Art Carney, Barbara Hershey, David

Keith, Tim Thomerson, Martin Mull, Eddie Albert, Penelope Milford. Hays returns to his hometown with orders from his conglomerate to modernize an old-fashioned brewery . . . but being with his old cronies, and one-time girlfriend, effects a change of attitude. Unpretentious film named after 70s hit record by Johnny Paycheck has Capraesque flavor at times, but eventually settles for obvious formula schtick.▼

Take Your Best Shot (1982) C-100m. TVM D: David Greene. Robert Urich, Meredith Baxter Birney, Jeffrey Tambor, Jack Bannon, Claudette Nevins, Susan Peretz. Struggling actor Urich juggles a failing marriage and a flagging career in this comedy, a change of pace for the writer-producer team of Richard Levinson and William Link. Average.▼

Taking Off (1971) C-93m. ***½ D: Milos Forman. Lynn Carlin, Buck Henry, Linnea Heacock, Audra Lindley, Paul Benedict, Georgia Engel. Forman's first American film is beguilingly funny look at American life-styles from two generations' point of view, centering on runaway girl (Heacock) who drives parents (Carlin, Henry) into new experiences of their own. Carly Simon seen as one of auditioning singers.

Taking of Flight 847, The: The Uli Derickson Story (1988) C-100m. TVM D: Paul Wendkos. Lindsay Wagner, Eli Danker, Sandy McPeak, Ray Wise, Leslie Easterbrook, Laurie Walters, Joseph Nasser. Taut drama about the real-life 1985 hijacking and the flight attendant credited with saving all but one of the passengers' lives. Wagner is surprisingly good heading a no-name cast, but keep an eye on Danker, chillingly on-target as the unstable leader of the hijackers who speaks no English. A number of Emmy nominations went to this film, but none to writer Norman Morrill. Above average.▼

Taking of Pelham One Two Three, The (1974) C-104m. ***½ D: Joseph Sargent. Walter Matthau, Robert Shaw, Martin Balsam, Hector Elizondo, Earl Hindman, Dick O'Neill, Jerry Stiller, Tony Roberts, Lee Wallace, Doris Roberts, Kenneth McMillan, Julius Harris, James Broderick, Sal Viscuso. Ruthless Shaw and three cohorts hijack N.Y.C. subway train, hold passengers for one million in cash—to be delivered *in one hour!* Outstanding thriller, laced with cynical comedy, bursts with heart-stopping excitement, terrific performances, and first-rate editing. Crackerjack Peter Stone screenplay greatly improves John Godey's bestseller; pulsating score by David Shire.▼

Talent for Loving, A (1969) C-110m. ** D: Richard Quine. Richard Widmark, Topol, Cesar Romero, Genevieve Page, Judd Hamilton, Caroline Munro. Rambunctious Western concerning a professional gambler

trapped into marrying within rich Mexican family cursed by the Aztecs with a talent for loving. From Richard Condon's novel.

Talent Scout (1937) 62m. *½ D: William Clemens. Donald Woods, Jeanne Madden, Fred Lawrence, Rosalind Marquis, Charles Halton. Tacky B musical about a Hollywood talent scout and the girl he promotes to stardom. The only fun is anticipating the clichéd dialogue scene by scene.

Tale of Africa, A SEE: **Afurika Monogatari**▼

Tale of Five Women, A (1951-British) 86m. *½ D: Romollo Marcellini, Geza von Cziffra, Wolfgang Staudte, E. E. Reinert, Montgomery Tully. Bonar Colleano, Barbara Kelly, Anne Vernon, Lana Morris, Karen Humbold, Lily Kahn, Eva Bartok, Gina Lollobrigida. Magazine editor Kelly accompanies amnesiac RAF officer to visit lovers in five cities, hoping to jar his memory. Disappointingly dull multiepisode film. Originally titled A TALE OF FIVE CITIES, running 99m.

Tale of Two Cities, A (1917) 70m. *** D: Frank Lloyd. William Farnum, Jewel Carmen, Joseph Swickard, Herschell Mayall, Rosita Marstini. Ambitious silent-film version of Dickens story was a big hit in 1917, and it's easy to see why: Farnum is an appealing hero, production is first-rate, and battle scenes are reminiscent of Griffith's INTOLERANCE.

Tale of Two Cities, A (1935) 128m. **** D: Jack Conway. Ronald Colman, Elizabeth Allan, Edna May Oliver, Reginald Owen, Basil Rathbone, Blanche Yurka, Isabel Jewell, Walter Catlett, Henry B. Walthall, H.B. Warner, Donald Woods. Dickens' panorama of the 1780s French Revolution becomes an MGM blockbuster, with Colman as carefree lawyer awakened to responsibility, aiding victims of the Reign of Terror. Stage star Blanche Yurka creates a memorable Mme. Defarge in her film debut. Tremendous cast in a truly lavish production. Written for the screen by W.P. Lipscomb and S.N. Behrman. Also shown in computer-colored version.▼

Tale of Two Cities, A (1958-British) 117m. *** D: Ralph Thomas. Dirk Bogarde, Dorothy Tutin, Cecil Parker, Stephen Murray, Athene Seyler, Christopher Lee, Donald Pleasence, Ian Bannen. Faithful retelling of Dickens story in this well-made British production, with Bogarde a good Sydney Carton. Remade again for TV.▼

Tale of Two Cities, A (1980) C-156m. TVM D: Jim Goddard. Chris Sarandon, Peter Cushing, Kenneth More, Barry Morse, Flora Robson, Billie Whitelaw, Alice Krige. Seventh filming of the Dickens classic has all the trimmings, but Sarandon can't hold a candle to Ronald Colman as either Sydney Carton or Charles Darnay. John Gay did the script for producer Norman Rosemont, who's been working his way through the literary favorites of the ages for TV. Average.

Tales from the Crypt (1972-British) **C-92m.** **½ D: Freddie Francis. Ralph Richardson, Peter Cushing, Joan Collins, Richard Greene, Patrick Magee, Ian Hendry, Nigel Patrick. Five stories of terror involving deceit, mayhem, and a few well-timed laughs. Nothing extraordinary, however; based on the old E. C. comics. Followed by VAULT OF HORROR.▼

Tales From the Crypt, Part II SEE: **Vault of Horror**

Tales from the Darkside: The Movie (1990) **C-93m.** ** D: John Harrison. Deborah Harry, Matthew Lawrence, Christian Slater, Robert Sedgwick, Julianne Moore, David Johansen (Buster Poindexter), William Hickey, James Remar, Rae Dawn Chong, Robert Klein. Boy imprisoned by suburban cannibal Harry tells her three horror stories—about a walking mummy, a supernatural cat, and a vow made to a gargoyle—to stave off being served as a main course. Good production values, but the stories are tepid; only the third one, by Michael McDowell, has a kick (the first two are by Arthur Conan Doyle and Stephen King). Connection to TV series of the same name is tenuous at best.▼

Tales of Beatrix Potter SEE: **Peter Rabbit and Tales of Beatrix Potter**▼

Tales of Hoffman (1951-British) **C-118m.** **½ D: Michael Powell, Emeric Pressburger. Moira Shearer, Robert Rounseville, Leonide Massine, Robert Helpmann, Pamela Brown. Jacques Offenbach's fantasy opera of student who engages in bizarre dreams, revealing three states of his life. Striking and offbeat film, not for all tastes. Cut from original 138m. release.

Tales of Manhattan (1942) **118m.** *** D: Julien Duvivier. Charles Boyer, Rita Hayworth, Henry Fonda, Ginger Rogers, Charles Laughton, Edward G. Robinson, Ethel Waters, Paul Robeson, Eddie "Rochester" Anderson, Thomas Mitchell, Cesar Romero, George Sanders. Charming film about the effect a dress tailcoat has on its various owners; five episodes, alternately amusing, poignant, ironic. Our favorite: down and out Robinson attending 25th class reunion. Pictorially stylish throughout; photographed by Joseph Walker.

Tales of Ordinary Madness (1983-Italian) **C-107m.** *½ D: Marco Ferreri. Ben Gazzara, Ornella Muti, Susan Tyrrell, Tanya Lopert, Roy Brocksmith. Pretentious swill about poet Gazzara who boozes endlessly and meets the oddest assortment of women. Gazzara, and especially Tyrrell, have never been worse. Based on stories by Charles Bukowski.▼

Tales of Robin Hood (1951) **60m.** *½ D: James Tinling. Robert Clarke, Mary Hatcher,

Paul Cavanagh, Wade Crosby. Minor account of folklore hero consisting of episodes of unsold TV series.

Tales of Terror (1962) **C-90m.** *** D: Roger Corman. Vincent Price, Peter Lorre, Basil Rathbone, Debra Paget, Maggie Pierce, Leona Gage, Joyce Jameson. Four Edgar Allan Poe stories distilled by Richard Matheson into three-part film, with Lorre's comic performance as vengeful husband walling up adulterous wife the standout. Price appears in all three segments. Odd Panavision and color effects will suffer on small screen.▼

Tales That Witness Madness (1973-British) **C-90m.** *½ D: Freddie Francis. Kim Novak, Georgia Brown, Joan Collins, Jack Hawkins, Donald Houston, Peter McEnery, Suzy Kendall, Donald Pleasence. Absurd collection of four *Twilight Zone*-like stories. A waste of time and talent.

Talk About a Stranger (1952) **65m.** ** D: David Bradley. George Murphy, Nancy Davis (Reagan), Billy Gray, Kurt Kasznar, Lewis Stone. Boy tries to find out more about a mysterious neighbor in OK programmer.

Talk of the Town, The (1942) **118m.** **** D: George Stevens. Jean Arthur, Ronald Colman, Cary Grant, Glenda Farrell, Edgar Buchanan, Charles Dingle, Rex Ingram, Emma Dunn, Tom Tyler, Lloyd Bridges. Intelligent comedy with brilliant cast; fugitive Grant hides out with unsuspecting professor Colman and landlady Arthur, and tries to convince legal-minded Colman there's a human side to all laws. Splendid film written by Irwin Shaw and Sidney Buchman.▼

Talk Radio (1988) **C-110m.** **½ D: Oliver Stone. Eric Bogosian, Alec Baldwin, Ellen Greene, Leslie Hope, John C. McGinley, John Pankow, Michael Wincott. Eric Bogosian's one-set play (written with Ted Savinar) is fleshed out for this feature film about an abrasive talk-show host who puts down his many callers but can't get his own life together. Well acted, extremely well shot and directed, but one's enjoyment may depend on one's tolerance for this kind of talk-radio program—and its hosts. Stone and Bogosian collaborated on the screenplay, which also incorporated elements of Steven Singular's book *Talked to Death: The Life and Murder of Alan Berg*.▼

Tall Blond Man With One Black Shoe, The (1972-French) **C-90m.** *** D: Yves Robert. Pierre Richard, Bernard Blier, Jean Rochefort, Mireille Darc, Jean Carmet. Engaging French farce with rival secret agents making life a shambles for the Tall Blond Man (Richard) who's been innocently pegged a spy. Followed by RETURN OF . . . in 1974 and an American remake (THE MAN WITH ONE RED SHOE) in 1985.▼

Tall Dark and Handsome (1941) **78m.** ****½** D: H. Bruce Humberstone. Cesar Romero, Virginia Gilmore, Charlotte Greenwood, Milton Berle, Sheldon Leonard. Amusing Runyonesque gangster comedy about an underworld bigwig who's really a softie. Remade as LOVE THAT BRUTE.

Tall in the Saddle (1944) **87m.** ******* Edwin L. Marin. John Wayne, Ella Raines, Ward Bond, Gabby Hayes, Elisabeth Risdon, Raymond Hatton. Cowboy Wayne avoids women until he goes to work at Raines' ranch; good, enjoyable Western. Also shown in computer-colored version.▼

Tall Lie, The SEE: For Men Only

Tall Man Riding (1955) **C-83m.** ****½** D: Lesley Selander. Randolph Scott, Dorothy Malone, Peggie Castle, John Dehner, Lane Chandler. Sturdy Western with Scott involved in outmaneuvering greedy ranchers during territorial land granting in Montana.

Tall Men, The (1955) **C-122m.** ****** D: Raoul Walsh. Clark Gable, Jane Russell, Robert Ryan, Cameron Mitchell, Juan Garcia, Harry Shannon, Emile Meyer, Mae Marsh. Large-scale Western with Gable and Mitchell as ex-Rebels who sign on for Ryan's cattle drive, and in short order all three are fighting Indians, blizzards, and each other (over Russell, of course). Pretty dull, considering stars and director.▼

Tall Story (1960) **91m.** ****½** D: Joshua Logan. Anthony Perkins, Jane Fonda, Ray Walston, Marc Connelly, Anne Jackson, Murray Hamilton, Elizabeth Patterson, Bob Wright, Bart Burns, Gary Lockwood. Fast-moving froth about man-hungry coed Fonda (in film debut) falling in love with college basketball star Perkins. Based on Howard Lindsay-Russel Crouse play.

Tall Stranger, The (1957) **C-81m.** ****** D: Thomas Carr. Joel McCrea, Virginia Mayo, Michael Ansara, Michael Pate. Standard fare of McCrea helping wagon convoy cross Colorado territory. Based on a Louis L'Amour novel.

Tall T, The (1957) **C-78m.** ******* D: Budd Boetticher. Randolph Scott, Richard Boone, Maureen O'Sullivan, Henry Silva, Skip Homeier, John Hubbard, Arthur Hunnicutt. Scott becomes involved with kidnapped O'Sullivan, and tries to undermine unity of outlaw gang holding them prisoner. Solid Western all the way, scripted by Burt Kennedy from an Elmore Leonard story.

Tall Target, The (1951) **78m.** ******* D: Anthony Mann. Dick Powell, Paula Raymond, Adolphe Menjou, Marshall Thompson, Ruby Dee, Will Geer. Gripping suspense as detective Powell follows tip that Abraham Lincoln is going to be assassinated during 1861 train ride. Interestingly, Powell's character is named John Kennedy!

Tall Texan, The (1953) **82m.** ****** D: Elmo

Williams. Lloyd Bridges, Lee J. Cobb, Marie Windsor, Luther Adler, Syd Saylor. Good cast cannot uplift this standard Western about a group seeking out a gold deposit in Indian territory. A tale of greed and gold that just doesn't pan out.

Tall Women, The (1966-Spanish) **C-101m.** ****** D: Sidney Pink. Anne Baxter, Maria Perschy, Rosella Como, John Clarke. Western about seven women making their way through Indian country. Foreign-made movie suffers from bad dubbing and mediocre acting.

Tamango (1957-French) **C-98m.** ****** D: John Berry. Dorothy Dandridge, Curt Jurgens, Jean Servais, Roger Hanin, Guy Mairesse. Offbeat misfire about Dutch captain Jurgens involved with slave trader, romancing native Dandridge and trying to quell slave mutiny abroad.

Tamarind Seed, The (1974) **C-123m.** ******* D: Blake Edwards. Julie Andrews, Omar Sharif, Anthony Quayle, Daniel O'Herlihy, Sylvia Sims, Oscar Homolka. Well-mounted espionage/romance story set in London, Paris and Barbados; shows what a capable director can do with sappy material.▼

Taming of the Shrew, The (1929) **66m.** ****** D: Sam Taylor. Mary Pickford, Douglas Fairbanks, Edwin Maxwell, Joseph Cawthorn, Clyde Cook, Geoffrey Wardell, Dorothy Jordan. Static version of the Shakespeare classic, with wild, shrewish Kate (Pickford) ardently pursued and "tamed" by swaggering, self-confident Petruchio (Fairbanks). Defeated by its lack of pacing and downright embarrassing performances, though it's undeniably fascinating to see Doug and Mary together in their only co-starring appearance. This is the film with the infamous credit, "By William Shakespeare, with additional dialogue by Sam Taylor." Original running time 73m. Remade in 1967 with E. Taylor and R. Burton.▼

Taming of the Shrew, The (1967-U.S.-Italian) **C-126m.** *****½** D: Franco Zeffirelli. Elizabeth Taylor, Richard Burton, Vernon Dobtcheff, Michael Hordern, Natasha Pyne, Michael York, Cyril Cusack, Alan Webb, Victor Spinetti. Colorful version of Shakespeare's romp is well served by Richard and Elizabeth, good supporting cast, lovely photography, and fine musical score by Nino Rota. Shakespeare purists may object, but Zeffirelli has succeeded in making a film instead of a photographed stage play. Scripted by Suso Cecchi d'Amico, Paul Dehn, and Zeffirelli. Filmed before in 1929 with another famous acting couple, Mary Pickford and Douglas Fairbanks.▼

Taming Sutton's Gal (1957) **71m.** ***½** D: Lesley Selander. John Lupton, Gloria Talbott, Jack Kelly, May Wynn, Verna

Felton. Tedious hokum involving moonshiner's amorous wife.

T.A.M.I. Show, The (1964) 100m. *** D: Steve Binder. The Rolling Stones, James Brown, Chuck Berry, Marvin Gaye, The Supremes, Jan and Dean, Gerry & The Pacemakers, Smokey Robinson & The Miracles, Leslie Gore, Billy J. Kramer & The Dakotas. Historic rock and r&b concert at the Santa Monica Civic Auditorium was covered by television cameras and kinescoped onto film by whiz-kid Binder. Invaluable document of music history, with great early Mick Jagger and electrifying footwork by Brown. (Two of those go-go dancers are Teri Garr and Toni Basil!) Originally 113m., with Beach Boys sequence that was later cut (although they're still visible in the finale). Title stands for Teenage Awards Music International. Followed by THE BIG T.N.T. SHOW; see also THAT WAS ROCK.▼

Tam-Lin SEE: **Devil's Widow, The**

Tammy and the Bachelor (1957) C-89m. *** D: Joseph Pevney. Debbie Reynolds, Walter Brennan, Leslie Nielsen, Mala Powers, Fay Wray, Sidney Blackmer, Mildred Natwick, Louis Beavers. Unpretentious if cutesy romantic corn of country girl Reynolds falling in love with pilot Nielsen whom she's nursed back to health after plane crash. Followed by two sequels and a TV series.▼

Tammy and the Doctor (1963) C-88m. **½ D: Harry Keller. Sandra Dee, Peter Fonda, Macdonald Carey, Beulah Bondi, Margaret Lindsay, Reginald Owen, Adam West. Sugary fluff involving homespun Tammy (Dee) courted by a doctor (Fonda, in his film debut); supporting cast adds touching cameos.▼

Tammy and the Millionaire (1967) C-87m. ** D: Sidney Miller, Ezra Stone, Leslie Goodwins. Debbie Watson, Frank McGrath, Denver Pyle, George Furth, Donald Woods, Dorothy Green. Four episodes of the TV series spliced into low-grade feature, diluting the fuzzy folksy charm of backwoods girl trying to better the world.

Tammy Tell Me True (1961) C-97m. ** D: Harry Keller. Sandra Dee, John Gavin, Virginia Grey, Beulah Bondi, Cecil Kellaway, Edgar Buchanan. Tired romance of girl coming to college for first time, makes name for herself by helping dean of women. Script and acting very uneven.

Tampico (1944) 75m. ** D: Lothar Mendes. Edward G. Robinson, Lynn Bari, Victor McLaglen, Marc Lawrence, Mona Maris. Merchant-marine skipper Robinson senses espionage on his boat, but suspects wrong party. Routine WW2 intrigue, partially salvaged by stars.

Tampopo (1986-Japanese) C-114m. ***½ D: Juzo Itami. Ken Watanabe, Tsutomu Yamakazi, Nobuko Miyamoto, Koji Yakusho. Funny, original comedy-satire about one of everybody's favorite subjects: food. The scenario, which unravels as a series of vignettes, concerns a truck driver who helps a widow make her noodle shop a viable business. A clever, irreverent delight.▼

Tanganyika (1954) C-81m. ** D: Andre de Toth. Van Heflin, Ruth Roman, Howard Duff, Jeff Morrow. OK adventure of explorer attempting land claim in East Africa with numerous perils along the way.

Tangier (1946) 76m. **½ D: George Waggner. Maria Montez, Preston Foster, Robert Paige, Louise Allbritton, Kent Taylor, Sabu, J. Edward Bromberg, Reginald Denny. Limp intrigue in Tangier with vengeful dancer Montez; it isn't even in color.

Tangier Incident (1953) 77m. *½ D: Lew Landers. George Brent, Mari Aldon, Dorothy Patrick, Bert Freed. Tame actioner with Brent a federal agent hunting an espionage ring.

Tango & Cash (1989) C-98m. ** D: Andrei Konchalovsky. Sylvester Stallone, Kurt Russell, Teri Hatcher, Jack Palance, Brion James, James Hong, Marc Alaimo. Rumored $55 million budget must have gone for male hairstyling in congenitally derivative narc caper about two competitive cops who take on Mr. Big. Surprisingly tolerable, though, with a nifty prison break sequence and a pleasingly relaxed Stallone performance.▼

Tango Bar (1988-Puerto Rican-Argentinian) C-90m. *** D: Marcos Zurinaga. Raul Julia, Valeria Lynch, Ruben Juarez. Perceptive, entertaining "political musical" about a tango dancer who left Argentina when the military coup occurred, and is now reunited with her longtime partner Julia after ten years in exile. Serves as both an anthology of the tango, and a tale of Argentina's recent political history. Crammed with clips of film and TV personalities, from Fred Astaire to Fred Flintstone, doing the tango.▼

Tank (1984) C-113m. ** D: Marvin Chomsky. James Garner, G.D. Spradlin, C. Thomas Howell, Shirley Jones, Jenilee Harrison, James Cromwell, Dorian Harewood. One-dimensional rehash of SUPPOSE THEY GAVE A WAR AND NOBODY CAME? turns that film's shades of gray into simplistic good-guy/bad-guy story. Teenage son of career military man is wrongfully jailed by vindictive redneck sheriff; Dad goes to rescue him with the help of his own Sherman tank. Odd to find Garner in such a cornball movie.▼

Tank Force (1958-British) C-81m. *½ D: Terence Young. Victor Mature, Leo Genn, Anthony Newley, Luciana Paluzzi. Clichéd dud of WW2 with assorted British prisoners escaping across Libyan desert. Originally titled NO TIME TO DIE.

Tanks Are Coming, The (1951) **90m.** **
D: Lewis Seiler, D. Ross Lederman. Steve
Cochran, Philip Carey, Mari Aldon, Paul
Picerni, Harry Bellaver, James Dobson.
Moderate WW2 actioner set during Allied
capture of Berlin.
Tap (1989) **C-110m.** *** D: Nick Castle.
Gregory Hines, Suzzanne Douglas, Sammy
Davis, Jr., Savion Glover, Joe Morton,
Dick Anthony Williams, Terrence McNally,
Sandman Sims, Bunny Briggs, Steve Condos, Jimmy Slyde, Pat Rico, Arthur Duncan, Harold Nicholas, Etta James. Slight,
old-fashioned but engaging story of a man
who shuns his tap-dancing heritage for the
good life and easy money he can make
pulling jewel robberies . . . until the call
of the tap is just too strong. A loving
tribute to tap, with some clever contemporary touches by writer-director Castle
(whose same-named father was a top choreographer). Hines has never been better,
and he's surrounded by an extremely talented cast. Davis is a standout as Little
Mo (in his final feature film), and the
challenge dance with old-time hoofers is a
special treat.▼
Tapeheads (1988) **C-97m.** ** D: Bill
Fishman. John Cusack, Tim Robbins, Doug
McClure, Connie Stevens, Clu Gulager,
Mary Crosby, Katy Boyer, Lyle Alzado,
Jessica Walter, Susan Tyrrell, Junior
Walker, Sam Moore. Energetic but pretentious and silly account of Cusack and Robbins' escapades and adventures as they try
to make it in the L.A. music world. Too
clever for its own good.▼
Tap Roots (1948) **C-109m.** **½ D: George
Marshall. Van Heflin, Susan Hayward,
Boris Karloff, Julie London, Whitfield
Connor, Ward Bond, Richard Long, Arthur Shields. Oddball venture into GWTW
territory, with Van and Susan as lovers in
progressive Mississippi county that says it
will secede from the state if the state
secedes from the Union! No big deal, but
watchable, with Karloff as an Indian medicine man.
Taps (1981) **C-118m.** **½ D: Harold
Becker. Timothy Hutton, George C. Scott,
Ronny Cox, Sean Penn, Tom Cruise,
Brendan Ward. Hutton leads fellow students in armed takeover of their military
academy, hoping their "clout" will keep
it from being torn down. Earnest performances help carry this film, which plays
all its cards too soon, leaving a lot of dead
space before its predictable outcome. Penn's
film debut.▼
Tarantula (1955) **C-80m.** *** D: Jack
Arnold. John Agar, Mara Corday, Leo G.
Carroll, Nestor Paiva, Ross Elliott, Eddie
Parker. Scientist Carroll's new growth formula works a little *too* well, and pretty
soon there's a humongous spider chewing
up the countryside. One of the best giant-

insect films, with fast pacing, convincing
special effects, and interesting subplot de-
tailing formula's effect on humans. That's
Clint Eastwood as the squadron leader in
final sequence.
Tarantulas: The Deadly Cargo (1977)
C-100m. TVM D: Stuart Hagmann. Claude
Akins, Charles Frank, Deborah Winters,
Pat Hingle, Sandy McPeak, Bert Remsen,
Howard Hesseman, Tom Atkins, Charles
Siebert. Horde of deadly tarantulas spreads
terror through small town. Would-be thriller
commits the unpardonable sin of being
dull. Below average.▼
Taras Bulba (1962) **C-122m.** **½ D: J.
Lee Thompson. Tony Curtis, Yul Brynner,
Christine Kaufmann, Sam Wanamaker,
George Macready. Cardboard costumer of
16th-century Ukraine, centering on Cos-
sack life and fighting. Nice photography
(on location in Argentina) by Joe MacDon-
ald and fine musical score by Franz Waxman. The Gogol novel was previously
filmed in 1936 in France (TARASS
BOULBA) and in 1939 in England (THE
REBEL SON).▼
Tarawa Beachhead (1958) **77m.** **½ D:
Paul Wendkos. Kerwin Mathews, Julie
Adams, Ray Danton, Karen Sharpe. Standard account of WW2 military assault with
usual focus on problems of troops.
Target (1985) **C-117m.** ** D: Arthur Penn.
Gene Hackman, Matt Dillon, Gayle Hunnicutt, Victoria Fyodorova, Josef Sommer,
Guy Boyd, Herbert Berghof. Ordinary guy
and his teenage son are suddenly plunged
into world of international intrigue when
they learn that wife/mom has been kidnapped while vacationing in Paris. Some
good action scenes help, but story is so
farfetched, key scenes so badly written,
and film so overlong that it has to count as
a misfire. Reteaming of Hackman and director Penn certainly promised better. ▼
Target Eagle (1984-Spanish-Mexican)
C-99m. **½ D: Jose Antonio de la Loma.
George (Jorge) Rivero, Maud Adams,
George Peppard, Max von Sydow, Chuck
Connors. Fine cast perks up routine programmer with Rivero as an eagle-tattooed
mercenary hired by Spanish police chief
von Sydow(!) to infiltrate a drug-smuggling
ring. Peppard is excellent in unusual casting as a suave but ruthless villain. ▼
Target Earth (1954) **75m.** **½ D: Sherman Rose. Richard Denning, Virginia Grey,
Kathleen Crowley, Richard Reeves, Robert Ruark, Steve Pendleton. People in deserted city trapped by invading robot force.
Competently acted movie starts off beautifully but bogs down too soon.▼
Target for Killing (1966-Austrian) **C-93m.**
*½ D: Manfred Kohler. Stewart Granger,
Curt Jurgens, Adolfo Celi, Klaus Kinski,
Rupert Davies, Scilla Gabel, Mollie Peters, Erika Remberg. Run-of-the-mill thriller

involving a secret agent trying to thwart the Mob's intended killing of a young heiress.

Target: Harry (1969) **C-81m.** *½ D: Henry Neill (Roger Corman). Vic Morrow, Suzanne Pleshette, Victor Buono, Cesar Romero, Stanley Holloway, Charlotte Rampling, Michael Ansara, Ahna Capri. Humdrum redoing of THE MALTESE FALCON, with the three stars mirroring Bogart, Astor, and Greenstreet. Originally shot for TV. Also known as HOW TO MAKE IT.

Target of an Assassin (1976-South African) **C-102m.** ** D: Peter Collinson. Anthony Quinn, John Phillip Law, Simon Sabela, Marius Weyers, Sandra Prinsloo. Fairish thriller story about two men who conspire against black African leader—one, a paid assassin, the other a desperate down-and-outer who kidnaps him for ransom. Original title: TIGERS DON'T CRY; also known as THE LONG SHOT.

Target Risk (1975) **C-78m.** **TVM** D: Robert Scheerer. Bo Svenson, Meredith Baxter, Robert Coote, Keenan Wynn, John P. Ryan, Philip Bruns. Gem courier Svenson is pressed into pulling off jewel heist to ransom his kidnapped girlfriend. Pilot for series that never materialized. Average.

✓ **Targets** (1968) **C-90m.** ***½ D: Peter Bogdanovich. Boris Karloff, Tim O'Kelly, Nancy Hsueh, James Brown, Sandy Baron, Arthur Peterson, Peter Bogdanovich, Randy Quaid. Karloff (as more or less himself) intends to retire, claiming his films can't compete with the horrors of everyday life; meanwhile, Vietnam veteran O'Kelly proves it by going out and shooting everybody in sight. Bogdanovich's first feature is incredibly suspenseful, with sweat-inducing climax at drive-in theatre; excellent photography by Laszlo Kovacs. Some prints still have brief gun-control prologue, which was added after Robert Kennedy's assassination.▼

Target, Sea of China (1954) **100m.** *½ D: Franklin Adreon. Harry Lauter, Aline Towne, Lyle Talbot, Robert Shayne, Fred Graham. Sloppy cliff-hanger nonsense of conspirators from unnamed foreign power aiding the rebellious natives. Reedited from Republic serial TRADER TOM OF THE CHINA SEAS.

Target Unknown (1951) **90m.** **½ D: George Sherman. Mark Stevens, Alex Nicol, Joyce Holden, Robert Douglas, Don Taylor, Gig Young. Imaginative handling of worn-out premise of group of Allied soldiers caught in Nazi-occupied France.

Target Zero (1955) **92m.** ** D: Harmon Jones. Richard Conte, Charles Bronson, Chuck Connors, L.Q. Jones, Peggie Castle. Unrewarding Korean War film.

Tarnished Angels, The (1958) **91m.** ***½ D: Douglas Sirk. Rock Hudson, Dorothy Malone, Robert Stack, Jack Carson, Robert Middleton. Compelling adaptation of William Faulkner's fatalistic drama *Pylon*, set in 1930s, with Hudson as newspaperman drawn to barnstorming pilot Stack—his curious life-style and ethics, his put-upon wife, and his frustrated mechanic.

Tarnished Lady (1931) **83m.** **½ D: George Cukor. Tallulah Bankhead, Clive Brook, Phoebe Foster, Osgood Perkins, Elizabeth Patterson. Bankhead marries Brook for his money but falls in love with him almost too late. Ornate triangle has good performances.

Tars and Spars (1946) **88m.** ** D: Alfred E. Green. Alfred Drake, Janet Blair, Sid Caesar, Marc Platt, Jeff Donnell, Ray Walker. Humdrum musical with Coast Guard backdrop, based very loosely on real-life camp show created by servicemen, one of whom, Sid Caesar, makes his movie debut doing a hilarious war-movie spoof. A rare film appearance for Broadway star Drake.

Tartars, The (1962-Italian) **C-83m.** ** D: Richard Thorpe. Orson Welles, Victor Mature, Folco Lulli, Liana Orfei. Welles' performance of Burundai, head of Tartar invasion of Volga River, plus appearance of Mature, are only distinguishing features of otherwise routine spectacle.

Tartu SEE: **Adventures of Tartu**▼

Tarzan Several generations of movie buffs have regarded Johnny Weissmuller as the definitive Tarzan, though Edgar Rice Burroughs' jungle king has been portrayed by numerous others since 1918, when beefy Elmo Lincoln first swung onto the screen. There were other silent-film versions of the Tarzan tale, but the next film to make a major impact was the early talkie TARZAN, THE APE MAN (1932), which starred Olympic swimming hero Weissmuller. Though it wasn't particularly faithful to Burroughs' book, it was an entertaining, well-made film that captured the imagination of a Depression-era audience, and led to a string of equally entertaining sequels. Buffs generally cite TARZAN AND HIS MATE (1934) as the best of all. This and the other 1930s entries in this series were "class" films with fine production values, plenty of action, and strong supporting casts, led, of course, by lovely Maureen O'Sullivan as Jane. (The success of these films inspired other producers to try and cash in with their own Tarzan projects, most of which were second-rate endeavors, though they all starred good-looking men who, like Weissmuller, had been Olympic medal winners: Buster Crabbe, Herman Brix, and Glenn Morris.) The later MGM outings such as TARZAN'S NEW YORK ADVENTURE became more contrived, like other series films, with often-excessive comedy relief supplied by

Cheetah the chimp, and family interest sparked by the arrival of Johnny Sheffield as Boy. When MGM lost interest in the series, Weissmuller continued making Tarzan movies for producer Sol Lesser at RKO, without O'Sullivan and without that MGM production sheen. Lex Barker took over the role in 1949, and the series became progressively more routine; Barker did his last jungle outing in 1955. Since then a number of people have played Tarzan, including Denny Miller (who starred in a 1959 remake of Weissmuller's 1932 film, filled with tinted stock footage from the original), Jock Mahoney (who also played supporting roles in two other Tarzan films), Mike Henry, and Gordon Scott, the latter faring best in some well-produced British-made adventure stories (including TARZAN'S GREATEST ADVENTURE, an excellent jungle tale shot in color, with young Sean Connery in the cast). Ron Ely took on the role for a Mexican-filmed TV series, and some of these episodes have been strung together into ersatz feature films. But the most recent theatrical ventures involving Tarzan have all been unusual: an unappealing animated spoof called SHAME OF THE JUNGLE featuring the voice of Johnny Weissmuller, Jr.; a live-action farce called TARZAN, THE APE MAN designed as a showcase for sexy Bo Derek; a television update, with tongue in cheek, called TARZAN IN MANHATTAN; and the most ambitious of them all, GREYSTOKE: THE LEGEND OF TARZAN, LORD OF THE APES, which purported to return to Edgar Rice Burroughs' original concept but (for all its dramatic success) deviated from the source in its own way. Compared to a film like GREYSTOKE, the old series films might look simplistic and even quaint— but they're unpretentious and certainly entertaining. And faithful or not, Johnny Weissmuller's Tarzan may still represent the indelible image in most people's minds of Burroughs' legendary jungle character.

Tarzan and His Mate (1934) **93m.** D: Cedric Gibbons, Jack Conway. Johnny Weissmuller, Maureen O'Sullivan, Neil Hamilton, Paul Cavanagh, Forrester Harvey.

Tarzan and the Amazons (1945) **76m.** D: Kurt Neumann. Johnny Weissmuller, Brenda Joyce, Johnny Sheffield, Henry Stephenson, Maria Ouspenskaya, Barton MacLane.

Tarzan and the Great River (1967) **C-99m.** D: Robert Day. Mike Henry, Jan Murray, Manuel Padilla Jr., Diana Millay, Rafer Johson.

Tarzan and the Green Goddess (1938) **72m.** D: Edward Kull. Herman Brix (Bruce Bennett), Ula Holt, Frank Baker, Don Castello, Lewis Sargent. Feature version

of THE NEW ADVENTURES OF TARZAN serial. SEE: Tarzan series.▼

Tarzan and the Huntress (1947) **72m.** D: Kurt Neumann. Johnny Weissmuller, Brenda Joyce, Johnny Sheffield, Patricia Morison, Barton MacLane.

Tarzan and the Jungle Boy (1968) **C-99m.** D: Robert Day. Mike Henry, Alizia Gur, Ronald Gans, Rafer Johnson, Ed Johnson, Steven Bond.

Tarzan and the Leopard Woman (1946) **72m.** D: Kurt Neumann. Johnny Weissmuller, Brenda Joyce, Johnny Sheffield, Acquanetta, Edgar Barrier, Tommy Cook.

Tarzan and the Lost Safari (1957-British) **C-84m.** D: H. Bruce Humberstone. Gordon Scott, Yolande Donlan, Betta St. John, Wilfrid Hyde-White, George Coulouris.

Tarzan and the Mermaids (1948) **68m.** D: Robert Florey. Johnny Weissmuller, Brenda Joyce, Linda Christian, George Zucco, John Laurenz, Fernando Wagner.

Tarzan and the She-Devil (1953) **76m.** D: Kurt Neumann. Lex Barker, Joyce MacKenzie, Raymond Burr, Monique Van Vooren, Tom Conway.

Tarzan and the Slave Girl (1950) **74m.** D: Lee Sholem. Lex Barker, Vanessa Brown, Robert Alda, Denise Darcel, Hurd Hatfield.

Tarzan and the Trappers (1958) **74m.** D: Charles Haas and Sandy Howard. Gordon Scott, Eve Brent, Rickie Sorensen, Lesley Bradley, Maurice Marsac.▼

Tarzan and the Valley of Gold (1966) **C-90m.** D: Robert Day. Mike Henry, David Opatoshu, Manuel Padilla Jr., Nancy Kovack, Don Megowan.

Tarzan Escapes (1936) **95m.** D: Richard Thorpe. Johnny Weissmuller, Maureen O'Sullivan, John Buckler, Benita Hume, William Henry, Herbert Mundin.

Tarzan Finds a Son! (1939) **90m.** D: Richard Thorpe. Johnny Weissmuller, Maureen O'Sullivan, Johnny Sheffield, Ian Hunter, Frieda Inescort, Laraine Day, Henry Wilcoxon.

Tarzan Goes to India (1962-British) **C-86m.** D: John Guillermin. Jock Mahoney, Mark Dana, Simi, Leo Gordon.

Tarzan in Manhattan (1989) **C-100m.** TVM D: Michael Schultz. Joe Lara, Kim Crosby, Tony Curtis, Jan-Michael Vincent, Jimmy Medina Taggert. Tarzan hits the Big Apple when he finds that some no-good guys have been monkeying around with Cheetah, chimpnapping the little guy in Africa on behalf of nasty vivisectionists. Lighthearted pilot to a prospective new series featuring male model Lara as moviedom's 18th Tarzan and Crosby as a Brooklynese cabbie named Jane. Average.

Tarzan of the Apes (1918) **55m.** ****½** D: Scott Sidney. Elmo Lincoln, Enid Markey, True Boardman, Kathleen Kirkham, Gordon Griffith. The very first Tarzan film is a surprisingly watchable and straightforward telling of the Greystoke tale, though Lincoln looks like he's about fifty years old, with a beer belly to boot.▼

Tarzan's Deadly Silence (1970) **C-99m.** D: Robert L. Friend. Ron Ely, Manuel Padilla Jr., Jock Mahoney, Woody Strode, Gregorio Acosta, Nichelle Nichols.

Tarzan's Desert Mystery (1943) **70m.** D: William Thiele. Johnny Weissmuller, Nancy Kelly, Johnny Sheffield, Otto Kruger, Joseph Sawyer, Lloyd Corrigan, Robert Lowery.

Tarzan's Fight for Life (1958) **C-86m.** D: H. Bruce Humberstone. Gordon Scott, Eve Brent, Rickie Sorensen, Jil Jarmyn.

Tarzan's Greatest Adventure (1959-British) **C-88m.** D: John Guillermin. Gordon Scott, Anthony Quayle, Sara Shane, Niall MacGinnis, Scilla Gabel, Sean Connery.

Tarzan's Hidden Jungle (1955) **73m.** D: Harold Schuster. Gordon Scott, Vera Miles, Peter Van Eyck, Jack Elam, Rex Ingram.

Tarzan's Jungle Rebellion (1970) **C-92m.** D: William Witney. Ron Ely, Manuel Padilla Jr., Ulla Stromstedt, Sam Jaffe, William Marshall, Lloyd Haynes.

Tarzan's Magic Fountain (1949) **73m.** D: Lee Sholem. Lex Barker, Brenda Joyce, Evelyn Ankers, Albert Dekker, Alan Napier, Charles Drake, Henry Brandon.

Tarzan's New Adventure SEE: New Adventures of Tarzan, The

Tarzan's New York Adventure (1942) **71m.** D: Richard Thorpe. Johnny Weissmuller, Maureen O'Sullivan, Johnny Sheffield, Virginia Grey, Charles Bickford, Paul Kelly, Russell Hicks, Miles Mander.

Tarzan's Peril (1951) **79m.** D: Byron Haskin. Lex Barker, Virginia Huston, George Macready, Douglas Fowley.

Tarzan's Revenge (1938) **70m.** D: D. Ross Lederman. Glenn Morris, Eleanor Holm, George Barbier, C. Henry Gordon, Hedda Hopper, George Meeker.▼

Tarzan's Savage Fury (1952) **80m.** D: Cyril Endfield. Lex Barker, Dorothy Hart, Patric Knowles, Charles Korvin.

Tarzan's Secret Treasure (1941) **81m.** D: Richard Thorpe. Johnny Wessmuller, Maureen O'Sullivan, Johnny Sheffield, Reginald Owen, Barry Fitzgerald, Tom Conway.

Tarzan's Three Challenges (1963) **C-92m.** D: Robert Day. Jock Mahoney, Woody Strode, Ricky Der, Tsuruko Kobayashi.

Tarzan, the Ape Man (1932) **99m.** D: W. S. Van Dyke. Johnny Weissmuller, Maureen O'Sullivan, C. Aubrey Smith, Neil Hamilton, Doris Lloyd. Also shown in computer-colored version.▼

Tarzan, the Ape Man (1959) **C-82m.** D: Joseph M. Newman. Dennis Miller, Joanna Barnes, Cesare Danova, Robert Douglas, Thomas Yangha.

Tarzan, The Ape Man (1981) **C-112m.** BOMB D: John Derek. Bo Derek, Richard Harris, Miles O'Keeffe, John Phillip Law, Wilfrid Hyde-White. Deranged "remake" of original Tarzan film lacks action, humor, and charm—and nearly forced editors of this book to devise a rating lower than BOMB. Forget about Weissmuller comparisons: O'Keeffe makes *Elmo Lincoln* look like Edwin Booth. If you really want to see Derek unclothed, buy a pinup calendar.▼

Tarzan the Fearless (1933) **85m.** D: Robert F. Hill. Buster Crabbe, Jacqueline Wells (Julie Bishop), E. Alyn Warren, Eddie Woods, Philo McCullough, Mathew Betz, Frank Lackteen, Mischa Auer. (Adapted from serial.)▼

Tarzan the Magnificent (1960-British) **C-88m.** D: Robert Day. Gordon Scott. Jock Mahoney, Betta St. John, John Carradine, Alexandra Stewart, Lionel Jeffries, Earl Cameron.

Tarzan Triumphs (1943) **78m.** D: William Thiele. Johnny Weissmuller, Frances Gifford, Johnny Sheffield, Stanley Ridges, Sig Ruman.

Task Force (1949) **116m.** **½** D: Delmer Daves. Gary Cooper, Jane Wyatt, Wayne Morris, Walter Brennan, Julie London, Bruce Bennett, Stanley Ridges, Jack Holt. Well-made but unremarkable story of a Naval officer's career, tracing aircraft carrier development. Originally shown with some scenes in color.

Taste of Evil, A (1971) **C-73m.** TVM D: John Llewellyn Moxey. Barbara Parkins, Barbara Stanwyck, Roddy McDowall, William Windom, Arthur O'Connell, Bing Russell. Young woman's return from mental institution after traumatic rape incident predictably slides into near-total relapse: is it her imagination? Mechanical plot line should have been far, far better. Average.

Taste of Honey, A (1961-British) **100m.** ***½** D: Tony Richardson. Rita Tushingham, Robert Stephens, Dora Bryan, Murray Melvin, Paul Danquah. Homely young girl who has affair with black sailor and becomes pregnant, is cared for by homosexual friend. Shelagh Delaney's London and Broadway stage hit is poignant and uncompromising film with fine, sensitive performances.▼

Taste the Blood of Dracula (1970-British) **C-95m.** **½** D: Peter Sasdy. Christopher Lee, Geoffrey Keen, Gwen Watford, Linda Hayden, Roy Kinnear, Ralph Bates. Fourth in Hammer series (after DRACULA HAS RISEN FROM THE GRAVE) with Lee as famed vampire out to avenge death of Black Magic wizard by affluent thrill seekers in Victorian England. Direction, acting, production not bad, but what was point of having Dracula in film? Beginning and end best parts. Sequel: SCARS OF DRACULA.

Tattered Dress, The (1957) **93m.** **½** D:

Jack Arnold. Jeff Chandler, Jeanne Crain, Jack Carson, Gail Russell, George Tobias. Slowly paced but watchable account of lawyer Chandler defending society couple accused of murder; Crain is his sympathetic wife.

Tattered Web, A (1971) **C-73m. TVM** D: Paul Wendkos. Lloyd Bridges, Frank Converse, Broderick Crawford, Murray Hamilton, Sallie Shockley, Anne Helm. Good supporting cast bolsters so-so morality play of police detective trying to restore his dignity. Average.▼

Tattoo (1981) **C-103m.** *½ D: Bob Brooks. Bruce Dern, Maud Adams, Leonard Frey, Rikke Borge, John Getz, Peter Iachangelo. Mentally ill tattoo-artist Dern kidnaps fashion model Adams so he can use her body as a canvas. Improbable, sleazy melodrama; screenplay by Joyce Bunuel (Luis's daughter-in-law) from a story by director Brooks.▼

Tawny Pipit (1944-British) **85m.** **½ D: Bernard Miles, Charles Saunders. Bernard Miles, Rosamund John, Niall MacGinnis, Jean Gillie, George Carney, Christopher Steele, Lucie Mannheim, Wylie Watson, Ian Fleming. Slight but appealing story of some English villagers' fight to save the title rare breed of birds, who have nested in a nearby field. Miles and Saunders also scripted.

Taxi! (1932) **70m.** **½ D: Roy Del Ruth. James Cagney, Loretta Young, George E. Stone, Dorothy Burgess, Guy Kibbee, Leila Bennett, Cotton Club Orchestra. Hokey but colorful Depression melodrama of warring N.Y.C. cab drivers, with Cagney fine as a hotheaded hack. Yes, that's George Raft as his dance-contest rival . . . but nothing can top Jimmy's opening bit in Yiddish!

Taxi (1953) **77m.** ** D: Gregory Ratoff. Dan Dailey, Constance Smith, Neva Patterson, Blanche Yurka, Stubby Kaye. Mild little comedy of N.Y.C. cab driver Dailey trying to help an Irish girl find her husband. John Cassavetes' film debut.

√ **Taxi Driver** (1976) **C-113m.** ** D: Martin Scorsese. Robert De Niro, Cybill Shepherd, Harvey Keitel, Peter Boyle, Jodie Foster, Albert Brooks, Leonard Harris, Joe Spinell, Martin Scorsese. To some, Scorsese and writer Paul Schrader's perception of hell—as a crazed taxi driver's vision of N.Y.C.—was brilliant. To us, this gory, cold-blooded story of sick man's supposed catharsis through violence is ugly and unredeeming. Judge for yourself. Searing performances and Bernard Herrmann's final music score are among film's few virtues.▼

Taxi For Tobruk (1965-French) **90m.** **½ D: Denys De La Patelliere. Lino Ventura, Hardy Kruger, Charles Aznavour, German Cobos. Engaging study of French soldiers and their German prisoner crossing the desert during WW2.

Taxing Woman, A (1987-Japanese) **C-126m.** ***½ D: Juzo Itami. Nobuko Miyamoto, Tsutomo Yamazaki. Disarming contemporary comedy about a tireless, single-minded investigator for the Japanese Revenue Service, and her confrontation with a hotshot businessman who thinks he knows all the angles when it comes to cheating the government. Somewhat overlong, but delightful, with a winning performance by Miyamoto (writer-director Itami's wife) in the lead. Followed by a sequel.▼

Taxing Woman Returns, A (1988-Japanese) **C-127m.** *** D: Juzo Itami. Nobuko Miyamoto, Rentaro Mikuni, Masahiko Tsugawa, Tetsuro Tamba, Toru Masuoka, Takeya Nakamura, Hosei Komatsu, Mihoko Shibata. Miyamoto "returns" as the dedicated tax investigator; here, she takes on a gaggle of industrialists, politicians, mobsters, and other assorted hypocrites who've conspired to grossly inflate Tokyo's real estate values. On-the-mark satire is as pointed and knowing as it is funny.▼

Taza, Son of Cochise (1954) **C-79m.** **½ D: Douglas Sirk. Rock Hudson, Barbara Rush, Gregg Palmer, Bart Roberts, Morris Ankrum, Joe Sawyer. Actually two sons: one wants to live peacefully with the white man, the other thinks Geronimo has a better idea. Sirk's only Western is uneven followup to BROKEN ARROW—with Jeff Chandler popping in just long enough to die—but sweeping action scenes and sympathetic treatment of Indians help. Originally in 3-D.

√ **Tea and Sympathy** (1956) **C-122m.** *** D: Vincente Minnelli. Deborah Kerr, John Kerr, Leif Erickson, Edward Andrews, Darryl Hickman, Dean Jones, Norma Crane. Glossy but well-acted version of Robert Anderson play about prep school boy's affair with a teacher's wife, skirting homosexual issues. Both Kerrs give sensitive portrayals. Scripted by the playwright. All three stars (including Erickson) recreate their Broadway roles.

Teacher, The (1974) **C-98m.** ** D: Hikmet Avedis. Angel Tompkins, Jay North, Anthony James, Marlene Schmidt, Sivi Aberg, Barry Atwater, Med Flory. Trashy but enjoyable film has "older" woman Tompkins introducing North (TV's *Dennis the Menace* all grown up) to sex, while a psychopathic killer (James) threatens both their lives. John Cassavetes' and Gena Rowlands' mommies have cute cameos as disapproving bystanders in a restaurant scene.▼

Teacher and the Miracle, The (1961-Italian) **88m.** **½ D: Aldo Fabrizi. Eduardo Nevola, Marco Paolette, Mary Lamar, Jose Calvo. Good tear-jerker of man broken by death of son who had inspired him to start art school. Cast gives adequate performance.

Teachers (1984) **C-106m.** ** D: Arthur Hiller. Nick Nolte, JoBeth Williams, Judd Hirsch, Ralph Macchio, Lee Grant, Richard Mulligan, Allen Garfield, Royal Dano, Laura Dern, Morgan Freeman, William Schallert, Crispin Glover, Zohra Lampert, Art Metrano. "Outrageous" blend of comedy-drama set in urban high school (and filmed in Columbus, Ohio). Seemingly patterned after Paddy Chayefsky's THE HOSPITAL and NETWORK but nowhere near as good. Slick, well cast, but dramatically disjointed and obvious at every turn.▼

Teacher's Pet (1958) **120m.** *** D: George Seaton. Clark Gable, Doris Day, Gig Young, Mamie Van Doren, Nick Adams, Charles Lane. Self-educated city editor Gable clashes with journalism teacher Day in this airy, amusing comedy. Young is memorable as Doris' intellectual boyfriend. Written by Fay and Michael Kanin.▼

Tea for Two (1950) **C-98m.** **½ D: David Butler. Doris Day, Gordon MacRae, Gene Nelson, Eve Arden, Billy DeWolfe. One of Day's better Warner Bros. musicals, loosely based on *No, No, Nanette*; Doris must say "no" to every question for 24 hours in order to win enough money to finance a Broadway musical she wants to star in.

Teahouse of the August Moon, The (1956) **C-123m.** ***½ D: Daniel Mann. Marlon Brando, Glenn Ford, Machiko Kyo, Eddie Albert, Paul Ford. Outstanding comedy scripted by John Patrick from his hit play of army officers involved with Americanization of post-WW2 Okinawa. A warm and memorable film.▼

Tears in the Rain (1988-British) **C-101m.** TVM D: Don Sharp. Sharon Stone, Christopher Cazenove, Leigh Lawson, Anna Massey, Maurice Denham, Paul Daneman. *Harlequin Romance* soap opera of forbidden love between a young American woman, in England to fulfill her mother's dying wish, and the wealthy son of the man who was her mother's lover. Average.

Teckman Mystery, The (1954-British) **89m.** ** D: Wendy Toye. Margaret Leighton, John Justin, Meier Tzelniker, Roland Culver, George Coulouris, Michael Medwin. Justin is writer commissioned to do a biography of Medwin, presumably dead war hero, with surprising results. Capably acted.

Ted Kennedy Jr. Story, The (1986) **C-100m.** TVM D: Delbert Mann. Craig T. Nelson, Susan Blakely, Kimber Shoop, Michael J. Shannon, Dennis Creaghan. Well-realized true-life story of young Teddy Kennedy's overcoming the loss of a leg to cancer at age 12. This one's the story of a courageous youth—not simply a Kennedy (played by natural newcomer

Shoop). The real Ted Kennedy, Jr., appears in an epilogue. Written con brio by veteran Roger O. Hirson. Above average.

Teenage Bad Girl SEE: **Bad Girl**▼

Teenage Caveman (1958) **66m.** ** D: Roger Corman. Robert Vaughn, Darrah Marshall, Leslie Bradley, Frank De Kova. Vaughn, light years away from THE YOUNG PHILADELPHIANS or S.O.B., is the title character, a prehistoric adolescent hankering for greener pastures, in this AIP quickie with predictable "surprise" ending.

Teen-age Crime Wave (1955) **77m.** BOMB D: Fred F. Sears. Tommy Cook, Sue English, Molly McCart, Frank Griffin, James Bell, Ray Riehl. Adolescent hoodlums terrorize farm family after a robbery and shooting. Bad.

Teenage Devil Dolls (1952) **58m.** BOMB D: B. Lawrence Price, Jr. Barbara Marks, Robert A. Sherry, Robert Norman, Elaine Lindenbaum, Joel Climenhaga. Yet another entry in the REEFER MADNESS school of filmmaking, about an insecure, discontented teen girl's descent into drug addiction and crime. Presented as a case history and without dialogue; there's only narration and special effects.▼

Teenage Doll (1957) **68m.** ** D: Roger Corman. June Kenney, Fay Spain, Richard Devon, Dorothy Neumann. Title dish doesn't want to spend school nights at home in her room, gets involved with punk peers. This above-average sleazy B won't obscure memory of Dreyer and Ozu, but is true to its era.

Teen-age Millionaire (1961) **84m.** BOMB D: Lawrence Doheny. Jimmy Clanton, ZaSu Pitts, Rocky Graziano, Diane Jergens, Chubby Checker, Jackie Wilson, Dion, Marv Johnson, Bill Black, Jack Larson, Vicki Spencer, Sid Gould, Maurice Gosfield. Deadening musical about teenager Clanton, with a huge inheritance, who becomes a pop star. The rock acts are unusually and annoyingly tame here.

Teenage Mutant Ninja Turtles (1990) **C-93m.** ** D: Steve Barron. Judith Hoag, Elias Koteas, voices of Robbie Rist, Kevin Clash, Brian Tochi, David McCharen, Corey Feldman. Four mutated turtles who live in the sewers of N.Y.C. with their ninja master (an oversized rat from Japan) befriend a plucky TV reporter and help crack an insidious crime wave. The wacked-out comic book creation of Kevin Eastman and Peter Laird (which led to a hit animated TV series) should have inspired a much better movie. Badly written, flatly directed, and murky-looking, it jump-starts every now and then—but not often enough. Strongest asset is the design and articulation of the Turtles by Jim Henson's Creature Shop.▼

Teenage Psycho Meets Bloody Mary,

The SEE: **Incredibly Strange Creatures Who Stopped Living and Became Mixed-Up Zombies, The▼**

Teen-age Rebel (1956) **94m. **½** D:** Edmund Goulding. Ginger Rogers, Michael Rennie, Betty Lou Keim, Mildred Natwick, Rusty Swope, Warren Berlinger, Lilli Gentle, Louise Beavers, Irene Hervey. Pat yet provocative film of divorcée Rogers, now remarried, trying to reestablish understanding with her daughter.

Teenagers From Outer Space (1959) **86m.** BOMB **D:** Tom Graeff. David Love (Tom Graeff), Dawn Anderson, Harvey B. Dunn, Bryant Grant, Tom Lockyear. Ridiculous sci-fi about alien youths who bring monster to Earth, shown as the shadow of a lobster! Very, very cheap; besides directing and starring, Graeff wrote, produced, photographed, and edited!▼

Teenage Zombies (1958) **73m.** BOMB **D:** Jerry Warren. Don Sullivan, Steve Conte, Katherine Victor, Paul Pepper, Bri Murphy, Mitzi Albertson. Victor captures teenagers snooping around her island, imprisons them for experiments. Typically awful Warren horror film with long stretches in which nothing happens . . . and incidentally, no teenage zombies! Remade as FRANKENSTEIN ISLAND.▼

Teen Witch (1989) **C-105m.** ** **D:** Dorian Walker. Robyn Lively, Dan Gauthier, Joshua Miller, Dick Sargent, Zelda Rubinstein, Lisa Fuller, Shelley Berman. Teen comedy with a moral, about a girl who, one week before her sixteenth birthday, learns that she's a descendant of some bona fide Salem witches . . . and uses her newfound magical powers to snare a football hero as boyfriend. Some nice ideas, but mostly falls flat. Berman is funny as a stuffy English teacher who becomes a victim of the teenage witch's black magic.▼

Teen Wolf (1985) **C-91m.** ** **D:** Rod Daniel. Michael J. Fox, James Hampton, Scott Paulin, Susan Ursitti, Jerry Levine, Jim MacKrell. Teenager with usual growing pains discovers that he's also a werewolf—and that this finally makes him popular at school. Pleasant at best, but anemic comedy has nowhere to go. Best moments come from TV comedy writer-producer (and former comic) Jay Tarses as Fox's athletic coach. Followed by an animated TV series and TEEN WOLF TOO.▼

Teen Wolf Too (1987) **C-95m.** BOMB **D:** Christopher Leitch. Jason Bateman, Kim Darby, John Astin, Paul Sand, James Hampton, Mark Holton. Limp comedy, chronicling the adventures of the Teen Wolf's cousin (Bateman), makes the original seem like Preston Sturges in his prime. Excruciating.▼

Telefon (1977) **C-102m.** *** **D:** Don Siegel. Charles Bronson, Lee Remick, Donald Pleasence, Tyne Daly, Patrick Magee, Alan Badel, Sheree North. Slick espionage thriller from Walter Wager's ingenious novel; Bronson is Russian agent sent to stop crazy defector from triggering hypnotized spies to commit sabotage throughout U.S. Daly is terrific as wisecracking computer expert. Script by Stirling Silliphant and original director Peter Hyams.▼

Telephone, The (1988) **C-82m.** BOMB **D:** Rip Torn. Whoopi Goldberg, Severn Darden, Amy Wright, Elliott Gould, John Heard. Goldberg may have hit rock bottom with this clinker in which she's cast as an out-of-work actress with major psychological problems. Goldberg had real-life problems with the finished film too; she sued to prevent this version from being released. Terrible script by Harry Nilsson and Terry Southern. Hang up on this wrong number.▼

Telethon (1977) **C-100m.** TVM **D:** David Lowell Rich. Polly Bergen, Lloyd Bridges, Red Buttons, Edd Byrnes, Dick Clark, Janet Leigh, Kent McCord, David Selby, Jill St. John, Jimmie Walker, Sugar Ray Robinson. Take any of those all-star TV disaster flicks, move it to Vegas, lay on a Jerry Lewis-style fundraiser, and you get this. Below average.

Tell It to the Judge (1949) **87m.** **½ **D:** Norman Foster. Rosalind Russell, Robert Cummings, Gig Young, Marie McDonald, Harry Davenport, Douglass Dumbrille. Flyweight marital farce with Russell and Cummings in and out of love every ten minutes; enjoyable if you like the stars.

Tell Me a Riddle (1980) **C-90m.** **½ **D:** Lee Grant. Melvyn Douglas, Lila Kedrova, Brooke Adams, Dolores Dorn, Bob Elross, Joan Harris, Zalman King. Thoughtful but static filmization of Tillie Olsen's novella chronicling the relationship between a dying woman and her husband of 40 years. Well acted by Douglas and Kedrova; Grant's first feature as director. That's Peter Coyote as the young Douglas.▼

Tell Me Lies (1968-British) **C-118m.** ** **D:** Peter Brook. Glenda Jackson, The Royal Shakespeare Company, Kingsley Amis, Stokely Carmichael, Paul Scofield. Strange, unsuccessful combination of songs, skits, and newsreel footage attacking U.S. involvement in Vietnam wasn't even liked by doves. Interesting now merely as historical document.

Tell Me My Name (1977) **C-80m.** TVM **D:** Delbert Mann. Arthur Hill, Barbara Barrie, Barnard Hughes, Valerie Mahaffey. Weeper about mother forced to reveal her past after being confronted by illegitimate 19-year-old daughter. Formula soap opera for which even the fine performers cannot work up much enthusiasm. Below average.

Tell Me That You Love Me, Junie Moon (1970) **C-112m.** ***½ **D:** Otto Preminger.

Liza Minnelli, Ken Howard, Robert Moore, James Coco, Kay Thompson, Fred Williamson, Nancy Marchand, Anne Revere. Moving story of three misfits who decide to live together: facially scarred Minnelli, epileptic Howard, wheelchair-bound homosexual Moore. Moments of comedy, melodrama, compassion expertly blended by Preminger in one of his best films; adapted from her novel by Marjorie Kellogg.

Tell Me Where It Hurts (1974) **C-78m.** TVM D: Paul Bogart. Maureen Stapleton, Paul Sorvino, Doris Dowling, Fay Kanin, Rose Gregorio, John Randolph, Ayn Ruymen, Louise Latham. Unhappy homemaker Stapleton starts a discussion group with her closest friends to find new meaning. Fay Kanin's incisive script won an Emmy, but the going's plodding. Average.

Tell No Tales (1938) **69m.** **½ D: Leslie Fenton. Melvyn Douglas, Louise Platt, Gene Lockhart, Douglass Dumbrille, Sara Haden, Florence George, Halliwell Hobbes, Zeffie Tilbury. Editor tries to save his dying newspaper by capturing notorious kidnappers himself. Good B picture with some telling vignettes (particularly a black boxer's wake), though it doesn't hold up to the finish.

Tell-Tale Heart, The (1963-British) **81m.** ** D: Ernest Morris. Laurence Payne, Adrienne Corri, Dermot Walsh, Selma Vaz Dias. Edgar Allan Poe yarn elaborated into tale of jealous love murder; not sufficiently atmospheric.▼

Tell Them Willie Boy Is Here (1969) **C-96m.** *** D: Abraham Polonsky. Robert Redford, Katharine Ross, Robert Blake, Susan Clark, Barry Sullivan, Charles McGraw, John Vernon. Massive manhunt for Indian who killed in self-defense pretends to be more important than it is, but is so well-crafted the preaching can be overlooked. Moodily photographed by Conrad Hall. The blacklisted Polonsky's first film since FORCE OF EVIL twenty-one years before.▼

Tempest (1928) **102m.** *** D: Sam Taylor. John Barrymore, Camilla Horn, Louis Wolheim, George Fawcett, Ullrich Haupt, Michael Visaroff. Lushly filmed tale of Russian Revolution, with peasant Barrymore rising to rank of sergeant, controlling fate of Princess (Horn) who had previously scorned him.▼

Tempest (1959-Italian) **C-125m.** **½ D: Alberto Lattuada. Silvana Mangano, Van Heflin, Viveca Lindfors, Geoffrey Horne, Oscar Homolka, Robert Keith, Agnes Moorehead, Finlay Currie, Vittorio Gassman, Helmut Dantine. Turgid, disjointed costumer set in 18th-century Russia, loosely based on Pushkin novel about peasant uprising to dethrone Catherine the Great (Lindfors).

Tempest (1982) **C-140m.** ** D: Paul Mazursky. John Cassavetes, Gena Rowlands, Susan Sarandon, Vittorio Gassman, Raul Julia, Molly Ringwald, Sam Robards, Paul Stewart, Anthony Holland. Aimless comedy, loosely based on Shakespeare's play, has Cassavetes as a N.Y.C. architect who tries to solve his midlife crisis by moving to a Greek island with his teenage daughter. Appealing cast, beautiful scenery, some engaging scenes . . . but they don't quite add up.▼

Temptation (1946) **92m.** **½ D: Irving Pichel. Merle Oberon, George Brent, Paul Lukas, Charles Korvin, Lenore Ulric, Ludwig Stossel. Woman-with-a-past Oberon marries archeologist Brent, then falls in love with unscrupulous Korvin. Nothing new, but smoothly done.

Tempter, The (1974-Italian) **C-96m.** BOMB D: Alberto de Martino. Carla Gravina, Mel Ferrer, Arthur Kennedy, George Coulouris, Alida Valli, Umberto Orsini. Frenzied but pointless rip-off of THE EXORCIST with Gravina as Ferrer's demonized daughter. Blecch.▼

Temptress, The (1926) **117m.** **½ D: Fred Niblo. Greta Garbo, Antonio Moreno, Roy D'Arcy, Marc MacDermott, Lionel Barrymore, Virginia Brown Faire. Garbo's second American film is dated curio about wicked woman who drives men to death and destruction, only to have her own life ruined by falling in love with Moreno. Adapted from Blasco-Ibanez; some prints run 95m.

10 (1979) **C-122m.** ** D: Blake Edwards. Dudley Moore, Julie Andrews, Bo Derek, Robert Webber, Dee Wallace, Sam Jones, Brian Dennehy, Max Showalter, Don Calfa, Nedra Volz, James Noble. Middle-aged songwriter finds himself hung up on sex, especially when he sets eyes on beautiful Derek. Blake Edwards' idea of a real sophisticated movie; sporadically funny but tiresome, glib, and pompous. Doug Sheehan is one of the policemen at Moore's house.▼

Tenafly (1972) **C-100m.** TVM D: Richard Colla. James McEachin, Mel Ferrer, Ed Nelson, John Ericson, Lillian Lehman. Unusual mixture of whodunit suspense narrative and slice-of-life comedy as black private-eye investigates death of talk-show host's wife. Written by Richard Levinson and William Link. Average; pilot for the series.

Tenant, The (1976-French-U.S.) **C-125m.** ***½ D: Roman Polanski. Roman Polanski, Isabelle Adjani, Melvyn Douglas, Jo Van Fleet, Shelley Winters, Bernard Fresson, Lila Kedrova, Claude Dauphin. Unique, bizarrely cast horror film about a timid clerk who rents an apartment whose previous inhabitant attempted suicide. Critically drubbed upon release, but a sure bet to become cult item over the years; fine photography by Sven Nykvist.▼

Ten Cents a Dance (1931) **80m.** *½ D: Lionel Barrymore. Barbara Stanwyck, Ricardo Cortez, Monroe Owsley, Sally Blane, Blanche Frederici. Dreary, slow-moving drama about a taxi dancer's unfortunate marriage to a worthless wimp, who turns out to be a crook and a cheat, as well.

Ten Commandments, The (1923) **146m.** *** D: Cecil B. DeMille. Theodore Roberts, Charles de Roche, Estelle Taylor, Richard Dix, Rod La Rocque, Leatrice Joy, Nita Naldi, Agnes Ayres. Biblical story, told in compact form (but on a gargantuan scale—with several scenes in two-color Technicolor) is only first portion of this silent film. The rest is a modern-day parable involving two brothers, one a saint, the other a sinner—and it's anything but subtle. Still, it's good entertainment in the best DeMille style.▼

Ten Commandments, The (1956) **C-220m.** **** D: Cecil B. DeMille. Charlton Heston, Yul Brynner, Anne Baxter, Edward G. Robinson, Yvonne De Carlo, Debra Paget, John Derek, Cedric Hardwicke, H.B. Warner, Henry Wilcoxon, Nina Foch, Martha Scott, Judith Anderson, Vincent Price, John Carradine, Woodrow "Woody" Strode. Vivid storytelling at its best. Biblical epic follows Moses' life from birth and abandonment through manhood, slavery, and trials in leading the Jews out of Egypt. Few subtleties in DeMille's second handling of this tale (first filmed in 1923) but few lulls, either. Parting of the Red Sea, writing of the tablets are unforgettable highlights. Oscar-winning special effects.▼

Ten Days That Shook the World SEE: **October**▼

Ten Days to Tulara (1958) **77m.** BOMB D: George Sherman. Sterling Hayden, Grace Raynor, Rodolfo Hoyos, Carlos Muzquiz. Dud adventure account of Hayden at al pursued across Mexico by police for the gold they carry.

Ten Days Wonder (1972-French) **C-101m.** **½ D: Claude Chabrol. Orson Welles, Anthony Perkins, Marlene Jobert, Michel Piccoli, Guido Alberti. Ellery Queen meets Claude Chabrol in erratic but moody mystery concerning Perkins' love affair with stepmother Jobert. Film doesn't work, but is often fascinating to watch.▼

Tender Age, The SEE: **Little Sister, The**▼

Tender Comrade (1943) **C-102m.** **½ D: Edward Dmytryk. Ginger Rogers, Robert Ryan, Ruth Hussey, Patricia Collinge, Mady Christians, Kim Hunter, Jane Darwell. Rogers and friends live communally while their men are out fighting the war, a situation that caused this Dmytryk-Dalton Trumbo collaboration to be labeled as Com-

munist propaganda by HUAC in later years. Some unbearable—and ironically, pro-American—speechifying, but occasionally fascinating as social history.

Tender Flesh SEE: **Welcome to Arrow Beach**

Tenderfoot, The (1932) **70m.** **½ D: Ray Enright. Joe E. Brown, Ginger Rogers, Lew Cody, George Chandler, Allan Lane, Vivien Oakland. Brown's a naive cowboy who wants to back a Broadway show in the worst way—and does.

Tender Is the Night (1962) **C-146m.** **½ D: Henry King. Jennifer Jones, Jason Robards, Jr., Joan Fontaine, Tom Ewell, Jill St. John, Paul Lukas. Sluggish, unflavorful version of F. Scott Fitzgerald novel with Jones unsatisfactory as mentally unstable wife of psychiatrist Robards; Fontaine is her chic sister; set in 1920s Europe.

Tender Mercies (1983) **C-89m.** *** D: Bruce Beresford. Robert Duvall, Tess Harper, Allan Hubbard, Betty Buckley, Ellen Barkin, Wilford Brimley. Winning but extremely low-key film about a country singer who finds the inspiration to put his life back together when he meets an attractive young widow and her little boy. Duvall's Oscar-winning performance is the real attraction here, though the whole cast is excellent; Horton Foote's screenplay (also an Oscar winner) is not so much a story as a series of vignettes. Incidentally, Duvall wrote his own songs for the film.▼

Tender Scoundrel (1966-French-Italian) **C-94m.** *½ D: Jean Becker. Jean-Paul Belmondo, Nadja Tiller, Robert Morley, Genevieve Page. Dumb story of delightful rogue and ladies' man who is constantly on the hustle.

Tender Trap, The (1955) **C-111m.** ***½ D: Charles Walters. Frank Sinatra, Debbie Reynolds, Celeste Holm, David Wayne, Carolyn Jones, Lola Albright, Tom Helmore. Delightful romp of swinging bachelor Sinatra who stumbles into marriage with determined Debbie in N.Y.C.; impeccable support from Holm and Wayne, plus memorable Cahn-Van Heusen title tune. Julius J. Epstein adapted Max Shulman's and Robert Paul Smith's play.

Tender Years, The (1947) **81m.** ** D: Harold Schuster. Joe E. Brown, Richard Lyon, Noreen Nash, Charles Drake, Josephine Hutchinson. Warm drama of minister trying to protect dog his son is attached to; notable mainly for rare dramatic performance by Brown.▼

Tenebrae SEE: **Unsane**▼

Ten from Your Show of Shows (1973) **92m.** **** D: Max Liebman. Sid Caesar, Imogene Coca, Carl Reiner, Howard Morris, Louis Nye. Incomparable collection from early 50s TV show displaying comic genius of four stars, working with classic material by Mel Brooks, among others. Ten skits include FROM HERE TO ETERNITY spoof, silent-movie sendup, Swiss clock, and final, unbearably funny takeoff on *This Is Your Life*. A must.▼

Ten Gentlemen From West Point (1942) 102m. *** D: Henry Hathaway. George Montgomery, Maureen O'Hara, John Sutton, Laird Cregar, Victor Francen, Harry Davenport, Ward Bond, Tom Neal, Ralph Byrd, Douglass Dumbrille. Early years of West Point, with focus on vicious commander Cregar and other assorted military film clichés; somehow, it's still entertaining.

Ten Little Indians (1966-British) 92m. **½ D: George Pollock. Hugh O'Brian, Shirley Eaton, Fabian, Leo Genn, Stanley Holloway, Wilfrid Hyde-White, Daliah Lavi, Dennis Price. Fair remake of Agatha Christie's whodunit AND THEN THERE WERE NONE, with suspects trapped in remote Alpine village. Originally released with gimmick of murder-minute for audience to guess killer. Remade again in 1975 and 1989.

Ten Little Indians (1975-British) C-98m. *½ D: Peter Collinson. Oliver Reed, Elke Sommer, Herbert Lom, Richard Attenborough, Charles Aznavour, Stephane Audran, Gert Frobe, Adolfo Celi, voice of Orson Welles. Third (and arguably weakest) rendering of Agatha Christie whodunit, set this time in Iran. Great plot cannot survive such tired retelling.▼

Ten Little Indians (1989) C-98m. *½ D: Alan Birkinshaw. Donald Pleasence, Frank Stallone, Sarah Maur Thorp, Brenda Vaccaro, Herbert Lom, Warren Berlinger, Paul L. Smith, Moira Lister. Producer Harry Alan Towers' *third* redo of the Christie classic is his worst yet. This time he isolates an uninteresting cast in an African safari camp in the 1930s, and boringly plods through this once-intriguing, nowweary plot. Stop Towers before he remakes again!▼

Tennessee Champ (1954) C-73m. **½ D: Fred M. Wilcox. Shelley Winters, Keenan Wynn, Dewey Martin, Earl Holliman, Dave O'Brien. Good performances highlight average story of boxer who reforms crooked employer.

Tennessee Johnson (1942) 103m. **½ D: William Dieterle. Van Heflin, Lionel Barrymore, Ruth Hussey, Marjorie Main, Charles Dingle, Regis Toomey, Grant Withers, Lynne Carver, Noah Beery, Sr., Morris Ankrum. Sincere historical drama of President Andrew Johnson's rise and subsequent conflicts with Congress, given a glossy MGM production.

Tennessee's Partner (1955) C-87m. **½ D: Allan Dwan. John Payne, Rhonda Fleming, Ronald Reagan, Coleen Gray, Morris

Ankrum. Offbeat little Western with Payne excellent in an unusual "heel" characterization, Reagan accidentally becoming his pal. Based on a Bret Harte story.▼

Ten North Frederick (1958) 102m. *** D: Philip Dunne. Gary Cooper, Diane Varsi, Suzy Parker, Geraldine Fitzgerald, Tom Tully, Stuart Whitman. Grasping wife (Fitzgerald) prods her husband (Cooper) into big-time politics, with disastrous results. He finds personal solace in love affair with much younger woman (Parker). Good performances in somewhat soapy adaptation of John O'Hara novel.▼

Ten Rillington Place (1971-British) C-111m. *** D: Richard Fleischer. Richard Attenborough, Judy Geeson, John Hurt, Gabrielle Daye, Andre Morell. Low-key presentation of famous John Christie-Timothy Evans murder case that rocked Great Britain in the late 1940s. No overt editorializing but psychological undertone exists; outstanding performances by entire cast and location filming inseparable with film's total effect.▼

Ten Seconds to Hell (1959) 93m. **½ D: Robert Aldrich. Jeff Chandler, Jack Palance, Martine Carol, Robert Cornthwaite, Dave Willock, Wesley Addy. Chandler and Palance are almost believable as Germans involved in defusing bombs in Berlin, while competing for Carol's affection.

Tension (1949) 95m. **½ D: John Berry. Richard Basehart, Audrey Totter, Cyd Charisse, Barry Sullivan, Tom D'Andrea. Timid Basehart methodically plans to murder his wife's lover, only to have someone beat him to it in this intriguing melodrama.

Tension at Table Rock (1956) C-93m. ** D: Charles Marquis Warren. Richard Egan, Dorothy Malone, Cameron Mitchell, Billy Chapin, Angie Dickinson. Soaper Western with Egan on the lam for a murder committed in self-defense.

Tentacles (1977-Italian) C-90m. *½ D: Oliver Hellman (Ovidio Assonitis). John Huston, Shelley Winters, Henry Fonda, Bo Hopkins, Delia Boccardo, Cesare Danova. Giant octopus threatens a seaside community in this rip-off of JAWS. Some unexpected casting and the spectacle of having killer whales emerge the heroes save the picture from total decay.▼

Ten Tall Men (1951) C-97m. **½ D: Willis Goldbeck. Burt Lancaster, Jody Lawrance, Gilbert Roland, Kieron Moore. Tongue-in-cheek Foreign Legion tale, with dynamic Lancaster pushing the action along.

Tenth Avenue Angel (1948) 74m. BOMB D: Roy Rowland. Margaret O'Brien, Angela Lansbury, George Murphy, Phyllis Thaxter, Warner Anderson. Capable cast lost in terrible script about street urchin who prevents young man from becoming gangster.

Tenth Man, The (1988) C-100m. TVM

D: Jack Gold. Anthony Hopkins, Kristin Scott Thomas, Derek Jacobi, Cyril Cusack, Brenda Bruce, Paul Rogers. A once-prosperous French lawyer becomes a Nazi prisoner during WW2, and gives all his worldly possessions to a fellow captive to take his place in front of a firing squad; after the war, he secures a job as servant in his own villa, now the property of the dead man's family. Slow-moving version of Graham Greene's parable, given the usual first-class Hallmark Hall of Fame treatment. Average.

Tenth Month, The (1979) **C-130m.** TVM D: Joan Tewkesbury. Carol Burnett, Keith Michell, Dina Merrill, Melissa Converse, Cristina Raines, Richard Venture. Overlong drama that addresses the question: should a middle-aged divorcee who has an affair with a married man and becomes pregnant keep and raise the child alone? Based on Laura Z. Hobson's novel about single parenthood. Average.▼

Ten Thousand Bedrooms (1957) **C-114m.** ** D: Richard Thorpe. Dean Martin, Anna Maria Alberghetti, Eva Bartok, Walter Slezak, Paul Henreid, Jules Munshin, Marcel Dalio. Dean's first film without Jerry Lewis seemed to spell doom for his career; it's a lightweight but overlong musical romance with Dino as a playboy hotel-manager in Rome.

Tenth Victim, The (1965-Italian) **C-92m.** *** D: Elio Petri. Marcello Mastroianni, Ursula Andress, Elsa Martinelli, Salvo Randone, Massimo Serato. Cult sci-fi of futuristic society where violence is channeled into legalized murder hunts. Here, Ursula hunts Marcello. Intriguing idea, well done. Based on Robert Sheckley's story "The Seventh Victim."▼

Ten To Midnight (1983) **C-100m.** ** D: J. Lee Thompson. Charles Bronson, Andrew Stevens, Gene Davis, Lisa Eilbacher, Wilford Brimley, Geoffrey Lewis. Handsome psycho-killer does his woman-killing in the nude, but runs afoul of police detective Bronson, whose daughter he terrorizes. Kicked off the force for falsifying evidence against the killer, Bronson goes on his usual Death Wish rampage. Ultraviolent, kinkier-than-average Bronson vehicle.▼

Ten Wanted Men (1955) **C-80m.** ** D: Bruce Humberstone. Randolph Scott, Jocelyn Brando, Richard Boone, Skip Homeier, Leo Gordon, Donna Martell. Conventional Western programmer with cattleman Scott's dream of law and order smashed by ambitions of ruthless rival Boone.▼

Ten Who Dared (1960) **C-92m.** BOMB D: William Beaudine. Brian Keith, John Beal, James Drury, R. G. Armstrong, Ben Johnson, L. Q. Jones. Dreadful Disney film based on true story of Major John Wesley Powell's exploration of Colorado

River in 1869; cast is drowned in clichés, while action is sparse. Forget it.▼

Teorema (1968-Italian) **C-98m.** ** D: Pier Paolo Pasolini. Terence Stamp, Silvana Mangano, Massimo Girotti, Anna Wiazemsky, Laura Betti, Andres Jose Cruz. Pointed but obvious, occasionally hokey political/ sexual fable, with Stamp cast as a young stranger who may be Christ—or Satan. He leaves an irrevocable impression on a bourgeois family by sleeping with its every member.▼

Tequila Sunrise (1988) **C-116m.** **½ D: Robert Towne. Mel Gibson, Michelle Pfeiffer, Kurt Russell, Raul Julia, J.T. Walsh, Arliss Howard, Ann Magnuson, Arye Gross. Lifelong friends, one a supposedly retired drug dealer, the other a fast-rising L.A. cop, are forced to confront each other, both in business and in vying for the affections of a sleek restaurant owner. Star power is high here, and all three leads exude considerable charisma, but after a snappy start the script leads them nowhere. Veteran director Budd Boetticher plays a judge. Disappointing result for writer-director Towne.▼

Teresa (1951) **102m.** ** D: Fred Zinnemann. John Ericson, Pier Angeli, Patricia Collinge, Richard Bishop, Peggy Ann Garner. Intriguing, but superficially told story of WW2 veteran Ericson who returns to U.S. with his Italian bride, encountering home-town prejudice. Rod Steiger plays psychiatrist in film debut.▼

Terminal Choice (1985-Canadian) **C-97m.** *½ D: Sheldon Larry. Joe Spano, Diane Venora, David McCallum, Robert Joy, Don Francks, Nicholas Campbell, Ellen Barkin. Deadly doings at a hospital; good cast wasted in this unsavory thriller.▼

Terminal Island (1973) **C-88m.** *½ D: Stephanie Rothman. Phyllis Elizabeth Davis, Don Marshall, Barbara Leigh, Sean Kenney, Roger Mosley, Tom Selleck, Jo Morrow. Cynical exploitation film about futuristic offshore California penal colony where murderers are sent in lieu of abolished death penalty. Reissued a decade later to capitalize on the presence of several future stars, including *Magnum P.I.*'s Selleck and Mosley.▼

Terminal Man, The (1974) **C-107m.** *** D: Mike Hodges. George Segal, Joan Hackett, Richard A. Dysart, Jill Clayburgh, Donald Moffat, Matt Clark. Cold but engrossing thriller has computer scientist Segal coming under influence of computers in his brain which cause violence. Well-acted; based on the Michael Crichton novel.▼

Terminal Station SEE: **Indiscretion of an American Wife**▼

Terminator, The (1984) **C-108m.** ***½ D: James Cameron. Arnold Schwarzenegger, Michael Biehn, Linda Hamilton, Paul Winfield, Lance Henriksen, Rick Rossovich,

[1154]

Earl Boen, Dick Miller, Bill Paxton. A cyborg is sent here from the future to kill a seemingly innocent woman. Schwarzenegger is perfectly cast as violence-prone robot who cannot be stopped. Terrific action picture never lets up for a minute—a model for others to follow. Director Cameron cowrote with producer Gale Anne Hurd (with echoes of ideas from an old *Outer Limits* episode).▼

Term of Trial (1963-British) 113m. **½ D: Peter Glenville. Laurence Olivier, Simone Signoret, Sarah Miles, Terence Stamp, Roland Culver, Hugh Griffith. Talky story of schoolmaster charged with assault by young Miles, and subsequent trial's effect on Olivier's wife, Signoret. Despite fine cast, a wearisome film. Miles' film debut.

Terms of Endearment (1983) C-132m. **** D: James L. Brooks. Shirley MacLaine, Debra Winger, Jack Nicholson, John Lithgow, Jeff Daniels, Lisa Hart Carroll, Danny DeVito. Wonderful mix of humor and heartache follows the relationship of a mother and daughter over the years. Consistently offbeat and unpredictable, with exceptional performances by all three stars; first-time director Brooks also wrote the screenplay from Larry McMurtry's novel. Won Oscars for MacLaine, Nicholson, Screenplay, Director, and Best Picture.▼

Terraces (1977) C-78m. TVM D: Lila Garrett. Lloyd Bochner, Jane Dulo, Arny Freeman, Eliza Garrett, Bill Gerber, Kit McDonough, Julie Newmar, Lola Albright. Soap opera dealing with various people sharing adjoining terraces in an expensive highrise. Below average.

Terrible Beauty, A SEE: **Night Fighters**
Terrible Joe Moran (1984) C-100m. TVM D: Joseph Sargent. James Cagney, Art Carney, Ellen Barkin, Peter Gallagher, Joseph Sirola, Edward I. Koch, Floyd Patterson. In his last film (and only TV movie), Cagney's a feisty old wheelchair-bound former boxing champ, sharing his Big Apple brownstone with loyal Carney, reestablishing contact with his estranged granddaughter and discovering she's romantically involved with a guy heavily in debt to the mob. A talky but satisfying "kitchen" drama by Frank Cucci lovingly tailored to its star. Above average.

Terrible People, The (1960-German) 95m. ** D: Harald Reinl. Eddi Arent, Karin Dor, Elizabeth Flickenschildt, Fritz Rasp, Joachim Fuchsberger. Fair action story of condemned bank crook vowing to return from dead to punish those who prosecuted him. Retitled: HAND OF THE GALLOWS.

Terror, The (1963) C-81m. **½ D: Roger Corman. Boris Karloff, Jack Nicholson, Sandra Knight, Dick Miller. Engaging chiller nonsense with Karloff the mysterious owner of a castle where eerie deeds occur; set on Baltic coast in 1800s. This is the legendary Corman quickie for which all of Karloff's scenes were shot in less than three days as the sets (from THE RAVEN) were being torn down around them!▼

Terror Among Us (1981) C-100m. TVM D: Paul Krasny. Don Meredith, Sarah Purcell, Jennifer Salt, Ted Shackelford, Tracy Reed, Kim Lankford, Sharon Spelman, Rod McCary. Parole officer and police sergeant vs. convicted rapist who is back on the streets; looks like a leftover script from *Police Story*. Average.

Terror at Alcatraz (1982) C-100m. TVM D: Sidney Hayers. Tom Smothers, Dick Smothers, Diana Muldaur, Mike Kellin, Lynette Mettey, Jack Albertson, Tom Ewell, Roger C. Carmel, Marc Lawrence, Elisha Cook, Titos Vandis, Kathrine Baumann. Melodramatic title masks a sitcom about two TV newsmen who get involved in search for treasure supposedly buried on Alcatraz Island by Al Capone. This pilot for the Smothers Brothers' short-lived *Fitz and Bones* series aired long after the show's demise. Average.

Terror at London Bridge SEE: **Bridge Across Time**▼
Terror at Midnight (1956) 70m. ** D: Franklin Adreon. Scott Brady, Joan Vohs, Frank Faylen, John Dehner. Undynamic telling of Vohs being blackmailed and her law-enforcer boyfriend (Brady) helping out.

Terror Beneath the Sea (1970-Japanese) C-85m. *½ D: Hajimo Sato. Peggy Neal, Andrew Hughes, Shinichi (Sonny) Chiba, Mike Daneen, Eric Nielson. Mad scientist creates monsters from human prisoners in an underwater city. The usual.▼

Terror by Night (1946) 60m. D: Roy William Neill. Basil Rathbone, Nigel Bruce, Alan Mowbray, Dennis Hoey, Renee Godfrey, Mary Forbes. SEE: **Sherlock Holmes** series. Also shown in computer-colored version.▼

Terror Castle SEE: **Horror Castle**▼
Terror from Under the House SEE: **Inn of the Frightened People**▼
Terror House (1942) SEE: **Night Has Eyes, The**▼
Terror House (1972) C-98m. *½ D: Bud Townsend. Linda Gillin, Arthur Space, John Neilson, Mary Jackson, Michael Macready. A young woman gets more than she bargained for when she wins a "vacation" trip to an old mansion. Predates other cannibalism efforts, and doesn't take itself that seriously—but still not very good. Also known as THE FOLKS AT RED WOLF INN and TERROR AT RED WOLF INN. Some prints run 83m.

Terror in a Texas Town (1958) 80m. **½ D: Joseph H. Lewis. Sterling Hayden, Sebastian Cabot, Carol Kelly, Eugene Martin, Ned Young, Victor Millan. Offbeat Western drama about Scandinavian whaler (Hayden) who comes to his father's farm in Texas, finds town terrorized by Cabot, who's forcing everyone to sell their oil-rich land. Incredible final shootout.

Terror in the Aisles (1984) C/B&W-85m. *½ D: Andrew J. Kuehn. Nancy Allen, Donald Pleasence. Endless collage of film clips from almost 75 terror movies, from ALIEN to WAIT UNTIL DARK, with the kitchen sink in between. There's silly commentary from Allen and Pleasence, sitting in a simulated movie house, and just too much footage for it all to make any sense. For diehard genre addicts only.▼

Terror in the Sky (1971) C-72m. TVM D: Bernard Kowalski. Leif Erickson, Doug McClure, Roddy McDowall, Keenan Wynn, Lois Nettleton. Pilots and several passengers on commercial flight are felled by food poisoning; ex-combat-helicopter-pilot (McClure) must land plane. Negligible suspense, despite good performances. A remake of ZERO HOUR, later spoofed in AIRPLANE! Average.

Terror in the Wax Museum (1973) C-93m. *½ D: Georg Fenady. Ray Milland, Broderick Crawford, Elsa Lanchester, Maurice Evans, Shani Wallis, John Carradine, Louis Hayward, Patric Knowles, Mark Edwards. Low-budget and low-grade murder mystery takes little advantage of wax museum horror potential; a good cast wasted. If you look closely you can see the "wax figures" moving.▼

Terror in Toyland SEE: **You Better Watch Out** ▼

Terror Is a Man (1959) 89m. ** D: Gerry DeLeon. Francis Lederer, Greta Thyssen, Richard Derr, Oscar Keesee. On Blood Island, doctor experiments with panther to turn him into a human. Filmed in the Philippines, this sci-fi horror story comes to life in last third of picture. Clearly inspired by H. G. Wells' *Island of Dr. Moreau.* Also known as BLOOD CREATURE.▼

Terrorists, The (1975-British) C-97m. *½ D: Caspar Wrede. Sean Connery, Ian McShane, Jeffrey Wickham, Isabel Dean, John Quentin. Muddled thriller about political terrorism and airline hijacking is indifferently acted by Connery and McShane, amateurishly directed, and tediously unspooled. Pity, because premise is sound and photography (by Sven Nykvist) is smashing. Filmed in Norway.

Terrorist on Trial: The United States vs. Salim Ajami (1988) C-140m. TVM D: Jeff Bleckner. Sam Waterston, Ron Leibman, Robert Davi, Joe Morton, Jo Henderson, Stephen Lee, Frances Conroy, James Greene. Speculative drama about a captured Arab terrorist extradited to the U.S. for trial, and defended by a Jewish lawyer. The final collaboration by the estimable team of Richard Levinson (who died shortly before the project's comple-

tion) and William Link—and a worthy companion to their other excellent, thought-provoking television films. Above average.

Terrornauts, The (1967-British) C-75m. *½ D: Montgomery Tully. Simon Oates, Zena Marshall, Charles Hawtrey, Patricia Hayes, Stanley Meadows, Max Adrian. Alien forces kidnap an entire building on Earth, people and all. Based on Murray Leinster's novel *The Wailing Asteroid,* this sci-fi flick is hampered by low budget.▼

Terror of Dr. Hichcock SEE: **Horrible Dr. Hichcock, The**

Terror of Frankenstein (1975-Swedish-Irish) C-91m. *** D: Calvin Floyd. Leon Vitali, Per Oscarsson, Nicholas Clay, Stacey Dorning, Jan Ohlsson. Literate, well-made adaptation of the classic story, definitely worth a look for horror buffs. This is the most faithful of all film versions of the novel.▼

Terror of Mechagodzilla (1975-Japanese) C-83m. *½ D: Inoshiro Honda. K. Sasaki, Tomoko Ai, Akihiko Hirata, Kenji Sahara. Mechagodzilla is restored by villains and sent to destroy Godzilla again, aided by the remote-controlled Titanosaurus. Colorful but oddly grim.

Terror of Sheba, The SEE: **Persecution**▼

Terror of the Red Mask (1960-Italian) C-90m. ** D: Piero Pierotti. Lex Barker, Chelo Alonso, Massimo Serato. Costumer strains to have air of a chiller as hero Barker swordfights his way through castle of horror.

Terror of the Tongs (1961-British) C-90m. **½ D: Anthony Bushell. Geoffrey Toone, Burt Kwouk, Brian Worth, Christopher Lee, Richard Leech. Atmospheric British thriller of captain searching for killers of daughter; eventually breaks entire Tong society in Hong Kong. Good acting but may be a little gruesome for some viewers. Released theatrically in b&w.

Terror of Tiny Town, The (1938) 63m. *½ D: Sam Newfield. Billy Curtis, Yvonne Moray, Little Billy, John Bambury. If you're looking for a midget musical Western, look no further. A typical sagebrush plot is enacted (pretty badly) by a cast of little people, and the indelible impression is that of characters sauntering into the saloon *under* those swinging doors!▼

Terror on a Train (1953-British) 72m. **½ D: Ted Tetzlaff. Glenn Ford, Anne Vernon, Maurice Denham, Victor Maddern. Tense little film of Ford defusing time bomb placed aboard train full of high explosives.

Terror on Highway 91 (1989) C-100m. TVM D: Jerry Jameson. Ricky Schroder, George Dzundza, Matt Clark, Brad Dourif, Lara Flynn Boyle, Frederic Lehne. Schroder's hard to believe as a rookie Southern cop who decides to blow the whistle on police corruption in his small town. The story's supposedly true—only the highway was changed to protect something (?). Average.

Terror on the Beach (1973) **C-74m. TVM** D: Paul Wendkos. Dennis Weaver, Estelle Parsons, Scott Hylands, Kristoffer Tabori, Susan Dey, Michael Christian, Henry Olek. Middle-class family harassed for no apparent reason during seaside vacation. Plot's resolution weakest point of otherwise interestingly directed thriller. Above average.

Terror on the 40th Floor (1974) **C-100m. TVM** D: Jerry Jameson. John Forsythe, Anjanette Comer, Joseph Campanella, Lynn Carlin, Don Meredith, Laurie Heineman, Kelly Jean Peters, Pippa Scott. Road company TOWERING INFERNO has fire engulfing a skyscraper, trapping a group of people in a penthouse. Average.▼

Terror Out of the Sky (1978) **C-100m. TVM** D: Lee H. Katzin. Efrem Zimbalist, Jr., Tovah Feldshuh, Dan Haggerty, Bruce French, Lonny Chapman, Ike Eisenmann. Those pesky bugs return in this sequel to THE SAVAGE BEES, with the little stingers threatening a new invasion and two bee specialists and a free-lance pilot determined to thwart it. Several notches below its predecessor. Average.▼

Terror Train (1980-Canadian) **C-97m. ** D: Roger Spottiswoode. Ben Johnson, Jamie Lee Curtis, Hart Bochner, David Copperfield, Derek Mackinnon, D. D. Winters (Vanity). Fraternity hires a train for a night-long graduation costume party only to have an ex-member, emotionally scarred by an initiation prank, come aboard, disguised and uninvited, to seek revenge. Stylish photography (by John Alcott, of all people) and novelty of killer donning the costume of each successive victim lift this above most of the others in this disreputable genre.▼

TerrorVision (1986) **C-85m. BOMB** D: Ted Nicolaou. Diane Franklin, Mary Woronov, Gerrit Graham, Chad Allen, Bert Remsen, Alejandro Rey, Randi Brooks, Sonny Carl Davis. Inept direction and overacting sink this cartoonish tale of a family and friends' reactions when a monster from outer space emerges from their TV set. Watch an old *Outer Limits* episode instead.▼

Terror Within, The (1988) **C-88m. ** D: Thierry Notz. Andrew Stevens, Starr Andreeff, Terri Treas, George Kennedy, John LaFayette, Tommy Hinchley. Grim horror/sci-fi concoction set after plague has wiped out 99 percent of humanity. An underground medical center is attacked by hybrid monsters born of human women and bent on creating more of the same. Low-budget Roger Corman production is a cross between ALIEN and THE DAY THE WORLD ENDED, with a routine, predictable plot.▼

Terry Fox Story, The (1983-Canadian) **C-97m. TVM** D: Ralph Thomas. Eric Fryer, Robert Duvall, Rosalind Chao, Chris Makepeace, Michael Zelniker, Elva Mai Hoover, Frank Adamson. Inspiring, lovingly made true story of the Canadian athlete who lost a leg to cancer and then undertook a one-man fund-raising marathon across Canada. First-time actor Fryer, a real life amputee, is perfectly cast as Fox. Above average.▼

Tess (1979-French-British) **C-170m. ***½** D: Roman Polanski. Nastassia Kinski, Peter Firth, John Bett, Tom Chadbon, Rosemary Martin, Leigh Lawson, Sylvia Coleridge. Handsome, evocative adaptation of Thomas Hardy's *Tess of the D'Urbervilles,* with Kinski in her star-making performance as the strong-willed girl from a poor family whose fortunes rise and fall when she is foisted onto polite society. Long but engrossing. Oscar-winner for Cinematography, Costume Design, and Art Direction.▼

Tess of the Storm Country (1960) **C-84m. **½** D: Paul Guilfoyle. Diane Baker, Jack Ging, Lee Philips, Wallace Ford, Robert F. Simon, Bert Remsen. Fifth screen version (since 1914) of Grace White's period novel of Scottish girl and uncle coming to America and adjusting to life in Pennsylvania Dutch country; leisurely paced, nicely done.

Testament (1983) **C-89m. ***½** D: Lynne Littman. Jane Alexander, William Devane, Roxana Zal, Ross Harris, Lukas Haas, Philip Anglim, Lilia Skala, Leon Ames, Rebecca DeMornay, Mako, Lurene Tuttle, Kevin Costner. Admirably understated drama about a small town contending with nuclear holocaust, focusing on one tight-knit family. Restrained and effective, with a heartrending performance by Alexander. Screenplay by John Sacret Young, from a story by Carol Amen. Originally made for PBS' *American Playhouse.*▼

Testament of Dr. Mabuse, The (1933-German) **120m. ***½** D: Fritz Lang. Rudolf Klein-Rogge, Otto Wernicke, Gustav Diesl, Karl Meixner. Criminal mastermind controls his underworld empire even while confined to an insane asylum! Fabled character from Lang's silent-film epic returns in less stylized but no less entertaining crime story—which even incorporates supernatural elements. Film was a subject of controversy during Nazi era. Lang returned to this character once more for THE THOUSAND EYES OF DR. MABUSE in 1960, but other hands remade this script in 1962. Also known as THE LAST WILL OF DR. MABUSE. Many TV prints run 75m. Retitled THE CRIMES OF DR. MABUSE.▼

Testimony (1987-British) **C/B&W-157m. ** D: Tony Palmer. Ben Kingsley, Terence Rigby, Ronald Pickup, John Shrap-

[1157]

nel, Sherry Baines, Robert Stephens, Murray Melvin, Robert Urquhart. Ambitious, overlong biopic of composer Dmitri Shostakovich focuses on his political problems in the Soviet Union. Kingsley brings depth to the leading role, and Nic Knowland provides fabulous widescreen camerawork in black and white (with flashes of color), but these attributes cannot overcome a turgid narrative.

Test of Love, A (1984-Australian) **C-93m.** *** D: Gil Brealey. Angela Punch McGregor, Drew Forsythe, Wallas Eaton, Simon Chilvers, Liddy Clark, Tina Arhondis. Moving, inspirational, if a bit too predictable story of a young teacher (Punch McGregor), and her attempts to reach a disabled girl (Arhondis, whose performance is truly wonderful). Based on a true story; originally titled ANNIE'S COMING OUT.▼

Test Pilot (1938) **118m.** *** D: Victor Fleming. Clark Gable, Myrna Loy, Spencer Tracy, Lionel Barrymore, Samuel S. Hinds, Marjorie Main, Gloria Holden, Louis Jean Heydt. Blend of romantic comedy and drama doesn't always work, but with those stars it's well worth watching. Tracy steals film as Gable's pal in story of daredevils who try out new aircraft. Based on a Frank Wead story.

Tex (1982) **C-103m.** *** D: Tim Hunter. Matt Dillon, Jim Metzler, Meg Tilly, Bill McKinney, Frances Lee McCain, Ben Johnson, Emilio Estevez, Jack Thibeau. First of S. E. Hinton's young-adult best sellers to reach the screen (via the Disney company) is an understated but likable tale of a boy whose mother has died, whose father is away, whose brother is trying to raise him with no money and little patience . . . and whose self-esteem is nil. Straightforward little drama. Hinton has a cameo as a teacher.▼

Texan Meets Calamity Jane, The (1950) **C-71m.** BOMB D: Ande Lamb. Evelyn Ankers, James Ellison, Jack Ingram, Lee "Lasses" White. Ankers is too subdued as famed cowgirl of yesteryear, involved in fight to prove claim to prosperous saloon.

Texans, The (1938) **92m.** **½ D: James Hogan. Randolph Scott, Joan Bennett, May Robson, Walter Brennan, Robert Cummings, Robert Barrat. Post-Civil War Texas is setting for average Western with good cast.

Texas (1941) **93m.** *** D: George Marshall. William Holden, Glenn Ford, Claire Trevor, George Bancroft, Edgar Buchanan. High-level Western of two friends, one a rustler, the other a cattleman, competing for Trevor's affection.

Texas Across the River (1966) **C-101m.** *** D: Michael Gordon. Dean Martin, Alain Delon, Joey Bishop, Rosemary Forsyth, Peter Graves, Tina Marquand (Aumont), Andrew Prine, Michael Ansara. Diverting takeoff on cowboy-and-Indian films, with Bishop hilarious as a deadpan Indian and Marquand cute as a young squaw.

Texas, Brooklyn and Heaven (1948) **76m.** ** D: William Castle. Guy Madison, Diana Lynn, James Dunn, Lionel Stander, Florence Bates, Roscoe Karns. Stale "comedy" of cowboy who falls in love with city girl who loves horses. Good cast helps a little.

Texas Carnival (1951) **C-77m.** ** D: Charles Walters. Esther Williams, Howard Keel, Red Skelton, Ann Miller, Keenan Wynn, Tom Tully, Red Norvo. Emptier than usual, this flabby MGM musical about penniless carny mistaken for millionaire leaves fine cast high and dry with no fresh material.

Texas Chainsaw Massacre, The (1974) **C-83m.** *** D: Tobe Hooper. Marilyn Burns, Gunner Hansen, Ed Neal, Allen Danzinger, Paul A. Partain, William Vail. Travelers in rural Texas encounter crazed family of bizarros who have a committed though unusual sense of what cuts of meat you need for good barbecue. Sweatinducing, claustrophobic, unrelenting suspense-comic-horror film. Classic and influential—and nowhere nearly as violent as it's reputed to be. Narrated by an unbilled John Larroquette. Followed by two sequels.▼

Texas Chainsaw Massacre 2, The (1986) **C-95m.** BOMB D: Tobe Hooper. Dennis Hopper, Caroline Williams, Bill Johnson, Jim Siedow, Bill Moseley. Hooper returns to his hit property with a mind-numbing, pretentious sequel. Hopper plays a nutty ex-Texas Ranger obsessed with revenge against the crazed family of Texas cannibals, while deejay Williams is simply looking to save her own skin when the cannibals go after her following a broadcast that angers them. Frenetic overacting and unfunny attempts at black humor sink this mess. Followed by LEATHERFACE: TEXAS CHAINSAW MASSACRE III.▼

Texas Detour (1978) **C-92m.** ** D: Hikmet Avedis. Patrick Wayne, Mitch Vogel, Lindsay Bloom, R. G. Armstrong, Priscilla Barnes, Cameron Mitchell. Typical low-grade action picture about a macho stunt driver.▼

Texas Lady (1955) **C-86m.** ** D: Tim Whelan. Claudette Colbert, Barry Sullivan, Greg Walcott, Horace McMahon, John Litel. Genteel oater with Colbert lovely as crusading newspaper editor in old West. Mediocre script.▼

Texas Rangers, The (1936) **95m.** *** D: King Vidor. Fred MacMurray, Jack Oakie, Jean Parker, Lloyd Nolan, Edward Ellis. Fine, elaborate Western of three comrades who split up; MacMurray and Oakie become rangers, Nolan an outlaw. Remade as STREETS OF LAREDO; sequel: THE TEXAS RANGERS RIDE AGAIN.

Texas Rangers, The (1951) C-74m. ** D: Phil Karlson. George Montgomery, Gale Storm, Jerome Courtland, Noah Beery, Jr. Aimless Western involving Texas law enforcers against gang of outlaws.

Texas Rangers Ride Again (1940) 68m. ** D: James Hogan. John Howard, Jack Oakie, Akim Tamiroff, Ellen Drew, May Robson, Robert Ryan. Sequel is standard Western fare of lawmen involved with cattle rustlers in the modern-day West.

Texican, The (1966) C-91m. ** D: Lesley Selander. Audie Murphy, Broderick Crawford, Diana Lorys, Luz Marquez, Antonio Casas, Antonio Perel. Routine Spanish-made Western pits ex-lawman Murphy against ruthless frontier town boss Crawford.

Thaddeus Rose and Eddie (1978) C-100m. TVM D: Jack Starrett. Johnny Cash, Diane Ladd, Bo Hopkins, June Carter Cash, James Hampton, Noble Willingham. Ho-hum comedy-drama about two irresponsible good ol' boys from Texas, and the gals they love. Marks the TV acting debuts of country singers Johnny and June Carter Cash. Average.

Thank God, It's Friday (1978) C-90m. BOMB D: Robert Klane. Donna Summer, Valerie Landsburg, Terri Nunn, Chick Vennera, Ray Vitte, Jeff Goldblum, Paul Jabara, Debra Winger, Andrea Howard, The Commodores (with Lionel Richie). Perhaps the worst film ever to have won some kind of Oscar (for Summer's hit song, "Last Dance"), this one-night-in-the-life-of-a-disco comedy is about as monotonous and uninventive as disco music itself. A must-see for morons, cast notwithstanding.▼

Thanks a Million (1935) 87m. *** D: Roy Del Ruth. Dick Powell, Ann Dvorak, Fred Allen, Patsy Kelly, Alan Dinehart, Margaret Irving, Paul Whiteman and Orchestra, Yacht Club Boys. Very entertaining musical of crooner Powell running for governor, with help of wisecracking manager Allen, sweetheart Dvorak, and blustery politician Raymond Walburn. Good fun, with several breezy tunes and specialties by Whiteman and Yacht Club Boys. Script by Nunnally Johnson. Remade as IF I'M LUCKY.▼

Thanksgiving Promise, The (1986) C-100m. TVM D: Beau Bridges. Beau Bridges, Lloyd Bridges, Jordan Bridges, Millie Perkins, Ed Lauter, Jason Bateman, Courtney Travis-Smith, Dorothy Dean Bridges. Atmospheric Disney charmer about a young boy and the pet goose he is fattening for his neighbor's dinner table. Distinguished for bringing together the entire Bridges family: patriarch Lloyd, wife Dorothy (her belated film debut), son Beau (who directed and coproduced with Mel

Ferrer), Beau's son Jordan (in his acting debut), and even—unbilled—Jeff Bridges. Based on the warm novel by Blaine and Brenton Yorgason. Above average.

Thank You All Very Much (1969-British) C-105m. *** D: Waris Hussein. Sandy Dennis, Ian McKellen, Eleanor Bron, John Standing. Absorbing study of unwed mother who decides to have her baby. Realistic and touching.

Thank You, Aunt (1967-Italian) 93m. ** D: Salvatore Samperi. Lisa Gastoni, Lou Castel, Gabriele Ferzetti. Utterly perverse tale of psychopathic young man (Castel) who comes to live with attractive young aunt (Gastoni) whom he torments with sex games and rituals. Ugh. Released here as GRAZIE, ZIA in 1969.

Thank You, Jeeves (1936) 68m. **½ D: Arthur Collins. Arthur Treacher, Virginia Field, David Niven, Lester Matthews. Treacher is at peak form playing P.G. Wodehouse's impeccable butler whose love of decorum leads him on merry chase. Retitled: THANK YOU, MR. JEEVES. Followed by STEP LIVELY, JEEVES.

Thank You, Mr. Jeeves SEE: **Thank You, Jeeves**

Thank You, Mr. Moto (1937) 67m. D: Norman Foster. Peter Lorre, Pauline Frederick, Sidney Blackmer, Sig Ruman, John Carradine, Nedda Harrigan, Philip Ahn. SEE: **Mr. Moto** series.

Thank Your Lucky Stars (1943) 127m. *** D: David Butler. Eddie Cantor, Dennis Morgan, Joan Leslie; guest stars Humphrey Bogart, Bette Davis, Olivia de Havilland, Errol Flynn, John Garfield, Ida Lupino, Ann Sheridan, etc. Very lame plot (Cantor plays both himself and lookalike cabbie) frames all-star Warner Bros. show, with Davis singing "They're Either Too Young Or Too Old," Flynn delightfully performing "That's What You Jolly Well Get," other staid stars breaking loose.▼

That Certain Age (1938) 95m. **½ D: Edward Ludwig. Deanna Durbin, Melvyn Douglas, Jackie Cooper, Irene Rich, Nancy Carroll, John Halliday, Jack Searl. Deanna develops crush on her parents' houseguest, sophisticated Douglas, leaving boyfriend Cooper out in the cold—and saddled with responsibility for putting on amateur show. Silly script made bearable by smooth stars.

That Certain Feeling (1956) C-103m. BOMB D: Norman Panama, Melvin Frank. Bob Hope, Eva Marie Saint, George Sanders, Pearl Bailey, Al Capp. Incredibly bad Hope comedy with Bob as neurotic cartoonist; Sanders gives only life to stale film. Pearl sings title song.

That Certain Summer (1972) C-74m. TVM D: Lamont Johnson. Hal Holbrook, Hope Lange, Martin Sheen, Joe Don Baker, Scott Jacoby, Marlyn Mason, James McEachin. Divorcé Holbrook must find way to discuss homosexuality with son during one of their usual reunions in San Francisco. Outstanding performances by entire cast in sensibly scripted, carefully crafted film, well done by any medium's standards. A television landmark from the estimable producing/writing team of Richard Levinson and William Link. Above average.

That Certain Woman (1937) 93m. **½ D: Edmund Goulding. Bette Davis, Henry Fonda, Donald Crisp, Ian Hunter, Minor Watson, Sidney Toler, Anita Louise. Remake of Goulding's early talkie THE TRESPASSER (with Gloria Swanson) features Bette as a gangster's widow who's trying to start life fresh, falling in love for real with Fonda. Well-acted soaper.

That Championship Season (1982) C-110m. ** D: Jason Miller. Bruce Dern, Stacy Keach, Robert Mitchum, Martin Sheen, Paul Sorvino, Arthur Franz. Disappointing adaptation of Miller's Pulitzer Prize-winning play (which took 10 years to reach the screen), about the 24th annual reunion of a high school basketball squad and their paternalistic coach. Whatever made it work on stage is missing here; the movie never catches fire, and its characters come off more as caricatures.▼

That Cold Day in the Park (1969) C-113m. *½ D: Robert Altman. Sandy Dennis, Michael Burns, Susanne Benton, John Garfield, Jr., Luana Anders, Michael Murphy. Strange, plodding film with frustrated spinster taking in young man she sees in the park. What follows is bizarre and unmoving; a far cry from Altman's later work. Filmed in Canada. TV print runs 92m.▼

That Dangerous Age SEE: **If This Be Sin**

That Darn Cat (1965) C-116m. *** D: Robert Stevenson. Hayley Mills, Dean Jones, Dorothy Provine, Roddy McDowall, Neville Brand, Elsa Lanchester, William Demarest, Frank Gorshin, Ed Wynn. Long but entertaining suspense comedy from Disney, about a cat that leads FBI man Jones on trail of kidnapped woman. Slapstick scenes and character vignettes highlight this colorful film.▼

That Forsyte Woman (1949) C-114m. **½ D: Compton Bennett. Errol Flynn, Greer Garson, Walter Pidgeon, Robert Young, Janet Leigh, Harry Davenport. Rather superficial adaptation of John Galsworthy novel of a faithless woman (Garson) who finds herself attracted by her niece's fiancee; good-looking, but no match for the later BBC-TV series, *The Forsyte Saga.*

That Funny Feeling (1965) C-93m. **½ D: Richard Thorpe. Sandra Dee, Bobby Darin, Donald O'Connor, Nita Talbot, Larry Storch, Leo G. Carroll, Robert Strauss. Funny only if you adore Darin and Dee, and even then story of footloose playboy and maid who pretends she lives with him wears thin.

That Gang of Mine (1940) 62m. D: Joseph H. Lewis. Bobby Jordan, Leo Gorcey, Clarence Muse, Dave O'Brien, Joyce Bryant, Donald Haines, David Gorcey. SEE: **Bowery Boys** series.

That Girl from Paris (1936) 105m. **½ D: Leigh Jason. Lily Pons, Jack Oakie, Gene Raymond, Herman Bing, Mischa Auer, Frank Jenks, Lucille Ball. Breezy Pons vehicle. She flees Continental wedding and runs to America. Tuneful songs, fine supporting cast. A remake of STREET GIRL; remade as FOUR JACKS AND A JILL.▼

That Hagen Girl (1947) 83m. BOMB D: Peter Godfrey. Shirley Temple, Ronald Reagan, Rory Calhoun, Lois Maxwell, Dorothy Peterson, Conrad Janis. The prospect of Reagan and Temple as costars may sound amusing today—but this film is atrocious, with suicidal Shirley believing Ron to be her illegitimate father!

That Hamilton Woman (1941) 128m. *** D: Alexander Korda. Vivien Leigh, Laurence Olivier, Alan Mowbray, Sara Allgood, Gladys Cooper, Henry Wilcoxon, Heather Angel. Olivier and Leigh—both breathtakingly beautiful—enact ill-fated historical romance of Lord Admiral Nelson and Lady Emma Hamilton in American-made film intended to spur pro-British feelings. P.S.: It was Winston Churchill's favorite movie. Also known as LADY HAMILTON.▼

That Kind of Woman (1959) 92m. *** D: Sidney Lumet. Sophia Loren, Tab Hunter, George Sanders, Jack Warden, Keenan Wynn, Barbara Nichols. Soldier Hunter and dishy Loren are attracted to each other on a train, but she's the mistress of elegant fatcat Sanders. Surprisingly adult comedy-drama for its era; excellent performances from all but Hunter, and even he's better than usual. Well shot by Boris Kaufman. Remake of SHOPWORN ANGEL, scripted by Walter Bernstein.

That Lady (1955) C-100m. **½ D: Terence Young. Olivia de Havilland, Gilbert Roland, Paul Scofield, Dennis Price, Christopher Lee. Unemotional costumer set in 16th-century Spain, with de Havilland a widowed noblewoman involved in court intrigue. Scofield's film debut.

That Lady From Peking (1970-U.S.-Australian) C-86m. *½ D: Eddie Davis. Carl Betz, Nancy Kwan, Bobby Rydell, Sid Melton, Don Reid, Eva von Feilitz. Dull drama of writer Betz on the trail of a murdered Russian diplomat's diary.

That Lady in Ermine (1948) C-89m. *** D: Ernst Lubitsch, Otto Preminger. Betty Grable, Douglas Fairbanks, Jr., Cesar Romero, Walter Abel, Reginald Gardiner, Harry Davenport. Entertaining if overblown musical of mythical kingdom where ancestors magically return. Lubitsch died during production; Preminger completed the film. Script by Samson Raphaelson.

That'll Be the Day (1974-British) **C-90m.** *** D: Claude Whatham. David Essex, Ringo Starr, Rosemary Leach, James Booth, Billy Fury, Keith Moon. Compelling story traces British working-class youth (Essex) from adolescence to early adulthood in the 1950's, as his growing frustrations find their eventual outlet in rock music. First half of dynamic story, continued in STAR-DUST, where character's resemblance to John Lennon crystallizes.▼

That Man Bolt (1973) **C-105m.** ** D: Henry Levin, David Lowell Rich. Fred Williamson, Byron Webster, Teresa Graves, Jack Ging, Miko Mayama. Scenic actioner, filmed in Hong Kong, Las Vegas and L.A., mixes kung fu, some comedy and two songs by Graves. Plot has Williamson as international courier of syndicate money.

That Man from Rio (1964-French) **C-114m.** *** D: Philippe De Broca. Jean-Paul Belmondo, Françoise Dorleac, Jean Servais, Adolfo Celi, Simone Renant. Engaging spoof of Bond-type movies features Belmondo as hero, chasing double-crosser and thief in search for Brazilian treasure. Nice color photography by Edmond Séchan complements fast-moving script. Enjoyed great international success and spawned many imitations.

That Man George (1966-French-Spanish-Italian) **C-90m.** ** D: Jacques Deray. George Hamilton, Claudine Auger, Alberto De Mendoza, Daniel Ivernel. Routine tale of robbery of armored van transporting bullion from gold mine.

That Man in Istanbul (1966) **C-117m.** **½ D: Anthony (Antonio) Isasi. Horst Buchholz, Sylva Koscina, Mario Adorf, Klaus Kinski. Fairly engaging spy romp featuring Koscina as FBI agent with Buchholz as playboy in search for missing scientist.

That Midnight Kiss (1949) **C-96m.** **½ D: Norman Taurog. Kathryn Grayson, Mario Lanza, Jose Iturbi, Ethel Barrymore, Keenan Wynn, J. Carrol Naish, Jules Munshin. Flimsy musical romance between Lanza and Grayson salvaged by pleasant musical interludes and glossy production.

That Night (1957) **88m.** **½ D: John Newland. John Beal, Augusta Dabney, Malcolm Brodrick, Shepperd Strudwick, Rosemary Murphy. Straightforward account of writer suffering a heart attack, and the effect it has on his family.

That Night in Rio (1941) **C-90m.** **½ D: Irving Cummings. Alice Faye, Don Ameche, Carmen Miranda, S. Z. Sakall, J. Carrol Naish, Curt Bois, Leonid Kinsky, Frank Puglia. Standard 20th Century-Fox musical of mistaken identities, uses Miranda to best advantage; Maria Montez has a tiny role.

Filmed before as FOLIES BERGERE, and again as ON THE RIVIERA.

That Night with You (1945) **84m.** ** D: William A. Seiter. Franchot Tone, Susanna Foster, David Bruce, Louise Allbritton, Jacqueline de Wit, Buster Keaton. OK vehicle for soprano Foster who connives her way to show biz break via producer Tone.

That Obscure Object of Desire (1977-Spanish-French) **C-103m.** *** D: Luis Buñuel. Fernando Rey, Carole Bouquet, Angela Molina, Julien Bertheau, Andre Weber. Buñuel's last film is as audacious as any of his classics; wealthy sadomasochist Rey falls hard for a young maid, and she's only too happy to make him "suffer." Buñuel's bizarrest stroke is having Bouquet and Molina alternate playing the girl! Shot in French, with Rey dubbed by Michel Piccoli. Based on Pierre Louys novel, filmed several times, most notably as THE DEVIL IS A WOMAN (1935).▼

That's Dancing! (1985) **C/B&W-105m.** **½ D: Jack Haley, Jr. Narrated and hosted by Gene Kelly, Sammy Davis, Jr., Mikhail Baryshnikov, Liza Minnelli, Ray Bolger. Too many mediocre selections, flat introductions by five guest hosts . . . but there's still much to enjoy in this dance compilation, from Fred and Ginger's "Pick Yourself Up" to WEST SIDE STORY. Added curio: a Bolger number cut from THE WIZARD OF OZ. 1980s selections that end the film seem lumbering and ludicrous compared to the marvels of movement that precede them.▼

That Secret Sunday (1986) **C-100m.** TVM D: Richard Colla. James Farentino, Parker Stevenson, Daphne Ashbrook, George Grizzard, William Lucking, Dan Hedaya, Michael Lerner. A serial murder, a police cover-up, and the irresponsible press. Average.

That's Entertainment! (1974) **C-132m.** **** D: Jack Haley, Jr. Fred Astaire, Bing Crosby, Gene Kelly, Peter Lawford, Liza Minnelli, Donald O'Connor, Debbie Reynolds, Mickey Rooney, Frank Sinatra, James Stewart, Elizabeth Taylor. Stars host nostalgia bash with scenes from nearly 100 MGM musicals. There are many cherished moments with the above-named stars plus unexpectedly delightful numbers with Esther Williams, Clark Gable (singing and dancing!), Jimmy Durante, and Eleanor Powell, whose challenge dance with Astaire is unforgettable. Only complaint: why shorten the final AMERICAN IN PARIS ballet?▼

That's Entertainment, Part 2 (1976) **C-133m.** ***½ D: Gene Kelly. Fred Astaire and Gene Kelly host this inevitable sequel and do some engaging song-and-dance work. Film hasn't cohesion or momentum of its predecessor, but the material is irresistible. This time, comedy and drama are included along with musical numbers—

Tracy and Hepburn, Marx Brothers, etc. Most imaginative segment of all is title sequence by Saul Bass. Cut to 126m. after initial showings.▼

That Sinking Feeling (1979-Scottish) **C-92m.** *** D: Bill Forsyth. Robert Buchanan, John Hughes, Billy Greenlees, Gordon John Sinclair, Janette Rankin. Forsyth's initial feature is a witty little comedy about a gang of bored teens unable to find work in dreary Glasgow. Their leader comes up with a scheme to boost their morale: pilfering sinks from a warehouse. Released in U.S. after the success of Forsyth's subsequent films (GREGORY'S GIRL, LOCAL HERO).▼

That's Life! (1986) **C-102m.** *** D: Blake Edwards. Jack Lemmon, Julie Andrews, Sally Kellerman, Robert Loggia, Jennifer Edwards, Rob Knepper, Matt Lattanzi, Chris Lemmon, Cynthia Sikes, Emma Walton, Felicia Farr. Deeply felt observation of an affluent family and its members' personal crises— including Lemmon's anxiety over turning sixty and his loving wife's fear that she may have cancer. Far from perfect, but mostly believable and quite moving. Filmed at Edwards' and wife Andrews' actual Malibu home, with most of their (and Lemmon's) real-life family onscreen . . . including at least one pet!▼

That's My Boy (1951) **98m.** ** D: Hal Walker. Dean Martin, Jerry Lewis, Marion Marshall, Eddie Mayehoff, Ruth Hussey, Polly Bergen, John McIntire. Ex-football star Mayehoff wants klutzy son Lewis to follow in his footsteps, induces Martin to coach him. Supposed comic idea is played straight, with very few laughs, maudlin situations . . . yet it was considered quite funny in 1951 when M&L were in their heyday. Later a TV series.

That's the Spirit (1945) **93m.** ** D: Charles Lamont. Peggy Ryan, Jack Oakie, June Vincent, Gene Lockhart, Johnny Coy, Andy Devine, Arthur Treacher, Irene Ryan, Buster Keaton. Whimsy is too studied in this syrupy fantasy of Oakie returning from heaven to make explanations to wife on Earth. Songs include "How Come You Do Me Like You Do?"

That's The Way of the World SEE: **Shining Star**▼

That Touch of Mink (1962) **C-99m.** **½ D: Delbert Mann. Cary Grant, Doris Day, Gig Young, Audrey Meadows, John Astin, Dick Sargent. Attractive cast in nice piece of fluff with wealthy playboy Grant pursuing Day. Amusing at times, but wears thin; Astin is memorable as a creep with designs on poor Doris.▼

That Uncertain Feeling (1941) **84m.** *** D: Ernst Lubitsch. Merle Oberon, Melvyn Douglas, Burgess Meredith, Alan Mowbray, Olive Blakeney, Harry Davenport, Sig Rumann, Eve Arden. Chic little Lubitsch comedy about married couple with problems, and their absurd pianist friend. Stolen hands down by Meredith as the musical malcontent. Filmed before (in 1925) by Lubitsch as KISS ME AGAIN. Also shown in computer-colored version.▼

That Was Rock (1984) **92m.** ***½ The best rock and R&B numbers from THE T.A.M.I. SHOW (1964) and THE BIG T.N.T. SHOW (1966) with remixed soundtrack and new connecting footage (in color) of Chuck Berry. Of inestimable value as history, and not too shabby as entertainment, either, but who put Ray Charles directly after James Brown?▼

That Was Then, This Is Now (1985) **C-100m.** **½ D: Christopher Cain. Emilio Estevez, Craig Sheffer, Kim Delaney, Barbara Babcock, Jill Schoelen, Frank Howard, Larry B. Scott, Ramon Sheen, Morgan Freeman. Delinquent kid, alienated from society, clings to his relationship with adoptive brother—and freaks out when the older boy takes on a girlfriend, whom he sees as a threat. Estevez wrote the script, from S. E. Hinton's young-adult novel, but its intense emotions probably read better than they play out on screen. A variable film with some strong moments.▼

That Way with Women (1947) **84m.** ** D: Frederick de Cordova. Dane Clark, Martha Vickers, Sydney Greenstreet, Alan Hale, Craig Stevens. Tired reworking of George Arliss' MILLIONAIRE, with Greenstreet as wealthy man who plays Cupid for Clark and Vickers.

That Woman Opposite SEE: **City After Midnight**

That Wonderful Urge (1948) **82m.** **½ D: Robert B. Sinclair. Tyrone Power, Gene Tierney, Arleen Whelan, Reginald Gardiner, Lucile Watson, Gene Lockhart, Gertrude Michael, Porter Hall. Fairly entertaining remake of LOVE IS NEWS about heiress getting back at nasty reporter. Power repeats his role from the 1937 film.

Theatre of Blood (1973-British) **C-104m.** **½ D: Douglas Hickox. Vincent Price, Diana Rigg, Robert Morley, Ian Hendry, Harry Andrews, Coral Browne, Robert Coote, Michael Hordern, Jack Hawkins, Diana Dors, Dennis Price, Milo O'Shea. A one-joke film, albeit a great joke: hammy Shakespearean actor Price vows revenge on critics who've blasted him, murders them one by one by recreating famous death scenes from the plays. Somewhat spoiled by incredibly gory killings; great cast has fun with it, though.▼

Theatre of Death (1967-British) **C-90m.** **½ D: Samuel Gallu. Christopher Lee, Julian Glover, Lelia Goldoni, Jenny Till, Evelyn Laye, Ivor Dean. Vampire-like murders revolving around Paris' Grand Guignol stage sensation and its beautiful young starlet under sinister hypnotic trance. Solid, low-budget mystery-thriller benefits from believable performances.▼

Thelma Jordon SEE: **File on Thelma Jordon, The**

Thelonious Monk: Straight No Chaser (1988) **C/B&W-90m.** *** D: Charlotte Zwerin. Comprehensive documentary portrait of the legendary, innovative jazz pianist-composer, crammed with footage of Monk in performance. Much of the material was shot during the late 1960s by Christian Blackwood. Executive producer is Clint Eastwood; released the same year as the latter's Charlie Parker biography, BIRD.

Them! (1954) **94m.** ***½ D: Gordon Douglas. James Whitmore, Edmund Gwenn, Joan Weldon, James Arness, Onslow Stevens. First-rate '50s sci-fi about giant ant mutations running wild in the Southwest. Intelligent script (by Ted Sherderman, from George Worthing Yates' story) extremely well directed, with memorable climax in L.A. sewers. Fess Parker has small but memorable role. Look fast for Leonard Nimoy at a teletype machine.▼

Then Came Bronson (1969) **C-100m.** TVM D: William Graham. Michael Parks, Bonnie Bedelia, Akim Tamiroff, Martin Sheen, Sheree North, Gary Merrill. Young newspaper reporter (Parks) shaken up after suicide of friend, buys friend's motorcycle and sets out on shore road journey, meeting runaway bride (Bedelia), befriending her. Soft, somber film with a couple of OK episodes, fair performances. Above average; pilot for the series.

Then There Were Three (1961-Italian) **82m.** ** D: Alex Nicol. Frank Latimore, Alex Nicol, Barry Cahill, Sid Clute. Routine WW2 actioner concerning Nazi officer going behind Allied lines to hunt down Italian partisans.

Theodora Goes Wild (1936) **94m.** ***½ D: Richard Boleslawski. Irene Dunne, Melvyn Douglas, Thomas Mitchell, Thurston Hall, Rosalind Keith, Spring Byington. Dunne's first starring comedy is a delightful story about small-town woman who writes scandalous best-seller and falls in love with sophisticated New Yorker who illustrated the book. Lots of funny twists in this engaging farce, scripted by Sidney Buchman from a Mary McCarthy story.

Theodora, Slave Empress (1954-Italian) **88m.** ** D: Riccardo Freda. Gianna Maria Canale, Georges Marchal, Renato Baldini, Henri Guisol, Irene Papas. Better-than-average production values are only asset in standard plot of hero thwarting plan of Roman generals to overthrow empress.

There Goes My Heart (1938) **84m.** *** D: Norman Z. McLeod. Fredric March, Virginia Bruce, Patsy Kelly, Alan Mowbray, Nancy Carroll, Eugene Pallette, Claude Gillingwater, Harry Langdon, Arthur Lake.

Typical 30s fluff about runaway heiress Bruce spotted by reporter March; good cast makes one forget trite story-line.

There Goes The Bride (1979-British) **C-88m.** BOMB D: Terence Marcel. Tom Smothers, Twiggy, Martin Balsam, Sylvia Syms, Michael Witney, Hermione Baddeley, Broderick Crawford, Phil Silvers, Jim Backus. Addle-brained father-of-the-bride Smothers throws the wedding party into a tizzy when he has a fling with 1920's-flapper magazine model, Twiggy, whom he has conjured up and only he can see. Unfunny slapstick that comes alive for about 45 seconds when Smothers and Twiggy do an on-target, extravagantly staged Astaire-Rogers routine. Based on Ray Cooney's and John Chapman's 1974 West End farce.

There Goes the Groom (1937) **65m.** ** D: Joseph Santley. Burgess Meredith, Ann Sothern, Louise Henry, Mary Boland, Onslow Stevens, William Brisbane. Strained screwball comedy about newly rich Meredith suddenly courted by Sothern and her wacky family; a smile or two but little else.

There Must Be a Pony (1986) **C-100m.** TVM D: Joseph Sargent. Elizabeth Taylor, Robert Wagner, James Coco, William Windom, Chad Lowe, Edward Winter, Ken Olin. Once-celebrated star (guess who?) returns from mental hospital, attempts a comeback, and risks a romance with a handsome stranger despite her teenage son's misgivings. Svelte Liz has the role played on stage by Myrna Loy (on tour—it never made it to Broadway). James Kirkwood's novel was adapted by Mart Crowley. Average.

There's A Girl in My Soup (1970-British) **C-95m.** *½ D: Roy Boulting. Goldie Hawn, Peter Sellers, Tony Britton, Nicky Henson, Diana Dors. Middle-aged Sellers groping for youth, woos kookie Hawn. Silly story, just a few real laughs.▼

There's Always a Price Tag (1958-French) **102m.** **½ D: Denys de la Patelliere. Michele Morgan, Daniel Gelin, Peter Van Eyck, Bernard Blier. Morgan is excellent in DOUBLE INDEMNITY-type plot about wife who conspires to murder her husband, but film drags and loses credibility after promising start.

There's Always a Woman (1938) **82m.** *** D: Alexander Hall. Joan Blondell, Melvyn Douglas, Mary Astor, Frances Drake, Jerome Cowan, Robert Paige, Thurston Hall. Fine blend of mystery and comedy as D.A. Douglas and detective-wife Blondell try to solve same crime.

There's Always Tomorrow (1956) **84m.** **½ D: Douglas Sirk. Barbara Stanwyck, Fred MacMurray, Joan Bennett, William Reynolds, Pat Crowley, Gigi Perreau, Jane Darwell. MacMurray is in a rut, at work and at home, making him particularly susceptible to old-flame Stanwyck, who comes back into his life. Sudsy but well-acted soap opera, filmed before in 1934.

Therese (1986-French) **C-91m.** *** D: Alain Cavalier. Catherine Mouchet, Aurore Prieto, Sylvie Habault, Ghislane Mona, Helene Alexandridis. Stark, stylistically directed, fact-based story of a dreamy, intense 15-year-old girl (Mouchet) and her desire to become a Carmelite nun, to be wedded to Christ.▼

Therese Desqueyroux (1962-French) **107m.** **½ D: Georges Franju. Emmanuele Riva, Philippe Noiret, Edith Scob, Sami Frey. Bored Riva tries to poison rich husband Noiret; she's acquitted in court, but still does not escape punishment. Riva stands out in this otherwise gloomy drama adapted from a Francois Mauriac novel.

There's Magic in Music (1941) **79m.** ** D: Andrew L. Stone. Allan Jones, Susanna Foster, Diana Lynn, Margaret Lindsay, Lynne Overman, Grace Bradley. Adequate showcase for Foster, an ex-burlesque singer who becomes an opera diva at a summer music camp.

There's No Business Like Show Business (1954) **C-117m.** **½ D: Walter Lang. Ethel Merman, Dan Dailey, Donald O'Connor, Marilyn Monroe, Johnnie Ray, Mitzi Gaynor, Hugh O'Brian, Frank McHugh. Gaudy (and seemingly interminable) hokum about a show-biz family, built around catalog of Irving Berlin songs. Entertaining if not inspired, with several expensive numbers designed to fill CinemaScope screen. Merman and Dailey are fine, Marilyn's at her sexiest, and O'Connor is in top form throughout. Then there's Johnnie Ray deciding to become a priest . . . ▼

There's One Born Every Minute (1942) **59m.** ** D: Harold Young. Hugh Herbert, Tom Brown, Peggy Moran, Guy Kibbee, Gus Schilling, Edgar Kennedy, Carl "Alfalfa" Switzer, Elizabeth Taylor. Contrived comedy of nutty family whose erstwhile head (Herbert) runs a pudding company. Notable as screen debut of 10-year-old Liz as junior member of the clan.

There Was A Crooked Man . . . (1970) **C-125m.** ***½ D: Joseph L. Mankiewicz. Kirk Douglas, Henry Fonda, Hume Cronyn, Warren Oates, Burgess Meredith, John Randolph, Michael Blodgett, Arthur O'Connell, Martin Gabel, Alan Hale, Victor French, Barbara Rhoades, Lee Grant. Bawdy, entertaining Western-comedy-prison-film with Douglas as cocky inmate at territorial prison circa 1883 who matches wits with progressive warden Fonda towards one goal: escape. Powerhouse cast, handsome production. Written by David Newman and Robert Benton.▼

These Are the Damned (1962-British) **96m.** **½ D: Joseph Losey. Macdonald Carey, Shirley Anne Field, Viveca Lindfors, Alexander Knox, Oliver Reed, James Villiers. Film begins as unusual love story set against background of violent "Teddy boys" in England, then halfway through, switches to *Twilight Zone*-like sci-fi. First shown in U.S. with severe editing; now restored for TV. Original British title: THE DAMNED.

These Glamour Girls (1939) **80m.** **½ D: S. Sylvan Simon. Lew Ayres, Lana Turner, Richard Carlson, Anita Louise, Marsha Hunt, Ann Rutherford, Mary Beth Hughes, Jane Bryan, Tom Brown. Turner is effective as nonsocialite who turns the tables on sneering girls at swank college weekend; naive but polished gloss.

These Thousand Hills (1959) **C-96m.** *** D: Richard Fleischer. Don Murray, Richard Egan, Lee Remick, Patricia Owens, Stuart Whitman, Albert Dekker, Harold J. Stone. Adult Western with Murray a rancher who learns to accept responsibility and maintain loyalty to dependent friends; sturdy cast. Based on a novel by A.B. Guthrie, Jr.

These Three (1936) **93m.** **** D: William Wyler. Miriam Hopkins, Merle Oberon, Joel McCrea, Catherine Doucet, Alma Kruger, Bonita Granville, Marcia Mae Jones, Margaret Hamilton, Walter Brennan. Penetrating drama of two young women (Oberon, Hopkins) running school, ruined by lies of malicious student Granville; loosely based on Lillian Hellman's *The Children's Hour*. Superb acting by all, with Granville especially impressive; scripted by the playwright. Remade in 1961 by same director as THE CHILDREN'S HOUR.▼

These Wilder Years (1956) **91m.** **½ D: Roy Rowland. James Cagney, Barbara Stanwyck, Walter Pidgeon, Betty Lou Keim, Don Dubbins. Unusual to see Cagney in this kind of soap opera, about a man who wants to find his illegitimate son, and becomes involved with teenage unwed mother (Keim) through intervention of foundling home director Stanwyck.

They All Died Laughing SEE: **Jolly Bad Fellow, A**

They All Kissed the Bride (1942) **85m.** **½ D: Alexander Hall. Joan Crawford, Melvyn Douglas, Roland Young, Billie Burke, Allen Jenkins. Good stars in fairly amusing film of man being arrested for kissing bride at wedding.

They All Laughed (1981) **C-115m.** **½ D: Peter Bogdanovich. Audrey Hepburn, Ben Gazzara, John Ritter, Colleen Camp, Dorothy Stratten, Blaine Novak, Patti Hansen, George Morfogen, Sean Ferrer, Glenn Scarpelli, Elizabeth Pena. Quirky romantic comedy, long on style, short on substance, follows the adventures and amours of four private detectives. Spotlights some sharp-looking ladies, makes excellent use of N.Y.C. locations, but personal taste will have to judge its degree of success. Ferrer is the son of Hepburn and Mel Ferrer. Stratten was killed prior to film's release.▼

They Call It Murder (1971) **C-100m.** TVM D: Walter Grauman. Jim Hutton, Lloyd Bochner, Jessica Walter, Carmen Matthews, Leslie Nielsen, Jo Ann Pflug, Nita Talbot, Edward Asner, Vic Tayback. Miscasting and unimaginative dialogue abounds in adaptation of Erle Stanley Gardner novel *The D.A. Draws a Circle,* with Hutton hard pressed to link swimming pool murder, car crash fatality, and large insurance claim. Average.

They Call It Sin (1932) **75m.** ** D: Thornton Freeland. Loretta Young, David Manners, George Brent, Louis Calhern, Una Merkel, Elizabeth Patterson. Typical, standard soaper of Young's unhappy love affair while silent suitor stands by.

They Call Me Bruce? (1982) **C-88m.** *½ D: Elliot Hong. Johnny Yune, Ralph Mauro, Pam Huntington, Margaux Hemingway. Unfunny, frequently obnoxious kung fu parody with Korean comedian Yune a doltish cook who is constantly mistaken for Bruce Lee. About two-thirds of the gags are based on TV commercials. Also known as A FISTFUL OF CHOPSTICKS and followed by THEY STILL CALL ME BRUCE.▼

They Call Me MISTER Tibbs! (1970) **C-108m.** ** D: Gordon Douglas. Sidney Poitier, Barbara McNair, Martin Landau, David Sheiner, Anthony Zerbe, Jeff Corey, Ed Asner. Weak follow-up to IN THE HEAT OF THE NIGHT finds black detective Virgil Tibbs (now married and living in San Francisco) investigating murder of girl, with priest-friend Landau implicated. Followed by THE ORGANIZATION.▼

They Call Me Trinity (1971-Italian) **C-109m.** **½ D: E. B. Clucher (Enzo Barboni). Terence Hill, Bud Spencer, Farley Granger, Gisela Hahn, Stephen Zacharias, Dan Sturkie. Wild spoof of THE MAGNIFICENT SEVEN made international superstars of Hill and Spencer; they play half-brothers who try to help Mormon settlement protect itself from the inevitable band of Mexican marauders. Virtually nonstop slapstick spiced with gentle ribbing of the spaghetti Western genre; good fun. Sequel: TRINITY IS STILL MY NAME.▼

They Came from Beyond Space (1967-British) **C-85m.** BOMB D: Freddie Francis. Robert Hutton, Jennifer Jayne, Zia Mohyeddin, Bernard Kay, Michael Gough. Hutton is free to combat spacemen because the silver plate he carries inside his skull makes him immune to their powers.▼

They Came From Within (1975-Canadian) **C-87m.** *½ D: David Cronenberg. Paul Hampton, Joe Silver, Lynn Lowry, Allen Magicovsky, Barbara Steele, Susan Petrie.

Bizarre, sexually-oriented parasites run rampant through dwellers in high-rise apartment building with plenty of gory violence quick to ensue. First "major" film by cult favorite Cronenberg sets the disgusting pattern for most of his subsequent pictures. Originally titled SHIVERS, then THE PARASITE MURDERS. Cut to 77m. for TV.▼

They Came to Blow Up America (1943) **73m.** ** D: Edward Ludwig. George Sanders, Anna Sten, Ward Bond, Dennis Hoey, Sig Ruman, Ludwig Stossel, Robert Barrat. Overzealous espionage yarn designed for WW2 audiences, dated now. Good cast is only virtue.

They Came to Cordura (1959) **C-123m.** **½ D: Robert Rossen. Gary Cooper, Rita Hayworth, Van Heflin, Tab Hunter, Richard Conte, Michael Callan, Dick York. Soapy oater set in 1916 Mexico. Cooper is Army officer accused of cowardice, sent to find five men worthy of Medal of Honor. Hayworth is shady lady he meets on the way.▼

They Came to Rob Las Vegas (1968-Spanish-French-Italian) **C-128m.** ** D: Antonio Isasi. Gary Lockwood, Elke Sommer, Lee J. Cobb, Jack Palance. Big heist is small potatoes as armed robbers plot to intercept Vegas gambling money.

They Dare Not Love (1941) **76m.** *½ D: James Whale. George Brent, Martha Scott, Paul Lukas, Egon Brecher, Roman Bohnen, Edgar Barrier. Good story idea submerged by silly script and Brent's miscasting as dashing Austrian prince, who tries to bargain with Gestapo officer Lukas on behalf of his country. Lloyd Bridges has small role as Nazi seaman.

They Died with Their Boots On (1941) **138m.** *** D: Raoul Walsh. Errol Flynn, Olivia de Havilland, Arthur Kennedy, Charley Grapewin, Gene Lockhart, Anthony Quinn, Stanley Ridges, Sydney Greenstreet, Regis Toomey, Hattie McDaniel. Sweeping Hollywood version of Little Bighorn battle, with Flynn flamboyant as Custer. Fine vignettes amidst episodic buildup to exciting "Last Stand" scene. Errol and Olivia's final film together. Also available in computer-colored version.▼

They Drive By Night (1940) **93m.** ***½ D: Raoul Walsh. George Raft, Ann Sheridan, Ida Lupino, Humphrey Bogart, Gale Page, Alan Hale, Roscoe Karns. Marvelous melodrama of truck-driving brothers battling crooked bosses, with appealing Sheridan and bravura Lupino sparking cast. Unforgettable dialogue by Jerry Wald and Richard Macaulay. Partial reworking of BORDERTOWN. Also shown in computer-colored version.▼

They Gave Him a Gun (1937) **94m.** ** D: W. S. Van Dyke II. Spencer Tracy, Gladys George, Franchot Tone, Edgar

Dearing, Charles Trowbridge. Fine cast does more than justice to weak psychological story of war-hardened Tone turning to crime, Tracy trying to stop him.

They Got Me Covered (1943) 95m. ** D: David Butler. Bob Hope, Dorothy Lamour, Lenore Aubert, Otto Preminger, Eduardo Ciannelli, Marion Martin, Donald MacBride, Walter Catlett, Donald Meek. Spy yarn (by Harry Kurnitz) set in Washington was topical at the time, awkward now; not up to Hope standards.▼

They Knew What They Wanted (1940) 96m. *** D: Garson Kanin. Carole Lombard, Charles Laughton, William Gargan, Harry Carey, Frank Fay. Laughton and Lombard are excellent in this flawed adaptation by Robert Ardrey of Sidney Howard's play (filmed twice before). He's an Italian grape-grower in California who conducts correspondence with waitress and asks her to marry him. Fay is too sanctimonious for words as local priest.▼

They Live (1988) C-97m. ** D: John Carpenter. Roddy Piper, Keith David, Meg Foster, George "Buck" Flower, Peter Jason, Raymond St. Jacques, Jason Robards III, Larry Franco. Lonely drifter arrives in L.A., discovers that consumerist society is being dominated by aliens, whose human disguises and subliminal advertising messages are visible only through special glasses. Satiric sci-fi adventure begins well, degenerates into standard urban action piece, not helped by awful alien makeup. Screenwriter "Frank Armitage" (working from a short story by Ray Faraday Nelson) is actually director Carpenter.▼

They Live by Night (1949) 95m. ***½ D: Nicholas Ray. Farley Granger, Cathy O'Donnell, Howard da Silva, Jay C. Flippen, Helen Craig. Director Ray's first film is sensitive, well-made story of young lovers who are fugitives from the law. Set in 1930s, it avoids clichés and builds considerable impact instead. Based on Edward Anderson's *Thieves Like Us*, remade in 1974 under that name.▼

They Loved Life SEE: Kanal▼

They Made Me a Criminal (1939) 92m. **½ D: Busby Berkeley. John Garfield, Claude Rains, Gloria Dickson, May Robson, Billy Halop, Huntz Hall, Leo Gorcey, Bobby Jordan, Gabriel Dell, Barbara Pepper, Ward Bond, Ann Sheridan. Garfield takes it on the lam when he thinks he's killed a reporter, stays out West with Robson and Dead End Kids. Enjoyable, with Rains miscast as a Dick Tracy type. Remake of THE LIFE OF JIMMY DOLAN.▼

They Made Me a Fugitive (1947-British) 103m. *** D: Cavalcanti. Trevor Howard, Sally Gray, Griffith Jones, Rene Ray, Mary Merrall, Charles Farrell. Dilettante crook is double-crossed by his boss and seeks revenge while on the lam from po-

lice. Potent (yet little-known) British *film noir* packs a real punch, with no holds barred in terms of brutality (and refusal to provide a pat, happy ending). Strikingly photographed by Otto Heller. Look sharp and you'll spot young Peter Bull and Sebastian Cabot. Originally cut when released in U.S. as I BECAME A CRIMINAL, also trimmed for British reissue, so finding a complete print today is difficult.

They Meet Again (1941) 67m. *½ D: Erle C. Kenton. Jean Hersholt, Dorothy Lovett, Robert Baldwin, Neil Hamilton, Maude Eburne, Anne Bennett, Barton Yarborough, Arthur Hoyt. Boring entry in Hersholt's *Dr. Christian* series, with the good doctor attempting to prove the innocence of bank teller Yarborough, accused of pilfering $3,000. A real drag, except for little Leon Tyler's jive musical number during a birthday party, a real pip.▼

They Met In Argentina (1941) 77m. *½ D: Leslie Goodwins, Jack Hively. Maureen O'Hara, James Ellison, Alberto Vila, Buddy Ebsen. Limp musical of O'Hara, a Latin heiress caught between U. S. engineer and local sportsman. Skip it.

They Met in Bombay (1941) 93m. **½ D: Clarence Brown. Clark Gable, Rosalind Russell, Peter Lorre, Jessie Ralph, Reginald Owen, Eduardo Ciannelli. Two jewel thieves team up in ordinary romantic comedy-actioner, spiced by Lorre as money-hungry cargo-ship captain.

They Might Be Giants (1971) C-98m. *** D: Anthony Harvey. Joanne Woodward, George C. Scott, Jack Gilford, Lester Rawlins, Al Lewis, Rue McClanahan, Theresa Merritt, Eugene Roche, James Tolkan, Kitty Winn, Sudie Bond, F. Murray Abraham, Paul Benedict, M. Emmet Walsh. Fun yarn of slightly daffy gentleman who believes he is Sherlock Holmes, and his psychiatrist tagalong whose real name is Dr. Watson. Expanded for TV; Theatrical version ran only 88m. See also THE RETURN OF THE WORLD'S GREATEST DETECTIVE.▼

They Only Come Out at Night (1975) C-78m. TVM D: Daryl Duke. Jack Warden, Charles Ynfante, Madeline Thornton-Sherwood, Tim O'Connor, Joe Mantell, Lili Valenty, Barbara Luna. Veteran detective Warden investigates slayings of several elderly women. Standard whodunit served as pilot to Warden's *Jigsaw John*. Average.

They Only Kill Their Masters (1972) C-97m. **½ D: James Goldstone. James Garner, Katharine Ross, Hal Holbrook, Harry Guardino, June Allyson, Christopher Connelly, Tom Ewell, Peter Lawford, Edmond O'Brien, Arthur O'Connell, Ann Rutherford. Great cast in complicated modern-day whodunit set in coastal California town; tries for Dashiell Hammett feeling, doesn't quite make it. Policeman Garner tries to solve murder of pregnant woman, with formidable Doberman pinscher figuring prominently. Not bad, but a letdown.

They Ran for Their Lives (1969) C-92m. ** D: Oliver Drake (John Payne). John Payne, Jim Davis, Luana Patten, John Carradine. Fair drama featuring Payne as nobody coming to aid of young woman who's being pursued by thugs after classified documents which once belonged to her father.

They're Playing With Fire (1984) C-96m. BOMB D: Howard (Hikmet) Avedis. Eric Brown, Sybil Danning, Andrew Prine, Paul Clemens, K. T. Stevens. What starts off as rehash of Brown's PRIVATE LESSONS quickly turns into sick, ugly slasher film. Danning (as a college English professor!) lures Brown into helping her with a let's-kill-Mom-and-make-off-with-my-inheritance plot—except that someone else is killing everybody in sight. Not even Danning's formidable nude scenes are reason enough to sit through this slop.▼

They Rode West (1954) C-84m. **½ D: Phil Karlson. Robert Francis, Donna Reed, May Wynn, Phil Carey, Onslow Stevens. Camp commander prevents army surgeon from attempting to treat Indian epidemic. Good cast highlights better than average Western.

They Saved Hitler's Brain (1963) 74m. BOMB D: David Bradley. Walter Stocker, Audrey Caire, Carlos Rivas, John Holland, Dani Lynn, Marshall Reed, Nestor Paiva. Daughter of kidnapped scientist traces him to isle of Mandoras, where Nazis still flourish under the leadership of Hitler's still-living head. Unbelievably muddled plot results from intercutting 1950s studio potboiler, beautifully photographed by Stanley Cortez (MAGNIFICENT AMBERSONS) with super-cheap 1960s footage involving completely different cast. Originally titled MADMEN OF MANDORAS.▼

They Shall Have Music (1939) 101m. *** D: Archie Mayo. Jascha Heifetz, Joel McCrea, Andrea Leeds, Walter Brennan, Gene Reynolds, Marjorie Main, Porter Hall, Dolly Loehr (Diana Lynn), Terry Kilburn. Cornerstone of Samuel Goldwyn's efforts to bring classical music to the masses and make a movie star out of Heifetz. Plot involves disadvantaged kids who help Brennan save his settlement music school by convincing Heifetz to give a benefit.▼

They Shoot Horses, Don't They? (1969) C-121m. ***½ D: Sydney Pollack. Jane Fonda, Michael Sarrazin, Susannah York, Gig Young, Red Buttons, Bonnie Bedelia, Bruce Dern, Allyn Ann McLerie. 1930s marathon dance becomes microcosm of life, with myriad of subplots, characters' lives intertwining. Fonda is self-destructive girl who attracts aimless Sarrazin with tragic results; Young won Oscar as oily promoter of grueling "contest." Fascinating. Based on Horace McCoy's novel.▼

They Still Call Me Bruce (1987) C-91m. *½ D: Johnny Yune, James Orr. Johnny Yune, David Mendenhall, Pat Paulsen, Joey Travolta, Robert Guillaume, Bethany Wright, Carl Bensen. In-name-only sequel to THEY CALL ME BRUCE has at least one thing in common with its predecessor: it's awful. This time Yune plays a Korean searching for the American GI who saved him years ago, winding up instead as a big-brother figure for orphan Mendenhall.▼

They've Kidnapped Anne Benedict SEE: **Abduction of Saint Anne, The**▼

They Went That-A-Way and That-A-Way (1978) C-95m. *½ D: Edward Montagne, Stuart E. McGowan. Tim Conway, Chuck McCann, Richard Kiel, Dub Taylor, Reni Santoni, Lenny Montana. Lame prison escape comedy (with script by Conway) puts Conway and McCann through lackluster routines as a road-company Laurel and Hardy.▼

They Were Expendable (1945) 135m. **** D: John Ford. Robert Montgomery, John Wayne, Donna Reed, Jack Holt, Ward Bond, Louis Jean Heydt, Marshall Thompson, Leon Ames, Cameron Mitchell. One of the finest (and most underrated) of all WW2 films, based on the true story of America's PT boat squadron in the Philippines during the early days of the war. Moving, exquisitely detailed production (photographed by Joseph August) under Ford's distinctive hand, with real-life Naval officer Montgomery a convincing lead. Screenplay by Frank "Spig" Wead. Also shown in computer-colored version.▼

They Were Sisters (1945-British) 110m. **½ D: Arthur Crabtree. Phyllis Calvert, James Mason, Hugh Sinclair, Dulcie Gray, Pamela Kellino (Mason). Fresh approach to stock drama of trio of sisters with contrasting marriages and lives.

They Were So Young (1955-German) 80m. *** D: Kurt Neumann. Scott Brady, Raymond Burr, Johanna Matz, Ingrid Stenn. Nicely produced, grim melodrama of girls sent to South America to be used by crooks. Even without "names" in cast, film would be good.

They Who Dare (1953-British) C-101m. **½ D: Lewis Milestone. Dirk Bogarde, Denholm Elliott, Akim Tamiroff, Eric Pohlmann, David Peel. Effective WW2 actioner with good character delineation, tracing commando raid on German-controlled Aegean air fields.

They Won't Believe Me (1947) 79m. ***½ D: Irving Pichel. Susan Hayward, Robert Young, Jane Greer, Rita Johnson, Tom Powers, Don Beddoe, Frank Ferguson. Fine James Cain-type melodrama about a philanderer who gets involved with three women, leading to tragedy (and a terrific twist ending). Young excels in his unsympathetic role; Johnson does wonders with her scenes as his wife.▼

They Won't Forget (1937) 95m. **** D: Mervyn LeRoy. Claude Rains, Gloria Dickson, Otto Kruger, Allyn Joslyn, Elisha Cook, Jr., Edward Norris. Electrifying drama begins when pretty high school student is murdered in Southern town. A man is arrested, and a big-time Northern lawyer takes the case, but everyone seems more interested in exploiting personal interests than in seeing justice triumph. No punches are pulled in this still-powerful film. Lana Turner plays the unfortunate girl, in her first important role. Script by Robert Rossen and Aben Kandel, from the book *Death in the Deep South* by Ward Greene, based on notorious 1913 incident later dramatized for TV as THE MURDER OF MARY PHAGAN.▼

Thief, The (1952) 85m. **½ D: Russell Rouse. Ray Milland, Rita Gam, Martin Gabel, Harry Bronson. Spy yarn set in N.Y.C. with a difference: no dialogue. Gimmick grows wearisome, script is tame.

Thief (1971) C-74m. TVM D: William Graham. Richard Crenna, Angie Dickinson, Cameron Mitchell, Hurd Hatfield, Robert Webber. Ex-con finds himself unable to repay debt, must obtain sum of money very quickly. Uneven performances in formula drama, enlivened by crisp direction. Average.▼

Thief (1981) C-122m. *** D: Michael Mann. James Caan, Tuesday Weld, Willie Nelson, James Belushi, Robert Prosky, Tom Signorelli, Dennis Farina. Arresting drama about a professional thief, inventively realized by writer-director Mann (in his feature debut). Caan is excellent as the man with one drive: survival. Stylishly photographed (by Donald Thorin) and scored (by Tangerine Dream).▼

Thief of Bagdad, The (1924) 155m. *** D: Raoul Walsh. Douglas Fairbanks, Julanne Johnston, Anna May Wong, Sojin, Snitz Edwards, Charles Belcher, Brandon Hurst. Dashing Fairbanks is sent on magic quest in Arabian Nights-type fantasy/adventure with lovely Johnston the princess who rides off with Doug on his magic carpet. Quite long, but never dull; one of the most imaginative of all silent films, with awesome sets by William Cameron Menzies. Remade three times (so far).▼

Thief of Bagdad, The (1940-British) C-106m. **** D: Ludwig Berger, Tim Whelan, Michael Powell. Sabu, John Justin, June Duprez, Conrad Veidt, Rex Ingram, Miles Malleson, Mary Morris. Remarkable fantasy of native boy Sabu outdoing

evil magician Veidt in Arabian Nights fable with incredible Oscar-winning Technicolor photography by Georges Perinal and Osmond Borradaile, special effects and art direction. Ingram gives splendid performance as a genie; vivid score by Miklos Rozsa.▼

Thief of Baghdad (1961-Italian) C-90m. ** D: Arthur Lubin. Steve Reeves, Giorgia Moll, Arturo Dominici, Edy Vessel. Reeves searches for enchanted blue rose so he can marry Sultan's daughter. Nothing like Sabu version, but occasionally atmospheric.▼

Thief of Baghdad, The (1978-British-French) C-100m. TVM D: Clive Donner. Roddy McDowall, Peter Ustinov, Kabir Bedi, Frank Finlay, Marina Vlady, Terrence Stamp, Pavla Ustinov, Ian Holm. More flying carpet and genie-in-the-magic-lamp fantasy in this fourth filming of the Arabian Nights adventure that's handsome enough but nowhere near the definitive 1940 version. Average.▼

Thief of Damascus (1952) C-78m. ** D: Will Jason. Paul Henreid, John Sutton, Jeff Donnell, Lon Chaney, Elena Verdugo. Jumbled costume spectacle featuring Aladdin, Sinbad and Ali Baba out to rescue princess; typical Sam Katzman quickie reuses much footage from JOAN OF ARC!

Thief of Hearts (1984) C-100m. ** D: Douglas Day Stewart. Steven Bauer, Barbara Williams, John Getz, David Caruso, Christine Ebersole, George Wendt. While ransacking a house Bauer steals woman's diaries, reads them through, and then determines to woo her—using the "secret" knowledge he's learned. Slick but curiously unappealing film written by first-time director Stewart. Reworked slightly for homevideo, with potentially X-rated shots added.▼

Thief of Paris, The (1967) C-119m. *** D: Louis Malle. Jean-Paul Belmondo, Genevieve Bujold, Marie Dubois, Francoise Fabian, Julien Guiomar. Solid comedy-drama with personal setbacks turning Belmondo to thievery for revenge on society; soon he finds that robbery has become his whole life.

Thief Who Came to Dinner, The (1973) C-105m. ** D: Bud Yorkin. Ryan O'Neal, Jacqueline Bisset, Warren Oates, Jill Clayburgh, Charles Cioffi, Ned Beatty, Austin Pendleton, Gregory Sierra, Michael Murphy, John Hillerman. Disappointing caper comedy (considering cast and director) about a computer expert who becomes a jewel thief in Houston's top social circles. Clayburgh (pre-stardom) has small but telling role as O'Neal's ex-wife; script by Walter Hill.▼

Thieves (1977) C-92m. BOMB D: John Berry. Marlo Thomas, Charles Grodin, Irwin Corey, Hector Elizondo, Mercedes McCambridge, John McMartin, Gary

Merrill, Ann Wedgeworth. Pretentious, boring adaptation of Herb Gardner's play about crazy couple trying to recapture their innocence in a corrupt N.Y.C. Corey (as Thomas' cabbie father) adds only life to so-called comedy. Bob Fosse has a brief role.

Thieves Fall Out (1941) 72m. ** D: Ray Enright. Eddie Albert, Joan Leslie, Alan Hale, William T. Orr, John Litel, Anthony Quinn, Edward Brophy. Innocuous drama of rival mattress factory families and their problems.

Thieves' Highway (1949) 94m. *** D: Jules Dassin. Richard Conte, Valentina Cortese, Lee J. Cobb, Barbara Lawrence, Jack Oakie, Millard Mitchell. Exciting drama of underworld mobsters moving in on the California trucking business; fast-moving film has Cortese's American debut. Adapted by A.I. Bezzerides from his novel.

Thieves' Holiday (1946) 100m. *** D: Douglas Sirk. George Sanders, Signe Hasso, Carole Landis, Akim Tamiroff, Gene Lockhart. Famous French thief and rogue, beautifully played by Sanders, works his way into position as prefect of police. Delightful romantic adventure. Originally titled SCANDAL IN PARIS.

Thieves Like Us (1974) C-123m. ***½ D: Robert Altman. Keith Carradine, Shelley Duvall, John Schuck, Bert Remsen, Louise Fletcher, Ann Latham, Tom Skerritt. Three misfits escape from prison camp in 1930s Midwest, go on a crime spree; the youngest (Carradine) falls in love with a simple, uneducated girl (Duvall). Despite familiar trappings, Altman digs deep into period atmosphere and strong characterizations; this film gets better every time you look at it. Remake of THEY LIVE BY NIGHT. Scripted by Calder Willingham, Joan Tewkesbury, and Altman.

Thin Air (1969-British) C-91m. *½ D: Gerry Levy. George Sanders, Maurice Evans, Patrick Allen, Neil Connery, Hilary Dwyer, Robert Flemyng. Parachutists keep disappearing, due to unseen forces; routine sci-fi with little to recommend it. Originally titled THE BODY STEALERS (INVASION OF THE BODY STEALERS).▼

Thin Blue Line, The (1988) C-96m. **** D: Errol Morris. Remarkable, perhaps even landmark, documentary, as Morris sets out to prove that a convicted hitchhiker did *not* kill a Dallas policeman in 1976—and that the lowlife who fingered him (and who wound up on Death Row for a subsequent murder) did. Very subjective but totally convincing, so convincing that the case was reopened after the film's premiere, and the defendant was exonerated. Philip Glass's score adds to the hypnotic effect.▼

Thing, The (1982) C-108m. *½ D: John Carpenter. Kurt Russell, A. Wilford Brimley, Richard Dysart, Richard Masur, Donald Moffat, T.K. Carter, David Clennon. Remake of the 1951 film about Antarctic outpost terrorized by an alien organism. More faithful to the original story, but nonstop parade of slimy, repulsive special effects turns this into a freak show and drowns most of the suspense.▼

Thing (From Another World), The (1951) 87m. ***½ D: Christian Nyby. Kenneth Tobey, Margaret Sheridan, Robert Cornthwaite, Douglas Spencer, James Arness, Dewey Martin, William Self, George Fenneman. Classic blend of science-fiction and horror, loosely based on John W. Campbell, Jr.'s *Who Goes There?* Scientists at lonely Arctic outpost dig up alien (Arness) from the permafrost and must fight for their lives when it's accidentally thawed. Tense direction (often credited to producer Howard Hawks), excellent performances, eerie score by Dmitri Tiomkin. Screenplay by Charles Lederer. Watch out for 81m. reissue prints. Remade in 1982. Also shown in computer-colored version.▼

Things Are Tough All Over (1982) C-92m. ** D: Tom Avildsen. Cheech Marin, Thomas Chong, Shelby Fiddis, Rikki Marin, Evelyn Guerrero. Besides their standard characterizations, the boys play two Arab brothers whose paths cross C & C's as the latter drive a ritzy car to California, one that happens to have $5 million hidden inside. Superb makeup and mimicry give evidence to the team's genuine talent, but the laughs just aren't there most of the time.▼

Things Change (1988) C-100m. **½ D: David Mamet. Don Ameche, Joe Mantegna, Robert Prosky, J.J. Johnson, Ricky Jay, Mike Nussbaum, Jack Wallace, Dan Conway, J.T. Walsh. Simple Italian shoemaker (Ameche) agrees to take the rap for a Chicago mob murder for a fee, but the man assigned to baby-sit him for a weekend (Mantegna) decides to take the old man on a final fling before he goes to jail. Slight, sometimes flat comic fable by Mamet and Shel Silverstein is buoyed by some wonderful vignettes and endearing performances by the stars. Ameche is a joy to watch.▼

Things in Their Season (1974) C-75m. TVM D: James Goldstone. Patricia Neal, Ed Flanders, Marc Singer, Meg Foster, Charles Haid, Doreen Lang, Med Flory. Touching, beautifully acted drama of Wisconsin farm family, with wife-mother Neal discovering she is terminally ill with leukemia. Screenplay by John Gay. Above average.

Things to Come (1936-British) 92m. *** D: William Cameron Menzies. Raymond Massey, Cedric Hardwicke, Ralph Richardson, Maurice Braddell, Edward Chapman, Ann Todd. Stunning visualization of H. G. Wells's depiction of the future.

Massey portrays leader of new world, Richardson despotic wartime ruler. Aloof but always interesting, enhanced by Menzies' sets. Vibrant music by Arthur Bliss; Wells himself wrote the screenplay. Some prints of the original 113m. version still exist. Remade in 1979 as THE SHAPE OF THINGS TO COME (actually the name of Wells' 1933 book).▼

Thing That Couldn't Die, The (1958) 69m. ** D: Will Cowan. Andra Martin, William Reynolds, Robin Hughes, Carolyn Kearney, Jeffrey Stone. You never know what a dowsing rod will find. In this thriller one finds the still living, decapitated head of a Spanish wizard who's looking for his body. Cheap, and looks it, but Hughes is good in title role.

Thing with Two Heads, The (1972) C-93m. ** D: Lee Frost. Ray Milland, Rosie Grier, Don Marshall, Roger Perry, Chelsea Brown. Fantastic tale of bigot who finds his head transplanted onto black man's body. Played partially for laughs, which helps a little.

Thin Ice (1937) 78m. *** D: Sidney Lanfield. Sonja Henie, Tyrone Power, Arthur Treacher, Joan Davis, Alan Hale, Raymond Walburn, Sig Ruman. Early Sonja Henie, and very good, with dashing prince Power in love with commoner Henie.

Thin Ice (1981) C-100m. TVM D: Paul Aaron. Kate Jackson, Lillian Gish, Gerald Prendergast, Louise Latham, Mimi Kennedy, James Greene, Barton Heyman. Widowed high-school teacher Jackson drifts into a love affair with one of her teenaged students. Gish continues her remarkable film career, as Jackson's loving grandmother. Average.

Think Dirty (1970-British) C-94m. *½ D: Jim Clark. Marty Feldman, Shelley Berman, Judy Cornwell, Julie Ege, Patrick Cargill, Jack Watson. Leering, obnoxious comedy-fantasy with adman Feldman having to use sex to promote a cereal on TV; meanwhile, his prudish wife is mounting a campaign to purify the airwaves. Original British title: EVERY HOME SHOULD HAVE ONE.▼

Think Fast, Mr. Moto (1937) 66m. D: Norman Foster. Peter Lorre, Virginia Field, Sig Ruman, Murray Kinnell, Lotus Long, J. Carrol Naish, Frederick Vogeding, George Cooper SEE: **Mr. Moto** series.

Thin Man, The One series stands apart from the others; its episodes were filmed two and three years apart, its stars were those of the major rank, and the films were *~t l~~k~d down at as Grade-B efforts.

THE THIN MAN, a highly l series launched quite unexin 1934 with a delightfully unpreblend of screwball comedy and nystery, from a story by Dashiell :. William Powell and Myrna Loy

starred as Nick and Nora Charles, a perfectly happy, sophisticated couple whose marriage never stood in the way of their having fun and going off on detective capers. This blithe, carefree portrayal of a modern American couple was beautifully handled by Loy and Powell, and audiences loved it. Five Thin Man films followed, from 1936 to 1947. None of them fully captured the essence of the original, although they retained much of the charm and had the infallible byplay of the two stars, aided by their dog Asta, who soon became a star in his own right. AFTER THE THIN MAN featured an upcoming actor named James Stewart as a suspect, and Sam Levene in the detective role played in the original by Nat Pendleton (and repeated in ANOTHER THIN MAN). ANOTHER THIN MAN also introduced Nick Charles, Jr. as a baby, who grew up in each successive film. SHADOW OF THE THIN MAN was next in the series, and featured Nick and Nora sleuthing at the race track. THE THIN MAN GOES HOME presented Nick's parents (Harry Davenport and Lucile Watson), who never wanted him to be a detective in the first place. The final film, SONG OF THE THIN MAN, had Nick and Nora frequenting many jazz hangouts (à la *Peter Gunn*) for some offbeat sequences. While the original THIN MAN rated above its followups, even the weakest entries were fresh and enjoyable, thanks mainly to the two stars. By the way, "The Thin Man" really wasn't Powell—he was a character in the first film, played by Edward Ellis.

Thin Man, The (1934) 93m. D: W. S. Van Dyke II. William Powell, Myrna Loy, Maureen O'Sullivan, Nat Pendleton, Minna Gombell, Cesar Romero, Natalie Moorhead, Edward Ellis, Porter Hall.▼

Thin Man Goes Home, The (1944) 100m. D: Richard Thorpe. William Powell, Myrna Loy, Lucile Watson, Gloria De Haven, Anne Revere, Helen Vinson, Harry Davenport, Leon Ames, Donald Meek, Edward Brophy.▼

Thin Red Line, The (1964) 99m. **½ D: Andrew Marton. Keir Dullea, Jack Warden, James Philbrook, Kieron Moore. James Jones' novel about relationship between sergeant Warden and private Dullea, who cannot come to terms, is focus of WW2 tale, set in Guadalcanal.

Third Day, The (1965) C-119m. **½ D: Jack Smight. George Peppard, Elizabeth Ashley, Roddy McDowall, Arthur O'Connell, Mona Washbourne, Herbert Marshall, Robert Webber, Charles Drake, Sally Kellerman, Vincent Gardenia, Arte Johnson. Capable cast helps standard amnesia tale about Peppard's inability to remember events that have caused him to be accused of murder.

Third Degree Burn (1989) **C-97m. TVM**
D: Roger Spottiswoode. Treat Williams,
Virginia Madsen, Richard Masur, CCH
Pounder, Michael Chapman, Robert Nadir. Nickle-and-dime detective hired to keep
an eye on a wealthy businessman's sexy
but bored wife finds himself being seduced
by her and then framed for her husband's
murder. Languid suspense thriller that's
hole-ier than Swiss cheese. Made for cable. Average.
Third Finger, Left Hand (1940) **96m. ★★**
D: Robert Z. Leonard. Myrna Loy, Melvyn Douglas, Raymond Walburn, Lee
Bowman, Bonita Granville. Mediocre comedy with attractive stars swallowed up.
Loy dissuades romance by pretending to be
married, so Douglas claims to be her husband!
Third Generation, The (1979-German)
C-111m. ★★★½ D: Rainer Werner Fassbinder. Eddie Constantine, Hanna Schygulla,
Volker Spengler, Margit Carstensen, Bulle
Ogier, Udo Kier, Hark Bohm. Pitch-black
comedy about upper-middle class German
terrorists, their cops-and-robbers antics,
and how they provide excuse for government oppression. Superb ensemble cast in
one of Fassbinder's best films.
Third Girl from the Left, The (1973)
C-74m. TVM D: Peter Medak. Kim
Novak, Tony Curtis, Michael Brandon,
George Furth, Barbi Benton, Louis Guss,
Michael Conrad, Anne Ramsey. Embar-
rassing, clichéd dialogue all but spoils
old-fashioned melodrama featuring Novak
as "the last of the chorus girl troupers,"
experiencing second thoughts over impend-
ing marriage to singer Jordan (Curtis).
Dory Previn wrote both the script and
music. Average.
Third Key, The (1956-British) **96m. ★★★**
D: Charles Frend. Jack Hawkins, John
Stratton, Dorothy Alison, Geoffrey Keen,
Ursula Howells. Exciting story of Scotland
Yard investigation, as Inspector Hawkins
and rookie sergeant (Stratton) diligently
pursue safecracking incident to its surprising conclusion. Original British title: THE
LONG ARM.
Third Man, The (1949-British) **104m.**
★★★★ D: Carol Reed. Orson Welles, Joseph Cotten, (Alida) Valli, Trevor Howard,
Bernard Lee, Wilfrid Hyde-White. Graham Greene's account of mysterious Harry
Lime (Welles) in post-WW2 Vienna is a
bona fide classic, with pulp-writer Cotten
on a manhunt for Harry. Anton Karas'
zither rendition of "The Third Man Theme"
adds just the right touch; cinematographer
Robert Krasker won an Oscar. Note: there
are two versions of this film. The British
version features introductory narration by
director Reed; the American print is narrated by Cotten, and runs 93m. Little of
substance was actually cut, but the film

was tightened somewhat by coproducer
David O. Selznick. Also shown in com-
puter-colored version.▼
Third Man on the Mountain (1959)
C-105m. ★★★ D: Ken Annakin. James
MacArthur, Michael Rennie, Janet Munro,
James Donald, Herbert Lom, Laurence
Naismith. Fine Disney adventure about
Swiss boy (MacArthur) determined to climb
the Matterhorn (here called the Citadel)
who learns more than just mountain-climbing
in his dogged pursuit. Look quickly to spot
MacArthur's mother Helen Hayes in a
cameo as tourist.▼
Third Secret, The (1964-British) **103m.**
★★½ D: Charles Crichton. Stephen Boyd,
Jack Hawkins, Richard Attenborough, Diane
Cilento, Pamela Franklin, Paul Rogers,
Alan Webb. Episodic whodunit with Boyd
tracking down the murderer of his psychoanalyst; no real surprises here.
Third Voice, The (1960) **79m. ★★★** D: Hubert Cornfield. Edmond O'Brien, Laraine
Day, Julie London, Ralph Brooks, Roque
Ybarra, Henry Delgado. Neat suspense
film involving murder, impersonation and
double-crossing.
Thirst (1979-Australian) **C-90m. ★★★** D:
Rod Hardy. Chantal Contouri, David
Hemmings, Henry Silva, Max Phipps, Shir-
ley Cameron, Rod Mullinar. Strange,
stylish, thoroughly chilling tale of secret
society trying to brainwash Contouri and
transform her into a baroness-vampire.
Minimum of plot and characterization but
maximum suspense in this well-directed
shocker.▼
Thirsty Dead, The (1975) **C-90m.** BOMB
D: Terry Becker. John Considine, Jennifer
Billingsley, Judith McConnell, Tani Guthrie.
Guide abducts actress and friends to jungle
Shangri-La, where strange tribe drinks
human blood to regain youth. Boring
Philippine-made junk.▼
Thirteen at Dinner (1985) **C-100m. TVM**
D: Lou Antonio. Peter Ustinov, Faye
Dunaway, David Suchet, Lee Horsley,
Amanda Pays, Jonathan Cecil, Diane Keen,
Benedict Taylor. Hercule Poirot's investigation of a British lord's murder brings
him face-to-face with the dead man's actress wife and a talented impersonator (giving Dunaway double the chance for scenery
chewing). Adapted from the Agatha Christie novel by Rod Browning. Made in England. Average.
13 Fighting Men (1960) **69m. ★½** D:
Harry Gerstad. Grant Williams, Brad Dexter, Carole Mathews, Peter Dix, Richard Garland, Rayford Barnes, John Erwin.
Minor film about Union soldiers fighting
off Rebel troops to protect gold shipment.
13 Frightened Girls (1963) **C-89m.**
BOMB D: William Castle. Murray Hamilton,
Joyce Taylor, Hugh Marlowe, Khigh Dhiegh.
One of Castle's weirdest films (no mean

feat), set in Swiss boarding school catering to daughters of diplomats; after trading bits of info they picked up from Daddy during the holidays, the girls decide to go off and do spy stuff. Castle held a worldwide talent search to find his "stars," for whom this was their first—and no doubt last—film. A side-splitting camp classic awaiting rediscovery.

13 Ghosts (1960) **C-88m.** **½ D: William Castle. Charles Herbert, Donald Woods, Martin Milner, Jo Morrow, Rosemary DeCamp, Margaret Hamilton, John Van Dreelen. Typically tongue-in-cheek Castle spook opera, about nice, all-American family (with children named Buck and Medea!) that inherits a haunted house. Plenty of chills and chuckles, with Hamilton cleverly cast as sinister housekeeper. TV prints run 85m., minus footage of Castle introducing "Illusion-O"—movie patrons were given "ghost viewers" enabling them to see (or not see) the spirits.▼

Thirteen Hours By Air (1936) **80m.** **½ D: Mitchell Leisen. Fred MacMurray, Joan Bennett, ZaSu Pitts, John Howard, Bennie Bartlett, Grace Bradley, Alan Baxter, Ruth Donnelly, Dean Jagger. Dated but diverting tale of transcontinental flight, with romance, murder, and intrigue surrounding mysterious passengers.

13 Rue Madeleine (1946) **95m.** **½ D: Henry Hathaway. James Cagney, Annabella, Richard Conte, Frank Latimore, Walter Abel, Melville Cooper, Sam Jaffe. OK documentary-style story of O.S.S. agents' attempt to locate German missile site in France during WW2. Good cast also includes young E. G. Marshall, Karl Malden, Red Buttons.▼

Thirteenth Guest, The (1932) **69m.** **½ D: Albert Ray. Ginger Rogers, Lyle Talbot, J. Farrell MacDonald, Paul Hurst, James C. Eagles. Guests are reassembled from dinner party that took place 13 years ago—at which the host fell dead—in order to solve mystery of unnamed 13th guest to whom the deceased bequeathed his estate. Enjoyable antique chiller complete with hooded murderer. Remade as THE MYSTERY OF THE THIRTEENTH GUEST.▼

13th Hour, The (1947) **65m.** D: William Clemens. Richard Dix, Karen Morley, Mark Dennis, John Kellogg, Bernadene Hayes, Jim Bannon, Regis Toomey. SEE: **The Whistler** series.

13th Letter, The (1951) **85m.** **½ D: Otto Preminger. Linda Darnell, Charles Boyer, Michael Rennie, Constance Smith, Judith Evelyn. Interesting account of effect of series of poison pen letters on townsfolk, set in Canada. Remake of H. G. Clouzot's LE CORBEAU.

13 West Street (1962) **80m.** **½ D: Philip Leacock. Alan Ladd, Rod Steiger, Jeanne Cooper, Michael Callan, Dolores Dorn.

Early version of DEATH WISH has Ladd out to get gang of hoodlums; taut actioner with most capable cast. Based on novel *The Tiger Among Us* by Leigh Brackett.

Thirteen Women (1932) **73m.** ** D: George Archainbaud. Irene Dunne, Ricardo Cortez, Myrna Loy, Jill Esmond, Florence Eldridge, Kay Johnson. Silly tripe with Loy as a half-caste with hypnotic powers who has sworn revenge on sorority sisters who rejected her years ago in school.

—30— (1959) **96m.** *½ D: Jack Webb. Jack Webb, William Conrad, David Nelson, Whitney Blake, Louise Lorimer, Joe Flynn, James Bell. Hackneyed, over-written tale of a typical night on a big-city newspaper. Conrad chews the scenery as city editor, but the script's the main villain, abetted by atrocious music score. Title, by the way, is journalists' way of indicating "the end."

Thirty Day Princess (1934) **75m.** **½ D: Marion Gering. Sylvia Sidney, Cary Grant, Edward Arnold, Vince Barnett, Lucien Littlefield. Pleasant minor account of Sidney substituting for an ill princess who must make a good-will tour in U. S., with expected results. Cowritten by Preston Sturges.

30 Foot Bride of Candy Rock, The (1959) **75m.** ** D: Sidney Miller. Lou Costello, Dorothy Provine, Gale Gordon, Charles Lane, Jimmy Conlin, Peter Leeds. Lou Costello's only starring film without Bud Abbott is nothing much, mildly entertaining, with Provine enlarged to gigantic proportions.▼

30 Is a Dangerous Age, Cynthia (1968-British) **C-98m.** **½ D: Joseph McGrath. Dudley Moore, Eddie Foy, Jr., Suzy Kendall, John Bird. Man who has frittered away his life decides that within 6 weeks he wants to be married and famous. Funny, but sometimes falls flat. Dudley also composed the score and cowrote the screenplay.▼

39 Steps, The (1935-British) **87m.** **** D: Alfred Hitchcock. Robert Donat, Madeleine Carroll, Lucie Mannheim, Godfrey Tearle, Peggy Ashcroft, Wylie Watson. Classic Hitchcock mystery with overtones of light comedy and romance, as innocent Donat is pulled into spy-ring activities. Memorable banter between Donat and Carroll, who thinks he's a criminal, set style for sophisticated dialogue for years. Remade twice.▼

39 Steps, The (1959-British) **C-93m.** **½ D: Ralph Thomas. Kenneth More, Taina Elg, Brenda de Banzie, Barry Jones, Reginald Beckwith, Sidney James, James Hayter. Young man is accidentally involved in murder and espionage and ensnares the aid of disbelieving young woman. More and Elg are delightful in this replica of

1935 classic; though not nearly as good, it's still entertaining.▼

Thirty-Nine Steps, The (1978-British) **C-102m.** **½ D: Don Sharp. Robert Powell, David Warner, Eric Porter, Karen Dotrice, John Mills, George Baker. Based more on John Buchan's book than Hitchcock adaptation, remake isn't bad but lacks panache; Powell plays innocent man pursued by villains who believe he's obtained details of their plot to hatch WW1.▼

Thirty Seconds Over Tokyo (1944) **138m.** *** D: Mervyn LeRoy. Van Johnson, Robert Walker, Spencer Tracy, Phyllis Thaxter, Scott McKay, Robert Mitchum, Don DeFore, Stephen McNally, Louis Jean Heydt, Leon Ames, Paul Langton. Exciting WW2 actioner of first American attack on Japan with sturdy cast, guest appearance by Tracy as General Doolittle. Script by Dalton Trumbo. Oscar-winning special effects.▼

36 Hours (1964) **115m.** **½ D: George Seaton. James Garner, Eva Marie Saint, Rod Taylor, Werner Peters, Celia Lovsky, Alan Napier. Intriguing WW2 yarn with Garner as captured spy brainwashed into thinking the war is over begins well, but peters out fast. Taylor as German officer is interesting casting. Remade for cable TV as BREAKING POINT. Also shown in computer-colored version.

30 Years of Fun (1963) **85m.** **** Compiled by Robert Youngson. Charlie Chaplin, Buster Keaton, Laurel and Hardy, Harry Langdon, Sydney Chaplin, Charley Chase, etc. Without repeating from previous films, Youngson presents hilarious silent comedy footage. Included is rare sequence of Laurel and Hardy performing together for the first time in 1917's LUCKY DOG.

This Above All (1942) **110m.** *** D: Anatole Litvak. Tyrone Power, Joan Fontaine, Thomas Mitchell, Nigel Bruce, Gladys Cooper, Sara Allgood, Phillip Merivale, Alexander Knox. Timely WW2 film shows its age, but is still good, with strong cast in Eric Knight tale of embittered soldier Power finding courage and love with patriotic Britisher Fontaine; adapted by R.C. Sherriff.

This Angry Age (1958-Italian-U.S.) **C-111m.** ** D: Rene Clement. Silvana Mangano, Anthony Perkins, Alida Valli, Richard Conte, Jo Van Fleet, Nehemiah Persoff. Ludicrous mishmash set in Indo-China with Van Fleet a stereotyped, dominating mother who's convinced that her children (Perkins and Mangano) can make their rice fields a going proposition. Originally titled THE SEA WALL.

This Child Is Mine (1985) **C-100m.** TVM D: David Greene. Lindsay Wagner, Chris Sarandon, Nancy McKeon, Michael Lerner, Kathleen York, Matthew Faison. Drama about the struggles, both emotional and legal, between a teenager who gave up

her child for adoption and now wants the infant back, and the caring, adoptive parents who've gained legal custody. Average.

This Could Be the Night (1957) **103m.** **½ D: Robert Wise. Jean Simmons, Paul Douglas, Anthony Franciosa, Joan Blondell, Neile Adams, ZaSu Pitts, J. Carrol Naish. Forced, frantic comedy of prim teacher Simmons working as secretary to gangster Douglas, who runs a nightclub; Franciosa is the young associate who romances her.

This Day and Age (1933) **85m.** *** D: Cecil B. DeMille. Charles Bickford, Judith Allen, Richard Cromwell, Harry Green, Eddie Nugent, Ben Alexander, Bradley Page. Fascinating story of high-schoolers taking law into their own hands to pin mobster Bickford for murder of tailor Green. Hardly subtle, yet powerfully effective.

This Earth Is Mine (1959) **C-125m.** **½ D: Henry King. Rock Hudson, Jean Simmons, Dorothy McGuire, Claude Rains, Kent Smith, Anna Lee, Ken Scott. Disjointed soaper set in 1930s California vineyards about intertwining family romances, with Hudson-Simmons love story the focal point.

This Girl for Hire (1983) **C-100m.** TVM D: Jerry Jameson. Bess Armstrong, Celeste Holm, Cliff De Young, Hermione Baddeley, Scott Brady, Jose Ferrer, Howard Duff, Beverly Garland, Roddy McDowall, Percy Rodrigues, Ray Walston, Elisha Cook. Terrific cast of veterans and saucy Bess as a lady private eye, enliven this takeoff of 40s detective flicks; our heroine investigates the murder of egotistical mystery writer Ferrer. Clever, but ultimately too cute. Average.

This Gun for Hire (1942) **80m.** *** D: Frank Tuttle. Alan Ladd, Veronica Lake, Robert Preston, Laird Cregar, Tully Marshall, Marc Lawrence, Pamela Blake. Ladd came into his own as paid gunman seeking revenge on man who double-crossed him, with Lake as a fetching vis-à-vis. Script by W.R. Burnett and Albert Maltz, from Graham Greene's novel; remade as SHORT CUT TO HELL.▼

This Happy Breed (1944-British) **C-114m.** ***½ D: David Lean. Robert Newton, Celia Johnson, John Mills, Kay Walsh, Stanley Holloway. Splendidly acted saga follows British family from 1919 to 1939 in this adaptation of Noel Coward play.

This Happy Feeling (1958) **C-92m.** *** D: Blake Edwards. Debbie Reynolds, Curt Jurgens, John Saxon, Alexis Smith, Estelle Winwood, Mary Astor. Most engaging cast gives zip to simple yarn of Reynolds enthralled by actor Jurgens, but sparked by suitor Saxon; Winwood fine as eccentric housekeeper.▼

This House Possessed (1981) **C-100m.** TVM D: William Wiard. Parker Stevenson, Lisa Eilbacher, Joan Bennett, Slim

[1173]

Pickens, Shelley Smith, K. Callan. Rock star has a nervous breakdown and seeks solitude in a secluded house with his young, nubile nurse. Veteran star Joan Bennett gives some distinction to this pedestrian haunted-house chiller as an old rag-lady who seems to know its horrifying secret. Average.

This Is Elvis (1981) **C/B&W-101m.** **½ D: Malcolm Leo, Andrew Solt. David Scott, Paul Boensh III, Johnny Harra, Lawrence Koller, Rhonda Lyn, Debbie Edge, Larry Raspberry, Furry Lewis. Unusual examination of Elvis's life combines documentary footage with sequences of actors playing Presley at various stages of his life. The film is both fascinating and phony, an insightful portrayal of a tragic legend and yet another excuse to rake in profits by trading on his memory. Videocassette version runs 144m.▼

This Is Kate Bennett . . . (1982) **C-78m.** TVM D: Harvey Hart. Janet Eilber, David Haskell, Greg Mullavey, Kyle Richards, Granville Van Dusen, James Noble, Larry Breeding, David Groh, Dick Anthony Williams. Pedestrian look at a woman juggling a career as a TV news reporter and single parent and finding herself the prey of a sniper whose story she's chasing. Another pilot that never made it to series. Below average.

This Island Earth (1954) **C-86m.** *** D: Joseph Newman. Jeff Morrow, Rex Reason, Faith Domergue, Russell Johnson, Lance Fuller, Douglas Spencer. Suspenseful, intelligent science fiction about scientists lured to mysterious project, only to find they've been recruited—or more appropriately, shanghaied—by aliens to help them defend their invasion-torn planet. Existentialism of Raymond F. Jones' novel has been muted, but it's still thoughtful and exciting, with excellent visuals.▼

This Is My Affair (1937) **101m.** *** D: William A. Seiter. Barbara Stanwyck, Robert Taylor, Victor McLaglen, Brian Donlevy, Sidney Blackmer, John Carradine, Sig Ruman. Exciting film of Taylor joining gang of robbers on order from President McKinley to expose powerful mob; Stanwyck is saloon singer who loves Taylor (they married in real-life two years later).

This Is My Love (1954) **C-91m.** ** D: Stuart Heisler. Linda Darnell, Rick Jason, Dan Duryea, Faith Domergue, Hal Baylor, Jerry Mathers. Darnell and her sister Domergue (who's married to invalid Duryea) compete for affections of Jason in this murky soap-drama.

This Is Spinal Tap (1984) **C-82m.** *** D: Rob Reiner. Michael McKean, Christopher Guest, Harry Shearer, Rob Reiner, Tony Hendra, June Chadwick, R.J. Parnell, David Kaff. Admirably precise parody of a rock documentary, with Reiner as director Marty Di Bergi, who chronicles latest American tour of aging British rock group that's a working definition of the term "loser." Collaborative effort improvised by Reiner and his cast of colleagues; cunning satire through and through, though not always terribly funny. Our favorite bit: the amplifier that goes to "11." Many familiar faces appear in cameos.▼

This Is the Army (1943) **C-121m.** *** D: Michael Curtiz. George Murphy, Joan Leslie, George Tobias, Alan Hale, Ronald Reagan, Joe Louis, Kate Smith, Irving Berlin, many others. Soldiers who staged Irving Berlin's WW1 musical *Yip Yip Yaphank* reunite to help mount similar WW2 effort; corny but enjoyable framework (with Warner Bros. cast) for filmed record of legendary 1940s show, a topical melange of songs and skits. P.S.: This is the film where George Murphy plays Ronald Reagan's father!▼

This Is the Life (1944) **87m.** ** D: Felix E. Feist. Donald O'Connor, Peggy Ryan, Susanna Foster, Patric Knowles. Spunky cast of versatile performers with Foster torn between swank Knowles and performer O'Connor. Based on a play by Sinclair Lewis and Fay Wray!

This Is the Night (1932) **78m.** **½ D: Frank Tuttle. Lily Damita, Charlie Ruggles, Roland Young, Thelma Todd, Cary Grant, Irving Bacon. Enjoyable if somewhat strained romantic comedy in the Lubitsch mold, set in Paris and Venice, with Young hiring Damita to pose as his wife to help cover up his amorous pursuit of Todd. Grant has a wonderful entrance (as Todd's athletic husband) in his feature debut.

This Is the West That Was (1974) **C-78m.** TVM D: Fielder Cook. Ben Murphy, Kim Darby, Jane Alexander, Matt Clark, Tony Franciosa, Stuart Margolin, Stefan Gierasch, Luke Askew. Light-hearted look at the Wild Bill Hickok-Calamity Jane-Buffalo Bill Cody legend. Western spoof that never gets going, despite game cast. Average.

This Land Is Mine (1943) **103m.** ** D: Jean Renoir. Charles Laughton, Maureen O'Hara, George Sanders, Walter Slezak, Kent Smith, Una O'Connor, Philip Merivale, George Counouris, Nancy Gates. Meek French teacher Laughton, aroused by Nazi occupation, becomes hero. Patriotic wartime film is dated and disappointing today; written by Dudley Nichols.▼

This Love of Ours (1945) **90m.** **½ D: William Dieterle. Merle Oberon, Charles Korvin, Claude Rains, Carl Esmond, Sue England, Jess Barker, Harry Davenport, Ralph Morgan. Sudsy soaper of Korvin leaving wife Oberon, meeting twelve years later, falling in love again. Rains steals show in supporting role. Remade in 1956 as NEVER SAY GOODBYE.

This Man Is Mine (1934) **76m.** ** D:

John Cromwell. Irene Dunne, Ralph Bellamy, Constance Cummings, Kay Johnson, Sidney Blackmer, Charles Starrett, Vivian Tobin. Lightweight script does in this lesser Dunne vehicle, with Irene vying with Cummings for the love of Bellamy.

This Man Is News (1938-British) **77m.** *** D: David MacDonald. Barry K. Barnes, Valerie Hobson, Alastair Sim, John Warwick, Garry Marsh. Framed newspaperman goes after jewel thieves in this crisp, stylish little comedy-thriller. Sequel: THIS MAN IN PARIS.

This Man Must Die (1970-French) **C-115m.** ***½ D: Claude Chabrol. Michel Duchaussoy, Jean Yanne, Caroline Cellier, Lorraine Rainer, Marc DiNapoli, Guy Marly. Outstanding film about man who sets out to find the person who killed his young son in hit-and-run accident and the complications which ensue. This may be the best of many fine Chabrol dramas; Yanne and Cellier are unforgettable, the photography beautiful.▼

This Man's Navy (1945) **100m.** *** D: William Wellman. Wallace Beery, Tom Drake, James Gleason, Jan Clayton, Selena Royle, Noah Beery, Sr., Henry O'Neill, Steve Brodie. Usual Beery service-story nicely rehashed; Beery treats Drake as a son, gets vicarious pleasure out of his navy career.

This Man Stands Alone (1979) **C-78m.** TVM D: Jerrold Freedman. Louis Gossett, Jr., Clu Gulager, Mary Alice, Barry Brown, James McEachin, Lonny Chapman, Philip Michael Thomas. Based on true story of a black civil rights activist who runs for sheriff in a southern town and beats a popular segregationist. Compromised by cardboard characterizations, despite the earnest efforts of the always-fine Gossett. Average.

This Modern Age (1931) **76m.** ** D: Nick Grinde. Joan Crawford, Neil Hamilton, Marjorie Rambeau, Hobert Bosworth, Emma Dunn. Upper-class Hamilton loves Crawford, but his family doesn't take to the poor working-girl. Standard predictable plot.

This Property Is Condemned (1966) **C-110m.** ** D: Sydney Pollack. Natalie Wood, Robert Redford, Charles Bronson, Kate Reid, Mary Badham, Robert Blake, Alan Baxter, Dabney Coleman, Jon Provost. Often absurd film version of Tennessee Williams' one-act play has doe-eyed Wood falling for Redford, the out-of-towner staying in her mama's boarding house. Except for James Wong Howe's photography, this is trash without the style that often makes trash enjoyable. Francis Ford Coppola was one of the screenwriters.▼

This Rebel Age SEE: **Beat Generation, The**

This Rebel Breed (1960) **90m.** **½ D: Richard L. Bare. Rita Moreno, Mark Damon, Diane (Dyan) Cannon, Gerald Mohr, Jay Novello, Eugene Martin, Tom Gilson, Richard Rust. Above-average melodrama detailing the apprehension of teenage gangs. Retitled: THREE SHADES OF LOVE.

This Savage Land (1968) **C-98m.** **½ D: Vincent McEveety. Barry Sullivan, Glenn Corbett, Kathryn Hays, Andrew Prine, George C. Scott, John Drew Barrymore. Widower and family sell Ohio spread, head West for new start, ride into town embroiled in vigilante dispute. Excellent performances (especially Scott) in surprisingly believable script. Comprised of episodes of *The Road West* TV series, but given theatrical release.

This Side of the Law (1950) **74m.** ** D: Richard L. Bare. Viveca Lindfors, Kent Smith, Janis Paige, Monte Blue. Hokey script has Smith hired by crooked lawyer to impersonate missing wealthy man.

This Sporting Life (1963-British) **129m.** ***½ D: Lindsay Anderson. Richard Harris, Rachel Roberts, Alan Badel, William Hartnell, Colin Blakely, Arthur Lowe. Yorkshire coal-miner "betters" himself by becoming professional rugby player. Powerful film (written by David Storey) about love, success, and disillusionment; also serves to illustrate what a grueling game rugby is. Originally 134m.▼

This Thing Called Love (1941) **98m.** *** D: Alexander Hall. Rosalind Russell, Melvyn Douglas, Binnie Barnes, Allyn Joslyn, Gloria Dickson, Lee J. Cobb. Adult comedy of newlyweds who set up three-month trial run for their marriage. Stars' expertise puts it over.

This Time for Keeps (1947) **C-105m.** **½ D: Richard Thorpe. Esther Williams, Lauritz Melchior, Jimmy Durante, Johnnie Johnston, Xavier Cugat. Empty-headed, enjoyable Williams bathing-suit musical with Durante around to relieve tedium.

This Way Please (1937) **75m.** **½ D: Robert Florey. Charles "Buddy" Rogers, Betty Grable, Mary Livingstone, Ned Sparks, Jim Jordan, Marion Jordan, Porter Hall, Lee Bowman, Rufe Davis. Second-string musical about movie theater usherette with a crush on bandleader Rogers; amusing specialty material by Davis, engaging moments with radio's Fibber McGee and Molly (Jim & Marion Jordan).

This Wife for Hire (1985) **C-100m.** TVM D: James R. Drake. Pam Dawber, Robert Klein, Laraine Newman, Dick Gautier, Ann Jillian, Sam Jones, Tim Kazurinsky. Amiable froth about the domestic complications that arise when a happily married woman hires herself out—purely platonically—as a surrogate wife. Average.

This Woman Is Dangerous (1952) **100m.** **½ D: Felix E. Feist. Joan Crawford,

Dennis Morgan, David Brian, Richard Webb, Sherry Jackson. In typical tough-girl role, Crawford finds true love after countless mishaps, including an eye operation.

This Woman Is Mine (1941) 91m. ** D: Frank Lloyd. Franchot Tone, John Carroll, Walter Brennan, Carol Bruce, Nigel Bruce, Leo G. Carroll. Standard love triangle on merchant boat in northern waters plying the fur trade.

This Year's Blonde (1980) C-100m. TVM D: John Erman. Constance Forslund, Lloyd Bridges, Norman Fell, Vic Tayback, Michael Lerner, John Marley. The Marilyn Monroe chapter of Garson Kanin's *Moviola* tells of her relationship with her ambitious agent, Johnny Hyde (vividly portrayed by Bridges). Another TV movie MARILYN: THE UNTOLD STORY, tops this one, as does its star, Catherine Hicks, who's more persuasive as MM than Forslund. Retitled: THE SECRET LOVE OF MARILYN MONROE.

Thomas Crown Affair, The (1968) C-102m. *** D: Norman Jewison. Steve McQueen, Faye Dunaway, Paul Burke, Jack Weston, Biff McGuire, Yaphet Kotto. Glittery production complements story of supercool millionaire McQueen who plots perfect bank robbery, as insurance investigator Dunaway coldly determines to nab the gentleman-thief. Perfect nonthink entertainment; Jewison and cinematographer Haskell Wexler's use of multi-image screens may suffer on TV. Oscar-winning song, "The Windmills of Your Mind," by Michel Legrand and Alan & Marilyn Bergman.▼

Thomasine & Bushrod (1974) C-95m. **½ D: Gordon Parks, Jr. Max Julien, Vonetta McGee, George Murdock, Glynn Turman, Juanita Moore. OK mixture of black exploitation and Western action with comedy, as a black "Bonnie and Clyde" team operate in 1911 Texas. Julien scripted and co-produced, along with the classy-looking McGee. Shot in New Mexico.

Thompson's Last Run (1986) C-100m. TVM D: Jerrold Freedman. Robert Mitchum, Wilford Brimley, Kathleen York, Guy Boyd, Royce Wallace, Susan Tyrrell. Two pros easily mesh in this contemporary update of the well-worn Western about old buddies on opposite sides of the law—one an escaped con, the other his longtime adversary bent on bringing him in. Average.

Thornwell (1981) C-100m. TVM D: Harry Moses. Glynn Turman, Vincent Gardenia, Craig Wasson, Todd Susman, Julius Harris, Paul Lieber, Edward Bell, Howard E. Rollins, Jr. The true story of James Thornwell and his years of mental anguish after being given LSD by the U.S. Army. A dramatized version of the story that documentary producer Moses first brought

to light on the *60 Minutes* TV show. Above average.

Thoroughbreds Don't Cry (1937) 80m. **½ D: Alfred E. Green. Judy Garland, Mickey Rooney, Sophie Tucker, C. Aubrey Smith, Frankie Darro, Henry Kolker, Helen Troy. Fairly good racetrack story with jockey Rooney involved in crooked deals, young Garland adding some songs. Mickey and Judy's first film together.

Thoroughly Modern Millie (1967) C-138m. **½ D: George Roy Hill. Julie Andrews, James Fox, Mary Tyler Moore, Carol Channing, Beatrice Lillie, John Gavin, Jack Soo, Pat Morita, Philip Ahn. Up to a point this Ross Hunter attempt to recapture some of Andrews' *Boy Friend* magic is successful, but after nearly two and a half hours, one begins to yawn. 1920s farce has a fatal case of the cutes. Elmer Bernstein's score won an Oscar.▼

Those Calloways (1965) C-131m. *** D: Norman Tokar. Brian Keith, Vera Miles, Brandon de Wilde, Walter Brennan, Ed Wynn, Linda Evans, Philip Abbott. Long, episodic but rewarding Disney film about an eccentric New England man (Keith) and his family, focusing on his determined efforts to use nearby lake for bird sanctuary before it's bought up by business interests.▼

Those Daring Young Men in Their Jaunty Jalopies (1969-British-U.S.) C-93m. **½ D: Ken Annakin. Tony Curtis, Susan Hampshire, Terry-Thomas, Eric Sykes, Gert Frobe, Peter Cook, Dudley Moore, Jack Hawkins. Slapstick adventures of participants in 1500 mile car race to Monte Carlo. Despite funny routines, 1920s period-piece backfires a bit too much. British title: MONTE CARLO OR BUST.

Those Endearing Young Charms (1945) 81m. **½ D: Lewis Allen. Robert Young, Laraine Day, Bill Williams, Ann Harding, Marc Cramer, Anne Jeffries, Lawrence Tierney. Surprisingly effective romance finds Day torn between nice-guy Williams and smooth-talking heel Young. Nothing special, but some amusing dialogue, nicely played.

Those Fantastic Flying Fools (1967) C-95m. **½ D: Don Sharp. Burl Ives, Troy Donahue, Gert Frobe, Terry-Thomas, Hermione Gingold, Daliah Lavi, Lionel Jeffries. Lightweight tale of Victorian England moon race, loosely adapted from Jules Verne story (previously filmed as FROM THE EARTH TO THE MOON). Originally titled BLAST-OFF.▼

Those Lips, Those Eyes (1980) C-107m. *** D: Michael Pressman. Frank Langella, Glynnis O'Connor, Thomas Hulce, Kevin McCarthy, Jerry Stiller, Herbert Berghof. Stagestruck adolescent learns about love the hard way while interning in Cleveland summer stock during the early '50s. Hulce is too nerdish in the key role, but Langella as down-on-his-luck actor, O'Connor as company's resident dish, are quite good. A sleeper, written by David Shaber.▼

Those Magnificent Men In Their Flying Machines (1965) **C-132m.** *** D: Ken Annakin. Stuart Whitman, Sarah Miles, James Fox, Alberto Sordi, Robert Morley, Gert Frobe, Jean-Pierre Cassel, Terry-Thomas, Irina Demick, Benny Hill, Flora Robson, Sam Wanamaker, Gordon Jackson, Millicent Martin, Red Skelton. Long but enjoyable film of great airplane race involving international conflicts, cheating, and romance. Skelton has funny cameo in amusing prologue, tracing history of aviation.▼

Those Redheads from Seattle (1953) **C-90m.** ** D: Lewis R. Foster. Rhonda Fleming, Gene Barry, Agnes Moorehead, Teresa Brewer, Guy Mitchell. Modestly produced musical nonsense set in gold-rush era with Moorehead the mother of four girls who takes her brood to Alaska.

Those She Left Behind (1989) **C-100m.** TVM D: Waris Hussein. Gary Cole, Joanna Kerns, Mary Page Keller, Colleen Dewhurst, George Coe, Maryedith Burrell. A businessman's life is shattered when his wife dies in childbirth and he's confronted with the responsibility of bringing up his newborn daughter alone. Good performances in this near-tearjerker. Average.

Those Were the Days (1940) **76m.** ** D: J. Theodore Reed. William Holden, Bonita Granville, Ezra Stone, Judith Barrett, Vaughan Glaser, Lucien Littlefield, Richard Denning. Light-hearted (and headed) comedy from George Fitch's *Siwash* stories, with Holden as a college hell-raiser (circa 1904) who woos judge's daughter Granville to avoid a jail sentence. We give it a C-minus. Alan Ladd has a small role as a student.

Thousand and One Nights, A (1945) **C-93m.** *** D: Alfred E. Green. Cornel Wilde, Evelyn Keyes, Phil Silvers, Adele Jergens, Dusty Anderson, Dennis Hoey, Rex Ingram. Good escapism based on Arabian Nights fables; colorful production with serviceable cast including Ingram repeating genie-ish role from THIEF OF BAGDAD.

Thousand and One Nights, A (1968-Spanish) **C-86m.** ** D: Joe Lacy (Jose Maria Elorrieta). Jeff Cooper, Raf Vallone, Luciana Paluzzi, Perla Christal, Reuben Rojo. Tongue-in-cheek Arabian Nights fantasy with the familiar tapestry: a flying carpet, a handsome swordsman, a beautiful part-time genie, a sinister vizier. Not to be confused with the similarly titled Cornel Wilde movie of the '40s.

Thousand Clowns, A (1965) **118m.** ***½ D: Fred Coe. Jason Robards, Barbara Harris, Martin Balsam, Barry Gordon, Gene Saks, William Daniels. Faithful adaptation by Herb Gardner of his Broadway comedy about society dropout who's being pressured to drop in again for the sake of young nephew who lives with him. Perfectly cast, filmed in N.Y.C., with Balsam's Oscar-winning performance as Robards' brother.▼

Thousand Eyes of Dr. Mabuse, The (1960-German) **103m.** **½ D: Fritz Lang. Dawn Addams, Peter Van Eyck, Gert Frobe, Wolfgang Preiss. Fast-moving if unconvincing revival of arch-villain of 1920s, with Frobe the police agent tracking down the reincarnated Mabuse in Berlin; gimmicky, complex plot line. Lang's directorial swan song. Also known as THE SECRET OF DR. MABUSE and THE DIABOLICAL DR. MABUSE.▼

Thousand Plane Raid, The (1969) **C-94m.** *½ D: Boris Sagal. Christopher George, Laraine Stephens, J. D. Cannon, Gary Marshall, Michael Evans. Thoroughly routine suspenser about plot to bomb German aircraft factory near end of WW2.

Thousands Cheer (1943) **C-126m.** **½ D: George Sidney. Mickey Rooney, Judy Garland, Gene Kelly, Red Skelton, Eleanor Powell, Ann Sothern, Lucille Ball, Virginia O'Brien, Frank Morgan, Kathryn Grayson, Lena Horne, many others. Grayson lives with officer-father John Boles at army base, falls for hotheaded private Kelly and decides to prepare an all-star show for the soldiers. Dubious plot is an excuse for specialty acts by top MGM stars.▼

Thou Shalt Not Commit Adultery (1978) **C-100m.** TVM D: Delbert Mann. Louise Fletcher, Wayne Rogers, Bert Convy, Robert Reed. Tepid contemporary interpretation of one of the Ten Commandments, sudsed-up by having a paralytic's wife having extramarital affairs with his permission. Followed by THOU SHALT NOT KILL (1982). Below average.

Thou Shalt Not Kill (1961-Italian) **129m.** **½ D: Claude Autant-Lara. Laurent Terzieff, Horst Frank, Suzanne Flon, Mica Orlovic. Too-often sterile narrative dealing with trial of French conscientious objector, with side-plot of German priest facing penalty for having killed Frenchman during WW2.

Thou Shalt Not Kill (1982) **C-100m.** TVM D: I. C. Rappaport. Lee Grant, Gary Graham, Diana Scarwid, Robert Culp, James Keach, Michael C. Gwynne, Scott Marlowe, Albert Salmi. Lawyer Grant takes on innocent defendant accused of murder whose troubles just begin when he's put in jail. Second in a never-was series of contemporary interpretations of the Ten Commandments, following the equally pedestrian THOU SHALT NOT COMMIT ADULTERY. Filmed in 1979. Average.

Thrashin' (1986) **C-90m.** ** D: David

Winters. Josh Brolin, Robert Rusler, Pamela Gilday, Brooke McCarter, Brett Marx. Skateboard-riding youth gangs are pitted against each other in this WEST SIDE STORY on wheels . . . minus the spirit and originality, not to mention music.▼

Threads (1984-British) **C-110m.** *** D: Mick Jackson. Karen Meagher, Reece Dinsdale, Rita May, Nicholas Lane, Victoria O'Keefe. Britain's answer to THE DAY AFTER is a powerful, if a bit overlong, drama about effect of nuclear holocaust on working-class town of Sheffield, with the focus on a pair of families whose son and daughter are about to wed. Unrelentingly graphic and grim, sobering, and shattering—as it should be. Originally produced for British television.▼

Threat, The (1949) **65m.** *** D: Felix Feist. Charles McGraw, Michael O'Shea, Virginia Grey, Julie Bishop, Robert Shayne, Anthony Caruso. Thug McGraw escapes prison, kidnaps cop and D.A. who put him away, plus singer he suspects of having squealed. Fast, rugged little "B" keeps action hopping until tough conclusion.▼

Threat, The (1960) **66m.** ** D: Charles R. Rondeau. Robert Knapp, Linda Lawson, Lisabeth Hush, James Seay, Mary Castle, Barney Phillips. Standard find-the-real-murderer yarn.

¡Three Amigos! (1986) **C-105m.** ** D: John Landis. Steve Martin, Chevy Chase, Martin Short, Patrice Martinez, Alfonso Arau, Tony Plana, Joe Mantegna, Jon Lovitz. Silent film Western heroes are summoned to Mexico for what they think will be a public appearance, find out they're really supposed to rid a village of its bandit chieftain. Smarmy one-joke comedy has its moments but not too many; buffs may be amused to note that villain Arau was one of the key bad guys in THE WILD BUNCH. Coscripter Randy Newman wrote the songs.▼

Three Avengers, The (1964-Italian) **C-97m.** *½ D: Gianfranco Parolini. Alan Steel, Mimmo Palmara, Lisa Gastoni, Rosalba Neri. Below par Ursus (Steel) adventure tale, dealing with evil ruler of Atra.▼

Three Bad Men (1926) **92m.** ***½ D: John Ford. George O'Brien, Lou Tellegen, J. Farrell MacDonald, Tom Santschi, Frank Campeau. Three gruff outlaws become benevolent protectors of young girl whose father is killed during Western settlement period. Beautiful mixture of action, drama, comedy, and sentiment in one of Ford's best silents.

Three Bad Sisters (1956) **76m.** *½ D: Gilbert L. Kay. Marla English, Kathleen Hughes, Sara Shane, John Bromfield, Jess Barker, Madge Kennedy. Aimless account of title figures fighting among themselves to outdo the others, fighting over their father's estate.

Three Bites of the Apple (1967) **C-105m.** *½ D: Alvin Ganzer. David McCallum, Sylva Koscina, Tammy Grimes, Harvey Korman, Domenico Modugno, Aldo Fabrizi. Good scenery is only plus of flimsy comedy about McCallum's attempts to avoid heavy taxation of money he's won in a casino on the Riviera.

Three Blind Mice (1938) **75m.** **½ D: William A. Seiter. Loretta Young, Joel McCrea, David Niven, Stuart Erwin, Marjorie Weaver, Pauline Moore, Jane Darwell, Binnie Barnes. Familiar idea of three fortune-hunting girls going after well-heeled male prospects; slickly done. Remade, reworked many times.

Three Blondes In His Life (1960) **81m.** ** D: Leon Chooluck. Jock Mahoney, Greta Thyssen, Anthony Dexter, Jesse White. Occasionally tangy rehash of romances and misconduct of now-deceased insurance investigator.

Three Brave Men (1957) **88m.** **½ D: Philip Dunne. Ray Milland, Frank Lovejoy, Ernest Borgnine, Nina Foch, Dean Jagger, Virginia Christine, Edward Andrews, Andrew Duggan, Joseph Wiseman. Navy clerk Borgnine is fired as a security risk because of alleged Communist leanings; lawyer Milland tries to get him reinstated. Adapted by Dunne from Pulitzer Prize-winning articles by Anthony Lewis, courtroom drama is interesting but unexceptional.

Three Broadway Girls SEE: **Greeks Had a Word for Them, The**▼

Three Brothers (1980-Italian-French) **C-113m.** *** D: Francesco Rosi. Philippe Noiret, Charles Vanel, Michele Placido, Vittorio Mezzogiorno, Andrea Ferreol, Maddalena Crippa, Sara Tafuri, Marta Zoffoli. Wise, touching, but slow-moving account of three very different brothers who return to the country village of their youth for their mother's funeral. The recollections of their elderly peasant father (Vanel) and scenes with his young granddaughter (Zoffoli) are particularly moving. Adapted from Platonov's *The Third Son.*▼

Three Caballeros, The (1945) **C-70m.** *** D: Norman Ferguson. Aurora Miranda, Carmen Molina, Dora Luz, voices of Sterling Holloway, Clarence Nash, Jose Oliveira, Joaquin Garay. Colorful Disney pastiche that followed 1940s Good Neighbor Policy by saluting Latin America, through the eyes of Donald Duck. Filled with infectious music (including "Baia," "You Belong to My Heart"), eye-popping visuals, amusing cartoon sequences, and clever combinations of live-action and animation. Donald, Jose Carioca, and Panchito perform title song in a dazzling display of cartoon wizardry. ▼

Three Came Home (1950) **106m.** ***½

D: Jean Negulesco. Claudette Colbert, Patric Knowles, Florence Desmond, Sessue Hayakawa, Sylvia Andrew, Phyllis Morris. Stunning performances by Colbert and Hayakawa make this a must. British and American families living on Borneo during WW2 are sent to prison camps by Japanese, but cultured officer Hayakawa takes an interest in authoress Colbert. Producer Nunnally Johnson adapted Agnes Newton Keith's autobiographical book.▼

Three Cases of Murder (1954-British) **99m.** *** D: David Eady, Wendy Toye, George More O'Ferrall. Alan Badel, Hugh Pryse, John Gregson, Elizabeth Sellars, Emrys Jones, Orson Welles. Three offbeat murder stories; opener "In the Picture" is genuinely eerie, closer "Lord Mountdrago" (from Somerset Maugham story) has Welles in absorbing tale of a government official haunted by rival.

Three Cheers for the Irish (1940) **100m.** **½ D: Lloyd Bacon. Thomas Mitchell, Dennis Morgan, Priscilla Lane, Alan Hale, Virginia Grey, Irene Hervey. Breezy little comedy of family feud when Irish Mitchell's daughter Lane falls for Scottish Morgan.

Three Coins in the Fountain (1954) **C-102m.** *** D: Jean Negulesco. Clifton Webb, Dorothy McGuire, Jean Peters, Louis Jourdan, Maggie McNamara, Rossano Brazzi. Splashy romance yarn made ultrapleasing by Rome locations. Three women make wishes for romance at Fountain of Trevi, spurring several amorous adventures. Won Oscars for Milton Krasner's photography and the Jule Styne-Sammy Cahn title song. Remade by same director as THE PLEASURE SEEKERS.

Three Comrades (1938) **98m.** ***½ D: Frank Borzage. Robert Taylor, Margaret Sullavan, Franchot Tone, Robert Young, Guy Kibbee, Lionel Atwill. Beautifully poignant film of Erich Maria Remarque's tale of post-WW1 Germany, and three life-long friends who share a love for dying Sullavan. Excellent performances all around; coscripted by F. Scott Fitzgerald.

Three-Cornered Moon (1933) **77m.** *** D: Elliott Nugent. Claudette Colbert, Richard Arlen, Mary Boland, Wallace Ford, Hardie Albright, Lyda Roberti. Predates golden age of screwball comedies, but tops many of them; Boland is head of wacky family combating Depression.

Three Daring Daughters (1948) **C-115m.** **½ D: Fred M. Wilcox. Jeanette MacDonald, Jose Iturbi, Elinor Donahue, Ann B. Todd, Jane Powell, Edward Arnold, Harry Davenport. Woman magazine editor tells her daughters that she's remarrying. Despite predictable results, well-acted MGM comedy succeeds.

Three Days of the Condor (1975) **C-117m.** *** D: Sydney Pollack. Robert Redford, Faye Dunaway, Cliff Robertson, Max von

Sydow, John Houseman, Carlin Glynn. Redford, a reader for U.S. intelligence office, learns more than he should, and suddenly finds himself a hunted man. Dunaway is excellent as innocent woman who shelters him. Good suspense yarn.▼

Three Desperate Men (1951) **71m.** *½ D: Sam Newfield. Preston Foster, Virginia Grey, Jim Davis, Ross Latimer. Flabby little oater about three brothers who become outlaws.

Three Faces of Eve, The (1957) **91m.** ***½ D: Nunnally Johnson. Joanne Woodward, David Wayne, Lee J. Cobb, Nancy Kulp, Vince Edwards. Narrated by Alistair Cooke. Academy Award tour de force by Woodward as schizophrenic with three contrasting personalities and three separate lives. Cobb is psychiatrist who tries to cure her. Johnson also produced and wrote the screenplay.▼

Three Faces West (1940) **79m.** **½ D: Bernard Vorhaus. John Wayne, Sigrid Gurie, Charles Coburn, Spencer Charters, Roland Varno, Russell Simpson. Offbeat WW2-era drama about group of Austrian refugees heading for Oregon under Wayne's guidance. Guric is hardly typical leading lady for the Duke, but film's odd mix of frontier and Nazi elements make it worth a look.▼

3:15 (1986) **C-95m.** ** D: Larry Gross. Adam Baldwin, Deborah Foreman, Rene Auberjonois, Ed Lauter, Scott McGinnis, Danny De La Paz, John Scott Clough, Mario Van Peebles. Good cast in lackluster, low-budget teenage gang film, filmed in 1984.▼

Three for Bedroom C (1952) **C-74m.** ** D: Milton Bren. Gloria Swanson, Fred Clark, James Warren, Steve Brodie, Hans Conried, Margaret Dumont. Sadly uneven comedy of romance between movie star and scientist aboard transcontinental train heading to L.A. A derailment for Swanson after her triumph in SUNSET BOULEVARD.▼

Three for Jamie Dawn (1956) **81m.** ** D: Thomas Carr. Laraine Day, Ricardo Montalban, Richard Carlson, June Havoc. Diverting story poorly executed, about jury members being pressured to swing a not-guilty verdict for the defendant.

Three for the Road (1987) **C-88m.** *½ D: B. W. L. Norton. Charlie Sheen, Kerri Green, Alan Ruck, Sally Kellerman, Blair Tefkin, Raymond J. Barry, Alexa Hamilton. Anachronistic youth movie about the spoiled-brat daughter of a senator who travels to boarding school with Sheen and Ruck—and hits more than a few detours. Dull in the extreme.▼

Three for the Show (1955) **C-93m.** ** D: H. C. Potter. Betty Grable, Marge and Gower Champion, Jack Lemmon, Myron McCormick. Tuneful music is only thing

[1179]

that holds slight plot together in this dud remake of Maugham's TOO MANY HUSBANDS. Some bright dance numbers staged for CinemaScope really suffer on TV.

Three Fugitives (1989) **C-93m.** ****½** D: Francis Veber. Nick Nolte, Martin Short, Sarah Rowland Doroff, James Earl Jones, Alan Ruck, Kenneth McMillan, Bruce McGill. Bumbling bank robber—who's only pulling the heist to support his little daughter—takes a hostage with him, little dreaming that the guy is a notorious holdup man who's just finished a long stretch in prison. Fast-paced farce doesn't quite hang together, despite energetic performances; Veber's first American film is a remake of his own French comedy, LES FUGITIFS.▼

Three Girls About Town (1941) **73m.** ****½** D: Leigh Jason. Joan Blondell, Binnie Barnes, Janet Blair, John Howard, Robert Benchley, Eric Blore, Hugh O'Connell, Una O'Connor. Wacky but amusing comedy of three sisters encountering a corpse in N.Y.C. hotel and the frantic consequences.

Three Godfathers (1936) **82m.** ******* D: Richard Boleslawski. Chester Morris, Lewis Stone, Walter Brennan, Irene Hervey, Willard Robertson, Sidney Toler. Little-seen and underrated version of Peter B. Kyne's story (filmed twice before) about three bad guys who adopt a foundling in the desert. Beautifully shot and warmly acted. Retitled MIRACLE IN THE SAND.

3 Godfathers (1948) **C-105m.** ******* D: John Ford. John Wayne, Pedro Armendariz, Harry Carey, Jr., Ward Bond, Mae Marsh, Jane Darwell, Ben Johnson, Mildred Natwick. Sturdy, sentimental, sometimes beautiful rendition of Peter B. Kyne's oft-filmed saga of three bandits who "adopt" a baby born in the desert. Final scene doesn't ring true, but Ford makes up for it in balance of film. Dedicated to the director's first star, Harry Carey, Sr. Remade for TV as THE GODCHILD.▼

Three Guns for Texas (1968) **C-99m.** ****** D: David Lowell Rich, Paul Stanley, Earl Bellamy. Neville Brand, Peter Brown, Martin Milner, William Smith, Philip Carey. Boring exploits of three Texas Rangers, strung together from three episodes of *Laredo* TV series. Forgettable action, fair repartee between leads. This actually received theatrical release!

Three Guys Named Mike (1951) **90m.** ****** D: Charles Walters. Jane Wyman, Van Johnson, Barry Sullivan, Howard Keel, Phyllis Kirk, Jeff Donnell. Enthusiastic (to the point of nausea) stewardess Wyman has her choice of the title trio of nice, handsome, eligible bachelors. Only in the movies . . . Scripted by Sheldon Leonard.

Three Hearts for Julia (1943) **83m.** ****** D: Richard Thorpe. Ann Sothern, Melvyn Douglas, Lee Bowman, Richard Ainley, Felix Bressart, Marta Linden, Reginald Owen. Only debonair Douglas could seem right as husband romancing his wife (Sothern) who is divorcing him, but he can't support whole film.

Three Hours to Kill (1954) **C-77m.** ******* D: Alfred L. Werker. Dana Andrews, Donna Reed, Dianne Foster, Stephen Elliot. Andrews plays stagecoach driver unjustly accused of killing fiancé's brother; he returns to find real killer. Tight, well-done movie.

Three Hundred Miles for Stephanie (1981) **C-100m.** **TVM** D: Clyde Ware. Tony Orlando, Edward James Olmos, Pepe Serna, Julie Carmen, Gregory Sierra, Peter Graves. Orlando made his dramatic acting debut as a San Antonio cop who vows to run more than 300 miles in five days as an act of faith for his young, brain-damaged daughter. Director Ware based his screenplay on a true story. Above average.

300 Spartans, The (1962) **C-114m.** ***½** D: Rudolph Maté. Richard Egan, Ralph Richardson, Diane Baker, Barry Coe. Events leading up to heroic Greek stand against Persians at Thermopylae; strictly cardboard, except for location filming by Geoffrey Unsworth.

300 Year Weekend, The (1971) **C-123m.** ***½** D: Victor Stoloff. William Devane, Michael Tolan, Sharon Laughlin, Roy Cooper, Gabriel Dell, M'el Dowd. Dreary drama about a marathon group-encounter session *does* seem to go on for about 300 years.

Three Husbands (1950) **78m.** ****½** D: Irving Reis. Eve Arden, Ruth Warrick, Howard da Silva, Vanessa Brown, Shepperd Strudwick, Billie Burke, Emlyn Williams, Jane Darwell. Pleasing comedy of three husbands trying to find out whether or not deceased playboy spent time with their wives. Undoubtedly inspired by the 1949 hit, A LETTER TO THREE WIVES, and cowritten by Vera Caspary, who adapted the earlier film.

Three in the Attic (1968) **C-92m.** ****½** D: Richard Wilson. Christopher Jones, Judy Pace, Yvette Mimieux, Maggie Thrett. Silly tale of youth with so much style that he works three girls at once until they get wise and decide to lock him in and drain him of his potency.▼

Three in the Cellar SEE: **Up in the Cellar**▼

Three Into Two Won't Go (1969-British) **C-93m.** ****** D: Peter Hall. Rod Steiger, Claire Bloom, Judy Geeson, Peggy Ashcroft, Paul Rogers. Marriage of Steiger and Bloom breaks up when he becomes infatuated with sexy hitchhiker Geeson. Originally an OK drama, but Universal shot extra footage and reedited original film to 100m. for television.

Three Is a Family (1944) **81m.** ****½** D:

Edward Ludwig. Fay Bainter, Marjorie Reynolds, Charlie Ruggles, Helen Broderick, Arthur Lake, Hattie McDaniel, Jeff Donnell, Walter Catlett, Cheryl Walker. Above-par fluff of hectic homelife in apartment filled with family, friends, and new babies.

Three Kinds of Heat (1987) **C-87m.** BOMB D: Leslie Stevens. Robert Ginty, Victoria Barrett, Shakti, Barry Foster, Sylvester McCoy. Dreadful excuse for an action film teams Ginty with Amazonian Barrett and Shakti on an Interpol mission to London. Quite a comedown for filmmaker Stevens, who created the classic TV series *The Outer Limits.*▼

Three Kings, The (1987) **C-100m.** TVM D: Mel Damski. Jack Warden, Stan Shaw, Lou Diamond Phillips, Jane Kaczmarek, Vic Tayback, Charles Nelson Reilly, Rick Lenz, Tiana Alexandra. The estimable Stirling Silliphant wrote this misfired contemporary parable about three misfits who escape from a mental hospital dressed as the three wise men of old, and search for the spirit of Christmas on camelback in downtown L.A. Below average.

Three Little Girls in Blue (1946) **C-90m.** *** D: Bruce Humberstone. June Haver, George Montgomery, Vivian Blaine, Celeste Holm, Vera-Ellen, Frank Latimore, Charles Smith. Colorful tale of three sisters out to trap wealthy husbands; familiar plot with good tunes like "You Make Me Feel So Young." A remake of THREE BLIND MICE and MOON OVER MIAMI, set in turn of the century Atlantic City. Holm's film debut.

Three Little Words (1950) **C-102m.** *** D: Richard Thorpe. Fred Astaire, Vera-Ellen, Red Skelton, Arlene Dahl, Keenan Wynn, Gloria De Haven, Debbie Reynolds, Carleton Carpenter. Standard MGM musical about famous songwriters Kalmar and Ruby and their climb to fame; bouncy cast, fine tunes, including "Who's Sorry Now?" "Thinking of You," title song. Debbie plays Helen Kane, but the real Helen dubbed "I Wanna Be Loved By You."▼

Three Lives of Thomasina, The (1964) **C-97m.** *** D: Don Chaffey, Patrick McGoohan, Susan Hampshire, Karen Dotrice, Vincent Winter, Denis Gilmore, Laurence Naismith, Finlay Currie. Charming Disney film made in England from Paul Gallico's story about a heartless veterinarian, his daughter's devotion to her pet cat, and a mystical young woman with lifegiving "powers." A winner.▼

Three Loves Has Nancy (1938) **69m.** **½ D: Richard Thorpe. Janet Gaynor, Robert Montgomery, Franchot Tone, Guy Kibbee, Claire Dodd, Reginald Owen. Naive country girl Gaynor goes to N.Y.C. to find the man who left her at the altar, finds admirers Tone and Montgomery instead.

3 Men and a Baby (1987) **C-102m.** *** D: Leonard Nimoy. Tom Selleck, Steve Guttenberg, Ted Danson, Nancy Travis, Margaret Colin, Philip Bosco, Celeste Holm. Enjoyable remake of France's big hit THREE MEN AND A CRADLE, about a trio of swinging bachelor roommates who suddenly find themselves custodians of an infant. Winning performances all around help keep this buoyant comedy on-track from start to finish.▼

Three Men and a Cradle (1985-French) **C-100m.** *** D: Coline Serreau. Roland Giraud, Michel Boujenah, Andre Dussolier, Philippine Leroy Beaulieu, Dominique Lavanat, Marthe Villalonga. Very entertaining comedy about three swinging bachelors who find themselves stuck with a baby, which one of them fathered. Compassionate and funny; a real charmer. A box-office sensation in France, it went on to win three César awards. Remade in U.S. as 3 MEN AND A BABY.▼

Three Men in a Boat (1956-British) **C-84m.** *½ D: Ken Annakin. Laurence Harvey, Jimmy Edwards, David Tomlinson, Shirley Eaton, Jill Ireland, Martita Hunt, Adrienne Corri, Lisa Gastoni. Third filming of the Jerome K. Jerome book is a frantic, frequently annoying comedy about womanizer Harvey and bumbling pals Edwards and Tomlinson constantly finding trouble while on a boat trip up the Thames.▼

Three Men in White (1944) **85m.** D: Willis Goldbeck. Lionel Barrymore, Van Johnson, Marilyn Maxwell, Keye Luke, Ava Gardner, Alma Kruger, Rags Ragland. SEE: **Dr. Kildare** series.

Three Men On a Horse (1936) **88m.** *** D: Mervyn LeRoy. Frank McHugh, Sam Levene, Joan Blondell, Teddy Hart, Guy Kibbee, Carol Hughes, Allen Jenkins, Edgar Kennedy, Eddie Anderson. First-rate comedy of timid McHugh who always picks winning race-horses; stagy but funny. Blondell's fun as Levene's Brooklynese girlfriend. Adapted from Broadway play by George Abbott and John Cecil Holm.

3 Murderesses (1960-French) **C-96m.** **½ D: Michel Boisrond. Alain Delon, Mylene Demongeot, Pascale Petit, Jacqueline Sassard, Anita Ruf, Simone Renant. Most diverting cast in standard playboy yarn with Delon romancing trio of contrasting females. Originally titled WOMEN ARE WEAK.

Three Musketeers, The (1935) **90m.** ** D: Rowland V. Lee. Walter Abel, Paul Lukas, Ian Keith, Onslow Stevens, Ralph Forbes, Margot Grahame, Heather Angel. Dullest version of Dumas story, with Abel miscast as D'Artagnan.▼

Three Musketeers, The (1939) **73m.** *** D: Allan Dwan. Don Ameche, Ritz Brothers, Lionel Atwill, Binnie Barnes, Miles Mander, Gloria Stuart, Pauline Moore,

John Carradine, Joseph Schildkraut. Spirited musical, generally faithful to Dumas story; Ameche flavorful as D'Artagnan, Barnes lovely as Lady DeWinter, Ritz Brothers funny substitutes for unsuspecting musketeers.

Three Musketeers, The (1948) C-125m. **½ D: George Sidney. Lana Turner, Gene Kelly, June Allyson, Van Heflin, Angela Lansbury, Robert Coote, Frank Morgan, Vincent Price, Keenan Wynn, Gig Young. Oddball, lavish production of Dumas tale with Kelly as D'Artagnan. Occasional bright moments, but continual change of tone, and Heflin's drowsy characterization as Athos, bog down the action. Lana makes a stunning Lady DeWinter.▼

Three Musketeers, The (1974-British) C-105m. ***½ D: Richard Lester. Oliver Reed, Raquel Welch, Richard Chamberlain, Michael York, Frank Finlay, Christopher Lee, Geraldine Chaplin, Faye Dunaway, Charlton Heston, Jean-Pierre Cassel, Roy Kinnear, Spike Milligan. Delightful tongue-in-cheek version of Dumas classic, artfully mixing swashbuckling adventure and romance with broad slapstick. One of Raquel Welch's finest hours. Followed by THE FOUR MUSKETEERS, which was actually filmed simultaneously.▼

Three O'Clock High (1987) C-101m. *½ D: Phil Joanou. Casey Siemaszko, Anne Ryan, Richard Tyson, Jeffrey Tambor, Philip Baker Hall, John P. Ryan, Stacey Glick, Jonathan Wise. High school journalist is assigned to do a welcome-wagon profile on the new psycho-in-class, finds himself challenged by this behemoth to duke it out in the parking lot after school. Steven Spielberg protégé Joanou is to the camera what James Brown is to shoes, but it's a lot of energy expended over nothing. Siemaszko is underwhelming in the lead.▼

Three on a Couch (1966) C-109m. *½ D: Jerry Lewis. Jerry Lewis, Janet Leigh, Mary Ann Mobley, Gila Golan, Leslie Parrish, James Best, Kathleen Freeman. For psychiatrist Leigh to marry him, Lewis has to play five roles; one of them is "straight" but unintentionally funny, the other four zany, but unintentionally unfunny. The women are attractive.

Three on a Date (1978) C-100m. TVM D: Bill Bixby. June Allyson, Ray Bolger, Loni Anderson, John Byner, Gary Crosby, Carol Lawrence, Rick Nelson, Patrick Wayne, Didi Conn. TV game show winners, plus chaperone, on a Hawaiian holiday in this *Love Boat* variation that's equally as inspired in concept and execution. Average.

Three on a Match (1932) 64m. *** D: Mervyn LeRoy. Warren William, Joan Blondell, Bette Davis, Ann Dvorak, Humphrey Bogart, Lyle Talbot, Glenda Farrell, Anne Shirley, Edward Arnold. Fine, fast-moving melodrama of three girls who renew childhood friendship, only to find suspense and tragedy. Dvorak is simply marvelous. Remade as BROADWAY MUSKETEERS.

Three on a Match (1987) C-100m. TVM D: Donald P. Bellisario. Patrick Cassidy, Bruce A. Young, David Hemmings, Lance LeGault, Mitch Pileggi, Dendrie Allyn Taylor. Three escapees from a brutal Southern prison join up for an unlikely cross-country trip in this lighthearted prospective pilot. Written and directed by the creator of *Magnum, P.I.* Average.

Three on a Spree (1961-British) 83m. *½ D: Sidney J. Furie. Jack Watling, Carole Lesley, Renee Houston, John Slater. Disconcerting, poorly directed comedy of man forced to spend a million pounds in sixty days to inherit eight million, à la BREWSTER'S MILLIONS.

Threepenny Opera, The (1931-German) 112m. ***½ D: G. W. Pabst. Rudolph Forster, Lotte Lenya, Carola Neher, Reinhold Schunzel, Fritz Rasp, Valeska Gert. Fine musical satire chronicling activities of dashing gangster Forster, his cohorts, and antagonists, with Lenya outstanding as Pirate Jenny. From Bertolt Brecht's play, with music by Kurt Weill, adapted from John Gay's *The Beggar's Opera*. Remade many times since.▼

Three Ring Circus (1954) C-103m. ** D: Joseph Pevney. Dean Martin, Jerry Lewis, Joanne Dru, Zsa Zsa Gabor, Wallace Ford, Sig Ruman, Nick Cravat, Elsa Lanchester. So-so Martin and Lewis comedy has them as discharged servicemen up to trouble in a circus. Reissued in shorter version as JERRICO, THE WONDER CLOWN.

Three's a Crowd (1969) C-75m. TVM D: Harry Falk. Larry Hagman, Jessica Walter, E. J. Peaker, Harvey Korman, Michael Lerner, Norman Fell. Pilot Hagman remarries after his first wife's death in plane crash—then she turns up alive and well. Formula complications abound in spirited comedy rehash of MY FAVORITE WIFE, with resolution taking place in hotel. Look for Farrah Fawcett. Average.

Three Sailors and a Girl (1953) C-95m. ** D: Roy Del Ruth. Jane Powell, Gordon MacRae, Gene Nelson, Sam Levene, Jack E. Leonard. Bland musical of three gobs who invest ship's surplus funds in a musical show starring Powell. Based on George S. Kaufman's *The Butter and Egg Man*.

Three Secrets (1950) 98m. *** D: Robert Wise. Eleanor Parker, Patricia Neal, Ruth Roman, Frank Lovejoy, Leif Erickson. Sturdy melodrama; three women wait anxiously for word of which one's child survived plane crash.▼

Three Shades of Love SEE: **This Rebel Breed**

Three Sisters, The (1966) 168m. **½ D:

Paul Bogart. Kim Stanley, Geraldine Page, Shelley Winters, Kevin McCarthy, Sandy Dennis. Taped recreation of Actors Studio Broadway production of Chekhov's play about 19th-century Russia and relationships amidst a most unhappy family.

Three Sisters (1970-British) **C-165m.** ******** D: Laurence Olivier, John Sichel. Laurence Olivier, Joan Plowright, Alan Bates, Jeanne Watts, Louise Purnell, Derek Jacobi. Brilliant rendering of Chekhov play about three daughters of deceased Russian colonel living in provinces, circa 1900. Olivier's vibrant production is definitive screen version of this classic. Released here in 1974 by American Film Theater.

Three Smart Girls (1936) **84m.** *****½** D: Henry Koster. Deanna Durbin, Binnie Barnes, Alice Brady, Ray Milland, Barbara Read, Mischa Auer, Nan Grey, Charles Winninger. Delightful musicomedy with Deanna's feature-film debut as matchmaking young girl who brings parents back together. Songs: "Someone To Care For Me," "My Heart Is Singing." Sequel: THREE SMART GIRLS GROW UP.

Three Smart Girls Grow Up (1939) **90m.** ******* D: Henry Koster. Deanna Durbin, Charles Winninger, Nan Grey, Helen Parrish, Robert Cummings, William Lundigan. Little Deanna is still matchmaking for sisters, warming up stern father, singing "Because," winning over everyone in sight.

Threesome (1984) **C-100m. TVM** D: Lou Antonio. Stephen Collins, Deborah Raffin, Joel Higgins, Susan Hess, Addison Powell, Dana Delany. Adaptation of Herbert Gold's novel about a romantic triangle set amid the singles scene of the Big Apple. Comes within a whisker of making it as swinger Collins and best pal Higgins parry for the affections of their other buddy, Raffin. Average.

Three Sovereigns for Sarah (1985) **C-180m. TVM** D: Philip Leacock. Vanessa Redgrave, Phyllis Thaxter, Kim Hunter, Patrick McGoohan, Shay Duffin, Ronald Hunter, Will Lyman. Riveting, beautifully filmed drama of the Salem witch trials, focusing on a witch-hunt survivor (Redgrave), who attempts to reverse the judgment against herself and her older sisters (Thaxter, Hunter), who have already been hanged. Fine performances all around, with a special nod to Vanessa. Originally presented over several evenings on PBS' *American Playhouse*. Above average.▼

Three Stooges Go Around the World in a Daze, The (1963) **94m.** ****½** D: Norman Maurer. Three Stooges, Jay Sheffield, Joan Freeman, Walter Burke, Peter Forster. Even those who dislike the Stooges may enjoy this funny updating of Jules Verne's tale, replete with sight gags and world travel.

Three Stooges in Orbit, The (1962) **87m.** ****½** D: Edward Bernds. The Three Stooges,

Carol Christensen, Edson Stroll, Emil Sitka. Nutty scientist Sitka invents contraption that flies and floats. The Stooges accidentally launch it and run headlong into the Army, with usual slapstick results for younger audiences.

Three Stooges Meet Hercules, The (1962) **89m.** ****½** D: Edward Bernds. The Three Stooges, Vicki Trickett, Quinn Redcker, George N. Neise. Time machine takes the Stooges back to era of Roman legions; they are trapped on galley ship, battle cyclops, and wind up with chariot chase. Good slapstick for kids and fans.▼

Three Strangers (1946) **92m.** *****½** D: Jean Negulesco. Sydney Greenstreet, Geraldine Fitzgerald, Peter Lorre, Joan Lorring, Robert Shayne, Marjorie Riordan. Greenstreet and Lorre team up with Fitzgerald as partners holding winning sweepstakes ticket under unusual circumstances. Bizarre John Huston-Howard Koch script makes fascinating viewing.

Three Stripes in the Sun (1955) **93m.** ****½** D: Richard Murphy. Aldo Ray, Phil Carey, Dick York, Chuck Connors, Mitsuko Kimura. Good film of American GI falling in love with Japanese orphanage worker after years of hating enemy; based on a true story.

3:10 to Yuma (1957) **92m.** *****½** D: Delmer Daves. Van Heflin, Glenn Ford, Felicia Farr, Leora Dana, Henry Jones, Richard Jaeckel, Robert Emhardt. Extremely suspenseful Western, one of the best of the 1950s. Farmer Heflin, needing the money, agrees to hold captured outlaw Ford until the train arrives, but Ford starts to psych him out. Gripping every step of the way, with memorable George Duning theme sung by Frankie Laine. Script by Halsted Welles from an Elmore Leonard story.▼

Three the Hard Way (1974) **C-93m.** ****½** D: Gordon Parks, Jr. Jim Brown, Fred Williamson, Jim Kelly, Sheila Frazier, Jay Robinson, Alex Rocco, Corbin Bersen. Top black action cast in nonstop, nearly bloodless thriller of white supremist Robinson's insane plot to eliminate blacks with a serum in the water supply. Produced by Harry Bernsen (Corbin's father).

3,000 Mile Chase, The (1977) **C-100m. TVM** D: Russ Mayberry. Cliff DeYoung, Glenn Ford, Blair Brown, David Spielberg, Priscilla Pointer, Brendan Dillon. Professional courier's efforts to deliver the key witness in narcotics czar's trial come under attack by latter's hit men. DeYoung is earnest; Ford's along for the ride in familiar chase plot. Average.

Three Tough Guys (1974-Italian-U.S.) **C-92m.** ****½** D: Duccio Tessari. Lino Ventura, Fred Williamson, Isaac Hayes, Paula Kelly. Oddball but fast-moving actioner, with tough priest Ventura and ex-cop Hayes solving million-dollar bank robbery. Hayes, who also did the music, is nicely subdued as an actor.

Three Violent People (1956) **C-100m.** ****½ D: Rudolph Maté.** Charlton Heston, Anne Baxter, Gilbert Roland, Tom Tryon, Forrest Tucker, Elaine Stritch, Bruce Bennett, Barton MacLane. Adequately paced Western set in post-Civil War Texas; Heston, returning home with bride Baxter, is forced to fight carpetbaggers and deal with wife's shady past.

Three Wise Fools (1946) **90m.** **** D:** Edward Buzzell. Margaret O'Brien, Lionel Barrymore, Lewis Stone, Edward Arnold, Thomas Mitchell, Jane Darwell, Cyd Charisse. Intended as fanciful, this turns out mawkish with adorable O'Brien winning over three crusty old men.

Three Wise Girls (1931) **66m.** **** D:** William Beaudine. Jean Harlow, Mae Clarke, Walter Byron, Jameson Thomas, Marie Prevost, Andy Devine, Lucy Beaumont. Brassy comedy-drama of Harlow as a small-town soda jerk who heads to N.Y. where Clarke shows her the ropes of being a fashion model. Odd mixture of moods and ironies with a solid cast.

Three Wishes for Jamie (1987) **C-100m. TVM D:** Robert William Young. Jack Warden, Stevan Rimkus, Anna Livia Ryan, David Healy, Peter Marinker, Ed Bishop. Flavorsome adaptation of Charles O'Neal book about love-struck young Irishman's adventures after being granted three wishes by a Fairy Queen. Warden romps through his matchmaker role in the very best "top o' the mornin' " Barry Fitzgerald style, in this tale that 35 years earlier had become a minor musical hit on Broadway. Average.

Three Wishes of Billy Grier, The (1984) **C-100m. TVM D:** Corey Blechman. Ralph Macchio, Betty Buckley, Hal Holbrook, Season Hubley, Lawrence Pressman, Conchata Ferrell, Ed Lauter, Viveca Lindfors. Teenager stricken with disease that rapidly accelerates aging sets out to realize three ambitions in life in his remaining few months. Well acted by "The Karate Kid" himself and those supporting him, and intelligently written by the director. Above average.

3 Women (1977) **C-125m.** *****½ D:** Robert Altman. Sissy Spacek, Shelley Duvall, Janice Rule, Robert Fortier, Ruth Nelson, John Cromwell. Brilliant, moody, thought-provoking film about a strange young girl (Spacek) who gets a job in an old-age convalescent home and attaches herself to coworker Duvall, who fancies herself a social butterfly. Their interrelationship, and involvement with a quiet, embittered woman (Rule) forms the "plot." Hypnotic film for Altman fans, heavy going for others; a completely unconventional movie.

3 Worlds of Gulliver, The (1960-British)

C-100m. ***** D:** Jack Sher. Kerwin Mathews, Jo Morrow, June Thorburn, Lee Patterson, Gregoire Aslan, Basil Sydney, Peter Bull. Hero is washed overboard and finds himself in the Land of Lilliput . . . but that's just the beginning. Well-made adventure/ fantasy designed for kids, fun for older viewers, too. Fine special effects by Ray Harryhausen, charming Bernard Herrmann score.▼

Three Young Texans (1954) **C-78m.** **** D.** Henry Levin. Mitzi Gaynor, Keefe Brasselle, Jeffrey Hunter, Harvey Stephens, Dan Riss. Standard Western has Hunter pulling railroad robbery to prevent crooks from forcing his father to do same job, expected complications.

Threshold (1981-Canadian) **C-97m.** ***** D:** Richard Pearce. Donald Sutherland, John Marley, Sharon Ackerman, Mare Winningham, Jeff Goldblum, Michael Lerner, Allan Nicholls, Paul Hecht, Robert Joy. Excellent, surprisingly low-key drama about the first artificial heart transplant, with more humanism and offbeat touches than you'd find in typical TV treatment of this sort of thing. Goldblum and Winningham score as, respectively, the biologist who invents the artificial heart and its first recipient. Unreleased in the U.S. until 1983, when Barney Clark's real-life operation made headlines.▼

Thrill of a Romance (1945) **C-105m.** **** D:** Richard Thorpe. Van Johnson, Esther Williams, Frances Gifford, Henry Travers, Spring Byington, Lauritz Melchior, Tommy Dorsey, Xavier Cugat. Typical Williams swim-romance vehicle with one good song, "I Should Care."

Thrill of Brazil, The (1946) **91m.** ****½ D:** S. Sylvan Simon. Evelyn Keyes, Keenan Wynn, Ann Miller, Allyn Joslyn, Tito Guizar. Pleasant South-of-the-border romance with music and spirited cast giving life to ordinary script.

Thrill of It All, The (1963) **C-108m.** ***** D:** Norman Jewison. Doris Day, James Garner, Arlene Francis, Edward Andrews, Reginald Owen, ZaSu Pitts, Elliott Reid. Enjoyable spoof of TV and commercials by Carl Reiner; good vehicle for Day as housewife-turned-TV-spokeswoman and Garner as her neglected husband. Reiner has a particularly funny series of cameos.▼

Throne of Blood (1957-Japanese) **108m.** ****** D:** Akira Kurosawa. Toshiro Mifune, Isuzu Yamada, Takashi Shimura, Minoru Chiaki. Graphic, powerful adaptation of *MacBeth* in a samurai setting. Gripping finale, with Taketoki Washizu (the Macbeth character, masterfully played by Mifune) attacked by arrows.▼

Through a Glass, Darkly (1962-Swedish) **91m.** *****½ D:** Ingmar Bergman. Harriet Andersson, Gunnar Bjornstrand, Max von Sydow, Lars Passgard. Four-character drama about just-released mental patient, her husband, her father and her younger brother who spend summer together on secluded island. Moody, evocative story of insanity—well-deserved Oscar winner, one of Bergman's best. The first in the filmmaker's "faith" trilogy, followed by WINTER LIGHT and THE SILENCE.▼

Through Naked Eyes (1983) **C-100m.** TVM D: John Llewellyn Moxey. David Soul, Pam Dawber, Fionnula Flanagan, William Schallert, Dick Anthony Williams, Rod McCary. Kinky thriller about voyeurism in an apartment complex where people are being bumped off. He's watching her through binoculars only to learn that she's watching him through a telescope; then they both discover somebody else is watching them. Average.▼

Through the Magic Pyramid (1981) **C-100m.** TVM D: Ron Howard. Chris Barnes, Hans Conried, Vic Tayback, Olivia Barash, Jo Ann Worley, James Hampton, Elaine Giftos, Eric Greene. Juvenile comedy-adventure about a youngster who goes back in time to ancient Egypt to help young Prince Tut become Pharaoh. Ron Howard's dad, Rance, co-wrote and co-produced. Average.

Throw Momma from the Train (1987) **C-88m.** **½ D: Danny DeVito. Danny DeVito, Billy Crystal, Anne Ramsey, Kim Greist, Kate Mulgrew, Branford Marsalis, Rob Reiner, Bruce Kirby. Black comedy spin-off of Hitchcock's STRANGERS ON A TRAIN, with DeVito (in an excellent performance) as a childish man who tries to persuade his writing professor (Crystal) to "exchange murders" with him so he can bump off his harridan of a mother (Ramsey, who's incredible). Uneven, to be sure, and not as all-out funny as you might expect from the starring duo. Director DeVito has many offbeat ideas, and cinematographer Barry Sonnenfeld (who did those wild gags in RAISING ARIZONA) leaves a distinctive stamp on this film—particularly the runaway car sequence. Written by Stu Silver.▼

Thumb Tripping (1972) **C-94m.** **½ D: Quentin Masters. Michael Burns, Meg Foster, Mariana Hill, Bruce Dern, Michael Conrad, Joyce Van Patten. Amusing as a period piece on the hippie era, with Burns and Foster as hitchhikers who decide to travel together and share experiences.▼

Thunder Afloat (1939) **94m.** **½ D: George B. Seitz. Wallace Beery, Chester Morris, Virginia Grey, Clem Bevans, John Qualen, Regis Toomey. Above-average Beery vehicle of old salt pitted against rival (Morris) when he joins the Navy.

Thunder Alley (1967) **C-90m.** *½ D: Richard Rush. Annette Funicello, Fabian, Diane McBain, Warren Berlinger, Jan Murray, Maureen Arthur. Fabian's inept stock-car driving gets him suspended from racing, but unfortunately, the acting profession doesn't have the same rules.▼

Thunder and Lightning (1977) **C-95m.** **½ D: Corey Allen. David Carradine, Kate Jackson, Roger C. Carmel, Sterling Holloway, Ed Barth, Ron Feinberg. Amiable moonshine picture with attractive pairing of Carradine and Jackson and lots of expected car smash-ups.▼

Thunderball (1965-British) **C-129m.** **½ D: Terence Young. Sean Connery, Claudine Auger, Adolfo Celi, Luciana Paluzzi. Rik Van Nutter, Martine Beswick, Bernard Lee, Lois Maxwell, Desmond Llewelyn, Roland Culver. Fourth James Bond film isn't as lively as the others. Plenty of gimmicks, and Oscar-winning special effects, as world is threatened with destruction, but film tends to bog down—especially underwater. Celi makes a formidable Bond villain. Remade eighteen years later—with Connery—as NEVER SAY NEVER AGAIN.▼

Thunder Bay (1953) **C-102m.** *** D: Anthony Mann. James Stewart, Joanne Dru, Gilbert Roland, Dan Duryea, Jay C. Flippen, Henry (Harry) Morgan. Action-packed account of oil-drillers vs. Louisiana shrimp fishermen, with peppery cast.▼

Thunder Below (1932) **67m.** **½ D: Richard Wallace. Tallulah Bankhead, Charles Bickford, Paul Lukas, Eugene Pallette, James Finlayson, Edward Van Sloan. Tallulah loves Lukas, but when husband Bickford goes blind, she can't bear to leave him. Melodramatic triangle story, well-acted by all.

Thunder Birds (1942) **C-78m.** ** D: William Wellman. Gene Tierney, Preston Foster, John Sutton, Dame May Whitty, Reginald Denny, Iris Adrian. Tame adventure as two rival fliers romance Tierney between air exploits.

Thunderbirds (1952) **98m.** **½ D: John H. Auer. John Derek, John Barrymore, Jr., Mona Freeman, Gene Evans. Standard tale of training aviators for WW2, with typical romantic interludes.

Thunderboat Row (1989) **C-100m.** TVM D: Thomas J. Wright. Chad Everett, Jason Adams, Nick Corri, Robert Estes, Dennis Boutsikaris. Formula cop vs. drug smugglers actioner with state-of-the-art speedboats substituting for black-and-whites with screeching tires. Pilot for prospective series. Average.

Thunderbolt and Lightfoot (1974) **C-114m.** *** D: Michael Cimino. Clint Eastwood, Jeff Bridges, George Kennedy, Geoffrey Lewis, Catherine Bach, Gary Busey, Jack Dodson, Vic Tayback, Dub Taylor, Bill McKinney. Thief Eastwood and drifter Bridges team up with Clint's ex-partners (Kennedy and Lewis) to retrieve loot from previous robbery. Colorful, tough melodrama-comedy with good characterizations; Lewis is particularly fine, but Bridges steals the picture. Cimino's directorial debut.▼

Thundercloud SEE: **Colt .45**

Thunderhead—Son of Flicka (1945) C-78m. **½ D: Louis King. Roddy McDowall, Preston Foster, Rita Johnson, James Bell, Diana Hale, Carleton Young. Good, colorful attempt to repeat MY FRIEND FLICKA's success; doesn't match original, but it's enjoyable. Followed by GREEN GRASS OF WYOMING.

Thunder in Carolina (1960) C-92m. ** D: Paul Helmick. Rory Calhoun, Alan Hale, Connie Hines, John Gentry, Ed McGrath, Troyanne Ross. Programmer account of stockcar racing in the South.

Thundering Jets (1958) 73m. *½ D: Helmut Dantine. Rex Reason, Dick Foran, Audrey Dalton, Robert Dix. Still another account of flight officer trying to reevaluate his handling of servicemen.

Thunder in the City (1937-British) 86m. *** D: Marion Gering. Edward G. Robinson, Luli Deste, Nigel Bruce, Constance Collier, Ralph Richardson, Arthur Wontner. Amusing film about a go-getting American promoter who visits England and gambles on a long-shot: hitherto unknown mineral known as Magnelite, which he proceeds to "ballyhoo." Tailor-made for an ebullient Robinson.▼

Thunder in the East (1953) 98m. **½ D: Charles Vidor. Alan Ladd, Deborah Kerr, Charles Boyer, Corinne Calvet, Cecil Kellaway. Melodramatic hodgepodge with Ladd a gunrunner mercenary involved in India with local political upheavals.

Thunder in the Sun (1959) C-81m. **½ D: Russell Rouse. Susan Hayward, Jeff Chandler, Jacques Bergerac, Blanche Yurka, Carl Esmond, Fortunio Bonanova. Hayward is romanced by wagon train scout Chandler and Bergerac, head of French Basque immigrants on way to California.

Thunder in the Valley (1947) C-103m. **½ D: Louis King. Lon McCallister, Peggy Ann Garner, Edmund Gwenn, Reginald Owen. Usual tale of boy in love with his dog, cruel father who doesn't share his feelings; colorful but standard.

Thunder Island (1963) 65m. ** D: Jack Leewood. Gene Nelson, Fay Spain, Brian Kelly, Miriam Colon, Art Bedard. A hit man is hired to kill the former dictator of a Latin country who's now living in exile on a nearby island. Unexceptional programmer co-written by Jack Nicholson.

Thunder of Drums, A (1961) C-97m. **½ D: Joseph M. Newman. George Hamilton, Luana Patten, Richard Boone, Charles Bronson, Richard Chamberlain, Slim Pickens. Better than average cast saves average story of new lieutenant having rough time in cavalry.

Thunder on the Hill (1951) 84m. *** D: Douglas Sirk. Claudette Colbert, Ann Blyth, Robert Douglas, Anne Crawford, Gladys Cooper. Nun Colbert can't believe visitor Blyth, about to be hanged, is murderess, sets out to prove her innocent; Cooper fine as Mother Superior. Sincere, interesting drama.

Thunder Over Arizona (1956) C-75m. ** D: Joseph Kane. Skip Homeier, Kristine Miller, George Macready, Wallace Ford. Undemanding minor Western showing the corruption and greed of people incited by a rich silver ore discovery.▼

Thunder Over Hawaii SEE: **Naked Paradise**

Thunder Over Tangier (1957-British) 66m. *½ D: Lance Comfort. Robert Hutton, Martin Benson, Derek Sydney, Lisa Gastoni. Flabby account of refugees being conned with phony passports.

Thunder Over the Plains (1953) C-82m. ** D: Andre de Toth. Randolph Scott, Lex Barker, Phyllis Kirk, Henry Hull, Elisha Cook, Jr., Richard Benjamin, Charles McGraw, Fess Parker. Routine Western set in post-Civil War Texas, with Scott as army officer sent to prevent carpetbaggers from harassing all. Benjamin's film debut.

Thunder Pass (1954) 76m. ** D: Frank McDonald. Dane Clark, Andy Devine, Dorothy Patrick, John Carradine, Raymond Burr. Usual story of resolute army officer (Clark) pushing settlers onward in face of Indian attack.▼

Thunder Road (1958) 92m. *** D: Arthur Ripley. Robert Mitchum, Gene Barry, Jacques Aubuchon, Keely Smith, James Mitchum. Rural bootlegger takes on Feds *and* the Mob in cult favorite that even today continues to play in drive-ins; for many this remains the definitive moonshine picture. Jim Mitchum makes screen debut playing Bob's *brother;* the elder Mitchum got a hit record out of the title tune!▼

Thunder Rock (1942-British) 112m. *** D: Roy Boulting. Michael Redgrave, Barbara Mullen, Lilli Palmer, James Mason, Frederick Valk. Allegorical fable of discouraged newspaperman given renewed faith by visions of various drowned people. Excellent cast makes this most enjoyable; based on Robert Ardrey's play.

Thunderstorm (1956-Spanish) 81m. *½ D: John Guillermin. Carlos Thompson, Linda Christian, Charles Korvin, Gary Thorne. Warmed-over trivia concerning Christian's provocative arrival in a small fishing village on the Spanish coast.

Thursday's Child (1943-British) 81m. **½ D: Rodney Ackland. Sally Ann Howes, Wilfrid Lawson, Kathleen O'Regan, Eileen Bennett, Stewart Granger, Marianne Davis, Gerhardt Kempinski, Felix Aylmer. Melodramatic soap opera of twelve-year-old girl from middle-class family who becomes child film star, to the detriment of all around her. Howes, making her film debut, is excellent as the level-headed youngster. Recommended mainly for buffs, and fans of dashing Granger (in an early supporting role).

Thursday's Child (1983) **C-100m. TVM** D: David Lowell Rich. Gena Rowlands, Don Murray, Jessica Walter, Rob Lowe, Tracey Gold, Janet MacLachlan, Robin Gammell, Alan Fudge, Susan Ruttan. Good cast elevates this drama about a family whose teenaged son undergoes a heart transplant. Gwen Bagni-Dubov adapted Victoria Poole's factual book. Above average.

Thursday's Game (1974) **C-100m. TVM** D: Robert Moore. Gene Wilder, Bob Newhart, Ellen Burstyn, Cloris Leachman, Martha Scott, Nancy Walker, Valerie Harper, Rob Reiner, Norman Fell, Richard Schaal, Dick Gautier, John Archer. Sparkling adult comedy about pokerplaying buddies Wilder and Newhart and their marital and business problems. Absolutely tops with dandy cast and a gloriously intelligent, often hilarious script by James L. Brooks. Filmed in 1971. Above average.▼

THX-1138 (1971) **C-88m. **½ D: George Lucas. Robert Duvall, Donald Pleasence, Maggie McOmie, Don Pedro Colley, Ian Wolfe. Futuristic tale in the 1984 vein about robotlike society where sex is forbidden and everyone looks the same. Dull script, but visually impressive; Lucas' first feature is expanded version of prize-winning featurette he made at USC.▼

Thy Kingdom Come . . . Thy Will Be Done (1988-U.S.-British) **C-107m. ***½** D: Antony Thomas. Provocative documentary about born-again Christianity, which examines everything from the type of person who becomes involved in the movement, to its ties to right-wing politics. A controversial production that almost didn't get seen in this country. Among the highlights: a revealing sequence filmed in Jim and Tammy Bakker's Heritage, USA park.

Tiara Tahiti (1962-British) **C-100m. ** D: William (Ted) Kotcheff. James Mason, John Mills, Claude Dauphin, Herbert Lom. Mild comedy-drama involving Mason and Mills as two former Army officers who have an old grudge to settle; establishment of a Tahiti resort hotel sets wheels in motion.▼

Ticket to Heaven (1981-Canadian) **C-107m. *** D: Ralph L. Thomas. Nick Mancuso, Saul Rubinek, Meg Foster, Kim Cattrall, R. H. Thomson, Jennifer Dale, Guy Boyd. Mancuso, strung out from bad relationship, is seduced into becoming a "heavenly child" in a Moonie-like cult. Pointed drama is frightening in its relevancy. Mancuso is excellent, Rubinek and

Thomson lend fine support as his best friend and a deprogrammer.▼

Ticket to Tomahawk, A (1950) **C-90m.** *** D: Richard Sale. Dan Dailey, Anne Baxter, Rory Calhoun, Walter Brennan, Charles Kemper, Connie Gilchrist, Arthur Hunnicutt, Mauritz Hugo, Chief Yowlachie, Victor Sen Yung. Engaging comedy-Western about stagecoach company that hires gunslinger Calhoun to keep dreaded railroad from running on time. Good fun; one of the chorus girls with Dailey in his one musical number is Marilyn Monroe.▼

Tickle Me (1965) **C-90m. **½ D: Norman Taurog. Elvis Presley, Jocelyn Lane, Julie Adams, Jack Mullaney, Merry Anders, Connie Gilchrist. That's the only way to get any laughs out of this one: Elvis works at all-girl dude ranch singing his usual quota of songs. Written by Elwood Ullman and Edward Bernds, both of whom worked with The Three Stooges in better days.▼

Ticklish Affair, A (1963) **C-89m. ** D: George Sidney. Shirley Jones, Gig Young, Red Buttons, Carolyn Jones, Edgar Buchanan. Amiable film of Navy commander Young falling in love with widow Jones; all it lacks is wit, sparkle and a fresh script.

. . . tick . . . tick . . . tick . . . (1970) **C-100m. ** D: Ralph Nelson. Jim Brown, George Kennedy, Fredric March, Lynn Carlin, Don Stroud, Clifton James, Janet MacLachlan. Poor man's IN THE HEAT OF THE NIGHT with black man (Brown) replacing white sheriff (Kennedy) in Southern town, flaring local hostilities. March adds film's only spice as aging, cantankerous mayor.

Tidal Wave (1975) **C-82m.** *½ D: Shiro Moriana, Andrew Meyer. Lorne Greene, Kiliu Kobayashi, Rhonda Leigh Hopkins, Hiroshi Fujioka. Laughable Americanization of big-budget (and much superior) Japanese film, SUBMERSION OF JAPAN; epic special effects dwarfed by idiotic new footage with Greene, and horrible dubbing. For diehard disaster buffs only.▼

Tiefland (1954-German) **98m. **½ D: Leni Riefenstahl. Leni Riefenstahl, Franz Eichberger, Bernard Minetti, Maria Koppenhofer, Luis Rainer. Blonde, dreamy shepherd Eichberger and arrogant marquis Minetti vie for Spanish dancer Riefenstahl. Atmospheric, visually poetic drama, even though the characters lack depth. Filmed between 1942 and 1945; editing wasn't completed until 1954.▼

Tie Me Up! Tie Me Down! (1990-Spanish) **C-101m. **½ D: Pedro Almodovar. Victoria Abril, Antonio Banderas, Francsico Rabal, Loles Leon, Julieta Serrano, Maria Barranco. Mental patient kidnaps a former porn star-junkie, slaps her around some, then ties her to a bed; actually, he just wants to get married and have kids. Potential NOW nightmare comes off as surprisingly tame for Almodovar, though it still has his unpredictable black humor. Thought-provoking and energetically performed. Two scenes (one a loud but fairly explicit sex scene) earned this an X rating, so the distributor decided to release it unrated instead.

Tiger and the Pussycat, The (1967-Italian-U.S.) **C-105m.** **½ D: Dino Risi. Ann-Margret, Vittorio Gassman, Eleanor Parker, Antonella Stani, Fiorenzo Fiorentini. Innocuous sex-comedy of middle-aged businessman Gassman unintentionally getting involved with promiscuous young Ann-Margret. Italian and American players work well together.▼

Tiger Bay (1959-British) **105m.** *** D: J. Lee Thompson. John Mills, Horst Buchholz, Hayley Mills, Yvonne Mitchell, Megs Jenkins, Anthony Dawson. Lonely Cardiff child witnesses a murder and is abducted by the Polish sailor-killer. A poignant, sensitive, and very different police chase story. Hayley steals the film in first major acting role.▼

Tiger By the Tail (1968) **C-99m.** ** D: R. G. Springsteen. Christopher George, Tippi Hedren, Dean Jagger, Charo, Glenda Farrell, Lloyd Bochner, Alan Hale, Skip Homeier, R. G. Armstrong. Vietnam war hero is accused of murdering his brother and recruits his socialite girlfriend in hunt for the real killer. Overly talkative thriller.

Tiger Makes Out, The (1967) **C-94m.** **½ D: Arthur Hiller. Eli Wallach, Anne Jackson, Bob Dishy, John Harkins, David Burns, Ruth White, Rae Allen, Charles Nelson Reilly. One-man crusader against society (Wallach) symbolically kidnaps suburban housewife (Jackson). Originally a one-act, two-character play by Murray Schisgal, his expanded screenplay loses focus, relies on vivid N.Y. locations and funny cameos by character actors. Dustin Hoffman's film debut.

Tiger of Eschnapur, The (1958-German) **C-101m.** ** D: Fritz Lang. Debra Paget, Paul Hubschmid, Walther Reyer, Rene Deltman, Luciana Paluzzi. Exotic dancer Paget is desired by dastardly maharajah Reyer, but she loves architect Hubschmid; meanwhile, Reyer's subjects are plotting revolution. Slow-moving, disappointing adventure-romance of interest mostly for Lang's participation. The first of the director's Indian diptych, followed by THE INDIAN TOMB; both were originally edited down to 95m., dubbed and released as JOURNEY TO THE LOST CITY.

Tiger of the Seven Seas (1962-Italian) **C-90m.** ** D: Luigi Capuano. Gianna Maria Canale, Anthony Steel, Grazia Maria Spina, Ernesto Calindri. Follow-up to QUEEN OF THE PIRATES, with Canale the center of romance and swordfighting in this OK pirate yarn.▼

Tiger Shark (1932) **80m.** *** D: Howard Hawks. Edward G. Robinson, Richard Arlen, Zita Johann, J. Carrol Naish, Vince Barnett. Robinson gives rich, colorful performance as Portuguese tuna fisherman who marries wayward girl out of pity, then sees her fall in love with his best friend—a plot gambit Warner Bros. reused several times (SLIM, MANPOWER, etc.). Authentically filmed amid fisheries on Monterey coast.

Tigers in Lipstick (1979-Italian) **C-83m.** ** D: Luigi Zampa. Ursula Andress, Laura Antonelli, Sylvia Kristel, Monica Vitti, Michele Placido, Roberto Benigni, Orazio Orlando. Veteran comedy director Zampa pilots a fun but overly tame throwback to '60s sex comedies that spotlight four beautiful actresses (individually) in seven separate segments, emphasizing aggressive women who take advantage of men. Best segment: ''The Pickup,'' in which Antonelli is a frantic businesswoman who disrupts the life of an orchestra conductor. Originally titled: WILD BEDS.▼

Tiger's Tale, A (1987) **C-97m.** *½ D: Peter Douglas. Ann-Margret, C. Thomas Howell, Charles Durning, Kelly Preston, William Zabka, Ann Wedgeworth, James Noble, Tim Thomerson, Steven Kampmann, Angel Tompkins. Unbelievable romantic comedy about a high school senior who gets involved with his girlfriend's mother, a nurse named Rose Butts. Need we say more? Debuting writer-director Douglas (Kirk's son) has bitten off more than he can chew—or we can swallow. Ann-Margret is watchable, as always, but miscast. ▼

Tiger Town (1983) **C-95m.** **TVM** D: Alan Shapiro. Roy Scheider, Justin Henry, Ron McLarty, Bethany Carpenter, Noah Moazezi, Mary Wilson. Heartwarming baseball tale involving a young Detroit Tigers fan and the fading ball player he finds he is able to ''will'' one final chance at a championship. A home run for first time writer/director Shapiro. Made for cable by Disney. Above average.▼

Tiger Walks, A (1964) **C-91m.** **½ D: Norman Tokar. Brian Keith, Vera Miles, Pamela Franklin, Sabu, Kevin Corcoran, Peter Brown, Una Merkel, Frank McHugh, Edward Andrews. Oddball Disney film about young girl (Franklin) whose compassion for tiger which has broken away from circus stirs controversy and political wheeling-and-dealing. Surprisingly bitter portrait of small-town America.▼

Tiger Warsaw (1988) **C-93m.** *½ D: Amin Q. Chaudhri. Patrick Swayze, Piper Laurie, Lee Richardson, Mary McDonnell, Barbara Williams, Bobby DiCicco, Jenny Chrisinger, Kaye Ballard. Muddled melodrama about troubled ex-junkie Swayze and what happens when he comes home and attempts to sort out his life. Hokey and highly improbable.▼

Tiger Woman, The SEE: **Jungle Gold**▼

Tight Little Island (1949-British) **82m.** **** D: Alexander Mackendrick. Basil Radford, Joan Greenwood, James Robertson Justice, Jean Cadel, Gordon Jackson, Wylie Watson, John Gregson. Hilarious, fast-paced comedy about WW2 ship sinking while loaded with whiskey and the antics of local Scottish islanders thirsting for its cargo. A solid hit. Compton MacKenzie, the author of the novel, has a small role as Captain Buncher. British title: WHISKY GALORE! Followed by MAD LITTLE ISLAND.▼

Tightrope (1984) **C-114m.** **½ D: Richard Tuggle. Clint Eastwood, Genevieve Bujold, Alison Eastwood, Dan Hedaya. New Orleans cop finds he has much in common with the sex murderer he's pursuing. Intriguing Eastwood vehicle undone by sleaziness—and darkness.▼

Tight Shoes (1941) **68m.** ** D: Albert S. Rogell. Broderick Crawford, Binnie Barnes, John Howard, Anne Gwynne. Cast pushes hard to make this Damon Runyon yarn amusing at times; Crawford is big-shot crook who has big feet.

Tight Spot (1955) **97m.** ***½ D: Phil Karlson. Ginger Rogers, Edward G. Robinson, Brian Keith, Lorne Greene, Katherine Anderson. Solid little film, with Rogers in one of her best performances as a former gangster's moll who's on the spot because she has agreed to testify against him. Tense script by William Bowers.

Tijuana Story, The (1957) **72m.** BOMB D: Leslie Kardos. James Darren, Jean Willes, Robert McQueeney, Rodolfo Acosta, Robert Blake. Juvenile melodrama of Darren a victim of narcotic addiction, set in Mexico.

Till Death (1978) **C-89m.** *** D: Walter Stocker. Keith Atkinson, Belinda Balaski, Marshall Reed, Bert Freed, Jonathan Hole. Neat little shocker, virtually a two-character thriller. Atkinson refuses to believe that Balaski was killed on their wedding night, finds her alive in her crypt. Made in 1972.

Tillie and Gus (1933) **58m.** ***½ D: Francis Martin. W.C. Fields, Alison Skipworth, Baby LeRoy, Edgar Kennedy, Jacqueline Wells (Julie Bishop), Clifford Jones, Barton MacLane, Clarence Wilson. Fields and Skipworth are perfectly matched as card hustlers in this very entertaining comedy, which also pits W.C. against Baby LeRoy for the first time. Nominal plot has them helping niece Wells win a crucial riverboat race.

Tillie's Punctured Romance (1914) **73m.** **½ D: Mack Sennett. Charlie Chaplin, Marie Dressler, Mabel Normand, Mack Swain, Charles Bennett, Chester Conklin, Keystone Kops. A comic curio, the first full-length comedy feature film, with Dressler repeating stage role as farm girl fleeced by city-slicker Chaplin (appearing out of his usual character). Not terribly funny, or coherent, but there are good moments; mainly interesting for historical purposes. Dressler starred in a pair of sequels, TILLIE'S TOMATO SURPRISE and TILLIE WAKES UP.▼

Till Marriage Do Us Part (1974-Italian) **C-97m.** **½ D: Luigi Comencini. Laura Antonelli, Alberto Lionello, Michele Placido, Jean Rochefort, Karin Schubert. A naive young woman unable to consummate her marriage seeks and finds sexual fulfillment elsewhere. Light forgettable farce featuring Antonelli at her sexiest.▼

Till the Clouds Roll By (1946) **C-137m.** **½ D: Richard Whorf. Robert Walker, Van Heflin, Lucille Bremer, Dorothy Patrick, many guest stars including Judy Garland, Kathryn Grayson, Lena Horne, Tony Martin, Dinah Shore, Frank Sinatra, June Allyson, Angela Lansbury, Cyd Charisse, Virginia O'Brien. Soggy biography of songwriter Jerome Kern uplifted by song numbers featuring some high-powered MGM talent. Highlights include Lansbury's "How D'Ya Like to Spoon With Me," Lena's "Why Was I Born?," Judy's "Look for the Silver Lining," and mini production of *Show Boat.*▼

Till the End of Time (1946) **105m.** *** D: Edward Dmytryk. Dorothy McGuire, Guy Madison, Robert Mitchum, Bill Williams, Tom Tully, William Gargan, Jean Porter, Ruth Nelson. Solid, sympathetic drama of three returning WW2 veterans was released months before THE BEST YEARS OF OUR LIVES; the focus is on Madison falling for troubled war widow McGuire. Screenplay by Allen Rivkin, based on Niven Busch's novel *They Dream of Home*. Title song (based on Chopin's Polonaise in A-flat Major) was a big hit.▼

Till We Meet Again (1944) **88m.** ** D: Frank Borzage. Ray Milland, Barbara Britton, Walter Slezak, Lucile Watson, Mona Freeman. Fair wartime drama of nun Britton helping pilot Milland return to Allied lines; elements don't always click in this one.

Till We Meet Again (1989) **C-250m.** TVM D: Charles Jarrott. Bruce Boxleitner, Barry Bostwick, Mia Sara, Courteney Cox, Lucy Gutteridge, Hugh Grant, Maxwell Caulfield, Juliet Mills, Michael York. Lavish but tiresome adaptation of Judith Krantz's sprawling novel spanning 50 years in the lives and loves of three women—a mother who was a pre-WWI Paris music-hall star (Gutteridge) and two daughters (film actress Sara, aviatrix Cox). Originally shown in two parts. Average.

Tilt (1978) **C-111m.** ** D: Rudy Durand. Brooke Shields, Ken Marshall, Charles Durning, John Crawford, Gregory Walcott, Geoffrey Lewis. Meandering tale of pinball wizard Shields and musician Marshall traveling cross-country, eventually challenging champion Durning. Only value of film (aside from Durning) is dazzling point-of-view photography inside pinball machine. Recut by director Durand to 100m.▼

'Til We Meet Again (1940) **99m.** **½ D: Edmund Goulding, Merle Oberon, George Brent, Pat O'Brien, Geraldine Fitzgerald, Binnie Barnes, Frank McHugh, Eric Blore, George Reeves. Overblown remake of ONE WAY PASSAGE recounts romance between suave crook Brent and fatally ill Oberon; McHugh repeats comedy-relief role from 1932 original.

Tim (1979-Australian) **C-108m.** **½ D: Michael Pate. Piper Laurie, Mel Gibson, Alwyn Kurts, Pat Evison, Peter Gwynne, Deborah Kennedy. Lush, well-meaning if a bit schmaltzy chronicle of the relationship between older woman (Laurie) and younger, retarded man (nicely played by Gibson). Pate wrote the screenplay from Colleen McCullough's first novel.▼

Timberjack (1955) **C-94m.** ** D: Joseph Kane. Vera Ralston, Sterling Hayden, David Brian, Adolphe Menjou, Hoagy Carmichael. Young man fights crooks taking over lumber mill who also killed his father. Harmless potboiler.

Timber Queen (1943) **66m.** *½ D: Frank McDonald. Richard Arlen, Mary Beth Hughes, June Havoc, Sheldon Leonard. Static programmer with pilot Arlen helping Hughes solve her business problems and romancing her.

Timbuktu (1959) **91m.** ** D: Jacques Tourneur. Victor Mature, Yvonne De Carlo, George Dolenz, John Dehner, Marcia Henderson, James Foxx. Mature plays adventurer involved in African story of plot to overthrow government. Script is below average; cast is uneven.

Time After Time (1979) **C-112m.** **½ D: Nicholas Meyer. Malcolm McDowell, David Warner, Mary Steenburgen, Charles Cioffi, Kent Williams, Patti D'Arbanville, Joseph Maher, Corey Feldman, Shelley Hack. Fanciful tale of H. G. Wells following Jack the Ripper from Victorian England to 1979 America in his time machine. Engaging premise eroded by story loopholes, and halfhearted attempts at social comment. Best is Steenburgen in an appealing, star-making performance as Wells' modern American girlfriend. Vivid score by Miklos Rozsa.▼

Time After Time (1985-British) **C-103m.** *** D: Bill Hays. John Gielgud, Googie Withers, Helen Cherry, Ursula Howells, Brenda Bruce, Freddie Jones, Fiona Walker, Trevor Howard. Very funny comedy about Gielgud, living on an estate with his three elderly sisters (named April, May, and Baby June)—their eccentricities, memories, and what happens when they are

visited by their manipulative, long-lost cousin (Withers). Great script by Andrew Davies, from Molly Keane's novel; hampered only by occasionally awkward direction.

Time Bandits (1981-British) **C-110m.** **½ D: Terry Gilliam. Sean Connery, Shelley Duvall, John Cleese, Katherine Helmond, Ian Holm, Michael Palin, Ralph Richardson, Peter Vaughan, David Warner, Kenny Baker, David Rappaport. Six dwarfs, assisted by the Supreme Being (Richardson), escort a young English schoolboy through time. They meet Robin Hood (Cleese), Napoleon (Holm), King Agamemnon (Connery). Imaginative, but not as funny or as thrilling as it should be. Written by Gilliam and Palin, of Monty Python fame. British running time 116m.▼

Time Bomb (1961-French) **92m.** ** D: Yves Ciampi. Curt Jurgens, Mylene Demongeot, Alain Saury, Robert Porte, Jean Durand. So-so story of captain plotting to collect insurance by planting bomb on ship.

Time Bomb (1984) **C-100m.** TVM D: Paul Krasny. Morgan Fairchild, Billy Dee Williams, Joseph Bottoms, Merlin Olsen. Female terrorist Fairchild—lip gloss and all—leads a band of hijackers across Texas to nab a cargo of nuclear weapons-grade plutonium. Standard bonehead TV-action flick; busted pilot for cop series to have starred Williams and Bottoms. Average.

Time Flyer SEE: **Blue Yonder, The▼**

Time for Killing, A (1967) **C-88m.** ** D: Phil Karlson. Glenn Ford, Inger Stevens, George Hamilton, Paul Petersen, Max Baer, Timothy Carey, Kenneth Tobey, Dick Miller, (Harry) Dean Stanton. Fair Civil War drama pits Union Captain Ford against Confederate Major Hamilton, when the latter kidnaps Ford's bride-to-be. Director Karlson has done some good minor films in the past, but this isn't one of them. Look for a young Harrison Ford. Also known as THE LONG RIDE HOME.

Time for Love, A (1973) **C-100m.** TVM D: George Schaefer, Joseph Sargent. Jack Cassidy, John Davidson, Lauren Hutton, Christopher Mitchum, Bonnie Bedelia, Joanna K. Cameron. Two stories: meeting uninhibited girl at business convention, junior executive decides to dump plans of marrying wealthy socialite; pop star can't take crazy professional pressures, hitchhikes to small coastal town, meets simple teacher of deaf children. Not as bad as it sounds, with occasionally good dialogue, no-nonsense direction. Above average.

Time for Loving, A (1971-British) **C-104m.** **½ D: Christopher Miles. Mel Ferrer, Joanna Shimkus, Britt Ekland, Philippe Noiret, Susan Hampshire, Mark Burns, Lila Kedrova, Robert Dhery, Michel Legrand. Sophisticated Jean Anouilh liaison trilogy in the LA RONDE style. Sometimes called PARIS WAS MADE FOR LOVERS.

Time for Miracles, A (1980) **C-100m.** TVM D: Michael O'Herlihy. Kate Mulgrew, Jean-Pierre Aumont, Rossano Brazzi, John Forsythe, Lorne Greene, Jean LeClerc, Leonard Mann, Robin Clarke, Milo O'Shea, William Prince. Reverent dramatization of the story of Elizabeth Bayley Seton, 18th-century widow who became America's first native-born saint. Henry Denker wrote the teleplay. Average.▼

Time Guardian, The (1987-Australian) **C-105m.** ** D: Brian Hannant. Tom Burlinson, Nikki Coghill, Dean Stockwell, Carrie Fisher, Tim Robertson, Peter Merrill, Wan Thye Liew, Damon Sanders. A city from the year 4039 travels through time to evade army of killer cyborgs from the 40th century; Burlinson and Fisher are sent to the 1988 Australian desert, where he teams up with geologist Coghill to battle arriving cyborgs. Confusing sci-fi adventure has poor dialogue and too many unanswered questions.▼

Time Limit (1957) **96m.** *** D: Karl Malden. Richard Widmark, Richard Basehart, Dolores Michaels, June Lockhart, Rip Torn, Martin Balsam, Carl Benton Reid, James Douglas. Imaginative direction and acting spark this courtroomer concerning the trial of American military officer suspected of collaborating with enemy while P.O.W. in North Korea. Malden's sole foray behind the camera; Widmark co-produced.

Time Lost and Time Remembered (1966-British) **91m.** *** D: Desmond Davis. Sarah Miles, Cyril Cusack, Julian Glover, Sean Caffrey. Thoughtful study of Miles' unhappy marriage to older man, emphasized by visit home where she discovers new set of values. Original British title: I WAS HAPPY HERE.

Time Machine, The (1960) **C-103m.** *** D: George Pal. Rod Taylor, Alan Young, Yvette Mimieux, Sebastian Cabot, Tom Helmore, Whit Bissell, Doris Lloyd. H. G. Wells' fantasy reduced to comic book level, but still entertaining, with Taylor as single-minded scientist who invents time-travel device and has vivid, frustrating experiences in the future. Oscar-winning special effects. Remade for TV in 1978.▼

Time Machine, The (1978) **C-100m.** TVM D: Henning Schellerup. John Beck, Priscilla Barnes, Andrew Duggan, Rosemary DeCamp, Jack Kruschen, Whit Bissell. Updated version of the H. G. Wells classic, given a "Classics Illustrated" treatment. Average.

Time of Destiny, A (1988) **C-118m.** ** D: Gregory Nava. William Hurt, Timothy Hutton, Melissa Leo, Stockard Channing, Megan Follows, Francisco Rabal. Major disappointment from the makers of EL NORTE. Plodding soaper, set in the WW2 era, with tragedy and revenge coming between close friends and fellow GIs Hurt and Hutton (whose performances are far from their best). Written and produced by Anna Thomas.▼

Time of Indifference (1964-Italian) **84m.** ** D: Francesco Maselli. Rod Steiger, Shelley Winters, Claudia Cardinale, Paulette Goddard, Tomas Milian. Turgid melodrama of moral and social decay in Italy during late 1920s, focusing on one nouveau-poor family; from novel by Alberto Moravia.▼

Time of the Gypsies (1989-Yugoslav) **C-142m.** **½ D: Emir Kusturica. Davor Dujmovic, Bora Todorovic, Ljubica Adzovic, Sinolicka Trpkova, Husnija Hasimovic. Fair chronicle of the coming of age of a naive young gypsy (Dujmovic) and his initiation into the ways of petty crime. Sometimes effective, but way overlong and in no way as magical or memorable as Kusturica's WHEN FATHER WAS AWAY ON BUSINESS. However, he did earn the Best Director prize at the Cannes Film Festival. Shot in a Gypsy language called Romany, this may be the first film ever to require subtitles in every country in which it plays!▼

Time of Their Lives, The (1946) **82m.** *** D: Charles Barton. Bud Abbott, Lou Costello, Marjorie Reynolds, Binnie Barnes, John Shelton, Gale Sondergaard, Jess Barker. Most unusual film for A&C, and one of their best. Costello and Reynolds are killed during Revolutionary times, and their ghosts haunt a country estate where Abbott and friends come to live. Imaginative, funny, and well done. Based on a Broadway play, *Gramercy Ghost*, by John Cecil Holm.▼

Time of Your Life, The (1948) **109m.** ** D: H. C. Potter. James Cagney, William Bendix, Wayne Morris, Jeanne Cagney, Broderick Crawford, Ward Bond, James Barton, Paul Draper, James Lydon, Gale Page, Richard Erdman. Uninspired version of William Saroyan's prizewinning morality play about the various characters who populate Nick's Saloon, Restaurant and Entertainment Palace, which is actually a waterfront dive. Interesting cast, but it just doesn't come together.▼

Time Out for Love (1961-French) **91m.** **½ D: Philippe De Broca. Jean Seberg, Maurice Ronet, Micheline Presle, Françoise Prevost. Amusing adult study of Yank Seberg engulfed by seemingly immoral world of new acquaintances, with their own code of standards. Retitled: FIVE DAY LOVER.

Time Out for Rhythm (1941) **75m.** ** D: Sidney Salkow. Rudy Vallee, Ann Miller, Rosemary Lane, Allen Jenkins, The Three Stooges. Mediocre show-biz musical turns out to be a wonderful showcase for the Stooges, who do some of their best material (including the "Maja? Aha!" routine).

One good production number, "Boogie Woogie Man," features Glen Gray and his Casa Loma Orchestra.

Time Out of Mind (1947) **88m. **** D: Robert Siodmak. Phyllis Calvert, Robert Hutton, Ella Raines, Eddie Albert, Leo G. Carroll. Plodding period-piece of girl in love above her station seeing her lover live unhappy life. From a Rachel Field novel.

Timerider (1983) **C-93m. **** D: William Dear. Fred Ward, Belinda Bauer, Peter Coyote, Ed Lauter, Richard Masur, Tracey Walter, L. Q. Jones. Motocross bike racer is accidentally sent back in time to the Old West, circa 1875 . . . and that's where the writers fell asleep. Good premise and cast are left hanging as film crawls downhill. Produced and co-written by Michael Nesmith.▼

Times of Harvey Milk, The (1984) **C-87m. ***½** D: Robert Epstein. Narrated by Harvey Fierstein. Extremely moving documentary about Harvey Milk, the first gay supervisor elected in San Francisco; mayor George Moscone; and clean-cut, respectable supervisor Dan White, who assassinated them both. Eerie, fascinating, sad, funny; as dramatic and involving as the most carefully plotted fiction. This deservedly earned a Best Documentary Academy Award.▼

Times Square (1980) **C-111m.** BOMB D: Alan Moyle. Tim Curry, Trini Alvarado, Robin Johnson, Peter Coffield, Herbert Berghof, Miguel Pinero, Elizabeth Pena. A pair of teenage runaways, one (Alvarado) upper class, the other (Johnson) "of the streets," romp around a curiously unmenacing Times Square. Illogical, unrealistic scenario, frantic direction, music score for the hard of hearing. Script by film critic Jacob Brackman.▼

Timestalkers (1987) **C-100m.** TVM D: Michael Schultz. William Devane, Lauren Hutton, Klaus Kinski, John Ratzenberger, Forrest Tucker, Gail Youngs. Imaginative time-travel adventure with a modern-day college professor falling under the spell of a determined woman from the 26th century, helping track down her scientist dad's villainous associate who has fled back to the 18th century. Adapted by Brian Clemens from Ray Brown's unpublished novel *The Tintype*, it offers the ubiquitous Klaus Kinski in his American TV movie debut and veteran actor Forrest Tucker in his acting swan song. Average.▼

Time Stands Still (1981-Hungarian) **C/ B&W-99m. **½** D: Peter Gothar. Istvan Znamenak, Henrik Pauer, Sandor Soth, Peter Galfy, Aniko Ivan, Agi Kakassy, Lojos Oze, Maria Ronyecz. Budapest's alienated adolescents of the early 1960s, in the aftershock of revolution, focusing on sullen Znamenak and comrades. Down-

beat, enigmatic, but intriguing—with American "oldies" on the soundtrack.▼

Timetable (1956) **79m. **** D: Mark Stevens. Mark Stevens, King Calder, Felicia Farr, Marianne Stewart, Jack Klugman, Wesley Addy. Small-scale account of insurance detective involved in investigation of robbery he engineered. Klugman's film debut.

Time, the Place and the Girl, The (1946) **C-105m. **½** D: David Butler. Dennis Morgan, Martha Vickers, Jack Carson, Janis Paige, S. Z. Sakall, Alan Hale, Florence Bates, Carmen Cavallero. Best thing about this flimsily plotted put-on-a-show musical is the Arthur Schwartz-Leo Robin score, including "A Gal in Calico" and "Rainy Night in Rio." No relation to 1929 musical of same name.

Time to Die, A (1983) **C-91m. *½** D: Matt Cimber. Rex Harrison, Rod Taylor, Edward Albert, Jr., Raf Vallone, Linn Stokke. Deadening time-waster with WW2 veteran Albert seeking out the six killers of his wife. Based on a story by Mario Puzo, and filmed in 1979. Originally titled SEVEN GRAVES FOR ROGAN.▼

Time to Kill (1942) **61m. **** D: Herbert I. Leeds. Lloyd Nolan, Ralph Byrd, Heather Angel, Doris Merrick, Richard Lane. Michael Shayne (Nolan) versus counterfeiters of rare coins. Adequate entry in the series, sparked by Nolan's tough-guy performance. Though a Mike Shayne movie, it's based on a Raymond Chandler story; remade as THE BRASHER DOUBLOON.

Time to Live, A (1985) **C-100m.** TVM D: Rick Wallace. Liza Minnelli, Jeffrey DeMunn, Swoosie Kurtz, Scott Schwartz, Corey Haim. Liza made her TV-movie debut with a riveting performance as a mother who must cope with her young son's struggles with muscular dystrophy. John McGreevey's sensitive script was adapted from the touching book *Intensive Care* by Mary-Lou Weisman (whom Minnelli plays). Above average.▼

Time to Love and a Time to Die, A (1958) **C-132m. ***** D: Douglas Sirk. John Gavin, Lilo Pulver, Jock Mahoney, Don DeFore, Keenan Wynn, Thayer David, Dana (Jim) Hutton, Klaus Kinski. Intensely dramatic love story set against background of WW2. German soldier on furlough from battle falls in love, inevitably must return to the trenches. Well-directed version of Erich Maria Remarque novel (with the author in a small role). Hutton's film debut.▼

Time To Sing, A (1968) **C-92m. *½** D: Arthur Dreifuss. Hank Williams, Jr., Ed Begley, Shelley Fabares, Charles Robinson, D'Urville Martin, Donald Woods, Clara Ward. Down-home tale of Williams suppressing love for singing to please uncle-guardian (Begley). Script aimed at 10-year-old mentality, matched by Williams' wooden performance.

Time to Triumph, A (1986) **C-100m.** TVM D: Noel Black. Patty Duke, Joseph Bologna, Julie Bovasso, Denise B. Mickelbury, Dara Modglin, Jackie Welch. Duke plays real-life Concetta Hassan, who's forced to become family breadwinner when her construction worker husband is felled by a heart attack . . . and earns her way as an Army helicopter pilot. Average.

Time Trackers (1989) **C-87m.** *½ D: Howard R. Cohen. Ned Beatty, Wil Shriner, Kathleen Beller, Bridget Hoffman, Alex Hyde-White, Lee Bergere, Robert Cornthwaite. Tepid sci-fi tale about group from the future chasing down evil genius determined to use time travel to alter history in his favor. Beatty is a 20th-century cop accidentally picked up along the way. Some laughs at the beginning, but spends far too long (most of the film in fact) in medieval England.

Time Travelers, The (1964) **C-82m.** **½ D: Ib Melchior. Preston Foster, Philip Carey, Merry Anders, John Hoyt, Steve Franken. Spirited flashes of imagination heighten this sci-fi story about scientists who journey into the future and find their actions there will affect the past. Not bad, with downbeat ending; one of the first American films photographed by Vilmos Zsigmond.▼

Time Travelers (1976) **C-78m.** TVM D: Alexander Singer. Sam Groom, Tom Hallick, Richard Basehart, Trish Stewart, Francine York, Booth Coleman. Producer Irwin Allen's attempt to resurrect his flop series, *Time Tunnel,* has two scientists searching for cure to a mysterious epidemic and finding themselves in Chicago 1871 on the eve of the great fire. Footage from IN OLD CHICAGO is better than any of the new stuff. Taken from an original, unpublished short story by Rod Serling. Average.

Time Walker (1982) **C-83m.** BOMB D: Tom Kennedy. Ben Murphy, Nina Axelrod, Kevin Brophy, James Karen, Shari Belafonte-Harper, Antoinette Bower. Alien, buried in King Tut's tomb, is unwrapped and wreaks havoc. Low-budget junk.▼

Time Without Pity (1956-British) **88m.** **½ D: Joseph Losey. Michael Redgrave, Alec McCowen, Ann Todd, Peter Cushing, Leo McKern, Renee Houston, Lois Maxwell, Joan Plowright. Tense little film of father's effort to prove son's innocence of murder charge; occasionally overly talky. From an Emlyn Williams play.

Tin Drum, The (1979-German) **C-142m.** **** D: Volker Schlondorff. David Bennent, Mario Adorf, Angela Winkler, Daniel Olbrychski, Katharina Thalbach, Heinz Bennent, Andrea Ferreol, Charles Aznavour. Mesmerizing adaptation of the Gunter Grass novel. Three-year-old Oskar (David Bennent) ceases to grow physically as the Nazis take power in Germany and beats out his anger on his drum. A "realistic fantasy" with superb acting, particularly by 12-year-old Bennent. Memorable sequence after memorable sequence; deservedly won a Best Foreign Film Academy Award.▼

Tingler, The (1959) **82m.** **½ D: William Castle. Vincent Price, Judith Evelyn, Darryl Hickman, Philip Coolidge, Patricia Cutts. Preposterous but certainly original shocker: coroner Price discovers that fear causes a creepy-crawly creature to grow on people's spines; it can only be subdued by screaming. This is the infamous picture that got moviegoers into the spirit with electrical buzzers under selected theater seats! Also noteworthy as likely the earliest film depicting someone taking a trip on LSD. Most TV prints are missing crucial color sequence.

Tin Men (1987) **C-112m.** **½ D: Barry Levinson. Richard Dreyfuss, Danny DeVito, Barbara Hershey, John Mahoney, Jackie Gayle, Stanley Brock, Seymour Cassel, Bruno Kirby, J. T. Walsh, Michael Tucker. Writer-director Levinson returns to DINER territory (literally—it's set in 1963 Baltimore) for a melancholy comedy-drama about a hustler (Dreyfuss) and a loser (DeVito), both in the aluminum-siding business, whose lives converge after their cars meet in an accident. Some fine comedy and pointed observations on human nature are undermined by unresolved ideas and inconsistencies in the way the characters behave. Stand-up comic Gayle is hilarious as DeVito's partner, who has *Bonanza* on the brain.▼

Tin Pan Alley (1940) **94m.** *** D: Walter Lang. Alice Faye, Betty Grable, Jack Oakie, John Payne, Esther Ralston, Allen Jenkins, Nicholas Brothers, John Loder, Elisha Cook, Jr. Predictable plot of struggling pre-WW1 songwriters enlivened by Alfred Newman's Oscar-winning score and colorful numbers including "Sheik of Araby" with Billy Gilbert as sultan. Oakie is in top form. Remade as I'LL GET BY.

Tin Star, The (1957) **93m.** *** D: Anthony Mann. Henry Fonda, Anthony Perkins, Betsy Palmer, Neville Brand, Lee Van Cleef, John McIntire, Michel Ray. Fledgling sheriff Perkins turns to bounty hunter Fonda to help combat outlaws preying on his town; solid, well-acted Western. Scripted by Dudley Nichols.▼

Tintorera (1977-British-Mexican) **C-91m.** BOMB D: Rene Cardona, Jr. Susan George, Hugo Stiglitz, Andres Garcia, Fiona Lewis, Jennifer Ashley, Priscilla Barnes, Laura Lyons. Can two Mexican shark hunters find satisfaction with an assortment of vacationing beauties from England and the

U.S.? That's the main issue of this listless JAWS ripoff, loaded with gore and nude scenes.▼

Tip Off, The (1931) 75m. **½ D: Albert Rogell. Eddie Quillan, Robert Armstrong, Ginger Rogers, Joan Peers, Ralf Harolde, Charles Sellon, Mike Donlin. Naive Quillan, with the help of boxer Armstrong and spunky Rogers, manages to avoid trouble after he commences a romance with a gangster's girl. Zippy little programmer.

Tip on a Dead Jockey (1957) 99m. *** D: Richard Thorpe. Dorothy Malone, Robert Taylor, Gia Scala, Martin Gabel, Jack Lord. Neat account of Taylor tied in with smuggling syndicate in Madrid, romancing Malone. Good Charles Lederer adaptation of Irwin Shaw story.

Titan Find SEE: **Creature**▼

Titanic (1953) 98m. *** D: Jean Negulesco. Clifton Webb, Barbara Stanwyck, Robert Wagner, Richard Basehart, Audrey Dalton, Thelma Ritter, Brian Aherne. Hollywoodized version of sea tragedy centers on shipboard story. Not bad, but events better told in A NIGHT TO REMEMBER. Oscarwinning script by producer Charles Brackett, Walter Reisch, and Richard Breen.

Titan—Story of Michelangelo, The (1950) 68m. *** D: Richard Lyford. Narrated by Fredric March. Evocative documentary portrait of the great artist, capturing the man through his work. Originally a Swiss film made in 1940, it was reedited for U.S. release by Robert Snyder, and won an Oscar as Best Documentary. ▼

Titfield Thunderbolt, The (1953-British) C-84m. *** D: Charles Crichton. Stanley Holloway, George Relph, Naunton Wayne, John Gregson, Godfrey Tearle, Edie Martin, Hugh Griffith, Sid James, Jack MacGowran. Boisterous Ealing comedy about villagers who are attached to their antiquated railway line and run it themselves in competition with the local bus line. Lovely photography by Douglas Slocombe. Script by T.E.B. Clarke.

T-Men (1947) 96m. *** D: Anthony Mann. Dennis O'Keefe, June Lockhart, Alfred Ryder, Charles McGraw, Wallace Ford, Mary Meade. Semidocumentary-style story of undercover treasury agents trying to get to the bottom of counterfeit ring. Vividly exciting; director Mann and cameraman John Alton went out of their way to use unusual, effective lighting and compositions in this A-1 film.▼

T.N.T. Jackson (1974) C-73m. ** D: Cirio Santiago. Jeanne Bell, Stan Shaw, Pat Anderson, Ken Metcalf, OK Filipinoshot black actioner with statuesque former Playmate Bell as karate expert searching for her missing brother and kicking the hell out of anyone who gets in her way. A blaxploitation favorite, no doubt for the curious way Bell's shirts get torn off at the start of every fight scene.▼

To All My Friends On Shore (1971) C-74m. TVM D: Gilbert Cates. Bill Cosby, Gloria Foster, Dennis Hines, Ray Mason, Dennis Pate. Problems confronted in fatherson relationship when they get word that child has incurable disease. Uneven performances, but film's conception and point of view exceptionally strong, refreshing. Above average.▼

Toast of New Orleans, The (1950) C-97m. **½ D: Norman Taurog. Kathryn Grayson, Mario Lanza, David Niven, Rita Moreno, J. Carrol Naish. Lanza plays fisherman transformed into operatic star. Rest of cast good, and Lanza sings "Be My Love."▼

Toast of New York, The (1937) 109m. *** D: Rowland V. Lee. Edward Arnold, Cary Grant, Frances Farmer, Jack Oakie, Donald Meek, Clarence Kolb, Billy Gilbert, Stanley Fields. Arnold is in fine form as rags-to-riches businessman Jim Fisk in late 19th century. Grant is his partner in hokey but entertaining biographical fiction; good showcase for spirited Farmer.▼

Tobacco Road (1941) 84m. **½ D: John Ford. Charley Grapewin, Marjorie Rambeau, Gene Tierney, William Tracy, Elizabeth Patterson, Dana Andrews, Ward Bond. Southern degradation is theme of cleaned-up filmization of Erskine Caldwell hit play, well directed by Ford with good cast; punch isn't always there, though. Script by Nunnally Johnson.

To Bed . . . Or Not To Bed (1963-Italian) 103m. **½ D: Gian Luigi Polidoro. Alberto Sordi, Bernhard Tarschys, Inger Sjostrand, Ulf Palme. Saucy sex romp with Sordi expecting to find free love on business trip to Stockholm, discovering home sweet home is best. Retitled: THE DEVIL.

To Begin Again (1982-Spanish) C-93m. *** D: Jose Luis Garci. Antonio Ferrandis, Encarna Paso, Jose Bodalo, Agustin Gonzalez, Pablo Hoyo. Distinguished—and dying—professor Ferrandis revisits Spain, where he journeys through his past and romances old flame Paso. Sweetly sentimental; Oscar winner for Best Foreign Film.

To Be or Not To Be (1942) 99m. ***½ D: Ernst Lubitsch. Jack Benny, Carole Lombard, Robert Stack, Lionel Atwill, Felix Bressart, Sig Ruman, Tom Dugan, Helmut Dantine, Stanley Ridges. Benny has the role of a lifetime as "that great, great actor" Joseph Tura, whose Polish theatre troupe is put out of business by invading Nazis—until they become involved in espionage and find their thespian skills being put to the ultimate test. Superb black comedy scripted by Edwin Justus Mayer; the opening gag with Dugan is a gem.

Lombard's final film, released after her death. Remade in 1983.▼

To Be or Not To Be (1983) **C-108m.** **½ D. Alan Johnson. Mel Brooks, Anne Bancroft, Charles Durning, Tim Matheson, Jose Ferrer, James Haake, Christopher Lloyd, George Gaynes, George Wyner, Jack Riley, Lewis J. Stadlen. Remake of 1942 classic follows the original almost scene for scene, with Brooks and Bancroft—in fine comic form—as stars of Polish theater who become involved with invading Nazis. Offers more laughs than the original film, but less substance; incessant schtick undermines occasional attempts at poignancy.▼

Tobor the Great (1954) 77m. *½ D: Lee Sholem. Charles Drake, Karin Booth, Billy Chapin, Taylor Holmes, Steven Geray. Weak sci-fi adventure of enemy agents plotting to capture secret robot plans; terrible acting and dialogue. A botched attempt at a heartwarming sci-fi comedy-thriller.▼

Tobruk (1967) **C-110m.** **½ D: Arthur Hiller. Rock Hudson, George Peppard, Nigel Green, Guy Stockwell, Jack Watson, Leo Gordon, Norman Rossington, Percy Herbert, Liam Redmond. WW2 actioner of Allies trying to destroy Rommel's fuel supply in the Sahara, bogs down in pretentiousness, much social comment, etc. Gordon also wrote the screenplay.▼

Toby Tyler, or Ten Weeks with a Circus (1960) **C-96m.** **½ D: Charles Barton. Kevin Corcoran, Henry Calvin, Gene Sheldon, Bob Sweeney, Richard Eastham, James Drury. Likable Disney fare about a young boy who runs away to join the circus at the turn of the century.▼

To Catch a King (1984) **C-113m.** **TVM D: Clive Donner. Robert Wagner, Teri Garr, Horst Janson, Barbara Parkins, John Standing, Marcel Bozzuffi, Jane Lapotaire, Barry Foster. So-so espionage thriller, written by Harry Patterson (also known as novelist Jack Higgins), about a fanciful Nazi plot to kidnap the Duke and Duchess of Windsor from Lisbon in 1940, and the efforts of nightclub singer Garr and cafe owner Wagner to thwart it. Made for cable. Average.▼

To Catch a Spy (1971-British-French) **C-94m.** *½ D: Dick Clement. Kirk Douglas, Marlene Jobert, Trevor Howard, Tom Courtenay, Patrick Mower, Bernadette Lafont, Bernard Blier. Feeble comedy-mystery of events resulting when Jobert's new husband is arrested by the Russians as a spy; Douglas is a mystery man, Courtenay a bumbling British agent. Also known as CATCH ME A SPY.▼

To Catch a Thief (1955) **C-106m.** *** D: Alfred Hitchcock. Grace Kelly, Cary Grant, Jessie Royce Landis, John Williams, Charles Vanel, Brigitte Auber. The French Riviera serves as picturesque backdrop for this entertaining (if fluffy) Hitchcock caper with Grant as reformed cat burglar suspected in new wave of jewel robberies. Chic and elegant in every way—and Kelly never looked more ravishing. Script (including much-imitated fireworks scene) by John Michael Hayes; Oscar-winning photography by Robert Burks.▼

To Commit a Murder (1967-French) **C-91m.** *½ D: Edouard Molinaro. Louis Jourdan, Senta Berger, Edmond O'Brien, Bernard Blier, Fabrizzio Capucci. Playboy/writer Jourdan gets involved with a plot to abduct French nuclear scientist; interesting idea poorly handled.

Today We Live (1933) 113m. ** D: Howard Hawks. Joan Crawford, Gary Cooper, Robert Young, Franchot Tone, Roscoe Karns. Stilted William Faulkner story of WW1 romance and heroism; despite star-studded cast, not much. Faulkner cowrote the screenplay.

Todd Killings, The (1971) **C-93m.** ** D: Barry Shear. Robert F. Lyons, Richard Thomas, Barbara Bel Geddes, Sherry Miles, Gloria Grahame, Edward Asner, Belinda Montgomery. Good cast in sleazy story of hip girl-getter Lyons actually involved in series of murders. Retitled A DANGEROUS FRIEND.▼

To Die For (1989) **C-90m.** *½ D: Deran Sarafian. Brendan Hughes, Sydney Walsh, Amanda Wyss, Scott Jacoby, Micah Grant, Steve Bond. Dracula legend is updated to modern-day, morally decadent L.A., but the results are strictly second-rate. Vampire "Vlad Tepish" sets his sights on sexy real-estate agent Walsh—apparently unaware that realtors in L.A. are a bloodless lot.▼

To Die in Madrid (1965-French) 87m. **** D: Frederic Rossif. Narrated by John Gielgud and Irene Worth. Masterpiece in documentary filmmaking dealing with bloody civil war in Spain in which more than a million people died.

To Die in Paris (1968) **C-100m.** **TVM D: Charles Dubin, Allen Reisner. Louis Jourdan, Kurt Krueger, Robert Ellenstein, John Marley, Ludwig Donath, Letitia Roman. Exploits of head of resistance in Paris during WW2 who, imprisoned during ordinary round up of suspicious characters, must prevent captors from realizing who he is and be on look-out for assassin sent by underground. Good tension. Average.

To Die of Love (1972-French) **C-110m.** **½ D: Andre Cayatte. Annie Girardot, Bruno Pradal, Francois Simon, Monique Melinand, Nathalie Nell, Nicolas Dumayet. Girardot's superb performance carries true story about French schoolteacher who was driven to suicide after she was forced to abandon 16-year-old student she loved.

More interesting for subject matter than for actual execution.

To Each His Own (1946) **122m.** *** D: Mitchell Leisen. Olivia de Havilland, John Lund, Mary Anderson, Roland Culver, Philip Terry, Griff Barnett. Well-turned soaper of unwed mother giving up baby, lavishing love on him as his "aunt" without revealing truth. Fine support by Culver as aging Olivia's beau. De Havilland won Best Actress Oscar. Lund's film debut.

To Elvis, With Love SEE: **Touched by Love**▼

To Find a Man (1972) **C-90m.** *** D: Buzz Kulik. Pamela (Sue) Martin, Darren O'Connor, Lloyd Bridges, Phyllis Newman, Tom Ewell, Tom Bosley. Solid comedy-drama about two high-schoolers' attempts to find an abortionist. Study of friendships is good, and exceedingly fine acting of youthful leads is a definite plus.

To Find My Son (1980) **C-100m. TVM** D: Delbert Mann. Richard Thomas, Justin Dana, Molly Cheek, Julie Cobb, Steve Kanaly, Allyn Ann McLerie. Poignant story (written by Sandor Stern) about a single man's battle to adopt a handicapped 7-year-old orphan. Average.

To Forget Venice (1979-Italian) **C-110m.** ** D: Franco Brusati. Erland Josephson, Mariangela Melato, Elenora Giorgi, David Pontremoli. Two pairs of homosexuals (male and female) come to grips with each other at the country estate of a dying opera star. So-so drama managed an Oscar nomination for Best Foreign Film.▼

Together? (1979-Italian) **C-100m.** *½ D: Armenia Balducci. Jacqueline Bisset, Maximilian Schell, Terence Stamp, Monica Guerritore. Bisset and neurotic lover Schell argue, eat, argue, talk about sex, argue, have sex, argue some more. And the viewer gets a migraine. Originally titled I LOVE YOU, I LOVE YOU NOT.▼

Together Again (1944) **100m.** *** D: Charles Vidor. Irene Dunne, Charles Boyer, Charles Coburn, Mona Freeman, Elizabeth Patterson. Little bit of nothing carried off beautifully by Dunne, widow mayor of small town, and Boyer, suave New Yorker whom she hires to sculpt a statue of her late husband; charming comedy.

Together Brothers (1974) **C-94m.** **½ D: William A. Graham. Anthony Wilson, Ahmad Nurradin, Glynn Turman, Richard Yniguez, Lincoln Kilpatrick, Owen Pace. Suspense thriller with five young blacks scouring ghetto for the killer of their policeman friend. Violent treatment balanced by sensitive character studies.

Togetherness (1970) **C-103m.** ** D: Arthur Marks. George Hamilton, Peter Lawford, John Banner, Olinka Berova, Jesse White. American playboy Hamilton woos Communist athlete Berova in this dated comedy filmed in Greece.

To Have and Have Not (1944) **100m.** ***½ D: Howard Hawks. Humphrey Bogart, Walter Brennan, Lauren Bacall, Hoagy Carmichael, Dan Seymour, Marcel Dalio, Dolores Moran, Sheldon Leonard. Hemingway's "worst novel" forms the basis for Hawks' version of CASABLANCA: tough skipper-for-hire Bogart reluctantly becomes involved with French Resistance, less reluctantly woos even tougher Bacall (in her film debut). Their legendary love scenes make the movie, but there are also solid performances, taut action, and a couple of songs. (Andy Williams was hired to dub Bacall's singing, but that's her voice, after all.) Super dialogue by William Faulkner and Jules Furthman; remade as THE BREAKING POINT and THE GUN RUNNERS. Also shown in computer-colored version.▼

To Heal a Nation (1988) **C-100m. TVM** D: Michael Pressman. Eric Roberts, Glynnis O'Connor, Marshall Colt, Scott Paulin, Lee Purcell, Laurence Luckinbill, Linden Chiles, Brock Peters. Earnest drama about Vietnam vet Jan Scruggs, who spearheaded the campaign to build the Vietnam Veterans Memorial in Washington. Talky but powerful script by Lionel Chetwynd (based on the book by Scruggs and Joel L. Swerdlow), with closing scenes that pack a wallop. Above average.

To Hell and Back (1955) **C-106m.** *** D: Jesse Hibbs. Audie Murphy, Marshall Thompson, Susan Kohner, Charles Drake, Gregg Palmer, Jack Kelly, David Janssen. Murphy (the most decorated soldier of WW2) stars in very good war film based on his autobiography, with excellent battle sequences making up for uneven script.▼

To Joy (1949-Swedish) **95m.** **½ D: Ingmar Bergman. Stig Olin, Maj-Britt Nilsson, John Ekman, Margit Carlquist, Victor Seastrom, Birger Malmsten. Early Bergman drama is of interest mostly because it offers a thematic prelude of what was to come from the filmmaker. Otherwise, it's a modest, occasionally insightful chronicle of Olin and Nilsson's failing marriage.▼

To Kill a Clown (1972) **C-104m.** ** D: George Bloomfield. Alan Alda, Blythe Danner, Heath Lamberts, Eric Clavering. Couple whose marriage is on the rocks get trapped on island off New England coast by crippled, deranged Vietnam veteran. Weird mixture of traditional chiller film elements and topical considerations.▼

To Kill a Cop (1978) **C-200m. TVM** D: Gary Nelson. Joe Don Baker, Louis Gossett, Jr., Patrick O'Neal, Desi Arnaz, Jr., Christine Belford, Eartha Kitt, Rosey Grier. Police action drama about a maverick chief of detectives, a string of cop killings, and a black revolutionary leader plotting a police massacre. Based on the best-seller by

Robert Daley, it became the pilot to the *Eischied* series. Average.

To Kill a Mockingbird (1962) **129m.** ***½ D: Robert Mulligan. Gregory Peck, Mary Badham, Philip Alford, John Megna, Brock Peters, Robert Duvall, Frank Overton, Rosemary Murphy, Paul Fix, Collin Wilcox, Alice Ghostley, William Windom. Peck won Oscar as Southern lawyer who defends black (Peters) accused of rape, and tries to explain proceedings to his children and their friends. Leisurely paced, flavorful adaptation of Harper Lee novel; Horton Foote's screenplay also earned an Oscar. Duvall's film debut.▼

To Kill a Priest (1988-U.S.-French) **C-117m.** ** D: Agnieska Holland. Ed Harris, Christopher Lambert, David Suchet, Joss Ackland, Tim Roth, Joanne Whalley, Peter Postlethwaite, Timothy Spall, Cherie Lunghi. Well-intentioned but inept drama about ill-fated Polish priest Lambert (a character based on Father Jerzy Popieluszko, who supported the country's trade unionists and paid for his activism with his life); here he tangles with bullying secret policeman Harris. Director Holland may be a Polish exile, but the film only superficially explores the plight of her country.▼

Tokyo After Dark (1959) **80m.** ** D: Norman Herman. Michi Kobi, Richard Long, Lawrence Dobkin, Paul Dubov, Butch Yamaoto. Uninspired account of military cop Long on the lam in Tokyo from unintentional homicide.

Tokyo Joe (1949) **88m.** **½ D: Stuart Heisler. Humphrey Bogart, Florence Marly, Sessue Hayakawa, Alexander Knox, Jerome Courtland. Lesser Bogart film about American in post-war Tokyo pulled into smuggling and blackmail for the sake of his ex-wife and child.▼

Tokyo Olympiad (1966-Japanese) **C-93m.** **½ D: Kon Ichikawa. If you're lucky enough to see the superb original version of this documentary about the 1964 Olympics, shoot this rating to ***½. This one was cut down for U.S. release and virtually destroyed by insipid narration; however, the original 170m. print did play the 1984 New York Film Festival and is now available on video.▼

Tokyo Pop (1988) **C-99m.** **½ D: Fran Rubel Kazui. Carrie Hamilton, Yutaka Tadokoro, Taiji Tonoyama, Tetsuro Tamba, Masumi Harukawa. Trifling if occasionally amusing tale of what happens when punk rocker Hamilton treks off to Japan in search of celebrity. The West-meets-East theme has possibilities, but the result is curiously slight (despite Hamilton's winning performance). By the way, she's the daughter of Carol Burnett.▼

Tokyo Rose (1945) **69m.** ** D: Lew Landers. Byron Barr, Osa Massen, Don Douglas, Richard Loo, Keye Luke, Grace Lem,

Leslie Fong, H. T. Tsiang. Timid drama of slinky female propagandist for Axis during WW2.

Tokyo Story (1953-Japanese) **134m.** **** D: Yasujiro Ozu. Chishu Ryu, Chieko Higashiyama, So Yamamura, Haruko Sugimura, Setsuko Hara. An elderly couple (Ryu, Higashiyama) visit their children in Tokyo, who are too busy living their lives and treat them tactlessly. Quietly powerful story of old age, the disappointments parents experience with their children, and the fears the young have of time passing. A masterpiece.▼

Tol'able David (1921) **80m.** **½ D: Henry King. Richard Barthelmess, Gladys Hulette, Ernest Torrence, Warner Richmond, Walter P. Lewis. Celebrated silent film is a little faded now but still fairly charming backwoods tale of young Barthelmess standing up to trouble from three convicts who move to town. Remade in 1930.

To Live and Die in L.A. (1985) **C-116m.** *½ D: William Friedkin. William L. Petersen, Willem Dafoe, John Pankow, Debra Feuer, John Turturro, Darlanne Fluegel, Dean Stockwell. Gritty movie equivalent of TV's *Miami Vice* makes it hard to root for anyone, since the good guys are as sleazy as the bad guys! Petersen plays hotshot Secret Service agent going after slimy counterfeiter—but for a crack federal agent he acts pretty dumb! Friedkin supplies one spectacular car chase, but it's not enough to counteract bad taste the film leaves behind.▼

Toll Gate, The (1920) **59m.** *** D: Lambert Hillyer. William S. Hart, Anna Q. Nilsson, Jack Richardson, Joseph Singleton, Richard Headrick. One of Hart's best films, casting him as fleeing outlaw who stops to save young boy's life, becomes involved with the child's widowed mother.

Toma (1973) **C-74m.** TVM D: Richard Heffron. Tony Musante, Simon Oakland, Susan Strasberg, Nicholas Colasanto, Robert Yuro, Abe Vigoda, Dave Toma, Philip Michael Thomas. Leader of syndicate numbers racket stalked by disguise-master undercover policeman. Excellent lead performance by Musante in challenging role, as he pleads with superiors for less interference and sweats it out when his family becomes syndicate hostages. Written by Edward Hume, Gerald DiPago, based on a true story. Pilot for brief series which later transmogrified into *Baretta*. Above average.

Tomahawk (1951) **C-82m.** **½ D: George Sherman. Yvonne De Carlo, Van Heflin, Preston Foster, Jack Oakie, Alex Nicol, Tom Tully, Rock Hudson. Colorful Western spiked with sufficient action to overcome bland account of friction between redskins and the army.

To Mary—With Love (1936) **86m.** **½ D: John Cromwell. Warner Baxter, Myrna

[1197]

Loy, Ian Hunter, Claire Trevor, Jean Dixon, Pat Somerset. Dated drama of Baxter and Loy having stormy period of marriage but ending up loving each other more than ever.

Tomb of Ligeia (1965-British) **C-81m.** *** D: Roger Corman. Vincent Price, Elizabeth Shepherd, John Westbrook, Richard Johnson, Derek Francis. Price's late wife seems to be manifesting herself all over the place, both as a cat and in new bride Shepherd. Super-stylish chiller with superb location work. The last of Corman's eight Poe adaptations; screenplay by Robert Towne.▼

Tomb of the Living Dead SEE: **Mad Doctor of Blood Island**▼

Tomboy (1985) **C-92m.** BOMB D: Herb Freed. Betsy Russell, Jerry Dinome, Dinome (Gerard Christopher), Kristi Somers, Richard Erdman, Cynthia Ann Thompson. Bottom-of-the-barrel formula teenage sex tease film. Role reversal is stressed as Russell is an automotive wiz determined to outrace and win the romantic favor of handsome Dinome. ▼

Tomboy and the Champ (1961) **C-92m.** ** D: Francis D. Lyon. Candy Moore, Ben Johnson, Jesse White, Jess Kirkpatrick, Rex Allen. Mild B film about a young girl and her prize cow; strictly for children, who will probably enjoy it, despite standard plot devices.▼

Tom Brown of Culver (1932) **82m.** **½ D: William Wyler. Tom Brown, H. B. Warner, Richard Cromwell, Slim Summerville, Ben Alexander, Sidney Toler, Russell Hopton, Andy Devine. Well-made but corny military-school picture has Tom Brown in namesake role of American who goes from rebel to role model at famed British academy. Tyrone Power (billed as Jr.) makes his screen debut here, and reportedly Alan Ladd can be spotted in a bit part. Remade as SPIRIT OF CULVER.

Tom Brown's School Days (1940) **86m.** **½ D: Robert Stevenson. Cedric Hardwicke, Freddie Bartholomew, Gale Storm, Jimmy Lydon, Josephine Hutchinson, Billy Halop, Polly Moran. Occasionally overbaked but still entertaining, fast-paced account of life at a Victorian boys' school. Although most of cast is American, British flavor seeps through. Retitled: ADVENTURES AT RUGBY.▼

Tom Brown's Schooldays (1951-British) **93m.** ***½ D: Gordon Parry. John Howard Davies, Robert Newton, James Hayter, John Charlesworth, Hermione Baddeley. Well-acted film of Victorian England school life with exceptional British cast and good direction.▼

Tom, Dick and Harry (1941) **86m.** ***½ D: Garson Kanin. Ginger Rogers, George Murphy, Alan Marshal, Burgess Meredith, Joe Cunningham, Jane Seymour, Phil Silvers. Spirited comic dilemma as wide-eyed Ginger chooses among three anxious suitors: sincere Murphy, wealthy Marshal, nonconformist Meredith. Silvers has hilarious role as obnoxious ice-cream man. Written by Paul Jarrico. Remade as THE GIRL MOST LIKELY.▼

Tom Horn (1980) **C-98m.** *½ D: William Wiard. Steve McQueen, Linda Evans, Richard Farnsworth, Billy Green Bush, Slim Pickens, Elisha Cook. McQueen's next-to-last film is beautifully shot, otherwise deadly Western about the final days of real-life Wyoming bounty hunter. See also MR. HORN, a TVM with David Carradine in the title role.▼

Tom Jones (1963-British) **C-129m.** **** D: Tony Richardson. Albert Finney, Susannah York, Hugh Griffith, Edith Evans, Joyce Redman, Diane Cilento, Joan Greenwood, David Tomlinson, Peter Bull, David Warner. High-spirited adaptation of the Henry Fielding novel about a young man's misadventures and bawdy experiences in 18th-century England; rowdy, randy, and completely disarming. Academy Award winner as Best Picture, it also won Oscars for Richardson, who directed with great flair and imagination, screenwriter John Osborne, who caught the gritty flavor of the period to perfection, and composer John Addison, whose infectious score suits the picture to a tee. Film debut of Lynn Redgrave. Richardson cut the film by seven minutes for its 1989 reissue.▼

Tommy (1975-British) **C-111m.** *** D: Ken Russell. Roger Daltrey, Ann-Margret, Oliver Reed, Elton John, Eric Clapton, Keith Moon, Robert Powell, Tina Turner, Jack Nicholson. Energetic rendering of The Who's best-selling rock opera, with standout musical performances by Clapton, John (who sings "Pinball Wizard") and Turner. Loss of multi-channel sound on TV may diminish effectiveness.▼

Tommy Steele Story, The SEE: **Rock Around the World**

Tomorrow (1972) **103m.** ***½ D: Joseph Anthony. Robert Duvall, Olga Bellin, Sudie Bond, Richard McConnell, Peter Masterson, William Hawley. Overlooked Faulkner story about a handyman who cares for and eventually falls in love with an abandoned pregnant woman. Bellin is excellent, Duvall astonishingly good in best-ever screen presentation of the author's work. Screenplay by Horton Foote.▼

Tomorrow at Ten (1964-British) **80m.** **½ D: Lance Comfort. John Gregson, Robert Shaw, Alec Clunes, Alan Wheatley. Taut drama involving kidnapper who dies, leaving boy in house (whereabouts unknown) with time bomb set to explode.

Tomorrow Is Another Day (1951) **90m.** **½ D: Felix E. Feist. Ruth Roman, Steve Cochran, Lurene Tuttle, Ray Teal, Morris

Ankrum. Frank little film of ex-con Cochran marrying dime-a-dance girl Roman, heading for California, thinking he's killed her old boyfriend.

Tomorrow Is Forever (1946) **105m.** *** D: Irving Pichel. Claudette Colbert, Orson Welles, George Brent, Lucile Watson, Richard Long, Natalie Wood. Weepy rehash of *Enoch Arden*, with Welles as man listed dead in war, returning with new face to find wife Colbert remarried to Brent. Bravura work by Welles with good support by Wood as his adopted daughter.

Tomorrow Never Comes (1977-Canadian-British) **C-109m.** ** D: Peter Collinson. Oliver Reed, Susan George, Raymond Burr, John Ireland, Stephen McHattie, Donald Pleasence. Young man goes bananas when he learns his girlfriend has been unfaithful, leading to violent standoff with police in busy resort town. Uninvolving melodrama.▼

Tomorrow's Child (1982) **C-100m.** TVM D: Joseph Sargent. Stephanie Zimbalist, William Atherton, Bruce Davison, Ed Flanders, Salome Jens, James Shigeta, Susan Oliver, Arthur Hill. So-so drama about surrogate motherhood and test-tube babies, written by Jerry McNeely. Original title, GENESIS, said it better. Average.▼

Tomorrow the World (1944) **86m.** ***½ D: Leslie Fenton. Fredric March, Betty Field, Agnes Moorehead, Skippy Homeier, Joan Carroll, Boots Brown. Thoughtful drama based on Broadway play of American couple adopting German boy, trying to undo rigid Nazi influence in him.

Tom Sawyer (1930) **86m.** **½ D: John Cromwell. Jackie Coogan, Mitzi Green, Junior Durkin, Jackie Searle, Clara Blandick, Lucien Littlefield. Enjoyable but slow-moving adaptation of the Mark Twain classic. Coogan, Green, Durkin, and Searle are, respectively, Tom, Becky Thatcher, Huck Finn, and Sid Sawyer; they all repeated their roles the following year in HUCKLEBERRY FINN. Remade in 1938 (as THE ADVENTURES OF TOM SAWYER) and twice in 1973.

Tom Sawyer (1973) **C-104m.** *** D: Don Taylor. Johnnie Whitaker, Celeste Holm, Warren Oates, Jeff East, Jodie Foster. Well-crafted musical remake of Tom Sawyer, the boy wonder of Hannibal, Mo., and his friends Huckleberry Finn and Becky Thatcher. Songs by Richard M. and Robert B. Sherman.▼

Tom Sawyer (1973) **C-78m.** TVM D: James Neilson. Josh Albee, Jeff Tyler, Jane Wyatt, Buddy Ebsen, Vic Morrow, John McGiver, Karen Pearson, Chris Wiggins. Tom and Huck exude their ever-lovin' charm in this acceptable retelling of their now-familiar tale, with Morrow a particularly nasty Injun Joe in one of the best of his evil turns. This version premiered several weeks before the musicalized theatrical one. Video title: THE ADVENTURES OF TOM SAWYER. Average.▼

Tom Sawyer, Detective (1938) **68m.** **½ D: Louis King. Billy Cook, Donald O'Connor, Porter Hall, Phillip Warren, Janet Waldo, Elizabeth Risdon, William Haade. Pleasant little family film based on Mark Twain's novella that turns Tom (Cook) and Huck (O'Connor) into backwoods detectives investigating a mysterious murder involving a long-lost twin, and attempting to clear the name of local preacher Hall.

tom thumb (1958) **C-98m.** ***½ D: George Pal. Russ Tamblyn, June Thorburn, Peter Sellers, Terry-Thomas, Alan Young, Jessie Matthews, Bernard Miles. Excellent children's picture with Tamblyn as tiny tom thumb, taken in by kindly couple but exploited by villainous Terry-Thomas and henchman Sellers. Charming Puppetoons sequences, Oscar-winning special effects, perfect Peggy Lee-Sonny Burke score.▼

Tonight and Every Night (1945) **C-92m.** *** D: Victor Saville. Rita Hayworth, Janet Blair, Lee Bowman, Marc Platt, Leslie Brooks, Professor Lamberti, Florence Bates. Entertaining wartime musical of British theater that never misses a performance, despite bombings and personal hardships. Try spotting Shelley Winters as one of the chorines.▼

Tonight at 8:30 (1952-British) **C-81m.** *** D: Anthony Pelissier. Valerie Hobson, Nigel Patrick, Jack Warner, Kay Walsh, Ted Ray, Martita Hunt, Stanley Holloway, Betty Ann Davies. Three Noel Coward one-act plays ideally transferred to film. Original British title: MEET ME TONIGHT.

Tonight's the Night (1954) **C-88m.** *** D: Mario Zampi. David Niven, Yvonne De Carlo, Barry Fitzgerald, George Cole, Robert Urquhart. Good British cast bolsters appealing comedy about house in Ireland which natives claim is haunted.

Tonight's the Night (1987) **C-100m.** TVM D: Bobby Roth. Ed Marinaro, Ken Olin, Max Gail, Robert Rusler, Belinda Bauer, Tracy Nelson, Janet Margolin. Three generations of males spend a weekend cruising singles bars looking for girls. Distant cousin to WHERE THE LADIES GO and SINGLE BARS, SINGLE WOMEN. Average.

Tonight We Raid Calais (1943) **70m.** **½ D: John Brahm. Annabella, John Sutton, Lee J. Cobb, Beulah Bondi, Blanche Yurka, Howard da Silva, Marcel Dalio. Fast-paced if undistinguished WW2 tale of sabotage mission in France with good performances; written by Waldo Salt.

Tonight We Sing (1953) **C-109m.** **½ D: Mitchell Leisen. David Wayne, Ezio Pinza, Roberta Peters, Anne Bancroft, Tamara Toumanova, Isaac Stern, Jan Peerce.

Hodgepodge supposedly based on impresario Sol Hurok's life, allowing for disjointed string of operatic/musical interludes. Produced by George Jessel.

Tonka (1958) **C-97m.** **½ D: Lewis R. Foster. Sal Mineo, Philip Carey, Jerome Courtland, Rafael Campos, H. M. Wynant, Joy Page. Mineo stands out in this modest Disney film about an Indian brave's attachment to a wild horse, which he captures and tames. Weak resolution and cut-rate version of Custer's Last Stand detract from promising story. Retitled A HORSE NAMED COMANCHE.▼

Tony Draws a Horse (1951-British) **90m.** **½ D: John Paddy Carstairs. Cecil Parker, Anne Crawford, Derek Bond, Barbara Murray. Witty little film about parents bickering over proper psychology in dealing with their undisciplined child.

Tony Rome (1967) **C-110m.** **½ D: Gordon Douglas. Frank Sinatra, Jill St. John, Richard Conte, Sue Lyon, Gena Rowlands, Simon Oakland, Jeffrey Lynn, Lloyd Bochner. Good cast in moderately diverting detective caper. Private-eye Rome (Sinatra) hired by millionaire (Oakland) to find out why his daughter would wind up drunk and unconscious in low-class Miami hotel. Sequel: LADY IN CEMENT.▼

Too Bad She's Bad (1955-Italian) **95m.** ** D: Alessandro Blasetti. Sophia Loren, Vittorio De Sica, Marcello Mastroianni, Lina Furia. Unremarkable little comedy about life and love among happy-go-lucky crooks, set in Rome.

Too Beautiful for You (1989-French) **C-91m.** ** D: Bertrand Blier. Gerard Depardieu, Josiane Balasko, Carole Bouquet, Roland Blanche, Francois Cluzet. Car dealer Depardieu cheats on beautiful, cultured wife Bouquet; the object of his affection is his plain, pudgy temporary receptionist (Balasko). Starts off brightly, but then goes absolutely nowhere.

Too Far to Go (1979) **C-100m. TVM** D: Fielder Cook. Michael Moriarty, Blythe Danner, Kathryn Walker, Ken Kercheval, Josef Sommer, Glenn Close. Moriarty and Danner bring distinction to this middling study of the dissolution of a marriage. Taken from seventeen short stories by John Updike. Released theatrically in 1982 with a new credit sequence, score by Elizabeth Swados, sound-effects track, and several smaller alterations. This was Close's first appearance on film. Average.

Too Good to Be True (1988) **C-100m. TVM** D: Christian I. Nyby II. Loni Anderson, Patrick Duffy, Glynnis O'Connor, Julie Harris, Larry Drake, James B. Sikking. Sub-par remake of LEAVE HER TO HEAVEN with Loni playing the old Gene Tierney part as a maniacally possessive wife. Average.

Too Hot to Handle (1938) **105m.** *** D:

Jack Conway. Clark Gable, Myrna Loy, Walter Pidgeon, Leo Carrillo, Johnny Hines, Virginia Weidler. Gable and Pidgeon are rival newsreel photographers vying for aviatrix Loy in this fast-paced action-comedy; Gable's scene faking enemy attack on China is a gem.

Too Hot to Handle (1959-British) **C-92m.** ** D: Terence Young. Jayne Mansfield, Leo Genn, Carl Boehm, Christopher Lee. Seamy study of chanteuse Mansfield involved with one man too many in the nightclub circuit.

Too Hot To Handle (1976) **C-90m.** BOMB D: Don Schain. Cheri Caffaro, Sharon Ipale, Corinne Calvet, John van Dreelen, Vic Diaz, Jordan Rosengarten. Trashy sex-adventure film has Caffaro as international hit lady involved in James Bondish escapades in Manila. Pros van Dreelen and Calvet look embarrassed. Made by husband-and-wife team Schain and Caffaro. Hugo Montenegro, of all people, did the score.▼

Too Late Blues (1962) **100m.** ** D: John Cassavetes. Bobby Darin, Stella Stevens, John Cassavetes, Rupert Crosse, Vince Edwards, Cliff Carnell, Seymour Cassel. Pretentious nonsense about jazz musician Darin involved with selfish dame Stevens.

Too Late for Tears (1949) **99m.** **½ D: Byron Haskin. Lizabeth Scott, Don DeFore, Dan Duryea, Arthur Kennedy, Kristine Miller. Atmospheric but muddled drama detailing what happens when a bag filled with cash is dropped into the car of greedy bad-girl Scott and nice-guy husband Kennedy. DeFore is a mystery man; Duryea is at his best as a heavy. Also known as KILLER BAIT.▼

Too Late the Hero (1970) **C-133m.** *** D: Robert Aldrich. Michael Caine, Cliff Robertson, Henry Fonda, Ian Bannen, Harry Andrews, Denholm Elliott, Ronald Fraser. Two reluctant soldiers (Robertson, Caine) sent on suicide mission on Pacific island during WW2; turns into battle of wits between them and Japanese officer. Action-packed film builds to pulsating finale. Shown on network TV as SUICIDE RUN.▼

Toolbox Murders, The (1978) **C-93m.** *½ D: Dennis Donnelly. Cameron Mitchell, Pamelyn Ferdin, Wesley Eure, Nicholas Beauvy, Aneta Corsaut, Tim Donnelly, Evelyn Guerrero. A film that delivers exactly what its title promises: graphic slayings of young women by means of various pieces of hardware. Yecch.▼

Too Many Crooks (1958-British) **85m.** **½ D: Mario Zampi. Terry-Thomas, George Cole, Brenda De Banzie, Sydney Tafler. OK satire on racketeer films buoyed by Terry-Thomas' presence.▼

Too Many Girls (1940) **85m.** *** D: George Abbott. Lucille Ball, Richard Carlson, Eddie Bracken, Ann Miller, Hal

LeRoy, Desi Arnaz, Frances Langford. Engaging Rodgers-Hart musical comedy with winning cast, sharp dialogue. Four boys are hired to keep an eye on footloose Lucy at Pottawatomie College in Stopgap, New Mexico. Stagey presentation of musical numbers seems to work fine here; Van Johnson very noticeable as one of the chorus boys (it was his film debut, as well as Arnaz and Bracken's). Incidentally, this is where Lucy and Desi met.▼

Too Many Husbands (1940) **84m.** ******* D: Wesley Ruggles. Jean Arthur, Fred Mac-Murray, Melvyn Douglas, Harry Davenport, Dorothy Peterson, Edgar Buchanan. Jean is married to Douglas when husband #1 (MacMurray), thought dead, turns up. Excellent comedy from W. Somerset Maugham's play *Home and Beauty*. Remade as THREE FOR THE SHOW.

Too Many Suspects SEE: **Ellery Queen** (1975)

Too Many Thieves (1966) **C-100m.** ****** D: Abner Biberman. Peter Falk, Britt Ekland, Joanna Barnes, Nehemiah Persoff, David Carradine, George Coulouris, Elaine Stritch, Ludwig Donath. Falk is lawyer hired to retrieve national treasure stolen from Macedonian shrine. Thieves abound in theatrical feature comprised of two episodes from Falk's *Trials of O'Brien* TV series.

Too Much (1987) **C-89m.** BOMB D: Eric Rochat, Bridgette Andersen, Masato Fukazama, Hiroyuki Watanabe, Char Fontana. Threadbare comedy about an adorable (to the point of nausea) little girl (Andersen), her robot friend, and their experiences in Japan. Bottom-of-the-barrel fare.

Too Much Harmony (1933) **76m.** ****½** D: A. Edward Sutherland. Bing Crosby, Jack Oakie, Grace Bradley, Judith Allen, Lilyan Tashman, Ned Sparks. Pleasant, if plotty, backstage musical with some good song numbers, including "Thanks," "The Day You Came Along."

Too Much, Too Soon (1958) **121m.** ****** D: Art Napoleon. Dorothy Malone, Errol Flynn, Efrem Zimbalist, Jr., Ray Danton, Neva Patterson, Martin Milner, Murray Hamilton. But not enough, in sensationalistic tale of Diana Barrymore's decline. Flynn steals the show as John Barrymore.

Too Outrageous! (1987-Canadian) **C-100m.** ****½** D: Richard Benner. Craig Russell, Hollis McLaren, David McIlwraith, Ron White, Lynne Cormack, Michael J. Reynolds. Russell shines in this disappointing sequel to OUTRAGEOUS! as female impersonator Robin Turner, who's become a smash in N.Y.C.—but will he go mainstream? Unfortunately, the scenario is too hackneyed to make you care. Best moments are his impersonations of Streisand, Mae West, etc.

Too Scared to Scream (1985) **C-104m.** ***½** D: Tony Lo Bianco. Mike Connors,

Anne Archer, Leon Isaac Kennedy, Ian McShane, Ruth Ford, John Heard, Carrie Nye, Maureen O'Sullivan, Murray Hamilton. Good cast stuck in dreary film about attempts to catch a psycho killer. Filmed in 1982.▼

Too Soon to Love (1960) **85m.** ****** D: Richard Rush. Jennifer West, Richard Evans, Warren Parker, Ralph Manza, Jack Nicholson. Mildly interesting period piece about illicit teenage love, pregnancy, and abortion. An early credit for Nicholson and writer-director Rush.

Tootsie (1982) **C-116m.** ******** D: Sydney Pollack. Dustin Hoffman, Jessica Lange, Teri Garr, Dabney Coleman, Charles Durning, Bill Murray, Sydney Pollack, George Gaynes, Geena Davis, Estelle Getty, Christine Ebersole. Smashing comedy about an obnoxious N.Y. actor who finally lands a job—disguised as a woman—and soon finds himself a better person female than he ever was male! Farcical premise becomes totally credible thanks to razor-sharp script (credited to Larry Gelbart and Murray Schisgal, from Gelbart and Don McGuire's story), fine direction, and superlative performances all around—including director Pollack's as Hoffman's harried agent. Lange won Best Supporting Actress Oscar. Bill Murray's performance was unbilled in film.▼

Too Young the Hero (1988) **C-100m.** TVM D: Buzz Kulik. Ricky Schroder, Jon DeVries, Debra Mooney, Mary-Louise Parker, Rick Warner. Dramatization of Calvin Graham's real-life WW2 adventures when he enlisted in the Navy at 12, became a war hero at Guadalcanal, and then was mistakenly branded a deserter back home as he was being released from service. Schroder's first "grown-up" role (though ironically he plays a pre-teenager). Bland war drama. Average.

Too Young to Die (1990) **C-100m.** TVM D: Robert Markowitz. Michael Tucker, Juliette Lewis, Brad Pitt, Alan Fudge, Emily Longstreth, Michael O'Keefe. Unpleasant fact-based drama about a teenage girl forced to stand trial for murder as an adult. Downbeat tale fights a losing battle for our sympathy. Average.

Too Young to Kiss (1951) **91m.** ****½** D: Robert Z. Leonard. June Allyson, Van Johnson, Gig Young, Paula Corday, Hans Conried. Allyson is fetching as pianist posing as child prodigy to get her big break falling in love with Johnson.

Too Young to Know (1945) **86m.** ****** D: Frederick de Cordova. Joan Leslie, Robert Hutton, Rosemary DeCamp, Dolores Moran. Slick, empty drama of career girl Leslie torn between husband and job.

To Paris with Love (1955-British) **C-78m.** ****½** D: Robert Hamer. Alec Guinness, Odile Versois, Vernon Gray, Elina Labourdette, Claude Romain, Jacques Francois, Austin Trevor. Middle-aged widower Guinness and son (Gray) try to marry each other off while on holiday in Paris. So-so comedy should amuse Guinness fans and Francophiles.▼

Topaz (1969) **C-127m.** *** D: Alfred Hitchcock. John Forsythe, Frederick Stafford, Dany Robin, John Vernon, Karin Dor, Michel Piccoli, Philippe Noiret, Claude Jade, Roscoe Lee Browne. French Intelligence agent Stafford works with American official Forsythe to dig out info on Russia's involvement in Cuba. Whirlwind plot circles globe, maintains intrigue level; good, not great Hitchcock, scripted by Samuel Taylor from Leon Uris' best-seller. Laserdisc video release includes not one but two alternate endings Hitchcock shot and then decided not to use!▼

Topaze (1933) **78m.** *** D: Harry D'Arrast. John Barrymore, Myrna Loy, Albert Conti, Luis Alberni, Reginald Mason, Jobyna Howland. Delightful film adapted from Marcel Pagnol's play about an impeccably honest but naive schoolteacher in France who unwittingly becomes a dupe for wealthy baron's business scheme. Barrymore is perfect. Remade as I LIKE MONEY.▼

Top Banana (1954) **C-100m.** *** D: Alfred E. Green. Phil Silvers, Rose Marie, Danny Scholl, Judy Lynn, Jack Albertson, Herbie Faye. Literally a filmed version of Silvers' Broadway hit (shot in N.Y.C.'s Winter Garden Theatre) about a Milton Berle-like TV comic. Full of burlesque chestnuts, plus new Johnny Mercer score. Filmed (believe it or not) in 3-D.

Top Gun (1955) **73m.** **½ D: Ray Nazarro. Sterling Hayden, William Bishop, Karin Booth, Regis Toomey, Rod Taylor, Denver Pyle. OK Western about man cleared of murder and elected marshal.

Top Gun (1986) **C-110m.** **½ D: Tony Scott. Tom Cruise, Kelly McGillis, Val Kilmer, Anthony Edwards, Tom Skerritt, Michael Ironside, John Stockwell, Barry Tubb, Rick Rossovich, Tim Robbins, James Tolkan, Meg Ryan. Young studs vie for glory, on the ground and in the air, at elite naval aviation training school. Contrived beyond belief, with dogfights that play like video games, and total lack of sexual chemistry between the two leads . . . but slickly calculated to please '80s audiences (and fans of ever-smiling Cruise). Edwards, as Cruise's sidekick, steals the show. Giorgio Moroder and Tom Whitlock won an Oscar for the song "Take My Breath Away," performed by Berlin.▼

Top Hat (1935) **99m.** **** D: Mark Sandrich. Fred Astaire, Ginger Rogers, Edward Everett Horton, Helen Broderick, Eric Blore, Erik Rhodes. What can we say? Merely a knock-out of a musical being doing Astaire and Rogers at their brightest doing

"Cheek to Cheek," "Isn't This a Lovely Day to Be Caught in the Rain," "Top Hat, White Tie, and Tails," other Irving Berlin songs, as the duo goes through typical mistaken-identity plot. Wonderful support from rest of cast; that's Lucille Ball as the flower shop clerk. Scripted by Dwight Taylor and Allan Scott, from a play by Alexander Farago and Aladar Laszlo. Originally 101m.; some prints are 93m.▼

Topkapi (1964) **C-120m.** **** D: Jules Dassin. Melina Mercouri, Peter Ustinov, Maximilian Schell, Robert Morley, Akim Tamiroff, Despo Diamantidou. First-rate entertainment of would-be thieves who plan perfect crime in Constantinople museum; lighthearted caper has inspired many imitations. Filmed in Istanbul, with Ustinov's delightful performance copping an Academy Award. Written by Monja Danischewsky, from Eric Ambler's novel *The Light of Day*; memorable score by Manos Hadjidakis.▼

To Please a Lady (1950) **91m.** **½ D: Clarence Brown. Clark Gable, Barbara Stanwyck. Adolphe Menjou, Roland Winters, Will Geer, Emory Parnell, Frank Jenks. Unremarkable love story of reporter Stanwyck and race-car driver-heel Gable.

Top Man (1943) **74m.** ** D: Charles Lamont. Donald O'Connor, Susanna Foster, Peggy Ryan, Richard Dix, Anne Gwynne, Lillian Gish, Noah Beery, Jr. Youthful O'Connor heads the family when Dad goes off to war; typical assembly-line musical comedy from Universal, with guest spots by Count Basie, Borrah Minnevitch's Harmonica Rascals.

Top of the Hill, The (1980) **C-200m.** TVM D: Walter Grauman. Wayne Rogers, Elke Sommer, Adrienne Barbeau, Sonny Bono, Peter Brown, J. D. Cannon, Macdonald Carey, Mel Ferrer, Gary Lockwood, Paula Prentiss. Love and sex at Lake Placid with the 1980 Winter Olympics as an excuse for high-living Rogers to find snow bunnies. From the Irwin Shaw novel. Originally shown in two parts. Average.

Top of the World (1955) **90m.** ** D: Lewis R. Foster. Dale Robertson, Evelyn Keyes, Frank Lovejoy, Nancy Gates. Set in Alaska, movie revolves around jet pilot Robertson, his ex-wife Keyes and her new boyfriend Lovejoy.

Top o' the Morning (1949) **100m.** **½ D: David Miller. Bing Crosby, Barry Fitzgerald, Ann Blyth, Hume Cronyn, John McIntire, Eileen Crowe. Crosby-Fitzgerald malarkey is wearing thin in this fanciful musical of Bing searching for thief hiding the Blarney Stone.

Topper (1937) **97m.** ***½ D: Norman Z. McLeod. Constance Bennett, Cary Grant, Roland Young, Billie Burke, Alan Mowbray, Eugene Pallette, Arthur Lake, Hedda Hopper. Delightful gimmick comedy with ghosts Grant and Bennett dominating life of meek Young; sparkling cast in adaptation of Thorne Smith novel, scripted by Jack Jevne, Eddie Moran, and Eric Hatch. Followed by two sequels, a TV series, and a TV remake. Also shown in computer-colored version.▼

Topper (1979) **C-100m.** **TVM** D: Charles S. Dubin. Kate Jackson, Andrew Stevens, Jack Warden, Rue McClanahan, James Karen, Charles Siebert. Breezy updating of the 1937 classic. The two leads (then married) also produced this one, aiming for a new *Topper* TV series. Average.

Topper Returns (1941) **88m.** ******* D: Roy Del Ruth. Joan Blondell, Roland Young, Carole Landis, Billie Burke, Dennis O'Keefe, Patsy Kelly, Eddie "Rochester" Anderson. Topper helps ghostly Blondell solve her own murder in the last of this series, with hilarious results. Also shown in computer-colored version.▼

Topper Takes a Trip (1939) **85m.** ******* D: Norman Z. McLeod. Constance Bennett, Roland Young, Billie Burke, Alan Mowbray, Verree Teasdale, Franklin Pangborn. Cary Grant is missing (except in a flashback), but rest of cast returns for repeat success as Young is frustrated on Riviera vacation by ghostess Bennett. Also shown in computer-colored version.▼

Top Secret (1978) **C-100m.** **TVM** D: Paul Leaf. Bill Cosby, Tracy Reed, Gloria Foster, Sheldon Leonard. Dated spy caper that even Cosby, as a hip American agent on the trail of stolen plutonium in Italy, cannot pump life into. Below average.

Top Secret! (1984) **C-90m.** ****½** D: Jim Abrahams, David Zucker, Jerry Zucker. Val Kilmer, Lucy Gutteridge, Christopher Villiers, Jeremy Kemp, Michael Gough, Omar Sharif, Peter Cushing, Harry Ditson, Jim Carter. Likably silly comedy from the writing-directing team that brought you AIRPLANE!, about an Elvis-like rock star who becomes embroiled in espionage work while touring East Germany—with Nazis as bad guys and French resistance fighters as allies! Lots of laughs but no real momentum—and where's the ending?▼

Top Secret Affair (1957) **100m.** ****½** D: H. C. Potter. Susan Hayward, Kirk Douglas, Paul Stewart, Jim Backus, John Cromwell. John P. Marquand's *Melville Goodwin, U.S.A.* becomes fair comedy, with most credit going to Hayward as fiery publisher who knows all about Senate appointee's (Douglas) past.

Tops Is the Limit SEE: **Anything Goes** (1936)

To Race the Wind (1980) **C-105m.** **TVM** D: Walter Grauman. Steve Guttenberg, Randy Quaid, Mark L. Taylor, Lisa Eilbacher, Barbara Barrie, Catherine Hicks. Lighthearted, well-acted story of a blind law student's struggle to lead a normal life in a sighted world; from the autobiography of Harold (BUTTERFLIES ARE FREE) Krents. Above average.▼

Tora! Tora! Tora! (1970-U.S.-Japanese) **C-143m.** ******* D: Richard Fleischer, Toshio Masuda, Kinji Fukasaku. Martin Balsam, Soh Yamamura, Jason Robards, Joseph Cotten, Tatsuya Mihashi, E. G. Marshall, James Whitmore, Wesley Addy, Leon Ames, George Macready. Events leading up to Pearl Harbor attack, from both American and Japanese points of view. Well-documented screenplay shows major and minor blundering on both sides, then recreates attack with frightening realism. Well-made film creates incredible tension. Oscar-winning special effects.▼

Torch, The (1950-Mexican) **90m.** ****** D: Emilio Fernandez. Paulette Goddard, Pedro Armendariz, Gilbert Roland, Walter Reed. Mexican revolutionary captures town and falls for daughter of nobility. Rare English-language effort by Mexico's top director; a shame it isn't better. Beautifully photographed by Gabriel Figueroa.

Torchlight (1984) **C-90m.** ****** D: Tom Wright. Pamela Sue Martin, Steve Railsback, Ian McShane, Al Corley, Rita Taggart. Married couple Martin and Railsback's world is wrecked when he becomes a cocaine addict. Below-average morality tale: its message may be important, but its dramatics are muddled.▼

Torch Song (1953) **C-90m.** ****½** D: Charles Walters. Joan Crawford, Michael Wilding, Marjorie Rambeau, Gig Young, Henry (Harry) Morgan, Dorothy Patrick, Benny Rubin, Nancy Gates. Crawford is hard as nails as a Broadway musical star who chews up people for lunch—until she comes into contact with blind pianist Wilding, who isn't cowed by her. Glossy, often hilariously clichéd drama reminds us that It's Lonely At the Top. There's one absurd musical number in which Crawford appears in blackface! Her "clumsy" dance partner in the opening number is in fact the film's director, himself a former dancer and choreographer.▼

Torch Song Trilogy (1988) **C-117m.** ****½** D: Paul Bogart. Anne Bancroft, Matthew Broderick, Harvey Fierstein, Brian Kerwin, Karen Young, Charles Pierce. Fierstein rewrote (and considerably compressed) his landmark Broadway play about a drag queen, and lost something in the process. Changing sensibilities in the AIDS era also affect the original material, though there are still fine moments. Fierstein reprises his stage performance as Arnold Beckoff, and Bancroft scores strongly as his mother.▼

Torment (1944-Swedish) **100m.** *****½** D: Alf Sjoberg. Mai Zetterling, Stig Jarrel, Alf Kjellin, Olaf Winnerstrand. Schoolboy Kjellin and girl he falls in love with (Zetterling) are hounded by sadistic teacher

Jarrel. Moody and evocative, with a script by Ingmar Bergman.▼

Tormented (1960) **75m.** BOMB D: Bert I. Gordon. Richard Carlson, Juli Reding, Susan Gordon, Lugene Sanders, Joe Turkel, Lillian Adams. Low-budget hogwash of guilt-ridden pianist dubious over his forthcoming marriage to society woman. Weak ghost story.

Torn Apart (1989) **C-96m.** **½ D: Jack Fisher. Andrian Pasdar, Cecilia Peck, Barry Primus, Machram Huri, Arnon Zadok, Margit Polak. Boy and girl grow up together and fall in love—but he's Jewish, she's Arab, and the setting is Israel. A new slant on *Romeo and Juliet* with a topical backdrop, this humanist drama has convincing performances and a timely message. Peck is the daughter of Gregory Peck.

Torn Between Two Lovers (1979) **C-100m.** TVM D: Delbert Mann. Lee Remick, Joseph Bologna, George Peppard, Giorgio Tozzi, Molly Cheek. Romantic drama graced by ever-lovely Remick as married socialite who has an affair with a dashing architect she meets on a trip. Title comes from hit song of the late '70s. Average.▼

√ **Torn Curtain** (1966) **C-128m.** **½ D: Alfred Hitchcock. Paul Newman, Julie Andrews, Lila Kedrova, David Opatoshu, Ludwig Donath. Oddly unmoving Hitchcock thriller about American scientist pretending to be defector. Slick but empty film. Some TV prints are cut to 121m., excising violent scenes.▼

Torpedo Alley (1953) **84m.** ** D: Lew Landers. Dorothy Malone, Mark Stevens, Charles Winninger, Bill Williams. Typical Korean War actioner involving U.S. submarine offensives.▼

Torpedo Bay (1964-Italian-French) **91m.** **½ D: Charles Frend. James Mason, Lilli Palmer, Gabriele Ferzeti, Alberto Lupo, Geoffrey Keen. British and Italian naval crews meet on neutral territory during WW2; modest but fairly interesting drama.

Torpedo of Doom, The (1938) **100m.** *** D: William Witney, John English. Lee Powell, Herman Brix (Bruce Bennett), Eleanor Stewart, Montagu Love, Hugh Sothern. Superior cliff-hanger from Republic's golden age of serials, involving dynamic duo of Marines undergoing innumerable obstacles to subdue a world-hungry scientist; quite actionful. Reedited from FIGHTING DEVIL DOGS.▼

Torpedo Run (1958) **C-98m.** **½ D: Joseph Pevney. Glenn Ford, Ernest Borgnine, Diane Brewster, Dean Jones. Sluggish WW2 revenge narrative of sub-commander Ford whose family was aboard Jap prison ship he had to blow up.▼

Torrent, The (1926) **68m.** *** D: Monta Bell. Ricardo Cortez, Greta Garbo, Gertrude Olmstead, Edward Connelly, Lucien

Littlefield, Martha Mattox, Tully Marshall, Mack Swain, Lucy Bennett. Garbo stars in her first American film as a Spanish peasant girl who becomes a famous prima donna after being deserted by nobleman Cortez, whose life is ruled by his mother. A still entertaining tale of lost love, based on a Blasco-Ibanez novel.

Torrents of Spring (1990-Italian-French) **C-101m.** **½ D: Jerzy Skolimowski. Timothy Hutton, Nastassia Kinski, Valeria Golino, William Forsythe, Urbano Barberini, Francesca De Sapio, Jacques Herlin. No disgrace, but an almost inevitably stilted film version of an Ivan Turgenev story. Russian Hutton (!), engaged to German Golino, gets roving glands for married Kinski, who's negotiating to purchase his estate. Nicely shot (with a good duel scene), but Hutton's regal bearing falls apart whenever he's asked to open his mouth.▼

Torrid Zone (1940) **88m.** ***½ D: William Keighley. James Cagney, Ann Sheridan, Pat O'Brien, Andy Devine, Helen Vinson, Jerome Cowan, George Tobias, George Reeves. South-of-the-border comedy, action and romance with nightclub star Sheridan helping plantation owner O'Brien keep Cagney from leaving. Zesty dialogue (scripted by Richard Macauley and Jerry Wald) in this variation on THE FRONT PAGE.

Torso (1974-Italian) **C-90m.** *½ D: Sergio Martino. Suzy Kendall, Tina Aumont, John Richardson, Luc Merenda. A killer is carving up beautiful co-eds in this bloody potboiler.▼

Tortilla Flat (1942) **105m.** *** D: Victor ✓ Fleming. Spencer Tracy, Hedy Lamarr, John Garfield, Frank Morgan, Akim Tamiroff, Sheldon Leonard, Donald Meek, John Qualen, Allen Jenkins. Steinbeck's salty novel of California fishing community vividly portrayed by three top stars, stolen by Morgan as devoted dog lover.

Torture Chamber of Baron Blood, The SEE: **Baron Blood**▼

Torture Chamber of Dr. Sadism, The (1967-German) **C-90m.** **½ D: Harald Reinl. Christopher Lee, Lex Barker, Karin Dor, Carl Lange, Vladimir Medar. A resurrected Lee seeks revenge on Barker and Dor; after luring them to his castle they are mentally and physically tortured. Based on Poe's *Pit and the Pendulum*. Atmospheric, but not for the squeamish. Also known as THE BLOOD DEMON. Released on video as CASTLE OF THE WALKING DEAD at 75m.▼

Torture Garden (1968-British) **C-93m.** **½ D: Freddie Francis. Jack Palance, Burgess Meredith, Beverly Adams, Peter Cushing, Barbara Ewing, Michael Bryant, Maurice Denham. Anthology horror film revolving around sideshow weirdo Dr. Diabolo (Meredith) with power to let curious visitors see and experience their near-future. Good cast and production, but stories uneven; first and last tales best. Written by Robert Bloch.▼

To Sir with Love (1967-British) **C-105m.** ***½ D: James Clavell. Sidney Poitier, Judy Geeson, Christian Roberts, Suzy Kendall, Faith Brook, Geoffrey Bayldon, Patricia Routledge, Adrienne Posta, Lulu, Michael Des Barres. Excellent film of novice Poitier assigned to roughhouse London school, gradually earning respect from his students. Well acted, with nice work by British newcomers; Lulu also sings hit title song. Written and produced by Clavell, from E.R. Braithwaite's novel.▼

Total Recall (1990) **C-109m.** *** D: Paul Verhoeven. Arnold Schwarzenegger, Rachel Ticotin, Sharon Stone, Ronny Cox, Michael Ironside, Marshall Bell, Mel Johnson, Jr. Schwarzenegger learns he's a victim of mind-tampering in this 21st century tale—and once he discovers his true identity, journeys to Mars to help fight a power-hungry madman there. Riveting yarn (based on Phillip K. Dick's short story "We Can Remember It for You Wholesale") offers endless twists and intriguing ideas . . . and the kind of over-the-top violence for which director Verhoeven is known. Dazzling special effects throughout.

To the Devil—A Daughter (1976-British-German) **C-95m.** **½ D: Peter Sykes. Richard Widmark, Christopher Lee, Honor Blackman, Denholm Elliott, Nastassja Kinski, Michael Goodliffe. Occult novelist Widmark is enlisted to help young girl (Kinski) who's being pursued by defrocked priest Lee for satanic ritual. Hammer Films adaptation of Dennis Wheatley book is well made but lacks punch.▼

To the Ends of the Earth (1948) **109m.** ***½ D: Robert Stevenson. Dick Powell, Signe Hasso, Ludwig Donath, Vladimir Sokoloff, Edgar Barrier. Fast-moving thriller of government agent tracking down narcotics smuggling ring has good acting and ironic ending.

To the Shores of Tripoli (1942) **C-86m.** **½ D: H. Bruce Humberstone. John Payne, Maureen O'Hara, Randolph Scott, Nancy Kelly, William Tracy, Maxie Rosenbloom, Iris Adrian. Spoiled rich-boy Payne joins Marines with off-handed attitude, doesn't wake up until film's end. Routine material.▼

To the Victor (1948) **100m.** **½ D: Delmer Daves. Dennis Morgan, Viveca Lindfors, Victor Francen, Bruce Bennett, Dorothy Malone, Eduardo Ciannelli, William Conrad. Story of collaborators standing trial in France for war crimes sadly could have been much better; script by Richard Brooks.

To Trap a Spy (1966) **C-90m.** **½ D: Don Medford. Robert Vaughn, David McCallum, Leo G. Carroll, Luciana Paluzzi, Patricia Crowley. Expanded from initial segment of

The Man From U.N.C.L.E. TV series, this reflects small budget and cast's newness at formula action-espionage type plot.

Touch, The (1971-U.S.-Swedish) **C-112m.** *½ D: Ingmar Bergman. Elliott Gould, Bibi Andersson, Max von Sydow, Sheila Reid. Bergman's first English-language film should be called THE TETCHED, in view of the fact that Andersson leaves doctor-husband von Sydow for boorish Gould. The two Bergman regulars are fine, but Gould is miscast and dialogue embarrassingly awkward.▼

Touchables, The (1968-British) **C-97m.** BOMB D: Robert Freeman. Judy Huxtable, Esther Anderson, Marilyn Richard, Kathy Simmonds. Dreary tale of four girls and a guy who try to kidnap pop singing idol. Terrible. TV print runs 88m.

Touch and Go (1955-British) **C-85m.** **½ D: Michael Truman. Jack Hawkins, Margaret Johnston, Roland Culver, June Thorburn. Wry study of sturdy English family trying to overcome obstacles upsetting their planned emigration to Australia.

Touch and Go (1980-Australian) **C-92m.** ** D: Peter Maxwell. Wendy Hughes, Chantal Contouri, Carmen Duncan, Jeanie Drynan, Liddy Clark. Sexy female Robin Hoods steal for worthy causes. A well-meaning comedy-caper film that is slight and forgettable.▼

Touch and Go (1986) **C-101m.** **½ D: Robert Mandel. Michael Keaton, Maria Conchita Alonso, Ajay Naidu, Maria Tucci, Max Wright, Lara Jill Miller. Self-centered hockey star becomes involved with delinquent kid and his mother. Aptly titled film has persuasive performances but unconvincing story line.▼

Touched (1983) **C-93m.** ** D: John Flynn. Robert Hays, Kathleen Beller, Ned Beatty, Gilbert Lewis, Lyle Kessler. Uninspired, poorly scripted latter-day DAVID AND LISA with Hays and Beller escaping from mental institution and trying to build a "normal" life for themselves. Good performances, anyway.▼

Touched by Love (1980) **C-95m.** **½ D: Gus Trikonis. Deborah Raffin, Diane Lane, Michael Learned, Cristina Raines, Mary Wickes, Clu Gulager, John Amos, Clive Shalom. Sentimental drama, based on nursing trainee Lena Canada's memoir, of cerebral palsy victim's pen-pal relationship with Elvis Presley. Fine performances by Lane and Raffin. Originally titled TO ELVIS, WITH LOVE.▼

Touch Me Not (1974-British) **C-84m.** ** D: Douglas Fifthian. Lee Remick, Michael Hinz, Ivan Desny, Ingrid Garbo. Unexciting thriller with industrial spy Hinz using neurotic secretary Remick to gather information on boss Desny. Also known as THE HUNTED.▼

Touch of Class, A (1973) **C-105m.** ** D:

Melvin Frank. George Segal, Glenda Jackson, Paul Sorvino, Hildegard Neil, Cec Linder, K. Callan, Mary Barclay. Undeniable chemistry of Segal and Jackson can only occasionally breathe life into this stale comedy about married man who intends nothing more than having a carefree affair, only to fall genuinely in love. Jackson won Best Actress Oscar.▼

Touch of Evil (1958) 93m. **** D: Orson Welles. Charlton Heston, Orson Welles, Janet Leigh, Joseph Calleia, Akim Tamiroff, Marlene Dietrich, Dennis Weaver, Valentin de Vargas, Mort Mills, Victor Milian, Joanna Moore, Zsa Zsa Gabor. Narc Heston and corrupt cop Welles tangle over murder investigation in sleazy Mexican border town, with Heston's bride Leigh the pawn of their struggle. Fantastic, justifiably famous opening shot merely commences stylistic masterpiece, dazzlingly photographed by Russell Metty. Great Latin rock score by Henry Mancini; neat unbilled cameos by Joseph Cotten, Ray Collins, and especially Mercedes McCambridge. Most revival theatres now show Welles' original 108m. version, discovered in 1976.
▼

Touch of Larceny, A (1959-British) 93m. *** D: Guy Hamilton. James Mason, George Sanders, Vera Miles, Oliver Johnston, William Kendall, Duncan Lamont. Ingenious comedy of officer who uses availability of military secrets to his advantage in off-beat plan.

Touch of Scandal, A (1984) C-100m. TVM D: Ivan Nagy. Angie Dickinson, Tom Skerritt, Jason Miller, Don Murray, Robert Loggia. Angie's running for public office when a lurid scandal rears its ugly head. And Geraldine Ferraro thought she had troubles! Average.

Tough As They Come (1942) 61m. D: William Nigh. Billy Halop, Huntz Hall, Bernard Punsley, Gabriel Dell, Helen Parrish, Paul Kelly, Ann Gillis. See: **Bowery Boys** series.

Tough Enough (1983) C-106m. ** D: Richard Fleischer. Dennis Quaid, Carlene Watkins, Stan Shaw, Pam Grier, Warren Oates, Bruce McGill, Wilford Brimley, Fran Ryan. Numerous problems plagued production of this predictable tale of would-be Country-Western singer Quaid entering Tough Man amateur boxing competitions for exposure. Insipid ROCKY rip-off wastes good cast. Completed in 1981.▼

Tougher They Come, The (1950) 69m. *½ D: Ray Nazarro. Wayne Morris, Preston Foster, William Bishop, Kay Buckley. Trivial study of ruthless operators trying to take over lumber camp.

Toughest Gun in Tombstone (1958) 72m. *½ D: Earl Bellamy. George Montgomery, Beverly Tyler, Don Beddoe, Jim Davis. Weak shoot-out tale with Montgomery in the title role.

Toughest Man Alive, The (1955) 72m. ** D: Sidney Salkow. Dane Clark, Lita Milan, Ross Elliott, Myrna Dell, Syd Saylor, Anthony Caruso. Mild caper of tracking down gun-smuggling in South America.

Toughest Man in Arizona, The (1952) C-90m. **½ D: R. G. Springsteen. Vaughn Monroe, Joan Leslie, Edgar Buchanan, Victor Jory. While waging war on crime marshal Monroe falls for girl with expected results. Fairly well produced and acted.

Toughest Man in the World, The (1984) C-100m. TVM D: Dick Lowry. Mr. T, Dennis Dugan, John P. Navin, Peggy Pope, Lynne Moody. Streetwise nightclub bouncer (guess who?) becomes volunteer youth-center director for neighborhood youngsters—and he sings the title song, too. Average.

Tough Guys (1986) C-104m. **½ D: Jeff Kanew. Burt Lancaster, Kirk Douglas, Charles Durning, Alexis Smith, Dana Carvey, Darlanne Fluegel, Eli Wallach, Monty Ash, Billy Barty. A couple of former crooks—who staged America's last train robbery twenty-five years ago—are finally sprung from prison and gamely try to adjust to 1980s life. Watching Burt and Kirk (in this tailor-made comedy) is a joy, but the film gets more childish and predictable as it goes along. Still watchable but what a shame!▼

Tough Guys Don't Dance (1987) C-110m. **½ D: Norman Mailer. Ryan O'Neal, Isabella Rossellini, Debra Sandlund, Wings Hauser, Lawrence Tierney, Frances Fisher, John Bedford Lloyd, Clarence Williams III. Genuinely odd *film noir* cum black-comedy adapted by Mailer from his own novel, with O'Neal as a loser who may have committed murder—but can't remember. Peopled exclusively by weird characters who speak in purple prose . . . but it does have its moments, and a lively performance by Tierney as O'Neal's no-nonsense father who wants to "deep-six the heads." Filmed in Provincetown, Massachusetts.▼

Toughlove (1985) C-100m. TVM D: Glenn Jordan. Lee Remick, Bruce Dern, Piper Laurie, Eric Schiff, Dedee Pfeiffer, Dana Elcar, Beth Miller, Jason Patric. Manipulative script by Karen Hall undermines this promising drama concerning the organization that tries to help parents with children who are into drugs and alcohol. Sincere performances by Remick and Dern help greatly. Average.▼

Tourist (1980) C-100m. TVM D: Jeremy Summers. Lee Meriwether, Bradford Dillman, Lois Nettleton, Adrienne Barbeau, David Groh, James Stephens, Bonnie Bedelia, John Ireland, Marisa Berenson, John McCook, Laurette Spang-McCook. Vacationing couples tour Europe in a *Love Boat* plotting that, surprisingly, comes from the pen of Gerald Green (author of THE

LAST ANGRY MAN and HOLOCAUST). Below average.

Tourist Trap (1979) **C-85m.** *½ D: David Schmoeller. Chuck Connors, Jon Van Ness, Jocelyn Jones, Robin Sherwood, Tanya Roberts, Keith McDermott. Here's an original idea for a horror movie: those life-size dummies in Connors' "museum" are strangely lifelike, aren't they? Not so much that the idiots he lures there ever catch on. A couple of genuine scares, but mostly boring thriller.▼

Tovarich (1937) **98m.** *** D: Anatole Litvak. Claudette Colbert, Charles Boyer, Basil Rathbone, Anita Louise, Melville Cooper, Isabel Jeans, Morris Carnovsky. Boyer and Colbert, royal Russians, flee the Revolution with court treasury but nothing for themselves; they're finally reduced to working as servants. Enjoyable but dated romantic comedy set in Paris. Based on a French play Americanized by Robert E. Sherwood.

Toward the Unknown (1956) **C-115m.** **½ D: Mervyn LeRoy. William Holden, Lloyd Nolan, Virginia Leith, Charles McGraw, James Garner, Murray Hamilton, L.Q. Jones, Paul Fix, Karen Steele. Intelligent narrative about test pilots, focusing on a tarnished air officer (Holden) eager to regain the respect of his men. Garner's film debut.

Towering Inferno, The (1974) **C-165m.** **½ D: John Guillermin, Irwin Allen. Steve McQueen, Paul Newman, William Holden, Faye Dunaway, Fred Astaire, Susan Blakely, Richard Chamberlain, Jennifer Jones, O. J. Simpson, Robert Vaughn, Robert Wagner, Susan Flannery, Gregory Sierra, Dabney Coleman. All-star idiocy about a burning skyscraper. Purports to pay tribute to firemen but spends most of its time devising grisly ways for people to die. The pyrotechnics are gripping, but the movie is just another cold-blooded Hollywood "product." Oscar-winner for Cinematography, Editing and Song ("We May Never Love Like This Again").▼

Tower of Evil SEE: **Horror on Snape Island**▼

Tower of London (1939) **92m.** **½ D: Rowland V. Lee. Basil Rathbone, Boris Karloff, Barbara O'Neil, Ian Hunter, Vincent Price, Nan Grey, Leo G. Carroll, John Sutton, Miles Mander. Muddled historical melodrama (not a horror film, as many believe), with Rathbone as unscrupulous, power-hungry Richard III and Karloff as his dutiful executioner Mord. Court intrigue leads to uninspired battle scenes. Remade in 1962.

Tower of London (1962) **79m.** *½ D: Roger Corman. Vincent Price, Michael Pate, Joan Freeman, Robert Brown. Remake of 1939 film has Price, who played Duke of Clarence first time around, tack-

ling role of Richard III in a flat, papiermâché production.▼

Tower of Terror SEE: **In the Devil's Garden**▼

Town Bully, The (1988) **C-100m. TVM** D: Noel Black. Bruce Boxleitner, Pat Hingle, Isabella Hoffman, David Graf, Jerry Hardin, Timothy Scott. Prosecutor incurs the wrath of a town when he tries to bring to justice the killer of the violent ex-con who's been terrorizing the citizenry. Mild, contemporary reworking of HIGH NOON. Average.

Town Called Hell, A (1971-British-Spanish) **C-95m.** BOMB D: Robert Parrish. Robert Shaw, Telly Savalas, Stella Stevens, Martin Landau, Fernando Rey. A manhunt for Mexican revolutionary Shaw. The pits. Originally titled A TOWN CALLED BASTARD.▼

Town Like Alice, A (1956-British) **107m.** **½ D: Jack Lee. Virginia McKenna, Peter Finch, Maureen Swanson, Vincent Ball. Taut WW2 tale, well acted, about Japanese oppression of female British POWS in Malaysia. Based on Nevil Shute's novel, later remade as TV miniseries. Retitled: RAPE OF MALAYA.

Town on Trial (1956-British) **96m.** **½ D: John Guillermin. John Mills, Charles Coburn, Derek Farr, Barbara Bates, Alec McCowen. A murder investigation in a small British town, where there's no shortage of suspects. Low-key drama makes good use of natural locations.

Town Tamer (1965) **C-89m.** ** D: Lesley Selander. Dana Andrews, Terry Moore, Pat O'Brien, Lon Chaney, Bruce Cabot, Lyle Bettger, Coleen Gray, Barton MacLane, Richard Arlen, Sonny Tufts. As title indicates, Andrews cleans up community, and among the rubble are some veteran actors. Routine Western has minor nostalgia value, in light of the cast.

Town That Dreaded Sundown, The (1977) **C-90m.** **½ D: Charles B. Pierce. Ben Johnson, Andrew Prine, Dawn Wells, Christine Ellsworth, Charles B. Pierce. OK thriller made from true story of a hooded killer who terrorized town of Texarkana in the mid-40s. Ben Johnson's presence gives it some stature.▼

Town Went Wild, The (1944) **78m.** ** D: Ralph Murphy. Freddie Bartholomew, Jimmy Lydon, Edward Everett Horton, Tom Tully, Jill Browning, Minna Gombell. Fitfully amusing poverty-row comedy concerning two feuding families and the interesting possibility that their children were switched at birth.

Town Without Pity (1961) **105m.** **½ D: Gottfried Reinhardt. Kirk Douglas, E. G. Marshall, Christine Kaufmann, Robert Blake, Richard Jaeckel, Frank Sutton, Barbara Rutting. Courtroom drama of G.I.s accused of raping German girl. Decent cast, but could have been better handled. Title song, sung by Gene Pitney, was a big hit. Filmed in Germany.

Toxic Avenger, The (1985) **C-100m.** **½ D: Michael Herz, Samuel Weil. Andree Maranda, Mitchell Cohen, Jennifer Baptist, Cindy Manion, Robert Prichard, Mark Torgi. Funny spoof about 90-pound weakling Torgi, who is transformed into a monster who only does good deeds. Not without violence and gore but still entertaining; recommended mostly for fans of the genre. Followed by two sequels.▼

Toxic Avenger, Part II, The (1989) **C-96m.** **½ D: Michael Herz, Lloyd Kaufman. Ron Fazio, John Altamura, Phoebe Legere, Rick Collins, Rikiya Yasuoka, Tsutomu Sekine, Lisa Gaye. Sequel to 1985's surprise hit offers more of the same silliness, with Melvin Junko (a.k.a. The Toxic Avenger) going after the Japanese conglomerate responsible for destroying a home for the blind in Tromaville in order to build a toxic chemical depot. Exploitation movie spoof has some very funny moments. Shot simultaneously with Part III.▼

Toxic Avenger Part III, The—The Last Temptation of Toxie (1989) **C-86m.** *½ D: Michael Herz, Lloyd Kaufman. Ron Fazio, Phoebe Legere, Rick Collins, Lisa Gaye, Jessica Dublin, John Altamura. More crossed eyes, comically gruesome deaths, and cheerful vulgarity as Toxie, now an out-of-work superhero, is tempted by evil Apocalypse Inc. into becoming an ambitious yuppie, unaware that the boss (Collins) is the Devil himself. Heavily self-referential and goes on far too long; moronic rather than silly.▼

Toy, The (1982) **C-99m.** *½ D: Richard Donner. Richard Pryor, Jackie Gleason, Scott Schwartz, Teresa Ganzel, Ned Beatty, Wilfrid Hyde-White, Annazette Chase. Stultifying remake of the Pierre Richard comedy LE JOUET with Pryor as penniless writer hired by zillionaire Gleason as plaything for spoiled son Schwartz. A few good gags are lost in a sea of you-can't-buy-friends-you-gotta-earn-them lectures, not to mention dubious taste for an 80's film with a black in such a demeaning part.▼

Toys in the Attic (1963) **90m.** **½ D: George Roy Hill. Dean Martin, Geraldine Page, Yvette Mimieux, Wendy Hiller, Gene Tierney, Larry Gates, Nan Martin. Timid adaptation (by James Poe) of Lillian Hellman play about man returning home with childlike bride; Page and Hiller are Martin's overprotective sisters.▼

Toy Soldiers (1984) **C-91m.** ** D: David Fisher. Jason Miller, Cleavon Little, Rodolfo De Anda, Terri Garber, Tracy Scoggins. Fast-paced but forgettable adventure has a plot resembling HIGH RISK (which also starred Little): Miller and Little help kids rescue their young friends from captivity in rebellion-torn Latin American nation.▼

Toy Tiger (1956) **C-88m.** **½ D: Jerry Hopper. Jeff Chandler, Laraine Day, Tim Hovey, Cecil Kellaway, Richard Haydn, David Janssen. Pleasant remake of MAD ABOUT MUSIC with Hovey "adopting" Chandler as his father to back up tales to school chums about a real dad.

Toy Wife, The (1938) **95m.** ** D: Richard Thorpe. Luise Rainer, Melvyn Douglas, Robert Young, Barbara O'Neil, H. B. Warner, Alma Kruger, Libby Taylor. Southern belle Rainer is pursued by Young and Douglas, can't decide which one to marry; inconsequential confection.

T.P. Sloane SEE: **Death Ray 2000**▼

Trackdown (1976) **C-98m.** **½ D: Richard T. Heffron. Jim Mitchum, Karen Lamm, Anne Archer, Erik Estrada, Cathy Lee Crosby, Vince Cannon. Montana rancher Mitchum comes to L.A. in search of his runaway sister, who's fallen into seamy street life. Not much depth but lots of action.

Trackdown: Finding the Goodbar Killer (1983). **C-100m.** D: Bill Persky. George Segal, Shelley Hack, Alan North, Shannon Presby, Tracy Pollan, Steve Allie Collura. Segal is wonderfully average as the plodding cop investigating the murder of a real-life Manhattan schoolteacher that was fictionalized in LOOKING FOR MR. GOODBAR, but the thriller's tautness sags during gratuitous romantic interludes. Average.

Tracker, The (1988) **C-115m. TVM** D: John Guillermin. Kris Kristofferson, Mark Moses, Scott Wilson, David Huddleston, John Quade, Don Swayze, Brynn Thayer, Karen Kopins. Retired Old West tracker reunites with estranged college-educated son to hunt down a wild-eyed religious fanatic on a murder spree. Veteran British director Guillermin's first Western. Made for cable. Average.▼

Trackers, The (1971) **C-73m. TVM** D: Earl Bellamy. Sammy Davis, Jr., Ernest Borgnine, Julie Adams, Connie Kreski, Jim Davis. Fair chase drama sprinkled with character portraits: Borgnine as vengeful rancher, out to get men who killed son and kidnapped daughter, scornful of black professional tracker who doesn't mind telling employer what he thinks about him. Average.▼

Track of the Cat (1954) **C-102m.** ** D: William Wellman. Robert Mitchum, Teresa Wright, Tab Hunter, Diana Lynn, Beulah Bondi, William Hopper, Carl (Alfalfa) Switzer. Slow-moving film of cougar hunt and family difficulties. William H. Clothier's "colorless" color photography is main asset.

Track of the Moon Beast (1976) **C-90m.** BOMB D: Richard Ashe. Chase Cordell, Donna Leigh Drake, Gregorio Sala, Patrick Wright. Young man becomes a hideous monster because of meteor fragment lodged in his body. Good horror makeup, but lousy film.▼

Track of the Vampire SEE: **Blood Bath**

Track of Thunder (1968) **C-83m.** ** D: Joseph Kane. Tom Kirk, Ray Stricklyn, H. M. Wynant. Average melodrama of feuding small-time stock car racers.

Tracks (1977) **C-90m.** *½ D: Henry Jaglom. Dennis Hopper, Taryn Power, Dean Stockwell, Topo Swope, Michael Emil, Zack Norman. Hopper escorts dead Vietnam buddy across the country by train, eventually goes bonkers. We've seen it before and almost always in less muddled fashion. Emil's and Norman's characters later got their own feature, SITTING DUCKS.▼

Track the Man Down (1955-British) **75m.** ** D: R. G. Springsteen. Kent Taylor, Petula Clark, Renee Houston, George Rose. Dog-tracking background makes this standard Scotland Yard murder hunt above par.

Track 29 (1988-British) **C-90m.** *½ D: Nicolas Roeg. Theresa Russell, Gary Oldman, Christopher Lloyd, Colleen Camp, Sandra Bernhard, Seymour Cassel, Leon Rippy, Vance Colvig. Bizarre black comedy about a love-starved woman, her nerdy husband who's obsessed with model trains, and a stranger who claims to be her long lost son! Even allowing for the usual eccentricities of director Roeg and writer Dennis Potter, this is pretty weird and not terribly entertaining. British-produced but filmed in North Carolina.▼

Trader Horn (1931) **120m.** *** D: W. S. Van Dyke II. Harry Carey, Edwina Booth, Duncan Renaldo, Olive Golden (Carey), Mutia Omoolu, C. Aubrey Smith. Early talkie classic filmed largely in African jungles still retains plenty of excitement in tale of veteran native dealer Carey encountering tribal hostility. Remade in 1973.

Trader Horn (1973) **C-105m.** *½ D: Reza S. Badiyi. Rod Taylor, Anne Heywood, Jean Sorel, Don Knight, Ed Bernard, Stack Pierce. Laughable remake of 1931 version has Taylor famed explorer and trader of African interior, accompanied by young widow. Obvious use of stock footage and the fact that cast never leaves backlot ruin all notion of believability.

Trader Tom of the China Seas SEE: **Target, Sea of China**

Trade Winds (1938) **90m.** *** D: Tay Garnett. Fredric March, Joan Bennett, Ralph Bellamy, Ann Sothern, Sidney Blackmer, Thomas Mitchell. Debonair detective March goes after murder-suspect Bennett; by the end of the around-the-world chase, they fall in love and solve mystery. Director Garnett filmed background footage on round-the-world cruise, but the stars never left the studio! This is the film where Bennett went from blond to brunette—and never went back.

Trading Places (1983) **C-116m.** **½ D: John Landis. Dan Aykroyd, Eddie Murphy, Ralph Bellamy, Don Ameche, Denholm Elliott, Jamie Lee Curtis, Paul Gleason, Kristin Holby, Jim Belushi, Alfred Drake. Fine cast breathes life into time-worn comedy premise (remember those Three Stooges shorts?) testing heredity vs. environment by switching a "have" (preppie Aykroyd) and a "have-not" (street hustler Murphy). Murphy, in his second film, is a comic powerhouse, and makes up for director Landis's indulgences—like a subplot involving a gorilla.▼

Traffic (1972-French) **C-89m.** ** D: Jacques Tati. Jacques Tati, Maria Kimberly, Marcel Fraval, H. Bostel, Tony Kneppers. Initially enjoyable outing with M. Hulot (Tati) trying to transport car from France to Dutch auto show bogs down in aimless side trips. Bright spots overwhelmed by general lethargy.

Tragedy of a Ridiculous Man (1981-Italian) **C-116m.** ** D: Bernardo Bertolucci. Ugo Tognazzi, Anouk Aimee, Laura Morante, Victor Cavallo, Ricardo Tognazzi. Disappointing drama about cheese manufacturer Tognazzi coping with son's alleged kidnapping by political terrorists. Bertolucci seems to be commenting on modern social and familial stresses and upheavals, but his message is incredibly muddled.

Trail of the Lonesome Pine (1936) **C-102m.** *** D: Henry Hathaway. Sylvia Sidney, Henry Fonda, Fred MacMurray, Fred Stone, Fuzzy Knight, Beulah Bondi, Spanky McFarland, Nigel Bruce. Classic story of feuding families and changes that come about when railroad is built on their land. Still remarkably strong today, with fine performances. First outdoor film in full Technicolor. Previously filmed in 1915.

Trail of the Pink Panther (1982) **C-97m.** ** D: Blake Edwards. Peter Sellers, David Niven, Herbert Lom, Richard Mulligan, Joanna Lumley, Robert Wagner, Capucine, Robert Loggia, Harvey Korman, Burt Kwouk, Graham Stark, Peter Arne. Attempt to fashion a new Pink Panther film, despite the death of series star Sellers, using previously unseen footage and new linking material. It almost works—until the seams begin to show, as reporter Lumley seeks out people who knew Clouseau for a TV story. Lom *does* have a sidesplitting scene in which he tries to eulogize his long-time nemesis—and can't stop laughing. Filmed at the same time as subsequent CURSE OF THE PINK PANTHER.▼

Trail of the Vigilantes (1940) **78m.** **½ D: Allan Dwan. Franchot Tone, Warren William, Broderick Crawford, Peggy Moran, Andy Devine, Mischa Auer, Porter Hall.

Tone is Eastern law enforcer out West to hunt down outlaw gang; lively comedy-Western.

Trail Street (1947) **84m.** ** D: Ray Enright. Randolph Scott, Robert Ryan, Anne Jeffreys, George "Gabby" Hayes, Madge Meredith, Steve Brodie. Scott stars as Bat Masterson, saving local townspeople from corrupt rule; standard oater.▼

Train, The (1965) **133m.** **** D: John Frankenheimer. Burt Lancaster, Paul Scofield, Michel Simon, Jeanne Moreau, Albert Remy, Wolfgang Preiss. Gripping WW2 actioner of French Resistance trying to waylay train carting French art treasures to Germany. High-powered excitement all the way.▼

Trained to Kill (1975) **C-91m.** *½ D: Daniel J. Vance. Stephen Sandor, Rockne Tarkington, Richard X. Slattery, Heidi Vaughn, Michael Lane. A Vietnam vet is forced to confront a sadistic gang in his home town; low-grade, graphically violent drama, made in 1973 as THE NO MERCY MAN.

Train Robbers, The (1973) **C-92m.** **½ D: Burt Kennedy. John Wayne, Ann-Margret, Rod Taylor, Ben Johnson, Christopher George, Ricardo Montalban, Bobby Vinton, Jerry Gatlin. Interesting little chamber-Western, reminiscent of Kennedy's early Randolph Scott scripts. Outlaw's widow hires Wayne and his pals to locate buried gold so she can return it and clear family name. Low-key film emphasizes character instead of action; relaxed performances, twist ending.▼

Train Robbery Confidential (1962-Brazilian) **102m.** **½ D: Roberto Farias. Eliezer Gomes, Reginaldo Farias, Grande Otelo, Atila Iorio. Labored account of six men involved in railroad heist, with disintegration of friendship due to greed.

Traitors, The (1963-British) **71m.** **½ D: Robert Tronson. Patrick Allen, James Maxwell, Zena Walker, Harold Goodwin, Sean Lynch. Fair spy meller of U.S. and British agent assigned to catch source of security leak in NATO.

Traitor's Gate (1964-British) **80m.** **½ D: Freddie Francis. Gary Raymond, Albert Lieven, Margot Trooger, Klaus Kinski, Catherina (Catherine) Von Schell. Two brothers are involved at sea in plot to steal crown jewels. Based on Edgar Wallace novel, film has fair acting, good direction.

Tramplers, The (1966-Italian) **C-105m.** ** D: Albert Band. Joseph Cotten, Gordon Scott, James Mitchum, Ilaria Occhini. Foreign-made Western set in post-Civil War South, with Cotten the domineering father; all just an excuse for gun-play.▼

Tramp, Tramp, Tramp (1942) **70m.** *½ D: Charles Barton. Jackie Gleason, Florence Rice, Jack Durant, Bruce Bennett. Meager comedy as Gleason and Durant,

4-F rejects, protect the homefront, becoming involved in murder caper.

Trancers SEE: **Future Cop** (1985)▼

Transatlantic Merry-Go-Round (1934) **92m.** ** D: Ben Stoloff. Jack Benny, Nancy Carroll, Gene Raymond, Sidney Blackmer, Patsy Kelly, Mitzi Green, Boswell Sisters. Whodunit set against musical story of ocean-going radio troupe led by Benny. Just fair, with some odd production numbers, and a plot resolution that's for the birds.▼

Transatlantic Tunnel (1935-British) **70m.** **½ D: Maurice Elvey. Richard Dix, Leslie Banks, Madge Evans, Helen Vinson, C. Aubrey Smith, George Arliss, Walter Huston. Disappointing story about building of transatlantic tunnel bogs down in two-dimensional character conflicts. Futuristic sets are main distinction. Originally 94m. and titled THE TUNNEL.▼

Transformers, The (1986) **C-86m.** BOMB D: Nelson Shin. Voices of Orson Welles, Robert Stack, Leonard Nimoy, Eric Idle, Judd Nelson, Lionel Stander. Obnoxious animated feature about the title good guys, who defend the universe against an evil planet (which has a voice of its own . . . provided by Orson Welles). That deafening rock score certainly doesn't help. Little more than a feature-length toy commercial. ▼

Transplant (1979) **C-100m. TVM** D: William A. Graham. Kevin Dobson, Melinda Dillon, Granville Van Dusen, Ronny Cox, Helen Hunt, Bibi Besch. Hard-driving young executive with weak heart agonizes over whether to undergo a transplant. Script by John Gay. Average.

Transylvania 6-5000 (1985) **C-94m.** BOMB D: Rudy DeLuca. Jeff Goldblum, Joseph Bologna, Ed Begley, Jr., Carol Kane, Jeffrey Jones, John Byner, Geena Davis, Michael Richards, Norman Fell, Teresa Ganzel. Tediously unfunny horror-movie spoof that wastes a lot of talent. Shot in Yugoslavia, and should have stayed there. ▼

Trap, The (1947) **68m.** D: Howard Bretherton. Sidney Toler, Mantan Moreland, Victor Sen Yung, Tanis Chandler, Larry Blake, Kirk Alyn, Rita Quigley, Anne Nagel. SEE: **Charlie Chan** series.

Trap, The (1959) **C-84m.** **½ D: Norman Panama. Richard Widmark, Lee J. Cobb, Tina Louise, Earl Holliman, Carl Benton Reid, Lorne Greene. Turgid drama set in Southwest desert town, with gangsters on the lam intimidating the few townspeople.▼

Trap, The (1966-British) **C-106m.** *** D: Sidney Hayers. Rita Tushingham, Oliver Reed, Rex Sevenoaks, Barbara Chilcott, Linda Goranson. Fur trapper Reed, having missed annual wife auction after three winters in the snow, settles for orphaned mute

Rita. Vivid 1890s tale, well photographed by Robert Krasker.▼

Trapeze (1956) **C-105m.** *** D: Carol Reed. Burt Lancaster, Tony Curtis, Gina Lollobrigida, Katy Jurado, Thomas Gomez, Johnny Puleo. Moody love triangle with a European circus background; aerialist Lancaster and Curtis vie in the air and on the ground for Gina's attention.▼

Trapped (1949) **78m.** **½ D: Richard Fleischer. Lloyd Bridges, Barbara Paxton, John Hoyt, James Todd. The FBI's hot on the trail of a gang of counterfeiters in this so-so thriller, done in the semi-documentary style typical of that era.▼

Trapped (1973) **C-74m. TVM** D: Frank DeFilitta. James Brolin, Susan Clark, Earl Holliman, Tammy Harrington, Robert Hooks, Ivy Jones, Bob Hastings. Man mugged in department store bathroom awakens to find he's been locked in overnight, is then attacked by security dogs. Good premise gone awry, thanks to faulty script and subplot. Average.

Trapped (1989) **C-100m. TVM** D: Fred Walton. Kathleen Quinlan, Bruce Abbott, Ben Loggins, Katy Boyer. Effective thriller about a woman trapped in her computer-activated high-rise office building with an industrial spy and a killer: a cat-and-mouse game spanning 63 floors. If is sounds like a change-of-gender DIE HARD stripped of its glitz and nonstop action, well . . . Made for cable. Average.▼

Trapped Beneath the Sea (1974) **C-100m. TVM** D: William A. Graham. Lee J. Cobb, Martin Balsam, Paul Michael Glaser, Cliff Potts, Laurie Prange, Joshua Bryant. Drama about efforts to rescue crew of four stranded in a mini-sub off Florida coast. Based on an actual event of June 17, 1973, and tautly told. Above average.

Trapped by Boston Blackie (1948) **67m.** D: Seymour Friedman. Chester Morris, June Vincent, Richard Lane, Patricia White (Barry), Edward Norris, George E. Stone. SEE: **Boston Blackie** series.

Trapped in Silence (1986) **C-100m. TVM** D: Michael Tuchner. Marsha Mason, Kiefer Sutherland, John Mahoney, Stephen Pearlman, Ron Silver, Amy Wright. Kiefer Sutherland (Donald's look-alike son) is an elective mute (capable of speaking but refusing), and Marsha Mason is the psychologist intent on getting through to him. Average.▼

Trapped in Tangiers (1960-Italian) **74m.** BOMB D: Antonio Cervi. Edmund Purdom, Genevieve Page, Gino Cervi, Jose Guadiola, Felix Bafauce, Antonio Molino. Dubbed dialog kills otherwise unsophisticated actioner of American uncovering dope ring in Tangiers.

Trauma (1962) **92m.** ** D: Robert Malcolm Young. John Conte, Lynn Bari, Lorre Richards, David Garner, Warren Kemmer-

ling, William Bissell. Heavy-handed chiller about Richards' attempt to recover lost memory of past horrors in spooky mansion.▼

Traveling Executioner, The (1970) **C-95m.** *½ D: Jack Smight. Stacy Keach, Marianna Hill, Bud Cort, Graham Jarvis, James J. Sloyan. Story of a man's love for an electric chair (spiritual) and love for a woman prisoner (sexual) may or may not be intended for laughs; either way, film is dull and the usually fine Keach gives hammy performance.

Traveling Man (1989) **C-105m. TVM** D: Irvin Kershner. John Lithgow, John Glover, Jonathan Silverman, Chynna Phillips, Margaret Colin. Burned-out traveling salesman is teamed by his unscrupulous boss with a backstabbing young hotshot who filches his accounts. Good character studies by the three leads battle a leaden story. Made for cable. Average.

Traveling Saleslady (1935) **63m.** **½ D: Ray Enright. Joan Blondell, Glenda Farrell, William Gargan, Hugh Herbert, Grant Mitchell. Snappy Warner Bros. programmer, with Blondell helping to put over inventor Herbert's booze-flavored toothpaste—in order to teach her stubborn father (a rival toothpaste manufacturer) a lesson.

Traveling Saleswoman (1950) **75m.** ** D: Charles F. Riesner. Joan Davis, Andy Devine, Adele Jergens, Chief Thundercloud. Davis and Devine mug it up as soap saleswoman and fiancé in stale Western comedy.

Travelling North (1987-Australian) **C-98m.** **½ D: Carl Schultz. Leo McKern, Julia Blake, Henri Szeps, Graham Kennedy, Michele Fawdon, Diane Craig. Irascible retiree falls in love with a divorcee, and they move to an idyllic retirement home in North Queensland, Australia . . . but their life together is clouded almost immediately when he learns he has a serious heart condition. Fine performances highlight this simple, straightforward adaptation of David Williamson's play—which, ultimately, may be a bit *too* simple and straightforward.▼

Travels With Anita SEE: **Lovers and Liars**▼

Travels with My Aunt (1972) **C-109m.** **½ D: George Cukor. Maggie Smith, Alec McCowen, Lou Gossett, Robert Stephens, Cindy Williams. Stylish adaptation of Graham Greene book about straitlaced McCowen being swept into crazy world of his aunt (Smith) who takes him all over Europe on what turns out to be shady scheme. Deliberately paced film never really gets going, leaves viewer in midair like final tossed coin. Anthony Powell earned an Oscar for his costumes.

Travis Logan, D.A. (1970) **C-100m. TVM** D: Paul Wendkos. Vic Morrow, Hal

Holbrook, Brenda Vaccaro, George Grizzard, Scott Marlowe. Barely clever attempt by man to plan perfect murder thwarted by central character Logan (Morrow), enlivened by somewhat offbeat direction. Average.

Travis McGee (1983) **C-100m. TVM** D: Andrew V. McLaglen. Sam Elliott, Gene Evans, Katharine Ross, Vera Miles, Amy Madigan, Richard Farnsworth, Geoffrey Lewis. John D. MacDonald's macho sleuth gets enmeshed in a muddled case involving a drunken old salt, a neurotic pianist, and the sister of a presumably drowned land developer. Elliott's McGee is so somnambulent that by the first commercial break you'll be asleep, too. Any chances for a series were deep sixed with the land developer. Adapted by the usually adroit Stirling Silliphant from *The Empty Copper Sea*. Below average.

T. R. Baskin (1971) **C-90m.** **½ D: Herbert Ross. Candice Bergen, Peter Boyle, James Caan, Marcia Rodd, Erin O'Reilly, Howard Platt. Beautiful young small-town girl tries to make it in Chicago, finds problems in the big city. Wildly uneven comedy-drama has a few nice scenes, good acting by Caan in small role. Written and produced by Peter Hyams.

✓ **Treasure Island** (1934) **105m.** ***½ D: Victor Fleming. Wallace Beery, Jackie Cooper, Lewis Stone, Lionel Barrymore, Otto Kruger, Nigel Bruce, Douglass Dumbrille. Stirring adaptation of Robert Louis Stevenson pirate yarn of 18th-century England and journey to isle of hidden bounty; Beery is a boisterous Long John Silver in fine film with top production values. Only flaw is a stiff Cooper as Jim Hawkins. Also shown in computer-colored version.▼

✓ **Treasure Island** (1950) **C-96m.** ***½ D: Byron Haskin. Bobby Driscoll, Robert Newton, Basil Sydney, Walter Fitzgerald, Denis O'Dea, Ralph Truman, Finlay Currie. Vivid Disney version of Robert Louis Stevenson's classic, filmed in England, with Driscoll a fine Jim Hawkins and Newton the definitive Long John Silver. Changes the novel's original ending, but who's quibbling? "Objectionable" violence was deleted from 1975 reissue version.▼

Treasure Island (1972-British) **C-94m.** ** D: John Hough. Orson Welles, Kim Burfield, Walter Slezak, Lionel Stander. Weak retelling of classic tale finds very hammy Welles (who also co-scripted) in the role of Long John Silver.

Treasure Island (1990) **C-131m. TVM** D: Fraser Heston. Charlton Heston, Christian Bale, Julian Glover, Richard Johnson, Oliver Reed, Christopher Lee, Clive Wood, Nicholas Amer, Michael Halsey. Exciting, realistic, and beautifully photographed version of classic pirate adventure remains faithful in spirit to Robert Louis Stevenson's masterwork. Heston is effectively

cast against type as Long John Silver, with Bale as sturdy young Jim Hawkins. Reed and Lee have brief but vivid turns as the doomed Capt. Billy Bones and the hideous Blind Pew. Filmed on location in Cornwall and Port Antonio, Jamaica, aboard the H.M.S. *Bounty* (from the 1962 MUTINY ON THE BOUNTY), with a flavorful score by Paddy Maloney and The Chieftains. Directorial debut for Heston's son who also produced and scripted. Made for cable. Above average.▼

Treasure of Fear SEE: **Scared Stiff** (1945)▼

Treasure of Jamaica Reef, The (1974) **C-96m.** *½ D: Virginia Stone. Stephen Boyd, Chuck Woolery, Roosevelt Grier, David Ladd, Cheryl Stoppelmoor (Ladd). A search for gold buried deep in the Caribbean. Of interest only for the presence of Stoppelmoor/Ladd pre-*Charlie's Angels*. Originally titled EVIL IN THE DEEP.▼

Treasure of Lost Canyon, The (1952) **C-82m.** ** D: Ted Tetzlaff. William Powell, Julia (Julie) Adams, Rosemary DeCamp, Charles Drake, Tommy Ivo. Mild Western, uplifted by Powell as old prospector. Youth uncovers treasure which causes unhappiness to all. From a Robert Louis Stevenson story.

Treasure of Matecumbe (1976) **C-117m.** **½ D: Vincent McEveety. Robert Foxworth, Joan Hackett, Peter Ustinov, Vic Morrow, Jane Wyatt, Johnny Doran, Billy "Pop" Attmore. Two boys with treasure map are aided in their quest by Foxworth, Hackett, and Ustinov . . . and pursued by bad-guy Morrow. Ustinov adds life to Disney film, but the "quest" seems endless. Filmed in the Florida Keys.▼

Treasure of Monte Cristo (1949) **79m.** ** D: William Berke. Glenn Langan, Adele Jergens, Steve Brodie, Robert Jordan, Michael Whelan, Sid Melton. Jergens marries seaman Langan, a descendant of the Count of Monte Cristo, for his inheritance, then falls in love with him. Adequate programmer.

Treasure of Monte Cristo, The (1960-British) **C-95m.** ** D: Robert S. Baker, Monty Berman. Rory Calhoun, Patricia Bredin, Peter Arne, Gianna Maria Canale. Uninspired variation on Dumas tale, with Calhoun aiding Bredin unearth buried treasure: slow-moving yarn.

Treasure of Pancho Villa, The (1955) **C-96m.** *½ D: George Sherman. Rory Calhoun, Shelley Winters, Gilbert Roland, Joseph Calleia. Good cast wasted in plodding account of famed 1910s Mexican bandit.▼

Treasure of Ruby Hills (1955) **71m.** *½ D: Frank McDonald. Zachary Scott, Carole Matthews, Barton MacLane, Dick Foran, Lola Albright. Uninspired Western of land-grabbing ranchers.

good ✓

Treasure of San Gennaro, The (1966-Italian-German-French) **C-102m.** ** D: Dino Risi. Nino Manfredi, Senta Berger, Harry Guardino, Claudine Auger, Toto, Mario Adorf. American Guardino and girlfriend Berger plan to rob the treasure of Naples' patron saint, San Gennaro, in typical caper film occasionally redeemed by good comic bits. Poorly dubbed.

Treasure of Silver Lake, The (1965-German) **C-88m.** ** D: Harald Reinl. Lex Barker, Gotz George, Pierre Brice, Herbert Lom, Karin Dor, Marianne Hoppe. Dubbed dialogue almost ruins average Western based on Karl May novels with familiar characters Shatterhand and Winnetou.

Treasure of Tayopa (1974) **C-90m.** BOMB D: Bob Cawley. Gilbert Roland, Rena Winters, Bob Corrigan, Phil Trapani, Frank Hernandez, Andrew Farnsworth. Low-grade modern Western about an expedition led by Winters to find a centuries-lost treasure trove in the Mexican hills. Psycho Trapani turns it into a senseless bloodbath. Only professional connected with the film, Roland, appears in the prologue and epilogue to give credence to the Tayopa legend.

Treasure of the Amazon, The (1985-Mexican) **C-104m.** ** D: Rene Cardona, Jr. Stuart Whitman, Emilio Fernandez, Donald Pleasence, Bradford Dillman, Ann Sidney, John Ireland, Sonia Infante. Silly adventure film has Whitman leading South American expedition to recover treasure trove of diamonds. Mucho violence. ▼

Treasure of the Four Crowns (1983-Spanish) **C-97m.** BOMB D: Ferdinando Baldi. Tony Anthony, Ana Obregon, Gene Quintano, Francisco Rabal, Jerry Lazarus. Fortune hunters seek ancient prize. It's no accident that the title of this 3-D potboiler sounds suspiciously like RAIDERS OF THE LOST ARK. From the same folks who brought you COMIN AT YA!▼

Treasure of the Golden Condor (1953) **C-93m.** **½ D: Delmer Daves. Cornel Wilde, Constance Smith, Fay Wray, Anne Bancroft, Leo G. Carroll, Bobby (Robert) Blake. Predictable costumer set in 18th-century Latin America, with noble-born Wilde out to claim his fortune. Remake of SON OF FURY.▼

Treasure of the Sierra Madre, The (1948) **124m.** **** D: John Huston. Humphrey Bogart, Walter Huston, Tim Holt, Bruce Bennett, Barton MacLane, Alfonso Bedoya. Excellent adaptation of B. Traven's tale of gold, greed, and human nature at its worst, with Bogart, Huston, and Holt as unlikely trio of prospectors. John Huston won Oscars for Best Direction and Screenplay, and his father Walter won as Best Supporting Actor. That's John as an American tourist near the beginning, and young

Robert Blake selling lottery tickets. Also shown in computer-colored version.▼

Tree Grows in Brooklyn, A (1945) **128m.** **** D: Elia Kazan. Dorothy McGuire, Joan Blondell, James Dunn, Lloyd Nolan, Peggy Ann Garner, Ted Donaldson, James Gleason, Ruth Nelson, John Alexander. Splendid, sensitive film from Betty Smith's novel about a bright young girl trying to rise above the hardships of her tenement life in turn of the century Brooklyn, New York. Perfect in every detail. Dunn won an Oscar as ne'er-do-well father, Garner received a special Academy Award for her performance. Screenplay by Tess Slesinger and Frank Davis. An impressive Hollywood directorial debut by Kazan. Remade for TV.▼

Tree Grows in Brooklyn, A (1974) **C-78m.** TVM D: Joseph Hardy. Cliff Robertson, Diane Baker, James Olson, Pamelyn Ferdin, Nancy Malone, Allyn Ann McLerie, Michael-James Wixted. Lovingly made remake of the 1945 classic with a sterling performance by Robertson and fine work by the others. Blanche Hanalis updated the original screenplay. Above average

Tree of the Wooden Clogs, The (1978-Italian) **C-185m.** **** D: Ermanno Olmi. Luigi Ornaghi, Francesca Moriggi, Omar Brignoli, Antonio Ferrari. A year in the life of a community of peasants in Northern Italy, just before the turn of the century. Simple, quietly beautiful epic; a work of art.

Tremors (1990) **C-96m.** *** D: Ron Underwood. Kevin Bacon, Fred Ward, Finn Carter, Michael Gross, Reba McEntire, Bobby Jacoby, Charlotte Stewart, Tony Genaros, Victor Wong. Sharp, funny, and fast-paced, this is an effective updating of 1950s monster-movie themes. Bacon and Ward, amiable handymen, lead a misfit group in a desert valley battling against giant wormlike predators that burrow through the sand. Cast is good, the music appropriate, and special effects outstanding. A small winner all around.▼

Trenchcoat (1983) **C-91m.** ** D: Michael Tuchner. Margot Kidder, Robert Hays, Daniel Faraldo, Gila von Weitershausen, David Suchet, Ronald Lacey. Another attempt by the Disney studio to change image finds amateur mystery writer Kidder on vacation in Malta, suddenly involved in real murder and international intrigue with undercover agent Hays. Forced mystery-comedy is reminiscent of the company's juvenile outings of the '50s and '60s, but this one has no Shaggy Dog to redeem it.▼

Trenchcoat in Paradise (1989) **C-100m.** TVM D: Martha Coolidge. Dirk Benedict, Sydney Walsh, Bruce Dern, Catherine Oxenberg, Michelle Phillips, Jeremy Slate, Kim Zimmer. Small-time private eye from New Jersey hightails it to Hawaii after crossing the mob; he gets sucked into a murder case there involving a real estate scam and a couple of hot tomatoes. Cheeky P.I. pilot to prospective series. Average.

Trent's Last Case (1952-British) **90m.** **½ D: Herbert Wilcox. Michael Wilding, Margaret Lockwood, Orson Welles, Hugh McDermott. Superior cast in lukewarm tale of the investigation of businessman's suicide. Previously filmed (by Howard Hawks) in 1929.

Trespasses (1987) **C-100m.** BOMB D: Loren Bivens, Adam Roarke. Robert Kuhn, Van Brooks, Mary Pillot, Adam Roarke, Lou Diamond Phillips, Ben Johnson. A sleep-inducing waste, with cattleman Kuhn and rape victim Pillot becoming involved; her spineless husband and the pair of rapists are the heavies. Phillips coauthored this. Shot in 1983.▼

Trial (1955) **105m.** *** D: Mark Robson. Glenn Ford, Dorothy McGuire, John Hodiak, Arthur Kennedy, Katy Jurado, Rafael Campos. Intelligent filming of Don Mankiewicz novel, scripted by the author. Courtroomer involves Mexican boy accused of murder, but actually tied in with pro- vs. anti-Communist politics.

Trial, The (1963-French-Italian-German) **118m.** ***½ D: Orson Welles. Anthony Perkins, Jeanne Moreau, Romy Schneider, Elsa Martinelli, Orson Welles, Akim Tamiroff. Gripping, if somewhat muddled, adaptation of Kafka novel of man in nameless country arrested for crime that is never explained to him. Not for all tastes.▼

Trial by Combat SEE: **Dirty Knight's Work**

Trial and Error SEE: **Dock Brief, The**

Trial of Billy Jack, The (1974) **C-175m.** BOMB D: Frank Laughlin. Tom Laughlin, Delores Taylor, Victor Izay, Teresa Laughlin, William Wellman, Jr., Sacheen Littlefeather. Further adventures of Mr. Peacethrough-Violence prove that Laughlin is the only actor intense enough to risk a hernia from reading lines. Laughable until final, nauseating massacre scene that renders film's constant yammering about "peace" ludicrous.

Trial of Chaplain Jensen, The (1975) **C-78m.** TVM D: Robert Day. James Franciscus, Joanna Miles, Lynda Day George, Dorothy Tristan, Charles Durning, Harris Yulin. Franciscus is the only U.S. Navy officer ever court-martialed for adultery. True but trite. Average.

Trial of Lee Harvey Oswald, The (1977) **C-210m.** TVM D: David Greene. Ben Gazzara, Lorne Greene, John Pleshette, Mo Malone, Frances Lee McCain, Lawrence Pressman, Marisa Pavan. Intriguing courtroom drama from the "what if?" school of story-telling. Pleshette is quite good as Oswald, who may or may not have been involved in any of the Kennedy

assassination conspiracy theories (including several that are quite bizarre), which are explored here. Originally shown in two parts. Released on video at 192m. Above average.▼

Trial of the Incredible Hulk, The (1989) **C-100m.** TVM D: Bill Bixby. Bill Bixby, Lou Ferrigno, Rex Smith, John Rhys-Davies, Marta DuBois, Nancy Everhard, Nicholas Hormann, Joseph Mascolo. Second post-series Hulk movie has the big green guy joining forces with the blind Marvel Comics superhero, Daredevil, to do battle with a ruthless mobster who's out to control the crime underworld. Average.

Trial Run (1969) **C-98m.** TVM D: William Graham. James Franciscus, Leslie Nielsen, Diane Baker, Janice Rule, John Vernon, David Sheiner, Fred Beir. Cynical, near-brilliant look at high-priced modern-day lawyers. Franciscus will stop at nothing for status in high-powered firm. Some overly flashy direction, one lopsided sequence, but strong drama nonetheless. Above average.

Trials of Oscar Wilde, The (1960-British) **C-123m.** *** D: Ken Hughes. Peter Finch, Yvonne Mitchell, John Fraser, Lionel Jeffries, Nigel Patrick, James Mason. Fascinating, well-acted chronicle of Oscar Wilde's libel suit against the Marquis of Queensberry and the tragic turn his life takes because of it. Finch is superb as the once brilliant wit who winds up in prison; stylish widescreen photography by Ted Moore. Released at the same time as OSCAR WILDE with Robert Morley.

Triangle Factory Fire Scandal, The (1979) **C-100m.** TVM D: Mel Stuart. Tom Bosley, David Dukes, Tovah Feldshuh, Janet Margolin, Stephanie Zimbalist, Lauren Frost, Stacey Nelkin, Ted Wass, Charlotte Rae, Milton Selzer, Valerie Landsburg. How to turn a real-life catastrophe (the turn-of-the-century N.Y.C. fire that revolutionized working conditions and fire regulations) into a dull soap opera. Average.▼

Tribe, The (1974) **C-78m.** TVM D: Richard A. Colla. Victor French, Warren Vanders, Henry Wilcoxon, Adriana Shaw, Stewart Moss, Sam Gilman, Meg Wylie. Offbeat, unsatisfactory drama about cave men, with group of Cro-Magnons battling vicious Neanderthals at the dawn of history. Below average.

Tribes (1970) **C-74m.** TVM D: Joseph Sargent. Darren McGavin, Jan-Michael Vincent, Earl Holliman, John Gruber, Danny Goldman, Richard Yniguez. THE D.I. updated for the anti-war era, with tough marine drill instructor McGavin having his hands full with longhair Vincent. Incisive mix of comedy, drama, and social comment, with Emmy-winning script by Tracy Keenan Wynn and Marvin Schwartz. Shown theatrically overseas as THE SOL-

DIER WHO DECLARED PEACE. Above average.▼

Tribute (1980-Canadian) **C-121m.** ** D: Bob Clark. Jack Lemmon, Robby Benson, Lee Remick, Colleen Dewhurst, John Marley, Kim Cattrall, Gale Garnett. Mawkish adaptation of Bernard Slade's play about a life-of-the-party type who's dying of cancer and wants to work out a relationship with his estranged son. Badly directed, with sledgehammer approach to sentiment. Worked much better on stage (where Lemmon created the role). Exteriors filmed in N.Y.C.; scripted by Slade.▼

Tribute to a Bad Man (1956) **C-95m.** *** D: Robert Wise. James Cagney, Don Dubbins, Stephen McNally, Irene Papas, Vic Morrow, Royal Dano, Lee Van Cleef. Cagney is the whole show in this Western about a resourceful, ruthless land baron using any means possible to retain his vast possessions.

Trick Baby (1973) **C-89m.** ** D: Larry Yust. Kiel Martin, Mel Stewart, Dallas Edwards Hayes, Beverly Ballard. Con-man who passes for white uses trickery to cash in on society. Usual black exploitation film. Retitled DOUBLE CON.

Trick or Treat (1986) **C-97m.** ** D: Charles Martin Smith, Marc Price, Tony Fields, Lisa Orgolini, Doug Savant, Gene Simmons, Ozzy Osbourne. Hey kids, rock 'n' roll really *is* the Devil's music! Fan of recently killed rocker conjures the dead star by playing his unreleased last album backward—but finds his hero is evil and bent on the world's destruction. Clever and well made, but story becomes terribly trite. Debuting director Smith has a cameo as a high school teacher.▼

Trick or Treats (1982) **C-91m.** BOMB D: Gary Graver. Jackelyn Giroux, David Carradine, Carrie Snodgress, Steve Railsback, Peter Jason, Chris Graver, Paul Bartel. Giroux is far too old to be convincing as a terrorized baby-sitter in this cheap horror spoof. Orson Welles is credited as consultant; director Graver is better-known as the camerman Welles relied upon in his later film projects. ▼

Tricks of the Trade (1988) **C-100m.** TVM D: Jack Bender. Cindy Williams, Markie Post, Chris Mulkey, James Whitmore, Jr., Scott Paulin, John Ritter. Fetching odd-couple comedy teaming the pampered, insulated wife of a prosperous stockbroker with a high-priced hooker to find his killer. Attractive performances by the two actresses and inventive direction by Bender—leading up to a zany shootout in a sex shop!—give this lighthearted suspense tale all the right touches. Written by Noreen Stone. Above average.

Trilogy of Terror (1975) **C-78m.** TVM D: Dan Curtis. Karen Black, Robert Bur-

ton, John Karlen, George Gaynes, James Storm, Gregory Harrison, Kathryn Reynolds. Karen plays four tormented women in three exercises in the bizarre by writer Richard Matheson. Best: the third, "Prey," has devil doll hounding her almost to death. This segment alone is worth your time. Above average.▼

Trinity Is STILL My Name! (1972-Italian) **C-117m.** **½ D: E. B. Clucher (Enzo Barboni). Terence Hill, Bud Spencer, Harry Carey, Jr., Jessica Dublin, Yanti Somer. Sequel to THEY CALL ME TRINITY is even funnier, as Trinity and Bambino mosey their way through a clutch of archetypal Western situations with their usual aplomb; scene in a chic French restaurant is a hoot. Later cut to 101m.; original Italian running time 124m.▼

Trio (1950-British) **88m.** *** D: Ken Annakin, Harold French. James Hayter, Kathleen Harrison, Anne Crawford, Nigel Patrick, Jean Simmons, Michael Rennie. Following the success of QUARTET, three more diverting Somerset Maugham stories, "The Verger," "Mr. Knowall," and "Sanatorium." All beautifully acted.▼

Trip, The (1967) **C-85m.** ** D: Roger Corman. Peter Fonda, Susan Strasberg, Bruce Dern, Dennis Hopper, Salli Sachsi, Dick Miller, Luana Anders, Peter Bogdanovich. TV commercial director Fonda takes his first LSD trip. Definitely a relic of its era, with a screenplay by Jack Nicholson.▼

Triple Cross (1967-French-British) **C-126m.** ** D: Terence Young. Christopher Plummer, Yul Brynner, Romy Schneider, Trevor Howard, Gert Frobe, Claudine Auger. Adequate WW2 spy yarn features Plummer as real-life British safecracker Eddie Chapman, who works both sides of the fence. A bit too long.

Triplecross (1986) **C-100m.** TVM D: David Greene. Ted Wass, Markie Post, Gary Swanson, Shannon Wilcox, Barbara Horan. Three competitive millionaire private eyes vie with one another to solve a complicated murder case in this lighthearted but tired pilot to a prospective series. Below average.

Triple Deception (1956-British) **C-85m.** ** D: Guy Green. Michael Craig, Julia Arnall, Brenda De Banzie, Geoffrey Keen, Eric Pohlmann, Patrick Westwood. On-location filming in France enhances murder tale with Craig the wily imposter caught in his own web.

Triple Echo (1973-British) **C-90m.** *** D: Michael Apted. Glenda Jackson, Oliver Reed, Brian Deacon, Jenny Lee Wright. High-powered talent in sensitive story of transvestite in English countryside during WW2. Young Deacon, an army deserter, is persuaded by lonely farm woman Jackson to pose as her sister, then tough tank

Sergeant Reed becomes involved. Retitled SOLDIER IN SKIRTS.▼

Triple Trouble (1950) **66m.** D: Jean Yarbrough. Leo Gorcey, Huntz Hall, Gabriel Dell, Lyn Thomas, George Chandler, Bernard Gorcey. SEE: **Bowery Boys** series.

Tripoli (1950) **C-95m.** ** D: Will Price. John Payne, Maureen O'Hara, Howard da Silva, Connie Gilchrist. Good cast cannot save average script of U.S. marines battling Barbary pirates in 1805; sole standout is da Silva.

Trip to Bountiful, The (1985) **C-106m.** *** D: Peter Masterson. Geraldine Page, John Heard, Carlin Glynn, Richard Bradford, Rebecca De Mornay, Kevin Cooney. Leisurely, richly textured filmization of Horton Foote's 1953 television play (later done on Broadway) about a widow, living unhappily with her son and daughter-in-law, determined to make her way home to Bountiful, Texas, for one last look. Page won well-deserved Oscar for her heartbreaking performance, but entire cast is excellent. Fine filmmaking debut for stage director Masterson.▼

Tristana (1970-French-Spanish) **C-98m.** ***½ D: Luis Buñuel. Catherine Deneuve, Fernando Rey, Franco Nero, Jesus Fernandez, Lola Gaos, Vincent Solder. Deneuve is Tristana, a young woman who goes to live with her guardian (Rey) after her mother dies. Rey falls in love with her but faces competition from Nero. One of Buñuel's most serene, serious yet perverse studies of Catholicism, old age, death, desire, and deformity. Beautifully filmed in Toledo, Spain. Released in Europe at 105m.

Tristan and Isolde SEE **Lovespell** ▼

Triumph of Hercules, The (1964-Italian) **C-90m.** ** D: Alberto De Martino. Dan Vadis, Moira Orfei, Pierre Cressoy, Marilu Tolo, Piero Lupi. Average gymnastic runthrough with Vadis more resourceful than most Hercules.

Triumph of Sherlock Holmes, The (1935-British) **75m.** **½ D: Leslie Hiscott. Arthur Wontner, Ian Fleming, Lyn Harding, Leslie Perrins, Jane Carr, Charles Mortimer. Wontner and Fleming make a very acceptable team as Holmes and Watson in this minor British series entry about murder and a secret society among coal miners. Based on Conan Doyle's "The Valley of Fear." Original British running time: 84m.▼

Triumph of the Spirit (1989) **C-121m.** *** D: Robert M. Young. Willem Dafoe, Edward James Olmos, Robert Loggia, Wendy Gazelle, Kelly Wolf, Costas Mandylor, Kario Salem. Hard-hitting, heartbreaking, based-on-fact account of Salamo Arouch (Dafoe), Greek-Jewish boxer who is deported with his family to Auschwitz during WW2. Sometimes *too* grim, but

it's a story that needs to be told and remembered. Filmed on location at Auschwitz-Birkenau.▼

Triumph of the Ten Gladiators (1964-Italian) **C-94m.** ** D: Nick Nostro. Dan Vadis, Helga Line, Stanley Kent, Gianni Rizzo, Halina Zalewska, John Heston. If not strong on plot, film allows for exuberances of swordplay and knockout brawls; set in ancient Rome.

Triumph of the Will (1935-German) **110m.** **** D: Leni Riefenstahl. Riefenstahl's infamous documentary on Hitler's 1934 Nuremberg rallies is rightly regarded as the greatest propaganda film of all time. Fascinating and (of course) frightening to see.▼

Triumphs of a Man Called Horse (1983-U.S.-Mexican) **C-86m.** *½ D: John Hough. Richard Harris, Michael Beck, Ana De Sade, Vaughn Armstrong, Anne Seymour, Buck Taylor. Limp sequel to THE RETURN OF A MAN CALLED HORSE with Beck, as Harris' half-breed son, attempting to shelter Sioux from greedy white settlers. Fans of the two earlier HORSES will be disappointed.▼

Trog (1970-British) **C-91m.** BOMB D: Freddie Francis. Joan Crawford, Michael Gough, Kim Braden, David Griffin, John Hamill. Missing Link discovered by anthropologist Crawford naturally gets loose and does its thing. Do yours—don't watch it. Sadly, Crawford's last film.

Trojan Horse, The (1962-Italian) **C-105m.** **½ D: Giorgio Ferroni. Steve Reeves, John Drew Barrymore, Hedy Vessel, Juliette Mayniel. Above-average production values and Barrymore's presence in role of Ulysses inflates rating of otherwise stale version of Homer's epic.

Trojan Women, The (1972-Greek-U.S.) **C-105m.** ** D: Michael Cacoyannis. Katharine Hepburn, Irene Papas, Genevieve Bujold, Vanessa Redgrave, Patrick Magee, Brian Blessed. Euripides' tragedy about the plight of the women of Troy after its army is defeated gets a surprisingly flat (albeit faithful) rendering here, although any film which brings together four such great actresses can't be totally dismissed.▼

Troll (1986) **C-86m.** *½ D: John Buechler. Michael Moriarty, Shelley Hack, Noah Hathaway, Jenny Beck, Sonny Bono, June Lockhart, Anne Lockhart, Brad Hall, Julie-Louis Dreyfuss. If your idea of entertainment is seeing Sonny Bono metamorphose into an apartment of foliage, this is the movie for you. Angelic tyke is possessed by a troll, who takes over her body and starts turning the neighbors into seed pods that eventually turn into new trolls. Too close to GREMLINS; some viewers may get off on hearing June Lockhart swear. ▼

Tron (1982) **C-96m.** ** D: Steven Lisberger. Jeff Bridges, Bruce Boxleitner, David Warner, Cindy Morgan, Barnard Hughes, Dan Shor. A computer whiz is sucked inside a powerful computer, where he must fight for his life in a giant videogame competition. State-of-the-art special effects are stunning, but the story runs out of steam too soon, with only Bridges' charisma to keep it afloat. Disappointing Disney production.▼

Troop Beverly Hills (1989) **C-105m.** **½ D: Jeff Kanew. Shelley Long, Craig T. Nelson, Betty Thomas, Mary Gross, Stephanie Beacham, Audra Lindley, Edd Byrnes, Ami Foster, Jenny Lewis. Sometimes-amusing comedy about a spoiled, wealthy Beverly Hills housewife who leads her daughter's Girl Scout troop on unique outings on which everyone learns about self-esteem—and Gucci loafers. Predictable, to be sure, but undemanding fun.▼

Trooper Hook (1957) **81m.** **½ D: Charles Marquis Warren. Joel McCrea, Barbara Stanwyck, Earl Holliman, Susan Kohner, Sheb Wooley, Celia Lovsky. Woman scorned by whites for having lived with Indians and having child by the chief, begins anew with cavalry officer.

Tropic Holiday (1938) **78m.** **½ D: Theodore Reed. Dorothy Lamour, Ray Milland, Martha Raye, Bob Burns, Tito Guizar. Silly musical set in Mexico, with perky performances by all.

Tropic of Cancer (1970) **C-87m.** ***½ D: Joseph Strick. Rip Torn, James Callahan, Ellen Burstyn, David Bauer, Laurence Ligneres, Phil Brown. Director Strick is generally more successful with Henry Miller than he's been with James Joyce, thanks to Torn's earthy portrayal of the loose-living expatriate author amidst a string of amorous adventures in '20s Paris. Slapdash but invigorating; Burstyn makes a strong impression in tiny role as Henry's disgusted wife. Originally rated X.

Tropic Zone (1953) **C-94m.** *½ D: Lewis R. Foster. Ronald Reagan, Rhonda Fleming, Estelita, Noah Beery. Blah actioner set in South America with Reagan fighting the good cause to save a banana plantation from outlaws.

Trottie True SEE: **Gay Lady, The**▼

Trouble Along the Way (1953) **110m.** **½ D: Michael Curtiz. John Wayne, Donna Reed, Charles Coburn, Sherry Jackson, Marie Windsor. Unusually sentimental Wayne vehicle casts him as divorced man trying to maintain custody of his daughter (Jackson); he earns back self-respect by coaching football team for small Catholic school.

Trouble at 16 SEE: **Platinum High School**
Trouble Comes to Town (1972) **C-74m.** TVM D: Daniel Petrie. Lloyd Bridges, Pat Hingle, Hari Rhodes, Janet MacLachlan, Sheree North, Thomas Evans, Joseph Bottoms. Southern sheriff (Bridges), against protests of blacks and whites, takes in son of man who saved his life in Korea, eventually leading to strained situation. Better-than-average script by David Westheimer, good casting of important role, intelligent resolution. Above average.

Trouble for Two (1936) **75m.** *** D: J. Walter Ruben. Robert Montgomery, Rosalind Russell, Frank Morgan, Reginald Owen, Louis Hayward. Unique, offbeat black comedy of Montgomery and Russell joining London Suicide Club; based on Robert Louis Stevenson story.

Trouble in High Timber Country (1980) **C-100m.** TVM D: Vincent Sherman. Eddie Albert, Joan Goodfellow, Martin Kove, Robin Dearden, Belinda J. Montgomery, Kevin Brophy, Steve Doubet, Scott Yeager, James B. Sikking, Bettye Ackerman, Richard Sanders. Family's lumber and mining empire is threatened by conglomerate takeover in this middling pilot to the quickie series, *The Yeagers*, which had Andy Griffith stepping into Albert's shoes. Average.

Trouble in Mind (1985) **C-111m.** **½ D: Alan Rudolph. Kris Kristofferson, Keith Carradine, Lori Singer, Geneviève Bujold, Joe Morton, Divine, George Kirby, John Considine. Highly stylized, highly individual melodrama set in the near future, with Kristofferson as idealistic ex-cop, fresh from a stretch in jail, who gets involved with some young innocents who've just come to the big city. Odd, unusual, with 1940s *film noir* feeling but so determinedly vague and unreal that it also comes off rather cold. Still, it's an eyeful, and recommended for fans of the offbeat and Rudolph in particular. Title song sung by Marianne Faithful. ▼

Trouble in Paradise (1932) **83m.** **** D: Ernst Lubitsch. Miriam Hopkins, Kay Francis, Herbert Marshall, Charlie Ruggles, Edward Everett Horton, C. Aubrey Smith, Robert Grieg, Leonid Kinskey. Sparkling Lubitsch confection about two jewel thieves (Marshall and Hopkins) who fall in love, but find their relationship threatened when he turns on the charm to their newest (female) victim. This film is a working definition of the term "sophisticated comedy." Script by Samson Raphaelson and Grover Jones.

Trouble in Paradise (1988-U.S.-Australian) **C-100m.** TVM D: Di Drew. Raquel Welch, Jack Thompson, Nicholas Hammond, John Gregg. An elegantly tailored widow finds herself marooned on a tropical island with a carousing Aussie seaman and stalked by a gang of drug smugglers. Raquel sashays around seductively (and revealingly) at the head of an all-Australian cast in this harmless comedy that borrows generously from

Barrie's THE ADMIRABLE CRICHTON and Wertmuller's SWEPT AWAY. Average.

Trouble in Store (1953-British) **85m.** **½ D: John Paddy Carstairs. Margaret Rutherford, Norman Wisdom, Moira Lister, Megs Jenkins. Full of fun sight gags and good character actors, film traces ups-and-downs of naive department store worker. Wisdom's film debut.▼

Trouble in the Glen (1953-British) **C-91m.** ** D: Herbert Wilcox. Margaret Lockwood, Orson Welles, Forrest Tucker, Victor McLaglen. Scottish-based drama of feud over closing of road that has been used for a long time. Average-to-poor script benefits from Welles.▼

Troublemaker, The (1964) **80m.** ** D: Theodore Flicker. Tom Aldredge, Joan Darling, Theodore Flicker, Buck Henry, Godfrey Cambridge, Al Freeman, Jr. Terribly dated, independently made comedy about a country bumpkin's adventures in N.Y.C.; most interesting as an artifact of its time, made by the talented improvisational comedy troupe known as The Premise.

Trouble Makers (1948) **69m.** D: Reginald LeBorg. Leo Gorcey, Huntz Hall, Gabriel Dell, Helen Parrish, Lionel Stander, Frankie Darro. SEE: **Bowery Boys** series.

Trouble Man (1972) **C-99m.** ** D: Ivan Dixon. Robert Hooks, Paul Winfield, Ralph Waite, William Smithers, Paula Kelly, Julius W. Harris. Hooks is superslick black troubleshooter caught in gang warfare. Cliché-ridden script includes about four hundred killings, glorifying underworld life. Well-made but tasteless.

Trouble With Angels, The (1966) **C-112m.** **½ D: Ida Lupino. Rosalind Russell, Hayley Mills, June Harding, Binnie Barnes, Mary Wickes, Gypsy Rose Lee, Camilla Sparv. Cutesy study of Pennsylvania convent school, with students Mills and Harding driving mother superior Russell to distraction. Episodic, occasionally touching comedy. Sequel: WHERE ANGELS GO . . . TROUBLE FOLLOWS.▼

Trouble with Girls, The (1969) **C-104m.** **½ D: Peter Tewksbury. Elvis Presley, Marlyn Mason, Nicole Jaffe, Sheree North, Edward Andrews, John Carradine. Vincent Price, Joyce Van Patten. One of the better Presley vehicles has Elvis as manager of a Chautauqua company (medicine show) in the 1920s; film has nice feeling for the period.▼

Trouble With Harry, The (1955) **C-99m.** *** D: Alfred Hitchcock. Edmund Gwenn, John Forsythe, Shirley MacLaine, Mildred Natwick, Mildred Dunnock, Jerry Mathers, Royal Dano. Offbeat, often hilarious black comedy courtesy Mr. Hitchcock and scripter John Michael Hayes about bothersome corpse causing all sorts of problems

for peaceful neighbors in New England community. Gwenn is fine as usual, MacLaine appealing in her first film. Beautiful locations, whimsical score (his first for Hitch) by Bernard Herrmann.▼

Trouble With Spies, The (1987) **C-91m.** BOMB D: Burt Kennedy. Donald Sutherland, Ned Beatty, Ruth Gordon, Lucy Gutteridge, Michael Hordern, Robert Morley, Gregory Sierra. Awful spy comedy about incompetent British and Soviet secret agents. Some good actors are wasted; this one's as bad as they come. Filmed in 1984.▼

Trouble with Women, The (1947) **80m.** ** D: Sidney Lanfield. Ray Milland, Teresa Wright, Brian Donlevy, Rose Hobart, Charles Smith, Lewis Russell, Iris Adrian, Lloyd Bridges. Professor Milland announces that women like to be treated rough; you can guess the rest of this tame comedy.

Trout, The (1982-French) **C-105m.** ** D: Joseph Losey. Isabelle Huppert, Jacques Spiesser, Jeanne Moreau, Jean-Pierre Cassel, Daniel Olbrychski, Alexis Smith, Craig Stevens. Elaborate but muddled account of country girl Huppert and her encounters, sexual and otherwise, in the world of high finance. Moreau is wasted as the wife of businessman Cassel; Smith and Stevens appear in cameos. Original title: LA TRUITE. Also released at 116m.▼

Truck Stop Women (1974) **C-88m.** **½ D: Mark Lester. Lieux Dressler, Claudia Jennings, Dennis Fimple, Jennifer Burton. Sloppy but good-natured exploitation fare about women who run truck stop as front for prostitution and truck hijacking activities. Business is so good the Mob tries to move in. Jennings is a standout in this raucous sleaze romp.▼

Truck Turner (1974) **C-91m.** *½ D: Jonathan Kaplan. Isaac Hayes, Yaphet Kotto, Alan Weeks, Annazette Chase, Sam Laws, Nichelle Nichols. Extremely violent black exploiter, with Hayes only distinguishing feature as a skip-tracer (a detective who hunts bail jumpers). His original score is familiar.

True Believer (1989) **C-103m.** *** D: Joseph Ruben. James Woods, Robert Downey, Jr., Yuji Okumoto, Margaret Colin, Kurtwood Smith, Tom Bower, Miguel Ferenandes, Charles Hallahan. Woods gives his usual dynamic performance as a once-idealistic lawyer, a radical hero of the '60s who's lost his scruples—until his hero-worshipping clerk (Downey) goads him into taking the near-hopeless case of an Asian-American who was apparently railroaded into prison eight years before. Contrived, to be sure, but entertaining all the way.▼

True Confession (1937) **85m.** *½ D: Wesley Ruggles. Carole Lombard, Fred MacMurray, John Barrymore, Una Merkel, Porter Hall, Edgar Kennedy, Lynne Overman, Irving Bacon, Fritz Feld. Alarmingly unfunny "comedy" about pathological liar Lombard and the trouble she causes for herself and good-natured lawyer husband MacMurray when she confesses to a murder she didn't commit. Remade with Betty Hutton as CROSS MY HEART.

True Confessions (1981) C-108m. **½ D: Ulu Grosbard. Robert De Niro, Robert Duvall, Charles Durning, Ed Flanders, Burgess Meredith, Rose Gregorio, Cyril Cusack, Kenneth McMillan, Dan Hedaya, Jeanette Nolan. Methodically slow, complex, and provocative film (adapted by John Gregory Dunne and Joan Didion from Dunne's novel) about the uneasy bond and surprising similarities between two brothers, one a hardened police detective, the other a power-wielding monsignor in the Catholic Church. A meaty but somehow unsatisfying film (based on a true case previously filmed as a TVM, WHO IS THE BLACK DAHLIA?) with two characteristically fine performances by De Niro and Duvall.▼

True Grit (1969) C-128m. *** D: Henry Hathaway. John Wayne, Glen Campbell, Kim Darby, Jeremy Slate, Robert Duvall, Strother Martin, Dennis Hopper, Jeff Corey. Film version of Charles Portis's wonderful novel about an over-the-hill marshal who helps 14-year-old track down her father's killer. Not as good as the book, but Wayne's Oscar-winning performance and rousing last half-hour make it fine screen entertainment. Sequel: ROOSTER COGBURN. Followed by a TV movie in 1978.▼

True Grit (1978) C-100m. TVM D: Richard T. Heffron. Warren Oates, Lisa Pelikan, Lee Meriwether, James Stephens, Jeff Osterhage, Lee H. Montgomery, Ramon Bieri. The further adventures of Rooster Cogburn put Oates in the unfortunate position of trying to fill the Duke's boots in this busted series pilot. Average.

True Love (1989) C-104m. *** D: Nancy Savoca. Annabella Sciorra, Ron Eldard, Aida Turturro, Roger Rignack, Star Jasper, Michael J. Wolfe, Kelly Cinnante. Refreshing, low-budget slice-of-life sleeper about an Italian wedding in the Bronx. There's tons of atmosphere, and the script (by Savoca and her husband, Richard Guay) is never condescending. Fine performances all around, with Sciorra and Eldard perfectly cast as no-nonsense bride and immature groom.▼

True Stories (1986) C-111m. ** D: David Byrne. David Byrne, John Goodman, Swoosie Kurtz, Annie McEnroe, Spalding Gray, Alix Elias, Pops Staples. Smarmy, pseudo-hip tour of modern-day Texas by Talking Heads' Byrne; is there anything easier to satirize than eccentric Lone Star crazies? Photography, likable Goodman performance, and a couple of numbers make this worth a look if you're curious;

mostly, though, it's depressing. Playwright Beth Henley had a part in the screenplay.▼

True Story of Jesse James, The (1957) C-92m. **½ D: Nicholas Ray. Robert Wagner, Jeffrey Hunter, Hope Lange, Agnes Moorehead, Alan Hale, John Carradine, Alan Baxter, Frank Gorshin. Remake of 1939 Tyrone Power/Henry Fonda classic (JESSE JAMES) understandably lacks its star power, but there are enough offbeat Ray touches to keep things interesting (along with some stock footage from the original). Screenplay by Walter Newman.

True Story of Lynn Stuart, The (1958) 78m. **½ D: Lewis Seiler. Betsy Palmer, Jack Lord, Barry Atwater, Kim Spaulding. Modest, straightforward account of housewife Palmer posing as gun moll to trap gang.

True to Life (1943) 94m. *** D: George Marshall. Mary Martin, Franchot Tone, Dick Powell, Victor Moore, Mabel Paige, William Demarest, Ernest Truex, Clarence Kolb. Engaging comedy of radio writer Powell going to live with "typical" American family to get material for his soap opera.

True to the Army (1942) 76m. ** D: Albert S. Rogell. Allan Jones, Ann Miller, Judy Canova, Jerry Colonna. Zany nonsense erupts when military life and romance clash; loud WW2 escapism. This remake of SHE LOVES ME NOT was remade again as HOW TO BE VERY, VERY POPULAR.

True to the Navy (1930) 71m. ** D: Frank Tuttle. Clara Bow, Fredric March, Sam Hardy, Eddie Featherstone, Jed Prouty, Rex Bell. Silly early talkie about on-again, off-again romance between sailor March and soda-fountain waitress Bow. Buffs will get a kick out of it; Clara does one sexy dance number.

Truman Capote's The Glass House SEE: **Glass House, The**▼

Trunk, The (1960-British) 72m. *½ D: Donovan Winter. Phil Carey, Julia Arnall, Dermot Walsh, Vera Day. Programmer involving trumped-up murder charge and usual dose of red herrings; ill-conceived tale.

Trunk to Cairo (1966-Israeli) C-80m. *½ D: Menahem Golan. Audie Murphy, George Sanders, Marianne Koch, Hans Von Bosodi, Joseph Yadin. Murphy, in rare non-Western role, plays still another secret agent in Cairo to investigate Sanders' attempt to build a rocket bound for the moon.

Trust Me (1989) C-104m. **½ D: Bobby Houston. Adam Ant, David Packer, Talia Balsam, William DeAcutis, Joyce Van Patten, Barbara Bain. Some scattershot laughs cannot sustain this satire of the art scene. Ant plays a gallery owner who will do all he can to see artist Packer dead—so the value of his work will increase. Bright idea, uneven result.▼

Truth About Spring, The (1965-British) C-102m. *** D: Richard Thorpe. Hayley

Mills, John Mills, James MacArthur, Lionel Jeffries, Harry Andrews, Niall MacGinnis, David Tomlinson. Skipper Mills introduces daughter Hayley to first boyfriend, MacArthur, in enjoyable film geared for young viewers.

Truth About Women, The (1958-British) **C-98m.** **½ D: Muriel Box. Laurence Harvey, Julie Harris, Diane Cilento, Mai Zetterling, Eva Gabor, Wilfrid Hyde-White, Christopher Lee, Ernest Thesiger. Multiepisode tale about playboy Harvey's flirtations; well mounted and cast, but slow-going.▼

Try and Get Me SEE: **Sound of Fury, The**▼

Trygon Factor, The (1967-British) **C-87m.** *½ D: Cyril Frankel. Stewart Granger, Susan Hampshire, Robert Morley, Cathleen Nesbitt, James Robertson Justice. Impossible-to-follow Scotland Yard whodunit. Centers around bizarre old English family and series of interesting murders.

Tucker: The Man and His Dream (1988) **C-111m.** ***½ D: Francis Ford Coppola. Jeff Bridges, Joan Allen, Martin Landau, Frederic Forrest, Mako, Dean Stockwell, Elias Koteas, Nina Siemaszko, Christian Slater, Corky Nemec, Marshall Bell, Don Novello, Peter Donat, Dean Goodman, Patti Austin. Smart, sassy, stylish film about Preston Tucker, who tried to build "the car of the future" in the 1940s, only to be crushed by the Big Three automakers and their political cronies. Told with great flair by director Coppola (who obviously felt a kinship with the indomitable, family-minded visionary), and filled with fine performances, especially Landau in a poignant characterization as Tucker's unlikely partner. Lloyd Bridges (Jeff's dad) appears unbilled as an adversarial senator. Lively music score by Joe Jackson.▼

Tuck Everlasting (1980) **C-100m.** ***½ D: Frederick King Keller. Margaret Chamberlain, Paul Flessa, Fred A. Keller, James McGuire, Sonia Raimi, Bruce D'Auria. Lovely, sweet, entertaining fable about family, invulnerable to pain, aging, and death, and the young girl who learns their secret. Perfect for children who prefer books to video games. Produced independently in upstate New York; based on Natalie Babbitt's award-winning novel.▼

Tuff Turf (1985) **C-112m.** *½ D: Fritz Kiersch. James Spader, Kim Richards, Paul Mones, Matt Clark, Claudette Nevins, Robert Downey (Jr.), Olivia Barash, Jack Mack & the Heart Attack. Old-fashioned, unrealistic troubled-teen melodrama with overtones of WEST SIDE STORY, set in a fantasy version of the San Fernando Valley. Pre-*sex, lies and videotape* Spader, as preppie newcomer, is mannered, but Richards is good.▼

Tugboat Annie (1933) **87m.** **½ D: Mervyn LeRoy. Marie Dressler, Wallace Beery, Robert Young, Maureen O'Sullivan, Willard Robertson, Frankie Darro. Marie is skipper of the tugboat *Narcissus,* Beery her ner'er-do-well husband in this rambling, episodic comedy drama; inimitable stars far outclass their wobbly material. Followed by TUGBOAT ANNIE SAILS AGAIN, and a 1950s TV series.

Tugboat Annie Sails Again (1940) **77m.** ** D: Lewis Seiler. Marjorie Rambeau, Alan Hale, Jane Wyman, Ronald Reagan, Clarence Kolb, Charles Halton. Airy comedy with predictable plot about Annie's job in jeopardy. Rambeau takes up where Marie Dressler left off; Reagan saves the day for her.

Tulips (1981-Canadian) **C-92m.** *½ D: Stan Ferris. Gabe Kaplan, Bernadette Peters, Henry Gibson, Al Waxman, David Boxer. Weak romance, with Kaplan and Peters each attempting to commit suicide, then meeting and falling in love. "Stan Ferris" is a pseudonym for Mark Warren, Rex Bromfield, and Al Waxman—and the lack of directorial cohesion shows.▼

Tulsa (1949) **C-90m.** *** D: Stuart Heisler. Susan Hayward, Robert Preston, Pedro Armendariz, Lloyd Gough, Chill Wills, Ed Begley. Bouncy drama of oil-woman Hayward fighting for her property, forgetting about human values while involved in wildcat drilling.▼

Tumbleweed (1953) **C-79m.** ** D: Nathan Juran. Audie Murphy, Lori Nelson, Chill Wills, Lee Van Cleef. Bland oater with Murphy trying to prove he didn't desert wagon train under Indian attack.

Tumbleweeds (1925) **81m.** ***½ D: King Baggot. William S. Hart, Barbara Bedford, Lucien Littlefield, J. Gordon Russell, Richard R. Neill. One of the screen's most famous Westerns, with Hart deciding to get in on the opening of the Cherokee Strip in 1889, particularly if pretty Bedford is willing to marry him and settle there. Landrush scene is one of the great spectacles in silent films. Above running time does not include a poignant eight-minute introduction Hart made to accompany 1939 reissue of his classic.▼

Tuna Clipper (1949) **79m.** *½ D: William Beaudine. Roddy McDowall, Elena Verdugo, Ronald Winters, Rick Vallin, Dickie Moore. Flabby tale of youth (McDowall) who pushes himself into rugged fishing life to prove his worth.

Tunes of Glory (1960-British) **C-106m.** **** D: Ronald Neame. Alec Guinness, John Mills, Susannah York, Kay Walsh, Dennis Price, John Fraser, Duncan Macrae, Gordon Jackson, Allan Cuthbertson. Superbly acted character drama of conflict between callous colonel and younger replacement; set in Scotland. Written by

James Kennaway, from his novel. York's film debut.▼

Tunnel, The SEE: **Transatlantic Tunnel**▼

Tunnel of Love, The (1958) **98m.** ******* D: Gene Kelly. Doris Day, Richard Widmark, Gig Young, Gia Scala. Bright comedy of married couple Widmark and Day enduring endless red tape to adopt a child. Good cast spices adaptation of Joseph Fields-Peter de Vries play.

Tunnelvision (1976) **C-67m.** ****** D: Neal Israel, Brad Swirnoff. Phil Proctor, Howard Hesseman, Ernie Anderson, Edwina Anderson, James Bacon, Gerrit Graham, Betty Thomas, Chevy Chase, Roger Bowen, Al Franken, Tom Davis, Bill Schallert, Laraine Newman, Ron Silver. Crude, uneven parody of what TV programming will be like in the future. Of interest only for appearances by now famous performers.▼

Turkey Shoot SEE: **Escape 2000**▼

Turk 182! (1985) **C-98m.** ****** D: Bob Clark. Timothy Hutton, Robert Urich, Kim Cattrall, Robert Culp, Darren McGavin, Steven Keats, James Tolkan, Peter Boyle, Paul Sorvino, Dick O'Neill. Contrived attempt at Capra-esque comedy. Young Brooklynite turns into super-graffiti artist to protest N.Y.C.'s lack of support for his brother, an injured fireman. Hutton's brooding persona doesn't suit this comic setting.▼

Turnabout (1940) **83m.** ****** D: Hal Roach. John Hubbard, Carole Landis, Adolphe Menjou, Mary Astor, William Gargan, Joyce Compton, Verree Teasdale, Donald Meek. Certainly unique, but incredibly bad comedy, risque in its day, about husband and wife switching personalities thanks to magic Buddha; from a story by Thorne Smith, later a short-lived TV series in the 1970s.

Turn Back the Clock (1933) **77m.** ******* D: Edgar Selwyn. Lee Tracy, Mae Clarke Otto Kruger, George Barbier, Peggy Shannon, C. Henry Gordon, Clara Blandick. Fascinating Depression-era sleeper with an intriguing premise. Tracy is ideally cast as a middle-aged working man who gets to relive his life . . . and marry into wealth and power. Snappy script by director Selwyn and Ben Hecht. And watch for The Three Stooges!

Turn Back the Clock (1989) **C-100m.** TVM D: Larry Elikann. Connie Sellecca, Wendy Kilbourne, Jere Burns, David Dukes, Dina Merrill, Gene Barry. Acceptable remake of the '40s thriller REPEAT PERFORMANCE, in which a woman relives the past year following the shooting of her husband. Look for Joan Leslie, who starred in the original, as a New Year's Eve party guest. Average.

Turner & Hooch (1989) **C-97m.** ****** D: Roger Spottiswoode. Tom Hanks, Mare Winningham, Craig T. Nelson, Reginald VelJohnson, Scott Paulin, J.C. Quinn, John McIntire, Beasley. Detective Hanks' only means of catching some murderers is by extracting their identity from the sole murder witness: a dog named Hooch. Hanks (who plays a neatness freak) and Hooch (a lovably ugly dog who makes a mess of everything) squeeze all the humor they can out of a paper-thin script—but even they can't make up for a bummer of an ending.▼

Turning Point, The (1952) **85m.** ****½** D: William Dieterle. William Holden, Alexis Smith, Edmond O'Brien, Ed Begley, Don Porter. Love and intrigue with Holden investigating internal corruption within crime-investigation committee.

Turning Point, The (1977) **C-119m.** ****½** D: Herbert Ross. Anne Bancroft, Shirley MacLaine, Mikhail Baryshnikov, Leslie Browne, Tom Skerritt, Martha Scott, Marshall Thompson. Two friends who started in ballet are reunited after many years; Bancroft is now a star ballerina, MacLaine a Midwestern housewife/dance teacher whose daughter (Browne) is embarking on her own ballet career. Promising idea bogs down in clichés, with supposedly liberated treatment of women's relationships exemplified by wild catfight. Those few dance sequences presented intact give film its only value. Written by Arthur Laurents, photographed by Robert Surtees. Baryshnikov's film debut.▼

Turning Point of Jim Malloy, The (1975) **C-78m.** TVM D: Frank D. Gilroy. John Savage, Biff McGuire, Peggy McKay, Gig Young, Kathleen Quinlan, Janis Paige. Nostalgic drama based on John O'Hara's youth in a small Pennsylvania town and his first exposure to the world of journalism under the tutelege of an alcoholic reporter. Atmospheric, lovingly filmed version of O'Hara's *Gibbsville* adapted from his collection *The Doctor's Son* by Gilroy. Also called JOHN O'HARA'S GIBBS-VILLE and GIBBSVILLE: THE TURNING POINT OF JIM MALLOY, it later spun off a brief series. Above average.

Turning to Stone (1985-Canadian) **C-98m.** ******* D: Eric Till. Nicky Guadagni, Shirley Douglas, Anne Anglin, Jackie Richardson, Bernard Behrens. Riveting psychological drama about Guadagni, a nice young girl who's busted for smuggling drugs, and her adjustment to unhappy realities of life behind bars. For once, a nonexploitation women's prison drama. Fine performances all around; expert script by Judith Thompson.

Turnover Smith (1980) **C-78m.** TVM D: Bernard Kowalski. William Conrad, Belinda J. Montgomery, Hilly Hicks, James Darren, Michael Parks, Cameron Mitchell, Tracy Reed, Nehemiah Persoff, Nita Talbot. Famed criminologist vs. crazed killer in this unsold pilot movie. Average.

Turn the Key Softly (1953-British) **83m.** ** D: Jack Lee. Yvonne Mitchell, Terence Morgan, Joan Collins, Kathleen Harrison, Thora Hird, Geoffrey Keen. Film recounts incidents in lives of three women ex-convicts upon leaving prison; contrived dramatics.

Turtle Diary (1985-British) **C-97m.** *** D: John Irvin. Glenda Jackson, Ben Kingsley, Richard Johnson, Michael Gambon, Rosemary Leach, Eleanor Bron. Deliciously original (if low-key) fable of two repressed people who are drawn together—and ultimately freed—by an unusual common interest: they both become concerned about the fate of captive giant turtles at the zoo. Witty, decidedly offbeat script by Harold Pinter (who does a cameo as a bookstore customer). Johnson, who plays Jackson's jovial next-door neighbor, also produced the film.▼

Tuttles of Tahiti, The (1942) **91m.** *** D: Charles Vidor. Charles Laughton, Jon Hall, Peggy Drake, Florence Bates, Mala, Alma Ross, Victor Francen. Laughton and family lead leisurely life on South Seas island, avoiding any sort of hard labor. That's it . . . but it's good.▼

12 Angry Men (1957) **95m.** **** D: Sidney Lumet. Henry Fonda, Lee J. Cobb, Ed Begley, E. G. Marshall, Jack Klugman, Jack Warden, Martin Balsam, John Fiedler, George Voskovec, Robert Webber, Edward Binns, Joseph Sweeney. Brilliant film about one man who tries to convince 11 other jurors that their hasty conviction of a boy on trial should be reconsidered. Formidable cast (including several character-stars-to-be); Lumet's impressive feature film debut. Script by Reginald Rose, from his television play.▼

Twelve Chairs, The (1970) **C-94m.** *** D: Mel Brooks. Ron Moody, Frank Langella, Dom DeLuise, Mel Brooks, Bridget Brice, Robert Bernal. Impoverished Russian nobleman Moody seeks one of 12 dining chairs, now scattered, with jewels sewn into seat. DeLuise hilarious as his chief rival. Unsympathetic characters hamper film's success, though mastermind Brooks still provides many laughs. Filmed in Yugoslavia; versions of this same story have been made in Hollywood, Germany, Argentina, England, and Cuba!▼

Twelve Hours to Kill (1960) **83m.** *½ D: Edward L. Cahn. Nico Minardos, Barbara Eden, Grant Richards, Russ Conway, Art Baker, Gavin MacLeod. Poor crime melodrama of gangland murder witnessed by Greek immigrant in N.Y.C.

Twelve O'Clock High (1949) **132m.** **** D: Henry King. Gregory Peck, Hugh Marlowe, Gary Merrill, Millard Mitchell, Dean Jagger, Paul Stewart. Taut WW2 story of U.S. flyers in England, an officer replaced for getting too involved with his men (Merrill) and his successor who has same problem (Peck). Jagger won Oscar in supporting role; Peck has never been better. Written by Sy Bartlett and Beirne Lay, Jr., from their novel. Later a TV series.▼

12 to the Moon (1960) **74m.** BOMB D: David Bradley. Ken Clark, Michi Kobi, Tom Conway, Tony Dexter, John Wengraf, Anna-Lisa. International expedition to the moon encounters hostile aliens who freeze North America solid. An ambitious failure.

Twentieth Century (1934) **91m.** **** D: Howard Hawks. John Barrymore, Carole Lombard, Walter Connolly, Roscoe Karns, Etienne Girardot, Ralph Forbes, Charles Levison (Lane), Edgar Kennedy. Super screwball comedy in which egomaniacal Broadway producer Barrymore makes shopgirl Lombard a star; when she leaves him, he does everything he can to woo her back on lengthy train trip. Barrymore has never been funnier, and Connolly and Karns are aces as his long-suffering cronies. Matchless script by Ben Hecht and Charles MacArthur, from their play; later a hit Broadway musical, *On the Twentieth Century*.▼

28 Up (1985-British) **C/B&W-133m.** *** D: Michael Apted. Unique sociological documentary in which Apted interviews a diverse group of individuals at ages 7, 14, 21, and 28. A one-of-a-kind portrayal of dreams, aspirations, and realities; fascinating to see Apted's subjects literally age before your eyes. Raise this rating to ***½ if viewed in separate installments—the way it was originally made for TV.

25th Hour, The (1967-French-Italian-Yugoslavian) **C-119m.** ** D: Henri Verneuil. Anthony Quinn, Virna Lisi, Michael Redgrave, Gregoire Aslan, Marcel Dalio, Serge Reggiani. Story of Rumanian peasant's Nazi-enforced eight-year separation from his beautiful wife is indifferently done, in spite of capable acting by stars.

24 Hours of the Rebel SEE: **September 30, 1955**

Twenty-Four Hours to Kill (1965-British) **C-92m.** **½ D: Peter Bezencenet. Mickey Rooney, Lex Barker, Walter Slezak, Michael Medwin, Helga Somerfeld, Wolfgang Lukschy. OK suspenser with Rooney marked for execution by Slezak's smuggling ring when his plane is forced to land in Beirut for 24 hours.

20 Million Miles to Earth (1957) **82m.** **½ D: Nathan Juran. William Hopper, Joan Taylor, Frank Puglia, Thomas B. Henry. Venusian monster runs wild in Italy; intelligent script with good special effects by Ray Harryhausen.

Twenty Million Sweethearts (1934) **89m.** **½ D: Ray Enright. Dick Powell, Ginger Rogers, Pat O'Brien, Allen Jenkins, Grant Mitchell, The Mills Brothers. Contrived musical about unscrupulous promoter

[1222]

O'Brien building Powell into radio star, career coming between him and happy marriage to Ginger. Plot soon wears thin, as does constant repetition of Powell's "I'll String Along With You," but bright cast helps out. Two good songs by the Mills Bros. Remade as MY DREAM IS YOURS.

20 Mule Team (1940) 84m. ** D: Richard Thorpe. Wallace Beery, Leo Carrillo, Marjorie Rambeau, Anne Baxter, Douglas Fowley. Minor Western of borax-miners in Arizona with usual Beery mugging and standard plot. Baxter's first film.

21 Days Together (1938-British) 75m. **½ D: Basil Dean. Vivien Leigh, Laurence Olivier, Hay Petrie, Leslie Banks, Francis L. Sullivan. John Galsworthy's play of lovers with three weeks together before man goes on trial for murder; Olivier and Leigh are fine in worthwhile, but not outstanding, film. Script by Graham Greene. Original title: 21 DAYS.

21 Hours at Munich (1976) C-100m. TVM D: William A. Graham. William Holden, Shirley Knight, Franco Nero, Anthony Quayle, Noel Willman. Well-done re-creation of the events surrounding 1972 Munich Olympics massacre, despite Holden's being miscast as the Munich police chief. Above average.▼

Twenty Plus Two (1961) 102m. ** D. Joseph M. Newman. David Janssen, Jeanne Crain, Dina Merrill, Agnes Moorehead, Brad Dexter. Poor production values detract from potential of yarn with private eye Janssen investigating a murder, encountering a neat assortment of people.

27th Day, The (1957) 75m. **½ D: William Asher. Gene Barry, Valerie French, Arnold Moss, George Voskovec. Imaginative sci-fi study of human nature with five people given pellets capable of destroying the world. Based on John Mantley's novel.

20,000 Eyes (1961) 60m. *½ D: Jack Leewood. Gene Nelson, Merry Anders, John Banner, James Brown. Flabby robbery caper done on shoestring budget.

20,000 Leagues Under the Sea (1954) C-127m. **** D: Richard Fleischer. Kirk Douglas, James Mason, Paul Lukas, Peter Lorre, Robert J. Wilke, Carleton Young. Superb Disney fantasy-adventure on grand scale, from Jules Verne's novel. Scientist Lukas and sailor Douglas get involved with power-hungry Captain Nemo (Mason) who operates futuristic submarine. Memorable action sequences, fine cast make this a winner. Won Oscars for Art Direction and Special Effects.▼

20,000 Pound Kiss, The (1963-British) 57m. **½ D: John Moxey. Dawn Addams, Michael Goodliffe, Richard Thorp, Anthony Newlands. Edgar Wallace tale of blackmail, with a most intricate plot.

20,000 Years in Sing Sing (1933) 81m.

*** D: Michael Curtiz. Spencer Tracy, Bette Davis, Arthur Byron, Lyle Talbot, Warren Hymer, Louis Calhern, Grant Mitchell, Sheila Terry. Still-powerful prison drama has only teaming of Tracy and Davis. He's a hardened criminal, she's his girl. Based on Warden Lewis F. Lawes' book. Remade as CASTLE ON THE HUDSON.

23 Paces to Baker Street (1956) C-103m. *** D: Henry Hathaway. Van Johnson, Vera Miles, Cecil Parker, Patricia Laffan, Maurice Denham, Estelle Winwood. Absorbing suspenser filmed in London has blind playwright Johnson determined to thwart crime plans he has overheard.▼

Twice Dead (1988) C-85m. *½ D: Bert Dragin. Tom Breznahan, Jill Whitlow, Jonathan Chapin, Christopher Burgard, Sam Melville, Brooke Bundy, Todd Bridges. Boring horror programmer with an all-too-familiar setting: a mansion, haunted by a dead movie star whose spirit assists its new inhabitants in a battle against some punks.▼

Twice in a Lifetime (1974) C-78m. TVM D: Herschel Daugherty. Ernest Borgnine, Della Reese, Eric Laneuville, Slim Pickens, Herb Jeffries, Arte Johnson. Scruffy old salt operating a salvage tug clashes with unscrupulous yard foreman determined to retain control of the docks. Borgnine at his most bombastic is nicely balanced by Reese from her waterfront cafe. Another pilot film that never earned series status. Below average.

Twice in a Lifetime (1985) C-111m. *** D: Bud Yorkin. Gene Hackman, Ann-Margret, Ellen Burstyn, Amy Madigan, Ally Sheedy, Brian Dennehy, Stephen Lang, Darrell Larson. Middle-aged man, with a marriage that's become routine, falls in love with younger woman and must endure the pain he causes not only his wife but also his children—especially his oldest daughter. Realistic look at the way different people react to situation keeps this film away from cliché and predictability; superior acting, especially by Hackman, Burstyn, and Madigan (as the angry daughter) make it special. Written by Colin Welland.▼

Twice Round the Daffodils (1962-British) 89m. ** D: Gerald Thomas. Juliet Mills, Donald Sinden, Donald Houston, Kenneth Williams, Jill Ireland, Nanette Newman. Mills is charming nurse in a male TB ward, trying to avoid romantic inclinations of her patients; expected sex jokes abound.

Twice-Told Tales (1963) C-119m. *** D: Sidney Salkow. Vincent Price, Sebastian Cabot, Mari Blanchard, Brett Halsey, Richard Denning. Episodic adaptation of Hawthorne stories has good cast, imaginative direction, and sufficient atmosphere to keep one's interest. One of the TALES is an abbreviated HOUSE OF THE SEVEN

GABLES, which also starred Price in the 1940 version.▼

Twice Upon a Time (1983) **C-75m.** ***½ D: John Korty, Charles Swenson. Voices of Lorenzo Music, Judith Kahan Kampmann, Marshall Efron, James Cranna, Julie Payne, Hamilton Camp, Paul Frees. Captivating, hilarious animated feature done in a pseudo-cut-out style called "Lumage." Evil bosses of the Murkworks intend to blanket the world with perpetual nightmares; only a looney (and indescribable) bunch of would-be heroes can stop them. Too complex and fast-paced for small children, but a real treat for everyone else. Never given a full theatrical release, despite having George Lucas as executive producer.

Twilight for the Gods (1958) **C-120m.** **½ D: Joseph Pevney. Rock Hudson, Cyd Charisse, Arthur Kennedy, Leif Erickson, Charles McGraw, Ernest Truex, Richard Haydn, Wallace Ford. Ernest K. Gann book, adapted by the author, becomes turgid soaper of people on run-down vessel heading for Mexico, their trials and tribulations to survive when ship goes down.

Twilight of Honor (1963) **115m.** **½ D: Boris Sagal. Richard Chamberlain, Nick Adams, Joan Blackman, Claude Rains, Joey Heatherton, James Gregory, Pat Buttram, Jeanette Nolan. Routine drama of struggling lawyer Chamberlain who wins murder case with assistance of older expert Rains. Look for Linda Evans in a bit part.

Twilight People (1972-U.S.-Filipino) **C-84m.** BOMB D: Eddie Romero. John Ashley, Pat Woodell, Charles Macaulay, Pam Grier, Jan Merlin, Eddie Garcia. Incredibly inept rip-off of THE ISLAND OF LOST SOULS has former SS doctor performing hideous experiments resulting in beings half-human, half-creature. Not even a good bad movie. Will put insomniacs to sleep.▼

Twilight's Last Gleaming (1977-U.S.-German) **C-146m.** **½ D: Robert Aldrich. Burt Lancaster, Richard Widmark, Charles Durning, Melvyn Douglas, Paul Winfield, Burt Young, Joseph Cotten, Roscoe Lee Browne, Richard Jaeckel. Unstable Air Force officer seizes missile installation, threatens to start World War III unless U.S. comes clean on its former Vietnam policy. OK if overlong programmer based on Walter Wager's novel *Viper Three*.▼

Twilight Time (1983-U.S.-Yuglosav) **C-102m.** *½ D: Goran Paskaljevic. Karl Malden, Jodi Thelen, Damien Nash, Mia Roth, Pavle Vujisic, Dragon Maksimovic. Sincere but unsuccessful film about an old man saddled with the upbringing of two grandchildren in rural Yugoslavia. Malden's performance is first-rate, but uneasy blend

of American and Yugoslav elements, and snail's pace all but sink it.

Twilight Zone—The Movie (1983) **C-102m.** **½ D: John Landis, Steven Spielberg, Joe Dante, George Miller. Vic Morrow, Scatman Crothers, Bill Quinn, Selma Diamond, Kathleen Quinlan, Jeremy Licht, Kevin McCarthy, William Schallert, John Lithgow, Abbe Lane, John Larroquette, narrated by Burgess Meredith. Dan Aykroyd and Albert Brooks provide entertaining prologue for four unusual tales (three actual remakes from Rod Serling's classic TV series), but none of them provides all-important moment of revelation that made the show so memorable . . . and more tellingly, none improves on the original. Best—final segment, remake of "Nightmare at 20,000 Feet," with Lithgow as terrified airline passenger, though even this episode is more explicit (and therefore less intriguing) than '60s TV version.▼

Twin Beds (1942) **85m.** ** D: Tim Whelan. Joan Bennett, George Brent, Mischa Auer, Una Merkel, Glenda Farrell, Margaret Hamilton. Life of married couple Bennett and Brent is constantly interrupted by wacky neighbor Auer; and it's his film, too.

Twin Detectives (1976) **C-78m.** TVM D: Robert Day. Jim Hager, Jon Hager, Lillian Gish, Patrick O'Neal, Michael Constantine, Otis Young, Lynda Day George. Comedy-mystery involving identical twin private eyes, a spunky old lady, a psychic con group, and a murdered medium. The Hager Brothers are country singers/comics from *Hee Haw*, and should have stayed there. And whatever possessed dear Miss Gish to make her TV movie debut in this bit of fluff! Below average.

Twinkle and Shine SEE: **It Happened to Jane**

Twinkle in God's Eye, The (1955) **73m.** ** D: George Blair. Mickey Rooney, Coleen Gray, Hugh O'Brian, Joey Forman, Michael Connors. Simple yarn of clergyman Rooney trying to convert wrongdoers in Western town to God's faith via good humor.

Twinkle, Twinkle, Killer Kane SEE: **Ninth Configuration, The**▼

Twins (1988) **C-112m.** *** D: Ivan Reitman. Arnold Schwarzenegger, Danny DeVito, Kelly Preston, Chloe Webb, Bonnie Bartlett, Marshall Bell, Trey Wilson, Hugh O'Brian. Entertaining comedy about genetically designed twins (Schwarzenegger and DeVito!) who discover each other's existence at the age of 35. Effectively blends sentiment and roughhouse humor, with the two mismatched stars packing extra punch in their delightful performances.▼

Twins of Evil (1972-British) **C-85m.** **½ D: John Hough. Peter Cushing, Madeleine Collinson, Mary Collinson, Luan Peters, Dennis Price, Isobel Black, Harvey Hall. One of the twins is a vampire, but nobody can tell which is which. Engaging Hammer chiller makes inspired use of *Playboy*'s first twin playmates. Follow-up to VAMPIRE LOVERS and LUST FOR A VAMPIRE▼

Twirl (1981) **C-100m. TVM** D: Gus Trikonis. Stella Stevens, Charles Haid, Lisa Whelchel, Erin Moran, Edd Byrnes, Sharon Spelman, Matthew Tobin, Donna McKechnie. Made-for-TV clone of Michael Ritchie's SMILE focuses satirically on parental pressure on youngsters competing in national baton-twirling contest. Average.▼

Twist, The (1976-French) **C-105m.** *½ D: Claude Chabrol. Bruce Dern, Stephane Audran, Ann-Margret, Sydne Rome, Jean-Pierre Cassel, Curt Jurgens, Maria Schell, Charles Aznavour. Undistinguished chronicle of the infidelities of various boring upper-class characters. Lackluster direction, with a superior cast wasted. Originally titled FOLIES BOURGEOISES, and filmed in both English and French versions.▼

Twist All Night (1961) **78m. BOMB.** D: William Hole, Jr. Louis Prima, June Wilkinson, Sam Butera and The Witnesses, Gertrude Michael, David Whorf. Stupid comedy about Prima's attempts to keep his nightclub going; sexy Wilkinson is his girlfriend. Sometimes shown with a nineminute color prologue, TWIST CRAZE, directed by Allan David. Also known as THE CONTINENTAL TWIST.

Twist and Shout (1984-Danish) **C-99m.** *** D: Bille August. Adam Tonsberg, Lars Simonsen, Ulrikke Juul Bondo, Camilla Soeberg, Thomas Nielsen. Funny, endearing, pleasantly nostalgic tale of a pair of teen buddies in the era of The Beatles' heyday. One (Simonsen) is dominated by his stern, manipulative father, while the other (Tonsberg) experiences the joy and pain of love. Sequel to August's earlier ZAPPA. ▼

Twist Around the Clock (1961) **86m.** ** D: Oscar Rudolph. Chubby Checker, Dion, The Marcels, Vicki Spencer, Clay Cole, John Cronin, Mary Mitchell. Agent Cronin tries to book Twist performers; of course, by the finale, the dance is the rage of America. Dion, however, performs "The Wanderer" and "Runaround Sue." This was a remake of ROCK AROUND THE CLOCK.

Twisted Brain (1974) **C-85m. BOMB** D: Larry N. Stouffer. Pat Cardi, Rosie Holotik, John Niland, Austin Stoker, Joye Hash. Wimpy high-school kid discovers Jekyll & Hyde formula and kills those who picked on him. Low-budget crud with unbelievably amateurish acting. Also known as HORROR HIGH.▼

Twist of Fate (1954-British) **89m.** ** D: David Miller. Ginger Rogers, Herbert Lom, Stanley Baker, Jacques Bergerac, Margaret Rawlings. Lukewarm script benefits from good performances in story of Riviera-based actress who discovers that fiancé is dangerous criminal. Original British title: THE BEAUTIFUL STRANGER.

Twist of Fate (1989) **C-200m. TVM** D: Ian Sharp. Ben Cross, Veronica Hamel, Bruce Greenwood, Sarah Jessica Parker, John Glover, Ian Richardson, Nickolas Grace, Simon MacCorkindale. Numbingly improbable story of a Nazi bigwig who, near war's end, undergoes plastic surgery to allow him to pass as a Jew, gets himself tossed into the Bergen-Belsen concentration camp, and survives to become one of Israel's founding fathers! Even the actors don't appear to believe a word of the script, based on Robert L. Fish's 1978 novel. Originally shown in two parts. Below average.

Twist of Sand, A (1968-British) **C-90m.** ** D: Don Chaffey. Richard Johnson, Honor Blackman, Jeremy Kemp, Peter Vaughan, Roy Dotrice. Ex-submarine commander Johnson leads crew of smugglers on expedition for diamonds in ordinary programmer.

Two Against the World (1936) **64m.** ** D: William McGann. Humphrey Bogart, Beverly Roberts, Linda Perry, Carlyle Moore, Jr., Henry O'Neill, Helen MacKellar, Claire Dodd. Remake of FIVE STAR FINAL set in radio station is more contrived, not as effective. Retitled: ONE FATAL HOUR.

Two and Two Make Six (1961-British) **89m.** ** D: Freddie Francis. George Chakiris, Janette Scott, Alfred Lynch, Jackie Lane. Mild romantic yarn of A.W.O.L. soldier Chakiris falling in love with Scott.

Two Dollar Bettor (1951) **73m.** ** D: Edward L. Cahn. John Litel, Marie Windsor, Steve Brodie, Barbara Logan. Nifty little programmer showing the snowballing of businessman Litel's problems, once he gets racetrack fever.

Two English Girls (1972-French) **C-108m.** ***½ D: François Truffaut. Jean-Pierre Leaud, Kika Markham, Stacey Tendeter, Sylvia Marriott, Marie Mansart, Philippe Leotard. Profoundly moving tale of a young writer (Leaud), and his lengthy love affair with two sisters. Fine performances and superb Nestor Almendros cinematography; directed with great feeling by Truffaut. In 1984, he added additional footage, increasing the running time to 132m.—and this version rates ****, one of Truffaut's greatest achievements.▼

Two-Faced Woman (1941) **94m.** **½ D: George Cukor. Greta Garbo, Melvyn Douglas, Constance Bennett, Roland Young, Robert Sterling, Ruth Gordon, Frances Carson. Garbo's last film, in which MGM tried unsuccessfully to Americanize her personality. Attempted chic comedy of errors is OK, but not what viewer expects from the divine Garbo. Constance Bennett is much more at home in proceedings, stealing the film with her hilarious performance.▼

Two Faces of Dr. Jekyll, The (1960-British) **C-88m.** ** D: Terence Fisher. Paul Massie, Dawn Addams, Christopher Lee, David Kossoff, Francis De Wolff, Norma Marla. Uneven, sometimes unintentionally funny low-key psychological reworking of Stevenson story stresses Mr. and Mrs. relationship, plus fact that doctor himself is a weakling (and Hyde is suave and handsome!). Unfortunately, dialogue and situations are boring. Look for Oliver Reed as a bouncer. Originally shown in U.S. as HOUSE OF FRIGHT.

Two Fathers' Justice (1985) **C-100m.** TVM D: Rod Holcomb. Robert Conrad, George Hamilton, Brooke Bundy, Catherine Corkill, Whitney Kershaw, Greg Terrell. Revenge tale of two-fisted steelworker and stuffy executive teaming up to track down the men who killed their kids at a pre-wedding party. Average.▼

Two-Five, The (1978) **C-74m.** TVM D: Bruce Kessler. Don Johnson, Joe Bennett, Michael Durrell, George Murdock, John Crawford. Predictable cop show pilot has a couple of eager-beaver rookies out to save their harassed commander's hide by nabbing a drug kingpin in their own unorthodox ways. Average.

Two Flags West (1950) **92m.** ** D: Robert Wise. Joseph Cotten, Linda Darnell, Jeff Chandler, Cornel Wilde, Dale Robertson, Jay C. Flippen, Noah Berry, Jr. Very uneven Civil War Western. Battle scenes of good quality mixed with unappealing script and weak performances.

Two for the Money (1971) **C-73m.** TVM D: Bernard Kowalski. Robert Hooks, Stephen Brooks, Neville Brand, Walter Brennan, Catherine Burns, Mercedes McCambridge, Richard Dreyfuss. Two cops leave the department to track down a mass murderer who's been loose for twelve years. Well done. Average.

Two for the Road (1967-British) **C-112m.** *** D: Stanley Donen. Audrey Hepburn, Albert Finney, Eleanor Bron, William Daniels, Claude Dauphin, Nadia Gray, Jacqueline Bisset. Beautifully acted film of bickering couple Hepburn and Finney stopping to reminisce about their twelve years of marriage, trying to work to save their happiness. Perceptive, winning film, well directed by Donen. Lovely theme by Henry Mancini; script by Frederic Raphael.▼

Two for the Seesaw (1962) **120m.** *** D: Robert Wise. Robert Mitchum, Shirley MacLaine, Edmond Ryan, Elisabeth Fraser. Intelligent handling of William Gibson play. Mitchum is Midwest lawyer trying to rebuild life in N.Y.C., involved with eccentric MacLaine.

Two for Tonight (1935) **61m.** **½ D:

Frank Tuttle. Bing Crosby, Joan Bennett, Mary Boland, Lynne Overman, Thelma Todd, James Blakeley. Songwriter Crosby is forced to write musical play in one week. Entertaining slapstick musical with Boland as his mother, Bennett his girl.

Two Gals and a Guy (1951) **71m.** ** D: Alfred E. Green. Janis Paige, Robert Alda, James Gleason, Lionel Stander. Trials and tribulations of married vocal duo, caught up in the early days of TV performing; standard production.

Two Gentlemen Sharing (1969-British) **C-92m.** ** D: Ted Kotcheff. Robin Phillips, Judy Geeson, Hal Frederick, Esther Anderson, Norman Rossington. Unusual story of mixed racial couples is done more with the sensational in mind than honest portrayal.

Two Girls and a Sailor (1944) **124m.** *** D: Richard Thorpe. Van Johnson, June Allyson, Gloria DeHaven, Jose Iturbi, Jimmy Durante, Lena Horne, Donald Meek, Virginia O'Brien, Gracie Allen, Harry James and Xavier Cugat orchestras. Weak plot of Allyson-Johnson-DeHaven triangle doesn't interfere with large cast and many fine musical numbers; breezy entertainment.▼

Two Girls on Broadway (1940) **71m.** ** D: S. Sylvan Simon. Lana Turner, George Murphy, Joan Blondell, Kent Taylor, Wallace Ford. Sisters love same man (Murphy) but everything works out in this routine musical, sparked by snappy Blondell. Remake of THE BROADWAY MELODY.

Two Gun Lady (1956) **75m.** ** D: Richard Bartlett. Peggie Castle, Marie Windsor, William Talman. Simple oater of female sure-shot and law enforcer tracking down her father's murderer.

Two Guns and a Badge (1954) **69m.** *½ D: Lewis D. Collins. Wayne Morris, Morris Ankrum, Beverly Garland, Roy Barcroft. Poor script uplifted by competent cast in story of ex-convict who is mistakenly hired as deputy sheriff.

Two Guys from Milwaukee (1946) **90m.** **½ D: David Butler. Dennis Morgan, Jack Carson, Joan Leslie, Janis Paige, S. Z. Sakall, Patti Brady. Silly story of European prince Morgan Americanized by cabdriver Carson; cast is so engaging it doesn't matter. Look for Humphrey Bogart and Lauren Bacall in cameos.

Two Guys from Texas (1948) **C-86m.** **½ D: David Butler. Dennis Morgan, Jack Carson, Dorothy Malone, Penny Edwards, Fred Clark, Forrest Tucker. Average musical about two vaudevillians who find themselves on a Texas ranch. Highlight is an animated sequence with Bugs Bunny and caricatures of Morgan and Carson. Remake of THE COWBOY FROM BROOKLYN.

Two-Headed Spy, The (1958-British) **93m.**

*** D: Andre de Toth. Jack Hawkins, Gia Scala, Alexander Knox, Felix Aylmer, Donald Pleasence, Michael Caine, Laurence Naismith. Exciting true story of British spy (Hawkins) who operated in Berlin during WW2 is loaded with heart-stopping tension and suspense. Fine performances all around; one of Caine's earliest roles.

Two Hundred Motels (1971) C-98m. **½ D: Frank Zappa, Tony Palmer. Frank Zappa, Mothers of Invention, Theodore Bikel, Ringo Starr, Keith Moon. Visual, aural assault disguised as movie; completely berserk, freeform film (shot on videotape in England) featuring bizarre humor of Zappa and the Mothers. Some of it ingenious, some funny, but not spellbinding enough to maintain entire film. Funny X-rated animation sequence.▼

Two in a Crowd (1936) 85m. ** D: Alfred E. Green. Joan Bennett, Joel McCrea, Henry Armetta, Alison Skipworth, Nat Pendleton, Reginald Denny, Andy Clyde, Donald Meek, Elisha Cook, Jr. Down-and-out McCrea and Bennett find a stolen $1,000 note on New Year's Eve. Starts cute, but quickly fizzles.

Two Kinds of Love (1983) C-100m. TVM D: Jack Bender. Lindsay Wagner, Ricky Schroder, Peter Weller, Sydney Penny, Allyn Ann McLerie. Doting mom nurtures adolescent son to become a ladykiller when a broken arm puts the brakes on other sports. Then mom dies suddenly and he's left with his workaholic dad. Heartstrings are only lightly tugged in this adaption of Peggy Mann's novel *There Are Two Kinds of Terrible*. Average.▼

Two-Lane Blacktop (1971) C-101m. ***½ D: Monte Hellman. James Taylor, Warren Oates, Laurie Bird, Dennis Wilson, David Drake, Richard Ruth. Cult film about race across the Southwest between a '55 Chevy and a new GTO has intense direction to compensate for low-key script; Oates' performance is about as good as you'll ever see and should have had the Oscar. Watch for Harry Dean Stanton as a hitchhiker.

Two Little Bears, The (1961) 81m. ** D: Randall Hood. Eddie Albert, Jane Wyatt, Soupy Sales, Nancy Kulp, Brenda Lee. Harmless fable-comedy of Albert confused to discover that his two children turn into bears at night, cavorting around the house.

Two Lives of Carol Letner, The (1981) C-100m. TVM D: Philip Leacock. Meredith Baxter Birney, Don Johnson, Dolph Sweet, Salome Jens, Robert Webber, Kene Holliday, Mary Jackson, Graham Jarvis. Pedestrian drama about an ex-call girl who is cajoled by the cops into doing some undercover hustling. Average.

Two Lost Worlds (1950) 61m. *½ D: Norman Dawn. Laura Elliot, James Arness, Bill Kennedy, Gloria Petroff. Draggy story of shipwreck on uncharted island with prehistoric monsters; stock footage courtesy of ONE MILLION B.C. Cast doesn't reach island until last twenty minutes; you may not wait that long.▼

Two Loves (1961) C-100m. ** D: Charles Walters. Shirley MacLaine, Laurence Harvey, Jack Hawkins, Juano Hernandez, Nobu McCarthy. Plodding sudser set in New Zealand with spinster teacher MacLaine trying to decide between suitors Harvey and Hawkins.

Two Minute Warning (1976) C-115m. *½ D: Larry Peerce. Charlton Heston, John Cassavetes, Martin Balsam, Beau Bridges, David Janssen, Jack Klugman, Gena Rowlands. Pointless story of attempt to catch sniper in packed football stadium. Usual melange of hackneyed characters in this contrived Hollywood product. Merv Griffin sings the national anthem! (Film heavily doctored for network showing, with nearly one hour added including new cast and subplot; this review applies to original theatrical version.)

Two Moon Junction (1988) C-104m. **½ D: Zalman King. Sherilyn Fenn, Richard Tyson, Louise Fletcher, Burl Ives, Kristy McNichol, Millie Perkins, Don Galloway, Herve Villechaize, Dabbs Greer, Screamin' Jay Hawkins. Or, *Sorority Girl Goes Nympho*. Well-bred Dixie beauty gets an itch south of the navel to take off with a traveling carny hunk; rich grandma Fletcher and sheriff Ives conspire to halt the union. Camp fest is just funny enough and sexy enough to maintain interest; McNichol has a lively cameo as a bisexual cowgirl. The title may be a pun.▼

Two Mrs. Carrolls, The (1947) 99m. **½ D: Peter Godfrey. Humphrey Bogart, Barbara Stanwyck, Alexis Smith, Nigel Bruce, Isobel Elsom. Shrill murder drama with Bogie as psychopathic artist who paints wives as Angels of Death, then kills them; Stanwyck registers all degrees of panic as the next marital victim. Filmed in 1945.

Two Mrs. Grenvilles, The (1987) C-200m. TVM D: John Erman. Ann-Margret, Claudette Colbert, Stephen Collins, Elizabeth Ashley, John Rubinstein, Penny Fuller, Sam Wanamaker. Showgirl marries into socially proper N.Y. family to the dismay of the matriarch and brings scandal when she "accidentally" shoots her husband. Derek Marlowe's well-crafted adaptation of Dominick Dunne's novel, loosely based on the 1955 killing of Long Island socialite William Woodward, Jr., provides showy star turns for both leading ladies. Notable mainly for Colbert's return to film after twenty-five years. Originally shown in two parts. Above average.

Two Mules for Sister Sara (1970) C-105m. *** D: Don Siegel. Clint Eastwood, Shirley MacLaine, Manolo Fabregas, Alberto Morin, Armando Silvestre. Engaging story of drifter Eastwood helping nun MacLaine across Mexican desert, becoming wary of her un-pious nature. Beautifully shot (by Gabriel Figueroa), well-acted, good fun, marred by needlessly violent massacre climax. Albert Maltz wrote the screenplay, from a story by Budd Boetticher.▼

Twonky, The (1953) 72m. *½ D. Arch Oboler. Hans Conried, Gloria Blondell, Trilby Conried, Billy Lynn. Satirical sci-fi is misfire entertainment, when Conried's TV set actually takes charge of his life, possessed by a spirit from the future.

Two O'Clock Courage (1945) 68m. ** D: Anthony Mann. Tom Conway, Ann Rutherford, Richard Lane, Lester Matthews, Roland Drew, Emory Parnell, Jane Greer. Conway wakes up on a street corner with amnesia and finds himself the top suspect in a murder case, joins with cabbie Rutherford to solve mystery. Routine effort which looks and sounds like a typical SAINT or FALCON entry, but is actually a remake of a 1936 film TWO IN THE DARK.

Two of a Kind (1951) 75m. **½ D: Henry Levin. Edmond O'Brien, Lizabeth Scott, Terry Moore, Alexander Knox. Uninspired suspenser about con-artists plotting to dupe an elderly couple out of their inheritance fund.

Two of a Kind (1982) C-100m. TVM D: Roger Young. George Burns, Robby Benson, Barbara Barrie, Cliff Robertson, Frances Lee McCain, Geri Jewell, Peggy McKay. George's dramatic TV debut occurred in this "love" story between a failing, withdrawn old man and the retarded grandson who brings him back to life. Lovingly written by James Sadwith. Above average.▼

Two of a Kind (1983) C-87m. BOMB D: John Herzfeld. John Travolta, Olivia Newton-John, Charles Durning, Beatrice Straight, Scatman Crothers, Castulo Guerra, Oliver Reed, James Stephens, voice of Gene Hackman. Puerile fantasy-romance with a script that must have been scrawled on a gum wrapper. A quartet of angels try to persuade God to give the human race another chance—using two pretty unappealing subjects (an inventor-turned-bank robber and a not-so-innocent bank teller) as guinea pigs for the finer qualities of human nature. Just awful.▼

Two of Us, The (1968-French) 86m. ***½ D: Claude Berri. Michel Simon, Alain Cohen, Luce Fabiole, Roger Carel, Paul Preboist, Charles Denner. Charming film about growing relationship between young Jewish boy sent away from WW2 Paris and blustery, anti-Semitic guardian who lives in the country. Warm, funny, beautifully acted.▼

Two on a Bench (1971) C-73m. TVM D: Jerry Paris. Patty Duke, Ted Bessell, Andrew Duggan, John Astin, Alice Ghostley,

Terry Carter, Jeannie Berlin. Dull comedy throws Duke and Bessell at each other, hired to find out which one is working for spy. Boston locations only asset in listless, unimaginatively written and conceived comedy of errors by Richard Levinson and William Link. Below average.

Two on a Guillotine (1965) 107m. **½ D: William Conrad. Connie Stevens, Dean Jones, Cesar Romero, Parley Baer, Virginia Gregg, Connie Gilchrist. To receive inheritance from late father (Romero), Connie must spend night in haunted house. Familiar plot with some visual scares.

Two People (1973) C-100m. **½ D: Robert Wise. Peter Fonda, Lindsay Wagner, Estelle Parsons, Alan Fudge, Geoffrey Horne, Frances Sternhagen. Soapy, but oddly affecting drama about Army deserter returning home to face the consequences and fashion model with whom he falls in love. Beautiful photography by Gerald Hirschfeld and likable performance by Wagner in her first major role.

Two Rode Together (1961) C-109m. **½ D: John Ford. James Stewart, Richard Widmark, Linda Cristal, Shirley Jones, Andy Devine, John McIntire, Mae Marsh, Henry Brandon, Anna Lee. Fair Western with Stewart as cynical marshal hired to rescue pioneers captured by the Comanches years ago; Widmark is cavalry officer who accompanies him.▼

Two Seconds (1932) 68m. **½ D: Mervyn LeRoy. Edward G. Robinson, Vivienne Osborne, Preston Foster, J. Carrol Naish, Guy Kibbee, Berton Churchill. Offbeat and engrossing, if not entirely successful, melodrama tells Robinson's life as he sees it in two seconds it takes for him to die in electric chair. Often overplayed, sometimes unusually effective; a most interesting curio.

Two Sisters from Boston (1946) 112m. *** D: Henry Koster. Kathryn Grayson, June Allyson, Lauritz Melchior, Jimmy Durante, Peter Lawford, Ben Blue. Grayson and Allyson go to work in Durante's Bowery saloon in this entertaining turn-of-the-century musical; bright score helps.

Two Smart People (1946) 93m. ** D: Jules Dassin. Lucille Ball, John Hodiak, Lloyd Nolan, Hugo Haas, Lenore Ulric, Elisha Cook, Jr. Conniving couple involved in art forgery; laughs don't come very often. Co-written by Leslie Charteris.

2001: A Space Odyssey (1968-British) C-139m. **** D: Stanley Kubrick. Keir Dullea, William Sylvester, Gary Lockwood, Daniel Richter; voice of HAL, Douglas Rain. A milestone film: space travel is placed into context of man's history, from first confrontation with a Greater Power to future time warp where life cycle has no meaning. For now, it's man vs. machinery of his own making in an unforgettable space journey with computer HAL in control. A visual feast, film also boasts distinction of having put Richard Strauss into the Top 40 with "Thus Spake Zarathustra." Cut by 17 minutes after premiere, by Kubrick himself, to present length. Oscar-winning special effects. Screenplay by Arthur C. Clarke and the director, from Clarke's *The Sentinel.* Followed by 2010 in 1984.▼

2010 (1984) **C-114m.** *** D: Peter Hyams. Roy Scheider, John Lithgow, Helen Mirren, Bob Balaban, Keir Dullea, voice of Douglas Rain, Madolyn Smith, Dana Elcar, Elya Baskin, Savely Kramarov. Ambitious sequel to 2001: A SPACE ODYSSEY written by director Hyams from the follow-up novel by Arthur C. Clarke (who has a cameo on Washington park bench). Scheider is perfect Everyman who journeys into space on joint American-Soviet mission to solve mystery of what went wrong on original *Discovery* flight. More concrete and therefore less mystical than 2001, with an ending that's *much* too literal, but still an entertaining journey, with state-of-the-art visual effects by Richard Edlund.▼

2000 Years Later (1969) **C-80m.** ** D: Bert Tenzer. Terry-Thomas, Edward Everett Horton, Pat Harrington, Lisa Seagram. Amusing story of 20th century man exploiting a Roman soldier who comes back to life after 2000 years.

Two Tickets to Broadway (1951) **C-106m.** **½ D: James V. Kern. Tony Martin, Janet Leigh, Gloria De Haven, Eddie Bracken, Ann Miller, Barbara Lawrence, Smith and Dale, Bob Crosby, The Charlivels. Modest musical involving Martin et al trying to get on Crosby's TV show. Forget the hackneyed plot and enjoy the Jule Styne-Leo Robin score, along with standards like Rodgers & Hart's "Manhattan." Best bit: Crosby's musical spoof of brother Bing, "Let's Make Comparisons" (by Bob C. and Sammy Cahn).▼

Two Tickets to London (1943) **79m.** ** D: Edwin L. Marin. Michele Morgan, Alan Curtis, Barry Fitzgerald, C. Aubrey Smith. Passable drama of Curtis helped by Morgan in hunting down espionage agents.

Two Tickets to Paris (1962) **78m.** BOMB D: Greg Garrison. Joey Dee and The Starlighters, Gary Crosby, Kay Medford, Jeri Lynne Fraser, Lisa James, Charles Nelson Reilly. Engaged to be married teenagers Dee and Fraser sail for France, with each having a meaningless flirtation. Trifling musical comedy; originally released at 90m.

Two Way Stretch (1960-British) **87m.** *** D: Robert Day. Peter Sellers, Wilfrid Hyde-White, Lionel Jeffries, Liz Fraser, Maurice Denham. Wry shenanigans of Sellers, et al as prisoners who devise a means of escaping to commit a robbery and then return to safety of their cells.▼

Two Weeks in Another Town (1962) **C-107m.** *** D: Vincente Minnelli. Kirk Douglas, Edward G. Robinson, Cyd Charisse, George Hamilton, Claire Trevor, Daliah Lavi, Rossana Schiaffino, Constance Ford. Overly ambitious attempt to intellectualize Irwin Shaw novel, revolving around problems of people involved in moviemaking in Rome. Reunites much of the talent from THE BAD AND THE BEAUTIFUL, footage from which is used as the film-within-a-film here.

Two Weeks in September (1967-French) **C-96m.** **½ D: Serge Bourguignon. Brigitte Bardot, Laurent Terzieff, Michael Sarne, James Robertson Justice. Bardot, mistress to older man, has fling with younger lover, can't decide between the two. Location shooting in London and Scotland enhances OK story.

Two Weeks With Love (1950) **C-92m.** **½ D: Roy Rowland. Jane Powell, Ricardo Montalban, Louis Calhern, Ann Harding, Debbie Reynolds, Carleton Carpenter. Reynolds fans will enjoy her role as daughter vacationing in Catskills proving to her parents that she's grown up, and singing "Abba Dabba Honeymoon" with Carpenter.

Two Wives at One Wedding (1960-British) **66m.** *½ D: Montgomery Tully. Gordon Jackson, Christina Gregg, Lisa Daniely, Andre Maranne. Trite minor film involving Jackson confronted by extortion gang charging him with bigamy.

Two Women (1961-Italian) **99m.** **** D: Vittorio De Sica. Sophia Loren, Raf Vallone, Eleanora Brown, Jean-Paul Belmondo. Loren deservedly won Oscar for heartwrenching portrayal of Italian mother who, along with young daughter, is raped by Allied Moroccan soldiers during WW2. How they survive is an intensely moving story; based on an Alberto Moravia novel.▼

Two Worlds of Angelita, The (1982) **C-73m.** *** D: Jane Morrison. Marien Perez Riera, Rosalba Rolon, Angel Domenech Soto, Delia Esther Quinones, Roberto Juan Texidor. Perceptive drama of problems and pressures on Puerto Rican family when they move to N.Y.C. barrio, all seen through the eyes of nine-year-old daughter (Riera). Filmed independently in Puerto Rico and New York.

Two Worlds of Jennie Logan, The (1979) **C-100m.** TVM D: Frank DeFelitta. Lindsay Wagner, Marc Singer, Alan Feinstein, Linda Gray, Henry Wilcoxon, Joan Darling. Stylish murder mystery/romantic drama taking place simultaneously in two centuries. Based on David Williams' *Second Sight.* Above average.▼

Two Yanks in Trinidad (1942) **88m.** ** D: Gregory Ratoff. Brian Donlevy, Pat O'Brien, Janet Blair, Donald MacBride. Donlevy and O'Brien are hoods who join the army, turning their talents to fighting the enemy; flat patriotism.

Two Years Before the Mast (1946) 98m. *½ D: John Farrow. Alan Ladd, Brian Donlevy, William Bendix, Esther Fernandez, Howard da Silva, Barry Fitzgerald, Albert Dekker, Darryl Hickman. Badly scripted story of Richard Henry Dana's (Donlevy) crusade to expose mistreatment of men at sea. Da Silva is standout as tyrannical captain.

Tycoon (1947) C-128m. **½ D: Richard Wallace. John Wayne, Laraine Day, Cedric Hardwicke, Judith Anderson, James Gleason, Anthony Quinn, Grant Withers. Wayne plays determined young railroad builder in this overlong, but well-acted drama with fine cast. Also shown in computer-colored version.▼

Typhoon (1940) C-70m. **½ D: Louis King. Dorothy Lamour, Robert Preston, Lynne Overman, J. Carrol Naish, Chief Thundercloud, Jack Carson. Another Lamour sarong epic, typically romantic; Overman provides good comedy support.

Tyrant of the Sea (1950) 70m. ** D: Lew Landers. Rhys Williams, Ron Randell, Valentine Perkins, Doris Lloyd, Lester Matthews, Terry Kilburn, William Fawcett. Undistinguished melodrama set in 1803. Napoleon is ready to invade England and only retired tough sea captain (Williams) can destroy French landing barges and save the country. Meanwhile, romance blossoms between young Lt. Randell and captain's daughter Perkins.

UFO Incident, The (1975) C-100m. TVM D: Richard A. Colla. James Earl Jones, Estelle Parsons, Barnard Hughes, Dick O'Neill, Beeson Carroll, Terrence O'Connor. Absorbing, fact-based, semi-sci-fi drama tracing story of New England couple who claim to have been taken aboard a UFO and examined medically. Long on monologues, skimpy in action, it's kept afloat by two leads and Hughes, the doctor who probes their memories. Above average.

UFOria (1980) C-100m. **½ D: John Binder. Cindy Williams, Harry Dean Stanton, Fred Ward, Harry Carey, Jr., Beverly Hope Atkinson. Amiable if sometimes uneasy mix of MELVIN AND HOWARD and CLOSE ENCOUNTERS OF THE THIRD KIND with Williams as a kooky grocery store cashier who believes she has received a message from outer space and will become a female Noah on UFO ark. Long unreleased, this finally found a distributor (and an audience) in 1986.▼

UFO (Unidentified Flying Objects) (1956) C/B&W-92m. ** D: Winston Jones. Documentary-style account of unknown missiles, detailing various reports of unidentified flying objects being spotted. Film lacks excitement.

Ugetsu (1953-Japanese) 96m. ***½ D: Kenji Mizoguchi. Machiko Kyo, Masayuki Mori, Kinuyo Tanaka, Sakae Ozawa. Eerie ghost story set in 16th-century Japan tells of two peasants who leave their families; one seeks wealth in the city and the other wishes to become a samurai warrior. This superbly photographed film was a Venice Film Festival prize winner. Full title UGETSU MONOGATARI.▼

Ugly American, The (1963) C-120m. **½ D: George H. Englund. Marlon Brando, Sandra Church, Pat Hingle, Eiji Okada, Arthur Hill, Kukrit Pramoj, Jocelyn Brando. Brando is American ambassador to Asian country; his arrival stirs up pro-communist elements, leading to havoc. Political revelations of U.S. power struggle aren't meat for exciting film. Adapted by Stewart Stern from the Burdick-Lederer book.▼

Ugly Dachshund, The (1966) C-93m. ** D: Norman Tokar. Dean Jones, Suzanne Pleshette, Charlie Ruggles, Kelly Thordsen, Parley Baer. Silly, featherweight Disney comedy about husband and wife who train their respective dogs for competition at dog show. Fun for kids, but too contrived and silly for anyone else to enjoy.▼

UHF (1989) C-97m. ** D: Jay Levey. "Weird Al" Yankovic, Victoria Jackson, Kevin McCarthy, Michael Richards, David Bowe, Stanley Brock, Anthony Geary, Trinidad Silva, Gedde Watanabe, Billy Barty, John Paragon, Fran Drescher, Sue Ane Langdon, Emo Philips. Music video parodist Yankovic's starring feature debut casts him as the manager of a small-time TV station who inadvertently hits it big with his unconventional programming ideas. Story is threadbare, but some of the spoofs of commercials, movies, and TV shows are fun. Yankovic scripted with director Levey.

Ultimate Chase, The SEE: **Ultimate Thrill, The**▼

Ultimate Imposter, The (1979) C-97m. TVM D: Paul Stanley. Joseph Hacker, Keith Andes, Erin Gray, Tracy Brooks Swope, Bobby Riggs. Computer-age secret agent, using the latest gadgetry, sets out to help a Russian submarine commander defect. Silly premise that ended up as a busted series pilot. Below average.▼

Ultimate Solution of Grace Quigley, The SEE: **Grace Quigley**▼

Ultimate Thrill, The (1974) C-110m. ** D: Robert Butler. Eric Braeden, Britt Ekland, Barry Brown, Michael Blodgett, John Davis Chandler. Executive is drawn into murder by his paranoiac fears; undistinguished programmer retitled THE ULTIMATE CHASE for network showing.▼

Ultimate Warrior, The (1975) C-94m. **½ D: Robert Clouse. Yul Brynner, Max von Sydow, Joanna Miles, William Smith, Stephen McHattie, Lane Bradbury. Routine acting and directing spoil potentially intriguing futuristic fantasy. In the 21st century, Brynner and von Sydow each control a decreasing band of people fighting for whatever is left in N.Y.C. following ecological disasters.▼

Ulysses (1955-Italian) **C-104m.** ** D: Mario Camerini. Kirk Douglas, Silvana Mangano, Anthony Quinn, Sylvie, Rossana Podesta. Hokey, lumbering costumer with Douglas as Ulysses, on his Odyssey home to Penelope after the Trojan War. Watch Kirk speak in dubbed Italian, then English. Seven writers are credited for this, including Ben Hecht and Irwin Shaw.▼

Ulysses (1967) **140m.** **½ D: Joseph Strick. Barbara Jefford, Milo O'Shea, Maurice Roeves, T. P. McKenna, Martin Dempsey, Sheila O'Sullivan. Idea of putting James Joyce's massive novel on the screen seemed daring in 1967, but now seems like a stupid stunt. Lots of good prose makes it to the screen, but end result is interesting curio, not a film. Shot on location in Ireland; Strick far more successfully filmed Joyce's A PORTRAIT OF THE ARTIST AS A YOUNG MAN in 1979.▼

Ulysses Against Hercules (1961-Italian) **C-99m.** *½ D: Mario Caiano. Georges Marchal, Michael Lane, Alessandra Panaro, Gianni Santuccio. Childish blend of myth and muscleman antics with Hercules (Lane) sent to punish Ulysses (Marchal); special effects of bird-men not up to snuff.

Ulzana's Raid (1972) **C-103m.** ***½ D: Robert Aldrich. Burt Lancaster, Bruce Davison, Jorge Luke, Richard Jaeckel, Joaquin Martinez, Lloyd Bochner, Karl Swenson. Violent cavalry-and-Indians tale was well received by some of the more perceptive critics; one of Burt's best performances. Taut script by Alan Sharp.▼

Umberto D (1952-Italian) **89m.** **** D: Vittorio De Sica. Carlo Battisti, Maria Pia Casilio, Lina Gennari. Ex-bureaucrat on a meager fixed pension is about to be forced out into Rome streets with only his beloved mongrel to comfort him. De Sica is said to have considered this his greatest work, and he may have been right; subplot about Battisti's relationship with an unmarried, pregnant woman is as touching as predominant story line. Shattering, all the way up to the tear-jerking conclusion.▼

Umbrellas of Cherbourg, The (1964-French) **C-91m.** ***½ D: Jacques Demy. Catherine Deneuve, Nino Castelnuovo, Anne Vernon, Marc Michel, Ellen Farnen. Haunting music (score) by Michel Legrand, lyrics by Demy) and gorgeous photography make this an outstanding romantic drama. Try to catch original version with subtitles, as dubbing hurts original effect. All dialogue is sung. Followed by THE YOUNG GIRLS OF ROCHEFORT.▼

Umbrella Woman, The SEE: **Good Wife, The**▼

U.M.C. (1969) **C-100m. TVM** D: Boris Sagal. James Daly, Richard Bradford, Maurice Evans, Kevin McCarthy, Shelley Fabares, William Windom, J. D. Cannon, Edward G. Robinson. Excellent cast in moderately effective behind-the-scenes drama of university medical center; script and subplots strictly formula. Pilot for the *Medical Center* TV series. Retitled OPERATION HEARTBEAT. Average.

Unbearable Lightness of Being, The (1988) **C-171m.** ***½ D: Philip Kaufman. Daniel Day-Lewis, Juliette Binoche, Lena Olin, Derek de Lint, Erland Josephson, Pavel Landovsky, Donald Moffat. Extraordinarily well-made adaptation of the acclaimed novel by Milan Kundera about a young Czech doctor of the 1960s who has a way with women (lots of women) and an aversion to politics but who finds himself caught up in his country's political turmoil—and a crisis of commitment with the women in his life. Kaufman and Jean-Claude Carriere's adaptation unfolds just like a good book, taking its time but never meandering as it paints a vivid picture of the character's life and times. Sensual, intelligent, and beautifully acted by the three leads; strikingly photographed by Sven Nykvist.▼

Uncanny, The (1977-British-Canadian) **C-85m.** ** D: Denis Heroux. Peter Cushing, Ray Milland, Susan Penhaligon, Joan Greenwood, Alexandra Stewart, Chloe Franks, Donald Pleasence, Samantha Eggar, John Vernon. Lackluster trilogy of "supernatural" tales built around author Cushing's assertion that cats are conspiring against mankind.▼

Uncertain Glory (1944) **102m.** ** D: Raoul Walsh. Errol Flynn, Jean Sullivan, Paul Lukas, Lucile Watson, Faye Emerson, Douglass Dumbrille, Dennis Hoey, Sheldon Leonard. Wavering script about French philanderer Flynn deciding to give his life for his country.

Unchained (1955) **75m.** ** D: Hall Bartlett. Elroy "Crazylegs" Hirsch, Barbara Hale, Chester Morris, Johnny Johnston, Peggy Knudsen, Jerry Paris. Fair drama of life at prison farm at Chino, California; highlighted by Alex North-Hy Zarek theme song: "Unchained Melody." Saxophonist Dexter Gordon is seen briefly as a musician (though his playing was dubbed by George Auld).

Uncle Buck (1989) **C-100m.** **½ D: John Hughes. John Candy, Amy Madigan, Jean Louisa Kelly, Gaby Hoffman, Macaulay Culkin, Elaine Bromka, Garrett M. Brown, Laurie Metcalf, Jay Underwood. Ne'er-do-well bachelor Candy has to look after his brother's kids for a couple of days . . . and surprise! The perpetual foul-up turns out to be a caring and responsible uncle. Comedy with serious and sentimental strains gives

Candy one of his better vehicles, though writer-director Hughes' inconsistencies keep it from scoring a bull's-eye. Followed by a TV series.▼

Uncle Harry SEE: **Strange Affair of Uncle Harry, The**

Uncle Joe Shannon (1978) **C-115m.** BOMB D: Joseph C. Hanwright. Burt Young, Doug McKeon, Madge Sinclair, Jason Bernard, Bert Remsen, Allan Rich. Slobbering, self-indulgent film (written by Young) about down-and-out trumpet player and young boy who tries to resist his "charm." Several hands from ROCKY—including Young—were hoping to duplicate that film's success. Maynard Ferguson dubbed Young's trumpet licks.

Uncle Silas SEE: **Inheritance, The** (1947)

Uncle Tom's Cabin (1987) **C-110m.** TVM D: Stan Lathan. Avery Brooks, Kate Burton, Bruce Dern, Paula Kelly, Phylicia Rashad, Kathryn Walker, Edward Woodward, Frank Converse, George Coe, Albert Hall. Ambitious "contemporary adaptation" (i.e., slightly revisionist version) of the Harriet Beecher Stowe novel, adapted by John Gay. First American sound version of the classic (following a 1965 German production) doesn't have the Eliza-crossing-the-ice segment but does have a first-rate cast, including a standout Simon Legree in Edward Woodward. Above average.

Uncommon Love, An (1983) **C-100m.** TVM D: Steven Hilliard Stern. Barry Bostwick, Kathryn Harrold, Ed Begley, Jr., Holly Hunter, Cyril O'Reilly, Allison Argo, Phillip R. Allen. He's a college professor, she's in his marine biology class. They fall in love but he soon learns she's working her way through school turning tricks in a massage parlor. Now that's uncommon, but will their thing survive? Tune in next week. Below average.

Uncommon Valor (1983) **C-100m.** TVM D: Rod Amateau. Mitchell Ryan, Ben Murphy, Rick Lohman, Barbara Parkins, Norman Fell, Gregory Sierra, John Reilly, Salome Jens, Julie Cobb, Belinda Montgomery. A hospital is torched, but the actors lack any spark in this pedestrian series pilot that fizzled. Below average.

Uncommon Valor (1983) **C-105m.** **½ D: Ted Kotcheff. Gene Hackman, Robert Stack, Fred Ward, Reb Brown, Randall "Tex" Cobb, Patrick Swayze, Harold Sylvester, Tim Thomerson. Formula action film about a retired Army officer who gathers motley crew of Vietnam vets to invade Laos in search of his son, still Missing in Action. Solid performances down the line make this watchable.▼

Unconquered (1947) **C-146m.** **½ D: Cecil B. DeMille. Gary Cooper, Paulette Goddard, Howard da Silva, Boris Karloff, Cecil Kellaway, Ward Bond, Katherine de Mille, C. Aubrey Smith, Porter Hall, Mike Mazurki. Gargantuan DeMille colonists-vs.-Indians nonsense, one of his most ludicrous films but still fun.

Unconquered (1989) **C-100m.** TVM D: Dick Lowry. Peter Coyote, Dermot Mulroney, Tess Harper, Jenny Robertson, Bud Gunton, Larry Riley. Interlocking drama about Richmond Flowers, Sr. and Jr. The father is a crusading Alabama civil rights lawyer of the '60s, the son a 90-pound weakling who overcame physical disabilities to become a world-class hurdler and later a football star. Give writer Pat Conroy credit for attempting to cram two stories into one movie—but it doesn't do either one justice, in a saga that includes such real-life figures as Governor George Wallace, Coach Bear Bryant, and Reverend Martin Luther King, Jr. Average.

Undead, The (1957) **75m.** *** D: Roger Corman. Richard Garland, Pamela Duncan, Allison Hayes, Mel Welles, Billy Barty, Richard Devon, Bruno VeSota. One of Corman's best early films, coscripted by Charles Griffith. A scientist, investigating the possibility of reincarnation, manages to transport himself back into the Dark Ages. Lots of atmosphere and black humor, with a neat twist ending.▼

Undefeated, The (1969) **C-119m.** ** D: Andrew V. McLaglen. John Wayne, Rock Hudson, Tony Aguilar, Roman Gabriel, Bruce Cabot, Lee Meriwether, Ben Johnson, Merlin Olsen. Aside from interesting Wayne-Hudson teaming and the presence of football stars Gabriel and Olsen, this routine Western has little to offer. Post-Civil War tale casts two stars as Union and Confederate colonels. Best line: "The conversation sorta dried up."▼

Under Capricorn (1949-British) **C-117m.** ** D: Alfred Hitchcock. Ingrid Bergman, Joseph Cotten, Michael Wilding, Margaret Leighton, Cecil Parker. Stuffy costumer set in 19th-century Australia; Bergman is frail wife of hardened husband Cotten; Wilding comes to visit, upsetting everything. Leighton excellent in supporting role. One of Hitchcock's few duds.▼

Under Cover (1987) **C-94m.** *½ D: John Stockwell. David Neidorf, Jennifer Jason Leigh, Barry Corbin, Kathleen Wilhoite, David Harris. Neidorf is an out-of-town cop operating undercover with female narc Leigh to catch the drug pushers who killed another cop on the case. Best known as the pilot "Cougar" in TOP GUN, Stockwell here makes an uninspired directorial debut.▼

Undercover Girl (1950) **83m.** ** D: Joseph Pevney. Alexis Smith, Scott Brady, Richard Egan, Gladys George, Regis Toomey. Smith in title role joins police to locate her father's killer; George in cameo is outstanding.

Undercover Maisie (1947) **90m.** D: Harry Beaumont. Ann Sothern, Barry Nelson, Mark Daniels, Leon Ames, Clinton Sundberg. SEE: **Maisie** series.

Under-Cover Man (1932) **70m.** ** D: James Flood. George Raft, Nancy Carroll, Roscoe Karns, Gregory Ratoff, Lew Cody. Good but familiar tale of Raft devoting his life to finding father's killer. Well acted.

Undercover Man, The (1949) **85m.** *** D: Joseph II. Lewis. Glenn Ford, Nina Foch, James Whitmore, Barry Kelley, Howard St. John. Realistic drama of mob-leader (loosely based on Al Capone) being hunted down by secret service men who hope to nail him on tax-evasion charge. Whitmore's film debut.

Undercovers Hero (1975-British) **C-95m.** BOMB D: Roy Boulting. Peter Sellers, Lila Kedrova, Curt Jurgens, Beatrice Romand, Jenny Hanley, Rex Stallings. Inept WW2 "comedy," with Sellers in six roles, including Hitler; a total dud. Made in 1973, barely released here. British title: SOFT BEDS AND HARD BATTLES.

Undercover With the KKK (1979) **C-100m.** TVM D: Barry Shear. Don Meredith, James Wainwright, Ed Lauter, Albert Salmi, Maggie Blye, Slim Pickens, Michele Carey. Story of Gary Thomas Rowe, recruited by FBI to infiltrate the KKK around the time of Martin Luther King's march on Montgomery. Between completion of this film and its first showing, Rowe was indicted for murder of one of the Freedom Riders, forcing some re-editing, new prologue, and epilogue spoken by Robert Stack. Retitled THE FREEDOM RIDERS and MY UNDERCOVER YEARS WITH THE KKK. Average.

Undercurrent (1946) **116m.** **½ D: Vincente Minnelli. Katharine Hepburn, Robert Taylor, Robert Mitchum, Edmund Gwenn, Marjorie Main, Jayne Meadows. Stale melodramatics of woman realizing her husband is wicked, saved only by fine cast and usual high MGM production quality.

Under Fire (1957) **78m.** ** D: James B. Clark. Rex Reason, Steve Brodie, Jon Locke, Harry Morgan, Robert Levin. Bland war tale about soldiers alleged to have deserted under enemy fire.

Under Fire (1983) **C-128m.** ***½ D: Roger Spottiswoode. Nick Nolte, Gene Hackman, Joanna Cassidy, Ed Harris, Jean-Louis Trintignant, Richard Masur, Rene Enriquez, Hamilton Camp. First-rate political thriller about journalists on the line in Managua, Nicaragua, 1979, how their lives intertwine, and how two of them risk their professionalism by becoming involved in the revolutionary conflict. One of those rare films that manages to combine real-life politics and realistic romance with a no-nonsense story. Trio of stars are superb; so is Jerry Goldsmith's music. Only problem: It goes on too long. Screenplay by Ron Shelton and Clayton Frohman.▼

Undergrads, The (1985) **C-105m.** TVM D: Steven Hilliard Stern. Art Carney, Chris Makepeace, Len Birman, Lesleh Donaldson, Jackie Burroughs, Alfie Scopp. Feisty old fellow decides to enroll in college with his grandson. Bland and predictable but likable nevertheless, thanks in large part to Carney. Made for cable by Disney. Average.▼

Underground (1941) **95m.** *** D: Vincent Sherman. Jeffrey Lynn, Philip Dorn, Kaaren Verne, Mona Maris, Frank Reicher, Martin Kosleck. Gripping story of German underground movement, with Dorn shielding his activities from loyal soldier-brother Lynn. Kosleck is definitive Nazi swine.

Underground Man, The (1974) **C-100m.** TVM D: Paul Wendkos. Peter Graves, Jack Klugman, Judith Anderson, Celeste Holm, Jo Ann Pflug, Vera Miles, Kay Lenz, Jim Hutton, Sharon Farrell. Standard mystery-drama, with Graves as Ross MacDonald's private eye Lew Archer, searching for kidnapped son of an old girlfriend, and finding tangled web of infidelity, long hidden murder, and other standard elements. Below average.

Underground U.S.A. (1980) **C-85m.** *** D: Eric Mitchell. Patti Astor, Eric Mitchell, Rene Ricard, Tom Wright, Cookie Mueller, Jackie Curtis, Taylor Mead. Street hustler Mitchell forces his way into the life of has-been movie star Astor. Rambling but fascinating; a sort of punk rock SUNSET BOULEVARD.

Under Milk Wood (1973-British) **C-90m.** ** D: Andrew Sinclair. Richard Burton, Elizabeth Taylor, Peter O'Toole, Glynis Johns, Sian Phillips, Vivien Merchant. Rather obscure Dylan Thomas, not in terms of his work but in the film's ambitions. Beautiful images, but rather overbearing technique weighs down the acting.▼

Under My Skin (1950) **86m.** **½ D: Jean Negulesco. John Garfield, Micheline Presle, Luther Adler, Orley Lindgren, Noel Drayton. Pensive study of troubled, crooked jockey Garfield, attempting to reform for the sake of son Lindgren and pretty widow Presle. Based on Ernest Hemingway's *My Old Man*; remade for TV in 1979 under that title.

Under-Pup, The (1939) **81m.** **½ D: Richard Wallace. Gloria Jean, Robert Cummings, Nan Grey, Beulah Bondi, Virginia Weidler, Margaret Lindsay, C. Aubrey Smith, Billy Gilbert. Hokey but heartwarming tale of singing tenement child who attends exclusive summer camp as charity guest of a snobbish girls' club. Film debut for Gloria Jean, Universal Pictures' "successor" to Deanna Durbin. Originally released at 88m.

Under Satan's Sun (1987-French) **C-97m.**

[1233]

*** D: Maurice Pialat. Gerard Depardieu, Sandrine Bonnaire, Maurice Pialat, Alain Artur, Yann Dedet. A very demanding and difficult film, not for all tastes but most rewarding to those who can relate to the subject: the questions, conflicts, and torments of rural priest Depardieu. Adapted from a book by Georges Bernanos, author of *Diary of a Country Priest.* Also known as UNDER THE SUN OF SATAN.▼

Undersea Girl (1957) **75m. BOMB** D: John Peyser. Mara Corday, Pat Conway, Dan Seymour, Florence Marly, Myron Healey. Flabby murder yarn with all sides of law hunting for loot buried on ocean bottom.

Undersea Kingdom SEE: **Sharad of Atlantis**▼

Undersea Odyssey, An SEE: **Neptune Factor, The**▼

Under Siege (1986) **C-150m. TVM** D: Roger Young. Peter Strauss, Mason Adams, Lew Ayres, George Grizzard, Hal Holbrook, E. G. Marshall, Beatrice Straight, Victoria Tennant, Fritz Weaver, Paul Winfield. Imaginative thriller dealing with America's first battle with domestic terrorism, highlighted by graphic special effects that involve blowing the dome off the Capitol building in Washington, D.C. Drawback is the sometimes overly talky and suspiciously padded script by a battery of writers, one of whom was Pulitzer Prizewinner Bob Woodward (*All the President's Men*). Above average.

Under Ten Flags (1960-U.S.-Italian) 92m. **½ D: Duilio Coletti. Van Heflin, Charles Laughton, Mylene Demongeot, John Ericson, Cecil Parker, Liam Redmond, Alex Nicol. German attack-ship during WW2 uses a variety of dodges to elude British pursuers, in naval cat-and-mouse game, told from Axis point of view. Filmed in Italy.

Under the Biltmore Clock (1985) **C-90m. TVM** D: Neal Miller. Lenny Von Dohlen, Barnard Hughes, Sean Young, Mark Hulsey, Wayne Kneeland. Disappointing, paper-thin adaptation of an F. Scott Fitzgerald short story, "Myra Meets His Family," about a young fortune hunter (Young), out to snare herself a husband—wealthy preppy Van Dohlen, who's as superficial as this film. A PBS *American Playhouse* presentation. Below average.▼

Under the Boardwalk (1989) **C-104m.** *½ D: Fritz Kiersch. Richard Joseph Paul, Danielle Von Zerneck, Steve Monarque, Keith Coogan, Roxana Zal, Hunter Von Leer, Tracey Walter, Dick Miller, Sonny Bono, Elizabeth Kaitan. Surfers from the San Fernando Valley ("Vals") square off against Venice locals ("Lokes"), with Romeo-and-Juliet-like conflict of Val boy who loves Loke girl. Anemic teen picture is a major waste of time. Oddest element:

jargon-spouting narrator is 20 years in the future.▼

Under the Cherry Moon (1986) **98m.** *½ D: Prince. Prince, Jerome Benton, Kristin Scott-Thomas, Steven Berkoff, Francesca Annis, Emmanuelle Sallet, Alexandra Stewart, Victor Spinetti. Supremely silly vanity film with Prince self-cast as American gigolo/entertainer in the south of France who has a devastating effect on women (yes, it's a science-fiction story). Stylish-looking fairy-tale/fable, filmed in black & white, is a triumph of self-adoration, and overall embarrassment. Some music throughout, but in fragmented scenes.▼

Under the Gun (1950) **83m.** **½ D: Ted Tetzlaff. Richard Conte, Audrey Totter, Sam Jaffe, John McIntire, Royal Dano. Effective study of gangsters behind bars, played by competent cast.

Under the Gun (1989) **C-89m.** ** D: James Sbardellati. Sam Jones, Vanessa Williams, John Russell, Michael Halsey, Sharon Williams, Bill McKinney, Rockne Tarkington, Don Stark, Nick Cassavetes. Cop Jones teams up with lawyer Williams to go after plutonium thief who ordered the death of Jones' brother. Acceptable but familiar odd-couple crime melodrama; at least it keeps moving.▼

Under the Influence (1986) **C-100m. TVM** D: Thomas Carter. Andy Griffith, Season Hubley, Paul Provenza, Keanu Reeves, William Schallert, Joyce Van Patten. Griffith gives a rock-solid portrayal of a family man who refuses to acknowledge he's an alcoholic. Writer and recovered alcoholic Joyce Rebeta-Burditt's incisive script delivers a powerful statement. Above average.

Under the Rainbow (1981) **C-98m. BOMB** D: Steve Rash. Chevy Chase, Carrie Fisher, Eve Arden, Joseph Maher, Adam Arkin, Mako, Pat McCormick, Billy Barty. Even by today's standards this is an astoundingly unfunny and tasteless comedy about spies, undercover agents, and midgets who cross paths in a hotel during filming of THE WIZARD OF OZ. Is this film the Wicked Witch's revenge?▼

Under the Red Robe (1937-British) **82m.** **½ D: Victor Seastrom. Conrad Veidt, Raymond Massey, Annabella, Romney Brent, Sophie Stewart. Diverting costumer with Veidt as hero, Annabella lovely heroine, and Massey the cruel villain in story of French Cardinal Richelieu's oppression of the Huguenots. Offbeat sense of humor adds to film's enjoyment.▼

Under the Roofs of Paris (1930-French) **92m.** ***½ D: Rene Clair. Albert Prejean, Pola Illery, Gaston Modot, Edmond Greville, Paul Olivier. Mime and song, with a minimum of dialogue, tell the story in this wonderful film about two ordinary

[1234]

Parisians (Prejean, Greville) involved with the same woman (Illery). A ground-breaking link between silent and sound cinema; Lazare Meerson's sets are outstanding. Written by Clair.▼

Under the Sun of Satan SEE: **Under Satan's Sun**▼

Under the Volcano (1984) **C-109m.** ***½ D: John Huston. Albert Finney, Jacqueline Bisset, Anthony Andrews, Ignacio Lopez Tarso, Katy Jurado, James Villiers. Somber but striking adaptation of Malcolm Lowry's novel about alcoholic diplomat in Mexico during the late 1930s; rich in atmosphere and texture, with a great performance by Finney. Screenplay by Guy Gallo; music by Alex North.▼

Under the Yum Yum Tree (1963) **C-110m.** **½ D: David Swift. Jack Lemmon, Carol Lynley, Dean Jones, Edie Adams, Imogene Coca, Paul Lynde, Robert Lansing. Obvious sex comedy owes most of its enjoyment to Lemmon as love-hungry landlord trying to romance tenant Lynley who's living with her fiancé (Jones).

Undertow (1949) **71m.** **½ D: William Castle. Scott Brady, John Russell, Dorothy Hart, Peggy Dow, Bruce Bennett, Gregg Martell. Well-done if predictable account of innocent Brady framed on a murder rap, and how he brings the real culprits to justice. Rock Hudson is billed as "Roc" in this, his second film.

Under Two Flags (1936) **96m.** *** D: Frank Lloyd. Ronald Colman, Claudette Colbert, Victor McLaglen, Rosalind Russell, Gregory Ratoff, Nigel Bruce, Herbert Mundin, John Carradine, J. Edward Bromberg. Debonair Colman is caught between two women (aristocratic Russell and camp follower Colbert), and the envy of jealous commandant McLaglen in this unbelievable but entertaining Foreign Legion story, from the book by Ouida (filmed before in 1916 and 1922). Originally ran 110m.

✓ **Underwater!** (1955) **C-99m.** ** D: John Sturges. Jane Russell, Gilbert Roland, Richard Egan, Lori Nelson, Jayne Mansfield. Standard skin-diving fare, with Roland and Egan seeking out treasure in the deep. Russell in a bathing suit is the main attraction.▼

good
B grade

Underwater City, The (1962) **C-78m.** ** D: Frank McDonald. William Lundigan, Julie Adams, Roy Roberts, Carl Benton Reid, Chet Douglas, Paul Dubov. Mildly diverting sci-fi about engineer who builds experimental underwater city. Released theatrically in b&w.

Underwater Warrior (1958) **90m.** **½ D: Andrew Marton. Dan Dailey, Claire Kelly, James Gregory, Ross Martin. On-location filming in the Philippines adds zest to narrative-style account of frogmen in action during closing days of WW2.

Under Western Skies (1945) **83m.** *½ D: Jean Yarbrough. Martha O'Driscoll, Noah

Beery, Jr., Leon Errol. Uninspired blend of shoot-em-up and musical, with scatterbrained jokes tossed in.

Underworld (1985-British) **C-100m.** **½ D: George Pavlou. Denholm Elliott, Steven Berkoff, Larry Lamb, Miranda Richardson, Art Malik, Nicola Cowper, Ingrid Pitt. Fair thriller about mutants who live underground and who kidnap pretty hooker Cowper in order to obtain from Dr. Elliott the drug that will keep them alive. Retired gunman Lamb is hired by gang boss Berkoff to rescue her.▼

Underworld After Dark SEE **Big Town After Dark**

Underworld Informers (1965-British) **105m.** *** D: Ken Annakin. Nigel Patrick, Catherine Woodville, Margaret Whiting, Colin Blakely, Harry Andrews, Frank Finlay. Tight, taut crime tale as Scotland Yard inspector Patrick must clear his name by bringing in notorious gangland leaders. Vivid atmosphere, fine acting by all. Original British title: THE INFORMERS.

Underworld Story, The (1950) **90m.** *** D: Cy Endfield. Gale Storm, Dan Duryea, Herbert Marshall, Mary Anderson, Michael O'Shea. Surprisingly effective gangster yarn of reporter joining small town newspaper and uncovering corruption; cast is uniformly good.

Underworld, U.S.A. (1961) **99m.** **½ D: Samuel Fuller. Cliff Robertson, Dolores Dorn, Beatrice Kay, Robert Emhardt, Larry Gates. Robertson sees his father murdered and develops lifetime obsession to get even with the mob responsible. One of director Fuller's most visually striking films; unfortunately, his script goes astray and doesn't fulfill initial promise.▼

Undying Monster, The (1942) **60m.** **½ D: John Brahm. James Ellison, John Howard, Heather Angel, Bramwell Fletcher. OK chiller of a werewolf on the prowl around an English estate; nothing new, but atmospherically photographed by Lucien Ballard.

Unearthly, The (1957) **73m.** *½ D: Brooke L. Peters. John Carradine, Allison Hayes, Myron Healey, Sally Todd. Mad scientist Carradine's experiments in immortality have resulted only in a basement full of deformed morons. Don't you join them.▼

Unfaithful, The (1947) **109m.** **½ D: Vincent Sherman. Ann Sheridan, Lew Ayres, Zachary Scott, Eve Arden, Steven Geray, John Hoyt. Title refers to Sheridan, who gets tangled in murder while husband is out of town; good cast in fairly interesting drama. Remake of THE LETTER.

Unfaithfully Yours (1948) **105m.** **** D: Preston Sturges. Rex Harrison, Linda Darnell, Rudy Vallee, Barbara Lawrence, Kurt Kreuger, Lionel Stander, Robert Greig, Edgar Kennedy, Julius Tannen, Al Bridge. Brilliant Sturges comedy of symphony conductor Harrison, who suspects his wife of infidelity and considers three courses of action (including murder) during concert. Great moments from Vallee and Kennedy; often side-splittingly funny. Remade in 1984.▼

Unfaithfully Yours (1984) **C-96m.** **½ D: Howard Zieff. Dudley Moore, Nastassja Kinski, Armand Assante, Albert Brooks, Cassie Yates, Richard Libertini, Richard B. Shull. Remake of Preston Sturges' wonderful film about an orchestra conductor who suspects his wife of having an affair—and plans to murder her. Pretty funny, with a perfect cast, but loses steam somewhere along the way. Certainly no match for the witty original.▼

Unfaithfuls, The (1960-Italian) **89m.** **½ D: Stefano Steno. Mai Britt, Gina Lollobrigida, Pierre Cressoy, Marina Vlady, Anna Maria Ferrero, Tina Lattanzi, Carlo Romano. Multifaceted film of life among rich, corrupt society of Rome.

Unfaithful Wife SEE: **La Femme Infidele**

Unfinished Business (1941) **96m.** ** D: Gregory LaCava. Irene Dunne, Robert Montgomery, Preston Foster, Eugene Pallette, Dick Foran, Esther Dale, Walter Catlett. Ordinary romance about ambitious singer Dunne, loving Foster, marrying his brother Montgomery for spite—and promptly regretting it. Blah drama wastes good cast and director.

Unfinished Business (1984-Canadian) **C-99m.** *** D: Don Owen. Isabelle Mejias, Peter Spence, Leslie Toth, Peter Kastner, Julie Biggs, Chuck Shamata. Appealing sequel to Owen's NOBODY WAVED GOODBYE. It's twenty years later: Kastner and Biggs, now divorced, have a rebellious offspring of their own, 17-year-old Mejias. Story focuses on her problems and anxieties as she approaches adulthood.

Unfinished Business (1985-Australian) **C-78m.** *** D: Bob Ellis. John Clayton, Michele Fawdon, Norman Kaye, Bob Ellis, Andrew Lesnie. Touching, neatly acted comedy of middle-aged journalist Clayton, who meets up with Fawdon, the woman he once loved. She's married but childless—and proposes that he make her pregnant.

Unfinished Dance, The (1947) **C-101m.** **½ D: Henry Koster. Margaret O'Brien, Cyd Charisse, Karin Booth, Danny Thomas, Esther Dale. Sugar-sweet story of young dancer O'Brien whose idol is ballerina Charisse. Remake of French film BALLERINA.

Unfinished Journey of Robert Kennedy, The (1969) **C-75m. TVM** D: Mel Stuart. Excellent David Wolper documentary narrated by John Huston mixes survey of political career and interviews on private life. Above average.

Unforgiven, The (1960) **C-125m.** *** D:

John Huston. Burt Lancaster, Audrey Hepburn, Audie Murphy, John Saxon, Charles Bickford, Lillian Gish, Doug McClure, Joseph Wiseman, Albert Salmi. Western set in 1850s Texas tells of two families at odds with Indians over Hepburn, whom the latter claim as one of theirs. Gish and Bickford are outstanding in stellar-cast story, with rousing Indian attack climax.▼

Unguarded Hour, The (1936) **90m.** **½ D: Sam Wood. Loretta Young, Franchot Tone, Lewis Stone, Roland Young, Jessie Ralph, Dudley Digges, Henry Daniell, Aileen Pringle. Young is being blackmailed and cannot prove an accused murderer's innocence without damaging her own reputation—and embarrassing her prosecutor husband. Intriguing story comes to silly conclusion, but cast maintains interest (though the three leads are not terribly convincing as British subjects).

Unguarded Moment, The (1956) **C-95m.** **½ D: Harry Keller. Esther Williams, George Nader, John Saxon, Edward Andrews, Les Tremayne, Jack Albertson. Mild drama of school teacher whose emotional stability is endangered by lusting pupil. Film noteworthy only for Williams' non-aquatic role; based on a story by Rosalind Russell!

Unholy, The (1988) **C-100m.** ** D: Camilo Vila. Ben Cross, Hal Holbrook, Jill Carroll, William Russ, Trevor Howard, Ned Beatty, Claudia Robinson, Nicole Fortier. Ambitious horror film puts priest Cross to the test when archbishop Holbrook assigns him to cast out the devil from a New Orleans church. Veteran Philip Yordan's script (cowritten by film's designer Fernando Fonseca) is weird but unconvincing. Special effects are arresting, but highlight is Fortier as the supersexy demon.▼

Unholy Four, The (1953-British) **80m.** *½ D: Terence Fisher. Paulette Goddard, William Sylvester, Patrick Holt, Paul Carpenter, Jeremy Hawk. Muddled drama of amnesiac Sylvester caught up in a murder plot. Original British title: A STRANGER CAME HOME.

Unholy Garden, The (1931) **74m.** **½ D: George Fitzmaurice. Ronald Colman, Fay Wray, Estelle Taylor, Tully Marshall, Warren Hymer, Mischa Auer, Henry Armetta. Forgettable but very entertaining fluff with Colman an adventurer/thief in desert setting; murder, action, romance neatly blended, carried by Colman's effortless charm. Written by Ben Hecht and Charles MacArthur.

Unholy Matrimony (1988) **C-100m. TVM** D: Jerrold Freeman. Patrick Duffy, Charles Durning, Michael O'Keefe, Lisa Blount, Fred Thompson, Michael C. Gwynne. Duffy plays real-life cop John Dillman, who doggedly investigates mail-order minister Durning and a doctor (O'Keefe) with

[1236]

a double identity, both of whom are suspects in a "perfect" crime. Based on Dillman's book about the case. Average.
Unholy Night, The (1929) 94m. ** D: Lionel Barrymore. Ernest Torrence, Dorothy Sebastian, Roland Young, Natalie Moorhead, Sidney Jarvis, Polly Moran, Sojin. With the murder of several members of their regiment, veterans from the Indian war gather at Young's London home to ferret out the murderer. Stagy Ben Hecht melodrama with much hamming, especially by Boris Karloff.
Unholy Partners (1941) 94m. *** D: Mervyn LeRoy. Edward G. Robinson, Edward Arnold, Laraine Day, Marsha Hunt, William T. Orr, Don Beddoe, Walter Kingsford. Intriguing premise: Robinson starts sensationalistic newspaper after WWI, is forced to bargain with underworld king Arnold. Day gives fine performance as E.G.'s girl Friday; Hunt sings "After You've Gone."
Unholy Rollers (1972) C-88m. **½ D: Vernon Zimmerman. Claudia Jennings, Louis Quinn, Betty Anne Rees, Roberta Collins. Behind-the-scenes life on roller derby circuit, Roger Corman-style; raunchy low-budgeter offers some fun.▼
Unholy Three, The (1925) 86m. **½ D: Tod Browning. Lon Chaney, Mae Busch, Matt Moore, Victor McLaglen, Harry Earles. In departure from horrific roles, Chaney plays side-show ventriloquist who teams with strongman and midget to form underworld trio. Corny aspects of story can't mar fascination with basic idea, or Chaney's performance. Remade in 1930.
Unholy Three, The (1930) 72m. **½ D: Jack Conway. Lon Chaney, Lila Lee, Elliott Nugent, Harry Earles, John Miljan, Ivan Linow. Almost scene-for-scene remake of 1925 film was Chaney's only talkie; he's terrific, other players less so. Denouement rewritten for this remake to take advantage of sound. Midget Earles is largely incoherent.
Unholy Wife, The (1957) C-94m. *½ D: John Farrow. Rod Steiger, Diana Dors, Tom Tryon, Beulah Bondi, Marie Windsor. Muddled melodrama about farmer's wife attempting to kill husband and mistakenly shooting someone else.▼
Unidentified Flying Objects SEE: **UFOS: (Unidentified Flying Objects)**
Unidentified Flying Oddball (1979) C-93m. **½ D: Russ Mayberry. Dennis Dugan, Jim Dale, Ron Moody, Kenneth More, John LeMesurier, Rodney Bewes, Shelia White. Innocuous Disney update of Mark Twain's CONNECTICUT YANKEE IN KING ARTHUR'S COURT, with young Dugan (and a lookalike robot) catapulted back to medieval times. Retitled A SPACEMAN IN KING ARTHUR'S COURT.▼
Uninhibited, The (1965-Spanish) C-104m.

** D: Juan Antonio Bardem. Melina Mercouri, Hardy Kruger, James Mason, Didier Haudepin, Jose Maria Monpin. Good cast can't save muddled drama of troubled souls whose lives intertwine in picturesque seaside village on the Costa Brava.
Uninvited, The (1944) 98m. ***½ D: Lewis Allen. Ray Milland, Ruth Hussey, Donald Crisp, Gail Russell, Cornelia Otis Skinner, Dorothy Stickney, Barbara Everest, Alan Napier. Ghost suspenser about Russell haunted by dead mother's spectre; Milland and Hussey try to solve mystery. No trick ending in this ingenious film, which introduced Victor Young's melody "Stella by Starlight."
Union City (1980) C-87m. **½ D: Mark Reichert. Dennis Lipscomb, Deborah Harry, Irina Maleeva, Everett McGill, Pat Benatar, Tony Azito. Harry (of the rock group Blondie) makes her dramatic debut as the wife of neurotic businessman Lipscomb, who beats to death a vagrant. Low-budget *film noir* is enhanced by Lipscomb performance and moody, quirky direction.▼
Union Depot (1932) 75m. *** D: Alfred E. Green. Douglas Fairbanks, Jr., Joan Blondell, Guy Kibbee, Alan Hale, David Landau, Frank McHugh. Fast-paced, eventful yarn that brings sharpie Fairbanks and stranded chorus-girl Blondell together at a bustling train station where a hundred subplots crisscross. Great fun, brimming with early-1930s flavor.
Union Pacific (1939) 135m. *** D: Cecil B. DeMille. Barbara Stanwyck, Joel McCrea, Robert Preston, Akim Tamiroff, Brian Donlevy, Anthony Quinn, Lynne Overman, Evelyn Keyes, Fuzzy Knight, J. M. Kerrigan, Stanley Ridges, Regis Toomey. Brawling DeMille saga about building the first transcontinental railroad; McCrea the hero, Donlevy the villain, Stanwyck (with Irish brogue!) in between. Action scenes, including spectacular train wreck, are highlights.
Union Station (1950) 80m. **½ D: Rudolph Maté. William Holden, Nancy Olson, Barry Fitzgerald, Jan Sterling, Allene Roberts, Lyle Bettger. Dated police techniques, plus general implausibility, detract from well-made film about manhunt for kidnapper (Bettger) of young blind woman (Roberts).▼
Unknown, The (1946) 70m. ** D: Henry Levin. Jim Bannon, Barton Yarborough, Karen Morley, Jeff Donnell, Robert Scott, Robert Wilcox. So-so entry in brief *I Love a Mystery* series with Bannon as Jack Packard, Yarborough as Doc Young. This one involves odd-ball family, with amnesiac daughter Donnell coming home to see her deranged mother (Morley) after twenty years.
Unknown Guest, The (1943) 64m. **½ D: Kurt Neumann. Victor Jory, Pamela

Blake, Veda Ann Borg, Harry Hayden, Emory Parnell. Murder whodunit manages to create suspense and perk interest, largely due to Jory's performance in this programmer.

Unknown Island (1948) C-76m. *½ D: Jack Bernhard. Virginia Grey, Philip Reed, Richard Denning, Barton MacLane. Boring story of scientists searching for prehistoric monsters on strange island has unimaginative special effects, little else.▼

Unknown Man, The (1951) 86m. **½ D: Richard Thorpe. Walter Pidgeon, Ann Harding, Barry Sullivan, Keefe Brasselle, Lewis Stone, Eduard Franz, Richard Anderson, Dawn Addams. Most capable cast enhances this yarn of lawyer discovering client in murder trial was guilty, and the strange triumph of justice he plots.

Unknown Powers (1979) C-96m. *½ D: Don Como. Samantha Eggar, Jack Palance, Will Geer, Roscoe Lee Browne. Inept examination of such phenomena as astrology, mysticism, spiritual healing and psychic surgery, with the "stars" introducing each section.▼

Unknown Terror, The (1957) 77m. ** D: Charles Marquis Warren. John Howard, Paul Richards, May Wynn, Mala Powers, Sir Lancelot. Unremarkable chiller supposedly set in South America, involving uncontrollable fungus.

Unknown World (1951) 74m. ** D: Terrell O. Morse. Bruce Kellogg, Marilyn Nash, Victor Kilian, Otto Waldis, Jim Bannon. Mechanical mole called Cyclotram drills into earth to find a haven from the A-bomb. Typical moralistic 1950s sci-fi, and not terribly distinguished.▼

Unman, Wittering and Zigo (1971-British) C-102m. *** D: John Mackenzie. David Hemmings, Carolyn Seymour, Douglas Wilmer, Hamilton Dyce, Anthony Haygarth, Donald Gee. Nifty little sleeper with Hemmings as new boys' school teacher who is promptly informed by his class that they murdered his predecessor, and that he'd better stay in line . . . or else. Creepy, chilling mystery, loaded with twists and stylishly photographed by Geoffrey Unsworth. Actual killer's identity is not revealed until *after* the closing credits! Title refers to the last three names on the roll . . . but Zigo is always absent.

Unmarried Woman, An (1978) C-124m. **** D: Paul Mazursky. Jill Clayburgh, Alan Bates, Michael Murphy, Cliff Gorman, Pat Quinn, Kelly Bishop, Lisa Lucas, Michael Tucker, Jill Eikenberry. Intelligent, compassionate look at how a woman copes when her husband walks out on her. Mazursky (who also wrote script) pulls no punches and makes no compromises—his characters are living, breathing people and his film is a gem. Clayburgh is magnificent in title role.▼

Unnatural Causes (1986) C-100m. TVM D: Lamont Johnson. John Ritter, Alfre Woodard, Patti LaBelle, John Sayles, Sean McCann, John Vargas, Gwen E. Davis. Dynamite drama about a dedicated Veterans Administration benefits counselor and a stricken Vietnam vet who attempt to link the latter's illness to Agent Orange. Woodard mesmerizes as the real-life Maude DeVictor who battled the V.A. power structure; Ritter, as a fictional composite of several of those she attempted to help, is extremely good. Sayles scripted from the heart. Above average.▼

Unremarkable Life, An (1989) C-92m. *½ D: Amin Q. Chaudhri. Patricia Neal, Shelley Winters, Mako, Rochelle Oliver, Charles Dutton, Lily Knight, Jenny Chrisinger. A hokey script does in this dud about two aging, very different sisters who live under the same roof and share memories and disagreements, especially when Mako starts wooing Neal. Neal and Winters try their best, but this is no WHALES OF AUGUST.▼

Unsane (1982-Italian) C-100m. ** D: Dario Argento. Anthony Franciosa, John Saxon, Daria Nicolodi, Giuliano Gemma, Mirella D'Angelo, John Steiner. Not as interesting as most of horror stylist Argento's thrillers, story is about novelist Franciosa becoming the subject of death threats. Extremely bloody but featuring some arresting camerawork by Luciano Tovoli, who also photographed THE PASSENGER. Originally titled: TENEBRAE. Video version runs 91m.▼

Unseen, The (1945) 81m. ** D: Lewis Allen. Joel McCrea, Gail Russell, Herbert Marshall, Phyllis Brooks, Isobel Elsom, Norman Lloyd. Man who made THE UN-INVITED tries similar venture but doesn't succeed. Governess Russell haunted again by strange mystery, but film haunted by very weak ending. Screenplay by Raymond Chandler and Hagar Wilde.

Unseen, The (1981) C-89m. BOMB D: Peter Foleg. Barbara Bach, Sidney Lassick, Stephen Furst, Lelia Goldoni, Karen Lamm, Doug Barr, Lois Young. TV reporter Bach and crew—two other women, naturally—are harassed by "Junior" (Furst), product of incestuous affair between Lassick and Goldoni. Moronic horror film is not very horrifying.▼

Unsinkable Molly Brown, The (1964) C-128m. *** D: Charles Walters. Debbie Reynolds, Harve Presnell, Ed Begley, Jack Kruschen, Hermione Baddeley. Big, splashy, tuneful adaptation of Broadway musical. Debbie is entertaining as backwoods girl who knows what she wants, eventually gets to be wealthiest woman in Denver in the late 1800s. Based on a true story! Meredith Willson score includes "I

Ain't Down Yet,'' "Belly Up to the Bar, Boys."▼

Unspeakable Acts (1990) **C-100m. TVM** D: Linda Otto. Jill Clayburgh, Brad Davis, Gary Frank, Season Hubley, Valerie Landsburg, Bebe Neuwirth, Gregory Sierra, Terence Knox. Clayburgh and Davis play real-life husband and wife child advocates Laurie and Joe Braga in this powerful fact-based drama about mass child abuse. Alan Landsburg's potent script is based on journalist Jan Hollingsworth's book, and on court transcripts. Above average.

Unsuitable Job for a Woman, An (1981-British) **C-94m.** *** D: Christopher Petit. Pippa Guard, Billie Whitelaw, Paul Freeman, Dominic Guard, Elizabeth Spriggs. Moody, entertaining *film noir* thriller about a woman detective (P. Guard) and her investigation of an unusual murder case after her boss commits suicide. Based on a novel by P. D. James.▼

Unsuspected, The (1947) **103m.** **½ D: Michael Curtiz. Claude Rains, Joan Caulfield, Audrey Totter, Constance Bennett, Hurd Hatfield. Predictable melodrama with good cast; superficially charming radio star Rains has murder on his mind, with niece Caulfield the victim.

Untamed (1929) **88m.** ** D: Jack Conway. Joan Crawford, Robert Montgomery, Ernest Torrence, Holmes Herbert, John Miljan, Gwen Lee. Cornball early talkie with Crawford as Bingo, an oil heiress reared in the tropical wilds, who falls in love with poor boy Montgomery.

Untamed (1940) **C-83m.** *½ D: George Archainbaud. Ray Milland, Patricia Morison, Akim Tamiroff, William Frawley, Jane Darwell, Esther Dale. Technicolor is about the only thing this hokey "northern" Western has going for it. Milland is a brave doctor trying to get serum through a blizzard in this remake of Clara Bow's MANTRAP.

Untamed (1955) **C-111m.** *** D: Henry King. Tyrone Power, Susan Hayward, Agnes Moorehead, Richard Egan, Rita Moreno, John Justin. Quite vivid account of Boer trek through hostile South African country, with Power romancing Hayward.

Untamed Breed, The (1948) **C-79m.** ** D: Charles Lamont. Sonny Tufts, Barbara Britton, William Bishop, Edgar Buchanan. Routine trials and tribulations of breeding cattle in old Texas, amid romance and gunplay.

Untamed Frontier (1952) **C-75m.** **½ D: Hugo Fregonese. Joseph Cotten, Shelley Winters, Scott Brady, Suzan Ball, Antonio Moreno. Range war between Texan cattle owners is basis for this Western improved by good cast.

Untamed Heiress (1954) **70m.** *½ D: Charles Lamont. Judy Canova, Donald Barry, Taylor Holmes, George Cleveland.

Slight Canova shenanigans involving the search for daughter of woman who financed a now-wealthy man.

Untamed Women (1952) **70m.** *½ D: W. Merle Connell. Mikel Conrad, Doris Merrick, Richard Monahan, Mark Lowell, Midge Ware, Carol Brewster. Campy nonsense about Air Force flyers stranded on Pacific island ruled by strange women, last descendants of the Druids. Caveat emptor!

Untamed Youth (1957) **80m.** BOMB D: Howard W. Koch. Mamie Van Doren, Lori Nelson, John Russell, Don Burnett, Eddie Cochran, Lurene Tuttle, Robert Foulk. The Hollywood Rock and Rollers. Side-splitting camp masterpiece has sisters Mamie and Lori railroaded onto yucky prison work farm owned by hissably slimy Russell. You know something's wrong when Mamie sings four songs and Cochran only one. Best line: "Don't hit me in the mouth again! You'll break my dental plate!"

Until Hell Is Frozen (1960-German) **87m.** ** D: Leopold Lahola. Charles Millot, Gotz George, Anna Smolik, Pierre Parel. Rambling account of P.O.W.'s in Russian prison camp in 1950, detailing their vain efforts to escape; muddled drama.

Until September (1984) **C-95m.** ** D: Richard Marquand. Karen Allen, Thierry Lhermitte, Christopher Cazenove, Marie-Christina Conti, Nitza Saul, Hutton Cobb. Temporarily stranded in Paris, Allen falls in love with handsome (and married) banker Lhermitte. Utterly predictable romantic drama doesn't even make interesting use of Paris locations.▼

Until They Sail (1957) **95m.** **½ D: Robert Wise. Paul Newman, Joan Fontaine, Jean Simmons, Sandra Dee, Piper Laurie, Charles Drake. Soaper courtroom story set in WW2 New Zealand, with sisters (Fontaine, Simmons, Laurie and Dee) involved in love, misery and murder. From James Michener story.

Untouchables, The (1987) **C-119m.** **** D: Brian DePalma. Kevin Costner, Sean Connery, Charles Martin Smith, Andy Garcia, Robert De Niro, Richard Bradford, Jack Kehoe, Brad Sullivan, Billy Drago, Patricia Clarkson. High-energy entertainment that packs a wallop: writer David Mamet's update of the well-remembered TV series tells how an earnest but naive federal agent named Eliot Ness learns (the hard way) to deal with both underworld crime and police corruption in Prohibition-era Chicago. Fluidly (and often flamboyantly) filmed, with powerhouse performances by Connery (in his Oscar-winning role), as a seasoned street cop, and De Niro, as a grandiose Al Capone. Climactic shoot-out, with echoes of POTEMKIN, will have you on the edge of your seat! Photographed by Stephen H. Burum, with a rich music score by Ennio Morricone.▼

[1239]

Unvanquished, The SEE: **Aparajito**▼
Unwed Father (1974) C-78m. TVM D: Jeremy Paul Kagan. Joseph Bottoms, Kay Lenz, Joseph Campanella, Kim Hunter, Beverly Garland, William H. Bassett. Bottoms is a high-schooler battling to gain custody of his illegitimate baby. Unconvincing social drama additionally crippled by weak performances. Below average.
Unwed Mother (1958) 74m. *½ D: Walter Doniger. Norma Moore, Robert Vaughn, Diana Darrin, Billie Bird. Title tells all in this unsensational programmer.
Up from the Beach (1965) 99m. **½ D: Robert Parrish. Cliff Robertson, Red Buttons, Francoise Rosay, Irina Demick, Marius Goring, Slim Pickens, James Robertson Justice, Broderick Crawford. Static film of American sergeant Robertson involved with French civilians in love and war during Normandy invasion.
Up Front (1951) 92m. **½ D: Alexander Hall. David Wayne, Tom Ewell, Marina Berti, Jeffrey Lynn, Richard Egan. Sometimes amusing WW2 comedy based on Bill Mauldin's cartoon characters Willie and Joe, and their military shenanigans. Sequel: BACK AT THE FRONT.
Up Goes Maisie (1946) 89m. D: Harry Beaumont. Ann Sothern, George Murphy, Hillary Brooke, Stephen McNally, Ray Collins, Jeff York, Gloria Grafton. SEE: **Maisie** series.
Uphill All the Way (1985) C-86m. BOMB D: Frank Q. Dobbs. Roy Clark, Mel Tillis, Burl Ives, Glen Campbell, Trish Van Devere, Burt Reynolds, Frank Gorshin, Sheb Wooley. Teaming of singing stars Tillis and Clark as inept robbers in the Old West probably sounded like fun on paper but emerges as a mirthless chase film. Cameo contributions of pals Reynolds and Campbell add little. ▼
Up in Arms (1944) C-106m. **½ D: Elliott Nugent. Danny Kaye, Dana Andrews, Constance Dowling, Dinah Shore, Louis Calhern, Lyle Talbot, Margaret Dumont, Elisha Cook, Jr. Danny's first feature film (about a hypochondriac in the Army) doesn't wear well, biggest asset being vivacious Dinah Shore; Virginia Mayo is one of the chorus girls. Only those great patter songs—including "The Lobby Number" and "Melody in 4F"—hold up. Based on *The Nervous Wreck*, filmed before with Eddie Cantor as WHOOPEE!▼
Up in Central Park (1948) 88m. ** D: William A. Seiter. Deanna Durbin, Dick Haymes, Vincent Price, Albert Sharpe, Tom Powers. Disappointing screen version of Broadway musical hit (minus many of its songs) about an Irish colleen in turn of the century N.Y.C. who helps expose the crooked Tammany Hall tactics of Boss Tweed (Price).
Up in Mabel's Room (1944) 76m. *** D:

Allan Dwan. Dennis O'Keefe, Marjorie Reynolds, Gail Patrick, Mischa Auer, Charlotte Greenwood, Lee Bowman. Engaging comedy of innocent O'Keefe embarrassed by presence of old flame (Patrick) in front of his wife (Reynolds). Based on a stage play filmed before in 1926; director and star reteamed in 1945 for GETTING GERTIE'S GARTER.
Up in Smoke (1957) 64m. D: William Beaudine. Huntz Hall, Stanley Clements, Benny Rubin, Jack Mulhall, Judy Bamber. SEE: **Bowery Boys** series.
Up in Smoke (1978) C-86m. *** D: Lou Adler. Cheech Marin, Tommy Chong, Stacy Keach, Tom Skerritt, Edie Adams, Strother Martin. This silly pothead comedy breaks down all resistance with its cheerful vignettes about two dummies in search of "good grass." Nothing great, but undeniably funny; this was Cheech and Chong's first movie.▼
Up in the Cellar (1970) C-92m. *** D: Theodore J. Flicker. Wes Stern, Joan Collins, Larry Hagman, Judy Pace. Above-average story of alluring youth who knows how to turn women on. Flicker's screenplay is exceptionally sharp, which is why the film works. Made to cash in on success of THREE IN THE ATTIC, and in fact retitled THREE IN THE CELLAR.▼
Up In The World (1956-British) 91m. **½ D: John Paddy Carstairs. Norman Wisdom, Maureen Swanson, Jerry Desmonde, Colin Gordon, Lionel Jeffries. Typical Wisdom comedy, anticipating Jerry Lewis' solo vehicles. He's a bumbling window cleaner involved with aristocrats and kidnappers, and even gets to sing a song.
Upper Hand, The (1967-French) C-86m. **½ D: Denys de la Patelliere. Jean Gabin, George Raft, Gert Frobe, Nadja Tiller. Labored international underworld yarn, with wooden performances by cast involved in gold smuggling.
Up Periscope (1959) C-111m. **½ D: Gordon Douglas. James Garner, Edmond O'Brien, Andra Martin, Alan Hale, Carleton Carpenter, Frank Gifford. Garner is Navy Lieutenant transferred to submarine during WW2, with usual interaction among crew as they reconnoiter Japanese held island.
Upperworld (1934) 72m. *** D: Roy Del Ruth. Warren William, Mary Astor, Ginger Rogers, Dickie Moore, Andy Devine, J. Carrol Naish, Mickey Rooney, Sidney Toler. Rich businessman William, wed to Astor, becomes involved with burlesque performer Rogers—much to his regret. Entertaining Ben Hecht drama, uplifted by William's charm, Rogers' presence, marred only by an unsatisfying conclusion.
Upstairs and Downstairs (1961-British) C-100m. *** D: Ralph Thomas. Mylene

Demongeot, Michael Craig, Anne Heywood, James Robertson Justice, Daniel Massey, Claudia Cardinale. Witty study of human nature: Craig married boss' daughter (Heywood) and they must entertain firm's clients. Film traces chaos of party-giving, and odd assortment of servants who come and go.

Up the Academy (1980) C-88m. ** D: Robert Downey. Ron Leibman, Wendell Brown, Ralph Macchio, Tom Citera, Tom Poston, Stacey Nelkin, Barbara Bach, Leonard Frey. Crude, tasteless but occasionally lively comedy about misadventures in a boys' military school. Leibman had his name taken off credits and advertising, but film isn't *that* bad. Also known as *MAD MAGAZINE* PRESENTS UP THE ACADEMY, although for pay-TV release all references to *Mad* and Alfred E. Neuman were excised. Macchio's film debut.▼

Up the Creek (1958-British) 83m. **½ D: Val Guest. David Tomlinson, Wilfrid Hyde-White, Peter Sellers, Vera Day, Michael Goodliffe. Broad naval spoof à la MR. ROBERTS, which leans too much on slapstick rather than barbs; Hyde-White is best as nonplussed admiral. Previously filmed as OH, MR. PORTER.▼

Up the Creek (1984) C-95m. ** D: Robert Butler. Tim Matheson, Jennifer Runyon, Stephen Furst, Dan Monahan, Sandy Helberg, Jeff East, Blaine Novak, James B. Sikking, John Hillerman. Silly comedy—though far from the worst of its kind—about four college losers (played by graduates of PORKY'S and ANIMAL HOUSE) who battle dastardly preppies and gung-ho military cadets to win a raft race. Plenty of skimpily clad girls, plus a genuinely funny charade scene.▼

Up the Down Staircase (1967) C-124m. *** D: Robert Mulligan. Sandy Dennis, Patrick Bedford, Eileen Heckart, Ruth White, Jean Stapleton, Sorrell Booke, Roy Poole, Ellen O'Mara. Film version of Bel Kaufman's bestseller about N.Y.C. public schools is too slickly handled to be taken seriously, but generally entertaining. Good acting, especially by O'Mara as pathetic student.▼

Up the MacGregors (1967-Italian-Spanish) C-93m. *½ D. Frank Garfield. David Bailey, Agata Flori, Leo Anchoriz, Roberto Carmardiel. Sequel to SEVEN GUNS FOR THE MACGREGORS (but released here earlier) is distinguished from a million other Italian Westerns only by its relatively restrained use of violence.

Up the River (1930) 92m. **½ D: John Ford. Spencer Tracy, Claire Luce, Warren Hymer, Humphrey Bogart, William Collier, Sr. Silly but disarmingly funny comedy about a pair of habitual convicts, played by Tracy (dynamic in his feature-film debut) and Hymer, and their efforts to help

fellow inmate Bogart (in his *second* feature), who's fallen in love with female prisoner Luce. Needless to say, this is notable for its confluence of great talents at the beginnings of their careers—but it's also fun to watch.

Up the Sandbox (1972) C-97m. **½ D: Irvin Kershner. Barbra Streisand, David Selby, Jane Hoffman, John C. Becher, Jacobo Morales. Uneasy mixture of naturalism and fantasy somewhat redeemed by Streisand's performance, some funny sequences, and genuine feeling for plight of neglected young mother in N.Y.C.▼

Up Tight (1968) C-104m. *** D: Jules Dassin. Raymond St. Jacques, Ruby Dee, Frank Silvera, Julian Mayfield, Roscoe Lee Browne, Max Julien. Tough remake of THE INFORMER, ghetto-style. Black revolutionaries betrayed by one of their own.

Up to His Ears (1965-French-Italian) C-94m. *** D: Philippe De Broca. Jean-Paul Belmondo, Ursula Andress, Maria Pacome, Valerie Lagrange, Jess Hahn. Wealthy young man decides to end his troubles by hiring a killer to do him in, then changes his mind. Energetic comedy runs hot and cold, but has many delicious moments.

Uptown New York (1932) 80m. **½ D: Victor Schertzinger. Jack Oakie, Shirley Grey, Leon Waycoff (Ames), George Cooper, Raymond Hatton. Modest, occasionally entertaining soaper about pretty young Grey, who's loved by successful but slimy surgeon Waycoff and decent, enterprising bubble-gum salesman Oakie.▼

Uptown Saturday Night (1974) C-104m. **½ D: Sidney Poitier. Sidney Poitier, Bill Cosby, Harry Belafonte, Calvin Lockhart, Flip Wilson, Richard Pryor, Rosalind Cash, Roscoe Lee Browne, Paula Kelly. Undeniably entertaining, this film still looks like an *Amos 'n Andy* script dusted off. Broad, silly comedy about two pals (Poitier, Cosby) who try to retrieve a stolen winning lottery ticket and get involved with an underworld kingpin (Belafonte, in an uproarious Godfather parody). A pair of follow-ups: LET'S DO IT AGAIN and A PIECE OF THE ACTION.▼

Upturned Glass, The (1947-British) 89m. *** D: Lawrence Huntington. James Mason, Pamela Kellino (Mason), Rosamund John, Ann Stephens, Henry Oscar, Morland Graham. Mason stars as a doctor who is driven to murder to avenge the death of his lover. Somber psychological thriller that starts slowly but builds suspensefully to a powerful conclusion. Mason also coproduced.

Up Your Alley (1989) C-88m. **½ D: Bob Logan. Murray Langston, Linda Blair, Bob Zany, Kevin Benton, Ruth Buzzi, Glen Vincent, Jack Hanrahan, Melissa

Shear, Johnny Dark, Yakov Smirnoff. Ambitious low-budget comedy with dramatic underpinnings. Reporter Blair pretends to be homeless to write a story about cynical street person Langston, and his innocent friend Zany. Gags too often undermine this film's sensitive and serious moments. Cowritten by director Logan and star Langston (a.k.a. The Unknown Comic).▼

Uranium Boom (1956) **67m.** *½ D: William Castle. Dennis Morgan, Patricia Medina, William Talman, Tina Carver. Dull account of two ore prospectors striking it rich, but more concerned with who will win Medina's love.

Urban Cowboy (1980) **C-135m.** *** D: James Bridges. John Travolta, Debra Winger, Scott Glenn, Madolyn Smith, Barry Corbin, Brooke Alderson, Mickey Gilley, Charlie Daniels Band, Bonnie Raitt. A young hardhat new to Pasadena, Texas, gravitates to the incredible honky-tonk named Gilley's, with its easy women, macho ambience, and mechanical bull, perfecting an "image" of manhood that doesn't quite work out in real life. An evocative slice of life adapted from Aaron Latham's magazine story by Latham and director Bridges.▼

Ursus in the Land of Fire (1963-Italian) **C-87m.** *½ D: Giorgio Simonelli. Ed Fury, Claudia Mori, Adriano Micantoni, Luciana Gilli. Stupid muscleman mini-film, with Fury battling all odds to help Gilli regain her throne.

Ursus in the Valley of the Lions (1961-Italian) **C-82m.** ** D: Carlo Ludovico Bragaglia. Ed Fury, Moira Orfei, Mary Marlon, Alberto Lupo, Gerard Herter. Routine costumer with Fury teaming with friendly lions to overcome the barbarians.▼

Us SEE: **Benefit of the Doubt, The**

Used Cars (1980) **C-111m.** *** D: Robert Zemeckis. Kurt Russell, Jack Warden, Gerrit Graham, Frank McRae, Deborah Harmon, Joseph P. Flaherty, David L. Lander, Michael McKean, Andrew Duncan, Wendie Jo Sperber. Outrageous comedy about used car dealer rivalry that leads to spectacular and outlandish customer-getting schemes. Hilarious script by Bob Gale and Bob Zemeckis revels in bad taste, but does it so good-naturedly it's difficult to resist. And remember, $50 never killed anybody.▼

Users, The (1978) **C-125m. TVM** D: Joseph Hardy. Jaclyn Smith, Tony Curtis, Joan Fontaine, Red Buttons, George Hamilton, John Forsythe, Darren McGavin, Michelle Phillips. Smalltown girl with dark past masterminds a fading film star's comeback. It's Hollywood at its most deliciously decadent in this lavishly appointed adaptation of Joyce Haber's thinly veiled roman à clef. Average.▼

U.S. Marshals: Waco & Rhinehart (1987) **C-100m. TVM** D: Christian I. Nyby II.

Charles C. Hill, Justin Deas, William Hootkins, Bob Tzudiker, Kathleen Lloyd. Busted contemporary Western pilot about a couple of unorthodox lawmen on an anything-goes search for their colleague's killer. Produced by the good folks at Disney Studios. Below average.

Utah Blaine (1957) **75m.** *½ D: Fred F. Sears. Rory Calhoun, Angela Stevens, Max Baer, Paul Langton. Undistinguished Western about Calhoun helping to overcome land-grabbing outlaws.

Utilities (1981-Canadian) **C-91m.** *½ D: Harvey Hart. Robert Hays, Brooke Adams, John Marley, James Blendick, Ben Gordon, Jane Malett, Tony Rosato. Social worker Hays declares war on the gas, electric and phone companies in this undercooked satiric comedy.▼

Utopia (1950-French) **80m.** *½ D: Leo Joannon. Stan Laurel, Oliver Hardy, Suzy Delair, Max Elloy. L&H's final film saddles the great comics with poor script and production, despite decent premise of the duo inheriting a uranium-rich island. Also known as ATOLL K and ROBINSON CRUSOELAND.▼

Utu (1983-New Zealand) **C-104m.** *½ D: Geoff Murphy. Anzac Wallace, Bruno Lawrence, Tim Elliott, Kelly Johnson, Wi Kuki Kaa. Maori tribesman (and British army subordinate) in New Zealand goes on a ritualistic rampage after his family is wiped out in a senseless raid. Downbeat, dull, and full of stereotypical characters—without the compensating power of Australia's not dissimilar THE CHANT OF JIMMY BLACKSMITH. Originally released in New Zealand at 118m; this review is based on the shorter U.S. version.▼

U2: Rattle and Hum (1988) **C/B&W-99m.** **½ D: Phil Joanou. Title Irish rock band was the late 80s' most celebrated, but scattershot documentary never really explains why to the unknowing or unconverted. Music compensates to some degree, with some of the best numbers fortunately weighted near the end; a side trip to Elvis' Graceland seems out of place. For no apparent reason, film's first half is in grainy black-and-white and the second is in color.▼

U-238 and the Witch Doctor (1953) **100m.** *½ D: Fred C. Brannon. Clayton Moore, Phyllis Coates, Johnny Spencer (Sands), Roy Glenn, John Cason. Tedious cliffhanger utilizing an abundance of stock footage and minimum of action in tame account of uranium hunt in Africa, involving battles with natives and animals. Re-edited from Republic serial JUNGLE DRUMS OF AFRICA.

V (1983) **C-205m. TVM** D: Kenneth Johnson. Marc Singer, Faye Grant, Michael Durrell, Peter Nelson, Jane Badler,

Neva Patterson, Andrew Prine, Robert Englund, Richard Herd, Penelope Windust, Rafael Campos. Legions of alien visitors from space come to Earth on a peace mission and threaten to establish a Fascist dictatorship, singling out the world's scientists as scapegoats. Reportedly one of the most expensive television movies ever, and the great special effects bear it out. Imaginative sci-fi tale written by director-producer Kenneth Johnson. Originally shown in two parts. Above average. Followed by V: THE FINAL BATTLE and a series.

Vacation from Marriage (1945-British) **92m.** *** D: Alexander Korda. Robert Donat, Deborah Kerr, Glynis Johns, Ann Todd, Roland Culver, Elliot Mason. Donat and Kerr sparkle in story of dull couple separated by WW2, each rejuvenated by wartime romance. Johns is perky as Kerr's military friend. Clemence Dane won an Oscar for her original story. British version, titled PERFECT STRANGERS, ran 102m.

Vacation in Hell, A (1979) **C-100m.** TVM D: David Greene. Priscilla Barnes, Barbara Feldon, Andrea Marcovicci, Maureen McCormick, Michael Brandon. Vacationers at a posh island resort wander into the jungle and face terror. Wow. Average.

Vagabond (1985-French) **C-105m.** ***½ D: Agnes Varda. Sandrine Bonnaire, Macha Meril, Stephane Freiss, Elaine Cortadellas, Marthe Jarnias, Yolande Moreau. Haunting drama about young drifter Bonnaire, who wanders about hitching a ride here, sleeping there, and how those she encounters respond to her. A simple, powerful, superbly directed film about chance meetings, missed opportunities, and the price one must sometimes pay for one's lifestyle.▼

Vagabond King, The (1956) **C-86m.** ** D: Michael Curtiz. Kathryn Grayson, Oreste, Rita Moreno, Cedric Hardwicke, Walter Hampden, Leslie Nielsen. Bland remake of Rudolf Friml's operetta (filmed before in 1930), about poet-scoundrel Francois Villon. Oreste was touted as new musical star in 1956, but didn't quite make it. Story, sans music, filmed in 1928 (THE BELOVED ROGUE) and 1938 (IF I WERE KING).

Vagabond Lover, The (1929) **69m.** **½ D: Marshall Neilan. Rudy Vallee, Sally Blane, Marie Dressler, Charles Sellon, Norman Peck. Orchestra leader-crooner Vallee impersonates impresario; rich Dressler hires his band, and he falls for her niece (Blane). Pleasant musical-comedy antique is sparked by Dressler.▼

Valachi Papers, The (1972-Italian) **C-125m.** **½ D: Terence Young. Charles Bronson, Lino Ventura, Jill Ireland, Joseph Wiseman, Walter Chiari, Amedeo Nazzari. Sloppy but engrossing account of Mafia life as seen through eyes of famed informer Joseph Valachi (Bronson). Lots of blood will go for TV screening, but gangland flavor will remain. From the book by Peter Maas.

Valdez Is Coming (1971) **C-90m.** **½ D: Edwin Sherin. Burt Lancaster, Susan Clark, Jon Cypher, Barton Heyman, Frank Silvera, Hector Elizondo. OK intellectual Western with Lancaster a Mexican-American deputy sheriff forced to confront ruthless land baron after triggering local hostilities. Shot in Spain; first film for noted Broadway director Sherin.

Valentine (1979) **C-100m.** TVM D: Lee Philips. Mary Martin, Jack Albertson, Loretta Swit, Danny DeVito, Lloyd Nolan, Judy Norton Taylor, Philip Michael Thomas. Two young-at-heart senior citizens fall in love in this poignant drama that marked Mary Martin's TV-movie debut. Average.

Valentine Magic on Love Island (1980) **C-100m.** TVM D: Earl Bellamy. Janis Paige, Dominique Dunne, Christopher Knight, Adrienne Barbeau, Bill Daily, Lisa Hartman, Howard Duff, Dody Goodman. Paige and Dunne pretend they're Mr. Roarke and Tattoo in this blatant rip-off of *Fantasy Island* (with coproducer Dick Clark pretending to be Aaron Spelling). Later shown as MAGIC ON LOVE ISLAND. Average.

Valentino (1951) **C-102m.** *½ D: Lewis Allen. Anthony Dexter, Eleanor Parker, Richard Carlson, Patricia Medina, Joseph Calleia, Lloyd Gough, Otto Kruger. Undistinguished, superficial biography of famed star of American silent films.

Valentino (1977) **C-127m.** *½ D: Ken Russell. Rudolf Nureyev, Leslie Caron, Michelle Phillips, Carol Kane, Felicity Kendal, Seymour Cassel, Peter Vaughan, Anton Diffring. Typically excessive, visually flamboyant Ken Russell "biography" offers little insight on great screen lover, and suffers further from Nureyev's awkward performance. But any film that casts Huntz Hall as movie mogul Jesse Lasky can't be *all* bad.

Valentino Returns (1987) **C-102m.** **½ D: Peter Hoffman. Frederic Forrest, Veronica Cartwright, Barry Tubb, Jenny Wright, David Packer, Seth Isler, Miguel Ferrer. Meandering drama of young Tubb and his no-account father, frustrated mother, and his desperation to experience sex. "Valentino Returns" is the name of his shiny pink Cadillac, purchased on credit, which he thinks will make him a hit with the girls. Great atmosphere, so-so result. Set in 1950s California. Screenplay by Leonard Gardner, based on his short story; he's featured in the role of Lyle.▼

Valerie (1957) **84m.** *½ D: Gerd Oswald. Sterling Hayden, Anita Ekberg, Anthony Steel, Malcolm Atterbury. Unmemorable account (via flashbacks) of facts leading up to the wounding of Hayden's wife, and death of her parents.

Valiant Is the Word for Carrie (1936) **110m.** ****½** D: Wesley Ruggles. Gladys George, Arline Judge, John Howard, Dudley Digges, Harry Carey, Isabel Jewell, Jackie Moran. Get out your handkerchief for this one, the epitome of 1930s soapers as selfless Gladys George devotes herself to orphan children. She won an Oscar nomination for her performance.

Valley Girl (1983) **C-95m.** ****½** D: Martha Coolidge. Nicolas Cage, Deborah Foreman, Colleen Camp, Frederic Forrest, Elizabeth Daily, Lee Purcell. Refreshingly nonexploitative punker-suburbanite romance is several cuts above most contemporary teen pics, but the result is still distressingly mild. Attractive leads, amusing performances by Camp and Forrest as Foreman's hippieish parents, but film never really goes anywhere.▼

Valley of Decision, The (1945) **111m.** ******* D: Tay Garnett. Greer Garson, Gregory Peck, Donald Crisp, Lionel Barrymore, Preston Foster, Marsha Hunt, Gladys Cooper, Reginald Owen, Dan Duryea, Jessica Tandy. Not overpowering, as intended, but good film of housemaid Garson, master's son Peck. His family owned mine where her father and brother were killed. Romantic tension and workers' strike ensue. Set in 1870 Pittsburgh; from Marcia Davenport's novel.

Valley of Eagles (1951-British) **85m.** ****½** D: Terence Young. Jack Warner, Nadia Gray, Christopher Lee, Anthony Dawson. Above-par chase tale of Swedish scientist tracking down his wife and assistant who stole his research data and headed for the north country.

✓ **Valley of Gwangi** (1969) **C-95m.** ****½** D: James O'Connolly. James Franciscus, Gila Golan, Richard Carlson, Laurence Naismith, Dennis Kilbane. Standard reworking of King Kong theme; adventurers in Mexico stumble upon prehistoric monster, hit on idea to display their find in a traveling circus, make money. Script and production have holes, but film is sparked by Ray Harryhausen special effects. Based on a story by Willis O'Brien.

Valley of Headhunters (1953) **67m.** D: William Berke. Johnny Weissmuller, Christine Larson, Nelson Leigh, Vince Townsend, Steven Ritch. SEE: **Jungle Jim** series.

Valley of Mystery (1967) **C-90m.** ****** D: Josef Leytes. Richard Egan, Peter Graves, Joby Baker, Lois Nettleton, Harry Guardino, Julie Adams, Fernando Lamas. Lackluster drama pitting plane passengers and crew against jungle perils, personal conflict when flight crash lands. Made for TV but released to theaters first.

Valley of the Dolls (1967) **C-123m.** BOMB

D: Mark Robson. Barbara Parkins, Patty Duke, Sharon Tate, Susan Hayward, Paul Burke, Tony Scotti, Martin Milner, Lee Grant, Joey Bishop, George Jessel. Scattered unintentional laughs do not compensate for terribly written, acted, and directed adaptation of Jacqueline Susann novel about three young women in show biz. Author Susann has a bit role as a reporter. Look for Richard Dreyfuss in a quick backstage bit. Remade as a TV movie in 1981.

Valley of the Dolls (1981) SEE: **Jacqueline Susann's Valley of the Dolls**

Valley of the Dragons (1961) **79m.** ***½** D: Edward Bernds. Cesare Danova, Sean McClory, Joan Staley, Danielle De Metz, Roger Til. A comet carrying a fragment of prehistoric Earth picks up two 19th-century men. Tawdry, vulgar version of Jules Verne's novel *Off on a Comet*; laden with stock footage. Remade as ON THE COMET.

Valley of the Giants (1938) **C-79m.** ****** D: William Keighley. Wayne Morris, Claire Trevor, Charles Bickford, Alan Hale, Jack LaRue, Frank McHugh, Donald Crisp, John Litel. Stale actioner of Morris thwarting Bickford's attempt to rape Northern California of its redwoods, with saloon girl Trevor brightening the proceedings. Previously made in 1919 with Wallace Reid and 1927 with Milton Sills. Footage and story line were later used in THE BIG TREES.

Valley of the Kings (1954) **C-86m.** ****** D: Robert Pirosh. Robert Taylor, Eleanor Parker, Kurt Kasznar, Carlos Thompson. Meandering adventure yarn of excavations in Egypt for tombs of ancient pharaohs.

Valley of the Redwoods (1960) **63m.** ***½** D: William Witney. John Hudson, Lynn Bernay, Ed Nelson, Michael Forest, Robert Shayne, John Brinkley. Programmer involving payroll theft and escape of robbers to Canada.

Valley of the Sun (1942) **84m.** ******* D: George Marshall. Lucille Ball, Cedric Hardwicke, Dean Jagger, James Craig, Billy Gilbert, Antonio Moreno, Tom Tyler. Intrigue of the old West with crooked white man provoking Indian uprising as he is being hunted by colonial agent.▼

Valley of the Zombies (1946) **56m.** ***½** D: Philip Ford. Robert Livingston, Adrian Booth, Ian Keith, Thomas Jackson, LeRoy Mason. Witless horror epic of man-returned-from-dead bent on revenge. No zombies to be found—in a valley or elsewhere.

Valmont (1989-French-British) **C-137m.** ****½** D: Milos Forman. Colin Firth, Annette Bening, Meg Tilly, Fairuza Balk, Sian Phillips, Jeffrey Jones, Henry Thomas, Fabia Drake, Ian McNeice. Ah, the bedhopping of Choderlos de Laclos's *Les Liaisons Dangereuses*! Meticulous retelling—the third on film—of the sexual shenanigans of 18th-century French aristocrats (Firth and Bening). Youthful cast makes this seem more mischievous than other versions . . . but that very playfulness also softens some of its bite. Elderly Drake, who died shortly after film's release, steals every scene she's in. Previously filmed in 1959 (DANGEROUS LIAISONS 1960) and 1988 (DANGEROUS LIAISONS).▼

Value for Money (1955-British) **C-89m.** *** D: Ken Annakin. John Gregson, Diana Dors, Derek Farr, Donald Pleasence, Cyril Smith, Ernest Thesiger. Funny little comedy about young man inheriting father's money and his enjoyment of same.

Vamp (1986) **C-94m.** *½ D: Richard Wenk. Chris Makepeace, Sandy Baron, Robert Rusler, Dedee Pfeiffer, Gedde Watanabe, Grace Jones, Billy Drago. Fun-loving college guys run afoul of a female vampire in this dreary and distasteful horror outing. Starts out promisingly, with tongue-in-cheek, but soon drops the light touch in favor of the kinky. ▼

Vampira SEE: **Old Dracula**

Vampire, The (1957) **74m.** ** D: Paul Landres. John Beal, Coleen Gray, Dabbs Greer, Raymond Greenleaf. Minor chiller with scientist turned into blood-seeker. Not without some merit, Beal is excellent. Retitled: MARK OF THE VAMPIRE.▼

Vampire (1979) **C-100m. TVM** D: E. W. Swackhamer. Jason Miller, E. G. Marshall, Richard Lynch, Jessica Walter, Kathryn Harrold, Barrie Youngfellow, Jonelle Allen, Michael Tucker. Brooding architect and retired cop join forces to destroy a modern-day vampire who's stalking San Francisco taking vengeance on those who despoiled his resting place. Campy, and a pleasant surprise. Script by Steven Bochco and Michael Kozoll. Above average.

Vampire Bat, The (1933) **71m.** **½ D: Frank Strayer. Lionel Atwill, Melvyn Douglas, Fay Wray, Dwight Frye, Maude Eburne, George E. Stone, Lionel Belmore. Good cast helps average story along. Atwill stars as mad doctor forced to kill townsfolk in search of "blood substitute." Beware shorter prints.▼

Vampire Circus (1971-British) **C-87m.** **½ D: Robert Young. John Moulder Brown, Adrienne Corri, Laurence Payne, Thorley Walters, Lynne Frederick. Very weird Hammer horror with unique gimmick; 19th century European circus travels from town to town for good reason: everyone in it is a vampire—including the animals! Last-minute cuts muddled the film considerably, but still well worth a look.

Vampire Lovers, The (1971-British) **C-88m.** **½ D: Roy Ward Baker. Ingrid Pitt, Pippa Steele, Madeleine Smith, Peter Cushing, George Cole, Dawn Addams, Kate O'Mara. Rather erotic Hammer chiller about lesbian vampires faithfully adapted from Sheridan Lefanu's "Carmilla," filmed

many times before and since. Followed by LUST FOR A VAMPIRE and TWINS OF EVIL.▼

Vampire Men of the Lost Planet (1970) **C-85m.** BOMB D: Al Adamson. John Carradine, Robert Dix, Vicki Volante, Joey Benson, Jennifer Bishop. Scientist traces epidemic of vampire attacks on earth to strange, distant planet, with the aid of stock footage from other movies. A real mish-mash, released theatrically as HORROR OF THE BLOOD MONSTERS, CREATURES OF THE PREHISTORIC PLANET, HORROR CREATURES OF THE PREHISTORIC PLANET, and SPACE MISSION OF THE LOST PLANET.▼

Vampyr (1932-Danish) **60m.** *** D: Carl Theodor Dreyer. Julian West, Sybille Schmitz, Harriet Gerard. Dreyer's stylized use of light, shadow, and camera angles takes preference over the plot in this chilling vampire-in-a-castle tale, very loosely based on Lefanu's "Carmilla."▼

Van, The (1976) **C-92m.** *½ D: Sam Grossman. Stuart Getz, Deborah White, Danny DeVito, Harry Moses, Marcie Barkin, Bill Adler, Stephen Oliver. Shy Getz uses his fancy new van to seduce pretty girls. Innocuous idiocy of the California youth genre.▼

Vanessa, Her Love Story (1935) **74m.** ** D: William K. Howard. Helen Hayes, Robert Montgomery, Otto Kruger, May Robson, Lewis Stone. Soapy story of gypsy love with Hayes attracted to roguish Montgomery. Dated romance doesn't come off too well today. Hayes' last starring role until 1951's MY SON JOHN.

Vanished (1971) **C-200m. TVM** D: Buzz Kulik. Richard Widmark, Skye Aubrey, Tom Bosley, Larry Hagman, Murray Hamilton, James Farentino, Robert Hooks, E. G. Marshall, Eleanor Parker, William Shatner, Robert Young, Sheree North, Stephen McNally, Jim Davis. Strong cast in Fletcher Knebel's best seller about mysterious disappearance of Presidential advisor. FBI has information that he was homosexual; why won't President make statement? Interesting resolution, but film's point of view seems like standard mystery. Historically noteworthy as first TV-movie shown in two parts. Average.

Vanishing Act (1986) **C-100m. TVM** D: David Greene. Mike Farrell, Margot Kidder, Elliott Gould, Fred Gwynne, Graham Jarvis. A man searches for his missing bride, only to find a strange woman bearing her identity, insisting she's the one. Robert Thomas' play *The Trap for a Lonely Man* has the distinction of having been made into *two* previous TV movies, HONEYMOON WITH A STRANGER and ONE OF MY WIVES IS MISSING; this one boasts a script by Richard Levinson and William Link. Average.▼

Vanishing American, The (1955) **90m.** ** D: Joseph Kane. Scott Brady, Audrey Totter, Forrest Tucker, Gene Lockhart, Jim Davis, Jay Silverheels. Mild, minor film about landgrabbers trying to take Navajo territory.

Vanishing Point (1971) **C-107m.** ** D: Richard C. Sarafian. Barry Newman, Cleavon Little, Dean Jagger, Paul Koslo, Robert Donner, Severn Darden, Gilda Texter, Victoria Medlin. Told to drive a Dodge Challenger from Denver to San Francisco, Newman—for no apparent reason—decides to do it in 15 hours. Naturally, the cops are soon in hot pursuit, but Barry gets some help from blind d.j. Super Soul (Little). Existential chase thriller was a big drive-in hit, and remains a cult favorite, but is pretty much a disappointment. Exceptional rock score.▼

Vanishing Prairie, The (1954) **C-75m.** *** D: James Algar. Narrated by Winston Hibler. Disney's second True-Life Adventure feature provides astonishing footage of animal life in the great plains, including the birth of a buffalo calf. Fine presentation with little Disney gimmickry; Academy Award winner.▼

Vanishing Virginian, The (1942) **97m.** *** D: Frank Borzage. Frank Morgan, Kathryn Grayson, Spring Byington, Natalie Thompson, Douglas Newland, Mark Daniels, Juanita Quigley, Scotty Beckett, Dickie Jones, Louise Beavers. Sweet film full of nostalgia for the Old South (though it's set in the 20th century), based on Rebecca Yancey Williams' memoir of her father, a lifelong public servant in Lynchburg, Virginia. Works in elements of suffragette movement, women's rights, and the coming of Prohibition, but focuses mainly on the family, headed by the ever delightful Morgan. Also serves as showcase for young Grayson, who sings several numbers.

Vanishing Wilderness (1974) **C-93m.** *** D: Arthur Dubs, Heinz Seilmann. Cowboy actor Rex Allen narrates this stunningly photographed wildlife documentary which covers virtually all of North America—from the alligators of the Everglades to the polar bears of the Arctic. Topnotch but for excessive narration and heavenly choirs punctuating each scene.▼

Van Nuys Blvd. (1979) **C-93m.** ** D: William Sachs. Bill Adler, Cynthia Wood, Dennis Bowen, Melissa Prophet, David Hayward. Small-town boy Adler treks off to make the Southern California disco-drag-race-hamburger-stand scene. A bit better than average, but that's not saying very much.▼

Vanquished, The (1953) **C-84m.** *½ D: Edward Ludwig. John Payne, Jan Sterling, Coleen Gray, Lyle Bettger, Ellen

Corby. Bland little Western about corruption within a town's administration.

Varan, the Unbelievable (1962-Japanese-U.S.) **70m.** *½ D: Inoshiro Honda, Jerry Baerwitz. Myron Healy, Tsuruko Kobayashi, Kozo Nomura, Ayumi Sonoda. Typical Japanese rubber monster film except that creature defies clear definition. It's vaguely reptilian, but some insist it's a giant squirrel, since in Japanese prints it flies like a flying squirrel. Regardless, it stomps cities and scares the masses. Unbelievable is key word. Adapted (with new footage) from 1958 release.▼

Variety Girl (1947) **83m.** **½ D: George Marshall. Mary Hatcher, Olga San Juan, DeForest Kelley, William Demarest, Frank Faylen, Frank Ferguson. Hatcher and San Juan head for Hollywood with hopes of stardom; flimsy excuse for countless Paramount guest stars, including Bob Hope, Bing Crosby, Gary Cooper and Ray Milland. Hope and Crosby come off best in amusing golfing scene. Puppetoon segment in color.

Variety Lights (1950-Italian) **93m.** **½ D: Federico Fellini, Alberto Lattuada. Peppino De Filippo, Carla Del Poggio, Giulietta Masina, John Kitzmiller, Dante Maggio, Checco Durante. Fellini's first film (though codirected) is a rather ordinary tale of the lovely Del Poggio struggling through small-town music halls to become a star. Some funny and touching scenes featuring the usual Fellini eccentrics.▼

Varsity Show (1937) **81m.** *** D: William Keighley. Dick Powell, Priscilla Lane, Fred Waring, Walter Catlett, Ted Healy, Rosemary Lane. Powell is Broadway producer who agrees to stage a show at his alma mater; result is a parade of musical numbers, including fine specialties by Buck and Bubbles, and rousing finale staged by Busby Berkeley. Originally released at 121m.

Vasectomy: A Delicate Matter (1986) **C-90m.** BOMB D: Robert Burge. Paul Sorvino, Cassandra Edwards, Abe Vigoda, Ina Balin, June Wilkinson, William Marshall, Lorne Greene, Gary Raff. Bank executive Sorvino is the father of eight. His wife gives him an ultimatum: Get a vasectomy, or it's bye-bye sex life. Utterly inane comedy that's almost (but not quite) too stupid to be offensive.▼

Vatican Affair, The (1969-Italian) **C-94m.** ** D: Emilio Miraglia. Walter Pidgeon, Ira Furstenberg, Klaus Kinski, Tino Carraro. Pidgeon masterminds Vatican robbery in routine heist film.

Vault of Horror (1973-British) **C-87m.** **½ D: Roy Ward Baker. Daniel Massey, Anna Massey, Terry-Thomas, Glynis Johns, Curt Jurgens, Dawn Addams, Tom Baker, Denholm Elliott, Michael Craig, Edward Judd. Five horror tales interwoven by thin connecting thread, dealing with murder, torture, bloodthirsty vampires, voodoo; adapted from old E. C. Comics. Fine cast with so-so material. Follow-up to TALES FROM THE CRYPT; reissued as TALES FROM THE CRYPT, PART II.▼

Vega$ (1978) **C-74m.** TVM D: Richard Lang. Robert Urich, Tony Curtis, Red Buttons, Will Sampson, June Allyson, Edd Byrnes, Jack Kelly, Greg Morris, Phyllis Davis, Judy Landers. The pilot to the hit series about a flashy private eye who makes the Strip his beat and has scantily clad pretties in constant pursuit. Script by Michael Mann. Average.▼

Vegas Strip Wars, The (1984) **C-100m.** TVM D: George Englund. Rock Hudson, James Earl Jones, Noriyuki "Pat" Morita, Sharon Stone, Robert Costanzo, Tony Russel. Maverick casino owner Hudson wars against his ex-partners who've double-crossed him and becomes a rival by reopening a once-decaying joint across the street. It will be remembered if at all as Hudson's last TV movie and for Jones's outrageous fright-wig send-up of fight promoter Don King. Below average.▼

Veils of Bagdad (1953) **C-82m.** **½ D: George Sherman. Victor Mature, Virginia Field, James Arness, Nick Cravat. Standard Arabian nights costumer, with Mature zestier than most such cardboard heroes.

Velvet (1984) **C-100m.** TVM D: Richard Lang. Leah Ayres, Shari Belafonte-Harper, Mary-Margaret Humes, Sheree Wilson, Michael Ensign, Polly Bergen, Leigh McCloskey, William Windom, Andrea Marcovicci. Aerobics instructors as undercover spies, played by the numbers using *Charlie's Angels* as a TV role model. Prospective pilot written by Ned Wynn. Average.

Velvet Touch, The (1948) **97m.** **½ D: John Gage. Rosalind Russell, Leo Genn, Claire Trevor, Sydney Greenstreet, Leon Ames, Frank McHugh. Satisfying murder mystery features Russell as stage actress who commits perfect crime; good Leo Rosten script with a nifty ending.▼

Velvet Vampire, The (1971) **C-80m.** ** D: Stephanie Rothman. Michael Blodgett, Celeste Yarnall, Sherry Miles, Jerry Daniels. Stylish transfer of vampire legend to western U.S. with Yarnall as sexy bloodsucker. Later reissued as CEMETERY GIRLS.▼

Vendetta (1950) **84m.** ** D: Mel Ferrer. Faith Domergue, George Dolenz, Hillary Brooke, Nigel Bruce, Joseph Calleia, Hugo Haas. Florid but uneven costume melodrama about a woman who must avenge her family's honor when her father is murdered. Howard Hughes' expensive showcase for beautiful but inexperienced Domergue. Ferrer was film's fourth director, after Preston Sturges, Max Ophuls, and Hughes.

Venetian Affair (1967) **C-92m.** ** D: Jerry Thorpe. Robert Vaughn, Elke Sommer, Felicia Farr, Karl Boehm, Luciana Paluzzi, Boris Karloff. Limp spy vehicle not far removed from Vaughn's *Man from U.N.-C.L.E.* TV series. International intrigue isn't too intriguing in this one; Karloff is good in a supporting role.

Venetian Woman, The (1986-Italian) **C-84m.** *** D: Mauro Bolognini. Laura Antonelli, Jason Connery, Monica Guerritore, Claudio Amendola, Annie-Belle. Disarmingly straightforward 16th-century sex comedy-drama of Connery (son of Sean Connery and Diane Cilento) arriving in Venice and juggling affairs with lovely but frustrated older women Antonelli and Guerritore. Exquisite art direction, gorgeous Antonelli, and clever musical score by Ennio Morricone heighten this little gem. Original Italian title: LA VENEXIANA.

Vengeance (1937) **61m.** ** D: Del Lord. Lyle Talbot, Wendy Barrie, Wally Albright, Marc Lawrence, Eddie Acuff, Lucille Lund, Robert Rideout. Harmless little crime drama about police officer Talbot's act of cowardice during a bank robbery. He resigns from the force in shame and infiltrates the gang of sinister hoodlum Lawrence. Originally titled WHAT PRICE VENGEANCE.▼

Vengeance of Fu Manchu, The (1968-British) **C-91m.** ** D: Jeremy Summers. Christopher Lee, Douglas Wilmer, Tsai Chin, Horst Frank, Maria Rohm, Howard Marion Crawford. Third entry in low-budget series that keeps Sax Rohmer stories in period. Lee again stars as evil genius this time out to destroy world police organization, and discredit arch-nemesis Nayland Smith (Wilmer) with a double. Good cast working below capabilities; lousy script. Followed by BLOOD OF FU MANCHU.

Vengeance of She, The (1968-British) **C-101m.** ** D: Cliff Owen. John Richardson, Olinka Berova, Edward Judd, Colin Blakely. Not a sequel, but more like a remake of Hammer's 1965 version of Haggard's SHE; here, the spirit of Ayesha takes over young Berova. Pretty boring.

Vengeance: The Story of Tony Cimo (1986) **C-100m.** TVM D: Marc Daniels. Brad Davis, Roxanne Hart, Brad Dourif, William Conrad, Michael Beach, Wayne Tippet. Fact-based drama about a man who takes the law into his own hands to avenge the brutal killing of his parents. Two Brads here—vengeful Davis seethes; psycho con Dourif chews scenery. Average.

Vengeance Valley (1951) **C-83m.** ** D: Richard Thorpe. Burt Lancaster, Robert Walker, Joanne Dru, Sally Forrest, John Ireland, Carleton Carpenter, Hugh O'Brian. Sex in the West with Lancaster and Walker as battling brothers, Dru and Forrest their women. Walker plays slimy villain with gusto.▼

Venom (1982-British) **C-98m.** *½ D: Piers Haggard. Klaus Kinski, Nicol Williamson, Oliver Reed, Sarah Miles, Sterling Hayden, Cornelia Sharpe, Susan George, Michael Gough. World's deadliest snake terrorizes international terrorist-kidnapper and a houseful of hostages. Half the big-name cast appears to be drunk; the other half looks as though it wishes it were. Destined to become a camp classic.▼

Venus in Furs (1970-British-Italian-German) **86m.** *½ D: Jess Franco. James Darren, Barbara McNair, Maria Rohm, Klaus Kinski, Dennis Price, Margaret Lee. Musician is baffled to see a woman who had previously washed ashore in a mutilated state; poor mystery.▼

Vera Cruz (1954) **C-94m.** *** D: Robert Aldrich. Gary Cooper, Burt Lancaster, Denise Darcel, Cesar Romero, George Macready, Ernest Borgnine, Charles Bronson. Lumbering yet exciting Western set in 1860s Mexico with Cooper and Lancaster involved in plot to overthrow Emperor Maximilian.▼

Verboten! (1959) **93m.** **½ D: Samuel Fuller. James Best, Susan Cummings, Tom Pittman, Paul Dubov, Dick Kallman, Steven Geray. American soldier falls in love with embittered German girl in occupied Berlin after WW2. High-pitched drama, flamboyantly directed by Fuller.▼

Verdict, The (1946) **86m.** **½ D: Don Siegel. Peter Lorre, Sydney Greenstreet, Joan Lorring, George Coulouris, Arthur Shields, Rosalind Ivan, Holmes Herbert. Greenstreet and Lorre make the most of this "perfect crime" yarn, with Greenstreet as Scotland Yard inspector who's "retired" when his methods are thought to be outmoded. Director Siegel's first feature.

Verdict, The (1974) SEE: **Jury of One**

Verdict, The (1982) **C-129m.** **** D: Sidney Lumet. Paul Newman, Charlotte Rampling, Jack Warden, James Mason, Milo O'Shea, Edward Binns, Julie Bovasso, Lindsay Crouse, Roxanne Hart, James Handy. Newman gives one of his finest performances as Boston lawyer who's hit bottom, until a medical negligence case gives him a chance to restore his self-esteem—while fighting for the kind of justice he still believes in. Director Lumet uses silence as eloquently as dialogue, and turns a story with more than a few loopholes into an emotionally charged experience. Screenplay by David Mamet, from the novel by Barry Reed.▼

Verne Miller (1987) **C-92m.** BOMB D: Rod Hewitt. Scott Glenn, Barbara Stock, Thomas G. Waites, Lucinda Jenney, Sonny Carl Davis, Diane Salinger, Andrew Robinson, Joseph Carberry, Richard Bright. Dumb drama with Glenn in a one-note

performance as a real-life ex–South Dakota sheriff who became a notorious gangster during the 1920s and '30s. Film is all attitude and posturing, with no logic or depth.▼

Veronika Voss (1982-German) **105m.** *** D: Rainer Werner Fassbinder. Rosel Zech, Hilmar Thate, Cornelia Froboess, Annemarie Duringer, Doris Schade, Volker Spengler. Interesting saga of faded '40s movie star Zech, allegedly a friend of Goebbels, who ten years after the war's end is a morphine addict. Good, but not great, Fassbinder; the last of his trilogy about post-war Germany, following THE MARRIAGE OF MARIA BRAUN and LOLA.

Vertigo (1958) **C-128m.** **** D: Alfred Hitchcock. James Stewart, Kim Novak, Barbara Bel Geddes, Tom Helmore, Henry Jones, Ellen Corby, Raymond Bailey, Lee Patrick. One of Hitchcock's most discussed films. Retired police detective Stewart, who has a fear of heights, is hired by old school chum in San Francisco to keep an eye on his wife (Novak), eventually falls in love with his quarry . . . and that's just the beginning; to reveal more would be unthinkable. Haunting, dream-like thriller, with riveting Bernard Herrmann score to match; a genuinely great motion picture that demands multiple viewings.▼

Very Brady Christmas, A (1988) **C-100m.** TVM D: Peter Baldwin. Florence Henderson, Robert Reed, Ann B. Davis, Maureen McCormick, Eve Plumb, Jennifer Runyon, Barry Williams, Christopher Knight, Michael Lookinland, Jerry Houser, Caryn Richman. Reunion movie with holiday theme proved there was still ratings magic surrounding The Brady Bunch of the popular 1969–74 series. This led to yet another series (the fifth;) but, alas, *The Brady*s was short-lived. Average.

Very Close Quarters (1986) **C-101m.** BOMB D: Vladimir Rif. Shelley Winters, Paul Sorvino, Theodore Bikel, Farley Granger, Lee Taylor Allen, Ellen Barber, Frederick Allen. Astonishingly inept, obnoxious comedy about a group of rather vulgar individuals sharing a communal flat in Moscow. THE MORE THE MERRIER this isn't. Interesting cast wasted. Filmed in 1983. ▼

Very Edge, The (1962-British) **82m.** ** D: Cyril Frankel. Richard Todd, Anne Heywood, Nicole Maurey, Jack Hedley, Barbara Mullen, Jeremy Brett, Maurice Denham, Patrick Magee. Pregnant Heywood is assaulted by sex pervert Brett, with unfortunate repercussions. Unsavory and unexciting thriller.▼

Very Honorable Guy, A (1934) **62m.** *½ D: Lloyd Bacon. Joe E. Brown, Alice White, Alan Dinehart, Hobart Cavanaugh, Al Dubin. Flat comedy from Damon Runyon story about gambler who sells his body to science—ahead of time—in order to pay off debt. Change of pace for Brown doesn't work at all.

Very Important Person SEE: **Coming-Out Party** (1961)

Very Missing Person, A (1972) **C-73m.** TVM D: Russ Mayberry. Eve Arden, Julie Newmar, James Gregory, Skye Aubrey, Ray Danton. Arden recreates Hildegarde Withers character first played in 1930s by Edna May Oliver in standard detective thriller in which woman's disappearance leads to murder. Another busted pilot. Average.

Very Private Affair, A (1962-French-Italian) **C-95m.** ** D: Louis Malle. Brigitte Bardot, Marcello Mastroianni, Gregor von Rezzari, Eleonore Hirt, Dirk Sanders. Rather remote romantic drama in which Bardot plays a famous movie star (from Geneva) who is robbed of her privacy and retreats from the world. Mastroianni is her mom's former lover, a theater director now protecting Bardot. Well-photographed but dull film sports a flashy ending filmed against backdrop of the Spoleto Festival. Originally titled: LA VIE PRIVEE. ▼

Very Special Favor, A (1965) **C-104m.** **½ D: Michael Gordon. Rock Hudson, Leslie Caron, Charles Boyer, Walter Slezak, Dick Shawn, Larry Storch, Nita Talbot, Jay Novello. Too-often blah, forced comedy of Boyer asking Hudson to romance daughter Caron.

Very Thought of You, The (1944) **99m.** ** D: Delmer Daves. Eleanor Parker, Dennis Morgan, Dane Clark, Faye Emerson, Beulah Bondi. Flat romance of couple marrying during WW2, encountering family wrath when they return home; unusual Daves backfire.

Vibes (1988) **C-99m.** ** D: Ken Kwapis. Cyndi Lauper, Jeff Goldblum, Julian Sands, Googy Gress, Peter Falk, Michael Lerner, Ramon Bieri, Elizabeth Pena, Bill McCutcheon, Karen Akers. Unsatisfactory romantic adventure comedy about psychics Lauper (in her first starring role) and Goldblum, and their quest for a supposed city of gold in the mountains of Ecuador. Unfortunate misfire from comedy writers Lowell Ganz and Babaloo Mandel (NIGHT SHIFT, SPLASH). ▼

Vice Squad (1931) **80m.** ** D: John Cromwell. Paul Lukas, Kay Francis, Helen Johnson (Judith Wood), Esther Howard, William B. Davidson. Lukas is excellent in tale of corrupt vice squad, but production needs a shot of adrenalin. Good potential dissipated by slow presentation. ▼

Vice Squad (1953) **87m.** **½ D: Arnold Laven. Edward G. Robinson, Paulette Goddard, K. T. Stevens, Porter Hall, Lee Van Cleef. Well-paced account of events in typical day of police detective department.

Vice Squad (1982) **C-97m.** ** D: Gary A. Sherman. Season Hubley, Gary Swanson, Wings Hauser, Pepe Serna, Beverly Todd. Hooker helps Hollywood cops catch sadistic pimp who sexually mutilates other prostitutes. Both dull and sleazy, but Hauser is undeniably a great movie villain. ▼

Vice Versa (1948-British) **111m.** *** D: Peter Ustinov. Roger Livesey, Kay Walsh, David Hutcheson, Anthony Newley, James Robertson Justice, Petula Clark, Patricia Raine, Joan Young. Entertaining comedy about Victorian stockbroker Livesey and his schoolboy son Newley, who change places after wishing on a magic stone. Parts of it are silly, but much of it is inspired and hilarious. Justice is great as a hypocritical headmaster; Ustinov also wrote the script. Predates the father-son "comedies" of the 1980s.

Vice Versa (1988) **C-100m.** *** D: Brian Gilbert. Judge Reinhold, Fred Savage, Corinne Bohrer, Swoosie Kurtz, David Proval, Jane Kaczmarek, William Prince, Gloria Gifford. Second of four films released in 1987/1988 to concern generational identity switches; this time, an ill-gotten mystical Thai skull enables a department store workaholic and his 11-year-old son to become each other. Not up to BIG, but better than it ought to be; Reinhold and Savage appear to be having a whale of a time in their roles. ▼

Vicious Circle, The SEE: **Circle, The**

Vicki (1953) **85m.** **½ D: Harry Horner. Jeanne Crain, Jean Peters, Elliott Reid, Casey Adams, Richard Boone, Carl Betz, Aaron Spelling. Loose remake of I WAKE UP SCREAMING, with Boone the resolute cop convinced agent Reid killed chanteuse girlfriend Peters. Dramatic flair isn't always evident, but wait till you find out who the killer is.

Victim (1961-British) **100m.** ***½ D: Basil Dearden. Dirk Bogarde, Sylvia Sims, Dennis Price, Nigel Stock, Peter McEnery, Donald Churchill, Anthony Nicholls, Hilton Edwards, Norman Bird, John Barrie. Fine thriller with lawyer Bogarde risking reputation by trying to confront gang of blackmailers who murdered his onetime lover. Considered daring at the time for treatment of homosexuality. Screenplay by Janet Green and John McCormick. ▼

Victim, The (1972) **C-73m.** TVM D: Herschel Daugherty. Elizabeth Montgomery, George Maharis, Eileen Heckart, Sue Ane Langdon, Jess Walton, Ross Elliott. Unaware that after telephone conversation sister was murdered, wealthy Montgomery travels through rainstorm to be at her side. Slowly, she realizes something is definitely wrong. OK performances, but crazy direction ruins intended suspense. Average.

Victims (1982) **C-100m.** TVM D: Jerrold Freedman. Kate Nelligan, Ken Howard,

Howard Hesseman, Madge Sinclair, Jonelle Allen, Bert Remsen, Michael C. Gwynne. Rape victim recruits three others attacked by the same man to stalk him after the courts have set him free on a technicality. Nelligan is frighteningly good as the obsessed woman who takes the law into her own hands, and Hesseman is chillingly sadistic as the villain. Unfortunately, the holes in the script are too gaping to make this thriller as good as it should be. Average.▼

Victims for Victims: The Theresa Saldana Story (1984) C-100m. TVM D: Karen Arthur. Theresa Saldana, Adrian Zmed, Lelia Goldoni, Lawrence Pressman, Linda Carlson, Mariclare Costello. Harrowing recreation of actress Saldana's near fatal attack by a crazed admirer and her subsequent crusade to help victims of violent crime in the form of the therapeutic group, "Victims for Victims." The lead casting surely can't be faulted! Written by Arthur Heinemann. Above average.

Victoria the Great (1937-British) C/B&W-118m. *** D: Herbert Wilcox. Anna Neagle, Anton Walbrook, H. B. Warner, Walter Rilla, Mary Morris, C. V. France, Charles Carson, Felix Aylmer. Neagle is radiant as Queen Victoria in often-stodgy biopic emphasizing her romance with Prince Albert (Walbrook). Final reel, the jubilee celebration, is in Technicolor. Sequel: SIXTY GLORIOUS YEARS.

Victors, The (1963) 156m. *** D: Carl Foreman. George Hamilton, George Peppard, Vince Edwards, Eli Wallach, Melina Mercouri, Romy Schneider, Jeanne Moreau, Peter Fonda, Senta Berger, Elke Sommer, Albert Finney. Sprawling WW2 drama of Allied soldiers on the march through Europe, focusing on their loving and fighting. Good cast and direction overcome Foreman's ambling script. Originally released at 175m.

Victor/Victoria (1982) C-133m. ***½ D: Blake Edwards. Julie Andrews, James Garner, Robert Preston, Lesley Ann Warren, Alex Karras, John Rhys-Davies, Graham Stark, Peter Arne. Down-and-out singer Andrews masquerades as a man and becomes the toast of Paris cabarets in the 1930s, to the delight of her gay mentor (Preston) and the confusion of an American admirer (Garner). Stylish, sophisticated, often hilarious comedy, with Henry Mancini and Leslie Bricusse earning Oscars for their song score and adaptation. Blake Edwards' screenplay is based on VIKTOR UND VIKTORIA, a 1933 German film (remade in 1936 as FIRST A GIRL with Jessie Matthews).▼

Victory (1940) 78m. *** D: John Cromwell. Fredric March, Betty Field, Cedric Hardwicke, Jerome Cowan, Rafaela Ottiano, Sig Ruman. March is authentic in tale of loner whose idyllic island life is disrupted by band of cutthroats; flavorful adaptation of Joseph Conrad novel sags at the end. Filmed before in 1919 and in 1930 (as DANGEROUS PARADISE).

Victory (1981) C-110m. *½ D: John Huston. Sylvester Stallone, Michael Caine, Max von Sydow, Pele, Daniel Massey, Carole Laure. POWs get a chance to escape German prison camp but stick around to finish soccer game—just as it would have happened in real life. Only Pele's celebrated kicks save this silly bore from a BOMB rating.▼

Victory at Entebbe (1976) C-150m. TVM D: Marvin J. Chomsky. Kirk Douglas, Elizabeth Taylor, Burt Lancaster, Linda Blair, Helen Hayes, Anthony Hopkins, Helmut Berger, David Groh, Theodore Bikel, Richard Dreyfuss, Jessica Walter, Julius Harris, Harris Yulin. Cliché-ridden recreation by Ernest Kinoy of lightning raid by Israeli commandos to free Jewish hostages imprisoned by Arab terrorists in Uganda. Only Lancaster and Hopkins, as Israeli defense minister Shimon Peres and Prime Minister Yitzhak Rabin, manage anything like thoughtful impersonations, while Harris (a replacement for Godfrey Cambridge, who died during filming) does Idi Amin like a vaudeville turn (as written). Originally shown on tape for topicality, later transferred to film. See RAID ON ENTEBBE or OPERATION: THUNDERBOLT for better treatment of the subject. Average.

Victory at Sea (1954) 108m. *** Produced by Henry Salomon. Narrated by Alexander Scourby. Briskly edited version of popular TV documentary series, highlighting Allied fight during WW2. Excellent photography, rousing Richard Rodgers score.▼

Videodrome (1983-Canadian) C-90m. ** D: David Cronenberg. James Woods, Sonja Smits, Deborah Harry, Peter Dvorsky, Les Carlson, Jack Creley, Lynne Gorman. Genuinely intriguing story premise—about pirate cable-TV programmer (Woods, in a dynamic performance) who's mesmerized by bizarre, untraceable transmissions that have hallucinatory power. Unfortunately, story gets slower—and sillier—as it goes along, with icky special effects by Rick Baker.▼

Video Madness SEE: **Joysticks**▼

View from Pompey's Head, The (1955) C-97m. **½ D: Philip Dunne. Richard Egan, Dana Wynter, Cameron Mitchell, Marjorie Rambeau, Sidney Blackmer, Bess Flowers. Superficial gloss from Hamilton Basso novel about social and racial prejudice in small Southern town; Blackmer as aging novelist and Rambeau his wife come off best.

View from the Bridge, A (1962-French)

110m. *** D: Sidney Lumet. Raf Vallone, Maureen Stapleton, Carol Lawrence, Jean Sorel, Morris Carnovsky, Harvey Lembeck, Vincent Gardenia. Effective adaptation of Arthur Miller drama set near Brooklyn waterfront, involving dock worker Vallone's rejection of wife Stapleton and suppressed love of niece Lawrence; Sorel is smuggled-in immigrant Lawrence loves.

View to a Kill, A (1985-British) **C-131m.** ** D: John Glen. Roger Moore, Christopher Walken, Tanya Roberts, Grace Jones, Patrick Macnee, Patrick Bauchau, Fiona Fullerton, Alison Doody, Desmond Llewelyn, Robert Brown, Lois Maxwell, Walter Gotell, Dolph Lundgren. One of the weakest James Bond films saddles 007 with a bland villain (Walken, who wants to destroy California's lucrative Silicon Valley), a monotonous villainess (Jones), and a wimpy leading lady (Roberts). And it goes on forever. Only some spectacular stunt sequences keep it alive. (Oh, yes, there's also a gorgeous Russian spy—played by Fullerton—who disappears too soon.) Moore's final appearance as 007.▼

Vigil (1984-New Zealand) **C-90m.** **½ D: Vincent Ward. Bill Kerr, Fiona Kay, Gordon Shields, Penelope Stewart, Frank Whitten. Ward's first feature is an apt predecessor to his NAVIGATOR. It's a grim, thinly scripted, but visually arresting account of how a young farm girl reacts to the arrival of a stranger upon the death of her father.

Vigilante (1982) **C-90m.** BOMB D: William Lustig. Robert Forster, Fred Williamson, Richard Bright, Rutanya Alda, Willie Colon, Joe Spinell, Carol Lynley, Woody Strode. Forster is driven to join DEATH WISH-type vigilantes after his family is viciously attacked by degenerate punks. Script is full of holes, and so is some of the cast after various bloody attacks. Truly distasteful. Originally titled STREET GANG.▼

Vigilante Force (1976) **C-89m.** **½ D: George Armitage. Kris Kristofferson, Jan-Michael Vincent, Victoria Principal, Bernadette Peters, Brad Dexter, David Doyle, Andrew Stevens. Vietnam vet Kristofferson, hired to help restore order when small California town is overrun by workers from nearby oilfields, succeeds but then takes over town himself. Minor but interesting, fast-paced film.

Vigilantes Return, The (1947) **C-67m.** ** D: Ray Taylor. Margaret Lindsay, Jon Hall, Paula Drew, Andy Devine, Robert Wilcox, Jack Lambert. Standard Western with marshal Hall sent to bring law and order to untamed town.

Vigil in the Night (1940) **96m.** *** D: George Stevens. Carole Lombard, Brian Aherne, Anne Shirley, Rhys Williams, Peter Cushing, Rafaela Ottiano, Ethel Griffies. Compelling drama of provincial hospital life in England, with outstanding work by Lombard as dedicated nurse, Shirley as her flighty sister, Aherne as doctor. Potentially corny script made credible and exciting by good cast, fine direction pulling viewer into the story.

Viking Queen, The (1967-British) **C-91m.** ** D: Don Chaffey. Don Murray, Carita, Donald Houston, Andrew Keir, Adrienne Corri, Niall MacGinnis, Wilfrid Lawson. Empty-headed costumer of early England under Roman rule, with plenty of gore as anarchists incite a violent uprising among the people. Murray and fine British actors are lost.

Vikings, The (1958) **C-114m.** **½ D: Richard Fleischer. Kirk Douglas, Tony Curtis, Ernest Borgnine, Janet Leigh, Alexander Knox, Frank Thring; narrated by Orson Welles. Big-name cast and on-location photography in Norway and Brittany are only standouts in routine Viking adventure, sweepingly photographed by Jack Cardiff.▼

Viking Women and the Sea Serpent (1957) **66m.** BOMB D: Roger Corman. Abby Dalton, Susan Cabot, Brad Jackson, Richard Devon. The title ladies are held captive on an island. The original title of this Grade-Z hokum is THE VOYAGE OF THE VIKING WOMAN TO THE WATERS OF THE GREAT SEA SERPENT(!) By any name, it stinks.

Villa! (1958) **C-72m.** *½ D: James B. Clark. Brian Keith, Cesar Romero, Margia Dean, Rodolfo Hoyos. Dull recreation of events in life of Mexican bandit.

Village of the Damned (1960-British) **78m.** *** D: Wolf Rilla. George Sanders, Barbara Shelley, Michael Gwynne, Laurence Naismith, John Phillips, Richard Vernon. Fine adaptation of John Wyndham novel (*The Midwich Cuckoos*) about mishap in English village followed by birth of strange, emotionless children. Eerie, well-made chiller, followed by CHILDREN OF THE DAMNED.▼

Village of the Giants (1965) **C-80m.** BOMB D: Bert I. Gordon. Tommy Kirk, Johnny Crawford, Beau Bridges, Ronny Howard, Tisha Sterling, Tim Rooney, Joy Harmon. Poor special effects are just one problem with this silly film about teenagers growing to tremendous heights. Based on H. G. Wells story, refilmed by Gordon in 1976 as FOOD OF THE GODS.▼

Villain (1971-British) **C-98m.** *½ D: Michael Tuchner. Richard Burton, Ian McShane, Nigel Davenport, Joss Ackland, Fiona Lewis, Donald Sinden, Cathleen Nesbitt. Nasty, stomach-churning melodrama about British underworld, taken from James Barlow's novel *The Burden of Proof*. Burton plays vicious homosexual thug only a mother (Nesbitt) could love.

Villain, The (1979) **C-89m.** ** D: Hal Needham. Kirk Douglas, Ann-Margret, Arnold Schwarzenegger, Paul Lynde, Foster Brooks, Ruth Buzzi, Jack Elam, Strother Martin. Lynde plays an Indian chief named Nervous Elk, and so it goes. Combination Western spoof/Road Runner cartoon makes CAT BALLOU look subtle, but may make you laugh if it hits you in a silly frame of mind.

Villain Still Pursued Her, The (1940) **66m.** ** D: Edward F. Cline. Anita Louise, Richard Cromwell, Hugh Herbert, Alan Mowbray, Buster Keaton, Joyce Compton, Billy Gilbert, Margaret Hamilton. Laughs are few and far between in this full-length spoof of old-time melodramas in which boos and hisses are encouraged. Even pie-throwing sequence is dull. Keaton adds brightest moments.▼

Villa Rides (1968) **C-125m.** ** D: Buzz Kulik. Yul Brynner, Robert Mitchum, Charles Bronson, Herbert Lom, Jill Ireland. Witless retelling of Villa's Mexican campaign, with broadened focus on cohort Bronson, captured pilot Mitchum. Rare chance to see Brynner with hair; screenplay by Robert Towne and Sam Peckinpah.▼

Vincent (1987-Australian) **C-99m.** *** D: Paul Cox. Engrossing, thoughtfully directed documentary look at the life and letters of Vincent van Gogh. A rare and revealing celluloid examination of an artist and his creativity. The voice of John Hurt is heard as van Gogh. Originally titled VINCENT— THE LIFE AND DEATH OF VINCENT VAN GOGH.▼

Vincent, Francois, Paul and the Others (1974-French) **C-118m.** **** D: Claude Sautet. Yves Montand, Michel Piccoli, Gerard Depardieu, Stephane Audran. Melancholy, enormously satisfying life-goes-on drama about longtime male buddies who pursue their respective vocations during the week—medicine, boxing, factory ownership, etc.—then team up for food and drink on idyllic country weekends. Montand stands out in a dream French cast as a going-broke boss in perilous romantic and physical shape.▼

Vindicator, The (1986-Canadian) **C-88m.** ** D: Jean-Claud Lord. Terri Austin, Richard Cox, Pam Grier, Maury Chaykin, David McIlwraith. Updating of FRANKENSTEIN saga concerns infighting among scientists working on cyborg experiments. Highlights: an impressive metallic monster design by Stan Winston plus tough-girl troubleshooter role for guest star Grier. Originally titled: FRANKENSTEIN '88. ▼

Vintage, The (1957) **C-92m.** ** D: Jeffrey Hayden. Pier Angeli, Michele Morgan, John Kerr, Mel Ferrer, Theodore Bikel, Leif Erickson. Strangely cast melodrama set in vineyard of France involving two brothers on the lam.

Violated (1984) **C-88m.** BOMB D: Richard Cannistraro. J. C. Quinn, John Heard, D. Balin, April Daisy White, Kaye Dowd, Lisanne Falk, Carol Francis, Samantha Fox, Elizabeth Kaitan. Dreary exploitation film about N.Y.C. businessmen who prey on young party girls. White is a rape victim befriended by cop Quinn, who goes after the big boys. Contains a brief, standout performance by Heard as a fidgety intermediary who hires Quinn as a hit man. ▼

Violation of Sarah McDavid, The (1981) **C-100m.** TVM D: John Llewellyn Moxey. Patty Duke Astin, Ned Beatty, James Sloyan, Vernee Watson, Victoria Racimo, Richard Venture, Fran Bennett, Ally Sheedy, Eric Stoltz. Dedicated teacher is assaulted in her classroom, and her ambitious principal tries to keep the attack a secret. A graphic depiction of violence in schools, written by Arnold and Lois Peyser. Above average.

Violent City SEE: **Family, The** (1970)▼

Violent Enemy, The (1968-British) **C-94m.** *** D: Don Sharp. Tom Bell, Susan Hampshire, Ed Begley, Jon Laurimore, Michael Standing, Noel Purcell. Intense drama of IRA plot to blow up British power plant, and various motives involved.

Violent Four, The (1968-Italian) **C-98m.** ** D: Carlo Lizzani. Gian Maria Volonte, Tomas Milian, Margaret Lee, Carla Gravina, Don Backy. Unexceptional tale of notorious Italian robbery gang which stages massive bank holdup schemes, becoming police's number-one target.

Violent Men, The (1955) **C-96m.** **½ D: Rudolph Maté, Barbara Stanwyck, Glenn Ford, Edward G. Robinson, Dianne Foster, Brian Keith, Richard Jaeckel. Robinson is unscrupulous, wealthy rancher in conflict with good folk of the valley, Stanwyck his wife. Some good action sequences. From a Donald Hamilton novel.

Violent Ones, The (1967) **C-84m.** *½ D: Fernando Lamas. Fernando Lamas, Aldo Ray, Tommy Sands, David Carradine, Lisa Gaye, Melinda Marx. Junk about lawman Lamas' problems in getting Mexican community to refrain from lynching his prisoners when they are suspected of raping and murdering Marx.▼

Violent Professionals, The (1973-Italian) **C-92m.** ** D: Sergio Martino. Richard Conte, Luc Merenda, Silvana Tranquilli, Steffan Zaccharias. Mezza-mezza Italian action flick about a suspended cop who infiltrates the mob to get the goods on a notorious gang boss. Violent indeed.

Violent Road (1958) **86m.** **½ D: Howard W. Koch. Brian Keith, Dick Foran, Efrem Zimbalist, Jr., Merry Anders. Well-done programmer involving men driving explosives over bumpy road, allowing for each to reexamine his way of life.

Violent Saturday (1955) **C-91m.** ***** D:** Richard Fleischer. Victor Mature, Richard Egan, Stephen McNally, Lee Marvin, Sylvia Sidney, Ernest Borgnine, Tommy Noonan, J. Carrol Naish. Effective study of repercussion on small town when bank robbers carry out a bloody holdup.

Violent Stranger (1957-British) **83m.** ****½** D: Montgomery Tully. Zachary Scott, Faith Domergue, Faith Brook, Peter Illing, Gordon Jackson, Kay Callard. Domergue, wife of condemned killer, sets out to find the real culprit. Not bad little crime drama. Originally titled MAN IN THE SHADOW.

Violent Summer (1961-French) **85m.** ****** D: Michel Boisrond. Martine Carol, Jean Desailly, Dahlia Lavi, Henri-Jacques Huet. Unconvincing tale of murder of a halfwit girl, with most of the guests at a Riviera resort home prime suspects; too many loose threads.

Violent Years, The (1956) **57m.** BOMB D: William M. Morgan (Franz Eichorn). Jean Moorehead, Barbara Weeks, Arthur Millan, Theresa Hancock, Joanne Cangi, Gloria Farr. Tawdry, preachy juvenile delinquency trash about a rich teen girl, ignored by her parents, who heads up a gang. Wooden-Indian acting all around. Scripted by the one, the only, Edward Wood, Jr. Also known as FEMALE.▼

Violets Are Blue . . . (1986) **C-88m.** ****** D: Jack Fisk. Sissy Spacek, Kevin Kline, Bonnie Bedelia, John Kellogg, Jim Standford, Augusta Dabney. Romantic drama about onetime highschool sweethearts, reunited after many years, who try to pick up where they left off—though he's married and settled in their hometown and she's single and a globetrotting photojournalist. Pleasant, attractive, but dull.▼

Violette (1978-French) **C-122m.** ****** D: Claude Chabrol. Isabelle Huppert, Stephane Audran, Jean Carmet, Jean Francoise Garreaud, Bernadette Lafont. Slow-moving account, based on true incident of 14-year-old girl who led double life and poisoned her parents, killing her father. Huppert sleepwalks through the role, and Chabrol lacks his usual directorial flair. Full title VIOLETTE NOZIERE.▼

Violins Came With the Americans, The SEE: **Sun and the Moon, The**

V.I.P.s., The (1963-British) **C-119m.** ****½** D: Anthony Asquith. Elizabeth Taylor, Richard Burton, Louis Jourdan, Margaret Rutherford, Rod Taylor, Maggie Smith, Orson Welles, Linda Christian, Elsa Martinelli, Dennis Price, David Frost, Michael Hordern, Robert Coote. Glossy GRAND HOTEL plot, set in London airport. Everyone is terribly rich and beautiful; if you like watching terribly rich, beautiful people, fine. If not, it's all meaningless. Rutherford (who won an Oscar for this) is excellent, and so is Maggie Smith. Written by Terence Rattigan.

Virgin and the Gypsy, The (1970-British) **C-92m.** ****½** D: Christopher Miles. Joanna Shimkus, Franco Nero, Honor Blackman, Mark Burns, Maurice Denham, Fay Compton, Kay Walsh. D. H. Lawrence's novella comes to screen as interesting, atmospheric, but unbelievable love story. Priest's daughter falls for vagabond gypsy and suffers consequences. Miles later directed Lawrence biopic, PRIEST OF LOVE.▼

Virginia (1941) **C-110m.** ****** D: Edward H. Griffith. Madeleine Carroll, Fred MacMurray, Sterling Hayden, Helen Broderick, Marie Wilson, Carolyn Lee. Well-mounted but tedious film of Southern woman (Carroll) who must sacrifice her property and herself in order to raise money to live.

Virginia City (1940) **121m.** ****½** D: Michael Curtiz. Errol Flynn, Miriam Hopkins, Randolph Scott, Humphrey Bogart, Frank McHugh, Alan Hale, Guinn Williams, John Litel. Followup to DODGE CITY has big cast in lush Civil War Western, but tale of rebel spy Hopkins posing as dance hall girl doesn't live up to expectations; Bogart miscast as slimy Mexican bandido.▼

Virginia Hill Story, The (1974) **C-78m.** TVM D: Joel Schumacher. Dyan Cannon, Harvey Keitel, Allen Garfield, John Vernon, Herbert Anderson, Robby Benson, John Quade, Conrad Janis. Dramatized biography tracing life and loves of gangster Bugsy Siegel's moll and the testimony about organized crime she gave before the Kefauver committee. Cannon gives a florid portrayal in the title role, Keitel is properly sinister as Siegel, and Anderson is stentorian as Kefauver. Above average.

Virginian, The (1929) **90m.** ****½** D: Victor Fleming. Gary Cooper, Richard Arlen, Walter Huston, Mary Brian, Chester Conklin, Eugene Pallette. Owen Wister's novel becomes stiff but interesting Western, salvaged in good climactic shoot-out; Huston is slimy villain, and Cooper has one of his better early roles. Famous line: "Smile when you say that." Remade in 1946, followed by a hit TV series in the 1960s.▼

Virginian, The (1946) **C-90m.** ****½** D: Stuart Gilmore. Joel McCrea, Brian Donlevy, Sonny Tufts, Barbara Britton, Fay Bainter, Henry O'Neill, William Frawley, Vince Barnett, Paul Guilfoyle. Remake of '29 classic Western follows story closely. Good, not great, results due to story showing its age. McCrea is hero, Donlevy the villain, Tufts a good-guy-turned-bad.

Virgin Island (1959-British) **C-84m.** ****½** D: Pat Jackson. John Cassavetes, Virginia Maskell, Sidney Poitier, Colin Gordon. Leisurely study of author Cassavetes and bride Maskell moving to Caribbean isle; film lightly touches on racial issue.

Virgin of Nuremburg, The SEE: **Horror Castle**▼

Virgin President, The (1968) 71m. ** D: Graeme Ferguson. Severn Darden, Richard Neuweiler, Andrew Duncan, Richard Schaal, Paul Benedict, Sudie Bond, Peter Boyle. Darden is Fillard Millmore, the 43rd president of the United States. Occasionally funny but mostly silly spoof.

Virgin Queen, The (1955) C-92m. *** D: Henry Koster. Bette Davis, Richard Todd, Joan Collins, Herbert Marshall, Jay Robinson, Dan O'Herlihy, Rod Taylor. Davis is in full authority in her second portrayal of Queen Elizabeth I, detailing her conflicts with Walter Raleigh.▼

Virgin Soldiers, The (1969-British) C-96m. *** D: John Dexter. Hywel Bennett, Nigel Patrick, Lynn Redgrave, Nigel Davenport, Rachel Kempson, Tsai Chin, Jack Shepherd. Smooth comedy-drama about British recruits in Singapore; title refers to their lack of experience in battle as well as in bed. Solid Carl Foreman production, adapted by John Hopkins from Leslie Thomas' novel. Followed by STAND UP, VIRGIN SOLDIERS in 1977.▼

Virgin Spring, The (1959-Swedish) 88m. *** D: Ingmar Bergman. Max von Sydow, Brigitta Valberg, Gunnel Lindblom, Brigitta Pettersson, Axel Duberg. Brooding medieval fable of a deeply religious farming family whose daughter is raped and murdered by vagrants. Fascinating, beautifully made, an Oscar winner for Best Foreign Film. Remade as—or, more appropriately, ripped off by—LAST HOUSE ON THE LEFT.▼

Viridiana (1961-Spanish) 90m. ***½ D: Luis Buñuel. Francisco Rabal, Silvia Pinal, Fernando Rey, Margarita Lozano. Powerful psychological study of novice nun Pinal, who loses her innocence when forced by Mother Superior to visit nasty uncle Rey. Near-perfect direction by a master filmmaker; solid performances by all.▼

Virtuous Sin, The (1930) 82m. BOMB D: George Cukor, Louis Gasnier. Walter Huston, Kay Francis, Kenneth MacKenna, Jobyna Howland, Paul Cavanagh. Laughably bad production with alluring Francis giving herself to Russian general Huston so he will exempt her husband from death sentence. A real turkey.

Virus (1980-Japanese) C-155m. **½ D: Kinji Fukasaku. Sonny Chiba, Chuck Connors, Glenn Ford, Stephanie Faulkner, Masao Kusakari, Isao Natsuki, Stuart Gillard, Olivia Hussey, George Kennedy, Henry Silva, Bo Svenson, Cecil Linder, Robert Vaughn. Mankind is destroyed by a plague and nuclear war—except for 858 men and eight women. Beautiful sequences filmed in the Antarctic, adequate special effects, but overlong and meandering. Allegedly the biggest budgeted Japanese film ever.▼

Viscount, The (1967-French-Italian-Spanish) C-98m. BOMB D: Maurice Cloche. Kerwin Mathews, Edmond O'Brien, Jane Fleming, Yvelle Lebon, Jean Yanne, Fernando Rey. In spite of the presence of such well-known European actors as Yanne and Rey, grade-D spy film is a waste of time.

Vision Quest (1985) C-105m. ** D: Harold Becker. Matthew Modine, Linda Fiorentino, Michael Schoeffling, Ronny Cox, Harold Sylvester, Roberts Blossom, Charles Hallahan, Daphne Zuniga, Forest Whitaker, Raphael Sbarge. Muddled, overlong growing-pains movie with too many familiar elements. Modine is a high-school wrestler with a philosophical bent; Fiorentino is a tough-talking older woman who turns him on. Based on a novel by Terry Davis. Madonna appears briefly onscreen singing "Crazy for You."▼

Visions . . . (1972) C-73m. TVM D: Lee Katzin. Monte Markham, Telly Savalas, Barbara Anderson, Lonny Chapman, Tim O'Connor, Richard Erdman. College professor flashes on visions of someone planting explosives in buildings, relates experience to Denver police who keep surveillance on him for fear he may be mad bomber. Fairly tense situations, but film's pacing too hurried and sloppy. Average. Alternate title: VISIONS OF DEATH.

Visions of Eight (1973) C-110m. ** D: Juri Ozerov, Mai Zetterling, Arthur Penn, Michael Pfleghar, Kon Ichikawa, Milos Forman, Claude Lelouch, John Schlesinger. Seemingly good idea of having eight different directors give eight different views of 1972 Olympics results in strangely disappointing film, considering all the talent involved; with possible exception of Schlesinger's final chapter on the marathon, none of the episodes stay in the memory.▼

Visit, The (1964-German-French-Italian) 100m. **½ D: Bernhard Wicki. Ingrid Bergman, Anthony Quinn, Irina Demick, Paolo Stoppa, Hans-Christian Blech, Romolo Valli, Valentina Cortese, Eduardo Ciannelli. Intriguing but uneven film parable of greed and evil; wealthy Bergman returns to European home town, offering a fantastic sum to the people there if they will legitimately kill her first seducer (Quinn). Actors struggle with melodramatic script; results are interesting if not always successful. Bowdlerized version of Friedrich Durrenmatt's play.

Visiting Hours (1982-Canadian) C-103m. BOMB D: Jean Claude Lord. Michael Ironside, Lee Grant, Linda Purl, William Shatner, Harvey Atkin, Helen Hughes. Awful programmer, set in a hospital with demented Ironside stalking TV journalist

Grant, who hopefully was well paid for this junk.▼

Visitor, The (1979-Italian) **C-90m.** ** D: Michael J. Paradise (Giulio Paradisi). Mel Ferrer, Glenn Ford, Lance Henriksen, John Huston, Joanne Nail, Shelley Winters, Sam Peckinpah. Filmed Stateside by the BEYOND THE DOOR folks, this passable time-killer wastes a good cast in yet another OMEN rip-off; too bad Huston or Peckinpah couldn't have directed as well.▼

Visitors, The (1972) **C-88m.** BOMB D: Elia Kazan. Patrick McVey, Patricia Joyce, James Woods, Chico Martinez, Steve Railsback. Deplorable story of two Vietnam vets who, upon release from prison for sex crime, invade the house of third vet who testified at their trial. Woods' film debut.▼

Visit to a Chief's Son (1974) **C-92m.** **½ D: Lamont Johnson. Richard Mulligan, Johnny Sekka, Jean Philip Hogdon, Jesse Kinaru, Chief Lomoiro, Jock Anderson. OK family drama about a self-centered father and son who become humanized on an African safari.

Visit to a Small Planet (1960) **85m** **½ D: Norman Taurog. Jerry Lewis, Joan Blackman, Earl Holliman, Fred Clark, John Williams, Jerome Cowan, Lee Patrick, Gale Gordon. Gore Vidal satire becomes talky Lewis vehicle with Jerry the alien who comes to Earth to observe man's strange ways.

Vital Signs (1986) **C-100m. TVM** D: Stuart Millar. Edward Asner, Gary Cole, Kate McNeil, Barbara Barrie, John Randolph, James Sloyan. Crisis movie involving father and son surgeons—one an alcoholic, the other a drug addict. Sturdy performances, solid script (by Lee Hutson) give this one body. Above average.

Vital Signs (1990) **C-103m.** *½ D: Marisa Silver. Adrian Pasdar, Diane Lane, Jimmy Smits, Norma Aleandro, Jack Gwaltney, Laura San Giacomo, Jane Adams, Tim Ransom, Bradley Whitford, Lisa Jane Persky, William Devane, James Kanre, Telma Hopkins. Third-year medical students experience the usual clichés: performing rounds, undercutting rivals, questioning authority, and sneaking an occasional quickie in the hospital linen closet. Watchable, but of absolutely no distinction; stick with THE NEW INTERNS, where you can at least compare the acting styles of Dean Jones and Telly Savalas. Smits effectively projects quiet authority as the surgeon instructor.

Vivacious Lady (1938) **90m.** *** D: George Stevens. James Stewart, Ginger Rogers, James Ellison, Beulah Bondi, Charles Coburn, Frances Mercer, Grady Sutton, Jack Carson, Franklin Pangborn. Overlong but entertaining comedy of professor Stewart marrying nightclub singer Rogers, trying to break the news to his conservative family and fiancée back home. Bondi is fun in amusing variation on her usual motherly role.▼

Viva Knievel! (1977) **C-106m.** BOMB D: Gordon Douglas. Evel Knievel, Gene Kelly, Lauren Hutton, Marjoe Gortner, Red Buttons, Eric Shea, Leslie Nielsen, Cameron Mitchell, Frank Gifford, Albert Salmi, Dabney Coleman. The senses reel at this hilariously inept attempt to turn the infamous stunt driver into a movie hero. The Bad Guys plan to have Evel "accidentally" killed in Mexico, so they can use his truck to smuggle drugs back into the U.S.! Don't miss opening scene, in which Our Hero sneaks into orphanage at midnight to distribute Evel Knievel plastic model kits—whereupon one little boy miraculously throws away his crutches!▼

Viva Las Vegas (1964) **C-86m.** **½ D: George Sidney. Elvis Presley, Ann-Margret, Cesare Danova, William Demarest, Jack Carter. Elvis and Ann-Margret are well-teamed in this popular Presley vehicle, with Elvis a race car driver. Songs include "The Lady Loves Me," "What'd I Say?" "I Need Somebody to Lean On," and classic title tune.▼

Viva Maria! (1965-French-Italian) **C-119m.** ***½ D: Louis Malle. Brigitte Bardot, Jeanne Moreau, George Hamilton, Gregor Von Rezzori, Paulette Dubost. Rollicking tale of two beautiful entertainers/revolutionaries in Mexico has inconsistent first half, then takes off for hilarious finish. Lots of fun.

Viva Max! (1969) **C-92m.** **½ D: Jerry Paris. Peter Ustinov, Pamela Tiffin, Jonathan Winters, John Astin, Keenan Wynn, Harry Morgan, Alice Ghostley, Kenneth Mars, Ann Morgan Guilbert, Paul Sand. Mildly amusing yarn of eccentric Mexican general recapturing Alamo, sending equally inept American militia to rout him out. Forced humor doesn't always work, but not bad; Astin is excellent as Ustinov's loyal sergeant.▼

Viva Villa! (1934) **115m.** ***½ D: Jack Conway. Wallace Beery, Leo Carrillo, Fay Wray, Donald Cook, Stuart Erwin, George E. Stone, Henry B. Walthall, Joseph Schildkraut, Katherine DeMille. Viva Beery, in one of his best films as the rowdy rebel who led the fight for Madera's Mexican Republic. Ben Hecht's script plays with facts, but overall, film is entertaining.

Viva Zapata! (1952) **113m.** **** D: Elia Kazan. Marlon Brando, Jean Peters, Anthony Quinn, Joseph Wiseman, Margo, Mildred Dunnock. Vibrant film about Mexican peasant's rise to power and eventual Presidency. Brando is perfect in title role, Quinn equally fine in Oscar-winning performance as his brother. Script by John Steinbeck.▼

Vivement Dimanche SEE: **Confidentially Yours**▼

Vogues (1937) **C-108m.** ** D: Irving Cummings. Warner Baxter, Joan Bennett, Helen Vinson, Mischa Auer, Alan Mowbray, Jerome Cowan, Marjorie Gateson, Polly Rowles, Hedda Hopper, The Wiere Brothers. Minor musical with wealthy Bennett deciding to work as fashion model to chagrin of her boss Baxter. One good song, ''That Old Feeling.'' Original title: VOGUES OF 1938.▼

Voice in the Mirror, The (1958) 102m. **½ D: Harry Keller. Richard Egan, Julie London, Arthur O'Connell, Walter Matthau, Troy Donahue, Mae Clarke. Effective, unpretentious account of Egan trying to combat alcoholism, with help of wife London.

Voice in the Wind, A (1944) 85m. *** D: Arthur Ripley. Francis Lederer, Sigrid Gurie, J. Edward Bromberg, J. Carrol Naish. Low-key drama of pianist Lederer haunted by Nazi oppression, later rekindling old love affair; unusual film, well acted.

Voice of Bugle Ann, The (1936) 70m. **½ D: Richard Thorpe. Lionel Barrymore, Maureen O'Sullivan, Eric Linden, Dudley Digges, Spring Byington, Charles Grapewin. Sentimental tale of remarkable dog's owner taking revenge on person who kills the animal; not always convincing.

Voice of Merrill, The SEE: **Murder Will Out**

Voice of Terror SEE: **Sherlock Holmes and the Voice of Terror**▼

Voice of the Turtle, The (1947) 103m. ***½ D: Irving Rapper. Ronald Reagan, Eleanor Parker, Eve Arden, Wayne Morris, Kent Smith. Delightful wartime comedy of wide-eyed Parker letting soldier Reagan share her apartment. John van Druten adapted his own Broadway hit. Retitled ONE FOR THE BOOK.

Voice of the Whistler (1946) 60m. D: William Castle. Richard Dix, Lynn Merrick, Rhys Williams, James Cardwell, Donald Woods, Gigi Perreau. SEE: **Whistler** series.

Voices (1979) **C-107m.** ** D: Robert Markowitz. Michael Ontkean, Amy Irving, Alex Rocco, Barry Miller, Herbert Berghof, Viveca Lindfors. Aspiring rock singer falls for deaf woman (well played by Irving) who, never having heard him sing, is able to return his love. Sincerely intentioned drama is ultimately compromised by Hollywood formulas.▼

Voices of Sarafina! (1989) **C-85m.** ***½ D: Nigel Noble. Miriam Makeba, Mbongeni Ngema. Powerful, profound documentary of the young, black South African actors performing in the Broadway musical *Sarafina*, which chronicles the involvement of black schoolchildren in the 1976 Soweto

uprising. Also detailed is their relationship with Ngema, the show's controversial writer-director. Finale, in which exiled South African singer Makeba appears backstage after a performance, is especially moving.

Volcano (1953-Italian) 106m. ** D: William Dieterle. Anna Magnani, Rossano Brazzi, Geraldine Brooks, Eduardo Ciannelli. Slowly paced dramatics about two sisters involved with unprincipled diver.

Volcano (1969) SEE: **Krakatoa, East of Java**

Voltaire (1933) 72m. **½ D: John G. Adolfi. George Arliss, Margaret Lindsay, Doris Kenyon, Reginald Owen, Alan Mowbray, Douglass Dumbrille, Theodore Newton. Arliss offers another crafty, knowing portrayal as the writer, wit and ''great humanitarian of the 18th century'' who was the conscience of his country in pre-revolutionary France. Stagy production; Arliss is the whole show.

Volunteers (1985) **C-106m.** *½ D: Nicholas Meyer. Tom Hanks, John Candy, Rita Wilson, Tim Thomerson, Gedde Watanabe, George Plimpton. Dismal comedy about spoiled playboy who accidentally joins Peace Corps and tries running things his way in Thailand. Candy has a few good moments but not enough. What's more, it's a grimy-*looking* film. Hanks and costar Wilson later married in real life.▼

Von Richthofen and Brown (1971) **C-97m.** ** D: Roger Corman. John Phillip Law, Barry Primus, Peter Masterson, Karen Huston, Hurd Hatfield, Robert La Tourneaux. Weak historical drama of WW1 pilots and aerial dogfights. Aerial work is excellent; it's the ground work which crashes. Corman's last film as director to date.

Von Ryan's Express (1965) **C-117m.** *** D: Mark Robson. Frank Sinatra, Trevor Howard, Raffaella Carra, Brad Dexter, Sergio Fantoni, Edward Mulhare, James Brolin, Adolfo Celi, John Leyton, Vito Scotti. Exciting WW2 saga with Sinatra a POW colonel who leads daring escape by taking over freight train. Strong supporting cast helps.▼

Voodoo Island (1957) 76m. ** D: Reginald Le Borg. Boris Karloff, Beverly Tyler, Murvyn Vye, Elisha Cook. Boring horror-thriller has Karloff asked by businessmen to investigate strange doings on potential motel-island resort. Also known as SILENT DEATH.

Voodoo Man (1944) 62m. ** D: William Beaudine. Bela Lugosi, John Carradine, George Zucco, Michael Ames (Tod Andrews), Henry Hall, Wanda McKay, Louise Currie. With touching devotion to zombie-wife, Lugosi performs harrowing experiments with unsuspecting girls to cure her. Campy B film.

Voodoo Tiger (1952) 67m. D: Spencer Bennet. Johnny Weissmuller, Jean Byron,

Jeanne Dean, Robert Bray, Tamba. SEE: **Jungle Jim** series.

Voodoo Woman (1957) **77m.** *½ D: Edward L. Cahn. Marla English, Tom Conway, Michael Connors, Lance Fuller. Cheaterchiller with few scares in lowjinks about deranged scientist changing English into a monster. Incomprehensible film.

Voyage, The (1973-Italian) **C-95m.** ** D: Vittorio De Sica. Sophia Loren, Richard Burton, Ian Bannen, Barbara Pilavin, Annabella Incontera, Paolo Lena. Listless adaptation of Pirandello story about starcrossed lovers Burton and Loren, forbidden to marry and shadowed by tragedy. Attractive stars and surroundings, but a draggy film.

Voyage of the Damned (1976-British) **C-134m.** *** D: Stuart Rosenberg. Faye Dunaway, Oskar Werner, Max von Sydow, Orson Welles, Malcolm McDowell, Lynne Frederick, James Mason, Lee Grant, Wendy Hiller, Jose Ferrer, Luther Adler, Katharine Ross, Sam Wanamaker, Denholm Elliott, Nehemiah Persoff, Julie Harris, Maria Schell, Ben Gazzara. Absorbing drama based on fact. In 1939 a ship full of German-Jewish refugees bound for Havana was denied permission to land anywhere and forced to return to Germany. Picture almost dissolves into separate stories, but von Sydow as ship's captain holds it together. Originally released at 158m.▼

Voyage of the Yes, The (1972) **C-73m.** TVM D: Lee Katzin. Desi Arnaz, Jr., Mike Evans, Beverly Garland, Skip Homeier, Della Reese, Scoey Mitchlll. Two teenagers in small sailboat battle elements and their own prejudices. OK once they get into the boat; marginal material a waste. Average.▼

Voyage to the Bottom of the Sea (1961) **C-105m.** *** D: Irwin Allen. Walter Pidgeon, Joan Fontaine, Robert Sterling, Barbara Eden, Michael Ansara, Peter Lorre, Frankie Avalon, Henry Daniell, Regis Toomey. Entertaining, colorful nonsense about conflicts aboard massive atomic submarine, with Pidgeon the domineering admiral trying to keep the Earth from being fried by a burning radiation belt. No deep thinking, just fun. Later a TV series.▼

Voyage to the End of the Universe (1963-Czechoslavakian) **81m.** **½ D: Jack Pollack (Jindrich Polak). Dennis Stephans, Francis Smolen, Dana Meredith, Irene Kova, Rodney Lucas, Otto Lack. Twenty-fifth-century space crew is threatened by mysterious, radioactive dark star. Surprise ending is no surprise. Czech film originally titled IKARIE XB 1, with 90-minute runningtime.

Voyage to the Planet of Prehistoric Women (1968) **C-80m.** *½ D: Derek Thomas (Peter Bogdanovich). Mamie Van Doren, Mary Marr, Paige Lee, Aldo Roman,

Margot Hartman. Astronauts land on Venus and kill the creature worshiped by the planet's gill-women. Actually a 1962 Russian picture, PLANET OF STORMS, framed with new footage conceived (and narrated) by Bogdanovich in 1966. Still an awful movie, but of definite curio interest to film buffs.

Voyage to the Prehistoric Planet (1965) **80m.** *½ D: Jonathan Sebastian (Curtis Harrington). Basil Rathbone, Faith Domergue, Marc Shannon, Christopher Brand. Slow, ponderous saga of an expedition to Venus in the year 2020; made up mostly of footage from handsome Russian epic PLANET OF STORMS, involving a robot, dinosaurs, other monsters, and hidden, intelligent Venusians. Rathbone's scenes were shot on the sets for PLANET OF BLOOD, which he made at the same time.▼

Vulture, The (1967-British-Canadian) **C-91m.** *½ D: Lawrence Huntington. Robert Hutton, Akim Tamiroff, Broderick Crawford, Diane Clark, Phillip Friend, Patrick Holt. Disappointing, unsatisfying sci-fi horror with laughable mad scientist (Tamiroff) who becomes half-man, half-bird and avenges death of his ancestor. Released theatrically in b&w.▼

W (1974) **C-95m.** *½ D: Richard Quine. Twiggy, Michael Witney, Dirk Benedict, John Vernon, Eugene Roche, Alfred Ryder. Twiggy struggles through story in which sadistic Benedict, her ex-husband convicted of her supposed murder, menaces her and new husband Witney. Flamboyant but unsuccessful thriller, retitled I WANT HER DEAD.▼

Wabash Avenue (1950) **C-92m.** *** D: Henry Koster. Betty Grable, Victor Mature, Phil Harris, Reginald Gardiner, James Barton, Margaret Hamilton. Bright, colorful period piece with scoundrel Mature trying to break up romance between saloonowner Harris and his musical star, Grable. Done with conviction and enthusiasm; enjoyable remake of Grable's 1943 vehicle CONEY ISLAND.

WAC from Walla Walla, The (1952) **83m.** *½ D: William Witney. Judy Canova, Stephen Dunne, Allen Jenkins, Irene Ryan, George Cleveland. Lame-brained service adventure of perennial yokel Canova.

Wackiest Ship in the Army, The (1960) **C-99m.** *** D: Richard Murphy. Jack Lemmon, Ricky Nelson, John Lund, Chips Rafferty, Tom Tully, Joby Baker, Warren Berlinger. Comedy-drama sometimes has you wondering if it's serious or not; it succeeds most of the time. Offbeat WW2 story about broken-down sailing ship used as decoy doesn't make fun of the war, for a change, and is entertaining. Later a TV series.▼

Wacko (1981) **C-90m.** *½ D: Greydon Clark. Joe Don Baker, Stella Stevens, George Kennedy, Jeff Altman, Anthony James, Andrew (Dice) Clay. A dedicated cop goes after the dreaded "lawnmower killer" who last terrorized a town ten years ago. Heavy-handed spoof of HALLOWEEN-type horror films works hard for laughs but delivers very few.▼

Waco (1966) **C-85m.** **½ D: R.G. Springsteen. Howard Keel, Jane Russell, Brian Donlevy, Wendell Corey, Terry Moore, John Smith, John Agar, Gene Evans, Richard Arlen, Ben Cooper, Jeff Richards. Gunfighter Keel comes to clean up town, but former girl friend Russell is now married to Reverend Corey. Nice veteran cast, but film is only for Western addicts.

Wages of Fear, The (1952-French-Italian) **105m.** ***½ D: H. G. Clouzot. Yves Montand, Charles Vanel, Peter Van Eyck, Vera Clouzot, Folco Lulli, William Tubbs. Marvelous, gritty and extremely suspenseful epic set in South America, chronicling the personalities of and relationships among four men involved in long-distance driving of trucks filled with nitroglycerine. Originally 156m.; many other shorter versions exist. Remade as SORCERER.▼

Wagner (1983-British-Hungarian-Austrian) **C-300m.** ** D: Tony Palmer. Richard Burton, Vanessa Redgrave, Gemma Craven, Laszlo Galffi, John Gielgud, Ralph Richardson, Laurence Olivier, Ronald Pickup, Joan Plowright, Arthur Lowe, Franco Nero. Glossy but uninspired biography of the composer, monotonously acted by Burton. Overlong, to state the obvious. Originally a nine-hour British TV series.▼

Wagon Master (1950) **86m.** *** D: John Ford. Ben Johnson, Joanne Dru, Harry Carey, Jr., Ward Bond, Alan Mowbray, Jane Darwell, James Arness, Jim Thorpe. Good Ford Western about two roaming cowhands who join a Mormon wagon train heading for Utah frontier. Fine showcase for young stars Johnson and Carey. Beautifully filmed. Inspired the later *Wagon Train* TV series. Also shown in computer-colored version.▼

Wagons Roll at Night, The (1941) **84m.** **½ D: Ray Enright. Humphrey Bogart, Sylvia Sidney, Eddie Albert, Joan Leslie, Sig Ruman, Cliff Clark, Charley Foy, Frank Wilcox. KID GALAHAD in circus trappings is OK, thanks to cast: Bogie's the circus manager, Sidney his star, Albert the hayseed turned lion tamer.

Waikiki (1980) **C-105m.** TVM D: Ron Satlof. Dack Rambo, Steve Marachuk, Donna Mills, Darren McGavin, Cal Bellini, Robert F. Lyons, Mark Slade, Tanya Roberts. Pedestrian pilot revolving around a couple of dashing private detectives in Hawaii. Below average.▼

Waikiki Wedding (1937) **89m.** *** D: Frank Tuttle. Bing Crosby, Martha Raye, Shirley Ross, Bob Burns, Leif Erickson, Grady Sutton, Anthony Quinn. Press-agent Crosby promotes Ross as Pineapple Queen, sings "Blue Hawaii" and Oscar-winning "Sweet Leilani" in this pleasant musicomedy.

Waiting for the Moon (1987) **C-85m.** *½ D: Jill Godmilow. Linda Hunt, Linda Bassett, Bruce McGill, Jacques Boudet, Andrew McCarthy, Bernadette Lafont. Spiritless, sleep-inducing account of the complex relationship between an ailing Gertrude Stein (Bassett) and her companion, Alice B. Toklas (Hunt). Slow-moving, occasionally confusing, and very disappointing. A PBS *American Playhouse* presentation.▼

Waitress! (1982) **C-93m.** BOMB D: Samuel Weil, Michael Herz. Carol Drake, June Martin, Renata Majer, Jim Harris, David Hunt, Carol Bevar, Calvert DeForest. If watching a chef spit in soup is your idea of a fun way to spend an evening, then you might find a couple of laughs in this moronic comedy set in a restaurant.▼

Wait Till Your Mother Gets Home! (1983) **C-100m.** TVM D: Bill Persky. Paul Michael Glaser, Dee Wallace, Peggy McKay, David Doyle, Ray Buktenica, Lynne Moody, James Gregory. Perceptive if familiar tale of a football coach who has to run the household while his wife goes to work. Written by D. Eyre and director Persky. Above average.▼

Wait 'Til the Sun Shines, Nellie (1952) **C-108m.** *** D: Henry King. Jean Peters, David Wayne, Hugh Marlowe, Albert Dekker, Alan Hale, Warren Stevens. Nostalgic film of the hopes and disappointments of small town barber Wayne in the early 1900s. Produced by George Jessel.

Wait Until Dark (1967) **C-108m.** *** D: Terence Young. Audrey Hepburn, Alan Arkin, Richard Crenna, Efrem Zimbalist, Jr., Jack Weston, Samantha Jones. Solid shocker with Hepburn as blind woman left alone in apartment, terrorized by psychotic Arkin and henchmen looking for heroin they think is planted there. Memorable nail-biter, flashy role for Arkin; based on Frederick Knott's Broadway hit.▼

Wake in Fright SEE: **Outback**

Wake Island (1942) **87m.** *** D: John Farrow. Brian Donlevy, Robert Preston, Macdonald Carey, Albert Dekker, Walter Abel, Barbara Britton, William Bendix, Rod Cameron. Stirring war film of U.S.'s fight to hold Pacific island at outbreak of WW2. Nothing new here, but exciting and well-done.▼

Wake Me When It's Over (1960) **C-126m.** *** D: Mervyn LeRoy. Dick Shawn, Ernie Kovacs, Margo Moore, Jack Warden, Don Knotts. Entertaining comedy of hustling Shawn making the most of his army station in the Far East by building a fancy hotel with army supplies. Kovacs lends good support.

Wake Me When the War Is Over (1969) C-73m. TVM D: Gene Nelson. Ken Berry, Eva Gabor, Werner Klemperer, Danielle DeMetz, Jim Backus, Hans Conried, Parley Baer. Bumbling American officer (Berry) thinks WW2 is still on, thanks to efforts of odd German baroness (Gabor) and her friends. Fair comedy but for Berry. Average.

Wake of the Red Witch (1948) 106m. **½ D: Edward Ludwig. John Wayne, Gail Russell, Luther Adler, Gig Young, Adele Mara, Eduard Franz, Henry Daniell, Paul Fix. Rivalry between East Indies magnate and adventuresome ship's captain over pearls and women. Film is a bit confused, but nicely photographed by Reggie Lanning. Incidentally, Wayne took the name of his production company, Batjac, from this film's shipping firm. Also shown in computer-colored version. ▼

Wake Up and Dream (1946) C-92m. ** D: Lloyd Bacon. June Haver, John Payne, Charlotte Greenwood, Connie Marshall, John Ireland, Clem Bevans, Lee Patrick. Moody film from Robert Nathan's story about girl determined to find brother missing from WW2.

Wake Up and Live (1937) 91m. *** D: Sidney Lanfield. Alice Faye, Walter Winchell, Ben Bernie, Jack Haley, Patsy Kelly, Joan Davis, Grace Bradley, Warren Hymer, Ned Sparks, Walter Catlett. Fast-moving spoof of radio with battling Winchell and Bernie, mike-frightened singer Haley, and Faye singing "There's a Lull in My Life."

Walkabout (1971-Australian) C-95m. *** D: Nicolas Roeg. Jenny Agutter, Lucien John, David Gulpilil, John Meillon. Lost in wilderness of Australia, two children rely on young aborigine in order to survive. Roeg, in his first solo outing as director, also beautifully photographed the film; lush score by John Barry.

Walk a Crooked Mile (1948) 91m. **½ D: Gordon Douglas. Louis Hayward, Dennis O'Keefe, Louise Allbritton, Carl Esmond, Onslow Stevens, Raymond Burr. Average melodrama about secret service agent who breaks up mob with help of Scotland Yard.

Walk, Don't Run (1966) C-114m. *** D: Charles Walters. Cary Grant, Samantha Eggar, Jim Hutton, John Standing, Miiko Taka, Ted Hartley. Enjoyable fluff about Eggar unwittingly agreeing to share her apartment with businessman Grant and athlete Hutton during the Tokyo Olympics. Stars are most agreeable in this remake of THE MORE THE MERRIER. Grant's last film as an actor. ▼

Walker (1988) C-90m. BOMB D: Alex Cox. Ed Harris, Marlee Matlin, Richard Masur, René Auberjonois, Peter Boyle, Miguel Sandoval, Gerrit Graham. Juvenile, intentionally anachronistic comic history of William Walker, American soldier of fortune (previously played by Marlon Brando in BURN!) who became president of 19th-century Nicaragua thanks to an assist from Cornelius Vanderbilt. Matlin's follow-up to her Oscar is actually an inglorious cameo; the sorry screenplay is by Rudy Wurlitzer. A self-indulgent mess. ▼

Walk East on Beacon (1952) 98m. **½ D: Alfred L. Werker. George Murphy, Finlay Currie, Virginia Gilmore, George Roy Hill. Good documentary-style drama by Leo Rosten about FBI investigation of espionage; filmed on location in Boston.

Walking Dead, The (1936) 66m. *** D: Michael Curtiz. Boris Karloff, Edmund Gwenn, Marguerite Churchill, Ricardo Cortez, Barton MacLane, Warren Hull, Joe Sawyer. Karloff is framed and executed, but professor brings him back to life. As he regains his memory, he seeks out those who framed him. Good horror tale.

Walking Hills, The (1949) 78m. *** D: John Sturges. Randolph Scott, Ella Raines, William Bishop, Edgar Buchanan, Arthur Kennedy. Well-acted oater of Westerners searching for abandoned gold mine.

Walking My Baby Back Home (1953) C-95m. **½ D: Lloyd Bacon. Donald O'Connor, Buddy Hackett, Janet Leigh, Scatman Crothers, George Cleveland, Lori Nelson. Confused musical comedy about army buddies forming a Dixieland band; redeemed by Hackett's wacky humor.

Walking Stick, The (1970-British) C-101m. **½ D: Eric Till. Samantha Eggar, David Hemmings, Emlyn Williams, Phyllis Calvert, Ferdy Mayne, Francesca Annis. Potentially interesting story of beautiful polio victim coerced into assisting her worthless lover in a robbery is just too low-key to be consistently absorbing. Eggar's performance helps.

Walking Tall (1973) C-125m. ** D: Phil Karlson. Joe Don Baker, Elizabeth Hartman, Gene Evans, Rosemary Murphy, Noah Beery, Felton Perry. Sickeningly violent action-drama about determined Southern sheriff's one-man war against local corruption. Huge theatrical success, based on the exploits of real-life baseball-bat-wielding Buford Pusser, with a muscular performance by Baker. Followed by a couple of sequels, a TVM (A REAL AMERICAN HERO) and a series. ▼

Walking Tall, Part Two SEE: **Part 2, Walking Tall** ▼

Walking Through the Fire (1979) C-100m. TVM D: Robert Day. Bess Armstrong, Tom Mason, Richard Masur, Swoosie Kurtz, Bonnie Bedelia, June Lockhart, J. D. Cannon. Affecting dramatization by Sue Grafton of Laura Lee's personal chronicle of her struggle with Hodgkin's disease and its effect on her unborn child. Above average.

Walk in the Shadow (1966-British) 93m. *** D: Basil Dearden. Patrick McGoohan,

Janet Munro, Paul Rogers, Megs Jenkins. Fine courtroom melodrama, as emotions flare after a girl's drowning.

Walk in the Spring Rain (1970) **C-100m.** **½ D: Guy Green. Anthony Quinn, Ingrid Bergman, Fritz Weaver, Katherine Crawford. Happily married Bergman has extramarital affair in this low-key romantic drama. One expects more from such a cast. Scripted and produced by Stirling Silliphant.▼

Walk in the Sun, A (1945) **117m.** ***½ D: Lewis Milestone. Dana Andrews, Richard Conte, Sterling Holloway, George Tyne, John Ireland, Herbert Rudley, Norman Lloyd, Lloyd Bridges, Huntz Hall. Human aspect of war explored as American battalion attacks German hideout in Italy; good character studies of men in war. Adapted by Robert Rossen from Harry Brown's novel.▼

Walk into Hell (1957-Australian) **C-93m.** *½ D: Lee Robinson. Chips Rafferty, Francoise Christophe, Reginald Lye, Pierre Cressoy. Lumbering account of civilized Australians vs. native customs, filmed on location in New Guinea.▼

Walk Like a Dragon (1960) **95m.** **½ D: James Clavell. Jack Lord, Nobu McCarthy, James Shigeta, Mel Torme, Josephine Hutchinson, Rodolfo Acosta. Offbeat Western drama of Lord saving McCarthy from life of prostitution, taking her back to San Francisco, overcoming expected obstacles.

Walk Like a Man (1987) **C-86m.** BOMB D: Melvin Frank. Howie Mandel, Christopher Lloyd, Cloris Leachman, Colleen Camp, Amy Steel, Stephen Elliott, George DiCenzo. Mandel is returned to civilization after being raised by wolves, with the expected slapstick results. Puerile comedy with a cast that deserves much better.▼

Walk on the Wild Side (1962) **114m.** **½ D: Edward Dmytryk. Laurence Harvey, Capucine, Jane Fonda, Anne Baxter, Barbara Stanwyck. Lurid hodgepodge set in 1930's New Orleans, loosely based on Nelson Algren novel, of Harvey seeking lost love Capucine, now a member of bordello run by lesbian Stanwyck. Memorable titles by Saul Bass; fine score by Elmer Bernstein.▼

Walk Proud (1979) **C-102m.** ** D: Robert Collins. Robby Benson, Sarah Holcomb, Domingo Ambriz, Pepe Serna, Trinidad Silva. Sincerely intentioned but not very forceful gang picture about a Chicano (Benson) who falls for a WASP beauty who goes to his high school. Looks like a made-for-TV.

Walk Softly, Stranger (1950) **81m.** *** D: Robert Stevenson. Joseph Cotten, (Alida) Valli, Spring Byington, Paul Stewart, Jack Paar, Jeff Donnell, John McIntire. Small-time crook Cotten reforms because of the love and faith of crippled girl Valli.▼

Walk Tall (1960) **C-60m.** *½ D: Maury Dexter. Willard Parker, Joyce Meadows, Kent Taylor. Flabby oater about capture of outlaws who killed Indian squaws.

Walk the Dark Street (1956) **74m.** *½ D: Wyott Ordung. Chuck Connors, Don Ross, Regina Gleason, Eddie Kafafian. Uninspired revenge hunt, set in a metropolitan city, of two men stalking each other with rifles.

Walk the Proud Land (1956) **C-88m.** *** D: Jesse Hibbs. Audie Murphy, Anne Bancroft, Pat Crowley, Charles Drake, Jay Silverheels. Sturdy scripting makes this oater attractive; Murphy is Indian agent trying to quell strife between redskins and settlers, with the capture of Geronimo his major feat.

Walk With Love and Death, A (1969) **C-90m.** ** D: John Huston. Anjelica Huston, Assaf Dayan, Anthony Corlan, John Hallam, Robert Lang, Michael Gough. Fine period flavor but little else of note in story of young love set against turmoil of 14th-century France. Director Huston's daughter (in her first film) plays lead, Huston himself has small role.

Wall, The (1982) **C-150m. TVM** D: Robert Markowitz. Tom Conti, Lisa Eichhorn, Gerald Hiken, Rachel Roberts, Philip Sterling, Eli Wallach, Rosanna Arquette, Griffin Dunne, Dianne Wiest. Millard Lampell's adaptation of his 1960 play, which in turn came from John Hersey's book about the 1943 Jewish uprising in the Warsaw Ghetto. Confusing film translation and generally perfunctory acting reduces a never-to-be-forgotten historical happening to an off-the-assembly-line war movie, despite being shot entirely on location in Poland (just before the Solidarity movement overwhelmed that country). Average.

Wall, The (1982-British) SEE: **Pink Floyd—The Wall▼**

Wallenberg: A Hero's Story (1985) **C-200m. TVM** D: Lamont Johnson. Richard Chamberlain, Alice Krige, Bibi Andersson, Melanie Mayron, Stuart Wilson, Kenneth Colley. Powerful portrait by Chamberlain of the idealistic Swedish diplomat who outsmarted Adolph Eichmann (chillingly played by Colley) and rescued more than 100,000 Hungarian Jews during WW2, only to be captured by the Russians at war's end, never to be seen again. Johnson won an Emmy for directing, and there were many other nominations, including one for Gerald Green, whose incisive script stands beside the one he did for HOLOCAUST. Originally shown in two parts. Above average.

Wallflower (1948) **77m.** *** D: Frederick de Cordova. Joyce Reynolds, Robert Hutton, Janis Paige, Edward Arnold, Jerome

Cowan, Barbara Brown. Amusing comedy based on Broadway success; two stepsisters (Reynolds and Paige) vie for the same love.

Wall of Noise (1963) **112m.** **½ D: Richard Wilson. Suzanne Pleshette, Ty Hardin, Dorothy Provine, Ralph Meeker, Simon Oakland, Murray Matheson. Turgid racetrack drama with adultery, not horses, the focal point.

Walls (1985-Canadian) **C-88m.** *½ D: Tom Shandel. Winston Rekert, Andree Pelletier, Alan Scarfe, John Lord, Lloyd Berry. Perfectly awful fact-based account of how some convicts come to take hostages, with tragic results. A serious attempt to examine flaws in prison bureaucracy, but the result is preachy, one-dimensional, hopelessly inept.

Walls Came Tumbling Down, The (1946) **82m.** *** D: Lothar Mendes. Lee Bowman, Marguerite Chapman, Edgar Buchanan, Lee Patrick, J. Edward Bromberg. Detective Bowman goes to work when priest is murdered in fast-moving private eye film.

Walls of Glass (1985) **C-86m.** **½ D: Scott Goldstein. Philip Bosco, Geraldine Page, Linda Thorson, Olympia Dukakis, Brian Bloom, Steven Weber, Louis Zorich, William Hickey. Intriguing if uneven character study with Bosco nicely cast as a middle-aged, sonnet-spouting N.Y.C. cab driver who hates his job, and yearns for success as an actor. Occasionally slow, but still effective.▼

Walls of Gold (1933) **74m.** *½ D: Kenneth MacKenna. Sally Eilers, Norman Foster, Ralph Morgan, Rosita Moreno, Rochelle Hudson, Frederic Santley, Mary Mason. Terrible soaper about love conflicts among the well-to-do; Eilers does something to ruffle fiancé Foster, so to spite her he marries her sister, and she marries his uncle. Forget it.

Walls of Hell, The (1964) **88m.** ** D: Gerardo De Leon. Jock Mahoney, Fernando Poe, Jr., Mike Parsons, Paul Edwards, Jr. WW2 actioner set in Manila. Filmed in the Philippines, suffers from amateurish native casting.

Walls of Jericho, The (1948) **106m.** ** D: John M. Stahl. Cornel Wilde, Linda Darnell, Anne Baxter, Kirk Douglas, Ann Dvorak, Marjorie Rambeau, Henry Hull, Colleen Townsend, Barton MacLane. Good cast tries to perk up story of ambitious lawyer in Jericho, Kansas, whose marital problems stand in the way of success; pretty dreary going most of the way.

Wall Street (1987) **C-124m.** *** D: Oliver Stone. Michael Douglas, Charlie Sheen, Daryl Hannah, Hal Holbrook, Martin Sheen, Terence Stamp, Sean Young, Sylvia Miles, James Spader, John McGinley, Saul Rubinek, Franklin Cover, James Karen, Richard Dysart, Josh Mostel, Mil-

lie Perkins, Cecilia Peck, Grant Shaud. Young hotshot who's going nowhere in a N.Y. brokerage firm manages to buttonhole the highest roller on Wall Street (Douglas, in an Oscar-winning performance) and win his confidence—but he sells his soul, so to speak, in return for admittance to that high-powered world of wheeling and dealing. Modern-day morality tale by cowriter-director Stone (whose father was a broker, and to whom the film is dedicated) is short on subtlety but completely absorbing, especially in the wake of the real-life "insider trading" scandal of 1986. Oliver Stone, Monique Van Vooren, and Liliane Montevecchi can be glimpsed.▼

Waltz Across Texas (1982) **C-99m.** **½ D: Ernest Day. Terry Jastrow, Anne Archer, Richard Farnsworth, Noah Beery, Mary Kay Place, Josh Taylor, Ben Piazza, Jorge Cervera, Jr., Savannah Smith. Oilman Jastrow and geologist Archer fall in love. Predictable, but far from unpleasant. The leads are husband and wife offscreen; they wrote the story, coproduced the film.▼

Waltz King, The (1963) **C-95m.** **½ D: Steve Previn. Kerwin Mathews, Brian Aherne, Senta Berger, Peter Kraus, Fritz Eckhardt. Moderately entertaining Disney musical biopic stars Mathews as Johann Strauss, Jr. Features fine music and the usual excellent Disney Technicolor. Filmed in Germany; shown in the U.S. as two-part TV show.▼

Waltz of the Toreadors (1962-British) **C-105m.** *** D: John Guillermin. Peter Sellers, Dany Robin, Margaret Leighton, John Fraser. Jean Anouilh's saucy sex romp gets top notch handling with Sellers as the retired military officer who still can't keep his eye off the girls.▼

Wanda (1971) **C-105m.** ***½ D: Barbara Loden. Barbara Loden, Michael Higgins, Charles Dosinan, Frank Jourdano. Touching, original little drama about passive woman (Loden) who takes up with two-bit thief Higgins. Well acted.

Wanda Nevada (1979) **C-105m.** *½ D: Peter Fonda. Peter Fonda, Brooke Shields, Fiona Lewis, Luke Askew, Ted Markland, Severn Darden, Paul Fix, Henry Fonda. Fonda wins Shields in a poker game, and they set out together to prospect for gold in the Grand Canyon. If this film were any more laid-back it would be nonexistent. Peter and Henry's only film together.▼

Wanderers, The (1979) **C-113m.** ***½ D: Philip Kaufman. Ken Wahl, John Friedrich, Karen Allen, Toni Kalem, Alan Rosenberg, Linda Manz, Erland van Lidth de Jeude, Olympia Dukakis. Impressionistic look at Bronx-Italian high school life in 1963 isn't always consistent in tone, but there are dozens of privileged moments.

Understandably, it's become a cult favorite.▼

Wannsee Conference, The (1984-German-Austrian) **C-87m.** ***½ D: Heinz Schirk. Dietrich Mattausch, Gerd Bockmann, Friedrich Beckhaus, Gunter Spoerrie, Martin Luttge, Peter Fritz. Fascinating, chilling recreation of the infamous meeting, held in a Berlin suburb in January 1942, in which Nazi bigwigs discussed implementation of the Final Solution. Participants plot the destruction of millions with a casual air, which only adds to the terror. Based on minutes taken at the conference; film's length matches the event's actual running time.▼

Want a Ride, Little Girl? SEE: **Impulse** (1974)▼

Wanted: Babysitter SEE: **Babysitter, The** (1975)▼

Wanted: Dead or Alive (1987) **C-104m.** BOMB D: Gary Sherman. Rutger Hauer, Gene Simmons, Robert Guillaume, Mel Harris, William Russ, Susan McDonald, Jerry Hardin. Hauer plays Nick Randall, grandson of fellow bounty hunter Josh, the character Steve McQueen played in the identically named TV series. Link is mentioned, then ignored, in routine cheapo about the CIA's pursuit of an Arab terrorist. Bravura grenade-in-mouth finale.▼

Wanted for Murder (1946-British) **95m.** **½ D: Lawrence Huntington. Eric Portman, Dulcie Gray, Derek Farr, Roland Culver, Stanley Holloway. Engaging whodunit yarn, effectively underplayed by the cast; co-scripted by Emeric Pressburger.

Wanted: The Sundance Woman (1976) **C-100m.** TVM D: Lee Philips. Katharine Ross, Steve Forrest, Stella Stevens, Hector Elizondo, Michael Constantine, Katherine Helmond. Ross again is Etta Place in sequel to BUTCH CASSIDY AND THE SUNDANCE KID—or, what happened to Etta following their deaths—she's running guns for Pancho Villa. Sparkling humor of the original has fizzled. Retitled MRS. SUNDANCE RIDES AGAIN; Elizabeth Montgomery played the role in 1974's MRS. SUNDANCE. Average.

Wanton Contessa SEE: **Senso**▼

War Against Mrs. Hadley, The (1942) **86m.** ** D: Harold Bucquet. Edward Arnold, Fay Bainter, Richard Ney, Sara Allgood, Spring Byington, Jean Rogers, Frances Rafferty, Dorothy Morris, Rags Ragland, Isobel Elsom, Van Johnson. Mild WW2 human-interest tale by George Oppenheimer about matron Bainter who refuses to participate in war support.

War and Peace (1956-U.S.-Italian) **C-208m.** **½ D: King Vidor. Audrey Hepburn, Henry Fonda, Mel Ferrer, Vittorio Gassman, John Mills, Herbert Lom, Oscar Homolka, Anita Ekberg, Helmut Dantine, Mai Britt. Tolstoy's sprawling novel fails

to come alive in this overlong, oversimplified adaptation. Star-studded cast and spectacular battle scenes (directed by Mario Soldati) cannot compensate for clumsy script (by six writers, including Vidor) and some profound miscasting. Filmed far more successfully in 1968.▼

War and Peace (1968-Russian) **C-373m.** **** D: Sergei Bondarchuk. Ludmila Savelyeva, Vyacheslav Tihonov, Hira Ivanov-Golovko, Irina Gubanova, Antonia Shuranova. Sergei Bondarchuk. Even in theaters, poor English dubbing hurt this definitive film version of Tolstoy's novel, and on TV, the commercials and multiple-night showings may damage it more. Even so, it should be seen for production values alone; a dazzling film. Oscar-winner for Best Foreign Film. Originally 434m.▼

War Arrow (1953) **C-78m.** ** D: George Sherman. Maureen O'Hara, Jeff Chandler, Suzan Ball, Charles Drake, Jay Silverheels. Western story of U.S. Cavalry man Chandler coming to Texas to train Seminole Indians to subdue a Kiowa uprising. O'Hara is object of his love.

War Between Men and Women, The (1972) **C-110m.** **½ D: Melville Shavelson. Jack Lemmon, Barbara Harris, Jason Robards, Herb Edelman, Lisa Gerritsen, Severn Darden. Fans of James Thurber won't think much of this on-and-off mixture of famed writer-cartoonist's material and Hollywood schmaltz, but film occasionally makes for pleasant comedy-romance. Barbara Harris comes off best in likable cast. Material had previously inspired a TV series, *My World—And Welcome To It.*

War Between the Planets (1965-Italian) **C-80m.** BOMB D: Anthony Dawson (Antonio Margheriti). Jack Stuart (Giacomo Rossi-Stuarti), Amber Collins (Ombretta Colli), Peter Martell, Halina Zalewska. Alien planet is on collision course with earth, but valiant efforts by scientific forces snatch victory from the jaws of boredom. Fun only if you like spaghetti sci-fi. Made at same time as other losers such as WAR OF THE PLANETS, WILD WILD PLANET, etc. Also known as PLANET ON THE PROWL.▼

War Between the Tates, The (1977) **C-100m.** TVM D: Lee Philips. Elizabeth Ashley, Richard Crenna, Ann Wedgeworth, Annette O'Toole, Granville Van Dusen. Domestic drama has small-town professor trying to resolve crisis when his wife learns of his affair with one of his students. This adaptation of Alison Lurie's best-seller has lost some of its bite, but Ashley's rich portrait compensates. Average.

War Drums (1957) **C-75m.** **½ D: Reginald LeBorg. Lex Barker, Joan Taylor, Ben Johnson, Stuart Whitman. Sufficiently bloody Western set in Civil War days of

Indian uprisings against onslaught of gold miners.

War Game, The (1967-British) **47m.** **½ D: Peter Watkins. Originally intended as a straight BBC documentary, this filmed projection of nuclear holocaust's aftermath was more than the network bargained for; effective as propaganda and not bad as film.▼

War Games (1970) SEE: **Suppose They Gave a War and Nobody Came?**▼

WarGames (1983) **C-110m.** **½ D: John Badham. Matthew Broderick, Dabney Coleman, John Wood, Ally Sheedy, Barry Corbin, Juanin Clay. FAIL SAFE for the Pac-Man generation: a pop movie about a computer whiz-kid who taps into government early-warning system and nearly starts World War III. Entertaining to a point, but gets more contrived as it goes along, leading to finale straight out of an old B movie. Incidentally, it's easy to see why this was so popular with kids: most of the adults in the film are boobs.▼

War Gods of the Deep (1965-British) **C-85m.** **½ D: Jacques Tourneur. Vincent Price, Tab Hunter, David Tomlinson, Susan Hart, John LeMesurier. Gill-men invade remote seacoast town. Actually, two films in one: establishing menace, first half has odd, almost poetic feel to it, but second half deteriorates, with shoddy underwater city. Tourneur's final feature. British title: THE CITY UNDER THE SEA.

War Hunt (1962) **81m.** **½ D: Denis Sanders. John Saxon, Robert Redford, Charles Aidman, Sydney Pollack. Well-done Korean War story focusing on kill-happy soldier Saxon who tries to help an orphan boy. Redford's film debut.

War Is Hell (1963) **81m.** ** D: Burt Topper. Tony Russel, Baynes Barron, Tony Rich, Burt Topper. Korean War actioner with no new ideas to offer. Introduced by Audie Murphy.

War, Italian Style (1967-Italian) **C-84m.** ** D: Luigi Scattini. Buster Keaton, Franco and Ciccio, Martha Hyer, Fred Clark. Sloppy, meandering spy satire set in WW2 Italy, redeemed barely by Keaton's appearance. Unfortunately, this was his final film.

Warlock (1959) **C-121m.** *** D: Edward Dmytryk. Richard Widmark, Henry Fonda, Anthony Quinn, Dorothy Malone, Dolores Michaels, Wallace Ford, Tom Drake, Richard Arlen, Regis Toomey, DeForest Kelley. Intelligent, well-paced Western giving new depth to usual cowboys-vs.-outlaws shootout; script by Robert Alan Aurthur.▼

War Lord, The (1965) **C-123m.** *** D: Franklin Schaffner. Charlton Heston, Rosemary Forsyth, Richard Boone, Maurice Evans, Guy Stockwell, Niall McGinnis, James Farentino, Henry Wilcoxon, Michael Conrad. Intriguing, generally well-done adaptation of Leslie Stevens' *The Lovers*, with Heston as feudal knight invoking little-known law allowing him to have another man's bride on their wedding night. Title and medieval setting would seem to indicate sweeping spectacle . . . which this certainly isn't.

Warlords of Atlantis (1978-British) **C-96m.** **½ D: Kevin Connor. Doug McClure, Peter Gilmore, Shane Rimmer, Lea Brodie, Cyd Charisse, Daniel Massey. Monsters and mayhem abound in this palatable Saturday matinee item with McClure joining British scientists in search for underwater city.

Warlords of the 21st Century (1982) **C-91m.** ** D: Harley Cokliss. Michael Beck, Annie McEnroe, James Wainwright, John Ratzenberger, Bruno Lawrence. Routine action film set after WW3 in time of an oil shortage. Wainwright (as the ruthless, right-wing military villain) virtually repeated his role in the contemporary-set Robin Williams comedy THE SURVIVORS. Filmed in New Zealand; originally titled BATTLETRUCK. ▼

War Lover, The (1962-British) **105m.** **½ D: Philip Leacock. Steve McQueen, Robert Wagner, Shirley Anne Field, Gary Cockrell. John Hersey's thoughtful novel becomes superficial account of McQueen and Wagner, two WW2 pilots in England, both in love with Field; aerial photography is above par.▼

Warm December, A (1973) **C-100m.** ** D: Sidney Poitier. Sidney Poitier, Esther Anderson, Johnny Sekka, Yvette Curtis. George Baker, Earl Cameron. Story of Poitier's love for Anderson, who is dying of sickle cell anemia, isn't as sappy as it might be, but isn't particularly good, either. Anderson is attractive. Made in England.

Warm Hearts, Cold Feet (1987) **C-100m.** TVM D: James Frawley. Tim Matheson, Margaret Colin, Barry Corbin, George DiCenzo, Elizabeth Ashley. Cutesy yuppie comedy about young expectant marrieds who are columnists for competing newspapers, writing running commentaries on wifey's pregnancy. Average.

Warning Shot (1967) **C-100m.** ***½ D: Buzz Kulik. David Janssen, Ed Begley, Keenan Wynn, Lillian Gish, Eleanor Parker, Sam Wanamaker, Stefanie Powers, George Sanders, George Grizzard, Steve Allen, Carroll O'Connor, Joan Collins, Walter Pidgeon. Exciting action-filled melodrama about cop's attempt to clear his name after killing a supposedly innocent doctor. TV-vet Kulik made this one exciting for theaters, and it's even better on TV.

Warning Sign (1985) **C-100m.** *½ D: Hal Barwood. Sam Waterston, Kathleen

Quinlan, Yaphet Kotto, Jeffrey De Munn, Richard Dysart, G. W. Bailey, Jerry Hardin, Rick Rossovich, Cynthia Carle. Self-important, would-be CHINA SYNDROME about disastrous results of chemical spill at research lab that's secretly been working on germ warfare for the government. Unpleasant and ineffectual. Screenwriter Barwood's directing debut.▼

War of Children, A (1972) **C-73m. TVM** D: George Schaefer. Jenny Agutter, Vivien Merchant, John Ronane, Danny Figgis, Anthony Andrews, Aideen O'Kelly. Solid James Costigan-written script about mad warfare in modern-day Northern Ireland, centering around single family. Good cast, totally location-shot. Above average.

War of the Colossal Beast (1958) **68m.** *½ D: Bert I. Gordon. Sally Fraser, Roger Pace, Dean Parkin, Russ Bender, Charles Stewart. Sequel to THE AMAZING CO-LOSSAL MAN finds our oversized hero alive but not well; his face is a mess, and so is his mind, leading to the inevitable low-budget rampage. Forget it. Last scene originally in color.

War of the Gargantuas, The (1966-U.S.-Japanese) **C-93m. BOMB** D: Inoshiro Honda. Russ Tamblyn, Kumi Mizuno, Kipp Hamilton, Yu Fujiki. Japan is menaced by a mean, green "gargantua" (humanoid giant), with a friendly brown gargantua trying to make peace. Strange, even by Japanese monster-movie standards.

War of the Planets (1965-Italian) **C-99m.** BOMB D: Anthony Dawson (Antonio Margheriti). Tony Russel, Lisa Gastoni, Massimo Serato, Franco Nero, Carlo Giustini. Light creatures attack earth but are repelled. Cheap sets and plodding script make this a loser.

War of the Planets SEE: **Cosmos: War of the Planets**

War of the Roses, The (1989) **C-116m.** **½ D: Danny DeVito. Michael Douglas, Kathleen Turner, Danny DeVito, Marianne Sägebrecht, Sean Astin, Heather Fairfield, G. D. Spradlin, Peter Donat. The saga of a marriage that goes sour, to say the least; when Douglas and Turner can't agree on a property settlement in their divorce proceedings, war breaks out in (and over) their exquisitely appointed house. As satiric commentary on yuppie materialism, this very black comedy scores a bull's-eye—for about an hour. Then, having made its point, it continues for nearly an hour more as the couple grows increasingly vicious and irrational, literally destroying their home. Some people loved this film (the star performances *are* perfect), so obviously it's a matter of taste. DeVito's odd point of view and wild camera angles are an asset throughout.▼

War of the Satellites (1958) **66m.** ** D: Roger Corman. Dick Miller, Susan Cabot,

Richard Devon, Robert Shayne, Eric Sinclair. Ruthless combination of THE DAY THE EARTH STOOD STILL and KRONOS has unseen aliens warning Earth to cease their space exploration, brainwashing scientist Devon to make sure it's done. The day after the U.S. Explorer satellite went up, Corman told a studio he could have a film ready in two months . . . and he did. Understandably not so hot, but any movie with Dick Miller as a heroic scientist can't be *all* bad.

War of the Wildcats (1943) **102m.** **½ D: Albert S. Rogell. John Wayne, Martha Scott, Albert Dekker, Gabby Hayes, Marjorie Rambeau, Sidney Blackmer, Dale Evans. Slugger Wayne brooks no nonsense in this oil-drilling yarn; good action, obligatory romance. Originally titled IN OLD OKLAHOMA.▼

War of the Worlds (1953) **C-85m.** ***½ ✓ D: Byron Haskin. Gene Barry, Les Tremayne, Ann Robinson, Robert Cornthwaite, Henry Brandon, Jack Kruschen; narrated by Sir Cedric Hardwicke. Vivid, frightening adaptation of H. G. Wells' story about a Martian invasion. Dramatically sound and filled with dazzling, Oscar-winning special effects; superior sci-fi, produced by George Pal. Later a TV series.▼

War of the Zombies (1965-Italian) **C-85m.** ** D: Giuseppe Vari. John Drew Barrymore, Susy Anderson, Ettore Manni, Ida Galli. Standard European spectacle plot: Rome sends best legionnaire to quell disturbance in Eastern province in clutches of mad priest (Barrymore). Production values somewhat better than usual. Also known as NIGHT STAR GODDESS OF ELECTRA.

War Paint (1953) **C-89m.** **½ D: Lesley Selander. Robert Stack, Joan Taylor, Charles McGraw, Peter Graves. Action-packed film of U. S. cavalry detachment overcoming danger and villainous attempts to prevent delivery of peace treaty to an Indian chief.

War Party (1989) **C-97m.** ** D: Franc Roddam. Billy Wirth, Kevin Dillon, Tim Sampson, Jimmie Ray Weeks, M. Emmet Walsh, Dennis Banks, Kevyn Major Howard, Bill McKinney. Reenactment of a hundred-year-old battle between Blackfoot Indian tribe and U.S. Cavalry turns into the real thing once again when one white youth brings a loaded gun to the festivities. Basically an excuse for a cowboys and Indians movie, this intriguing premise becomes just another botched opportunity for Hollywood to shed light on the problems of the American Indian.▼

Warpath (1951) **C-95m.** **½ D: Byron Haskin. Edmond O'Brien, Dean Jagger, Forrest Tucker, Harry Carey, Jr., Wallace Ford, Polly Bergen. Nifty action Western with O'Brien hunting down outlaws who killed his girlfriend; an Indian attack is thrown in for good measure.

Warrior and the Slave Girl, The (1958-Italian) **C-84m.** ** D: Vittorio Cottafavi. Ettore Manni, Georges Marchal, Gianna Maria Canale, Rafael Calvo. Unsubtle costumer set in ancient Armenia, with Canale the evil princess, subdued by Roman Manni; usual amount of swordplay.

Warrior and the Sorceress, The (1984) **C-76m.** *½ D: John Broderick. David Carradine, Luke Askew, Maria Socas, Anthony DeLongis, Harry Townes, William Marin. Copycat version of both A FISTFUL OF DOLLARS and YOJIMBO transplants story of a lone fighter playing both ends against the middle to a mythical kingdom on a planet circling two suns. Lovely leading lady Socas plays the entire film topless; you also might note the very convincing makeup effects on a pretty dancer who has four breasts. ▼

Warrior Empress, The (1960-Italian) **C-87m.** ** D: Pietro Francisci. Kerwin Mathews, Tina Louise, Riccardo Garrone, Antonio Batistella, Enrico Maria Salerno. Senseless mixture of fantasy and adventure with Phaon (Mathews) falling in love with Sappho (Louise), overcoming treacherous Salerno.

Warrior Queen (1987) **C-69m.** BOMB D: Chuck Vincent. Sybil Danning, Donald Pleasence, Richard Hill, Josephine Jacqueline Jones, Tally Chanel, Stasia Micula (Samantha Fox), Suzanna Smith. Ridiculous made-in-Italy exploitation film emphasizes sex in recreating the decadence of ancient Pompeii. Pleasence is at his hammy worst as the mayor whose wife (porn star Fox) has eyes for other men. Relies extensively on footage from the '60 LAST DAYS OF POMPEII for an apocalyptic climax. Later released on videocassette in an unrated version running 79m., with several sex scenes restored. ▼

Warriors, The (1955-British) **C-85m.** **½ D: Henry Levin. Errol Flynn, Joanne Dru, Peter Finch, Patrick Holt, Yvonne Furneaux, Michael Hordern, Christopher Lee. Flynn's final swashbuckler casts him as British prince protecting French conquests (and lovely Dru) from attacks by Finch and his supporters. Well-made but awfully familiar. British title: THE DARK AVENGER.▼

Warriors, The (1979) **C-90m.** *** D: Walter Hill. Michael Beck, James Remar, Thomas Waites, Dorsey Wright, Brian Tyler, Deborah Van Valkenburgh. Comic book plot about N.Y.C. gang crossing rival turfs to get "home" is redeemed by lightning pace, tough action sequences, creative use of color. Notorious for the number of violent incidents it allegedly instigated, but worthy of some respect. Script by Hill and David Shaber; photographed by Andrew Laszlo.▼

Warriors Five (1962-Italian) **84m.** **½ D: Leopoldo Savona. Jack Palance, Giovanna Ralli, Serge Reggiani, Folco Lulli. Moderate actioner set in WW2 Italy with Palance behind enemy lines trying to combat the Germans.

Warriors of the Wasteland (1983-Italian) **C-87m.** *½ D: Enzo G. Castellari. Timothy Brent (Giancarlo Prete), Fred Williamson, Anna Kanakis, Venantino Venantini, Enzo G. Castellari. Two ROAD WARRIOR types try to protect innocent people from a wandering band of bad guys. 21st-century sci-fi on a 19th-century budget.▼

War Wagon, The (1967) **C-101m.** *** D: Burt Kennedy. John Wayne, Kirk Douglas, Howard Keel, Robert Walker, Keenan Wynn, Bruce Cabot, Joanna Barnes, Bruce Dern. Amiable tongue-in-cheek Western, with ex-con Wayne seeking to settle a score with villainous Cabot by plundering his gold-laden stagecoach—with the help of Douglas (who's been hired to kill Wayne on Cabot's behalf) and a motley band of associates. Keel is hilarious as wisecracking Indian.▼

Washington Affair, The (1977) **C-86m.** ** D: Victor Stoloff. Barry Sullivan, Carol Lynley, Tom Selleck, Arlene Banas, Kathleen Gaffney. Claustrophobic suspense film (shot almost entirely in just two rooms) has Sullivan as a corrupt businessman who uses a hidden camera and women to entrap government engineer Selleck into getting him an aircraft contract. Unreleased theatrically, it surfaced after Selleck's TV series *Magnum, P.I.,* became a hit. Remake of same director's INTIMACY.▼

Washington B.C. SEE: Hail to the Chief▼

Washington Merry-Go-Round (1932) **79m.** **½ D: James Cruze. Lee Tracy, Constance Cummings, Walter Connolly, Alan Dinehart, Jane Darwell. Dry run for MR. SMITH GOES TO WASHINGTON has idealistic young congressman Tracy out to do good for his Depression-ravaged constituents—only to find it ain't that easy, especially when he opposes an "important" appropriations bill. Remains surprisingly relevant today, with engaging performances and strong feel for the political arena, but peters out after great first half.

Washington Mistress (1982) **C-100m.** TVM D: Peter Levin. Lucie Arnaz, Richard Jordan, Tony Bill, Pat Hingle, Tarah Nutter, Charles Levin. Sudsy romantic drama about a bright, ambitious congressional aide who falls for a charming, married lobbyist and has a long, not-so-secret affair with him. Coldly played by the stars. Average.▼

Washington Story (1952) **81m.** ** D: Robert Pirosh. Van Johnson, Patricia Neal, Louis Calhern, Sidney Blackmer, Elizabeth Patterson. Newspaperwoman Neal assigned to harass Congress selects young

Congressman Johnson as her target; naturally, she falls in love with him. Romantic angle is better than political one—but neither is particularly interesting.

Wasn't That a Time! SEE: **Weavers, The: Wasn't That a Time!▼**

Wasp Woman, The (1960) **66m. **½ D: Roger Corman. Susan Cabot, Fred (Anthony) Eisley, Barboura Morris, Michael Marks, William Roerick, Frank Gerstle, Frank Wolff. Enjoyable Corman cheapie about cosmetics magnate Cabot, fearful of aging, using royal jelly from wasps to become young and beautiful. She also periodically turns into a wasp-monster that must kill. Minor camp classic; an unauthorized semi-remake, EVIL SPAWN, was made for video in 1987.▼

Watched! (1972) **C-95m. *½ D: John Parsons. Stacy Keach, Harris Yulin, Brigid Polk, Denver John Collins. Keach plays a former government lawyer who went underground, befriending dopers. Yulin is chief of the narcotics squad, using lots of surveillance filming in his war of wills with Keach. Haphazard structure of this low-budget film relies upon Keach's nearly one-man show, expressing the personal transition out of 1960s culture. ▼

Watcher in the Woods, The (1980) **C-84m. **½ D: John Hough. Bette Davis, Carroll Baker, David McCallum, Lynn-Holly Johnson, Kyle Richards, Ian Bannen, Richard Pasco. All-American family takes over British country house, where young Johnson is tormented by the spirit of owner Davis's long-missing daughter. Not bad, with atmospheric photography by Alan Hume, but awfully familiar stuff by now. First shown with an abrupt conclusion, then with special effects sequence that made things worse, then reworked again and improved (by Vincent McEveety)—for 1981 rerelease! Original running time 100m.▼

Watch It, Sailor! (1961-British) **81m. ** D: Wolf Rilla. Dennis Price, Liz Fraser, Irene Handl, Graham Stark, Marjorie Rhodes. Mildly amusing stage farce adapted to screen, with Price managing to outdo Fraser's mother (Rhodes), getting to the church on time.

✓ **Watch on the Rhine** (1943) **114m. ***½ D: Herman Shumlin. Bette Davis, Paul Lukas, Geraldine Fitzgerald, Lucile Watson, Beulah Bondi, George Coulouris, Donald Woods, Henry Daniell. Fine filmization of Lillian Hellman's timely WW2 play of German Lukas and wife Davis pursued and harried by Nazi agents in Washington. Lukas gives the performance of his career, which won him Academy Award; Bette somewhat overshadowed. Script by Dashiell Hammett.▼

Watch the Birdie (1950) **70m. **½ D: Jack Donohue. Red Skelton, Arlene Dahl, Ann Miller, Leon Ames, Pamela Britton,

Richard Rober, Mike Mazurki. Average Skelton comedy features him as photographer, silly father and grandfather. Rest of cast is also good with routine material, reworking of Buster Keaton's THE CAMERAMAN.

Watch Your Stern (1960-British) **88m. ** D: Gerald Thomas. Kenneth Connor, Eric Barker, Leslie Phillips, Joan Sims, Hattie Jacques. Amusing, obvious shenanigans on the seas, with Connor impersonating a scientist sent to perfect a Naval torpedo weapon.

Water (1985-British) **C-95m. BOMB D: Dick Clement. Michael Caine, Brenda Vaccaro, Leonard Rossiter, Valerie Perrine, Jimmie Walker, Billy Connelly, Dennis Dugan. Inept comedy of errors concerns a Caribbean British colony where the local governor (Caine) juggles greedy U.S. oil interests, a comical rebellion, and other assorted looneys as a valuable mineral water is discovered. Rossiter is funny as a diplomat sent from England to calm the situation, and Maureen Lipman is terrific in a nasty caricature of Prime Minister Thatcher, but Vaccaro is miscast in a strained Carmen Miranda impression. Pointless cameos by Dick Shawn, Fred Gwynne, film's executive producer George Harrison, Eric Clapton, and Ringo Starr.▼

Water Babies, The (1978-British-Polish) **C-92m. ** D: Lionel Jeffries. James Mason, Billie Whitelaw, Bernard Cribbins, Joan Greenwood, David Tomlinson, Tommy Pender, Samantha Gates. Combination live action and animated film for children, framing its fairy-tale undersea adventure with virtually unrelated story and characters in Dickensian London. Inoffensive for children, but downright boring at times.▼

Waterfront (1944) **66m. *½ D: Steve Sekely. John Carradine, J. Carrol Naish, Maris Wrixon, Edwin Maxwell, Terry Frost. Low-grade espionage tale of Nazi agents Carradine and Naish murdering and blackmailing in WW2 San Francisco.▼

Waterhole #3 (1967) **C-95m. **½ D: ✓ William Graham. James Coburn, Carroll O'Connor, Margaret Blye, Claude Akins, Bruce Dern, Joan Blondell, James Whitmore. Amusing Western comedy of three confederates who rob Army of a fortune in gold and bury it in desert waterhole. Produced by Blake Edwards.▼

Waterloo (1971-Italian-Russian) **C-123m. ** D: Sergei Bondarchuk. Rod Steiger, Christopher Plummer, Orson Welles, Jack Hawkins, Virginia McKenna, Dan O'Herlihy, Michael Wilding. Cumbersome historical film centering around Napoleon's defeat at Waterloo. Tremendous action but muddled plot. The original Russian version ran nearly four hours.

Waterloo Bridge (1940) **103m. ***½ D: Mervyn LeRoy. Vivien Leigh, Robert Taylor, Lucile Watson, Virginia Field, Maria Ouspenskaya, C. Aubrey Smith. Sentimental love story, well-acted, of soldier and ballet dancer meeting during London air raid, falling in love instantly. Cleaned-up version of the Robert E. Sherwood play, with beautiful performance by lovely Leigh. Screenplay by S.N. Behrman, Hans Rameau, and George Froeschel. First filmed in 1931, remade as GABY.▼

Waterloo Road (1944-British) 76m. ***
D: Sidney Gilliat. John Mills, Stewart Granger, Alastair Sim, Joy Shelton, Beatrice Varley, Alison Leggatt, Jean Kent. Enjoyable wartime drama about soldier who goes AWOL when he learns his wife has been seeing another man. Evocative of its period, film also benefits from spry touches of humor.

Watermelon Man (1970) C-97m. **½
D: Melvin Van Peebles. Godfrey Cambridge, Estelle Parsons, Howard Caine, D'Urville Martin, Kay Kimberly, Mantan Moreland. Provocative serio-comedy about bigoted white man who suddenly turns black and sees his life go upside down. Worth seeing, although Herman Raucher's one-joke script makes its point and then has nowhere to go. TV print edited to 91m.▼

Watership Down (1978-British) C-92m.
***½ D: Martin Rosen. Voices of John Hurt, Richard Briers, Ralph Richardson, Denholm Elliott, Harry Andrews, Joss Ackland; narrated by Michael Hordern. Stylish animated-cartoon from Richard Adams' best-selling book about a family of rabbits seeking a safe place to live, encountering many perils along the way; not a kiddie film by any means. Bird character voiced by Zero Mostel provides only comic relief. Excellent score by Angela Morley and Malcolm Williamson. One of the best non-Disney animated features ever made.▼

Watts Monster, The SEE: **Dr. Black, Mr. Hyde**▼

Wattstax (1973) C-98m. ***½ D: Mel Stuart. Isaac Hayes, The Staple Singers, Luther Ingram, Rev. Jesse Jackson, Richard Pryor, Rufus Thomas, Carla Thomas, Bar-Kays, Kim Weston, The Emotions, Johnnie Taylor. Exciting, vibrant documentary with music, centering around L.A. community of Watts, and the black experience. Pryor's monologues are exceptionally good.

Watusi (1959) C-85m. **½ D: Kurt Neumann. George Montgomery, Taina Elg, David Farrar, Rex Ingram, Dan Seymour. MGM fabricated a sequel to KING SOLOMON'S MINES to utilize leftover footage from its 1950 version of H. Rider Haggard yarn.

Wavelength (1983) C-87m. ** D: Mike Gray. Robert Carradine, Cherie Currie, Keenan Wynn. Cheap science-fiction film

about aliens on Earth and a government coverup steals liberally from earlier pictures for ideas. Best thing is a varied musical score by Tangerine Dream. ▼

Waxwork (1988) C-97m. *½ D: Anthony Hickox. Zach Galligan, Deborah Foreman, David Warner, Michelle Johnson, Patrick Macnee, Dana Ashbrook, Miles O'Keeffe, Charles McCaughan, J. Kenneth Campbell, John Rhys-Davies. Garbled, peculiar comedy-horror thriller set in evil magician's waxworks exhibit, with apocalyptic battle between humans and most of the famous monsters of history—Dracula (O'Keeffe), Frankenstein, the Mummy, a werewolf, Phantom of the Opera, Audrey II, etc. Characters are unpleasant, and film lacks irony, insight, and wit. One segment is in black and white.▼

Way Ahead, The (1944-British) 91m.
***½ D: Carol Reed. David Niven, Stanley Holloway, James Donald, John Laurie, Leslie Dwyer, Hugh Burden, Jimmy Hanley, Billy Hartnell, Raymond Huntley, Reginald Tate, Leo Genn, Penelope Dudley Ward, Renée Asherson, Raymond Lovell, Peter Ustinov, Trevor Howard. Exhilarating wartime British film showing how disparate civilians come to work together as a fighting unit; full of spirit and charm, with an outstanding cast, and fine script by Eric Ambler and Peter Ustinov. Film debut of Trevor Howard. Originally released in the U.S. in a shortened, more serious version called THE IMMORTAL BATTALION (with an introduction by journalist Quentin Reynolds). Most American prints are still short; original British running time 116m.▼

Way Down East (1920) 119m. *** D: D. W. Griffith. Lillian Gish, Richard Barthelmess, Lowell Sherman, Burr McItosh, Kate Bruce, Mary Hay, Creighton Hale. The ultimate stage melodrama—with a city slicker despoiling the innocence of a virginal heroine, who then must pay the price. Executed with conviction by Griffith and a fine cast, building up to famous climax with Gish drifting away on the ice floes. Often shown in shorter versions; restored to 148m. by the Museum of Modern Art in 1985. ▼

Way Down East (1935) 80m. *½ D: Henry King. Rochelle Hudson, Henry Fonda, Russell Simpson, Slim Summerville, Spring Byington, Edward Trevor. Romantic melodrama set in New England was hokey as a 1920 silent; the remake hasn't improved with age. Ridiculous script conquers all.

Way Down South (1939) 61m. **½ D: Bernard Vorhaus. Bobby Breen, Alan Mowbray, Clarence Muse, Ralph Morgan, Edwin Maxwell, Steffi Duna, Sally Blane, Robert Greig, Charles Middleton, Hall Johnson Choir. Hokey but fascinating musical curio (written by Muse and Langston Hughes!), set in the pre-Civil War South. Boy soprano Breen is the young master of a plantation, whose "happy" slaves are scheduled for sale by crooked lawyer Maxwell.

Way for a Sailor (1930) 83m. ** D: Sam Wood. John Gilbert, Wallace Beery, Leila Hyams, Jim Tully, Polly Moran. Early talkie with silent-star Gilbert as devoted sailor who loses girl for the sea. Mostly a curio for film buffs.

Way of a Gaucho (1952) C-91m. ** D: Jacques Tourneur. Gene Tierney, Rory Calhoun, Richard Boone, Hugh Marlowe, Everett Sloane. Soaper set in 1870's Argentina of Tierney and Calhoun trying to make a go of life on the Pampas.

Way of All Flesh, The (1940) 86m. ** D: Louis King. Akim Tamiroff, Gladys George, William Henry, Muriel Angelus, Berton Churchill, Roger Imhof. Overly sentimental tale of poor immigrant who is "taken" and must pay for his error; George is superlative as always. Remake of Emil Jannings silent film.

Way of Youth, The (1959-French) 81m. ** D: Michel Boisrond. Francoise Arnoul, Lino Ventura, Bourvil, Alain Delon. Obvious sensuality fails to arouse sufficient interest in contrived story of adultery and ill-gotten gains.

Way Out, The (1956-British) 90m. ** D: Montgomery Tully. Gene Nelson, Mona Freeman, John Bentley, Michael Goodliffe, Sydney Tafler. Lumbering story of husband who committed a crime going on the lam with wife.

Way Out West (1937) 65m. ***½ D: James W. Horne. Stan Laurel, Oliver Hardy, Sharon Lynn, James Finlayson, Rosina Lawrence, Stanley Fields, Vivien Oakland. Stan and Ollie are sent to deliver mine deed to daughter of late prospector, but crooked Finlayson leads them to wrong girl. One of their best features; moves well without resorting to needless romantic subplot. Another bonus: some charming musical interludes, and a wonderful soft-shoe dance. Also shown in computer-colored version.▼

Way to Love, The (1933) 80m. *** D: Norman Taurog. Maurice Chevalier, Ann Dvorak, Edward Everett Horton, Minna Gombell, Nydia Westman, Douglass Dumbrille, John Miljan. Chevalier falls in love with Dvorak, who works on the wrong end of a knife throwing act, in this pleasant romantic comedy with music; songs include title tune, "I'm A Lover of Paris."

Way to the Gold, The (1957) 94m. ** D: Robert D. Webb. Jeffrey Hunter, Sheree North, Barry Sullivan, Neville Brand, Walter Brennan. Meandering buried-loot-hunt story.

Way to the Stars, The (1945-British) 109m. **** D: Anthony Asquith. John Mills, Michael Redgrave, Douglass Montgomery, Rosamund John, Stanley Holloway, Trevor Howard, Felix Aylmer, Bonar Colleano. Excellent drama about a British airfield and the men stationed there, focusing mainly on personal relationships in wartime. Jean Simmons appears briefly as a singer. Script by Terence Rattigan and Anatole de Grunwald. Originally released in U.S. as JOHNNY IN THE CLOUDS, with a prologue set after the end of WW2.

Wayward Bus, The (1957) 89m. ** D: Victor Vicas. Joan Collins, Jayne Mansfield, Dan Dailey, Rick Jason. Low-brow version of John Steinbeck novel about passengers on bus in California, with trite interpretation of their interaction.

Wayward Girl, The (1957) 71m. *½ D: Lesley Selander. Marcia Henderson, Peter Walker, Whit Bissell, Ray Teal. Turgid nonsense about mother and stepdaughter vying for same lover, leading to murder.

Wayward Girl, The (1959-Norwegian) 91m. **½ D: Edith Carlmar. Liv Ullmann, Atle Merton, Rolf Soder, Tore Foss, Nana Stenersen. Moralistic romance tale of young lovers who seek refuge on a deserted farm, becoming involved with the returning owner.

Wayward Wife, The (1955-Italian) 91m. ** D: Mario Soldati. Gina Lollobrigida, Gabriele Ferzetti, Franco Interlenghi, Renato Baldini. Unimaginative, predictable film of blackmail. Lollobrigida, girl with a past, finds her marriage threatened.

Way . . . Way Out (1966) C-106m. BOMB D: Gordon Douglas. Jerry Lewis, Connie Stevens, Robert Morley, Dennis Weaver, Howard Morris, Brian Keith, Dick Shawn, Anita Ekberg, James Brolin. One of Jerry's worst. Plot concerns comedian's trip to the moon with sexy astronaut Stevens; hopefully they took the film's negative along.

Way West, The (1967) C-122m. *½ D: Andrew V. McLaglen. Kirk Douglas, Robert Mitchum, Richard Widmark, Lola Albright, Michael Witney, Stubby Kaye, Sally Field, Jack Elam. Despite cast, this version of A. B. Guthrie, Jr.'s epic novel fails completely. McLaglen's lackluster direction partially to blame, but big problem is script, which may hold all-time record for undeveloped sub-plots. Mitchum is good through it all; Sally Field's first feature.▼

Way We Were, The (1973) C-118m. *** D: Sydney Pollack. Barbra Streisand, Robert Redford, Bradford Dillman, Murray Hamilton, Patrick O'Neal, Viveca Lindfors, Lois Chiles, Allyn Ann McLerie, Herb Edelman, James Woods, Sally Kirkland. First-class love story about political activist Streisand and her opposite, Waspish Joe College-type Redford, from late 30s to early 50s. Prerelease cutting excised meatiest sequence on blacklist era in Hollywood, alas, leaving Hamilton and Lindfors with bit parts, and some confusion in last portion of plot. Still quite good, with literate Arthur Laurents script from his own novel. Marvin Hamlisch's score and title song (lyrics by Alan and Marilyn Bergman) won Oscars.▼

W.C. Fields and Me (1976) **C-111m.** *** D: Arthur Hiller. Rod Steiger, Valerie Perrine, John Marley, Jack Cassidy, Paul Stewart, Bernadette Peters, Billy Barty. Story of comedian's romance with Carlotta Monti is a cut above most Hollywood bios, thanks to Steiger's excellent performance, authentic atmosphere, good cast. Has little relation to the truth, but still entertaining.

Weak and the Wicked, The (1953-British) **81m.** **½ D: J. Lee Thompson. Glynis Johns, John Gregson, Diana Dors, Jane Hylton. Frank study of women's prison life, focusing on their rehabilitation.

Weaker Sex, The (1948-British) **89m.** ** D: Roy (Ward) Baker. Ursula Jeans, Cecil Parker, Joan Hopkins, Derek Bond, Thora Hird, Bill Owen. Jeans is staunch English housewife showing her patriotic zest during WW2; modest domestic comedy.

We All Loved Each Other So Much (1977-Italian) **C-124m.** ***½ D: Ettore Scola. Nino Manfredi, Vittorio Gassman, Aldo Fabrizi, Stefania Sandrelli, Stefano Satta Flores, Giovanna Ralli. Spirited, wistful comedy of three friends (Gassman, Manfredi, Satta Flores) who each love Sandrelli over the course of three decades. The latter, an actress, plays a bit role in LA DOLCE VITA; the shooting of Anita Ekberg's Trevi Fountain scene is recreated, complete with Mastroianni and Fellini! A loving homage to Fellini, De Sica, and post-war Italian cinema.▼

Weapon, The (1956-British) **81m.** **½ D: Val Guest. Steve Cochran, Lizabeth Scott, George Cole, Herbert Marshall, Nicole Maurey, Jon Whiteley. Minor but trim little story of youngster who accidentally shoots his pal and runs away.

We Are All Murderers (1957-French) **113m.** *** D: André Cayatte. Marcel Mouloudji, Raymond Pellegrin, Louis Seigner, Antoine Balpetre. Most effective social plea against capital punishment, focusing on youth bred to kill in war involved in murder after the armistice.

We Are in the Navy Now (1962-British) **C-102m.** ** D: Wendy Toye. Kenneth More, Lloyd Nolan, Joan O'Brien, Mischa Auer. Farcical service comedy without wit or slapstick to see it through. Original title: WE JOINED THE NAVY.

We Are Not Alone (1939) **112m.** ***½ D: Edmund Goulding. Paul Muni, Jane Bryan, Flora Robson, Una O'Connor, Henry Daniell, Cecil Kellaway, Alan Napier. Superb acting and overall production make tale of man in love with governess (Bryan), accused of murdering his wife (Robson) a must. From novel by James Hilton, coscripted by the author.

We Are the Children (1987) **C-100m.** TVM D: Robert M. Young. Ted Danson, Ally Sheedy, Judith Ivey, Zia Mohyeddin. Ethiopian famine serves as the backdrop for this mediocre drama intertwining the lives of an American TV journalist, an idealistic doctor who runs a local clinic, and a nun/nurse who's been living in Africa for many years. Danson coproduced. Average.

Weavers, The: Wasn't That a Time! (1982) **C-78m.** **** D: Jim Brown. Lee Hays, Pete Seeger, Fred Hellerman, Ronnie Gilbert. Simply wonderful documentary about a reunion of the much-loved folk-singing quartet of the 1940s and 50s, climaxed by footage of their Carnegie Hall concert. Irresistible film built on the foundation of Lee Hays' wit and indomitable spirit.▼

Web, The (1947) **87m.** *** D: Michael Gordon. Ella Raines, Edmond O'Brien, William Bendix, Vincent Price, Maria Palmer. Tough bodyguard engages in murder, then finds himself a patsy for boss' schemes. Exciting melodrama, one of O'Brien's best early roles.

Web of Evidence (1959 British) **88m.** **½ D: Jack Cardiff. Van Johnson, Vera Miles, Emlyn Williams, Bernard Lee, Jean Kent, Ralph Truman, Leo McKern. Sincere drama of Johnson in England finding clues to prove his father innocent of long-standing murder sentence. Original British title: BEYOND THIS PLACE.

Web of Fear (1963-French) **92m.** **½ D: Francois Villiers. Michele Morgan, Dany Saval, Claude Rich, George Rigaud. Morgan is music teacher set up as patsy by Saval and Rich in this moody drama of passion and murder.

Web of Passion (1959-French) **C-101m.** **½ D: Claude Chabrol. Madeleine Robinson, Antonella Lualdi, Jean-Paul Belmondo, Jacques Dacqmine. Non-conformist Belmondo insinuates himself into a family's graces, delighting in breaking down their standards, with murders resulting. Talky but intriguing drama. Retitled: LEDA.

Web of the Spider (1970-Italian) **C-94m.** ** D: Anthony Dawson (Antonio Margheriti). Anthony Franciosa, Michele Mercier, Peter Carsten, Karen Field, Silvano Tranquilli. Overly familiar thriller about the skeptic who accepts a wager that he cannot survive the night alone in a haunted house. Franciosa and associates try vainly to give it a fresh twist but are upstaged by shrieking spirits, howling winds, and assorted creepy crawlies. Previously made by the same director as CASTLE OF TERROR.▼

Wedding, A (1978) **C-125m.** **½ D: Robert Altman. Carol Burnett, Desi Arnaz,

Jr., Amy Stryker, Vittorio Gassman, Geraldine Chaplin, Mia Farrow, Paul Dooley, Lillian Gish, Lauren Hutton, John Cromwell, Pat McCormick, Howard Duff, Pam Dawber, Dennis Christopher, Peggy Ann Garner, Nina Van Pallandt, Dina Merrill, John Considine, Viveca Lindfors. Uneven, unfocused look at family intrigues surrounding a nouveau riche wedding; some amusing moments and pointed characterizations, but picture doesn't quite gel.▼

Wedding in Blood (1973-French-Italian) C-98m. **½ D: Claude Chabrol. Stephane Audran, Michel Piccoli, Claude Pieplu, Clothilde Joano, Eliana de Santis. Piccoli and Audran, each married to another, are having an affair. How soon will they murder their spouses? And get caught? Medium Chabrol.▼

Wedding in White (1972-Canadian) C-106m. *** D: William Fruet. Donald Pleasence, Carol Kane, Doris Petrie, Doug McGrath, Leo Phillips. Fine performances in sad tale of girl impregnated by brother's drunken pal during WW2 and her father's efforts to save the family's honor.▼

Wedding March, The (1928) 113m. **** D: Erich von Stroheim. Erich von Stroheim, Fay Wray, ZaSu Pitts, George Fawcett, Maude George, George Nicholls, Cesare Gravina. A roguish Viennese prince (played to perfection by von Stroheim) agrees to marry for money and position to help his family, then falls in love with a poor but beautiful girl. A masterpiece, blending romance and irony, with an unforgettable finale . . . though what we see is just the first half of the film von Stroheim completed (the second part no longer exists). One sequence in two-color Technicolor.▼

Wedding Night, The (1935) 84m. **½ D: King Vidor. Gary Cooper, Anna Sten, Ralph Bellamy, Walter Brennan, Helen Vinson, Sig Ruman. Study of romance and idealism; unbelievable love yarn but entertaining. Producer Samuel Goldwyn's third and final attempt to make Anna Sten a new Garbo.

Wedding Party, The (1969) 92m. *½ D: Cynthia Munroe, Brian De Palma, Wilford Leach. Jill Clayburgh, Charles Pfluger, Valda Satterfield, Raymond McNally, Jennifer Salt, John Braswell, Judy Thomas, Robert De Niro, William Finley. Talky, corny, boring comic oddity detailing events preceding marriage of Clayburgh and Pfluger; the bride and her family are boorish, and the groom grows ever more reluctant. Self-consciously directed; of interest only for De Palma's participation, and initial screen appearances of Clayburgh and De Niro (spelled "DeNero" in the credits). Shot in 1963, and barely released.▼

Weddings and Babies (1960) 81m. **½ D: Morris Engel. Viveca Lindfors, John Myhers. Charming love story between photographer and model, shot on-location in N.Y.C. modest but engaging production.

We Dive at Dawn (1943-British) 98m. *** D: Anthony Asquith. John Mills, Eric Portman, Niall MacGinnis, Reginald Purdell, Louis Bradfield, Ronald Millar. First-rate WW2 submarine saga, concentrating on personalities of men in the crew as much as on assignment to sink German battleship. Nicely understated drama.▼

Weeds (1987) C-115m. **½ D: John Hancock. Nick Nolte, Rita Taggart, Lane Smith, William Forsythe, John Toles-Bey, Joe Mantegna, Ernie Hudson, Anne Ramsey, Charlie Rich. San Quentin lifer/aspiring playwright is near-miraculously sprung from prison when a newspaper critic lobbies for his release, and goes on to form a "Barbed Wire Theatre" acting troupe of ex-cons. Odd, original mix of comedy and drama based on Rick Cluchey's real-life experiences with the San Quentin Drama Group. Earnest and well acted but never quite gels.▼

Wee Geordie (1956-British) C-93m. ***½ D: Frank Launder. Bill Travers, Alastair Sim, Norah Gorsen, Molly Urquhart, Francis De Wolff. Flavorful romp with Travers a Scottish hammer thrower who goes to the Olympics. Despite predictable sight gags and romance, film makes one relish each situation.

Weekend (1967-French-Italian) C-103m. ***½ D: Jean-Luc Godard. Mireille Darc, Jean Yanne, Jean-Pierre Kalfon, Valerie Lagrange, Jean-Pierre Leaud. Mind-expanding anti-Western diatribe about one woman's road to guerrillahood is among Godard's more fully realized works, with a long traffic-jam sequence that is justifiably regarded as one of the great set pieces in screen history. An essential 60s time-capsule entry.

Weekend at Bernie's (1989) C-97m. **½ D: Ted Kotcheff. Andrew McCarthy, Jonathan Silverman, Catherine Mary Stewart, Terry Kiser, Don Calfa, Louis Giambalvo. Two young hustlers, far down on the corporate ladder, win an invitation to their boss' sumptuous beach house for the weekend . . . only to find him dead upon arrival. Slim but agreeably silly farce, written by Robert Klane.▼

Weekend at Dunkirk (1965-France-Italy) C-101m. ** D: Henri Verneuil. Jean-Paul Belmondo, Catherine Spaak, Georges Geret, Jean-Pierre Marielle, Pierre Mondy. Dull war film, based on well-known French novel, about four French soldiers on the Dunkirk Beach around evacuation time early in WW2.

Weekend at the Waldorf (1945) 130m. *** D: Robert Z. Leonard. Ginger Rogers, Lana Turner, Walter Pidgeon, Van Johnson, Edward Arnold, Phyllis Thaxter, Keenan Wynn, Robert Benchley, Leon Ames, Porter Hall, George Zucco, Xavier Cugat. Glossy remake of GRAND HOTEL with Rogers and Pidgeon outshining others; very superficial, but entertaining.

Weekend for Three (1941) 61m. ** D: Irving Reis. Dennis O'Keefe, Jane Wyatt, Philip Reed, ZaSu Pitts, Edward Everett Horton, Franklin Pangborn, Hans Conried. Playboy Reed stops by to visit newlyweds Wyatt and O'Keefe—and is in no hurry to leave. Considering premise, cast, and writers (Dorothy Parker and Alan Campbell, from a Budd Schulberg story), it's astonishing this isn't better than it is.

Week-end In Havana (1941) C-80m. **½ D: Walter Lang. Alice Faye, Carmen Miranda, John Payne, Cesar Romero, Cobina Wright, Jr., George Barbier, Leonid Kinskey, Sheldon Leonard, Billy Gilbert. Colorful musical has Faye landing in Havana, torn between Payne and Romero; Miranda lends peppery support.

Week-end Marriage (1932) 66m. ** D: Thornton Freeland. Loretta Young, Norman Foster, Aline MacMahon, George Brent, Vivienne Osborne, Roscoe Karns. Comedy courtship leads to drama of moneyhungry husband after marriage; nothing special.

Weekend Nun, The (1972) C-78m. TVM D: Jeannot Szwarc. Joanna Pettet, Vic Morrow, Ann Sothern, James Gregory, Beverly Garland, Barbara Werle, Kay Lenz, Marion Ross. Sister Damian (Pettet) innocently assumes she can work as probation officer and remain true to her vows, but experiences on job and with realistic partner Jardine (Morrow), culminating in tragic accident, make her realize she must make major vocational decision. Well-conceived, smoothly executed morality play, complete with fine performances by entire cast. Ken Trevey's script is based on fact. Above average.

Weekend of Terror (1970) C-73m. TVM D: Jud Taylor. Robert Conrad, Lee Majors, Lois Nettleton, Carol Lynley, Jane Wyatt, Kevin Hagen. Three nuns taken hostage by kidnappers searching for girl who resembles original hostage killed accidentally. If you can get by embarrassing dialogue, fair suspense with predictable resolution. Average.

Weekend Pass (1984) C-92m. BOMB D: Lawrence Bassoff. Patrick Hauser, D. W. Brown, Chip McAllister, Peter Ellenstein, Hilary Shapiro, Pamela G. Kay. Intolerable drive-in comedy lifts its premise from ON THE TOWN: having completed basic training, four stereotypical naval recruits set off for 72 "wild" hours in L.A. 92 minutes of mine sweeping would be more entertaining.▼

Weekend War (1988) C-100m. TVM D: Steven Hilliard Stern. Stephen Collins, Daniel Stern, Evan Mirand, Michael Beach, Scott Paulin, James Tolkan, Charles Haid. A company of weekend warriors finds itself caught up in real guerrilla warfare while pulling two weeks of National Guard

duty in Honduras. Cogent TV drama, the first involving the Central American conflict, makes its points while cribbing from both THE BRIDGE ON THE RIVER KWAI and PLATOON. Average.

Weekend Warriors (1986) C-85m. *½ D: Bert Convy. Chris Lemmon, Vic Tayback, Lloyd Bridges, Graham Jarvis, Daniel Greene, Marty Cohen, Brian Bradley. Low-level, sloppily made comedy about some goof-offs who join the National Guard, and their subsequent hijinks. Convy's debut as director.▼

Weekend with Father (1951) 83m. **½ D: Douglas Sirk. Van Heflin, Patricia Neal, Virginia Field, Gigi Perreau, Richard Denning. Pleasant frou-frou of widow and widower courting despite their children's interference.

Week's Vacation, A (1980-French) C-102m. *** D: Bertrand Tavernier. Nathalie Baye, Gerard Lanvin, Michel Galabru, Philippe Noiret, Philippe Leotard. Subtle drama of schoolteacher Baye briefly escaping her problems by visiting her parents in Lyons. Sensitive depiction of inter-personal relations is director Tavernier's strong suit. Colorful widescreen photography will suffer on TV.

Wee Willie Winkie (1937) 99m. *** D: John Ford. Shirley Temple, Victor McLaglen, C. Aubrey Smith, June Lang, Michael Whalen, Cesar Romero, Constance Collier, Douglas Scott. Shirley and her widowed mother come to live at a British Army outpost in India, where the moppet works hard to win over her crusty grandfather, the Colonel (Smith), and is quickly adopted by a soft-hearted sergeant (McLaglen). One of Shirley's best vehicles, "inspired" (it says here) by the Rudyard Kipling story. Beware 77m. prints.▼

Weird Science (1985) C-94m. *½ D: John Hughes. Anthony Michael Hall, Kelly LeBrock, Ilan Mitchell-Smith, Bill Paxton, Suzanne Snyder, Judie Aronson. Two nerdy teens use computer to conjure up woman of their dreams (sexy LeBrock), but writer-director Hughes doesn't follow through on his own premise! Appalling excuse for comedy; tasteless and endless, unredeemed by Hughes's sharp teenage dialogue and Hall's engaging performance.▼

Weird Woman (1944) 64m. **½ D: Reginald LeBorg. Lon Chaney, Jr., Anne Gwynne, Evelyn Ankers, Ralph Morgan, Lois Collier. Chaney's ex-girlfriend objects to his Tropic-Isle bride, connives to get even. Way-out entry in the *Inner Sanctum* series, based on Fritz Leiber's *Conjure Wife*, is good fun, with Ankers in nice change-of-pace villainess role. Remade as BURN, WITCH, BURN and WITCHES' BREW.

We Joined the Navy SEE: **We Are in the Navy Now**

Welcome Home (1989) C-96m. ** D:

Franklin J. Schaffner. Kris Kristofferson, JoBeth Williams, Sam Waterston, Brian Keith, Thomas Wilson Brown, Trey Wilson. Please, not again. Presumed dead Air Force officer Kristofferson, 17 years in Cambodia with a new wife and two children, returns home to remarried spouse number one and their teenage son. Tolerably sincere at best, embalmed at worst. Director Schaffner's final film.

Welcome Home, Bobby (1986) **C-100m.** **TVM** D: Herbert Wise. Tony Lo Bianco, Timothy Williams, Adam Baldwin, Nan Wood, Stephen James, John Karlen, John Pleshette, Gisela Caldwell. High school senior has a sexual identity crisis; his blue-collar father nearly disowns him, his peers shun him. Newcomer Williams is the sensitive student, veteran Lo Bianco the insensitive dad. Average.

Welcome Home, Johnny Bristol (1971) **C-100m. TVM** D: George McCowan. Martin Landau, Jane Alexander, Brock Peters, Forrest Tucker, Martin Sheen, Pat O'Brien. Returning Vietnam vet in flashback-ridden thriller dealing with bizarre reactions to Vermont home town and ways in which it has changed. Unconvincing characters in forgettable drama. Below average.

Welcome Home, Soldier Boys (1972) **C-91m.** ** D: Richard Compton. Joe Don Baker, Paul Koslo, Alan Vint, Elliott Street, Jennifer Billingsley, Billy "Green" Bush, Geoffrey Lewis, Francine York. Sensationalistic melodrama about four ex-Green Berets who adjust to civilian life by gang-raping a girl and burning down a town. Yet another one-dimensionally violent depiction of Vietnam veterans.

Welcome in Vienna (1986-Austrian) **126m.** *** D: Axel Corti. Gabriel Barylli. Nicolas Brieger, Claudia Messner, Hubert Mann, Liliana Nelska. Intriguing, uncompromising account of Austrian Jew Barylli and German intellectual Brieger, who've fled to America, and return to their homeland as U.S. soldiers during the final months of WW2. A thought-provoking look at the Austrian people's less than honorable response to Nazi aggression. The conclusion of Corti's "Where To and Back" trilogy, preceded by GOD DOESN'T BELIEVE IN US ANYMORE and SANTA FE.

Welcome Stranger (1947) **107m.** *** D: Elliott Nugent. Bing Crosby, Barry Fitzgerald, Joan Caulfield, Wanda Hendrix, Frank Faylen, Elizabeth Patterson. Entertaining musical of Crosby filling in for vacationing doctor in small community, getting involved with local girl and lovely little town.

Welcome to Arrow Beach (1974) **C-99m.** ** D: Laurence Harvey. Laurence Harvey, Joanna Pettet, Stuart Whitman, John Ireland, Meg Foster, Jesse Vint, Gloria LeRoy. Harvey's final film (edited by phone from his deathbed) is strange but watchable

shocker. He plays a war veteran who returns to California and kills passersby to feed his newly acquired taste for human flesh (though shortened TV prints seriously alter the story). Good cast helps, especially spellbinding Foster in an early role. Retitled: TENDER FLESH.

Welcome to 18 (1987) **C-89m.** ** D: Terry Carr. Courtney Thorne-Smith, Mariska Hargitay, Jo Ann Willette, Cristen Kaufman, E. Erich Anderson, John Putch. Tired teen titillation yarn about three girlfriends who spend their first summer out of high school experiencing life in the fast lane in Nevada. Attractive newcomers (including brunette Hargitay, daughter of Jayne Mansfield) muddle through preachy, plot-heavy nonsense.▼

Welcome to Hard Times (1967) **C-105m.** *** D: Burt Kennedy. Henry Fonda, Janice Rule, Keenan Wynn, Janis Paige, John Anderson, Aldo Ray, Warren Oates, Fay Spain, Edgar Buchanan, Lon Chaney, Jr., Elisha Cook, Jr. Intriguing, symbol-laden account of run-down Western town victimized by outlaw Ray, with Fonda finally forced to shoot it out to save what's left. Adapted by Kennedy from E. L. Doctorow novel.

Welcome to L.A. (1977) **C-106m.** **½ D: Alan Rudolph. Keith Carradine, Sally Kellerman, Geraldine Chaplin, Harvey Keitel, Lauren Hutton, Viveca Lindfors, Sissy Spacek, Denver Pyle, John Considine, Richard Baskin. This chronicle of lost, lonely Southern Californians who can only connect for fleeting moments between the sheets is occasionally intriguing, but pales beside some of Rudolph's later, better work. A major debit: Baskin's music, which quickly becomes monotonous. Produced by Robert Altman.▼

Welcome to the Club (1971) **C-88m.** ** D: Walter Shenson. The Warblers, Jack Warden, Brian Foley, Lee Meredith, Andy Jarell. Navy morale officer tries to find quarters for USO entertainers in Japan. Forgettable comedy.

We Live Again (1934) **82m.** ** D: Rouben Mamoulian. Fredric March, Anna Sten, Sam Jaffe, C. Aubrey Smith, Jane Baxter, Ethel Griffies. Cumbersome costumer with March a Russian nobleman in love with peasant girl Sten. Based on Leo Tolstoy's *Resurrection*, filmed several times before; Preston Sturges and Maxwell Anderson were among the writers.

Well, The (1951) **85m.** *** D: Leo Popkin, Russell Rouse. Richard Rober, Henry (Harry) Morgan, Barry Kelley, Christine Larson, Maidie Norman, Ernest Anderson. Incisive study of crowd psychology, focusing on effects on townfolk when black child becomes lodged in deep well. Fine score by Dimitri Tiomkin.

Well-Digger's Daughter, The (1941-French) **142m.** ***½ D: Marcel Pagnol.

Raimu, Fernandel, Josette Day, Charpin, George Grey. Naive Day is seduced and abandoned—with child—and peasant father Raimu isn't very pleased. Both touching and hilarious.▼

Well-Groomed Bride, The (1946) 75m. ** D: Sidney Lanfield. Olivia de Havilland, Ray Milland, Sonny Tufts, James Gleason, Percy Kilbride. Fine cast suffers with ridiculous comedy of stubborn girl insisting on champagne for her wedding.

Wells Fargo (1937) 94m. *** D: Frank Lloyd. Joel McCrea, Frances Dee, Bob Burns, Lloyd Nolan, Ralph Morgan, Johnny Mack Brown, Porter Hall, Robert Cummings, Harry Davenport. McCrea, struggling to build famous express service, loses love of his wife (Dee) in process. Large-scale Western is long, but filled with action. Originally released at 115m.

We of the Never Never (1983-Australian) C-132m. *** D: Igor Auzins. Angela Punch McGregor, Arthur Dignam, Tony Barry, Tommy Lewis, Lewis Fitz-Gerald. True story based on memoirs of first white woman to travel into Australian wilderness known as the Never Never is visually stunning but never develops narrative momentum or dramatic punch. Still, it's a pleasure to look at.▼

We're Fighting Back (1981) C-98m. TVM D: Lou Antonio. Kevin Mahon, Paul McCrane, Joe Morton, Ellen Barkin, Stephen Lang, Brian Tochi. The exploits of N.Y.C.'s Guardian Angels inspired this movie about a youth group that has banded together to fight subway crime. Scripted by T.S. Cook (of CHINA SYNDROME fame). Average.

We're Going to Be Rich (1938-British) 78m. **½ D: Monty Banks. Gracie Fields, Victor McLaglen, Brian Donlevy, Coral Browne, Ted Smith, Gus McNaughton. Entertainer Fields finds herself in the midst of an African oil boom in this OK story with musical numbers; Donlevy and McLaglen in contrived rivalry supply much of the plot.

We're No Angels (1955) C-106m. **½ D: Michael Curtiz. Humphrey Bogart, Peter Ustinov, Aldo Ray, Joan Bennett, Basil Rathbone, Leo G. Carroll. Mild entertainment as three escapees from Devil's Island find refuge with French family and extricate them from various predicaments. Remade in 1989.▼

We're No Angels (1989) C-106m. *½ D: Neil Jordan. Robert De Niro, Sean Penn, Demi Moore, Hoyt Axton, Bruno Kirby, Ray McAnally, James Russo, Wallace Shawn, John C. Reilly. Lumbering comedy about a couple of dimwitted convicts who inadvertently escape from prison and find refuge pretending to be priests visiting a nearby shrine. De Niro, who also served as executive producer, mugs as never be-

fore, playing Leo Gorcey to Penn's Huntz Hall. Handsome production design is no compensation for a lugubrious script by David Mamet, "suggested by" the play that was filmed before in 1955.▼

We're Not Dressing (1934) 77m. *** D: Norman Taurog. Bing Crosby, Carole Lombard, George Burns, Gracie Allen, Ethel Merman, Leon Errol, Ray Milland. Musical *Admirable Crichton* with rich-girl Lombard falling in love with sailor Crosby when entourage is ship-wrecked on desert isle. Merman is man-chasing second fiddle, with Burns and Allen on tap as local expeditionists. Great fun; Bing sings "Love Thy Neighbor."

We're Not Married (1952) 85m. *** D: Edmund Goulding. Ginger Rogers, Fred Allen, Victor Moore, Marilyn Monroe, Paul Douglas, David Wayne, Eve Arden, Louis Calhern, Zsa Zsa Gabor, James Gleason, Jane Darwell, Eddie Bracken, Mitzi Gaynor. Fine froth served up in several episodes as six married couples discover their weddings weren't legal. Segments vary in quality but the top-notch cast generally delivers the goods. Written and produced by Nunnally Johnson.

We're Rich Again (1934) 71m. ** D: William A. Seiter. Edna May Oliver, Billie Burke, Marian Nixon, Reginald Denny, Joan Marsh, Larry "Buster" Crabbe, Grant Mitchell, Gloria Shea, Edgar Kennedy. Screwball farce with rich Denny about to marry into Marsh's once-wealthy family, having to put up with usual assortment of eccentric relatives, including polo-playing grandma Oliver (who steals the film). Amiable cast defeated by hopelessly silly story.

Werewolf, The (1956) 83m. *½ D: Fred F. Sears. Steven Ritch, Don Megowan, Joyce Holden, Eleanore Tanin, Harry Lauter. Yet another telling of the half-man, half-wolf breed. Scientists, seeking cure for radiation poisoning, inject man with serum and he becomes a werewolf. Loses a lot in the retelling.

Werewolf in a Girl's Dormitory (1961-Italian-Austrian) 84m. BOMB D: Richard Benson (Paolo Heusch). Carl Schell, Barbara Lass, Curt Lowens, Maurice Marsac. Superintendent at school for problem girls doubles as a werewolf. Strictly bottom-of-the-barrel.

Werewolf of London (1935) 75m. **½ D: Stuart Walker. Henry Hull, Warner Oland, Valerie Hobson, Lester Matthews, Spring Byington. The first film about werewolves is dated but still effective. Scientist Hull stumbles onto curse of lycanthropy and terrorizes London as a mad killer. Oland is fun as mysterious man who warns Hull of impending doom.

Werewolf of Washington, The (1973) C-90m. *½ D: Milton Moses Ginsberg. Dean Stockwell, Biff McGuire, Clifton

James, Beeson Carroll, Thayer David, Jane House, Michael Dunn. Juvenile attempt to mix Watergate horrors with the more traditional kind. For the curious only.▼

Westbound (1959) **C-72m.** **½ D: Budd Boetticher. Randolph Scott, Virginia Mayo, Karen Steele, Michael Dante, Andrew Duggan, Michael Pate. Trim sagebrush tale of Yankee officer Scott organizing a stage coach line to bring in gold from California.

West 11 (1963-British) **93m.** *½ D: Michael Winner. Alfred Lynch, Kathleen Breck, Eric Portman, Diana Dors, Kathleen Harrison. Lumbering account of out-of-work Lynch agreeing to murder Portman's aunt, with the crime bringing about a reformation of his character.▼

Westerner, The (1940) **100m.** ***½ D: William Wyler. Gary Cooper, Walter Brennan, Fred Stone, Doris Davenport, Forrest Tucker, Chill Wills, Dana Andrews, Tom Tyler, Lillian Bond. Excellent tale of land disputes getting out of hand in the old West, with Brennan's Judge Roy Bean winning him his third Oscar. Tucker's film debut.▼

Western Union (1941) **C-94m.** *** D: Fritz Lang. Robert Young, Randolph Scott, Dean Jagger, Virginia Gilmore, John Carradine, Slim Summerville, Chill Wills, Barton MacLane. Big-scale Western, in gorgeous Technicolor, focuses on renegade attempts to thwart Western Union on the last leg of its westward expansion in the 1860s. Entertaining, if not terribly inspired.▼

We Still Kill the Old Way (1967-Italian) **C-92m.** ** D: Elio Petri. Irene Papas, Gian Maria Volonte, Luigi Pistilli. Crimes of honor in old Sicily purport to show old-world Mafia methods; actually nothing more than a small revenge film.

West of Shanghai (1937) **64m.** ** D: John Farrow. Boris Karloff, Gordon Oliver, Beverly Roberts, Ricardo Cortez, Sheila Bromley, Vladimir Sokoloff, Richard Loo. Cheap programmer of Chinese warlord Karloff holding Cortez and others prisoner in a remote Chinese outpost.

West of Suez SEE: **Fighting Wildcats**

West of Zanzibar (1928) **63m.** *** D: Tod Browning. Lon Chaney, Lionel Barrymore, Mary Nolan, Warner Baxter, Jacqueline Gadsdon. Crippled Chaney rules a jungle monarchy and lives for one thing: revenge on the man who ruined his life. His scheme: to despoil the man's beautiful young daughter (Nolan). Hokey ending mars seamy, bizarre story; remade as KONGO. Originally released at 69m.

West of Zanzibar (1954-British) **C-84m.** ** D: Harry Watt. Anthony Steel, Sheila Sim, Edric Connor, Orlando Martins. Ivory hunters meet up with jungle obstacles and native tribes; Steel and Sim share the adventures.

West Point of the Air (1935) **100m.** **½ D: Richard Rosson. Wallace Beery, Robert Young, Maureen O'Sullivan, Lewis Stone, James Gleason, Rosalind Russell, Robert Taylor. Commander Beery pushes reluctant son Young through army air-training for his own satisfaction. Good cast enlivens standard drama.

West Point Story (1950) **107m.** **½ D: Roy Del Ruth. James Cagney, Virginia Mayo, Doris Day, Gordon MacRae, Gene Nelson, Alan Hale, Jr. Silly but watchable musical about a Broadway director staging a revue at West Point. Wait till you hear "The Military Polka."

West Side Story (1961) **C-151m.** **** D: Robert Wise, Jerome Robbins. Natalie Wood, Richard Beymer, George Chakiris, Rita Moreno, Russ Tamblyn, Tucker Smith, David Winters, Tony Mordente, Simon Oakland, John Astin. Vivid film adaptation of the landmark Broadway musical, updating Romeo and Juliet story to youth-gang atmosphere of late 1950s N.Y.C. Wood and Beymer lack charisma, but everything surrounding them is great: Robbins' choreography, Leonard Bernstein-Stephen Sondheim score (including "Maria," "America," and "Something's Coming"). Script by Ernest Lehman, from Arthur Laurents' play. Winner of 10 Academy Awards including Best Picture, Direction, Supporting Actor and Actress (Chakiris, Moreno), Cinematography, Costumes, Art Direction-Set Decoration, Editing, Scoring; Robbins earned a special award for his choreography.▼

Westward Ho, The Wagons (1956) **C-90m.** ** D: William Beaudine. Fess Parker, Kathleen Crowley, Jeff York, David Stollery, Sebastian Cabot, George Reeves, Juliette Compton. Lackluster pioneer saga has Disney polish but no excitement as wagon train travels West. Four Mouseketeers from the *Mickey Mouse Club* appear—Karen, Cubby, Tommy, and Doreen.▼

Westward Passage (1932) **73m.** ** D: Robert Milton. Ann Harding, Laurence Olivier, Irving Pichel, ZaSu Pitts, Juliette Compton, Irene Purcell, Don Alvarado, Florence Lake, Edgar Kennedy, Ethel Griffies. Acting uplifts clichéd tale of girl who divorces to marry for true love, despite sacrifices. Film debut of child actress Bonita Granville.

Westward the Women (1951) **118m.** *** D: William Wellman. Robert Taylor, Denise Darcel, Beverly Dennis, John McIntire, Hope Emerson, Lenore Lonergan, Julie Bishop, Marilyn Erskine. Intriguing Western with Taylor heading wagon train full of females bound for California to meet mail-order husbands. Based on a story

[1274]

by Frank Capra. Also shown in computer-colored version.

Westworld (1973) **C-88m.** *** D: Michael Crichton. Richard Benjamin, Yul Brynner, James Brolin, Norman Bartold, Alan Oppenheimer, Victoria Shaw, Steve Franken. Adult vacation resort of the future offers opportunity to live in various fantasy worlds serviced by robots. Benjamin chooses old-time Western town, but begins to fear when one of the robots malfunctions. Engaging story by Crichton; followed by FUTUREWORLD.▼

Wetbacks (1956) **C-89m.** *½ D: Hank McCune. Lloyd Bridges, Nancy Gates, John Hoyt, Barton MacLane. Tawdry study of smuggling Mexicans across Texas border.

Wet Gold (1984) **C-100m.** TVM D: Dick Lowry. Brooke Shields, Burgess Meredith, Tom Byrd, Brian Kerwin, William Bronder, David Kass. Brooke and three guys search for sunken treasure in this thinly disguised update of THE TREASURE OF THE SIERRA MADRE. Brooke has the old Tim Holt role and Meredith is in Walter Huston's. Under water and below average.▼

We the Living (1942-Italian) **170m.** *** D: Goffredo Alessandrini. Alida Valli, Rossano Brazzi, Fosco Giachetti, Giovanni Grasso, Emilio Cigoli, Mario Pisu. Still involving, and recently rediscovered, romantic drama of young Russian Valli, an anticommunist who becomes involved with party official Giachetti in order to obtain medical treatment for fugitive lover Brazzi. Based on an Ayn Rand novel and banned soon after its release because its scenario is as antiauthoritarian as it is anticommunist.▼

Wetherby (1985-British) **C-97m.** **½ D: David Hare. Vanessa Redgrave, Joely Richardson, Judi Dench, Ian Holm, Tim McInnery, Suzanna Hamilton. Uninvited guest shows up for dinner at a Yorkshire schoolteacher's, then returns the next day to blow his brains out. Writer David Hare's first film as director has some excellent performances and occasionally biting dialogue but is far too self-consciously gloomy. Richardson, radiant as the younger Redgrave in the flashbacks, is real-life daughter of Vanessa and director Tony Richardson.▼

We Think the World of You (1988-British) **C-94m.** *** D: Colin Gregg. Alan Bates, Gary Oldman, Frances Barber, Liz Smith, Max Wall, Kerry Wise. In 1950s London, middle-aged Bates becomes entwined in the lives of imprisoned boyfriend Oldman's working-class family, and Oldman's pet dog in particular. Diverting comedy-drama of unrequited love, adapted by Hugh Stoddart from Joseph R. Ackerley's semi-autobiographical novel. A must for animal lovers . . . and romantics.▼

Wet Parade, The (1932) **120m.** **½ D: Victor Fleming. Walter Huston, Myrna Loy, Neil Hamilton, Lewis Stone, Dorothy Jordan, Robert Young, Jimmy Durante, Wallace Ford. Extremely long diatribe about the Devil's Brew which manages to be both anti-liquor and anti-Prohibition. First half features Stone as an alcoholic Southern gentleman; second half moves North to focus on Prohibition agents (including Durante, of all people!). Strange but interesting; script by John Lee Mahin, from the Upton Sinclair novel.

We've Never Been Licked (1943) **103m.** ** D: John Rawlins. Richard Quine, Noah Beery, Jr., Robert Mitchum, Anne Gwynne, Martha O'Driscoll. Jingoistic, melodramatic account of American youth brought up in Japan, and his involvement in WW2.

We Were Dancing (1942) **94m.** ** D: Robert Z. Leonard. Norma Shearer, Melvyn Douglas, Gail Patrick, Marjorie Main, Reginald Owen, Connie Gilchrist, Sig Ruman. Hokey adaptation of Noel Coward's play *Tonight at 8:30*, about princess running off with another man at her engagement party. Shearer et al try, but material defeats them. Ava Gardner's first film.

We Were Strangers (1949) **106m.** *** D: John Huston. Jennifer Jones, John Garfield, Pedro Armendariz, Gilbert Roland, Ramon Novarro. Intense, intriguing political drama of Garfield and Jones joining with the Cuban underground in a plot to overthrow the government. Well-directed by Huston; Garfield is fine, but Roland steals the film as one of the revolutionaries. Scripted by Huston and Peter Viertel.

We Who Are Young (1940) **79m.** ** D: Harold S. Bucquet. Lana Turner, John Shelton, Gene Lockhart, Grant Mitchell, Henry Armetta, Jonathan Hale, Clarence Wilson. Turner marries Shelton though his company's policy forbids it; aimless comedy-drama.

We Will All Meet in Paradise (1977-French) **C-110m.** **½ D: Yves Robert. Jean Rochefort, Claude Brasseur, Guy Bedos, Victor Lanoux, Daniele Delorme, Daniel Gelin. The trials and hangups of four boyish middle-aged Frenchmen. Cheerful but slight sex comedy; follow-up to PARDON MON AFFAIRE, and not as good. Also known as PARDON MON AFFAIRE, TOO.▼

Whale for the Killing, A (1981) **C-150m.** TVM D: Richard T. Heffron. Peter Strauss, Richard Widmark, Dee Wallace, Kathryn Walker, Bruce McGill, Ken James, David Ferry. Strauss' personal statement about the slaughter of whales off Newfoundland. Powerful if somewhat talky drama written by Lionel Chetwynd from Farley Mowat's book. Above average.▼

Whales of August, The (1987) **C-90m.** ***½ D: Lindsay Anderson. Bette Davis,

Lillian Gish, Vincent Price, Ann Sothern, Harry Carey, Jr., Margaret Ladd, Tisha Sterling, Mary Steenburgen. Two elderly sisters live together in a cottage in Maine, with ever-patient Gish forced to care for blind and irascible Davis . . . who may be turning senile. Sothern is their ebullient friend and neighbor, Carey their veteran handyman, and Price a courtly Russian émigré who works his charms on the ladies; they're all terrific, but Gish and Davis dominate the film with their sheer screen presence, a lifetime of movie memories in each classic face. An exquisitely delicate film, adapted by David Berry from his play, and beautifully directed by Anderson (in his American debut). Tisha Sterling, Sothern's real-life daughter, plays Sothern as a young woman in opening scene.▼

What? (1973-Italian) **C-112m.** **½ D: Roman Polanski. Sydne Rome, Marcello Mastroianni, Hugh Griffith, Romolo Valli, Guido Alberti, Roman Polanski. Ribald comedy about gorgeous innocent who stays at mansion of eccentric millionaire and can't understand all the commotion she causes. Change-of-pace for Polanski is agreeable, if not outstanding; good cast—especially underrated Rome—keeps things bubbling. Later cut to 94m. and reissued as DIARY OF FORBIDDEN DREAMS.▼

What a Carve Up! SEE: **No Place Like Homicide**▼

What a Life (1939) **75m.** D: Jay Theodore Reed. Jackie Cooper, Eddie Bracken, Betty Field, John Howard, Janice Logan, Vaughan Glaser, Lionel Stander, Hedda Hopper. See: **Henry Aldrich** series.

What Are Best Friends For? (1973) **C-78m.** TVM D: Jay Sandrich. Ted Bessell, Lee Grant, Larry Hagman, Barbara Feldon, Nita Talbot, George Furth, Corinne Camacho. Bouncy comedy about the efforts of a married couple to find companionship for their recently divorced friend. Sparkling performances make something out of almost nothing. Average.

What a Way to Go! (1964) **C-111m.** *** D: J. Lee Thompson. Shirley MacLaine, Paul Newman, Robert Mitchum, Dean Martin, Gene Kelly, Bob Cummings, Dick Van Dyke, Reginald Gardiner, Margaret Dumont, Fifi D'Orsay. Lavish, episodic black comedy by Betty Comden and Adolph Green stars MacLaine as jinx who marries succession of men, each of whom promptly dies, leaving her even wealthier than before. Series of movie parodies is amusing, and performances are uniformly charming, especially Newman as obsessed painter and Kelly as egotistical film star. Based on a story by Gwen Davis.

What a Woman! (1943) **94m.** **½ D: Irving Cummings. Rosalind Russell, Brian

Aherne, Willard Parker, Alan Dinehart, Ann Savage. Literary agent Russell sells film rights to spicy novel, and unwillingly becomes involved with its bookish author (Parker) in this lightweight comedy vehicle.

What Became of Jack and Jill? (1972-British) **C-93m.** **½ D: Bill Bain. Vanessa Howard, Paul Nicholas, Mona Washbourne, Peter Copley, Peter Jeffrey. Game attempt at detailing modern day, no-holds-barred love affair twisted by intrusion of grandmother; defeated by smug script, odd point of view.

What Changed Charley Farthing SEE: **Bananas Boat, The**▼

What Did You Do in the War, Daddy? (1966) **C-119m.** *** D: Blake Edwards. James Coburn, Dick Shawn, Sergio Fantoni, Aldo Ray, Harry Morgan, Carroll O'Connor, Leon Askin, Giovanna Ralli. A not too funny but quite pleasant film about group of misfit American soldiers trying to tame wacky Italian town into surrender. Written by William Peter Blatty; O'Connor's blustery performance led to his being cast in *All in the Family*.

What Do You Say to a Naked Lady? (1970) **C-90m.** *** D: Allen Funt. Amusing X-rated *Candid Camera* effort. Accent is on sex, and some of the reactions to stunts, and queries, are hilarious. Look for Richard Roundtree!▼

Whatever Happened to Aunt Alice? (1969) **C-101m.** *** D: Lee H. Katzin. Geraldine Page, Ruth Gordon, Rosemary Forsyth, Robert Fuller, Mildred Dunnock. Eccentric Page stays wealthy by murdering her housekeepers, stealing their savings. Gordon hires on as next "victim," trying to solve missing-persons mystery. Played to the hilt; most enjoyable.▼

What Ever Happened to Baby Jane? (1962) **132m.** ***½ D: Robert Aldrich. Bette Davis, Joan Crawford, Victor Buono, Marjorie Bennett, Anna Lee. Far-fetched, thoroughly engaging black comedy of two former movie stars; Joan's a cripple at the mercy of demented sister Baby Jane Hudson (Davis). Bette has a field day in her macabre characterization, with Buono a perfect match. Triggered a decade-long spate of older female stars in horror films. Script by Lukas Heller, from Henry Farrell's novel.▼

What Every Woman Knows (1934) **92m.** ***½ D: Gregory La Cava. Helen Hayes, Brian Aherne, Madge Evans, Lucile Watson, Dudley Digges, Donald Crisp. Charming, funny adaptation of James Barrie's play about a woman who is "the brains" behind her well-meaning but none-too-bright politician husband. Beautifully acted and surprisingly contemporary. Filmed before in 1921.

What Every Woman Wants (1962-British) **69m.** *½ D: Ernest Morris. William (James) Fox, Hy Hazell, Dennis Lotis, Elizabeth

Shepherd. Dull marital comedy of wives trying to reform husbands.

What Have I Done to Deserve This? (1985-Spanish) **C-100m.** *** D: Pedro Almodóvar. Carmen Maura, Chus Lampreave, Veronica Forque, Kiti Manver. Off-the-wall black comedy about an off-the-wall housewife (delightfully played by Maura) and her various trials and escapades. A fresh, original film, featuring a feminist heroine of classic proportions.▼

What Next, Corporal Hargrove? (1945) **95m.** **½ D: Richard Thorpe. Robert Walker, Keenan Wynn, Jean Porter, Chill Wills, Hugo Haas, William Phillips, Fred Essler, Cameron Mitchell. Hargrove (Walker) is in France with con-man buddy (Wynn) in OK sequel to SEE HERE, PRIVATE HARGROVE; trivial and episodic.

What! No Beer? (1933) **66m.** ** D: Edward Sedgwick. Buster Keaton, Jimmy Durante, Roscoe Ates, Phyllis Barry, John Miljan, Edward Brophy, Henry Armetta. Mediocre prohibition comedy about dim-witted bootleggers Keaton and Durante; plot makes no sense, Durante is incredibly overbearing. Best scenes involve Buster and leading-lady Barry. Keaton's last starring feature in America.

What Price Glory? (1926) **120m.** *** D: Raoul Walsh. Victor McLaglen, Edmund Lowe, Dolores Del Rio, William V. Mong, Phyllis Haver, Leslie Fenton, Barry Norton. Boisterous rivalry between Capt. Flagg (McLaglen) and Sgt. Quirt (Lowe) centers on lovely Charmaine (Del Rio) when they go to France during WW1. Zesty comedy, with plenty of fireworks for lip-readers, abruptly turns grim as focus shifts to horrors of war, only to return to Flagg-Quirt hijinks for finale. Fine entertainment, from Laurence Stallings-Maxwell Anderson play; two main characters reappeared in a handful of follow-ups, none of them as good as this. Remade in 1952.

What Price Glory? (1952) **C-111m.** **½ D: John Ford. James Cagney, Corinne Calvet, Dan Dailey, Robert Wagner, Marisa Pavan, James Gleason. Classic silent film becomes shallow Cagney-Dailey vehicle of battling Army men Flagg and Quirt in WW1 France.▼

What Price Hollywood? (1932) **88m.** *** D: George Cukor. Constance Bennett, Lowell Sherman, Neil Hamilton, Gregory Ratoff, Brooks Benedict. Soused movie director Sherman helps waitress Bennett fulfill her ambition to become a movie star—while he sinks into alcoholic ruin. Surprisingly sharp-eyed look at Hollywood—both comic and dramatic—that served as inspiration for later A STAR IS BORN. From a story by Adela Rogers St. John.

What Price Murder (1958-French) **105m.** **½ D: Henri Verneuil. Henri Vidal, Mylene Demongeot, Isa Miranda, Alfred Adam. Well-turned murder mystery of hubby and secretary planning to do away with wife.

What Price Vengeance SEE: **Vengeance**▼

What's a Nice Girl Like You . . .? (1971) **C-73m. TVM** D: Jerry Paris. Brenda Vaccaro, Jack Warden, Vincent Price, Roddy McDowall, Edmond O'Brien, Jo Anne Worley. Entertaining comedy by Howard Fast about Bronx ugly-duckling drawn into elaborate extortion plot which calls for her to impersonate rich socialite. Some good bits, but film lags in wrong places. Average.

What Price Victory (1988) **C-100m. TVM** D: Kevin Connor. Mac Davis, George Kennedy, Robert Culp, Susan Hess, Guy Boyd, Warren Berlinger, Eriq La Salle, Brian Wimmer. Lumpy drama about unscrupulous college football recruiting practices fumbles the ball. Below average.

What's Good for the Goose (1969-British) **C-105m.** BOMB D: Menahem Golan. Norman Wisdom, Sally Geeson, Sally Bazely, Sarah Atkinson, Terence Alexander. Weak, unfunny, sex romp wherein the object is to score as often as possible. Skip it.

What's New, Pussycat? (1965) **C-108m.** ** D: Clive Donner. Peter Sellers, Peter O'Toole, Romy Schneider, Capucine, Paula Prentiss, Woody Allen, Ursula Andress. Disturbed fashion editor O'Toole goes to psychiatrist Sellers for help with his romantic problems, but Sellers is even crazier than he. Woody Allen's first feature as actor and writer, and like many of his later comedies, one sits through a lot of misfired gags to get to a few undeniable gems. Hit title song by Burt Bacharach and Hal David.▼

What's So Bad About Feeling Good? (1968) **C-94m.** **½ D: George Seaton. George Peppard, Mary Tyler Moore, Dom DeLuise, John McMartin, Don Stroud, Nathaniel Frey, Susan Saint James, Charles Lane, Thelma Ritter. Amiable attempt at old-fashioned Capraesque comedy, with pixillated toucan spreading good feeling throughout N.Y.C. Doesn't hit bullseye, but has its moments. Written by Seaton and Robert Pirosh. Look for Cleavon Little, Moses Gunn.

What's the Matter with Helen? (1971) **C-101m.** *** D: Curtis Harrington. Debbie Reynolds, Shelley Winters, Dennis Weaver, Agnes Moorehead, Michael MacLiammoir. Campy murder tale set in 1930s. Reynolds and Winters try to erase their sordid past, start anew in Hollywood with school for talented kids. Good fun; Debbie ideal in period setting. Written by Henry Farrell.

What's Up, Doc? (1972) **C-94m.** *** D: Peter Bogdanovich. Barbra Streisand, Ryan O'Neal, Kenneth Mars, Austin Pendleton, Madeline Kahn, Sorrell Booke, Michael Murphy, Liam Dunn, John Hillerman, M. Emmet Walsh. Modern-day screwball comedy with impish Streisand making life miserable for stuffy musicologist O'Neal and his fiancée (Kahn, in feature debut), becoming involved in mixup over stolen jewels. Great comic chase scenes highlight overpowering farce, Bogdanovich's bouquet to 1930s Hollywood (and BRINGING UP BABY in particular). Look for John Byner and Randy Quaid at the hotel banquet.▼

What's Up, Tiger Lily? (1966) C-80m. *** Compiled by Woody Allen. Tatsuya Mihashi, Miya Hana, Eiko Wakabayashi, Tadao Nakamura, Woody Allen, China Lee. Slick Japanese imitation James Bond movie (KAGI NO KAG, or KEY OF KEYS, released in 1964) is redubbed by Allen into one long, very funny joke. The object of international intrigue is a valued egg-salad recipe, and the main characters are named Phil Moskowitz, Terri Yaki and Suki Yaki. Music by The Lovin' Spoonful (who also appear in the film). One of the new voices is Louise Lasser.▼

What Waits Below (1985) C-88m. ** D: Don Sharp. Robert Powell, Lisa Blount, Timothy Bottoms, Richard Johnson, Anne Heywood, Liam Sullivan. Disappointing fantasy thriller of archaeologists stumbling upon a lost race of Lemurians living in South American caves. Effects aren't very special; a good cast is wasted. Filmed in 1983.▼

Wheeler Dealers, The (1963) C-106m. *** D: Arthur Hiller. Lee Remick, James Garner, Jim Backus, Phil Harris, Shelley Berman, Chill Wills, John Astin, Louis Nye. Funny, fast-moving spoof of Texas millionaires who play with investments just for fun. Garner also catches Lee Remick along the way.

Wheel of Fortune SEE: **Man Betrayed, A**▼

When a Stranger Calls (1979) C-97m. *½ D: Fred Walton. Carol Kane, Charles Durning, Colleen Dewhurst, Tony Beckley, Rachel Roberts, Ron O'Neal. Psycho murders two children after terrorizing their babysitter, returns seven years later to extend his crime. Unpleasant, improbable melodrama falls apart after OK opening 11 minutes. Based on a short-subject called THE SITTER.▼

When a Woman Loves (1959-Japanese) C-97m. **½ D: Heinosuke Gosho. Ineko Arima, Shin Saburi, Yatsuko Tan-ami, Nobuko Otowa. Utilizing flashbacks, film recalls love affair between Saburi and older man Arima, a war correspondent; sentimental weeper with almost enough class.

When Comedy Was King (1960) 81m. **** Compiled by Robert Youngson. Charlie Chaplin, Buster Keaton, Laurel and Hardy, Ben Turpin, Fatty Arbuckle, Wallace Beery, Gloria Swanson. Second Youngson compilation of silent comedy clips has many old favorites in classic scenes. Chaplin, Keaton, Laurel & Hardy, Keystone Kops,

Charley Chase and others shine in this outstanding film.▼

When Dinosaurs Ruled the Earth (1970-British) C-96m. *** D: Val Guest. Victoria Vetri, Robin Hawdon, Patrick Allen, Drewe Henley, Imogen Hassall, Magda Konopka, Patrick Holt. Fast-paced, enjoyable prehistoric actioner with Vetri and Hawdon lovers ostracized by respective tribes. Beautiful locations, very good special effects by Jim Danforth, and honorable attempt to simulate period. Story by J.G. Ballard.

When Dreams Come True (1985) C-100m. TVM D: John Llewellyn Moxey. Cindy Williams, David Morse, Jessica Harper, Stan Shaw, Lee Horsley. Bland suspense tale of a nightmare-ridden woman who discovers that the killer in her dreams actually exists but can't convince her disbelieving detective boyfriend. Below average.

When Eight Bells Toll (1971-British) C-94m. ** D: Etienne Perier. Anthony Hopkins, Robert Morley, Nathalie Delon, Jack Hawkins, Ferdy Mayne, Corin Redgrave, Derek Bond. Alistair MacLean adapted his best-seller of gold piracy at sea, but the production lacks flash and finesse and Hopkins is too disagreeable a hero.

When Every Day Was the Fourth of July (1978) C-100m. TVM D: Dan Curtis. Katy Kurtzman, Dean Jones, Louise Sorel, Harris Yulin, Chris Peterson, Geoffrey Lewis, Scott Brady, Henry Wilcoxon, Michael Pataki. Touching period piece, fictionalized from events in Curtis' childhood (but reminiscent of TO KILL A MOCKINGBIRD), about a young girl who begs her lawyer father to defend the town weirdo—a shell-shocked, mute handyman—on homicide charges, thus incurring the scorn of the community. Curtis himself narrates this drama. Followed by THE LONG DAYS OF SUMMER. Above average.▼

When Father Was Away on Business (1985-Yugoslav) C-144m. ***½ D: Emir Kusturica. Moreno D'E Bartolli, Miki Manojlovic, Mirjana Karanovic, Mustafa Nadarevic, Mira Furian. Captivating story about a family's efforts to get along when the head of the household is sent to a labor camp for making an indiscreet remark. Told mostly through the eyes of a six-year-old boy (D'E Bartolli), whose concerns and flights of fancy are irresistible. Set in Sarajevo in the early 1950s, but like all good films, it's timeless and universal.

When Gangland Strikes (1956) 70m. ** D: R. G. Springsteen. Raymond Greenleaf, Marjie Millar, John Hudson, Anthony Caruso. Blasé handling of law enforcer's dilemma between duty and protecting family when he's blackmailed. Remake of 1939 film MAIN STREET LAWYER.▼

When Harry Met Sally . . . (1989) C-95m. ***½ D: Rob Reiner. Billy Crystal, Meg Ryan, Carrie Fisher, Bruno Kirby,

Steven Ford, Lisa Jane Persky, Michelle Nicastro, Harley Kozak. Delightful Woody Allen-ish romantic comedy set in N.Y.C. about a man and woman who carve out a genuine friendship, and struggle to keep it from becoming a romantic attachment. Full of great dialogue and knowing remarks about the way men and women view each other. Screenplay by Nora Ephron (with some distinctive Billy Crystalisms throughout). Director Reiner's mother has the movie's single funniest line, at the end of the delicatessen scene.▼

When Hell Broke Loose (1958) 78m. ** D: Kenneth Crane. Charles Bronson, Violet Rensing, Richard Jaeckel, Arvid Nelson. Low-keyed trim episode involving assassination attempt on General Eisenhower, set in WW2 Europe.

When Hell Was in Session (1979) C-100m. TVM D: Paul Krasny. Hal Holbrook, Eva Marie Saint, Mako, Ronny Cox, Renne Jarrett, Richard Evans, William Kirby Cullen. Holbrook gives a harrowing portrayal of Navy Commander Jeremiah Denton in this dramatization of the officer's experience as a Vietnam POW for seven-and-a-half years. Not for the squeamish. Above average.

When He's Not a Stranger (1989) C-100m. TVM D: John Gray. Annabeth Gish, John Terlesky, Kevin Dillon, Kim Meyers, Paul Dooley. Intense date-rape drama set on a college campus. On-target performance by Gish, complementing the sensible script of director Gray and Beth Sullivan. Above average.

When I Grow Up (1951) 80m. *** D: Michael Kanin. Bobby Driscoll, Robert Preston, Martha Scott, Sherry Jackson, Charley Grapewin, Henry (Harry) Morgan. Effective low-key study of the generation gap, with Driscoll most appealing as a boy who finds that he and his grandfather have much in common.

When In Rome (1952) 78m. **½ D: Clarence Brown. Van Johnson, Paul Douglas, Joseph Calleia, Mimi Aguglia, Tudor Owen. Tasteful yet unrestrained tale of con-artist Douglas disguising himself as priest attending Holy Year pilgrimage in Italy; through American priest Johnson, et al. he finds new faith.

When Ladies Meet (1933) 85m. *** D: Harry Beaumont. Ann Harding, Robert Montgomery, Myrna Loy, Alice Brady, Frank Morgan. Harding and Loy meet and discuss the characters of a new book, unaware that they both love the same man . . . just like the characters in the novel. Talky but unusual, intelligent film, with a powerhouse cast and that MGM gloss. Remade in 1941.

When Ladies Meet (1941) 108m. ** D: Robert Z. Leonard. Joan Crawford, Robert Taylor, Greer Garson, Herbert Marshall, Spring Byington. Attractive performers in plodding remake of 1933 movie based on

Rachel Crothers' play. Authoress Crawford loves Marshall, who's married to Garson; Taylor loves Joan. Talk marathon on woman's rights is vastly outdated. Taylor and Garson try to bring life to film, but can't. Retitled STRANGE SKIRTS for TV.

When Lovers Meet SEE: **Lover Come Back** (1946)

When Michael Calls (1971) C-73m. TVM D: Philip Leacock. Elizabeth Ashley, Ben Gazzara, Michael Douglas, Karen Pearson. Thriller-mystery of mother receiving strange phone calls from voice sounding like dead son, with subplot about divorce. Tame, predictable resolution in film that can't even build tension convincingly. Written by James Bridges. Video title: SHATTERED SILENCE. Below average.▼

When My Baby Smiles at Me (1948) C-98m. **½ D: Walter Lang. Betty Grable, Dan Dailey, Jack Oakie, June Havoc, James Gleason, Richard Arlen. Strictly routine musical about burlesque team that breaks up when one member gets job on Broadway. Eventually they're reteamed, of course. Based on famous play *Burlesque.* Filmed before as DANCE OF LIFE and SWING HIGH, SWING LOW.

When She Says No (1984) C-100m. TVM D: Paul Aaron. Kathleen Quinlan, Jeffrey DeMunn, George Dzundza, David Huffman, Kenneth McMillan, Rip Torn, Jane Alexander. Dowdyish college professor lives it up at a teacher's convention, invites three male colleagues to her room, and later hauls them into court for rape, though they insist it was seduction. Quinlan is absolutely fine as usual, but the unresolved plot will leave the viewer cold. Average.

When She Was Bad . . . (1979) C-100m. TVM D: Peter H. Hunt. Cheryl Ladd, Robert Urich, Eileen Brennan, Dabney Coleman, Marcia Lewis, Ramon Bieri, Nicole Eggert. Pretty young housewife and mother, unable to cope with marriage, becomes a child beater. Below average.

When Strangers Marry (1944) 67m. *** D: William Castle. Robert Mitchum, Kim Hunter, Dean Jagger, Neil Hamilton, Lou Lubin, Milton Kibbee. Hunter finds out she may have married a murderer, in this exceptional B picture. It was Mitchum's first important role. Reissued as BETRAYED.

When's Your Birthday? (1937) 77m. **½ D: Harry Beaumont. Joe E. Brown, Marian Marsh, Edgar Kennedy, Margaret Hamilton, Frank Jenks. Entertaining Brown vehicle of timid boxer whose prowess depends on position of stars; good supporting cast.

When the Bough Breaks (1986) C-100m. TVM D: Waris Hussein. Ted Danson, Richard Masur, Rachel Ticotin, David Huddleston, James Noble, Kim Miyori, Merritt Butrick. Thriller about a child psychologist's obsessive investigation into a series of murders involving a clique of well-heeled professional men. Writer Phil Penningroth's adaptation of Jonathan Kellerman's Edgar Allan Poe Award-winning book unravels before the finale but maintains its grip. Danson coproduced this one. Above average.

When the Boys Meet the Girls (1965) **C-110m.** ** D: Alvin Ganzer. Connie Francis, Harve Presnell, Herman's Hermits, Louis Armstrong, Liberace, Sue Ane Langdon, Fred Clark, Frank Faylen, Sam the Sham. Rehash of GIRL CRAZY, turned into a dull guest-star showcase.

When the Circus Comes to Town (1981) **C-100m. TVM** D: Boris Sagal. Elizabeth Montgomery, Christopher Plummer, Eileen Brennan, Gretchen Wyler, Ann Shropshire, Tommy Madden, Timothy Hill. Romantic comedy (Montgomery's first, following a long string of dramas) about a Southern spinster who decides to recharge her life by running away and joining a flea-bitten traveling circus. Above average.

When the Daltons Rode (1940) **80m.** *** D: George Marshall. Randolph Scott, Kay Francis, Brian Donlevy, George Bancroft, Andy Devine, Broderick Crawford, Stuart Erwin. Fine Western actioner with good cast, typical plot; Francis and Scott provide romantic relief.

When the Legends Die (1972) **C-105m.** *** D: Stuart Millar. Richard Widmark, Frederic Forrest, Luana Anders, Vito Scotti, Herbert Nelson. Offbeat story of aging rodeo cowboy who cannot accept fact that years are creeping up on him, and young Indian he befriends.▼

When the North Wind Blows (1974) **C-113m.** **½ D: Stewart Raffill. Henry Brandon, Herbert Nelson, Dan Haggerty. A hermit trapper protects snow tigers in Siberia. Beautiful scenery; OK fare for children.▼

When the Redskins Rode (1951) **C-78m.** *½ D: Lew Landers. Jon Hall, Mary Castle, James Seay, John Ridgley. Lame-brained Western set during French and Indian War of 1750s.

When the Whales Came (1989-British) **C-100m.** ** D: Clive Rees. Paul Scofield, Helen Mirren, Helen Pearce, Max Rennie, David Suchet, David Threlfall, Barbara Jefford, Jeremy Kemp. Dull dud set in 1914 with Scofield, in a performance that's not among his best, cast as a deaf old hermit who loves birds; he lives alone on a remote island and is befriended by youngsters Rennie and Pearce (the latter a nonactor discovered on Britain's Scilly Isles, where film was made).▼

When Time Ran Out . . . (1980) **C-121m.** BOMB D: James Goldstone. Paul Newman, Jacqueline Bisset, William Holden, James Franciscus, Edward Albert, Red Buttons, Ernest Borgnine, Burgess Meredith, Valentina Cortesa, Veronica Hamel, Alex Karras, Barbara Carrera. WHEN IDEAS RAN OUT, or, THE BLUBBERING INFERNO: Irwin Allen's shameless rehash of all his disaster-movie clichés is a monumental bore that even a volcanic eruption cannot save. Written by Carl Foreman and Stirling Silliphant—who were hopefully well-paid. Retitled EARTH'S FINAL FURY for TV.▼

When Tomorrow Comes (1939) **90m.** **½ D: John M. Stahl. Irene Dunne, Charles Boyer, Barbara O'Neil, Nydia Westman, Onslow Stevens. Standard soapy story (by James M. Cain!) enhanced by leading players; Boyer loves Dunne, although he's already married. Remade twice as INTERLUDE.

When We Were Young (1989) **C-100m. TVM** D: Daryl Duke. Ronny Cox, Jace Alexander, Lindsay Frost, Cynthia Gibb, Jane Krakowski, Eriq LaSalle. High school seniors examine their relationships with one another at their 1959 graduation party as they prepare to enter adulthood. Mediocre TV pilot from the people involved with *Dynasty*. Average.

When Willie Comes Marching Home (1950) **82m.** **½ D: John Ford. Dan Dailey, Corinne Calvet, Colleen Townsend, William Demarest, Mae Marsh. Schmaltzy WW2 adventures of West Virginia youth Dailey, including interlude with French underground leader Calvet.

When Wolves Cry SEE: **Christmas Tree, The**▼

When Women Had Tails (1970-Italian) **C-110m.** *½ D: Pasquale Festa Campanile. Senta Berger, Giuliano Gemma, Frank Wolff, Lando Buzzanca, Aldo Giuffre. Cute, harmless but unfunny slapstick comedy with Berger a most attractive cavewoman. Lina Wertmuller co-wrote the screenplay. Sequel: WHEN WOMEN LOST THEIR TAILS.▼

When Worlds Collide (1951) **C-81m.** **½ D: Rudolph Maté. Richard Derr, Barbara Rush, Peter Hanson, Larry Keating, John Hoyt. Cardboard characters and corny dialogue detract from story of scientists preparing for the end of the world. Special effects (including submersion of Manhattan) won Oscar for this George Pal production.▼

When You Comin' Back, Red Ryder? (1979) **C-118m.** *½ D: Milton Katselas. Marjoe Gortner, Hal Linden, Lee Grant, Peter Firth, Candy Clark, Pat Hingle, Stephanie Faracy, Audra Lindley, Bill McKinney. Stagy, unpleasant film of Mark Medoff's play about a psycho terrorizing a disparate group of people in roadside diner. Has its moments, but not enough to justify nearly two hours of viewing.

When You're In Love (1937) **104m.** **½ D: Robert Riskin. Grace Moore, Cary Grant, Aline MacMahon, Thomas Mitchell, Emma Dunn. Overlong but enjoyable vehicle for

opera star Moore who "hires" Grant as her husband. Most 98m. TV prints are missing film's highlight, where star sings "Minnie the Moocher." Celebrated screenwriter Riskin's only fling at directing.
When Your Lover Leaves (1983) C-100m. TVM D: Jeff Bleckner. Valerie Perrine, Betty Thomas, David Ackroyd, Edward O'Neill, Dwight Schultz, Shannon Wilcox. Comedy-drama produced by Henry Winkler and Ron Howard involves a recent divorcee who takes up with a kinky cop when her married boyfriend dumps her. A complete misfire. Below average.▼
Where Angels Go, Trouble Follows (1968) C-95m. **½ D: James Neilson. Rosalind Russell, Stella Stevens, Binnie Barnes, Mary Wickes, Dolores Sutton, Susan Saint James, Barbara Hunter; guest stars Milton Berle, Arthur Godfrey, Van Johnson, William Lundigan, Robert Taylor. For *Flying Nun* fans only; contrived comedy followup to TROUBLE WITH ANGELS with Mother Superior Russell pitted against young, progressive nun Stevens.
Where Are the Children? (1986) C-92m. *½ D: Bruce Malmuth. Jill Clayburgh, Max Gail, Harley Cross, Elisabeth Harnois, Elizabeth Wilson, Barnard Hughes, Frederic Forrest. Clayburgh's two children are kidnapped—just as, nine years before, her first two kids (by a previous marriage) also vanished. Manages to create some suspense but becomes more ludicrous as it unfolds. Despite a raging storm, the Cape Cod location is the most attractive aspect of the film. Based on Mary Higgins Clark's novel. ▼
Where Are Your Children? (1943) 73m. *½ D: William Nigh. Jackie Cooper, Patricia Morison, Gale Storm, Gertrude Michael, John Litel, Evelynne Eaton. Thoughtless study of juvenile delinquency.
Where Danger Lives (1950) 84m. ** D: John Farrow. Robert Mitchum, Faith Domergue, Claude Rains, Maureen O'Sullivan. Young physician Mitchum becomes involved with woman (Domergue) who is bordering on insanity.
Where Does It Hurt? (1972) C-88m. BOMB D: Rod Amateau. Peter Sellers, Jo Ann Pflug, Rick Lenz, Harold Gould, Hope Summers, Eve Bruce, Kathleen Freeman. Abysmal, tasteless "comedy" about hospital run by corrupt Sellers, staffed by money-hungry incompetents. Good cast wasted.
Where Do We Go From Here? (1945) C-77m. **½ D: Gregory Ratoff. Fred MacMurray, June Haver, Joan Leslie, Gene Sheldon, Anthony Quinn, Carlos Ramirez, Otto Preminger. Engaging but ultimately silly musical comedy about genie enabling MacMurray to travel backwards into American history. Ira Gershwin-Kurt Weill score

includes wonderful mini-opera involving Christopher Columbus. Fred and June later married in real life.
Where Eagles Dare (1969) C-158m. ***½ D: Brian G. Hutton. Richard Burton, Clint Eastwood, Mary Ure, Michael Hordern, Patrick Wymark, Robert Beatty, Ferdy Mayne, Anton Diffring, Donald Houston, Ingrid Pitt. Modern-day version of Republic serial, with slam-bang cliff-hanger action that never lets up. Burton and company assigned to free American officer held captive in German mountain castle during WW2. Terrific; script by Alistair MacLean, from his best-selling novel.▼
Where Have All the People Gone? (1974) C-78m. TVM D: John Llewellyn Moxey. Peter Graves, Verna Bloom, George O'Hanlon, Jr., Kathleen Quinlan, Michael-James Wixted. Graves and his family are among survivors of a radiation explosion. "End of the world" tale by Lewis John Carlino; unevenly spun, indifferently acted. Average.▼
Where It's At (1969) C-104m. **½ D: Garson Kanin. David Janssen, Robert Drivas, Rosemary Forsyth, Brenda Vaccaro, Don Rickles, Edy Williams. Pleasant but undistinguished comedy about strained relationship between Las Vegas casino owner Janssen and Princeton-graduate son Drivas.
Where Love Has Gone (1964) C-114m. **½ D: Edward Dmytryk. Bette Davis, Susan Hayward, Michael Connors, Jane Greer, Joey Heatherton, George Macready. Glossy drama of Heatherton killing mother Hayward's lover; Davis is the domineering grandmother, Greer is a sympathetic probation officer. Script by John Michael Hayes, from Harold Robbins' novel.▼
Where No Vultures Fly SEE: **Ivory Hunter**
Where Pigeons Go to Die (1990) C-100m. TVM D: Michael Landon. Michael Landon, Art Carney, Robert Hy Gorman, Cliff De Young, Ronne Troup, Bruce French. A man recalls his boyhood relationship with his loving grandfather, when the two of them trained and raced homing pigeons. Agreeable adaptation of R. Wright Campbell's book. Average.
Where's Charley? (1952) C-97m. *** D: David Butler. Ray Bolger, Allyn Ann McLerie, Robert Shackleton, Mary Germaine, Horace Cooper, Margaretta Scott. Bolger recreates Broadway role in musical adaptation of CHARLEY'S AUNT, as Oxford student whose face-saving impersonation of dowdy dowager leads to endless complications. Frank Loesser score includes "Once in Love with Amy." One of the principal dancers is Jean Marsh. Filmed in England.
Where's Jack? (1969-British) C-119m. **½ D: James Clavell. Tommy Steele, Stanley Baker, Fiona Lewis, Alan Badel, Dudley Foster, Sue Lloyd, Noel Purcell.

Despite good cast and production values, surprisingly unengrossing historical adventure tale of Britain's most celebrated highwayman and escape artist, Jack Sheppard (Steele), wanted by British government and notorious mercenary (Baker).

Where's Picone? (1984-Italian) **C-122m.** *** D: Nanni Loy. Giancarlo Giannini, Lina Sastri, Aldo Giuffre, Clelia Rondinelli, Carlo Croccolo. Giannini is hilarious in a role tailor-made for his talent: a sleazy, two-bit, ultimately hapless conniver who must live by his wits to survive on the fringes of Neapolitan society. A biting black comedy about bureaucracy and corruption Italian-style.▼

Where's Poppa? (1970) **C-82m.** **½ D: Carl Reiner. George Segal, Ruth Gordon, Trish Van Devere, Ron Leibman, Rae Allen, Vincent Gardenia, Barnard Hughes, Rob Reiner, Garrett Morris, Paul Sorvino. Absurdist comedy has cult following, but grisly subject matter makes it an acquired taste; Segal plays a repressed N.Y.C. lawyer whose senile mother dominates his life. Outlandish gags involve mugging, rape, nursing homes and other ills. Original ending was *too* potent, and changed. Script by Robert Klane, from his novel. Reissued as GOING APE.▼

Where the Boys Are (1960) **C-99m.** **½ D: Henry Levin. Dolores Hart, George Hamilton, Yvette Mimieux, Jim Hutton, Barbara Nichols, Paula Prentiss, Connie Francis, Frank Gorshin, Chill Wills. Notbad film about teenagers during Easter vacation in Ft. Lauderdale. Connie Francis, in her first film, is pretty good, and sings the hit title tune; other young players seen to good advantage. Nichols is hilarious as usual as a flashy blonde. Ineptly remade in 1984.▼

Where the Boys Are '84 (1984) **C-93m.** BOMB D: Hy Averback. Lisa Hartman, Lorna Luft, Wendy Schaal, Lynn-Holly Johnson, Russell Todd, Howard McGillin, Louise Sorel, Alana Stewart. Tacky remake of 1960 film about four college girls (three horny, one virginal) who descend on Ft. Lauderdale, Florida in search of cheap sex. This Allan Carr production has all the appeal of an oil slick.▼

Where the Buffalo Roam (1980) **C-96m.** BOMB D: Art Linson. Peter Boyle, Bill Murray, Bruno Kirby, Rene Auberjonois, R. G. Armstrong, Rafael Campos, Leonard Frey, Mark Metcalf, Craig T. Nelson. Intended celebration of famed "Gonzo" journalist Hunter S. Thompson will baffle those unfamiliar with his work and insult those who are. Even Neil Young's music can't save dreadful comedy.▼

Where the Bullets Fly (1966-British) **C-88m.** **½ D: John Gilling. Tom Adams, Dawn Addams, Tim Barrett, Michael Ripper. Well-paced super spy satire involv-

ing Adams tracking down special fuel formula.▼

Where the Green Ants Dream (1984-German) **C-100m.** **½ D: Werner Herzog. Bruce Spence, Wandjuk Marika, Roy Marika, Ray Barrett, Norman Kaye, Colleen Clifford. Rambling account of a group of wise, noble Australian aborigines who must go up against a mining company set on bulldozing their sacred land in a quest for uranium. The theme—a clash of civilizations—is characteristic of Herzog, but the result just doesn't gel. ▼

Where the Heart Is (1990) **C-94m.** ** D: John Boorman. Dabney Coleman, Uma Thurman, Joanna Cassidy, Crispin Glover, Suzy Amis, Christopher Plummer, Maury Chaykin, David Hewlett. Disappointing farce about wealthy N.Y.C. demolitions expert Coleman, who decides to teach his family humility—and the value of money—by shutting them out and making them homeless. Well-intended hodgepodge that's too silly and outlandish to be taken seriously. Scripted by Boorman and his daughter, Telsche; some saw this as an update of the director's earlier LEO THE LAST.

Where the Hell's That Gold?!!? (1988) **C-100m.** TVM D: Burt Kennedy. Willie Nelson, Jack Elam, Delta Burke, Gerald McRaney, Alfonso Arau, Gregory Sierra. Flaccid comedy-Western about the search for a cache of stolen gold, camped up by eye-rolling Elam and buxom Burke, while Nelson plays alternately crusty and bemused. Western veteran Kennedy produced, directed, and wrote this one—and ought to have a posse on his tail. Below average.

Where the Hot Wind Blows (1958-French-Italian) **120m.** ** D: Jules Dassin. Gina Lollobrigida, Pierre Brasseur, Marcello Mastroianni, Melina Mercouri, Yves Montand, Paolo Stoppa. Artsy film that meanders around subject of legalized immorality in small Italian village.▼

Where the Ladies Go (1980) **C-100m.** TVM D: Theodore J. Flicker. Candy Clark, Karen Black, Earl Holliman, Lisa Hartman, Janette Lane Bradbury, Mary Jo Catlett, Lou Antonio. Humorous tale about a special little bar (hours 9AM to 3PM) to which the ladies go to live out their fantasies and find some adventure. Flicker's offbeat touches bring to mind his early feature film work. Script by Carol Sobieski. Average.

Where the Lilies Bloom (1974) **C-96m.** *** D: William A. Graham. Julie Gholson, Jan Smithers, Matthew Burril, Helen Harmon, Harry Dean Stanton, Rance Howard, Sudie Bond. Four Appalachian children carry on by themselves when their father dies—and keep the news of his death a secret, so they won't be taken away by the state. First-rate family drama scripted by

Earl Hamner, Jr. and filmed on location in North Carolina.

Where the Red Fern Grows (1974) **C-90m.** *** D: Norman Tokar. James Whitmore, Beverly Garland, Jack Ging, Lonny Chapman, Stewart Peterson. Appealing family drama about a boy's devotion to two hunting dogs, and how his experiences teach him about responsibility and growing up. Set in 1930's Oklahoma.▼

Where the River Runs Black (1986) **C-100m.** **½ D: Chris Cain. Charles Durning, Alessandro Rabelo, Marcelo Rabelo, Conchata Ferrell, Peter Horton, Dana Delaney, Castulo Guerra. Orphaned boy raised in the Amazon jungle is brought to civilization by a well-meaning priest (Durning) who knew his father. Slow-moving story starts well but loses its grip as it leaves behind mystical elements and focuses more on child's-eye view of good guys and bad guys. Nicely filmed on location in Brazil.▼

Where There's Life (1947) **75m.** *** D: Sidney Lanfield. Bob Hope, Signe Hasso, William Bendix, George Coulouris. Wacky comedy with radio star Hope earmarked as new king of mythical European country, trying to elude the menacing "messengers" who have come for him.

Where the Sidewalk Ends (1950) **95m.** *** D: Otto Preminger. Dana Andrews, Gene Tierney, Gary Merrill, Karl Malden, Bert Freed, Tom Tully, Ruth Donnelly, Craig Stevens, Neville Brand. While investigating a murder, brutal N.Y.C. cop (Andrews) inadvertently kills a man, then tries to conceal his own guilt while continuing his search for murderer. Moody crime melodrama is a good illustration of *film noir*. Fine characterizations, pungent script by Ben Hecht from William Stuart's novel *Night Cry*. Oleg Cassini (film's costume designer and Tierney's then-husband) has a cameo.

Where the Spies Are (1965-British) **C-110m.** *** D: Val Guest. David Niven, Françoise Dorleac, John Le Mesurier, Cyril Cusack, Eric Pohlmann, Reginald Beckwith. Well made mixture of dry comedy and suspense in tale of doctor forced into spying. Good cast names enhance already fine movie.

Where Time Began (1978-Spanish) **C-86m.** ** D: Piquer Simon. Kenneth More, Pep Munne, Jack Taylor. Mundane retelling of Jules Verne's JOURNEY TO THE CENTER OF THE EARTH, with predictable parade of sea serpents, giant turtles, and prehistoric dinosaurs.▼

Where Were You When the Lights Went Out? (1968) **C-94m.** *½ D: Hy Averback. Doris Day, Robert Morse, Terry-Thomas, Steve Allen, Lola Albright, Jim Backus, Patrick O'Neal, Pat Paulsen, Ben Blue, Earl Wilson. Below average

Doris Day comedy centering around the massive N.Y.C. blackout on November 9, 1965.

Which Way Is Up? (1977) **C-94m.** **½ D: Michael Schultz. Richard Pryor, Lonette McKee, Margaret Avery, Dolph Sweet, Morgan Woodward. Americanization of Lina Wertmuller's very funny THE SEDUCTION OF MIMI doesn't quite make it. Pryor gets to play three roles—a cotton-picking orange picker, a minister, and a dirty old man—and gets the most laughs as the latter.▼

Which Way to the Front? (1970) **C-96m.** BOMB D: Jerry Lewis. Jerry Lewis, John Wood, Jan Murray, Kaye Ballard, Robert Middleton, Paul Winchell, Sidney Miller, Gary Crosby. One of Jerry's worst has him a 4-F millionaire playboy who enlists other 4-Fs to fight Hitler. His last completed film until HARDLY WORKING. Co-scripted by Dick Miller.▼

Whiffs (1975) **C-91m.** *½ D: Ted Post. Elliott Gould, Eddie Albert, Harry Guardino, Godfrey Cambridge, Jennifer O'Neill, Alan Manson. Gould is guinea pig for Army Chemical Corps who has outlived his usefulness . . . but the military isn't rid of him so easily. Another sorry attempt to recapture the lunacy of M*A*S*H.▼

While the City Sleeps (1956) **100m.** *** D: Fritz Lang. Dana Andrews, Ida Lupino, Rhonda Fleming, George Sanders, Vincent Price, John Drew Barrymore, Thomas Mitchell, Sally Forrest, Howard Duff, Mae Marsh. Veteran cast and intertwining story-lines keep interest in account of newspaper reporters and police on the track of a berserk killer.▼

Whip Hand, The (1951) **82m.** *½ D: William Cameron Menzies. Elliott Reid, Carla Balenda, Raymond Burr, Edgar Barrier, Lurene Tuttle. Communists with germ-warfare intentions have taken over an abandoned resort town, but do these slimes *really* think they can tangle with Elliott Reid? Howard Hughes RKO Special is campy, but not campy enough.

Whiplash (1948) **91m.** ** D: Lewis Seiler. Dane Clark, Alexis Smith, Zachary Scott, Eve Arden, Jeffrey Lynn, S.Z. Sakall, Alan Hale. Unmoving melodrama about artist turning into grim prizefighter. Script is main defect; acting OK.

Whipsaw (1935) **83m.** **½ D: Sam Wood. Myrna Loy, Spencer Tracy, Harvey Stephens, William Harrigan, Clay Clement. Tracy uses bad-girl Loy to lead him to band of thieves; predictable complications follow in familiar but well-done crime drama.

Whirlpool (1949) **97m.** *** D: Otto Preminger. Gene Tierney, Richard Conte, Jose Ferrer, Charles Bickford, Eduard Franz, Fortunio Bonanova, Constance Collier. Tense melodrama of nefarious hypnotist

Ferrer using innocent Tierney to carry out his evil schemes. Script by Ben Hecht (using a pseudonym) and Andrew Solt, from a Guy Endore novel.

Whisky Galore SEE: **Tight Little Island**▼

Whisperers, The (1966-British) **106m.** ** D: Bryan Forbes. Edith Evans, Eric Portman, Nanette Newman, Avis Bunnage, Gerald Sim, Ronald Fraser. Dame Edith is the whole show in this mediocre melodrama about dotty old lady who is sure she is being spied upon; things get worse when her scummy son and husband drop by. Too restrained to be really absorbing, but worth catching just for her performance; moody score by John Barry.

Whispering Ghosts (1942) **75m.** ** D: Alfred L. Werker. Brenda Joyce, Milton Berle, John Shelton, John Carradine. Berle is effective as bumbling performer trying to live up to radio role as crackerjack detective.

Whispering Smith (1948) **C-88m.** *** D: Leslie Fenton. Alan Ladd, Brenda Marshall, Robert Preston, Donald Crisp, William Demarest. Well-acted Western about soft-spoken special agent investigating robberies who finds friend involved with crooks.

Whispering Smith Vs. Scotland Yard (1951-British) **77m.** ** D: Francis Searle. Richard Carlson, Greta Gynt, Rona Anderson, Herbert Lom, Dora Bryan. Famed detective proves conclusively that suicide was actually well-staged murder. Good cast in below-average mystery. Original British title: WHISPERING SMITH HITS LONDON.

Whisper Kills, A (1988) **C-100m.** TVM D: Christian I. Nyby II. Loni Anderson, Joe Penny, June Lockhart, James Sutorius, Jeremy Slate. A serial killer terrorizes a small town when he uses the telephone to intimidate his victims, one of whom is local editor Anderson. Average.

Whistle at Eaton Falls, The (1951) **96m.** **½ D: Robert Siodmak. Lloyd Bridges, Dorothy Gish, Carleton Carpenter, Murray Hamilton, Anne Francis, Ernest Borgnine, Doro Merande, Arthur O'Connell. Set in New Hampshire, this documentary-style film deals with labor relation problems in a small town when new plant manager has to lay off workers. Gish is factory owner in interesting supporting role.

Whistle Blower, The (1986-British) **C-100m.** *** D: Simon Langton. Michael Caine, James Fox, Nigel Havers, Felicity Dean, John Gielgud, Gordon Jackson, Barry Foster. Deftly handled thriller about a middle-aged former intelligence officer (an effectively subtle Caine), whose linguist son has a high-security government position . . . and is a bit too bright and idealistic for his own good. A literate, multileveled story, adapted by Julian Bond from John Hale's novel.▼

Whistle Down the Wind (1961-British) **99m.** ***½ D: Bryan Forbes. Hayley Mills, Alan Bates, Bernard Lee, Norman Bird, Elsie Wagstaffe. Fugitive murderer seeking refuge in a North Country barn is discovered by three children who think him to be Christ. Mills and Bates are excellent in this poignant, believable, and well-produced story of childhood innocence. Adapted from novel by Mary Hayley Bell (Hayley's mother). Forbes' directorial debut.▼

Whistle Stop (1946) **85m.** ** D: Leonide Moguy. George Raft, Ava Gardner, Victor McLaglen, Tom Conway, Jorja Curtright, Florence Bates, Charles Drake. Minor Philip Yordan drama of good girl Ava caught between restless, no-account Raft and corrupt nightclub owner Conway. Has its moments but ultimately is forgettable.▼

Whistler, The One of the most unusual—and one of the best—mystery series of the 30s and 40s was based on a popular radio show called "The Whistler." The premise of the show, and at least one of the films, was a mysterious figure who walked along whistling a haunting tune. "I am the Whistler," he would say. "And I know many things." He would introduce the current mystery and reappear from time to time to bridge gaps from one setting to another. Veteran Richard Dix starred in all but one of the eight Whistler films, but in keeping with the series' flexibility in presenting a new story every time, he alternated from hero to villain in various entries in the series. In the initial film, THE WHISTLER, Dix was a victim of circumstances about to be killed; in THE POWER OF THE WHISTLER he was an amnesiac murderer; in THE MYSTERIOUS INTRUDER he was a private eye; and in THE 13TH HOUR an innocent man framed for a murder he didn't commit. The one non-Dix film, RETURN OF THE WHISTLER, followed the radio format of the mysterious narrator with excellent results. That entry, and several others, had stories written by Cornell Woolrich, while others were written by Eric Taylor; they were all tightly knit, engrossing little mysteries, competently acted by contract players and directed in several cases by William Castle. One of the few series to gain acceptance with the public and critics alike, the Whistler films hold up quite well today as examples of the kind of mystery film "they just don't make any more."

Whistler, The (1944) **59m.** D: William Castle. Richard Dix, Gloria Stuart, Alan Dinehart, Joan Woodbury, J. Carrol Naish, Byron Foulger, Trevor Bardette.

Whistling in Brooklyn (1943) **87m.** **½ D: S. Sylvan Simon. Red Skelton, Ann Rutherford, Jean Rogers, "Rags" Ragland, Ray Collins, Henry O'Neill, William

Frawley, Sam Levene. Skelton, again as radio sleuth "The Fox," mixed up in murder and pretending to be a member of the Dodgers ball team.

Whistling in Dixie (1942) **74m.** ******* D: S. Sylvan Simon. Red Skelton, Ann Rutherford, George Bancroft, Guy Kibbee. Red, as radio's "Fox" marries Ann, but their Southern honeymoon is interrupted by murder and mystery. Funny Skelton vehicle.

Whistling in the Dark (1941) **77m.** ******* D: S. Sylvan Simon. Red Skelton, Ann Rutherford, Virginia Grey, Conrad Veidt, "Rags" Ragland, Eve Arden. Faithful remake of 1933 film isn't as wacky as subsequent outings with Skelton as radio sleuth "The Fox," but still enjoyable; Red is held by fiendish Veidt and forced to spell out plans for "perfect murder." Followed by two sequels.

White Angel, The (1936) **75m.** ****** D: William Dieterle. Kay Francis, Ian Hunter, Donald Woods, Nigel Bruce, Donald Crisp, Henry O'Neill, Billy Mauch, Halliwell Hobbes. Lavish but unsuccessful biography of Florence Nightingale with Francis miscast in reworked history of 19th-century British nursing pioneer.

White Buffalo, The (1977) **C-97m.** ****** D. J. Lee Thompson. Charles Bronson, Jack Warden, Will Sampson, Kim Novak, Clint Walker, Stuart Whitman, Slim Pickens, Cara Williams, John Carradine. Wild Bill Hickok is haunted by the image of a buffalo that symbolizes his fear of death; strange, murky film, with atypical Bronson role, good support from Warden and Novak. Retitled HUNT TO KILL for network TV.▼

White Cargo (1942) **90m.** ****** D: Richard Thorpe. Hedy Lamarr, Walter Pidgeon, Frank Morgan, Richard Carlson, Reginald Owen. Lamarr, in one of her best-known roles, is the seductive Tondelayo who entrances all at British plantation post in Africa, with Pidgeon the expeditionist who really falls for her. Exotic love scenes, corny plot. Previously filmed in 1929.

White Christmas (1954) **C-120m.** ****** D: Michael Curtiz. Bing Crosby, Danny Kaye, Rosemary Clooney, Vera-Ellen, Dean Jagger, Mary Wickes, Sig Ruman, Grady Sutton. Nice Irving Berlin score is unfortunately interrupted by limp plot of army buddies Crosby and Kaye boosting popularity of winter resort run by their ex-officer Jagger. "What Can You Do With a General" stands out as Berlin's least memorable tune. Partial reworking of HOLIDAY INN, not half as good.▼

White Cliffs of Dover, The (1944) **126m.** ******* D: Clarence Brown. Irene Dunne, Alan Marshal, Van Johnson, Frank Morgan, C. Aubrey Smith, Dame May Whitty, Roddy McDowall, Gladys Cooper, Peter Lawford. American Dunne marries Britisher Marshal in patriotic WW1 romancer that boasts wonderful cast (including young Elizabeth Taylor). Slick but shallow.

White Comanche (1968-Spanish) **C-90m.** *½ D: Gilbert Kay (Jose Briz). Joseph Cotten, William Shatner, Perla Cristal, Rossana Yanni. Boring time-killer detailing the conflict between twin boys whose mother is Indian and whose father is white.▼

White Cradle Inn SEE: **High Fury**

White Dawn, The (1974) **C-109m.** ****½** D: Philip Kaufman. Warren Oates, Timothy Bottoms, Lou Gossett, Simonie Kopakik, Joanasie Salomonie. OK adventure about three whalers in 1896 who become lost in the Arctic and their subsequent exploitation of the Eskimos who save them. Brilliant photography by Michael Chapman partially compensates for rambling narrative.▼

White Dog (1982) **C-89m.** ****½** D: Samuel Fuller. Kristy McNichol, Paul Winfield, Burl Ives, Jameson Parker, Lynn Moody, Marshall Thompson, Paul Bartel, Dick Miller, Parley Baer. Young actress takes in a white dog, unaware that it's been trained to attack black people on sight; professional animal trainer Winfield takes on challenge to retrain him. Interesting but downbeat drama, undeserving of the controversy and preposterous charges of racism that kept it from being released. Script by director Fuller (who has a cameo as Kristy's agent) and Curtis Hanson, loosely based on the Romain Gary novel.

White Fang (1972-Italian-Spanish-French) **C-97m.** ****½** D: Lucio Fulci. Franco Nero, Virna Lisi, Fernando Rey, Rik Battaglia, Harry Carey, Jr. Scenic but needlessly violent tale of a boy and his dog in the wilds of Alaska, based on the Jack London adventure.▼

White Feather (1955) **C-102m.** ****½** D: Robert D. Webb. Robert Wagner, Jeffrey Hunter, Debra Paget, John Lund, Eduard Franz, Noah Beery, Hugh O'Brian. Pat Western film with some good action scenes of government agent Wagner attempting to convince Indian tribe to move to reservation; Paget and Hunter are members of Cheyenne tribe who resist.

White Girl, The (1990) **C-88m.** BOMB D: Tony Brown. Troy Beyer, Taimak, Teresa Farley, Dianne Shaw, O.L. Duke, Michael Spinks, George Kirby. Brown (of PBS' *Tony Brown's Journal*) scripted this preachy, embarrassingly bad home movie about a light-skinned black women (Beyer) and her flirtation with cocaine addiction. Well-intentioned in its anti-drug message, but amateurish. Filmed in 1987. "White Girl," if you care, is slang for cocaine.

White Heat (1949) **114m.** *****½** D: Raoul Walsh. James Cagney, Virginia Mayo, Edmond O'Brien, Margaret Wycherly, Steve Cochran. Cagney returned to gangster films, older but forceful as ever, as psychopathic hood with mother obsession; Mayo is his ne-

[1285]

glected wife, O'Brien the cop out to get him. "Top of the World" finale is now movie legend. Written by Ivan Goff and Ben Roberts, from a Virginia Kellogg story. Also shown in computer-colored version.▼

White Lightning (1973) **C-101m.** **½ D: Joseph Sargent. Burt Reynolds, Jennifer Billingsley, Ned Beatty, Bo Hopkins, Matt Clark, Louise Latham, Diane Ladd. Formula melodrama with moonshiner Burt going after crooked sheriff who drowned his brother; pleasant cast helps this OK action pic. Sequel: GATOR.▼

White Line Fever (1975) **C-92m.** *** D: Jonathan Kaplan. Jan-Michael Vincent, Kay Lenz, Slim Pickens, L. Q. Jones, Leigh French, Don Porter. A B-picture that hits bull's-eye. Vincent is a young trucker who battles corruption on the road and off, with a diesel truck as his "good buddy."▼

White Lions, The (1981) **C-96m.** ** D: Mel Stuart. Michael York, Glynnis O'Connor, Donald Moffat, J. A. Preston, Roger E. Mosley. Slight tale of life in an African wildlife preserve with naturalist York and his family. Mainly for the kids.

White Mama (1980) **C-105m. TVM** D: Jackie Cooper. Bette Davis, Ernest Harden, Eileen Heckart, Virginia Capers, Lurene Tuttle, Anne Ramsey. Prime latter-day Davis. A penniless widow, as a means of survival, strikes a bargain with a streetwise black youth to provide a home for him. Script by Robert C. S. Downs. Above average.▼

White Mischief (1988-British) **C-106m.** *** D: Michael Radford. Sarah Miles, Joss Ackland, John Hurt, Greta Scacchi, Charles Dance, Susan Fleetwood, Jacqueline Pearce, Murray Head, Geraldine Chaplin, Trevor Howard. Elegantly kinky tale based on James Fox's book about the British colony living in Kenya's Happy Valley during the early days of WW2, and the true story of a husband's response to the local stud stealing his beautiful wife. Sensual and quietly bizarre, with meticulous production detail and a fine cast, headed by Scacchi at her most stunning.▼

White Nights (1957-Italian) **94m.** *** D: Luchino Visconti. Maria Schell, Jean Marais, Marcello Mastroianni. Elaborately interwoven love tale arising from casual meeting; based on Dostoyevsky story.▼

White Nights (1985) **C-135m.** **½ D: Taylor Hackford. Mikhail Baryshnikov, Gregory Hines, Isabella Rossellini, Jerzy Skolimowski, Helen Mirren, Geraldine Page, John Glover, Shane Rimmer. Prominent ballet star who defected from Russia to U.S. finds himself back in the U.S.S.R. after a forced plane landing . . . while American expatriate tap dancer is used as bait to wear down his resistance about fleeing the country again. Baryshnikov's powerful presence (as actor and dancer) almost makes up for contrived story; Hines's characterization isn't nearly as believable or appealing. Nicest surprise is surefooted performance by director Skolimowski as KGB agent who hounds Baryshnikov. ▼

White of the Eye (1987-British) **C-110m.** *** D: Donald Cammell. David Keith, Cathy Moriarty, Art Evans, Alan Rosenberg, Alberta Watson, Michael Greene, Mark Hayashi. Bizarre thriller set in a small Arizona town about psycho Keith, who besides being on a killing spree is (understandably) having marital squabbles with wife Moriarty. Dazzling technique recalling the experimental films of the 1960s marks this disturbing picture, a smashing return to films for director Cammell (PERFORMANCE, DEMON SEED) and Moriarty (RAGING BULL, NEIGHBORS).▼

White Savage (1943) **C-75m.** **½ D: Arthur Lubin. Jon Hall, Maria Montez, Sabu, Don Terry, Turhan Bey, Thomas Gomez, Sidney Toler. Standard escapist fare, in glorious Technicolor, with island princess Montez trying to remove obstacles that bar marriage to shark-hunter Hall. Richard Brooks' first screenplay!

White Sheik, The (1951-Italian) **83m.** **½ D: Federico Fellini. Alberto Sordi, Brunella Bova, Leopoldo Trieste, Giulietta Masina. Fellini's first solo film as director is a minor chronicle of the adventures of a provincial couple honeymooning in Rome and the wife's involvement with a cartoon hero, The White Sheik (Sordi). Remade, more or less, as THE WORLD'S GREATEST LOVER.▼

White Sister, The (1933) **110m.** **½ D: Victor Fleming. Helen Hayes, Clark Gable, Lewis Stone, Louise Closser Hale, May Robson, Edward Arnold. Dated but interesting remake of 1923 silent with Lillian Gish and Ronald Colman; this time Hayes is woman who enters convent when she thinks her lover (Gable) has been killed in the war. Fine performances provide major interest today, not the predictable story line.

White Sister (1973-Italian) **C-104m.** **½ D: Alberto Lattuada. Sophia Loren, Adriano Celentano, Fernando Rey. Strange love story of hospital Mother Superior and self-professed young Communist who helps run the wards.

White Slave Ship (1962-Italian) **C-92m.** *½ D: Silvio Amadio. Pier Angeli, Edmund Purdom, Armand Mestral, Ivan Desny. Childish hokum, set in 18th century, of rebellion aboard vessel carrying women to the colonies.

White Squaw, The (1956) **75m.** *½ D: Ray Nazarro. David Brian, May Wynn, William Bishop, Nancy Hale. Tedious narrative and a reverse situation; government taking away land from white rancher to give back to the Indians.

White Tie and Tails (1946) **81m.** **½ D: Charles Barton. Dan Duryea, William Bendix, Ella Raines, Clarence Kolb, Frank Jenks, John Miljan, Scotty Beckett. Breezy film with usual-villain Duryea in good comedy form as butler who pretends to be master of house while boss is away.

✓ **White Tower, The** (1950) **C-98m.** *** D: Ted Tetzlaff. Glenn Ford, Claude Rains, (Alida) Valli, Oscar Homolka, Cedric Hardwicke, Lloyd Bridges. Heavily symbolic but well-done drama about people risking their lives to climb Swiss Alps.▼

White Voices (1965-Italian) **C-93m.** *** D: Pasquale Festa Campanile, Massimo Franciosa. Paolo Ferrari, Sandra Milo, Anouk Aimee, Graziella Granata, Barbara Steele, Jeanne Valerie. Good lusty adventure à la TOM JONES concerns exploits of castrati-singers who have retained high singing voices by means of operation.

White Warrior, The (1961-Italian) **C-86m.** *½ D: Riccardo Freda. Steve Reeves, Giorgia Moll, Renato Baldini, Gerard Herter. Tiring spectacle about tribal chieftain leading rebellion against advancing troops of Czar, set in 19th century.

White Water Rebels (1983) **C 100m.** TVM D: Reza S. Badiyi. Catherine Bach, James Brolin, Pepe Serna, Richard Lynch, Kai Wulff, Michael C. Gwynne. White water kayaker Brolin and photojournalist Bach versus unscrupulous developers who want to dam up a wild mountain river, with a water-soaked outline of DELIVERANCE probably tucked in their life preservers. Average.

White Water Summer (1987) **C-90m.** *½ D: Jeff Bleckner. Kevin Bacon, Sean Astin, Jonathan Ward, K.C. Martel, Matt Adler, Caroline McWilliams, Charles Siebert. Feeble account of Bacon teaching city lad Astin and his pals the ways of the wilderness. Filmed in 1985 and barely released theatrically.▼

White Wilderness (1958) **C-73m.** *** D: James Algar. Narrated by Winston Hibler. Typically good Disney True-Life feature takes a look at the Arctic region, its flora and fauna; highlight is extended sequence on lemmings and their yearly suicide ritual.▼

White Witch Doctor (1953) **C-96m.** **½ D: Henry Hathaway. Susan Hayward, Robert Mitchum, Walter Slezak, Timothy Carey. Bakuba territory is scene of diverse interests of nurse Hayward who wants to bring modern medicine to natives and adventurers Mitchum and Slezak bent on finding hidden treasure.

✓ **White Zombie** (1932) **73m.** *** D: Victor Halperin. Bela Lugosi, Madge Bellamy, Robert Frazer, Brandon Hurst. Eerily made film about army of zombies at sugar mill working for white leader; unique low-budget chiller.▼

Who? (1974-British) **C-93m.** **½ D: Jack Gold. Elliott Gould, Trevor Howard, Joseph Bova, Ed Grover, James Noble, John Lehne. Gould plays FBI agent investigating American scientist's car crash in Russia, and subsequent reappearance with a strangely restructured face. Intriguing if not completely satisfying spy/sci-fi mix.

Who Dares Wins SEE: **Final Option, The**▼

Who Done It? (1942) **75m.** *** D: Erle C. Kenton. Bud Abbott, Lou Costello, Patric Knowles, Louise Allbritton, William Gargan, William Bendix, Mary Wickes, Don Porter, Thomas Gomez, Jerome Cowan, Ludwig Stossel. One of A&C's best finds the boys as would-be radio writers who pretend to be detectives when the network's president is murdered, and everyone believes them—including the killer! Great supporting cast is topped by Wickes as wise-cracking secretary and Bendix as real cop who's even dumber than Lou.▼

Who Done It? (1956-British) **85m.** **½ D: Basil Dearden. Benny Hill, Belinda Lee, David Kossoff, Garry Marsh, George Margo, Ernest Thesiger. Hill's only star vehicle movie is a Red Skelton-type comedy about a novice private eye involved with foreign spies. No double-entendre jokes, but lots of slapstick, much of it labored and obvious. Best for kids.▼

Whoever Slew Auntie Roo? SEE: **Who Slew Auntie Roo?**▼

Who Framed Roger Rabbit (1988) **C-103m.** ***½ D: Robert Zemeckis. Bob Hoskins, Christopher Lloyd, Joanna Cassidy, Stubby Kaye, Alan Tilvern, and the voices of Charles Fleischer, Lou Hirsch, Mel Blanc, Mae Questel, Tony Anselmo, June Foray, Wayne Allwine. Staggering special-effects comedy places down-and-out detective Hoskins on the trail of a murderer, with cartoon star Roger Rabbit (the chief suspect) at his side. Flaws in story and characterization pale alongside the incredible blend of live-action and animation, but the ultimate feat is making us believe that Roger and his cartoon colleagues actually exist. Extra fun: spotting the many cartoon stars who make cameo appearances, looking as they did in 1947, when the story takes place. Jessica Rabbit's speaking voice was done by Kathleen Turner (unbilled) and her singing voice by Amy Irving. A coproduction of the Steven Spielberg and Walt Disney companies. The animation was directed by Richard Williams, who received a special Academy Award; three other Oscars included one for Special Visual Effects.▼

Who Gets the Friends? (1988) **C-100m.** TVM D: Lila Garrett. Jill Clayburgh, James Farentino, Lucie Arnaz, Leigh Taylor-Young, Robin Thomas, James Sloyan, Greg Mullavey. There's a nice sensibility to this sophisticated comedy about a (seemingly) happily married couple's divorce and its effect on the twosome's close-knit circle of friends. Script by producer/director Garrett and Sandy Krinski. Above average.

Who Goes There? SEE: **Passionate Sentry, The**

Who Has Seen the Wind (1977-Canadian) C-100m. **½ D: Allan King. Brian Painchaud, Douglas Junor, Gordon Pinsent, Chapelle Jaffe, Jose Ferrer, Helen Shaver. OK chronicle of young Painchaud and Junor's life in Saskatchewan during the Depression. Ferrer is amusing as a bootlegger.▼

Who Is Harry Kellerman and Why Is He Saying Those Terrible Things About Me? (1971) C-108m. ** D: Ulu Grosbard. Dustin Hoffman, Barbara Harris, Jack Warden, David Burns, Gabriel Dell, Dom DeLuise, Betty Walker. Muddled comedy-drama by Herb Gardner casts Dustin as successful rock composer-singer who finds money doesn't answer all of life's questions. Harris comes along late in film to save this debacle with an outstanding performance.

Who Is Julia? (1986) C-100m. TVM D: Walter Grauman. Mare Winningham, Jameson Parker, Jeffrey DeMunn, Jonathan Banks, Bert Remsen, Mason Adams. Woman undergoes a brain transplant. An unexpectedly literate adaptation by James S. Sadwith of Barbara S. Harris' novel. Above average.

Who Is Killing the Great Chefs of Europe? (1978) C-112m. *** D: Ted Kotcheff. George Segal, Jacqueline Bisset, Robert Morley, Jean-Pierre Cassel, Philippe Noiret, Jean Rochefort, Madge Ryan, Joss Ackland, Nigel Havers. Slick comedy whodunit with self-explanatory title has luscious views of European scenery and food, plus a magnificently funny role for Morley as the world's premier gourmet. Script by Peter Stone, based on Nan and Ivan Lyons' novel.

Who Is Killing the Stuntmen? SEE: **Stunts**▼

Who Is the Black Dahlia? (1975) C-100m. TVM D: Joseph Pevney. Efrem Zimbalist, Jr., Ronny Cox, Macdonald Carey, Lucie Arnaz, Tom Bosley, Gloria DeHaven, Rick Jason, June Lockhart, Mercedes McCambridge, Donna Mills. Veteran L.A. detective Zimbalist attempts to piece together clues in the murder of a woman in 1947. Based on a true unsolved murder case, this atmospheric crime drama is intriguingly written and well cast down to the cameos. Source material later used for TRUE CONFESSIONS. Above average.

Who Killed Gail Preston? (1938) 60m. **½ D: Leon Barsha. Don Terry, Rita Hayworth, Robert Paige, Wyn Cahoon, Gene Morgan, Marc Lawrence, Arthur Loft. Minor whodunit fairly well played; murder in a nightclub is the premise.

Who Killed Mary What's'ername? (1971) C-90m. **½ D: Ernie Pintoff. Red Buttons, Alice Playten, Sylvia Miles, Sam Waterston, Dick Williams, Conrad Bain. Diabetic ex-boxer sets out to find a prostitute's murderer when he becomes angered at everyone's indifference. Whodunit isn't bad, but nothing special; acting is generally good.▼

Who Killed Teddy Bear? (1965) 91m. *½ D: Joseph Cates. Juliet Prowse, Sal Mineo, Jan Murray, Elaine Stritch, Dan Travanty (Daniel J. Travanti). Sleazy, leering low-budget suspenser about psychopathic busboy Mineo preying on discotheque hostess Prowse. A waste of talent.

Who Killed the Mysterious Mr. Foster? SEE: **Sam Hill: Who Killed Mr. Foster?**

Whole Shootin' Match, The (1978) 101m. *** D: Eagle Pennell. Lou Perry, Sonny Davis, Doris Hargrave, Eric Henshaw, David Weber. A pair of hapless Texas buddies on the darker side of 30 grasp at life and constantly come up empty yet still trust they will reach the end of their rainbow. Humorous, melancholy portrait of two very human beings; an independent feature shot on a budget of $30,000.

Whole Town's Talking, The (1935) 95m. *** D: John Ford. Edward G. Robinson, Jean Arthur, Wallace Ford, Arthur Hohl, Edward Brophy, Arthur Byron, Donald Meek. Entertaining comedy with meek clerk Robinson a lookalike for notorious gangster; fine performances by E. G. and Arthur. Script by Jo Swerling and Robert Riskin, from a W.R. Burnett novel.

Whole Truth, The (1958-British) 84m. **½ D: John Guillermin. Stewart Granger, Donna Reed, George Sanders, Gianna Maria Canale. Good cast lends strength to fair plot of almost perfect attempt to pin murder of movie starlet on producer Granger.

Whole World Is Watching, The (1969) C-97m. TVM D: Richard Colla. Joseph Campanella, James Farentino, Burl Ives, Hal Holbrook, Steve Ihnat, Rick Ely, Stephen McNally, Carrie Snodgress. Young lawyer brothers defend student radical accused of murdering policeman during campus riot. OK tension during trial, but major characters come across as stereotypes. Predecessor of "The Lawyers" segment of *The Bold Ones*, written by the ubiquitous Levinson-Link team. Average.

Who'll Save Our Children? (1978) C-100m. TVM D: George Schaefer. Shirley Jones, Len Cariou, Cassie Yates, Conchata Ferrell, Frances Sternhagen. Well-acted drama about foster parents who battle to keep the youngsters they have raised when the natural parents, who deserted the children years earlier, sue to reclaim them. Based on Rachel Maddux' *The Orchard Children*. Above average.

Who'll Stop the Rain (1978) **C-126m.**
*** D: Karel Reisz. Nick Nolte, Tuesday
Weld, Michael Moriarty, Anthony Zerbe,
Richard Masur, Ray Sharkey, David Opa-
toshu, Gail Strickland, Charles Haid. Rob-
ert Stone's National Book Award-winning
Dog Soldiers suffers from excessively gen-
teel treatment in telling its truly mean story
about the smuggling of heroin from Viet-
nam to California. Strong performances in
virtually every role. Also known as DOG
SOLDIERS.▼
Wholly Moses! (1980) **C-109m.** *½ D:
Gary Weis. Dudley Moore, Laraine New-
man, James Coco, Paul Sand, Jack Gilford,
Dom DeLuise, John Houseman, Madeline
Kahn, David L. Lander, Richard Pryor,
John Ritter. Great cast flounders in this
stale saga of "savior" Moore, who thinks
God has ordained him to lead the Jews out
of Egypt. Some amusing bits, notably by
DeLuise; otherwise, an appalling waste.▼
Whoopee! (1930) **C-93m.** *** D: Thorn-
ton Freeland. Eddie Cantor, Eleanor Hunt,
Paul Gregory, John Rutherford, Ethel
Shutta, Spencer Charters. Antique movie
musical sparked by Cantor's performance
as a hyper-hypochondriac, and Busby
Berkeley's wonderful production numbers.
Cantor sings "Making Whoopee" and "My
Baby Just Cares for Me"; the girl who
sings the first chorus of the opening song
is a very young Betty Grable. Filmed in
early two-color Technicolor. Remade as
UP IN ARMS.▼
Whoopee Boys, The (1986) **C-88m.**
BOMB D: John Byrum. Michael O'Keefe,
Paul Rodriguez, Denholm Elliott, Carole
Shelley, Andy Bumatai, Eddie Deezen,
Marsha Warfield, Joe Spinell, Dan
O'Herlihy. Awful comedy about a couple of
wiseguys who try to break into Palm Beach
society. Crude, to say the least.▼
Who's Afraid of Virginia Woolf? (1966)
129m. ***½ D: Mike Nichols. Elizabeth
Taylor, Richard Burton, George Segal,
Sandy Dennis. Two couples get together
for an all-night session of bitter conver-
sation; Burton and Taylor's finest hour
(together) in searing Edward Albee drama.
Taylor and Dennis won Oscars, as did
Haskell Wexler's incisive b&w photography, Richard Sylbert's art direction, and
Irene Sharaff's costumes. Film broke Hollywood taboos for adult material, would
cause lesser furor today. Script by producer Ernest Lehman. Nichols' first film
as director.▼
Who Says I Can't Ride a Rainbow?
(1971) **C-85m.** **½ D: Edward Mann.
Jack Klugman, Norma French, Reuben
Figueroa, David Mann, Morgan Freeman,
Esther Rolle. Offbeat story of man who
feels it is the children of the world who
will determine its future.
Who's Been Sleeping in My Bed? (1963)

C-103m. **½ D: Daniel Mann. Dean Martin, Elizabeth Montgomery, Carol Burnett,
Martin Balsam, Jill St. John, Richard Conte,
Louis Nye. Undemanding fluff about TV
star Martin being urged altar-ward by fian-
ceé Montgomery. Burnett, in her film
debut, is his psychiatrist's nurse.
Whose Life Is It Anyway? (1981) **C-
118m.** ***½ D: John Badham. Richard
Dreyfuss, John Cassavetes, Christine Lahti,
Bob Balaban, Kenneth McMillan, Kaki
Hunter, Janet Eilber, Thomas Carter. Searing black comedy in which sculptor Drey-
fuss is paralyzed from the neck down in an
auto accident, argues for his right to die.
Remarkable performance by Dreyfuss, ex-
cellent ones by hospital chief of staff
Cassavetes, doctor Lahti, judge McMillan,
nurse trainee Hunter. From Brian Clark's
hit play, with a script by the author and
Reginald Rose.▼
Who's Got the Action? (1962) **C-93m.**
**½ D: Daniel Mann. Dean Martin, Lana
Turner, Eddie Albert, Nita Talbot, Walter
Matthau, Paul Ford, Margo, John McGiver.
Strained froth of Turner combatting hubby
Martin's horse-racing fever by turning
bookie.
Who's Harry Crumb? (1989) **C-98m.** **
D: Paul Flaherty. John Candy, Jeffrey
Jones, Annie Potts, Tim Thomerson, Barry
Corbin, Shawnee Smith, Valri Bromfield,
Renee Coleman, Joe Flaherty, Lyle Alzado,
James Belushi, Stephen Young. Candy is
ideally cast as an inept private detective
attempting to unearth a kidnapper in this
uneven comedy. Has some very funny
moments, but too much outright silliness.
▼
Who Slew Auntie Roo? (1971) **C-89m.**
** D: Curtis Harrington. Shelley Winters,
Mark Lester, Chloe Franks, Ralph Rich-
ardson, Lionel Jeffries, Hugh Griffith. Sickie
about daffy old lady who steers unwitting
children into her lair. Made in England;
intended to be a travesty of *Hansel and
Gretel!* Also known as WHOEVER SLEW
AUNTIE ROO?▼
Who's Minding the Mint? (1967) **C-97m.**
***½ D: Howard Morris. Jim Hutton,
Dorothy Provine, Milton Berle, Joey Bish-
op, Bob Denver, Walter Brennan, Victor
Buono, Jack Gilford, Jamie Farr, Jackie
Joseph. Hilarious comedy, neglected at
time of release, is tremendous fun in the
classic comedy tradition, with motley gang
of thieves helping U.S. Mint worker Hutton
replace money he accidentally destroyed.
Buono is especially funny as pompous
ex-skipper.▼
Who's Minding the Store? (1963) **C-90m.**
**½ D: Frank Tashlin. Jerry Lewis, Agnes
Moorehead, Jill St. John, John McGiver,
Ray Walston, Nancy Kulp, Francesca
Bellini. Jerry Lewis vehicle with bumbling
idiot (guess who?) set loose in department

store. Great supporting cast in stereotyped comic foil roles, plus one good inventive bit.

Who's That Girl? (1987) **C-94m.** BOMB D: James Foley. Madonna, Griffin Dunne, Haviland Morris, John McMartin, Robert Swan, Drew Pillsbury, John Mills. Atrocious attempt at screwball comedy with Dunne as the hapless hero whose life is turned inside out when he's assigned to escort Madonna (just sprung from jail) out of town. Derivative film is missing just two things: charm and humor.▼

Who's That Knocking at My Door? (1968) **90m.** *** D: Martin Scorsese. Zina Bethune, Harvey Keitel, Anne Collette, Lennard Kuras, Michael Scala, Harry Northrup, Bill Minkin. Crude but fascinating autobiographical drama from Scorsese, his first feature, focusing on relationship between streetwise Keitel, hung up by his strict Catholic upbringing, and independent young woman (Bethune). Keitel's film debut. Also released as J.R.

Who Stole the Body? (1962-French) **92m.** ** D: Jean Girault. Francis Blanche, Darry Cowl, Clement Harari, Daniel Ceccaldi, Mario David. Weak farce on horror films, with Blanche and Cowl two dimwits trying to solve a crime.

Who Was That Lady? (1960) **115m.** *** D: George Sidney. Tony Curtis, Dean Martin, Janet Leigh, James Whitmore, John McIntire, Barbara Nichols, Joi Lansing. Spicy shenanigans move along at lively pace as Curtis and Martin pretend to be secret agents to confuse Tony's jealous wife Leigh; script by Norman Krasna, from his play.

Who Will Love My Children? (1983) **C-100m.** TVM D: John Erman. Ann-Margret, Frederic Forrest, Cathryn Damon, Donald Moffat, Lonny Chapman, Patricia Smith, Christopher Allport, Tracey Gold, Soleil Moon Frye, Robbie Kiger. Dying mother (Ann-Margret in her TV-movie debut) strives to have her ten children placed with loving families in this poignant weeper, based by writer Michael Bortman on the true story of Iowa farm wife Lucile Fray. Above average.

Why Bother to Knock (1964-British) **88m.** *½ D: Cyril Frankel. Elke Sommer, Richard Todd, Nicole Maurey, Scot Finch. Trashy smut about Todd traipsing around Europe giving out keys to his pals, with the girls all turning up unexpectedly.

Why Me? (1984) **C-100m.** TVM D: Fielder Cook. Glynnis O'Connor, Armand Assante, Craig Wasson, Annie Potts, Michael Sacks, William Windom. Sensitively handled but graphic drama about Air Force nurse whose face, life and marriage are shattered in a head-on collision. O'Connor turns in another sterling performance despite the fact that her character's mouth is literally stitched shut through much of the film. True story of Leola Mae Harmon was the basis of Dalene Young's incisive script. Above average.▼

Why Must I Die? (1960) **86m.** ** D: Roy Del Ruth. Terry Moore, Debra Paget, Bert Freed, Julie Reding. Similar to I WANT TO LIVE except in quality. Moore is singer falsely convicted of murder, with expected histrionics.

Why Not! (1979-French) **C-93m.** *** D: Coline Serreau. Sami Frey, Christine Murillo, Mario Gonzalez, Michel Aumont, Nicole Jamet, Mathe Souverbie. Frey, Murillo and Gonzalez, trying to leave their pasts behind, are roommates—and share the same bed. Then Frey becomes involved with Jamet. Sometimes funny and touching, but not as involving as it should be. Original French title: POURQUOI PAS!

Why Shoot the Teacher? (1977-Canadian) **C-101m.** *** D: Silvio Narizzano. Bud Cort, Samantha Eggar, Chris Wiggins, Gary Reineke, John Friesen, Michael J. Reynolds. Simple, warm, enjoyable story of Cort's experiences when he takes a teaching job in a small, isolated farming town during the Depression.▼

Why Worry? (1923) **77m.** ***½ D: Fred Newmeyer, Sam Taylor. Harold Lloyd, Jobyna Ralston, John Aasen, Leo White, James Mason. Hilarious story of millionaire playboy Lloyd who stumbles into revolution-ridden country and inadvertently becomes involved. Packed with belly-laugh sight-gags. Edited for TV and paired with abridged version of 1921 daredevil short NEVER WEAKEN.

Why Would Anyone Want to Kill a Nice Girl Like You? (1969-British) **C-99m.** ** D: Don Sharp. Eva Renzi, David Buck, Peter Vaughan, Paul Hubschmid, Sophie Hardy, Kay Walsh. A young tourist on the French Riviera thinks someone is trying to kill her, but none of the local officials will believe her. Familiar storyline handled in routine fashion.

Why Would I Lie? (1980) **C-105m.** ** D: Larry Peerce. Treat Williams, Lisa Eichhorn, Gabriel Swann, Susan Heldfond, Anne Byrne, Valerie Curtin, Jocelyn Brando, Nicolas Coster, Severn Darden. Irrational dud about compulsive liar Williams, who tries to unite Swann with ex-con mother Eichhorn. Film is also odiously reactionary; the villainess (Heldfond) is a one-dimensionally manipulative, man-hating feminist.

Wichita (1955) **C-81m.** **½ D: Jacques Tourneur. Joel McCrea, Vera Miles, Lloyd Bridges, Wallace Ford, Peter Graves. Action-filled Western; good cast helps Wyatt Earp (McCrea) restore order to Western town overrun with outlaws.▼

Wicked as They Come (1957-British) **94m.** ** D: Ken Hughes. Arlene Dahl, Phil Carey, Herbert Marshall, David Kossoff.

Dahl cavorts nicely in this minor story of a girl from the poor part of town involved with the wrong people.

Wicked City, The (1950-French) **76m.** *½ D: Francois Villiers. Maria Montez, Jean-Pierre Aumont, Lilli Palmer, Marcel Dalio. Even exotic Montez can't spice lazy telling of unscrupulous woman and the gob she involves in her sordid life.

Wicked Dreams of Paula Schultz, The (1968) **C-113m.** BOMB D: George Marshall. Elke Sommer, Bob Crane, Werner Klemperer, Joey Forman, John Banner, Maureen Arthur. Laughless dud about beautiful East German Olympic hopeful who polevaults over Berlin Wall to freedom; unengaging cast was mostly recruited from *Hogan's Heroes.*

Wicked Lady, The (1945-British) **104m.** **½ D: Leslie Arliss. Margaret Lockwood, James Mason, Patricia Roc, Michael Rennie, Martita Hunt, Felix Aylmer. Title refers to Lockwood, in this unconvincing costumer of female outlaw who teams with robber Mason in evil doings. Remade in 1983.▼

Wicked Lady, The (1983-British) **C-98m.** *½ D: Michael Winner. Faye Dunaway, Alan Bates, John Gielgud, Denholm Elliott, Prunella Scales, Oliver Tobias, Glynis Barber. Remake of 1945 film, coscripted by its director, Leslie Arliss, about a scheming vixen who becomes a "highwayman" by night; hasn't the panache to turn its campy material into the romp it's intended to be. Heavy-handed stuff—including the periodic nudity.▼

Wicked, Wicked (1973) **C-95m.** BOMB D: Richard L. Bare. Tiffany Bolling, Scott Brady, David Bailey, Edd Byrnes. Disastrous mystery-thriller centering around series of hotel murders. Film was released in Duo-vision split-screen process with two things happening at once. Pity there was not enough material for even one.

Wicked Woman (1954) **77m.** *½ D: Russell Rouse. Richard Egan, Beverly Michaels, Percy Helton, Evelyn Scott. Lumbering drama about no-good waitress leading assorted men astray.

Wicker Man, The (1973-British) **C-103m.** ***½ D: Robin Hardy. Edward Woodward, Christopher Lee, Britt Ekland, Diane Cilento, Ingrid Pitt, Lindsay Kemp. Harrowing, absorbing thriller by Anthony Shaffer; not really a horror film as many believe. Scot police sergeant Woodward comes to small island investigating disappearance of a child, discovers a society of modern pagans. Eerie and erotic, with seemingly authentic local color and folk music; a must-see. Shown only in truncated versions for many years; beware the 87m. and 95m. prints, which may still be in circulation.▼

Wide Blue Road, The (1956-Italian) **100m.** **½ D: Gillo Pontecorvo. Yves Montand,

Alida Valli, Francisco Rabal, Peter Carsten, Ronaldino. Montand is non-plussed playboy taking pleasure where he finds it until Valli comes into picture. Performers outshine dialogue.

Wide Open Faces (1938) **67m.** **½ D: Kurt Neumann. Joe E. Brown, Jane Wyman, Alison Skipworth, Lyda Roberti, Alan Baxter, Lucien Littlefield, Sidney Toler. Enjoyable Brown vehicle with top-notch supporting cast; innocent soda jerk mixed up with gangster.

Widow, The (1955-Italian) **89m.** ** D: Lewis Milestone. Patricia Roc, Anna Maria Ferrero, Massimo Serrato, Akim Tamiroff. Uneven soaper of Roc involved with lover Serrato, a sports car racer, who falls for Ferrero; film meanders.

Widow (1976) **C-100m.** TVM D: J. Lee Thompson. Michael Learned, Bradford Dillman, Farley Granger, Louise Sorel, Robert Lansing, Carol Rossen, Eric Olson. Dreary soap opera about a woman with two children trying to adjust emotionally after her husband's death, taken from Lynn Caine's best-seller. Below average.

Widow From Chicago, The (1930) **64m.** ** D: Edward L. Cline. Alice White, Neil Hamilton, Edward G. Robinson, Frank McHugh, Lee Shumway. Robinson plays a beer baron targeted for revenge by White, whose brother he rubbed out, in this antiquated gangster film, interesting only for Robinson's pre-LITTLE CAESAR performance.

Wife, Doctor and Nurse (1937) **85m.** **½ D: Walter Lang. Loretta Young, Warner Baxter, Virginia Bruce, Jane Darwell, Sidney Blackmer, Minna Gombell, Elisha Cook, Jr., Lon Chaney, Jr. Baxter is caught between two women, but seems uninterested in both. Bright comedy with expert cast.

Wife, Husband and Friend (1939) **80m.** *** D: Gregory Ratoff. Loretta Young, Warner Baxter, Binnie Barnes, George Barbier, Cesar Romero, J. Edward Bromberg, Eugene Pallette. Renie Riano. Entertaining comedy about aspiring singer Young whose husband Baxter tries to show her up; fun, but better as EVERYBODY DOES IT. Produced and scripted by Nunnally Johnson, from a story by James M. Cain(!)

Wifemistress (1977-Italian) **C-110m.** **½ D: Marco Vicario. Marcello Mastroianni, Laura Antonelli, Leonard Mann, Annie-Belle, Gastone Moschin, William Berger. Antonelli, repressed by philandering husband Mastroianni, sets out to explore his secret lives after he is forced into hiding. Sometimes erotic but mostly murky comedy-drama.▼

Wife of Monte Cristo, The (1946) **80m.** ** D: Edgar G. Ulmer. John Loder, Lenore Aubert, Charles Dingle, Eduardo Ciannelli, Eva Gabor, Martin Kosleck. Corruption in the medical profession proves a formidable match for the Count; standard low-budget swashbuckler.

Wife Takes a Flyer, The (1942) 86m. ** D: Richard Wallace. Joan Bennett, Franchot Tone, Allyn Joslyn, Cecil Cunningham, Chester Clute. Weak WW2 espionage comedy of Tone pretending to be Bennett's husband to escape from Holland.

Wife vs. Secretary (1936) 88m. **½ D: Clarence Brown. Clark Gable, Jean Harlow, Myrna Loy, May Robson, George Barbier, James Stewart, Hobart Cavanaugh. Perfect example of Hollywood gloss, with three topnotch stars towering over inferior material. Harlow is particularly good in tale of secretary who becomes invaluable to her boss (Gable), causing complications in both of their lives.

Wife Wanted (1946) 73m. ** D: Phil Karlson. Kay Francis, Paul Cavanagh, Robert Shayne, Veda Ann Borg. In her last film, Francis is film star innocently hooked up with lonely-heart crooks; low production values.

Wilby Conspiracy, The (1975) C-101m. *** D: Ralph Nelson. Sidney Poitier, Michael Caine, Nicol Williamson, Prunella Gee, Persis Khambatta, Saeed Jaffrey. Slick chase movie about black African political activist and the reluctant white companion he drags with him on cross-country flight from the law. Memories of Poitier's earlier THE DEFIANT ONES keep focusing throughout, but the two stars maintain a light touch. Sinister Williamson steals it from them both.▼

Wild and the Free, The (1980) C-100m. TVM D: James Hill. Granville Van Dusen, Linda Gray, Frank Logan, Ray Forchion, Sharon Anderson, Bill Gribble. Comical adventure involving scientists working in chimpanzee research and a group of home-raised chimps which are returned to the jungle. Average.▼

Wild and the Innocent, The (1959) C-84m. **½ D: Jack Sher. Audie Murphy, Joanne Dru, Gilbert Roland, Jim Backus, Sandra Dee, George Mitchell, Peter Breck. Murphy and Dee make an engaging duo as trapper and untamed country girl involved in gunplay in town during July 4th holiday.

Wild and the Willing, The (1962-British) 112m. ** D: Ralph Thomas. Virginia Maskell, Paul Rogers, Samantha Eggar, Ian McShane, John Hurt, Richard Warner. Life and love at a provincial university, with over-earnest attempt to be realistic and daring in story of student who seduces professor's wife.

Wild and Wonderful (1964) C-88m. **½ D: Michael Anderson. Tony Curtis, Christine Kaufmann, Larry Storch, Marty Ingels, Jacques Aubuchon, Jules Munshin. Empty slapstick froth involving French poodle movie star with Curtis and Kaufmann romancing.

Wild and Wooly (1978) C-100m. TVM D: Philip Leacock. Chris DeLisle, Susan Bigelow, Jessica Walter, Doug McClure, David Doyle, Ross Martin, Vic Morrow. It's *Charlie's Angels* in the Old West, with three women breaking out of prison to try to thwart the assassination of Teddy Roosevelt. A pilot that led nowhere. Average.▼

Wild Angels, The (1966) C-93m. *½ D: Roger Corman. Peter Fonda, Nancy Sinatra, Bruce Dern, Diane Ladd, Buck Taylor, Norman Alden, Michael J. Pollard, Joan Shawlee, Gayle Hunnicutt, Dick Miller. Predecessor of EASY RIDER without that film's class; Charles Griffith's story of destructive motorcycle gang is OK after about 24 beers. Peter Bogdanovich worked extensively on this film: writing, editing, second unit, etc.; he also can be glimpsed in one of the rumbles.▼

Wild Beds SEE: Tigers in Lipstick▼

Wild Blue Yonder, The (1951) 98m. **½ D: Allan Dwan. Wendell Corey, Vera Ralston, Forrest Tucker, Phil Harris, Walter Brennan, Ruth Donnelly. Standard WW2 aviation yarn, saluting the B-29 bomber, detailing friendship of Corey and Tucker, rivalry for nurse Ralston, etc. And just for change of pace, Harris sings "The Thing."

Wild Boys of the Road (1933) 68m. *** D: William A. Wellman. Frankie Darro, Rochelle Hudson, Dorothy Coonan, Edwin Philips, Ann Hovey, Arthur Hohl, Sterling Holloway. Darro, Philips, and Coonan are unable to find work during the Depression, so they ride the rails, panhandle, steal. Dated but still provocative Warner Bros. "social conscience" drama.

Wild Bunch, The (1969) C-134m. **** D: Sam Peckinpah. William Holden, Ernest Borgnine, Robert Ryan, Edmond O'Brien, Warren Oates, Ben Johnson, Jaime Sanchez, Strother Martin, L. Q. Jones, Albert Dekker, Bo Hopkins, Emilio Fernandez, Dub Taylor. Peckinpah's best film won instant notoriety for its "beautiful" bloodletting, but seems almost restrained alongside today's films. Aging outlaws with their own code of ethics find themselves passe in 1913 and decide to retire after one final haul. Acting, dialogue, direction, score, photography, and especially editing are world class; an authentic American classic. Reissued in 1981 at 142m., with two deleted sequences restored. European theatrical version running 144m. now available on homevideo.▼

Wildcat (1942) 70m. ** D: Frank McDonald. Richard Arlen, Arline Judge, Buster Crabbe, William Frawley, Arthur Hunnicutt, Elisha Cook, Jr. Crabbe and Arlen are rival oilmen dueling to see who can bring in the first well. Another Pine–Thomas production with the usual quota of thrills and romance.

Wildcats (1986) **C-107m.** *** D: Michael Ritchie. Goldie Hawn, Swoosie Kurtz, Robyn Lively, Brandy Gold, James Keach, Jan Hooks, Bruce McGill, Nipsey Russell, Mykel T. Williamson, M. Emmet Walsh, Woody Harrelson. Football-crazy phys-ed teacher Hawn finally gets her wish—to coach a junior varsity team—at a rough inner-city high school. Never strays from formula but manages to deliver the laughs. Entertaining.▼

Wild Cats on the Beach (1959-Italian) **C-96m.** **½ D: Vittorio Sala. Elsa Martinelli, Alberto Sordi, Georges Marchal, Antonio Cifariello. Quartet of love tales set at resort area of Cote D'Azur; varying in quality.

Wild Child, The (1969-French) **85m.** *** D: Francois Truffaut. Francois Truffaut, Jean-Pierre Cargol, Jean Daste, Paul Ville. Initially absorbing true story of wild boy raised alone in French woods and the doctor who tries to civilize him. Simply told, deliberately old-fashioned in technique; film loses steam half-way through. Truffaut is ideal as the doctor. Set in 1700s.

Wild Company (1930) **73m.** *½ D: Leo McCarey. H. B. Warner, Frank Albertson, Sharon Lynn, Joyce Compton, Claire McDowell, Bela Lugosi. Badly dated melodrama of flaming youth and generation-gap; devil-may-care Albertson ignores parents' warnings about company he keeps, gets into trouble over underworld murder. Lugosi plays nightclub owner.

Wild Country, The (1971) **C-100m.** **½ D: Robert Totten. Steve Forrest, Vera Miles, Ronny Howard, Jack Elam, Frank deKova, Morgan Woodward, Clint Howard. Standard Disney fare, adapted from Ralph Moody's *Little Britches*, about joys and hardships faced by family which moves from Pittsburgh to Wyoming in 1880s. Magnificent scenery.▼

Wild Drifter SEE: **Cockfighter**▼

Wild Duck, The (1983-Australian) **C-96m.** *½ D: Henri Safran. Liv Ullmann, Jeremy Irons, Lucinda Jones, John Meillon, Arthur Dignam, Michael Pate. Dreary, disappointing adaptation of the Ibsen play, centering on two days in the lives of the Ackland (anglicized from "Ekdal") family members and updating the story by twenty-odd years. The question is: Why? Performances are OK, but it's oh so slow and pretentious.▼

Wilderness Family, Part 2 SEE: **Further Adventures of the Wilderness Family**▼

Wild for Kicks (1962-British) **92m.** ** D: Edmond T. Greville. David Farrar, Noelle Adam, Christopher Lee, Gillian Hills, Shirley Anne Field, Oliver Reed. Strange little drama of rebellious teenager involved in murder. Original British title: BEAT GIRL.▼

Wild Geese, The (1978-British) **C-134m.**

**½ D: Andrew V. McLaglen. Richard Burton, Roger Moore, Richard Harris, Hardy Kruger, Stewart Granger, Jack Watson, Frank Finlay, Jeff Corey, Winston Ntshona. Silly but entertaining action yarn by Reginald Rose with Burton miscast as leader of mercenaries who rescue kidnapped African leader. Better (and shorter) script would have helped. Sequel followed in 1985.▼

Wild Geese II (1985-British) **C-125m.** ** D: Peter Hunt. Scott Glenn, Barbara Carrera, Edward Fox, Laurence Olivier, Robert Webber, Robert Freitag, Kenneth Haigh. Cluttered action-adventure about a much-wanted mercenary hired to spring arch-Nazi Rudolf Hess from Berlin's Spandau prison and the incidents this triggers. Uncomfortable mix of straight action and tongue-in-cheek further hinders overly busy script.▼

Wild Geese Calling (1941) **77m.** ** D: John Brahm. Henry Fonda, Joan Bennett, Warren William, Ona Munson, Barton MacLane, Russell Simpson. Action and romance in 1890s Oregon and Alaska, but not enough of either to push this one over the hump.

Wild Gold (1934) **75m.** ** D: George Marshall. John Boles, Claire Trevor, Harry Green, Roger Imhof, Monroe Owsley, Ruth Gillette. Strange blend of comedy, melodrama, romance, and music in hodgepodge story of miner Boles infatuated with singer Trevor, facing irate husband, unexpected disaster in remote forest cabin. Uses stock footage from silent film THE JOHNSTOWN FLOOD.

Wild Guitar (1962) **87m.** BOMB D: Ray Dennis Steckler. Arch Hall, Jr., Nancy Czar, William Watters (Arch Hall, Sr.), Cash Flagg (Ray Dennis Steckler). Guitar-playing, motorcycle-riding Hall is exploited by a deceitful record executive. Perfectly awful melodrama.▼

Wild Harvest (1947) **92m.** *½ D: Tay Garnett. Alan Ladd, Dorothy Lamour, Robert Preston, Lloyd Nolan, Richard Erdman, Allen Jenkins. Pretty dismal film of traveling grain-harvesters with Preston and Ladd rivaling for Lamour's love.

Wild Heart, The (1950-British) **C-82m.** ** D: Michael Powell, Emeric Pressburger. Jennifer Jones, David Farrar, Cyril Cusack, Sybil Thorndike, Edward Chapman, George Cole, Hugh Griffith, Esmond Knight. Muddled tale of strange Welsh girl in late 19th century whose life is dominated by superstitions; she marries minister but is stirred by lusty squire. Beautiful color location photography by Christopher Challis. Re-edited from 110m. British release called GONE TO EARTH, which plays much better.

Wild Heritage (1958) **C-78m.** **½ D: Charles Haas. Will Rogers, Jr., Maureen O'Sullivan, Rod McKuen, Casey Tibbs. Soaper involving events in the intertwining lives of two westward-bound pioneer families.

Wild Horse Hank (1979-Canadian) **C-94m.** **½ D: Eric Till. Linda Blair, Michael Wincott, Al Waxman, Pace Bradford, Richard Crenna. Inoffensive adventure of college student Blair trying to save horses from being butchered for dog food. A bit overlong, even at 94m., and Blair walks through her role; still, older children may enjoy it.▼

Wild Horses (1985) **C-100m.** TVM D: Dick Lowry. Kenny Rogers, Pam Dawber, Ben Johnson, David Andrews, Richard Masur, Karen Carlson, Richard Farnsworth. Ex-rodeo champ turns his back on his family and his humdrum blue-collar life to join a wild-horse roundup. Rogers's personable charm and a couple of his songs carry it, but special thanks should go to veteran actors (both onetime rodeo wranglers) Ben Johnson and Richard Farnsworth, who add to the flavor. Average.▼

Wild in the Country (1961) **C-114m.** **½ D: Philip Dunne. Elvis Presley, Hope Lange, Tuesday Weld, Millie Perkins, John Ireland, Gary Lockwood. Can *you* resist Elvis in a Clifford Odets script about a back-country hothead with literary aspirations? Cliched if earnest, but an undeniable curiosity with some good performances, Elvis' among them. That's young Christina Crawford as Lockwood's girlfriend.▼

Wild in the Sky (1972) **C-87m.** **½ D: William T. Naud. Georg Stanford Brown, Brandon de Wilde, Keenan Wynn, Tim O'Connor, James Daly, Dick Gautier, Robert Lansing. Zany idea doesn't quite come off in story of three prisoners who hijack a B-52 bomber. Written by Naud and Gautier. Original title: BLACK JACK.

Wild in the Streets (1968) **C-97m.** **½ D: Barry Shear. Christopher Jones, Shelley Winters, Diane Varsi, Hal Holbrook, Millie Perkins, Ed Begley, Richard Pryor, Bert Freed. Dark satire about millionaire singing idol/drug pusher who is elected President after voting age is lowered to 14. Wildly overrated by some critics, film is nonetheless enjoyable on a nonthink level.▼

Wild Is the Wind (1957) **114m.** **½ D: George Cukor. Anna Magnani, Anthony Quinn, Anthony Franciosa, Dolores Hart, Joseph Calleia. Turgid soaper set in the West, with Quinn marrying the sister of his dead wife, not able to separate the two. Good acting helps script along; both leads won Oscar nominations.

Wild Life, The (1984) **C-96m.** *½ D: Art Linson. Christopher Penn, Ilan Mitchell-Smith, Eric Stoltz, Jenny Wright, Lea Thompson, Rick Moranis, Hart Bochner, Randy Quaid. Unfunny youth comedy about straight-arrow high school grad Stoltz deciding to leave home and move into "swinging singles" apartment. Meager attempt to clone FAST TIMES AT RIDGEMONT HIGH with same writer and producer (doubling here as director), and Christopher Penn trying to ape brother Sean's flaky character—unsuccessfully.▼

Wild Man of Borneo, The (1941) **78m.** ** D: Robert B. Sinclair. Frank Morgan, Mary Howard, Billie Burke, Donald Meek, Marjorie Main, Connie Gilchrist, Bonita Granville, Walter Catlett, Phil Silvers, Dan Dailey. Good cast in weak sideshow comedy; Morgan masquerades as title character in one of his less memorable roles.

Wild McCullochs, The (1975) **C-93m.** ** D: Max Baer. Forrest Tucker, Max Baer, Julie Adams, Janice Heiden, Dennis Redfield, Don Grady, William Demarest. Forgettable QUIET MAN rip-off has Tucker as self-made Texas millionaire who tries to raise his sons in his two-fisted image, with Baer eventually forced to prove he is "a man." Yawn.

Wild North, The (1952) **C-97m.** ** D: Andrew Marton. Stewart Granger, Cyd Charisse, Wendell Corey, J. M. Kerrigan, Ray Teal. Undazzling account of accused murderer hunted by Mountie, with the expected proving of innocence before finale; Charisse is love interest.

Wild One, The (1954) **79m.** ***½ D: Laslo Benedek. Marlon Brando, Mary Murphy, Robert Keith, Lee Marvin, Jay C. Flippen, Jerry Paris, Alvy Moore. THE original motorcycle film with Brando's renowned performance as packleader terrorizing small town; dated, but well worth viewing. Script by John Paxton; produced by Stanley Kramer.▼

Wild on the Beach (1965) **77m.** *½ D: Maury Dexter. Frankie Randall, Sherry Jackson, Jackie & Gayle, Sonny & Cher, Sandy Nelson. Randall and Jackson fight over the rights to a beachhouse—and fall in love. Dreary comedy notable only for the appearance of Mr. and Mrs. Bono.

Wild Orchids (1929) **102m.** **½ D: Sidney Franklin. Greta Garbo, Lewis Stone, Nils Asther. Standard love triangle with married Garbo falling for wealthy, charming Asther on a trip to Java. Garbo's charisma elevates typical soaper. Silent film with music score. ▼

Wild Pack, The (1971) **C-102m.** **½ D: Hall Bartlett. Kent Lane, Tisha Sterling, John Rubinstein, Butch Patrick, Mark de Vries, Peter Nielsen. Fairly interesting drama, set in Brazil, about day-to-day life of a group of black and white orphans who steal food; film won grand prize at Moscow Film Festival. Originally titled THE SANDPIT GENERALS.

Wild Pair, The (1987) **C-88m.** *½ D: Beau Bridges. Beau Bridges, Bubba Smith, Lloyd Bridges, Gary Lockwood, Raymond St. Jacques, Danny De La Paz, Lela

[1294]

Rochon, Ellen Geer. Trite police thriller, with cop Smith and FBI agent Beau Bridges teaming up to bring some drug dealing racists to justice. Utterly ordinary in all departments. Bridges' first theatrical film as director.▼

Wild Party, The (1929) 76m. **½ D: Dorothy Arzner. Clara Bow, Fredric March, Shirley O'Hara, Marceline Day, Joyce Compton, Jack Oakie. Fascinating antique about dishy new prof at all-girls' school and his on-again, off-again relationship with a sexy student who thinks college is just a lark. Absolutely awful by any objective standards, but great fun to watch.▼

Wild Party, The (1956) 81m. *½ D: Harry Horner. Anthony Quinn, Carol Ohmart, Arthur Franz, Jay Robinson, Kathryn Grant (Crosby), Nehemiah Persoff, Paul Stewart. Blah attempt at naturalistic drama with Quinn the has-been football star going mildly berserk at a sleazy roadside dance hall.

Wild Party, The (1975) C-95m. ** D: James Ivory. James Coco, Raquel Welch, Perry King, Tiffany Bolling, David Dukes, Royal Dano, Dena Dietrich. Uneven evocation of 1920s Hollywood with Coco as a Fatty Arbuckle-type comedian who throws a lavish party to try and save his failing career. Film has definite assets (notably its performances) but just doesn't come off. Based on the narrative poem by Joseph Moncure March; cut by its distributor, later restored by Ivory to 107m.▼

Wild Racers, The (1968) C-79m. *½ D: Daniel Haller. Fabian, Mimsy Farmer, Judy Cornwall, David Landers. Dumb racer Fabian loves his work and one-night stands; Farmer is his latest challenge.

Wild Ride, The (1960) 63m. *½ D: Harvey Berman. Jack Nicholson, Georgianna Carter, Robert Bean. Amateurish low-budgeter about a hedonistic hot-rodder who's as casual about killing people as he is about stealing his buddy's girlfriend. Worth seeing only if you're curious about this early Nicholson performance.▼

Wild River (1960) C-110m. ***½ D: Elia Kazan. Montgomery Clift, Lee Remick, Jo Van Fleet, Albert Salmi, Jay C. Flippen, James Westerfield. Clift plays Tennessee Valley Authority official trying to convince elderly Van Fleet to sell her property for new projects. Kazan's exquisite evocation of 1930s Tennessee—and moving romance between Clift and Remick—give this film its strength. Bruce Dern makes his film debut in supporting role.

Wildrose (1984) C-95m. ***½ D: John Hanson. Lisa Eichhorn, Tom Bower, Jim Cada, Cinda Jackson, Dan Nemanick, Bill Schoppert. Eichhorn excels in this wonderfully vivid tale of a female iron pit worker, both strong and insecure, who must deal with the resentment of her male co-workers;

meanwhile, she commences a romance with one of them (Bower). Filmed in Minnesota, with the landscape and its inhabitants carefully, almost lovingly, etched.▼

Wild Rovers (1971) C-109m. ***½ D: Blake Edwards. William Holden, Ryan O'Neal, Karl Malden, Lynn Carlin, Tom Skerritt, Joe Don Baker, Rachel Roberts, Moses Gunn. Underrated Western about two cowpokes who become fugitives after they rob a bank on whim. Choppy script seems unimportant in light of Holden's performance, incredibly lyrical scenes. Edwards' original 136m. version has finally been restored and released, which may boost the film's maligned reputation.▼

Wild Seed, The (1965) 99m. *** D: Brian Hutton. Michael Parks, Celia Kaye, Ross Elliott, Woodrow Chambliss, Eva Novak. Arty yet gripping story of runaway Kaye traveling to California, guided by road bum Parks.

Wild Side, The (1983) C-96m. BOMB D: Penelope Spheeris. Chris Pederson, Bill Coyne, Jennifer Clay, Timothy Eric O'Brien, Andrew Pece, Don Allen. Poorly staged, perfectly awful drama about alienated suburban teenagers, angry kids who cut their hair instead of growing it long and live in abandoned, rat-infested crash pad. Tries to "make a statement" while wallowing in gratuitous violence. Also known as SUBURBIA.▼

Wild Stallion (1952) C-72m. *½ D: Lewis D. Collins. Martha Hyer, Edgar Buchanan, Hugh Beaumont, Ben Johnson. Shoddy military academy saga interlaced with soapish romance, told via flashbacks.

Wild Strawberries (1957-Sweden) 90m. **** D: Ingmar Bergman. Victor Sjostrom, Ingrid Thulin, Bibi Andersson, Gunnar Bjornstrand, Folke Sundquist, Bjorn Bjelvenstam. Elderly Stockholm professor reviews the disappointments of his life, while traveling by car to receive an honorary degree. Superb use of flashbacks and brilliant performance by Sjostrom make this Bergman classic an emotional powerhouse. Still a staple of any serious filmgoer's education.▼

Wild Style (1982) C-82m. ** D: Charlie Ahearn. "Lee" Quinones, Sandra "Pink" Fabara, Fred Brathwaite, Patti Astor, Busy Bee, Grand Master Flash. Independent filmmaker's ode to such contemporary street-life phenomena as graffiti art, break dancing, and rap music, centering on Zoro (Quinones), who spray-paints subway cars in the South Bronx. Sociologically interesting, but dramatically naive—and a little "rapping" goes a long way.▼

Wild Thing (1987) C-92m. *½ D: Max Reid. Rob Knepper, Kathleen Quinlan, Robert Davi, Maury Chaykin, Betty Buckley. Misguided mishmash about a boy whose parents are murdered and who grows up into a "wild thing" who protects street people from the likes of arch-villain Davi. One would like to think that screenwriter John Sayles had more in mind for this fable than what turned out on screen. The Troggs' rock 'n' roll hit "Wild Thing" is used as the movie's theme.▼

Wild Times (1980) **C-200m.** TVM D: Richard Compton. Sam Elliott, Ben Johnson, Bruce Boxleitner, Penny Peyser, Dennis Hopper, Cameron Mitchell, Pat Hingle, Harry Carey, Jr., Gene Evans, Leif Erickson, Trish Stewart. Engaging version of Brian Garfield's tale about a dime novel hero who becomes America's first Wild West Show impressario. Originally shown in two parts, then shortened for its second run. Average.▼

Wild Westerners, The (1962) **C-70m.** *½ D: Oscar Rudolph. James Philbrook, Nancy Kovack, Duane Eddy, Guy Mitchell. Humdrum account of marshal and new wife overcoming obstacles to bring gold east for Yankee cause.

Wild, Wild Planet (1965-Italian) **C-93m.** *½ D: Anthony Dawson (Antonio Margheriti). Tony Russel, Lisa Gastoni, Massimo Serato, Franco Nero, Carlo Giustini. Female alien uses robots to gain control of earth scientists by shrinking them. Fairly good ending does not redeem lackluster film. Made at same time as WAR OF THE PLANETS and other losers.

Wild Wild West Revisited, The (1979) **C-100m.** TVM D: Burt Kennedy. Robert Conrad, Ross Martin, Paul Williams, Harry Morgan, Rene Auberjonois, Robert Shields, Lorene Yarnell, Wilford Brimley. The resourceful duo of the old-time series (1965-69) come out of retirement in this proposed series pilot to hunt down the baddy who has been cloning world leaders in his scheme to dominate the planet. Average. Followed by MORE WILD WILD WEST.▼

Wild, Wild Winter (1966) **C-80m.** ** D: Lennie Weinrib. Gary Clarke, Chris Noel, Steve Franken, Don Edmonds. Light-headed ski-slope musical froth, with guest stars Jay and The Americans, The Beau Brummels, Dick and Dee Dee.

Wild Women (1970) **C-73m.** TVM D: Don Taylor. Hugh O'Brian, Anne Francis, Marilyn Maxwell, Marie Windsor, Sherry Jackson, Cynthia Hall. Army engineers, mapping crucial Texas trails during 1840s, travel disguised as a wagon train; their "wives" are recruited from federal prisons. Tame mixture of comedy and adventure. Average.▼

Wild Women of Chastity Gulch, The (1982) **C-100m.** TVM D: Philip Leacock. Priscilla Barnes, Lee Horsley, Joan Collins, Howard Duff, Pamela Bellwood, Phyllis Davis, Jeanette Nolan, Morgan Brittany, Donny Osmond, Lisa Whelchel. Sitcom level Western pitting a band of women-

hungry renegades against the good ladies and barroom belles of Chastity Gulch whose men have marched off to war. Average.

Wild Youth SEE: **Naked Youth**▼

Willa (1979) **C-100m.** TVM D: Joan Darling, Claudio Guzman. Deborah Raffin, Clu Gulager, Cloris Leachman, Diane Ladd, John Amos, Nancy Marchand, Mary Wickes. Hash-slinging waitress embarks on a new career as a lady trucker after being abandoned by her husband. Average.▼

Willard (1971) **C-95m.** ** D: Daniel Mann. Bruce Davison, Elsa Lanchester, Ernest Borgnine, Sondra Locke, Michael Dante, J. Pat O'Malley, Jody Gilbert, Joan Shawlee. Touching story of a boy and his rats captured public's fancy at the box office, but film's lack of style prevents it from being anything more than a second-rate thriller. Sequel: BEN.▼

Will, G. Gordon Liddy (1982) **C-100m.** TVM D: Robert Lieberman. Robert Conrad, Katherine Cannon, Gary Bayer, Peter Ratray, James Rebhorn, Red West, Maurice Woods, Danny Lloyd. Conrad is right on target as convicted Watergate conspirator Liddy, but the real Liddy remains an enigma in this emasculated film version of his autobiography (originally three hours but severely cut, reportedly over producer Conrad's objections). Average.▼

Willie and Joe Back at the Front SEE: **Back at the Front**

Willie and Phil (1980) **C-115m.** *** D: Paul Mazursky. Michael Ontkean, Margot Kidder, Ray Sharkey, Jan Miner, Tom Brennan, Julie Bovasso, Louis Guss, Kathleen Maguire, Kaki Hunter, Natalie Wood. Affectionate, perceptive, underrated retelling of JULES AND JIM. Ontkean and Sharkey meet after a screening of the Truffaut classic, become fast pals, then friends and lovers of the free-spirited Kidder. A wistful tale of how chance encounters alter lives, how camaraderie between friends is everlasting, how men always do the asking but women do the deciding.

Willie Dynamite (1974) **C-102m.** *** D: Gilbert Moses. Roscoe Orman, Diana Sands, Thalmus Rasulala, Roger Robinson, George Murdock. Multi-ingredients mix well in a good black actioner set in N.Y.C., with Orman as a pimp out to topple big-shot Robinson, an outrageous homosexual. Sands is fine in her last film.

Will James' Sand SEE: **Sand**

Willow (1988) **C-125m.** *** D: Ron Howard. Val Kilmer, Joanne Whalley, Warwick Davis, Jean Marsh, Patricia Hayes, Billy Barty, Pat Roach, Gavan O'Herlihy. Rollicking fantasy-adventure, from a story by George Lucas (not hard to guess, since it follows a definite STAR WARS formula) about a little person (Davis) who takes on the challenge of shepherding an abandoned baby to its place of destiny—

where it will destroy the evil powers of Queen Bavmorda (Marsh). Plenty of action, humor, and eye-filling special effects, though it seems a bit intense at times for the youngsters at whom it's targeted.▼

Will Penny (1968) **C-108m.** ***½ D: Tom Gries. Charlton Heston, Joan Hackett, Donald Pleasence, Lee Majors, Bruce Dern, Ben Johnson, Slim Pickens, Anthony Zerbe, Clifton James. One of the best films on the cowboy/loner ever to come out of Hollywood. Heston's character is one of great strength; supporting actors are exceptional. Written by director Gries. Memorable score by David Raksin.▼

Will Success Spoil Rock Hunter? (1957) **C-94m.** ***½ D: Frank Tashlin. Tony Randall, Jayne Mansfield, Betsy Drake, Joan Blondell, John Williams, Henry Jones, Mickey Hargitay. Guest star, Groucho Marx. Clever satire uses George Axelrod play about ad man who tries to persuade glamorous star to endorse Stay-Put Lipstick as springboard for scattershot satire on 1950s morals, television, sex, business, et al. Director-writer Tashlin in peak form.

Will There Really Be a Morning? (1983) **C-150m. TVM** D: Fielder Cook. Susan Blakely, Lee Grant, John Heard, Melanie Mayron, Royal Dano, Joseph Maher, Madeline Thornton-Sherwood. Blakely and Grant give scorching performances as the ill-fated Frances Farmer and her monstrous mother in this "other" (purportedly more factual) movie on the long-ago screen and stage actress. Adapted by Dalene Young from Farmer's autobiography. For comparison, see the theatrical film FRANCES and the independent feature COMMITTED. Above average.

Willy McBean and his Magic Machine (1965-Japanese) **C-94m.** **½ D: Arthur Rankin, Jr. Voices of Larry Mann, Billie Richards, Alfie Scopp, Paul Ligman, Bunny Cowan, Paul Soles. Puppet novelty item about mad professor and his time machine; OK for kids.▼

Willy Milly SEE: **Something Special**▼

Willy Wonka and the Chocolate Factory (1971) **C-98m.** **½ D: Mel Stuart. Gene Wilder, Jack Albertson, Peter Ostrum, Roy Kinnear, Aubrey Woods, Michael Bollner, Ursula Reit. Adaptation of Roald Dahl's book, *Charlie and the Chocolate Factory*, has all the ingredients of classic fantasy. Enigmatic Wilder gives kids a tour of his mystery-shrouded candy factory, but cruel edge taints film's enjoyment. Anthony Newley-Leslie Bricusse score includes "Candy Man." Scripted by Dahl, with eye-popping sets by Harper Goff.▼

Wilma (1977) **C-100m. TVM** D: Bud Greenspan. Cicely Tyson, Shirley Jo Finney, Jason Bernard, Joe Seneca, Denzel Washington. Uninspired drama about the early years of Wilma Rudolph (Finney) who beat polio to become the gold medal-winning Olympic track star. Lackluster performances generated by so-so script. Below average.▼

Wilson (1944) **C-154m.** ***½ D: Henry King. Alexander Knox, Charles Coburn, Geraldine Fitzgerald, Thomas Mitchell, Cedric Hardwicke, Vincent Price, Mary Anderson, Sidney Blackmer, Stanley Ridges, Eddie Foy, Jr., Francis X. Bushman. Superb biography of WW1-era President whose League of Nations idea became an obsession; one of Hollywood's solid films . . . but beware of cutting. Amazingly a notorious box-office flop, even after winning five Oscars (including Lamar Trotti's script and Leon Shamroy's photography).

Winchester '73 (1950) **92m.** ***½ D: Anthony Mann. James Stewart, Shelley Winters, Dan Duryea, Stephen McNally, Charles Drake, Millard Mitchell, John McIntire, Will Geer, Jay C. Flippen, Rock Hudson, Anthony (Tony) Curtis. Exceptional Western story of Stewart tracking down a man—and his stolen gun—through series of interrelated episodes, leading to memorable shootout among rock-strewn hills. First-rate in every way, this landmark film was largely responsible for renewed popularity of Westerns in the 1950s. Script by Robert L. Richards and Borden Chase, from a story by Stuart N. Lake. Beautifully photographed by William Daniels; remade for TV in 1967.▼

Winchester '73 (1967) **C-97m. TVM** D: Herschel Daugherty. Tom Tryon, John Saxon, Dan Duryea, Joan Blondell, John Drew Barrymore, Ned Romero. OK remake of 1950 version with Saxon returning home from prison seething hate, eventually stealing priceless rifle from brother sheriff Tryon. Action mostly good; only resolution seems poorly handled. Average.

Wind, The (1928) **88m.** **** D: Victor Seastrom. Lillian Gish, Lars Hanson, Montagu Love, Dorothy Cumming, Edward Earle, William Orlamond. Virgin Virginian Gish battles the elements in a barren dustbowl town—marrying on the rebound a man who disgusts her, shooting the lout who rapes her. Probably Gish's greatest vehicle—and one of the last great silents—with a splendidly staged climactic desert storm sequence. Written by Frances Marion, from Dorothy Scarborough's novel.▼

Wind, The (1987) **C-92m. BOMB** D: Nico Mastorakis. Meg Foster, Wings Hauser, David McCallum, Robert Morley, Steve Railsback. Good cast is wasted in old-fashioned thriller about mystery writer Foster terrorized by Hauser in her spooky house in Greece. Unconvincing structure has hero Railsback injected artificially into the story in later reels. Released directly to videocassette.▼

Wind Across the Everglades (1958) **C-93m.** **½ D: Nicholas Ray. Burl Ives, Christopher Plummer, Gypsy Rose Lee, George Voskovec, Tony Galento. Oddball cast in even odder story of boozy turn-of-the-century Florida game warden (Plummer) who takes it upon himself to rid the area of poachers. Matchup of director Ray and writer-producer Budd Schulberg makes this a genuine curio. Peter Falk makes his film debut in a small role.

Wind and the Lion, The (1975) **C-119m.** **½ D: John Milius. Sean Connery, Candice Bergen, Brian Keith, John Huston, Geoffrey Lewis, Steve Kanaly, Vladek Sheybal. Milius brings modern sensibilities to an old-fashioned adventure-romance, with uneven results. Connery is Moroccan sheik who kidnaps American woman and her son, sparking international incident in which Teddy Roosevelt (Keith) becomes involved. Loosely based on a true incident.▼

Wind Cannot Read, The (1958-British) **C-110m.** **½ D: Ralph Thomas. Dirk Bogarde, Yoko Tani, Ronald Lewis, John Fraser, Anthony Bushell, Michael Medwin. Tidy tale of Bogarde escaping from Japanese prison camp during WW2 to find his ailing wife Tani.

Windmills of the Gods (1988) **C-200m.** TVM D: Lee Philips. Jaclyn Smith, Robert Wagner, Franco Nero, Christopher Cazenove, David Ackroyd, Jean-Pierre Aumont, Ruby Dee, Jeffrey DeMunn, Michael Moriarty, Ian McKellen, Susan Tyrrell. Sidney Sheldon's bestselling pastiche about a lady ambassador who finds herself the target of assassins. John Gay's script, weaving international intrigue with performances that are a hoot, gives this one its spin. Originally shown in two parts. Average.

Windom's Way (1957-British) **C-108m.** *** D: Ronald Neame. Peter Finch, Mary Ure, Natasha Parry, Robert Flemyng, Michael Hordern, Gregoire Aslan. Dedicated doctor (Finch) working in Malayan village tries to encourage resistance to Communist takeover. Strong performances in this intelligent film.▼

Window, The (1949) **73m.** *** D: Ted Tetzlaff. Bobby Driscoll, Barbara Hale, Arthur Kennedy, Paul Stewart, Ruth Roman. Sleeper film less impressive now than in 1949; still good, with young Driscoll earning a special Academy Award for his performance as a little boy who witnesses a murder and is unable to convince his parents he's not lying. Parents' dialogue weakens credibility, but suspense still mounts; extremely well photographed (by William Steiner) and staged. Based on a story by Cornell Woolrich. Remade as THE BOY CRIED MURDER and CLOAK AND DAGGER (1984).▼

Window in London, A SEE: **Lady in Distress**▼

Windows (1980) **C-96m.** BOMB D: Gordon Willis. Elizabeth Ashley, Talia Shire, Joseph Cortese, Kay Medford. Homicidal lesbian Ashley is in love with mousy neighbor Shire, who is in turn in love with bland detective Cortese. Reactionary, offensive thriller whose only element of mystery is why it was ever filmed. Heavy-handed directorial debut by gifted cinematographer Willis.

Windrider (1986-Australian) **C-92m.** **½ D: Vincent Monton. Tom Burlinson, Nicole Kidman, Charles Tingwell, Jill Perryman, Simon Chilvers. Windsurfer Burlinson and rock star Kidman become romantically involved. Occasionally appealing, but slight and forgettable.▼

Winds of Kitty Hawk, The (1978) **C-100m.** TVM D: E. W. Swackhamer. Michael Moriarty, David Huffman, Tom Bower, Eugene Roche, Scott Hylands, John Randolph, Kathryn Walker. Stunningly photographed but tediously talky dramatization about the Wright Brothers, their efforts to fly, and their feud with Glenn Curtiss and his patron, Alexander Graham Bell. Stacy and James Keach covered much of the same ground in half the time some years earlier in their production on public television. Off the ground, there's magic. Above average.▼

Windwalker (1980) **C-108m.** **½ D: Kieth Merrill. Trevor Howard, Nick Ramus, James Remar, Serene Hedin, Dusty Iron Wing McCrea. Indian patriarch Howard returns to life to save his family from the vengeance of his son, a twin who was stolen at birth and raised by an enemy tribe. Curious casting of Howard; however, the Utah scenery is glorious in this unusual Western. Filmed in the Cheyenne and Crow languages, and subtitled.▼

Windy City (1984) **C-102m.** ** D: Armyan Bernstein. John Shea, Kate Capshaw, Josh Mostel, Jim Borrelli, Jeffrey DeMunn, Lewis J. Stadlen. Promising but uneven film flashes back to last hurrah for some youthful pals whose lives haven't turned out quite as they'd hoped or planned. Writer Bernstein (making directorial debut) invades BIG CHILL/SECAUCUS 7 territory with extremely mixed results.▼

Wing and a Prayer (1944) **97m.** *** D: Henry Hathaway. Don Ameche, Dana Andrews, William Eythe, Richard Jaeckel, Charles Bickford, Sir Cedric Hardwicke, Henry (Harry) Morgan, Richard Crane, Glenn Langan. Fine WW2 actioner of brave pilots aboard aircraft carrier. Excellent cast does well in exciting story.

Winged Serpent, The SEE: **Q**▼

Winged Victory (1944) **130m.** **½ D: George Cukor. Lon McCallister, Jeanne Crain, Edmond O'Brien, Don Taylor, Judy Holliday, Lee J. Cobb, Peter Lind Hayes, Red Buttons, Barry Nelson, Karl Malden, Gary Merrill, Martin Ritt. WW2 saga is less

stirring today than in 1944, but graphic depiction of young men's training for pilot duty is still quite interesting. So is the opportunity of seeing future stars early in their careers. Script by Moss Hart, from his play.
Wings (1927) **139m.** **½ D: William A. Wellman. Clara Bow, Charles "Buddy" Rogers, Richard Arlen, Jobyna Ralston, Gary Cooper, Arlette Marchal, El Brendel. One of the most famous silent films is, alas, not one of the best, despite rose-colored memories. Story of two all-American boys (in love with the same girl) who enlist in the Army Air Corps during WW1 is much too thin to sustain such a long movie. What's important here are the combat flying sequences, among the best in Hollywood history. First Oscar winner as Best Picture.▼
Wings for the Eagle (1942) **85m.** ** D: Lloyd Bacon. Ann Sheridan, Dennis Morgan, Jack Carson, George Tobias, Don DeFore. Sincere tribute to aircraft workers during WW2 has little meaning today, but Sheridan, et al give good performances.
Wings in the Dark (1935) **77m.** **½ D: James Flood. Cary Grant, Myrna Loy, Dean Jagger, Roscoe Karns, Hobart Cavanaugh, Bert Hanlon. Sky-writing stunt flier Loy falls for flier Grant, who's blinded in a gas explosion. Attractive performers left dangling without a script in this implausible soap opera; fine aerial photography.
Wings of Chance (1961-Canadian) **C-76m.** *½ D: Edward Dew. Frances Rafferty, Jim Brown, Richard Tretter, Patrick Whyte. Tame tale of plane crash in the northern woods and rescue attempts.
Wings of Desire (1988-West German-French) **C/B&W-130m.** ***½ D: Wim Wenders. Bruno Ganz, Solveig Dommartin, Otto Sander, Curt Bois, Peter Falk. Haunting, lyrical, thoroughly fascinating meditation/fairy tale about a pair of angels who wander through the streets of West Berlin. They observe life around them and ponder what it would be like to be human. Scripted by Wenders and Peter Handke and inspired in part by some Rainer Maria Rilke poems. A must-see.▼
Wings of Eagles, The (1957) **C-110m.** **½ D: John Ford. John Wayne, Maureen O'Hara, Dan Dailey, Ward Bond, Ken Curtis, Edmund Lowe, Kenneth Tobey, Sig Ruman. Biography of Frank "Spig" Wead, pioneer WW1 aviator who later turned to screenwriting after an accident; first half is slapstick comedy, with no sense of period detail, then abruptly changes to drama for balance of film. Very mixed bag; film buffs will have fun watching Bond play "John Dodge," spoofing director Ford.▼
Wings of Fire (1967) **C-100m. TVM** D: David Lowell Rich. Suzanne Pleshette, James Farentino, Ralph Bellamy, Juliet Mills, Jeremy Slate, Lloyd Nolan. Headstrong flier

Pleshette enters air race to save floundering freight service run by father and associate. Hokey melodrama has climax and resolution unusually contrived. Below average.
Wings of the Hawk (1953) **C-80m.** ** D: Budd Boetticher. Van Heflin, Julia Adams, George Dolenz, Pedro Gonzales-Gonzales, Abbe Lane, Antonio Moreno, Noah Beery. Heflin is hero of thwarted attempt of renegades to overthrow Mexican government; Adams and Lane help him. Originally in 3-D.
Wings of the Morning (1937-British) **C-89m.** **½ D: Harold Schuster. Annabella, Henry Fonda, John McCormack, Irene Vanbrugh, Philip Frost, Leslie Banks, Sam Livesey. Trifling story of gypsies, crucial horserace, blossoming love between Fonda and Annabella, initially disguised as a boy. Much ado about nothing. England's first Technicolor film still boasts beautiful pastel hues (by Ray Rennahan and Jack Cardiff) as major attraction, along with sequence of famed tenor McCormack doing several songs.
Wings of the Navy (1939) **89m.** ** D: Lloyd Bacon. George Brent, Olivia de Havilland, John Payne, Frank McHugh, John Litel, Victor Jory, Henry O'Neill, John Ridgely. Standard semidocumentary of pilots being trained for fighting while de Havilland is vied for by brothers Brent and Payne. Typical Warners prewar propaganda, but watchable.
Winner Never Quits, A (1986) **C-100m. TVM** D: Mel Damski. Keith Carradine, Mare Winningham, G. W. Bailey, Dennis Weaver, Fionnula Flanagan, Huckleberry Fox, Dana Delany, Charles Hallahan. Amiable family drama about Pete Gray, the one-armed outfielder who played for the St. Louis Browns briefly during WW2, and the effect he had on a handicapped youngster who idolized him. An interesting slice of bygone Americana, well acted, well written (by Burt Prelutsky), and co-produced by actor James Keach. Above average.
Winner Take All (1932) **68m.** **½ D: Roy Del Ruth. James Cagney, Virginia Bruce, Marian Nixon, Guy Kibbee, Alan Mowbray, Dickie Moore. Minor but engaging Cagney vehicle with Jimmy as a thick-witted, cocky prizefighter torn between good-girl Nixon and fickle society-girl Bruce. Look fast for George Raft as night club bandleader.
Winner Take All (1975) **C-100m. TVM** D: Paul Bogart. Shirley Jones, Laurence Luckinbill, Sam Groom, Joan Blondell, Sylvia Sidney, Joyce Van Patten. Drama about a compulsive woman gambler. The cast doesn't cut it, but then the script didn't offer much. Below average.
Winnie (1988) **C-100m. TVM** D: John Korty. Meredith Baxter Birney, David Morse, Jenny O'Hara, Peggy McKay, Bar-

bara Barrie. A vivid star turn for Birney as a woman, institutionalized for 30 years, determined to prove she can make it on the outside. The based-on-fact story was adapted by Joyce Eliason from Jamie Paster Bolnick's book *Winnie: My Life in the Institution*. Above average.

Winning (1969) **C-123m.** *** D: James Goldstone. Paul Newman, Joanne Woodward, Richard Thomas, Robert Wagner, David Sheiner, Clu Gulager. Above average racing story of man who will let nothing stand in the way of track victory.▼

Winning Team, The (1952) **98m.** **½ D: Lewis Seiler. Doris Day, Ronald Reagan, Frank Lovejoy, Eve Miller, James Millican, Russ Tamblyn. Biography of baseball pitching great Grover Cleveland Alexander isn't bad, but never veers too far from Hollywood formula. Good showcase for Reagan.

Win, Place or Steal (1975) **C-81m.** ** D: Richard Bailey. Dean Stockwell, Russ Tamblyn, Alex Karras, McLean Stevenson, Alan Oppenheimer, Kristina Holland. OK racetrack caper comedy, with Tamblyn and Karras doing a Laurel and Hardy.▼

Winslow Boy, The (1950-British) **117m.** ***½ D: Anthony Asquith. Robert Donat, Margaret Leighton, Cedric Hardwicke, Francis L. Sullivan, Frank Lawton, Basil Radford, Wilfrid Hyde-White, Ernest Thesiger. Superior courtroom melodrama from Terence Rattigan's play, headed by Donat as barrister defending innocent Naval cadet (Neil North) accused of school theft. Script by Rattigan and Anatole de Grunwald.▼

Winter à Go-Go (1965) **C-88m.** ** D: Richard Benedict. James Stacy, William Wellman, Jr., Beverly Adams, Jill Donohue, Julie Parrish. Lowbrow shenanigans at a ski resort run by Stacy for the young, affluent set.

Winter Carnival (1939) **105m.** **½ D: Charles F. Riesner. Richard Carlson, Ann Sheridan, Helen Parrish, James Corner, Virginia Gilmore, Robert Walker, Joan Leslie, Peggy Moran. Contrived romance flick (co-written by Budd Schulberg) set at Dartmouth College during festive weekend; Sheridan is divorcée in love with professor Carlson.

Winterhawk (1976) **C-98m.** ** D: Charles B. Pierce. Michael Dante, Leif Erickson, Woody Strode, Denver Pyle, Elisha Cook Jr., L. Q. Jones, Arthur Hunnicutt, Dawn Wells. Well-meaning but overly melodramatic story of Blackfoot Indian brave (Dante) who comes to white man for smallpox serum, is attacked instead, and gets revenge by kidnapping two white youngsters. Quite violent at times.

Winter Kill (1974) **C-100m. TVM** D: Jud Taylor. Andy Griffith, John Larch, Tim O'Connor, Sheree North, Nick Nolte, Elayne Heilviel, Charles Tyner, Louise Latham. Resort-town sheriff Griffith tracks murderer, who leaves spray-painted messages at the scene. Another Griffith pilot that failed to catch on. Average.

Winter Kills (1979) **C-97m.** **½ D: William Richert. Jeff Bridges, John Huston, Anthony Perkins, Sterling Hayden, Eli Wallach, Belinda Bauer, Richard Boone, Ralph Meeker, Dorothy Malone, Toshiro Mifune, Tomas Milian, Elizabeth Taylor. Younger brother of an assassinated U.S. President tries to solve the case, opens up several cans of political worms. A failure in 1979, it was reedited, revived in 1983 (with original ending restored) and newly appreciated as a black comedy, which not everybody recognized the first time around. Still wildly uneven, but worth a look, if only for Huston's wonderful performance as Bridges' kingpin father.▼

Winter Light (1962-Swedish) **80m.** ***½ D: Ingmar Bergman. Ingrid Thulin, Gunnar Bjornstrand, Max von Sydow, Gunnel Lindblom, Allan Edwall. A difficult film for non-Bergman buffs, this look at a disillusioned priest in a small village is the second of Bergman's trilogy on faith (the first, THROUGH A GLASS DARKLY; the third, THE SILENCE). Powerful, penetrating drama.▼

Winter Meeting (1948) **104m.** **½ D: Bretaigne Windust. Bette Davis, Janis Paige, James (Jim) Davis, John Hoyt, Florence Bates. Sluggish script of disillusioned poetess who loves embittered war hero, prevents well-acted film from achieving greater heights. Notable as only romantic lead for Jim Davis, better known for his westerns and TV series *Dallas*.

Winter of Our Discontent, The (1983) **C-100m. TVM** D: Waris Hussein. Donald Sutherland, Teri Garr, Tuesday Weld, Michael Gazzo, Richard Masur, E. G. Marshall. Top-notch cast mired in muddled version of Steinbeck's final novel about the compromising of an honorable man. Michael de Guzman's adaptation doesn't capture the guts of Steinbeck but gives it a valiant effort. Average.

Winter of Our Dreams, The (1981-Australian) **C-90m.** **½ D: John Duigan. Judy Davis, Bryan Brown, Cathy Downes, Baz Luhrmann, Peter Mochrie, Mervyn Drake. Davis is fine as a lonely prostitute who becomes involved with dissatisfied bookshop-owner Brown, married to Downes. Intriguing drama is a bit disjointed, particularly near the finale.▼

Winter People (1989) **C-110m.** ** D: Ted Kotcheff. Kurt Russell, Kelly McGillis, Lloyd Bridges, Mitchell Ryan, Amelia Burnette, Eileen Ryan, Jeffrey Meek. Turgid tale of backwoods clans and a blood feud that flares up when McGillis bears a child with the wrong father. Set in the 1930s, but extremely odd by any period's standards; how it came to be made in 1989 is anyone's guess. Overwrought, to say the least.▼

Winter Rates SEE: **Out of Season**▼

Winterset (1936) **78m.** ** D: Alfred Santell. Burgess Meredith, Margo, Eduardo Ciannelli, Paul Guilfoyle, John Carradine, Edward Ellis, Stanley Ridges, Myron McCormick, Mischa Auer. Meredith, in screen debut, plays young man determined to find the man responsible for crime his father paid for with his life. Once-powerful film (with stars of Maxwell Anderson's Broadway play recreating their stage roles) seems artificial and pretentious today.▼

Winter's Tale, The (1968-British) **C-151m.** ** D: Frank Dunlop. Laurence Harvey, Jane Asher, Diana Churchill, Moira Redmond, Jim Dale. Filmed record of 1966 Edinburgh Festival presentation of Shakespeare's play is as static as a photographed stage play can be; may play better on TV.

Wintertime (1943) **82m.** ** D: John Brahm. Sonja Henie, Jack Oakie, Cesar Romero, Carol Landis, Cornel Wilde, S.Z. Sakall, Woody Herman. Henie gives her all to save uncle's hotel from bankruptcy. Innocuous, below par for her vehicles.

Wipeout! (1972-Italian) **C 100m.** *½ D: Fernando Di Leo. Henry Silva, Richard Conte, Vittorio Caprioli, Gianni Garko, Howard Ross, Marino Mase. Predictably violent Italian-made Mafia movie. Conte is a capo who hires hit-man Silva to wipe out his rivals, then plans to turn him over to the law.

Wired (1989) **C-108m.** BOMB D: Larry Peerce. Michael Chiklis, Ray Sharkey, J. T. Walsh, Patti D'Arbanville, Lucinda Jenney, Alex Rocco, Gary Groomes, Jere Burns, Billy Preston. The film fiasco of its year, a numbingly wrongheaded adaptation of Bob Woodward's best-selling cautionary bio of John Belushi—complete with a cab-driving guardian angel (Sharkey). Chiklis looks a little like Belushi but conveys none of his comic genius in some clumsy *Saturday Night Live* recreations. Walsh, as Woodward, is an unintentional howl with the decade's most constipated performance. Sole cast survivor: D'Arbanville as Cathy Smith, the woman who administered the star's fatal drug overdose.▼

Wiretappers (1956) **80m.** BOMB D: Dick Ross. Bill Williams, Georgia Lee, Douglas Kennedy, Phil Tead. Obnoxious little film blending crime and religion. Williams is seedy character working for two rival syndicates.

Wisdom (1986) **C-109m.** BOMB D: Emilio Estevez. Emilio Estevez, Demi Moore, Tom Skerritt, Veronica Cartwright, William Allen Young, Richard Minchenberg, Ernie Brown. Recent grad Estevez can't find work because of a long-ago felony on his record; frustration launches him and

girlfriend Moore on a cross-country series of bank heists to aid the American farmer's plight. Robert Wise assisted Estevez on the direction, which is certainly more competent than his wretched script; film has one of the most self-defeating wrapups you'll ever see.▼

Wise Blood (1979) **C-108m.** ***½ D: John Huston. Brad Dourif, Daniel Shor, Amy Wright, Harry Dean Stanton, Ned Beatty, Mary Nell Santacroce. Brilliant translation of Flannery O'Connor's peculiar hell-and-salvation tale. Flawless cast, led by Dourif as obsessed preacher of The Church Without Christ, inhabits Southern Gothic world as though born in it. Huston (who bills himself here as *Jhon* Huston) appears as a preacher.▼

Wise Girl (1937) **70m.** **½ D: Leigh Jason. Miriam Hopkins, Ray Milland, Walter Abel, Guinn Williams, Henry Stephenson. Pleasant screwball comedy about rich-girl Hopkins pretending to be poor in order to track down her late sister's kids, who are living with starving Greenwich Village artist Milland.

Wise Guys (1986) **C-91m.** *½ D: Brian DePalma. Danny DeVito, Joe Piscopo, Harvey Keitel, Ray Sharkey, Dan Hedaya, Captain Lou Albano, Julie Bovasso, Patti LuPone. Whimsical black comedy (that's what we said) about two losers who work for small-time hood in Newark, N.J. When their efforts to double-cross him fail, he sets them up to kill each other. Unsuccessful change of pace for director DePalma is an almost total misfire; buoyed only by DeVito's comic energy.▼

Wish You Were Here (1987-British) **C-92m.** *** D: David Leland. Emily Lloyd, Tom Bell, Clare Clifford, Barbara Durkin, Geoffrey Hutchings, Charlotte Barker, Chloe Leland, Jesse Birdsall, Geoffrey Durham, Pat Heywood. A troubled teenage girl expresses herself by being sexually outrageous—without understanding what the consequences might be. Bittersweet film set in early 1950s England with a knockout performance by 16-year-old Lloyd. Strong directing debut for screenwriter Leland, who based his central character on Cynthia Payne, the young madam depicted in PERSONAL SERVICES, which he wrote.▼

Wistful Widow of Wagon Gap, The (1947) **78m.** **½ D: Charles Barton. Bud Abbott, Lou Costello, Marjorie Main, George Cleveland, Gordon Jones, William Ching, Peter Thompson, Glenn Strange. Unusual Western spoof for A&C, inspired by real-life law: Lou accidentally kills a man, and is required to take care of his wife (Main) and children (seven). He then becomes sheriff, convinced that no one will dare kill him. Some slow spots, but overall, bright fun.

Witchboard (1985) **C-98m.** ** D: Kevin

S. Tenney. Todd Allen, Tawny Kitaen, Stephen Nicholas, Kathleen Wilhoite, Burke Byrnes, James W. Quinn, J.P. Luebsen, Rose Marie, Susan Nickerson. Standard low-budget horror film with a few twists. An evil spirit, contacted by means of a Ouija board (a "witchboard"), impersonates the ghost of a small boy to kill its victims. Well-plotted but routinely directed and acted.▼

Witchcraft (1964-British) **79m.** ** D: Don Sharp. Lon Chaney, Jack Hedley, Jill Dixon, Viola Keats. Standard plot of witch cult happenings in English village after grave of 300-year-old witch is unearthed.

Witch Doctor SEE: **Men of Two Worlds**

Witchery (1989-Italian) **C-96m.** BOMB D: Martin Newlin (Fabrizio Laurenti). Linda Blair, David Hasselhoff, Catherine Hickland, Annie Ross, Hildegard Knef, Leslie Cumming, Bob Champagne, Rick Farnsworth, Michael Manchester. Competently made but ponderous, underplotted horror tale of people isolated at old hotel on island, killed one by one by vengeful witch Knef. Horror scenes emphasize torture. Uncomfortable, predictable, and boring. Filmed in Massachusetts.▼

Witches' Brew (1980) **C-99m.** **½ D: Richard Shorr, Herbert L. Strock. Lana Turner, Richard Benjamin, Teri Garr, Kathryn Leigh Scott, Jordan Charney, Kelly Jean Peters. After a dull first half, this turns into an enjoyable spoof of the horror classic BURN, WITCH, BURN (also done as WEIRD WOMAN). College prof Benjamin's wife Garr resorts to witchcraft to further his career. Lana good as the veteran witch who has selfish reasons for helping Benjamin's cause.▼

Witches' Mountain (1970-Mexican) **98m.** BOMB D: Raul Artigot. Patty Shepard, John Caffari, Monica Randall. A reporter ventures to a "haunted" spot and finds its reputation may not be unearned. Boring.▼

Witches of Eastwick, The (1987) **C-118m.** *** D: George Miller. Jack Nicholson, Cher, Susan Sarandon, Michelle Pfeiffer, Veronica Cartwright, Richard Jenkins, Keith Jochim, Carel Struycken. Lively, colorful fantasy about three man-hungry women in picture-postcard New England town who, unaware of their witchly powers, conjure up the ultimate man: the devil. Magnetic performances and handsome production keep it entertaining throughout, though it careens wildly from sensual fantasy to black-comic farce to full-throttle horror, and ends up not making a lot of sense. Buoyed by an infectious John Williams score. Loosely based on John Updike's novel.▼

Witches of Salem, The SEE: **Crucible, The**
Witchfinder General, The SEE: **Conqueror Worm, The**▼
Witching, The SEE: **Necromancy**▼
Witchmaker, The (1969) **C-99m.** BOMB

D: William O. Brown. John Lodge, Alvy Moore, Thordis Brandt, Anthony Eisley, Shelby Grant. Satanism and supernatural elements are behind a series of grisly murders of young women in Louisiana swamp; bloody, and bloody awful.▼

Witch Without a Broom, A (1968-Spanish) **C-78m.** *½ D: Joe Lacy (Jose Maria E. Lorrieta). Jeffrey Hunter, Maria Perschy, Perla Cristal, Gustavo Rojo. Jeff finds himself bewitched by a 15th-century apprentice sorceress who takes him on an odyssey from the Stone Age to a futuristic Martian jaunt. Pointless fantasy.▼

With a Song in My Heart (1952) **C-117m.** *** D: Walter Lang. Susan Hayward, Rory Calhoun, David Wayne, Thelma Ritter, Robert Wagner, Una Merkel. Well-intentioned schmaltz based loosely on events in life of singer Jane Froman with Hayward earnest as songstress struggling to make comeback after crippling plane crash. Alfred Newman won an Oscar for Scoring.

With Fire and Sword (1961-Italian) **C-96m.** *½ D: Fernando Cerchio. Jeanne Crain, John Drew Barrymore, Pierre Brice, Akim Tamiroff. Costume spaghetti about Cossacks vs. Poles; embarrassing minor epic. Retitled: DAGGERS OF BLOOD.

With Intent to Kill (1984) **C-100m.** TVM D: Mike Robe. Karl Malden, Paul Sorvino, Shirley Knight, Timothy Patrick Murphy, Catherine Mary Stewart, Holly Hunter, Alex McArthur, William Devane. A father vows vengeance on the boyfriend of his murdered daughter following a not-guilty-by-reason-of-insanity verdict. Malden gives another must-watch performance in this script by director Robe. Above average.

Within These Walls (1945) **71m.** ** D: H. Bruce Humberstone. Thomas Mitchell, Mary Anderson, Edward Ryan, Mark Stevens, B. S. Pully, Roy Kelly, Harry Shannon. Fairly good but predictable prison drama with warden Mitchell faced with his own son as a prisoner.

With Love and Kisses (1936) **66m.** *½ D: Les Goodwins. Pinky Tomlin, Toby Wing, Kane Richmond, Arthur Houseman, Russell Hopton, Fuzzy Knight, Kenneth Thomson. Incredibly hokey comedy with music about naive farmboy Tomlin, an aspiring songwriter whose composition is stolen by conniving crooner Richmond. Tomlin, by the way, can only write music when in the company of his cow Minnie.

Withnail & I (1987-British) **C-105m.** **½ D: Bruce Robinson. Richard E. Grant, Paul McGann, Richard Griffiths, Ralph Brown, Michael Elphick. "I" is a young longhair, living in London in the last months of 1969; Withnail is his eccentric, self-absorbed roommate. Both are unemployed actors, children of their times, who endure a disastrous vacation in the country. Director Robinson wrote this autobiographical

film, which has its amusing moments but eventually becomes monotonous. Best laugh: consultant credit for "Richard Starkey, M.B.E." Fellow Beatle George Harrison coexecutive produced the film.▼
Without a Clue (1988-British) **C-106m.** **½ D: Thom Eberhardt. Michael Caine, Ben Kingsley, Jeffrey Jones, Lysette Anthony, Paul Freeman, Nigel Davenport, Pat Keen, Peter Cook. Mild farce built on the premise that Sherlock Holmes was a fictional creation of wily Dr. John Watson, who is forced to hire a second-rate actor (Caine) to impersonate the now famous and sought-after detective. Scattered laughs, engaging performances by star duo.▼
Without Apparent Motive (1972-French) **C-102m.** ** D: Philippe Labro. Jean-Louis Trintignant, Dominique Sanda, Sacha Distel, Carla Gravina, Paul Crauchet, Laura Antonelli, Jean-Pierre Marielle. Powerhouse European cast can't do much for Ed McBain tale about detective Trintignant's attempts to solve series of unpredictable killings; Erich Segal plays an astrologer.
Without a Trace (1983) **C-120m.** **½ D: Stanley R. Jaffe. Kate Nelligan, Judd Hirsch, David Dukes, Stockard Channing, Jacqueline Brookes, Kathleen Widdoes. Story of one woman's ordeal when her six-year-old son disappears while walking to school one morning. Genteel, well-made film keeps an arm's-length emotionally, especially in Nelligan's cold portrayal of the mother. Then there's a resolution that's not to be believed. Based on a real-life N.Y.C. incident that had a much different outcome. Directorial debut of producer Jaffe.▼
Without Her Consent (1990) **C-100m.** TVM D: Sandor Stern. Melissa Gilbert, Scott Valentine, Barry Tubb, Bebe Neuwirth, Crystal Bernard, Brooke Bundy, Madison Mason, William Allen Young. Young woman is raped by a new acquaintance; her boyfriend, finding justice none too swift, takes the law into his own hands. Average.
Without Honor (1949) **69m.** ** D: Irving Pichel. Laraine Day, Dane Clark, Franchot Tone, Agnes Moorehead, Bruce Bennett. Good cast talks endlessly in melodrama of woman who thinks she's killed a man.
Without Love (1945) **111m.** *** D: Harold S. Bucquet. Spencer Tracy, Katharine Hepburn, Lucille Ball, Keenan Wynn, Carl Esmond, Patricia Morison, Felix Bressart, Gloria Grahame. Tracy and Hepburn have never been livelier, but script (by Donald Ogden Stewart, from Philip Barry's play) lets them down in story of inventor and widow who marry for convenience, later fall in love. Wynn and Ball are excellent second leads.
Without Pity (1948-Italian) **94m.** *** D: Alberto Lattuada. Carla Del Poggio, John

Kitzmiller, Giulietta Masina, Folco Lulli, Pierre Luigi. Moving neo-realist classic about a black G.I. (Kitzmiller) and his love affair with a prostitute (Del Poggio) in liberated WW2 Italy. Superb supporting performance by Masina; film was cowritten by her husband, Federico Fellini. Originally titled: SENZA PIETA.
Without Reservations (1946) **107m.** *** D: Mervyn LeRoy. Claudette Colbert, John Wayne, Don Defore, Anne Triola, Frank Puglia, Phil Brown, Thurston Hall, Louella Parsons, Dona Drake. Authoress Colbert meets perfect man to play hero in movie version of her new book: soldier Wayne. Engaging comedy-romance, with some amusing swipes at Hollywood, several surprise guest stars.▼
Without Warning (1980) **C-89m.** *½ D: Greydon Clark. Jack Palance, Cameron Mitchell, Martin Landau, Ralph Meeker, Tarah Nutter, Sue Ane Langdon, Neville Brand, Larry Storch. Very silly horror film. Alien launches carnivorous disks at various citizens. A few scattered laughs and shudders, some intense acting, and a flagrantly bad job by Landau as a militant ex-sergeant named Fred Dobbs. Also known as IT CAME WITHOUT WARNING.
With Six You Get Eggroll (1968) **C-95m.** ** D: Howard Morris. Doris Day, Brian Keith, Pat Carroll, Barbara Hershey, George Carlin, Alice Ghostley. Oft-told tale of a widow and widower who try to move their children under the same roof. Amiable but slow on laughs; look for Vic Tayback as the Chicken Truck Driver, Jamie Farr and William Christopher as, respectively, JoJo and Zip. Day's last film to date.▼
With This Ring (1978) **C-100m.** TVM D: James Sheldon. Tony Bill, Tom Bosley, Diana Canova, John Forsythe, Scott Hylands, Donny Most, Dick Van Patten, Betty White. Formula sitcom approach to the wedding game, with all the predictability of a *Love Boat* episode. Mary Frances Crosby, Bing's daughter, made her TV acting debut in this one. Average.
Witness (1985) **C-112m.** *** D: Peter Weir. Harrison Ford, Kelly McGillis, Josef Sommer, Lukas Haas, Jan Rubes, Alexander Godunov, Danny Glover, Patti LuPone. A big-city cop on the lam hides out on an Amish farm, where he and a young widow are attracted to each other. Entertaining film is marred by jarring shifts in tone, especially toward the end. Oscar winner for writers Earl W. Wallace, William Kelley, Pamela Wallace. ▼
Witness Chair, The (1936) **64m.** *½ D: George Nicholls. Ann Harding, Walter Abel, Douglass Dumbrille, Frances Sage, Moroni Olsen, Margaret Hamilton. Faithful secretary tries to take the rap for the boss she's secretly in love with in this

unbelievable courtroom/whodunit; polished but dull.

Witness for the Prosecution (1957) **114m.** **** D: Billy Wilder. Marlene Dietrich, Tyrone Power, Charles Laughton, Elsa Lanchester, John Williams, Henry Daniell, Una O'Connor. Fantastically effective London courtroom suspenser from Agatha Christie play. Dietrich is peerless as wife of alleged killer (Power). Laughton at his best as defense attorney, and Lanchester delightful as his long-suffering nurse. Scripted by Wilder and Harry Kurnitz. Remade as a TVM.▼

Witness for the Prosecution (1982) **C-100m. TVM** D: Alan Gibson. Ralph Richardson, Deborah Kerr, Beau Bridges, Donald Pleasence, Wendy Hiller, Diana Rigg. Great cast has a ball with Agatha Christie's memorable suspense drama about a London murder trial. Kerr's performance as barrister Richardson's garrulous nurse marked her TV acting debut, but Rigg, as defendant Bridges's enigmatic wife, walks off with the show. Adapted by John Gay from the Christie play and the Billy Wilder/Harry Kurnitz 1957 screenplay. That version of it, though, remains untouched. Above average.

Witness in the Dark (1959-British) **62m.** *½ D: Wolf Rilla. Patricia Dainton, Conrad Phillips, Madge Ryan, Nigel Green, Enid Lorimer. Uncommonly obvious suspenser with murderer seeking to kill blind girl who was present when crime was committed.

Witness to Murder (1954) **83m.** *** D: Roy Rowland. Barbara Stanwyck, George Sanders, Gary Merrill, Jesse White. Solid suspenser of Stanwyck witnessing act of murder and trying to convince police of what she saw.

Wives and Lovers (1963) **103m.** **½ D: John Rich. Janet Leigh, Van Johnson, Shelley Winters, Martha Hyer, Ray Walston, Jeremy Slate. Surface, slick entertainment; newly famous writer Johnson, wife Leigh and child move to suburbia. Literary agent Hyer on the make almost causes divorce; Winters is wise-cracking neighbor. Script by Edward Anhalt, from Jay Presson Allen's play.

Wives Never Know (1936) **75m.** **½ D: Elliott Nugent. Charlie Ruggles, Mary Boland, Adolphe Menjou, Vivienne Osborne, Claude Gillingwater, Fay Holden, Louise Beavers. Flimsy tale of couple trying to awaken each other's love; Ruggles and Boland are always worth watching, and Menjou adds dash.

Wives Under Suspicion (1938) **69m.** **½ D: James Whale. Warren William, Gail Patrick, Constance Moore, William Lundigan, Ralph Morgan. Minor but interesting drama of callous D.A. William waking up when he thinks his wife (Patrick) is seeing another man. Remake of Whale's THE KISS BEFORE THE MIRROR.▼

Wiz, The (1978) **C-133m.** ** D: Sidney Lumet. Diana Ross, Michael Jackson, Nipsey Russell, Ted Ross, Mabel King, Theresa Merritt, Thelma Carpenter, Lena Horne, Richard Pryor. Diana Ross weeps and whines her way through modern black variation on THE WIZARD OF OZ, from the Broadway show by William F. Brown and Charlie Smalls. Some good musical numbers, fine supporting cast, but dreary finale—and drearier performance by Ross—really weigh it down. Music arranged and conducted by Quincy Jones.▼

Wizard, The (1989) **C-99m.** ** D: Todd Holland. Fred Savage, Luke Edwards, Jenny Lewis, Beau Bridges, Christian Slater, Will Seltzer, Jackey Vinson, Wendy Phillips, Sam McMurray. A road movie for kids, with Savage, his traumatized brother Edwards, and Lewis pursued across the Southwest by various relatives and other grown-ups. Limp, overplotted comedy suffers from heavy product plugs. ROCKY-like finish, dealing with Edwards' video-game wizardry, may thrill preteens but few others.▼

Wizard of Baghdad, The (1960) **C-92m.** ** D: George Sherman. Dick Shawn, Diane Baker, Barry Coe, John Van Dreelen, Robert F. Simon, Vaughn Taylor. Blah satire on costumers, with Shawn a lazy genie.

Wizard of Loneliness, The (1988) **C-111m.** ** D: Jenny Bowen. Lukas Haas, Lea Thompson, John Randolph, Anne Pitoniak, Dylan Baker, Lance Guest, Jeremiah Warner. Topnotch acting (especially by precocious young star Haas) fails to save a haphazardly constructed adaptation of John Nichols' novel about a youngster growing up with his grandparents in New England during WW2. His aunt (Thompson in an unusual character role) carries a dark secret that leads to a melodramatic climax. A coproduction of PBS' *American Playhouse* that will probably play better on the small screen.▼

Wizard of Oz, The (1939) **C/B&W-101m.** **** D: Victor Fleming. Judy Garland, Ray Bolger, Bert Lahr, Jack Haley, Frank Morgan, Billie Burke, Margaret Hamilton, Charley Grapewin, Clara Blandick, The Singer Midgets. A genuine American classic, based on L. Frank Baum's story of a Kansas girl who goes "Over the Rainbow" to a land of colorful characters and spirited adventure. A perfect cast in the perfect fantasy, with Harold Arlen and E. Y. Harburg's unforgettable score. Just as good the fifteenth time as it is the first time. Won Oscars for "Over the Rainbow" and Herbert Stothart's scoring, plus a special miniature award for Judy. Previously filmed in 1925; remade as THE WIZ (set in N.Y.C.) and OZ (Australia). A pair of sequels: JOURNEY BACK TO OZ and RETURN TO OZ.▼

Wizard of Speed and Time, The (1988) C-95m. **½ D: Mike Jittlov. Mike Jittlov, Paige Moore, Richard Kaye, David Conrad, John Massari, Steve Brodie, Frank LaLoggia, Philip Michael Thomas. A young special-effects whiz and his pals buck the Hollywood system and try to make a movie. This completely self-referential low-budget comedy scores big points for gumption and enthusiasm, which helps make up for some amateurish qualities. Best of all are Jittlov's eye-popping, one-of-a-kind visual effects. Expanded from a popular short subject of the same name.▼

Wizards (1977) C-80m. *½ D: Ralph Bakshi. Voices of Bob Holt, Jesse Wells, Richard Romanus, David Proval, Mark Hamill. Animated sci-fi tale of future world after devastation, with warring factions that conjure up Hitler's armies. Turgid, unappealing film for adults or children.▼

Wolf at the Door (1987-French-Danish) C-90m. *** D: Henning Carlsen. Donald Sutherland, Max von Sydow, Valerie Morea, Sofie Grabol, Fanny Bastin, Merete Voldstedlund. Sutherland is more subdued as Gauguin than Anthony Quinn was in LUST FOR LIFE; generally interesting bio covers the middle period of the artist's life, when he returned to Paris from Tahiti—then struggled to raise the money to go back. Arouses your interest in the subject.▼

Wolf Dog (1958-Canadian) 61m. *½ D: Sam Newfield. Jim Davis, Allison Hayes, Tony Brown, Austin Willis. Low-jinks about farm life in the north country involving land-hungry ranchers.

Wolfen (1981) C-115m. *** D: Michael Wadleigh. Albert Finney, Diane Venora, Edward James Olmos, Gregory Hines, Tom Noonan, Dick O'Neill. Detective Finney tracks mysterious beasts that are terrorizing N.Y.C. Surreal, allegorical mystery is satisfying—and could have been great. Hines stands out as coroner; Gerry Fisher's ingenious cinematography is also noteworthy.▼

Wolf Lake (1978) C-87m. *½ D: Burt Kennedy. Rod Steiger, David Huffman, Robin Mattson, Jerry Hardin, Richard Herd, Paul Mantee. Dull revenge film. Steiger (intense as ever) and four old army buddies stay at Canadian hunting lodge run by Huffman, a Vietnam deserter who fled to Canada. Steiger lost his son in the Vietnam war and tries to take out his grief (violently) on Huffman, with tragic results.▼

Wolf Larsen (1958) 83m. **½ D: Harmon Jones. Barry Sullivan, Peter Graves, Gita Hall, Thayer David. Nicely done version of Jack London's THE SEA WOLF with Sullivan effective as the tyrannical captain of the eerie ship.▼

Wolf Larsen (1975-Italian) C-92m. ** D: Giuseppi Vari. Chuck Connors, Barbara Bach, Giuseppi Pambieri. Tired new version of Jack London's SEA WOLF with Connors chewing up scenery as the sadistic sea captain. Video titles: LEGEND OF THE SEA WOLF and LARSEN, WOLF OF THE SEVEN SEAS.▼

Wolf Man, The (1941) 70m. ***½ D: George Waggner. Lon Chaney, Jr., Evelyn Ankers, Claude Rains, Maria Ouspenskaya, Ralph Bellamy, Patric Knowles, Warren William, Bela Lugosi, Fay Helm. One of the finest horror films ever made: Larry Talbot (Chaney) is bitten by werewolf Lugosi, survives to carry the curse himself. Outstanding cast includes Rains as unknowing father, Ankers as perplexed girl friend, Ouspenskaya as wizened gypsy woman who foretells his fate and attempts to care for him. Literate and very engrossing, with superb makeup by Jack Pierce, atmospheric music (re-used in many other Universal chillers) by Charles Previn and Hans J. Salter. Sequel: FRANKENSTEIN MEETS THE WOLF MAN.▼

Woman and the Hunter, The (1957) 79m. *½ D: George Breakston. Ann Sheridan, David Farrar, John Loder. Tedious love triangle set in the jungles of Kenya; Sheridan tries hard but material defeats all.

Woman-Bait SEE: **Inspector Maigret**

Woman Called Golda, A (1982) C-200m. TVM D: Alan Gibson. Ingrid Bergman, Judy Davis, Leonard Nimoy, Anne Jackson, Ned Beatty, Barry Foster, Robert Loggia. Bergman's memorable, Emmy-winning swan song as Golda Meir, following the Israeli prime minister's life and career through her historic meeting with Anwar Sadat in 1977. Written by Harold Gast and Steven Gethers. Originally shown in two parts. Above average.▼

Woman Called Moses, A (1978) C-200m. TVM D: Paul Wendkos. Cicely Tyson, Will Geer, Robert Hooks, James Wainwright, Dick Anthony Williams, Jason Bernard, Hari Rhodes. Dramatization of the life of Harriet Tubman, who founded the underground railway that helped fellow former slaves to freedom in the antebellum South. There's the expected exceptional performance by Tyson and the last work of Will Geer, but the whole project nearly goes down the tube because of an irrelevant narration provided by Orson Welles at his most imperious. Adapted by Lonne Elder III from Marcy Heldish's novel. Average.

Woman Chases Man (1937) 71m. **½ D: John G. Blystone. Miriam Hopkins, Joel McCrea, Charles Winninger, Ella Logan, Erik Rhodes, Broderick Crawford. Sometime hilarious, often strained screwball comedy with Hopkins trying to fleece wealthy McCrea, falling in love in the process.

Woman Eater (1959-British) 70m. *½ D: Charles Saunders. George Coulouris, Rob-

[1305]

ert MacKenzie, Norman Claridge, Marpessa Dawn, Jimmy Vaughan. Mad scientist Colouris feeds women to a stolen Amazonian tree that he keeps in the dungeon of his British manor, hoping to derive a substance that will revive the dead. And they say that scientific research lacks imagination!▼

Woman Hater (1949-British) **70m.** ** D: Terence Young. Stewart Granger, Edwige Feuillere, Ronald Squire, Mary Jerrold. Contrived battle of wits between confirmed bachelor and single girl leads to predictable romance.▼

Woman He Loved, The (1988) **C-100m.** TVM D: Charles Jarrott. Jane Seymour, Anthony Andrews, Olivia de Havilland, Lucy Gutteridge, Julie Harris, Robert Hardy, Phyllis Calvert. Lackadaisical retelling of the romance of Wallis Warfield Simpson and the Prince of Wales, with Seymour and Andrews uncanny in their resemblance to the subjects. William Luce penned this version of the tale, told from Simpson's viewpoint; not to be confused with a 1972 TV drama called THE WOMAN I LOVE, which starred Richard Chamberlain and Faye Dunaway. Average.

Woman Hunt (1972-U.S.-Philippine) **C-81m.** BOMB D: Eddie Romero. John Ashley, Sid Haig, Laurie Rose, Lisa Todd, Eddie Garcia, Pat Woodell. Wretched knock-off of THE MOST DANGEROUS GAME, using kidnapped women as prey. Todd's dull performance as a black-leather-clad lesbian sadist wouldn't even amuse her *Hee Haw* fans.▼

Woman Hunter, The (1972) **C-73m. TVM** D: Bernard Kowalski. Barbara Eden, Robert Vaughn, Stuart Whitman, Sydney Chaplin, Larry Storch, Enrique Lucero. Wealthy, unstable Dina Hunter (Eden) on Mexican holiday is fearful that murderer is stalking her and jewels. Unconvincing climax in suspense film that seems excuse for Eden to show off fashions. Average.▼

Woman in a Dressing Gown (1957-British) **93m.** *** D: J. Lee Thompson. Yvonne Mitchell, Anthony Quayle, Sylvia Syms, Andrew Ray, Carole Lesley. Excellent British drama about middle-aged man lured away from his unkempt wife by an attractive young woman at his office. Mature, intelligent, and moving.

Woman in Bondage (1943) **70m.** ** D: Steve Sekely. Gail Patrick, Nancy Kelly, Gertrude Michael, Anne Nagel, Tala Birell, Alan Baxter, H. B. Warner. Exploitation patriotism hammering away at Nazi maltreatment of conquered people. Dates badly.

Woman in Flames, A (1982-German) **C-106m.** *** D: Robert Van Ackeren. Gudrun Landgrebe, Mathieu Carriere, Gabriele Lafari, Hanns Zischler. Landgrebe, after leaving her pompous husband, becomes a high-class hooker and falls for aging, bisexual gigolo Carriere. Provoca-

tive, but certainly not optimistic, chronicle of the manner in which men and women perceive of and treat each other and the effect of constant sex without passion, caring, love.▼

Woman in Green, The (1945) **68m.** D: Roy William Neill. Basil Rathbone, Nigel Bruce, Hillary Brooke, Henry Daniell, Paul Cavanagh, Matthew Boulton, Eve Amber. Also shown in computer-colored version. SEE: Sherlock Holmes series.▼

Woman in Hiding (1949) **92m.** ** D: Michael Gordon. Ida Lupino, Howard Duff, Stephen McNally, Peggy Dow, John Litel, Joe Besser. Overdone dramatics of wife discovering husband is killer, fleeing before it's too late; some restraint would have been most helpful.

Woman in Question, The (1952-British) **82m.** *** D: Anthony Asquith. Dirk Bogarde, Jean Kent, Susan Shaw, Hermione Baddeley. Police inspector, investigating murder of a fortune teller, turns up with questions of character and mystery surrounding her life. Retitled: FIVE ANGLES ON MURDER.

Woman in Red (1935) **68m.** ** D: Robert Florey. Barbara Stanwyck, Gene Raymond, Genevieve Tobin, John Eldredge, Philip Reed, Dorothy Tree. Routine courtroom drama of Stanwyck and Raymond marriage interrupted by charge that she's been seeing Eldredge.

Woman in Red, The (1984) **C-87m.** *** D: Gene Wilder. Gene Wilder, Kelly Le-Brock, Gilda Radner, Joseph Bologna, Charles Grodin, Judith Ivey. Broad remake of French farce PARDON MON AFFAIRE with happily married Wilder going ga-ga over beautiful LeBrock. Stevie Wonder score includes Oscar-winning "I Just Called to Say I Love You."▼

Woman Inside, The (1981-Canadian) **C-94m.** BOMB D: Joseph Van Winkle. Gloria Manon, Dane Clark, Joan Blondell, Michael Champion, Marlene Tracy. Vietnam veteran Manon has sex change operation. Flimsy and flaky, with a budget of $32.95; destined to become a midnight camp classic. Sadly, Blondell's last screen role, as Manon's aunt.▼

Woman in the Dunes (1964-Japanese) **123m.** ***½ D: Hiroshi Teshigahara. Eiji Okada, Kyoko Kishida, Koji Mitsui, Hiroko Ito, Sen Yano. Entomologist Okada becomes trapped in a sandpit and the prisoner of Kishida. Moving, memorable allegory, with striking direction and cinematography (by Hiroshi Segawa).▼

Woman in the Moon (1929-German) **156m.** ** D: Fritz Lang. Klaus Pohl, Willy Fritsch, Gustav von Wangenheim, Gerda Maurus, Fritz Rasp. This lesser Lang effort, his last silent film, is about a spaceship and its trip to the moon. It's slow and way overlong, and it pales beside his brilliant METROPOLIS. Also known as BY ROCKET TO THE MOON and GIRL IN THE MOON.▼

Woman in the Window, The (1944) **99m.** ***½ D: Fritz Lang. Joan Bennett, Edward G. Robinson, Dan Duryea, Raymond Massey, Bobby (Robert) Blake, Dorothy Peterson. High-grade melodrama about Robinson meeting subject of alluring painting (Bennett), becoming involved in murder and witnessing his own investigation. Surprise ending tops exciting film. Scripted and produced by Nunnally Johnson.

Woman in White, The (1948) **109m.** *** D: Peter Godfrey. Eleanor Parker, Alexis Smith, Sydney Greenstreet, Gig Young, Agnes Moorehead, John Emery, John Abbott. Florid gothic thriller from Wilkie Collins book about strange household and tormented Parker.

Woman Is a Woman, A (1960-French) C-83m. **½ D: Jean-Luc Godard. Jean-Paul Belmondo, Jean-Claude Brialy, Anna Karina, Noel Pacquin. Pert stripper Karina wants a baby; boyfriend Belmondo is not interested in fatherhood, so she approaches his best friend (Brialy). Occasionally spirited, but mostly a self-indulgent trifle.▼

Woman Next Door, The (1981-French) C-106m. *** D: Francois Truffaut. Gerard Depardieu, Fanny Ardant, Henri Garcin, Michele Baumgartner, Veronique Silver. Depardieu's new neighbor is ex-lover Ardant. Both are now married; still, they revive their relationship. Somber, compassionate study of human nature and emotions, nicely acted by the two leads.▼

Woman Obsessed (1959) C-102m. **½ D: Henry Hathaway. Susan Hayward, Stephen Boyd, Barbara Nichols, Dennis Holmes, Theodore Bikel, Ken Scott. Energetic stars try hard in Canadian ranch-life soaper of widow Hayward who marries Boyd, with predictable clashing and making up.

Woman of Affairs, A (1928) **108m.** *** D: Clarence Brown. Greta Garbo, John Gilbert, Lewis Stone, John Mack Brown, Douglas Fairbanks, Jr., Hobart Bosworth, Dorothy Sebastian. Smooth, entertaining late-silent with Garbo as reckless socialite who undertakes serious burden of making good her late husband's thefts. Fine cast; story is diluted from Michael Arlen's *The Green Hat.*

Woman of Distinction, A (1950) **85m.** *** D: Edward Buzzell. Rosalind Russell, Ray Milland, Edmund Gwenn, Janis Carter, Francis Lederer. Minor but very enjoyable slapstick, as visiting professor Milland causes scandal involving college dean Russell. Energetic cast puts this over; brief guest appearance by Lucille Ball.▼

Woman of Dolwyn SEE: **Last Days of Dolwyn, The**

Woman of Paris, A (1923) **81m.** *** D: Charles Chaplin. Edna Purviance, Adolphe Menjou, Carl Miller, Lydia Knott, Charles French. French girl Purviance is set to marry her sweetheart (Miller), but a misunderstanding causes her to move to Paris, where she becomes the mistress of wealthy Menjou. Chaplin's one attempt to make a serious film (without himself as star) was quite sophisticated for its time, and remains interesting, even moving, today. It was a box-office flop in 1923; Chaplin reedited it, but waited until 1977 to reissue it, with his newly composed music score. Chaplin does a cameo as a railway porter, but he's virtually unrecognizable.▼

Woman of Rome (1956-Italian) **93m.** ** D: Luigi Zampa. Gina Lollobrigida, Daniel Gelin, Franco Fabrizi, Raymond Pellegrin. Old stuff of girl of easy virtue with Lollobrigida for scenery.▼

Woman of Straw (1964-British) C-117m. **½ D: Basil Dearden. Sean Connery, Gina Lollobrigida, Ralph Richardson, Johnny Sekka, Alexander Knox. Muddled suspenser of Connery and Lollobrigida plotting the "perfect murder" of old Richardson with ironic results.

Woman of the North Country (1952) C-90m ** D: Joseph Kane. Gale Storm, Ruth Hussey, Rod Cameron, Jim Davis, John Agar, J. Carrol Naish. Predictable love and fight tale set in the mining lands; Storm's last film to date.

Woman of the River (1955-Italian) C-92m. ** D: Mario Soldati. Sophia Loren, Gerard Oury, Lise Bourdin, Rik Battaglia. Seamy, gloomy account of Loren involved with passion and criminals. Still, this was the film that really got her career going.

Woman of the Rumor, The (1954-Japanese) **95m.** **½ D: Kenji Mizoguchi. Kinuyo Tanaka, Yoshiko Kuga, Tomoemon Otani, Eitaro Shindo. Melodramatic account of Geisha house operator Tanaka, whose lover really prefers her daughter. Minor Mizoguchi.

Woman of the Town, The (1943) **90m.** *** D: George Archainbaud. Claire Trevor, Albert Dekker, Barry Sullivan, Henry Hull, Marion Martin. First-class Western with Dekker as Bat Masterson, who must choose between love for dance-hall girl Trevor or law and order.▼

Woman of the Year (1942) **112m.** ***½ D: George Stevens. Spencer Tracy, Katharine Hepburn, Fay Bainter, Dan Tobin, Reginald Owen, Roscoe Karns, William Bendix. First teaming of Tracy and Hepburn is a joy; Kate's a world-famed political commentator brought down to earth by sports reporter Tracy, whom she later weds. Unforgettable scene of Hepburn trying to understand her first baseball game. Oscar-winning screenplay by Ring Lardner, Jr. and Michael Kanin; later a hit Broadway musical. Remade for TV in 1976. Also shown in computer-colored version.▼

Woman of the Year (1976) **C-100m. TVM** D: Jud Taylor. Renee Taylor, Joseph Bologna, Dick O'Neill, Anthony Holland, Dick Bakalyan, Virginia Christine. Breezy comedy about the improbable marriage of an easy-going sports columnist and a celebrated society reporter. Taylor and Bologna are surprisingly comfortable in the shoes of Hepburn and Tracy. Above average.

Woman on Pier 13 SEE: **I Married a Communist**

Woman on the Beach, The (1947) **71m.** *½ D: Jean Renoir. Robert Ryan, Joan Bennett, Charles Bickford, Nan Leslie, Walter Sande, Irene Ryan. Overheated melodrama wastes clever gimmick: Coast Guard officer isn't completely convinced his lover's husband is really blind. Loaded with laughable dialogue and sledgehammer music cues; easy to see why this was Renoir's American swan song.

Woman on the Run (1950) **77m.** *** D: Norman Foster. Ann Sheridan, Dennis O'Keefe, Robert Keith, Ross Elliott, Frank Jenks. Sheridan is most convincing as wife trying to find her husband, witness to gangland murder, before the underworld does.

Woman Rebels, A (1936) **88m.** *** D: Mark Sandrich. Katharine Hepburn, Herbert Marshall, Elizabeth Allan, Donald Crisp, Doris Dudley, David Manners, Lucile Watson, Van Heflin. Hepburn is marvelous as young girl whose experiences in Victorian England lead to her crusading for Women's Rights. Well-mounted soap opera remains surprisingly timely.

Woman's Devotion, A (1956) **C-88m.** ** D: Paul Henreid. Ralph Meeker, Janice Rule, Paul Henreid, Rosenda Monteros. Choppy mystery of artist Meeker and wife Rule, involved in a murder while in Mexico. Also known as BATTLE SHOCK.

Woman's Face, A (1941) **105m.** *** D: George Cukor. Joan Crawford, Melvyn Douglas, Conrad Veidt, Osa Massen, Reginald Owen, Albert Basserman, Marjorie Main. Crawford has one of her most substantial roles in this exciting yarn of woman whose life changes when she undergoes plastic surgery. Taut climax spotlights villain Veidt. Originally filmed in 1938 in Sweden, as EN KVINNAS ANSIKTE, with Ingrid Bergman; script by Donald Ogden Stewart.▼

Woman's Secret, A (1949) **85m.** **½ D: Nicholas Ray. Maureen O'Hara, Melvyn Douglas, Gloria Grahame, Bill Williams, Victor Jory. Intriguing flashback drama of woman coming to hate singer she built up to success; good performances by two female stars. Just a bit too sloppy. Produced and scripted by Herman J. Mankiewicz, from a Vicki Baum novel.

Woman's Vengeance, A (1947) **96m.**

***½ D: Zoltan Korda. Charles Boyer, Ann Blyth, Jessica Tandy, Cedric Hardwicke, Mildred Natwick. Outstanding drama of philandering Boyer put on trial when his wife is found dead; brilliant cast gives vivid realistic performances. Script by Aldous Huxley, from his story.

Woman's World (1954) **C-94m.** *** D: Jean Negulesco. Clifton Webb, June Allyson, Van Heflin, Arlene Dahl, Lauren Bacall, Fred MacMurray, Cornel Wilde, Elliott Reid. Sophisticated look at big business, the men and women involved, with arch Webb the corporation boss choosing a new successor.

Woman They Almost Lynched, The (1953) **90m.** ** D: Allan Dwan. John Lund, Joan Leslie, Audrey Totter, Brian Donlevy, Ellen Corby, Minerva Urecal, Jim Davis. Civil War period film about refined young woman Leslie who comes to Western town and learns to tote gun; title tells the rest.

Woman Times Seven (1967) **C-99m.** *** D: Vittorio De Sica. Shirley MacLaine, Peter Sellers, Rossano Brazzi, Vittorio Gassman, Lex Barker, Elsa Martinelli, Robert Morley, Patrick Wymark, Adrienne Corri, Alan Arkin, Michael Caine, Anita Ekberg, Philippe Noiret. A seven-episode film with MacLaine showing seven types of women; some funny moments, some perceptive comments, but with that cast and director, it should have been much better.▼

Woman Under the Influence, A (1974) **C-155m.** ** D: John Cassavetes. Peter Falk, Gena Rowlands, Katherine Cassavetes, Lady Rowlands, Fred Draper. Typically overlong, overindulgent Cassavetes film, vaguely delineating relationship of woman who's cracking up and her hardhat husband, who can't handle it. Strong performances by Rowlands and Falk are chief virtue of this one.

Woman Wanted (1935) **68m.** ** D: George B. Seitz. Maureen O'Sullivan, Joel McCrea, Lewis Stone, Louis Calhern, Edgar Kennedy, Adrienne Ames, Robert Greig. Unremarkable programmer has O'Sullivan hunted by police and mobsters, McCrea out to prove her innocence.

Woman Who Came Back, The (1945) **68m.** ** D: Walter Colmes. John Loder, Nancy Kelly, Otto Kruger, Ruth Ford, Harry Tyler. Fair yarn of woman (Kelly) who is convinced she has received witches' curse from ancient forebear.▼

Woman Who Cried Murder, The SEE: **Death Scream**

Wombling Free (1978-British) **C-96m.** *½ D: Lionel Jeffries. David Tomlinson, Frances De La Tour, Bonnie Langford, Bernard Spear, Yasuko Nagazumi, John Junkin, Reg Lye. Silly kiddie pic has the Wombles (actors in creature suits) cleaning up after man's litter and leading a protest against pollution. They're invisible to mankind except for a little girl (Langford) who believes. Objectionable use of stereotypes; best segment has big production-number tributes to Gene Kelly and Fred Astaire. Based on a BBC-TV series, never released in U.S. but later adapted as a U.S. TV series featuring Frank Gorshin.▼

Women, The (1939) 132m. ***½ D: George Cukor. Joan Crawford, Norma Shearer, Rosalind Russell, Mary Boland, Joan Fontaine, Paulette Goddard, Lucile Watson, Marjorie Main, Virginia Weidler, Phyllis Povah, Ruth Hussey, Mary Beth Hughes, Virginia Grey, Hedda Hopper, Butterfly McQueen. All-star (and all-female) cast shines in this hilarious adaptation of Clare Boothe play about divorce, cattiness, and competition in circle of "friends." Crawford has one of her best roles as bitchy Crystal Allen. Fashion show sequence is in color; script by Anita Loos and Jane Murfin. Remade as THE OPPOSITE SEX.▼

Women Are Like That (1938) 78m. **½ D: Stanley Logan. Kay Francis, Pat O'Brien, Ralph Forbes, Melville Cooper. Smooth fluff: Francis is daughter of ad executive in love with copywriter O'Brien.

Women Are Weak SEE: **3 Murderesses**

Women at West Point (1979) C-100m. TVM D: Vincent Sherman. Linda Purl, Leslie Ackerman, Jameson Parker, Andrew Stevens, Edward Edwards, Jack Blessing, Robert Townsend, Ken Olin. Fictionalized drama about the first women to enter the U.S. Military Academy in 1976 emerges, unfortunately, as "Gidget Becomes a Plebe." Below average.

Women in Cages (1972-U.S.-Philippine) C-78m. BOMB D: Gerry De Leon. Judy Brown, Pam Grier, Roberta Collins. Lurid prison melodrama, with the emphasis on sadism, has the switcheroo of Grier cast as lesbian guard who tortures prisoners in her gothic chamber, known as "The Playpen."▼

Women in Chains (1971) C-73m. TVM D: Bernard Kowalski. Ida Lupino, Lois Nettleton, Jessica Walter, Belinda Montgomery, John Larch, Penny Fuller. Probation officer wants to see prison system first hand, arranges fake identity, finds herself in tough situation when only person aware of scheme dies. Good production tries hard, but script is unbelievable, performances uneven. Average.

Women in Limbo SEE: **Limbo**

Women in Love (1969-British) C-129m. ***½ D: Ken Russell. Alan Bates, Oliver Reed, Glenda Jackson, Eleanor Bron, Jennie Linden, Alan Webb. Fine adaptation of D. H. Lawrence novel about two interesting love affairs. Tends to bog down toward the end, but acting and direction

are really impressive, as is memorable nude wrestling scene. Jackson won her first Oscar for this performance. Followed in 1989 by Russell's THE RAINBOW, a "prequel" in which Jackson plays the mother of her character in this film.▼

Women of Brewster Place, The (1989) C-200m. TVM D: Donna Deitch. Oprah Winfrey, Mary Alice, Olivia Cole, Robin Givens, Moses Gunn, Jackée, Paula Kelly, Lonette McKee, Paul Winfield, Cicely Tyson. Ambitious filming of Gloria Naylor's novel spanning several decades in the lives of seven black women who live in a tenement on a walled-off street and struggle to overcome racism, violence, and poverty. Well-acted ensemble drama with everyone getting at least one star turn, thanks to Karen Hall's multi-dimensional script. TV acting debut for top-billed Oprah, who was also executive producer. Originally shown in two parts. Followed by a weekly TV series, *Brewster Place* (also featuring Winfrey and Cole). Above average.

Women of Devil's Island (1961-Italian) C-95m. *½ D: Domenico Paolella. Guy Madison, Michele Mercier, Frederica Ranchi. Humdrum mini-epic with Madison helping aristocratic woman held prisoner on swamp-surrounded island.

Women of Pitcairn Island, The (1956) 72m. *½ D: Jean Yarbrough. James Craig, Lynn Bari, John Smith, Arleen Whelan, Sue England, Carol Thurston, Charlita. Low-budget garbage about families developing from people who remained on island after MUTINY ON THE BOUNTY.

Women of San Quentin (1983) C-100m. TVM D: William A. Graham. Stella Stevens, Debbie Allen, Hector Elizondo, Amy Steel, Rosana DeSoto, Gregg Henry, Yaphet Kotto. No sadistic matrons out of old Ida Lupino prison flicks here. The women are guards, but the originality stops there. Stevens puts down a riot among the males by strolling into the yard unarmed and ordering them to drop their tire irons and two-by-fours! Below average.

Women of the Prehistoric Planet (1966) C-87m. *½ D: Arthur C. Pierce. Wendell Corey, Keith Larsen, John Agar, Irene Tsu, Paul Gilbert, Merry Anders, Adam Roarke, Stuart Margolin. One of many studio-bound sci-fi pix from the '60s, a strange lot indeed. Spaceship crashes on mysterious planet full of prehistoric inhabitants. Agar gives best performance, and there's a twist ending, if you stick around for it.

Women of Valor (1986) C-100m. TVM D: Buzz Kulik. Susan Sarandon, Kristy McNichol, Alberta Watson, Valerie Mahaffey, Suzanne Lederer, Neva Patterson, Patrick Bishop. Curiously old-fashioned war movie about Army nurses taken captive in the Philippines by the Japanese during WW2. Looks like 1943's CRY HAVOC in a time capsule. Below average.▼

Women on the Verge of a Nervous Breakdown (1988-Spanish) C-88m. ***½ D: Pedro Almodovar. Carmen Maura, Antonio Banderas, Julieta Serrano, Maria Barranco, Rossy De Palma. Witty, outrageous, and highly stylized comedy about charmingly off-kilter actress Maura and how she responds when suddenly abandoned by her longtime lover. A real audience-pleaser, with plenty of laughs; crammed with a colorful array of supporting characters (most memorably a taxi driver with a bleached-blond pompadour whose car is a combination drugstore/bar).▼

Women's Prison (1955) 80m. ** D: Lewis Seiler. Ida Lupino, Jan Sterling, Cleo Moore, Audrey Totter, Phyllis Thaxter, Howard Duff, Mae Clarke, Gertrude Michael, Juanita Moore. Campy 1950s programmer, with Lupino as a vicious prison superintendent riding herd over a cast that no B movie lover could resist.

Women's Room, The (1980) C-150m. TVM D: Glenn Jordan. Lee Remick, Colleen Dewhurst, Patty Duke Astin, Kathryn Harrold, Tovah Feldshuh, Tyne Daly, Lisa Pelikan, Mare Winningham, Ted Danson, Gregory Harrison, Jenny O'Hara, Al Corley. Talky adaptation by Carol Sobieski of Marilyn French's feminist novel about the evolution of several '50s women as they make it into the '70s. Emmy-nominated as Outstanding Drama Special, as were both Dewhurst and Astin as Outstanding Supporting Actress. Above average.

Wonder Bar (1934) 84m. **½ D: Lloyd Bacon. Al Jolson, Kay Francis, Dolores Del Rio, Dick Powell, Ricardo Cortez, Louise Fazenda, Hugh Herbert, Hal LeRoy, Guy Kibbee. Very strange, often tasteless musical drama set in Paris nightclub with murder, romance, and Busby Berkeley's incredible "Goin' to Heaven on a Mule" production number, sure to be cut by most TV stations.

Wonderful Country, The (1959) C-96m. **½ D: Robert Parrish. Robert Mitchum, Julie London, Gary Merrill, Pedro Armendariz, Jack Oakie, Albert Dekker. Brooding Western involving Mitchum running guns along Mexico-Texas line, romancing London; script by Robert Ardrey.

Wonderful World of the Brothers Grimm, The (1962) C-129m. *** D: Henry Levin, George Pal. Laurence Harvey, Claire Bloom, Karl Boehm, Oscar Homolka, Martita Hunt, Jim Backus, Yvette Mimieux, Barbara Eden, Walter Slezak, Russ Tamblyn, Buddy Hackett, Beulah Bondi, Terry-Thomas. Fanciful adaptations of Grimm tales offset by OK look at famed brothers' lives. Best of all are Puppetoons sequences in toy shop, Hackett battling fire-breathing

dragon. Colorful George Pal entertainment, originally shown in Cinerama, with Oscar-winning costumes by Mary Wills.▼

Wonderland SEE: Fruit Machine, The▼

Wonder Man (1945) C-98m. *** D: H. Bruce Humberstone. Danny Kaye, Virginia Mayo, Vera-Ellen, Donald Woods, S. Z. Sakall, Allen Jenkins, Ed Brophy, Steve Cochran, Otto Kruger, Natalie Schafer. Kaye's fun as twins, the serious one forced to take the place of his brash entertainer brother when the latter is killed. Big, colorful production with Oscar-winning special effects.▼

Wonders of Aladdin, The (1961-U.S.-Italian) C-93m. ** D: Henry Levin, Mario Bava. Donald O'Connor, Noelle Adam, Vittorio De Sica, Aldo Fabrizi. Few wonders to behold in this mild children's fantasy which the kids might enjoy.▼

Wonder Woman (1974) C-78m. TVM D: Vincent McEveety. Cathy Lee Crosby, Kaz Garas, Ricardo Montalban, Andrew Prine, Charlene Holt, Richard X. Slattery. Live-action cartoon—the one that didn't make it—about a superhuman female who uses her powers to stalk an elusive espionage agent. Unlike Lynda Carter, Crosby doesn't even resemble WW. Set in present-day. Below average. Followed by THE NEW, ORIGINAL WONDER WOMAN.

Won Ton Ton, the Dog Who Saved Hollywood (1976) C-92m. ** D: Michael Winner. Bruce Dern, Madeline Kahn, Art Carney, Phil Silvers, Teri Garr, Ron Leibman. Fine cast struggles through inept spoof of 1920s Hollywood. Dog comes off better than dozens of veteran stars who make pointless cameo appearances (from Rhonda Fleming to the Ritz Brothers).

Wooden Horse, The (1950-British) 101m. *** D: Jack Lee. Leo Genn, David Tomlinson, Anthony Steel, Peter Burton, David Greene, Anthony Dawson, Bryan Forbes, Peter Finch. Sturdy, exciting P.O.W. drama of men who determine to tunnel their way out of Nazi prison camp.

Woodstock (1970) C-184m. **** D: Michael Wadleigh. Joan Baez, Richie Havens, Crosby, Stills and Nash, Jefferson Airplane, Joe Cocker, Sly and the Family Stone, Ten Years After, Santana, Country Joe and the Fish, John Sebastian, The Who, Jimi Hendrix, Arlo Guthrie. 1970 Oscar-winner as Best Documentary, film brilliantly captures unique communal experience of outdoor rock festival, along with great performances which highlighted unusual weekend bash. Among highlights: Cocker, Sly Stone, The Who. Unfortunately, effect of multiscreen images and stereophonic sound will be lost on TV. Martin Scorsese was one of the editors.▼

Word of Honor (1981) C-100m. TVM D: Mel Damski. Karl Malden, Rue McClanahan, Ron Silver, Largo Woodruff,

Alexa Kenin, Jacqueline Brookes, Henderson Forsythe, John Marley, Alex Karras, John Malkovich. Small-town reporter Malden takes a stand and refuses to divulge the name of a confidential source. Strong performance by the always reliable Malden in this newspaper story produced by Alex Karras and Susan Clark. Above average.

Words and Music (1948) **C-119m.** ****½** D: Norman Taurog. Mickey Rooney, Tom Drake, June Allyson, Ann Sothern, Judy Garland, Gene Kelly, Lena Horne, Vera-Ellen, Cyd Charisse, Allyn Ann McLerie, Mel Torme, Betty Garrett, Perry Como, Janet Leigh. Sappy biography of songwriters Rodgers (Drake) and Hart (Rooney) is salvaged somewhat by their wonderful music, including Kelly's dance to "Slaughter on Tenth Avenue."▼

Working Girl (1988) **C-113m.** ******* D: Mike Nichols. Harrison Ford, Sigourney Weaver, Melanie Griffith, Alec Baldwin, Joan Cusack, Philip Bosco, Nora Dunn, Oliver Platt, James Lally, Kevin Spacey, Robert Easton, Olympia Dukakis, Ricki Lake. Cute comedy about a naive but ambitious secretary who tries to outfox her wily boss by closing a big deal—with the help of a man she just happens to fall in love with. Star-making showcase for Griffith also gives Ford an ideal opportunity to play light comedy, and Weaver a sly supporting role as the villainess. Carly Simon's music was scored by Rob Mounsey; her song "Let the River Run" won an Oscar. Later a TV series.▼

Working Girls, The (1973) **C-81m.** ****½** D: Stephanie Rothman. Sarah Kennedy, Laurie Rose, Lynne Guthrie, Solomon Sturges, Mary Beth Hughes, Cassandra Peterson. One of the better drive-in comedies, with three attractive girls struggling to make a success of themselves in a male-oriented world; Kennedy and Sturges (Preston's son) make an endearing couple. Lately popping up on cable-TV because of nifty strip-tease performed by Peterson (better known as TV's Elvira).▼

Working Girls (1986) **C-90m.** *****½** D: Lizzie Borden. Louise Smith, Ellen McElduff, Amanda Goodwin, Marusia Zach, Janne Peters, Helen Nicholas. Beautifully realized, on-target account of a day in a N.Y.C. brothel; the sex is more humorous and businesslike than erotic, and the profession is depicted as an economic alternative to other traditional "women's" work. First-rate all the way.▼

Working Man, The (1933) **75m.** ****½** D: John G. Adolfi. George Arliss, Bette Davis, Hardie Albright, Theodore Newton, Gordon Westcott. Charming story of ambitious businessman Arliss becoming interested in the children of his long-time rival.

Work Is a 4-Letter Word (1967-British) **C-93m.** ****½** D: Peter Hall. David Warner, Cilla Black, Elizabeth Spriggs, Zia Mohyeddin, Joe Gladwyn. Zany, but hit-and-miss comedy based on the play *Eh?* about young man who raises giant mushrooms that produce euphoria when eaten. Warner is well cast.

World According to Garp, The (1982) **C-136m.** ******** D: George Roy Hill. Robin Williams, Mary Beth Hurt, Glenn Close, John Lithgow, Hume Cronyn, Jessica Tandy, Swoosie Kurtz, Amanda Plummer. Dazzling (if somewhat loose) adaptation of John Irving's novel, about an unusual young man's journey through life—an adventure shaped in large part by his unorthodox (and unmarried) mother. Absorbing, sure-footed odyssey through vignettes of social observation, absurdist humor, satire, and melodrama; beautifully acted by all, especially Close (in her feature debut) as Garp's mother and Lithgow as a transsexual. Script by Steve Tesich. Director Hill has cameo as pilot who crashes into Garp's house.▼

World and the Flesh (1932) **75m.** ****** D: John Cromwell. George Bancroft, Miriam Hopkins, Alan Mowbray, George E. Stone. Labored drama of soldier-of-fortune Bancroft asking price of Hopkins to save her wealthy friends from Russian Revolution; moves very slowly.

World Apart, A (1988) **C-112m.** ****½** D: Chris Menges. Barbara Hershey, David Suchet, Jeroen Krabbe, Paul Freeman, Tim Roth, Jodhi May. Personal story of South African apartheid as seen through the eyes of a teenage girl whose mother, a Communist activist, is jailed under the notorious 90-day detention act in 1963. Both a story of government abuse and a look at one mother's neglect of her family because of her involvement with a larger cause. Unfortunately, it becomes too diffuse to succeed completely on either count. Young May is remarkable as the girl, however. Autobiographical script was written by Shawn Slovo. Directorial debut for cinematographer Menges.▼

World Changes, The (1933) **90m.** ******* D: Mervyn LeRoy. Paul Muni, Mary Astor, Aline MacMahon, Donald Cook, Alan Dinehart, Guy Kibbee, Margaret Lindsay, Henry O'Neill, Jean Muir. Extremely watchable Edna Ferber–like saga of farm boy Muni, who pursues his ambitions to Chicago in the late 1800s and becomes a meat-packing baron and multimillionaire—only to see his family life crumble before his very eyes. Astor is excellent as his selfish wife, MacMahon her usual tower of strength as his mother. Cast is brimming with familiar faces, including young Mickey Rooney, and pre–*Charlie Chan* Sidney Toler.

World for Ransom (1954) **80m.** ****½** D: Robert Aldrich. Dan Duryea, Gene Lockhart, Patric Knowles, Reginald Denny,

Nigel Bruce, Marian Carr. Duryea has his hands full when he pokes his nose into high-tension scheme to kidnap nuclear scientist in Singapore. Offbeat programmer traded on popularity of Duryea's *China Smith* TV series.

World Gone Mad, The (1932) **74m.** ** D: Christy Cabanne. Pat O'Brien, Evelyn Brent, Neil Hamilton, Mary Brian, Louis Calhern, J. Carrol Naish, Buster Phelps, Richard Tucker. District attorney about to uncover stock swindle is framed and murdered; his intrepid reporter pal (who else but O'Brien) and the new D.A. (Hamilton) investigate. Then-topical programmer has its moments, but is too talky and meandering.▼

World Gone Wild (1988) **C-95m.** ** D: Lee H. Katzin. Bruce Dern, Michael Paré, Catherine Mary Stewart, Adam Ant, Rick Podell, Anthony James. Post-apocalyptic science-fiction saga set in the 21st century, in the desolate village of Lost Wells, which is threatened by evil plunderers (led by Adam Ant). Who will come to the villagers' rescue? THE SEVEN SAMURAI meets MAD MAX in this marginally successful, futuristic action yarn. ▼

World in His Arms, The (1952) **C-104m.** *** D: Raoul Walsh. Gregory Peck, Ann Blyth, John McIntire, Anthony Quinn, Andrea King, Eugenie Leontovich, Sig Ruman. Unlikely but entertaining tale of skipper Peck romancing Russian Blyth, set in 1850s San Francisco.

World in My Corner (1956) **82m** **½ D: Jesse Hibbs. Audie Murphy, Barbara Rush, Jeff Morrow, John McIntire, Tommy Rall, Howard St. John. Murphy is poor boy who rises to fame via boxing, almost ruined by rich life with Rush standing by.

World Is Full of Married Men, The (1979-British) **C-107m.** ** D: Robert Young. Anthony Franciosa, Carroll Baker, Sherrie Cronn, Gareth Hunt, Georgina Hale, Anthony Steel. The sexual escapades—and downfall—of advertising executive Franciosa. Slick and sleazy exploitation melodrama that ultimately gives feminism a bad name, from a novel and screenplay by Jackie Collins.▼

World Moves On, The (1934) **90m.** **½ D: John Ford. Madeleine Carroll, Franchot Tone, Reginald Denny, Stepin Fetchit, Lumsden Hare, Raul Roulien, Louise Dresser, Sig Ruman. Long but interesting family saga covering 100 years as Louisiana family is split, three sons heading business operations in England, France, Germany, experiencing tremendous changes from peaceful 19th century through WW1.

World of Abbott and Costello, The (1965) **75m.** ** Narrated by Jack E. Leonard. Bud Abbott, Lou Costello, Marjorie Main, Bela Lugosi, Tom Ewell, others. Inept compilation of A&C footage, with

curious selection of scenes, senseless narration. Still, there's "Who's on First?" and other fine routines that survive even this lackluster treatment.

World of Apu, The (1959-Indian) **103m.** ***½ D: Satyajit Ray. Soumitra Chatterjee, Sharmila Tagore, Alok Chakravarty, Swapan Mukherji. Sadly poetic tale of the shy Apu (Chatterjee) marrying and fathering a child. Magnificently acted; last of the director's "Apu" trilogy.▼

World of Henry Orient, The (1964) **C-106m.** ***½ D: George Roy Hill. Peter Sellers, Tippy Walker, Merrie Spaeth, Paula Prentiss, Angela Lansbury, Phyllis Thaxter, Tom Bosley. Marvelous comedy of two teenage girls who idolize eccentric pianist (Sellers) and follow him around N.Y.C. Bosley and Lansbury are superb as Walker's parents, with Thaxter appealing as Spaeth's understanding mother. Screenplay by Nunnally and Nora Johnson, from her novel.▼

World of Suzie Wong, The (1960) **C-129m.** **½ D: Richard Quine. William Holden, Nancy Kwan, Sylvia Syms, Michael Wilding, Laurence Naismith. Holden's sluggish performance as American artist in love with prostitute Kwan doesn't help this soaper, lavishly filmed in Hong Kong. Script by John Patrick from Paul Osborn's Broadway play.▼

World of Tomorrow, The (1984) **C/B&W-83m.** *** D: Lance Bird, Tom Johnson. Lovely documentary about 1939 New York World's Fair, a compilation of newsreels, home movies, promotional films, and various other period graphics . . . much of it in color! Occasionally teeters on the edge of pretentiousness, especially in narration spoken by Jason Robards. Cut to one hour for some showings.

World Premiere (1941) **70m.** *½ D: Ted Tetzlaff. John Barrymore, Frances Farmer, Eugene Pallette, Virginia Dale, Ricardo Cortez, Sig Ruman, Fritz Feld. Poor excuse for comedy involves idiotic producer Barrymore, jealous movie stars, outlandish publicity stunts, and Nazi saboteurs. A real waste.

World's Greatest Athlete, The (1973) **C-93m.** *** D: Robert Scheerer. John Amos, Jan-Michael Vincent, Tim Conway, Roscoe Lee Browne, Dayle Haddon, Howard Cosell. Hard-luck coach Amos returns to his roots in Africa and discovers superathlete Vincent; enjoyable Disney comedy with excellent special effects. Conway particularly funny in sequence in which he shrinks to Tom Thumb size. Cosell's classic line: "I've never seen anything like this in my entire illustrious career!"▼

World's Greatest Lover, The (1977) **C-89m.** **½ D: Gene Wilder. Gene Wilder, Carol Kane, Dom DeLuise, Fritz Feld, Carl Ballantine, Michael Huddleston, Matt Collins, Ronny Graham. Sporadically funny comedy set in 1920s Hollywood, with Wilder screen-testing as new movie sheik and wife Kane deserting him for real-life Valentino. Wild slapstick combines with occasional vulgarities and moments of poignancy in this uneven film. Inspired by Fellini's THE WHITE SHEIK.▼

World, the Flesh, and the Devil, The (1959) **95m.** **½ D: Ranald MacDougall. Harry Belafonte, Inger Stevens, Mel Ferrer. Belafonte and Stevens are only survivors of worldwide nuclear explosion; their uneasy relationship is jarred by arrival of Ferrer. Intriguing film starts well, bogs down halfway through, and presents ridiculous conclusion. Best scenes are at beginning, when Belafonte is alone in an impressively deserted Manhattan.▼

World War III (1982) **C-200m. TVM** D: David Greene. Rock Hudson, David Soul, Brian Keith, Cathy Lee Crosby, Jeroen Krabbe, Katherine Helmond, Robert Prosky, James Hampton, Richard Yniguez, Herbert Jefferson, Jr. Doomsday thriller, written by Robert L. Joseph, revolving around a Russian military unit's invasion of Alaska to seize the pipeline in retaliation for a U.S. grain embargo circa Christmas, 1987. Keith is great as a world-weary Secretary General of the USSR, and Hudson plays the U.S. President by accident on whose decision a possible nuclear holocaust rests. The original director, Boris Sagal, was killed during location filming, most of which was then moved to Zoctrope Studios, where obvious indoor work vitiates much of the military tension. Originally shown in two parts. Above average.▼

World Was His Jury, The (1958) **82m.** *½ D: Fred F. Sears. Edmond O'Brien, Mona Freeman, Karin Booth, Robert McQueeney. Routine account of ship's captain proven innocent of negligence in sea disaster.

World Without End (1956) **C-80m.** **½ D: Edward Bernds. Hugh Marlowe, Nancy Gates, Nelson Leigh, Rod Taylor. Space flight headed for Mars breaks the time barrier and ends up on Earth in the 26th century. Pretty good sci-fi owes more than a little to H.G. Wells' *The Time Machine.*

World Without Sun (1964) **C-93m.** **** D: Jacques Cousteau. Excellent, Oscar-winning documentary of Cousteau and his oceanauts, creating an underwater adventure that challenges any fiction.

Worst Secret Agents SEE: **Oh! Those Most Secret Agents**

Worst Woman in Paris?, The (1933) **78m.** **½ D: Monta Bell. Benita Hume, Adolphe Menjou, Harvey Stephens, Helen Chandler, Margaret Seddon. Glossy Lubitsch-like comedy of chic Hume walking out on wealthy husband Menjou, returning to America, falling in love with naive young Stephens.

Worth Winning (1989) **C-102m.** *½ D: Will Mackenzie. Mark Harmon, Madeleine Stowe, Lesley Ann Warren, Maria Holvöe, Mark Blum, Andrea Martin, David Brenner. Smug, successful Harmon bets that he can hustle a trio of women into agreeing to marry him. Occasionally obnoxious (and predictable) comedy.▼

Woyzeck (1978-German) **C-82m.** **½ D: Werner Herzog. Klaus Kinski, Eva Mattes, Wolfgang Reichmann, Willy Semmelrogge, Josef Bierbichler, Paul Burian. Minor Herzog features the usual wide-eyed performance by Kinski as an ostensibly normal man who goes insane and becomes a murderer. Based on Georg Buchner's drama.

Wraith, The (1986) **C-92m.** ** D: Mike Marvin. Charlie Sheen, Nick Cassavetes, Randy Quaid, Sherilyn Fenn, Griffin O'Neal, David Sherrill, Jamie Bozian, Clint Howard. A Dodge Turbo Interceptor—it's a car—strangely appears one day and takes on some auto thieves. For those who favor fast cars and lots of noise. Of note only for the number of famous actors' siblings and offspring in the cast.▼

Wrath of God, The (1972) **C-111m.** ** D: Ralph Nelson. Robert Mitchum, Rita Hayworth, Frank Langella, John Colicos, Victor Buono, Ken Hutchison, Paula Pritchett, Gregory Sierra. If you take this film—about a defrocked priest in a revolution-ridden country south of the border seriously, it's an OK action yarn. If you accept it as tongue-in-cheek, it may yield greater enjoyment. Hayworth's final film.

Wreck of the Hesperus, The (1948) **70m.** ** D: John Hoffman. Willard Parker, Edgar Buchanan, Patricia White (Barry). Loosely based on Longfellow poem, this low-budget flick suffers from lack of production values to enhance special effects of storms at sea.

Wreck of the Mary Deare, The (1959-U.S.-British) **C-105m.** **½ D: Michael Anderson. Gary Cooper, Charlton Heston, Michael Redgrave, Emlyn Williams, Cecil Parker, Alexander Knox, Virginia McKenna, Richard Harris. Sticky going: skipper of sunken ship accused of negligence, cleared at inquest by testimony of salvage boat captain. Special effects are real star. Script by Eric Ambler.

Wrecking Crew, The (1969) **C-105m.** *½ D: Phil Karlson. Dean Martin, Sharon Tate, Elke Sommer, Nancy Kwan, Tina Louise, Nigel Green. Fourth and final theatrical Matt Helm epic, while hardly a good film, is at least a step up from the last two, thanks to a return to the original director and the re-creation (in Tate) of an engaging klutz a la Stella Stevens in THE SILENCERS. Story has Helm after crime ring that's hijacked a train carrying a

[1313]

billion in gold. Chuck Norris has one line with Matt Helm in a bar.

Written on the Wind (1956) **C-99m.** *** D: Douglas Sirk. Rock Hudson, Lauren Bacall, Robert Stack, Dorothy Malone, Robert Keith, Grant Williams. Florid melodrama of playboy-millionaire Stack, his nymphomaniac sister Malone, and how they destroy themselves and others around them. Irresistible kitsch. Malone won Oscar for her performance.▼

Wrong Arm of the Law, The (1962-British) **94m.** *** D: Cliff Owen. Peter Sellers, Lionel Jeffries, Bernard Cribbins, Davy Kaye, Nanette Newman, John Le Mesurier, Dennis Price. Wacky comedy spoof has Australian trio being chased by police as well as crooks because they've been dressing as cops and confiscating loot from apprehended robbers. Some very funny moments.▼

Wrong Box, The (1966-British) **C-105m.** ***½ D: Bryan Forbes. John Mills, Ralph Richardson, Michael Caine, Peter Cook, Dudley Moore, Nanette Newman, Wilfred Lawson, Tony Hancock, Peter Sellers. Scramble for inheritance is basis for wacky black comedy set in Victorian England; aging Mills attempts to do in brother Richardson (with help from family cohorts) in order to be sole survivor. Sellers has hilarious cameo as oddball doctor. Based on a Robert Louis Stevenson story, scripted by Larry Gelbart and Burt Shevelove.▼

Wrong Guys, The (1988) **C-86m.** *½ D: Danny Bilson. Louie Anderson, Richard Lewis, Richard Belzer, Franklyn Ajaye, Tim Thomerson, Brion James, Bill Manard, Ernie Hudson. Clumsy and unfunny comedy about a Cub Scout reunion campout that goes awry; cast of stand-up comics do battle with a stupid script.▼

Wrong Is Right (1982) **C-117m.** **½ D: Richard Brooks. Sean Connery, George Grizzard, Robert Conrad, Katharine Ross, G. D. Spradlin, John Saxon, Henry Silva, Leslie Nielsen, Robert Webber, Rosalind Cash, Hardy Kruger, Dean Stockwell, Ron Moody, Jennifer Jason Leigh. Broad, bizarre, free-swinging satire of our TV-dominated culture, keyed to superstar reporter Connery's involvement with an international terrorist group, and the U.S. government's possible ties to it. Scattershot script manages to hit a few targets, and benefits from Brooks' breathless pace.▼

Wrong Kind of Girl, The SEE: **Bus Stop**▼

Wrong Man, The (1956) **105m.** *** D: Alfred Hitchcock. Henry Fonda, Vera Miles, Anthony Quayle, Harold J. Stone, Nehemiah Persoff. Unusual Hitchcock film done as semidocumentary, using true story of N.Y.C. musician (Fonda) falsely ac-

cused of robbery. Miles is excellent as wife who cracks under strain; offbeat and compelling. Written by Maxwell Anderson and Angus MacPhail.▼

WUSA (1970) **C-115m.** **½ D: Stuart Rosenberg. Paul Newman, Joanne Woodward, Anthony Perkins, Laurence Harvey, Pat Hingle, Cloris Leachman, Don Gordon, Leigh French, Moses Gunn, Bruce Cabot, Lou Gossett, Jr. One of Newman's pet projects casts him as a cynical drifter who becomes a d.j. for an ultra-rightwing New Orleans radio station and struggles with his own apathy as he gradually becomes aware of WUSA's true (and sinister) intentions. Film's obvious sincerity is undercut by simplistic, overwritten script; still, the acting is uniformly fine and there are a couple of truly memorable scenes.

Wuthering Heights (1939) **103m.** **** D: William Wyler. Merle Oberon, Laurence Olivier, David Niven, Flora Robson, Donald Crisp, Geraldine Fitzgerald, Leo G. Carroll, Cecil Kellaway, Miles Mander, Hugh Williams. Stirring adaptation of Emily Brontë's novel stops at chapter 17, but viewers won't argue: sensitive direction and sweeping performances propel this magnificent story of doomed love in pre-Victorian England. Haunting, a must-see film. Gregg Toland's moody photography won an Oscar; script by Ben Hecht and Charles MacArthur. Remade in 1954 and 1970.▼

Wuthering Heights (1954-Mexican) **90m.** **½ D: Luis Buñuel. Iraseme Dilian, Jorge Mistral, Lilia Prado, Ernesto Alonso, Luis Aceves Castaneda. Strikingly directed but talky, overbaked, ultimately unsuccessful version of the Brontë classic: bitter, coldhearted former servant Mistral, now rich, returns to disrupt the life of true love Dilian, now married to another.▼

Wuthering Heights (1970-British) **C-105m.** *** D: Robert Fuest. Anna Calder-Marshall, Timothy Dalton, Harry Andrews, Pamela Browne, Judy Cornwell, Ian Ogilvy, Hugh Griffith, Julian Glover. Good, realistic treatment of Brontë's novel with authentic locations and atmosphere, Dalton and Calder-Marshall believable looking as Heathcliff and Cathy, but film's point of view indistinct and pace too fast.▼

W.W. and the Dixie Dancekings (1975) **C-91m.** **½ D: John G. Avildsen. Burt Reynolds, Art Carney, Conny Van Dyke, Jerry Reed, James Hampton, Ned Beatty. Lightly likable film about a conman who hooks up with struggling country-western group and stops at nothing to promote their success; Carney has oddball role as religious lawman pursuing Burt. Script by Thomas Rickman.

Wyatt SEE: **Return of the Gunfighter**

Wyoming (1940) **89m.** ** D: Richard

Thorpe. Wallace Beery, Leo Carrillo, Ann Rutherford, Marjorie Main, Lee Bowman, Joseph Calleia, Bobs Watson. OK oater with Beery and Carrillo fun as on-again, off-again outlaw pals tempted by honesty.

Wyoming (1947) **84m.** **½ D: Joseph Kane. William Elliott, Vera Ralston, John Carroll, "Gabby" Hayes, Albert Dekker, Virginia Grey. Not-bad Wild Bill Elliott Western of ranchers vs. homesteaders in Wyoming territory.▼

Wyoming Kid, The SEE: **Cheyenne**

Wyoming Mail (1950) **C-87m.** **½ D: Reginald LeBorg. Stephen McNally, Alexis Smith, Ed Begley, Richard Egan, James Arness, Frankie Darro. Postal robbery in old West, with capable cast shining up script's dull spots.

Wyoming Renegades (1955) **C-73m.** *½ D: Fred F. Sears. Phil Carey, Gene Evans, Martha Hyer, William Bishop, Aaron Spelling. Confused Western portraying the story of ex-bandit Carey who wants to go straight; Hyer helps him.

Xanadu (1980) **C-88m.** *½ D: Robert Greenwald. Olivia Newton-John, Gene Kelly, Michael Beck, James Sloyan, Dimitra Arliss, Katie Hanley, Sandahl Bergman, Marilyn Tokuda, John "Fee" Waybill, voices of Wilfred Hyde-White and Coral Browne. Flashy but empty-headed remake of DOWN TO EARTH, with Olivia as muse who pops in to inspire young roller-boogie artist. Designed as a showcase for the singer, but the only thing it showcases is her total lack of screen charisma. Kelly (using his character name from COVER GIRL) tries his best to perk things up; even a brief animated sequence by Don Bluth doesn't help. Newton-John's future husband, Matt Lattanzi, plays Kelly as a young man. Songs include "Magic," by John Farrar and title tune by Electric Light Orchestra. Cable-TV version runs 96m.▼

X-15 (1961) **C-106m.** ** D: Richard Donner. David McLean, Charles Bronson, Ralph Taeger, Brad Dexter, Mary Tyler Moore, Patricia Owens. Mild narrative of pilots testing the experimental space plane of the title, and their romantic and family lives. Unusual role for Bronson, even then.

Xica (1978-Brazilian) **C-107m.** **½ D: Carlos Diegues. Zeze Motta, Walmor Chagas, Jose Wilker, Marcus Vinicius, Altair Lima. Saucy, if a bit overspiced, tale of strong-willed black slave Motta who seduces the new Royal Diamond Contractor (Chagas) in corrupt, repressive colonial Brazil. Nicely directed and acted—particularly by Motta—but curiously unmemorable. Filmed in 1976; released in the U.S. in 1982.

X—the Man with the X-Ray Eyes (1963) **C-80m.** **½ D: Roger Corman. Ray Milland, Diana Van Der Vlis, Harold J. Stone, John Hoyt, Don Rickles. Not-bad little film about scientist Milland developing serum that enables him to see through things.▼

X The Unknown (1956-British) **80m.** **½ D: Leslie Norman. Dean Jagger, Leo McKern, William Lucas, Edward Chapman, Anthony Newley, Peter Hammond. Well-thought-out sci-fi production set in Scotland. Radioactive mud from the earth's center grows and absorbs anything in its path. Effective chiller written by Jimmy Sangster.

X, Y and Zee (1972-British) **C-110m.** ** D: Brian G. Hutton. Elizabeth Taylor, Michael Caine, Susannah York, Margaret Leighton, John Standing. Contrived, often perverse tale of woman, her husband, another woman and the way the three are interchangeable in relationships. Taylor-York love scene ranks high in the annals of poor taste. Original British title: ZEE AND COMPANY.▼

Yakuza, The (1975) **C-112m.** *** D: Sydney Pollack. Robert Mitchum, Takakura Ken, Brian Keith, Herb Edelman, Richard Jordan, Kishi Keiko. Mitchum tries to rescue pal Keith's kidnapped daughter by returning to Japan after several years; he gets more than he bargains for from title organization, a kind of Oriental Mafia. Mitchum and Ken are fine in suspenseful action pic, written by Paul Schrader and Robert Towne. Retitled: BROTHERHOOD OF THE YAKUZA.▼

Yank at Eton, A (1942) **88m.** ** D: Norman Taurog. Mickey Rooney, Freddie Bartholomew, Tina Thayer, Ian Hunter, Edmund Gwenn, Alan Mowbray, Peter Lawford, Terry Kilburn. Rooney goes to school in England and it's a wonder he's not ejected immediately.

Yank at Oxford, A (1938-U.S.-British) **100m.** *** D: Jack Conway. Robert Taylor, Lionel Barrymore, Maureen O'Sullivan, Vivien Leigh, Edmund Gwenn. Attractive cast, including young Leigh, in familiar story of cocky American trying to adjust to Oxford, and vice versa. Remade in 1984 as OXFORD BLUES.

Yankee Buccaneer (1952) **C-86m.** **½ D: Frederick de Cordova. Jeff Chandler, Scott Brady, Suzan Ball, David Janssen. Standard pirate tale, buoyed by healthy cast.

Yankee Doodle Dandy (1942) **126m.** **** D: Michael Curtiz. James Cagney, Joan Leslie, Walter Huston, Irene Manning, Rosemary DeCamp, Richard Whorf, Jeanne Cagney, S. Z. Sakall, Walter Catlett, Frances Langford, Eddie Foy, Jr., George Tobias. Cagney wraps up film in neat little package all his own with dynamic recreation of George M. Cohan's life and times; he deservedly won Oscar for rare song-and-dance performance, as did music directors Ray Heindorf and Heinz Roemheld. Two computer-colored versions exist—one of which is edited down for TV!▼

Yankee Pasha (1954) **C-84m.** **½ D: Joseph Pevney. Jeff Chandler, Rhonda Fleming, Mamie Van Doren, Bart Roberts (Rex Reason), Lee J. Cobb, Hal March. Nicely paced costumer set in 1800's with Chandler crossing the ocean to France and beyond to find his true love, captured by pirates.

Yank in Indo-China, A (1952) **67m.** *½ D: Wallace Grissell. John Archer, Douglas Dick, Jean Willes, Don Harvey. Just adequate yarn of American pilots involved in guerilla warfare.

Yank in Korea, A (1951) **73m.** *½ D: Lew Landers. Lon McCallister, William Phillips, Brett King, Larry Stewart. Corny war actioner.

Yank in the RAF, A (1941) **98m.** *** D: Henry King. Tyrone Power, Betty Grable, John Sutton, Reginald Gardiner, Donald Stuart, Richard Fraser. Power's only there so he can see London-based chorine Grable; they make a nice team. Songs: "Another Little Dream Won't Do Us Any Harm," "Hi-Ya Love."

Yank in Viet-Nam, A (1964) **80m.** ** D: Marshall Thompson. Marshall Thompson, Enrique Magalona, Mario Barri, Urban Drew. Low-budget topical actioner set in Saigon, with marine Thompson attempting to help the South Vietnamese. Retitled: YEAR OF THE TIGER.

Yanks (1979) **C-139m.** **½ D: John Schlesinger. Richard Gere, Lisa Eichhorn, Vanessa Redgrave, William Devane, Chick Vennera, Wendy Morgan, Rachel Roberts, Joan Hickson, John Ratzenberger, Antony Sher. Lavish production about WW2 romances between U.S. soldiers and British women doesn't really deliver the goods, due to choppy structure and flabby direction. Gere's so-called star power seems to be a casualty of energy crisis cutbacks.

Yaqui Drums (1956) **71m.** *½ D: Jean Yarbrough. Rod Cameron, J. Carrol Naish, Mary Castle, Robert Hutton. Soggy account of rancher vs. criminal saloon owner in old West.

Yearling, The (1946) **C-128m.** ***½ D: Clarence Brown. Gregory Peck, Jane Wyman, Claude Jarman, Jr., Chill Wills, Margaret Wycherly, Henry Travers, Jeff York, Forrest Tucker, June Lockhart. Marjorie Kinnan Rawling's sensitive tale of a boy attached to a young deer was exquisitely filmed in Technicolor on location in Florida, with memorable performances. Oscar-winner for Cinematography and Art Direction, and a special Oscar for newcomer Jarman. Beware 94m. reissue print.▼

Year My Voice Broke, The (1987-Australian) **C-103m.** *** D: John Duigan. Noah Taylor, Loene Carmen, Ben Mendelsohn,

Graeme Blundell, Lynette Curran, Malcolm Robertson, Judi Farr. Affecting story of a teenage boy's friendship and infatuation with a troubled girl; set in a small town in the early 1960s. A cut above the usual coming-of-age film, thanks to director Duigan's touching script and amazingly natural performances by his young actors.▼

Year of Living Dangerously, The (1983-Australian) **C-115m.** *** D: Peter Weir. Mel Gibson, Sigourney Weaver, Linda Hunt, Michael Murphy, Bill Kerr, Noel Ferrier. Fascinating political drama set in strife-ridden Indonesia just before Sukarno's fall in 1965 . . . much more successful as a mood-piece than as romance, however, with Weaver's flimsy character (and flimsier accent) a detriment. Diminutive Hunt—a woman playing a man—is mesmerizing and most deservedly won an Academy Award.▼

Year of the Dragon (1985) **C-136m.** **½ D: Michael Cimino. Mickey Rourke, John Lone, Ariane, Leonard Termo, Ray Barry, Caroline Kava, Eddie Jones. Highly charged, arresting melodrama scripted by Oliver Stone (from Robert Daley's book) about a Vietnam vet who's still fighting his own private war, as a N.Y.C. cop whose current target is corruption in Chinatown, and crime czar Lone in particular. Companion piece to Cimino's THE DEER HUNTER has same intensity but nearly drowns in a sea of excess and self-importance. Still worth watching. Incidentally, virtually all New York settings (including Mott Street) were recreated on location in North Carolina!▼

Year of the Tiger SEE: **Yank in Viet-Nam, A**

Years Between, The (1946-British) **88m.** **½ D: Compton Bennett. Michael Redgrave, Valerie Hobson, Flora Robson, James McKechnie. Sensitively handled story of oft-told tale of man returning from war to discover wife thought him dead and is now about to remarry and has taken his place in Parliament!

Yellow Balloon, The (1952-British) **80m.** **½ D: J. Lee Thompson. Andrew Ray, Kenneth More, Veronica Hurst, William Sylvester, Bernard Lee. Sensible suspenser of small boy who thinks he accidentally killed a chum and is exploited by cheap crook.

Yellowbeard (1983) **C-101m.** BOMB D: Mel Damski. Graham Chapman, Peter Boyle, Richard "Cheech" Marin, Tommy Chong, Peter Cook, Marty Feldman, Martin Hewitt, Michael Hordern, Eric Idle, Madeline Kahn, James Mason, John Cleese, Susannah York, Stacey Nelkin. Appalling waste of talent in a startlingly inept and unfunny pirate comedy. Written by costars Chapman and Cook with Bernard McKenna;

they all ought to walk the plank for this one. This was Feldman's final film.▼

Yellow Cab Man, The (1950) 85m. *** D: Jack Donohue. Red Skelton, Gloria De Haven, Walter Slezak, Edward Arnold, James Gleason, Jay C. Flippen, Polly Moran. Fine Skelton romp with Red as would-be inventor of unbreakable glass, involved with gangsters and crooked businessman; Slezak is perfect as bad-guy.

Yellow Canary, The (1943-British) 98m. **½ D: Herbert Wilcox. Anna Neagle, Richard Greene, Albert Lieven, Margaret Rutherford, Valentine Dyall. Above average WW2 spy drama with Neagle feigning Nazi loyalty to obtain secrets for the Allies.

Yellow Canary (1963) 93m. BOMB D: Buzz Kulik. Pat Boone, Barbara Eden, Steve Forrest, Jack Klugman, Jesse White, Milton Selzer, John Banner, Jeff Corey, Harold Gould. If you've lain awake nights hoping to see Pat Boone as an obnoxious pop singer in a movie written by Rod Serling, your wish has come true. But don't fret; Pat turns into a nice guy when his infant son is kidnapped and he has to go rescue him. And you thought *The Twilight Zone* was just a TV show!

Yellow Jack (1938) 83m. ** D: George B. Seitz. Robert Montgomery, Virginia Bruce, Lewis Stone, Stanley Ridges, Henry Hull, Charles Coburn, Buddy Ebsen, Andy Devine, John O'Neill, Sam Levene, Alan Curtis, William Henry. Story of Dr. Walter Reed's determination to find cure for yellow fever is artificial, dramatically stale. Based on Sidney Howard play.

Yellow Mountain, The (1954) C-78m. *½ D: Jesse Hibbs. Lex Barker, Mala Powers, Howard Duff, William Demarest. Unremarkable tale of Barker rivaling Duff for gold and love of Powers.

Yellow Rolls-Royce, The (1965-British) C-122m. *** D: Anthony Asquith. Rex Harrison, Shirley MacLaine, Ingrid Bergman, Jeanne Moreau, Edmund Purdom, George C. Scott, Omar Sharif, Art Carney, Alain Delon, Roland Culver, Wally Cox. Slick Terence Rattigan drama involving trio of owners of title car, focusing on how romance plays a part in each of their lives; contrived but ever-so-smoothly handled.

Yellow Sky (1948) 98m. *** D: William Wellman. Gregory Peck, Anne Baxter, Richard Widmark, Robert Arthur, John Russell, Harry Morgan, James Barton. Exciting Western with exceptional cast in story of confrontation in Arizona ghost town. Script by Lamar Trotti from a W.R. Burnett story.

Yellowstone (1936) 65m. **½ D: Arthur Lubin. Henry Hunter, Judith Barrett, Andy Devine, Alan Hale, Ralph Morgan, Monroe Owsley, Raymond Hatton, Paul Harvey, Paul Fix. Nifty programmer of murder,

greed, and stolen money buried in the title park. Ambitious direction and a solid supporting cast elevate this one.▼

Yellowstone Kelly (1959) C-91m. **½ D: Gordon Douglas. Clint Walker, Edward Byrnes, John Russell, Ray Danton, Claude Akins, Rhodes Reason, Warren Oates. Rugged Western involving Indian uprising, with Walker the burly hero trying to keep peace; written by Burt Kennedy.

Yellow Submarine (1968-British) C-85m. **** D: George Dunning. Pure delight, a phantasmagorical animated feature with as much to hear as there is to see: Beatles' songs, puns, non sequitur jokes combined with surreal pop-art visions in story of Beatles trying to save Pepperland from the Blue Meanies. Unique, refreshing. Songs include "Lucy in the Sky With Diamonds," "When I'm Sixty-four," "All You Need Is Love."▼

Yellow Ticket (1931) 81m. *** D: Raoul Walsh. Elissa Landi, Laurence Olivier, Lionel Barrymore, Walter Byron, Sarah Padden, Mischa Auer, Boris Karloff. Colorful melodrama set in czarist Russia, with peasant girl Landi coming under lecherous eye of officer Barrymore. Handsome production, lusty storytelling add up nicely; Karloff has good bit as drunken orderly.

Yellow Tomahawk, The (1954) C-82m. ** D: Lesley Selander. Rory Calhoun, Peggie Castle, Noah Beery, Warner Anderson. Calhoun is Indian guide who goes to any length to prevent redskin attack on settlers.

Yellow Winton Flyer, The SEE: The Reivers▼

Yentl (1983) C-134m. **½ D: Barbra Streisand. Barbra Streisand, Mandy Patinkin, Amy Irving, Nehemiah Persoff, Steven Hill. A young woman in Eastern Europe at the turn of the century disguises as a boy in order to fulfill her dream and get an education. Isaac Bashevis Singer's simple short-story is handled with love and care by first-time director/producer/cowriter Streisand, but goes on far longer than necessary, with twelve (count 'em) soliloquy songs by Alan and Marilyn Bergman and Michel Legrand (who also earned Oscars for their score) and a finale uncomfortably reminiscent of FUNNY GIRL. A star vehicle if there ever was one; no wonder Streisand fans love it.▼

Yes, Giorgio (1982) C-110m. *½ D: Franklin J. Schaffner. Luciano Pavarotti, Kathryn Harrold, Eddie Albert, Paolo Borboni, James Hong, Beulah Quo. Opera superstar Pavarotti plays . . . an opera superstar, who pursues an independent-minded lady doctor during American tour. So-called romantic comedy gives the phrase "old fashioned" a bad name; missing ingredient is a parade of character actors like Mischa Auer and Herman Bing to make it palatable. Only saving grace: Pavarotti sings.▼

Yes, My Darling Daughter (1939) **86m.** **½ D: William Keighley. Priscilla Lane, Fay Bainter, Roland Young, May Robson, Jeffrey Lynn, Genevieve Tobin, Ian Hunter. Everybody is enthused about young lovers running off together except young man in question (Lynn). Mildly amusing comedy.

Yes, Sir, That's My Baby (1949) **C-82m.** **½ D: George Sherman. Donald O'Connor, Charles Coburn, Gloria De Haven, Joshua Shelley, Barbara Brown. Flimsy musical of football-crazy O'Connor on college campus, rescued by spirit and verve of cast.

Yesterday (1980-Canadian) **C-97m.** *½ D: Larry Kent. Claire Pimpare, Vincent Van Patten, Eddie Albert, Cloris Leachman, Nicholas Campbell. Hackneyed story of love between American Van Patten and French-Canadian Pimpare may appeal to the most undiscriminating adolescent.

Yesterday's Child (1977) **C-78m.** TVM D: Corey Allen, Bob Rosenbaum. Shirley Jones, Ross Martin, Claude Akins, Geraldine Fitzgerald, Stephanie Zimbalist, Patrick Wayne. Wealthy family is stunned when teen-aged girl turns up claiming to be their child kidnapped 14 years earlier. Melodramatic nonsense adapted from Doris Miles Disney's fine mystery novel *Night of Clear Choice.* And two directors were needed to put this one together! Below average.

Yesterday's Enemy (1959-British) **95m.** *½ D: Val Guest. Stanley Baker, Guy Rolfe, Leo McKern, Gordon Jackson, David Oxley, Philip Ahn, Bryan Forbes. Mild WW2 actioner set in Burma.

Yesterday, Today and Tomorrow (1964-Italian) **C-119m.** **** D: Vittorio De Sica. Sophia Loren, Marcello Mastroianni, Tina Pica, Giovanni Ridolfi. Oscar-winner for Best Foreign Film is impeccable trio of comic tales, with Loren never more beautiful than as Italian women who use sex in various ways to get what they want. Striptease for Marcello is among the most famous scenes in her career (and remains pretty steamy).▼

Yojimbo (1961-Japanese) **110m.** **** D: Akira Kurosawa. Toshiro Mifune, Eijiro Tono, Seizaburo Kawazu, Isuzu Yamada. Superb tongue-in-cheek samurai picture, the plot of which resembles a Western; Mifune is perfection as samurai up for hire in town with two warring factions, both of whom he teaches a well-deserved lesson. Beautiful on all accounts; the inspiration for A FISTFUL OF DOLLARS. Sequel: SANJURO.▼

Yokel Boy (1942) **69m.** *½ D: Joseph Santley. Albert Dekker, Joan Davis, Eddie Foy, Jr., Alan Mowbray. Silly slapstick satire on gangster movies.

Yol (1982-Turkish-Swiss) **C-111m.** *** D: Serif Goren. Tarik Akan, Serif Sezer, Halil Ergun, Meral Orhonsoy, Necmettin Cobanoglu. Incisive chronicle of the experiences of a convict who returns home while on "leave" from jail. Screenplay by Yilmaz Guney, written while he was himself in prison.▼

Yolanda and the Thief (1945) **C-108m.** **½ D: Vincente Minnelli. Fred Astaire, Lucille Bremer, Frank Morgan, Leon Ames, Mildred Natwick, Mary Nash. Opulent musical fantasy about a con-man (Astaire) who tries to convince rich convent-bred girl (Bremer) that he's her guardian angel. Unusual film that you'll either love or hate. Best musical number: "Coffee Time." ▼

Yor, the Hunter from the Future (1983-Italian) **C-88m.** BOMB D: Anthony M. Dawson (Antonio Margheriti). Reb Brown, Corinne Clery, John Steiner, Carole Andre, Alan Collins. Shamelessly idiotic muscleman movie with a nuclear-age twist. Humorously tacky at first, then just plain boring.▼

You and Me (1938) **90m.** **½ D: Fritz Lang. Sylvia Sidney, George Raft, Barton MacLane, Harry Carey, Roscoe Karns, George E. Stone, Warren Hymer, Robert Cummings. Genuinely odd but likable film about an ex-con who falls in love with Sidney and marries her, unaware that she's a former jailbird herself. Unusual mix of gangsterism, sentiment, Damon Runyonesque comedy, and music (by Kurt Weill) —with even some rhythmic dialogue! Story by Norman Krasna, screenplay by Virginia Van Upp.

You Are What You Eat (1968) **C-75m.** ** D: Barry Feinstein. Tiny Tim, Peter Yarrow, Paul Butterfield, Barry McGuire, Father Malcom Boyd, The Electric Flag, Harper's Bizarre, Super Spade. Documentary of the mid-60s does, by the mere appearance of some of the era's luminaries, carry one back a few years; however, film is ill-conceived, haphazardly put together. Not much compared to some later social documents.

You Belong to Me (1941) **94m.** ** D: Wesley Ruggles. Barbara Stanwyck, Henry Fonda, Edgar Buchanan, Roger Clark, Ruth Donnelly, Melville Cooper, Maude Eburne. Weak comedy of doctor Stanwyck and hubby Fonda who's wary of her male patients. Looks as though it was made in three days. Coscripted by Dalton Trumbo. Remade as EMERGENCY WEDDING.

You Better Watch Out (1980) **C-100m.** *** D: Lewis Jackson. Brandon Maggart, Dianne Hull, Scott McKay, Joe Jamrog, Peter Friedman, Ray Barry, Bobby Lesser, Sam Gray. Gripping, well-made little thriller about a killer disguised as Santa Claus, with Maggart excellent as the psychopathic Kris Kringle. A sleeper, with cult status possibilities. Also known as CHRISTMAS EVIL and TERROR IN TOYLAND.▼

You Came Along (1945) 103m. **½ D: John Farrow. Robert Cummings, Lizabeth Scott, Don DeFore, Charles Drake, Kim Hunter, Julie Bishop. Effective drama of three army buddies on bond-selling tours, their romantic involvements. Scott's first film.

You Can't Beat Love (1937) 82m. ** D: Christy Cabanne. Preston Foster, Joan Fontaine, Herbert Mundin, William Brisbane, Alan Bruce, Paul Hurst. Slow, trivial story of eccentric playboy Foster dabbling in politics and tangling with mayor's daughter Fontaine. Of interest only for the presence of Fontaine, who is very young and most attractive.

You Can't Cheat an Honest Man (1939) 76m. ***½ D: George Marshall. W. C. Fields, Edgar Bergen, Constance Moore, James Bush, Mary Forbes, Thurston Hall, Edward Brophy, Grady Sutton, Eddie "Rochester" Anderson. Fields (as Larson E. Whipsnade) runs circus with interference from Bergen and Charlie McCarthy in frantic comedy classic with loads of snappy one-liners and memorable ping-pong game. Most of Fields' scenes were directed by Eddie Cline.▼

You Can't Fool Your Wife (1940) 68m. ** D: Ray McCarey. Lucille Ball, James Ellison, Robert Coote, Emma Dunn, Virginia Vale, Elaine Shepard. Ball and Ellison are dull married couple until hubby takes a fling and wife makes herself glamorous to win him back. Adequate comedy filler, made palatable by Lucy's charms in dual role.▼

You Can't Get Away With Murder (1939) 78m. **½ D: Lewis Seiler. Humphrey Bogart, Billy Halop, Gale Page, John Litel, Henry Travers, Joe Sawyer. Standard but well-acted crime tale of young Halop (minus the other Dead End Kids) teaming with gangster Bogart, taking rap with him in Sing Sing.

You Can't Go Home Again (1979) C-100m. TVM D: Ralph Nelson. Lee Grant, Chris Sarandon, Hurd Hatfield, Tammy Grimes, Roland Winter, Malachy McCourt. Mediocre adaptation of the Thomas Wolfe classic about the struggles of a young writer in the 20s and the affair he has with an older married woman. Average.

You Can't Have Everything (1937) 99m. *** D: Norman Taurog. Alice Faye, Ritz Bros., Don Ameche, Charles Winninger, Tony Martin, Louise Hovick (Gypsy Rose Lee), Arthur Treacher, Tip, Tap and Toe. Good show-biz musical as Faye writes drama which only succeeds as musical. Ritz Bros. have good material, Louis Prima adds music.▼

You Can't Hurry Love (1988) C-92m.

*½ D: Richard Martini. David Packer, Scott McGinnis, Bridget Fonda, David Leisure, Anthony Geary, Frank Bonner, Lu Leonard, Merete Van Kamp, Sally Kellerman, Charles Grodin, Kristy McNichol. Paper-thin, predictable fare about the adventures of young Packer, who's lost in the L.A. single scene. This one looks as if it came off an assembly line. Bridget is Peter's daughter.▼

You Can't Run Away from It (1956) C-95m. ** D: Dick Powell. June Allyson, Jack Lemmon, Charles Bickford, Paul Gilbert, Jim Backus, Stubby Kaye, Henny Youngman. Slight musical remake of IT HAPPENED ONE NIGHT with Lemmon the reporter, Allyson the madcap heiress.

You Can't Steal Love SEE: **Live a Little, Steal a Lot**▼

You Can't Take It With You (1938) 127m. ***½ D: Frank Capra. Jean Arthur, Lionel Barrymore, James Stewart, Edward Arnold, Mischa Auer, Ann Miller, Spring Byington, Eddie "Rochester" Anderson, Donald Meek, Halliwell Hobbes, Dub Taylor, Samuel S. Hinds, Harry Davenport. George S. Kaufman-Moss Hart play about eccentric but blissfully happy household becomes prime Capra-corn, not quite as compelling today as MR. DEEDS or MR. SMITH (due to Robert Riskin's extensive rewriting), but still highly entertaining. Oscar winner for Best Picture and Director. Followed a half-century later by a TV series.▼

You Can't Win 'Em All (1970) C-95m. *½ D: Peter Collinson. Tony Curtis, Charles Bronson, Michele Mercier, Patrick Magee, Gregoire Aslan. Bronson and Curtis are friendly rivals caught in war-torn Turkey during the early 1920s. Bantering stars make the most of tired script by Leo Gordon (who also has supporting role). Filmed on location.

You for Me (1952) 71m. **½ D: Don Weis. Peter Lawford, Jane Greer, Gig Young, Paula Corday, Elaine Stewart. Unpretentious romantic comedy with Greer as well-intentioned nurse involved with a variety of suitors.

You Gotta Stay Happy (1948) 100m. **½ D: H. C. Potter. Joan Fontaine, James Stewart, Eddie Albert, Roland Young, Willard Parker, Percy Kilbride, Porter Hall. OK comedy about millionairess who runs off on wedding night to find new marriage. Could have been much better.

You Know What Sailors Are (1954-British) C-89m. ** D: Ken Annakin. Akim Tamiroff, Donald Sinden, Sarah Lawson, Naunton Wayne. Attempted cold-war spoof of British navy officer, jokingly telling cohorts that salvaged scrap is a new secret weapon.

You Lie So Deep, My Love (1975) C-78m. TVM D: David Lowell Rich. Don Galloway, Barbara Anderson, Angel Tompkins, Walter Pidgeon, Anne Schedeen, Russell Johnson. Wealthy woman tries to save her failing marriage while philandering husband is willing to murder to get out of it (with her money). Standard drama packed with unpleasant characters. Below average.

You Light Up My Life (1977) **C-90m.** **½ D: Joseph Brooks. Didi Conn, Joe Silver, Michael Zaslow, Stephen Nathan, Melanie Mayron. Oscar-winning title song may be best remembered thing about this film, but Conn and Silver are worth watching in loosely structured story of show-business-oriented girl trying to break loose and establish herself while putting her life in order. Produced, directed, written, and musically supervised by Brooks.▼

You'll Find Out (1940) **97m.** ** D: David Butler. Kay Kyser, Boris Karloff, Peter Lorre, Bela Lugosi, Dennis O'Keefe, Ginny Simms, Helen Parrish, Alma Kruger, Harry Babbitt, Ish Kabibble. Kay and his Band spend the night in a debutante's haunted house with three suspicious characters on hand. Obvious and overlong (to say the least); a real disappointment to anyone anxious to savor the Karloff/Lugosi/Lorre team; more suited for fans of Ish Kabibble. ▼

You'll Like My Mother (1972) **C-92m.** **½ D: Lamont Johnson. Patty Duke, Rosemary Murphy, Sian Barbara Allen, Richard Thomas, Dennis Rucker. Offbeat thriller with psychological undertones. Duke plays pregnant widow journeying to visit mother-in-law she's never met. Some good moments, but doesn't add up.

You'll Never Get Rich (1941) **88m.** *** D: Sidney Lanfield. Fred Astaire, Rita Hayworth, John Hubbard, Robert Benchley, Osa Massen, Frieda Inescort, Guinn Williams. Delicious musicomedy has Astaire drafted at inconvenient time, but show he's doing still goes on, and he manages to get Hayworth, too. Cole Porter score includes "So Near and Yet So Far."▼

You'll Never See Me Again (1973) **C-73m.** **TVM** D: Jeannot Szwarc. David Hartman, Joseph Campanella, Jane Wyatt, Ralph Meeker, Jess Walton, Colby Chester, Bill Zuckert. Marital quarrel results in chance nosebleed, angry exit by wife. Husband follows to in-laws' house, discovers wife never arrived, eventually arrested by police. Straightforward suspense film (from a Cornell Woolrich story) with few novel ingredients, adequate performances, predictable resolution. Average.

You Must Be Joking! (1965-British) **C-100m.** *** D: Michael Winner. Michael Callan, Lionel Jeffries, Terry-Thomas, Denholm Elliott, Wilfrid Hyde-White, James Robertson Justice, Bernard Cribbins, Gabriella Licudi. Engaging poke at British

army as zany psychologist (Jeffries) rounds up five weirdos to establish, via special testing, the "complete, quick thinking" exemplary British soldier.

You Never Can Tell (1951) **78m.** *** D: Lou Breslow. Dick Powell, Peggy Dow, Charles Drake, Joyce Holden, Frank Nelson, Albert Sharpe. Amusing fantasy of a murdered dog returning to Earth as a human (Powell) to find his killer. Holden is a delight as his sidekick—who used to be a horse. Storyline reversed in OH, HEAVENLY DOG!

Young Again (1986) **C-100m. TVM** D: Steven Hilliard Stern. Robert Urich, Lindsay Wagner, Jack Gilford, Keanu Reeves. Footloose bachelor is granted his wish to be a teenager again in this engaging variation on BACK TO THE FUTURE, done by the Disney Studio. Average.

Young Americans (1967) **C-104m.** ** D: Alex Grasshoff. Although this documentary about the "Young Americans" singing group won an Academy Award (which it was forced to relinquish when it was discovered that it had played theatrically before the year of its contention), not everyone will be able to take it; production is smooth, but the kids sell America like those guys on TV sell machines that slice carrots 144 different ways.

Young and Dangerous (1957) **78m.** ** D: William Claxton. Mark Damon, Edward Binns, Lili Gentle, Ann Doran, Connie Stevens. Damon, a footloose youth, turns respectable for love of a nice girl. The usual.

Young and Innocent (1937-British) **80m.** *** D: Alfred Hitchcock. Derrick de Marney, Nova Pilbeam, Percy Marmont, Edward Rigby, Mary Clare, Basil Radford. A Hitchcock thriller with charm and humor; young girl helps runaway man innocently accused of murder to find the real culprit. Pleasant echoes of 39 STEPS; nightclub revelation scene is especially memorable. Based on a novel by Josephine Tey; first shown in U.S. as THE GIRL WAS YOUNG.▼

Young and the Damned, The SEE: **Los Olvidados**▼

Young and the Immoral, The SEE: **Sinister Urge, The**

Young and Wild (1958) **69m.** *½ D: William Witney. Gene Evans, Scott Marlowe, Carolyn Kearney, Robert Arthur. Trashy account of thrill-seeking teenagers on the loose with a stolen car.

Young and Willing (1943) **82m.** **½ D: Edward H. Griffith. William Holden, Eddie Bracken, Barbara Britton, James Brown, Martha O'Driscoll, Robert Benchley, Susan Hayward. Perennial summer-stock comedy *Out of the Frying Pan* becomes naive but zany comedy of show biz hopefuls trying to make good.▼

Young at Heart (1954) **C-117m.** *** D: Gordon Douglas. Doris Day, Frank Sinatra, Gig Young, Ethel Barrymore, Dorothy Malone, Alan Hale, Jr. Musical remake of Fannie Hurst's FOUR DAUGHTERS with Sinatra romancing Day amid much tear-shedding. Slickly done.▼

Young Bess (1953) **C-112m.** *** D: George Sidney. Jean Simmons, Stewart Granger, Charles Laughton, Deborah Kerr, Cecil Kellaway, Leo G. Carroll, Kay Walsh. Splashy costumer with Simmons as Elizabeth I; Laughton repeating role of Henry VIII. Fine cast does quite well in historical setting.

Young Billy Young (1969) **C-89m.** **½ D: Burt Kennedy. Robert Mitchum, Angie Dickinson, Robert Walker, David Carradine, Jack Kelly, John Anderson, Paul Fix. Sheriff Mitchum, seeking the killer of his son, takes young Walker under his wing as a surrogate. Peculiar Western, adapted by Kennedy from Will Henry's *Who Rides With Wyatt*, is based on the alleged friendship between Wyatt Earp and Billy Clanton; interesting, but nothing special.

Youngblood (1986) **C-109m.** *½ D: Peter Markle. Rob Lowe, Cynthia Gibb, Patrick Swayze, Ed Lauter, Eric Nesterenko, George Finn, Fionnula Flanagan. Boring, utterly predictable story of Lowe joining small-time Canadian hockey team, falling in love with the daughter of his no-nonsense coach. This movie has no energy, on the ice or off!▼

√ **Youngblood Hawke** (1964) **137m.** **½ D: Delmer Daves. James Franciscus, Genevieve Page, Suzanne Pleshette, Eva Gabor, Mary Astor, Lee Bowman, Edward Andrews, Don Porter. Clichéd but somehow compelling trash from Herman Wouk's novel about a naive Southerner who writes a novel and becomes the toast of N.Y.C. literary society—with several women vying for his attention.

Young Captives, The (1959) **61m.** ** D: Irvin Kershner. Steven Marlo, Tom Selden, Luana Patten, Ed Nelson, Joan Granville. Lurid melodrama of newly-weds involved with psychopathic killer.

Young Cassidy (1965-British) **C-110m.** *** D: Jack Cardiff, John Ford. Rod Taylor, Julie Christie, Maggie Smith, Flora Robson, Michael Redgrave, Edith Evans, Jack MacGowran. Taylor's best role ever as the earthy intellectual Sean O'Casey, set in 1910 Dublin; filled with rich atmosphere and fine supporting players.

Young Country, The (1970) **C-73m. TVM** D: Roy Huggins. Roger Davis, Joan Hackett, Walter Brennan, Wally Cox, Skip Young, Pete Deuel. Offbeat casting in comedy Western about likable gambler Moody (Davis) hard pressed to track down money once belonging to mysterious gunman (Cox). Granted film's unconvincing tran-

sitions, characters are given decent dialogue and there's a most acceptable resolution. Above average.

Young Daniel Boone (1950) **C-71m.** *½ D: Reginald LeBorg. David Bruce, Kristine Miller, Mary Treen, Don Beddoe. Programmer adventure involving historical figure in conflict with Indians and settlers.

Young Dillinger (1965) **102m.** **½ D: Terry O. Morse. Nick Adams, Mary Ann Mobley, Robert Conrad, John Ashley, Victor Buono, John Hoyt, Reed Hadley. Adams gives force to chronicle of gangster John Dillinger, his rise and seemingly inevitable fall; sufficient gunplay.▼

Young Doctors, The (1961) **100m.** *** D: Phil Karlson. Fredric March, Ben Gazzara, Dick Clark, Eddie Albert, Ina Balin, Aline MacMahon, Edward Andrews, Arthur Hill, George Segal, Rosemary Murphy, Dick Button, Dolph Sweet. Sturdy cast uplifts soaper set in large city hospital. Based on an Arthur Hailey novel. Segal's first film.

Young Doctors in Love (1982) **C-95m.** ** D: Garry Marshall. Michael McKean, Sean Young, Harry Dean Stanton, Patrick Macnee, Hector Elizondo, Dabney Coleman, Pamela Reed, Michael Richards, Taylor Negron, Saul Rubinek, Titos Vandis. Hospital comedy has plenty of scattershot gags, but not enough laughs—and certainly not enough substance—to maintain a feature film. Many daytime soap opera stars appear in camcos. Feature directing debut of TV comedy writer-producer Marshall.▼

Young Don't Cry, The (1957) **89m.** ** D: Alfred L. Werker. Sal Mineo, James Whitmore, J. Carrol Naish, Paul Carr. OK drama of loner youth Mineo who takes pity on an escaped murderer.

Young Dracula (1974-Italian-French) SEE: **Andy Warhol's Dracula**▼

Young Dracula (1974-British) SEE: **Son of Dracula**

Young Dr. Kildare (1938) **81m.** D: Harold S. Bucquet. Lew Ayres, Lionel Barrymore, Lynne Carver, Nat Pendleton, Jo Ann Sayers, Samuel S. Hinds. SEE: **Dr. Kildare** series.

Young Einstein (1988-Australian) **C-90m.** **½ D: Yahoo Serious. Yahoo Serious, Odile Le Clezio, John Howard, Pee Wee Wilson, Su Cruickshank. Nutty comedy from Down Under based on the premise that Albert Einstein not only developed the theory of relativity, but also invented rock 'n' roll! The silliness continues from there . . . though any movie with "cat pies" can't be all bad. Aptly named Yahoo (born Greg Pead) wrote, produced, directed, and stars in this slapstick epic.

Younger Brothers, The (1949) **C-77m.** **½ D: Edwin L. Marin. Wayne Morris,

Janis Paige, Bruce Bennett, Geraldine Brooks, Robert Hutton, Alan Hale, Fred Clark. OK Western of notorious Younger brothers and the incident that drives them to renewed violence and terror.

Younger Generation, The (1929) 88m. **½ D: Frank Capra. Jean Hersholt, Lina Basquette, Ricardo Cortez, Rosa Rosanova, Rex Lease. Ethnic heart-tugger by Fannie Hurst about a Jewish family that suffers because of one son's determination to abandon his roots and break into N.Y.C. society. (Cortez played a similar role in SYMPHONY OF SIX MILLION.) Director Capra pulls out all the stops in this silent film with talkie sequences.

Youngest Profession, The (1943) 82m. **½ D: Edward Buzzell. Virginia Weidler, Jean Porter, EdwardArnold, John Carroll, Agnes Moorehead, Scotty Beckett. Weidler and Porter are incurable (and obnoxious) autograph hounds in innocent little film with many MGM guest stars (including Lana Turner, William Powell, Robert Taylor, Greer Garson and Walter Pidgeon).

Youngest Spy, The SEE: **My Name Is Ivan**

Young Frankenstein (1974) 105m. ***½ D: Mel Brooks. Gene Wilder, Peter Boyle, Marty Feldman, Teri Garr, Madeline Kahn, Cloris Leachman, Kenneth Mars, Richard Haydn. Finely tuned parody of old FRANKENSTEIN pictures, scripted by Wilder and Brooks, with appropriate music (by John Morris), sets, laboratory equipment (some of it from the 1930s), and b&w camerawork (by Gerald Hirschfeld). Plus vivid characterizations by mad doctor Wilder, monster Boyle, hunchback assistant Feldman, et al. Spoof of blind-man sequence from BRIDE OF FRANKENSTEIN with Gene Hackman is uproarious.▼

Young Fury (1965) C-80m. **½ D: Christian Nyby. Rory Calhoun, Virginia Mayo, Lon Chaney, John Agar, Richard Arlen, Linda Foster. Tired gunslinger returns home to discover son leading gang of young hellions terrorizing countryside. Standard formula plot highlighted by a cast chockfull of old stars. William Bendix's last film.

Young Girls of Rochefort, The (1968-French) C-124m. ** D: Jacques Demy. Catherine Deneuve, Francoise Dorleac, Gene Kelly, George Chakiris, Danielle Darrieux, Grover Dale, Michel Piccoli. Director Demy's follow-up to THE UMBRELLAS OF CHERBOURG is a homage to the Hollywood musical, but what it has in style it lacks in substance; contrived story and repetitive Michel Legrand music score surely wear thin, and even Gene Kelly can't save it.

Young Graduates, The (1971) C-99m. BOMB D: Robert Anderson. Patricia Wymer, Tom Stewart, Gary Rist, Jennifer Rist, Dennis Christopher. Idiotic update of 1950's youth films; heroine falls in love with her teacher amid other dumb high school adventures. A chance to see Christopher paying his dues in his first feature.▼

Young Guns, The (1956) 84m. ** D: Albert Band. Russ Tamblyn, Gloria Talbott, Perry Lopez, Scott Marlowe. Routine account of Tamblyn trying to erase everyone's memory of gunslinger father so he can live peaceful life.

Young Guns (1988) C-107m. **½ D: Christopher Cain. Emilio Estevez, Kiefer Sutherland, Lou Diamond Phillips, Charlie Sheen, Dermot Mulroney, Casey Siemaszko, Terence Stamp, Jack Palance, Terry O'Quinn, Sharon Thomas, Brian Keith, Patrick Wayne. Six young punks, taken under the wing of a civilized British gentleman (Stamp), find it hard to retain their equilibrium when they're left on their own, and whipped into a frenzy of violence by their newest recruit—William Bonney, soon to be known as Billy the Kid (Estevez). Contemporary-minded Western adopts 1980s-style language and sensibilities, and asks us to accept a plot with as many holes as some of Billy's victims . . . but it's still watchable, and features several strong performances. Followed by a sequel.▼

Young Guns of Texas (1962) C-78m. **½ D: Maury Dexter. James Mitchum, Alana Ladd, Jody McCrea, Chill Wills. Second generation of movie stars perform satisfactorily in account of gold and girl hunt in old West, tied in with Indian raid.

Young Harry Houdini (1987) C-100m. TVM D: James Orr. Wil Wheaton, Jeffrey DeMunn, Kerri Green, Barry Corbin, Roy Dotrice, Jose Ferrer. From the house of Disney comes this amiable, fictionalized recounting of how a 12-year-old who was to become Harry Houdini ran away from home to join a traveling medicine show to start a life as a magician. DeMunn is the older Houdini, who narrates the tale; Dotrice is Arthur Conan Doyle, with whom Houdini shared a fascination with the supernatural. Written by director Orr and Jim Cruickshank. Above average.

Young Hellions SEE: **High School Confidential**▼

Young Ideas (1943) 77m. *½ D: Jules Dassin. Susan Peters, Herbert Marshall, Mary Astor, Elliott Reid, Richard Carlson. Dismal comedy about writer who disappears and shows up later at resort spot, married to man her family considers unsuitable.

Young in Heart, The (1938) 90m. ***½ D: Richard Wallace. Janet Gaynor, Douglas Fairbanks, Jr., Paulette Goddard, Roland Young, Billie Burke, Minnie Dupree, Richard Carlson. Refreshing comedy about wacky family of con artists going straight under influence of unsuspecting Dupree.

Written by Paul Osborn and Charles Bennett from an I.A.R. Wylie novel.

Young Jesse James (1960) 73m. *½ D: William Claxton. Ray Stricklyn, Willard Parker, Merry Anders, Robert Dix, Emile Meyer, Jacklyn O'Donnell. Title tells all in this routine oater.

Young Joe, The Forgotten Kennedy (1977) C-97m. TVM D: Richard T. Heffron. Peter Strauss, Barbara Parkins, Stephen Elliott, Darleen Carr, Simon Oakland, Lance Kerwin. Strauss gives sincere performance in tear-stained drama that strives to fulfill the public's never-ending fascination with the legendary Kennedy family. Average.

Young Land, The (1959) C-89m. **½ D: Ted Tetzlaff. Pat Wayne, Yvonne Craig, Dennis Hopper, Dan O'Herlihy, Cliff Ketchum. Sincere Western of pre-Mexican war Texas.

Young Lawyers, The (1969) C-75m. TVM D: Harvey Hart. Jason Evers, Judy Pace, Zalman King, Tom Fielding, Anjanette Comer, Keenan Wynn, James Shigeta, Richard Pryor. Three law students, working for famous Boston attorney who gave up practice to direct neighborhood law office, defend two musicians charged with robbing and beating cab driver. Extensive location work and script which tackles legal problems squarely are film's major assets, but watch out for resolution. Pilot for the series. Above average.

Young Lions, The (1958) 167m. ***½ D: Edward Dmytryk. Marlon Brando, Montgomery Clift, Dean Martin, Hope Lange, Barbara Rush, Maximilian Schell, Mai Britt, Lee Van Cleef. One of the all-time best WW2 studies, adapted by Edward Anhalt from the Irwin Shaw novel. Martin and Clift play U.S. soldiers, Brando a confused Nazi officer; effectively photographed by Joe MacDonald, with Hugo Friedhofer's fine score.▼

Young Love, First Love (1979) C-100m. TVM D: Steven Hilliard Stern. Valerie Bertinelli, Timothy Hutton, Arlen Dean Snyder, Fionnula Flanagan, Leslie Ackerman. Title tells all in this routine story that asks the burning question: Should Valerie go "all the way"? Average.▼

Young Lovers, The (1964) 105m. ** D: Samuel Goldwyn, Jr. Peter Fonda, Nick Adams, Sharon Hugueny, Deborah Walley, Kent Smith. Amateurish, meandering drama of college youths involved in romance.

Young Man with a Horn (1950) 112m. *** D: Michael Curtiz. Kirk Douglas, Lauren Bacall, Doris Day, Juano Hernandez, Hoagy Carmichael, Mary Beth Hughes. Effective drama of trumpet-player Douglas compulsively drawn to music, with Bacall the bad girl, Day the wholesome one. Carl Foreman-Edmund H. North script was adapted from Dorothy Baker's

book, and inspired by Bix Beiderbecke's life; Harry James dubbed Douglas' licks.▼

Young Man With Ideas (1952) 84m. **½ D: Mitchell Leisen. Glenn Ford, Ruth Roman, Denise Darcel, Nina Foch, Donna Corcoran, Ray Collins, Sheldon Leonard. Modest comedy-drama about a young Montana lawyer who moves to California with his wife and kids for a fresh start and encounters various problems while studying for the state bar exam.

Young Mr. Lincoln (1939) 100m. ***½ D: John Ford. Henry Fonda, Alice Brady, Marjorie Weaver, Donald Meek, Richard Cromwell, Eddie Quillan, Milburn Stone, Ward Bond, Francis Ford. Fine Ford Americana with Abraham Lincoln (Fonda) facing years of struggle as a beginning lawyer in the 1800s. Brady lends solid support.▼

Young Mr. Pitt, The (1942-British) 118m. ***½ D: Carol Reed. Robert Donat, Robert Morley, Phyllis Calvert, John Mills, Max Adrian. Long, only occasionally moving historical drama of young British prime minister during Napoleonic era; thinly veiled WW2 morale-booster. Written by Frank Launder and Sidney Gilliatt.

Young Nurses, The (1973) C-77m. ** D: Clinton Kimbrough. Jean Manson, Ashley Porter, Angela Gibbs, Zack Taylor, Jack LaRue, Jr., Dick Miller, Sally Kirkland, Allan Arbus. Fourth of Roger Corman's "nurse" movies is OK, focusing on drug ring working out of the hospital. Neat appearance by director Samuel Fuller as a villain, and a rather sad one by aged Mantan Moreland (in his final film). Followed by CANDY STRIPE NURSES.▼

Young One, The (1960-Mexican) 96m. *½ D: Luis Buñuel. Zachary Scott, Bernie Hamilton, Key Meersman, Crahan Denton. Turgid melodramatics with Scott keeping Meersman, conflicting with a black musician on the run who comes to their deserted island.

Young People (1940) 78m. ** D: Allan Dwan. Shirley Temple, Jack Oakie, Charlotte Greenwood, Arleen Whelan, George Montgomery, Kathleen Howard. Show-biz team Oakie and Greenwood raise orphaned Shirley and try to settle down in this weak musical, a later and lesser Temple vehicle. Good dance routine at the finish.

Young Philadelphians, The (1959) 136m. *** D: Vincent Sherman. Paul Newman, Barbara Rush, Alexis Smith, Brian Keith, Diane Brewster, Billie Burke, John Williams, Robert Vaughn, Otto Kruger, Adam West. Newman and Rush have memorable roles as poor lawyer who schemes to the top, and society girl he hopes to win; Vaughn is army buddy Newman defends on murder charge, Smith quite good as frustrated wife of attorney Kruger.▼

Young Pioneers (1976) C-100m. TVM D: Michael O'Herlihy. Roger Kern, Linda

[1323]

Purl, Robert Hays, Shelly Juttner, Robert Donner, Frank Marth. Homesteading adventures of newlyweds in Dakota wilderness of the 1870s. Uncluttered, occasionally interesting family-style Western. Followed by YOUNG PIONEERS' CHRISTMAS. Average.

Young Pioneers' Christmas (1976) C-100m. TVM D: Michael O'Herlihy. Roger Kern, Linda Purl, Robert Hays, Kay Kimler, Robert Donner, Britt Leach. Further adventures of those pioneering young folks in poignant sequel to YOUNG PIONEERS. More of the same—with tinsel added. A short-lived series followed. Average.

Young Racers, The (1963) C-87m. ** D: Roger Corman. Mark Damon, William Campbell, Patrick Magee, Luana Anders, Robert Campbell. Juvenile nonsense about sports car racing involving ex-racer turned exposé writer, trying to do a book on the sport.

Young Rebel (1967-French-Italian-Spanish) C-111m. ** D: Vincent Sherman. Horst Buchholz, Gina Lollobrigida, Jose Ferrer, Louis Jourdan, Francisco Rabal. Despite cast, ordinary historical claptrap about Buchholz being sent to Spain by Pope Pius V to obtain help in fighting the Moors. Also known as CERVANTES.

Young Runaways, The (1968) C-91m. ** D: Arthur Dreifuss. Brooke Bundy, Kevin Coughlin, Lloyd Bochner, Patty McCormack, Lynn Bari, Norman Fell. Silly B-picture about restless teenagers and how they are swept up into sordid lifestyles. Interesting mainly for early look at Richard Dreyfuss as cocky car thief.

Young Savages, The (1961) 110m. *** D: John Frankenheimer. Burt Lancaster, Dina Merrill, John David Chandler, Shelley Winters, Telly Savalas, Edward Andrews, Chris Robinson, Pilar Seurat, Milton Selzer. Lancaster is idealistic D.A. battling all odds to see justice done in street-gang slaying; at times brutal, too often pat. Adapted by Edward Anhalt and JP Miller from Evan Hunter's novel *A Matter of Conviction*. Savalas' film debut.

Young Scarface SEE: **Brighton Rock**
Young Sherlock Holmes (1985) C-109m. ** D: Barry Levinson. Nicholas Rowe, Alan Cox, Sophie Ward, Anthony Higgins, Susan Fleetwood, Freddie Jones, Nigel Stock, Michael Hordern. Promising film speculates about Conan Doyle's detective when he was a boy, introduces him to Watson, and involves him in his first great case. Knowing references to Holmes's later life, perfect Victorian atmosphere all give way to jarring 1980s special effects, inappropriate INDIANA JONES-type subplot, and action climax that doesn't make much sense. If you *do* watch it through, be sure to stay through the *very* end. Written by Chris

Columbus (GREMLINS). Steven Spielberg was one of the executive producers.▼

Young Stranger, The (1957) 84m. *** D: John Frankenheimer. James MacArthur, James Daly, Kim Hunter, James Gregory, Marian Seldes, Whit Bissell. Excellent drama about a teenage boy's brush with delinquency and strained relationship with his wealthy, neglectful father. Surprisingly undated, sincere little film; MacArthur's impressive screen debut (and director Frankenheimer's, too).

Young Swingers, The (1963) 71m. BOMB D: Maury Dexter. Molly Bee, Rod Lauren, Gene McDaniels, Jack Larson, Jo Helton. Singer Lauren tries to keep nightclub operating, despite interference of greedy realestate agent Helton. Grade Z all the way.

Young, the Evil, and the Savage, The (1968-Italian) C-82m. *½ D: Antonio Margheriti. Michael Rennie, Mark Damon, Eleanora Brown, Sally Smith, Pat Valturri, Ludmilla Lvova. Standard story of strangler on the loose at fashionable girls college with Rennie wooden as police inspector assigned to case.

Young Tom Edison (1940) 82m. *** D: Norman Taurog. Mickey Rooney, Fay Bainter, George Bancroft, Virginia Weidler, Eugene Palette, Victor Kilian. Inventor's early life depicted with flair by effective Rooney, who could tone down when he had to; followed by Spencer Tracy's EDISON THE MAN.

Young Warriors, The (1967) C-93m. ** D: John Peyser. James Drury, Steve Carlson, Jonathan Daly, Robert Pine, Michael Stanwood. Clichéd WW2 yarn filled with Universal Pictures contract players; loosely derived from Richard Matheson novel.

Young Warriors (1983) C-103m. *½ D: Lawrence D. Foldes. Ernest Borgnine, Richard Roundtree, Lynda Day George, James Van Patten, Anne Lockhart, Mike Norris, Dick Shawn, Linnea Quigley. Self-righteous, violent exploitation film has students turning vigilantes to put local criminals out of business. Features several second-generation actors (Van Patten, Lockhart, Norris). Semi-sequel to MALIBU HIGH. ▼

Young Widow (1946) 100m. ** D: Edwin L. Marin. Jane Russell, Marie Wilson, Louis Hayward, Faith Domergue, Kent Taylor, Penny Singleton, Cora Witherspoon. Soap-opera was not Russell's forte and she can't support teary WW2 tale of woman who can't forget her late husband.

Young Winston (1972-British) C-145m. *** D: Richard Attenborough. Simon Ward, Anne Bancroft, Robert Shaw, John Mills, Jack Hawkins, Patrick Magee, Ian Holm, Robert Flemyng, Jane Seymour, Edward Woodward, Anthony Hopkins, Laurence Naismith. Entertaining account of Churchill's early life, from school days, through journalistic experience in Africa, up to first election to Parliament. Handsome production, good performances, and rousing battle scenes. Scripted and produced by Carl Foreman.▼

Young Wives' Tale (1951-British) **78m.** **½ D: Henry Cass. Joan Greenwood, Nigel Patrick, Audrey Hepburn, Derek Farr. Comedy of situations deriving from postwar housing shortage and fabricated mistaken relationships.

You Only Live Once (1937) **86m.** *** D: Fritz Lang. Sylvia Sidney, Henry Fonda, William Gargan, Barton MacLane, Jean Dixon, Jerome Cowan, Margaret Hamilton, Ward Bond, Guinn Williams. Beautifully crafted drama about ex-convict Fonda trying to go straight, finding that fate is against him. Loosely based on the Bonnie and Clyde legend, but impressive on its own.▼

You Only Live Twice (1967-British) **C-116m.** **½ D: Lewis Gilbert. Sean Connery, Akiko Wakabayashi, Tetsuro Tamba, Mie Hama, Karin Dor, Bernard Lee, Lois Maxwell, Desmond Llewellyn, Donald Pleasence. Big James Bond production with first look at arch-nemesis Blofeld (Pleasence), Japanese locales, but plot (SPECTRE out to cause major powers to declare war on each other) and lack of convincing, clever crisis situations are liabilities film can't shake off. Script by Roald Dahl (!), spectacular sets by Ken Adam.▼

Your Cheatin' Heart (1964) **99m.** *** D: Gene Nelson. George Hamilton, Susan Oliver, Red Buttons, Arthur O'Connell, Rex Ingram. One of Hamilton's best roles, as legendary country-western singer Hank Williams, who couldn't cope with fame on the ole opry circuit; songs dubbed by Hank Williams, Jr. Oliver most effective as Hank's wife.

You're a Big Boy Now (1966) **C-96m.** ***½ D: Francis Ford Coppola. Peter Kastner, Elizabeth Hartman, Geraldine Page, Julie Harris, Rip Torn, Michael Dunn, Tony Bill, Karen Black. Beguiling, wayout film of young man with overprotective parents learning about life from callous young actress Hartman. Will not appeal to everyone, but acting is marvelous, with Dolph Sweet hilarious as tough cop. Location filming in N.Y.C. adds to film, too. Title song by The Lovin' Spoonful.▼

You're a Sweetheart (1937) **96m.** ** D: David Butler. Alice Faye, George Murphy, Ken Murray, Andy Devine, William Gargan, Charles Winninger, Donald Meek, Bobby Watson. Routine musical with go-getter Murphy dreaming up publicity stunt for show which stars Faye. Title song became a standard.

You're in the Army Now (1941) **79m.** **

D: Lewis Seiler. Jimmy Durante, Phil Silvers, Donald MacBride, Jane Wyman, Regis Toomey, Joe Sawyer. Rather obvious service comedy, with Durante and Silvers trying hard to rise above their material. Some funny scenes, with finale copied from Chaplin's THE GOLD RUSH. Trivia note: features the longest kiss (between Toomey and Wyman) in screen history, clocked at 3 min., 5 sec.

You're in the Navy Now (1951) **93m.** ** D: Henry Hathaway. Gary Cooper, Jane Greer, Millard Mitchell, Eddie Albert, John McIntire, Ray Collins, Harry Von Zell, Lee Marvin, Jack Webb. Flat naval comedy set in WW2 with Cooper commanding a dumb crew on the U.S.S. *Teakettle* (the ship is outfitted with a steam engine). Film debuts for Marvin and Charles Buchinski (Bronson). Originally screened with the title U.S.S TEAKETTLE.

You're My Everything (1949) **C-94m.** *** D: Walter Lang. Dan Dailey, Anne Baxter, Anne Revere, Stanley Ridges, Buster Keaton, Alan Mowbray, Selena Royle. Musical about socialite Baxter becoming a movie star runs hot and cold, spoofing Hollywood of the 20s and 30s, but bogging down in slurpy romance; worthwhile for first half.

You're Never Too Young (1955) **C-102m.** *** D: Norman Taurog. Dean Martin, Jerry Lewis, Diana Lynn, Raymond Burr, Nina Foch, Veda Ann Borg. Fast, funny remake of THE MAJOR AND THE MINOR (which also featured Lynn) with Jerry disguised as 12-year-old, involved in jewel robbery. Script by Sidney Sheldon.

You're Not So Tough (1940) **71m.** D: Joe May. Nan Grey, Henry Armetta, Rosina Galli, Billy Halop, Huntz Hall, Gabriel Dell. SEE: Bowery Boys series.

You're Only Young Once (1938) **78m.** D: George B. Seitz. Lewis Stone, Cecilia Parker, Mickey Rooney, Fay Holden, Frank Craven, Ann Rutherford, Eleanor Lynn. See: **Andy Hardy** series.

You're Telling Me (1934) **67m.** ***½ D: Erle C. Kenton. W. C. Fields, Joan Marsh, Larry "Buster" Crabbe, Louise Carter, Kathleen Howard, Adrienne Ames. Hilarious remake of Fields' silent film SO'S YOUR OLD MAN, with thin storyline (about a friendly foreign princess giving lowly, browbeaten Fields respectability in his home town) a perfect excuse for some of his funniest routines—including classic golf game.

You're Telling Me (1942) **60m.** *½ D: Charles Lamont. Hugh Herbert, Jane Frazee, Robert Paige, Richard Davies, Anne Gwynne, Mischa Auer, Ernest Truex. Tired comedy vehicle for Hugh as bumbler given job with radio advertising agency, involved with matchmaking on the side.

Your Money or Your Wife (1972) **C-73m.** **TVM** D: Allen Reisner. Ted Bessell, Elizabeth Ashley, Jack Cassidy, Betsy von Furstenberg. Good premise gone awry in novel-based story of two scriptwriters cooking up imaginary kidnap plot, then putting it to work. Unconvincing character development, sloppy direction, passable performances. Script by JP Miller. Average.

Your Mother Wears Combat Boots (1989) **C-100m.** **TVM** D: Anson Williams. Barbara Eden, Hector Elizondo, Meagan Fay, Maria O'Brien, Conchata Ferrell, David Kaufman. Overprotective mother follows her teenage son into airborne training, attempting to steer him back to college. Silly service comedy that plays like a bus-and-truck production of PRIVATE BENJAMIN. Below average.

Your Past Is Showing (1957-British) **92m.** *** D: Mario Zampi. Terry-Thomas, Peter Sellers, Peggy Mount, Dennis Price, Shirley Eaton. Droll hijinks of a strange grouping of folks brought together to rid themselves of the editor of a smut-exposé magazine. Original British title: THE NAKED TRUTH.▼

Your Place or Mine (1983) **C-100m.** **TVM** D: Robert Day. Bonnie Franklin, Robert Klein, Peter Bonerz, Tyne Daly, Penny Fuller. Warmhearted but typical romantic comedy about a couple of mature "singles" and the problems their best friends have in getting them together. Average.▼

Yours, Mine and Ours (1968) **C-111m.** *** D: Melville Shavelson. Lucille Ball, Henry Fonda, Van Johnson, Tom Bosley, Tim Matheson. For once, a wholesome "family" picture with some intelligent scripting. Based on real situation of widowed mother of eight marrying widower with ten more children. Lucy's drunk scene is a delight in warm, well-made comedy. Among Fonda's brood: Suzanne Cupito (who grew up to be Morgan Brittany) and a very young Tracy Nelson.▼

Your Three Minutes Are Up (1973) **C-92m.** ***½ D: Douglas N. Schwartz. Beau Bridges, Ron Leibman, Janet Margolin, Kathleen Freeman, David Ketchum, Stu Nisbet, Read Morgan. Overlooked comedy with serious undertones vividly captures two American lifestyles in story of ultra-straight Bridges hanging out with swinging buddy Leibman, who's out to beat the system. Unpretentious film says more about our society than many more "important" movies of recent vintage; solid performances. Written by James Dixon.

Your Ticket Is No Longer Valid (1979-Canadian) **C-91m.** BOMB D: George Kaczender. Richard Harris, George Peppard, Jeanne Moreau, Jennifer Dale, Alexandra Stewart, Winston Rekert. Trashy adaptation of a Romain Gary novel is an embarrassment for its cast: Harris is struggling to raise cash for his failed, inherited family business while suffering from impotency and recurring fantasies of a gypsy stud making love to his girlfriend Dale; Peppard is a foulmouthed banker who is also impotent; and Moreau is a Parisian brothel madam who procures the gypsy boy for Harris's and Dale's eventual amusement. Lurid junk. ▼

Your Turn, Darling (1963-French) **93m.** ** D: Bernard Borderie. Eddie Constantine, Henri Cogan, Gaia Germani, Elga Andersen. Constantine is Lemmy Caution, U.S. secret agent involved with gang of spies; lumbering account.

You Ruined My Life (1987) **C-100m.** **TVM** D: David Ashwell. Soleil Moon Frye, Paul Reiser, Mimi Rogers, Allen Garfield, Tony Burton, Todd Susman. Rambunctious preteen who grew up on the Las Vegas strip escapes her overbearing aunt's clutches by forging an unlikely alliance with an unorthodox math professor. Disney fluff starring TV's "Punky Brewster." Average.

You Said a Mouthful (1932) **75m.** *** D: Lloyd Bacon. Joe E. Brown, Ginger Rogers, Preston Foster, Guinn Williams, Sheila Terry, Selmer Jackson. One of Brown's best vehicles, about inventor of unsinkable bathing suit; Rogers is his vivacious leading lady.

Youth Runs Wild (1944) **67m.** ** D: Mark Robson. Bonita Granville, Kent Smith, Tessa Brind (Vanessa Brown), Lawrence Tierney, Jean Brooks, Dickie Moore. With parents and older siblings at war in defense plants, teenagers do just what the title implies. Rare non-horror entry from producer Val Lewton is interesting as time capsule, routine as drama.

Youth Takes a Fling (1938) **79m.** ** D: Archie Mayo. Andrea Leeds, Joel McCrea, Frank Jenks, Dorothea Kent, Isabel Jeans, Virginia Grey. Working girl Leeds sets out to snare sea-crazy McCrea, who couldn't care less. Slick Joe Pasternak production never hits the mark.

You've Got To Walk It Like You Talk It Or You'll Lose That Beat (1971) **C-85m.** **½ D: Peter Locke. Zalman King, Richard Pryor, Bob Downey, Liz Torres, Roz Kelly, Allen Garfield. Uneven, often crude satire focusing on the sorry escapades of a young loser, a product of the 60s. Filmed in 1968.

You Were Meant for Me (1948) **92m.** *** D: Lloyd Bacon. Jeanne Crain, Dan Dailey, Oscar Levant, Barbara Lawrence, Selena Royle. Nice combination of musical score and script of girl who marries band leader; their experiences in Depression are basis of film.

You Were Never Lovelier (1942) **97m.** ***½ D: William A. Seiter. Fred Astaire, Rita Hayworth, Adolphe Menjou, Leslie Brooks, Adele Mara, Xavier Cugat, Gus Schilling, Larry Parks. Astaire pursuing

Hayworth via matchmaking father Menjou becomes lilting musical with such lovely Jerome Kern-Johnny Mercer songs as title tune, "Dearly Beloved," "I'm Old-Fashioned."▼

Yuma (1970) **C-73m.** TVM D: Ted Post. Clint Walker, Barry Sullivan, Edgar Buchanan, Kathryn Hays, Peter Mark Richman, Morgan Woodward. Marshal of frontier town center of plot to discredit him, stalked by brother of prisoner, must unravel chain of events to unmask plan's creator. Old-fashioned Western lacks script with punch, but fair direction and actionful resolution make up for lulls. Average.▼

Yum-Yum Girls, The (1976) **C-93m.** ** D: Barry Rosen. Judy Landers, Tanya Roberts, Michelle Dawn, Carey Poe, Stan Bernstein. Entertainingly trashy film, made before Landers' and Roberts' TV success, about young girls coming to N.Y.C. to become fashion models. OK cook's tour of the business, marred by unfunny script.▼

Yuri Nosenko, KGB (1986-U.S.-British) **C-85m.** TVM D: Mick Jackson. Tommy Lee Jones, Oleg Rudnik, Josef Sommer, Ed Lauter, George Morfogen, Stephen Newman. Cold War spy thriller based on fact, involving a burned-out CIA agent and a defecting KGB member who may or may not be a Russian plant. Produced for British television and for American cable. Above average.▼

Z (1969-French) **C-127m.** *** D: Costa-Gavras. Yves Montand, Irene Papas, Jean-Louis Trintignant, Charles Denner, Georges Geret, Jacques Perrin, Francois Perier, Marcel Bozzufi. Oscar-winner for Best Foreign Film and Editing, based on true-life incident, concerns political assassination of Montand and chilling aftermath. Talky film praised more for its topicality than cinematics is nonetheless gripping; good acting.▼

Zabriskie Point (1970) **C-112m.** **½ D: Michelangelo Antonioni. Mark Frechette, Daria Halprin, Rod Taylor, Paul Fix, Harrison Ford. Rambling study by a foreigner of the aggressive, materialistic, unflinching American lifestyle. Worth watching but difficult to stay with, though there's a real eye-opening finale. Sam Shepard was one of the scriptwriters.▼

Zachariah (1971) **C-93m.** **½ D: George Englund. John Rubinstein, Pat Quinn, Don Johnson, Country Joe and The Fish, Elvin Jones, New York Rock Ensemble, The James Gang, Dick Van Patten. Audacious rock Western with elements of a morality play and moments of sharp satire; co-scripted by members of Firesign Theater. Certainly offbeat, but how much you like it is strictly personal taste.▼

Zamba (1949) **75m.** *½ D: William Berke. Jon Hall, June Vincent, George Cooper,

Jane Nigh, George O'Hanlon. Juvenile adventure story of boy raised by gorillas; rough going.

Zandy's Bride (1974) **C-116m.** *½ D: Jan Troell. Gene Hackman, Liv Ullmann, Eileen Heckart, Harry Dean Stanton, Susan Tyrrell, Sam Bottoms, Joe Santos. Two frequently wasted stars in tepid romance of a mail-order bride and her pioneer husband; no one needs *these* scenes from a marriage. Also known as FOR BETTER, FOR WORSE.

Zany Adventures of Robin Hood, The (1984) **C-100m.** TVM D: Ray Austin. George Segal, Morgan Fairchild, Roddy McDowall, Janet Suzman, Kenneth Griffith, Michael Hordern, Tom Baker. It might have looked funny on paper, but aside from one or two bright spots this spoof fizzles and makes the viewer pine for another go at Mel Brooks' short-lived series *When Things Were Rotten.* Average.▼

Zapped! (1982) **C-96m.** *½ D: Robert J. Rosenthal. Scott Baio, Willie Aames, Felice Schachter, Heather Thomas, Robert Mandan, Greg Bradford, Scatman Crothers, Sue Ane Langdon. Attractive cast is wasted in this stupid spoof of CARRIE, in which Baio acquires telekinetic powers . . . which he's most anxious to use in undressing Thomas (or rather, her stand-in). Followed by a sequel.▼

Zarak (1957-British) **C-99m.** **½ D: Terence Young. Victor Mature, Michael Wilding, Anita Ekberg, Bernard Miles, Finlay Currie. Hokum set in India with Mature the head of native outlaws, Wilding the British officer sent to get him.

Zardoz (1974-British) **C-105m.** **½ D: John Boorman. Sean Connery, Charlotte Rampling, Sara Kestelman, Sally Anne Newton, John Alderton, Niall Buggy. Weird sci-fi entry, set in 2293, about technology gone wild in society run by group of eternally young intellectuals. Visually striking cult film will probably leave most viewers dissatisfied.▼

Zaza (1939) **83m.** ** D: George Cukor. Claudette Colbert, Herbert Marshall, Bert Lahr, Helen Westley, Constance Collier, Genevieve Tobin, Walter Catlett. Colbert, doing her own singing, is the French music hall performer who falls for married Marshall, playing the role in his sleep. Remake of Gloria Swanson silent vehicle has well-mounted novelty value, but the drama simply never gets into gear.

Zebra Force (1977) **C-100m.** ** D: Joe Tornatore. Mike Lane, Richard X. Slattery, Rockne Tarkington, Glenn Wilder, Anthony Caruso. A band of Vietnam vets uses military tactics against the Mob to fatten their own pockets and "rid society of scum." Straightforward low-budgeter suffers from Grade Z performances. Director Tornatore scripted and coproduced.▼

Zebra in the Kitchen (1965) **C-93m.** **½ D: Ivan Tors. Jay North, Martin Milner, Andy Devine, Joyce Meadows, Jim Davis, Dorothy Green. Wholesome family fare of young North involved with wild pets and the city zoo's attempt to keep its inmates locked up.

Zed & Two Noughts, A (1985-British-Dutch) **C-115m.** *** D: Peter Greenaway. Andrea Ferreol, Brian Deacon, Eric Deacon, Frances Barber, Joss Ackland. Extremely provocative examination of birth, life, and death, focusing on Ferreol, who has lost a leg in a car crash, and two zoologist brothers (the Deacons) whose wives have been killed in the same accident and who become obsessed with decay. Difficult to watch but well worthwhile for those willing to be challenged. Not so much a film as a visual essay, exquisitely directed and photographed (by Sacha Vierny).▼

Zeisters SEE: Fat Guy Goes Nutzoid ▼

Zelig (1983) **C/B&W-79m.** *** D: Woody Allen. Woody Allen, Mia Farrow, Garrett Brown, Stephanie Farrow, Will Holt, Sol Lomita, Mary Louise Wilson. Pseudo-documentary using remarkable recreations of old newsreels and recordings, about a chameleonlike man named Leonard Zelig (Allen), who became a celebrity in the fad-crazy '20s. A supremely well-executed joke, more clever than funny; it might have worked even better in a shorter format. Gordon Willis's cinematography and Dick Hyman's music are standouts.▼

Zelly and Me (1988) **C-87m.** **½ D: Tina Rathborne. Isabella Rossellini, Glynis Johns, Alexandra Johnes, Kaiulani Lee, David Lynch, Joe Morton. Uneven account of the trials and stresses in the life of wealthy, overprotected orphan Johnes. Occasionally insightful but far too introspective—with too much left unexplained.▼

Zenobia (1939) **71m.** **½ D: Gordon Douglas. Oliver Hardy, Harry Langdon, Billie Burke, Alice Brady, James Ellison, Jean Parker, June Lang, Stepin Fetchit, Hattie McDaniel. Small-town doctor agrees to treat an ailing elephant—and the grateful pachyderm refuses to leave his side! Amiable comedy set in the Old South, with some dated (and mildly tol'able) subplots. This was Hardy's only starring venture without Stan Laurel, and he's quite good, in a fairly straight nonslapsticky performance.

Zeppelin (1971-British) **C-101m.** *** D: Etienne Perier. Michael York, Elke Sommer, Peter Carsten, Marius Goring, Anton Diffring, Andrew Keir. Colorful cast and atmosphere (including interesting special effects) click in entertaining story of German-born British aviator emotionally torn by duty and homeland during World War I.

Zero for Conduct (1933-French) **44m.** **** D: Jean Vigo. Jean Daste, Robert le Flon, Louis Lefebvre, Constantin Kelber, Gerard de Bedarieux. Life in a French boarding school, where the authorities attempt to regiment the students—unsuccessfully. The kids are all wonderfully spontaneous; one of the best films ever about children among children. The inspiration for IF. . . . Written by the director.▼

Zero Hour (1957) **81m.** **½ D: Hall Bartlett. Dana Andrews, Linda Darnell, Sterling Hayden, Elroy "Crazylegs" Hirsch, Geoffrey Toone, Jerry Paris, Peggy King, John Ashley. Effective suspense story (based on Arthur Hailey teleplay) of potential airplane disaster when pilots are felled by ptomaine poisoning. Remade for TV as TERROR IN THE SKY, and then spoofed in 1980 as AIRPLANE!

Zero to Sixty (1978) **C-100m.** *½ D: Don Weis. Darren McGavin, Sylvia Miles, Joan Collins, Denise Nickerson, The Hudson Brothers, Lorraine Gary. McGavin is improbably cast as a schnook who hooks up with a strident, street-smart 16-year-old girl who makes her living repossessing cars. Loud, stupid comedy with more car-chase thrills than humor.▼

Ziegfeld Follies (1946) **C-110m.** *** D: Vincente Minnelli. William Powell, Judy Garland, Lucille Ball, Fred Astaire, Fanny Brice, Lena Horne, Red Skelton, Victor Moore, Virginia O'Brien, Cyd Charisse, Gene Kelly, Edward Arnold, Esther Williams. Variable all-star film introduced by Powell as Ziegfeld in heaven. Highlights are Brice-Hume Cronyn sketch, Astaire-Kelly dance, Moore-Arnold comedy routine, Skelton's "Guzzler's Gin," Horne's solo, Garland's "The Interview." Various segments directed by George Sidney, Roy Del Ruth, Norman Taurog, Lemuel Ayers, Robert Lewis, Merril Pye. Filmed mostly in 1944.▼

Ziegfeld Girl (1941) **131m.** *** D: Robert Z. Leonard. James Stewart, Lana Turner, Judy Garland, Hedy Lamarr, Tony Martin, Jackie Cooper, Ian Hunter, Edward Everett Horton, Al Shean, Eve Arden, Dan Dailey, Philip Dorn, Charles Winninger. Large-scale musical drama opens brightly, bogs down into melodrama and preposterous subplot resolutions, as the lives of three girls (Turner, Garland, Lamarr) are changed by being recruited as Ziegfeld Follies girls. Busby Berkeley's "You Stepped Out of a Dream" is most famous number, but somewhat overshadowed by Judy's "I'm Always Chasing Rainbows," "Minnie from Trinidad." The MGM glitter has never been brighter.▼

Ziegfeld: The Man and His Women

(1978) **C-150m. TVM** D: Buzz Kulik.
Paul Shenar, Samantha Eggar, Barbara
Parkins, Pamela Peadon, Valerie Perrine,
Inga Swenson, Ron Hussman, Nehemiah
Persoff, David Opatoshu. Flashy, sump-
tuously mounted account of the life and
time of Flo Ziegfeld, as told by the women
in his life: Billie Burke (Eggar) Anna Held
(Parkins), Marilyn Miller (Peadon) and
Lillian Lorraine (Perrine). Shenar is mis-
cast in the pivotal title role. Script by
Joanna Lee. Average.

**Ziggy Stardust and The Spiders from
Mars** (1983) **C-91m.** *½ D: D. A. Pennebaker. David Bowie. Bowie in concert as
Ziggy Stardust, his androgynous alter ego.
Practically unwatchable, and unlistenable:
cinema verite at its worst. Shot in 1973; of
interest to Bowie fans only.▼

Zigzag (1970) **105m.** **½ D: Richard A.
Colla. George Kennedy, Anne Jackson,
Eli Wallach, Steve Ihnat, William Marshall, Joe Maross. Dying insurance investigator (Kennedy) plans a complicated
scheme to pin a murder on himself and be
executed, so his family will collect a big
insurance settlement, but his plans go awry.
Good performances in moderately interesting drama.

Zina (1985-British) **C/B&W-90m.** **½
D: Ken McMullen. Domiziana Giordano,
Ian McKellen, Philip Madoc, Ron Anderson, Micha Bergese. Extremely (and deliberately) slow exploration of the problems
and obsessions of Leon Trotsky's daughter
(Giordano) while in psychoanalysis in pre-
war Berlin. Bryan Loftus' cinematography
is exceptional. Not for all tastes.

Zita (1968-French) **C-91m.** *** D: Robert
Enrico. Joanna Shimkus, Katina Paxinou,
Suzanne Flon, Jose Marie Flotats, Paul
Crauchet. Delicate story of young girl who
learns about life as her beloved aunt is
dying; love blossoms, as she breaks away
from mother-figure to become an adult
herself. Charming.

Zoltan, Hound of Dracula SEE: **Dracula's
Dog**▼

Zombie (1979-Italian) **C-91m.** BOMB D:
Lucio Fulci. Tisa Farrow, Ian McCulloch,
Richard Johnson, Al Cliver, Annetta Gay.
A zombie epidemic on a small Caribbean
island. A poor imitation of George Rome-
ro's horror films, and pretty repellent.▼

Zombie High (1987) **C-91m.** BOMB D:
Ron Link. Virginia Madsen, Richard Cox,
Kay Kuter, James Wilder, Sherilynn Fenn,
Paul Williams. Ridiculous, Grade Z chiller
about students at a sleepaway academy
who are being lobotomized by their teachers. Which, come to think of it, would
make them perfect candidates to sit through
this picture.▼

Zombie Island Massacre (1984) **C-95m.**
BOMB D: John N. Carter. David Broadnax,
Rita Jenrette, Tom Cantrell, Diane Clayre

Holub. Ex-Abscam Congressional spouse
(and *Playboy* subject) Jenrette has three
gratuitous nude scenes in the opening 20
minutes—and then they have to ruin everything by going to the stupid island. The
corpses keep a-comin' in this cheapo outing. Rita warbles title tune, "Di Reggae
Picnic."▼

Zombies of Mora Tau (1957) **70m.** *½
D: Edward L. Cahn. Gregg Palmer, Allison Hayes, Autumn Russell, Joel Ashley.
Juvenile hodgepodge about zombies guarding diamonds hidden in a sunken ship.▼

Zombies of Sugar Hill, The: SEE **Sugar
Hill**

Zombies of the Stratosphere SEE: **Satan's
Satellites**▼

Zombies on Broadway (1945) **68m.** **
D: Gordon Douglas. Wally Brown, Alan
Carney, Bela Lugosi, Anne Jeffreys, Shel-
don Leonard, Frank Jenks. Press agents
Brown and Carney (cut-rate version of
Abbott and Costello) search for zombie to
use in nightclub stunt. Lugosi adds only
spice as zombie expert.

Zontar, the Thing from Venus (1968)
C-80m. BOMB D: Larry Buchanan. John
Agar, Anthony Houston, Susan Bjurman,
Patricia De Laney, Warren Hammack. Ti-
tle alien, resembling a bat, arrives to take
over with INVASION OF THE BODY
SNATCHERS-like methods; it's Agar to
the rescue. Crude, Texas-filmed remake of
IT CONQUERED THE WORLD.▼

Zoo in Budapest (1933) **85m.** ***½ D:
Rowland V. Lee. Gene Raymond, Loretta
Young, O. P. Heggie, Paul Fix, Wally
Albright. Wonderfully whimsical love story
set in famous Budapest zoo where Raymond, who has spent his life there, falls in
love with runaway Young, who's hiding
inside zoo grounds. Beautifully filmed by
Lee Garmes.

Zoot Suit (1981) **C-103m.** *** D: Luis
Valdez. Daniel Valdez, Edward James
Olmos, Charles Aidman, Tyne Daly, John
Anderson. Fascinating, powerful, if too
theatrical "stylized musical" based on railroading of Chicano gang members to San
Quentin for murder in 1942 and efforts to
obtain their release; adding commentary is
the gang's leader (Valdez) and his zoot-
suited alter ego (Olmos). Filmed on stage,
with shots of an audience that is presumably watching the performance—a major
distraction. Written by Luis Valdez, with
music by Daniel Valdez.

Zorba the Greek (1964) **146m.** ***½ D:
Michael Cacoyannis. Anthony Quinn, Alan
Bates, Irene Papas, Lila Kedrova, George
Foundas. Brooding, flavorful rendering of
Kazantzakis novel. Quinn is zesty in title
role of earthy peasant, Bates his intellectual British cohort. Kedrova won an Oscar
as a dying prostitute, as did cinematographer Walter Lassally and the art direc-

tion-set decoration. Memorable Mikis Theodorakis score.▼

Zorro (1961-Spanish) **C-90m.** **½ D: Joaquin Luis Romero Marchent. Frank Latimore, Mary Anderson, Ralph Marsch, Howard Vernon. Foreign-made Western with salty flavor of old California; Latimore is appropriately zealous as Zorro.

Zorro (1975-Italian-French) **C-100m.** *** D: Duccio Tessari. Alain Delon, Stanley Baker, Ottavia Piccolo, Moustache, Enzo Cerusico, Adriana Asti. Zesty retelling of saga of legendary masked rider and hero of the oppressed, not as distinctive as earlier versions (and set in South America rather than old California) but fun on its own terms.

Zorro Rides Again (1937) **68m.** ** D: William Witney, John English. John Carroll, Helen Christian, Reed Howes, Duncan Renaldo, Noah Beery. Edited from vintage Republic serial, recounting adventures of Carroll in old West to help railroad; just fair.

Zorro, The Gay Blade (1981) **C-93m.** ** D: Peter Medak. George Hamilton, Lauren Hutton, Brenda Vaccaro, Ron Leibman, Donovan Scott, James Booth. Hamilton is Don Diego Vega, foppish son of the legendary Zorro, and look-alike gay brother Bunny Wigglesworth. So-so, with Leibman overacting outrageously as the villain. Dedicated to Rouben Mamoulian!▼

Zotz! (1962) **87m.** ** D: William Castle. Tom Poston, Julia Meade, Jim Backus, Fred Clark, Cecil Kellaway, Margaret Dumont. Goofy attempt at humorous chiller with Poston a teacher who finds strange coin that gives him mystical power over others.▼

Zouzou (1934-French) **92m.** **½ D: Marc Allegret. Josephine Baker, Jean Gabin, Yvette Leblon, Illa Meery, Madeleine Guitty. FORTY-SECOND STREET meets FOOTLIGHT PARADE French-style, with Baker cast as a Creole laundress. In the best backstage musical tradition, she replaces a tempermental performer in a stage revue and captivates the crowd in a star-making turn. Overly familiar story line is helped by fast pace, and engaging musical numbers: how can you top Baker, covered in feathers and perched on a swing?▼

Z.P.G. (1972-British) **C-95m.** ** D: Michael Campus. Oliver Reed, Geraldine Chaplin, Don Gordon, Diane Cilento. Sci-fi tale with style but no class. Reproduction becomes crime punishable by death in the future, but some people try to defy the law. Title, of course, stands for Zero Population Growth.

Zulu (1964-British) **C-138m.** *** D: Cy Endfield. Stanley Baker, Jack Hawkins, Ulla Jacobsson, Michael Caine, Nigel Green, James Booth. Narrated by Richard Burton. True story about undermanned British forces trying to defend their African mission from attack by hordes of Zulu warriors. Dramatic elements tend toward cliche, but virtually half the film is taken up by massive battle, which is truly spectacular and exciting. Followed 15 years later by prequel, ZULU DAWN.▼

Zulu Dawn (1979-U.S.-Dutch) **C-121m.** *** D: Douglas Hickox. Burt Lancaster, Peter O'Toole, Simon Ward, John Mills, Nigel Davenport, Michael Jayston, Denholm Elliott, Ronald Lacey, Freddie Jones, Bob Hoskins. A prequel to 1964's ZULU (cowritten by that film's writer-director Cy Endfield), showing the British command's bull-headed and ineffectual handling of the Zulu nation—first in diplomacy, then in battle. Solid war drama of the period, outstanding locations (dwarfed on TV), though there's nothing new here. Released theatrically in U.S. at 98m.▼

Zuma Beach (1978) **C-100m. TVM** D: Lee H. Katzin. Suzanne Somers, Steven Keats, Michael Biehn, Mark Wheeler, Kimberly Beck, Perry Lang, Rosanna Arquette, Timothy Hutton, Tanya Roberts, P.J. Soles. Fading rock star becomes involved with high schoolers at a beach party. OK if watching Suzanne in a bathing suit is enough to keep you interested for 100m. Cowritten by John Carpenter! Average.

EXCITING CONTEMPORARY PLAYS

☐ **THE COLLECTED PLAYS OF NEIL SIMON, VOL 2, by Neil Simon.** From the most prolific and probably the most popular American playwright of our time come some of the best loved plays of today. Includes *Little Me; The Gingerbread Lady; The Prisoner of Second Avenue; The Sunshine Boys; The Good Doctor; God's Favorites; California Suite;* and *Chapter Two.* With a special Introduction by the author. (263581—$14.95)

☐ **PLENTY by David Hare.** This superbly crafted, razor-edged drama takes its remarkable heroine, a former French Resistance fighter, through twenty years of postwar changes. "David Hare is the most fascinating playwright since Harold Pinter. The play is unforgettable, an enigma wrapped in mystery with repressed and smoldering sexuality and high drama."—Liz Smith, *The New York Daily News.* (259568—$7.95)

☐ **FENCES: A Play by August Wilson.** The author of the 1984-85 Broadway season's best play, *Ma Rainey's Black Bottom,* returns with another powerful, stunning dramatic work. "Always absorbing . . . The work's protagonist—and greatest creation—is a Vesuvius of rage. . . . The play's finest moments perfectly capture that inky almost imperceptible agitated darkness just before the fences of racism, for a time, came crashing down."—Frank Rich, *The New York Times* (264014—$7.95)

☐ **THE HOUSE OF BLUE LEAVES AND TWO OTHER PLAYS by John Guare.** Artie Shaughnessy, a zoo-keeper and aspiring songwriter, is a man with a dream—which is put on a collision course with a devastating, wildly funny reality. THE HOUSE OF BLUE LEAVES, along with two other of Guare's fierce farces, form a trio of acerbic tragicomedies that painfully and hilariously reflect our world. "Mr. Guare . . . is in a class by himself."—*The New York Times* (264596—$9.95)

☐ **FOB AND OTHER PLAYS by David Henry Hwang.** From the Tony-award winning author of *M. Butterfly* comes a collection of six plays that capture the spirit, the struggles, and the secret language of the Chinese-American while exploring universal human issues. "Hwang is fast becoming the wunderkind of the American theater."—*San Francisco Chronicle* (263239—$8.95)

Prices slightly higher in Canada.

**Buy them at your local
bookstore or use this coupon
on next page for ordering.**